MIDDLE AND JUNIOR HIGH
CORE COLLECTION

TWELFTH EDITION

CORE COLLECTION SERIES

FORMERLY
STANDARD CATALOG SERIES

MARIA HUGGER, GENERAL EDITOR

CHILDREN'S CORE COLLECTION
MIDDLE AND JUNIOR HIGH CORE COLLECTION
SENIOR HIGH CORE COLLECTION
FICTION CORE COLLECTION
NONFICTION CORE COLLECTION
GRAPHIC NOVELS CORE COLLECTION

MIDDLE AND JUNIOR HIGH
CORE COLLECTION

TWELFTH EDITION

EDITED BY

JULIE CORSARO

KENDAL SPIRES

AND

GABRIELA TOTH

H. W. Wilson
A Division of EBSCO Information Service, Inc.
Ipswich, Massachusetts
2015
GREY HOUSE PUBLISHING

Printed in the United States of America

ISBN 978-1-61925-706-1

Abridged Dewey Decimal Classification and Relative Index, Edition 15 is © 2004-2012 OCLC Online Computer Library Center, Inc. Used with Permission. DDC, Dewey, Dewey Decimal Classification, and WebDewey are registered trademarks of OCLC.

Middle and Junior High Core Collection, 2015, published by Grey House Publishing, Inc., Amenia, NY, under exclusive license from EBSCO Information Services, Inc.

A catalog record for this title is available from the Library of Congress.

PRINTED IN CANADA

TABLE OF CONTENTS

PREFACE

MIDDLE AND JUNIOR HIGH CORE COLLECTION is a selective list of books recommended for young people in grades five through nine, together with professional aids for librarians and library media specialists. This list is available in full as an EBSCO*host*, updated weekly. Printed versions are published approximately every two years and contain *Most Highly Recommended* and *Core Collection* books, the top recommended titles in the database. Additional metadata for these titles, plus all of the *Supplementary* and *Archival Materials* levels, appear only in the database available via EBSCO. Go to www.ebscohost.com/public/core-collections for more information or for a trial.

What's New in this Edition?

This edition features library science titles specifically addressing children's librarianship in public and school libraries, collection development for the age group, or related issues. To find books on library services for adults and the general public, please refer to the Nonfiction Core Collection. EBSCO invites feedback from Core Collections customers at corecollections@ebsco.com.

This edition includes more than 11,000 book titles, over 1,000 more than the 11th edition.

History

JUNIOR HIGH SCHOOL LIBRARY CATALOG, first published in 1965, was developed to address the unique needs of younger adolescents. It developed from the STANDARD CATALOG FOR HIGH SCHOOL LIBRARIES, which was subsequently modified in scope and renamed SENIOR HIGH SCHOOL LIBRARY CATALOG. With the seventh edition in 1995, the title of the Catalog was changed from JUNIOR HIGH SCHOOL LIBRARY CATALOG to MIDDLE AND JUNIOR HIGH SCHOOL CATALOG to reflect the prevalence of middle school programs and the extension of coverage to grades five and six. With the ninth edition in 2009, the title was changed to MIDDLE AND JUNIOR HIGH CORE COLLECTION to emphasize the function of the database in establishing and maintaining the solid core of a library, which can be expanded in many ways, according to the library's individual needs. The 11th edition contained broad revisions in the areas of computers, math, and the sciences. In addition, it offered an expanded list of works for librarians and media specialists including bibliographies and other resources for the selection and evaluation of materials for the age range.

Scope

All books listed are published in the United States, or published in Canada or the United Kingdom and distributed in the United States.

The Core Collection excludes the following: non-English-language materials, with the exception of bilingual materials, dictionaries, and similar items; works of adult fiction other than books originally written for adults but read by young people or books widely used in the curriculum; textbooks; and books about individual computer programs or versions of programs, and other topics that quickly become outdated. This volume includes a generous selection of graphic novels, even though a more comprehensive collection of recommended graphic novels can be found in GRAPHIC NOVELS CORE COLLECTION on EBSCO*host*. This collection also excludes most works widely known as "classic literature." This was done as an effort to both save space and to concentrate on recommending titles that are perhaps less well known. Additionally, extensive conversations with high school librarians indicated that additions of classics to the collection were primarily based on local curricula, not on recommendations from the Core Collection. While some classics remain in the collection, the removed titles can still be found on EBSCO*host*.

Preparation

Books included in this edition were selected by experienced librarians representing public library systems and academic libraries across the United States who also act as a committee of advisors on library policy and trends. The names of participating librarians and their affiliations are listed in the Acknowledgments.

Organization

The Core Collection is organized into two parts: the Classified Collection; and an Author, Title, and Subject Index.

Part 1. Classified Collection. This is arranged according to the Dewey Decimal Classification. Within classes, arrangement is by main entry, with complete bibliographical and cataloging information given for each book. The classified arrangement, along with the descriptive and critical annotations, provides a useful guide to book selection. Entries include such information as price and ISBN to facilitate acquisitions.

Part 2. Author, Title, and Subject Index. This is a comprehensive key to the Classified List with entries for authors, titles, and subjects.

ACKNOWLEDGMENTS

H. W. Wilson and EBSCO Information Services express special gratitude to the following librarians who both advised the company in editorial matters and assisted in the selection and weeding of titles for this Core Collection:

Advisory Board

Betty Carter
Library Consultant
Coppell, Texas

Julie Corsaro
Library Consultant
Williamsburg, VA

Gail de Vos
SLIS University of Alberta
Edmonton, Alberta, Canada

Crystal Faris
Kansas City Public Library
Kansas City, Missouri

Laura Harrington
North Andover High School
North Andover, Massachusetts

Pam Spencer Holley
Library Consultant
Hallwood, Virginia

Joquetta Johnson
Randallstown High School
Randallstown, Maryland

John Peters
Children's Literature Specialist
Bronx, New York

Linda Ward-Callaghan
Joliet Public Library
Joliet, Illinois

The editors would like to thank EBSCO librarian Christi Showman Farrar whose help was instrumental in the creation of this collection.

DIRECTIONS FOR USE OF THE
CORE COLLECTION

USES OF THE COLLECTION

MIDDLE AND JUNIOR HIGH CORE COLLECTION is designed to serve a number of purposes:

As an aid in purchasing. The Core Collection is designed to assist in the selection and ordering of titles. Annotations are provided for each title along with information concerning the publisher, ISBN, price, and availability. Since Part 1, Classified Collection, is arranged according to the Dewey Decimal Classification, the Core Collection may be used to identify parts of the library collection that should be updated or strengthened. In evaluating the suitability of a work each library will want to consider the special character of the school and community it serves.

As an aid to the reader's advisor. The work of the reader's advisor is furthered by the information about sequels and companion volumes and the descriptive and critical annotations in the Classified Collection, and by the subject access in the Index.

As an aid in verification of information. For this purpose full bibliographical data are provided in the Classified Collection. Entries also include recommended subject headings based upon *Sears List of Subject Headings* and a suggested classification derived from the *Abridged Dewey Decimal Classification and Relative Index*. Notes describe editions available, awards, publication history, and other titles in the series.

As an aid in curriculum support. The classified approach, subject indexing, and annotations are helpful in identifying materials appropriate for classroom use.

As an aid in collection maintenance. Information about titles available on a subject facilitates decisions to rebind, replace, or discard items. If a book has been deleted from the Core Collection in this edition because it is no longer in print, that deletion is not intended as a sign that the book is no longer valuable or that it should necessarily be weeded from the collection.

As an instructional aid. The Core Collection is useful in courses that deal with literature and book selection for young people.

ORGANIZATION

The Core Collection consists of two parts: a Classified Collection, and an Author, Title, and Subject Index.

Part 1. Classified Collection

The Classified Collection is arranged with nonfiction books first, classified according to the Dewey Decimal Classification in numerical order from 000 to 999. Individual biographies are classed at 92 and precede the 920s (collective biography). Fiction books (Fic) follow the nonfiction. Short story collections (S C) follow fiction. The information supplied for each book includes bibliographic description, suggested subject headings, an annotation, and frequently, an evaluation from a quote source.

An Outline of Classification, which serves as a table of contents for the Classified Collection, is reproduced below. It should be noted that many topics can be classified in more than one discipline. If a particular title is not found where it might be expected, the Index should be consulted to determine if it is classified elsewhere.

Within classes, works are arranged alphabetically under main entry, usually the author. Works of individual biography are arranged alphabetically under the biography's subject.

Each listing consists of a full bibliographical description. Prices, which are always subject to change, have been obtained from the publisher, when available, and are as current as possible. Entries include recommended subject headings derived from the *Sears List of Subject Headings,* a suggested classification number from the *Abridged Dewey Decimal Classification and Relative Index,* a brief description of the contents, and, whenever possible, an evaluation from a quoted source. The following is an example of a typical entry and a description of its components:

★**Gourley, Catherine, 1950-**
Flappers and the new American woman; perceptions of women from 1918 through the 1920s. Twenty-first Century Books 2008 144p il (Images and issues of women in the twentieth century) lib bdg $38.60
Grades 7 8 9 10 **305.4**
1. Women—United States—History 2. United States—History—1919-1933
ISBN 978-0-8225-6060-9; 0-8225-6060-7
LC 2001-8530

This describes images of women in the United States from 1918- through the 1920s.
"The sparkling and engaging [text is] generously expanded by numerous, well-placed black-and-white photographs and period reproductions. ...Great for research or browsing." SLJ
Includes bibliographical references

The star at the start of the entry indicates this is a "most highly recommended" title. The name of the author, Catherine Gourley, is given in conformity with *Anglo-American Cataloguing Rules, 2nd edition,* 2002 revision. The title of the book is *Flappers and the new American woman; perceptions of women from 1918 through the 1920s.* The book was published by Twenty-first Century Books in 2008.

The book has 144 pages and contains illustrations. It is published in the "Images and issues of women in the twentieth century" series, in a library binding, and sells for $38.60. (Prices given were current when the Collection went to press.) The book is recommended for any of the following grade levels: 7 8 9 10.

At the end of the last line of type in the body entry is the figure 305.4 in bold face type. This is the classification number derived from the fifteenth edition of the *Abridged Dewey Decimal Classification.* The number 305.4 is the classification number for "Women".

The numbered terms "1. Women—United States—History" and "2. United States—History—1919-1933" are recommended subject headings for this book based on *Sears List of Subject Headings.*

The ISBN (International Standard Book Number) is included to facilitate ordering. The Library of Congress control number is provided when available.

Following are three notes supplying additional information about the book. The first is a description of the book's content. The second is a critical note from *School Library Journal*. Such annotations are useful in evaluating books for selection and in determining which of several books on the same subject is best suited for the individual reader. The final note describes special features, in this case a bibliography. Notes are also made to describe sequels and companion volumes, editions available, awards, and publication history.

Part 2. Author, Title, and Subject Index

The Index is a single alphabetical list of all the books entered in the Core Collection. Each book is entered under author; title (if distinctive); and subject. The classification number, displayed in boldface type, is the key to the location of the main entry for the book in the Classified Collection.

Appropriate added entries are made for joint authors and editors. "See" references are made from forms of names or subjects that are not used as headings. "See also" references are made to related or more specific headings.

The following are examples of Index entries for the book cited above:

Author	**Gourley, Catherine, 1950-**	
	Flappers and the new American woman	**305.4**
Title	**Flappers** and the new American woman. Gourley, C.	**305.4**
Subject	**Women—United States—History**	
	Gourley, C. Flappers and the new American woman	
		305.4

Standards Used

Anglo-American Cataloguing Rules, 2nd ed., 2002 revision, 2005 update. Chicago: American Library Association, 2005.

Dewey, Melvil. *Abridged Dewey Decimal Classification and Relative Index.* 15th ed. Edited by Joan S. Mitchell, et al. Dublin, Ohio: OCLC, 2012.

Bristow, Barbara and Christi Showman Farrar, eds. *Sears List of Subject Headings.* 21st ed. Ipswich, MA: H. W. Wilson, 2014.

OUTLINE OF CLASSIFICATION

Reproduced below is the Second Summary of the Dewey Decimal Classification. * As Part 1 of this Core Collection is arranged according to this classification, the outline will serve as a table of contents for it. Please note, however, that the inclusion of this outline is not to be considered a substitute for consulting the Dewey Decimal Classification itself.

000	**Computer science, knowledge & systems**		**500**	**Science**
010	Bibliographies		510	Mathematics
020	Library & information sciences		520	Astronomy
030	Encyclopedias & books of facts		530	Physics
040	[Unassigned]		540	Chemistry
050	Magazines, journals & serials		550	Earth sciences & geology
060	Associations, organizations & museums		560	Fossils & prehistoric life
070	News media, journalism & publishing		570	Life sciences; biology
080	Quotations		580	Plants (Botany)
090	Manuscripts & rare books		590	Animals (Zoology)
100	**Philosophy**		**600**	**Technology**
110	Metaphysics		610	Medicine & health
120	Epistemology		620	Engineering
130	Parapsychology & occultism		630	Agriculture
140	Philosophical schools of thought		640	Home & family management
150	Psychology		650	Management & public relations
160	Logic		660	Chemical engineering
170	Ethics		670	Manufacturing
180	Ancient, medieval & eastern philosophy		680	Manufacture for specific uses
190	Modern western philosophy		690	Building & construction
200	**Religion**		**700**	**Arts**
210	Philosophy & theory of religion		710	Landscaping & area planning
220	The Bible		720	Architecture
230	Christianity & Christian theology		730	Sculpture, ceramics & metalwork
240	Christian practice & observance		740	Drawing & decorative arts
250	Christian pastoral practice & religious orders		750	Painting
260	Christian organization, social work & worship		760	Graphic arts
270	History of Christianity		770	Photography & computer art
280	Christian denominations		780	Music
290	Other religions		790	Sports, games & entertainment
300	**Social sciences, sociology & anthropology**		**800**	**Literature, rhetoric & criticism**
310	Statistics		810	American literature in English
320	Political science		820	English & Old English literatures
330	Economics		830	German & related literatures
340	Law		840	French & related literatures
350	Public administration & military science		850	Italian, Romanian & related literatures
360	Social problems & social services		860	Spanish & Portuguese literatures
370	Education		870	Latin & Italian literatures
380	Commerce, communications & transportation		880	Classical & modern Greek literatures
390	Customs, etiquette & folklore		890	Other literatures
400	**Language**		**900**	**History**
410	Linguistics		910	Geography & travel
420	English & Old English languages		920	Biography & genealogy
430	German & related languages		930	History of ancient world (to ca. 499)
440	French & related languages		940	History of Europe
450	Italian, Romanian & related languages		950	History of Asia
460	Spanish & Portuguese languages		960	History of Africa
470	Latin & Italic languages		970	History of North America
480	Classical & modern Greek languages		980	History of South America
490	Other languages		990	History of other areas

* Reproduced from Edition 15 of the Abridged Dewey Decimal Classification and Relative Index, published in 2012, by permission of OCLC Online Computer Library Center, Inc., owner of copyright.

MIDDLE AND JUNIOR HIGH CORE COLLECTION
TWELFTH EDITION
CLASSIFIED COLLECTION

000 COMPUTER SCIENCE, KNOWLEDGE & SYSTEMS

001.4 Research; statistical methods

Cefrey, Holly

Researching people, places, and events. Rosen Central 2010 48p il (Digital and information literacy) lib bdg $26.50

Grades: 5 6 7 8   **001.4**

1. Research 2. Report writing 3. Internet research
ISBN 978-1-4358-5317-1 lib bdg; 1-4358-5317-2 lib bdg

LC 2008-46785

Describes researching people, places, and events on the Internet, including using primary and secondary sources, evaluating source material, and avoiding plagiarism

"Colorful photos, diagrams, and sidebars and [a] lively [text creates an] appealing, user-friendly [presentation]. . . . . Students and teachers will find [this title] useful in keeping up-to-date on and utilizing online resources and today's technology in a rapidly changing digital world." SLJ

Includes glossary and bibliographical references

Randolph, Ryan P.

New research techniques; getting the most out of search engine tools. [by] Ryan Randolph. Rosen Central 2011 48p il (Digital and information literacy) lib bdg $27.95; pa $11.75

Grades: 5 6 7 8   **001.4**

1. Internet resources 2. Internet searching 3. Web search engines
ISBN 978-1-4488-1321-6 lib bdg; 1-4488-1321-2 lib bdg; 978-1-4488-2292-8 pa; 1-4488-2292-0 pa

LC 2010016912

Explains new research techniques and tools that are available for online searching. Among the topics covered are browser tools and search engine toolbars, browser add-ons, Web mashups, e-mail and text alerts, RSS feeds and readers, Boolean operators, and refining research results.

"Color illustrations, large fonts, clearly defined subheadings, and easy to read content encourage access to copious information. . . . Teachers and librarians should find this . . . to be a highly versatile teaching tool." Libr Media Connect

Includes glossary and bibliographical references

Worek, Michael

The **Nobel** Prize; the story of Alfred Nobel and the most famous prize in the world. Firefly 2010 79p il $19.95

Grades: 7 8 9 10   **001.4**

1. Chemists 2. Inventors 3. Nobel Prizes 4. Philanthropists 5. Manufacturing executives
ISBN 978-1-55407-711-3; 1-55407-711-7

"Starting with a biography of Alfred Nobel, this current (to 2009) title is thorough, well-written, and interesting. The text is broken down by discipline—science, literature, peace, and economics. The works of each Nobel laureate . . . are explained. Photographs pepper the book, and time lines of awards and an extensive index complete the text. This is a fine effort, especially useful for reports." SLJ

001.9 Controversial knowledge

Allen, Judy

Unexplained. Kingfisher 2006 144p il $19.95

Grades: 5 6 7 8   **001.9**

1. Parapsychology 2. Curiosities and wonders
ISBN 978-0-7534-5950-8; 0-7534-5950-7

This addresses such topics as ghosts, psychic phenomena, superstitions, mysterious natural phenomena, alleged monsters, disappearances, secrets and mysteries of ancient history, and possible extraterrestrials.

"A seamless combination of absorbing fact-filled text and stunning visuals in an investigation of mysteries that continue to baffle, tantalize, and spark endless debate." SLJ

Includes glossary

Ape-men; Kelly Wand, book editor. Greenhaven Press/Thomson/Gale 2006 174p (Fact or fiction?) $29.95

Grades: 6 7 8 9   **001.9**

1. Yeti 2. Monsters 3. Sasquatch
ISBN 0-7377-1892-7; 978-0-7377-1892-8

LC 2005046293

"Five essays offer proof of the existence of large apelike creatures around the world, while another five refute it. In an epilogue, readers are guided through the process of analyzing the arguments critically. Materials for further research include a fairly good selection of monographs, periodical articles, and three annotated Web sites." SLJ

Includes bibliographical references

Barton, Chris

Can I see your I.D.? true stories of false identities. illustrated by Paul Hoppe. Dial Books for Young Readers 2011 121p il $16.99

Grades: 6 7 8 9   **001.9**

1. Identity (Psychology) 2. Impostors and imposture 3. Impersonation

ISBN 978-0-8037-3310-7; 0-8037-3310-0

LC 2010-11878

"In 10 impeccably crafted profiles, Barton . . . shares the stories of individuals—many just teenagers—who adopted false identities for amusement, profit, or survival. . . . Barton reveals the motivations behind and the consequences of each deception. The use of second-person narration is very effective, allowing readers to assume the identities of each individual. Barton's prose captures the daring, ingenuity, and quick thinking required of each imposter. . . . Hoppe contributes dynamic comic book style panel art." Publ Wkly

Includes bibliographical references

Gee, Joshua

Encyclopedia horrifica; the terrifying truth! about vampires, ghosts, monsters, and more. Scholastic Inc. 2007 129p il $14.99

Grades: 4 5 6 7   **001.9**

1. Ghosts 2. Monsters 3. Vampires

ISBN 978-0-439-92255-5; 0-439-92255-0

LC 2007061733

A visual reference contains true stories of such creatures as vampires, aliens, werewolves, and ghosts, accompanied by photographic evidence, eyewitness accounts, and original interviews.

"Each topic is replete with color illustrations and photos and is accompanied by a light, readable text that tries to separate fact from fiction." Voice Youth Advocates

Includes bibliographical references

Halls, Kelly Milner

★ **Tales** of the cryptids; mysterious creatures that may or may not exist. by Kelly Milner Halls, Rick Spears, Roxyanne Young; [illustrated by Rick Spears] Darby Creek 2006 72p il map $18.95

Grades: 4 5 6 7   **001.9**

1. Monsters

ISBN 1-58196-049-2

This considers the existance of creatures such as Bigfoot, the Loch Ness Monster, Marozi of Kenya, the Orangpendek of Sumatra, and the Thylacine of Tasmania.

"The conversational text makes for fun reading, and a plethora of pictures . . . will prove enticing." SLJ

Karst, Ken

Area 51; Ken Karst. Creative Education 2014 48 p. color illustrations, map (Enduring mysteries) (hardcover : alk. paper) $35.65

Grades: 5 6 7 8   **001.9**

1. Air bases 2. Unidentified flying objects 3. Area 51 (Nev.) 4. Air bases -- Nevada 5. Research aircraft -- United States 6. Unidentified flying objects -- Sightings

and encounters -- Nevada

ISBN 1608183998; 9781608183999

LC 2013036073

This book, by Ken Karst, part of the "Enduring Mysteries" series, "takes an investigative approach to the curious phenomena and mysterious circumstances surrounding Area 51, from conspiracy theories to claims of extraterrestrial sightings to hard facts." (Publisher's note)

"With only the barest dashes of skepticism, these handsomely produced surveys present budding cryptozoologists and conspiracy theorists with rich arrays of historical anecdotes and encounters, supposed evidence, "scientific" explanations of varying plausibility, and tantalizing speculations...Karst goes beyond standard issue recaps—ensuring, for instance, that readers will come away from Atlantis knowing more than they did about Madame Blavatsky, as well as Mu and Lemuria, and also expanding his topics with references to, at best, tangentially relevant mysteries such as the fate of Amelia Earhart in Loch Ness Monster." SLJ

Includes bibliographical references and index

Other titles in the series are:

Atlantis (2014)

Bigfoot (2014)

Loch Ness Monster (2014)

Bermuda Triangle (2015)

Matthews, Rupert

Strange animals. QEB Pub. 2011 30p il (Unexplained) lib bdg $28.50

Grades: 4 5 6 7   **001.9**

1. Monsters

ISBN 978-1-59566-856-1; 1-59566-856-X

LC 2010017915

This discusses the possible existance of cryptids such as Bigfoot, the Loch Ness monster, the Bunyip, sea monsters, the Orang Pendek, and the Marozi.

"This well-written and thoughtfully designed [book] features [an] engrossing [topic]. . . . Though the pages are profusely illustrated with large, well-reproduced photographs and drawings, the layout is not cluttered. This [book] just might inspire kids to seek out more in-depth materials." SLJ

Includes glossary and bibliographical references

Miller, Ron

Is the end of the world near? from crackpot predictions to scientific scenarios. Twenty-First Century Books 2011 120p il

Grades: 6 7 8 9 10   **001.9**

1. End of the world

ISBN 0-7613-7396-9; 978-0-7613-7396-4

LC 2010051963

"The author devotes most of his presentation to a selective tally of our possible ends, from religious and pseudoscientific predictions (including the supposed Mayan apocalypse 'scheduled' for December 21, 2012) to an array of more feasible pandemics, ecological breakdowns, nuclear conflagrations, supervolcanoes, and other natural catastrophes. . . . He also tucks in references to prominent end-of-days novels and films, and takes his eschatological narrative to the universe-ending 'Big Crunch' before closing on a perversely optimistic note. Capped with generous annotated

2

lists of multimedia resources and illustrated throughout with dramatic photographed or digitally rendered disasters." SLJ

Includes bibliographical references

Stewart, Gail

UFOs; by Gail B. Stewart. ReferencePoint Press 2007 96p il (The mysterious & unknown) lib bdg $24.95

Grades: 6 7 8 9   **001.9**

1. Unidentified flying objects
ISBN 978-1-60152-030-2; 1-60152-030-1

This book "combines numerous stories of [UFO] sightings with historical and scientific details about investigations, providing a balanced view of a controversial topic. . . . Colorful illustrations and appealing design will encourage readers." SLJ

Includes bibliographical references

001.94   Mysteries

Hawkins, John

Atlantis and other lost worlds; by John Hawkins. PowerKids Press 2012 32 p. col. ill. (Mystery hunters) (library) $25.25; (paperback) $10.60

Grades: 4 5 6 7   **001.94**

1. Extinct cities 2. Cities and towns 3. Atlantis (Legendary place)
ISBN 1448864291; 9781448864294; 9781448864416; 9781448864423

LC 2011021292

This book by John Hawkins is part of the Mystery Hunters series and focuses on lost and legendary cities. "The sunken city of Atlantis is a popular myth, and is just one of the many myths of lost worlds featured in this . . . volume. This book explores the history behind these . . . stories. It presents readers with evidence that lost worlds are real and evidence that they are all made up, so that they can gather the information and make up their own minds." (Publisher's note)

004   Computer science; computer programming, programs, data; special computer methods

Flath, Camden

Tomorrow's enterprising scientists; computer software designers and specialists. Mason Crest Publishers 2010 64p il (New careers for the 21st century: finding your role in the global renewal) lib bdg $22.95

Grades: 7 8 9 10   **004**

1. Vocational guidance 2. Computer software industry
ISBN 978-1-4222-1822-8 lib bdg; 1-4222-1822-8 lib bdg

LC 2010019187

"Chapters identify and emphasize specific careers—important strengths, necessary aptitudes and interests, education and training, projected earnings, closely related occupations, type of work environment, and predictions for the future of the field. . . . Color photos have a small role amid the many statistics, figures, graphs and charts that support and supplement the . . . [text]." SLJ

Includes bibliographical references

Lohr, Steve

Digital revolutionaries; the men and women who brought computing to life. Flash Point 2009 165p il pa $11.99

Grades: 5 6 7 8   **004**

1. Computer industry 2. Computers -- History
ISBN 978-1-59643-532-2 pa; 1-59643-532-1 pa

"This text will be a fascinating read for students who are curious about the development of the technology present in every aspect of their lives and the many people behind it. The five chapters are written in a lively, conversational voice. Lohr describes how many independent and creative thinkers helped to develop computers as we know them today. His history includes topics from software programs to animation, from FORTRAN to BASIC, and from Bill Gates to Steve Jobs, bringing technology to life along the way. . . . A positive, upbeat, and enlightening read." SLJ

Includes bibliographical references

004.068   Computer science--management

Hollander, Barbara Gottfried

The next big thing; developing your digital business idea. Barbara Gottfried Hollander. 1st ed. Rosen Pub. 2013 64 p. col. ill. (Digital entrepreneurship in the age of apps, the web, and mobile devices) (library) $31.95; (paperback) $12.95

Grades: 8 9 10 11 12   **004.068**

1. Entrepreneurship 2. Internet industry 3. New products 4. Electronic commerce 5. New business enterprises
ISBN 1448869269; 9781448869268; 9781448869312; 9781448869718

LC 2012003029

This book is part of the Digital Entrepreneurship in the Age of Apps, the Web, and Mobile Devices series and focuses on digital businesses. "These how-to titles lead teens through building a digital business. Each volume uses real-world examples from current Internet companies such as Facebook, Twitter, and Netflix to explain the various steps involved in building a website, blog, app, etc." (School Library Journal)

Includes bibliographical references and index.

004.6   Interfacing and communications

Cornwall, Phyllis

Online etiquette and safety. Cherry Lake Pub. 2010 32p il (Super smart information strategies) lib bdg $27.07

Grades: 3 4 5 6   **004.6**

1. Etiquette 2. Internet -- Social aspects 3. Internet

-- Security measures

ISBN 978-1-60279-956-1 lib bdg; 1-60279-956-3 lib bdg

LC 2010002023

This "teaches valuable lessons on why it's important to be responsible online citizens despite the misleading anonymity of the Web and offers tips on how to deal with cyberbullies and other online dangers." Booklist

Includes bibliographical references

Grayson, Robert

Managing your digital footprint. Rosen Central 2011 48p il (Digital and information literacy) lib bdg $26.50; pa $11.75

Grades: 5 6 7 8　　　　　　　　　　　　**004.6**

1. Internet 2. Etiquette 3. Right of privacy

ISBN 978-1-4488-1319-3 lib bdg; 1-4488-1319-0 lib bdg; 978-1-4488-2290-4 pa; 1-4488-2290-4 pa

LC 2010025746

Though this "title is a broad overview of a sometimes-complex subject, the detail is significant.... Touches of blue enhance the clean design, . . . [This] discusses the permanence of impulsively posted material online, contrasting it with more retro forms of self-expression, such as keeping a paper diary." Booklist

Includes bibliographical references

Mooney, Carla

Online predators. ReferencePoint Press 2011 96p il (Issues in the digital age)

Grades: 7 8 9 10 11 12　　　　　　　　　**004.6**

1. Cyberbullying 2. Computer crimes 3. Child sexual abuse 4. Internet -- Safety measures

ISBN 1-60152-193-6; 978-1-60152-193-4

LC 2011020180

"Packed with frightening cases of online attacks by sexual predators, financial predators, and bullies, this detailed, up-to-date, highly readable guide is a warning to young people—and adults—about Internet-based crime and identity theft. . . . Computer-savvy teens will especially welcome the coverage of emerging careers in cybersecurity and forensics. . . . A clean design with color photos and extensive back matter . . . further add to this title's appeal." Booklist

Includes bibliographical references

Sandler, Corey

Living with the Internet and online dangers. Facts on File 2010 ix, 165p il (Teen's guides) $34.95; pa $14.95

Grades: 6 7 8 9　　　　　　　　　　　　**004.6**

1. Computer security 2. Internet and teenagers 3. Internet -- Security measures

ISBN 978-0-8160-7874-5; 0-8160-7874-2; 978-0-8160-7875-2 pa; 0-8160-7875-0 pa

LC 2009023137

"Sandler acknowledges the importance of the Internet, cell phones, and digital devices for communication but also wants to inform readers about safety and security. Chapters cover social networking, shopping, online job hunting, file-sharing, email scams and Internet fraud, online drugstores, and online meeting and dating. The author also addresses protecting one's identity, viruses, cell phones, IMs and text

messaging, wireless security, and helping friends cope with Internet and online dangers. Written in an informative and respectful manner, this book is sure to be useful for teens' informational reading." SLJ

Includes glossary and bibliographical references

005.3　Programs

Gregory, Josh

Apps; from concept to consumer. by Josh Gregory. Children's Press, an imprint of Scholastic Inc. 2015 64 p. illustrations (color) (library binding : alk. paper) $30

Grades: 6 7 8 9 10　　　　　　　　　　**005.350**

1. Computer applications 2. Mobile computing 3. Application software 4. Application software -- Development -- Vocational guidance

ISBN 0531205398; 053121236X; 9780531205396; 9780531212363

LC 2014030460

With this book, by Josh Gregory, part of the "Calling all innovators: A career for you?" series, "[r]eaders will learn how the first mobile apps were created and find out which apps are making the biggest splash today. They will also see how easy it is to get started creating their own apps and what it takes to score the next big hit on the app stores." (Publisher's note)

"Despite a few flaws, [the titles in this series] are recommended for their in-depth descriptions of the histories of different careers." SLJ

Includes bibliographical references and index

005.8　Data security

Hunter, Nick

Internet safety; Nick Hunter. Heinemann Library 2012 56 p. col. ill.

Grades: 6 7 8 9 10　　　　　　　　　　**005.8**

1. Internet users 2. Internet -- Safety measures 3. Computer crimes -- Prevention

ISBN 9781432948719; 9781432962050

LC 2010046905

"...Discusses types of crime, cyber bullying, phishing, and scams and viruses, ending with ways to protect yourself. Statistics and websites provide information for both individual research and for educators wishing to lead discussion on the topic... Good choices for student research and debate. "SLJ

Includes bibliographical references (p. 54-55) and index

006.3　Artificial intelligence

Henderson, Harry

Artificial intelligence; mirrors for the mind. Chelsea House 2007 190p il (Milestones in discovery and invention) $35

Grades: 7 8 9 10 11 12   **006.3**
   1. Artificial intelligence
   ISBN 0-8160-5749-4; 978-0-8160-5749-8
                              LC 2006-16639
   This book includes "portraits of the men and women in the vanguard of this innovative field. Subjects include Alan Turing, who made the connection between mathematical reasoning and computer operations; Allen Newell and Herbert Simon, who created a program that could reason like a human being; Pattie Maes, who developed computerized agents to help people with research and shopping; and Ray Kurzweil, who, besides inventing the flatbed scanner and a reading machine for the blind, has explored relationships between people and computers that may exceed human intelligence." Publisher's note
   Includes glossary and bibliographical references

Pearce, Q. L.
   Artificial intelligence. Lucent Books 2011 112p il (Technology 360) $33.45
Grades: 7 8 9 10   **006.3**
   1. Robots 2. Artificial intelligence
   ISBN 978-1-4205-0384-5; 1-4205-0384-7
                              LC 2011006362
   This offers "clean design with clear explanations of sometimes-complicated scientific subjects. . . . Artificial Intelligence covers the history of how people have tried to teach machines to think and move, concluding with a chapter on the ethics surrounding AI. . . . A strong [title] for report writers and students with a serious interest in technology and its inventions." Booklist
   Includes glossary and bibliographical references

006.7   Multimedia systems

Fontichiaro, Kristin
   Podcasting 101. Cherry Lake Pub. 2010 32p il (Super smart information strategies) lib bdg $27.07
Grades: 3 4 5 6   **006.7**
   1. Podcasting
   ISBN 978-1-60279-953-0 lib bdg; 1-60279-953-9 lib bdg
                              LC 2010004533
   "A knockout resource for media-fair projects, Podcasting 101 doles out page after page of useful information, from the equipment required to content ideas for those who might need a creative spark to tips for structuring and adding effects to a successful podcast." Booklist
   Includes bibliographical references

Gilbert, Sara D., 1943-
   The **story** of Twitter; Sara Gilbert. Creative Education 2014 46 p. (Built for success) (hardcover : alk. paper) $37.10
Grades: 6 7 8 9   **006.7**
   1. Twitter (Web site) 2. Twitter 3. Twitter (Firm) 4. Microblogs -- United States
   ISBN 160818398X; 9781608183982
                              LC 2013029614
   This book, by Sara Gilbert, presents a "look at the origins, leaders, and innovations of Twitter, the online social

networking and microblogging service founded in 2006, which has hundred of millions of users worldwide." (Publisher's note)
   "This series that profiles well-known businesses (previous books include The Story of Google, The Story of Microsoft, The Story of Amazon, and The Story of Nike, which SLJ called "interesting and well written") continues with some more winners. Though books on corporate America sound like a hard sell, the large, attractive photos and beautiful design will pull in readers, and these companies—focusing on music, movies, and social media—have a fairly high "cool" quotient. Well written and well organized, the text flows smoothly, providing comprehensive coverage." SLJ
   Includes bibliographical references and index
   Other titles in this series include:
   The Story of Amazon.com (2013)
   The Story of Apple (2012)
   The Story of CNN (2013)
   The Story of Coca-Cola (2009)
   The Story of Disney (2009)
   The Story of eBay (2012)
   The Story of Facebook (2012)
   The Story of Ford (2009)
   The Story of Google (2009)
   The Story of McDonald's (2009)
   The Story of Microsoft (2009)
   The Story of MTV (2015)
   The Story of Nike (2009)
   The Story of Starbucks (2008)
   The Story of Target (2015)
   The Story of the NFL (2012)
   The Story of Wal-Mart (2011)
   The Story of Pixar (2015)

Kling, Andrew A.
   Web 2.0. Lucent Books 2011 128p il map (Technology 360) $33.45
Grades: 7 8 9 10   **006.7**
   1. Internet 2. Online social networks
   ISBN 978-1-4205-0171-1; 1-4205-0171-2
                              LC 2010028893
   This offers "clean design with clear explanations of sometimes-complicated scientific subjects. . . . The history of the Internet and how people interact with it is the focus in Web 2.0, which discusses groundbreaking sites from Napster to Facebook, with a concluding chapter that tries to foresee the future. . . . A strong [title] for report writers and students with a serious interest in technology and its inventions." Booklist
   Includes bibliographical references

Nakaya, Andrea C.
   Thinking critically; by Andrea C. Nakaya. ReferencePoint Press, Inc. 2013 80 p. (hardback) $28.95
Grades: 7 8 9 10 11 12   **006.7**
   1. Social media 2. Social networking 3. Internet and teenagers 4. Online social networks 5. Internet -- Safety measures
   ISBN 1601525885; 9781601525888
                              LC 2012043628

This book, by Andrea C. Nakaya, is a "well-researched examination" of social networking. "The first page of each chapter, 'The Debate at a Glance,' offers bullet points that summarize common arguments pro and con. The design is spare, with understated graphics; bright, compelling photos; and text boxes that pull out interesting quotes. Easy-to-read graphs and charts add another layer of visual information." (School Library Journal)

"Diagrams and sidebars support these well-organized models for classroom discourse. First chapters introduce the debates surrounding . . . social networking. . . subsequent chapters present pro and con responses to four key questions. Despite lots of graphic elements, the text-heavy pages may be off-putting. Two pages of facts and a list of related organizations are appended." Horn Book.

Includes bibliographical references and index
Social networking

Rowell, Rebecca
YouTube; the company and its founders. ABDO Pub. Co. 2011 112p il (Technology pioneers) lib bdg $32.44

Grades: 5 6 7 8   **006.7**
1. Internet 2. YouTube, Inc.
ISBN 978-1-61714-813-2 lib bdg; 1-61714-813-X lib bdg; 978-1-61758-971-3 e-book
LC 2010043379

This is an introduction to YouTube and its founders.

"Written in a clear, linear fashion, this series offers vivid, well-researched details about the development of technological advancements considered essential in today's society. . . . Readers who are interested in technology and inventions will be thoroughly engrossed." SLJ

Includes glossary and bibliographical references

Selfridge, Benjamin
A **teen's** guide to creating Web pages and blogs; [by] Benjamin Selfridge, Peter Selfridge, and Jennifer Osburn. Prufrock Press 2009 148p il pa $16.95; OP

Grades: 5 6 7 8 9 10   **006.7**
1. Weblogs 2. Internet and teenagers 3. Web sites -- Design
ISBN 978-1-59363-345-5; 1-59363-345-9
LC 2008-40044

First published 2004 by Zephyr Press with title: Kid's guide to creating Web pages for home and school

"This guide begins with basic step-by-step information about HTML, fonts, images, lists, and tables. . . . The book's last half introduces more advanced techniques, such as JavaScript, functions, loops, and applications like Flash and Instant Messenger. . . . Illustrated, with references and a glossary, this attractive paperback has lots of practical content." Voice Youth Advocates

Includes glossary and bibliographical references

Truesdell, Ann
Wonderful wikis; by Ann Truesdell. Cherry Lake Publishing 2013 32 p. (Information explorer) (library) $28.50; (paperback) $14.21

Grades: 4 5 6 7   **006.7**
1. Wikis (Computer science)
ISBN 1610804805; 9781610804806; 9781610806541
LC 2012001758

This juvenile nonfiction book, by Ann Truesdell, as part of the publisher's "Explorer Library" series, presents a profile and guidelines for school children to make use of wikis online for educational purposes. Topics addressed include definitions of what a wiki is, how to contribute to them properly, and what ways they are most useful.

Includes bibliographical references and index

011.6   General bibliographies and catalogs of works for young people and people with disabilities; for specific types of libraries

Barnhouse, Rebecca
The **Middle** Ages in literature for youth; a guide and resource book. Scarecrow Press 2004 183p (Literature for youth) pa $30

Grades: Adult Professional   **011.6**
1. Reference books 2. Middle Ages -- Bibliography 3. Children's literature -- Bibliography 4. Young adult literature -- Bibliography
ISBN 0-8108-4916-X
LC 2004-74

"Searchable by subject, title, location, or author, this is a comprehensive guide to books about the period. Each chapter presents a topic, such as Vikings or Crusades, and then gives annotated lists of both fiction and nonfiction titles. Added features include classroom activities such as creative-writing prompts, medieval measurements using tools from the time period, and math involving computations using Roman numerals. . . . Professional sources for educators round out this useful bibliography." SLJ

Gillespie, John Thomas, 1928-
★ The **children's** and young adult literature handbook; a research and reference guide. Libraries Unlimited 2005 393p (Children's and young adult literature reference series) $55

Grades: Adult Professional   **011.6**
1. Reference books 2. Children's literature -- Bibliography 3. Young adult literature -- Bibliography 4. Children's literature -- History and criticism 5. Young adult literature -- History and criticism
ISBN 1-56308-949-1

This is "a selection guide and collection development aid for librarians, as well as a navigation tool for researchers. Describing and evaluating more than 1,000 publications, the book covers . . . general reference, bibliographies, and biographies to review sources, literary awards, professional organizations, and special library collections. Internet and other nonprint media are included, as are major English-language resources from Britain, Canada, Australia, and South Africa." Publisher's note

"This reference should meet the needs of librarians, teachers, and scholars." Choice

Classic teenplots; a booktalk guide to use with readers ages 12-18. [by] John T. Gillespie and Corinne J. Naden. Libraries Unlimited 2006 348p (Children's and young adult literature reference series) $55

Grades: Adult Professional **011.6**

1. Book talks 2. Young adult literature 3. Teenagers -- Books and reading

ISBN 1-59158-312-8

LC 2006017624

"Prefaced by a brief guide to booktalking are one hundred entries for in-print classic titles for teens, taken from the out-of-print Juniorplots and Seniorplots series. Additional titles have been added to round out the eight theme/genre-based sections, which include topics such as Teenage Life and Concerns, Historical Fiction and Other Lands, and Important Nonfiction. . . . This excellent resource offers from sixteen to twenty titles per section." Voice Youth Advocates

Includes bibliographical references

Matthew, Kathryn I.

Neal-Schuman guide to recommended children's books and media for use with every elementary subject; by Kathryn I. Matthew and Joy L. Lowe. 2nd ed; Neal-Schuman Publishers 2010 356p pa $75

Grades: Adult Professional **011.6**

1. Best books 2. Books and reading 3. Audiovisual materials -- Catalogs 4. Children's literature -- Bibliography

ISBN 978-1-55570-688-3; 1-55570-688-6

LC 2010014082

First published 2002

"Listing more than 1,000 books, videos, software, CDs, and Web sites up through early 2010, this book offers elementary (and middle-school) librarians a wonderful collection-development and collaboration tool. Each chapter covers one elementary subject area. . . . The chapters are broken down into narrower topics; each section covers the book and media choices plus ideas for exploring many of the resources listed. Each chapter begins with relevant national standards and ends with teacher resources and references including books, professional organizations, and Web sites. The annotated listings are arranged by grade level from pre–K up through middle school and include full bibliographic information." Booklist

Includes bibliographical references

Meese, Ruth Lyn

Family matters; adoption and foster care in children's literature. Libraries Unlimited 2010 147p pa $35

Grades: Adult Professional **011.6**

1. Adoption -- Bibliography 2. Foster home care -- Bibliography 3. Children's literature -- Bibliography

ISBN 978-1-59158-782-8 pa; 1-59158-782-4 pa

LC 2009040750

"Meese's goal is to help adults, particularly educators, select high-quality children's books about adoption and foster care and to raise awareness about the unique issues that adoptees often face. . . . Charts, Venn diagrams, and extensive annotations supplement the annotated list of books

for children in kindergarten through grade eight. Meese explains her rationale for choosing these books so that readers have the tools to evaluate other selections." SLJ

Includes bibliographical references

Nieuwenhuizen, Agnes

Right book, right time; 500 great books for teenagers. Allen & Unwin 2008 355p il pa $19.95

Grades: 7 8 9 10 11 12 Adult Professional **011.6**

1. Reference books 2. Teenagers -- Books and reading 3. Young adult literature -- Bibliography

ISBN 978-174114-883-1; 174114-883-9

"This Australian reader's guide offers detailed annotations of 200 recent young adult and adult books divided into twelve thematic sections ranging from 'Actions, Adventure & Crime' to 'When You Want to Laugh.' . . . Titles from Australia intermingle with books from the UK and the U.S. . . . With its open format and direct address to the reader, this will be a useful reference for those YAs looking to expand their reading horizons, but enterprising YA librarians will also find this a useful new dimension for expanding or promoting a collection. Interspersed with the annotations are essays championing a variety of literatures ranging from graphic novels to chick-lit." Bull Cent Child Books

Includes bibliographical references

Reid, Rob

Reid's read-alouds; selections for children and teens. American Library Association 2009 xiii, 121p pa $45

Grades: Adult Professional **011.6**

1. Books and reading 2. Children's literature -- Bibliography 3. Young adult literature -- Bibliography

ISBN 978-0-8389-0980-5 pa; 0-8389-0980-9 pa

LC 2008045376

"Reid has collected 200 titles published between 2000 and 2008 that have both readability and general kid appeal. The titles are organized alphabetically by author, and the book includes subject and age-level indexes. Each selection has a cursory summary, grade-level range, and a suggestion for a 10-minute read-aloud, which either provides an introduction to the main characters or a glimpse into the story. . . . This last part is what makes the book so useful." SLJ

Includes bibliographical references

Reid's read-alouds 2; modern day classics from C.S. Lewis to Lemony Snicket. American Library Association 2011 160p

Grades: Adult Professional **011.6**

1. Books and reading 2. Children's literature -- Bibliography 3. Young adult literature -- Bibliography

ISBN 0-8389-1072-6; 978-0-8389-1072-6

LC 2010028985

"The very successful first edition of Reid's Read-Alouds (ALA, 2009) profiled children's and young adult books published between the years 2000 and 2008. This companion volume showcases 200 strong titles that were published from 1950 to 1999. Reid offers a variety of genres and age levels, and a good balance between male and female protagonists. . . . The focus is on books that are great to read to groups of young people. Each entry includes a brief plot summary, suggested grade level, and Reid's signature '10

Minute Selections,' which are engaging episodes from the books that can be read in one sitting. These alone make the book a valuable resource." SLJ

Includes bibliographical references

Safford, Barbara Ripp

Guide to reference materials for school library media centers; 6th ed; Libraries Unlimited 2010 236p $60

Grades: Adult Professional   **011.6**
1. Instructional materials centers 2. School libraries -- Catalogs 3. Reference books -- Bibliography
ISBN 978-1-59158-277-9; 1-59158-277-6

LC 2009-51190

First edition by Christine Gehrt Wynar published 1973 with title: Guide to reference books for school media centers

"This volume has been updated to include web-based reference offerings as well as listings of older sources, provided that their content is still valid. . . . This title profiles resources recommended for use by school librarians for collection management, readers' advisory, teaching, general reference materials, the social sciences and humanities, and science and technology. This volume is an excellent starting point for new school librarians, as well as for those who are building a library from scratch." SLJ

Includes bibliographical references

Schon, Isabel

Recommended books in Spanish for children and young adults, 2004-2008. Scarecrow Press 2009 414p $55

Grades: Adult Professional   **011.6**
1. Reference books 2. Spanish literature -- Bibliography 3. Children's literature -- Bibliography 4. Young adult literature -- Bibliography 5. Latin American literature -- Bibliography
ISBN 978-0-8108-6386-6; 0-8108-6386-3

LC 2008-33390

"Schon evaluates 1231 reference books, fiction, and nonfiction. . . . Entries are arranged alphabetically by author and include a grade level for each book. . . . Schon examines and recommends materials based on the quality of the Spanish language, literary appeal, and the versatility of the translators, paying special attention to the effective use of Peninsular Spanish or the Spanish from the Americas. This annotated bibliography will help selectors in public libraries and media centers to develop existing Spanish-language collections." SLJ

Spiegel, Carol

Book by book; an annotated guide to young people's literature with peacemaking and conflict resolution themes. Educators for Social Responsibility 2010 186p pa $35

Grades: Adult Professional   **011.6**
1. Peace -- Bibliography 2. Conflict management -- Bibliography 3. Children's literature -- Bibliography 4. Young adult literature -- Bibliography
ISBN 978-0-942349-93-1 pa; 0-942349-93-8 pa

"More than 900 books for preschool through high school have been organized by title into two sections, picture and chapter books; described; and assigned behavioral headings.

Thematic clusters include making connections, emotional literacy, caring and effective communication, cultural competence and social responsibility, and conflict management and responsible decision making. . . . Useful especially in elementary and middle schools where character education is part of the curriculum without the explicit mandate." SLJ

Welch, Rollie James

A **core** collection for young adults; 2nd ed; Neal-Schuman Publishers 2011 416p (Teens @ the library series) pa $80

Grades: Adult Professional   **011.6**
1. Young adult literature 2. Young adults' libraries 3. Teenagers -- Books and reading 4. Young adult literature -- Bibliography
ISBN 978-1-55570-692-0; 1-55570-692-4

LC 2010-46693

First published 2003 under the authorship of Patrick Jones

Provides information meant to be a practical manual for developing collections that appeal to teens. Includes a guide to more than 100 "Best" lists, tips for maintaining a core collection, and selection tips for major YA genres.

"The book is a wide-reaching resource that introduces literature with appeal to young adults to an audience new to library work with teens." Voice Youth Advocates

Includes bibliographical references

Young Adult Library Services Association

The **official** YALSA awards guidebook; compiled and edited by Tina Frolund for the Young Adult Library Services Association. Neal-Schuman Publishers 2008 171p pa $55

Grades: Adult Professional   **011.6**
1. Reference books 2. Young adults' libraries 3. Teenagers -- Books and reading 4. Young adult literature -- Awards 5. Young adult literature -- Bibliography
ISBN 978-1-55570-629-6; 1-55570-629-0

LC 2008-17584

This "volume offers one-stop shopping for an overview of the Alex, Printz, and Edwards awards. In addition to annotated bibliographies of winners and honor books, the title includes acceptance speeches for the Printz and Edwards awards and award interviews from YALSA starwarts Mary Arnold, Michael Cart, and Betty Carter." Bull Cent Child Books

Includes bibliographical references

016 Bibliographies and catalogs of works on specific subjects

Al-Hazza, Tami Craft

★ **Books** about the Middle East; selecting and using them with children and adolescents. [by] Tami Craft Al-Hazza and Katherine T. Bucher. Linworth Pub. 2008 168p pa $39.95

Grades: Adult Professional   **016**
1. Reference books 2. Middle East -- Bibliography 3. Children's literature -- Bibliography 4. Young adult

literature -- Bibliography
ISBN 978-1-58683-285-8; 1-58683-285-9
LC 2007-40149
"This book examines the body of literature about the diverse groups of people who inhabit the Middle East, and it also explores a variety of ways in which this literature can be used. . . . It fills a huge gap and should not be overlooked. This powerhouse book will be tremendously helpful to media specialists, educators, and public librarians." Voice Youth Advocates

Includes bibliographical references

Crew, Hilary S.

Women engaged in war in literature for youth; a guide to resources for children and young adults. Scarecrow Press 2007 303p (Literature for youth) pa $51

Grades: Adult Professional **016**
1. Reference books 2. War -- Bibliography 3. Women -- Bibliography 4. Children's literature -- Bibliography 5. Young adult literature -- Bibliography
ISBN 978-0-8108-4929-7; 0-8108-4929-1
LC 2006-101112
"Crew's guide to print and online sources documents women's roles in wars over the centuries and throughout the world, divided by time periods. . . . This is a great addition for libraries looking for a way to move Women's Studies beyond the month of March." SLJ

Includes bibliographical references

Fichtelberg, Susan

★ **Encountering** enchantment; a guide to speculative fiction for teens. Libraries Unlimited 2007 328p (Genreflecting advisory series) $48

Grades: Adult Professional **016**
1. Reference books 2. Fantasy fiction -- Bibliography 3. Science fiction -- Bibliography 4. Young adult literature -- Bibliography
ISBN 1-59158-316-0; 978-1-59158-316-5
LC 2006-33739
"This useful guide should be in every YA collection." SLJ
"This guide organizes by genre, subgenre, and theme some 1,400 titles of fantasy, science fiction and paranormal titles, most published within the last decade. Chapters cover such subgenres as epic fantasy, wizardry, romance, and mystery, which are further broken down by subgenres and themes. Annotations offer bibliographic information, brief plot summaries, reading levels, alternative media formats (including large print and Braille), and awards information." Publisher's note

Includes bibliographical references

Garcha, Rajinder

The **world** of Islam in literature for youth; a selective annotated bibliography for K-12. [by] Rajinder Garcha, Patricia Yates Russell. Scarecrow Press 2006 xx, 221p (Literature for youth) pa $35

Grades: Adult Professional **016**
1. Reference books 2. Islam -- Bibliography 3. Children's literature -- Bibliography 4. Young adult

literature -- Bibliography
ISBN 978-0-8108-5488-8; 0-8108-5488-0
LC 2005-26645
"This annotated bibliography has more than 700 selected print and electronic resources. Each numbered entry includes complete bibliographic information, a recommended grade level, and a one-paragraph summary and critique." SLJ
"This highly useful bibliography fills a conspicuous gap in a much-needed cultural area." Voice Youth Advocates

Includes bibliographical references

Hall, Susan

Using picture storybooks to teach literary devices; recommended books for children and young adults. Libraries Unlimited 2007 282p (Using picture books to teach) pa $42

Grades: Adult Professional **016**
1. Literature -- Study and teaching
ISBN 978-1-59158-493-3 pa; 1-59158-493-0 pa
"This fourth volume of the series, . . . gives teachers and librarians the . . . tool to teach literary devices in grades K–12. With this volume, the author has added: colloquialism; counterpoint; solecism; archetype; and others to the list of devices. The entries have been reorganized to include all the information under the book listing itself. Each entry includes an annotation, a listing of curricular tie-ins for the book and the art style used, and a listing and explanation of all the literary devices taught by that title." Publisher's note

Includes bibliographical references

Halsall, Jane

Visual media for teens; creating and using a teen-centered film collection. [by] Jane Halsall and R. William Edminster. Libraries Unlimited 2009 xxii, 158p (Libraries Unlimited professional guides for young adult librarians) pa $40

Grades: Adult Professional **016**
1. Young adults' libraries 2. Libraries and motion pictures 3. Motion pictures -- Catalogs
ISBN 978-1-59158-544-2; 1-59158-544-9
LC 2009-20300
"This is an excellent guide for librarians interested in building a popular film collection to satisfy their teen audiences. It offers professionals an organized look at current films that have young adult appeal and provides analysis of the importance of such a collection." SLJ

Includes filmographies and bibliographical references

Herald, Diana Tixier

Teen genreflecting 3; a guide to reading interests. Libraries Unlimited 2011 xxiv, 377p (Genreflecting advisory series) $48

Grades: Adult Professional **016**
1. Reference books 2. Teenagers -- Books and reading 3. Young adult literature -- Bibliography
ISBN 978-1-59158-729-3; 1-59158-729-3
LC 2010-40791
First published 1997 with title: Teen genreflecting
"The chapters and subchapters provide a brief overview of the topic and are organized by genre, subgenre, or an overall theme. Each entry is annotated and includes a

concise subject list, and some entries include a list of read-alikes. Herald also includes books written for children and those for adults that have teen appeal. . . . Herald suggests using this volume to identify read-alikes, to beef up genre collections, and for library staff to familiarize themselves with the literature. . . . A worthy addition to reference or professional-development collection." SLJ

Includes bibliographical references

Mosley, Shelley

The **suffragists** in literature for youth; the fight for the vote. [by] Shelley Mosley, John Charles. The Scarecrow Press, Inc. 2006 326p (Literature for youth) pa $45

Grades: Adult Professional   016
1. Reference books   2. Women -- Suffrage -- Bibliography 3. Children's literature -- Bibliography 4. Young adult literature -- Bibliography
ISBN 978-0-8108-5372-0 pa; 0-8108-5372-8 pa
LC 2006-17542

"This book would be a tremendous resource to any library or classroom collection." Voice Youth Advocates

Includes bibliographical references

Rabey, Melissa

Historical fiction for teens; a genre guide. Libraries Unlimited 2011 324p (Genreflecting advisory series) $45

Grades: Adult Professional   016
1. Teenagers -- Books and reading 2. Historical fiction -- Bibliography 3. Young adult literature -- Bibliography 4. Historical fiction
ISBN 978-1-59158-813-9; 1-59158-813-8
LC 2010041101

This "includes more than 300 novels popular with teen readers. Limited to titles written for grades 5 and up, from 1975 to 2010 (with some notable exceptions), the book is divided by regions, time periods, and subgenres. . . . This volume would be especially useful for readers' advisory and for browsing in school and public libraries." Booklist

Includes bibliographical references

Rosen, Philip

Bearing witness; a resource guide to literature, poetry, art, music, and videos by Holocaust victims and survivors. [by] Philip Rosen and Nina Apfelbaum. Greenwood Press 2002 210p $52.95

Grades: Adult Professional   016
1. Reference books   2. Holocaust, 1933-1945 -- Bibliography
ISBN 0-313-31076-9
LC 00-69153

"This volume will be valuable to all who are researching the Holocaust. Its strength lies in the inclusion of materials not often found elsewhere." Booklist

Includes bibliographical references

Thomas, Rebecca L.

Popular series fiction for middle school and teen readers; a reading and selection guide. [by] Rebecca L. Thomas and Catherine Barr. 2nd ed; Libraries Unlimited 2009 710p (Children's and young adult literature reference series) $65

Grades: Adult Professional   016
1. Reference books   2. Children's literature -- Bibliography 3. Young adult literature -- Bibliography
ISBN 978-1-59158-660-9
LC 2008-38125

First published 2005

"The authors have identified nearly 2,200 in-print series . . . (including manga, Cine-Manga, and illustrated novels) that will appeal to readers in grades 6-12. Entries are arranged by the series title and contain author, most recent publisher, grade level, notation for availability of accelerated-reader resources, genre, a descriptive three- to five-sentence annotation, and a list of individual titles in the series, arranged by publication date." Booklist

Includes bibliographic references

Wadham, Rachel

This is my life; a guide to realistic fiction for teens. [by] Rachel L. Wadham. Libraries Unlimited 2010 431p (Genreflecting advisory series) $55

Grades: Adult Professional   016
1. Teenagers -- Books and reading 2. Young adult literature -- Bibliography
ISBN 978-1-59158-942-6; 1-59158-942-8
LC 2010-24074

This "surveys contemporary realistic fiction for young adults (middle through high school). Wadham . . . annotates some 1,300 titles published for young adults between 1999 and 2009. Arranged by theme, titles represent real-life issues of broad interest (friendship, love, family, work) as well as specific issues faced in 'problem novels' (pregnancy, homelessness, eating disorders, crime and violence, abuse, drugs and alcohol, death, racism). Annotations include plot summaries, availability in audio, awards, grade-level designations, and subject keywords. . . . This is a useful tool for its intended audience of librarians and instructors seeking issue-related fiction." Booklist

Includes bibliographical references

Walter, Virginia A.

★ **War** & peace; a guide to literature and new media, grades 4-8. [by] Virginia A. Walter. Libraries Unlimited 2007 276p (Children's and young adult literature reference series) pa $40

Grades: Adult Professional   016
1. Reference books 2. War -- Bibliography 3. Peace -- Bibliography 4. Children's literature -- Bibliography 5. Young adult literature -- Bibliography
ISBN 1-59158-271-7 pa; 978-1-59158-271-7 pa
LC 2006030671

"Walter addresses the issue of war—and peace—by examining the information needs of children and how we as professionals can meet them. . . . The bulk of the book is the annotated listing of resources that is divided topically. . . . The well-annotated bibliography includes books, DVDs, Web sites, and CDs, as well as suggestions for using the materials. . . . This book should be a 'must purchase.'" SLJ

Includes bibliographical references

Wee, Patricia Hachten

World War II in literature for youth; a guide and resource book. [by] Patricia Hachten Wee, Robert James Wee. Scarecrow Press 2004 391p (Literature for youth) pa $48

Grades: Adult Professional   **016**
1. Reference books 2. World War, 1939-1945 -- Bibliography 3. Children's literature -- Bibliography 4. Young adult literature -- Bibliography
ISBN 0-8108-5301-9

LC 2004-11087

This "offers more than 3,000 annotated bibliographies for resources on the Second World War. Entries are arranged according to well-thought-out subjects and cover multiple genres (biographies, memoirs, fiction, eyewitness accounts, technical reports, etc.) and formats (monographs, reference sets, periodicals, Web sites, CDs, videos, DVDs). Annotations are succinct but informative and include both positive and negative comments." Booklist

Includes bibliographical references

Wesson, Lindsey Patrick

Green reads; best environmental resources for youth, K-12. Libraries Unlimited 2009 219p (Children's and young adult literature reference series) $50

Grades: Adult Professional   **016**
1. Reference books 2. Children's literature -- Bibliography 3. Young adult literature -- Bibliography 4. Environmental protection -- Bibliography 5. Conservation of natural resources -- Bibliography
ISBN 978-1-59158-834-4; 1-59158-834-0

LC 2009-17353

"This well-organized bibliography offers 450 annotated resources that can be integrated into the classroom to introduce students to environmental concepts. The five chapters focus on global warming, pollution, the Earth's resources, recycling, and conservation. Subchapters follow a uniform organization, including fiction; DVDs and CDs; nonfiction; seminal works, which are labeled 'Recycled Favorites'; and a storytime lesson plan with a variety of activities including songs and tactile learning activities. . . . This reference will delight educators and professionals interested in making students aware of environmental issues and to help youngsters rediscover the outside and natural worlds around them." SLJ

Includes bibliographical references

016.098   Challenged books – United States -- Bibliography

★ **Books** under fire; a hit list of banned and challenged children's books. Pat Scales. ALA Editions, an imprint of the American Library Association 2015 xvi, 208 p.p illustrations (pbk.) $47
Grades: Adult Professional   **016.098**
1. Books -- Censorship 2. Children -- Books and reading -- United States 3. School libraries -- Censorship -- United States 4. Challenged books -- United States -- Bibliography 5. Prohibited books -- United States -- Bibliography 6. Children's literature -- Censorship

-- United States
ISBN 0838911099; 9780838911099

LC 2014023945

This book on banned and challenged books, by Pat R. Scales, "covers both children's and young adult books. The main section profiles 34 books (and series such as 'Harry Potter' and 'Captain Underpants') that have recently been challenged for library or curriculum suitability in the US. . . . Each entry includes a . . . synopsis, quotations from some reviews, details of known challenges, awards/accolades, and a 'Further Reading' section." (Choice: Current Reviews for Academic Libraries)

"Like death and taxes, book challenges are always with us, as noted intellectual-freedom advocate Scales implies in her splendid new book about censorship. . . . Books under Fire contains a veritable arsenal of information . . . this one is clearly indispensable and belongs in every library collection." Booklist

Includes bibliographical references and index

020   Library and information sciences

Fontichiaro, Kristin

Go straight to the source. Cherry Lake Pub. 2010 32p il (Super smart information strategies) lib bdg $27.07

Grades: 3 4 5 6   **020**
1. Research 2. Information resources 3. History -- Sources
ISBN 978-1-60279-640-9 lib bdg; 1-60279-640-8 lib bdg

LC 2009028057

"The appealing layout includes manageable paragraphs, a variety of engaging illustrations, and examples that clearly guide reader through each topic. . . . [This] provides an excellent introduction to primary sources and will create enthusiasm in readers for examining old photographs and ads." SLJ

Includes glossary and bibliographical references

021   Relationships of libraries, archives, information centers

York, Sherry

Booktalking authentic multicultural literature; fiction and history for young readers. Linworth Pub. 2009 112p pa $39.95
Grades: Adult Professional   **021**
1. Book talks 2. Multicultural education 3. Youth -- Books and reading 4. Teenagers -- Books and reading 5. Multiculturalism -- Bibliography 6. Young adult literature -- Bibliography
ISBN 978-1-58683-300-8 pa; 1-58683-300-6 pa

LC 200843798

This title "highlights 101 contemporary books by a variety of U.S. authors. Arranged alphabetically by title, entries include the cultural background of author, illustrator, and translator; their Web sites when available; reading and interest levels; genre; related titles; and the single-paragraph booktalk itself. Over 20 ethnic groups are represented. . . .

Librarians will find this book helpful in expanding their collections to reflect our global society." SLJ

021.2   Relationships with the community

Gillespie, Kellie M.

Teen volunteer services in libraries. VOYA Books 2004 133p il (VOYA guides) pa $26.95

Grades: Adult Professional   **021.2**
1. Libraries 2. Volunteer work
ISBN 0-8108-4837-6

LC 2003-17932

"If you are even considering starting a teen volunteer program, you must read this book. If you already have one in your library, this volume still has much to offer." SLJ
Includes bibliographical references

Squires, Tasha

Library partnerships; making connections between school and public libraries. Information Today, Inc. 2009 203p pa $39.50

Grades: Adult Professional   **021.2**
1. Public libraries 2. School libraries 3. Library cooperation 4. Libraries and schools 5. Libraries and students
ISBN 978-1-57387-362-8; 1-57387-362-4

LC 2008-51647

The author "delves into the many possible avenues for partnership [between school and public libraries], from summer reading programs to book talks to resource sharing and more." Publisher's note

"Squires's confident advice can get beleaguered librarians through . . . difficulties and into mutually productive partnerships." Voice Youth Advocates
Includes bibliographical references

021.7   Promotion of libraries, archives, information centers

Cole, Sonja

Booktalking around the world; great global reads for ages 9-14. Libraries Unlimited 2010 155p pa $35

Grades: Adult Professional   **021.7**
1. Book talks 2. Children's literature 3. Ethnology 4. Geography 5. World history 6. Children's literature -- Bibliography
ISBN 1-59884-613-2 pa; 978-1-59884-613-3 pa; 978-1-59884-614-0 ebook

LC 2010036580

"In this authoritative and highly readable text, [Cole] presents booktalks and reading lists of interest to children. The titles chosen are set in Africa, Asia, Europe, the Americas, Australia, New Zealand and the South Pacific Islands, and the Arctic and Antarctic. Each booktalk contains an enticing description of the book, bibliographic information, interest and reading levels, and awards. Those that have videos available are noted." SLJ
Includes bibliographical references

Keane, Nancy J.

The **tech** -savvy booktalker; a guide for 21st-century educators. [by] Nancy J. Keane and Terence W. Cavanaugh. Libraries Unlimited 2009 162p il pa $35

Grades: Adult Professional   **021.7**
1. Book talks 2. Information technology
ISBN 978-1-59158-637-1 pa; 1-59158-637-2 pa

LC 2008-38988

"Keane offers a way to enhance booktalks with technology and to invite students to explore new ways to talk about books using Web 2.0 tools. The volume is divided into 11 chapters from booktalking concepts to more advanced uses of technology including scanners, digital cameras, computer software, and audio recording. Also included are chapters on software programs such as PowerPoint and iMovie as well as Internet sites such as YouTube and Amazon. The sequence of chapters is designed to allow easy access to information for both novice and experienced computer users. . . . This excellent resource shows ways to use existing technology to augment booktalks and to expand the experience beyond the classroom." SLJ
Includes bibliographical references

Langemack, Chapple

★ The **booktalker's** bible; how to talk about the books you love to any audience. [by] Chapple Langemack. Libraries Unlimited 2003 199p pa $30

Grades: Adult Professional   **021.7**
1. Book talks
ISBN 1-56308-944-0

LC 2003-47543

"This book reminds readers that booktalks . . . are an effective way to present books and can be aimed at all types of settings . . . and age groups. It explains why booktalks are needed, tells how to hold one, and offers tips for a failsafe presentation. Each chapter provides practical examples and closes with additional reading. Appendixes include sample talks and ideas for titles as well as other helpful resources." Booklist
Includes bibliographical references

Mahood, Kristine

Booktalking with teens. Libraries Unlimited 2010 289p (Libraries Unlimited professional guides for young adult librarians) pa $45

Grades: Adult Professional   **021.7**
1. Book talks 2. Teenagers -- Books and reading 3. Young adult literature -- Bibliography
ISBN 978-1-59158-714-9; 1-59158-714-X

LC 2009-49893

This "provides advice about preparing, developing, writing, performing and justifying booktalks. . . . Mahood's expertise and enthusiasm are contagious and challenge all of us who work with youth to be as inspiring while sharing books as she is." Booklist
Includes bibliographical references

Skaggs, Gayle

Look, it's books! marketing your library with displays and promotions. [by] Gayle Skaggs. Mc-Farland & Co. 2008 188p il pa $45

Grades: Adult Professional **021.7**

1. School libraries 2. Books and reading 3. Libraries -- Exhibitions

ISBN 978-0-7864-3132-8 pa; 0-7864-3132-6 pa

LC 2007049517

022 Administration of physical plant

Bolan, Kimberly

Teen spaces; the step-by-step library makeover. 2nd ed; American Library Association 2009 225p il pa $40

Grades: Adult Professional **022**

1. Young adults' libraries

ISBN 978-0-8389-0969-0

LC 2008-26621

First published 2003

"An essential guide for any library planning a teen-space project. . . . After an introductory chapter on teens and their needs within a library, all aspects of teen areas are explained. From the analysis and planning to design and decoration, Bolan outlines the steps to take and the pitfalls to avoid. . . . This book truly is a guide to step-by-step library makeovers." SLJ

Includes bibliographical references

025.04 Information storage and retrieval systems

Barnett, Diana

Putting it all together; teaching the research process. Upstart 2009 74p pa $17.95

Grades: Adult Professional **025.04**

1. Research 2. Information literacy

ISBN 978-1-932146-99-8 pa; 1-932146-99-7 pa

"This well-organized and to-the-point title focuses on practical application of the AASL standards of information literacy for student learning in middle and high schools. The research process is broken down into eight integrated steps, with teacher modeling ideas and printable student exercises for each one. . . . An excellent starting point for teaching research." SLJ

Berger, Pam

★ Choosing Web 2.0 tools for learning and teaching in a digital world; [by] Pam Berger and Sally Trexler; foreword by Joyce Valenza. Libraries Unlimited 2010 221p il map pa $40

Grades: Adult Professional **025.04**

1. Web 2.0 2. Internet in education 3. Internet searching -- Study and teaching 4. Information literacy -- Study and teaching

ISBN 978-1-59158-706-4; 1-59158-706-9

LC 2009-54069

"This guide offers a plethora of ideas for incorporating digital learning into schools in an accessible and reader-friendly manner." Voice Youth Advocates

Includes glossary and bibliographical references

Porterfield, Jason

Conducting basic and advanced searches. Rosen Central 2010 48p il (Digital and information literacy) lib bdg $26.50

Grades: 5 6 7 8 **025.04**

1. Internet resources 2. Internet searching

ISBN 978-1-4358-5316-4 lib bdg; 1-4358-5316-4 lib bdg

LC 2008-46783

Describes how to conduct both basic and advanced searches on the Internet, from the basics of online search engines, boolean search terms, and evaluating the content of search results

"Colorful photos, diagrams, and sidebars and [a] lively [text creates an] appealing, user-friendly [presentation]. . . . Students and teachers will find [this title] useful in keeping up-to-date on and utilizing online resources and today's technology in a rapidly changing digital world." SLJ

Includes glossary and bibliographical references

Rabbat, Suzy

Find your way online. Cherry Lake Pub. 2010 32p il (Super smart information strategies) lib bdg $27.07

Grades: 3 4 5 6 **025.04**

1. Internet searching

ISBN 978-1-60279-639-3 lib bdg; 1-60279-639-4 lib bdg

LC 2009024549

"The appealing layout includes manageable paragraphs, a variety of engaging illustrations, and examples that clearly guide readers through each topic. . . . [This] begins with keywords, narrowing the search, and search engines. Then it shows students how to 'drill down' using subject directories and databases." SLJ

Scheeren, William O.

Technology for the school librarian; theory and practice. Libraries Unlimited 2010 223p il $50

Grades: Adult Professional **025.04**

1. School libraries 2. Digital libraries 3. Information technology 4. Libraries -- Special collections

ISBN 978-1-59158-900-6; 1-59158-900-2

LC 2009-51922

"This title provides information on the practical aspects of technology in the school library as well as the theoretical framework to spark continued learning. Sharing actual case studies as well as practical tips on technology implentation and terminology, this title will be a valuable resource to any school librarian." Libr Media Connect

Includes bibliographical references

Truesdell, Ann

Find the right site. Cherry Lake Pub. 2010 32p il (Super smart information strategies) lib bdg $27.07

Grades: 3 4 5 6   **025.04**
1. Internet searching
ISBN 978-1-60279-638-6 lib bdg; 1-60279-638-6
lib bdg
                                        LC 2009027083
"The appealing layout includes manageable paragraphs,
a variety of engaging illustrations, and examples that clearly
guide readers through each topic. . . . [This] is an excellent
introduction to Web site evaluation and related pitfalls." SLJ
Includes glossary and bibliographical references

025.042   World Wide Web

Bodden, Valerie
   Using the Internet; Valerie Bodden. Creative
Education 2012 48 p. (Research for writing) (library) $35.65
Grades: 8 9 10 11 12   **025.042**
1. Internet resources 2. Internet searching 3. Internet
in education 4. Internet research 5. Computer network
resources 6. Electronic information resource literacy
ISBN 160818207X; 9781608182077
                                        LC 2011040493
This book is part of the Research for Writing series and
focuses on using the Internet for research. The titles within
the series "explain information such as the difference between qualitative and quantitative data, how to evaluate
sources (both in print and online), and the importance of
reference librarians." (School Library Journal)
   Includes bibliographical references and index.

Devine, Jane
   Going beyond Google again; strategies for using and teaching the Invisible Web. Jane Devine and
Francine Egger-Sider. Amer Library Assn"||"Neal-
Schuman, an imprint of the American Library Assn
2013 160 p. (paperback) $72
Grades: Adult Professional   **025.042**
1. Internet in education 2. Internet searching -- Study
and teaching 3. Invisible Web 4. Database searching
5. Internet searching 6. Invisible Web -- Study and
teaching
ISBN 1555708986; 9781555708986
                                        LC 2013010867
This book is a follow-up volume to book "Going Beyond
Google" by Jane Devine and Francine Egger-Sider, "which
placed teaching the Invisible Web into information literacy
programs. [This volume] expands on the teaching foundation laid in the first book and continues to document the Invisible Web's existence and evolution, and suggests ways of
teaching students to use it." (Publisher's note)
   Includes bibliographical references and index

Harris, Frances Jacobson
   ★ **I** found it on the Internet; coming of age online. Frances Jacobson Harris. 2nd ed. American
Library Association 2010 xi, 234 p.p ill. (paperback) $45
Grades: Adult Professional   **025.042**
1. Internet searching 2. Internet in education 3. Internet

and teenagers 4. Young adults' libraries
ISBN 0838910661; 9780838910665
                                        LC 2010013644
This book is an "analysis of the fundamental differences
in how teens . . . and adults . . . view information and communication. . . . The book opens with a description of the
current state of library affairs, wherein information retrieval
has become primarily a computerized event and the collision
between information technology and communication technology has literally forged a new, merged reality that Harris
terms ICT (information community technology)." (School
Library Journal)
This is an "analysis of the fundamental differences in
how teens (for whom the Internet is a primary language) and
adults (who will always be second-language learners) view
information and communication." SLJ
   Includes bibliographical references and index

025.1   Administration

Farmer, Lesley S. Johnson
   Neal -Schuman technology management hand-
book for school library media centers; by Lesley S.
Johnson Farmer and Marc E. McPhee. Neal-Schuman
Publishers 2010 289p il pa $59.95
Grades: Adult Professional   **025.1**
1. School libraries 2. Instructional materials centers
ISBN 978-1-55570-659-3; 1-55570-659-2
                                        LC 2010-9301
"This informative, well-researched text is perfect for
those in the early stages of integrating technology into their
programs. The first chapter begins with an overview of the
impact technology has had on society and defines technology and its role in the library, including past, present, and
possible future changes, as well as managerial roles of the
librarian. Other chapters examine planning for management,
assessing, researching, developing a technology plan, acquiring all types of tech resources, and managing the physical space to accommodate equipment and networking." SLJ
   Includes bibliographical references

The **frugal** librarian; thriving in tough economic
times. edited by Carol Smallwood. American Library Association 2011 277p il
Grades: Adult Professional   **025.1**
1. Library finance 2. Libraries and community 3.
Libraries -- United States
ISBN 0-8389-1075-0; 978-0-8389-1075-7
                                        LC 2010034317
"The thirty-four chapters in Smallwood's collection address a myriad of issues faced by libraries and librarians
when times get tough and money is tight. Written by practicing librarians from academic, public, and school libraries,
the concise essays are easy to read, sometimes personal, and
highly practical. . . . This issue is certainly timely, but in reality, sound management and creative budgeting never van-
ish from the library environment. The table of contents and
descriptive title chapters, coupled with the index, allow for
ease of use for the browser. This inexpensive volume from

ALA will be particularly helpful to public and academic librarians." Voice Youth Advocates

Includes bibliographical references

Fullner, Sheryl Kindle

The **shoestring** library. Linworth Publishing 2010 139p il pa $30

Grades: Adult Professional   025.1
1. Library finance
ISBN 978-1-58683-520-0 pa; 1-58683-520-3 pa
                                               LC 2010-718

"The book is divided into two sections. 'Library Management for Tough Times' has hints for taking advantage of free continuing-education opportunities, using volunteers, networking, and more. 'The Physical Plant' contains suggestions for sprucing up the library at little or no cost (for example: request mismatched or clearance paints from paint stores; then get students to do the painting)." (Booklist)

"Fullner has put together 300 ideas for the cash-strapped school librarian. The book is divided into two sections. 'Library Management for Tough Times' has hints for taking advantage of free continuing-education opportunities, using volunteers, networking, and more. 'The Physical Plant' contains suggestions for sprucing up the library at little or no cost (for example: request mismatched or clearance paints from paint stores; then get students to do the painting)." Booklist

Harvey, Carl A.

★ **No** school library left behind; leadership, school improvement, and the media specialist. [by] Carl A. Harvey II. Linworth Pub. 2008 106p pa $39.95

Grades: Adult Professional   025.1
1. School libraries 2. Instructional materials centers 3. Libraries -- Administration
ISBN 978-1-58683-233-9; 1-58683-233-6
                                               LC 2007-42178

"The content [of this book] constitutes a crash course in school improvement, covering definitions, history, legislation, research, best practices, assessment, profiles of accreditation associations, and most importantly, a strong rationale for why media specialists should lead the way in school improvement efforts. . . . Of major interest to novice and seasoned practitioners, this guide is timely and relevant." Libr Media Connect

Includes bibliographical references

Independent school libraries; perspectives on excellence. Dorcas Hand, editor. Libraries Unlimited 2010 369p il (Libraries Unlimited professional guides in school librarianship) pa $45

Grades: Adult Professional   025.1
1. Private schools 2. School libraries
ISBN 978-1-59158-803-0 pa; 1-59158-803-0 pa; 978-1-59158-812-2 ebook
                                               LC 2010-14567

"Twenty-one essays by prominent independent school librarians both address the current state of independent school librarianship in the United States and offer suggestions for the future. Pieces cover the library's role in the school, statistical comparisons, staffing, advocacy, assessment, technol-

ogy, information commons, collaboration, college preparation, programming, traditions, collection development, minors' rights, budgeting, facilities, accreditation, and disaster planning. . . . Librarians from all schools will find a wealth of information here." Voice Youth Advocates

Includes bibliographical references

Johnson, Doug

★ The **indispensable** librarian; surviving and thriving in school libraries in the information age. Doug Johnson ; illustrations by Brady Johnson. Linworth, an imprint of ABC-CLIO, LLC 2013 xix, 207 p.p illustrations (pbk.) $40

Grades: Adult Professional   025.1
1. Librarians 2. School libraries 3. School librarians -- United States 4. School libraries -- United States -- Administration
ISBN 161069239X; 9781610692397
                                               LC 2012051394

This book, by Doug A. Johnson, "defines and clarifies the role of the school library media specialist in a technologically enhanced school, providing relevant examples and useful advice on a variety of topics; and underscores the importance of strong management skills, especially regarding collaborative planning and communications. The book is written especially for K-12 school librarians, both new and experienced, and is also suitable for pre-service librarians as a textbook." (Publisher's note)

"Johnson offers both theory and practical suggestions on ways to embed [librarians] and [their] jobs into the fabric of a school's culture and curriculum." Lib Med Con

Includes bibliographical references and index

MacDonell, Colleen

★ **Essential** documents for school libraries; 2nd ed.; Linworth 2010 xxiv, 156p il $50

Grades: Adult Professional   025.1
1. Libraries -- Administration
ISBN 978-1-58683-400-5
                                               LC 2010-21241

First published 2004

"Each chapter begins with why the documents are needed, followed by practical advice for writing the documents, and examples of how the documents make an effective change in the library media program." Libr Media Connect [review of 2004 edition]

Includes bibliographical references

Marek, Kate

Organizational storytelling for librarians; using stories for effective leadership. American Library Association 2011 105p pa $50

Grades: Adult Professional   025.1
1. Leadership 2. Storytelling 3. Communication
ISBN 978-0-8389-1079-5; 0-8389-1079-3
                                               LC 2010033485

"This professional offering teaches librarians to use storyteling as an effective leadership tool. . . . Marek has written a clear and thorough introduction to organizational storytelling for librarians. Carefully researched, the book includes notes at the end of each chapter. A comprehensive resource list encourages further study. Controlling own's own story and the story of one's library is a useful skill, especially during times of budgetary turbulence. Individual librarians and library leaders need to be able to convey personal and shared values effectively; this title provides a wealth of information on the topic." Voice Youth Advoactes

Includes bibliographical references

Martin, Barbara Stein

★ **Fundamentals** of school library media management; a how-to-do-it manual. [by] Barbara Stein Martin and Marco Zannier. Neal-Schuman Publishers 2009 172p il (How-to-do-it manuals for librarians) pa $59.95

Grades: Adult Professional   025.1
 1. School libraries 2. Instructional materials centers
 ISBN 978-1-55570-656-2; 1-55570-656-8
                                        LC 2009-7930
This book "contains useful information to help school librarians manage a myriad of tasks and roles. . . . [The authors] have created a book that is helpful, accessible, and full of down-to-earth, concrete examples." Booklist

Includes bibliographical references

McGhee, Marla W.

The **principal's** guide to a powerful library media program; a school library for the 21st century. [by] Marla W. McGhee and Barbara A. Jansen. 2nd ed.; Linworth 2010 xxviii, 149p pa $45

Grades: Adult Professional   025.1
 1. School libraries 2. Instructional materials centers 3. School superintendents and principals
 ISBN 978-1-58683-526-2 pa; 1-58683-526-2 pa; 978-1-58683-527-9 ebook
                                        LC 2010-21243
First published 2005
"With focused and well-organized topics from understanding the research and standards to supporting and sustaining them through collaborative processes, this . . . offers a great deal of concrete information. . . . This book gives administrators a clear idea of what is required in the media center and the role of the librarian as a specialist. . . . An excellent choice for the professional media specialist's or principal's shelf." SLJ

Includes bibliographical references

★ **School** library management; [edited by] Judi Repman and Gail Dickinson. 6th ed.; Linworth Pub. 2007 200p il pa $44.95

Grades: Adult Professional   025.1
 1. School libraries 2. Libraries -- Administration
 ISBN 1-58683-296-4; 978-1-58683-296-4
                                        LC 2006-103468
First published 1987 with title: School library management notebook
"This collection of more than 35 articles written for Library Media Connection from 2003 to 2006 is a virtual treasure trove for library media specialists. . . . The book covers the very practical everyday issues such as scheduling and overdues, and also provides invaluable information on data gathering, facilities planning, professional development, the

role of the library in the world of standardized testing, the technological future of libraries, and much more." SLJ

Includes bibliographical references

Tips and other bright ideas for elementary school libraries. Volume 4 Kate Vande Brake, editor. Linworth 2010 134p Volume 4 pa $35

Grades: Adult Professional   025.1
 1. Elementary school libraries 2. Libraries -- Administration
 ISBN 978-1-58683-416-6 pa; 1-58683-416-9 pa; 978-1-58683-417-3 ebook
                                        LC 2010011049
This title includes "fun and informative management advice from fellow librarians. All of it has been taken from 2006-2009 Library Media Connection magazine. . . . [The introduction] reviews some of the many jobs and responsibilities in a librarian's day. Section one includes management hints to help maximize effectiveness, followed by sections on working with students, teaching skills, . . . working with teachers, technology, reading promotion, public relations, and working with helpers." SLJ

The **whole** library handbook; teen services. edited by Heather Booth and Karen Jensen. ALA Editions, an imprint of the American Library Association 2014 xi, 204 p.p illustrations (alk. paper) $60

Grades: Adult Professional   025.1
 1. Young adults' libraries 2. Teenagers -- Books and reading 3. Libraries and teenagers 4. Young adult services librarians 5. Young adults' libraries -- Administration 6. Young adults' libraries -- United States -- Administration
 ISBN 0838912249; 9780838912249
                                        LC 2014004303
This book, edited by Heather Booth and Karen Jensen, part of the Whole Library Handbook series from the American Library Association, is "specifically geared towards those who serve young adults, gathering . . . articles and commentary from . . . innovative and successful teen services librarians. Sections focusing on practice, theory, and the philosophical underpinnings of the profession are supported by current research and historical perspectives." (Publisher's note)

"This guide to providing teen services in public libraries is quite comprehensive, earning its place as part of The Whole Library Handbook series." VOYA

Includes bibliographical references and index

025.2   Acquisitions and collection development

Baumbach, Donna

★ **Less** is more; a practical guide to weeding school library collections. American Library Association 2006 194p il pa $32

Grades: Adult Professional   025.2
 1. Libraries -- Collection development
 ISBN 978-0-8389-0919-5; 0-8389-0919-1
                                        LC 2006-7490

"This outstanding, easy-to-use guide makes weeding realistic and achievable. . . . This is an indispensable resource for every school library." Booklist

Includes bibliographical references

Brenner, Robin E.

★ **Understanding** manga and anime. Libraries Unlimited 2007 335p il pa $40

Grades: Adult Professional   **025.2**

1. Anime 2. Manga -- Study and teaching 3. Libraries -- Collection development 4. Libraries -- Special collections -- Graphic novels

ISBN 978-1-59158-332-5; 1-59158-332-2

LC 2007-9773

The author "provides thorough explanations of manga and anime vocabulary, potential censorship issues because of cultural disparities, and typical Manga conventions. . . . No professional collection could possibly be complete without this all-inclusive and exceptional work." Voice Youth Advocates

Fagan, Bryan D.

Comic book collections for libraries; [by] Bryan D. Fagan and Jody Condit Fagan; foreword by Stan Sakai; cover art by Derek Steed. Libraries Unlimited 2011 162p pa $45; e-book $45

Grades: Adult Professional   **025.2**

1. Graphic novels -- Bibliography 2. Comic books, strips, etc. -- Bibliography 3. Libraries -- Special collections -- Graphic novels

ISBN 978-1-59884-511-2 pa; 1-59884-511-X pa; 978-1-59884-512-9 e-book

LC 2010052532

"The book begins by introducing the structure of the comic book, industry players, and genres. The bulk of the guide, however, is comprised of actionable advice on such things as creating and maintaining the collection, cataloging for effective access, and promoting the collection, including how to feature comics with other library materials, such as movies and games." Publisher's note

"Armed with this book, librarian should feel confident about knowledgeably creating and maintaining a successful comic-book collection." SLJ

Includes bibliographical references

Fletcher-Spear, Kristin

Library collections for teens: manga and graphic novels; [by] Kristen Fletcher-Spear and Merideth Jenson-Benjamin. Neal-Schuman Publishers 2010 175p pa $55

Grades: Adult Professional   **025.2**

1. Young adults' libraries 2. Graphic novels 3. Young adult literature 4. Comic books, strips, etc. 5. Graphic novels -- Bibliography 6. Graphic novels -- History and criticism 7. Libraries -- Special collections -- Graphic novels

ISBN 1-55570-745-9; 978-1-55570-745-3

LC 2010040895

"This informative, comprehensive handbook is perfect for any librarian, whether new to graphic novels and manga or already familiar with the format. The first chapter explains how to use the book. . . . The chapter then goes on to give a brief history of graphic novels and manga for those interested in gaining a better understanding of their evolution. Other topics featured include the literacy benefits of graphic novels, how to create and maintain a collection and selection policy, and how to develop programming with graphic novels as the focus. The last chapter lists recommended books by genre. . . . This all-inclusive guide will enable librarians to better serve teens through a more diverse collection." SLJ

Includes glossary and bibliographical references

Franklin, Patricia

School library collection development; just the basics. Claire Gatrell Stephens and Patricia Franklin. Libraries Unlimited 2012 x, 71 p.p ill. (Just the basics) (paperback) $35

Grades: Adult Professional   **025.2**

1. School libraries 2. Libraries -- Collection development 3. Collection management (Libraries) -- United States 4. School libraries -- Collection development -- United States

ISBN 1598849433; 9781598849431

LC 2012016990

This book, by Claire Gatrell Stephens and Patricia Franklin, discusses collection development for school librarians. This volume offers a "manual that explains the fundamentals of purchasing, developing, and managing a collection. Containing information useful to anyone from a paraprofessional working under the guidance of a certified school librarian to a newcomer to the field to a certified media specialist, this book covers all of the basics through best practices." (Publisher's note)

Gallaway, Beth

★ **Game** on! gaming at the library. Neal-Schuman Publishers 2009 306p il pa $55

Grades: Adult Professional   **025.2**

1. Video games 2. Video games and children 3. Video games and teenagers 4. Multimedia library services 5. Electronic games -- Collections 6. Libraries -- Special collections

ISBN 1-55570-595-2; 978-1-55570-595-4

LC 2009-14110

"An essential guide for any librarian who plans on embracing the video-game phenomenon, or at the very least, understanding it. . . . [The chapters] are well organized and contain an abundance of practical information. The sections on selection, collection, and circulation of video games include relevant advice on policy, cataloging, marketing, storage, and displays. . . . The annotated list of video games for a core collection is wonderful for selection purposes." SLJ

Includes bibliographical references

Goldsmith, Francisca

The **readers'** advisory guide to graphic novels. American Library Association 2010 124p (ALA readers' advisory series) pa $45

Grades: Adult Professional   **025.2**

1. Graphic novels -- Bibliography 2. Libraries -- Special collections -- Graphic novels

ISBN 978-0-8389-1008-5; 0-8389-1008-4

LC 2009-25239

"After dispelling the two main myths that ghettoize graphic novels—they are just for adolescents and they are far less complex than texts without pictures—Goldsmith emphasizes that GNs are a format and not a genre. She suggests active and passive ways to offer readers' advisory (RA) from face-to-face encounters with patrons to book displays and book groups and offers guidance on helping established GN readers to find new titles they might enjoy. . . . All in all it is a valuable and quite readable resource that belongs in every library's professional collection." Voice Youth Advocates

Includes glossary and bibliographical references

Graphic novels beyond the basics; insights and issues for libraries. Martha Cornog and Timothy Perper, editors. Libraries Unlimited 2009 xxx, 281p il pa $45

Grades: Adult Professional   **025.2**
1. Graphic novels -- History and criticism 2. Comic books, strips, etc. -- History and criticism 3. Libraries -- Special collections -- Graphic novels
ISBN 978-1-59158-478-0; 1-59158-478-7
         LC 2009-16189

Editors Cornog and Perper have collected essays by experts Robin Brenner, Francisca Goldsmith, Trina Robbins, Michael R. Lavin, Gilles Poitras, Lorena O'English, Michael Niederhausen, Erin Byrne, and Cornog herself, all about graphic novels in libraries. Topics covered range from the appeal of superheroes to manga, the appeal of comics to women and girls, anime, independent comics, dealing with challenges to the material, and more. Appendices provide resource information on African American-interest graphic novels, Latino-Interest graphic novels, LGBT-interest graphic novels, religious-themed graphic novels, a bibliography of books about graphic novels in libraries, and online resources.

"Whether you are serious about the genre, interested in the history, or looking for ammunition, this book should be on your shelf. The wealth of knowledge and research that went into these essays is impressive, and reading this book will put you on the road to becoming an expert." Libr Media Connect

Includes bibliographical references

Herald, Nathan

Graphic novels for young readers; a genre guide for ages 4-14. Libraries Unlimited 2011 188p (Genreflecting advisory series) $40

Grades: Adult Professional   **025.2**
1. Graphic novels 2. Children's literature 3. Graphic novels -- Bibliography
ISBN 1-59884-395-8; 978-1-59884-395-8
         LC 2010044947

"Librarians looking to beef up their graphic-novel collections will do well to get their hands on this valuable volume. The annotated entries are laid out in eight chapters organized by major genre, and from action and adventure to educational. Within chapters, the titles, 600 in all, are arranged alphabetically into popular subgenres such as superheroes, mythology, sports, and many more. . . . The intended audience for each title is clear, with bold icons providing an age range. Herald's writing style lends personality to what

could easily be a dry overview. . . . A thorough, well-organized, one-stop shop for quality graphic novels." SLJ

Includes bibliographical references

★ **Intellectual** Freedom Manual; Trina Magi, Martin Garnar, Office for Intellectual Freedom of the American Library Association. 9th ed. ALA Editions, An imprint of the American Library Association 2015 434 p. $70

Grades: Adult Professional   **025.2**
1. Censorship 2. Library science 3. Intellectual freedom 4. Freedom of information -- United States -- Handbooks, manuals, etc. 5. Libraries -- Censorship -- United States -- Handbooks, manuals, etc.
ISBN 0838912923; 9780838912928
         LC 2014037437

First published 1974

This newest edition "is more than just an invaluable compendium of guiding principles and policies. It's also an indispensable resource for day-to-day guidance on maintaining free and equal access to information for all people. Fortifying and emboldening professionals and students from across the library spectrum, this manual includes . . . 34 ALA policy statements and documents [and] explanations of legal points." (Publisher's note)

"All libraries should have a copy of this book to use when writing or revising policies; indispensable." Libr J

Includes bibliographical references and index

Mayer, Brian

Libraries got game; aligned learning through modern board games. [by] Brian Mayer and Christopher Harris. American Library Association 2010 134p il pa $45

Grades: Adult Professional   **025.2**
1. Board games 2. Libraries -- Special collections
ISBN 978-0-8389-1009-2; 0-8389-1009-2
         LC 2009-26839

"This is a valuable resource for K-12 librarians interested in building curriculum-aligned 'designer' game collections. The authors . . . explain how specific games enhance language-arts, social-studies, and math units, and build literacy skills. The two chapters devoted to promoting and justifying the inclusion of games in the library are well documented and a wonderful source to have to convince skeptical administrators. Suggestions for building a core collection, which highlights top recommended games for elementary school, middle school, and high school; a list of game publishers; a list of games discussed; and a glossary of terminology are included." SLJ

Includes bibliographical references

Reichman, Henry

★ **Censorship** and selection; issues and answers for schools. 3rd ed; American Library Association 2001 223p pa $37

Grades: Adult Professional   **025.2**
1. Censorship 2. Academic freedom 3. School libraries
ISBN 0-8389-0798-9
         LC 00-67657

First published 1988

"Reichman's manual provides sound practical advice on how to handle this complex and emotionally charged subject." Voice Youth Advocates

Includes bibliographical references

Scales, Pat R.

★ **Protecting** intellectual freedom in your school library; scenarios from the front lines. [by] Pat R. Scales for the Office for Intellectual Freedom. American Library Association 2009 148p (Intellectual freedom front lines) pa $55

Grades: Adult Professional   **025.2**

1. School libraries 2. Intellectual freedom

ISBN 978-0-8389-3581-1; 0-8389-3581-8

LC 2008-39893

"Scales uses court opinions, federal and state laws, and ALA documents to offer solutions for responding to infringements. A broad range of potential scenarios—from challenges to materials in both the library and the classroom, the legality of film rating systems, using computerized reading programs as selection tools and labeling books by reading levels, policies for interlibrary loans and reserves to confidentiality of children's and teens' circulation records—are covered. . . . This resource should be in every school library's professional collection." Voice Youth Advocates

Includes bibliographical references

025.3   Bibliographic analysis and control

★ **Cataloging** correctly for kids; an introduction to the tools. edited by Sheila S. Intner, Joanna F. Fountain, and Jean Weihs. 5th ed.; Association for Library Collections and Technical Services, American Library Association 2011 224p pa $55

Grades: Adult Professional   **025.3**

1. Cataloging 2. Reference books 3. Children's literature -- Cataloging

ISBN 978-0-8389-3589-7 pa; 0-8389-3589-3 pa

LC 2010012945

First published 1989 by the Cataloging for Children's Materials Committee

Among the topics discussed are: guidelines for standardized cataloging for children; how children search; using AACR2 and MARC 21; copy cataloging; using RDA; Sears List of Subject Headings; LC Children's headings; sources for Dewey numbers; cataloging nonbook materials; authority control; how the CIP program helps children; cataloging for kids in the academic library; cataloging for non-English-speaking children and preliterate children; automating the children's catalog; vendors of cataloging for children's materials.

Includes bibliographical references

025.43   General classification systems

★ **Sears** List of Subject Headings; Barbara A. Bristow, editor; Christi Showman Farrar, associate

editor. 21st edition Grey House Publishing/H.W. Wilson 2014 946 pp. (hardcover) $165.00

Grades: Adult Professional   **025.43**

1. Cataloging 2. Library science 3. Subject headings

ISBN 9781619251908

LC 2013498263

This book, edited by Barbara A. Bristow and Christi Showman Farrar, presents the frameworks for the Sears List of Subject Headings cataloging system. "This resource lists subject headings used by small and medium-sized libraries, with patterns, examples, and notes on usage. The subject headings are listed alphabetically and aligned with the Dewey Decimal Classification system and include a list of canceled and replacement headings, as well as a discussion of the theoretical foundations of the list and the general principles of subject cataloging." (Book News)

025.5   Services for users

American Association of School Librarians

Standards for the 21st-century learner in action. American Association of School Librarians 2009 120p pa $39

Grades: Adult Professional   **025.5**

1. Information literacy 2. Libraries -- Standards

ISBN 978-0-8389-8507-6 pa; 0-8389-8507-6 pa

"Standards in Action attempts to expand upon AASL's Standards for the 21st Century Learner by providing benchmarks and action examples. The original document was a nine-page brochure that outlined nine common beliefs, four learning standards, four strands, and indicators under each strand. It was an excellent starting point, but the addition of benchmarks at grades two, five, eight, ten, and twelve helps flesh out the original vision. . . . School libraries should own a copy of this professional, which has a role within any program." Voice Youth Advocates

Includes glossary and bibliographical references

Grassian, Esther S.

Information literacy instruction; theory and practice. [by] Esther S. Grassian and Joan R. Kaplowitz. 2nd ed; Neal-Schuman Publishers 2009 xxvii, 412p pa $75

Grades: Adult Professional   **025.5**

1. Information literacy 2. Information literacy -- Study and teaching 3. Information retrieval -- Study and teaching 4. Bibliographic instruction -- College and university students

ISBN 978-155570-666-1; 1-55570-666-5

LC 2009-23647

First published 2001

This "is designed for anyone involved in the creation and management of information literacy programming. Sixteen well-written chapters, organized into five sections, provide both theory and practical applications, with the emphasis on the practical. . . . Several extras appear in the accompanying CD-ROM. . . . A timely, thorough, and endlessly useful must-have title for librarians, teaching librarians, and library schools." Booklist

Includes bibliographical references

Harper, Meghan

Reference sources and services for youth. Neal-Schuman Publishers 2011 307p $65

Grades: Adult Professional 025.5

1. School libraries 2. Children's libraries 3. Young adults' libraries 4. Reference services (Libraries)

ISBN 978-1-55570-641-8; 1-55570-641-X

LC 2011004987

"The concept of school and public library collaboration is thoroughly explored in this excellent volume on providing reference services. The chapter on information literacy includes web links with information about standards, models, instruction and assessment, rubrics, web quests, graphic organizers, evaluation tools, and assessment. Additional chapters provide a discussion of online resources, government resources for youth, evaluation and marketing reference services, and managing them." SLJ

Includes bibliographical references

Intner, Carol F.

Homework help from the library; in person and online. American Library Association 2011 202p il pa $47

Grades: Adult Professional 025.5

1. Homework 2. Library resources 3. Libraries and students

ISBN 978-0-8389-1046-7; 0-8389-1046-7

LC 2010042096

"Building on the concept that information services and education converge with homework help, the author sketches in the history of youth services and current learning theories. She offers practical suggestions for needs assessment and determining a guiding philosophy. Speaking to the public librarian, Intner outlines the points to consider in designing a homework help program and training staff. Possible workshop topics include an overview of student needs and available resources, creating a comfortable and inviting space, considering the needs of different ages, understanding youth culture, and responding to various learning styles. . . . Youth librarians will want this comprehensive and practical guide within easy reach. " Voice Youth Advocates

Includes bibliographical references

Lanning, Scott

Essential reference services for today's school media specialists; [by] Scott Lanning and John Bryner. 2nd ed.; Libraries Unlimited 2010 141p il pa $45

Grades: Adult Professional 025.5

1. School libraries 2. Reference services (Libraries)

ISBN 978-1-59158-883-2; 1-59158-883-9

LC 2009-39375

"The content focuses on core reference skills, electronic resources, and leadership. The first few chapters discuss information literacy, evaluation of resources, the role of print resources, and the reference interview. These are followed by chapters on the library catalog, electronic resources, and the Web as a reference tool. Finally, there are several chapters dealing with the teacher-librarians' instructional and leadership roles. The authors use a very accessible tone while providing the basics." Booklist

Includes bibliographical references

Lenburg, Jeff

The **Facts** on File guide to research; 2nd ed; Facts on File 2010 xxxvi, 720p (Facts on File library of language and literature) $50; pa $18.95

Grades: 8 9 10 11 12 025.5

1. Research 2. Information resources

ISBN 978-0-8160-8121-9; 0-8160-8121-2; 978-0-8160-8122-6 pa; 0-8160-8122-0 pa

LC 2009-48200

First published 2005

This guide includes "lists of thousands of resources and explains general research methods and proper citation of sources. . . . [It features] discussions of Google and other search engines, subject-specific keyword search strategies, a cautionary note about Wikipedia, and . . . more." Publisher's note

Includes bibliographical references

Smith, Susan S.

★ **Web** -based instruction; a guide for libraries. [by] Susan Sharpless Smith. 3rd ed.; American Library Association 2010 236p il pa $65

Grades: Adult Professional 025.5

1. Bibliographic instruction 2. Library information networks 3. Computer-assisted instruction 4. Web sites -- Design

ISBN 978-0-8389-1056-6; 0-8389-1056-4

LC 2010-6452

First published 2001

This book covers "tools and trends, including current browsers, access methods, hardware, and software. [The author] also supplies tips to secure project funding and provides strategic guidance for all types of libraries." Publisher's note

Includes bibliographical references

Tallman, Julie I.

Making the writing and research connection with the I-search process; a how-to-do-it manual. [by] Julie I. Tallman, Marilyn Z. Joyce. 2nd ed.; Neal-Schuman Publishers 2006 xx, 167p il (How-to-do-it manuals for librarians) pa $55

Grades: Adult Professional 025.5

1. Research 2. Report writing 3. Young adults' libraries 4. Bibliographic instruction

ISBN 1-55570-534-0; 978-1-55570-534-3

LC 2005-32473

First published 1997

This volume "covers the I-Search process for middle and high-school students and . . . includes a detailed explanation of I-Search in the context of content units. Although it is useful for the media specialist and teacher who are familiar with I-Search, novices will also find valuable information. . . . The accompanying CD-ROM contains all of the figures found in the book (templates, handouts, etc.), which can be reproduced and adapted." Booklist

Includes bibliographical references

Wichman, Emily T.

Librarian's guide to passive programming; easy and affordable activities for all ages. Emily T. Wichman. Libraries Unlimited Inc. 2012 xvii, 152 p.p ill. (pbk. : acid-free paper) $40

Grades: Adult Professional   **025.5**

1. Librarians 2. Library finance 3. Library services 4. Libraries -- Activity programs -- United States

ISBN 159884895X; 9781598848953; 9781598848960

LC 2011045419

In her book, author Emily T. Wichman discusses library budget cuts, and how "librarians are seeking new ways to stretch their programming dollars and maximize staff resources. Passive programming allows libraries to inexpensively showcase their services while inviting visitors of all ages to enjoy the value that libraries bring to the community." (Publisher's note)

Includes bibliographical references and index.

027   General libraries, archives, information centers

Trumble, Kelly

The **Library** of Alexandria; illustrated by Robina MacIntyre Marshall. Clarion Bks. 2003 72p il maps $17

Grades: 5 6 7 8   **027**

1. Ancient civilization 2. Egypt -- Civilization 3. Alexandrian Library (Egypt)

ISBN 0-395-75832-7

LC 2003-150

An introduction to the largest and most famous library in the ancient world, discussing its construction in Alexandria, Egypt, its vast collections, rivalry with the Pergamum Library, famous scholars, and destruction by fire

This is a "well-organized and thorough resource." SLJ

Includes bibliographical references (p. 68-69) and index

027.6   Libraries for special groups and organizations

Alire, Camila

★ **Serving** Latino communities; a how-to-do-it manual for librarians. [by] Camila Alire, Jacqueline Ayala. 2nd ed; Neal-Schuman Publishers 2007 229p il (How-to-do-it manuals for librarians) pa $59.95

Grades: Adult Professional   **027.6**

1. Libraries and Hispanic Americans

ISBN 978-1-55570-606-7; 1-55570-606-1

LC 2007-7783

First published 1998

"The information covered helps library staff understand the needs of their library's Latino community; develop successful programs and services; obtain funding for projects and programs; prepare staff to work more effectively with Latinos; establish partnerships with relevant external agencies and organizations; improve collection development; and perform effective outreach and public relations. . . . There are few resources widely available on this topic and none as complete." Libr Media Connect

Includes bibliographical references

Klipper, Barbara

Programming for children and teens with autism spectrum disorder; Barbara Klipper. ALA Editions 2014 168 p. illustrations (pbk) $45

Grades: Adult Professional   **027.6**

1. Autism 2. Autistic children 3. Libraries and people with disabilities 4. Children's libraries -- Activity programs 5. Youth with autism spectrum disorders -- Services for 6. Children with autism spectrum disorders -- Services for

ISBN 9780838912065; 0838912060

LC 2013044207

This book, by Barbara Klipper, is "[f]or librarians who offer or are thinking about offering programming to children and/or teens with autism spectrum disorders (ASD). . . . There are storytime models; programming for school-age children, teens, and families; and program plans for school libraries. Helpful side boxes include tips on ways to supplement or adapt existing programs and library spaces. . . . The appendixes include valuable resources such as vendors, websites, and publishers." (School Library Journal)

Includes bibliographical references and index

Lerch, Maureen T.

Serving homeschooled teens and their parents. Libraries Unlimited 2004 242p (Libraries Unlimited professional guides for young adult librarians) pa $39

Grades: Adult Professional   **027.6**

1. Home schooling 2. Young adults' libraries

ISBN 0-313-32052-7

LC 2004-46518

"After introductory chapters that dispel many myths about homeschooling and delve into adolescent psychology, the two experts give sound advice and great examples for service plan creation, collection development, programming, and promotion of services." Libr Media Connect

Includes bibliographical references

027.62   Libraries for specific age groups

Alessio, Amy J.

A **year** of programs for teens. American Library Association 2007 159p il pa $35

Grades: Adult Professional   **027.62**

1. Young adults' libraries 2. Teenagers -- Books and reading 3. Young adults' library services -- Activity projects

ISBN 0-8389-0903-5; 978-0-8389-0903-4

LC 2006-13758

"Following an overview of the planning component of successful teen programming, this guide is presented as a calendar of ideas for each month of the year. Each month offers three to four programs with the preparation time, the length of the program, the recommended number of teen participants, age range, a shopping list, the setup required, variations or extra activities, and resources. . . . Librarians working with teens will find plenty of fresh ideas here." Booklist

Includes bibliographical references

A **year** of programs for teens 2; [by] Amy J. Alessio and Kimberly A. Patton. American Library Association 2011 pa $45

Grades: Adult Professional   **027.62**

1. Young adults' libraries 2. Teenagers -- Books and reading 3. 3. Young adults' library services -- Activity projects

ISBN 978-0-8389-1051-1; 0-8389-1051-3

LC 2010013661

"The authors offer great suggestions to public and school librarians who either need more ideas or to those who just want to spice up their current routines. The book includes plenty of real-life examples and variety. Part one offers ideas for core programming—those that can be scheduled on a regular basis. The authors give great advice for starting monthly clubs as well as introducing or revamping reading programs. Great book lists and ideas for displays are included, and passive activities like puzzles and quizzes round out this section. The second section lays out a year's worth of possible programming, with multiple options for each month." SLJ

Includes bibliographical references

Braafladt, Keith

Technology and literacy; 21st century library programming for children and teens. by Jennifer Nelson and Keith Braafladt. American Library Association 2012 129 p. (alk. paper) $50.00

Grades: Adult Professional   **027.62**

1. Library services 2. Literacy programs 3. Literature and technology 4. Children's libraries -- Activity programs 5. Scratch (Computer program language) 6. Computer literacy -- Study and teaching 7. Technological literacy -- Study and teaching 8. Young adults' libraries -- Activity programs

ISBN 0838911080; 9780838911082

LC 2011035104

This book by Jennifer Nelson presents a "guide for creating and implementing technology-based programming in public libraries. . . . Beginning chapters explain and present a plan for offering such programs, providing steps on how to execute them. . . . The author explains the value of this type of programming and the process involved with adoption, and covers planning, gathering support from both administration and staff, marketing . . . managing time, etc." (School Library Journal)

Includes bibliographical references and index.

Braun, Linda W.

Risky business; taking and managing risks in library services for teens. [by] Linda W. Braun, Hillias Jack Martin, and Connie Urquhart for the Young Adult Library Services Association. American Library Association 2010 151p

Grades: Adult Professional   **027.62**

1. Young adults' libraries 2. Risk-taking (Psychology) 3. Teenagers -- Books and reading 4. Libraries --

Collection development

ISBN 0-8389-3596-6; 978-0-8389-3596-5

LC 201005995

"This thought-provoking title will pique awareness and present some 'ah ha!' moments. It involves a degree of risk to provide exemplary library services to young adults in terms of collection building, programming, and technology. This book encourages librarians to take the necessary risks and describes factors to consider in different situations. . . . Of particular interest are chapters devoted to developing a mature, appealing, high-interest YA collection. This section alone makes the book a worthwhile addition." SLJ

Includes bibliographical references

Brehm-Heeger, Paula

Serving urban teens. Libraries Unlimited 2008 229p (Libraries Unlimited professional guides for young adult librarians) pa $40

Grades: Adult Professional   **027.62**

1. Young adults' libraries 2. Teenagers -- Books and reading 3. Young adults' library services 4. Public libraries -- Metropolitan areas

ISBN 978-1-59158-377-6; 1-59158-377-2

LC 2007045415

This book "begins with definitions and a brief history of library services to urban teens, followed by a description of issues concerning this special group. The remaining chapters detail every aspect of making positive connections with teens, from training staff—the entire library staff—to making space, developing the collection, designing programs, and developing partnerships within the community. . . . It is not only the mission of libraries but also in their self-interest to capture the minds and hearts of youth while they can. This book provides the tools to accomplish the job." Voice Youth Advocates

Includes bibliographical references

Burek Pierce, Jennifer

Sex, brains, and video games; a librarian's guide to teens in the twenty-first century. American Library Association 2008 130p pa $35

Grades: Adult Professional   **027.62**

1. Adolescence 2. Young adults' libraries 3. Teenagers -- United States

ISBN 978-0-8389-0951-5; 0-8389-0951-5

LC 2007-21926

"This guide provides new and reevaluated ideas and insights about the sociological, neurological, emotional, and sexual perspectives of adolescence. The author's purpose is to assist librarians as they try to engage teens through relevant and attractive responses to their recreational, informational, and technological needs and interests. . . . It is filled with a great deal of pertinent and thought-provoking advice and information." SLJ

Includes bibliographical references

Cannon, Tara C.

Cooler than fiction; a planning guide for teen nonfiction booktalks. [by] Jill S. Jarrell and Tara C. Cannon. McFarland & Company, Inc., Publishers 2011 189p il pa $45

Grades: Adult Professional **027.62**
1. Book talks 2. Young adults' libraries 3. Teenagers -- Books and reading
ISBN 978-0-7864-4886-9; 0-7864-4886-5

LC 2010040710

"This wonderful professional resource for teen librarians and school media specialists focuses on the art of booktalking with a twist. . . . The authors' take on talking up nonfiction books to teens is refreshing and creative and shows their love of reading and teens. Each title receives a summary, along with extra discussion questions and activities for awesome interactive appeal. Each chapter groups an assortment of nonfiction titles into unique categories like 'Funny, Gross, and Disturbing,' 'Food and Crafts,' 'Knowing Your World,' 'Science,' and 'History.'. . . This book is a much-needed tool for public librarians serving teens, as well as school media specialists, to develop excellent booktalking programs and partnerships while getting more teens to read and fun have doing so. It is a must-have for professional collections in public and school libraries." Voice Youth Advocates

Includes bibliographical references

Coleman, Tina

Teen craft projects 2; Tina Coleman and Peggie Llanes ; foreword by Amy Alessio and Katie LaMantia. ALA Editions, an imprint of the American Library Association 2013 xiv, 93 p.p (alk. paper : paperback) $45
Grades: Adult Professional **027.62**
1. Handicraft for children 2. Handicraft 3. Libraries and teenagers 4. Young adults' libraries -- Activity programs
ISBN 0838911528; 9780838911525

LC 2012041728

This book, by Tina Coleman and Peggie Llanes, features a "selection of innovative ideas. These projects have been chosen especially to engage tweens and teens and have been field-tested by YA librarian Amy Alessio's Teen Corps, students in grades 6 [through] 12 at the Schaumburg Township (IL) Public Library." (Publisher's note)

"The follow-up to The Hipster Librarian's Guide to Teen Craft Projects (2009) features 12 teen-tested activities, such as "No-Sew Organizers" and "Rock Star Jewelry." Going beyond the traditional craft book or blog post, this volume includes library-programming-specific tips for success by discussing difficulty, time expectations, supervision requirements, group-size recommendations, and mess factor...Although the price tag may be hard to swallow for the thriftiest among us, which often lines up with those also considered the "craftiest," the hand-holding may prove invaluable to the DIY-shy and librarians new to the overwhelming realm of teen crafts." (Booklist)

Includes bibliographical references (page 93) and index
Teen craft projects two

Colston, Valerie

Teens go green! tips, techniques, tools, and themes for YA programming. Valerie Colston. Libraries Unlimited 2012 xiii, 142 p.p ill. (acid-free paper) $40
Grades: Adult Professional **027.62**
1. School libraries -- Activity projects 2. Environmental education -- Activity projects 3. Libraries and teenagers -- United States 4. Environmental education -- Activity programs -- United States 5. Young adults' libraries -- Activity programs -- United States
ISBN 1591589290; 1591589304; 9781591589297; 9781591589303

LC 2011029006

This book is a reference resource "for librarians or high school teachers looking for low-cost, environmentally themed art projects and programs that teens will relate to and find fun. In Part 1, the author explains the needs for these programs, offers tips for teaching them, and suggests ways to expand teen involvement in the library. Part 2 provides dozens of . . . art project ideas that demonstrate how simple teaching green teen art projects can be." (Publisher's note)

"...A nice resource to have on hand for librarians whose community is ecominded or for those who want affordable programming options to consult." Booklist

Includes bibliographical references and index

Flowers, Sarah

Evaluating teen services and programs; Sarah Flowers. Neal-Schuman, an imprint of the American Library Association 2012 xv, 119 p.p (pbk.) $49.95
Grades: Adult Professional **027.62**
1. Library services 2. Young adults' libraries 3. Libraries -- United States 4. Libraries and teenagers -- United States 5. Young adults' libraries -- Evaluation -- United States
ISBN 1555707939; 9781555707934

LC 2012015105

Author Sarah Flowers presents "a guide that provides basic information to help teen/youth services librarians, library directors, library school students studying teen services, and middle/high school librarians examine all aspects of their teen programs and services to determine where improvement is needed. Find out what you need to develop goals and objectives for evaluation, and learn how to collect the data that will give you a realistic picture of your library's strengths and weaknesses." (Publisher's note)

Includes bibliographical references and index

Young adults deserve the best; YALSA's competencies in action. [by] Sarah Flowers for the Young Adult Library Services Association. American Library Association 2011 126p pa $45
Grades: Adult Professional **027.62**
1. Librarians 2. Young adults' libraries
ISBN 978-0-8389-3587-3; 0-8389-3587-7

LC 2010-14148

This "guide to the professional competencies developed by the Young Adult Library Services Association of ALA aims to 'outline the skills, the knowledge, and the philosophy that should be a part of the makeup of every librarian who serves teens.' Flowers begins by elaborating on and demonstrating how to execute the YALSA competencies. From there she discusses how to advocate for a teen-services department when none exists. The final section is a compilation of various resources, including the Library Bill of Rights and ALA interpretations of them with regard to labels and rating systems, Internet activity, ethics, and nonprint materials.. . . The information is presented in a clear, concise, and conversational manner, making this resource both easy to navigate and a pleasure to read." SLJ

Includes bibliographical references

Gorman, Michele

Connecting young adults and libraries; a how-to-do-it manual. [by] Michele Gorman and Tricia Suellentrop. 4th ed; Neal-Schuman Publishers Inc. 2009 xxxiii, 450p il (How-to-do-it manuals for librarians) pa $85

Grades: Adult Professional   **027.62**

1. Young adults' libraries 2. Teenagers -- Books and reading 3. Young adult literature -- Bibliography
ISBN 978-1-55570-665-4

LC 2009-17657

First published 1992 under the authorship of Patrick Jones

"This useful, comprehensive handbook on how to best serve young adult library patrons is a must-have for any librarian's professional library. . . . All key topics are covered here—customer service (affirming the fact that young adults are our customers), information literacy, collection development, booktalking, outreach, programming, technology, and more. Each chapter is well organized and includes background on the topic, suggestions to improve services, useful ideas, advice, sources, and works cited. . . . [This] is an excellent professional resource." Voice Youth Advocates

Includes bibliographical references

Hardesty, Constance

The **teen** -centered writing club; bringing teens and words together. Libraries Unlimited 2008 174p il (Libraries Unlimited professional guides for young adult librarians) pa $40

Grades: Adult Professional   **027.62**

1. Creative writing 2. Young adults' libraries 3. English language -- Composition and exercises
ISBN 978-1-59158-548-0; 1-59158-548-1

LC 2008-11519

"Hardesty encourages librarians to listen to teens and assist them in their search for identity through the written word. . . . From starting a club and the writing activities to share, to grand finales and how to evaluate the program's effectiveness, the author details all the information needed to create such a club. Particularly useful are chapters on the four roles of facilitators, creating a nonfiction writing club, and how to take your efforts online. Many handouts are included, a boon to any busy librarian. An appendix includes resources for publishing. All this information is laid out in a straightforward, positive manner. An essential resource for planning or presenting writing clubs." SLJ

Includes bibliographical references

Jones, Ella W.

Start -to-finish YA programs; hip-hop symposiums, summer reading programs, virtual tours, poetry slams, teen advisory boards, term paper clinics, and more! Neal-Schuman Publishers 2009 217p il pa $75

Grades: Adult Professional   **027.62**

1. Cultural programs 2. Young adults' libraries
ISBN 978-1-55570-601-2; 1-55570-601-0

LC 2008-50853

"Jones's creativity, twenty-five years of experience, and her genuine love for teenagers is obvious in the meticulous and creative programming ideas and materials. This valuable resource will be appreciated by librarians in public and school settings." Voice Youth Advocates

Includes bibliographical references

Kan, Katharine

★ **Sizzling** summer reading programs for young adults; [by] Katharine L. Kan for the Young Adult Library Services Association. 2nd ed.; American Library Association 2006 110p il pa $30

Grades: Adult Professional   **027.62**

1. Young adults' libraries 2. Teenagers -- Books and reading
ISBN 0-8389-3563-X

First published 1998

This "presents more than 50 summer reading programs that have been used successfully with preteens and teenagers. . . . Submissions represent a cross section of themes, incentives, activities and budgets. . . . Children and young adult services librarians will find a wealth of practical, hands-on information." Booklist

Kunzel, Bonnie Lendermon

The **teen** -centered book club; readers into leaders. [by] Bonnie Kunzel and Constance Hardesty. Libraries Unlimited 2006 xxi, 211p (Libraries Unlimited professional guides for young adult librarians) pa $40

Grades: Adult Professional   **027.62**

1. Young adults' libraries 2. Book clubs (Discussion groups) 3. Teenagers -- Books and reading
ISBN 1-59158-193-1

"Two experienced youth-services librarians introduce the idea of teen-centered book clubs. . . . In clear prose supported by research, the authors cover every aspect of the program, from assessing the needs of the library and teens to conducting successful meetings to evaluating activities. . . . An excellent reference." SLJ

Includes bibliographical references

Ludwig, Sarah

Starting from scratch; building a teen library program. Libraries Unlimited 2011 xiv, 202p pa $40; ebook $40

Grades: Adult Professional   **027.62**

1. Young adults' libraries
ISBN 978-1-59884-607-2 pa; 1-59884-607-8 pa; 978-1-59884-608-9 ebook; 1-59884-608-6 ebook

LC 2011020103

This book offers a practical, comprehensive guide to creating a successful, vibrant, and youth-centered teen services program with limited resources.

"Ludwig provides plenty of real-world advice and ideas. . . . This well-written and helpful book will be invaluable to both new and seasoned teen librarians as well as those thinking about pursuing a career working with teens." SLJ

Includes bibliographical references

Mahood, Kristine

A **passion** for print; promoting reading and books to teens. Libraries Unlimited 2006 239p il (Libraries Unlimited professional guides for young adult librarians) pa $40

Grades: Adult Professional   **027.62**

1. Young adults' libraries 2. Teenagers -- Books and reading

ISBN 1-59158-146-X; 978-1-59158-146-8

LC 2006-3716

"Beginning with research on reading, Mahood moves on to merchandising principles; developing teen collections, spaces, and Web sites; and finally to booktalking, readers' advisory, and events scheduling. The author's enthusiasm and experience, coupled with citing current studies, other professional books, articles, and Web sites, make her suggestions appealing and attainable. She provides everything from lists of YA genres to easy design principles for displays to suggestions for questions to ask for better readers' advisory." Booklist

Martin, Hillias J.

★ **Serving** lesbian, gay, bisexual, transgender, and questioning teens; a how-to-do-it manual for librarians. [by] Hillias J. Martin, Jr., James R. Murdock. Neal-Schuman Publishers 2007 267p bibl (How-to-do-it manuals for librarians) pa $55

Grades: Adult Professional   **027.62**

1. Gay men 2. Lesbians 3. Bisexuality 4. Transsexualism 5. Young adults' libraries

ISBN 978-1-55570-566-4; 1-55570-566-9

LC 2006-39469

"This volume offers abundant useful guidance not only for reaching the target audience, but also for planning and promoting library services to teens in general. . . . The tone is friendly and largely free of jargon. . . . All librarians should turn to this book for pertinent insight on the needs of 5 to 10 percent of the teen population." SLJ

Includes bibliographical references

Miller, Donna P.

Crash course in teen services. Libraries Unlimited 2008 128p (Crash course) pa $30

Grades: Adult Professional   **027.62**

1. Young adults' libraries

ISBN 978-1-59158-565-7; 1-59158-565-1

LC 2007-32758

"Designed for public librarians new to teen service, the book offers advice on relating to teens and creating teen-friendly space as well as tips on teen-centered reference, collection development, readers' advisory, programming, and 'the three Ps': professional resources, professional development, and public relations." Booklist

Includes bibliographical references

Ott, Valerie A.

Teen programs with punch; a month-by-month guide. Libraries Unlimited 2006 282p il (Libraries Unlimited professional guides for young adult librarians) pa $40

Grades: Adult Professional   **027.62**

1. Young adults' libraries 2. Teenagers -- Books and reading

ISBN 1-59158-293-8

LC 2006012775

"Ott has gathered together less-than-conventional program ideas arranged by month. She provides clear instructions, lists of supplemental materials, promotional ideas, reading lists, costs, and suggested grade levels for each one. For librarians with limited budgets, and who may be pressed for time, there are quick and easy ideas that cost little or no money. . . . Many of the programs are designed to draw underserved populations, such as goths, GLBTQ teens, and vegetarians, into the library. . . . This highly informative guide would make a great addition to any YA librarian's professional collection." SLJ

Includes bibliographical references

Reid, Rob

★ **What's** black and white and Reid all over? something hilarious happened at the library. Rob Reid. American Library Association 2012 xii, 175 p.p (softbound) $45

Grades: Adult Professional   **027.62**

1. Storytelling 2. Humorous fiction 3. Children's libraries 4. Storytelling -- United States 5. Wit and humor, Juvenile -- Bibliography 6. Children's libraries -- Activity programs -- United States

ISBN 0838911471; 9780838911471

LC 2011043233

This book presents "10 humorous story programs -- five aimed at preschoolers and five for school-aged children. . . . Each one provides read-aloud suggestions and movement activities. There are also . . . storytelling tips that include everything from how to hold the book to what props to use. . . . Reid also includes an additional list of titles that can be substituted, jokes, call-and-response chants, short storybooks, songs, and musical activities." (School Library Journal)

"Those new to interactive book talking will appreciate his instructions for hamming up particular titles. Seasoned users will be grateful for the flexibility Reid provides to tailor programs to the tastes, time slots, and collection at hand." VOYA

Includes bibliographical references and index

Schneider, Elizabeth

Create, relate & pop @ the library; services & programs for teens & tweens. [by] Erin Helmrich and Elizabeth Schneider. Neal-Schuman Publishers 2011 218p il

Grades: Adult Professional   **027.62**

1. Cultural programs 2. Young adults' libraries

ISBN 1-55570-722-X; 978-1-55570-722-4

LC 2011-4986

The authors show "how to capitalize on the latest trends—from TV, movies, and music to indie and niche interests—by incorporating them into compelling, creative programs. . . . The book encompasses both traditional and Web 2.0 participatory programming, offering . . . ideas, program templates, and step-by-step outlines of methods, supplies, and resources."

"This is a handy guide." SLJ

Includes bibliographical references

Sima, Judy

Raising voices; creating youth storytelling groups and troupes. [by] Judy Sima, Kevin Cordi. Libraries Unlimited 2003 xxviii, 241p pa $32.50

Grades: Adult Professional   **027.62**
1. Storytelling
ISBN 1-56308-919-X

LC 2003-47631

This offers a "blueprint for beginning and sustaining a successful group or troupe of storytellers from grades 4 to 12. . . . The book includes reproducible forms that will save a lot of work and lists of valuable resources. . . . Raising Voices is the complete, and essential, handbook for this special group of storytellers." SLJ

Includes bibliographical references

Teaching Generation M; a handbook for librarians and educators. edited by Vibiana Bowman Cvetkovic and Robert J. Lackie. Neal-Schuman Publishers 2009 368p il pa $85

Grades: Adult Professional   **027.62**
1. Technology 2. Information literacy 3. Internet and teenagers 4. Young adults' libraries
ISBN 978-1-55570-667-8; 1-55570-667-3

LC 2009-17658

"This professional handbook tackles three important topics—who is the millennial generation, what kind of world do millennials live in, and what can we do to teach them? Chapter topics include media literacy, the information search process, Facebook, YouTube, Google, and Wikipedia, gaming, webcomics, mobile technology, cooperative learning, screencasting, and the new generation of research papers. . . . In-text citations make this book more of a resource than a pleasure read, but it is a must-read for non-M-generation librarians new to young adult services and for those new teachers or anyone wanting to understand Web 2.0." Voice Youth Advocates

Includes bibliographical references

Tuccillo, Diane

Teen -centered library service; putting youth participation into practice. [by] Diane P. Tuccillo. Libraries Unlimited 2010 xxii, 259p il (Libraries Unlimited professional guides for young adult librarians) pa $45

Grades: Adult Professional   **027.62**
1. School libraries 2. Young adults' libraries
ISBN 978-1-59158-765-1; 1-59158-765-4

LC 2009-45692

This offers "guidelines to YA librarians for getting teens to play a part in their libraries. . . . The book begins with a description of this philosophy and places it into context within the history of YA librarianship. Each chapter then deals with specifics: teen advisory groups, writing and per-

formance ideas, ways to meld teens and technology, ideas for community outreach, ways to combine teen and adult library groups, ideas to involve teens who are only around for limited time, and a chapter on assessing your YA participation. . . . This well-organized title is aimed at public librarians and might also be useful to show administrators how important YA services are to the library as a whole." SLJ

Includes bibliographical references

Urban teens in the library; research and practice. edited by Denise E. Agosto and Sandra Hughes-Hassell. American Library Association 2010 208p bibl il pa $60

Grades: Adult Professional   **027.62**
1. Young adults' libraries 2. Teenagers -- Books and reading
ISBN 978-0-8389-1015-3; 0-8389-1015-7

LC 2009-25147

"This work does much to explain who urban teens are and what they need from their libraries. The authors examine the existing research—some of which they have performed—that provides a wealth of data for public and school libraries." SLJ

Includes bibliographical references

Walter, Virginia A.

Twenty -first-century kids, twenty-first-century librarians. American Library Association 2010 104p pa $45

Grades: Adult Professional   **027.62**
1. Librarians 2. Children's libraries 3. Young adults' libraries
ISBN 978-0-8389-1007-8 pa; 0-8389-1007-6 pa

LC 2009016972

"This volume more than updates Walter's 2001 Children and Libraries; it revisits the nature of children, addressing social changes and encouraging a new generation of children's librarians. Chapter 1 provides a fine history about U.S. library services to children, primarily in public libraries. Subsequent chapters detail six enduring core values of children's library services and add two emerging themes: the need for information (and information literacy) and collaboration. Walter's main contribution lies in her description of five models of children relative to the library: as reader, as a child of the information age, as a community member, as global, and as an empowered person. Another chapter focuses on management principals. . . . Walter's core values are worth reading and implementing." Booklist

Includes bibliographical references

Welch, Rollie James

The guy -friendly YA library; serving male teens. Libraries Unlimited 2007 xxi, 196p (Libraries Unlimited professional guides for young adult librarians) pa $40

Grades: Adult Professional   **027.62**
1. Young adults' libraries 2. Boys -- Books and reading
3. Teenagers -- Books and reading
ISBN 978-1-59158-270-0; 1-59158-270-9

LC 2006-102882

"The first chapter offers key components for quality service for teen males, while the second chapter explains the characteristics and developmental issues of this population. The book emphasizes reading, with three chapters dedicated to male teen reading habits, topics of interest, and detailed genre coverage. . . . The sixth chapter deals with programming and also explains how the establish an effective teen advisory board. . . . The seventh chapter covers school visits and emphasizes the importance of booktalks. The eighth chapter discusses creating a teen area in the library." Booklist

Includes bibliographical references

027.8   School libraries

Adams, Helen R.

★ **Ensuring** intellectual freedom and access to information in the school library media program. Libraries Unlimited 2008 xxi, 254p il map pa $40

Grades: Adult Professional   **027.8**

1. Censorship 2. School libraries 3. Freedom of information

ISBN 978-1-59158-539-8; 1-59158-539-2

LC 2008-16753

This is "an extremely helpful guide for dealing with intellectual-freedom and information-access issues. In chapters geared to school situations and covering topics including selection of resources, the First Amendment, privacy, challenges to resources, the Internet, and access for students with disabilities, Adams offers background on the topic and bulleted lists of strategies for dealing with the issue. . . . This is a book that every school librarian needs to keep handy and share with administrators, colleagues, and parents." Booklist

Includes bibliographical references

Baule, Steven M.

Facilities planning for school library and technology centers; 2nd ed.; Linworth Pub. 2007 134p il pa $39.95

Grades: Adult Professional   **027.8**

1. School libraries -- Design and construction 2. Instructional materials centers -- Design and construction

ISBN 978-1-58683-294-0; 1-58683-294-8

LC 2006-34179

First published 1992

The author "provides information on how to put together a planning team; how to perform a needs assessment for the library media center or technology lab; how to create bid documents and specification charts; how to develop time lines; and how to plan to move into the new facility once construction is complete. . . . Anyone who is going to build or renovate a facility will want this book." Booklist

Includes bibliographical references

Bishop, Kay

The **collection** program in schools; concepts, practices, and information sources. 4th ed. Libraries Unlimited 2007 xx, 269p il (Library and information science text series) pa $50; $65

Grades: Adult Professional   **027.8**

1. School libraries 2. Libraries -- Collection development 3. School libraries -- Collection development 4. Children's literature -- Bibliography of

bibliographies 5. Young adult literature -- Bibliography of bibliographies

ISBN 1-59158-360-8 pa; 1-59158-583-X; 978-1-59158-360-8 pa; 978-1-59158-583-1

LC 2007-9005

First published 1988 under the authorship of Phyllis J. Van Orden

"Media specialists who read this book will be renewed in their quest for excellence in their collections. . . . The book covers A-Z: Acquisitions, Evaluation, Ethical Issues, Inventory, Procedure Manual, Selection, Special Groups of Students, Weeding, etc. . . . This is a must purchase for every school library media center." Libr Media Connect

Includes bibliographical references

Buzzeo, Toni

The **collaboration** handbook. Linworth Pub. 2008 132p il pa $42.95

Grades: Adult Professional   **027.8**

1. School libraries

ISBN 978-1-58683-298-8 pa; 1-58683-298-0 pa

LC 2008-18119

"In this succinct guide, Buzzeo paints a picture of how media specialists can use instructional collaboration to transform a media program and increase student achievement. . . . Those new to the field will appreciate the step-by-step approach to increasing collaboration, while experienced media specialists will likely benefit most from the chapters on data-driven collaboration and assessment. The book concludes with a substantial amount of information on how to overcome common barriers to collaboration, the role of advocacy, and the importance of integrating new technologies into collaborative projects." SLJ

Includes bibliographical references

Erikson, Rolf

Designing a school library media center for the future; [by] Rolf Erikson and Carolyn Markuson. 2nd ed; American Library Association 2007 117p il pa $45

Grades: Adult Professional   **027.8**

1. School libraries -- Design and construction 2. Instructional materials centers -- Design and construction

ISBN 978-0-8389-0945-4; 0-8389-0945-0

LC 2006-37644

First published 2000

"The first chapter offers an overview of the various steps involved in any project. Succeeding chapters cover technology planning, space allocations, furniture and placement, lighting and acoustics, ADA requirements, specifications, and bids." Booklist

Includes bibliographical references

Grimes, Sharon

★ **Reading** is our business; how libraries can foster reading comprehension. American Library Association 2006 155p il pa $35

Grades: Adult Professional   **027.8**

1. School libraries 2. Books and reading 3. Reading comprehension

ISBN 0-8389-0912-4

LC 2005028263

Grimes "led a school-wide research study with classroom teachers to transform the reading program at Lansdowne Elementary School in Baltimore. The study resulted in dramatic and measurable gains in student reading achievement. This book can be used as a toolkit to duplicate those results. Grimes's work is informed by solid educational research in the field of reading comprehension. The text is lively and clearly written, accessible to teachers and librarians." SLJ

Includes bibliographical references

Harada, Violet H.

Assessing for learning; librarians and teachers as partners. [by] Violet H. Harada and Joan M. Yoshina. 2nd ed.; Libraries Unlimited 2010 242p il pa $45

Grades: Adult Professional   **027.8**
1. School libraries 2. Instructional materials centers
ISBN 978-1-59884-470-2; 1-59884-470-9
First published 2055 with title: Assessing learning

"Using assessment tools familiar to the classroom teacher, the authors show how to use them in the library setting. Starting with the challenges that face 21st century schools, the rationale for schools as learning organizations is laid out. The tools for assessment are the main points of this title and include checklists, rubrics, rating scales, conferences, logs, personal correspondence, exit passes, graphic organizers, and student portfolios. . . . The tools for better instruction and assessment of learning need to be used by all educators, and this title provides examples and models for all librarians." Libr Media Connect

Includes bibliographical references

Hughes-Hassell, Sandra

School reform and the school library media specialist; [by] Sandra Hughes-Hassell and Violet H. Harada. Libraries Unlimited 2007 xxiii, 204p il (Principles and practice series) pa $40

Grades: Adult Professional   **027.8**
1. School libraries
ISBN 978-1-59158-427-8; 1-59158-427-2
LC 2007-16437

"This volume covers critical issues impacting school libraries today and offers practical solutions to meet these challenges. Written by leaders in the field such as Pam Berger, Carol Gordon, Barbara Stripling, and Ross Todd, the articles expound on implications of No Child Left Behind legislation, 21st-century literacy requirements, population diversity, and professional growth. . . . This volume will empower current and future school librarians as they embrace its guidelines." SLJ

Morris, Betty J.

★ **Administering** the school library media center; 5th ed.; Libraries Unlimited 2010 580p il $75; pa $60

Grades: Adult Professional   **027.8**
1. School libraries 2. Instructional materials centers
ISBN 978-1-59158-685-2; 1-59158-685-2; 978-1-59158-689-0 pa; 1-59158-689-5 pa
LC 2010015939

First published 1973 under the authorship of John T. Gillespie and Diana L. Spirt with title: Creating a school media program

"This updated edition provides a comprehensive and current examination of the multiple and varied jobs media specialists do to manage today's school library media centers. . . . Sample job description statements, media center budgets, and budget justification tools are thorough and valuable references. Morris addresses the proactive and visible leadership role that today's media specialists must take on to remain viable and support student learning. . . . The title supports concepts on current standards. It is a forward thinking text for new or future library media specialists and a realistic, functional reference for practitioners." Libr Media Connect

Includes bibliographical references

Stephens, Claire Gatrell

Library 101; a handbook for the school library media specialist. [by] Claire Gatrell Stephens and Patricia Franklin. Libraries Unlimited 2007 233p il pa $35

Grades: Adult Professional   **027.8**
1. School libraries 2. Instructional materials centers 3. Libraries -- Handbooks, manuals, etc.
ISBN 978-1-59158-324-0; 1-59158-324-1
LC 2007-18420

"This handbook provides information for brand-new and inexperienced librarians preparing for a first job in a school library media center. Articles are divided into four subcategories covering day-to-day operations (library organization, circulation policies, media management, scheduling, staffing, and media center arrangement); collaboration with teachers; collection development and management; and equipment." Booklist

Includes bibliographical references

Sykes, Judith A.

Conducting action research to evaluate your school library; Judith Anne Sykes. Libraries Unlimited, an imprint of ABC-CLIO, LLC 2013 118 p. illustrations (hard copy) $40

Grades: Adult Professional   **027.8**
1. School libraries 2. Librarians -- Rating 3. Educational evaluation 4. School librarians 5. Teacher-librarians 6. Action research in education 7. School libraries -- Evaluation
ISBN 161069077X; 9781610690775
LC 2012051277

In this book, author Judith Anne Sykes "coalesces current expert opinions on the topic of action research in the school library environment and highlighting what other teacher librarians in the field have identified as the pros and cons of using the process. Readers are directed to focus on mitigating the 'cons' through the use of specific working pages and templates and by initially exploring 'five favorite' links." (Publisher's note)

"When budget issues hit, school librarianship can be in danger, and this text provides tools for professionals to evaluate their programs and make necessary changes to stay a vital part of their schools. . . This purchase would be worthwhile for any teacher-librarian interested in evaluating his or her program and taking advantage of Sykes' extensive research and expertise." Booklist

Includes bibliographical references and index

Valenza, Joyce Kasman

★ **Power** tools recharged; 125+ essential forms and presentations for your school library information program. illustrated by Emily Valenza. American Library Association 2004 various paging il pa $55

Grades: Adult Professional   **027.8**
1. School libraries 2. Libraries -- Public relations
ISBN 0-8389-0880-2

LC 2004-5853

First published 1998 with title: Power tools

This offers a compilation of customizable, reproducible forms and handouts for school library administration and assessment, teaching information literacy, making presentations. Included are such items as templates for a gift book program, letters to parents and faculty members, a checklist of tasks, library equipment sign-out forms, and a reading interest survey.

Includes bibliographical references

Van Deusen, Jean Donham

Enhancing teaching and learning; a leadership guide for school library media specialists. [by] Jean Donham. rev. ed.; Neal-Schuman Publishers 2008 353p il pa $65

Grades: Adult Professional   **027.8**
1. School libraries 2. Instructional materials centers
ISBN 978-1-55570-647-0; 1-55570-647-9

LC 2008-23321

First published 1998

"This title is well-written, well-researched, and informative. Donham masterfully weaves together current AASL standards and the real world of today's media specialist." Voice Youth Advocates

Includes bibliographical references

Woolls, E. Blanche

The **school** library media manager; [by] Blanche Woolls. 4th ed; Libraries Unlimited 2008 279p il (Library and information science text series) $55; pa $45

Grades: Adult Professional   **027.8**
1. School libraries 2. Instructional materials centers
ISBN 978-1-59158-648-7; 1-59158-648-8; 978-1-59158-643-2 pa; 1-59158-643-7 pa

LC 2008-18081

First published 1994

Provides information "for teaching the administration of school library media centers. . . . Readers learn how to choose a credential program, how to find the requirements for working in each of the 50 states, what to do when looking for and choosing a job, and how to survive the first week in that new position. . . . Sections also cover: collaborating with teachers, how to write a proposal, and how to accept leadership responsibilities, including the role of a media specialist in the legislative process." Publisher's note

Includes bibliographical references

028   Reading and use of other information media

Ross, Val

You can't read this; forbidden books, lost writing, mistranslations, & codes. Tundra Books 2006 140p il $19.95

Grades: 7 8 9 10   **028**
1. Books -- Censorship 2. Books and reading -- History
ISBN 0-88776-732-X

The author "offers a unique historical survey based around a broadly interpreted theme: the power of reading. The chronologically arranged chapters touch on censorship, literacy, and the influence of political texts. . . . The accounts are fascinating, and Ross is an accomplished storyteller who brings history right into the present. Scattered black-and-white photos and art illustrate this timely, powerful text." Booklist

Includes bibliographical references

028.1   Reviews

Baxter, Kathleen A.

★ **From** cover to cover; evaluating and reviewing children's books. rev ed.; Collins 2010 229p $14.99

Grades: Adult Professional   **028.1**
1. Books -- Reviews 2. Children's literature -- History and criticism
ISBN 978-0-06-077757-9; 0-06-077757-5

First published 1997

The author addresses the distinctions between evaluation and review, and what makes a good children's book. She discusses categories of children's books including nonfiction; traditional literature (folktales, myths, legends, etc.); poetry, verse, rhymes, and songs; picture books; easy readers and transitional books; and fiction. She then describes the process of writing a review.

This is a "very complete resource that will continue to be the venerable reference tool and required reading for education and library-science students, youth librarians, teachers, and anyone else interested in kids, reading, and children's literature." SLJ

Naidoo, Jamie Campbell

★ **Rainbow** family collections; selecting and using children's books with lesbian, gay, bisexual, transgender, and queer content. Jamie Campbell Naidoo. Libraries Unlimited, an imprint of ABC-CLIO, LLC 2012 xvii, 260 p.p ill. (hardback) $50

Grades: Adult Professional   **028.1**
1. Libraries and sexual minorities 2. Sexual minorities in literature 3. Libraries and sexual minorities -- United States 4. Libraries -- Special collections -- Sexual minorities 5. Sexual minorities -- Bibliography 6. Children's libraries -- Collection development -- United States 7. Children's libraries -- Services to minorities -- United States 8. Children of sexual minority parents

-- Books and reading -- United States
ISBN 1598849603; 9781598849608

LC 2012008362

This book by Jamie Campbell Naidoo "highlight[s] titles for children from infancy to age 11" featuring lesbian, gay, bisexual, transgender, and queer content. It "supplies a synopsis of the title's content, lists awards it has received, cites professional reviews, and provides suggestions for librarians considering acquisition. The book also provides a brief historical overview of LGBTQ children's literature along with the major book awards for this genre." (Publisher's note)

Includes bibliographical references and index

Schall, Lucy

Value -packed booktalks; genre talks and more for teen readers. Libraries Unlimited 2011 261p pa $45; e-book $45

Grades: Adult Professional   **028.1**

1. Book talks 2. Young adult literature 3. Fiction genres 4. Values -- Bibliography 5. Teenagers -- Books and reading 6. Young adult literature -- Bibliography
ISBN 978-1-59884-735-2 pa; 978-1-59884-736-9 e-book

LC 2010053243

"This volume provides an in-depth break-down of nearly 100 books in a variety of categories. Each selection features a title summary, suggested page numbers for read-aloud moments, a sample booktalk, invaluable connections to the school curriculum, and related works. Each category, such as 'Problem Solving: Mystery' and 'Heritage: Historical Books,' also includes several helpful subcategories, including 'Loyalty' and 'Equality.' . . . While this book will prove to be a useful tool, it should be used in tandem with other guides that include more classics." SLJ

Includes bibliographical references

Young Adult Library Services Association

★ **Best** books for young adults; edited by Holly Koelling; foreword by Betty Carter. 3rd ed; American Library Association 2007 346p il pa $42

Grades: Adult Professional   **028.1**

1. Best books 2. Reference books 3. Teenagers -- Books and reading 4. Young adult literature -- Bibliography
ISBN 978-0-8389-3569-9; 0-8389-3569-9

LC 2007-26009

First published 1994 under the editorship of Betty Carter

This "is a classic, standard resource for collection building and on-the-spot readers' advisory. . . . Absolutely indispensable for school and public libraries." Booklist

Includes bibliographical references

**028.5   Reading and use of other information
media by young people**

Barr, Catherine, 1951-

Best books for middle school and junior high readers; grades 6-9. [by] Catherine Barr and John T. Gillespie. 2nd ed; Libraries Unlimited 2009 1242p (Children's and young adult literature reference series) lib bdg $85

Grades: Adult Professional   **028.5**

1. Books and reading 2. Teenagers -- Books and reading 3. Children's literature -- Bibliography 4. Young adult literature -- Bibliography
ISBN 978-1-59158-573-2 lib bdg; 1-59158-573-2 lib bdg

LC 2008-50755

First published 2004

"This guide to books for readers in grades six through nine lists approximately 15,000 titles, now including those published from 2004 through 2008. Titles were selected primarily on the basis of reviews in Booklist, School Library Journal, VOYA, and other review journals. Arrangement is first by subject or genre and then alphabetically by author. In addition to author and title, each listing contains reading level, publication data, a brief annotation, Dewey decimal classification number, and citations for reviews. . . . Best Books titles are valuable collection-development tools for school and public libraries." Booklist

Bartel, Julie

Annotated book lists for every teen reader; the best from the experts at YALSA-BK. [by] Julie Bartel and Pam Spencer Holley for the Young Adult Library Services Association. Neal-Schuman Publishers 2011 270p pa $65

Grades: Adult Professional   **028.5**

1. Best books 2. Young adult literature 3. Teenagers -- Books and reading 4. Young adult literature -- Bibliography 5. Young adult literature -- Stories, plots, etc.
ISBN 1-55570-658-4; 978-1-55570-658-6

LC 2010-33312

"Bartel and Holley have scoured the YALSA-BK archives to find more than 1100 books with broad teen readership. While the book's primary purpose is for readers' advisory, the authors also suggest it will be useful in creating displays as well as igniting creativity. . . .The scope is wide ranging with a good mix of standards, classics, and newer titles. With a highly appropriate title, this volume hits the mark." SLJ

Includes bibliographical references

Baxter, Kathleen A.

Gotcha again for guys! more nonfiction books to get boys excited about reading. [by] Kathleen A. Baxter and Marcia Agness Kochel. Libraries Unlimited 2010 248p il pa $35

Grades: Adult Professional   **028.5**

1. Book talks 2. Boys -- Books and reading 3. Children's literature -- Bibliography
ISBN 978-1-59884-376-7 pa; 1-59884-376-1 pa; 978-1-59884-377-4 e-book

LC 2010036577

This "highlights books published mainly between 2007 and 2009. Twelve chapters cover themes such as sports, animals, gross/disgusting stuff, mysteries/disasters, and machines. Each one features anywhere from a few to two dozen ready-touse booktalks, most aimed at grades 3-8, along with extensive bibliographies (not annotated) of other titles that have received good reviews in Booklist, Horn Book Guide, and School Library Journal. New to this volume are enlightening interviews with male authors such as Kadir Nelson, Nic Bishop, and Seymour Simon, whose books are featured in the text. The introduction also lists ideas for promoting books to boys in public libraries and school media centers." SLJ

Includes bibliographical references

Gotcha good! nonfiction books to get kids excited about reading. [by] Kathleen A. Baxter and Marcia Agness Kochel. Libraries Unlimited 2008 259p pa $35

Grades: Adult Professional **028.5**

1. Books and reading 2. Children's literature -- Bibliography 3. Young adult literature -- Bibliography
ISBN 978-1-59158-654-8 pa; 1-59158-654-2 pa
LC 2008010350

"In addition to annotations for over 1000 nonfiction titles, [the authors] profile eight prolific authors and provide fun top-10 features for the various subjects covered. . . . The titles chosen are truly high quality, relevant, and up-to-date, with suggested ages provided, most ranging from grades three through eight. . . . A must-have for all librarians who want to get kids excited about nonfiction." SLJ

Includes bibliographical references

Bodart, Joni Richards

Radical reads 2; working with the newest edgy titles for teens. Scarecrow Press 2010 479p pa $45

Grades: Adult Professional **028.5**

1. Teenagers -- Books and reading 2. Young adult literature -- Bibliography
ISBN 978-0-8108-6908-0; 0-8108-6908-X
LC 2009-25724

Bodart "offers insight into writing book reports and booktalks that secondary school English teachers and library media specialists can share with students. . . . The detailed book entries include citations with suggested reading and interest levels designated by middle school, younger high school, and older high school. Also included are subject areas, character descriptions, a booktalk and booktalk ideas, a list of major themes and ideas, book report ideas, risks, strengths, awards, and full-text reviews. The entries' detail will be an asset in readers' advisory and a quick resource to check the content and reviews for a title that is being questioned." Voice Youth Advocates

Includes bibliographical references

Booth, Heather

★ **Serving** teens through readers' advisory. American Library Association 2007 159p (ALA readers' advisory series) pa $36

Grades: Adult Professional **028.5**

1. Young adults' libraries 2. Teenagers -- Books and reading 3. Young adult literature -- Bibliography
ISBN 0-8389-0930-2; 978-0-8389-0930-0
LC 2006-36134

"The first few chapters discuss teen reading habits and why readers' advisory for this group is different and also provide 'tips for the generalist' who may not be an expert in teen fiction. Other chapters cover elements of the readers' advisory interaction . . . and survey the appropriate books. Two unique chapters offer well-thought-out and practical

advice on making reading-related homework assignments less painful for staff and students as well as suggestions for providing readers' advisory services to teens through their parents or other adults. . . . [This] is essential reading for all readers' advisors and any library staff who work with teens." Booklist

Includes bibliographical references

Brooks, Wanda M.

Embracing, evaluating, and examining African American children's and young adult literature; edited by Wanda M. Brooks, Jonda C. McNair; foreword by Rudine Sims Bishop. Scarecrow Press 2008 251p pa $45

Grades: Adult Professional **028.5**

1. African Americans in literature 2. Children -- Books and reading 3. Children's literature -- History and criticism 4. Young adult literature -- History and criticism 5. American literature -- African American authors -- History and criticism
ISBN 978-0-8108-6027-8 pa; 0-8108-6027-9 pa
LC 2007025703

"Brooks and McNair have compiled 12 scholarly studies about the use of books by and about African-American children and young adults in classrooms across the United States. Selections include a detailed textual analysis of the work of Arna Bontemps and Langston Hughes; a sociolinguistic perspective on readers' response to books containing African-American Vernacular English; and a detailed study of the books used as classroom read-alouds by teachers in rural schools, which found that only three percent were about African Americans. While each study is complete in and of itself, the text as a whole gives a broad picture of what is currently being done in this field, both in K-12 classrooms and college classes that emphasize children's literature." SLJ

Includes bibliographical references

Cart, Michael

★ **Young** adult literature: from romance to realism; rev ed.; American Library Association 2010 242p pa $60

Grades: Adult Professional **028.5**

1. Teenagers -- Books and reading 2. Young adults' literature -- History 3. Young adult literature -- History and criticism
ISBN 978-0-8389-1045-0; 0-8389-1045-9
LC 2010-13674

A revised edition of: From romance to realism: 50 years of growth and change in young adult literature, published 1996 by HarperCollins Pub.

"This updated and expanded second edition of Cart's already lively and comprehensive history of young adult literature (1996) is an essential resource. It is divided into two sections ('That Was Then' and 'This Is Now'), and the author once again discusses the history and current moment to offer a broad and loving overview of the rich literature. . . . Highly accessible and thorough, the text is a staple for any study of the canon." SLJ

Includes bibliographical references

Collins, Joan

Motivating readers in the middle grades; [by] Joan Collins. Linworth Pub. 2008 128p il pa $36.95

Grades: Adult Professional   **028.5**

1. Middle schools 2. Youth -- Books and reading

ISBN 978-1-58683-297-1; 1-58683-297-2

LC 2007-51426

"This workbook describes three six-week projects for inciting reading motivation in grades six through eight, developed by Massachusetts middle school educators. . . . This resource is supremely teacher-friendly; projects are presented by grade with concise rationales, instructions, suggestions, and caveats. Suggested novels are annotated, varied, and age appropriate." Voice Youth Advocates

Includes bibliographical references

★ **Dear** author; letters of hope. edited by Joan F. Kaywell; with an introduction by Catherine Ryan Hyde. Philomel Books 2007 222p $14.99

Grades: 8 9 10 11 12   **028.5**

1. Authors, American 2. Teenagers -- Books and reading

ISBN 978-0-399-23705-8; 0-399-23705-4

LC 2006-21050

"Chris Lynch, Nancy Garden, and Christopher Paul Curtis and are just a few of the well-known authors who respond to real teens' letters in this powerful compilation. Not mere fan mail, the selections speak about teens' gravest concerns—bullying, derailed friendships, racism, date rape, incest, illness, divorce, and more—and they describe how the authors' books helped them face the heartaches. . . . For some readers, this dialogue between writers and readers will be inspiring; for those harboring their own wounding secrets, it may be lifesaving." Booklist

Includes bibliographical references

Diamant-Cohen, Betsy

Booktalking bonanza; ten ready-to-use multimedia sessions for the busy librarian. American Library Association 2009 240p il pa $40

Grades: Adult Professional   **028.5**

1. Book talks 2. Books and reading 3. Children's literature

ISBN 978-0-8389-0965-2; 0-8389-0965-5

LC 2008-15371

"This volume is a collection of scripts for multimedia-enriched booktalks. After an introductory chapter that explains the reasoning for this approach, 10 scripts are outlined. Books, music, video, and Web sites are included for each one. The programs are geared toward elementary-aged children, although suggestions for adapting them for a middle or high school audience are included." SLJ

Includes bibliographical references

Embracing, evaluating, and examining African American children's and young adult literature; edited by Wanda M. Brooks, Jonda C. McNair; foreword by Rudine Sims Bishop. Scarecrow Press 2008 251p pa $45

Grades: Adult Professional   **028.5**

1. African Americans in literature 2. Children --

Books and reading 3. Children's literature -- History and criticism 4. Young adult literature -- History and criticism 5. American literature -- African American authors -- History and criticism

ISBN 978-0-8108-6027-8 pa; 0-8108-6027-9 pa

LC 2007025703

"Brooks and McNair have compiled 12 scholarly studies about the use of books by and about African-American children and young adults in classrooms across the United States. Selections include a detailed textual analysis of the work of Arna Bontemps and Langston Hughes; a sociolinguistic perspective on readers' response to books containing African-American Vernacular English; and a detailed study of the books used as classroom read-alouds by teachers in rural schools, which found that only three percent were about African Americans. While each study is complete in and of itself, the text as a whole gives a broad picture of what is currently being done in this field, both in K-12 classrooms and college classes that emphasize children's literature." SLJ

Includes bibliographical references

Fraser, Elizabeth

Reality rules II; a guide to teen nonfiction reading interests. Elizabeth Fraser. Libraries Unlimited 2012 xvii, 230 p.p (Genreflecting advisory series) (cloth) $48

Grades: Adult Professional   **028.5**

1. Best books 2. Teenagers -- Books and reading 3. Young adult literature -- Bibliography 4. Young adult literature -- Stories, plots, etc 5. Teenagers -- Books and reading -- United States

ISBN 1598847902; 9781598847901

LC 2012020232

In this book, Elizabeth Fraser "recommends nonfiction books published after 2007 that will appeal to a wide range of young adults, including reluctant and ESL readers. Sections include 'Adventure,' 'Memoirs and Autobiographies,' 'Biography,' 'Sports,' 'All About You,' and 'The Arts,'" (School Library Journal)

"This is another wonderful research and reference work, a follow-up to Reality Rules I...As a reader's advisory, for collection development, and for helping the classroom teacher get the best resources, this is an excellent and well-researched book for use with the teen reader." (Library Media Connection)

Includes bibliographical references and indexes

Reality rules! a guide to teen nonfiction reading interests. Libraries Unlimited 2008 246p (Genreflecting advisory series)

Grades: Adult Professional   **028.5**

1. Reference books 2. Young adult literature 3. Teenagers -- Books and reading 4. Young adult literature -- Bibliography

ISBN 9781591585633

LC 2007-51063

"This guide focuses on titles created for teens and those with strong teen appeal. The author covers more than 500 titles published since 2000, also including benchmarks and perennial classics." Publisher's note

Includes bibliographical references

Gilmore, Barry

★ **Speaking** volumes; how to get students discussing books, and much more. Heinemann 2006 128p pa $17.95

Grades: Adult Professional   **028.5**
1. Books and reading
ISBN 978-0-325-00915-5 pa; 0-325-00915-5 pa
                    LC 2005-28371

"Gilmore provides practical, hands-on methods to involve students in oral and written classroom conversations that encourage reflection and ultimately polished, coherent expression. . . . Both new and seasoned discussion leaders will want a copy for repeated reference." Voice Youth Advocates

Includes bibliographical references

Handbook of research on children's and young adult literature; edited by Shelby A. Wolf . . . [et al.] Routledge 2010 555p $295; pa $119.95

Grades: Adult Professional   **028.5**
1. Children's literature -- History and criticism 2. Young adult literature -- History and criticism
ISBN 978-0-415-96505-7; 0-415-96505-5; 978-0-415-96506-4 pa; 0-415-96506-3 pa; 978-0-203-84354-3 e-book
                    LC 2010-16339

"The book examines readers, texts, and cultural contexts of children's literature and across the three intersecting disciplines of Education, English, and Library and Information Science, in an effort to model a multidisciplinary approach to children's literature research. Thirty-seven scholarly articles, by figures such as Eliza Dresang, Rudine Sims Bishop, and Roderick McGillis . . . are counterpointed by responses that often provide more personal perspectives, including insights from noted authors such as Lois Lowry, M. T. Anderson, and Markus Zusak." Bull Cent Child Books

Honnold, RoseMary

The **teen** reader's advisor. Neal-Schuman Publishers 2006 491p (Teens @ the library series) pa $75

Grades: Adult Professional   **028.5**
1. Young adults' libraries 2. Teenagers -- Books and reading 3. Young adult literature -- Bibliography
ISBN 1-55570-551-0
                    LC 2006-12640

"The first part deals with the challenges of working with teens, from developing a rapport and dealing with the more conservative adults in their lives, to marketing a YA collection to its audience. The author's descriptions of the major awards and lists relating to the literature as well as the list of print and online reader's advisory resources are sure to be helpful. Part two consists of subject and genre lists. Each one has at least 10 titles. The annotations are excellent." SLJ

Includes bibliographical references

Jones, Patrick

★ **Connecting** with reluctant teen readers; tips, titles, and tools. [by] Patrick Jones, Maureen L. Hartman, Patricia Taylor. Neal-Schuman Publishers 2006 xxi, 314p $59.95

Grades: Adult Professional   **028.5**
1. Young adults' libraries 2. Teenagers -- Books and reading 3. Young adult literature -- Bibliography
ISBN 1-55570-571-5; 978-1-55570-571-8
                    LC 2006-12355

"Well written and well researched, this practical hands-on guide to defining and wooing reluctant readers is a must-read for librarians and teachers who work with adolescents. It is divided into three parts: 'Tips That Work,' 'Titles That Work,' and 'Tools That Work.'" SLJ

Includes bibliographical references

Kajder, Sara B.

Bringing the outside in; visual ways to engage reluctant readers. [by] Sara B. Kajder; foreword by Linda Rief. Stenhouse Publishers 2006 105p il $18.50

Grades: Adult Professional   **028.5**
1. Reading
ISBN 1-57110-401-1; 978-1-57110-401-4
                    LC 2005056415

The author "demonstrates myriad ways to employ students' outside talents in the classroom. . . . She shows how she adapts the curriculum to incorporate an expanded definition of literacy tools. Sara offers teachers guidance on how to extend their repertoire of teaching strategies, and help kids connect their natural curiosity and skills as readers and writers of both print and electronic texts." Publisher's note

"Teachers, especially those working with at-risk students, will be thankful for hands-on methods to engage teens through technology." Voice Youth Advocates

Includes bibliographical references

Keane, Nancy J.

101 great, ready-to-use book lists for children; Nancy J. Keane. Libraries Unlimited, an imprint of ABC-CLIO, LLC 2012 xiv, 246 p.p (paperback) $45

Grades: Adult Professional   **028.5**
1. Best books 2. Children -- Books and reading 3. School libraries -- Book lists 4. Children's libraries -- Book lists 5. Children's literature -- Bibliography 6. Children -- Books and reading -- United States
ISBN 1610690834; 9781610690836
                    LC 2011051429

"Keane uses her vast knowledge of children's literature to create book lists for children K-8th grade. They are broken into seven parts that are subdivided into subject areas. . . . Each entry includes the title, author, publisher, publication date, number of pages, an annotation, Lexile level when available, and interest level by grade or age range. The easily reproducible lists will be useful for curriculum and collection development as well as for interesting book displays." SLJ

Includes bibliographical references and index

101 great, ready-to-use book lists for teens; Nancy J. Keane. Libraries Unlimited, an imprint of ABC-CLIO, LLC 2012 xiv, 263 p.p (paperback) $40; (ebook) $40

Grades: Adult Professional   028.5
1. Book selection 2. Books and reading 3. Young adult literature -- Bibliography 4. High school libraries -- Book lists 5. Young adults' libraries -- Book lists 6. Teenagers -- Books and reading -- United States
ISBN 1610691342; 9781610691345; 9781610691352
LC 2011051428

This book offers a "compilation of YA [Young Adult] materials . . . published prior to August 2011. The book is divided . . . into themed lists such as 'Genres,' 'Readalikes,' and 'Teaching Literary Elements.' The themes . . . include . . . topics such as 'Romance,' 'Autism & Asperger's Syndrome,' 'Different Belief Systems,' and 'Crossing the Border.' Each entry includes the title, author, publisher, publication date, page numbers, an annotation, Lexile level when available, and interest level by grade or age range." (School Library Journal)

"This is a useful resource for new librarians and may also be helpful to seasoned librarians. The emphasis is on books published within the last ten years, but some older titles are included." Lib Med Con

Includes bibliographical references and index

The **big** book of teen reading lists; 100 great, ready-to-use book lists for educators, librarians, parents, and teens. Libraries Unlimited 2006 297p pa $35

Grades: Adult Professional   028.5
1. Teenagers -- Books and reading 2. Young adult literature -- Bibliography
ISBN 1-59158-333-0; 978-1-59158-333-2
LC 2006-17627

"Keane has produced another great resource for teachers, librarians, and students, especially reluctant readers." SLJ
Includes bibliographical references

Krashen, Stephen D.
★ The **power** of reading; insights from the research. by Stephen D. Krashen. 2nd ed; Libraries Unlimited 2004 199p bibl diag tab $25
Grades: Adult Professional   028.5
1. Reading 2. Literacy
ISBN 1-59158-169-9 pa
LC 2004-44207

First published 1993
The author presents research for "the argument that free voluntary reading (FVR) is the most effective tool available for increasing literacy. . . . Some of the topics he explores include the research surrounding second language acquisition, reading rewards and incentives programs, and some of today's popular 'electronic reading products.'" Publisher's note
Includes bibliographical references

McDaniel, Deanna
Gentle reads; great books to warm hearts and lift spirits, grades 5-9. [by] Deanna J. McDaniel. Libraries Unlimited 2008 318p (Children's and young adult literature reference series) $45
Grades: Adult Professional   028.5
1. Children's literature -- Bibliography 2. Young adult

literature -- Bibliography
ISBN 978-1-59158-491-9
LC 2008018878

This includes "500 recommended titles. Here readers will find books with divorce, drug use, attempted suicides, and more but they all meet the criteria the author has set by being either inspiring, heartwarming, or in some way uplifting. . . . Arranged by genres, the entries include full bibliographic information, an annotation, and a description of why the book fits the 'gentle criteria.'" SLJ
Includes bibliographical references

Nilsen, Alleen Pace
★ **Literature** for today's young adults; [by] Alleen Pace Nilsen, Kenneth L. Donelson. 8th ed; Allyn and Bacon/Pearson 2008 xx, 491p il $122.20
Grades: Adult Professional   028.5
1. Books and reading 2. Young adult literature -- History and criticism
ISBN 978-0-205-59323-1; 0-205-59323-2
LC 2008-2625

First published 1980
This is an "introduction to young adult literature framed within a literary, historical, and social context. The authors provide teachers with criteria for evaluating books of all genres, from poetry and nonfiction to mysteries, science fiction, and graphic novels. . . . [It also includes coverage of] issues such as pop culture and mass media." Publisher's note
Includes bibliographical references

Quick and popular reads for teens; edited by Pam Spencer Holley for the Young Adult Library Services Association. American Library Association 2009 228p pa $45
Grades: Adult Professional   028.5
1. Teenagers -- Books and reading 2. Young adult literature -- Bibliography 3. Young Adult Library Services Association
ISBN 978-0-8389-3577-4; 0-8389-3577-X
LC 2008-49691

"This practical guide pulls together the Quick Picks for the Reluctant Young Adult Reader lists and the Popular Paperbacks for Young Adults lists created by the Young Adult Library Services Association (YALSA), a division of the American Library Association (ALA) from 1999 to 2008. . . . [The editor] assembles the lists into separate Nonfiction and Fiction categories, with an additional chapter containing Theme-Oriented Booklists that is useful for putting together displays, bookmarks, or readers' advisory. . . . This essential tool for librarians will help them find that popular book to turn a reluctant reader into a teen who appreciates the enjoyment one comes from reading." Voice Youth Advocates
Includes bibliographical references

Saccardi, Marianne
Books that teach kids to write; [by] Marianne C. Saccardi. Libraries Unlimited 2011 150p pa $30; e-book $30
Grades: Adult Professional   028.5
1. Creative writing 2. Books and reading 3. Literature

-- Study and teaching
ISBN 978-1-59884-451-1 pa; 978-1-59884-452-8 e-book
LC 2011001866
"Divided into sections such as 'Making Stories Unique,' 'Creating Memorable Characters,' and 'Putting Passion and Voice into Nonfiction Writing,' this book gives countless recommendations for teaching various skills. Saccardi offers short, annotated summaries of mentor texts and describes how they can be used to model good writing techniques. . . . After reading this resource, educators will have a long wish list of materials to purchase." SLJ
Includes bibliographical references

Schall, Lucy
Genre talks for teens; booktalks and more for every teen reading interest. Libraries Unlimited 2009 309p pa $40
Grades: Adult Professional   028.5
1. Book talks 2. Teenagers -- Books and reading
ISBN 978-1-59158-743-9; 1-59158-743-3
LC 2008-54984
"Schall has chosen about 100 books published since 2003 for inclusion in this volume. . . . Each book includes a summary, a booktalk, a read-aloud/reader response sampling, supporting learning activities, and related works. Books are keyed by theme, reading level, and audience. . . . Because of its varied ways to engage readers and its current coverage, the book is a welcome addition." Booklist
Includes bibliographical references

Silvey, Anita
500 great books for teens. Houghton Mifflin Co. 2006 397p $26
Grades: Adult Professional   028.5
1. Teenagers -- Books and reading 2. Young adult literature -- Bibliography
ISBN 978-0-618-61296-3; 0-618-61296-3
LC 2006-3350
"Silvey selects and annotates five hundred titles for young adults, arranging them loosely in twenty-one chapters by genre and/or area of interest, from 'Adventure and Survival' to 'War and Conflict.' Each book is coded for either younger (12-14) or older (14-18) teens and gets a couple hundred words or so. . . . The selections are both sturdy and wide-ranging." Horn Book
Includes bibliographical references

Sullivan, Michael
★ Connecting boys with books 2; closing the reading gap. American Library Association 2009 119p il pa $40
Grades: Adult Professional   028.5
1. School libraries 2. Children's libraries 3. Young adults' libraries 4. Boys -- Books and reading
ISBN 978-0-8389-0979-9 pa; 0-8389-0979-5 pa
LC 2008-34925
Sullivan "looks at developmental differences between boys and girls and how our culture views reading as a leisure activity. He also looks at materials that will attract male readers. His concern is not necessarily the boy who cannot

read but the aliterate boy—the one who can read but chooses not to." Booklist
"A must-read for all librarians and media specialists." SLJ
Includes bibliographical references (p. 105-110)

Serving boys through readers' advisory. American Library Association 2010 152p (ALA readers' advisory series) pa $48
Grades: Adult Professional   028.5
1. Children's literature 2. Reference services (Libraries) 3. Boys -- Books and reading 4. Boys
ISBN 978-0-8389-1022-1; 0-8389-1022-X
LC 2009-26841
"This volume was created to give a general direction when helping most boys select books. . . . Sullivan challenges us to throw out our preconceived notions about how to conduct such an interview. Methods of performing indirect readers' advisory with parents and teachers are included. The excellent booktalks for elementary, middle school, and high school boys alone make this a worthwhile purchase." SLJ
Includes bibliographical references

Temple, Charles A.
Children's books in children's hands; an introduction to their literature. [by] Charles Temple, Mariam Martinez, Junko Yokota; with contributions by Evelyn B. Freeman. 3rd ed.; Pearson Allyn and Bacon 2006 xxv, 630p il $129.33
Grades: Adult Professional   028.5
1. Books and reading 2. Children's literature -- History and criticism
ISBN 0-205-42043-5; 978-0-205-42043-8
LC 2006272616
First published 1998
Part I covers the intellectual development of children, literary elements of children's literature, and reader response criticism. Part II surveys the literature by genre. Part III shows how to create a literature-based classroom through activities, classroom libraries, and book discussions. Appendices list award-winning titles, professional organizations, publishers, children's periodicals and Web sites. This edition has been updated to include coverage of such topics as technology in the classroom, visual literacy, and the influence of the No Child Left Behind Act of 2000 on reading instruction in the public schools.
Includes bibliographical references

Zbaracki, Matthew D.
Best books for boys; a resource for educators. foreword by Jon Scieszka. Libraries Unlimited 2008 189p il (Children's and young adult literature reference series)
Grades: Adult Professional   028.5
1. Best books 2. Young adult literature 3. Reading interests 4. Boys -- Books and reading 5. Children's literature -- Book lists 6. Children's literature -- Bibliography 9. Young adult literature -- Bibliography
ISBN 1-59158-599-6; 978-1-59158-599-2
LC 2007-51065
"Good source notes guide readers to additional writings on the topic and speak to the author's significant research

in his field. Nicely indexed by author, title, and subject, this [is an] easy-to-navigate resource." Voice Youth Advocates

Includes bibliographical references

028.7   Use of books and other information media as sources of information

Callison, Daniel

★ The **blue** book on information age inquiry, instruction and literacy; [by] Daniel Callison and Leslie Preddy. Libraries Unlimited 2006 643p il pa $45

Grades: Adult Professional   **028.7**

    1. Information literacy

    ISBN 978-1-59158-325-7; 1-59158-325-X

LC 2006-23645

A revised edition of Key Words, Concepts and Methods for Information Age Instruction, published 2003 by LMS Associates

"Part 1 introduces the concepts of information inquiry, providing foundational documents and exploring search and use models, information literacy, standards, the instructional role of library media specialists, online inquiry learning, and resource management. Part 2 offers concrete examples of inquiry applied to the middle-school student research process and supplies reproducible pages for classroom use. Part 3 discusses and defines 51 key terms. Entries here are several pages in length and include citations and references. Indispensable for all school media specialists, this book will also appeal to other readers, who will be impressed by its well-organized design, thoroughness, and practicality." Booklist

Includes bibliographical references

Riedling, Ann Marlow

Learning to learn; a guide to becoming information literate in the 21st century. 2nd ed.; Neal-Schuman Publishers 2006 148p il pa $35

Grades: Adult Professional   **028.7**

    1. Research 2. Internet resources 3. Internet searching 4. Information literacy

    ISBN 978-1-55570-556-5; 1-55570-556-1

LC 2006-13721

First published 2002

This is a "guide to the research/learning process. Chapters lead researchers step-by-step through the information maze to find what they are looking for. Numerous URLs and exercises are included, as is material on copyright, plagiarism, and basic citation styles. . . . The section on evaluating Web sites is particularly valuable. As an added bonus, all mentioned sites are updated and hyperlinked at the publisher's Web site. This is a practical guide for all librarians, but particularly for those teaching research skills." SLJ [review of 2002 edition]

Includes bibliographical references

030   General encyclopedic works

Anderson, Jennifer Joline

Wikipedia; the company and its founders. ABDO Pub. Co. 2011 112p il (Technology pioneers) lib bdg $34.22

Grades: 5 6 7 8   **030**

    1. Electronic encyclopedias 2. Wikis (Computer science) 3. Wikimedia Foundation

    ISBN 978-1-61714-812-5 lib bdg; 1-61714-812-1 lib bdg; 978-1-61758-970-6 e-book

LC 2010037886

This is an introduction to Wikipedia and its founders.

"Written in a clear, linear fashion, this series offers vivid, well-researched details about the development of technological advancements considered essential in today's society. . . . Readers who are interested in technology and inventions will be thoroughly engrossed." SLJ

Includes glossary and bibliographical references

★ The **World** Almanac and Book of Facts 2015; edited by Sarah Janssen. Simon & Schuster 2014 1008 p. $13.99

Grades: 6 7 8 9 10 11 12 Adult   **030**

    1. Almanacs 2. Geography 3. Popular culture

    ISBN 1600571905; 9781600571909

Annual. First published 1868. Publisher varies

"The World Almanac and Book of Facts is America's top-selling reference book of all time, with more than 82 million copies sold. Published annually since 1868, this compendium of information is the authoritative source for all your entertainment, reference, and learning needs. The 2015 edition of The World Almanac [edited by Sarah Janssen] reviews the events of 2014 and will be your go-to source for any questions on any topic." (Publisher's note)

"This is the most comprehensive and well-known of almanacs. . . . Contains a chronology of the year's events, consumer information, historical anniversaries, annual climatological data, and forecasts. Color section has flags and maps. Includes detailed index." N Y Public Libr Book of How & Where to Look It Up

031   General encyclopedic works in specific languages and language families

DK Publishing, Inc.

DK children's illustrated encyclopedia; 7th ed.; DK Pub. 2010 600p il map $34.99

Grades: 4 5 6 7   **031**

    1. Encyclopedias and dictionaries

    ISBN 978-0-7566-5759-8; 0-7566-5759-8

LC 2010279636

First published 1991 with title: Random House children's encyclopedia; a revised edition of Dorling Kindersley's children's illustrated encyclopedia 6th ed. published 2006

A highly illustrated one-volume encyclopedia containing entries ranging from Abolitionist movement to Zoos.

"This handsome revision features more than 3000 photographs, maps, time lines, and illustrations. . . . The attractive format encourages browsing." SLJ

Guinness world records 2015; by Guinness World Records. St. Martin's Press 2014 255 p. ill. (some col.) $28.95

Grades: 3 4 5 6 7 8 9 10 11 12 **031**

1. World records 2. World records -- Periodicals 3. Curiosities and wonders -- Periodicals

ISBN 1908843632; 9781908843630

This 2015 edition of the Guinness World Records book "presents thousands of new and updated records. . . . [It] showcases the very best of the most recent world records, with new subjects as diverse as castles, 3D printing, the search for alien life and the latest developments in AI and robotics. Plus, the Flashback features offer a look back at the archives to bring you the best of the classic and iconic records from the past 60 years." (Publisher's note)

The **Kingfisher** children's encyclopedia. Kingfisher 2012 480 p. (hardcover) $29.99

Grades: 3 4 5 6 7 8 **031**

1. Picture books for children 2. Encyclopedias and dictionaries

ISBN 075346814X; 9780753468142

The entries in this updated children's encyclopedia "range from one to four pages in length each, feature full-color illustrations and photos and subheadings in a large, easy-to-read font and sidebars and fact boxes of thought-provoking information." Topics include "continents and countries, technology, transportation, animal and plant life, religion, and space." (School Library Journal)

Knowledge Encyclopedia. Dk Pub 2013 360 p. $29.99

Grades: 4 5 6 7 8 **031**

1. Encyclopedias and dictionaries

ISBN 1465414177; 9781465414175

This book, by the Smithsonian Institution, is a "family reference using 3-D rendered images to explore the wonders of the world . . . . Divided into six chapters . . . , a wide range of topics come to life. Illustrated with fascinating facts, maps, timelines, and graphics, the Knowledge Encyclopedia makes complex subjects easy to understand and is the perfect resource for kids, whether to help with homework or to pique their curiosity." (Publisher's note)

Turner, Tracey

World of the weird. Firefly Books 2009 144p il $14.95

Grades: 5 6 7 8 **031**

1. Curiosities and wonders

ISBN 978-1-55407-481-5; 1-55407-481-9

"A first-rate browsing item, from the bicycle-riding frog on the front cover to the recipe for chocolate-covered crickets at the end. . . . Turner presents barrages of snippets on extreme sports ('chessboxing'), uncommon maladies ('exploding head syndrome'), oddball festivals, bizarre beliefs ('Eating stolen bacon is a cure for constipation.' Do tell!), strange creatures real or otherwise, supernatural phenomena and . . . more. . . . Illustrated with photos that are often startling but never gory or gross, this compact page-turner will light up the imaginations of motivated young readers and jaded nonreaders alike." Kirkus

The **World** Book Encyclopedia. World Book, Inc 22 v col ill, col maps

Grades: 4 5 6 7 8 9 10 11 12 Adult **031**

1. Reference books 2. Encyclopedias and dictionaries

New editions published yearly; revised frequently

"A 22-volume, highly illustrated, A-Z general encyclopedia for all ages, featuring sections on how to use World Book, other research aids, pronunciation key, a student guide to better writing, speaking, and research skills, and comprehensive index." (Publisher's note)

031.02 Books of miscellaneous facts

Aronson, Marc

For boys only; the biggest, baddest book ever. [by] Marc Aronson [and] H.P. Newquist. Feiwel and Friends 2007 157p il map $14.95

Grades: 4 5 6 7 **031.02**

1. Boys 2. Curiosities and wonders

ISBN 978-0-312-37706-9; 0-312-37706-1

LC 2007-32847

"In a tone both light and humorous, Newquist and Aronson aim to please by assembling a tantalizing miscellany—codes, puzzles, best lists, brief history and science facts, instructions for making fake blood and playing Ultimate Frisbee. . . . This offers lots of good fun." Booklist

Farndon, John

Do not open; written by John Farndon. DK Publishing 2007 256p il $24.99

Grades: 4 5 6 7 **031.02**

1. Curiosities and wonders

ISBN 978-0-7566-3205-2; 0-7566-3205-6

LC 2007300131

This encyclopedic tome catalogues "the mysterious and unusual. . . . Flaps, foldout pages and varied styles of illustration—from photomontage to digital cartoons and more conventional line art—keep the book visually fresh and ably complement the subject matter. . . . Taking in everything from weird weather like St. Elmo's fire and raining frogs to possible locations of Atlantis, the book incites curiosity—and expansively rewards it." Publ Wkly

Iggulden, Conn

The **dangerous** book for boys; [by] Conn Iggulden, Hal Iggulden. Collins 2007 270p il map $24.95

Grades: 4 5 6 7 **031.02**

1. Boys 2. Amusements 3. Recreation 4. Curiosities and wonders

ISBN 0-06-124358-2; 978-0-06-124358-5

LC 2006-491918

"This eclectic collection addresses the undeniable boy-appeal of certain facts and activities. Dozens of short chapters, in fairly random order, cover a wide range of topics in conversational prose. Simple instructions for coin tricks and paper airplanes alternate with excerpts from history such as Famous Battles and facts about ancient wonders of the world and astronomy. . . . Tongue-in-cheek humor emerges throughout." SLJ

Kane, Joseph Nathan

Famous first facts; a record of first happenings, discoveries, and inventions in American history. [by] Joseph Nathan Kane, Steven Anzovin, & Janet Podell. 6th ed.; Wilson, H.W. 2006 1307p il $185

Grades: 5 6 7 8 9 10 11 12 Adult   **031.02**

1. Reference books 2. Encyclopedias and dictionaries 3. United States -- History -- Dictionaries

ISBN 978-0-8242-1065-6; 0-8242-1065-4

LC 2006-3096

First published 1933

Over 7500 entries cover first occurences in American history, organized into 16 chapters each divided into sections. Sections are alphabetically organized, and individual entries are organized chronologically within each section. Includes five indexes: subject index, index by years, index by days, index to personal names, and geographical index

"Besides serving as an essential ready-reference source, the book is also fun to read out loud to colleagues—when was bubble gum first manufactured in the U.S.? When was the spray can introduced?" Booklist

The **World** almanac for kids. World Almanac il maps

Grades: 4 5 6 7   **031.02**

1. Almanacs 2. Reference books

Annual. First published 1995 for 1996

This volume contains information on animals, art, religion, sports, books, law, language, science and computers. Includes a section of full-color maps and flags. Illustrated throughout with pictures, diagrams, and charts

050   General serial publications

Botzakis, Stergios

Pretty in print; questioning magazines. by Stergios Botzakis. Fact Finders 2007 32p il (Media literacy) lib bdg $22.60; pa $7.95

Grades: 4 5 6 7   **050**

1. Periodicals 2. Publishers and publishing

ISBN 978-0-7368-6764-1 lib bdg; 0-7368-6764-3 lib bdg; 978-0-7368-7860-9 pa; 0-7368-7860-2 pa

LC 2006021443

This is "written in a breezy style and [has] plenty of popping colors and photos. . . . Useful and attractive." SLJ

Includes bibliographical references

070.1   Documentary media, educational media, news media

Garner, Joe

We interrupt this broadcast; the events that stopped our lives--from the Hindenburg explosion to the Virginia Tech shooting. [foreword by Walter Cronkite; afterword by Brian Williams; narrated by Bill Kurtis] 10th anniversary ed.; Sourcebooks MediaFusion 2008 194p il $49.95

Grades: 7 8 9 10 11 12 Adult   **070.1**

1. Disasters 2. Broadcast journalism 3. Television broadcasting of news

ISBN 978-1-4022-1319-9; 1-4022-1319-0

LC 2008-20015

First published 1998

This book and 3 CD set "documents, in text, audio and black-and-white photographs, the moments when history, for better or for worse (though usually for worse), was made in an instant. . . . In addition to the CDs' reports and sound bites dramatically introduced and explained . . . each event gets about four pages of coverage, with an efficient summary and at least half a dozen photos. . . . These are the kinds of moments that still shock and amaze. This moving book is 'a tribute of sorts' to the events that defined eras, the journalists who reported on them and the media television, radio that made us all witnesses." Publ Wkly

070.4   Journalism

Bausum, Ann

★ **Muckrakers**; how Ida Tarbell, Upton Sinclair, and Lincoln Steffens helped expose scandal, inspire reform, and invent investigative journalism. by Ann Bausum; foreword by Daniel Schorr. National Geographic 2007 111p il $21.95; lib bdg $32.90

Grades: 6 7 8 9   **070.4**

1. Authors 2. Novelists 3. Historians 4. Journalism 5. Journalists 6. Essayists 7. Biographers 8. Social reformers 9. Socialist leaders 10. Writers on politics

ISBN 978-1-4263-0137-7; 1-4263-0137-5; 978-1-4263-0138-4 lib bdg; 1-4263-0138-3 lib bdg

LC 2007-11391

This describes "muckrakers, 20th-century journalists who investigated corruption and called for reform. . . . The well-captioned, black-and-white illustrations, mainly photos, are sometimes reproduced with a sepia tone. . . . Clearly written, this offers a very readable and informative introduction to American muckrakers." Booklist

Includes bibliographical references

Reeves, Diane Lindsey

TV journalist; [by] Diane Lindsey Reeves. Ferguson 2007 64p il (Virtual apprentice) $29.95

Grades: 6 7 8 9   **070.4**

1. Vocational guidance 2. Television broadcasting of news

ISBN 978-0-8160-6753-4; 0-8160-6753-8

LC 2006-36570

This book about becoming a TV journalist is "written with engaging language capable of drawing even reluctant readers into the prose. . . . Pop quizzes, information boxes, quotes from famous people in the field, and on-the-job description make these books highly attractive to the target audience." Libr Media Connect

070.5   Publishing

Todd, Mark
Whatcha mean, what's a zine? the art of making zines and mini comics. [by] Mark Todd + Esther Peal Watson; with contributions by more than 20 creators of Indie-comics and magazines. Houghton Mifflin 2006 110p il pa $12.99
Grades: 7 8 9 10   **070.5**
1. Desktop publishing 2. Comic books, strips, etc. 3. Zines
ISBN 978-0-618-56315-9; 0-618-56315-6
LC 2005-55026
"A zine is a mini-magazine or homemade comic about any topic of the creator's choice, designed for maximum creativity and expression. The authors present a history of self-publishing. . . . Other topics include ideas for zine subjects; copying, binding, and printing tips, including easy-to-understand silk-screening and gocco instruction. . . . Throughout, technical terms are deftly used and advice is dispensed in an accessible, rousing format that includes comics, drawings, and cut-and-paste zine techniques. This well-designed and entertaining resource is sure to find an audience among hip, artistic, and do-it-yourself enthusiasts." SLJ

081   General collections in specific languages and language families

Hudson, Wade
Powerful words; more than 200 years of extraordinary writing by African Americans. illustrated by Sean Qualls; foreword by Marian Wright Edelman. Scholastic Nonfiction 2004 178p il $19.95
Grades: 5 6 7 8   **081**
1. African Americans -- History 2. African Americans -- Biography 3. American literature -- African American authors
ISBN 0-439-40969-1
LC 2003-42792
A collection of speeches and writings by African Americans, with commentary about the time period in which each person lived, information about the speaker/writer, and public response to the words.
"Short enough to hold attention, the selections . . . are also long enough to show the writers' tone and style. Many sensitive full-page portraits are included. . . . This well-designed volume will be an excellent addition to many library collections." Booklist
Includes bibliographical references

098   Prohibited works, forgeries, hoaxes

Scales, Pat R.
Teaching banned books; 12 guides for young readers. American Library Association 2001 134p pa $28
Grades: Adult Professional   **098**
1. School libraries 2. Books -- Censorship 3. Children's

literature -- Study and teaching
ISBN 0-8389-0807-1
LC 01-22340
"Scales knows her material inside out. She also knows how to inspire others to take up this cause and gives them an effective handbook to do just that." Booklist
Includes bibliographical references

100   PHILOSOPHY

100   Philosophy, parapsychology and occultism, psychology

Law, Stephen
Really, really big questions; about the weird, the wonderful, and everything else. illustrated by Nishant Choksi. Kingfisher 2009 62p il $16.99
Grades: 5 6 7 8   **100**
1. Philosophy
ISBN 978-0-7534-6309-3; 0-7534-6309-1
An introduction to philosophy which uses clear analogies to explore some of life's biggest moral and scientific questions, including the origins of the universe and the meaning of life
"Through a combination of vibrant colors; hip, retro illustrations; and interesting quotes, Law has produced a stimulating work for young minds that is sure to spark conversation and, of course, more questions." SLJ

130   Parapsychology and occultism

Steiger, Brad
Gale encyclopedia of the unusual and unexplained; [by] Brad E. Steiger and Sherry Hansen Steiger. Thomson/Gale 2003 3v il map set $205
Grades: 7 8 9 10 11   **130**
1. Reference books 2. Occultism -- Encyclopedias 3. Supernatural -- Encyclopedias
ISBN 0-7876-5382-9
LC 2003-3995
"These volumes cover broad concepts from 'Afterlife Mysteries' to 'Invaders from Outer Space.' . . . [This is] an encyclopedia for believers. The volumes are meant to 'explore and describe the research of those who take such phenomena seriously.'. . . The work covers material of interest to a large segment of the public in a way that is clear and readable." Booklist
Includes bibliographical references

133   Specific topics in parapsychology and occultism

★ Paranormal phenomena: opposing viewpoints; Mary E. Williams, book editor. Greenhaven

Press/Thomson Gale 2003 205p il (Opposing
viewpoints series) lib bdg $21.95; pa $14.96
Grades: 7 8 9 10   **133**
1. Ghosts 2. Future life 3. Parapsychology 4.
Extrasensory perception 5. Unidentified flying objects
ISBN 0-7377-1238-4 lib bdg; 0-7377-1237-6 pa
LC 2002-66461
Replaces the edition published 1997 under the editorship
of Paul A. Winters

"Four chapters of four to six essays each offer opinions
on the reality of ghosts, psychic ability, extraterrestrial life,
UFO's, near-death experiences, reincarnation, and changing concepts of eternal life. Each essay is preceded by an
introduction, which poses questions to be answered in the
article." SLJ

Includes bibliographical references

133.1   Apparitions

Gudgeon, Christopher

Ghost trackers; the unreal world of ghosts, ghost-
hunting, and the paranormal. by Chris Gudgeon;
foreword by Joe MacLeod. Tundra Books 2010 75p
il pa $14.95
Grades: 4 5 6 7   **133.1**
1. Ghosts 2. Parapsychology
ISBN 978-0-88776-950-4; 0-88776-950-0

"Gudgeon thoroughly discusses all things ghostly. Chapters take on the history of sightings, scientists and paranormal research, haunted places around the world, and ghost
tracking. . . . Side boxes offer other assorted information,
and photographs and illustrations, some quite eerie, are
sprinkled throughout. The writing is clear and the subject is
presented in an evenhanded manner." SLJ

Hawes, Jason

Ghost hunt; chilling tales of the unknown. [by]
Jason Hawes & Grant Wilson; with Cameron Dokey.
Little Brown & Co. 2010 218p il $16.99
Grades: 4 5 6 7 8 9   **133.1**
1. Ghosts
ISBN 978-0-316-09959-2; 0-316-09959-7

"This collection of stories is based on case files from The
[Atlantic] Paranormal Society, TAPS, founded by Hawes
and Wilson. Each of the eight selections describes the sightings and paranormal activity from the perspective of the
observer, then describes how members of TAPS researched,
set up equipment, and discovered explanations for what happened. . . . The stories have enough elements of the unknown
to make them spine-tingling, but they are more mystery than
horror. . . . The easy-to-read format and subject matter will
keep even the most reluctant readers interested." SLJ

Followed by: Ghost hunt 2: more chilling tales of the
unknown (2011)

Ghost hunt 2; more chilling tales of the unknown.
by Jason Hawes and Grant Wilson; with Cameron
Dokey. Little Brown & Co. 2011 297p il $16.99

Grades: 4 5 6 7 8   **133.1**
1. Ghosts
ISBN 978-0-316-09958-5; 0-316-09958-9

"From ghostly spirits roaming Alcatraz to glowing red
eyes in the woods, The Atlantic Paranormal Society (aka the
popular reality television series Ghost Hunters) is back with
a compilation of even more chilling and terrifying tales. Selections include a restless spirit terrorizing a house-sitting
victim through her dreams, ghosts reappearing in the O.K.
Corral in Tombstone, AZ, and a saddened ghost revisiting a
lighthouse where her family was eradicated long ago." SLJ

Matthews, Rupert

Ghosts and spirits. QEB Pub. 2011 32p il (Un-
explained) lib bdg $28.50
Grades: 4 5 6 7   **133.1**
1. Ghosts 2. Apparitions
ISBN 978-1-59566-857-8; 1-59566-857-8
LC 2010014205
This discusses stories about ghosts and poltergeists.

"This well-written and thoughtfully designed [book] features [an] engrossing [topic]. . . . Though the pages are profusely illustrated with large, well-reproduced photographs
and drawings, the layout is not cluttered. This [book] just
might inspire kids to seek out more in-depth materials." SLJ

Includes glossary

Stefoff, Rebecca

Ghosts and spirits; [by] Rebecca Stefoff. Marshall Cavendish Benchmark 2007 94p il (Secrets of
the supernatural) lib bdg $32.79
Grades: 5 6 7 8   **133.1**
1. Ghosts
ISBN 978-0-7614-2634-9 lib bdg; 0-7614-2634-5
lib bdg
LC 2006031652
This is a history of beliefs in ghosts and spirits throughout the world, including haunted houses, spiritualism, haux-
es, and investigations into paranormal phenomena.

"Nearly every other page has an illustration. . . . The text
is accessible." Libr Media Connect

Includes glossary and bibliographical references

Wetzel, Charles

Haunted U.S.A. written by Charles Wetzel; il-
lustrated by Josh Cochran. Sterling 2008 86p il
(Mysteries unwrapped) pa $5.95
Grades: 5 6 7 8   **133.1**
1. Ghosts
ISBN 978-1-4027-3735-0 pa; 1-4027-3735-1 pa
LC 2007045905
"Wetzel tells stories of haunted America from the White
House to Hollywood. Although some of the places and people mentioned, such as the Amityville house and Rudolph
Valentino, might be unfamiliar to younger readers, the selections are still good ghost stories. . . . [The book has] an ample
number of clear black-and-white and full-color photographs
and illustrations. . . . Perfect for libraries that need a boost or
an update to their scary-story collections." SLJ

Includes bibliographical references

133.3 Divinatory arts

Stefoff, Rebecca

Prophets and prophecy; [by] Rebecca Stefoff. Marshall Cavendish Benchmark 2007 79p il (Secrets of the supernatural) lib bdg $32.79

Grades: 5 6 7 8   **133.3**
  1. Prophets 2. Prophecies
  ISBN 978-0-7614-2638-7 lib bdg; 0-7614-2638-8 lib bdg
                              LC 2007008779

This is a history of prophecy and fortune-telling from ancient times to the present, discussing such topics as tarot cards, the Oracle of Delphi, astrology, fate, Nostradamus, Jean Dixon, omens, and the I Ching.

"Nearly every other page has an illustration. . . . The text is accessible." Libr Media Connect

Includes glossary and bibliographical references

133.4 Demonology and witchcraft

Black magic and witches; Tamara L. Roleff, book editor. Greenhaven Press 2003 127p (Fact or fiction) $29.95; pa $21.20

Grades: 6 7 8 9   **133.4**
  1. Magic 2. Witchcraft
  ISBN 0-7377-1318-6; 0-7377-1319-4 pa
                              LC 2002-378

Explores both sides of the question of whether or not witchcraft is destructive, looking at issues related to the Harry Potter books, wiccans serving in the military, and the validity of magic

"This is a useful introduction to current debate over witchcraft." SLJ

Includes bibliographical references

Hirschmann, Kris

Demons. ReferencePoint Press 2011 80p il (Monsters and mythical creatures) $26.95

Grades: 5 6 7 8   **133.4**
  1. Demonology
  ISBN 978-1-60152-147-7; 1-60152-147-2
                              LC 2010029905

"Beginning with an introduction that explains the origins of the devilish creatures, the book discusses demon-like entities throughout cultures and religions. . . . The book's visuals, which include contemporary photos of ceremonies and artists' rendering of demons, can be quite startling. Excellent sidebars . . . cover topics such as the number of exorcists in the Catholic Church." Booklist

Includes bibliographical references

Kerns, Ann

Wizards and witches. Lerner Publications 2010 48p il (Fantasy chronicles) lib bdg $27.93

Grades: 4 5 6 7   **133.4**
  1. Witches
  ISBN 978-0-8225-9983-8 lib bdg; 0-8225-9983-X lib bdg
                              LC 2008050757

"The explanations and history behind . . . witches [and wizards] . . . will provide satisfaction for readers who want to know more about these familiar characters from myth, fantasy, and folk and fairy tales. Brief and concise." SLJ

Includes bibliographical references

Schanzer, Rosalyn

★ **Witches!** the absolutely true tale of disaster in Salem. National Geographic Society 2011 144p il $16.95; lib bdg $27.99

Grades: 6 7 8 9   **133.4**
  1. Witchcraft 2. Salem (Mass.) -- History
  ISBN 978-1-4263-0869-7; 1-4263-0869-8; 978-1-4263-0870-3 lib bdg; 1-4263-0870-1 lib bdg; 978-1-4263-0888-8 e-book
                              LC 2011012989

"With text that flows like a dramatic novel, Schanzer brings readers into the famous Salem trials, asking them to ponder the motivations of the accusers and the tribulations of the accused. Black-and-white ink prints and red accents are wonderfully evocative and set an appropriately horrific tone." SLJ

150 Psychology

Fullick, Ann

★ **Understanding** health and behavior. Heinemann Library 2009 56p il (Why science matters) lib bdg $32.86; pa $9.49

Grades: 7 8 9 10   **150**
  1. Health 2. Human behavior 3. Animal behavior
  ISBN 978-1-4329-1840-8 lib bdg; 1-4329-1840-0 lib bdg; 978-1-4329-1853-8 pa; 1-4329-1853-2 pa
                              LC 2008-14349

This book discusses various behaviors, including reactions to hunger and social interactions, observations of people and animals in laboratories and natural environments, the role of nature and nurture on the development of humans and animals, and the effects of exercise, diet, and drug use

"The layout is bright and engaging. . . . This book should be engaging to its target readers and will provide them with a behavioral perspective on topics that will be both relevant and critically important to them throughout their teen and adult years." Sci Books & Films

Includes glossary and bibliographical references

Gardner, Robert

★ **Health** science projects about psychology; [by] Robert Gardner and Barbara Gardner Conklin. Enslow Pubs. 2002 112p il (Science projects) $26.60

Grades: 7 8 9 10   **150**
  1. Psychology 2. Science projects
  ISBN 0-7660-1439-8
                              LC 2001-3425

Uses science projects to explore such areas of psychology as personality, emotions, perception, learning, memory, and parapsychology

"Schools with psychology classes should find this title helpful as well as schools whose students participate in science fair competitions." Book Rep

Includes bibliographical references

Kincher, Jonni

Psychology for kids vol. 1: 40 fun tests that help you learn about yourself; [by] Jonni Kincher; [edited by Julie Bach and Pamela Espeland] updated ed.; Free Spirit Pub. Inc. 2008 132p il pa $21.95

Grades: 6 7 8 9   **150**

1. Personality 2. Psychological tests
ISBN 978-1-57542-283-1

LC 2008020660

First published 1990

"Are you an extrovert or an introvert? An optimist or a pessimist? Can you predict the future? Are you creative? Left-brained or right-brained? What body language do you speak? Do you have ESP? Based on . . . psychological concepts, these 40 . . . tests help kids explore their interests and abilities." Publisher's note

Includes bibliographical references

Psychology for kids vol. 2: 40 fun experiments that help you learn about others. Free Spirit Pub. 2008 132p il pa $21.95

Grades: 6 7 8 9   **150**

1. Psychology
ISBN 978-1-57542-284-8

LC 2008020663

First published 1995

"Are people more logical or emotional? How do people make judgments? Do males and females see things differently? Can we shape other people's behavior? Are we more alike or more different? Based on science and . . . psychological concepts and research, 40 . . . experiments make it fun for kids to learn about what makes people tick." Publisher's note

Includes bibliographical references

152.1   Sensory perception

Jackson, Donna M.

Phenomena; secrets of the senses. Little, Brown and Company 2008 174p il $16.99

Grades: 6 7 8 9   **152.1**

1. Senses and sensation 2. Extrasensory perception
ISBN 978-0-316-16649-2; 0-316-16649-9

LC 2008-31215

"Students with an interest in the weird and unusual will find this book fascinating. It begins with an introduction to human senses and continues with chapters devoted to phenomena such as the 'sixth sense,' synethesia, and intuition. One of the most interesting sections discusses animals that use their senses in unusual ways. . . . The black-and-white illustrations and photographs are plentiful enough to make the text accessible to reluctant readers. Accurate, entertaining nonfiction." SLJ

Includes glossary and bibliographical references

152.14   Visual perception

Vry, Silke

Trick of the eye; art and illusion. Prestel 2010 89p il $14.95

Grades: 4 5 6   **152.14**

1. Art appreciation 2. Optical illusions
ISBN 978-3-7913-7026-2; 3-7913-7026-X

"From the Parthenon to the Mona Lisa to the Op-Art of the 1960s, images and text reveal the many ways our eyes play tricks on us. Perception of size and color is discussed using standard optical illusions, but this book includes much more. Anecdotes, such as the story of dueling Greek painters Zeuxis and Parrhasius, and unique reproductions, like portraits with altered facial features, lend excitement. The author has taken an interactive approach, filling the pages with questions, puzzles, and project ideas. . . . Text explains the images, which are large and clear. The broad range of styles represented and the fun of the interactive approach will no doubt appeal to young art lovers and curious kids alike." SLJ

Wick, Walter

★ **Walter** Wick's optical tricks; by Walter Wick. 10th anniversary edition; Cartwheel Books 2008 43p il $14.99

Grades: 4 5 6 7   **152.14**

1. Optical illusions
ISBN 978-0-439-85520-4; 0-439-85520-9

First published 1998

Presents a series of optical illusions and explains what is seen.

The author "has produced a stunning picture book of optical illusions. With crystal-clear photographs, he creates a series of scenes that fool the eye and the brain." Booklist [review of 1998 ed.]

152.4   Emotions

Andrews, Linda Wasmer

Emotional intelligence. Franklin Watts 2004 80p il (Life balance) $19.50

Grades: 5 6 7 8 9   **152.4**

1. Emotions
ISBN 0-531-12335-9

LC 2003-19772

"This book explains that the ability to manage one's emotions and to understand those of others is important for success in life. . . . This title will help young people to understand themselves and others better, and the tools for managing relationships and one's own emotions will promote maturity and development of social skills." SLJ

Includes glossary and bibliographical references

DiConsiglio, John

Out of control; how to handle anger--yours and everyone else's. Franklin Watts 2008 112p il (Scholastic choices) lib bdg $22.50

Grades: 7 8 9 10 **152.4**
1. Anger
ISBN 978-0-531-18846-0 lib bdg; 0-531-1-8846-9 lib bdg

LC 2007008648

This book has "a magazine-like feel to [it], with glossy pages, lots of photos and graphics, an eye-catching layout with sidebars and boxes, and even tests and quizzes. There is solid content behind the slick facade, though. [The book] delves into the physical and emotional roots of anger, exploring the differences between healthy and unhealthy reactions, and discussing anger-management techniques." Voice Youth Advocates

Includes glossary and bibliographical references

Guarino, Robert

Me and my feelings; what emotions are and how we can manage them. written by Robert Guarino; illustrated by Jeff Jackson; foreword by Robert Ornstein. Hoopoe Books 2011 162p il pa $15.99
Grades: 7 8 9 10 **152.4**
1. Emotions
ISBN 978-1-933779-71-3; 1-933779-71-3

This "title devotes a chapter each to the 'primary' emotions—fear, anger, sadness, happiness, surprise, and disgust—and how to handle them, along with an easy-to-understand discussion. . . . 'Secondary' emotions like pride, jealousy, and love are briefly explored in a separate section. With cartoonlike illustrations throughout, interesting situations, and concise scientific explanations, the book offers a wealth of information in an accessible format." SLJ

Tym, Kate

Coping with your emotions; [by] Kate Tym and Penny Worms. Raintree 2005 48p il (Get real) $29.93
Grades: 6 7 8 9 **152.4**
1. Emotions
ISBN 1-4109-0575-6

LC 2004-8069

"Chapters consist of a spread presenting an overview of a topic such as depression . . . followed by three case studies about teens dealing with the problem. On the same page, three 'experts' . . . offer advice. . . . The advice of professionals lends credibility to the information presented. . . . Sure to appeal to readers looking for advice." SLJ

Inlcudes glossary and bibliographical references

153.1 Memory and learning

Hudmon, Andrew

★ **Learning** and memory. Chelsea House Publishers 2005 136p il (Gray matter) $32.95
Grades: 8 9 10 11 12 **153.1**
1. Brain 2. Memory 3. Psychology of learning
ISBN 0-7910-8638-0

LC 2005-11699

This "volume provides fascinating insights into various processes involved in how we learn different things in different ways. Particularly enlightening is the section differenti-

ating explicit memory (learning facts) and implicit memory (learning processes) . . . The [book features] colorful historical photos and illustrations, process models, and shaded insets." SLJ

Includes bibliographical references

153.4 Thought, thinking, reasoning, intuition, value, judgment

Watanabe, Ken

No problem! an easy guide to getting what you want. illustrated by Elwood H. Smith; adapted by Sarah L. Thomson. Viking 2010 70p il $16.99; pa $9.99
Grades: 4 5 6 **153.4**
1. Problem solving
ISBN 978-0-670-01203-9; 0-670-01203-3; 978-0-670-01254-1 pa; 0-670-01254-8 pa

Adaptation of: Problem solving 101, published 2009 for adults

"This little gem explains how to approach intimidating goals or jobs by breaking them down into simple tasks. Realistic scenarios such as finding money for a big purchase or choosing a high school are approached with data-driven evaluation tools. The author defines the steps involved along with terms such as hypotheses, logic trees, matrixes, and evaluation charts." SLJ

153.6 Communication

Jackson, Donna M.

★ **Every** body's talking; what we say without words. by Donna M. Jackson. Twenty-First Century Books 2014 64 p. illustrations (lib. bdg. : alk. paper) $30.60
Grades: 5 6 7 8 9 **153.6**
1. Body language 2. Nonverbal communication
ISBN 1467708585; 9781467708586

LC 2013019674

This book, by Donna M. Jackson, "explores the complexities of body language. Discover what is really being expressed when people stand, sit, or move in certain ways and learn how you can use your body and facial expressions to communicate more effectively in a variety of situations." (Publisher's note)

"Nonverbal clues including stance, facial expression, posture, eye contact, and others add meaning to our words, or sometimes contradict them. Using second-person narration to engage readers, suggestions for interpreting body language is followed by a chapter explaining how cultural differences affect interpretations. A final chapter encourages readers to practice physical positions to increase confidence. Plentiful full-color pictures illustrate concepts." Horn Book

Includes bibliographical references and index

153.8   Will (Volition)

Bachel, Beverly K.

★ **What** do you really want? how to set a goal and go for it! A guide for teens. Free Spirit 2000 134p il pa $12.95

Grades: 7 8 9 10 11 12   **153.8**

1. Success 2. Motivation (Psychology)

ISBN 1-57542-085-6

LC 00-57286

The book discusses various ways for teenagers to set goals, build support networks, keep themselves motivated in the process and reap the harvest of their successes

Bachel's "helpful advice is well supported by quotations from teens who have tried some of the techniques, and simple, appealing graphics keep things light. . . . Back matter includes goal-setting resources and some helpful organizations and Web sites." Booklist

Sobel, David

What's the catch? how to avoid getting hooked and manipulated. illustrated by Jeff Jackson; foreword by Robert Ornstein. Hoopoe Books 2011 138p il pa $15.99

Grades: 7 8 9 10   **153.8**

1. Mass media 2. Advertising 3. Persuasion (Psychology)

ISBN 978-1-933779-78-2; 1-933779-78-2

This "is a guide for teens to understand how they are influenced by parents, peers, and the media, often without knowing it. Chapters explain advertising methods and their effect on consumers, and a discussion of Internet safety is included. . . . Although [this] clearly written, well-organized [book] could be read independently, [it includes] questions for discussion and classroom activities, making [it an] excellent [resource] for group discussions." SLJ

153.9   Intelligence and aptitudes

Armstrong, Thomas

You're smarter than you think; a kid's guide to multiple intelligences. edited by Jennifer Brannen. Free Spirit 2003 186p il pa $15.95

Grades: 7 8 9 10 11 12   **153.9**

1. Intellect

ISBN 1-57542-113-5

LC 2002-2687

The author "covers eight different intelligences—word, music, logic, picture, body, people, self, and nature—and talks about what they mean." Booklist

"A self-help book that's clear, concise, and fun to peruse." SLJ

Includes bibliographical references

155.3   Sex psychology; psychology of people by gender or sex, by sexual orientation

Rosen, Michael J.

Girls vs. guys; surprising differences between the sexes. by Michael J. Rosen. Twenty-First Century Books 2015 72 p. color illustrations (lib. bdg. : alk. paper) $33.27

Grades: 6 7 8 9 10   **155.3**

1. Gender role 2. Sex differences (Psychology) 3. Gender identity

ISBN 1467716103; 9781467716109

LC 2013021833

In this book "author Michael J. Rosen explores the ways in which environment and experience, as well as neurology, physiology, and genetics come together to shape personality and gender behavior - in both expected and unexpected ways." (Publisher's note)

"Approachable format, attractive design, and breezy writing make this look at the science of sex differences both appealing and informative. Rosen highlights current research around varied intriguing topics such as what makes each gender laugh, which is more likely to be struck by lightning, and which sex is more attractive to mosquitoes." Horn Book

Includes bibliographical references and index

155.45   Exceptional children; children by social and economic levels, by ethnic or national group

Fonseca, Christine

101 success secrets for gifted kids; the ultimate guide. Prufrock Press 2011 xi, 191p pa $14.95

Grades: 4 5 6 7 8   **155.45**

1. Gifted children

ISBN 978-1-59363-544-2; 1-59363-544-3

LC 2011004912

"Fonseca explains what it means to be labeled 'gifted,' how to cope in school, and how to interact with friends and family. Information is delivered in a friendly, conversational manner with firsthand advice from gifted kids and their parents. The myriad tips include how to deal with stress, how to complete homework assignments effectively, how to be respectful of others, how to accept oneself, and even how to deal with bullies. All are incredibly useful." SLJ

Includes bibliographical references

155.5   Psychology of young people twelve to twenty

Hugel, Bob

I did it without thinking; true stories about impulsive decisions that changed lives. Franklin Watts 2008 112p il (Scholastic choices) lib bdg $27; pa $8.95

Grades: 6 7 8 9 10   **155.5**

1. Decision making 2. Adolescent psychology 3. Risk-

taking (Psychology)

ISBN 978-0-531-13868-7 lib bdg; 0-531-13868-2 lib bdg; 978-0-531-20526-6 pa; 0-531-20526-6 pa

LC 2008-690

Teenagers give their stories of impulsive decisions, their reasons for making them, and the consequences—whether good or bad.

This book is "colorful and compact, with . . . an appealing layout. . . . The stories, while not overly preachy, are brief and generally upbeat. . . . [The] book has excellent black-and-white photographs of a diverse array of teens." SLJ

Includes glossary and bibliographical references

Saval, Malina

The **secret** lives of boys; inside the raw emotional world of male teens. Basic Books 2009 257p $25.95

Grades: Adult Professional 155.5

1. Boys -- Psychology

ISBN 978-0-465-00254-2; 0-465-00254-4

LC 2008-49703

The author "sought to find out if teen boys really were seriously at risk, and to offer, if possible, a more nuanced portrayal of young males. On both counts, she has succeeded. Through in-depth interviews and research, she portrays the lives of 10 young males. . . . It is a fascinating take on the subject, written in a clear and lively style with a useful index and interesting endnotes that can lead to further exploration." SLJ

Includes bibliographical references

Van Wagenen, Maya

★ **Popular**; Vintage wisdom for a modern geek. Maya Van Wagenen. Dutton Juvenile 2014 272 p. illustrations (hardback) $18.99

Grades: 7 8 9 10 155.5

1. Popularity 2. Middle schools 3. Autobiographies 4. Teenage girls 5. Self-confidence 6. Life skills -- Humor

ISBN 0525426817; 9780525426813

LC 2014000236

YALSA Award for Excellence in Nonfiction for Young Adults (2015)

This memoir by Maya Van Wagenen tells how "stuck near the bottom of the social ladder at 'pretty much the lowest level of people at school who aren't paid to be here,' Maya has never been popular. But before starting eighth grade, she decides to begin a unique social experiment: spend the school year following a 1950s popularity guide, written by former teen model Betty Cornell." (Publisher's note)

"The clash of eras and cultures is funny—the author wears a girdle, hat, and pearls to class; learns how to apply makeup; improves her posture and poise; and tries a diet. But the best lessons she learns . . . are about how to talk to and understand the people around her." SLJ

155.9 Environmental psychology

De la Bedoyere, Camilla

Balancing work and play. Amicus 2010 46p il (Healthy lifestyles) lib bdg $32.80

Grades: 7 8 9 10 11 12 155.9

1. Stress (Psychology)

ISBN 978-1-60753-083-1; 1-60753-083-X

This book is "well-written and satisfyingly informative. . . . [The] magazine-like format includes numerous sidebars, color photos, and charts." SLJ

Includes glossary

Gootman, Marilyn E.

★ **When** a friend dies; a book for teens about grieving & healing. edited by Pamela Espeland. Rev. and updated ed.; Free Spirit Pub. 2005 118p pa $9.95

Grades: 7 8 9 10 155.9

1. Death 2. Bereavement

ISBN 1-57542-170-4

LC 2005-447

First published 1994

This offers "information on subjects including: How can I stand the pain? How should I be acting? What is 'normal'? What if I can't handle my grief on my own? and How can I find a counselor or a therapist? Interspersed throughout the book . . . are quotes by teenagers who have experienced grief. . . . Quotes from well-known writers and philosophers give insight into the grieving process and healing." SLJ

Harmon, Dan

Frequently asked questions about overscheduling and stress; [by] Daniel E. Harmon. Rosen Pub. 2010 64p il (FAQ: teen life) lib bdg $29.25

Grades: 7 8 9 10 155.9

1. Stress (Psychology)

ISBN 978-1-4358-3514-6; 1-4358-3514-X

LC 2009-17825

"Common stressors such as multi-tasking and over-filling one's schedule are discussed, along with how too much stress can cause damage to one's body. Suggestions are made on how to rethink scheduling and de-stress one's life. . . . This is a good resource for teens struggling to understand what is happening to themselves or to their friends." Voice Youth Advocates

Includes glossary and bibliographical references

Myers, Edward

★ **When** will I stop hurting? teens, loss, and grief. illustrations by Kelly Adams. Scarecrow Press 2004 159p il (It happened to me) $34.50

Grades: 7 8 9 10 155.9

1. Bereavement 2. Loss (Psychology)

ISBN 0-8108-4921-6

LC 2003-23698

This book "will be extremely helpful for teens struggling to understand their emotions following the loss of a loved one. Grieving is well explained and the individual nature of grief is stressed." Libr Media Connect

Includes bibliographical references

Phillips, Tracy A.

Losing someone you love; dealing with death and dying. Enslow Publishers 2009 104p il (Issues in focus today) lib bdg $31.93

Grades: 7 8 9 10   **155.9**
1. Death 2. Bereavement
ISBN 978-0-7660-3067-1 lib bdg; 0-7660-3067-9
lib bdg

LC 2008042872

"The final chapters are most helpful, detailing typical
responses and reactions to grief as well as how to find support and to be supportive.... Bold subheads, interior color
photos, and pull quotes break up the text.... Keep this title
on the assignment shelf." SLJ
Includes glossary and bibliographical references

Simons, Rae
   Survival skills; how to handle life's catastrophes.
Mason Crest Publishers 2009 128p il (Survivors:
ordinary people, extraordinary circumstances) lib
bdg $24.95
Grades: 5 6 7 8   **155.9**
1. Life skills 2. Survival skills
ISBN 978-1-4222-0456-6 lib bdg; 1-4222-0456-1
lib bdg

LC 2008-50320

"Begins with a brief and accessible discussion of the
psychology of stress and its role in adolescence, and offers
twelve pieces of advice for overcoming difficult experiences
and catastrophes.... [This book features] important, and
sometimes complex, information in an easy-to-read format,
offering high gloss photographs, marginal glossary notes,
concept definitions, a bibliography, and further reading
reccommendations." Voice Youth Advocates
Includes glossary and bibliographical references

158   Applied psychology

Amblard, Odile
   Friends forever? why your friendships are so important. by Odile Amblard; illustrated by Andree Pri-
gent; edited by Andrea Bussell. Amulet Books 2008
112p il (Sunscreen) $9.95
Grades: 5 6 7 8   **158**
1. Friendship 2. Interpersonal relations
ISBN 978-0-8109-9480-5; 0-8109-9480-1

LC 2007-43138

"The importance of friendship is stressed in the opening of Friends Forever?, followed by brief discussions on
the types of friendships and how they are formed and maintained.... The tone of the [book] is breezy and light without
being flippant. The [author] never [talks] down to the teen
reader." Voice Youth Advocates

Andrews, Linda Wasmer
   Meditation; [by] Linda Wasmer Andrews. F.
Watts 2004 79p (Life balance) $19.50; pa $6.95
Grades: 5 6 7 8   **158**
1. Meditation
ISBN 0-531-12219-0; 0-531-16609-0 pa

LC 2003-7153

"Andrews emphasizes that meditation is not a flaky practice, or a particularly religious one, but one that's designed to
reduce stress and help individuals manage their lives. Four

chapters explain the why and how of meditating.... [This
offers] solid, easy-to-understand information" SLJ
Includes bibliographical references

Auderset, Marie-Josee
   Walking tall; how to build confidence and be the
best you can be. by Marie-Jose Auderset; illustrated
by Gaetan de Seguin; edited by N.B. Grace. Amulet
Books 2008 112p il (Sunscreen) $9.95
Grades: 5 6 7 8   **158**
1. Self-confidence
ISBN 978-0-8109-9479-9; 0-8109-9479-8

LC 2007-43416

This "addresses issues of self-confidence and section one
deals with feelings of high and low self-esteem, acceptance
of oneself, and body image issues. It includes an exercise to
help the reader realize her strengths and use that realization
to build self-confidence.... The tone of the [book] is breezy
and light without being flippant. The [author] never [talks]
down to the teen reader." Voice Youth Advocates
Includes bibliographical references

Bezdecheck, Bethany
   Relationships; 21st-century roles. Rosen Pub.
2010 112p il (A young woman's guide to contemporary issues) lib bdg $31.95
Grades: 7 8 9 10   **158**
1. Family 2. Friendship 3. Interpersonal relations
ISBN 978-1-4358-3540-5; 1-4358-3540-9

LC 2009-12065

"Facts are shared in a conversational tone, creating the
sense of a chat with a big sister.... [Though] designed for
personal reading and browsing, the data provided are accurate and also lend themselves to use in reports. This ... will
be of great interest." SLJ
Includes glossary and bibliographical references

Canfield, Jack
   Chicken soup for the teenage soul [I-IV] [by]
Jack Canfield, Mark Victor Hansen, Kimberly Kir-
berger. Health Communications 1997 4v il hardcover o.p. v1 pa $14.95; v2 pa $9.99; v3 pa $14.95;
v4 pa $14.95
Grades: 7 8 9 10 11 12   **158**
1. Emotions 2. Interpersonal relations
ISBN 1-55874-468-1 [I]; 1-55874-463-0 [I pa];
1-55874-615-3 [II]; 1-55874-616-1 [II pa]; 1-55874-
761-3 [III]; 0-7573-0233-5 [IV]
These books cover "teenage subjects running the gamut
from love, family ties, and self-esteem to developing values
and life crises, such as a death in the family.... Teenagers
not only helped select the poems, stories, and accounts that
have been included but also have written some of them .
. . with a few contributions by well-known people, including Sandra Cisneros, Helen Keller, and Robert Fulghum. .
. . This isn't a religious book, but it is an inspirational and
motivational one, sometimes funny, sometimes poignant."
Booklist [review of 1997 volume]
Includes bibliographical references

Chicken soup for the teenage soul's the real deal; school: cliques, classes, clubs, and more. [compiled by] Jack Canfield, Mark Victor Hansen, Deborah Reber. Health Communications 2005 292p pa $12.95

Grades: 7 8 9 10   **158**
1. Emotions 2. Interpersonal relations
ISBN 0-7573-0255-6

LC 2005046051

"The stories included here were submitted by students and are based on their own experiences. Almost every page includes a fun fact, a statistic, or a quiz." SLJ

Crist, James J.

What to do when you're sad & lonely; a guide for kids. [by] James J. Crist. Free Spirit Pub. 2006 124p il pa $9.95

Grades: 4 5 6 7   **158**
1. Solitude 2. Depression (Psychology)
ISBN 978-1-57542-189-6 pa; 1-57542-189-5 pa

LC 2005021794

"Advising his audience to read this book and work through negative feelings with an adult, Crist describes sad and lonely feelings, distinguishes them from more serious conditions such as depression, and then suggests 'Blues Busters' and ways to ask for help. . . . Crist's clear explanations and simple techniques . . . are relevant for both children and adults." Voice Youth Advocates

Includes bibliographical references

★ **What** to do when you're scared & worried; a guide for kids. [by] James Crist. Free Spirit Pub. 2004 128p il pa $9.95

Grades: 4 5 6 7   **158**
1. Fear 2. Worry
ISBN 1-57542-153-4

"Part one deals with normal anxiety, offering detailed steps for developing 10 coping mechanisms. Expert help is needed to deal with the more serious problems discussed in Part two (e.g., phobias, separation anxiety, obsessive-compulsive disorder). Throughout, the author provides information, case histories, and coping skills in a manner that is both reassuring and encouraging. . . . Illustrations lighten the tone of the subject matter." SLJ

Includes bibliographical references

Fox, Annie

Be confident in who you are; [by] Annie Fox. Free Spirit Pub. 2008 92p il (Middle school confidential) pa $9.95

Grades: 5 6 7 8   **158**
1. Self-confidence
ISBN 978-1-57542-302-9; 1-57542-302-2

LC 2008-4754

"The book contains quizzes, is chock-full of helpful hints, and lists other resources to help readers increase their self-esteem. Kindt's cartoons include several great panels that move the teens' story forward. The graphic-novel-like design will make this self-help tool stand out and appeal to fans of that format." SLJ

Real friends vs. the other kind. Free Spirit Pub. 2009 90p il

Grades: 5 6 7 8   **158**
1. Friendship 2. Interpersonal relations
ISBN 1-57542-319-7 pa; 978-1-57542-319-7 pa

LC 2008031368

"Jack, Abby, Mateo, Jen, Chris, and Michelle are the middle school students of various ethnicities who take readers through this slim, interactive guide. Chapters cover such topics as friendship dilemmas, so-called friends, when friendships aren't working, crushes, and making new friends. Each chapter opens with a scene played out by the students in cartoon panels. Next, bits of text, along with a multitude of side boxes, address the topic at hand. . . . Lists of questions are offered, along with the answers. There's a lot packed into this colorful title that falls somewhere between self-help and peer advice." SLJ

★ **Too** stressed to think? a teen guide to staying sane when life makes you crazy. by Annie Fox and Ruth Kirschner; edited by Elizabeth Verdick. Free Spirit Pub. 2005 163p il pa $14.95

Grades: 7 8 9 10   **158**
1. Stress (Psychology)
ISBN 1-57542-173-9

LC 2005018484

"This well-organized, upbeat book discusses what stress is and how it affects the body and brain, talks about tools to reduce and control it, and gives suggestions for recognizing the myriad situations that can trigger stress at home and at school and seeking help when necessary. Best of all, each one of these scenarios includes information on how the situation might be addressed." SLJ

Includes bibliographical references

Hantman, Clea

30 days to getting over the dork you used to call your boyfriend; a heartbreak handbook. by Clea Hantman. Delacorte Press 2008 161p il pa $7.99

Grades: 8 9 10 11 12   **158**
1. Loss (Psychology)
ISBN 978-0-385-73549-0 pa; 0-385-73549-9 pa

LC 2007005945

"Hautman outlines a thirty-day process to help teens get through the five stages of a break-up—denial, anger, bargaining, depression, and acceptance. . . . Each day involves exercises to help put events, one's ex, and oneself in perspective. Each day also has a song of the day, which highlights the day's theme, and a bonus inspirational haiku. . . . The process and activities are helpful and even fun." Voice Youth Advocates

Harris, Ashley Rae

★ **Cliques,** crushes & true friends; developing healthy relationships. ABDO Pub. Co. 2009 112p il (Essential health: strong, beautiful girls) lib bdg $22.95

Grades: 6 7 8 9   **158**
1. Friendship 2. Interpersonal relations 3. Girls --

Psychology
ISBN 978-1-60453-099-5; 1-60453-099-5
                                            LC 2008-12103
This guide to healthy relationships covers the social
world of adolescent girls.

"Each chapter tells a personal narrative, with a consulting doctor giving insight and making suggestions. The topics are well selected, the design is attractive, and the stories feature girls from a variety of cultures." Booklist

Includes glossary and bibliographical references

★ **Girl** in the mirror; understanding physical changes. ABDO Pub. 2009 112p il (Essential health: strong, beautiful girls) lib bdg $22.95
Grades: 6 7 8 9   158
1. Puberty 2. Self-esteem
ISBN 978-1-60453-100-8; 1-60453-100-2
                                            LC 2008-11903
This features fictional narratives paired with firsthand advice from a licensed psychologist to help preteen and teen girls feel comfortable with their changing bodies and know that they are not alone. Situations include developing early and "late-bloomers".

Includes glossary and bibliographical references

Jones, Jami Biles
Bouncing back; dealing with the stuff life throws at you. [by] Jami L. Jones. Franklin Watts 2007 112p il (Choices) lib bdg $22.50; pa $8.95
Grades: 6 7 8 9 10 11 12   158
1. Personality 2. Problem solving
ISBN 0-531-12404-5 lib bdg; 978-0-531-12404-8 lib bdg; 0-531-17730-0 pa; 978-0-531-17730-3 pa
                                            LC 2004018426
"The image of a bouncing ball is used effectively throughout this book to discuss the concept of resiliency in the context of adjusting to life's problems. Each chapter begins with a short vignette of a teen facing a stressful situation and ends by reminding readers of the story and hypothesizing solutions. . . . The advice given is psychologically sound, the writing is clear and easy to read, the pages are visually appealing, and photos show teens of both genders and various racial backgrounds." SLJ

Includes glossary and bibliographical references

McIntyre, Thomas
★ The **behavior** survival guide for kids; how to make good choices and stay out of trouble. [by] Thomas McIntyre. Free Spirit Pub. 2003 167p pa $14.95
Grades: 5 6 7 8   158
1. Conduct of life 2. Interpersonal relations
ISBN 1-57542-132-1
                                            LC 2003-4565
"The author provides skills and activities to learn and practice so that new behaviors can replace those that have resulted in getting students into trouble. . . . Those motivated to make better choices for how they behave in school or with friends and family will find much to help them." Voice Youth Advocates

Moss, Wendy
Being me; a kid's guide to boosting confidence and self-esteem. by Wendy L. Moss. Magination Press 2010 112p il $14.95; pa $9.95
Grades: 5 6 7 8   158
1. Self-esteem 2. Self-confidence
ISBN 978-1-4338-0883-8; 1-4338-0883-8; 978-1-4338-0884-5 pa; 1-4338-0884-6 pa
                                            LC 2010014384
"Moss encourages her young audience to concentrate on two areas: focusing on inner self-esteem and building social confidence. Through procedure and practice . . . Moss reminds kids that real confidence doesn't come from being the smartest, prettiest, or the most popular one in the room but from the comfort one has with him- or herself. . . . Moss' offering gives great tips for the truly interested." Booklist

Orr, Tamra
★ **Beautiful** me; finding personal strength & self acceptance. ABDO Pub. 2009 112p il (Essential health: Strong, beautiful girls) lib bdg $22.95
Grades: 6 7 8 9   158
1. Self-esteem 2. Depression (Psychology)
ISBN 978-1-60453-098-8; 1-60453-098-7
                                            LC 2008-11902
This is "about girls who have dealt with depression, let their self-esteem waffle, and even engaged in dangerous behaviors in the process of finding themselves." Publisher's note

"The topics are well selected, the design is attractive, and the stories feature girls from a variety of cultures." Booklist

Includes glossary and bibliographical references

Owens, L. L.
★ **Frenemies**; dealing with friend drama. content consultant, Robyn J. A. Silverman. ABDO Pub. 2010 112p il (Essential health: strong, beautiful girls) lib bdg $32.79
Grades: 6 7 8 9   158
1. Friendship 2. Interpersonal relations 3. Girls -- Psychology
ISBN 978-1-60453-750-5; 1-60453-750-7
                                            LC 2009-2132
In this book about friendships "each chapter tells a personal narrative, with a consulting doctor giving insight and making suggestions. The topics are well selected, the design is attractive, and the stories feature girls from a variety of cultures." Booklist

Perrier, Pascale
Flying solo; how to soar above your lonely feelings, make friends, and find the happiest you. by Pascale Perrier with Erin Zimring; illustrated by Klaas Verplancke. Amulet Books 2007 112p il pa $9.95
Grades: 5 6 7 8   158
1. Solitude 2. Friendship
ISBN 978-0-8109-9281-8 pa; 0-8109-9281-7 pa
                                            LC 2006023609
"A self-help book with solid, practical advice. The text is divided into three sections or, as they are called here, phases: 'Why do I feel alone?,' 'How to stop feeling lonely,' and

'Finding solitude.' Each section has a series of subsections with quick discussions of mini-topics designed to hold readers' attention while imparting the necessary information. For the most part, the presentation is clear, understandable, and immediate. . . . The cartoon drawings are colorfully bright and match the text in its attempt to keep the tone light." SLJ

Piquemal, Michel

When life stinks; how to deal with your bad moods, blues, and depression. [by] Michel Piquemal with Melissa Daly; illustrated by Olivier Tossan ; [translated by Jane Moseley] Amulet Books 2004 112p il pa $9.95
Grades: 7 8 9 10   158
1. Depression (Psychology)
ISBN 0-8109-4932-6
                                         LC 2004-13001
"The pleasing use of blocks of color and cartoon illustrations enhances the text. . . . Using the common-sense suggestions provided, readers will more successfully navigate the turmoil of adolescence." SLJ
Includes bibliographical references

Romain, Trevor

★ **Cliques,** phonies & other baloney. Free Spirit 1998 129p il pa $9.95
Grades: 7 8 9 10   158
1. Friendship 2. Social groups 3. Interpersonal relations
ISBN 1-57542-045-7
                                         LC 98-36248
Discusses cliques, what they are and their negative aspects, and gives advice on forming healthier relationships and friendships
"With a sense of ease and lighthearted humor . . . the author serves up solid advice in friendly, reassuring prose." SLJ
Includes bibliographical references

Webber, Diane

Your space; dealing with friends and peers. F. Watts 2008 112p il (Scholastic choices) lib bdg $27; pa $8.95
Grades: 6 7 8 9   158
1. Friendship 2. Peer pressure
ISBN 978-0-531-18849-1 lib bdg; 0-531-18849-3 lib bdg; 978-0-531-14774-0 pa; 0-531-14774-6 pa
                                         LC 2007006579
Provides advice and tips for teenagers on making and maintaining worthwhile friendships, evaluating friendships and clique behavior, handling peer pressure, bullying, and staying safe on the Internet.
Includes bibliographical references

158.1   Personal improvement and analysis

Weeks, Marcus

Heads up psychology; Marcus Weeks. First American edition Dk Pub 2014 160 p. illustrations (some color) hbk $15.99

Grades: 7 8 9 10   158.1
1. Psychology 2. Psychologists 3. Human behavior
ISBN 1465419934; 9781465419934
In this book by Marcus Weeks, "psychological theories are explained with the help of cleverly conceived graphic illustrations and diagrams to show how they relate to everyday life. Biography spreads give interesting insights into the lives and work of Freud, Pavlov, and more, while other psychologists and their big ideas are profiled in a comprehensive directory, and case study panels describe groundbreaking experiments in the field." (Publisher's note)
"By interspersing explanations of topics and research studies with biographies of great thinkers, psychological pioneers, and researchers, Weeks helps readers connect fields of psychological study with names they may have heard or read. In true DK fashion, format, graphics, text boxes, pixelated portraits of scientists, bubbles, and balloons all contribute to making this a busy but appealing companion for high-school psychology textbooks." Booklist

170   Ethics (Moral philosophy)

Weinstein, Bruce D.

★ **Is** it still cheating if I don't get caught? [by] Bruce Weinstein; illustrations by Harriet Russell. Roaring Brook 2009 160p il pa $12.95
Grades: 8 9 10 11 12   170
1. Ethics
ISBN 978-1-59643-306-9; 1-59643-306-X
The author "addresses adolescent ethical dilemmas using a set of five 'Life Principles' (Do No Harm, Make Things Better, Respect Others, Be Fair, Be Loving)." Publ Wkly
"This appealing guide speaks to the ethical dilemmas that all young people experience in their daily lives, and it should prompt considerable conversation and reflection." Kirkus

174   Occupational ethics

★ **Ethics** in school librarianship; a reader. edited by Carol Simpson. Linworth Pub. 2003 164p pa $44.95
Grades: Adult Professional   174
1. School libraries 2. Librarians -- Ethics
ISBN 1-58683-084-8
                                         LC 2003-7956
This is a compilation of "articles dealing with the ethical aspects of collection development, access, confidentiality, technology, intellectual freedom, intellectual property, administration, Internet use, and professional relationships. . . . School librarians and administrators would do well to have this thought and discussion-provoking book on hand." SLJ
Includes bibliographical references

Hartman, Eve

Science ethics and controversies; [by] Eve Hartman and Wendy Meshbesher. Raintree 2009 48p il (Sci-hi: life science) $31.43; pa $8.99

Grades: 5 6 7 8　　　　　　　　　　　　　　**174**
　　1. Science -- Ethical aspects
　　ISBN 978-1-4109-3330-0; 1-4109-3330-X; 978-1-
　　4109-3338-6 pa; 1-4109-3338-5 pa
　　　　　　　　　　　　　　　　LC 2009003475
　　In this introduction to science ethics and controversies
"clear language, embedded definitions, and interesting examples illustrate abstract concepts through both text and
well-chosen photographs. . . . [It] discusses topics such as
global warming and animal research, and their implications
for decision-making by scientists, policy makers, and voters. Because so many issues are raised in this book, it will
be especially useful as a research starter in both science and
social-studies classes. . . . [The] book also includes suggested activities to test ideas as well as a thorough glossary and
a Webliography." SLJ
　　Includes glossary and bibliographical references

174.2　　Medical and health professions

Altman, Linda Jacobs
　　★ **Bioethics**; who lives, who dies, and who decides? Enslow Publishers 2006 112p il (Issues in
focus today) lib bdg $23.95
Grades: 7 8 9 10 11 12　　　　　　　　　**174.2**
　　1. Bioethics
　　ISBN 0-7660-2546-2; 978-0-7660-2546-2
　　　　　　　　　　　　　　　　LC 2006-07002
　　This "provides an overview of the big moral issues
brought about by breakthroughs in biotechnology. Altman is fair to all sides, whether the passionate argument is
about abortion, the cloning of animals, assisted suicide, artificial life support, or organ transplants. . . . The readable
style and clear, abundantly illustrated design will stimulate
debate." Booklist
　　Includes glossary and bibliographical references

Boskey, Elizabeth
　　America debates genetic DNA testing. Rosen
Central 2008 64p il (America debates) lib bdg
$29.25
Grades: 7 8 9 10　　　　　　　　　　　　**174.2**
　　1. Genetic screening
　　ISBN 978-1-4042-1926-7 lib bdg; 1-4042-1926-9
　　lib bdg
　　　　　　　　　　　　　　　　LC 2006-102516
　　The issues "are debated in a clear, concise manner. Col-
or photographs and boxed information highlighted in red
break up the [text]." SLJ
　　This "book explains genetic testing and examines the
debate over prenatal and adult testing, and the effects that
genetic DNA testing can potentially have on society." Publisher's note
　　Includes glossary and bibliographical references

Freedman, Jeri
　　America debates stem cell research. Rosen Central 2008 64p il map (America debates) lib bdg
$29.25

Grades: 7 8 9 10　　　　　　　　　　　　**174.2**
　　1. Stem cell research
　　ISBN 978-1-4042-1928-1 lib bdg; 1-4042-1928-5
　　lib bdg
　　　　　　　　　　　　　　　　LC 2007-1036
　　This book is an "overview of the issues surrounding
stem cells and their potential to revolutionize medicine and
provide cures, with a focus on the use of embryonic stem
cells. The ethical and moral debates over how cells are obtained, the definition of 'personhood,' and various religious
perspectives are explored, as well as how politics play a part
in the discussion of this issue. It includes a look at stem cell
research around the world." Publisher's note
　　Includes glossary and bibliographical references

Lovegrove, Ray
　　Health; ethical debates in modern medicine.
Black Rabbit Books 2008 46p il map (Dilemmas in
modern science) lib bdg $34.25
Grades: 7 8 9 10　　　　　　　　　　　　**174.2**
　　1. Medical ethics
　　ISBN 978-1-59920-095-8; 1-59920-095-3
　　　　　　　　　　　　　　　　LC 2007-35690
　　This title is "easy to navigate as evocative photographs,
charts, and sidebars help break down complicated arguments
into manageable parts for easy digestion." SLJ
　　Includes glossary and bibliographical references

Marzilli, Alan
　　Stem cell research and cloning. Chelsea House
2007 144p il (Point/counterpoint) lib bdg $35
Grades: 7 8 9 10　　　　　　　　　　　　**174.2**
　　1. Cloning 2. Stem cell research
　　ISBN 978-0-7910-9230-5 lib bdg; 0-7910-9230-5
　　lib bdg
　　　　　　　　　　　　　　　　LC 2006017148
　　"This book explores the legal and political ramifications
of the debates about [stem cell research and cloning], including federal funding for stem cell research, privately funded
research, and the government's role in limiting scientific inquiry." Publisher's note
　　Includes bibliographical references

Schafer, Susan
　　Cloning. M.E. Sharpe 2009 88p il (Genetics:
the science of life) $38.95
Grades: 6 7 8 9　　　　　　　　　　　　**174.2**
　　1. Cloning
　　ISBN 978-0-7656-8138-6; 0-7656-8138-2
　　　　　　　　　　　　　　　　LC 2008-8115
　　This discusses what cloning is, how it works, its ethics
and future.
　　"Chock-full of information. . . . Interest is maintained
through countless fascinating examples. . . . Illustrations and
color photographs enhance [the text]." SLJ
　　Includes bibliographical references

Uschan, Michael V., 1948-
　　Forty years of medical racism; the Tuskegee experiments. Lucent Books 2005 112p il map (Lucent
library of Black history) lib bdg $28.70

Grades: 8 9 10 11 12   **174.2**
1. Syphilis 2. Human experimentation in medicine 3. African Americans -- Health and hygiene
ISBN 1-59018-486-6

This is an account of "the Tuskegee Study of Untreated Syphilis in the Negro Male. . . . Halftone photographs of participants and of the persons who designed, conducted, or criticized the project supplement the text. Informational sidebars provide additional descriptions and photographs of some of the damage done by untreated syphilis." SLJ

Includes bibliographical references

Wittenstein, Vicki Oransky
For the good of mankind? the shameful history of human medical experimentation. Vicki Oransky Wittenstein. Twenty-First Century Books 2014 96 p. (lib. bdg. : alk. paper) $35.93
Grades: 7 8 9 10 11 12   **174.2**
1. Medical ethics 2. Science -- Experiments 3. Human experimentation in medicine -- History 4. Medical sciences -- Research -- Methodology -- History
ISBN 1467706590; 9781467706599
LC 2012043413

In this book, Vicki Oransky Wittenstein "describes many cringe-inducing examples of the ways doctors have exploited the marginalized, powerless and voiceless of society as human guinea pigs over the centuries. . . . Some experiments did lead to important discoveries and breakthroughs, but readers are challenged to consider the costs of violating individual rights for the cause of advancing medical knowledge." (Kirkus Reviews)

Includes bibliographical references (page 89) and index

176   Ethics of sex and reproduction

Cloning; William Dudley, book editor. Greenhaven Press 2005 112p il (Writing the critical essay) $26.20
Grades: 7 8 9 10   **176**
1. Cloning
ISBN 0-7377-3196-6

This presents essays representing various points of view on the ethics of cloning and includes questions designed to aid the reader in analyzing each essay.

Includes bibliographical references

178   Ethics of consumption

Kerr, Jim
★ Food; ethical debates on what we eat. Smart Apple Media 2009 46p il map (Dilemmas in modern science) lib bdg $34.25
Grades: 7 8 9 10   **178**
1. Food industry 2. Genetic engineering
ISBN 978-1-59920-094-1; 1-59920-094-5
LC 2007-39651

This title is "easy to navigate as evocative photographs, charts, and sidebars help break down complicated arguments into manageable parts for easy digestion." SLJ

"Presents both sides of food production issues, including animal welfare, high-tech farming, genetically modified foods, organic farming, food distribution, and world hunger." Publisher's note

Includes glossary and bibliographical references

179   Other ethical norms

Animal testing; life-saving research vs. animal welfare. by Lois Sepahban. First edition Compass Point Books 2015 30 p. (hardcover : alk. paper) $33.32
Grades: 6 7 8 9 10   **179**
1. Animal rights 2. Animal experimentation
ISBN 0756549965; 9780756549961; 9780756550455; 9780756550493
LC 2014026544

This book, by Lois Sepahban, is "like two books in one: Start from one end and learn why some people argue animal testing is needed. Then flip it over and discover why others argue it should be banned. Critical thinking questions help you analyze both perspectives and form your own opinions about the issue." (Publisher's note)

"There's tons of text here, but it's clear and engaging, featuring charts, real-life examples, color photos, and text boxes that supplement the narrative . . . [a] pertinent series for personal or academic use." SLJ

Includes bibliographical references

Belanger, Jeff
What it's like; to climb Mount Everest, blast off into space, survive a tornado, and other extraordinary stories. Sterling Pub. Co. 2010 136p il pa $9.95
Grades: 5 6 7 8   **179**
1. Courage 2. Anecdotes 3. Adventure and adventurers
ISBN 978-1-4027-6711-1; 1-4027-6711-0
LC 2009040875

"This illustrated collection presents short, first-person accounts of high-octane adventures—and, in some cases, personal disasters—by the people who actually experienced them. . . . The stories are told in present-tense, straightforward language, filled in with many pertinent and fascinating details. . . . The exciting action and the entries' short length will draw reluctant readers, as will the many color photographs, which are imaginatively laid out. This attractive package will be an easy sell." Booklist

Cheating; Stefan Kiesbye, book editor. Greenhaven Press 2010 107p (Social issues firsthand) $31.80
Grades: 7 8 9 10   **179**
1. Ethics 2. Honesty 3. Cheating (Education)
ISBN 978-0-7377-5009-6; 0-7377-5009-X
LC 2010000920

"The 13 entries in this book were written from the perspective of those who have cheated, for example, an 'economic hit man,' and those who have observed cheating, such as college professors. The selections are organized in several sections, including the school setting, the workplace, and sports. A list of organizations is included. This collection is particularly interesting because of the use of the personal narrative, and it is a good addition for libraries." SLJ

Includes bibliographical references

Factory farming; Debra A. Miller, book editor. Greenhaven Press 2010 183p (Current controversies) lib bdg $38.50; pa $26.75

Grades: 8 9 10 11 12   **179**

1. Livestock industry
ISBN 0-7377-4909-1 lib bdg; 0-7377-4910-5 pa;
978-0-7377-4909-0 lib bdg; 978-0-7377-4910-6 pa
LC 2009053380

"This solid volume looks at the economics, ethics, environmental impact, and future of factory farming. The issues are explored through diverse pro and con articles that have been edited for brevity, highlighting various points in the discussion surrounding the large-scale production and slaughter of animals for food. . . . This is a valuable addition to collections needing information on the state of modern food production." SLJ

Includes bibliographical references

Ravilious, Kate

Power; ethical debates about resources and the environment. Black Rabbit Books 2009 46p il map (Dilemmas in modern science) lib bdg $29.25

Grades: 7 8 9 10   **179**

1. Conservation of natural resources 2. Natural resources -- Management
ISBN 978-1-59920-096-5; 1-59920-096-1
LC 2007-35691

This title is "easy to navigate as evocative photographs, charts, and sidebars help break down complicated arguments into manageable parts for easy digestion." SLJ

"Presents both sides of environmental issues involving natural resources, including environmental ethics, power and energy, renewable resources, transportation and travel, and wood and water use." Publisher's note

Includes glossary and bibliographical references

179.7   Respect and disrespect for human life

Death and dying; Jane Langwith, book editor. Greenhaven Press 2008 128p il (Introducing issues with opposing viewpoints) lib bdg $33.70

Grades: 7 8 9 10   **179.7**

1. Death 2. Bereavement 3. Future life 4. Right to die 5. Terminal care -- Ethical aspects
ISBN 978-0-7377-3974-9; 0-7377-3974-6

Presents essays covering different viewpoints on death, including the role of religion in death, the possibility of the afterlife, and whether physicians should assist in the process of dying.

Includes bibliographical references

Euthanasia: opposing viewpoints; Carrie L. Snyder, book editor. Greenhaven Press 2006 269p il

(Opposing viewpoints series) lib bdg $34.95; pa $23.70

Grades: 7 8 9 10   **179.7**

1. Euthanasia
ISBN 0-7377-2933-3 lib bdg; 0-7377-2934-1 pa
LC 2005-55110

"The four chapters explore whether euthanasia is ethical, if it should be legalized, if legalization would lead to involuntary killing, and under what circumstances, if any, doctors should assist in suicide." Booklist [review of 2000 edition]

Includes bibliographical references

Rebman, Renee C.

Euthanasia and the right to die; a pro/con issue. Enslow Pubs. 2002 64p il (Hot pro/con issues) lib bdg $27.93

Grades: 7 8 9 10   **179.7**

1. Euthanasia 2. Right to die
ISBN 0-7660-1816-4
LC 2001-5251

The author discusses "the right to die by choice rather than by nature. . . . Rebman steps into the debate by asking what is a 'good death.' . . . She goes on to offer a variety of possible answers without bias, and she paints a historic picture of the controversy and how technology has complicated our definitions of life and death. . . . Objectivity makes this a good reference." Booklist

Includes bibliographical references and index

Stefoff, Rebecca

The **right** to die. Marshall Cavendish Benchmark 2009 126p il (Open for debate) lib bdg $29.95

Grades: 7 8 9 10   **179.7**

1. Suicide 2. Euthanasia 3. Right to die 4. Medical ethics
ISBN 978-0-7614-2948-7 lib bdg; 0-7614-2948-4 lib bdg
LC 2008000361

This presents arguments for and against euthanasia and assisted suicide in ancient and modern times

Includes bibliographical references

181   Eastern philosophy

Whitfield, Susan

Philosophy and writing. Sharpe Focus 2009 80p il map (Inside ancient China) $34.95

Grades: 7 8 9 10   **181**

1. Chinese literature 2. Chinese philosophy 3. China -- Civilization
ISBN 978-0-7656-8168-3; 0-7656-8168-4
LC 2008-31167

"Whitfield covers religion and philosophy [of ancient China] and how they have been passed down using various precursors to books and printing. . . . [This is illustrated with] fine and frequent color photographs and reproductions. Readers will be rewarded . . . with clear, accessible writing, peppered liberally with entertaining stories from history." SLJ

Includes glossary and bibliographical references

183 Sophistic, Socratic, related Greek philosophies

Jun Lim

Socrates; the public conscience of Golden Age Athens. by Jun Lim. 1st ed. Rosen Pub. 2006 112 p. col. ill., col. map (library) $34.60

Grades: 5 6 7 8   **183**

1. Philosophers
ISBN 1404205640; 9781404205642

LC 2005012259

This book by Jun Lim is part of the Library of Greek Philosophers series and looks at Socrates. "This series introduces students to the great philosophers and mathematicians who helped shape the intellectual world in modern times." Examples are given "of the kinds of knowledge these men taught to their students. The early years, travels, and education of each man are told, and the contributions to society are detailed in the context of the times." (Library Media Connection)

Includes bibliographical references (p. 107-108) and index.

200 RELIGION

200 Religion

Bowker, John

World Religions; The Great Faiths Explored & Explained. Dorling Kindersley 2006 216 p. ill. (chiefly col.) $27.95

Grades: 8 9 10 11 12 Adult   **200**

1. Religion 2. Religions -- Handbooks, manuals, etc.
ISBN 9780756617721; 0756617723

LC bl2006011130

This book, by John Bowker, takes a "new approach to understanding different faiths. . . . [It] looks at the beliefs and practices of many different religions, including Christianity, Judaism, Hinduism, Buddhism, Jainism, Sikhism and Islam." (Publisher's note)

"This book is a bold attempt to meld religious information with expressive art and to use the art as a tool for pedagogy. . . . World Religions has generous discussions of the ancient Egyptian, Greek, Roman, Norse, and Celtic religions, topics not even included in the Oxford Dictionary. . . . Ultimately, World Religions is the more commendable publication, though both books are recommended for most libraries." LJ

Breuilly, Elizabeth

★ **Religions** of the world; the illustrated guide to origins, beliefs, traditions & festivals. [by] Elizabeth Breuilly, Joanne O'Brien, Martin Palmer; consultant editor, Martin E. Marty. rev ed; Facts on File 2005 160p il map $29.95

Grades: 7 8 9 10   **200**

1. Religions
ISBN 0-8160-6258-7

LC 2005051101

First published 1997

This "is a valuable resource, covering the beliefs and practices of 10 major religions and lavishly illustrated with color photos, maps, diagrams, and charts." SLJ

Includes bibliographical references

The **encyclopedia** of world religions; Robert S. Ellwood, general editor; Gregory D. Alles, associate editor. Rev. ed.; Facts on File 2006 514p il map (Facts on File library of religion and mythology) $50

Grades: 7 8 9 10 11 12   **200**

1. Reference books 2. Religions -- Encyclopedias
ISBN 978-0-8160-6141-9; 0-8160-6141-6

LC 2005-56750

First published 1998

This encyclopedia "covers all the major and minor religions of the world, including the religions of the ancient world; the major religions practiced around the world today; religions of contemporary indigenous peoples; definitions of religious symbols and ideas; key leaders and thinkers; and terms and definitions." Publisher's note

Includes bibliographical references

Hackney Blackwell, Amy

Lent, Yom Kippur, and other Atonement days. Chelsea House 2009 112p il (Holidays and celebrations) $40

Grades: 6 7 8 9   **200**

1. Lent 2. Yom Kippur 3. Religious holidays
ISBN 978-1-60413-100-0; 1-60413-100-4

LC 2009010109

This "presents a welcome worldview of various atonement days, headlined by Lent, Yom Kippur, and the Buddhist holiday Rains Retreat. . . . Each gets an introduction to its associated religion, a brief history of the holiday, and a rundown of the significant days, rituals, and practices of observation. Then, readers are treated to a trip around the world . . . to investigate the unique ways in which different cultures observe similar holidays. The layout is text-dominated but dotted with colorful quality photos and a few informational insets. A good choice to help explain the significance behind holidays, . . . illuminating the many similarities lurking behind cultural and religious differences." Booklist

Includes glossary and bibliographical references

Langley, Myrtle

Religion; written by Myrtle Langely; special photography by Ellen Howden . . . [et al.] Rev. ed.; DK Pub. 2005 72p il (DK eyewitness books) $15.99; lib bdg $19.99

Grades: 4 5 6 7   **200**

1. Religion
ISBN 978-0-7566-1087-6; 0-7566-1087-7; 978-0-7566-1088-3 lib bdg; 0-7566-1088-5 lib bdg

LC 2005-278287

First published 1996 by Knopf

Introduces the history, philosophies, and rituals of various world religions including Hinduism, Buddhism, Shintoism, Zoroastrianism, and Christianity.

"Text consists of comprehensive, elucidative captions for the eye-catching, full-color photographs, drawings, and reproductions of paintings clustered on the pages. . . . This is a superb, succinct overview of the founders, tenets, and ways of worship of the world's major religions." SLJ

Murphy, Larry

★ **African** -American faith in America; [by] Larry G. Murphy. Facts on File 2003 128p il (Faith in America) $30

Grades: 7 8 9 10   **200**
   1. African Americans -- Religion
ISBN 0-8160-4990-4

LC 2002-28593

"In-depth coverage of diverse religious worship practiced among African Americans is presented. Murphy examines popular Christian religions, but also explores Judaism, Islam, Buddhism, and more. The well-written account begins with the religious experiences of the first Africans in America, moves to the establishment of pioneer religious institutions, and culminates with a chapter on the current status of diverse congregations. . . . Students will find ample material on well-known historical figures and current leaders" SLJ

Includes bibliographical references

National Geographic concise history of world religions; an illustrated time line. edited by Tim Cooke. National Geographic 2011 352 p. col. ill. (hardcover) $40.00

Grades: 8 9 10 11 12 Adult   **200**
   1. World history 2. Religious institutions 3. Religions -- Encyclopedias 4. Religion -- History -- Chronology 5. Religion and ethics 6. Religions -- History
ISBN 1426206984; 9781426206986

LC 2011276808

This book "continues the 'Concise History' series with [a] . . . take on major religions and lesser-known faiths of all times and nations." It offers a "global perspective on the history of faith in the Americas, Europe, Asia and Oceania, and Africa and the Middle East. . . . 50 feature essays explore in detail the origins, development and influence of faith." (Publisher's Note)

Includes bibliographical references (p. 343-344) and index

Osborne, Mary Pope

★ **One** world, many religions; the ways we worship. Knopf 1996 86p il map $19.95

Grades: 4 5 6 7   **200**
   1. Islam 2. Taoism 3. Judaism 4. Buddhism 5. Hinduism 6. Religions 7. Christianity 8. Confucianism
ISBN 0-679-83930-5

LC 96-836

"The presentation is notable for its respect to each group, succinctness, and clarity. . . . The artful, full-page, color and black-and-white photographs tell much of the story." SLJ

Includes glossary and bibliographical references

What do you believe? religion and faith in the world today. DK Pub. 2011 96p il map $16.99

Grades: 4 5 6 7   **200**
   1. Religions 2. Philosophy
ISBN 978-0-7566-7228-7; 0-7566-7228-7

"This extensive guidebook covers the beliefs and history of the world's major religions. Focusing in particular on Buddhism, Christianity, Hinduism, Islam, Judaism, and Sikhism, the book also explores atheism and agnosticism, indigenous belief systems, East Asian religions, philosophy, and morality. . . . The graphically bold format—which mixes photographs, cartoons, and sidebars—will keep kids' attention, whether they are seeking truth, knowledge, or more to ponder." Publ Wkly

200.9   History, geographic treatment, biography

Braude, Ann

★ **Women** and American religion; Jon Butler & Harry S. Stout, general editors. Oxford University Press 2000 141p il (Religion in American life) lib bdg $28

Grades: 7 8 9 10   **200.9**
   1. Women -- Religious life 2. United States -- Religion
ISBN 0-19-510676-8

LC 99-32968

Braude discusses "how women from various groups, including African Americans, immigrants, and social crusaders, shaped the face of religion in the U.S. . . . Included are individuals such as colonist Margaret Winthrop and African American preacher Jarena Lee, as well as religious leaders such as Mary Baker Eddy and Mother Elizabeth Seaton. Black-and-white illustrations and historical engravings pepper the text." Booklist

Includes bibliographical references

Fridell, Ron

Religious fundamentalism. Marshall Cavendish Benchmark 2009 144p il (Open for debate) $29.95

Grades: 7 8 9 10   **200.9**
   1. Islam 2. Christianity 3. Religious fundamentalism
ISBN 978-0-7614-2945-6; 0-7614-2945-X

LC 2008000364

This examines religious fundamentalism in Christianity and Islam.

Includes bibliographical references

★ **Religion** in America: opposing viewpoints; David Haugen and Susan Musser, book editors. Greenhaven Press 2011 237p il (Opposing viewpoints series) $39.70; pa $27.50

Grades: 8 9 10 11 12   **200.9**
   1. United States -- Religion
ISBN 978-0-7377-4988-5; 0-7377-4988-1; 978-0-7377-4989-2 pa; 0-7377-4989-X pa

LC 2010016975

This volume explores the topics relating to religion in the United States by presenting varied expert opinions that examine many of the different aspects that comprise these issues.

Includes bibliographical references

200.973 Religion – United States

Capaccio, George

Religion; George Capaccio. Cavendish Square Publishing 2014 80 p. (library binding) $35.64

Grades: 6 7 8 **200.973**

1. United States -- Religion 2. United States -- History -- 1600-1775, Colonial period 3. United States -- Religion -- To 1800

ISBN 1627128883; 9781627128889; 9781627128896

LC 2013050650

In this book on religion in Colonial America, author George Capaccio "launches his narrative with a description of the state of religious affairs in both the Old and New Worlds. He explores the failure of John Winthrop's goal to achieve Puritan perfection, the controversy over Anne Hutchinson's tenacious faith, the evangelizing stamina of ex-slave and Methodist preacher Absalom Jones, and the spiritual resilience of the Catawba Indians." (Publisher's note)

"Thoroughly researched and expertly executed, this series describes in rich detail the lives of Native Americans, African Americans, and white settlers, including children, women, and criminals. The introductory material that prefaces each title is of particular value, as it demonstrates that the colonists were part of a larger world picture. For instance, Religion takes readers back to Jerusalem to chronicle the expansion of Protestantism and Catholicism there and abroad...Strong, attractive titles for those looking for more coverage of Colonial America." SLJ

201 Specific aspects of religion

Glick, Susan

War and peace; by Susan Glick. Lucent Books 2004 112p il map (Discovering mythology) $28.70

Grades: 6 7 8 9 **201**

1. War 2. Peace 3. Mythology

ISBN 1-56006-903-1

LC 2004-6290

This examines the meaning and cultural significance behind the myths concerning war and peace in ancient world cultures

Includes bibliographical references

Hamilton, Virginia

★ **In** the beginning; creation stories from around the world; told by Virginia Hamilton; illustrated by Barry Moser. Harcourt Brace Jovanovich 1988 161p il hardcover o.p. pa $20

Grades: 5 6 7 8 **201**

1. Creation 2. Mythology

ISBN 0-15-238740-4; 0-15-238742-0 pa

LC 88-6211

A Newbery Medal honor book, 1989

"Hamilton has gathered 25 creation myths from various cultures and retold them in language true to the original. Images from the tales are captured in Moser's 42 full-page illustrations, tantalizing oil paintings that are rich with somber colors and striking compositions. Included in the collection are the familiar stories (biblical creation stories, Greek and Roman myths), and some that are not so familiar (tales from the Australian aborigines, various African and native American tribes, as well as from countries like Russia, China, and Iceland). At the end of each tale, Hamilton provides a brief commentary on the story's origin and originators." Booklist

Includes bibliographical references

Kallen, Stuart A.

Shamans; by Stuart A. Kallen. Lucent Books 2004 112p il (Mystery library) $28.70

Grades: 6 7 8 9 **201**

1. Shamanism

ISBN 1-59018-628-1

LC 2004-12665

"The methods employed by shamans to visit the realm of spirits in order to learn how to effect cures are described in some detail. . . . Activities of Siberian and North, Central, and South American shamans receive the most attention. Chinese, Australian aboriginal, Greenlander, ancient Greek, and a few other practitioners are mentioned. . . . Halftone photographs make textual descriptions real while numerous shaded sidebars offer considerable supplementary material. . . . This title provides a varied, understandable introduction to the spiritual side of many human cultures." SLJ

Includes bibliographical references

Mass, Wendy

Gods and goddesses. Lucent Bks. 2002 112p (Discovering mythology) $27.45

Grades: 6 7 8 9 **201**

1. Mythology 2. Gods and goddesses

ISBN 1-56006-852-3

LC 2001-5775

Examines the origins and nature of Egyptian, Hindu, Celtic, Greek, Roman, Viking, and Aztec gods and goddesses as revealed in the mythologies of these cultures

"This is a good overview for study of mythology that may spark interest in further study." Book Rep

Includes bibliographical references

★ **U-X-L** encyclopedia of world mythology. UXL 2009 5v il set $314

Grades: 7 8 9 10 11 12 **201**

1. Reference books 2. Mythology -- Encyclopedias

ISBN 978-1-41443-030-0; 1-41443-030-2

LC 2008-12696

"In A-Z format, the set provides more than 300 entries for five content areas: characters, deities, myths, themes, and cultures. . . . The entries generally range from three to four pages. . . . Recommended for middle- and high-school libraries." Booklist

World mythology; the illustrated guide. Roy Willis, general editor. Oxford University Press 2006 311p il map pa $22.50

Grades: 8 9 10 11 12 **201**

1. Mythology

ISBN 0-19-530752-6; 978-0-19-530752-8

LC 2005-30779

First published 1993 by Holt & Co.

This book describes "the myths of Egypt, the Middle East, India, China, Tibet, Mongolia, Japan, Greece, Rome, the Celtic lands, Northern and Eastern Europe, the Arctic,

North and South America, Mesoamerica, Africa, Australia, Oceania, and Southeast Asia." Libr J [review of 1993 edition]

Includes bibliographical references

204   Religious experience, life, practice

Philip, Neil

★ **In** the house of happiness; a book of prayers and praise. selected by Neil Philip; illustrated by Isabelle Brent. Clarion Bks. 2003 un il $17

Grades: 6 7 8 9   **204**
1. Prayers
ISBN 0-618-23481-0

LC 2002-10269

A collection of short prayers from major religions— Christianity, Judaism, Hinduism, Buddhism, and Islam— along with tribal chants, folk rhymes, and poems of praise and devotion

"The beautiful art encourages readers to pick up the book. Brent, who was inspired by the Book of Hours, lavishly employs illumination to highlight her pictures of nature. . . . This book offers the opportunity for quiet moments of reflection in a lovely setting." Booklist

209   Sects and reform movements

Stein, Stephen J.

Alternative American religions. Oxford Univ. Press 1999 156p il (Religion in American life) lib bdg $28

Grades: 7 8 9 10   **209**
1. Cults 2. Sects 3. United States -- Religion
ISBN 0-19-511196-6

LC 99-42370

Examines various alternative religions, or New Religious Movements, that have existed in the United States from colonial times through the twentieth century and from the perspectives of both insiders and outsiders

"The tone throughout is nonjudgmental and the emphasis is on people and their ideas. Black-and-white photos and reproductions add information and perspective to the presentation." SLJ

220   Bible

Atkinson, Peter

The **Lion** encyclopedia of the Bible; illustrated by Peter Dennis. Lion 2009 127p il map $19.99

Grades: 7 8 9 10 11 12   **220**
1. Reference books 2. Bible -- Encyclopedias
ISBN 978-0-7459-6010-4; 0-7459-6010-3

Taking a chronological approach to the story line of the Bible, this resource integrates and explores the Bible's historical, geographical, and social origins. It also overviews the different types of writing found within the texts and shows how they relate to Christian beliefs.

This is "thematically immense but skillfully distilled in presentation. . . . Complex and potentially confusing material is explained succinctly. . . . Maps and colorful and dramatic drawings, paintings, and photographs appear throughout. . . . With its inviting format and unaffected writing, this is a welcome resource." SLJ

Brown, Alan

The **Bible** and Christianity; by Alan Brown. Smart Apple Media 2003 30p il (Sacred texts) $27.10

Grades: 5 6 7 8   **220**
1. Christianity 2. Bible (as subject)
ISBN 1-58340-243-8

LC 2003-41645

Explains how the Old and New Testaments came to be part of the Bible used by Christians and discusses some of the important messages found in the holy scriptures.

"Colorful strips of symbolic patterns adorn the pages and accent the informative text boxes. . . . The clear captioned . . . illustrations (photos and historical art) provide additional background." Horn Book Guide
Includes glossary

220.3   Encyclopedias and topical dictionaries

Oxford University Press

The **Oxford** companion to the Bible; edited by Bruce M. Metzger, Michael D. Coogan. Oxford Univ. Press 1993 xxi, 874p il map $70

Grades: 8 9 10 11 12 Adult   **220.3**
1. Reference books 2. Bible (as subject) -- Dictionaries
ISBN 0-19-504645-5

LC 93-19315

This volume "contains more than 700 signed entries treating the formation, transmission, circulation, sociohistorical situation, interpretation, theology, uses, and influence of the Bible." Libr J

220.5   Bible - Modern versions and translations

The **Bible**: Authorized King James Version; with an introduction and notes by Robert Carroll and Stephen Prickett. Oxford University Press 2008 lxxiv, 1039, 248, 445p il map (Oxford world's classics) pa $18.95

Grades: 5 6 7 8 9 10 11 12 Adult   **220.5**
ISBN 978-0-19-953594-1

LC 2008-273825

This Oxford World's Classics version first published 1997

The authorized or King James Version originally published 1611.

Includes bibliographical references

Good news Bible; today's English version. American Bible Soc. 2006 $10.99

Grades: 8 9 10 11 12 Adult   **220.5**
ISBN 978-1-58516-154-6; 1-58516-154-3

"Begun in 1964 with the Gospel of Mark, The New Testament was completed in 1966, with rev. eds. in 1971 and 1976. The whole Bible was published in 1976. An extremely popular, inexpensive translation using contemporary American English. . . . Especially useful for youth or lay Bible study as well as for private reading." Bollier. Lit of Theology

The **Holy** Bible; containing the Old and New Testaments with the Apocryphal/Deuterocanonical books: New Revised Standard Version. Oxford University Press 1989 xxi, 996, 298, 284p map $29.99
Grades: 5 6 7 8 9 10 11 12 Adult **220.5**
ISBN 0-19-528330-9; 978-0-19-528330-3
LC 90-222105
"Intended for public reading, congregational worship, private study, instruction, and meditation, it attempts to be as literal as possible while following standard American English usage, avoids colloquialism, and prefers simple, direct terms and phrases." Sheehy. Guide to Ref Books. 10th edition. suppl

The **New** American Bible; translated from the original languages with critical use of all the ancient sources including the revised Psalms and the revised New Testament. authorized by the Board of Trustees of the Confraternity of Christian Doctrine and approved by the Administrative Committee Board of the National Conference of Catholic Bishops and the United States Catholic Conference. Oxford University Press 2006 xxiii, 1514p $39.99
Grades: 8 9 10 11 12 Adult **220.5**
ISBN 978-0-19-528904-6; 0-19-528904-8
First published 1970 by Kenedy
"Roman Catholic version based on modern English translations; replaces the Douay edition." N Y Public Libr Book of How & Where to Look It Up

The **new** Jerusalem Bible; [general editor: Henry Wansbrough] Doubleday 1985 2108p map $45; pa $29.95
Grades: 7 8 9 10 11 12 Adult **220.5**
ISBN 0-385-14264-1; 978-0-385-14264-9; 0-385-24833-4 pa; 978-0-385-24833-4 pa
LC 85-16070
First published in this format 1966 with title: The Jerusalem Bible
"Derives from the French version edited at the Dominican Ecole Biblique de Jerusalem and known as 'La Bible de Jerusalem.' The introductions and notes are 'a direct translation from the French, though revised and brought up to date in some places' but translation of the Biblical text goes back to the original languages." Guide to Ref Books. 11th edition

220.9 Geography, history, chronology, persons of Bible lands in Bible times

Lottridge, Celia Barker
Stories from Adam and Eve to Ezekiel; retold from the Bible. by Celia Barker Lottridge; illustrated by Gary Clement. Douglas & McIntyre/Groundwood 2004 192p il $24.95
Grades: 4 5 6 7 **220.9**
1. Bible stories
ISBN 0-88899-490-7
"Lottridge uses her storyteller's ear to bring ancient stories from the Hebrew Bible to a young audience, tailoring them to make them more age appropriate.... The numerous, well-drawn ink-and-watercolor illustrations are reminiscent of Warwick Hutton's work. Some pictures . . . are quite spectacular." Booklist

Murphy, Claire Rudolf
★ **Daughters** of the desert; stories of remarkable women from Christian, Jewish, and Muslim traditions. [by] Claire Rudolf Murphy . . . [et al.] SkyLight Paths Pub. 2003 178p $19.95
Grades: 7 8 9 10 **220.9**
1. Bible 2. Bible stories 3. Women in the Bible 4. Women in the Qur'an
ISBN 1-89336-172-1
LC 2002-153821
"Using sacred writings as their basis, the five women authors have reshaped the stories of such individuals as Sarah, Mary Magdalene, Eve, and Khadiji, the wife of Mohammed. . . . The stories are short and simply told, but they are intriguing and invite discussion." Booklist
Includes bibliographical references

Tubb, Jonathan N.
Bible lands. Dorling Kindersley 2000 63p il map (DK eyewitness books) $15.99; lib bdg $19.99
Grades: 4 5 6 7 **220.9**
1. Bible -- Antiquities
ISBN 0-7894-5770-9; 0-7694-6579-5 lib bdg
Photographs and text document life in Biblical times, surveying the clothing, food, and civilizations of a wide variety of cultures, including the Israelites, Babylonians, Persians, and Romans.

220.95 Bible - History

Ehrlich, Amy, 1942-
With a mighty hand; the story of the Torah. Amy Ehrlich, Daniel Nevins. Candlewick Press 2013 224p. $29.99
Grades: 2 3 4 5 6 7 8 **220.95**
1. Bible 2. Bible stories 3. Picture books for children
ISBN 0763643955; 9780763643959
LC 2012947723
This book is an interpretation of the Torah for children. Amy Ehrlich has "changed the traditional phrasing" of the Bible's first five books. She "describes Moses' basket as "a little ark of papyrus," reminding readers of how much danger the baby was in, floating in the middle of the Nile. . . . Not every word of the Bible has been included, the text having been pared down to a series of interconnected stories." (Kirkus Reviews)

221.9   Geography, history, chronology, persons of Old Testament lands in Old Testament times

Ward, Elaine M.

Old Testament women; [by] Elaine Ward. Enchanted Lion 2004 32p il (Art revelations) $18.95
Grades: 5 6 7 8   221.9
    1. Bible stories 2. Women in the Bible
    ISBN 1-59270-011-X

These Old Testament stories about women include "explanatory paragraphs, sidebars, and captions by the author. Art masterpieces . . . illustrate each story. . . . The captions provide background on the artist and the significance of each painting or mosaic. . . . The 18 women . . . include Rachel, Leah, Ruth, and Bathsheba. . . . Bosch, Botticelli, and Poussin are among the painters whose work appears here. . . . Visually stunning." SLJ

222   Historical books of Old Testament

The **contemporary** Torah; a gender-sensitive adaptation of the JPS translation. revising editor, David E.S. Stein; consulting editors, Adele Berlin, Ellen Frankel, and Carol L. Meyers. Jewish Publication Society 2006 xlii, 412p $28
Grades: 8 9 10 11 12 Adult   222
    1. Bible. Pentateuch
    ISBN 0-8276-0796-2; 978-0-8276-0796-5
                                    LC 2006-40608

A modern adaptation of the Jewish Publication Society's translation of the Torah. "In places where the ancient audience probably would not have construed gender as pertinent to the text's plain sense, the editors changed words into gender-neutral terms; where gender was probably understood to be at stake, they left the text as originally translated, or even introduced gendered language where none existed before. They made these changes regardless of whether words referred to God, angels, or human beings." Publisher's note

Feiler, Bruce S.

★ **Walking** the Bible; an illustrated journey for kids through the greatest stories ever told. by Bruce Feiler; illustrated by Sasha Meret. HarperCollinsPublishers 2004 108p il map $16.99; lib bdg $17.89
Grades: 5 6 7 8   222
    1. Bible (as subject) 2. Middle East
    ISBN 0-06-051117-6; 0-06-051118-4 lib bdg
                                    LC 2003-15861

The author describes his journey through places mentioned in the Old Testament

"In this version of his adult book with the same title (Morrow, 2001), Feiler largely succeeds in slimming rather than dumbing down his account of his trip across the 10,000-mile setting of the earliest Bible stories. The author's unpretentious . . . tone and astute pacing help make the volume accessible, and his sincerity is palpable." SLJ

Fischer, Chuck

★ **In** the beginning: the art of Genesis; a pop-up book. by Chuck Fischer. Little, Brown 2008 un il $35
Grades: 5 6 7 8   222
    1. Bible stories 2. Religious art 3. Pop-up books 4. Bible -- O.T. -- Genesis
    ISBN 978-0-316-11842-2; 0-316-11842-7
                                    LC 2007045411

Fischer "presents an impressive, three-dimensional view of the Book of Genesis. . . . Fischer and his collaborators offer a Garden of Eden scene executed in an artistic style that recalls ancient tile work; a huge Noah's Ark landed atop a mountain; and a Tower of Babel impressively high. . . . The text, more commentary than story, is hidden in inset mini-books and is accompanied by reproductions of biblical masterpieces. . . . This book becomes more amazing as the pages are turned." Booklist

The **Torah**: the five books of Moses; a new translation of the Holy Scriptures according to the Masoretic text; first section. Jewish Publication Society 1963 393p $20; pa $15
Grades: 8 9 10 11 12 Adult   222
    1. Bible. Pentateuch
    ISBN 0-8276-0015-1; 0-8276-0680-X pa

This "translation of Genesis, Exodus, Leviticus, Numbers, and Deuteronomy was prepared . . . to present a version of the Bible that takes into account modern insights and knowledge of ancient times. . . . Of chief value to persons of the Jewish religion but of interest to Bible scholars of any religion." Booklist

223   Poetic books of Old Testament

Dillon, Leo

★ **To** every thing there is a season; verses from Ecclesiastes. illustrations by Leo and Diane Dillon. Blue Sky Press (NY) 1998 un il $16.95
Grades: 4 5 6 7 8   223
    1. Bible -- Pictorial works
    ISBN 0-590-47887-7
                                    LC 97-35124

"The words of Ecclesiastes I:4 and III:1-8, adapted from the King James Version of the Bible, are . . . {illustrated here in} 16 full- and double-page paintings. . . . Kindergarten and up." (SLJ)

"The Dillons compellingly convey the relevance of the Ecclesiastes verse throughout history, via a stunning array of artwork that embraces motifs from cultures the world over." Publ Wkly

226   Gospels and Acts

Connolly, Sean

New Testament miracles; 1st American ed; Enchanted Lion Books 2004 32p il (Art revelations) $18.95

Grades: 7 8 9 10 **226**
1. Christian art 2. Miracles -- Christianity
ISBN 1-59270-012-8

LC 2003-49414

"The 12 miracles discussed . . . include Jesus healing the man born blind, Jesus raising Lazarus from the dead, and the conversion of Paul. Each one is told from verses in the four Gospels or the Book of Acts, with explanatory paragraphs, sidebars, and captions by the author. Art masterpieces . . . illustrate each story. Works by El Greco, Rembrandt, Tintoretto, and Witz, among others, are featured. . . . Visually stunning." SLJ

230 Christianity

Hale, Rosemary Drage
Christianity. Rosen Pub. 2010 112p il (Understanding religions) lib bdg $31.95
Grades: 7 8 9 10 **230**
1. Christianity
ISBN 978-1-4358-5621-9; 1-4358-5621-X

LC 2009-10295

This book about Christianity "discusses origins and historical development; aspects of the divine; sacred texts, persons, space, and time; ethical principles; death and the afterlife; and society and religion." SLJ

Includes glossary and bibliographical references

Nardo, Don
Christianity. Compass Point Books 2010 48p il map (World religions) lib bdg $27.99
Grades: 5 6 7 8 **230**
1. Christianity
ISBN 978-0-7565-4237-5 lib bdg; 0-7565-4237-5 lib bdg

LC 2009-15811

"The colorful, attractive layout includes high-quality reproductions of photographs, maps, and paintings. Students who are new to religious studies, as well as those doing reports, will find that this . . . meets their needs." SLJ

Includes glossary and bibliographical references

Self, David
★ **Christianity**; [by] David Self. World Almanac Library 2005 48p il map (Religions of the world) lib bdg $30
Grades: 5 6 7 8 **230**
1. Christianity
ISBN 0-8368-5866-2

LC 2005041712

This is a summary of the Christian religion including history, beliefs, worship, festivals, practice, and current disagreements.

"Wonderfully colorful in images, language, and fact. . . . [This is] enumerated with full-color photographs on every page, charts, maps, and tables." SLJ

Includes bibliographical references

232.9 Family and life of Jesus

Lottridge, Celia Barker
Stories from the life of Jesus; retold from the Bible by Celia Barker Lottridge; illustrated by Linda Wolfsgruber. Doulgas & McIntyre 2004 140p il $24.95
Grades: 4 5 6 7 **232.9**
1. Bible stories
ISBN 0-88899-497-4

A retelling of selected events from the life of Christ based on biblical accounts

This is an "exceptional collection. . . . Each story is retold in three or four pages of clear, concise prose that is meant to be read aloud. . . . Each selection is enhanced by dramatic and atmospheric, mixed-media illustrations that are executed in warm earth tones." SLJ

Spirin, Gennady
★ **Jesus**; his life in verses from the King James Holy Bible. art by Gennady Spirin. Marshall Cavendish Children 2010 un il $21
Grades: 5 6 7 8 **232.9**
ISBN 978-0-7614-5630-8; 0-7614-5630-9

LC 2009005956

"In an unusual project, a tempera painting by Spirin has been digitally dissected to create individual images for this picture book that portrays 13 events from the life of Jesus. . . . Details from the larger work illustrate key moments—including the Annunciation, Jesus' baptism, and the raising of Lazarus, among others—beside passages from the King James Bible (Jesus' words are printed in red). The result is an elegant, large-format volume that offers a reverent and arresting visual interpretation of biblical events." Publ Wkly

270 History, geographic treatment, biography of Christianity; Church history; Christian denominations and sects

Nardo, Don
The **birth** of Christianity. Morgan Reynolds Pub. 2011 112p il (World religions and beliefs) lib bdg $28.95
Grades: 7 8 9 10 **270**
1. Christianity 2. Church history
ISBN 978-1-59935-145-2; 1-59935-145-5

LC 2010038443

This covers the beginnings of Christianity "in an impartial way. The [context] in which the [religion] developed [is] explained, offering insight into how [Christianity] came to be and introducing major concepts from the [religion]." SLJ

Includes glossary and bibliographical references

274 Christianity by specific continents, countries, localities in modern world

Schomp, Virginia

The **church**. Marshall Cavendish Benchmark 2010 80p il (Life in Victorian England) lib bdg $34.21

Grades: 6 7 8 9   **274**

1. Church of England 2. Great Britain -- Religion 3. Great Britain -- History -- 19th century

ISBN 978-1-60870-031-8 lib bdg; 1-60870-031-3 lib bdg

LC 2010006901

Describes the role of religion in the lives of Victorians, including how it influenced the way they lived, how they observed special occasions, and how they coped with the many changes and challenges of their times

This "is clearly written, thorough, and informative. The visually rich layout includes photographs and paintings from the time period, full-page illustrations, and attention-grabbing sidebars. Most appealing are the primary source quotations, which are plentiful and relevant." Libr Media Connect

Includes glossary and bibliographical references

280 Denominations and sects of Christian church

Brown, Stephen F.

Catholicism & Orthodox Christianity; by Stephen F. Brown and Khaled Anatolios. 3rd ed.; Chelsea House 2009 144p il (World religions) $40

Grades: 7 8 9 10 11 12   **280**

1. Catholic Church 2. Orthodox Eastern Church

ISBN 978-1-60413-106-2; 1-60413-106-3

LC 2008-43046

First published 2002 by Facts and File

This "traces the roots of [Catholicism and Orthodox Christianity] from the early Christian churches to today. The historical passage of the Catholic and Orthodox faiths is recounted, from the original teachings of Jesus Christ to the separation of the Eastern and Western Churches to recent attempts at reconciliation." Publisher's note

Includes glossary and bibliographical references

Protestantism; 3rd ed.; Chelsea House 2009 144p il map (World religions) $40

Grades: 7 8 9 10 11 12   **280**

1. Protestantism

ISBN 978-1-60413-112-3; 1-60413-112-8

LC 2008-29659

First published 1991 by Facts on File

This "explores the origins, customs, and history of Protestantism, from its beginnings in the Middle Ages to its role in today's world. Current issues, such as the development of new religious denominations, its stance on abortion, the ordination of gays and women, and the relationship between religion and politics, are explored within the framework of the fundamental moral tenets of the faith." Publisher's note

Includes glossary and bibliographical references

Noll, Mark A.

★ **Protestants** in America; general editors, Jon Butler and Harry S. Stout. Oxford University Press 2000 155p il (Religion in American life) lib bdg $28

Grades: 7 8 9 10   **280**

1. Protestantism 2. Protestant churches

ISBN 0-19-511034-X

LC 00-27271

Discusses the origins of Protestantism, the diversity of Protestant churches in the United States, and the role of Protestants in American life from colonial times to the present

"This volume is especially valuable for its discussion of the church in the African-American community and its coverage of smaller sects, like the Shakers. The many black-and-white photographs and reproduction add immensely to the text." SLJ

Includes bibliographical references

289.3 Latter-Day Saints (Mormons)

Bial, Raymond

Nauvoo; Mormon city on the Mississippi River. [by] Raymond Bial. Houghton Mifflin Co. 2006 44p il map $17

Grades: 5 6 7 8   **289.3**

1. Mormons 2. Church of Jesus Christ of Latter-day Saints 3. Illinois -- History

ISBN 978-0-618-39685-6; 0-618-39685-3

LC 2005027528

"Bial introduces readers to a city that was established by the Church of Jesus Christ of Latter Day Saints in 1839. . . . This effectively written account provides a sympathetic but balanced introduction to Mormon beliefs. . . . Excellent color photographs grace almost every page." SLJ

Book of Mormon

★ The **Book** of Mormon; another testament of Jesus Christ. [translated by Joseph Smith, Jr.] Doubleday 2004 586p $24.95

Grades: 8 9 10 11 12 Adult   **289.3**

1. Mormons 2. Church of Jesus Christ of Latter-day Saints

ISBN 0-385-51316-X

LC 2004-51982

First published 1830

"Based on golden plates which Joseph Smith claimed were revealed to him, and which he unearthed from Cumorah Hill, New York, this book is roughly similar in structure to the Bible. . . . Emphasized are the doctrines of pre-existence, perfection, the afterlife, and Christ's second coming." Haydn. Thesaurus of Book Dig

Bushman, Claudia L.

★ **Mormons** in America; [by] Claudia Lauper Bushman and Richard Lyman Bushman. Oxford Univ. Press 1998 142p il (Religion in American life) $28

Grades: 7 8 9 10   **289.3**

1. Mormons 2. Church of Jesus Christ of Latter-day

Saints
ISBN 0-19-510677-6
LC 98-18605

Chronicles the history of the Church of Jesus Christ of Latter-Day Saints beginning in America in the early 1800s and continuing to the present day throughout the world

"A solid resource for libraries. Illustrated with historical material and black-and-white photos. Time line and bibliography appended." Booklist

Includes bibliographical references

292 Classical religion (Greek and Roman religion)

Bryant, Megan E.

Oh my gods! a look-it-up guide to the gods of mythology. Franklin Watts 2009 128p il map (Mythlopedia) lib bdg $39; pa $13.95
Grades: 4 5 6 7   **292**
1. Gods and goddesses 2. Classical mythology
ISBN 978-1-60631-026-7 lib bdg; 1-60631-026-7 lib bdg; 978-1-60631-058-8 pa; 1-60631-058-5 pa
LC 2009-17169

Presents a guide to Greek mythology, providing profiles of gods and goddesses along with information on monsters, heroes, and the underworld.

"The book is organized around entries on major gods and titans, each with vital stats and a Top 10 Things to Know about Me, followed by a few highlights from their lore and sidebars that delve into their cultural relevance. Illustrations abound, from embellished stock images to original cartoons, and the pastel-heavy color scheme may entice readers otherwise resistant to the grays and ivories that tend to dominate classicism." Booklist

Includes glossary and bibliographical references

She's all that! a look-it-up guide to the goddesses of mythology. Franklin Watts 2009 128p il map (Mythlopedia) lib bdg $39; pa $13.95
Grades: 4 5 6 7   **292**
1. Gods and goddesses 2. Classical mythology
ISBN 978-1-60631-027-4 lib bdg; 1-60631-027-5 lib bdg; 978-1-60631-059-5 pa; 1-60631-059-3 pa
LC 2009-17168

Presents a guide to Greek mythology, providing profiles of goddesses and the myths surrounding them.

This "spices things up with sassy artwork, a pastel color scheme, and an OMG sensibility. . . . Aside from the heaps of information coming from all angles on just about every page, . . . [this] book also contains a decent family tree, a rudimentary star chart, and lists of further reading. . . . For kids unconvinced that anything so old and gray could have any bearing on their lives, . . . [this provides] a feisty . . . guide to the many cultural references lingering from antiquity." Booklist

Includes glossary and bibliographical references

Daly, Kathleen N.

Greek and Roman mythology, A to Z; [by] Kathleen N. Daly; revised by Marian Rengel. 3rd ed.; Chelsea House Publishers 2009 162p il (Mythology A to Z) lib bdg $45
Grades: 8 9 10 11 12   **292**
1. Classical mythology
ISBN 978-1-60413-412-4; 1-60413-412-7
LC 2009-8243

First published 1992 by Facts on File

Alphabetically listed entries identify and explain the characters, events, important places, and other aspects of Greek and Roman mythology

"The format is accessible, making the book useful for school assignments, as well as enjoyable for general reading. Each entry provides a clear definition, and retells the stories associated with the character or place. The broad coverage, ample cross-references, and extensive index enable readers to recognize the many connections and interrelationships between characters and myths." SLJ [review of 1992 edition]

Includes bibliographical references

Fleischman, Paul

★ **Dateline** : Troy; [by] Paul Fleischman; collages by Gwen Frankfeldt & Glenn Morrow. new updated ed.; Candlewick Press 2006 80p il $18.99
Grades: 7 8 9 10   **292**
1. Trojan War
ISBN 978-0-7636-3083-6; 0-7636-3083-7

First published 1996

A retelling of the story of the Trojan War illustrated with collages featuring newspaper clippings of modern events from World War I through the Iraq War

Hamilton, Edith

Mythology; illustrated by Steele Savage. Little, Brown 1942 497p il $27.95; pa $13.95
Grades: 8 9 10 11 12 Adult   **292**
1. Trojan War 2. Norse mythology 3. Gods and goddesses 4. Classical mythology
ISBN 0-316-34114-2; 0-316-34151-7 pa

A retelling of Greek, Roman and Norse myths

McCaughrean, Geraldine

★ **Hercules**; retold by Geraldine McCaughrean. Cricket Books 2005 142p il (Heroes) $16.95
Grades: 5 6 7 8   **292**
1. Classical mythology 2. Hercules (Legendary character)
ISBN 978-0-8126-2737-4; 0-8126-2737-7
LC 2005004524

First published 2003 by Oxford University Press

This is a retelling of the twelve labors of Hercules including his battles with the Cretan Bull, the many-headed Hydra, the Nemean Lion, and the three-headed guardian of hell, Cerberus.

"This volume does a creditable job of making Hercules a dimensional character whose struggles against fate and the vindictiveness of the gods arouse readers' sympathy. . . . McCaughrean enlivens the familiar story with arresting imagery." SLJ

★ **Odysseus**; retold by Geraldine McCaughrean. Cricket Books 2004 148p il (Heroes) $16.95

Grades: 5 6 7 8   **292**
1. Classical mythology 2. Odysseus (Greek mythology)
ISBN 978-0-8126-2721-3; 0-8126-2721-0
                  LC 2004-10734

"With mounting suspense, wild action, and simple, rhythmic prose, this dramatic retelling of Homer's classic makes a gripping read-aloud as well as an exciting introduction to the story." Booklist

★ **Perseus**; retold by Geraldine McCaughrean. Cricket Books 2005 118p il (Heroes) $16.95
Grades: 5 6 7 8   **292**
1. Classical mythology 2. Perseus (Greek mythology)
ISBN 978-0-8126-2735-0; 0-8126-2735-0

This "makes a thrilling read-aloud. . . . McCaughrean blends the colloquial and contemporary into the heroic quest." Booklist

Mitchell, Adrian, 1941-

★ **Shapeshifters**; tales from Ovid's Metamorphoses. retold by Adrian Mitchell; illustrated by Alan Lee. Frances Lincoln Children's 2010 143p il
Grades: 7 8 9 10   **292**
1. Classical mythology
ISBN 1-84507-536-6; 978-1-84507-536-1

This is a "marvelous re-creation of myth from Ovid. . . . The language is simple and contemporary, moving from rhyme to free verse to prose and back again. . . . All of these stories explore mystery: the origins of flowers, mountains, lakes. Pygmalion, Persephone, Midas and Arachne all appear here . . . [Lee] makes men and women, gods and beasts, sea, sky and leaf shimmer." Kirkus

Nardo, Don

The **Greenhaven** encyclopedia of Greek and Roman mythology; Don Nardo, author; Barbette Spaeth, consulting editor. Greenhaven Press 2002 304p il (Greenhaven encyclopedia of) lib bdg $76.20
Grades: 7 8 9 10   **292**
1. Classical mythology
ISBN 0-7377-0719-4
                  LC 2001-40864

This is an overview of classical mythology, its heroes, and its influence on the history of Western civilization
Includes bibliographical references

Otfinoski, Steven

All in the family; a look-it-up guide to the in-laws, outlaws, and offspring of mythology. F. Watts 2009 128p il (Mythlopedia) lib bdg $39; pa $13.95
Grades: 4 5 6 7   **292**
1. Classical mythology
ISBN 978-1-60631-025-0 lib bdg; 1-60631-025-9 lib bdg; 978-1-60631-057-1 pa; 1-60631-057-7 pa
                  LC 2009-20999

"Jam-packed with trivia, brief profiles, god and goddess relationships, stories, 'Top 10 Things to Know About Me' facts, and entertaining illustrations, this title explores 20 heroes and mortals of classic Greek mythology. The selections include the well-known Achilles, Heracles, Odysseus, and Pandora and the more obscure Meleager, Orion, Atalanta,

and Bellerophon; each one is given lively treatment. . . . The lighthearted style and humorous collage and cartoon illustrations may draw even the most reluctant of readers. " SLJ
Includes glossary and bibliographical references

Rylant, Cynthia

The **beautiful** stories of life; six Greek myths, retold. illustrated by Carson Ellis. Harcourt 2009 71p il $16
Grades: 5 6 7 8   **292**
1. Classical mythology
ISBN 978-0-15-206184-5; 0-15-206184-3
                  LC 2007-34808

"Rylant retells the stories of Pandora, Persephone, Orpheus, Pygmalion, Narcissus, and Psyche in this trim, handsome book. Written in a modern style with an old-fashioned feel, the selections sit well with other titles in the genre. . . . Accompanied by full-page black-and-white illustrations and sprinkled with decorations, the whole package is nicely done." SLJ

Schomp, Virginia

The **ancient** Greeks; [by] Virginia Schomp. Marshall Cavendish Benchmark 2007 96p il map (Myths of the world) lib bdg $22.95
Grades: 6 7 8 9   **292**
1. Classical mythology 2. Greece -- Civilization
ISBN 978-0-7614-2547-2
                  LC 2006028375

"With [its] beautiful illustrations, high-quality production, and focus on source material, the [book] should whet the interest of readers." SLJ
Includes glossary and bibliographical references

Steer, Dugald

The **mythology** handbook; a course in ancient Greek myths. by Hestia Evans; edited by Dugald A. Steer and Clint Twist. Candlewick Press 2009 71p il map $12.99
Grades: 4 5 6 7   **292**
1. Classical mythology
ISBN 978-0-7636-4291-4

"This follow-up to Mythology (Candlewick, 2007) again uses the voice of a fictional 19th-century scholar. Here, Lady Hestia Evans offers a guide to elements of Greek myth for her two children, providing information in 'lessons' . . . with exercises based on each topic. Some of the activities encourage students to do further research . . . while others suggest that they draw new monsters, write hymns with the Muses' help, or design a new pentathlon for the Olympics. Mazes and a word search (using Greek letters) are also included. . . . The activities are engaging, and the illustrations of creatures and maps of the ancient world will add to the knowledge of even more experienced myth fans." SLJ

Turnbull, Ann

★ **Greek** myths; retold by Ann Turnbull; illustrated by Sarah Young. Candlewick Press 2011 165p il

Grades: 5 6 7 8 9 10   **292**
  1. Classical mythology 2. Mythology, Greek
  ISBN 0-7636-5111-7; 978-0-7636-5111-4
                      LC 2010-39178

Turnbull divides sixteen Greek myths "under three headings: Earth, the Heavens, and the Underworld; Monsters and Heroes; Gods and Mortals. . . . Grades five to ten." (Bull Cent Child Books)

"Sixteen Greek myths . . . are retold here with stylistic grace well matched to beautiful visual presentation. . . . Turnbull narrates with . . . vibrancy. . . . Sarah Young's mixed-media artwork—regal, yet sensuous compositions in richly textured earthtones touch[ed] with gold—is sufficiently representational to assist younger readers with context clues, and sufficiently elegant and sophisticated to satisfy seasoned readers." Bull Cent Child Books

293   Germanic religion

Daly, Kathleen N.

  Norse mythology A to Z; [by] Kathleen N. Daly; revised by Marian Rengel. 3rd ed.; Chelsea House 2009 128p il map (Mythology A to Z) lib bdg $45
Grades: 8 9 10 11 12   **293**
  1. Reference books 2. Norse mythology -- Dictionaries
  ISBN 978-1-60413-411-7; 1-60413-411-9
                      LC 2009-13338
  First published 1991

Alphabetically listed entries identify and explain the characters, events, and important places of Norse mythology

  Includes bibliographical references

Porterfield, Jason

  Scandinavian mythology; [by] Jason Porterfield. Rosen Pub. Group 2008 64p il map (Mythology around the world) lib bdg $29.95
Grades: 5 6 7 8   **293**
  1. Norse mythology 2. Scandinavia -- Civilization
  ISBN 978-1-4042-0740-0 lib bdg; 1-4042-0740-6 lib bdg
                      LC 2005037508

The author describes the history of "the Scandinavian nations, introducing concepts and characters central to Norse myths. . . . The most remarkable part of [this book] . . . is the respect [it shows] for the mythological customs, treating them throughout with the same care that writers of books on major religions might offer. The illustrations show both ancient and modern incarnations of the deities and heroes described in the [text]." SLJ

  Includes glossary and bibliographical references

Schomp, Virginia

  The **Norsemen**; [by] Virginia Schomp. Marshall Cavendish Benchmark 2007 96p il map (Myths of the world) lib bdg $22.95
Grades: 6 7 8 9   **293**
  1. Norse mythology 2. Scandinavia -- Civilization
  ISBN 978-0-7614-2548-9
                      LC 2007002772

"With [its] beautiful illustrations, high-quality production, and focus on source material, the [book] should whet the interest of readers." SLJ

  Includes bibliographical references

294   Religions of Indic origin

Mann, Gurinder Singh

  Buddhists, Hindus, and Sikhs in America; [by] Gurinder Singh Mann, Paul David Numrich & Raymond B. Williams. Oxford University Press 2001 158p il (Religion in American life) hardcover o.p. pa $12.95
Grades: 7 8 9 10   **294**
  1. Sikhism 2. Buddhism 3. Hinduism 4. Asian Americans -- Religion
  ISBN 0-19-512442-1; 0-19-533311-X pa
                      LC 2001-45151

Presents the basic tenets of these three Asian religions and discusses the religious history and experience of their practitioners after immigration to the United States

"Solid information, a large selection of historical and contemporary photographs, interesting readings from primary sources, and accounts from school-age Buddhists, Hindus, and Sikhs combine to make this is a valuable resource." Booklist

  Includes bibliographical references

Ollhoff, Jim

  Indian mythology. ABDO Pub. 2012 32 p. il map lib bdg $27.07
Grades: 5 6 7 8   **294**
  1. Hinduism 2. Indic mythology 3. India -- Religion
  ISBN 978-1-61714-722-7; 1-61714-722-2
                      LC 2010041628

'This book offers information about Indian mythology, answering questions such as "Who is Devi? What is Ganesha? Why are myths so important in our lives? Myths are a rich source of history. People use them to make sense of our world. Even before myths were written down, people told and retold the stories of the gods and goddesses of their homeland. Readers of Indian Mythology will learn the history of myths, as well as their deeper meaning." (Publisher's note) The book "introduces Brahma, Vishnu, Shiva, Kali, and other Hindu gods and goddesses while also discussing how the deities often took on different forms called avatars." (Booklist)

"Ollhoff writes in a clear and engaging fashion, presenting complex issues in a way that will be easy for youngsters to grasp. . . . The photographs and reproductions of art tie directly to the [text]." SLJ

294.3   Buddhism

Demi

  ★ **Buddha**. Holt & Co. 1996 un il $21.95

Grades: 4 5 6　　　　　　　　　　　**294.3**
　1. Philosophers　2. Buddhist leaders
　ISBN 0-8050-4203-2

LC 95-16906

Demi "uses clear, uncomplicated storytelling to present complex philosophical concepts. . . . The gilded illustrations (based, according to the jacket, on 'Indian, Chinese, Japanese, Burmese, and Indonesian paintings, sculptures, and sutra illustrations') are delicate, yet the colors and composition are bold, with central figures and action cascading beyond the careful borders." Bull Cent Child Books

★ The **Dalai** Lama; a biography of the Tibetan spiritual and political leader. Henry Holt & Co. 1998 un il $18.95
Grades: 4 5 6 7　　　　　　　　　**294.3**
　1. Buddhism　2. Tibet (China)　3. Buddhist leaders　4. Political leaders　5. Nobel laureates for peace
　ISBN 0-8050-5443-X

LC 97-30654

In this biography of the Buddhist spiritual leader, Demi "uses straightforward prose and fluid, eastern-influenced art—small pen-and-ink and watercolor images with fine, intricate detail. . . . Told with respect and devotion, this is an inspirational picture-book biography." Horn Book

Eckel, Malcolm David
　Buddhism. Rosen Pub. 2010 112p il (Understanding religions) lib bdg $31.95
Grades: 7 8 9 10　　　　　　　　**294.3**
　1. Buddhism
　ISBN 978-1-4358-5619-6; 1-4358-5619-8

LC 2009-10083

Subjects covered in this book include "buddhas and bodhisattvas, Zen meditation, Tantric scriptures, pilgrimage, temples, and festivals and rites." Publisher's note
　Includes glossary and bibliographical references

Ganeri, Anita
　★ **Buddhism**; [by] Anita Ganeri. World Almanac Library 2006 48p il map (Religions of the world) lib bdg $30.60
Grades: 5 6 7 8　　　　　　　　　**294.3**
　1. Buddhism
　ISBN 0-8368-5865-4

LC 2005041708

The author "presents a survey of Buddhist history, beliefs, sacred texts, festivals, and lifecycle events. . . . There is discussion of the art and folk literature associated with the religious tradition. Colorful photographs, illustrations, and art reproductions appear throughout." SLJ
　Includes bibliographical references

Lee, Jeanne M.
　I once was a monkey; stories Buddha told. Farrar, Straus & Giroux 1999 un il $16
Grades: 4 5 6 7　　　　　　　　　**294.3**
　1. Jataka stories
　ISBN 0-374-33548-6

LC 98-17651

A retelling of six Jatakas, or birth stories, which illustrate some of the central tenets of Buddha's teachings, such as compassion, honesty, and thinking clearly before acting
　"The appealing character of the monkey will pull children into the tales, which convey lessons in a direct yet gentle way that is never preachy. The accompanying linocut illustrations are lovely." Booklist

Nardo, Don
　Buddhism. Compass Point Books 2009 48p il map (World religions) lib bdg $27.99
Grades: 5 6 7 8　　　　　　　　　**294.3**
　1. Buddhism
　ISBN 978-0-7565-4236-8 lib bdg; 0-7565-4236-7 lib bdg

LC 2009-11453

"The colorful, attractive layout includes high-quality reproductions of photographs, maps, and paintings. Students who are new to religious studies, as well as those doing reports, will find that this . . . meets their needs." SLJ
　Includes glossary and bibliographical references

Wangu, Madhu Bazaz
　Buddhism; 4th ed.; Chelsea House 2009 144p il (World religions) $40
Grades: 7 8 9 10 11 12　　　　　　**294.3**
　1. Buddhism
　ISBN 978-1-60413-105-5; 1-60413-105-5

LC 2008-51265

First published 1993 by Facts on File
　This "tells the story of Buddhism's origins and its development into three major schools of thought—and presents the particular beliefs and practices of those schools of Buddhism. . . . [This] title explores the concept of the 'socially engaged Buddhist,' the growth and practice of Buddhism in America, and the recent revival of Buddhism in Asia." Publisher's note
　Includes glossary and bibliographical references

Winston, Diana
　★ **Wide** awake: a Buddhist guide for teens. Perigee Bk. 2003 290p pa $13.95
Grades: 7 8 9 10 11 12　　　　　　**294.3**
　1. Buddhism
　ISBN 0-399-52897-0

LC 2002-192666

"Switching between anecdotes of her own journey in Buddhism and advice on how teens can apply the Buddha's teachings to their lives, Winston offers a personal and thoughtful introduction to Buddhist thought and practice." Booklist

294.5　Hinduism

Ganeri, Anita
　The **Ramayana** and Hinduism. Smart Apple Media 2003 30p il (Sacred texts) $27.10

Grades: 5 6 7 8 9   **294.5**
  1. Hinduism
  ISBN 1-58340-242-X
             LC 2003-42352
Explains the history and practices of the religion of Hinduism, especially as revealed through its sacred book, the Ramayana

Narayanan, Vasudha
  Hinduism. Rosen Pub. 2010 112p il (Understanding religions) lib bdg $31.95
Grades: 7 8 9 10   **294.5**
  1. Hinduism
  ISBN 978-1-4358-5620-2; 1-4358-5620-1
             LC 2009-11026
This book about Hinduism "discusses origins and historical development; aspects of the divine; sacred texts, persons, space, and time; ethical principles; death and the afterlife; and society and religion." SLJ
Includes glossary and bibliographical references

Plum-Ucci, Carol
  Celebrate Diwali; [by] Carol Plum-Ucci. Enslow Publishers 2008 128p il map (Celebrate holidays) $31.93
Grades: 5 6 7 8   **294.5**
  1. Divali
  ISBN 978-0-7660-2778-7; 0-7660-2778-3
             LC 2006028106
This describes the history, cultural significance, customs, symbols and celebrations around the world of the Hindu holiday of Diwali.
  "Captioned photographs, maps, drawings, and sidebars combine with accessible text to present a thorough discussion of [Diwali]. . . . This . . . is a useful resource." Horn Book Guide
  Includes glossary and bibliographical references

Rasamandala Das
  ★ **Hinduism**. World Almanac Library 2006 48p il map (Religions of the world) $30.60
Grades: 5 6 7 8   **294.5**
  1. Hinduism
  ISBN 0-8368-5867-0
Hinduism is "explored in an accessible introductory manner, including information on [its] history, teachings, religious practices, culture and lifestyle, and the [faith's role] in today's global society. Vibrant full-color photographs are appropriately placed within the [text]. Ideal for . . . school reports or for general interest." SLJ
  Includes bibliographical references

Rosinsky, Natalie M.
  Hinduism. Compass Point Books 2009 48p il map (World religions) lib bdg $27.99
Grades: 5 6 7 8   **294.5**
  1. Hinduism
  ISBN 978-0-7565-4238-2 lib bdg; 0-7565-4238-3 lib bdg
             LC 2009-9349

"The colorful, attractive layout includes high-quality reproductions of photographs, maps, and paintings. Students who are new to religious studies, as well as those doing reports, will find that this . . . meets their needs." SLJ
  Includes glossary and bibliographical references

Schomp, Virginia
  Ancient India. Marshall Cavendish Benchmark 2009 96p il (Myths of the world) lib bdg $34.21
Grades: 6 7 8 9   **294.5**
  1. Buddhism 2. Hindu mythology 3. Indic mythology
  ISBN 978-0-7614-4213-4 lib bdg; 0-7614-4213-8 lib bdg
             LC 2008034952
"The language is straightforward but has enough variation in sentence structure to keep the reading lively. . . . Liberally illustrated with large and vibrant reproductions of artwork in diverse media, the [book reflects] the grace and opulence of [this] ancient [culture] as well as the more vividly grotesque expressions of imagination." SLJ
  Includes glossary and bibliographical references

Wangu, Madhu Bazaz
  Hinduism; 4th ed.; Chelsea House 2009 144p il (World religions) $40
Grades: 7 8 9 10 11 12   **294.5**
  1. Hinduism
  ISBN 978-1-60413-108-6; 1-60413-108-X
             LC 2008-43047
First published 1991 by Facts on File
This describes the history of Hinduism, its customs, beliefs, and rites of passage, the Hindu nationalist movement in India, Hinduism and the interfaith movement, and Hinduism and the environmental movement.
  Includes glossary and bibliographical references

294.6   Sikhism

Singh, Nikky-Guninder Kaur
  Sikhism; 3rd ed.; Chelsea House 2009 144p il (World religions) $40
Grades: 7 8 9 10 11 12   **294.6**
  1. Sikhism
  ISBN 978-1-60413-114-7; 1-60413-114-4
             LC 2008-29662
First published 1993 by Facts on File
This "describes the basic tenets of Sikhism, examines the recent move toward greater political independence within the Indian nation, and covers issues of cultural adaptation, persecution, and subsequent education now taking place in the West." Publisher's note
  Includes glossary and bibliographical references

295   Zoroastrianism (Mazdaism, Parseeism)

Hartz, Paula
  Zoroastrianism; by Paula R. Hartz. 3rd ed.; Chelsea House 2009 144p il (World religions) $40

Grades: 7 8 9 10 11 12   **295**
1. Zoroastrianism
ISBN 978-1-60413-116-1; 1-60413-116-0
                LC 2008-35811
First published 1999 by Facts on File
This "analyzes how [Zoroastrianism] has a crucial place in religious history and continues to maintain a devoted following today." Publisher's note
Includes glossary and bibliographical references

Schomp, Virginia
The **ancient** Persians. Marshall Cavendish Benchmark 2009 96p il (Myths of the world) lib bdg $34.21
Grades: 6 7 8 9   **295**
1. Poets 2. Zoroastrianism 3. Iran -- Civilization
ISBN 978-0-7614-4218-9 lib bdg; 0-7614-4218-9 lib bdg
               LC 2009011876
"The language is straightforward but has enough variation in sentence structure to keep the reading lively. . . . Liberally illustrated with large and vibrant reproductions of artwork in diverse media, the [book reflects] the grace and opulence of [this] ancient [culture] as well as the more vividly grotesque expressions of imagination." SLJ
Includes glossary and bibliographical references

296   Judaism

Buxbaum, Shelley M.
Jewish faith in America; {by} Shelley M. Buxbaum, Sara E. Karesh. Facts on File 2003 128p il (Faith in America) $30
Grades: 7 8 9 10   **296**
1. Judaism 2. Jews -- United States 3. United States -- Ethnic relations
ISBN 0-8160-4986-6
               LC 2002-29392
"Thoroughly researched and heavily illustrated." Libr Media Connect
This offers a history of the Jewish people in America "from the early days . . . and their participation in the Revolutionary and Civil Wars, to the impact of World War II and the Holocaust on Jewish life in America. . . . {It also covers} the various ways Judaism is practiced in the U.S. as well as the contributions Jews have made to American society." Publisher's note
Includes bibliographical references (p. 123) and index

Ehrlich, Carl S.
Judaism. Rosen Pub. 2010 112p il (Understanding religions) lib bdg $31.95
Grades: 7 8 9 10   **296**
1. Judaism
ISBN 978-1-4358-5622-6; 1-4358-5622-8
               LC 2009-10055
This "book provides students with an overview of the great religious tradition of Judaism. Readers learn about the covenant with God, the Bible, the Mishnah, and the Talmud. They also read about sects, messianic movements, mysti-

cism, and the Kabbalah. Rabbinical systems of law and custom are covered as are various principles and practices, holy days, and contemporary movements in Judaism." Publisher's note
Includes glossary and bibliographical references

Morrison, M. A.
Judaism; by Martha A. Morrison and Stephen F. Brown. 4th ed.; Chelsea House 2009 144p il (World religions) $40
Grades: 7 8 9 10 11 12   **296**
1. Judaism
ISBN 978-1-60413-110-9; 1-60413-110-1
               LC 2008-29657
First published 1991 by Facts on File under the authorship of Fay Carol Gates
This "presents the basic beliefs of the Jewish religious heritage and highlights the different manners in which these traditions can be upheld. Both Orthodox Judaism and the religious practices and movements within Reformed Judaism, including Reform Judaism, Conservative Judaism, and Reconstructionist Judaism, are explored." Publisher's note
Includes glossary and bibliographical references

The **Oxford** dictionary of the Jewish religion; editor in chief, Adele Berlin. 2nd ed. Oxford University Press 2011 xxiv, 934 p.p (hardcover) $195
Grades: 8 9 10 11 12 Adult   **296**
1. Judaism -- Dictionaries 2. Judaism -- Encyclopedias
ISBN 0199730040; 9780199730049; 9780199759279
               LC 2010035774
This book, by Maxine Grossman, edited by Adele Berlin, presents an updated, second edition of its original 1997 publication. It "focuses on recent and changing rituals in the Jewish community. . . . Nearly 200 internationally renowned scholars have created a new edition that incorporates updated bibliographies, biographies of 20th-century individuals who have shaped the recent thought and history of Judaism, and an index with alternate spellings of Hebrew terms." (Publisher's note)
Includes bibliographical references and index.

Rosinsky, Natalie M.
Judaism. Compass Point Books 2009 48p il map (World religions) lib bdg $27.99
Grades: 5 6 7 8   **296**
1. Judaism
ISBN 978-0-7565-4240-5 lib bdg; 0-7565-4240-5 lib bdg
               LC 2009-15813
"The colorful, attractive layout includes high-quality reproductions of photographs, maps, and paintings. Students who are new to religious studies, as well as those doing reports, will find that this . . . meets their needs." SLJ
Includes glossary and bibliographical references

296.1 Sources

Chaikin, Miriam

★ **Angels** sweep the desert floor; Bible legends about Moses in the wilderness. illustrated by Alexander Koshkin. Clarion Bks. 2002 102p il $19

Grades: 4 5 6 7 **296.1**
1. Prophets 2. Bible stories 3. Jewish legends 4. Angels -- Fiction 5. Biblical characters
ISBN 0-395-97825-4
LC 2001-47501

A collection of eighteen stories based on the Bible which tell how angels respond to God's commands to ease the way for Moses and the Israelites as they cross the wilderness after being freed from slavery in Egypt

"The full-page watercolor, tempera, and gouache illustrations have a fanciful formality that complements the narrative. Capable of exciting the creative, as well as the spiritual imagination, these wonderful stories make great read-alouds." SLJ

Includes bibliographical references

Pinsker, Marlee

In the days of sand and stars; illustrated by Fran¿cois Thisdale. Tundra Books 2006 87p il $22.95

Grades: 5 6 7 8 **296.1**
1. Bible stories 2. Jewish legends 3. Women in the Bible
ISBN 978-0-88776-724-1; 0-88776-724-9

This is a collection of stories from the Midrash about women including Eve, Naamah, Sarai, Sarah, Rebecca, Leah, Rachel, Dina, and Yocheved.

"Pinsker works like a musician, playing with words instead of notes, but the result is just as lilting and lyrical. The stories are matched by unusual illustrations. Thisdale blends traditional artwork with digital technology. Pieces of photographs mix with ancient elements, giving the pictures a fresh, compelling look." Booklist

296.4 Traditions, rites, public services

Kimmel, Eric A.

★ **Wonders** and miracles; a Passover companion. illustrated with art spanning three thousand years; written and compiled by Eric A. Kimmel. Scholastic Press 2004 136p il $18.95

Grades: 4 5 6 7 **296.4**
1. Passover
ISBN 0-439-07175-5
LC 2002-4732

Presents the steps performed in a traditional Passover Seder, plus stories, songs, poetry, and pictures that celebrate the historical significance of this holiday to Jews all over the world.

"The marvelous selection of art—paintings, photographs, artifacts, and illustrations from historical Haggadahs—illuminates each step in the service. . . . Both the presentation of information and the overall design attest to the careful and loving attention given to every detail. This

inviting, handsome, and informative compendium should find a place of honor in every library." SLJ

Includes bibliographical references

Metter, Bert

Bar mitzvah, bat mitzvah; the ceremony, the party, and how the day came to be. by Bert Metter; illustrated by Joan Reilly. Clarion Books 2007 un il $16; pa $5.95

Grades: 4 5 6 7 **296.4**
1. Bar mitzvah 2. Bat mitzvah
ISBN 978-0-618-76772-4; 0-618-76772-X; 978-0-618-76773-1 pa; 0-618-76773-8 pa
LC 2006032942

The author "describes a typical ceremony and explains how this custom began for boys during the Middle Ages and how it was adapted for girls beginning in 1922. He also discusses the recent custom of adult bar and bat mitzvahs and celebratory parties. The writing is clear and concise; ink illustrations . . . help break up the text." Booklist

Includes bibliographical references

297 Islam, Babism, Bahai Faith

Alkouatli, Claire

Islam. Marshall Cavendish 2006 143p il (World religions) lib bdg $39.93

Grades: 7 8 9 10 **297**
1. Islam
ISBN 978-0-7614-2120-7 lib bdg; 0-7614-2120-3 lib bdg
LC 2005026862

"Provides an overiew of the history and origins, basic tenets and beliefs, organization, traditions, customs, rites, societal and historical influences, and modern-day impact of Islam." Publisher's note

This offers a "fine, well-detailed overview of the second largest religion in the world." Booklist

Includes glossary and bibliographical references

Aslan, Reza, 1972-

No god but God; the origins and evolution of Islam. Delacorte Press 2011 166p $16.99; lib bdg $19.99

Grades: 7 8 9 10 **297**
1. Islam -- History
ISBN 0-385-73975-3; 0-385-90805-9 lib bdg; 978-0-385-73975-7; 978-0-385-90805-4 lib bdg
LC 2010020408

Adaptation of: No god but God: the origins, evolution, and future of Islam, published 2006 by Random House for adults

"Packing in a formidable amount of research, legend, and critical analysis, Aslan condenses his adult book of the same name to create a concise introduction to Islam. By breaking up chapters with clear subheadings, maintaining a conversational tone, and incorporating numerous anecdotes that both inform and entertain, Aslan makes 15 centuries of religious history digestible without oversimplifying complex material. . . . This welcome addition to Islamic studies provides a valuable context for reflection about the origins of issues facing Muslims and their neighbors today." Publ Wkly

Barnard, Bryn

★ The **genius** of Islam; how Muslims made the modern world. Alfred A. Knopf 2011 37p il map $17.99; lib bdg $20.99

Grades: 4 5 6 7   297

1. Islamic civilization 2. Islam -- History

ISBN 978-0-375-84072-2; 0-375-84072-9; 978-0-375-94072-9 lib bdg; 0-375-94072-3 lib bdg

LC 2010-12777

This is a "concise and eloquent exploration of the far-reaching influence of Islam over the centuries. Each spread is devoted to a different subject (writing, Arabic numerals, architecture, astronomy, agriculture), while captioned spot art homes in on specific inventions and innovations (the zither, the astrolabe, advanced medical knowledge)." Publ Wkly

Includes bibliographical references

Demi

★ **Muhammad**; written and illustrated by Demi. Margaret K. McElderry Bks. 2003 un il $19.95

Grades: 4 5 6 7   297

1. Islam 2. Prophets 3. Islamic leaders 4. Writers on religion

ISBN 0-689-85264-9

LC 2002-2985

"With dramatic scenes extending past the borders of the intricately patterned frames, the art will be a continual source of interest for young people. . . . [An] excellent retelling of the Prophet's life that combines beauty and scholarship." Booklist

Includes bibliographical references

Gordon, Matthew

Islam; by Matthew S. Gordon. 4th ed. Chelsea House 2009 144 p. col. ill., map (World religions) (library) $40.00

Grades: 7 8 9 10 11 12   297

1. Islam

ISBN 978-1-60413-109-3; 1-60413-109-8

LC 2008035810

First published 1991 by Facts on File

This describes the founding of Islam and its spread, The Koran, Hadith, and Islamic law, branches of Islam and their basic beliefs, Muslim customs and rituals, the pattern of Islamic life, and the place of Islam in the modern world.

Includes bibliographical references (p. 138-139) and index.

Hafiz, Dilara

★ The **American** Muslim teenager's handbook; by Dilara Hafiz, Imran Hafiz, and Yasmine Hafiz. [new ed.]; Atheneum Books for Young Readers 2009 168p il pa $11.99

Grades: 7 8 9 10 11 12   297

1. Islam 2. Conduct of life 3. Muslims -- United States 4. Teenagers -- Religious life

ISBN 978-1-4169-8578-5; 1-4169-8578-6

A revised edition of the title first published 2007 by Acacia Pub.

"Casual, colloquial, joking, contemporary, and passionate, this interactive handbook by two Arizona teens and their mom talks about their faith, about what it is like to be both proud Americans and proud Muslims, and about misunderstandings and stereotypes. . . . There are also step-by-step guides on how to pray, how to read the Qur'an, and how to fast at Ramadan. Muslim and non-Muslim teens alike will be caught by the candor, the humor, and the call for interfaith dialogue and tolerance." Booklist

Includes bibliographical references

Hinds, Kathryn, 1962-

★ **Faith**; [by] Kathryn Hinds. Marshall Cavendish Benchmark 2008 96p il map (Life in the Medieval Muslim world) lib bdg $23.95

Grades: 6 7 8 9 10   297

1. Middle Ages 2. Medieval civilization 3. Islam -- History 4. Islamic countries

ISBN 978-0-7614-3092-6 lib bdg; 0-7614-3092-X lib bdg

LC 2008019268

"A social history of the Muslim world from the eighth through the mid-thirteenth century, with a focus on the religion of Islam." Publisher's note

"Richly illustrated with art reproductions, maps, photos, and ornate Islamic border designs, [this] . . . . will entice visual learners." Libr Media Connect

Includes glossary and bibliographical references

Illustrated dictionary of the Muslim world; [editor, Felicity Crowe and others] Marshall Cavendish Reference 2010 192p il (Muslim world) $85.64

Grades: 7 8 9 10   297

1. Reference books 2. Islam -- Dictionaries 3. Islamic civilization -- Dictionaries

ISBN 978-0-7614-7929-1; 0-7614-7929-5

LC 2010008613

Contains hundreds of short entries on Islamic concepts, religious practices, historical events and personalities, geographical places, and fact files of nations with large Muslim populations.

"Attractive trim on the pages, colorful fonts, quality illustrations, and framed (often illustrated) sideboxes create a pleasing layout. Excellent for assignments." SLJ

Includes glossary and bibliographical references

Is Islam a religion of war or peace? Jann Einfeld, book editor. Greenhaven Press 2005 108p (At issue) hardcover o.p. pa $19.95

Grades: 7 8 9 10   297

1. Islam 2. War -- Religious aspects 3. Terrorism -- Religious aspects

ISBN 0-7377-3099-4 lib bdg; 0-7377-3100-1 pa

LC 2004-59678

"Eleven opinions are presented here. The book begins with Osama bin Laden's justification for his attacks on Americans. The portrayal of Islam as a predominantly peaceful religion by President George W. Bush is countered by evangelist Pat Robertson. Additional perspectives are offered by Islamic scholars, a former Muslim, a female Muslim reformer, and a rabbi who is an expert on Islam." SLJ

Includes bibliographical references

Islam in America; Laura K. Egendorf, book editor. Greenhaven Press 2006 112p (At issue) lib bdg $28.70; pa $19.95

Grades: 7 8 9 10 11 12   **297**
1. Islam 2. Muslims -- United States
ISBN 0-7377-2727-6 lib bdg; 0-7377-2728-4 pa
        LC 2005046317

The selections in this collection "treat such subjects as whether American Muslims support terrorist groups and whether or not they experience discrimination. The pieces on African-American Muslims and the growing popularity of Islam among Hispanic Americans are particularly interesting." SLJ

Includes bibliographical references

Islamic beliefs, practices, and cultures. Marshall Cavendish Reference 2010 352p il (Muslim world) lib bdg $114.21

Grades: 7 8 9 10   **297**
1. Islamic civilization 2. Islam -- Customs and practices
ISBN 978-0-7614-7926-0; 0-7614-7926-0
        LC 2010008611

"Attractive trim on the pages, colorful fonts, quality illustrations, and framed (often illustrated) sideboxes create a pleasing layout. Excellent for assignments." SLJ

"In addition to exploring the beliefs, teachings, and practices of Islam and its holy places, calendar, and festivals, this volume covers Muslim contributions to the arts, architecture, science, literature, philosophy, and the role of the media." Booklist

Luxenberg, Alan
Radical Islam. Mason Crest 2009 64p il (World of Islam) lib bdg $22.95

Grades: 7 8 9 10 11 12   **297**
1. Islam 2. Radicalism
ISBN 978-1-4222-0536-5 lib bdg; 1-4222-0536-3 lib bdg

Luxenberg "describes Islam's historical background, its rise to world prominence, its decline, the factions that have arisen, and the move of some toward radicalism. . . . In examining specific radical arms (and their leaders), the book suggests ways for U.S. leaders to interpret intentions and future implications. . . . The book . . . would be a good addition for world-religion collections." Booklist

Includes glossary and bibliographical references

Modern Muslim societies. Marshall Cavendish Reference 2010 416p il (Muslim world) lib bdg $114.21

Grades: 7 8 9 10   **297**
1. Islam -- Customs and practices
ISBN 978-0-7614-7927-7; 0-7614-7927-9
        LC 2010008612

"Attractive trim on the pages, colorful fonts, quality illustrations, and framed (often illustrated) sideboxes create a pleasing layout. Excellent for assignments." SLJ

This book "covers marriage and family life, education and employment, organizations, law and politics, and civil and human rights in its first half. 'Focus' features treat topics such as 'Wearing the Veil' and 'Al-Qaeda.' Each chapter of the second half, 'Regional and National Surveys,' covers a different part of the world and its Muslim population." Booklist

Nardo, Don
The **birth** of Islam. Morgan Reynolds Pub. 2011 112p (World religions and beliefs) lib bdg $28.95

Grades: 7 8 9 10   **297**
1. Islamic civilization 2. Islam -- History
ISBN 978-1-59935-146-9; 1-59935-146-3
        LC 2010038442

This covers the beginnings of Islam "in an impartial way. The [context] in which the [religion] developed [is] explained, offering insight into how [Islam] came to be and introducing major concepts the [religion]." SLJ

Includes glossary and bibliographical references

Raatma, Lucia
Islam. Compass Point Books 2010 48p il map (World religions) lib bdg $27.99

Grades: 5 6 7 8   **297**
1. Islam
ISBN 978-0-7565-4239-9 lib bdg; 0-7565-4239-1 lib bdg
        LC 2009-15812

"The colorful, attractive layout includes high-quality reproductions of photographs, maps, and paintings. Students who are new to religious studies, as well as those doing reports, will find that this . . . meets their needs." SLJ

Includes glossary and bibliographical references

297.1 Islam

The **meaning** of the glorious Koran; an explanatory translation by Marmaduke Pickthall; with an introduction by William Montgomery Watt. A.A. Knopf 1992 xxiv, 693p il $22

Grades: 7 8 9 10 11 12 Adult   **297.1**
1. Qur'an
ISBN 0-679-41736-2; 978-0-679-41736-1
        LC 92-52928

This translation first published 1930

"The sacred scripture of Islam, regarded by Muslims as the Word of God, and except in sura I.—which is a prayer to God—and some few passages in which Muhammad or the angels speak in the first person, the speaker throughout is God." Ency Britannica

The **Qur'an**; English translation and parallel Arabic text. translated, with an introduction and notes, by M.A.S. Abdel Haleem. Oxford University Press 2010 xxxix, 624 p.p maps (hardcover) $45

Grades: 7 8 9 10 11 12 Adult   **297.1**
1. Qur'an
ISBN 019957071X; 9780199570713
        LC 2010281328

This book, by M. A. S. Abdel Haleem, offers an English translation of the Qur'an with Arab text presented in parallel. "This translation is written in contemporary language . . . , set page-for-page against the most widespread traditional calligraphic Arabic text. . . . Furthermore, Haleem includes notes that explain geographical, historical, and personal allusions as well as an index in which Qur'anic material is arranged into topics for easy reference." (Publisher's note)

"Because the Koran stresses its Arabic nature, devout Muslims believe that only an Arabic version is the actual Koran and insist that its translation cannot be more than an approximate interpretation. . . Yet anyone wishing to understand Islamic civilization and global affairs may find this Koran very useful. . . . Highly recommended." LJ

Includes bibliographical references and index

297.3   Islamic worship

Jeffrey, Laura S.

Celebrate Ramadan; [by] Laura S. Jeffrey. Enslow Publishers 2007 112p il (Celebrate holidays) lib bdg $31.93

Grades: 5 6 7 8   **297.3**

1. Islam 2. Ramadan 3. Id al-Adha
ISBN 978-0-7660-2774-9 lib bdg; 0-7660-2774-0 lib bdg

LC 2006028107

"This book opens by introducing a contemporary Muslim, Bushra, who celebrated Ramadan as a girl growing up in England [and] later immigrated to the United States. . . . An informative chapter surveys the history, beliefs, and practices of Islam. . . . The remainder of the book offers a detailed discussion of Ramadan, prayer, and spiritual awareness, and of l'Id al Fitr. . . . Punctuated by sidebars and illustrated with color photos, this clearly written book offers a good overview of how the holidays of Islam are celebrated." Booklist

Includes glossary and bibliographical references

297.9   Babism and Bahai Faith

Hartz, Paula

Baha'i Faith; 3rd ed.; Chelsea House 2009 144p il (World religions) $40

Grades: 7 8 9 10 11 12   **297.9**

1. Bahai Faith
ISBN 978-1-60413-104-8; 1-60413-104-7

LC 2008043045

First published 2002 by Facts on File

This "explores all aspects of the Baha'i faith, from the original teachings of its founder, Baha'u'llah, to the modern-day communities that exist in 236 countries and territories throughout the world." Publisher's note

Includes glossary and bibliographical references

299   Religions not provided for elsewhere

Harpur, James

Celtic myth; a treasury of legends, art, and history. [by] James Harpur. M.E. Sharpe 2008 96p il (The world of mythology) $35.95

Grades: 8 9 10 11 12   **299**

1. Celtic mythology 2. Celtic civilization
ISBN 978-0-7656-8102-7

LC 2007006015

"With lots of heroic adventures and exciting, sometimes gruesome detail, Harpur retells stories of the Irish and Welsh Celts and weaves in facts about their culture and the history of their struggle for dominence. The dense text is broken up with beautiful, color images on every page, including paintings and photos of the settings, sculptures, weapons, and other artifacts." Booklist

Includes glossary and bibliographical references

Matson, Gienna

Celtic mythology A to Z; [by] Gienna Matson. Facts on File 2004 114p il map (Mythology A to Z) $40

Grades: 8 9 10 11 12 Adult   **299**

1. Celtic mythology
ISBN 0-8160-4890-8

LC 2004-47111

"This title is an excellent introduction to the mythology of Celtic cultures and should be in most public and school libraries." Booklist

This is an "illustrated guide to the characters, objects, and places that make up the mythic lore of the Celtic peoples." Publisher's note

Includes bibliographical references

Taylor, Rodney Leon

Confucianism; Rodney L. Taylor. Chelsea House Publishers 2004 151p il (Religions of the world) **299**

1. Confucianism
ISBN 0-7910-7857-4

LC 2003-23920

"Taylor discusses the elements of Confucian tradition in culture and in the arts as well as its specification of differing roles for men, women, and children in society. He devotes one chapter to significant developments through the centuries and another to the place of the tradition's ancient practices and ideas in the world today. Full-page sidebars feature selections from Confucian writings and teachings, which serve to both break up and add flavor to the long sections of text." SLJ

299.31   Ancient Egyptian Religion

Hinds, Kathryn, 1962-

★ **Religion**; by Kathryn Hinds. Marshall Cavendish Benchmark 2007 vii, 72 p.p col. ill., col. maps (Life in ancient Egypt) (library) $8.66

Grades: 6 7 8 9   **299.31**

1. Egyptian mythology 2. Egypt -- Religion 3. Egypt

-- Civilization
ISBN 9780761421863; 0761421866

LC 2006011086

"Describes the role of religion in ancient Egypt during the New Kingdom period, from about 1550 BCE to about 1070 BCE, including the diverse gods and goddesses the people worshipped, their creation myths, and the role of priesthood." Publisher's note

Includes bibliographical references (p. 67-68) and index.

Napoli, Donna Jo

★ **Treasury** of Egyptian Mythology; Classic Stories of Gods, Goddesses, Monsters & Mortals. by Donna Jo Napoli and illustrated by Christina Balit. National Geographic Children's books 2013 192 p. $24.95

Grades: 3 4 5 6   **299.31**

1. Egyptian mythology 2. Gods and goddesses
ISBN 1426313802; 9781426313806

Author Donna Jo Napoli presents a "tableau of Egyptian myths, including those of pharaohs, queens, the boisterous Sun God Ra, and legendary creatures like the Sphinx. The stories are embellished with sidebars that provide historical, cultural, and geographic context and a mapping feature that adds to the fun and fascination. Resource notes and ample back matter direct readers to discover more about ancient Egypt." (Publisher's note)

Schomp, Virginia

The **ancient** Egyptians; [by] Virginia Schomp. Marshall Cavendish Benchmark 2007 95p il map (Myths of the world) lib bdg $22.95

Grades: 6 7 8 9   **299.31**

1. Egyptian mythology 2. Egypt -- Civilization
ISBN 978-0-7614-2549-6

LC 2006037686

"With [its] beautiful illustrations, high-quality production, and focus on source material, the [book] should whet the interest of readers." SLJ

"A retelling of several key ancient Egyptian myths, with background information describing the history, geography, belief systems, and customs of the ancient Egypt." Publisher's note

Includes glossary and bibliographical references

299.5   Religions of East and Southeast Asian origin

Demi

★ The **legend** of Lao Tzu and the Tao te ching. Margaret K. McElderry Books 2007 un il $21.99

Grades: 4 5 6 7   **299.5**

1. Taoism 2. Philosophers
ISBN 1-4169-1206-1; 978-1-4169-1206-4

LC 2005029695

"This is the legend of Lao Tzu . . . who may or may not have founded Taoism, one of the greatest religions of the world. Demi's elegant picture-book introduction to the legendary Chinese philosopher . . . combines nuggets of his purported life with 20 verses from the Tao Te Ching. . . .

The narrative and graceful paintings are contained in a gold circular frame on each parchment shaded page." SLJ

Hartz, Paula

Daoism; by Paula R. Hartz. 3rd ed.; Chelsea House 2009 144p il (World religions) $40

Grades: 7 8 9 10 11 12   **299.5**

1. Taoism
ISBN 978-1-60413-115-4; 1-60413-115-2

LC 2008-35809

First published 1993 by Facts on File with title: Taoism

This "traces the history of Daoism and explains its basic thoughts, traditions, and practices. It also details the Daoist movement worldwide and how the limitations of consumerism are leading a younger generation to search for their own spiritual harmony." Publisher's note

Includes glossary and bibliographical references

Shinto; by Paula R. Hartz. 3rd ed.; Chelsea House 2009 144p il (World religions) $40

Grades: 7 8 9 10 11 12   **299.5**

1. Shinto
ISBN 978-1-60413-113-0; 1-60413-113-6

LC 2008-29661

First published 1997 by Facts on File

This "examines the basic tenets of Shinto, its evolution in response to other religious influences, and how the original Shinto religion—rooted in an agrarian society—survives in contemporary Japan." Publisher's note

Includes glossary and bibliographical references

Helft, Claude

Chinese mythology; stories of creation and invention. [by] Claude Helft; illustrations by Chen Jiang Hong; translated from the French by Michael Hariton and Claudia Bedrick. 1st American ed.; Enchanted Lion Books 2007 78p il $14.95

Grades: 7 8 9 10   **299.5**

1. Chinese mythology
ISBN 978-1-59270-074-5; 1-59270-074-8

LC 2007031297

"This slim book offers high visual interest along with concise introductions to an important body of myths. Helft deftly organizes what can be confusing anecdotes about gods who often occupy themselves with governing and making war. . . . Interleaved pages describe a dozen cultural items (jade, yin/yang, dragons, etc.). . . . Full-page and vignette illustrations in traditional style with strong ink lines emphasize vitality and movement. Chen's evocative and richly colored paintings add value to this compact collection." SLJ

Kallen, Stuart A.

Shinto. Lucent Bks. 2002 128p il map (Religions of the world) lib bdg $27.45

Grades: 6 7 8 9   **299.5**

1. Shinto
ISBN 1-56006-988-0

LC 2001-6120

Discusses historical origins, the teachings, practices, and the spread of Shinto into modern times

Includes glossary and bibliographical references

Levin, Judith

Japanese mythology; [by] Judith Levin. The Rosen Pub. Group 2008 64p il map (Mythology around the world) $29.95

Grades: 5 6 7 8   **299.5**

1. Shinto 2. Buddhism 3. Japanese mythology 4. Japan -- Civilization

ISBN 978-1-4042-0736-3; 1-4042-0736-8

LC 2005035279

This "presents not only an introduction to Shinto and Buddhist beliefs, but also Japanese history and mythology in general. . . . The most remarkable part of [this book] . . . is the respect [it shows] for the mythological customs, treating them throughout with the same care that writers of books on major religions might offer. The illustrations show both ancient and modern incarnations of the deities and heroes." SLJ

Includes glossary and bibliographical references

Roberts, Jeremy

Chinese mythology A to Z; 2nd ed.; Chelsea House 2009 172p il (Mythology A to Z) lib bdg $45

Grades: 8 9 10 11 12   **299.5**

1. Chinese mythology 2. China -- Religion

ISBN 978-1-60413-436-0; 1-60413-436-4

LC 2009-10176

First published 2004

"Coverage includes: Buddhist deities and legendary characters; animal stories, such as the fox legends; important locations, such as shrines and sacred places; [and] allegorical figures, such as the Jade Emperor, the Rain Master, and the Lord of the Granary." Publisher's note

Includes bibliographical references

299.6 Religions originating among Black Africans and people of Black African descent

Lugira, Aloysius Muzzanganda

African traditional religion; by Aloysius M. Lugira. 3rd ed.; Chelsea House 2009 144p il map (World religions) $40

Grades: 7 8 9 10 11 12   **299.6**

1. Africa -- Religion

ISBN 978-1-60413-103-1; 1-60413-103-9

LC 2008-51188

First published 1999 by Facts on File with title: African religion

"The African continent is home to more than 6,000 different ethnic and cultural groups, each with its own religious traditions. Yet these many traditions have much in common. . . . [This book] offers a . . . perspective on the beliefs that are a permanent part of Africa's history and future." Publisher's note

Includes glossary and bibliographical references

Lynch, Patricia Ann

African mythology, A to Z; revised by Jeremy Roberts. 2nd ed.; Chelsea House 2010 xxiv, 149p il map (Mythology A to Z) lib bdg $45

Grades: 8 9 10 11 12   **299.6**

1. African mythology 2. Africa -- Religion

ISBN 978-1-60413-415-5; 1-60413-415-1

LC 2009-33612

First published 2004

This is a "reference to the deities, places, events, animals, beliefs, and other subjects that appear in the myths of various African peoples." Publisher's note

Includes bibliographical references

Schomp, Virginia

The **ancient** Africans; [by] Virginia Schomp. Marshall Cavendish Benchmark 2009 96p il map (Myths of the world) $23.95

Grades: 6 7 8 9   **299.6**

1. African mythology 2. Ethnology -- Africa 3. Africa -- Civilization

ISBN 978-0-7614-3099-5; 0-7614-3099-7

LC 2008011695

"A retelling of several ancient African myths, with background information describing the history, geography, belief systems, and customs of various peoples of Africa." Publisher's note

Includes bibliographical references

299.7 Religions of North American native origin

Hartz, Paula

Native American religions; [by] Paula R. Hartz. 3rd ed.; Chelsea House 2009 144p il (World religions) $40

Grades: 7 8 9 10 11 12   **299.7**

1. Native Americans -- Religion

ISBN 978-1-60413-111-6; 1-60413-111-X

LC 2008051197

First published 1997 by Facts on File

This "presents the history of the Native American religions, starting from their roots as tribal religions, and then details the detrimental effects of European colonization, the annihilation of the Native Americans that threatened the religions, and their sudden restoration in the 20th century." Publisher's note

Includes glossary and bibliographical references

Martin, Joel

★ **Native** American religion. Oxford University Press 1999 157p il (Religion in American life) $28

Grades: 7 8 9 10   **299.7**

1. Native Americans -- Religion

ISBN 0-19-511035-8

LC 98-50155

An "examination of religious life and practices from ancient times through the Colonial period and the Western Expansion, and into the 20th century. Martin acknowledges the importance of religion in all aspects of Native American daily life and explores some of the differences among the various cultures. He also explores the impact of the arrival of Europeans on spiritual life." SLJ

Includes bibliographical references

300 SOCIAL SCIENCES, SOCIOLOGY & ANTHROPOLOGY

302 Specific topics in sociology and anthropology

Teens and volunteerism; Hal Marcovitz. 2nd edition Mason Crest Publishers 2014 112 p. color illustrations (hc) $24.95

Grades: 9 10 11   **302**

1. Volunteer work 2. Teenagers -- United States 3. Teenage volunteers in social service -- United States

ISBN 1422229602; 9781422229606

LC 2013007185

In this book, by Hal Marcovitz, a "recent report showed that each year an estimated 13 million teenagers donate more than 2.4 billion hours of their time to charitable causes, and the Gallup Youth Survey has found that roughly one-third of all teens participate in volunteer work. This volume examines the opportunities young people have for volunteering, and explores the issue of school-mandated community service." (Publisher's note)

Includes bibliographical references and index

302.23 Media (Means of communication)

Social media; like it or leave it. Rebecca Rowell. Compass Point Books, a Capstone imprint 2015 30 p. (Perspectives flip books: issues) (hardcover : alk. paper) $33.32

Grades: 6 7 8 9 10   **302.23**

1. Internet -- Social aspects 2. Social media

ISBN 0756549949; 9780756549947; 9780756550240; 9780756550479

LC 2014026596

This book, by Rebecca Rowell, is an entry of the "Perspectives flip books: issues" series exploring social media. "Perspectives Flip Books are like two books in one: Start from one end and learn why people are logging off. Then flip it over and discover why others believe responsible social media use can be beneficial. Critical thinking questions help you analyze both perspectives and form your own opinions about the issue." (Publisher's note)

"This cleverly designed Perspectives Flip Book shows the pros and cons of social media . . . students will likely find this book a helpful guide to understanding and safely using this exciting technology." Booklist

Includes bibliographical references

302.3 Social interaction within groups

Bullying; Beth Rosenthal, book editor. Greenhaven Press 2008 120p il (Introducing issues with opposing viewpoints) lib bdg $33.70

Grades: 7 8 9 10   **302.3**

1. Bullies

ISBN 978-0-7377-3801-8; 0-7377-3801-4

LC 2007-32382

"Topics covered in this book range from the causes of bullying, what role society plays in encouraging bullying, the roles of TV and/or video games in violence and bullying, the responsibility of parents, the value of anti-bullying programs, and the ways that the behavior can be reduced. . . . Articles are presented in a pro/con format; 'active reading' questions preface each viewpoint and are designed to help students focus on the main points and to read carefully. Full-color photos and other graphics appear throughout." SLJ

Includes bibliographical references

Dear bully; seventy authors tell their stories. edited by Carrie Jones and Megan Kelley Hall. HarperTeen 2011 369p $17.99; pa $9.99

Grades: 7 8 9 10 11 12   **302.3**

1. Bullies

ISBN 978-0-06-206098-3; 0-06-206098-8; 978-0-06-206097-6 pa; 0-06-206097-X pa

LC 2011010166

"In brief, true stories about bullying victims, perpetrators, and bystanders, 70 children's authors look back at what was often the hell of growing up, especially in junior high. . . . This timely collection is an excellent resource, especially for group discussion." Booklist

DiPiazza, Francesca Davis

Friend me! six hundred years of social networking in America. by Francesca Davis DiPiazza. Twenty-First Century Books 2012 112 p.

Grades: 6 7 8 9   **302.3**

1. Social networking -- History 2. Social groups -- United States -- History 3. Community life -- United States -- History 4. United States -- Social life and customs -- History 5. Communities -- United States -- History 6. Social networks -- United States -- History

ISBN 0761358692; 9780761358695

LC 2011021268

This book's title makes [it] appear to be about the recent phenomena of electronic social networks. However, the subtitle is a clue that the scope includes so much more. The whole of the American history of socializing is covered, beginning with the Iroquois and their method of weaving beads into wampum belts. Early religious groups, colonial coffeehouses, broadsides, secret gatherings of slaves, circuit riders, telegraphs, mail orders, and groups such as the YMCA and NAACP are profiled as examples of social networking. Today's online communities (Facebook, Twitter, blogs, e-mail, etc.) are touched upon with the supposition that face-to-face socializing is still important. (Booklist)

Includes bibliographical references and index

Ellis, Deborah

★ **We** want you to know; kids talk about bullying. Coteau Books 2010 120p il $19.95; pa $15.95
Grades: 5 6 7 8 9 10   **302.3**
   1. Bullies
   ISBN 978-1-55050-417-0; 1-55050-417-7; 978-1-
   55050-463-7 pa; 1-55050-463-0

"As part of her work with an anti-bullying campaign
in her local Canadian community, Ellis interviewed young
people between the ages of 9 and 19 about their experiences.
In honest, straightforward prose, she shares their stories,
many as targets and some as perpetrators or bystanders. .
. . Each story is written from the first-person point of view,
some with real names and photos, providing an intimacy and
immediacy that are critical with these kinds of issues. Readers will find at least one or two stories they can relate to, and
educators should be able to use many of the narratives to
jumpstart conversation." SLJ

Includes bibliographical references

Golus, Carrie

Take a stand! what you can do about bullying. illustrated by Jack Desrocher. Lerner Publications Co.
2009 64p il (Health zone) hardcover o.p. lib bdg
$30.60   **302.3**
   1. Bullies
   ISBN 978-0-8225-7554-2; 0-8225-7554-X
                 LC 2007-49659

This offers advice about stopping bullying.

"The format is beyond lively, with lots of color, cartoons, and an informal writing style, but it manages to present sometimes frightening material in a non-threatening and
browsable way." Booklist

Includes glossary and bibliographical references

Hillstrom, Laurie Collier

Online social networks. Lucent Books 2010 96p
il (Technology 360) $32.45
Grades: 8 9 10 11 12   **302.3**
   1. Online social networks
   ISBN 978-1-4205-0167-4; 1-4205-0167-4
                 LC 2009045044

This book explores "the early development and advances of [online social network] technology, its impact on society both positive and negative, and the importance it plays
in our lives. . . . [It] begins with the history of the Internet.
It explains the early purpose of the ARPANET, its expansion, the changes from text-based to the graphic interface
of the World Wide Web, email communication, the features
of some of the first social sites, and the differentiating characteristics of MySpace, Facebook, and Twitter. . . . Numerous color photos, diagrams, 'Bits & Bytes' boxes as well as
many other additional text boxes create appeal and provide
beneficial informative and complementary material to aid in
understanding the technical details of the [text]." SLJ

Includes glossary and bibliographical references

Kevorkian, Meline

101 facts about bullying; what everyone should
know. [by] Meline Kevorkian and Robin D'Antona.
Rowman & Littlefield Pub. 2008 148p $32.95

Grades: Adult Professional   **302.3**
   1. Bullies
   ISBN 978-1-57886-849-0; 1-57886-849-1

"A user-friendly, accessible, and well-organized resource. . . . The format will lend itself well to group discussions and give teachers and others who work with young
people a solid basis upon which to explore the issues surrounding this prevalent problem." SLJ

Lusted, Marcia Amidon

Social networking: MySpace, Facebook, & Twitter. ABDO Pub. Co. 2011 112p il (Technology
pioneers) lib bdg $34.22
Grades: 5 6 7 8   **302.3**
   1. Online social networks   2. Facebook Inc.   3.
   MySpace, Inc. 4. Twitter, Inc.
   ISBN 978-1-61714-811-8 lib bdg; 1-61714-811-3 lib
   bdg; 978-1-61758-969-0 e-book
                 LC 2010037885

This is an introduction to social networking sites,
MySpace, Facebook, and Twitter.

"Written in a clear, linear fashion, this series offers vivid,
well-researched details about the development of technological advancements considered essential in today's society. .
. . Readers who are interested in technology and inventions
will be thoroughly engrossed." SLJ

Includes glossary and bibliographical references

Shapiro, Ouisie

Bullying and me; schoolyard stories. illustrated
by Steven Vote. Albert Whitman & Company 2010
un il $16.99
Grades: 4 5 6 7   **302.3**
   1. Bullies
   ISBN 978-0-8075-0921-0; 0-8075-0921-3
                 LC 2010000754

"Thirteen individuals, including some adults, who have
been bullied at school share their painful experiences. . . .
Vote's full-color portraits sensitively depict the faces at the
receiving end of abuse. . . . An educational psychologist specifically addresses each individual's dilemma, but the book's
strength lies in the honestly conveyed through the personal
stories." Publ Wkly

Solomon, Laura

Doing social media so it matters; a librarian's
guide. American Library Association 2011 65p pa
$37
Grades: Adult Professional   **302.3**
   1. Online social networks 2. Libraries and community
   ISBN 978-0-8389-1067-2; 0-8389-1067-X
                 LC 2010034319

"This slim manual is packed with useful advice. Solomon, a library services manager for the Ohio Public Information Network, sprinkles her account with real-world
examples of the power of libraries leveraging social media.
She makes a strong case for establishing social-media accounts. . . . Discussions about branding, social capital, and
other strategies for success are especially important. Wrapping up with chapters on statistics and whether the invest-

ment of time and effort is worthwhile, Solomon gives libraries the knowledge they need to proceed on their own." SLJ

Includes bibliographical references

302.302 Computer applications

Schwartz, Heather E.

Safe social networking; by Heather E. Schwartz. Capstone Press 2013 32 p. col. ill. (Fact finders. Tech safety smarts) (library) $26.65

Grades: 4 5 6 7 **302.302**

1. Online social networks 2. Internet -- Security measures 3. Social networking 4. Social networks 6. Online social networks -- Security measures

ISBN 1429699434; 9781429699433; 9781620658024

LC 2012026027

This children's resource book, by Heather E. Schwartz, is part of the publisher's "Fact Finders" series, providing guidance for young children to safely use and navigate online social media. "If a strange person asks to be your online friend, do you know what to do? . . . This book is here to help! Learn tech-savvy ways to keep your social networking sites safe sites without taking away all the fun!" (Publisher's note)

Includes bibliographical references (p. 31) and index.

302.34 Social interaction in primary groups

Bazelon, Emily

★ **Sticks** and stones; defeating the culture of bullying and rediscovering the power of character and empathy. by Emily Bazelon. Random House 2013 viii, 386 p.p ill. (hardcover) $27

Grades: Adult Professional **302.34**

1. Bullies 2. Adolescence 3. Social media 4. Bullying 5. Bullying in schools 6. Bullying -- Prevention 7. Bullying in schools -- Prevention

ISBN 0812992806; 9780679644002; 9780812992809

LC 2012022773

This book, by Emily Bazelon, discusses teen culture in the U.S., focusing on bullying. "Being a teenager has never been easy, but in recent years, with the rise of the Internet and social media, it has become exponentially more challenging. . . . Bazelon defines what bullying is and, just as important, what it is not. She explores when intervention is essential and when kids should be given the freedom to fend for themselves. She also dispels persistent myths." (Publisher's note)

"While less prescriptive than other books on the topic, very useful FAQs are included, as are resource lists for readers. Masterfully written, Bazelon's book will increase understanding, awareness, and action." Pub Wkly

Includes bibliographical references and index

Strauss, Susan L.

★ **Sexual** harassment and bullying; a guide to keeping kids safe and holding schools accountable. Susan L. Strauss. Rowman & Littlefield Publishers 2012 290 p. (cloth : alk. paper) $34.95

Grades: Adult Professional **302.34**

1. Bullies 2. Social media 3. Sexual harassment 4. Bullying 5. Bullying -- Prevention 6. Sexual harassment in education 7. Sexual harassment -- Prevention

ISBN 1442201622; 9781442201620

LC 2011031731

In this book, "[Susan L.] Strauss draws on her experiences as consultant, former high-school teacher, and parent of a child who was sexually harassed to advise parents, teachers, and other adults on how to protect children" from bullying and harassment. She gives definitions of bullying and harassment, "offers a particular focus on the kind of harassment of gay, bisexual, and transgendered students," and examines "how social media . . . have ramped up bullying and harassment." (Booklist)

Includes bibliographical references and index.

Vicious; true stories by teens about bullying. edited by Hope Vanderberg. Free Spirit Pub. Inc. 2012 167 p. (Real teen voices) (paperback) $11.99

Grades: 6 7 8 **302.34**

1. Bullies 2. Teenagers' writings 3. Bullying -- Case studies 4. Self-esteem in adolescence -- Case studies 5. Aggressiveness in adolescence -- Case studies 6. Interpersonal conflict in adolescence -- Case studies

ISBN 1575424134; 9781575424132

LC 2012015908

This book is a collection of "autobiographical essays" from teenagers involved with the New York-based organization Youth Communication in which they detail "their struggles with bullies, anger about bad home situations and unfair treatment, and pressure to conform or be successful." (School Library Journal)

Includes bibliographical references and index

303.3 Coordination and control

Tarshis, Thomas Paul

Living with peer pressure and bullying. Facts on File 2010 167p (Teen's guides) $34.95; pa $14.95

Grades: 6 7 8 9 **303.3**

1. Bullies 2. Peer pressure 3. Adolescent psychology

ISBN 978-0-8160-7914-8; 0-8160-7914-5; 978-0-8160-7915-5 pa; 0-8160-7915-3 pa

LC 2009024521

"Tarshis examines topics such as peer pressure, managing difficult situations, the risks and rewards of telling the truth, mental-health problems, cyberbullying, and finding and paying for medical care. Each chapter begins with a personal account about a teen facing the chapter topic; includes explanations presented in clear language, at times accompanied by questionnaires and explanatory charts; and ends with 'What You Need to Know,' which summarizes the main ideas. [This book is an] important [addition] for most libraries." SLJ

Includes glossary and bibliographical references

Webber, Diane

Totally tolerant; spotting and stopping prejudice. [by] Diane Webber and Laurie Mandel. Franklin

Watts 2008 112p il (Scholastic choices) lib bdg $27; pa $8.95

Grades: 5 6 7 8   **303.3**

1. Prejudices 2. Toleration

ISBN 978-0-531-13867-0 lib bdg; 0-531-13867-4 lib bdg; 978-0-531-20525-9 pa; 0-531-20525-8 pa

LC 2007-51873

This book about tolerance contains "vignettes and quotes from teens. . . . Statistics, quizzes, historical photos that illustrate prejudice in the 1950s and even recent news stories such as the Jena Six are peppered throughout for a professional perspective. The young reader is also motivated to think critically and use other tools such as journaling or volunteering to create change in their own lives. . . . Plenty of photos accompany . . . [this] book, and words are defined not only in a glossary but used clearly in context as well, providing a great introduction to the topic for the beginning reader." Voice Youth Advocates

Includes glossary and bibliographical references

303.4   Social change

Harris, Ashley Rae

★ **Txt** me l8r; using technology responsibly. content consultant, Robyn J. A. Silverman. ABDO Pub. Co. 2010 112p il (Essential health: strong, beautiful girls) $34.22

Grades: 6 7 8 9   **303.4**

1. Technology 2. Information technology 3. Technological innovations 4. Internet -- Social aspects

ISBN 978-1-60453-754-3; 1-60453-754-X

LC 2009-2138

Using personal narratives, with a consulting doctor giving insight and making suggestions, this discusses the responsible use of technology and the dangers of over-use of cell phones, social websites, texting, and other online communication.

"The topics are well selected, the design is attractive, and the stories feature girls from a variety of cultures." Booklist

Includes bibliographical references

Hill, Laban Carrick

★ **America** dreaming; how youth changed America in the sixties. Little, Brown & Company 2007 165p il pa $12.99

Grades: 6 7 8 9 10   **303.4**

1. Social change 2. Youth movement 3. Baby boom generation 4. United States -- History -- 1961-1974

ISBN 978-0-316-00904-1; 0-316-00904-0; 978-0-316-07148-2 pa; 0-316-07148-X pa

LC 2006-27898

"An excellent textbook for the children and, probably, grandchildren of baby boomers who want to know what the youth culture of the time as all about." NY Times Book Rev

"Covering subjects such as the civil rights movement, hippie culture, black nationalism, and the feminist movement, Hill paints a . . . picture of life in the '60's and shows how teenagers were on the forefront of the societal changes that occurred during this . . . decade." Publisher's note

Includes bibliographical references

Solway, Andrew

Communication; the impact of science and technology. Gareth Stevens Pub. 2010 64p il (Pros and cons) lib bdg $35

Grades: 5 6 7 8   **303.4**

1. Communication 2. Telecommunication 3. Information technology

ISBN 978-1-4339-1986-2 lib bdg; 1-4339-1986-9 lib bdg

LC 2009-12435

An "active layout that features color photographs, maps, graphs or charts on every spread, this . . . [book] has much to offer. . . . It conveniently outlines the range of views . . . helping students to learn how to view both sides of [the] issue[s]." SLJ

Includes glossary and bibliographical references

Turney, Jon

Technology; ethical debates about the application of science. Smart Apple Media 2009 46p il (Dilemmas in modern science) $34.25

Grades: 7 8 9 10   **303.4**

1. Technology 2. Science -- Ethical aspects

ISBN 978-1-59920-097-2; 1-59920-097-X

LC 2007-35692

This title is "easy to navigate as evocative photographs, charts, and sidebars help break down complicated arguments into manageable parts for easy digestion." SLJ

"Presents both sides of issues arising from how we use technology, including Internet use, identity theft, technology and the military, nanotechnology, and robots and automation." Publisher's note

Includes glossary and bibliographical references

303.48   Causes of change

Changemakers; rebels and radicals who changed US history. edited by Michele Bollinger and Dao X. Tran. Haymarket Books 2012 210 p. (alk. paper) $19.95

Grades: 6 7 8   **303.48**

1. Change 2. Radicalism 3. Social justice 4. United States -- Biography 5. Social movements -- United States 6. Social reformers -- United States -- Biography

ISBN 1608461564; 9781608461561

LC 2012034044

This book, edited by Michele Bollinger and Dao X Tran, "offers a 'people's history' version of the individuals who have shaped [the U.S.] for middle school students. In the place of founding fathers, presidents, and titans of industry, are profiles of those who . . . fought for social justice in America: Tecumseh, Harriet Tubman, Mark Twain, César Chávez, Rachel Carson, Harvey Milk, Henry Wallace, and many more." (Publisher's note)

Gentry, Sarah E.

Living with the Internet; Samuel C. McQuade, III and Sarah Gentry. Chelsea House Publishers 2011 152 p. (Cybersafety)

76

Grades: 7 8 9 10 11 12 **303.48**

1. Internet forums 2. Internet -- Social aspects 3. Internet -- Safety measures 4. Online social networks
ISBN 1604136979; 9781604136975

LC 2011005646

"Backed by recent statistics and facts, this straightforward series educates teens about online safety." Booklist

Includes bibliographical references and index

Mooney, Carla

Thinking critically; Cell phones. by Carla Mooney. ReferencePoint Press, Inc. 2014 80 p. illustrations (Thinking critically) (hardback) $28.95

Grades: 7 8 9 10 11 12 **303.48**

1. Cell phones and teenagers 2. Cell phones -- Social aspects
ISBN 160152580X; 9781601525802

LC 2013011853

This book about cell phones, written by Carla Mooney, is part of the Thinking Critically series, which "encourage[s] teens to view important social issues from different perspectives. . . . [It] examines such questions as whether the device poses a health hazard, if concerns about teen usage are justified, and if stronger laws are needed to prevent drivers' usage." (Booklist)

"Diagrams and sidebars (Social includes one stock photo) support these well-organized models for classroom discourse. First chapters introduce the debates surrounding cell phones, social networking, and gun control; subsequent chapters present pro and con responses to four key questions. Despite lots of graphic elements, the text-heavy pages may be off-putting. Two pages of facts and a list of related organizations are appended." Horn Book

Includes bibliographical references and index
Cell phones

Scandiffio, Laura

People who said no; courage against oppression. Laura Scandiffio. Annick Press 2012 168 p. $24.95

Grades: 5 6 7 **303.48**

1. Demonstrations 2. Protest movements 3. Civil disobedience 4. Resistance to government
ISBN 1554513839; 9781554513833

This book, by Laura Scandiffio, profiles activists who broke the law to protest injustices. "Sometimes it's okay to ignore the rules or break the law. . . . This . . . book features people who did just that: Sophie and Hans Scholl . . . and Andrei Sakharov. . . . Also included are Helen Suzman, . . . Aung San Suu Kyi, . . . and the people of Egypt, who recently brought down the repressive government of Hosni Mubarak." (Publisher's note)

303.49   Social forecasts

Schutten, Jan Paul

Hello from 2030; the science of the future and you. Jan Paul Schutten. Beyond Words Publishing Company 2014 224 p. color illustrations (hardcover : alk. paper) $15.99

Grades: 4 5 6 7 **303.49**

1. Forecasting 2. World history -- 21st century 3. Social prediction 4. Science -- Forecasting 5. Technological forecasting
ISBN 1582704740; 9781582704746

LC 2013044906

In this book on the science of the future, Jan Paul Schutten "asserts that the future is nothing to fear and that while 2030 might present some daunting challenges, what happens is largely within our control in the present. He highlights the potential for longer and healthier lives, faster technology, and smarter homes. Yet the book retains a cautionary tone regarding environmental issues like water usage and energy consumption." (Booklist)

"Extremely detailed source notes for each chapter draw on current research and news articles and include links to further reading. The engaging text is supported by plenty of full-color visuals presented in a dynamic format. Presenting an overwhelmingly optimistic outlook on the future, the book reminds us that we might as well welcome change with open arms." Booklist

Includes bibliographical references and index

303.6   Conflict and conflict resolution

Drew, Naomi

★ The **kids'** guide to working out conflicts; how to keep cool, stay safe, and get along. Naomi Drew. Free Spirit Pub. 2004 146p il pa $13.95

Grades: 6 7 8 9 **303.6**

1. Conflict management
ISBN 1-57542-150-X

LC 2003-21108

Describes common forms of conflict, the reasons behind conflicts, and various positive ways to deal with and defuse tough situations at school, at home, and in the community without getting physical.

"In clean, respectful language, [the author] offers youth a highly doable eight-step plan to overcome anger issues. . . . The thoughtful encouraging tone of this important book . . . embraces children all along the conflict spectrum, from tortured victims of bullying to those who endure sustained stress and from moderate levels of conflict to full-blown bullies. . . . Highly recommended." Voice Youth Advocates

Includes bibliographical references

Ellis, Deborah

★ **Off** to war; voices of soldiers' children. Groundwood Books/House of Anansi Press 2008 175p il $15.95; pa $9.95

Grades: 5 6 7 8 **303.6**

1. Children and war 2. Iraq War, 2003-2011 3. Afghanistan
ISBN 978-0-88899-894-1; 0-88899-894-5; 978-0-88899-895-8 pa; 0-88899-895-3 pa

The wars in Iraq and Afghanistan have impacted the children of soldiers—men and women who have been called away from their families to fight in a faraway war. In their own words, some of these children describe how their experience has marked and shaped their lives

"Accessible and utterly readable. . . . The book is an excellent resource for opening discussions about the current events." SLJ

Includes glossary and bibliographical references

Gottfried, Ted

★ The **fight** for peace; a history of antiwar movements in America. 21st Century Bks. 2006 136p il (People's history) $26.60
Grades: 7 8 9 10   303.6
1. War 2. Peace 3. Pacifism
ISBN 0-7613-2932-3

"Gottfried starts out by explaining that a group in Connecticut rallied together in 2003 to peacefully protest the war against Iraq. . . . Then the author discusses the antiwar movement during the Civil War and proceeds through history, beginning with the ancient Greek play Lysistrata. . . . The pictures, political cartoons, and quotes are an excellent addition. . . . This is a book that can be read for general interest as well as for reports." SLJ

Includes bibliographical references

Judson, Karen

★ **Resolving** conflicts; how to get along when you don't get along. Enslow Pubs. 2005 112p il (Issues in focus today) $31.93
Grades: 7 8 9 10 11 12   303.6
1. Conflict management
ISBN 0-7660-2359-1

                                                LC 2004-28119
The author "describes different kinds of conflicts and how they can be resolved, with a special focus on teens and building their conflict-resolution skills and understanding." Publisher's note

Includes bibliographical references

O'Brien, Anne Sibley

After Gandhi; one hundred years of nonviolent resistance. [by] Anne Sibley O'Brien and Perry Edmond O'Brien. Charlesbridge 2009 181p il map $15.95
Grades: 7 8 9 10   303.6
1. Nonviolence 2. Passive resistance
ISBN 978-1-58089-129-5; 1-58089-129-2

                                                LC 2008-10660
"Using Gandhi as its starting point, this large-format book traces the history of nonviolent resistance by looking at significant adherents from 1908 to 2003 including Martin Luther King, Jr., Nelson Mandela, Charles Perkins, César Chávez, Aung San Suu Kyi, Vaclav Havel, and Wangari Maathi and groups such as the student activists of Tiananmen Square and the Madres de Plaza de Mayo (Mothers of the Disappeared) in Argentina. . . . The handsome design and striking black-and-white illustrations are strong visuals that complement the story of nonviolent resistance in action." Booklist

Includes bibliographical references

Senker, Cath

Violence. Smart Apple Media 2010 46p il (Voices) lib bdg $34.25

Grades: 7 8 9 10 11 12   303.6
1. Violence
ISBN 978-1-59920-280-8 lib bdg; 1-59920-280-8 lib bdg

                                                LC 2008050432
This book about violence "addresses the causes, possible solutions, and outlooks, both good and bad, of . . . [the] issue. Each brief chapter covers basic questions, answered with a simple definition or explanation, then supported by pertinent quotes and statistics from well-known experts and organizations. Color photographs, sidebars, graphs, and charts pull the content together in a busy but cohesive presentation. . . . Students assigned research on . . . [the topic] will appreciate the quotes and statistics plus commentary that address the . . . [issue] from several angles." Libr Media Connect

Includes glossary

Walker, Niki

Why do we fight? conflict, war, and peace. Niki Walker. Owlkids Books 2013 80 p. $16.95
Grades: 5 6 7 8   303.6
1. War 2. Culture conflict 3. Conflict management
ISBN 1926973860; 9781926973869

                                                LC 2013930981
In this book, Niki Walker explains "different types of conflict and then contemplat[es] ways conflict can escalate." (Kirkus Reviews) "Using real-world examples, such as the 1979 peace deal between Egypt and Israel or the history of Afghanistan over multiple centuries, Walker offers . . . explanations of power and resource inequities, cultural divisions, the global role of the United Nations, bias, prejudice, and more." (Publishers Weekly)

Weinberg, Leonard

★ **What** is terrorism? [by] Leonard Weinberg and William Eubank. Chelsea House Publishers 2006 104p il (The roots of terrorism) lib bdg $35
Grades: 7 8 9 10   303.6
1. Terrorism
ISBN 0-7910-8305-5

                                                LC 2005027569
This "gives a history of terrorism from its early beginnings through current events. This volume describes the actions and goals of numerous terrorist groups. . . . This . . . has a great deal of information. . . . The glossy pages show off an eye-pleasing color format with neat sections and well-placed pictures." Voice Youth Advocates

Includes bibliographical references

304.6   Population

Altman, Linda Jacobs

Genocide; the systematic killing of a people. rev. and expanded; Enslow Publishers 2009 128p il map (Issues in focus today) lib bdg $31.93
Grades: 6 7 8 9   304.6
1. Genocide
ISBN 978-0-7660-3358-0 lib bdg; 0-7660-3358-9 lib bdg

                                                LC 2007050697

First published 1995

This is written in "short accessible chapters." Horn Book Guide

"Examines the history of genocide throughout the world, including the Holocaust, and explores the definition of the term, the importance of bearing witness, and the necessary steps to prevent genocide in the future." Publisher's note

Includes glossary and bibliographical references

Barber, Nicola

Coping with population growth; Nicola Barber. Raintree 2011 48 p. col. ill.

Grades: 4 5 6 7   **304.6**

1. Population 2. Population -- Environmental aspects

ISBN 9781410942968; 9781410943033

LC 2010052702

"Barber examines the pressures exerted on the environment and global resources due to population growth... Color photographs add interest, and helpful diagrams effectively convey statistical concepts." Horn Book

Includes bibliographical references (p. 46-47) and index

Bellamy, Rufus

Population growth. Amicus 2010 44p il map (Sustaining our environment) lib bdg $31.35

Grades: 6 7 8 9   **304.6**

1. Population 2. Overpopulation 3. Environmental protection

ISBN 978-1-60753-137-1 lib bdg; 1-60753-137-2 lib bdg

LC 2009-30032

Discusses how population expansion taxes our resources and poses a treat to the environment.

"The tone is refreshingly optimistic with its examples of specific steps being taken to reduce harm to the environment. Sidebars highlight case studies and campaigns from around the world and from the individual to the national levels. Clear, informative captions accompany the excellent selection of color photographs, charts and graphs." SLJ

Includes glossary

January, Brendan

★ **Genocide**; modern crimes against humanity. Twenty-First Century Books 2007 160p il map lib bdg $31.93

Grades: 8 9 10 11 12   **304.6**

1. Genocide

ISBN 978-0-7613-3421-7 lib bdg; 0-7613-3421-1 lib bdg

LC 2005032850

"January gives young readers a sensitive, solid framework with which to comprehend multiple facets of genocide, from etymology of the term to acknowledging deniers of the Holocaust. The slim volume devotes chapters to separate examples of genocide, historic and contemporary: Armenians of the Ottoman Empire, European Jews, Cambodians, Tutsis of Rwanda, Muslims of Bosnia, and tribes of Darfur. . . . This outstanding book sparks thoughtful inquiry." Voice Youth Advocates

Includes bibliographical references

Springer, Jane

★ **Genocide**. Groundwood Books 2006 144p (Groundwork guides) hardcover o.p. pa $9.95

Grades: 8 9 10 11 12   **304.6**

1. Genocide

ISBN 978-0-88899-681-7; 0-88899-681-0; 978-0-88899-682-4 pa; 0-88899-682-9 pa

"This disturbing history of mass ethnic killings across the world examines the why, when, where, and how genocide takes place. . . . In a lucid, informal text, Springer ably documents particular crimes against humanity, including the transatlantic slave trade, the slaughter of America's Native peoples, the Turkish massacre of the Armenians, the Nanking massacre, the Holocaust, and the Khmer Rouge slaughter in Cambodia." Booklist

304.8 Movement of people

Daniels, Roger

American immigration; a student companion. Oxford Univ. Press 2000 303p (Oxford student companions to American history) lib bdg $60

Grades: 7 8 9 10   **304.8**

1. Immigrants -- United States 2. United States -- Immigration and emigration

ISBN 0-19-511316-0

LC 00-56673

"This resource would be ideal for young adults seeking brief overviews of particular ethnic groups." Voice Youth Advocates

"Following an essay that provides an overview of the book, students find immigration statistics, areas of settlement, major periods of immigration, and the predominant religion of the immigrant groups. Key pieces of legislation . . . are discussed. . . . The appendices cover important dates in immigration history; immigration, ethnic, and refugee organizations." Book Rep

Includes bibliographical references

Hammerschmidt, Peter A.

History of American immigration. Mason Crest Publishers 2009 64p il (Major American immigration) lib bdg $22.95; pa $9.95

Grades: 6 7 8 9   **304.8**

1. Immigrants -- United States 2. United States -- Immigration and emigration

ISBN 978-1-4222-0613-3 lib bdg; 1-4222-0613-0 lib bdg; 978-1-4222-0680-5 pa; 1-4222-0680-7 pa

LC 2008-28222

"Hammerschmidt's book makes a point of mentioning the importation of slaves as one way in which people came to the United States. . . . Both legal and illegal immigration are given a reasonable amount of space. . . . Overall the coverage is solid. . . . [This] accessible [book] will primarily be used for reports, but [is a] good [choice] to round out a collection on immigration and citizenship topics." SLJ

Includes glossary and bibliographical references

Lawlor, Veronica

I was dreaming to come to America; memories from the Ellis Island Oral History Project. selected and illustrated by Veronica Lawlor; foreword by Rudolph W. Giuliani. Viking 1995 38p il hardcover o.p. pa $6.99

Grades: 4 5 6 7   304.8
    1. Ellis Island Immigration Station 2. United States -- Immigration and emigration
    ISBN 0-670-86164-2; 0-14-055622-2 pa
                                        LC 95-1281

"Begun in 1975, the Ellis Island Oral History Project is . . . {a} collection of interviews with individuals who immigrated to the U.S. through Ellis Island. Short selections— each 1 or 2 paragraphs long—from 15 of those interviews are reprinted here. The subjects were for the most part children when they arrived in the period 1900-1925. . . . Grades four to six." (SLJ)

"There is a flavor of Chagall in the peasant figures dancing above the ship or hopping ashore near the turreted towers of the huge building on Ellis Island. The elegant rendering offers a timeless view of this significant journey that is at once personal and universal." Horn Book

Ollhoff, Jim

Exploring immigration. ABDO Pub. Co. 2011 32p il (Your family tree) $18.95

Grades: 4 5 6 7   304.8
    1. Genealogy 2. Immigrants 3. United States -- Immigration and emigration
    ISBN 978-1-61613-463-1; 1-61613-463-1
                                    LC 2009050807

This book about immigration is "great . . . for kids interested in genealogy. [It does] a wonderful job of presenting the fundamentals of genealogical research in a clear and exciting manner. . . . Understanding and properly using primary documents is stressed throughout. . . . [An] attractive, spacious [layout]; full-color, sharp images; clearly labeled diagrams; and scattered maps add information and appeal." SLJ

Includes glossary

Senker, Cath

Immigrants and refugees; Cath Senker. Smart Apple Media 2012 46 p. (Mapping global issues) (library) $35.65

Grades: 6 7 8   304.8
    1. Internal migration 2. Immigration and emigration 3. Refugees 4. Immigrants 5. Emigration and immigration
    ISBN 1599205092; 9781599205090
                                    LC 2011000248

This "entry in the Mapping Global Issues series tracks movement of people throughout the world as they search for a better life, whether fleeing from poverty or war, and goes into surprising detail about the methods by which they move. Beginning with sub-Saharan Africa, this title reminds readers of the amount of in-country migration that occurs. . . . Frequent large maps outline migration patterns regionally and globally." (Booklist)

Includes bibliographical references (p. 45) and index

305   Groups of people

Stewart, Sheila

Growing up in religious communities. Mason Crest 2009 64p il (The changing face of modern families) $22.95

Grades: 6 7 8 9   305
    1. Family 2. Religious communities
    ISBN 978-1-4222-1500-5; 1-4222-1500-8

This describes some of the unique challenges facing families in religious communities, which may be set apart from others by what they wear, their rituals, what they are not allowed to eat or do, or else by not mixing at all with those outside the community, but which may have their own strengths.

"Colorful photographs and sidebars appear throughout. [This book is a] good [introduction] to the study of sociology and interpretation of data." SLJ

Includes bibliographical references

305.23   Young people

Bedell, J. M.

Teens in Pakistan. Compass Point Books 2009 96p il map (Global connections) lib bdg $33.26

Grades: 6 7 8 9   305.23
    1. Teenagers 2. Pakistan
    ISBN 978-0-7565-4043-2; 0-7565-4043-7
                                    LC 2008-38332

Discusses the similarities and differences of teenagers in Pakistan.

Includes glossary

Burton, Bonnie

Girls against girls; why we are mean to each other and how we can change. Zest Books 2009 128p il pa $12.95

Grades: 7 8 9 10   305.23
    1. Bullies 2. Girls -- Psychology
    ISBN 978-0-9790173-6-0; 0-9790173-6-X

This guide for teenage girls explains why girls can sometimes be mean to each other, what to do if you are a victim of bullying, and the importance of treating other girls with respect.

This offers "excellent coping techniques. . . . Burton never talks down to her readers, nor does she pull her punches. Readers will respond to the author's clear respect for the painful nature of the problem." Booklist

★ The Courage to be yourself; true stories by teens about cliques, conflicts, and overcoming peer pressure. edited by Al Desetta with Educators for Social Responsibility. Free Spirit Pub. 2005 145p pa $13.95

Grades: 7 8 9 10 11 12   305.23
    1. Teenagers 2. Conduct of life
    ISBN 1-57542-185-2
                                    LC 2005-5173

"There is certainly some value in hearing teens of many ethnicities and orientations speaking plainly about being fat, or being from India in a school full of blond, blue-eyed folk, or being Arab after 9/11." Booklist

"In 26 first-person stories, real teens write about their lives." Publisher's note

Includes bibliographical references

Donovan, Sandra, 1967-

Teens in Thailand; by Sandy Donovan. Compass Point Books 2009 96p il map (Global connections) lib bdg $33.26

Grades: 6 7 8 9   **305.23**
   1. Teenagers 2. Thailand
   ISBN 978-0-7565-4046-3; 0-7565-4046-1
                                          LC 2008-35714
Uncovers the challenges, pastimes, customs and culture of teens in Thailand.

Includes glossary and bibliographical references

Edge, Laura Bufano, 1953-

From jazz babies to generation next; the history of the American teenager. by Laura B. Edge. Twenty-First Century Books 2011 112p il (People's history) lib bdg $33.26

Grades: 6 7 8 9 10   **305.23**
   1. Teenagers -- United States
   ISBN 978-0-7613-5868-8; 0-7613-5868-4
                                          LC 2010031144
Traces the history of teenagers in the United States, including their influence on the economy, fashion, and entertainment.

"The writing is smooth, informative, and interesting. Although the subject matter may not translate directly into a report topic, it does provide sociocultural, historical, and political overviews of the 1900s. Almost every two-page spread contains a photograph." Voice Youth Advocates

Includes bibliographical references

Farrell, Courtney

Children's rights. ABDO Pub. 2010 112p il (Essential issues) lib bdg $22.95

Grades: 7 8 9 10   **305.23**
   1. Child labor 2. Child sexual abuse
   ISBN 978-1-60453-952-3; 1-60453-952-6
                                          LC 2009-29938
The text is "well-written, providing examples that put a human face to each problem. Quotes and facts are clearly attributed, and their sources are noted in the extensive back matter. . . . . . . [This] will be of great assistance to students writing reports." SLJ

Includes glossary and bibliographical references

Freedman, Russell

Children of the Great Depression. Clarion Books 2005 118p il lib bdg $20

Grades: 4 5 6 7   **305.23**
   1. Great Depression, 1929-1939 2. Children -- United States 3. United States -- Social conditions
   ISBN 0-618-44630-3
                                          LC 2005-06506
"This stirring photo-essay combines . . . unforgettable personal details with a clear historical overview of the pe-

riod and black-and-white photos by Dorothea Lange, Walker Evans, and many others." Booklist

"Eight chapters cover the causes of the Great Depression, schooling, work life, migrant work, the lives of children who rode the rails, entertainment, and the economic resurgence of the early '40s." SLJ

Mangan, Tricia

How to feel good; 20 things teens can do. by Tricia Mangan. Magination Press 2012 125 p. (pbk. : alk. paper) $12.95

Grades: 8 9 10 11 12   **305.23**
   1. Teenagers 2. Life skills 3. Adolescent psychology
   ISBN 1433810409; 9781433810404
                                          LC 2011020623
This book offers advice to teenagers in areas of psychological health in order "to feel good about . . . [themselves] and . . . [their] abilities. For teens, new relationships and experiences are happening all around them, and can make them feel overwhelmed and stressed. Being confident and secure can seem miles away. . . . [This book] provides interactive exercises and questions to help teens recognize and understand why they feel the way they do and to change hurtful thought patterns and habits. With these 20 . . . steps, teens can use this book to learn how to be confident and happy with themselves." (Publisher's note)

"With a gentle, firm but never condescending tone . . . clinical psychologist Mangan leads anxious teens through the A's (activating events), B's (beliefs), and C's (consequences) of taking control of spiraling and self-defeating moods." Booklist

Musolf, Nell

Teens in Greece. Compass Point Books 2009 96p il map (Global connections) lib bdg $33.26

Grades: 6 7 8 9   **305.23**
   1. Teenagers 2. Greece
   ISBN 978-0-7565-4040-1; 0-7565-4040-2
                                          LC 2008-35713
Discusses the similarities and differences of teenagers in Greece.

Includes glossary

Smith, David J.

This child, every child; a book about the world's children. written by David J. Smith; illustrated by Shelagh Armstrong. Kids Can Press 2011 36p il (CitizenKid) $18.95

Grades: 4 5 6 7   **305.23**
   1. Children
   ISBN 978-1-55453-466-1; 1-55453-466-6
This title "takes a global look at the lives of contemporary children. Balancing statistics with fictional profiles of kids, Smith's concise narrative focuses on such topics as families, homes, health, work, war, and play. Each spread contains accessible summaries of articles from 1989's United Nations Convention on the Rights of the Child, underscoring the disparity between many children's lives and that document's vision and goals. . . . Rendered in acrylics with digital textures, Armstrong's gauzy paintings sometimes span multiple cultures in a single illustration . . . reinforcing the universal nature of children's needs." Publ Wkly

Smith-Llera, Danielle

Teens in Argentina. Compass Point Books 2009 96p il map (Global connections) lib bdg $33.26

Grades: 6 7 8 9   **305.23**

1. Teenagers 2. Argentina

ISBN 978-0-7565-4037-1; 0-7565-4037-2

LC 2008-35712

Discusses the similarities and differences of teenagers in Argentina.

Includes glossary and bibliographical references

Wilson, Janet

One peace; true stories of young activists. written and illustrated by Janet Wilson. Orca Book Publishers 2008 43p il $19.95

Grades: 4 5 6 7   **305.23**

1. Peace 2. Children and war

ISBN 978-1-55143-892-4; 1-55143-892-5

"The stories of young people who have been refugees from war, injured by land mines, or learned about the consequences of violence through other means are interspersed with children's poems, quotes, artwork, and photographs. The brief, powerful accounts document how these children ages 8 to 15 worked for or became symbols of peace." SLJ

305.235   Young people twelve to twenty

Donovan, Sandra, 1967-

Teens in Morocco; by Sandy Donovan. Compass Point Books 2008 96 p. col. ill., col. maps (Global connections) (library) $33.99

Grades: 7 8 9 10   **305.235**

1. Teenagers -- Morocco -- Social conditions 2. Morocco -- Social conditions -- 21st century

ISBN 075653402X; 9780756534028

LC 2007032692

Uncovers the challenges, pastimes, customs and culture of teens in Morocco

"Information is solid, giving readers an informed and realistic view of life in that country. A historical timeline is included, and suggestions for other nonfiction and fiction titles for further reading." Voice Youth Advocates

Includes bibliographical references (p. 92-93) and index.

Ellis, Deborah

Kids of Kabul; living bravely through a never-ending war. Deborah Ellis. Groundwood Books 2012 143 p. $15.95

Grades: 6 7 8 9 10 11 12   **305.235**

1. Taliban 2. Interviews 3. Children -- Afghanistan

ISBN 1554981816; 9781554981816

This book is a collection of interviews with Afghani children who "mostly don't remember the Taliban's fall more than a decade ago, but they can't help but be shaped by the damage the Taliban did to their country. . . . One girl is imprisoned for fleeing a forced child marriage, while another's mother is a member of Parliament; one boy's damaged by a landmine, and another's proud to be a Scout. . . . [I]ntroductions to each young person provide historical, legal and social context." (Kirkus Reviews)

Jukes, Mavis

★ The guy book; an owner's manual for teens: safety, maintenance, and operating instructions for teens. Crown 2002 152p il hardcover o.p. pa $12.95

Grades: 7 8 9 10   **305.235**

1. Boys 2. Adolescence 3. Sex education

ISBN 0-679-99028-3 lib bdg; 0-679-89028-9 pa

LC 2001-47073

Provides information for boys on changes that occur in their bodies during puberty and offering advice on sexual topics, nutrition, drugs, girls, and more.

"In a jokey premise that will appeal to teens, the book follows the format of a car owner's manual with a retro look. . . . Much of this information is available in other sources, but the added sense of fun will make this a first choice for a lot of young men." Booklist

Includes bibliographical references

Lilly, Alexandra

Teens in Turkey; by Alexandra Lilly. Compass Point Books 2008 96 p. ill., maps (library) $33.99

Grades: 7 8 9 10   **305.235**

1. Teenagers 2. Teenagers -- Turkey -- Social conditions

ISBN 9780756534141; 0756534143

LC 2007033090

Uncovers the challenges, pastimes, customs and culture of teens in Turkey

"Information is solid, giving readers an informed and realistic view of life in that country. A historical time line is included, and suggestions for other nonfiction and fiction titles for further reading." Youth Voice Advocates

Includes bibliographical references (p. 90-91) and index.

Shandler, Sara

Ophelia speaks; adolescent girls write about their search for self. HarperPerennial 1999 285p pa $12.95

Grades: 7 8 9 10   **305.235**

1. Girls 2. Adolescence

ISBN 0-06-095297-0

LC 99-13534

"Shandler collected writings from adolescent girls all over the country on topics that include sexuality, eating disorders, feminism, family dynamics, and friendship; their words, framed by Shandler's own reflections, are riveting and revealing." Libr J

305.3   People by gender or sex

Bornstein, Kate

My gender workbook; how to become a real man, a real woman, the real you, or something else entirely. Kate Bornstein ; with illustrations by Diane DiMassa. Routledge 1998 292p il

Grades: 7 8 9 10 11 12   **305.3**

1. Gender role 2. Transgender people

ISBN 0-415-91672-0; 0-415-91673-9 (pbk)

LC 98-134184

Written by Kate Bornstein and illustrated by Diane Di-Masa, this book "brings theory down to Earth and provides a practical approach to living with or without a gender. Bornstein starts from the premise that there are not just two genders performed in today's world, but countless genders lumped under the two-gender framework. Using a . . . workbook format, Bornstein gently but firmly guides you to discover your own unique gender identity." (Publisher's note)

"Artist and trans activist Bornstein (Gender Outlaw: On Men, Women, and the Rest of Us) has updated her 1997 introduction to gender, sexuality, and making your way in a world that has a lot of opinions about both. Goofy..., practical..., this updated workbook is full of clipart, tweets, and interactive exercises and quizzes...Bornstein dismantles some of the social mores we take the most for granted, and we are all the better for it." (Library Journal)

My new gender workbook; a step-by-step guide to achieving world peace through gender anarchy and sex positivity. Kate Bornstein. Routledge 2013 xiii, 293 p.p ill. (paperback) $39.95

Grades: 7 8 9 10 11 12 **305.3**
    1. Sex 2. Gender role 3. Sex education 4. Sex -- Psychological aspects 5. Gender identity 6. Sex (Psychology)
    ISBN 0415538653; 9780203109038; 9780415538640; 9780415538657
                       LC 2012033355
"Since its first publication in 1997, My Gender Workbook has been challenging, encouraging, questioning, and helping those trying to figure out how to become a 'real man,' a 'real woman,' or 'something else entirely.' In this exciting new edition of her classic text, Bornstein re-examines gender in light of issues like race, class, sexuality, and language. With new quizzes, new puzzles, new exercises, and plenty of Kate's playful and provocative style, My New Gender Workbook promises to help a new generation create their own unique place on the gender spectrum." (Publisher's note)

"It makes a sometimes-intimidating set of theories accessible and friendly for any reader, not just those already working on their gender. Bornstein dismantles some of the social mores we take the most for granted, and we are all the better for it. " LJ

305.4   Women

Bausum, Ann
   ★ **With** courage and cloth; winning the fight for a woman's right to vote. by Ann Bausum. National Geographic 2004 111 p. ill. (some col.), maps $32.90

Grades: 5 6 7 8 9 **305.4**
    1. Women -- Suffrage 2. Women's rights -- History 3. Women -- United States -- History
    ISBN 0792269969; 0792276477; 9780792269960
                       LC 2004001191
This book, by Ann Bausum, is a history of the movement for women's suffrage in the United States. "After covering the importance of familiar issues, she devotes the bulk of the book to the events of 1906 to 1920, when a new group

of young women emerged who were willing to truly suffer for suffrage. The movement split into two camps-Carrie Chapman Catt's larger National American Woman Suffrage Association, . . . and a smaller . . . National Woman's Party led by Alice Paul." (School Library Journal)

"Bausum's lucid and nuanced study focuses on 1913-20, the last years of the more than seven decades when women in the US fought for the right to vote. She summarizes what went before and she teases out, remarkably clearly, how hard it was. . . . Bausum focuses on Alice Paul and some other lesser-known lights of the movement, and all the while she makes the history live as she explains, exhorts, and lets nothing drop by the wayside. The entire volume is put together wonderfully, using some never-before-published photos and a lively layout. . . . Excellent." Kirkus

Bingham, Jane
   Women at war; the progressive era, World War I and women's suffrage, 1900-1920. Chelsea House 2011 il (A cultural history of women in America) $35

Grades: 5 6 7 8 **305.4**
    1. World War, 1914-1918 2. Women -- Employment 3. Women -- Social conditions 4. Women -- United States -- History
    ISBN 978-1-6041-3932-7; 1-6041-3932-3
                    LC 2010044828
An "eye-catching [layout] with good use of color, photographs, and informative sidebars, many of which use primary-source quotations, are the highlights of [this] appealing [volume]. . . . After a succinct overview of contemporary events, the chapters describe women's lives at home, at work, in education, in politics, in the arts, and their role in the general culture. . . . [This book] explores the changing role of women during the Progressive Era, the impact of World War I on their lives, and the struggle for voting rights." SLJ

Includes glossary and bibliographical references

Coppens, Linda Miles
   ★ **What** American women did, 1789-1920; a year-by-year reference. McFarland & Co. 2001 259p il hardcover o.p. pa $49.95

Grades: 7 8 9 10 **305.4**
    1. Women -- Social conditions 2. Women -- United States -- History
    ISBN 0-7864-0899-5; 0-7864-3245-4 pa
                     LC 00-64010
"A chronological account of women's accomplishments in the areas of domesticity, work, education, religion, the arts, law and politics, and reform efforts. . . . This work will prove useful for students wishing to gain a better perspective of history, particularly social history, as it pertained to women." SLJ

Includes bibliographical references

Gelletly, LeeAnne
   A **woman's** place in early America; LeeAnne Gelletly. Mason Crest Publishers 2013 64 p. (Finding a voice : women's fight for equality in U.S. society) (hc) $22.95

Grades: 4 5 6 7 8   **305.4**
1. Women -- United States -- History 2. United States
-- Social conditions 3. United States -- Politics and
government 4. Women's rights -- United States
ISBN 1422223558; 9781422223550; 9781422223659
    LC 2011043480

Author LeeAnne Gelletly's book focuses on women in
Early America. "In early America, married women had no
rights under law. They belonged to their husbands. Their
voices were not heard in public. But with the War of Independence, women found a voice as patriots. They supported
the rebellion with boycotts. During wartime, women spied
on the enemy. They served as messengers. They tended the
wounded. Some even served as soldiers. Women performed
daring feats of bravery. And they proved they were capable
of doing much more than 18-century society allowed them."
(Publisher's note)

Includes bibliographical references and index

Gorman, Jacqueline Laks
The **modern** feminist movement; sisters under
the skin, 1961-1979. Chelsea House 2011 il (A cul-
tural history of women in America) $35
Grades: 5 6 7 8   **305.4**
1. Feminism 2. Women -- Social conditions 3. Women
-- United States -- History
ISBN 978-1-6041-3935-8; 1-6041-3935-8
    LC 2010045990

An "eye-catching [layout] with good use of color, photographs, and informative sidebars, many of which use primary-source quotations, are the highlights of [this] appealing
[volume]. . . . After a succinct overview of contemporary
events, the chapters describe women's lives at home, at
work, in education, in politics, in the arts, and their role in
the general culture. . . . [This book] delves into the years of
protest and quest for equal rights." SLJ

Includes glossary and bibliographical references

Gourley, Catherine
★ **Flappers** and the new American woman;
perceptions of women from 1918 through the 1920s.
Twenty-First Century Books 2008 144p il (Images
and issues of women in the twentieth century) lib bdg
$38.60
Grades: 7 8 9 10   **305.4**
1. Women -- United States -- History 2. United States
-- History -- 1919-1933
ISBN 978-0-8225-6060-9; 0-8225-6060-7
    LC 2006-28983

This describes images of women in the United States
from 1918 through the 1920s.

"The sparkling and engaging [text is] generously expanded by numerous, well-placed black-and-white photographs and period reproductions. . . . Great for research or
browsing." SLJ

Includes bibliographical references

★ **Gibson** girls and suffragists; perceptions of
women from the turn of the century through 1918.
Twenty-First Century Books 2008 144p il (Images

and issues of women in the twentieth century) lib bdg
$38.60
Grades: 7 8 9 10   **305.4**
1. Women -- United States -- History 2. United States
-- History -- 1898-1919
ISBN 978-0-8225-7150-6; 0-8225-7150-1
    LC 2007-1689

This describes the images of women in United States at
the beginning of the twentienth century.

"The sparkling and engaging [text is] generously expanded by numerous, well-placed black-and-white photographs and period reproductions. . . . Great for research or
browsing." SLJ

Includes bibliographical references

★ **Gidgets** and women warriors; perceptions of
women in the 1950s and 1960s. by Catherine Gourley. Twenty-First Century Books 2008 144p il (Images and issues of women in the twentieth century)
$38.60
Grades: 7 8 9 10   **305.4**
1. Women -- United States -- History 2. United States
-- History -- 20th century
ISBN 978-0-8225-6805-6; 0-8225-6805-5
    LC 2006036103

This "examines women after World War II. Chapters explore varied aspects of the lives of white women as teens,
consumers, wives, mothers, and burgeoning activists. . . . .
Most images and discussions of minority women are confined to the chapter on the Civil Rights movement. . . . Text
is accessible and interesting for teens fascinated with wom-
en's history." Youth Voice Advocates

Includes bibliographical references (p. 132-139)

★ **Rosie** and Mrs. America; perceptions of wom-
en in the 1930s and 1940s. Twenty-First Century
Books 2008 144p il (Images and issues of women
in the twentieth century) lib bdg $38.60
Grades: 7 8 9 10   **305.4**
1. Women -- United States -- History 2. United States
-- History -- 20th century
ISBN 978-0-8225-6804-9; 0-8225-6804-7
    LC 2006-28984

This describes images of women in the United States in
the 1930s and 1940's.

"The sparkling and engaging [text is] generously expanded by numerous, well-placed black-and-white photographs and period reproductions. . . . Great for research or
browsing." SLJ

Includes bibliographical references

Marsico, Katie
Women's right to vote; America's suffrage
movement. Marshall Cavendish Benchmark 2010
112p il (Perspectives on) $39.93
Grades: 7 8 9 10   **305.4**
1. Women -- Suffrage 2. Women -- United States --
History
ISBN 978-0-7614-4980-5; 0-7614-4980-9

This discusses the history of the women's suffrage
movement in the United States.

This "well-written [book begins] with [an overview] and some historical background, and then [proceeds] chronologically to the current decade. . . . Marsico engages readers especially well, particularly when recounting the tenuous hours before the 19th Amendment ratification vote in Tennessee. It is evident that . . . [the author has] done [her] research. [The book contains] information that is perhaps less well-known to student researchers, including . . . the treatment of imprisoned suffragists. Black-and-white and color photographs along with some period cartoons place readers in the time period, and sidebars interspersed throughout present issues that aren't easily covered within the main [text]." SLJ

Includes bibliographical references

Mills, J. Elizabeth

Expectations for women; confronting stereotypes. Rosen Pub. 2010 112p il (A young woman's guide to contemporary issues) lib bdg $31.95
Grades: 7 8 9 10   **305.4**
1. Women 2. Body image 3. Self-perception
ISBN 978-1-4358-3543-6; 1-4358-3543-3
LC 2009-14429
"Facts are shared in a conversational tone, creating the sense of a chat with a big sister. . . . [Though] designed for personal reading and browsing, the data provided are accurate and also lend themselves to use in reports. This . . . will be of great interest." SLJ

Includes glossary and bibliographical references

Senker, Cath

Strength in numbers; industrialization and political activism, 1861-1899. Chelsea House 2011 il (A cultural history of women in America) $35
Grades: 7 8 9 10   **305.4**
1. Feminism 2. Women's rights 3. Women -- United States -- History 4. United States -- Social conditions
ISBN 978-1-60413-931-0; 1-60413-931-5
LC 2010045964
This is a history of American women from 1861-1899.

This book offers a "comprehensive, vivid, and thought-provoking [look] at the struggles and triumphs of . . . the women who [participated] in shaping our nation. Through succinct, informative text, [this] heavily illustrated volume incorporates the history of three major groups of people: the Natives, European settlers, and African slaves. Featured quotes from books, articles, letters, and speeches bring the history to life." SLJ

Includes glossary and bibliographical references

Stearman, Kaye

Feminism; [by] Kaye Stearman. Raintree 2004 64p il (Ideas of the modern world) lib bdg $32.79
Grades: 7 8 9 10   **305.4**
1. Feminism
ISBN 0-7398-6415-7
LC 2003-2068
"Stearman discusses the history of women's rights with connections made to other political movements such as abolitionism and temperance. . . . The author looks at new interpretations of feminism and issues such as sweatshop labor, countries with controversial social laws against women's

rights, and female genital mutilation. [This book has] a balance of ideas and nonjudgmental language. Black-and-white and full-color photos appear throughout." SLJ

Includes bibliographical references

Women of today; contemporary issues and conflicts, 1980-present. [by] Kaye Stearman and Patience Coster. Chelsea House 2011 il (A cultural history of women in America) $35
Grades: 5 6 7 8   **305.4**
1. Feminism 2. Women -- United States 3. Women -- Social conditions
ISBN 978-1-6041-3936-5; 1-6041-3936-6
LC 2010046014
An "eye-catching [layout] with good use of color, photographs, and informative sidebars, many of which use primary-source quotations, are the highlights of [this] appealing [volume]. . . . After a succinct overview of contemporary events, the chapters describe women's lives at home, at work, in education, in politics, in the arts, and their role in the general culture. . . . [This book] highlights women's achievements, including U.S. Supreme Court justices, Speaker of the U.S. House of Representatives, and presidential candidates." SLJ

Includes glossary and bibliographical references

Taschek, Karen

Daughters of liberty; the American Revolution and the Early Republic, 1775-1827. Chelsea House 2011 64p il (A cultural history of women in America) $35
Grades: 7 8 9 10   **305.4**
1. Women -- United States -- History 2. United States -- Social conditions 3. United States -- History -- 1775-1783, Revolution
ISBN 978-1-60413-928-0; 1-60413-928-5
LC 2010033717
This is a history of women in America from 1775-1827.

This book offers a "comprehensive, vivid, and thought-provoking [look] at the struggles and triumphs of . . . the women who [participated] in shaping our nation. Through succinct, informative text, [this] heavily illustrated volume incorporates the history of three major groups of people: the Natives, European settlers, and African slaves. Featured quotes from books, articles, letters, and speeches bring the history to life." SLJ

Includes glossary and bibliographical references

VanMeter, Larry A.

Women win the vote; the hard-fought battle for women's suffrage. Enslow Publishers 2009 128p il map (America's living history) lib bdg $31.93
Grades: 5 6 7 8   **305.4**
1. Women -- Suffrage 2. Women -- United States -- History
ISBN 978-0-7660-2940-8 lib bdg; 0-7660-2940-9 lib bdg
LC 2008024900
"Archival photographs, maps, and sidebars combine with . . . informative [text]." Horn Book Guide

"Discusses the history of the women's suffrage movement in the United States, including the origins of the movement, the key figures in the struggle for suffrage, and the Nineteenth Amendment granting women the right to vote." Publisher's note

Includes glossary and bibliographical references

Woolf, Alex, 1964-

Finding an identity; early America and the Colonial Period, 1492-1774. Chelsea House 2011 64p il (A cultural history of women in America) $35

Grades: 7 8 9 10   **305.4**

1. Women -- United States -- History 2. United States -- History -- 1600-1775, Colonial period

ISBN 978-1-6041-3927-3; 1-6041-3927-7

LC 2010029225

This is a history of women in America from 1492-1774.

This book offers a "comprehensive, vivid, and thought-provoking [look] at the struggles and triumphs of . . . the women who [participated] in shaping our nation. Through succinct, informative text, [this] heavily illustrated volume incorporates the history of three major groups of people: the Natives, European settlers, and African slaves. Featured quotes from books, articles, letters, and speeches bring the history to life." SLJ

Includes glossary and bibliographical references

305.5 People by social and economic levels

Horn, Geoffrey M.

Sojourner Truth; speaking up for freedom. by Geoffrey Michael Horn. Crabtree Pub. Co. 2010 64 p. ill. (some col.) (pbk. : alk. paper) $10.95

Grades: 4 5 6 7 8   **305.5**

1. Abolitionists -- United States -- Biography 2. African American women -- Biography 3. African American abolitionists -- Biography 4. Social reformers -- United States -- Biography

ISBN 0778748405; 9780778748243; 9780778748403

LC 2009022428

This children's picture book by Geoffrey M. Horn in the Voices for Freedom: Abolitionist Views series looks at abolitionist Sojourner Truth. It "relates and details Truth's life and times, from her often-brutal treatment as a slave, named Isabella at birth, to her freedom, religious influences, and self-determination . . . and path to outspoken, sometimes provocative, and influential traveling speaker on a mission to raise awareness of and support for abolitionism." (Booklist)

"Combining accessible, lively prose and abundant visuals, this title . . . offers an engaging, informative introduction to the early advocate for the rights of African Americans and women." Booklist

305.8 Ethnic and national groups

★ The **African** American almanac; Christopher A. Brooks, editor; foreword by Benjamin Jealous.

11th ed; Gale Cengage Learning 2011 1601p il map $297

Grades: 8 9 10 11 12 Adult   **305.8**

1. Reference books 2. African Americans

ISBN 978-1-4144-4547-2

First edition under the editorship of Harry A. Ploski published 1967 by Bellwether with title: The Negro almanac. Periodically revised. Editors vary

"Reference covering the cultural and political history of Black Americans. Includes generous amount of statistical information and biographies of Black Americans, both historical and contemporary." N Y Public Libr. Book of How & Where to Look It Up

The **Black** experience in America; from civil rights to the present. edited by Jeff Wallenfeldt. Britannica Educational Pub. 2010 230p il (African American history and culture) lib bdg $45

Grades: 8 9 10 11 12   **305.8**

1. African Americans -- History 2. United States -- Race relations 3. African Americans -- Civil rights

ISBN 978-1-61530-146-1; 1-61530-146-1

LC 2010-14639

This "is notable for the depth and breadth of its coverage. Beginning with WWII events that led to integration, the book, illustrated with black-and-white photos, chronologically follows the history of the civil rights movement as well as introducing black influences on literature, sports, and music. . . . It's hard to find a single-volume title that covers so much." Booklist

Includes glossary and bibliographical references

Bolden, Tonya

★ **Tell** all the children our story; memories and mementos of being young and Black in America. Abrams 2001 128p il $24.95

Grades: 5 6 7 8   **305.8**

1. African American children 2. United States -- Race relations

ISBN 0-8109-4496-0

LC 2001-1353

"This compilation of the African American experience, from colonial times through the twentieth century, reads and looks like a family scrapbook. . . . Photographs, excerpts from diaries and memoirs, and reproductions of artwork by black artists such as Charles Altson beautifully bring the story of each generation to life. Bolden vibrantly delivers her historical message through a contemporary perspective." Booklist

Includes bibliographical references

Discrimination: opposing viewpoints; Jacqueline Langwith, book editor. Greenhaven Press 2008 247p il (Opposing viewpoints series) $36.20; pa $24.95

Grades: 8 9 10 11 12   **305.8**

1. Minorities 2. Discrimination 3. Affirmative action programs

ISBN 978-0-73773-739-4; 0-73773-739-5; 978-0-73773-740-0 pa; 0-73773-740-9 pa

LC 2007-933224

This covers the topic of discrimination "in pro and con articles written by experts in the field or journalists with relevant experience. Clearly written, well researched, and far reaching, Discrimination explores the problem in its many forms." SLJ

Includes bibliographical references

Doak, Robin S.

Struggling to become American; [by] Robin Doak. Chelsea House 2007 106p il map (Latino American history) $35

Grades: 5 6 7 8 **305.8**
1. Latinos (U.S.) 2. Hispanic Americans 3. Immigrants -- United States
ISBN 0-8160-6443-1; 978-0-8160-6443-4
LC 2006017140

"Topics such as U.S. policy decisions regarding Puerto Rico and Cuba, racism experienced by immigrants and those who became American when the U.S. Mexican border shifted in 1848, Latino culture in the United States, and the repatriation of Mexicans during the Great Depression are covered in a reasonable amount of detail. Plenty of captioned photographs, political cartoons, and colorful subheads and informational sidebars keep the book visually interesting." SLJ

Includes bibliographical references

Hernandez, Roger E.

1898 to World War II. Marshall Cavendish Benchmark 2009 78p il (Hispanic America) lib bdg $34.21

Grades: 4 5 6 7 **305.8**
1. Hispanic Americans -- History 2. United States -- History -- 1898-1919 3. United States -- History -- 1919-1933 4. United States -- History -- 1933-1945
ISBN 978-0-7614-4176-2 lib bdg; 0-7614-4176-X lib bdg
LC 2008041140

"Provides comprehensive information on the history of the Spanish coming to the United States, focusing on the time from 1898 to the start of World War II." Publisher's note

Includes glossary and bibliographical references

Horst, Heather A.

Jamaican Americans; [by] Heather A. Horst and Andrew Garner; series editor, Robert D. Johnston. Chelsea House 2007 144p il map (The new immigrants) lib bdg $27.95

Grades: 7 8 9 10 11 12 **305.8**
1. West Indian Americans 2. Immigrants -- United States
ISBN 0-7910-8790-5; 978-0-7910-8790-9
LC 2006-25904

The "chatty narrative style may engage readers." Horn Book Guide

"Drawing on personal stories and historical fact, this . . . book focuses on [Jamaican Americans] and assesses their lasting impact." Publisher's note

Includes bibliographical references

Horton, James Oliver

Landmarks of African American history. Oxford University Press 2004 207p (American landmarks) $30

Grades: 8 9 10 11 12 **305.8**
1. Historic sites 2. African Americans -- History
ISBN 0-19-514118-0
LC 2004-2798

"Horton discusses 13 historic places, beginning with Jamestown, VA, and ending with the Woolworth department store in Greensboro, NC, the site of the first student sit-in in 1960. Clearly written and well organized, the text enriches the study of African-American history, providing a context and a look at its artifacts. . . . Well-placed illustrations of archival and current photographs and maps make for an attractive presentation." SLJ

Includes bibliographical references

It's not all black and white; multiracial youth speak out. St. Stephen's Community House. Annick Press 2012 109 p. $12.95

Grades: 8 9 10 11 12 **305.8**
1. Prejudices 2. Minority youth 3. Identity (Psychology) 4. Racially mixed people
ISBN 1554513804; 9781554513802

In this collection of "poems, interviews, and short essays, a group of young people describe being biracial, multiracial, or of mixed race. . . . Themes include navigating mixed-race relationships, dealing with prejudice and the assumptions people make based on appearances, and working through identity confusion to arrive at a strong and positive sense of self." (Publisher's note)

Katz, William Loren

Black Indians; a hidden heritage. Atheneum Pubs. 1986 198p il $17.95; pa $10

Grades: 8 9 10 11 12 **305.8**
1. Native Americans 2. African Americans
ISBN 0-689-31196-6; 0-689-80901-8 pa
LC 85-28770

Traces the history of relations between blacks and American Indians, and the existence of black Indians, from the earliest foreign landings through pioneer days.

The author "has provided a valuable addition to titles on American Indians. Excellent for assignments, it contains important information many history instructors may be unaware of. His sections on black Indians and the Seminoles of Florida and their views about living together are particularly good." Child Book Rev Serv

Includes bibliographical references

Miller, Calvin Craig

Backlash; race riots in the Jim Crow Era. Calvin Craig Miller. Morgan Reynolds Pub. 2012 128 p.

Grades: 8 9 10 11 12 **305.8**
1. Racism -- History 2. Riots -- United States 3. African Americans -- History 4. Cities and towns -- United States 5. United States -- Race relations -- History 6. United States -- Race relations 7. African Americans -- Crimes against 8. Riots -- United States -- History -- 20th century 9. United States -- Race relations -- History -- 20th century 10. African Americans -- Crimes against

-- History -- 20th century
ISBN 1599351838; 9781599351834

LC 2011005673

This book details the history of 'violence against African Americans in the Jim Crow era. . . . In cities, without the protection of secrecy, violence manifested itself in white mob attacks against black communities. This . . . [book] recognizes seven of the worst attacks that occurred in cities across the United States. Starting with the 1898 riot in Wilmington, North Carolina, in which white supremacists overturned an elected government . . . and killed 30 blacks, the . . . text goes on to cover similar events in Atlanta, Springfield, East St. Louis, Chicago, Tulsa, and Detroit. In each case, [Calvin Craig] Miller notes numerous similarities, including rage among working-class whites over competition with blacks for jobs and affordable housing, and rumors fueled by racist media.' (Booklist)

Includes bibliographical references (p. 123-124) and index

Ochoa, George

Atlas of Hispanic-American history; [by] George Ochoa and Carter Smith. Rev ed; Facts on File 2008 250p il map (Facts on File library of American history) $95; pa $21.95

Grades: 7 8 9 10   305.8

1. Reference books 2. Hispanic Americans -- History
ISBN 978-0-8160-7092-3; 978-0-8160-7736-6 pa

LC 2008-20664

First published 2001

This reference chronicles the "cultural, historical, political, and social experiences of Hispanic Americans through the years. . . . [It] examines Spanish, Native American, and African influences and how they combine in different ways to form the varied cultures of Hispanic America." Publisher's note

Includes bibliographical references

Petrillo, Valerie

A **kid's** guide to Latino history; more than 70 activities. Chicago Review Press 2009 214p il pa $14.95

Grades: 4 5 6 7   305.8

1. Hispanic Americans -- History
ISBN 978-1-55652-771-5 pa; 1-55652-771-3 pa

LC 2008040433

"This big, lively overview examines the history of Latinos in the U.S. . . . The chatty, informative text, presented in readable, spacious layouts, will draw kids with lots of fun, illustrated instructions for related activities. . . . The accessible facts and the individual portraits of notable authors, athletes, entertainers, and politicians portray Latinos' rich contribution to U.S. heritage, and kids will want to talk about the well-presented issues." Booklist

Includes bibliographical references

Race relations: opposing viewpoints; Karen Miller, book editor. Greenhaven Press 2011 204p il

(Opposing viewpoints series) lib bdg $39.70; pa $26.50

Grades: 8 9 10 11 12   305.8

1. United States -- Race relations
ISBN 978-0-7377-4986-1 lib bdg; 0-7377-4986-5 lib bdg; 978-0-7377-4987-8 pa; 0-7377-4987-3 pa

LC 2010028939

Articles in this anthology present opposing views on the nature of race, the impact of society and the government on race relations, and what the future holds.

Includes bibliographical references

Rodger, Marguerite

Racism and prejudice; [by] Marguerite Rodger and Jessie Rodger. Crabtree Pub. Co. 2010 48p il (Straight talk about. . .) lib bdg $29.27; pa $9.95

Grades: 7 8 9 10   305.8

1. Racism 2. Prejudices
ISBN 978-0-7787-2129-1 lib bdg; 0-7787-2129-9 lib bdg; 978-0-7787-2136-9 pa; 0-7787-2136-1 pa

LC 2010019132

The authors "cover topics ranging from overt racism to homophobia to the treatment of people with mental and physical disabilities. They discuss the history of hate and include personal accounts from those who've dealt with being stereotyped. The book is well laid out and easy to read. . . . Readers will appreciate the relevant photos of teens, the quotes, and the honest writing style." SLJ

Includes glossary

Sanna, Ellyn

We shall all be free; survivors of racism. Mason Crest Publishers 2009 128p il (Survivors: ordinary people, extraordinary circumstances) lib bdg $24.95

Grades: 7 8 9 10   305.8

1. Racism 2. Minorities 3. Prejudices
ISBN 978-1-4222-0458-0; 1-4222-0458-8

LC 2008-50326

"Sanna covers racism of all kinds, including genocide in parts of Africa; the deplorable conditions of Native Americans; anti-Semitism; racism against the Roma, better known as Gypsies, and against African Americans; and the conditions faced by some immigrants. . . . [This title exposes] the underbelly of society, explaining terms that might be unfamiliar and providing multiple examples of the issues." SLJ

Includes bibliographical references

Szulhan, Rebecca

Contemporary achievements. Weigl Publishers 2009 48p il (African American history) lib bdg $29.05; pa $10.95

Grades: 6 7 8 9   305.8

1. African Americans -- History 2. African Americans -- Biography
ISBN 978-1-59036-884-8 lib bdg; 1-59036-884-3 lib bdg; 978-1-59036-885-5 pa; 1-59036-885-1 pa

LC 2008-42473

"Combines short biographies and quick facts about academics, athletics, politics and literature. . . . This . . . is fabulous for students interested in or researching history. Glossy pictures, quick facts, techonology links, and sidebars of information interrupt the text, giving readers interesting and important information without overwhelming them." Voice Youth Advocates

Includes glossary and bibliographical references

Wright, Simeon

Simeon's story; an eyewitness account of the kidnapping of Emmett Till. [by] Simeon Wright; with Herb Boyd. Lawrence Hill Books 2010 144p il map $19.95

Grades: 6 7 8 9 10   **305.8**

1. Racism 2. Children 3. Lynching 4. Trials (Homicide) 5. Murder victims 6. Mississippi -- Race relations 7. African Americans -- Mississippi

ISBN 978-1-55652-783-8; 1-55652-783-7

LC 2009-33631

"Simeon Wright was 12 years old when his cousin Emmett 'Bobo' Till came from Chicago to visit relatives in Mississippi.... One hot August night in 1955, Till whistled at a white female store clerk, setting off a chain of events that left an indelible mark not only on our nation's history, but also on the cousin who witnessed Till's gaffe and eventual kidnapping. Wright's story is chilling, and his honest account will hook readers from the beginning." SLJ

305.896   Africans and people of African descent

Osborne, Linda Barrett

★ Miles to go for freedom; segregation and civil rights in the Jim Crow years. by Linda Barrett Osborne. Abrams Books for Young Readers 2011 118 p.

Grades: 6 7 8   **305.896**

1. United States -- History 2. United States -- Race relations 3. African Americans -- Segregation 4. African Americans -- Civil rights 5. African Americans -- Segregation -- History -- 20th century

ISBN 9781419700200

LC 2011022854

In this book, the "companion volume to 'Traveling the Freedom Road' (2009), Osborne ... offers a[n] ... overview of African American history, focusing here on both the South and the North during the late nineteenth-century through the mid-twentieth century.... Period images, including photos of public events, such as lynchings; magazine illustrations; and prints fill every double-page spread. After the first section on the South, the following section about the North focuses on the Great Migration, exploring not only the reasons why African Americans left but also the often chilly reception they received when they arrived. The final short section about the nation as a whole ends with the triumph of Brown v. Board of Education." (Booklist)

Includes bibliographical references and index

306   Culture and institutions

Bales, Kevin

Slavery today; [by] Kevin Bales and Becky Cornell. Groundwood Books 2008 141p il (Groundwork guides) $18.95; pa $10

Grades: 7 8 9 10   **306**

1. Slavery

ISBN 978-0-88899-772-2; 0-88899-772-8; 978-0-88899-773-9 pa; 0-88899-773-6 pa

"Easy to read and extremely engaging, the work traces the existence and occurrence of slavery in modern factories, jungles, and farms around the world, and discusses prostitution and strategies for ending slavery in the global market.... Students will find this book of great use for research papers, but it is also highly readable for personal enrichment. The language used is not complicated, the prose is understandable, and the personal narratives are passionate, even when describing awful, inhumane acts." Libr Media Connect

Includes bibliographical references

Bowling, beatniks, and bell-bottoms; pop culture of 20th-century America. Sara Pendergast and Tom Pendergast, editors. U.X.L 2002 5v il set $250

Grades: 8 9 10 11 12 Adult   **306**

1. United States -- Civilization 2. Popular culture -- United States

ISBN 0-7876-5675-5

LC 2002-1829

The editors "track trends in American popular culture through 750 entries arranged chronologically by decade over five volumes. Within decades, entries are divided into nine major areas: 'Commerce,' 'Fashion,' 'Film and Theater,' 'Food and Drink,' 'Music,' 'Print Culture,' 'Sports and Games,' Television and Radio,' and 'The Way We Lived.... . Informative, entertaining, and clearly presented." Libr J

Includes bibliographical references

Brownell, Richard

American counterculture of the 1960s. Lucent Books 2010 96p il (World history) lib bdg $33.45

Grades: 6 7 8 9   **306**

1. Counter culture 2. Demonstrations -- United States 3. United States -- Social conditions

ISBN 978-1-4205-0263-3; 1-4205-0263-8

LC 2010010503

This is an introduction to the counterculture of the 1960s, including personal stories and important personalities.

This "shines as it provides a contemporaneous writing as well as work by scholars that offer plenty of drama—and lots of facts too.... [It also] provides a solid time line, plenty of photographs, sourced quotes, and a list of books and websites for further investigation. Excellent for reports and research." Booklist

Includes bibliographical references

Mark, Joan T.

Margaret Mead; coming of age in America. [by] Joan Mark. Oxford Univ. Press 1998 110p il (Oxford portraits in science) $28

Grades: 7 8 9 10   **306**
1. Anthropologists 2. Curators 3. Writers on science
ISBN 0-19-511679-8

LC 98-18604

This is a biography of the American anthropologist who wrote Coming of Age in Samoa. Bibliography. Index. "Grades six to ten." (Libr J)

An "account of the life and works of the influential, pioneering anthropologist. . . . Mark does a fine job of abstracting Mead's research and published works and showing why they were both critically acclaimed and criticized. The reader-friendly prose is peppered with fascinating anecdotes and photos. Mead herself is presented as a complex, intriguing figure, with fascinating, often contradictory, public and private lives." Booklist

Includes bibliographical references

306.3   Economic institutions

Lester, Julius
★ **From** slave ship to freedom road; paintings by Rod Brown. Dial Bks. 1998 40p il hardcover o.p. pa $6.99
Grades: 5 6 7 8   **306.3**
1. Slavery -- United States
ISBN 0-8037-1893-4; 0-14-056669-4 pa

LC 96-44422

"Lester's impassioned questions grow from his visceral response to Brown's narrative paintings. . . . The combination of history, art, and commentary demands interaction." Booklist

"Lester uses empathy-provoking exercises, open-ended questions, and the paintings of Rod Brown to help readers understand the experience of African-American slaves." Bull Cent Child Books

306.362   Slavery

Conkling, Winifred
Passenger on the Pearl; the true story of Emily Edmonson's flight from slavery. Winifred Conkling. First edition Algonquin Young Readers 2015 176 p. illustrations, maps $17.95
Grades: 7 8 9 10   **306.362**
1. Fugitive slaves 2. Pearl (Schooner) 3. Underground Railroad -- Washington Region 4. Fugitive slaves -- Washington Region -- History -- 19th century 5. Antislavery movements -- United States -- History -- 19th century
ISBN 1616201967; 9781616201968

LC 2014029246

This book presents a "historical narrative concerning several people involved in an attempted slave escape in 1848. The Pearl was to ferry 13-year-old Emily Edmonson and scores of other runaway slaves from Washington DC down the Potomac River and up the Chesapeake Bay. However, the ship was captured before reaching free soil. [Winifred] Conkling narrates the tumultuous stories of Edmonson, her family, and the others involved." (School Library Journal)

"By examining the intersecting experiences of enslaved people, abolitionists, free people of color, slave owners, and slave traders, this book provides an effective antidote to the oversimplified picture of slavery in America painted by some outdated textbooks." Booklist

Includes bibliographical references

306.4   Specific aspects of culture

Palad, Thea
★ **Mixed** messages; interpreting body image & social norms. ABDO Pub. Co. 2009 112p il (Essential health: strong, beautiful girls) lib bdg $22.95
Grades: 6 7 8 9   **306.4**
1. Self-esteem 2. Self-acceptance 3. Girls -- Psychology
ISBN 978-1-60453-102-2 lib bdg; 1-60453-102-9 lib bdg

LC 2008-19351

This features fictional narratives paired with firsthand advice from a licensed psychologist to help preteen and teen readers better understand the countless media messages that are presented to them daily. Topics include body image, stereotypes, and feeling comfortable in one's own skin.

"The topics are well selected, the design is attractive, and the stories feature girls from a variety of cultures." Booklist

Includes glossary and bibliographical references

306.7   Sexual relations

Burningham, Sarah O'Leary
Boyology; a teen girl's crash course in all things boy. illustrations by Keri Smith. Chronicle Books 2009 167p il pa $12.99
Grades: 6 7 8 9 10   **306.7**
1. Dating (Social customs) 2. Interpersonal relations 3. Boys -- Psychology
ISBN 978-0-8118-6436-7; 0-8118-6436-7

LC 2008-5277

"Adolescent girls seeking a deeper understanding of the opposite sex will appreciate this appealing, entertaining guide full of useful facts and sound advice. Burningham . . . explores a wide range of subjects, including how to determine which 'breed' of boy you're dealing with, first dates and the rules of the dating game, setting boundaries, peer conflicts and pressures, dealing with parents, the difference between having a boyfriend and boy friends and coping with the inevitable breakup." Kirkus

Feinstein, Stephen
Sexuality and teens; what you should know about sex, abstinence, birth control, pregnancy, and stds. Enslow Publishers 2010 104p il (Issues in focus today) lib bdg $31.93
Grades: 7 8 9 10   **306.7**
1. Youth -- Sexual behavior
ISBN 978-0-7660-3312-2; 0-7660-3312-0

LC 2009-1373

"This text provides a well-balanced look at sexual attitudes and behaviors as they relate to today's youth. . . . The book could be useful for basic report and debate information or as a jumping-off point for class discussions." SLJ

Includes glossary and bibliographical references

Forssberg, Manne

★ **Sex** for guys; translated by Maria Lundin. Groundwood Books/House of Anansi 2007 142p il (Groundwork guides) $15.95; pa $9.95

Grades: 7 8 9 10 11 12   **306.7**

1. Sex education 2. Men -- Sexual behavior
ISBN 978-0-88899-770-8; 978-0-88899-771-5 pa

This "will prove invaluable to guys bombarded with less sensitive and comprehensive media messages. . . . This is a witty, sane treatment of the things that drive guys crazy—a must read for teens with questions." Bull Cent Child Books

Includes bibliographical references

306.76 Sexual orientation, transgenderism, intersexuality

Bausum, Ann

★ **Stonewall**; breaking out in the fight for gay rights. Ann Bausum. Viking Books for Young Readers 2015 128 p. illustrations (hardback) $16.99

Grades: 8 9 10 11 12   **306.76**

1. Gay rights 2. Stonewall Riots, New York, N.Y., 1969 3. Gay men -- United States -- History -- 20th century 4. Lesbians -- United States -- History -- 20th century 5. Greenwich Village (New York, N.Y.) -- History -- 20th century 6. Gay liberation movement -- United States -- History -- 20th century
ISBN 9780670016792

LC 2014039812

"Bausum begins her history of the gay rights movement with a careful, detailed exposition of the June 1969 Stonewall riots, laying out the events leading up to the clash between the Greenwich Village gay community and the police and putting those events in the context of time and place. She dedicates the first half of the book to the riots themselves, drawing on reports, interviews, and other first-person accounts to put together a candid linear narrative that takes into consideration the perspectives of both sides of the conflict. . . . Bausum writes with the precision of a journalist; there is never any doubt as to what she wonders, what she conjectures, and what she knows." Horn Book

Includes filmography and bibliographical references (pages 111-115) and index

★ The **Full** spectrum; a new generation of writing about gay, lesbian, bisexual, transgender, questioning, and other identities. edited by David Levithan & Billy Merrell. Knopf 2006 272p il hardcover o.p. pa $9.95

Grades: 8 9 10 11 12   **306.76**

1. Gay men 2. Lesbians 3. Gender role 4. Homosexuality 5. Sex role
ISBN 0-375-93290-9; 0-375-83290-4 pa

LC 2005-23435

"The 40 contributions to this invaluable collection about personal identity have two things in common: all are nonfiction and all are by writers under the age of 23. Beyond that, diversity is the order of the day, and the result is a vivid demonstration of how extraordinarily broad the spectrum of sexual identity is among today's gay, lesbian, bisexual, transgender, and questioning youth. . . . Insightful, extraordinarily well written, and emotionally mature, the selections offer compelling, dramatic evidence that what is important is not what we are but who we are." Booklist

Huegel, Kelly

★ **GLBTQ**; the survival guide for gay, lesbian, bisexual, transgender, and questioning teens. rev & updated 2nd ed.; Free Spirit Pub. 2011 229p il

Grades: 7 8 9 10 11 12   **306.76**

1. Lesbianism 2. Bisexuality 3. Homosexuality 4. Transsexualism
ISBN 1-57542-363-0; 978-1-57542-363-0

LC 2010-48196

First published 2003

Describes the challenges faced by gay, lesbian, bisexual, and transgendered teens, offers practical advice, real-life experiences, and accessible resources and support groups.

"The information . . . [this] provides for GLBTQ teens makes it a valuable addition to any high school or public library collection." Voice Youth Advcocates

Includes bibliographical references

Marcus, Eric

What if someone I know is gay? answers to questions about what it means to be gay and lesbian, by Eric Marcus. Rev. and updated 1st Simon Pulse ed Simon & Schuster 2008 183 p. (prebind) $17.99; (paperback) $9.99

Grades: 7 8 9 10 11 12   **306.76**

1. Homosexuality
ISBN 9781435285101; 9781416949701
First published in 2000 by Price/Stern/Sloan
Includes bibliographical references.

"The content . . . stands strong, and readers will appreciate Marcus's gentle tone and the careful candor that he uses to describe the sometimes-rocky LGB experience. Helpful information about gay-straight alliances and marriage and partnership issues are all addressed." SLJ

Sanna, Emily

Gay believers; homosexuality and religion. Mason Crest Publishers 2010 64p il (Gallup's guide to modern gay, lesbian, and transgender lifestyle) $22.95; pa $9.95

Grades: 8 9 10 11 12   **306.76**

1. Religions 2. Homosexuality
ISBN 978-1-4222-1749-8; 978-1-4222-1868-6 pa

LC 2010012747

This discusses homosexuality in Christianity, Judaism, Islam, Hinduism, and Buddhism.

"The advice is solid. . . . The [book is] easy to read, up-to-date, and [includes] personal stories that many readers will relate to." SLJ

Includes bibliographical references

Seba, Jaime

Coming out; telling family and friends. Mason Crest Publishers 2010 64p il (Gallup's guide to modern gay, lesbian, and transgender lifestyle) $22.95; pa $9.95

Grades: 8 9 10 11 12	**306.76**

1. Homosexuality

ISBN 978-1-4222-1745-0; 978-1-4222-1865-5 pa

LC 2010017052

This discusses revealing one's homosexuality to friends and family.

"The advice is solid. . . . The [book is] easy to read, up-to-date, and [includes] personal stories that many readers will relate to." SLJ

Includes bibliographical references

Gallup guides for youth facing persistent prejudice; The LGBT community. by Jaime Seba. Mason Crest Publishers 2013 64 p. col. ill., photographs (library) $22.95

Grades: 5 6 7 8	**306.76**

1. LGBT people -- Civil rights 2. Homophobia 3. Gay youth -- United States 4. Sexual minorities -- Civil rights -- United States

ISBN 1422224678; 9781422224670

LC 2012017108

This book by Jaime Seba on the LGBT community "discusses the history of prejudice toward this group, the laws that protect people against discrimination-and what you can do to fight the prejudice you find in the world." (Publisher's note) As part of the "Gallup Guides for Youth Facing Persistent Prejudice" series, it "emphasiz[es] recent violence and other problems, such as bullying and depression, which are, unfortunately, still routine for many LGBT youth." (Booklist)

Includes bibliographical references (p. 62) and index.

Homosexuality around the world; safe havens, cultural challenges. by Jaime A. Seba. Mason Crest Publishers 2011 64 p. ill. (chiefly col.) (hardcover) $22.95; (paperback) $9.95

Grades: 6 7 8 9 10	**306.76**

1. Gay rights 2. Homosexuality 3. Depression, Mental 4. Gays 5. Gay rights 6. Gays -- Legal status, laws, etc.

ISBN 1422217531; 1422218724; 9781422217535; 9781422218723

LC 2010017917

This book looks at global views on homosexuality. Readers can "explore different countries and learn about their cultural attitudes toward lesbian, gay, bisexual, and transgender people, as gay men and women from around the globe share their personal stories and experiences. Find out how American policies compare with our North American neighbors, Canada and Mexico, [and] discover how gay equal rights are beginning to emerge in places such as India and South Africa." (Publisher's note)

Includes bibliographical references (p. 60-61) and index.

306.8 Marriage and family

Fields, Julianna

Gay and lesbian parents. Mason Crest 2009 64p il map (The changing face of modern families) $22.95

Grades: 6 7 8 9	**306.8**

1. Gay parents

ISBN 978-1-4222-1495-4; 1-4222-1495-8

This describes the challenges facing gay and lesbian parents.

This is "informative [and] nonjudgmental. . . . Including color photos, plentiful sidebars, and interesting headline stories, the accessible [text presents] real-life experiences and numerous supporting facts, definitions, graphs, charts, and statistics." SLJ

Includes glossary and bibliographical references

Multiracial families. Mason Crest Publishers 2010 64p il (The changing face of modern families) lib bdg $22.95

Grades: 6 7 8 9	**306.8**

1. Family 2. Interracial marriage 3. Racially mixed people

ISBN 978-1-4222-1494-7 lib bdg; 1-4222-1494-X lib bdg

This describes the challenges that multi-racial families face.

This is "informative [and] nonjudgmental. . . . Including color photos, plentiful sidebars, and interesting headline stories, the accessible [text presents] real-life experiences and numerous supporting facts, definitions, graphs, charts, and statistics." SLJ

Includes glossary and bibliographical references

Fox, Annie

What's up with my family? illustrated by Matt Kindt. Free Spirit 2010 90p il (Middle school confidential) pa $9.99

Grades: 6 7 8 9	**306.8**

1. Family

ISBN 978-1-57542-333-3 pa; 1-57542-333-2 pa

"Using a magazine-style format that is part graphic novel and part nonfiction advice, Fox helps teens work out family problems like sibling rivalry, blended families, overprotective parents, and dealing with loss. . . . The book is full of tips on strengthening family relationships while working through the challenges every family faces. . . . This short, readable book will attract even reluctant readers with the format and give practical advice for all teens on improving family life." Voice Youth Advocates

Lynette, Rachel

★ **What** makes us a family? living in a nontraditional family. content consultant, Robyn J. A. Silverman. ABDO Pub. Co. 2009 112p il (Essential health: strong beautiful girls) lib bdg $32.79

Grades: 6 7 8 9   **306.8**
1. Family
ISBN 978-1-60453-756-7 lib bdg; 1-60453-756-6
lib bdg

                   LC 2009004416
"The topics are well selected, the design is attractive, and the stories feature girls from a variety of cultures." Booklist

This "explores various types of families including adoptive and foster; kids being raised by grandparents, two moms, and single parents; and families that are biracial, or that have a stepparent or a parent who abuses alcohol." SLJ

The **sibling** slam book; what it's really like to have a brother or sister with special needs. Woodbine House 2005 152p il pa $15.95
Grades: 6 7 8 9   **306.8**
1. Siblings 2. Children with disabilities
ISBN 1-890627-52-6
"This multifaceted vehicle for eliciting some unique and many universal emotions is designed specifically for siblings of special-needs children. An adolescent mainstay, the slam book is the chosen venue for encouraging the venting of opinions, hopes, fears, frustrations, and triumphs. Comments by 81 young people display the recurring theme of optimism, complicated by hard work, dedication, resentment, and fierce protection, all as by-products of love." SLJ

Simons, Rae
    Blended families. Mason Crest 2009 64p il (The changing face of modern families) lib bdg $22.95
Grades: 6 7 8 9   **306.8**
1. Stepfamilies
ISBN 978-1-4222-1492-3 lib bdg; 1-4222-1492-3
lib bdg
"Colorful photographs and sidebars appear throughout. [This book is a] good [introduction] to the study of sociology and interpretation of data." SLJ
    Includes glossary and bibliographical references

    Grandparents raising kids. Mason Crest Publishers 2010 64p il (The changing face of modern families) lib bdg $22.95
Grades: 6 7 8 9   **306.8**
1. Grandparents 2. Child rearing
ISBN 978-1-4222-1496-1 lib bdg; 1-4222-1496-6
lib bdg
This describes the challenges facing families in which children are raised by their grandparents.
    "There are questions directed at the reader to encourage deeper consideration of their opinions and synthesis of the knowledge they have gained from the book. . . . This . . . would be very helpful for students writing reports or simply seeking information." SLJ

    Teen parents. Mason Crest 2009 64p il (The changing face of modern families) lib bdg $22.95
Grades: 6 7 8 9   **306.8**
1. Teenage fathers 2. Teenage mothers
ISBN 978-1-4222-1491-6 lib bdg; 1-4222-1491-5
lib bdg

This describes the challenges facing teen parents.
    This is "informative [and] nonjudgmental. . . . Including color photos, plentiful sidebars, and interesting headline stories, the accessible [text presents] real-life experiences and numerous supporting facts, definitions, graphs, charts, and statistics." SLJ
    Includes glossary and bibliographical references

Stewart, Sheila
    What is a family? Mason Crest 2009 64p il (The changing face of modern families) lib bdg $22.95
Grades: 6 7 8 9   **306.8**
1. Family
ISBN 978-1-4222-1528-9 lib bdg; 1-4222-1528-8
lib bdg
This discusses traditional and non-traditional families, including single-parent families, blended families, gay or lesbian-parent families, and grandparents raising grandchildren and addresses questions such as: 'Are non-traditional families new?' 'What makes some families strong, while others struggle?' and 'Are some families so non-traditional that they can't really even be considered families?'
    "Colorful photographs and sidebars appear throughout. [This book is a] good [introduction] to the study of sociology and interpretation of data." SLJ
    Includes glossary and bibliographical references

Worth, Richard
    Frequently asked questions about teen fatherhood. Rosen Pub. 2010 64p il (FAQ: teen life) lib bdg $29.25
Grades: 7 8 9 10   **306.8**
1. Teenage fathers
ISBN 978-1-4358-5325-6; 1-4358-5325-3

                   LC 2008-51938
    "While conversational, [this volume is] surprisingly helpful—even emotive. . . . [This book greets] its intended audience with encouragement and aplomb. Dealing with feelings of disbelief and blame quickly segue into preparing for a birth, staying in school, and considering part-time jobs. Adoption and abortion are given only brief mentions." Booklist
    Includes glossary and bibliographical references

306.84   Types of marriage and relationships

Spilsbury, Louise
    Same -sex marriage; Louise Spilsbury. Rosen Central 2012 48 p. col. ill.
Grades: 7 8 9 10   **306.84**
1. Same-sex marriage
ISBN 1448870135; 9781448860203; 9781448870134;
9781448870141
                   LC 2011032847
This book by Louise Spilsbury "[d]iscusses the legal debate of same-sex marriage, including the history of the gay rights movement, the arguments both in support and opposition of same-sex marriage, and how same-sex marriage is treated around the world." (WorldCat)
    Includes bibliographical references and index

306.87 Intrafamily relationships

Apelqvist, Eva

LGBTQ families; the ultimate teen guide. Eva Apelqvist. Scarecrow Press, Inc. 2013 208 p. (It happened to me) (cloth : alk. paper) $50

Grades: 7 8 9 10 11 12   **306.87**
  1. LGBT people 2. Families 3. Children of gay parents 4. Gays -- Family relationships 5. Sexual minorities -- Family relationships
  ISBN 0810885360; 9780810885363

LC 2013015488

This book by Eva Apelqvist is part of the It Happened to Me series. This entry "begins with an overview of each letter of the iconic acronym and progresses into a more thorough look at LGBTQ adolescents, LGBTQ parents, and how trans individuals may affect family dynamics. Other chapters investigate same-sex marriage, other issues (e.g., rights of sperm donors), LGBTQ rights around the world, bullying, . . . and the ongoing debate between the LGBTQ community and various religious, political, and business groups." (Booklist)

Includes bibliographical references and index

306.874 Parent-child relationship

Buscemi, Karen

Split in two; keeping it together when your parents live apart. Karen Buscemi. Zest 2009 120 p. ill. (paperback) $12.95

Grades: 7 8 9 10 11 12   **306.874**
  1. Children of divorced parents
  ISBN 0980073219; 9780980073218

LC 2008936059

"Provides advice to children of divorced parents on living in two homes simultaneously, including how to organize during moves, managing different lifestyles, and coping with the emotional stress of separation." Publisher's note

"Written in a casual, genuine tone, the substantive chapters begin with valuable questions that help kids assess whether their basic needs for privacy and comfort are met in each household. . . . Like the text, Mucha's quirky cartoon illustrations find humor in the complicated situations and feelings, adding further appeal to this hip, reassuring guide filled with straightforward, honest advice." Booklist

Littlefield, Bruce

My two moms; lessons of love, strength, and what makes a family. by Zach Wahls ; with Bruce Littlefield. Gotham Books 2012 xix, 233 p.p ill. (hardcover) $26; (paperback) $16

Grades: 7 8 9 10 11 12   **306.874**
  1. Same-sex marriage 2. Children of gay parents 3. Gay rights -- United States 4. Lesbian mothers -- United States 5. Same-sex marriage -- United States
  ISBN 1592407137; 1592407633; 9781592407132; 9781592407637

LC 2011053087

In this book, "[Zach] Wahls writes about growing up as the son of gay parents in the heartland. In January 2011, the author, then a student at the University of Iowa, testified before the Iowa House Judiciary Committee as they considered a state constitutional amendment to ban same-sex marriage. . . . The speech was aimed at dismantling the myth that kids are damaged by having gay parents . . . Here the author expands on his speech, discussing the values that his parents helped to instill in him." (Kirkus)

306.89 Separation and divorce

Trueit, Trudi Strain

Surviving divorce; teens talk about what helps and what hurts. [by] Trudi Strain Trueit. 1st ed.; Scholastic 2007 112p il (Choices) lib bdg $22.50; pa $8.95

Grades: 6 7 8 9   **306.89**
  1. Divorce
  ISBN 0-531-12368-5 lib bdg; 978-0-531-12368-3 lib bdg; 0-531-16726-7 pa; 978-0-531-16726-7 pa

LC 2004018423

This "is an inviting guide to the facts and feelings of parental divorce. Personal stories and photos of kids begin each chapter, and frequent statistics and quizzes will help readers assess their feelings and put them into context. The solid advice is well presented, as are the messages that readers are not alone and that there are many ways to seek help." Booklist

Includes glossary and bibliographical references

306.9 Institutions pertaining to death

Noyes, Deborah

★ **Encyclopedia** of the end; mysterious death in fact, fancy, folklore, and more. Houghton Mifflin Co. 2008 143p il $25

Grades: 7 8 9 10 11 12   **306.9**
  1. Death 2. Reference books 3. Funeral rites and ceremonies
  ISBN 978-0-618-82362-8; 0-618-82362-X

LC 2008-1872

"This stylish A-to-Z encounter with all things related to death and dying shows Noyes . . . at her liveliest. . . . The author offers a broad illumination of spiritual, historical and biological aspects of death. Photos, paintings and engravings in homage to 'the end' make the book dynamic visually, too." Publ Wkly

Thornhill, Jan

I found a dead bird; the kids' guide to the cycle of life & death. Maple Tree Press 2006 64p il $21.95; pa $9.95

Grades: 4 5 6   **306.9**
  1. Death 2. Bereavement
  ISBN 1-897066-70-8; 1-897066-71-6 pa

Explores the cycle of life and death, and how the process is necessary in nature, while also commenting on how death effects people personally, and the skills they use to cope with such a trauma when it occurs.

"This straightforward, no holds barred approach to the subject will captivate children. Chock-full of color photographs, the well-designed book contains boxes with tidbits of information on a wide variety of topics, such as death of a species, human destruction, plant decomposition, trapped in time, and learning from death." SLJ

307 Communities

Anderson, Judith

★ **Looking** at settlements; by Judith Anderson. Smart Apple Media 2007 il map (Geography skills) $22.95

Grades: 6 7 8 9   307
1. Human settlements
ISBN 978-1-59920-052-1; 1-59920-052-X
                          LC 2006036142

"The text is easy to follow. . . . The examples given in the text that involve places are almost always accompanied by excellent photographs. . . . Maps, block diagroams, tables, and graphs are clearly presented and easy to interpret." Sci Books Films

Includes glossary and bibligraphical references

Dyer, Hadley

Watch this space; designing, defending and sharing public space. written by Hadley Dyer; illustrated by Marc Ngui. Kids Can Press 2010 80p il $18.95

Grades: 5 6 7 8   307
1. Public spaces
ISBN 978-1-55453-293-3

"With provocative questions and an informative, casual tone, this heavily illustrated title addresses a rare topic in books for youth: city planning and public spaces. From basic definitions of public space, Dyer moves on to ethical questions about safety and privacy, art and beautification, and community-friendly design elements of publicly owned spaces. Throughout, Dyer uses personal anecdotes and global examples, from Peoples' Park in Berkeley, California, to Al-Azhar Park in Cairo, Egypt, to emphasize the impact of public spaces around the world." Booklist

Hopkinson, Deborah

Shutting out the sky; life in the tenements of New York, 1880-1924. Orchard Bks. 2003 134p il $17.95

Grades: 5 6 7 8 9 10   307
1. Poor 2. Immigrants -- United States 3. Lower East Side (New York, N.Y.)
ISBN 0-439-37590-8
                          LC 2002-44781

Photographs and text document the experiences of five individuals who came to live in the Lower East Side of New York City as children or young adults from Belarus, Italy, Lithuania, and Romania at the turn of the twentieth century.

"The text is supported by numerous tinted archival photos of living and working conditions. Although this book will appeal to students looking for material for projects, the

writing lends immediacy and vivid images make it simply a fascinating read." SLJ

Includes bibliographical references

307.2 Movement of people to, from, within communities

Harris, Laurie Lanzen

The **great** migration north, 1910-1970; by Laurie Lanzen Harris. Omnigraphics, Inc. 2012 xvi, 241 p.p

Grades: 7 8 9 10 11 12   307.2
1. Internal migration 2. African Americans -- History 3. United States -- History -- 20th century 4. African Americans -- Migrations -- History -- 20th century 5. Rural-urban migration -- United States -- History -- 20th century
ISBN 0780811860; 9780780811867
                          LC 2011033540

This historical survey by Laurie Lanzen Harris "explains the social and economic factors that drove the African-American exodus out of the rural South to the industrial cities of the North during the first half of the twentieth century. The book also details the transformative impact of this migration on U.S. industry, culture, and race relations, as well as the daily experiences of the men, women, and children who built new lives for themselves in New York, Chicago, Philadelphia, Detroit, and other cities of the North. Finally, it explains how this multi-generational flight from oppression to opportunity changed the internal dynamics of African-American families and communities across America." (Publisher's note)

Includes bibliographical references and index.

307.7 Specific kinds of communities

Laidlaw, Jill A.

Cities; by Jill Laidlaw. Amicus 2011 44p il map (Sustaining our environment) lib bdg $31.35

Grades: 6 7 8 9   307.7
1. Urban ecology 2. Sustainable architecture 3. Renewable energy resources
ISBN 978-1-60753-135-7 lib bdg; 1-60753-135-6 lib bdg
                          LC 2009040708

"The tone is refreshingly optimistic with its examples of specific steps being taken to reduce harm to the environment. Sidebars highlight case studies and campaigns from around the world and from the individual to the national levels. Clear, informative captions accompany the excellent selection of color photographs, charts and graphs." SLJ

Includes glossary

Lorinc, John

Cities. Groundwood Books/House of Anansi Press 2008 144p (Groundwork guides) $18.95; pa $10

Grades: 7 8 9 10 11 12   307.7
   1. Urbanization 2. Cities and towns
   ISBN 978-0-88899-820-0; 0-88899-820-1; 978-0-
   88899-819-4 pa; 0-88899-819-8 pa
   "This packed, highly readable [title] . . . does an excellent job of tracing urban history worldwide, raising the big
social, political, and economic issues of poverty, migration,
conservation, public health, crime, transportation, and much
more, always rooted in specific examples of the problems
and riches of city life." Booklist
   Includes bibliographical references

307.76   Urban communities

Reilly, Kathleen M.
   Cities; Discover How They Work. by Kathleen
M. Reilly, illustrated by Tom Casteel. Pgw 2014 128
p. $16.95
Grades: 4 5 6   307.76
   1. Urban ecology 2. Cities and towns 3. City planning
   4. Civil engineering
   ISBN 1619302136; 1619302179; 9781619302136;
   9781619302174
   This book, by Kathleen M. Reilly and illustrated by Tom
Casteel, "will give kids a view into the inner functioning of
. . . urban areas. They'll learn about all the parts that come
together to make cities work and how they've grown and
changed since the very first riverside settlements. . . . Sidebars, unique illustrations, . . . and fun . . . facts combine with
age-appropriate hands-on activities to make learning about
complex urban environments fun and reinforce learning."
(Publisher's note)
   "According to the 2010 Census, 80% of Americans live
in urban areas." But do they know what it takes to make a
city run? From this well-organized and engaging text, readers will learn how cities developed and grew...The simple
black-and-white illustrations are helpful, but young readers
accustomed to photos might pass on it when leafing through
the book. Even so, this is a worthy title for any library
collection." SLJ

Spilsbury, Richard
   Towns and cities; by Richard Spilsbury. Heinemann Library 2012 64 p. (The impact of environmentalism) (library) $35.00; (paperback) $9.99
Grades: 6 7 8   307.76
   1. Environmental protection 2. City planning 3. Cities
   and towns 5. Urban ecology (Sociology)
   ISBN 1432965190; 9781432965198; 9781432965259
                                      LC 2012001039
   This book by Richard Spilsbury is part of the Impact
of Environmentalism series and looks at cities and towns.
The series provides "a global overview of environmentalism
from different, often overlapping, perspectives." This entry
"supplies insights into sustainable urbanization, including
information about solar-energy efforts in cities worldwide."
(School Library Journal)
   Includes bibliographical references and index.

320   Political science (Politics and government)

Anderson, Jodi Lynn
   ★ **Americapedia**; taking the dumb out of freedom. [by] Jodi Anderson, Daniel Ehrenhaft, Andisheh Nouraee. Walker Books for Young Readers
2011 240p il $24.99; pa $16.99
Grades: 7 8 9 10   320
   1. Citizenship 2. World politics 3. United States --
   Politics and government
   ISBN 978-0-8027-9792-6; 0-8027-9792-X; 978-0-
   8027-9793-3 pa; 0-8027-9792-X pa
                                      LC 2010-38028
   "This examination of the state of the union uses edgy
humor to discuss pertinent matters in the worlds of politics,
international relations, religion, and culture. Bullet points,
footnotes, sidebars, and tongue-in-cheek graphics . . . lighten
heady topics like nuclear proliferation and the Israel-Pales-
tine conflict. Despite the irreverent tone . . . discussions of
such topics as the stem cell debate, global warming, and ger-
rymandering remind readers of the seriousness behind the
issues." Publ Wkly
   Includes bibliographical references

Bukovac, Matthew
   Failed states; unstable countries in the 21st century. Rosen Pub. 2011 64p il map (In the news) lib
bdg $29.95; pa $12.95
Grades: 7 8 9 10   320
   1. Financial crises
   ISBN 978-1-4358-9447-1 lib bdg; 1-4358-9447-2 lib
   bdg; 978-1-4488-1679-8 pa; 1-4488-1679-3 pa
                                      LC 2009045686
   This book "tackles in simple terms what exactly constitute a failed state and how a country lands in such a predicament. Further chapters cover countries presently in the
media, including Iraq, Somalia, and Pakistan, among others. . . . With numerous photos, concise and manageable
chapters, and a glossary, . . . [this book provides] an excellent background for students with an interest in social sciences or a jumping off point for school assignments." Voice
Youth Advocates
   Includes glossary and bibliographical references

320.01   Philosophy and theory

The **politics** book; Big ideas simply explained. edited by Rebecca Warren and Kate Johnsen ; illustrated by James Graham. 1st American ed. DK
   Pub. 2013 352 p. ill. (some col.) (Big ideas
   simply explained) (hardcover) $25.00
Grades: 8 9 10 11 12 Adult   320.01
   1. Political philosophy
   ISBN 1465402144; 9781465402141
                                      LC 2012533724
   This book, part of the Big Ideas Simply Explained series, looks at political philosophy. "More than 100 political
philosophers, among them Confucius, Plato, Machiavelli,
Mary Wollstonecraft, Karl Marx, Ito Hirobumi, Emiliano
Zapata, Jomo Kenyatta, and Mao Zedong, are covered in

seven chronological sections ranging from 'Ancient Political Thought' to 'Postwar Politics.'" (Library Journal)

320.4 Structure and functions of government

Han, Lori Cox

Handbook to American democracy; Lori Cox Han and Tomislav Han. Facts On File 2011 224 p.
Grades: 8 9 10 11 12 Adult   **320.4**
1. United States -- History 2. Democracy -- United States -- History 3. United States -- Politics and government 4. United States -- Politics and government -- Handbooks, manuals, etc
ISBN 0816078548; 9780816078547

LC 2011005185

The authors "address the foundations of American democracy and the three branches of American government. The books introduce offices, history, and issues in eight chapters each (e.g., 'The Founding Fathers and the American Revolution,' 'How Congress Is Organized,' and 'Vice Presidents, Presidential Advisers, and America's First Ladies'). The material is complemented by black-and-white photos and sidebars on legal cases, laws and legislation, statistics, maps, biographies of major figures such as Henry VIII, and other primary materials, and chapters close with a summary. . . . [The volumes] each include an individual glossary, index, selected bibliography, and table of contents." (Libr J)

Includes bibliographical references and index

321 Systems of governments and states

Davidson, Tish

★ **Theocracy**; Tish Davidson. Mason Crest 2013 64 p. col. ill. (Major forms of world government) (library) $22.95; (ebook) $28.95
Grades: 6 7 8 9 10   **321**
1. Theocracy 2. Political science
ISBN 1422221431; 9781422221433; 9781422294604

LC 2012027863

This book, by Tish Davidson, as part of the publisher's "Major Forms of World Government" series, "examines theocratic governments, from ancient Egypt to present-day Iran. It explores how different theocracies arose, how their leaders maintained authority, and what it was like for ordinary people living under religious rule." (Publisher's note)

Includes bibliographical references and index.

Perl, Lila

Theocracy. Marshall Cavendish Benchmark 2007 158p il (Political systems of the world) lib bdg $27.95
Grades: 7 8 9 10 11 12   **321**
1. Theocracy
ISBN 978-0-7614-2631-8

LC 2006-26055

"Gives an overview of theocracy as a political system, including and historical discussion of theocratic regimes throughout the world." Publisher's note

Includes bibliographical references

321.8 Democratic government

Laxer, James

Democracy. Groundwood Books 2009 143p (Groundwork guides) $18.95; pa $10
Grades: 8 9 10 11 12   **321.8**
1. Democracy
ISBN 978-0-88899-912-2; 0-88899-912-7; 978-0-88899-913-9 pa; 0-88899-913-5 pa

This title "stands out for its accessible introduction to historical and contemporary democracy across the globe. Laxer skillfully supports his arguments with examples and avoids pat definitions." Booklist

Includes bibliographical references

322.4 Political action groups

Bartoletti, Susan Campbell

★ **They** called themselves the K.K.K. the birth of an American terrorist group. Houghton Mifflin 2010 172p il map $19
Grades: 7 8 9 10   **322.4**
1. Racism 2. Ku Klux Klan 3. White supremacy movements 4. Reconstruction (1865-1876) 5. United States -- Race relations
ISBN 0-618-44033-X; 978-0-618-44033-7

LC 2009-45247

This is a history of the Ku Klux Klan. Bibliography. Index. "Middle school, high school." (Horn Book)

"In this comprehensive, accessible account, . . . [the author] draws from documentary histories, slave narratives, newspapers, congressional testimony, and other sources to chronicle the origins and proliferation of the Ku Klux Klan against the charged backdrop of Reconstruction politics and legislation. . . . The author lives up to her introductory promise to avoid censoring racist language and images, and includes some horrifying descriptions of lynchings and murders perpetuated during KKK raids. . . . Her account of attending a Klan meeting while researching the book is chilling to the core." Publ Wkly

Includes bibliographical references

323 Civil and political rights

Bausum, Ann

★ **Marching** to the mountaintop; how poverty, labor fights, and civil rights set the stage for Martin Luther King, Jr.'s final hours. by Ann Bausum. National Geographic 2012 104 p.
Grades: 7 8 9 10   **323**
1. Memphis (Tenn.) -- History 2. African Americans -- Civil rights 3. Strikes -- United States -- History 4. African Americans -- Economic conditions 5. Sanitation Workers Strike, Memphis, Tenn., 1968 6. Memphis (Tenn.) -- Race relations -- History -- 20th century 7. Labor movement -- Tennessee -- Memphis -- History --

20th century
ISBN 1426309392; 1426309406; 9781426309397;
9781426309403

LC 2011024661

"In this . . . [book about] the 1968 Memphis Sanitation Workers Strike, [author Ann] Bausum . . . handles both the labor action itself--born of institutionalized racial injustice within the public works system and the tragic deaths of two African-American workers in a faulty compactor--and what would be the final civil rights action of Dr. King's storied career. . . . She . . . [covers] the African-American workers who accepted . . . dangerous sanitation jobs, and . . . the ploys to cut back their already minimal pay. . . . [T]he focus shifts to follow Kings involvement, as he hoped the national focus on labor injustice would draw attention to his broader plans for an attack on poverty itself as the next great civil rights issue." (Bulletin of the Center for Children's Books)

Includes bibliographical references (p. 100-102) and index

Civil liberties; Lauri S. Friedman, book editor. Greenhaven Press 2010 144p il map (Introducing issues with opposing viewpoints) lib bdg $34.70

Grades: 7 8 9 10 11 12　　　　　　　　**323**

1. Terrorism 2. Civil rights 3. National security
ISBN 978-0-7377-4732-4; 0-7377-4732-3

LC 2009-51887

This book "of pro/con essays . . . [is] intended to stimulate discussion of critical social issues and to open readers' minds to divergent opinions. Civil Liberties includes discussions of the Patriot Act, the rights of Muslims and Arab Americans, and racial profiling. . . . Active-reading questions preface the essays, which are followed by directions for evaluating the arguments presented. Color photos and other graphics throughout enliven the reading experience." SLJ

Includes bibliographical references

National Geographic Society (U.S.)

★ **Every** human has rights; a photographic declaration for kids. based on the United Nations Universal Declaration of Human Rights; with poetry from the ePals community; foreword by Mary Robinson. National Geographic 2009 30p il $26.90

Grades: 4 5 6 7 8　　　　　　　　**323**

1. Human rights
ISBN 978-1-4263-0511-5; 1-4263-0511-7

"On the sixtieth anniversary of the Universal Declaration of Human Rights, this full-color photo-essay combines prize-winning poems by young people with beautiful photographs from all over the world. . . . The stirring pictures will stimulate classroom discussion about the declaration, which is quoted in full at the back." Booklist

Stewart, Gail

Human rights in the Middle East; by Gail B. Stewart. Lucent Books 2004 112p il map (Lucent library of conflict in the Middle East) $28.70

Grades: 6 7 8 9　　　　　　　　**323**

1. Human rights 2. Middle East
ISBN 1-59018-488-2

LC 2004-10836

This discusses such human rights issues in the Middle East as the forced labor of children, discrimination against women and ethnic minorities, torture and executions, and censorship.

Includes bibliographical references

323.1　Civil and political rights of nondominant groups

Archer, Jules

★ **They** had a dream; the civil rights struggle from Frederick Douglass to Marcus Garvey to Martin Luther King and Malcolm X. Viking 1993 258p il (Epoch biographies) hardcover o.p. pa $7.99

Grades: 6 7 8 9　　　　　　　　**323.1**

1. Clergy 2. Slaves 3. Authors 4. Abolitionists 5. Memoirists 6. Nonfiction writers 7. Writers on politics 8. Black Muslim leaders 9. Civil rights activists 10. Nobel laureates for peace 11. African Americans -- Biography 12. African Americans -- Civil rights
ISBN 0-14-034954-5 pa

LC 92-40071

Traces the progression of the civil rights movement and its effect on history through biographical sketches of four prominent and influential African Americans: Frederick Douglass, Marcus Garvey, Martin Luther King, Jr., and Malcolm X

"This discussion of the contributions of four pivotal civil rights activists is balanced and substantive." Publ Wkly

Includes bibliographical references

Aretha, David

Freedom Summer. Morgan Reynolds Pub. 2007 128p (The civil rights movement) lib bdg $27.95

Grades: 7 8 9 10 11 12　　　　　　　　**323.1**

1. Mississippi Freedom Project 2. Mississippi -- Race relations 3. African Americans -- Civil rights
ISBN 978-1-59935-059-2; 1-59935-059-9

LC 2007-23815

This "discusses the collaborative strategies black and white Americans . . . devised to dismantle the restrictive, often violent measures used in the South to prevent most African Americans from voting. . . . [This title is] visually appealing with generous white space around the [text]. Throughout, mostly black-and-white historical photos . . . enhance the [narrative]. Also adding impact are numerous dramatic accounts by participants in the struggle." SLJ

Includes bibliographical references

Montgomery bus boycott. Morgan Reynolds Pub. 2009 128p il (The civil rights movement) $28.95

Grades: 7 8 9 10　　　　　　　　**323.1**

1. African Americans -- Civil rights 2. Montgomery (Ala.) -- Race relations
ISBN 978-1-59935-020-2; 1-59935-020-3

LC 2008-18679

"The wrenching consequences of Rosa Parks's decision that sparked the Civil Rights Movement are depicted in this well-written book. Descriptions of civil rights activism dating back to 1865 . . . provide historical context and a sense of the fervor surrounding discrimination and segregation. The facts of the boycott are documented with supportive news articles, relevant quotations, moving individual stories, and significant court cases. . . . [Photographs] depict significant figures and document incidents such as meetings and carpooling to avoid buses." SLJ

Includes bibliographical references

Sit -ins and freedom rides. Morgan Reynolds Pub. 2009 128p il lib bdg $28.95

Grades: 5 6 7 8　　　　　　　　　　　　**323.1**

1. African Americans -- Civil rights 2. Southern States -- Race relations

ISBN 978-1-59935-098-1 lib bdg; 1-59935-098-X lib bdg

LC 2008039600

"Aretha opens with an introduction to the four college students who orchestrated the famous sit-in at Woolworth's in Greensboro, NC, in 1960. He follows that with chapters that describe slavery, Reconstruction, and Jim Crow in terms of how they set the stage for the resistance efforts. . . , [The book] offers insight into to workings of the protests at the grassroots level. Individual anecdotes interspersed thoughout the detailed narrative provide personal and effective accounts that go beyond mere facts. Black-and-white and some color photographs appear on almost every page." SLJ

Includes bibliographical references

Bausum, Ann

★ **Freedom** Riders; John Lewis and Jim Zwerg on the front lines of the civil rights movement. by Ann Bausum; forewords by Freedom Riders Congressman John Lewis and Jim Zwerg. National Geographic 2006 79p il por $18.95; lib bdg $28.90

Grades: 5 6 7 8　　　　　　　　　　　　**323.1**

1. Members of Congress 2. Civil rights activists 3. African Americans -- Civil rights 4. Southern States -- Race relations

ISBN 0-7922-4173-8; 0-7922-4174-6 lib bdg

LC 2005012947

"Bausum's narrative style, fresh, engrossing, and at times heart-stopping, brings the story of the turbulent and often violent dismantling of segregated travel alive in vivid detail. The language, presentation of material, and pacing will draw readers in and keep them captivated." SLJ

Includes bibliographical references

Bowers, Rick

★ The **spies** of Mississippi; the true story of the spy network that tried to destroy the Civil Rights Movement. National Geographic 2010 120p il $16.95; lib bdg $26.90

Grades: 7 8 9 10　　　　　　　　　　　　**323.1**

1. Mississippi -- Race relations 2. African Americans -- Civil rights 3. Mississippi State Sovereignty Commission

ISBN 978-1-4263-0595-5; 1-4263-0595-8; 978-1-4263-0596-2 lib bdg; 1-4263-0596-6 lib bdg

LC 2009-18944

"Bowers draws upon archival material, supplemented with his own extensive research, to document the activities

of the Mississippi State Sovereignty Commission, a Civil Rights-era state agency that disseminated segregationist propaganda and used Soviet-style methods to spy upon, harass, and harm those who challenged white supremacy. . . . This book's unique perspective will help students understand the previously unknown history of the despicable actions of Mississippi leaders who opposed civil rights and the silent citizens who supported their activities." SLJ

Includes bibliographical references

Brimner, Larry Dane, 1949-

Birmingham Sunday. Calkins Creek 2010 48p il

Grades: 5 6 7 8　　　　　　　　　　　　**323.1**

1. Bombings 2. Hate crimes 3. Racism 4. African Americans -- Civil rights 5. Birmingham (Ala.) -- Race relations 6. Sixteenth Street Baptist Church (Birmingham, Ala.)

ISBN 1590786130; 9781590786130

LC 2009035716

This book describes the bombing of the Sixteenth Street Church in 1963 by Ku Klux Klan members, which killed four girls, and discusses how the event contributed to the civil rights movement. "Grades five to eight." (Bull Cent Child Books)

"This moving photo-essay covers much more than just an account of the Birmingham, Alabama, Baptist Church bombing that killed four young girls in 1963. The detailed text, illustrated with black-and-white photos on every spacious double-page spread, sets the shocking assassination of the children within a general overview of both the racist segregation of the times and the struggle against it." Booklist

★ **Black** & white; the confrontation of Reverend Fred L. Shuttlesworth and Eugene Bull O'Connor. Calkins Creek 2011 109p il

Grades: 7 8 9 10 11 12　　　　　　　　　　　　**323.1**

1. Clergy 2. Police officials 3. Civil rights activists 4. Organization officials 5. African Americans -- Civil rights 6. Birmingham (Ala.) -- Race relations

ISBN 1-59078-766-8; 978-1-59078-766-3

"Reverend Fred L. Shuttlesworth led the civil rights struggle for equality in Birmingham, Alabama. . . . Eugene 'Bull' Connor, backed by the Ku Klux Klan, became a symbol of racist hatred and violence against Shuttlesworth. With a spacious design that includes archival pictures and primary-source documents on almost every page, this accessible photo-essay recounts the events in three sections, which focus first on the preacher, then on the commisioner, and finally, on their confrontation. . . . Never simplistic in his depictions, Brimner shows the viewpoints from all sides. . . . A penetrating look at elemental national history." Booklist

Includes bibliographical references

Bullard, Sara

Free at last; a history of the Civil Rights Movement and those who died in the struggle. introduction by Julian Bond. Oxford Univ. Press 1993 112p il map $28; pa $12.95

Grades: 8 9 10 11　　　　　　　　　　　　**323.1**

1. United States -- Race relations 2. African Americans

-- Civil rights
ISBN 0-19-508381-4; 0-19-509450-6 pa

             LC 92-38174

An illustrated history of the civil rights movement, including a timeline and profiles of forty people who gave their lives in the movement

Includes bibliographical references

Civil rights; Jill Karson, book editor. Greenhaven Press 2003 238p il map (Great speeches in history series) lib bdg $33.70; pa $22.45

Grades: 7 8 9 10   **323.1**
1. Speeches 2. United States -- Race relations 3. African Americans -- Civil rights
ISBN 0-7377-1593-6 lib bdg; 0-7377-1594-4 pa

             LC 2002-32209

"A collection of the speeches of well-known individuals who participated in or supported the American Civil Rights Movement from early pioneers through the 1960s up until today. Selections from Frederick Douglass, Malcolm X, Fannie Lou Hamer, Jesse Jackson, and Nelson Mandela emphasize the power of oratory to inform, persuade, and make an impact." SLJ

Includes bibliographical references

Cooper, John
     Season of rage; Hugh Burnett and the struggle for civil rights. [by] John Cooper. Tundra Books 2005 71p il pa $9.95

Grades: 7 8 9 10   **323.1**
1. Race discrimination 2. Carpenters 3. Civil rights activists 4. Canada -- Race relations
ISBN 0-88776-700-1

"Cooper has chosen the small town of Dresden, Ontario, to paint a picture of what life was like for black Canadians in the middle of the last century. One Sunday in the early 1930s, when 12-year-old Hugh Burnett and his younger brother had a hankering for ice cream, they entered a restaurant. The boys were told that they would have to eat in the kitchen. . . . The event in the restaurant sparked a lifelong crusade for Burnett, who spearheaded the formation of the National Unity Association. . . . A number of archival photos enhance the text. . . . An eye-opening story." SLJ

Des Chenes, Betz
     American civil rights: primary sources; [compiled by] Phillis Engelbert; edited by Betz Des Chenes. U.X.L 1999 xl, 200p il $58

Grades: 8 9 10 11 12   **323.1**
1. Civil rights
ISBN 0-7876-3170-1

             LC 99-27167

Presents fifteen documents, including speeches, autobiographical texts, and proclamations, related to the civil rights movement and arranged by category under economic rights, desegregation, and human rights

"The uniqueness of this set lies in the range of people covered. Students will find it an excellent resource for reports and interesting reading." Booklist

Includes bibliographical references

Freedman, Russell
     ★ **Freedom** walkers; the story of the Montgomery bus boycott. Holiday House 2006 114p il $18.95

Grades: 4 5 6 7   **323.1**
1. Clergy 2. Historians 3. College teachers 4. Nonfiction writers 5. Civil rights activists 6. Nobel laureates for peace 7. African Americans -- Civil rights 8. Montgomery (Ala.) -- Race relations
ISBN 978-0-8234-2031-5; 0-8234-2031-0

             LC 2006-41148

This account of the Montgomery bus boycott of 1955 focuses on Jo Ann Robinson, Claudette Colvin, Rosa Parks, Martin Luther King, and other participants.

This offers "expertly paced text, balanced but impassioned. . . . The narrative arc is compelling; well-captioned black-and-white photographs enhance the impact." Horn Book

Includes bibliographical references

Hynson, Colin
     The **civil** rights movement. Arcturus 2010 48p il (Timelines) lib bdg $34.25

Grades: 5 6 7 8   **323.1**
1. United States -- Race relations 2. African Americans -- Civil rights
ISBN 978-1-84837-638-0 lib bdg; 1-84837-638-3 lib bdg

             LC 2009051261

"This title offers a succinct overview of the civil rights movement in the U.S., beginning with the country's first-ever Civil Rights Act, signed by Congress in 1866. The picture-book-sized format is dynamic: each neatly laid-out spread combines short, informative paragraphs with a time line of landmark dates; well-chosen boxed quotes and archival images; and cross-referenced notes that link to related spreads and help students synthesize the events into a bigger historical picture." Booklist

Includes glossary and bibliographical references

Johnson, Troy R.
     Red power; the Native American civil rights movement. [by] Troy R. Johnson. Chelsea House 2007 112p il (Landmark events in Native American history) lib bdg $35

Grades: 7 8 9 10   **323.1**
1. United States -- Race relations 2. Native Americans -- Civil rights
ISBN 978-0-7910-9341-2 lib bdg; 0-7910-9341-7 lib bdg

             LC 2006102264

This "describes and defines what has come to be known as the American Indian Movement. . . . Early resistance . . . is summarized briefly and includes a chapter on the massacre at Wounded Knee Creek in 1890. The remaining six chapters focus on pivotal events such as the murders at Pine Ridge Reservation, the occupations of Alcatraz in 1969 and Wounded Knee in 1973, and the subsequent changes in government policy toward Native self-governance. . . . [This book is an excellent [tool] for first-time researchers and history buffs alike." SLJ

Includes bibliographical references

Kallen, Stuart A.

Women of the civil rights movement; [by] Stuart A. Kallen. Lucent Books 2005 112p il map (Women in history) $28.70

Grades: 7 8 9 10 **323.1**
1. Women -- Biography 2. African Americans -- Civil rights
ISBN 1-59018-569-2

LC 2004023822

"Kallen spotlights the unsung women who played a significant role in the Civil Rights movement. Short chapters are divided into various aspects of the struggle, including organizations, protests, education, voting rights, political office, radicals, and creative expression. Upclose black-and-white photographs and vignettes highlight key people." SLJ

Includes bibliographical references

Kasher, Steven

The **civil** rights movement: a photographic history, 1954-68; [by] Steven Kasher; foreword by Myrlie Evers-Williams. Abbeville Press 1996 255p il $45; pa $29.95

Grades: 8 9 10 11 12 Adult **323.1**
1. African Americans -- Civil rights
ISBN 0-7892-0123-2; 0-7892-0656-0 pa

LC 96-4337

"This book contains images by more than 50 photographers, whose images were borrowed from photo agencies, galleries, and private collections. Ten accompanying essays break the Civil Rights movement into chronological periods. Kasher's research, writing, and photo selection are impeccable and engaging." Libr J

Includes bibliographical references

King, Martin Luther

The **words** of Martin Luther King, Jr. selected by Coretta Scott King. Newmarket Press 1983 112p il $15.95; pa $11.95

Grades: 8 9 10 11 12 Adult **323.1**
1. United States -- Race relations 2. African Americans -- Civil rights
ISBN 0-937858-28-5; 1-55704-483-X pa

LC 83-17306

This "volume of selections from Dr. King's speeches and writings . . . focuses on seven areas of his concerns: 'The Community of Man, Racism, Civil Rights, Justice and Freedom, Faith and Religion, Nonviolence, and Peace'" Publisher's note

Includes bibliographical references

Levinson, Cynthia Y.

We've got a job; the 1963 Birmingham Children's March. written by Cynthia Levinson. Peachtree Publishers 2012 176 p.

Grades: 6 7 8 9 **323.1**
1. Political activists 2. African American youth 3. African Americans -- Civil rights 4. Birmingham (Ala.) -- Race relations 5. Civil rights demonstrations -- Alabama 6. African American youth -- Alabama --

Birmingham -- History -- 20th century
ISBN 9781561456277

LC 2011031738

YALSA Award for Excellence in Nonfiction for Young Adults Finalist (2013)

In this book, "[c]overing the history of the Birmingham Children's March from inception to full impact, [author Cynthia Y.] Levinson traces the stories of four young people between the ages of 9 and 15 in 1963. Audrey Hendricks, Washington Booker III, Arnetta Streeter, and James Stewart came from very different segments of the city's black community, but all risked their lives and spent time in jail to fight for their freedom." (School Library Journal)

Living through the Civil Rights Movement; Charles George, book editor. Greenhaven Press 2007 117p il (Living through the Cold War) lib bdg $32.35

Grades: 7 8 9 10 **323.1**
1. United States -- Race relations 2. African Americans -- Civil rights
ISBN 978-0-7377-2919-1 lib bdg; 0-7377-2919-8 lib bdg

LC 2006017184

"This title does an excellent job of chronicling the movement by using primary-source documents. Excerpts from speeches by government officials, such as Lyndon Baines Johnson, George Wallace, and John F. Kennedy, appear as well as speeches or statements from Malcolm X, Martin Luther King, Jr., and Stokely Carmichael." SLJ

Includes bibliographical references

Malaspina, Ann

The **ethnic** and group identity movements; earning recognition. Chelsea House 2007 176p il map (Reform movements in American history) lib bdg $30

Grades: 6 7 8 9 10 **323.1**
1. Minorities 2. Civil rights 3. Multiculturalism 4. Social movements 5. United States -- Ethnic relations
ISBN 978-0-7910-9571-3; 0-7910-9571-1

LC 2007-21721

"Malaspina explains how leaders within the Asian, disability, Chicano, senior, gay, American Indian, and Muslim communities drew on models of the successful civil and women's rights movements to build group identity and improve the political and social treatment of their members. . . . Illustrations include black-and-white and color photos and period art." SLJ

Includes bibliographical references

Mayer, Robert H.

★ **When** the children marched; the Birmingham civil rights movement. Enslow Publishers 2008 176p il map (Prime) $34.60

Grades: 7 8 9 10 **323.1**
1. African American children 2. African Americans -- Civil rights 3. Birmingham (Ala.) -- Race relations
ISBN 978-0-7660-2930-9; 0-7660-2930-1

LC 2007-25590

"Children played a significant role in Birmingham's crucial civil rights struggle, and this stirring history of the movement, with many photos, news reports, and quotes from all sides, emphasizes the connections between the young people's power and that of the big leaders. . . . From the cover picture of police escorting African American children to jail, the numerous photos of youth in nonviolent confrontation—marching, attacked by dogs and fire hoses, crammed in prisons—will draw readers with their gripping drama." Booklist

Includes glossary and bibliographical references

McWhorter, Diane

A **dream** of freedom; the Civil Rights Movement from 1954 to 1968. foreword by Reverend Fred Shuttlesworth. Scholastic Nonfiction 2004 160p il $19.95

Grades: 5 6 7 8   **323.1**
1. United States -- Race relations 2. African Americans -- Civil rights
ISBN 0-439-57678-4

The author discusses "the national civil rights movement from Brown v. the Board of Education to the assassination of Martin Luther King Jr. . . . This account is both factual and personal. She discusses her feelings as a white child in the South, and she focuses in on the many ways in which both white and black children were involved in the movement. . . . The breadth and depth of McWhorter's book is exemplary." Booklist

Mitchell, Don

The **Freedom** Summer Murders; Don Mitchell. Scholastic 2014 256 p. $18.99

Grades: 7 8 9 10   **323.1**
1. Homicide 2. African Americans -- Civil rights 3. Mississippi Freedom Project 4. Civil rights workers -- Mississippi -- Biography 5. Mississippi -- Race relations -- History -- 20th century 6. Murder -- Mississippi -- Neshoba County -- History -- 20th century
ISBN 0545477255; 9780545477253

This young adult book by Don Mitchell tells how "In June of 1964, three idealistic young men . . . were lynched by the Ku Klux Klan in Mississippi. They were trying to register African Americans to vote as part of the Freedom Summer effort to bring democracy to the South. Their disappearance and murder caused a national uproar and was one of the most significant incidents of the Civil Rights Movement, and contributed to the passage of the Civil Rights Act of 1964." (Publisher's note)

"The murders of three young civil rights workers--James Chaney, Andrew Goodman, and Michael Schwerner--are the focus of Mitchell's absorbing book. He conducted interviews with friends and family members of the men, and provides a fascinating biographical sketch of each, along with a thorough account of the police investigation. This compelling book will grab you from its opening paragraphs and won't let go. Bib., ind." Horn Book

Nardo, Don

Birmingham 1963; how a photograph rallied Civil Rights support. Compass Point 2011 64p il (Captured history) lib bdg $33.99

Grades: 6 7 8 9   **323.1**
1. Documentary photography 2. Photojournalists 3.

African Americans -- Civil rights 4. Birmingham (Ala.) -- Race relations
ISBN 978-0-7565-4398-3; 0-7565-4398-3

This book about Charles Moore's 1963 photograph of young African American civil rights protesters being blasted with a fire hose places the photo "in historical context, profiles the photographer, describes the conditions under which it was taken, and analyzes both its immediate and its continuing impact. The [text includes] ample background information and details and [is] enhanced by large photos and sidebars." SLJ

Includes glossary and bibliographical references

Partridge, Elizabeth

★ **Marching** for freedom; walk together, children, and don't you grow weary. Viking 2009 72p il $19.99

Grades: 6 7 8 9 10 11 12   **323.1**
1. Selma (Ala.) -- Race relations 2. African Americans -- Civil rights 3. Civil rights movements 4. African American children
ISBN 978-0-670-01189-6; 0-670-01189-4
LC 2009-9696

Boston Globe-Horn Book Award: Nonfiction (2010)

An examination of the march from Selma to Montgomery in 1965 led by Dr. Martin Luther King, Jr., this book focuses on the children who faced terrifying violence in order to walk alongside him in their fight for freedom and the right to vote.

This is a "stirring photo-essay. . . . The vivid text is filled with quotes collected from Partridge's personal interviews with adults who remember their youthful experiences. . . . Filled with large black-and-white photos, every spread brings readers up close to the dramatic, often violent action." Booklist

Includes bibliographical references

Turck, Mary

★ **Freedom** song; young voices and the struggle for civil rights. [by] Mary C. Turck. Chicago Review Press 2009 146p il pa $18.95

Grades: 7 8 9 10   **323.1**
1. African American music 2. Chicago Children's Choir 3. Freedom Singers (Musical group) 4. African Americans -- Civil rights
ISBN 978-1-55652-773-9; 1-55652-773-X
LC 2008-29673

"The book is divided into chapters that represent the history of the Civil Rights Movement. 'Sunday of Song,' 'Singing in the Churches,' and 'South Africa,' for example, contain information about the factual events while including how the evolution of the music captured the mood and sentiment of the time. The importance of music in the lives of African Americans is described in depth. . . . The accompanying CD allows students to internalize the words and their emotional impact as they listen. Overall, this informative and well-written book is an excellent addition to any collection." SLJ

Includes bibliographical references

Walsh, Frank

The **Montgomery** bus boycott. World Almanac Library 2003 48p il map (Landmark events in American history) lib bdg $26.60; pa $11.95

Grades: 5 6 7 8 **323.1**

1. African Americans -- Civil rights 2. Montgomery (Ala.) -- Race relations

ISBN 0-8368-5375-X lib bdg; 0-8368-5403-9 pa

LC 2002-36020

Describes how the black community of Montgomery, Alabama, staged the 1955 boycott to end segregation on public buses and discusses that struggle in the context of the Civil Rights Movement

"Brief but informative. . . . [The book is] heavily illustrated with well-chosen and carefully placed archival photographs and . . . reproductions of historical documents." SLJ

Includes glossary and bibliographical references

Wexler, Sanford

The **civil** rights movement; an eyewitness history. introduction by Julian Bond. Facts on File 1993 356p il maps (Eyewitness history series) $75

Grades: 7 8 9 10 **323.1**

1. United States -- Race relations 2. African Americans -- Civil rights

ISBN 0-8160-2748-X

LC 92-28674

Uses speeches, articles, and other writings of those involved to trace the history of the civil rights movement in the United States, primarily from 1954 to 1965

"This very readable source deserves a place in every public and middle and high school library, though it may fit better in the circulating collection." Booklist

Includes bibliographical references

Williams, Juan

Eyes on the prize: America's civil rights years, 1954-1965; [by] Juan Williams with the Eyes on the prize production team; introduction by Julian Bond. Viking 1987 300p il hardcover o.p. pa $20

Grades: 7 8 9 10 **323.1**

1. United States -- Race relations 2. African Americans -- Civil rights

ISBN 0-670-81412-1; 0-14-009653-1 pa

LC 86-40271

"Highly recommended both as a socio-historical document and as a heartfelt, poignant remembrance of a movement and its activists." Booklist

Includes bibliographical references

Williams, Mary E.

Civil rights; edited by Mary E. Williams. Greenhaven Press 2002 94p il (Examining issues through political cartoons) lib bdg $24.95; pa $16.20

Grades: 7 8 9 10 **323.1**

1. Affirmative action programs 2. African Americans -- Civil rights -- Cartoons and caricatures

ISBN 0-7377-1100-0 lib bdg; 0-7377-1099-3 pa

LC 2001-55743

The author provides "readers with an overview of African Americans' struggle for those rights enjoyed by other

citizens and of the historical role of the political cartoon. . . . Four chapters ('The Struggle for Justice,' 'Has the Civil Rights Movement Benefited Minorities?' 'How Has Affirmative Action Affected Civil Rights?' and 'What Is the Legacy of the Civil Rights Movement?') examine three to six cartoons each. All are reproduced in the book, and information about the artist is provided." SLJ

Includes bibliographical references (p. 89-91) and index

323.11 Ethnic and national groups

Freedman, Russell, 1929-

★ **Because** they marched; the people's campaign for voting rights that changed America. Russell Freedman. Holiday House 2014 83 p. (hardcover) $20

Grades: 6 7 8 9 10 **323.11**

1. Selma (Ala.) 2. African Americans -- Civil rights 3. Civil rights demonstrations -- Alabama 4. Selma (Ala.) -- Race relations 5. Civil rights movements -- Alabama -- Selma -- History -- 20th century 6. African Americans -- Suffrage -- Alabama -- Selma -- History -- 20th century 7. African Americans -- Civil rights -- Alabama -- Selma -- History -- 20th century

ISBN 0823429210; 9780823429219

LC 2013038991

This book, by Russell Freedman, celebrates "the 50th anniversary of the 1965 march for voting rights from Selma to Montgomery, Alabama. . . . [The author] has written a riveting account of this pivotal event in the history of civil rights. . . . In the early 1960s, tensions in the segregated South intensified. Tired of reprisals for attempting to register to vote, Selma's black community began to protest." (Publisher's note)

"With characteristically clear prose sprinkled liberally with primary source quotes and carefully selected photographs, Freedman documents the historic 1965 Selma-to-Montgomery march that sparked the passing of the Voting Rights Act, "the crowning achievement of the civil rights movement." Freedman's opening chapter is particularly effective because it focuses on the teachers' march to the courthouse to register as a major trigger for the movement."

Includes bibliographical references and index

Lowery, Lynda Blackmon

Turning 15 on the road to freedom; my story of the 1965 Selma to Montgomery March. by Lynda Blackmon Lowery ; as told to Elspeth Leacock and Susan Buckley. Dial Books, an imprint of Penguin Group (USA) LLC 2015 128 p. (hardcover) $19.99

Grades: 7 8 9 10 11 12 **323.11**

1. African Americans -- Civil rights 2. Selma (Ala.) -- Race relations 3. Civil rights movements -- Alabama -- Selma -- History -- 20th century 4. African Americans -- Suffrage -- Alabama -- Selma -- History -- 20th century

ISBN 0803741235; 9780803741232

LC 2013047316

This book, by Lynda Blackmon Lowery, is "a memoir of the Civil Rights Movement from one of its youngest heroes. As the youngest marcher in the 1965 voting rights march from Selma to Montgomery, Alabama, Lynda Blackmon Lowery proved that young adults can be heroes. Jailed eleven times before her fifteenth birthday, Lowery fought alongside Martin Luther King, Jr. for the rights of African-Americans." (Publisher's note)

"By the time I was fifteen years old, I had been in jail nine times." So opens Lowery's account of growing up in Selma, Alabama, during the troubled 1960s, as the African American community struggled for voting rights. At 13, Lynda and other students began slipping out of school to participate in marches...A concluding page comments that the Supreme Court recently struck down part of the Voting Rights Act, and notes that "who has the right to vote is still being decided today." This inspiring personal story illuminates pivotal events in America's history." Booklist

Turning fifteen on the road to freedom

Rubin, Susan Goldman

Freedom Summer; the 1964 Struggle for Civil Rights in Mississippi. by Susan Rubin. Holiday House 2014 120 p. illustrations (hardcover) $18.95
Grades: 5 6 7 8 9 10   **323.11**
1. African Americans -- Civil rights 2. Mississippi Freedom Project 3. African Americans -- Suffrage 4. Civil rights workers -- Mississippi 5. Civil rights movements -- Mississippi
ISBN 0823429202; 9780823429202
LC 2013020208
"Rubin has created a narrative retelling of the events and occurrences from the summer of 1964. Chock-full of primary sources, such as photographs, memos sent to applicants regarding the growing tensions in Mississippi, and pencil drawings depicting various settings from Neshoba County, Mississippi, Freedom Summer is organized in a time-line fashion, from June 1964 until late August 1964." (VOYA)

"This work gives a real sense of the time and place, the issues and the opposing sides, and the impact on the nation. Including myriad period photos and drawings, facsimiles of reports and records, meticulous source notes, an extensive bibliography, picture credits, and an extensive index, this title is the epitome of excellent historical reporting, with the human element never forgotten." SLJ

Includes bibliographical references and index

323.3   Civil and political rights of other social groups

Serres, Alain

I have the right to be a child; author, Alain Serres ; illustrator, Aurélia Fronty ; translator, Helen Mixter. Groundwood Books 2012 48 p.
Grades: 3 4 5 6 7   **323.3**
1. Treaties 2. Human rights 3. Children -- Civil rights
ISBN 1554981492; 9781554981496
In this children's book, "a young narrator describes what it means to be a child with rights -- from the right to food, water and shelter, to the right to go to school, to the right to be free from violence, to the right to breathe clean air, and much more. The book emphasizes that these rights belong to every child on the planet. . . . A brief afterword explains that the rights outlined in the book come from the Convention on the Rights of the Child." (Publisher's note)

323.44   Freedom of action (Liberty)

Carson, Brian

Understanding your right to freedom from searches; [by] Brian Carson and Catherine Ramen. Rosen Pub. 2011 160p il (Personal freedom & civic duty) lib bdg $33.25
Grades: 6 7 8 9   **323.44**
1. Searches and seizures
ISBN 978-1-44884-670-2; 1-44884-670-6
LC 2010044135
This "offers a balanced, engagingly lucid summary of the legal history behind the Fourth Amendment to the U.S. Constitution and the reasoning behind a number of subsequent Supreme Court rulings that have helped to define the amendment's ambiguous wording. . . . This survey will leave readers with both a greater understanding of how the amendment's interpretation has developed over time and an enhanced appreciation of the entire Constitution's vital significance in our lives." Booklist

Includes bibliographical references

Dougherty, Terri

Freedom of expression and the Internet. Lucent Books 2010 112p il map $33.45
Grades: 7 8 9 10   **323.44**
1. Copyright 2. Freedom of speech 3. Intellectual freedom 4. Internet -- Social aspects
ISBN 978-1-4205-0227-5; 1-4205-0227-1
LC 2010-1547
"This book explores the parameters of freedom of speech and the responsibility that accompanies it, explaining as well the difference between the presentation of fact and opinion. The remainder of the volume is devoted to child-protection policies, concerns about anonymity, copyright issues, trademark violations, 'School Speech and Cyberbullies,' and 'International Free Speech.' The text is well organized and clearly written, outlining the issues in such a way as to be understandable to teens. Color photos, sidebars, discussion questions, and a list of organization contacts are included. This is a good source for report writers." SLJ

Includes bibliographical references

Senker, Cath

Privacy and surveillance; Cath Senker. Rosen Central 2012 48 p. (Ethical debates)
Grades: 7 8 9 10   **323.44**
1. Right of privacy 2. Electronic surveillance 3. Privacy, Right of 4. Privacy, Right of -- Case studies 5. Electronic surveillance -- Case studies
ISBN 1448870119; 9781448860227; 9781448870110; 9781448870127
LC 2011028565
This book by Cath Senker, part of the Ethical Debates series, "[d]iscusses the controversies regarding privacy and surveillance, including the ethical aspects of electronic surveillance of citizens by the government, security of identity over the Internet, and students under surveillance at schools." (WorldCat)

Includes bibliographical references and index

323.6   Citizenship and related topics

Maury, Rob

    Citizenship; rights and responsibilities. Mason Crest Publishers 2009 64p il (Major American immigration) lib bdg $22.95; pa $9.95

Grades: 6 7 8 9   **323.6**

    1. Citizenship 2. United States -- Immigration and emigration

    ISBN 978-1-4222-0618-8 lib bdg; 1-4222-0618-1 lib bdg; 978-1-4222-0685-0 pa; 1-4222-0685-8 pa

                                    LC 2008-28223

    Presents the rights and responsibilities held by United States citizens, and describes the U.S. naturalization process.

    "The chapters are short and easy to read, the sidebars are informative, and the chronology is helpful." Voice of Youth Advocates

    Includes glossary and bibliographical references

Raatma, Lucia

    Citizenship; by Lucia Raatma. Children's Press 2012 64 p. ill. (chiefly col.), col. map (Cornerstones of freedom) (library) $30; (paperback) $8.95

Grades: 4 5 6   **323.6**

    1. Citizenship -- United States

    ISBN 0329917374; 0531230643; 0531281647; 9780329917371; 9780531230640; 9780531281642

                                    LC 2011031340

    This book on citizenship by Lucia Raatma "covers everything from basic facts about naturalization to debates over hot issues such as gun control." It is part of the "Cornerstones of Freedom" series for students in grades 4 to 6. Included are "a two-page map of 'What Happened Where?'; a two-page epilogue; glossary-style identifications of significant people; a page of primary sources; a bibliography of books; a glossary; and an index plus author bio." (Booklist)

    Includes bibliographical references (p. 61) and index.

324   The political process

Morris-Lipsman, Arlene

    Presidential races; campaigning for the White House. Rev. ed.; Twenty-First Century Books 2012 112p il (People's history) lib bdg $33.26

Grades: 6 7 8 9 10   **324**

    1. Presidents -- United States -- Election

    ISBN 978-0-7613-7395-7; 0-7613-7395-0

                                    LC 2011001304

    First published 2007

    Describes how election campaigns for the office of president of the United States have changed from the time of George Washington to the Obama vs. McCain campaign of 2008.

    Includes bibliographical references

324.6   Election systems and procedures; suffrage

Aretha, David

    Selma and the Voting Rights Act. Morgan Reynolds Pub. 2007 128p il (The civil rights movement) lib bdg $27.95

Grades: 7 8 9 10 11 12   **324.6**

    1. Voting Rights Act of 1965 2. African Americans -- Suffrage 3. Selma (Ala.) -- Race relations 4. African Americans -- Civil rights

    ISBN 978-1-59935-056-1; 1-59935-056-4

                                  LC 2007-24655

    The author discusses "mid-1960s Alabama and the black struggle to exercise the constitutional right to vote. Even those who know the story of the famous protest marches will be interested in the details here. . . . There are quotes from and photos of the famous as well as the unknown, as well as excerpts from speeches and news photos." Booklist

    Includes bibliographical references

Hollihan, Kerrie Logan

    Rightfully ours; how women won the vote : 21 activities. Kerrie Logan Hollihan. 1st ed. Chicago Review Press 2012 xiii, 130 p.p ill. (some col.) (paperback) $16.95

Grades: 4 5 6 7 8   **324.6**

    1. Women -- Suffrage 2. Women -- United States -- History 3. Suffragists -- United States -- History 4. Women's rights -- United States -- History 5. Women -- Suffrage -- United States -- History

    ISBN 1883052890; 9781883052898

                                  LC 2012006044

    This book is an "account of the struggle for women's suffrage. The first three chapters focus on notable activists Lucy Stone, Elizabeth Cady Stanton, and Susan B. Anthony. [Kerrie Logan] Hollihan recounts how this battle was inexorably tied to the antislavery movement and the role played by women of color in both movements, including Harriett Tubman, Sojourner Truth, and Ida Wells-Barnett." (School Library Journal)

    Includes bibliographical references (p. 121-124) and index

Marzilli, Alan

    Election reform; 2nd ed.; Chelsea House 2010 119p il map (Point-counterpoint) lib bdg $35

Grades: 7 8 9 10   **324.6**

    1. Politics 2. Elections -- United States 3. Campaign funds -- United States

    ISBN 978-1-60413-691-3; 1-60413-691-X

                                  LC 2009-51401

    First published 2004

    This book "examines ongoing debates over voting rights and election laws and asks how the United States might reach the ideal of 'one person, one vote.'" Publisher's note

    Includes bibliographical references

Monroe, Judy

    The **Susan** B. Anthony women's voting rights trial; a headline court case. Enslow Pubs. 2002 112p il (Headline court cases) lib bdg $26.60

Grades: 7 8 9 10   **324.6**
1. Suffragists 2. Abolitionists 3. Women -- Suffrage
ISBN 0-7660-1759-1

LC 2001-4528

Examines the efforts to gain the right for women in the United States to vote, focusing on the trial of Susan B. Anthony for illegally voting in the presidential election in 1872

"Simple syntax, insightful quotes, and logical organization make the information easily accessible." SLJ

Includes glossary and bibliographical references

Senker, Cath

Women claim the vote; the rise of the women's suffrage movement, 1828-1860. Chelsea House 2011 64p il (A cultural history of women in America) $35
Grades: 7 8 9 10   **324.6**
1. Feminism 2. Women -- Suffrage 3. Women -- United States -- History 4. United States -- Social conditions
ISBN 978-1-60413-930-3; 1-60413-930-7

LC 2010045960

This is a history of the women's suffrage movement in America from 1828-1860 .

This book offers a "comprehensive, vivid, and thought-provoking [look] at the struggles and triumphs of . . . the women who [participated] in shaping our nation. Through succinct, informative text, [this] heavily illustrated volume incorporates the history of three major groups of people: the Natives, European settlers, and African slaves. Featured quotes from books, articles, letters, and speeches bring the history to life." SLJ

Includes glossary and bibliographical references

---

325   International migration and colonization

Anderson, Dale

Arriving at Ellis Island. World Almanac Library 2002 48p il map (Landmark events in American history) lib bdg $26.60; pa $11.95
Grades: 5 6 7 8   **325**
1. Ellis Island Immigration Station 2. United States -- Immigration and emigration
ISBN 0-8368-5337-7 lib bdg; 0-8368-5351-2 pa

LC 2002-24627

Discusses immigration to the United States during the nineteenth and early twentieth centuries and describes the small island in New York harbor that served as the point of entry for millions of immigrants from 1892 to 1954

The "design is attractive, with drawings, maps, paintings, and photos; primary sources, such as excerpts from diaries, letters, and newspapers, support and enhance the [text]. . . . Informative, competently written." Booklist

Includes glossary and bibliographical references

Bausum, Ann

★ **Denied,** detained, deported; stories from the dark side of American immigration. National Geographic 2009 111p il $21.95; lib bdg $32.90
Grades: 6 7 8 9 10 11 12   **325**
1. Essayists 2. Anarchists 3. Memoirists 4. Writers on politics 5. Family planning advocates 6. Immigrants

-- United States 7. United States -- Immigration and emigration
ISBN 978-1-4263-0332-6; 1-4263-0332-7; 978-1-4263-0333-3 lib bdg; 1-4263-0333-5 lib bdg

"This volume deals frankly with the more troubling aspects of United States immigration policy. The author chose the stories of three immigrants. . . . Twelve-year-old German-Jew Herb Karliner was denied entry to the United States at the border when he attempted to escape Nazi Germany. Sixteen-year-old Japanese-American Mary Matsuda was detained with the rest of her family during World War II. Labor-activist Emma Goldman was deported for her 'un-American' views. . . . The themes of the three stories are unified by the introduction and conclusion, which deal with Chinese immigration during the late 19th century and the history of immigration across the southern border of the United States, respectively. Photographs throughout will help students relate to the narrative. . . . This is an interesting and readable book." SLJ

Includes bibliographical references

Bial, Raymond

Ellis Island; coming to the land of liberty. Houghton Mifflin Books for Children 2009 56p il $18
Grades: 4 5 6 7   **325**
1. Ellis Island Immigration Station 2. United States -- Immigration and emigration
ISBN 978-0-618-99943-9; 0-618-99943-4

LC 2008-36794

"Bial examines the history of the famed immigration station. . . . He looks at the socio-historical roots of the mass exodus to America and provides a detailed look at the immigrant experience from ship to shore, with Ellis Island in between. Primary-source quotes and period photos pair eloquently with the modern narrative voice and color photographs of the museum exhibits. . . . The generously sized period photos and Bial's museum shots tell a vivid and poignant tale." SLJ

Includes bibliographical references

Conway, Lorie

Forgotten Ellis Island; the extraordinary story of America's immigrant hospital. [by] Lorie Conway. 1st Smithsonian Books ed.; Smithsonian Books/Collins 2007 185p il map $26.95
Grades: 7 8 9 10 11 12   **325**
1. Hospitals 2. Ellis Island Immigration Station 3. Immigrants -- Health and hygiene 4. United States -- Immigration and emigration
ISBN 978-0-06-124196-3; 0-06-124196-2

LC 2007022913

"Conway details the medical inspection that immigrants went through after disembarking and shows how thousands of people were treated at the island's hospitals, sometimes against their will. . . . Each chapter contains dozens of interesting archival photographs and large blocks of quotes from doctors and immigrants. . . . [The book] will add depth to any report on U.S. immigration." SLJ

Includes bibliographical references

Fields, Julianna

First -generation immigrant families. Mason Crest 2009 64p il map (The changing face of modern families) $22.95

Grades: 6 7 8 9   **325**

1. Family 2. Immigrants -- United States
ISBN 978-1-4222-1499-2; 1-4222-1499-0

This describes the unique set of challenges facing first-generation immigrant families as they live with two cultures and, often, two languages.

"Colorful photographs and sidebars appear throughout. [This book is a] good [introduction] to the study of sociology and interpretation of data." SLJ

Solway, Andrew

Graphing immigration. Raintree 2010 32p il (Real world data) $28.21; pa $7.99

Grades: 4 5 6 7   **325**

1. Statistics 2. Graphic methods 3. Immigrants -- United States 4. United States -- Immigration and emigration
ISBN 978-1-4329-2617-5; 1-4329-2617-9; 978-1-4329-2626-7 pa; 1-4329-2626-8 pa

LC 2009001185

"A line graph in [this] title shows the estimated number of illegal immigrants in the U.S. from 1980 to 2005. Arguments about costs and benefits of all kinds of immigrants include a pie chart that shows where immigrants in the U.S. come from and pairs thoughts on why people migrate with a discussion of costs and benefits. . . . The clear design, with lots of full-color photos and sidebars, will encourage browsers as much as the up-to-date examples and the clear directions for remaining 'chart smart.'" Booklist

Includes glossary and bibliographical references

Stefoff, Rebecca

★ **American** voices from a century of immigration: 1820-1924. Marshall Cavendish Benchmark 2006 115p (American voices from--) lib bdg $37.07

Grades: 6 7 8 9   **325**

1. Immigrants -- United States 2. United States -- Immigration and emigration
ISBN 978-0-7614-2172-6 lib bdg; 0-7614-2172-6 lib bdg

LC 2005035963

"Describes the diverse peoples who came to the United States from 1820, when records began to be kept, to 1924, when the gates were nearly closed to immigrants. The reactions of Americans to the new arrivals, laws that were passed, and the experiences of the immigrants themselves are covered through the use of primary sources." Publisher's note

Includes glossary and bibliographical references

326 Slavery and emancipation

Bial, Raymond

The **Underground** Railroad. Houghton Mifflin 1995 48p il map hardcover o.p. pa $6.95

Grades: 4 5 6 7   **326**

1. Underground railroad 2. Slavery -- United States
ISBN 0-395-69937-1; 0-395-97915-3 pa

LC 94-19614

"Although the text covers ground often trodden by other works on this popular subject, Bial's shots of places and things which now appear tidy and innocent conjure spirits of desperate freedom-seekers as handily as do more detailed narratives." Bull Cent Child Books

Includes bibliographical references

DeFord, Deborah H.

★ **Life** under slavery; [by] Deborah H. DeFord. Chelsea House 2006 112p il map (Slavery in the Americas) $35

Grades: 6 7 8 9   **326**

1. Slavery -- United States
ISBN 978-0-8160-6135-8; 0-8160-6135-1

LC 2005034651

This describes the treatment of slaves in the United States, life expectancies, entertainments, and family lives of slaves, and the cultural elements introduced into the New World by enslaved Africans.

"Clearly written, accessible, and well organized . . . [this] is illustrated with black-and-white drawings, period photographs, and explanatory text boxes." SLJ

Includes bibliographical references

Fradin, Judith Bloom

★ **5,000** miles to freedom; Ellen and William Craft's flight from slavery. [by] Judith Bloom Fradin and Dennis Brindell Fradin. National Geographic 2006 96p il $19.95; lib bdg $29.90

Grades: 5 6 7 8 9 10   **326**

1. Slaves 2. Memoirists 3. Slavery -- United States
ISBN 0-7922-7885-2; 0-7922-7886-0 lib bdg

"In 1848, light-skinned Ellen Craft, dressed in the clothing of a rich, white man, assumed the identity of Mr. William Johnson and, escorted by his black slave, William, traveled by railroad and boat to reach the North. With the passage of a more stringent Fugitive Slave Law in 1850, the couple . . . decided to travel to England. . . . In 1869, they returned to the United States, opening a school and operating a farm in Georgia. . . . This lively, well-written volume presents the events in their lives in an exciting, page-turner style that's sure to hold readers attention. Black-and-white photographs, illustrations, and reproductions enhance the text." SLJ

Includes bibliographical references

Gann, Marjorie

★ **Five** thousand years of slavery; [by] Marjorie Gann and Janet Willen. Tundra Books 2011 168p il map $27.95

Grades: 7 8 9 10   **326**

1. Slavery 2. Slavery -- History
ISBN 978-0-88776-914-6; 0-88776-914-4

"This well-researched global survey introduces readers to slavery practices, customs, suffering, uprisings, and revolts as well as antislavery efforts from ancient Greece and Rome to today's world. . . . Informative documentary photos and factually rich sidebars enhance the text. . . . [This is a] groundbreaking title." SLJ

Includes bibliographical references

Gold, Susan Dudley

United States v. Amistad; slave ship mutiny. Marshall Cavendish Benchmark 2006 144p il (Supreme Court milestones) lib bdg $39.93

Grades: 7 8 9 10   **326**

1. Amistad (Schooner) 2. Slavery -- United States
ISBN 978-0-7614-2143-6; 0-7614-2143-2

This is an account of the 1841 Supreme Court case involving the mutiny aboard the slave ship Amistad and the circumstances which surrounded it.

Includes bibliographical references

Grayson, Robert

The **Amistad**. ABDO Pub. 2011 112p il (Essential events) lib bdg $23.95

Grades: 7 8 9 10 11 12   **326**

1. Slave trade 2. Amistad (Schooner)
ISBN 978-1-61714-761-6; 1-61714-761-3

LC 2010044662

This "is dramatic history, focusing on the 1839-40 trial of the kidnapped Africans who rebelled on the slave ship from Cuba and were captured and tried in the U.S. on charges of piracy. Were the Africans property? . . . The spacious . . . design is inviting, with many color illustrations and screens, and the extensive back matter includes a detailed time line, glossary, bibliography and source notes." Booklist

Includes glossary and bibliographical references

Nardo, Don

The **Atlantic** slave trade; [by] Don Nardo. Thomson/Gale 2008 104p il (Lucent library of black history) lib bdg $32.45

Grades: 6 7 8 9   **326**

1. Slavery 2. Slave trade
ISBN 978-1-4205-0007-3 lib bdg; 1-4205-0007-4 lib bdg

LC 2007-22999

"Nardo examines [slave trade and] its impact on West Africa, its implication for the economic and social health of the entire African continent, the role that black Africans played in the sale of their countrymen, and the continuing shadow slavery still casts over this country's race relations. . . . Include[s] extensive bibliographies, period illustrations, and primary-source documents." SLJ

Includes bibliographical references

Slavery; James D. Torr, book editor. Greenhaven Press 2004 240p map (Opposing viewpoints in world history) hardcover o.p. pa $22.45

Grades: 8 9 10 11 12   **326**

1. Slavery -- United States
ISBN 0-7377-1705-X; 0-7377-1706-8 pa

LC 2003-44812

This book offers "perspectives on American slavery through a selection of primary sources. The excerpts, culled from speeches, pamphlets, and scholarly texts, are divided into four sections that cover moral issues, slave resistance,

abolitionists, and events that led to the Civil War. . . . The entries that are included . . . will greatly enhance students' understanding of the issues. . . . An important, useful addition to the high-school history curriculum." Booklist

Includes bibliographical references

Worth, Richard

The **slave** trade in America; cruel commerce. foreword by series advisor Dr. Henry Louis Gates, Jr. Enslow Publishers 2004 128p il map (Slavery in American history) lib bdg $26.60

Grades: 7 8 9 10   **326**

1. Slave trade 2. Slavery -- United States
ISBN 0-7660-2151-3

LC 2003-12079

This is a history of the slave trade in America from colonial times to emancipation

This "clearly written, well-researched {book presents} solid coverage of the subject." SLJ

Includes glossary and bibliographical references

327   International relations

Renehan, Edward J.

The **Monroe** doctrine; the cornerstone of American foreign policy. [by] Edward J. Renehan Jr. Chelsea House 2007 122p il map (Milestones in American history) lib bdg $35

Grades: 7 8 9 10   **327**

1. Monroe Doctrine 2. United States -- Foreign relations
ISBN 0-7910-9353-0 lib bdg; 978-0-7910-9353-5 lib bdg

LC 2006034126

This description of the Monroe Doctrine is "accessible, lively. . . . Many quotations, sidebars, art reproductions, and maps support the [text]. Excerpts from primary source materials also help give readers a sense of time and place." Horn Book Guide

Includes bibliographical references

327.12   Espionage and subversion

Earnest, Peter

The **real** spy's guide to becoming a spy; by Peter Earnest and Suzanne Harper, in association with the Spy Museum. Abrams Books for Young Readers 2009 144p il $16.95

Grades: 4 5 6 7   **327.12**

1. Spies 2. Espionage 3. Intelligence service
ISBN 978-0-8109-8329-8; 0-8109-8329-X

LC 2009-00518

"This guide, written by the executive director of the International Spy Museum, gives readers a glimpse at how spies work. Along with descriptions of the different types of intelligence officers and agencies and the tasks they perform, the text includes brief stories of spies in action." Horn Book Guide

Goodman, Michael E.

The **KGB** and other Russian spies; Michael E. Goodman. Creative Education 2012 48 p. col. ill. (Spies around the world) (library) $35.65

Grades: 6 7 8 9   **327.12**

1. Spies 2. Russia 3. Espionage, Soviet 4. Spies -- Soviet Union 5. Intelligence service -- Soviet Union 6. Soviet Union. Komitet gosudarstvennoĭ bezopasnosti

ISBN 1608182274; 9781608182275

LC 2011035790

This book is part of the Spies Around the World series and focuses on Russian spies. "Each title contains an introduction to that particular country's spying apparatus plus chapters covering origins and famous individuals, and an explanation of this shadowy occupation. Each table of contents lists eight special features under the 'Evolution of Espionage' heading, where a particular event or spy-related item is highlighted." (Library Media Connection)

Includes bibliographical references (p. 47) and index

The **SIS** and other British spies; Michael E. Goodman. Creative Education 2012 48 p. ill. (library) $35.65

Grades: 6 7 8 9   **327.12**

1. Intelligence service 2. Spies 3. Espionage, British 4. Great Britain. MI6 5. Spies -- Great Britain 6. Intelligence service -- Great Britain

ISBN 1608182290; 9781608182299

LC 2011035791

This book is part of the Spies Around the World series and focuses on the British SIS and other British spies. "Each title contains an introduction to that particular country's spying apparatus plus chapters covering origins and famous individuals, and an explanation of this shadowy occupation. Each table of contents lists eight special features under the 'Evolution of Espionage' heading, where a particular event or spy-related item is highlighted." (Library Media Connection)

Includes bibliographical references (p. 47) and index

Janeczko, Paul B.

The **dark** game; true spy stories. Candlewick Press 2010 248p il $16.99

Grades: 5 6 7 8   **327.12**

1. Espionage

ISBN 978-0-7636-2915-1; 0-7636-2915-4

"From Benedict Arnold and Mata Hari to the lesser-known Elizabeth Van Lew and Juan Pujol, Janeczko delves into [spies'] stories with delicious detail, drawing readers into a world of intrigue and danger. Did you ever wonder why invisible ink works? How a code breaker deciphers a message? Or whether dentistry could affect a secret agent's success? The answers to these questions and more can be found here. Each chapter covers a historical era and chronicles the maturation of spying, while primary-source photographs are interspersed throughout, lending an authentic feel to each section." SLJ

Mitchell, Susan K.

Spies and lies; famous and infamous spies. Enslow Publishers 2011 48p il (The secret world of spies) lib bdg $23.93

Grades: 4 5 6   **327.12**

1. Spies 2. Espionage

ISBN 978-0-7660-3713-7

LC 2010044126

"Archival photographs, sidebars, and multiple fact-filled features (sidebars, text boxes, etc.) combine with accessible texts to present a thorough (albeit busy) introduction to the history and current enterprise of spies and spying." Horn Book

Includes glosssary and bibliographical references

Spies, double agents, and traitors. Enslow Publishers 2011 48p il (The secret world of spies) lib bdg $23.93

Grades: 4 5 6   **327.12**

1. Spies 2. Espionage

ISBN 978-0-7660-3711-3

LC 2010006178

Discusses double agents and traitors throughout history, such as Benedict Arnold, Dusan Popov, Kim Philby, and Robert Hanssen, and includes information on becoming a spy catcher (counterintelligence agent).

Includes glossary bibliographical references

Spy gizmos and gadgets. Enslow Publishers 2011 48p il (The secret world of spies) lib bdg $23.93

Grades: 4 5 6   **327.12**

1. Espionage 2. Electronic surveillance

ISBN 978-0-7660-3710-6

LC 2010006177

Discusses different gadgets used by spies, such as invisible ink, hidden cameras, small guns made to look like ordinary objects, and bugs, and includes career information.

Includes glossary and bibliographical references

327.1273   CIA (Intelligence agency)

Goodman, Michael E.

The **CIA** and other American spies; Michael E. Goodman. Creative Eduation 2012 48 p. ill. (Spies around the world) (library) $35.65

Grades: 6 7 8 9   **327.1273**

1. Intelligence service -- United States 2. United States. Central Intelligence Agency 3. Espionage, American 4. Spies -- United States

ISBN 1608182266; 9781608182268

LC 2011035789

This book is part of the Spies Around the World series. "Focused more on the histories of spying organizations, each title looks at a different agency, making references to popular culture (e.g., the work of the CIA is compared to the 'Bourne' trilogy) and showing the difference between reality and movies. While not adding career how-to's, the volumes showcase famous spies from history, going back to the origins of each agency, as well as 'Tools of the Trade' and major cases." (School Library Journal)

Includes bibliographical references and index

328.73   Legislative process – United States

Bow, James

    What is the legislative branch? by James Bow. Crabtree Publishing Company 2013 32 p. (Your guide to government) (reinforced library binding) $26.60

Grades: 4 5 6 7   **328.73**

    1. Legislative bodies   2. United States. Congress   3. United States -- Politics and government

    ISBN 0778708799; 9780778708797; 9780778709053

                    LC 2013001277

    This book, by James Bow "provide[s] solid introductory material about the U.S. government. [The] book discusses the purpose of [the legislative] branch; the different positions, . . . the work done; and the strengths and the challenges of each branch and how they interact." (School Library Journal)

330   Economics

Hlinka, Michael

    Follow Your Money; Who Gets It, Who Spends It, Where Does It Go? by Kevin Sylvester and Michael Hlinka ; illustrated by Kevin Sylvester. Annick Press 2013 56 p. col. ill. (paperback) $14.95; (hardcover) $24.95

Grades: 5 6 7 8   **330**

    1. Pricing   2. Money

    ISBN 1554514800; 1554514819; 9781554514809; 9781554514816

    This book by Kevin Sylvester and Michael Hlinka answers the questions "what happens to your money after you hand it to the cashier? Who actually pockets it or puts it into the bank? Was the price you paid fair? Why do things cost what they do? Kids will also discover the trail their money takes through advertising, banks [and] charitable giving. [It is an] introduction to the . . .people and companies that we influence and are influenced by when we pay for a product or service." (Publisher's note)

Hollander, Barbara

    Money matters; an introduction to economics. [by] Barbara Gottfried Hollander. Heinemann Library 2010 56p il map (The global marketplace) $33.50

Grades: 6 7 8 9   **330**

    1. Money   2. Economics

    ISBN 978-1-4329-3929-8; 1-4329-3929-7

                    LC 2010003996

    This introduction to economics covers "a wealth of material in concise paragraphs with pertinent sub-headings. . . . [It includes] excellent photos, charts, maps, and tables

that help with the understanding of some sophisticated concepts." SLJ

    Includes glossary and bibliographical references

Outman, James L.

    Industrial Revolution: biographies; [by] James L. Outman, Elisabeth M. Outman. U.X.L 2003 218p il (Industrial revolution reference library) $55

Grades: 8 9 10 11 12   **330**

    1. Industrial revolution

    ISBN 0-7876-6514-2

                    LC 2002-155421

    "The 25 essays in [this volume] provide biographical information with an emphasis on each person's contribution or impact on the Industrial Revolution. . . . More than 50 black-and-white photographs complement the text. . . . This is an excellent adjunct to American and world history units and classes on economics and labor movements." Booklist

    Includes bibliographical references

330.9   Economic situation and conditions

Arnold, James R.

    The **industrial** revolution; [by] James R. Arnold and Roberta Weiner. Grolier 2005 10v il map set $299

Grades: 5 6 7 8   **330.9**

    1. Reference books   2. Industrial revolution

    ISBN 0-7172-6031-3

                    LC 2004-54243

    "The Industrial Revolution spanned several centuries and continents, and this set covers developments and their impact in a well-organized fashion. . . . The set is copiously illustrated, with a variety of art reproductions, diagrams, and historical photographs. . . . With worldwide scope and coverage from the 18th century through the early 1900s, this is more comprehensive than single-volume histories, while the logical structure and appealing layout make it accessible to a wide range of students." SLJ

    Includes glossary and bibliographical references

Brezina, Corona

    America's recession; the effects of the economic downturn. Rosen Pub. 2011 64p il (Headlines!) lib bdg $29.25

Grades: 7 8 9 10   **330.9**

    1. Recessions   2. Global Financial Crisis, 2008-2009   3. Economic policy -- United States   4. United States -- Economic conditions

    ISBN 978-1-4488-1296-7; 1-4488-1296-8

                    LC 2010016915

    This "volume addresses the . . . topic of America's economic recession. Beginning with the housing boom that peaked in 2006, Brezina discusses predatory lending and other causes, then government efforts to combat recession. She also addresses topics such as foreclosure and unemployment, concluding with possible patterns of recovery. Good organization, clear writing, captioned photos, and sidebars deliver the information clearly." Horn Book Guide

    Includes glossary and bibliographical references

Doak, Robin S.

Black Tuesday; prelude to the Great Depression. by Robin S. Doak. Compass Point Books 2008 96p il map (Snapshots in history) lib bdg $31.93

Grades: 6 7 8 9   **330.9**

1. Stock market crash, 1929 2. Great Depression, 1929-1939 3. United States -- Economic conditions -- 1919-1933

ISBN 978-0-7565-3327-4 lib bdg; 0-7565-3327-9 lib bdg

LC 2007004911

This "explains how the decade's economic boom and un-regulated markets created the speculative bubble that burst when the stock market crashed in 1929. Doak concludes that growing investor panic and inadequate government response to the crash contributed to the Great Depression. . . . [The text incorporates] primary-source material and [includes] numerous period photos and political cartoons." SLJ

Grant, R. G.

Why did the Great Depression happen? Gareth Stevens Pub. 2010 il map (Moments in history) lib bdg $31.95; pa $14.05

Grades: 6 7 8 9   **330.9**

1. Stock market crash, 1929 2. Great Depression, 1929-1939 3. Europe -- Economic conditions 4. United States -- Economic conditions

ISBN 978-1-4339-4169-6 lib bdg; 1-4339-4169-4; 978-1-4339-4170-2 pa; 1-4339-4170-8 pa

LC 2010012461

This "explains the before, during and after of [the Great Depression] in a clear, unbiased manner. . . . Sidebars include meticulously cited eyewitness quotes or extra insight on particularly important events. Even more information is contained in the maps, period photographs, and well-placed captions that grace every page." SLJ

Includes glossary and bibliographical references

Heinrichs, Ann

★ The **great** recession. Children's Press 2011 il (Cornerstones of freedom) lib bdg $30; pa $8.95

Grades: 4 5 6 7   **330.9**

1. Recessions 2. Financial crises 3. Economic policy -- United States

ISBN 978-0-531-25035-8 lib bdg; 0-531-25035-0 lib bdg; 978-0-531-26560-4 pa; 0-531-26560-9 pa

LC 2011010824

This "offers simplified but not simplistic explanations of the current great recession's course and immediate causes. The . . . design has . . . visually stimulating pages that combine big color photos, boxed side essays, and blocks of large text with bright-red headers and highlights. In simple language and a judicious, matter-of-fact tone, Heinrichs describes the origins and growth of the housing bubble and the trade in mortgage-backed securities that magnified the effects of its eventual collapse; summarizes the federal government's palliative measures; surveys the effects of hard times on general patterns of living and spending; and notes the creation of a 'Generation R,' for whom high unemployment and financial insecurity are likely to become ways of life." Booklist

Includes bibliographical references

Lange, Brenda

The **Stock** Market Crash of 1929; the end of prosperity. [by] Brenda Lange. Chelsea House 2007 114p il (Milestones in American history) lib bdg $35

Grades: 7 8 9 10   **330.9**

1. Stock market crash, 1929 2. Great Depression, 1929-1939 3. United States -- Economic conditions -- 1919-1933

ISBN 0-7910-9354-9 lib bdg; 978-0-7910-9354-2 lib bdg

LC 2006038868

This describes the Stock Market Crash of October 29, 1929, also known as Black Tuesday, and its consequences.

This is "accessible, lively. . . . Many quotations, sidebars, art reproductions, and maps support the [text]. Excerpts from primary source materials also help give readers a sense of time and place." Horn Book Guide

Includes bibliographical references

Mooney, Carla

The **Industrial** Revolution; investigate how science and technology changed the world with 25 projects. illustrated by Jen Vaughn. Nomad Press 2011 120p il (Build it yourself) $21.95; pa $15.95

Grades: 4 5 6 7   **330.9**

1. Industrial revolution

ISBN 978-1-936313-81-5; 1-936313-81-2; 978-1936313-80-8; 1-936313-80-4 pa

This "gives on overview of the era known as the Industrial Revolution as well as the consequences, good and bad, of each new development upon the average citizen. Topics covered include the transformation of textiles from home-spun to manufactured, the birth of labor unions, advances in transportation and communication, the inventions of Thomas Edison, and brief profiles of 'Captains of Industry,' such as Carnegie, Vanderbilt, and Rockefeller. Each chapter ends with enticing projects related to the topic. . . . The crisp, clear format, featuring ample black-and-white sketches and diagrams and pleasingly arranged type in a large font, is in sync with the straightforward text." Booklist

Outman, James L.

Industrial Revolution: almanac; [by] James L. Outman, Elisabeth M. Outman. U.X.L 2003 242p il (Industrial revolution reference library) $55

Grades: 8 9 10 11 12   **330.9**

1. Reference books 2. Industrial revolution

ISBN 0-7876-6513-4

LC 2002-155422

"This is an excellent adjunct to American and world history units and classes on economics and labor movements." Booklist

Includes bibliographical references

331.3   Labor force by personal attributes

Bartoletti, Susan Campbell

★ **Growing** up in coal country. Houghton Mifflin 1996 127p il $17; pa $7.95

Grades: 5 6 7 8   **331.3**

1. Child labor 2. Coal mines and mining 3. Immigrants 4. Children -- Employment -- United States
ISBN 0-395-77847-6; 0-395-97914-5 pa

LC 96-3142

This is an "account of working and living conditions in Pennsylvania coal towns. The first half of the volume . . . {describes} various duties in the mines, from jobs performed by the youngest boys to the tasks of adult miners, while the second half describes the company village, common customs and recreational activities, and the accidents and diseases that frequently beset the workers. Preceding each chapter and within the text {are} quotes from personal interviews with miners, as well as taped interviews and transcripts." (Horn Book) Bibliography. "Grade five and up." (Booklist)

"With compelling black-and-white photographs of children at work in the coal mines of northeastern Pennsylvania about 100 years ago, this handsome, spacious photo-essay will draw browsers as well as students doing research on labor and immigrant history." Booklist

Includes bibliographical references

Burgan, Michael

★ **Breaker** boys; how a photograph helped end child labor. Compass Point Books 2011 64p il (Captured history) lib bdg $33.99; pa $8.95

Grades: 6 7 8 9   **331.3**

1. Photographers 2. Coal mines and mining 3. Documentary photography 4. Child labor -- United States
ISBN 978-0-7565-4439-3 lib bdg; 0-7565-4439-4; 978-0-7565-4510-9 pa; 0-7565-4510-2 pa

LC 2011003316

This book explains how Lewis Hine's photographs of children who worked in coal mines in Pennsylvania helped lead to the passage of child labor laws.

This "is model nonfiction. . . . The design is fresh and inviting, the writing clear, and the back matter . . . is useful and extensive. An all-around winner." Booklist

Includes glossary and bibliographical references

Freedman, Russell

★ **Kids** at work; Lewis Hine and the crusade against child labor. with photographs by Lewis Hine. Clarion Bks. 1994 104p il $20; pa $9.95

Grades: 5 6 7 8   **331.3**

1. Child labor 2. Photographers
ISBN 0-395-58703-4; 0-395-79726-8 pa

LC 93-5989

Freedman "does an outstanding job of integrating historical photographs with meticulously researched and highly readable prose." Publ Wkly

Includes bibliographical references

Gifford, Clive

Child labor. Smart Apple Media 2010 46p il (Voices) lib bdg $34.25

Grades: 7 8 9 10 11 12   **331.3**

1. Child labor
ISBN 978-1-59920-279-2 lib bdg; 1-59920-279-4 lib bdg

LC 2008-50429

The "text offers statistics, graphs, quotations (from politicians and scientists to children and laborers), and many photographs to make clear how . . . [child labor affects] the world today. An eye to how the issue affects young people—and how young people can help—is also a priority. . . . [This] book is quick to read and stocked with quotations and statistics that will assist in research as well as general interest." Voice Youth Advocates

Includes glossary and bibliographical references

331.4   Women workers

Colman, Penny

★ **Rosie** the riveter; women working on the home front in World War II. Crown 1995 120p il hardcover o.p. pa $10.99

Grades: 5 6 7 8   **331.4**

1. Women -- Employment 2. World War, 1939-1945 -- United States
ISBN 0-517-59790-X; 0-517-88567-0 pa

LC 94-3614

"A thoughtfully prepared look at women's history and wartime society, this dynamic book is characterized by extensive research." Horn Book

This is an account of women's employment in wartime industry during the Second World War. "Colman looks at the jobs women took, the impact women had on the workplace, and what happened to working women at war's end. . . . [She also discusses] the public relations campaign that not only 'wooed' women into the workplace, but also sought to change firmly entrenched attitudes about women's role in society." Booklist

Includes bibliographical references

331.6   Workers by ethnic and national origin

Ouellette, Jeannine

A **day** without immigrants; rallying behind America's newcomers. by Jeannine Ouellette. Compass Point Books 2008 96p il map (Snapshots in history) $31.93

Grades: 6 7 8 9   **331.6**

1. Migrant labor 2. Illegal aliens 3. Immigrants -- United States
ISBN 978-0-7565-2498-2 lib bdg; 0-7565-2498-9 lib bdg

LC 2007004679

This book "uses the rallies of May 1, 2006 to address issues about immigration, both legal and illegal. . . . [This] volume includes a minimal glossary, a helpful time line, and suggestions for further reading." Voice Youth Advocates

Includes glossary and bibliographical references

331.7 Labor by industry and occupation

Farrell, Courtney

Green jobs. ABDO Pub. 2011 112p il (Inside the industry) lib bdg $34.22

Grades: 8 9 10 11 12   **331.7**

1. Occupations 2. Vocational guidance 3. Environmental protection

ISBN 978-1-61714-801-9; 1-61714-801-6

LC 2010039122

"This book contains an interesting overview of jobs that fall beneath the 'green' umbrella. Farrell writes in clear prose about the wide range of career opportunities that students with environmental interests can pursue. She focuses on four fields: green architect, organic farmer, professional conservationist, and alternative-energy expert." SLJ

Includes glossary and bibliographical references

Hopkinson, Deborah

★ Up before daybreak; cotton and people in America. Scholastic Nonfiction 2005 120p il $18.99

Grades: 5 6 7 8   **331.7**

1. Cotton 2. Working class 3. Textile industry -- History

ISBN 0-439-63901-8

LC 2005-8128

"From the industrial revolution to the 1950s demise of the Lowell cotton mills, Hopkinson discusses the history and sociology of king cotton, frequently emphasizing the children who labored under slave masters, endured dead-end mill jobs, or helped sharecropping parents claw out a living. . . . Stories of real people . . . sharply focus the dramatic history, as do arresting archival photos of stern youngsters manipulating hoes, cotton sags, or bobbins." Booklist

J.G. Ferguson Publishing Company

Encyclopedia of careers and vocational guidance; 15th ed.; Ferguson 2010 5v il set $249.95

Grades: 8 9 10 11 12 Adult   **331.7**

1. Reference books 2. Occupations -- Encyclopedias 3. Vocational guidance -- Encyclopedias

ISBN 978-0-8160-8313-8; 0-8160-8313-4

LC 2010-17724

First published 1967

"These five volumes contain more than 700 . . . [articles] on careers in nearly 100 industries. Each three to five-page entry provides a concise and engaging profile of fields like accounting, animal care, computers, the environment, publishing, sales, and the visual arts. Included in each job entry are an overview, a history, a description, requirements, employers, advancement, earnings, work environment, outlook, and more." Libr J [review of 2008 edition]

Includes bibliographical references

United States. Dept. of Labor

Young person's occupational outlook handbook; 5th ed; Jist Works 2005 319p il $19.95

Grades: 6 7 8 9   **331.7**

1. Occupations 2. Reference books 3. Vocational

guidance

ISBN 1-59357-125-9

LC 2004-13091

This "career reference includes 277 jobs employing 88 percent of the workforce. . . . Each entry includes a short description of duties and working conditions; suggested academic preparation; hands-on activites simulating actual job aspects; related personal habits and preferences or sources for further investigation; and additional related jobs. . . . The book is a strong starting point for student research." Voice Youth Advocates

331.8 Labor unions, labor-management bargaining and disputes

Baker, Julie

The Bread and Roses strike of 1912. Morgan Reynolds Pub. 2007 160p il (American workers) $27.95

Grades: 6 7 8 9 10   **331.8**

1. Strikes 2. Lawrence (Mass.) -- History 3. Textile industry -- History

ISBN 978-1-59935-044-8; 1-59935-044-0

LC 2006101826

A history of the 1912 strike of textile workers in Lawrence, Massachusetts.

"Baker's style is readable, and the well-chosen, well-reproduced photos make the subject all the more real." SLJ

Includes bibliographical references

Laughlin, Rosemary

The Ludlow massacre of 1913-14; [by] Rosemary Laughlin. 1st ed.; Morgan Reynolds Pub. 2006 144p il (American workers) lib bdg $27.95

Grades: 6 7 8 9   **331.8**

1. Strikes 2. Coal mines and mining 3. Labor movement -- History

ISBN 978-1-931798-86-0; 1-931798-86-9

LC 2005030050

"In the autumn of 1913, coal miners working for the Colorado Fuel and Iron Company walked off the job, demanding recognition of their union. This . . . chronicles the long strike that frequently erupted into armed combat between the Colorado state militia and the miners. Vivid portraits are presented of the protagonists in the struggle. . . . Laughlin presents the facts with a storyteller's flair, supplemented by frequent quotes, period photographs, and engravings that show what life was like for the miners." Booklist

Includes bibliographical references

The Pullman strike of 1894; [by] Rosemary Laughlin. Morgan Reynolds Pub. 2006 144p il (American workers) lib bdg $27.95

Grades: 6 7 8 9   **331.8**

1. Strikes 2. Railroads -- History 3. Labor movement -- History

ISBN 978-1-931798-89-1; 1-931798-89-3

LC 2005028637

First published 2000 in the series Great events

This "tells the story of the strike and explains its long-term effects on the labor movement and the nation. The author examines the arguments made by labor and management and explains how the strike affected all of those involved. . . . [This is] a good choice for report material on industrialization, labor history, or the Gilded Age." SLJ

Includes bibliographical references

Skurzynski, Gloria

Sweat and blood; a history of U.S. labor unions. Twenty-First Century Books 2008 112p il (People's history) lib bdg $31.93

Grades: 7 8 9 10   331.8

1. Labor unions 2. Working class
ISBN 978-0-8225-7594-8; 0-8225-7594-9

LC 2007-50270

This "begins with the roots of unionization in colonial America, cruises through the frenzy of industrialization in the twentieth century, and ends in the present day. . . . The period prints and photographs are well chosen to highlight and comment on the text. Classes studying any part of the industrial or social history of this country will be well served by this valuable resource." Booklist

Includes bibliographical references

Whitelaw, Nancy

The **Homestead** Steel Strike of 1892; [by] Nancy Whitelaw. 1st ed.; Morgan Reynolds Pub. 2006 144p il (American workers) lib bdg $27.95

Grades: 6 7 8 9   331.8

1. Strikes 2. Steel industry 3. Philanthropists 4. Homestead Strike, 1892 5. Art collectors 6. Labor movement -- History 7. Metal industry executives
ISBN 978-1-931798-88-4; 1-931798-88-5

LC 2005027113

This is the story of the 1892 strike against the Homestead Steel company owned by Andrew Carnegie and Henry Clay Frick which led to bloodshed and a breaking of the union.

"This is a riveting story told in 11 well-written, lively chapters, with well-placed, good-quality reproductions and drawings throughout the text." SLJ

Includes bibliographical references

331.89 Labor-management bargaining and disputes

Bartoletti, Susan Campbell

★ **Kids** on strike! Houghton Mifflin 1999 208p il $20; pa $8.95

Grades: 5 6 7 8   331.89

1. Strikes 2. Child labor 3. Centenarians 4. Labor leaders
ISBN 0-395-88892-1; 0-618-36923-6 pa

LC 98-50575

Describes the conditions and treatment that drove workers, including many children, to various strikes, from the mill workers strikes in 1828 and 1836 and the coal strikes at the turn of the century to the work of Mother Jones on behalf of child workers

"This well-researched and well-illustrated account creates a vivid portrait of the working conditions of many American children in the 19th and early 20th centuries." SLJ

Includes bibliographical references

Brimner, Larry Dane, 1949-

Strike! the farm workers' fight for their rights. Larry Dane Brimner. Calkins Creek 2014 172 p. ill. (some col.), maps hbk $16.95

Grades: 6 7 8 9   331.89

1. Agricultural industry 2. Strikes -- United States -- History
ISBN 1590789970; 9781590789971

LC 2014935299

"Author Larry Dane Brimner follows the five-year-long strike through the rise of César Chávez and the United Farm Workers. . . . In the 1960s, while the United States was at war and racial tensions were boiling over, Filipino American workers were demanding fair wages and decent living conditions in California's vineyards. When the workers walked out of the fields in September 1965, the great Delano grape strike began." (Publisher's note)

"Brimner's inclusion of information about the Filipino workers who began the movement, quotes and balanced discussion of Chavez's strengths and weaknesses provides a fresh perspective on the movement, making this book a first-purchase choice for middle-level researchers." SLJ

Includes bibliographical references and index

332 Financial economics

Bostick, Nan

Managing Money. Saddleback Educational Pub. 2012 120 p. ill.

Grades: 8 9 10 11 12   332

1. Life skills 2. Banks and banking 3. Household budgets 4. Teenagers -- Personal finance 5. Economics -- Handbooks, manuals, etc. 6. Adult education 7. Finance, Personal 8. Life skills--Handbooks, manuals, etc.
ISBN 1616516593; 9781616516598

This book is a part of the "Life Skills Handbooks" series. "With the text split into four main topics—controlling your spending, banking basics, buying now and paying later, and improving your budgeting skills—young adults get a comprehensive look at the world of personal finance. . . . When it comes to sticking to a budget, teens are encouraged to keep their needs and wants in sharp focus. There's even a chapter devoted to unexpected purchases and variable spending. . . . There are also helpful hints for paying those expenses without credit cards. Credit-card debt, loans, and spending more than one earns are issues that are addressed . . . . Basic advice, such as how to write out a check and read a bank statement, is included." (Booklist) Index.

"This entry in Saddleback's Life Skills Handbooks series is a keeper... Young adults get a comprehensive look at the world of personal finance in digestible doses." Booklist

332.024   Personal finance

Bochner, Rose

The **new** totally awesome money book for kids (and their parents) [by] Arthur Bochner & Rose Bochner; foreword by Adriane G. Berg. 3rd ed., rev & updated.; Newmarket Press 2007 189p il pa $9.95

Grades: 4 5 6 7   **332.024**
1. Personal finance
ISBN 978-1-55704-738-0
     LC 2006038930

First published 1993 with title: The totally awesome money book for kids (and their parents)

An introduction to money for kids including the basics of saving, investing, working, and taxes.

"Using an easy and comfortable style that young people will find unthreatening, the book presents a wealth of information. . . . The cute illustrations are also fun." Voice Youth Advocates

Includes bibliographical references

Chatzky, Jean

Not your parents' money book; making, saving, and spending your own money. [by Jean Sherman Chatzky]; illustrated by Erwin Haya. Simon & Schuster Books for Young Readers 2010 162p il pa $12.99

Grades: 5 6 7 8   **332.024**
1. Money 2. Personal finance
ISBN 978-1-4169-9472-5 pa; 1-4169-9472-6 pa
     LC 2010008840

"Written in a light, somewhat jocular tone and sprinkled with amusing but eye-opening and conversation-starting quotes from 12, 13, and 14-year-olds, this book is sure to hold readers' attention. The content includes how you get money, via allowances and jobs, and notes the difference between cash-only and paychecks. Tracking typical teen expenditures, both long-term and short, is juxtaposed against keeping money in checking, savings, and money-market accounts. . . . Chatzky's presentation is engaging. . . . Cartoons appear on almost every page, adding humor and some additional material." SLJ

Includes bibliographical references

Hall, Alvin

★ **Show** me the money; [by] Alvin Hall. DK 2008 96p il $15.99

Grades: 4 5 6   **332.024**
1. Money 2. Personal finance
ISBN 978-0-7566-3762-0; 0-7566-3762-7

"Four main sections cover the history of money, expenses/income, the basics of economics, and the world of work and business. Brief profiles of eight wealthy entrepreneurs and their paths to prosperity and eight significant economists and their theories are included. The lively writing features real-life examples that will be meaningful to students and is presented in a balanced, nonjudgmental style that encourages them to decide for themselves among the various ideas concerning economic policies. . . . Color photos and graph-

ics excel at conveying the concepts presented and represent diversity well." SLJ

Includes glossary

Roderick, Stacey

Centsibility; the Planet Girl guide to money. [by] Stacey Roderick and Ellen Warwick; illustrated by Monika Melnychuk. Kids Can Press 2008 80p il (Planet girl) $12.95

Grades: 5 6 7 8   **332.024**
1. Personal finance
ISBN 978-1-55453-208-7

"This book presents handy methods for managing money. . . . Chapters are broken down into subsections . . . which are peppered with quizzes and craft projects to keep readers engaged. . . . The book's sound advice is both practical and approachable." Horn Book Guide

Wiseman, Blaine

Budgeting. Weigl Publishers 2009 32p il (Everyday economics) lib bdg $26; pa $9.95

Grades: 5 6 7   **332.024**
1. Budget
ISBN 978-1-60596-643-4 lib bdg; 1-60596-643-6 lib bdg; 978-1-60596-644-1 pa; 1-60596-644-4 pa
     LC 2009018439

This "informative [book introduces budgeting in] U.S. economic theory and practices using everyday language and real-life examples. [It] includes history, a brief annotated chronology, sidebar and intext explanations of terminology, and helpful diagrams. . . . With brief paragraphs; large, captioned photographs; ample margins; and well-organized graphics, the [book's] design makes economics accessible without sacrificing content. . . . [This is] easy to navigate and full of solid information and interesting facts." SLJ

Includes glossary

332.1   Banks

Fischer, James

Banking basics. Mason Crest Publishers 2010 il (Junior library of money) $22.95; pa $9.95

Grades: 6 7 8 9   **332.1**
1. Banks and banking
ISBN 978-1-4222-1761-0; 1-4222-1761-2; 978-1-4222-1880-8 pa; 1-4222-1880-5 pa
     LC 2010021814

This offers a history of banking and describes how banks operate.

This title presents "solid information and [has] eye-catching and relevant illustrations. . . . [The book is] clearly written, making understandable connections between daily life and financial concepts." SLJ

Includes glossary and bibliographical references

332.4   Money

Brezina, Corona

    How deflation works. Rosen Pub. 2011 80p il (Real world economics) lib bdg $30.60

Grades: 7 8 9 10   **332.4**

    1. Deflation (Finance)

    ISBN 978-1-4358-9465-5; 1-4358-9465-0

                         LC 2009045292

This "discusses the possible correlations between a recession and deflation, expanding at length about why deflation, expanding at length about why deflation is ultimately unhealthy for the economy." SLJ

    Includes bibliographical references

Cribb, Joe

    ★ **Money**; written by Joe Cribb. rev ed; DK Pub. 2005 72p il (DK eyewitness books) lib bdg $15.99

Grades: 4 5 6 7   **332.4**

    1. Money

    ISBN 0-7566-1389-2

    First published 1990 by Knopf

    Examines, in text and photographs, the symbolic and material meaning of money, from shekels, shells, and beads to gold, silver, checks, and credit cards. Also discusses how coins and banknotes are made, the value of money during wartime, and how to collect coins

Jenkins, Martin

    The **history** of money; from bartering to banking. Martin Jenkins, illustrated by Satoshi Kitamura. First U.S. Edition   Candlewick Press   2014   64 p. color illustrations $16.99

Grades: 4 5 6 7 8   **332.4**

    1. Money -- History

    ISBN 0763667633; 9780763667634

                         LC 2013952840

"Martin Jenkins and Satoshi Kitamura take readers on a . . . tour of the history of money. What can take the form of a stone with a hole in the middle, a string of shells, a piece of paper, or a plastic card? The answer is money, of course. But when did we start using it? And why? What does money have to do with writing? And how do taxes and interest work?" (Publisher's note)

"This cleverly designed picture book uses just the right balance of information and explanation to guide students through both the global history of currency and the application of market pressures on exchange methods." Booklist

    Includes bibliographical references and index

Simons, Rae

    All about money; the history, culture, and meaning of modern finance. Mason Crest Publishers 2010 64p il $22.95; pa $9.95

Grades: 6 7 8 9   **332.4**

    1. Money 2. Economics

    ISBN 978-1-4222-1760-3; 1-4222-1760-4; 978-1-4222-1879-2 pa; 1-4222-1879-1 pa

                         LC 2010021818

This describes the history currency and how money is used in various economic systems.

This title presents "solid information and [has] eye-catching and relevant illustrations. . . . [The book is] clearly written, making understandable connections between daily life and financial concepts." SLJ

    Includes glossary and bibliographical references

332.6   Investment

Connolly, Sean

    The **stock** market. Amicus 2010 46p il (World economy explained) lib bdg $34.25

Grades: 7 8 9 10   **332.6**

    1. Stocks 2. Stock exchanges 3. Financial crises

    ISBN 978-1-60753-082-4; 1-60753-082-4

                         LC 2009-29073

"Explains the functions and history of the Stock Market and its involvement with the 2007 credit crunch." Publisher's note

    Includes glossary

Furgang, Kathy

    How the stock market works. Rosen Pub. 2011 80p il (Real world economics) lib bdg $30.60

Grades: 7 8 9 10   **332.6**

    1. Stocks 2. Stock exchanges

    ISBN 978-1-4358-9466-2; 1-4358-9466-9

                         LC 2009045687

This "includes a history of Wall Street and discusses the ups and downs of the stock market and its impact on people's everyday lives in a general and accessible manner for students." SLJ

    Includes glossary and bibliographical references

Healey, Aaron

    Making the trade; stocks, bonds, and other investments. Heinemann Library 2011 56p il (The global marketplace) lib bdg $33.50

Grades: 6 7 8 9   **332.6**

    1. Investments 2. Stock exchanges 3. Saving and investment

    ISBN 978-1-4329-3931-1; 1-4329-3931-9

                         LC 2010004094

This title covers "a wealth of material in concise paragraphs with pertinent subheadings. . . . [The book] reinforces the concept of balancing stock investments with an umbrella-versus-suntan-lotion example that has the great subtext of suggesting stock investment can be as risky as the weather." SLJ

    Includes glossary and bibliographical references

Thompson, Helen

    Investing money. Mason Crest Publishers 2010 64p il (Junior library of money) $22.95; pa $9.95

Grades: 6 7 8 9   **332.6**

    1. Money 2. Personal finance 3. Saving and investment

    ISBN 978-1-4222-1766-5; 1-4222-1766-3; 978-1-4222-1885-3 pa; 1-4222-1885-6 pa

                         LC 2010027815

This title presents "solid information and [has] eye-catching and relevant illustrations. . . . Investing Money includes a 'risk/reward' pyramid and touches on diversified investments with a nice piggy-bank analogy about hiding your full piggy banks in different spots around the house in case of disaster or theft. . . . [The book is] clearly written, making understandable connections between daily life and financial concepts." SLJ

Includes glossary and bibliographical references

Understanding the stock market. Mason Crest Publishers 2010 64p il (Junior library of money) $22.95; pa $9.95

Grades: 6 7 8 9   **332.6**
1. Investments 2. Stock exchanges
ISBN 978-1-4222-1773-3; 1-4222-1773-6; 978-1-4222-1892-1 pa; 1-4222-1892-9 pa
LC 2010028431

This is an introduction to how the stock market works, including concepts such as shares, investing, The Dow Jones Industrial Average, bull markets and bear markets, and the stock market's effect on the economy.

This title presents "solid information and [has] eye-catching and relevant illustrations. . . . [It is] clearly written, making understandable connections between daily life and financial concepts." SLJ

Includes glossary and bibliographical references

332.64 Exchange of securities and commodities; speculation

Blumenthal, Karen
Six days in October; the stock market crash of 1929. Atheneum Bks. for Young Readers 2002 156p il $17.95

Grades: 7 8 9 10   **332.64**
1. Great Depression, 1929-1939 2. New York Stock Exchange, Inc. 3. United States -- Economic conditions -- 1919-1933
ISBN 0-689-84276-7
LC 2001-46360

A comprehensive review of the events, personalities, and mistakes behind the Stock Market Crash of 1929, featuring photographs, newspaper articles, and cartoons of the day

"This fast-paced, gripping . . . account of the market crash of October 1929 puts a human face on the crisis." Publ Wkly

Includes bibliographical references

332.7 Credit

Byers, Ann
First credit cards and credit smarts. Rosen Pub. 2010 64p il (Get smart with your money) lib bdg $29.95; pa $12.95

Grades: 7 8 9 10 11 12   **332.7**
1. Credit cards 2. Consumer credit
ISBN 978-1-4358-5271-6 lib bdg; 1-4358-5271-0 lib bdg; 978-1-4358-5548-9 pa; 1-4358-5548-5 pa
LC 2008-54969

This offers advice on managing credit, including topics such as credit scores, interest, and money management.

This offers "practical information and advice. The writing is accessible. . . . [The book is] heavily illsutrated with large, clear, up-to-date photographs of teens." SLJ

Includes glossary and bibliographical references

Tomljanovic, Tatiana
Borrowing. Weigl Pubs. 2009 32p il (Everyday economics) lib bdg $26; pa $9.95

Grades: 5 6 7   **332.7**
1. Credit
ISBN 978-1-60596-645-8 lib bdg; 1-60596-645-2 lib bdg; 978-1-60596-646-5 pa; 1-60596-646-0 pa
LC 2009018444

This "informative [book introduces borrowing in] U.S. economic theory and practices using everyday language and real-life examples. [It] includes history, a brief annotated chronology, sidebar and intext explanations of terminology, and helpful diagrams. . . . With brief paragraphs; large, captioned photographs; ample margins; and well-organized graphics, the [book's] design makes economics accessible without sacrificing content. . . . [This is] easy to navigate and full of solid information and interesting facts." SLJ

Includes glossary

333.7 Natural resources and energy

Cunningham, Kevin
Soil. Morgan Reynolds Pub. 2010 111p il (Diminishing resources) $28.95

Grades: 8 9 10 11 12   **333.7**
1. Soils 2. Soil conservation
ISBN 978-1-59935-114-8; 1-59935-114-5
LC 2009-10487

"The first chapter of Soil discusses how depletion of this resource began as far back as the Neolithic age, and the book continues through time, closing with today's efforts to conserve soil in places such as Iceland. In addition to being great research resources, [this title is] interesting enough for pleasure reading. [It contains] beautiful, full-page photographs, as well as a helpful time line." SLJ

Includes bibliographical references

Gazlay, Suzy
Managing green spaces; careers in wilderness and wildlife management. Crabtree 2010 64p il (Green-collar careers) lib bdg $30.60; pa $10.95

Grades: 4 5 6 7   **333.7**
1. Wildlife 2. Wilderness areas 3. Vocational guidance
ISBN 978-0-7787-4855-7 lib bdg; 0-7787-4855-3 lib bdg; 978-0-7787-4866-3 pa; 0-7787-4866-9 pa
LC 2009-28145

"Passions often lead to professions, as this upbeat title . . . shows. . . . There is inevitable overlap among the categories: government-run parks and forestry, outdoor adventure, science, and wildlife sanctuaries. The browsable format, combining many crisp color photos with blocks of narrative texts and sidebars featuring specific ecoprofessionals, will easily lead students through the survey of nature-focused careers." Booklist

333.72   Conservation and protection

Dell, Pamela

Protecting the planet; environmental activism. Compass Point Books 2010 64p il (Green generation) lib bdg $31.99; pa $6.95

Grades: 5 6 7 8 9   **333.72**
   1. Environmental movement   2. Environmental protection
   ISBN 978-0-7565-4248-1 lib bdg; 0-7565-4248-0 lib bdg; 978-0-7565-4295-5 pa; 0-7565-4295-2 pa
                   LC 2009-8782

"The cover design, layout, and graphics feel hip and of the moment. The clear writing is easy to understand and includes many concrete examples of environmentally friendly practices. . . . [A] good choice[s] for both leisure reading and reports." SLJ

Includes glossary and bibliographical references

Fuoco, Gina Dal

Earth. Compass Point Books 2009 40p il (Mission: science) lib bdg $26.60

Grades: 4 5 6   **333.72**
   1. Earth
   ISBN 978-0-7565-4070-8 lib bdg; 0-7565-4070-4 lib bdg
                   LC 2008-37575

Discusses the basic parts systems (atmosphere, hydrosphere, and geosphere) of Earth and how important it is to protect Earth's resources

Includes glossary

The **green** movement; Debra A. Miller, book editor. Greenhaven Press 2010 219p (Current controversies) lib bdg $39.70; pa $27.50

Grades: 7 8 9 10   **333.72**
   1. Environmental movement
   ISBN 978-0-7377-4913-7 lib bdg; 0-7377-4913-X lib bdg; 978-0-7377-4914-4 pa; 0-7377-4914-8 pa
                   LC 2010003354

"This book presents varying opinions concerning the [green] movement. Proponents view green efforts as necessary to guarantee a sustainable future and advocate for current change in this direction. . . . Opponents view these opinions as merely hype and offer counter perspectives. Readers are given a balanced view of the subject through pro and con arguments presented in a question-and-response format. . . . A useful purchase for school and public libraries." SLJ

Includes bibliographical references

Green, Jen

Conservation; Jen Green. Heinemann Library 2012 64 p. (The impact of environmentalism) (hb) $35

Grades: 6 7 8   **333.72**
   1. Environmental movement   2. Biodiversity conservation 3. Conservation of natural resources   4. Environmentalism 5. Conservation of natural resources
   ISBN 1432965166; 9781432965167; 9781432965228
                   LC 2012000824

This book by Jen Green is part of the series "The Impact of Environmentalism". It "addresses biodiversity and efforts to assist endangered animals" (Booklist) and "looks at the way changing ideas about the environment and sustainability have affected our attitudes to conservation, and will do so in the future." (Publisher's note)

Includes bibliographical references and index.

Kelsey, Elin

★ **Not** your typical book about the environment; illustrated by Clayton Hammer. Owlkids 2010 64p il $22.95; pa $10.95

Grades: 4 5 6 7   **333.72**
   1. Environmental protection 2. Ecology 3. Sustainable living
   ISBN 978-1-897349-79-3; 1-897349-79-3; 978-1-897349-84-7 pa; 1-897349-84-X pa

Written to allay children's fears about the environment, this book shows how smart technologies, innovative ideas, and a growing commitment to alternative lifestyles are exploding around the world, creating a future that will be brighter than we sometimes might think. Includes profiles of unexpected personalities.

"Imaginative, comic-booklike illustrations add to a lively layout that will keep readers moving from one paragraph to the next, and funny wordplay prevents the facts from becoming overwhelming or dry. . . . This hilarious, information-packed work is an excellent addition." SLJ

Kriesberg, Daniel A.

Think green, take action; books and activities for kids. illustrated by Kathleen A. Price. Libraries Unlimited 2010 136p il pa $30; e-book $30

Grades: Adult Professional   **333.72**
   1. Environmental sciences -- Study and teaching
   ISBN 978-1-59884-378-1 pa; 1-59884-378-8 pa; 978-1-59884-379-8 e-book
                   LC 2010014409

"A resource for teaching environmental understanding and activism through stewardship, this book outlines teaching strategies for ages 6-10, provides resources for understanding environmental concerns for ages 10-13, and promotes action and growth for ages 13+. Chapters focus on local ecology, endangered species, resource depletion, and pollution. Extensive annotated bibliographies of both recent and older fiction and nonfiction selections . . . supplement the activities." SLJ

Includes bibliographical references

Leardi, Jeanette

Making cities green. Bearport Pub. 2009 32p il (Going green) lib bdg $25.27

Grades: 4 5 6 7 **333.72**

1. Urban ecology 2. Renewable energy resources
ISBN 978-1-59716-961-5 lib bdg; 1-59716-961-7
lib bdg

LC 2009-19166

"Color photographs (most full page) and a few diagrams accompany the informative text[s]. . . . Overall, the [book] . . . is user-friendly and covers topics that are not easily found elsewhere." SLJ

Includes glossary and bibliographical references

McKay, Kim

True green kids; 100 things you can do to save the planet. [by] Kim McKay and Jenny Bonnin. National Geographic 2008 143p il $15.95

Grades: 4 5 6 7 **333.72**

1. Environmental protection
ISBN 978-1-4263-0442-2; 1-4263-0442-0

Presents an overview of global warming and describes 100 simple ways to be more environmentally friendly in the bedroom, in the house, at school, and on vacation.

"Accompanied by attractive, up-to-date pictures in a lively design, the one hundred suggestions are direct . . . and generally practical." Horn Book Guide

Includes glossary

Nagle, Jeanne

Living green; [by] Jeanne Nagle. Rosen Pub. 2009 64p il (In the news) lib bdg $21.95

Grades: 7 8 9 10 **333.72**

1. Environmental protection
ISBN 978-1-43585037-8; 1-435-85037-8

"Accessible and up-to-date. . . . Living Green presents theories of climate change and short biographies of green pioneers before examining the role of government and NGOs in environmental protection, as well as basic, earth-friendly lifestyle changes that individuals can make. Throughout, Nagle addresses the controversies that surround issues, encouraging readers to take a wide, nuanced view." Booklist

Petronis, Lexi

47 things you can do for the environment. Zest 2011 il pa $10.99

Grades: 6 7 8 9 **333.72**

1. Environmental protection
ISBN 978-0-9827322-1-2; 0-9827322-1-X

"Divided into categories revolving around habits at home, school, in the community, or on the road, [this book] offers such suggestions as shopping at vintage or second-hand stores, eating less meat, donating old cellphones, and carpooling. Each green venture is followed by concrete ideas . . . that encourage direct action. Cheerful cartoon spot art underscores the positive tone." Publ Wkly

Raatma, Lucia

Green living; no action too small. Compass Point Books 2009 64p il (Green generation) lib bdg $31.99; pa $6.95

Grades: 5 6 7 8 9 **333.72**

1. Environmental movement 2. Environmental

protection
ISBN 978-0-7565-4245-0 lib bdg; 0-7565-4245-6 lib bdg; 978-0-7565-4293-1 pa; 0-7565-4293-6 pa

LC 2009-8779

Shows children how can they make a difference. From fighting global warming to protecting wildlife, this book contains the information young environmentalists need to change the world

"The cover design, layout, and graphics feel hip and of the moment. The clear writing is easy to understand and includes many concrete examples of environmentally friendly practices. . . . [A] good [choice] for both leisure reading and reports." SLJ

Includes glossary and bibliographical references

Rapp, Valerie

Protecting Earth's land; by Valerie Rapp. Lerner Publications 2009 72p il map (Saving our living Earth) lib bdg $30.60

Grades: 5 6 7 8 **333.72**

1. Environmental protection
ISBN 978-0-8225-7559-7 lib bdg; 0-8225-7559-0 lib bdg

LC 2008-3549

"Provides a thorough, interesting discussion of multiple aspects of [land protection], including historical origins, the current situation, and potential solutions. . . . Photos from around the world accompany discussions. . . . [This is a] solid choice to replace outdated books." SLJ

Includes glossary and bibliographical references

★ **Recycle** this book; 100 top children's book authors tell you how to go green. edited by Dan Gutman. Yearling 2009 267p pa $5.99

Grades: 5 6 7 8 **333.72**

1. Authors 2. Recycling 3. Environmental protection
ISBN 978-0-385-73721-0 pa; 0-385-73721-1 pa

LC 2008-10800

"This lively collection of brief essays (and a poem) by 100 outstanding children's and young adult authors teaches through example. Each selection highlights a small step (or steps) taken by the writer toward a greener Earth. . . . The essays also provide insight into the lives and thoughts of many familiar and beloved authors such as Laurie Halse Anderson, Ralph Fletcher, Gary Schmidt, Lois Lowry, Susan Patron, and Rick Riordan. Several pages of Web sites offer a starting point for action and information. Highly useful for classroom and family discussions and science-project ideas." SLJ

Reilly, Kathleen M.

Planet Earth; 25 environmental projects you can build yourself. Nomad Press 2008 122p il (Projects you can build yourself) $21.95; pa $14.95

Grades: 4 5 6 7 **333.72**

1. Science projects 2. Environmental sciences
ISBN 978-1-934670-05-7; 1-934670-05-7; 978-1-934670-04-0 pa; 1-934670-04-9 pa

"Both comprehensive and approachable, this title . . . combines explanations of science concepts and environmental issues with hands-on projects. . . . Elementary- and middle-school students will find the succinct overview of the facts very useful, and they'll welcome the clearly presented projects." Booklist

Rohmer, Harriet

★ **Heroes** of the environment; true stories of people who are helping to protect our planet. illustrated by Julie McLaughlin. Chronicle Books 2009 109p il map $16.99

Grades: 4 5 6   **333.72**

1. Environmentalists

ISBN 978-0-8118-6779-5; 0-8118-6779-X

LC 2009004366

"Engaging graphics and clear writing combine to provide a compelling reading experience." Sci Books Films

Sivertsen, Linda

Generation green; the ultimate teen guide to living an eco-friendly life. written by Linda Sivertsen and Tosh Sivertsen. Simon Pulse 2008 248p pa $10.99

Grades: 5 6 7 8   **333.72**

1. Environmental movement

ISBN 978-1-4169-6122-2; 1-4169-6122-4

"A thorough yet accessible manual on green living. . . . The book's incisive voice, using teen idioms, is accessible to those who have little or no background in environmental issues, yet the standards within will likewise engage readers already committed to being green. . . . [This book is] unique, for its central focus is not to explain the science behind current environmental challenges, but rather to reveal how young people can work to solve those problems in their everyday lives." SLJ

Includes bibliographical references

Smalley, Carol Parenzan

Green changes you can make around your home. Mitchell Lane Publishers 2010 47p il (Tell your parents) lib bdg $21.50

Grades: 4 5 6 7   **333.72**

1. Environmental movement   2. Environmental protection

ISBN 978-1-58415-764-9 lib bdg; 1-58415-764-X lib bdg

LC 2009-4527

This book that explains how to be environmentally friendly "offers numerous facts and statistics, all of which are cited. . . . Chapters cover present-day issues and . . . are interspersed with full-color photographs and short 'Did You Know' trivia boxes. . . . Back matter includes detailed resource lists and 'Try This!' experiments." SLJ

Includes glossary and bibliographical references

Strange, Cordelia

Environmental science & protection; keeping our planet green. Mason Crest Publishers 2011 64p il map (New careers for the 21st century: finding your role in the global renewal) lib bdg $22.95; pa $9.95

Grades: 7 8 9 10   **333.72**

1. Vocational guidance   2. Environmental sciences   3.

Environmental protection

ISBN 978-1-4222-1813-6 lib bdg; 1-4222-1813-9 lib bdg; 978-1-4222-2034-4 pa; 1-4222-2034-6 pa

LC 2010011418

"Chapters identify and emphasize specific careers–important strengths, necessary aptitudes and interests, education and training, projected earnings, closely related occupations, type of work environment, and predictions for the future of the field. . . . Color photos have a small role amid the many statistics, figures, graphs and charts that support and supplement the . . . [text]." SLJ

Includes bibliographical references

Try this at home; planet-friendly projects for kids. Jackie Farquhar, D.I.Y. editor. Owlkids 2009 93p il pa $10.95

Grades: 5 6 7 8   **333.72**

1. Environmental protection

ISBN 978-2-89579-192-8 pa; 2-89579-192-9 pa

"Many of these projects are unique or innovative, featuring ideas like growing your own pizza ingredients and making a foosball game out of recycled corks, clothespins, and plastic fruit baskets. One of the best projects provides tips on making sure a bike is road ready, offering advice on checking the cables, gears, and oiling the chain. The book also includes sections designed to increase environmental awareness, including information on carbon footprint and 'eco all-stars.' Interactive elements, like a game board, should appeal to children. Illustrations are hip collages of full-color photographs and cartoons." SLJ

Includes bibliographical references

333.73   Land

Casper, Julie Kerr

Lands; taming the wilds. Chelsea House 2007 226p il (Natural resources) $39.50

Grades: 8 9 10 11 12   **333.73**

1. Land use

ISBN 978-0-8160-6356-7; 0-8160-6356-7

LC 2006-37262

This "addresses human impacts on all types of landscapes and how people can become responsible caretakers of these vital repositories of nature's bounty." Publisher"s note

Includes bibliographical references

Desonie, Dana

Geosphere; the land and its uses. Chelsea House 2008 200p il map (Our fragile planet) $35

Grades: 7 8 9 10   **333.73**

1. Land use   2. Human influence on nature

ISBN 978-0-8160-6217-1; 0-8160-6217-X

LC 2007-25453

Outlines the causes and effects of the human impact on the environment, discussing such topics as agriculture, mining, energy production, urbanization, and overpopulation, and describes ways to achieve sustainable environmental practices.

Includes glossary and bibliographical references

333.75 Forest lands

Casper, Julie Kerr

Forests; more than just trees. Chelsea House Publishers 2007 194p il map (Natural resources) $39.50

Grades: 8 9 10 11 12 **333.75**
1. Forests and forestry
ISBN 978-0-8160-6355-0; 0-8160-6355-9
LC 2006100042

This "focuses on the importance of all types of forests, why it is necessary to protect and conserve these natural resources, and what people can do to maintain healthy forest ecosystems." Publisher's note
Includes bibliographical references

Littlewood, Antonia

Rain forest destruction; Peter and Antonia Littlewood. Smart Apple Media 2012 46 p. col. ill., col. maps (Mapping global issues) (library) $35.65

Grades: 6 7 8 **333.75**
1. Rain forests 2. Forest conservation 3. Deforestation 4. Rain forest ecology 5. Rain forest conservation
ISBN 1599205122; 9781599205120
LC 2011017067

This book is part of the Mapping Global Issues series and it focuses on rainforest destruction. "Colorful layouts with numerous maps and graphs dominate this series, which provides an international perspective on important issues. Brief chapters frame problems, discuss their causes, and suggest possible solutions, using maps to illustrate the locations and extent of threats." (School Library Journal)
Includes bibliographical references (p. 45) and index

Stenstrup, Allen

Forests. Morgan Reynolds Pub. 2009 112p il (Diminishing resources) lib bdg $28.95

Grades: 8 9 10 11 12 **333.75**
1. Forest conservation 2. Forests and forestry
ISBN 978-1-59935-116-2; 1-59935-116-1
LC 2009-31025

"This highly readable [book] provides a unique viewpoint on the utilization of natural resources, as scientific and environmental concerns are discussed from a historical perspective. . . . [It contains] beautiful, full-page photographs, as well as a helpful time line." SLJ
Includes bibliographical references

333.76 Rural lands

Morris, Neil

The **landscape**; Neil Morris. Heinemann Library 2012 64 p. (The impact of environmentalism) (library) $35.00; (paperback) $9.99

Grades: 6 7 8 **333.76**
1. Landscape protection 2. Environmental movement 3. Landscape changes 4. Landscape assessment 5. Landscapes -- Environmental aspects
ISBN 1432965247; 9781432965181; 9781432965242
LC 2012001036

This book by Neil Morris is part of the "Impact of Environmentalism" series. It "looks at the way changing ideas about the environment and sustainability have affected our attitudes to the landscape, and will do so in the future." (Publisher's note) "Visual evidence shows how lands have been changed by human activities." The "book also discusses . . . efforts by humankind to protect the environment and create sustainable smaller environments." (School Library Journal)
Includes bibliographical references and index

333.78 Recreational and wilderness areas

Carson, Mary Kay

The **park** scientists; Mary Kay Carson ; with photographs by Tom Uhlman. Houghton Mifflin Harcourt 2014 80 p. (Scientists in the field) $18.99

Grades: 4 5 6 7 8 9 **333.78**
1. Science 2. National parks and reserves -- United States 3. Park rangers -- United States 4. Interpretation of cultural and natural resources -- United States
ISBN 0547792689; 9780547792682
LC 2013039895

Written by Mary Kay Carson and illustrated by Tom Uhlman, this children's book describes how "America's National Parks are protected places and have become living museums for as many as 270 million visitors per year! In addition, researchers are able to perform long term studies of a wide number of subjects from salamanders the size of thumbnails to gigantic geothermal geysers. These parks are natural laboratories for scientists." (Publisher's note)

"The National Park System is often known as the nation's own backyard due to the possibilities it provides for leisure, recreation, and scientific study. This entry into the long-running Scientists in the Field series celebrates this by focusing on three specific parks: Yellowstone, Saguaro, and the Great Smoky Mountains... With a conservationist bent, Carson describes just how accessible these real-life "natural laboratories and living museums" are and how each individual can act with the same spirit of inquiry as the scientist-explorers detailed here." Booklist

McHugh, Erin

National Parks; A Kid's Guide to America's Parks, Monuments and Landmarks. Erin McHugh ; Art by Neal Aspinall, Doug Leen, and Brian Maebius. Black Dog & Leventhal Publishers 2012 128 p. col. ill., col. map (hbk.) $19.95; (hbk.) $19.95

Grades: 4 5 6 **333.78**
1. National parks and reserves -- United States
ISBN 157912884X; 9781579128845

This book, "arranged alphabetically by state . . . tours more than 75 U.S. parks, monuments, and landmarks, from the rocky shores of Maine's Acadia National Park to the ancient redwood groves of Northern California. Also included is a removable, fold-out collector map to house" the commemorative quarters from the America the Beautiful series. (Publisher's note)

333.79 Energy

Bowden, Rob, 1973-

Energy sources; the impact of science and technology. Gareth Stevens Pub. 2010 64p il (Pros and cons) lib bdg $35

Grades: 5 6 7 8   **333.79**

1. Energy resources

ISBN 978-1-4339-1987-9 lib bdg; 1-4339-1987-7 lib bdg

LC 2009-12434

"Looks at how scientific and technological advances in recent decades have dramatically altered the way we live—and examines both positive and negative impacts of these changes." Publisher's note

Includes glossary and bibliographical references

Brezina, Corona

Jobs in sustainable energy. Rosen Pub. 2010 80p il (Green careers) lib bdg $30

Grades: 5 6 7 8   **333.79**

1. Vocational guidance 2. Renewable energy resources

ISBN 978-1-4358-3569-6 lib bdg; 1-4358-3569-7 lib bdg

LC 2009021855

This "well-conceived [introduction focuses] on various jobs in [sustainable energy], the education and experience required, and expected earnings. The [book is] well organized, making it easy to gain an overview of the major aspects of the work. . . . [This book] will make [a] good [addition] to career collections. Photographs from the field and website and contact information for professional organizations add value." SLJ

Includes glossary and bibliographical references

Caduto, Michael J.

★ **Catch** the wind, harness the sun; 22 supercharged science projects for kids. Storey Pub. 2011 223p il $26.95; pa $16.95

Grades: 5 6 7 8   **333.79**

1. Energy conservation 2. Renewable energy resources 3. Science -- Experiments

ISBN 978-1-60342-971-9; 1-60342-971-9; 978-1-60342-794-4 pa; 1-60342-794-5 pa; 1603427945 pa; 1603429719; 9781603427944 pa; 9781603429719

LC 2010051169

"The eco-themed activities that Caduto lays out here are only the beginning, as he embeds them in short but clear explanations of relevant scientific facts, profiles of young eco-activists, provocative follow-up questions, photos and cartoon spot art aplenty, folktales, and other enhancements." Booklist

Flath, Camden

Careers in green energy; fueling the world with renewable resources. Mason Crest Publishers 2010 64p il map (New careers for the 21st century: finding your role in the global renewal) lib bdg $22.95; pa $9.95

Grades: 7 8 9 10   **333.79**

1. Vocational guidance 2. Renewable energy resources

ISBN 978-1-4222-1812-9 lib bdg; 1-4222-1812-0 lib bdg; 978-1-4222-2033-7 pa; 1-4222-2033-8 pa

LC 2010020683

"Chapters identify and emphasize specific careers—important strengths, necessary aptitudes and interests, education and training, projected earnings, closely related occupations, type of work environment, and predictions for the future of the field. . . . Color photos have a small role amid the many statistics, figures, graphs and charts that support and supplement the . . . [text]." SLJ

Includes bibliographical references

Friedman, Lauri S.

Energy alternatives; Lauri S. Friedman, book editor. Greenhaven Press 2011 154p il map (Introducing issues with opposing viewpoints) $36.82

Grades: 7 8 9 10   **333.79**

1. Renewable energy resources

ISBN 978-0-7377-5198-7; 0-7377-5198-3

LC 2011000872

Essays examine both sides of the questions raised about energy alternatives.

This is is an "excellent [resource] both for student research and for personal interest." Booklist

Includes bibliographical references

Gardner, Robert

Energy; green science projects about solar, wind, and water power. Enslow Publishers 2011 128p il (Team Green science projects) lib bdg $31.93

Grades: 6 7 8 9 10   **333.79**

1. Energy resources 2. Science projects 3. Science -- Experiments

ISBN 978-0-7660-3643-7; 0-7660-3643-X

This book offers science experiments about energy resources and energy conservation.

"Gardner provides plenty of information, well-designed experiments, and demonstrations, and then shares brief science-fair ideas. . . . Experiments and demonstrations are presented with clear step-by-step instructions and occasional illustrations and represent a wide range of complexity." SLJ

Includes glossary and bibliographical references

Gunderson, Jessica

The **energy** dilemma. Creative Education 2010 48p il (Earth issues) lib bdg $34.25

Grades: 6 7 8 9 10   **333.79**

1. Pollution 2. Energy resources

ISBN 978-1-58341-980-9 lib bdg; 1-58341-980-2 lib bdg

LC 2009-28048

"Unfamiliar words are printed in bold type and defined in the glossary for students. . . . Written in a straightforward manner, with photographs that are clearly captioned, . . . [this] is a welcome addition for libraries." Libr Media Connect

"An examination of the resources humans use to create energy, exploring fossil fuels' impacts on the environment and discussing cleaner, more sustainable options that may contribute to a healthier planet." Publisher's note

Includes glossary and bibliographical references

Kallen, Stuart A.

Renewable energy research. ReferencePoint Press 2010 96p il (Inside science) lib bdg $26.95

Grades: 7 8 9 10 **333.79**

1. Renewable energy resources

ISBN 978-1-60152-129-3; 1-60152-129-4

LC 2010-18102

This "offers the necessary information for stellar reports. Politics, debates, and ethical concerns are briefly and fairly mentioned, but the . . . [book concentrates] on consistent, documented, and well-balanced scientific coverage. The human stories sprinkled throughout will help kids identify with both scientists and patients." SLJ

Includes bibliographical references

Laidlaw, Jill A.

Energy; by Jill Laidlaw. Amicus 2011 44p il map (Sustaining our environment) lib bdg $31.35

Grades: 6 7 8 9 **333.79**

1. Energy resources 2. Renewable energy resources

ISBN 978-1-60753-136-4 lib bdg; 1-60753-136-4 lib bdg

LC 2009-29985

"The tone is refreshingly optimistic with its examples of specific steps being taken to reduce harm to the environment. Sidebars highlight case studies and campaigns from around the world and from the individual to the national levels. Clear, informative captions accompany the excellent selection of color photographs, charts and graphs." SLJ

Includes glossary

McPherson, Stephanie Sammartino

★ **Arctic** thaw; climate change and the global race for energy resources. Stephanie Sammartino McPherson. Twenty-First Century Books 2015 64 p. color illustrations, color map (library binding : alkaline paper) $34.60

Grades: 6 7 8 9 10 **333.79**

1. Global warming 2. International relations 3. Arctic regions -- Exploration 4. Climate change -- Arctic regions 5. Power resources -- Arctic regions 6. Natural resources -- Arctic regions 7. Economic development -- Arctic regions

ISBN 1467720437; 9781467720434

LC 2013025164

In this book on climate change, author Stephanie Sammartino McPherson "describe[s] the changes in polar ice cover that are encouraging exploration and allowing access to previously inaccessible energy resources. Subsequent chapters describe new, shorter ocean passages, the jockeying for territory as nearby nations lay claim and others look for ways to get involved, and the likely difficulties of development." (Kirkus Reviews)

"Succinct and clearly written, the text offers up-to-date information, illustrated with clear color photos and useful maps. An articulate introduction to the Arctic in a time of profound, striking changes." Booklist

Includes bibliographical references (pages 59-60) and index

Miller, Debra A.

Energy production and alternative energy; Michael E. Miller consulting editor. Greenhaven Press 2011 123p il map (Confronting global warming) lib bdg $37.10

Grades: 7 8 9 10 11 12 **333.79**

1. Electric power 2. Renewable energy resources

ISBN 978-0-7377-5106-2; 0-7377-5106-1

LC 2010024976

Discusses the world's history of energy production and consumption, and explains how alternative energy sources may help with the coming fossil fuel energy crisis and protecting the worldwide environment.

"Presented in a scholarly design that will appeal to older readers. . . . The illustrations and pictures support the text, and the graphics and sidebars are well placed." Libr Media Connect

Includes glossary and bibliographical references

Rau, Dana Meachen

Alternative energy beyond fossil fuels. Compass Point Books 2010 64p il (Green generation) lib bdg $31.99; pa $6.95

Grades: 5 6 7 8 9 **333.79**

1. Energy resources 2. Renewable energy resources

ISBN 978-0-7565-4247-4 lib bdg; 0-7565-4247-2 lib bdg; 978-0-7565-4289-4 pa; 0-7565-4289-8 pa

LC 2009-08778

"This great little book introduces the topics of fossil fuel usage, the limited nature of fossil fuels, and alternative energy options. It is particularly praiseworthy for its refreshingly objective, but still enthusiastic, presentations on solar, wind, geothermal, hydro, and biomass energy. . . . Interesting, well-written, and appropriately illustrated, the book is entertaining enough for general reading, but factual enough for use as a science text." Sci Books Films

Includes glossary and bibliographical references

Rigsby, Mike

Doable renewables; 16 alternative energy projects for young scientists. Chicago Review Press 2010 196p il pa $16.95

Grades: 6 7 8 9 10 **333.79**

1. Renewable energy resources 2. Science -- Experiments

ISBN 978-1-56976-343-8 pa; 1-56976-343-7 pa

LC 2010019520

This is a "collection of science-oriented projects, focused . . . on renewable energy sources. From a windmill . . . to a human-powered LED light that relies on a hand-cranked generator, this activities range in complexity and skill, but all use simple technology to show basic and fascinating processes." Booklist

Sobey, Ed

Solar cell and renewable energy experiments. Enslow Publishers 2011 128p il (Cool science projects with technology) lib bdg $31.93

Grades: 6 7 8 9 **333.79**

1. Renewable energy resources 2. Science --

Experiments
ISBN 978-0-7660-3305-4; 0-7660-3305-8

LC 2010027430

This explains what solar cells do and how they work, how wind and water power electronics, and offers experiments in renewable energy.

Includes glossary and bibliographical references

Solway, Andrew

Renewable energy sources. Raintree 2010 48p il (Sci-hi: Earth and space science) lib bdg $31.43; pa $8.99

Grades: 4 5 6 7   333.79

1. Renewable energy resources

ISBN 978-1-4109-3351-5 lib bdg; 1-4109-3351-2 lib bdg; 978-1-4109-3361-4 pa; 1-4109-3361-X pa

LC 2009-3535

"Multiple colorful sidebars and large and small diagrams and photographs will help students to grasp the fundamentals being discussed, and the easy but interesting science experiments will act as further reinforcements." SLJ

Includes glossary and bibliographical references

Thaddeus, Eva

Powering the future; new energy technologies. with illustrations by Catherine Paplin. University of New Mexico Press 2010 125p il map (Worlds of wonder) $24.95

Grades: 6 7 8 9 10   333.79

1. Renewable energy resources

ISBN 978-0-8263-4901-9; 0-8263-4901-3

LC 2009044300

The author tackles "environmental issues with depth and rigor, attuned to both current events and the concerns of today's teens. . . . The excellent [text is] enhanced by color photographs and diagrams that further explain scientific ideas." Horn Book Guide

Includes glossary

333.8   Subsurface resources

Gardner, Timothy

Oil. Morgan Reynolds Pub. 2009 111p il (Diminishing resources) lib bdg $28.95

Grades: 8 9 10 11 12   333.8

1. Petroleum 2. Energy conservation 3. Greenhouse effect

ISBN 978-1-59935-117-9; 1-59935-117-X

LC 2009-10245

This book about oil "will draw activists, but even readers who do not think they care that much will find the facts devastating. Quotes from authoritative sources . . . about both the historic overview and the contemporary crisis accompany full-color double-page photos that show what is happening now. . . . [The book] discusses in detail the role of the Middle East, the effects of America's addiction to cars, and always, the current focus on global warming." Booklist

Includes bibliographical references

Gorman, Jacqueline Laks

Fossil fuels. Gareth Stevens Pub. 2009 48p il map (What if we do nothing?) lib bdg $31

Grades: 5 6 7 8   333.8

1. Coal 2. Petroleum 3. Environmental protection

ISBN 978-1-4339-0087-7 lib bdg; 1-4339-0087-4 lib bdg

LC 2008-29214

This "examines a potential crisis, its historical causes, scientific background, and possible outcome if no action is taken. . . . [The book] makes the connection between climate change and the use of polluting energy sources, and the Kyoto Protocol's plans for the reduction of globe-warming emissions are considered. . . . Full-color photographs, charts, and maps help illustrate some of the ideas and problems." SLJ

Includes glossary and bibliographical references

Hartman, Eve

Fossil fuels; [by] Eve Hartman and Wendy Meshbesher. Raintree 2010 48p il map (Sci-hi: Earth and space science) lib bdg $31.43; pa $8.99

Grades: 4 5 6 7   333.8

1. Coal 2. Oils and fats

ISBN 978-1-4109-3350-8 lib bdg; 1-4109-3350-4 lib bdg; 978-1-4109-3360-7 pa; 1-4109-3360-1 pa

LC 2009-3548

"Multiple colorful sidebars and large and small diagrams and photographs will help students to grasp the fundamentals being discussed, and the easy but interesting science experiments will act as further reinforcements." SLJ

Includes glossary and bibliographical references

Mooney, Carla

Oil spills and offshore drilling. ReferencePoint Press 2011 96p il map (Compact research: energy and the environment) lib bdg $26.95

Grades: 7 8 9 10 11 12   333.8

1. Oil spills 2. Offshore oil well drilling

ISBN 978-1-60152-141-5; 1-60152-141-3

LC 2010037325

This volume has "up-to-date information with frequent references to . . . the Deepwater Horizon disaster in the Gulf of Mexico. . . . [It] asks if the U.S. needs to drill offshore, if it's an environmental risk, if regulations are adequate, and discusses the future of offshore drilling. . . . Each chapter is followed by a section of primary-source quotes espousing pro and con views. . . . [This is a] first-rate ready-reference [book] and excellent to use in teaching research with primary documents." SLJ

Includes bibliographical references

333.9   Other natural resources

Dobson, Clive

Wind power; 20 projects to make with paper. Firefly Books 2010 96p il $24.95; pa $12.95

Grades: 5 6 7 8   333.9

1. Wind power 2. Paper crafts

ISBN 978-1-55407-659-8; 1-55407-659-5; 978-1-55407-749-6 pa; 1-55407-749-4 pa

"In this informative craft book, a celebration of wind and of innovative efforts to harness its energy, Dobson describes the geometric and aerodynamic principles behind windmills, sails, and wind turbines, then implements these concepts via 20 paper projects, ranging from a two-blade pinwheel to a dramatic 'Squirrel Cage' turbine. . . . Readers should gain a more palpable understanding of the subject matter by building and watching the graceful compositions function." Publ Wkly

333.91 Water and lands adjoining bodies of water

Currie, Stephen

Hydropower. ReferencePoint Press 2011 96p il map (Compact research: energy and the environment) $26.95

Grades: 7 8 9 10 11 12 **333.91**
1. Hydroelectric power plants 2. Renewable energy resources
ISBN 978-1-60152-122-4; 1-60152-122-7
LC 2010017393

This volume has "up-to-date information with frequent references to the Three Gorges Dam in China. . . . [It] poses questions concerning the possibility of reducing dependency on fossil fuels, the impact of hydropower on the environment, how developing countries can benefit from its use, and if the oceans represent the future of hydropower. . . . [This volume is a] first-rate ready-reference [book] and excellent to use in teaching research with primary documents." SLJ

Includes bibliographical references

Kallen, Stuart

Running dry; the global water crisis. by Stuart A. Kallen. Twenty-First Century Books 2015 64 p. illustrations (chiefly color) (lib. bdg. : alk. paper) $33.32

Grades: 5 6 7 8 **333.91**
1. Water supply 2. Water conservation 3. Water-supply 4. Water consumption 5. Water -- Pollution
ISBN 146772646X; 9781467726467; 9781467763080
LC 2014003223

This book, by Stuart A. Kallen "provides information on the growing water crisis. Looking at the subject globally, the discussion includes matters such as the dwindling supply of fresh water, its pollution by agriculture and industry, the dramatic effects of climate change, and the increasing competition for water. . . . Sidebars and full-page features spotlight pertinent topics such as the desalination of sea water." (Booklist)

"This title provides a clear and concise look at the importance of fresh water in sustaining life on earth . . . the book will appeal to those with little or no background on the subject. An excellent source for student research." SLJ

Includes bibliographical references and index

Kaye, Cathryn Berger

★ **Going** blue; a teen guide to saving our oceans & waterways. by Cathryn Berger Kaye; with Philippe Cousteau and Earth Echo International. Free Spirit Pub. 2010 151p il map pa $14.95

Grades: 6 7 8 9 10 **333.91**
1. Marine ecology 2. Marine pollution 3. Environmental protection
ISBN 978-1-57542-348-7; 1-57542-348-0
LC 2010-16589

Teaches young people about the Earth's water crisis and provides practical suggestions on how readers can identify water-related needs in the community and transform their ideas into action.

"This valuable how-to manual is suitable for an individual student, a family, a youth group, or a school wishing to protect our precious resource of water. This upbeat treasure will challenge anyone interested in environmental activism, whether water related or not. It is a must for any library serving youth." Voice Youth Advocates

Includes bibliographical references

Laidlaw, Jill A.

Water; by Jill Laidlaw. Amicus 2011 44p il map (Sustaining our environment) lib bdg $31.35

Grades: 6 7 8 9 **333.91**
1. Water 2. Water supply
ISBN 978-1-60753-140-1; 1-60753-140-2
LC 2009028258

This book looks at key environmental and social issues that are linked with water and highlights what is being done to try to make water sustainable for all.

"The tone is refreshingly optimistic with its examples of specific steps being taken to reduce harm to the environment. Sidebars highlight case studies and campaigns from around the world and from the individual to the national levels. Clear, informative captions accompany the excellent selection of color photographs, charts and graphs." SLJ

Includes glossary

Mulder, Michelle, 1976-

★ **Every** last drop; bringing clean water home. Michelle Mulder. Orca Book Pub 2014 48 p. illustrations (some color) (Orca footprints) (hardcover) $19.95

Grades: 4 5 6 7 **333.91**
1. Water conservation 2. Water resources development 3. Water quality management
ISBN 9781459802247; 9781459807129; 1459802233; 9781459802230
LC 2013951377

This book, by Michelle Mulder, "looks at why the world's water resources are at risk and how communities around the world are finding innovative ways to quench their thirst and water their crops. Maybe you're not ready to drink fog, as they do in Chile, or use water made from treated sewage, but you can get a low-flush toilet, plant a tree, protect a wetland or just take shorter showers." (Publisher's note)

"Divided into four chapters, this book explores the history of water use by humans; the natural cycle of water on earth; how people access, clean, and desalinate water; and ways in which we can conserve and preserve our water resources. Plenty of well-captioned photos, including some from the author's own travels, illustrate and personalize the accessible text." Horn Book

333.95   Biological resources

Endangered oceans: opposing viewpoints; Louise I. Gerdes, book editor. Greenhaven Press 2009 234p il (Opposing viewpoints series) lib bdg $38.50; pa $26.75

Grades: 8 9 10 11 12   **333.95**

1. Marine ecology 2. Marine pollution 3. Environmental policy

ISBN 978-0-7377-4210-7 lib bdg; 978-0-7377-4211-4 pa

LC 2008-36462

Articles in this anthology cover such topics as overfishing and loss of coral reefs, government policies to protect ocean life, sustainable fishing, and the effects of human activities on marine mammals.

Includes bibliographical references

Guerive, Gaelle

Extraordinary endangered animals; by Sandrine Silhol & Gaëlle Guérive; illustrated by Marie Doucedame. Abrams 2011 il $24.95

Grades: 5 6 7 8   **333.95**

1. Endangered species

ISBN 978-1-4197-0034-7; 1-4197-0034-0

"Detailed, large-scale photographs and intricate drawings depict 35 endangered species from around the globe, including the California condor, the sea otter, the golden lion tamarin, and the sawfish. Silhol and Guérive describe the habitat, behavior, and endangered status of each animal, while sidebars place each in human context, implicating our role in their endangerment. . . . Honest but not downbeat, this informative collection encourages readers to take action before these species disappear." Publ Wkly

Kurlansky, Mark, 1948-

The **world** without fish; how could we let this happen? illustrations by Frank Stockton. Workman Pub. 2011 183p il $16.95

Grades: 5 6 7 8 9 10   **333.95**

1. Water pollution 2. Commercial fishing

ISBN 978-0-7611-5607-9; 0-7611-5607-0

LC 2011-15516

It was the author's intent to communicate that "our 'enduring misconception' about nature's bounty may lead to the extinction of many of the fish we eat (such as cod, salmon, swordfish, and tuna) and the subsequent collapse of marine ecosystems . . . . To avoid the dystopia he fears, Kurlansky stresses the importance of supporting sustainable fishing and hopes to enlist his readers to act to help 'change the way we do things!'" (Science)

"Brief sections in graphic-novel format follow a young girl, Ailat, and her father over a couple of decades as the condition of the ocean grows increasingly dire, eventually an orange, slimy mess mostly occupied by jellyfish and leatherback turtles. At the end, Ailat's young daughter doesn't even know what the word fish means. This is juxtaposed against nonfiction chapters with topics including types of fishing equipment and the damage each causes, a history of the destruction of the cod and its consequences, the international politics of the fishing industry and the effects of pollution

and global warming. . . . Depressing and scary yet grimly entertaining." Kirkus

Laidlaw, Rob

★ **Saving** lives & changing hearts; animal sanctuaries and rescue centres. Fitzhenry & Whiteside 2012 62 p. $19.95

Grades: 4 5 6 7 8   **333.95**

1. Wildlife refuges 2. Wildlife rehabilitation

ISBN 1554552125; 9781554552122

This book "profiles a variety of sanctuaries throughout the world and the people who work to safeguard the wildlife. . . . The author offers the . . . stories behind the founding of many of these sanctuaries and presents . . . conclusions to the many . . . stories of rescued animals. A section showing the difference between true sanctuaries and those neither meeting the needs of animals in their care nor preparing them for rehabilitation into the wild is" included. (School Library Journal)

Mackay, Richard

The **atlas** of endangered species; Rev and updated; University of California Press 2009 128p il map pa $19.95

Grades: 6 7 8 9   **333.95**

1. Endangered species

ISBN 978-0-520-25862-4 pa; 0-520-25862-2 pa

First published 2002 in the United Kingdom

Catalogs the inhabitants of a wide variety of ecosystems, including forests, mangroves, and coral reefs. It examines the major threats to biodiversity, from loss of habitat to hunting, and describes the steps being taken toward conservation.

"More than 40 topics, among them 'Human Environmental Impact,' 'Temperate Forests,' 'Dolphins and Whales,' and 'Conserving Domestic Breeds,' are presented on double-page spreads containing full-color maps, charts, graphs, small photographs, and text. The presentation is clear and attractive." Booklist

Includes bibliographical references

Mills, Andrea

Animals like us; written and edited by Andrea Mills. DK Pub. 2005 79p il map $19.99

Grades: 5 6 7 8   **333.95**

1. Rare animals 2. Endangered species 3. Wildlife conservation

ISBN 978-0-7566-1008-1; 0-7566-1008-7

LC 2005299478

Colorful introduction to animals around the world details physical attributes, geographic distribution, and habitat.

"Captivating digital photo layouts are interspersed with 'fact files' that point out loss of habitat and dwindling animal populations." Horn Book Guide

Reptiles and amphibians; edited by Tim Harris. Brown Bear Books 2012 64 p. (Facts at your fingertips: endangered animals) (library binding) $35.65

Grades: 5 6 7 8   **333.95**

1. Reptiles 2. Amphibians 3. Endangered species 4.

Rare reptiles 5. Rare amphibians
ISBN 1936333368; 9781936333363

LC 2010053968

This book "profiles a global sampling of reptiles and amphibians in various degrees of endangerment . . . . Twenty-one species are described in . . . detail that includes information on their classification, distribution, physical characteristics, habitat, diet, and reproduction." The book is part of "the 'Facts at Your Fingertips: Endangered Animals' series, which profiles various groups of endangered species from all parts of the planet." (National Science Teachers Association)

Includes bibliographical references and index

Salmansohn, Pete, 1947-

Saving birds; heroes around the world. [by] Pete Salmansohn and Stephen W. Kress. Tilbury House 2003 39p il $16.95; pa $7.95

Grades: 5 6 7 8   **333.95**

1. Endangered species 2. Wildlife conservation 3. Birds -- Protection
ISBN 0-88448-237-5; 0-88448-276-6 pa

LC 2002-6710

Profiles adults and children working in six habitats around the world to save wild birds, some of which are on the brink of extinction.

"As a teaching aid, this volume is an exceptional supplement. The six articles relating the heroic rescue of the endangered birds are accurate and enhanced by appropriate color photographs." Sci Books Films

Sheehan, Sean

Endangered species; by Sean Sheehan. Gareth Stevens Pub. 2009 48p il map (What if we do nothing?) lib bdg $31

Grades: 5 6 7 8   **333.95**

1. Endangered species
ISBN 978-1-4339-0086-0 lib bdg; 1-4339-0086-6 lib bdg

LC 2008029167

"Using intelligent, focused text; an open design; vivid photos; and excellent maps, [this] book demands attention." Booklist

Includes bibliographical references

Should drilling be permitted in the Arctic National Wildlife Refuge? David M. Haugen, book editor. Greenhaven Press 2008 92p (At issue) lib bdg $29.95; pa $21.20

Grades: 7 8 9 10 11 12   **333.95**

1. Oil well drilling 2. Arctic National Wildlife Refuge (Alaska)
ISBN 978-0-7377-3930-5 lib bdg; 0-7377-3930-4 lib bdg; 978-0-7377-3931-2 pa; 0-7377-3931-2 pa

LC 2007-51383

"This collection of essays, . . . examines the current issue of drilling for oil in the Arctic National Wildlife Refuge (ANWR). . . . Having these essays collected into one volume makes this book a valuable option for young adults in speech and debate activities. Additional strengths are the list of organizations to contact and a bibliography of recent books and articles on this hot topic." Booklist

Includes bibliographical references

Walker, Niki

Biomass; fueling change. [by] Niki Walker. Crabtree Pub. 2007 32p il (Energy revolution) lib bdg $19.95; pa $8.95

Grades: 5 6 7 8   **333.95**

1. Biomass energy
ISBN 978-0-7787-2914-3 lib bdg; 0-7787-2914-1 lib bdg; 978-0-7787-2928-0 pa; 0-7787-2928-1 pa

LC 2006016035

This "book presents a range of historical uses of the various forms of biomass, from charcoal smelters in ancient Egypt to ethanol-fueled lanterns in the 19th century and gasifiers during World War II. Vivid color photographs with informative captions extend the [text]." SLJ

Includes glossary

336.2   Taxes

La Bella, Laura

How taxation works. Rosen Pub. 2011 80p il (Real world economics) lib bdg $30.60

Grades: 7 8 9 10   **336.2**

1. Taxation -- United States
ISBN 978-1-4358-9463-1; 1-4358-9463-4

LC 2009047165

This describes how taxation works.

Includes glossary and bibliographical references

338   Production

Rankin, Kenrya

Start it up; the complete guide to turning your passions into pay. [illustrated by Eriko Takada and Marissa Fiend] Zest Books 2011 155p il pa $14.95

Grades: 7 8 9 10 11 12   **338**

1. Entrepreneurship 2. Business enterprises
ISBN 978-0-9819733-5-7; 0-9819733-5-3

"Combining a conversational style with a systematic approach, [this book] walks teens through starting their own business. . . . Rankin gives a good overview of such difficult concepts as start-up and operating costs and asks readers to consider potentially overlooked topics like the pros and cons of publicizing prices and things to consider when working with family and friends." Booklist

338.1   Specific kinds of industries

Green, Jen

Food and farming; Jen Green. 1st ed. Heinemann Library 2012 64 p. (The impact of environmentalism) (hardcover) $35

Grades: 6 7 8 9 10   **338.1**

1. Environmental movement 2. Agriculture -- Environmental aspects 3. Food supply 4. Environmentalism 5. Agriculture -- Environmental

aspects

ISBN 1432965174; 9781432965174; 9781432965235

LC 2012001033

This book by Jen Green is part of the Impact on Environmentalism series. In "discussing the impact of the environmental movement on food and farming, Green also explores controversies surrounding modern agriculture and its distribution practices. A brief history of farming . . . leads to a discussion of more recent trends, including high-yield varieties of crops, monoculture, genetically modified foods, pesticides, water management, factory farming, organic farming, [and] fair trade." (Booklist)

Pollan, Michael

★ The **omnivore's** dilemma; the secrets behind what you eat. adapted by Richie Chevat. Young readers ed.; Dial Books 2009 298p il $17.99

Grades: 5 6 7 8 9 10   338.1

1. Food supply 2. Food chains (Ecology) 3. Food habits 4. Sustainable agriculture

ISBN 0-8037-3415-8; 978-0-8037-3415-9

LC 2009-9283

Adapted from: The omnivore's dilemma: a natural history of four meals, published 2006 by Penguin Press

This volume is adapted from Pollan's 2006 work for adults, The Omnivore's Dilemma: A Natural History of Four Meals. It presents information about food production in the United States and "encourages kids to consider the personal and global health implications of their food choices." (Publisher's note) Bibliography. Index. "Grades seven to ten." (Bull Cent Child Books)

"Adopting the role of food detective, the author 'peers behind the curtain' of the modern food industry and finds that the industrial approach to the food chain imperils our health and planet. The four sections of the volume describe differing types of meals: industrial; industrial organic; local sustainable; and hunted, gathered and found. Clear organization and lively writing rooted in fascinating examples make this accessible and interesting." Kirkus

Includes bibliographical references

338.5   General production economics

Brezina, Corona

How stimulus plans work. Rosen Pub. 2011 80p il (Real world economics) lib bdg $30.60

Grades: 7 8 9 10   338.5

1. Recessions 2. Economic policy -- United States

ISBN 978-1-4358-9464-8; 1-4358-9464-2

LC 2009045557

This "gives a simple yet comprehensive summary of a complex and expansive topic. It makes the point that all economies are cyclical and that recessions may be caused by different events. It covers deficits and Roosevelt's New Deal and Obama's stimulus plan at length, as well as the Marshall Plan and Japan's response to its recession of the 1990s." SLJ

Includes glossary and bibliographical references

Hollander, Barbara

Booms, bubbles, and busts; the economic cycle. [by] Barbara Gottfried Hollander. Heinemann Li-

brary 2010 56p il map (The global marketplace) lib bdg $33.50

Grades: 6 7 8 9   338.5

1. Business cycles 2. Financial crises

ISBN 978-1-4329-3932-8; 1-4329-3932-7

LC 2010004095

This title about the economic cycle covers "a wealth of material in concise paragraphs with pertinent subheadings. . . . [It] includes an informative time line from 2001 to 2009. . . and . . . excellent photos, charts, maps, and tables that help with the understanding of some sophisticated concepts." SLJ

Includes glossary and bibliographical references

338.6   Organization of production

Bezdecheck, Bethany

Bailout! government intervention in business. Rosen Pub. 2011 64p il (In the news) lib bdg $29.95; pa $12.95

Grades: 7 8 9 10   338.6

1. Bankruptcy 2. Corporations 3. Industrial policy -- United States

ISBN 978-1-4358-9449-5 lib bdg; 1-4358-9449-9 lib bdg; 978-1-4488-1681-1 pa; 1-4488-1681-5 pa

LC 2009052247

This " succinctly and objectively covers corporate bailouts and includes a history of government intervention in business dating back to 1970, when the government provided the Penn Central Transportation Company with $700 million to pay its creditors. . . . With numerous photos, concise and manageable chapters, and a glossary, . . . [this provides] an excellent background for students with an interest in social sciences or a jumping off point for school assignments." Voice Youth Advocates

Includes glossary and bibliographical references

338.7   Business enterprises

Buckley, A. M.

Pixar; the company and its founders. ABDO Pub. Co. 2011 112p il (Technology pioneers) lib bdg $34.22

Grades: 5 6 7 8   338.7

1. Animated films 2. Computer animation 3. Pixar Animation Studios

ISBN 978-1-61714-810-1 lib bdg; 1-61714-810-5 lib bdg; 978-1-61758-968-3 e-book

LC 2010044831

An introduction to Pixar Animation Studios and its founders.

"Written in a clear, linear fashion, this series offers vivid, well-researched details about the development of technological advancements considered essential in today's society. . . Readers who are interested in technology and inventions will be thoroughly engrossed." SLJ

Includes glossary and bibliographical references

Other titles in the series include:

Apple (2012)

Craigslist (2011)

eBay (2011)
Facebook (2013)
Google (2011)
Microsoft (2013)
Netflix (2013)
Nintendo (2011)
Sony (2013)
Tivo (2013)
Twitter (2013)

Ehrenhaft, Daniel

Larry Ellison; sheer nerve. 21st Cent. Bks. (Brookfield) 2001 80p il (Techies) lib bdg $23.93   **338.7**
1. Businesspeople 2. Computer software industry 3. Oracle Corp. 4. Computer software executives
ISBN 0-7613-1962-X

LC 2001-27167

This is a profile of the computer software executive who founded the Oracle Corporation

This "will appeal not only to report writers, but also to recreational readers." SLJ

Includes bibliographical references

Marc Andreessen; Web warrior. 21st Cent. Bks. (Brookfield) 2001 77p il (Techies) lib bdg $23.90 Grades: 6 7 8 9   **338.7**
1. Internet 2. Businesspeople 3. Computer programmers 4. Computer software executives 5. Netscape Communications Corporation
ISBN 0-7613-1964-6

LC 00-57710

This offers "a breezy style, short length, large font, numerous photographs, and attractive page design." Voice Youth Advocates

Includes bibliographical references

Firestone, Mary

Nintendo; the company and its founders. ABDO Pub. Co. 2011 112p il (Technology pioneers) lib bdg $34.22
Grades: 5 6 7 8   **338.7**
1. Video games 2. Nintendo of America Inc.
ISBN 978-1-61714-809-5 lib bdg; 1-61714-809-1 lib bdg; 978-1-61758-967-6 e-book

LC 2010044664

This is an introduction to the Nintendo video game company and its founders.

"Written in a clear, linear fashion, this series offers vivid, well-researched details about the development of technological advancements considered essential in today's society. . . Readers who are interested in technology and inventions will be thoroughly engrossed." SLJ

Includes glossary and bibliographical references

Gitlin, Marty

EBay; the company and its founder. ABDO Pub. Co. 2011 112p il (Technology pioneers) lib bdg $34.22
Grades: 5 6 7 8   **338.7**
1. Auctions 2. Executives 3. Businesspeople 4. Internet marketing 5. eBay Inc. 6. Software engineers

7. Internet executives
ISBN 978-1-61714-807-1 lib bdg; 1-61714-807-5 lib bdg; 978-1-61758-965-2 e-book

LC 2010044663

This is an introduction to eBay internet auction site and its founder, Pierre Omidyar.

"Written in a clear, linear fashion, this series offers vivid, well-researched details about the development of technological advancements considered essential in today's society. . . Readers who are interested in technology and inventions will be thoroughly engrossed." SLJ

Includes glossary and bibliographical references

Hamen, Susan E.

Google; the company and its founders. ABDO Pub. Co. 2011 112p il (Technology pioneers) lib bdg $34.22
Grades: 5 6 7 8   **338.7**
1. Computer industry 2. Web search engines 3. Computer scientists 4. Google, Inc. 5. Internet executives 6. Information technology executives
ISBN 978-1-61714-808-8; 1-61714-808-3

LC 2010037884

This book about Google and its founders "provides a compact, direct, well-researched, and relevant explanation of how Sergey Brin, Larry Page, and their brand have changed the world. . . . This title presents just the right amount of background on the two men . . . before it moves into more thorough explorations of how the founders' creation has grown far beyond providing basic Web searching. . . . Dynamically designed with clear and colorful photographs, sidebars, and wide margins, this is at once a dual biography, Internet history, and business primer." Booklist

Includes bibliographical references

Segall, Grant

John D. Rockefeller; anointed with oil. Oxford University Press 2000 125p il (Oxford portraits) $28
Grades: 7 8 9 10   **338.7**
1. Philanthropists 2. Capitalists and financiers 3. Standard Oil Company 4. Energy industry executives
ISBN 0-19-512147-3

LC 00-44616

"Included in the biography are some primary documents, such as letters, photos, and cartoons, as well as references to some of the other giants of industry, such as Flagler, Carnegie, and Gould." Book Rep

Includes bibliographical references

338.9   Economic development and growth

Belmont, Helen

★ **Planning** for a sustainable future; [by] Helen Belmont. Smart Apple Media 2008 46p il map (Geography skills) $22.95
Grades: 6 7 8 9   **338.9**
1. City planning 2. Human ecology
ISBN 978-1-59920-051-4; 1-59920-051-1

LC 2006100028

"The text is easy to follow. . . . The examples given in the text that involve places are almost always accompanied by excellent photographs. . . . Maps, block diagrams, tables, and graphs are clearly presented and easy to interpret." Sci Books Films

Includes glossary and bibliographical references

339.4   Factors affecting income and wealth

Thompson, Helen

Cost of living. Mason Crest Publishers 2010 63p il (Junior library of money) $22.95; pa $9.95

Grades: 6 7 8 9   **339.4**

    1. Prices 2. Personal finance 3. Cost and standard of living

    ISBN 978-1-4222-1762-7; 1-4222-1762-0; 978-1-4222-1866-2 pa; 1-4222-1866-X pa

                     LC 2010029402

This defines the cost of living as the amount of money a person needs to spend on housing, food, transportation, clothing, and other items that people need to live and explains how it can go up and down based on the conditions in the economy, and depending on where you live.

This title presents "solid information and [has] eye-catching and relevant illustrations. . . . [The book is] clearly written, making understandable connections between daily life and financial concepts." SLJ

Includes glossary and bibliographical references

341.242   European regional organizations

Ponsford, Simon

The European Union today; [by] Simon Ponsford. Sea-to-Sea Publications 2009 48p il (Today) lib bdg $32.80

Grades: 4 5 6   **341.242**

    1. European Union 2. European federation

    ISBN 978-1-59771-124-1 lib bdg; 1-59771-124-1 lib bdg

                     LC 2008-4573

This "is a good choice for readers who may be a bit hazy, for instance, on the organization's structure and purpose—not to mention the significant differences between the European Council, the Council of the European Union, and the Council of Europe. [The book is] well stocked with color photos, fact boxes, and statistics." SLJ

Includes glossary

341.6   Law of war

Kenney, Karen Latchana

Korematsu v. the United States; World War II Japanese-American internment camps. by Karen Latchana Kenney ; content consultant Richard D. Friedman. ABDO Pub. Co. 2013 160 p. ill. (some col.) (library) $35.64

Grades: 8 9 10 11 12   **341.6**

    1. Korematsu v. United States (Supreme Court case) 2.

Japanese Americans -- Evacuation and relocation, 1942-1945 3. United States -- Trials, litigation, etc.

ISBN 1617834734; 9781617834738

                     LC 2012001277

This book by Karen Latchana Kenney is part of the Landmark Supreme Court Cases series and focuses on the case of Korematsu v. the United States. It "looks at the historical impact of World War II and the internment of Japanese American citizens out of fear and hysteria following the bombing of Pearl Harbor." (School Library Journal)

Includes bibliographical references (p. 146-154) and index.

342   Branches of law; laws, regulations, cases; law of specific jurisdictions, areas, socioeconomic regions

The Constitutional Convention; Richard Haesly, book editor. Greenhaven Press 2002 240p il maps (History firsthand) lib bdg $34.95; pa $23.70

Grades: 7 8 9 10   **342**

    1. Constitutional history -- United States

    ISBN 0-7377-1072-1 lib bdg; 0-7377-1071-3 pa

                     LC 2001-23832

This is a "study of the historical and political events that led up to the ratification of the U.S. Constitution. Using accounts and opinions by actual delegates and other prominent figures such as Patrick Henry and Thomas Jefferson, Haesly outlines the concepts of the Declaration of Independence, the Articles of Confederation, and the Constitution/Bill of Rights. The volume is enlivened by personal stories of those who lived through and influenced the events depicted, and includes discussions on slavery and the nature of the presidency. . . . Well suited for reports." SLJ

Includes bibliographical references

Feinberg, Barbara Silberdick

The Articles of Confederation; the first constitution of the United States. 21st Cent. Bks. (Brookfield) 2002 110p il maps lib bdg $24.90

Grades: 7 8 9 10   **342**

    1. Constitutional history -- United States 2. United States -- Articles of Confederation 3. United States -- Politics and government -- 1775-1783, Revolution

    ISBN 0-7613-2114-4

                     LC 2001-27441

"Feinberg introduces the history and text of 'The Articles of Confederation and Perpetual Union,' the constitution that guided the U.S. government from 1776 to 1787. . . . Attractively laid out, this solid choice includes many black-and-white illustrations, including portrait paintings, engravings, and maps." Booklist

Includes bibliographical references

Furgang, Kathy

The Ninth Amendment; rights retained by the people. Rosen Central 2011 64p il (Amendments to the United States Constitution: The Bill of Rights) $29.25; pa $12.95

Grades: 5 6 7 8   **342**
  1. Civil rights 2. Constitutional law -- United States
  3. United States -- Constitution -- 1st-10th amendments
  ISBN 978-1-4488-1264-6; 1-4488-1264-X; 978-1-
  4488-2310-9 pa; 1-4488-2310-2 pa
                      LC 2010020091
This book about the Ninth Amendment to the U.S. Constitution is "well-written, objective and informative. . . . [It discusses] the historical reasons for [the] amendment, its basis in British and American common law, and the statutory and case law that shaped its implementation and development. . . . While primarily useful for reports, [this book] will also give students perspective on current events." SLJ
  Includes glossary and bibliographical references

Gold, Susan Dudley
  The **Pentagon** papers; national security or the right to know. by Susan Dudley Gold. Benchmark Books 2004 144p il lib bdg $25.95
Grades: 7 8 9 10   **342**
  1. Freedom of the press 2. Pentagon Papers 3. New York Times Company v. United States
  ISBN 0-7614-1843-1
                      LC 2004-8583
An examination of the Supreme Court decision regarding the New York Times decision to publish articles about United States government's "secret war" in Cambodia and Vietnam
  "The format of the [book] makes [it] easy to read and understand. [A] valuable [resource] for reports." SLJ
  Includes bibliographical references

  Roberts v. Jaycees; women's rights. Marshall Cavendish Benchmark 2009 144p il (Supreme Court milestones) $29.95
Grades: 7 8 9 10   **342**
  1. Sex discrimination
  ISBN 978-0-7614-2952-4; 0-7614-2952-2
                   LC 2007043021
First published 1984 by Twenty-First Century Books with title: Roberts v. U.S. Jaycees
  This examines the Supreme Court case regarding sex discrimination against women members of the the Jaycees organization.
  Includes bibliographical references

Haynes, Charles C.
  First freedoms; a documentary history of the First Amendment Rights in America. [by] Charles C. Haynes, Sam Chaltain, Susan M. Glisson. Oxford University Press 2005 255p il $40
Grades: 8 9 10 11 12   **342**
  1. Freedom of speech 2. Freedom of religion 3. Freedom of the press 4. Constitutional history -- United States 5. United States -- Constitution -- 1st-10th amendments
  ISBN 978-0-19-515750-5; 0-19-515750-8
                 LC 2005-31880
This book features "information and primary documents concerning the origins and attacks on the First Amendment. The various documents go from the Charter of Rhode Island

and Providence Plantations in 1663 through the Patriot Act of 2001." Libr Media Connect
  This is "an excellent resource for all libraries, as well as enjoyable reading for history buffs." SLJ

Jones, Molly
  The **First** Amendment; freedom of speech, the press, and religion. Rosen Central 2011 64p il (Amendments to the United States Constitution: The Bill of Rights) lib bdg $29.25; pa $12.95
Grades: 5 6 7 8   **342**
  1. Freedom of speech 2. Freedom of religion 3. Freedom of the press 4. United States -- Constitution -- 1st-10th amendments
  ISBN 978-1-4488-1252-3 lib bdg; 1-4488-1252-6 lib bdg; 978-1-4488-2302-4 pa; 1-4488-2302-1 pa
                 LC 2010023234
This book about the First Amendment to the U.S. Constitution is "well-written, objective and informative. . . . [It discusses] the historical reasons for [the] amendment, its basis in British and American common law, and the statutory and case law that shaped its implementation and development. . . . While primarily useful for reports, [this book] will also give students perspective on current events." SLJ
  Includes glossary and bibliographical references

Krull, Kathleen
  A **kid's** guide to America's Bill of Rights; curfews, censorship, and the 100-pound giant. illustrated by Anna DiVito. Avon Bks. 1999 226p il $15.99
Grades: 4 5 6 7   **342**
  1. Civil rights 2. United States -- Constitution -- 1st-10th amendments
  ISBN 0-380-97497-5
                 LC 99-17324
  "After describing how the first 10 amendments came to be added to the Constitution, the book considers each one from a historical point of view, examining Supreme Court cases and famous challenges, and explaining in what ways each amendment applies to children and teenagers. Anna Divito's cartoonlike drawings add a visually appealing touch." Booklist
  Includes bibliographical references

Orr, Tamra
  The **Tenth** Amendment; limiting federal powers. Rosen Central 2011 64p il (Amendments to the United States Constitution: The Bill of Rights) lib bdg $29.25; pa $12.95
Grades: 5 6 7 8   **342**
  1. Federal government 2. State rights 3. United States -- Constitution -- 1st-10th amendments
  ISBN 978-1-4488-1265-3 lib bdg; 1-4488-1265-8 lib bdg; 978-1-4488-2311-6 pa; 1-4488-2311-0 pa
                 LC 2010021852
This book about the Tenth Amendment to the U.S. Constitution is "well-written, objective and informative. . . . [It discusses] the historical reasons for [the] amendment, its basis in British and American common law, and the statutory and case law that shaped its implementation and develop-

ment. . . . While primarily useful for reports, [this book] will also give students perspective on current events." SLJ

Includes glossary and bibliographical references

Patrick, John J.

The **Bill** of Rights; a history in documents. Oxford Univ. Press 2003 205p il map (Pages from history) lib bdg $32.95

Grades: 7 8 9 10   342

1. Civil rights 2. United States -- Constitution -- 1st-10th amendments

ISBN 0-19-510354-8

LC 2002-6294

Uses contemporary documents to explore the history of the first ten amendments to the U.S. Constitution, the British traditions on which they were based, and their impact on American society

"This attractive and informative volume will be a valuable resource for most collections." SLJ

Includes bibliographical references

Pendergast, Tom

Constitutional amendments: from freedom of speech to flag burning; [by] Tom Pendergast, Sara Pendergast, and John Sousanis; Elizabeth Shaw Grunow, editor. U.X.L 2001 3v set $165

Grades: 7 8 9 10   342

1. Civil rights 2. Constitutional law -- United States 3. United States -- Constitution -- 1st-10th amendments

ISBN 0-7876-4865-5

LC 00-67236

"Presentation is very clear. . . . This is definitely a set that belongs in school and public libraries." Booklist

"Covering each of the 27 amendments, this 3-vol. resource provides the history and social context of the amendment process. Entries range in length from 10 to 15 pages and begin with the full text of the amendment followed by an essay on the social and political climate that gave rise to its proposal." Publisher's note

Includes glossary and bibliographical references

Porterfield, Jason

The **Third** Amendment; the right to privacy in the home. Rosen Central 2011 64p il (Amendments to the United States Constitution: The Bill of Rights) lib bdg $29.25; pa $12.95

Grades: 5 6 7 8   342

1. Right of privacy 2. United States -- Constitution -- 1st-10th amendments

ISBN 978-1-4488-1256-1 lib bdg; 1-4488-1256-9 lib bdg; 978-1-4488-2304-8 pa; 1-4488-2304-8 pa

LC 2010015855

This book about the Third Amendment to the U.S. Constitution is "well-written, objective and informative. . . . [It discusses] the historical reasons for [the] amendment, its basis in British and American common law, and the statutory and case law that shaped its implementation and development. . . . While primarily useful for reports, [this book] will also give students perspective on current events." SLJ

Includes glossary and bibliographical references

Ritchie, Donald A.

★ **Our** Constitution. Oxford University Press 2006 255p il map $40

Grades: 7 8 9 10   342

1. United States -- Constitution 2. Constitutional history -- United States

ISBN 978-0-19-522385-9; 0-19-522385-3

LC 2005031885

This "volume begins with five chapters of background (Why have a constitution? How has it changed?) and then goes on to discuss the preamble, articles, and amendments, using a What It Says (word for word) and What It Means format. Every spread contains photos, reproductions, and sidebars, all of which invite students to read and understand this living document. . . . This is an excellent, well-documented addition for most libraries." SLJ

Includes glossary and bibliographical references

Stearman, Kaye

Freedom of information; Kaye Stearman. Rosen Central Pub. 2012 48 p. (pbk.) $11.75

Grades: 7 8 9 10   342

1. Secrecy 2. Political ethics 3. United States -- Politics and government 4. Freedom of information -- United States

ISBN 1448860199; 1448870089; 1448870100; 9781448860197; 9781448870080; 9781448870103

LC 2011034070

Author Kaye Stearman presents "explanations of how freedom of information laws work and how they have been framed in different countries. . . . Most countries' laws contain limits on disclosure, and there are many debates about where the lines should be drawn. . . . Chapters explore the debate about how these laws should be applied so that they work well for both government officials and the public." (Publisher's note)

Includes bibliographical references and index.

Stefoff, Rebecca

U.S. v. Nixon; the limits of presidential privilege. Marshall Cavendish Benchmark 2009 127p il (Supreme Court milestones) lib bdg $29.95

Grades: 7 8 9 10   342

1. Presidents 2. Vice-presidents 3. Watergate Affair, 1972-1974 4. Senators 5. Nonfiction writers 6. Members of Congress

ISBN 978-0-7614-2955-5 lib bdg; 0-7614-2955-7 lib bdg

LC 2007031607

This examines the Supreme Court regarding the Watergate scandal.

Includes bibliographical references

Van Zee, Amy

Dred Scott v. Sandford; slavery and freedom before the American civil war. by Amy Van Zee ; content consultant, Earl Maltz. ABDO Pub. Co. 2013 160 p. ill. (some col.) (Landmark Supreme Court cases) (hbk. : alk. paper) $35.64

Grades: 8 9 10 11 12   342

1. Slavery -- United States 2. United States. Supreme

Court 3. Slavery -- Law and legislation -- United States -- History -- 19th century
ISBN 1617834726; 9781617834721

LC 2012001276

This book is part of the Landmark Supreme Court Cases Series. This title focuses on Dred Scott v. Sandford and explains how "the origins of slavery in the United States in regard to societal acceptance and black inferiority, deeply ingrained throughout the growth and development of the country, played a major role in every aspect of the developing nation with the continuing struggle between both sides of the issue." (School Library Journal)

Includes bibliographical references (p. 146-153) and index

Vile, John R.

The **United** States Constitution; questions and answers. Greenwood Press 1998 316p il $39.95

Grades: 8 9 10 11 12   **342**

1. United States -- Constitution 2. Constitutional law -- United States
ISBN 0-313-30643-5

LC 97-32008

The author examines each section of the U.S. Constitution "and provides a question-and-answer format that allows for easy explanation of a complicated document. The amendments are addressed in detail. . . . The book is easy to read and well laid out." Book Rep

Includes bibliographical references

342.73 Constitutional law – United States

Baxter, Roberta

The **Bill** of Rights; by Roberta Baxter. Heinemann Library 2012 48 p. (hbk) $32

Grades: 4 5 6 7   **342.73**

1. Legislation 2. United States -- Politics and government 3. Constitutional history -- United States 4. Civil rights -- United States -- History 5. United States. Constitution. 1st-10th Amendments
ISBN 1432967517; 9781432967512; 9781432967604

LC 2011037780

In this book, Roberta Baxter, readers can "learn about the Bill of Rights, one of the most significant documents in U.S. history. [They can] find out about those who were involved in its creation and why studying this primary source is [considered] so important." (Publisher's note)

Includes bibliographical references (p. 47) and index

Judson, Karen

The **Constitution** of the United States; its history, Bill of Rights, and amendments. by Karen Judson. Enslow Publishers, Inc. 2012 104 p. (Constitution and the United States government) (hbk. : alk. paper) $31.93

Grades: 6 7 8   **342.73**

1. United States. Constitution. 1st-10th amendments 2. Constitutional history -- United States
ISBN 0766040674; 9780766040670

LC 2011030976

This book, by Karen Judson, "discusses the history and importance of the United States Constitution and how it is applied to decision making and laws in America. Judson [gives] readers . . . historical background on the constitutional convention and the issues that had to be resolved in order to write an effective constitution." (Publisher's note)

Includes bibliographical references (p. 97-101) and index

Sonneborn, Liz

The **Articles** of Confederation; by Liz Sonneborn. Heinemann Library 2013 48 p. (Documenting U.S. history) (hb) $32

Grades: 4 5 6 7   **342.73**

1. United States -- Politics and government -- 1775-1783, Revolution 2. Constitutional history -- United States 3. United States. Articles of Confederation 4. United States -- Politics and government -- 1775-1783
ISBN 1432967495; 9781432967499; 9781432967581

LC 2011037709

In this book, written by Liz Sonneborn, readers can "learn about the Articles of Confederation, one of the most significant documents in U.S. history. [They can] find out about those who were involved in its creation and why studying this primary source is [considering] so important." (Publisher's note)

Includes bibliographical references and index

The **United** States Constitution; by Liz Sonneborn. Heinemann-Raintree 2012 48 p. (hb) $32

Grades: 4 5 6 7   **342.73**

1. United States. Constitution 2. Constitutional law -- United States 4. Constitutional history -- United States
ISBN 1432967525; 9781432967529; 9781432967611

LC 2011037781

In this book, by Liz Sonneborn, readers can "learn about the United States Constitution, one of the most significant documents in U.S. history. [They can also] find out about those who were involved in its creation and why studying this primary source is [considered] so important." (Publisher's note)

Includes bibliographical references and index

344 Labor, social service, education, cultural law

Anderson, Wayne

★ **Brown** v. Board of Education; the case against school segregation. Rosen Pub. Group 2004 64p il (Supreme Court cases through primary sources) lib bdg $29.95

Grades: 6 7 8 9   **344**

1. Clergy 2. Segregation in education 3. Welders 4. Railroad workers 5. Civil rights activists 6. Topeka (Kan.) -- Board of Education
ISBN 0-8239-4009-8

LC 2003-219

This is a discussion of the Supreme Court decision which ended racial segregation in public schools.

This "deserves a place in every library. . . . Copious and well-chosen primary source documents give extra value to this [book]. . . . Each document adds human drama to the already engaging text." Lib Media Connect

Includes glossary and bibliographical references

Bodden, Valerie

Environmental law. Creative Education 2011 48p il (Earth issues) lib bdg $23.95

Grades: 6 7 8 9   344

1. Environmental law

ISBN 978-1-58341-981-6; 1-58341-981-0

"Unfamiliar words are printed in bold type and defined in the glossary for students. . . . Written in a straightforward manner, with photographs that are clearly captioned, . . . [this] is a welcome addition for libraries." Libr Media Connect

Includes glossary and bibliographical references

Fridell, Ron

Cruzan v. Missouri and the right to die debate; debating Supreme Court decisions. Enslow Publishers 2005 128p il (Debating Supreme Court decisions) lib bdg $26.60

Grades: 7 8 9 10   344

1. Metalworkers 2. Accident victims 3. Right to die -- Law and legislation

ISBN 0-7660-2356-7

LC 2004-20028

This examines both sides of the debate concerning assisted suicide and related Supreme Court decisions.

Includes glossary and bibliographical references

Gerber, Larry

The **Second** Amendment; the right to bear arms. Rosen Central 2011 64p il (Amendments to the United States Constitution: The Bill of Rights) lib bdg $29.25; pa $12.95

Grades: 5 6 7 8   344

1. Gun control 2. United States -- Constitution -- 1st-10th amendments

ISBN 978-1-4488-1253-0 lib bdg; 1-4488-1253-4 lib bdg; 978-1-4488-2303-1 pa; 1-4488-2303-X pa

LC 2010015854

This book about the Second Amendment to the U.S. Constitution is "well-written, objective and informative. . . . [It discusses] the historical reasons for [the] amendment, its basis in British and American common law, and the statutory and case law that shaped its implementation and development. . . . While primarily useful for reports, [this book] will also give students perspective on current events." SLJ

Includes glossary and bibliographical references

Gold, Susan Dudley

Brown v. Board of Education; separate but equal? by Susan Dudley Gold. Benchmark Books 2004 143p il (Supreme Court milestones) lib bdg $25.95

Grades: 6 7 8 9   344

1. Clergy 2. Segregation in education 3. Welders 4. Railroad workers 5. Civil rights activists 6. Topeka (Kan.) -- Board of Education

ISBN 0-7614-1842-3

LC 2004-5866

An overview of the Supreme Court decision which struck down racial segregation in schools.

"The format of the [book] makes [it] easy to read and understand. [A] valuable [resource] for reports." SLJ

Hayhurst, Chris

Jobs in environmental law. Rosen Pub. 2010 80p il (Green careers) lib bdg $30.60

Grades: 7 8 9 10   344

1. Environmental law 2. Vocational guidance

ISBN 978-1-4358-3567-2 lib bdg; 1-4358-3567-0 lib bdg

LC 2009025276

This "offers broad descriptions of the work of lawyers, paralegals, and legal secretaries and the professional requirements and mindset necessary to succeed in this field. Environmental police officers, lobbyists, and regulations and communications specialists are also included. . . . [This] slim [title is] well organized and [contains] informatively captioned color photos." SLJ

Includes glossary and bibliographical references

Mountjoy, Shane

Engel v. Vitale; school prayer and the establishment clause. Chelsea House 2007 128p il (Great Supreme Court decisions) lib bdg $30

Grades: 7 8 9 10   344

1. Church and state 2. Religion in the public schools

ISBN 0-7910-9241-0; 978-0-7910-9241-5

LC 2006-7328

This describes the 1962 Supreme Court case which ruled that official prayers in public schools were unconstitutional.

"Excellent period photos, magazine covers, and portraits of historical figures are closely cued to the [text]. . . . Handsomely packaged, accessible." SLJ

Includes glossary and bibliographical references

Perl, Lila

Cruzan v. Missouri; the right to die? Marshall Cavendish Benchmark 2007 143p il (Supreme Court milestones) $27.95

Grades: 7 8 9 10   344

1. Metalworkers 2. Accident victims 3. Right to die -- Law and legislation

ISBN 978-0-7614-2581-6; 0-7614-258-0

LC 2006-25740

"Perl discusses Nancy Cruzan's parents quest for her right to die following an auto accident and her resulting vegetative state. Highlights include the discussion of religious arguments, physician-assisted suicide, and the cases of Karen Ann Quinlan and Terry Schiavo. . . . Additional information is presented in sidebars. Occasional black-and-white photos add interest." SLJ

Includes bibliographical references

345 Criminal law

Aretha, David

The **trial** of the Scottsboro boys. Morgan Reynolds Pub. 2007 128p il (The civil rights movement) lib bdg $27.95

Grades: 7 8 9 10 11 12   345

1. Trials 2. Scottsboro case 3. African Americans -- Civil rights

ISBN 978-1-59935-058-5; 1-59935-058-0

LC 2007-23818

This describes the case of nine young black men between the ages of 13 and 20 who were accused of rape in the 1930s in Alabama by two white women and were sentenced to death.

"Aretha writes clearly, with objectivity and compassion." SLJ

Includes bibliographical references

Brezina, Corona

The **Fifth** Amendment; double jeopardy, self-incrimination, and due process of law. Rosen Central 2011 64p il (Amendments to the United States Constitution: The Bill of Rights) lib bdg $29.25; pa $12.95

Grades: 5 6 7 8   345

1. Criminal procedure 2. United States -- Constitution -- 1-10th amendments

ISBN 978-1-4488-1260-8 lib bdg; 1-4488-1260-7 lib bdg; 978-1-4488-2306-2 pa; 1-4488-2306-4 pa

LC 2010018820

This book about the Fifth Amendment to the U.S. Constitution is "well-written, objective and informative. . . . [It discusses] the historical reasons for [the] amendment, its basis in British and American common law, and the statutory and case law that shaped its implementation and development. . . . While primarily useful for reports, [this book] will also give students perspective on current events." SLJ

Includes glossary and bibliographical references

Burgan, Michael

The **Scopes** trial; faith, science, and American education. Marshall Cavendish Benchmark 2010 112p il (Perspectives on) $39.93

Grades: 7 8 9 10   345

1. Geologists 2. Science teachers 3. Evolution -- Study and teaching

ISBN 978-0-7614-4981-2; 0-7614-4981-7

An account of the trial of John T. Scopes, prosecuted in 1925 for teaching evolution.

This "well-written [book begins] with [an overview] and some historical background, and then [proceeds] chronologically to the current decade. . . . Burgan presents both sides with respect and objectivity. . . . It is evident that . . . the author [has] done [his] research. [The book contains] information that is perhaps less well-known to student researchers, including the preliminary events leading up to the Scopes trial. . . . Black-and-white and color photographs along with some period cartoons place readers in the time period, and sidebars interspersed throughout present issues that aren't easily covered within the main [text]." SLJ

Cates, David

The **Scottsboro** boys; by David Cates. ABDO Pub. Co. 2012 112 p. ill. $34.22

Grades: 6 7 8 9   345

1. Scottsboro case 2. Civil rights -- United States -- History 3. Trials (Rape) -- Alabama -- Scottsboro 4. Scottsboro Trial, Scottsboro, Ala., 1931 5. African Americans -- Civil rights -- History

ISBN 161783310X; 9781617833106

LC 2011036128

This book "tells the story of the nine African American teenagers accused of raping two white women on a train in Scottsboro, Alabama in 1931, covering the arrests and . . . . legal proceedings." The book "explores the history of America at the time of the trials, the accounts of the nine men on trial regarding their train ride from Tennessee to Alabama, their sentences, and the effects of this event on society." (Publisher's notes)

"These titles are excellent introductions to these important topics, particularly for developing an analytical framework for debate.—" SLJ

Includes bibliographical references (p. 104-109) and index

Coleman, Wim

Racism on trial; From the Medgar Evers murder case to 'Ghosts of Mississippi' [by] Wim Coleman and Pat Perrin. Enslow Publishers 2009 112p il (Famous court cases that became movies) lib bdg $31.93

Grades: 5 6 7 8   345

1. Lynching 2. Trials (Homicide) 3. Murderers 4. White supremacists 5. Civil rights activists 6. Mississippi -- Race relations

ISBN 978-0-7660-3059-6; 0-7660-3059-8

LC 2008-21483

"Examines the Byron De La Beckwith murder trials, including the mistrials and his eventual conviction, key figures in the case, and the inspiration for the movie Ghosts of Mississippi." Publisher's note

Includes glossary and bibliographical references

Galiano, Dean

The **Fourth** Amendment; unreasonable search and seizure. Rosen Central 2011 64p il (Amendments to the United States Constitution: The Bill of Rights) lib bdg $29.25; pa $12.95

Grades: 5 6 7 8   345

1. Searches and seizures 2. United States -- Constitution -- 1st-10th amendments

ISBN 978-1-4488-1259-2 lib bdg; 1-4488-1259-3 lib bdg; 978-1-4488-2305-5 pa; 1-4488-2305-6 pa

LC 2010017394

This book about the Fourth Amendment to the U.S. Constitution is "well-written, objective and informative. . . . [It discusses] the historical reasons for [the] amendment, its basis in British and American common law, and the statutory and case law that shaped its implementation and development. . . . While primarily useful for reports, [this book] will also give students perspective on current events." SLJ

Includes glossary and bibliographical references

Hinds, Maurene J.

   Furman v. Georgia and the death penalty debate; [by] Maurene J. Hinds. Enslow Publishers 2005 128p il (Debating Supreme Court decisions) lib bdg $26.60

Grades: 7 8 9 10   **345**

   1. Capital punishment

   ISBN 0-7660-2390-7

                    LC 2004-18943

   The author "examines the arguments on both sides of the [death penalty] debate, and she shows how the courts—especially the Supreme Court—have played a part in the evolution of capital punishment in the United States." Publisher's note

   Includes glossary and bibliographical references

Jacobs, Thomas A.

   ★ **They** broke the law, you be the judge; true cases of teen crime. edited by Al Desetta. Free Spirit Pub. 2003 213p il pa $15.95

Grades: 7 8 9 10   **345**

   1. Juvenile courts 2. Administration of criminal justice

   ISBN 1-57542-134-8

                    LC 2003-4814

   "An excellent introduction to how juvenile justice works, this will be a great resource for classroom and group discussions." Booklist

   "This book details 21 cases ranging from truancy to auto theft. Following a description of events leading up to and including the crime itself, readers are given background about the individual, sentencing options, and questions to consider before sentencing, and then asked to make a decision about the case." SLJ

   Includes bibliographical references

Kelly-Gangi, Carol

   Miranda v. Arizona and the rights of the accused; debating Supreme Court decisions. [by] Carol Kelly-Gangi. Enslow Publishers 2006 128p il (Debating Supreme Court decisions) lib bdg $26.60

Grades: 7 8 9 10   **345**

   1. Criminals 2. Right to counsel

   ISBN 0-7660-2477-6

                    LC 2006011737

   This discusses the Supreme Court case involving a suspect's rights while being questioned by police.

   Includes bibliographical references

Rosaler, Maxine

   ★ The **devil** on trial; witches, anarchists, atheists, communists, and terrorists in America's courtrooms. by Phillip Marguiles and Maxine Rosaler. Houghton Mifflin Co. 2008 218 p. ill., ports $22

Grades: 7 8 9 10 11 12   **345**

   1. Lawyers 2. Trials -- History 3. Administration of criminal justice -- United States 4. Diplomats 5. Trials -- United States 6. Criminal justice, Administration of -- Social aspects -- United States 7. Discrimination in criminal justice administration -- United States -- History

   ISBN 061871717X; 9780618717170

                    LC 2008001870

   The authors examine cases such as the Scopes 'monkey' trial, the two trials of Alger Hiss trials, and the witch trials in Salem, Mass. Glossary. Bibliography. Index. "Grades seven to ten." (Bull Cent Child Books)

   The authors "examine five highly emotional court cases, each of which served as a litmus test for the health of America's justice system at the time it occurred. . . . Each chapter gives historical context of the court proceeding, describes its progression in some detail, and comments on the political and intellectual aftermath. . . . [This is] a highly relevant and riveting book." SLJ

   Includes bibliographical references (p. [203] - 207) and index

Roza, Greg

   The **Eighth** Amendment; preventing cruel and unusual punishment. Rosen Central 2011 64p il (Amendments to the United States Constitution: The Bill of Rights) lib bdg $29.25; pa $12.95

Grades: 5 6 7 8   **345**

   1. Punishment 2. United States -- Constitution -- 1st-10th amendments

   ISBN 978-1-4488-1263-9 lib bdg; 1-4488-1263-1 lib bdg; 978-1-4488-2309-3 pa; 1-4488-2309-9 pa

                    LC 2010015857

   This book about the Eighth Amendment to the U.S. Constitution is "well-written, objective and informative. . . . [It discusses] the historical reasons for [the] amendment, its basis in British and American common law, and the statutory and case law that shaped its implementation and development. . . . While primarily useful for reports, [this book] will also give students perspective on current events." SLJ

   Includes glossary and bibliographical references

Shea, Therese

   The **Sixth** Amendment; the rights of the accused in criminal cases. Rosen Central 2011 64p il (Amendments to the United States Constitution: The Bill of Rights) lib bdg $29.25; pa $12.95

Grades: 5 6 7 8   **345**

   1. Criminal procedure 2. United States -- Constitution -- 1st-10th amendments

   ISBN 978-1-4488-1261-5 lib bdg; 1-4488-1261-5 lib bdg; 978-1-4488-2307-9 pa; 1-4488-2307-2 pa

                    LC 2010021318

   This book about the Sixth Amendment to the U.S. Constitution is "well-written, objective and informative. . . . [It discusses] the historical reasons for [the] amendment, its basis in British and American common law, and the statutory and case law that shaped its implementation and development. . . . While primarily useful for reports, [this book] will also give students perspective on current events." SLJ

   Includes glossary and bibliographical references

Sorensen, Lita

   The **Scottsboro** Boys Trial; a primary source account. Rosen Pub. Group 2004 64p il (Great trials of the 20th century) lib bdg $29.25

Grades: 8 9 10 11 12   **345**

   1. Trials 2. Scottsboro case 3. African Americans

-- Civil rights
ISBN 0-8239-3975-8

LC 2002-153356

An account of the 1931 trial in which African American youths were charged with rape.

This is "packed with information. . . . [An] attractive, intelligent offering." SLJ

Includes bibliographical references

346   Private law

Butler, Rebecca P.

★ **Copyright** for teachers & librarians in the 21st century. Neal-Schuman Publishers 2011 274p il pa $70

Grades: Adult Professional   346

1. Copyright 2. Fair use (Copyright)
ISBN 978-1-55570-738-5

LC 2011012600

First published 2004 with title: Copyright for teachers and librarians

"Library educator Rebecca Butler explains fair use, public domain, documentation and licenses, permissions, violations and penalties, policies and ethics codes, citations, creation and ownership, how to register copyrights, and gives tips for staying out of trouble." Publisher's note

Includes bibliographical references

Jacobs, Thomas A.

What are my rights? 95 questions and answers about teens and the law. rev. ed; Free Spirit Pub. 2006 199p il pa $14.95

Grades: 7 8 9 10 11 12   346

1. Youth -- Law and legislation
ISBN 1-57542-028-7

LC 97-8599

First published 1997

This "presents answers to questions about laws that affect teens, encouraging youths to understand both their rights and responsibilities in order to make sound decisions. The book is organized into chapters on family, school, work, teens and their bodies, growing up, criminal behavior, and the legal system. . . . An accessible, current resource." SLJ

Includes bibliographical references

Popek, Emily

Copyright and digital ethics. Rosen Central 2011 48p il (Digital and information literacy) lib bdg $26.50; pa $11.75

Grades: 5 6 7 8   346

1. Ethics 2. Internet 3. Copyright
ISBN 978-1-4488-1323-0 lib bdg; 1-4488-1323-9; 978-1-4488-2294-2 pa; 1-4488-2294-7 pa

LC 2010027018

Though this "title is a broad overview of a sometimes-complex subject, the detail is significant. . . . Touches of blue enhance the clean design. . . . [This] explains concepts like fair use and tries to persuade readers of the damage done by digital piracy and plagiarism." Booklist

Includes bibliographical references

346.04   Property

Crews, Kenneth D.

★ **Copyright** law for librarians and educators; creative strategies and practical solutions. with contributions from Dwayne K. Buttler . . . [et al.] 2nd ed; American Library Association 2012 xii, 192 p.p ill. (alk. paper) $57

Grades: Adult Professional   346.04

1. Copyright 2. Sound recordings 3. Fair use (Copyright) 4. Copyright -- United States 5. Fair use (Copyright) -- United States 6. Teachers -- United States -- Handbooks, manuals, etc 7. Librarians -- United States -- Handbooks, manuals, etc
ISBN 0838910920; 9780838910924

LC 2011027604

First published 2000 with title: Copyright essentials for librarians and educators

Author Kenneth D. Crews' book "allows readers to get up to speed on current interpretations of the Digital Millennium Copyright Act from a librarian-educator viewpoint." It also "draws on cutting-edge case law in 18 discrete areas of copyright, including specialized and controversial music and sound recording issues. [This guide offers] information professionals . . . the tools they need to take control of their rights and responsibilities as copyright owners and users." (Publisher's note)

The author "addresses 18 areas of copyright in 5 parts. He begins with the scope of protectable works as well as works without copyright protection. Next, he discusses the rights of ownership, including duration and exceptions. He then explains fair use and its related guidelines. Part 4 focuses on the TEACH Act, Section 108, and responsibilities and liabilities. Lastly, Crews examines special issues such as the Digital Millennium Copyright Act." Booklist

Includes bibliographical references and index.

Russell, Carrie

Complete copyright for K-12 librarians and educators; Carrie Russell. American Library Association 2012 xi, 173 p.p ill. (chiefly col.) (alk. paper) $50

Grades: Professional   346.04

1. Copyright 2. Fair use (Copyright) 3. Segregation -- Law and legislation 4. Copyright -- United States 5. Fair use (Copyright) -- United States 6. Librarians -- Legal status, laws, etc. -- United States 7. School libraries -- Law and legislation -- United States
ISBN 0838910831; 9780838910832

LC 2012016674

This book by Carrie Russell "is designed as a resource for educators, offering guidance for providing material to students while carefully observing copyright law. The book offers detailed advice on distinctive issues of intellectual property in the school setting; explores scenarios often encountered by educators . . . and precisely defines 'fair use,' by showing readers exactly what's possible within the law." (Education Digest)

Includes bibliographical references and index

347   Procedure and courts

Brannen, Daniel E.

★ **Supreme** Court drama; cases that changed America. [by] Daniel E. Brannen & Richard Clay Hanes; Elizabeth M. Shaw, editor. U.X.L 2001 4v il set $215

Grades: 7 8 9 10   347

1. United States -- Supreme Court 2. Constitutional law -- United States
ISBN 0-7876-4877-9

LC 00-56380

"This set will be an especially useful reference when students need to retrieve concise information on Supreme Court cases." Book Rep

"The 159 cases included span the years 1803 to 2000 and are organized under major legal topics such as 'Individual Liberties' and 'Equal Protection and Civil Rights.' Each entry, ranging from three to five pages, is introduced by a profile listing the appellant and appellee or petitioner and respondent, attorneys, and justices along with a brief description of the case and its significance. . . . Each volume contains alphabetical and chronological lists of the cases, a guide to how the Supreme Court works, a list of Supreme Court Justices, and the text of the U.S. Constitution." SLJ

Includes glossary and bibliographical references

Panchyk, Richard

Our Supreme Court; a history with 14 activities. Chicago Review Press 2006 195p il $16.95

Grades: 7 8 9 10   347

1. United States -- Supreme Court 2. Constitutional law -- United States
ISBN 978-1-55652-607-7; 1-55652-607-5

LC 2006009018

"The history and evolution of the court and how it works are discussed in the first chapter. Thematic sections follow, covering such topics as free speech, privacy, and civil rights, with significant decisions included. . . . This a solid work that makes a complex and important subject accessible to students." SLJ

Includes bibliographical references

347.73   Civil procedure and courts of the United States

Jost, Kenneth

★ The **Supreme** Court A to Z; Kenneth Jost. 5th ed. CQ Press 2012 xvii, 668 p.p ill. (hardcover : alk. paper) $125.00

Grades: 8 9 10 11 12 Adult   347.73

1. United States. Supreme Court -- Biography 2. United States. Supreme Court -- Encyclopedias
ISBN 1608717445; 9781608717446

LC 2012000642

This book by Kenneth Jost "offers . . . information about the Supreme Court, including its history, traditions, organization, dynamics, and personalities. The entries in The Supreme Court A to Z are arranged alphabetically and are . . . cross-referenced to related information. This volume also

has a detailed index, reference materials on Supreme Court nominations, a seat chart of the justices, the U.S. Constitution, online sources of decisions, and a bibliography." (Publisher's note)

Includes bibliographical references (p. 617-630) and index.

Rodger, Ellen

What is the judicial branch? by Ellen Rodger. Crabtree Publishing Company 2013 32 p. (Your guide to government) (reinforced library binding) $26.60

Grades: 4 5 6 7   347.73

1. Law -- United States 2. Courts -- United States 3. Procedure (Law) -- United States
ISBN 0778708802; 9780778708803; 9780778709060

LC 2013001275

This book, by Ellen Rodger "provide[s] solid introductory material about the U.S. government. [The] book discusses the purpose of [the judicial] branch; the different positions, . . . the work done; and the strengths and the challenges of each branch and how they interact." (School Library Journal)

The **Supreme** Court justices; illustrated biographies, 1789-2012. edited by Clare Cushman, the Supreme Court Historical Society ; foreword by Chief Justice John G. Roberts, Jr. 3rd ed. CQ Press, an imprint of SAGE Publications 2013 xx, 562 p.p ill., ports. (hardcover) $135

Grades: 8 9 10 11 12 Adult   347.73

1. Judges -- Biography 2. Judges -- United States -- Biography 3. United States. Supreme Court -- History 4. United States. Supreme Court -- Officials and employees -- Biography
ISBN 1608718328; 9781608718320

LC 2012031502

This book, edited by Clare Cushman, is "a single-volume reference profiling every Supreme Court justice from John Jay through Elena Kagan. An original essay on each justice paints a . . . picture of his or her individuality as shaped by family, education, pre-Court career, and the times in which he or she lived. Each biographical essay also presents the major issues on which the justice presided. Essays are arranged in the order of the justices' appointments." (Publisher's note)

"Written by leading constitutional scholars, the well-researched essays are arranged in chronological order of the justices' appointment to the Court. The volume includes a revised bibliography organized by individual justices, and a thorough index. . . . Recommended." Choice

Includes bibliographical references (pages 516-538) and index.

351   Public administration

Bow, James

What is the executive branch? by James Bow. Crabtree Publishing Company 2013 32 p. (Your guide to government) (reinforced library binding) $26.60

Grades: 4 5 6 7 **351**

1. Presidents -- United States 2. Executive power -- United States 3. Executive departments -- United States
ISBN 0778709027; 9780778709022; 9780778709077

LC 2013001276

This book, by James Bow "provide[s] solid introductory material about the U.S. government. [The] book discusses the purpose of [the executive] branch; the different positions, . . . the work done; and the strengths and the challenges of each branch and how they interact." (School Library Journal)

355 Military science

Chapman, Caroline

★ **Battles** & weapons: exploring history through art; [by] Caroline Chapman. Two-Can 2007 64p il (Picture that!) $19.95

Grades: 5 6 7 8 **355**

1. War in art 2. Military history 3. Military art and science
ISBN 978-1-58728-588-2

LC 2006033229

"High quality reproductions of paintings, murals, sculptures, and artifacts show military customs and equipment over the centuries. . . . The lively, informative text creates a 'you are there' sense that will engage even reluctant readers." SLJ

Includes bibliographical references

Chrisp, Peter

Warfare; by Peter Chrisp. Lucent Books 2004 48p il map (Medieval realms) $28.70

Grades: 6 7 8 9 **355**

1. Military history 2. Medieval civilization 3. Knights and knighthood
ISBN 1-59018-537-4

LC 2003-18308

This briefly describes wars and warfare in the Middle Ages, including the Norman invasions, the Crusades, knighthood and chivalry, the Hundred Years War, the campaign of Crécy, the Black Prince's War, and the Wars of the Roses
Inlcudes glossary and bibliographical references

Solway, Andrew

Graphing war and conflict. Raintree 2010 32p il (Real world data) $28.21; pa $7.99

Grades: 4 5 6 7 **355**

1. Graphic methods 2. Military history
ISBN 978-1-4329-2620-5; 1-4329-2620-9; 978-1-4329-2629-8 pa; 1-4329-2629-2 pa

LC 2009001188

This "uses graphs and charts to talk about global conflicts between 1990 and 2005, from guerilla warfare and civil war to nuclear attacks, with a special section on terrorism, including 9/11 and suicide bombers. . . . The clear design, with lots of full-color photos and sidebars, will encourage browsers as much as the up-to-date examples and the clear directions for remaining 'chart smart.'" Booklist

Includes glossary and bibliographical references

War: opposing viewpoints; Louise Gerdes, book editor. Greenhaven Press 2005 239p il (Opposing viewpoints series) lib bdg $34.95; pa $23.70

Grades: 8 9 10 11 12 **355**

1. War 2. Intervention (International law) 3. Military policy -- United States 4. United States -- Foreign relations
ISBN 0-7377-2591-5 lib bdg; 0-7377-2592-3 pa

LC 2004-54283

In this anthology the authors "debate controversies surrounding the causes and conduct of war, including under what circumstances war is justified, how prisoners and civilians should be treated, and what measures, if any, will prevent wars." Publisher's note

Includes bibliographical references

355.02 War and warfare

Benoit, Peter

The **nuclear** age; by Peter Benoit. Children's Press 2012 64 p. ill. (chiefly col.), col. map (Cornerstones of freedom) (library) $30.00; (paperback) $8.95

Grades: 4 5 6 **355.02**

1. Nuclear weapons -- History 2. Nuclear energy -- History
ISBN 0531230627; 0531281620; 9780531230626; 9780531281628

LC 2011031341

This book by Peter Benoit, part of the "Cornerstones of Freedom" series, "offers comprehensive coverage of all concepts related to the nuclear age beginning in the late 1800s through current times. . . . Four chapters highlight issues that emerge--birth of the new age, cold war, atom's legacy and human dilemma." Topics include "the atomic bomb, [Adolf] Hitler versus allies, international competitions, precautions, peaceful pursuits and cleaner sources of energy." (Children's Literature)

Includes bibliographical references (p. 61) and index.

355.1 Military life and customs

Hart, Joyce

Frequently asked questions about being part of a military family. Rosen Pub. 2009 64p il (FAQ: teen life) lib bdg $29.25

Grades: 6 7 8 9 **355.1**

1. Family life 2. Military personnel 3. United States -- Armed forces
ISBN 978-1-4358-5328-7 lib bdg; 1-4358-5328-8 lib bdg

LC 2008055612

"While conversational, [this volume is] surprisingly helpful—and even emotive. [This] starts big: who's in the military, what are the branches, etc. Mostly, though, this is mentor-to-friend reassurance." Booklist

Includes glossary and bibliographical references

355.4   Military operations

Durman, Laura

Siege; by Laura Durman. Arcturus Pub. 2012
32 p. col. ill. (Knights and castles) (library) $28.50
Grades: 4 5 6   **355.4**
1. Middle Ages 2. Military art and science 3. Sieges
4. Castles 5. Siege warfare
ISBN 1848585624; 9781848585621

LC 2011051446

This book by Laura Durman is part of the Knights and
Castles series and looks at sieges. In "two-page spreads
filled with photos, staged reenactments, diagrams, and line
drawings, Durman . . . outlines how both sides prepared and
fared in a siege. Chapters on castle defense, defense tactics,
and personal protection" are included as is an "in-depth look
at the precision and force at work with such siege machines
as the trebuchet, mangonel, battering ram, and belfry."
(Children's Literature)

Includes bibliographical references (p. 31) and index.

Grayson, Robert

Military. Marshall Cavendish Benchmark 2010
62p il (Working animals) lib bdg $28.50
Grades: 4 5 6 7   **355.4**
1. Animals -- War use
ISBN 978-1-60870-164-3 lib bdg; 1-60870-164-6
lib bdg

"Attractively designed and packed with information. . . .
The composition of each page is attractively set up with well-
selected and reproduced stock and historical photos." SLJ

Includes glossary and bibliographical references

McIntosh, J. S.

Escape and evasion; by Jack Montana. Mason
Crest Publishers 2011 il (Special forces: protecting,
building, teaching and fighting) lib bdg $22.95
Grades: 6 7 8 9   **355.4**
1. Survival skills 2. Military art and science 3. United
States -- Army -- Special Forces
ISBN 978-1-4222-1840-2; 1-4222-1840-6

LC 2010020680

The book covers all the essential skills of an undercover
soldier. Infiltration by land, sea, and air are described in detail. The unique physical demands of night fighting are explained. Tracking techniques are also revealed.

"The well-chosen color photographs help make this series a fun armchair experience for military enthusiasts as
well as a good resource for reports and for males considering
military careers." Booklist

Includes bibliographical references

355.8   Military equipment and supplies
(Material)

Byam, Michele

Arms & armor; written by Michéle Byam. rev
ed; DK Pub. 2004 72p il (DK eyewitness books)
$15.99

Grades: 4 5 6 7   **355.8**
1. Armor 2. Weapons
ISBN 0-7566-0654-3

LC 2004-558979

First published 1988 by Knopf

A photo essay examining the design, construction, and
uses of hand weapons and armor from a Stone Age axe to the
revolvers and rifles of the Wild West

Sullivan, Edward T.

The ultimate weapon; the race to develop the
atomic bomb. Holiday House 2007 182p il $24.95
Grades: 6 7 8 9   **355.8**
1. Atomic bomb 2. Manhattan Project
ISBN 978-0-8234-1855-8; 0-8234-1855-3

LC 2005-50330

This history of the Manhattan Project "effectively distills
the science behind the development of the atomic bomb into
understandable terms that turns the human story behind the
project into compelling drama." Booklist

Includes bibliographical references

Vander Hook, Sue

The Manhattan Project. ABDO Pub. 2011
112p il map (Essential events) lib bdg $23.95
Grades: 7 8 9 10 11 12   **355.8**
1. Atomic bomb 2. Manhattan Project
ISBN 978-1-61714-767-8; 1-61714-767-2

LC 2010041429

This describes the project that developed the first atomic
bomb, and discusses the political, social, and technical issues pertaining to it.

Includes glossary and bibliographical references

356   Specific kinds of military forces and warfare

Earl, C. F.

Army Rangers; by Gabrielle Vanderhoof and
C.F. Earl. Mason Crest Publishers 2011 96p il
(Special forces: protecting, building, teaching and
fighting) lib bdg $22.95
Grades: 6 7 8 9   **356**
1. United States -- Army -- Rangers
ISBN 978-1-4222-1838-9; 1-4222-1838-4

LC 2010023795

This describes the Army Rangers unit and its history,
training, weapons, modern missions.

"The well-chosen color photographs help make this series a fun armchair experience for military enthusiasts as
well as a good resource for reports and for males considering
military careers." Booklist

Includes bibliographical references

Green Berets. Mason Crest Publishers 2011 64p
il (Special forces: protecting, building, teaching and
fighting) lib bdg $22.95

Grades: 6 7 8 9   356

1. United States -- Army -- Special Forces
ISBN 978-1-4222-1841-9; 1-4222-1841-4

LC 2010025293

This is an overview of the training, duties, and characteristics of Green Beret personnel.

"The well-chosen color photographs help make this series a fun armchair experience for military enthusiasts as well as a good resource for reports and for males considering military careers." Booklist

Includes bibliographical references

Haney, Eric L.

Inside Delta Force; the story of America's elite counterterrorist unit. Delacorte Press 2006 246p il hardcover o.p. pa $17

Grades: 8 9 10 11 12   356

1. United States -- Army -- Delta Force
ISBN 0-385-73251-1; 0-385-33936-4 pa

LC 2004-30945

"In this adaptation of an adult book, Retired Command Sergeant Major Haney relates a . . . story of the 1977 founding of the ultrasecret counterterrorist unit of the U.S. Army known as Delta Force. . . . Better stock up on copies; you won't want to ration this one." Booklist

McIntosh, J. S.

Elite forces selection; by Jack Montana. Mason Crest Publishers 2011 64p il (Special forces: protecting, building, teaching and fighting) lib bdg $22.95

Grades: 6 7 8 9   356

1. United States -- Army -- Special Forces
ISBN 978-1-4222-1839-6; 1-4222-1839-2

LC 2010016871

This describes how special forces are selected and trained.

"The well-chosen color photographs help make this series a fun armchair experience for military enthusiasts as well as a good resource for reports and for males considering military careers." Booklist

Includes bibliographical references

358 Air and other specialized forces and warfare; engineering and related services

Marcovitz, Hal

Biological & chemical warfare. ABDO Pub. Co. 2010 112p il (Essential issues) lib bdg $22.95

Grades: 7 8 9 10   358

1. Chemical warfare 2. Biological warfare
ISBN 978-1-60453-951-6; 1-60453-951-8

LC 2009-29947

The text is "well-written, providing examples that put a human face to each problem. Quotes and facts are clearly attributed, and their sources are noted in the extensive back matter. . . . Sidebars provide further information, or, more compellingly, offer stories about those touched by the topic.

[This] will be of great assistance to students writing reports." SLJ

Includes glossary and bibliographical references

358.4 Air forces and warfare

Schwartz, Heather E.

Women of the U.S. Air Force; aiming high. Capstone Press 2011 32p (Women in the U.S. Armed Forces) lib bdg $26.65

Grades: 4 5 6 7   358.4

1. Women air pilots 2. Women in the armed forces 3. United States -- Air Force
ISBN 978-1-4296-5449-4; 1-4296-5449-X

LC 2010040749

Describes the past, present, and future of women in the U.S. Air Force.

The book has "a snappy design and eye-catching photographs, and the [text is] written with struggling readers in mind. The content is engaging, the material is worthy, and the [package is] attractive." SLJ

Includes glossary and bibliographical references

Vanderhoof, Gabrielle

Air Force. Mason Crest Publishers 2011 64p il (Special forces: protecting, building, teaching and fighting) lib bdg $22.95

Grades: 6 7 8 9   358.4

1. United States -- Air Force
ISBN 978-1-4222-1837-2; 1-4222-1837-6

LC 2010019186

"The well-chosen color photographs help make this series a fun armchair experience for military enthusiasts as well as a good resource for reports and for males considering military careers." Booklist

"Air Force introduces the history and core values of this specialized branch, along with a description of pararescuers, combat controllers, special operations weather technicians, and tactical air controllers. Recent roles in Haiti and Afghanistan are explored, and such innovations as biofuel and bird radars are mentioned. The last chapter examines the requirements to join the Air Force and provides a suggested training regimen for those interested in pursuing this opportunity." Voice Youth Advocates

Includes bibliographical references

359 Sea forces and warfare

Dolan, Edward F.

Careers in the U.S. Navy. Marshall Cavendish Benchmark 2009 80p il (Military service) lib bdg $24.95

Grades: 6 7 8 9   359

1. Vocational guidance 2. United States -- Navy
ISBN 978-0-7614-4210-3 lib bdg; 0-7614-4210-3 lib bdg

LC 2008035919

Discusses service in the U.S. Navy, including training, educational benefits, and career opportunities.

"Young people interested in exploring a career in [the U. S. Navy] will find solid information. . . . Colored photographs, acronymns, Web sites, and a detail index will add to the appeal." Booklist
Includes bibliographical references

Llanas, Sheila Griffin

Women of the U.S. Navy; making waves. Capstone Press 2011 32p il (Women in the U. S. Armed Forces) lib bdg $26.65

Grades: 4 5 6 7   **359**

1. Sailors 2. United States -- Navy 3. Women in the armed forces
ISBN 978-1-4296-5448-7; 1-4296-5448-1

LC 2010040801

This book explains "how women's roles in the U.S. [Navy] have evolved over the years. [The] volume starts with an account of one specific servicewoman and then delves into her branch's history. [The book has] a snappy design and eye-catching photographs, and the [text is] written with struggling readers in mind. The content is engaging, the material is worthy, and the [package is] attractive." SLJ
Includes glossary and bibliographical references

359.9   Specialized combat forces; engineering and related services

Gray, Judy Silverstein

The **U.S.** Coast Guard and military careers; [by] Judy Silverstein Gray. Enslow Publishers 2007 128p il (The U.S. Armed Forces and military careers) lib bdg $31.93

Grades: 6 7 8 9   **359.9**

1. Vocational guidance 2. United States -- Coast Guard
ISBN 978-0-7660-2493-9 lib bdg; 0-7660-2493-8 lib bdg

LC 2006001744

This offers a history of the U.S. Coast Guard, describes what the Coast Guard does and outlines career opportunities.
Includes glossary and bibliographical references

McIntosh, J. S.

Marines; by Jack Montana. Mason Crest Publishers 2011 64p il (Special forces: protecting, building, teaching and fighting) lib bdg $22.95

Grades: 6 7 8 9   **359.9**

1. United States -- Marine Corps
ISBN 978-1-4222-1842-6; 1-4222-1842-2

LC 2010020681

Briefly describes the history, training, and missions of the United States Marine Corps.
"The well-chosen color photographs help make this series a fun armchair experience for military enthusiasts as well as a good resource for reports and for males considering military careers." Booklist
Includes bibliographical references

Navy SEALs; by Jack Montana. Mason Crest Publishers 2011 96p il (Special forces: protecting, building, teaching and fighting) lib bdg $22.95

Grades: 6 7 8 9   **359.9**

1. United States -- Navy -- Sea Air Land Team
ISBN 978-1-4222-1843-3; 1-4222-1843-0

LC 2010021842

This describes the history of the Navy SEALs, their training and selection, their survival tactics and modern missions around the world.
"The well-chosen color photographs help make this series a fun armchair experience for military enthusiasts as well as a good resource for reports and for males considering military careers." Booklist
Includes bibliographical references

361.2   Social action

Drake, Jane

Yes you can! your guide to becoming an activist. [by] Jane Drake & Ann Love. Tundra Books 2010 136p pa $12.95

Grades: 7 8 9 10   **361.2**

1. Social action
ISBN 978-0-88776-942-9; 0-88776-942-X pa

"Young people who want to effect change are guided by a sequence of nine steps and inspirational examples of grassroots activism. . . . Each step, or chapter, includes a story, strategies, skills, and a time line of milestones and setbacks. . . . The style is conversational and the tone offers realistic encouragement to teens looking to solve problems. . . . This title will primarily serve as a how-to, although the time lines, an accessible index, and factual information about anti-smoking campaigns, recycling, and children's rights make it a useful historical perspective of activism." SLJ

Halpin, Mikki

★ **It's** your world--if you don't like it, change it; activism for teenagers. Simon Pulse 2004 305p pa $8.99

Grades: 7 8 9 10   **361.2**

1. Social action
ISBN 0-689-87448-0

"Animal rights, racism, war protest, AIDS, school violence and bullying, women's rights, and promoting tolerance are among the topics covered here. Halpin provides basic information about each one and then makes myriad suggestions for action at home, in the community, the 'five-minute activist,' etc. The ideas are easy to implement. . . .This is an important book that will empower any young adult who would like to make a difference." SLJ
Includes bibliographical references

361.3   Social work

Flath, Camden

Social workers; finding solutions for tomorrow's society. Mason Crest Publishers 2011 64p il (New careers for the 21st century: finding your role in the global renewal) lib bdg $22.95; pa $9.95

Grades: 7 8 9 10 **361.3**
1. Social work 2. Vocational guidance
ISBN 978-1-4222-1821-1 lib bdg; 1-4222-1821-X lib
bdg; 978-1-4222-2042-9 pa; 1-4222-2042-7 pa
LC 2010017920

"Chapters identify and emphasize specific careers—important strengths, necessary aptitudes and interests, education and training, projected earnings, closely related occupations, type of work environment, and predictions for the future of the field. . . . Color photos have a small role amid the many statistics, figures, graphs and charts that support and supplement the . . . [text]." SLJ
Includes bibliographical references

Gay, Kathlyn
★ **Volunteering**; the ultimate teen guide. Scarecrow Press 2004 127p il (It happened to me)
$37.50; pa $14.95
Grades: 7 8 9 10 **361.3**
1. Volunteer work
ISBN 0-8108-4922-4; 978-0-8108-4922-8; 0-8108-5833-9 pa; 978-0-8108-5833-6 pa
LC 2004-8174

"This is a useful tool in that it provides a one-stop resource for teens interested in locating volunteer opportunities." SLJ
Includes bibliographical references

O'Neal, Claire
Volunteering in your school. Mitchell Lane Publishers 2011 47p (How to help: a guide to giving back) lib bdg $29.95
Grades: 4 5 6 **361.3**
1. Volunteer work
ISBN 978-1-58415-920-9; 1-58415-920-0
LC 2010011982

This suggests ways in which young people can volunteer to do such tasks as participating in a clean-up day, setting up a recycling center, or planting a garden to enhance and contribute to the school community.

This "well-organized [book] will encourage children to contribute to the world around them. [The] title is filled with examples of volunteer opportunities that can be accomplished with some adult involvement and supervision to guide, steer, and maintain focus so that youngsters will have varied and successful experiences." SLJ
Includes bibliographical references

Ways to help in your community. Mitchell Lane 2010 47p il (How to help: a guide to giving back) lib bdg $29.95
Grades: 4 5 6 **361.3**
1. Community life 2. Volunteer work
ISBN 978-1-58415-921-6 lib bdg; 1-58415-921-9 lib bdg

This "well-organized [book] will encourage children to contribute to the world around them. [The] title is filled with examples of volunteer opportunities that can be accomplished with some adult involvement and supervision to guide, steer, and maintain focus so that youngsters will have varied and successful experiences. . . . [The book] offers specific examples and steps for making a neighborhood safer, organizing yard sales, spending time with an elderly person,

helping at a soup kitchen, or offering to do storyhours at a library." SLJ
Includes bibliographical references

361.7 Private action

Reusser, Kayleen
Celebrities giving back. Mitchell Lane Publishers 2011 47p (How to help: a guide to giving back) lib bdg $29.95
Grades: 4 5 6 **361.7**
1. Charities 2. Celebrities 3. Philanthropists
ISBN 978-1-58415-922-3 lib bdg; 1-58415-922-7 lib bdg
LC 2010014904

"Reusser writes about 17 people, including Bono and his interest in eliminating world hunger and poverty, President Carter's dreams of building homes for the homeless, and charitable works by Rihanna, Shakira, Tony Hawk, and others." SLJ
Includes bibliographical references

361.9 History, geographic treatment, biography

Slavicek, Louise Chipley, 1956-
Jane Addams. Chelsea House 2011 126 p. ill (some col.) (Women of achievement) lib bdg $35
Grades: 6 7 8 9 **361.9**
1. Authors 2. Philanthropists 3. Hull House (Chicago, Ill.) 4. Essayists 5. Pacifists 6. Social welfare leaders 7. Nobel laureates for peace 8. Chicago (Ill.) -- Social conditions
ISBN 978-1-60413-907-5; 1-60413-907-2
LC 2011000038

This book "traces [Jane] Addams' life and considerable accomplishments in social welfare, labor reform, and women's suffrage . . . [and] portrays Addams' difficult path to good education and her determination to use her life well." It is "supplemented with sidebars and illustrations . . . [and] includes a chronology, notes for the many quotes, a source bibliography, and lists of recommended books and websites." (Booklist) Details on her role in "found[ing] the pioneering settlement house, Hull House, where she and a dedicated staff of volunteers, most of them college-educated women like herself, lived and worked among some of Chicago's most destitute residents" are also presented. (Publisher's note)

This "traces Addams' life and considerable accomplishments in social welfare, labor reform, and women's suffrage. Slavicek vividly portrays Addams' difficult path to good education and her determination to use her life well. . . . Solid fare for the biography collection." Booklist
Includes bibliographical references and index.

362.1   People with illnesses and disabilities

Dreyer, ZoAnn

Living with cancer; ZoAnn Dreyer. Facts On
File 2008 202p $34.95

Grades: 8 9 10 11 12   **362.1**
1. Cancer
ISBN 978-0-8160-6484-7

LC 2007-10675

"Although written for teens with these conditions, these
titles will have more general appeal... Material in both titles
is presented in a straightforward manner. "SLJ
Includes bibliographical references (p. 192-194)
and index.

Farrell, Courtney

Mental disorders. ABDO Pub. Co. 2010 112p il
(Essential issues) lib bdg $22.95

Grades: 7 8 9 10   **362.1**
1. Mental illness
ISBN 978-1-60453-956-1; 1-60453-956-9

LC 2009-29942

"This title examines the world's critical issues surrounding mental disorders. Readers will learn the historical background of mental disorders, leading up to the current and
future impact on society." Publisher's note
Includes glossary and bibliographical references

Fast food; Lauri S. Friedman, book editor. Greenhaven Press 2010 122p il map (Introducing issues with opposing viewpoints) $34.70

Grades: 7 8 9 10 11 12   **362.1**
1. Obesity 2. Restaurants 3. Convenience foods
ISBN 978-0-7377-4733-1; 0-7377-4733-1

LC 2009-51963

This is a collection of essays arguing various viewpoints
about fast foods and their effects on health, and whether or not fast food restaurants should be banned, taxed,
or regulated.

This "contains some fascinating arguments, including
the central question of whether or not fast food makes people fat and sick. Active-reading questions preface the essays,
which are followed by directions for evaluating the arguments presented. Color photos and other graphics throughout enliven the reading experience." SLJ
Includes bibliographical references

Fleischman, John

★ **Phineas** Gage: a gruesome but true story about
brain science. Houghton Mifflin 2002 86p il $16;
pa $8.95

Grades: 5 6 7 8 9   **362.1**
1. Railroad workers 2. Brain -- Wounds and injuries
ISBN 0-618-05252-6; 0-618-49478-2 pa

LC 2001-39253

"The author deftly introduces readers to a diverse range
of relevant scientific history as well as more specific beliefs
that influenced the medical establishment's understanding of
Gage, then goes on to examine subsequent neurological discoveries that have changed and enhanced our understanding
of Gage's fate. The book's present-tense narrative is invit-

ing and intimate, and the text is crisp and lucid." Bull Cent
Child Books
Includes glossary and bibliographical references

Jones, Molly

Health care for everyone. Rosen Pub. 2011 64p
il (Headlines!) lib bdg $29.95

Grades: 7 8 9 10   **362.1**
1. Medical care 2. Health insurance
ISBN 978-1-4488-1290-5; 1-4488-1290-9

LC 2010024137

This book "begins with President Obama's 2010 [health
care] legislation then discusses problems within the industry.
. . . Good organization, clear writing, captioned photos, and
sidebars deliver the information cleanly." Horn Book Guide
Includes glossary and bibliographical references

Naden, Corinne J.

Patients' rights; [by] Corinne Naden. Marshall
Cavendish Benchmark 2008 144p il (Open for debate) lib bdg $27.95

Grades: 7 8 9 10   **362.1**
1. Medical care
ISBN 978-0-7614-2576-2; 0-7614-2576-4

LC 2006-21786

This book maintains a "balanced tone while providing
an abundance of examples and factual information. Many
captioned color photos enhance the text." SLJ
Includes bibliographical references

Parks, Peggy J

HPV; Peggy J. Parks. 2nd edition Reference-
Point Press 2015 96 p. col. ill., col. map (Compact
research. Diseases and disorders) hbk $28.95

Grades: 7 8 9 10 11 12   **362.1**
1. Papillomaviruses
ISBN 9781601526908

LC 2014007191

Presents an overview of the causes, symptoms, and various types of the Human Papillomavirus; and provides information on available vaccines, health risks of genital HPV,
and organizations and advocacy groups.
Includes bibliographical references and index

What can I do now?: Health care. Ferguson 2007
222p $29.95

Grades: 8 9 10 11 12   **362.1**
1. Medicine 2. Vocational guidance
ISBN 0-8160-6031-2; 978-0-8160-603-1

LC 2006030410

"This volume offers an overview of the health-care industry, a look at different careers, ideas for getting experience, and additional resources. . . . The layout is attractive,
the font a good size, and the information accessible. . . . An
excellent addition." SLJ

Winick, Judd

Pedro & me; friendship, loss, & what I learned.
Henry Holt and Co. 2009 187p il pa $16.99

Grades: 7 8 9 10 11 12   **362.1**
1. Graphic novels 2. Television personalities 3.

Biographical graphic novels 4. AIDS patients 5. AIDS activists 6. Friendship -- Graphic novels 7. AIDS (Disease) -- Graphic novels 8. Real world (Television program) -- Graphic novels
ISBN 978-0-8050-8964-6
First published 2000
2001 Robert F. Sibert Honor Book for informational books for youth
In this "volume—part graphic novel, part memoir—professional cartoonist Winick pays tribute to his Real World housemate and friend Pedro Zamora, an AIDS activist who died of the disease in 1994." Publ Wkly

362.196 Specific conditions

Therrien, Patricia
An **enemy** within; overcoming cancer and other life-threatening diseases. by Patty Therrien. Mason Crest Publishers 2009 128 p. col. ill. (library) $24.95
Grades: 7 8 9 10   **362.196**
1. Terminally ill 2. Cancer patients 3. Cancer in children -- Patients -- Biography 4. Catastrophic illness -- Patients -- Biography
ISBN 1422204502; 9781422204504
LC 2008033776
This book offers a collection of "stories of courageous young people and how their lives have changed due to such a diagnosis [which] are told from their own viewpoint." The volume "includes full-color photographs, table of contents, for further reading and for more information sections, bibliography, index, and author and consultant profiles." (Publisher's note)
Includes bibliographical references (p. 125) and index.

362.2 People with mental illness and disabilities

Scott, Celicia
Caffeine; energy drinks, coffee, soda, & pills. Celicia Scott. Mason Crest 2015 48 p. (Downside of drugs) $20.95
Grades: 6 7 8   **362.2**
1. Caffeine 2. Drugs -- Physiological effect 3. Drug abuse 4. Caffeine habit
ISBN 142223018X; 9781422230183
LC 2014466074
This juvenile book, by Celicia Scott, part of the "Downside of Drugs" series, explores how "people around the world consume . . . drinks . . . and pills that contain caffeine, without a thought for the consequences the caffeine may have on their lives. . . . With a vast industry targeting its marketing at young people, educating yourself is the essential first step to counter caffeine's possible effects on your life, from sleep problems to addiction." (Publisher's note)
"Written with a Harvard Medical School consultant, this series discusses drugs in a tone that is appropriately sober yet not alarmist or condescending...Despite some awkward moments, this series is mostly well written and expertly researched." SLJ

Flath, Camden
21st -century counselors; new approaches to mental health & substance abuse. Mason Crest Publishers 2011 64p il (New careers for the 21st century: finding your role in the global renewal) lib bdg $22.95
Grades: 7 8 9 10   **362.2**
1. Counseling 2. Vocational guidance 3. Drug abuse counseling
ISBN 978-1-4222-1825-9 lib bdg; 1-4222-1825-2 lib bdg
LC 2010021812
"Chapters identify and emphasize specific careers—important strengths, necessary aptitudes and interests, education and training, projected earnings, closely related occupations, type of work environment, and predictions for the future of the field. . . . Color photos have a small role amid the many statistics, figures, graphs and charts that support and supplement the . . . [text]." SLJ
Includes bibliographical references

Mental Illness; Roman Espejo, Book Editor. Greenhaven Press 2012 215 p. pa $30.95
Grades: 9 10 11 12   **362.2**
1. Mental illness
ISBN 9780737757354
LC 2011011655
This book, edited by Roman Espejo, focuses on the topic of mental illness. Questions raised include: "Is Mental Illness a Serious Problem?; How Should Society Address Mental Illness?; What Mental Health Issues Do Youths Face Today?; What Treatments for Mental Illness Are Effective?" (Publisher's note)

362.28 Suicide

Galas, Judith C.
★ The **power** to prevent suicide; a guide for teens helping teens. [by] Richard E. Nelson, Judith C. Galas; foreword by Bev Cobain; edited by Pamela Espeland. Updated ed; Free Spirit 2006 115p pa $13.95
Grades: 7 8 9 10 11 12   **362.28**
1. Suicide
ISBN 1-57542-206-9; 978-1-57542-206-0
First published 1994
"The authors' premise is that, as trusted and caring friends, YAs have a special role in the prevention of suicide among their peers, and discuss what to do if they observe the danger signals. . . . This book provides clear, practical information and advice." SLJ

Marcovitz, Hal
Suicide. ABDO Pub. Co. 2010 112p il (Essential issues) lib bdg $22.95
Grades: 7 8 9 10   **362.28**
1. Suicide
ISBN 978-1-60453-958-5; 1-60453-958-5
LC 2009-30354

This is "well-written, providing examples that put a human face to each problem. Quotes and facts are clearly attributed, and their sources are noted in the extensive back matter. . . . Sidebars provide further information, or, more compellingly, offer stories about those touched by the topic. . . . [This] will be of great assistance to students writing reports." SLJ

Includes glossary and bibliographical references

Suicide: opposing viewpoints; Jacqueline Langwith, book editor. Greenhaven Press 2008 268p (Opposing viewpoints series) lib bdg $38.50; pa $26.75

Grades: 8 9 10 11 12   **362.28**

1. Suicide 2. Euthanasia

ISBN 978-0-7377-4012-7 lib bdg; 0737740124 lib bdg; 978-0-7377-4013-4 pa; 0-7377-4013-2 pa

LC 2008-1007

The articles in this anthology cover topics such as suicide among teens and other types of people, what causes suicide, assisted suicide, and how suicide can be prevented.

Includes bibliographical references

362.29   Substance abuse

Addiction: opposing viewpoints; Christina Fisanick, book editor. Greenhaven Press 2009 228p il (Opposing viewpoints series) lib bdg $39.70; pa $27.50

Grades: 8 9 10 11 12   **362.29**

1. Alcoholism 2. Drug abuse

ISBN 978-0-7377-4352-4 lib bdg; 0-7377-4352-2 lib bdg; 978-0-7377-4351-7 pa; 0-7377-4351-4 pa

LC 2008-53997

Articles in this anthology discuss the nature of addiction, including how addictions can be prevented and treated.

Includes bibliographical references

Berne, Emma Carlson

Methamphetamine. ReferencePoint Press 2007 102p il map (Compact research) $24.95

Grades: 8 9 10 11 12   **362.29**

1. Drug abuse 2. Methamphetamine

ISBN 978-1-60152-004-3; 1-60152-004-2

LC 2006032206

"Berne explores whether methamphetamine usage in the U.S. has reached epidemic proportions, its dangers, the link between addiction and crime, and abuse prevention." SLJ

Includes bibliographical references

Bjornlund, Lydia

Marijuana; by Lydia Bjornlund. ReferencePoint Press 2012 136 p. (Compact research series) (hardcover) $27.95

Grades: 7 8 9 10 11 12   **362.29**

1. Marijuana 2. Drug education 3. Medical botany 4. Drugs -- Physiological effect 5. Drugs -- Law and legislation -- United States 6. Marijuana -- United States

7. Marijuana -- Law and legislation -- United States

ISBN 160152160X; 9781601521606

LC 2011007743

This book on marijuana is a part of the Compact Research: Drugs series and "focus[es] on three types of information: "objective single-author narratives, opinion-based primary source quotations, and facts and statistics." What this translates to on the page is an overview of the topic and an in-depth chapter-by chapter discussion of the points raised in the overview." Lydia Bjornlund "looks at questions such as whether marijuana is a dangerous drug, whether it should be legalized, and the most pressing dilemma: Should the drug be readily available for medical use?" (Booklist)

Includes bibliographical references and index.

Teen smoking. Reference Point Press 2010 104p il (Compact research. Current issues) $25.95

Grades: 8 9 10 11 12   **362.29**

1. Smoking

ISBN 978-1-60152-098-2; 1-60152-098-0

LC 2009-28008

This addresses the following questions: How serious a problem is teen smoking?; Who is to blame for teen smoking?; How should teen smoking be regulated?; How can we prevent teen smoking?

"The straightforward presentation of serious subject matter, graphics, and easy access to facts . . . [make this book] excellent . . . for reports and debates." SLJ

Breguet, Amy

Vicodin, OxyContin, and other pain relievers; [by] Amy E. Breguet. Chelsea House 2008 112p il (Junior drug awareness) $30

Grades: 6 7 8 9   **362.29**

1. Narcotics 2. Analgesics 3. Drug abuse

ISBN 978-0-7910-9700-7; 0-7910-9700-5

LC 2007032350

This describes the effects of Vicodin and OxyContin and other pain relievers, how they are used and abused, and how to get help for addiction.

Includes glossary and bibliographical references

Cobb, Allan B.

Heroin. Chelsea House Publishers 2009 109p il (Junior drug awareness) lib bdg $30

Grades: 6 7 8 9   **362.29**

1. Heroin 2. Drug abuse

ISBN 978-0-7910-9749-6 lib bdg; 0-7910-9749-8 lib bdg

LC 2007043662

This "describes the uses and abuses of [heroin]. . . . The reasons people might take drugs, their dangers, signs of addiction, and treatment options are covered. . . . The content is reliable and comprehensive." Horn Book Guide

Includes glossary and bibliographical references

Drugs, alcohol, and tobacco; learning about addictive behavior. Rosalyn Carson-DeWitt, editor in chief. Macmillan Ref. USA 2003 3v set $295

Grades: 7 8 9 10 **362.29**

1. Reference books 2. Drug abuse -- Encyclopedias
ISBN 0-02-865756-X

LC 2002-9270

Based on the Encyclopedia of drugs, alcohol & addictive behavior, 2nd edition, published 2001

"The 190 alphabetically arranged articles range from one to six pages in length and yield a comprehensive look at the nature of, treatments for, and social issues surrounding addictive substances and behaviors. Topics include specific drugs, diagnoses, treatments, legal and social implications, drug trafficking, cultural pressures, and related compulsive behaviors." SLJ

Includes bibliographical references

Egendorf, Laura K.

Performance -enhancing drugs. Reference point 2007 96p il (Compact research) lib bdg $24.95

Grades: 8 9 10 11 12 **362.29**

1. Drugs 2. Athletes -- Drug use
ISBN 978-1-60152-003-6 lib bdg; 1-60152-003-4 lib bdg

This "well-organized [volume presens] general information that report writers, particularly reluctant readers, will find useful. Brightly colored illustrated facts and statistics charts invite perusal. Thought-provoking questions introduce most of the chapters. . . . [This book] covers ethical issues and dangers in usage, effectiveness of testing, and prevention. . . . Primary-source quotes are well documented." SLJ

Freedman, Jeri

Professional wrestling; steroids in and out of the ring. Rosen Central 2009 48p il (Disgraced! the dirty history of performance-enhancing drugs in sports) lib bdg $26.50

Grades: 5 6 7 8 **362.29**

1. Steroids 2. Wrestling 3. Athletes -- Drug use
ISBN 978-1-4358-5305-8 lib bdg; 1-4358-5305-9 lib bdg

LC 2009-1041

Discusses professional wrestlers who died relatively young due to steroid use, the reason why it is common in professional wrestling, efforts at control, the effects of the drugs, related scandals, and steroids in other types of wrestling

"Amazing statements from athletes giving reasons why they took illegal drugs are good for discussion topics. . . . Concludes with thoughts regarding future additional legislation. [A] useful [update]." SLJ

Includes glossary and bibliographical references

Gottfried, Ted

Marijuana; by Ted Gottfried with Lisa Harkrader. Marshall Cavendish Benchmark 2010 32p il (Drug facts) $19.95

Grades: 4 5 6 7 **362.29**

1. Marijuana
ISBN 978-0-7614-4351-3; 0-7614-4351-7

LC 2008-52761

"Provides clear explanations about effects, followed by diagrams of the body to clarify the specific organs/body systems that suffer the most damage. . . . An excellent starting point." SLJ

Includes glossary

Ingram, Scott

Marijuana; [by] W. Scott Ingram. Chelsea House 2008 110p il (Junior drug awareness) lib bdg $30

Grades: 6 7 8 9 **362.29**

1. Marijuana 2. Drug abuse
ISBN 978-0-7910-9695-6 lib bdg; 0-7910-9695-5

LC 2007-24826

This "provides useful, balanced, and comprehensive information." Horn Book Guide

Includes glossary and bibliographical references

Koellhoffer, Tara

Ecstasy and other club drugs; [by] Tara Koellhoffer. Chelsea House 2008 120p il (Junior drug awareness) $30

Grades: 6 7 8 9 **362.29**

1. Drug abuse 2. Ecstasy (Drug)
ISBN 978-0-7910-9697-0; 0-7910-9697-1

LC 2007017789

This describes the effects of Ecstasy (MDMA), GHB, Rohypnol, Ketamine, LSD, and other drugs, why people take them, and addiction and treatment.

This "provides useful, balanced, and comprehensive information." Horn Book Guide

Includes glossary and bibliographical references

Inhalants and solvents; [by] Tara Koellhoffer. Chelsea House 2008 112p il (Junior drug awareness) lib bdg $30

Grades: 6 7 8 9 **362.29**

1. Inhalant abuse
ISBN 978-0-7910-9698-7 lib bdg; 0-7910-9698-X lib bdg

LC 2007024824

This "provides useful, balanced, and comprehensive information." Horn Book Guide

This "examines the many household products—approximately 1,400 of them in all—that can be abused and explains the damage they can do to the brain and body." Publisher's note

Includes glossary and bibliographical references

Kreske, Damian P.

How to say no to drugs. Chelsea House Publishers 2008 112p il (Junior drug awareness) lib bdg $30

Grades: 6 7 8 9 **362.29**

1. Drug abuse
ISBN 978-0-7910-9699-4 1; 0-7910-9699-8

LC 2007043664

This "explains how drug use affects the body and can lead to addiction, as well as how young people can avoid peer pressure to use drugs. The book also includes the personal stories of teenagers who have gone through treatment to repair the damage their drug use did." Publisher's note

Includes glossary and bibliographical references

Landau, Elaine

Meth; America's drug epidemic. [by] Elaine Landau. Twenty-First Century Books 2007 120p il lib bdg $30.60

Grades: 7 8 9 10   **362.29**
1. Drug abuse 2. Methamphetamine
ISBN 978-0-8225-6808-7

LC 2006030923

"This excellent exposé explains the facts about methamphetamine: its effects upon addicts, the impact of the drug's widespread manufacture and use upon society as a whole, and the efforts of government and law enforcement to curtail its spread." Booklist

Includes bibliographical references

Let's clear the air: 10 reasons not to start smoking; with a foreword by Christy Turlington; [illustrations by Deanne Staffo] Lobster Press 2007 192p il pa $14.95

Grades: 5 6 7 8   **362.29**
1. Smoking
ISBN 978-1-897073-66-7 pa; 1-897073-66-6 pa

"Young people ranging in ages from 9 to 14 offer sound arguments for not taking up cigarettes. . . . Interspersed throughout the accessible text are boxes and sidebars with facts and statistics, photos, and spot art. . . . The antismoking message here is all the more effective coming directly from a diverse group of young people." Booklist

LeVert, Suzanne

Ecstasy; by Suzanne LeVert with Jeff Hendricks. Marshall Cavendish Benchmark 2010 32p il (Drug facts) $19.95

Grades: 4 5 6 7   **362.29**
1. Drug abuse 2. Designer drugs 3. Ecstasy (Drug)
ISBN 978-0-7614-4349-0; 0-7614-4349-5

LC 2008-52753

"Provides clear explanations about effects, followed by diagrams of the body to clarify the specific organs/body systems that suffer the most damage. . . . An excellent starting point." SLJ

Includes glossary

★ The **facts** about ecstasy; [by] Suzanne LeVert. Benchmark Books 2004 96p il (Drugs) lib bdg $$2.79; pa $6.99

Grades: 6 7 8 9   **362.29**
1. Ecstasy (Drug)
ISBN 978-0-7614-1807-8 lib bdg; 0-7614-1807-5 lib bdg; 978-0-7614-3588-4 pa; 0-7614-3588-3 pa

LC 2004-9341

The author describes the drug MDMA, commonly known as ecstasy, and how it is abused, its health risks, the laws against it, and how to recover from the habit

Inlcudes glossary and bibliographical references

★ The **facts** about heroin; [by] Suzanne LeVert. Marshall Cavendish Benchmark 2005 95p il (Drugs) lib bdg $42.79; pa $6.99

Grades: 7 8 9 10   **362.29**
1. Heroin 2. Drug abuse
ISBN 978-0-7614-1975-4 lib bdg; 0-7614-1975-6 lib bdg; 978-0-7614-3595-2 pa; 0-7614-3595-6 pa

LC 2005001728

"Describes the history, characteristics, legal status, and abuse of the drug Heroin." Publisher's note

Includes glossary and bibliographical references

★ The **facts** about steroids; [by] Suzanne LeVert. Benchmark Books 2004 96p il (Drugs) lib bdg $42.79

Grades: 6 7 8 9   **362.29**
1. Steroids 2. Athletes -- Drug use
ISBN 978-0-7614-1808-5 lib bdg; 0-7614-1808-3 lib bdg

LC 2004-11852

The author "discusses the effects of steroids on the body, health risks, the law, prevention, and treatment. The medicinal use of steroids is very briefly mentioned. . . . [This title has a] readable, well-organized [text], and good use of color, graphics, photographs, tables, diagrams, and labels helps to spark readers' interest." SLJ

Includes glossary and bibliographical references

Menhard, Francha Roffe

★ The **facts** about inhalants; [by] Francha Roffe Menhard. Benchmark Books 2004 92p il (Drugs) lib bdg $$42.79

Grades: 6 7 8 9   **362.29**
1. Solvent abuse
ISBN 978-0-7614-1809-2 lib bdg; 0-7614-1809-1 lib bdg

LC 2004-11858

The author "addresses the types of inhalants, the history, dangers, effects, available help for abuse of these drugs, and the laws regulating them. . . . [This title has a] readable, well-organized [text], and good use of color, graphics, photographs, tables, diagrams, and labels helps to spark readers' interest." SLJ

Includes glossary and bibliographical references

Merino, Noel

Smoking; Noël Merino, book editor. Greenhaven Press 2010 143p il (Introducing issues with opposing viewpoints) $35.75

Grades: 8 9 10 11 12   **362.29**
1. Smoking 2. Tobacco habit
ISBN 978-0-7377-5101-7; 0-7377-5101-0

LC 2010-26766

Replaces the edition published 2006 under the editorship of Laurie S. Friedman

"The articles in this anthology expose multiple sides of . . . [the smoking] debate." Publisher's note

Includes bibliographical references

Naff, Clay Farris

Nicotine and tobacco; by Clay Farris Naff. ReferencePoint Press, Inc. 2007 110p il (Compact research) $24.95

Grades: 8 9 10 11 12   **362.29**

1. Smoking 2. Tobacco habit

ISBN 978-1-60152-006-7; 1-60152-006-9

     LC 2006033962

This "well-organized [volume presents] general information that report writers, particularly reluctant readers, will find useful. Brightly colored illustrated facts and statistics charts invite perusal. Thought-provoking questions introduce most of the chapters. . . . [This book] addresses the dangers of smoking and chewing tobacco and of exposure to secondhand smoke, why young people use tobacco, and how numbers can be reduced. Primary-source quotes are well documented." SLJ

Includes bibliographical references

Parks, Peggy J.

Bath salts and other synthetic drugs; by Peggy J. Parks. ReferencePoint Press, Inc. 2014 96 p. (Compact research series) (hardback) $28.95

Grades: 8 9 10 11 12   **362.29**

1. Drugs 2. Designer drugs 3. Drugs of abuse 4. Synthetic drugs

ISBN 1601525168; 9781601525161

     LC 2013015820

This book, by Peggy J. Parks, "describes the rise in use of these newer and perhaps lesser known but potentially deadly drugs, as well as problems associated with elusive marketing and hard-to-track Internet sales. Additional back matter comprises lists of key people, advocacy groups, and related organizations." (Booklist)

"Backed by current facts, statistics, and first-person experiences, every chapter includes further documentation with concluding "Primary Source Quotes," from former addicts and law enforcement to health care workers and government officials. In this visual, by-the-numbers era, the series responds with end-of-chapter charts and graphs that display drug-related information." (Booklist)

Includes bibliographical references and index

Methamphetamine; by Peggy J. Parks. ReferencePoint Press, Inc. 2013 96 p. (Compact research series) (hardback) $28.95

Grades: 8 9 10 11 12   **362.29**

1. Drug abuse 2. Methamphetamine 3. Methamphetamine abuse

ISBN 1601525206; 9781601525208

     LC 2013009272

This book, by Peggy J. Parks, "looks at the serious dangers of meth production and abuse and the difficulties in treating meth addiction and passing laws to regulate the drug. Backed by current facts, statistics, and first-person experiences, every chapter includes further documentation with concluding 'Primary Source Quotes,' from former ad-

dicts and law enforcement to health care workers and government officials." (Booklist)

"In this visual, by-the-numbers era, the series responds with end-of-chapter charts and graphs that display drug-related information. Additional back matter comprises lists of key people, advocacy groups, and related organizations; a bibliography; and a chronology. This series is the next go-to resource for drug-abuse research." (Booklist)

Includes bibliographical references and index

Porterfield, Jason

Doping; athletes and drugs. [by] Jason Porterfield. 1st ed.; Rosen Pub. 2008 64p il (In the news) $29.95

Grades: 5 6 7 8   **362.29**

1. Steroids 2. Drug abuse 3. Athletes -- Drug use

ISBN 978-1-4042-1917-5; 1-4042-1917-X

     LC 2007015919

"Overview of the sports and sports figures most often connected with drug scandals, why athletes resort to drug use, the different types of drugs used for physical enhancement, and the methods used to police doping. . . . [This] short [volume is] packed full of information." Voice Youth Advocates

Includes glossary and bibliographical references

Major League Baseball; the great steroid scandals. Rosen Central 2010 48p il (Disgraced! the dirty history of performance-enhancing drugs in sports) lib bdg $26.50

Grades: 5 6 7 8   **362.29**

1. Baseball 2. Steroids 3. Athletes -- Drug use

ISBN 978-1-4358-5302-7 lib bdg; 1-4358-5302-4 lib bdg

     LC 2008-55581

Discusses drug abuse by professional baseball players, with an emphasis on the widespread use of steroids since the late 1980s, revelations of the extent of the problem, and the effects of steroids on the players and on the game and its records

"Amazing statements from athletes giving reasons why they took illegal drugs are good for discussion topics. . . . Concludes with thoughts regarding future additional legislation. [A] useful [update]." SLJ

Includes glossary and bibliographical references

Powell, Jillian

Alcohol and drug abuse; by Jillian Powell; health consultant, John G. Samanich. Gareth Stevens Pub. 2009 48p il (Emotional health issues) lib bdg $31

Grades: 6 7 8 9   **362.29**

1. Alcoholism 2. Drug abuse

ISBN 978-0-8368-9199-7; 0-8368-9199-6

     LC 2008-5459

First published 2008 in the United Kingdom

This book about alcohol and drug abuse has "clear language and explanations. . . . [It is] suitable for fact-finding missions, but the abundant graphics and case studies are likely to draw in browsers as well. Throughout, unfamiliar vocabulary is highlighted in bold and explained in context and in the glossary. . . . Fact boxes and case study sidebars add information." SLJ

Includes glossary and bibliographical references

Schaefer, Adam

Steroids; [by] A.R. Schaefer. Cherry Lake Pub. 2009 32p il (Health at risk) lib bdg $27.07

Grades: 4 5 6 7   362.29

1. Steroids 2. Athletes -- Drug use

ISBN 978-1-60279-287-6 lib bdg; 1-60279-287-9 lib bdg

LC 2008017502

This describes how steroids affect the body and what sports groups are doing to halt their use.

"Great for reports or reluctant readers." Booklist

Includes bibliographical references

Sommers, Annie Leah

College athletics; steroids and supplement abuse. Rosen Pub. Group 2010 48p il (Disgraced! the dirty history of performance-enhancing drugs in sports) lib bdg $26.50

Grades: 5 6 7 8   362.29

1. Steroids 2. College sports 3. Athletes -- Drug use 4. Sports -- Corrupt practices

ISBN 978-1-4358-5303-4 lib bdg; 1-4358-5303-2 lib bdg

LC 2008-55408

Discusses efforts to enhance performance in sports, the use of steroids and supplements by college athletes, including the case of football player Tommy Chaikin, college players as role models, and the influence of the NCAA

"Amazing statements from athletes giving reasons why they took illegal drugs are good for discussion topics. . . . Concludes with thoughts regarding future additional legislation. Useful updates." SLJ

Includes glossary and bibliographical references

Sommers, Michael A.

The NFL; steroids and human growth hormone. Rosen Central 2010 48p il (Disgraced! the dirty history of performance-enhancing drugs in sports) lib bdg $26.50

Grades: 5 6 7 8   362.29

1. Football 2. Steroids 3. Athletes -- Drug use 4. National Football League

ISBN 978-1-4358-5304-1 lib bdg; 1-4358-5304-0 lib bdg

LC 2008-56131

Discusses the uses of performance enhancing drugs, particularly anabolic steroids, by professional football players, their effects on the players and the sport, and the successes and failures of efforts to control their use

"Amazing statements from athletes giving reasons why they took illegal drugs are good for discussion topics. . . . Concludes with thoughts regarding future additional legislation. [A] useful [update]." SLJ

Includes glossary and bibliographical references

Sterngass, Jon

Steroids. Marshall Cavendish Benchmark 2011 112p il (Controversy!) lib bdg $25.95

Grades: 8 9 10 11 12   362.29

1. Steroids

ISBN 9780761449034; 0761449035

Discusses what steroids are, how they are used in sports, how they can be used in other areas, and the debate surrounding them.

This is "written in clear, sophisticated language and will serve well . . . . for research papers or debates." Voice Youth Advocates

Includes bibliographical references

Tobacco and Smoking; edited by Roman Espejo. Greenhaven Pr 2015 242 p. illustrations (Opposing viewpoints) pbk $33.80; library binding $48.80

Grades: 8 9 10 11 12   362.29

1. Smoking 2. Tobacco industry

ISBN 0737772956; 9780737772951 ; 9780737772944 ; 0737772948

Articles in this anthology discuss topics such as smokeless tobacco, teen smoking, government regulation of smoking, and tobacco advertising.

Includes bibliographical references and index

Tobacco information for teens; health tips about the hazards of using cigarettes, smokeless tobacco, and other nicotine products: including facts about nicotine addiction, nicotine delivery systems, secondhand smoke, health consequ. edited by Karen Bellenir, 2nd ed.; Omnigraphics 2010 440p il (Teen health series) $69

Grades: 7 8 9 10 11 12   362.29

1. Smoking 2. Tobacco habit

ISBN 978-0-7808-1153-9; 0-7808-1153-4

LC 2010023716

First published 2007

"Provides basic consumer health information for teens on tobacco use, addiction, and related diseases, along with tips for quitting smoking. Includes index and resource information." Publisher's note

Includes bibliographical references

Warburton, Lianne

Amphetamines and other stimulants; [by] Lianne Warburton and Diana Callfas. Chelsea House 2008 120p il (Junior drug awareness) lib bdg $30

Grades: 6 7 8 9   362.29

1. Drug abuse 2. Stimulants 3. Amphetamines

ISBN 978-0-7910-9712-0 lib bdg; 0-7910-9712-9 lib bdg

LC 2007018860

This "provides useful, balanced, and comprehensive information." Horn Book Guide

This "explores the science and history behind commonly used stimulants, and provides information about addiction and treatment options." Publisher's note

Includes glossary and bibliographical references

West, Krista

Cocaine and crack; [by] Krista West. Chelsea House Publishers 2008 119p il map (Junior drug awareness) lib bdg $30

Grades: 6 7 8 9 **362.29**

1. Cocaine 2. Drug abuse 3. Crack (Drug)

ISBN 978-0-7910-9704-5 lib bdg; 0-7910-9704-8 lib bdg

LC 2007024971

This "provides useful, balanced, and comprehensive information." Horn Book Guide

This "examines how cocaine became an illegal drug after many years of legal use in commercial products, and explains why crack was formulated in the 1980s to make a cheaper and more powerful version of the addictive drug. Information about these drugs' effects on the body and mind and advice on how to overcome addiction to them are also included." Publisher's note

Includes glossary and bibliographical references

Steroids and other performance-enhancing drugs. Chelsea House 2009 118p il (Junior drug awareness) lib bdg $30

Grades: 6 7 8 9 **362.29**

1. Steroids

ISBN 978-0-7910-9748-9 lib bdg; 0-7910-9748-X lib bdg

LC 2008-14062

"The content is reliable and comprehensive." Horn Book Guide

This "explores the facts and science behind steroid use, as well as efforts to keep the problem under control, particularly among professional sports stars and young people." Publisher's note

Includes glossary and bibliographical references

362.292 Alcohol

Bjornlund, Lydia D.

Alcohol; [by] Lydia Bjornlund. Cherry Lake Pub. 2009 32p il (Health at risk) lib bdg $27.07

Grades: 4 5 6 7 **362.292**

1. Alcohol 2. Alcoholism

ISBN 978-1-60279-280-7 lib bdg; 1-60279-280-1 lib bdg

LC 2008017495

This describes the effects of alcohol, the dangers of driving drunk, how to get help, and how to make good choices. "Great for reports or reluctant readers." Booklist

Includes bibliographical references

Gottfried, Ted

Alcohol; by Ted Gottfried with Katherine Follett. Marshall Cavendish Benchmark 2010 32p il (Drug facts) $19.95

Grades: 4 5 6 7 **362.292**

1. Alcoholism 2. Drinking of alcoholic beverages 3. Alcohol -- Physiological effect

ISBN 978-0-7614-4348-3; 0-7614-4348-7

LC 2008-52751

"Provides clear explanations about effects, followed by diagrams of the body to clarify the specific organs/body systems that suffer the most damage. . . . An excellent starting point." SLJ

Includes glossary

★ The **facts** about alcohol; [by] Ted Gottfried. Benchmark Books 2004 111p il (Drugs) lib bdg $$2.79; pa $6.99

Grades: 6 7 8 9 **362.292**

1. Alcoholism 2. Drinking of alcoholic beverages 3. Teenagers -- Alcohol use

ISBN 978-0-7614-1805-4 lib bdg; 0-7614-1805-9 lib bdg; 978-0-7614-3587-7 pa; 0-7614-3587-5 pa

LC 2004-5388

The author "includes historical aspects of alcohol and society, including humans' first experimentations with fermentation, Prohibition, and the temperance movement; related laws and legislation; and definition, causes, treatment, and effects. . . . [This title has a] readable, well-organized [text], and good use of color, graphics, photographs, tables, diagrams, and labels helps to spark readers' interest." SLJ

Includes glossary and bibliographical references

Smith, Terri Peterson

Alcohol. Chelsea House Publishers 2008 110p il (Junior drug awareness) lib bdg $30

Grades: 6 7 8 9 **362.292**

1. Alcoholism

ISBN 978-0-7910-9764-9 lib bdg; 0-7910-9764-1 lib bdg

LC 2008014066

This "describes the uses and abuses of [alcohol]. . . . The reasons people [drink alcohol, its] dangers, signs of addiction, and treatment options are covered. . . . The content is reliable and comprehensive." Horn Book Guide

Includes glossary and bibliographical references

Youngerman, Barry

The **truth** about alcohol; Robert N. Golden, general editor; Fred L. Peterson, general editor; Barry Youngerman, principal author; Heath Dingwell, contributing author; Richelle Rennegarbe, adviser. 2nd ed.; Facts on File 2010 230p (Truth about series) $35

Grades: 8 9 10 11 12 **362.292**

1. Alcoholism 2. Teenagers -- Alcohol use

ISBN 978-0-8160-7639-0; 0-8160-7639-1

LC 2009-53476

First published 2004

This discusses such topics as binge drinking, underage drinking, the prevalence of drinking on college campuses, drunken driving, dealing with alcohol abuse in the family, alcohol advertising and counter-advertising, and seeking help for an alcohol problem.

Includes glossary and bibliographical references

362.4   People with physical disabilities

The **Center** for Cartoon Studies presents Annie Sullivan and the trials of Helen Keller; by Joseph Lambert ; with an introduction by TK. Disney Hyperion Books 2012 96 p.

Grades: 5 6 7   **362.4**
1. Women authors -- Biography 2. Female friendship -- Graphic novels 3. People with disabilities -- Graphic novels 4. Graphic novels 5. Women -- United States -- History 6. Women -- United States -- Biography 7. Female friendship -- United States -- History
ISBN 9781423113362

LC 2011036324

This nonfiction graphic novel about Annie Sullivan and Helen Keller "focuses on the trials both Annie and Helen struggle with in their lives," particularly the incident when Helen was accused of plagiarism in her story 'The Frost King' and interrogated at the Perkins Institution. "Helen's perspective is . . . communicated in dialogue-free black panels in which she is represented as only a gray silhouette" by author/illustrator Joseph Lambert. (Kirkus) Bibliography.

Martin, Claudia
Helpers. Marshall Cavendish Benchmark 2010 64p il (Working animals) lib bdg $28.50

Grades: 4 5 6 7   **362.4**
1. Animals and people with disabilities
ISBN 978-1-60870-163-6 lib bdg; 1-60870-163-8 lib bdg

"Attractively designed and packed with information. . . . The composition of each page is attractively set up with well-selected and reproduced stock and historical photos." SLJ

"Describes animals that help people who are blind or deaf, or who have physical handicaps." Publisher's note

Thornton, Denise
Physical disabilities; the ultimate teen guide. Scarecrow Press 2007 162p il (It happened to me) $42

Grades: 7 8 9 10 11 12   **362.4**
1. People with physical disabilities
ISBN 978-0-8108-5300-3; 0-8108-5300-0

LC 2006-29235

"Thornton interviewed hundreds of young people to help readers understand disabilities from a personal viewpoint. She divides this very broad subject into eight areas—school, technologies and tools, getting around, sports, the arts, relationships, independence, and advocacy. In each section, she includes personal stories plus essential information helpful to the disabled. . . . Well-organized and helpful." SLJ

Includes bibliographical references

362.5   Poor people

Fields, Julianna
Kids growing up without a home. Mason Crest 2009 64p il (The changing face of modern families) $22.95

Grades: 6 7 8 9   **362.5**
1. Homeless persons
ISBN 978-1-4222-1498-5; 1-4222-1498-2

This describes the challenges facing homeless families. This is "informative [and] nonjudgmental. . . . Including color photos, plentiful sidebars, and interesting headline stories, the accessible [text presents] real-life experiences and numerous supporting facts, definitions, graphs, charts, and statistics." SLJ

Lusted, Marcia Amidon
Poverty. ABDO Pub. Co. 2010 112p il map (Essential issues) lib bdg $22.95

Grades: 7 8 9 10   **362.5**
1. Poverty
ISBN 978-1-60453-957-8; 1-60453-957-7

LC 2009-30333

The text is "well-written, providing examples that put a human face to each problem. Quotes and facts are clearly attributed, and their sources are noted in the extensive back matter. . . . Sidebars provide further information, or, more compellingly, offer stories about those touched by the topic. . . . [This] will be of great assistance to students writing reports." SLJ

Includes glossary and bibliographical references

Senker, Cath
Poverty; [by] Cath Senker. World Almanac Library 2007 48p il (What if we do nothing?) lib bdg $30.60; pa $11.95

Grades: 5 6 7 8   **362.5**
1. Poor 2. Poverty
ISBN 978-0-8368-7757-1 lib bdg; 978-0-8368-8157-8 pa

LC 2006030447

"After discussing patterns of poverty, each chapter raises specific 'What would you do?' questions, with brief suggested answers at the back of the book. Whether the issue is increased taxation of the wealthy, cancellation of unpayable debts, improving primary health care, or more, student activists will want to talk about it, and social-studies teachers will find this a strong curriculum title." Booklist

Includes bibliographical references

Poverty and hunger; Cath Senker. Smart Apple Media 2012 46 p. col. ill., col. maps (Mapping global issues) (library) $35.65

Grades: 6 7 8   **362.5**
1. Hunger 2. Poverty 3. Poor 4. Food security
ISBN 1599205114; 9781599205113

LC 2011017066

This book is part of the Mapping Global Issues series and it focuses on poverty and hunger. "Colorful layouts with numerous maps and graphs dominate this series, which provides an international perspective on important issues. Brief chapters frame problems, discuss their causes, and suggest possible solutions, using maps to illustrate the locations and extent of threats." (School Library Journal)

Includes bibliographical references (p. 45) and index.

362.7 Young people

★ **Adoption**; David M. Haugen and Matthew J. Box, book editors. Greenhaven Press 2005 108p (Social issues firsthand) lib bdg $28.70

Grades: 8 9 10 11 12   362.7

1. Adoption
ISBN 0-7377-2881-7

LC 2005-46075

"The book explores such diverse issues as gay adoptive parents, open and transracial adoptions, the search for and reunion with birthparents, custody battles, and more. The editors have done an excellent job of selecting 16 lively, articulate, and poignant essays by birthparents, adoptive parents, and adoptees, all offering different perspectives on the process." SLJ

Includes bibliographical references

Ellis, Deborah

Our stories, our songs; African children talk about AIDS. Fitzhenry & Whiteside 2005 104p il $18.95

Grades: 6 7 8 9   362.7

1. Orphans 2. AIDS (Disease) 3. Malawi 4. Tanzania
ISBN 1-55041-913-7

"In the summer of 2003, Ellis traveled to Malawi and Zambia and met with children and teens whose lives have been touched by AIDS. In short, autobiographical vignettes, the young people, many of whom are orphans or living on the street, discuss their families, their favorite pastimes, their fears, and their dreams. . . . Ellis presents the stories in a matter-of-fact and compassionate manner that maintains the children's dignity. . . . An impressive offering whose chilling accounts remain with readers long after the book is finished." SLJ

Fields, Julianna

Foster families. Mason Crest 2009 64p il (The changing face of modern families) $22.95

Grades: 6 7 8 9   362.7

1. Foster home care
ISBN 978-1-4222-1497-8; 1-4222-1497-4

This describes the challenges facing foster families.

This is "informative [and] nonjudgmental. . . . Including color photos, plentiful sidebars, and interesting headline stories, the accessible [text presents] real-life experiences and numerous supporting facts, definitions, graphs, charts, and statistics." SLJ

Gordon, Sherri Mabry

Beyond bruises; the truth about teens and abuse. Enslow 2009 128p il (Issues in focus today) lib bdg $31.93

Grades: 7 8 9 10   362.7

1. Date rape 2. Invective 3. Child abuse 4. Domestic violence
ISBN 978-0-7660-3064-0; 0-7660-3064-4

LC 2008-12273

"Discusses the various types of abuse teenagers face, including both domestic and dating abuse, the impact abuse

has on teens, and several ways to help teens who suffer from some form of abuse." Publisher's note

Includes glossary and bibliographical references

Jocelyn, Marthe

A **home** for foundlings. Tundra Books 2005 128p il pa $15.95

Grades: 7 8 9 10   362.7

1. Abandoned children 2. Foundling Hospital (London, England)
ISBN 0-88776-709-5

"Black-and-white reproductions of early admission documents and ledgers as well as period photographs and engravings appear throughout. This is a useful resource." SLJ

McAlpine, Margaret

Working with children. Gareth Stevens Pub 2005 64p il (My future career) lib bdg $26

Grades: 6 7 8 9   362.7

1. Teaching 2. Child care 3. Child development 4. Vocational guidance
ISBN 0-8368-4241-3

LC 2004-45226

This describes seven occupations related to children, including a description of the job and the responsibilities, qualifications, and best personality type for each one.

"The writing is clear and interesting, and the [book is] visually well organized." SLJ

Includes bibliographical references

Medina, Sarah

Abuse and neglect; by Sarah Medina; health consultant, John G. Samanich. G. Stevens Pub. 2009 48p il (Emotional health issues) lib bdg $31

Grades: 6 7 8 9   362.7

1. Child abuse 2. Child sexual abuse
ISBN 978-0-8368-9198-0 lib bdg; 0-8368-9198-8 lib bdg

LC 2008-5458

First published 2008 in the United Kingdom

This book about abuse has "clear language and explanations. . . . [It is] suitable for fact-finding missions, but the abundant graphics and case studies are likely to draw in browsers as well. Throughout, unfamiliar vocabulary is highlighted in bold and explained in context and in the glossary. . . Fact boxes and case study sidebars add information." SLJ

Includes glossary and bibliographical references

Saul, Laya

Ways to help disadvantaged youth. Mitchell Lane Publishers 2011 47p (How to help: a guide to giving back) lib bdg $29.95

Grades: 4 5 6   362.7

1. Poor 2. Social action
ISBN 978-1-58415-918-6; 1-58415-918-9

LC 2010006536

This "well-organized [book] will encourage children to contribute to the world around them. [This] title is filled with examples of volunteer opportunities that can be accomplished with some adult involvement and supervision to guide, steer, and maintain focus so that youngsters will have varied and successful experiences. . . . [The book] suggests tutoring, having a toy or food drive, etc." SLJ

Includes bibliographical references

Simons, Rae

Adoptive parents. Mason Crest Publishers 2009 64p il map (The changing face of modern families) $22.95

Grades: 6 7 8 9   **362.7**
1. Adoption
ISBN 978-1-4222-1502-9; 1-4222-1502-4

LC 2009026372

This discusses some the questions facing adoptive parents such as 'What role do birth families play? Are they going to be a part of the child's life?' and 'What do you tell the child about his birth and adoption?'

"Colorful photographs and sidebars appear throughout. These books are good introductions to the study of sociology and interpretation of data." SLJ

Includes bibliographical references

Stewart, Sheila

A **house** between homes; kids in the foster care system. by Sheila Stewart and Camden Flath. Mason Crest Publishers 2010 48p il lib bdg $19.95; pa $7.95

Grades: 3 4 5 6   **362.7**
1. Foster home care
ISBN 978-1-4222-1692-7 lib bdg; 1-4222-1692-6 lib bdg; 978-1-4222-1905-8 pa; 1-4222-1905-4 pa

LC 2010012756

"The prose is respectable in its dialogue, character development, and pacing... This series will be well placed in a school media center, as well as in any institution that serves high-risk children." SLJ

Discusses the foster care system, including the reasons why children enter the system, what happens in foster care, the types of children, foster parents, and what happens next, and provides a story about siblings who are placed in foster care.

Warren, Andrea

Orphan train rider; one boy's true story. Houghton Mifflin 1996 80p il hardcover o.p. pa $7.95

Grades: 4 5 6 7   **362.7**
1. Orphans 2. Adoption 3. Abandoned children
ISBN 0-395-69822-7; 0-395-91362-4 pa

LC 94-43688

"Between 1854 and 1930, more than 200,000 orphaned and abandoned children from the cities of the eastern seaboard were 'placed out' to new homes and families in the midwest and western states. . . . {This is an} account of the 'orphan-train' phenomena, and of one man's story of how it affected his life. . . . The chapters alternate information about the largest agency, the Children's Aid Society, and its history, with the story of Lee Nailling, from whom the author has gathered the facts of his own childhood journey to Texas and his eventual reunion, late in life, with some of his long-lost siblings. {Bibliography. Index.} Grades four to eight." (SLJ)

"An excellent introduction to researching or discussing children-at-risk in an earlier generation. The book is clearly

written and illustrated with numerous black-and-white photographs and reproductions." SLJ

Includes bibliographical references

362.73   Institutional and related services

Warren, Andrea

We rode the orphan trains. Houghton Mifflin 2001 132p il $18; pa $8.95

Grades: 4 5 6 7   **362.73**
1. Orphans
ISBN 0-618-11712-1; 0-618-11712-1 pa

LC 00-47279

"This is powerful nonfiction for classroom and personal reading and for discussion." Booklist

The author "interviews eight orphan train riders concerning their childhood experiences during 'the largest children's migration in history' between 1854 and 1929 as part of a 'placing out' program run by the Children's Aid Society of New York City." Publ Wkly

Includes bibliographical references

362.82   Families

★ **Domestic** violence: opposing viewpoints; Mike Wilson, book editor. Greenhaven Press 2008 217p (Opposing viewpoints series) lib bdg $39.70; pa $27.50

Grades: 8 9 10 11 12   **362.82**
1. Domestic violence
ISBN 978-0-7377-4206-0 lib bdg; 0-7377-4206-2 lib bdg; 978-0-7377-4207-7 pa; 0-7377-4207-0 pa

LC 2008-28517

Articles in this anthology discuss domestic violence, including its causes and possible remedies.

Includes bibliographical references

Stewart, Sheila

When Daddy hit Mommy; by Sheila Stewart and Rae Simons. Mason Crest Publishers 2011 48p il lib bdg $19.95; pa $7.95

Grades: 3 4 5   **362.82**
1. Child abuse 2. Domestic violence
ISBN 978-1-4222-1696-5 lib bdg; 1-4222-1696-9 lib bdg; 978-1-4222-1909-6 pa; 1-4222-1909-7 pa

LC 2010029346

Discusses domestic violence, including its causes, its effects on the family, how to get help, life in a shelter, and help for the abuser, and provides a story about a girl whose father gets violent.

Zehr, Howard

What will happen to me? by Howard Zehr and Lorraine Stutzman Amstutz; portraits by Howard Zehr. Good Books 2010 94p il pa $14.95

Grades: 7 8 9 10   **362.82**
1. Children of prisoners
ISBN 978-1-56148-689-2

LC 2010-12419

This discusses issues facing "children of incarcerated parents. . . . In part one, the statements from the children interviewed are accompanied by full-color photo portraits. What comes through is that they all love their parents unequivocally, but here it is tangible and poignant both in their words and faces. . . . Part two offers advice for caregivers and includes 10 questions often asked by children whose parents are in jail." SLJ

Includes bibliographical references

362.87   Displaced persons

Nelson, Sheila

In defense of our country; survivors of military conflict. by Sheila Stewart with Joyce Zoldak. Mason Crest Publishers 2009 128p il map (Survivors: ordinary people, extraordinary circumstances) lib bdg $24.95

Grades: 7 8 9 10 **362.87**
1. War 2. Soldiers 3. Ethnic relations 4. Military history
ISBN 978-1-4222-0452-8 lib bdg; 1-4222-0452-9 lib bdg
LC 2008-50556

The title "looks at wars in Africa, Southeast Asia, Eastern Europe, and the Middle East, though plenty of inset boxes cover other topics such as trench warfare in World War I, the Red Cross, and the American Civil War. . . . [This book] will be valued for . . . [its] ability to generate empathy for survivors and their strengths and resilience in difficult situations." SLJ

Includes bibliographical references

362.88   Victims of crimes and war

Bickerstaff, Linda

Violence against women; public health and human rights. Rosen Pub. 2010 112p il (A young woman's guide to contemporary issues) lib bdg $31.95

Grades: 7 8 9 10 **362.88**
1. Violence 2. Abused women
ISBN 978-1-4358-3539-9; 1-4358-3539-5
LC 2009-12062

"Facts are shared in a conversational tone, creating the sense of a chat with a big sister. . . . [Though] designed for personal reading and browsing, the data provided are accurate and also lend themselves to use in reports." SLJ

Includes glossary and bibliographical references

Landau, Elaine

★ **Date** violence; [by] Elaine Landau. Franklin Watts 2004 80p (Life balance) $20.50; pa $6.95

Grades: 5 6 7 8 **362.88**
1. Violence 2. Date rape 3. Dating (Social customs)
ISBN 0-531-12214-X; 0-531-16613-9 pa
LC 2003-19480

"Landau helps those who are new to dating to distinguish between healthy and unhealthy relationships by providing

understandable warning signs of emotional, physical, and sexual abuse. . . . This book will help young people make informed decisions and more wisely navigate the emotionally charged, confusing issues associated with adolescent relationships." SLJ

Includes glossary and bibliographical references

Simons, Rae

Gender danger; survivors of rape, human trafficking, and honor killings. by Rae Simons with Joyce Zoldak. Mason Crest Publishers 2009 128p il (Survivors: ordinary people, extraordinary circumstances) lib bdg $24.95

Grades: 7 8 9 10 **362.88**
1. Rape 2. Violence 3. Sex crimes 4. Abused women 5. Women -- Social conditions
ISBN 978-1-4222-0451-1; 1-4222-0451-0
LC 2008-50322

The author discusses "the issues faced by women in this and other cultures. The book looks at rape as a weapon of war, honor killings, female circumcision, and the complex and often dangerous world of transgender individuals." SLJ

Includes bibliographical references

362.883   Rape

Wilkins, Jessica

Date rape. Crabtree Pub. 2011 48p il (Straight talk about . . .) $29.27; pa $9.95

Grades: 7 8 9 10 **362.883**
1. Date rape
ISBN 978-0-7787-2128-4; 0-7787-2128-0; 978-0-7787-2135-2 pa; 0-7787-2135-3 pa
LC 2010-16397

This book about date rape "also spends a good deal of its pages covering dating violence, both verbal and physical, which girls don't always understand to be problematic. . . . The information . . . is strong and far reaching." Booklist

363   Other social problems and services

Esherick, Joan

The **FDA** & Psychiatric Drugs; how a drug is approved. Joan Esherick. revised edition Mason Crest 2013 128 p. library binding $24.95

Grades: 7 8 9 10 **363**
1. Psychotropic drugs
ISBN 9781422228265

Describes how a psychiatric drug is approved for use by the FDA, as well as some historical background on the agency.

363.1 Public safety programs

Aronson, Marc

★ **Trapped**; how the world rescued 33 miners from 2,000 feet below the Chilean desert. Atheneum 2011 144p il

Grades: 4 5 6 7   **363.1**

1. Rescue work 2. Gold mines and mining 3. Copper mines and mining 4. Mine accidents -- Chile

ISBN 1-4169-1397-1; 978-1-4169-1397-9

LC 2011000777

This title is about thirty-three miners trapped in a copper-gold mine in San Jose, Chile and how experts from around the world, from drillers, to astronauts, to submarine specialists, came together to make their remarkable rescue possible.

This is "a riveting, in-depth recounting of the events that held the world rapt. . . . Twelve short chapters with photos and diagrams keep the story well-paced." Publ Wkly

Includes bibliographical references

Ballard, Carol

Food safety. Gareth Stevens Pub. 2010 48p il (What if we do nothing?) lib bdg $31

Grades: 7 8 9 10   **363.1**

1. Food poisoning 2. Food contamination

ISBN 978-1-4339-1982-4 lib bdg; 1-4339-1982-6 lib bdg

LC 2008-52284

This describes the precautions taken by food producers, retailers, and food safety organizations to guard against food-borne illnesses from such causes as pesticides, microbes, pollution, and chemical additives.

"Meaningful illustrations include color photos and text-enhancing charts. . . . [This is] well written and useful for reports." SLJ

Includes glossary and bibliographical references

Bennie, Paul

The **great** Chicago fire of 1871; [by] Paul Bennie. Chelsea House 2008 128p il (Great historic disasters) $35

Grades: 7 8 9 10   **363.1**

1. Fires -- Chicago (Ill.)

ISBN 978-0-7910-9638-3; 0-7910-9638-6

LC 2007-36550

"On October 8, 1871, a fire started in the O'Learys' barn in Chicago. . . . [This occurence] brought about lasting changes in fire prevention and building codes. . . . [This book], which [describes] the [disaster] and [its] aftermath in detail, [is] well written and informative. . . . [This is] first-rate for reports and general browsing." SLJ

Includes bibliographical references

Chernobyl; David Erik Nelson, book editor. Greenhaven Press 2010 220p il map (Perspectives on modern world history) $38.50

Grades: 8 9 10 11 12   **363.1**

1. Chernobyl Nuclear Accident, Chernobyl, Ukraine, 1986

ISBN 978-0-7377-4555-9; 0-7377-4555-X

LC 2009-27203

"This volume contains a wealth of relevant information representing many viewpoints of the current discussions surrounding the 1986 disaster at the Chernobyl nuclear power plant in Ukraine, which led to an official death toll of 56 people. Each article, skillfully drawn from multinational secondary sources, provides researchers with an admirable base for reports." SLJ

Includes glossary and bibliographical references

Lace, William W.

The **Hindenburg** disaster of 1937. Chelsea House Publishers 2008 120p il (Great historic disasters) lib bdg $35

Grades: 6 7 8 9 10   **363.1**

1. Aircraft accidents 2. Hindenburg (Airship)

ISBN 978-0-7910-9739-7; 0-7910-9739-0

LC 2008004890

On May 6, 1937, the celebrated airship Hindenburg caught fire during its landing in Lakehurst, New Jersey, killing 36 people. This describes the disaster and its aftermath.

The book covers its topic "thoroughly and [includes] high-quality photographs and occasional sidebars. Lace's account of the airship has a good deal of intrigue and drama and could be useful for reports or recreational reading." SLJ

Includes glossary and bibliographical references

Lusted, Marcia Amidon

The **Chernobyl** Disaster. ABDO Pub. 2011 112p il (Essential events) lib bdg $23.95

Grades: 7 8 9 10 11 12   **363.1**

1. Nuclear power plants 2. Chernobyl Nuclear Accident, Chernobyl, Ukraine, 1986

ISBN 978-1-6171-4763-0; 1-6171-4763-X

LC 2010045019

This describes "the technology and engineering detail of how a nuclear power plant generates electricity and why it is dangerous, as well as the politics of why the disaster happened. . . . The spacious . . . design is inviting, with many color illustrations and screens, and the extensive back matter includes a detailed time line, glossary, bibliography and source notes." Booklist

Includes glossary and bibliographical references

The **Three** Mile Island nuclear disaster; by Marcia Amidon Lusted. ABDO Pub. Company 2012 112 p. il (Essential events)

Grades: 6 7 8   **363.1**

1. Nuclear energy 2. Nuclear power plants 3. Nuclear power plants -- Accidents 4. Three Mile Island Nuclear Power Plant (Pa.)

ISBN 1617833118; 9781617833113

LC 2011036182

This children's educational book by Marcia Amidon Lusted "examines an important historic event — the Three Mile Island nuclear disaster near Middletown, Pennsylvania. . . . [It] explores the history of nuclear power in the United States, how a nuclear plant works, details of the emergency at Metropolitan Edison Company's nuclear power plant, handling of the disaster by the Nuclear Regulatory Commission, President Jimmy Carter's visit to Three Mile Island, the investigation into the disaster, and the effects of this event on society. Features include a table of contents, glossary, selected bibliography, Web links, source notes, and an index, plus a timeline and essential facts." (Publisher's note)

Includes glossary and bibliographical references.

Mara, Wil

The **Chernobyl** disaster; legacy and impact on the future of nuclear energy. Marshall Cavendish Benchmark 2010 112p il (Perspectives on) $39.93

Grades: 7 8 9 10   **363.1**

1. Chernobyl Nuclear Accident, Chernobyl, Ukraine, 1986

ISBN 978-0-7614-4984-3; 0-7614-4984-1

"Briefly outlines the nuclear disaster in an easy-to-read format. It examines the nuclear crisis from the moment it occurred to the fallout afterwards. The volume begins with a moment-by-moment account of the disaster itself. Color illustrations of the reactor provide a detailed explanation of the process behind its failure. . . . This is a recommended addition to any school or public library." Voice Youth Advocates

Parks, Peggy J., 1951-

Drunk driving. ReferencePoint Press 2009 96p il (Compact research. Current issues) lib bdg $25.95

Grades: 7 8 9 10   **363.1**

1. Drunk driving

ISBN 978-1-60152-072-2; 1-60152-072-7

LC 2008-48499

This "title has an overview of [drunk driving] as well as topic-specific chapters such as 'Who Drives Drunk?' and 'How Should Drunk Drivers Be Punished?' It offers differing ideas on questions that have more than one answer. The colorful graphs and charts contain current information." SLJ

Includes bibliographical references

Sherman, Jill

The **Hindenburg** disaster. ABDO Pub. Co. 2010 112p il (Essential events) lib bdg $34.22

Grades: 6 7 8 9   **363.1**

1. Airships 2. Aircraft accidents 3. Hindenburg (Airship)

ISBN 978-1-60453-944-8; 1-60453-944-5

LC 2009-30427

This book offers "vivid detail as well as historical and political context. . . . Recounting the [Hindenburg] crash, Sherman captures readers' attention with an opening chapter devoted to the actual crash. She then paints a full picture of the invention of the zeppelin and its uses and development. The author then works her way back to a full description of the crash and a discussion of the theories around its cause. [This title has] pertinent sidebars with primary source material. Archival photos add to the dramatic [narrative]." SLJ

Includes bibliographical references

363.11 Occupational and industrial hazards

Scott, Elaine

★ **Buried** alive! how 33 miners survived 69 days deep under the Chilean desert. Elaine Scott. Houghton Mifflin Harcourt 2012 80 p. col. ill., col. maps (hardcover) $17.99; (ebook) $17.99

Grades: 4 5 6 7 8   **363.11**

1. Miners 2. Disasters 3. Industrial accidents 4. San José Mine Accident, Chile, 2010 5. Mine rescue work -- Chile -- Copiapó Region 6. San José Mine Accident, Chile, 2010 7. Gold mines and mining -- Accidents -- Chile -- Copiapó Region 8. Copper mines and mining -- Accidents -- Chile -- Copiapó Region

ISBN 0547707789; 9780547707785; 9780547691787

LC 2011025945

Author Elaine Scott chronicles the events that took place "[o]n August 5, 2010, [when] a copper mine in Chile collapsed, trapping 33 miners nearly half a mile underground . . . [The author] describes the choices the miners' strong leader advised that prolonged their survival long enough to be rescued and the creative solutions that effected that rescue. They drilled through over 2,000 feet of especially hard rock, delivered supplies to the trapped men through a tiny bore hole and then invented a way to carry the men, one at a time, to the surface in a very small capsule." (Kirkus)

Includes bibliographical references (p. 78) and index.

363.17 Hazardous materials

Kops, Deborah

The **Great** Molasses Flood; Boston, 1919. Deborah Kops. Charlesbridge 2012 102 p.

Grades: 6 7 8 9   **363.17**

1. Molasses 2. Industrial accidents 3. Boston (Mass.) -- History 4. Floods -- Massachusetts -- Boston -- History -- 20th century 5. Industrial accidents -- Massachusetts -- Boston -- History -- 20th century 6. Alcohol industry -- Accidents -- Massachusetts -- Boston -- History -- 20th century 7. Molasses industry -- Accidents -- Massachusetts -- Boston -- History -- 20th century

ISBN 1580893481; 9781580893480; 9781580893497

LC 2011000655

This historical survey by Deborah Kops follows the events of "January 15, 1919 . . . an unseasonable warm day in Boston, Massachusetts, and a day that would go down in history. One minute it was business as usual on the waterfront and the next - KABOOM! A large tank holding molasses exploded, sending shards of metal hundreds of feet away, collapsing buildings, and coating the harborfront community with a thick layer of sticky-sweet sludge." (Publisher's note)

"The combination of the sepia-toned photographs, the use of brown to highlight the chapter headings, and the choice of cream-colored paper gives this book a rich, elegant quality while staying consistent with the subject matter." Booklist

363.2 Police services

Allman, Toney

★ The **medical** examiner. Gale 2006 104p il (Crime scene investigations) lib bdg $31.20

Grades: 7 8 9 10   **363.2**

1. Forensic sciences 2. Medical jurisprudence

ISBN 1-59018-912-4

Discusses what medical examiners do.

This "book has fascinating, factual information and quotes taken from interviews with professionals. . . . [This] well-organized [title has] clear subheadings, tables of statistics, and well-chosen color photos." SLJ

Arroyo, Sheri L.

How crime fighters use math; math curriculum consultant: Rhea A. Stewart. Chelsea Clubhouse 2010 32p il (Math in the real world) lib bdg $28

Grades: 4 5 6   **363.2**

1. Mathematics 2. Vocational guidance 3. Criminal investigation

ISBN 978-1-60413-602-9 lib bdg; 1-60413-602-2 lib bdg

LC 2009-23330

"The layout for [this] slim [title] is bright and colorful with a photograph and a 'You Do the Math' problem to solve and large, easy-to-read text on every spread. An answer key is included in the back matter, along with a page detailing the career choices and the educational requirements. [It] touches on crime-scene grids, the importance of shoe prints in tracking a criminal, cracking secret codes, and more. . . . [This title] would be useful to supplement lessons on mathematics. [It] will also appeal to students wanting to learn more about math as it relates to specific careers." SLJ

Includes glossary and bibliographical references

Ballard, Carol

At the crime scene! collecting clues and evidence. Enslow Publishers 2009 48p il (Solve that crime!) lib bdg $23.93

Grades: 5 6 7 8   **363.2**

1. Forensic sciences 2. Criminal investigation

ISBN 978-0-7660-3373-3 lib bdg; 0-7660-3373-2 lib bdg

LC 2008-33306

This "title boasts in-depth information, sidebars detailing events of true crime, and activities that will increase understanding. . . . Photographs are colorful, well-captioned, and related to the text." SLJ

Includes glossary and bibliographical references

Crime under the microscope! in the forensics lab. Enslow Publishers 2009 48p il (Solve that crime!) lib bdg $23.93

Grades: 5 6 7 8   **363.2**

1. Forensic sciences 2. Criminal investigation

ISBN 978-0-7660-3374-0 lib bdg; 0-7660-3374-0 lib bdg

LC 2008-33307

This describes how forensics solves crimes in the laboratory

This "title boasts in-depth information, sidebars detailing events of true crime, and activities that will increase understanding. . . . Photographs are colorful, well-captioned, and related to the text." SLJ

Includes glossary and bibliographical references

Crimebusting! identifying criminals and victims. Enslow Publishers 2010 48p il lib bdg $23.93

Grades: 5 6 7 8   **363.2**

1. Criminals -- Identification

ISBN 978-0-7660-3375-7 lib bdg; 0-7660-3375-9 lib bdg

LC 2008-34803

This "title boasts in-depth information, sidebars detailing events of true crime, and activities that will increase understanding. . . . Photographs are colorful, well-captioned, and related to the text." SLJ

Bell, Suzanne

Encyclopedia of forensic science; foreword by Barry A.J. Fisher; preface by Robert C. Shaler. rev ed; Facts on File 2008 402p il (Facts on File science library) $85

Grades: 8 9 10 11 12 Adult   **363.2**

1. Reference books 2. Forensic sciences -- Encyclopedias

ISBN 978-0-8160-6799-2; 0-8160-6799-6

LC 2008-5862

First published 2003

"In addition to explaining the science of forensics, Bell . . . reviews various disciplines related to forensic science, among them entomology, odontology, and psychology. Other entries cover professional organizations, government agencies, famous names in the field of forensics, evidence, and legal issues. . . . With its clear language and brief entries [this] volume will provide readers with a nuts-and-bolts understanding of the real world of forensic science." Booklist [review of 2003 edition]

Includes bibliographical references

Fakes and forgeries. Facts On File 2008 108p il (Essentials of forensic science) $35

Grades: 7 8 9 10 11 12   **363.2**

1. Fraud 2. Forgery

ISBN 978-0-8160-5514-2; 0-8160-5514-9

LC 2008-4502

This is a "fascinating introduction to how scientists identify fraudulent copies, from signatures to oil paintings. . . . Bell moves from examples of the crime that date back to ancient Mesopotamian civilizations all the way through to today's high-tech counterfeiting cases." Booklist

Includes glossary and bibliographical references

Denega, Danielle

Skulls and skeletons; true life stories of bone detectives. Franklin Watts 2007 64p il map (24/7: Science behind the scenes) lib bdg $26; pa $7.95

Grades: 6 7 8 9   **363.2**

1. Forensic sciences 2. Forensic anthropology

ISBN 978-0-531-12064-4 lib bdg; 0-531-12064-3 lib bdg; 978-0-531-17527-9 pa; 0-531-17527-8 pa

LC 2006-21229

Explains how forensic anthropologists figure out a victim's profile and examines three case studies in which forensic anthropologists help identify the victims.

Includes glossary and bibliographical references

Dolan, Edward F.

Careers in the U.S. Coast Guard. Marshall Cavendish Benchmark 2008 80p il (Military service) lib bdg $24.95

Grades: 6 7 8 9   **363.2**

1. Vocational guidance 2. United States -- Coast Guard

ISBN 978-0-7614-4207-3 lib bdg; 0-7614-4207-3 lib bdg

LC 2008039819

Discusses service in the U.S. Coast Guard, including training, educational benefits, and career opportunities.

"Young people interested in exploring a career in [the U. S. Coast Guard] will find solid information. . . . Colored photographs, acronyms, Web sites, and detailed index will add to the appeal." Booklist

Includes bibliographical references

Evans, Colin

★ **Crime** lab. Chelsea House 2011 134p il (Law enforcement agencies) lib bdg $35

Grades: 6 7 8 9   **363.2**

1. Forensic sciences 2. Criminal investigation

ISBN 978-1-60413-612-8; 1-60413-612-X

LC 2010043271

This describes the work of crime labs from the 19th century to the present, including the technology used such as ballistics, toxicology, atomic evidence, radio carbon dating, DNA, and fingerprints.

"The Law Enforcement Agencies series is as formidable as the various groups it introduces. Solidly and comprehensively researched. . . . An attractive design, plenty of photos, and solid back matter complete each package. Extremely useful for students and appealing for browsers." Booklist

Includes bibliographical references

Evidence. Chelsea House 2010 132p il (Criminal justice) lib bdg $35

Grades: 6 7 8 9   **363.2**

1. Forensic sciences 2. Criminal investigation

ISBN 978-1-60413-615-9 lib bdg; 1-60413-615-4 lib bdg

The author "describes with authority how varieties of direct and circumstantial evidence . . . are gathered and analyzed. . . . He explains how crime-scene reconstructions, autopsies, and careful observation—as well as traces of blood, skin, poison, carpet fiber, and other substances—played central roles in obtaining convictions. . . . This makes a compelling introduction to a perennially popular topic." Booklist

★ **Interpol**. Chelsea House Publishers 2011 112p il (Law enforcement agencies) lib bdg $35

Grades: 6 7 8 9   **363.2**

1. Law enforcement 2. Criminal investigation 3. International Criminal Police Organization

ISBN 978-1-60413-613-5; 1-60413-613-8

LC 2010048099

This is a history of Interpol from 1914 to the present, covering some of its international cases.

Includes bibliographical references

★ **New** York Police Department. Chelsea House Publishers 2011 120p il (Law enforcement agencies) lib bdg $35

Grades: 6 7 8 9   **363.2**

1. Law enforcement 2. Police -- New York (N.Y.) 3. New York (N.Y.) -- Police Dept.

ISBN 978-1-60413-614-2; 1-60413-614-6

LC 2010049866

This is a history of the New York City Police Department from 1800 to the present, covering such topics as The Mafia, fingerprints, The Son of Sam, police corruption, John Gotti, and the attacks of September 11, 2001.

Includes bibliographical references

Gardner, Robert

Forensic science projects with a crime lab you can build; [by] Robert Gardner. Enslow Publishers 2007 128p il (Build-a-lab! science experiments) $23.95

Grades: 6 7 8 9   **363.2**

1. Science projects 2. Forensic sciences 3. Criminal investigation

ISBN 978-0-7660-2806-7; 0-7660-2806-2

LC 2006039026

Describes how to build a crime lab out of everyday materials so that things like fingerprints and handwriting can be analyzed.

"Gardner creatively handles the challenging task of assembling activities that connect strongly with his often grisly theme. . . . While the forensics information will draw students' interest, the potential dangers may lead some recommenders to set this aside for use in classrooms, where adult supervision can be ensured." Booklist

Includes bibliographical references

Graham, Ian

Forensic technology. Smart Apple Media 2011 il (New technology) lib bdg $34.25

Grades: 4 5 6 7   **363.2**

1. Forensic sciences 2. Criminal investigation

ISBN 978-1-599-20532-8; 1-599-20532-7

LC 2010044238

Describes the technology used by forensic scientists to gather and analyze evidence from crime scenes.

This "offers a fine overview for reports, and its attractive design may also entice middle-grade readers to learn more." Booklist

Gray, Leon

Virtual crime! solving cybercrime. Enslow Publishers 2009 48p il (Solve that crime!) lib bdg $23.93

Grades: 5 6 7 8   **363.2**

1. Computer crimes

ISBN 978-0-7660-3376-4 lib bdg; 0-7660-3376-7 lib bdg

LC 2008-33308

This "title boasts in-depth information, sidebars detailing events of true crime, and activities that will increase understanding. . . . Photographs are colorful, well-captioned, and related to the text." SLJ

Includes glossary and bibliographical references

Harris, Elizabeth Snoke

★ **Crime** scene science fair projects. Lark Books 2006 112p il $25.95

Grades: 6 7 8 9 10   **363.2**

1. Science projects 2. Forensic sciences 3. Criminal investigation

ISBN 1-57990-765-2

LC 2006-16803

"Harris begins with an explanation of forensic science and how it's applied in the everyday world, followed by a discussion of how to plan for a successful project. The projects involve lie detection, lifting fingerprints, recovering data from burned documents, and so on. . . . The author's concise, lively style will even engage students who aren't fond of reading nonfiction." SLJ

Harris, Nathaniel

Crime fighting; the impact of science and technology. Gareth Stevens Pub. 2010 64p il (Pros and cons) lib bdg $35

Grades: 5 6 7 8   **363.2**

1. Criminal investigation

ISBN 978-1-4339-1985-5 lib bdg; 1-4339-1985-0 lib bdg

LC 2009-12433

An "active layout that features color photographs, maps, graphs or charts on every spread, this . . . [book] has much to offer. . . . It conveniently outlines the range of views . . . helping students to learn how to view both sides of [the] issue[s]." SLJ

Includes glossary and bibliographical references

Innes, Brian

DNA and body evidence. Sharpe Focus 2008 96p il (Forensic evidence) $39.95

Grades: 7 8 9 10 11 12   **363.2**

1. Forensic sciences 2. DNA fingerprinting 3. Criminal investigation

ISBN 978-0-7656-8115-7

LC 2007-6749

This "book begins with the history of DNA and fluid analysis, continues with DNA fingerprinting and gathering evidence, and highlights landmark usage of DNA evidence as well as its routine uses in both the judicial and penal systems. . . . The [book is] comprehensive enough for students with prior knowledge of forensics but approachable for beginners. . . . [It weaves] technical terms and anecdotal evidence into a seamless presentation." SLJ

Includes glossary and bibliographical references

Fingerprints and impressions. Sharpe Focus 2008 96p il (Forensic evidence) $39.95

Grades: 7 8 9 10 11 12   **363.2**

1. Fingerprints 2. Forensic sciences 3. Criminal investigation

ISBN 978-0-7656-8114-0

LC 2007-6751

This "covers the origins of fingerprinting and the analysis and usage of fingerprinting data and concludes with its use as admissible evidence in court. . . . [The book is] comprehensive enough for students with prior knowledge of forensics but approachable for beginners. . . . [It weaves] technical terms and anecdotal evidence into a seamless presentation." SLJ

Includes glossary and bibliographical references

Kops, Deborah

★ **Racial** profiling. Marshall Cavendish Benchmark 2006 127p il (Open for debate) lib bdg $39.93

Grades: 7 8 9 10   **363.2**

1. Law enforcement 2. Racial profiling in law enforcement 3. Racial profiling 4. War on terrorism 5. Japanese Americans -- Evacuation and relocation, 1942-1945

ISBN 978-0-7614-2298-3; 0-7614-2298-6

This is "well organized and . . . clearly and plainly written." SLJ

Includes bibliographical references

Lane, Brian

Crime and detection; written by Brian Lane. Dorling Kindersley 2005 61p il (DK eyewitness books) $15.99

Grades: 4 5 6 7   **363.2**

1. Crime 2. Forensic sciences 3. Criminal investigation

ISBN 0-7566-1386-8

First published 1998 by Knopf

Explores the many different methods used to solve crimes, covering such topics as criminal, detectives, and forensics

Mezzanotte, Jim

Police. Marshall Cavendish Benchmark 2010 64p il (Working animals) lib bdg $28.50

Grades: 4 5 6 7   **363.2**

1. Animals in police work

ISBN 978-1-60870-166-7 lib bdg; 1-60870-166-2 lib bdg

LC 2010007006

Describes animals, such as dogs and horses, which work with police in such areas as search-and-rescue, tracking criminals, and sniffing out explosives

"Attractively designed and packed with information. . . . The composition of each page is attractively set up with well-selected and reproduced stock and historical photos." SLJ

Newton, Michael

★ **Bomb** squad. Chelsea House Publishers 2010 127p il (Law enforcement agencies) lib bdg $35

Grades: 6 7 8 9   **363.2**

1. Bombs 2. Police

ISBN 978-1-60413-624-1; 1-60413-624-3

LC 2010022102

"Solidly and comprehensively researched. . . . Bomb Squad shows that explosives have always been a means of striking terror throughout history. The volume covers the making and defusing of bombs, nuclear devices, and headline-making acts of terror. . . . An attractive design, plenty of photos, and solid back matter complete [the] package. Extremely useful for students and appealing for browsers." Booklist

Includes bibliographical references

★ **Drug** Enforcement Administration. Chelsea House Publishers 2011 128p il (Law enforcement agencies) lib bdg $35

Grades: 6 7 8 9   363.2
1. Drug traffic 2. Drugs -- Law and legislation 3. United States -- Drug Enforcement Administration
ISBN 978-1-60413-641-8; 1-60413-641-3
LC 2010036940

This describes the work of the Drug Enforcement Administration, including some of its cases concerning marijuana, cocaine, heroin, and methamphetamine.

"The Law Enforcement Agencies series is as formidable as the various groups it introduces. Solidly and comprehensively researched. . . . An attractive design, plenty of photos, and solid back matter complete each package. Extremely useful for students and appealing for browsers." Booklist

Includes bibliographical references

★ **SWAT** teams. Chelsea House Publishers 2010 127p il (Law enforcement agencies) lib bdg $35

Grades: 6 7 8 9   363.2
1. Police 2. Law enforcement
ISBN 978-1-60413-625-8; 1-60413-625-1
LC 2010026511

This describes the work of SWAT (Special Weapons and Tactics) teams in law enforcement, including missions ranging from hostage rescue and apprehension of violent felons to drug raids and natural-disaster relief. The book traces the history of special police teams worldwide, examining their techniques, tools, successes, and failures.

Includes bibliographical references

★ **U.S.** marshals. Chelsea House Publishers 2011 128p il (Law enforcement agencies) lib bdg $35

Grades: 6 7 8 9   363.2
1. Law enforcement 2. United States -- Marshals Service
ISBN 978-1-60413-627-2; 1-60413-627-8
LC 2010038195

This describes the U. S. Marshals Service, its history, and its work in fighting counterfeiting, in court security, the Witness Security Program, and fugitive investigations.

"The Law Enforcement Agencies series is as formidable as the various groups it introduces. Solidly and comprehensively researched. . . . An attractive design, plenty of photos, and solid back matter complete each package. Extremely useful for students and appealing for browsers." Booklist

Includes bibliographical references

Orr, Tamra
Racial profiling. ABDO Pub. Co. 2010 112p il (Essential viewpoints) lib bdg $32.79

Grades: 7 8 9 10   363.2
1. Racial profiling in law enforcement 2. Racial profiling
ISBN 978-1-60453-535-8; 1-60453-535-0
LC 2008-34915

"This timely book covers racial profiling as practiced in the United States since the terrorist attacks of 9/11, when it has come to center on young men of Middle Eastern extraction. . . . Orr presents arguments for and against the practice in focused, clearly written essays that will help students become informed. . . . There are plenty of color photographs. This book will enhance most collections." SLJ

Includes bibliographical references

Perritano, John
Science beats crime. Marshall Cavendish Benchmark 2010 48p il (Cool science) lib bdg $28.50

Grades: 5 6 7 8   363.2
1. Forensic sciences 2. Criminal investigation
ISBN 978-1-60870-078-3 lib bdg; 1-60870-078-X lib bdg
LC 2009053774

"Perritano briefly traces the history of forensic science, . . . discusses different subspecialities, such as toxicology and forensic anthropology, and then gets into the good stuff—fingerprinting, DNA profiling, ballistics, splatter patterns, even a gross-out spread of how studying maggots can determine time of death. Interspersed throughout are real-life case studies. . . . This solid, amply illustrated, and easy-reading introduction to forensic science ends with a look at the future of the field." Booklist

Includes glossary and bibliographical references

Rainis, Kenneth G.
★ **Blood** & DNA evidence; crime-solving science experiments. science consultant, Brian Gestring. Enslow Publishers 2006 104p il (Forensic science projects) lib bdg $31.93

Grades: 7 8 9 10   363.2
1. Forensic sciences 2. DNA fingerprinting
ISBN 0-7660-1958-6
LC 2005029214

This "invites readers to complete scientific experiments that emulate the solution to actual murders. . . . Following each real-life scenario, the book provides a checklist of materials and a step-by-step experiment to get the same results as the detectives. . . . The format is easy to follow, the scenarios intriguing, and the experiments complex enough for real science buffs to feel challenged." Booklist

Includes glossary and bibliographical references

Ricciuti, Edward R.
★ **Federal** Bureau of Investigation. Chelsea House Publishers 2010 144p il (Law enforcement agencies) lib bdg $35

Grades: 6 7 8 9   363.2
1. Criminal investigation 2. United States -- Federal Bureau of Investigation
ISBN 978-1-60413-636-4; 1-60413-636-7

"Solidly and comprehensively researched. . . . Federal Bureau of Investigation is a broad and deep look at the agency from its inception. Many of its most famous cases, including the Rosenbergs' arrest, terror cases, and the fight against organized crime, are discussed. Common criticisms, such as the overreach of the agency (J. Edgar Hoover in particular) are included. . . . An attractive design, plenty of photos, and solid back matter complete [the] package. Extremely useful for students and appealing for browsers." Booklist

Includes bibliographical references

Ryan, Bernard

★ The **Secret** Service. Chelsea House Publishers 2010 128p il (Law enforcement agencies) lib bdg $35

Grades: 6 7 8 9   **363.2**

1. United States -- Secret Service
ISBN 978-1-60413-623-4; 1-60413-623-5

This describes the work of The Secret Service including protecting the president, other key government figures, and visiting foreign leaders, investigating financial fraud and protecting crowds, buildings, and locations from potential threats.

"The Law Enforcement Agencies series is as formidable as the various groups it introduces. Solidly and comprehensively researched. . . . An attractive design, plenty of photos, and solid back matter complete each package. Extremely useful for students and appealing for browsers." Booklist

Includes bibliographical references

Schindler, Howard

Science sleuths; solving mysteries using scientific inquiry. [by] Howard Schindler and Dennis Mucenski. Prufrock Press Inc. 2010 vii, 195p il pa $19.95

Grades: Adult Professional   **363.2**

1. Forensic sciences 2. Science -- Methodology
ISBN 978-1-59363-397-4 pa; 1-59363-397-1 pa
LC 2009042622

"This professional resource uses [the] field [of forensics] to develop skills in scientific inquiry. The book features three activities in which students, working in groups or individually, analyze the evidence presented to them to solve a case. The activities are keyed to national standards for scientific inquiry. The tasks for 3-4 days of activities, culminating in a final essay, assist the teacher in planning the solution. . . . This is a most valuable resource for the science teacher of grades 6-9." Voice Youth Advocates

Includes bibliographical references

Spilsbury, Richard

Counterfeit! stopping fakes and forgeries. Enslow Publishers 2009 48p il (Solve that crime!) lib bdg $23.93

Grades: 5 6 7 8   **363.2**

1. Fraud 2. Forgery
ISBN 978-0-7660-3378-8 lib bdg; 0-7660-3378-3 lib bdg
LC 2008-33310

This "title boasts in-depth information, sidebars detailing events of true crime, and activities that will increase understanding. . . . Photographs are colorful, well-captioned, and related to the text." SLJ

Includes glossary and bibliographical references

Stefoff, Rebecca

Crime labs. Marshall Cavendish Benchmark 2010 95p il (Forensic science investigated) $23.95

Grades: 6 7 8 9 10   **363.2**

1. Forensic sciences 2. Graphologists 3. Criminologists
ISBN 978-0-7614-4140-3; 0-7614-4140-9
LC 2010-10536

The "titles in the Forensic Science Investigated series stand out not only for their thorough overviews of how forensic science is practiced today but also for their fascinating historical perspectives. . . . Crime labs introduces nineteenth-century Frenchman Edmond Locard, creator of the world's first forensic lab." Booklist

Includes bibliographical references

Criminal profiling. Marshall Cavendish Benchmark 2010 93p il (Forensic science investigated) $23.95

Grades: 6 7 8 9   **363.2**

1. Physicians 2. Criminal investigation 3. Criminologists 4. Writers on medicine
ISBN 978-0-7614-4141-0; 0-7614-4141-7
LC 2010010535

The "titles in the Forensic Science Investigated series stand out not only for their thorough overviews of how forensic science is practiced today but also for their fascinating historical perspectives. . . . Criminal Profiling spotlights early criminologists, such as Cesare Lombroso, who believed that criminal instincts manifested in physical features." Booklist

Includes bibliographical references

Forensic anthropology. Marshall Cavendish Benchmark 2010 95p il (Forensic science investigated) $19.95

Grades: 6 7 8 9   **363.2**

1. Forensic anthropology 2. Criminal investigation
ISBN 978-0-7614-4142-7; 0-7614-4142-5
LC 2010010534

The "titles in the Forensic Science Investigated series stand out not only for their thorough overviews of how forensic science is practiced today but also for their fascinating historical perspectives. . . . Forensic Anthropology starts off with a riveting account of scientists who cracked an 1849 Harvard murder case by finding clues among the victim's remains." Booklist

Includes bibliographical references

Stewart, Gail

Bombings; by Gail B. Stewart. Thomson/Gale 2006 104p il (Crime scene investigations series) $28.70

Grades: 7 8 9 10   **363.2**

1. Bombings 2. Criminal investigation
ISBN 1-59018-620-6
LC 2005026125

An examination of criminal investigations of bombings. This scrutinizes "current, highly publicized criminal cases that young readers will recognize. . . . Case studies are accompanied by actual, clearly labeled, color case photos showing just enough to fascinate the reader without unneeded gore." Voice Youth Advocates

Includes bibliographical references

K -9 police units; by Gail B. Stewart. Lucent Books 2010 104p il (Crime scene investigations) lib bdg $32.45

Grades: 7 8 9 10 **363.2**

1. Working dogs 2. Animals in police work
ISBN 978-1-4205-0137-7 lib bdg; 1-4205-0137-2 lib bdg

LC 2009-27456

This describes "the rigorous selection and training process of both dog and handler. Also discussed are the many different types of applications for these brave animals, as well as the bond of mutual trust that is required between the police officer and his canine companion while working in true life-and-death situations. . . . [This] should not only be a popular addition to any collection but will also go a long way in setting the record straight regarding who does what within a criminal investigation." Voice Youth Advocates

Includes bibliographical references

Townsend, John

Famous forensic cases. Amicus 2011 il (Amazing crime scene science) $19.95

Grades: 4 5 6 7 **363.2**

1. Forensic sciences 2. Criminal investigation
ISBN 978-1-60753-169-2; 1-60753-169-0

In this book "readers will find a straight presentation of fascinating information. Loosely organized by era, the book opens with a history of fingerprinting . . . which focuses on the 1920s and 1930s. Other topics include hair science in the 1950s, voiceprints in the 1970s, and recent advancements in DNA forensics. Scatter throughout are case studies. . . . This entry features an eye-catching layout, plenty of sidebars, and well-chosen photos. . . . Kids will go for this one." Booklist

Walker, Pamela

Forensic science experiments; [by] Pamela Walker, Elaine Wood. Facts on File 2009 150p il (Facts on File science experiments) $35

Grades: 7 8 9 10 **363.2**

1. Forensic sciences 2. Science -- Experiments
ISBN 978-0-8160-7804-2; 0-8160-7804-1

LC 2008-39900

This "contains 20 experiments that allow students to actively engage in scientific inquiry. Projects are presented in a uniform format, with an introduction to the topic, time requirements (35 minutes to 2 weeks), a materials list, numbered procedures, and several analysis questions. . . . The experiments themselves are timely and fascinating. . . . In [this book], a banana autopsy, blood-spatter inquiry, and 'Glitter as Trace Evidence' will hook CSI fans. Despite detailed instructions, close teacher supervision is a must." SLJ

Includes glossary and bibliographical references

Webber, Diane

Do you read me? famous cases solved by handwriting analysis! [by] Diane Webber. Franklin Watts 2007 64p il map (24/7, science behind the scenes) lib bdg $27; pa $7.95

Grades: 5 6 7 8 **363.2**

1. Graphology 2. Forensic sciences
ISBN 978-0-531-12066-8 lib bdg; 0-531-12066-X lib bdg; 978-0-531-15456-4 pa; 0-531-15456-4 pa

LC 2006006797

"Cases such as the infamous Lindbergh kidnapping and the discovery of Hitler's lost diaries are used to explore how handwriting can be used to solve a mystery. Subsequent sections tackle questions such as the validity of handwriting analysis as well as explore some of the nuances of the science." Voice Youth Advocates

Includes glossary and bibliographical references

Weir, William

★ **Border** patrol. Chelsea House 2010 125p il (Law enforcement agencies) lib bdg $35

Grades: 6 7 8 9 **363.2**

1. Smuggling 2. Illegal aliens 3. United States -- Border Patrol 4. United States -- Immigration and emigration
ISBN 978-1-60413-635-7; 1-60413-635-9

LC 2010030051

"Solidly and comprehensively researched. . . . Border Patrol takes on a topic much in the news. The hottest issues of border control are all examined: drugs, bandits, and smuggling of goods and people. There is also great information on the technology used, as well as a levelheaded discussion on the terror threat presented by illegal immigrants. . . . An attractive design, plenty of photos, and solid back matter complete [the] package. Extremely useful for students and appealing for browsers." Booklist

Includes glossary and bibliographical references

Worth, Richard

★ **Los** Angeles Police Department. Chelsea House Publishers 2011 128p il (Law enforcement agencies) lib bdg $35

Grades: 6 7 8 9 **363.2**

1. Law enforcement 2. Police -- Los Angeles (Calif.) 3. Los Angeles (Calif.) -- Police Dept.
ISBN 978-1-60413-656-2; 1-60413-656-1

LC 2010040906

This is a history of the Los Angeles Police Department from the early days of California to the present, including such cases as The Sleepy Lagoon Murder and the Zoot Suit Riots, The Black Dahlia murder, the Watts riots, and the Charles Manson case.

"The Law Enforcement Agencies series is as formidable as the various groups it introduces. Solidly and comprehensively researched. . . . An attractive design, plenty of photos, and solid back matter complete each package. Extremely useful for students and appealing for browsers." Booklist

Includes bibliographical references

Young, Karen Romano

Crime scene science; 20 projects and experiments about clues, crimes, criminals, and other mysterious things. illustrations by David Goldin. National Geographic 2009 80p il (Science fair winners) $12.95; lib bdg $24.90

Grades: 6 7 8 9 **363.2**

1. Science projects 2. Forensic sciences 3. Criminal

investigation

ISBN 978-1-4263-0521-4; 1-4263-0521-4; 978-1-4263-0522-1 lib bdg; 1-4263-0522-2 lib bdg

LC 2009-20387

This is a "collection of 20 science fair show-stoppers. . . . Significantly deeper than most science-fair tutorials. . . . High-interest topics abound: footprint casting, crime scene mapping, lie detection, and even compelling tricks like decoding those weird little bars the postal service stamps onto letters." Booklist

Includes bibliographical references

363.25 Detection of crime (Criminal investigation)

MacLeod, Elizabeth

Bones Never Lie; How Forensics Helps Solve History's Mysteries. Elizabeth MacLeod. Firefly Books Ltd 2013 iv, 156 p.p (hardcover) $24.95

Grades: 4 5 6 7 8   **363.25**

1. Forensic sciences -- Encyclopedias

ISBN 1554514835; 9781554514830

This children's book, by Elizabeth MacLeod, explores how through "forensics--the scientific way of examining physical evidence--we now know what killed Napoleon and whether Anastasia survived the massacre of the Russian royal family. Seven intriguing stories about historical royal figures whose demise was suspicious, and hard scientific facts about crime-solving techniques make each event seem like an episode of CSI rather than a history lesson." (Publisher's note)

"In real life, forensics can be slow and tedious, but MacLeod invests these high-profile deaths with considerable vim and drama. A good selection of staged and archival photographs and artwork accompany the stories. A fully fleshed and crisply told story of forensics at its romantic best." Kirkus

363.3 Other aspects of public safety

Cunningham, Kevin

Wildfires. Morgan Reynolds Pub. 2009 112p il (Extreme threats) lib bdg $28.95

Grades: 7 8 9 10   **363.3**

1. Wildfires

ISBN 978-1-59935-120-9; 1-59935-120-X

LC 2009-25709

This book about wildfires has "black-and-white and color photographs on almost every page. . . . Frequent sidebars, covering as much as a spread, discuss peripheral and often unusual information. The conclusion . . . explains what scientists are doing, or what they anticipate doing, to ameliorate the threat." SLJ

Includes glossary and bibliographical references

363.31 Censorship

Gottfried, Ted

★ **Censorship**. Benchmark Books 2005 143p il (Open for debate) $37.07

Grades: 7 8 9 10   **363.31**

1. Censorship

ISBN 0-7614-1883-0

This discusses censorship issues in regard to such topics as pornography, the internet, motion pictures, politics, and literature.

Includes bibliographical references

363.32 Social conflict

Bedell, J. M.

Combating terrorism. Compass Point Books 2010 48p il (Terrorism) lib bdg $27.99

Grades: 6 7 8 9   **363.32**

1. Terrorism

ISBN 978-0-7565-4309-9 lib bdg; 0-7565-4309-6 lib bdg

LC 2009-38908

"The style stays consistently clear and strightforward throughout , and the tone remains objective. A well-designed layout, with plenty of white space and well-placed sidebars, adds to the acessibility. . . . A great choice." SLJ

Includes glossary and bibliographical references

Burgan, Michael

Terrorist groups. Compass Point Books 2010 48p il (Terrorism) lib bdg $27.99

Grades: 6 7 8 9   **363.32**

1. Terrorism 2. Terrorists

ISBN 978-0-7565-4311-2 lib bdg; 0-7565-4311-8 lib bdg

Discusses terrorist groups such as al-Qaida, the Colombian FARC, and the Palestinian PFLP.

"The style stays consisently clear and straightforward throughout, and the tone remains objective. A well-designed layout, with plenty of white space and well-placed sidebars, adds to the acessibility. . . . A great choice." SLJ

Includes glossary and bibliographical references

Can the War on Terrorism be won? David Haugen and Susan Musser, book editors. Greenhaven Press 2007 109p (At issue: National security) $29.95; pa $21.20

Grades: 6 7 8 9   **363.32**

1. Terrorism 2. War on terrorism

ISBN 978-0-7377-1973-4; 978-0-7377-1974-1 pa

LC 2006039099

This "gathers 13 excerpted articles and speeches. . . . Readers encounter a spectrum of opinions about the War on Terror. . . . Each extract is headed with a straightforward title . . . and prefaced with a helpful abstract. Capped by an extensive reading list and annotated list of organizations, this is a strong option for assignment or debate-team research." Booklist

Includes bibliographical references

Fremont-Barnes, Gregory

Rescue at the Iranian Embassy; the most daring SAS raid. Rosen Pub. 2011 64p il map (The most daring raids in history) lib bdg $29.25

Grades: 7 8 9 10   **363.32**

1. Iran -- History -- 1979- 2. Great Britain -- Army -- Special Air Service Regiment

ISBN 978-1-4488-1869-3; 1-4488-1869-9

LC 2010029625

First published 2009 in the United Kingdom with title: Who dares wins

On May 5, 1980, the world watched as the SAS performed a daring raid on the Iranian Embassy in London. The raid was a huge success for the SAS, rescuing nineteen hostages with near-perfect military execution, although two were killed by the terrorists.

This book is "packed with facts, covering the details of the action, the people involved, and the tools used, in engaging prose. The authors cite their sources thoroughly. . . . Diagrams, photos, . . . and maps make the action easy to follow and provide visual context for the raids. . . . This . . . is sure to find a large readership." SLJ

Includes glossary and bibliographical references

Friedman, Lauri S.

Terrorist attacks. ReferencePoint Press 2008 128p il map (Compact research. Current issues) lib bdg $24.95

Grades: 7 8 9 10 11 12   **363.32**

1. Terrorism

ISBN 978-1-60152-022-7; 1-60152-022-0

LC 2007-9907

This "introduces theories as to why people carry out terrorist attacks, how they are executed, and how the attacks might be prevented. . . . [The] volume includes people and groups associated with the issue, a chronology of events, related organizations, and suggestions for further research. Chapters open and end with an array of quotes that argue for or against a particular argument or aspect of the issue, complete with full citation." SLJ

Includes glossary and bibliographical references

Gupta, Dipak K.

★ **Who** are the terrorists? Chelsea House 2006 116p il map (The roots of terrorism) lib bdg $35

Grades: 7 8 9 10   **363.32**

1. Islam 2. Terrorism

ISBN 0-7910-8306-3

LC 2005021627

This "volume discusses the world history as well as the groups and individuals behind today's headlines. . . . Gupta emphasizes that equating Islam with the barbaric acts of a few terrorists is like making the burning crosses of the Ku Klux Klan the essence of Christianity. He also points out the role of the American invasion of Iraq and the images from Abu Ghraib. . . . This is sure to spark vehement group discussion." Booklist

Includes bibliographical references

Nardo, Don

The **history** of terrorism. Compass Point Books 2010 48p il (Terrorism) lib bdg $27.99

Grades: 6 7 8 9   **363.32**

1. Terrorism

ISBN 978-0-7565-4310-5 lib bdg; 0-7565-4310-X lib bdg

Discusses the use of terrorism throughout history, and examines the individuals and groups who have resorted to violent actions in order to generate fear

"The style stays consistently clear and straightforward throughout, and the tone remains objective. A well-designed layout, with plenty of white space and well-placed sidebars, adds to the accessibility. . . . A great choice." SLJ

Includes glossary and bibliographical references

Terrorism; an opposing viewpoints guide. Stephen Currie, book editor. Greenhaven Press 2006 111 p. ill. (chiefly col.) (Opposing viewpoints series) (library) $33.75

Grades: 8 9 10 11 12   **363.32**

1. Terrorism 2. Authorship

ISBN 9780737732061; 0737732067

LC 2005049314

This title "makes use of the . . . . Opposing Viewpoints format (with selections that argue crucial issues from many sides), adding exercises, suggestions, and models for students' writing. More than half the book is published articles from alternative viewpoints, and the vital contemporary questions (Are terrorist attacks inevitable? Is the threat of terrorism exaggerated? etc.) will spark debate and discussion." Booklist

Includes bibliographical references (p. 104-106) and index.

Tougas, Shelley

What makes a terrorist? Compass Point Books 2010 48p il (Terrorism) lib bdg $27.99

Grades: 6 7 8 9   **363.32**

1. Terrorism 2. Terrorists

ISBN 978-0-7565-4312-9 lib bdg; 0-7565-4312-6 lib bdg

Discusses terrorism and the traits of terrorists.

"The style stays consistently clear and straightforward throughout, and the tone remains objective. A well-designed layout, with plenty of white space and well-placed sidebars, adds to the accessibility. . . . A great choice." SLJ

Includes glossary and bibliographical references

363.33   Control of firearms

Atkin, S. Beth

★ **Gunstories**; life-changing experiences with guns. interviews and photographs by S. Beth Atkin. HarperCollins Publishers 2006 245p il $16.99; lib bdg $17.89

Grades: 7 8 9 10 11 12   **363.33**

1. Guns 2. Firearms

ISBN 0-06-052659-9; 0-06-052660-2 lib bdg

LC 2005-2076

"This book should be useful for students involved in the debate about guns in our culture as well as for those with a general interest in the subject." SLJ

Nakaya, Andrea C.

Thinking critically; Gun Control & Violence. by Andrea C. Nakaya. ReferencePoint Press, Inc. 2014 80 p. illustrations (Thinking critically) (hardback) $28.95

Grades: 7 8 9 10 11 12   **363.33**
1. Violence 2. Gun control 3. Gun control -- United States 4. Violent crimes -- United States
ISBN 1601526067; 9781601526069
LC 2013012392

This book about gun control and violence, written by Andrea C. Nakaya, is part of the Thinking Critically series, which "encourage[s] teens to view important social issues from different perspectives. . . . [It] considers whether Americans have a constitutional right to own guns and if stronger gun control measures might prevent mass shootings." (Booklist)

"Diagrams and sidebars (Social includes one stock photo) support these well-organized models for classroom discourse. First chapters introduce the debates surrounding cell phones, social networking, and gun control; subsequent chapters present pro and con responses to four key questions. Despite lots of graphic elements, the text-heavy pages may be off-putting. Two pages of facts and a list of related organizations are appended." Horn Book

Includes bibliographical references and index

363.34   Disasters

Bailey, Gerry

Fragile planet. Gareth Stevens Pub. 2011 48p il map (Planet SOS) lib bdg $31.95; pa $14.05

Grades: 4 5 6   **363.34**
1. Natural disasters
ISBN 978-1-4339-4974-6 lib bdg; 1-4339-4974-1 lib bdg; 978-1-4339-4975-3 pa; 1-4339-4975-X pa
LC 2010032886

This "well-designed [book]. . . . discusses natural events and disasters, such as avalanches, earthquakes, floods, hurricanes, lightning, volcanoes, and windstorms. . . . The many large, colorful photos will engage readers and assist them in understanding the important concepts introduced." SLJ

Includes glossary

Butts, Edward

SOS : stories of survival; true tales of disaster, tragedy, and courage. by Ed Butts. Tundra Books 2007 119p il pa $12.95

Grades: 6 7 8 9   **363.34**
1. Disasters
ISBN 978-0-88776-786-9 pa

"Butts writes with taut excitement about 13 devastating events—floods, fires, explosions, mountain slides, and more—from the 1891 Canadian Springhill Mine Disaster and the Triangle Shirtwaist Fire to Chernobyl, the Tsunami of 2004, and Hurricane Katrina. . . . The personal eyewitness accounts and occasional archival photos dramatize the cataclysmic events." Booklist

Includes bibliographical references

Engelbert, Phillis

Dangerous planet; the science of natural disasters. U.X.L 2001 3v il maps set $165

Grades: 6 7 8 9   **363.34**
1. Natural disasters
ISBN 0-7876-2848-4
LC 98-54422

"The science is accurate, and the technical terms are explained well. The illustrations are clear and well placed." Booklist

This set "explains the science behind earthquakes, volcanoes, tornadoes, avalanches, mudslides and other devastating natural disasters. Alphabetically arranged entries typically include a definition of the type of disaster; a summary, including coverage of particularly well-known or destructive occurrences; a discussion of the causes of the disaster; technology's role in predicting and measuring a disaster; [and] a list of further reading." Publisher's note

Includes bibliographical references

Fradin, Judith Bloom

★ **Droughts**; [by] Judy & Dennis Fradin. National Geographic 2008 48p il map (Witness to disaster) $16.95; lib bdg $20.90

Grades: 4 5 6 7   **363.34**
1. Droughts
ISBN 978-1-4263-0339-5; 1-4263-0339-4; 978-1-4263-0340-1 lib bdg; 1-4263-0340-8 lib bdg
LC 2008020424

"This book examines the lessons from the Dust Bowl droughts for farmers, including the importance of topsoil. The history of droughts around the world compares impacts on a wide variety of societies. The final chapter looks at the latest tools and technologies developed to help us survive future droughts." Publisher's note

Includes glossary and bibliographical references

Garbe, Suzanne

The **Worst** wildfires of all time; by Suzanne Garbe. Capstone Press 2013 32 p. ill. (chiefly col.), col. maps (library) $27.32

Grades: 4 5 6 7   **363.34**
1. Wildfires 2. Natural disasters
ISBN 1429684186; 9781429684187
LC 2011053150

This book by Suzanne Garbe is part of the Epic Disasters series and looks at the worst wildfires of all time. "These uncontrolled fires can strike in the blink of an eye and spread just as quickly. Put out the flames and read about the worst wildfires in history." The series allows readers to "witness the destructive power of hurricanes, earthquakes, and more." (Publisher's note)

Includes bibliographical references and index.

Karwoski, Gail

Tsunami; the true story of an April Fools' Day disaster. [by] Gail Langer Karwoski; illustrated by John MacDonald. Darby Creek Pub. 2006 64p il $17.95

Grades: 4 5 6 7   **363.34**
　1. Tsunamis　2. Hawaii -- History　3. Hawaii
　ISBN 1581960441

The author "opens with a description of the tsunami waves that struck the northern coast of the Hawaiian Islands in 1946, destroying a school and sweeping many children and adults out to sea. The book goes on to provide broader information about tsunamis, from scientific understanding of how they occur to ongoing efforts at early warning systems. . . . Clearly written and informative." Booklist

Langley, Andrew

　Hurricanes, tsunamis, and other natural disasters; [by] Andrew Langley. Kingfisher 2006 63p il map (Kingfisher knowledge) $12.95
Grades: 5 6 7 8   **363.34**
　1. Natural disasters
　ISBN 978-0-7534-5975-1; 0-7534-5975-2
　　　　　　　　　　　　　　　　LC 2005027200

This briefly describes such natural disasters as hurricanes, tsunamis, avalanches, brush fires, earthquakes, floods, tornadoes, drought and famine, pandemics, with many color illustrations and maps

"This book presents a high-interest topic in an attractively designed format that features colorful, eye-catching graphics and a solidly written text." Booklist

Includes glossary and bibliographical references

Markle, Sandra

　Rescues! Millbrook Press 2006 88p il map lib bdg $25.26
Grades: 4 5 6 7   **363.34**
　1. Rescue work　2. Survival after airplane accidents, shipwrecks, etc.
　ISBN 978-0-8225-3413-6 lib bdg; 0-8225-3413-4 lib bdg
　　　　　　　　　　　　　　　　LC 2005-09707

"From the collapse of a Pennsylvania coal mine in 2002 to the tsunami that struck 11 countries in 2004 to Hurricane Katrina in 2005, the 11 disasters Markle describes are straight from news headlines. In this full-color photo-essay, she uses individual experiences of rescue and survival to bring each drama close." Booklist

Includes bibliographical references

Miller, Mara

　Hurricane Katrina strikes the Gulf Coast; disaster & survival. [by] Mara Miller. Enslow Publishers 2006 48p il map (Deadly disasters) $23.93
Grades: 4 5 6 7   **363.34**
　1. Hurricanes　2. Rescue work　3. Hurricane Katrina, 2005
　ISBN 0-7660-2803-8
　　　　　　　　　　　　　　　　LC 2005030989

"Miller begins with an account of the development of Hurricane Katrina as it struck Florida and then threatened the Gulf Coast. She discusses the subsequent flooding of New Orleans, the damage it caused, rescue and recovery attempts, and planning for the aftermath of future hurricanes. The author includes a clear scientific description of hurricanes, defining key terms. Color photos and graphics help

explain concepts such as the structure of a hurricane, Katrina's path, and the conditions endured by the victims." SLJ
　Includes glossary and bibliographical references

Mooney, Carla

　Surviving in cold places; by Carla Mooney. Lerner Publications Company 2014 32 p. (Shockzone--True survival stories) (lib. bdg. : alk. paper) $26.60
Grades: 5 6 7 8   **363.34**
　1. Survival skills　2. Wilderness survival　3. Cold -- Physiological effect　4. Survival -- Polar regions　5. Polar regions -- Environmental conditions
　ISBN 1467714348; 9781467714341
　　　　　　　　　　　　　　　　LC 2013019868

This book on survival in cold climates, by Carla Mooney, is part of the "Shock Zone: True Survival Stories" series. It presents "historic accounts of incidents in the Andes, Antarctic, and Alaska." The book provides "survival tips . . . an extended bibliography, and gateways to more information." (Voice of Youth Advocates)

"Each thin volume shares six to eight (mostly) contemporary stories of extreme survival, including a 2005 grizzly bear attack on a father and daughter and a boy's eight-day ordeal buried in rubble in the 2010 Haiti earthquake. Readers will be grabbed by a mix of harrowing details and eye-catching color photographs. The stories and appended safety tips are superficially presented but are nonetheless fascinating.' Horn Book

Includes bibliographical references (pages 30, 32) and index

Other titles in the series include:
Surviving in the Wilderness (2014)
Surviving Natural Disasters (2014)

Pietras, Jamie

　Hurricane Katrina; [by] Jamie Pietras. Chelsea House 2008 128p il map (Great historic disasters) $35
Grades: 7 8 9 10   **363.34**
　1. Hurricane Katrina, 2005
　ISBN 978-0-7910-9639-0; 0-7910-9639-4
　　　　　　　　　　　　　　　　LC 2007036551

"This book details the meteorological, political, and social circumstances that came together so fatally during 2005's Hurricane Katrina. Mostly objective, the writing is occasionally peppered with commentary on the local and federal governments' missteps and inaction following the storm and ensuing floods. Gripping photographs support the text." Horn Book Guide

Includes glossary and bibliographical references

Reilly, Kathleen M.

　Natural disasters; investigate Earth's most destructive forces. by Kathleen M. Reilly ; illustrated by Tom Casteel. Nomad Press 2012 121 p. (paperback) $15.95
Grades: 4 5 6 7   **363.34**
　1. Weather　2. Natural disasters
　ISBN 1619301466; 9781619301467

In this book, "spiraling winds, surging waters, eruptions, blazing forests, and chilling snows are discussed." Topics include "the MMS Scale and the Enhanced Fujita Scale."

In addition to an "explanation of each type of phenomenon, safety tips, historical incidences, pen-and-ink line drawings, and correlative projects using simple materials are included." (School Library Journal)

Robson, David

Disaster response. ReferencePoint Press 2009 96p il map (Compact research. Current issues) lib bdg $25.95

Grades: 7 8 9 10   **363.34**
1. Disaster relief
ISBN 978-1-60152-081-4; 1-60152-081-6
LC 2009-2283

"Robson covers disasters ranging from manmade to weather-related and bioterrorism. . . . Hurricane Katrina is discussed in the overview and leads into chapters that question the ability of the United States to handle natural disasters and how it can be improved. . . . Colorful graphs and up-to-date statistics are included. [This title] would be [a] great [addition] for students needing print materials to help with research projects, and for those who require some kind of first-person account included in their research." SLJ

Includes bibliographical references

Rusch, Elizabeth

★ Eruption! volcanoes and the science of saving lives. text by Elizabeth Rusch ; illustrated by Tom Uhlman. Houghton Mifflin Harcourt 2013 76 p. col. ill. (hardcover) $18.99

Grades: 5 6 7 8   **363.34**
1. Disaster response and recovery 2. Volcanoes 3. Natural disasters 4. Volcanic eruptions
ISBN 0547503504; 9780547503509
LC 2012034055

This book by Elizabeth Rusch contains "photographs and sidebars [which] reveals the perilous . . . life-saving work of an international volcano crisis team (VDAP) and the sleeping giants they study, from Colombia to the Philippines, from Chile to Indonesia. [It presents an] stunning account of volcanologists Andy Lockhart, John Pallister, and their group of scientists who risk their lives, investigating deadly volcanoes that remain constant threats to people around the world." (Publisher's note)

Includes bibliographical references (pages 74-75) and index.

Sanna, Ellyn

Nature's wrath; surviving natural disasters. Mason Crest Publishers 2009 128p il map (Survivors: ordinary people, extraordinary circumstances) lib bdg $24.95

Grades: 7 8 9 10   **363.34**
1. Natural disasters 2. Hurricane Katrina, 2005 3. Indian Ocean earthquake and tsunami, 2004
ISBN 978-1-4222-0454-2 lib bdg; 1-4222-0454-5 lib bdg
LC 2008-33334

Describes how natural disasters have decimated areas and lives, and how people have worked to reclaim their lives in the aftermath

Saul, Laya

Ways to help after a natural disaster; by Laya Saul. Mitchell Lane Publishers 2011 47 p. col. ill. (library) $29.95

Grades: 4 5 6   **363.34**
1. Volunteer work 2. Disaster relief
ISBN 1584159170; 9781584159179
LC 2010006538

"This focuses on various activities in which children can participate to help families be prepared in the event of a natural disaster or in its aftermath, when citizens experience the devastating results. The brief sections on teaching preparedness include advice for putting together supply kits and a sample list for collecting emergency numbers. The bulk of the information is sound, practical, commonsense recommendations. . . . Included are simple measures, such as offering emotional support, as well as those that are more complicated, such as organizing drives for collecting blood or food and clothing. The design is inviting, with text appealingly laid out and offset by blocks of color." Booklist

Includes bibliographical references and index.

Stefoff, Rebecca

Forensics and modern disasters. Marshall Cavendish Benchmark 2010 95p il (Forensic science investigated) $23.95

Grades: 6 7 8 9 10   **363.34**
1. Disasters 2. Forensic sciences 3. Criminal investigation
ISBN 978-0-7614-4144-1; 0-7614-4144-1
LC 2010-10533

The "titles in the Forensic Science Investigated series stand out not only for their thorough overviews of how forensic science is practiced today but also for their fascinating historical perspectives. . . . Forensics and Modern Disasters dives directly into contemporary practices and shows how techniques . . . have helped identify victims of large-scale tragedies, including 9/11." Booklist

Includes bibliographical references

363.37   Fire hazards

Cooper, Michael L., 1950-

Fighting fire! ten of the deadliest fires in American history and how we fought them. Michael L. Cooper. Henry Holt and Co. 2014 224 p. illustrations, maps (hardback) $19.99

Grades: 5 6 7 8   **363.37**
1. Fires 2. Fire fighting 3. Fire extinction -- United States -- History
ISBN 0805097147; 9780805097146
LC 2013043580

This book, by Michael L. Cooper, "brings to life ten of the deadliest infernos . . . [the United States] has ever endured: the great fires of Boston, New York, Chicago, Baltimore, and San Francisco, the disasters of the Triangle Shirt-waist Factory, the General Slocum, and the Cocoanut Grove nightclub, the wildfire of Witch Creek in San Diego County, and the catastrophe of 9/11." (Publisher's note)

"Throughout history, fires have wreaked destruction but have also sparked innovation and reform. The Great Chicago Fire (1871) destroyed a third of the city but brought about a new architecture style; the Triangle Shirtwaist Factory Fire (1911) killed 146 people but led to the passage of laws protecting workers. Entries are lively, with dramatic illustrations to match." Horn Book

Includes bibliographical references and index

363.4 Controversies related to public morals and customs

Blumenthal, Karen

★ **Bootleg**: murder, moonshine, and the lawless years of Prohibition. Roaring Brook Press 2011 154p il $18.99

Grades: 8 9 10 11 12 **363.4**
1. Temperance 2. Prohibition 3. United States -- History -- 1919-1933 5. Alcholic beverage industry
ISBN 978-1-59643-449-3; 1-59643-449-X
LC 2010032687

The author "offers a highly readable, well-shaped look at the Eighteenth Amendment. . . . She provides concise, clearly written insights into the seeds of temperance movements in the late eighteenth century. . . . The section on Al Capone will satisfy readers hungry for the gangster-warfare side of Prohibition. A closing chapter makes an argument that despite the mostly disastrous results, there were bright points to Prohibition. . . . Plenty of archival images lend to the book's pleasant design, and an ample bibliography and source notes close out this top-notch resource." Booklist

Includes bibliographical references

Hill, Jeff

Prohibition. Omnigraphics 2004 xxv, 201p il (Defining moments) $38

Grades: 7 8 9 10 **363.4**
1. Prohibition
ISBN 0-7808-0768-5
LC 2004-22643

This book provides an "historical analysis of the Prohibition era (1920-33), including the politics of the Eighteenth Amendment; the Mob wars; the roles played by important public figures, from mobster Al Capone to Prohibition activist Carry Nation to President Warren Harding; and much more. . . . With a detailed glossary, a chronology, and an annotated bibliography, this is an important curriculum resource on the social and political history of an era." Booklist

Includes glossary and bibliographical references

Worth, Richard

Teetotalers and saloon smashers; the temperance movement and prohibition. Enslow Publishers 2009 128p il map (America's living history) lib bdg $31.93

Grades: 5 6 7 8 **363.4**
1. Temperance 2. Prohibition
ISBN 978-0-7660-2908-8 lib bdg; 0-7660-2908-5 lib bdg
LC 2008-13905

"Discusses the temperance movement in American history, including important figures in the movement, the history of temperance, and the period of Prohibition in the United States." Publisher's note

Includes glossary and bibliographical references

363.45 Drug traffic

Harris, Nathaniel

Drug trafficking. Gareth Stevens Pub. 2010 48p il (What if we do nothing?) lib bdg $31

Grades: 7 8 9 10 **363.45**
1. Drug abuse 2. Drug traffic
ISBN 978-1-4339-1981-7 lib bdg; 1-4339-1981-8 lib bdg
LC 2008-52495

This "explains how drugs are grown, created, and distributed, and the problems individuals face when they become addicted. Meaningful illustrations include color photos and text-enhancing charts. . . . [This title is] well written and useful for reports." SLJ

Includes glossary and bibliographical references

Sherman, Jill

Drug trafficking. ABDO Pub. Co. 2010 112p il (Essential issues) lib bdg $22.95

Grades: 7 8 9 10 **363.45**
1. Drug abuse 2. Drug traffic
ISBN 978-1-60453-953-0; 1-60453-953-4
LC 2009-29935

This is "well-written, providing examples that put a human face to each problem. Quotes and facts are clearly attributed, and their sources are noted in the extensive back matter. . . . [This] will be of great assistance to students writing reports." SLJ

Includes glossary and bibliographical references

363.46 Abortion

★ **Abortion**: opposing viewpoints; David Haugen, Susan Musser, and Kacy Lovelace, book editors. Greenhaven Press 2010 206p (Opposing viewpoints series) lib bdg $39.70; pa $27.50

Grades: 8 9 10 11 12 **363.46**
1. Abortion
ISBN 978-0-7377-4747-8 lib bdg; 0-7377-4747-1 lib bdg; 978-0-7377-4748-5 pa; 0-7377-4748-X pa
LC 2009-41649

Provides opposing viewpoints on the topic of abortion.
Includes bibliographical references

Haney, Johannah

The **abortion** debate; understanding the issues. Enslow Publishers 2009 112p il (Issues in focus today) lib bdg $31.93

Grades: 6 7 8 9   363.46

1. Abortion

ISBN 978-0-7660-2916-3 lib bdg; 0-7660-2916-6 lib bdg

LC 2008013900

"Examines the debate over abortion, discussing both the pro-life and pro-choice sides of the argument, the history and laws on abortion in the United States, and finding a middle ground on the issue." Publisher's note

Includes bibliographical references

363.5   Housing

Rubel, David

If I had a hammer; building homes and hope with Habitat for Humanity. with a foreword by Jimmy Carter. Candlewick Press 2009 148p il $19.99

Grades: 6 7 8 9 10   363.5

1. Housing 2. Social action 3. Habitat for Humanity International Inc.

ISBN 978-0-7636-4701-8; 0-7636-4701-2

LC 2009025691

"Technology and faith are the subjects in this hands-on account of Habitat for Humanity, the organization that helps create safe, decent housing for those in need in the U.S. and across the globe. . . . The book's open design, with clear type on thick, quality paper, includes many color photos. . . . The text's details about the essentials of providing shelter, fresh water, electricity, and effective sewage systems for all combine into a powerful message that will inspire many readers." Booklist

363.6   Public utilities and related services

Brown, Cynthia Light

Discover National Monuments, National Parks; natural wonders. illustrated by Blair Shedd. Nomad Press 2009 106p il (Discover your world) pa $19.95

Grades: 5 6 7 8   363.6

1. National parks and reserves

ISBN 978-1-9346702-8-6 pa; 1-9346702-8-6 pa

"With an inviting, browsable design and a chatty style, this large-sized volume . . . covers 15 national monuments and parks in the U.S. that celebrate and protect natural phenomena . . . The science will excite readers, with detailed explanations of tectonic plates, radiometric dating, and dendrochronology." Booklist

Burgan, Michael

Not a drop to drink; water for a thirsty world. Peter H. Gleick, consultant. National Geographic 2008 64p il map (National Geographic investigates) $17.95

Grades: 4 5 6 7   363.6

1. Water 2. Water supply

ISBN 978-1-4263-0360-9; 1-4263-0360-2

Explores the important connections between human activity and the water cycle and shows how researchers are working to understand such issues as how climate change affects water supplies and how the oceans can help solve the water crisis.

Workman, James G.

Water. Morgan Reynolds Pub. 2009 111p il (Diminishing resources) lib bdg $28.95

Grades: 8 9 10 11 12   363.6

1. Water supply 2. Water conservation

ISBN 978-1-59935-115-5; 1-59935-115-3

LC 2009-28708

This discussion of world water supply and conservation "will draw activists, but even readers who do not think they care that much will find the facts devastating. Quotes from authoritative sources—environmentalists, scientists, and survivors—about both the historic overview and the contemporary crisis accompany full-color double-page photos that show what is happening now. . . . The discussion ranges from the pros and cons of dams to the price of bottled water." Booklist

Includes bibliographical references

363.7   Environmental problems

Albee, Sarah

Poop happened! a history of the world from the bottom up. illustrated by Robert Leighton. Walker 2010 170p il lib bdg $20.89; pa $15.99

Grades: 4 5 6 7   363.7

1. Feces 2. Toilets 3. Sanitation 4. Refuse and refuse disposal

ISBN 978-0-8027-9825-1 lib bdg; 0-8027-9825-X lib bdg; 978-0-8027-2077-1 pa; 0-8027-2077-3 pa

"Albee deposits a heaping history of human sanitation— or rather lack thereof— and its effects. . . . She pumps out a steady stream of comments on the miasmic effects of urbanization, waste disposal, and the roles of (not) bathing in ancient Greece, Rome, medieval Europe, . . . and the 'Reeking Renaissance.' She then digs into the gradual adoption of better practices in the nineteenth century. . . . The cartoon illustrations feature sludgy green highlights." Booklist

Bellamy, Rufus

Tourism. Amicus 2010 44p il map (Sustaining our environment) lib bdg $31.35

Grades: 6 7 8 9   363.7

1. Tourist trade

ISBN 978-1-60753-138-8 lib bdg; 1-60753-138-0 lib bdg

LC 2009-28236

"The tone is refreshingly optimistic with its examples of specific steps being taken to reduce harm to the environment. Sidebars highlight case studies and campaigns from around the world and from the individual to the national levels. Clear, informative captions accompany the excellent selection of color photographs, charts and graphs." SLJ

Includes glossary

Waste and pollution. Amicus 2010 44p il map (Sustaining our environment) lib bdg $31.35

Grades: 6 7 8 9   **363.7**

1. Pollution 2. Waste products 3. Industrial waste 4. Refuse and refuse disposal

ISBN 978-1-60753-139-5 lib bdg; 1-60753-139-9 lib bdg

LC 2009-40709

Introduces problems associated with pollution and waste disposal and how we may be able to ease the bad effects on the environment.

"The tone is refreshingly optimistic with its examples of specific steps being taken to reduce harm to the environment. Sidebars highlight case studies and campaigns from around the world and from the individual to the national levels. Clear, informative captions accompany the excellent selection of color photographs, charts and graphs." SLJ

Includes glossary

Berne, Emma Carlson

Global warming and climate change. ReferencePoint Press 2008 112p il (Compact research) $24.95

Grades: 8 9 10 11 12   **363.7**

1. Greenhouse effect 2. Climate -- Environmental aspects

ISBN 978-1-60152-019-7; 1-60152-019-0

LC 2007-8371

This discusses global warming and climate change, its consequences and controversies and possible solutions.

"Useful for reports. . . . [This] presents pertinent questions with appropriate and well-documented quotations from a variety of viewpoints and basic facts and diagrams." SLJ

Includes bibliographical references

Bryan, Nichol

Danube; cyanide spill. by Nichol Bryan. World Almanac Library 2004 48p il map (Environmental disasters) lib bdg $29.27; pa $11.95

Grades: 5 6 7 8   **363.7**

1. Chemical spills 2. Water pollution

ISBN 0-8368-5505-1 lib bdg; 0-8368-5512-4 pa

LC 2003-57694

Discusses the disastrous year 2000 overflow of a Romanian reservoir that held heavy metals and cyanide, pouring the deadly mix into rivers that feed the Danube and killing all living creatures in its path.

Includes glossary and bibliographical references

Love Canal; pollution crisis. World Almanac Library 2004 48p il map (Environmental disasters) hardcover o.p. lib bdg $29.27

Grades: 5 6 7 8   **363.7**

1. Pollution 2. Love Canal Chemical Waste Landfill (Niagara Falls, N.Y.)

ISBN 0-8368-5508-6 lib bdg; 0-8368-5515-9 pa

LC 2003-57162

Traces the history and eventual cleanup of the ecological disaster known as Love Canal, which resulted from building a neighborhood over a chemical dumpsite that poisoned the environment and endangered the health of residents.

This is "well-illustrated. . . . [It does] a fine job of placing [the] disaster within a larger context by including detailed background about America's industrial and environmental history; quotes from eyewitnesses, politicians, and journalists; and clear explanations of the changes in policy that [the] disaster instigated." Booklist

Includes glossary and bibliographical references

Byrnes, Patricia

Environmental pioneers. Oliver Press (Minneapolis) 1998 160p il (Profiles) lib bdg $19.95

Grades: 7 8 9 10   **363.7**

1. Authors 2. Governors 3. Cartoonists 4. Naturalists 5. Conservationists 6. Environmentalists 7. Senators 8. Feminists 9. Centenarians 10. College teachers 11. Marine biologists 12. State legislators 13. Writers on nature 14. Writers on science 15. Organization officials

ISBN 1-881508-45-5

LC 97-30233

Profiles people who have been influential in the environmental movement: John Muir, Jay Norwood "Ding" Darling, Rosalie Edge, Aldo Leopold, Olaus and Margaret Murie, Rachel Carson, David Brower, and Gaylord Nelson

"Unlike most authors of books on this topic for a young audience, Byrnes is an experienced environmental writer, and takes an affectionate tone in describing her subjects." SLJ

Includes bibliographical references

Cherry, Lynne

★ **How** we know what we know about our changing climate; scientists and kids explore global warming. by Lynne Cherry and Gary Braasch; with a foreword by David Sobel. Dawn Publications 2008 66p il $18.95; pa $11.95

Grades: 4 5 6 7   **363.7**

1. Greenhouse effect 2. Climate -- Environmental aspects

ISBN 978-1-58469-103-7; 0-1-58469-103-4; 978-1-58469-130-3 pa; 1-58469-130-1 pa

LC 2007-37255

"The can-do emphasis helps to make the topic less depressing, and the intriguing color photographs are thoughtful and upbeat." Booklist

"This volume describes where scientists look to find evidence of climate change—from changes in bird migration patterns and fruit blossom dates, to obtaining tree rings and mud cores—and especially how students and other citizen-scientists are assisting to monitor climate change, as well as what can be done to mitigate global warming." Publisher's note

Collard, Sneed

Global warming; a personal guide to causes and solutions. Lifelong Learning 2011 il $18

Grades: 6 7 8 9   **363.7**

1. Greenhouse effect 2. Climate -- Environmental

aspects
ISBN 978-0-97853677-0

"After a quick introduction and opening discussion of the basics and impacts of global warming, Collard identifies the causes, challenges, and related issues and examines the complex issue of what needs to be done. He suggests various solutions and gives global examples to support his arguments. His knowledgeable and persuasive tone convinces readers that change is necessary and achievable. . . . The informative text is broken into columns, making the extra-wide-page format easy to read. More than eight pages of references give students many further-research options. . . . An excellent resource for reports and debates." SLJ

David, Laurie

★ The **down** -to-earth guide to global warming; [by] Laurie David and Cambria Gordon. Orchard Books 2007 112p il map pa $15.99
Grades: 4 5 6 7   363.7
1. Greenhouse effect 2. Climate -- Environmental aspects
ISBN 978-0-439-02494-5 pa; 0-439-02494-3 pa
LC 2006-35705

The authors "put forth the basics on global warming, climate change, and how readers can green up the environment. They temper the book's often troubling subject matter with kid-friendly humor, some celebrity shout-outs, and explanations of the scientific underpinnings. An amply illustrated layout, featuring attention-grabbing sidebars, dramatic photos, and diagrams, will sustain reader interest." Booklist
Includes bibliographical references

Davies, Nicola

Gaia warriors; urgent; the fight is on! with an afterword by James Lovelock. Candlewick Press 2011 192p il $14.99
Grades: 5 6 7 8   363.7
1. Gaia hypothesis 2. Environmental protection 3. Greenhouse effect 4. Climate -- Environmental aspects
ISBN 978-0-7636-4808-4; 0-7636-4808-6
LC 2010-40126

This "offers a dynamic overview of global warming's causes and concerns. Davies . . . devotes half the book to exciting profiles of individuals . . . who are working to slow climate change. . . . They include scientists, rock musicians, food distributors, architects, and youth organizers, and their broad variety reinforces the sense that every creative individual effort matters. Highly browsable layouts combine color photos and quotes printed in varied, eye-catching fonts. . . . [This has a] humorous, conversational tone." Booklist
Includes glossary

Delano, Marfe Ferguson

★ **Earth** in the hot seat; bulletins from a warming world. National Geographic 2009 63p il (Preserve our planet) $19.95; lib bdg $28.90
Grades: 5 6 7 8   363.7
1. Greenhouse effect 2. Climate -- Environmental aspects
ISBN 978-1-4263-0434-7; 1-4263-0434-X; 978-1-4263-0435-4 lib bdg; 1-4263-0435-8 lib bdg
LC 2008029317

"This book lays out . . . the evidence for global warming and the part that human activity plays in it. Five chapters lay out the signs and evidences of a warming world. . . . Subsequent chapters of the book are devoted to what humankind can expect in a warming world and steps that must be taken to avert catastrophe for humans and the planet. . . . The illustrative photos are fully up to National Geographic high standards. This [is a] fine book, reasonably priced and carefully researched." Voice Youth Advocates
Includes bibliographical references

Dorion, Christiane

Pollution. Gareth Stevens Pub. 2010 48p il (What if we do nothing?) lib bdg $31
Grades: 7 8 9 10   363.7
1. Pollution 2. Environmental protection
ISBN 978-1-4339-1984-8 lib bdg; 1-4339-1984-2 lib bdg
LC 2008-52494

This "title covers the main sources of air, water, and ground pollution and offers some suggestions for reducing it. . . . Meaningful illustrations include color photos and text-enhancing charts. . . . [This title is] well written and useful for reports." SLJ
Includes glossary and bibliographical references

The **environment**: opposing viewpoints; Louise I. Gerdes, book editor. Greenhaven Press 2009 224p il (Opposing viewpoints series) $39.70; pa $27.50
Grades: 8 9 10 11 12   363.7
1. Environmental sciences
ISBN 978-0-7377-4362-3; 978-0-7377-4361-6 pa
LC 2008-55846

This collection of essays offers varying viewpoints on environmental pollution and protection.
Includes bibliographical references

Evans, Kate

Weird weather; everything you didn't want to know about climate change but probably should find out. [with an introduction by George Monbiot] Groundwood Books 2007 95p il $15.95; pa $9.95
Grades: 8 9 10 11 12   363.7
1. Graphic novels 2. Weather -- Graphic novels 3. Greenhouse effect -- Graphic novels 4. Climate -- Environmental aspects -- Graphic novels
ISBN 978-0-88899-838-5; 978-0-88899-841-5 pa

First published 2006 in the United Kingdom with title: Funny weather

This book, in graphic novel format, presents "the history of global warming, likely outcomes of current pollution patterns, and what can be done if we hope to survive as a species. Cleverly, the narrative unfolds through the voices of three main characters: an outraged young idealist, a scientist fascinated by the challenges of the situation, and a greedy consumer who is only interested in himself. Accessible and entertaining, this book will be adored by science teachers. . . . Important reading for secondary students and adults." SLJ
Includes bibliographical references

Farrell, Courtney

The **Gulf** of Mexico oil spill. ABDO Pub. 2011 112p il (Essential events) lib bdg $23.95

Grades: 7 8 9 10 11 12   **363.7**

1. Gulf of Mexico oil spill, 2010
ISBN 978-1-61714-765-4; 1-61714-765-6

LC 2010044976

This describes the political, social, and technical issues concerning the 2010 oil spill in the Gulf of Mexico.

Includes glossary and bibliographical references

Fleischman, Paul

★ **Eyes** wide open; what's behind the environmental headlines. Paul Fleischman. Candlewick Press 2014 208 p. illustrations hbk $17.99; pbk $9.99

Grades: 8 9 10 11 12   **363.7**

1. Environmental sciences 2. Environmental degradation 3. Environmental quality 4. Environmental protection
ISBN 0763671029; 0763675458 ; 9780763671020; 9780763675455

LC 2013953458

This book by Paul Fleischman describes how "we're living in an Ah-Ha moment. Take 250 years of human ingenuity. Add abundant fossil fuels. The result: a population and lifestyle never before seen. The downsides weren't visible for centuries, but now they are. Suddenly everything needs rethinking--suburbs, cars, fast food, cheap prices. It's a changed world. This book explains it." (Publisher's note)

"With simple, matter-of-fact language, an attractive layout and an abundance of references, this compact guide to addressing climate change is a must-read for millennials and for all who seek solutions to global warming. . . . Readers are offered advice on how to analyze and interpret what they hear in person and discover through the media." Kirkus

Includes bibliographical references, filmography and index

Fridell, Ron

Protecting Earth's water supply; by Ron Fridell. Lerner Publications Co. 2009 72p il (Saving our living Earth) lib bdg $30.60

Grades: 5 6 7 8   **363.7**

1. Water pollution 2. Water conservation
ISBN 978-0-8225-7557-3 lib bdg; 0-8225-7557-4 lib bdg

LC 2007-35924

"Provides a thorough, interesting discussion of multiple aspects of [water supply protection], including historical origins, the current situation, and potential solutions. . . . Photos from around the world accompany discussions. . . . [This is a] solid choice to replace outdated books." SLJ

Includes glossary and bibliographical references

Geiger, Beth

Clean water. Roaring Brook Press 2009 40p il (Sally Ride science) pa $7.99

Grades: 5 6 7 8   **363.7**

1. Water supply 2. Water pollution
ISBN 978-1-59643-577-3 pa; 1-59643-577-1 pa

This is a "well-written, engaging book. . . . The [book']s best feature is the conversational tone that simply and clearly conveys important, and sometimes complicated, scientific concepts. Illustrations and layout are well done, and include colorful photographs and charts. Excellent." SLJ

★ **Global** warming: opposing viewpoints; David Haugen, Susan Musser, and Kacy Lovelace, book editors. Greenhaven Press 2010 249p il map (Opposing viewpoints series) $39.70; pa $27.50

Grades: 8 9 10 11 12   **363.7**

1. Greenhouse effect
ISBN 978-0-7377-4631-0; 0-7377-4631-9; 978-0-7377-4632-7 pa; 0-7377-4632-7 pa

LC 2009-38723

"Explores whether global warming is a real phenomenon or a myth, addressing possible causes like carbon dioxide, deforestation, melting permafrost, and livestock agriculture. Examines the effects of global warming on the polar ice caps, polar bears and human health, and discusses some proposed strategies to mitigate the impact." Publisher's note

Includes bibliographical references

Gore, Al

★ **An** **inconvenient** truth; the crisis of global warming. adapted for young readers by Jane O'Connor. rev ed.; Viking 2007 191p il map $23; pa $16

Grades: 5 6 7 8   **363.7**

1. Greenhouse effect 2. Climate -- Environmental aspects
ISBN 978-0-670-06271-3; 978-0-670-06272-0 pa

Adapted from the title for adults published 2006 by Rodale Press

This explains what global warming is, what causes it, and explains how to take action to stop this crisis.

This is illustrated with "easy-to-grasp graphics and revealing before-and-after photos. . . . O'Connor rephrases Gore's arguments in briefer, simpler language without comprising their flow." SLJ

Our choice; how we can solve the climate crisis. [text adapted by Richie Chevat] Young readers ed.; Puffin Books 2009 207p il map $24.99; pa $16.99

Grades: 6 7 8 9 10   **363.7**

1. Human ecology 2. Environmental policy 3. Environmental protection 4. Greenhouse effect
ISBN 978-0-670-01248-0; 0-670-01248-3; 978-0-14-240981-7 pa; 0-14-240981-2 pa

LC 2010-455157

"This colorful, well-designed volume presents the climate crisis in an easy-to-understand format. Covering many aspects of this complex problem, it addresses the effects of pollution on the environment, the search for alternative energy sources, and offers suggestions for conserving power and reducing the impact of human habitation on the planet. . . . Although the urgency of the current global situation is stressed, the chapters are also laced with hope. Suggestions for change offer positive steps that anyone can take to reduce his carbon footprint, and extend a call to unite globally to save the planet for future generations." Voice Youth Advocates

Gunderson, Jessica

Global warming. Creative Education 2011 48p il (Earth issues) lib bdg $23.95

Grades: 6 7 8 9 10 **363.7**

1. Climate 2. Greenhouse effect

ISBN 978-1-58341-982-3; 1-58341-982-9

"An examination of the causes and potential effects of increasing global temperatures, exploring how humans and natural phenomena are involved, as well as how people can contribute to a healthier planet." Publisher's note

Includes glossary and bibliographical references

Hanel, Rachael

Climate fever; stopping global warming. Compass Point Books 2010 64p il (Green generation) lib bdg $31.99; pa $6.95

Grades: 5 6 7 8 9 **363.7**

1. Greenhouse effect 2. Climate -- Environmental aspects

ISBN 978-0-7565-4246-7 lib bdg; 0-7565-4246-4 lib bdg; 978-0-7565-4291-7 pa; 0-7565-4291-X pa

LC 2009-11448

"The cover design, layout, and graphics feel hip and of the moment. The clear writing is easy to understand and includes many concrete examples of environmentally friendly practices. . . . [A] good choice[s] for both leisure reading and reports." SLJ

Includes glossary and bibliographical references

Henningfeld, Diane Andrews

Health and disease; Michael E. Mann, consulting editor. Greenhaven Press 2011 136p il map (Confronting global warming) lib bdg $37.10

Grades: 7 8 9 10 11 **363.7**

1. Weather 2. Environmentally induced diseases 3. Greenhouse effect

ISBN 978-0-7377-4858-1; 0-7377-4858-3

LC 2010014227

"Presented in a scholarly design that will appeal to older readers. . . . The illustrations and pictures support the text, and the graphics and sidebars are well placed." Libr Media Connect

"Explores the effects of global warming on human health, examining the impacts of extreme cold snaps; issues arising from aridity; the health dangers posed by hurricanes and floods; diminished air capacity from smog, pollution, the ozone, and aero-allergens." Publisher's note

Includes glossary and bibliographical references

Hirschmann, Kris

Pollution. Kidhaven Press 2004 48p il (Our environment) lib bdg $23.70

Grades: 5 6 7 8 **363.7**

1. Pollution

ISBN 0-7377-1563-4

This briefly describes the sources and effects of air and water pollution and refuse disposal and suggests possible solutions

Includes glossary and bibliographical references

Hodge, Susie

Global warming. New Forest Press 2010 64p il map (Cutting-edge science) lib bdg $34.25

Grades: 7 8 9 10 **363.7**

1. Greenhouse effect 2. Climate -- Environmental aspects

ISBN 978-1-84898-320-5; 1-84898-320-4

This book covers "the topical science [issue] of climate change. . . . [It] includes contemporary scientific findings, the more stable science underlying the [issue], and the social [context]. The color photographs throughout are mainly stock images. Sidebars profile scientists in action or delve deeper into the research methods and studies producting this information." Horn Book Guide

Includes bibliographical references

Jakab, Cheryl

Waste management. Marshall Cavendish Benchmark 2010 32p il map (Environment in focus) lib bdg $28.50

Grades: 4 5 6 **363.7**

1. Refuse and refuse disposal

ISBN 978-1-60870-093-6; 1-60870-093-3

"The layout gives each topic the look of a file folder, with the first spread going to a case-study problem and the second going to a 'Toward a Sustainable Future' case-study solution. . . . Photos bring home the heartbreaking litter, human-waste treatment plants, etc." Booklist

Includes glossary

Jankeliowitch, Anne

Kids who are changing the world; photographs by Yann Arthus-Bertrand ; text by Anne Jankéliowitch. Sourcebooks Jabberwocky 2014 144 p. (tp : alk. paper) $14.99

Grades: 4 5 6 7 **363.7**

1. Child environmentalists 2. Environmental protection -- Fiction 3. Nature conservation -- Citizen participation

ISBN 9781402295324; 9781492608462; 1402295324

LC 2014011237

This book, by by Anne Jankéliowitch, photographs by Yann Arthus-Bertrand, offers "inspiring stories of 45 young heroes who have made an impact on our planet. . . . With skills ranging from singing, drawing, and painting to fundraising, public demonstrations, and events, they have fought climate change and pollution, and worked to protect animals and their natural habitats." (Publisher's note)

"Each story is styled as an interview with direct quotes from the kids involved. Photographs are dynamic and stunning, and background information and statistics on environmental issues are included in the margins." - Booklist

Includes bibliographical references and index

Johnson, Rebecca L.

Understanding global warming; by Rebecca L. Johnson. Lerner Publications 2009 72p il map (Saving our living Earth) lib bdg $30.60

Grades: 5 6 7 8 **363.7**

1. Greenhouse effect 2. Climate -- Environmental

aspects
ISBN 978-0-8225-7561-0 lib bdg; 0-8225-7561-2
lib bdg

LC 2007-48358

"Provides a thorough, interesting discussion of multiple aspects of [global warming], including historical origins, the current situation, and potential solutions. . . . Photos from around the world accompany discussions. . . . [This is a] solid choice to replace outdated books." SLJ

Includes glossary and bibliographical references

Macgillivray, Alex

Understanding Rachel Carson's Silent Spring. Rosen Pub. 2011 128p il (Words that changed the world) lib bdg $31.95

Grades: 7 8 9 10 **363.7**

1. Authors 2. Insect pests 3. Conservationists 4. Pesticides and wildlife 5. College teachers 6. Marine biologists 7. Writers on nature 8. Writers on science 9. Pesticides -- Environmental aspects
ISBN 978-1-4488-1670-5; 1-4488-1670-X

LC 2010-9260

"This focused title examines Rachel Carson's Silent Spring, zeroing in on the content and enduring impact of the watershed 1962 work. . . . The text begins with a brief introduction to Carson and her times before moving into an analysis of the text and its indictment of pesticide use, . . . the immediate postpublication response, and its hugely influential legacy today. . . . A useful supplement to environmental-science units, this will easily support student research." Booklist

Includes glossary and bibliographical references

Marcovitz, Hal

How serious a threat is climate change? ReferencePoint Press 2011 96p il (In controversy) lib bdg $26.95

Grades: 7 8 9 10 **363.7**

1. Environmental protection 2. Greenhouse effect
ISBN 978-1-60152-142-2; 1-60152-142-1

LC 2010033916

Discusses the scientific evidence for climate change, what countries around the world are doing to combat it, and why some people are skeptical.

"The author presents substantial amounts of information in a readable, student-friendly manner. Useful for reports." SLJ

Includes bibliographical references

Is offshore oil drilling worth the risks? ReferencePoint Press 2011 96p il (In controversy) lib bdg $26.95

Grades: 7 8 9 10 **363.7**

1. Oil spills 2. Offshore oil well drilling
ISBN 978-1-60152-143-9; 1-60152-143-X

LC 2010037854

Discusses the issues surrounding offshore oil drilling.

"The author presents substantial amounts of information in a readable, student-friendly manner. Useful for reports." SLJ

Includes bibliographical references

McCutcheon, Chuck

What are global warming and climate change? answers for young readers. University of New Mexico Press 2010 103p il map (Worlds of wonder) $24.95

Grades: 6 7 8 9 10 **363.7**

1. Greenhouse effect 2. Climate -- Environmental aspects
ISBN 978-0-8263-4745-9; 0-8263-4745-2

The author tackles "environmental issues with depth and rigor, attuned to both current events and the concerns of today's teens. . . . The excellent [text is] enhanced by color photographs and diagrams that further explain scientific ideas." Horn Book Guide

Mileham, Rebecca

Global pollution. New Forest Press 2010 64p il map (Cutting-edge science) lib bdg $34.25

Grades: 7 8 9 10 **363.7**

1. Pollution
ISBN 978-1-84898-322-9; 1-84898-322-0

This book covers "the topical science [issue] of . . . pollution. . . . [It] includes contemporary scientific findings, the more stable science underlying the [issue], and the social [context]. The color photographs throughout are mainly stock images. Sidebars profile scientists in action or delve deeper into the research methods and studies producing this information." Horn Book Guide

Inlcudes bibliographical references

Miller, Debra A.

Garbage and recycling. Lucent Books 2009 112p il map (Hot topics) $32.45

Grades: 7 8 9 10 **363.7**

1. Recycling 2. Refuse and refuse disposal
ISBN 978-1-4205-0147-6; 1-4205-0147-X

LC 2009-18371

This is a "standout survey of what happens to what we throw away and how those decisions affect the globe. . . . This overview offers a balance of viewpoints in its clear comparison of traditional methods of waste management with more sustainable technologies, such as recycling and new landfill techniques. . . . [Sidebars] make for compelling reading, while numerous color photos, charts, and maps will further attract readers' attention." Booklist

Includes bibliographical references

Miller, Malinda

Tomorrow's transportation; green solutions for air, land & sea. Mason Crest Publishers 2011 64p il (New careers for the 21st century: finding your role in the global renewal) lib bdg $22.95

Grades: 7 8 9 10 **363.7**

1. Transportation 2. Vocational guidance
ISBN 978-1-4222-1824-2 lib bdg; 1-4222-1824-4
lib bdg

LC 2010021833

"Chapters identify and emphasize specific careers–important strengths, necessary aptitudes and interests, education and training, projected earnings, closely related occupations, type of work environment, and predictions for the future of the field. . . . Color photos have a small role amid the many statistics, figures, graphs and charts that support and supplement the . . . [text]." SLJ

Includes bibliographical references

Morris, Neil

★ **Global** warming. World Almanac Library 2007 48p il (What if we do nothing?) lib bdg $22.95; pa $11.95

Grades: 5 6 7 8   **363.7**

1. Greenhouse effect 2. Climate -- Environmental aspects

ISBN 978-0-8368-7755-7 lib bdg; 0-8368-7755-1 lib bdg; 978-0-8368-155-4 pa; 0-8368-8155-9 pa

LC 2006-30444

This "boasts an attractive format, with large pages that allow room for pictures, excellent charts and graphs, as well as a thoughtful, clear discussion of the topic." Booklist

Includes bibliographical references

Nardo, Don

Climate crisis; the science of global warming. by Don Nardo. Compass Point Books 2009 47p il map (Headline science) lib bdg $27.93; pa $7.95

Grades: 5 6 7   **363.7**

1. Greenhouse effect 2. Climate -- Environmental aspects

ISBN 978-0-7565-3571-1 lib bdg; 0-7565-3571-9 lib bdg; 978-0-7565-3948-1 pa; 0-7565-3948-X pa

LC 2008-7259

"Color photos and graphics provide visual information; a timeline is helpful to find fast facts, and the Facthound Web site provides students with additional information." Libr Media Connect

"Presents an introduction to global warming, discussing the impact of rising temperatures, melting ice, water shortages, increased rate of animal extinctions, and the current human efforts underway to lessen the effects." Publisher's note

Includes glossary and bibliographical references

Oil spill; disaster. Scholastic Press 2010 31p il pa $5.99

Grades: 4 5 6 7 8   **363.7**

1. Oil spills 2. Gulf of Mexico oil spill, 2010

ISBN 978-0-545-31776-4; 0-545-31776-2

Explores the immediate and future consequences of the Gulf of Mexico oil spill in April 2010, when the offshore oil rig Deepwater Horizon exploded, causing major environmental and economical damage along the Gulf coast of the United States.

"While text and color photographs convey the extent of the devastation to the Gulf, the book also highlights some innovative attempts to clean up oil spills and profiles two middle school students, who researched cleaning up oil in their own neighborhood." Publ Wkly

Oxlade, Chris

Climate change. Smart Apple Media 2010 44p il map (Science in the news) lib bdg $34.25

Grades: 6 7 8 9   **363.7**

1. Greenhouse effect

ISBN 978-1-59920-319-5 lib bdg; 1-59920-319-7 lib bdg

LC 2008-41437

The narrative "move[s] smoothly, occasionally pausing for the definition of a term. [The title] boast[s] plenty of attractive photos, and a clean layout allows the information to be easily consumed. . . . Provides the information that younger teens need." SLJ

Includes glossary

Parker, Steve, 1952-

Population. QEB Pub. 2010 32p il (QEB changes in . . .) lib bdg $28.50

Grades: 3 4 5 6   **363.7**

1. Human ecology 2. Human influence on nature

ISBN 978-1-59566-774-8 lib bdg; 1-59566-774-1 lib bdg

LC 2008-56070

"The information is presented in brief paragraphs and sidebars. Suggestions for kids to help improve the planet are sprinkled throughout. . . . Students will enjoy this appealing layout and the information can spark further research on the topic[s]. . . . Either digitally or on paper, students could make fantastic presentations using a similar design." Libr Media Connect

Includes glossary

Pollution: opposing viewpoints; Louise I. Gerdes, book editor. Greenhaven Press 2011 262p il (Opposing viewpoints series) lib bdg $39.70; pa $26.50

Grades: 8 9 10 11 12   **363.7**

1. Pollution

ISBN 978-0-7377-5231-1 lib bdg; 0-7377-5231-9 lib bdg; 978-0-7377-5232-8 pa; 978-0-7377-5232-7 pa

LC 2010-51681

"The authors in this . . . anthology debate several controversial questions, including whether various forms of pollution continue to be a serious problem, whether pollution poses a public health threat, and what policies and programs will best reduce pollution." Publisher's note

Includes bibliographical references

Rapp, Valerie

Protecting Earth's air quality; by Valerie Rapp. Lerner Publications 2009 72p il map (Saving our living Earth) lib bdg $30.60

Grades: 5 6 7 8   **363.7**

1. Air pollution

ISBN 978-0-8225-7558-0 lib bdg; 0-8225-7558-2 lib bdg

LC 2008-907

"Provides a thorough, interesting discussion of multiple aspects of [protecting Earth's air quality], including historical origins, the current situation, and potential solutions. . . . Photos from around the world accompany discussions. . . . [This is a] solid choice to replace outdated books." SLJ

Includes glossary and bibliographical references

Robinson, Matthew

America debates global warming; crisis or myth? Rosen Central 2008 64p il (America debates) lib bdg $29.25

Grades: 5 6 7 8 9 10 11 12 **363.7**

1. Greenhouse effect 2. Climate -- Environmental aspects

ISBN 978-1-4042-1925-0 lib bdg; 1-4042-1925-0 lib bdg

LC 2007-10931

This "is especially effective in laying out the information in a simple, logical format." SLJ

This is a "presentation of the debate on global warming. . . . Scientists, world leaders, and political leaders weigh in." Publisher's note

Includes glossary and bibliographical references

Scarborough, Kate

★ **Nuclear** waste. Bridgestone Bks. 2003 32p il (Our planet in peril) lib bdg $22.60

Grades: 5 6 7 8 **363.7**

1. Nuclear energy 2. Radioactive waste disposal

ISBN 0-7368-1362-4

LC 2002-10139

"Chapters introduce topics such as . . . 'What is nuclear power?' through brief paragraphs of information. Numerous colorful photographs, graphs, and diagrams with informative captions add details on each spread." SLJ

Includes glossary and bibliographical references

Silverstein, Alvin

Global warming; by Alvin Silverstein, Virginia Silverstein, Laura Silverstein Nunn. rev. ed.; Twenty-First Century Books 2009 112p il (Science concepts, second series) $31.93

Grades: 5 6 7 8 **363.7**

1. Greenhouse effect 2. Climate -- Environmental aspects

ISBN 978-0-7613-3935-9; 0-7613-3935-3

First published 2003

The authors "explain how human activity and the greenhouse effect have changed the climate on Earth and the effect this has on people and animals. The authors also explore ways that everyone can 'go green' to help fight global warming." (Publisher's note)

Includes bibliographical references

Stille, Darlene R.

The **greenhouse** effect; warming the planet. Compass Point Books 2006 48p il map (Exploring science) $26.60

Grades: 7 8 9 10 **363.7**

1. Greenhouse effect 2. Climate -- Environmental aspects

ISBN 978-0-7565-1956-8; 0-7565-1956-X

LC 2006-06763

"The book provides a brief, yet thorough, explanation and overview of the greenhouse effect. . . . The text . . . is straightforward and clearly written. The illustrations and

diagrams . . . further clarify the explanations in the text." Sci Books Films

Includes glossary and bibliographical references

Townsend, John

Predicting the effects of climate change. Heinemann Library 2009 56p il map (Why science matters) $31.43; pa $9.49

Grades: 6 7 8 9 **363.7**

1. Greenhouse effect 2. Climate -- Environmental aspects

ISBN 978-1-4329-1839-2; 1-4329-1839-7; 978-1-4329-1852-1 pa; 1-4329-1852-4 pa

LC 2008-14309

Provides an overview of climate change, discussing evidence, causes, and effects, and examines what can be done to stop its progression.

This book "would be a good addition to middle school libraries." Sci Books Films

Includes filmography, glossary and bibliographical references

Wilcox, Charlotte

Earth -friendly waste management; by Charlotte Wilcox. Lerner 2009 72p il (Saving our living Earth) lib bdg $30.60

Grades: 5 6 7 8 **363.7**

1. Recycling 2. Refuse and refuse disposal

ISBN 978-0-8225-7560-3 lib bdg; 0-8225-7560-4 lib bdg

LC 2008-1883

"Provides a thorough, interesting discussion of multiple aspects of [waste management], including historical origins, the current situation, and potential solutions. . . . Photos from around the world accompany discussions. . . . [This is a] solid choice to replace outdated books." SLJ

Includes glossary and bibliographical references

Recycling. Lerner Publications 2008 48p il (Cool science) lib bdg $26.60

Grades: 4 5 6 **363.7**

1. Salvage 2. Recycling

ISBN 978-0-8225-6768-4 lib bdg; 0-8225-6768-7 lib bdg

LC 2006102423

"This book explains the many amazing ways people use science to recycle garbage into great things." Publisher's note

Includes glossary and bibliographical references

363.73   Pollution

Solway, Andrew

Transportation; by Andrew Solway. Heinemann Library 2013 64 p. (The impact of environmentalism) (library) $35.00; (paperback) $9.99

Grades: 6 7 8 **363.73**

1. Environmental movement 2. Transportation -- Environmental aspects 3. Pollution 4.

Environmentalism
ISBN 1432965204; 9781432965204; 9781432965266
LC 2012001043

This book Andrew Solway is part of the "Impact of Environmentalism" series. It "discusses global warming, climate change, and energy alternatives such as biofuels and renewable energies." It "also discusses the history of human activities and its environmental impact, and efforts by humankind to protect the environment and create sustainable smaller environments. Sidebars and full-color photos appear throughout." (School Library Journal)

Includes bibliographical references and index.

363.738 Pollutants

Global warming; Mary E. Williams, book editor. Greenhaven Press 2006 96 p. ill. (chiefly col.) (Writing the critical essay) (library) $26.20
Grades: 8 9 10 11 12   363.738
1. Essays 2. Authorship 3. Greenhouse effect
ISBN 0737732105; 9780737732108

LC 2005055066

"Section one presents five opposing excerpts from recent periodicals, each one beginning with a short summary and questions for readers to consider and including relevant illustrations, political cartoons, and color photographs. Section two offers information on essay writing and includes annotated examples. . . . This volume provides a useful way for English composition, science, and social science teachers to integrate library research into their classrooms." SLJ

Includes bibliographical references (p. 92-93) and index.

Newman, Patricia

Plastic, ahoy! investigating the great Pacific garbage patch. Patricia Newman ; photographs by Annie Crawley. Millbrook Press 2014 48 p. (lib. bdg. : alk. paper) $30.60
Grades: 5 6 7 8 9 10   363.738
1. Plastics 2. Marine pollution 3. Refuse and refuse disposal 4. Waste disposal in the ocean 5. Marine pollution -- Pacific Ocean
ISBN 1467712833; 9781467712835

LC 2013017773

This book, by Patricia Newman, focuses on "what happens when [plastic] ends up where it doesn't belong--like in the Pacific Ocean? How does it affect ocean life? Is it dangerous? And exactly how much is out there? A team of researchers went on a scientific expedition to find out. They explored the Great Pacific Garbage Patch, where millions of pieces of plastic have collected. The plastic has drifted there from rivers, beaches, and ocean traffic all over the world." (Publisher's note)

"Here readers travel to the Pacific Garbage Patch with three graduate-student scientists as they try to determine the effect of plastics on the sea. There's solid explanation of their hypotheses and research, and emphasis on the researchers' experiences lends a personal feel. Questions of how plastic may harm the oceans, its inhabitants, and even humans encourage further inquiry." Horn Book

363.8 Food supply

Barker, Geoff P.

Hunger; by Geoff Barker. Smart Apple Media 2010 46p il (Voices) lib bdg $34.25
Grades: 7 8 9 10 11 12   363.8
1. Famines 2. Food relief
ISBN 978-1-59920-281-5 lib bdg; 1-59920-281-6 lib bdg

LC 2008-50430

This book about hunger "addresses the causes, the possible solutions, and outlooks, both good and bad, of . . . [the] issue. Each brief chapter covers basic questions, answered with a simple definition or explanation, then supported by pertinent quotes and statistics from well-known experts and organizations. Color photographs, sidebars, graphs and charts pull the content together in a busy but cohesive presentation. . . . Students . . . will appreciate the quotes and statistics plus commentary that addresses the . . . [issue] from several angles." Libr Media Connect

Includes glossary

Morris, Neil

Do you know where your food comes from? [by] Neil Morris. Heinemann Library 2006 56p il (Making healthy food choices) $32.86; pa $9.49
Grades: 6 7 8 9   363.8
1. Nutrition 2. Food industry
ISBN 978-1-4034-8575-5; 1-4034-8575-5; 978-1-4034-8581-6 pa; 1-4034-8581-X pa

LC 2006003973

This "not only teaches adolescents about how and where food is produced but also about how to make sensible food choices. Also addressed are issues that move beyond personal health (such as the environmental impact of limiting 'food miles,' the distance foods travel from where they are produced to where they are consumed). Straightforward paragraphs are nicely supported by colorful fact boxes and sidebars, covering information as diverse as the world's top producers of milk and the omega-3 content of various fish. An attractive layout and full-color photos enhance the content." Booklist

363.9 Population problems

McLeish, Ewan

Overcrowded world. Gareth Stevens Pub. 2009 48p il map (What if we do nothing?) lib bdg $31
Grades: 5 6 7 8   363.9
1. Overpopulation
ISBN 978-1-4339-0088-4 lib bdg; 1-4339-0088-2 lib bdg

LC 2008029182

"Using intelligent, focused text; an open design; vivid photos; and excellent maps, [this] book demands attention." Booklist

"This book looks at the issue of overpopulation, its causes, and its impact on people and the environment. It also discusses the strategies adopted by different governments to deal with the problem." Publisher's note

Includes bibliographical references

364   Criminology

Somervill, Barbara A.

Graphing crime. Raintree 2010 32p il (Real world data) $28.21; pa $7.99

Grades: 4 5 6 7   **364**

1. Crime 2. Statistics 3. Graphic methods
   ISBN 978-1-4329-2623-6; 1-4329-2623-3; 978-1-4329-2632-8 pa; 1-4329-2632-2 pa

LC 2009001292

This "discusses juvenile offenders, drug money, terrorism, and more, and teaches readers how to evaluate statistics in the various charts, such as the difference between crimes committed and crimes reported, or between total numbers and rate per population. . . . The clear design, with lots of full-color photos and sidebars, will encourage browsers as much as the up-to-date examples and the clear directions for remaining 'chart smart.'" Booklist

Includes glossary and bibliographical references

Townsend, John

Crime through time. Raintree 2006 48p il (Painful history of crime) lib bdg $31.43

Grades: 6 7 8 9   **364**

1. Crime -- History
   ISBN 1-4109-2051-8

This "looks at violations of the law from ancient times to the present, giving insight into criminals, types of crime, and methods of solving it. . . . The subject, format, and presentation of material in [this book] will inform students, including reluctant readers." SLJ

Includes bibliographical references

364.1   Criminal offenses

Blackwood, Gary L.

Gangsters. Benchmark Bks. 2002 72p il (Bad guys) lib bdg $29.93

Grades: 4 5 6   **364.1**

1. Criminals
   ISBN 0-7614-1016-3

LC 00-57154

This profiles Monk Eastman, James Colosimo, Al Capone, Clyde Barrow, John Dillinger, and Alvin Karpis

"Useful for research and pleasure reading. . . . There is an attractive mix of illustrations, photos, maps, and reproductions." Book Rep

Includes glossary and bibliographical references

Fooks, Louie

The **drug** trade; the impact on our lives. [by] Louie Fooks. Raintree 2003 64p il (21st century debates) lib bdg $32.79

Grades: 6 7 8 9   **364.1**

1. Drug traffic 2. Drugs and crime
   ISBN 0-7398-6033-X

LC 2003-3593

This "looks at global drug production and trafficking, types of illegal drugs, who uses them, and possible solutions. The book includes information about drug crops and the economic implications that make it difficult for governments around the world to control their sale and abuse. . . . Color photographs are plentiful and color-keyed boxes include opposing viewpoints, facts, and topics to debate." SLJ

Hanel, Rachael

Identity theft. Marshall Cavendish Benchmark 2011 143p il (Controversy!) lib bdg $25.95

Grades: 8 9 10 11 12   **364.1**

1. Identity theft
   ISBN 978-0-7614-4901-0; 0-7614-4901-9

"Hanel explores types of identity theft, common scams, and prevention, which is a contentious point. Many argue that governmental proposals to secure data are invading people's privacy and civil liberties. . . . With rapid changes in technology and legislation, [this book is] recommended for all libraries seeking quality and current materials on [this topic]." SLJ

Haugen, Brenda

The **Great** Train Robbery; history-making heist. Compass Point Books 2011 96p il (True crime) lib bdg $33.99

Grades: 6 7 8 9   **364.1**

1. Thieves 2. Railroads
   ISBN 978-0-7565-4360-0; 0-7565-4360-6

LC 2010017722

This is an account of the Great Train Robbery of 1963. Its loot was, at that time, the largest amount of cash ever stolen in Britain.

"The chapters are short and will keep students engaged." Libr Media Connect

Includes bibliographical references

Jacobs, Thomas A.

★ **Teen** cyberbullying investigated; where do your rights end and consequences begin? Free Spirit Pub. 2010 195p il pa $15.99

Grades: 7 8 9 10 11 12   **364.1**

1. Bullies 2. Computer crimes
   ISBN 978-1-57542-339-5; 1-57542-339-1

LC 2009-43293

This title deals with the "topic of online teen harassment, by both teens and by adults. The author, a former judge, focuses on recent landmark court cases, many of them still pending, and in an informal, interactive style, each chapter discusses one case in detail, bringing together the rights of the victim as well as those of the perpetrator." Booklist

Includes glossary and bibliographical references

Johnson, Julie

Why do people join gangs? Raintree Steck-Vaughn Pubs. 2001 48p il (Exploring tough issues) lib bdg $29.93

Grades: 6 7 8 9   **364.1**

1. Gangs
   ISBN 0-7398-3236-0

LC 00-51750

This attempts to explain the attraction of gangs with sections on bullying, rites and rituals, gang mentality, and drug and protection rackets

"Concise and well written, this book provides an overview of the problem, focusing on the United States, but discussing other countries as well." SLJ

Includes glossary and bibliographical references

MacNee, Marie J.

Outlaws, mobsters & crooks; from the Old West to the Internet. edited by Jane Hoehner. U.X.L 1998 5v il v1-3 set $225; v4 & v5 ea $83

Grades: 8 9 10 11 12   **364.1**

1. Reference books 2. Criminals -- Dictionaries
ISBN 0-7876-2803-4 v1-3; 0-7876-6482-0 v4; 0-7876-6483-9 v5

      LC 98-14861

Presents the lives of seventy-five North American criminals including the nature of their crimes, their motivations, and information relating to the law officers who challenged them

"Browsers and researchers alike will make good use of this enjoyable reference set due to its fact-filled content and peek into the lives of such a wide variety of outlaws." Voice Youth Advocates

Marcovitz, Hal

Gangs. ABDO Pub. Co. 2010 112p il (Essential issues) lib bdg $22.95

Grades: 7 8 9 10   **364.1**

1. Gangs
ISBN 978-1-60453-954-7; 1-60453-954-2

      LC 2009-29862

The text is "well-written, providing examples that put a human face to each problem. . . . [This] will be of great assistance to students writing reports." SLJ

Includes glossary and bibliographical references

Marsico, Katie

The **Texas** polygamist raid; religious freedom versus child welfare. Marshall Cavendish Benchmark 2011 il (Perspectives on) $39.93

Grades: 8 9 10 11 12   **364.1**

1. Polygamy 2. Child welfare 3. Religious fundamentalism
ISBN 978-1-60870-449-1; 1-60870-449-1

      LC 2010016038

Provides comprehensive information on the Texas polygamist raid and the differing perspectives accompanying it.

This title offers "excellent, thorough, and accurate information for reports or for general reading. . . . [It] contrasts child welfare with the importance of freedom of religion." SLJ

Includes bibliographical references

Miller, Debra A.

Political corruption; by Debra A. Miller. Lucent Books 2007 112p il (Hot topics) $32.45

Grades: 7 8 9 10   **364.1**

1. Political corruption
ISBN 978-1-59018-982-5; 1-59018-982-5

      LC 2007007793

This "offers a historical overview of political misdeeds and current efforts to curb them. Miller knows her [sub-

ject] and offers enough intrigue to hold readers' attention. Sidebars and relevant photos appear throughout." Horn Book Guide

Includes bibliographical references

Olson, Kay Melchisedech

The **D.B.** Cooper hijacking; vanishing act. Compass Point Books 2011 96p il (True crime) lib bdg $33.99

Grades: 6 7 8 9   **364.1**

1. Criminals 2. Missing persons 3. Hijacking of airplanes
ISBN 978-0-7565-4359-4; 0-7565-4359-2

      LC 2010006550

This is an account of the hijacking of a Boeing 727 in November of 1971 by a man known as D.B. Cooper, who was carrying $200,000 and a briefcase he said contained a bomb. No trace of the man has ever been found.

Includes bibliographical references

Schroeder, Andreas

★ **Scams!** ten stories that explore some of the most outrageous swindlers and tricksters of all time. Annick Press 2004 154p (True stories from the edge) $18.95; pa $7.95

Grades: 5 6 7 8   **364.1**

1. Fraud 2. Swindlers and swindling
ISBN 1-55037-853-8; 1-55037-852-X pa

This is a "collection of stories about forgers, con artists, and other individuals who duped the public for fame, money, love, or power. . . . Schroeder's lively narration with undocumented dialogue breathes life into characters whom readers can't help but marvel at for their sheer ingenuity. . . . Schroeder's page-turning stories are suspenseful." SLJ

Includes bibliographical references

Swift, Richard

★ **Gangs**; Richard Swift. Groundwood 2011 144 p. (Groundwork guides)

Grades: 7 8 9 10 11 12   **364.1**

1. Gangs 2. Ethnic groups 3. Urban sociology 4. Crime -- History
ISBN 088899978X pa; 0888999798; 9780888999788 pa; 9780888999795

In this book, "[a] short history, definition, and insight into the romantic idea of gangs as opposed to the actual reality of gang life, provide an overview of the book's focus. The role of poverty, family and home environment, communities and schools is explained. An explanation of the hierarchy that governs their world, code of conduct, gang locations throughout the world, differences in ethnic gangs, and an explanation for institutionalized groups . . . [is provided]. Supplementary information, such as gray pages and sidebars within chapters, provide additional material. A page of unique gang vocabulary and a timeline, complete chapter notes, further reading, viewing, and web lists, and a detailed index complete this . . . book." (Library Media Connection)

"This riveting volume, which is both comprehensive and concise, explores a complex and potentially controversial issue. Swift frames the issue against the gross social inequities that create gangs and discusses the factors that contribute to their existence, such as racism, poverty, drug use and trafficking, lack of jobs, crumbling global economies, etc. . . . Despite its conveniently compact size, the book is packed with information. . . . This interesting and accessible volume is an essential purchase." SLJ

364.15 Offenses against the person

Bascomb, Neal

★ The **Nazi** hunters; How a Team of Spies and Survivors Captured the World's Most Notorious Nazi. Neal Bascomb. Arthur A. Levine Books, an imprint of Scholastic Inc. 2013 256 p. (hardcover : alk. paper) $16.99

Grades: 6 7 8 9 10   **364.15**
1. War crimes 2. War criminals 3. Nazi hunters 4. Nazis -- Biography 5. Secret service -- Israel 6. Holocaust, Jewish (1939-1945) 7. World War, 1939-1945 -- Atrocities 8. War criminals -- Germany -- Biography 9. Fugitives from justice -- Argentina -- Biography
ISBN 0545430992; 9780545430999; 9780545431002; 9780545562393

LC 2012041757
YALSA Award for Excellence in Nonfiction for Young Adults (2014)

In this book, by Neal Bascomb, "Adolf Eichmann was among the Gestapo war criminals who managed to escape from Europe and establish new lives in Argentina. The search for him involved an international group of Nazi hunters who left no stone unturned to determine where and how he had fled, find him and bring him to justice." (Kirkus Reviews)

"This is a splendid example of fascinating storytelling blended with significant historical events." Booklist

Blackwood, Gary L.

Highwaymen. Benchmark Bks. 2002 72p il (Bad guys) lib bdg $29.93

Grades: 4 5 6   **364.15**
1. Thieves
ISBN 0-7614-1017-1

LC 99-86663
Describes the lives and careers of such European and American highwaymen as Claude Duval, Mary Frith, and Joseph Thompson Hare

"Well written and well designed. . . . {This book is} illustrated with reproductions of period artwork, documents, and photographs." Booklist

Includes glossary and bibliographical references

Outlaws. Benchmark Bks. 2002 72p il (Bad guys) lib bdg $29.93

Grades: 4 5 6   **364.15**
1. Thieves 2. West (U.S.) -- History
ISBN 0-7614-1015-5

LC 00-57161
This profiles seven outlaws of the Old West including Joaquin Murieta, Jesse James, John Wesley Hardin, Billy the Kid, Black Bart, Pearl Hart, and Henry Starr

"Vivid photographs, reproductions, and illustrations effectively complement the text. . . . Entertaining and informative reading." SLJ

Includes glossary and bibliographical references

Broyles, Janell

Frequently asked questions about hate crimes; Barbara Dunkell, Janell Broyles. Rosen Pub. 2012 64 p. col. ill. (FAQ: teen life) (library) $31.95

Grades: 7 8 9 10 11 12   **364.15**
1. Hate crimes 2. Discrimination 3. Hate crimes -- United States
ISBN 1448855624; 9781448855629

LC 2011015910
This book, which looks at hate crimes, is part of the FAQ: Teen Life series, which "focuses on a wide variety of timely, high-interest issues for adolescents. . . . Each title provides excellent contextual information about the topic, dispels common myths, and answers key questions concerning each issue. The authors also provide lists of vital questions to ask teachers, guidance counselors, and other specialists." (Voice of Youth Advocates)

Includes bibliographical references and index

Draper, Allison Stark

The **assassination** of Malcolm X. Rosen Pub. Group 2002 64p il (Library of political assassinations) lib bdg $26.50

Grades: 5 6 7 8   **364.15**
1. Black Muslims 2. Black Muslim leaders 3. Civil rights activists 4. African Americans -- Biography
ISBN 0-8239-3542-6

LC 2001-3323
"Draper confronts the important issues with exceptional candor and clarity, including the ongoing controversy of who ordered the murder." Booklist

Includes glossary and bibliographical references

364.152 Homicide

Aretha, David

The **murder** of Emmett Till. Morgan Reynolds Pub. 2007 160p il (The civil rights movement) lib bdg $27.95

Grades: 7 8 9 10 11 12   **364.152**
1. Children 2. Lynching 3. Murder victims 4. Mississippi -- Race relations 5. African Americans -- Civil rights
ISBN 978-1-59935-057-8; 1-59935-057-2

LC 2007-26250
"The heinous murder of Emmett Till galvanized the civil rights movement and raised the nation's awareness of the extreme racism in the South. . . . This title . . . details the events surrounding Till's murder, the trial and acquittal of his killers, and the nation's racial climate before and after this milestone in civil rights history." Booklist

Includes bibliographical references

Crowe, Chris

Getting away with murder: the true story of the Emmett Till case. Phyllis Fogelman Bks. 2003 128p il map $18.99

Grades: 7 8 9 10   **364.152**

1. Racism 2. Children 3. Lynching 4. Trials (Homicide) 5. Murder victims 6. Mississippi -- Race relations

ISBN 0-8037-2804-2

LC 2002-5736

This is the story of "the black 14-year-old from Chicago who was brutally murdered while visiting relatives in the Mississippi Delta in 1954. . . . The gruesome, racially motivated crime and the court's failure to convict the white murderers was a powerful national catalyst for the civil rights movement. . . . Crowe's powerful, terrifying account does justice to its subject in bold, direct telling, supported by numerous archival photos and quotes from those who remember." Booklist

Includes bibliographical references

Faryon, Cynthia J.

Guilty of being weird; the story of Guy Paul Morin. Cynthia J. Faryon. James Lorimer & Co. 2013 144 p. (Lorimer Real Justice) (hardcover) $18.95

Grades: 7 8 9 10 11 12   **364.152**

1. False accusation

ISBN 1459400933; 9781459400931

This book, by Cynthia J. Faryon, is part of the "Lorimer Real Justice" series. "At twenty-four, Guy Paul Morin was considered a bit strange. . . . So when the nine-year-old girl next door went missing, the police were convinced that Morin was responsible. . . . This book tells his story, showing how the justice system not only failed to help an innocent young man, but conspired to convict him." (Publisher's note)

"Structured like a data log, each chapter covers a specific date. . . . Teens interested in CSI can turn a critical eye to badly executed procedures and biased criminal investigation. . . . However, the choppy organization by date and the differences between the Canadian and American legal system will limit the book's appeal." SLJ

Haugen, Brenda

The **Black** Dahlia; shattered dreams. Compass Point Books 2010 96p il (True crime) lib bdg $33.99

Grades: 6 7 8 9   **364.152**

1. Homicide 2. Murder victims

ISBN 978-0-7565-4358-7; 0-7565-4358-4

LC 2010011206

This is an account of the 1947 the murder of aspiring actress Elizabeth Short, who became known as the Black Dahlia.

Includes bibliographical references

★ The **Zodiac** killer; terror and mystery. Compass Point Books 2010 96p il lib bdg $33.99

Grades: 6 7 8 9   **364.152**

1. Homicide 2. Criminal investigation

ISBN 978-0-7565-4357-0 lib bdg; 0-7565-4357-6 lib bdg

LC 2010-11205

"The serial killer who terrorized California in the late 1960s and early 1970s—he called himself Zodiac—is the subject of this heart-stopper of a book. . . . Haugen goes briskly through the details with a curt efficiency well suited for teen readers. . . . Photographs are few, but the reproductions of Zodiac's letters pack a punch, and sidebars . . . add to the overall strong design. Zodiac was never captured, but Haugen's conclusions on his impact are savvy." Booklist

Houser, Aimee

Tragedy in Tucson; the Arizona shooting rampage. by Aimee Houser. ABDO Pub. Co. 2012 112 p. col. ill., col. map (hc) $34.22

Grades: 6 7 8 9 10   **364.152**

1. Gun control 2. Schizophrenia 3. Murder -- Arizona -- Tucson 4. Mental health laws -- United States 5. Firearms and crime -- Arizona -- Tucson 6. Firearms -- Social aspects -- United States

ISBN 1617833126; 9781617833120

LC 2011038452

This book "examines . . . the shooting of Representative Gabrielle Giffords and 18 others in Tucson, Arizona." It "explores the man behind the shooting, Jared Loughner, and his history of mental illness, the disease schizophrenia, Giffords's rise in politics, [and] the political climate in America, including the hot button issue of health-care reform, Giffords's fight for her life, and the effects of this event on society. Also discussed are the gun laws in America." (Publisher's note)

"...These titles are excellent introductions to these important topics, particularly for developing an analytical framework for debate." SLJ

Includes bibliographical references (p. 104-109, 112) and index

Mackay, Jenny

The **Columbine** School shooting. Lucent Books 2010 96p il (Crime scene investigations) lib bdg $32.45

Grades: 7 8 9 10   **364.152**

1. School shootings 2. Columbine High School (Littleton, Colo.)

ISBN 978-1-4205-0138-4; 1-4205-0138-0

LC 2009-36532

Discusses the Columbine High School Massacre in Littleton, Colorado, on April 20, 1999, focusing on the crime itself as well as the tools and techniques used to process the scene. Also features crime stats, facts versus fiction sections, full-color photos and more.

This book is "both interesting and easily readable . . . [and includes] vivid color photography, charts, graphs, sidebar commentaries, highlighted facts (including career information), an annotated bibliography, and an index. . . . [This] should not only be a popular addition to any collection but will also go a long way in setting the record straight regarding who does what within a criminal investigation." Voice Youth Advocates

Includes bibliographical references

Marsico, Katie

The **Columbine** High School massacre; murder in the classroom. Marshall Cavendish Benchmark 2010 128p il (Perspectives on) lib bdg $39.93

Grades: 7 8 9 10   **364.152**

 1. School shootings 2. Columbine High School (Littleton, Colo.)

 ISBN 978-0-7614-4985-0; 0-7614-4985-X

            LC 2009020590

This "is a well-written examination of this violent school shooting and the controversies it inspired. The roles of society and the controversial effect s of violent video games are discussed, as well as the evolution of school security. . . . The title provides a complete and concise examination of the issue at hand, from its occurrence to the impact on society. It also contains a timeline of events and well-chosen illustrations. This is a recommended addition to any school or public library." Voice Youth Advocates

Includes bibliographical references

Robson, David

The **murder** of Emmett Till. Lucent Books 2010 104p il (Crime scene investigations) lib bdg $32.45

Grades: 7 8 9 10   **364.152**

 1. Racism 2. Children 3. Homicide 4. Murder victims 5. African Americans -- Mississippi

 ISBN 978-1-4205-0213-8; 1-4205-0213-1

            LC 2009-33485

"Explores the 1955 landmark case of egregious racial injustice that is largely credited with igniting a nationwide social movement against segregation, bigotry, and hate crime. . . . [This book is] both interesting and easily readable . . . [and includes] vivid color photography, charts, graphs, sidebar commentaries, highlighted facts (including career information), an annotated bibliography, and an index. . . . [This] should not only be a popular addition to any collection but will also go a long way in setting the record straight regarding who does what within a criminal investigation." Voice Youth Advocates

Includes bibliographical references

Uschan, Michael V., 1948-

Lynching and murder in the deep South; [by] Michael V. Uschan. Lucent Books 2007 104p il map (Lucent library of Black history) $32.45

Grades: 8 9 10 11 12   **364.152**

 1. Lynching 2. African Americans -- Civil rights 3. Southern States -- Race relations

 ISBN 1-59018-845-4

            LC 2005037807

"Uschan deals honestly with this important historical topic . . . that occurred from the end of Reconstruction through the 1920s, '30s, and into the '40s and '50s. Writing in clear and telling prose, the author chronicles the horrific history of this practice in the South, why it was so pervasive, and how it was eventually brought to an end. This is a book

that fills a gap. . . . Black-and-white photos and reproductions appear throughout." SLJ

Includes bibliographical references

Worth, Richard

Massacre at Virginia Tech; disaster & survival. [by] Richard Worth. Enslow Publishers 2008 48p il map (Deadly disasters) $23.93

Grades: 4 5 6 7   **364.152**

 1. Students 2. School violence 3. Virginia Tech (Blacksburg, Va.) shootings, 2007 4. Murderers 5. Virginia Polytechnic Institute and State University

 ISBN 978-0-7660-3274-3; 0-7660-3274-4

            LC 2007025592

Examines the tragic school shooting at Virginia Tech University, detailing the horrifying massacre, the lives of the killer and victims, and the sociological problems surrounding school shootings.

"The sequence of events, profiles of pertinent figures, and related topics such as gun control are all discussed. Photographs of the killer, victims, and survivors lend chilling immediacy." Horn Book Guide

Includes glossary and bibliographical references

364.16   Offenses against property

Blackwood, Gary L.

Swindlers. Benchmark Bks. 2002 72p il (Bad guys) lib bdg $29.93

Grades: 4 5 6   **364.16**

 1. Swindlers and swindling

 ISBN 0-7614-1031-7

            LC 00-57153

"Swindlers traces the concept of cheating to the biblical story of Jacob and Esau but focuses on historical personages such as William Henry Ireland, an English forger of Shakespearean plays; Soapy Smith, a con artist of the American West; and Joseph 'Yellow Kid' Weil, a swindler on a grand scale. Well written and well designed. . . . Illustrated with reproductions of period artwork, documents, and photographs." Booklist

Includes glossary and bibliographical references

Guillain, Charlotte

Great art thefts; by Charlotte Guillain. Capstone Raintree 2013 48 p. col. ill. (Treasure hunters) (library) $29.33; (paperback) $8.99

Grades: 5 6 7 8   **364.16**

 1. Theft -- History 2. Art thefts

 ISBN 1410949583; 9781410949516; 9781410949585

            LC 2012012759

This book by Charlotte Guillain, part of the Treasure Hunters series, looks at art thefts. "After . . . introductions that lay foundations so children will understand why thieves might want to steal art or treasure hunters take such risks, each volume contains chapters that follow the discovery and/ or quests for objects such as 'Roman Riches' or locations such as the legendary city of Troy." (School Library Journal)

Includes bibliographical references and index.

Hynson, Colin

Cyber crime; by Colin Hynson. Smart Apple Media 2012 44 p. col. ill. (Inside crime) (library) $35.65

Grades: 7 8 9 10   **364.16**
1. Computer crimes 2. Computer crimes -- Prevention
ISBN 1599203960; 9781599203966
LC 2010043232

This book, part of the Crime and Detection Series, focuses on cyber crime. "These titles examine the diversity of crimes committed around the world. Each . . . illustrated, oversized volume has a photograph or reproduction on every spread, many times taking up a full page." Andrew Grant-Adamson "looks at hackers, viruses, and computer crimes that have come to light in the age of the Internet." (School Library Journal)

Includes bibliographical references (p. 43) and index

Juettner, Bonnie

Blackmail and bribery; by Bonnie Juettner. Lucent Books 2009 104 p. col. ill. (Crime scene investigations) (hardcover) $35.45

Grades: 7 8 9 10   **364.16**
1. Bribery 2. Forensic sciences 3. Extortion 4. White collar crimes
ISBN 1420500686; 9781420500684
LC 2008025864

This book, part of the Crime Scene Investigations series, focuses on blackmail and bribery. This series "unveils the tools and techniques used by today's (and yesterday's) professionals. . . . Each title focuses on a particular type of crime, and includes features like crime stats, facts versus fiction sections, full-color photos and more." (Publisher's note)

Includes bibliographical references (p. 92-95) and index.

364.3   Offenders

Stemple, Heidi E. Y.

Bad girls; sirens, Jezebels, murderesses, thieves, and other female villains. Jane Yolen and Heidi E. Y. Stemple ; illustrated by Rebecca Guay. Charlesbridge 2012 176 p. (reinforced for library use) $18.95

Grades: 6 7 8 9 10 11 12   **364.3**
1. Women criminals 2. Criminals -- Biography 3. Femmes fatales -- Biography 4. Women murderers -- Biography 5. Female offenders -- Biography
ISBN 1580891853; 9781580891851
LC 2012000783

This book, by Jane Yolen and Heidi E. Stemple, illustrated by Rebecca Guay, examines the history of "twenty-six . . . notorious women. Each bad girl has a rotten reputation, but there are two sides to every tale. Decide whether Tituba was really a conspiring witch or just a humble housemaid. Analyze the evidence stacked for and against Lizzie Borden. And what made the brazen Cleopatra so dishonorable . . . or honorable?" (Publisher's note)

Includes bibliographical references and index

364.6   Penology

Gerber, Larry

Torture. Rosen Pub. 2011 64p il (Headlines!) lib bdg $29.95

Grades: 7 8 9 10   **364.6**
1. Torture
ISBN 978-1-4488-1291-2; 1-4488-1291-7
LC 2010018898

This book "looks at the history and modern practice of torture, ending with discussion of Abu Ghraib and Guantanamo. Good organization, clear writing, captioned photos, and sidebars deliver the information cleanly." Horn Book Guide

Includes glossary and bibliographical references

Kerrigan, Michael

The history of punishment; [by] Michael Kerrigan. Mason Crest Publishers 2003 96p il (Crime and detection) $22.95

Grades: 7 8 9 10   **364.6**
1. Punishment
ISBN 1-59084-386-X
LC 2003-488

This covers punishment "from the beginning of time, taking into account secular and religious laws and rules of conduct, and the various means people have employed to punish those who violate the laws, including corporal punishment, imprisonment, capital punishment, and rehabilitation efforts. . . . [This book provides] no-nonsense, straightforward, gritty information, accompanied by good-quality, full-color photos, reproductions, and illustrations." SLJ

Torture; Lauri S. Friedman, book editor. Greenhaven Press 2011 147p il (Introducing issues with opposing viewpoints) $36.75

Grades: 7 8 9 10   **364.6**
1. Torture
ISBN 978-0-7377-5203-8; 0-7377-5203-3
LC 2011005638

This is an "excellent [resource] both for student research and for personal interest. . . . Torture discusses the ethics of state-approved torture, particularly of terrorism suspects, and covers the Geneva Conventions, the death penalty, and whether torture produces good information." Booklist

Includes bibliographical references

Townsend, John

Punishment and pain; [by] John Townsend. Raintree 2006 48p il (Painful history of crime) lib bdg $31.43; pa $8.90

Grades: 6 7 8 9   **364.6**
1. Punishment
ISBN 1-4109-2054-2 lib bdg; 1-4109-2059-3 pa
LC 2005012517

This "shows the painful consequences of crime through torture and death, from the 1500s to the present. . . . The subject, format, and presentation of material in [this book] will inform students, including reluctant readers." SLJ

Includes bibliographical references

364.66   Capital punishment

The **death** penalty: opposing viewpoints; Diane Andrews Henningfeld, book editor; Bonnie Szumski, publisher; Helen Cothran, managing editor. Greenhaven Press 2006 223p il (Opposing viewpoints series) hardcover o.p. pa $23.70

Grades: 8 9 10 11 12   **364.66**

1. Capital punishment

ISBN 0-7377-2929-5; 0-7377-2930-9 pa

LC 2005-52743

"Powerful people and organizations contribute essays to the death-penalty debate. Supreme Court Justice Antonin Scala argues that the death penalty is just, and his former colleague, Sandra Day O'Connor, debates whether juveniles should be exempt from it. This nonbiased, comprehensive look at one of today's most difficult issues will be helpful for students writing persuasive essays and for debate groups." SLJ

Includes bibliographical references

Kuklin, Susan

★ **No** choirboy; murder, violence, and teenagers on death row. Henry Holt and Co. 2008 212p il $17.95

Grades: 8 9 10 11 12   **364.66**

1. Capital punishment 2. Juvenile delinquency

ISBN 978-0-8050-7950-0; 0-8050-7950-5

LC 2007-46940

"The book opens with candid interviews that introduce three inmates, all of them teenagers when they committed their crimes. . . . This eye-opening account will likely open minds. . . . The book concludes with solid back matter—notes, glossary, bibliography, and index." Horn Book

Includes glossary and bibliographical references

365   Penal and related institutions

America's prisons: opposing viewpoints; Noah Berlatsky, book editor. Greenhaven Press 2010 224p il map (Opposing viewpoints series) $39.70; pa $27.50

Grades: 8 9 10 11 12   **365**

1. Prisons -- United States

ISBN 978-0-7377-4956-4; 0-7377-4956-3; 978-0-7377-4957-1 pa; 0-7377-4957-1 pa

LC 2009-50927

"This collection of opposing viewpoints provides students an opportunity to weigh the merits of arguments that support or oppose the operation of America's prisons." Publisher's note

Includes bibliographical references

Edge, Laura Bufano

Locked up; a history of the U.S. prison system, by Laura B. Edge. Twenty-First Century Books 2009 112p il (People's history) lib bdg $31.93

Grades: 6 7 8 9 10   **365**

1. Prisons -- United States

ISBN 978-0-8225-8750-7; 0-8225-8750-5

LC 2008-26883

"Using primary resources, photographs, and solid research, Edge has written a well-organized and engaging history of our prison system. . . . This book can serve as an excellent resource for reports." SLJ

Includes bibliographical references

Lock, Joan

Famous prisons; [by] Joan Lock. Mason Crest Publishers 2003 96p il (Crime and detection) $22.95

Grades: 7 8 9 10   **365**

1. Prisons

ISBN 1-59084-380-0

LC 2003-477

"Lock takes readers on a tour of famous U.S. prisons . . . as well as one in England . . . and another in Ireland. . . She includes a history of each one, and the conditions over time, as well as interesting stories about each prison, and some of its famous inmates. . . . [The book provides] no-nonsense, straightforward, gritty information, accompanied by good-quality, full-color photos, reproductions, and illustrations." SLJ

Includes bibliographical references

Rabiger, Joanna

Daily prison life; [by] Joanna Rabiger. Mason Crest Publishers 2003 96p il (Crime and detection) $22.95

Grades: 7 8 9 10   **365**

1. Prisons 2. Prisoners

ISBN 1-59084-384-3

LC 2003-364

"Rabiger concentrates on the U.S. prison system and gives readers a closeup and grimly realistic view of living in one. . . . [This book provides] no-nonsense, straightforward, gritty information, accompanied by good-quality, full-color photos, reproductions, and illustrations." SLJ

Includes bibliographical references

Townsend, John

Prisons and prisoners; [by] John Townsend. Raintree 2006 48p il (Painful history of crime) lib bdg $31.45; pa $8.90

Grades: 6 7 8 9   **365**

1. Prisons 2. Prisoners

ISBN 1-4109-2053-4 lib bdg; 1-4109-2058-5 pa

LC 2005012516

This "looks at the history of [prisons] and the reforms that have taken place over the years from the days of the medieval castle dungeon to modern Supermax prisons. . . . The subject, format, and presentation of material in [this book] will inform students, including reluctant readers." SLJ

Includes bibliographical references

369.463   Girl Scouts and Girl Guides

Wadsworth, Ginger

★ **First** Girl Scout; Ginger Wadsworth. Clarion Books 2012 xiii, 210p ill. $17.99

Grades: 7 8 9 10 11 12   **369.463**

1. Biography 2. Girl Scouts 3. Philanthropists 4. Scout leaders 5. Girl Scouts of the United States of America

ISBN 978-0-547-24394-8; 0-547-24394-4

LC 2011009642

This book offers a biography of the founder of the Girl Scouts organization. "Juliette (Daisy) Gordon Low [who] was a . . . woman with ideas that were ahead of her time. She witnessed important eras in U.S. history, from the Civil War and Reconstruction to westward expansion to post–World War I. And she made history by founding the first national organization to bring girls from all backgrounds into the out-of-doors. Daisy created controversy by encouraging them to prepare not only for traditional homemaking but also for roles as professional women—in the arts, sciences, and business—and for active citizenship outside the home. Her group also welcomed girls with disabilities at a time when they were usually excluded." (Publisher's note)

"This well-documented biography introduces readers to the founder of the Girl Scouts. . . . Low's personality really comes to life through the details in the narrative. Wadsworth shows readers that this remarkable woman was a skilled leader and hostess in spite of having suffered severe hearing loss that made conversation difficult. . . . The attractive book design features chapter headings that look like Girl Scout badges, and most spreads include period photos or reproductions of primary-source documents. Exemplary nonfiction." SLJ

Includes bibliographical references (p. 201-204) and index.

370.15   Educational psychology

Wilson, David

★ **Strategies** for evaluation; forming judgments about information for classroom, homework, and test success. [by] David Wilson. Rosen Pub. Group 2006 48p il (The library of higher order thinking skills) lib bdg $25.25; pa $11.95

Grades: 5 6 7 8   **370.15**

1. Critical thinking 2. Evaluation

ISBN 1-4042-0473-3 lib bdg; 1-4042-0656-6 pa

LC 2004030620

"In an effort to help students improve their ability to think critically, this slim, colorful volume discusses how to evaluate and form judgments about information so that one can be successful in the classroom, with homework, and on tests. . . . While the information is basic, the book is easy to read for students who need some help learning how to tap into those higher-order thinking skills." SLJ

Includes bibliographical references

370.2   Miscellany

The **Handbook** of private schools; an annual descriptive survey of independent education. 89th ed; Sargent Pubs. 2008 1296p il map $99

Grades: Adult Professional   **370.2**

1. Reference books 2. Private schools -- Directories 3. Education -- United States -- Directories

ISBN 978-0-87558-165-1; 0-87558-165-X

Annual. First published 1915 with title: Handbook of the best private schools of the United States and Canada

"Describes more than 1,700 boarding and day schools, providing information on age and grade ranges, whether co-educational or for boys or girls, enrollment, faculty size and background, academic orientation and curriculum, and where graduates attend college. 'Features classified' section lists institutions offering military programs, elementary boarding divisions, programs for students with learning differences, international and bilingual schools, and schools with more than 500 or fewer than 100 students." Guide to Ref Books. 11th edition

370.71   Education

Growing schools; librarians as professional developers. Debbie Abilock, Kristin Fontichiaro, and Violet H. Harada, editors. Libraries Unlimited 2012 390 p. (pbk.) $45

Grades: Professional   **370.71**

1. Teachers -- Training 2. Educational technology 3. School libraries -- Information technology 4. Libraries and teachers -- United States -- Case studies 5. Teachers -- Training of -- United States -- Case studies 6. Educational technology -- Study and teaching -- Case studies 7. Information technology -- Study and teaching -- Case studies 8. Technological literacy -- Study and teaching -- Case studies 9. Teachers -- In-service training -- United States -- Case studies 10. School librarian participation in curriculum planning -- Case studies 11. Academic libraries -- Relations with faculty and curriculum -- Case studies

ISBN 1610690419; 9781610690416

LC 2012016191

In this book, "editors [Debbie] Abilock, [Kristin] Fontichiaro, and [Violet H.] Harada examine ways school librarians can act as professional developers within their pedagogical communities. Thirty-two articles in sixteen thematic chapters offer real-world examples of how teacher librarians have leveraged their skills and expertise to provide learning experiences for other teachers, community members, and students." (Voice of Youth Advocates)

"This book promotes the role of the school librarian as a leader in school, district, and online professional development in 16 essays written by school librarians, school district personnel, and professors...A rich smorgasbord of ideas, this book would be invaluable for an individual librarian looking to become a professional development leader, and for district librarians to use in planning and implementing meaningful district-wide professional development." (Library Media Connection)

Includes bibliographical references and index

McKeown, Rosalyn

Into the classroom; a practical guide for starting student teaching. Rosalyn McKeown. University of Tennessee Press 2011 xv, 165 p.p (pbk.) $14.95

Grades: Adult Professional **370.71**

1. Teaching 2. Student teaching 3. Student teaching -- United States

ISBN 1572338164; 9781572338166

LC 2011011282

This book offers suggestions to those "just starting out in a secondary school classroom. . . . After exploring the pitfalls of inexperience and providing . . . guidance on maintaining order in the classroom, [Rosalyn] McKeown focuses on teaching skills. She advises readers on writing objectives and lesson plans, creating interesting ways to start and end class, introducing variety into the classroom, lecturing, asking meaningful questions, and using visual aids." (Amazon. com)

Includes bibliographical references and index.

370.973   Schools – United States

Capaccio, George

Schools in Colonial America; George Capaccio. Cavendish Square Publishing 2015 80 p. (library binding) $35.64

Grades: 6 7 8 **370.973**

1. Schools -- United States -- History 2. United States -- History -- 1600-1775, Colonial period 3. Schools -- United States -- History -- Colonial period, ca. 1600-1775

ISBN 1627128948; 9781627128940; 9781627128957

LC 2014003452

This book on schools in Colonial America, by George Cappacio, "describes in rich detail the lives of Native Americans, African Americans, and white settlers, including children, women, and criminals." (School Library Journal)

"Thoroughly researched and expertly executed, this series describes in rich detail the lives of Native Americans, African Americans, and white settlers, including children, women, and criminals. The introductory material that prefaces each title is of particular value, as it demonstrates that the colonists were part of a larger world picture...Content in each title incorporates quotes from period letters and journals as well as a plethora of well-chosen, colorful illustrations. Strong, attractive titles for those looking for more coverage of Colonial America." SLJ

371.1   Schools and their activities

Harada, Violet H.

Inquiry learning through librarian-teacher partnerships; [by] Violet H. Harada and Joan M. Yoshina. Linworth Pub. 2004 172p il pa $39.95

Grades: Adult Professional **371.1**

1. Teaching teams 2. School libraries

ISBN 1-58683-134-8

LC 2004-662

"The authors describe what happens in an inquiry-based classroom and library media center and show teachers/librarians how to develop a curriculum that incorporates essential questions and important habits of mind, all aligned with content standards. . . . The volume contains everything a teacher-librarian team would need to create, teach, research, and assess major interdisciplinary units." SLJ

Includes bibliographical references

Miller, Malinda

Tomorrow's teachers; urban leadership, empowering students & improving lives. Mason Crest Publishers 2011 64p il (New careers for the 21st century: finding your role in the global renewal) lib bdg $22.95

Grades: 7 8 9 10 **371.1**

1. Teaching 2. Vocational guidance 3. Academic achievement

ISBN 978-1-4222-1823-5 lib bdg; 1-4222-1823-6 lib bdg

LC 2010021832

"Chapters identify and emphasize specific careers–important strengths, necessary aptitudes and interests, education and training, projected earnings, closely related occupations, type of work environment, and predictions for the future of the field. . . . Color photos have a small role amid the many statistics, figures, graphs and charts that support and supplement the . . . [text]." SLJ

Includes bibliographical references

371.2   School administration; administration of student academic activities

Odden, Allan R.

Improving student learning when budgets are tight; Allan R. Odden. Corwin 2012 xxi, 184 p.p

Grades: Adult Professional **371.2**

1. Schools -- Finance 2. Academic achievement 3. Schools -- Administration 4. School budgets -- United States 5. School improvement programs -- United States

ISBN 1452217084; 9781452217086

LC 2011045908

This book by Allan R. Odden "offers a comprehensive framework to enhance student achievement in good times and in bad. . . . Odden outlines a school improvement action plan focused sharply on student learning and then shows how to target resources to implement each strategy in that plan. . . . Educators will find a wide range of real-life examples of schools and districts that have implemented these strategies and significantly improved student learning." (Publisher's note)

Includes bibliographical references and index

371.3   Methods of instruction and study

Fox, Janet S.

★ **Get** organized without losing it; by Janet S. Fox; edited by Pamela Espeland. Free Spirit Pub. 2006 105p il (Laugh & learn) pa $8.95

Grades: 5 6 7 8 **371.3**
1. Life skills 2. Study skills 3. Time management
ISBN 978-1-57542-193-3 pa; 1-57542-193-3 pa
LC 2005032809
"In this handbook for students, Fox uses humor to provide practical, easy-to-follow ideas for organizing desks, backpacks, and lockers; managing time for homework and after school activities; planning long-term projects; and taking better notes. . . . Fox writes in a conversational style. . . . Humorous illustrations complement the text." Voice Youth Advocates

Includes bibliographical references

Green, Julie
Write it down. Cherry Lake Pub. 2010 32p il
(Super smart information strategies) lib bdg $27.07
Grades: 3 4 5 6 **371.3**
1. Note-taking
ISBN 978-1-60279-645-4 lib bdg; 1-60279-645-9
lib bdg
LC 2009024741
"The appealing layout includes manageable paragraphs, a variety of engaging illustrations, and examples that clearly guide readers through each topic. . . . Effective note taking and highlighting are the focus of [this book], but the book also suggests using sticky notes and creating diagrams and charts." SLJ

Includes glossary and bibliographical references

Greenberg, Michael
Painless study techniques; illustrations by Michele Earle-Bridges. Barron's Educational Series 2009 234p il pa $9.99
Grades: 6 7 8 9 10 **371.3**
1. Study skills
ISBN 978-0-7641-4059-4 pa; 0-7641-4059-0 pa
LC 2008-42609
"This book provides helpful information on topics such as time management, homework organization, note taking, creating outlines, studying for tests and quizzes, grammar, and writing a research paper. Greenberg breaks down each main topic into smaller, more manageable subtopics, giving examples to help illustrate his ideas. . . . Greenberg's writing style is clear and interesting. . . . A solid resource for most libraries." SLJ

Includes bibliographical references

Johnson, Steve
Digital tools for teaching; 30 e-tools for collaborating, creating, and publishing across the curriculum.
Maupin House Pub. 2011 $23.95
Grades: Adult Professional **371.3**
1. Internet in education 2. Computer-assisted instruction
ISBN 978-1-934338-84-1; 1-934338-84-2
LC 2010037430
"Considering the vast number of e-tools now available, . . . Johnson does an excellent job of sorting through them, listing his top choices, and even including ideas for using them. The book is divided into two parts. Part one provides information on today's tech-driven student, the importance of utilizing new technology, ways to start using the technology, and how to assess student products. Part two describes

the e-tools, giving the following for each: a brief overview, how to get started, ways to use the tool in the classroom, and any other issues that need to be considered. . . . [This] provides a wealth of information in a user-friendly, practical format that would benefit all educators regardless of grade level or content area." Voice Youth Advocates

Includes bibliographical references

November, Alan C.
Empowering students with technology; 2nd ed.;
Corwin Press 2010 115p il pa $25.95
Grades: Adult Professional **371.3**
1. Internet in education 2. Computer-assisted instruction
ISBN 978-1-4129-7425-7; 1-4129-7425-9
LC 2009-43649
First published 2001 by Skylight Professional Development
"Discusses the relationship of technology to today's learning environment and the potential for technology to encourage students to learn collaboratively. This . . . edition emphasizes current topics such as information literacy, global connectivity, and the educational applications of utilities such as digital cameras and cell phones. The book's usefulness is as a reasource for teachers and librarians to consult in creating, planning, and assisting with school projects in all subjects." Libr Media Connect

Includes bibliographical references

Richardson, Will
Blogs, wikis, podcasts, and other powerful Web tools for classrooms; 3rd ed.; Corwin 2010 171p il pa $31.95
Grades: Adult Professional **371.3**
1. Weblogs 2. Podcasting 3. Internet in education 4. Online social networks 5. Wikis (Computer science) 6. Teaching -- Aids and devices
ISBN 978-1-4129-7747-0; 1-4129-7747-9
LC 2009-51376
First published 2006
"The book is well-written and comprehensive. The author's engaging writing style will instill confidence in readers that they will be able to easily integrate the same technologies with the same results in their classrooms. Readers will not want to stop reading this eye-opening and inspirational book. It is jam-packed with proven ideas, and individuals, especially educators, will want to try out these technologies." Libr Media Connect

Includes bibliographical references

Teehan, Kay
Wikis; the educator's power tool. Linworth 2010 78p il pa $30
Grades: Adult Professional **371.3**
1. Internet in education 2. Electronic encyclopedias 3. Wikis (Computer science) 4. Computer-assisted instruction
ISBN 978-1-58683-530-9 pa; 1-58683-530-0 pa; 978-1-58683-531-6 e-book; 1-58683-531-9 e-book
LC 2010020285
"This book breaks down three types of wikis: library wikis, which are usually content and link-to-content focused; reciprocal wikis, which are collaborative in nature; and

student-produced wikis that are developed to share projects and research. . . . There is also a wiki to complement the guidelines in the book. This is a simple to use quick-start guide and a great resource for school technology teachers and librarians." Libr Media Connect

Includes bibliographical references

371.33 Teaching aids, equipment, materials

Baule, Steven M.

Social networking for schools; by Steven M. Baule and Julie E. Lewis. Linworth 2012 220 p. (hardcopy : alk. paper) $45

Grades: Professional   **371.33**
1. Schools 2. Social media 3. Educational technology 4. Students -- Social networks 5. Educational technology -- Social aspects 6. Education -- Effect of technological innovations on

ISBN 1586835378; 9781586835378; 9781586835385
LC 2012014933

This book by Steven M. Baule and Julie E. Lewis "take[s] a comprehensive look at the topic of social media use in schools. Starting with the numerous justifications for integrating social media into schools, it provides real-world examples of how to seamlessly integrate social media within your classroom or library, examines the methodologies for crafting the necessary policies and procedures to ensure that staff members." (Publisher's note)

"This detailed book will help schools incorporate social media tools into communication, curriculum, and professional development...This is an excellent resource that provides a blueprint for utilizing social media to facilitate teaching and learning." (Library Media Connection)

Includes bibliographical references and index

371.5 School discipline and related activities

Beaudoin, Marie-Nathalie

Responding to the culture of bullying and disrespect; new perspectives on collaboration, compassion, and responsibility. [by] Marie-Nathalie Beaudoin, Maureen Taylor. rev 2nd ed.; Corwin Press 2009 281p il $76.95; pa $36.95

Grades: Adult Professional   **371.5**
1. Bullies 2. School discipline
ISBN 978-1-4129-6853-9; 1-4129-6853-4; 978-1-4129-6854-6 pa; 1-4129-6854-2 pa
LC 2008-55933

First published 2004 with title: Breaking the culture of bullying and disrespect

"This profound resource explores the behaviors that cultivate a culture of bullying and disrespect. . . . Concrete solutions to issues are offered, and the authors make sure to load this title with practical suggestions for affecting change. They delve into ways to work directly with young people to better address their concerns. . . . This purchase is essential for any educator, counselor, or parent. It should be a staple of the school library reference collection because the information provided should be used daily. It will be a title that can

be referenced for years to come and will help with adults struggling to overcome bullying." Voice Youth Advocates

Includes glossary and bibliographical references

Bott, C. J.

More bullies in more books. Scarecrow Press 2009 197p il pa $35

Grades: Adult Professional   **371.5**
1. Bullies 2. Reference books 3. Children's literature -- Bibliography 4. Young adult literature -- Bibliography
ISBN 978-0-8108-6654-6 pa; 0-8108-6654-4 pa
LC 2009-923

This "offers more than 350 annotated titles published since 2000 to create awareness of the many types of harassment and bullying. . . . Although the text is written for educators and librarians for use in classroom settings, the information is equally helpful for parents, caregivers, and public librarians." SLJ

Includes bibliographical references

★ **Bully**; an action plan for teachers and parents to combat the bullying crisis. edited by Lee Hirsch and Cynthia Lowen ; with Dina Santorelli. Perseus Books Group 2012 viii, 295 p.p ill. $15.99

Grades: Adult Professional   **371.5**
1. Bullies 2. Bullying 3. Bullying -- Prevention 4. Cyberbullying -- Prevention 5. Bullying in schools -- Prevention
ISBN 1602861846; 1602861854; 9781602861848; 9781602861855
LC 2012289039

"This companion book to the documentary film Bully was edited by filmmaker [Lee]Hirsch and writer/producer [Cynthia] Lowen, with contributing chapters by a number of celebrities, authors, experts, government officials, and educators. Part homage to the film, part resource, the book interweaves the stories of children who have been bullied with practical information and advice for parents and other readers." (Publishers Weekly)

Includes bibliographical references (p. 281-289) and index

Myers, Jill J.

Responding to cyber bullying; an action tool for school leaders. [by] Jill J. Myers, Donna S. McCaw, Leaunda S. Hemphill. Corwin Press 2011 195p pa $33.95

Grades: Adult Professional   **371.5**
1. Bullies 2. Cyberbullying 3. School violence
ISBN 978-1-4129-9484-2; 1-4129-9484-5
LC 2010040679

"The book's introduction addresses the nature of 'digital generation' students. The problem of cyberbullying is introduced in light of the generational reality. The book covers decisions made to resolve real-life situations, practical principles about censorship, and the capacity and limitations of school authority. Included is a matrix that serves as a decision-making tool for administration. This resource is a healthy blend of the theoretical and practical." Libr Media Connect

Includes bibliographical references

371.7   Student welfare

Flath, Camden

Therapy jobs in educational settings; speech, physical, occupational & audiology. Mason Crest Publishers 2010 64p il (New careers for the 21st century: finding your role in the global renewal) lib bdg $22.95; pa $9.95

Grades: 7 8 9 10   **371.7**

1. Speech therapy 2. Physical therapy 3. Vocational guidance 4. Occupational therapy
ISBN 978-1-4222-1826-6 lib bdg; 1-4222-1826-0 lib bdg; 978-1-4222-2047-4 pa; 1-4222-2047-8 pa

LC 2010021727

"Chapters identify and emphasize specific careers—important strengths, necessary aptitudes and interests, education and training, projected earnings, closely related occupations, type of work environment, and predictions for the future of the field. . . . Color photos have a small role amid the many statistics, figures, graphs and charts that support and supplement the . . . [text]." SLJ

Includes bibliographical references

Hester, Joseph P.

★ **Public** school safety; a handbook, with a resource guide. McFarland & Co. 2003 200p pa $35

Grades: Adult Professional   **371.7**

1. School violence 2. Education -- Government policy
ISBN 0-7864-1483-9

LC 2003-2511

This "begins by discussing a number of important government reports that have identified the problems and causes of youth violence and some ideas for combating it. . . . The myriad strategies involving the community, parents, and teachers are discussed and both ineffective and effective programs are evaluated. . . . This is a solid and thorough guide." SLJ

Includes bibliographical references

Lily, Henrietta M.

School violence and conflict resolution; Marilyn E. Smith, Matthew Monteverde, Henrietta M. Lily. Rosen Pub. 2013 48 p.

Grades: 9 10 11 12   **371.7**

1. School violence 2. Conflict management 3. Conflict management -- United States 4. School violence -- United States -- Prevention
ISBN 9781448868919

LC 2012003027

"These newest additions to the Teen Mental Health series tackle topics that are at once timely and timeless in adolescents' lives. Filled with statistics on the recent history of violence in schools, School Violence and Conflict Resolution explains potential warning signs of violent offenders and how schools are combating violence, particularly through peer mediation. All of these easy-to-read books emphasize seeking support from friends, family, and counselors and even suggest "10 Great Questions to Ask a Guidance Counselor." Other features include "Myths and Facts" (such as the myth that only females worry about their bodies and self-image), a glossary, and a list of related organizations.

These titles are good beginning resources for both health reports and personal research." (Booklist)
Includes bibliographical references and index

McPherson, Stephanie Sammartino

Stressed out in school? learning to deal with academic pressure. Enslow Publishers 2009 112p il (Issues in focus today) lib bdg $31.93

Grades: 7 8 9 10   **371.7**

1. Students 2. Stress (Psychology)
ISBN 978-0-7660-3069-5 lib bdg; 0-7660-3069-5 lib bdg

LC 2008-40339

"Examines the stress and academic pressure students of all ages encounter, including early education, homework, standardized tests, college applications, peer pressure, and alternative learning styles." Publisher's note

Includes glossary and bibliographical references

Parks, Peggy J., 1951-

School violence. ReferencePoint Press 2008 104p il map (Compact research. Current issues) $25.95

Grades: 8 9 10 11 12   **371.7**

1. School violence
ISBN 978-1-60152-057-9; 1-60152-057-3

LC 2008-18372

The introduction "looks at the prevalence of [school violence]; causes such as bullying and gangs; the influence of the media, including online sources, on behavior; and the roles of alcohol and drugs, etc. The '. . . at a glance' spread and 'Overview' prepare readers for the more detailed information to come and provide facts about safety issues. Each of four chapters then addresses both sides of a question, followed by four pages of quotes and a section of colorful graphs, charts, and illustrations." SLJ

Includes bibliographical references

Schier, Helga

The **causes** of school violence; by Helga Schier. ABDO Publishing 2008 112 p. ill. (chiefly col.) (library) $34.22

Grades: 7 8 9 10   **371.7**

1. School violence 2. School violence -- United States
ISBN 160453060X; 9781604530605

LC 2007031920

This book is part of the Essential Viewpoints series and looks at the causes of school violence. The series "examines critical debates occurring today, including the legislation that has shaped the issue as well as the numerous sides of each argument. Color photos, detailed maps, and informative sidebars accompany" the text. (Publisher's note)

Includes bibliographical references (p. 102-103) and index.

Simons, Rae

Students in danger; survivors of school violence. Mason Crest Publishers 2009 128p il (Survivors: ordinary people, extraordinary circumstances) lib bdg $24.95

Grades: 7 8 9 10 **371.7**

1. Bullies 2. School violence 3. School shootings
ISBN 978-1-4222-0455-9 lib bdg; 1-4222-0455-3
lib bdg

LC 2008-50333

"This book is dedicated to explaining the psychology of
school violence through real-life examples and stories. . . .
It also discusses bullying as another, and often overlooked,
form of school violence. . . . [This book features] important, and sometimes complex information in an easy-to-read
format, offering high gloss photographs, marginal glossary
notes, concept definitions, a bibliography, and further reading recommendations." Voice Youth Advocates

Includes glossary and bibliographical references

Student drug testing; Patty Jo Sawvel, book editor.
Greenhaven Press 2007 136p il (Issues that concern you) lib bdg $33.70

Grades: 7 8 9 10 11 12 **371.7**

1. Drug testing 2. Youth -- Drug use 3. Students --
Civil rights
ISBN 0-7377-2424-2 lib bdg; 978-0-7377-2424-0
lib bdg

LC 2006043352

"This title compiles articles and essays that take opposing viewpoints on the issues of teen drug testing. A range of
opinions is introduced, from students and educators to journalists, government officials, and experts specializing in this
topic. . . . Color illustrations are attractive and effective in
emphasizing points, and cartoons add humor and interest. . .
. A well-rounded presentation." SLJ

Includes bibliographical references

371.8   Students

Tym, Kate

School survival; a guide to taking control of your
life. [by] Kate Tym and Penny Worms. Raintree
2005 48p il (Get real) $29.93

Grades: 7 8 9 10 **371.8**

1. Schools 2. Peer pressure 3. Socialization
ISBN 1-4109-0577-2

LC 2004-8070

"Chapters consist of a spread presenting an overview of
a topic such as . . . peer pressure, followed by three case
studies about teens dealing with the problem. On the same
page, three 'experts' . . . offer advice. . . . The advice of
professionals lends credibility to the information presented.
. . . [This volume is] sure to appeal to readers looking for
advice." SLJ

371.82   Specific groups of students; schools for
specific groups of students

Cahill, Sean

LGBT youth in America's schools; Jason Cianciotto and Sean Cahill. The University of Michigan
Press 2012 236 p. (pbk. : alk. paper) $30

Grades: Adult Professional **371.82**

1. Bullies 2. Gay youth 3. Discrimination 4. Schools
-- Administration 5. Gay students -- United States 6.
Sexual minorities -- Education 7. Lesbian students
-- United States 8. Bisexual students -- United States
9. Homosexuality and education -- United States 10.
Transgender youth -- Education -- United States
ISBN 0472031406; 9780472028320; 9780472031405;
9780472118229

LC 2011045478

In this book, "[Jason] Cianciotto and [Sean] Cahill use
statistics and real-life anecdotes to show the pervasiveness of gender- and sexual orientation-based harassment in
American schools, and argue for institutional reform and
policy changes. . . . [R]esearch shows that . . . more young
people are coming out . . . while still technically a minor, and
thus subject to the rules of their educational institutions, and
increasingly the abuse of their peers, teachers, and school
administrators." (Publishers Weekly)

Includes bibliographical references and index.

Finkelstein, Norman H.

Schools of hope; the Rosenwald Schools of the
American South. Norman H. Finkelstein. Calkins
Creek 2014 80 p. illustrations $16.95

Grades: 5 6 7 8 **371.82**

1. African Americans -- History 2. African Americans
-- Education
ISBN 1590788419; 9781590788417

LC 2013951346

"When Booker T. Washington, the famed African American educator, asked Julius Rosenwald, the wealthy president
of Sears, Roebuck and Company and noted philanthropist, to
help him build well-designed and fully equipped schools for
black children, the face of education in the South changed
for the better. . . . In this inspiring story, noted nonfiction
writer Norman H. Finkelstein spotlights one man's legacy
and the power of community action." (Publisher's note)

"This straightforward narrative is substantially supported with many photographs of the period, especially of
the schools and the students. Source notes, a bibliography
(which could have used a few more titles for the target readership), a list of websites, an index and picture credits add to
its authenticity. Clean layout and design augment a quality
introduction to an important chapter in the history of American education." -Kirkus

Mortenson, Greg

Three cups of tea; one man's mission to promote
peace--one school at a time. [by] Greg Mortenson
and David Oliver Relin; adapted for young readers
by Sarah Thomson. Dial Books for Young Readers
2009 209p il $16.99; pa $8.99

Grades: 4 5 6 7 **371.82**

1. Humanitarian intervention 2. Schools -- Pakistan 3.
Schools -- Afghanistan
ISBN 978-0-8037-3392-3; 0-8037-3392-5; 978-0-14-
241412-5 pa; 0-14-241412-3 pa

Based on Three cups of tea: one man's mission to fight
terrorism and build nations one school at a time, published
2006 by Viking for adults

"In 1993, while climbing one of the world's most difficult peaks, Mortenson became lost and ill, and eventually
found aid in the tiny Pakistani village of Korphe. He vowed
to repay his generous hosts by building a school; his efforts
have grown into the Central Asia Institute. . . . Retold for
middle readers, the story remains inspirational and compelling. . . . Illustrated throughout with b&w photos, it also
contains two eight-page insets of color photos." Publ Wkly

371.9   Special education

Brinkerhoff, Shirley

   Why can't I learn like everyone else? youth with
learning disabilities. by Shirley Brinkerhoff. Mason
Crest Publishers 2004 127p il (Youth with special
needs) $24.95; pa $14.95
Grades: 5 6 7 8   **371.9**
   1. Learning disabilities
   ISBN 1-59084-730-X; 1-42220-432-0 pa
                                                            LC 2003-18438
"Charlie Begay, an eighth-grade Navajo student in New
Mexico who cannot read due to dyslexia, describes his personal journey of embarrassment, frustration, and low self-
esteem. Following the fictional narrative is factual material
about learning disabilities, covering terminology, possible
signs, diagnosis, the law, coping strategies, and success
stories." SLJ
   Includes bibliographical references

Kent, Deborah

   Athletes with disabilities. Watts 2003 63p il
(Watts library) hardcover o.p. lib bdg $24
Grades: 4 5 6 7   **371.9**
   1. Sports for people with disabilities
   ISBN 0-531-12019-8 lib bdg; 0-531-16664-3 pa
                                                            LC 2002-8883
Explores the people and events involved in sports com-
petitions for people with disabilities and discusses people
with disabilities who play professional sports
   "Information is effectively conveyed through clear,
straightforward prose and accounts of individual athletes.
. . . [This is] informative, often inspirational and thought-
provoking." Booklist
   Includes bibliographical references

Paquette, Penny Hutchins

   ★ **Learning** disabilities; the ultimate teen guide.
[by] Penny Hutchins Paquette, Cheryl Gerson Tuttle.
Scarecrow Press 2003 301p il (It happened to me)
lib bdg $32.50; pa $17.95
Grades: 7 8 9 10   **371.9**
   1. Learning disabilities
   ISBN 0-8108-4261-0 lib bdg; 0-8108-5643-3 pa
                                                            LC 2002-17588
"Far more detailed than similiar books from other publishers." Voice Youth Advocates
   This provides an "overview of the most common disabilities. . . . The book also teaches students how to advocate
for themselves, informing them of their rights under law
both during the school years and after high school gradua-

tion. . . . Assistive technology that can help students improve
their learning abilities such as Optical Character Recognition (OCR) systems, screen reading software, books on tape,
electronic notebooks, and other tools that aid student learning are covered." Publisher's note
   Includes bibliographical references

Parks, Peggy J., 1951-

   Learning disabilities. ReferencePoint Press
2009 96p il (Compact research. Diseases and disorders) lib bdg $25.95
Grades: 7 8 9 10   **371.9**
   1. Learning disabilities
   ISBN 978-1-60152-077-7; 1-60152-077-8
                                                            LC 2009-13445
"Parks explains what learning disabilities are and discusses the causes and overcoming them. The book's strength
is that it explains how learning disabilities differ from other
types of disorders. . . . Teens will find the overall organization of [this] succinct and easy-to-read [book] useful and
attractive." SLJ
   Includes bibliographical references

Stanley, Jerry

   Children of the Dust Bowl; the true story of the
school at Weedpatch Camp. Crown 1992 85p il map
hardcover o.p. pa $9.95
Grades: 5 6 7 8   **371.9**
   1. Migrant labor 2. Great Depression, 1929-1939 3.
   Education -- Social aspects
   ISBN 0-517-88094-6; 0-517-58782-3 pa
                                                            LC 92-393
Describes the plight of the migrant workers who traveled
from the Dust Bowl to California during the Depression and
were forced to live in a federal labor camp and discusses the
school that was built for their children
   "Stanley's text is a compelling document. . . . The story
is inspiring and disturbing, and Stanley has recorded the details with passion and dignity." Booklist
   Includes bibliographical references

371.91   Students with physical disabilities

Hauser, Peter C.

   ★ **How** deaf children learn; what parents and
teachers need to know. Marc Marschark Peter C.
Hauser. Oxford University Press 2012 156 p. $26.50
Grades: Adult Professional   **371.91**
   1. Teaching 2. Deaf children 3. Elementary education
   4. Deaf -- Education 5. Deaf -- Means of communication
   ISBN 0195389751; 9780195389753
                                                            LC 2011012553
This book is "about teaching deaf children. Written primarily for parents and teachers of deaf or hard-of-hearing
children, this work covers general information about their
education, gives insights into their cognitive development,
and provides steps to their school success. The authors also
discuss issues such as the value of cochlear implants and the
debate over signing vs. speaking." (Library Journal)
   Includes bibliographical references.

371.95 Gifted students

Karnes, Frances A.

★ **Competitions** for talented kids; win scholarships, big prize money, and recognition. [by] Frances A. Karnes & Tracy L. Riley. Prufrock Press 2005 245p pa $17.95

Grades: 7 8 9 10 11 12 **371.95**

1. Contests 2. Gifted children

ISBN 1-59363-156-1

"Featuring more than 140 competitions focused on a wide range of academic subjects, studio arts, performing arts, leadership, and service learning, this volume encourages students to seek scholarships, prize money, and recognition for their talents." Booklist

Includes bibliographical references

372 Specific levels of education

Brooks-Young, Susan

Teaching with the tools kids really use; learning with Web and mobile technologies. Corwin 2010 137p pa $26.95

Grades: Adult Professional **372**

1. Web 2.0 2. Teachers -- Training

ISBN 978-1-4129-7275-8 pa; 1-4129-7275-2 pa

LC 2009-43856

"In this book, we see how technology can be used, but we also see the reponsibility of the educator to make sure it is done appropriately, so 21st-century skills are addressed. The author addresses technologies and applications, and also discusses their ethical uses and how to think ahead to make adjustments for the future. . . . This book will be incredibly useful for those who are unsure about Web 2.0 tools, want to explore their possibilities, and would like to educate themselves further about usage in their own schools." Libr Media Connect

Includes bibliographical references

Gates, Pamela

Cultural Journeys; Multicultural Literature for Elementary and Middle School Students. Rowman & Littlefield Pub Inc 2010 258 p. (paperback) $29.95

Grades: Adult Professional **372**

1. Best books 2. Multicultural literature

ISBN 144220687X; 9781442206878

This book looks at multicultural literature for elementary and middle school students. The first chapter asks "the question of 'why.' Why use multicultural literature? . . . The 'why' is further developed as the chapter continues with a definition of multicultural literature." The seventh chapter looks at "works that challenge stereotypes and go beyond the common one-dimensional diversity theme." (Alberta Journal of Educational Research)

Lukenbill, W. Bernard

Health information in a changing world; practical approaches for teachers, schools, and school librarians. [by] W. Bernard Lukenbill and Barbara Froling Immroth. Libraries Unlimited 2010 244p il $45

Grades: Adult Professional **372**

1. Health education 2. Youth -- Health and hygiene 3. Health -- Information services

ISBN 978-1-59884-398-9; 1-59884-398-2

LC 2010-7505

"This is quite an impressive book and a real treasure for any professional involved with health education, whether for the classroom, public health, or personal counseling." Voice Youth Advocates

"In promoting a holistic approach to teaching, Lukenbill and Immroth assert that health information need not be limited to physical-education classes or specific classroom units. Rather, it can be integrated throughout the curriculum, and school librarians are in the unique position to facilitate and advocate for this change. What follows are suggestions for developing health-information literacy throughout the standard subjects, guides for planning health fairs and other outreach activities, and an overview of search strategies for educators to impart to students." SLJ

Includes bibliographical references

Mackey, Bonnie

A **librarian's** guide to cultivating an elementary school garden; [by] Bonnie Mackey and Jennifer Mackey Stewart. Linworth Pub. 2009 124p il pa $39.95

Grades: Adult Professional **372**

1. Gardening 2. School libraries -- Activity projects

ISBN 978-1-58683-328-2 pa; 1-58683-328-6 pa

LC 2008-34963

"Its unusual topic makes this book a standout." Libr Media Connect

"In this comprehensive guide to designing and implementing a school garden, Mackay and Stewart offer practical advice on acquiring funding sources and developing community partnerships, as well as specific instructions for developing various types of gardens: vegetable, butterfly, natural habitat, etc. A wide variety of activities is included, each one linked to the National Science Standards. Annotated book lists and webliographies of appropriate material for both students and faculty are presented throughout." SLJ

Includes bibliographical references

Mary Elizabeth

Painless spelling; Mary Elizabeth. 3rd edition Barrons Educational Series, Inc. 2011 284 p. ill. pbk $9.99

Grades: 7 8 9 10 **372**

1. Spelling 2. English language -- Spelling

ISBN 0764147137; 9780764147135

LC 2010941464

First published 1998

Provides guidelines for spelling American English words; explains visual and sound patterns, letter combinations, syllables, compound words, and hyphenation; and includes practical exercises.

372.4   Reading

Bernadowski, Carianne

Research -based reading strategies in the library for adolescent learners; [by] Carianne Bernadowski and Patricia Liotta Kolencik. Libraries Unlimited 2010 108p il pa $40

Grades: Adult Professional   **372.4**
1. Reading 2. School libraries
ISBN 978-1-58683-347-3; 1-58683-347-2
LC 2009-21198

"This book explains six proven strategies—question/answer, think-alouds, reciprocal teaching, anticipation guides, questioning the author, and SQR3 (survey, question, read, recite, and review)—for reading comprehension and three strategies (Semantic Feature Analysis, word maps/journals, and Frayer Models/word sorts) for vocabulary building. . . . Although the strategies are standard approaches, weaving in librarian roles makes this book useful for librarians who serve teens." Booklist

Includes bibliographical references

Teaching literacy skills to adolescents using Coretta Scott King Award winners. Libraries Unlimited 2009 136p il pa $35

Grades: Adult Professional   **372.4**
1. Coretta Scott King Award 2. African Americans in literature 3. Teenagers -- Books and reading
ISBN 978-1-58683-337-4; 1-58683-337-5
LC 2009-15279

"The book includes award-winning book selections and Coretta Scott King Honor Books. It is a showcase for African-American authors' works, and helps educators working with adolescent students and their reading needs. . . . Each chapter covers one title and contains an annotation, grade level discussion starters, writing prompts, pre-reading activities, literary strategies for reading, post-reading activities, additional information about the author, and additional resources. This book would be a great professional resource, and a must have for those educators that teach adolescents." Libr Media Connect

Includes bibliographical references

Grover, Sharon

Listening to learn; audiobooks supporting literacy. by Sharon Grover and Lizette D. Hannegan. American Library Association 2011 xi, 188 p.p (alk. paper) $45

Grades: Adult Professional   **372.4**
1. Literacy 2. Audiobooks 3. Educational technology 4. Reading -- United States 5. Children -- Books and reading 6. Libraries -- Special collections -- Audiobooks 7. Literacy -- Study and teaching -- United States 8. School librarian participation in curriculum planning
ISBN 0838911072; 9780838911075
LC 2011041814

Authors Sharon Grover and Lizette D. Hannegan "make the case that audiobooks not only present excellent opportunities to engage the attention of young people but also advance literacy. 'Listening to Learn' connects audiobooks with K-12 curricula and demonstrates how the format can support national learning standards and literacy skills." (Publisher's note)

"This informative resource establishes the literacy benefits of audiobooks as an alternate reading delivery method... Discussions of audiobook formats and recommended sources for building an audiobook collection are also included. The authors provide a collaborative resource that would benefit a classroom, library, or home setting." (Library Media Connection)

Includes bibliographical references (p. 175-178) and index

Moreillon, Judi

Collaborative strategies for teaching reading comprehension; maximizing your impact. [by] Judi Moreillon. American Library Association 2007 170p il $38

Grades: Adult Professional   **372.4**
1. Reading comprehension
ISBN 978-0-8389-0929-4; 0-8389-0929-9
LC 2006036132

This "begins by emphasizing the importance of collaboration between classroom teachers and teacher-librarians. . . . The bulk of the book focuses on seven reading comprehension strategies and how to teach them. . . . Overall this book is a cut above other 'how-to' books with its plethora of suggestions and resources for teachers and librarians." Voice Youth Advocates

Includes glossary and bibliographical references

372.6   Language arts (Communication skills)

Cavanaugh, Terence W.

Bookmapping; lit trips and beyond. [by] Terence W. Cavanaugh, Jerome Burg. International Society for Technology in Education 2011 228p il pa $34.95

Grades: Adult Professional   **372.6**
1. Audiovisual education 2. Literature -- Study and teaching 3. Maps -- Study and teaching -- Activities and projects
ISBN 978-1-56484-283-1; 1-56484-283-5
LC 2010051664

This book "provides ideas on how teachers can use elements from different disciplines in their own classrooms. . . . Other information includes using Google Earth, sources for images, Bing maps, information on creating your own bookmaps, instruction for bookmaps done individually and in cooperation with another teacher's class or classes, how to set up mapping in the classroom, and exploring existing bookmaps available on the Web. . . . This book should be in the professional collection of every middle and high school library, preferably in every classroom." Voice Youth Advocates

Includes bibliographical references

Chatton, Barbara

Using poetry across the curriculum; learning to love language. 2nd ed; Libraries Unlimited 2010 241p pa $40

Grades: Adult Professional **372.6**
1. Poetry -- Study and teaching
ISBN 978-1-59158-697-5; 1-59158-697-6
LC 2009-36711
First published 1993

"With the emphasis in most schools on improving literacy, fluency, and reading and writing test scores, this book is extremely valuable. Sections are divided into various curricula areas. Each section begins with the national standards for that discipline, then a few paragraphs explain how the poetry in the extensive listing can be used. . . . Because all teachers must incorporate writing into their teaching, having relevant poetry for their curriculum and ideas on how to use it, will make this book popular." Libr Media Connect

Includes bibliographical references

Hamilton, Martha

Children tell stories; teaching and using storytelling in the classroom. [by] Martha Hamilton and Mitch Weiss. 2nd ed.; Richard C. Owen Publishers 2005 xx, 264p il pa $29.95

Grades: Adult Professional **372.6**
1. Storytelling
ISBN 978-1-57274-663-3 pa; 1-57274-663-7 pa
LC 2005021667
First published 1990

"Combining enthusiasm and inspiration with practical tips, handouts, and resources, Hamilton and Weiss offer a comprehensive second edition that will be useful to both novice and experienced tellers. . . . The accompanying high-quality DVD shows children and adults telling stories, gives Web links, and includes 25 stories to download and print." SLJ

Includes bibliographical references

Hopkins, Lee Bennett

★ **Pass** the poetry, please! 3rd ed; HarperCollins Pubs. 1998 277p $25; pa $5.99

Grades: Adult Professional **372.6**
1. Poetry -- Study and teaching
ISBN 0-06-027746-7; 0-06-446199-8 pa
LC 98-19617
First published 1972

"This a must-purchase." SLJ

"Written for teachers and librarians seeking ways of getting poetry into the lives of children. . . . Throughout, many poets are cited, from Langston Hughes to Nikki Giovanni and from Jack Prelutsky to Robert Frost." Booklist

Includes bibliographical references

Hostmeyer, Phyllis

Storytelling and QAR strategies; [by] Phyllis Hostmeyer and Marilyn Adele Kinsella. Libraries Unlimited 2010 123p pa $30

Grades: Adult Professional **372.6**
1. Storytelling
ISBN 978-1-59884-494-8 pa; 1-59884-494-6 pa; 978-1-59884-495-5 e-book
LC 2010036576

"The authors, both storytellers with backgrounds in education and library work, present 18 stories based on six aspects of character development. These selections, which include folktales, fables, and myths, are just right for youngsters in third through eighth grades. Each one is followed by telling tips, a story path, and questions using the QAR (Question-Answer Relationships) model." SLJ

Includes bibliographical references

Literacy development in the storytelling classroom; Sherry Norfolk, Jane Stenson, and Diane Williams, editors. Libraries Unlimited 2009 342p il $40

Grades: Adult Professional **372.6**
1. Storytelling 2. Language arts
ISBN 978-1-59158-694-4; 1-59158-694-1
LC 2009-11550

"This excellent essay collection connects storytelling to music, poetry, art, social studies, math, science, and physical education and provides sample stories and hands-on lesson plans for preschool through middle school-plus classrooms. Opening articles use research and anecdotal experience to tell why a multiple sensory activity like storytelling trumps teach-to-the-test exercises. Chapters two through five present the 'how-to' and for each lesson, include the appropriate national standards met, objectives, materials, instructional plans, some adaptations, assessments, and bibliography. The extensive suggested resource section includes book, nonbook, professional, and student materials. . . . It is a fascinating collection with useful, creative surprises for classrooms and library programs." Voice Youth Advocates

Includes bibliographical references

Miller, Donalyn

★ The **book** whisperer; awakening the inner reader in every child. [by] Donalyn Miller; foreword by Jeff Anderson. Jossey-Bass 2009 227p

Grades: Adult Professional **372.6**
1. Books and reading
ISBN 0-4703-7227-3; 978-0-4703-7227-2
LC 2008055666

Donalyn Miller's approach to reading promotion "is simple yet provocative: affirm the reader in every student, allow students to choose their own books, carve out extra reading time, model authentic reading behaviors, discard time-worn reading assignments such as book reports and comprehension worksheets, and develop a classroom library filled with high-interest books. . . . Miller provides many tips for teachers and parents and includes a useful list of ultimate reading suggestions picked by her students. This outstanding contribution to the literature is highly recommended." Libr J

Includes bibliographical references

Monnin, Katie

Teaching graphic novels; practical strategies for the secondary ELA classroom. Maupin House Pub. 2010 xx, 236p il pa $24.95

Grades: Adult Professional **372.6**
1. Literacy 2. Graphic novels -- Study and teaching 3. English language -- Study and teaching
ISBN 978-1-934338-40-7 pa; 1-934338-40-0 pa
LC 2009040723

"Responding to the growth of all forms of graphic novels and nonfiction, Monnin advocates using the material that students willingly read to improve literacy, not just in reading classrooms but also as part of the English/Language Arts curriculum. . . . The examples and book titles will be a help to teachers unfamiliar with graphic novels and suggestions for comparison units using a graphic novel with a traditional novel will support those more at ease with conventional selections. The appendixes alone are worth the cost of the book. This should be in the professional collections of all secondary school libraries." SLJ

Includes bibliographical references

Roth, Rita

The **story** road to literacy; [by] Rita Roth. Teacher Ideas Press 2006 176p il pa $30

Grades: Adult Professional   **372.6**

1. Language arts 2. Children of immigrants 3. English language -- Study and teaching

ISBN 1-59158-323-3

LC 2005030835

"Roth advances the idea that using traditional literature with students who are learning English will help them acquire critical communication skills while tying unfamiliar new places to familiar elements of their own heritages. The author provides practical, ready-to-use lesson plans, story samples, and suggested activities." SLJ

Includes bibliographical references

372.62   Written and spoken expression

★ **Breakfast** on Mars and 37 Other delectable Essays; Edited by Rebecca Stern and Brad Wolfe. Roaring Brook Press 2013 xii, 211p.p ill. (hardcover) $16.99

Grades: 6 7 8 9 10 11 12   **372.62**

1. American essays 2. Authorship -- Handbooks, manuals, etc. 3. Essay -- Authorship 4. English language -- Composition and exercises -- Study and teaching (Elementary) 5. English language -- Composition and exercises -- Study and teaching (Middle school)

ISBN 1596437375; 9781596437371

LC 2012040918

This book, edited by Rebecca Stern and Brad Wolfe, is a collection of essays meant for middle- and high-school students. "Thirty-eight short essays . . . come from Sloane Crosley, Sarah Prineas, Ned Vizzini, Scott Westerfeld, Rita Williams-Garcia, and more. Assigned a genre . . . and topic . . . ., the contributors [wrote essays meant to] inspire and entertain." (Publishers Weekly)

"This handy volume fills a gap. Thirty-eight essays for young readers by contemporary writers demonstrate that "essays can be just as enjoyable to read as fiction"...An important collection that ought to become a staple in writing classes." Kirkus

Ellis, Sarah

From reader to writer; teaching writing through classic children's books. Douglas & McIntyre 2000 176p hardcover o.p. pa $14.95

Grades: Adult Professional   **372.62**

1. Poets 2. Artists 3. Authors 4. Novelists 5. Dramatists 6. Librarians 7. Theologians 8. Illustrators 9. Mathematicians 10. Editors 11. Essayists

12. Linguists 13. Satirists 14. Biographers 15. Philologists 16. Travel writers 17. Fantasy writers 18. Literary critics 19. Children's authors 20. Nonfiction writers 21. Writers on science 22. Short story writers 23. Young adult authors 24. Science fiction writers 25. Rhetoric -- Study and teaching 26. Children's literature -- Study and teaching

ISBN 0-88899-372-2; 0-88899-440-0 pa

The author discusses the work of seventeen British, Canadian and American authors of children's literature. "With each classic book, there's a 'sneak preview' (i.e., booktalk), a suggested read-aloud, exercises to help students and adult writers find their own stories, and a short annotated bibliography of related children's books." Booklist

372.63   Spelling and handwriting

Cunha, Stephen F.

How to ace the National Geographic Bee; official study guide. by Stephen F. Cunha. 4th ed. National Geographic 2012 127 p. ill., maps (library) $18.90; (paperback) $9.95

Grades: 4 5 6 7 8   **372.63**

1. Maps 2. Geography 3. Examinations -- Study guides 4. Contests 5. Geography -- Competitions 6. School contests -- United States

ISBN 1426309856; 1426309864; 9781426309854; 9781426309861

LC 2012419185

This book "is a study guide to prepare the reader for test questions in geographic trivia. . . . The book then separates into six distinct chapters. It begins with defining geography and giving the reader an overall understanding of how the bee is conducted. Chapter 3 . . . defines the various types of maps and how they should be interpreted and also explains map features and landforms." (Voice of Youth Advocates)

Includes bibliographical references (p. 109-117).

372.64   Literature appreciation

Pellowski, Anne

The **storytelling** handbook; a young people's collection of unusual tales and helpful hints on how to tell them. illustrated by Martha Stoberock. Simon & Schuster Bks. for Young Readers 1995 129p il hardcover o.p. pa $7.99

Grades: Adult Professional   **372.64**

1. Storytelling

ISBN 0-689-80311-7; 978-1-4169-7598-4 pa; 1-4169-7598-5 pa

LC 95-2991

This work "addresses the young person who wants to tell stories in a public setting. It is similar in format to many adult books on storytelling how-tos, with sections on getting started and selecting and preparing stories, as well as a selection of sample tales. Pellowski's notes are extensive and will be very useful to novices looking for ways to research stories." Booklist

Includes bibliographical references

373 Secondary education

Somerlott, Robert

The **Little** Rock school desegregation crisis in American history. Enslow Pubs. 2001 128p il (In American history) lib bdg $26.60

Grades: 7 8 9 10   **373**

1. School integration 2. Segregation in education 3. Arkansas -- Race relations 4. African Americans -- Education 5. Central High School (Little Rock, Ark.)

ISBN 0-7660-1298-0

LC 00-11444

This book discusses the desegregation of Central High School in Little Rock Arkansas in 1957

This is a "well-researched and well-documented account. . . . Somerlott clearly captures the courage of the students and their families in the face of violent threats. He also presents a broader view of the impact of this event on the city of Little Rock, the state of Arkansas, and the nation." SLJ

Includes bibliographical references

373.1 Organization and activities in secondary education

Barron's SSAT/ISEE; Secondary School Admission Test/Independent School Entrance Exam. 3rd edition Barron's Educational Series, Inc. 2013 494 p. $16.99

Grades: 6 7 8 9   **373.1**

1. High schools -- Entrance requirements

ISBN 9781438002255

"This updated manual prepares students to pass either the Secondary School Admissions Test (SSAT) or the Independent School Entrance Exam (ISEE), nationally administered tests used as admission requirements by many private secondary schools. Students can improve their test-taking skills by taking the book's two practice SSAT exams or its two practice ISEE exams. All test questions are answered and explained. The book also includes extensive practice and review exercises." (Publisher's note)

Braun, Linda W.

★ **Teens,** technology, and literacy; or, Why bad grammar isn't always bad. Libraries Unlimited 2007 105p il pa $30

Grades: Adult Professional   **373.1**

1. Literacy 2. Information technology 3. Bibliographic instruction 4. Computer-assisted instruction 5. Teenagers -- Books and reading

ISBN 1-59158-368-3; 978-1-59158-368-4

LC 2006-31714

"Braun shows teachers, administrators, and librarians how to incorporate today's technologies into the development of literacy skills. The author backs up the grammar used in IMs and text messaging by explaining how these technologies promote better literacy in the classroom. . . . This book is a must for most collections." SLJ

Includes bibliographical references

Erlbach, Arlene

The **middle** school survival guide; illustrations by Helen Flook. Walker & Co. 2003 150p il pa $8.95

Grades: 5 6 7 8   **373.1**

1. Teenagers 2. Life skills 3. Middle schools

ISBN 0-8027-8852-1

LC 2002-34784

A guidebook to help deal with changes in school, families, social lives, and bodies that come during the middle school years, with specific advice for a variety of situations

"Erlbach's advice is sound, but the real gems are the quotes from kids. There are some explicit content and frank discussion, with Erlbach using the same no-nonsense language whether covering drugs, sexual harassment, crushes, cheating, oral sex, or pregnancy. . . . Strong, and well-delivered, often necessary medicine." Booklist

Gagliardi, Tina

★ **School** survival; keeping your cool at school. ABDO Pub. Co. 2009 112p il (Essential health: strong, beautiful girls) lib bdg $22.95

Grades: 6 7 8 9   **373.1**

1. Education -- Social aspects

ISBN 978-1-60453-104-6 lib bdg; 1-60453-104-5 lib bdg

LC 2008-11904

This features fictional narratives paired with firsthand advice from a licensed psychologist to help preteen and teen girls find new ways to face everyday challenges at school. Situations include handling test anxiety, and dealing with bullies.

"The topics are well selected, the design is attractive, and the stories feature girls from a variety of cultures." Booklist

Includes glossary and bibliographical references

Glasser, Debbie

New kid, new scene; a guide to moving and switching schools. by Debbie Glasser and Emily Schenck. Magination Press 2012 112p il $14.95; pa 9.95

Grades: 5 6 7 8   **373.1**

1. Moving 2. Students

ISBN 978-1-4338-1039-8; 1-4338-1039-5; 978-1-4338-1038-1 pa; 1-4338-1038-7 pa

LC 2011013608

"Students making the transition to new schools, new communities, or new homes will always experience a bit of anxiety, and this self-help book offers practical advice on how to make those changes smoother. The ideas and suggestions are sound and practical. . . . The eye-catching layout will keep students flipping through the pages." SLJ

Katz, Eric D.

High school's not forever; [by] Jane Bluestein and Eric Katz. HCI Teens 2005 302p il pa $12.95

Grades: 7 8 9 10 11 12   **373.1**

1. High school students

ISBN 0-7573-0256-4

LC 2005-50232

"Culled from the responses of some 2000 high and post-high school students, this title gives voice to young people who have lived through the experience and who offer both affirming and cautionary tales as they attempted to navigate the uncertain seas of friendship, depression, academic achievement, drugs, and sexuality. . . . There is no question that this book will enhance most YA collections." SLJ

Includes bibliographical references

Serritella, Judy

Look again! appealing bulletin board ideas for secondary students. Linworth Pub. 2002 160p pa $36.95

Grades: Adult Professional   **373.1**
    1. Bulletin boards 2. Teenagers -- Books and reading
    ISBN 1-58683-053-8

                 LC 2002-16181

"Basic practical tips suggest ways to liven up board displays, for example, by using three-dimensional materials such as corrugated cardboard or wallpaper. Ideas focus on providing students with information they need, as well as on promoting reading and library services." Book Rep

Includes bibliographical references

375   Curricula

Bishop, Kay

Connecting libraries with classrooms; the curricular roles of the media specialist. 2nd. ed.; Linworth 2011 122p pa $45

Grades: Adult Professional   **375**
    1. Librarians 2. School libraries 3. Instructional materials centers
    ISBN 978-1-59884-599-0; 1-59884-599-3

                 LC 2010051623

This book provides an . . . exploration of the topics that are currently relevant in K-12 curricula, including the school librarian's role in dealing with these issues, collaborating with teachers, and connecting to classrooms.

"Kay Bishop's book covers a wide range of topics and issues within the school library field. . . . Collaborative planning between classroom teacher, principal, students, and the community is also addressed. This material will be a welcome addition to the Library Media Specialist's arsenal of resources to stay current and involved." Libr Media Connect

Includes bibliographical references

Nichols, Beverly

Managing curriculum and assessment; a practitioner's guide. [by] Beverly Nichols . . . [et al.] Linworth Publishing 2006 170p pa $49.95

Grades: Adult Professional   **375**
    1. Evaluation 2. Education -- Curricula
    ISBN 1-58683-216-6

                 LC 2006003202

"This is a guide by practitioners who give advice on how to respond to the laws and requirements of No Child Left Behind. It is an invaluable resource that provides new insights. . . . There are three sections to the guide with an accompanying CD that contains everything in the book and

more. . . . This guide is loaded with examples and is a must have for your professional library." Libr Media Connect

Includes bibliographical references

379   Public policy issues in education

Magoon, Kekla

Today the world is watching you; the Little Rock Nine and the fight for school integration, 1957. Twenty-First Century Books 2011 160p il map lib bdg $38.60

Grades: 6 7 8 9   **379**
    1. School integration 2. Segregation in education 3. Arkansas -- Race relations 4. African Americans -- Education 5. Central High School (Little Rock, Ark.)
    ISBN 978-0-7613-5767-4; 0-7613-5767-X

                 LC 2010028443

On September 4, 1957, nine African American teenagers made their way toward Central High School in Little Rock, Arkansas. Armed soldiers of the Arkansas National Guard blocked most of them at the edge of campus. The three students who did make it onto campus faced an angry mob. But the U.S. Supreme Court had ruled in 1955 that school segregation—that is, separate schools for black children and white children—was unconstitutional.

"Well-paced and engaging, the book is broken up into manageable chapters and gives background information on racial tensions in America starting with slavery. The information is carefully documented. . . . Black-and-white photographs and text boxes give additional information and context. . . . An ideal purchase for research purposes." SLJ

Includes glossary and bibliographical references

Miller, Mara

School desegregation and the story of the Little Rock Nine; [by] Mara Miller. Enslow Publishers 2008 128p il map (From many cultures, one history) lib bdg $31.93

Grades: 6 7 8 9   **379**
    1. School integration 2. Segregation in education 3. Arkansas -- Race relations 4. African Americans -- Education 5. Central High School (Little Rock, Ark.)
    ISBN 978-0-7660-2835-7; 0-7660-2835-6 lib bdg

                 LC 2007023376

"Through the 1950s, segregation was a way of life in the Deep South. But in 1957, after the U.S. Supreme Court ruling in the case of Brown v. Board of Education, nine courageous African-American students, the Little Rock Nine, prepared to integrate Central High School in Little Rock, Arkansas." Publisher's note

Includes glossary and bibliographical references

Sharp, Anne Wallace

Separate but equal; the desegregation of America's schools. [by] Anne Wallace Sharp. Lucent Books 2007 104p il (Lucent library of black history) $28.70

Grades: 7 8 9 10   **379**
    1. School integration 2. Segregation in education 3.

African Americans -- Education
ISBN 1-59018-953-1; 978-1-59018-953-5

LC 2006008269

"This simple and direct overview begins with the ban against educating slaves and the efforts of Prudence Crandall to provide black girls with schooling in Connecticut in 1832. Following a history of segregation, the major battles to desegregate public schools in the North and in the South, as well as those to desegregate universities and colleges, are highlighted. The violent white backlash that occurred in both Southern and Northern states in the 1960s and '70s is also covered." SLJ

Includes bibliographical references

Stokes, John

★ **Students** on strike; Jim Crow, civil rights, Brown, and me; a memoir. by John A. Stokes with Lois Wolfe, and Herman J. Viola. National Geographic 2008 127p il $15.95; lib bdg $23.90

Grades: 4 5 6 7   379

1. Segregation in education 2. African Americans -- Education
ISBN 978-1-4263-0153-7; 1-4263-0153-7; 978-1-4263-0154-4 lib bdg; 1-4263-0154-5 lib bdg

"In 1951, a group of African-American high school students in Prince Edward County, VA, went on strike to protest the substandard conditions in their segregated schools. They eventually became plaintiffs in a lawsuit that was one of the five that were part of the 1954 Brown decision . . . Fear of retribution and lingering bitterness has kept the strike leaders silent, but Stokes, who was among them, has decided that the story of the strike and its aftermath need to be told. . . . Stoke's inspiring story reveals an almost completely unreported part of one of the most important court cases of the 20th century." SLJ

Tougas, Shelley

★ **Little** Rock girl 1957; how a photograph changed the fight for integration. Compass Point Books 2011 64p il (Captured history) lib bdg $33.99; pa $8.95

Grades: 6 7 8 9   379

1. Students 2. School integration 3. Documentary photography 4. Segregation in education 5. Photojournalists 6. Arkansas -- Race relations 7. African Americans -- Education 8. Central High School (Little Rock, Ark.)
ISBN 978-0-7565-4440-9 lib bdg; 0-7565-4440-8; 978-0-7565-4512-3 pa; 0-7565-4512-9 pa

LC 2010054303

This explains how Will Counts' 1957 photograph of an African American student, Elizabeth Eckford, attempting to enter the all-white Central High School in Little Rock, Arkansas while surrounded by an angry mob, helped focus national attention on racial segregation.

This "is model nonfiction. . . . The design is fresh and inviting, the writing clear, and the back matter . . . is useful and extensive. An all-around winner." Booklist

Includes glossary and bibliographical references

Walker, Paul Robert

★ **Remember** Little Rock; the time, the people, the stories. by Paul Robert Walker. National Geographic 2008 61p il map $17.95; lib bdg $27.90

Grades: 5 6 7 8 9   379

1. School integration 2. Segregation in education 3. Arkansas -- Race relations 4. African Americans -- Education 5. Central High School (Little Rock, Ark.)
ISBN 978-1-4263-0402-6; 1-4263-0402-1; 978-1-4263-0403-3 lib bdg; 1-4263-0403-X lib bdg

LC 2008-24959

"The story of the battle to integrate Central High School in 1957 Little Rock, Arkansas, is presented through photographs and firsthand accounts from those who were there. . . . The multitude of eyewitness accounts, the poignant photographs, and the contextual background make this text a must-have addition to any classroom or library." Voice Youth Advocates

Includes bibliographical references

379.2   Specific policy issues in public education

Aretha, David

With all deliberate speed; court-ordered busing and American schools. David Aretha. Morgan Reynolds Pub. 2012 128 p. ill. (some col.) (The civil rights movement) (lib. bdg.) $28.95

Grades: 7 8 9 10   379.2

1. School integration 2. Busing (School integration) 3. Boston (Mass.) -- Race relations 4. School integration -- History
ISBN 1599351811; 1599352176; 9781599351810; 9781599352176

LC 2011019530

This book, part of the "Civil Rights Movement" series, "details the slow, painful, unpopular, and often ineffective process of integrating public schools by busing students outside their neighborhoods in the decades following the 1954 landmark Brown v. Board of Education decision. In addition to a detailed account of experiences in Boston, [David] Aretha includes specific information on busing in numerous large and small metropolitan areas around the country." (Booklist)

"The latest books from the Civil Rights Movement series offer well-researched and clearly-written discussions of events and issues that helped define their times." Booklist

Includes bibliographical references (p. 122-124) and index

381   Commerce (Trade)

Freese, Susan M.

Craigslist; the company and its founder. ABDO Pub. Co. 2011 112p il (Technology pioneers) lib bdg $34.22

Grades: 5 6 7 8   381

1. Advertising 2. Businessmen 3. Internet marketing 4. Online social networks 5. Webmasters 6. Craigslist

Inc. 7. Software engineers

ISBN 978-1-61714-806-4 lib bdg; 1-61714-806-7 lib bdg; 978-1-61758-964-5 e-book

LC 2010042448

This is an introduction to Craigslist and its founder, Craig Newmark.

"Written in a clear, linear fashion, this series offers vivid, well-researched details about the development of technological advancements considered essential in today's society. . . . Readers who are interested in technology and inventions will be thoroughly engrossed." SLJ

Includes glossary and bibliographical references

Gilbert, Sara

★ The **story** of eBay. Creative Education 2011 il (Built for success) $23.95

Grades: 6 7 8 9   381

1. eBay Inc.

ISBN 978-1-60818-062-2; 1-60818-062-X

LC 2010031226

A look at the origins, leaders, growth, and holdings of eBay, the online auction and shopping company that was founded in 1995 and today sells a multitude of collectibles and other consumer products.

This book is "written in a lively style, yet with a minimum of fuss. . . . The slim, gleaming format, well-chosen photos, and the effort to explore what makes a company successful today [makes this title] unique." Booklist

Includes bibliographical references

The **story** of Wal-Mart. Creative Education 2011 48p il (Built for success) lib bdg $23.95

Grades: 6 7 8 9   381

1. Retail trade 2. Retail executives 3. Wal-Mart Stores, Inc.

ISBN 978-1-60818-064-6; 1-60818-064-6

LC 2010031370

A look at the origins, leaders, growth, and operations of Wal-Mart, the discount retailing company whose first store opened in 1962 and which today is one of the largest corporations in the world.

This book is "written in a lively style, yet with a minimum of fuss. . . . The slim, gleaming format, well-chosen photos, and the effort to explore what makes a company successful today [makes this title] unique." Booklist

Includes bibliographical references

382 International commerce (Foreign trade)

Gifford, Clive

The **arms** trade. Chrysalis Education 2004 61p il (World issues) $29.95

Grades: 7 8 9 10   382

1. Defense industry 2. Firearms industry

ISBN 1-59389-154-7

"This book packs in copious information from a well-rounded perspective. . . . Very effective color photos . . . add a startling and engrossing element." Booklist

Includes glossary and bibliographical references

Major, John S.

The **Silk** Route; 7,000 miles of history. illustrated by Stephen Fieser. HarperCollins Pubs. 1995 32p il maps hardcover o.p. pa $6.99

Grades: 4 5 6 7   382

1. Trade routes 2. China -- History

ISBN 0-06-443468-0

LC 92-38169

"The pictures and short segments make the book a teaching tool as well as a resource when learning about China and its silk industry." Child Book Rev Serv

384 Communications

Henderson, Harry

★ **Communications** and broadcasting; from wired words to wireless Web. rev ed.; Facts on File 2006 201p il (Milestones in discovery and invention) $35

Grades: 7 8 9 10 11 12   384

1. Telecommunication

ISBN 0-8160-5748-6; 978-0-8160-5748-1

LC 2006-5577

First published 1997

This is a "look at the development and interconnection of [the following] scientific ideas: electromagnetism, leading to the telegraph and telephone; Maxwell's wave theory, leading to radio and television; and communications and information theory, from Claude Shannon to the World Wide Web and beyond. In addition, there are . . . portraits of the inventors themselves." Publisher's note

Includes glossary and bibliographical references

384.5 Wireless communication

Byers, Ann

Communications satellites. Rosen Pub. Group 2003 58p il (Library of satellites) lib bdg $26.50

Grades: 4 5 6 7   384.5

1. Artificial satellites in telecommunication

ISBN 0-8239-3851-4

LC 2002-7527

This discusses the history, development, and applications of communications satellites

"Clear and topical photographs enliven the [presentation]. While packed with information, the [text is] easy to read." SLJ

Includes bibliographical references

385 Railroad transportation

Gimpel, Diane

The **transcontinental** railroad. ABDO Pub. Co. 2011 112p il (Essential events) lib bdg $23.95

Grades: 7 8 9 10 11 12   **385**
  1. Railroads -- History 2. West (U.S.) -- History
  ISBN 978-1-61714-768-5; 1-61714-768-0
                      LC 2010044830
Describes how and why the Transcontinental Railroad
was built and tells how it affected the westward expansion
of settlers.
  Includes glossary and bibliographical references

Landau, Elaine
  The **transcontinental** railroad; [by] Elaine Lan-
dau. Franklin Watts 2005 63p il (Watts library)
$25.50
Grades: 5 6 7 8   **385**
  1. Frontier and pioneer life 2. Railroads -- History
  3. Central Pacific Railroad 4. Union Pacific Railroad
  Company
  ISBN 0-531-12326-X
                      LC 2005000914
"Landau describes how people traveled prior to the
building of the railroads and how the concept of Manifest
Destiny influenced the development of the railroads. . . .
Black-and-white and color illustrations, maps, sidebars, and
time lines enhance the well-organized [text]." SLJ
  Includes bibliographical references

McMahon, Peter
  Ultimate trains. Kids Can Press 2010 40p il
(Machines of the future) $16.95
Grades: 4 5 6 7   **385**
  1. Railroads 2. Science -- Experiments
  ISBN 978-1-55453-366-4; 1-55453-366-X
"In simple engaging text and illustrations, McMahon
and Mora present a brief history of [railroads]. Integral to the
book are five experiments children can create. . . . Each ex-
periment ties in well with a particular type of train, features
clear instructions, and offers safety precautions." Booklist
  Includes glossary

Murphy, Jim
  ★ **Across** America on an emigrant train. Clarion
Bks. 1993 150p il hardcover o.p. pa $10.95
Grades: 5 6 7 8   **385**
  1. Poets 2. Authors 3. Novelists 4. Authors, Scottish
  5. Essayists 6. Travel writers 7. Short story writers
  8. Railroads -- History 9. United States -- Description
  and travel
  ISBN 0-395-63390-7; 0-395-76483-1 pa
                      LC 92-38650
"Murphy presents a forthright and thoroughly engrossing history of the transcontinental railway, with entries from
Robert Louis Stevenson's 1879 journal as he rode cross
country. It's also an inviting introduction to Stevenson, with
a romance in the bargain." SLJ
  Includes bibliographical references

Renehan, Edward J.
  The **Transcontinental** Railroad; the gateway to
the West. [by] Edward J. Renehan, Jr. Chelsea House
2007 120p il (Milestones in American history) lib
bdg $35

Grades: 7 8 9 10   **385**
  1. Railroads -- History 2. West (U.S.) -- History 3.
  Central Pacific Railroad 4. Union Pacific Railroad
  Company
  ISBN 0-7910-9351-4 lib bdg; 978-0-7910-9351-1
  lib bdg
                      LC 2006-38870
This history of the transcontinental railroad is "accessi-
ble, lively. . . . Many quotations, sidebars, art reproductions,
and maps support the [text]. Excerpts from primary source
materials also help give readers a sense of time and place."
Horn Book Guide
  Includes bibliographical references

Zimmermann, Karl R.
  ★ **All** aboard! passenger trains around the world.
[by] Karl Zimmermann; photography by the author.
Boyds Mills Press 2006 48p il $19.95
Grades: 5 6 7 8   **385**
  1. Railroads
  ISBN 1-59078-325-5
                      LC 2005-24990
Zimmermann "has traveled by train across six continents, and his beautiful, big color photos appear on every
double-page spread of this enthusiastic account, which
blends history, geography, business, and engineering with
his personal focus." Booklist

  ★ **Steam** locomotives; whistling, chugging,
smoking iron horses of the past. Boyds Mills Press
2004 48p il $19.95
Grades: 4 5 6 7   **385**
  1. Locomotives 2. Steam engines
  ISBN 1-59078-165-1
"In this photo-essay, Zimmermann shares his excitement
for steam locomotives with young readers, tracing the development of the early engines and their impact on the history of the U.S. He includes a clear explanation . . . of how
a steam engine works. The photographs, some archival and
some from the present day, are excellent. . . . The engaging
text clearly imparts the author's enthusiasm and love for the
subject." SLJ
  Includes glossary

386 Inland waterway and ferry transportation

Bial, Raymond
  The **canals**. Benchmark Bks. 2002 56p il map
(Building America) lib bdg $27.07
Grades: 6 7 8 9   **386**
  1. Canals
  ISBN 0-7614-1336-7
                      LC 00-65078
This describes the history of canals in America from co-
lonial times to the 19th century
  This book is "marked by strong research, clear
writing, good organization, and very handsome color
photographs." Booklist
  Includes glossary and bibliographical references

Coleman, Wim

The **amazing** Erie Canal and how a big ditch opened up the West; [by] Wim Coleman & Pat Perrin. MyReportLinks.com Books 2006 128p il map (The wild history of the American West) lib bdg $33.27
Grades: 6 7 8 9   **386**
    1. Erie Canal (N.Y.)
    ISBN 1-59845-017-4
             LC 2005029389
This book "shares a brief, informative history of canals; the geographic need for the Erie Canal; and an explanation of how its creation impacted American commerce and history. . . . Throughout the text, illustrations of Web pages invite readers to search online for more detailed information. The book's text is clear, and the format is attractive, with excellent black-and-white photos and color illustrations on nearly every page." Booklist
    Includes bibliographical references

Roop, Peter

River roads west; America's first highways. [by] Peter and Connie Roop. Calkins Creek 2007 64p il map $19.95
Grades: 6 7 8 9   **386**
    1. Canals 2. Rivers 3. United States -- History 4. Transportation -- History
    ISBN 1-59078-430-8; 978-1-59078-430-3
"The role of transportation in national history has seldom been more clearly delineated than in this meticulous treatment. Spanning prehistory to the 19th century, the sparkling text, inflected with wry humor, focuses sequentially on the Hudson River and Erie Canal, the Ohio, Mississippi, Missouri, Rio Grande, and the Colorado Rivers, and the Columbia River." SLJ
    Includes bibliographical references

387.1   Ports

House, Katherine L.

Lighthouses for kids; history, science, and lore with 21 activities. [by] Katherine L. House. Chicago Review Press 2008 118p il pa $14.95
Grades: 4 5 6 7 8   **387.1**
    1. Lighthouses
    ISBN 978-1-55652-720-3 pa; 1-55652-720-9 pa
             LC 2007-27093
"This book is noteworthy for the way in which the activities are related to the information in the text. . . . Readers learn about the challenges of building . . . [lighthouses], inventions to make them more reliable, and how lighthouses function as historical relics today." SLJ
    Includes glossary and bibliographical references

387.2   Ships

Zimmermann, Karl R.

Ocean liners; crossing and cruising the seven seas. photographs by the author. Boyds Mills Press 2008 48p il $17.95

Grades: 5 6 7 8   **387.2**
    1. Ocean liners 2. Ocean travel
    ISBN 978-1-59078-552-2; 1-59078-552-5
             LC 2007049323
This is "a comprehensive overview of ships from sail to steam to diesel, from the important modes of transportation to the modern resorts at sea. The information is organized in chapters about the history and development of the ships, the star ships of the Atlantic crossings and the conversion to modern cruising. . . . All is accompanied by photographs taken over the years by the author and supplemented by historic drawings, photos and documents. . . . A fascinating voyage." Kirkus
    Includes glossary

387.7   Air transportation

Parker, Steve

By air. Marshall Cavendish Benchmark 2011 il (Future transport)
Grades: 4 5 6   **387.7**
    1. Aeronautics 2. Forecasting
    ISBN 1608707776; 9781608707775
             LC 2011000998
"Beginning with a speculative illustration featuring people of the future traveling through the air in carlike personal jets, this title . . . offers a fascinating look at prototypes for all sorts of aircraft, from small planes to passenger airliners to lighter-than-air vehicles. . . . The various possibilities for future aircraft are covered in double-page spreads that are well laid out and easy to digest. Illustrated with plenty of striking, digitally enhanced color pictures, this will probably be of equal interest to those doing reports and browsers." Booklist
    Includes bibliographical references

388   Transportation

Harris, Joseph

Transportation; the impact of science and technology. Gareth Stevens Pub. 2010 64p il (Pros and cons) lib bdg $35
Grades: 5 6 7 8   **388**
    1. Transportation 2. Transportation -- History
    ISBN 978-1-4339-1990-9 lib bdg; 1-4339-1990-7 lib bdg
             LC 2009-12437
An "active layout that features color photographs, maps, graphs or charts on every spread, this . . . [book] has much to offer. . . . It conveniently outlines the range of views . . . helping students to learn how to view both sides of [the] issue[s]." SLJ
    Includes glossary and bibliographical references

Mulder, Michelle, 1976-

Pedal it! how bicycles are changing the world. Michelle Mulder. Orca Book Publishers 2013 48 p. (Footprints) (hardcover) $19.95

Grades: 3 4 5 6 7 8 **388**
1. Cycling 2. Bicycles
ISBN 1459802195; 9781459802193

LC 2012953464

This book, by Michelle Mulder, "celebrates the humble bicycle--from the very first boneshakers to the sleek racing bikes of today, from handlebars to spokes to gear sprockets--and shows you why and how bikes can make the world a better place. Not only can bikes be used to power computers and generators, they can also reduce pollution, promote wellness and get a package across a crowded city--fast!" (Publisher's note)

388.3 Vehicular transportation

Bjornlund, Lydia
What is the future of alternative energy cars? by Lydia Bjornlund. ReferencePoint Press, Inc. 2014 80 p. color illustrations (Future of renewable energy series) (hardback) $28.95
Grades: 6 7 8 9 **388.3**
1. Alternative fuel vehicles 2. Automobiles -- Fuel consumption 3. Automobiles -- Technological innovations
ISBN 1601526105; 9781601526106

LC 2013036244

This book on alternative energy cars, by Lydia Bjornlund, is "organized around a narrative-driven, pro-con [design]. . . . [It] examine[s] . . . cost, environmental impact, practicality when measured against fossil fuels, and the role of government in renewable energy's future. Important ideas are supported throughout each book by current and relevant facts, quotes, full-color statistical illustrations, and anecdotes." (Publisher's note)

"Well written and understandable, the authors use a wide variety of source material to present each side fairly and completely. The question/answer format of the chapters breaks the topics into simplified arguments that can easily be absorbed." VOYA

Includes bibliographical references and index

388.4 Local transportation

Reis, Ronald A.
The **New** York City subway system. Chelsea House 2009 136p il (Building America: then and now) lib bdg $35
Grades: 6 7 8 9 **388.4**
1. Subways 2. New York (N.Y.) 3. Transportation -- History
ISBN 978-1-60413-046-1 lib bdg; 1-60413-046-6 lib bdg

LC 2008-25550

This is a history of New York City's subway system
Includes glossary and bibliographical references

Sandler, Martin W.
★ **Secret** subway; the fascinating tale of an amazing feat of engineering. National Geographic 2009 96p il map $17.95; lib bdg $26.90
Grades: 5 6 7 8 **388.4**
1. Subways 2. New York (N.Y.) -- History
ISBN 978-1-4263-0462-0; 1-4263-0462-5; 978-1-4263-0463-7 lib bdg; 1-4263-0463-3 lib bdg

LC 2008-39831

"Sandler takes an in-depth look at the building of New York's first subway. . . . [He] writes about the subway in a well-put-together book with interesting information, great pictures, and a compelling true story." Voice Youth Advocates

Includes bibliographical references

391 Customs

Albee, Sarah
Why'd They Wear That? Fashion As the Mirror of History. by Sarah Albee ; foreword by Timothy Gunn. Natl Geographic Soc Childrens books 2015 192 p. $19.99
Grades: 5 6 7 8 9 **391**
1. Fashion -- History 2. Clothing and dress -- History
ISBN 1426319193; 9781426319198

In this book, by Sarah Albee, "kids will learn about outrageous, politically-perilous, funky, disgusting, regrettable, and life-threatening creations people have worn throughout the course of human history, all the way up to the present day. From spats and togas to hoop skirts and hair shirts, why people wore what they did is an illuminating way to look at the social, economic, political, and moral climates throughout history." (Publisher's note)

"What a good idea for a book. And what a smart way to do it. As the subtitle says, this hefty, extensively illustrated book uses fashion to discuss the ways and whys people dress and how it reflects what's happening in their civilization... the many photographs are well chosen and reproduced, and Albee writes in a conversational style that, though occasionally repetitive, is instantly appealing to readers. Tim Gunn writes the foreword, and a time line and bibliography conclude. Dressed to impress!" Booklist

Bailey, Diane
Tattoo art around the world. Rosen Pub. 2011 64p il (Tattooing) lib bdg $30.60; pa $12.95
Grades: 7 8 9 10 **391**
1. Tattooing
ISBN 978-1-4488-4618-4 lib bdg; 1-4488-4618-8 lib bdg; 978-1-4488-4622-1 pa; 1-4488-4622-6 pa

LC 2010048428

This book "discusses how different cultures have used tattoos. . . . The design and the reading level are accessible without talking down to the audience, so this is a good choice for enticing reluctant readers with an interest in body art." Booklist

Includes bibliographical references

Baker, Patricia

Fashions of a decade, The 1940s. Chelsea House Publishers 2006 64p il $35

Grades: 7 8 9 10 11 12 **391**

    1. Costume

    ISBN 0-8160-6720-1; 978-0-8160-6720-6

                    LC 2006-49934

First published 1992

Chronicles clothing trends of the 1940s and the influence of World War II on styles of dress, availability of many fabrics, and the new ideas of "designers at war"

Includes glossary and bibliographical references

Fashions of a decade, The 1950s. Chelsea House Publishers 2006 64p il $35

Grades: 7 8 9 10 11 12 **391**

    1. Costume

    ISBN 0-8160-6721-X; 978-0-8160-6721-3

                    LC 2006-50142

First published 1992

Surveys the fads, fashions, trends, and cultural and intellectual preoccupations of the 1950s

Includes glossary and bibliographical references

Behnke, Alison

The **little** black dress and zoot suits; Depression and wartime fashions from the 1930s to 1950s. Twenty-First Century Books 2011 64p il (Dressing a nation: the history of U.S. fashion)

Grades: 7 8 9 10 **391**

    1. Fashion 2. Clothing and dress 3. United States -- Social life and customs

    ISBN 0-7613-5892-7; 978-0-7613-5892-3

                    LC 2010035444

This "covers a time of rapid change in the American fashion industry, from an era of frugal thriftiness necessary in the face of the Great Depression and WWII to one informed by a brand-new youth culture, movie stars, and postwar leisure time. . . . There's plenty for fashion-savy readers to digest. . . . The book's sharp, bold, rather tidy design features eye-catching art from the period. . . . . [This is an] engaging title." Booklist

Includes bibliographical references

Bix, Cynthia Overbeck

Petticoats and frock coats; revolution and Victorian Age fashions from the 1770s to the 1860s. Twenty-First Century Books 2011 64p il (Dressing a nation: the history of U.S. fashion) lib bdg $31.93

Grades: 7 8 9 10 **391**

    1. Fashion 2. American national characteristics 3. Clothing and dress -- History 4. United States -- Social life and customs 5. United States -- History -- 1600-1775, Colonial period

    ISBN 978-0-7613-5888-6; 0-7613-5888-9

                    LC 2010053384

This is a history of fashion in the U.S. from the 1770s to the 1860s.

Includes bibliographical references

Bliss, John

Preening, painting, and piercing; body art. Raintree 2010 32p il (Culture in action) lib bdg $29

Grades: 5 6 7 8 **391**

    1. Body art 2. Cosmetics 3. Tattooing 4. Theatrical makeup

    ISBN 978-1-4109-3924-1; 1-4109-3924-1

                    LC 2009051182

"This book covers different looks achieved through makeup, body painting, tattoos, and piercing. Photographs, advertisements, paintings, and artifacts show a variety of cultures and time periods and help readers see the huge changes in the fashion of physical appearance. . . . The author does a good job of explaining that some cultures have negative stereotypes of tattooed people being criminals and some piercing can be dangerous to people with allergies. Fun activities are included. . . . This book . . . is well written and has few biases." SLJ

Includes glossary and bibliographical references

Carnegy, Vicky

Fashions of a decade, The 1980s. Chelsea House Publishers 2006 64p il $35

Grades: 7 8 9 10 11 12 **391**

    1. Costume

    ISBN 978-0-8160-6724-4; 0-8160-6724-4

                    LC 2006-49458

First published 1992

A pictorial survey chronicling the international clothing fashions of the 1980s

This "provides an accessible overview of the decade, placing fashion trends within their appropriate political and historical contexts. . . . Browsers and fashion design students alike will be intrigued." Booklist

Includes glossary and bibliographical references

Clancy Steer, Deirdre

The **1980s** and 1990s. Chelsea House 2009 64p il (Costume & fashion source books) $35

Grades: 6 7 8 9 **391**

    1. Costume -- History 2. Fashion -- History 3. Clothing and dress -- History 4. United States -- Social life and customs

    ISBN 978-1-60413-386-8; 1-60413-386-4

                    LC 2009-6700

This describes how gender, occasion, class, and social clime affected fashion during the 1980s and 1990s.

This is written "in a clear, engaging style. . . . [The] volume is profusely and gorgeously illustrated with period paintings and photographs, movie and TV stills, design sketches, and photographs from period reenactments. Each illustration is captioned with intriguing, relevant facts that enhance the text." SLJ

Includes glossary and bibliographical references

Colonial America; [by] Deirdre Clancy Steer and Amela Baksic. Chelsea House 2009 64p il (Costume & fashion source books) $35

Grades: 6 7 8 9 **391**

    1. Costume -- History 2. Fashion -- History 3. Clothing and dress -- History 4. United States -- Social life and

customs -- 1600-1775, Colonial period
ISBN 978-1-60413-380-6; 1-60413-380-5

A look at what kinds of clothing people in colonial America wore.

This is written "in a clear, engaging style. . . . [The] volume is profusely and gorgeously illustrated with period paintings and photographs, movie and TV stills, design sketches, and photographs from period reenactments. Each illustration is captioned with intriguing, relevant facts that enhance the text." SLJ

Connikie, Yvonne
 Fashions of a decade, The 1960s. Chelsea House Publishers 2006 64p il $35
 Grades: 7 8 9 10 11 12   **391**
   1. Costume
  ISBN 0-8160-6722-8; 978-0-8160-6722-0
  First published 1992
  A pictorial survey chronicling the international fashions of the 1960s

  This is "not for serious students of fashion, but will be fun for browsers and those interested in an introduction to the concept of clothing design in the context of contemporary events." SLJ

  Includes glossary and bibliographical references

Costantino, Maria
 Fashions of a decade, The 1930s. Chelsea House Publishers 2006 64p il $35
 Grades: 7 8 9 10 11 12   **391**
   1. Costume
  ISBN 0-8160-6719-8; 978-0-8160-6719-0
                                    LC 2006-49933
  First published 1992
  Chronicles trends in 1930s styles such as lower hemlines and broader shoulders; the introduction of synthetic fabrics; and new views of fitness, health, and personal beauty
  Includes glossary and bibliographical references

Elgin, Kathy
 Elizabethan England. Chelsea House 2009 64p il (Costume & fashion source books) $35
 Grades: 6 7 8 9   **391**
   1. Costume -- History 2. Fashion -- History 3. Clothing and dress -- History 4. Great Britain -- History -- 1485-1603, Tudors
  ISBN 978-1-60413-379-0; 1-60413-379-1
                                    LC 2008-47258
  This describes how gender, occasion, class, and social clime affected fashion in Elizabethan England.

  This is written "in a clear, engaging style. . . . [The] volume is profusely and gorgeously illustrated with period paintings and photographs, movie and TV stills, design sketches, and photographs from period reenactments. Each illustration is captioned with intriguing, relevant facts that enhance the text." SLJ

  Includes glossary and bibliographical references

 The **medieval** world. Chelsea House 2009 64p il (Costume & fashion source books) $35
 Grades: 6 7 8 9   **391**
   1. Medieval civilization 2. Costume -- History 3.

Fashion -- History 4. Clothing and dress -- History
ISBN 978-1-60413-378-3; 1-60413-378-3
                                    LC 2008-47259
This describes how gender, occasion, class, and social clime affected clothing and dress during the Middle Ages.

This is written "in a clear, engaging style. . . . [The] volume is profusely and gorgeously illustrated with period paintings and photographs, movie and TV stills, design sketches, and photographs from period reenactments. Each illustration is captioned with intriguing, relevant facts that enhance the text." SLJ

Includes glossary and bibliographical references

★ **Fashions** of a decade [series] Chelsea House Publishers 2006 8v il set $280
 Grades: 7 8 9 10 11 12   **391**
   1. Costume
  ISBN 0-8160-7059-8; 978-0-8160-7059-6
  First published 1991-1992
  This set describes clothing styles of the 20th century in the context of world events, social movements, and cultural movements of each decade.

  "These titles provide colorful and fascinating information. . . . Attractive black-and-white illustrations, color photos, reproductions, sketches from magazines and newspapers, and fact boxes enhance and bring to life these lively and accessible texts." SLJ

Gerber, Larry
 Getting inked; what to expect when you get a tattoo. Rosen Pub. 2011 64p il (Tattooing) lib bdg $30.60; pa $12.95
 Grades: 7 8 9 10   **391**
   1. Tattooing
  ISBN 978-1-4488-4616-0 lib bdg; 978-1-4488-4621-4 pa
                                    LC 2010045970
  This book "details how to find a competent tattoo artist, what the inking process is like, and how to care for the tattoo afterward. . . . Illustrations . . . are of high quality. . . . The design and the reading level are accessible without talking down to the audience, so this is a good choice for enticing reluctant readers with an interest in body art." Booklist
  Includes bibliographical references

Graydon, Shari
 In your face; the culture of beauty and you. Annick 2004 176p il hardcover o.p. pa $14.95
 Grades: 7 8 9 10   **391**
   1. Body image 2. Personal appearance
  ISBN 1-55037-857-0; 1-55037-856-2 pa
  The author "looks at fashion across time and cultures, and analyzes the underlying messages in today's focus . . . on thinness, long nails, and high heels. Along the way, she warns both young men and women of the very real dangers of eating disorders, plastic surgery, liposuction, and other body-image 'solutions.' . . . Graydon will make readers laugh as well as think about the issues." Booklist
  Includes bibliographical references

Havelin, Kate

Buckskin dresses and pumpkin breeches; colonial fashions from the 1580s to 1760s. Twenty-First Century Books 2011 64p il (Dressing a nation: the history of U.S. fashion) lib bdg $31.93

Grades: 7 8 9 10   **391**

1. Native Americans -- History 2. Clothing and dress -- History 3. United States -- Social life and customs 4. United States -- History -- 1600-1775, Colonial period
ISBN 978-0-7613-5887-9; 0-7613-5887-0

LC 2011001176

This is a history of Colonial U.S. fashion from 1580s to 1760s.

Includes bibliographical references

Hoopskirts, Union blues, and Confederate grays; Civil War fashions from 1861 to 1865. Twenty-First Century Books 2011 64p il (Dressing a nation: the history of U.S. fashion) lib bdg $31.93

Grades: 7 8 9 10   **391**

1. Fashion 2. Clothing and dress -- History 3. United States -- Social life and customs 4. United States -- History -- 1861-1865, Civil War
ISBN 978-0-7613-5889-3; 0-7613-5889-7

LC 2010048808

This is a history of fashion in the U.S. from 1861 to 1865.

Includes bibliographical references

Herald, Jacqueline

Fashions of a decade, The 1920s. Chelsea House Publishers 2006 64p il $35

Grades: 7 8 9 10 11 12   **391**

1. Costume
ISBN 0-8160-6718-X; 978-0-8160-6718-3

LC 2006-49932

First published 1992

Surveys the fads, fashions, trends, and cultural and intellectual preoccupations of the 1920s

"Students interested in fashion and societal changes, as well as those in need of a good outline reference, will find this volume . . . helpful." Booklist

Includes glossary and bibliographical references

Fashions of a decade, The 1970s. Chelsea House Publishers 2006 64p il $35

Grades: 7 8 9 10 11 12   **391**

1. Costume
ISBN 0-8160-6723-6; 978-0-8160-6723-7

LC 2006-46807

First published 1992

This volume in the series looks at how the fashions of the 1970s reflected the social, historical and cultural events of that decade

This "includes chapters on 'Black is Beautiful,' 'Dressed to Clash,' 'Trash Culture,' etc. . . . An abundance of full-color and black-and-white illustrations and photographs amplify the text with generally appropriate placement and captions." SLJ

Includes glossary and bibliographical references

Krohn, Katherine E.

Calico dresses and buffalo robes; American West fashions from the 1840s to the 1890s. Twenty-first Century Books 2011 64p il (Dressing a nation: the history of U.S. fashion) lib bdg $31.93

Grades: 7 8 9 10   **391**

1. West (U.S.) -- History 2. Native Americans -- History 3. Clothing and dress -- History 4. West (U.S.) -- Social life and customs 5. Frontier and pioneer life -- West (U.S.)
ISBN 978-0-7613-5890-9; 0-7613-5890-0

LC 2011003036

This is a history of clothing and dress in the American West from the 1840s to 1890s.

Includes bibliographical references

Kyi, Tanya Lloyd

★ The **blue** jean book; the story behind the seams. Annick Press 2005 79p il $24.95; pa $12.95 **391**

1. Jeans (Clothing)
ISBN 1-55037-917-8; 1-55037-916-X pa

"Kyi traces the history of these pants from the early life of Levi Strauss and the patented riveted pocket to the stiff competition and controversy of production in our modern world. . . . History and social issues are intertwined to show how activities, jobs, and the economy influence the development and production of clothing. . . . This is an enjoyable read for anyone wishing to know more about this fashion item and an excellent resource for an introduction to product development and economy." SLJ

Mason, Paul, 1967-

★ **Body** piercing and tattooing. Heinemann Lib. 2003 56p il (Just the facts) lib bdg $25.64

Grades: 6 7 8 9   **391**

1. Tattooing 2. Body piercing
ISBN 1-4034-0817-3

LC 2002-10936

Describes the history of body piercing and tattooing, as well as what motivates people to get a piercing or a tattoo, how to care for them, problems that can arise, and legal issues surrounding them

"The writing is clear and frank. . . . Students will find much to like and make use of in [this book]." Libr Media Connect

Includes glossary and bibliographical references

McEvoy, Anne

The **1920s** and 1930s. Chelsea House 2009 64p il (Costume & fashion source books) $35

Grades: 6 7 8 9   **391**

1. Fashion -- History 2. Clothing and dress -- History 3. United States -- Social life and customs
ISBN 978-1-60413-383-7; 1-60413-383-X

LC 2009-1236

This describes how gender, occasion, class, and social clime affected fashion during the 1920s and 1930s.

This is written "in a clear, engaging style. . . . [The] volume is profusely and gorgeously illustrated with period paintings and photographs, movie and TV stills, design sketches, and photographs from period reenactments. Each illustration is captioned with intriguing, relevant facts that enhance the text." SLJ

Includes glossary and bibliographical references

The **American** West. Chelsea House 2009 64p il (Costume & fashion source books) $35

Grades: 6 7 8 9   391

1. Native American costume 2. Frontier and pioneer life 3. Costume -- History 4. Fashion -- History 5. Clothing and dress -- History 6. West (U.S.) -- Social life and customs

ISBN 978-1-60413-382-0; 1-60413-382-1

LC 2008-47261

A look at what was worn by pioneers and settlers as well as Native Americans as the West opened up.

This is written "in a clear, engaging style. . . . [The] volume is profusely and gorgeously illustrated with period paintings and photographs, movie and TV stills, design sketches, and photographs from period reenactments. Each illustration is captioned with intriguing, relevant facts that enhance the text." SLJ

Includes glossary and bibliographical references

Fashions of a decade, The 1990s. Chelsea House Publishers 2006 64p il $35

Grades: 7 8 9 10 11 12   391

1. Costume

ISBN 0-8160-6725-2; 978-0-8160-6725-1

LC 2006-41268

First published 1992

A pictorial survey of the 1990s fashion trends

"The major flaw is that the book understandably includes only two years' worth of information; certainly the years 19921999 deserve treatment before a volume may purport to be about the entire decade." SLJ

Includes glossary and bibliographical references

Nagle, Jeanne

Why people get tattoos and other body art. Rosen 2011 64p il (Tattooing) lib bdg $30.60; pa $12.95

Grades: 7 8 9 10   391

1. Tattooing

ISBN 978-1-4488-4617-7 lib bdg; 978-1-4488-4620-7 pa

LC 2011000276

This book "explains the appeal of tattoos for a wide variety of people as a way of expressing themselves aesthetically, religiously, or for other reasons. Illustrations . . . are of high quality. . . . The design and the reading level are accessible without talking down to the audience, so this is a good choice for enticing reluctant readers with an interest in body art." Booklist

Includes bibliographical references

Pendergast, Sara

Fashion, costume, and culture; clothing, headwear, body decoration, and footwear through the ages. [by] Sara Pendergast and Tom Pendergast. U.X.L 2004 5v il set $275

Grades: 6 7 8 9   391

1. Fashion 2. Clothing and dress 3. Costume -- History

ISBN 0-7876-5417-5

This set "surveys how people have covered and adorned themselves through the ages and around the world. . . . There are 430 entries in all, ranging from a paragraph or two to a page. . . . The work is notable for its organization, breadth of coverage, and attractive design. Strongly recommended for school and public libraries." Booklist

Platt, Richard

They wore what?! the weird history of fashion and beauty. [by] Richard Platt. Two-Can 2007 48p il $16.95; pa $9.95

Grades: 4 5 6   391

1. Personal appearance 2. Fashion -- History

ISBN 978-1-58728-582-0; 1-58728-582-7; 978-1-58728-584-4 pa; 1-58728-584-3 pa

LC 2006039159

Published in the United Kingdom with title: Would you believe in 1500, platform shoes were outlawed?

"Busy, colorful pages recount the historical, social, and political sides of clothing, hair, hats, and shoes, from legal and moral issues such as wearing fur to dangerous practices like cinched waists and bound feet. . . . Ever-fluctuating ideas of beauty and body image are also explored." Horn Book Guide

Includes glossary and bibliographical references

Rooney, Anne

The **1950s** and 1960s. Chelsea House 2009 64p il (Costume & fashion source books) $35

Grades: 6 7 8 9   391

1. Costume -- History 2. Fashion -- History 3. Clothing and dress -- History 4. United States -- Social life and customs

ISBN 978-1-60413-385-1; 1-60413-385-6

LC 2008-47260

This describes how gender, occasion, class, and social clime affected fashion during the 1950s and 1960s

This is written "in a clear, engaging style. . . . [The] volume is profusely and gorgeously illustrated with period paintings and photographs, movie and TV stills, design sketches, and photographs from period reenactments. Each illustration is captioned with intriguing, relevant facts that enhance the text." SLJ

Includes glossary and bibliographical references

Rowland-Warne, L.

Costume; written by L. Rowland-Warne; [special photography, Liz McAulay] Dorling Kindersley 2000 63p il (DK eyewitness books) $15.99; lib bdg $19.99

Grades: 4 5 6 7   391

1. Costume 2. Clothing and dress 3. Fashion -- History

ISBN 0-7894-5586-2; 0-7894-6584-1 lib bdg

First published 1992 by Knopf

Photographs and text document the history and meaning of clothing, from loincloths to modern children's clothes

Spalding, Frank

Erasing the ink; getting rid of your tattoo. Rosen Pub. 2011 64p il (Tattooing) lib bdg $30.60; pa $12.95

Grades: 7 8 9 10   **391**
1. Skin 2. Tattooing
ISBN 978-1-4488-4615-3 lib bdg; 978-1-4488-4619-1 pa

LC 2010045920

This book "focuses . . . on the negatives of getting a tattoo and the difficulties of removing them. . . . Illustrations . . . are of high quality. . . . The design and the reading level are accessible without talking down to the audience, so this is a good choice for enticing reluctant readers with an interest in body art." Booklist

Includes bibliographical references

Taschek, Karen

The **Civil** War. Chelsea House 2009 64p il (Costume & fashion source books) $35

Grades: 6 7 8 9   **391**
1. Costume -- History 2. Fashion -- History 3. Clothing and dress -- History 4. United States -- History -- 1861-1865, Civil War
ISBN 978-1-60413-381-3; 1-60413-381-3

LC 2008-47262

A look at the clothing and styles on both sides of the Civil War.

This is written "in a clear, engaging style. . . . [The] volume is profusely and gorgeously illustrated with period paintings and photographs, movie and TV stills, design sketches, and photographs from period reenactments. Each illustration is captioned with intriguing, relevant facts that enhance the text." SLJ

Includes glossary and bibliographical references

391.4   Kinds of garments; accessories; buttons

Kyi, Tanya Lloyd

50 underwear questions; a bare-all history. by Tanya Kyi and illustrated by Ross Kinnaird. Annick Press 2011 116 p. $21.95

Grades: 4 5 6 7   **391.4**
1. Underwear 2. Clothing and dress -- History
ISBN 1554513537; 9781554513536

This book, by Tanya Kyi and illustrated by Ross Kinnaird, examines the history of underwear. "The format, as the title indicates, is question-and-answer. Beginning with 'ancient undies,' the questions cover everything from what's worn under certain kinds of dress to how the modern bra came into being, and reasons for wearing underclothes in the first place." (Booklist)

393   Death customs

Colman, Penny

★ **Corpses,** coffins, and crypts; a history of burial. Holt & Co. 1997 212p il $17.95

Grades: 7 8 9 10   **393**
1. Death 2. Burial 3. Funeral rites and ceremonies
ISBN 0-8050-5066-3

LC 97-7842

Documents the burial process throughout the centuries and in different cultures.

The author "is both candid and detailed in her handling of the gruesome nitty-gritty. . . . Many of the photographs in the liberally illustrated text are from her own explorations, and all are captioned, some in great detail. . . . She's filled her sensitive, solid book with answers to questions people often need and want to know but are too reluctant to ask." Booklist

Includes glossary and bibliographical references

Deem, James M.

★ **Bodies** from the ice; melting glaciers and the recovery of the past. Houghton Mifflin 2008 58p il map $17

Grades: 5 6 7 8 9 10   **393**
1. Mummies 2. Glaciers
ISBN 978-0-618-80045-2; 0-618-80045-X

LC 2008-01868

A Sibert Medal honor book, 2009

This describes the discovery of human remains preserved in glaciers in the Alps, the Andes, The Himalayas, and other places around the world and what can be learned from them

"Full-color photographs, reproductions, and maps are clearly captioned; grand images of glaciated mountain peaks span entire pages, and detailed pictures of recovered objects . . . are presented. . . . [This] is a fantastic resource. Deem superbly weaves diverse geographical settings, time periods, and climate issues into a readable work that reveals the increasing interdisciplinary dimensions of the sciences." SLJ

Includes bibliographical references

Greene, Meg

Rest in peace; a history of American cemeteries. Twenty-First Century Books 2008 112p il map (People's history) lib bdg $30.60

Grades: 8 9 10 11 12   **393**
1. Burial 2. Cemeteries 3. United States -- Social life and customs
ISBN 978-0-8225-3414-3 lib bdg; 0-8225-3414-2 lib bdg

LC 2007022093

"This account of cemeteries in the U.S. offers a sweeping history . . . as well as plenty of noteworthy details, illustrated throughout with black-and-white photos shaded in sepia tones. . . . This book . . . presents many aspects of an unusual topic." Booklist

Includes bibliographical references

Halls, Kelly Milner

Mysteries of the mummy kids. Darby Creek Pub. 2007 72p il map $18.95

Grades: 4 5 6 7   **393**
1. Mummies
ISBN 978-1-58196-059-4; 1-58196-059-X

"Halls presents an eerily fascinating exploration of mummified children and teens found in South and North America, Europe, and Asia. . . . The writing style is plain yet absorbing, presenting scientific and historical information in simple terms." Voice Youth Advocates

Includes bibliographical references

Knapp, Ron

Mummy secrets uncovered. Enslow Publishers 2011 48p il (Bizarre science) lib bdg $23.93

Grades: 5 6 7 8   **393**

  1. Mummies

  ISBN 978-0-7660-3670-3; 0-7660-3670-7

                    LC 2010000976

First published 1996 with title: Mummies

This describes mummies such as the Iceman found in the Italian Alps in 1991, King Tut of Egypt, the people of Pompeii killed by the eruption of Mount Vesuvius, Tollund Man found in Denmark in 1950, and the Ice Maiden found in the Siberian Steppes.

"Aimed at reluctant readers, [this title is] sure to disgust and delight in equal measure. . . . [The title] will pique interest and get kids lining up at the reference desk looking for more. The text is complemented by illustrations and magnified photos of things that you would hope never to see." SLJ

Includes glossary and bibliographical references

Malam, John

Mummies; foreword by Ron Beckett and Gerald Conlogue. Kingfisher 2003 63p il (Kingfisher knowledge) $11.95

Grades: 5 6 7 8   **393**

  1. Mummies

  ISBN 0-7534-5623-0

                    LC 2003-44630

"Malam covers Egyptian mummies; the discovery of a variety of preserved bodies throughout history and the world in bogs, deserts, and ice; animal mummies; and mummies today. [The title includes] stunning, captioned photos and illustrations that emphasize the many intriguing factual details in the text." SLJ

Includes glossary and bibliographical references

Markle, Sandra

★ **Outside** and inside mummies. Walker & Co. 2005 40p il $17.95; lib bdg $18.85

Grades: 4 5 6 7   **393**

  1. Mummies

  ISBN 0-8027-8966-8; 0-8027-8967-6 lib bdg

                    LC 2004-66128

"Markle explores a global smorgasbord of mummy varieties, both those created by human procedures and those caused by nature. Crisp (if gruesome) color photos accompany the readable, informative text, which discusses not only the mummification process, but also the cutting-edge technologies used by forensic anthropologists and others to study the mummies themselves." SLJ

Includes glossary

Perl, Lila

Mummies, tombs, and treasure; secrets of ancient Egypt. drawings by Erika Weihs. Clarion Bks. 1987 120p il lib bdg $16; pa $8.95

Grades: 4 5 6 7   **393**

  1. Mummies 2. Funeral rites and ceremonies 3. Egypt -- Antiquities

  ISBN 0-89919-407-9 lib bdg; 0-395-54796-2 pa

                    LC 86-17646

This "book is attractive, readable, plentifully illustrated with drawings and black-and-white photographs. . . . Phonetic pronunciations throughout make this easily accessible." Appraisal

Includes bibliographical references

Robson, David

The **mummy**. ReferencePoint Press 2011 il (Monsters and mythical creatures) $27.95

Grades: 6 7 8 9   **393**

  1. Mummies

  ISBN 978-1-60152-182-8; 1-60152-182-0

                    LC 2011022437

This is "an ideal starting point for young researchers interested in the weird, mysterious, and paranormal. Using fleet, descriptive prose to communicate the impressively researched (and sourced) information, [this] medium-length [work manages] to rope in just about everything, from folklore to history to pop culture. . . . TheMummy begins with the seminal 1932 Boris Karloff film before backtracking into the worldwide 'mummy lust' that began with the 1922 discovery of King Tut's tomb and and the subsequent curses and legends. . . . The illustrations are fine and varied, the sidebars always illuminating, and the back matter robust." Booklist

Includes bibliographical references

Sloan, Christopher

Mummies. National Geographic 2010 48p il (National Geographic Kids) $17.95; lib bdg $26.90

Grades: 4 5 6 7   **393**

  1. Mummies

  ISBN 978-1-4263-0695-2; 1-4263-0695-4; 978-1-4263-0696-9 lib bdg; 1-4263-0696-2 lib bdg

                    LC 2010-08498

"A gratifyingly grisly album of choice photos accompanies Sloan's lucid, informative text as he describes not only the mummification processes but also individual mummies produced whether by intent or by chance. From the dried Beauty of Kroran in China to the bundled Lady of Cao in a Peruvian pyramid or the familiar Boy King Tut in Egypt, a global variety is offered to fascinated readers. . . . [This is a] well-written, heavily illustrated glimpse into the world of after-death preservation, either by accident or design." SLJ

Includes glossary and bibliographical references

394.1   Eating, drinking; using drugs

Augustin, Byron

The **food** of Mexico. Marshall Cavendish Benchmark 2011 il (Flavors of the world) $21.95

Grades: 4 5 6 7   **394.1**

  1. Mexican cooking 2. Festivals -- Mexico 3. Mexico -- Social life and customs

  ISBN 978-1-6087-0237-4

                    LC 2010013830

"Explores the culture of Mexico through its food." (Publisher's note)

Includes bibliographical references

Kras, Sara Louise

The **food** of Italy. Marshall Cavendish Benchmark 2011 il (Flavors of the world) $21.95

Grades: 4 5 6 7　　394.1

1. Italian cooking 2. Festivals -- Italy 3. Italy -- Social life and customs

ISBN 978-1-6087-0236-7

LC 2010021542

This explores the culture, traditions, and festivals of Italy through its food.

Includes bibliographical references

Kummer, Patricia K.

The **food** of Thailand. Marshall Cavendish Benchmark 2011 il (Flavors of the world) $21.95

Grades: 4 5 6 7　　394.1

1. Thai cooking 2. Festivals -- Thailand 3. Thailand -- Social life and customs

ISBN 978-1-6087-0238-1

LC 2010023508

This explores the culture, traditions, and festivals of Thailand through its food.

Includes bibliographical references

Orr, Tamra

The **food** of Greece; [by] Tamra B. Orr. Marshall Cavendish Benchmark 2011 il (Flavors of the world) $21.95

Grades: 4 5 6 7　　394.1

1. Greek cooking 2. Festivals -- Greece 3. Greece -- Social life and customs

ISBN 978-1-6087-0235-0; 978-1-6087-0688-4 e-book

LC 2010035820

This explores the culture, traditions, and festivals of Greece through its food.

Includes bibliographical references

Orr, Tamra B.

The **food** of China; [by] Tamra B. Orr. Marshall Cavendish Benchmark 2011 il (Flavors of the world)

Grades: 4 5 6 7　　394.1

1. Chinese cooking 2. Festivals -- China 3. China -- Social life and customs

ISBN 1-608-70234-0; 978-1-608-70234-3; 978-1-608-70687-7 e-book

LC 2010039293

This explores the culture, traditions, and festivals of China through its food.

"Numerous high-quality, close-up color photos of outdoor vegetable markets, food in various stages of preparation, and families gathering around the table will keep readers engaged (and hungry) throughout the accessible and enlightening food tour." Booklist

Includes bibliographical references

Schlosser, Eric

★ **Chew** on this; everything you don't want to know about fast food. by Eric Schlosser and Charles Wilson. Houghton Mifflin Co. 2006 304p il $16; pa $9.99

Grades: 6 7 8 9 10　　394.1

1. Eating habits 2. Food industry 3. Convenience foods

ISBN 0-618-71031-0; 0-618-59394-2 pa

LC 2005-27527

"An adaptation of Schlosser's Fast Food Nation (Houghton, 2001), Chew on This covers the history of the fast-food industry and delves into the agribusiness and animal husbandry methods that support it. . . . Equally disturbing is his revelation of the way that the fast-food giants have studied childhood behavior and geared their commercials and free toy inclusions to hook the youngest consumers. The text is written in a lively, layout-the-facts manner. Occasional photographs add bits of visual interest." SLJ

Silverstein, Alvin

Chocolate ants, maggot cheese, and more; the yucky food book. by Alvin and Virginia Silverstein and Laura Silverstein Nunn; illustrated by Gerald Kelley. Enslow Publishers 2010 48p il (Yucky science) lib bdg $23.93

Grades: 4 5 6 7　　394.1

1. Eating customs

ISBN 978-0-7660-3315-3 lib bdg; 0-7660-3315-5 lib bdg

LC 2009012283

"Written in an engaging and conversational style and full of revolting descriptions and entertaining cartoon illustrations . . . [this is] sure to turn even the strongest stomach. An introduction . . . puts 'yucky' in perspective, reminding kids that our world is diverse and that everyone has a different definition of repulsive." SLJ

Includes glossary and bibliographical references

Whitman, Sylvia

What's cooking? the history of American food. Lerner Publs. 2001 88p il (People's history) lib bdg $22.60

Grades: 5 6 7 8　　394.1

1. Food -- History 2. United States -- Social life and customs

ISBN 0-8225-1732-9

LC 00-9168

A look at food in the United States from colonial times to the present, describing what we have eaten, where it came from, and how it reflected events in American history

"The text is very accessible, and there are many interesting black-and-white photographs. . . . Intriguing as well as informative." Booklist

Includes bibliographical references

394.12　Eating and drinking

Mogren, Molly

Andrew Zimmern's field guide to exceptionally weird, wild, & wonderful foods; an intrepid eater's digest. by Andrew Zimmern. 1st ed. Feiwel & Friends 2012 197 p. ill. (paperback) $14.99; (hardcover) $19.99

Grades: 5 6 7 **394.12**
1. Food 2. Cooking
ISBN 0312606613; 125001929X; 9780312606619; 9781250019295

LC 2012289475

This book is a "guide to world cuisine." The authors Andrew Zimmern and Molly Mogren "focus on 40 unusual foodstuffs including cockroaches, guinea pigs, headcheese, lutefisk, turducken, and Twinkies. Recipes, interviews, and a great many facts . . . lead to . . . digressions, including suggestions on how to survive a zombie outbreak . . . and a time line of popular dances, following a discussion of eating 'dancing' (live) shrimp." (Publishers Weekly)

394.2 Special occasions

Heath, Alan
Windows on the world; multicultural festivals for schools and libraries. Scarecrow Press 1995 392p il hardcover o.p. pa $47.95
Grades: Adult Professional **394.2**
1. Festivals 2. Multiculturalism
ISBN 0-8108-2880-4; 0-8108-3958-X pa

LC 94-10032

This guide "promotes reading through thematic festive activities centered around diverse cultural celebrations. Students explore varied art forms, from sculpture, print-making, batik, and puppetry to drama, music, dancing, cooking, and writing. . . . The book is profusely illustrated with photographs, diagrams, activity sheets, maps, bulletin board ideas, and . . . instructions for arts and crafts projects." Publisher's note
Includes bibliographical references

394.26 Holidays

Bowler, Gerald
The **world** encyclopedia of Christmas; [by] Gerry Bowler. McClelland & Stewart 2000 257p il hardcover o.p. pa $12.95
Grades: 8 9 10 11 12 **394.26**
1. Reference books 2. Christmas -- Encyclopedias
ISBN 0-7710-1531-3; 0-7710-1535-6 pa

This "provides more than 1,000 entries on worldwide secular and religious Christmas practices expressed in song, literature, events, film, arts, and trivia and is aimed at young adult and adult readers as well as researchers. Entries are primarily descriptive, but a number of them, especially those on films, contain critical commentary. . . . The book is enticing reading with its many descriptions of exotic customs and its blend of the ancient and the modern. It is written well and concisely." Booklist

Breuilly, Elizabeth
Festivals of the world; the illustrated guide to celebrations, customs, events, and holidays. [by] Elizabeth Breuilly, Joanne O'Brien, Martin Palmer. Checkmark Bks. 2002 160p il maps $29.95

Grades: 6 7 8 9 **394.26**
1. Festivals 2. Reference books 3. Religious holidays
ISBN 0-8160-4481-3

LC 2001-59876

The religions featured include Judaism, Christianity, Islam, Hinduism, Buddhism, Sikhism, Taoism, and Zoroastrianism

"A unique approach to holidays, organized by religion rather than alphabet, marks this thoughtful reference book. The introduction relates world festivals to the universal human search for meaning, and offers thematic relationships between seemingly disparate events. . . . Beautiful full-color photographs, diagrams, and maps bring the celebrations to life, and informative text boxes offer additional facts. . . . This book deserves to be in every reference collection." SLJ
Includes glossary and bibliographical references

Colman, Penny
Thanksgiving; the true story. [by] Penny Colman. Henry Holt 2008 149p il $18.95
Grades: 5 6 7 8 **394.26**
1. Thanksgiving Day 2. United States -- Social life and customs
ISBN 978-0-8050-8229-6; 0-8050-8229-8

LC 2007046943

"Drawing on historical research and the results of a written questionnaire, Colman first retraces the growth of Thanksgiving as a national holiday and then surveys the wide range of customs and mouthwatering comestibles associated with the celebration. Both tracks are illuminating. . . . A selection of old photos and prints illustrate this engagingly presented [title]." Booklist
Includes bibliographical references

Henderson, Helene
Patriotic holidays of the United States; an introduction to the history, symbols, and traditions behind the major holidays and days of observance. by Helene Henderson; foreword by Matthew Dennis. Omnigraphics 2006 408p il map $63
Grades: 7 8 9 10 11 12 **394.26**
1. Holidays 2. Patriotism 3. United States -- Social life and customs
ISBN 0-7808-0733-2

LC 2005024870

"Henderson defines patriotic holidays as those dealing with aspects of democratic civic rights, responsibilities, and values consistent with the ideals laid out in the nation's founding documents. . . . The book begins with a fascinating look at patriotism. Along with several definitions and views on it, the author explores different symbols of the U.S., including those of political parties, the cornucopia, the eagle, and the flag. She then considers each holiday in alphabetical order, describing any customs, songs, and foods associated with it; the history behind the observance; and a sampling of activities and observances around the country. . . . The volume also contains almost 100 pages of useful primary documents related to holidays, including The Mayflower Compact; The Declaration of Independence; flag laws; and excerpts from diaries, letters, and speeches." SLJ
Includes bibliographical references

★ **Holidays**, festivals, and celebrations of the world dictionary; detailing more than 3,000 observances from all 50 states and more than 100 nations: a compendious reference guide to popular, ethnic, religious, national, and ancient holidays... edited by Cherie D. Abbey. 4th ed.; Omnigraphics 2010 1323p $144

Grades: 8 9 10 11 12 Adult   **394.26**
1. Reference books 2. Holidays -- Dictionaries 3. Festivals -- Dictionaries
ISBN 978-0-7808-0994-9

LC 2009-41138

First edition published 1994 compiled by Sue Ellen Thompson and Barbara W. Carlson

"A comprehensive dictionary that describes more than 3,000 holidays and festivals celebrated around the world. Features both secular and religious events from many different cultures, countries, and ethnic groups. Includes contact information for events; multiple appendices with background information on world holidays; extensive bibliography; multiple indexes." Publisher's note

Jeffrey, Laura S.

Celebrate Martin Luther King, Jr., Day; [by] Laura S. Jeffrey. Enslow 2006 104p il (Celebrate holidays) lib bdg $31.93

Grades: 5 6 7 8   **394.26**
1. Clergy 2. Martin Luther King Day 3. Nonfiction writers 4. Civil rights activists 5. Nobel laureates for peace 6. African Americans -- Civil rights
ISBN 0-7660-2492-X

LC 2005028110

This offers a brief introduction to the life of Martin Luther King and the Civil Rights movement in the United States and how Martin Luther King Day became a holiday and is celebrated.

Includes glossary and bibliographical references

Celebrate Tet; [by] Laura S. Jeffrey. Enslow Publishers 2008 104p il map (Celebrate holidays) lib bdg $31.93

Grades: 5 6 7 8   **394.26**
1. Vietnamese New Year
ISBN 978-0-7660-2775-6 lib bdg; 0-7660-2775-9 lib bdg

LC 2006031922

"Captioned photographs, maps, drawings, and sidebars combine with an accessible text to present a thorough discussion of the Vietnamese New Year celebration. Jeffrey discusses the holiday's legendary origins and ancient traditions along with people's modern-day observances." Horn Book Guide

Includes glossary and bibliographical references

Marks, Diana F.

Let's celebrate today; calendars, events, and holidays. illustrated by Donna L. Farrell. 2nd ed; Libraries Unlimited 2003 340p il pa $38.95

Grades: Adult Professional   **394.26**
1. Holidays 2. Calendars 3. Festivals
ISBN 1-59158-060-9

LC 2003-47723

First published 1998

This is a "day-by-day calendar... for planning... activities and classroom units based on national and international holidays, multicultural and historic events, famous firsts, inventions, birthdays of important individuals (including authors), and more. The entries are annotated and include contact information and Web site addresses to facilitate further research and learning. In addition, three suggested learning activities are provided for each day of the year." Publisher's note

Includes bibliographical references

Mattern, Joanne

Celebrate Christmas; [by] Joanne Mattern. Enslow Publishers 2007 112p il (Celebrate holidays) lib bdg $31.93

Grades: 5 6 7 8   **394.26**
1. Christmas
ISBN 978-0-7660-2776-3 lib bdg; 0-7660-2776-7 lib bdg

LC 2006025258

The author "devotes several pages to the origins of Christmas, first as a pagan holiday, then as a celebration of Jesus' birth, and its evolution into the holiday as it is observed today. Symbols of Christmas, important people, and traditions from around the world are explored, and there is a fair amount of discussion about the commercialization of the holiday.... Full-color photos and reproductions appear throughout. There is plenty here for reports." SLJ

Includes glossary and bibliographical references

Celebrate Cinco de Mayo; [by] Joanne Mattern. Enslow Pub. 2006 104p il map (Celebrate holidays) lib bdg $31.93

Grades: 5 6 7 8   **394.26**
1. Cinco de Mayo 2. Mexico -- History 3. Mexico -- Social life and customs
ISBN 0-7660-2579-9

LC 2005028107

This describes the history of Cinco de Mayo and how it is celebrated.

Includes glossary and bibliographical references

Paterson, Katherine

★ **Giving** thanks; poems, prayers, and praise songs of thanksgiving. edited and with reflections by Katherine Paterson ; illustrated by Pamela Dalton. Chronicle Books LLC 2013 56 p. (alk. paper) $18.99

Grades: 3 4 5 6 7 8 9 10 11 12   **394.26**
1. Thanksgiving Day 2. Picture books for children 4. Children's poetry 5. Children -- Prayers and devotions 6. Religious poetry 7. Gratitude -- Religious aspects
ISBN 1452113394; 9781452113395

LC 2013009517

In this illustrated children's book, Wilder Award winner Katherine Paterson presents a collection of speeches, songs, and prayers related to giving thanks. She "offers an essay before each section: 'Gather Around the Table,' 'A Celebration of Life,' 'The Spirit Within' and 'Circle of Community.'" (Kirkus Reviews)

Rajtar, Steve

United States holidays and observances; by date, jurisdiction, and subject, fully indexed. McFarland & Co. 2003 165p $45

Grades: 11 12 Adult **394.26**

1. Holidays 2. Festivals

ISBN 0-7864-1446-4

LC 2002-154293

This "concentrates on observances and holidays established by statute in the U.S. and American Samoa, District of Columbia, Guam, the Northern Mariana Islands, Puerto Rico, and the U.S. Virgin Islands. In addition, UN-designated holidays are included. . . . The text is arranged by month, and chapters for each month are divided into 'Observances with Variable Dates' and 'Observances with Fixed Dates.' Each entry identifies the observance as federal or specific to a state and offers a description that ranges in length from three or four lines to a quarter page. . . . [This] would be a good addition to ready-reference desks in public libraries and information centers in schools." Booklist

395 Etiquette (Manners)

Aboukhair, Rachel

The **grumpy** girl's guide to good manners. New Chapter Pub. 2011 93p il pa $14.95

Grades: 6 7 8 9 **395**

1. Etiquette

ISBN 978-0-9827918-4-4; 0-9827918-4-4

"In this hilarious and satirical memoir, written when the author was 16, readers meet Rachel, a uncooperative teen whose mother decreed a week of etiquette lessons in the middle of the Texas desert. What follows is an account of the 15-year-old's trials: a cousin who never stops talking about her ex-boyfriend and instructions on how to hold silverware, apply makeup, dress properly, walk in high heels, and dance with a boy. . . . Occasional bullet point tips are offered on such topics as manicuring nails and a proper handshake. Readers will enjoy the author's conversational style and sympathize with her plight, and, who knows, they just might learn a few manners along the way." SLJ

Post, Peggy

Emily Post's table manners for kids. Collins 2009 96p $15.99

Grades: 4 5 6 7 **395**

1. Etiquette

ISBN 978-0-06-111709-1; 0-06-111709-9

LC 2008010655

"This deceptively slim guide teems with advice about everything from meal courses to table settings, from the art of conversation to dining out. The tone is measured and mildly proscriptive, offset by Bjorkman's amusing cartoons. . . . A strength: the excellent troubleshooting for specific concerns, such as eating fondue and using chopsticks." Kirkus

Emily Post's The guide to good manners for kids; by Peggy Post & Cindy Post Senning. HarperCollins 2004 144p il $15.99; lib bdg $16.89

Grades: 4 5 6 7 **395**

1. Etiquette

ISBN 0-06-057196-9; 0-06-057197-7 lib bdg

LC 2003-26426

This offers advice on etiquette at home, at school, and other places, including letter writing and on-line communication, table manners, phone answering, and behavior at social gatherings, and public places.

"The writing is clear, friendly, and sometimes clever. . . . The advice is consistently practical and simple." SLJ

Senning, Cindy Post

Emily Post prom and party etiquette. Collins 2010 134p il $15.99

Grades: 7 8 9 10 11 12 **395**

1. Parties 2. Etiquette

ISBN 978-0-06-111713-8; 0-06-111713-7

LC 2009-2795

"Covering parties and special occasions like prom, homecoming, quinceañera, and graduation, the authors have developed a modern set of rules for navigating today's more relaxed social customs with finesse and confidence. Myriad issues are tackled, from how to rent a tuxedo and who pays for what on prom night to table settings and crafting the perfect thank-you note, with important points highlighted. The comprehensive guide gives proper respect to religious occasions and thoughtfully explains how to determine from an invitation whether bringing a date is acceptable or not. Witty line drawings complement the text." SLJ

Teen manners; from malls to meals to messaging and beyond. by Cindy Post Senning and Peggy Post. 1st ed.; Collins 2007 134p il $15.99; lib bdg $16.89

Grades: 7 8 9 10 **395**

1. Etiquette

ISBN 978-0-06-088198-6; 0-06-088198-4; 978-0-06-088199-3 lib bdg; 0-06-088199-2 lib bdg

LC 2007010991

This offers advice on etiquette in personal relationships, in communication, dining, school, getting a job or getting into college, parties and dating, and other social situations.

395.1 Etiquette for people by gender or sex; for age groups

Packer, Alex J.

★ **How** Rude! the teen guide to good manners, proper behavior, and not grossing people out. Alex J. Packer, Ph.D. Rev. and updated ed. Free Spirit Pub 2014 489 p. illustrations $23.99

Grades: 7 8 9 10 **395.1**

1. Etiquette

ISBN 1575424541; 9781575424545

LC 2014001602

"It is difficult to make a topic like etiquette seem relevant and appealing to teenagers, but that is exactly what

Packer accomplishes. Drawing heavily on surveys of teens, parents, and teachers to target which situations were most pertinent, the opening chapters successfully sell the importance of manners to both the individual and society. . . . The text acknowledges social mores for other cultures and discusses the changeable nature of etiquette depending on context." Booklist

Includes bibliographical references and index

398 Folklore

Allen, Judy

    Fantasy encyclopedia; 1st ed.; Kingfisher 2005 144p il $19.95

Grades: 4 5 6 7   **398**

    1. Fairies 2. Mythical animals

    ISBN 0-7534-5847-0

                       LC 2004-29475

"This highly visual presentation introduces readers to fantasy characters within their habitats and genres. . . . More than 50 types of characters are arranged in nine chapters covering topics such as 'The Little People,' 'Mysterious Animals,' and 'Ghosts and Spirits.' . . . Student fans of the fantasy genre will find this tool exceedingly browsable, and school and public libraries will want to purchase reference and circulating copies." Booklist

    Includes glossary

Curran, Robert

    The **zombie** handbook; an essential guide to zombies and more importantly, how to avoid them. Barron's 2011 il $14.99

Grades: 6 7 8 9   **398**

    1. Zombies

    ISBN 978-0-7641-6409-5; 0-7641-6409-0

"This compact book does a good job of introducing zombies: what they are, how they look, where you find them. . . . The text is highly readable, the interspersed artwork is creepy and plentiful." Booklist

Etingoff, Kim

    Howling at the moon; vampires & werewolves in the New World. Mason Crest Publishers 2011 63p il (The making of a monster: vampires & werewolves) lib bdg $22.95; pa $9.95

Grades: 7 8 9 10   **398**

    1. Vampires 2. Werewolves

    ISBN 978-1-4222-1805-1 lib bdg; 1-4222-1805-8 lib bdg; 978-1-4222-1958-4 pa; 1-4222-1958-5 pa

                       LC 2010022670

Explores New World variants of myths and folklore about werewolves and vampires.

"The writing is engaging and accessible, and peppered easily with teen vernacular. . . . Large, clear photographs and period and contemporary drawings appear on every other page or so. . . . First-rate entertainment." SLJ

    Includes glossary and bibliographical references

    The **science** of the beast; the facts behind the fangs. Mason Crest Publishers 2011 63p il (The

making of a monster: vampires & werewolves) lib bdg $22.95; pa $9.95

Grades: 7 8 9 10   **398**

    1. Vampires 2. Werewolves

    ISBN 978-1-4222-1808-2 lib bdg; 1-4222-1808-2 lib bdg; 978-1-4222-1961-4 pa; 1-4222-1961-5 pa

                       LC 2010023660

Describes medical conditions and other observable phenomena that may have influenced early belief in vampires and werewolves.

"The writing is engaging and accessible, and peppered easily with teen vernacular. . . . Large, clear photographs and period and contemporary drawings appear on every other page or so. . . . First-rate entertainment." SLJ

    Includes glossary and bibliographical references

Indovino, Shaina Carmel

    Transylvania and beyond; vampires & werewolves in old Europe. Mason Crest Publishers 2011 63p il (The making of a monster: vampires & werewolves) lib bdg $22.95; pa $9.95

Grades: 7 8 9 10   **398**

    1. Vampires 2. Werewolves

    ISBN 978-1-4222-1809-9 lib bdg; 1-4222-1809-0 lib bdg; 978-1-4222-1962-1 pa; 1-4222-1962-3 pa

                       LC 2010021831

Explores European variants of myths and folklore about werewolves and vampires.

"The writing is engaging and accessible, and peppered easily with teen vernacular. . . . Large, clear photographs and period and contemporary drawings appear on every other page or so. . . . First-rate entertainment." SLJ

    Includes glossary and bibliographical references

Kallen, Stuart A.

    The **sphinx**; part of the Monsters and mythical creatures series. by Stuart A. Kallen. ReferencePoint Press 2012 80 p. ill. (chiefly col.) (Monsters and mythical creatures series) (hardback) $27.95

Grades: 4 5 6 7 8   **398**

    1. Sphinxes (Mythology)

    ISBN 1601522223; 9781601522221

                       LC 2011026636

This book, part of the "Monsters and Mythical Creatures" series, looks at the "history . . . [and] associated mythology" of the Sphinx. (School Library Journal). It "reveals the significant symbolic role this creature has played in human civilization from ancient Egypt through classical Greece and the Renaissance into the twenty-first century. . . . The ancient mythical creature has been an inspiration for artists, writers, architects, scholars, and theologians for millennia." (Publisher's note)

"Children will get a well-rounded look at the featured subjects and how they have evolved into the creatures that still fascinate many today.—" SLJ

    Includes bibliographical references and index

    Vampire history and lore. ReferencePoint Press 2010 80p il (The vampire library) lib bdg $26.95

Grades: 7 8 9 10 **398**

1. Vampires
ISBN 978-1-60152-132-3; 1-60152-132-4
LC 2010005866

Explores vampire beliefs from the blood sucking beasts of ancient times to the immortal teen heartthrobs of the twenty first century.

"Energetic and surprisingly educational, this lively [book] seizes upon a zeitgeist topic and takes it as far as possible." Booklist

Werewolves. Reference Point Press 2010 104p il (The mysterious & unknown) $25.95
Grades: 4 5 6 7 **398**

1. Werewolves
ISBN 978-1-60152-097-5; 1-60152-097-2

Describes the history and lore surrounding the topic of werewolves, examining how the shape-shifting beast has been feared by various cultures around the world, and its continuing influence on popular culture

This is "surprisingly exhaustive. . . . Breakout summaries and quotes enliven the layout. . . . There is . . . plenty of creepy stuff to scrutinize." Booklist

Includes bibliographical references

Kelly, Sophia

What a beast! a look-it-up guide to the monsters and mutants of mythology. Scholastic 2010 128p il map (Mythlopedia) lib bdg $39; pa $13.95
Grades: 4 5 6 7 **398**

1. Monsters 2. Classical mythology
ISBN 978-1-60631-028-1 lib bdg; 1-60631-028-3 lib bdg; 978-1-60631-060-1 pa; 1-60631-060-7 pa
LC 2009-20998

Describes some of the creatures and monsters in Greek mythology.

This "spices things up with sassy artwork, a pastel color scheme, and an OMG sensibility. . . . [This title is] loaded with information on the inspired methods with which various nasty creatures could put an end to bothersome heroes. Aside from the heaps of information coming from all angles on just about every page, . . . [the] book also contains a decent family tree, a rudimentary star chart, and lists of further reading. . . . For kids unconvinced that anything so old and gray could have any bearing on their lives, . . . [this book provides] a feisty . . . guide to the many cultural references lingering from antiquity." Booklist

Includes glossary and bibliographical references

Knudsen, Shannon

Fairies and elves. Lerner 2010 48p il (Fantasy chronicles) lib bdg $27.93
Grades: 4 5 6 7 **398**

1. Fairies
ISBN 978-0-8225-9979-1 lib bdg; 0-8225-9979-1 lib bdg
LC 2008050207

"The explanations and history behind . . . fairies [and elves] . . . will provide satisfaction for readers who want to know more about these familiar characters from myth, fantasy, and folk and fairy tales. Brief and concise." SLJ

Includes bibliographical references

Losure, Mary

The **Fairy** Ring, or, Elsie and Frances Fool the World; Mary Losure. Candlewick Press 2012 184 p. ill.
Grades: 5 6 7 8 **398**

1. Deception 2. Fairies 3. Fairies -- England
ISBN 9780763656706; 0763656704
LC 2011046081

This book offers explores an event that occurred "[t]owards the end of World War I, [when] two girls in Yorkshire took photographs that purported to capture the fairies they regularly saw, and these pictures . . . became a national sensation when . . . Sir Arthur Conan Doyle . . . championed them as authentic. . . . [The] book . . . conveys the widening of the ripples from the event and . . . the impulses behind the creation of the photographs." (Bulletin of the Center for Children's Books)

Martin, Nicholas

Fighting the fangs; a guide to vampires and werewolves. Mason Crest Publishers 2011 63p il (The making of a monster: vampires & werewolves) lib bdg $22.95; pa $9.95
Grades: 7 8 9 10 **398**

1. Vampires 2. Werewolves
ISBN 978-1-4222-1804-4 lib bdg; 1-4222-1804-X lib bdg; 978-1-4222-1957-7 pa; 1-4222-1957-7 pa
LC 2010025187

A guide to identifying and defeating vampires and werewolves.

"The writing is engaging and accessible, and peppered easily with teen vernacular. . . . Large, clear photographs and period and contemporary drawings appear on every other page or so. . . . First-rate entertainment." SLJ

Includes glossary and bibliographical references

Myths and legends. Macmillan Lib. Ref. USA 2000 436p (Macmillan profiles) $95
Grades: 7 8 9 10 **398**

1. Reference books 2. Folklore -- Dictionaries 3. Mythology -- Dictionaries
ISBN 0-02-865376-9
LC 99-51558

This volume "contains informative, accurate, and detailed information." SLJ

Entries in this volume "are drawn from the mythologies of numerous cultures, ranging from antiquity (Astarte) to more modern times (Paul Bunyan). Some articles focus on groups: Centaurs Leprechauns, Mermaids. Some profile real-life heroes: Casey Jones and Davy Crockett among others. More than 40 of the articles cover classical Greek and Roman mythology." Booklist

Nelson, Sheila

The **psychology** of our dark side; humans' love affair with vampires & werewolves. by Sheila Stewart. Mason Crest Publishers 2011 63p il (The making of a monster: vampires & werewolves) lib bdg $22.95; pa $9.95

Grades: 7 8 9 10   **398**
1. Vampires 2. Werewolves 3. Superstition
ISBN 978-1-4222-1807-5 lib bdg; 1-4222-1807-4 lib
bdg; 978-1-4222-1960-7 pa; 1-4222-1960-7 pa
LC 2010025294
Explores some of the reasons that many people, both past
and present, are fascinated by vampires and werewolves.
"The writing is engaging and accessible, and peppered
easily with teen vernacular. . . . Large, clear photographs and
period and contemporary drawings appear on every other
page or so. . . . First-rate entertainment." SLJ
Includes glossary and bibliographical references

Regan, Sally
The **vampire** book. DK Pub. 2009 93p il
$19.99
Grades: 5 6 7 8   **398**
1. Vampires
ISBN 978-0-7566-5551-8; 0-7566-5551-X
"This guide covers the origins and evolution of vampires throughout history, giving a worldwide perspective on
legends, mythology, and lore, from African tales of terror
to blood-drinking witches of Southeast Asia. It also covers
vampires in literature, film, and television. . . . The vivid
colors in the often full-page art leap from the pages, and the
bold font demands attention." SLJ

Robson, David
Encounters with vampires. ReferencePoint
Press 2010 80p il (Vampire library) lib bdg $26.95
Grades: 7 8 9 10   **398**
1. Vampires
ISBN 978-1-6015-2133-0; 1-6015-2133-2
LC 2010-10100
The author "lays out both folklore and real-world reports
of bloodsucking beings. Expanding beyond familiar Transyl-
vanian tales and stories of vampires in strictly human form,
the author's survey is global, from the Malaysian langsuyar,
believed to be responsible for many newborn deaths, to the
red-eyed, monstrous Latin American chupacabra, notorious
for preying on livestock. . . . Young vampire-fiction fans will
find much to ponder here, while the accounts of contemporary murders with purported vampire links may emerge as
the most chilling and grisly." Booklist
Includes bibliographical references

Sanna, Emily
Pop monsters; the modern-day craze for vampires and werewolves. Mason Crest Publishers 2011
63p il (The making of a monster: vampires & werewolves) lib bdg $22.95; pa $9.95
Grades: 7 8 9 10   **398**
1. Vampires 2. Werewolves
ISBN 978-1-4222-1806-8 lib bdg; 1-4222-1806-6 lib
bdg; 978-1-4222-1959-1 pa; 1-4222-1959-3 pa
LC 2010025186
Describes the current phenomenon of vampires and
werewolves in popular culture, from books, television, and
movies, to computer games.
"The writing is engaging and accessible, and peppered
easily with teen vernacular. . . . Large, clear photographs and

period and contemporary drawings appear on every other
page or so. . . . First-rate entertainment." SLJ
Includes glossary and bibliographical references

Stewart, Gail
Vampires : do they exist? [by] Gail B. Stewart.
ReferencePoint Press 2010 80p il (The vampire
library) $26.95
Grades: 7 8 9 10   **398**
1. Vampires
ISBN 978-1-60152-110-1; 1-60152-110-3
Examines the legends about the forms vampires can
take, how they feed on the living, and the dangers of
encountering them.
"Energetic and surprisingly educational, this lively
[book] seizes upon a zeitgeist topic and takes it as far as
possible." Booklist

Vande Velde, Vivian
Tales from the Brothers Grimm and the Sisters
Weird. Harcourt Brace & Co. 1995 128p il hard-
cover o.p. pa $5.95
Grades: 7 8 9 10   **398**
1. Fairy tales 2. Short stories
ISBN 0-15-200220-0; 0-15-205572-X pa
LC 94-26341
This collection presents alternative versions of such fa-
miliar fairy tales as Rumpelstiltskin, Hansel and Gretel, and
The Princess and the Pea.
"Vande Velde challenges readers' notions of good, bad,
and ugly. . . . Modern references and sensibilities . . . add to
the humor (often the gallows variety). Entertaining and provocative, these selections make good read-alouds and can be
used to spark discussion or creative writing exercises." SLJ

398.2   Folk literature

Abrahams, Roger D.
African folktales; traditional stories of the black
world. selected and retold by Roger D. Abrahams.
Pantheon Bks. 1983 354p il (Pantheon fairy tale &
folklore library) hardcover o.p. pa $18
Grades: 8 9 10 11 12 Adult   **398.2**
1. Folklore -- Africa
ISBN 0-394-72117-9 pa
LC 83-2474
These stories are arranged in five groupings. "The first
section, by way of introduction, is given over to a few wonder tales of the kind that Europeans and Americans are most
accustomed to, but that are found here in typically African
renderings. The sections that then follow are: shorter stories
used to introduce a subject for moral discussions; moral stories specific to the problems of keeping family and community together (and which, therefore, might be called domestic dramas); tales told in praise of great deeds; and finally, a
large section of outrageous stories, told primarily to entertain, about the antisocial doings of one or another trickster
figure." (Preface) Bibliography. Index of tales.
Includes bibliographical references

American Indian myths and legends; selected and edited by Richard Erdoes and Alfonso Ortiz. Pantheon Bks. 1984 527p il hardcover o.p. pa $18

Grades: 8 9 10 11 12 Adult   **398.2**

1. Native Americans -- Folklore 2. Native Americans -- Religion

ISBN 0-394-74018-1

LC 84-42669

"This volume comprises 160 tales of native folklore and myth ranging from one geographical end of our continent to the other. The book is organized according to type of myth. . . . Erdoes and Ortiz seek to keep Indian myth intact and pure through their retellings, using, as often as possible, primary sources." Booklist

Includes bibliographical references

The **August** House book of scary stories; spooky tales for telling out loud. edited by Liz Parkhurst. August House 2009 144p $15.95

Grades: 4 5 6 7 8   **398.2**

1. Folklore 2. Storytelling 3. Short stories 4. Horror fiction

ISBN 978-0-87483-915-9; 0-87483-915-7

LC 2009008711

An anthology of spooky stories drawn from folklore, local history, and the storytellers' imaginations, and divided into the categories "Just Desserts and Lessons Learned," "Ghostly Guardians," "Dark Humor," "Urban Legends and Jump Tales," and "Fearless Females."

"Each of these 20 chilling tales is meant to be told out loud and includes author notes about how to maximize the spooky effect. Middle schoolers will relish reading and sharing these tales, hoping to creep each other out." SLJ

Baynes, Pauline

Questionable creatures; a bestiary. [by] Pauline Baynes. Eerdmans Books for Young Readers 2006 47p il $18

Grades: 4 5 6 7   **398.2**

1. Bestiaries 2. Mythical animals

ISBN 978-0-8028-5284-7; 0-8028-5284-X

LC 2005033658

"Baynes introduces readers to the creatures and myths found in medieval bestiaries and explains how the books were made and how they were viewed by the general public. The rest of the volume details the commonly held beliefs that both peasants and scholars embraced about specific animals. . . . Baynes's detailed gouache and colored-pencil illustrations . . . are done in the style of medieval illuminations. . . . The artist shows great respect for the early bestiary creators while also giving the stories relevance for modern readers." SLJ

Includes bibliographical references

Bedard, Michael

The **painted** wall and other strange tales; selected and adapted from the Liao-chai of Pu Sung-ling by Michael Bedard. Tundra Books 2003 109p $16.95

Grades: 7 8 9 10   **398.2**

1. Folklore -- China

ISBN 0-88776-652-8

"Known as the Liao-chai, these . . . stories were first collected by a scholar named Pu Sung-ling. . . . Wildly popular in China but little known in the West, they draw on the supernatural or unusual to cast their spell. . . . The stories are short and accessible to reluctant readers." SLJ

Bennett, Adelaide

Ancient werewolves and vampires; the roots of the teeth. Mason Crest Publishers 2011 63p il (The making of a monster: vampires & werewolves) lib bdg $22.95; pa $9.95

Grades: 7 8 9 10   **398.2**

1. Vampires 2. Werewolves

ISBN 978-1-4222-1802-0 lib bdg; 1-4222-1802-3 lib bdg; 978-1-4222-1955-3 pa; 1-4222-1955-0 pa

LC 2010023796

Explores the earliest tales and folklore about werewolves and vampires.

"The writing is engaging and accessible, and peppered easily with teen vernacular. . . . Large, clear photographs and period and contemporary drawings appear on every other page or so. . . . First-rate entertainment." SLJ

Includes glossary and bibliographical references

Global legends and lore; vampires and werewolves around the world. Mason Crest Publishers 2011 63p il (The making of a monster: vampires & werewolves) lib bdg $22.95; pa $9.95

Grades: 7 8 9 10   **398.2**

1. Vampires 2. Werewolves

ISBN 978-1-4222-1810-5 lib bdg; 1-4222-1810-4 lib bdg; 978-1-4222-1963-8 pa; 1-4222-1963-1 pa

LC 2010025778

Presents legends about vampires and werewolves from around the world.

"The writing is engaging and accessible, and peppered easily with teen vernacular. . . . Large, clear photographs and period and contemporary drawings appear on every other page or so. . . . First-rate entertainment." SLJ

Includes glossary and bibliographical references

Blackwood, Gary L.

Legends or lies? Marshall Cavendish Benchmark 2006 72p il (Unsolved history) lib bdg $34.21

Grades: 4 5 6 7   **398.2**

1. Legends

ISBN 978-0-7614-1891-7 lib bdg; 0-7614-1891-1 lib bdg

Describes several legends that have intrigued people for centuries: the lost civilization of Atlantis, the Amazons, King Arthur, St Brendon, Pope Joan, and El Dorado

This collection "of tidbits about lingering mysteries of the past . . . [offers] more substance than most. . . . [It offers] a full-page illustration opening each chapter; reproductions, many in color; and a generously spaced format." SLJ

Includes glossary and bibliographical references

Boughn, Michael

Into the world of the dead; astonishing adventures in the underworld. Annick Press 2006 56p il lib bdg $24.95; pa $12.95

Grades: 5 6 7 8   **398.2**
  1. Death -- Folklore 2. Future life -- Folklore
  ISBN 1-55037-959-3 lib bdg; 1-55037-958-5 pa

"Boughn retells stories from many cultures on every continent except South America, including quite a few from Mesoamerica, Asia, Africa, and Oceania. Readers will find heroes who have traveled to and returned from the underworld as well as the gods and monsters who dwell there. Full-color and black-and-white illustrations, including reproductions, photos, and plenty of graphics of skulls, appear on every page. . . . This is a book that many young people may find appealing." SLJ

Brown, Dee Alexander

Dee Brown's folktales of the Native American; retold for our times. Holt & Co. 1993 174p pa $12
Grades: 7 8 9 10   **398.2**
  1. Native Americans -- Folklore
  ISBN 0-8050-2607-X
                     LC 93-12449

First published 1979 by Holt, Rinehart & Winston with title: Teepee tales of the American Indian

This is a collection of 36 folktales from Native American tribes, including the Seneca, Hopi, Navaho, Creek, Cheyenne, Cherokee, and Blackfoot, grouped by themes such as tricksters and magicians, heroes and heroines, and ghost stories

Includes bibliographical references

Bryan, Ashley

★ **Ashley** Bryan's African tales, uh-huh. Atheneum Bks. for Young Readers 1998 198p $22
Grades: 4 5 6   **398.2**
  1. Folklore -- Africa
  ISBN 0-689-82076-3
                     LC 97-77743

This volume combines three previously published titles: The ox of the wonderful horns and other African folktales (1971), Beat the story-drum, pum-pum (1980), Lion and the ostrich chicks and other African folktales (1986)

This collection of African folktales is "told with Bryan's distinctive rhythmic word patterns and filled with humor, life lessons, and the antics of trickster Ananse. . . . Quality reproductions of the original woodcuts enrich this handsome volume." Horn Book Guide

Burns, Batt

★ The **king** with horse's ears and other Irish folktales; [by] Batt Burns; illustrated by Igor Oleynikov. Sterling Pub. Co. 2009 96p il (Folktales of the world) $14.95
Grades: 4 5 6 7   **398.2**
  1. Fairy tales 2. Folklore -- Ireland
  ISBN 978-1-4027-3772-5; 1-4027-3772-6
                 LC 2007035258

"These 13 Irish tales retold by storyteller Burns follow fairies and warriors, heroes and clever thieves. . . . The stories are cleanly retold in contemporary, accessible language, and each is introduced with a short paragraph providing cultural or other information. . . . Oleynikov's paintings have a rough texture that suits the energy of the retellings and adds to the lively tone. This is a hearty collection, handsomely

produced with Celtic-knot borders and gouache full-page and spot illustrations." Booklist
  Includes glossary

Chase, Richard

The **Jack** tales; told by R.M. Ward and his kindred in the Beech Mountain section of western North Carolina and by other descendants of Council Harmon (1803-1896) elsewhere in the southern mountains; with three tales from Wise County, Virginia; set down from these sources and edited by Richard Chase; with an appendix compiled by Herbert Halpert; and illustrated by Berkeley Williams, Jr. Houghton Mifflin 2003 216p il pa $7.95
Grades: 5 6 7 8 Adult Professional   **398.2**
  1. Folklore -- Southern States
  ISBN 978-0-618-34692-9 pa; 0-618-34692-9 pa
                LC 2003276676

First published 1943

A collection of folk tales from the southern Appalachians that center on a single character, the irrepressible Jack

"Humor, freshness, colorful American background, and the use of one character as a central figure in the cycle mark these 18 folk tales, told here in the dialect of the mountain country of North Carolina. A scholarly appendix by Herbert Halpert, giving sources and parallels, increases the book's value as a contribution to American folklore. Black-and-white illustrations in the spirit of the text." Booklist

Includes bibliographical references

Currie, Stephen

African American folklore. Lucent Books 2008 104p il (Lucent Library of Black History) $32.45
Grades: 7 8 9 10   **398.2**
  1. African Americans -- Folklore
  ISBN 978-1-4205-0082-0; 1-4205-0082-1
               LC 2008020201

Examines African American folklore in context so that readers will understand the connection between black history and the broad sweep of America's story.

The book is "highly accessible and [provides] cultural context to help readers understand [the] topic. . . . [The] book includes captioned color and black-and-white photographs and reproductions on every spread. Well-organized and clearly written." SLJ

Includes bibliographical references

Curry, Jane Louise

Hold up the sky: and other Native American tales from Texas and the Southern Plains; illustrated by James Watts. Margaret K. McElderry Bks. 2003 159p il $17.95
Grades: 4 5 6 7   **398.2**
  1. Folklore -- Southern States 2. Native Americans -- Folklore
  ISBN 0-689-85287-8
                LC 2002-16519

Retells twenty-six tales from Native Americans whose traditional lands were in Texas and the Southern Plains, and provides a brief introduction to the history of each tribe

"Curry has carefully researched and sensitively retold tales from fourteen Native American nations. Attractive pencil drawings enhance the stories." Horn Book Guide

Includes bibliographical references

DiPrimio, Pete

The **sphinx**. Mitchell Lane Publishers 2010 48p il map (Monsters in myth) lib bdg $29.95

Grades: 4 5 6 7   398.2

1. Sphinxes (Mythology)

ISBN 978-1-58415-931-5; 1-58415-931-6

LC 2010006560

This describes the mythic Sphinx that has appeared in both Egyptian and Greek myth.

This book is "thorough and respectful of a number of ancient and modern sources and [bends] over backward to navigate often contradictory, interlinked legends. . . . A number of paintings and photos break up the otherwise text-heavy pages, and copious chapter notes and reading suggestions conclude. This is by no means entry-level stuff, but for kids handy with the basics and ready to delve deeper, [this book] will be of great use." Booklist

Includes glossary and bibliographical references

English folktales; edited by Dan Keding and Amy Douglas. Libraries Unlimited 2005 231p il map (World folklore series) $35

Grades: Adult Professional   398.2

1. Folklore -- Great Britain

ISBN 1-59158-260-1

LC 2005016075

"This collection of more than 50 English folktales contains a variety of stories arranged by common themes: The Fool in All His Glory, Wily Wagers and Tall Tales, Dragons and Devils, etc. The work of 22 storytellers is represented and their tellings are lively and inflected with the rhythms and speech of the regions from which their stories emanate. It is a delightful compendium for storytellers." SLJ

Forest, Heather

Wisdom tales from around the world; retold by Heather Forest. August House 1996 156p $28; pa $17.95

Grades: 7 8 9 10   398.2

1. Folklore

ISBN 0-87483-478-3; 0-87483-479-1 pa

LC 96-31141

A collection of traditional stories from around the world, reflecting the cumulative wisdom of Sufi, Zen, Taoist, Buddhist, Jewish, Christian, African, and Native American cultures

"Forest retells folktales, proverbs, and parables in a thoughtful and satisfying style that amuses as it deftly imparts lessons for living." SLJ

Includes bibliographical references

Gavin, Jamila

Tales from India; illustrated by Amanda Hall. Candlewick Press 2011 il

Grades: 5 6 7 8   398.2

1. Hindu mythology 2. Folklore -- India

ISBN 0-7636-5564-3; 978-0-7636-5564-8

LC 2010047651

"Gavin, . . . presents 10 classic Hindu stories, accompanied by Hall's lush and elegant gouache illustrations. . . . . Readers should be drawn toward the valor, action, and dramatic transformations in these powerful tales." Publ Wkly

Grimm, Jacob, 1785-1863

Tales from the Brothers Grimm; selected & illustrated by Lisbeth Zwerger. Lisbeth Zwerger. Minedition 2013 96 p. (hbk.) $29.99

Grades: 4 5 6 7 8   398.2

1. Fairy tales 2. Fairy tales -- Germany

ISBN 9789888240531; 9888240536

In this book, Lisbeth Zwerger selects and illustrates stories "from the well-known collection of fairy tales by the Brothers Grimm. Old favorites such as 'Hansel and Gretel' and 'The Bremen Town Musicians' are included as are some lesser-known stories such as 'The Seven Ravens' and 'Hans My Hedgehog.'" (Publisher's note)

"High production values give this mix of new and recycled translations and illustrations a suitably sumptuous air...Like Zwerger's figures, which are nearly all small on the page and tend to look off into the distance, Bell's translations are more often lyrical than intimate or earthy: "Once upon a time, when wishes could still come true, there was a king whose daughters were all beautiful, but the youngest was so lovely that the sun itself, although it had seen so much, marveled at her beauty whenever it shone on her face."...A belated companion to Zwerger's Hans Christian Andersen's Fairy Tales (1992, 2006), similarly elegant of design and equally fine for reading alone or aloud." (Kirkus)

Hamilton, Virginia

★ The **people** could fly: American Black folktales; told by Virginia Hamilton; illustrated by Leo and Diane Dillon. 2009 178p il $24.99; pa $13

Grades: 5 6 7 8   398.2

1. African Americans -- Folklore

ISBN 978-0-394-86925-4; 0-394-86925-7; 978-0-679-84336-8 pa; 0-679-84336-1 pa

A reissue of the title first published 1985

Coretta Scott King honor book for illustration, 1986

The author "has been successful in her efforts to write these tales in the Black English of the slave storytellers. Her scholarship is unobtrusive and intelligible. She has provided a glossary and notes concerning the origins of the tales and the different versions in other cultures. Handsomely illustrated." NY Times Book Rev

Includes bibliographical references

Hausman, Gerald

Horses of myth; [by] Gerald and Loretta Hausman; pictures by Robert Florczak. Dutton Children's Books 2004 100p il $12

Grades: 4 5 6 7   398.2

1. Folklore 2. Horses -- Folklore

ISBN 0-525-46964-8

LC 2002-40809

"These five tales each feature a different type of horse, remarkable for both its individuality and the qualities representative of its breed. . . . Florczak's illustrations adapt characteristics appropriate to the locations and time periods of each selection's origins. . . . This is an attractive volume, useful to teachers and librarians for read-alouds and of interest to horse-loving youngsters." SLJ

Hayes, Joe

Dance, Nana, dance; Cuban folktales in English and Spanish. retold by Joe Hayes; illustrated by Mauricio Trenard Sayago. Cinco Puntos Press 2008 128p il $20.95

Grades: 5 6 7 8 9   **398.2**

1. Folklore -- Cuba 2. Bilingual books -- English-Spanish

ISBN 978-1-933693-17-0; 1-933693-17-7

LC 2007-38295

A collection of stories from Cuban folklore, representing the cultures of Spain, Africa, and the Caribbean.

"Each tale is accompanied by a full-page illustration that is colorful and contributes to the text. This book is a great addition to folktale and Spanish language collections. Students will enjoy these stories that could easily be incorporated into the curriculum." Libr Media Connect

Helbig, Alethea

Myths and hero tales; a cross-cultural guide to literature for children and young adults. [by] Alethea K. Helbig and Agnes Regan Perkins. Greenwood Press 1997 288p $49.95

Grades: 8 9 10 11 12 Adult   **398.2**

1. Reference books 2. Mythology -- Bibliography

ISBN 0-313-29935-8

LC 97-8778

"Brief, incisive critical reviews of 189 books, published between 1985 and 1996, that contain 1455 myths and hero tales form the heart of this . . . sourcebook. Scholarly accuracy and literary quality are the authors' chief criteria for inclusion, but they also comment trenchantly on illustrations. Indexes list stories by writer, tale type, culture, character and place name, grade level, title, or illustrator." SLJ

Hirschmann, Kris

Medusa. ReferencePoint Press 2011 il (Monsters and mythical creatures) $27.95

Grades: 6 7 8 9   **398.2**

1. Medusa (Greek mythology)

ISBN 978-1-60152-181-1; 1-60152-180-4

LC 2011020993

This is "an ideal starting point for young researchers interested in the weird, mysterious, and paranormal. Using fleet, descriptive prose to communicate the impressively researched (and sourced) information, [this] medium-length [work manages] to rope in just about everything, from folklore to history to pop culture. . . . Medusa goes into the monster's roots in Greek storytelling before delving more deeply into Homer's Iliad, the story of Perseus, and the Gorgan's appearance in art, theater, opera, and more. . . . The illustrations are fine and varied, the sidebars always illuminating, and the back matter robust." Booklist

Includes bibliographical references

Horowitz, Anthony

Death and the underworld; illustrated by Thomas Yeates. Kingfisher 2011 133p il (Legends) $9.99

Grades: 6 7 8   **398.2**

1. Folklore 2. Death -- Folklore 3. Future life -- Folklore

ISBN 978-07534-6542-4; 0-7534-6542-6

This retells classic myths and legends of afterlife.

"Balancing the heroic and the macabre, these dryly humorous, sometimes gory retellings hold particular appeal for reluctant readers. The conversational language also lends itself well to reading aloud. Black-and-white illustrations provide occasional breaks in the text while adding visual interest." Horn Book Guide

Heroes and villains; illustrated by Thomas Yeates. Kingfisher 2011 165p il (Legends) $9.99

Grades: 6 7 8   **398.2**

1. Folklore

ISBN 978-0-7534-6546-2; 0-7534-6546-9

This retells classic myths and legends of heroes and villains.

"Balancing the heroic and the macabre, these dryly humorous, sometimes gory retellings hold particular appeal for reluctant readers. The conversational language also lends itself well to reading aloud. Black-and-white illustrations provide occasional breaks in the text while adding visual interest." Horn Book Guide

Houston, James A.

James Houston's Treasury of Inuit legends. Harcourt 2006 268p $18; pa $8.95

Grades: 5 6 7 8   **398.2**

1. Inuit -- Folklore

ISBN 978-0-15-205924-8; 978-0-15-205930-9 pa

LC 2006043577

"This collection includes four previously published stories: 'Tiktaliktak' (1965), 'The White Archer' (1967), 'Akavak' (1968), and 'Wolf Run' (1971). Noted artist Houston lived among the Inuit people for fourteen years and brought their culture to life through his books and artwork." Horn Book Guide

Jaffe, Nina

The **cow** of no color: riddle stories and justice tales from around the world; [by] Nina Jaffe and Steve Zeitlin; pictures by Whitney Sherman. Holt & Co. 1998 159p il $17

Grades: 4 5 6 7   **398.2**

1. Folklore

ISBN 0-8050-3736-5

LC 98-14167

In each of these stories, collected from around the world, a character faces a problem situation which requires that he make a decision about what is fair or just

"Sherman's black-and-white line drawings have a stark gracefulness that complements the tales' form and structure; the tales themselves are simply told with little embellishment." Bull Cent Child Books

Includes bibliographical references

Krasno, Rena

Cloud weavers; ancient Chinese legends. [by] Rena Krasno and Yeng-Fong Chiang; illustrations from the collection of Yeng-Fong Chiang. Pacific View Press 2003 96p il $22.95

Grades: 5 6 7 8   **398.2**

1. Folklore -- China

ISBN 1-881896-26-9

LC 2002-35911

Presents legends and tales from China, including ancient folktales, stories that reflect Chinese traditions and virtues, historical tales, and selections from literature

This collection "provides a showcase for some remarkable pieces of Chinese calendar art and advertising posters from the 1920s and 1930s. . . . Prefaces provide cultural insight for some stories, and the brisk retellings weave important background unobtrusively into the narrative." Booklist

Lester, Julius

★ Uncle Remus, the complete tales; with a new introduction. as told by Julius Lester; illustrated by Jerry Pinkney. 1999 xxi, 686p il lib bdg $35

Grades: 4 5 6 7   **398.2**

1. Animals -- Folklore 2. African Americans -- Folklore

ISBN 0-8037-2451-9

LC 99-17121

Reprint in one volume of works originally published separately, 1987-1994

Lester retells stories of the trickster rabbit from African American folklore collected by Joel Chandler Harris

"This is a landmark collection. . . . Lester's retellings are sharp and flavorful and grounded in the here and now." [review of book 1] Booklist

Livo, Norma J.

Folk stories of the Hmong; peoples of Laos, Thailand, and Vietnam. [by] Norma J. Livo and Dia Cha. Libraries Unlimited 1991 135p il $26

Grades: 8 9 10 11 12 Adult   **398.2**

1. Hmong Americans

ISBN 0-87287-854-6

LC 91-370

This is a collection of folktales of the Hmong people of Asia which also includes a description of Hmong history and culture, with 16 pages of color photographs of Hmong dress and needlework

Includes bibliographical references

Marshall, James Vance

Stories from the Billabong; retold by James Vance Marshall; illustrated by Francis Firebrace. Frances Lincoln Children's Books 2009 61p il $19.95

Grades: 3 4 5 6   **398.2**

1. Aboriginal Australians -- Folklore

ISBN 978-1-84507-704-4; 1-84507-704-0

"With the help of Aboriginal storytellers who have collected the tales and myths of their people, Marshall has assembled 10 fascinating stories of the Dreamtime. . . . Each selection is beautifully told and is illustrated by a traditional artist who uses the distinctive symbols and colors of the Ab-

original people. . . . This is an engaging, colorful book that belongs in most libraries." SLJ

Martin, Rafe

★ The world before this one; a novel told in legend. with paper sculpture by Calvin Nicholls. Levine Bks. 2002 195p il hardcover o.p. pa $5.99

Grades: 4 5 6 7   **398.2**

1. Seneca Indians -- Folklore

ISBN 0-590-37976-3; 978-0-590-37980-9 pa; 0-590-37980-1 pa

LC 2001-23403

"Written in the style of a novel, this collection of 14 Seneca tales is presented through the retelling of one central story into which all of the others are artfully woven. . . . Martin offers sources for the tales along with an introductory note by Seneca Elder Peter Jemison. Each chapter includes a painstakingly detailed white paper sculpture of a character (often an animal) from one of the stories." SLJ

McCaughrean, Geraldine

★ The epic of Gilgamesh; retold by Geraldine McCaughrean; illustrated by David Parkins. Eerdmans Bks. for Young Readers 2003 95p il $18

Grades: 5 6 7 8   **398.2**

1. Gilgamesh 2. Folklore -- Iraq

ISBN 0-8028-5262-9

LC 2003-1086

A retelling, based on seventh-century B.C. Assyrian clay tablets, of the wanderings and adventures of the god king, Gilgamesh, who ruled in ancient Mesopotamia (now Iraq) in about 2700 B.C., and of his faithful companion, Enkidu

This is "clearly a telling for our time, but one that honors its source. Parkins captures the epic's primitive power and universal emotions in rough, broadly rendered portraits." Horn Book

McKinley, Robin

★ The outlaws of Sherwood. Greenwillow Bks. 1988 282p hardcover o.p. pa $14

Grades: 8 9 10 11 12   **398.2**

1. Robin Hood (Legendary character)

ISBN 0-688-07178-3; 0-441-01325-2 pa

LC 88-45227

"McKinley takes a fresh look at a classic, changing some of the events or deviating from standard characterization to gain new dimensions. Her afterword explains her artistic compromise with myth and history, her wish to write a version that is 'historically unembarrassing.' With a few exceptions, she has done that admirably, creating a story that has pace and substance and style, and that is given nuance and depth by the characterization." Bull Cent Child Books

Menchu, Rigoberta

The secret legacy; [by] Rigoberta Menchu with Dante Liano; pictures by Domi; translated by David Unger. Groundwood Books/House of Anansi Press 2008 64p il $19.95

Grades: 4 5 6 7 8   **398.2**

1. Mayas -- Folklore 2. Folklore -- Guatemala

ISBN 978-0-88899-896-5; 0-88899-896-1

"On her first day watching over her Mayan grandfather's cornfields, young Ixkem is invited by the b'e'n, spirits in the form of small humans, to visit them underground. They feed her generously and she tells them stories that explain Mayan customs and include bits of folklore. . . . The Mexican artist Domi has provided bright paintings in a naturalistic, folk-art style. The lyrical translation preserves the storyteller's voice." SLJ

Mhlophe, Gcina

African tales; a Barefoot collection. written by Gcina Mhlophe; illustrated by Rachel Griffin. Barefoot Books 2009 95p il map

Grades: 5 6 7 8   **398.2**

1. Folklore -- Africa

ISBN 1-84686-118-7; 978-1-84686-118-5

LC 2008028042

"Each of these eight tales is preceded by information and interesting facts about the country from which it originated. A basic map of Africa helps orient readers to the location of the various countries represented. Extensive source notes are appended. . . . There are many choices that could be read aloud or told using a call-and-response format. The book design . . . is a feast for the eyes. Griffin employs a collage technique using colored beads, sewn fabric, and textured papers, and incorporates them into shapes and faces of animals and humans. . . . This compilation contains a wealth of information and will enhance folklore collections." SLJ

Includes bibliographical references

Mitton, Tony

The **storyteller's** secrets; illustrated by Peter Bailey. David Fickling Books 2010 118p il $15.99

Grades: 4 5 6   **398.2**

1. Folklore 2. Storytelling -- Fiction

ISBN 978-0-385-75190-2; 0-385-75190-7

"In a handsome volume profusely illustrated with a mix of silhouettes and vigorous line drawings, Mitton presents verse renditions of European tales and legends. . . . Written in ballad-style quatrains with unforced, natural sounding rhymes and cadences, the stories offer enthralling, easy-to-follow plots with clear themes. . . . Mitton links all of his selections with prose encounters between two marveling children and a mysterious old Storyteller. . . . This gathering will cast the same sort of profound spell on readers and listeners." Booklist

Monte, Richard

The **mermaid** of Warsaw; and other tales from Poland. illustrated by Paul Hess. Frances Lincoln 2011 il pa $8.95

Grades: 4 5 6 7   **398.2**

1. Folklore -- Poland

ISBN 978-1-84780-164-7; 1-84780-164-1

"A gratifying and unusual collection of folktales from Poland. There are a number of good stock characters in these pages: beautiful princesses who get themselves into trouble, warty-nosed ogres, . . . buffoons who overstep themselves or commit one-too-many deadly sins. There are also talking trees, dark forests, miraculous springs and . . . monsters. . . . The tales are told . . . in an unwavering voice, with portent enough to keep an audience listening close, and Hess' art-

work has the right spidery look and sinister atmosphere. . . . That the locales are ancient and real gives the whole collection added wallop." Kirkus

Morpurgo, Michael

★ **Beowulf**; illustrated by Michael Foreman. Candlewick Press 2006 92p il $17.99

Grades: 5 6 7 8   **398.2**

1. Beowulf 2. Folklore -- Europe 3. Monsters -- Folklore

ISBN 978-0-7636-3206-9; 0-7636-3206-6

"Morpurgo retells the classic story of the courageous young warrior . . . who used his brute strength to save the neighboring Danes, then his own kinsmen, by slaying two horrible monsters, a sea serpent, and a massive dragon. . . . Many attractive full-page watercolor and pastel paintings illustrate important action-filled scenes. . . . This is a fine retelling." SLJ

Sir Gawain and the Green Knight; as told by Michael Morpurgo; illustrated by Michael Foreman. Candlewick Press 2004 114p il $18.99

Grades: 5 6 7 8   **398.2**

1. Arthurian romances 2. Gawain (Legendary character)

ISBN 0-7636-2519-1

LC 2003-65527

The quest of Sir Gawain for the Green Knight teaches him a lesson in pride, humility, and honor

"Morpurgo's sprightly writing brings out all the humor as well as the horror of the original tale, and Foreman's profuse, evocative watercolor-and-pastel illustrations highlight the drama in each scene." SLJ

Napoli, Donna Jo, 1948-

★ **Treasury** of Greek mythology; classic stories of gods, goddesses, heroes & monsters. National Geographic Society 2011 191p il map $24.95; lib bdg $33.90

Grades: 5 6 7 8   **398.2**

1. Greek mythology

ISBN 978-1-4263-0844-4; 1-4263-0844-2; 978-1-4263-0845-1 lib bdg; 1-4263-0845-0 lib bdg

LC 2011024327

"Napoli presents 25 tales introducing the major players of the Greek pantheon along with an assortment of celebrated heroes and mortals. . . . At once eloquent and elemental, these lyrically written portraits deftly detail each character's origins, realm of power, and legendary story lines. Filled with sensual imagery, the language is poetic, yet balanced by amusing asides and wry observations that add a contemporary, almost conversational accessibility. . . . Stunning stylized paintings featuring luminous colors, rich patterns, and star-infused motifs add depth and drama to the text. . . . Interesting sidebars appear throughout, providing historical, scientific, and cultural information." SLJ

Norman, Howard

★ **Between** heaven and earth; bird tales from around the world. illustrated by Leo & Diane Dillon. Harcourt 2004 78p il lib bdg $22

Grades: 4 5 6 7 **398.2**
1. Folklore 2. Birds -- Folklore
ISBN 0-15-201982-0

LC 2003-7874

A collection of folktales from around the world, all of which have a bird as a main character

This is "a collection of stories that are rich in cultural references from the lands of their origins. . . . The Dillons' luminous watercolor-and-pencil illustrations, detailed with patterns drawn from each tale's culture of origin, will draw readers and listeners back to the stories." Booklist

Oberman, Sheldon

★ **Solomon** and the ant; and other Jewish folktales. retold by Sheldon Oberman; introduction and commentary by Peninnah Schram. Boyds Mills Press 2006 165p $19.95
Grades: 5 6 7 8 **398.2**
1. Jews -- Folklore
ISBN 1-59078-307-7

LC 2005020115

"This collection of 43 traditional Jewish stories is authoritative as well as immensely entertaining. . . . The stories, from both Ashkenazi and Sephardic traditions, are arranged more or less chronologically—from biblical days through the talmudic period to more contemporary times. There are legends, medieval fables, trickster tales, and more. . . . The stories, wonderful for storytelling and sharing, are accessible even to listeners younger than the target audience, and the notes and commentary will provide older children with context and history." Booklist

Includes bibliographical references

Ollhoff, Jim

Japanese mythology. ABDO Pub. 2011 32p il (The world of mythology) lib bdg $27.07
Grades: 5 6 7 8 **398.2**
1. Japanese mythology
ISBN 978-1-61714-723-4

LC 2010042019

'This book offers information about Japanese mythology, answering questions such as "Who is Hachiman? What is the Seven Gods of Fortune? Why are myths so important in our lives? Myths are a rich source of history. People use them to make sense of our world. Even before myths were written down, people told and retold the stories of the gods and goddesses of their homeland. Readers of Japanese Mythology will learn the history of myths, as well as their deeper meaning." (Publisher's note) "A Shinto creation story forms the backbone of [this book], which also introduces the sun goddess Amaterasu; the fabled first emperor of Japan, Jimmu; and the impish Oni." (Booklist)

"Ollhoff writes in a clear and engaging fashion, presenting complex issues in a way that will be easy for youngsters to grasp. . . . The photographs and reproductions of art tie directly to the [text]." SLJ

Olson, Arielle North

Ask the bones: scary stories from around the world; selected and retold by Arielle North Olson and Howard Schwartz; illustrated by David Linn. Viking 1999 145p il hardcover o.p. pa $5.99

Grades: 4 5 6 7 **398.2**
1. Folklore
ISBN 0-670-87581-3; 0-14-230140-X pa

LC 98-19108

A collection of scary folktales from countries around the world including China, Russia, Spain, and the United States

"David Linn's bone-chilling black-and-white illustrations . . . will stay with the reader long after the book is closed. Excellent for reading aloud, this collection will satisfy even jaded genre fans." Booklist

Includes bibliographical references

More bones; scary stories from around the world. selected and retold by Arielle North Olson and Howard Schwartz; illustrated by E.M. Gist. Viking 2008 162p il $15.99
Grades: 4 5 6 7 **398.2**
1. Folklore
ISBN 978-0-670-06339-0; 0-670-06339-8

"This tour of the world's shadowy corners is full of dark wizards, unkind witches, and other untrustworthy creatures. . . . The 22 tales, as retold by Olson and Schwartz, give a vivid glimpse into unfamiliar, unnerving territory. . . . The atmospheric illustrations, while not intricately detailed, are somewhat startling in their imagery." Booklist

Orr, Tamra

The **monsters** of Hercules. Mitchell Lane Publishers 2011 48p il map (Monsters in myth) lib bdg $29.95
Grades: 4 5 6 7 **398.2**
1. Monsters 2. Hercules (Legendary character)
ISBN 978-1-58415-927-8; 1-58415-927-8

LC 2010028764

This book about the monsters of Hercules is "thorough and respectful of a number of ancient and modern sources and [bends] over backward to navigate often contradictory, interlinked legends. . . . A number of paintings and photos break up the otherwise text-heavy pages, and copious chapter notes and reading suggestions conclude. This is by no means entry-level stuff, but for kids handy with the basics and ready to delve deeper, [this book] will be of great use." Booklist

Includes glossary and bibliographical references

The **sirens**. Mitchell Lane Publishers 2011 48p il map (Monsters in myth) lib bdg $29.95
Grades: 4 5 6 7 **398.2**
1. Sirens (Mythology)
ISBN 978-1-58415-930-8; 1-58415-930-8

LC 2010026965

This book examines the various stories that surround the myths of the Sirens.

This book is "thorough and respectful of a number of ancient and modern sources and [bends] over backward to navigate often contradictory, interlinked legends. . . . A number of paintings and photos break up the otherwise text-heavy pages, and copious chapter notes and reading suggestions conclude. This is by no means entry-level stuff, but for kids handy with the basics and ready to delve deeper, [this book] will be of great use." Booklist

Includes glossary and bibliographical references

Philip, Neil

★ **Celtic** fairy tales; retold with an introduction by Neil Philip; illustrated by Isabelle Brent. Viking 1999 137p il $21.99

Grades: 4 5 6 7   **398.2**
1. Fairy tales 2. Celts -- Folklore 3. Folklore -- Great Britain

ISBN 0-670-88387-5

LC 98-50081

An illustrated collection of twenty stories from many Celtic regions, including "The Battle of the Birds," "Finn MacCool and the Scotch Giant," and "The Ship that Went to America."

"There's a mix of the almost familiar and nicely exotic in this collection, which is lavishly illustrated with a glowing full-page painting for each tale and Celtic motifs on every page." Booklist

Pyle, Howard

The **merry** adventures of Robin Hood; [by] Howard Pyle; illustrated by Scott McKowen. Sterling Pub. 2004 335p il (Sterling unabridged classics) $9.95

Grades: 8 9 10 11 12   **398.2**
1. Robin Hood (Legendary character) 2. Folklore -- Great Britain

ISBN 978-1-4027-1456-6; 1-4027-1456-4

LC 2004016213

Recounts the legend of Robin Hood, who plundered the king's purse and poached his deer and whose generosity endeared him to the poor.

The **story** of King Arthur and his knights; written and illustrated by Howard Pyle. Scribner 1984 312p il $22.95

Grades: 1 2 8 9 10 11   **398.2**
1. Arthurian romances 2. Kings

ISBN 0-684-14814-5

LC 84-50167

A reissue of the title first published 1903

This is an account of the times "when Arthur, son of Uther-Pendragon, was Overlord of Britain and Merlin was a powerful enchanter, when the sword Excalibur was forged and won, when the Round Table came into being." Publisher's note

The **story** of Sir Launcelot and his companions. Dover Publications 1991 340p il pa $13.95

Grades: 8 9 10 11 12   **398.2**
1. Arthurian romances 2. Lancelot (Legendary character)

ISBN 0-486-26701-6

LC 90-22326

A reissue of the title first published 1907 by Scribner

This third book of the series follows "Sir Launcelot's adventures as he rescues Queen Guinevere from the clutches of Sir Mellegrans, does battle with the Worm of Corbin, wanders as a madman in the forest and is finally returned to health by the Lady Elaine." Best Sellers

The **story** of the champions of the Round Table; written and illustrated by Howard Pyle. Dover Publications 1968 328p il pa $11.95

Grades: 8 9 10 11 12   **398.2**
1. Arthurian romances

ISBN 0-486-21883-X

A reissue of the title first published 1905 by Scribner

"Pyle's second volume of Arthurian legends will be of interest to motivated students of literature and history, as well as useful in professional collections for comparisons and source work. In spite of the archaic language . . . the narrative depth and graphic force . . . will draw in readers." Booklist

The **story** of the Grail and the passing of Arthur. Dover Publications 1992 258p il pa $12.95

Grades: 8 9 10 11 12   **398.2**
1. Arthurian romances 2. Kings 3. Grail -- Fiction

ISBN 0-486-27361-X

LC 92-29058

A reissue of the title first published 1910 by Scribner

This fourth volume of the series follows the adventures of Sir Geraint, Galahad's quest for the holy Grail, the battle between Launcelot and Gawaine, and the slaying of Mordred

Rapunzel and other magic fairy tales; selected and illustrated by Henriette Sauvant; translated by Anthea Bell. Trafalgar Square 2008 157p il $15.95

Grades: 5 6 7 8   **398.2**
1. Folklore 2. Fairy tales

ISBN 1-4052-2702-8

"Sauvant has selected 14 tales of German, English, and French origin, many of them written down by the Grimm brothers. While most of them are familiar . . . others will be unknown to most readers. . . . The illustrations, which range in size from tiny fillers to full-page and double-page pictures, appear to be painted in watercolor or acrylic on a textured surface. While some are painted in classic fairy-tale style, others are best described as surreal. . . . The sophistication of both stories and artwork makes this collection most suitable for older readers." SLJ

Raven, Nicky

★ **Beowulf**; a tale of blood, heat, and ashes. retold by Nicky Raven; illustrated by John Howe. 1st U.S. ed.; Candlewick Press 2007 72p il $18.99

Grades: 7 8 9 10 11 12   **398.2**
1. Beowulf 2. Folklore -- Europe 3. Monsters -- Folklore

ISBN 978-0-7636-3647-0; 0-7636-3647-9

LC 2007027094

A modern, illustrated retelling of the Anglo-Saxon epic about the heroic efforts of Beowulf, son of Ecgtheow, to save the people of Heorot Hall from the terrible monster, Grendel.

This is "a gripping rendition of the Anglo-Saxon epic. . . . Raven takes some liberties that add welcome nuance to the story. . . . Howe's artwork . . . is . . . spectacular, easily capturing the heroic grandeur and horrific gruesomeness of the tale." Booklist

Rumford, James

★ **Beowulf**; a hero's tale retold. Houghton Mifflin Company 2007 un il $17

Grades: 4 5 6 7   **398.2**

1. Beowulf 2. Folklore -- Europe 3. Monsters -- Folklore

ISBN 0-618-75637-X; 978-0-618-75637-7

A simplified and illustrated retelling of the exploits of the Anglo-Saxon warrior, Beowulf, and how he came to defeat the monster Grendel, Grendel's mother, and a dragon that threatened the kingdom.

"Superb on all counts—from the elegant bookmaking to the vigorous, evocative prose . . . to the pen-and-ink and watercolor illustrations that strikingly recall the work of Edmund Dulac." Horn Book

San Souci, Robert

★ **Cut** from the same cloth; American women of myth, legend, and tall tale. collected and told by Robert D. San Souci; illustrated by Brian Pinkney; introduction by Jane Yolen. Philomel Bks. 1993 140p il hardcover o.p. pa $6.99

Grades: 4 5 6 7   **398.2**

1. Tall tales 2. Women -- Folklore 3. Folklore -- United States

ISBN 0-399-21987-0; 0-698-11811-1 pa

LC 92-5233

A collection of fifteen stories about legendary American women from Anglo-American, African American, and Native American folklore

"San Souci's language is vigorous and action verbs abound; Pinkney's black-and-white block prints match the strength of the telling. The inclusion of notes on the sources and a general bibliography make this an academic resource as well as a good collection of rolicking stories." Child Book Rev Serv

★ A **terrifying** taste of short & shivery; thirty creepy tales. retold by Robert D. San Souci; illustrated by Lenny Wooden. Delacorte Press 1998 159p il $14.95; pa $10.95

Grades: 4 5 6 7   **398.2**

1. Folklore 2. Ghost stories

ISBN 0-385-32635-1; 0-385-32255-0 pa

LC 98-5551

"Drawing on urban legends, myths, folktales, and ghost stories from around the world and across time, the reteller serves up 30 tales of the supernatural that range from eerie to downright scary. . . . Suspenseful, accessible, and energetic, the tales are uniformly brief and gripping." SLJ

Includes bibliographical references

Sanna, Ellyn

★ **Latino** folklore and culture; stories of family, traditions of pride. [by] Ellyn Sanna. Mason Crest Publishers 2005 112p il (Hispanic heritage) $22.95

Grades: 7 8 9 10   **398.2**

1. Folklore -- Latin America 2. Latin Americans -- Social life and customs

ISBN 1-59084-932-9

LC 2004024248

This "book begins with a description of the place of folklore in culture and the differences between the terms Latino and Hispanic. Specific folktales, such as the many versions of 'La Llorona,' and dominant themes, such as machismo, strong women, and religion, are described in subsequent chapters. . . . [This is] an excellent resource both for students researching Latino arts for reports and for general readers." SLJ

Includes bibliographical references

Schwartz, Alvin, 1927-1992

★ **More** scary stories to tell in the dark; collected from folklore and retold by Alvin Schwartz; illustrated by Brett Helquist. Reillustrated Harper Trophy ed Harper 2010 111 p. ill. (hardcover) $15.99

Grades: 4 5 6 7   **398.2**

1. Ghost stories 2. Horror fiction 3. Folklore -- United States

ISBN 9780060835217; 0060835214

LC 2010922248

Originally published in 1984 by Lippincott, with illustrations by Stephen Gammell.

This volume contains stories of ghosts, murders, graveyards and other horrors.

"Helquist's new illustrations for Schwartz's classic [collection] of ghost stories inhabit an altogether more benign universe than the nightmarish Stephen Gammell originals. [This edition is] handsome and accessible, ceding the stories themselves pride of place." Horn Book Guide

Includes bibliographical references (pages 105-111).

★ **Scary** stories 3; more tales to chill your bones. collected from folklore and retold by Alvin Schwartz; drawings by Stephen Gammell. HarperCollins Pubs. 1991 115p il music $15.99; lib bdg $16.89; pa $5.99

Grades: 4 5 6 7   **398.2**

1. Ghost stories 2. Horror fiction 3. Folklore -- United States

ISBN 0-06-021794-4; 0-06-021795-2 lib bdg; 0-06-440418-8 pa

LC 90-47474

Traditional and modern-day stories of ghosts, haunts, superstitions, monsters, and horrible scary things

"The book is well paced and continually captivates, surprises, and entices audiences into reading just one more page. Gammell's gauzy, cobwebby, black-and-white pen-and-ink drawings help to sustain the overall creepy mood." SLJ

Includes bibliographical references

Schwartz, Howard

The **day** the Rabbi disappeared: Jewish holiday tales of magic; retold by Howard Schwartz; illustrated by Monique Passicot. Viking 2000 80p il hardcover o.p. pa $9.95

Grades: 4 5 6 7   **398.2**

1. Jews -- Folklore 2. Jewish holidays -- Fiction

ISBN 0-670-88733-1; 0-8276-0757-1 pa

LC 99-42061

Retellings of twelve traditional tales from Jewish folklore featuring elements of magic and relating to holidays, including Rosh Hodesh, Sukkot, Tu bi-Shevat, and Shabbat

"Schwartz follows these brief, clear, and simply told tales with rich and highly readable notes about the history of the holiday, the importance of the rabbi, and the sources of the story." Horn Book

Shelby, Anne

The **adventures** of Molly Whuppie and other Appalachian folktales; [by] Anne Shelby; illustrations by Paula McArdle. The University of North Carolina Press 2007 88p il $14.95

Grades: 4 5 6 7 **398.2**

1. Folklore -- Appalachian Mountains
ISBN 978-0-8078-3163-2

LC 2007013789

A collection of Appalachian folktales featuring Molly Whuppie and her adventures.

"Shelby has captured the language of Appalachia. . . Her adaptations are true to the traditional folktales. . . . Young readers and listeners will make these stories their own and enjoy retelling them." SLJ

Includes bibliographical references

Stewart, Gail

Trolls. ReferencePoint Press 2011 il (Monsters and mythical creatures) $27.95

Grades: 6 7 8 9 **398.2**

1. Trolls
ISBN 978-1-60152-183-5; 1-60152-183-9

LC 2011016391

This is "an ideal starting point for young researchers interested in the weird, mysterious, and paranormal. Using fleet, descriptive prose to communicate the impressively researched (and sourced) information, [this] medium-length [work manages] to rope in just about everything, from folklore to history to pop culture. . . . Trolls [twines] together the various strands of Norse legends into a coherent, readable, eye-opening narrative that begins in the ninth century and ends with Harry Potter. . . . The illustrations are fine and varied, the sidebars always illuminating, and the back matter robust." Booklist

Includes bibliographical references

Talk that talk: an anthology of African-American storytelling; edited by Linda Goss & Marian E. Barnes. Simon & Schuster 1989 521p hardcover o.p. pa $32.95

Grades: 8 9 10 11 12 Adult **398.2**

1. African Americans -- Folklore
ISBN 0-671-67167-7; 0-671-67168-5 pa

LC 89-10582

The selections included range "from slave stories and the animal legends of Brer Rabbit and Brer Fox to the comedy monologues of Dick Gregory and rap routines. . . . Interspersed throughout are brief sections of commentary and analysis." Booklist

Includes bibliographical references

Tarnowska, Wafa'

★ **Arabian** nights; written by Wafa' Tarnowska; illustrated by Carole Hénaff. Barefoot Books 2010 125p il $24.99

Grades: 5 6 7 8 **398.2**

1. Fairy tales 2. Arabs -- Folklore
ISBN 978-1-84686-122-2; 1-84686-122-5

LC 2008028159

"With bright, lush, stylized acrylic illustrations, this collection of eight stories from A Thousand and One Nights is designed for reading aloud. . . . Throughout, the spacious paintings capture the sense of the supernatural in daily life, including magical images of people taking flight above city, trees, and desert." Booklist

Taylor, C. J.

Peace walker; the legend of Hiawatha and Tekanawita. Tundra Books 2004 45p il $15.95

Grades: 6 7 8 9 **398.2**

1. Indian leaders 2. Iroquois Indians -- Folklore
ISBN 0-88776-547-5

Using sources from her own Mohawk oral tradition, Taylor relates a historical legend about "the Iroquois Confederacy and its Great Law of Peace . . . (which still guides the Grand Council of the People of the Longhouse today). Nine chapters portray a period of internal warring that led to domination by Atotarho, a cruel Onondaga sorcerer chief. The narrative concludes with the successful efforts of Hiawatha, [an] . . . Onondaga chief, and Tekanawita, a . . . Huron, who converted a culture of accusation, suspicion, and revenge to one of virtue, honesty, and patience. . . . Age eight and up." (Quill Quire)

"The events surrounding the collaboration of two chiefs, the Onandaga Hiawatha and Tekanawita of the Mohawk, to upset the tyrant Atotarho are related simply and abound with graphic details of Native life. . . . Each chapter includes one full-page illustration done in acrylic on canvas in a slightly naive style. . . . The writing is eloquent and poetically rhythmic." SLJ

Tchana, Katrin Hyman

★ **Changing** Woman and her sisters; stories of goddesses from around the world. retold by Katrin Hyman Tchana; illustrated by Trina Schart Hyman. Holiday House 2006 80p il $18.95

Grades: 5 6 7 8 **398.2**

1. Folklore 2. Gods and goddesses
ISBN 978-0-8234-1999-9; 0-8234-1999-1

LC 2005-52504

An illustrated collection of traditional tales which feature goddesses from different cultures, including Navajo, Mayan, and Fon. Notes explain each goddess's place in her culture, the reason for the book, and how the illustrations were developed

"This large, handsome volume assembles well-chosen, well-told stories. . . . Hyman . . . contributed distinctive portrayals of the goddesses using a technique that melded photographs and found materials into full-page ink and acrylic paintings." Booklist

Includes bibliographical references

Thomas, Joyce Carol

★ The **skull** talks back and other haunting tales; collected by Zora Neale Hurston; adapted by Joyce Carol Thomas; illustrated by Leonard Jenkins. HarperCollins 2004 56p $15.99; lib bdg $16.89

Grades: 4 5 6 7   **398.2**

1. Authors 2. Novelists 3. Dramatists 4. Horror fiction 5. Memoirists 6. Folklorists 7. Short story writers 8. African Americans -- Folklore

ISBN 0-06-000631-5; 0-06-000634-X lib bdg

LC 2003-22215

"Using a direct style that loses none of the colloquial immediacy of the original voices, Thomas has done a great job of retelling six of Hurston's supernatural tales, and Jenkins' monochromatic collages and silhouettes capture the delicious, shivery glow of skeletons and graveyards." Booklist

Tingle, Tim

Spirits dark and light; supernatural tales from the five civilized tribes. [by] Tim Tingle. August House 2006 192p $15.95

Grades: 6 7 8 9   **398.2**

1. Supernatural -- Fiction 2. Native Americans -- Folklore

ISBN 0-87483-778-2

LC 2006042709

"Choctaw storyteller Tingle tells 25 deliciously scary tales collected from the five major Native American tribes of the southeastern U.S.the Cherokee, Chickasaw, Choctaw, Creek, and Seminole. . . . For each tribe, Tingle begins with background on history, culture, and folklore. The language is clear and informal, and the dialogue is immediate." Booklist

Walking the Choctaw road. Cinco Puntos Press 2003 142p il $24.95; pa $10.95

Grades: 7 8 9 10   **398.2**

1. Choctaw Indians -- Folklore 2. Folklore -- Southern States

ISBN 0-938317-74-1; 0-938317-73-3 pa

LC 2003-1069

A collection of stories of the Choctaw people, including traditional lore arising from beliefs and myths, historical tales passed down through generations, and personal stories of contemporary life

"Sophisticated narrative devices and some subtle character nuances give these stories a literary cast, but the author's evocative language, expert pacing, and absorbing subject matter will rivet readers and listeners both." Booklist

Tracy, Kathleen

Cerberus. Mitchell Lane Publishers 2011 48p il map (Monsters in myth) lib bdg $29.95

Grades: 4 5 6 7   **398.2**

1. Classical mythology

ISBN 978-1-58415-924-7; 1-58415-924-3

LC 2010026968

This describes myths of Cerberus, Hades three-headed watchdog who guarded the gates of the Greek Underworld.

This book is "thorough and respectful of a number of ancient and modern sources and [bends] over backward to navigate often contradictory, interlinked legends. . . . A number

of paintings and photos break up the otherwise text-heavy pages, and copious chapter notes and reading suggestions conclude. This is by no means entry-level stuff, but for kids handy with the basics and ready to delve deeper, [this book] will be of great use." Booklist

Includes glossary and bibliographical references

★ **Trickster**: Native American tales; a graphic collection. edited by Matt Dembicki. Fulcrum 2010 231p il pa $22.95

Grades: 5 6 7 8   **398.2**

1. Graphic novels 2. Folklore -- Graphic novels 3. Native Americans -- Folklore

ISBN 978-1-55591-724-1 pa; 1-55591-724-0 pa

LC 2009-49668

"More than 40 storytellers and cartoonists have contributed to this original and provocative compendium of traditional folklore presented in authentic, colorful, and engaging sequential art. The stories are drawn from a variety of Native peoples across North America, and so the trickster character appears variously as Rabbit, a raccoon, Coyote, and in other guises; landscapes, clothing and rhythms of speech and action also vary in keeping with distinct traditions. Realistic, impressionistic, painterly, and cartoon styles of art are employed to echo and announce the tone of each tale and telling style, making this a rich visual treasure as well as cultural trove." SLJ

Valentino, Serena

How to be a werewolf; the claws-on guide for the modern lycanthrope. Candlewick Press 2011 144p il $14.99

Grades: 7 8 9 10   **398.2**

1. Werewolves

ISBN 978-0-7636-5387-3; 0-7636-5387-X

LC 2010039173

"This handbook is divided into three distinct segments: 'Unleashing Your Wild Side,' 'The Stylish Lycanthrope,' and 'Moonlight Mystery.' Each chapter quizzes readers or is full of helpful tips to advise them on their path toward lycanthropy. The guide sheds light on understanding your werewolf self, hunting strategies and lunar charts, living quarters, party recipes, and music to howl by. The volume . . . includes research on werewolf legends and lore as well as movies, TV shows, comics, games, books, and further study. An entertaining read full of color photos and illustrations that add to the book's charm." SLJ

Yep, Laurence, 1948-

★ The **rainbow** people; [retold by] Laurence Yep; illustrated by David Wiesner. Harper & Row 1989 194p il hardcover o.p. pa $6.99

Grades: 4 5 6 7   **398.2**

1. Folklore -- China

ISBN 0-06-026760-7; 0-06-026761-5; 0-06-440441-2 pa

LC 88-21203

"Twenty Chinese folktales, selected and retold by Yep from those collected in the 1930s in the Oakland Chinatown as part of a WPA project. . . . The tales, while drawn from the depicting Chinese culture, present a variety of familiar motifs and types: wizards and saints, shape changing and magical objects, pourquoi tales and lessons. An 'Afterword' provides suggestions for further reading on Chinese folktales. This is an excellent introduction to Chinese and Chinese-American folklore." SLJ

Includes bibliographical references

Yolen, Jane

★ **Mightier** than the sword; world folktales for strong boys. collected and told by Jane Yolen; with illustrations by Raul Colón. Silver Whistle/Harcourt 2003 112p il $19

Grades: 4 5 6 7   **398.2**

1. Folklore
ISBN 0-15-216391-3

LC 2002-9886

A collection of folktales from around the world which demonstrate the triumph of brains over brawn

Yolen's "versions of these stories are lively, expressively written, ready for reading aloud or telling, and illustrative of her point." SLJ

Includes bibliographical references

398.209   Folklore -- History, geographic treatment, biography

Delacre, Lulu

Golden tales; myths, legends, and folktales from Latin America. [retold by] Lulu Delacre. Scholastic 1996 73p hardcover o.p. pa $5.99

Grades: 5 6 7 8   **398.209**

1. Folklore -- Latin America 2. Native Americans -- Folklore
ISBN 0-439-24398-X pa

LC 94-36724

This includes 12 "stories from four native cultures (Taino, Zapotec, Muisca, and Quechua), including pourquoi tales, legends of the conquistadores, and folktales from before and after the age of Columbus. . . . [The author's] . . . retellings are done in a clear and confident voice and are accompanied by her robust, colorful oil paintings. . . . This impressively presented and referenced collection will inspire readers and tellers alike." Booklist

Includes bibliographical references

Ollhoff, Jim

Middle Eastern Mythology; by Jim Ollhoff. ABDO Publishing Company 2011 32p il (The world of mythology) lib bdg $27.07

Grades: 5 6 7 8   **398.209**

1. Mythology 2. Middle East 3. Children -- Books and reading 4. Mythology -- Middle East
ISBN 1617147257; 9781617147258; 1-61714-725-7; 978-1-61714-725-8

LC 2010042977

This describes the history of myths of the Middle East, their meaning, and their gods and goddesses including Mithra, Mot, the Mesopotamian goddess Ishtar, and the Canaanite thunder god, Baal.

"Ollhoff writes in a clear and engaging fashion, presenting complex issues in a way that will be easy for youngsters

to grasp. . . . The photographs and reproductions of art tie directly to the [text]." SLJ

Smith, Charles R., 1969-

The **mighty** 12; superheroes of Greek myth. by Charles R. Smith, Jr. ; illustrated by P. Craig Russell. 1st ed. Little, Brown 2008 48 p. col. ill. (hardcover) $16.99; (paperback) $7.99

Grades: 5 6 7 8   **398.209**

1. Gods and goddesses 2. Classical mythology
ISBN 031601043X; 9780316010436 out of print; 9780316073660; 0316073660

LC 2007048729

"Future students of Homer get a handy checklist of musclebound Greek gods in this combo of mythology, comics and loose rhyme. . . . Smith and Russell make the pairing of classical material and a comics-like format look completely natural, with a gee-why-didn't-we-think-of-that simplicity." Publ Wkly

Includes bibliographical references (p. 48).

398.21   Tales and lore on a specific topic

Hearne, Betsy Gould

Beauties and beasts; by Betsy Hearne; illustrated by Joanne Caroselli. Oryx Press 1993 179p il (Oryx multicultural folktale series) pa $33.95

Grades: 8 9 10 11 12 Adult   **398.21**

1. Folklore 2. Mythology 3. Fairy tales
ISBN 0-89774-729-1

LC 93-16

"Professionals will be very grateful for this sensitively written, thoughtful, and accessible interpretive collection." J Youth Serv Libr

"The theme of a lonely beast who is transformed by the magic of human love is threaded throughout worldwide variations of the 'Beauty and the Beast' folktale. Author Betsy G. Hearne presents 28 versions of the beloved fable with minimal adaptations from around the world." Publisher's note

Includes bibliographical references

398.24   Tales and lore of plants and animals

Drake, Ernest

Drake's comprehensive compendium of dragonology; by Ernest Drake and edited by Dugald A. Steer. Candlewick Press 2009 182 p. $19.99

Grades: 4 5 6 7   **398.24**

1. Dragons
ISBN 0763646237; 9780763646233

LC 2009016525

This book, by Ernest Drake and edited by Dugald A. Steer, presents an encyclopedia of dragonology. It features "a guide to dragon species, with entries on everything from the well-known European dragon to the lesser-known hydra — as well as pseudo-species such as the phoenix and the incognito, insight into dragon biology, from flight to reproduction [and] an in-depth look at dragons' habits, including migration, communication, camouflage, and notorious hoarding practices." (Publisher's note)

Hirschmann, Kris

The **werewolf**; by Kris Hirschmann. Reference-Point Press 2012 80 p. (hardback) $27.95

Grades: 4 5 6 7 8 **398.24**
1. Werewolves
ISBN 160152238X; 9781601522382

LC 2011036347

This book on werewolves "examines these legendary creatures . . . . describing their bodies, their behavior, and their monstrous transformations. It also goes snout to snout with some of history's most infamous real-life werewolves and discusses the many books and films these encounters have inspired." (Publisher's note)

"Children will get a well-rounded look at the featured subjects and how they have evolved into the creatures that still fascinate many today.— SLJ

Includes bibliographical references and index

Mayor, Adrienne

The **Griffin** and the Dinosaur; How Adrienne Mayor Discovered a Fascinating Link Between Myth and Science. Natl Geographic Soc Childrens books 2014 48 p. col. ill. $18.99

Grades: 5 6 7 8 **398.24**
1. Griffins 2. Dinosaurs
ISBN 1426311087; 9781426311086

"Could Griffins have been real? When [author] Adrienne Mayor carefully read the ancient Greek and Roman descriptions, this mythic hybrid of a lion and an eagle sounded like something people had actually seen." Co-written by Mayor and Marc Aronson, with illustrations by Chris Muller, "Here is the story of one insightful, curious, and determined woman who solved the mystery of the Griffin, and invented a new science. Now she and others travel the world matching myths and fossils." (Publisher's note)

"With the suspense of a detective story, the narrative details Mayor's research process as she consults with experts, conducts fieldwork, and seeks out ancient documents, artifacts, and stories." - PM reviews

Nigg, Joe

Wonder beasts; tales and lore of the phoenix, the griffin, the unicorn, and the dragon. Libraries Unlimited 1995 160p il $27.50

Grades: 7 8 9 10 **398.24**
1. Dragons 2. Unicorns 3. Animals -- Folklore
ISBN 1-56308-242-X

LC 94-46797

The author "has compiled material ranging from Herodotus, Ovid, Pliny the Elder, to Chinese and Native American folk tales, and fantasies by Edith Nesbit. Each entry is carefully documented and a reference list at the end provides dozens of full citations for those who'd like to delve deeper. Wonder Beasts will be useful to students who are researching myth and folklore, and to librarians and scholars who are looking for a comprehensive source list on the topic." Voice Youth Advocates

398.25   Ghost stories

Schwartz, Alvin, 1927-1992

★ **Scary** stories to tell in the dark; collected from folklore by Alvin Schwartz; edited by Rachel Abrams; illustrated by Brett Helquist.   Newly illustrated ed. Harper 2010 113 p. ill. (paperback) $5.99; (hardcover) $16.99

Grades: 4 5 6 7 **398.25**
1. Ghost stories 2. Horror fiction 3. Folklore -- United States
ISBN 9780060835200; 0060835192; 0060835206; 9780060835194

Stories of ghosts and witches, "jump" stories, scary songs, and modern-day scary stories.

"Helquist's new illustrations for Schwartz's classic [collection] of ghost stories inhabit an altogether more benign universe than the nightmarish Stephen Gammell originals. [This edition is] handsome and accessible, ceding the stories themselves pride of place." Horn Book Guide

398.8   Rhymes and rhyming games

Bodden, Valerie

Nursery rhymes. Creative Education 2010 32p il (Poetry basics) $28.50

Grades: 5 6 7 8 **398.8**
1. Nursery rhymes
ISBN 978-1-58341-778-2; 1-58341-778-8

LC 2008009157

This book describes nursery rhymes' "history, characteristics, and variations. Many examples are provided as well as ideas for how children can write their own pieces. The information is accessible, and the writing is sufficiently lively to engage readers. The well-designed pages feature a variety of art reproductions from different literary eras and some photographs." Horn Book Guide

Includes glossary and bibliographical references

400   LANGUAGE

401   Philosophy and theory

Lunge-Larsen, Lise

★ **Gifts** from the gods; written by Lise Lunge-Larsen; illustrated by Gareth Hinds. Houghton Mifflin Harcourt/Childrens 2011 90p. $18.99

Grades: 4 5 6 7 **401**
1. Vocabulary 2. Classical mythology
ISBN 978-0-547-15229-5; 0-547-15229-9

LC 2010031635

In this book "[Lise] Lunge-Larsen and [Gareth] Hinds explain what words like echo, grace, hypnotize, and janitor have in common, tracing the origins of common words and expressions to Greek and Roman myths. Readers may know that 'arachnid' derives from the story of Arachne and that modern-day 'sirens' have mythical antecedents, but this collection . . . [also explains] the roots of 'nemesis' (the goddess of justice) or 'tantalize,' after doomed Tantalus. Lunge-Larsen provides additional context, including dictionary definitions, and quotes from children's literature. Hinds incorporates graphic novel–style elements into his .... illustrations, including dialogue balloons and filmic perspectives." (Publishers Weekly)

411   Writing systems of standard forms of languages

Donoughue, Carol

The **story** of writing; [by] Carol Donoughue. Firefly Books 2007 48p il map $19.95

Grades: 4 5 6 7   **411**

1. Writing -- History 2. Alphabet -- History

ISBN 978-1-55407-306-1; 1-55407-306-5

This is an "introduction to the history of the Roman alphabet. . . . Beginning sections about early civilizations' alphabets, starting with Sumerian cuniforms, include a you-are-there narrative. . . . Later spreads cover European illuminated manuscripts and the development of printing technology. A final section [covers] Chinese characters. . . . Numerous carefully chosen color photos of artifacts . . . greatly enhance the book's appeal." Booklist

Includes bibliographical references

Robb, Don

★ **Ox,** house, stick; the history of our alphabet. illustrated by Anne Smith. Charlesbridge 2007 48p il $16.95; pa $7.95

Grades: 4 5 6 7   **411**

1. Writing -- History 2. Alphabet -- History

ISBN 978-1-57091-609-0; 978-1-57091-610-6 pa

LC 2005-06015

"Robb traces the history of each letter from its origin to its modern appearance in the Roman alphabet. He explains the birth of writing in pictogram form and the eventual transition to written symbols that stand for sounds. . . . Smith's whimsical paintings are a fitting companion to Robb's light-hearted text." SLJ

418   Standard usage (Prescriptive linguistics)

Ostenson, Jonathan W.

Integrating young adult literature through the common core standards; Rachel L. Wadham and Jonathan W. Ostenson. Libraries Unlimited, an imprint of ABC-CLIO, LLC 2013 x, 260 p.p (paperback) $45

Grades: Adult Professional   **418**

1. Reading 2. Reading (Secondary) 3. Reading comprehension 4. Teenagers -- Books and reading -- United States 5. Language arts (Secondary) -- Standards -- United States

ISBN 1610691180; 9781610691185

LC 2012036269

This text "examines the various components to be considered when determining the complexity of YA texts. The book is divided into two sections with the first part deal-

ing with the various elements that make texts complex and the second section providing specific instructional suggestions for integrating the CCSS [common core standards] with YAL [young adult literature]." (New England Reading Association Journal)

Includes bibliographical references and indexes

419   Sign languages

Butterworth, Rod R.

The **Perigee** visual dictionary of signing; an A-to-Z guide to over 1,350 signs of American Sign Language. [by] Rod R. Butterworth and Mickey Flodin. rev & expanded 3rd ed; Berkley Pub. Group 1995 478p il pa $15.95

Grades: 8 9 10 11 12 Adult   **419**

1. Reference books 2. Sign language -- Dictionaries

ISBN 0-399-51952-1

LC 95-1380

First published 1983

This guide to American Sign Language features more than 1,350 alphabetically arranged signs with directions on how to form them. Illustrations show precise hand positions and movements. Includes memory aids

Costello, Elaine

Random House Webster's American Sign Language dictionary: unabridged. Random House Reference 2008 xxxii, 1200p $55

Grades: 8 9 10 11 12 Adult   **419**

1. Reference books 2. Sign language -- Dictionaries

ISBN 978-0-375-42616-2; 0-375-42616-7

First published 1994 with title: Random House American Sign Language dictionary

This dictionary includes "over 5,600 signs for the novice and experienced user alike. It includes complete descriptions of each sign, plus full-torso illustrations. There is also a subject index for easy reference as well as alternate signs for the same meaning." Publisher's note

Gallaudet University

★ The **Gallaudet** dictionary of American Sign Language; Clayton Valli, editor in chief; illustrated by Peggy Swartzel Lott, Daniel Renner, and Rob Hills. Gallaudet University Press 2005 xli, 558p il $49.95

Grades: 8 9 10 11 12 Adult   **419**

1. Reference books 2. Sign language -- Dictionaries

ISBN 1-56368-282-6; 978-1-56368-282-7

LC 2005-51129

"This is a very valuable language resource for parents, students, and teachers learning ASL as a first language and as a second language." Choice

Includes bibliographical references

Sternberg, Martin L. A.

★ **American** Sign Language; a comprehensive dictionary. illustrated by Herbert Rogoff. Unabridged; HarperCollins Pubs. 1998 xxi, 983p il $60; pa $24

Grades: 8 9 10 11 12 Adult **419**

1. Reference books 2. Sign language -- Dictionaries

ISBN 0-06-271608-5; 0-06-273634-5 pa

LC 98-26649

First published 1981

Arranged alphabetically, this dictionary features 7,000 sign entries, with cross-references and more than 12,000 illustrations

Includes bibliographical references

Warner, Penny

Signing fun; American sign language vocabulary, phrases, games & activities. illustrated by Paula Gray. Gallaudet Univ. Press 2006 225p il pa $19.95

Grades: 4 5 6 7 8 **419**

1. Sign language

ISBN 1-56368-292-3

"This book is a great resource for readers who want to learn more signs, or for teachers and librarians looking for fun ways to share them with kids." SLJ

420 Specific languages

Dubosarsky, Ursula

The **word** snoop; illustrated by Tohby Riddle. Dial Books 2009 246p il $16.99

Grades: 5 6 7 8 **420**

1. English language -- History

ISBN 978-0-8037-3406-7; 0-8037-3406-9

LC 2009-8306

First published 2008 in Australia with title: The word spy

A tour of the English language from the beginning of the alphabet in 4000 BC to modern text messaging and emoticons

"Short chapters, clear explanations, and humorous examples bring the subject to life, while word puzzles and coded messages at the end of each section invite reader participation. The attractive design adds to the appeal." Booklist

421 Writing system, phonology, phonetics of standard English

Truss, Lynne

Eats, shoots & leaves; the zero tolerance approach to punctuation. Gotham Books 2004 xxvii, 209p $19.95; pa $12

Grades: 8 9 10 11 12 Adult **421**

1. Punctuation

ISBN 1-59240-087-6; 1-59240-203-8 pa

LC 2004-40646

First published 2003 in the United Kingdom

The author "dissects common errors that grammar mavens have long deplored (often, as she readily points out, in isolation) and makes . . . arguments for increased attention to punctuation correctness. . . . Truss serves up delightful, unabashedly strict and sometimes snobby little book, with cheery Britishisms ('Lawks-a-mussy!') dotting pages

that express a more international righteous indignation." Publ Wkly

Includes bibliographical references

422 Etymology of standard English

Baker, Rosalie F.

In a word; 750 words and their fascinating stories and origins. by Rosalie Baker; illustrated by Tom Lopes. Cobblestone Pub. 2003 221p il $17.95

Grades: 5 6 7 8 **422**

1. English language -- Etymology

ISBN 0-8126-2710-5

LC 2003-25582

"The entries in this book discuss the meanings and derivations of 750 words and phrases. . . . While exploring word origins, Baker also touches on interesting facets of European history and Greek mythology. The jaunty illustrations are reproduced in black and shades of gray. . . . This informative book fosters an appreciation for the richness of the English language." Booklist

Gorrell, Gena K.

Say what? the weird and mysterious journey of the English language. Tundra Books 2009 146p il pa $10.95

Grades: 7 8 9 10 11 12 **422**

1. English language -- Etymology

ISBN 978-0-88776-878-1; 0-88776-878-4

"Gorrell takes readers on a quick and amusing historical tour of the English language, looking at how it has been influenced by Latin, Old English, French, and German. . . . This clever and funny book also integrates explanations for tricky grammar and spelling problems as part of the historical explanation for our changing language. Readers are not only given examples of malapropisms but also a list of several words that are often confused. . . . Supplementary materials including a time line and a large number of illustrations will make this book a valuable addition to both public and school libraries." Voice Youth Advocates

Hitchings, Henry

The **secret** life of words; how English became English. Farrar, Straus and Giroux 2008 440p $27

Grades: 8 9 10 11 12 Adult **422**

1. English language -- Etymology

ISBN 978-0-374-25410-0; 0-374-25410-9

LC 2008-26055

"Hitchings here provides a colorful, thematic history of the English language. Treating borrowings and coinages as psychological windows to history, the author takes the reader on a tour of the lexicon from Anglo-Saxon to the present day and shows how new words answer linguistic needs. . . . Hitchings treats the reader to some 3,000 word histories. . . . With 90-plus pages of notes, sources, and useful indexes, this is a fine choice for libraries and a 'smorgasbord' for language aficionados." Choice

Includes bibliographical references

More word histories and mysteries; from aardvark to zombie. from the editors of the American Heritage dictionaries. Houghton Mifflin 2006 288p il pa $12.95

Grades: 8 9 10 11 12 Adult   **422**

1. Reference books 2. English language -- Etymology
ISBN 978-0-618-71681-4; 0-618-71681-5

LC 2006020835

This "emphasizes the huge number of source languages from which English draws its vast vocabulary—from Sanskrit to French and beyond. The introductory pages give the reader a brief overview of the methods and aims of etymology and a potted history of the origins of English. . . . The editors then present an alphabetical listing of words and their etymology. Each of the 300-plus entries is about half a page to a page long and briefly outlines the origins of the word, its use, and the evolution of its meaning. . . . The book's informative yet informal writing style would appeal to the amateur enthusiast, and accessibility is further enhanced by a useful glossary of linguistic terms." Libr J

Morris, William

Morris dictionary of word and phrase origins; [by] William and Mary Morris; foreword by Isaac Asimov. 2nd ed; Harper & Row 1988 669p $38

Grades: 8 9 10 11 12 Adult   **422**

1. English language -- Etymology 2. English language -- Terms and phrases
ISBN 0-06-015862-X

LC 87-45651

Original three volume edition published 1962-1971; one volume edition first published 1977

"Traces the origins of several thousand words and phrases commonly used in the English language, including slang terms and clichés not usually found in more formal works. Entries are listed alphabetically by the first word in the phrase, with an index at the end." Ref Sources for Small & Medium-sized Libr. 6th edition

Word histories and mysteries; from abracadabra to Zeus. from the editors of the American Heritage dictionaries. Houghton Mifflin Co. 2004 xvi, 348p il pa $12.95

Grades: 8 9 10 11 12 Adult   **422**

1. Reference books 2. English language -- Etymology
ISBN 978-0-618-45450-1; 0-618-45450-0

LC 2004014798

"The 400 alphabetically arranged entries here illustrate the diversity from which the English language draws its vocabulary, particularly from the prehistoric base that linguists call Proto-Indo-European. As a result, the editors aim to demonstrate links between the ancient base and modern English. . . . An overall quality resource." Libr J

423   Dictionaries of standard English

★ The **American** Heritage student dictionary; Updated ed.; Houghton Mifflin 2007 xx, 1068p il $19.95

Grades: 6 7 8 9   **423**

1. Reference books 2. English language -- Dictionaries
ISBN 978-0-618-70149-0; 0-618-70149-4

LC 2006277388

First published 1977 with title: The American Heritage school dictionary

Contains more than 65,000 entries, including hundreds of notes on usage, word histories, accompanied by 2000 color photo and illustrations.

Little, Brown & Co. Inc.

★ **Bartlett's** Roget's thesaurus. Little, Brown 1996 xxxii, 1415p $21.95; pa $16.95

Grades: 8 9 10 11 12 Adult   **423**

1. Americanisms 2. Reference books 3. English language -- Synonyms and antonyms
ISBN 0-316-10138-9; 0-316-73587-6 pa

LC 96-18343

This thesaurus "reflects the current state of American English, including terminology from the worlds of composers and television, with such sub-categories as 'Living Things,' 'The Arts,' 'Feelings.' But what really makes the book a joy to use is the tremendously useful lists—everything from phobias to styles and periods of furniture." Am Libr

McCutcheon, Marc

★ The **Facts** on File student's thesaurus. Facts on File 2005 592p $60

Grades: 6 7 8 9   **423**

1. Reference books 2. English language -- Synonyms and antonyms
ISBN 0-8160-6038-X

LC 2004061966

This provides synonyms and antonyms for more than 9,000 words listed in alphabetical order

The **Merriam**-Webster dictionary of synonyms and antonyms. Merriam-Webster 1992 443p pa $4.99

Grades: 8 9 10 11 12 Adult   **423**

1. Reference books 2. English language -- Synonyms and antonyms
ISBN 0-87779-906-7

LC 93-119503

First published 1942 with title: Webster's dictionary of synonyms

"This synonym dictionary is an outstanding work. . . . Synonyms and similar words, alphabetically arranged, are carefully defined, discriminated, and illustrated with thousands of quotations. The entries also include antonyms and analogous words." Nichols. Guide to Ref Books for Sch Media Cent. 4th edition

★ **Merriam**-Webster's intermediate dictionary. Merriam-Webster 2011 18a, 1005 p.p $18.95

Grades: 5 6 7 8 **423**

1. Vocabulary 2. Encyclopedias and dictionaries 3. English language -- Dictionaries
ISBN 0877796793; 9780877796794

LC 2011534122

This dictionary is "written especially for the needs of students grades 6-8, ages 11-14" and has "nearly 70,000 entries including new words and definitions from the fields of science, technology, entertainment, and health" as well as "more than 22,000 usage examples." The book also "provides definitions, pronunciation, etymology, part of speech designation, and other appropriate information." (Publisher's note)

Merriam-Webster's school thesaurus. Merriam-Webster 1994 690p $15.95

Grades: 7 8 9 10 **423**

1. Reference books 2. English language -- Synonyms and antonyms
ISBN 0-87779-178-3

First published 1978 with title: Webster's student thesaurus

This alphabetically arranged volume includes more than 43,000 synonyms, antonyms, idiomatic phrases, related words, and contrasted words

★ **Merriam**-Webster's visual dictionary. Merriam-Webster, Inc. 2012 1112 p. (hbk.) $39.95

Grades: 6 7 8 9 10 11 12 Adult **423**

1. English language -- Dictionaries
ISBN 0877791511; 9780877791515

This visual dictionary, edited by Jean-Claude Corbeil, has "more than 8,000 highly detailed, full-color illustrations, organized by subject in specialized fields from all aspects of life, . . . [and] nearly 25,000 . . . technical and everyday terms with clear, concise definitions. . . . Themes include a wide variety of fields: astronomy, the earth, human beings, the animal kingdom, plants and gardening, . . . food, arts and architecture, . . . sports and games" and more. (Publisher's note)

Princeton Language Institute

Roget's 21st century thesaurus in dictionary form; the essential reference for home, school, or office. edited by the Princeton Language Institute; Barbara Ann Kipfer, head lexicographer. 3rd ed; Bantam Dell 2005 962p $15; pa $5.99

Grades: 8 9 10 11 12 Adult **423**

1. Reference books 2. English language -- Synonyms and antonyms
ISBN 0-385-33895-3; 0-440-24269-X pa

First published 1992

This thesaurus, cross referencing each word with the same concept, provides 500,000 synonyms and antonyms in a dictionary format and includes recently coined and common slang terms and commonly used foreign terms.

★ **Random** House Webster's unabridged dictionary; 2nd ed.; Random House 2005 xxvi, 2230p il map $59.95

Grades: 8 9 10 11 12 Adult **423**

1. Reference books 2. English language -- Dictionaries
ISBN 0-375-42599-3

First published 1966 with title: The Random House dictionary of the English language

This dictionary contains over 315,000 entries. A new-words section and an essay on the growth of English are included. 2,400 spot maps and illustrations complement the text

Roget's II; the new thesaurus. by the editors of The American Heritage Dictionaries. 3rd ed.; Houghton Mifflin 2003 1200p $21

Grades: 8 9 10 11 12 Adult **423**

1. Reference books 2. English language -- Synonyms and antonyms
ISBN 0-618-25414-5

First published 1980

The work uses a dictionary format, with words and numbered definitions on the left column of a page, and corresponding numbered synonyms, near-synonyms, antonyms and near-antonyms on the right column.

Roget's international thesaurus; 6th ed; HarperResource 2001 xxv, 1248p $20.95; pa $16.95

Grades: 8 9 10 11 12 Adult **423**

1. Reference books 2. English language -- Synonyms and antonyms
ISBN 0-06-273693-0; 0-06-093544-8 pa

LC 2002-276277

First copyright edition published 1911 with title: The standard thesaurus of English words and phrases classified and arranged so as to facilitate the expression of ideas and assist in literary composition

This edition includes 330,000 words and phrases organized into 1,075 categories and a pinpoint reference system that directs the user from a comprehensive index to the numbered category of the right word. Cross-references throughout lead to other categories. Also included are supplemental word lists that supply the names of things which have no synonyms (measurements, wines, state mottoes) as well as quotations that amplify the meanings of selected words

Scholastic dictionary of synonyms, antonyms, and homonyms. Scholastic Reference 2001 220p pa $5.99

Grades: 7 8 9 10 11 12 **423**

1. Reference books 2. English language -- Homonyms 3. English language -- Synonyms and antonyms
ISBN 0-439-25415-9

LC 2001-278627

A revised edition of Webster's synonyms, antonyms, homonyms, published 1962

"Most of the book is dedicated to the dictionary of synonyms and antonyms; the final 25 pages or so list homonyms. This is good for browsing or for a writer's quick reference." KLIATT

Terban, Marvin

★ **Scholastic** dictionary of idioms; new & updated; Scholastic 2006 298p il pa $19.85

Grades: 4 5 6 7　　**423**

1. Reference books 2. English language -- Idioms

ISBN 978-0-439-77083-5 pa; 0-439-77083-1 pa

First published 1996

This "introduction to American slang and phrase origins identifies and defines more than six hundred commonly used idioms, complementing the entries with . . . sample sentences and . . . illustrations." Publisher's note

427 Historical and geographic variations, modern nongeographic variations of English

Dictionary of American slang; Barbara Ann Kipfer, editor; Robert L. Chapman, founding editor. 4th ed., fully rev. and updated; Collins 2007 592p $45

Grades: 8 9 10 11 12 Adult　　**427**

1. Americanisms 2. Reference books 3. English language -- Slang -- Dictionaries

ISBN 978-0-06-117646-3; 0-06-117646-X

First published 1960 by Crowell. Variant title: New dictionary of American slang

This dictionary of American slang terms "features pronunciation guides, word origins, examples of appropriate usage as well as a . . . highlighting system that lets you know which terms should be used with caution, and never in polite company." Publisher's note

428 Standard English usage (Prescriptive linguistics)

Bacon, Pamela S.

100 + literacy lifesavers; a survival guide for librarians and teachers K-12. [by] Pamela S. Bacon and Tammy K. Bacon. Libraries Unlimited 2009 363p il pa $40

Grades: Adult Professional　　**428**

1. Reading 2. Teaching teams

ISBN 978-1-59158-669-2 pa; 1-59158-669-0 pa

LC 2008-45514

"This wonderful professional resource's focus is mainly school librarians and teachers, but it could be used by public librarians to generate ideas for educational programs. . . . This book is an insightful tool that provides the skills and plans for successful collaboration and evaluation of literacy efforts between teachers and librarians." Voice Youth Advocates

Includes glossary and bibliographical references

Budzik, Mary

Punctuation : the write stuff! [created by Basher; written by Mary Budzik] Kingfisher 2010 64p il (Basher basics) pa $7.99

Grades: 4 5 6 7　　**428**

1. Punctuation

ISBN 978-0-7534-6420-5 pa; 0-7534-6420-9 pa

"This slim volume uses catchy graphic design and an informal narrative to spark interest in the subject. In a presentation reminiscent of manga and Saturday-morning cartoons, each punctuation mark is introduced as a unique character who conveys his job through chatty dialogue. . . . The book explains the various uses of each mark and some basics of sentence structure." SLJ

Includes glossary

Farwell, Sybil M.

Supporting reading in grades 6-12; a guide. by Sybil M. Farwell and Nancy L. Teger. Libraries Unlimited 2012 xiii, 358 p.p

Grades: Professional　　**428**

1. Motivation (Psychology) 2. Children -- Books and reading 3. Reading (Secondary) 4. Motivation in education 5. School librarian participation in curriculum planning

ISBN 9781598848038; 9781598848045

LC 2012010826

This book, by Sybil M. Farwell and Nancy L. Teger, "addresses head-on the disturbing trend of declining leisure reading among students and demonstrates how school librarians can contribute to the development of lifelong reading habits as well as improve students' motivation and test scores. The book provides a comprehensive framework for achieving this: the READS curriculum, which stands for Read as a personal activity." (Publisher's note)

Includes bibliographical references and index

Fogarty, Mignon

Grammar girl presents the ultimate writing guide for students; with illustrations by Erwin Haya. Henry Holt and Co. 2010 294p il $19.99; pa $12.99

Grades: 6 7 8 9 10　　**428**

1. Rhetoric 2. Report writing 3. English language -- Grammar

ISBN 978-0-8050-8943-1; 0-8050-8943-8; 978-0-8050-8944-8 pa; 0-8050-8944-6 pa

LC 2010011699

"This text is evenly divided into five sections: parts of speech, sentence structure, punctuation, usage, and a final segment on how readers can improve their writing. Fogarty's style mimics her podcasts with pithy but helpful rules and advice laced with examples. Pop quizzes and cartoon illustrations are also included. Libraries should purchase this book for reference use if nothing else, but budding writers will find it invaluable." SLJ

Includes bibliographical references

Fuhrken, Charles

What every middle school teacher needs to know about reading tests (from someone who has written them) Charles Fuhrken. Stenhouse Publishers 2012 vii, 237 p.p ill. (pbk. : alk. paper) $24

Grades: Professional　　**428**

1. Achievement tests 2. Examinations -- Study guides 3. Educational tests and measurements 4. Reading

(Middle school) -- Ability testing
ISBN 1571108858; 1571109455; 9781571108852; 9781571109453

LC 2011037287

This book's author, "Charles Furhrken, has spent years working with several major testing companies and contributing to the reading assessments of various testing programs." He "offers . . . strategies to help students perform well on test day." Particular focus is given to "information about reading tests, including . . . preparation materials, samples of the most frequently assessed reading standards, and . . . core-reading activities." (Publisher's note)

Includes bibliographical references and index.

Hellweg, Paul

★ The **American** Heritage student thesaurus; Paul Hellweg, Joyce LeBaron, Susannah LeBaron. Houghton Mifflin Harcourt 2012 vi, 378 p.p $18.95
Grades: 5 6 7 8 9 10   428
  1. Vocabulary 2. English language -- Synonyms and antonyms
ISBN 0547659164; 9780547659169

LC 2012462955

This newly updated student thesaurus "includes advice to teen writers about choosing the best word for their purpose, how synonyms are presented in the text, and the use of other words like antonyms. . . . Pages are large, with the entry word in a blue sans-serif type, while the synonyms appear in a smaller black boldface type. An even smaller type is used for each explanatory sentence, followed by antonyms (marked with a blue arrow) where appropriate." (Children's Literature)

L is for lollygag; quirky words for a clever tongue. Chronicle Books 2008 125p $12.99
Grades: 4 5 6 7   428
  1. Vocabulary
ISBN 978-0-8118-6021-5; 0-8118-6021-3

LC 2007021061

"Budding and accomplished wordsmiths will delight in this specialized dictionary showcasing oft-overlooked gems of the English language. . . . Each definition is related with humor, sometimes including word origination and listing equally interesting synonyms. . . . Black-and-white engravings juxtaposed with cartoons in Picassoesque profile give an old-fashioned yet offbeat air to this unusual compendium." SLJ

Includes bibliographical references

O'Conner, Patricia T.

Woe is I Jr; the junior grammarphobes' guide to better English in plain English. [by] Patricia O'Conner; drawings by Tom Stiglich. G.P. Putnam's Sons 2007 152p il $16.99
Grades: 4 5 6 7 8   428
  1. English language -- Usage 2. English language -- Grammar
ISBN 978-0-399-24331-8

LC 2006020575

An adaptation of Woe is I, published 2003 for adults by Riverhead Books

The author "covers pronouns, plurals, possessives, verb usage, subject-verb agreement, capitalization, and punctuation with jargon-free explanations and entertaining examples. . . . She knows her subject, can convey her message with wit and ease, and does it all in a compact, easy-to-read format." SLJ

Ostler, Rosemarie

Dewdroppers, waldos, and slackers; a decade-by-decade guide to the vanishing vocabulary of the twentieth century. Oxford University Press 2003 239p il hardcover o.p. pa $23
Grades: 8 9 10 11 12   428
  1. Reference books 2. English language -- Slang
ISBN 978-0-19-516146-5; 0-19-516146-7; 978-0-19-518254-5 pa; 0-19-518254-5 pa

LC 2003-8302

"This reference work is not simply a slang dictionary. Along with definitions . . . Ostler includes in each decade's chapter both brief discussions of relevant cultural topics and a few photos. These short, often humorous essays are a way to provide examples for the terms defined. . . . Ostler's work is fun for browsing; it offers a unique presentation of recent cultural history." Libr J

Includes bibliographical references

Terban, Marvin

★ **Scholastic** dictionary of spelling; rev ed; Scholastic Reference 2006 272p il pa $9.99
Grades: 4 5 6   428
  1. Spellers 2. Reference books
ISBN 978-0-439-76421-6; 0-439-76421-1
First published 1998

This spelling dictionary gives instructions for looking up a word the reader does not know how to spell, offers more than 150 memory tricks to correct commonly misspelled words, explains general spelling rules and their exceptions, and includes sections such as "The Four Longest Words in the English Language" and "The Spelling Words That Made Kids Champions." To aid pronunciation, each word is divided into syllables with the accented syllable in boldface.

Scholastic guide to grammar; [by] Marvin Terban as Professor Grammar. Scholastic Inc. 2011 255p il pa $9.99
Grades: 4 5 6 7   428
  1. English language -- Grammar
ISBN 978-0-545-35669-5; 0-545-35669-5

This guide to English language grammar covers the parts of speech, sentences and paragraphs, spelling, capitalization, punctuation, communicating ideas through vocabulary, homonyms, homophones, homographs, figures of speech, alliteration, hyperbole, similes, personification, and idioms, and includes a thesaurus.

433   Dictionaries of standard German

Betteridge, Harold T.

Cassell's German-English, English-German dictionary; completely revised by Harold T. Betteridge. Websters New World 1978 1580p 2v in 1 $27

Grades: 8 9 10 11 12 Adult   **433**

1. Reference books 2. German language -- Dictionaries
ISBN 9780025229303

First compiled 1888 by Elizabeth Weir and published by Heath. Periodically revised. Previous American editions published by Funk & Wagnalls with title: The New Cassell's German dictionary

This dictionary incorporates "many new words and usages. Gives phonetic transcriptions of headwords. One of the most useful bilingual dictionaries." Guide to Ref Books. 11th edition

443   Dictionaries of standard French

Girard, Denis

Cassell's French dictionary; French-English, English-French. completely revised by Denis Girard with the assistance of Gaston Dulong, Oliver Van Oss, and Charles Guinness. Wiley 2002 762, 655p thumb-indexed $24.95

Grades: 8 9 10 11 12 Adult   **443**

1. Reference books 2. French language -- Dictionaries
ISBN 0-02-522620-7

First published 1920 with title: Cassell's French-English, English-French dictionary. Previous American editions published by Funk & Wagnalls with title: The New Cassell's French dictionary

"New words including colloquialisms, slang, American English and French-Canadian terms [are included]. . . . There are also sections on French verbs and French and English abbreviations. Reliable, standard dictionary. A first choice." N Y Public Libr. Ref Books for Child Collect. 2d edition

453   Dictionaries of standard Italian

Cassell's Italian dictionary; Italian-English, English-Italian. compiled by Piero Rebora, with the assistance of Francis M. Guercio and Arthur L. Hayward. Wiley 2002 xxi, 1128p thumb-indexed $24.95

Grades: 8 9 10 11 12 Adult   **453**

1. Reference books 2. Italian language -- Dictionaries
ISBN 0-02-522540-5

First published 1958 in the United Kingdom with title: Cassell's Italian-English, English-Italian dictionary. Previous United States editions published by Funk & Wagnalls

"A general dictionary of the Italian language as currently written and spoken." Ref Sources for Small & Medium-sized Libr. 5th edition

463   Dictionaries of standard Spanish

Gooch, Anthony

Cassell's Spanish-English, English-Spanish dictionary; completely revised by Anthony Gooch, Angel Garcia de Paredes. Wiley 2002 xxv, 1109p $22.95

Grades: 8 9 10 11 12 Adult   **463**

1. Reference books 2. Spanish language -- Dictionaries
ISBN 0-02-522910-9

Previously published in 1978 by Macmillan

This dictionary emphasizes the Spanish of Latin America, and includes both classical and literary Spanish as well as the language of the modern Spanish-speaking world.

473   Dictionaries of classical Latin

Simpson, D. P.

Cassell's Latin dictionary; Latin-English, English-Latin. by D. P. Simpson. Macmillan 1977 883p thumb-indexed $24.95

Grades: 8 9 10 11 12 Adult   **473**

1. Reference books 2. Latin language -- Dictionaries
ISBN 0-02-522580-4

LC 77-7670

First published 1854. This edition first published 1959. Previous United States editions published by Funk & Wagnalls with title: Cassell's New Latin dictionary

"Cassell's incorporates current English idiom and Latin spelling into the traditional presentation of classical Latin. The 30,000 entries include generic terms, geographical and proper nouns. Etymological notes and illustrative quotations are provided within entries." Wynar. Guide to Ref Books for Sch Media Cent. 3d edition

493   Non-Semitic Afro-Asiatic languages

Giblin, James

The riddle of the Rosetta Stone; key to ancient Egypt. [by] James Cross Giblin. Crowell 1990 85p il hardcover o.p. pa $7.99

Grades: 5 6 7 8   **493**

1. Hieroglyphics 2. Rosetta stone 3. Egyptian language
ISBN 0-06-446137-8 pa

LC 89-29289

Describes how the discovery and deciphering of the Rosetta Stone unlocked the secret of Egyptian hieroglyphics

"Suspense keeps the reader glued to this fine piece of nonfiction as the mystery of hieroglyphs is slowly unraveled. . . . The author has done a masterful job of distilling information, citing the highlights, and fitting it all together in an interesting and enlightening look at a puzzling subject." Horn Book

Includes bibliographical references

500 SCIENCE

500 Natural sciences and mathematics

★ The **big** idea science book; incredible concepts that show how science works in the real world. editor, Matilda Gollon; consultant, Lisa Burke. DK Pub. 2010 304p il $29.99

Grades: 4 5 6 7   500

1. Science

ISBN 978-0-7566-6287-5; 0-7566-6287-7

LC 2010-281143

"Aimed at grabbing readers' general interest in science, this lively overview is split into sections on life, earth, and physical science; within each category, specific subjects are plainly labeled for easy reference. . . . Full-color photographs, drawings, and diagrams further inform, and readers can visit an interactive Web site for more exploration. For breadth of material and clarity, it's hard to beat." Publ Wkly

Bryson, Bill

A **really** short history of nearly everything. Delacorte Press 2009 169p il $19.99

Grades: 4 5 6 7   500

1. Science

ISBN 978-0-385-73810-1; 0-385-73810-2

A newly illustrated, abridged and adapted edition of A short history of nearly everything, published 2003 by Broadway Books for adults; this edition first published in the United Kingdom 2008

Bryson "whirls through mind-numbing notions such as the creation of the universe and the life span of an atom with good cheer and accessible, even exciting, writing. The two-page speads meander their way through the various recesses of science with a combination of explanatory prose, historical anecdotes, wry asides, and illustrations that range from helpful to comical." Booklist

Currie, Stephen

African American inventors; Stephen Currie. Lucent Books 2010 104 p. ill. (some col.) (hardcover) $36.10

Grades: 6 7 8 9 10   500

1. Inventions 2. African American inventors 3. Inventions -- United States -- History 4. African American inventors -- Biography

ISBN 1420501216; 9781420501216

LC 2009038456

This book is part of the Lucent Library of Black History and focuses on African-American Inventors and Inventions. "Each volume in the Lucent Library of Black History examines an event or time period of particular significance in African American history. . . . Each chapter contains sidebars that highlight relevant personalities and events. Numerous photos and illustrations" are included. (Publisher's note)

Particular attention is given to historical, social, and political contexts and challenges faced by the inventors (e.g., institutionalized racism; difficulties with the patent system). The text is dense but informative." Horn Book

Includes bibliographical references (p. 93-98) and index.

Hillman, Ben

How weird is it; a freaky book all about strangeness. Scholastic 2009 47p il $15.99

Grades: 5 6 7 8   500

1. Science

ISBN 978-0-439-91868-8; 0-439-91868-5

LC 2008-09787

Strange but facinating facts about everyday things that turn out to be extraordinary.

"Humor adds interest to the random but readable text. Large, vivid computer-manipulated photographs illustrate the information." Horn Book Guide

Isabella, Jude

Hoaxed! fakes & mistakes in the world of science. by the editors of YES mag; illustrated by Howie Woo. Kids Can Press 2009 48p il lib bdg $16.95; pa $8.95

Grades: 5 6 7 8   500

1. Fraud 2. Science

ISBN 978-1-55453-206-3 lib bdg; 1-55453-206-X lib bdg; 978-1-55453-207-0 pa; 1-55453-207-8 pa

This title examines hoaxes, fakes and mistakes from the world of science, including crop circles, Bigfoot and the Loch Ness monster, and UFOs reported at Roswell, New Mexico. Index. "Ages nine to twelve." (Quill Quire)

"Piltdown man, Richard Meinertzhagen the light-fingered bird collector, 'Stone Age' Tasaday in the Philippines, crop circles in England, cold fusion energy and UFOs in Roswell, N.M., are the fakes and mistakes described in this lively introduction to fraud in science. The breezy text opens with a clear description of the scientific process of hypothesis, experiment, publication in professional magazines and replication of results before proceeding to the many colorful fakes exposed." Kirkus

Includes index.

Murphy, Glenn

Why is snot green; and other extremely important questions (and answers) Roaring Brook Press 2009 236p il pa $9.95

Grades: 4 5 6 7   500

1. Science 2. Technology

ISBN 978-1-59643-500-1 pa; 1-59643-500-3 pa

"Conservation, evolution, technology, animal life, space travel, physics, and much more are discussed in this lively science book. . . . [This offers] chatty questions and answers . . . with text that is compelling, never intimidating, and sometimes deliberately outrageous. . . . Children will have fun browsing the spacious pages and sharing what they read with adults." Booklist

O'Meara, Stephen James

Are you afraid yet? the science behind scary stuff; written by Stephen James O'Meara; illustrated by Jeremy Kaposy. Kids Can Press 2009 78p il $17.95; pa $9.95

Grades: 5 6 7 8   500

1. Science 2. Supernatural

ISBN 978-1-55453-294-0; 1-55453-294-9; 978-1-55453-295-7 pa; 1-55453-295-7 pa

"This book cleverly weaves together the supernatural and the scientific in an entertaining read that answers questions about ghosts, UFOs, vampires, werewolves, and how long a decapitated head can remain conscious. Examples depicting such things in classical fiction and popular movies are seamlessly interjected between the factual explanations. Each page is filled with detailed black-and-white illustrations, emphasizing the sometimes-humorous, yet often-macabre descriptions." SLJ

Richardson, Gillian

Kaboom! explosions of all kinds. Annick Press 2009 83p il $22.95; pa $12.95

Grades: 4 5 6 7   **500**

1. Science 2. Explosions
ISBN 978-1-55451-204-1; 1-55451-204-2; 978-1-55451-203-4 pa; 1-55451-203-4 pa

"With comic-style sound-effect headings and fact boxes galore, Kaboom! highlights the supercharged of the natural and manmade worlds, from astronomy, geology, biology, herbology, and entomology to chemistry, mechanics, pyrotechnics, and art. Text is broken into asymmetrical panels for bite-size explanations. Some explosions are captured in sequence and detail with historical and high-speed photography and illustrations in comic-style panel frames. . . . Kaboom! is an engrossing attention-getter, effectively tapping the sensationalism of all types of blasts." SLJ

Williams, Brian

Science across cultures. Raintree 2010 48p il (Sci-hi: Earth and space science) lib bdg $31.34; pa $8.99

Grades: 6 7 8 9   **500**

1. Science 2. Scientists
ISBN 978-1-4109-3353-9 lib bdg; 1-4109-3353-9 lib bdg; 978-1-4109-3363-8 pa; 1-4109-3363-6 pa

LC 2009-13461

"This . . . makes science high impact and electric. . . . There are full-color pictures and eye-popping illustrations on quality paper. With no white spaces, every page is an attention-grabbing feast of color and design. Information is dispensed in large type with key words in bold. Interesting facts appear in pop-up balloons making this book an enjoyable read." Libr Media Connect

Includes glossary and bibliographical references

Wollard, Kathy

How come? in the neighborhood; illustrated by Debra Solomon. Workman Pub. 2007 292p il pa $12.95

Grades: 5 6 7   **500**

1. Science
ISBN 978-0-7611-4429-8

"Wollard explains hundreds of phenomena commonly encountered at home, at school, or in the yard—from boiling water to blushing, from why a yo-yo comes back to how the body makes and uses fat. Even taking on such knotty issues as whether the chicken or the egg came first, she answers each query with a specific, closely reasoned answer, animated by lively turns of phrase and intriguing observations. . . . Decorated with small, comical line drawings and supplemented by a healthy list of relevant Web sites, this volume

will draw both browsers and serious-minded students like bugs to a porch light." Booklist

500.5 Space sciences

Parks, Peggy J., 1951-

Space research. ReferencePoint Press 2010 96p il (Inside science) $26.95

Grades: 8 9 10 11 12   **500.5**

1. Astronautics 2. Space sciences 3. Outer space -- Exploration
ISBN 978-1-60152-111-8; 1-60152-111-1

LC 2009-48159

"Parks piles on the research, digging deep into interstellar study, programs that reach into space, and what it all means to the common person, never shying away from detail and onerous proper nouns. . . . The color layout features plenty of photos, boxes, and charts, while Parks delivers a surprisingly spry text." Booklist

Includes bibliographical references

502 Miscellany

Murphy, Glenn

How loud can you burp? more extremely important questions (and answers!) Roaring Book Press 2009 284p il pa $10.99

Grades: 4 5 6 7   **502**

1. Science 2. Questions and answers
ISBN 978-1-59643-506-3 pa; 1-59643-506-2 pa

"'Why does pollen give you hay fever?' 'Why don't big metal ships just sink?' These are but a couple of the questions that Murphy received on the Web site he set up to solicit inquiries from kids. Written in an informal, question-and-answer format, he delivers serious scientific information in an easygoing, humorous manner, with several pages dedicated to each topic. . . . A few line drawings break up the text and sidebars highlight interesting facts or are, at times, simply funny. . . . This is an entertaining, accessible approach to science that's sure to appeal to science buffs and general browsers alike." SLJ

502.8 Auxiliary techniques and procedures; apparatus, equipment, materials

Kramer, Stephen

★ **Hidden** worlds: looking through a scientist's microscope; photographs by Dennis Kunkel. Houghton Mifflin 2001 57p il (Scientists in the field) $16; pa $5.95

Grades: 4 5 6 7   **502.8**

1. Microscopes 2. Microscopists
ISBN 0-618-05546-0; 0-618-35405-0 pa

LC 00-58083

This book takes a "look at the work of a microscopist. Kunkel works with microscopes to explore science. . . . This book contains many of his photos, most taken with electron microscopes. . . . Several opening pages, along with the front and back endpapers, are visually dazzling. The heart of the book, though, is what readers learn about how Kunkel produces these images, and to what uses scientists put them. . . . This title offers a wealth of scientific information along with an insightful look at the world of an individual scientist." SLJ

Includes bibliographical references

Levine, Shar

★ The **ultimate** guide to your microscope; [by] Shar Levine & Leslie Johnstone. Sterling Pub. 2008 143p il pa $9.95

Grades: 5 6 7 8 9   **502.8**

1. Microscopes

ISBN 978-1-4027-4329-0 pa; 1-4027-4329-7 pa

LC 2006-100967

"Through this fun and inviting book, readers can begin to explore the world using a microscope. Students are encouraged to learn the basics in the two first chapters and then undertake the 41 hands-on activities in the next eight chapters. Activities are presented in manageable one or two-page uniformly formatted modules." SLJ

503 Dictionaries, encyclopedias, concordances

Jakab, Cheryl

★ The **encyclopedia** of junior science; [by] Cheryl Jakab, David Keystone. Chelsea Clubhouse 2009 10v il map set $230

Grades: 4 5 6 7   **503**

1. Reference books 2. Science -- Encyclopedias

ISBN 978-1-60413-554-1 set; 1-60413-554-9 set

LC 2008-38113

"This set introduces students to basic science concepts. Approximately 270 entries are arranged alphabetically. . . . The writing is basic, and much of the information is presented in the form of charts and bulleted lists. . . . This set would be useful for school and public libraries seeking a science encyclopedia." Booklist

The **Kingfisher** science encyclopedia; general editor, Charles Taylor. 3rd ed. Kingfisher 2011 vii, 488 p.p ill. (some col.) (hardcover) $34.99

Grades: 5 6 7 8   **503**

1. Science -- Encyclopedias 3. Science

ISBN 0753466880; 9780753466889

LC 2011047026

This book is a science encyclopedia edited by Charles Taylor. The book is arranged thematically and "most topics are presented on . . . two-page spreads, with relevant charts, timelines, and other illustrations surrounding the text. In the bottom right corner of the spread is a 'See Also Pages' box that directs readers to related topics with their page numbers." (Voice of Youth Advocates)

Topical chapters present "basic surveys of physics, geology, chemistry, biology, anatomy, the environment, and space. . . . Articles are generally, though not rigidly, confined to a spread each, and all have see-also references. . . . The illustrations are a plus; they are crisply reproduced, finely detailed, and labeled, enhancing the text rather than competing with it." SLJ

507.8 Use of apparatus and equipment in study and teaching

Bonnet, Robert L.

46 science fair projects for the evil genius. McGraw-Hill 2009 194p il (Evil genius series) pa $19.95

Grades: 6 7 8 9   **507.8**

1. Science projects 2. Science -- Experiments

ISBN 978-0-07-160027-9; 0-07-160027-2

LC 2008008078

Provides instructions and plans for science projects across various disciplines, including physics, astronomy, energy, environmental science and economics.

Churchill, E. Richard

365 more simple science experiments with everyday materials; by E. Richard Churchill, Louis V. Loeschnig, and Muriel Mandell ; illustrated by Frances Zweifel. Black Dog & Leventhal Pub 2014 320 p. ill. $12.95

Grades: 4 5 6 7   **507.8**

1. Experiments 2. Science -- Experiments 3. Scientific recreations

ISBN 1579129676; 9781579129675

LC 96053239

In this book "kids ages 9 through 12 get a year's worth of fun and educational hands-on experiments while gaining knowledge of the fundamentals of science. . . . The hundreds of experiments are divided into 32 chapters, . . . which focus on . . . basic principles of physics, . . . science using common foods, . . . concepts having to do with time and space, and . . . some puzzling ideas about nature. The final chapters explore the science of outer space." (Publisher's note)

"The projects are diverse, considering that some experiments take just minutes to complete, while others are more involved and even require days to see complete results. However, all of the included experiments are inquiry-based and dynamic, making the book perfect for formal instructional settings or entertaining curious minds with scientific fundamentals." Booklist

Three hundred sixty five simple science experiments with everyday materials

Simple science experiments with everyday materials

Cobb, Vicki

See for yourself; more than 100 amazing experiments for science fairs and school projects. illustrated by Dave Klug. 2nd ed; Skyhorse Pub. 2010 192p il pa $14.95

Grades: 4 5 6 7   **507.8**

1. Science -- Experiments

ISBN 978-1-61608-083-9; 1-61608-083-3

LC 2010020800

First published 2001 by Scholastic

This is an "accessible and often intriguing collection of activities and experiments. . . . The experiments are grouped by their source of inspiration: humans, the supermarket, the toy store, drugstore, and hardware and stationery stores. . . . Cartoon-style illustrations are . . . in full color." SLJ

★ **We** dare you! hundreds of science bets, challenges, and experiments you can do at home. [by] Vicki Cobb and Kathy Darling. Skyhorse Pub. 2007 321p il hardcover o.p. pa $14.94

Grades: 4 5 6 7   **507.8**
1. Science -- Experiments
ISBN 978-1-60239-225-0; 1-60239-225-0; 978-1-60239-775-0 pa; 1-60239-775-9 pa
LC 2007-51236

"Divided into chapters with titles such as 'The Human Wonder,' 'Fluid Feats,' 'Energy Entrapments,' and 'Mathematical Duplicity,' this volume has more than 200 experiments with clear how-to instructions. All of the projects are doable and the science behind them is explained in a kid-accessible manner. . . . Black-and-white line drawings add humor and clarify instructions. This is a great resource for teachers, parents, and budding scientists—and for any youngster who can't resist a challenge." SLJ

Includes bibliographical references

Connolly, Sean

The **book** of potentially catastrophic science; 50 experiments for daring young scientists. Workman Pub. 2010 305p il

Grades: 5 6 7 8   **507.8**
1. Science -- Experiments
ISBN 0-7611-5687-9; 978-0-7611-5687-1
LC 2010-07044

This book presents thirty-four experiments. "Each chapter starts with a brief outline of the scientific advances of the time, followed by a clarification of the science and then one or more hands-on experiments to illustrate the object or concept presented. . . . Grades five to eight." (Sci Books Films)

"This volume approaches science historically, spotlighting certain periods, processes, individuals, discoveries, and inventions. Each of the 34 chapters includes a discussion and one or two related activities, such as making a Stone Age tool, creating an earthquake in Jell-O, building a parachute for an egg drop, and extracting a banana's DNA. Safety concerns are addressed for each project, and adult help will be necessary to complete some of the experiments successfully. . . . Connolly's writing is engaging, and the historical approach works well, offering kids a quick introduction to science history and the opportunity to explore certain ideas along the way." Booklist

Gardner, Robert

Light, sound, and waves science fair projects; revised and expanded using the scientific method. Enslow Publishers 2010 160p il (Physics science projects using the scientific method) lib bdg $34.60

Grades: 7 8 9 10   **507.8**
1. Light 2. Sound 3. Waves 4. Science projects 5. Science -- Experiments
ISBN 978-0-7660-3416-7 lib bdg; 0-7660-3416-X lib bdg
LC 2009006493

First published 2004 with title: Light, sound, and waves science fair projects using sunglasses, guitars, CDs, and other stuff

"Explains how to use the scientific method to conduct several science experiments about light, sound, and waves. Includes ideas for science fair projects." Publisher's note

Includes bibliographical references

Planet Earth science fair projects; revised and expanded using the scientific method. Robert Gardner. Enslow Publishers 2010 160 p. il (Earth science projects using the scientific method) $35.94

Grades: 7 8 9 10   **507.8**
1. Science projects 2. Geology 3. Astronomy 4. Earth sciences 5. Science -- Experiments
ISBN 0766034232; 9780766034235
LC 2009026546

A revised edition of Planet Earth Science Fair Projects Using the Moon, Stars, Beach Balls, Frisbees, and Other Far-out Stuff, published 2005

This book, by Robert Gardner, presents "simple projects . . . [that] will help young scientists begin to understand Earth, including its place in the solar system, its atmosphere, its only natural satellite—the Moon, and its resources and geology. For students interested in competing in science fairs, the book contains lots of great suggestions and ideas for further experiments." (Publisher's note)

"Explains how to use the scientific method to conduct several science experiments about earth science. Includes ideas for science fair projects." Publisher's note

Includes bibliographical references and index

Goodstein, Madeline

Ace your sports science project; great science fair ideas. [by] Madeline Goodstein, Robert Gardner, and Barbara Gardner Conklin. Enslow Publishers 2009 128p il (Ace your physics science project) lib bdg $31.93

Grades: 5 6 7 8   **507.8**
1. Sports 2. Physics 3. Science projects 4. Science -- Experiments
ISBN 978-0-7660-3229-3 lib bdg; 0-7660-3229-9 lib bdg
LC 2008-4689

"Presents several science experiments and project ideas dealing with the physics of sports." Publisher's note

Includes bibliographical references

Goal! science projects with soccer. Enslow Publishers 2009 104p il (Score! Sports science projects) lib bdg $31.93

Grades: 5 6 7 8   **507.8**
1. Motion 2. Soccer 3. Force and energy 4. Science projects 5. Science -- Experiments
ISBN 978-0-7660-3106-7 lib bdg; 0-7660-3106-3 lib bdg
LC 2008-2999

"Introductions include information about the history of the sport, safety steps to follow, and the scientific method. . . . Detailed diagrams help clarify many of the directions." SLJ

Includes glossary and bibliographical references

Graham, Ian

Science rocks! written by Ian Graham; additional text by Dr. Mike Goldsmith; step illustrations by Dan Wright. DK Pub. 2011 144p il $19.99

Grades: 6 7 8 9 **507.8**

1. Science -- Experiments

ISBN 978-0-7566-7198-3; 0-7566-7198-1

"Physics, chemistry, biology, and human physiology are the subjects covered in this huge, lavishly illustrated volume, packed with detailed suggestions for experiments to perform at home, at school, and for science-fair projects. The tone is relaxed but never cute, and the browsable design blends how-to with explanations of the forces at play." Booklist

Leavitt, Loralee

Candy experiments; Loralee Leavitt. Andrews McMeel Pub., LLC 2012 146 p. $14.99

Grades: 4 5 6 **507.8**

1. Candy 2. Science -- Experiments

ISBN 1449418368; 9781449418366

LC 2011944678

This book presents science activities for children involving candy. "Grouped by physical properties that include 'Color,' 'Secret Ingredients,' and 'Sticky' or processes like 'Blow It Up,' 'Squash It,' and 'Dissolve This,' the activities begin with an introductory question and tend to flow incrementally. Each one includes the time required, a list of ingredients . . . step-by-step directions, and a discussion, including a cursory scientific explanation." (School Library Journal)

Margles, Samantha

Mythbusters science fair book. Scholastic 2011 128p il pa $9.99

Grades: 4 5 6 7 **507.8**

1. Science projects 2. Science -- Experiments

ISBN 978-0-545-23745-1; 0-545-23745-9

This offers "50 original ideas for science fair projects or long, boredom-riddled summer days. Much like the popular television program on which it's based, the book stays true to the scientific method. . . . Divided into chapters on chemical reactions, temperature, energy and force, and more, the two- to three-page experiments on busily designed pages feature easy step-by-step procedures." Booklist

McCallum, Ann

Eat your science homework; recipes for inquiring minds. Ann McCallum ; illustrated by Leeza Hernandez. Charlesbridge 2014 48 p. colored illustrations (reinforced for library use) $16.95

Grades: 5 6 7 8 **507.8**

1. Science -- Experiments 2. Cooking 3. Food -- Composition 4. Food -- Experiments 5. Cooking -- Experiments 6. Science -- Experiments

ISBN 157091298X; 9781570912986; 9781570912993

LC 2013022070

This book, by Ann McCallum, illustrated by Leeza Hernandez, helps "readers discover delicious and distinct recipes. . . . A main text explains upper-elementary science concepts, including subatomic particles, acids and bases, black holes, and more. Alongside simple recipes, side-bars

encourage readers to also experiment and explore outside of the kitchen. A review, glossary, and index make the entire book easy to digest." (Publisher's note)

"Scientific terms are explained in each chapter, and recipes are given and reinforced with a glossary. Bright illustrations and clear instructions will appeal to younger readers, while older readers will find the concepts and vocabulary educational; the recipes will appeal to a wide range of ages." SLJ

Science activities for all students; edited by Aviva Ebner. Facts on File 2009 2v il loose-leaf $370

Grades: Adult Professional **507.8**

1. Science projects 2. Science -- Experiments

ISBN 978-0-8160-7396-2 loose-leaf; 0-8160-7396-1 loose-leaf

LC 2008043827

Replaces Science Projects for All Students and More Science Projects for All Students, published 1998 and 2002 respectively

These "binders enable students in grades 4 through 9 with developmental or physical challenges to join their classmates in . . . hands-on [science] activities. There are 60 experiments in each binder—designed to be as inclusive as possible—in the areas of basic skills, Earth science, weather, space science, life science, and physical science. Each binder is also enhanced by approximately 250 black-and-white line illustrations." Publisher's note

Includes glossary and bibliographical references

VanCleave, Janice Pratt

Janice VanCleave's engineering for every kid; easy activities that make learning science fun. Jossey-Bass 2007 205p il (Science for every kid series) pa $14.95

Grades: 4 5 6 7 **507.8**

1. Engineering 2. Science projects 3. Science -- Experiments

ISBN 978-0-471-47182-0 pa; 0-471-47182-8 pa

LC 2006-10540

Explains some of the basic physical principles of engineering, accompanied by activities that illustrate those principles

Vickers, Tanya M.

Teen science fair sourcebook; winning school science fairs and national competitions. Enslow Publishers 2009 160p il lib bdg $34.60

Grades: 7 8 9 10 **507.8**

1. Science projects 2. Science -- Exhibitions 3. Science -- Experiments

ISBN 978-0-7660-2711-4; 0-7660-2711-2

LC 2008-30779

"The book is clearly written, and its page design, which includes the occasional photo, is colorful. . . . A useful resource for highly motivated students." Booklist

Includes glossary and bibliographical references

Walker, Pamela

Environmental science experiments; [by] Pamela Walker, Elaine Wood. Facts on File 2010 153p il (Facts on File science experiments) $35

Grades: 7 8 9 10   **507.8**

1. Environmental science 2. Science -- Experiments

ISBN 978-0-8160-7805-9; 0-8160-7805-X

LC 2008-53715

This "contains 20 experiments that allow students to actively engage in scientific inquiry. Projects are presented in a uniform format, with an introduction to the topic, time requirements (35 minutes to 2 weeks), a materials list, numbered procedures, and several analysis questions. . . . Line drawings, colorful images, and data tables enhance instructions. . . . The experiments themselves are timely and fascinating. [The book] includes high-interest investigations into what people throw away, the safety of reusing water bottles, and a 'bottled versus tap water' taste test." SLJ

Includes glossary and bibliographical references

Williams, Jennifer

★ **Oobleck,** slime, & dancing spaghetti; twenty terrific at-home science experiments inspired by favorite children's books. by Jennifer Williams. Bright Sky Press 2009 192 p. ill. (paperback) $14.95

Grades: 4 5 6   **507.8**

1. Science/Experiments

ISBN 1933979348; 9781933979342

LC 2009000876

This book "provides a series of science experiments designed to explore concepts and ideas that spring from various stories. At the beginning of each chapter, a children's book is . . . summarized. The author then explains a related science concept, suggests discussion questions that connect the experiment to the story, and offers ideas for taking the project further. . . . The experiments cover concepts including polymers, chemical reactions, and non-Newtonian fluids." (School Library Journal)

"Using children's literature as a springboard, this title provides a series of science experiments designed to explore concepts and ideas that spring from various stories. At the beginning of each chapter, a children's book is nicely summarized. The author then explains a related science concept, suggests discussion questions that connect the experiment to the story, and offers ideas for taking the project further. This is serious science. . . . The experiments do a really wonderful job of emphasizing the importance of observation and data collection. The writing is relatively clear. . . . This book is great choice for home use and science units." SLJ

Includes bibliographical references.

Young, Karen Romano

Junkyard science; 20 projects and experiments about junk, garbage, waste, things we don't need anymore, and ways to recycle or reuse it--or lose it. illustrations by David Goldin. National Geographic 2010 80p il (Science fair winners) $24.90; pa $12.95

Grades: 3 4 5 6   **507.8**

1. Recycling 2. Environmental sciences 3. Science

-- Experiments

ISBN 978-1-4263-0690-7; 1-4263-0690-3; 978-1-4263-0689-1 pa; 1-4263-0689-X pa

This volume provides "outlines for science fair projects in the . . . environmental . . . sciences. The procedures include just enough structure to help novice experimenters get started. . . . Well-placed questions encourage creativity and further thinking. [The] volume includes humorous cartoon spot illustrations and a section on preparing presentations." Horn Book Guide

508   Natural history

Art, Henry Warren

Woodswalk; peepers, pikas, and exploding puff balls. [by] Henry W. Art and Michael W. Robbins. Storey Books 2003 122p il map $21.95; pa $14.95

Grades: 4 5 6   **508**

1. Seasons 2. Nature study 3. Forest plants 4. Forest animals

ISBN 1-58017-477-9; 1-58017-452-3 pa

"This inviting introduction to forests describes the sights, sounds, and smells that await young explorers. The accessible text details the wonders of each season in both eastern and western locales, while full-color photos depict the flora and fauna that inhabit these intriguing environments." SLJ

Baker, Stuart

In the Antarctic. Marshall Cavendish Benchmark 2009 32p il map (Climate change) lib bdg $19.95

Grades: 5 6 7 8   **508**

1. Antarctica 2. Greenhouse effect

ISBN 978-0-7614-4438-1 lib bdg; 0-7614-4438-6 lib bdg

LC 2009-5766

The book about climate change in the Antarctic "is perfectly organized for students. . . . Unique layout features serve as signposts and will help focus readers' attention. . . . [The book] features an outstanding chart of possible effects of global warming on the area in question, listing 'Possible Event', 'Predicted Result', and 'Impact' in short, bulleted statements." SLJ

Includes glossary

In the tropics. Marshall Cavendish Benchmark 2010 32p il map (Climate change) lib bdg $19.95

Grades: 5 6 7 8   **508**

1. Tropics 2. Greenhouse effect

ISBN 978-0-7614-4440-4 lib bdg; 0-7614-4440-8 lib bdg

LC 2009-5768

The book about climate change in the Tropics "is perfectly organized for students. . . . Unique layout features serve as signposts and will help focus readers' attention. . . . [The book] features an outstanding chart of possible effects of global warming on the area in question, listing 'Possible Event', 'Predicted Result', and 'Impact' in short, bulleted statements." SLJ

Includes glossary

Bardhan-Quallen, Sudipta

Nature science experiments; what's hopping in a dust bunny? illustrated by Edward Miller. Sterling 2010 64p il (Mad science) $12.95

Grades: 4 5 6   **508**

1. Nature study 2. Science -- Experiments
ISBN 978-1-4027-2412-1; 1-4027-2412-8

"The first chapter of this attractive book, 'The Stuff of Life,' jumps right in by outlining the materials needed and the step-by-step process to follow to collect and isolate DNA by rinsing one's mouth out with salt water. . . . Youngsters can turn to the table of contents or detailed index to choose experiments based on interest and availability of resources. . . . The chapters on bacteria and protists include color photomicrographs of the organisms, and amusing cartoon illustrations appear throughout. This exploration of the natural world will spark readers' interest in experimenting and questioning results." SLJ

Chin, Jason

★ **Island**; a story of the Galapagos. Jason Chin. 1st ed. Roaring Brook Press 2012 40 p. (alk. paper) $16.99

Grades: 3 4 5 6   **508**

1. Birds 2. Droughts 3. Reptiles 4. Natural history -- Galapagos Islands 5. Galapagos Islands
ISBN 1596437162; 9781596437166

LC 2011033797

The author, Jason Chin, explains "how species of reptiles and birds on the Galapagos have evolved. He begins with the birth of the islands themselves, a process in which volcanic eruptions punch successive holes in the Earth's surface as tectonic plates move over them, [and] the adaptations of the islands' animals. . . . [Chin also provides information on the] droughts [that] become more common [due to the] climate and geology." (Publishers Weekly)

Includes bibliographical references and index.

Hamilton, Neil A.

Scientific exploration and expeditions; from the age of discovery to the twenty-first century. [by] Neil Hamilton. M.E. Sharpe 2011 2v il map set $165

Grades: 7 8 9 10 11 12   **508**

1. Reference books 2. Scientific expeditions
ISBN 978-0-7656-8076-1; 0-7656-8076-9

LC 2010-12118

"Hamilton's 115 entries in this set describe the courses and discoveries of significant scientific expeditions from the early 15th century to mid 2009. . . , The presentations are systematic, carefully detailed, not exclusively Eurocentric, and when appropriate, skeptical. The currency of information and focus on science will make this work particularly useful." SLJ

Includes bibliographical references

Lynch, Wayne

The **Everglades**; text and photographs by Wayne Lynch. NorthWord Books for Young Readers 2007 64p il (Our wild world: ecosystems) $16.95; pa $8.95

Grades: 4 5 6 7   **508**

1. Everglades (Fla.) 2. Natural history -- Florida
ISBN 978-1-55971-970-4; 1-55971-970-2; 978-1-55971-971-1 pa; 1-55971-971-0 pa

LC 2006-101497

This "provides an up-close look at the fascinating flora and fauna of the world-famous Everglades. . . . Lynch . . . smoothly pairs engaging prose with numerous color photographs that capture the beauty of the region in both sweeping panorama and close-up detail." Booklist

Wadsworth, Ginger

John Burroughs; the sage of Slabsides. Clarion Bks. 1997 95p il $16.95

Grades: 5 6 7 8   **508**

1. Authors 2. Naturalists 3. Writers on nature
ISBN 0-395-77830-1

LC 95-48400

A photobiography of the naturalist, ornithologist, author, poet, teacher, and pioneer of the conservation movement who lived and worked in his rustic cabin in the Catskill Mountains

"The pictures are mostly informal and candid, taken from personal collections, with a few studio portraits interspersed. Written with a familiar, almost intimate tone, the text is liberally sprinkled with quotes from Burroughs's publications." SLJ

Includes bibliographical references

Wood, A. J.

Charles Darwin and the Beagle adventure; countries visited during the voyage round the world of HMS Beagle under the command of Captain Fitzroy, Royal Navy, including extracts from the works of Charles Darwin. written by A.J. Wood & Clint Twist. Candlewick Press 2009 un il map $19.99

Grades: 4 5 6 7 8   **508**

1. Evolution 2. Naturalists 3. Travel writers 4. Writers on science 5. Beagle Expedition (1831-1836)
ISBN 978-0-7636-4538-0; 0-7636-4538-9

LC 2009-921214

"This beautifully illustrated large-format book immediately appeals to both the eye and the mind. Imitating a 19th-century scrapbook to a certain extent, including various pull-outs . . . the book draws the young reader in. . . . Included are copious quotes from Darwin's journals and other writings, as well as reproductions . . . . of numerous 19th-century engravings, drawings, and watercolors, some from the Beagle voyage itself. . . . Integrated into the 19th-century material are modern illustrations and well-written narratives relating background information, the story of the Beagle's voyage . . . and notes on Darwin's life and work. . . . This volume provides an excellent introduction to Darwin and his accomplishments." Sci Books Films

Woods, Michael

Seven natural wonders of Africa; by Michael Woods and Mary B. Woods. Twenty-First Century Books 2009 80p il map (Seven natural wonders) lib bdg $33.26

Grades: 5 6 7 8   **508**

1. Curiosities and wonders 2. Africa 3. Natural history
-- Africa

ISBN 978-0-8225-9071-2; 0-8225-9071-9

LC 2008-21867

This book "takes seven noteworthy wonders in [Africa]
and spotlights them in separate chapters. The text introduces
each one from a historical perspective, and beautiful color
photographs offer inviting views, while maps, sidebars, and
featured quotes add variety to the pages. [This book] looks
at mountain gorillas, the Nile, Victoria Falls, the Sahara
Desert, Mount Kilimanjaro, the Seychelles Islands and the
Serengeti Plain." Booklist

Includes bibliographical references

Seven natural wonders of Asia and the Middle
East; by Michael Woods and Mary B. Woods. Twenty-First Century Books 2009 80p il (Seven natural
wonders) lib bdg $33.26

Grades: 5 6 7 8   **508**

1. Curiosities and wonders 2. Asia 3. Middle East 4.
Natural history -- Asia 5. Natural history -- Middle East

ISBN 978-0-8225-9073-6; 0-8225-9073-5

LC 2008027605

Chapters in this book describe Mount Everest, the Gobi
Desert, Mount Fuji, Sumatra rain forests, the Dead Sea, Cap-
padocia, and the Chocolate Hills, including historical perspectives and color photographs.

Includes bibliographical references

Seven natural wonders of Australia and Oceania;
by Michael Woods and Mary B. Woods. Twenty-First
Century Books 2009 80p il (Seven natural wonders)
lib bdg $33.26

Grades: 5 6 7 8   **508**

1. Curiosities and wonders 2. Australia 3. Natural
history -- Australia

ISBN 978-0-8225-9074-3 lib bdg; 0-8225-9074-3
lib bdg

LC 2008014003

Chapters in this book describe the Australian outback,
Aoraki/Mount Cook, Mount Kilauea, the Bungle Bungles,
the Tasmanian wilderness, Bora Bora, and New Caledonia,
including historical perspectives and color photographs.

Includes bibliographical references

Seven natural wonders of Central and South
America; by Michael Woods and Mary B. Woods.
Twenty-First Century Books 2009 80p il map (Sev-
en natural wonders) lib bdg $33.26

Grades: 5 6 7 8   **508**

1. Curiosities and wonders 2. Natural history -- South
America 3. Natural history -- Central America

ISBN 978-0-8225-9070-5 lib bdg; 0-8225-9070-0
lib bdg

LC 2008027203

This book "takes seven noteworthy wonders in [Cen-
tral and South America] . . . and spotlights them in separate chapters. The text introduces each one from a historical
perspective, and beautiful color photographs offer inviting
views, while maps, sidebars, and featured quotes add vari-

ety to the pages. . . . [This book] discusses Angel Falls, the
Amazon River, the Atacama Desert, the Galápagos Islands,
the Montecristo Cloud Forest, Poás Volcano, and the Andes
Mountains." Booklist

Includes glossary and bibliographical references

Seven natural wonders of Europe; by Michael
Woods and Mary B. Woods. Twenty-First Century
Books 2009 80p il (Seven natural wonders) lib
bdg $33.26

Grades: 5 6 7 8   **508**

1. Curiosities and wonders 2. Natural history -- Europe
3. Europe -- Description and travel

ISBN 978-0-8225-9072-9 lib bdg; 0-8225-9072-7
lib bdg

LC 2008027604

Chapters in this book describe Loch Ness, Westmann
Islands, Lake Baikal, Black Forest, Mons Klint, Fjords of
Norway, and The Alps, including historical perspectives and
color photographs.

Includes bibliographical references

Seven natural wonders of North America; by
Michael Woods and Mary B. Woods. Twenty-First
Century Books 2009 80p il map (Seven natural
wonders) lib bdg $33.26

Grades: 5 6 7 8   **508**

1. Curiosities and wonders 2. North America 3.
Natural history -- North America

ISBN 978-0-8225-9069-9; 0-8225-9069-7

LC 2008021864

This book "takes seven noteworthy wonders in [North
America] . . . and spotlights them in separate chapters. The
text introduces each one from a historical perspective, and
beautiful color photographs offer inviting views, while
maps, sidebars, and featured quotes add variety to the pages.
. . . [This book] takes readers to Dinosaur Provincial Park,
Pacific Rim National Park, the redwood forests, Niagara
Falls, the Grand Canyon, Yellowstone National Park, and
the Paricutin Volcano." Booklist

Includes glossary and bibliographical references

509 Science -- History, geographic treatment, biography

Baxter, Roberta

John Dalton and the development of atomic theory; by Roberta Baxter. Morgan Reynolds Pub. 2012
144 p. ill. (library) $28.95

Grades: 7 8 9 10 11 12   **509**

1. Atomic theory 2. Chemists -- Great Britain --
Biography

ISBN 1599351226; 9781599351223; 9781599352763

LC 2010038610

This children's nonfiction book, by Roberta Baxter, is
part of the "Profiles in Science" series, profiling the 19th-
century physicist and chemist John Dalton and his contributions to the development of atomic theory. Topics include
a profile of his personal life, his work researching atomic

theory at the turn of the 19th century, and the legacy of his theories after his death.

"The reading level is high, some of the more advanced scientific concepts are not adequately illustrated, and the author assumes reader familiarity with British currency, history, and geography. . . . [T]his title should be considered as a supplementary choice for secondary readers who possess a basic understanding of chemistry and need report material on Dalton or his revolutionary work." SLJ

Includes bibliographical references

Blanchard, Anne

★ **Arab** science and invention in the golden age; [illustrated by Emmanuel Cerisier; translated by R.M. Brent] Enchanted Lion Books 2008 65p il map $19.95

Grades: 6 7 8 9 **509**
1. Arab civilization 2. Science -- History 3. Islamic countries -- History
ISBN 978-1-59270-080-6; 1-59270-080-2
LC 2008-26431

"The Muslim world led an amazing scientific revolution for hundreds of years with breakthroughs in math, geography, physics, astronomy, and medicine. This large-size, attractive volume packs in a wealth of information about the rise and fall of the immense empire. . . . The open format, with lots of boxed inserts and detailed illustrations on each double-page spread, is dense with information." Booklist

Includes glossary and bibliographical references

Eamer, Claire

Before the World Was Ready; Stories of Daring Genius in Science. by Claire Eamer. Firefly Books Ltd 2013 125 p. (paperback) $14.95; $24.95

Grades: 5 6 7 8 **509**
1. Inventions 2. Scientists
ISBN 1554515351; 9781554515356; 9781554515363

This book looks at eight scientists and inventors. "Alfred Wegener struggled to convince geologists that the ground beneath our feet is moving. . . . Nikola Tesla's futuristic ideas about electricity were dismissed. Charles Darwin delayed publishing his controversial theory of evolution for decades." Also included are Charles Babbage, Ada Lovelace, Rachel Carson, and George Cayley. (Publisher's note)

Hakim, Joy

★ The **story** of science: Aristotle leads the way. Smithsonian Books 2004 282p (Story of science) $24.95

Grades: 8 9 10 11 12 **509**
1. Ancient civilization 2. Science -- History
ISBN 1-58834-160-7

"Hakim has interwoven creation myths, history, physics, and mathematics to present a seamless, multifaceted view of the foundation of modern science. . . . The entire volume is beautifully organized." SLJ

Includes bibliographical references

★ The **story** of science: Einstein adds a new dimension. Smithsonian Books 2007 468p il (Story of science) $27.95

Grades: 8 9 10 11 12 **509**
1. Cosmology 2. Quantum theory 3. Science -- History
ISBN 978-1-58834-162-4; 1-58834-162-3
LC 2007-14096

Hakim delivers a "brisk, intellectually challenging account of the development of quantum theory and modern cosmology. . . . She introduces a teeming cast of deep thinkers who . . . delivered a series of brilliant experiments and insights. . . . Supplemented by a digestible resource list and a generous assortment of illustrations." Booklist

Includes bibliographical references

★ The **story** of science: Newton at the center. Smithsonian Books 2005 463p (Story of science) $24.95

Grades: 8 9 10 11 12 **509**
1. Physics 2. Astronomy 3. Science -- History
ISBN 1-58834-161-5
LC 2004-58465

This "is an account of the history of astronomy and physics from c.1500 to 1900."

"Teachers will find anecdotal information to enliven their lessons; browsers will be fascinated by the sidebars and captioned illustrations that enhance the text or show related information." SLJ

Includes bibliographical references

Jackson, Donna M.

★ **Extreme** scientists; exploring nature's mysteries from perilous places. Houghton Mifflin Harcourt 2009 63p il (Scientists in the field) $18

Grades: 5 6 7 8 **509**
1. Botanists 2. Explorers 3. Scientists 4. Spelunkers 5. Meteorologists 6. Microbiologists 7. College teachers
ISBN 978-0-618-77706-8; 0-618-77706-7
LC 2008-36796

This volume "profiles three scientists working far out in the field. Hurricane hunter Paul Flaherty, . . . Hazel Barton, a microbiologist specializing in single-cell organisms living in extreme conditions, . . . [and] ecologist and college professor Steve Sillett, who . . . climbs into the canopies to study redwoods. While the clearly written text includes vivid passages about the dangers these scientists face, it goes on to discuss what drives them to pursue their subjects and what they have discovered along the way. . . . The many excellent color photos portray these adventures as scientists intently focused on their work." Booklist

Includes glossary and bibliographical references

Moser, Diane

The **birth** of science: ancient times to 1699; [by] Ray Spangenburg and Diane Kit Moser. Facts on File 2004 256p (History of science) $35

Grades: 7 8 9 10 **509**
1. Science -- History
ISBN 0-8160-4851-7
LC 2003-19470

First published 1993 with title: The history of science from the ancient Greeks to the scientific revolution

Discusses major scientists as well as scientific knowledge and discoveries from ancient times through the seventeenth century

"Very well written and thoroughly understandable, the book succeeds hugely in its objective to introduce the development of science in an interesting fashion to the intended audience without patronizing or oversimplifying." Sci Books Films [review of 1993 edition]

Includes glossary and bibliographical references

Mullins, Lisa

   Science in the Renaissance; [by] Lisa Mullins. Crabtree Pub. 2009 32p pa $8.95; lib bdg $26.60
Grades: 6 7 8 9   **509**
   1. Science 2. Renaissance
   ISBN 978-0-7787-4614-0 pa; 0-7787-4614-3 pa; 978-07787-4594-5 lib bdg; 0-7787-4594-5 lib bdg
                LC 2008-52602

"Ideal introductions to concepts, people, and events of the Renaissance... succinct and thorough." SLJ

Nardo, Don

   The scientific revolution; by Don Nardo. Lucent Books 2011 104 p. ill. (World history series) (library) $34.95
Grades: 6 7 8 9   **509**
   1. Science -- History 2. Discoveries in science -- Europe 3. Discoveries in science -- Europe
   ISBN 1420506137; 9781420506136
                LC 2011006556

This book by Don Nardo is part of the World History series and looks at the Scientific Revolution. The series entries offer an "overview of an important historical event or period. The series is designed both to acquaint readers with the basics of history and to make them aware that their lives and their own historical era are an intimate part of the ongoing human saga." (Publisher's note)

Includes bibliographical references (p. 96-98) and index.

Reynolds, Moira Davison

   American women scientists; 23 inspiring biographies, 1900-2000. McFarland & Co. 1999 149p il hardcover o.p. pa $24.95
Grades: 7 8 9 10   **509**
   1. Women scientists
   ISBN 0-7864-0649-6; 0-7864-2161-4 pa
                LC 99-14603

"Four-to-six page profiles of 23 of the century's premier women scientists, representing a wide variety of disciplines. The entries are arranged chronologically beginning with Cornelia Clapp (1849-1934) and ending with Mary Good (1931-). . . . Each entry includes a black-and-white portrait." SLJ

Includes bibliographical references

Spangenburg, Ray

   Science frontiers, 1946 to the present; [by] Ray Spangenburg and Diane Kit Moser. Facts on File 2004 272p (History of science) $35

Grades: 7 8 9 10   **509**
   1. Science -- History
   ISBN 0-8160-4855-X
                LC 2003-24290

First published 1994 with title: The history of science from 1946 to the 1990s

The authors provide "descriptions of complex scientific theories and lines of research in the latter part of the 20th century—but only in the natural sciences: physics (new particles, lasers, and superconductors), astronomy (quasars, black holes, cosmology, dark matter, planetary geology, and SETI), geology (evolution, plate tectonics, and environmental change), and biology (DNA, biotechnology, the human genome, and retroviruses)." Sci Books Films [review of 1994 edition]

Includes glossary and bibliographical references

Stefoff, Rebecca, 1951-

   Flat Earth and Round Earth; Rebecca Stefoff. Cavendish Square 2014 48 p. color illustrations (It Is Science) $29.93
Grades: 6 7 8   **509**
   1. Pseudoscience 2. Literature and science 3. Science -- Popular works
   ISBN 1627125124; 9781627125123

This middle grades book by Rebecca Stefoff "explores the historical relationships between science and pseudoscience. Though she explains the scientific method in detail and injects healthy doses of skepticism . . . she shows how . . . alchemy split into . . . practical and spiritual approaches before the former evolved into modern chemistry. In contrast, . . . astrology and astronomy continue to coexist as active pursuits, and so do conventional and alternative medicine." (School Library Journal)

"What sets this series apart is its comparative approach to "hard" and "soft" science. Each title contains a chapter covering pseudoscience and how the scientific method works. Illustrations are practical, often images of scientists or scientific instruments. The writing is clear, concise, and matter-of-fact. Content is occasionally recycled throughout the series." Lib Med Con

509.2   Scientists

Davidson, Tish

   African American scientists and inventors; by Tish Davidson. Mason Crest Publishers 2013 64 p. ill. (some col.) (Major Black contributions from Emancipation to civil rights) (library) $22.95
Grades: 4 5 6   **509.2**
   1. African American inventors 2. African American scientists 3. African American inventors -- Biography 4. African American scientists -- Biography
   ISBN 1422223752; 9781422223758
                LC 2011051942

This book by Tish Davidson profiles African American scientists and inventors. "Some of them were elementary school dropouts. Others became medical doctors or college professors. Some were famous, while some toiled in obscurity. . . . Lewis Latimer devised a manufacturing process that made electric lights affordable for ordinary people. Charles

Drew did pioneering work in blood storage, helping save countless lives. Garrett Woods figured out how to send messages from moving trains." (Publisher's note)

Includes bibliographical references (pages 60-61) and index.

Di Domenico, Kelly

Women scientists who changed the world; by Kelly Di Domenico. Rosen Pub. 2012 106 p. col. ill. (library) $34.60

Grades: 5 6 7 8   **509.2**

1. Women scientists -- Biography 2. Women in science -- Biography

ISBN 1448859999; 9781448859993

LC 2011032120

In this collective biography by Kelly Di Domenico, "readers meet eleven women scientists, whose research and discoveries are outstanding in their fields. . . . Readers are introduced to each scientist's life and work, including the obstacles each woman had to overcome to achieve success. Profiles include biologist Rachel Carson, orangutan researcher Birute Galdikas, and Nobel Prize-winning biochemist Ada Yonath." (Publisher's note)

Includes bibliographical references (p. 101) and index.

Krull, Kathleen

Lives of the scientists; experiments, explosions (and what the neighbors thought) Kathleen Krull, Illustrated by Kathryn Hewitt. Houghton Mifflin Harcourt 2013 96 p. $20.99

Grades: 4 5 6 7   **509.2**

1. Science -- History 2. Scientists -- Biography

ISBN 0152059091; 9780152059095

LC 2012953333

The author Kathleen Krull's book focuses on the history of science. "This latest in the Lives of . . . series is summed up by the subtitle's 'What the Neighbors Thought.' The authors delve into intriguing, obscure, and peculiar facts about 20 famous scientists from all fields of study, regions of the globe, and eras of history." Topics include James D. Watson, Francis Crick, Marie Curie, Edwin Hubble, Barbara McClintock, and Grace Murray Hopper." (Booklist)

Miles, Liz

Louis Pasteur; by Liz Miles. Raintree 2009 48 p. ill. (chiefly col.) (Great scientists) (library) $32.00

Grades: 4 5 6   **509.2**

1. Science -- History -- 19th century 2. Scientists -- France -- Biography 3. Microbiologists -- France -- Biography

ISBN 141093229X; 9781410932297

LC 2007050125

This book by Liz Miles is part of the Leveled Biographies series and looks at Louis Pasteur. "What is Pasteurization? How has Pasteur's work helped treat many diseases? The 'Leveled Biographies' series offers leveled, high-interest nonfiction in a range of text genres. Each title tells the story of one memorable life, using pictures, maps, sidebars, and engaging text to make each person's story come alive." (Publisher's note)

Includes bibliographical references (p. 46) and index.

509.56   Science – Islamic Empire -- History

Romanek, Trudee

Science, medicine, and math in the early Islamic world; Trudee Romanek. Crabtree Pub. Company 2012 48 p. (reinforced library binding : alk. paper) $30.60

Grades: 4 5 6 7   **509.56**

1. Science -- History 2. Medicine -- History 3. Mathematics -- History 4. Islamic civilization 5. Science -- Islamic Empire -- History

ISBN 0778721701; 9780778721703; 9780778721772; 9781427195630; 9781427198402

LC 2012000077

This children's educational book, by Trudee Romanek, describes "the scientific contributions of the early Islamic empires to science, medicine, and mathematics. . . . This . . . book explores their public hospitals, libraries, and universities; their achievements in mathematics and astronomy, and the pursuit of alchemy; Arabic numbers; optics; music and musical instruments; poetry; and education." (Publisher's note)

510   Mathematics

Bazin, Maurice

★ **Math** and science across cultures; activities and investigations from the Exploratorium. [by] Maurice Bazin, Modesto Tamez, and the Exploratorium Teacher Institute. New Press 2002 176p il maps pa $19.95

Grades: Adult Professional   **510**

1. Science 2. Mathematics

ISBN 1-56584-541-2

LC 00-136455

This book provides "activities that integrate geography, math, and science into a multicultural curriculum. . . . Each topic provides a hands-on, minds-on activity that enriches thinking skills and the application-research-based process." Sci Books Films

Includes bibliographical references

Henderson, Harry

Mathematics : powerful patterns in nature and society. Facts on File 2007 170p il (Milestones in discovery and invention) $35

Grades: 7 8 9 10 11 12   **510**

1. Mathematics

ISBN 0-8160-5750-8; 978-0-8160-5750-4

LC 2006-24680

"Some mathematicians have discovered relatively simple yet exceedingly powerful patterns that yield insight into aspects of natural and human behavior. . . . [This book] presents 10 essays that profile the minds behind such patterns, many of which have surfaced in recent popular culture." Publisher's note

Includes glossary and bibliographical references

Lee, Cora

The **great** number rumble; [a story of math in surprising places] [by] Cora Lee & Gillian O'Reilly; illustrations by Virginia Gray. Annick Press 2007 104p il $24.95; pa $14.95

Grades: 4 5 6   **510**

1. Mathematics

ISBN 978-1-55451-032-0; 1-55451-032-5; 978-1-55451-031-3 pa; 1-55451-031-7 pa

"When the schools in Jeremy's town ban math, there are loud cheers from the kids. . . . But Jeremy's best friend Sam, a self-proclaimed mathnik, sets out to prove that math is not only important, but fun. In the chapters that follow, Sam reveals math's presence in everyday places, including sports (types of triangles determine how a bike functions), art (artist M.C. Escher combined math patterns with imagination), even in nature (ants instinctively calculate dead reckoning—a navigation tool also used by astronauts). . . . In the end, Jeremy, his teachers, and even the Director of Education have to admit that school minus math equals all sorts of trouble." (Publisher's note) Index. "Ages nine to eleven." (Quill Quire)

"Interspersed with the story line are one-page biographies of Pythagoras, Archimedes, Hypatia of Alexandria, Sophie Germain, Charles Ludwig Dodgson, Srinivasa Ramanujan, and Andrew Wiles. Sidebars with Jeremy's thoughts on chaos theory, cash prizes for new prime numbers, laws of probability, and palindrome numbers add to the information. Full-color cartoons, diagrams, and photos appear throughout." SLJ

McKellar, Danica

★ **Math** doesn't suck; how to survive middle school math without losing your mind or breaking a nail. [by] Danica McKellar. Hudson Street Press 2007 297p il $23.95

Grades: 5 6 7 8   **510**

1. Mathematics

ISBN 978-1-59463-039-2; 1-59463-039-9

LC 2007017091

This "covers some of the most basic ideas of middle-grade math, including concepts relating to fractions, decimals, and ratios, making each comprehensible, interesting, and fun. Using real-world constructions, such as tangled necklaces, boyfriends, and pizza, concepts are thoroughly explained." Voice Youth Advocates

Salvadori, Mario George

★ **Math** games for middle school; challenges and skill-builders for students at every level. [by] Mario Salvadori and Joseph P. Wright. Chicago Review Press 1998 168p il pa $16.95

Grades: 6 7 8 9   **510**

1. Mathematics -- Study and teaching

ISBN 1-55652-288-6

LC 97-51422

Uses explanations, word problems, and games to cover some mathematical topics that middle school students need to know, including the invention of numerical notations, basic arithmatical operations, measurements, geometry, graphs, and probability

512   Algebra

Caron, Lucille

Pre -algebra and algebra smarts! [by] Lucille Caron, Philip M. St. Jacques. Enslow Publishers 2011 64p il (Math smarts!) lib bdg $27.93

Grades: 6 7 8   **512**

1. Algebra 2. Mathematics

ISBN 978-0-7660-3938-4

LC 2011006928

This helps re-inforce classroom learning of important pre-algebra and algebra skills such as positive and negative rational numbers, absolute value, and solving equations

Includes bibliographical references

Schwartz, Richard Evan

You can count on monsters; the first 100 numbers and their characters. A.K. Peters 2010 un il pa $24.95

Grades: 5 6 7 8   **512**

1. Counting 2. Prime numbers 3. Factoring (Mathematics)

ISBN 978-1-56881-578-7 pa; 1-56881-578-6 pa

LC 2009-38661

"This hybrid math/art book is both ambitious and imaginative. An introductory section explains the colored-dot configurations and factor trees for numbers 1 to 100, which appear on the verso of each spread. These factor trees are 'all the way grown out' to the lowest common factors, or prime numbers. On the opposite page is a monster scene that represents the number. Schwartz has created a creature for each prime number. . . . Thus, the monster for 5 is a five-featured, five-pointed star, and the 13 monster sports a pink-and-white eye-patch with 13 segments. . . . Readers will need patience and an open, undaunted mind to deconstruct the monster scenes. This is a book for math lovers who want to have some fun. Challenge these students to create their own prime monsters and combinations." SLJ

513   Arithmetic

Caron, Lucille

Fraction and decimal smarts! [by] Lucille Caron, Philip M. St. Jacques. Enslow Publishers 2011 64p il (Math smarts!) lib bdg $27.93

Grades: 5 6 7 8   **513**

1. Fractions 2. Decimal fractions

ISBN 978-0-7660-3936-0

LC 2011008382

"This clearly written series provides definitions and examples of many concepts... examples are realistic and appropriate for the target age group." SLJ

Includes bibliographical references

Percent and ratio smarts! [by] Lucille Caron, Philip M. St. Jacques. Enslow Publishers 2011 64p il (Math smarts!) lib bdg $27.93

Grades: 5 6 7 8 **513**
1. Fractions 2. Ratios (Statistics)
ISBN 978-0-7660-3940-7

LC 2011008164

This helps re-inforce classroom learning of important percent and ratio skills including reducing ratios, the golden rectangle, and the meaning of percents

Includes bibliographical references

Julius, Edward H.
Arithmetricks; 50 easy ways to add, subtract, multiply, and divide without a calculator. illustrations by Dale M. Gladstone. Wiley 1995 142p il pa $12.95
Grades: 7 8 9 10 **513**
1. Arithmetic
ISBN 0-471-10639-9

LC 94-41836

This book "offers fifty ways to do simple arithmetic calculations in one's head. . . . Each trick is covered on two facing pages. The first page presents the problem and gives two examples of how to use the trick. The facing page has a black and white cartoon and extra exercises to practice. The correct answers are given at the end of the book. This would be a fun book for mathematically inclined Middle-Schoolers and up. Math teachers will enjoy using this book for extra-curricular activities." Appraisal

516   Geometry

Caron, Lucille
Geometry smarts! [by] Lucille Caron, Philip M. St. Jacques. Enslow Publishers 2011 64p il (Math smarts!) lib bdg $27.93
Grades: 5 6 7 8 **516**
1. Geometry
ISBN 978-0-7660-3935-3

LC 2011008384

This helps re-inforce classroom learning of geometry skills such as points, lines, planes, triangles, circles, quadrilaterals, perimeter, area, and circumference

Includes bibliographical references

516.2   Euclidean geometry

Blatner, David
★ **Joy** of [pi] Walker and Co. 1997 129p il hardcover o.p. pa $12
Grades: 8 9 10 11 12 **516.2**
1. Numbers 2. Geometry
ISBN 0-8027-1332-7; 0-8027-7562-4 pa

"Why does an irrational number impel rational people to do irrational things—like calculating pi to several billion digits? That's what's happening with a pair of characters in Blatner's delightful excursion through the history of pi. . . . Even numerically challenged readers will find Blatner's tale immensely appealing, both for the graphic layout, in day-glo colors, no less, and for the amusing and informative anecdotes Blatner relates." Booklist

Green, Dan
Algebra & geometry; anything but square. illustrated by Simon Basher. Kingfisher 2011 il (Basher science) $14.99; pa $8.99
Grades: 4 5 6 **516.2**
1. Algebra 2. Geometry
ISBN 978-0-7534-6627-8; 978-0-7534-6597-4 pa

"This creative team introduces the components of algebra and geometry as cartoon-style characters. The book begins with a brief introduction to the subject of mathematics and Pythagoras. . . . Each chapter begins with an introduction and then the concepts are presented on a spread. One page features a drawing of the concept's character, while the opposing page provides a brief introduction to its characteristics and personality." (School Library Journal)

Wingard-Nelson, Rebecca
Trigonometry smarts! Enslow Publishers 2012 64p il (Math smarts!) lib bdg $27.93
Grades: 5 6 7 8 **516.2**
1. Trigonometry
ISBN 978-0-7660-3944-5

LC 2011006492

This helps re-inforce classroom learning of important trigonometry topics such as square roots, the Pythagorean Theorem, tangents, radians, and degrees.

Includes bibliographical references

519.2   Probabilities

Wingard-Nelson, Rebecca
Graphing and probability word problems; no problem! Enslow Publishers 2010 64p il (Math busters word problems) lib bdg $27.93
Grades: 6 7 8 9 **519.2**
1. Mathematics 2. Problem solving
ISBN 978-0-7660-3372-6; 0-7660-3372-4

LC 2010003281

This offers ways to tackle word math problems with graphing and probability using real world examples.

520   Astronomy and allied sciences

Aguilar, David A.
★ **Planets,** stars, and galaxies; a visual encyclopedia of our universe. written and illustrated by David A. Aguilar; contributing writers Christine Pulliam & Patricia Daniels. National Geographic 2007 191p il $24.95; lib bdg $38.90
Grades: 5 6 7 8 9 10 11 12 **520**
1. Galaxies 2. Astronomy 3. Solar system
ISBN 978-1-4263-0170-4; 1-4263-0170-7; 978-1-4263-0171-1 lib bdg; 1-4263-0171-5 lib bdg

LC 2007061234

"This text introduces readers to the most current information available about the universe. Informatiion is presented is a clear and easy-to-understand manner. . . . The book features bright, eye-catching illustrations that Aguilar created on his computer. In addition, there are many vibrant photographs in the book that were taken by cameras here on Earth as well as by satellites and telescopes." Booklist

Includes glossary and bibliographical references

Boerst, William J.

Johannes Kepler; discovering the laws of celestial motion. Morgan Reynolds 2003 144p il maps (Renaissance scientists) lib bdg $23.95

Grades: 7 8 9 10   520

1. Astronomers 2. Mathematicians
ISBN 1-88384-698-6

LC 2003-708

A biography of Johannes Kepler, the seventeenth-century German astronomer and mathematician who formulated the three laws of planetary motion

"Boerst not only offers a good portrait of the astronomer and his work but also shows the effects of the contentious political and religious forces that created upheaval in his society and made scholarship anything but a safe haven. The well-designed pages feature excellent color illustrations." Booklist

Includes bibliographical references

Carson, Mary Kay

★ **Beyond** the solar system; exploring galaxies, black holes, alien planets, and more : a history with 21 activities. by Mary Kay Carson. Chicago Review Press 2013 vii, 127 p.p col. ill. (paperback) $18.95

Grades: 5 6 7 8   520

1. Creative activities 2. Astronomy -- History
ISBN 1613745443; 9781613745441

LC 2012046330

In this book, "Mary Kay Carson traces the evolution of humankind's astronomical knowledge, from the realization that we are not at the center of the universe to recent telescopic proof of planets orbiting stars outside our solar system. . . . This book contains 21 hands-on projects to further explore the subjects discussed" as well as "minibiographies of famous astronomers, a time line of major scientific discoveries . . .[and] a glossary of technical terms." (Publisher's note)

Includes bibliographical references (p. 121) and index.

The **Facts** on File dictionary of astronomy; edited by John Daintith, William Gould. 5th ed.; Facts on File 2006 550p il (Facts on File science library) $59.50

Grades: 7 8 9 10 11 12   520

1. Reference books 2. Astronomy -- Dictionaries
ISBN 0-8160-5998-5; 978-0-8160-5998-0

LC 2006-40860

First published 1979 under the editorship of Valerie Illingworth

This dictionary includes "more than 3,700 entries . . . that reflect all aspects of astronomy, together with associated terms in spectroscopy, photometry, and particle physics." Publisher's note

Includes bibliographical references

Gardner, Robert

Ace your space science project; great science fair ideas. [by] Robert Gardner and Madeline Goodstein. Enslow Publishers 2009 128p il (Ace your science project) lib bdg $31.93

Grades: 5 6 7 8   520

1. Space sciences 2. Science projects 3. Science -- Experiments
ISBN 978-0-7660-3230-9 lib bdg; 0-7660-3230-2 lib bdg

LC 2008-04688

"Informative, practical, and not without dry wit, this is a good bet for replacing older books of science projects related to astronomny." Booklist

Includes bibliographical references

Garlick, Mark A.

Atlas of the universe. Simon & Schuster Books for Young Readers 2008 128p il map (Insiders) $19.99

Grades: 5 6 7 8   520

1. Astronomy 2. Cosmology
ISBN 978-1-4169-5558-0; 1-4169-5558-5

"Seamlessly commingling luscious, color space photographs and dramatic, sharply detailed digital imagery, this tour of the universe earns high marks for visual impact. It's not too shabby in breadth of coverage either." SLJ

Gater, Will

The **practical** astronomer; [by] Will Gater and Anton Vamplew; consultant Jacqueline Mitton. DK Pub. 2010 256p il map pa $19.95

Grades: 7 8 9 10 11 12   520

1. Astronomy 2. Astronomy -- Observers' manuals
ISBN 978-0-7566-6210-3; 0-7566-6210-9

LC 2010-281460

"This beautifully illustrated volume is a valuable and accurate guide to observing and understanding the wide variety and essential characteristics of fascinating astronomical objects that are visible from Earth. . . . [It enables] the reader to learn about coordinate systems; solar system motions; the nature of light; and how to use the eye, binoculars, telescopes, cameras, and astronomical atlases and catalogues to explore the heavens directly and efficiently." Sci Books Films

Green, Dan

Astronomy; out of this world! illustrated by Simon Basher. Kingfisher 2009 128p il pa $8.95

Grades: 5 6 7 8   520

1. Astronomy
ISBN 978-0-7534-6290-4 pa; 0-7534-6290-7 pa

"Basher has created a portrait gallery of personified planets, comets, space probes, galaxies, several kinds of stars, and an array of other celestial bodies in a hyper-cute, pastel cartoon style. . . . Along with short bulleted lists of additional information, each figure offers a fact-based self-description. . . . Green's astro-narrative is both accurate and spiced with seldom-mentioned details." SLJ

Includes glossary

Jankowski, Connie

Space exploration. Compass Point Books 2009 40p il (Mission: science) lib bdg $26.60

Grades: 4 5 6   **520**

1. Astronomy 2. Outer space -- Exploration

ISBN 978-0-7565-3958-0 lib bdg; 0-7565-3958-7 lib bdg

LC 2008-7722

Discusses outer space exploration and examines future possibilities such as a permanent space station, colonies in space, and journeys outside the solar system

Includes glossary

★ **NightWatch**: a practical guide to viewing the universe; foreword by Timothy Ferris; illustrations by Adolf Schaller, Victor Costanzo, Roberta Cooke, Glenn LeDrew; principal photography by Terence Dickinson. 4th ed.; Firefly Books 2006 192p il $35

Grades: 8 9 10 11 12   **520**

1. Astronomy

ISBN 978-1-55407-147-0; 1-55407-147-X

LC 2006-491527

First published 1983

This "handbook for amateur astronomers combines a text both meaty and hard to put down with a great array of charts, boxes, tables, and dazzling full-color photos of the sky." SLJ [review of 1998 edition]

Includes bibliographical references

Silverstein, Alvin

★ The **universe**; by Alvin & Virginia Silverstein & Laura Silverstein Nunn. rev. ed.; Twenty-First Century Books 2009 112p il (Science concepts, second series) lib bdg $31.93

Grades: 6 7 8 9   **520**

1. Universe 2. Astronomy

ISBN 978-0-7613-3937-3; 0-7613-3937-X

LC 2007052245

First published 2003

This book explores the universe and its elements, including the Milky Way, the solar system, the stars, and other astronomical bodies.

"Authoritative, objective, and broadly based. . . . Beautifully designed and well illustrated." SLJ [review of 2003 edition]

Includes bibliographical references

Space: a visual encyclopedia. DK Pub. 2010 254p il $24.99

Grades: 5 6 7 8   **520**

1. Astronomy 2. Astronautics 3. Space sciences

ISBN 978-0-7566-6277-6; 0-7566-6277-X

"Any reader wishing to gain a fair introductory understanding of astronomy in one concise book will find much satisfaction in this work. An abundance of fascinating information is contained within these pages, and the format is such that excellent and attractive related photographs and diagrams directly accompany the text. . . . The book is very well organized and very well written." Sci Books & Films

Stefoff, Rebecca, 1951-

Astrology and Astronomy; Rebecca Stefoff. Cavendish Square 2014 48 p. color illustrations (Is it Science?) $29.93

Grades: 6 7 8   **520**

1. Astrology 2. Astronomy 3. Science -- Popular works

ISBN 162712506X; 9781627125062

LC 2015015837

This middle grades book by Rebecca Stefoff, part of the Is It Science? series, "explores the historical relationships between science and pseudoscience." It discusses how, "along with similarly shared ancient origins, astrology and astronomy continue to coexist as active pursuits. . . . There are even still a few geocentrists around, Stefoff notes." (Publisher's note)

"Each volume is heavily illustrated with period images and modern photographs, and each closes with particularly generous lists of further resources."

VanCleave, Janice Pratt, 1942-

Step -by-step science experiments in astronomy; by Janice VanCleave. Rosen Pub. 2013 80 p. col. ill. (Janice Vancleave's first-place science fair projects) (library) $33.25; (paperback) $14.15

Grades: 5 6 7 8   **520**

1. Astronomy 2. Science -- Experiments 3. Science projects 4. Astronomy -- Experiments

ISBN 1448869781; 9781448869787; 9781448884612

LC 2012000715

This book by Janice VanCleave presents 22 science experiments in astronomy for children. "Van Cleave states the basic goal of the experiments, followed by a list of necessary materials. . . . Step-by-step instructions are . . . accompanied by diagrams where needed. The results section states exactly what is expected to happen and the 'Why?' section explains in accessible terms why those specific results were achieved." (School Library Journal)

Includes bibliographical references (p. 77-78) and index

Walker, Pamela

★ **Space** and astronomy experiments; [by] Pamela Walker, Elaine Wood. Facts on File 2010 xx, 152p il (Facts on File science experiments) $35

Grades: 7 8 9 10 11 12   **520**

1. Astronomy 2. Space sciences 3. Science -- Experiments

ISBN 978-0-8160-7809-7; 0-8160-7809-2

LC 2009-32825

This book "presents experiments designed to foster understanding of space science and astronomy. Geared to middle and high-school students and their teachers, the 20 experiments convey basic astronomy principles, draw from historic experiments, or explore new technologies. . . . Schools and libraries where students and teachers are looking for science experiments on space and astronomy will find this volume a useful addition to the collection." Booklist

Includes glossary and bibliographical references

Ward, D. J.

Seven wonders of space phenomena; by D.J. Ward. Twenty-First Century Books 2011 80 p. ill. (chiefly col.) (library) $33.26

Grades: 5 6 7 8   **520**
1. Universe 2. Astronomy 3. Astronomy -- Miscellanea
ISBN 0761354522; 9780761354529

LC 2010028447

This book by D.J. Ward looks at "space phenomena, such as dark matter, dark energy, and the beginning of the universe. Read what astronomers and space scientists have discovered about these amazing wonders—and what they have yet to learn." (Publisher's note)

Includes bibliographical references (p. 76-78) and index.

Yount, Lisa

Edward Pickering and his women "computers" analyzing the stars. Lisa Yount. Chelsea House 2011 130 p. (Trailblazers in science and technology) (library) $35

Grades: 7 8 9 10 11 12   **520**
1. Women astronomers 2. Pickering, Edward C. (Edward Charles), 1846-1919 3. Physicists -- United States -- Biography 4. Astronomers -- United States -- Biography
ISBN 1604136642; 9781604136647

LC 2011002792

This book, by Lisa Yount, is part of the "Trailblazers in Science and Technology" series. "In the 42 years that Edward Pickering directed the Harvard College Observatory, he and his team of women 'computers' made strides in promoting the new field of astrophotography.... The advances these women made under Pickering's direction broadened the window of professional opportunity for women as well as our greater understanding of the universe." (Publisher's note)

Includes bibliographical references and index

Modern astronomy; expanding the universe. Facts on File 2006 204p il (Milestones in discovery and invention) $35

Grades: 7 8 9 10 11 12   **520**
1. Astronomy
ISBN 0-8160-5746-X; 978-0-8160-5746-7

LC 2005-25113

This book profiles "12 men and women whose research and work in new technologies brought about a revolution in the understanding of time and space during the 20th century." Publisher's note

Includes glossary and bibliographical references

520.92 Astronomers

Saucier, C. A. P.

Explore the cosmos like Neil DeGrasse Tyson; a space science journey. by C.A.P. Saucier. Prometheus Books 2015 177 p. color illustrations (pbk.) $14.99

Grades: 4 5 6   **520.92**
1. Astronomy 2. Cosmology 3. Astronomy -- Popular works 4. Astronomers -- United States -- Biography 5.

Astrophysicists -- United States -- Biography
ISBN 1633880141; 9781633880146

LC 2014039219

In this book author "CAP Saucier interweaves up-to-date information about the universe and the science of astrophysics with a biographical portrait of the famous astrophysicist. Quotes from [Neil deGrasse] Tyson appear throughout each chapter, personalizing the science." (Publisher's note)

"Perhaps a bit overly ambitious, this guide is nonetheless an excellent jumping-off point for those pursuing a deeper interest in space, while its level of detail may deter others. Its focus is brought back to Earth in Tyson's belief that knowledge and curiosity are of the utmost importance, challenging readers to grab some binoculars, go outside, and start asking questions." Booklist

Includes bibliographical references and index

522   Techniques, procedures, apparatus, equipment, materials

Cole, Michael D.

Eye on the universe; the incredible hubble space telescope. Michael D. Cole. Enslow Publishers 2013 48 p. $23.93

Grades: 4 5 6 7 8   **522**
1. Hubble Space Telescope 2. Outer space -- Exploration 3. Picture books for children 4. Astronomy -- Research 5. Astronautics in astronomy 6. Hubble Space Telescope (Spacecraft)
ISBN 0766040771; 9780766040779

LC 2011047074

This book looks at the Hubble Space Telescope. "Orbiting high above Earth, the Hubble Telescope captures ... wonders of space.... Photographs are relayed back to Earth, allowing scientists and astronomers to study parts of space that were once completely unknown. Michael D. Cole explores the ... journey of launching this telescope into space and how it has unlocked many of the ... mysteries in the universe." (Publisher's note)

Includes bibliographical references and index

DeVorkin, David H.

Hubble imaging space and time; [by] David Devorkin & Robert W. Smith. Smithsonian National Air and Space Museum in association with National Geographic 2008 223p il $50

Grades: 8 9 10 11 12 Adult   **522**
1. Astronomy 2. Hubble Space Telescope
ISBN 978-1-4262-0322-0; 1-4262-0322-5

LC 2008018242

"This handsome volume celebrates the technological and scientific breakthroughs that have made the Hubble such a resounding success. The full, up-to-date story is told in glorious photographs and the equally sparkling commentary of Hubble experts DeVorkin and Smith.... The authors cover the people, science, and aesthetics of the stellar Hubble era. Not only are the telescope's contributions to science beyond quantification, DeVorkin and Smith aver, the images the Hubble has gathered have also had profound effects on our imagination and spiritual growth." Booklist

Includes bibliographical references

Gardner, Robert

Astronomy projects with an observatory you can build; [by] Robert Gardner. Enslow Publishers 2007 128p il (Build-a-lab! science experiments) lib bdg $31.93

Grades: 7 8 9 10 **522**

1. Astronomy 2. Science projects 3. Science -- Experiments
ISBN 978-0-7660-2808-1 lib bdg; 0-7660-2808-9 lib bdg

LC 2006032807

This describes the scientific method and offers instructions in building an observatory and projects in observing Earth, the moon, the sun, the stars, and the planets.

"The digitally rendered diagrams are helpful in clarifying the written directions. [This volume is] involving and entertaining." SLJ

Includes bibliographical references

Matloff, Gregory L.

More telescope power; all new activities and projects for young astronomers. with drawings by C. Bangs. Wiley 2002 118p il pa $12.95 **522**

1. Astronomy 2. Telescopes 3. Science -- Experiments
ISBN 0-471-40985-5

LC 2001-46738

Presents various astronomy activities using a telescope, including constructing a simple telescope, tracking satellites, and sketching details of the moon

This "book is well-written, interesting, and suitable for anyone who wants to learn more about astronomy." Book Rep

Includes glossary and bibliographical references

Scott, Elaine

★ **Space,** stars, and the beginning of time; what the Hubble telescope saw. Clarion Books 2011 66p il $17.99

Grades: 5 6 7 8 **522**

1. Astronomy 2. Hubble Space Telescope 3. Outer space -- Exploration
ISBN 0-547-24189-5; 978-0-547-24189-0

LC 2010-08040

This book examines data collected from the Hubble Space Telescope. Index. "Grades four to eight." (Bull Cent Child Books)

This examines "some of the data that has been collected over the two decades of the Hubble Telescope's operation. Opening chapters discuss the satellite's instrumentation and its 2009 repairs, and then the real fun begins with sections on calculating the age of the universe and its speed of expansion; the nature of dark matter, dark energy, and black holes; star formation; and planet formation, particularly outside our solar system. . . . Gasp-worthy photographs should fire up the most sluggish imaginations." Bull Cent Child Books

523   Specific celestial bodies and phenomena

Pasachoff, Jay M.

A **field** guide to the stars and planets; 4th ed; Houghton Mifflin 2000 578p il map (Peterson field guide series) $30; pa $19

Grades: 8 9 10 11 12 Adult **523**

1. Stars 2. Astronomy
ISBN 0-395-93432-X; 0-395-93431-1 pa

LC 99-27354

First published 1964 under the authorship of Donald H. Menzel and Jay M. Pasachoff

This guide contains 24 monthly sky maps, 54 atlas charts, information and numerous color photographs from NASA and other sources, and time-sensitive material through 2010

Includes bibliographical references

523.1   The universe, galaxies, quasars

Aguilar, David A.

Space encyclopedia; a tour of our solar system and beyond. written & illustrated by David A. Aguilar ; contributing writers Christine Pulliam & Patricia Daniels. National Geographic 2013 191 p. color illustrations (National Geographic kids) (reinforced library binding) $24.95

Grades: 7 8 9 10 11 12 **523.1**

1. Planets 2. Astronomy 3. Cosmology 4. Outer space 5. Solar system
ISBN 1426309481; 1426315600; 1426316291; 9781426309489; 9781426315602; 9781426316296

LC 2013444119

This book on outer space by David A. Aguilar is "broken up into five sections. . . . Aguilar moves from the origins of the universe, to the planets and bodies of our Solar System, and then to the impressive phenomena from all corners of the universe. Everything from black holes to dark matter and theories about multiple universes is touched upon." (Children's Literature)

"This attractive compendium of information about space is encyclopedic in the sense that its scope is broad. The facts are presented in two- to eight-page highly illustrated articles within five thematic sections. . . . The articles are clearly written and informative, but the visuals steal the show." Booklist

Includes bibliographical references (page 191) and index

Dunbar, James Lu

The **Universe** Verse; James Lu Dunbar. James & Kenneth Pub 2014 112 p. color illustrations $24.95

Grades: 5 6 7 8 9 10 **523.1**

1. Science -- Popular works 2. Universe -- Comic books strips, etc. 3. Science 4. Cosmology 5. Human beings 6. Life -- Origin 7. Comic books, strips, etc.
ISBN 1888047259; 9781888047257

This comic book, by James Lu Dunbar, "is a scientifically-accurate rhyming comic book about the origins of the universe, life on Earth and the human race. It introduces and illuminates the most fundamental features of our existence in a way that is engaging and accessible to a wide audience.

. . . This book contains most major scientific milestones known to humanity." (Publisher's note)

"The images slowly transition from black and white in the first section to unobtrusive color in last section.... Young students will revel in the artwork, while older kids could use the text as an introduction to advanced high school science." SLJ

Goldsmith, Mike

Universe; journey into deep space. Mike Goldsmith ; illustrated by Mark A. Garlick. Kingfisher 2012 48 p. (hardcover) $17.99

Grades: 4 5 6 7   **523.1**

1. Universe 2. Astronomy 3. Outer space
ISBN 075346876X; 9780753468760

This book, by Mike Goldsmith, illustrated by Mark A. Garlick, profiles "some of the Universe's most intriguing places, and along the way . . . [describes] the amazing history of the Cosmos. A series of . . . spreads give . . . snapshots of distant galactic locations as the reader journeys . . . from red cold Mars (3 light minutes away) to a massive Supernova (10,000 light years away) and beyond." (Publisher's note)

523.2   Planetary systems

Aguilar, David A.

13 planets; the latest view of the solar system. David A. Aguilar. National Geographic Books 2011 60 p. il $16.95

Grades: 5 6 7 8   **523.2**

1. Planets 2. Astronomy 3. Solar system
ISBN 1426307705; 1426307713; 9781426307706; 9781426307713

LC 2010032510

Updated and revised edition of: 11 planets: A new view of the Solar System (2008)

This book by David A. Aguilar is designed to "update young readers on the high-interest topic of space. Using simple text and spectacular photorealistic computer art by the author, this book profiles all 13 planets in their newly created categories--plus the sun, the Oort Cloud, comets, and other worlds being discovered." (Publisher's note)

"Aguilar offers an amended volume reflecting the findings of the International Astronomical Union, which currently classifies eight objects in the solar system as planets and, with the addition of Haumea and Makemake, five as dwarf planets. . . . Aguilar has not only added sections on Haumea and Makemake, he has also used this opportunity to rewrite portions of the text and captions throughout the book and, in some cases, to substitute new illustrations or improve old ones for the new volume. The result is a more readable, more accurate, and more handsome edition of the previous work." Booklist

Includes bibliographical references and index
Thirteen planets
Latest view of the solar system

Benson, Michael

★ **Beyond**; a solar system voyage. Abrams Books for Young Readers 2009 121p il $19.95

Grades: 5 6 7 8 9 10   **523.2**

1. Astronomy 2. Solar system
ISBN 0-8109-8322-2; 978-0-8109-8322-9

LC 2008-22297

This book presents the solar system from the perspective of the space probes sent there. Glossary. Index. "Ages nine to twelve." (Sci Books Films)

"The book's focus is the exploration of the solar system by space probes, with many full-page photos. . . . The author skillfully blends lively narrative with the photos to contribute to the excitement of the explorations. . . . It is an inexpensive but valuable addition for any library." Voice Youth Advocates

Includes glossary and bibliographical references

Carson, Mary Kay

Exploring the solar system; a history with 22 activities. by Mary Kay Carson. Chicago Review Press 2008 vii, 168 p.p ill. (paperback) $17.95

Grades: 4 5 6 7   **523.2**

1. Astronomy 2. Solar system
ISBN 1556527152; 9781556527159

This book by Mary Kay Carson is a "mix of facts, history, and hands-on activities [about the solar system]. Beginning with a two-page table of contents with chapters arranged as planets in our solar system and an introductory time line, the author takes readers on a historical journey of what was known and/or discovered in each of eight time periods." (School Library Journal)

Greathouse, Lisa E.

Solar system. Compass Point Books 2009 40p il (Mission: science) lib bdg $26.60

Grades: 4 5 6   **523.2**

1. Solar system
ISBN 978-0-7565-4071-5 lib bdg; 0-7565-4071-2 lib bdg

LC 2008-35728

Introduces the solar system and the specific characteristics of its planets

Includes glossary

Stefoff, Rebecca, 1951-

The **Sun** and the Earth; Rebecca Stefoff. Cavendish Square 2014 48 p. color illustrations (Is It Science?) $29.93

Grades: 6 7 8   **523.2**

1. Sun 2. Earth 3. Astronomy -- History
ISBN 1627125213; 9781627125215

LC 2015015844

This book, by Rebecca Stefoff, explores the astronomical relationship between the Earth and the Sun. Topics addressed include the history and politics surrounding various scientific models throughout history, the science behind the rising and setting of the sun as seen from the Earth, and the unique features of the Earth's solar orbit compared to other planets.

"Each volume is heavily illustrated with period images and modern photographs, and each closes with particularly generous lists of further resources." SLJ

Tourville, Amanda Doering

Exploring the solar system. Rourke Pub. 2010
48p il (Let's explore science) $32.79; pa $9.95
Grades: 4 5 6 7   **523.2**
1. Solar system
ISBN 978-1-61590-323-8; 1-61590-323-2; 1-61590-
562-6 pa; 9781615905621 pa
                                 LC 2010009910
This "moves from basic definitions . . . to more technical
information, such as the formula for calculating the speed of
light. Also included is up-to-date coverage of Pluto's demo-
tion from planet to plutoid, as well as a section on dwarf
planets. . . . In [this] title, well-chosen boxed examples,
abundant color photos, diagrams, and an appended glossary
add interest and support the engaging [text]." Booklist
Includes glossary and bibliographical references

Wittenstein, Vicki Oransky

Planet hunter; Goeff Marcy and the search for
other earths. Boyds Mills Press 2010 48p il $17.95
Grades: 5 6 7 8   **523.2**
1. Extrasolar planets 2. Life on other planets 3.
Astrophysicists 4. College teachers
ISBN 978-1-59078-592-8; 1-59078-592-4
"The profound thrill of searching for (and finding!) planets orbiting stars other than our own is deftly captured in this
profile of Geoff Marcy, one of the great hunt's most successful practitioners. Matched to big, sharp color photos of scientists (mostly) at work and compelling speculative views of
exotic suns and landscapes, Wittenstein's matter-of-fact narrative first introduces readers to Marcy and his team on the
night shift . . . at the W. M. Keck Observatory atop Hawaii's
Mauna Kea. . . . This handsomely packaged introduction is
just the ticket for turning earthbound (for now) children into
budding skywatchers." SLJ
Includes glossary and bibliographical references

523.3   Specific parts of solar system

Carlowicz, Michael J.

The **moon**; [by] Michael Carlowicz. Abrams
2007 240p il $19.95
Grades: 8 9 10 11 12   **523.3**
1. Moon 2. Moon -- Exploration
ISBN 978-0-8109-9307-5; 0-8109-9307-4
                                 LC 2006102611
A collection of photographs celebrate the moon, its influence on Earth and society, and the scientific expeditions to
the satellite
Includes bibliographical references

Simon, Seymour

★ The **moon**; rev ed.; Simon & Schuster Bks.
for Young Readers 2003 un il $17.95
Grades: 4 5 6 7   **523.3**
1. Moon 2. Moon -- Exploration
ISBN 0-689-83563-9
                                 LC 2001-31303
First published 1984 by Four Winds Press

A basic introduction to Earth's closest neighbor, its composition, and man's missions to it
"The digitally remastered color photographs in this
update are incredible. . . . The text has undergone minimal
change. . . . The facts remain true and relevant, and the writing reflects the graphics: beautiful. This is a must-have for
astronomy sections." SLJ

**523.4   Planets, asteroids, trans-Neptunian
objects of solar system**

Capaccio, George

Jupiter. Marshall Cavendish Benchmark 2009
64p il (Space!) lib bdg $22.95
Grades: 4 5 6 7   **523.4**
1. Jupiter (Planet)
ISBN 978-0-7614-4244-8 lib bdg; 0-7614-4244-8 lib
bdg; 9780761445555
                                 LC 2008037276
"Describes Jupiter, including its history, its composition,
and its role in the solar system." Publisher's note
Includes glossary and bibliographical references

Mars. Marshall Cavendish Benchmark 2010
64p il (Space!) lib bdg $22.95
Grades: 4 5 6 7   **523.4**
1. Mars (Planet)
ISBN 978-0-7614-4247-9 lib bdg; 0-7614-4247-2 lib
bdg; 9780761445579
                                 LC 2008037280
Describes Mars, including its history, its composition,
and its role in the solar system
Includes glossary and bibliographical references

Colligan, L. H.

Mercury. Marshall Cavendish Benchmark 2009
64p il (Space!) lib bdg $22.95
Grades: 4 5 6 7   **523.4**
1. Mercury (Planet)
ISBN 0-7614-4239-1 lib bdg; 9780761442394 lib
bdg; 9780761445517
                                 LC 2008037278
"Describes Mercury, including its history, its composition, and its role in the solar system." Publisher's note
Includes glossary and bibliographical references

Hicks, Terry Allan

Saturn. Marshall Cavendish Benchmark 2010
64p il (Space!) lib bdg $22.95
Grades: 4 5 6 7   **523.4**
1. Saturn (Planet)
ISBN 978-0-7614-4249-3 lib bdg; 0-7614-4249-9 lib
bdg; 9780761445593
                                 LC 2008037453
"Describes Saturn, including its history, its composition,
and its role in the solar system." Publisher's note
Includes glossary and bibliographical references

Jones, Thomas D.

★ **Planetology**; unlocking the secrets of the solar system. [by] Tom Jones and Ellen Stofan. National Geographic 2008 217p il $35

Grades: 7 8 9 10 11 12   **523.4**

1. Planets 2. Astrogeology

ISBN 978-1-4262-0121-9; 1-4262-0121-4

LC 2008-10726

"This beautifully produced book provides an introduction to comparative planetology for a general audience. The large-format volume focuses on comparing and contrasting different processes that shape and form the primary planets in the solar system. . . . The writing is crisp and clear, and the choice of imagery and examples is very strong." Choice

Includes bibliographical references

Miller, Ron

Mars; [by] Ron Miller. Twenty-First Century Books 2006 95p il (Worlds beyond) lib bdg $27.90

Grades: 7 8 9 10   **523.4**

1. Mars (Planet)

ISBN 0-7613-2362-7

LC 2003-10139

Chronicles the discovery and explorations of the planet Mars and discusses each of its moons, its place in the solar system, and more.

"Chock full of stunning photographs and illustrations. . . . Written clearly and concisely. . . . A valuable resource." Voice Youth Advocates

Includes bibliographical references

Seven wonders of the gas giants and their moons. Twenty-First Century Books 2011 80p il (Seven wonders) lib bdg $33.26

Grades: 5 6 7 8   **523.4**

1. Planets

ISBN 978-0-7613-5449-9 lib bdg; 0-7613-5449-2 lib bdg; 9780761372813

LC 2010-15558

This book describes seven phenomena about the outer planets of the solar system and their moons, including the great red spot of Jupiter and the underground sea of Europa. Index. "Grades five to eight." (Sci Books Films)

This "celebrates the most unique features of Jupiter, Saturn, Uranus and Neptune, including companion moons and Saturn's mysterious rings. . . . [This] volume makes basic concepts clear in lively, energetic language that, along with the mesmerizing color photos and artists' renderings of space, will easily captivate a young audience, while up-to-date examples, including discoveries made in the last five years, will only increase the sense of immediacy and excitement." Booklist

Includes glossary and bibliographical references

Seven wonders of the rocky planets and their moons. Twenty-First Century Books 2011 80p il (Seven wonders) lib bdg $33.26

Grades: 4 5 6   **523.4**

1. Planets

ISBN 978-0-7613-5448-2 lib bdg; 0-7613-5448-4 lib bdg; 9780761372837

LC 2010-15553

This book shows "views of features on Mercury, Venus, Earth (and its moon), and Mars. [Glossary. Index.] Grades five to eight." (Sci Books Films)

This "compares the fascinating diversity of Earth's land masses with those on Mars, Venus and Mercury. . . . [This] volume makes basic concepts clear in lively, energetic language that, along with the mesmerizing color photos and artists' renderings of space, will easily captivate a young audience, while up-to-date examples, including discoveries made in the last five years, will only increase the sense of immediacy and excitement." Booklist

Includes glossary and bibliographical references

Nardo, Don

Asteroids and comets. Morgan Reynolds Pub. 2009 112p il (Extreme threats) lib bdg $28.95

Grades: 7 8 9 10   **523.4**

1. Comets 2. Asteroids

ISBN 978-1-59935-121-6; 1-59935-121-8

LC 2009-26295

This book covers "evidence of impacts, types of impactors, giant impacts and mass extinctions, recent impacts and near misses, the current and future danger of near-earth-objects (NEOs), and scientific research on how to address the threat. . . . Features high-gloss pages in mottled green, full-color pictures, and informative sidebars. . . . [It is] well written, nicely designed, and interesting." Voice Youth Advocates

Includes glossary and bibliographical references

Poynter, Margaret

Doomsday rocks from space. Enslow Publishers 2011 48p il (Bizarre science) lib bdg $23.93

Grades: 5 6 7 8   **523.4**

1. Comets 2. Asteroids 3. Meteorites

ISBN 978-0-7660-3673-4; 0-7660-3673-1

LC 2009053601

First published 1996 with title: Killer asteroids

"Aimed at reluctant readers, [this title is] sure to disgust and delight in equal measure. . . . [The title] will pique interest and get kids lining up at the reference desk looking for more. The text is complemented by illustrations and magnified photos of things that you would hope never to see." SLJ

Includes glossary and bibliographical references

Scott, Elaine

When is a planet not a planet? the story of Pluto. Clarion Books 2007 43p il $17

Grades: 3 4 5 6   **523.4**

1. Planets

ISBN 978-0-618-89832-9; 0-618-89832-8

"Scott takes the 2006 downgrading of Pluto from planet to dwarf planet as a teachable moment for discussing questions such as how the number of planets has changed through the centuries, what can be called a planet, and how scientists come to conclusions—and occasionally change their minds. . . . Beautifully designed, the book includes many well-captioned, color illustrations, from period portraits to NASA images to artist's conceptions." Booklist

Sherman, Josepha

Neptune. Marshall Cavendish Benchmark 2009 63p il (Space!) lib bdg $22.95

Grades: 4 5 6 7   **523.4**

1. Neptune (Planet)

ISBN 978-0-7614-4246-2 lib bdg; 0-7614-4246-4 lib bdg; 9780761445562

LC 2008037279

"Describes Neptune, including its history, its composition, and its role in the solar system." Publisher's note

Includes glossary and bibliographical references

Sparrow, Giles

Destination Uranus, Neptune, and Pluto. PowerKids Press 2010 32p il lib bdg $23.95; pa $10

Grades: 3 4 5 6   **523.4**

1. Uranus (Planet) 2. Neptune (Planet) 3. Pluto (Dwarf planet)

ISBN 978-1-4358-3446-0 lib bdg; 978-1-4358-3463-7 pa

LC 2009-2985

Examines the outer planets, and discusses their moons, interiors, atmospheres, locations, and exploration.

Tyson, Neil De Grasse

The **Pluto** files; the rise and fall of America's favorite planet. W.W. Norton 2009 194p il $23.95; pa $15.95

Grades: 8 9 10 11 12 Adult   **523.4**

1. Pluto (Dwarf planet)

ISBN 978-0-393-06520-6; 0-393-06520-0; 978-0-393-33732-7 pa; 0-393-33732-4 pa

LC 2008-40436

The author, who is the director of the Hayden Planetarium and the Rose Center for Earth and Space at the American Museum of Natural History in New York City, discusses the "history of Pluto and the debate over its planethood. . . [Tyson cites Pluto's] entrenchment in America's cultural and patriotic view of the cosmos to explain its considerable popularity and the reasons why so many people campaigned for the preservation of its status." (Publisher's note)

The author "uses an engaging mix of facts, photographs, cartoons, illustrations, songs, e-mails, and humor to explain what's up (and down) with Pluto." Christ Sci Monit

Includes bibliographical references

523.43   Mars

Miller, Ron

Curiosity's mission on Mars; exploring the red planet. by Ron Miller. TFCB, Twenty-First Century Books 2014 64 p. color illustrations (lib. bdg. : alk. paper) $33.26

Grades: 7 8 9 10 11 12   **523.43**

1. Mars (Planet) -- Exploration

ISBN 1467710873; 9781467710879

LC 2013009290

This book, by Ron Miller, "provides a . . . basic introduction to the Curiosity rover, which NASA launched into space on November 26, 2011. It landed on Mars in August 2012, began drilling into rocks, and has found many key ingredients necessary for life. . . . Sidebars provide additional information on related topics, such as the . . . the likelihood of ice beneath the surface of Mars, and the layers of the planet's atmosphere." (Booklist)

"This clearly written book provides a solid, basic introduction to the Curiosity rover, which NASA launched into space on November 26, 2011. It landed on Mars in August 2012, began drilling into rocks, and has found many key ingredients necessary for life...Sidebars provide additional information on related topics, such as the naming of Curiosity by Kansas sixth-grader Clara Ma, the likelihood of ice beneath the surface of Mars, and the layers of the planet's atmosphere. Rather small color photos and diagrams illustrate this succinct introduction." (Booklist)

Includes bibliographical references (pages 55-56) and index

Rusch, Elizabeth

★ The **mighty** Mars rovers; the incredible adventures of Spirit and Opportunity. by Elizabeth Rusch. Houghton Mifflin Books for Children 2012 79 p. ill. (chiefly col.) (hardcover) $18.99; (hardcover) $18.99

Grades: 4 5 6   **523.43**

1. Mars probes 2. Mars (Planet) -- Exploration 3. Astronautics 4. Roving vehicles (Astronautics)

ISBN 054747881X; 9780547478814

LC 2011012159

In this book, "[Elizabeth] Rusch covers not only the scientific aspects of Mars exploration but also the personalities of the people who made it happen, and profiles the rovers themselves, Spirit and Opportunity." She looks at "the behind-the-scenes efforts of launching a scientific mission." Also included are "[f]ull-color photographs," a glossary, and a list of further resources. (School Library Journal)

Includes bibliographical references (p. 76), discography (p. 78), filmograophy (p. 78), and index.

523.45   Jupiter

Miller, Ron

Jupiter. 21st Cent. Bks. (Brookfield) 2002 72p il (Worlds beyond) lib bdg $27.90

Grades: 5 6 7 8   **523.45**

1. Jupiter (Planet)

ISBN 0-7613-2356-2

LC 2001-36790

Chronicles the discovery and explorations of the planet Jupiter and discusses each of its moons, its place in the solar system, and more

Illustrated "with a mix of NASA photos and big, amazingly realistic, digitally produced, color images." SLJ

Includes glossary and bibliographical references

523.46   Saturn

Miller, Ron

Saturn; Ron Miller. Twenty-First Century Books 2003 80p ill. (library) $27.93

Grades: 5 6 7 8   523.46

1. Saturn (Planet)

ISBN 9780761323600; 0761323600

Chronicles the discovery and exploration of the planet Saturn and discusses its rings and moons, its place in the solar system, and more.

"Concepts are explained clearly, and helpful diagrams and carefully chosen illustrations assist understanding." SLJ

Includes bibliographical references

523.5   Meteors, solar wind, zodiacal light

Koppes, Steven N.

Killer rocks from outer space; asteroids, comets, and meteorites. Lerner Publications Co. 2004 112p il (Discovery!) $26.60

Grades: 6 7 8 9   523.5

1. Comets 2. Asteroids 3. Meteorites

ISBN 0-8225-2861-4

LC 2003-10077

Describes the role that collisions with meteors, comets, and asteroids have played in the history of Earth and other planets in the solar system and examines what is being done to protect Earth from future collisions

"A catchy title, colorful cover, and well-written and interesting information combine to make this unusual science book one that students will find to be very readable and extremely useful for research projects. . . . This book will find many readers and should inspire students to further study astronomy." Lib Media Connect

Includes bibliographical references

Spangenburg, Ray

Meteors, meteorites, and meteoroids; [by] Ray Spangenburg and Kit Moser. Watts 2002 112p il (Out of this world) $33.50; pa $14.95

Grades: 6 7 8 9   523.5

1. Meteors 2. Meteorites

ISBN 0-531-11925-4; 0-531-15567-6 pa

LC 2002-17

Explores the mysteries of rocks that travel vast distances through space, sometimes passing through Earth's atmosphere and sometimes landing on the surface

This "includes scientific facts and personal touches that give the text warmth. The conversational style makes for easy reading and high interest. The illustrations are accurate and colorful and significantly provide understanding to the text." Book Rep

Includes glossary and bibliographical references

523.8   Stars

Abramson, Andra Serlin

Inside stars; by Andra Serlin Abramson and Mordecai-Mark Mac Low. Sterling Children's Books 2011 48p il (Inside . . .) $16.95; pa $9.95

Grades: 5 6 7 8   523.8

1. Stars

ISBN 978-1-4027-7709-7; 1-4027-7709-4; 978-1-4027-8162-9 pa; 1-4027-8162-8 pa

LC 2011283564

Presents an illustrated overview of stars, including information on how they affect the Earth, how scientists study them, how they are classified, how they form and die, and specific information about our star, the Sun.

"On full but not crowded-looking pages, the captions, vocabulary words and digestible blocks of text are set into and around an engagingly diverse mix of cutaway views, digital paintings and eye-widening deep-space photographs. . . . There's plenty here to stimulate both random browsers and confirmed young sky watchers." Kirkus

Includes bibliographical references

Aguilar, David A.

Super stars; the biggest, hottest, brightest, and most explosive stars in the Milky Way. National Geographic 2010 48p il $16.95; lib bdg $27.90

Grades: 4 5 6 7   523.8

1. Stars

ISBN 978-1-4263-0601-3; 1-4263-0601-6; 978-1-4263-0602-0 lib bdg; 1-4263-0602-4 lib bdg

LC 2009-37124

"Pairing dramatic space art with souped-up prose, Aguilar introduces more than a dozen types of stars and stellar phenomena. . . . Aside from the occasional alien or interstellar spacecraft set against glowing star fields, the information in both pictures and texts sticks to the facts, accurately reflecting current knowledge without ever coming close to turning into a dry recitation of data. . . . [This is an] unusually exuberant ticket to ride for young sky watchers and armchair space travelers." SLJ

Includes glossary and bibliographical references

Croswell, Ken

★ The lives of stars. Boyds Mills Press 2009 72p il $19.95

Grades: 5 6 7 8   523.8

1. Stars 2. Astronomy

ISBN 978-1-59078-582-9; 1-59078-582-7

LC 2008033913

"Extensive, detailed information about stars is coupled with amazing colorful photographs, many from the Hubble Space Telescope, in this stunning book. Packed with facts about the stars and their life cycle, the text often relates them to situations or objects familiar to readers." SLJ

Includes glossary

DeCristofano, Carolyn Cinami

★ A black hole is not a hole; Carolyn Cinami DeCristofano ; Illustrated by Michael Carroll.

Charlesbridge 2012 v, 74 p.p col ill. (reinforced for library use) $18.95

Grades: 4 5 6 7 **523.8**

1. Stars 2. Universe 3. Black holes (Astronomy)
ISBN 9781570917837; 9781570917844

LC 2010022764

In this non-fiction children's book, Carolyn Cinami DeCristofano discusses black holes. "Covering the life cycles of stars; the formation of black holes and weird optical and physical effects associated with them; more recent revelations of super-sized black holes at the centers of galaxies; and the general effects of mass on space, light, and matter, she presents a . . . picture of the strange structure and stranger physics of black holes." (Booklist)

Jackson, Ellen B.

★ The **mysterious** universe; supernovae, dark energy, and black holes. text by Ellen Jackson; photographs and illustrations by Nic Bishop. Houghton Mifflin 2008 60p il (Scientists in the field) $18

Grades: 5 6 7 8 9 **523.8**

1. Supernovas 2. Black holes (Astronomy)
ISBN 978-0-618-56325-8; 0-618-56325-3

LC 2007-41165

"Splitting its attention evenly between the scientist and his field, this handsomely designed volume displays the joys of being fascinated by one's work in a way that will encourage students to seek similar professional satisfaction for themselves." Booklist

Includes glossary and bibliographical references

Mack, Gail

The **stars**. Marshall Cavendish Benchmark 2009 64p il (Space!) lib bdg $32.79

Grades: 4 5 6 7 **523.8**

1. Stars 2. Galaxies
ISBN 978-0-7614-4250-9 lib bdg; 0-7614-4250-2 lib bdg

LC 2009014655

This stands out for its "clear, accurate [presentation] of basic facts punctuated by lively turns of phrase and, sometimes, details not commonly found in the plethora of similar tours of the solar system and beyond." SLJ

Includes glossary and bibliographical references

Miller, Ron

Seven wonders beyond the solar system. Twenty-First Century Books 2011 80p il (Seven wonders) lib bdg $33.26

Grades: 5 6 7 8 **523.8**

1. Extrasolar planets 2. Solar system
ISBN 978-0-7613-5454-3; 0-7613-5454-9

LC 2010028446

This "discusses how stars and galaxies form and how scientists search for 'the most Earthlike planet,' as well as the noteworthy nebulae, pulsars, and superclusters. . . . [This] volume makes basic concepts clear in lively, energetic language that, along with the mesmerizing color photos and artists' renderings of space, will easily captivate a young audience, while up-to-date examples, including discoveries

made in the last five years, will only increase the sense of immediacy and excitement." Booklist

Includes glossary and bibliographical references

Ridpath, Ian

The **monthly** sky guide; Ian Ridpath ; illustrated by Wil Tirion. 9th ed. Cambridge University Press 2012 71 p. col. ill. (paperback) $17.99

Grades: 8 9 10 11 12 Adult **523.8**

1. Astronomy 2. Stars -- Atlases 4. Stars -- Identification 5. Stars -- Observers' manuals
ISBN 1107683157; 9781107683150

LC 2012033599

This book, the ninth edition of Ian Ridpath and Wil Tirion's guide to the night sky, "is updated with planet positions and forthcoming eclipses to the end of the year 2017. It contains twelve chapters describing the main sights visible in each month of the year, providing" information for anyone "wanting to identify prominent stars, constellations, star clusters, nebulae and galaxies; to watch out for meteor showers . . . ; or to follow the movements of the four brightest planets." (Publisher's note)

Includes bibliographical references and index.

525 Earth (Astronomical geography)

Bell, Trudy E.

Earth's journey through space; by Trudy E. Bell. Chelsea House Publishers 2008 80p il (Scientific American) lib bdg $30

Grades: 5 6 7 8 **525**

1. Astronomy 2. Earth 3. Solar system
ISBN 978-0-7910-9050-3 lib bdg; 0-7910-9050-7 lib bdg

LC 2007032351

The author "describes in some detail just how our planet's axial tilt, rotation, and orbital path were discovered and measured, as well as how external forces affect all three. She then goes on to explain how scientists use parallax and other physical effects to determine distances and movements in our galaxy and the universe at large. . . . In general, the old prints, modern space photos, and clear digital images are well chosen to clarify and enhance the presentation." SLJ

Includes bibliographical references

Ride, Sally K.

Mission : planet Earth; our world and its climate--and how humans are changing them. [by] Sally Ride & Tam O'Shaughnessy. Roaring Brook Press 2009 80p il map (Sally Ride science) $19.95

Grades: 5 6 7 8 **525**

1. Earth 2. Climate -- Environmental aspects
ISBN 978-1-59643-310-6; 1-59643-310-8

LC 2009-29253

"This environmental-science primer introduces a range of important concepts necessary to understand climate change and global warming. Topics include the carbon cycle, water cycle, long-range carbon emissions data, biological evidence of climate change, and much more. The authors have an extensive background in science education, and

their text exhibits an excellent balance of concept thoroughness with ease of comprehension. Attractive photographs
and colorful graphics, including many charts and diagrams,
are incorporated throughout." SLJ

Simon, Seymour

★ **Earth** : our planet in space; rev ed; Simon &
Schuster Bks. for Young Readers 2003 un il $17.95
Grades: 4 5 6 7　　　　　　　　　　　　　　**525**
　1. Earth
　ISBN 0-689-83562-0

LC 2001-31304

First published 1984 by Four Winds Press

This describes the relationship between the Earth, the
sun, and the moon and explains the seasons, day and night,
the atmosphere, and changes in the planet's surface. Illustrated with photographs taken from space

525.022　Earth -- Illustrations, models, miniatures

Nardo, Don

The **Blue** marble; how a photograph revealed
Earth's fragile beauty. by Don Nardo. Compass Point
Books 2014 64 p. (Compass point books. Captured
history) (library binding) $33.99
Grades: 5 6 7 8 9　　　　　　　　　　　　**525.022**
　1. Earth 2. Photographs 3. Apollo project 4. Apollo
17 (Spacecraft) 5. Photographs -- History 6. Earth
(Planet) -- Photographs from space
　ISBN 0756547326;　9780756547325;　9780756547882

LC 2013031184

"The astronauts headed to the moon in December 1972
thought they knew what to expect. . . . But what they didn't
expect came as a huge bonus. The astronauts of Apollo 17
would produce an amazing photograph of planet Earth--a
lonely globe floating in inky black space. Their stunning
Blue Marble image was destined to become one of the most
reproduced and recognizable photos in history." (Publisher's note)

"This outstanding follow-up to Capstone's 'Captured
History' series continues the same format, focusing on a single, emblematic photograph that defines an era or event. . . .
This set will show students how a single image can 'capture'
history and influence the perceptions and actions of those
who see it. The books will certainly draw a large readership and are must-buys for all middle-level and secondary
collections." SLJ

　Includes bibliographical references (page 63) and index
　Other titles in this series include:
　Assassination and its Aftermath (2014)
　Breaker Boys (2012)
　Civil War Witness (2014)
　The Golden Spike (2015)
　Hitler in Paris (2014)
　Little Rock Girl 1957 (2012)
　Man on the Moon (2011)
　Migrant Mother (2011)
　Raising the Flag (2011)
　Shadow Catcher (2015)
　Summiting Everest (2014)

Tank Man (2014)

526.9　Surveying

Anderson, Judith

★ **Ways** to do surveys; [by] Judith Anderson.
Smart Apple Media 2008 32p il map (Geography
skills) $22.95
Grades: 6 7 8 9　　　　　　　　　　　　　**526.9**
　1. Surveying
　ISBN 978-1-59920-053-8;　1-59920-053-8

LC 2006036140

"The text is easy to follow. . . . The examples . . . are
almost always accompanied by excellent photographs. . . .
Maps, block diagrams, tables, and graphs are clearly presented and easy to interpret." Sci Books Films

　Includes glossary and bibliographical references

529　Chronology

Formichelli, Linda

Timekeeping; Explore the History and Science of
Telling Time With 15 Projects. by Linda Formichelli,
W. Eric Martin ; illustrated by Sam Carbaugh. Inde-
pendent Pub Group 2012 128 p. (hardcover) $21.95
Grades: 4 5 6 7 8　　　　　　　　　　　　　　**529**
　1. Time 2. Science -- Experiments
　ISBN 1619301369;　9781619301368

This juvenile activity book, by Linda Formichelli, W.
Eric Martin, with illustrations by Sam Carbaugh, is part of
the "Build It Yourself" series. It teaches "the cultural history of time" through providing several activities and projects such as "making a shadow clock, tracking time like
an ancient Egyptian, using a protractor to create a sundial,
measuring time with water, and making a candle clock."
(Publisher's note)

Kagayame, Johnny

Discovering the construct of time; [by] Johnny
Kagayame, Josepha Sherman. Rosen Pub. 2011
112p il (The scientist's guide to physics)
Grades: 7 8 9 10　　　　　　　　　　　　　　**529**
　1. Time 2. Calendars 3. Space and time 4. Clocks
and watches
　ISBN 1448847036;　9781448847037

LC 2010042035

"Beginning with a brief discussion of the concept of time
and its meaning in different cultures, this book presents the
history of time measurement. . . . A section of the chapter
'Time in Modern Times' introduces Einstein's theories of
relativity. . . . Illustrated chiefly with clearly reproduced
color photos, this volume provides an accessible, basic introduction to its subject." Booklist

　Includes glossary and bibliographical references

Kummer, Patricia K.

★ The **calendar**; by Patricia K. Kummer.
Franklin Watts 2005 80p il (Inventions that shaped
the world) $30.50; pa $9.95

Grades: 4 5 6 7 **529**
1. Calendars
ISBN 0-531-12340-5; 0-531-16720-8 pa

LC 2004-6914

This "book presents the origins and history of the calendar. . . . The illustrations include clear reproductions of period paintings, engravings, and drawings as well as photos of artifacts, sculpture, and contemporary scenes. . . . A good basic introduction." Booklist

Includes bibliographical references

Sullivan, Navin

Time; [by] Navin Sullivan. Marshall Cavendish Benchmark 2007 48p il (Measure up!) lib bdg $20.95
Grades: 4 5 6 7 **529**
1. Time 2. Calendars 3. Clocks and watches
ISBN 978-0-7614-2321-8 lib bdg; 0-7614-2321-4 lib bdg

This is "engaging and informative. . . . The excellent blend of photographs, charts, and diagrams complements the [text]." SLJ

Includes glossary and bibliographical references

530 Physics

Baxter, Roberta

The **particle** model of matter. Raintree 2009 48p il (Sci-hi: physical science) lib bdg $31.43; pa $8.99
Grades: 4 5 6 7 **530**
1. Atoms 2. Matter
ISBN 978-1-4109-3244-0 lib bdg; 978-1-4109-3259-4 pa

LC 2008030582

This takes a look at atoms, the building blocks of matter. It describes the different kinds of atoms, the particles that make up an atom, and the different states that matter can take

Includes bibliographical references

Bonnet, Robert L.

Home run! science projects with baseball and softball. [by] Robert L. Bonnet and Dan Keen. Enslow Publishers 2009 104p il (Score! Sports science projects) lib bdg $31.93
Grades: 5 6 7 8 **530**
1. Motion 2. Baseball 3. Force and energy 4. Science projects 5. Science -- Experiments
ISBN 978-0-7660-3365-8 lib bdg; 0-7660-3365-1 lib bdg

LC 2008-3005

"In addition to colorful, digital drawings illustrating the projects, a few photos and period prints also brighten the pages. . . . [This] will appeal to those looking for fresh science-project ideas." Booklist

Includes glossary and bibliographical references

Christianson, Gale E.

Isaac Newton and the scientific revolution. Oxford Univ. Press 1996 155p il (Oxford portraits in science) lib bdg $28
Grades: 7 8 9 10 **530**
1. Physicists 2. Scientists 3. Mathematicians 4. Writers on science
ISBN 0-19-509224-4

LC 96-13179

Explores the life and scientific contributions of the famed English mathematician and natural philosopher

This book "reads easily and with a pleasant and comfortable flow. Structured around pivotal moments in Newton's life, the book is an excellent reference for biographical data on the great English scientist; in addition, it affords a fine historical perspective of the scientific revolution." Sci Books Films

Includes bibliographical references

Farndon, John

Experimenting with physics. Marshall Cavendish Benchmark 2009 112p il (Experimenting with science) $35.64
Grades: 7 8 9 10 **530**
1. Physics 2. Science -- Experiments
ISBN 978-0-7614-3929-5; 0-7614-3929-3

LC 2008017568

"Explores and explains physics concepts—including energy, motion, simple machines, gravity, flight, electricity, and magnetism—and provides experiments to aid in understanding physics." Publisher's note

Gardner, Robert

Ace your physical science project; great science fair ideas. [by] Robert Gardner, Madeline Goodstein, and Thomas R. Rybolt. Enslow Publishers 2009 128p il (Ace your physics science project) lib bdg $31.93
Grades: 5 6 7 8 **530**
1. Physics 2. Science projects 3. Science -- Experiments
ISBN 978-0-7660-3225-5 lib bdg; 0-7660-3225-6 lib bdg

LC 2008-29637

"Dozens of . . . science activities are presented with background information, step-by-step instructions, and suggestions for extending to the science fair level. . . . Color illustrations and important safety information are included." Horn Book Guide

Includes bibliographical references

Science fair projects about the properties of matter; revised and expanded using the scientific method. Enslow Publishers 2010 160p il (Physics science projects using the scientific method) lib bdg $34.60
Grades: 7 8 9 10 **530**
1. Matter 2. Science projects 3. Science -- Experiments
ISBN 978-0-7660-3417-4 lib bdg; 0-7660-3417-8 lib bdg

LC 2009014804

First published 2004 with title: Science fair projects about the properties of matter using marbles, water, balloons, and more

"Explains how to use the scientific method to conduct several science experiments about the properties of matter. Includes ideas for science fair projects." Publisher's note

Includes bibliographical references

Slam dunk! science projects with basketball; [by] Robert Gardner and Dennis Shortelle. Enslow Publishers 2009 104p il (Score! sports science projects) lib bdg $31.93

Grades: 5 6 7 8   **530**
1. Physics 2. Basketball 3. Science projects 4. Science -- Experiments
ISBN 978-0-7660-3366-5 lib bdg; 0-7660-3366-X lib bdg

     LC 2008-24879

"Introductions include information about the history of the sport, safety steps to follow, and the scientific method. . . . Detailed diagrams help clarify many of the directions." SLJ

Includes glossary and bibliographical references

Green, Dan

Physics; why matter matters! [by] Dan Green; Simon Basher, illustrator. Kingfisher 2008 128p il pa $8.95

Grades: 5 6 7 8   **530**
1. Physics
ISBN 978-0-7534-6214-0 pa; 0-7534-6214-1 pa

     LC 2007-31805

This "introduces the elements of physics as anthropomorphic, cartoon-style characters. . . . Each of the groupings begins with an introduction and each concept is given its own spread that shows the cartoon figure and describes its 'personality.' The information is presented in a chatty and conversational tone. . . . Along with the narrative, which is written in the first person from the concept's point of view, other key facts are presented. This book would be handy as a supplement to a physics curriculum." SLJ

Includes glossary

Hartman, Eve

Light and sound; [by] Eve Hartman and Wendy Meshbesher. Raintree 2008 48p il (Sci-hi: physical science) lib bdg $22; pa $8.99

Grades: 5 6 7 8   **530**
1. Light 2. Sound
ISBN 978-1-4109-3378-2 lib bdg; 1-4109-3378-4 lib bdg; 978-1-4109-3383-6 pa; 1-4109-3383-0 pa

     LC 2009-3506

A "compelling read for both browsers and science buffs. . . . Information is clearly presented and flows smoothly. . . . A treasure trove of information." SLJ

Includes glossary and bibliographical references

Lee, Cora

The **great** motion mission; a surprising story of physics in everyday life. illustrated by Steve Rolston. Annick Press 2009 114p il $24.95; pa $14.95

Grades: 4 5 6   **530**
1. Physics
ISBN 978-1-55451-185-3; 1-55451-185-2; 978-1-55451-184-6 pa; 1-55451-184-4 pa

"This book is a combination of narrative and concepts about physics. . . . Jeremy and his friends are distraught when the local summer fair is canceled in order to host a physics conference. While Jeremy helps his uncle campaign to save the fair, his new neighbor, Aubrey, sets out to prove that physics isn't only necessary, but also fun. The text is chatty and accessible to students. Topics include 'Physics and Sight,' 'Physics and Sound,' and 'Physics in Motion.' Each chapter profiles a featured physicist, from Albert Einstein to Richard Feynman. . . . Cartoon illustrations help to explain concepts such as the water cycle and wave patterns. Photographs are scattered throughout, and boxed areas highlight specific topics. This title would be especially useful for students wanting a good introduction to physics." SLJ

Includes glossary and bibliographical references

Matter; edited by Andrea R. Field. 1st ed. Britannica Educational Pub. in association with Rosen Educational Services 2013 77 p. ill. (some col.) (Introduction to physics) (library) $31.70

Grades: 7 8 9 10   **530**
1. Matter 2. Physics
ISBN 1615308393; 9781615308392

     LC 2011052216

This book by Andrea R. Field is part of the Introduction to Physics series and focuses on Matter. The entry "covers the basic properties and states of matter; its relationship to energy, including Einstein's theory of special relativity; and physicists' quandaries with dark matter and antimatter." (Booklist)

Includes bibliographical references (p. 73) and index.

Mercer, Bobby

Junk drawer physics; 50 awesome experiments that don't cost a thing. Bobby Mercer. First edition Chicago Review Press, Inc. 2014 208 p. (trade paper) $14.95

Grades: 5 6 7 8   **530**
1. Physics 2. Science -- Experiments 3. Physics -- Experiments
ISBN 1613749201; 9781613749203

     LC 2013046726

In this book, Bobby Mercer "provides readers with more than 50 . . . hands-on experiments. . . . Turn a plastic cup into a pinhole camera using waxed paper, a rubber band, and a thumbtack. Build a swinging wave machine using a series of washers suspended on strings from a yardstick. . . . Each project has a materials list, detailed step-by-step instructions with illustrations, and a brief explanation of the scientific principle being demonstrated." (Publisher's note)

"This book is filled with practical and easy experiments that demonstrate many different principles of physics. Though it joins a crowded market of similar at-home science books, this title offers experiments that are fresh and different." SLJ

Morgan, Sally

From Greek atoms to quarks; discovering atoms. by Sally Morgan. Heinemann Library 2007 64p il (Chain reactions) lib bdg $34.29

Grades: 6 7 8 9   530

1. Atoms 2. Matter

ISBN 978-1-4034-9551-8 lib bdg; 1-4034-9551-3 lib bdg

LC 2006037044

"Morgan tells the story of the atom, including its discovery, structure, power, and future in subatomic particles. . . . Archival and full-color photos and reproductions appear on nearly every page." SLJ

Includes glossary and bibliographical references

The **science** of physics; edited by Andrea Field. Britannica Educational Pub. 2012 80 p. (Introduction to physics) (library binding) $31.70

Grades: 7 8 9 10   530

1. Physics

ISBN 1615306765; 9781615306763

LC 2011026548

This children's book, edited by Andrea R. Field, is part of the Introduction to Physics series. It "surveys some of the major branches of physics, the laws, and theories significant to each. Also chronicled are some of the historical milestones in the field by such great minds as Galileo and Isaac Newton." (Publisher's note)

Includes bibliographical references and index

Weir, Jane

Matter. Compass Point Books 2009 40p il (Mission: science) lib bdg $26.60

Grades: 4 5 6   530

1. Matter

ISBN 978-0-7565-4069-2 lib bdg; 0-7565-4069-0 lib bdg

LC 2008-37624

An introduction to the scientific concept of matter, including elements, atoms, and molecules

Includes glossary

530.092   Physicists

Baxter, Roberta

Ernest Rutherford and the birth of the atomic age; by Roberta Baxter. Morgan Reynolds Pub. 2011 ill. (Profiles in science) (library) $28.95

Grades: 7 8 9 10 11 12   530.092

1. Nuclear physics 2. Nuclear physics -- History 3. Physicists -- New Zealand -- Biography

ISBN 1599351714; 9781599351711; 9781599352756

LC 2010049096

This children's nonfiction book, by Roberta Baxter, is part of the "Profiles in Science" series, profiling the nuclear physicist Ernest Rutherford. Topics include a profile of his life as a child growing up in New Zealand, his work researching physics in Canada, his Nobel Prize, and the legacy of his work after his death.

"This is a well-rounded portrait of the 20th century's greatest experimental scientists. Baxter not only explains Rutherford's major accomplishments . . . in lucid but not oversimplified terms, but she also paints a vivid picture of an ambitious but not egotistical man with a big personality and close family ties. Enlightening diagrams and plenty of photographs . . . add solid visual elements. . . ." SLJ

Includes bibliographical references and index

Pohlen, Jerome

Albert Einstein and relativity for kids; his life and ideas with 21 activities and thought experiments. Jerome Pohlen. Chicago Review Press 2012 xv, 126 p.p (pbk.) $16.95

Grades: 5 6 7   530.092

1. Physicists 2. Relativity (Physics) 3. Physicists -- Biography 4. Relativity (Physics) -- Experiments

ISBN 161374028X; 9781613740286

LC 2012021342

This biography of physicist Albert Einstein "includes the science, politics, and people that surrounded the" scientist. "Einstein's role in the development of the atomic bomb is included along with an explanation of how nuclear fission works. His humanitarian efforts, including his regret at being the instigator behind the bomb are described along with his marriages, his relationships with his children, his eccentricities, and his scientific shortcomings." (School Library Journal)

Includes bibliographical references (page 117) and index

530.11   Relativity theory

Whiting, Jim

Space and time; Jim Whiting ; photographs by Getty Images ; folio illustration, Alex Ryan. 1st ed. Creative Education 2013 48 p. col. ill., col. maps (library) $35.65

Grades: 4 5 6 7   530.11

1. Physics 2. Space and time 3. Relativity (Physics)

ISBN 1608181928; 9781608181926

LC 2011040146

This book, by Jim Whiting, explores the concepts of space and time as part of the "Mysteries of the Universe" series. It appeals "to report writers and serious astronomy students. Each book carefully examines the history behind attempts to unravel explanations for the subjects, going back to Anaxagoras's work on energy in 450 B.C. all the way up to the contemporary findings of Stephen Hawking." (School Library Journal)

Includes bibliographical references (p. 46-47) and index

530.4   States of matter

Claybourne, Anna

The **nature** of matter; [by] Anna Claybourne. Gareth Stevens Pub. 2007 48p il (Gareth Stevens vital science: physical science) lib bdg $26.60; pa $11.95

Grades: 4 5 6 7   **530.4**
 1. Matter
 ISBN 978-0-8368-8088-5 lib bdg; 978-0-8368-8097-7 pa

               LC 2006033732

This describes uses for matter and what happens when it changes from one form to another, the basic physical laws and properties of matter, and the various ways in which we control how matter behaves.

This is "straightforward and clear. . . . The layout is bright and colorful, with photographs and illustrations on almost every page." SLJ

Includes glossary and bibliographical references

Meyer, Susan

 Gases and their properties. Rosen Central 2011 64p il (Science made simple) lib bdg $29.25; pa $12.95

Grades: 5 6 7 8   **530.4**
 1. Gases
 ISBN 978-1-4488-1233-2 lib bdg; 1-4488-1233-X lib bdg; 978-1-4488-2243-0 pa; 1-4488-2243-2 pa

               LC 2010015858

This introduction to gases and their properties includes "a lot of detailed information, making [it] useful as [a] resource . . . for science projects and reports. . . . The [book] also [includes a] brief discussion of scientists important in the field, the history of the topic, and current and future applications. . . . The straightforward, no-nonsense [narrative] and simple design make this . . . a nice package for basic science." SLJ

Includes glossary and bibliographical references

Oxlade, Chris

 States of matter; [by] Chris Oxlade. rev. and updated; Heimemann Library 2007 48p il (Chemicals in action) lib bdg $31.43; pa $8.95

Grades: 6 7 8 9   **530.4**
 1. Matter
 ISBN 978-1-4329-0055-7 lib bdg; 978-1-4329-0062-5 pa
 First published 2002

"Explanations are concise and clear without being oversimplified, and the arrangement is attractive and open. Colorful diagrams, drawings, and photographs appear on every page." SLJ

Includes glossary and bibliographical references

Reilly, Kathleen M.

 Explore solids and liquids! With 25 Great Projects. by Kathleen M. Reilly ; illustrated by Bryan Stone. Nomad Press 2014 92 p. color illustrations $14.95

Grades: 4 5 6   **530.4**
 1. Solids 2. Liquids 3. Science projects 4. Matter -- Properties -- Experiments
 ISBN 1619301717; 1619302373; 9781619301719; 9781619302372

In this book, by Kathleen M. Reilly and illustrated by Bryan Stone, "kids experience the wonder of different states of matter. They'll learn what matter is made of, how it can change, and how these interactions really work in our uni-

verse. With plenty of activities and projects, young readers gain a solid understanding of the matter they touch, see, feel, and experience every single day." (Publisher's note)

"This is an attractive presentation, easy to navigate, that encourages young readers to learn through text and experimentation." Library Media Connection Reviews

530.8   Measurement

Ball, Johnny

 Why pi; how math applies to everyday life. DK Pub. 2009 93p il map $16.99

Grades: 4 5 6 7   **530.8**
 1. Pi 2. Mathematics 3. Measurement
 ISBN 978-0-7566-5164-0; 0-7566-5164-6

"Author Johnny Ball focuses on how people have used numbers to measure things through the ages, from the ways the ancient Egyptians measured the pyramids to how modern scientists measure time and space." Publisher's note

Gardner, Robert

 Ace your math and measuring science project; great science fair ideas. Enslow Publishers 2009 128p il (Ace your physics science project) lib bdg $31.93

Grades: 5 6 7 8   **530.8**
 1. Measurement 2. Science projects 3. Weights and measures 4. Science -- Experiments
 ISBN 978-0-7660-3224-8 lib bdg; 0-7660-3224-8 lib bdg

               LC 2008-23926

"Dozens of . . . science activities are presented with background information, step-by-step instructions, and suggestions for extending to the science fair level. . . . Color illustrations and important safety information are included." Horn Book Guide

Includes bibliographical references

531   Classical mechanics

Claybourne, Anna

 Forms of energy. Raintree 2008 48p il (Sci-hi: physical science) lib bdg $22; pa $8.99

Grades: 5 6 7 8   **531**
 1. Force and energy
 ISBN 978-1-4109-3377-5 lib bdg; 1-4109-3377-6 lib bdg; 978-1-4109-3382-9 pa; 1-4109-3382-2 pa

               LC 2009-3504

A "compelling read for both browsers and science buffs. . . . Information is clearly presented and flows smoothly. . . . A treasure trove of information." SLJ

Includes glossary and bibliographical references

 Gut-wrenching gravity and other fatal forces; Anna Claybourne. Crabtree Publishing Company 2013 32 p. (Disgusting & dreadful science) (pbk. : alk. paper) $9.95

Grades: 4 5 6 **531**
1. Gravity 2. Physics 3. Force and energy
ISBN 0778709574; 9780778709503; 9780778709572
LC 2012043529

This book by Anna Claybourne is part of the Disgusting & Dreadful Science series and focuses on gravity and other physical forces. It shares facts including that "a mouse can survive a 328-foot fall, black holes have superstrong gravity that causes 'spaghettification,' and" more. Illustrations are included. (Booklist)
Includes bibliographical references and index

Energy; edited by Andrea R. Field. Britannica Educational Pub. in association with Rosen Educational Services 2012 79 p. ill. (some col.) (Introduction to physics)
Grades: 7 8 9 10 **531**
1. Force and energy -- Study and teaching (Middle school)
ISBN 9781615306732
LC 2011021493

"...With attractive, lively graphics, [this] will make a good supplement in libraries needing lots of science-experiment background information." Booklist

"This series fills a gap in the high school library by truly being an introduction to physics, electronics, and energy. It introduces readers to the major figures who discovered the laws of physics, and gives definitions of terms while providing common examples of such things as electrostatic induction, applications of magnetism, or conductivity and resistance in a circuit." (Library Media Connection)
Includes bibliographical references (p. 72-75) and index

Gardner, Robert
Ace your forces and motion science project; great science fair ideas. [by] Robert Gardner and Madeline Goodstein. Enslow Publishers 2009 128p il (Ace your physics science project) lib bdg $31.93
Grades: 5 6 7 8 **531**
1. Force and energy 2. Science projects 3. Science -- Experiments
ISBN 978-0-7660-3222-4 lib bdg; 0-7660-3222-1 lib bdg
LC 2008-49778

"Presents several science experiments and project ideas about forces and motion." Publisher's note
Includes bibliographical references

Forces and motion science fair projects; revised and expanded using the scientific method. Enslow Publishers 2010 160p il (Physics science projects using the scientific method) lib bdg $34.60
Grades: 7 8 9 10 **531**
1. Force and energy 2. Science projects 3. Science -- Experiments
ISBN 978-0-7660-3415-0 lib bdg; 0-7660-3415-1 lib bdg
LC 2008050066

First published 2004 with title: Forces and motion science fair projects using water balloons, pulleys, and other stuff

"Explains how to use the scientific method to conduct several physics experiments with forces and motion. Includes ideas for science fair projects." Publisher's note
Includes bibliographical references

Nardo, Don
Force and motion; laws of movement. by Don Nardo. Compass Point Books 2008 48p il (Exploring science) lib bdg $26.60
Grades: 7 8 9 10 **531**
1. Motion 2. Force and energy 3. Motion. 4. Force and energy.
ISBN 978-0-7565-3264-2 lib bdg; 0-7565-3264-7 lib bdg
LC 2007004604

"Each of these volumes contains five or six chapters of varying length, punctuated with 'Did you know' boxes, and an extensive resource list including books, Web sites, and museums. The concise chapters make for quick reading, and the bottom of each page has an interesting side note. The artwork is exciting and varied with photos, diagrams, and computerized images." (Library Media Connection)
Includes glossary and bibliographical references

O'Leary, Denyse
What are Newton's laws of motion? Crabtree Pub. Co. 2011 64p il (Shaping modern science) lib bdg $30.60; pa $10.95
Grades: 5 6 7 8 **531**
1. Motion 2. Physicists 3. Mathematicians 4. Writers on science
ISBN 978-0-7787-7200-2 lib bdg; 0-7787-7200-4 lib bdg; 978-0-7787-7207-1 pa; 0-7787-7207-1 pa
LC 2010-52629

This book examines how Sir Isaac Newton developed three basic laws that govern the way in which objects move. It explains how Newton expanded on the work of other scientists, including Galileo and Copernicus, to make his discovery. The book also explains how Newton's laws have influenced modern science and technology in areas such as sports and transportation.

This title is "not only written and organized well, but [it is] also gorgeous in design. Full-color photographs and illustrations are set over colorful backgrounds that add depth but not distraction. [The title] includes thought-provoking quotes from famous authors and scientists and some eyebrow-raising 'Quick Facts' throughout." SLJ
Includes glossary and bibliographical references

Orr, Tamra
Motion and forces. Rosen Central 2011 64p il (Science made simple) lib bdg $29.25; pa $12.95
Grades: 5 6 7 8 **531**
1. Motion 2. Force and energy
ISBN 978-1-4488-1232-5 lib bdg; 1-4488-1232-1 lib bdg; 978-1-4488-2240-9 pa; 1-4488-2240-8 pa
LC 2010020535

This introduction to motion and forces includes "a lot of detailed information, making [it] useful as [a] resource . . . for science projects and reports. . . . The [book] also [includes a] brief discussion of scientists important in the field, the history of the topic, and current and future applications.

... The straightforward, no-nonsense [narrative] and simple design make this ... a nice package for basic science." SLJ

Includes glossary and bibliographical references

Phelan, Glen

Invisible force; the quest to define the laws of motion. [by] Glen Phelan. National Geographic 2006 59p il (Science quest) $17.95; lib bdg $25.90

Grades: 5 6 7 8   **531**

1. Motion 2. Gravity

ISBN 0-7922-5539-9; 0-7922-5540-2 lib bdg

        LC 2005027350

This "traces the historical and scientific path to man's understanding of motion and gravity." Publisher's note

Includes glossary and bibliographical references

Pinna, Simon de

Transfer of energy; by Simon de Pinna. Gareth Stevens Pub. 2007 48p il (Gareth Stevens vital science: physical science) lib bdg $26.60; pa $11.95

Grades: 4 5 6 7   **531**

1. Force and energy

ISBN 978-0-8368-8091-5 lib bdg; 978-0-8368-8100-4 pa

        LC 2006033733

This explains such terms and concepts as kinetic and potential energy, chain reactions, energy pyramid, and power grid; the uses for the varying wavelengths of the electromagnetic spectrum; the ways that plants and animals use energy; and concepts such as conduction, convection, reflection, and transmission

This is "straightforward and clear. . . . The layout is bright and colorful, with photographs and illustrations on almost every page." SLJ

Includes bibliographical references

Silverstein, Alvin

Forces and motion; [by Alvin & Virginia Silverstein & Laura Silverstein Nunn] Twenty-First Century Books 2008 112p il (Science concepts) lib bdg $31.93

Grades: 5 6 7 8   **531**

1. Motion 2. Force and energy

ISBN 978-0-8225-7514-6 lib bdg; 0-8225-7514-0 lib bdg

        LC 2007-48826

"The breadth of material the authors cover in this volume is impressive. They discuss energy (kenetic and potential), forces (friction, gravity, electricity, and magnetism), simple machines (lever, wheel, pulley, ramp, and wedge), motion in fluids, and Newton's laws of motion. . . . [This offers] simple writing, many colorful pictures, and lots of examples." Sci Books Films

Includes glossary and bibliographical references

Solway, Andrew

Exploring forces and motion. Rosen Central 2008 48p il (Exploring physical science) lib bdg $26.50

Grades: 5 6 7 8   **531**

1. Motion 2. Force and energy

ISBN 978-1-4042-3747-6; 1-4042-3747-X

        LC 2006036680

Describes what force is and how it can be harnessed, and explains the relationship between force, mass, and acceleration.

Includes glossary and bibliographical references

Sullivan, Navin

Speed. Marshall Cavendish Benchmark 2007 48p il (Measure up!) lib bdg $20.90

Grades: 4 5 6 7   **531**

1. Speed 2. Measurement

ISBN 978-0-7614-2325-6 lib bdg; 0-7614-2325-7 lib bdg

"Have you ever wondered how we measure different speeds? How do we know how fast an airplane travels or how much speed a shuttle needs to travel to outer space? What does speed have to do with satellites? How does the speed of light compare with the speed of sound? Speed answers these questions and explores the history of humankind's discoveries about speed." Publisher's note

Includes glossary and bibliographical references

VanCleave, Janice Pratt, 1942-

Step -by-step science experiments in energy; by Janice VanCleave. Rosen Pub. 2013 80 p. col. ill. (Janice VanCleeve's first-place science fair projects) (library) $33.25; (paperback) $14.15

Grades: 5 6 7 8   **531**

1. Energy 2. Science -- Experiments 3. Science projects 4. Force and energy -- Experiments

ISBN 144886979X; 9781448869794; 9781448884711

        LC 2012006835

This book by Janice VanCleave is part of the First-Place Science Fair Projects series. The books have an introduction to the subject—here, energy, followed by 22 simple . . . experiments. Van Cleave states the basic goal of the experiments, followed by a list of necessary materials, most of which can be found around the house or easily acquired with minimal cost. Step-by-step instructions are clearly detailed and accompanied by diagrams where needed." (School Library Journal)

Includes bibliographical references and index.

Viegas, Jennifer

★ **Kinetic** and potential energy; understanding changes within physical systems. [by] Jennifer Viegas. 1st ed.; Rosen Pub. Group 2005 48p il (Library of physics) lib bdg $25.25

Grades: 7 8 9 10   **531**

1. Dynamics 2. Force and energy

ISBN 1-4042-0333-8

        LC 2004019126

"Viegas begins by explaining kinetic and potential energy and the history of their discoveries. Mechanical energy, momentum, and the laws of energy are also presented. . . . The [layout is] open and appealing and [includes] well-captioned photographs and simple diagrams." SLJ

Includes bibliographical references

532 Fluid mechanics

Parker, Steve, 1952-

The **science** of water; projects with experiments with water and power. [by] Steve Parker. Heinemann Library 2005 32p il (Tabletop scientist) lib bdg $29.29; pa $7.85

Grades: 4 5 6 7   **532**

1. Water 2. Science -- Experiments

ISBN 1-4034-7282-3 lib bdg; 1-4034-7289-0 pa

LC 2005007027

This "has experiments on the water cycle, water density, water as a solvent, surface tension, capillary action, buoyancy, water power, and water propulsion. . . . The colorful illustrations, organization, and ease of use of [this title makes it an] excellent [addition]." SLJ

Includes glossary

533 Pneumatics (Gas mechanics)

Gardner, Robert

Air; green science projects for a sustainable planet. Enslow Publishers 2011 128p il (Team Green science projects) lib bdg $31.93

Grades: 6 7 8 9 10   **533**

1. Air 2. Air pollution 3. Science projects 4. Science -- Experiments

ISBN 978-0-7660-3646-8; 0-7660-3646-4

LC 2010-1120

This book offers science experiments that explain the properties of air, how to conserve energy while heating and cooling air, and how to reduce air pollution.

"Gardner provides plenty of information, well-designed experiments, and demonstrations, and then shares brief science-fair ideas. . . . Experiments and demonstrations are presented with clear step-by-step instructions and occasional illustrations and represent a wide range of complexity." SLJ

Includes glossary and bibliographical references

Parker, Steve, 1952-

The **science** of air; projects and experiments on air and flight. [by] Steve Parker. Heinemann Library 2005 32p il (Tabletop scientist) lib bdg $29.29; pa $7.85

Grades: 4 5 6 7   **533**

1. Air 2. Science -- Experiments

ISBN 1-4034-7280-7 lib bdg; 1-4034-7287-4 pa

LC 2005006940

"The 12 experiments in [this] book have a materials list and step-by-step photo instructions. Boxed text explains the scientific ideas in each project and the processes that make it work, and offer ideas for further experimentation. The activities are followed by a history of the topic. . . . [This] title introduces air movement, air pressure, wind resistance, lift, flight, and energy from the wind. . . . The colorful illustrations, organization, and ease of use [this title makes it an] excellent [addition]." SLJ

Includes glossary

534 Specific forms of energy

Gardner, Robert

★ **Sound** projects with a music lab you can build. Enslow Publishers 2008 128p il (Build-a-lab! science experiments) lib bdg $31.93

Grades: 6 7 8 9   **534**

1. Music 2. Sound 3. Science projects 4. Science -- Experiments

ISBN 978-0-7660-2809-8 lib bdg; 0-7660-2809-7 lib bdg

LC 2007-19458

This describes science experiments and projects about music and sound such as making a washtub bass, a two-string bottle banjo, a shoe-box guitar, or pan pipes.

"The author does an excellent job presenting a balance of open-ended questions and supporting information that provide a solid foundation for successful experimentation." Sci Books Films

Includes bibliographical references

Sound; edited by Sherman Hollar. Britannica Educational Pub. in association with Rosen Educational Services 2013 79 p. ill. (Introduction to physics) (library) $31.70

Grades: 7 8 9 10   **534**

1. Sound

ISBN 1615308415; 9781615308415

LC 2012010563

This book on sound, edited by Sherman Hollar, is part of the "Introduction to Physics" series. It "describes how sound is produced, carried, and processed and features a chapter on acoustical engineers' applications in the life sciences, earth sciences, architecture, and the arts." (Booklist) "Also covered are functions and diseases of the human ear." (Publisher's note)

Includes bibliographical references and index.

535 Light and related radiation

Caes, Charles J.

★ **Discovering** the speed of light; by Charles J. Caes. 1st ed. Rosen Pub. 2012 112 p. ill. (chiefly col.) (Scientist's guide to physics) (library) $34.60

Grades: 5 6 7 8   **535**

1. Light -- Speed 2. Light -- Study and teaching -- History 3. Light -- Speed -- Measurement

ISBN 1448846994; 9781448846993

LC 2010048426

This book by Charles J. Caes is part of the "Scientist's Guide to Physics" series. It "uncovers the earliest study of the speed of light, around 550 BCE in classical Greece. From classical Greece to Galileo and later Albert Einstein, this title also details the history of the discovery of light speed measurement and theories." (VOYA)

Includes bibliographical references (p. 107-108) and index.

Light; edited by Michael Anderson. Britannica Educational Pub. in association with Rosen Educational Services 2013 77 p. ill. (some col.) (Introduction to physics) (library) $31.70

Grades: 7 8 9 10   **535**

1. Light 2. Light -- Speed

ISBN 1615308407; 9781615308408

LC 2012010241

This book "teaches the reader about light's many properties. It illuminates the path between light and matter, focusing in on reflection. refraction/dispersion, and light speed." Some chapters "explain light as a wave and as a particle. This book connects the past and present theories of light" and "explains in no-nonsense terms and real life applications the hows, the whats, and the whys of light theory." (NSTA Recommends)

Includes bibliographical references (p. 74) and index.

Meiani, Antonella

Light. Lerner Publs. 2003 40p il (Experimenting with science) lib bdg $23.93

Grades: 4 5 6 7   **535**

1. Light 2. Science -- Experiments

ISBN 0-8225-0084-1

LC 2001-38947

Experiments with light explain shadows and colors, and demonstrate such concepts as reflection and refraction

This offers "straightforward, well-designed experiments. . . . Numerous clear diagrams, some photos, and occasional historical sidebars extend this material, which is notable for its substance." Horn Book Guide

Includes glossary and bibliographical references

Stille, Darlene R.

★ **Manipulating** light; reflection, refraction, and absorption. by Darlene R. Stille. Compass Point Books 2006 48p il (Exploring science) $25.27

Grades: 6 7 8 9   **535**

1. Light

ISBN 0-7565-1258-1

LC 2005003903

This "book examines how light behaves, the law of reflection, mirrors, refraction, and absorption. . . . Full-color photographs, illustrations, or diagrams appear on almost every page, accompanied by captions that complement the text." SLJ

Includes glossary and bibliographical references

536   Heat

Gardner, Robert

Easy genius science projects with temperature and heat; great experiments and ideas. by Robert Gardner and Eric Kemer. Enslow Publishers 2009 128p il (Easy genius science projects) lib bdg $31.93

Grades: 5 6 7 8   **536**

1. Heat 2. Temperature 3. Science projects 4. Science -- Experiments

ISBN 978-0-7660-2939-2 lib bdg; 0-7660-2939-5 lib bdg

LC 2008-4675

"Presents several science experiments and science project ideas dealing with temperature and heat." Publisher's note

Includes glossary and bibliographical references

Heat; edited by Andrea R. Field. Britannica Educational Pub. 2013 76 p. ill. (some col.) (library) $31.70

Grades: 7 8 9 10   **536**

1. Heat 2. Physics

ISBN 1615308385; 9781615308385

LC 2011053232

This book looks at heat, or "the energy that is transferred from one object to another because of a difference in temperature," as well as "the related concepts of temperature, thermal energy, and thermodynamics and introduces readers to some of the great minds that furthered our understanding of this . . . area of physics." (Publisher's note)

Includes bibliographical references (p. 73) and index.

537   Electricity and electronics

Claybourne, Anna

Electric shocks and other energy evils; Anna Claybourne. Crabtree Publishing Company 2013 32 p. (Disgusting & dreadful science) (reinforced library binding) $27.60

Grades: 4 5 6   **537**

1. Electricity 2. Electric shock

ISBN 0778709264; 9780778709268; 9780778709534; 9781427191731; 9781427192493

LC 2012043527

This book, by Anna Claybourne, is part of the Disgusting and Dreadful Science series. It "features a look at the weird, revolting and shocking aspects of science for children. . . . From electricity to sound and from light to forces, the books offer . . . fascinating facts, fun examples and true-life stories to provide ways in to understanding solid scientific principles." (Publisher's note)

"These brief and lively introductions provide a plethora of fun and gross facts. Sounds explains the science behind sound, how ears work, ultrasound, and more. It also includes a scientific explanation of how whoopee cushions work. Shocks covers electrical current, circuits, lightning, etc. In both volumes, each subject is presented on a spread with a brief introduction. The explanations are clear and concise..." SLJ

Includes index

Other titles in the series include:

Ear-splitting sounds and other vile noises (2013)

Glaring light and other eye-burning rays (2013)

Gut-wrenching gravity and other fatal forces (2013)

Dreier, David Louis

Electrical circuits; harnessing electricity. by David Dreier; illustrator Ashlee Schultz. Compass Point Books 2007 48p il (Exploring science: physical science) lib bdg $19.95

Grades: 6 7 8 9 537
1. Electricity 2. Electric circuits
ISBN 978-0-7565-3267-3 lib bdg; 0-7565-3267-1
lib bdg

LC 2007004603

"This straightforward introduction to electricity . . . covers all the bases. It begins with what electricity is, how it appears in nature, and how it has been harnessed for public use. Atoms, the concept of electric charge, and magnetism are explained clearly. . . . Dreier tries to make a complex subject more understandable by using familiar examples. . . . This helps, as does the book's clean format, illustrated with sharp, bright color photographs." Booklist

Includes glossary and bibliographical references

Electricity; edited by Michael Anderson. Britannica Educational Pub. in association with Rosen Educational Services 2012 79 p. ill. (some col.) (Introduction to physics)
Grades: 7 8 9 10 537
1. Electricity
ISBN 161530665X; 9781615306657

LC 2011017090

"...Features clear diagrams and is a narrow enough topic to be well covered, with chapters on circuits, magnetic fields, and generators." Booklist

Includes bibliographical references (p. 76) and index

Galiano, Dean

Electric and magnetic phenomena. Rosen Central 2011 64p il (Science made simple) lib bdg $29.25; pa $12.95
Grades: 5 6 7 8 537
1. Magnetism 2. Electricity
ISBN 978-1-4488-1231-8 lib bdg; 1-4488-1231-3 lib bdg; 978-1-4488-2239-3 pa; 1-4488-2239-4 pa

LC 2010014546

This introduction to electric and magnetic phenomena includes "a lot of detailed information, making [it] useful as [a] resource . . . for science projects and reports. . . . The [book] also [includes a] brief discussion of scientists important in the field, the history of the topic, and current and future applications. . . . The straightforward, no-nonsense [narrative] and simple design make this . . . a nice package for basic science." SLJ

Includes glossary and bibliographical references

Gardner, Robert

Easy genius science projects with electricity and magnetism; great experiments and ideas. Enslow Publishers 2009 128p il (Easy genius science projects) lib bdg $31.93
Grades: 5 6 7 8 537
1. Magnetism 2. Electricity 3. Science projects 4. Science -- Experiments
ISBN 978-0-7660-2923-1 lib bdg; 0-7660-2923-9
lib bdg

LC 2007-38470

"Science projects and experiments about electricity and magnetism." Publisher's note

Includes glossary and bibliographical references

Easy genius science projects with light; great experiments and ideas. [by] Robert Gardner. Enslow Publishers 2008 128p il (Easy genius science projects) lib bdg $31.93
Grades: 6 7 8 9 537
1. Light 2. Science projects 3. Science -- Experiments
ISBN 978-0-7660-2926-2; 0-7660-2926-3

LC 2007-38468

This includes science projects and experiments about such light-related topics as colors, lenses, mirages, reflections, refraction, particle theory, polarization, and after images.

"The physics involved are . . . fascinating and will grab curious readers. . . . The inviting and chatty text for each project includes a boxed list of 'things you will need,' all of them commonly available, followed by detailed step-by-step instructions with clear diagrams." Booklist

Includes glossary and bibliographical references

Electricity and magnetism science fair projects; revised and expanded using the scientific method. Enslow Publishers 2010 160p il (Physics science projects using the scientific method) lib bdg $34.60
Grades: 7 8 9 10 537
1. Magnetism 2. Electricity 3. Science projects 4. Science -- Experiments
ISBN 978-0-7660-3418-1 lib bdg; 0-7660-3418-6
lib bdg

First published 2004 with title: Electricity and magnetism science fair projects: using batteries, balloons, and other hair-raising stuff

"This describes experiments on such topics as static electricity, moving charges, magnets and magnetic fields, and electricity and chemistry. Includes suggestions for science projects." Publisher's note

Includes bibliographical references

Parker, Steve, 1952-

Electricity and magnetism; [by] Steve Parker. Gareth Stevens Pub. 2007 48p il (Gareth Stevens vital science: physical science) lib bdg $26.60; pa $11.95
Grades: 4 5 6 7 537
1. Magnetism 2. Electricity
ISBN 978-0-8368-8085-4 lib bdg; 978-0-8368-8094-6 pa

LC 2006034188

This is "straightforward and clear. . . . The layout is bright and colorful, with photographs and illustrations on almost every page." SLJ

This explains "terms and concepts such as superconductor, static electricity, magnetic repulsion, and the piezoelectric effect; [the use of] electricity and magnetism [in] electrolysis, electromagnetic induction, and medical diagnostics and imaging; . . . lightning, auroras, St. Elmo's fire, animal navigation, and other electromagnetic phenomena." Publisher's note

Includes glossary and bibliographical references

Tomecek, Steve

Electromagnetism, and how it works; [by] Stephen M. Tomecek. Chelsea House 2007 72p il (Scientific American) $30

Grades: 6 7 8 9　　　537

1. Electromagnetism

ISBN 978-0-7910-9052-7; 0-7910-9052-3

LC 2007-17744

This describes the history of magnets including the discoveries of such scientists as Gilbert, Volta, Sturgeon, Edison, Westinghouse, and Tesla. It discusses inventions which depended on the understanding of magnets and electricity such as the telegraph, Morse Code, the telephone, the wireless radio, radar, the microwave, x-rays, and MRIs. The author explains how magnets work and how they can be used to create electricity.

Includes glossary and bibliographical references

Woodford, Chris

Experiments with electricity and magnetism. Gareth Stevens Pub. 2010 32p il (Cool science) lib bdg $28; pa $10.50

Grades: 4 5 6 7　　　537

1. Magnetism 2. Electricity 3. Science -- Experiments

ISBN 9781433934445 lib bdg; 1433934442 lib bdg; 9781433934452 pa; 1433934450 pa

LC 2009037141

"The book [is] written in an easy-to-understand, straightforward style with helpful real-life photographs... Students who need simple experiments or those who need more advanced projects will find [it] helpful." Library Media Connection

Includes bibliographical references

539　Modern physics

Claybourne, Anna

Who split the atom? Arcturus Pub. 2010 46p il (Breakthroughs in science and technology) lib bdg $32.80

Grades: 5 6 7 8　　　539

1. Atoms 2. Matter

ISBN 978-1-84837-683-0 lib bdg; 1-84837-683-9 lib bdg

LC 2010-11015

This book explores the ways in which scientists uncovered the atom.

The book is "divided into easy to read short chapters with large, colorful photographs and graphics on every page. . . . The added inserts provide additional information to engage readers and help them connect with the scientific details." Libr Media Connect

Includes glossary and bibliographical references

Willett, Edward

The **basics** of quantum physics; understanding the photoelectric effect and line spectra. Rosen Pub. Group 2005 48p il (Library of physics) lib bdg $25.25

Grades: 7 8 9 10　　　539

1. Quantum theory 2. Spectrum analysis

ISBN 1-4042-0334-6

"Willett introduces readers to the nature of light and of the atom. The ultraviolet catastrophe, the photoelectric effect, and line spectra are also addressed. [This title is] especially useful for reluctant readers or those new to the [topic]. The [layout is] open and appealing and [includes] well-captioned photographs and simple diagrams." SLJ

Includes bibliographical references

539.7　Atomic and nuclear physics

Campbell, Margaret Christine

★　**Discovering** atoms; Margaret Christine Campbell, Natalie Goldstein. 1st ed. Rosen Pub. 2012 112 p. ill. (The scientist's guide to physics) (library) $34.60

Grades: 5 6 7 8 9　　　539.7

1. Atoms 2. Atomic theory -- History 3. Atomic structure 4. Matter -- Constitution

ISBN 1448847001; 9781448847006

LC 2010048416

This book by Margaret Christine Campbell is part of the "Scientist's Guide to Physics" series. It "presents the . . . story of the atom's discovery, which is full of bizarre theories, false starts, dead ends, and . . . intellectual insight." (Publisher's note) "Campbell includes a . . . chronological foundation upon which the discovery of elements and the creation of the periodic table build up to the discovery of the atom, atomic rays, particles, models . . . and subatomic particles." (VOYA)

Includes bibliographical references and index.

Chaffee, Joel

Atomic and molecular structure. Rosen Central 2011 64p il (Science made simple) lib bdg $29.25; pa $12.95

Grades: 5 6 7 8　　　539.7

1. Atoms 2. Molecules

ISBN 978-1-4488-1230-1 lib bdg; 1-4488-1230-5 lib bdg; 978-1-4488-2238-6 pa; 1-4488-2238-6 pa

LC 2010015454

This introduction to atomic and molecular structure includes "a lot of detailed information, making [it] useful as [a] resource . . . for science projects and reports. . . . The [book] also [includes a] brief discussion of scientists important in the field, the history of the topic, and current and future applications. . . . The straightforward, no-nonsense [narrative] and simple design make this . . . a nice package for basic science." SLJ

Includes glossary and bibliographical references

Cregan, Elizabeth R.

The **atom.** Compass Point Books 2009 40p il (Mission: science) lib bdg $26.60

Grades: 4 5 6   **539.7**
    1. Atoms 2. Atomic theory 3. Nuclear energy
    ISBN 978-0-7565-3953-5 lib bdg; 0-7565-3953-6
    lib bdg
                                            LC 2008007724
"Cregan discusses the structure of the atom, key scientists, cathode rays and electrons, radioactivity, and atom smashers. . . . The [book has an] open [layout] and large, easy-to-read type. . . . Large eye-catching and colorful photographs and illustrations appear on every page. The [book] includes a simple activity." SLJ
    Includes glossary and bibliographical references

Henderson, Harry

The **Curie** family; exploring radioactivity. Harry Henderson. Chelsea House 2012 117 p. (Trailblazers in science and technology) $35
Grades: 7 8 9 10 11 12   **539.7**
    1. Radioactivity 2. Curie, Marie, 1867-1934 3. Curie, Pierre, 1859-1906 4. Radioactivity -- History 5. Physicists -- France -- Biography 6. Physicists -- Poland -- Biography
    ISBN 1604136758; 9781604136753
                                            LC 2011011800
This book, by Harry Henderson, is part of the "Trailblazers in Science and Technology" series. "Marie and Pierre Curie, their daughter Irène Joliot-Curie, and her husband Frédéric Joliot-Curie were one of science's most remarkable and influential families. Their painstaking research into the mysteries of radioactivity allowed scientists to reach a new understanding about the structure of atoms and opened a new field of medical treatment." (Publisher's note)
    Includes bibliographical references and index

Jerome, Kate Boehm

Atomic universe; the quest to discover radioactivity. by Kate Boehm Jerome. National Geographic 2006 59p il (Science quest) $17.95; lib bdg $25.90
Grades: 5 6 7 8   **539.7**
    1. Radioactivity 2. Nuclear physics
    ISBN 0-7922-5543-7; 0-7922-5544-5 lib bdg
                                            LC 2006001316
The text offers "key concepts in a pleasing and readable format that would appeal to reluctant readers." SLJ
    This "traces the path to the discovery of radioactivity and places this major scientific breakthrough in the context of history." Publisher's note
    Includes glossary and bibliographical references

Lepora, Nathan

Atoms and molecules. Marshall Cavendish Benchmark 2010 48p il (Invisible worlds) lib bdg $28.50
Grades: 4 5 6 7   **539.7**
    1. Atoms 2. Molecules 3. Nanotechnology
    ISBN 978-0-7614-4192-2 lib bdg; 0-7614-4192-1
    lib bdg
                                            LC 2008037237
This describes the details and characteristics of atoms and molecules that are too small for the unaided eye to see.
    The narrative is "clear, well written, broken down into manageable pieces, and peppered with eye-opening facts.

The numerous photographs are so phenomenal that they will inspire kids to read the text . . . so that they can wrap their minds around what they see." SLJ
    Includes glossary and bibliographical references

Manning, Phillip

★ **Atoms,** molecules, and compounds. Chelsea House 2008 137p il (Essential chemistry) $35
Grades: 7 8 9 10   **539.7**
    1. Atoms 2. Matter 3. Molecules 4. Chemical reactions
    ISBN 978-0-7910-9534-8; 0-7910-9534-7
                                            LC 2007-11403
"In relatively few pages, and with lots of colorful, clear illustrations, Manning takes us from Thompson's plum-pudding model of the atom to Rutherford's model to the quantum model, and through the discovery of atomic particles and the teasing out of atomic forces, in a very clear, compelling path. . . . The clear linkages he makes between the different types of chemical bonds and the nature of various materials will remain with the reader." Sci Books Films
    Includes glossary and bibliographical references

McLean, Adam

What is atomic theory? Crabtree Pub. Co. 2011 64p il (Shaping modern science) lib bdg $30.60; pa $10.95
Grades: 5 6 7 8   **539.7**
    1. Atoms 2. Chemists 3. Physicists 4. Atomic theory 5. Nuclear energy 6. Writers on science
    ISBN 978-0-7787-7197-5 lib bdg; 0-7787-7197-0 lib bdg; 978-0-7787-7204-0 pa; 0-7787-7204-7 pa
This title is "not only written and organized well, but [it is] also gorgeous in design. Full-color photographs and illustrations are set over colorful backgrounds that add depth but not distraction. [The title] includes thought-provoking quotes from famous authors and scientists and some eyebrow-raising 'Quick Facts' throughout." SLJ
    Includes glossary and bibliographical references

540   Chemistry and allied sciences

Coelho, Alexa

Why Is Milk White? & 200 Other Curious Chemistry Questions. Alexa Coelho and Simon Quellen Field. Independent Pub Group 2013 288 p. ill. (paperback) $14.95
Grades: 4 5 6 7 8   **540**
    1. Chemistry 2. Chemistry -- Miscellanea
    ISBN 1613744528; 9781613744529
                                            LC 2012040205
    This juvenile chemistry book, by Alexa Coelho and Simon Quellen Field, is a "question-and-answer primer [that] provides straightforward, easy-to-understand explanations for inquisitive young scientists' questions. . . . From lifting latent fingerprints from a 'crime scene' using super glue (for smooth surfaces) or iodine (for paper) to hollowing out the zinc interior of a penny using muriatic acid . . . , this handy guide is [a] . . . resource for the budding chemist." (Publisher's note)

The **Facts** on File chemistry handbook; the Diagram Group. Facts On File 2006 272 p. ill. (hardcover) $40; (ebook) $42.00

Grades: 8 9 10 11 12   **540**

1. Chemistry -- Dictionaries 2. Chemistry 3. Chemistry -- Handbooks, manuals, etc

ISBN 0816058784; 9780816058785 out of print; 9781438109558 pdf

LC 2005055496

This fact book for middle-grade readers, part of the Facts on File Handbook series, looks at chemistry. Each series entry "contains, in separate sections, a dictionary of around 1500 entries; 250-400 thumbnail biographies; a multipage chronology; and an array of field-specific charts, tables, and diagrams." (School Library Journal)

Includes bibliographical references (p. 262-264) and index

Farndon, John

Experimenting with chemistry. Marshall Cavendish Benchmark 2009 104p il (Experimenting with science) $35.64

Grades: 7 8 9 10   **540**

1. Chemistry 2. Science -- Experiments

ISBN 978-0-7614-3928-8; 0-7614-3928-5

LC 2008017570

"Explores and explains chemistry concepts and provides experiments to aid in understanding chemistry." Publisher's note

Gardner, Robert

Chemistry projects with a laboratory you can build. Enslow Publishers 2007 128p il (Build-a-lab! science experiments) $23.95

Grades: 6 7 8 9   **540**

1. Chemistry 2. Science -- Experiments

ISBN 978-0-7660-2805-0; 0-7660-2805-4

LC 2006-21071

This "is a guide to creating an at-home laboratory for conducting chemistry experiments. . . . Safety rules and ample warnings are provided. . . . The book describes 28 experiments, organized into four chapters. . . . The experiments are ongoing and would be fun activities for children who are curious about science." Sci Books Films

Includes bibliographical references

Chemistry science fair projects using inorganic stuff; revised and expanded using the scientific method. Enslow Publishers 2010 160p il (Chemistry science projects using the scientific method) lib bdg $34.60

Grades: 7 8 9 10   **540**

1. Chemistry 2. Science projects 3. Science -- Experiments

ISBN 978-0-7660-3413-6 lib bdg; 0-7660-3413-5 lib bdg

LC 2008046505

First published 2004 with title: Chemistry Science Fair Projects Using Acids, Bases, Metals,Salts, and Inorganic Stuff

"Colorful drawings complement the material and illustrations of chemical structures help to convey chemical processes. . . . Useful." SLJ

Includes bibliographical references

Green, Dan

Chemistry; getting a big reaction. created by Basher; written by Dan Green. Kingfisher 2010 128p il $14.99; pa $8.99

Grades: 4 5 6 7   **540**

1. Chemistry

ISBN 978-0-7534-6615-5; 0-7534-6615-5; 978-0-7534-6413-7 pa; 0-7534-6413-6 pa

This "begins with a short overview of [chemistry] and information on Antoine Lavoisier's 18th-century scientific findings. Concepts are grouped by associations: 'Basic States' (solid, liquid, etc.), 'Nuts and Bolts' (atom, ion, etc.), 'Nasty Boys' (acid, base, etc.), and more. The individual concepts are each introduced over a spread that features a computer-generated cartoon of a character representing the idea and a brief introduction to its characteristics and personality. . . . The information is presented in a chatty, first-person voice." SLJ

Hager, Thomas

Linus Pauling and the chemistry of life. Oxford University Press 1998 142p il (Oxford portraits in science) $28

Grades: 7 8 9 10   **540**

1. Chemists 2. College teachers 3. Writers on science 4. Nobel laureates for peace 5. Nobel laureates for chemistry

ISBN 0-19-510853-1

LC 97-43403

"Pauling's research achievements in chemistry, physics, biology, and medicine are . . . discussed in relation to his life. {Chronology. Bibliography. Index.} Grade seven and up." (SLJ)

"Students with a strong science background will get the most out of this biography, but even young people who don't like science will be able to identify with a man whose scientific curiosity and political principles led him to try to change the world. Chronology and recommended readings." Booklist

Includes bibliographical references

Newmark, Ann

Chemistry; written by Ann Newmark. rev ed; DK Pub. 2005 72p il (DK eyewitness books) $15.99

Grades: 4 5 6 7   **540**

1. Chemistry

ISBN 0-7566-1385-X

First published 1993

Explores the world of chemical reactions and shows the role that chemistry plays in our world.

Oxlade, Chris

Material changes and reactions; [by] Chris Oxlade. rev. and updated; Heinemann Library 2007 48p il (Chemicals in action) lib bdg $31.43; pa $8.99

Grades: 6 7 8 9 **540**

1. Chemical reactions
ISBN 978-1-4329-0053-3 lib bdg; 978-1-4329-0053-3 pa
First published 2002

"This title explores how elements melt, boil, and freeze; how they combine with each other to make new substances; and how chemical reactions take place every day in factories and in your home. [It also includes] several experiments that can be done at home." Publisher's note

Includes glossary and bibliographical references

Stefoff, Rebecca, 1951-

Alchemy and Chemistry; Rebecca Stefoff. Cavendish Square 2014 48 p. ill. (Is it Science?) $29.93

Grades: 6 7 8 **540**

1. Alchemy 2. Chemistry 3. Science -- Popular works
ISBN 1627125094; 9781627125093

LC 2014054653

This middle grades book by Rebecca Stefoff, part of the Is It Science? series, "explores the historical relationships between science and pseudoscience. Though she explains the scientific method in detail and injects healthy doses of skepticism into her accounts, rather than just denigrate pseudosciences as superstition, she shows how . . . alchemy split into equally serious practical and spiritual approaches before the former evolved into modern chemistry." (Publisher's note)

"Each volume is heavily illustrated with period images and modern photographs, and each closes with particularly generous lists of further resources." SLJ

Van Gorp, Lynn

Elements. Compass Point Books 2009 40p il (Mission: science) lib bdg $26.60

Grades: 4 5 6 **540**

1. Chemical elements
ISBN 978-0-7565-3951-1 lib bdg; 0-7565-3951-X lib bdg

LC 2008007284

"Van Gorp provides an overview of matter and the elements and how the latter combine to form compounds; ionic and covalent bonds; the periodic table of the elements; reactions; and mixtures and solutions. The [book has an] open [layout] and large, easy-to-read type. . . . Large eye-catching and colorful photographs and illustrations appear on every page. . . . The [book] includes a simple activity." SLJ

Includes glossary and bibliographical references

540.7   Education, research, related topics

Gardner, Robert

Ace your chemistry science project; great science fair ideas. [by] Robert Gardner, Salvatore Tocci, and Kenneth G. Rainis. Enslow Publishers 2009 112p il (Ace your science project) lib bdg $31.93

Grades: 5 6 7 8 **540.7**

1. Chemistry 2. Science projects 3. Science --

Experiments
ISBN 978-0-7660-3227-9 lib bdg; 0-7660-3227-2 lib bdg

LC 2008-30800

"Presents several science projects and science project ideas about chemistry." Publisher's note

Includes bibliographical references

Ace your science project using chemistry magic and toys; great science fair ideas. Enslow Publishers 2009 128p il (Ace your science project) lib bdg $31.93

Grades: 5 6 7 8 **540.7**

1. Toys 2. Chemistry 3. Science projects 4. Science -- Experiments
ISBN 978-0-7660-3226-2 lib bdg; 0-7660-3226-4 lib bdg

LC 2008-4685

"Dozens of . . . science activities are presented with background information, step-by-step instructions, and suggestions for extending to the science fair level. . . . Color illustrations and important safety information are included." Horn Book Guide

Includes bibliographical references

★ **Easy** genius science projects with chemistry; great experiments and ideas. Enslow Publishers 2009 112p il (Easy genius science projects) lib bdg $31.93

Grades: 5 6 7 8 **540.7**

1. Chemistry 2. Science projects 3. Science -- Experiments
ISBN 978-0-7660-2925-5 lib bdg; 0-7660-2925-5 lib bdg

LC 2007-38469

This book offers science projects and experiments about chemistry divided into the following chapters: atoms, molecules, elements, and compounds; chemical reactions; oxygen and oxidation; separating and testing substances

"Illustrations are bright and useful in explaining the techniques presented. . . . An excellent resource." Sci Books Films

Includes glossary and bibliographical references

Goodstein, Madeline

Plastics and polymers science fair projects; revised and expanded using the scientific method. Enslow Publishers 2010 160p il (Chemistry science projects using the scientific method) lib bdg $34.60

Grades: 7 8 9 10 **540.7**

1. Plastics 2. Polymers 3. Science projects 4. Science -- Experiments
ISBN 978-0-7660-3412-9 lib bdg; 0-7660-3412-7 lib bdg

LC 2008046504

"Explains how to use the scientific method to conduct several science experiments with plastics and polymers. Includes ideas for science fair projects." Publisher's note

Includes bibliographical references

541 Chemistry

Ballard, Carol

   Mixtures and solutions. Raintree 2010 48p il (Sci-hi: physical science) lib bdg $22; pa $8.99
Grades: 5 6 7 8   **541**
   1. Chemistry 2. Molecules
   ISBN 978-1-4109-3376-8 lib bdg; 1-4109-3376-8 lib bdg; 978-1-4109-3381-2 pa; 1-4109-3381-4 pa
                     LC 2009-13452
A "compelling read for both browsers and science buffs. . . . Information is clearly presented and flows smoothly. . . . A treasure trove of information." SLJ
   Includes glossary and bibliographical references

Manning, Phillip

   Chemical bonds. Chelsea House 2009 134p il (Essential chemistry) lib bdg $35
Grades: 7 8 9 10   **541**
   1. Chemistry
   ISBN 978-0-7910-9740-3; 0-7910-9740-4
                     LC 2008-1981
Examines the nature of the chemical bonds, answering questions about how they form, how they are broken, and how they help define life as we know it
   Includes glossary and bibliographical references

Wolny, Philip

   Chemical reactions. Rosen Central 2011 64p il (Science made simple) lib bdg $29.25; pa $12.95
Grades: 5 6 7 8   **541**
   1. Chemistry 2. Chemical reactions
   ISBN 978-1-4488-1235-6 lib bdg; 1-4488-1235-6 lib bdg; 978-1-4488-2242-3 pa; 1-4488-2242-4 pa
                     LC 2010018818
This introduction to chemical reactions includes "a lot of detailed information, making [it] useful as [a] resource . . . for science projects and reports. . . . The [book] also [includes a] brief discussion of scientists important in the field, the history of the topic, and current and future applications. . . . The straightforward, no-nonsense [narrative] and simple design make this . . . a nice package for basic science." SLJ
   Includes glossary and bibliographical references

546 Inorganic chemistry

Angliss, Sarah

   Gold; [by] Sarah Angliss. Benchmark Bks. 2000 32p il (The elements) lib bdg $28.50
Grades: 5 6 7 8   **546**
   1. Gold
   ISBN 978-0-7614-0887-1; 0-7614-0887-8
                     LC 98-46800
Explores the history of the precious metal gold and explains its chemistry, how it reacts, its uses, and its importance in our lives.
   Includes glossary

Beatty, Richard

   Boron; [by] Richard Beatty. Marshall Cavendish Benchmark 2005 32p il (The elements) lib bdg $28.50
Grades: 5 6 7 8   **546**
   1. Boron
   ISBN 978-0-7614-1921-1; 0-7614-1921-7
                     LC 2005-42159
"Included in the discussion are the uses of boron in pottery, in the nuclear industry, in living organisms, and in glassmaking. A review of the periodic table and boron's place in it, including the element's relationship to other elements, is provided." Sci Books Films
   Includes glossary

   The **lanthanides**; [by] Richard Beatty. Marshall Cavendish Benchmark 2008 32p il (The elements) lib bdg $28.50
Grades: 5 6 7 8   **546**
   1. Lanthanides
   ISBN 978-0-7614-2687-5; 0-7614-2687-6
                     LC 2006-53053
Introduces the lanthanide elements, also known as the rare earth metals, discussing their physical and chemical properties, where they are found, and how they are used.
"Provides a comprehensive, yet easy-to-read overview. . . . The explanations are succinct and clear, without being oversimplified, and the layout is attractive. Diagrams and photographs complement the text on every page." SLJ
   Includes glossary

   Phosphorus; by Richard Beatty. Benchmark Books 2001 32p il (The elements) lib bdg $28.50
Grades: 5 6 7 8   **546**
   1. Phosphorus
   ISBN 978-0-7614-0946-5; 0-7614-0946-7
                     LC 99-88821
Explores the history of the nonmetallic element phosphorus and explains its chemistry, its reactions with other substances, its uses, and its importance in our lives
   Offers "clear, basic information, without oversimplification, in an appealing format." SLJ
   Includes glossary

   Sulfur; [by] Richard Beatty. Benchmark Books 2000 32p il (The elements) lib bdg $28.50
Grades: 5 6 7 8   **546**
   1. Sulphur
   ISBN 978-0-7614-0948-9; 0-7614-0948-3
                     LC 99-86992
Explores the history of the element sulfur and explains its chemistry, its reactions with other substances, its uses, and its importance in our lives
   Offers "clear, basic information, without oversimplification, in an appealing format." SLJ
   Includes glossary

Dingle, Adrian

   ★ The **periodic** table; elements with style! [created by Simon Basher; written by Adrian Dingle] Kingfisher 2007 128p il pa $8.95

Grades: 4 5 6 7 **546**
1. Chemical elements
ISBN 978-0-7534-6085-6 pa; 0-7534-6085-8 pa
LC 2006022515

"After a brief introduction to Mendeleev's famous table and a spread on the chart-topping loner, hydrogen, Dingle presents the elements by group. . . . Data on featured elements includes symbol, atomic number and weight, color, standard state, classification, density, boiling and melting points, . . . a diagram of the position in the periodic table, a full-page original anime-styled icon, . . . and descriptive paragraphs that rise from informative all the way to entertaining." Bull Cent Child Books

Farndon, John
Aluminum; [by] John Farndon. Benchmark Books 2001 32p il (The elements) lib bdg $28.50
Grades: 5 6 7 8 **546**
1. Aluminum
ISBN 978-0-7614-0947-2; 0-7614-0947-5

Describes the discovery, versatility and other special characteristics, various uses, and affect on the human body of this most common metal in the world.
Includes glossary

Oxygen; [by] John Farndon. Benchmark Bks. 1999 32p il (The elements) lib bdg $28.50
Grades: 5 6 7 8 **546**
1. Oxygen
ISBN 978-0-7614-0879-6; 0-7614-0879-7
LC 97-52236

Explores the history of the chemical element oxygen and explains its chemistry, how it works in the body, and its importance in our lives.
"The captioned, full-color drawings, photographs, and diagrams clarify the text. . . . [This] will be of interest for both general reading and report writing." SLJ
Includes glossary

Furgang, Adam
The **noble** gases; helium, neon, argon, krypton, xenon, radon. Rosen Central 2010 48p il (Understanding the elements of the periodic table) lib bdg $26.50
Grades: 7 8 9 10 **546**
1. Gases 2. Periodic law 3. Chemical elements
ISBN 978-1-4358-3558-0 lib bdg; 1-4358-3558-1 lib bdg
LC 2009014409

This overview discusses "the history of each element, where it can be found, and how it is used in everyday life. . . . Charts show each element's chemical symbol, atomic number, atomic weight, melting point, and boiling point. Colorful photographs and illustrations are included on most pages. Lengthy sidebars highlight key information—some . . . present boxed information on helium versus hydrogen and on the Hindenburg disaster." SLJ
Includes bibliographical references

Goodstein, Madeline
Water science fair projects; revised and expanded using the scientific method. Enslow Publishers

2010 160p il (Chemistry science projects using the scientific method) lib bdg $34.60
Grades: 7 8 9 10 **546**
1. Water 2. Science projects 3. Science -- Experiments
ISBN 978-0-7660-3411-2 lib bdg; 0-7660-3411-9 lib bdg
LC 2008026265

First published 2004 with title: Water science fair projects using ice cubes, super soakers, and other wet stuff
"Explains how to use the scientific method to conduct several science experiments with water. Includes ideas for science fair projects." Publisher's note
Includes bibliographical references

Gray, Leon
Iodine; [by] Leon Gray. Benchmark Books 2005 32p il (The elements) lib bdg $28.50
Grades: 5 6 7 8 **546**
1. Iodine
ISBN 978-0-7614-1812-2; 0-7614-1812-1
LC 2004-47644

"After discussing the structure of the iodine atom and its place on the periodic table, Gray considers its special characteristics, the history of its discovery, and its production and uses, particularly in the medical field. . . . The color illustrations include well-designed, clearly labeled diagrams and many excellent photographs. A solid choice for science collections." Booklist
Includes glossary

Tin; [by] Leon Gray. Benchmark Books 2003 32p il (The elements) lib bdg $28.50
Grades: 5 6 7 8 **546**
1. Tin
ISBN 978-0-7614-1551-0; 0-7614-1551-3
LC 2003-52083

Examines the characteristics, sources, and uses of the element tin, as well as tin's importance in our lives
"Numerous captioned color photos and sidebars augment the accurate and well-organized but information-dense text." Horn Book GUide
Includes glossary

Zinc; [by] Leon Gray. Marshall Cavendish Benchmark 2006 32p il (The elements) lib bdg $28.50
Grades: 5 6 7 8 **546**
1. Zinc
ISBN 978-0-7614-1922-8; 0-7614-1922-5
LC 2005-42163

Discusses zinc and where it can be found, how it was discovered, its special characteristics, and their importance.
"Numerous captioned photos and sidebars augment the accurate and well-organized text." Horn Book Guide
Includes glossary

Green, Dan
The **elements**; Dan Green. Scholastic 2012 105 p. col. ill. (pbk.) $15.99

Grades: 7 8 9 10 11 12   **546**
1. Chemical elements
ISBN 054533019X; 9780545330190

LC 2011278730

This book on the elements, part of the "Discover More" series, is "arranged in single-topic spreads grouped in five chapters based on sections of the Periodic Table." It "highlights either selected single elements or related groups. The layout includes color photos, digital diagrams and images, fact boxes, explanatory captions, and other text in a variety of sizes and weights. . . . A downloadable ebook supplement . . . extends the overall topic." (School Library Journal)

"...This broad introduction is current enough to include mention of Element #117 (probably observed in 2010) and chock-full of basic information cranked up with a generous admixture of "gosh-wow" facts about our universe's building blocks.—" SLJ

Hall, Linley Erin

The **transactinides**; rutherfordium, dubnium, seaborgium, bohrium, hassium, meitnerium, darmstadtium, roentgenium. Rosen Central 2010 48p il (Understanding the elements of the periodic table) lib bdg $26.50
Grades: 5 6 7 8   **546**
1. Periodic law 2. Chemical elements
ISBN 978-1-4358-3559-7 lib bdg; 1-4358-3559-X lib bdg

LC 2009014943

This overview discusses "the history of each element, where it can be found, and how it is used in everyday life. . . . Charts show each element's chemical symbol, atomic number, atomic weight, melting point, and boiling point. Colorful photographs and illustrations are included on most pages. Lengthy sidebars highlight key information. . . . [The book] devotes a chapter to the controversies surrounding naming its elements." SLJ
Includes bibliographical references

Hasan, Heather

Iron; by Heather Hasan. Rosen Pub. Group 2004 48p il (Understanding the elements of the periodic table) lib bdg $26.50
Grades: 5 6 7 8   **546**
1. Iron 2. Periodic law
ISBN 978-1-4042-0157-6; 1-4042-0157-2

LC 2003-22262

Explains the characteristics of iron, where it is found, how it is used by humans, and its relationship to other elements found in the periodic table
Includes bibliographical references

★ **Just** add water; science projects you can sink, squirt, splash & sail. Children's Press 2008 32p il (Experiment with science) lib bdg $25; pa $7.95
Grades: 5 6 7 8   **546**
1. Water 2. Science -- Experiments
ISBN 978-0-531-18545-2 lib bdg; 0-531-18545-1 lib bdg; 978-0-531-18762-3 pa; 0-531-18762-4 pa

LC 2007-21682

"The book consists of nine hands-on activities that target physical science concepts inherent in water (e.g. density, buoyancy, and hardness.) . . . Students . . . will likely find the age-appropriate activities engaging and purposeful. . . . The colorful photos augment the narrative and the science is sound." Sci Books Films
Includes glossary and bibliographical references

La Bella, Laura

The **oxygen** elements; oxygen, sulfur, selenium, tellurium, polonium. Rosen Central 2010 48p il (Understanding the elements of the periodic table) lib bdg $26.50
Grades: 7 8 9 10   **546**
1. Periodic law 2. Chemical elements
ISBN 978-1-4358-3555-9 lib bdg; 1-4358-3555-7 lib bdg

LC 2009012541

This overview discusses "the history of each element, where it can be found, and how it is used in everyday life. . . . Charts show each element's chemical symbol, atomic number, atomic weight, melting point, and boiling point. Colorful photographs and illustrations are included on most pages. Lengthy sidebars highlight key information. . . . [The book] details the use of sulfur in rubber and gunpowder for example." SLJ
Includes bibliographical references

Lepora, Nathan

Chromium; [by] Nathan Lepora. Marshall Cavendish Benchmark 2005 32p il (The elements) lib bdg $28.50
Grades: 5 6 7 8   **546**
1. Chromium
ISBN 978-0-7614-1920-4; 0-7614-1920-9

LC 2005-42160

Discusses chromium and where it can be found, how it was discovered, its special characteristics, and its importance to the human body.

"Numerous captioned photos and sidebars augment the accurate and well-organized text." Horn Book Guide
Includes glossary

Molybdenum; [by] Nathan Lepora. Marshall Cavendish Benchmark 2007 32p il (The elements) lib bdg $28.50
Grades: 5 6 7 8   **546**
1. Molybdenum
ISBN 978-0-7614-2201-3; 0-7614-2201-3

LC 2005-57096

Introduces the element of molybdenum, discussing its physical and chemical properties, where it is found, and what processes or objects it is used in.

"Provides a comprehensive, yet easy-to-read overview in large, bold print. Explanations are concise and clear without being oversimplified, and the arrangement is attractive." SLJ
Includes glossary

Lew, Kristi

The **15** lanthanides and the 15 actinides. Rosen Central 2010 48p il (Understanding the elements of the periodic table) lib bdg $26.50

Grades: 7 8 9 10   **546**

1. Periodic law 2. Chemical elements

ISBN 978-1-4358-3557-3; 1-4358-3557-3

LC 2009014416

This overview discusses "the history of each element, where it can be found, and how it is used in everyday life. . . . Charts show each element's chemical symbol, atomic number, atomic weight, melting point, and boiling point. Colorful photographs and illustrations are included on most pages. Lengthy sidebars highlight key information." SLJ

Includes bibliographical references

Acids and bases. Chelsea House 2008 124p il (Essential chemistry) $35

Grades: 7 8 9 10   **546**

1. Acids 2. Bases (Chemistry)

ISBN 978-0-7910-9783-0; 0-7910-9783-8

LC 2008-24015

"Annotated, colorful photographs and illustrations appear on most spreads, and boxed areas and sidebars highlight specific subjects and areas. The explanations are clear and detailed." SLJ

Includes glossary and bibliographical references

Miller, Ron

★ The **elements**. Twenty-First Century Books 2006 135p il lib bdg $28.90

Grades: 8 9 10 11 12   **546**

1. Chemical elements

ISBN 0-7613-2794-0

LC 2003-20874

Discusses the history of the periodic table of the elements, includes biographies of major figures in the field of chemistry, and provides information on each element.

"A useful overview." SLJ

Includes bibliographical references

O'Daly, Anne

Sodium; [by] Anne O'Daly. Benchmark Books 2001 32p il (The elements) lib bdg $28.50

Grades: 5 6 7 8   **546**

1. Sodium

ISBN 978-0-7614-1271-7; 0-7614-1271-9

LC 2001-25253

Discusses the characteristics, sources, and uses of sodium.

Includes glossary

Oxlade, Chris

Elements and compounds; [by] Chris Oxlade. rev. and updated; Heinemann Library 2007 48p il (Chemicals in action) lib bdg $31.43; pa $8.99

Grades: 6 7 8 9   **546**

1. Chemical elements

ISBN 978-1-4329-0052-6 lib bdg; 978-1-4329-0059-5 pa

First published 2002

"Explanations are concise and clear without being oversimplified, and the arrangement is attractive and open. Colorful diagrams, drawings, and photographs appear on every page." SLJ

Includes glossary and bibliographical references

Metals; [by] Chris Oxlade. rev. and updated; Heinemann Library 2007 48p il (Chemicals in action) lib bdg $31.43; pa $8.99

Grades: 6 7 8 9   **546**

1. Metals

ISBN 978-1-4329-0054-0 lib bdg; 978-1-4329-0061-8 pa

First published 2002

"This title explores what metals are like, how they are mixed with each other to form alloys, and how they are used to make everything from paper clips to skyscrapers. [It also includes] several experiments that can be done at home." Publisher's note

Includes glossary and bibliographical references

Roza, Greg

The **halogen** elements; fluorine, chlorine, bromine, iodine, astatine. Rosen Central 2010 48p il (Understanding the elements of the periodic table) lib bdg $26.50

Grades: 7 8 9 10   **546**

1. Periodic law 2. Chemical elements

ISBN 978-1-4358-3556-6 lib bdg; 1-4358-3556-5 lib bdg

LC 2009012539

This overview discusses "the history of each element, where it can be found, and how it is used in everyday life. . . . Charts show each element's chemical symbol, atomic number, atomic weight, melting point, and boiling point. Colorful photographs and illustrations are included on most pages. Lengthy sidebars highlight key information." SLJ

Includes bibliographical references

Saunders, N.

Who invented the periodic table? [by] Nigel Saunders. Arcturus Pub. 2010 46p il (Breakthroughs in science and technology) lib bdg $32.80

Grades: 5 6 7 8   **546**

1. Chemists 2. Periodic law

ISBN 978-1-84837-680-9; 1-84837-680-4

LC 2010011016

"After a very brief presentation of atoms and elements, and a short, but comprehensive, view of the modern periodic table, the author presents a series of vignettes, starting with alchemy. Through these vignettes, the reader gets an appreciation of the personalities of, and challenges faced by, key contributors. . . . [This] presents an engaging story behind the story of the discovery of the periodic table." Sci Books & Films

Includes glossary

Sparrow, Giles

Iron; [by] Giles Sparrow. Benchmark Bks. 1999 32p il (The elements) lib bdg $28.50

Grades: 5 6 7 8   **546**
1. Iron
ISBN 978-0-7614-0880-2; 0-7614-0880-0
LC 97-48524

Discusses the origin, discovery, special characteristics, and uses of iron.

Includes glossary

Uttley, Colin

Magnesium; [by] Colin Uttley. Benchmark Bks. 2000 32p il (The elements) lib bdg $28.50
Grades: 5 6 7 8   **546**
1. Magnesium
ISBN 978-0-7614-0889-5; 0-7614-0889-4
LC 98-53200

Explores the history of the bright-colored metal magnesium and explains its chemistry, how it reacts, its uses, and its importance in our lives.

Includes glossary

Watt, Susan

Zirconium; [by] Susan Watt. Marshall Cavendish Benchmark 2008 32p il (The elements) lib bdg $28.50
Grades: 5 6 7 8   **546**
1. Zirconium
ISBN 978-0-7614-2688-2; 0-7614-2688-4
LC 2007-60885

Introduces the element of zirconium, discussing its physical and chemical properties, where it is found, and how it is used.

"Provides a comprehensive, yet easy-to-read overview. . . . The explanations are succinct and clear, without being oversimplified, and the layout is attractive." SLJ

Includes glossary

West, Krista

Bromine; [by] Krista West. Marshall Cavendish Benchmark 2008 32p il (The elements) lib bdg $28.50
Grades: 5 6 7 8   **546**
1. Bromine
ISBN 978-0-7614-2685-1; 0-7614-2685-X
LC 2006-51812

Introduces the element of bromine and its compoinds, discussing its physical and chemical properties, where it is found, and how it is used.

"Provides a comprehensive, yet easy-to-read overview. . . . The explanations are succinct and clear, without being oversimplified, and the layout is attractive. Diagrams and photographs complement the text on every page." SLJ

Includes glossary

Carbon chemistry. Chelsea House 2008 117p il (Essential chemistry) lib bdg $35
Grades: 7 8 9 10   **546**
1. Carbon
ISBN 978-0-7910-9708-3; 0-7910-9708-0
LC 2007-51318

Explains how carbon is integrated into all facets of life as we know it and discusses the unique properties of this essential element.

"Annotated, colorful photographs and illustrations appear on most spreads, and boxed areas and sidebars highlight specific subjects and areas. The explanations are clear and detailed." SLJ

Includes glossary and bibliographical references

Woodford, Chris

Titanium; [by] Chris Woodford. Benchmark Books 2003 32p il (The elements) lib bdg $28.50
Grades: 5 6 7 8   **546**
1. Titanium
ISBN 978-0-7614-1461-2; 0-7614-1461-4
LC 2001-8743

Discusses the characteristics, sources, and uses of the element titanium.

"The well-selected photographs and diagrams are appropriate to the text." Horn Book Guide

Includes glossary

547   Organic chemistry

Gardner, Robert

Organic chemistry science fair projects; revised and expanded using the scientific method. [by] Robert Gardner and Barbara Gardner Conklin. Enslow Publishers 2010 160p il (Chemistry science projects using the scientific method) lib bdg $34.60
Grades: 7 8 9 10   **547**
1. Science projects 2. Organic chemistry 3. Science -- Experiments
ISBN 978-0-7660-3414-3 lib bdg; 0-7660-3414-3 lib bdg
LC 2008050078

First published 2004 with title: Chemistry science fair projects using french fries, gumdrops, soap, and other organic stuff

"Colorful drawings complement the material and illustrations of chemical structures help to convey chemical processes. . . . Useful." SLJ

Includes bibliographical references

549   Mineralogy

Casper, Julie Kerr

Minerals; gifts from the Earth. Chelsea House 2007 194p il map (Natural resources) $39.50
Grades: 8 9 10 11 12   **549**
1. Minerals 2. Mines and mineral resources
ISBN 978-0-8160-6357-4; 0-8160-6357-5
LC 2006102275

Explains how minerals and formed and how they are used in technology.

Includes bibliographical references

Chesterman, Charles W.

The **Audubon** Society field guide to North American rocks and minerals; scientific consultant, Kurt E. Lowe. Knopf 1979 850p il $19.95

Grades: 8 9 10 11 12 Adult   **549**
  1. Rocks 2. Minerals
  ISBN 0-394-50269-8

                                 LC 78-54893

"Pocket guide providing color photos and descriptions of some 232 mineral species and forty types of rocks. Includes guide to mineral environments, glossary, bibliography, and indexes by name and locality." Ref Sources for Small & Medium-sized Libr. 5th edition

Pellant, Chris

Rocks and minerals; Helen Pellant, editorial consultant; photography by Harry Taylor. 2nd American ed; Dorling Kindersley 2002 256p il (Smithsonian handbooks) pa $20

Grades: 11 12 Adult   **549**
  1. Rocks 2. Minerals
  ISBN 0-7894-9106-0; 978-0-7894-9106-0

First published 1992 as part of the Eyewitness handbooks series

This field guide to identification of rocks and minerals includes techniques for collection and classification, and facts about physical and chemical composition and formation.

Simon and Schuster's guide to rocks and minerals; edited by Martin Prinz, George Harlow, and Joseph Peters. Simon & Schuster 1978 607p il hardcover o.p. pa $17

Grades: 8 9 10 11 12 Adult   **549**
  1. Rocks 2. Minerals
  ISBN 0-671-24417-5 pa

                                 LC 78-8610

Original Italian edition, 1977

"Half of this book consists of color plates; the other half is an authoritative text which describes the elements of mineralogy and petrology. Crystal system or family, physical and chemical properties, occurrence, uses, and rarity are included for each species." Libr J

550 Earth sciences

Allaby, Michael

★ **Visual** encyclopedia of earth. National Geographic 2008 256p il map $24.95; lib bdg $32.90

Grades: 7 8 9 10   **550**
  1. Reference books 2. Earth sciences -- Encyclopedias
  ISBN 978-1-4263-0366-1; 1-4263-0366-1; 978-1-4263-0367-8 lib bdg; 1-4263-0367-X lib bdg

                                 LC 2008-301484

"This overview of the earth . . . cover[s] all aspects of earth science. . . . [This] is a feast for the eyes and an exceptional introduction to earth science. It will be a useful resource for science teachers who want to engage their students in this subject matter." Libr Media Connect

Bow, James

Earth's secrets. Marshall Cavendish Benchmark 2010 48p il (Invisible worlds) lib bdg $28.50

Grades: 4 5 6 7   **550**
  1. Earth sciences
  ISBN 978-0-7614-4196-0 lib bdg; 0-7614-4196-4 lib bdg

The narrative is "clear, well written, broken down into manageable pieces, and peppered with eye-opening facts. The numerous photographs are so phenomenal that they will inspire kids to read the text . . . so that they can wrap their minds around what they see." SLJ

Includes glossary and bibliographical references

Calhoun, Yael

Earth science fair projects; revised and expanded using the scientific method. Enslow Publishers 2010 160p il (Earth science projects using the scientific method) lib bdg $34.60

Grades: 7 8 9 10   **550**
  1. Earth sciences 2. Science projects 3. Science -- Experiments
  ISBN 978-0-7660-3425-9 lib bdg; 0-7660-3425-9 lib bdg

First published 2005 with title: Earth science fair projects using rocks, minerals, magnets, mud, and more

"Each volume begins with an overview of the scientific method and safety, then presents a collection of activities encouraging readers to explore central concepts in the featured fields. The activities include step-by-step instructions and helpful color diagrams, interspersed with extended coverage of scientific ideas. The "Results" sections ask questions rather than giving away the answers. Reading list, websites." (Horn Book)

Includes glossary and bibliographical references

Diagram Group

★ The **Facts** on File Earth science handbook; [by] the Diagram Group. Rev. ed.; Facts on File 2006 272p il (Facts on File science library) $35

Grades: 8 9 10 11 12   **550**
  1. Earth sciences
  ISBN 0-8160-5879-2

                                 LC 2005-44692

First published 2000

This guide to earth sciences contains a dictionary with around 1400 entries, a chronology, thumbnail biographies, an A to Z list of over 150 advances in earth science, and a list of Tyler Prize winners.

Includes bibliographical references

Earth; the definitive visual guide. editors-in-chief, James F. Luhr. Revised and updated ed. DK Publishing 2013 528 p. ill. (chiefly col.) (hc) $50

Grades: 8 9 10 11 12 Adult   **550**
  1. Earth
  ISBN 9781465414373; 1465414371

                                 LC 2013444093

First published 2003

This book, edited by James F. Luhr, presents "insight into the forces and processes that formed our environment and which continue to influence its evolution. With thousands of . . . photographs and unique visual catalogues of the features and phenomena that take place on Earth -- such as rocks, minerals, and mountains to tropical rain forests and the different types of clouds -- [it] contains the most up-to-date ideas on how our world works." (Publisher's note)

"Specially commissioned new 3-D digital artwork provides a striking, informative guide to the features of our planet, explains the scientific processes that govern our world, and looks at the complex relationship between humans and the natural environment." Publisher's note

Gardner, Robert

Earth's cycles; green science projects about the water cycle, photosynthesis, and more. Enslow Publishers 2011 112p il (Team Green science projects) lib bdg $31.93

Grades: 6 7 8 9 10   550
    1. Earth sciences 2. Science projects 3. Science -- Experiments
    ISBN 978-0-7660-3644-4; 0-7660-3644-8
                                            LC 2010-25816

"Gardner takes familiar experiments geared toward motivated science learners and gives them an eco-twist. Some are straightforward demonstrations of basic science while others explore aspects of alternative and sustainable science and technologies. Sections of background information further expand the green science coverage. Photographs and diagrams help illustrate the necessary equipment and setups"

Includes glossary and bibliographical references

Gilpin, Daniel

Planet Earth; what planet are you on? created by Basher; written by Dan Gilpin. Kingfisher 2010 128p il $14.99; pa $8.99

Grades: 5 6 7 8   550
    1. Earth sciences
    ISBN 978-0-7534-6616-2; 0-7534-6616-3; 978-0-7534-6412-0 pa; 0-7534-6412-8 pa
                                            LC 2010015976

Presents concepts in earth sciences using lively descriptions and cartoon illustrations personifying each concept.

"The authors blend a surprising wealth of facts into the chatty, humorous text, which is filled with analogies kids can relate to. . . . The highly approachable language, animated cast of characters, awe-inspiring facts, and conservation messages make this an appealing starting point for students seeking basic earth-science information." Booklist

Rybolt, Thomas R.

Environmental science fair projects; revised and expanded using the scientific method. [by] Thomas R. Rybolt and Robert C. Mebane. Enslow Publishers 2010 160p il (Earth science projects using the scientific method) lib bdg $34.60

Grades: 7 8 9 10   550
    1. Earth sciences 2. Science projects 3. Environmental sciences 4. Science -- Experiments
    ISBN 978-0-7660-3426-6 lib bdg; 0-7660-3426-7 lib bdg

First published 2005 with title: Environmental science fair projects using water, feathers, sunlight, balloons, and more

"Each book focusing on earth science will be helpful to middle school students and contains a section about the scientific method as well as experiments that are outlined to cover the experimental question, hypothesis, materials, procedures, results and conclusions." (Publisher's Note)

Includes bibliographical references

Solway, Andrew

Understanding cycles and systems. Raintree 2008 48p il map (Sci-hi: Earth and space science) lib bdg $31.43; pa $8.99

Grades: 4 5 6 7   550
    1. Earth sciences 2. Earth
    ISBN 978-1-4109-3348-5 lib bdg; 1-4109-3348-2 lib bdg; 978-1-4109-3358-4 pa; 1-4109-3358-X pa
                                            LC 2009-3531

"Multiple colorful sidebars and large and small diagrams and photographs will help students to grasp the fundamentals being discussed, and the easy but interesting science experiments will act as further reinforcements." SLJ

"Explores the constant processes that surround us. . . . Learn about everything from the movement of rocks to the changing forms of water. . . . Discover how invisible elements and the Sun's energy are the keys to all living things." Publisher's note

Includes glossary and bibliographical references

Woodward, John

Planet Earth; written by John Woodward; consultant Kim Bryan. DK Pub. 2009 123p il (One million things) $18.99

Grades: 5 6 7 8   550
    1. Earth
    ISBN 978-0-7566-5235-7; 0-7566-5235-9

This book features "photographic spreads that . . . showcase the rocks, minerals, streams, oceans, layers, clouds, ancient sediments, and brand-new islands that make up our planet." Publisher's note

550.78   Earth sciences – experiments

VanCleave, Janice Pratt, 1942-

Step -by-step science experiments in earth science; by Janice VanCleave. Rosen Pub. 2013 80 p. col. ill. (library) $33.25; (paperback) $14.15

Grades: 5 6 7 8   550.78
    1. Earth sciences 2. Science -- Experiments 3. Earth sciences -- Experiments
    ISBN 1448869838; 9781448869831; 9781448884674
                                            LC 2012007944

This book by Janice VanCleave is part of the First-Place Science Fair Projects series. The books have an introduction to the subject—here, earth science, followed by 22 simple . . . experiments. Van Cleave states the basic goal of the experiments, followed by a list of necessary materials, most of which can be found around the house or easily acquired with minimal cost. Step-by-step instructions are clearly detailed and accompanied by diagrams where needed." (School Library Journal)

Includes bibliographical references (p. 78) and index.

551 Geology, hydrology, meteorology

Cobb, Allan B.

Earth chemistry. Chelsea House 2008 130p il map (Essential chemistry) $35

Grades: 7 8 9 10 **551**

1. Chemistry 2. Environmental sciences

ISBN 978-0-7910-9677-2; 0-7910-9677-7

LC 2007-51317

"Annotated, colorful photographs and illustrations appear on most spreads, and boxed areas and sidebars highlight specific subjects and areas. The explanations are clear and detailed." SLJ

This book explains "chemical or physical changes on Earth, exploring how the atmosphere, hydrosphere, lithosphere, and biosphere relate to and interact with one another." Publisher's note

Includes glossary and bibliographical references

Kelly, Erica

★ Evolving planet; [by] Erica Kelly & Richard Kissel. Harry N. Abrams 2008 136p il map $19.95

Grades: 5 6 7 8 **551**

1. Evolution 2. Earth 3. Field Museum of Natural History

ISBN 978-0-8109-9486-7; 0-8109-9486-0

LC 2007-36342

"Based on a exhibit at Chicago's Field Museum, this big spacious volume packs in a wealth of information about evolution over four billion years. . . . There are detailed, beautiful photographs and glorious paintings on every double-page spread and the chatty text is accessible for grade-schoolers." Booklist

Includes glossary and bibliographical references

Plate tectonics, volcanoes, and earthquakes; edited by John P. Rafferty. Britannica Educational Pub. in association with Rosen Educational Services 2010 312p il map (Dynamic Earth) lib bdg $45

Grades: 6 7 8 9 10 **551**

1. Volcanoes 2. Earthquakes 3. Plate tectonics

ISBN 978-1-61530-106-5; 1-61530-106-2

LC 2009042303

"The 2010 earthquake in Haiti, threats to aviation from clouds of volcanic ash and aerosols, and recent changes in the Antarctic make . . . [this] a very updated resource. The process of plate tectonics and prior explanations of the dynamic nature of the earth is followed by explanations of volcanism and seismology. Charts and text describe significant volcanoes and earthquakes that have impacted humans throughout history. . . . [Recommended] for younger youth as well as high school youth since they are highly readable, with details concerning activities of interest to all ages." Voice Youth Advocates

Includes bibliographical references

551.1 Gross structure and properties of the earth

Saunders, Craig

What is the theory of plate tectonics? Crabtree Pub. Co. 2011 64p il (Shaping modern science) lib bdg $30.60; pa $10.95

Grades: 5 6 7 8 **551.1**

1. Plate tectonics 2. Geophysicists 3. Meteorologists 4. College teachers

ISBN 978-0-7787-7202-6 lib bdg; 0-7787-7202-0 lib bdg; 978-0-7787-7209-5 pa; 0-7787-7209-8 pa

LC 2010-52622

This title is "not only written and organized well, but [it is] also gorgeous in design. Full-color photographs and illustrations are set over colorful backgrounds that add depth but not distraction. [The title] includes thought-provoking quotes from famous authors and scientists and some eyebrow-raising 'Quick Facts' throughout." SLJ

Includes glossary and bibliographical references

Silverstein, Alvin

Plate tectonics; by Alvin & Virginia Silverstein & Laura Silverstein Nunn. rev. ed.; Twenty-First Century Books 2009 120p il map (Science concepts, second series) lib bdg $31.93

Grades: 6 7 8 9 **551.1**

1. Plate tectonics

ISBN 978-0-7613-3936-6; 0-7613-3936-1

LC 2007051039

First published 1998

The authors "explain the theory of plate tectonics and how moving plates can cause . . . natural disasters: earthquakes, volcanoes, and tsunamis. The authors also explore how plate tectonics are changing our planet, and how they could affect our future on Earth." Publisher's note

Includes glossary and bibliographical references

Snedden, Robert

Earth's shifting surface. Raintree 2010 48p il (Sci-hi: Earth and space science) lib bdg $31.43; pa $8.99

Grades: 4 5 6 7 **551.1**

1. Plate tectonics 2. Earth -- Surface

ISBN 978-1-4109-3349-2 lib bdg; 1-4109-3349-0 lib bdg; 978-1-4109-3359-1 pa; 1-4109-3359-8 pa

LC 2009-3532

"Multiple colorful sidebars and large and small diagrams and photographs will help students to grasp the fundamentals being discussed, and the easy but interesting science experiments will act as further reinforcements." SLJ

Includes glossary and bibliographical references

Stille, Darlene R.

★ Plate tectonics; earth's moving crust. Compass Point Books 2006 48p il (Exploring science) $26.60

Grades: 7 8 9 10 **551.1**

1. Plate tectonics

ISBN 978-0-7565-1957-5; 0-7565-1957-8

LC 2006-06764

This describes the shifting of the earth's crust and its consequences.

Includes glossary and bibliographical references

Vogt, Gregory

Earth's core and mantle; heavy metal, moving rock. by Gregory L. Vogt. Twenty-First Century Books 2007 80p il map (Earth's spheres) lib bdg $29.27

Grades: 6 7 8 9   **551.1**

1. Earth -- Internal structure
ISBN 978-0-7613-2837-7 lib bdg; 0-7613-2837-8 lib bdg

LC 2003-23969

This "explores the makeup of the universe, the origin of the planet and its moon, and the layers under Earth's surface. . . . Each of these complex topics is made understandable by the use of colorful photographs, graphs, charts, and other illustrations. Captions include new and useful information, and the sidebars and fact pages are helpful." SLJ

Includes bibliographical references

The **lithosphere**; Earth's crust. by Gregory L. Vogt. Twenty-First Century Books 2007 80p il map (Earth's spheres) lib bdg $29.27

Grades: 6 7 8 9   **551.1**

1. Earth -- Crust
ISBN 978-0-7613-2838-4 lib bdg; 0-7613-2838-6 lib bdg

LC 2006-14882

This "explains the [Earth's] crust and how land is built and eroded, covering such subjects as plate tectonics, volcanoes, and geysers. Each of these complex topics is made understandable by the use of colorful photographs, graphs, charts, and other illustrations. Captions include new and useful information, and the sidebars and fact pages are helpful." SLJ

Includes bibliographical references

551.2   Volcanoes, earthquakes, thermal waters and gases

Dwyer, Helen

Earthquakes! Marshall Cavendish Benchmark 2010 32p il map (Eyewitness disaster) lib bdg $28.50

Grades: 4 5 6   **551.2**

1. Earthquakes
ISBN 978-1-60870-001-1; 1-60870-001-1

Provides information about earthquakes through eyewitness accounts from survivors and rescue workers.

"Bold subheadings and color captions break information into readable chunks for the younger learner. Important vocabulary is in bold print. . . . An excellent addition to your science collection." Libr Media Connect

Includes glossary and bibliographical references

Fradin, Judith Bloom

★ **Earthquakes**; witness to disaster. by Judy and Dennis Fradin. National Geographic 2008 48p map (Witness to disaster) $16.95; lib bdg $26.90

Grades: 4 5 6 7   **551.2**

1. Earthquakes
ISBN 978-1-4263-0211-4; 1-4263-0211-8; 978-1-4263-0212-1 lib bdg; 1-4263-0212-6 lib bdg

LC 2007044164

"The combination of good writing and excellent graphics paired with archival and personal perspectives makes this book a valuable addition." SLJ

"The first chapter documents the 1964 Alaskan quake that shook Prince William Sound with a 9.2 magnitude force, and set off a tsunami that ultimately caused most of the deaths attributed to this frightening act of nature. The following chapters explore the deadly history of earthquakes and the seismic and geological science of this phenomenon." Publisher's note

Includes glossary and bibliographical references

Volcano! the Icelandic eruption of 2010 and other hot, smoky, fierce, and fiery mountains. [by] Judy & Dennis Fradin. National Geographic 2010 48p il map (National Geographic kids) pa $6.95

Grades: 4 5 6 7   **551.2**

1. Volcanoes
ISBN 978-1-4263-0815-4 pa; 1-4263-0815-9 pa

"The format includes text, quotes, and facts in sidebars, as well as photographs on each page, with a colorful layout. The photographs and maps that are shown are of good quality." Sci Books & Films

This offers "a historical perspective on the human experience of volcanoes and a scientific perspective on why they occur and what scientists are doing to help people stay out of the way." Publisher's note

Includes glossary and bibliographical references

★ **Volcanoes**; by Judy and Dennis Fradin. National Geographic 2007 48p il map (Witness to disaster) $16.95; lib bdg $26.90

Grades: 4 5 6 7   **551.2**

1. Volcanoes
ISBN 978-0-7922-5376-1; 0-7922-5376-0; 978-0-7922-5377-8 lib bdg; 0-7922-5377-9 lib bdg

LC 2006-102817

This "introduces readers to these violent eruptions, using eyewitness accounts to explain the history and science involved. They begin with a report of the 1943 birth of a volcano in Paricutín, Mexico. . . . Subsequent chapters describe other celebrated volcanoes, explain their causes and types, note the benefits of these eruptions, and clarify how they are currently predicted. . . . Numerous clear, well-chosen photographs and diagrams help to convey the great power of volcanic activity and the consequences to humans. . . . This will be useful for report writers, and a fascinating pick for browsers." Booklist

Includes bibliographical references

Hague, Bradley

Alien deep; Revealing the Mysterious Living World at the Bottom of the Ocean. by Bradley Hague. National Geographic 2012 48 p. col. ill. (hardcover : alk. paper) $17.95

Grades: 5 6 7 8   **551.2**
1. Oceanography -- Research 2. Hydrothermal vent ecology 3. Natural history -- Galapagos Islands 4. Hydrothermal vents 5. Hydrothermal vent animals
ISBN 1426310676; 9781426310676; 9781426310683
LC 2012012939

This book by Bradley Hague "depicts adventurous and thrilling elements in oceanographic fieldwork in conjunction with a National Geographic television show." (Publisher's note) "The book takes readers along on the 2011 exploration of vents in the Galapagos Reef area of the Pacific Ocean. . . . Future scientists will be hooked by the excitement of finding newly developing vents and the disappointment of finding older vents that once disappeared under layers of magma." (Booklist)

Includes bibliographical references and index.

Latta, Sara L.

Lava scientist; careers on the edge of volcanoes. Enslow Publishers 2009 128p il (Wild science careers) lib bdg $31.93

Grades: 5 6 7 8   **551.2**
1. Volcanoes 2. Vocational guidance
ISBN 978-0-7660-3049-7 lib bdg; 0-7660-3049-7 lib bdg
LC 2008-4679

The book's "greatest strength is in the variety of first-hand accounts and the scientists' breadth of experience. [The book has] appealing color photographs and an attractive design." SLJ

"Explores careers in volcano science using examples of real-life scientists." Publisher's note

Includes glossary and bibliographical references

Levy, Matthys

Earthquakes, volcanoes, and tsunamis; projects and principles for beginning geologists. [by] Matthys Levy and Mario Salvadori. Chicago Review Press 2009 136p il pa $14.95

Grades: 5 6 7 8   **551.2**
1. Tsunamis 2. Volcanoes 3. Earthquakes
ISBN 978-1-55652-801-9 pa; 1-55652-801-9 pa
LC 2008040143

This "is an excellent introduction for young minds to the subject of earthquakes, volcanoes, and related phenomena. . . . The book is filled with projects to help young people understand the occurrence and consequences of earthquakes, volcanoes, and tsunamis." Sci Books Films

McCollum, Sean

Volcanic eruptions, earthquakes, and tsunamis. Chelsea House 2007 80p il (Scientific American) lib bdg $30

Grades: 5 6 7 8   **551.2**
1. Tsunamis 2. Volcanoes 3. Earthquakes
ISBN 978-0-7910-9047-3 lib bdg; 0-7910-9047-7 lib bdg
LC 2007017740

"Following an introduction that focuses on the formation of a volcano off the coast of Iceland in 1963 and presents the principles of seismology, geology, and the structure of the Earth, individual chapters on volcanoes, earthquakes, and tsunamis describe these phenomena, how they happen, and their characteristics. . . . The workmanlike writing is clear, with glossary terms highlighted in the text. Major events, such as Mount St. Helens, the 2004 tsunami, and the 1906 San Francisco earthquake, are used as examples, while good color diagrams and photos effectively illustrate ideas presented." SLJ

Includes bibliographical references

Nardo, Don

Volcanoes. Morgan Reynolds Pub. 2009 112p il map (Extreme threats) lib bdg $28.95

Grades: 7 8 9 10   **551.2**
1. Volcanoes
ISBN 978-1-59935-118-6; 1-59935-118-8
LC 2009-25705

This book "begins with a vivid account of the 79 CE eruption of Vesuvius, the cataclysm that buried Pompeii and Herculaneum. Later chapters explore the development of volcanology, formation and location of volcanoes, volcanic avalanches, supervolcanoes and mass extinctions, and the bleak future of humanity with regard to volcanoes. Throughout, Nardo references specific volcanoes and eruptions and brings the disasters to life by including primary source quotes from witnesses and scientists." Voice Youth Advocates

Includes glossary and bibliographical references

Person, Stephen

Devastated by a volcano! Bearport Pub. 2010 32p il map (Disaster survivors) lib bdg $25.27

Grades: 4 5 6 7   **551.2**
1. Volcanoes
ISBN 978-1-936087-50-1 lib bdg; 1-936087-50-2 lib bdg

"Captivating photos and illustrations and sidebars present interesting facts or brief anecdotes. . . . [This] should be purchased for all school and public libraries as . . . [it gives] a new perspective on the topic." Libr Media Connect

"Introduces volcanoes, describing how they are formed and why they become active, along with the experiences of actual survivors of a volcanic eruption and some wellknown volcanic eruptions of the past." Publisher's note

Includes glossary and bibliographical references

Prager, Ellen J.

Earthquakes and volcanoes; [by] Ellen Prager. Chelsea House Publishers 2009 118p il map (The restless Earth) lib bdg $32.95

Grades: 6 7 8 9   **551.2**
1. Volcanoes 2. Earthquakes
ISBN 978-0-7910-9705-2 lib bdg; 0-7910-9705-6 lib bdg
LC 2008-8777

"The high level of detail, perspective in world history, and solid organization provide an excellent foundation for students to throughly understand the cataclysmic events of earthquakes and tornadoes." Libr Media Connect

Includes glossary and bibliographical references

Reingold, Adam

Leveled by an earthquake! Bearport Pub. 2010 32p il map (Disaster survivors) lib bdg $25.27

Grades: 4 5 6 7   551.2
    1. Earthquakes
    ISBN 978-1-936087-53-2 lib bdg; 1-936087-53-7 lib bdg

LC 2009-36961

"Captivating photos and illustrations and sidebars present interesting facts or brief anecdotes. . . . [This] should be purchased for all school and public libraries as . . . [it gives] a new perspective on the topic." Libr Media Connect

"Introduces earthquakes, describing what causes them to occur and how they are measured, along with stories of survivors who were the victims of famous earthquakes of the past." Publisher's note

Includes glossary and bibliographical references

Rooney, Anne

Volcanoes. New Forest Press 2010 64p il map (Cutting-edge science) lib bdg $34.25

Grades: 7 8 9 10   551.2
    1. Volcanoes
    ISBN 978-1-84898-319-9; 1-84898-319-0

This guide to volcanoes covers plate tectonics, super volcanoes, tsunamis, scientific methods for detection and prediction, case studies of real volcanoes past and present, and the effects of volcanoes on the environment.

"Both books present basic information about these natural disasters, including explanations of plate tectonics, the categories and causes of each, and historical examples of prominent events. Stock color photographs and diagrams help to illustrate the concepts. Additional information about current scientific research projects and the scientists leading them can be found in the numerous sidebars." (Horn Book)

Includes glossary and bibliographical references

Silverstein, Alvin

Earthquakes; the science behind seismic shocks and tsunamis. [by] Alvin Silverstein, Virginia Silverstein, and Laura Silverstein Nunn. Enslow Publishers 2010 48p il map (The science behind natural disasters) lib bdg $23.93

Grades: 4 5 6   551.2
    1. Tsunamis 2. Earthquakes
    ISBN 978-0-7660-2975-0 lib bdg; 0-7660-2975-1 lib bdg

LC 2008-38589

"Scientific explanations are accompanied by plentiful color diagrams that will help students to grasp causes and effects. . . . Photos . . . are effective, and are sometimes turned into helpful, lively diagrams by the addition of such features as wind-direction arrows." SLJ

"Examines the science behind earthquakes and tsunamis, including what makes them happen, where they occur, how they are measured, and tips to stay safe during an earthquake." Publisher's note

Includes glossary and bibliographical references

Volcanoes; the science behind fiery eruptions. [by] Alvin Silverstein, Virginia Silverstein, and Laura Silverstein Nunn. Enslow Publishers 2010 48p il map (The science behind natural disasters) lib bdg $23.93

Grades: 4 5 6   551.2
    1. Volcanoes
    ISBN 978-0-7660-2972-9 lib bdg; 0-7660-2972-7 lib bdg

LC 2008-42866

"Scientific explanations are accompanied by plentiful color diagrams that will help students to grasp causes and effects. . . . Photos . . . are effective, and are sometimes turned into helpful, lively diagrams by the addition of such features as wind-direction arrows." SLJ

"Examines the science behind volcanoes, including what causes them to erupt, the inner-workings of a volcano, underwater volcanoes, and how to stay safe during an eruption." Publisher's note

Includes glossary and bibliographical references

Stewart, Melissa

Inside Earthquakes. Sterling Publishing Co., Inc. 2011 48p il map (Inside . . .) $16.95; pa $9.95

Grades: 5 6 7 8   551.2
    1. Earthquakes
    ISBN 978-1-4027-5877-5; 978-1-4027-8163-6 pa

LC 2010046452

This book about earthquakes "explores its topic in an engaging way, and the many illustrations work well with adjacent text and captions. . . . The [book's] varied page layouts and attractive and the quality of photos, computer-generated images, original illustrations, and charts is . . . excellent. . . . [The book] looks at the geology of the earth's crust as well as the effects of quakes on people and cities, landforms and coastlines." Booklist

Includes bibliographical references

Inside Volcanoes. Sterling Publishing Co. 2011 48p il map (Inside . . .) $16.95; pa $9.95

Grades: 5 6 7 8   551.2
    1. Volcanoes
    ISBN 978-1-4027-5876-8; 1-4027-5876-6; 978-1-4027-8164-3 pa; 1-4027-8164-4 pa

LC 2010046451

Examines the nature of volcanoes, how they are formed, what they look like, and how they are measured, in a text with ten foldout pages.

"With pages that fold out or flip up, well-reproduced photographs of volcanoes at rest and in action, diagrams, maps, charts, timelines and short explanations, there is much to look at and to learn. . . . Appropriately for a book that is clearly designed to stimulate interest, there are solid suggestions for both books and websites for further exploration. A good starting-place for volcano explorations." Kirkus

Stille, Darlene R.

Great shakes; the science of earthquakes. Compass Point Books 2009 43p il map (Headline science) lib bdg $27.93; pa $7.95

Grades: 5 6 7 8 **551.2**

1. Earthquakes

ISBN 978-0-7565-3947-4 lib bdg; 0-7565-3947-1 lib bdg; 978-0-7565-3368-7 pa; 0-7565-3368-6 pa

LC 2008-05739

This "is an accessible, technically accurate introduction to [earthquakes]. . . . In addition to the ludic writing, this slim volume offers . . . readers comprehensive coverage of the fundamentals of earthquakes, including the effects, plate tectonics, fault systems, seismic waves, forecasting, and safer building designs. . . . The many charts and graphs enrich the volume and clarify technical issues." Sci Books Films

Includes glossary and bibliographical references

Winchester, Simon

The **day** the world exploded; the earthshaking catastrophe at Krakatoa. adaptation by Dwight Jon Zimmerman; illustrated by Jason Chin. Collins 2008 96p il map $22.99; lib bdg $23.89

Grades: 5 6 7 8 **551.2**

1. Volcanoes

ISBN 978-0-06-123982-3; 0-06-123982-8; 978-0-06-123983-0 lib bdg; 0-06-123983-6 lib bdg

Adapted from: Krakatoa: the day the world exploded, August 27, 1883, published 2003 for adults

This presents an account of the catastrophic eruption off the coast of Java of the volcano-island of Krakatoa in 1883 and its effects

"Chin's full-color cartoon illustrations enhance the many archival and contemporary photographs, historical illustrations, and maps that accompany the text. . . . In addition to this work's educational and reference potential, it lends a human face to a natural disaster and will attract general readers as well." SLJ

Includes glossary and bibliographical references

551.3   Surface and exogenous processes and their agents

Glaciers, sea ice, and ice formation; edited by John P. Rafferty. Britannica Educational Pub. in association with Rosen Educational Services 2010 253p il map (Dynamic Earth) lib bdg $45

Grades: 6 7 8 9 10 **551.3**

1. Ice 2. Glaciers

ISBN 978-1-61530-119-5; 1-61530-119-4

LC 2010000226

This book "examines the dynamic processes of [glaciers, sea ice, and ice formation]. . . . [It] provides the reader with an understanding of basic processes, historical background, and current phenomena. . . . [Recommended] for younger youth as well as high school youth." Voice Youth Advocates

Includes bibliographical references

Stille, Darlene R.

★ **Erosion**; how land forms, how it changes. by Darlene R. Stille. Compass Point Books 2005 48p il map (Exploring science) $25.27

Grades: 6 7 8 9 **551.3**

1. Erosion

ISBN 0-7565-0854-1

LC 2004-23077

Examines the dangers, causes, and control of erosion.

"A few maps and many clear, color photos illustrate the book." Booklist

Includes glossary and bibliographical references

551.4   Geomorphology and hydrosphere

Aleshire, Peter

Deserts. Chelsea House 2007 178p il map (The extreme Earth) $35

Grades: 8 9 10 11 12 **551.4**

1. Deserts

ISBN 978-0-8160-6434-2; 0-8160-6434-2

This describes desert locations, their plants and animals, their indigenous peoples, ecology, and history.

Mountains; foreword by Geoffrey H. Nash. Chelsea House Publishers 2008 144p il map (The extreme Earth) $35

Grades: 8 9 10 11 12 **551.4**

1. Mountains

ISBN 978-0-8160-5918-8; 0-8160-5918-7

LC 2007-20692

This describes how mountains were formed, how they have changed over the span of geologic time, and their contributions to the environment, and goes on to describe specific mountains and mountain ranges including Mount Everest, the Appalachians, the Alps, the Mid-Atlantic Ridge of North America, the Sierra Nevadas, the Andes, Mauna Kea in Hawaii, Mount Saint Helens, Mount Kilimanjaro, and Humphreys Peak, in the southwestern United States.

Includes bibliographical references

Berlatsky, Noah

Water and ice; Michael E. Mann, consulting editor. Greenhaven Press 2011 120p il map (Confronting global warming) lib bdg $37.10

Grades: 7 8 9 10 11 **551.4**

1. Ice 2. Glaciers 3. Greenhouse effect

ISBN 978-0-7377-4861-1; 0-7377-4861-3

LC 2010011348

"After useful introductions to climate change science and background information on related atmospheric and oceanic sciences, the volumes examine the rise of average global and ocean temperatures. Evidence for and against causal relationships between these increases and extreme weather events such as hurricanes, droughts, and heat waves are then thoughtfully discussed. Some color photographs and diagrams are included." (Horn Book)

Includes glossary and bibliographical references

Hanson, Erik A.

Canyons; [by] Erik Hanson; foreword by Geoffrey H. Nash. Chelsea House 2007 206p il map (The extreme Earth) $35

Grades: 8 9 10 11 12   **551.4**

1. Canyons 2. Plate tectonics

ISBN 0-8160-6435-0; 978-0-8160-6435-9

LC 2006-15810

Profiles canyons around the world including the Grand Canyon, the Columbia River Gorge, Fish River Canyon, and Monterey Canyon; and describes how and when they were formed, how the landscape has changed over time, and the contribution of each to the environment.

"The story in this book may generate a longing within the reader to visit vistas and hike into canyons for an intimate view of earth history." Sci Books Films

Includes glossary and bibliographical references

Hanson, Jeanne K.

Caves; foreword by Geoffrey H. Nash. Chelsea House 2007 142p il map (The extreme Earth) $35

Grades: 8 9 10 11 12   **551.4**

1. Caves

ISBN 978-0-8160-5917-1; 0-8160-5917-9

LC 2006-11718

The describes types of caves and how they are formed, their exploration, and some specific caves including Mammoth Cave of Kentucky; the caves of Yucatan, Mexico; Lascaux Cave of southwestern France; Lubang Nasib Bagus and the Sarawak Chamber of Borneo, Malaysia; Kazumura Cave of Hawaii; Waitomo Cave of New Zealand; and Wind Cave of South Dakota.

Includes bibliographical references

551.46 Oceanography and submarine geology

Aleshire, Peter

Ocean ridges and trenches; foreword by Geoffrey H. Nash. Chelsea House 2007 148p il map (The extreme Earth) $35

Grades: 8 9 10 11 12   **551.46**

1. Ocean bottom 2. Marine ecology

ISBN 978-0-8160-5919-5; 0-8160-5919-5

LC 2006-32058

Provides information about the formation of ocean ridges and trenches. Includes ten examples of ridges and trenches from around the world.

Includes bibliographical references

Aronin, Miriam

Slammed by a tsunami! Bearport Pub. 2010 32p il map (Disaster survivors) lib bdg $25.27

Grades: 4 5 6 7   **551.46**

1. Tsunamis

ISBN 978-1-936087-48-8 lib bdg; 1-936087-48-0 lib bdg

LC 2009-34574

"Captivating photos and illustrations and sidebars present interesting facts or brief anecdotes. . . . [This] should be

purchased for all school and public libraries as . . . [it gives] a new perspective on the topic." Libr Media Connect

Includes glossary and bibliographical references

Basher, Simon

Oceans; [making waves!] designed and created by Simon Basher ; text written by Dan Green. Kingfisher 2012 128 p. ill. (paperback) $8.99; (hardcover) $14.99

Grades: 5 6 7 8   **551.46**

1. Oceanography 2. Marine ecology 3. Aquatic animals

ISBN 0753468220; 9780753468227; 9780753468210

"Following a brief introduction to oceans, the text employs an easy-to-navigate field guide like format, where facts and figures about ocean habitats, processes, and animals that live in various areas (e.g., shore, reef, deep water) face illustrations in manga style" Horn Book

"A rewarding wade, particularly for readers who think oceanography is a dry study." Booklist

Bodden, Valerie

To the ocean deep; by Valerie Bodden. Creative Education 2011 48 p. col. ill. (Great expeditions) (library) $34.25

Grades: 5 6 7 8   **551.46**

1. Ocean 2. Underwater exploration 3. Explorers -- Biography 4. Trieste (Bathyscaphe) -- History 5. Bathyscaphe -- History -- 20th century 6. Underwater exploration -- History -- 20th century

ISBN 1608180670; 9781608180677

LC 2010033416

This book by Valerie Bodden is part of the Great Expeditions series and looks at oceanic exploration expeditions. "Bodden includes brief biographies of major people involved in each expedition, interspersed with the text. There are also numerous photographs or reproductions of paintings and woodcuts from the time of the expeditions." (Library Media Connection)

Includes bibliographical references (p. 46-47) and index.

Burns, Loree Griffin

★ Tracking trash; flotsam, jetsam, and the science of ocean motion. Houghton Mifflin 2007 56p il map (Scientists in the field) $18

Grades: 5 6 7 8   **551.46**

1. Pollution 2. Ocean currents 3. Oceanographers

ISBN 0-618-58131-6; 978-0-618-58131-3

LC 2006-11534

This book describes "Curt Ebbesmeyer's ongoing work. . . . The oceanographer has been tracing the surface currents of the seas via the movement of plastic rubbish that has escaped from broken cargo containers. [Index.] Grades five to nine." (Bull Cent Child Books)

"The book profiles two oceanographers who devised experiments using computer-modeling programs of ocean surface current movement to predict the landfall of . . . drifting objects. . . . Spacious layout, exceptionally fine color photos, and handsome maps give this book an inviting look. . . . A unique and often fascinating book." Booklist

Includes glossary and bibliographical references

Day, Trevor

Oceans; illustrations by Richard Garratt. rev ed; Facts on File 2008 318p il map (Ecosystem) $70

Grades: 8 9 10 11 12 Adult   **551.46**

1. Ocean 2. Oceanography

ISBN 0-8160-5932-2; 978-0-8160-5932-4

LC 2006-100769

First published 1999

This volume describes the oceans of the world with regard to their geography, geology, history, chemistry, biology, ecology, exploration, relationship to the atmosphere, economic resources, and management.

Includes glossary and bibliographical references

Desonie, Dana

Oceans; how we use the seas. Chelsea House 2007 215p il map (Our fragile planet) $35

Grades: 8 9 10 11 12   **551.46**

1. Ocean 2. Oceanography 3. Marine ecology

ISBN 978-0-8160-6216-4; 0-8160-6216-1

LC 2007-13560

An introduction to how life in our oceans works, and how we are threatening it with pollution and depletion of fisheries.

The author "offers a comprehensive, detailed introduction to ocean science and conservation in this amply illustrated volume." Booklist

Includes glossary and bibliographical references

Dwyer, Helen

Tsunamis! Marshall Cavendish Benchmark 2010 32p il map (Eyewitness disaster) lib bdg $28.50

Grades: 4 5 6   **551.46**

1. Tsunamis

ISBN 978-1-60870-005-9; 1-60870-005-4

LC 2010001801

Provides information about tsunamis through eyewitness accounts from survivors and rescue workers.

"Bold subheadings and color captions break information into readable chunks for the younger learner. Important vocabulary is in bold print. . . . An excellent addition to your science collection." Libr Media Connect

Includes glossary and bibliographical references

Fradin, Judith Bloom

★ Tsunamis; witness to disaster. [by] Judy & Dennis Fradin. National Geographic 2008 48p il map (Witness to disaster) $16.95; lib bdg $20.90

Grades: 4 5 6 7   **551.46**

1. Tsunamis

ISBN 978-0-7922-5380-8; 0-7922-5380-9; 978-0-7922-5381-5 lib bdg; 0-7922-5381-7 lib bdg

LC 2008010536

This "explores the science, history, and personal experience of tsunamis and shows kids what scientists are doing to develop early warning systems so we can survive such disasters in the future." Publisher's note

Includes glossary and bibliographical references

Friedman, Lauri S.

Oceans; Lauri S. Friedman, book editor. Greenhaven Press 2011 (Introducing issues with opposing viewpoints) $36.82

Grades: 7 8 9 10   **551.46**

1. Ocean 2. Marine pollution

ISBN 978-0-7377-5200-7; 0-7377-5200-9

LC 2011005910

"These volumes present previously published articles and essays from journals, magazines, and websites to provide opposing viewpoints about alternative energy sources and environmental threats to Earth's oceans. Though the many photographs, sidebars, and charts make the books visually approachable, the lack of contextual information about primary sources makes for texts that are more inflammatory than useful." (Horn Book)

Includes bibliographical references

Kusky, Timothy M.

Tsunamis; giant waves from the sea. [by] Timothy Kusky. Facts on File 2008 134p il (The hazardous Earth) $39.50

Grades: 8 9 10 11 12   **551.46**

1. Tsunamis

ISBN 978-0-8160-6464-9; 0-8160-6464-4

LC 2007-23477

"This detailed study of the causes and physics of massive waves covers not only the oceanic sort but also similar phenomena, 'seiches,' that occur in closed bodies of water. . . . After analyzing tsunamis' various forms and behaviors, Kusky delivers harrowing accounts of over a dozen disasters, from those centuries past to the devastating Indian Ocean tsunami in 2004. He then closes with a discussion of early-warning systems. Occasional photos capture the devastation of which these waves are capable." Booklist

Includes bibliographical references

Lindop, Laurie

★ Venturing the deep sea. Twenty-First Century Books 2006 80p il map (Science on the edge) lib bdg $27.93

Grades: 5 6 7 8   **551.46**

1. Ocean bottom 2. Underwater exploration

ISBN 0-7613-2701-0

LC 2004-29729

"The science is intriguing here. . . . The photos of undersea projects, creatures, weird cave and underwater tube formations are all intriguing." Voice Youth Advocates

Includes bibliographical references

MacQuitty, Miranda

Eyewitness ocean; written by Miranda MacQuitty ; photographed by Frank Greenaway. DK Publishing 2008 72 p. illustrations (chiefly color) $9.99

Grades: 4 5 6 7   **551.46**

1. Ocean 2. Marine animals 3. Marine biology 4. Marine ecology 5. Ocean

ISBN 1465420541; 1465420967; 9780756637767; 9781465420541

LC 2008276032

In this book, by Miranda MacQuitty, "dive in and discover the watery world covering most of our earth and the amazing wildlife in its depths. . . . Through images, maps and informative text learn about life on the shore to the darkest depths of the ocean floor, including predators and prey, gas and oil exploration, products of the ocean, brave explorers and what the human race can do to help preserve one of the earth's most valuable resources." (Publisher's note)

"The DK Eyewitness series exemplifies what the publisher does best: taking a broad topic and slicing it into two-page chapters that, while they contain no narrative thread, make for excellent museum-type browsing... The photos are stunning and wonderfully arranged. Each book rounds out the guided tour with an FAQ of sorts, profiles, and plenty of places for interested readers to keep looking. Just the thing to whet appetites before trucking down to the local real-life museum." Booklist

Ocean

Part of the DK Eyewitness series.

Mallory, Kenneth

Adventure beneath the sea; living in an underwater science station. [photographs by Brian Skerry] Boyds Mills Press 2010 48p il map $18.95
Grades: 4 5 6 7   551.46
1. Underwater exploration
ISBN 978-1-59078-607-9; 1-59078-607-6

The author "invites readers to squeeze into Aquarius, a venerable science-station habitat resting on the sea floor at a depth of 60 feet in the Florida Keys. The readable text explains the complexities of training for a weeklong stay, the aims of the scientists on the team, and what it is like to spend 24/7 in squashed companionship in a 43' × 9' cylinder as part of a crew of seven. . . . Sidebars contain interesting information. . . . Full-color photos abound." SLJ

Includes glossary and bibliographical references

★ **Diving** to a deep-sea volcano. Houghton Mifflin Company 2006 60p il map (Scientists in the field) $17
Grades: 5 6 7 8   551.46
1. Ocean bottom 2. Marine biology 3. Underwater exploration
ISBN 978-0-618-33205-2; 0-618-33205-7
LC 2005-25449

This describes the exploration by marine biologist Rich Lutz and his crew of deep sea hydrothermal vents and the creatures that survive there.

"The profile of an enthusiastic scientist injects excitement into even unassuming facts." Booklist

Includes glossary and bibliographical references

McMillan, Beverly

Oceans; [by] Beverly McMillan and John N. Musick. Simon & Schuster Books for Young Readers 2007 64p il map (Insiders) $16.99
Grades: 4 5 6 7   551.46
1. Ocean 2. Marine biology 3. Marine ecology
ISBN 978-1-4169-3859-0; 1-4169-3859-1
LC 2007-61730

This book will "assault the reader with vibrant colors and eye-popping graphics. The illustrations range in size from

full-page background art to thumbnails. Even the smallest pictures are clear, with easy to distinguish details; all are either labeled or captioned. . . . You may want to purchase more than one copy." Libr Media Connect

"This first half of this richly illustrated guide introduces general concepts: how the ocean was formed, what lives in it, and how scientists have collected this information. The book then focuses on the various bio-zones and ecosystems supported by and within the ocean." Horn Book

Includes glossary

Rizzo, Johnna

Oceans; dolphins, sharks, penguins, and more!: meet 60 cool sea creatures and explore their amazing watery world. introduction by Sylvia A. Earle. National Geographic 2010 64p il $14.95; lib bdg $24.90
Grades: 4 5 6   551.46
1. Ocean 2. Marine animals
ISBN 978-1-4263-0686-0; 1-4263-0686-5; 978-1-4263-0724-9 lib bdg; 1-4263-0724-1 lib bdg

"A colorful olio of marine animals in eye-catching photos accompanies a cheerful conversational text. . . . Information boxes pop up all over the place as well, but it is the bright photos that steal the show. . . . This splashy volume is a nice introduction to a salty water-world." SLJ

Includes glossary

Simon, Seymour

Seymour Simon's extreme oceans; Seymour Simon. Chronicle Books 2013 60 p. col. ill. (reinforced) $17.99
Grades: 4 5 6   551.46
1. Ocean
ISBN 1452108331; 9781452108339
LC 2012012590

In this work of children's nonfiction, author "[Seymour] Simon examines the things that are 'most,' pertaining to oceans: the tallest sea mounts, the largest waves, the highest tides in the world, the most dangerous and largest animals, the coldest and warmest waters, the biggest storms and tsunamis, and the longest journeys, as well as a closing chapter predicting scenarios if sea levels continue to rise." (School Library Journal)

Yount, Lisa

Modern marine science; exploring the deep. Chelsea House 2006 204p il map (Milestones in discovery and invention) $35
Grades: 7 8 9 10 11 12   551.46
1. Marine sciences
ISBN 0-8160-5747-8
LC 2005-30562

This book "profiles 12 men and women who led the way into the oceans' deepest waters through research and new technologies. From Charles Darwin to Henry Stommel to Robert Ballard, this volume explores the lives and accomplishments of these scientific revolutionaries." Publisher's note

Includes glossary and bibliographical references

551.48 Hydrology

Burnham, Laurie

Rivers; foreword by Geoffrey H. Nash. Chelsea House 2007 176p il map (The extreme Earth) $35

Grades: 8 9 10 11 12 **551.48**

1. Rivers

ISBN 0-8160-5916-0; 978-0-8160-5916-4

LC 2006-31302

This is a "portrait of 10 of the most unusual rivers that examines what was on-site before the river, how it was formed, how and why it has changed over time, and its contributions to the environment." Publisher's note

Includes glossary and bibliographical references

Carrigan, Patricia

Waterfalls. Chelsea House 2007 146p il (The extreme Earth) $35

Grades: 8 9 10 11 12 **551.48**

1. Waterfalls

ISBN 978-0-8160-6436-6; 0-8160-6436-9

Presents an introduction to waterfalls, describing how they develop and how they are used to generate power, and providing the history and current formation of ten of the world's most famous waterfalls

Desonie, Dana

Hydrosphere; freshwater systems and pollution. Chelsea House 2008 194p il map (Our fragile planet) $35

Grades: 7 8 9 10 **551.48**

1. Water pollution 2. Water purification

ISBN 978-0-8160-6215-7; 0-8160-6215-3

LC 2007-22398

"Looks at the environmental and health effects of water pollution." Publisher's note

Includes glossary and bibliographical references

Dwyer, Helen

Floods! Marshall Cavendish Benchmark 2010 32p il map (Eyewitness Disaster) lib bdg $28.50

Grades: 4 5 6 **551.48**

1. Floods

ISBN 978-1-60870-002-8; 1-60870-002-X

Provides information about floods through eyewitness accounts from survivors and rescue workers.

"Bold subheadings and color captions break information into readable chunks for the younger learner. Important vocabulary is in bold print. . . . An excellent addition to your science collection." Libr Media Connect

Includes glossary and bibliographical references

Gardner, Robert

Water; green science projects for a sustainable planet. Enslow Publishers 2011 128p il (Team Green science projects) lib bdg $31.93

Grades: 6 7 8 9 10 **551.48**

1. Water 2. Science projects 3. Science -- Experiments

ISBN 978-0-7660-3645-1; 0-7660-3645-6

LC 2009-37902

This book offers science experiments that explain the properties of water, the water cycle, and how you can conserve water.

"Gardner takes familiar experiments geared toward motivated science learners and gives them an eco-twist. Some are straightforward demonstrations of basic science while others explore aspects of alternative and sustainable science and technologies. Sections of background information further expand the green science coverage. Photographs and diagrams help illustrate the necessary equipment and setups.' (Horn Book)

Includes glossary and bibliographical references

Hanson, Jeanne K.

Lakes; foreword, Geoffrey H. Nash. Facts on File 2007 146p il map (The extreme Earth) $35

Grades: 8 9 10 11 12 **551.48**

1. Lakes

ISBN 978-0-8160-5914-0; 0-8160-5914-4

LC 2005-34327

This describes how lakes are formed, the current environmental health of the lakes and their future prognosis, and some specific bodies of water including the Caspian Sea in the Middle East, the Aral Sea in Western Asia, Lake Superior in North America, Lake Baikal in Central Asia, and Lake Titicaca in South America.

Includes bibliographical references

551.5 Meteorology

Banqueri, Eduardo

Weather. Enchanted Lion Books 2006 33p il (Field guides) $16.95

Grades: 4 5 6 7 **551.5**

1. Weather

ISBN 1-59270-059-4

LC 2006-42864

This "book is filled with information about all aspects of weather, from why there are seasons to predicting the weather. Complementing the scientifically accurate text is an excellent mix of drawings and photographs." Sci Books and Films

Carson, Mary Kay

Weather projects for young scientists; experiments and science fair ideas. Chicago Review Press 2007 134p il $14.95

Grades: 4 5 6 7 **551.5**

1. Weather 2. Science -- Experiments

ISBN 978-1-55652-629-9; 1-55652-629-6

LC 2006-16430

This "presents difficult concepts in a very concrete, basic manner." Sci Books Films

Cosgrove, Brian

Weather; written by Brian Cosgrove. rev ed; DK Publishing 2007 72p il map (DK eyewitness books) $15.99; lib bdg $19.99

Grades: 4 5 6 7   **551.5**
1. Climate 2. Weather 3. Atmosphere
ISBN 978-0-7566-3006-5; 0-7566-3006-1; 978-0-
7566-0737-1 lib bdg; 0-7566-0737-X lib bdg
                                    LC 2007-281112
First published 1991 by Knopf

"Discover the world's weather—from heat waves and droughts to blizzards and floods"—Cover. Includes discussion of why the climate may change in the future.

"Accompanying the book are a poster, additional images on CD-ROM, and a useful glossary. Altogether, this book and its supplements are well crafted to motivate young learners about the importance of weather, to deepen their conceptual understanding of it, and to pique their interest in participating in its study." Sci Books Films

Includes glossary

DeLallo, Laura

Hammered by a heat wave! consultants, Daphne Thompson, Keith C. Heidorn. Bearport Pub. 2010 32p il map (Disaster survivors) lib bdg $25.27
Grades: 4 5 6 7   **551.5**
1. Meteorology
ISBN 978-1-936087-51-8 lib bdg; 1-936087-51-0 lib bdg

"Captivating photos and illustrations and sidebars present interesting facts or brief anecdotes. . . . [This] should be purchased for all school and public libraries as . . . [it gives] a new perspective on the topic." Libr Media Connect

Includes glossary and bibliographical references

Gaffney, Timothy R.

Storm scientist; careers chasing severe weather. Enslow Publishers 2009 112p il (Wild science careers) lib bdg $31.93
Grades: 5 6 7 8   **551.5**
1. Weather 2. Meteorology 3. Vocational guidance
ISBN 978-0-7660-3050-3 lib bdg; 0-7660-3050-4 lib bdg

"The day-today experiences along with the educational requirements are included in the clear, easy-to-read [text]. . . . Full-color photographs show the scientists in action." SLJ

Includes glossary and bibliographical references

Gardner, Robert

Ace your weather science project; great science fair ideas. [by] Robert Gardner and Salvatore Tocci. Enslow Publishers 2009 104p il (Ace your physics science project) lib bdg $31.93
Grades: 5 6 7 8   **551.5**
1. Weather 2. Science projects 3. Science -- Experiments
ISBN 978-0-7660-3223-1 lib bdg; 0-7660-3223-X lib bdg

                                    LC 2008-49779
"Presents several science experiments and project ideas about weather." Publisher's note

Includes bibliographical references

Easy genius science projects with weather; great experiments and ideas. Enslow Publishers 2009 128p il (Easy genius science projects) lib bdg $31.93
Grades: 5 6 7 8   **551.5**
1. Weather 2. Science projects 3. Science -- Experiments
ISBN 978-0-7660-2924-8 lib bdg; 0-7660-2924-7 lib bdg

                                    LC 2008-23972
"Science experiments and science project ideas about weather." Publisher's note

Includes glossary and bibliographical references

Meteorology projects with a weather station you can build; by Robert Gardner. Enslow Publishers 2008 128p il (Build-a-lab! science experiments) lib bdg $31.93
Grades: 6 7 8 9   **551.5**
1. Meteorology 2. Science projects 3. Weather forecasting 4. Science -- Experiments
ISBN 978-0-7660-2807-4 lib bdg; 0-7660-2807-0 lib bdg

                                    LC 2007010614
This describes science experiments and projects on such topics as wind, temperature, rain, clouds, climate and other aspects of weather.

Includes bibliographical references

Streissguth, Thomas

Extreme weather; [by] Tom Streissguth; Michael E. Mann, consulting editor. Greenhaven Press/Gale, Cengage Learning 2011 116p il map (Confronting global warming) lib bdg $37.10
Grades: 7 8 9 10 11 12   **551.5**
1. Weather 2. Climate -- Environmental aspects
ISBN 978-0-7377-4859-8; 0-7377-4859-1

                                    LC 2010-24973
"Presented in a scholarly design that will appeal to older readers. . . . The illustrations and pictures support the text, and the graphics and sidebars are well placed." Libr Media Connect

"Explores the relationship between global climate change and extreme weather, including air and water chemistry; solar radiation; hurricanes and tropical cyclones; heat waves and other potential future warming; drought, from the Dust Bowl of the 1930s to the current water crisis in California; and the impacts of rainfall, flooding, and El Niño." Publisher's note

Includes glossary and bibliographical references

Vogt, Gregory

The **atmosphere**; planetary heat engine. by Gregory L. Vogt. Twenty-First Century Books 2007 80p il map (Earth spheres) lib bdg $29.27
Grades: 6 7 8 9   **551.5**
1. Weather 2. Atmosphere
ISBN 978-0-76132-841-4 lib bdg; 0-76132-841-6 lib bdg

                                    LC 2006-07391
"The book covers a wide range of topics, including air currents, the water cycle, . . . meteorology, and climate

change, and explores how they affect our daily lives. A good deal of discussion is devoted to scientists' use of satellites and other high-tech tools to study the atmosphere. Color graphs, photographs, and sidebars . . . supplement the accessible text." Booklist

Includes bibliographical references

551.55 Atmospheric disturbances and formations

Aronin, Miriam

Mangled by a hurricane! consultant, James L. Franklin. Bearport Pub. 2010 32p il map (Disaster survivors) lib bdg $25.27

Grades: 4 5 6 7   **551.55**

1. Hurricanes 2. Hurricane Katrina, 2005
ISBN 978-1-936087-49-5 lib bdg; 1-936087-49-9 lib bdg

"Captivating photos and illustrations and sidebars present interesting facts or brief anecdotes. . . . [This] should be purchased for all school and public libraries as . . . [it gives] a new perspective on the topic." Libr Media Connect

Includes glossary and bibliographical references

Carson, Mary Kay

★ **Inside** hurricanes. Sterling 2010 48p il map (Inside) $16.95; pa $9.95

Grades: 5 6 7 8   **551.55**

1. Hurricanes
ISBN 978-1-4027-5880-5; 1-4027-5880-4; 978-1-4027-7780-6 pa; 1-4027-7780-9 pa

"This trip into the eye of the storm is enveloping in more ways than one. . . . The pages fold up, or down, or left, or right, with every turn guided by an icon familiar to anyone who lives in a storm zone: a circular blue 'Hurricane Evacuation Route' road sign. This constant motion can't help but engage. . . . The design and layout is well above par, featuring excellent cutaways of storm systems, meteorological maps, thrilling photography, and a spectacular foldout Saffir-Simpson Hurricane Scale. The text is packed with info, data, and case studies broken into digestible chunks, and boxes and sidebars . . . make this . . . very appealing." Booklist

★ **Inside** tornadoes. Sterling 2010 48p il map (Inside) $16.95; pa $9.95

Grades: 5 6 7 8   **551.55**

1. Tornadoes
ISBN 978-1-4027-5879-9; 1-4027-5879-0; 978-1-4027-7781-3 pa; 1-4027-7781-7 pa

"This visually tempting title defines and explains the storms people call twisters, gives examples of four particularly devastating ones in this country, describes tornado watchers at work, offers hands-on activity and suggests precautions for tornado safety. . . . It includes step-by-step explanatory text, striking images and helpful graphics." Kirkus

Includes glossary and bibliographical references

Fleisher, Paul

Lightning, hurricanes, and blizzards; the science of storms. Lerner Publications 2011 48p il (Weatherwise) lib bdg $29.27

Grades: 4 5 6 7   **551.55**

1. Blizzards 2. Lightning 3. Hurricanes
ISBN 978-0-8225-7536-8; 0-8225-7536-1

LC 2009044918

This describes how storms form, where they strike, and what makes them so powerful.

"Chapters are well-organized and contain clear explanations. The crisp layout contains plenty of captioned photos and diagrams, as well as sidebars that feature interesting facts and suggestions for observations readers can record in their backyards." Horn Book Guide

Includes glossary and bibliographical references

Fradin, Dennis Brindell

Tornado! the story behind these twisting, turning, spinning, and spiraling storms. by Judith Bloom Fradin & Dennis Brindell Fradin. National Geographic 2011 63p il map (National Geographic kids) $16.95; lib bdg $26.90

Grades: 4 5 6 7   **551.55**

1. Tornadoes
ISBN 978-1-4263-0779-9; 1-4263-0779-9; 978-1-4263-0780-5 lib bdg; 1-4263-0780-2 lib bdg

LC 2010042813

"Two of the four chapters describe deadly twisters in the U.S., while the others discuss the science and predictability of tornadoes. Throughout, there are first-person accounts. . . . Excellent color photos make this book a magnet for browsers, while the informative text and diagrams bring meaning to the images and provide content that students will find helpful for reports." Booklist

Includes glossary and bibliographical references

Fradin, Judith Bloom

★ **Hurricanes;** by Judy and Dennis Fradin. National Geographic 2007 48p il (Witness to disaster) $16.95; lib bdg $26.90

Grades: 4 5 6 7   **551.55**

1. Hurricanes
ISBN 978-1-4262-0111-0; 1-4262-0111-7; 978-1-4262-0112-7 lib bdg; 1-4262-0112-5 lib bdg

LC 2006-103003

This describes Hurricane Katrina, the science of hurricanes, some hurricanes of the past, and the prediction of hurricanes.

This offers "dramatic first-person quotes and an array of impressive photographs." Horn Book Guide

Includes glossary and bibliographical references

Longshore, David

Encyclopedia of hurricanes, typhoons, and cyclones; New ed; Facts on File 2008 468p il map (Facts on File science library) $75

Grades: 8 9 10 11 12 Adult   **551.55**

1. Reference books 2. Cyclones -- Encyclopedias 3. Typhoons -- Encyclopedias 4. Hurricanes --

Encyclopedias
ISBN 978-0-8160-6295-9; 0-8160-6295-1

LC 2007-32336

First published 1998

This encyclopedia describes named hurricanes, ty-phoons and cyclones, explains meteorological terms and instruments, and includes biographical data, a chronology, and a list of hurricane safety procedures.

"This is an excellent basic reference work that belongs in all school, public, and academic libraries." Sci Books Films

Includes bibliographical references

Markovics, Joyce L.
  Blitzed by a blizzard! by Joyce Markovics; con-sultant, Daphne Thompson. Bearport Pub. 2010 32p il map (Disaster survivors) lib bdg $25.27

Grades: 4 5 6 7   551.55
  1. Blizzards
  ISBN 978-1-936087-54-9 lib bdg; 1-936087-54-5 lib bdg

LC 2009-36960

"Captivating photos and illustrations and sidebars pres-ent interesting facts or brief anecdotes. . . . [This] should be purchased for all school and public libraries as . . . [it gives] a new perspective on the topic." Libr Media Connect

"Introduces blizzards, describing how they are formed and become hazardous, the experiences of actual survivors who became trapped in a storm, and some of the well known blizzards of the past." Publisher's note

Includes glossary and bibliographical references

Miller, Ron
  Chasing the storm; tornadoes, meteorology, and weather watching. by Ron Miller. Twenty-First Cen-tury Books 2014 64 p. color illustrations (lib. bdg. : alk. paper) $33.26

Grades: 6 7 8   551.55
  1. Storm chasers 2. Tornadoes
  ISBN 1467712841; 9781467712842

LC 2013009291

This book "offers a window into the world of scientists and lay enthusiasts who follow violent storms, particularly tornadoes." Author Ron Miller "explains how tornadoes are formed, discusses climate change and its probable connec-tion to the increase in extreme weather events, describes the work of meteorologists and others who watch the weather . . . and concludes by suggesting ways readers can prepare to become storm chasers themselves." (Kirkus Reviews)

"This pleasing book on storm chasers is packed with in-formation. Supported by colorful visuals and succinct expla-nations, the book takes a multimedia approach to presenting the phenomena of storms and the people who chase them. Hurricanes, tornadoes, and weather in general, are some of the topics covered, as well as tips on meteorology as a ca-reer. Included is a hands-on experience to build a weather station. The reading level is rigorous but not inaccessible to struggling readers, as comprehension is aided by the graphs and illustrations." Lib Med Con

Includes bibliographical references and index

Prokos, Anna
  Tornadoes; by Anna Prokos. Gareth Stevens Pub. 2009 48p il map (The ultimate 10. Natural disasters) lib bdg $31

Grades: 5 6 7 8   551.55
  1. Tornadoes
  ISBN 978-0-8368-9153-9 lib bdg; 0-8368-9153-8 lib bdg

LC 2008-18949

Tornadoes "are described, while color photos illustrate the resulting damage, conveying a significant part of the in-formation through their captions. . . . Explanations of weath-er terms . . . are included; additional facts are boxed off from the text; and preparation/safety tips are appended. . . . An especially useful book." SLJ

Includes glossary and bibliographical references

Royston, Angela
  Hurricanes!   Marshall Cavendish Benchmark 2010 32p il map (Eyewitness disaster) lib bdg $28.50

Grades: 4 5 6   551.55
  1. Hurricanes
  ISBN 978-1-60870-003-5; 1-60870-003-8

LC 2010001800

Provides information about hurricanes through eyewit-ness accounts from survivors and rescue workers.

"Bold subheadings and color captions break information into readable chunks for the younger learner. Important vo-cabulary is in bold print. . . . An excellent addition to your science collection." Libr Media Connect

Includes glossary and bibliographical references

  Storms! Marshall Cavendish Benchmark 2010 32p il map (Eyewitness disaster) lib bdg $28.50

Grades: 4 5 6   551.55
  1. Storms
  ISBN 978-1-60870-004-2; 1-60870-004-6

LC 2009041697

Provides information about storms through eyewitness accounts from survivors and rescue workers.

"Bold subheadings and color captions break information into readable chunks for the younger learner. Important vo-cabulary is in bold print. . . . An excellent addition to your science collection." Libr Media Connect

Includes glossary and bibliographical references

Rudolph, Jessica
  Erased by a tornado! Bearport Pub. 2010 32p il map (Disaster survivors) lib bdg $25.27

Grades: 4 5 6 7   551.55
  1. Tornadoes
  ISBN 978-1-936087-52-5 lib bdg; 1-936087-52-9 lib bdg

LC 2009-34363

"Captivating photos and illustrations and sidebars pres-ent interesting facts or brief anecdotes. . . . [This] should be purchased for all school and public libraries as . . . [it gives] a new perspective on the topic." Libr Media Connect

"Introduces tornadoes, describing how they are formed, where they occur, and how to stay safe when a storm hits, along with stories of survivors who were caught in famous tornadoes of the past." Publisher's note

Includes glossary and bibliographical references

Ryback, Carol

Hurricanes; by Carol Ryback and Jayne Keedle. Gareth Stevens Pub. 2009 48p il map (The ultimate 10. Natural disasters) lib bdg $31

Grades: 5 6 7 8 **551.55**

1. Hurricanes

ISBN 978-0-8368-9152-2 lib bdg; 0-8368-9152-X lib bdg

LC 2008-24628

Hurricanes "are described, while color photos illustrate the resulting damage, conveying a significant part of the information through their captions. . . . Explanations of weather terms . . . are included; additional facts are boxed off from the text; and preparation/safety tips are appended. . . . An especially useful book." SLJ

Includes glossary and bibliographical references

Silverstein, Alvin

Hurricanes; the science behind killer storms. [by] Alvin Silverstein, Virginia Silverstein, and Laura Silverstein Nunn. Enslow Publishers 2009 48p il map (The science behind natural disasters) lib bdg $23.93

Grades: 4 5 6 **551.55**

1. Hurricanes

ISBN 978-0-7660-2971-2 lib bdg; 0-7660-2971-9 lib bdg

LC 2008-26264

"Scientific explanations are accompanied by plentiful color diagrams that will help students to grasp causes and effects. . . . Photos . . . are effective, and are sometimes turned into helpful, lively diagrams by the addition of such features as wind-direction arrows." SLJ

Includes glossary and bibliographical references

Tornadoes; the science behind terrible twisters. [by] Alvin Silverstein, Virginia Silverstein, and Laura Silverstein Nunn. Enslow Publishers 2009 48p il map (The science behind natural disasters) lib bdg $23.93

Grades: 4 5 6 **551.55**

1. Tornadoes

ISBN 978-0-7660-2976-7 lib bdg; 0-7660-2976-X lib bdg

LC 2008-29635

"Scientific explanations are accompanied by plentiful color diagrams that will help students to grasp causes and effects. . . . Photos . . . are effective, and are sometimes turned into helpful, lively diagrams by the addition of such features as wind-direction arrows." SLJ

Includes glossary and bibliographical references

Stewart, Mark

Blizzards and winter storms. Gareth Stevens Pub. 2009 48p il map (The ultimate 10. Natural disasters) lib bdg $31

Grades: 5 6 7 8 **551.55**

1. Storms 2. Blizzards

ISBN 978-0-8368-9150-8 lib bdg; 0-8368-9150-3 lib bdg

LC 2008-28230

Blizzards and winter storms "are described, while color photos illustrate the resulting damage, conveying a significant part of the information through their captions. . . . An especially useful book." SLJ

Includes glossary and bibliographical references

Treaster, Joseph B.

★ Hurricane force; in the path of America's deadliest storms. Kingfisher 2007 128p il map $16.95

Grades: 4 5 6 7 8 **551.55**

1. Storms 2. Hurricanes

ISBN 978-0-7534-6086-3

LC 2006-22517

Describes how violent storms and hurricanes are formed and notes some of history's greatest storms to hit the U.S. such as Hurricane Katrina.

This is a "gripping photo-essay. . . . There are lots of full-color photographs that bring close the high winds and surging seas of hurricanes, the shattered homes, and pictures of people rescued or lost. The extensive back matter is an integral part of the book." Booklist

Includes bibliographical references

551.56 Atmospheric electricity and optics

Person, Stephen

Struck by lightning! Bearport Pub. 2010 32p il map (Disaster survivors) lib bdg $25.27

Grades: 4 5 6 7 **551.56**

1. Lightning

ISBN 978-1-936087-47-1 lib bdg; 1-936087-47-2 lib bdg

"Introduces lightning, discussing how it is formed and where it tends to strike, and describing some of the experiences of survivors who have been hit by lightning." Publisher's note

Includes glossary and bibliographical references

Stewart, Melissa

★ Inside lightning; illustrations by Cynthia Shaw. Sterling 2011 48p il (Inside . . .) $16.95

Grades: 5 6 7 8 **551.56**

1. Lightning

ISBN 978-1-4027-5878-2; 1-4027-5878-2

This book about lightning "explores its topic in an engaging way, and the many illustrations work well with adjacent text and captions. . . . The [book's] varied page layouts and attractive and the quality of photos, computer-generated images, original illustrations, and charts is . . . excellent. . . . Featuring a step-by-step, illustrated explanation of lightning formation as well as comments from people who have had close encounters with the phenomenon, Inside Lightning provides a vivid and unusually informative introduction to the subject." Booklist

Includes bibliographical references

551.6　Climatology and weather

Aitken, Stephen

Ecosystems at risk; Stephen Aitken. Marshall Cavendish Benchmark 2013 63 p. (Climate crisis) (print) $31.36

Grades: 4 5 6 7　　　　　　　　　　　　**551.6**
1. Ecology 2. Climate change 3. Biodiversity conservation 4. Climatic changes 5. Climatic changes -- Environmental aspects
ISBN 1608704637; 9781608704637; 9781608706341
　　　　　　　　　　　　　　　　LC 2011025243

In this book, by Stephen Aitken, "readers are introduced to topics relating to climatology, thermal expansion, and biodiversity. . . . The case studies . . . provide a global perspective on the ecological concepts being presented. In addition, teachers may find the book helpful in meeting several Common Core literacy standards. . . .The book concludes with . . . ways that individuals can take action to prevent species extinctions, followed by a glossary of conservation-related terms." (Science & Children)

"These sobering overviews present current observable results of climate change and offer scientific predictions about its future effects on the Earth's ecosystems and inhabitants...Suggested websites from educational and action-oriented organizations offer more options. These books should be considered to update collections on this important topic." SLJ

Includes bibliographical references and index
Other titles include:
Animal Life
People
Ocean Life
Plants and Insects

Arnold, Caroline

El Nino; stormy weather for people and wildlife. by Caroline Arnold. Clarion Bks 1998 48 p. col. ill. (reinforced) $16.00; (paperback) $5.95

Grades: 4 5 6 7　　　　　　　　　　　　**551.6**
1. Climate 2. El Nino Current
ISBN 0395776023; 0618551107; 9780618551101
　　　　　　　　　　　　　　　　LC 98004826

In this book, Caroline Arnold "explains how the warm current along the Peruvian coast can have a devastating impact on weather across the globe. Photographs of locations from California to Botswana to India document the effects on animals and plants and the increase in floods and hurricanes. Diagrams illustrate El Niño's formation, and a chart shows the recurring pattern in the past half century as well as the occurrence of its 'twin,' La Niña." (School Library Journal)

Includes bibliographical references (p. 45) and index.

Bailey, Gerry

Changing climate. Gareth Stevens Pub. 2011 48p il map (Planet SOS) lib bdg $31.95; pa $14.05

Grades: 4 5 6　　　　　　　　　　　　　**551.6**
1. Climate -- Environmental aspects
ISBN 978-1-4339-4962-3 lib bdg; 1-4339-4962-8 lib bdg; 978-1-4339-4963-0 pa; 1-4339-4963-6 pa
　　　　　　　　　　　　　　　　LC 2010032885

This "well-designed [book presents changing climate] . . . and how [it affects] human beings. With information about water supplies and melting ice and their impact on ecosystems, the discussion . . . of global water levels is especially enlightening. . . . The many large, colorful photos will engage readers and assist them in understanding the important concepts introduced." SLJ

Includes glossary

Baker, Stuart

In temperate zones. Marshall Cavendish Benchmark 2009 32p il map (Climate change) lib bdg $19.95

Grades: 5 6 7 8　　　　　　　　　　　　**551.6**
1. Forest ecology 2. Greenhouse effect
ISBN 978-0-7614-4441-1 lib bdg; 0-7614-4441-6 lib bdg
　　　　　　　　　　　　　　　　LC 2009-5769

The book about climate change in the temperate zones "is perfectly organized for students. . . . Unique layout features serve as signposts and will help focus readers' attention. . . . [The book] features an outstanding chart of possible effects of global warming on the area in question, listing 'Possible Event', 'Predicted Result', and 'Impact' in short, bulleted statements." SLJ

Includes glossary

Christie, Peter

The **curse** of Akkad; climate upheavals that rocked human history. Annick Press 2008 144p il map $19.95; pa $11.95

Grades: 6 7 8 9　　　　　　　　　　　　**551.6**
1. Climate 2. World history
ISBN 978-1-55451-119-8; 1-55451-119-4; 978-1-55451-118-1 pa; 1-55451-118-6 pa

"Christie discusses the ways in which environmental conditions have shaped human history. The chapters, each discussing a different aspect of climate change, are arranged in loose chronological order. Every section opens with a fictionalized account featuring either an imagined or a real historical figure. The author then explains how climate change caused the events to occur. . . . The book is well researched. . . . The text is readable." SLJ

Includes bibliographical references

Desonie, Dana

Climate; causes and effects of climate change. Chelsea House 2008 199p il map (Our fragile planet) $35

Grades: 7 8 9 10　　　　　　　　　　　**551.6**
1. Greenhouse effect 2. Climate -- Environmental aspects
ISBN 978-0-8160-6214-0; 0-8160-6214-5
　　　　　　　　　　　　　　　　LC 2007-27825

"Discusses how human-related activities are contributing to the warming of the Earth's climate, describes the effects of climate change on people and the environment, and outlines measures that can be taken to help manage the problem." Publisher's note

Includes glossary and bibliographical references

Evans, Bill

It's raining fish and spiders; by Bill Evans. Forge 2012 xiv, 223 p.p col. ill. (paperback) $18.99

Grades: 5 6 7 8   **551.6**
   1. Extreme weather 2. Weather forecasting 3. Weather 4. Severe storms
   ISBN 0765321327; 9780765321329
                       LC 2011278417

This book offers "information, lists, and accounts of personal experiences involving extreme weather by meteorologist and TV personality [Bill] Evans. Included are sections on tornadoes, hurricanes, and blizzards, with a good amount of information on each and . . . photos and diagrams sprinkled throughout." (Booklist)

Includes bibliographical references (p.221-222)

Flannery, Tim F.

★ We are the weather makers; the history of climate change. [by] Tim Flannery; adapted by Sally M. Walker. Candlewick Press 2009 303p il map $17.99

Grades: 7 8 9 10   **551.6**
   1. Greenhouse effect 2. Climate -- Environmental aspects
   ISBN 978-0-7636-3656-2; 0-7636-3656-8
                       LC 2008-939840

An adaptation of The weather makers, published 2005 for adults by Atlantic Monthly Press

"Arguing that climate change and global warming affect us all and that we can be part of the solution, this comprehensive look at the issue includes a clear explanation of the mechanism of the carbon cycle, the role of greenhouse gases on Earth, historical instances of climate change and their causes, descriptions of effects on a variety of habitats, future scenarios and suggestions—both personal and global—about what might be done. . . . A copy belongs in every middle and high-school library." Kirkus

Includes bibliographical references

Gardner, Robert

Weather science fair projects; revised and expanded using the scientific method. Enslow Publishers 2010 160p il (Earth science projects using the scientific method) lib bdg $34.60

Grades: 7 8 9 10   **551.6**
   1. Weather 2. Science projects 3. Science -- Experiments
   ISBN 978-0-7660-3424-2 lib bdg; 0-7660-3424-0 lib bdg

First published 2005 with title: Weather science fair projects using sunlight, rainbows, ice cubes, and more

"Each volume begins with an overview of the scientific method and safety, then presents a collection of activities encouraging readers to explore central concepts in the featured fields. The activities include step-by-step instructions and helpful color diagrams, interspersed with extended coverage of scientific ideas. The "Results" sections ask questions rather than giving away the answers." (Horn Book)

Includes bibliographical references

George, Charles

Climate change research; [by] Charles George and Linda George. ReferencePoint Press 2010 96p il (Inside science) lib bdg $26.95

Grades: 7 8 9 10 11 12   **551.6**
   1. Climate -- Environmental aspects
   ISBN 978-1-60152-128-6; 1-60152-128-6
                       LC 2009-53704

"This title examines the science behind climate change research in the following chapters: What is Climate Change?; Reading Climate Change in the Earth; Temperature and Precipitation; Climate Models; and Climate Technology of the Future." Publisher's note

Includes bibliographical references

Hartman, Eve

Climate change; [by] Eve Hartman and Wendy Meshbesher. Raintree 2010 48p il map (Sci-hi: Earth and space science) lib bdg $31.43; pa $8.99

Grades: 4 5 6 7   **551.6**
   1. Greenhouse effect 2. Climate -- Environmental aspects
   ISBN 978-1-4109-3352-2 lib bdg; 1-4109-3352-0 lib bdg; 978-1-4109-3362-1 pa; 1-4109-3362-8 pa
                       LC 2009-3538

Examine the causes of climate change, and how scientists gather data about global warming. Learn about the different ways people and nations are combating climate change, and how people and animals adapt to a new climate.

"Multiple colorful sidebars and large and small diagrams and photographs will help students to grasp the fundamentals being discussed, and the easy but interesting science experiments will act as further reinforcements." SLJ

Includes glossary and bibliographical references

Johnson, Rebecca L.

Investigating climate change; scientists' search for answers in a warming world. by Rebecca L. Johnson. Twenty-First Century Books 2008 111p il map (Discovery) lib bdg $30.60

Grades: 7 8 9 10   **551.6**
   1. Greenhouse effect 2. Climate -- Environmental aspects
   ISBN 978-0-8225-6792-9; 0-8225-6792-X
                       LC 2007-38566

This "presents contemporary scientific research into the causes of climate change. . . . Johnson . . . lays out complex scientific data and theories in an engaging, straightforward narrative that will not overwhelm readers. Complementing the text are numerous color diagrams, graphs, maps, and photographs." Booklist

Includes bibliographical references

Nardo, Don

Climate change. Morgan Reynolds Pub. 2009 112p il (Extreme threats) lib bdg $28.95

Grades: 7 8 9 10   **551.6**
   1. Greenhouse effect 2. Climate -- Environmental aspects
   ISBN 978-1-59935-119-3; 1-59935-119-6
                       LC 2009-25704

This book about climate change has "black-and-white and color photographs on almost every page. . . . Frequent sidebars, covering as much as a spread, discuss peripheral and often unusual information. The conclusion . . . explains what scientists are doing, or what they anticipate doing, to ameliorate the threat." SLJ

Includes glossary and bibliographical references

Parker, Steve, 1952-

Climate. QEB Pub. 2010 32p il (QEB changes in . . .) lib bdg $28.50

Grades: 3 4 5 6   **551.6**

1. Climate

ISBN 978-1-59566-776-2 lib bdg; 1-59566-776-8 lib bdg

LC 2008-56068

"The information is presented in brief paragraphs and sidebars. Suggestions for kids to help improve the planet are sprinkled throughout. . . . Students will enjoy this appealing layout and the information can spark further research on the topic[s]. . . . Either digitally or on paper, students could make fantastic presentations using a similar design." Libr Media Connect

Includes glossary

Simpson, Kathleen

★ **Extreme** weather; science tackles global warming and climate change. by Kathleen Simpson; Jonathan D.W. Kahl, consultant. National Geographic 2008 64p il map (National Geographic investigates) $17.95; lib bdg $27.90

Grades: 4 5 6 7   **551.6**

1. Greenhouse effect 2. Climate -- Environmental aspects

ISBN 978-1-4263-0359-3; 1-4263-0359-9; 978-1-4263-0281-7 lib bdg; 1-4263-0281-9 lib bdg

This "is a well-written and engaging book. . . . Excellent descriptions of how and why these various weather patterns occur are presented. The book includes dramatic photographs and clear diagrams." Sci Books Films

Includes glossary and bibliographical references

551.609   History, geographic treatment, biography

Christie, Peter

50 climate questions; a blizzard of blistering facts. Peter Christie ; illustrated by Ross Kinnaird. Annick Press 2012 117 p. ill. (50 Questions) (paperback) $14.95; (hardcover) $22.95; (ebook) $10.99

Grades: 4 5 6 7   **551.609**

1. Climate 2. Climate change 3. Climate -- History

ISBN 155451374X; 9781554513741; 9781554513758; 9781554515165

This book by Peter Christie presents a "survey of the effects of climate through history and prehistory." (Kirkus Reviews) "Topics include global warming's effect on the Arctic . . . and how a cooling climate 2.5 million years ago forced early humans to diversify their diets. Christie also provides insight into weather events throughout history --

for example, how weather change contributed to civil unrest that spawned the French Revolution." (Publishers Weekly)

551.63   Weather forecasting and forecasts, reporting and reports

Fleisher, Paul

Doppler radar, satellites, and computer models; the science of weather forecasting. Lerner Publications 2010 48p il map (Weatherwise) lib bdg $29.27

Grades: 4 5 6   **551.63**

1. Weather forecasting

ISBN 978-0-8225-7535-1; 0-8225-7535-3

LC 2009-44919

This describes how scientists predict the weather, the tools and instruments that help them make forecasts, and how far in advance can they make good predictions.

"Chapters are well-organized and contain clear explanations. The crisp layout contains plenty of captioned photos and diagrams, as well as sidebars that feature interesting facts and suggestions for observations readers can record in their backyards." Horn Book Guide

Includes glossary and bibliographical references

551.7   Historical geology

Gallant, Roy A.

History; journey through time. Benchmark Bks. 2002 80p il (Earthworks) lib bdg $19.95

Grades: 5 6 7 8   **551.7**

1. Evolution 2. Stratigraphic geology

ISBN 0-7614-1367-7

LC 2001-43253

An overview of the history of the Earth, the life that evolved on it, and known periods of mass extinctions, from the planet's origin to the present

Includes glossary and bibliographical references

552   Petrology

Davis, Barbara J.

Minerals, rocks, and soil. Raintree 2010 48p il map (Sci-hi: Earth and space science) lib bdg $31.43; pa $8.99

Grades: 4 5 6 7   **552**

1. Rocks 2. Minerals 3. Petrology

ISBN 978-1-4109-3347-8 lib bdg; 1-4109-3347-4 lib bdg; 978-1-4109-3357-7 pa; 1-4109-3357-1 pa

LC 2009-13459

"Multiple colorful sidebars and large and small diagrams and photographs will help students to grasp the fundamentals being discussed, and the easy but interesting science experiments will act as further reinforcements." SLJ

This title "shows . . . how minerals, soil, and rocks form." Publisher's note

Includes glossary and bibliographical references

Green, Dan

Rocks and minerals; a gem of a read! by Dan Green and Simon Basher; illustrated by Simon Basher. Kingfisher 2009 128p il pa $8.99

Grades: 5 6 7 8 **552**

1. Rocks 2. Minerals

ISBN 978-0-7534-6314-7 pa; 0-7534-6314-8 pa

This "presents a portrait gallery of 56 rocks and minerals (plus four kinds of fossils) composed of smiling, round-headed, usually peanut-shaped cartoon figures wearing or bearing distinctive identifiers. . . . The entries make light-hearted but unexpectedly meaty reading." Booklist

Hynes, Margaret

Rocks & fossils; foreword by Jack Horner. Kingfisher 2006 63p il (Kingfisher knowledge) $12.95

Grades: 5 6 7 8 **552**

1. Rocks 2. Fossils

ISBN 978-0-7534-5974-4; 0-7534-5974-4

LC 2005-23897

This is a "lavishly illustrated book. . . . The well-written text is pithy and comprehensible." Voice Youth Advocates

This covers "the history of rock, . . . the minerals that make them, and . . . their different uses, from building materials to pigments for paints and dyes. The formation of fossils is also explained." Publisher's note

Includes glossary and bibliographical references

Rocks and minerals; facts at your fingertips. DK Pub. 2012 156 p. col. ill., map (Pocket genius) (hardcover) $7.99

Grades: 5 6 7 8 **552**

1. Rocks 2. Minerals

ISBN 0756692857; 9780756692858

LC 2011277725

This book, part of the "Pocket Genius" encyclopedia series, "profiles nearly 200 types of rocks and minerals from volcanic rocks and granite to sparkling diamonds and explosive sulfur, and tells what they are made of, how they are formed and what they are used for." It "offers a . . . catalog-style presentation, which clearly lays out individual subcategories." (Publisher's note)

Smithsonian Institution

Extreme rocks & minerals! Q & A. Collins 2007 47p il $17.99; pa $6.99

Grades: 4 5 6 **552**

1. Rocks 2. Minerals

ISBN 978-0-06-089982-0; 0-06-089982-4; 978-0-06-089981-3 pa; 0-06-089981-6 pa

LC 2007001760

This describes types of rocks and minerals, how they are formed, and how people use them.

"It's hard to beat this title for a clear, accurate, and appealing survey. Illustrations are key to this subject, and the range of crisp photos is excellent." SLJ

Includes bibliographical references

Symes, R. F.

Rocks & minerals; written by R.F. Symes and the staff of the Natural History Museum, London ; special photography by Colin Keates and Andreas Einsiedel. Revised ed. DK Pub. 2008 72 p. ill. (some col.) (hardcover: boxed; package) $29.99; (hardcover) $16.99

Grades: 5 6 7 8 **552**

1. Gems 2. Rocks 3. Geology

ISBN 9780756631321 out of print; 0756637775; 9780756637774

LC 2009499083

This book is a guide to "rocks, fossils, minerals, precious metals, crystals, jewels and gemstones." Readers "see rocks that have come from outer space, stalactites as old as dinosaurs, the strange and beautiful shapes of natural crystals and priceless nuggets of gold, silver and platinum. Learn what the Earth is made of and how its rocks were formed, how early humans made the first flint tools and how diamonds and precious stones are cut, polished, and made into jewelry." (Publisher's note)

Trueit, Trudi Strain

Rocks, gems, and minerals. Watts 2003 63p il (Watts library) $24; pa $8.95

Grades: 4 5 6 7 **552**

1. Rocks 2. Minerals 3. Precious stones

ISBN 0-531-12195-X; 0-531-16241-9 pa

LC 2001-7222

This includes "attention-grabbing photography, excellent charts and diagrams, short articles with or without photographs, and vocabulary terms that appear in bold and are explained in context." Sci Books Films

Includes glossary and bibliographical references

553.2 Carbonaceous materials

Marcovitz, Hal

What is the future of fossil fuels? by Hal Marcovitz. ReferencePoint Press, Inc. 2013 80 p. color illustrations, maps (Future of renewable energy series) (hardback) $28.95

Grades: 6 7 8 9 **553.2**

1. Fossil fuels

ISBN 1601526121; 9781601526120

LC 2013029017

This book, by Hal Marcovitz, "examines the future of fossil fuels. Topics include: Are Fossil Fuels Affordable? Can Fossil Fuels Be Compatible with the Environment? Can Alternative Energy Take the Place of Fossil Fuels? Should the Government Continue to Support Fossil Fuels as an Energy?" (Publisher's note)

"Well written and understandable, the authors use a wide variety of source material to present each side fairly and completely. The question/answer format of the chapters breaks the topics into simplified arguments that can easily be absorbed. The author's style is rather dispassionate which elevates the quality of the works by allowing reader to come to their own conclusions." VOYA

Includes bibliographical references and index

553.7   Water

Casper, Julie Kerr

Water and atmosphere; the lifeblood of natural systems. Chelsea House 2007 207p il map (Natural resources) $39.50

Grades: 8 9 10 11 12   **553.7**

1. Atmosphere 2. Water supply

ISBN 978-0-8160-6359-8; 0-8160-6359-1

LC 2007-261

This covers such topics as the roles of water and atmospheric resources in exploration and trade; climate change and global warming; renewable and nonrenewable resources; surface and ground water, aquifers, and other natural water reservoirs; management and environmental issues; effects on endangered species; future issues and the importance of public education; and marine exploration.

Includes bibliographical references

Woodward, John

Water; written by John Woodward. DK Pub. 2009 72p il (DK eyewitness books) $16.99; lib bdg $19.99

Grades: 4 5 6 7   **553.7**

1. Water

ISBN 978-0-7566-4537-3; 0-7566-4537-9; 978-0-7566-4538-0 lib bdg; 0-7566-4538-7 lib bdg

Takes a look at the role of water in our bodies, our cultures, and our world.

557   Earth sciences of North America

Collier, Michael

★ **Over** the mountains; an aerial view of geology. foreword by John S. Shelton. Mikaya Press 2007 un il map (An aerial view of geology) $29.95

Grades: 8 9 10 11 12   **557**

1. Mountains 2. Aerial photography 3. Geology -- North America

ISBN 1-931414-18-1; 978-1-931414-18-0

LC 2006-47151

The author "expresses his passion for geology through awe-inspiring aerial photographs that reveal how mountains were formed and modified across the eons of time. . . . The four sections of this book explore what mountains are, why some are peaked and others rounded, and why they are often strung together in ranges. . . . Collier's love for the land is contagious, and his flying field trips over the mountains are thrilling." Voice Youth Advocates

Includes bibliographical references

560   Paleontology

Bradley, Timothy J.

★ **Paleo** bugs; survival of the creepiest. written and illustrated by Timothy J. Bradley. Chronicle Books 2008 44p il $15.99

Grades: 4 5 6 7   **560**

1. Fossils 2. Insects 3. Prehistoric animals

ISBN 978-0-8118-6022-2; 0-8118-6022-1

LC 2007-18174

This offers an "eye-widening gallery of extinct arthropods, from the mayfly-like heptagenia to a seven-foot-long arthropleura. . . . Bradley decks out each of his painted figures in bright hues, poses them in natural settings . . . and sets them aside a human hand or body in silhouette to suggest scale. . . . Readers will . . . pore over the pictures and come away knowing more about both these extinct animals and their modern descendants." Booklist

Includes glossary and bibliographical references

Holmes, Thom

★ **Dinosaur** scientist; careers digging up the past. Enslow Publishers 2009 128p il (Wild science careers) lib bdg $31.93

Grades: 5 6 7 8   **560**

1. Fossils 2. Vocational guidance

ISBN 978-0-7660-3053-4 lib bdg; 0-7660-3053-9 lib bdg

LC 2008-19634

"A great read for middle school students, the book provides vocational guidance while introducing the reader to a challenging, but very exciting, career as a paleontologist." Sci Books Films

Includes glossary and bibliographical references

Sabuda, Robert

★ **Sharks** and other sea monsters; [by] Robert Sabuda & Matthew Reinhart. Candlewick Press 2006 un il (Encyclopedia prehistorica) $27.99

Grades: 3 4 5 6 7   **560**

1. Prehistoric animals 2. Pop-up books

ISBN 0-7636-2229-X

LC 2005-44866

This pop-up book introduces such prehistoric creatures as giant sharks, sea scorpions, and squids

"Gatefolds and inset minibooks expand the capacity of the book's seven spreads. . . . The sheer wonder generated by the collaborators' dimensional sleight-of-hand will more than justify purchase." Booklist

Taylor, Paul D.

★ **Fossil**; written by Paul D. Taylor. rev ed; DK Pub. 2004 72p il map (DK eyewitness books) $15.99; lib bdg $19.99

Grades: 4 5 6 7   **560**

1. Fossils

ISBN 0-7566-0682-9; 0-7566-0681-0 lib bdg

First published 1990 by Knopf

This book describes different types of fossils, from algae to birds and mammals

560.973   Paleontology – United States -- History

Johnson, Rebecca L.

Battle of the dinosaur bones; Othniel Charles Marsh vs. Edward Drinker Cope. by Rebecca L.

Johnson. Twenty-First Century Books 2013 64 p. ill., plates, charts (Scientific rivalries and scandals) (library) $33.27

Grades: 5 6 7 8 **560.973**

1. Paleontology -- History 2. Paleontologists -- United States -- Biography 3. Paleontology -- United States -- History -- 19th century

ISBN 0761354883; 9780761354888

LC 2011045648

"This entry in the Scientific Rivalries and Scandals series focuses on the bitter antagonism between two pioneering nineteenth-century paleontologists. Marsh and Cope. Their contentious rivalry to discover the largest and most unusual dinosaur fossils of the American West became know as the Bone Wars and was at the forefront of American science for decades. The moral of the story is clear, revealing how rivalry can be positive and detrimental." (Booklist)

Includes bibliographical references (p. 58 - 60) and index.

567 Fossil cold-blooded vertebrates

Holmes, Thom

The **first** vertebrates; oceans of the Paleozoic era. Chelsea House 2008 188p il (The prehistoric Earth) lib bdg $35

Grades: 7 8 9 10 **567**

1. Fossils 2. Vertebrates

ISBN 978-0-8160-5958-4; 0-8160-5958-6

LC 2007-45329

Describes the first instances of vertebrate life in the oceans of the Paleozoic Era, tracing the development of early fish from jawless species to sharks and bony fish.

This "is a comprehensive, well-written, and easily readable text. . . . The chapters are well-organized." Sci Books Films

Includes glossary and bibliographical references

567.9 Reptiles

Abramson, Andra Serlin

Inside dinosaurs; by Andra Serlin Abramson, Jason Brougham, and Carl Mehling; illustrated by Jason Brougham. Sterling Innovation 2010 48p il (Inside) $16.95; pa $9.95

Grades: 5 6 7 8 **567.9**

1. Birds 2. Fossils 3. Dinosaurs

ISBN 978-1-4027-7074-6; 1-4027-7074-X; 978-1-4027-7778-3 pa; 1-4027-7778-7 pa

LC 2010010122

"This pleasantly specific overview covers not only the dinosaurs' distinctive physical characteristics (the authors include modern birds in the group), but the work of paleontologists in both field and lab, the types and typical life cycles of what are carefully dubbed 'non-avian' dinos within each 'clade,' the mass extinction of 65,000,000 years ago . . . and how new discoveries have refined theories about wings and feathers. . . . The art mixes small color photos with soft-edged paint-and-pencil reconstructions of bones, individual

live portraits and prehistoric herds in natural settings. . . . [This is an] above average series entry." Kirkus

Includes glossary and bibliographical references

Bacchin, Matteo

Giant vs. giant; Argentinosaurus and Giganotosaurus. drawings and story, Matteo Bacchin; essays, Marco Signore; translated from the Italian by Marguerite Shore. Abbeville Kids 2010 61p il (Dinosaurs) $15.95

Grades: 4 5 6 7 **567.9**

1. Fossils 2. Dinosaurs

ISBN 978-0-7892-1013-5; 0-7892-1013-4

LC 2010-21120

This "book is split into two sections: the first contains parts . . . of a serial graphic novel about dinosaur survival, complete with dramatic narrative and grisly, to-the-death battles. The second half is a higher-level traditional nonfiction text with color photographs and diagrams, focusing on the science behind the comics. The unique format is generally engaging and effective." Horn Book Guide

T. rex and the great extinction; drawings and story, Matteo Bacchin; essays, Marco Signore; translated from the Italian by Marguerite Shore. Abbeville Kids 2010 il (Dinosaurs) $15.95

Grades: 4 5 6 7 **567.9**

1. Fossils 2. Dinosaurs

ISBN 9780789210142; 0789210142

LC 2010021123

This "book is split into two sections: the first contains parts . . . of a serial graphic novel about dinosaur survival, complete with dramatic narrative and grisly, to-the-death battles. The second half is a higher-level traditional nonfiction text with color photographs and diagrams, focusing on the science behind the comics. The unique format is generally engaging and effective." Horn Book Guide

Barrett, Paul M.

★ **National** Geographic dinosaurs; illustrated by Raul Martin; introduction by Kevin Padian. National Geographic Soc. 2001 192p il $29.95

Grades: 6 7 8 9 **567.9**

1. Dinosaurs

ISBN 0-7922-8224-8

LC 00-45263

"Clearly distinguishing fact from theory, this book provides an exciting guide to the life and times of the dinosaurs." Sci Child

Includes glossary

Berkowitz, Jacob

★ **Jurassic** poop; what dinosaurs (and others) left behind. written by Jacob Berkowitz; illustrated by Steve Mack. Kids Can Press 2006 40p il $14.95; pa $7.95

Grades: 4 5 6 7 **567.9**

1. Feces 2. Fossils 3. Dinosaurs

ISBN 978-1-55337-860-0; 1-55337-860-1; 978-1-55337-867-9 pa; 1-55337-867-9 pa

This describes fossilized feces, or coprolites, and what we can learn from them

"Berkowitz' style is goofy and lighthearted, but there's plenty of real information. . . . The browsable format combines cartoony digital art, photographs . . . and design elements such a spiky borders and background shading." Bull Cent Child Books

Includes glossary

Bonner, Hannah

When dinos dawned, mammals got munched, and Pterosaurs took flight; a cartoon pre-history of life in the Triassic. Hannah Bonner. National Geographic Children's Books 2012 44 p. col. ill., col. maps (hardback) $25.90

Grades: 3 4 5 6 7   567.9
1. Dinosaurs 2. Triassic Period 3. Graphic novels 4. Paleontology -- Triassic -- Comic books, strips, etc.
ISBN 9781426308628; 9781426308635
LC 2011029212

In this book Hannah Bonner "chronicles developments in the Triassic Period, during which life got a fresh lease on the planet in the wake of the massive Permian extinction. She tracks an explosion of biological diversity as the oceans were repopulated, lush forests grew and the dominant kinds of land animals went from clumsy-looking therapsids to sleek archosaurian dinosaurs and proto-crocodiles. Early mammals are already waiting in the wings." (Kirkus Reviews)

Includes bibliographical references and index

Collard, Sneed B.

★ **Reign** of the sea dragons; illustrated by Andrew Plant. Charlesbridge 2008 61p il $17.95; pa $8.95

Grades: 5 6 7 8 9   567.9
1. Marine animals 2. Prehistoric animals
ISBN 978-1-58089-124-0; 978-1-58089-125-7 pa
LC 2007-26201

"An arresting dust jacket depicting a humongous pliosaur snapping huge toothy jaws at a small, long-necked plesiosaur is an attention-grabber, but it is the informative text that brings these real sea monsters to life. Collard follows his usual pattern of careful organization, with a readable text and up-to-date information. . . . Plant has provided five full-color paintings, but it is his numerous black-and-white drawings that lend sturdy anatomical and physical information. . . . Collard's discussion on extinction theories is cogent." SLJ

Includes glossary, bibliographical references, and websites

Dingus, Lowell

★ **Dinosaur** eggs discovered! unscrambling the clues. [by] Lowell Dingus, Luis M. Chiappe [and] Rodolfo Coria. Twenty-First Century Books 2008 112p il map (Discovery!) lib bdg $30.60

Grades: 8 9 10 11 12   567.9
1. Eggs 2. Fossils 3. Dinosaurs
ISBN 978-0-8225-6791-2 lib bdg; 0-8225-6791-1 lib bdg
LC 2006-102636

Recounts the discovery of a dinosaur nesting field containing a large number of eggs, describing the field work done to classify them, calculate the period of prehistory they came from, and identify the reasons why many of them never hatched.

This is "a valuable, unusually authoritative presentation for serious students of prehistoric life." Booklist

Includes glossary and bibliographical references

Dixon, Dougal

Plant -eating dinosaurs; by Dougal Dixon. North American ed. New Forest Press 2010 48 p. col. ill., col. maps (library) $28.50

Grades: 4 5 6 7   567.9
1. Fossils 2. Dinosaurs 3. Herbivores
ISBN 1848983336; 9781848983335
LC 2010925201

This volume "contains detailed information about dinosaurs and other prehistoric life, covering species development in chronological order. Careful links to the fossil finds that helped scientists with their explanations are found throughout. Additional text boxes cover topics from structure-function to footprints, and interpretive color illustrations and photographs further enhance the [text]." Horn Book Guide

Includes bibliographical references (p. 44-45) and index.

Prehistoric oceans. New Forest Press 2010 48p il map (Dinosaur files) lib bdg $28.50

Grades: 4 5 6 7   567.9
1. Fossils 2. Dinosaurs 3. Marine animals
ISBN 978-1-8489-8332-8; 1-8489-8332-8

This volume "contains detailed information about dinosaurs and other prehistoric life, covering species development in chronological order. Careful links to the fossil finds that helped scientists with their explanations are found throughout. Additional text boxes cover topics from structure-function to footprints, and interpretive color illustrations and photographs further enhance the [text]." Horn Book Guide

Includes glossary

Prehistoric skies. New Forest Press 2010 48p il map (Dinosaur files) lib bdg $28.50

Grades: 4 5 6 7   567.9
1. Fossils 2. Dinosaurs 3. Prehistoric animals
ISBN 978-1-8489-8331-1; 1-8489-8331-X

Discusses the physical characteristics, behavior, diet, and fossil evidence of prehistoric animals that lived in the sky.

This volume "contains detailed information about dinosaurs and other prehistoric life, covering species development in chronological order. Careful links to the fossil finds that helped scientists with their explanations are found throughout. Additional text boxes cover topics from structure-function to footprints, and interpretive color illustrations and photographs further enhance the [text]." Horn Book Guide

Includes glossary

Everhart, Michael J.

Sea monsters; prehistoric creatures of the deep. [by] Mike Everhart. National Geographic 2007 191p il map $30

Grades: 7 8 9 10 **567.9**

1. Fossils 2. Marine animals 3. Prehistoric animals

ISBN 978-1-4262-0085-4; 1-4262-0085-4

LC 2007-18671

Featuring "computer-generated images and 3D film clips—with 3D glasses—field photography by National Geographic cameramen, and much more, the book interweaves dramatic scenes of the far, far distant past; up-to-the-minute scientific profiles of nearly two dozen sea monsters; and a group portrait of the eccentric Sternberg family, Kansas-bred pioneers of marine paleontology." Publisher's note

Funston, Sylvia

★ Dino -why? the dinosaur question and answer book. updated and rev.; Maple Tree Press 2008 64p il $22.95; pa $10.95

Grades: 4 5 6 7 **567.9**

1. Dinosaurs

ISBN 978-1-897349-24-3; 1-897349-24-6; 978-1-897349-25-0 pa; 1-897349-25-4 pa

LC 2007-939082

First published 1992 by Joy Street Books with title: The dinosaur question and answer book

"This book is an excellent and highly readable introduction to dinosaurs. . . . The questions are well conceived, and the answers . . . are scientifically sound and up to date. . . . The illustrations, a few of them cartoon-like, are nicely drawn and useful." Sci Books Films

Holtz, Thomas R.

★ Dinosaurs; the most complete, up-to-date encyclopedia for dinosaur lovers of all ages. by Dr. Thomas R. Holtz, Jr.; illustrated by Luis V. Rey. Random House 2007 427p il $34.99; lib bdg $37.99

Grades: 7 8 9 10 **567.9**

1. Dinosaurs

ISBN 978-0-375-82419-7; 0-375-82419-7; 978-0-375-92419-4 lib bdg; 0-375-92419-1 lib bdg

LC 2006-102491

This "covers everything from dinosaur eggs to taxonomy and cladistics to the history of paleontology, glued together with chapters on the dinosaurs themselves. . . . The illustrations range from small photos to larger sepia-toned drawings to even larger full-color paintings. . . . This eye-catching imagination grabber will be enjoyed (on different levels) by dinophiles of all ages." SLJ

Includes glossary

Kelsey, Elin

Canadian dinosaurs; Elin Kelsey. Reprint Maple Tree Press 2009 96 p. ill. (prebind) $28.95

Grades: 4 5 6 **567.9**

1. Fossils 2. Dinosaurs

ISBN 1442060409; 9781442060401

This book offers a "history of fossil hunting north of the border, including bio-material on dino-hunters past and present, followed by a compendium of carnivores and herbivores.

. . . Illustrations, mainly in color, appear on every page. . . . The whole is rounded out with a list of dino locations, a time line, and a listing of institutions where these splendid fossils may be examined at leisure." (School Library Journal)

Lessem, Don

The ultimate dinopedia; the most complete dinosaur reference ever. illustrated by Franco Tempesta; with a foreword by Rodolfo Coria. National Geographic 2010 272p il map $24.95; lib bdg $34.90

Grades: 3 4 5 6 **567.9**

1. Dinosaurs

ISBN 978-1-4263-0164-3; 1-4263-0164-2; 978-1-4263-0165-0 lib bdg; 1-4263-0165-0 lib bdg

LC 2010-07146

In the opening chapter, Lessem "presents broad basics on [dinosaur] behavior and habitats as well as a look at major discoveries in paleontology. However, it's the later chapters, which devote two pages each to specific dinosaurs, that will hook hard-core dino lovers. . . . Tempesta's full-page illustrations appear on every spread and jump off the page, and the dynamic layout . . . is immensely appealing. . . . Lessem's comprehensive overview will satisfy the interested browser as much as the ardent dinosaur enthusiast." Booklist

Includes bibliographical references

Long, John A.

★ Dinosaurs; [by] John Long. Simon & Schuster Books for Young Readers 2007 64p il (Insiders) lib bdg $16.99

Grades: 4 5 6 7 **567.9**

1. Dinosaurs

ISBN 978-1-4169-3857-6 lib bdg; 1-4169-3857-5 lib bdg

LC 2007-61735

"Richly hued, crisp computer-generated art and 3D model imagery serve as a stunning and sophisticated graphic counterpoint to the educational text." Publ Wkly

"The first section includes paleontological periods, extinction theories, and a . . . pictorial time line tracing the first bird archaeopteryx to the earliest feathered dinosaurs. The second section contains profiles of a diverse selection of species." Booklist

Includes glossary

Feathered dinosaurs; the origin of birds. foreword by Luis M. Chiappe. Oxford University Press 2008 193p il $39.95

Grades: 7 8 9 10 **567.9**

1. Birds 2. Fossils 3. Dinosaurs

ISBN 978-0-19-537266-3; 0-19-537266-2

LC 2008-1232

A "record of feathered dinosaurs illuminates the evolutionary march from these . . . prehistoric creatures through to the first true flying birds and includes . . . text that places these feathered dinosaurs within the larger family of dinosaurs." Publisher's note

Includes bibliographical references

Malam, John

Dinosaur atlas; authors, John Malam and John Woodward; consultant Michael Benton. Dorling Kindersley 2006 96p il map $19.99

Grades: 5 6 7 8   **567.9**

1. Dinosaurs

ISBN 978-0-7566-2235-0; 0-7566-2235-2

LC 2006-285529

"The atlas is organized by continent. Each section is prefaced with a large map showing where various species are found, with a picture and a brief synopsis of each species on the facing page. . . . Each introductory map is followed by several regional maps, surveying important local fossil sites and formations. Each section provides attractive diorama snapshots for a wide range of periods and locations." Sci Books Films

Includes glossary

Manning, Phillip Lars

★ **Dinomummy**; the life, death, and discovery of Dakota, a dinosaur from Hell Creek. foreword by Tyler Lyson. Kingfisher 2007 64p il map $18.95

Grades: 4 5 6 7   **567.9**

1. Dinosaurs 2. North Dakota

ISBN 978-0-7534-6047-4; 0-7534-6047-5

LC 2007-02878

Tells about the discovery of the fossil remains of a hadrosaur in the hills of the Hell Creek Formation in North Dakota.

"The color photographs and simple text offer a detailed account of carefully unearthing the fossil and transporting it safely to the laboratory, where many tests were performed. Dinosaurs buffs and young scientists will love this book. It is a thrilling story that is part narrative, part mystery, and part science lesson." Voice Youth Advocates

McGowan, Chris

Dinosaur discovery; everything you need to be a paleontologist. illustrated by Erica Lyn Schmidt. Simon & Schuster Books for Young Readers 2011 48p il $17.99

Grades: 4 5 6 7   **567.9**

1. Fossils 2. Dinosaurs

ISBN 978-1-4169-4764-6; 1-4169-4764-7; 1416947647; 9781416947646

LC 2009044604

"In-depth facts about 13 dinosaurs are interspersed with activities that teach readers about anatomy and how paleontologists understand body structure. . . . The 27 activities and experiments illustrate the concepts presented and focus on the featured dinosaurs. By following the well-written directions as well as the picture steps, budding paleontologists will explore how a tail affects balance, discover binocular vision and learn how the two parts of a bone make them both stiff and elastic. . . . Schmidt's acrylic illustrations give life to the dinosaurs, and her scientific renderings of bones could have come straight out of an anatomy textbook. . . . A thinking, active alternative for readers who fall between adult nonfiction and all the rhyming dino fare meant for the younger set." Kirkus

Peterson, Sheryl

Pterodactyl. Creative Education 2010 48p il (Age of dinosaurs) lib bdg $34.25

Grades: 5 6 7 8   **567.9**

1. Dinosaurs

ISBN 978-1-58341-975-5 lib bdg; 1-58341-975-6 lib bdg

LC 2009025175

"Peterson nicely balances the known with conjecture. . . . The inviting design, on glossy pages, elegantly detours from the main text into details tantalizing . . . ; informative . . . ; and incredible. . . . The illustrations, from sharp diagrams to dramatic paintings to B-movie-worthy recreation scenes, add some nice flair to this solid entry." Booklist

Sloan, Christopher

Bizarre dinosaurs; some very strange creatures and why we think they got that way. [by] Christopher Sloan; with a foreword by James Clark and Cathy Forster. National Geographic 2008 31p il $16.95; lib bdg $25.90

Grades: 4 5 6 7   **567.9**

1. Dinosaurs

ISBN 978-1-4263-0330-2; 1-4263-0330-0; 978-1-4263-0331-9 lib bdg; 1-4263-0331-9 lib bdg

This "book should engage children of all ages who are fascinated by dinosaurs. . . . The illustrations are of uniformly high quality. . . . Each species gets two pages of text, including a full-page illustration; an inset with basic facts such as range, diet, and geological period in which it lived; a silhouette comparing their size with that of humans; and a paragraph of text." Sci Books Films

Thimmesh, Catherine

★ **Scaly** spotted feathered frilled; how do we know what dinosaurs really looked like? by Catherine Thimmesh. Houghton Mifflin Books for Children, Houghton Mifflin Harcourt 2013 64 p. $17.99

Grades: 4 5 6 7   **567.9**

1. Dinosaurs 2. Paleontology 3. Paleoart

ISBN 0547991347; 9780547991344

LC 2012048466

Author Catherine Thimmesh "explores the border between science and speculation in this [book about] how paleontologists . . . reconstruct prehistoric creatures from fossil evidence. . . . [She] explains how surviving evidence—including fossilized bone fragments, plant matter, bits of skin and, recently, feathers, prehistoric 'trackways' (preserved pathways of dino footprints) and similar physical features in modern animals—is assembled and interpreted by scientists." (Kirkus Reviews)

Includes bibliographical references (page 55) and index

Woodward, John

3 -D dinosaur; by John Woodward ; consultant, Darren Naish. 1st American ed. DK 2011 71 p. ill. (chiefly col.), col. maps (hardcover: interactive) $17.99

Grades: 6 7 8   **567.9**

1. Fossils 2. Dinosaurs 3. Fossils4. Dinosaurs 5.

Paleontology
ISBN 0756672155; 9780756672157

LC 2011282389

This children's book on dinosaurs by John Woodward includes "special activating boxes that indicate the presence of digital pop outs that when held up to a webcam attached to your PC, feature . . . 3D digital animation." It explores "the anatomy, diet, and behavior of dinosaurs and how paleontologists piece together the past." (Publisher's note)

Includes bibliographical references (p. [72]) and index.

Dinosaur! dinosaurs and other amazing prehistoric creatures as you've never seen them before. written by John Woodward ; consultant, Darren Naish ; illustrators, Peter Minister, Arran Lewis, Andrew Kerr, Peter Bull, Vlad Konstantinov. First American edition DK Publishing 2014 208 p. color illustraions, color maps (hardcover) $24.99
Grades: 5 6 7 8   567.9
1. Dinosaurs 2. Dinosaurs -- Pictorial works
ISBN 1465420479; 9781465420473

LC 2012287452

This book, by John Woodward, "[p]rofiles a range of dinosaur and prehistoric animal species from the Triassic, Jurassic, and Cretaceous Eras, featuring such animals as allosaurus, diplodocus, and mosasaurus." (Publisher's note)

"For those budding paleontologists and dinosaur fans willing to dig a little, there's a wealth of material on this ever-evolving subject." Booklist

DK Smithsonian Dinosaur!

567.91   Specific dinosaurs and other archosaurs

Sloan, Christopher
  Tracking Tyrannosaurs; meet T. rex's fascinating family, from tiny terrors to feathered giants. by Christopher Sloan. National Geographic 2013 48 p. (trade hard cover) $18.95
Grades: 5 6 7 8   567.91
1. Tyrannosaurus rex 2. Dinosaurs 3. Tyrannosaurus rex
ISBN 1426313748; 9781426313745; 9781426313752

LC 2013004988

This book, by Christopher Sloan, "highlights a newly discovered T. rex relative in China with a coat of downy feathers! This one-ton predator is the largest known animal to ever have walked the Earth. [Readers] meet 19 kinds of tyrannosaurs--including seven new species discovered in the last two years--that came before T. rex." (Publisher's note)

567.912   Specific dinosaurs

Dixon, Dougal
  Meat -eating dinosaurs; by Dougal Dixon. North American ed. New Forest Press 2010 47 p. col. ill., col. maps (Dinosaur files) (library) $28.50

Grades: 4 5 6 7   567.912
1. Fossils 2. Dinosaurs 3. Carnivorous animals
ISBN 9781848983342; 1848983344

LC 2010925204

This volume "contains detailed information about dinosaurs and other prehistoric life, covering species development in chronological order. Careful links to the fossil finds that helped scientists with their explanations are found throughout. Additional text boxes cover topics from structure-function to footprints, and interpretive color illustrations and photographs further enhance the [text]." Horn Book Guide

Includes bibliographical references (p. 44-45) and index.

569   Fossil mammals

Bardoe, Cheryl
  Mammoths and mastodons; titans of the Ice Age. Abrams Books for Young Readers 2010 43p il map
Grades: 4 5 6 7   569
1. Fossils 2. Mammoths 3. Mastodon 4. Mastodons
ISBN 0-8109-8413-X lib bdg; 978-0-8109-8413-4 lib bdg

LC 2009-22006

The author presents a "case study in how paleontologists examine both ancient and modern clues for insights into the diets, physical development and behavior of extinct animals. Cousins to modern elephants, mammoths and mastodons once roamed large portions of the Earth, but for reasons that are not completely understood . . . vanished relatively suddenly. Focusing particularly on . . . remnants like the 55 fossilized skeletons found near one sinkhole in South Dakota and 'Lyuba,' the well preserved 'prehistoric popsicle' discovered in 2007 in Siberia, the author presents both facts and educated guesses--while leaving it clear that there is much still to be learned." (Kirkus)

"This well-designed book opens with two boys finding a strange animal dead on the arctic tundra. Their father hikes four days to a village where the news can be spread; then scientists take away the frozen baby mammoth, the first example found intact, and study it intensively. The book intersperses accounts of the scientists' research and deductions with general information about mammoths and mastodons as well as imagined scenes taking place when they walked the earth. . . . A handsome introduction." Booklist

Includes glossary and bibliographical references

Turner, Alan
  ★ **National** Geographic prehistoric mammals; illustrated by Mauricio Antón. National Geographic 2004 192p il map $29.95; lib bdg $49.90
Grades: 5 6 7 8   569
1. Fossil mammals
ISBN 0-7922-7134-3; 0-7922-6997-7 lib bdg

LC 2004-1189

This describes the Age of Mammals and profiles over 100 prehistoric mammals, including time lines, fact boxes, distribution maps, photos of fossils, and illustrations

"Dramatic full-color pictures . . . and captions enhance the brief, informative text." SLJ

569.9   Humans and related genera

Aronson, Marc

★ The **skull** in the rock; how a scientist, a boy, and Google Earth opened a new window on human origins. by Marc Aronson and Lee Berger. National Geographic 2012 64 p. (hardcover : alk. paper) $18.95

Grades: 5 6 7 8 9 10   **569.9**

1. Human origins 2. Fossil hominids 3. Excavations (Archeology) 4. Paleoanthropology 5. Human beings -- Origin 6. Fossil hominids -- South Africa -- Witwatersrand Region 7. Human evolution -- South Africa -- Witwatersrand Region 8. Excavations (Archaeology) -- South Africa -- Witwatersrand Region

ISBN 1426310102; 9781426310102; 9781426310539

LC 2012012943

This book by Marc Aronson and Lee R. Berger tells the story of how "in 2008 [Berger]--with the help of his curious 9-year-old son--discovered two remarkably well preserved, two-million-year-old fossils . . . known as 'Australopithecus sediba'; a previously unknown species of ape-like creatures that may have been a direct ancestor of modern humans." (Publisher's note)

Includes bibliographical references and index.

Deem, James M.

★ **Bodies** from the bog. Houghton Mifflin 1998 42p il hardcover o.p. pa $5.95

Grades: 4 5 6 7   **569.9**

1. Mummies 2. Archeology 3. Prehistoric peoples

ISBN 0-395-85784-8; 0-618-35402-6 pa

LC 97-12010

Describes the discovery of bog bodies in northern Europe and the evidence which their remains reveal about themselves and the civilizations in which they lived

"The text is engaging and accessible, and the starkly dramatic photos are given dignity by the spacious and understated page design." Horn Book Guide

Includes bibliographical references

570   Biology

★ **Biology** matters! Grolier 2004 10v il set $389

Grades: 5 6 7 8 9 10   **570**

1. Biology 2. Reference books

ISBN 0-7172-5979-X

LC 2003-56942

"This set presents the fundamentals of the life sciences in a clear format. . . . Volumes contain between six and eight articles in 80 pages . . . introducing its subject, presenting a brief history, and covering many aspects of its current study and applications. . . . The text is large and easy to read, and the writing is straightforward. . . . This title . . . would be a useful addition for public and school libraries." Booklist

Green, Dan

Extreme biology; from superbugs to clones... get to the edge of science. written and illustrated by Simon Basher. Kingfisher 2013 64 p. col. ill. (hardcover) $12.99

Grades: 4 5 6 7   **570**

1. Biology

ISBN 0753470519; 9780753470510

This book written and illustrated by Simon Basher is designed to help readers "learn about the amazing research that is revolutionizing biology, from advances in medicine to genetic engineering. [Readers will] meet the world's toughest bacterium and a biologically immortal flatworm whilst learning about epigenetics, superbugs, nanomedicine and cloning. 'Extreme Biology' is a compelling guide to developments at the very forefront of science." (Publisher's note)

McManus, Lori

Cell systems. Heinemann Library 2011 48p il (Investigating cells) lib bdg $32

Grades: 5 6 7 8   **570**

1. Cells 2. Life (Biology)

ISBN 978-1-4329-3879-6; 1-4329-3879-7

LC 2009049974

This book looks at cell systems, including the cell, tissues, organ, and organ system hierarchy.

"The abundant graphic matter—photographs, diagrams, charts and graphs—work together with the text to create visually appealing pages. . . . [This] would be very useful in any kind of formal investigation of the topic and yet attractive enough to encourage browsing. . . . [This] . . . is exceptionally well done." Libr Media Connect

Includes glossary and bibliographical references

VanCleave, Janice Pratt, 1942-

Step -by-step science experiments in biology; by Janice VanCleave. Rosen 2013 80 p. col. ill. (Janice Vancleave's first-place science fair projects) (library) $33.25; (paperback) $14.15

Grades: 5 6 7 8   **570**

1. Biology 2. Science -- Experiments 3. Biology -- Experiments

ISBN 144886982X; 9781448869824; 9781448884636

LC 2012007943

This book by Janice VanCleave presents 22 science experiments in biology for children. "Van Cleave states the basic goal of the experiments, followed by a list of necessary materials. . . . Step-by-step instructions are . . . accompanied by diagrams where needed. The results section states exactly what is expected to happen and the 'Why?' section explains in accessible terms why those specific results were achieved." (School Library Journal)

Includes bibliographical references and index.

Winston, Robert

Life as we know it; Robert Winston. 1st American ed. DK Publishing 2012 96 p. col. ill. (hardcover) $16.99

Grades: 4 5 6   **570**

1. Ecology 2. Zoology 3. Food chains (Ecology) 4. Life (Biology)

ISBN 0756691699; 9780756691691

LC 2011277462

Author Robert Winston "begins with Earth's formation billions of years ago and continues to the present day, exploring cells, the animal kingdom, ecosystems, food chains, and creatures that tolerate extreme conditions (including bacteria that thrive in volcanic pools and coffinfish that live under high pressure on the sea floor). The book's . . . design incorporates numerous photographs, sidebars, . . . digital art, and light humor, usually in the form of speech-bubble captions for the animals." (Publishers Weekly)

570.7 Education, research, related topics

Calhoun, Yael

Plant and animal science fair projects; revised and expanded using the scientific method. Enslow Publishers 2010 160p il (Biology science projects using the scientific method) lib bdg $34.60

Grades: 7 8 9 10 **570.7**
  1. Natural history 2. Science projects 3. Science -- Experiments
  ISBN 978-0-7660-3421-1 lib bdg; 0-7660-3421-6 lib bdg

LC 2009-14805

First published 2005 with title: Plant and animal science fair projects using beetles, weeds, seeds, and more

"Each volume begins with an overview of the scientific method and safety, then presents a collection of activities encouraging readers to explore central concepts in the featured fields. The activities include step-by-step instructions and helpful color diagrams, interspersed with extended coverage of scientific ideas. The "Results" sections ask questions rather than giving away the answers." (Horn Book)

Includes bibliographical references

570.78 Biology - Student experiments

Latham, Donna

★ **Backyard** Biology; Investigate Habitats Outside Your Door With 25 Projects. by Donna Latham ; illustrated by Beth Hetland. Nomad Press 2013 128 p. ill. (Build it yourself) (paperback) $15.95

Grades: 4 5 6 7 **570.78**
  1. Biology 2. Front yards and backyards
  ISBN 1619301512; 9781619301511

This book, part of the Built It Yourself series, "incorporates 25 projects for kids to try as they explore the 'ecosystems that are outside your door.' The book's eight chapters cover biology (and microbiology), cells, and the life cycles of both plants and animals, among other topics; definitions of key terms appear throughout, as do [illustrator Beth] Hetland's cartoons and diagrams." (Publishers Weekly)

570.9 History, geographic treatment, biography

Yount, Lisa

Craig Venter; dissecting the genome. by Lisa Yount. Chelsea House 2011 xix, 134 p.p col. ill.

(Trailblazers in science and technology) (library) $35

Grades: 7 8 9 10 11 12 **570.9**
  1. Human genome 2. Biologists -- United States -- Biography
  ISBN 1604136626; 9781604136623

LC 2010050561

This book by Lisa Yount, part of the Trailblazers in Science and Technology series, looks at scientist Craig Venter. It "details the life and accomplishments of this trailblazing scientist, describing his early days in California and military service in Vietnam, his . . . work to map the human genome, and his other numerous scientific achievements." (Publisher's note)

Includes bibliographical references and index

571 Internal biological processes and structures

Green, Jen

Inside animals. Marshall Cavendish Benchmark 2010 48p il (Invisible worlds) $28.50

Grades: 4 5 6 7 **571**
  1. Cells 2. Anatomy 3. Physiology 4. Microorganisms
  ISBN 978-0-7614-4195-3; 0-7614-4195-6

LC 2008037241

This describes the animal details that are too small for the unaided eye to see, and how these microscopic systems work to keep the animal alive and healthy.

The narrative is "clear, well written, broken down into manageable pieces, and peppered with eye-opening facts. The numerous photographs are so phenomenal that they will inspire kids to read the text . . . so that they can wrap their minds around what they see." SLJ

Includes glossary and bibliographical references

571.4 Biophysics

Winner, Cherie

Cryobiology. Lerner Publications Co. 2006 48p il (Cool science) lib bdg $26.60

Grades: 4 5 6 **571.4**
  1. Cryobiology
  ISBN 978-0-8225-2907-1 lib bdg; 0-8225-2907-6 lib bdg

LC 2005006158

This book "discusses how different life forms survive low temperatures, e.g., hibernating animals. . . . [The book provides] clear explanations of the science and [covers] possible benefits to humans. A variety of photos and information boxes provide an eye-catching . . . layout." Horn Book Guide

Includes glossary and bibliographical references

571.6 Cell biology

Ballard, Carol

Cells and cell function. Rosen Central 2010 46p il (Living processes) lib bdg $26.50; pa $11.75

Grades: 5 6 7   **571.6**
1. Cells
ISBN 978-1-61532-342-5 lib bdg; 1-61532-342-2 lib bdg; 978-1-61532-349-4 pa; 1-61532-349-X pa
Describes what cells are and how they work.
"With colorful, quality photography, the well-organized content is divided into short chapters with bold subheadings making information easy to find. Clear and interesting writing distinguishes this . . . from older titles. The captions for pictures are used to provide identification and additional explanation for topics not included in the text." Libr Media Connect
Includes glossary and bibliographical references

Cohen, Marina
What is cell theory? Crabtree Pub. Co. 2011 64p il (Shaping modern science) lib bdg $30.60; pa $10.95
Grades: 5 6 7 8   **571.6**
1. Cells
ISBN 978-0-7787-7199-9 lib bdg; 0-7787-7199-9 lib bdg; 978-0-7787-7206-4 pa; 0-7787-7206-3 pa
LC 2010052633
This title is "not only written and organized well, but [it is] also gorgeous in design. Full-color photographs and illustrations are set over colorful backgrounds that add depth but not distraction. [The title] includes thought-provoking quotes from famous authors and scientists and some eyebrow-raising 'Quick Facts' throughout." SLJ
Includes glossary and bibliographical references

Lee, Kimberly Fekany
Cells. Compass Point Books 2009 40p il (Mission: science) lib bdg $26.60
Grades: 4 5 6   **571.6**
1. Cells
ISBN 978-0-7565-3954-2 lib bdg; 0-7565-3954-4 lib bdg
LC 2008007719
"Lee describes the difference between plant and animal cells, and their contents; diffusion; and cell storage, movement, and reproduction. . . . Large eye-catching and colorful photographs and illustrations appear on every page. . . . The [book] includes a simple activity." SLJ
Includes glossary and bibliographical references

Rainis, Kenneth G.
Cell and microbe science fair projects; revised and expanded using the scientific method. Enslow Publishers 2010 160p il (Biology science projects using the scientific method) lib bdg $34.60
Grades: 7 8 9 10   **571.6**
1. Cells 2. Biology 3. Microbiology 4. Science projects 5. Science -- Experiments
ISBN 978-0-7660-3420-4 lib bdg; 0-7660-3420-8 lib bdg
LC 2009019374
First published 2005 with title: Cell and microbe science fair projects using microscopes, mold, and more
"Each book focusing on biology will be helpful to middle school students and contains a section about the scientific method as well as experiments that are outlined to cover the experimental question, hypothesis, materials, procedures, results and conclusions." (Publisher's Note)
Includes bibliographical references

Silverstein, Alvin
Cells; by Alvin & Virginia Silverstein and Laura Silverstein Nunn. Twenty-First Century Books 2009 112p il (Science concepts, second series) lib bdg $31.93
Grades: 6 7 8 9   **571.6**
1. Cells
ISBN 978-0-7613-3934-2; 0-7613-3934-5
LC 2007051038
A presentation of the structure and function of different types of cells and of research into developing technologies such as cloning and the use of stem cells.
Includes glossary and bibliographical references

Somervill, Barbara A.
Animal cells and life processes. Heinemann Library 2011 48p il (Investigating cells) lib bdg $32
Grades: 5 6 7 8   **571.6**
1. Cells 2. Life (Biology)
ISBN 978-1-4329-3877-2; 1-4329-3877-0
LC 2009049971
Overview of animal cells and how they function.
"The abundant graphic matter—photographs, diagrams, charts and graphs—work together with the text to create visually appealing pages. . . . [This] would be very useful in any kind of formal investigation of the topic and yet attractive enough to encourage browsing. . . . [This] . . . is exceptionally well done." Libr Media Connect
Includes glossary and bibliographical references

Plant cells and life processes. Heinemann Library 2010 48p il (Investigating cells) lib bdg $32
Grades: 5 6 7 8   **571.6**
1. Cells 2. Plant physiology
ISBN 978-1-4329-3878-9; 1-4329-3878-9
LC 2009049973
This book explores the features of the plant cell and their life processes.
"The abundant graphic matter—photographs, diagrams, charts and graphs—work together with the text to create visually appealing pages. . . . [This] would be very useful in any kind of formal investigation of the topic and yet attractive enough to encourage browsing. . . . [This] . . . is exceptionally well done." Libr Media Connect
Includes glossary and bibliographical references

Stewart, Melissa
Cell biology; by Melissa Stewart. Revised ed. Twenty-First Century Books 2013 80 p. col. ill. (chiefly col.) ebook $31.95
Grades: 5 6 7 8   **571.6**
1. Cells 2. Science -- History 3. Cytology
ISBN 9781467703666; 1467703664
LC 2006028542
This book looks at cells. "From the nucleus, the cell's control center, to the tiny ribosomes, which help manufacture proteins, each part of a cell plays an essential role. This

book tells the story of how biologists unlocked the secrets of cells and revolutionized the way we look at living things." (Publisher's note)

Includes bibliographical references (p. 76-77) and index

Stimola, Aubrey

Cell biology. Rosen Pubs. 2011 64p il (Science made simple) lib bdg $29.25; pa $12.95

Grades: 5 6 7 8   571.6

1. Cells

ISBN 978-1-4488-1234-9 lib bdg; 1-4488-1234-8 lib bdg; 978-1-4488-2241-6 pa; 1-4488-2241-6 pa

LC 2010021319

This introduction to cell biology includes "a lot of detailed information, making [it] useful as [a] resource . . . for science projects and reports. . . . The [book] also [includes a] brief discussion of scientists important in the field, the history of the topic, and current and future applications. . . . The straightforward, no-nonsense [narrative] and simple design make this . . . a nice package for basic science." SLJ

Includes glossary and bibliographical references

571.8   Reproduction, development, growth

Morgan, Sally

From sea urchins to dolly the sheep; discovering cloning. [by] Sally Morgan. Heinemann Library 2006 64p il (Chain reactions) $34.29

Grades: 6 7 8 9   571.8

1. Cloning

ISBN 1-4034-8838-X

LC 2006009962

This "addresses cloning, from its beginnings in the 1890s to Dolly the sheep in 2003. The [book features] clear, straightforward writing and [a] bright and open [layout] with colorful photographs and illustrations on every spread." SLJ

Includes bibliographical references

Silverstein, Virginia B.

★ Growth and development; by Alvin Silverstein, Virginia Silverstein, and Laura Silverstein Nunn. Twenty-First Century Books 2008 112p il (Science concepts) lib bdg $31.93

Grades: 4 5 6 7   571.8

1. Growth 2. Biology

ISBN 978-0-8225-6057-9 lib bdg; 0-8225-6057-7 lib bdg

LC 2006030299

This "considers the growth process, animals with and without skeletons, human and plant growth, and future trends as a result of medical technology. Clear organization, engaging anecdotes, and generally good photos and diagrams are strengths of the [volume]." Horn Book Guide

Includes glossary and bibliographical references

Spilsbury, Richard

Plant growth; [by] Richard & Louise Spilsbury. Rev. and updated.; Heinemann Library 2008 48p il (The life of plants) $27.50; pa $7.99

Grades: 5 6 7 8   571.8

1. Plants -- Growth

ISBN 978-1-4329-1500-1; 1-4329-1500-2; 978-1-4329-1507-0 pa; 1-4329-1507-X pa

LC 2008275394

First published 2003

Describes plant growth and development.

This book "contains many bright and colorful photographs and diagrams to support the text, boldface vocabulary terms, a series of experiments and activities to provide further investigation, a complete glossary, an index, and a list of sources for additional information. . . . [This] volume is a complete and well-rounded unit." Sci Books Films

Includes glossary and bibliographical references

571.9   Diseases

Somervill, Barbara A.

Cells and disease. Heinemann Library 2011 48p il (Investigating cells) lib bdg $32

Grades: 5 6 7 8   571.9

1. Cells 2. Bacteria 3. Diseases

ISBN 978-1-4329-3881-9; 1-4329-3881-9

LC 2009-49981

This book describes cells and diseases.

"The abundant graphic matter—photographs, diagrams, charts and graphs—work together with the text to create visually appealing pages. . . . [This] would be very useful in any kind of formal investigation of the topic and yet attractive enough to encourage browsing. . . . [This] . . . is exceptionally well done." Libr Media Connect

Includes glossary and bibliographical references

572   Biochemistry

Silverstein, Alvin

Photosynthesis; [by] Alvin Silverstein, Virginia Silverstein, and Laura Silverstein Nunn. rev ed.; Twenty-First Century Books 2008 79p il (Science concepts, second series) lib bdg $31.93

Grades: 6 7 8 9   572

1. Photosynthesis

ISBN 978-0-8225-6798-1; 0-8225-6798-9

LC 2006022566

First published 1998

"Photosynthesis explains the process; the history of discoveries leading to current understanding of photosynthesis; and related issues such as acid rain, the greenhouse effect, and the use of basic materials that are directly or indirectly dependent on photosynthesis. . . . [This book is] well researched and interesting and the format is inviting for both general-interest reading and research. . . . The high-quality, full-color photographs have informative captions." SLJ

Includes glossary and bibliographical references

Sitarski, Anita

★ Cold light; creatures, discoveries, and inventions that glow. Boyds Mills Press 2007 48p il $16.95

Grades: 5 6 7 8   **572**
1. Light 2. Bioluminescence
ISBN 1-59078-468-5; 978-1-59078-468-6
"A clearly written, chatty text not only discusses the
expected bioluminescent critters (think fireflies), but delves
into the realms of chemiluminescence, photoluminescence,
and LEDs (light-emitting diodes) as well. . . . The text lays
out the historical hows and whys of cold light, its success in
the natural world, and its application in medicine and do-
mestic/industrial illumination. Clear color photos and information boxes abound." SLJ

572.8   Biochemical genetics

Johnson, Rebecca L.
Amazing DNA; [by] Rebecca L. Johnson; illustrations by Jack Desrocher; diagrams by Jennifer
E. Fairman. Millbrook Press 2008 48p il (Microquests) lib bdg $29.27
Grades: 4 5 6   **572.8**
1. DNA 2. Genetics
ISBN 978-0-8225-7139-1 lib bdg; 0-8225-7139-0
lib bdg
               LC 2006-102324
This describes DNA structure, cell replication and
genetic transmission.
"Johnson builds one scientific concept at a time using
authentic terminology and connecting new information to
familiar things. . . . Full-color microscope images, drawings,
and cartoons appear in a clean, uncluttered format, combining solid science with humor." Horn Book Guide
Includes glossary and bibliographical references

Parker, Steve, 1952-
Cocci, spirilla & other bacteria. Compass Point
Books 2009 48p il (Kingdom classification) lib
bdg $29.32
Grades: 6 7 8 9   **572.8**
1. Bacteria 2. Microorganisms
ISBN 978-0-7565-4225-2 lib bdg; 0-7565-4225-1
lib bdg
               LC 2009-7524
Discusses physical characteristics of bacteria; different
types; how they move, feed, and reproduce; how people use
them; how they can harm humans; and how the human body
defends itself against harmful bacteria
"With its compelling facts and visuals, this is a quality
choice." SLJ
Includes glossary

Rand, Casey
DNA and heredity. Heinemann Library 2011
48p il (Investigating cells) lib bdg $32
Grades: 5 6 7 8   **572.8**
1. DNA 2. Cells 3. Heredity
ISBN 978-1-4329-3880-2; 1-4329-3880-0
               LC 2009049978
Learn about cells, DNA and scientists who made an im-
pact in cell research.

"The abundant graphic matter—photographs, diagrams,
charts and graphs—work together with the text to create visually appealing pages. . . . [This] would be very useful in
any kind of formal investigation of the topic and yet attractive enough to encourage browsing. . . . [This] . . . is exceptionally well done." Libr Media Connect
Includes glossary and bibliographical references

Silverstein, Alvin
DNA; by Alvin Silverstein, Virginia Silverstein,
Laura Silverstein Nunn. rev ed.; Twenty-First Cen-
tury Books 2009 104p il (Science concepts, second
series) lib bdg $31.93
Grades: 6 7 8 9   **572.8**
1. DNA 2. Genetics
ISBN 978-0-8225-8654-8; 0-8225-8654-1
               LC 2007048819
First published 2002
Introduces DNA and discusses such topics as how hered-
ity works, what can happen when the code goes wrong, and
the science and technology that is being developed based on
cells and DNA, including gene therapy and cloning.
Includes glossary and bibliographical references

Vaughan, Jenny
Who discovered DNA? Arcturus Pub. 2010 46p
il (Breakthroughs in science and technology) lib bdg
$32.80
Grades: 5 6 7 8   **572.8**
1. DNA
ISBN 978-1-84837-679-3; 1-84837-679-0
               LC 2010011021
"This brief well-done book presents accurate information in an interesting way, using appropriate and appealing
graphics. . . . The book not only tells us that Frederick Mi-
esche discovered DNA in 1869, but presents many relevant
discoveries before that time and, especially, after it. Applications of the discoveries are also presented, as are controversies related to the genetic knowledge of our day. . . . [This]
would be useful as reference and should be available to all
interested students." Sci Books & Films
Includes glossary and bibliographical references

Yount, Lisa
Rosalind Franklin; photographing biomolecules.
by Lisa Yount. Chelsea House 2011 xix, 125 p.p
col. ill. (Trailblazers in science and technology) (library) $35.00
Grades: 7 8 9 10 11 12   **572.8**
1. Women scientists 2. DNA -- History 3. Molecular
biologists -- Great Britain -- Biography 4. Women
molecular biologists -- Great Britain -- Biography
ISBN 160413660X; 9781604136609
               LC 2010048229
This book by Lisa Yount is part of the Trailblazers in Science and Technology series and looks at Rosalind Franklin.
"Tracing her life from her birth in Great Britain to her education at Cambridge, to her groundbreaking research [in X-ray
crystallography], and to her tragic and untimely death," this
book offers an "overview of the life and career of one of

the most influential scientific figures of the 20th century." (Publisher's note)

Includes bibliographical references and index.

575 Specific parts of and physiological systems in plants

Stefoff, Rebecca

Charles Darwin and the evolution revolution. Oxford Univ. Press 1996 126p il (Oxford portraits in science) $28; pa $11.95

Grades: 7 8 9 10   **575**

1. Evolution 2. Naturalists 3. Travel writers 4. Writers on science

ISBN 0-19-508996-0; 0-19-512028-0 pa

LC 95-35802

"Extensive photos of Darwin and his family, friends, and colleagues, as well as reproductions of public notices and cartoons, are handsome additions to the nicely laid-out text. . . . It offers generally thorough, clear explanations of Darwin's scientific theories and sheds light on his personality." Booklist

Includes glossary and bibliographical references

575.6   Reproductive organs

Spilsbury, Richard

Plant reproduction; [by] Richard & Louise Spilsbury. Rev. and updated.; Heinemann Library 2008 48p il (Life of plants) $27.50; pa $7.99

Grades: 5 6 7 8   **575.6**

1. Plants

ISBN 978-1-4329-1501-8; 1-4329-1501-0; 978-1-4329-1508-7 pa; 1-4329-1508-8 pa

LC 2008275393

First published 2003

Discusses the different ways that plants reproduce, including pollination and spores.

This book "contains many bright and colorful photographs and diagrams to support the text, boldface vocabulary terms, a series of experiments and activities to provide further investigation, a complete glossary, an index, and a list of sources for additional information . . . . [This] volume is a complete and well-rounded unit." Sci Books Films

Includes glossary and bibliographical references

576   General and external biological phenomena

Gardner, Robert

Genetics and evolution science fair projects; revised and expanded using the scientific method. Enslow Publishers 2010 160p il (Biology science projects using the scientific method) lib bdg $34.60

Grades: 7 8 9 10   **576**

1. Genetics 2. Evolution 3. Science projects 4.

Science -- Experiments

ISBN 978-0-7660-3422-8 lib bdg; 0-7660-3422-4 lib bdg

LC 2009-14803

First published 2004 with title: Genetics and evolution science fair projects using skeletons, cereal, earthworms, and more

"Each volume begins with an overview of the scientific method and safety, then presents a collection of activities encouraging readers to explore central concepts in the featured fields. The activities include step-by-step instructions and helpful color diagrams, interspersed with extended coverage of scientific ideas. The "Results" sections ask questions rather than giving away the answers." (Horn Book)

Includes bibliographical references

Walker, Denise

Inheritance and evolution. Smart Apple Media 2007 48p il (Basic biology) $34.25

Grades: 8 9 10 11 12   **576**

1. Genetics 2. Evolution

ISBN 978-1-58340-989-3

LC 2006000346

This explains genetics, DNA, natural selection and cloning, and the process of extinction.

This "is well written and visually appealing enough to entice a few kids who aren't normally interested in science. There's plenty of information, supported by excellent, full-color photos, charts, and graphs, as well as numerous examples that clarify facts." Booklist

576.5   Genetics

Day, Trevor

Genetics; investigating the function of genes and the science of heredity. Trevor Day. 1st ed. Rosen Central 2013 48 p. ill. (chiefly col.) (Scientific pathways) (library) $29.25

Grades: 6 7 8 9   **576.5**

1. Genetics 2. Scientists 3. Heredity

ISBN 1448871999; 9781448871995

LC 2011047887

This book by Trevor Day is part of the Scientific Pathways series and looks at genetics. The series authors "look at science as a process of discovery and explain how each discipline developed in different cultures over time. Significant names and important terms are printed in bold . . . . Brief biographies of thinkers, inventors, and scientists are provided along with important experiments and the conclusions that were made in relation to them." (School Library Journal)

Includes bibliographical references and index.

Duke, Shirley Smith

You can't wear these genes. Rourke Pub. LLC 2010 48p il (Let's explore science) $32.79

Grades: 4 5 6 7   **576.5**

1. Genetics

ISBN 978-1-61590-324-5; 1-61590-324-0

LC 2010009911

This "offers a clear introduction to the complexities of genetics while inviting students to think about how their own DNA shaped who they are. In [this] title, well chosen boxed examples, abundant color photos, diagrams, and an appended glossary add interest and support the engaging [text]." Booklist

Includes glossary and bibliographical references

Hand, Carol

    Introduction to genetics. Rosen Pub. 2010 80p il lib bdg $30.60

Grades: 6 7 8 9 10 11 12   **576.5**
    1. Genetics 2. Heredity
    ISBN 978-1-4358-9531-7

                  LC 2009-40364

"The moderately technical language in the other titles discusses significant discoveries, current directions in research and—superficially—ethical and other issues. Illustrations include helpful charts, microphotos, portraits of scientists, and color photos; extensive back matter provides plenty of support for further research." SLJ

Mooney, Carla

    Genetics; Breaking the Code of Your DNA. by Carla Mooney ; illustrated by Samuel Carbaugh. Nomad Press 2014 128 p. illustrations (Inquire and Investigate) $21.95

Grades: 6 7 8 9 10 11   **576.5**
    1. Genetics 2. DNA 3. Genes
    ISBN 161930208X; 9781619302082

This book on genetics, by Carla Mooney, illustrated by Samuel Carbaugh, "presents the main concepts of the science, including what a chromosome does, how DNA is structured, and how genetic inheritance works. Students learn about new discoveries in the field of genetics and how those discoveries have helped to cure or even prevent certain diseases, as well as examine controversial issues in genetics such as genetically modified foods and stem cell research." (Publisher's note)

"Although the book can be used independently, it will be better appreciated with some background knowledge. A solid resource that shows life science and biology students the practicalities and marvels of genetics." Booklist

Morgan, Sally

    From Mendel's peas to genetic fingerprinting; discovering inheritance. Heinemann Library 2007 64p il (Chain reactions) $34.29

Grades: 6 7 8 9   **576.5**
    1. Genetics 2. Heredity
    ISBN 1-4034-8837-1; 978-1-4034-8837-4

                  LC 2006-11043

This book "informs students about genetics and its many applications, including the Human Genome Project and genetic fingerprinting. . . . The [book features] clear, straightforward writing and [a] bright and open [layout] with colorful photographs and illustrations on every spread." SLJ

Includes bibliographical references

Schafer, Susan

    Heredity. M.E. Sharpe 2009 96p il (Genetics: the science of life) $38.95

Grades: 6 7 8 9   **576.5**
    1. Genetics 2. Heredity
    ISBN 978-0-7656-8136-2; 0-7656-8136-6

                  LC 2008-8105

This discusses the history of genetics, genetic dominance, hybrid animals, and the role of heredity in disease.

"Chock-full of information. . . . The material is well organized and accessible. . . . Interest is maintained through countless fascinating examples. . . . Illustrations and color photographs enhance [the text]." SLJ

Includes bibliographical references

Simpson, Kathleen

    ★ **Genetics**; from DNA to designer dogs. Sarah Tishkoff, consultant. National Geographic 2008 64p il map (National Geographic investigates) $27.90

Grades: 4 5 6 7   **576.5**
    1. Genetics
    ISBN 978-1-4263-0361-6; 1-4263-0361-0; 978-1-4263-0327-2 lib bdg; 1-4263-0327-0 lib bdg

This discusses topics in genetics such as the identification of an Egyptian mummy by DNA testing, the genetics of pea plants studied by Gregor Mendel, cloning, the Human Genome Project, and stem cell research.

"The content is fairly exciting and should grab the attention of its target audience. . . . The photographs throughout are of high quality. . . . An engaging look at a complex topic." Booklist

Vaughan, Jenny

    Genetics. Smart Apple Media 2010 45p il (Science in the news) lib bdg $34.25

Grades: 6 7 8 9   **576.5**
    1. Genetics
    ISBN 978-1-59920-317-1 lib bdg; 1-59920-317-0 lib bdg

                  LC 2008-49275

This book about genetics "move[s] smoothly, occasionally pausing for the definition of a term. [The title] boast[s] plenty of attractive photos, and a clean layout allows the information to be easily consumed. . . . Provides the information that younger teens need." SLJ

Includes glossary

Yount, Lisa

    Modern genetics; engineering life. rev ed.; Facts on File 2006 204p il map (Milestones in discovery and invention) $35

Grades: 7 8 9 10 11 12   **576.5**
    1. Genetics 2. Genetic engineering
    ISBN 0-8160-5744-3; 978-0-8160-5744-3

                  LC 2005-18152

First published 1997 with title: Genetics and genetic engineering

This book "profiles 14 men and women who were among the leaders in making important genetic discoveries in research and new technologies. Profiles include James Watson, Francis Crick, Herbert Boyer, Stanley N. Cohen, Michael Bishop, and Harold Varmus." Publisher's note

Includes glossary and bibliographical references

576.8   Evolution

Andryszewski, Tricia

Mass extinction; examining the current crisis. Twenty-First Century Books 2008 111p il lib bdg $30.60

Grades: 7 8 9 10 11 12   **576.8**
1. Mass extinctions 2. Mass extinction of species
ISBN 978-0-8225-7523-8; 0-8225-7523-X
LC 2007-25620

"After noting the natural causes of previous mass extinctions, this book focuses on the human element of environment destruction, especially in North America. The earnest writing is convincing and accessible. . . . Vibrant photographs, illustrations, and sidebars supplement the text." Horn Book Guide

Includes glossary and bibliographical references

Berkowitz, Jacob

Out of this world; the amazing search for an alien earth. Kids Can Press 2009 48p il $16.95; pa $8.95

Grades: 4 5 6 7   **576.8**
1. Life on other planets 2. Outer space -- Exploration
ISBN 978-1-55453-197-4; 1-55453-197-7; 978-1-55453-198-1 pa; 1-55453-198-5 pa

The author "has written a miniencyclopedic, profusely illustrated, picture book that describes, in much detail, what we all know about the universe in which we live and about the conditions that must be present on any planet in our solar system, or on an exoplanet . . . for life as we know it to exist." Sci Books Films

Bortz, Alfred B.

Astrobiology. Lerner Publications 2008 48p il map (Cool science) lib bdg $26.60

Grades: 4 5 6   **576.8**
1. Space biology 2. Life on other planets
ISBN 978-0-8225-6771-4 lib bdg; 0-8225-6771-7 lib bdg
LC 2006033268

This describes "the search for life in the universe. Astrobiologists compare life on Earth to signs of life on other planets. They test meteorites for evidence of alien bacteria. They collect soil and atmospheric samples from other planets. They study photographs taken on space missions. And they listen for signals from alien civilizations on enormous radio dishes." Publisher's note

Includes bibliographical references

Brake, Mark

Alien Hunter's Handbook; How to Look for Extra-terrestrial Life. by Mark Brake ; illustrated by Colin Jack and Geriant Ford. Kingfisher 2012 111 p. (paperback) $10.99

Grades: 4 5 6 7   **576.8**
1. Extraterrestrial beings
ISBN 0753468859; 9780753468852

This book on extra-terrestrial life by Mark Brake "opens with an overview of the defining characteristics of life and some of Earth's remarkable creatures, such as the microscopic tardigrade, which can exist in the vacuum of space.

Topics like the development of solar systems, the speed of evolution, and the formation of language also get attention, laying factual groundwork for suppositions about what alien life could look like." (Publishers Weekly)

Claybourne, Anna

Who discovered natural selection? Arcturus Pub. 2010 46p il (Breakthroughs in science and technology) lib bdg $32.80

Grades: 5 6 7 8   **576.8**
1. Heredity 2. Naturalists 3. Natural selection 4. Travel writers 5. Writers on science
ISBN 978-1-84837-682-3; 1-84837-682-0
LC 2010011020

"Earning high marks for clarity, organization, and visual appeal, this introduction to evolution and natural selection takes a historical approach, beginning with the philosophies of the ancients and tracing the development of evolution theory through the 19th century naturalists who set the stage for the conceptualization of natural selection. . . . Short narrative sections are interspersed with high-interest sidebars to keep the pace lively. The book ends with examples of rapid natural selection in viral strains and in antibiotic-resistant bacteria, and it raises the question of how mutually supportive behaviors evolve among social species. Colorful photographs and illustrations, each carefully chosen and placed, support the book's central theme. . . . Claybourne has made evolution theory accessible to young learners in a fresh and accurate way. This is a must buy for school libraries." Sci Books & Films

Includes glossary and bibliographical references

★ **Evolution;** Clay Farris Naff, book editor. Greenhaven Press 2005 222 p. (Exploring science and medical discoveries) lib bdg $34.95

Grades: 8 9 10 11 12   **576.8**
1. Evolution
ISBN 9780737728231
LC 2004-60590

In this anthology, "nineteen selections are arranged in roughly chronological order, beginning with ancient Greek philosophers whose ideas about nature hinted at evolutionary theories to come. . . . This solid survey provides a good overview with manageable amounts of primary-source materials that would be dauntingly difficult to comprehend in their entirety." SLJ

Includes bibliographical references

Fleisher, Paul

Evolution; by Paul Fleisher. Lerner Publications Co. 2005 80 p. ill. (chiefly col.), col. maps (library) $27.93; (ebook) $20.95

Grades: 5 6 7 8   **576.8**
1. Evolution 2. Darwin, Charles, 1809-1882
ISBN 0822521342; 9780822521341; 9781467703697
LC 2004028897

In this book, Paul Fleisher "summarizes some of the ideas about evolution before Darwin's Origin of Species. He goes on to describe the observations Darwin made while on his famous Beagle voyage. A map of the ship's course accompanies this section. . . . Objections to Darwin's theory in the 1800s and developments and discoveries in the field since then lead to a step-by-step description of how life may have come about and changed through billions of years." (School Library Journal)

Includes bibliographical references (p. 76-77) and index.

Gamlin, Linda

Evolution; written by Linda Gamlin. rev ed.; DK Pub. 2009 72p il (DK eyewitness books) $16.99
Grades: 4 5 6 7   **576.8**
1. Evolution
ISBN 978-0-7566-5028-5; 0-7566-5028-3
First published 1993

Text about and photography of experiments, animals, plants, bones, and fossils reveal the ideas and discoveries that have changed our understanding of the natural world and how life began. Includes a CD and wall chart.

Gordon, Sherri Mabry

The **evolution** debate; Darwinism vs. intelligent design. Enslow Publishers 2009 128p il (Issues in focus today) lib bdg $31.93
Grades: 7 8 9 10   **576.8**
1. Evolution 2. Intelligent design theory
ISBN 978-0-7660-2911-8 lib bdg; 0-7660-2911-5 lib bdg

LC 2008-17416

"This book is most notable for its unbiased presentation of the arguments on each side of this contentious debate." SLJ

Includes glossary and bibliographical references

Hartman, Eve

Changing life on Earth; [by] Eve Hartman and Wendy Meshbesher. Raintree 2009 48p il (Sci-hi: life science) lib bdg $31.43; pa $8.99
Grades: 5 6 7 8   **576.8**
1. Evolution
ISBN 978-1-4109-3324-9 lib bdg; 1-4109-3324-5 lib bdg; 978-1-4109-3332-4 pa; 1-4109-3332-6 pa

LC 2009003459

In this introduction to evolution "clear language, embedded definitions, and interesting examples illustrate abstract concepts through both text and well-chosen photographs. . . . [The book] provides a clear and useful explanation of the theory of evolution, with multiple sources of evidence and a discussion of how it helps scientists to predict the implications of changes to the environment. . . . [The] book also includes suggested activities to test ideas as well as a thorough glossary and a Webliography." SLJ

Includes glossary and bibliographical references

Holmes, Thom

Evolution. Chelsea House 2010 109p il (Science foundations) lib bdg $35
Grades: 7 8 9 10   **576.8**
1. Evolution
ISBN 978-1-60413-338-7; 1-60413-338-4

LC 2010015738

"—A solid, competent history of the evolution of ideas and the theory of evolution itself...Certainly not for brows-

ing or easy light reading, but definitely of use to teachers or serious researchers.—" (School Library Journal)

Includes glossary and bibliographical references

Johnson, Sylvia A.

★ **Shaking** the foundation; Charles Darwin and the theory of evolution. by Sylvia A. Johnson. Twenty-First Century Books 2013 88 p. (library) $33.27
Grades: 6 7 8 9   **576.8**
1. Evolution 2. Evolution (Biology)
ISBN 0761354867; 9780761354864

LC 2012018075

This book offers an "overview of how [Charles] Darwin's theories of natural selection and evolution shook the foundations of religious beliefs and long-held scientific views. . . .[Sylvia A.] Johnson devotes the first half of her book to discussing the intellectual, philosophical and societal changes brought by the Enlightenment and Industrial Revolution that would make people receptive to Darwin's ideas. . . . The second half chronicles how Darwin formulated his theories." (Kirkus Reviews)

"In this thoughtful history of both Darwin and his theories of evolution, Johnson explains how the scientist lived and worked, religious and scientific challenges to his theories, and American legal challenges to evolution that continue in contemporary times. Numerous historical photographs and scientific illustrations, many from scientists of his time, greatly enhance the text." (Horn Book)

Includes bibliographical references and index

Mehling, Randi

Great extinctions of the past; by Randi Mehling. Chelsea House 2007 72p il (Scientific American) lib bdg $30
Grades: 5 6 7 8   **576.8**
1. Dinosaurs 2. Mass extinctions 3. Prehistoric animals 4. Mass extinction of species
ISBN 978-0-7910-9049-7 lib bdg; 0-7910-9049-3 lib bdg

LC 2006014851

Examines extinctions of prehistoric species including the dinosaurs, looks at the five largest extinctions ever, and explores the idea of a future mass extinction.

"The ideas in this book are . . . clearly explained. . . . [The book has] captioned color photos thoughout." SLJ

Includes glossary and bibliographical references

Newland, Sonya

Extinction! by Jim Pipe. Crabtree Publishing Company 2013 48 p. col. ill. (Crabtree chrome) (library) $30.60; (paperback) $9.95
Grades: 4 5 6   **576.8**
1. Extinct animals 2. End of the world 3. Mass extinctions
ISBN 0778779254; 9780778779254; 9780778779346

LC 2012032046

This book by Sonya Newland "explores both the history of extinction--dating back to the mass extinction of the Ordovician period 450 million years ago and the extinction of the dinosaurs 65 million years ago--as well as the possibility of the extinction of species in existence today. . . . In addition . . . Newland considers possible scenarios that might end life on Earth: an asteroid colliding with our planet . . . or an exploding nuclear bomb that blocks out the sun." (School Library Journal)

Includes bibliographical references and index

Pringle, Laurence P.

★ **Billions** of years, amazing changes; the story of evolution. Boyds Mills Press 2011 102p il $17.95

Grades: 4 5 6 7   **576.8**

1. Evolution

ISBN 978-1-59078-723-6; 1-59078-723-4

"Pringle provides an accessible introduction to complex concepts such as natural selection and genetics, paired with Jenkins's characteristically elegant collages. . . . Compelling photographs of fossils and living creatures, as well as Jenkins's paper collages, augment the substantial text. The presentation should help children gain a confident grasp on the fundamentals of evolution." Publ Wkly

Scott, Elaine

★ **Mars** and the search for life. Clarion Books 2008 60p il $17

Grades: 4 5 6 7   **576.8**

1. Life on other planets 2. Mars (Planet)

ISBN 978-0-618-76695-6; 0-618-76695-2

LC 2008-07243

The author discusses "the Mars Exploration Rover (MER) and tantalizing findings that suggest that conditions on the red planet may once have been hospitable to life. . . . Illustrations are arresting and clearly captioned." Bull Cent Child Books

Includes glossary and bibliographical references

Solway, Andrew

Why is there life on Earth? Raintree 2012 48p il (Earth, space, and beyond) $32; pa $8.99

Grades: 5 6 7 8   **576.8**

1. Life on other planets 2. Earth 3. Life -- Origin

ISBN 978-1-4109-4160-2; 978-1-4109-4166-4 pa

LC 2010040160

"Delivering compact but broad summations about...life on Earth, [this] survey [is] well suited for review or reinforcement reading." SLJ

Includes glossary and bibliographical references

Turner, Pamela S.

★ **Life** on earth--and beyond; an astrobiologist's quest. Charlesbridge 2008 109p il map lib bdg $19.95; pa $11.95

Grades: 5 6 7 8   **576.8**

1. Space biology 2. Life on other planets 3. Astrophysicists

ISBN 978-1-58089-133-2 lib bdg; 1-58089-133-0 lib bdg; 978-1-58089-134-9 pa; 1-58089-134-9 pa

LC 2007-01475

"Astrobiologists look outward from the Earth seeking evidence of life elsewhere in the universe. But, as this fascinating book shows, they also travel to places on Earth where extreme conditions may be similar to those on distant worlds. Turner follows astrobiologist Chris McKay as he looks for

life in apparently hostile environments. . . . Illustrated with many excellent color photos and other images." Booklist

Includes bibliographical references

Walker, Robert

What is the theory of evolution? Crabtree Pub. Co. 2011 64p il (Shaping modern science) lib bdg $30.60; pa $10.95

Grades: 5 6 7 8   **576.8**

1. Evolution 2. Naturalists 3. Travel writers 4. Writers on science

ISBN 978-0-7787-7198-2 lib bdg; 0-7787-7198-9 lib bdg; 978-0-7787-7205-7 pa; 0-7787-7205-5 pa

LC 2010052628

This title is "not only written and organized well, but [it is] also gorgeous in design. Full-color photographs and illustrations are set over colorful backgrounds that add depth but not distraction. [The title] includes thought-provoking quotes from famous authors and scientists and some eyebrow-raising 'Quick Facts' throughout." SLJ

Includes glossary and bibliographical references

Winston, Robert M. L.

★ **Evolution** revolution; [by] Robert Wilson. DK Pub. 2009 96p il $16.99

Grades: 5 6 7 8   **576.8**

1. Evolution

ISBN 978-0-7566-45243-; 0-7566-4524-7

"The first two thirds of the book are devoted to the history of thought and research on evolution, from stories of Creation, through Darwin, to genetics. The last third looks at 'Evolution in Action.' Information on the fetuses of related species rubs shoulders with variations within species and a time line of the Earth. Visually, the book snaps with colored backgrounds, cool graphics, topflight photos, and clever word balloons coming from vintage black-and-white reproductions." SLJ

577 Ecology

Ballard, Carol

Food webs. Rosen Central 2010 46p il (Living processes) lib bdg $26.50; pa $11.75 **577**

1. Food chains (Ecology)

ISBN 978-1-61532-340-1 lib bdg; 1-61532-340-6 lib bdg; 978-1-61532-351-7 pa; 1-61532-351-1 pa

LC 2009-28379

"With colorful, quality photography, the well-organized content is divided into short chapters with bold subheadings making information easy to find. Clear and interesting writing distinguishes this . . . from older titles. The captions for pictures are used to provide identification and additional explanation for topics not included in the text." Libr Media Connect

Includes glossary and bibliographical references

Ecology; the delicate balance of life on earth. edited by Sherman Hollar. Rosen Educational Services, LLC 2012 87 p. col. ill. (library) $31.70
Grades: 5 6 7 8   577
1. Ecology 2. Environmentalism
ISBN 1615305076; 9781615305070
LC 2010052490
This book on ecology, edited by Sherman Hollar, "explores the formation of ecological communities and examines the biological diversity that forms the backbone of life on the planet. . . . By parsing the natural world into various ecosystems and biomes" it looks at "interaction among species and between organisms and their natural habitats". (Publisher's note)
Includes bibliographical references (p. 84) and index.

Gardner, Robert
Ace your ecology and environmental science project; great science fair ideas. [by] Robert Gardner, Phyllis J. Perry, and Salvatore Tocci. Enslow Publishers 2009 128p il (Ace your science project) lib bdg $31.93
Grades: 5 6 7 8   577
1. Ecology 2. Science projects 3. Environmental sciences 4. Science -- Experiments
ISBN 978-0-7660-3216-3 lib bdg; 0-7660-3216-7 lib bdg
LC 2008-4683
"Dozens of . . . science activities are presented with background information, step-by-step instructions, and suggestions for extending to the science fair level. . . . Color illustrations and important safety information are included." Horn Book Guide
Includes bibliographical references

Housel, Debra J.
Ecosystems. Compass Point Books 2009 40p il map (Mission: science) lib bdg $26.60
Grades: 4 5 6   577
1. Ecology
ISBN 978-0-7565-4068-5 lib bdg; 0-7565-4068-2 lib bdg
LC 2008-35730
An introduction to the ways in which plants and animals interact with each other
Includes glossary

Latham, Donna
Amazing biome projects you can build yourself; illustrated by Farah Rizvi. Nomad Press 2009 122p il map (Build it yourself) pa $15.95
Grades: 4 5 6 7   577
1. Ecology 2. Handicraft 3. Earth sciences 4. Science -- Experiments
ISBN 978-1-934670-40-8; 1-934670-40-5
"Although the text addresses young 'eco explorers' directly, this book will likely be used as much by teachers, parents, and organization leaders in planning group activities. Offering an overview of eight terrestrial biomes as well as the ocean, Latham crams a lot of information about climate, plants, animals, soil, and other characteristics onto every

page. . . . Instructions for hands-on activities related to different biomes include craft projects such as pictographs and a cornhusk doll. Students can learn how to make a glacier, an erupting volcano, and a tornado in a bottle." SLJ
Includes glossary and bibliographical references

Ecology. Raintree 2009 48p il (Sci-hi: life science) lib bdg $31.43; pa $8.99
Grades: 5 6 7 8   577
1. Ecology
ISBN 978-1-4109-3328-7 lib bdg; 1-4109-3328-8 lib bdg; 978-1-4109-3336-2 pa; 1-4109-3336-9 pa
LC 2009003465
In this introduction to ecology "clear language, embedded definitions, and interesting examples illustrate abstract concepts through both text and well-chosen photographs. . . . [It] includes suggested activities to test ideas as well as a thorough glossary and a Webliography." SLJ
Includes glossary and bibliographical references

Rompella, Natalie
Ecosystems; [by] Natalie Rompella. Heinemann Library 2008 48p il (Science fair projects) $30
Grades: 5 6 7 8   577
1. Ecology 2. Science projects 3. Science -- Experiments
ISBN 978-1-4034-7915-0
LC 2006039543
This "describes 10 inquiry-based science projects related to life science and ecosystems. . . . Students from mid-elementary through middle school would find little difficulty following the clearly written instructions and suggestions. . . . The illustrations consist of colorful photographs and well-labeled diagrams." Sci Books Films
Includes bibliographical references

Shaw, Daniel
Eco -tracking; on the trail of habitat change. with photographs by Melanie Keithley, Jon Livingston MacLake, and the author. University of New Mexico Press 2010 85p il (Worlds of wonder) $19.95
Grades: 6 7 8 9 10   577
1. Ecology 2. Environmental protection
ISBN 978-0-8263-4531-8; 0-8263-4531-X
LC 2010010319
"The authors tackle environmental issues with depth and rigor, attuned to both current events and the concerns of today's teens. Global Warming and Powering look at the science and human impact of climate change and alternative energies, while Eco-tracking encourages citizen-science investigation for young environmentalists. The excellent texts are enhanced by color photographs and diagrams that further explain scientific ideas. " (Horn Book)
Includes glossary

Silverstein, Alvin
Food chains; [by] Alvin Silverstein, Virginia Silverstein, and Laura Silverstein Nunn. rev ed.; Twenty-First Century Books 2008 96p il (Science concepts, second series) $31.93

Grades: 6 7 8 9   **577**
1. Food chains (Ecology)
ISBN 978-0-8225-6797-4; 0-8225-6797-0
First published 1998

Explains various components of a food chain and discusses energy flows, food webs, food pyramids, recycling in nature, and the effect of humans on food chains.

Stille, Darlene R.

Nature interrupted; the science of environmental chain reactions. Compass Point Books 2009 48p il map (Headline science) lib bdg $27.93
Grades: 5 6 7 8   **577**
1. Ecology 2. Food chains (Ecology) 3. Environmental degradation
ISBN 978-0-7565-3949-8 lib bdg; 0-7565-3949-8 lib bdg

LC 2008007282

This "reviews the importance of subtle links in the environmental chain and the far-reaching consequences of its disruption. The possible harm to the food chain caused by the use of antibacterial soap is one case study. The flow of energy from one organism to the next in the food web and the unexpected results when this relationship is disrupted are shown in examinations of monarch butterflies, zebra mussels, and algal blooms. The color illustrations and charts . . . are clear and helpful, and the text, although information rich, is not overly difficult." SLJ

Includes glossary and bibliographical references

Suzuki, David T.

★ **You** are the Earth; know your world so you can make it better. [by] David Suzuki and Kathy Vanderlinden; art by Wallace Edwards; diagrams by Talent Pun. rev ed; Greystone Books 2010 159p il $16.95
Grades: 4 5 6 7   **577**
1. Ecology 2. Human ecology
ISBN 978-1-55365-476-6; 1-55365-476-5
First published 1999 with title: You are the Earth: from dinosaur breath to pizza from dirt

"After devoting a chapter to each of life's necessities—air, water, soil (earth), energy (fire), love, and a spiritual connection with the universe—the authors close with a look at three social and environmental initiatives by young people; a set of review questions (with answers); and 10 consciousness-raising activities, from science projects to storytelling. Sourced, briefly told versions of folktales from several traditions are interspersed throughout, and the plentiful illustrations include color diagrams, comics, and crisply reproduced photos. . . . [The authors'] eloquent plea to see ourselves and the Earth as interdependent will inspire readers to sit up, look around, and take a little less for granted." SLJ

Includes glossary

Walker, Pamela

Ecosystem science fair projects; revised and expanded using the scientific method. [by] Pam Walker and Elaine Wood. Enslow Publishers 2010 160p il (Biology science projects using the scientific method) lib bdg $34.60

Grades: 7 8 9 10   **577**
1. Ecology 2. Science projects 3. Science -- Experiments
ISBN 978-0-7660-3419-8 lib bdg; 0-7660-3419-4 lib bdg

LC 2009019375

First published 2005 with title: Ecosystem science fair projects using worms, leaves, crickets, and other stuff

This book "explains how to use the scientific method to conduct several science experiments about ecosystems." (Publisher's note)

"Explains how to use the scientific method to conduct several science experiments about ecosystems. Includes ideas for science fair projects." Publisher's note

Includes bibliographical references

Woodford, Chris

Arctic tundra and polar deserts; Revised ed. Raintree 2011 64p il map (Biomes atlases) $34
Grades: 5 6 7 8 9   **577**
1. Tundra ecology 2. Polar regions
ISBN 978-1-4329-4172-7; 1-4329-4172-0

LC 2010012428

Information about the animals and plants that typically make polar regions and tundra environments their homes.

"...Provides detailed information suitable for middle school research projects, and browsing potential is high due to the colorful, graphic nature." Library Media Connection

Includes bibliographical references

577.078   Ecology - Experiments

VanCleave, Janice Pratt, 1942-

Step -by-step science experiments in ecology; by Janice VanCleave. Rosen Pub. 2013 80 p. col. ill. (Janice VanCleave's first-place science fair projects) (library) $33.25; (paperback) $14.15
Grades: 5 6 7 8   **577.078**
1. Ecology 2. Science -- Experiments 3. Ecology -- Experiments
ISBN 1448869803; 9781448869800; 9781448884698

This book by Janice VanCleave is part of the First-Place Science Fair Projects series. The books have an introduction to the subject—here, ecology, followed by 22 simple . . . experiments. Van Cleave states the basic goal of the experiments, followed by a list of necessary materials, most of which can be found around the house or easily acquired with minimal cost. Step-by-step instructions are clearly detailed and accompanied by diagrams where needed." (School Library Journal)

Includes bibliographical references (p. 76-78) and index.

577.2   Specific factors affecting ecology

Simon, Seymour

★ **Wildfires.** Morrow Junior Bks. 1996 un il hardcover o.p. pa $6.99

Grades: 4 5 6 7   **577.2**
1. Forest fires 2. Forest ecology
ISBN 0-688-17530-9 pa

LC 95-12653

"Exploring the place of fire in nature, Simon explains that . . . forest fires have important functions in the ecosystem. With a brilliantly clear and colorful photograph facing each page of text, the book describes the causes and the progression of the wildfires that burned areas of Yellowstone National Park in 1988, explains how the fires were beneficial in many ways. . . . Lucid writing and excellent book design." Booklist

577.3 Ecology of specific environments

Allaby, Michael
Temperate forests; illustrations by Richard Garratt. rev ed; Facts on File 2008 336p il map (Ecosystem) $70
Grades: 7 8 9 10   **577.3**
1. Forest ecology 2. Forests and forestry
ISBN 0-8160-5930-6; 978-0-8160-5930-0

LC 2006-28859

First published 1999

"Those who are curious about or who are studying the environment and ecosystems . . . will find this book both fascinating and enlightening." Sci Books Films
Includes glossary and bibliographical references

Burnie, David
Shrublands; David Burnie. Raintree 2011 64 p. col. ill., col. maps (Biomes atlases) (library) $34
Grades: 6 7 8   **577.3**
1. Biomes 2. Habitat (Ecology) 3. Shrublands 4. Shrubland ecology
ISBN 143294178X; 9781432941789

LC 2010013019

This book is from the Biomes Atlases Series and focuses on shrublands. Each book offers an introduction to a different biome. "Brief notes for 10 to 12 highlights appear on each one, commenting on the diversity of flora, fauna, and landforms that occurs. Longer overviews of climate, plants, animals, people, and future prospects for the biome alternate with the regional close-ups." (School Library Journal)
Includes bibliographical references (p. 63) and index

Greenaway, Theresa
Jungle; written by Theresa Greenaway; photographed by Geoff Dann. rev ed.; DK Pub. 2004 71p il map (DK eyewitness books) $15.99
Grades: 4 5 6 7   **577.3**
1. Rain forest ecology
ISBN 0-7566-0694-2

LC 2004558978

First published 1994
Color photographs, drawings, and brief text describe the animals, plants, and ecology of tropical forests of the world

Jackson, Kay
Rain forests; by Kay Jackson. KidHaven Press 2007 48p il (Our environment) lib bdg $23.70
Grades: 5 6 7 8   **577.3**
1. Rain forests 2. Rain forest ecology
ISBN 978-0-7377-3624-3

LC 2007006892

"Jackson defines rain forests. . . . She explains why rain forests are important, . . . the causes of rain forest destruction, and current efforts to save diverse ecosystems. The writing is clear and succinct. . . . Full-color, captioned photographs and drawings appear on nearly every page." Booklist
Includes bibliographical references

Miller-Schroeder, Patricia
Boreal forests; [by] Patricia Miller-Schroeder. Weigl Publishers 2005 32p il map (Biomes) $26; pa $7.99
Grades: 4 5 6 7   **577.3**
1. Forest ecology
ISBN 1-59036-345-0; 1-59036-351-5 pa

LC 2005005436

This discusses the ecosystem of "the northern, coniferous forests or taigas. . . . The [volume contains] succinct text and [is] full of pictures, maps, graphs, and sidebars of interesting facts." Voice Youth Advocates
Includes bibliographical references

Quinlan, Susan E.
The **case** of the monkeys that fell from the trees; and other mysteries in tropical nature. Boyds Mills Press 2003 171p il map $15.95
Grades: 6 7 8 9   **577.3**
1. Natural history 2. Rain forest ecology
ISBN 1-56397-902-0

LC 2002-108914

"Quinlan's book is well organized and clearly written. . . . Besides presenting some fascinating case studies in a style that conveys the thrill of the scientific chase, it also provides information on the different kinds of tropical forests and how they function." SLJ
Includes bibliographical references

Tocci, Salvatore
The **chaparral**; life on the scrubby coast. Franklin Watts 2003 63p il map (Biomes and habitats) lib bdg $25.50; pa $8.95
Grades: 4 5 6 7   **577.3**
1. Chaparral ecology
ISBN 0-531-12303-0 lib bdg; 0-531-16671-6 pa

LC 2003-16574

A look at the plants, animals, locations, and various habitats that make up the chaparral ecosystems of the world

Life in the tropical forests. Franklin Watts 2005 63p il map (Biomes and habitats) lib bdg $25.50
Grades: 4 5 6 7   **577.3**
1. Rain forest ecology
ISBN 0-531-12364-2

LC 2004027054

Describes the animals, plants, and people that live in rainforests and the threats to their existence

Includes glossary and bibliographical references

Vogt, Richard Carl

Rain forests. Simon & Schuster Books for Young Readers 2009 64p il (Insiders) $16.99

Grades: 4 5 6 7   **577.3**

1. Rain forests

ISBN 978-1-4169-3866-8; 1-4169-3866-4

LC 2008061111

"The layers of a rain forest are drawn with exacting detail in every imaginable shade of green, while circular inserts zoom in on flora with accompanying stats. Running down the length of the spread are markers delineating the cutoff points for each layer—emergent, canopy, and so on. The rest of the book is similarly fine, bringing animals, reptiles, and insects into the mix. . . . Some photographs join the mostly hand-illustrated affair. . . . What will grab browsers are the 3D cover and vivid drawings on thick, oversize pages, but what will keep them reading is a cumulative sense of the rain forest as a verdant universe nearly festering with life." Booklist

Warhol, Tom

Chaparral and scrub; [by] Tom Warhol. Marshall Cavendish Benchmark 2006 80p il (Earth's biomes) lib bdg $32.79

Grades: 6 7 8 9   **577.3**

1. Chaparral ecology 2. Forests and forestry

ISBN 978-0-7614-2195-5 lib bdg; 0-7614-2195-5 lib bdg

LC 2006015824

"Explores chaparral and scrub biomes and covers where they are located as well as the plants and animals that inhabit them." Publisher's note

Includes glossary and bibliographical references

577.34   Rain forest ecology

Jackson, Tom

Tropical forests; Tom Jackson. Revised ed. Raintree 2011 64 p. col. ill., col. maps (Biomes atlases) (library) $34.00

Grades: 6 7 8   **577.34**

1. Rain forests 2. Rain forest animals 3. Rain forest ecology

ISBN 1432941771; 9781432941772

LC 2010012915

This children's nonfiction book, by Tom Jackson, profiles tropical forests as part of the publisher's "Biomes Atlases" series. "Each volume opens with a colorful world map featuring the eleven biomes of the world; individual books then diverge into a specific biome. Five topics are covered in each book: climate, plants, animals, people, and future of the biome." (Publisher's note)

Includes bibliographical references (p. 63) and index.

Welsbacher, Anne

. **Protecting** Earth's rain forests; by Anne Welsbacher. Lerner Publications 2009 72p il map (Saving our living Earth) lib bdg $30.60

Grades: 5 6 7 8   **577.34**

1. Rain forests 2. Environmental protection

ISBN 978-0-8225-7562-7 lib bdg; 0-8225-7562-0 lib bdg

LC 2007-38859

"Provides a thorough, interesting discussion of multiple aspects of [rain forest protection], including historical origins, the current situation, and potential solutions. . . . Photos from around the world accompany discussions. . . . Solid choice to replace outdated books." SLJ

Includes glossary and bibliographical references

577.4   Grassland ecology

Collard, Sneed B.

★ The **prairie** builders; reconstructing America's lost grasslands. written and photographed by Sneed B. Collard III. Houghton Mifflin Co. 2005 66p il (Scientists in the field) $17; pa $8.95

Grades: 4 5 6 7   **577.4**

1. Prairies 2. Nature conservation

ISBN 978-0-618-39687-0; 0-618-39687-X; 978-0-547-01441-8 pa; 0-547-01441-4 pa

LC 2004-13201

This describes an effort to restore part of the native tallgrass prairie in the the 8,000-acre Neal Smith National Wildlife Refuge in Iowa

"The engaging text is accompanied by large, inviting color photographs. . . . An essential purchase for libraries in prairie regions and a worthwhile choice for others." SLJ

Includes bibliographical references

Hoare, Ben

Temperate grasslands; Ben Hoare. Raintree 2011 64 p. col. ill., col. maps (Biomes atlases) (library) $34.00

Grades: 6 7 8 9   **577.4**

1. Prairies 2. Grasslands 3. Prairie animals 4. Prairie ecology 5. Grassland ecology

ISBN 143294181X; 9781432941819

LC 2010013034

This book, by Ben Hoare, is part of the publisher's "Biomes Atlases" nonfiction series. "Untouched temperate grasslands can be hard to find, since the fertile soil is often converted to farmland." This book presents a profile of the wild flora and fauna which does exist in these areas. (Publisher's note)

"Each volume opens with a colorful world map featuring the eleven biomes of the world; individual books then diverge into a specific biome. Five topics are covered in each book: climate, plants, animals, people, and future of the biome. Each of these main sections is separated by a two-page layout featuring a specific example of the region...While the majority of the information is available online, students will enjoy learning with these books much more than an electronic search." (Library Media Connection)

Includes bibliographical references (p. 63) and index.

Lynch, Wayne

Rocky Mountains; text and photographs by Wayne Lynch; assisted by Aubrey Lang. NorthWord Books for Young Readers 2006 64p il map (Our wild world ecosystems) $16.95; pa $8.95

Grades: 6 7 8 9   **577.4**
1. Mountain ecology 2. Rocky Mountains 3. Natural history -- Rocky Mountains
ISBN 1-55971-948-6; 1-55971-949-4 pa
            LC 2005-38014

"Introductory chapters explain the physical science that forms mountains and their weather. Each subsequent chapter zeros in on different mountain habitats (rivers and lakes, meadows and forests, and so on), introducing facts about the animals and plants in each. The authors . . . write in vivid, clear prose that, together with the quality of the beautiful images, sets this title apart from other . . . books on the topic." Booklist

Includes bibliographical references

Martin, Patricia A. Fink

Prairies, fields, and meadows. Watts 2002 144p il map (Exploring ecosystems) lib bdg $24.50; pa $6.95

Grades: 7 8 9 10   **577.4**
1. Prairie ecology 2. Grassland ecology
ISBN 978-0-531-11859-7; 0-531-11859-2 lib bdg; 978-0-531-16604-8 pa; 0-531-16604-X pa
            LC 2001-17570

"One can glean a great deal of useful information from this text." Libr Media Connect

Includes glossary and bibliographical references

Toupin, Laurie

★ **Life** in the temperate grasslands. Franklin Watts 2005 63p il map (Biomes and habitats) lib bdg $25.50

Grades: 4 5 6 7   **577.4**
1. Grassland ecology
ISBN 0-531-12385-5
            LC 2004-13282

This describes the ecology of grasslands such as the North American prairie, the South American pampas, the African veldt and the European steppes

This is "written in an accessible and interesting, conversational style. The [author conveys] a good deal of information about topics such as adaptation, environmental threats, seasonal changes, and other essentials important to report writers and general readers." SLJ

Includes bibliographical references

★ **Savannas**; life in the tropical grasslands. [by] Laurie Peach Toupin. Franklin Watts 2005 63p il map (Biomes and habitats) lib bdg $25.50

Grades: 4 5 6 7   **577.4**
1. Grassland ecology
ISBN 0-531-12386-3
            LC 2004-13281

This introduces "readers to the climate characteristics as well as plants and animals of [tropical grasslands. It is] written in an accessible and interesting, conversational style. The authors convey a good deal of information about topics such as adaptation, environmental threats, seasonal changes, and other essentials important to report writers and general readers." SLJ

Includes bibliographical references

577.5   Ecology of miscellaneous environments

Allaby, Michael

★ **Deserts**; illustrations by Richard Garratt. rev ed; Facts on File 2008 320p il map (Ecosystem) $70

Grades: 7 8 9 10   **577.5**
1. Deserts 2. Desert ecology
ISBN 0-8160-5929-2; 978-0-8160-5929-4
            LC 2007-00477
First published 2001

"This book is a good mix of text, excellent maps, photographs, and scientific information." Sci Books Films

This book provides "information on the climatic conditions that produce deserts and the climate cycles that make them expand and contract. . . . [It] also explores the locations and general types of deserts, and provides detailed accounts of the most important deserts." Publisher's note

Includes glossary and bibliographical references

Banting, Erinn

Caves; Erinn Banting. AV2 by Weigl 2012 32 p. col. ill., col. map (Ecosystems) (hardcover) $28.55; (paperback) $13.95

Grades: 4 5 6   **577.5**
1. Caves 2. Cave ecology 3. Ecology 4. Cave ecology
ISBN 1616906391; 1616906456; 9781616906399; 9781616906450
            LC 2010050985

This book by Erinn Banting is part of the "Biomes" series. "Caves are unique ecosystems that are found on all seven continents. This book explores the plants and animals that have adapted to life in this unique environment." (Publisher's note) "Explanations of climate and physical characteristics are accompanied by appropriate diagrams and illustrations." (School Library Journal)

Fridell, Ron

Life in the desert. Franklin Watts 2005 63p il map (Biomes and habitats) lib bdg $25.50

Grades: 4 5 6 7   **577.5**
1. Deserts 2. Desert ecology
ISBN 0-531-12384-7
            LC 2004027254

Presents an introduction to desert environments, in simple text with illustrations, providing information on its average temperature, climate, plant and animal life, and people
Includes glossary and bibliographical references

Lynch, Wayne
Sonoran Desert; text and photographs by Wayne Lynch; assisted by Aubrey Lang. NorthWord Books 2009 64p il (Our wild world ecosystems) $16.95
Grades: 5 6 7 8   577.5
1. Desert ecology 2. Sonoran Desert 3. Natural history -- Sonoran Desert
ISBN 978-1-58979-389-7; 1-58979-389-7
LC 2008036635
"An in-depth look at a vibrant ecosystem. Spilling over the Mexican border into Arizona and New Mexico, the Sonoran Desert is especially rich in varied plants, animals, insects, and other critters that call it home. Lynch shares his expertise and experiences in a clearly written, conversational text, lavishly illustrated with his own crisp color photos." SLJ

Warhol, Tom
Desert; [by] Tom Warhol. Marshall Cavendish Benchmark 2006 80p il (Earth's biomes) lib bdg $34.21
Grades: 6 7 8 9   577.5
1. Deserts 2. Desert ecology
ISBN 978-0-7614-2194-8 lib bdg; 0-7614-2194-7 lib bdg
LC 2006015823
"Explores desert biomes and covers where they are located as well as the plants and animals that inhabit them." Publisher's note
Includes glossary and bibliographical references

Tundra; [by] Tom Warhol. Marshall Cavendish Benchmark 2006 80p il (Earth's biomes) lib bdg $34.21
Grades: 6 7 8 9   577.5
1. Tundra ecology
ISBN 978-0-7614-2193-1 lib bdg; 0-7614-2193-9 lib bdg
LC 2006015822
"The clarity of the narrative and the spectacular photographs . . . make this . . . an appealing, useful addition to the . . . school." Voice of Youth Advocates
Includes glossary and bibliographical references

577.6 Aquatic ecology

Lynette, Rachel
River food chains. Heinemann Library 2011 48p il map (Protecting food chains) lib bdg $32; pa $8.99
Grades: 4 5 6 7   577.6
1. River ecology 2. Food chains (Ecology)
ISBN 978-1-4329-3861-1 lib bdg; 1-4329-3861-4 lib bdg; 978-1-4329-3868-0 pa; 1-4329-3868-1 pa
LC 2009049552

This book explores the species found in river food chains and webs, and discusses why these food chains and webs need to be protected.
"Featuring colorful, glossy images and accessible prose, this . . . offers a good introduction to the web of life in rivers. . . . Conservation issues are highlighted throughout, with specific suggestions for youth to get involved. . . . An informative, thought-provoking resource that conveys the fragile, interconnected web that holds ecosystems together." Booklist
Includes glossary and bibliographical references

Toupin, Laurie
Freshwater habitats; life in freshwater ecosystems. F. Watts 2005 63p il map (Biomes and habitats) lib bdg $25.50; pa $8.95
Grades: 4 5 6 7   577.6
1. Freshwater ecology
ISBN 0-531-12305-7 lib bdg; 0-531-16675-9 pa
LC 2003-16572
A look at the plants, animals, locations, and various habitats that make up the freshwater ecosystems of the world

Warhol, Tom
Water; [by] Tom Warhol. Marshall Cavendish Benchmark 2006 80p il (Earth's biomes) lib bdg $34.21
Grades: 6 7 8 9   577.6
1. Marine ecology 2. Freshwater biology
ISBN 978-0-7614-2192-4 lib bdg; 0-7614-2192-0 lib bdg
LC 2006011979
"Explores water biomes and covers where they are located as well as the plants and animals that inhabit them." Publisher's note
Includes glossary and bibliographical references

577.7 Marine ecology

Carson, Rachel
The **edge** of the sea; with illustrations by Bob Hines. Houghton Mifflin 1955 276p il hardcover o.p. pa $14
Grades: 7 8 9 10 11 12 Adult   577.7
1. Seashore 2. Marine biology
ISBN 0-395-92496-0 pa
"The seashores of the world may be divided into three basic types: the rugged shores of rock, the sand beaches, and the coral reefs and all their associated features. Each has its typical community of plants and animals. The Atlantic coast of the United States [provides] clear examples of each of these types. I have chosen it as the setting for my pictures of shore life." Preface

Cousteau, Philippe, 1980-
Make a splash! a kid's guide to protecting our oceans, lakes, rivers & wetlands. by Cathryn Berger Kaye ; with Philippe Cousteau and EarthEcho International. Free Spirit Pub. Inc. 2013 125 p. ill. (chiefly col.) (paperback) $13.99

Grades: 3 4 5 6   **577.7**

1. Environmentalists 2. Water conservation 3. Marine ecology 4. Environmentalism 5. Marine pollution -- Prevention

ISBN 1575424177; 9781575424170

LC 2012032120

This book for elementary-age readers has "colorful photos and digital drawings [that] illustrate many aspects of water on Earth, while the text provides information and tells stories of children in elementary schools around the world who have translated their own environmental concerns into action." (Booklist)

O'Neill, Michael Patrick

Wild waters photo journal. Batfish Books 2010 106p il $29.95

Grades: 6 7 8 9 10   **577.7**

1. Marine animals 2. Marine ecology

ISBN 978-0-9728653-6-4; 0-9728653-6-5

"This personal collection of stunning, full-color photographs highlights unique underwater habitats and the life found in select natural communities around the world. Full spreads provide either an overview of an ecosystem, e.g., Komodo National Park or Bali in Indonesia, or a signature animal, e.g., the great white shark at Guadalupe Island, Mexico, or a dwarf caiman in Brazil. . . . The photographs are compelling by themselves and beautiful to browse. This book informs readers and gives them a deeper understanding of the ever-present threats to the ecological diversity and beauty of the planet." SLJ

Parker, Steve, 1952-

★ **Seashore**; written by Steve Parker. rev ed; DK Pub. 2004 72p il (DK eyewitness books) $15.99

Grades: 4 5 6 7   **577.7**

1. Seashore 2. Marine plants 3. Marine animals

ISBN 0-7566-0721-3; 0-7566-0720-5 lib bdg

First published 1989 by Knopf

Brief text and photos introduce the animal inhabitants of the seashore, including fish, crustaceans, snails, and shorebirds

Pyers, Greg

The **biodiversity** of coral reefs. Marshall Cavendish 2010 32p il map lib bdg $28.50

Grades: 4 5 6 7   **577.7**

1. Coral reefs and islands

ISBN 978-1-60870-070-7 lib bdg; 1-60870-070-4 lib bdg

"Discusses the variety of living things in a coral reef's ecosystem." Publisher's note

Walker, Pamela

★ The **coral** reef; [by] Pam Walker and Elaine Wood. Facts on File 2005 140p (Life in the sea) $35

Grades: 6 7 8 9 10   **577.7**

1. Coral reefs and islands

ISBN 0-8160-5703-6

"An opening chapter gives detailed coverage of how reefs are formed. Later chapters examine the reefs' inhab-

itants, from essential microbes to the larger, showier fish, reptiles, and other animals. The final chapter . . . mentions environmental hazards and conservation efforts. . . . The range and depth of information . . . make this a fine addition for science collections." Booklist

577.8   Synecology and population biology

Silverstein, Alvin

★ **Symbiosis**; [by] Alvin Silverstein, Virginia Silverstein, and Laura Silverstein Nunn. rev ed.; Twenty-First Century Books 2008 96p il (Science concepts, second series) lib bdg $31.93

Grades: 6 7 8 9   **577.8**

1. Symbiosis

ISBN 978-0-8225-6799-8 lib bdg; 0-8225-6799-7 lib bdg

LC 2007003184

First published 1998

Discusses the three kinds of symbiosis—mutualism, commensalism, and parasitism—and describes examples of these relationships.

"Well researched and interesting and the format is inviting for both general-interest reading and research." SLJ [review of 1998 edition]

Includes bibliographical references

U-X-L encyclopedia of biomes; [editor] Marlene Weigel. 2nd ed.; U-X-L 2009 3v il map set $214

Grades: 7 8 9 10   **577.8**

1. Reference books 2. Ecology -- Encyclopedias

ISBN 978-1-4144-5516-7

LC 2008-14502

First published 1999

"Entries range from 35 to 45 pages and cover an overview and description, climate, elevation, soil, water bodies, vegetation, animal life, food web, plant and animal adaptations, endangered species, human effects on the biome and the effects of the environment on humans' culture and economy." Publisher's note

Includes bibliographical references

578   Natural history of organisms and related subjects

Kelsey, Elin

★ **Strange** new species; astonishing discoveries of life on earth. Maple Tree Press 2005 96p il $24.95; pa $16.95

Grades: 5 6 7 8   **578**

1. Biology 2. Scientists 3. Natural history

ISBN 1-897066-31-7; 1-897066-32-5 pa

"This large-format book showcases new species . . . and the scientists who have discovered them. . . . The discussion ends with information on cloning, genetically modified food, and the future of life. . . . With many excellent photos, this introductory book on new species will be an intriguing addition to classroom units on classification or biology." Booklist

Wildlife and plants; 3rd ed.; Marshall Cavendish 2007 20v il set $359.95

Grades: 4 5 6 7 **578**

1. Reference books 2. Plants -- Encyclopedias 3. Animals -- Encyclopedias
ISBN 978-0-7614-7693-1

First published 1994 with title: Wildlife and plants of the world

This set includes "more than 500 entries covering animals, plants, microorganisms, fungi, habitats, biomes, and overviews. . . . Entries provide a concise introduction followed by more detailed information including behavior, reproduction, characteristics, and survival tactics. . . . With its captivating information and photographs, students are sure to come to this easy-to-use set again and again." Booklist

578.4 Adaptation

Fullick, Ann

★ **Adaptation** and competition; [by] Ann Fullick. Heinemann Library 2006 64p il map (Life science in depth) lib bdg $34.29; pa $9.90

Grades: 6 7 8 9 **578.4**

1. Heredity 2. Adaptation (Biology)
ISBN 1-4034-7518-0 lib bdg; 1-4034-7526-1 pa

LC 2005023560

This "provides a detailed overview of how living organisms compete with one another to survive and how they adapt to climate and habitat. The style makes some complex science accessible, and the attractive book design breaks up the dense text. . . . The examples are lively." Booklist

Includes bibliographical references

Schafer, Susan

Adaptations. M.E. Sharpe 2009 96p il (Genetics: the science of life) $38.95 **578.4**

1. Adaptation (Biology)
ISBN 978-0-7656-8137-9; 0-7656-8137-4

LC 2008-8106

This discusses genetic adaptations in regard to defenses, feeding, and reproduction.

"Chock-full of information. . . . The material is well organized and accessible. . . . Interest is maintained through countless fascinating examples. . . . Illustrations and color photographs enhance [the text]." SLJ

Includes bibliographical references

Silverstein, Alvin

★ **Adaptation**; by Alvin Silverstein, Virginia Silverstein, and Laura Silverstein Nunn. Twenty-First Century Books 2008 112p il (Science concepts) lib bdg $31.93

Grades: 4 5 6 7 **578.4**

1. Adaptation (Biology)
ISBN 978-0-8225-3434-1 lib bdg; 0-8225-3434-7 lib bdg

LC 2007-02862

This "provides an accessible introduction to how living beings adapt to survive in diverse habitats. . . . The narrative gains clarity from abundant examples, colorful photos and diagrams, and fascinating sidebars." Booklist

Includes bibliographical references

Spilsbury, Richard

Adaptation and survival. Rosen Central 2010 46p il map (Living processes) lib bdg $26.50; pa $11.75

Grades: 5 6 7 **578.4**

1. Ecology 2. Adaptation (Biology)
ISBN 978-1-61532-343-2 lib bdg; 1-61532-343-0 lib bdg; 978-1-61532-348-7 pa; 1-61532-348-1 pa

LC 2009-30418

"With colorful, quality photography, the well-organized content is divided into short chapters with bold subheadings making information easy to find. Clear and interesting writing distinguishes this . . . from older titles. The captions for pictures are used to provide identification and additional explanation for topics not included in the text." Libr Media Connect

Includes glossary and bibliographical references

578.6 Miscellaneous nontaxonomic kinds of organisms

Collard, Sneed B.

Science warriors; the battle against invasive species. written by Sneed B. Collard III. Houghton Mifflin 2008 48p il (Scientists in the field) $17

Grades: 5 6 7 8 **578.6**

1. Nonindigenous pests 2. Biological invasions
ISBN 978-0-618-75636-0; 0-618-75636-1

LC 2008-01867

"Collard focuses on four major invader species in the U.S.: the brown tree snake, . . . the red imported fire ant, . . . the melaleuca tree, . . . and the zebra mussel. . . . These are useful and thought-provoking case studies of a very large problem." Bull Cent Child Books

Includes glossary and bibliographical references

Fleisher, Paul

★ **Parasites**; latching on to a free lunch. Twenty-First Century Books 2006 112p il (Discovery!) lib bdg $29.27

Grades: 7 8 9 10 **578.6**

1. Parasites
ISBN 978-0-8225-3415-0; 0-8225-3415-0

LC 2005-10521

This is "well organized and quite up to date. The photos . . . are plentiful, colorful, and excellent. . . . Clear, concise, and interesting." Voice Youth Advocates

This book describes "all sorts of unpleasant creatures that can feed on your body—head lice, fleas, ticks, tapeworms, and fungi—as well as the huge variety of parasites that feed on animals and plants all around you." Publisher's note

Includes bibliographical references

578.68   Rare and endangered species

Endangered species: opposing viewpoints; Viqi Wagner, book editor. Greenhaven Press 2008 230p map (Opposing viewpoints series) lib bdg $38.50; pa $26.75

Grades: 8 9 10 11 12   **578.68**
1. Endangered species 2. Nature conservation
ISBN 978-0-7377-2931-3 lib bdg; 978-0-7377-2932-0 pa

LC 2007-38314

This collection of articles offers varying viewpoints on extinction, preservation, property rights, and international cooperation.

Includes bibliographical references

Pobst, Sandy

★ **Animals** on the edge; science races to save species threatened with extinction. by Sandra Pobst; Todd K. Fuller, consultant. National Geographic 2008 64p il (National Geographic investigates) $17.95; lib bdg $27.90

Grades: 4 5 6 7   **578.68**
1. Endangered species 2. Wildlife conservation
ISBN 978-1-4263-0358-6; 1-4263-0358-0; 978-1-4263-0265-7 lib bdg; 1-4263-0265-7 lib bdg

This "eye-catching [title features] full-color photographs.... The approach is to understand the challenges to protecting endangered animals, including global warming, destruction of habitat, tagging and tracking, poaching, captive breeding, and cloning." Voice Youth Advocates

Includes glossary and bibliographical references

578.7   Organisms characteristic of specific kinds of environments

Conlan, Kathy

Under the ice. Kids Can Press 2002 55p il $16.95; pa $8.95

Grades: 4 5 6 7   **578.7**
1. Marine biology 2. Marine pollution 3. Polar regions
ISBN 1-55337-001-5; 1-55337-060-0 pa

"The first-person text creates a feeling of immediacy... . Well-captioned, color photos appear throughout the book. ... Conlan ... offers readers an engaging account of her adventurous career in scientific field research." Booklist

Kirby, Richard R.

Ocean drifters; a secret world beneath the waves. Firefly Books 2011 192p il $29.95

Grades: 5 6 7 8 9 10 11 12 Adult   **578.7**
1. Marine plankton
ISBN 978-1-55407-982-7; 1-55407-982-9

LC 2011284690

"Kirby (Marine Inst. Research Fellow, Plymouth Univ., UK), who has published widely in scientific journals, combines in this book his area of expertise-plankton-with magnificent color photography of each species. He details the importance of the ocean's plankton layer to the health of the globe and its effects on sea and human life in the photos'

descriptions...Recommended for readers interested in the smaller denizens of the natural world, the ocean, or microphotography." (Library Journal)

Includes bibliographical references

Kummer, Patricia K.

The **Great** Barrier Reef; by Patricia K. Kummer. Marshall Cavendish Benchmark 2008 96p il map (Nature's wonders) lib bdg $24.95

Grades: 5 6 7 8   **578.7**
1. Coral reefs and islands 2. Great Barrier Reef (Australia)
ISBN 978-0-7614-2852-7 lib bdg; 0-7614-2852-6 lib bdg

LC 2007026661

"Provides comprehensive information on the geography, history, wildlife, peoples, and environmental issues of the Great Barrier Reef." Publisher's note

Includes glossary and bibliographical references

Moore, Peter D.

Wetlands; illustrations by Richard Garratt. rev ed.; Facts on File 2008 270p il map (Ecosystem) $70

Grades: 7 8 9 10   **578.7**
1. Wetlands
ISBN 0-8160-5931-4; 978-0-8160-5931-7

LC 2006-37399

First published 2000

This book "examines the diversity of wetlands in the past, present, and future, how they work, and how they can be conserved." Publisher's note

Includes glossary and bibliographical references

Somervill, Barbara A.

Marine biologist. Cherry Lake Pub. 2009 32p il (Cool science careers) lib bdg $27.07

Grades: 3 4 5 6   **578.7**
1. Marine biology 2. Vocational guidance
ISBN 978-1-60279-504-4 lib bdg; 1-60279-504-5 lib bdg

LC 2008045234

This describes the career of marine biologist, including ways to become involved in the profession, the interests and skills required, and activities for learning more

This is "highly readable.... Colorful photographs illustrate [the] book." SLJ

Includes glossary and bibliographical references

Thomas, William David

Marine biologist. Gareth Stevens Pub. 2010 32p il (Cool careers: cutting edge) lib bdg $26; pa $8.95

Grades: 4 5 6   **578.7**
1. Marine biology 2. Vocational guidance
ISBN 978-1-4339-1957-2 lib bdg; 1-4339-1957-5 lib bdg; 978-1-4339-2156-8 pa; 1-4339-2156-1 pa

LC 2009000239

Describes the work of a marine biologist.

This title offers "clear, solid information in a large font. . . . [This] short [book is] packed with relevant, current material." SLJ

Includes glossary and bibliographical references

Walker, Pamela

★ The **continental** shelf; [by] Pam Walker & Elaine Wood. Facts on File 2005 142p (Life in the sea) $35

Grades: 6 7 8 9   **578.7**

1. Marine biology 2. Continental shelf

ISBN 0-8160-5704-4

This "title presents a comprehensive discussion of the physical aspects of the continental shelf; the variety of life beneath, on, and above the waters; and the many dangers to the health of these realms. . . . [This title has] helpful color photos and black-and-white charts and drawings. [This] important [work is] accessible to a variety of student abilities and should be considered for all collections." SLJ

Includes bibliographical references

★ The **open** ocean; [by] Pam Walker and Elaine Wood. Facts on File 2005 132p il (Life in the sea) $35

Grades: 6 7 8 9   **578.7**

1. Oceanography 2. Marine animals 3. Marine ecology

ISBN 0-8160-5705-2

     LC 2004-24228

In this title "the areas beyond the continental shelf are profiled, and food chains, the diversity of life forms, and the anatomy of sea animals are discussed. . . . [This book includes] helpful color photos and black-and-white charts and drawings. [This] important [work is] accessible to a variety of student abilities and should be considered for all collections." SLJ

Includes bibliographical references

Wallace, Marianne D.

America's forests; guide to plants and animals. Fulcrum Pub. 2009 47p il (America's ecosystems) pa $11.95

Grades: 5 6 7 8   **578.7**

1. Forest plants 2. Forest animals 3. Forest ecology 4. Forests and forestry

ISBN 978-1-55591-595-7 pa; 1-55591-595-7 pa

     LC 2008041005

This "is a guide to plants and animals within the context of forest communities. Marianne Wallace . . . expertly crafts this introduction to forests. . . . The book contains abundant illustrations." Sci Books Films

Includes glossary

Wechsler, Doug

Marvels in the muck; life in the salt marshes. Boyds Mills Press 2008 48p il $17.95

Grades: 4 5 6 7   **578.7**

1. Salt marshes 2. Marsh ecology

ISBN 978-1-59078-588-1

     LC 2007052583

"A season-by-season look at the ecology of an oft-over-looked habitat. Wechsler's lucid text introduces the insects,

birds, reptiles, crustaceans, and other critters that claim this salty expanse as home. . . . Clear color photos present species mentioned in the text." SLJ

Includes glossary and bibliographical references

Winner, Cherie

Life on the edge. Lerner Publications Co. 2006 48p il (Cool science) lib bdg $26.60

Grades: 4 5 6   **578.7**

1. Adaptation (Biology)

ISBN 978-0-8225-2499-1 lib bdg; 0-8225-2499-6 lib bdg

     LC 2005011071

This book "introduces creatures in extreme conditions such as thermal pools, Antarctica, and the deep sea. [The book provides] clear explanations of the science and [covers] possible benefits to humans. A variety of photos and information boxes provide an eye-catching . . . layout." Horn Book Guide

Includes glossary and bibliographical references

579   Natural history of microorganisms, fungi, algae

Arato, Rona

Protists; algae, amoebas, plankton, and other protists. Crabtree Pub. Co. 2010 48p il (A class of their own) lib bdg $29.27; pa $9.95

Grades: 5 6 7 8   **579**

1. Algae 2. Protists 3. Protozoa

ISBN 978-0-7787-5377-3 lib bdg; 0-7787-5377-8 lib bdg; 978-0-7787-5391-9 pa; 0-7787-5391-3 pa

     LC 2009-51386

Looks at the protist kingdom, providing information and examples of species from the major phyla, as well as information about the role of protists in the food chain and in various diseases.

"Lively section headings . . . and notes on uncommon achievements, . . . lighten the substantial load of biological terminology. Illustrated with a plethora of closeup color photos and microphotos, and closing with annotated lists of recommended Web sites, . . . [this captures] the remarkable diversity of life." SLJ

Includes glossary and bibliographical references

Bardhan-Quallen, Sudipta

Kitchen science experiments; how does your mold garden grow? illustrated by Edward Miller. Sterling 2010 64p il (Mad science) $12.95

Grades: 4 5 6   **579**

1. Biology 2. Microbiology 3. Science -- Experiments

ISBN 978-1-4027-2413-8; 1-4027-2413-6

     LC 2010003749

"The language is as much fun as the science, including wordplay warnings . . . and the design is inviting, with colorful diagrams on each spacious, double-page spread. . . . Many students will be hooked by the fascinating revelations about the world around them." Booklist

Includes bibliographical references

Brown, Jordan

Micro mania; a really close-up look at bacteria, bedbugs & the zillions of other gross little creatures that live in, on & all around you! [by] Jordan D. Brown. Imagine! 2010 80p il $19.95

Grades: 4 5 6   579

1. Microorganisms

ISBN 978-0-9823064-2-0; 0-9823064-2-3

"This engrossing book goes into squirm-inducing detail about the bacteria, microbes, and other assorted mini-organisms that dwell in our bodies and our homes. Each spread is well laid out with plenty of white space, large text, and colorful photos of these little critters . . . and the havoc they wreak. The writing is vivid without being breathless." SLJ

Latta, Sara L.

★ The good, the bad, the slimy; the secret life of microbes. [by] Sara Latta; photographs by Dennis Kunkel. Enslow Publishers 2006 128p il lib bdg $31.93

Grades: 5 6 7 8 9   579

1. Microorganisms

ISBN 0-7660-1294-8

LC 2005-35405

"Explanations are simple and clear, and the layout is appeling, open, and colorful." SLJ

Includes glossary and bibliographical references

May, Suellen

Invasive microbes. Chelsea House 2007 112p il (Invasive species) $30

Grades: 8 9 10 11 12   579

1. Microorganisms 2. Biological invasions

ISBN 0-7910-9131-7; 978-0-7910-9131-9

LC 2006011031

"An increase in global transportation has helped even the tiniest of organisms—microbes—find their way to new environments. . . . This . . . resource . . . [explains] the . . . impact . . . of invasive viruses, bacteria, protists, and fungi. This book evaluates scenarios for success in the escalating battle for containment." Publisher's note

Includes glossary and bibliographical references

Micro monsters. Kingfisher 2010 47p il (Kingdom) $14.99; pa $8.99

Grades: 3 4 5 6   579

1. Insects 2. Microorganisms

ISBN 978-0-7534-3014-9; 0-7534-3014-2; 978-0-7534-6455-7 pa; 0-7534-6455-1 pa

This book illustrates the unseen world of microscopic monsters and shows the reader how they survive and triumph. Some pages have movable flaps to show different pictures.

"Hyper-close-up photos detail all manner of stingers, stabbers, pincers, and chompers poking out from plated exoskeletons and hairy abdomens. This . . . is a great way to sneak in some basic science learning amid the din of death and destruction." Booklist

Parker, Steve, 1952-

Protozoans, algae & other protists. Compass Point Books 2009 48p il (Kingdom classification) lib bdg $29.32

Grades: 6 7 8 9   579

1. Algae 2. Protozoa

ISBN 978-0-7565-4224-5 lib bdg; 0-7565-4224-3 lib bdg

LC 2009-8783

Discusses the parts of protists, different types, their life cycles, and how they can be harmful to humans

"With its compelling facts and visuals, this is a quality choice." SLJ

Includes glossary

Stefoff, Rebecca

The Moneran kingdom; by Rebecca Stefoff. Marshall Cavendish Benchmark 2008 96p il (Family trees) $23.95

Grades: 6 7 8 9   579

1. Microorganisms

ISBN 978-0-7614-3076-6; 0-7614-3076-8

LC 2008-23210

"Explores the habitats, life cycles, and other characteristics of organisms in the Moneran kingdom." Publisher's note

Includes bibliographical references

Walker, Richard, 1951-

Microscopic life; [by] Richard Walker; foreword by Peter C. Doherty. Kingfisher 2004 63p il (Kingfisher knowledge) $12.95

Grades: 4 5 6 7   579

1. Microorganisms

ISBN 0-7534-5778-4

LC 2004-1321

"Double-page spreads introduce viruses, bacteria, 'mini animals' (e.g., Hydra and dust mites), and other microorganisms and explain how these unseen entities affect humanity in both harmful and helpful ways. The accompanying photographic enlargements . . . are fascinating." Horn Book Guide

Wearing, Judy

Fungi; mushrooms, toadstools, molds, yeasts, and other fungi. Crabtree 2010 48p il (A class of their own) lib bdg $29.27; pa $9.95

Grades: 5 6 7 8   579

1. Fungi

ISBN 978-0-7787-5375-9 lib bdg; 0-7787-5375-1 lib bdg; 978-0-7787-5389-6 pa; 0-7787-5389-1 pa

Features an examination of the four major groups of fungi: yeasts, toadstools, chytrids, and bread molds.

"Lively section headings . . . and notes on uncommon achievements, . . . lighten the substantial load of biological terminology. Illustrated with a plethora of closeup color photos and microphotos, and closing with annotated lists of recommended Web sites, . . . [thi scaptures] the remarkable diversity of life." SLJ

Includes glossary and bibliographical references

Zabludoff, Marc

★ The **protoctist** kingdom. Benchmark Books 2006 95p il (Family trees) lib bdg $29.92

Grades: 5 6 7 8 **579**

1. Protoctista

ISBN 0-7614-1818-0

LC 2004-21821

This examines the physical traits, adaptations, diets, habitats, and life cycles of such life forms as bacteria, amoebas, slime nets, molds, algae, coccoliths, forams, and diatoms.

"Fact-filled, yet surprisingly readable. . . . [This] title contains a wide variety of excellent-quality, full-color photographs; interesting sidebars; and diagrams." SLJ

Zamosky, Lisa

Simple organisms. Compass Point Books 2009 40p il (Mission: science) lib bdg $26.60

Grades: 4 5 6 **579**

1. Microorganisms

ISBN 978-0-7565-3955-9 lib bdg; 0-7565-3955-2 lib bdg

LC 2008-7723

An introduction to microscopic organisms, including germs

Includes glossary and bibliographical references

579.3   Prokaryotes (Bacteria)

Barker, David M.

Archaea; salt-lovers, methane-makers, thermophiles, and other archaeans. by David Barker. Crabtree Pub. 2010 48p il (A class of their own) lib bdg $29.27; pa $9.95

Grades: 5 6 7 8 **579.3**

1. Bacteria

ISBN 978-0-7787-5373-5 lib bdg; 0-7787-5373-5 lib bdg; 978-0-7787-5387-2 pa; 0-7787-5387-5 pa

LC 2009-51393

Looks at the archaea domain, providing information and examples of species from the three major phyla, as well as information about why so little is known about this diverse domain.

"Lively section headings . . . and notes on uncommon achievements, . . . lighten the substantial load of biological terminology. Illustrated with a plethora of closeup color photos and microphotos, and closing with annotated lists of recommended Web sites, . . . [this captures] the remarkable diversity of life." SLJ

Includes glossary and bibliographical references

Gardy, Jennifer

It's catching; the infectious world of germs and microbes. Jennifer Gardy, PhD, Josh Holinaty. Owlkids Books, Inc. 2014 63 p. $18.95

Grades: 5 6 7 **579.3**

1. Viruses 2. Bacteria 3. Germ theory of disease 4. Microorganisms

ISBN 1771470011; 9781771470018; 9781771470537

LC 2013949230

In this book, author Jennifer Gardy "picks up her microscope to bring expert insight to the microbes that are all around us but are too small to see. [She] discusses a range of germs and the diseases they cause, from the common cold to food poisoning to the Ebola virus." (Publisher's note)

"An amusing but information-packed look at all things infectious. The cartoon illustrations and chatty text with terms like "tummy" and "cooties" and phrases such as "a quick pit stop in the liver" might lead some to assume this is a lightweight read, but there's plenty to offer in this complex but comprehensible work...This readable, slender introduction to the world of microbial life is an entertaining and informative eye-opener." SLJ

Wearing, Judy

Bacteria; staph, strep, clostridium, and other bacteria. Crabtree 2010 48p il (A class of their own) lib bdg $29.27; pa $9.95

Grades: 5 6 7 8 **579.3**

1. Bacteria

ISBN 978-0-7787-5374-2 lib bdg; 0-7787-5374-3 lib bdg; 978-0-7787-5388-9 pa; 0-7787-5388-3 pa

Examines bacteria that are found in virtually every environment-including those that are characterized by extreme heat, cold, and depth-and, of course, bacteria that are found inside our bodies.

"Lively section headings . . . and notes on uncommon achievements, . . . lighten the substantial load of biological terminology. Illustrated with a plethora of closeup color photos and microphotos, and closing with annotated lists of recommended Web sites, . . . [this captures] the remarkable diversity of life." SLJ

Includes glossary and bibliographical references

579.5   Fungi

Parker, Steve, 1952-

Molds, mushrooms & other fungi. Compass Point Books 2009 48p il (Kingdom classification) lib bdg $29.32

Grades: 6 7 8 9 **579.5**

1. Fungi 2. Mushrooms

ISBN 978-0-7565-4223-8 lib bdg; 0-7565-4223-5 lib bdg

LC 2009-10749

Discusses the parts of fungi, different types, folklore about them, where they grow, how people use them, and how they can be harmful to humans, plants, and animals

"With its compelling facts and visuals, this is a quality choice." SLJ

Includes glossary

Stefoff, Rebecca

The **fungus** kingdom. Marshall Cavendish Benchmark 2008 95p il (Family trees) lib bdg $32.79

Grades: 6 7 8 9 **579.5**

1. Fungi

ISBN 978-0-7614-2696-7; 0-7614-2696-5

LC 2007003485

"Explores the habitats, life cycles, and other characteristics of organisms in the Fungus Kingdom." Publisher's note

Includes bibliographical references

579.6 Mushrooms

Lincoff, Gary

★ The **Audubon** Society field guide to North American mushrooms; [by] Gary H. Lincoff; visual key by Carol Nehring. Knopf 1981 926p il $19.95

Grades: 7 8 9 10 11 12 Adult   **579.6**

1. Mushrooms

ISBN 0-394-51992-2

LC 81-80827

This guide to 703 species of common mushrooms provides 762 color photographs and descriptions as keys to identifying these plants.

"The author is an expert on mushroom toxins and instills responsible cautions. The photos are uncommonly beautiful." SLJ

580 Natural history of plants and animals

Ballard, Carol

Plant variation and classification. Rosen Central 2010 46p il (Living processes) lib bdg $26.50; pa $11.75

Grades: 5 6 7   **580**

1. Plants 2. Variation (Biology) 3. Biology -- Classification

ISBN 978-1-61532-345-6 lib bdg; 1-61532-345-7 lib bdg; 978-1-61532-346-3 pa; 1-61532-346-5 pa

Explains how our plant classification system works and looks at how scientists use it to identify and group plant species. The book also examines the variation between and within plants species and discusses how and why such variations have occurred.

"With colorful, quality photography, the well-organized content is divided into short chapters with bold subheadings making information easy to find. Clear and interesting writing distinguishes this . . . from older titles. The captions for pictures are used to provide identification and additional explanation for topics not included in the text." Libr Media Connect

Includes glossary and bibliographical references

Casper, Julie Kerr

Plants; life from the earth. Chelsea House 2007 194p il (Natural resources) $39.50

Grades: 8 9 10 11 12   **580**

1. Botany 2. Plants

ISBN 978-0-8160-6358-1; 0-8160-6358-3

LC 2006-28965

This "examines the many plants that exist and the role they play in biodiversity. It focuses on key preservation issues affecting plant life, and the ways everyone can become a 'backyard conservationist.'" Publisher's note

Includes bibliographical references

Gibson, J. Phil

Plant diversity; [by] J. Phil Gibson and Terri R. Gibson. Chelsea House 2006 136p il (The green world) $37.50

Grades: 7 8 9 10 11 12   **580**

1. Plants

ISBN 0-7910-8960-6; 978-0-7910-8960-6

LC 2006-23234

Explores the diversity and natural history of green plants throughout the world.

This book is "lavishly illustrated with full-color photographs and illustrative diagrams . . . written in a clear but not condescending style. . . . An excellent series of sidebars presents questions and then supports the reader in reasoning to the answers. . . . [It is] well worth the investment." Libr Media Connect

Includes glossary and bibliographical references

Levine, Shar

Plants; flowering plants, ferns, mosses, and other plants. by Shar Levine and Leslie Johnstone. Crabtree Pub. 2010 48p il (A class of their own) lib bdg $29.27; pa $9.95

Grades: 5 6 7 8   **580**

1. Plants

ISBN 978-0-7787-5376-6 lib bdg; 0-7787-5376-X lib bdg; 978-0-7787-5390-2 pa; 0-7787-5390-5 pa

LC 2009-51342

Describes the main groups of plants, including mosses, ferns, conifers, and flowering plants.

"Lively section headings . . . and notes on uncommon achievements, . . . lighten the substantial load of biological terminology. Illustrated with a plethora of closeup color photos and microphotos, and closing with annotated lists of recommended Web sites, . . . [this captures] the remarkable diversity of life." SLJ

Includes glossary and bibliographical references

Stefoff, Rebecca

★ The **flowering** plant division. Benchmark Books 2006 91p il (Family trees) $20.95

Grades: 6 7 8 9   **580**

1. Plants

ISBN 0-7614-1817-2

This examines the physical traits, adaptations, habitats, and life cycles of flowering plants.

Includes glossary and bibliographical references

Taylor, Barbara

Inside plants. Marshall Cavendish Benchmark 2010 48p il (Invisible worlds) lib bdg $28.50

Grades: 4 5 6 7   **580**

1. Plants

ISBN 978-0-7614-4189-2 lib bdg; 0-7614-4189-1 lib bdg

LC 2008037247

This describes the plant details that are too small for the unaided eye to see, and how these microscopic systems work to keep the plant alive and healthy.

The narrative is "clear, well written, broken down into manageable pieces, and peppered with eye-opening facts.

The numerous photographs are so phenomenal that they will inspire kids to read the text . . . so that they can wrap their minds around what they see." SLJ

Includes glossary and bibliographical references

580.7 Education, research, related topics

Gardner, Robert

Ace your plant science project; great science fair ideas. [by] Robert Gardner and Phyllis J. Perry. Enslow Publishers 2009 104p il (Ace your biology science project) lib bdg $31.93

Grades: 5 6 7 8 **580.7**

1. Plants 2. Science projects 3. Science -- Experiments
ISBN 978-0-7660-3221-7 lib bdg; 0-7660-3221-3 lib bdg

LC 2008-4687

"Presents several science experiments and project ideas using plants." Publisher's note

Includes bibliographical references

Whitehouse, Patricia

Plants; [by] Patricia Whitehouse. Heinemann Library 2008 48p il (Science fair projects) $30

Grades: 5 6 7 8 **580.7**

1. Plants 2. Science projects 3. Science -- Experiments
ISBN 978-1-4034-7918-1

LC 2006039547

This guide to science fair projects about plants "is one of the better 'how-to-do-a-science-fair project' books on the market. . . . [It] guides students with initial concrete suggestions and ideas for projects, but continues to challenge students to extend their investigations. . . . The content is presented in a colorful and engaging format." Sci Books Films

Includes glossary and bibliographical references

580.75 Museum activities and services

Silvey, Anita

The plant hunters; true stories of their daring adventures to the far corners of the Earth. Anita Silvey. Farrar Straus Giroux 2012 88 p. col. ill. $19.99

Grades: 6 7 8 9 10 **580.75**

1. Botanists 2. Collectors and collecting 3. Plants -- Collection and preservation 4. Plant collecting -- History 5. Plant collectors -- Biography
ISBN 0374309086; 9780374309084

LC 2011005161

This book "introduces European and North American plant hunters, primarily from the nineteenth and twentieth centuries. Driven by curiosity, commerce, and 'botonomania,' they sought to collect valuable plant specimens around the world. Likening Baron Alexander von Humboldt to Indiana Jones and calling the plant hunters' experiences 'amazing escapades,' [Anita] Silvey . . . recount[s] horrific experiences reported by various plant hunters." (Booklist)

"The slim, engaging narrative paints vivid portraits of these botanic adventurers. It is smoothly written, smartly

paced and filled with exciting tales of risk taking and derring-do." Kirkus

581 Specific topics in natural history of plants

Munoz, William

Plants on the trail with Lewis and Clark; photographs by William Muñoz. Clarion Bks. 2003 104p il map $18

Grades: 4 5 6 7 **581**

1. Lewis and Clark Expedition (1804-1806) 2. Plants -- United States 3. West (U.S.) -- Exploration
ISBN 0-618-06776-0

LC 2002-10383

Describes the journey of Lewis and Clark through the western United States, focusing on the plants they cataloged, their uses for food and medicine, and the plant lore of Native American people

"Good-quality, full-color photos and reproductions clearly extend the text. . . . The author's knowledge of and keen interest in her subject matter is very evident in this fascinating account." SLJ

Includes bibliographical references (p. 88-90) and index

581.6 Miscellaneous nontaxonomic kinds of plants

Farrell, Courtney

Plants out of place. Rourke Pub. 2010 48p il (Let's explore science) $32.79

Grades: 4 5 6 7 **581.6**

1. Plants 2. Biological invasions 3. Food chains (Ecology)
ISBN 978-1-61590-322-1; 1-61590-322-4

LC 2010009909

This "takes a lively look at invasive plants . . . and shows both the destruction that non-native plants cause and what can be done about it. . . . In [this] title, well-chosen boxed examples, abundant color photos, diagrams, and an appended glossary add interest and support the engaging [text]." Booklist

Includes glossary and bibliographical references

Young, Kim J.

Ethnobotany; series editor William G. Hopkins. Chelsea House 2006 112p il (The green world) lib bdg $37.50

Grades: 7 8 9 10 **581.6**

1. Ethnobotany 2. Economic botany
ISBN 0-7910-8963-0 lib bdg

This is "a primer on plant and human relationships and interactions. . . . The reader is given insight into the importance of plants to both ancient and modern cultures and into how people's of particular cultures make use of plants." Sci Books Films

Includes glossary and bibliographical references

581.7   Plant ecology, plants characteristic of specific environments

Bodden, Valerie

Critical plant life. Creative Education 2010 48p il (Earth issues) $23.95

Grades: 7 8 9 10   **581.7**

1. Plant ecology

ISBN 978-1-58341-984-7; 1-58341-984-5

"The scientific information is up to date, well written for a lay audience, and presented in a highly engaging and visually appealing format." Sci Books Films

Includes glossary and bibliographical references

Johnson, Rebecca L.

Powerful plant cells; [by] Rebecca L. Johnson; illustrations by Jack Desrocher; diagrams by Jennifer E. Fairman. Millbrook Press 2008 48p il (Microquests) lib bdg $29.27

Grades: 5 6 7 8   **581.7**

1. Cells 2. Plants

ISBN 978-0-8225-7141-4; 0-8225-7141-2

LC 2006-36387

Explains what plant cells are, how they were discovered, their components, how they divide, different kinds, and what they do.

Includes bibliographical references

Spilsbury, Richard

Plant habitats; Richard & Louise Spilsbury. Rev. and updated; Heinemann Library 2008 48p il (Life of plants) $27.50; pa $7.99

Grades: 5 6 7 8   **581.7**

1. Plants 2. Plant ecology

ISBN 978-1-4329-1502-5; 1-4329-1502-9; 978-1-4329-1509-4 pa; 1-4329-1509-6 pa

LC 2008275392

First published 2003

Explains the different ways plants adapt to their environment in order to survive in a particular habitat.

This book "contains many bright and colorful photographs and diagrams to support the text, boldface vocabulary terms, a series of experiments and activities to provide further investigation, a complete glossary, an index, and a list of sources for additional information. . . . [This] volume is a complete and well-rounded unit." Sci Books Films

Includes glossary and bibliographical references

582.13   Plants noted for their flowers

Duncan, Wilbur Howard

Wildflowers of the eastern United States; by Wilbur H. Duncan and Marion B. Duncan. University of Georgia Press 1999 380p il $34.95; pa $24.95

Grades: 7 8 9 10 11 12 Adult   **582.13**

1. Wild flowers

ISBN 978-0-8203-2107-3; 0-8203-2107-9; 978-0-8203-2747-1 pa; 0-8203-2747-6 pa

LC 98-43314

"The eastern deciduous forest biome, . . . contains a variety of habitats supporting several thousand species of wildflowers. . . . The Duncans . . . have compiled a useful guide to more than 1,000 species. . . . A strength of the book is the photography, and although priority was given to showing diagnostic features, most photos are also very appealing visually. The 20-page introductory section includes a fine glossary and illustrations of necessary terminology." Choice

Niehaus, Theodore F.

★ A **field** guide to Pacific states wildflowers; illustrated by Charles L. Ripper. Houghton Mifflin 1976 xxxii, 432p il map (The Peterson field guide) hardcover o.p. pa $19

Grades: 7 8 9 10 11 12 Adult   **582.13**

1. Wild flowers

ISBN 0-395-21624-9; 0-395-91095-1 pa

LC 76-5873

"This offering identifies 1492 common wildflowers. . . . Common and scientific name, habitat, and recognition features are given for each plant." Libr J

Parker, Steve, 1952-

Sunflowers, magnolia trees & other flowering plants. Compass Point Books 2009 48p il (Kingdom classification) lib bdg $29.32

Grades: 6 7 8 9   **582.13**

1. Plants 2. Flowers

ISBN 978-0-7565-4222-1 lib bdg; 0-7565-4222-7 lib bdg

LC 2009-13696

Discusses the parts of flowering plants, the parts of flowers, the life cycle of flowering plants, different types that exist in different climates, how people use them, and efforts to conserve them

"With its compelling facts and visuals, this is a quality choice." SLJ

Includes glossary

Souza, D. M.

Freaky flowers. Watts 2002 63p il (Watts library) lib bdg $24.50; pa $8.95

Grades: 5 6 7 8   **582.13**

1. Flowers

ISBN 0-531-11981-5 lib bdg; 0-531-16221-4 pa

LC 2001-17573

"The book begins with a short course in botany that stresses vocabulary and processes. Subsequent chapters discuss different ways plants attract pollinators through colors, odors, and habitats. The last chapter acts as a warning that many plants are endangered because their pollinators are threatened, emphasizing the balance of nature. The outstanding full-color photos feature some of the most spectacular flowers found anywhere. Small sidebars offer interesting bits of trivia about similar plants. The text is packed with biological information and pertinent vocabulary." SLJ

Includes bibliographical references

Spellenberg, Richard

★ **National** Audubon Society field guide to North American wildflowers, western region; 2nd ed rev; Knopf 2001 862p il map $19.95

Grades: 7 8 9 10 11 12 Adult **582.13**

1. Wild flowers
ISBN 0-375-40233-0

LC 2001-269242

First published 1979

"More than 940 . . . full-color images show the wildflowers of western North America close-up and in their natural habitats. . . . Images are grouped by flower color and shape and keyed to . . . descriptions that reflect current taxonomy." Publisher's note

Thieret, John W.

★ **National** Audubon Society field guide to North American wildflowers: eastern region; revising author, John W. Thieret; original authors, William A. Niering and Nancy C. Olmstead. Knopf 2001 879p il map (National Audubon Society field guide series) $19.95

Grades: 7 8 9 10 11 12 Adult **582.13**

1. Wild flowers
ISBN 0-375-40232-2

LC 2001-269241

First published 1979 under the authorship of William A. Niering and Nancy C. Olmstead

"Covers the area east of the Rockies and east of the Big Bend area of Texas to the Atlantic. Color photographs together with family and species descriptions make this a most useful field guide." Sci News {review of 1979 edition}

Venning, Frank D.

Wildflowers of North America; a guide to field identification. illustrated by Manabu C. Saito. rev ed.; St. Martin's Press 2001 340p il (Golden field guides) pa $14.95

Grades: 8 9 10 11 12 Adult **582.13**

1. Wild flowers
ISBN 978-1-58238-127-5; 1-58238-127-5

First published 1984 by Golden Press

Accurate information on size, appearance, habitat, and known ranges and full-color illustrations constitute a guide to more than fifteen hundred native and naturalized species.

Includes bibliographical references

582.16 Trees

Brockman, C. Frank

Trees of North America; a field guide to the major native and introduced species north of Mexico. by C. Frank Brockman; illustrated by Rebecca Merrilees; revised by Jonathan P. Latimer and Karen Stray Nolting with David Challinor. rev and updated ed.; St. Martin's Press 2001 280p il map (Golden field guides) pa $14.95

Grades: 8 9 10 11 12 Adult **582.16**

1. Trees -- North America
ISBN 978-1-58238-092-6 pa; 1-58238-092-9 pa

LC 2001272405

First published 1968 by Golden Press

This "field guide features . . . characteristics—tree shape, bark, leaf, flower, fruit and twig—for quick identification. . . . [It includes] over 730 species in 76 families and 160 range maps." Publisher's note

Includes bibliographical references

Galat, Joan Marie

Branching out; How Trees Are Part of Our World. Joan Marie Galat. Owlkids Books, Inc. 2014 64 p. color illustrations (hardcover) $18.95

Grades: 4 5 6 7 **582.16**

1. Trees
ISBN 1771470496; 9781771470490; 9781771470827

LC 2014932714

This book, by Joan Marie Galat, " takes an in-depth look at [trees], introducing the basics of tree biology and profiling 11 different trees from around the world, including familiar ones such as the Red Maple and lesser-known trees like the Tall-Stilted Mangrove. Showcasing the inextricable ways in which trees are part of our society, culture, and economy, this illustrated volume also outlines how animals need trees and how, sometimes, they even help trees survive through symbiosis." (Publisher's note)

"This short, lively introduction to the subject focuses on 11 trees from all over the world...This title is truly worldwide in its coverage; only one tree, the Red Maple, is a native of North America. Appended glossary and index are extensive and complete. A solid overview." SLJ

Petrides, George A.

A **field** guide to western trees; eastern [i.e. western] United States and Canada. illustrated by Olivia Petrides. 1st ed., expanded.; Houghton Mifflin 1998 428p il map (The Peterson field guide) pa $20

Grades: 7 8 9 10 11 12 Adult **582.16**

1. Trees -- North America
ISBN 978-0-395-90454-1 pa; 0-395-90454-4 pa

LC 98013624

First published 1992

This "guide features detailed descriptions of 387 species, arranged in six major groups by visual similarity." Publisher's note

Includes bibliographical references

Ridsdale, Colin

Trees; [by] Colin Ridsdale, John White, Carol Usher; foreword by David Mabberley. DK 2005 360p il (Eyewitness companions) pa $25

Grades: 7 8 9 10 **582.16**

1. Trees
ISBN 978-0-7566-1359-4; 0-7566-1359-0

LC 2005296635

"From identification and anatomy to commercial exploitation and conservation, this is [a] . . . guide to more than 500 species of trees from around the world." Publisher's note

Williams, Michael D.

Identifying trees; an all-season guide to Eastern North America. Stackpole Books 2007 406p il pa $29.95

Grades: 7 8 9   **582.16**

1. Trees -- North America

ISBN 978-0-8117-3360-1; 0-8117-3360-2

LC 2006-10857

"Describes common locations and identifying characteristics [of trees]. . . . Covers every common tree in eastern North America." Publisher's note

583 Dicotyledons

Aaseng, Nathan

Weird meat-eating plants. Enslow Publishers 2011 48p il (Bizarre science) lib bdg $23.93

Grades: 5 6 7 8   **583**

1. Carnivorous plants

ISBN 978-0-7660-3672-7; 0-7660-3672-3

LC 2010016602

First published 1996 with title: Meat-eating plants

This describes meat-eating plants such as butterworts, sundews, byblis, pitcher plants, cobra lilies, venus flytraps, and bladderworts.

"Aimed at reluctant readers, [this title is] sure to disgust and delight in equal measure. . . . [The title] will pique interest and get kids lining up at the reference desk looking for more. The text is complemented by illustrations and magnified photos of things that you would hope never to see." SLJ

Includes glossary and bibliographical references

Pascoe, Elaine

Carnivorous plants; text by Elaine Pascoe; photographs by Dwight Kuhn. Blackbirch Press 2005 48p il (Nature close-up) $23.70

Grades: 4 5 6 7   **583**

1. Carnivorous plants

ISBN 1-4103-0309-8

LC 2005-276141

This describes such plants as venus flytraps, pitcher plants, cobra plants, and blatterworts, with instructions for growing and investigating them

Includes glossary and bibliographical references

584 Monocotyledons

Brown, Lauren

Grasses, an identification guide; written & illustrated by Lauren Brown. Houghton Mifflin 1979 240p il (Peterson nature library) hardcover o.p, pa $16

Grades: 7 8 11 12 Adult   **584**

1. Grasses

ISBN 978-0-395-27624-2; 0-395-27624-1; 978-0-395-62881-2 pa; 0-395-62881-4 pa

LC 78-24545

Identifies "135 of the most common species of North American grasses, sedges, and rushes, with their economic and ecological importance. " Publisher's note

Includes bibliographical references

585 Gymnosperms

Parker, Steve, 1952-

Redwoods, hemlocks & other cone-bearing plants. Compass Point Books 2010 48p il (Kingdom classification) lib bdg $29.32

Grades: 6 7 8 9   **585**

1. Cones 2. Redwood

ISBN 978-0-7565-4221-4 lib bdg; 0-7565-4221-9 lib bdg

LC 2009-12608

Discusses how conifers grow, their parts, the different types that grow in different climates, how people use them, and efforts to conserve them

"With its compelling facts and visuals, this is a quality choice." SLJ

Includes glossary

Stefoff, Rebecca

The conifer division; [by] Rebecca Stefoff. Marshall Cavendish Benchmark 2008 96p il (Family trees) $23.95

Grades: 6 7 8 9   **585**

1. Evergreens 2. Biology -- Classification

ISBN 978-0-7614-3077-3; 0-7614-3077-6

LC 2008-23373

"Explores the life cycles and other characteristics of plants, trees, and shrubs in the Conifer division." Publisher's note

Includes glossary and bibliographical references

587 Vascular seedless plants

Parker, Steve, 1952-

Ferns, mosses & other spore-producing plants. Compass Point Books 2010 48p il (Kingdom classification) lib bdg $29.32

Grades: 6 7 8 9   **587**

1. Ferns 2. Mosses

ISBN 978-0-7565-4220-7 lib bdg; 0-7565-4220-0 lib bdg

LC 2009-12060

Discusses how spore-producing plants grow and reproduce, different types, where they live, their life cycles, and how people use them

"This series gives an overview of a few of the main classifications of living things. Packed with text, photos, micrographs, and insets, these titles will compel readers to look closely. The main text meanders through the loaded pages providing background information, while visuals with italicized captions provide examples and detail. Scientific terms are often defined in the text and used again in later pages. Each spread focuses on a single aspect of the life-form and either moves through the life cycle or presents variations of the classification. Final spreads examine beneficial and harmful varieties. The books close with an overview of scientific classification with a specific example. With its compelling facts and visuals, this is a quality choice." (School Library Journal)

Includes glossary and bibliographical references

590 Animals

Amazing animals of the world 1. Grolier 2008 10v il map set $199
Grades: 6 7 8 9 **590**
1. Reference books 2. Animals -- Encyclopedias
ISBN 978-0-7172-6225-0 set; 0-7172-6225-1 set
LC 2007012982
This "is a 10-volume set featuring 400 animals from around the globe. Each page highlights one animal with an interesting description and full-color picture. The pictures are beautiful and visually engaging. . . . The information is concise and appealing enough for reading for personal information or for use in basic research." Sci Books Films
Includes glossary and bibliographical references

BishopRoby, Joshua
Animal kingdom. Compass Point Books 2009 40p il (Mission: science) lib bdg $26.60
Grades: 4 5 6 **590**
1. Animals -- Classification
ISBN 978-0-7565-4057-9 lib bdg; 0-7565-4057-7 lib bdg
LC 2008-37574
An introduction to the animal kingdom, which is made up of a variety of animals that are organized into categories based on physical attributes or ancestors
Includes glossary

Broom, Jenny
Animalium; Jenny Broom, illustrated by Katie Scott. Candlewick Press 2014 112 p. color illustrations (reinforced) $35
Grades: 3 4 5 6 7 **590**
1. Animals 2. Museums
ISBN 9780763675080; 0763675083
LC 2013952848
"Open 365 days a year and unrestricted by the constraints of physical space, each title in this series is organized into galleries that display more than 200 full-color specimens accompanied by lively, informative text. Offering hours of learning, this first title within the series--[Jenny Broom's book] Animalium--presents the animal kingdom in glorious detail with illustrations from Katie Scott." (Publisher's note)
"Each basic group includes several spreads offering examples from subgroups within the class as well as a spread with a connected habitat: coastal waters, coral reefs, rain forest, deserts, woodlands and tundra. No information sources are given, but there are good suggestions for general websites for further learning." Kirkus

Campbell, Jeff
Daisy to the Rescue; True Stories of Daring Dogs, Paramedic Parrots, and Other Animal Heroes. by Jeff Campbell, illustrated by Ramsey Beyer. Houghton Mifflin Harcourt 2014 336 p. illustrations $17.99
Grades: 6 7 8 9 10 **590**
1. Human-animal relationship 2. Animal behavior 3. Cognition in animals 4. Animal heroes -- Anecdotes
ISBN 1936976625; 9781936976621
This book, by Jeff Campbell, illustrated by Ramsey Beyer, "celebrates over fifty . . . heroic animals with stunning illustrated portraits and detailed accounts of their exploits. The book asks important questions about why these animals act the way they do . . . often putting themselves in harm's way in the process." (Publisher's note)
"Inherent animal abilities are discussed alongside the accounts, as are animal traits and scientific theories in layman's terms. Individual stories of animal derring-do, illustrated with pencil portraits, make for quick, compelling reads that prompt the reader to wonder what really goes on in an animal's head and heart." Booklist

Casper, Julie Kerr
Animals; creatures that roam the planet. Chelsea House Publishers 2007 179p il map (Natural resources) $39.50
Grades: 8 9 10 11 12 **590**
1. Animals
ISBN 978-0-8160-6353-6; 0-8160-6353-2
LC 2006030227
This describes how animals have adapted to various environments on Earth and how they have evolved, the causes of animal extinctions in the past and the present, the importance of animals to humans, and the conservation of animal resources.
Includes bibliographical references

Davies, Nicola, 1958-
Extreme animals; the toughest creatures on Earth. illustrated by Neal Layton. Candlewick Press 2006 61p il $12.99; pa $7.99
Grades: 3 4 5 6 **590**
1. Animals 2. Adaptation (Biology)
ISBN 978-0-7636-3067-6; 0-7636-3067-5; 978-0-7636-4127-6 pa; 0-7636-4127-8 pa
LC 2005-43544
"There is life everywhere on Earth . . . and much of that life thrives in conditions that humans could not endure for five minutes or less. This funny and appealing little book describes who these amazing life-forms are and how they manage to survive. Simple and inviting cartoon drawings enliven the text and convey the types of extremes in an easy-to-understand manner." SLJ
Includes glossary

Johnson, Jinny
★ **Animal** tracks & signs. National Geographic Society 2008 192p il $24.95; lib bdg $32.90
Grades: 5 6 7 8 **590**
1. Animals 2. Animal tracks 3. Tracking and trailing
ISBN 978-1-4263-0253-4; 1-4263-0253-3; 978-1-4263-0254-1 lib bdg; 1-4263-0254-1 lib bdg
"This attractive book describes the tracks (paw prints, bird claw prints, slimy trails) and signs (molted skin, food remains, scat, tree markings) that animals leave in their wake. .

. . A typical two-page layout includes a photo and short paragraph about the animal category, three or four colored boxes containing a photo or drawing of a specific animal (serval, bobcat), and a description of its size, geographic range, habitat, food, tracks and signs, and comments. . . . The beautiful photos vary from action . . . to informational. . . . The language is simple and readable." Voice Youth Advocates

Includes glossary and bibliographical references

Levine, Shar

Animals; mammals, birds, reptiles, amphibians, fish, and other animals. by Shar Levine and Leslie Johnstone. Crabtree Pub. 2010 48p il (A class of their own) lib bdg $29.27; pa $9.95

Grades: 5 6 7 8   **590**

1. Animals -- Classification

ISBN 978-0-7787-5372-8 lib bdg; 0-7787-5372-7 lib bdg; 978-0-7787-5386-5 pa; 0-7787-5386-7 pa

Looks at the animal kingdom, providing information and examples of species from the major phyla and classes, as well as case histories of newly discovered endangered species.

"Lively section headings . . . and notes on uncommon achievements, . . . lighten the substantial load of biological terminology. Illustrated with a plethora of closeup color photos and microphotos, and closing with annotated lists of recommended Web sites, . . . [this captures] the remarkable diversity of life." SLJ

Includes glossary and bibliographical references

Lewin, Ted

★ Tooth and claw; animal adventures in the wild. HarperCollins Pubs. 2003 97p il maps $15.99; lib bdg $16.89

Grades: 4 5 6 7   **590**

1. Wildlife 2. Dangerous animals

ISBN 0-688-14105-6; 0-688-14106-4 lib bdg

LC 2002-4588

Author/illustrator Ted Lewin relates fourteen of his experiences with wild animals while travelling the world, following each anecdote with facts about the featured animal and its habitat

"This is outstanding nature storytelling, related in a distinctive voice imbued with humor and personality; it's even better when read aloud." Horn Book

Includes glossary

McGhee, Karen

★ Encyclopedia of animals; [by] Karen McGhee, George McKay. National Geographic 2007 192p il map $24.95; lib bdg $38.90

Grades: 4 5 6 7 8   **590**

1. Reference books 2. Animals -- Encyclopedias

ISBN 0-7922-5936-X; 0-7922-5937-8 lib bdg

LC 2006299476

"This lavish, ambitious volume contains full-color illustrations of more than 1500 species. Each brief entry includes common and scientific names and mention of an interesting physical or behavioral trait. Range maps show where each animal is found, and conservation data notes which species are extinct, endangered, or vulnerable. In addition to the realistic drawings, there are dramatic photos of animals in their habitats." SLJ

Montgomery, Heather L.

★ Wild discoveries; wacky new animals. by Heather L. Montgomery. Scholastic, Inc. 2013 62 p. (pbk.) $6.99

Grades: 3 4 5 6 7   **590**

1. Discoveries in science 2. Animals

ISBN 0545477670; 9780545477673

LC 2012285070

This book by Heather Montgomery features "newly discovered species from around the world--such as the Shocking Pink Dragon and the Green Bomber. These . . . species are organized by region with . . . facts about each one's . . . abilities and traits. The book . . . has a special section featuring new species discovered by kids." (Publisher's note)

Noyes, Deborah

★ One kingdom; our lives with animals--the human-animal bond in myth, history, science, and story. Houghton Mifflin Company 2006 128p il $18

Grades: 7 8 9 10   **590**

1. Animals

ISBN 0-618-49914-8

LC 2005-25446

In this "photo-essay, Noyes examines the ways that human lives have overlapped with animals and how our beliefs, culture, and science have been impacted throught history by the essential but frequently paradoxical human-animal connection. . . . Readers will find the provocative questions Noyes raises compelling and challenging, and the lyrical, urgent prose, along with beautiful black-and-white photos of the animals up close, will draw serious students and browsers alike." Booklist

Includes bibliographical references

Silverstein, Alvin

Dung beetles, slugs, leeches, and more; the yucky animal book. by Alvin and Virginia Silverstein, and Laura Silverstein Nunn; illustrated by Gerald Kelley. Enslow Publishers 2010 48p il (Yucky science) lib bdg $23.93

Grades: 4 5 6 7   **590**

1. Insects 2. Invertebrates 3. Animal behavior

ISBN 978-0-7660-3317-7 lib bdg; 0-7660-3317-1 lib bdg

LC 2009012281

"Explores 'yucky' things animals do, including slime-producing animals, blood-ingesting animals, and more." Publisher's note

Includes glossary and bibliographical references

Siwanowicz, Igor

Animals up close; zoom in on the world's most incredible creatures. DK Pub. 2009 96p il $19.99

Grades: 4 5 6   **590**

1. Animals

ISBN 978-0-7566-4513-7; 0-7566-4513-1

"An eye-catching cover will attract readers to this amazing look at some of the world's insects, fish, mammals, reptiles, amphibians, and birds. The focus is on animals small enough to fit in a child's hand. Siwanowicz showcases each creature with a spread containing a full-color, high-quality, close-up photo surrounded by multiple factual asides. . . . The book is packed with interesting material that captures the author's fascination for small creatures." SLJ

Includes glossary

Spilsbury, Richard

Animal variation and classification. Rosen Central 2010 46p il (Living processes) lib bdg $26.50; pa $11.75

Grades: 5 6 7   **590**

1. Variation (Biology) 2. Animals -- Classification

ISBN 978-1-61532-344-9 lib bdg; 1-61532-344-9 lib bdg; 978-1-61532-347-0 pa; 1-61532-347-3 pa

LC 2009-30564

Explains how our animal classification system works and looks at how scientists use it to identify and group animal species, explores the variation between and within animal species and discusses how and why such variations have occurred.

"With colorful, quality photography, the well-organized content is divided into short chapters with bold subheadings making information easy to find. Clear and interesting writing distinguishes this . . . from older titles. The captions for pictures are used to provide identification and additional explanation for topics not included in the text." Libr Media Connect

Includes glossary and bibliographical references

Staub, Frank J.

★ The **signs** animals leave; [by] Frank Staub. Watts 2001 63p il (Watts library) $24.50; pa $8.95

Grades: 4 5 6   **590**

1. Animal tracks 2. Animal behavior

ISBN 0-531-11863-0; 0-531-16575-2 pa

LC 00-43603

This describes traces left by animals which reveal their behavior including tracks and scents

Includes bibliographical references

Zoology for kids; understanding and working with animals : with 21 activities. Josh and Bethanie Hestermann. Chicago Review Press, Incorporated 2015 144 p. color illustrations $18.95

Grades: 5 6 7 8 9   **590**

1. Zoology 2. Vocational guidance 3. Zoology -- Vocational guidance 4. Zoology -- Study and teaching -- Activity programs

ISBN 1613749619; 9781613749616

LC 2014042745

This book, by Josh and Bethanie Hestermann, "invites the next generation of zoologists to discover the animal kingdom through clear, entertaining information and anecdotes, lush color photos, hands-on activities, and peer-reviewed research. Young minds are introduced to zoology as a science by discussing animals' forms, functions, and behaviors as well as the history behind zoos and aquariums." (Publisher's note)

"Studded with fun activities and attractive animal photos, this comprehensive resource will excite those not already smitten with the animal world to enthusiastically join in the delightful exploration of what it means to study and care for animals in today's world...Charming photos, hand-

drawn graphics, highlighted words, and a correlative glossary enhance the clear-cut writing style." SLJ

Includes bibliographical references and index

590.7 Education, research, related topics

Gardner, Robert

Ace your animal science project; great science fair ideas. [by] Robert Gardner . . . [et al.] Enslow Publishers 2009 128p il (Ace your biology science project) lib bdg $31.93

Grades: 5 6 7 8   **590.7**

1. Animal behavior 2. Science projects 3. Science -- Experiments

ISBN 978-0-7660-3220-0 lib bdg; 0-7660-3220-5 lib bdg

LC 2008-4234

"Dozens of . . . science activities are presented with background information, step-by-step instructions, and suggestions for extending to the science fair level. . . . Color illustrations and important safety information are included." Horn Book Guide

Includes bibliographical references

590.72 Animals -- Research

Burns, Loree Griffin

Citizen scientists; be a part of scientific discovery from your own backyard. Loree Griffin Burns ; photographs by Ellen Harasimowicz. H. Holt 2012 80 p. col. ill., col. maps

Grades: 3 4 5 6 7 8   **590.72**

1. Suburbs 2. Animals -- Classification 3. Research -- Citizen participation 4. Wildlife -- Geographical distribution

ISBN 0805090622; 9780805090628; 9780805095173

LC 2011021673

AAAS/Subaru SB&F Prize for Excellence in Science Books: Hands On Science Book (2013)

In this children's book, Loree Griffin Burns "brings . . . attention to four . . . scientific projects that enlist regular people in data collection. . . . The projects include . . . the Monarch Watch butterfly tagging project, . . . the Audubon Christmas Bird Count," and a "project documenting ladybug species . . . . For each project, Burns gives detailed accounts of the procedures employed by citizen scientists." (Horn Book Magazine)

Includes bibliographical references and index

590.73 Collections and exhibits of living mammals

Zoehfeld, Kathleen Weidner

Wild lives; a history of the people & animals of the Bronx Zoo. with photographs from the Wildlife Conservation Society. Alfred A. Knopf 2006 86p il $18.95; lib bdg $20.99

Grades: 5 6 7 8   **590.73**
1. Zoos 2. Animals 3. Bronx Zoo
ISBN 0-375-80630-X; 0-375-90630-4 lib bdg
             LC 2005-18943
"Zoehfeld tells the story of the Bronx Zoo, from the preparations for its opening in 1899 to its current efforts in the areas of conservation and education. Along with information on the zoo, she discusses trends in thinking about wildlife, the ethics of removing animals from their habitats for their safety or for public display, and ongoing threats to the existence of many species. . . . The many photos, attractive layout, and use of color contribute to the visual appeal of this informative zoo story." Booklist
     Includes bibliographical references

590.9   Animals -- History, geographic treatment, biography

Historical animals; the dogs, cats, horses, snakes, goats, rats, dragons, bears, elephants, rabbits, and other creatures that changed the world. by Julia Moberg; illustrated by Jeff Albrecht Studios. Charlesbridge Publishing 2015 91 p. color illustrations $15.95
Grades: 4 5 6   **590.9**
1. Animals and civilization 2. Animals and history 3. Animals and civilization -- History
ISBN 1623540488; 9781623540487
            LC 2014018171
This book, by Julia Moberg abd illustrated by Jeff Albrecht Studios, is an "inside look at history's most famous animals. . . . Meet Alexander the Great's horse Bucephalus, who was his battle companion for nearly 30 years. Learn about Mozart's starling bird that helped him write music by singing along as he composed. Read about the Ethiopian goats that discovered the coffee bean, Marco Polo seeing dragons in China, and a dog named Boatswain that saved Napoleon's life." (Publisher's note)
     "While adults might groan at the sometimes forced humor and poetry, the intended audience will eat this one up. Historical fluff? Maybe, but if nothing else, this silly yet persuasive effort will coax readers into enjoying history." SLJ

590.92   Biographies of animals

Roop, Connie
     Tales of Famous Animals; Peter Roop and Connie Roop. Scholastic 2012 112 p. (reinforced) $17.99
Grades: 4 5 6 7 8   **590.92**
1. Pets 2. Animals
ISBN 0545430291; 9780545430296
This children's book, by Peter and Connie Roop, illustrated by Zachary Pullen, offers an "illustrated introduction to some of the most fascinating and admirable animals we've ever known! Everyone knows about President Obama's first dog Bo, but would you believe President Adams had a pet alligator . . . ? . . . Readers will also learn about heroic animals like Balto the sled dog and unique animals like Koko the gorilla." (Publisher's note)

590.94   Animals -- Europe

Johnson, Rebecca L.
     Chernobyl's wild kingdom; life in the dead zone. Rebecca L. Johnson. Twenty-First Century Books 2015 64 p. illustrations (some color) (lib. bdg. : alk. paper) $34.60
Grades: 7 8 9 10 11 12   **590.94**
1. Chernobyl Nuclear Accident, Chernobyl, Ukraine, 1986 2. Radioecology -- Ukraine -- Chornobyl
ISBN 1467711543; 9781467711548
            LC 2013039471
This book, by Rebecca L. Johnston, describes how "some wildlife flourishes in Chernobyl, Ukraine, more than 25 years after the explosion at the nuclear power plant there. After opening with a background chapter describing the 1986 disaster, evacuation and cleanup efforts, Johnson goes on to describe scientific studies on the wildlife in the area from which humans have been excluded." (Kirkus Reviews)
     "This clear presentation is supplemented with captioned photographs, explanatory boxes and a helpful map. The appropriate background and clear, easy-to-understand explanations make this one-of-a-kind title both accessible and interesting. An important story clearly and engagingly told by an experienced science writer." Kirkus
     Includes bibliographical references (pages 59-61) and index

590.99   Animals -- Australasia and Pacific Ocean islands

Hawaii's animals do the most amazing things! Marion Coste ; illustrated by Rena Ekmanis. University of Hawaii Press 2015 47 p. color illustrations (cloth : alk. paper) $14.99
Grades: 5 6 7 8   **590.99**
1. Hawaii 2. Animals -- Habitations 3. Animals -- Hawaii
ISBN 0824839625; 9780824839628
            LC 2014014460
This book on the animals of Hawaii, by Marion Coste and illustrated by Rena Ekmanis, "includes 12 endemic and indigenous animals, covering both rare and more well known creatures, such as the great frigate bird, fisher bird, fairy tern, pacific golden plover, Hawaiian green sea turtle, spinner dolphin, humpback whale, and mountain shrimp." (School Library Journal)
     "Middle school students will find useful material to extract for report writing, but the text is complex enough to entice older readers, too. A well-written overview of Hawaiian animals." SLJ
     Includes bibliographical references (page 47)

591   Specific topics in natural history of animals

Stemple, Adam
     National Geographic animal stories; heartwarming true tales from the animal kingdom. by Jane Yolen, Heidi E.Y. Stemple, Adam Stemple, and Jason

Stemple. National Geographic 2014 160 p. illustrations (hardcover : alk. paper) $24.99

Grades: 5 6 7 8 **591**

1. Animals in literature 2. Animals -- Anecdotes
ISBN 1426317255; 9781426317255; 9781426317262
LC 2014015729

This children's book, by Jane Yolen, shares "animal stories that span the centuries. . . . Some are sweet, some funny, some surprising, but all are emotionally powerful -- the Capitolene geese who saved the Roman empire, Balto the Alaskan sled dog, Smoky the Bear, the passenger pigeon of WWI Cher Ami, and the latest internet sensation Christian the lion." (Publisher's note)

" In nineteen engaging short stories, Yolen and her children explore extraordinary animals from history and the connections they made with other creatures and people. Some stories will likely be familiar to readers (e.g., sled dog Balto), while others will be new discoveries. Ishida's colorful illustrations enliven the tales, and sidebars give further information. Reading list, timeline, websites." Horn book

Includes bibliographical references and index

591.03   Encyclopedia of animals

Spelman, Lucy

Animal encyclopedia; 2,500 animals with photos, maps, and more! National Geographic 2012 303 p. col. ill., col. maps (hardcover) $24.95; (library) $33.90

Grades: 5 6 7 **591.03**

1. Animals -- Encyclopedias 2. Animals
ISBN 1426310226; 9781426310225; 9781426310232
LC 2012023783

This encyclopedia about animals "is separated into vertebrate and invertebrate animals and then further subdivided by phylum. Each species gets its own page with dynamic color photos of creatures in their natural habitat, while . . . information on variations within the species celebrates the diversity of animals across the globe." (Booklist)

Includes bibliographical references (p. 295) and index.

591.3   Genetics, evolution, age characteristics

Eamer, Claire

Spiked scorpions & walking whales; modern animals, ancient animals, and water. Annick Press 2009 100p il $19.95; pa $9.95

Grades: 6 7 8 9 **591.3**

1. Animals 2. Evolution
ISBN 978-1-55451-206-5; 1-55451-206-9; 978-1-55451-205-8 pa; 1-55451-205-0 pa

Describes how six different water-loving species evolved from how they appear in early fossil records to their appearance today, discussing segmented worms, platypus, and Canada geese.

"Eamer's information-packed text, often lively and conversational, can also be challenging. . . . The book features brightly colored, busy pages with sidebars, 'Fun Facts,' and small full-color photographs rimmed in bold shades. . . . Ca-

pable readers with a serious interest in animal science will find it enjoyable and even fascinating." SLJ

Super crocs & monster wings; modern animals' ancient past. [by] Claire Eamer. Annick Press 2008 93p il $19.95; pa $9.95

Grades: 4 5 6 7 **591.3**

1. Animals 2. Evolution 3. Prehistoric animals
ISBN 978-1-55451-130-3; 1-55451-130-5; 978-1-55451-129-7 pa; 1-55451-129-1 pa

"The author's conversational and often-humorous voice slides readers effortlessly through a great deal of fascinating scientific information in this title on animal evolution. After a brief but clear introduction to geologic time and Linnaean taxonomy, six chapters compare ancient and modern dragonflies, crocodilians, camelids, sloths, glyptodonts (armadillos), and beavers. . . . Jazzy fonts; crisp photos and paintings; and tilted illustrations, titles, and captions create an up-to-the-minute feel." SLJ

591.4   Physical adaptation

Burnie, David

How animals work. Dorling Kindersley 2010 132p il $24.99

Grades: 5 6 7 8 **591.4**

1. Animals 2. Animal behavior
ISBN 978-0-7566-5897-7; 0-7566-5897-7

Describes the anatomy of many animal species and explains how their bodies work to help them survive. Covers such animals as birds, butterflies, elephants, crocodiles, and wolves, and includes color photos, illustrations, and diagrams.

"This beautifully photographed encyclopedia of animals is divided into categories that include movement, diet, senses, and animal families. . . . Diagrams showing internal organs and intimate closeups of eyes, skin, fur, and wings, should engage budding biologists." Publ Wkly

Rodriguez, Ana Maria

Secret of the puking penguins . . . and more! Enslow Publishers 2008 48p il (Animal secrets revealed!) lib bdg $23.93

Grades: 5 6 7 8 **591.4**

1. Birds 2. Reptiles
ISBN 978-0-7660-2955-2 lib bdg; 0-7660-2955-7 lib bdg
LC 2007-39490

In this title "readers learn not only why King penguin fathers regurgitate food to feed their newborn chicks, but also how chameleons grip prey with their powerful tongue, along with some unusual information about alligators, cuckoos, and peacock feathers. Each topic is covered in six to nine pages with a short Meet the Scientists section. The methodology used by each scientist or team of scientists to make the discoveries is carefully explained is a lively and accessible manner. . . . The photo illustrations . . . are of excellent quality, well placed, and helpful." Booklist

Includes glossary and bibliographical references

591.47   Protective and locomotor adaptations, color

Johnson, Rebecca L.

★ **When** lunch fights back; wickedly clever animal defenses. by Rebecca L. Johnson. Millbrook Press 2015 48 p. (lib. bdg. : alk. paper) $29.27

Grades: 4 5 6 7   **591.47**

1. Animal defenses 2. Animals

ISBN 1467721093; 9781467721097

LC 2013046646

This book, by Rebecca L. Johnson, explains that "in nature, good defenses can mean the difference between surviving a predator's attack and becoming its lunch. Some animals rely on sharp teeth and claws or camouflage. But that's only the beginning. Meet creatures with some of the strangest defenses known to science." (Publisher's note)

"HAlong with the ever popular hagfish (aka "snot eel") and the horned lizard—which can indeed squirt blood from one or both eyes—Johnson... profiles 10 animals with particularly noxious defense mechanisms... This is an outstanding way for readers to meet scientists at work in both field and lab, as well as to learn that, for instance, fulmar chicks can project vomit up to 6 feet and, creepily, that a school of the Amazonian two-spot astyanax will attack and eject one of its own to distract an approaching predator.Thrilling reading for budding biologists." Kirkus

Includes bibliographical references and index

Wilsdon, Christina

Animal defenses. Chelsea House 2009 136p il (Animal behavior) lib bdg $32.95

Grades: 6 7 8 9   **591.47**

1. Animal defenses

ISBN 978-1-60413-089-8 lib bdg; 1-60413-089-X lib bdg

LC 2008-40116

"The detailed information is well organized. . . . Color photographs appear throughout." SLJ

This "presents the wide variety of physical and behavioral adaptations used by animals and insects in their struggle to survive and explores how scientists continue to make new discoveries about the age-old maneuvering between predator and prey." Publisher's note

Includes glossary and bibliographical references

591.5   Behavior

Creatures of the Night; Camilla Bedoyere. Firefly Books Ltd 2014 80 p. color illustrations $9.95

Grades: 4 5 6   **591.5**

1. Animal behavior 2. Nocturnal animals 3. Picture books for children

ISBN 1770854592; 9781770854598

This book by Camilla Bedoyere "features more than a dozen extraordinary animals that live in the dark. These are mammals, birds, insects and spiders whose unique physical features help them to survive in the pitch-black darkness of jungles, fields and in the air. Intricately drawn artworks give accurate details of each animal's anatomy and behavior, and

stunning photographs show how each animal hunts." (Publisher's note)

"This detailed look at creatures that go bump in the night is a reminder of just how amazing animal adaptations are." Booklist

Cusick, Dawn

Get the Scoop on Animal Puke; From Zombie Ants to Vampire Bats, 251 Cool Facts About Vomit, Regurgitation & More. Dawn Cusick. Random House Distribution childrens 2014 80 p. $14.95

Grades: 4 5 6   **591.5**

1. Animals 2. Vomiting 3. Animal behavior

ISBN 1623540453; 9781623540456

This children's book, by Dawn Cusick, describes how "animal puke serves many purposes in the natural world: it can scare and distract predators, feed family and neighbors, protect animals from poisoning (they can't call 911), aid with digestion, and so much more." (Publisher's note)

"What do hyenas, proboscis monkeys, and vampire bats have in common? Vomit. This companion to Cusick's Get the Scoop on Animal Poop! examines how and why various animals regurgitate their food...Cusick presents the material in a (very) immediate manner, providing readers with plenty of science, humor, and animal behavior facts to chew over—and even regurgitate." PW

Goldstein, Natalie

Animal hunting and feeding. Chelsea House 2009 110p il (Animal behavior) lib bdg $32.95

Grades: 6 7 8 9   **591.5**

1. Animals -- Food

ISBN 978-1-60413-143-7 lib bdg; 1-60413-143-8 lib bdg

LC 2008-40124

"All animals have to eat, but feeding behavior goes far beyond predators and prey. Animals have a variety of ways to find food. Some sit and wait for food to come to them. Others chase or trap their food. Other animals are scavengers and decomposers, breaking down the leftovers of other animals' meals. [This book] explains these various techniques as well as the importance of food chains and food webs." Publisher's note

Includes glossary and bibliographical references

Hile, Lori

Animal survival. Raintree 2011 56p il (Extreme survival) lib bdg $33.50

Grades: 4 5 6 7   **591.5**

1. Pets 2. Animals 3. Animal behavior 4. Natural disasters

ISBN 978-1-4109-3973-9; 1-4109-3973-1

LC 2010028842

This book is "fun and informative. [This] well-organized title starts with an overview [of animal survival], offers some specific examples, and includes additional facts or tips and resources. . . . [It features] dramatic archival and full-color photos on nearly every page. . . . The first chapter introduces resilient creatures that beat the odds and then follows with their journeys, animal heroes, and their work while surviving natural disasters. . . . [This is a book] that youngsters will enjoy and talk about." SLJ

Includes glossary and bibliographical references

Knapp, Ron

Bloodsucking creatures. Enslow Publishers 2011 48p il (Bizarre science) lib bdg $23.93

Grades: 5 6 7 8   **591.5**

1. Bloodsucking animals

ISBN 978-0-7660-3671-0; 0-7660-3671-5

LC 2010009761

First published 1996 with title: Bloodsuckers

This describes bloodsucking animals such as mosquitoes, vampire bats, and fleas.

"Aimed at reluctant readers, [this title is] sure to disgust and delight in equal measure. . . . [The title] will pique interest and get kids lining up at the reference desk looking for more. The text is complemented by illustrations and magnified photos of things that you would hope never to see." SLJ

Includes glossary and bibliographical references

Settel, Joanne

Exploding ants; amazing facts about how animals adapt. Atheneum Bks. for Young Readers 1999 40p il $16.95

Grades: 4 5 6 7   **591.5**

1. Animal behavior

ISBN 0-689-81739-8

LC 97-35395

Describes examples of animal behavior that may strike humans as disgusting, including the "gross" ways animals find food, shelter, and safety in the natural world

"This attractive volume presents its material as wondrous science instead of sensational effect." Booklist

Includes glossary and bibliographical references

Unlikely heroes; 37 inspiring stories of courage and heart from the animal kingdom. by Jennifer S. Holland. Workman Publishing 2014 246 p. illustrations (chiefly color) (pbk.) $13.95

Grades: 5 6 7 8   **591.5**

1. Altruism 2. Animal behavior 3. Animal behavior -- Anecdotes 4. Altruistic behavior in animals -- Anecdotes

ISBN 0761174419; 9780761174417

LC 2014033713

In this book, author Jennifer S. Holland "uncovers and celebrates . . . [a] side of animals that we often think belongs primarily to people—heroism, that indefinable quality of going above and beyond, often for altruistic reasons, often at great personal risk. These 37 inspiring true tales show animals whose quick acts have saved lives." (Publisher's note)

"In this heartwarming follow-up to Unlikely Friendships: 47 Remarkable Stories from the Animal Kingdom (2011) and Unlikely Loves: 43 Heartwarming True Stories from the Animal Kingdom (2013, both Workman), Holland whips up enthusiasm for the selfless acts of different animals . . . A sweet look at the animal kingdom." SLJ

Includes bibliographical references (pages 241-244) and index

591.518   Nocturnal behavior

Scott, Traer

★ **Nocturne**; creatures of the night. Traer Scott. Princeton Architectural Press 2014 128 p. (alk. paper) $19.95

        591.518

1. Animal behavior 2. Photography of animals 3. Nocturnal animals

ISBN 1616892889; 9781616892883

LC 2014006210

In this book "photographer Traer Scott takes the viewer on a journey through nighttime in the animal kingdom, revealing some of nature's most elusive creatures. Bats, big cats, flying squirrels, tarantula, owls, kangaroo mice, giant moths, sloth, several species of snakes, and a Madagascar hissing cockroach are only a few of the animals illuminated in these . . . portraits." (Publisher's note)

"In this exquisite collection of portraits of 42 nocturnal animals, photographer Scott sets her subjects against dark backgrounds that give the images quiet dignity and power, while making the animals' fur, feathers, quills, and skin all the more luminous...The brilliance of the photographs is in their minimalism, allowing the animals to dictate the mood of the compositions." PW

Creatures of the night

591.56   Behavior relating to life cycle

Allman, Toney

Animal life in groups. Chelsea House 2009 124p il (Animal behavior) lib bdg $32.95

Grades: 6 7 8 9   **591.56**

1. Animal behavior

ISBN 978-1-60413-142-0 lib bdg; 1-60413-142-X lib bdg

LC 2008-40120

This "explores the social lives of bees, meerkats, monkeys, and others, with a special emphasis on how different packs compare to one another and how living in groups benefits individual members." Publisher's note

Includes glossary and bibliographical references

Migration Nation; Animals on the Go from Coast to Coast. Joanne O'Sullivan. Imagine Publishing Incorporated 2015 96 p. col. illustrations, col. maps $15.95

Grades: 4 5 6 7 8   **591.56**

1. Animals 2. Animals -- Migration 3. Animal migrations

ISBN 162354050X; 9781623540500

This children's book, by Joanne O'Sullivan, "introduces the migratory habits of a dozen (mostly) North American animals. O'Sullivan explores migration by land (examining snakes, pronghorns, bison, and polar bears), by sea (salmon, manatees, and gray whales), and by sky (cranes and monarch butterflies)." (School Library Journal)

"Though many of the photographs go uncaptioned and so add little beyond eye candy, this broad and breezy overview will stimulate young animal lovers' "need to read" about one of the natural world's behavioral wonders." Kirkus

Schueller, Gretel H.

Animal migration; [by] Gretel H. Schueller and
Sheila K. Schueller. Chelsea House 2009 120p il
(Animal behavior) lib bdg $32.95

Grades: 6 7 8 9   **591.56**

1. Animals -- Migration

ISBN 978-1-60413-127-7 lib bdg; 1-60413-127-6
lib bdg

LC 2008-40125

This describes "why animals are compelled to migrate,
as well as the various patterns and cycles of their migrations." Publisher's note

Includes glossary and bibliographical references

Spilsbury, Richard

Life cycles. Rosen Central 2010 46p il (Life
processes) lib bdg $26.50; pa $11.75

Grades: 5 6 7   **591.56**

1. Life cycles (Biology)

ISBN 978-1-61532-341-8 lib bdg; 1-61532-341-4 lib
bdg; 978-1-61532-350-0 pa; 1-61532-350-3 pa

LC 2009-30414

"With colorful, quality photography, the well-organized
content is divided into short chapters with bold subheadings making information easy to find. Clear and interesting
writing distinguishes this . . . from older titles. The captions
for pictures are used to provide identification and additional explanation for topics not included in the text." Libr
Media Connect

Includes glossary and bibliographical references

West, Krista

Animal courtship. Chelsea House 2009 120p il
(Animal behavior) lib bdg $32.95

Grades: 6 7 8 9   **591.56**

1. Animal courtship

ISBN 978-1-60413-090-4 lib bdg; 1-60413-090-3
lib bdg

LC 2008-40121

This describes "the various ways species attract mates,
including by singing, dancing, glowing, and even attacking." Publisher's note

Includes glossary and bibliographical references

591.59   Communication

Sayre, April Pulley

★ **Secrets** of sound; studying the calls and songs
of whales, elephants, and birds. Houghton Mifflin
2002 63p il (Scientists in the field) pbk. $7.99

Grades: 4 5 6 7   **591.59**

1. Whales 2. Birdsongs 3. Elephants 4. Animal
communication

ISBN 9780618585465

LC 2001-51877

"The focus of this Scientists in the Field volume is scientists who study animal communication—whale songs,
elephant rumbles, and nocturnal bird calls. Bioacoustics,
the field encompassing their work, is a meld of biology,
technology, music, and physics. . . . Christopher Clark uses

underwater microphones to record whale songs. . . . Katy
Payne's familiarity with the vibrations of organ music led to
her discovery of the infrasound rumbles that elephants use to
communicate over long distances. Bill Evans records birds
at night to learn more about their migration patterns. {Glos-
sary. Bibliography. Index.} Intermediate." (Horn Book)

"This fascinating title shows the thrill of scientific discovery up close. . . . Lots of well-edited quotes from the
scientists convey their contagious enthusiasm for what they
do, and sharp color photos, sound charts, and activity boxes
break up the text, making it even more readable." Booklist

Includes glossary and bibliographical references

Tomecek, Steve

Animal communication; [by] Stephen M. Tomecek. Chelsea House 2009 104p il (Animal behavior) lib bdg $32.95

Grades: 6 7 8 9   **591.59**

1. Animal communication

ISBN 978-1-60413-091-1 lib bdg; 1-60413-091-1
lib bdg

LC 2008-40115

This explains "the many different ways in which animals
and insects express themselves and examines some of the
latest scientific discoveries involving animal intelligence."
Publisher's note

Includes glossary and bibliographical references

591.6   Miscellaneous nontaxonomic kinds of animals

Hammond, Paula

The **atlas** of the world's most dangerous animals;
mapping nature's born killers. Marshall Cavendish
2010 224p il map lib bdg $99.93

Grades: 7 8 9 10 11 12   **591.6**

1. Dangerous animals

ISBN 978-0-7614-7870-6 lib bdg; 0-7614-7870-1
lib bdg

LC 2008-44960

First published 2004 in the United Kingdom

Explores each of the world's continents, featuring deadly
species of animals.

"Each of these beautifully illustrated books features an
appealing layout; logical organization; and plenty of full-
color drawings, maps, and photographs. The volumes are
organized by continent, with an additional chapter covering
animals in the world's oceans...These volumes are ideal for
reports, but animal lovers will enjoy perusing them as well."
(School Library Journal)

Singer, Marilyn

★ **Venom**. Darby Creek 2007 96p il $19.95

Grades: 5 6 7 8   **591.6**

1. Poisonous animals

ISBN 978-1-58196-043-3; 1-58196-043-3

"Singer introduces a teeming menagerie of creatures . . .
that use venom for attack, defense, or, commonly, both. .
. . The close-up, color photos . . . include not only views of
many creepy crawlies but also such arresting scenes as wood
ants spraying formic acid. . . . Browsers and dedicated young

naturalists alike will enthusiastically dig their teeth into this substantial survey." Booklist

Tourville, Amanda Doering

Animal invaders. Rourke Pub. 2010 48p il (Let's explore science) $32.79

Grades: 4 5 6 7 **591.6**

1. Animals 2. Biological invasions
ISBN 978-1-61590-319-1; 1-61590-319-4

LC 2010009906

This describes non-native animal species.
Includes bibliographical references

Wilkes, Angela

Dangerous creatures; foreword by Steve Leonard. Kingfisher 2003 63p il (Kingfisher knowledge) $11.95

Grades: 5 6 7 8 **591.6**

1. Dangerous animals
ISBN 0-7534-5622-2

LC 2003-40063

Describes various kinds of dangerous animals, such as lions, piranhas, killer bees, and vampire bats

591.68   Rare and endangered animals

Hammond, Paula

The **atlas** of endangered animals; wildlife under threat around the world. Marshall Cavendish 2010 224p il map lib bdg $99.93

Grades: 7 8 9 10 11 12 **591.68**

1. Atlases 2. Reference books 3. Endangered species
ISBN 978-0-7614-7872-0; 0-7614-7872-8

LC 2008-44956

First published 2006 in the United Kingdom

This "beautifully illustrated . . . [book] features an appealing layout; logical organization; and plenty of full-color drawings, maps, and photographs. . . . Ideal for reports, but animal lovers will enjoy perusing them as well." SLJ

591.7   Animal ecology, animals characteristic of specific environments

Dawes, John

★ **Exploring** the world of aquatic life; [consultant editor, John P. Friel; authors, John Dawes and Andrew Campbell] Chelsea House Publishers 2009 6v il set $210

Grades: 5 6 7 8 **591.7**

1. Reference books 2. Marine animals -- Encyclopedias
ISBN 978-1-60413-255-7 set; 1-60413-255-8 set

LC 2008-30416

This set "offers an introduction to the diversity of animals that inhabit oceans, rivers, and lakes. . . . Entries are arranged alphabetically. . . . [The set includes] more than 100 articles. . . . Large photographs and illustrations appear on every two-page spread. . . . With its large typeface, clear explanations, and open layout, this set will appeal to younger

students and would be a useful addition to school and public libraries." Booklist

Includes bibliographical references

The **Deep;** Claire Nouvian [editor] University of Chicago Press 2007 252p il $60

Grades: 8 9 10 11 12 Adult **591.7**

1. Marine animals 2. Marine ecology
ISBN 978-0-226-59566-5; 0-226-59566-8

LC 2006-26921

"Readers will pick up science journalist Nouvian's book for its stunning, 200-plus full-page color photographs of dumbo octopi, vampire squid, frilled sharks, and hydrothermal vent worms; they will hang on to it for the well-written, extremely informative text. . . . Highly recommended for all types and sizes of libraries." Libr J

Includes bibliographical references

Johnson, Jinny

Simon & Schuster children's guide to sea creatures. Simon & Schuster Bks. for Young Readers 1998 80p il $21.95

Grades: 4 5 6 7 **591.7**

1. Marine animals
ISBN 0-689-81534-4

LC 97-8227

Describes the major groups of marine animals, including fish, birds, mammals, and crustaceans

"A beautifully illustrated guide, with a full-color drawing of each animal. . . . The book has enough information to be a useful research tool in the library. The organization, by habitat, is outstanding." Book Rep

Includes glossary

Johnson, Rebecca L.

★ **Journey** into the deep; discovering new ocean creatures. with a foreword by Sylvia A. Earle. Millbrook Press 2010 64p il lib bdg $31.93

Grades: 4 5 6 7 **591.7**

1. Ocean bottom 2. Marine animals 3. Scientific expeditions
ISBN 978-0-7613-4148-2 lib bdg; 0-7613-4148-X lib bdg

LC 2009049603

"This strikingly illustrated book takes its readers on a series of research voyages exploring the ocean from its shallow edges to unfathomable depths during the recently completed ten-year International Census of Marine Life. Clearly organized text and pictures combine to introduce newly discovered marine creatures of all kinds. . . . The excitement and challenge of discovery in tangible. Scientific photographs printed on blue-to-black background . . . illustrate animals mentioned in a nicely legible text. . . . Rich, revealing and rewarding." Kirkus

Includes glossary and bibliographical references

Miller, Sara Swan

Secret lives of burrowing beasts. Marshall Cavendish Benchmark 2010 48p il (Secret lives) lib bdg $29.93

Grades: 3 4 5 6   591.7
1. Burrowing animals
ISBN 978-0-7614-4221-9 lib bdg; 0-7614-4221-9
lib bdg
"The bright, sharp color photos . . . enhance, but take second fiddle to Miller's lively, well-knit [narrative]. . . . [This] volume closes with a generous selection of print and web resources." SLJ
Includes glossary

Secret lives of cave creatures. Marshall Cavendish Benchmark 2010 48p il (Secret lives) lib bdg $29.93
Grades: 3 4 5 6   591.7
1. Animals 2. Cave dwellers
ISBN 978-0-7614-4224-0 lib bdg; 0-7614-4224-3
lib bdg
"The bright, sharp color photos . . . enhance, but take second fiddle to Miller's lively, well-knit [narrative]. . . . [This] volume closes with a generous selection of print and web resources." SLJ
"Describes the life cycles and habits of the three kinds of animals that dwell in caves: those who use caves only for temporary shelter, those who live most of their lives in caves but go outside to find food, and those who are adapted to cave life and cannot live anywhere else." Publisher's note
Includes glossary

Secret lives of deep-sea creatures. Marshall Cavendish Benchmark 2010 48p il (Secret lives) lib bdg $29.93
Grades: 3 4 5 6   591.7
1. Marine animals
ISBN 978-0-7614-4226-4 lib bdg; 0-7614-4226-X
lib bdg
LC 2010000376
"The bright, sharp color photos . . . enhance, but take second fiddle to Miller's lively, well-knit [narrative]. . . . [This] volume closes with a generous selection of print and web resources." SLJ
"Describes the life cycles and habits of the strange creatures that make their homes deep below the surface of the sea." Publisher's note
Includes glossary

Secret lives of soil creatures. Marshall Cavendish Benchmark 2010 48p il (Secret lives) lib bdg $29.93
Grades: 3 4 5 6   591.7
1. Animals 2. Soil ecology
ISBN 978-0-7614-4229-5 lib bdg; 0-7614-4229-4
lib bdg
"The bright, sharp color photos . . . enhance, but take second fiddle to Miller's lively, well-knit [narrative]. . . . [This] volume closes with a generous selection of print and web resources." SLJ
"Describes the life cycles and habits of the three kinds of animals that live in and around the soil: the decomposers, the scavengers, and the predators." Publisher's note
Includes glossary

Turner, Pamela S.
Prowling the seas; exploring the hidden world of ocean predators. Walker & Co. 2009 39p il map $17.99; lib bdg $18.89
Grades: 4 5 6   591.7
1. Ocean 2. Marine animals 3. Predatory animals
ISBN 978-0-8027-9748-3; 0-8027-9748-2; 978-0-8027-9749-0 lib bdg; 0-8027-9749-0 lib bdg
"In each chapter, a clearly delineated map makes it easy to follow the animals' routes, and many clear color photos show the animals and the scientists who study them. . . . A clearly written presentation of an unusual topic." Booklist

Webb, Sophie
Far from shore; a naturalist explores the deep ocean. written and illustrated by Sophie Webb. Houghton Mifflin Books for Children 2011 80p il $17.99
Grades: 4 5 6 7   591.7
1. Dolphins 2. Water birds 3. Marine animals
ISBN 978-0-618-59729-1; 0-618-59729-8
LC 2010025121
Webb "returns with another richly detailed journal of her travels as a naturalist, combining scientific information, field guide-like illustrations, and a thorough account of the day-to-day experiments of a field scientist. The setting is a four-month-long research cruise on a National Ocean and Atmospheric Administration ship to study the impact of fishing on two dolphin populations that reside in the Eastern Tropical Pacific." Horn Book
Includes glossary

Woodward, John
Creatures of the deep; written by John Woodward. Barron's Educational Series 2009 30p il (Discoverology) $18.99
Grades: 5 6 7 8   591.7
1. Ocean 2. Marine animals 3. Pop-up books
ISBN 978-0-7641-6232-9; 0-7641-6232-2
"Flaps, foldouts, wheels, and pop-ups spill across the pages of this colorful title. . . . Each facing page unit . . . contains an introductory paragraph and a collection of color photos, realistic illustrations, and a sampling of the aforementioned doohickeys accompanied by brief, informative captions." SLJ

591.75   Urban animals

Downer, Ann
Wild animal neighbors; sharing our urban world. Ann Downer. Twenty-First Century Books 2014 64 p. (library binding : alkaline paper) $33.27
Grades: 5 6 7 8   591.75
1. Wildlife 2. Urban ecology 3. Suburban life 4. Urban animals 5. City and town life 6. Human-animal relationships 7. Nature -- Effect of human beings on
ISBN 0761390219; 9780761390213
LC 2012043817
This book, by Ann Downer, explains that "as the human population tops seven billion, animals are running out of

space. Their natural habitats are surrounded and sometimes even replaced by highways, shopping centers, office parks, and subdivisions. The result? A wildlife invasion of our urban neighborhoods. What kinds of animals are making cities their new home? How can they survive in our ecosystem of concrete, steel, and glass? And what does their presence there mean for their future and ours?" (Publisher's note)

"Although this book's editorial stance advocates for wild animals in city habitats, it's candid about problems such animals cause humans--from messy raccoons that may carry rabies to potentially dangerous mountain lions in Los Angeles. Accurate information unhampered by a rigid template and supported by good documentation is presented in readable, balanced prose; compelling photographs illustrate the text." (Horn Book)

Includes bibliographical references (page 62) and index

Read, Nicholas

City critters; wildlife in the urban jungle. Nicholas Read. Orca Book Publishers 2012 134 p. (pbk.) $19.95

Grades: 6 7 8   591.75

1. Urban ecology 2. Birds 3. Animals 4. Mammals 5. Urban animals

ISBN 1554693942; 9781554693948

LC 2011942577

This book, by Nicholas Read, offers "a closer look [that] . . . reveals . . . we share our urban environment with a great many untamed creatures. . . . [The book] examines how and why so many wild animals choose to live in places that, on first glance at least, seem contrary to their needs. How do those . . . [animals] manage to survive in the big city? . . . And what are our responsibilities in ensuring that these animals can continue to share our city lives?" (Publisher's note)

Includes bibliographical references and index.

591.77   Marine animals

Bedoyere, Camill

Monsters of the deep; by Camilla Bedoyere. Firefly Books Ltd. 2014 80 p. color illustrations (bound) $9.95

Grades: 4 5 6   591.77

1. Marine animals 2. Deep-sea animals

ISBN 1770854657; 9781770854659

LC 2014497405

In this book, by Camilla Bedoyere, "readers get a look into the watery deep and find 14 of nature's strangest creatures. Intricately drawn artworks and 200 stunning photographs highlight the extraordinary features of each animal's anatomy and survival tactics, such as bioluminescence to ward off predators and jet propulsion (in one case, jet vomit) to escape quickly." (Publisher's note)

"These attractive volumes cover a wide variety of unusual animals . . . [t]he layouts are dramatic, featuring fascinating, sometimes stunning, photos and drawings set against black backgrounds . . . [c]harming looks at some odd creatures." SLJ

Hoyt, Erich

★ Weird sea creatures; Erich Hoyt. Firefly Books 2013 63 p. (pbk.) $9.95; (bound) $19.95

Grades: 5 6 7 8 9 10   591.77

1. Marine biology 2. Abyssal zone 3. Deep-sea animals -- Pictorial works

ISBN 9781770851917; 1770851917; 1770851976; 9781770851979

LC 2012554415

This book celebrates "odd and recently discovered [undersea] species. Through 50 . . . photos, readers are introduced to a yeti crab; a spined pigmy shark; Dumbo, the octopod; and many other deep-sea dwellers." The introduction "presents the physical characteristics of the abyssal ocean— its cold darkness, its cruel pressure—and of the difficulties in finding, collecting, and photographing the creatures that call it home." (School Library Journal)

"Eerie, riveting eye candy for budding biologists and casual browsers alike." Kirkus

Johnson, Jinny

Coral reef life; Jinny Johnson. Smart Apple Media 2012 32 p. col. ill., col. map (Watery worlds) (library) $28.50

Grades: 4 5 6   591.77

1. Coral reef ecology 2. Coral reef animals

ISBN 1599205025; 9781599205021

LC 2011012947

This book by Jinny Johnson is part of the "Watery Worlds" series. "In this book, we find out how coral reefs are formed and learn why they are so important. We look at the amazing variety of fish around the reefs and discover why the reefs themselves are in danger." (Publishers note) It "contains a map and a 'facts' page." (Library Media Connection)

Woodward, John

Ocean; an amazing window on our world. written by John Woodward ; illustrations by Gary Hanna. DK Pub. 2012 59 p. col. ill. (Look closer) (hardcover) $10.99

Grades: 4 5 6   591.77

1. Picture books for children 2. Ocean 3. Marine biology 4. Marine animals

ISBN 0756692377; 9780756692377

LC 2011277622

This book is part of DK Publishing's Look Closer series and allows readers to "explore different perspectives of . . . underwater scenes as they zoom in, zoom out, and go sideways, forward, and backward. . . . Specially commissioned computer-generated imagery" is included. (Publisher's note)

592   Specific taxonomic groups of animals

Cerullo, Mary M.

★ Sea soup: zooplankton; [by] Mary M. Cerullo; photography by Bill Curtsinger. Tilbury House 2001 39p il $16.95

Grades: 5 6 7 8 **592**
1. Zooplankton
ISBN 0-88448-219-7

LC 00-46721

This book "opens a pellucid window into the drifting world of mostly minute animals that, along with phytoplankton, form an aqueous 'soup' that nourishes a wide variety of sea creatures. . . . Curtsinger's often extraordinary color photos allow readers to envision the often microscopically small creatures delineated in the text. . . . This is a fascinating look at a watery zoo of creatures whose ecological importance is far beyond the measure of their size." SLJ

Includes glossary and bibliographical references

Meinkoth, Norman August

★ The **Audubon** Society field guide to North American seashore creatures; [by] Norman A. Meinkoth. Knopf 1981 799p il maps flexible bdg $19.95

Grades: 7 8 9 10 11 12 Adult **592**
1. Invertebrates 2. Marine biology
ISBN 0-394-51993-0

LC 81-80828

This "unique field guide covers some 850 marine invertebrate animals living in or around the shallow waters of the temperate seacoasts of the United States and Canada. Excellent color photographs are grouped at the beginning of the book, followed by text that gives, for each animal, a short description, common and scientific names, habitat, range, and comments." Malinowsky. Best Sci & Technol Ref Books for Young People

Parker, Steve, 1952-

Sponges, jellyfish & other simple animals; by Steve Parker. Compass Point Books 2006 p. cm.

Grades: 5 6 7 8 **592**
1. Sponges. 2. Jellyfishes. 3. Invertebrates.
ISBN 0-7565-1614-5 (hard cover)

LC 2005029183

"Smoothly written, well-organized... With succinct text and colorful formats, [this] will appeal to students and browsers alike." SLJ

593 Miscellaneous marine and seashore invertebrates

Gilpin, Daniel

Starfish, urchins & other echinoderms; by Daniel Gilpin. Compass Point Books 2006 48 p.

Grades: 4 5 6 **593**
1. Starfishes 2. Sea urchins 3. Echinodermata
ISBN 0-7565-1611-0 (hard cover)

LC 2005029184

Introduces the physical characteristics, habitat, and types of echinoderms, including starfish, sea urchins, and sea cucumbers.

593.5 Coelenterates

Gray, Susan Heinrichs

Australian spotted jellyfish; [by] Susan H. Gray. Cherry Lake Pub. 2010 32p il map (Animal invaders) $27.07

Grades: 5 6 7 8 **593.5**
1. Jellyfishes 2. Biological invasions
ISBN 978-1-60279-628-7; 1-60279-628-9

LC 2009024168

This offers "an introduction to the problems caused by [the Australian spotted jellyfish], a discussion of its physical characteristics and habits, a history of how it arrived in its new habitat, and an analysis of challenges encountered by those trying to limit its spread. . . . [This] stinging jelly [was] brought by cargo ships to the Gulf of Mexico and some Atlantic coastal waters." Booklist

Includes glossary and bibliographical references

594 Mollusks and molluscoids

Arthur, Alex

Shell; written by Alex Arthur; special photography by Andreas von Einsiedel, Dave King and Colin Keates. Dk Pub 2013 72 p. (Eyewitness books) (library) $19.99

Grades: 6 7 8 **594**
1. Shells 2. Conchology
ISBN 1465409041; 9781465409041

This book is part of the DK Eyewitness Books series and focuses on shells. The titles in this series "focus on subjects that complement students' personal interests and areas of study to make learning simple and fun." Wall charts, clip art CDs, and photographs and illustrations are included. (Publisher's note)

Cerullo, Mary M.

Giant squid; searching for a sea monster. by Mary M. Cerullo with Clyde F.E. Roper. Capstone Press 2012 48 p. ill. (chiefly col.) (Smithsonian) (library) $26.86; (paperback) $8.95

Grades: 4 5 6 **594**
1. Giant squids
ISBN 1429680237; 9781429675413; 9781429680233

LC 2011029181

This book "recounts some of the legends and historical clues that led to the giant squid's identification in the 19th century before focusing on Dr. Clyde Roper, a renowned specialist on cephalopods. . . . The text describes how Roper gathered facts by autopsying the carcasses of giant squids and sperm whales (its chief predator), examining other squid species, etc.; it also outlines several expeditions he led in search of a live specimen." (School Library Journal)

Douglass, Jackie Leatherbury

★ **Peterson** first guide to shells of North America; illustrations by John Douglass. Houghton Mifflin 1989 128p il pa $5.95

Grades: 7 8 9 10 11 12 Adult   **594**
1. Shells
ISBN 0-395-91182-6

LC 88-32884

"Shell collectors will enjoy the basic descriptions of shell types. Douglass has included the 'most colorful, not necessarily the most common, shells.' . . . Filled with precise color drawings and concise identification information." Booklist

Gilpin, Daniel
  ★ **Snails,** shellfish & other mollusks; by Daniel Gilpin. Compass Point Books 2006 48 p.
Grades: 4 5 6   **594**
1. Snails. 2. Mollusks. 3. Shellfish.
ISBN 0-7565-1613-7 (hard cover)

LC 2005029182

"...Smoothly written, well-organized...With succinct texts and colorful formats, [this] will appeal to students and browsers alike." SLJ

Miller, Sara Swan
  Secret lives of seashell dwellers. Marshall Cavendish Benchmark 2010 48p il (Secret lives) lib bdg $29.93
Grades: 3 4 5 6   **594**
1. Mollusks
ISBN 978-0-7614-4228-8 lib bdg; 0-7614-4228-6 lib bdg

LC 2010000377

"The bright, sharp color photos . . . enhance, but take second fiddle to Miller's lively, well-knit [narrative]. . . . [This] volume closes with a generous selection of print and web resources." SLJ
  Includes glossary

Montgomery, Sy
  ★ The **Octopus** Scientists; exploring the mind of a mollusk. written by Sy Montgomery; photographs by Keith Ellenbogen. Houghton Mifflin Harcourt 2015 80 p. illustrations (chiefly color) $18.99
Grades: 5 6 7 8 9   **594**
1. Octopuses 2. Marine biology 3. Octopuses -- Research -- French Polynesia -- Morea
ISBN 0544232704; 9780544232709

This book by Sy Montogomery and illustrated by Keith Ellenborgen, "an inquiry into the mind of an intelligent invertebrate, is also a foray into our own unexplored planet. With three hearts and blue blood, its gelatinous body unconstrained by jointed limbs or gravity, the octopus seems to be an alien, an inhabitant of another world. But most intriguing of all, octopuses--classed as mollusks, like clams--are remarkably intelligent with quirky personalities." (Publisher's note)

"Amazing photographs reveal the octopuses' remarkable shape-changing abilities and help readers visualize this experience. Science in the field at its best." Kirkus

Newquist, H. P.
  Here there be monsters; the legendary kraken and the giant squid. Houghton Mifflin Harcourt 2010 73p il map $18

Grades: 4 5 6 7   **594**
1. Squids
ISBN 978-0-547-07678-2; 0-547-07678-9

"This intriguing book offers a chronological account of giant squids, beginning with sailors' tales about krakens and leading up to the groundbreaking discoveries of the past few decades.... The many illustrations, in color when available, include photos, engravings, and maps. ... An attractive, informative book on an underrepresented topic." Booklist

Rand, Casey
  Glass squid and other spectacular squid. Raintree 2011 32p il lib bdg $29; pa $7.99
Grades: 3 4 5 6   **594**
1. Squids
ISBN 978-1-4109-4194-7 lib bdg; 978-1-4109-4201-2 pa

LC 2010038186

"This informative and colorful series will engage younger children to learn more about the sea and its creatures." Library Media Connection

Rehder, Harald Alfred
  The **Audubon** Society field guide to North American seashells; {by} Harald A. Rehder; with photographs by James H. Carmichael, Jr.; visual key by Carol Nehring and Mary Beth Brewer. Knopf 1981 894p il flexible bdg $19.95
Grades: 7 8 9 10 11 12 Adult   **594**
1. Shells 2. Mollusks
ISBN 0-394-51913-2

LC 80-84239

"[T]his guide explores more than 705 seashells, living mollusks, abalone, periwinkles, conchs, limpets, oysters, clams, mussels, and cockles found on the Atlantic, Pacific, and Gulf coasts of North America and the West Indies. The photographs are arranged by shape and color, making identification quick and easy." Publisher's note

"The more than 700 color plates are arranged according to shape and color rather than family or genus, making identification very simple for even the rankest amateur.... The text gives the common name, scientific name, description, habitat, range, and comments for each species. This is the most comprehensive field guide to North American seashells." Libr J

595.3 Crustaceans

Gilpin, Daniel
  Lobsters, crabs & other crustaceans; by Daniel Gilpin. Compass Point Books 2006 48 p.
Grades: 4 5 6   **595.3**
1. Crabs 2. Lobster 3. Crustacea
ISBN 0-7565-1612-9 (hard cover)

LC 2005029180

Introduces the physical characteristics and habitats of crustaceans, from lobsters and shrimps to sow bugs and barnacles.

595.4   Chelicerates

Heos, Bridget

Stronger Than Steel; Spider Silk DNA and the Quest for Better Bulletproof Vests, Sutures, and Parachute Rope. Bridget Heos ; [illustrated by] Andy Comins. Houghton Mifflin Books for Children 2013 79 p. col. ill. (hardcover) $18.99

Grades: 5 6 7 8   **595.4**

1. Silk 2. Spiders 3. Inventions 4. Scientists 5. Spider webs 6. Nephila maculata

ISBN 0547681267; 9780547681269

LC 2012010992

This children's book, by Bridget Heos, illustrated by Andy Comis, is part of the "Scientists in the Field" series. In it "readers enter Randy Lewis' lab where they come face to face with golden orb weaver spiders, and transgenic alfalfa, silkworm silk, and goats, whose milk contains the proteins to spin spider silk--and to weave a nearly indestructible fiber." (Publisher's note)

Lasky, Kathryn

Silk & venom; searching for a dangerous spider. photographs by Christopher G. Knight. Candlewick Press 2011 57p il map

Grades: 4 5 6 7   **595.4**

1. Spiders 2. Biologists 3. Arachnologists 4. College teachers

ISBN 0-7636-4222-3; 978-0-7636-4222-8

LC 2010-41888

This book focuses on the the field work of arachnologist Greta Binford. "Binford's effort to trace the migration of Loxosceles from South American to North America . . . [led] her to field exploration in the Dominican Republic. [Glossary. Index.] Grades four to seven." (Bull Cent Child Books)

"Biology professor Greta Binford studies spiders in an Oregon lab and in the field in the Dominican Republic, where she searches for L. Taino, a Caribbean relative of the venomous brown recluse that might provide clues to how and when the recluse genus arrived in North America. . . . In leisurely, literary prose, Lasky presents the ancient class of arachnids before introducing the scientist and explaining her quest. . . . On most spreads, a full-bleed photograph is opposed by substantial text and one or two smaller pictures." Kirkus

Crab spiders; phantom hunters. Sandra Markle. Lerner Pub. Company 2012 48 p. col. ill. (Arachnid world)

Grades: 4 5 6 7   **595.4**

1. Spiders 2. Zoology 3. Predatory animals 4. Arachnids 5. Crab spiders 6. Crab spiders

ISBN 0761350454; 9780761350453

LC 2011020443

This book is part of Sandra Markle's "Arachnid World" series. "In this book, you will learn how crab spiders are similar to and different from other arachnids. Close-up photographs and diagrams reveal extraordinary details about the crab spider's body both inside and out. A hands-on activity illustrates how a crab spider can quickly ambush a flying insect. . . . Enter the . . . world of the arachnid family with award-winning science author Sandra Markle! Too often lumped together with insects, these fascinating animals have

distinctive characteristics and habits that are all their own." (Publisher's note)

Includes bibliographical references (p. 44-45) and index

Fishing spiders; water ninjas. Sandra Markle. Lerner Publications Company 2012 48 p. col. ill. (Arachnid world)

Grades: 4 5 6 7   **595.4**

1. Spiders 2. Aquatic animals 3. Predatory animals 4. Zoology -- Encyclopedias 5. Arachnids 6. Dolomedes

ISBN 9780761350446

LC 2011020442

This book is part of Sandra Markle's "Arachnid World" series. "In this book, you will learn how fishing spiders are similar to and different from other arachnids. Close-up photographs and diagrams reveal extraordinary details about the fishing spider's body both inside and out. A hands-on activity shows how the fishing spider's hairy coat helps it walk on water. . . . Enter the . . . world of the arachnid family with award-winning science author Sandra Markle! Too often lumped together with insects, these fascinating animals have distinctive characteristics and habits that are all their own." (Publisher's note)

Includes bibliographical references and index

Harvestmen; secret operatives. Lerner Publications 2011 48p il (Arachnid world) lib bdg $29.27

Grades: 5 6 7 8   **595.4**

1. Spiders

ISBN 978-0-7613-5042-2; 0-7613-5042-X

LC 2010023491

This describes how harvestmen are similar to and different from other arachnids. Close-up photographs and diagrams reveal details about the harvestmen's bodies, both inside and out. A hands-on activity reveals how harvestmen walk on long legs using only their sense of touch to get around.

Markle "presents a mix of common and less-common facts . . . and her commentary accompanies a particularly strong suite of illustrations featuring large, clear, labeled outside and inside views that display body parts. Photos go beyond the standard portraits. . . . First rate." SLJ

Includes glossary and bibliographical references

Jumping spiders; gold-medal stalkers. by Sandra Markle. Lerner Publications 2012 48 p. col. ill.

Grades: 4 5 6 7   **595.4**

1. Spiders 2. Animal behavior 3. Zoology -- Encyclopedias 4. Arachnids 5. Jumping spiders

ISBN 0761350470; 9780761350477

LC 2011021598

This book is part of Sandra Markle's "Arachnid World" series. "In this book, you will learn how jumping spiders are similar to and different from other arachnids. Close-up photographs and diagrams reveal extraordinary details about the jumping spider's body both inside and out. A hands-on activity compares the reader's jumping ability with that of a jumping spider. . . . Enter the . . . world of the arachnid family with award-winning science author Sandra Markle! Too often lumped together with insects, these fascinating animals have distinctive characteristics and habits that are all their own." (Publisher's note)

Includes bibliographical references (p. 44-45) and index

Markle, Sandra, 1946-

Black widows; deadly biters. Lerner Publications 2011 48p il (Arachnid world) lib bdg $29.27 Grades: 5 6 7 8 **595.4**

1. Spiders

ISBN 978-0-7613-5038-5; 0-7613-5038-1

This describes how black widows are similar to and different from other arachnids. Close-up photographs and diagrams reveal details about the black widow's body both inside and out. A hands-on activity compares the black widow's web to a human hair.

Markle "presents a mix of common and less-common facts . . . and her commentary accompanies a particularly strong suite of illustrations featuring large, clear, labeled outside and inside views that display body parts. Photos go beyond the standard portraits. . . . First rate." SLJ

Includes glossary and bibliographical references

Mites; master sneaks. by Sandra Markle. Lerner Publications 2012 48 p. (Arachnid world) Grades: 4 5 6 7 **595.4**

1. Mites 2. Animals -- Anatomy 3. Arachnids 4. Mites ISBN 9780761350460

LC 2011021462

In this book, a volume of the Arachnid World series, readers "will learn how mites are similar to and different from other arachnids. Close-up photographs, micrographs, and diagrams reveal . . . details about a mite's body both inside and out. A hands-on activity shows how quickly a few mites can multiply into hundreds." (Publisher's note) The book "discuss[es] . . . [their] physical structure, life cycle, and characteristic behaviors. . . . In "Mites," [author Sandra] Markle discusses a variety of these . . . creatures." (Booklist)

Includes bibliographical references and index

Orb weavers; hungry spinners. Lerner Publications 2011 48p il (Arachnid world) lib bdg $29.27 Grades: 5 6 7 8 **595.4**

1. Spiders

ISBN 978-0-7613-5039-2; 0-7613-5039-X

LC 2010023490

This describes how orb weavers are similar to and different from other arachnids. Close-up photographs and diagrams reveal details about the spider's body both inside and out. And a hands-on activity will give you an idea of how the orb weaver can detect prey caught in its web.

Markle "presents a mix of common and less-common facts . . . and her commentary accompanies a particularly strong suite of illustrations featuring large, clear, labeled outside and inside views that display body parts. Photos go beyond the standard portraits. . . . First rate." SLJ

Includes glossary and bibliographical references

Scorpions; armed stingers. Lerner Publications 2011 48p il (Arachnid world) lib bdg $29.27

Grades: 5 6 7 8 **595.4**

1. Scorpions

ISBN 978-0-7613-5037-8; 0-7613-5037-3

LC 2010004275

This describes how scorpions are similar to and different from other arachnids. Close-up photographs and diagrams reveal details about the scorpion's body both inside and out. And a hands-on activity reveals how a scorpion's senses help it find its prey.

Markle "presents a mix of common and less-common facts . . . and her commentary accompanies a particularly strong suite of illustrations featuring large, clear, labeled outside and inside views that display body parts. Photos go beyond the standard portraits. . . . First rate." SLJ

Includes glossary and bibliographical references

Tarantulas; supersized predators. by Sandra Markle. Lerner Publications Company 2012 48 p. (Arachnid world)

Grades: 4 5 6 7 **595.4**

1. Tarantulas 2. Predatory animals 3. Arachnids -- ISBN 9780761350439

LC 2011020437

In this book, a volume of the Arachnid World series, readers "will learn how tarantulas are similar to and different from other arachnids. Close-up photographs and diagrams reveal extraordinary details about the tarantula's body both inside and out. A hands-on activity illustrates how a tarantula grows bigger and bigger by molting." (Publisher's note) The book "discuss[es] . . . [their] physical structure, life cycle, and characteristic behaviors. . . . "Tarantulas" looks at the lives of these large, hairy spiders and points out that they help control insect populations." (Booklist)

Includes bibliographical references and index

Ticks; dangerous hitchhikers. Lerner Publications 2011 48p il (Arachnid world) lib bdg $29.27 Grades: 4 5 6 7 **595.4**

1. Ticks

ISBN 978-0-7613-5041-5; 0-7613-5041-1

LC 2010023484

This book about ticks offers "a clear, conversational text that will draw young people into the zoological facts with gripping, even gruesome examples that are well matched with unsparingly detailed photos. . . . The handsome design, featuring crisply magnified photos, and the approachable text from an experienced writer combine into a strong offering for both personal and classroom reading." Booklist

Includes bibliographical references

Wind scorpions; killer jaws. Sandra Markle. Lerner Publications 2012 48 p. (Arachnid world) (lib. bdg. : alk. paper) $30.60

Grades: 4 5 6 7 **595.4**

1. Scorpions 2. Animals -- Anatomy 3. Arachnids 4. Solpugida

ISBN 0761350489; 9780761350484

LC 2011021599

In this book, a volume of the Arachnid World series, readers "will learn how wind scorpions are similar to and very different from other arachnids. Close-up photographs and diagrams reveal extraordinary details about the wind scorpion's body both inside and out. A hands-on activity demonstrates how wind scorpions are able to pick up prey to eat it." (Publisher's note) The book "discuss[es] . . . [their] physical structure, life cycle, and characteristic behaviors . . . . 'Wind Scorpions' introduces a group of arachnids that use supersize jaws to defend themselves and to attack their prey." (Booklist)

Includes bibliographical references and index

Wolf spiders; mothers on guard. Lerner Publications 2010 48p il (Arachnid world) lib bdg $29.27

Grades: 5 6 7 8   **595.4**

1. Spiders

ISBN 978-0-7613-5040-8; 0-7613-5040-3

LC 2010004273

This describes how wolf spider mothers carry their young on their backs and how wolf spiders are similar to and different from other arachnids. Close-up photographs and diagrams reveal details about the spider's body both inside and out. And hands-on activities will let you experience how a wolf spider female keeps her eggs and young safe.

Markle "presents a mix of common and less-common facts . . . and her commentary accompanies a particularly strong suite of illustrations featuring large, clear, labeled outside and inside views that display body parts. Photos go beyond the standard portraits. . . . First rate." SLJ

Includes glossary and bibliographical references

Montgomery, Sy

★ The **tarantula** scientist. Houghton Mifflin Co. 2004 80p il map (Scientists in the field) $18; pa $7.95

Grades: 4 5 6 7   **595.4**

1. Tarantulas

ISBN 0-618-14799-3; 0-618-91577-X pa

LC 2003-20125

Describes the research that Samuel Marshall and his students are doing on tarantulas, including the largest spider on earth, the Goliath birdeating tarantula

"Enthusiasm for the subject and respect for both Marshall and his eight-legged subjects come through on every page of the clear, informative, and even occasionally humorous text. Bishop's full-color photos . . . are amazing." Booklist

Includes glossary and bibliographical references

Stefoff, Rebecca

The **arachnid** class. Marshall Cavendish Benchmark 2008 96p il (Family trees) $23.95

Grades: 6 7 8 9   **595.4**

1. Spiders

ISBN 978-0-7614-3075-9; 0-7614-3075-X

LC 2008017561

"Explores the habitats, life cycles, and other characteristics of arachnids, such as spiders, scorpions, mites, and ticks."

Includes glossary and bibliographical references

Zabludoff, Marc

★ **Spiders**; [by] Marc Zabludoff. Marshall Cavendish Benchmark 2006 112p il (Animalways) lib bdg $31.36

Grades: 7 8 9 10   **595.4**

1. Spiders

ISBN 0-7614-1747-8

LC 2004-16681

This discusses the evolution of spiders, their places in human culture, their life cycles, anatomy, and behavior

"Strong writing melds well with well-selected photos, all of which are clearly produced and of high quality. Some of the images are stunning." SLJ

Includes glossary and bibliographical references

595.7   Insects

Albee, Sarah

Bugged; How Insects Changed History. by Sarah Albee. Bloomsbury/Walker 2014 176 p. illustrations (some color) (pbk.) $17.99; (library edition) $23.89

Grades: 4 5 6 7   **595.7**

1. Insects 2. Human-animal relationship 3. Insects -- History 4. Human-animal relationships -- History

ISBN 0802734227; 0802734235; 9780802734228; 9780802734235

LC 2013025968

This book, by Sarah Albee, illustrated by Robert Leighton, focuses on the impact of insects on the world throughout history. According to the book, "beneficial bugs have built empires. Bad bugs have toppled them." The book is a "combination of world history, social history, natural science, epidemiology, public health, conservation, and microbiology." (Publisher's note)

"The shock value alone makes this worth the cover price, but once kids are pulled in, they will learn more than they bargained for about the impact of insects on human history... Overall, this title is astonishing, disgusting, revolting, and ultimately fascinating, making it perfect for emerging entomologists, budding historians, reluctant readers, and gross-out junkies alike.—" SLJ

How insects have changed human history

Anderson, Margaret Jean

Bugged -out insects; [by] Margaret J. Anderson. Enslow Publishers 2011 48p il (Bizarre science) lib bdg $23.93

Grades: 4 5 6 7   **595.7**

1. Insects

ISBN 978-0-7660-3674-1; 0-7660-3674-X

LC 2010006474

First published 1996 with title: Bizarre insects

This describes insects such as cicadas, butterflies, praying mantises, walkingsticks, beetles, stinkbugs, botflies, mayflies, mosquitoes, bees, ants, and locusts.

"Aimed at reluctant readers, [this title is] sure to disgust and delight in equal measure. . . . [The title] will pique interest and get kids lining up at the reference desk looking for more. The text is complemented by illustrations and magnified photos of things that you would hope never to see." SLJ

Includes glossary and bibliographical references

Beccaloni, George

Biggest bugs life-size. Firefly Books 2010 84p il $19.95

Grades: 4 5 6 7   **595.7**

1. Insects

ISBN 978-1-55407-699-4; 1-55407-699-4

"This book presents 35 of the world's biggest, longest, and heaviest bugs. . . . Double-page spreads feature each bug's statistics, a map with its area of distribution, and straightforward text that explains its living conditions, eating habits, and life cycle. . . . The highlights, of course, are the numerous life-size and up-close full-color photographs of the bugs. . . . The visual appeal alone will entice even the most reluctant readers." Booklist

Dixon, Norma

Focus on flies. Fitzhenry & Whiteside 2008 32p il $18.95

Grades: 4 5 6 7   **595.7**

1. Flies

ISBN 978-1-55005-128-5; 1-55005-128-8

This "chatty, informative title, illustrated with many clear color photos and diagrams, will hook readers with its fascinating view of a fly's 'creepy cool world.' . . . The gross details will appeal to middle-grade readers, who will then go on to learn about anatomy, metamorphosis, adaptation, diversity, classification, and flies' roles in plant pollination." Booklist

Includes bibliographical references

Evans, Arthur V.

National Wildlife Federation field guide to insects and spiders & related species of North America; written by Arthur Evans; foreword by Craig Tufts. Sterling Pub. 2007 496p il map pa $19.95

Grades: 7 8 9 10 11 12 Adult   **595.7**

1. Insects 2. Spiders

ISBN 978-1-4027-4153-1; 1-4027-4153-7

LC 2006-19491

"This guide presents a glimpse of the incredible array of colors, shapes, and forms found within the phylum Arthropoda. . . . Over 380 pages of color photographs follow, most showing two or three different species. . . . This is a very good guide that will find a wide audience." Choice

Includes bibliographical references

Gray, Susan Heinrichs

Emerald ash borer; by Susan H. Gray. Cherry Lake Pub. 2008 32p il map (Animal invaders) lib bdg $27.07

Grades: 3 4 5 6   **595.7**

1. Emerald ash borer 2. Biological invasions

ISBN 978-1-60279-112-1 lib bdg; 1-60279-112-0 lib bdg

LC 2007-34973

This describes the Emerald ash borers' "outstanding physical and behavioral characteristics at each stage in their life cycle, diet, and natural habitat, and then [explains] how they were introduced into areas outside their natural range . . . and the nature and extent of the ecological damage they have caused, and various attempts to eradicate or at least

control the animals. . . . Larvae of the emerald ash borer have infested and destroyed thousands of valuable ash trees in the Midwest. . . . Clear color photographs . . . accompany the texts on about every other page. . . . [This title is] clearly written and well organized, and [has] up-to-date information." SLJ

Includes glossary

Hamilton, Sue L.

Swarmed by bees; [by] Sue Hamilton. ABDO Pub. Co. 2010 32p il (Close encounters of the wild kind) lib bdg $27.07

Grades: 4 5 6 7   **595.7**

1. Bees 2. Animal attacks

ISBN 978-1-60453-933-2 lib bdg; 1-60453-933-X lib bdg

LC 2009-45598

Readers learn of actual human-bee encounters, information about bees, survival strategies, and attack statistics.

"Students will be drawn to the realistic full-color photographs, the realistic diagrams of the creatures' bodies, the real-life stories told by victims, and the interesting, attractive formatting that includes text, diagrams, photographs, and graphics on each page. . . . [This is] exciting and attractive in a 'gross' sort of way and will appeal particularly to boys for both leisure reading and research." Libr Media Connect

Includes glossary

Latimer, Jonathan P.

Caterpillars; [by] Jonathan P. Latimer, Karen Stray Nolting; illustrations by Amy Bartlett Wright; foreword by Virginia Marie Peterson. Houghton Mifflin 2000 48p il (Peterson field guides for young naturalists) pbk. $5.95

Grades: 4 5 6 7   **595.7**

1. Caterpillars

ISBN 9780395979457

LC 99-38944

Describes the physical characteristics, behavior, and habitat of a variety of caterpillars, arranged by the categories "Smooth," "Bumpy," "Sluglike," "Horned," "Hairy," "Bristly," and "Spiny"

Marshall, Stephen A.

Insects A to Z. Firefly 2009 32p il lib bdg $19.95; pa $7.95

Grades: 4 5 6   **595.7**

1. Insects

ISBN 978-1-55407-555-3 lib bdg; 1-55407-555-6 lib bdg; 978-1-55407-503-4 pa; 1-55407-503-3 pa

This is an illustrated dictionary of 26 insects which includes the Latin and common names of the order, family, genus and species, as well as information on geographic distribution. Fact boxes for each entry provide information detailing each insect's scientific name, diet, average size and the location at which each was photographed.

"The photography . . . is well composed and sharply focused, with a nicely varied layout from page to page. . . . The [text is] clearly written." SLJ

Milne, Lorus Johnson

★ The **Audubon** Society field guide to North American insects and spiders; [by] Lorus and Margery Milne; visual key by Susan Rayfield. Knopf 1980 989p il $19.95

Grades: 7 8 9 10 11 12 Adult   **595.7**

1. Insects 2. Spiders

ISBN 0-394-50763-0

LC 80-7620

The authors "have based their field guide on 702 excellent color photographs (75 of which are of spiders and other arachnids). In addition to some general information, the text (two thirds of the book) is made up of brief comments on each kind of arthropod pictured." Choice

Includes glossary

Pyle, Robert Michael

★ The **Audubon** Society field guide to North American butterflies; visual key by Carol Nehring and Jane Opper. Knopf 1981 916p il $19.95

Grades: 7 8 9 10 11 12 Adult   **595.7**

1. Butterflies

ISBN 0-394-51914-0

LC 80-84240

This guide "introduces more than 600 species of North American butterfly, including those native to the Hawaiian Islands. A section of brilliant color plates (more than 1,000 of them) featuring butterflies in their natural habitats, follows a general introduction and notes on text organization and use." Booklist

Rodriguez, Ana Maria

Secret of the plant-killing ants . . . and more! Enslow Publishers 2008 48p il (Animal secrets revealed!) lib bdg $23.93

Grades: 5 6 7 8   **595.7**

1. Ants 2. Insects

ISBN 978-0-7660-2953-8 lib bdg; 0-7660-2953-0 lib bdg

LC 2007039494

"Explains why ants in the Amazon rainforest kill all but one species of plant and details other strange abilities of different types of animals." Publisher's note

Includes glossary and bibliographical references

Schlaepfer, Gloria G.

Butterflies. Marshall Cavendish Benchmark 2006 112p il (Animalways) lib bdg $31.36

Grades: 6 7 8 9   **595.7**

1. Butterflies

ISBN 0-7614-1745-1

LC 2004-16682

This discusses the evolution of butterflies, their places in human culture, their life cycles, anatomy, and behavior

"Strong writing melds well with well-selected photos, all of which are clearly produced and of high quality. Some of the images are stunning." SLJ

Includes glossary and bibliographical references

Tait, Noel

Insects & spiders. Simon & Schuster Books for Young Readers 2008 64p il map (Insiders) $16.99

Grades: 5 6 7 8   **595.7**

1. Insects 2. Spiders

ISBN 978-1-4169-3868-2; 1-4169-3868-0

LC 2008-61110

Provides an overview of insects and spiders in a book that includes detailed three-dimensional illustrations.

"Sharp, hyper-realistic, larger-than-life drawings . . . are . . . set against a plain colored background or within a natural setting. . . . [This] title succinctly describes basic anatomy; physical and behavioral characteristics common to all [insects and spiders]." SLJ

Includes glossary

Young, Karen Romano

Bug science; 20 projects and experiments about arthropods: insects, arachnids, algae, worms, and other small creatures. illustrations by David Goldin. National Geographic 2009 80p il (Science fair winners) lib bdg $24.90; pa $12.95

Grades: 6 7 8 9   **595.7**

1. Insects 2. Arthropoda 3. Science projects 4. Science -- Experiments

ISBN 978-1-4263-0520-7 lib bdg; 1-4263-0520-6 lib bdg; 978-1-4263-0519-1 pa; 1-4263-0519-2 pa

LC 2009-12734

Twenty projects and experiments about arthropods: insects, arachnids, algae, worms, and other small creatures.

This book is "engaging, visually stimulating, and very student friendly. . . . Includes an introduction to the topic, suggestions for how to present the findings, and an index making the information really accessible. . . . The planning steps, guidance, and tips along the way for implementing projects are very sound." Libr Media Connect

Includes bibliographical references

Zabludoff, Marc

Beetles; by Marc Zabludoff. Marshall Cavendish Benchmark 2007 112p il (Animalways) lib bdg $34.21

Grades: 6 7 8 9   **595.7**

1. Beetles

ISBN 978-0-7614-2532-8

LC 2006038518

This describes the place of beetles in the animal kingdom, their evolution, anatomy, physiology, life cycle, diversity, and relationship to humans.

Includes glossary and bibliographical references

★ The **insect** class. Benchmark Books 2006 95p il (Family trees) lib bdg $29.93

Grades: 6 7 8 9   **595.7**

1. Insects

ISBN 0-7614-1819-9 lib bdg

LC 2004-21819

This examines physical traits, adaptations, diets, habitats, and life cycles of insects.

"Fact-filled, yet surprisingly readable. . . . [This] title contains a wide variety of excellent-quality, full-color photographs; interesting sidebars; and diagrams." SLJ

Includes glossary and bibliographical references

595.76 Beetles

Burns, Loree Griffin

★ **Beetle** busters; a rogue insect and the people who track it. Loree Griffin Burns ; photographs by Ellen Harasimowicz. Houghton Mifflin Harcourt 2014 64 p. color illustrations, color map (Scientists in the field) $18.99

Grades: 5 6 7 8   **595.76**

1. Beetles 2. Insects 3. Nonindigenous pests 4. Beetles 5. Asian longhorned beetle

ISBN 0547792670; 9780547792675

LC 2013050160

This book, by Loree Griffin Burns, focuses on the "Asian longhorned beetle (ALB). . . . These beetles came to America from China, living in wood turned into shipping material. At first the beetles invaded urban areas, where hardwood trees were in limited supply. . . . But . . . now . . . infestations have erupted in . . . hardwood forests, and these beetles, while bad at flying, are very good at killing trees. Clint McFarland's job? Stop the ALB at any cost." (Publisher's note)

"They arrived unseen, burrowed in wooden pallets, spools, and crates, aboard ships from China. The first group spotted in the United States, in Brooklyn, NY, was contained, and quickly taken care of, but since then infestations have been discovered from Massachusetts to Illinois, and as far north as Canada. They're Asian longhorned beetles, pests with "powerful jaws and a taste for wood" and the frightening potential to eat their way through North American forests...The author lives within the quarantined area in Massachusetts and has seen firsthand areas where swatches of infested (and other) trees have been cut down. Her questions about the method employed will leave readers asking some of their own—as they should. A timely, well-told story and a call to action." SLJ

Jenkins, Steve

★ The **beetle** book; Steve Jenkins. Houghton Mifflin Books for Children 2011 31 p. $16.99

Grades: 4 5 6 7   **595.76**

1. Beetles 2. Ecology -- Encyclopedias 3. Insects -- Encyclopedias

ISBN 9780547680842

LC 2011027129

This nonfiction natural history book presents pictures and information about an "array of beetles." Author/illustrator Steve Jenkins describes "the colors and patterns of this ubiquitous insect . . . [and] the details about the various adaptations that beetles have made over millennia in response to their environment, diet, and predators." Jenkins claims that "one out of four creatures on the planet is a beetle." (Kirkus Reviews)

595.78 Moths and butterflies

Pasternak, Carol

How to raise monarch butterflies; a step-by-step guide for kids. Carol Pasternak. Firefly Books 2012 48 p. col. ill. (bound) $19.95

Grades: 3 4 5 6 7   **595.78**

1. Caterpillars 2. Insects -- Care 3. Monarch butterflies 4. Monarch butterfly -- Life cycles

ISBN 1770850015; 1770850023; 9781770850019; 9781770850026

LC 2012419489

This book by Carol Pasternak presents a "detailed guide to locating and hatching. . . Monarch butterflies. . . . [R]eaders will learn about the life cycle of the Monarch and how to encourage populations in their own backyards, with tips on which plants to grow, as well as the care and feeding of their pet caterpillars. 'How to Raise Monarch Butterflies' explains what threats face Monarchs and how readers can help conserve the Monarch's feeding grounds from encroachment." (Publisher's note)

Includes bibliographical references and index.

Whalley, Paul

Butterfly & moth; written by Paul Whalley. Revised ed. DK Pub. 2012 72 p. ill. (chiefly col.), col. map (Eyewitness books) (hardcover) $16.99; (library) $19.99

Grades: 4 5 6 7   **595.78**

1. Butterflies 2. Moths

ISBN 0756692989; 0756692997; 9780756692988; 9780756692995

LC 2012418030

This book is part of the DK Eyewitness Books series and focuses on butterflies and moths. The titles in this series "focus on subjects that complement students' personal interests and areas of study to make learning simple and fun." Wall charts, clip art CDs, and photographs and illustrations are included. (Publisher's note)

595.79 Hymenoptera

Markle, Sandra, 1946-

The **case** of the vanishing honey bees; a scientific mystery. by Sandra Markle. Lerner Pub Group 2013 48 p. (lib. bdg. : alk. paper) $29.27

Grades: 4 5 6 7 8   **595.79**

1. Bees 2. Honey 3. Insects -- Behavior 4. Honeybee 5. Honeybee -- Health

ISBN 1467705926; 9781467705929

LC 2012046913

This book, by Sandra Markle, "explores the world of honeybees and the mysterious malady that threatens them. After an opening in which a beekeeper discovers that most of the bees in his 400 hives are gone due to colony collapse disorder (CCD), the book describes how healthy honeybees pollinate flowering plants, gather nectar, and raise their young." (Booklist)

597 Cold-blooded vertebrates

Benchley, Peter

Shark life; true stories about sharks & the sea. adapted for young people by Karen Wojtyla. Delacorte 2005 193p il $15.95; lib bdg $17.99

Grades: 5 6 7 8 **597**

1. Sharks 2. Dangerous animals

ISBN 0-385-73109-4; 0-385-90135-6 lib bdg

Adapted from the title for adults, Shark trouble, published in 2003.

"The presentation is divided into three sections, and the first revolves . . . around Benchley's own life-threatening experience in a shark-proof cage while making a documentary film on sharks immediately following his success with Jaws (book and movie). The following sections . . . [include] descriptions of the most dangerous sharks, advice on how to swim safely in the ocean, thoughts on how the media misrepresents shark attacks, observations on other . . . forms of marine life, and . . . more personal tales of Benchley's own close encounters of the carnivorous kind. . . . Grades four to eight." (Bull Cent Child Books)

"Benchley writes about his personal experiences with sharks as well as a variety of other sea creatures considered dangerous to humans." SLJ

Includes glossary

Capuzzo, Mike

Close to shore; the terrifying shark attacks of 1916. Crown 2003 140p il $16.95; lib bdg $18.99

Grades: 6 7 8 9 **597**

1. Sharks

ISBN 0-375-82231-3; 0-375-92231-8 lib bdg

LC 2002-29918

An adaptation of the title for adults published 2001 by Broadway Bks.

Details the first documented cases in American history of sharks attacking swimmers, which occured along the Atlantic coast of New Jersey in 1916

"This book has a rich assortment of photos and news clippings. . . . Capuzzo reconstructs events with a novelist's flair and a scientist's attention to detail, and his pacing is relentless." Booklist

Includes bibliographical references

Cerullo, Mary M.

★ The **truth** about great white sharks; written by Mary M. Cerullo; photographs by Jeffrey L. Rotman; illustrations by Michael Wertz. Chronicle Bks. 2000 48p il hardcover o.p. $14.95

Grades: 4 5 6 7 **597**

1. Sharks

ISBN 0-8118-2467-5; 0-8118-5759-X pa

LC 00-31506

This provides information "about shark anatomy, senses, eating habits, and their relationships with humans. . . . The book also contains unusual information such as how these fish are measured and photographed and why they are not able to survive in an aquarium. The attractive layout blends line drawings, full-color photographs, varied typefaces, and eye-catching graphics. Rotman's pictures are clear and in-

formative. . . . This title will be accessible to reluctant readers and is a must for most collections." SLJ

Includes bibliographical references

Gilbert, Carter Rowell

National Audubon Society field guide to fishes, North America; [by] Carter R. Gilbert, James D. Williams. rev ed, 2nd ed, fully rev; Alfred A. Knopf 2002 607p il maps pa $19.95

Grades: 7 8 9 10 11 12 Adult **597**

1. Fishes -- North America

ISBN 0-375-41224-7

LC 2002-20773

First published 1983 with title: The Audubon Society field guide to North American fishes, whales, and dolphins

This guide covers over 600 freshwater and saltwater species in detail, with notes on 771 more species.

Hamilton, Sue L.

Eaten by a shark; [by] Sue Hamilton. ABDO Pub. 2010 32p il (Close encounters of the wild kind) lib bdg $22.61

Grades: 4 5 6 7 **597**

1. Sharks 2. Animal attacks

ISBN 978-1-60453-931-8 lib bdg; 1-60453-931-3 lib bdg

LC 2009-37230

In this volume, readers learn of actual human-wildlife encounters, creature information, survival strategies, and attack statistics.

"Students will be drawn to the realistic full-color photographs, the realistic diagrams of the creatures' bodies, the real-life stories told by victims, and the interesting, attractive formatting that includes text, diagrams, photographs, and graphics on each page. . . . [This is] exciting and attractive in a 'gross' sort of way and will appeal particularly to boys for both leisure reading and research." Libr Media Connect

Includes glossary

Miller, Sara Swan

Seahorses, pipefishes, and their kin; Sara Swan Miller. Franklin Watts 2002 47 p. col. ill. (Animals in order) (library) $26.50; (paperback) $6.95

Grades: 4 5 6 **597**

1. Picture books for children 2. Marine biology 3. Marine animals 4. Gasterosteiformes

ISBN 9780531121719; 0531163792; 9780531163795

LC 2001003034

This book by Sara Swan Miller is part of the Animals in Order series and looks at seahorses, pipefishes, and related animals. "These colorful series entries present a wide variety of creatures that have been sorted by scientific classification into similar groupings called orders . . . . Family names, common names, genus, species, size, and/or location are given, and paragraphs describe various behaviors (food gathering, courtship, etc.)." (School Library Journal)

Includes bibliographical references (p. 46) and index.

Page, Lawrence M.

★ **Peterson** field guide to freshwater fishes of North America north of Mexico; [by] Lawrence M.

Page, Brooks M. Burr; illustrations by Eugene C. Beckham III . . . [et al.]; maps by Griffin E. Sheehy. 2nd ed.; Houghton Mifflin Harcourt 2011 663p il map pa $21

Grades: 7 8 9 10 11 12 Adult   **597**
  1. Fishes -- North America
  ISBN 978-0-547-24206-4; 0-547-24206-9
                  LC 2010-49219

First published 1991 with title: A field guide to freshwater fishes: North America north of Mexico

This guide to identifying different species of freshwater fish in North America includes "maps and information showing where to locate each species of fish—whether that species can be found in miles-long stretches of river or small pools that cover only dozens of square feet." Publisher's note

Includes glossary and bibliographical references

Rodriguez, Ana Maria
  Secret of the suffocating slime trap . . . and more! Enslow Publishers 2008 48p il (Animal secrets revealed!) lib bdg $23.93

Grades: 5 6 7 8   **597**
  1. Fishes
  ISBN 978-0-7660-2954-5 lib bdg; 0-7660-2954-9 lib bdg
                 LC 2007039493

This book offers "fascinating accounts of how scientists systematically analyzed, tested, and proved their theories or how their findings led to other, serendipitous discoveries. . . . Science experiments are thoughtfully placed to inspire exploration, and captioned, full-color photos appear throughout." SLJ

Includes glossary and bibliographical references

Stefoff, Rebecca
  ★ The **fish** classes; [by] Rebecca Stefoff. Marshall Cavendish Benchmark 2008 96p il (Family trees) $22.95

Grades: 6 7 8 9   **597**
  1. Fishes
  ISBN 978-0-7614-2695-0; 0-7614-2695-7
                 LC 2007003483

"Skillful weaving of engaging text and superb illustrations will incite interest." Voice Youth Advocates

Includes glossary and bibliographical references

Swinney, Geoff
  Fish facts; illustrated by Janeen Mason. Pelican Pub. Co. 2011 48p il $17.99

Grades: 5 6 7 8   **597**
  1. Fishes
  ISBN 978-1-58980-908-6; 1-58980-908-4
                 LC 2010046220

"This comprehensive collection of facts about fish is sure to educate as well as fascinate. . . . From fish that produce light and fish that are capable of powered flight, to fish that can change sex and fish that carry their offspring in their mouths, this is chock full of both the amazing and the weird. . . . While the rather advanced vocabulary and biology that Swinney delves into mark this as a book for older readers, younger ones can certainly enjoy both the illustrations and

the occasional factoid. Mason's artwork is both painstakingly detailed and realistically colored, even down to the muting effect that water has on colors. Few books come close to this one's inclusiveness." Kirkus

Turner, Pamela S.
  ★ **Project** Seahorse; [photographs by Scott Tuason] Houghton Mifflin Harcourt 2010 56p il (Scientists in the field) $18

Grades: 4 5 6 7   **597**
  1. Sea horses
  ISBN 978-0-547-20713-1; 0-547-20713-1
                 LC 2009-49707

"With striking images of coral-reef inhabitants, this photo-essay introduces Project Seahorse, an international effort to protect and rehabilitate the Danajon Bank, a double reef off a Philippine Island where seahorses once flourished . . . Tuason, a noted Asian marine photographer whose specialty is the Philippines, seems equally adept at photographing the land and people and the underwater world. This is another splendid demonstration of the work of Scientists in the Field." Kirkus

597.3   Selachii, Holocephali, fleshy-finned fishes

Cerullo, Mary M.
  Journey to shark island; a shark photographer's close encounters. by Mary M. Cerullo ; photographs by Jeffrey L. Rotman. Compass Point Books, a Capstone imprint 2015 40 p. color illustrations, color map (library binding) $31.32

Grades: 5 6 7   **597.3**
  1. Deep diving 2. Wildlife photography 3. Sharks
  ISBN 075654887X; 9780756548872; 9780756549107
                 LC 2014008678

This book, by Mary M. Cerullo, part of the "Shark Expedition" series, follows "photographer Jeff Rotmans diving team into the shark-infested waters of Cocos Island to discover sharks secrets, and perhaps to save their lives." (Publisher's note)

"With their focus on more spectacular species, Seeking Giant Sharks and Great White Shark have the highest appeal, but all four books are fresh looks at an always popular subject." SLJ

Includes bibliographical references

  Searching for Great white sharks; a shark diver's quest for Mr. Big. by Mary M. Cerullo. Compass Point Books, a Capstone imprint 2015 40 p. col. illustrations, col. map (Compass point books. Shark expedition) (library binding : alk. paper) $31.32

Grades: 5 6 7   **597.3**
  1. Sharks 2. Underwater photography 3. Deep diving 4. White shark 5. Wildlife photographers
  ISBN 0756548845; 9780756548841; 9780756549077
                 LC 2014006007

This juvenile book, by Mary M. Cerullo, illustrated by Jeffrey L. Rotman, profiles how "diver and photographer Jeff Rotman goes to extremes to find and photograph great whites in their natural habitats. It takes a shark cage, a blood and fish recipe, patience, and courage to get up close photos of these powerful hunters." (Publisher's note)

"Well-reproduced, close-up photos of sharks (and, trigger warning, one shark-attack victim) fill every dynamic, eye-catching page, and Cerullo's concise paragraphs present shark facts in a clear, engaging, and often suspenseful tone. With a high-interest topic and a graphics-heavy layout, this would be a hit with reluctant readers, as well as researchers." Booklist

Includes bibliographical references and index

Seeking giant sharks; a shark diver's quest for whale sharks, basking sharks, and manta rays. by Mary M. Cerullo ; photographs by Jeffrey L. Rotman. Compass Point Books, a Capstone imprint 2015 40 p. illustration (color) (library binding) $31.32

    Grades: 5 6 7	**597.3**
    1. Deep diving 2. Wildlife photography 3. Sharks 4. Underwater photography 5. Manta rays 6. Whale shark 7. Basking shark 8. Manta birostris
    ISBN 0756548853; 9780756548858; 9780756549084
                    LC 2014008991

This book, by Mary M. Cerullo, part of the "Shark Expedition" series, follows "photographer Jeff Rotmans . . . on his quest to reveal the quiet mysteries of filter feeders such as the whale shark and basking sharks, and why these giant creatures need our help." (Publisher's note)

"Centered on the experiences photographer and diver Jeff Rotman, this set offers exciting insight into the world of sharks . . . With their focus on more spectacular species, Seeking Giant Sharks and Great White Shark have the highest appeal, but all four books are fresh looks at an always popular subject." SLJ

Includes bibliographical references"||"Includes bibliographical references and index

Sharks; facts at your fingertips. DK Pub. 2012 156 p. col. ill., map (Pocket genius) (hc) $7.99

    Grades: 5 6 7 8	**597.3**
    1. Sharks 2. Rays (Fishes)
    ISBN 0756692865; 9780756692865
                    LC 2011277726

This book, part of the "Pocket Genius" encyclopedia series, "profiles more that 150 sharks and rays -- from the great white to the tiny dwarf lantern -- and tells what they eat, where they live and how fast they swim." It "offers a . . . catalog-style presentation, which clearly lays out individual subcategories." (Publisher's note)

Sharks of the deep; a shark photographer's search for sharks at the bottom of the sea. by Mary M. Cerullo ; photographs by Jeffrey L. Rotman. Compass Point Books, a Capstone imprint 2015 40 p. col. illustrations, col. map (library binding) $31.32

    Grades: 5 6 7	**597.3**
    1. Deep diving 2. Wildlife photography 3. Sharks 4. Underwater photography 5. Ocean bottom
    ISBN 0756548861; 9780756548865; 9780756549091
                    LC 2014009112

This book, by Mary M. Cerullo, part of the "Shark Expedition" series, follows "photographer Jeff Rotmans . . . to the ocean floor to see the sharks and other creatures he calls

living sculptures, from stingrays to the unusual wobbegong shark and other fascinating species. Look beyond the headlines and get to know the real story of sharks, their surprising beauty, and the important roles they play in their underwater world." (Publisher's note)

"Centered on the experiences photographer and diver Jeff Rotman, this set offers exciting insight into the world of sharks . . . all four books are fresh looks at an always popular subject." SLJ

Includes bibliographical references and index

Macquitty, Miranda

    Shark; written by Miranda MacQuitty. DK Pub. 2008 72 p. col. ill (Eyewitness books) (hardcover) $16.99

    Grades: 4 5 6 7	**597.3**
    1. Marine biology 2. Sharks
    ISBN 0756637783; 9780756637781
                    LC 2008276031

This book is part of the DK Eyewitness Books series and focuses on sharks. The titles in this series "focus on subjects that complement students' personal interests and areas of study to make learning simple and fun." Wall charts, clip art CDs, and photographs and illustrations are included. (Publisher's note)

Mallory, Kenneth

    ★ **Swimming** with hammerhead sharks. Houghton Mifflin 2001 48p il (Scientists in the field) pbk. $7.99

    Grades: 4 5 6 7	**597.3**
    1. Sharks
    ISBN 9780618250790
                    LC 00-61401

"Mallory, editor-in-chief of publishing programs at the New England Aquarium, uses the context of an IMAX film production on hammerhead sharks to explain how scientists—in particular, marine biologist Pete Klimley—are studying these {animals. Index.} Intermediate." (Horn Book)

This book follows "marine biologist Pete Klimley and an IMAX film team to seamounts off Cocos Island in the Pacific Ocean to observe and film schooling hammerhead sharks. . . . A fascinating record of research and investigation, this inviting book is larded with numerous dramatic color photos." SLJ

Includes bibliographical references

Walker, Sally M.

    ★ **Fossil** fish found alive; discovering the coelacanth. Carolrhoda Bks. 2002 72p il map lib bdg $17.95

    Grades: 5 6 7 8	**597.3**
    1. Coelacanth
    ISBN 1-57505-536-8
                    LC 2001-3815

Describes the 1938 discovery of the coelacanth, a fish previously believed to be extinct, and subsequent research about it

"Walker writes well, making this relatively unknown area of science history an exciting story of exploration and discovery. Excellent, full-color photos illustrate the text." Booklist

Includes bibliographical references

597.8 Amphibians

Beltz, Ellin

Frogs : inside their remarkable world. Firefly Books 2005 175p il $34.95

Grades: 5 6 7 8 9 10   597.8

1. Frogs 2. Toads

ISBN 1-55297-869-9

LC 2006-365517

The author gives a "picture of the history of the frog, its anatomical makeup, its place in the natural world and the threats that are seriously reducing its numbers around the world." Publisher's note

Crump, Marty

★ The **mystery** of Darwin's frog; by Marty Crump ; illustrated by Steve Jenkins and Edel Rodriquez. Boyds Mills Press 2013 40 p. ill. (reinforced) $16.95

Grades: 3 4 5 6 7   597.8

1. Picture books for children 2. Frogs

ISBN 1590788648; 9781590788646

LC 2012947844

In this book, Marty Crump, a researcher who has investigated the Rhinoderma darwinii, an inch-long frog discovered by Charles Darwin in Chile in 1834, "describes the earlier investigations of this intriguing frog and records her own efforts to document how it lives in the wild. She discusses her findings and goes on to present the problems facing not only Darwin's frogs, but also frogs in general-loss of habitat, pollution, and the assault of the lethal Bd fungus." (School Library Journal)

Gilpin, Daniel

Tree frogs, mud puppies, & other amphibians; by Daniel Gilpin. Compass Point Books 2006 48 p. col. ill. (Animal kingdom classification) (library) $29.99

Grades: 5 6 7 8   597.8

1. Picture books for children 2. Amphibians

ISBN 0756512492; 9780756512491

LC 2005003683

This book by Daniel Gilpin is part of the Families series and looks at tree frogs, mud puppies, and other amphibians. It "discusses the large diversity of amphibians, a typical amphibian's body, ancient amphibians, and an amphibian's skin and senses. It discusses hiding and warning, movement, prey, courtship, strange breeders, and the life-cycle." (Publisher's note)

Includes bibliographical references (p. 47) and index.

Markle, Sandra, 1946-

★ The **case** of the vanishing golden frogs. Milbrook Press 2011 48p il

Grades: 4 5 6   597.8

1. Frogs 2. Endangered species 3. Wildlife conservation

ISBN 0761351086; 9780761351085

LC 2010042642

"The golden frog, a Panamanian national symbol, began vanishing from its high mountain forests in the late 1990s, prompting a scientific investigation and rescue process that continues today. . . . Markle . . . describes a mission that has involved scientists from around the world." Kirkus

Includes glossary and bibliographical references

Pringle, Laurence

Frogs! strange and wonderful. Laurence Pringle ; illustrated by Meryl Henderson. Boyds Mills Press 2012 30 p. col. ill (reinf. trade ed.) $16.95

Grades: 3 4 5   597.8

1. Frogs 2. Poisonous animals 3. Camouflage (Biology) 4. Picture books for children 5. Amphibians

ISBN 1590783719; 9781590783719

LC 2011928834

In this book, author Laurence P. Pringle offers a "look at the similarities and differences among the many and varied species of frogs . . . The Reinwardt's flying frog glides between trees, the mantella and poison frogs come in all the colors of the rainbow and one can guess what makes the marsupial frog stand out. Camouflage, mating, development, coloring, size, locomotion, how and what they eat and how and why they make sounds are just some of the topics." (Kirkus)

Includes bibliographical references

Solway, Andrew

Poison frogs and other amphibians; by Andrew Solway. Heinemann Library 2006 48 p. col. ill. (Adapted for success) (library) $32.00; (paperback) $8.99

Grades: 5 6 7 8 9   597.8

1. Frogs 2. Animal defenses 3. Amphibians 4. Dendrobatidae

ISBN 140348225X; 9781403482259; 9781403482327 out of print

LC 2006014294

This book by Andrew Solway is part of the Adapted for Success series and looks at poison frogs. "Poison Frogs are among the most poisonous animals in the world, but how have they, and other amphibians, adapted to become so successful? The series explores how some of our favorite animals are uniquely adapted to their environment. Each book . . . covers habitat, defenses, camouflage, and the way animals find food." (Publisher's note)

Includes bibliographical references and index.

Somervill, Barbara A.

Cane toad; by Barbara A. Somervill. Cherry Lake Pub. 2008 32p il map (Animal invaders) lib bdg $26.26

Grades: 3 4 5 6   597.8

1. Toads 2. Biological invasions

ISBN 978-1-60279-115-2 lib bdg; 1-60279-115-5 lib bdg

LC 2007-33510

This describes the cane toads' "outstanding physical and behavioral characteristics at each stage in their life cycle, diet, and natural habitat, and then [explains] how they were introduced into areas outside their natural range . . . and the nature and extent of the ecological damage they have caused, and various attempts to eradicate or at least control the animals. . . . The prolific cane toads, which are fast supplanting native amphibians in Australia, excrete a toxin powerful enough to kill the animals, and some humans unfortunate enough to ingest them. . . . Clear color photographs . . . accompany the [text] on about every other page. . . . [This title is] clearly written and well organized, and [has] up-to-date information." SLJ

Includes glossary

Stefoff, Rebecca

★ The **amphibian** class; [by] Rebecca Stefoff. Marshall Cavendish Benchmark 2008 96p il (Family trees) lib bdg $22.95

Grades: 6 7 8 9   **597.8**

1. Amphibians

ISBN 978-0-7614-2692-9 lib bdg; 0-7614-2692-2

LC 2007003487

This is "meticulously detailed. . . . Sharp color photographs appear on about every other page. Other illustrations consist of classification charts and anatomical diagrams. . . . [This is] well-organized and clearly written." SLJ

Includes glossary and bibliographical references

Turner, Pamela S.

★ The **frog** scientist; photographs by Andy Comins. Houghton Mifflin Books for Children 2009 58p il (Scientists in the field) lib bdg $18

Grades: 5 6 7 8   **597.8**

1. Frogs 2. Biologists 3. College teachers

ISBN 978-0-618-71716-3 lib bdg; 0-618-71716-1 lib bdg

LC 2008-39770

This volume "opens with biologist Tyrone Hayes and his team collecting frogs at a pond in Wyoming. After a short chapter on Hayes' background, the discussion returns to his work: he addresses the general question of why amphibian populations world-wide are declining by studying the effects of atrizine, an agricultural pesticide, on the reproductive organs of leopard frogs from a particular pond. Well organized and clearly written. . . . Excellent color photos offer clear pictures of frogs and of this scientific team at work in the field and in the lab. . . . A vivid, realistic view of one scientist at work." Booklist

Includes glossary and bibliographical references

597.9 Reptiles

Conant, Roger

A **field** guide to reptiles & amphibians; eastern and central North America. [by] Roger Conant and Joseph T. Collins; illustrated by Isabelle Hunt Conant and Tom R. Johnson. 3rd ed, expanded; Houghton Mifflin 1998 616p il map (Peterson field guide series) pbk $21

Grades: 7 8 9 10 11 12 Adult   **597.9**

1. Reptiles 2. Amphibians

ISBN 9780395904527

LC 98-13622

First published 1958 with title: A field guide to reptiles and amphibians of the United States and Canada east of the 100th meridian

This guide describes 595 species and subspecies, featuring color photos, black and white drawings, and color distribution maps of reptiles and amphibians of the region. Also includes information on transporting live reptiles and amphibians

Includes glossary and bibliographical references

Hutchinson, Mark

Reptiles. Simon & Schuster Books for Young Readers 2011 64p il (Insiders) $16.99

Grades: 4 5 6 7   **597.9**

1. Reptiles

ISBN 978-1-4424-3276-5; 1-4424-3276-4

"Arranged around the digitally rendered, sharply focused central images . . . smaller inset pictures and blocks of text systematically present distinctive physical features, typical behaviors, habitats, ranges, diets, and other information about each type of reptile. . . . This book will wow casual browsers and budding herpetologists alike." Booklist

McCarthy, Colin

Reptile; written by Colin McCarthy; [special photography, Karl Shone . . . [et al.]] Dorling Kindersley 2000 63p il (DK eyewitness books) $15.99

Grades: 4 5 6 7   **597.9**

1. Reptiles

ISBN 0-7894-5786-5

First published 1991 by Knopf

Photographs and text depict the many different kinds of reptiles, their similarities and differences, habitats, and behavior

Stebbins, Robert C.

★ A **field** guide to Western reptiles and amphibians; text and illustrations by Robert C. Stebbins. 3rd ed newly rev; Houghton Mifflin 2003 533p il map (Peterson field guide series) pa $22

Grades: 7 8 9 10 11 12 Adult   **597.9**

1. Reptiles 2. Amphibians

ISBN 0-395-98272-3

LC 2002-27561

First published 1966

This "covers all the species of reptiles and amphibians found in western North America. More than 650 full-color paintings and photographs show key details for making accurate identifications. . . . Color range maps give species' distributions. . . . [Includes] information on conservation efforts and survival status." Publisher's note

Includes bibliographical references

Zabludoff, Marc

★ The **reptile** class. Benchmark Books 2005 95p il (Family trees) lib bdg $29.92

Grades: 6 7 8 9   **597.9**
  1. Reptiles
  ISBN 0-7614-1820-2
              LC 2004-21820

This examines physical traits, adaptations, diets, habitats, and life cycles of reptiles.

"Fact-filled, yet surprisingly readable. . . . [This] title contains a wide variety of excellent-quality, full-color photos; interesting sidebars; and diagrams." SLJ

597.92   Turtles

Lockwood, Sophie

  Sea turtles; by Sophie Lockwood. Child's World 2006 40p col. ill., col. maps (library) $29.93
Grades: 4 5 6   **597.92**
  1. Sea turtles
  ISBN 1592965504; 9781592965502
              LC 2005024792

"Conservation is the dominant theme of this attractive photo-essay. . . . which has beautiful full-page color photos that bring readers close to the subject. Fast-fact boxes focus on particular species, providing spot statistics on weight, length, color, habitat, threatened or endangered status, and more." Booklist

Includes bibliographical references (p. 39) and index.

Stefoff, Rebecca

  Turtles; [by] Rebecca Stefoff. Marshall Cavendish Benchmark 2007 110p il (Animalways) lib bdg $34.21
Grades: 6 7 8 9   **597.92**
  1. Turtles
  ISBN 978-0-7614-2539-7
              LC 2007013178

This describes the place of turtles in the animal kingdom, their evolution, anatomy, physiology, diversity, life cycle, and relationship to humans.

Includes glossary and bibliographical references

Stone, Lynn M.

  Box turtles; written and photographed by Lynn M. Stone. Lerner Publications 2007 48p il map lib bdg $25.26
Grades: 4 5 6 7   **597.92**
  1. Turtles
  ISBN 978-1-57505-869-6 lib bdg; 1-57505-869-3 lib bdg
              LC 2006012867

Describes the physical characteristics, behavior, habitat, and life cycle of box turtles and discusses their relationship with humans.

Swinburne, Stephen R.

  ★ **Sea** turtle scientist; by Stephen R. Swinburne. Houghton Mifflin Harcourt 2013 65 p. ill. (chiefly col.), col. map (Scientists in the field) $18.99

Grades: 5 6 7 8 9   **597.92**
  1. Biologists 2. Sea turtles
  ISBN 0547367554; 9780547367552
              LC 2012034045

"Dr. Kimberly Stewart, also known as the Turtle Lady of St. Kitts, is already waiting at midnight when an 800-pound leatherback sea turtle crawls out of the Caribbean surf and onto the sandy beach. The mother turtle has a vital job to do: dig a nest in which she will lay eggs that will hatch into part of the next generation of leatherbacks." (Publisher's note)

"This refreshing journey with a dedicated woman hard at work in her chosen field will resonate with readers." SLJ

Includes bibliographical references and index

597.95   Lizards

Collard III, Sneed B.

  Sneed B. Collard III's most fun book ever about lizards; Sneed B. Collard III. Charlesbridge 2012 47 p. (reinforced for library use) $16.95
Grades: 3 4 5 6 7   **597.95**
  1. Lizards 2. Lizards as pets 3. Wildlife photography 4. Children's literature 5. Lizards -- Miscellanea
  ISBN 9781580893244; 9781580893251
              LC 2011000809

This book offers an "introduction to the world of lizards [which] describes their . . . . variety and life in the wild and offers cautions from a long-time reptile fan for those who want to keep lizards as pets. [Author Sneed B.] Collard . . . turns his attention . . . to modern-day lizards. After presenting an exemplar, 'Joe Lizard,' a western fence lizard, he goes on to describe other well-known species, including Komodo dragons, Gila monsters, chameleons and iguanas, as well as some with unusual talents, including 'religious lizards' that can walk on water. He covers eating and being eaten, the ways saurians keep warm and reproduce, and threats to their survival. . . . [Photographs] show lizard characteristics. . . . Captions and sidebars add further information." (Kirkus)

Gish, Melissa

  Komodo dragons. Creative Education 2011 48p il (Living wild) lib bdg $23.95; pa $8.99
Grades: 5 6 7 8   **597.95**
  1. Komodo dragon
  ISBN 978-1-60818-080-6 lib bdg; 1-60818-080-8 lib bdg; 978-0-89812-672-3 pa; 0-89812-672-X pa
              LC 2010028307

A look at Komodo dragons, including their habitats, physical characteristics such as their sawlike teeth, behaviors, relationships with humans, and threatened status in the world today.

"Stunning, full-page photographs create immediate visual interest. A brief narrative introduction sets the scene for the richer, more scientific information in the rest of the text." Booklist

Includes glossary and bibliographical references

Somervill, Barbara A.

  Monitor lizard. Cherry Lake 2010 32p il (Animal invaders) lib bdg $27.07

Grades: 5 6 7 8   **597.95**
1. Lizards 2. Biological invasions
ISBN 978-1-60279-627-0 lib bdg; 1-60279-627-0
lib bdg

This offers "an introduction to the problems caused by [the monitor lizard], a discussion of its physical characteristics and habits, a history of how it arrived in its new habitat, and an analysis of challenges encountered by those trying to limit its spread. . . . [It] describes the threat posed by these aggressive 7-foot reptiles, sold as babies by pet vendors and now loose in Florida. . . . [This] well-focused [book is] clearly written. The uncluttered page design features at least one color photo on each page." Booklist

Includes glossary and bibliographical references

597.96   Snakes

Hamilton, Sue L.

Bitten by a rattlesnake; [by] Sue Hamilton. ABDO Pub. 2010 32p il (Close encounters of the wild kind) lib bdg $27.07

Grades: 4 5 6 7   **597.96**
1. Rattlesnakes 2. Animal attacks
ISBN 978-1-60453-930-1 lib bdg; 1-60453-930-5
lib bdg

LC 2009-45423

Readers learn of actual human-rattlesnake encounters, information about rattlesnakes, survival strategies, and attack statistics.

"Students will be drawn to the realistic full-color photographs, the realistic diagrams of the creatures' bodies, the real-life stories told by victims, and the interesting, attractive formatting that includes text, diagrams, photographs, and graphics on each page. . . . [This is] exciting and attractive in a 'gross' sort of way and will appeal particularly to boys for both leisure reading and research." Libr Media Connect

Includes glossary

Mattison, Christopher

Snake; by Chris Mattison. DK Pub. 1999 192p il hardcover o.p. pa $12.99

Grades: 7 8 9 10 11 12 Adult   **597.96**
1. Snakes
ISBN 0-7894-4660-X; 0-7566-1365-5 pa

LC 99-19957

An illustrated guide to "more than 60 types of snakes, ranging from adders to yellow anacondas. This richly formatted book features each snake in detailed entries with informative, readable text." Sci Child

Includes glossary

Menon, Sujatha

Discover snakes. Enslow Publishers 2008 47p il (Discover animals) lib bdg $23.93

Grades: 4 5 6 7   **597.96**
1. Snakes
ISBN 978-0-7660-3471-6 lib bdg; 0-7660-3471-2
lib bdg

LC 2008013867

First published 2005 in the United Kingdom

This "introduces readers to a variety of snakes, from pythons to boa constrictors and cobras. . . . Images and text explain about a snake's fangs, life cycle, senses, and how they fight and move. The book also discusses the different snake families and the hunting styles of each." Publisher's note

Includes glossary and bibliographical references

Montgomery, Sy

★ The **snake** scientist; photographs by Nic Bishop. Houghton Mifflin 1999 48p il map $16; pa $5.95

Grades: 4 5 6 7   **597.96**
1. Snakes
ISBN 0-395-87169-7; 0-618-11119-0 pa

LC 98-6124

Discusses the work of Bob Mason and his efforts to study and protect snakes, particularly red-sided garter snakes

"The lively text communicates both the meticulous measurements required in this kind of work and the thrill of new discoveries. Large, full-color photos of the zoologist and young students at work, and lots of wriggly snakes, pull readers into the presentation." SLJ

Includes bibliographical references

Somervill, Barbara A.

Python. Cherry Lake Pub. 2010 32p il map (Animal invaders) lib bdg $27.07

Grades: 5 6 7 8   **597.96**
1. Pythons 2. Biological invasions
ISBN 978-1-60279-629-4 lib bdg; 1-60279-629-7
lib bdg

LC 2009026013

This describes "the 19-foot nocturnal snake that has infiltrated the Florida Everglades, having no natural predators above it in the food chain. . . . [This] well-focused [book is] clearly written. The uncluttered page design features at least one color photo on each spread." Booklist

Includes glossary and bibliographical references

597.98   Crocodilians

Gish, Melissa

Alligators. Creative Education 2010 46p il (Living wild) $23.95; pa $9.95

Grades: 5 6 7 8   **597.98**
1. Alligators
ISBN 978-1-58341-967-0; 1-58341-967-5; 978-0-89812-550-4 pa; 0-89812-550-2 pa

LC 2010017372

The "book lucidly discusses conservation and the animals' often tenuous relationships with humans. The layout is uniformly simple but effective, constructed with a nice balance of main text for the report writers, smaller chunks of esoterica for browsers, and . . . killer photos." Booklist

Hamilton, Sue L.

Attacked by a crocodile; [by] Sue Hamilton. ABDO Pub. 2010 32p il (Close encounters of the wild kind) lib bdg $27.07

Grades: 4 5 6 7 **597.98**
1. Crocodiles 2. Animal attacks
ISBN 978-1-60453-929-5; 1-60453-929-1
LC 2009-45514
Readers learn of actual human-crocodile encounters, information about crocodiles, survival strategies, and attack statistics.

"Students will be drawn to the realistic full-color photographs, the realistic diagrams of the creatures' bodies, the real-life stories told by victims, and the interesting, attractive formatting that includes text, diagrams, photographs, and graphics on each page. . . . [This is] exciting and attractive in a 'gross' sort of way and will appeal particularly to boys for both leisure reading and research." Libr Media Connect

Includes glossary

Simon, Seymour
★ **Crocodiles** & alligators. HarperCollins Pubs. 1999 un il hardcover o.p. pa $6.99
Grades: 4 5 6 7 **597.98**
1. Alligators 2. Crocodiles
ISBN 0-06-027473-5; 0-06-443829-5 pa
LC 98-34705
Describes the physical characteristics and behavior of various members of the family of animals known as crocodilians

"The book is filled with interesting information, and the vivid, well-composed, full-color photographs and entertaining text will draw in browsers." SLJ

Snyder, Trish
Alligator & crocodile rescue; changing the future for endangered wildlife. Firefly Books 2006 64p il (Firefly animal rescue) lib bdg $19.95; pa $9.95
Grades: 5 6 7 8 **597.98**
1. Alligators 2. Crocodiles 3. Wildlife conservation
ISBN 1-55297-920-2 lib bdg; 1-55297-919-9 pa
This "outlines the various threats to survival of [alligators and crocodiles] and introduces readers to organizations and individuals trying to save them. . . . Numerous photographs document the work of scientists, conservationists, educators, and other people around the world who are committed to wildlife preservation." SLJ

598 Birds

Alderfer, Jonathan
National Geographic kids bird guide of North America; the best birding book for kids from National Geographic's bird experts. by Jonathan Alderfer. National Geographic 2013 176 p. (paperback) $15.95; (library) $23.90
Grades: 4 5 6 7 8 **598**
1. Birds -- North America 2. Birds -- Identification
ISBN 1426310943; 9781426310942; 9781426310959
LC 2012028615
Author "[Jonathan] Alderfer offers in-depth studies of 60 birds native to North America (plus 'mini-profiles' of another 60 specimens) in a guide for nascent birders. . . . The book is organized by region, and each bird's spread offers

color photographs, 'vital statistics' (including its call, diet, and habitat), maps of where it can be found, and other background." (Publishers Weekly)
Includes bibliographical references and index

★ **Birds** of the world; editorial adviser, Jason A. Mobley. Marshall Cavendish Reference 2008 11v il map set $359.95
Grades: 5 6 7 8 9 **598**
1. Reference books 2. Birds -- Encyclopedias
ISBN 978-0-7614-7775-4 set; 0-7614-7775-6 set
LC 2008-62300
"This encyclopedia, designed to introduce birds in all their varieties, contributes to and encourages student research. Nearly 140 . . . articles are arranged alphbetically. . . . Articles range in length from two to eight pages and include numerous full-color photographs, diagrams, and maps. . . . Clear and concise information is provided in an appealing layout most appropriate for upper-elementary through middle-school users." Booklist

Bull, John L.
★ The **National** Audubon Society field guide to North American birds, Eastern region; [by] John Bull and John Farrand, Jr.; revised by John Farrand, Jr.; visual key by Amanda Wilson and Lori Hogan. rev ed; Knopf 1994 797p il maps pa $19.95
Grades: 7 8 9 10 11 12 Adult **598**
1. Birds -- North America
ISBN 0-679-42852-6
LC 94-7768
Companion volume to National Audubon Society field guide to North American birds, Western region, by Miklos D. F. Udvardy
First published 1977
This pictorial guide to 508 eastern species arranges birds by color and shape to simplify identification. It also includes information on bird-watching and conservation status
Includes bibliographical references

Burnie, David
Bird; written by David Burnie. rev ed.; DK Pub. 2008 72p il (DK eyewitness books) $15.99
Grades: 4 5 6 7 **598**
1. Birds
ISBN 978-0-7566-3768-2; 0-7566-3768-6
First published 1988 by Knopf
A photo essay on the world of birds examining such topics as body construction, feathers and flight, the adaptation of beaks and feet, feeding habits, courtship, nests and eggs, and bird watching.
Includes glossary

Chu, Miyoko
Birdscapes; A pop-up celebration of birdsongs in stereo sound. by Miyoko Chu, with the Cornell Lab of Ornithology; paper engineering by Gene Vosough, Renee Jablow, and Andy Baron; illustrations by Julia Hargreaves. Chronicle Books 2008 un il $60

Grades: 5 6 7 8   **598**
   1. Birds 2. Pop-up books
   ISBN 978-0-8118-6428-2; 0-8118-6428-6

"With marvelously detailed pop-up spreads and high-quality sound, this look at various avian ecosystems is absolutely spectacular. Double-page sections depict the environmental characteristics and native species of the following North American habitats: the Sonoran Desert; a Pacific seabird colony; an eastern deciduous forest; the Arctic tundra; a cypress swamp; grasslands; and the Pacific rain forest. The paper sculptures, filled with colorful and realistic renderings of flora and local birdlife, are accompanied by a soundtrack of the species' calls and songs recorded . . . from the Cornell Lab of Ornithology's Macaulay Library collection." SLJ

Gish, Melissa
   ★ **Eagles**. Creative Education 2010 46p il (Living wild) lib bdg $23.95; pa $9.95
Grades: 5 6 7 8   **598**
   1. Eagles
   ISBN 978-1-58341-968-7 lib bdg; 1-58341-968-3 lib bdg; 978-0-89812-551-1 pa; 0-89812-551-0 pa
                   LC 2010-17373

This "book lucidly discusses conservation and the animals' often tenuous relationship with humans. The layout is uniformly simple but effective, constructed with a nice balance of main text for the report writers, smaller chunks of esoterica for browsers, and . . . killer photos." Booklist

   Hummingbirds. Creative Education 2011 46p il map (Living wild) lib bdg $23.95; pa $8.95
Grades: 5 6 7 8   **598**
   1. Hummingbirds
   ISBN 978-1-60818-078-3; 1-60818-078-6; 978-0-89812-670-9 pa; 0-89812-670-3 pa
                   LC 2010028314

A look at hummingbirds, including their habitats, physical characteristics such as their ability to hover, behaviors, relationships with humans, and admired status in the world today.

"Stunning, full-page photographs create immediate visual interest. A brief narrative introduction sets the scene for the richer, more scientific information in the rest of the text." Booklist

   Includes glossary and bibliographical references

   Owls. Creative Education 2011 46p il map (Living wild) lib bdg $23.95
Grades: 5 6 7 8   **598**
   1. Owls
   ISBN 978-1-60818-081-3; 1-60818-081-6
                   LC 2010028308

A look at owls, including their habitats, physical characteristics such as their large and observant eyes, behaviors, relationships with humans, and protected status in the world today.

"Stunning, full-page photographs create immediate visual interest. A brief narrative introduction sets the scene for the richer, more scientific information in the rest of the text." Booklist

   Includes glossary and bibliographical references

Griggs, Jack L.
   ★ **All** the birds of North America; American Bird Conservancy's field guide. concept and design by Jack L. Griggs. HarperPerennial 1997 172p il maps pa $19.95
Grades: 7 8 9 10 11 12 Adult   **598**
   1. Birds -- North America
   ISBN 0-06-52770-6
                   LC 96-49679

This identification guide to North American birds uses a system based on how and where birds collect food, with icons, color bars, key numbers, and color illustrations

Hanel, Rachael
   Penguins. Smart Apple Media 2009 46p il (Living wild) lib bdg $32.80
Grades: 4 5 6 7   **598**
   1. Penguins
   ISBN 978-1-58341-658-7 lib bdg; 1-58341-658-7 lib bdg
                   LC 2007008503

"The 17 species of penguins . . . fill [this] slim, informative [volume]. [The] overview is divided into several chapters . . . describing the shared and distinct physical characteristics of the various species, the location of their particular habitats, life cycle, social behavior, and the history of human awareness of and impact on these animals. Fine color photographs face pages of text with smaller views placed in colored sidebars or insets. The [book concludes] with current environmental threats and conservation efforts. . . . Handsome and appealing." SLJ

Helget, Nicole Lea
   Swans; by Nicole Helget. Smart Apple Media 2009 46p il (Living wild) lib bdg $32.80
Grades: 4 5 6 7   **598**
   1. Swans
   ISBN 978-1-58341-659-4 lib bdg; 1-58341-659-5 lib bdg
                   LC 2007015242

The "7 [species] of swans fill [this] slim, informative [volume]. [The] overview is divided into several chapters . . . describing the shared and distinct physical characteristics of the various species, the location of their particular habitats, life cycle, social behavior, and the history of human awareness of and impact on these animals. Fine color photographs face pages of text with smaller views placed in colored sidebars or insets. The [book concludes] with current environmental threats and conservation efforts. . . . Handsome and appealing." SLJ

   Includes bibliographical references

Hickman, Pamela M.
   Birds of prey rescue; changing the future for endangered wildlife. Firefly Books 2006 64p il (Firefly animal rescue) $19.95; pa $9.95
Grades: 5 6 7   **598**
   1. Birds of prey 2. Endangered species 3. Wildlife

conservation
ISBN 978-1-55407-145-6; 1-55407-145-3; 978-1-55407-144-9 pa; 1-55407-144-5 pa

LC 2007271465

Provides details about birds of prey from around the world, their endangerment, and conservation programs designed to save them.

Hoose, Phillip M.

★ The **race** to save the Lord God Bird; [by] Phillip Hoose. Farrar, Straus and Giroux 2004 196p il map $20

Grades: 7 8 9 10 **598**

1. Woodpeckers 2. Endangered species
ISBN 0-374-36173-8

Tells the story of the ivory-billed woodpecker's extinction in the United States, describing the encounters between this species and humans, and discussing what these encounters have taught us about preserving endangered creatures

"Sharp, clear, black-and-white archival photos and reproductions appear throughout. The author's passion for his subject and high standards for excellence result in readable, compelling nonfiction." SLJ

Includes glossary and bibliographical references

International Masters Publishers (Firm)

★ The **encyclopedia** of birds; edited by International Masters Publishers. Facts on File 2007 6v il set $425

Grades: 6 7 8 9 10 11 12 **598**

1. Reference books 2. Birds -- Encyclopedias
ISBN 0-8160-5904-7; 978-0-8160-5904-1

LC 2006-49526

"Each volume begins with the same general introduction, followed by a comprehensive list of the 250 species included. Entries feature several . . . closeup photographs of the bird and its home, and data on breeding, status, food, and habitat. A panel provides information on length and weight, wingspan, number of eggs, lifespan, and more. . . . Both browsers and budding ornithologists will enjoy learning about some intriguing creatures." SLJ

Includes glossary and bibliographical references

Larson, Jeanette C.

Hummingbirds; facts and folklore from the Americas. written by Jeanette Larson and Adrienne Yorinks; illustrated by Adrienne Yorinks. Charlesbridge 2011 64p il $16.95; pa $8.95

Grades: 5 6 7 8 **598**

1. Hummingbirds 2. Birds -- Folklore 3. Native Americans -- Folklore
ISBN 978-1-58089-332-9; 1-58089-332-5; 978-1-58089-333-6 pa; 1-58089-333-3 pa

LC 2010-07578

"In a narrative that flows easily between fact and lore, hummingbird behavior is thoroughly described and interwoven with the folktales it generated among Native American peoples. . . . All the stories show how ancient people answered the 'how and why' questions of the behaviors they observed, and these stories beautifully echo modern-day scientific observations. The full-color photos of quilts and embroidery by Yorinks invite readers to stop and savor each one." SLJ

Includes glossary and bibliographical references

Latimer, Jonathan P.

Backyard birds; [by] Jonathan P. Latimer, Karen Stray Nolting; illustrations by Roger Tory Peterson; foreword by Virginia Marie Peterson. Houghton Mifflin 1999 48p il (Peterson field guides for young naturalists) hardcover o.p. pa $5.95

Grades: 4 5 6 7 **598**

1. Birds
ISBN 0-395-92276-3

LC 98-35509

This is an identification guide to birds "'you are likely to see where you live.' . . . [It] includes a . . . selection of about 20 creatures . . . grouped by color. . . . Bright, full-color photographs and drawings clearly indicate distinguishing features. Useful, accessible." SLJ

Songbirds; [by] Jonathan P. Latimer, Karen Stray Nolting; illustrations by Roger Tory Peterson; foreword by Virginia Marie Peterson. Houghton Mifflin 2000 48p il (Peterson field guides for young naturalists) $15; pa $5.95

Grades: 4 5 6 7 **598**

1. Birds 2. Birdsongs
ISBN 0-395-97941-2; 0-395-97946-3 pa

LC 99-38293

Describes the physical characteristics, habitats, feeding habits, and voices of a variety of songbirds, arranged under the categories "Simple Songs," "Complex Songs," "Whistling Songs," "Warbling Songs," "Trilling Songs," "Name-sayers," and "Mimics"

Laubach, Christyna M.

Raptor! a kid's guide to birds of prey; by Christyna & Rene Laubach and Charles W.G. Smith. Storey Bks. 2002 118p il maps pbk $14.95

Grades: 4 5 6 7 **598**

1. Birds of prey
ISBN 9781580174459

LC 2001-54980

This is an "overview of North American raptors. . . . After describing their characteristics and behavior, the book introduces individual species within family groups: vultures, hawks, falcons, barn owls, and true owls. . . . There is also advice on bird-watching and efforts to save endangered species. Well-designed projects . . . are followed by a glossary and extensive lists of hawk-watching sites, raptor centers, banding demonstration sites, books, videos, organizations, and Web sites related to birds in general and raptors in particular." Booklist

Miller, Sara Swan

Woodpeckers, toucans, and their kin. Watts 2003 47p il lib bdg $25; pa $6.95

Grades: 4 5 6 **598**

1. Toucans 2. Woodpeckers 3. Honeyguides (Birds)
ISBN 0-531-12243-3 lib bdg; 0-531-16661-9 pa

LC 2002-1732

This book makes "fascinating reading. . . . Photographs are glorious." Libr Media Connect

"The author describes the distinguishing characteristics displayed by all members of its respective order; explains the principles of scientific classification; identifies the phylum and class to which each belongs; introduces 15 representative species; and offers tips for observing the creatures in the wild. The bulk of each title is devoted to the profiles of species, each of which consists of a page of text and a clear, color close-up photograph." (School Library Journal)

Peterson, Roger Tory

Peterson field guide to birds of Eastern and Central North America; [by] Roger Tory Peterson, with contributions from Michael DiGiorgio [et al.] 6th ed; Houghton Mifflin Harcourt 2010 445p il map (Peterson field guide series) $19.95

Grades: 5 6 7 8 9 10 11 12 Adult   598

1. Birds -- North America

ISBN 978-0-547-15246-2; 0-547-15246-9

LC 2009-37681

First published 1934 with title: A field guide to the birds

This guide to birds found east of the Rocky Mountains contains colored illustrations painted by the author, with a description of each species on the facing page. Views of young birds and seasonal variations in plumage are included.

★ **Peterson** field guide to birds of North America; with contributions from Michael DiGiorgio . . . [et al.] Houghton Mifflin Co. 2008 527p il map (Peterson field guide series) $26

Grades: 5 6 7 8 9 10 11 12 Adult   598

1. Birds -- North America

ISBN 0-618-96614-5; 978-0-618-96614-1

LC 2007-39803

First published 1934 with title: A field guide to the birds. Previously published in two separate parts as A field guide to western birds (1990) and A field guide to the birds of eastern and central North America (2002)

This guide to birds found in North America contains colored illustrations painted by the author, with a description of each species on the facing page. Views of young birds and seasonal variations in plumage are included. The book also includes a URL to video podcasts.

"This field guide is of high quality and should be in millions of birders' and other nature lovers' backpacks." Sci Books Films

Peterson field guide to birds of Western North America; with contributions from Michael DiGiorgio [et al.] 4th ed; Houghton Mifflin Harcourt 2010 493p il map (Peterson field guide series) pa $19.95

Grades: 5 6 7 8 9 10 11 12 Adult   598

1. Birds -- North America

ISBN 978-0-547-15270-7; 0-547-15270-1

LC 2009-39158

First published 1941 with title: A field guide to western birds

This guide illustrates over 600 species of birds on 176 color plates. In addition, over 588 range maps are included.

Stefoff, Rebecca

★ The **bird** class; [by] Rebecca Stefoff. 1st ed.; Marshall Cavendish Benchmark 2008 96p il (Family trees) $22.95

Grades: 6 7 8 9   598

1. Birds

ISBN 978-0-7614-2693-6; 0-7614-2693-0

LC 2007007706

"Skillful weaving of engaging text and superb illustrations will incite interest." Voice Youth Advocates

"Explores the habitats, life cycles, and other characteristics of organisms in the bird class." Publisher's note

Includes glossary and bibliographical references

Thompson, Bill

The **young** birder's guide to birds of eastern North America; [by] Bill Thompson III; illustrations by Julie Zickefoose. Houghton Mifflin Co. 2008 256p il map (Peterson field guide series) $14.95

Grades: 3 4 5 6   598

1. Birds 2. Bird watching

ISBN 978-0-547-11934-2; 0-547-11934-8

LC 2007-43904

This describes 200 species of birds of eastern North America, with color photos, black & white drawings, and range maps.

Includes glossary and bibliographical references

Udvardy, Miklos D. F.

★ **National** Audubon Society field guide to North American birds, Western region; revised by John Farrand, Jr.; visual key by Amanda Wilson and Lori Hogan. rev ed; Knopf 1994 822p il maps pa $19.95

Grades: 6 7 8 9 10 11 12 Adult   598

1. Birds -- North America

ISBN 0-679-42851-8

LC 94-7415

Companion volume to National Audubon Society field guide to North American birds, Eastern region by John L. Bull

First published 1977

In this guide, "virtually every bird found in North America is brought to life in a full-color photograph and with textual information on the bird's voice, nesting habits, habitat, range, and interesting behaviors. Accompanying range maps; overhead flight silhouettes; sections on birdwatching, accidental species, and endangered birds" are also included. (Publisher's note)

Includes bibliographical references

Vogel, Carole Garbuny

The **man** who flies with birds; [by] Carole G. Vogel and Yossi Leshem. Kar-Ben Pub. 2009 64p il map lib bdg $18.95

Grades: 5 6 7 8   598

1. Aircraft accidents 2. Birds -- Migration

ISBN 978-0-8225-7643-3 lib bdg; 0-8225-7643-0 lib bdg

LC 2008-31198

Discusses the work of the bird expert whose lifelong study of the patterns of bird migration in Israel has led to a significant reduction in the number of collisions between aircraft and bird flocks.

"The book is heavily illustrated with good-quality color photos, maps, and diagrams, many of them captioned with incredible facts about wildlife and migration. This inspiring title on a most timely topic will appeal to those who are fascinated with wildlife, Earth science, and technology." SLJ

Includes bibliographical references

Warhol, Tom

★ **Hawks**; [by] Tom Warhol. Marshall Cavendish Benchmark 2005 112p il (Animalways) lib bdg $31.36

Grades: 6 7 8 9   **598**
1. Hawks
ISBN 0-7614-1744-3
                                            LC 2003-22138

This describes the place of hawks in human culture and history, their evolution, anatomy, habits, life cycle, and protection.

Includes glossary and bibliographical references

Owls; [by] Tom Warhol. Marshall Cavendish Benchmark 2007 111p il (Animalways) lib bdg $34.21

Grades: 6 7 8 9   **598**
1. Owls
ISBN 978-0-7614-2537-3
                                            LC 2006019708

This describes the place of owls in the animal kingdom, owl lore and legend, owls' evolution, diversity, anatomy and behavior, life cycle, and endangered status.

This "will pique readers' curiosity, and the content will keep them hooked. Vivid color photographs and illustrations and a clear font make [this work] stand out." SLJ

Includes glossary and bibliographical references

Webb, Sophie

Looking for seabirds; journal from an Alaskan voyage. Houghton Mifflin Co. 2004 48p il $16

Grades: 4 5 6 7   **598**
1. Birds 2. Alaska
ISBN 0-618-21235-3
                                            LC 2003-12420

A journal of the author's observations and adventures while working on a research vessel counting seabirds through Alaska's Aleutian Island chain

The "immediacy of the narrative . . . and the clear and colorful watercolor-and-gouache landscapes and drawings of the birds form an appealing travelogue that is as exciting as it is informative." SLJ

Includes glossary and bibliographical references

Wolf, Sallie

★ The **robin** makes a laughing sound; a birder's journal. designed by Micah Bornstein. Charlesbridge 2010 43p il $11.95

Grades: 5 6 7 8   **598**
1. Birds 2. Bird watching
ISBN 978-1-58089-318-3; 1-58089-318-X
                                            LC 2008-7248

Presents observations made through every season of the year of different birds and their behavior, from robins taking a bath, to cardinals searching for food in the snow, to an owl perched on a tree at night.

"The charming, eye-catching format includes short dated nature notes written in script, some of them on glued or taped-in torn paper pieces; other paper scraps contain short typeset poems and small, labeled watercolors. . . . Pen-and-ink sketches capture a baby house sparrow, a V-formation of geese, a downy woodpecker at a suet feeder, and more. . . . This small, instructional guide may provide the inspiration for young authors with even a bit of artistic talent to begin keeping nature journals of their own." SLJ

598.072   Bird watching

Hoose, Phillip

★ **Moonbird**; a year on the wind with the great survivor B95. Phillip Hoose. Farrar Straus Giroux 2012 148 p. col. ill. (hardcover) $21.99

Grades: 5 6 7 8   **598.072**
1. Endangered species 2. Birds -- Protection 3. Wildlife conservation 4. Red knot 5. Bird watching 6. Red knot -- Migration
ISBN 0374304688; 9780374304683
                                            LC 2011035612

Robert F. Sibert Honor Book (2013)

YALSA Award for Excellence in Nonfiction for Young Adults Finalist (2013)

In this book, Phillip Hoose "explores the tragedy of extinction through a single bird species, but there is hope for survival in this story, and that hope is pinned on understanding the remarkable longevity of a single bird. . . . Hoose takes readers around the hemisphere, showing them the obstacles rufa red knots face, introducing a global team of scientists and conservationists, and offering insights about what can be done to save them before it's too late." (Kirkus Reviews)

598.3   Water birds

Gish, Melissa

Flamingos; Melissa Gish. Creative Education 2014 46 p. color illustrations (hardcover : alk. paper) $37.10

Grades: 5 6 7 8   **598.3**
1. Animals 2. Flamingos
ISBN 1608184161; 9781608184163
                                            LC 2013031813

This book, by Melissa Gish, is a "scientific look at flamingos, including their habitats, physical characteristics such as their coloration, behaviors, relationships with humans, and numbers of the tropical birds in the world today." (Publisher's note)

"Stewart continues with a topic near and dear to devotees of the 590s, once more providing both fascinating and well-written facts and some truly arresting images. Scientific material on each species is offered, along with pop cultural and historical information. Fans of previous books in this series, such as Sea Lions and Piranhas (both of which SLJ called "remarkable for their clear information and exceptional photography") and Bats, Crocodiles, and Killer Whales will flock to these new entries. Thorough in scope and elegant in design, these stellar titles will attract the browser and the report writer alike." SLJ

Includes bibliographical references and index

Part of recommended series "Living Wild," which includes 62 titles, each with details on different animals.

598.9   Falconiformes, Caprimulgiformes, owls

Latimer, Jonathan P.

Birds of prey; [by] Jonathan P. Latimer, Karen Stray Nolting; illustrations by Roger Tory Peterson; foreword by Virginia Marie Peterson. Houghton Mifflin 1999 48p il (Peterson field guides for young naturalists) $15; pa $5.95

Grades: 4 5 6 7   **598.9**

1. Birds of prey

ISBN 0-395-95211-5; 0-395-92277-1 pa

LC 98-35516

This illustrated volume introduces the physical characteristics, behavior, and habitats of such birds of prey as eagles, hawks, falcons, and owls.

Sattler, Helen Roney

The **book** of North American owls; illustrated by Jean Day Zallinger. Clarion Bks. 1995 64p il maps hardcover o.p. pa $7.95

Grades: 4 5 6 7   **598.9**

1. Owls

ISBN 0-395-60524-5; 0-395-90017-4 pa

LC 91-43626

This "is a superb ornithological primer. . . . The book is lavishly illustrated." Appraisal

This volume "includes owl classification and history, hunting and habitat, courtship and nesting, and the complex relationship between owls and humans. The comprehensive glossary includes all of the 21 North American species." Sci Child

Includes bibliographical references

599   Mammals

★ **Exploring** mammals. Marshall Cavendish 2007 20v il map set $399.95

Grades: 5 6 7 8 9 10   **599**

1. Reference books 2. Mammals -- Encyclopedias

ISBN 978-0-76147-719-8

LC 2007060864

"About 90 animals . . . are described in these volumes. Each article includes . . . a 'Profile,' with introductory information; a discussion of anatomy, with diagrams; a discussion of habitat; descriptions of various behaviors; and a consideration of factors determining survival. Each article also has numerous boxed sections . . . as well as many color

photographs and other illustrations. . . . This set has just about everything a student requires." Booklist

Includes bibliographical references

★ **Exploring** the world of mammals; [edited by Nancy Simmons, Richard Beatty, Amy Jane Beer] Chelsea House 2008 6v il map set $210

Grades: 5 6 7 8   **599**

1. Reference books 2. Mammals -- Encyclopedias

ISBN 978-0-7910-9651-2 set; 0-7910-9651-3 set

LC 2007028223

"This colorful and appealing set offers an introduction to the world of mammals. Most of entries are 2 to 4 pages in length. Sidebars offer extra details, and bright photographs and illustrations appear on every 2-page spread." Booklist

Mammals of the Northern Hemisphere; edited by Tim Harris. Brown Bear Books 2011 64 p. col. ill., col. maps (Facts at Your Fingertips: endangered animals) (library binding) $35.65

Grades: 7 8 9   **599**

1. Mammals 2. Endangered species 3. Wildlife conservation 4. Rare mammals -- Northern Hemisphere

ISBN 1936333341; 9781936333349

LC 2010053969

This book is part of the "Facts at Your Fingertips: Endangered Animals" series. "Each page has all benefits of a picture book with large, colorful photographs that accompany the encyclopedia-style text. Each new animal is accompanied by a 'data panel,' which summarizes . . . information such as location, size, habitat, population and diet. This series focuses on animals facing extinction all over the world. Factors contributing to the animal's endangered status as well as preservation techniques are also discussed." The book "talks about well-known animals like the Polar Bear and Giant Panda as well as lesser-known mammals such as the Ryukyu Flying Fox." (Children's Literature)

Includes bibliographical references (p. 63) and index.

Rodriguez, Ana Maria

Secret of the singing mice . . . and more! [by] Ana Maria Rodriguez. Enslow Publishers 2008 48p il (Animal secrets revealed!) lib bdg $23.93

Grades: 5 6 7 8   **599**

1. Mammals

ISBN 978-0-7660-2956-9 lib bdg; 0-7660-2956-5 lib bdg

LC 2007-39495

This book offers "fascinating accounts of how scientists systematically analyzed, tested and proved their theories or how their findings led to other, serendipitous discoveries. . . . Science experiments are thoughtfully placed to inspire exploration, and captioned, full-color photos appear throughout." SLJ

Includes glossary and bibliographical references

Whitaker, John O.

★ **National** Audubon Society field guide to North American mammals; rev ed; Knopf 1996 937p il maps pa $19.95

Grades: 6 7 8 9 10 11 12 Adult **599**
1. Mammals
ISBN 0-679-44631-1

LC 95-81456

First published 1980

This field guide describes 390 species of mammals of North America and includes keys for identification, range maps, information on tracks and anatomy, and 375 color photos

599.2 Marsupials and monotremes

Collard, Sneed B.

★ **Pocket** babies and other amazing marsupials. Darby Creek 2007 72p il map $18.95

Grades: 4 5 6 7 **599.2**
1. Marsupials
ISBN 978-1-58196-046-4; 1-58196-046-8

"This large-format book provides an attractive introduction to marsupials around the world. . . . Attractive, informative side-bars, excellent maps, and many-clear, color photos appear throughout the book. . . . This handsomely designed volume introduces marsupials with panache." Booklist

Includes glossary and bibliographical references

Gish, Melissa

Kangaroos. Creative Education 2010 46p il (Living wild) $23.95; pa $9.95

Grades: 5 6 7 8 **599.2**
1. Kangaroos
ISBN 978-1-58341-970-0; 1-58341-970-5; 978-0-89812-553-5 pa; 0-89812-553-7 pa

LC 2010017375

"A look at kangaroos, including their habitats, physical characteristics such as the females' pouches, behaviors, relationships with humans, and valued status in the world today." Publisher's note

Montgomery, Sy

★ **Quest** for the tree kangaroo; an expedition to the cloud forest of New Guinea. text by Sy Montgomery; photographs by Nic Bishop. Houghton Mifflin 2006 79p il map (Scientists in the field) $18

Grades: 5 6 7 8 **599.2**
1. Zoologists 2. Tree kangaroos 3. New Guinea
ISBN 0-618-49641-6

LC 2005-34849

"The writer and photographer of this exemplary description of science field work accompanied researcher Lisa Dabek on an expedition high in New Guinea's mountains to study tree kangaroos and promote the conservation of this elusive and endangered species. . . . Montgomery . . . paces her narrative well . . . keeping the reader engaged and concerned. . . . Bishop's photographs . . . are beautifully reproduced." Publ Wkly

Stefoff, Rebecca

★ The **marsupial** order; [by] Rebecca Stefoff. Marshall Cavendish Benchmark 2008 96p il (Family trees) lib bdg $22.95

Grades: 6 7 8 9 **599.2**
1. Marsupials
ISBN 978-0-7614-2697-4 lib bdg; 0-7614-2697-3 lib bdg

LC 2007007240

This is "meticulously detailed. . . . Sharp color photographs appear on about every other page. Other illustrations consist of classification charts and anatomical diagrams. . . . [This is] well-organized and clearly written. . . . In addition to discussing such well-known animals as kangaroos, koalas, and opossums, [this book] includes material on less-familiar species 'marsupial mice,' quolls, bandicoots, and bilbies. . . . [The book is] well-researched." SLJ

Includes glossary and bibliographical references

599.3 Miscellaneous orders of placental mammals

Markle, Sandra

Prairie dogs. Lerner Publications Company 2007 39p il map (Animal prey) lib bdg $25.26; pa $7.95

Grades: 4 5 6 **599.3**
1. Prairie dogs
ISBN 978-0-8225-6438-6 lib bdg; 0-8225-6438-6 lib bdg; 978-0-8225-6441-6 pa; 0-8225-6441-6 pa

LC 2006-598

Describes the behavior of prairie dogs in their native habitat, where they are the prey of larger animals and birds and where they must work together as a colony to create burrows and warning systems to protect themselves and their young

Includes glossary and bibliographical references

599.35 Rodents

Marrin, Albert

Oh, rats! the story of rats and people. illustrated by C.B. Mordan. Dutton Children's Books 2006 48p il $16.99

Grades: 3 4 5 6 **599.35**
1. Rats
ISBN 0-525-47762-4

LC 2004-24512

This is "lively and informative. . . . The nine short chapters are set in a handsome slim book with striking black-and-white scratchboard illustrations and muted red framing on many pages." SLJ

Includes bibliographical references

Stefoff, Rebecca

The **rodent** order; by Rebecca Stefoff. Marshall Cavendish Benchmark 2008 96p il (Family trees) $23.95

Grades: 6 7 8 9 **599.35**
1. Rodents
ISBN 978-0-7614-3073-5; 0-7614-3073-3

LC 2008-17555

"Explores the habitats, life cycles, and other characteristics of rodents." Publisher's note

Includes glossary and bibliographical references

599.37   Beavers

★ **Beavers;** Melissa Gish. Creative Education 2014 46 p. (Living Wild) (hardcover : alk. paper) $37.10

Grades: 5 6 7 8   **599.37**

1. Animals 2. Beavers 3. Beavers

ISBN 1608184145; 9781608184149

LC 2013031814

This book, by Melissa Gish, focuses on beavers. It provides "both fascinating and well-written facts and some truly arresting images. Scientific material . . . is offered, along with pop cultural and historical information." (School Library Journal)

" Fans of previous books in this series, such as Sea Lions and Piranhas (both of which SLJ called "remarkable for their clear information and exceptional photography") and Bats, Crocodiles, and Killer Whales will flock to these new entries. Thorough in scope and elegant in design, these stellar titles will attract the browser and the report writer alike." SLJ

Includes bibliographical references and index

599.4   Bats

Carson, Mary Kay

★ The **bat** scientists; with photographs by Tom Uhlman. Houghton Mifflin Books for Children 2010 79p il (Scientists in the field) $18

Grades: 4 5 6 7   **599.4**

1. Bats

ISBN 978-0-547-19956-6; 0-547-19956-2

LC 2010006767

This describes "patient field work, rescue and conservation efforts to save bats. . . . Woven into particular researchers' stories is an enormous amount of information about bat biology and behavior. Uhlman's photographs are clearly identified in context and the backmatter supports further research." Kirkus

Includes glossary and bibliographical references

Gish, Melissa

Bats. Creative Paperbacks 2010 46p il (Living wild) $23.95; pa $9.95

Grades: 5 6 7 8   **599.4**

1. Bats

ISBN 978-1-58341-966-3; 1-58341-966-7; 978-0-89812-549-8 pa; 0-89812-549-9 pa

LC 2010017371

The "book lucidly discusses conservation and the animals' often tenuous relationship with humans. The layout is uniformly simple but effective, constructed with a nice balance of main text for the report writers, smaller chunks of esoterica for browsers, and . . . killer photos." Booklist

Markle, Sandra, 1946-

The **case** of the vanishing little brown bats; a scientific mystery. Sandra Markle. Millbrook Press 2014 48 p. illustrations, maps (lib. bdg. : alk. paper) $29.27

Grades: 4 5 6   **599.4**

1. Bats 2. Animals -- Diseases 3. Little brown bat

ISBN 1467714631; 9781467714631

LC 2013030953

"This informative title sheds light on a mystery of nature: how little brown bats, nature's insect eaters, are mysteriously dying in their caves during hibernation. Each chapter takes readers into the problems that plague this endangered member of our ecosystem, describing how teams of scientists examined how 'white-nose syndrome,' caused by a fungus called Pd, is infecting the brown bat population." (School Library Journal)

"With plentiful details about the scientific work, photographs showing scientists and their tiny subjects, clear explanations, and an organization that is both topical and chronological, this title brings science to life." Kirkus

Includes bibliographical references and index

Taschek, Karen

Hanging with bats; ecobats, vampires, and movie stars. University of New Mexico Press 2008 94p il (Worlds of wonder) $16.95

Grades: 6 7 8 9   **599.4**

1. Bats

ISBN 978-0-8263-4403-8; 0-8263-4403-8

LC 2008-2076

"This book provides an all-inclusive look at the flying mammal many people do not understand well enough to appreciate. From the scientific discussion of where bats are found on the evolutionary tree to the whys and hows of building a bat house, there is little that cannot be learned from within these pages. . . . The text is written in a friendly style, with unusual words further defined or explained as needed, nicely allowing generous amounts of information to be absorbed without it feeling like work. The photographs and illustrations are fascinating, helping to lure in a reluctant reader. It should be noted that the photos of bats in action are particularly eye-catching. . . . It is a good choice for any library." Voice Youth Advocates

Includes glossary

Williams, Kim

Stokes beginner's guide to bats; [by] Kim Williams . . . [et al.] Little, Brown, and Co. 2002 159p il map $9.99

Grades: 6 7 8 9   **599.4**

1. Bats

ISBN 978-0-316-81658-8; 0-316-81658-2

LC 2001-38112

This book about bats gives "identification and behavior information in a portable pocket-sized format." Publisher's note

599.5 Cetaceans and sea cows

Baker, Molly

The **secret** world of whales; illustrated by Molly Baker. Chronicle Books 2011 108p il $16.99

Grades: 4 5 6 7   **599.5**

1. Whales

ISBN 978-0-8118-7641-4; 0-8118-7641-1

LC 2010-27355

"In this small-format volume, Siebert creates a concise introduction to whales, addressing myths and stories, the history of the whaling industry, communication and intelligence, and encounters between whales and humans. With playful, anthropomorphic cartoons, striking photographs, and a discussion of the dangers facing whales—noise pollution from boats, potentially lethal sonar—readers should gain a vivid impression of their behavior in the wild, as well as an appreciation for their majesty." Publ Wkly

Christopherson, Sara Cohen

Top 50 reasons to care about whales and dolphins; animals in peril. Enslow Publishers 2010 103p il (Top 50 reasons to care about endangered animals) lib bdg $31.93

Grades: 4 5 6 7   **599.5**

1. Whales 2. Dolphins 3. Endangered species

ISBN 978-0-7660-3453-2 lib bdg; 0-7660-3453-4 lib bdg

LC 2008-48695

This describes whales and dolphins—their life cycles, diets, young, habitats, and reasons why they are endangered animals

"The illustrations, mostly color photographs, represent a wonderful selection of the animals and their habitats. Reluctant readers may be enticed by this . . . simply because of the great images. This . . . would make a substantial supplement to the science curriculum when studying endangered animals." Libr Media Connect

Includes glossary and bibliographical references

Gish, Melissa

Killer whales. Creative Paperbacks 2010 46p il map (Living wild) $23.95; pa $9.95

Grades: 5 6 7 8   **599.5**

1. Whales

ISBN 978-1-58341-971-7; 1-58341-971-3; 978-0-89812-554-2 pa; 0-89812-554-5 pa

LC 2010017376

"A look at killer whales, including their habitats, physical characteristics such as their unique coloration, behaviors, relationships with humans, and protected status in the world today." Publisher's note

Whales. Creative Education 2011 46p il map (Living wild) lib bdg $23.95

Grades: 5 6 7 8   **599.5**

1. Whales

ISBN 978-1-60818-084-4

LC 2010028414

A look at whales, including their habitats, physical characteristics such as their streamlined bodies, behaviors,

relationships with humans, and threatened status in the world today.

Includes glossary and bibliographical references

Greenberg, Dan

★ **Whales**; by Dan Greenberg. Marshall Cavendish Benchmark 2009 24 p. ill. (Benchmark rockets) (library) $24.21

Grades: 3 4 5 6 7   **599.5**

1. Whales

ISBN 0761443460; 9780761443469

LC 0024390

This book is part of the Benchmark Rockets: Animals series and focuses on whales. Each title "tells about and illustrates the animal world. Each animal's lives and futures are revealed in . . . dialogue with photographs and charts. The text includes what each animal eats, how it communicates, and how it lives within a community." (Library Media Connection)

"Describes the physical characteristics, habitat, behavior, diet, life cycle, and conservation status of whales." Publisher's note

Includes glossary

Hall, Howard

A **charm** of dolphins; the threatened life of a flippered friend. 2nd ed.; London Town Press 2007 48p il map (Jean-Michel Cousteau presents) $8.95

Grades: 5 6 7 8   **599.5**

1. Dolphins

ISBN 978-0-9766134-8-0; 0-9766134-8-4

First published 1994 by Silver Burdett Press

Shows and describes species of dolphins around the world, depicts dolphin characteristics and behavior, and discusses the threats that human beings pose to the animals.

This "book covers the characteristics and unique traits of the . . . [dolphin] and includes colorful, awe-inspiring photos and immediate first-person narratives." SLJ

Includes glossary and bibliographical references

Hodgkins, Fran

★ The **whale** scientists; solving the mystery of whale strandings. Houghton Mifflin Co. 2007 63p il map (Scientists in the field) $18

Grades: 5 6 7 8   **599.5**

1. Whales

ISBN 978-0-618-55673-1; 0-618-55673-7

LC 2006-34634

This describes the evolution of whales and their relationship to humans and offers various scientific theories about their strandings.

"Hodgkins packs her text with an impressive amount of information. . . . Well-chosen color photographs amply illustrate the well-organized discussion." SLJ

Includes glossary and bibliographical references

Leon, Vicki

A **pod** of killer whales; the mysterious life of the intelligent orca. 2nd ed.; London Town Press 2007 48p il (Jean-Michel Cousteau presents) pa $8.95

Grades: 5 6 7 8   **599.5**
1. Whales
ISBN 978-0-9766134-7-3; 0-9766134-7-6
First published 1995 by Silver Burdett Press
Introduces killer whales, describing their social structure, eating habits, communication and hunting methods, and threats to their way of life.

This "book covers the characteristics and unique traits of . . . [killer whales] and includes colorful, awe-inspiring photos and immediate first-person narratives." SLJ
Includes bibliographical references

Lockwood, Sophie
Whales; by Sophie Lockwood. Child's World 2008 40p il map (World of mammals) lib bdg $29.93
Grades: 4 5 6   **599.5**
1. Whales
ISBN 978-1-59296-930-2 lib bdg; 1-59296-930-5 lib bdg
                                          LC 2007020890
This book about whales presents "all the basics for reports: an introduction to the creatures' challenges, the role humans play, physical traits and behaviors, habitats, and struggles for survival. Every part of their life [cycle], including sexual maturity, birth, and family relationships, is explained. . . . Clear bright photographs pump up the content. . . The detail that Lockwood imparts is startlingly high. The [text is] written in a dynamic and engaging style." SLJ
Includes glossary and bibliographical references

Lourie, Peter
★ The **manatee** scientists; saving vulnerable species. Houghton Mifflin Books for Children 2011 80p il map (Scientists in the field) $18.99
Grades: 4 5 6 7   **599.5**
1. Manatees 2. Scientists 3. Marine biology 4. Endangered species 5. Wildlife conservation
ISBN 978-0-547-15254-7; 0-547-15254-X
This book highlights the work scientists are doing to protect the manatee, including John Reynolds, who does an aerial count of manatees from the Florida sky; Lucy Keith who spends a weekend rescuing manatees trapped in a dam in Senegal; and Fernando Rosas who takes the author on an Amazonian boat trip, looking for a young manatee he released back into the wild.

"The manatees photographed by Lourie and others add plenty of visual appeal. . . . A sturdy addition to a standard-setting nonfiction series." Booklist

★ **Whaling** season; a year in the life of an arctic whale scientist. Houghton Mifflin Books for Children 2009 80p il map (Scientists in the field) $18
Grades: 4 5 6 7   **599.5**
1. Inuit 2. Whales 3. Biologists 4. Alaska
ISBN 978-0-618-77709-9; 0-618-77709-1
                                          LC 2009-18596
Profiles the work of John Craighead George, an Arctic whale scientist, as he studies the bowhead whale and works with the indigenous people of Alaska to better understand the history of the animal.

"Combining exemplary color photos and simple, vivid language, the chapters detail not only George's day-today methodology but also his motivation." Booklist
Includes glossary and bibliographical references

O'Connell, Jennifer
The **eye** of the whale; a rescue story. Jennifer O'Connell. 1st hardcover ed. Tilbury House, Publishers 2012 32 p. col. ill. (hardcover) $16.95
Grades: 5 6 7 8   **599.5**
1. Whales 2. Animal rescue 3. Humpback whale -- California -- San Francisco 4. Wildlife rescue -- California -- San Francisco
ISBN 0884483355; 9780884483359
                                          LC 2012031165
This true children's story, by Jennifer O'Connell, begins when, "near San Francisco, a distress call was radioed to shore by a local fisherman. He had discovered a humpback whale tangled in hundreds of yards of crab-trap lines. . . . A team of volunteers answered the call, and four divers risked their lives to rescue the enormous animal." (Publisher's note)

Rodriguez, Ana Maria
Secret of the sleepless whales . . . and more! by Ana Maria Rodriguez. Enslow Publishers 2008 48p il (Animal secrets revealed!) lib bdg $23.93
Grades: 5 6 7 8   **599.5**
1. Marine mammals
ISBN 978-0-7660-2957-6 lib bdg; 0-7660-2957-3 lib bdg
                                          LC 2007039479
This book "does a thorough job of explaining the behaviors of some marine mammals and the scientific methods used to investigate them. . . . The team that worked on the specific issue is identified, and the methodology they used to answer their scientific inquiry is described in detail. . . . The full-color photos are interesting. . . . The content is solid with seamless explanations of terms, and it's fun to read." SLJ
Includes glossary and bibliographical references

Stefoff, Rebecca
Sea mammals; by Rebecca Stefoff. Marshall Cavendish Benchmark 2008 96p il (Family trees) $23.95
Grades: 6 7 8 9   **599.5**
1. Marine animals
ISBN 978-0-7614-3072-8; 0-7614-3072-5
                                          LC 2008-11452
"Explores the habitats, life cycles, and other characteristics of sea mammals." Publisher's note
Includes glossary and bibliographical references

Swinburne, Stephen R.
Saving manatees; [by] Stephen Swinburne. Boyds Mills Press 2006 40p il map $16.95
Grades: 4 5 6 7   **599.5**
1. Manatees
ISBN 978-1-59078-319-1; 1-59078-319-0
                                          LC 2006000523
"In each chapter, Swinburne describes a different visit to a national wildlife refuge or other area in Florida's 'manatee

country,' where he consults with biologists and park rangers and joins a field trip of fourth-graders as they swim with the animals. . . . Swinburne weaves a great deal of information into his personal narrative, and his enthusiastic descriptions of his experiences with the animals are contagious and will draw children right into the subject, as will the many large color photos." Booklist

Includes bibliographical references

599.53 Dolphins and porpoises

Turner, Pamela S.

The **dolphins** of Shark Bay; by Pamela S. Turner. Houghton Mifflin Harcourt 2013 76 p. $18.99

Grades: 5 6 7 8   **599.53**

1. Dolphins 2. Bottlenose dolphin -- Behavior -- Australia -- Shark Bay (W.A.) 3. Bottlenose dolphin -- Research -- Australia -- Shark Bay (W.A.)

ISBN 0547716389; 9780547716381

     LC 2012048463

In this book, "ride alongside the author Pamela S. Turner and her scientific team . . . as they seek to answer the question: just why are dolphins so smart? And what does their behavior tell us about human intelligence, captive animals, and the future of the ocean?" (Publisher's note)

599.63 Even-toed ungulates

Lockwood, Sophie

Giraffes. Child's World 2006 40p il map (World of mammals) lib bdg $29.93

Grades: 4 5 6   **599.63**

1. Giraffes

ISBN 978-1-59296-496-3; 1-59296-496-6

     LC 2005-538

Explores the physical and behavioral characteristics of giraffes, examines their habitat and natural history, and discusses the role of humans in ensuring the continued survival of the species.

Includes glossary and bibliographical references

599.64 Bovids

Gish, Melissa

Bison. Creative Education 2011 46p il map (Living wild) $23.95

Grades: 5 6 7 8   **599.64**

1. Bison

ISBN 978-1-60818-077-6; 1-60818-077-8

     LC 2010028305

A look at bison, including their habitats, physical characteristics such as their shaggy coats, behaviors, relationships with humans, and threatened status in the world today.

This offers "an array of interesting facts. Photography is large and beautiful—a real draw." SLJ

Includes bibliographical references

Marrin, Albert

★ **Saving** the buffalo. Scholastic Nonfiction 2006 128p il $18.99

Grades: 4 5 6 7   **599.64**

1. Bison

ISBN 0-439-71854-6

     LC 2005-51827

"In characteristically robust prose, Marrin retraces the American bison's roller-coaster ride from Lord of the Great Plains to near extinction at the end of the 19th century, and slow recovery. Along with showing how the buffalo fit into the habitat's complex, interdependent ecology, he describes in vivid detail how the animals were hunted and utilized by indigenous peoples. . . . A generous array of accompanying illustrations includes crisply reproduced photos, both new and old; prints; paintings; and pictures of artifacts." SLJ

Includes glossary and bibliographical references

599.65 Deer

Gish, Melissa

Moose. Creative Education 2010 46p il map (Living wild) $23.95; pa $9.95

Grades: 5 6 7 8   **599.65**

1. Moose

ISBN 978-1-58341-973-1; 1-58341-973-X; 978-0-89812-556-6 pa; 0-89812-556-1 pa

     LC 2010017378

"A look at moose, including their habitats, physical characteristics such as their imposing antlers, behaviors, relationships with humans, and secure status in the world today." Publisher's note

Heuer, Karsten

★ **Being** caribou; five months on foot with a caribou herd. Walker & Co. 2007 48p il map $17.95; lib bdg $18.95

Grades: 4 5 6 7   **599.65**

1. Caribou 2. Arctic regions

ISBN 978-0-8027-9565-6; 0-8027-9565-X; 978-0-8027-9566-3 lib bdg; 0-8027-9566-8 lib bdg

     LC 2006-27651

This is an adaptation of an adult title by the same name, published 2005 by Mountaineers Books

"The caribou calving grounds in the Arctic National Wildlife Refuge are being threatened by oil exploration. [This title] will help make kids aware of what is at stake and give them a glimpse of an extraordinary part of the world and the lengths the caribou go to traverse it. It is an important book." Quill Quire

Includes bibliographical references

Stefoff, Rebecca

Deer; [by] Rebecca Stefoff. Marshall Cavendish Benchmark 2007 108p il (Animalways) lib bdg $34.21

Grades: 6 7 8 9   **599.65**

1. Deer

ISBN 978-0-7614-2534-2

     LC 2007016932

This describes the place of deer in the animal kingdom, their evolution, anatomy, life cycle, diversity, and relationship to humans.

This "will pique readers' curiosity, and the content will keep them hooked. Vivid color photographs and illustrations and a clear font make [this work] stand out." SLJ

Includes glossary and bibliographical references

599.66   Odd-toed ungulates

Carson, Mary Kay

★ **Emi** and the rhino scientist; [by] Mary Kay Carson; with photographs by Tom Uhlman. Houghton Mifflin Company 2007 57p il (Scientists in the field) $18

Grades: 5 6 7 8   599.66
1. Rhinoceros 2. Zoo employees 3. Animal scientists
ISBN 978-0-618-64639-5; 0-618-64639-6
LC 2006-34517

This describes "how Terri Roth, an expert in endangered-species reproduction at the Cincinnati Zoo, helped Emi to give birth to the first Sumatran rhino born in captivity in more than 100 years. . . . The text is full of important details, and the photographs are unfailingly crisp, bright, and full of variety." SLJ

Firestone, Mary

Top 50 reasons to care about rhinos; animals in peril. Enslow Publishers 2010 103p il (Top 50 reasons to care about endangered animals) lib bdg $31.93

Grades: 4 5 6 7   599.66
1. Rhinoceros 2. Endangered species
ISBN 978-0-7660-3457-0 lib bdg; 0-7660-3457-7 lib bdg
LC 2008048692

This describes the different types of rhino, their life cycle, diet, young, habitat, and reasons why they are endangered animals

"The illustrations, mostly color photographs, represent a wonderful selection of the animals and their habitats. Reluctant readers may be enticed by this . . . simply because of the great images. This . . . would make a substantial supplement to the science curriculum when studying endangered animals." Libr Media Connect

Includes glossary and bibliographical references

Frydenborg, Kay

The **wild** horse scientists; written by Kay Frydenborg. Houghton Mifflin Harcourt 2013 80 p. (Scientists in the field) $18.99

Grades: 7 8 9 10   599.66
1. Horses 2. Scientists 3. Conservationists 4. Assateague Island National Seashore (Md. and Va.) 5. Wild horses -- Assateague Island National Seashore (Md. and Va.) 6. Wildlife conservationists -- Assateague Island National Seashore (Md. and Va.)
ISBN 0547518315; 9780547518312
LC 2011039912

This book by Kay Frydenbourg, part of the "Scientists in the Field" series, "focuses on research leading to the use of porcine zona pellucida vaccine on wild horses for reliable, reversible birth control. Frydenborg introduces her readers to several scientists involved in this work. . . . Along the way are chapters on horse ancestry and the history of wild horses in this country, as well as information about color and size and other research and researchers." (Kirkus Reviews)

Includes bibliographical references.

Gish, Melissa

Rhinoceroses. Creative Education 2011 46p il map (Living wild) lib bdg $23.95

Grades: 5 6 7 8   599.66
1. Rhinoceros
ISBN 978-1-60818-083-7; 1-60818-083-2
LC 2010028316

A look at rhinoceroses, including their habitats, physical characteristics such as their horned noses, behaviors, relationships with humans, and protected status in the world today.

Includes glossary and bibliographical references

Halls, Kelly Milner

Wild horses; galloping through time. [by] Kelly Milner Halls; with illustrations by Mark Hallett. Darby Creek Pub. 2008 72p il $18.95

Grades: 3 4 5 6 7   599.66
1. Horses
ISBN 978-1-58196-065-5; 1-58196-065-4

Introduces the horse family tree including the relatives of today's modern horse that are now extinct, as well as the species of zebras and asses that still live in the wild

"Colorful illustrations of prehistoric horses, and descriptions of differences from modern horses in terms of their size and number of toes, will intrigue readers. . . . A visual and informational blue-ribbon winner." SLJ

Includes bibliographical references

Hamilton, Garry

Rhino rescue. Firefly Books 2006 64p il map (Firefly animal rescue) $19.95; pa $9.95

Grades: 5 6 7   599.66
1. Rhinoceros 2. Endangered species 3. Wildlife conservation
ISBN 978-1-55297-912-9; 1-55297-912-1; 978-1-55297-910-5 pa; 1-55297-910-5 pa
LC 2006275760

Provides details about rhinoceroses from Africa and Asia, their endangerment, and conservation programs designed to save them.

Lockwood, Sophie

Zebras; by Sophie Lockwood. Child's World 2008 40p il map (World of mammals) lib bdg $29.93

Grades: 4 5 6   599.66
1. Zebras
ISBN 978-1-59296-931-9 lib bdg; 1-59296-931-3 lib bdg
LC 2007-21689

This book about Zebras looks "at all aspects of the mammal's life including where they live, how they live, and their unique habits. . . . Detailed and labeled color photographs enhance the information provided. Enjoyable and full of information." Libr Media Connect

Includes glossary and bibliographical references

Montgomery, Sy

★ The **tapir** scientist; written by Sy Montgomery ; photographed by Nic Bishop. Houghton Mifflin Harcourt 2013 80 p. $18.99

Grades: 5 6 7 8   **599.66**

1. Brazil 2. Tapirs 3. Tapirs -- Brazil 4. Tapirs -- Research -- Brazil

ISBN 0547815484; 9780547815480

LC 2012018678

In this book, author Sy Montgomery and photographer Nic Bishop "experience long, hot days, cramped conditions, nervous waiting and itchy tick bites while searching for [tapirs]. . . . In less than a week, they see tapirs in the wild, find their tracks, take photographs, locate them through radio telemetry, collect 'samples of tapir poop, skin, fur, and blood,' and capture and collar two new tapirs, with more to come. This research matters, and the author . . . explains why." (Kirkus Reviews)

599.67   Elephants

Downer, Ann

Elephant talk; the surprising science of elephant communication. Twenty-First Century Books 2011 112p il map lib bdg $33.26

Grades: 4 5 6 7 8   **599.67**

1. Elephants 2. Animal communication

ISBN 978-0-7613-5766-7 lib bdg; 0-7613-5766-1 lib bdg

LC 2010-24880

"The complex behavior of wild elephants is introduced in a flowing narrative accompanied by full-color photographs, diagrams and maps. Downer provides an overview of elephant evolution, places the creatures in their African and Asian contexts, and describes the lives of these intelligent social animals. Her narrative then focuses on the elephants' inticate verbal and nonverbal communication techniques. . . . The illustrations and clearly labeled diagrams and maps are well placed to amplify the text. . . . Throughout this highly readable, informative title are profiles of individuals . . . who work with these animals." SLJ

Includes glossary and bibliographical references

Jackson, Donna M.

★ The **elephant** scientist; by Caitlin O'Connell and Donna M. Jackson; photographs by Caitlin O'Connell and Timothy Rodwell. Houghton Mifflin Books for Children 2011 70p il map $17.99

Grades: 4 5 6 7   **599.67**

1. Elephants 2. Biologists 3. Ecologists

ISBN 978-0-547-05344-8; 0-547-05344-4

LC 2010014134

In this book, "O'Connell traveled to Africa in 1992 to observe wild animals; the trip turned into a job offer to study elephants at Etosha National Park; the text focuses on the scientists' work, findings, and problems encountered. The authors offer [a] . . . look at new discoveries about elephant communication and how this knowledge can be used to slow the animal's slump into extinction. Combined with . . . full-color photographs by the scientists, the elephants' world is brought to the forefront. Readers enter the researchers' camp to see their setup, fieldwork, and takedown in action. They will learn how elephant anatomy and hierarchy work together to aid in communication." (School Library Journal)

O'Connell "worked with other scientists to [identify] the vibration-sensitive cells in elephants' feet and trunks that enabled to them to 'hear' sounds transmitted through the ground. Illustrated with many well-captioned, color photos, this eye-catching book provides a sometimes fascinating look at O'Connell's work with elephants in America and in Namibia." Booklist

Redmond, Ian

Elephant; written by Ian Redmond; photographed by Dave King. Dorling Kindersley 2000 63p il (DK eyewitness books) $15.99; lib bdg $19.99

Grades: 4 5 6 7   **599.67**

1. Elephants

ISBN 0-7894-6591-4; 0-7894-6591-4 lib bdg

First published 1993 by Knopf

Discusses elephants, their physiology, behavior, evolution, relatives, uses by humans, and conservation

599.7   Carnivores

Lockwood, Sophie

Sea otters. Child's World 2006 40p il map (World of mammals) lib bdg $29.93

Grades: 4 5 6   **599.7**

1. Otters

ISBN 978-1-59296-500-7; 1-59296-500-8

LC 2005-568

Explores the physical and behavioral characteristics of sea otters, examines their habitat and natural history, and discusses the role of humans in ensuring the continued survival of the species.

Includes glossary and bibliographical references

Skunks; by Sophie Lockwood. Child's World 2008 40p il map (World of mammals) lib bdg $29.93

Grades: 4 5 6   **599.7**

1. Skunks

ISBN 978-1-59296-929-6 lib bdg; 1-59296-929-1 lib bdg

LC 2007022219

This book about skunks presents "all the basics for reports: an introduction to the creatures' challenges, the role humans play, physical traits and behaviors, habitats, and struggles for survival. Every part of their life [cycle], including sexual maturity, birth, and family relationships, is explained. . . . Clear bright photographs pump up the content. .

.. The detail that Lockwood imparts is startlingly high. The [text is] written in a dynamic and engaging style." SLJ

Includes glossary and bibliographical references

599.74   Land carnivores

Read, Tracy C.

Exploring the world of raccoons. Firefly Books 2010 24p il (Exploring the world . . .) lib bdg $16.95; pa $6.95

Grades: 6 7 8 9   599.74
    1. Raccoons
    ISBN 978-1-55407-626-0 lib bdg; 1-55407-626-9 lib bdg; 978-1-55407-617-8 pa; 1-55407-617-X pa

"This slender book from the Exploring the World of . . . series introduces the raccoon. The discussion begins with its gradual migration, over the past 100 years, from disappearing North American forests into suburbs and cities. In illustrated two-page and four-page spreads, the book presents information on aspects of raccoon anatomy, habitat, food, seasonal cycle, care of young, and predators...The text is clearly written and informative, though its vocabulary would suit a high-school reader better than the elementary-school students who might be drawn to such a short, highly illustrated book. Still, capable middle-school readers looking for a succinct, informative introduction to raccoons will find it here." (Booklist)

Somervill, Barbara A.

Small Indian Mongoose. Cherry Lake Pub. 2010 32p il map (Animal invaders) lib bdg $27.07

Grades: 5 6 7 8   599.74
    1. Mongooses 2. Biological invasions
    ISBN 978-1-60279-630-0 lib bdg; 1-60279-630-0 lib bdg
                      LC 2009028179

This offers "an introduction to the problems caused by [the Small Indian Mongoose], a discussion of its physical characteristics and habits, a history of how it arrived in its new habitat, and an analysis of challenges encountered by those trying to limit its spread. . . . [This] considers the destructive effects of these mammals on islands (including several in Hawaii), where they were initially introduced to prey on rats. . . . [This] well-focused [book is] clearly written. The uncluttered page design features at least one color photo on each spread." Booklist

Includes glossary and bibliographical references

599.75   Cat family

Alderton, David

Wild cats of the world; photographs by Bruce Tanner. Facts on File 2002 192p il map $35

Grades: 7 8 9 10   599.75
    1. Wild cats
    ISBN 0-8160-5217-4
                      LC 2002-34736
    First published 1993

This "volume explores the development and behavior of wild cats, with chapters covering form and function, evolution, and distribution. It also examines each species in detail, providing information on distinctive features such as sight, hearing, hunting techniques, and locomotion." Publisher's note

Includes bibliographical references

Becker, John E.

★ **Wild** cats: past & present; illustrations by Mark Hallett. Darby Creek 2008 80p il $18.95

Grades: 5 6 7 8   599.75
    1. Wild cats
    ISBN 978-1-58196-052-5; 1-58196-052-2

"Becker provides an informative introduction to wild cats, including an account of their ancient ancestors, an overview of the family Felidae and its subdivisions, accounts of wild cats alive in the world today, and woven throughout, discussions of the endangered status of many species. . . . Clearly written and well organized, the text is enhanced by many side-bars, maps, photos, and paintings." Booklist

Bonar, Samantha

Small wildcats. Watts 2002 63p il (Watts library) $24; pa $8.95

Grades: 4 5 6   599.75
    1. Wild cats
    ISBN 0-531-11965-3; 0-531-16632-5 pa
                      LC 2001-17581

In this title "the reader learns terms, including species and genus, with various species examined more closely in chapters devoted to a particular region such as Africa, Europe and Asia, and the Americas. In addition, this book also provides conservation facts and ways in which the reader can help the endangered cats of the world." Libr Media Connect

Includes glossary and bibliographical references

Firestone, Mary

Top 50 reasons to care about tigers; animals in peril. Enslow Publishers 2010 103p il (Top 50 reasons to care about endangered animals) lib bdg $31.93

Grades: 4 5 6 7   599.75
    1. Tigers 2. Endangered species
    ISBN 978-0-7660-3452-5 lib bdg; 0-7660-3452-6 lib bdg
                      LC 2008-48689

This describes a tiger's life, how they hunt, the purpose of its stripes, caring for young, competing with people for space, and that these animals are very close to extinction

"The illustrations, mostly color photographs, represent a wonderful selection of the animals and their habitats. Reluctant readers may be enticed by this . . . simply because of the great images. This . . . would make a substantial supplement to the science curriculum when studying endangered animals." Libr Media Connect

Includes glossary and bibliographical references

Gamble, Cyndi

Leopards; natural history & conservation. text by Cyndi Gamble; photography by Rodney Griffiths.

Voyageur Press 2004 48p il map (World life library) pa $12.95

Grades: 7 8 9 10 **599.75**

1. Leopards

ISBN 0-89658-656-1

LC 2004-14316

"The text offers a comprehensive look at these endangered animals and raises awareness of various efforts to preserve their habitats and to save them from extinction. Excellent-quality photographs appear throughout. . . . An attractive and informative addition." SLJ

Inlcudes bibliographical references

Gish, Melissa

Jaguars. Creative Education 2011 46p il map (Living wild) lib bdg $23.95

Grades: 5 6 7 **599.75**

1. Jaguars

ISBN 978-1-60818-079-0; 1-60818-079-4

LC 2010028315

A look at jaguars, including their habitats, physical characteristics such as their powerful jaws, behaviors, relationships with humans, and threatened status in the world today.

This offers "an array of interesting facts. Photography is large and beautiful–a real draw." SLJ

Includes glossary and bibliographical references

Leopards. Creative Education 2010 46p il (Living wild) lib bdg $34.25; pa $8.99

Grades: 5 6 7 8 **599.75**

1. Leopards

ISBN 978-1-58341-972-4 lib bdg; 1-58341-972-1 lib bdg; 978-0-89812-555-9 pa; 0-89812-555-3 pa

LC 2010017377

"A look at leopards, including their habitats, physical characteristics such as their spotted fur, behaviors, relationships with humans, and threatened status in the world today." Publisher's note

Hamilton, Sue L.

Ambushed by a cougar; [by] Sue Hamilton. ABDO Pub. Co. 2010 32p il (Close encounters of the wild kind) lib bdg $27.07

Grades: 4 5 6 7 **599.75**

1. Pumas 2. Animal attacks

ISBN 978-1-60453-928-8 lib bdg; 1-60453-928-3 lib bdg

LC 2009-45521

Readers learn of actual human-cougar encounters, information about cougars, survival strategies, and attack statistics.

"Students will be drawn to the realistic full-color photographs, the realistic diagrams of the creatures' bodies, the real-life stories told by victims, and the interesting, attractive formatting that includes text, diagrams, photographs, and graphics on each page. . . . [This is] exciting and attractive in a 'gross' sort of way and will appeal particularly to boys for both leisure reading and research." Libr Media Connect

Includes glossary

Lockwood, Sophie

Lions; by Sophie Lockwood. Child's World 2008 40p il map (World of mammals) lib bdg $29.93

Grades: 4 5 6 **599.75**

1. Lions

ISBN 978-1-59296-933-3 lib bdg; 1-59296-933-X lib bdg

LC 2007013567

This book about lions presents "all the basics for reports: an introduction to the creatures' challenges, the role humans play, physical traits and behaviors, habitats, and struggles for survival. Every part of their life [cycle], including sexual maturity, birth, and family relationships, is explained. . . . Clear bright photographs pump up the content. . . . The detail that Lockwood imparts is startlingly high. The [text is] written in a dynamic and engaging style." SLJ

Includes glossary and bibliographical references

Montgomery, Sy

★ **Chasing** cheetahs; the race to save Africa's fastest cats. written by Sy Montgomery ; photographs by Nic Bishop. Houghton Mifflin Harcourt 2014 80 p. illustrations $18.99

Grades: 5 6 7 8 **599.75**

1. Cheetahs 2. Cheetah -- Africa 3. Cheetah Conservation Fund

ISBN 0547815492; 9780547815497

LC 2013017611

Scientists in the field

This book, by Sy Montgomery, focuses on cheetahs. "At the Cheetah Conservation Fund's (CCF) African headquarters in Namibia, Laurie Marker and her team save these . . . creatures from extinction. Since the organization's start in 1990, they've rescued more than 900 cheetahs. . . . But this arduous challenge continues. For most African livestock farmers, cheetahs are the last thing they want to see on their properties. In the 1980s, as many as 19 cheetahs per farmer died each year." (Publisher's note)

"Montgomery introduces readers to Laurie Marker and her team at the Cheetah Conservation Fund's site in Namibia. Scientific information about the cheetahs and profiles of the people who study them are interspersed with in-the-moment, journal-style accounts of activities at the site. Striking photographs capture the dedication of the scientists and the awesome power of the cheetahs." Horn Book

Includes bibliographical references and index.

★ **Saving** the ghost of the mountain; an expedition among snow leopards in Mongolia. text by Sy Montgomery; photographs by Nic Bishop. Houghton Mifflin Books for Children 2009 48p il map (Scientists in the field) $18

Grades: 5 6 7 8 **599.75**

1. Biologists 2. Snow leopard 3. Conservationists 4. Mongolia

ISBN 978-0-618-91645-0; 0-618-91645-8

LC 2008-36762

Author Sy Montgomery and photographer Nic Bishop accompany conservationist Tom McCarthy and his team as they travel to Mongolia's Altai Mountains to gather data about snow leopard populations in an attempt to save this endangered species

"Montgomery's enthusiasm translates well to the page and will have readers cheering for the entourage as they attempt to spot a snow leopard. This slender book abounds with information. Bishop's trademark stunning photography fills out the book with breathtaking views of the extreme environs of Central Asia and warm portraits of the charming people who live there." SLJ

Stefoff, Rebecca

★ **Lions.** Marshall Cavendish Benchmark 2006 112p il map (Animalways) lib bdg $31.36

Grades: 6 7 8 9   **599.75**

1. Lions

ISBN 0-7614-1746-X

LC 2004-11466

This describes the place of lions in human history and culture, their evolution, anatomy, habits, life cycle and possible future.

Includes glossary and bibliographical references

599.756   Tiger

Montgomery, Sy

★ The **man** -eating tigers of Sundarbans; with photographs by Eleanor Briggs. Houghton Mifflin 2001 57p il map hardcover o.p. pa $6.95

Grades: 4 5 6 7   **599.756**

1. Tigers

ISBN 0-618-07704-9; 0-618-49490-1 pa

LC 00-32031

"To draw readers into this scientific puzzle, Montgomery integrates science, storytelling, anthropology, and adventure in a unique treatment, illustrated with excellent color photos and diagrams." Horn Book Guide

Includes bibliographical references

599.77   Dog family

Halls, Kelly Milner

Wild dogs; past and present. Darby Creek Pub. 2005 64p il (World of animals) $18.95

Grades: 5 6 7 8   **599.77**

1. Wild dogs

ISBN 1-58196-027-1

This "book explains how fossils and DNA are used to show the evolutionary lines from prehistoric canids to the dogs we live with today. . . . The author presents a wealth of detail through the accessible text; the informative captions, charts, sidebars; and the simple but clear maps." SLJ

Includes bibliographical references

Imbriaco, Alison

The **red** wolf; help save this endangered species! MyReportLinks.com Books 2008 128p $33.27

Grades: 4 5 6 7   **599.77**

1. Wolves 2. Endangered species

ISBN 978-1-59845-038-5; 1-59845-038-7

LC 2006020825

This describes the red wolf "and the reasons for its decline, along with the steps being taken to reverse possible extinction. . . . The [book is a] strong research [tool] on [its] own, but the addition of vetted, linked Internet sites that are recommended throughout the text makes [it] even more valuable." Voice Youth Advocates

Includes glossary and bibliographical references

Lockwood, Sophie

Foxes. Child's World 2008 40p il map (World of mammals) lib bdg $29.93

Grades: 4 5 6   **599.77**

1. Foxes

ISBN 978-1-59296-932-6; 1-59296-932-1

LC 2007-21943

Explores the physical and behavioral characteristics of foxes.

Includes glossary and bibliographical references

McAllister, Ian

The **sea** wolves; living wild in the Great Bear Rainforest. written by Ian McAllister and Nicholas Read; photographs by Ian McAllister. Orca Book Publishers 2010 121p il $19.95

Grades: 5 6 7 8   **599.77**

1. Wolves 2. Rain forest ecology

ISBN 978-1-55469-206-4; 1-55469-206-7

The coastal wolf, a genetically distinct strain that swims and fishes, inhabits the Great Bear Rainforest on British Columbia's rugged west coast.

"This extensive, informative text is illustrated with remarkable photographs taken by McAllister, who has lived in and studied the area for years. They show the lush, old-growth forest and rocky shoreline and a variety of animals that share this habitat, but the wolves are the stars: at rest, at play, on the prowl and catching fish. . . . Fascinating and useful." Kirkus

599.78   Bears

Bortolotti, Dan

Panda rescue; changing the future for endangered wildlife. Firefly 2003 64p il map lib bdg $19.95; pa $9.95

Grades: 4 5 6 7   **599.78**

1. Giant panda 2. Wildlife conservation

ISBN 1-55297-598-3 lib bdg; 1-55297-557-6 pa

This describes the panda's "natural habitat, habits, physiology, and behavior in captivity. [It also includes] a time line of conservation efforts, profiles of conservationists in the field, and forecasts of the animals' future. Throughout, the author makes clear the factors that can threaten animal populations, and discusses human attitudes toward the animals throughout history. . . . Written in accessible, lively language and nicely illustrated with exciting color photos, [this] will be useful for reports and browsing." Booklist

Firestone, Mary

Top 50 reasons to care about giant pandas; animals in peril. Enslow Publishers 2010 103p il (Top

50 reasons to care about endangered animals) lib bdg $31.93

Grades: 4 5 6 7 **599.78**

1. Giant panda 2. Endangered species
ISBN 978-0-7660-3451-8 lib bdg; 0-7660-3451-8 lib bdg

LC 2008-48953

This describes the giant panda's life cycle, habitat, young, diet, living in the wild and in captivity, and why it is endangered

"The illustrations, mostly color photographs, represent a wonderful selection of the animals and their habitats. Reluctant readers may be enticed by this . . . simply because of the great images. This . . . would make a substantial supplement to the science curriculum when studying endangered animals." Libr Media Connect

Includes glossary and bibliographical references

Gish, Melissa

Brown bears; Melissa Gish. Creative Education 2014 46 p. (Living wild) (hardcover : alk. paper) $37.10

Grades: 5 6 7 8 **599.78**

1. Brown bear
ISBN 1608184153; 9781608184156

LC 2013031808

In this book, by Melissa Gish, "[v]ivid photographs help take readers on a virtual field study to observe the life cycle and behaviors of [brown bears]. . . . [It] also looks at past and present scientific research and includes a unique storytelling element in the form of an animal tale drawn from mythology or folklore." (Publisher's note)

"Thorough in scope and elegant in design, these stellar titles will attract the browser and the report writer alike." SLJ

Includes bibliographical references and index

Pandas. Creative Education 2011 48p il (Living wild) lib bdg $23.95; pa $8.95

Grades: 5 6 7 8 **599.78**

1. Giant panda
ISBN 978-1-60818-082-0 lib bdg; 1-60818-082-4 lib bdg; 978-1-60818-082-0 pa; 1-60818-082-4 pa

LC 2010028311

A look at pandas, including their habitats, physical characteristics such as their black-and-white fur, behaviors, relationships with humans, and threatened status in the world today.

Includes glossary and bibliographical references

Hamilton, Sue L.

Mauled by a bear; [by] Sue Hamilton. ABDO Pub. Co. 2010 32p il (Close encounters of the wild kind) lib bdg $27.07

Grades: 4 5 6 7 **599.78**

1. Bears 2. Animal attacks
ISBN 978-1-60453-932-5 lib bdg; 1-60453-932-1 lib bdg

LC 2009-35078

Readers learn of actual human-bear encounters, information about bears, survival strategies, and attack statistics.

"Students will be drawn to the realistic full-color photographs, the realistic diagrams of the creatures' bodies, the real-life stories told by victims, and the interesting, attractive formatting that includes text, diagrams, photographs, and graphics on each page. . . . [This is] exciting and attractive in a 'gross' sort of way and will appeal particularly to boys for both leisure reading and research." Libr Media Connect

Includes glossary

Hunt, Joni Phelps

A **band** of bears; the rambling life of a lovable loner. London Town Press 2007 48p il (Jean-Michel Cousteau presents) pa $8.95

Grades: 5 6 7 8 **599.78**

1. Bears
ISBN 978-0-9766134-5-9; 0-9766134-5-X

Offers an in-depth look at the survival and social skills of these creatures as they live, play, and raise their families in their natural habitats, featuring grizzlies, black bears, and polar bears.

This "book covers the characteristics and unique traits of . . . [bears] and includes colorful, awe-inspiring photos and immediate first-person narratives." SLJ

Includes bibliographical references

Lockwood, Sophie

Polar Bears. Child's World 2005 40p il (World of mammals) lib bdg $29.93

Grades: 4 5 6 **599.78**

1. Polar bear
ISBN 1-59296-501-6

"The first chapter of Polar Bears discusses the bond between the animal and the Inuit people, who have depended on hunting the bears for survival. Then the discussion turns to the bears themselves: their physical features, behaviors, and relatives as well as the threats to their survival." Booklist

Includes glossary and bibliographical references

McAllister, Ian

★ **Salmon** bears; giants of the Great Bear Rainforest. [by] Ian McAllister & Nicholas Read; photographs by Ian McAllister. Orca Book Publishers 2010 89p il map pa $18.95

Grades: 5 6 7 8 **599.78**

1. Bears 2. Salmon 3. Rain forest ecology
ISBN 978-1-55469-205-7 pa; 1-55469-205-9 pa

"Read's conversational text and McAllister's excellent photos provide a perfect framework for this evocative look at the big bears of the Great Bear Rainforest of British Columbia, and an intriguing investigation of its ecological pattern of dependency. The authors present a round of seasons from one winter to the next, touching upon such topics as the effects of fish farms on wild salmon populations, what happens during a salmon run, and what the future may hold for the fish, the bears, and the Great Bear Rainforest itself. . . . Superbly readable, informative, and attractive." SLJ

Includes bibliographical references

Montgomery, Sy

★ **Search** for the golden moon bear; science and adventure in the Asian tropics. Houghton Mifflin 2004 80p il $17

Grades: 5 6 7 8   **599.78**
1. Bears
ISBN 0-618-35650-9
LC 2004-5236

The author reports on an expedition into Laos and Thailand in search of a rare species of bear

"The exciting narrative is complemented by an array of full-color photos. . . . This attractive and informative offering is an intelligent reportage of science as it happens." SLJ

Includes bibliographical references

Ovsyanikov, Nikita
    Polar bears. Voyageur Press 1998 72p il maps (World life library) pa $17.95
Grades: 7 8 9 10   **599.78**
1. Polar bear
ISBN 0-89658-358-9; 978-0-89658-358-0
LC 98-3431

This describes the polar bear's habits, behavior, and biology

"Approachable. . . . Written by an expert on the species. . . . Well illustrated with many excellent photos." Booklist

Includes bibliographical references

Thomas, Keltie
    Bear rescue; changing the future for endangered wildlife. Firefly Books 2006 64p il (Firefly animal rescue series) $19.95
Grades: 5 6 7 8   **599.78**
1. Bears 2. Endangered species 3. Wildlife conservation
ISBN 1-55297-922-9

Provides details and facts about bears from around the world, their endangerment and a range of conservation programs to save them, including profiles of individual conservationsists and bear species

Ward, Paul
    ★ **Bears** of the world; [by] Paul Ward & Suzanne Kynaston. Facts on File 2002 191p il map $35
Grades: 6 7 8 9   **599.78**
1. Bears
ISBN 0-8160-5208-5
LC 2002034739

A revised edition of Wild bears of the world, published 1995

This "explains why bears have meant so much to humans, from early in evolutionary history to the present. It looks at how bears were depicted in ancient mythology and religion. . . . The primary focus is on introducing the living species; charting their evolutionary history; and showing how they live, what they eat, how they behave, and how they cope with their habitats." Publisher's note

Includes bibliographical references

599.8   Primates

Barker, David
    Top 50 reasons to care about great apes; animals in peril. Enslow Publishers 2010 103p il (Top 50

reasons to care about endangered animals) lib bdg $31.93
Grades: 4 5 6 7   **599.8**
1. Apes 2. Endangered species
ISBN 978-0-7660-3456-3 lib bdg; 0-7660-3456-9 lib bdg
LC 2008048691

This describes the great apes—their life cycle, habitats, young, and why these animals are endangered

"The illustrations, mostly color photographs, represent a wonderful selection of the animals and their habitats. Reluctant readers may be enticed by this . . . simply because of the great images." Libr Media Connect

Includes glossary and bibliographical references

Bow, Patricia
    Chimpanzee rescue; changing the future for endangered wildlife. Firefly Books 2004 64p il (Firefly animal rescue series) $19.95; pa $9.95
Grades: 5 6 7 8   **599.8**
1. Chimpanzees 2. Wildlife conservation
ISBN 1-55297-909-1; 1-55297-908-3 pa

This introduces chimpanzees, how and why they are in danger, and explains what efforts are being made to protect them.

This is "well-written. . . . Stunning, full-color photographs bring [this] species to life and depict a number of individuals in the field and laboratory working to save these animals." SLJ

Feinstein, Stephen
    The **chimpanzee**; help save this endangered species! [by] Stephen Feinstein. MyReportLinks.com Books 2007 128p il (Saving endangered species) $33.27
Grades: 5 6 7 8   **599.8**
1. Chimpanzees 2. Endangered species
ISBN 978-1-59845-039-2; 1-59845-039-5
LC 2006028079

"Focuses on the study of the primates, demonstrating how similar they are to humans and why they should be preserved. . . . Provide[s] an excellent tool for teaching students to do research using both books and legitimate online sources." Voice Youth Advocates

Includes glossary and bibliographical references

Gish, Melissa
    Gorillas. Creative Education 2010 46p il (Living wild) $23.95; pa $9.95
Grades: 5 6 7 8   **599.8**
1. Gorillas
ISBN 978-1-58341-969-4; 1-58341-969-1; 978-0-89812-552-8 pa; 0-89812-552-9 pa
LC 2010017374

This "book lucidly discusses conservation and the animals' often tenuous relationship with humans. The layout is uniformly simple but effective, constructed with a nice balance of main text for the report writers, smaller chunks of esoterica for browsers, and . . . killer photos." Booklist

Goodall, Jane

★ The **chimpanzees** I love; saving their world and ours. Scholastic Press 2001 80p il map $17.95

Grades: 4 5 6 7   **599.8**

1. Chimpanzees

ISBN 0-439-21310-X

LC 00-47080

"Striking an admirable balance between scientific reporting and deep affection, Goodall's . . . impassioned introduction to the creatures to whom she's dedicated her life's work may well ignite in readers a similar appreciation." Publ Wkly

Includes bibliographical references

Lockwood, Sophie

Baboons. Child's World 2006 40p il map (World of mammals) lib bdg $29.93

Grades: 4 5 6   **599.8**

1. Baboons

ISBN 978-1-59296-497-0; 1-59296-497-4

LC 2005-533

Explores the physical and behavioral characteristics of baboons, examines their habitat and natural history, and discusses the role of humans in ensuring the continued survival of the species.

"Lockwood's dynamic and engaging style and intriguing insight . . . [make the] book shine. . . . Will give children solid information for reports." SLJ

Includes glossary and bibliographical references

Ottaviani, Jim

Primates; The Fearless Science of Jane Goodall, Dian Fossey, and Biruté Galdikas. Jim Ottaviani ; illustrated by Maris Wicks. First edition First Second 2013 133 p. chiefly color illustrations (hardcover) $19.99

Grades: 5 6 7 8 9 10   **599.8**

1. Scientists -- Biography

ISBN 1596438657; 9781596438651

LC 2013427678

This nonfiction graphic novel, by Jim Ottaviani, illustrated by Maris Wicks, presents an "account of the three greatest primatologists of the last century: Jane Goodall, Dian Fossey, and Biruté Galdikas. These three ground-breaking researchers were all students of the great Louis Leakey, and each made profound contributions to primatology--and to our own understanding of ourselves." (Publisher's note)

"More story than study, the book provides an accessible introduction to Goodall's, Fossey's and Galdikas' lives and work." Kirkus

Includes bibliographical references, page 138

Russon, Anne E.

Orangutans : wizards of the rainforest; rev ed.; Firefly Books 2004 240p il map pa $24.95

Grades: 8 9 10 11 12   **599.8**

1. Orangutan

ISBN 1-55297-998-9

LC 2005-357221

First published 1999 in the United Kingdom

A firsthand account of the lives of orangutans including a scientific history of orangutans, a description of orangutans and their natural habitat, their behavior patterns, rehabilitation operations, the politics of orangutan rescue work, and a look at orangutans released back into the forest.

Includes bibliographical references

Sobol, Richard

Breakfast in the rainforest; a visit with mountain gorillas. with an afterword by Leonardo DiCaprio. Candlewick 2008 40p il map $18.99

Grades: 3 4 5 6   **599.8**

1. Gorillas 2. Rain forest ecology 3. Uganda

ISBN 978-0-7636-2281-7; 0-7636-2281-8

"Wildlife photographer Sobol recounts his travels to Uganda to observe gorillas living in the Virunga Mountains. In his personable text, he also touches on the creatures' habits, diet, and threats. Closeup photographs of the gorillas in addition to many pictures of the surrounding countryside and villagers help round out an understanding of the endangered animals' homeland." Horn Book Guide

Stefoff, Rebecca

★ The **primate** order. Benchmark Books 2005 92p il (Family trees) lib bdg $29.93

Grades: 6 7 8 9   **599.8**

1. Primates

ISBN 0-7614-1816-4

LC 2004-21404

This examines physical traits, adaptations, diets, habitats, and life cycles of primates.

"Fact-filled, yet suprisingly readable. . . . [This] title contains a wide variety of excellent-quality, full-color photographs; interesting sidebars; and diagrams." SLJ

Zabludoff, Marc

Monkeys; by Marc Zabludoff. Marshall Cavendish Benchmark 2007 108p il (Animalways) lib bdg $34.21

Grades: 6 7 8 9   **599.8**

1. Monkeys

ISBN 978-0-7614-2535-9

LC 2007013172

This describes the place of monkeys in the animal kingdom, their evolution, anatomy, life cycle, behavior, diversity, and relationship to humans.

This "will pique readers' curiosity, and the content will keep them hooked. Vivid color photographs and illustrations and a clear font make [this work] stand out." SLJ

Includes glossary and bibliographical references

599.9 Humans

Deem, James M.

Faces from the past; forgotten people of North America. by James M. Deem. Houghton Mifflin Harcourt 2012 154 p. $18.99

Grades: 6 7 8 9 10   **599.9**

1. Skeleton 2. Human body 3. Physical anthropology 4. North America -- Population 5. Radiocarbon dating

-- North America 6. Forensic anthropology -- North America 7. Human remains (Archaeology) -- North America 8. Facial reconstruction (Anthropology) -- North America

ISBN 0547370245; 9780547370248

LC 2012006819

This book by James M. Deem looks at "nine cases in which" facial "reconstructions help interpret a specific moment in American history. . . . This title brings to life such diverse figures as paleoamerican Spirit Cave Man; 'Pearl,' a slave from eighteenth-century upstate New York; a buffalo soldier whose corpse was reassembled and given an honorable burial; [and] nine persons among the 1,271 bodies found in pauper's graves in an almshouse cemetery." (Bulletin of the Center for Children's Books)

Szpirglas, Jeff

You just can't help it! your guide to the wild and wacky world of human behavior. Josh Holinaty, illustrator. Owlkids Books 2011 64p il $22.95; pa $10.95

Grades: 4 5 6 7   **599.9**

1. Human behavior 2. Human biology
ISBN 1-926818-07-5; 1-926818-08-3 pa; 978-1-926818-07-8; 978-1-926818-08-5 pa

"How many times have you been frightened and felt the hairs on the back of your neck stand up? Or been unable to hold back a laugh? Or flinched when an object whizzed by, too close for comfort? . . . [This] book provides a cultural, historical, and sociobiological perspective on human behavior. . . . [It is an] exploration of the basic human biology that determines our reactions, social interactions, and the ways we communicate with one another." (Publisher's note) Index. "Ages nine to twelve." (Quill Quire)

This is a "collection of curious facts and intriguing studies about human behavior. With a breezy text supported by a lively design, the author . . . presents science in a way certain to attract middle-grade and middle-school readers. Chapters on the senses, emotions, communication, and interactions with other human beings cover a variety of topics. . . . The digital art includes bits of photographs, line drawings, the use of color and shapes to help organize the print and plenty of symbols." Kirkus

Includes index

599.909   Physical anthropologists

Henderson, Harry, 1951-

The **Leakey** family; unearthing human ancestors. Harry Henderson. Chelsea House 2011 127 p. (Trailblazers in science and technology) (library) $35

Grades: 7 8 9 10 11 12   **599.909**

1. Olduvai Gorge (Tanzania) -- Antiquities 2. Fossil hominids -- Tanzania -- Olduvai Gorge 3. Excavations (Archaeology) -- Tanzania -- Olduvai Gorge 4. Paleoanthropolgists -- Tanzania -- Olduvai Gorge -- Biography 5. Physical anthropologists -- Tanzania -- Olduvai Gorge -- Biography
ISBN 160413674X; 9781604136746

LC 2011001972

This book, by Harry Henderson, profiles the Leakey family as part of the "Trailblazers in Science and Technology" series. "In the 20th century, the family name . . . became synonymous with paleoanthropology. . . . Louis S.B. Leakey explored East Africa and what is now Tanzania, finding skulls of human ancestors to fill in the evolutionary roadmap to modern man. Leakey worked alongside his wife, Mary, herself an experienced archaeologist and anthropologist." (Publisher's note)

Includes bibliographical references and index

599.93   Genetics, sex and age characteristics, evolution

Anderson, Dale

How do we know the nature of human origins. Rosen Pub. Group 2005 112p il (Great scientific questions and the scientists who answered them) lib bdg $31.95

Grades: 7 8 9 10   **599.93**

1. Evolution 2. Human origins 3. Fossil hominids
ISBN 978-1-4042-0077-7; 1-4042-0077-0

LC 2003-27875

Examines what is known about humankind's origins, and the scientists who have studied the topic

Anderson "enlivens the text by giving a little background information on the scientists involved. His presentation of controversies is quite well balanced [and] . . . the black-and-white photographs and charts are well chosen and well keyed to the text." SLJ

Includes bibliographical references

Goldenberg, Linda

★ **Little** people and a lost world; an anthropological mystery. Twenty-First Century Books 2007 112p il (Discovery!) lib bdg $31.93

Grades: 5 6 7 8   **599.93**

1. Pygmies 2. Fossil hominids 3. Excavations (Archeology) -- Indonesia
ISBN 978-0-8225-5983-2 lib bdg; 0-8225-5983-8 lib bdg

LC 2005-33431

This is an account of the 2003 discovery of small fossil hominids on Flores Island, Indonesia

"This will add important insights to the study of early humans as well as, more broadly, how science and politics interact." Booklist

Includes bibliographical references

Holmes, Thom

Early humans; the Pleistocene & Holocene epochs. Chelsea House 2009 151p il map (The prehistoric Earth) lib bdg $35

Grades: 7 8 9 10   **599.93**

1. Evolution 2. Human origins 3. Fossil hominids
ISBN 978-0-8160-5966-9; 0-8160-5966-7

LC 2008-38936

"The book consists of two sections. The first section describes the early hominins in Chapter 1 and the archaic species of Homo in Chapter 2. The second section reviews the origins and evolution of more modern Homo species in Chapters 3 and 4. The concluding chapter briefly discusses some contemporary topics, including the meaning of human races, the evolution of skin color, the human role in the evolution and extinction of other species, and the impact of the evolution of diseases. . . . [This] is an outstanding contribution to teaching junior high and high school students about evolution in general and human evolution in particular." Sci Books Films

Includes glossary and bibliographical references

La Pierre, Yvette

Neandertals; a prehistoric puzzle. Twenty-First Century Books 2008 112p il (Discovery!) lib bdg $30.60

Grades: 6 7 8 9   **599.93**
  1. Neanderthals 2. Fossil hominids 3. Prehistoric peoples
  ISBN 978-0-8225-7524-5; 0-8225-7524-8
                                            LC 2007-22066

When the first Neanderthal skeleton was discovered nearly 150 years ago, scientists presented the race as barely developed brutes. But recent findings indicate that Neanderthals made complex tools, organized group hunts, cared for their sick and injured, and buried their dead.

"Several theories about these prehistoric humans are discussed, including evolution, creationism, linear evolution, and natural selection. This balanced presentation is a valuable aspect of this well–formatted and visually appealing book." Voice Youth Advocates

Includes glossary and bibliographical references

Robertshaw, Peter

  ★ The **early** human world; by Peter Robertshaw and Jill Rubalcaba. Oxford University Press 2005 173p il map (World in ancient times) lib bdg $32.95
Grades: 7 8 9 10   **599.93**
  1. Human origins 2. Fossil hominids 3. Prehistoric peoples
  ISBN 0-19-516157-2
                                            LC 2004-9732

The author presents "information on human evolution as well as on early humanity in the New World. The text is matched with a great deal of supporting matter including time lines, maps, dramatis personae, high-quality photos, and artists' renderings." SLJ

Includes bibliographical references

Sloan, Christopher

The **human** story; our evolution from prehistoric ancestors to today. foreword by Meave Leakey and Louise Leakey; photographs by Kenneth L. Garrett; art by Kennis and Kennis. National Geographic Society 2004 80p il $21.95
Grades: 7 8 9 10   **599.93**
  1. Evolution 2. Human origins
  ISBN 0-7922-6325-1
                                            LC 2003-13978

Explores the origins of humans, including how such developments as Linnaeus' classification system and recent understanding of the human genome have improved scientists' comprehension of evolution

"What many . . . readers will find most exciting is how today's cutting-edge technology helps us learn about the prehistoric connections all humans share. Great for classroom discussion." Booklist

Includes glossary and bibliographical references

Stefoff, Rebecca

  ★ **First** humans. Marshall Cavendish Benchmark 2009 112p il map (Humans: an evolutionary history) lib bdg $37.07
Grades: 7 8 9 10   **599.93**
  1. Human origins 2. Fossil hominids
  ISBN 978-0-7614-4184-7; 0-7614-4184-0
                                            LC 2008-34330

"Stefoff provides an enlightening and entertaining history of the evolution of Homo sapiens, their ancestors, and cousins, from primitive origins to today. The clear, insightful [text is] accented by intriguing sidebars and colorful photos, maps, and graphs." SLJ

Includes glossary and bibliographical references

  ★ **Ice** age Neanderthals. Marshall Cavendish Benchmark 2009 112p il map (Humans: an evolutionary history) lib bdg $37.07
Grades: 7 8 9 10   **599.93**
  1. Neanderthals 2. Human origins 3. Fossil hominids
  ISBN 978-0-7614-4186-1; 0-7614-4186-7
                                            LC 2008-54830

"Stefoff provides an enlightening and entertaining history of the evolution of Homo sapiens, their ancestors, and cousins, from primitive origins to today. The clear, insightful [text is] accented by intriguing sidebars and colorful photos, maps, and graphs." SLJ

Includes glossary and bibliographical references

  ★ **Modern** humans. Marshall Cavendish Benchmark 2009 112p il map (Humans: an evolutionary history) lib bdg $37.07
Grades: 7 8 9 10   **599.93**
  1. Genetics 2. Evolution 3. Human origins 4. Fossil hominids
  ISBN 978-0-7614-4187-8; 0-7614-4187-5
                                            LC 2009-12364

"Stefoff provides an enlightening and entertaining history of the evolution of Homo sapiens, their ancestors, and cousins, from primitive origins to today. The clear, insightful [text is] accented by intriguing sidebars and colorful photos, maps, and graphs." SLJ

Includes glossary and bibliographical references

Tattersall, Ian

  ★ **Bones,** brains and DNA; the human genome and human evolution. by Ian Tattersall & Rob DeSalle; illustrated by Patricia J. Wynne. Bunker Hill Pub., Inc. 2007 47p il $16.95
Grades: 5 6 7 8   **599.93**
  1. Genetics 2. Evolution 3. Human origins
  ISBN 978-1-59373-056-7; 1-59373-056-X
                                            LC 2006931578

The "text follows the trail of human evolution, basing its factual content on current data exhibited in the New Hall of Human Origins in New York City's American Museum of Natural History. Using the skills of anthropologists, archaeologists, and paleontologists, the authors track clues laid down in the fossil record, and, more importantly, in our DNA. . . . The very unsimple concepts are presented clearly, in an attractive format, with splashings of small photos, colorful artwork, diagrams, and maps to attract the eye and elucidate the text." SLJ

Thimmesh, Catherine
★ **Lucy** long ago; uncovering the mystery of where we came from. Houghton Mifflin Harcourt 2009 63p il $18
Grades: 4 5 6 7   **599.93**
1. Human origins 2. Fossil hominids
ISBN 978-0-547-05199-4; 0-547-05199-9
LC 2008-36761

"The 1974 discovery of the fossilized partial skeleton of a small-brained primate who apparently walked upright 3.2 million years ago in what is now Ethiopia significantly changed accepted theories about human origins. Step by step, Thimmesh presents the questions the newly discovered bones raised and how they were answered. . . . Extensive research, clear organization and writing, appropriate pacing for new ideas and intriguing graphics all contribute to this exceptionally accessible introduction to the mystery of human origins." Kirkus

600   TECHNOLOGY

600   Technology (Applied sciences)

Macaulay, David
★ The **new** way things work; [by] David Macaulay with Neil Ardley. Houghton Mifflin 1998 400p il $35
Grades: 4 5 6 7 8 9 10 11 12 Adult   **600**
1. Machinery 2. Inventions 3. Technology
ISBN 0-395-93847-3
LC 98-14224

First published 1988 with title: The way things work
Arranged in five sections this volume provides information on "the workings of hundreds of machines and devices—holograms, helicopters, airplanes, mobile phones, compact disks, hard disks, bits and bytes, cash machines. . . . Explanations [are also given] of the scientific principles behind each machine—how gears make work easier, why jumbo jets are able to fly, how computers actually compute." Publisher's note

Piddock, Charles
Future tech; from personal robots to motorized monocycles. by Charles Piddock; Dr. James Lee, consultant. National Geographic 2009 64p il (National Geographic investigates) $17.95
Grades: 5 6 7 8   **600**
1. Technology 2. Forecasting
ISBN 978-1-4263-0468-2; 1-4263-0468-4

"This effort takes an appreciative, uncritical look at robots, transportation, bionics, nanotechnology and future life in general. It concludes with ten specific predictions for 2025. . . . Interesting color photographs appear on almost every page and entertaining text boxes with additional related information add appeal." Kirkus

Includes glossary and bibliographical references

Solway, Andrew
Inventions and investigations. Raintree 2008 48p il (Sci-hi: physical science) lib bdg $22; pa $8.99
Grades: 5 6 7 8   **600**
1. Inventors 2. Inventions
ISBN 978-1-4109-3379-9 lib bdg; 1-4109-3379-2 lib bdg; 978-1-4109-3384-3 pa; 1-4109-3384-9 pa
LC 2009-3508

This explores the scientific processes used by inventors throughout history.

A "compelling read for both browsers and science buffs. . . . Information is clearly presented and flows smoothly. . . . A treasure trove of information." SLJ

Includes glossary and bibliographical references

Woodford, Chris
★ **Cool** Stuff 2.0 and how it works; written by Chris Woodford and Jon Woodcock. DK Pub. 2007 256p il $24.99
Grades: 5 6 7 8 9 10   **600**
1. Inventions 2. Technology
ISBN 978-0-7566-3207-6; 0-7566-3207-2
LC 2007-299442

"More than 100 entries present a wide variety of topics with high child appeal, from robot cars to high-tech toilets. . . . Full but uncluttered layouts mix photos, text boxes, diagrams, and captions to highlight key elements. . . . Readers should have an easy time understanding the basics of what each item does, how it is used, and how it works. Along with up-to-date scientific information on high-interest topics, this title has very strong browsing appeal and great booktalk potential." SLJ

608   Patents

Lee, Dora
Biomimicry; Inventions inspired by nature. written by Dora Lee ; illustrated by Margot Thompson. Kids Can Press 2011 40 p. $18.95
Grades: 4 5 6   **608**
1. Inventions 2. Nature study 3. Human ecology 4. Technological innovations
ISBN 9781554534678

This book explores "modern innovations [that] have sprung from observation and imitation of the natural world. In topically organized double-page spreads, [Dora] Lee describes shapes and structures, materials and designs, as well as systems for exploration, communication, rescue and delivery. . . . Three or four specific examples, each with illustrative vignettes, follow or sometimes precede the general explanation. These topics range widely and include medical marvels, new power sources, [and] biological computers and robots. . . . [The book] includes a strong ecological message: The most important natural model is the sustainable ecosystem. Through biomimicry, humans can learn to live in balance on the Earth as well." (Kirkus)

609 Technology -- History, geographic treatment, biography

Bender, Lionel

Invention; written by Lionel Bender. rev ed; DK Pub. 2005 72p il (DK eyewitness books) $15.99; lib bdg $19.99

Grades: 4 5 6 7   **609**

1. Inventions

ISBN 0-7566-1076-1; 0-7566-1075-3 lib bdg

First published 1991 by Knopf

Photographs and text explore such inventions as the wheel, gears, levers, clocks, telephones, and rocket engines.

Cole, D. J.

Encyclopedia of modern everyday inventions; [by] David J. Cole, Eve Browning, and Fred E.H. Schroeder. Greenwood Press 2003 285p il $57.95

Grades: 7 8 9 10 11 12 Adult   **609**

1. Reference books 2. Inventions -- History

ISBN 0-313-31345-8

LC 2002-69620

"The analysis of each invention is thorough and lively. . . . This book . . . would make an excellent addition to any school or public library needing books on technology and inventions in the modern world." Voice Youth Advocates

Includes bibliographical references

Crowther, Robert

Robert Crowther's pop-up house of inventions; hundreds of fabulous facts about your home. Candlewick Press 2009 un il $17.99

Grades: 4 5 6 7   **609**

1. Inventions 2. Pop-up books

ISBN 978-0-7636-4253-2; 0-7636-4253-3

First published 2000 with title: Robert Crowther's amazing pop-up house of inventions

"As a beautifully engineered pop-up book, it is complex, highly visual, and inviting. . . . It is also durably manufactured. . . . The book is essentially an encyclopedic assortment of facts and anecdotes about the earliest forms of household appliances, furnishings, novelties, . . . games, clothing, and consumables such as soap, soda and candles. The author integrates history and science in a chatty, colorful, and humorous way that quickly draws readers into his subject." Sci Books Films

Diagram Group

Historical inventions on file; [by] the Diagram Group. Facts on File 1994 various paging il looseleaf $185

Grades: 6 7 8 9 10   **609**

1. Inventions -- History

ISBN 0-8160-2911-3

LC 94-7098

This volume uses an "On File format (i.e., three-ring binder with heavy bond paper suitable for reproduction), with 65 experiments re-creating {historical} . . . . inventions. The purpose of these re-creations is to assist students in understanding important concepts and innovations in science. . . . The beginning pages on safety procedures are followed by 11 sections. Section 1 is a 15-page chronology of key inventions from 9,000 B.C. to 1991. . . . Sections 2 through 9 cover experiments in various subject fields (e.g., 'Construction,' 'Transportation,' 'Electricity'). . . . Each subject section has a two-page chronology of inventions in that field. . . . Section 10, 'Our Findings,' is a list of the concepts discovered in each experiment. Section 11 consists of an appendix and index. The appendix lists the experiments by grade levels, the need for adult supervision, home or school setting, numbers of participants, and the amount of time to do the project. . . . Grades six to twelve." (Booklist)

This work contains "65 experiments re-creating famous inventions. The purpose of these re-creations is to assist students in understanding important concepts and innovations in science. Intended for grades 6-12, the work is multidisciplinary in approach, making use of history, science, mathematics, and abstract and applied thinking. . . . This will be a useful source for middle-and high-school students and teachers doing science projects and experiments." Booklist

Ferris, Julie

Ideas that changed the world; authors, Julie Ferris [et al.] DK Pub. 2010 256p il map $24.99

Grades: 6 7 8 9 10   **609**

1. Inventions -- History 2. Technology -- History

ISBN 978-0-7566-6531-9; 0-7566-6531-0

LC 2010282281

A guide to technological developments that changed the world describes each invention and explores its place in history and how it influenced civilization, discussing inventions from the wheel to computers.

"Brightly colored and packed with information, this reference volume delivers. . . . This book could be used in multiple subject areas. English classes might use it for general research or units on the decades, social studies for the major changes over time, and science due to the technological advancements." Libr Media Connect

Horne, Richard

101 things you wish you'd invented--and some you wish no one had; designed and illustrated by Richard Horne; written by Tracey Turner and Richard Horne. Walker & Co. 2008 un il pa $11.99

Grades: 6 7 8 9   **609**

1. Inventions

ISBN 978-0-80279-788-9; 0-80279-788-1

LC 2008-4990

"The authors have chosen interesting subjects and written concise and engaging histories and trivia. The quality of the book is quite impressive. With an appearance much like a field guide, this well-bound book is made with quality paper and has a very eye-catching layout." Voice Youth Advocates

"Offers explanations of how an array of both curious and common things came into existence in this . . . interactive book with checklists, adhesive stars, and activities." Publisher's note

Jedicke, Peter

Great inventions of the 20th century; by Peter Jedicke. Chelsea House 2007 72p il (Scientific American) $30

Grades: 5 6 7 8   **609**

1. Inventions -- History 2. Technology -- History
ISBN 978-0-7910-9048-0; 0-7910-9048-5

LC 2006014773

"The text is simple, clear, and concise. . . . [The book has] captioned color photos throughout." SLJ

This "presents a celebration of the inventors and inventions that transformed the world during the age of technology. Topics presented include cellophane, the microwave oven, liquid-filled rockets, ultrasound, and robotic machines, among many others." Publisher's note

Includes glossary and bibliographical references

Landau, Elaine

The history of everyday life. 21st Century Bks. 2005 56p il (Major inventions through history) $26.60

Grades: 5 6 7 8   **609**

1. Inventions -- History
ISBN 0-8225-3808-3

This "explores fireplaces and central heating, indoor plumbing, the washing machine, food and clothing production, and microwave ovens. . . . [It] presents information about daily living from ancient times to the present. . . . The text . . . is breezy but informative. . . . Illustrations are a mixture of period black-and-white and color photos." SLJ

Includes bibligraphical references

Lee, Richard B.

Africans thought of it! amazing innovations. [by] Bathseba Opini [and] Richard B. Lee. Annick Press 2011 48p il (We thought of it) $21.95; pa $11.95

Grades: 3 4 5 6   **609**

1. Inventions 2. Africa -- Civilization
ISBN 978-1-55451-277-5; 1-55451-277-8; 978-1-55451-276-8 pa; 1-55451-276-X pa

Describes the inventions created by the peoples of Africa in hunting, agriculture, architecture, metalwork, medicine, the arts, and other fields, and how they have spread through the world and continue to fit into modern African civilization.

"Vivid photographs feature authentic objects used . . . while people engaged in activities capture an enthusiastic look at the reliance on community. Colored backgrounds and borders present a busy, though uncluttered, dynamic portrayal of nuanced cultures. . . . Succinct definitions and compact descriptions provide a brief and interesting blend of the contemporary with the traditional." SLJ

Marshall Cavendish Corporation

★ Inventors and inventions. Marshall Cavendish 2008 5v il set $399.95

Grades: 6 7 8 9 10   **609**

1. Inventors 2. Reference books 3. Inventions -- History 4. Technology -- History
ISBN 978-0-7614-7761-7

LC 2007-60868

"Inventions and Inventors is designed to introduce students to an array of inventors from the past and present while encouraging 'interest in and knowledge of science' by exploring the history, development, and utility of a wide variety of inventions. This set contains 172 alphabetically arranged articles on a range of inventors as well as 21 overview articles. . . . The choice of inventors, the inclusion of more than 1,000 full-color illustrations, and the highly readable and engaging text all create a valuable reference for students and browsers alike." Booklist

Includes bibliographical references

Robinson, James

Inventions; foreword by James Dyson. Kingfisher 2006 63p il (Kingfisher knowledge) $12.95

Grades: 5 6 7 8   **609**

1. Inventions -- History 2. Technology -- History
ISBN 978-0-7534-5973-7; 0-7534-5973-6

"A slim, colorful overview of inventions." Kirkus

Includes glossary

Rossi, Ann

★ Bright ideas; the age of invention in America, 1870-1910. [by] Ann Rossi. National Geographic 2005 40p il (Crossroads America) $12.95

Grades: 4 5 6   **609**

1. Inventions -- History
ISBN 0-7922-8276-0

LC 2003-19834

This describes the history of late 19th and early 20th century inventions such as the light bulb, the telegraph, the telephone, and the automobile.

This "solid [title] for report writers may even pull in a few curious browsers because of [its] plentiful, full-color photos and reproductions. The [layout is] inviting, and the [text is] clear, informative, and readable." SLJ

Includes glossary

Strapp, James

Science and technology. Sharpe Focus 2009 80p il (Inside ancient China) $31.45

Grades: 7 8 9 10   **609**

1. Science and civilization 2. Science -- China 3. Technology -- History
ISBN 978-0-7656-8169-0; 0-7656-8169-2

LC 2008-31168

"This colorful book surveys science and technology developed by the ancient Chinese. Strapp discusses early compasses and mapmaking, the building of canals, and the invention of . . . the wheelbarrow, water clocks, gunpowder, and the harness. The last chapter looks at Chinese medicine and feng shui. . . . The writing is clear and the format is inviting, with many sidebars and pictures. Illustrations include photos of artifacts and maps as well as period artwork and line-and-wash pictures." Booklist

Includes bibliographical references

Tomecek, Steve

★ **What** a great idea! inventions that changed the world. [by] Stephen M. Tomecek; illustrated by Dan Stuckenschneider. Scholastic Ref. 2003 112p il $22.99

Grades: 4 5 6 7   **609**

1. Inventions -- History

ISBN 0-590-68144-3

LC 2001-20937

"Tomecek puts significant inventions and discoveries in a historical context. Dividing the text into five broad time periods, he offers a series of essays on important advances that occurred in each 'age'. . . . What emerges is a sense of interconnectedness that other books often lack. . . . Full-color diagrams and illustrations are well integrated into each spread." SLJ

Includes bibliographical references

Ye, Ting-xing

The **Chinese** thought of it; amazing inventions and innovations. Annick Press 2009 48p il map (We thought of it) $19.95; pa $9.95

Grades: 5 6 7 8   **609**

1. China -- Civilization 2. Inventions -- History 3. Technology -- History

ISBN 978-1-55451-196-9; 1-55451-196-8; 978-1-55451-195-2 pa; 1-55451-195-X pa

In this survey of Chinese inventions "at least one double-page spread is devoted to each of the eleven topics: farming, working with metal, transportation and exploration, canals and bridges, weapons and warfare, paper and printing, silk, and everyday innovations. . . . The layout of the book is appealing and just right for quick reading or browsing. . . . The author's personal story about her childhood in Shanghai effectively draws the reader in." Voice Youth Advocates

Includes bibliographical references

609.2   Technology -- Biography

Tucker, Tom

Brainstorm! the stories of twenty American kid inventors. with drawings by Richard Loehle. Farrar, Straus & Giroux 1995 148p il hardcover o.p. pa $6.95

Grades: 5 6 7 8   **609.2**

1. Inventors 2. Inventions

ISBN 0-374-40928-5 pa

LC 94-38780

The author looks at inventions devised by children since the 18th century. Ear muffs, water skis, the popsicle, colored car wax and the electronic television are among the products discussed. Includes a discussion of how the Patent Office works

Includes glossary and bibliographical references

610   Medicine and health

Auden, Scott

Medical mysteries; science researches conditions from bizarre to deadly. by Scott Auden; Elizabeth Brownell, consultant. National Geographic 2008 64p il (National Geographic investigates) $17.95; lib bdg $27.90

Grades: 4 5 6 7   **610**

1. Diseases 2. Medicine -- Research

ISBN 978-1-4263-0356-2; 1-4263-0356-4; 978-1-4263-0261-9 lib bdg; 1-4263-0261-4 lib bdg

This title features "full-color photographs that readers have come to expect from this publisher. . . . [It] focuses on diseases that are regarded as bizarre and are often deadly, including Creutzfeldt-Jakob, Progeria, and Morgellons. The approach is to examine the way in which these mysterious diseases were discovered and how they are being studied to find a cure. . . . [This book offers] explanations simple enough for middle school students but with enough content to make them a useful resource for high school students as well." Voice Youth Advocates

Includes glossary and bibliographical references

Dawson, Ian

★ **Renaissance** medicine. Enchanted Lion Books 2005 64p il (History of medicine) lib bdg $19.95

Grades: 6 7 8 9   **610**

1. Renaissance 2. Medicine -- History

ISBN 1-59270-038-1

This "offers a concise overview of the fascinating advancements in European medicine between 1450 and 1750. . . . Dawson carefully shows how inventions such as the printing press and microscope and the work of artists such as da Vinci influenced medical knowledge. Quotes from primary sources enhance the plainspoken language, and numerous reproductions of paintings and engravings vividly evoke the realities of surgery, leech treatments, and the horrors of the plague." Booklist

Includes glossary and bibliographical references

★ **Encyclopedia** of health; 4th ed.; Marshall Cavendish 2009 18v il set $514.21

Grades: 5 6 7 8 9 10   **610**

1. Reference books 2. Medicine -- Encyclopedias

ISBN 978-0-7614-7845-4; 0-7614-7845-0

LC 2008033014

First published 1995 with title: The Marshall Cavendish encyclopedia of health

This reference features alphabetically arranged entries on body function; diet and nutrition; human behavior; illness, injury and disorders; and prevention and care

"Easy-to-understand language, an attractive design, and content that supports student research and interest lend value to the set." Booklist

Includes bibliographical references

Goldsmith, Connie

Cutting -edge medicine. Lerner Publications Co. 2008 48p il (Cool science) lib bdg $26.60

Grades: 4 5 6   610
1. Medicine
ISBN 978-0-8225-6770-7 lib bdg; 0-8225-6770-9
lib bdg
                                          LC 2007001946
"This book explains the many amazing ways new medical techniques are helping people live longer, healthier
lives." Publisher's note
Includes glossary and bibliographical references

Kelly, Kate

Early civilizations; prehistoric times to 500 C.E.
Facts on File 2010 174p il map (The history of
medicine) $40
Grades: 6 7 8 9 10   610
1. Ancient civilization 2. Medicine -- History
ISBN 978-0-8160-7205-7; 0-8160-7205-1
                                          LC 2008-43441
"This eye-opening and information-rich [volume] . . .
shows that ancient human beings were quite knowledgeable
about health and well-being. This book discusses medical
advances from prehistoric times through the Roman Empire.
. . . Coverage is global. . . . Readers will gain a deepened
appreciation of and insights into modern medicine by examining this book. Because of its inclusion of new research, it
is recommended as a first purchase for most libraries." SLJ
Includes bibliographical references

Morley, David

★ **Healing** our world. Fitzhenry & Whiteside
2007 121p il map $18.95
Grades: 6 7 8 9   610
1. War relief 2. Disaster relief 3. Medical assistance 4.
Médecins Sans Frontières (Organization)
ISBN 978-1-55041-565-0
The author was the executive director of MSF Canada
from 1998 to 2005. "When children are caught in civil wars,
when earthquakes destroy homes and villages, when AIDS
and other diseases shatter families and communities—the
volunteers of Doctors Without Borders are there. . . . Médecins Sans Frontières, known in English as Doctors Without
Borders and by its volunteers as MSF, is the world's largest
independent medical humanitarian relief organization. . . .
In Healing Our World, David Morley presents his own story
and the stories of other MSFers who have volunteered in
. . . [places like] the Congo, El Salvador, Chechnya, Bangladesh, Mozambique, Afghanistan, [and] southern Africa."
(Publisher's note) "Age twelve and up." (Quill Quire)
"Morley is a former executive director of the Canadian
section of Doctors Without Borders, a humanitarian organization known throughout most of world as Medecins Sans
Frontieres (MSF). With clarity and passion, he introduces
the organization's history, charter, and current efforts to provide health care where it is needed most." Booklist

Rooney, Anne

Health and medicine; the impact of science and
technology. Gareth Stevens Pub. 2009 64p il (Pros
and cons) lib bdg $35

Grades: 5 6 7 8   610
1. Health 2. Medicine 3. Medical technology
ISBN 978-1-4339-1988-6 lib bdg; 1-4339-1988-5
lib bdg
                                          LC 2008-54133
An "active layout that features color photographs, maps,
graphs or charts on every spread, this . . . [book] has much
to offer. . . . It conveniently outlines the range of views . .
. helping students to learn how to view both sides of [the]
issue[s]." SLJ
"Looks at how scientific and technological advances in
recent decades have dramatically altered the way we live-
and examines both positive and negative impacts of these
changes." Publisher's note
Includes glossary and bibliographical references

Stefoff, Rebecca, 1951-

Magic and Medicine; Rebecca Stefoff. Caven-
dish Square 2014 48 p. illustrations (Is It Science?)
$29.93
Grades: 6 7 8   610
1. Magic 2. Medicine -- History 3. Science --
Methodology
ISBN 1627125159; 9781627125154
                                          LC 2014054661
This book, edited by Rebecca Stefoff, is part of the "Is
It Science?" series. The volume and the series explore the
history and methodology of science in various disciplines,
contrasting them with the older ideas and frameworks that
were proved wrong over time. This volume explores the history of medicine and the development from earlier magical
thinking to the contemporary scientific to the discipline.
"Each volume is heavily illustrated with period images
and modern photographs, and each closes with particularly
generous lists of further resources." SLJ

Woolf, Alex, 1964-

★ **Death** and disease; [by] Alex Woolf. Lucent
Books 2004 48p il map (Medieval realms) $29.95
Grades: 5 6 7 8   610
1. Medieval civilization 2. Medicine -- History
ISBN 1-59018-533-1
                                          LC 2003-61797
"Clear, well-organized [text] along with full-color reproductions of art and artifacts and photos of period structures
immerse readers in . . . medieval life and offer sufficient information for reports." SLJ
This "discusses topics such as medieval theories about
the body and disease, the influence of the Church on health
practices, the causes and effects of bubonic plague, and the
emergence of modern medicine as the medieval era drew to
an end." Booklist
Includes glossary and bibliographical references

**610.28   Auxiliary techniques and procedures;
apparatus, equipment, materials**

Strange, Cordelia

Medical technicians; health-care support for the
21st century. Mason Crest Publishers 2011 64p il

(New careers for the 21st century: finding your role in the global renewal) lib bdg $22.95

Grades: 7 8 9 10 **610.28**
1. Medical personnel 2. Vocational guidance
ISBN 978-1-4222-1817-4 lib bdg; 1-4222-1817-1 lib bdg

LC 2010014934

"Chapters identify and emphasize specific careers-important strengths, necessary aptitudes and interests, education and training, projected earnings, closely related occupations, type of work environment, and predictions for the future of the field. . . . Color photos have a small role amid the many statistics, figures, graphs and charts that support and supplement the . . . [text]." SLJ

Includes bibliographical references

610.73 Nursing and services of allied health personnel

Glasscock, Sarah
How nurses use math; math curriculum consultant: Rhea A. Stewart. Chelsea Clubhouse 2010 32p il (Math in the real world) lib bdg $28

Grades: 4 5 6 **610.73**
1. Nurses 2. Mathematics 3. Vocational guidance
ISBN 978-1-60413-607-4 lib bdg; 1-60413-607-3 lib bdg

LC 2009-20199

This describes how nurses use math in such tasks as giving eye tests, keeping records, taking the pulse, and measuring medicine and includes relevant math problems and information about how to become a nurse

Includes glossary and bibliographical references

Strange, Cordelia
Physicians assistants & nurses; new opportunities in the 21st-century health system. Mason Crest Publishers 2011 64p il (New careers for the 21st century: finding your role in the global renewal) lib bdg $22.95

Grades: 7 8 9 10 **610.73**
1. Nurses 2. Vocational guidance
ISBN 978-1-4222-1820-4 lib bdg; 1-4222-1820-1 lib bdg

LC 2010017919

"Chapters identify and emphasize specific careers-important strengths, necessary aptitudes and interests, education and training, projected earnings, closely related occupations, type of work environment, and predictions for the future of the field. . . . Color photos have a small role amid the many statistics, figures, graphs and charts that support and supplement the . . . [text]." SLJ

Includes bibliographical references

610.9 Medicine--history

Rooney, Anne
The history of medicine; Anne Rooney. Rosen Pub. Group 2013 208 p. (The history of science) (library) $42.60

Grades: 7 8 9 10 11 12 **610.9**
1. Medicine -- History 2. Medical innovations -- History
ISBN 1448872286; 9781448872282

LC 2012009971

This book, by Anne Rooney, is part of "The History of Science" series. "Organized thematically, this . . . entry . . . delves into the history of disease, diagnosis, treatment and surgery. Because of its broad scope, the book is able to make comparisons across eras, transforming . . . history into something relevant to today's teens. . . . Insets offer medical milestones, biographical sketches, and primary resources." (Booklist)

"Organized thematically, this enlightening entry into the History of Science series delves into the history of disease, diagnosis, treatment, and surgery... Rooney has crafted a highly readable tome about a dense topic." Booklist

Includes bibliographical references (p. 205) and index

Zuchora-Walske, Christine
Your head shape reveals your personality! science's biggest mistakes about the human body. by Christine Zuchora-Walske. Lerner Publishing Group 2015 32 p. color illustrations (lib. bdg. : alk. paper) $26.60

Grades: 4 5 6 7 **610.9**
1. Human body 2. Science -- History 3. Medicine -- History
ISBN 1467736619; 9781467736619

LC 2013041696

In this book, by Christine Zuchora-Walske, part of the "Science Gets It Wrong" series, "[d]iscover science's biggest mistakes and oddest assumptions about the human body, and see how scientific thought changed over time." (Publisher's note)

"Although each volume [in the Science Gets It Wrong series] has its merits, Your ead Shape Reveals Your Personality! stands out due in large part to the subject matter—the human body—and its gross-out potential." SLJ

Includes bibliographical references and index

611 Human anatomy, cytology, histology

Gold, Susan Dudley
Learning about the respiratory system; Susan Dudley Gold. Enslow Publishers 2013 48 p. (library) $23.93

Grades: 5 6 7 8 **611**
1. Picture books for children 2. Respiratory system 3. Respiratory organs
ISBN 0766041611; 9780766041615

LC 2012011104

This book by Susan Dudley Gold is part of the Learning About the Human Body Systems series and looks at the respiratory system. She "discusses what this body system is and what organs are involved in its various processes. She discusses the potential health problems that can affect the respiratory system, such as cancer, pneumonia, and emphysema, as well as ways to keep healthy and problem-free." (Publisher's note)

Includes bibliographical references and index.

Hall, Linley Erin

DNA and RNA. Rosen Pub. 2010 80p il lib bdg $30.60

Grades: 7 8 9 10 11 12   **611**

1. DNA 2. RNA

ISBN 978-1-4358-9532-4

LC 2009-46612

"...with the liberal use of color illustrations, color sidebars, subsections labeled in bold color fonts, and patterns of chemical bonds as backgrounds, will appeal to less able and reluctant readers." Libr Media Connect

"Introduces DNA and RNA, discussing how heredity works, what can happen when the code goes wrong, replication, and new advances in science and technology." (Publisher's note)

Haywood, Karen Diane

Skeletal system; [by] Karen Haywood. Marshall Cavendish Benchmark 2009 80p il (The amazing human body) lib bdg $34.21

Grades: 6 7 8 9   **611**

1. Skeleton

ISBN 978-0-7614-3056-8; 0-7614-3056-3

LC 2008-17574

"A good choice for students beginning to research the topic." Libr Media Connect

"Discusses the parts that make up the human skeletal system, what can go wrong, how to treat those illnesses and diseases, and how to stay healthy." Publisher's note

Includes glossary and bibliographical references

Morgan, Jennifer

Cells of the nervous system; [by] Jennifer R. Morgan and Ona Bloom. Chelsea House Publishers 2006 147p il (Gray matter) lib bdg $35

Grades: 8 9 10 11 12   **611**

1. Cells 2. Nervous system

ISBN 9781438119557; 978-0-7910-8512-7; 0-7910-8512-0

LC 2005-11690

An introduction to the human brain discusses how the nervous system relates and processes information, and how its parts can be damaged and repaired.

"Valuable addition[s] to an area where little is written for high school students." Libr Media Connect

Includes bibliographical references

612   Human physiology

Basher, Simon

Human body; a book with guts! by Simon Basher and Dan Green; illustrated by Simon Basher. Kingfisher 2011 128p il $14.95; pa $8.99

Grades: 5 6 7 8   **612**

1. Human body

ISBN 978-0-7534-6628-5; 0-7534-6628-7; 978-0-7534-6501-1 pa; 0-7534-6501-9 pa

"Basher brings his signature informative irreverence and smiley little cartoon icons to the world of human biology. Not a comprehensive resource, but supplemental science reading doesn't come much more fun." Booklist

Bruhn, Aron

Inside the human body; illustrations by Joel Ito and Kathleen Kemly. Sterling 2010 48p il (Inside) $19.95; pa $9.95

Grades: 4 5 6   **612**

1. Human body

ISBN 978-1-4027-7091-3; 1-4027-7091-X; 978-1-4027-7779-0 pa; 1-4027-7779-5 pa

LC 2010002503

"The illustrations in [this] cool . . . [title is] enhanced by 10 large gatefolds that allow kids to dig deeper into the topics and enjoy amazing illustrations. [The] title clearly defines fact and theory, leaving puzzles for the next generation of scientists to solve. . . . [The book] touches on each of the body systems and provides a highly detailed look at a human cell." SLJ

Includes glossary and bibliographical references

Buller, Laura

Open me up; written by Laura Buller . . . [et al.]; editorial consultant: Richard Walker. Dorling Kindersley 2009 256p il $24.99

Grades: 7 8 9 10 11 12   **612**

1. Human body

ISBN 978-0-7566-5532-7; 0-7566-5532-3

Provides details about the human body, from human cells and senses to brain structure and body systems.

"The juxtaposition of photographs, humor, . . . historical narratives and a variety of artwork should generate hours of gratifying discovery." Publ Wkly

Calabresi, Linda

Human body. Simon & Schuster Books for Young Readers 2008 un il (Insiders) $16.99

Grades: 4 5 6 7   **612**

1. Human body

ISBN 978-1-4169-3861-3; 1-4169-3861-3

LC 2007-61744

This volume "offers excellent pictures of systems, organs, and even individual cells in the human body. . . . A visually dynamic introduction to the human package." Booklist

★ The **complete** human body; the definitive visual guide. Alice Roberts [editor-in-chief] DK Publishing 2010 512p il $50

Grades: 8 9 10 11 12 Adult   **612**

1. Diseases 2. Human body
ISBN 978-0-7566-6733-7; 0-7566-6733-X

LC 2010-282438

This incorporates "hundreds of stunning images and clearly written text. . . . The extraordinary detail of these pictures will give students an excellent understanding of the body's structure and organization." SLJ

Gardner, Robert

Ace your human biology science project; great science fair ideas. [by] Robert Gardner and Barbara Gardner Conklin. Enslow Publishers 2009 128p il (Ace your biology science project) lib bdg $31.93

Grades: 5 6 7 8   **612**

1. Biology 2. Science projects 3. Science -- Experiments
ISBN 978-0-7660-3219-4 lib bdg; 0-7660-3219-1 lib bdg

LC 2008-30799

"Dozens of . . . science activities are presented with background information, step-by-step instructions, and suggestions for extending to the science fair level. . . . Color illustrations and important safety information are included." Horn Book Guide

Includes bibliographical references

Easy genius science projects with the human body; great experiments and ideas. Enslow Publishers 2009 112p il (Easy genius science projects) lib bdg $31.93

Grades: 7 8 9 10   **612**

1. Human body 2. Science -- Experiments
ISBN 978-0-7660-2927-9 lib bdg; 0-7660-2927-1 lib bdg

LC 2007-32315

"Both simple and complex science experiments involving the human body are included in this guide for young scientists. An introduction reviews the issues of safety and adult supervision, plus a quick review of the scientific method is included. . . . The high level vocabulary indicates that this is a book for more advanced science students. This would be a great book to put in the hands of a highly motivated student needing fresh ideas for a science fair." Libr Media Connect

Goddard, Jolyon

Inside the human body. Marshall Cavendish Benchmark 2010 48p il (Invisible worlds) lib bdg $28.50

Grades: 4 5 6 7   **612**

1. Human body 2. Physiology
ISBN 978-0-7614-4190-8 lib bdg; 0-7614-4190-5 lib bdg

LC 2008037254

This describes the details of the human body that are too small for the unaided eye to see, and how these microscopic systems work to keep the body alive and healthy.

The narrative is "clear, well written, broken down into manageable pieces, and peppered with eye-opening facts. The numerous photographs are so phenomenal that they will inspire kids to read the text . . . so that they can wrap their minds around what they see." SLJ

Includes glossary and bibliographical references

Human body from A to Z. Marshall Cavendish Reference 2011 480p $79.95

Grades: 6 7 8 9   **612**

1. Human anatomy
ISBN 978-0-7614-7946-8

LC 2011006783

Presents 168 entries that focus on all the elements that make up the human body, describing major body systems, physical features, and health issues.

"The writing is informal and readable, and... appropriate for upper-elementary through high-school readers." Booklist

Macaulay, David

★ The **way** we work; getting to know the amazing human body. [by] David Macaulay, with Richard Walker. Houghton Mifflin 2008 336p il $35

Grades: 6 7 8 9 10   **612**

1. Human body
ISBN 978-0-618-23378-6; 0-618-23378-4

LC 2008-25109

Boston Globe-Horn Book Award honor book: Nonfiction (2009)

"The opening chapter introduces basic concepts of biology and chemistry at the cellular level while subsequent chapters take us through the various systems of the body. . . . [Humor] occasionally leavens the information, which, though often complex and technical, is clearly and succintly presented in double-page spreads, accompanied by an illuminating array of illustrations." Horn Book

Nagel, Rob

★ **Body** by design; from the digestive system to the skeleton. U.X.L 2000 2v set $126

Grades: 7 8 9 10   **612**

1. Physiology 2. Human anatomy
ISBN 0-7876-3897-8

LC 99-14642

"Black-and-white and color photographs are plentiful, and color is used throughout to highlight headings and subheadings, sidebars, and other features." Booklist

"Each chapter examines one of the 11 organ systems of the body; the final chapter focuses on the senses. In addition to describing each system's structure and function, the diseases commonly associated with it and suggestions for keeping it healthy are also discussed." SLJ

Includes bibliographical references

Redd, Nancy Amanda

Body drama; real girls, real bodies, real issues, real answers. Gotham 2008 271p ebook $16.99

Grades: 6 7 8 9 10   **612**

1. Puberty 2. Human body 3. Physiology 4. Girls -- Health and hygiene
ISBN 9781101555002

Information for teenage girls about various issues pertaining to their changing physiology

"The author covers a myriad of physical as well as mental health issues, including cutting and depression. . . . It is likely to be a read-and-pass-along book not only for the helpful advice and accurate information but also for the gross-out pictures of head lice, warts, and keloid scars." Voice Youth Advocates

Includes bibliographical references

Reilly, Kathleen M.

The **human** body; 25 fantastic projects illuminate how the body works. illustrated by Shawn Braley. Nomad Press 2008 120p il $21.95; pa $15.95

Grades: 5 6 7 8   612

1. Human body

ISBN 978-1-934670-25-5; 1-934670-25-1; 978-1-934670-24-8 pa; 1-934670-24-3 pa

"The workings of the human body are expertly summarized in 11 tidy chapters, which include experiments that explain how the body works by creating models that either imitate or test its functions. . . . Many of the activities require adult supervision due to the materials required. . . . Simple drawings and cartoons enliven and illuminate the text. . . . The scientific explanations are superb." SLJ

Somervill, Barbara A.

★ The **human** body. Gareth Stevens Pub. 2008 48p il (Gareth Stevens vital science: life science) lib bdg $26.60; pa $11.95

Grades: 5 6 7 8   612

1. Human body

ISBN 978-0-8368-8441-8 lib bdg; 978-0-8368-8450-0 pa

LC 2007-16175

First published 2006 in the United Kingdom

This describes "human anatomy and physiology. . . . Factoids are scattered throughout the text in a fashion that captures the reader's attention and interest. . . . [The book offers] excellent graphics, namely photos and diagrams. The artwork complements and enhances the written content." Sci Books Films

Includes glossary and bibliographical references

Walker, Richard, 1951-

3 -D human body; written by Richard Walker. DK Pub. 2011 71p il $17.99

Grades: 3 4 5 6   612

1. Human body

ISBN 978-0-7566-7216-4; 0-7566-7216-3

"Lively and informative spreads, along with augmented reality technology, introduce readers to the human body. . . . Readers can download software from the publisher's Web site, which can be used in combination with a webcam to make six spreads turn into animated AR pop-ups on a computer screen. Those who don't use the multimedia effect can still learn plenty from the book's detailed mix of photographs, digital graphics, and engaging captions that illuminate how intricate bodily components work together." Publ Wkly

★ **Dr.** Frankenstein's human body book; the monstrous truth about how your body works. [author, Richard Walker; artist, Nick Abadzis] DK Pub. 2008 93p il $24.99

Grades: 4 5 6 7   612

1. Human body

ISBN 978-0-7566-4091-0; 0-7566-4091-1

"This anatomy book is as engrossing as any science fiction. Dr. Frankenstein, shown in a sepia photograph standing in a laboratory, gazing at a skull he holds in one hand, invites readers to join him as he creates a human being. . . . The story line is sustained with brief, pun-happy journal entries. . . . Gothic fonts and engraved illustrations and vignettes (in red and black and also hand-colored) blend with state-of-the-art images from MEG scans, gamma scans and other advanced technology. Clear explanations broken into easily assimilable captions and text blocks encourage the reader." Publ Wkly

Includes glossary

Human body; written by Richard Walker. DK Pub. 2009 72 p. ill. (chiefly col.) (DK eyewitness books) (hardcover) $16.99

Grades: 4 5 6 7   612

1. Human body

ISBN 9780756645458; 075664545X

LC 2009419529

In this book, text and illustrations present information on the parts of the body and how they work

Includes glossary and bibliographical references

Ouch! how your body makes it through a very bad day. written by Richard Walker. DK Pub. 2007 71p il $16.99

Grades: 4 5 6 7   612

1. Human body

ISBN 978-0-7566-2536-8; 0-7566-2536-X

"Tag along on a rotten day as a body copes with sneezing, getting cut, being stung by a bee, and vomiting, as well as performing more mundane actions such as urinating, tapping into its melanin supply, acting reflexively, and sweating. . . . Dramatic color graphics, both large and small, are accompanied by a multitude of informative captions. Researchers who find the information on the busy pages hard to grasp can pop in the accompanying CD-ROM and catch a ride up the esophagus on a wave of vomit. . . . Eye-catching, highly pictorial, informative, and with a megadose of ick! factor." SLJ

Includes glossary

612.1 Specific functions, systems, organs

Bjorklund, Ruth

Circulatory system. Marshall Cavendish Benchmark 2009 80p il (The amazing human body) lib bdg $34.21

Grades: 6 7 8 9   612.1

1. Cardiovascular system

ISBN 978-0-7614-3053-7; 0-7614-3053-9

LC 2007-50436

"A good choice for students beginning to research the topic." Libr Media Connect

"Discusses the parts that make up the human circulatory system, what can go wrong, how to treat those illnesses and diseases, and how to stay healthy." Publisher's note

Includes glossary and bibliographical references

Gold, John Coopersmith

Learning about the circulatory and lymphatic systems; by John C. Gold. Enslow Publishers 2013 48 p. (library) $23.93

Grades: 5 6 7 8   612.1

1. Picture books for children 2. Lymphatic system 3. Lymphatics 4. Cardiovascular system
ISBN 0766041565; 9780766041561

LC 2012011099

This book by John Coopersmith Gold is part of the Learning About the Human Body Systems series and looks at the circulatory and lymphatic systems. "The circulatory system runs through the body carrying oxygen and nutrients to our cells and removes waste. It's driven by the never-resting heart, which pumps blood through more than 60,000 miles of arteries and veins. The lymphatic system regulates the amount of liquid in the body among other tasks." (Publisher's note)

Includes bibliographical references and index.

Markle, Sandra

Faulty hearts; true survival stories. Lerner Pub. 2010 48p il (Powerful medicine) lib bdg $27.93

Grades: 5 6 7 8   612.1

1. Heart 2. Heart diseases 3. Cardiovascular system
ISBN 978-0-8225-8699-9 lib bdg; 0-8225-8699-1 lib bdg

LC 2009-33980

This book "is extremely well done, with a number of great examples of survival stories. The examples exemplify different and important heart diseases, symptoms, and treatments. . . . That the author is a former science teacher enables her to write clearly for the intended audience. The illustrations and photographs are perfect, adding to a full understanding of the diseases described." Sci Books & Films

Includes glossary and bibliographical references

Newquist, Hp

The **book** of blood; from legends and leeches to vampires and veins. HP Newquist. Houghton Mifflin Books for Children 2012 160 p. ill. (chiefly col.) (hardback) $17.99

Grades: 4 5 6   612.1

1. Blood
ISBN 0547315848; 9780547315843

LC 2011025134

In this book, "[H.P.] Newquist . . . demystifies one of the most elemental and (literally) vital components of life as we know it. After an overview of the complex makeup of blood, Newquist dives into humankind's history with, beliefs about, and study of blood, including missteps and misconceptions along the way . . . . Newquist goes into detail to explain how blood moves through the human body and the critical role it plays in keeping us alive." (Publishers Weekly)

Simon, Seymour

★ The **heart**; our circulatory system. [by] Seymour Simon. rev ed.; Collins 2006 30p il hardcover o.p. pa $6.99

Grades: 4 5 6 7   612.1

1. Heart 2. Cardiovascular system
ISBN 978-0-06-087720-0; 0-06-087720-0; 978-0-06-087721-7 pa; 0-06-087721-9 pa

LC 2006-279215

First published 1996

Describes the heart, blood, and other parts of the body's circulatory system and explains how each component functions

"The text is succinct and direct, making the details understandable without losing the sense that the whole process of circulation is 'strange and wonderful.' . . . The often striking pictures include many computer-enhanced photographs as well as diagrams and highly enlarged images made possible by electron microscopes. Handsome and well-conceived in every way." Booklist [review of 1996 edition]

612.2   Respiratory system

Siy, Alexandra

★ **Sneeze!** [by] Alexandra Siy and Dennis Kunkel. Charlesbridge 2007 45p il lib bdg $16.95; pa $6.95

Grades: 4 5 6 7   612.2

1. Allergy 2. Sneezing
ISBN 978-1-57091-653-3 lib bdg; 978-1-57091-654-0 pa

LC 2005-27567

"Kunkel's big, clear, beautiful color electron micrographs on every double-page spread show everything from dust mites, mildew, and pollen to the influenza A virus." Booklist

This describes some causes of sneezing, including "air-pollen, dust mites, mold spores, dust, goose down, cat hair, pepper, flu viruses, and bright light." Publisher's note

Includes glossary and bibliographical references

612.3   Digestive system

Allman, Toney

Nutrition and disease prevention. Chelsea House 2010 191p il map (Healthy eating: a guide to nutrition) lib bdg $35

Grades: 7 8 9 10 11 12   612.3

1. Nutrition 2. Preventive medicine
ISBN 978-1-60413-777-4; 1-60413-777-0

LC 2009-41337

This "volume uses boldface type to introduce important and unknown words to the reader and explains them in an easy to understand manner so the reader can grasp the concept being discussed. . . . [For] classes needing information about the importance of good nutrition . . . [this] would be valuable." Libr Media Connect

Includes glossary and bibliographical references

Brynie, Faith Hickman

101 questions about food and digestion that have been eating at you . . . until now. 21st Cent. Bks. (Brookfield) 2002 176p il (101 questions) lib bdg $30.60

Grades: 8 9 10 11 12　　　　　　　　**612.3**
　　1. Digestion 2. Nutrition
　　ISBN 0-7613-2309-0

　　　　　　　　　　　　　　　LC 2001-52250

Questions and answers explain the human digestive system and how it uses food for nutrition

"Presenting solid research with a lively writing style, this book provides a great deal of information and sound advice on the topic." Booklist

Includes glossary and bibliographical references

Donovan, Sandra, 1967-

Hawk & Drool; gross stuff in your mouth. by Sandy Donovan; illustrated by Michael Slack. Millbrook Press 2010 48p il (Gross body science) lib bdg $29.27

Grades: 4 5 6　　　　　　　　　　**612.3**
　　1. Saliva 2. Mouth -- Diseases
　　ISBN 978-0-8225-8966-2 lib bdg; 0-8225-8966-4 lib bdg

　　　　　　　　　　　　　　　LC 2008-50699

Presents disgusting facts about the human mouth, how it works to aid in digestion, the organisms that live there, and ways to keep it clean and healthy

"Solid information layered between sarcastic comments and kid-friendly terminology like fart, poop, barf, and puke will keep readers engaged. . . . Labeled, captioned (and graphic) photographs, cartoon-style illustrations, and micrographs add information." SLJ

Includes glossary and bibliographical references

Rumble & spew; gross stuff in your stomach and intestines. by Sandy Donovan; illustrated by Michael Slack. Millbrook Press 2010 48p il (Gross body science) lib bdg $29.27

Grades: 4 5 6　　　　　　　　　　**612.3**
　　1. Intestines
　　ISBN 978-0-8225-8899-3 lib bdg; 0-8225-8899-4 lib bdg

　　　　　　　　　　　　　　　LC 2008-37713

Presents disgusting facts about the human digestive system and its functions

"Solid information layered between sarcastic comments and kid-friendly terminology like fart, poop, barf, and puke will keep readers engaged. . . . Labeled, captioned (and graphic) photographs, cartoon-style illustrations, and micrographs add information." SLJ

Includes glossary and bibliographical references

Gold, Susan Dudley

Learning about the digestive and excretory systems; by Susan Dudley Gold. Enslow Publishers 2013 48 p. (Learning about the human body systems) (library) $23.93

Grades: 5 6 7 8　　　　　　　　　**612.3**
　　1. Picture books for children 2. Digestive system 3.

Urinary organs 4. Digestive organs
ISBN 0766041573; 9780766041578

　　　　　　　　　　　　　　　LC 2012011100

This book by Susan Dudley Gold is part of the Learning About the Human Body Systems series and looks at the digestive and excretory systems. She "explains why these systems are discussed together, how they work, and ways to keep healthy." Illustrations and color photographs are included. (Publisher's note)

Includes bibliographical references and index.

Hoffmann, Gretchen

Digestive system. Marshall Cavendish Benchmark 2009 80p il (The amazing human body) lib bdg $34.21

Grades: 6 7 8 9　　　　　　　　　**612.3**
　　1. Digestion
　　ISBN 978-0-7614-3058-2; 0-7614-3058-X

　　　　　　　　　　　　　　　LC 2008-17573

"A good choice for students beginning to research the topic." Libr Media Connect

"Discusses the parts that make up the human digestive system, what can go wrong, how to treat those illnesses and diseases, and how to stay healthy." Publisher's note

Includes glossary and bibliographical references

Simon, Seymour

★ **Guts**; our digestive system. [by] Seymour Simon. HarperCollins 2005 un il $16.99; lib bdg $17.89

Grades: 4 5 6 7　　　　　　　　　**612.3**
　　1. Digestion
　　ISBN 0-06-054651-4; 0-06-054652-2 lib bdg

　　　　　　　　　　　　　　　LC 2004-14508

"Simon's specialty of drawing in readers through large, detailed, breathtaking photos and then entertaining them with facts is again in evidence. . . . The text is enhanced with detailed colored X rays, computer-generated pictures, and microscopic photos." SLJ

612.4 Hematopoietic, lymphatic, glandular, urinary systems

Kim, Melissa

Learning about the endocrine and reproductive systems; by Melissa L. Kim. Enslow Publishers 2013 48 p. (Learning about the human body systems) (library) $23.93

Grades: 5 6 7 8　　　　　　　　　**612.4**
　　1. Picture books for children 2. Endocrine glands 3. Reproductive system 4. Generative organs
　　ISBN 0766041581; 9780766041585

　　　　　　　　　　　　　　　LC 2012011101

This book by Melissa L. Kim is part of the Learning About the Human Body Systems series and looks at the endocrine and reproductive systems. "The endocrine system is essential to human life. It enables a person to grow, respond to change and stress, and helps turn food into energy. The reproductive system has one crucial task: that of making the next generation of people." (Publisher's note)

Includes bibliographical references and index.

Klosterman, Lorrie

Endocrine system. Marshall Cavendish Benchmark 2009 79p il (The amazing human body) lib bdg $34.21

Grades: 6 7 8 9   **612.4**

1. Endocrine glands

ISBN 978-0-7614-3055-1; 0-7614-3055-5

LC 2007-50444

"A good choice for students beginning to research the topic." Libr Media Connect

"Discusses the parts that make up the human endocrine system, what can go wrong, how to treat those illnesses and diseases, and how to stay healthy." Publisher's note

Includes glossary and bibliographical references

Excretory system. Marshall Cavendish Benchmark 2010 77p il (The amazing human body) lib bdg $23.95

Grades: 6 7 8 9   **612.4**

1. Feces 2. Urine 3. Excretion

ISBN 978-0-7614-4037-6 lib bdg; 0-7614-4037-2 lib bdg

LC 2008037261

"Discusses the parts that make up the human excretory system, what can go wrong, how to treat those illnesses and diseases, and how to stay healthy." Publisher's note

Includes glossary and bibliographical references

612.6   Reproduction, development, maturation

Bailey, Jacqui

Sex, puberty, and all that stuff; a guide to growing up. illustrated by Jan McCafferty. Barron's 2004 112p il pa $12.95

Grades: 5 6 7 8   **612.6**

1. Puberty 2. Adolescence 3. Sex education

ISBN 0-7641-2992-9

"A large helping of straightforward, up-to-date information peppered with humor and bright, graphic illustrations make this book one of the best texts about sex for developing adolescents." Voice Youth Advocates

Includes bibliographical references

Brynie, Faith Hickman

★ **101** questions about reproduction; or how 1 + 1. Twenty-First Century Books 2006 176p il (101 questions) lib bdg $27.90

Grades: 7 8 9   **612.6**

1. Pregnancy 2. Childbirth 3. Sex education

ISBN 0-7613-2311-2

LC 2003-16350

Uses a question-and-answer format to present information about physical, medical, and social issues surrounding human reproduction, including birth control, pregnancy, and childbirth.

"This is a splendid companion to Brynie's 101 Questions about Sex and Sexuality (21st Century Bks, 2003); together the books present informative, complementary coverage for browsers and researchers." SLJ

Includes bibliographical references

Gravelle, Karen

The **period** book; everything you don't want to ask (but need to know) by Karen Gravelle & Jennifer Gravelle; illustrations by Debbie Palen. updated ed.; Walker & Co. 2006 126p il $16.95

Grades: 4 5 6 7   **612.6**

1. Menstruation

ISBN 978-0-8027-8072-0; 0-8027-8072-5

LC 2008270981

First published 1996

Explains what happens at the onset of menstruation, discussing what to wear, going to the gynecologist, and how to handle various problems

"The cartoonlike illustrations and conversational tone make this updated edition a friendly, reassuring resource as well as a thorough one." Horn Book Guide

Holmes, Melisa

Girlology's there's something new about you; a girl's guide to growing up. [by] Melisa Holmes & Trish Hutchison. Health Communications 2010 122p il pa $12.95

Grades: 6 7 8 9   **612.6**

1. Girls 2. Puberty

ISBN 978-0-7573-1526-8; 0-7573-1526-7

LC 2010021169

Written by physicians who are mothers of preteen and teen girls, this guide explains the changes girls will be facing as they grow up.

"The graphics are informative without being offensive, pictures of the friends are cute and appealing, giving a fresh lightheartedness to the book. This is a must-have book for all homes and libraries." Voice Youth Advocates

Katz, Anne

Girl in the know; your inside-and-out guide to growing up. written by Anne Katz; illustrated by Monika Melnychuk. Kids Can Press 2010 111p il $18.95

Grades: 4 5 6 7   **612.6**

1. Puberty 2. Girls -- Health and hygiene 3. Life skills guides 4. Girls -- Psychology

ISBN 978-1-55453-303-9; 1-55453-303-1

"This reassuring title is aimed at girls who want clear facts about puberty but who may not be ready to read in-depth specifics of sex and birth-control. The author . . . offers a holistic guide that covers the body changes puberty brings as well as tips about maintaining physical and emotional health. . . . The warm, straightforward, useful advice on a broad range of topics . . . will captivate both middle graders and middle-schoolers, and the frequent color drawings of stylish, diverse girls . . . reinforce the book's appeal to a wide age group." Booklist

Madaras, Lynda

The **what's** happening to my body? book for boys; [by] Lynda Madaras with Area Madaras; drawings by Simon Sullivan. 3rd rev ed.; Newmarket Press 2007 xx, 233p il $24.95; pa $12.95

Grades: 4 5 6 7　　**612.6**

1. Puberty 2. Adolescence 3. Sex education 4. Boys -- Health and hygiene
ISBN 978-1-55704-769-4; 1-55704-769-3; 978-1-55704-765-6 pa; 1-55704-765-0 pa

LC 2007009874

First published 1984

Discusses the changes that take place in a boy's body during puberty, including information on the body's changing size and shape, the growth spurt, reproductive organs, pubic hair, beards, pimples, voice changes, wet dreams, and puberty in girls

Includes bibliographical references

The **what's** happening to my body? book for girls; [by] Lynda Madaras with Area Madaras; drawings by Simon Sullivan. 3rd rev ed.; Newmarket Press 2007 xxvi, 259p il $24.95; pa $12.95

Grades: 4 5 6 7　　**612.6**

1. Puberty 2. Adolescence 3. Sex education 4. Girls -- Health and hygiene
ISBN 978-1-55704-768-7; 1-55704-768-5; 978-1-55704-764-9 pa; 1-55704-764-2 pa

LC 2007009862

Discusses the changes that take place in a girl's body during puberty, including information on the body's changing size and shape, pubic hair, breasts, reproductive organs, the menstrual cycle, and puberty in boys

Includes bibliographical references

Mar, Jonathan

The **body** book for boys; by Jonathan Mar and Grace Norwich. Scholastic 2010 128p il pa $8.99

Grades: 4 5 6　　**612.6**

1. Boys 2. Puberty 3. Adolescence
ISBN 978-0-545-23751-2 pa; 0-545-23751-3 pa

"In this reassuring title aimed at boys just entering adolescence, the authors present frank information on such topics as hygiene, the changes brought on by puberty, exercise, and dealing with girls. The tone is kept light, and the many bright illustrations also have a fun, jokey quality." Booklist

Parker, Steve

The **reproductive** system; by Steve Parker. Raintree Steck-Vaughn Pubs. 1999 48 p. ill. (some col.) (library) $27.14; (library) $32

Grades: 6 7 8 9　　**612.6**

1. Biology 2. Reproductive system
ISBN 0817248064 out of print; 143293421X; 9781432934217

LC 96029685

Includes bibliographical references (p. 47) and index.

This book for middle schoolers by Steve Parker looks at the reproductive system. It "addresses male and female anatomy, genes, fertility problems, contraception, STDs, and human development from conception to adolescence." Pho-

tographs, diagrams, and illustrations are included. (School Library Journal)

Plaisted, Caroline

Boy talk; a survival guide to growing up. illustrated by Chris Dickason. QEB Pub. 2011 il (Growing up)

Grades: 4 5 6 7　　**612.6**

1. Boys 2. Puberty
ISBN 1-60992-085-6; 978-1-60992-085-2

LC 2011009206

Discusses body changes that happen to boys during puberty, such as acne, body hair, body odor, mood swings, crushes, and more, and gives suggestions to teen boys for taking care of their hygiene and keeping good relationships.

"Using a colorful design featuring Dickason's wacky, mugging cartoon characters, this is about as appealing as a book on these topics can get, and it maintains a mildly funny, usually frank, and always healthy tone." Booklist

Rand, Casey

Human reproduction. Raintree 2009 48p il (Sci-hi: life science) lib bdg $31.43; pa $8.99

Grades: 5 6 7 8　　**612.6**

1. Reproduction 2. Sex education
ISBN 978-1-4109-3327-0 lib bdg; 1-4109-3327-X lib bdg; 978-1-4109-3335-5 pa; 1-4109-3335-0 pa

LC 2009003464

In this introduction to human reproduction "clear language, embedded definitions, and interesting examples illustrate abstract concepts through both text and well-chosen photographs. . . . [It] includes suggested activities to test ideas as well as a thorough glossary and a Webliography." SLJ

Includes glossary and bibliographical references

Schwartz, John

Short; walking tall when you're not tall at all. Roaring Brook Press 2010 132p il $16.99

Grades: 4 5 6 7 8　　**612.6**

1. Size 2. Growth 3. Body image 4. Prejudices
ISBN 978-1-59643-323-6; 1-59643-323-X

"In a humorous, personal voice, . . . Schwartz combines his own memories of growing up short with related discussions about physiology, statistics, popular culture, and societal prejudice, always returning to his own self-image. . . . Short kids will want every word. . . . and many readers will move on to the resource list of articles, Web sites, and scientific papers in the detailed, informal back matter." Booklist

Includes bibliographical references

Waters, Sophie

The **female** reproductive system. Rosen Central 2008 48p il (Girls' health) lib bdg $26.50

Grades: 5 6 7 8　　**612.6**

1. Pregnancy 2. Birth control 3. Reproductive system
ISBN 9781435844018; 978-1-4042-1950-2; 1-4042-1950-1

LC 2006101218

Describes the parts of the female reproductive system, explains how pregnancy occurs and the steps in embryo development, and discusses various forms of birth control

"Generously interspersed with color photographs and diagrams . . . [this book will] offer girls a safe, comfortable place to get straight, honest answers about their personal health issues." Libr Media Connect

Includes glossary and bibliographical references

612.7 Musculoskeletal system, integument

Brynie, Faith Hickman

★ **101** questions about muscles to stretch your mind and flex your brain; by Faith Hickman Brynie. Twenty-First Century Books 2008 176p il (101 questions) lib bdg $30.60

Grades: 8 9 10 11 12   **612.7**
1. Muscles
ISBN 978-0-8225-6380-8; 0-8225-6380-0

LC 2006-37041

This answers such questions as "What do tendons do? What causes muscle cramps? . . . [This book] makes human physiology accessible, with questions everyone has always wondered about and up-to-date, detailed answers that discuss the complex science in chatty but never condescending style. Like the text, the clear diagrams and photographs deal with everything from basic information . . . to the more advanced." Booklist

Includes glossary and bibliographical references

Colligan, L. H.

Muscles. Marshall Cavendish Benchmark 2010 78p il (The amazing human body) lib bdg $34.21

Grades: 6 7 8 9   **612.7**
1. Muscles
ISBN 978-0-7614-4038-3 lib bdg; 0-7614-4038-0 lib bdg

LC 2008037257

Discusses human musculature, what can go wrong, how to treat those diseases and injuries, and how to stay health

Includes glossary and bibliographical references

Gold, Susan Dudley

Learning about the musculoskeletal system and the skin; Susan Dudley Gold. Enslow Publishers 2013 48 p. (Learning about the human body systems) (library) $23.93

Grades: 5 6 7 8   **612.7**
1. Picture books for children 2. Musculoskeletal system 3. Skin
ISBN 076604159X; 9780766041592

LC 2012011102

This book by Susan Dudley Gold is part of the Learning About the Human Body Systems series and looks at the musculoskeletal system. "Bone and muscles join forces to move us from one place to another. The musculoskeletal system controls our breathing, allows our eyes to focus, and shapes our smiles. It enables us to talk and to eat. Our strong bones support our weight. Skin wraps our body in a tough layer of tissue that keeps moisture in and germs out." (Publisher's note)

Includes bibliographical references and index..

Hall, Margaret

Skin deep. Raintree 2007 32p il (Raintree fusion) lib bdg $28.21; pa $7.99

Grades: 5 6 7 8   **612.7**
1. Skin
ISBN 978-1-4109-2582-4 lib bdg; 1-4109-2582-X lib bdg; 978-1-4109-2611-1 pa; 1-4109-2611-7 pa

LC 2006-8771

Explains what skin is and why it is important, including protecting the body from germs, helping cool down the body when it gets too hot, and absorbing Vitamin D from sunlight.

Includes glossary and bibliographical references

Klosterman, Lorrie

Skin. Marshall Cavendish Benchmark 2009 79p il (The amazing human body) lib bdg $34.21

Grades: 6 7 8 9   **612.7**
1. Skin
ISBN 978-0-7614-3057-5; 0-7614-3057-1

LC 2008-17580

"A good choice for students beginning to research the topic." Libr Media Connect

"Discusses the parts that make up human skin, what can go wrong, how to treat those illnesses and diseases, and how to stay healthy." Publisher's note

Includes glossary and bibliographical references

Parker, Steve, 1952-

The **skeleton** and muscles; [by] Steve Parker. Raintree 2004 48p il (Our bodies) lib bdg $29.93

Grades: 5 6 7 8   **612.7**
1. Musculoskeletal system
ISBN 0-7398-6622-2

LC 2003-6594

This "takes a look at bones, muscles, and joints; how they are connected and function; and how to keep them healthy. The anatomy is accurate, and the format, with plenty of pictures, diagrams, and magnified photos, is very accessible. There are also lots of lively boxed facts." Booklist

Includes bibliographical references

612.8 Nervous system

Brynie, Faith Hickman

★ **101** questions about sleep and dreams that kept you awake nights . . . until now. Twenty-First Century Books 2006 176p il (101 questions) lib bdg $27.93

Grades: 7 8 9 10 11 12   **612.8**
1. Sleep 2. Dreams
ISBN 978-0-7613-2312-9; 0-7613-2312-0

LC 2005-17276

This book describes the physical and psychological aspects of sleep and dreams. Glossary. Index. "Grades nine to twelve." (Sci Books Films)

The author "presents sometimes rather complicated scientific material in a way that is not only easily understood, but also thoroughly enjoyable." Sci Books Films

Includes bibliographical references

Gardner, Robert

Ace your science project about the senses; great science fair ideas. [by] Robert Gardner . . . [et al.] Enslow Publishers 2009 112p il (Ace your biology science project) lib bdg $31.93

Grades: 5 6 7 8   **612.8**

1. Science projects 2. Senses and sensation 3. Science -- Experiments

ISBN 978-0-7660-3217-0 lib bdg; 0-7660-3217-5 lib bdg

LC 2008-30797

"Presents several science projects and science project ideas about the senses." Publisher's note

Includes glossary and bibliographical references

Gold, Martha V.

Learning about the nervous system; by Martha V. Gold. Enslow Publishers 2013 48 p. (Learning about the human body systems) (library) $23.93

Grades: 5 6 7 8   **612.8**

1. Picture books for children 2. Nervous system

ISBN 0766041603; 9780766041608

LC 2012011103

This book by Martha V. Gold is part of the Learning About the Human Body Systems series and looks at the nervous system. "The nervous system is made up of the brain, the spinal cord and nerves. It is responsible for telling the heart to beat, the lungs to breathe, and the muscles to move. The brain—the central command center—processes everything from understanding a teacher's instructions to enjoying a piece of chocolate cake." (Publisher's note)

Includes bibliographical references and index.

Larsen, C. S.

Crust and spray; gross stuff in your eyes, ears, nose, and throat. illustrated by Michael Slack. Millbrook Press 2010 48p il (Gross body science) lib bdg $29.27

Grades: 4 5 6   **612.8**

1. Ear 2. Eye 3. Nose 4. Throat

ISBN 978-0-8225-8964-8 lib bdg; 0-8225-8964-8 lib bdg

LC 2008-33777

"Solid information layered between sarcastic comments and kid-friendly terminology like fart, poop, barf, and puke will keep readers engaged. . . . Labeled, captioned (and graphic) photographs, cartoon-style illustrations, and micrographs add information." SLJ

Includes glossary and bibliographical references

Newquist, H. P.

★ The **great** brain book; an inside look at the inside of your head. illustrations by Keith Kasnot and Eric Brace. Scholastic Reference 2005 160p il $18.95

Grades: 5 6 7 8   **612.8**

1. Brain

ISBN 0-439-45895-1

LC 2004-42955

This describes the anatomy and physiology of the brain and covers such topics as the history of brain research, neu-

rons, learning and memory, brain diseases and mental illness, and the possible future of brain research

"With an appealing, colorful design and a flashy cover, this in-depth introduction to the human brain and its remarkable powers will attract browsers, but strong readers are its best audience. . . . The clever, kid-friendly anecdotes amid the anatomy lessons . . . enhance accessibility." Booklist

Rau, Dana Meachen

Freaking out! the science of the teenage brain. Compass Point Books 2011 64p il (Everyday science) lib bdg $33.32; pa $8.95

Grades: 7 8 9 10   **612.8**

1. Brain

ISBN 978-0-7565-4486-7 lib bdg; 0-7565-4486-6; 978-0-7565-4500-0 pa; 0-7565-4500-5 pa

LC 2010054302

This "offers a solid overview of the brain. The book begins with an explanation of what the brain does, how it looks, and its various components. It then goes on to discuss more specialized topics, such as mood changes, developmental skills, and memory. The attractive format, with easy-to-read print, features bright photographs . . . and plenty of sidebars on a variety of topics." Booklist

Includes glossary and bibliographical references

Scott, Elaine

All about sleep from A to ZZZZ; by Elaine Scott; illustrated by John O'Brien. Viking 2008 58p il $17.99

Grades: 5 6 7 8 9 10   **612.8**

1. Sleep

ISBN 978-0-670-06188-4; 0-670-06188-3

LC 2008-6074

"The book covers a range of topics, including circadian rhythms, dreams, and the functions and stages of sleep." Booklist

Simon, Seymour

★ The **brain**; our nervous system. [by] Seymour Simon. rev ed.; Collins 2006 30p il $17.99; pa $6.99

Grades: 4 5 6 7   **612.8**

1. Brain 2. Nervous system

ISBN 978-0-06-087718-7; 0-06-087718-9; 978-0-06-087719-4 pa; 0-06-087719-7 pa

LC 2007-272349

First published 1997

Describes the various parts of the brain and the nervous system and how they function to enable us to think, feel, move, and remember.

Simon's "clear, concise writing style is complemented by stunning color images taken with radiological scanners, such as CAT scans, MRIs, and SEMs (scanning electron microscopes.)" SLJ [review of 1997 edition]

Includes bibliographical references

★ **Eyes** and ears. HarperCollins Pubs. 2003 unil hardcover o.p. pa $6.99

Grades: 4 5 6 7 **612.8**
1. Ear 2. Eye 3. Vision 4. Hearing
ISBN 0-688-15303-8; 978-0-06-073302-5 pa; 0-06-073302-0 pa

LC 2002-19060

Describes the anatomy of the eye and ear, how those organs function and some ways in which they may malfunction, and how the brain is also involved in our seeing and hearing

"Simon is at his very best here. . . . The large, exquisitely reproduced photographs from a number of sources look like fiery planets, galaxies, and monster creatures. . . . The anatomy and physiology are detailed and accurate, with clear diagrams." Booklist

Simpson, Kathleen

The **human** brain; inside your body's control room. National Geographic 2009 64p il (National Geographic investigates) lib bdg $27.90
Grades: 5 6 7 8 **612.8**
1. Brain
ISBN 978-1-4263-0421-7 lib bdg; 1-4263-0421-8 lib bdg

"Readers will learn about . . . new brain research in this title, which includes a basic discussion of the parts of the brain, their functions, and how neurons send messages throughout the body. Information is also included about the role of the brain during sleep, dreaming, and various emotional states, as well as explanations of the various technologies available to measure brain activity. This is a well-organized, compelling introduction, sure to pique the curiosity of many children. Full-color photographs and illustrations enliven the text." SLJ

Includes bibliographical references

Wilson, M. R.

Frequently asked questions about how the teen brain works; [by] Michael R. Wilson. Rosen Pub. 2009 64p il (FAQ: teen life) lib bdg $29.25
Grades: 6 7 8 9 **612.8**
1. Brain 2. Teenagers -- Health and hygiene
ISBN 978-1-4358-5324-9 lib bdg; 1-4358-5324-5 lib bdg

LC 2008049322

Describes how the brains of adolescents differ from those of infants or adults, the structure and development of the human brain, the implications of recent discoveries for teen life and behavior, and possible future developments

"A conversational tone keeps the [book] readable, and specific topics have information relevant to teens' lives. . . . Illustrated throughout with captioned color photos." SLJ

Includes glossary and bibliographical references

Winston, Robert M. L., 1940-

What goes on in my head? how your brain works and why you do what you do. [by] Robert Winston. DK Pub. 2010 96p il $16.99
Grades: 4 5 6 7 **612.8**
1. Brain 2. Psychology
ISBN 978-0-7566-6885-3; 0-7566-6885-9

"The author presents a great deal of scientific content and supplements it with examples, anecdotes, and current

findings in the field. . . . In addition, interactive brain teasers and exercises make the science come alive. . . . The book combines vibrant colors and illustrations with explanations to keep young readers engaged." Sci Books Films

613 Personal health and safety

Complementary and alternative medicine information for teens; health tips about diverse medical and wellness systems. edited by Lisa Bakewell. 2nd ed. Omnigraphics, Inc. 2013 xiii, 389 p.p (hardcover) $69
Grades: 7 8 9 10 11 12 **613**
1. Alternative medicine 2. Teenagers -- Health and hygiene
ISBN 0780813111; 9780780813113

LC 2012047548

This book offers information about alternative medicine for teenagers. The "volume is divided into 60 chapters, each focusing on a specific natural medicine or therapy that can be used in combination with or in place of conventional drugs to enhance health . . . . The nine parts address major categories, such as whole-medicine systems, manipulative and body-based practices, dietary and herbal remedies, and energy medicines, as well as sensory and emotional-based therapies." (School Library Journal)

Includes bibliographical references and index.

Couwenhoven, Terri

The **boys'** guide to growing up; choices & changes during puberty. Terri Couwenhoven. Woodbine House 2012 viii, 64 p.p $16.95
Grades: 6 7 8 **613**
1. Puberty 2. Teenagers -- Sexual behavior 3. People with mental disabilities 4. Teenage boys -- Physiology 5. Sex instruction for children with mental disabilities
ISBN 1606130897; 9781606130896

LC 2012025776

This book on puberty by Terri Couwenhoven "is geared to boys with "developmental disabilities." It explains basic information that includes body changes in growth, hair, skin, voice, and feelings. It is not a sex guide though it does not shy away from emerging sexuality." (School Library Journal) Topics include "how to know when flirting is reciprocated (or not!) . . . what information is okay to share with others versus what should remain private, and how to stay safe." (Publisher's note)

De la Bedoyere, Camilla

Personal hygiene and sexual health. Amicus 2010 46p il (Healthy lifestyles) lib bdg $32.80
Grades: 7 8 9 10 **613**
1. Puberty 2. Teenagers -- Health and hygiene
ISBN 978-1-60753-087-9; 1-60753-087-2

LC 2009-47571

This book is "well-written and satisfyingly informative. . . . [The] magazine-like format includes numerous sidebars, color photos, and charts." SLJ

"Discusses the changes that come with puberty in the teenage years for both boys and girls, including personal hygiene issues, body changes, relationships, sexuality, and more." Publisher's note

Includes glossary

Dicker, Katie

Diet and nutrition. Amicus 2011 45p il (Healthy lifestyles) lib bdg $32.80

Grades: 7 8 9 10   **613**

1. Diet 2. Nutrition 3. Physical fitness 4. Teenagers -- Health and hygiene

ISBN 978-1-60753-085-5; 1-60753-085-6

LC 2009-44219

This book is "well-written and satisfyingly informative." SLJ

"Discusses the importance of having a balanced, healthy diet and a healthy body image in your teenage years, gives information on how the body digests various foods, and gives tips for making healthy choices to avoid eating disorders and obesity." Publisher's note

Includes glossary

Dunham, Kelli

The **girl's** body book; everything you need to know for growing up you! illustrated by Laura Tallardy. Applesauce Press 2008 115p il pa $9.95

Grades: 4 5 6 7   **613**

1. Puberty 2. Adolescence 3. Girls -- Health and hygiene

ISBN 978-1-60433-004-5; 1-60433-004-X

"The book's tone and lively cartoon illustrations are friendly and nonthreatening. . . . A solid choice for basic information about puberty." SLJ

Includes bibliographical references

Gardner, Robert

Ace your exercise and nutrition science project: great science fair ideas; [by] Robert Gardner, Barbara Gardner Conklin, and Salvatore Tocci. Enslow Publishers 2009 128p il (Ace your biology science project) lib bdg $31.93

Grades: 5 6 7 8   **613**

1. Exercise 2. Nutrition 3. Science projects 4. Science -- Experiments

ISBN 978-0-7660-3218-7 lib bdg; 0-7660-3218-3 lib bdg

LC 2008-30798

"Presents several science projects and science project ideas about exercise and nutrition." Publisher's note

Includes bibliographical references

Lehman, Robert

★ Will puberty last my whole life? real answers to real questions from preteens about body changes, sex, and other growing-up stuff. Julie Giesy Metzger and Robert Lehman ; illustrated by Cerizo. Sasquatch Books 2011 90 p. col. ill. (pbk.) $16.95

Grades: 4 5 6 7 8   **613**

1. Puberty 2. Questions and answers 3. Boys -- Health and hygiene 4. Girls -- Health and hygiene

ISBN 1570617392; 9781570617393

LC 2011038401

This book "for boys and girls between the ages of 9 and 12 has questions asked by girls in one half of the book" and "questions asked by boys are on the other side." The book contains "answers to questions pre-adolescents have about puberty, friends, feelings, sex, pimples, babies, body hair, menstruation, bras, and much more." (Amazon.com)

Libal, Autumn

★ Can I change the way I look? a teen's guide to the health implications of cosmetic surgery, makeovers, and beyond. Mason Crest Publishers 2005 128p il (Science of health) $24.95

Grades: 7 8 9 10   **613**

1. Personal grooming 2. Teenagers -- Health and hygiene

ISBN 1-59084-843-8

LC 2004-1883

"Framing her discussion within an examination of the media influence on our culture's definition of beauty, Libal does an excellent job of discussing the risks and benefits of cosmetics, piercing and tattooing, diet, exercise, and cosmetic surgery. . . . The author also considers, in some detail, the dangers of anorexia nervosa, bulimia, and steroid use." SLJ

Includes bibliographical references

McCoy, Kathleen

The **teenage** body book; [by] Kathy McCoy and Charles Wibbelsman; illustrations by Bob Stover and Kelly Grady. Rev and updated; Hatherleigh 2008 300p il pa $17.95

Grades: 7 8 9 10 11 12   **613**

1. Adolescence 2. Sex education 3. Teenagers -- Health and hygiene

ISBN 978-1-57826-277-9

LC 2009-368424

First published 1979 by Pocket Bks. with authors' names in reverse order

A handbook for teenagers discussing nutrition, health, fitness, emotions, and sexuality, including such topics as body image, drugs, STDs, fad diets and hazards and benefits of the Internet.

"This highly informative book . . . is at the same time easily readable, nonpreachy, and comprehensive. . . . This book should be not only in the library of every middle and high school, but also in the hands of every student and in health education classes." Sci Books Films

Natterson, Cara

The **care** & keeping of you 2; the body book for older girls. Dr. Cara Natterson ; illustrated by Josee Masse. American Girl 2013 96 p. (paperback) $12.99

Grades: 5 6 7 8   **613**

1. Puberty 2. Life skills -- Handbooks, manuals, etc. 3. Teenage girls -- Health and hygiene 4. Girls -- Life skills guides

ISBN 1609580427; 9781609580421

LC 2012045813

This book, by Cara Natterson, illustrated by Josee Masse, is a body image and physiology guide written for girls going through puberty. "This . . . advice book will guide you through the next steps of growing up. . . . This book covers new questions about periods, your growing body, peer pressure, personal care, and more." (Publisher's note)

"The friendly illustrations support the overall tone and style. . . . Its neutral, matter-of-fact approach will help show readers . . . that all the changes they may be feeling are perfectly normal." SLJ

Orr, Tamra

★ **Playing** safe, eating right; making healthy choices. ABDO Pub. 2009 112p il (Essential health: strong beautiful girls) lib bdg $22.95

Grades: 6 7 8 9   **613**
1. Health 2. Nutrition 3. Teenagers -- Health and hygiene
ISBN 978-1-60453-103-9 lib bdg; 1-60453-103-7 lib bdg

LC 2008-17015

This features fictional narratives paired with firsthand advice from a licensed psychologist to help preteen and teen girls evaluate options and choose healthy ways of living. Topics include diet and exercise, sleep, drugs and alcohol.

"The topics are well selected, the design is attractive, and the stories features girls from a variety of cultures." Booklist
Includes glossary and bibliographical references

Pfeifer, Kate Gruenwald

★ **American** Medical Assocation boy's guide to becoming a teen. Jossey-Bass 2006 128p il pa $12.95

Grades: 4 5 6 7   **613**
1. Puberty 2. Adolescence 3. Boys -- Health and hygiene
ISBN 0-7879-8343-8

"This guide addresses puberty's changes clearly. . . . The text's approach is straightforward, accessible, and nonjudgmental, whether the topic is same-sex attraction or divorcing parents. The volume closes with an extensive resource section, including hotlines." Booklist
Includes bibliographical references

★ **American** Medical Association girl's guide to becoming a teen. Jossey-Bass 2006 128p pa $12.95

Grades: 4 5 6 7   **613**
1. Puberty 2. Adolescence 3. Girls -- Health and hygiene
ISBN 0-7879-8344-6

This "covers the physical and emotional changes that puberty brings, along with solid tips about grooming, diet, exercise, and other health issues, such as eating disorders. . . . The clear text communicates concepts clearly . . . and girls will find plenty of useful information." Booklist
Includes bibliographical references

Reber, Deborah

Chill; stress-reducing techniques for a more balanced, peaceful you. Simon Pulse 2008 196p il pa $9.99

Grades: 8 9 10 11 12   **613**
1. Stress (Psychology) 2. Girls -- Health and hygiene
ISBN 978-1-4169-5526-9 pa; 1-4169-5526-7 pa

"This book has just the right combination of smart wit, know-it-all bravado, and advice from a pseudo big sister. The pages speed by, moving from topic to topic: time management, support systems, self-help therapy, exercise, nutrition, and more. Advice is free-flowing, complete with examples, exercises, and quizzes. . . . This helpful resource will appeal to a wide variety of young women." SLJ

613.2   Dietetics

Ballard, Carol

Food for feeling healthy; [by] Carol Ballard. Heinemann Library 2006 56p il (Making healthy food choices) $32.86; pa $9.49

Grades: 7 8 9 10   **613.2**
1. Nutrition
ISBN 978-1-4034-8571-7; 1-4034-8571-2; 978-1-4034-8577-9 pa; 1-4034-8577-1 pa

LC 2006003970

"Ballard incorporates the new food pyramid into a discussion of basic nutritional requirements. She considers obesity, malnutrition, and eating disorders and comments on various factors that influence eating choices, such as advertising and peer pressure. After helping readers decipher food labels, she provides a week's worth of menus." SLJ
Includes bibliographical references

Can diets be harmful? edited by Christine Watkins. Greenhaven Press 2012 101 p. (At issue) (library) $34.45; (paperback) $25.45

Grades: 8 9 10 11 12   **613.2**
1. Diet 2. Eating habits 3. Diet in disease 4. Reducing diets -- Heath aspects 5. Reducing diets -- Health aspects
ISBN 0737755563; 0737755571 pa; 9780737755565 lib bdg; 9780737755572

LC 2011020813

This book, edited by Christine Watkins, is part of the At Issue series and looks at diets. The series "provides a wide range of opinions on individual social issues. Each volume focuses on a specific issue and offers a variety of perspectives—eyewitness accounts, governmental views, scientific analysis, newspaper and magazine accounts, and many more—to illuminate the issue." (Publisher's note)
Includes bibliographical references (p. 93-97) and index.

Currie, Stephen

Junk food. Cherry Lake Pub. 2009 32p il (Health at risk) lib bdg $27.07

Grades: 4 5 6 7 8   **613.2**
1. Nutrition
ISBN 978-1-60279-284-5 lib bdg; 1-60279-284-4 lib bdg

LC 2008017498

This describes what junk food is, why it's not good for your body, and what's being done to help us control our junk food habit.

"Great for reports or reluctant readers." Booklist
Includes bibliographical references

Dieting; Claire Kreger Boaz, book editor. Greenhaven Press 2008 117p il (Issues that concern you) lib bdg $33.70

Grades: 8 9 10 11 12   **613.2**

1. Weight loss

ISBN 978-0-7377-3644-1 lib bdg; 0-7377-3644-5 lib bdg

LC 2007-35368

This title presents various views on dieting and weight loss.

Includes bibliographical references

Doeden, Matt

Eat right! how you can make good food choices. illustrations by Jack Desrocher. Lerner Publications 2008 64p il (Health zone) lib bdg $30.60

Grades: 4 5 6 7   **613.2**

1. Nutrition

ISBN 978-0-8225-7552-8; 0-8225-7552-3

LC 2007043322

"This offers a highly readable, never preachy exploration into the benefits of providing quality fuel for your body. It opens with an anecdote of a kid who snacks on soda and chips while playing volleyball. A friend challenges him to to eat better for a week, and he comes back with more sustained energy and a fresh outlook. . . . The following chapters do a great job of detailing everything from the food pyramid and benefits of different nutrients to warnings against following the faddish, ineffective diets." Booklist

Includes bibliographical references

Edwards, Hazel

Talking about your weight; by Hazel Edwards and Goldie Alexander. Gareth Stevens 2010 32p il (Healthy living) lib bdg $26

Grades: 4 5 6 7   **613.2**

1. Obesity 2. Nutrition 3. Weight loss

ISBN 978-1-4339-3655-5; 1-4339-3655-0

"This guidebook offers a simple look at healthy lifestyle choices involving exercise and diet. It examines people's relationships with food, body shape and genetics, eating disorders, and ways to combat obesity." Publisher's note

Etingoff, Kim

Building a healthy diet with the 5 food groups; Kim Etingoff. Mason Crest, an imprint of National Highlights 2015 48 p. (On my plate : building a healthy diet with the 5 food groups) (hardback) $20.95

Grades: 5 6 7   **613.2**

1. Diet 2. Health 3. Eating customs 4. Diet 5. Health 6. Food habits

ISBN 1422230953; 9781422230954

LC 2014010544

This book, by Kim Etingoff, "provides a thorough overview of different food groups: where they come from and what role they play in our overall health. Suggested research projects are strong and engaging. Students can do research to find out the closest place where beans, nuts, and seeds are grown." (School Library Journal)

"The sidebars and illustrations supplement the text well and the research project suggestions are especially useful for students and teachers." VOYA

Favor, Lesli J.

Weighing in; nutrition and weight management. Marshall Cavendish Benchmark 2007 128p il (Food and fitness) lib bdg $28

Grades: 7 8 9 10   **613.2**

1. Nutrition 2. Weight loss

ISBN 0761443673; 9780761443674

LC 2006-101930

This "offers an in-depth look at issues related to body weight. Chapters . . . discuss determining one's ideal weight; health risks associated with weight, from diabetes to anorexia; nutrition and wellness; teen dietary requirements and meal planning; and weight-loss strategies, with possible dangers highlighted. . . . Teens will find this a useful, often thought-provoking resource for personal or class research." Booklist

Includes bibliographical references

Furgang, Adam

Carbonated beverages; the incredibly disgusting story. Rosen Central 2011 48p il (Incredibly disgusting food) lib bdg $26.50; pa $11.75

Grades: 4 5 6 7   **613.2**

1. Carbonated beverages

ISBN 978-1-4488-1266-0 lib bdg; 1-4488-1266-6 lib bdg; 978-1-4488-2282-9 pa; 1-4488-2282-3 pa

LC 2010023227

This presents "straightforward information about why [carbonated beverages] are unhealthy without resorting to extreme gross-out factors. The [book contains] a breakdown of the foods' components . . . insight into how they are processed, and both short- and long-term effects of consumption. . . . Readers may or may not be disgusted, but they will definitely learn a thing or two about smart eating habits." SLJ

Includes glossary and bibliographical references

Salty and sugary snacks; the incredibly disgusting story. Rosen Central 2011 48p il (Incredibly disgusting food) lib bdg $26.50; pa $11.75

Grades: 4 5 6 7   **613.2**

1. Salt 2. Sugar 3. Nutrition 4. Snack foods

ISBN 978-1-4488-1267-7 lib bdg; 1-4488-1267-4 lib bdg; 978-1-4488-2283-6 pa; 1-4488-2283-1 pa

LC 2010025751

This book describes how salty and sugary snacks put dangerous amounts of sugar and salt into our bodies and how these unnecessary calories can have terrible effects on the body.

"Readers may or may not be disgusted, but they will definitely learn a thing or two about smart eating habits." SLJ

Includes glossary and bibliographical references

Gay, Kathlyn

The **scoop** on what to eat; what you should know about diet and nutrition. Enslow Publishers 2009 112p il (Issues in focus today) lib bdg $31.93

Grades: 7 8 9 10   **613.2**
1. Nutrition
ISBN 978-0-7660-3066-4; 0-7660-3066-0
LC 2008-40382
"Bolstered with well-integrated quotes and relevant statistics, [this book offers] an excellent starting point for students seeking [a] broad, thoroughly researched [introduction] to [diet and nutrition]. . . . Illuminating case studies, enhanced with multiple viewpoints, personalize the facts and place them in boarder context." Booklist
Includes glossary and bibliographical references

Heller, Tania
Overweight; a handbook for teens and parents. [by] Tania Heller; foreword by Mohsen Ziai. McFarland & Company 2005 180p pa $29.95
Grades: 7 8 9 10   **613.2**
1. Obesity 2. Weight loss 3. Teenagers -- Health and hygiene
ISBN 9781476603995; 0-7864-2082-0
LC 2005004360
"This work covers the causes and effects of the rise in childhood obesity while presenting . . . guidelines and recommendations for getting assessed and treated. Information is provided on healthy nutrition and physical activity for young people, tools for self-monitoring and medical conditions associated with weight gain." Publisher's note
Includes glossary and bibliographical references

Johanson, Paula
Fake foods; fried, fast, and processed: the incredibly disgusting story. Rosen Central 2011 48p il (Incredibly disgusting food) lib bdg $26.50; pa $11.75
Grades: 4 5 6 7   **613.2**
1. Nutrition 2. Natural foods 3. Convenience foods
ISBN 978-1-4488-1269-1 lib bdg; 1-4488-1269-0 lib bdg; 978-1-4488-2285-0 pa; 1-4488-2285-8 pa
LC 2010020534
This presents "straightforward information about why various junk foods are unhealthy without resorting to extreme gross-out factors. The [book contains] a breakdown of the foods' components . . . insight into how they are processed, and both short- and long-term effects of consumption. . . . Readers may or may not be disgusted, but they will definitely learn a thing or two about smart eating habits." SLJ
Includes glossary and bibliographical references

Juettner, Bonnie
Diet and disease. Lucent Books 2011 104p il (Nutrition & health) $30.85
Grades: 6 7 8 9   **613.2**
1. Nutrition 2. Preventive medicine
ISBN 978-1-4205-0269-5; 1-4205-0269-7
LC 2010035236
This "discusses the food choices that lead to the 'big four' diseases of cancer, heart disease, stroke, and type 2 diabetes and shows how good nutrition can help prevent deadly disease. . . . [This] volume is clearly written, addressing real-life concerns with solid information and perspec-

tive, and includes color photographs, notes, and [a list] of further resources." Booklist
Includes bibliographical references

Libal, Autumn
Fats, sugars, and empty calories; the fast food habit. Mason Crest Publishers 2006 104p il (Obesity: modern day epidemic) $23.95
Grades: 7 8 9 10   **613.2**
1. Health 2. Obesity 3. Nutrition
ISBN 978-1-59084-943-9; 1-59084-943-4
LC 2004-15660
Discusses the dangers of fast food.
Includes glossary and bibliographical references

Mooney, Carla
Junk food junkies. Lucent Books 2010 104p il (Nutrition & health) $30.85
Grades: 6 7 8 9   **613.2**
1. Nutrition
ISBN 978-1-4205-0271-8; 1-4205-0271-9
LC 2010016858
"A solid, detailed overview of the negative effects of a poor diet on health. Mooney livens up the dry subject matter with interesting nutrition facts, photographs, charts, tables, and anecdotes. She discusses health risks such as obesity and diabetes. The last chapter is particularly useful because it offers healthy alternatives for snacks and meals. It also explains how to read a nutrition label and tells readers what to avoid in terms of amounts of fat and calories. This book is useful for research and reports and as a teaching aid." SLJ
Includes glossary and bibliographical references

Morris, Neil
Food for sports; [by] Neil Morris. Heinemann Library 2006 56p il (Making healthy food choices) $32.86; pa $9.49
Grades: 7 8 9 10   **613.2**
1. Sports 2. Nutrition
ISBN 978-1-4034-8573-1; 1-4034-8573-9; 978-1-4034-8579-3 pa; 1-4034-8579-8 pa
LC 2006003971
This "talks about the types of foods that help athletes maximize their energy level. The information on sensible eating choices and calorie intake can help even non-athletes manage their health and weight. . . . [This is] well written. . . . There aren't many books out there that examine all aspects of food in such detail." SLJ
Includes bibliographical references

Rau, Dana Meachen, 1971-
Going organic; a healthy guide to making the switch. by Dana Meachen Rau. Compass Point Books 2012 64 p. col. ill. (paperback) $8.95; (hardcover) $33.99
Grades: 6 7 8 9   **613.2**
1. Diet 2. Nutrition 3. Natural foods 4. Organic farming 5. Health
ISBN 0756545234; 0756545285; 9780756545239; 9780756545284
LC 2011040704

"[Rau] outlines the perils of factory farms and industrial food lots, both on an environmental and personal scale; distinguishes the often interrelated terms organic, sustainable, and local; offers a rundown of potentially misleading marketing terms; and even tosses in a few recipes, charts, and other helpful sidebars. Readers who find their interest piqued by this informative and concise treatment..." Booklist

Includes bibliographical references (p. 62) and index.

Going vegetarian; a healthy guide to making the switch. by Dana Meachen Rau. Compass Point Books 2012 64 p. (hardcover) $33.99

Grades: 5 6 7 8 9   **613.2**
1. Nutrition 2. Vegetarianism 3. Vegetarian cooking
ISBN 0756545226; 9780756545222; 9780756545307
     LC 2011040836
Author Dana Meachen Rau presents a guide to becoming a vegetarian. "Learn about the benefits and challenges of a diet that does not include red meat, poultry, or fish. Helpful tips, delicious vegetarian recipes, and how tos will make the switch so much easier." The book also offers various organic, meatless, and vegan recipes and meal ideas. (Publisher"s note)

"Whether looking to go organic, ovo-lacto vegetarian, or vegan, kids will find the information necessary to make the switch in these titles...Organic focuses on the USDA's National Organic Program (NOP) regulations, making no mention of other certification programs. It does, however, warn kids about trusting organic labels implicitly and recommends that they go straight to the source when possible by researching and even visiting companies. Serve these up to budding health foodies.." (School Library Journal)

Includes bibliographical references (p. 62) and index

Schwartz, Ellen
I'm a vegetarian; amazing facts and ideas for healthy vegetarians. illustrated by Farida Zaman. Tundra Bks. 2002 112p il pa $9.95

Grades: 6 7 8 9   **613.2**
1. Vegetarianism
ISBN 0-88776-588-2; 9781770490604
     LC 2001-95376
"The author opens with an overview of the different types of vegetarians and the rationale behind their decisions, then moves into advice on handling parental concerns and sticky social situations that are sure to arise. A consideration of nutrition and how to achieve a healthy diet that provides all necessary nutrients follows, ending with a smattering of suggested menus and recipes. . . . She writes in a light, chatty tone, using a question-and-answer format, bulleted facts and lists, boxed information, and humor. Black-and-white drawings throughout add to the book's appeal." SLJ

Includes glossary and bibliographical references

Smolin, Lori A.
Nutrition and weight management; [by] Lori A. Smolin and Mary B. Grosvenor. 2nd ed.; Chelsea House 2010 184p il map (Healthy eating: a guide to nutrition) lib bdg $35

Grades: 7 8 9 10 11 12   **613.2**
1. Nutrition 2. Weight loss
ISBN 978-1-60413-803-0; 1-60413-803-3
     LC 2009-41335
First published 2005
This "volume uses boldface type to introduce important and unknown words to the reader and explains them in an easy to understand manner so the reader can grasp the concept being discussed. . . . [For] classes needing information about the importance of good nutrition . . . [this] would be valuable." Libr Media Connect

Includes glossary and bibliographical references

Waters, Rosa
My daily diet; dairy. Rosa Waters. Mason Crest, an imprint of National Highlights 2015 48 p. (hardback) $20.95

Grades: 5 6 7   **613.2**
1. Dairy products 2. Dairy products 3. Dairy products in human nutrition
ISBN 1422230961; 9781422230947; 9781422230961
     LC 2014010564
This book on dairy, by Rosa Waters, "gives young readers the health information and practical tools they need to make better food decisions and eat a balanced diet that includes all five food groups. . . . [It] give[s] young readers the tools they need to choose nutritious foods and begin a life-long commitment to health." (Publisher's note)

"Created with help from a consultant who is a pediatrician and professor at Harvard Medical School, this series provides a thorough overview of different food groups: where they come from and what role they play in our overall health. Suggested research projects are strong and engaging. Students can do research to find out the closest place where beans, nuts, and seeds are grown...the charts are phenomenal; one shows how many ounces of protein people need at different ages, while another lists the iron, carbohydrates, sugar, potassium, and other nutrients found in 20 different fruits. Despite the design, this is a very smart, readable series." SLJ

Includes bibliographical references and index
Other titles in the series include:
My Daily Diet: Fruits (2014)
My Daily Diet: Grains (2014)
My Daily Diet: Proteins (2014)
My Daily Diet: Vegetables (2014)

Watson, Stephanie
Mystery meat; hot dogs, sausages, and lunch meats: the incredibly disgusting story. Rosen Pub. Group 2011 48p il (Incredibly disgusting food) lib bdg $26.50; pa $11.75

Grades: 4 5 6 7   **613.2**
1. Meat 2. Sausages 3. Nutrition 4. Frankfurters
ISBN 978-1-4488-1268-4 lib bdg; 1-4488-1268-2 lib bdg; 978-1-4488-2284-3 pa; 1-4488-2284-X pa
     LC 2010013649
"The short but substantive chapters begin with a look at typical hot-dog ingredients and manufacturing practices, followed by discussions of how 'mystery meats,' including common, highly processed sandwich fillers, affect the body. A closing chapter about the components of a healthy diet

widens the book into an opportunity for adults and kids to discuss general nutrition and includes useful tips on reading food labels.... Young readers will find plenty of browsing and report fodder in these pages." Booklist

Includes bibliographical references

Woog, Adam

Food myths and facts. Lucent Books 2011 96p il (Nutrition & health) lib bdg $30.85

Grades: 6 7 8 9   **613.2**

1. Nutrition

ISBN 978-1-4205-0270-1; 1-4205-0270-0

LC 2010035960

This "aims to clear up nutritional misinformation on topics like metabolism, sports drinks, and fad diets.... [This] volume is clearly written, addressing real-life concerns with solid information and perspective, and includes color photographs, notes, and [a list] of further resources." Booklist

Includes bibliographical references

Zahensky, Barbara A.

Diet fads. Rosen 2007 64p il (Danger zone: dieting and eating disorders) lib bdg $27.95

Grades: 4 5 6 7 8   **613.2**

1. Obesity 2. Weight loss

ISBN 978-1-4042-1999-1

"This clearly written overview emphasizes the impact of super-thin celebrity images on general self-esteem. ... Zahensky considers the reasons people overeat and walks readers through practical steps to recognizing true hunger, making a weight-loss plan, and establishing good diet and exercise habits. She examines different types of fad and crash diets, pointing out their inherent dangers." SLJ

613.208 Young people

★ Diabetes information for teens; health tips about managing diabetes and preventing related complications, including facts about insulin, glucose control, healthy eating, physical activity, and learning to live with diabetes. edited by Karen Bellenir. Omnigraphics 2012 397 p. ill. (hardcover : alk. paper) $69.00

Grades: 7 8 9 10 11 12   **613.208**

1. Diabetes 2. Teenagers -- Health and hygiene 3. Diabetes 4. Diabetes in adolescence

ISBN 0780812182; 9780780812185

LC 2011038652

This book for teenagers on the topic of diabetes, edited by Karen Bellenir, "examines the alarming trends in diabetes prevalence, and it provides information about positive steps that can be taken. The book provides facts about the different types of diabetes, its medical management, and the roles of nutrition and physical activity in averting its consequences. Suggestions are included for handling problematic situations, such as caring for diabetes at school." (Publisher's note)

Includes bibliographical references and index

★ Diet information for teens; health tips about nutrition fundamentals and eating plans including facts about vitamins, minerals, food additives, and weight-related concerns. edited by Zachary Klimecki and Karen Bellenir. 3rd ed. Omnigraphics, Inc. 2012 xiii, 427 p.p ill. (Teen health series) (hardcover : alk. paper) $69

Grades: 8 9 10 11 12   **613.208**

1. Diet 2. Health 3. Teenagers -- Health and hygiene 4. Teenagers -- Nutrition

ISBN 0780811569; 9780780811560

LC 2011031595

This book is a "compendium of diet and nutrition" for teenagers comprising "articles on all facets of nutrition, drawn mainly from FDA documents.... Chapters of specialized appeal include 'Special Dietary Guidelines for Teenage Mothers' and 'Assessing School Lunches,' as well as coverage of teen snacking." (School Library Journal)

Includes bibliographical references and index

613.262 Vegetarian diet

Traugh, Susan M.

Vegetarianism. Lucent Books 2011 96p il (Nutrition & health) lib bdg $30.85

Grades: 6 7 8 9   **613.262**

1. Vegetarianism

ISBN 978-1-4205-0272-5; 1-4205-0272-7

LC 2010014015

This "explains the different types of vegetarians, from ovo-lacto to vegan, touches briefly on the lifestyle's difficulties, and depicts in an overall positive way why it is a healthy choice. [This] volume is clearly written, addressing real-life concerns with solid information and perspective, and includes color photographs, notes, and [a list] of further resources." Booklist

Includes bibliographical references

613.6 Personal safety and special topics of health

Champion, Neil

Finding food and water. Amicus 2010 32p il (Survive alive) lib bdg $28.50

Grades: 4 5 6 7   **613.6**

1. Wilderness survival

ISBN 978-1-60753-037-4 lib bdg; 1-60753-037-6 lib bdg

LC 2009030889

This offers survival tips for finding food and water in the wild, including how to know what is safe to eat or drink from land, plant, and animal sources.

This "colorful [book contains] numerous photos and illustrations that effectively break the [text] into small, readable chunks. There's lots of practical, everyday information here. ... Brief yet gripping real-life survival stories are interspersed throughout the [book]." SLJ

Includes glossary

Finding your way. Amicus 2011 32p il (Survive alive) lib bdg $28.50

Grades: 4 5 6 7   **613.6**

1. Orienteering 2. Wilderness survival

ISBN 978-1-60753-038-1 lib bdg; 1-60753-038-4 lib bdg

LC 2009030888

"With eye-catching photographs, clear explanations, a survival skills quiz, a glossary, Web sites, and 'True Survival' stories . . . this engaging text encourages readers to figure out where they are and where they want to go." Booklist

Includes glossary

In an emergency. Amicus 2010 32p il (Survive alive) lib bdg $28.50

Grades: 4 5 6 7   **613.6**

1. Survival skills

ISBN 978-1-60753-040-4; 1-60753-040-6

LC 2010002517

This offers survival tips on what to do in emergency situations. Includes scenarios about fire, bad weather, accidents, injuries, extreme conditions, and more.'

This "colorful [book contains] numerous photos and illustrations that effectively break the [text] into small, readable chunks. There's lots of practical, everyday information here. . . . Brief yet gripping real-life survival stories are interspersed throughout the [book]." SLJ

Includes glossary

Making shelter. Amicus 2010 32p il (Survive alive) lib bdg $28.50

Grades: 4 5 6 7   **613.6**

1. Wilderness survival

ISBN 978-1-60753-041-1 lib bdg; 1-60753-041-4 lib bdg

LC 2010001378

This offers survival tips for building shelter in the wild, including using natural means in different regions such as the desert, forest, jungle, and cold areas. Also includes information on what to bring for aid when building shelters.

Doeden, Matt

Safety smarts; how to manage threats, protect yourself, get help, and more. Matt Doeden. Twenty-First Century Books 2013 64 p. col. ill. (USA today teen wise guides : lifestyle choices) (library) $31.93

Grades: 8 9 10 11 12   **613.6**

1. Safety education 2. Teenagers -- Crimes against -- Prevention

ISBN 0761370226; 9780761370222

LC 2011044268

This book, by Matt Doeden, offers advice for teen safety as part of the "USA Today Teen Wise Guides: Lifestyle Choices" series. "In a perfect world, everyone would be safe all the time: in the car, at home, at school, and online. Well, . . . cars sometimes crash, burglars break into houses, kids get bullied at school, and cyberstalkers and sexual predators prowl the Internet. But that's no reason to hide in your room and worry. You can stay safe if you use some safety smarts." (Publisher's note)

Includes bibliographical references (p. 61-63) and index.

Hurley, Michael

Surviving the wilderness. Raintree 2011 56p il (Extreme survival) lib bdg $33.50

Grades: 4 5 6 7   **613.6**

1. Wilderness survival

ISBN 978-1-4109-3972-2; 1-4109-3972-3

LC 2010028839

This book is "fun and informative. [This] well-organized title starts with an overview [of wilderness survival], offers some specific examples, and includes additional facts or tips and resources. . . . [It features] dramatic archival and full-color photos on nearly every page. . . . [This is a book] that youngsters will enjoy and talk about." SLJ

Includes glossary and bibliographical references

Long, Denise

Survivor kid; a practical guide to wilderness survival. Chicago Review Press 2011 222p il $12.95

Grades: 4 5 6 7   **613.6**

1. Wilderness survival

ISBN 978-1-56976-708-5; 1-56976-708-4

LC 2011004952

"Long offers lessons on how to stay healthy and out of trouble while awaiting rescue. Her matter-of-fact, no-nonsense tone will play well with young readers, and the clear writing style is appropriate to the content. The engaging guide covers everything from building shelters to avoiding pigs and javelinas. . . . The volume invites browsing as much as studying. . . . An excellent bibliography will lead young readers to a host of fascinating websites, and 150 clipart-style line drawings complement the text." Kirkus

Includes bibliographical references

Nelson, Sara Kirsten

Stay safe! how you can keep out of harm's way. by Sara Nelson; illustrated by Jack Desrocher. Lerner Publications 2008 64p il (Health zone) lib bdg $30.60

Grades: 4 5 6 7   **613.6**

1. Safety education 2. Children and strangers 3. Child sexual abuse -- Prevention

ISBN 978-0-8225-7551-1; 0-8225-7551-5

The offers safety education on such subjects as bullying in schools, inappropriate touching by family members, internet solicitations and threats in public places (such as attempted abductions).

"The format is beyond lively, with lots of color, cartoons, and an informal writing style, but it manages to present sometimes frightening material in a non-threatening and browsable way." Booklist

Includes glossary and bibliographical references

Raatma, Lucia

Safety in your neighborhood. Child's World 2005 32p il (Living well) lib bdg $25.64

Grades: 4 5 6 7   **613.6**

1. Crime prevention 2. Safety education

ISBN 1-59296-240-8

LC 2003-27214

This book teaches young readers how to keep their neighborhood a safe place and what to do if that safety is compromised.

This "clearly written [title has] an appealing layout with plenty of full-color photos and a triple-spaced text. . . . [It] provides solid tips." SLJ

Includes glossary and bibliographical references

613.7 Physical fitness

Aikman, Louise

Pilates step-by-step; [by] Louise Aikman and Matthew Harvey. Rosen Central 2011 93p il (Skills in motion) lib bdg $31.95

Grades: 5 6 7 8   613.7

1. Pilates method
ISBN 978-1-4488-1549-4; 1-4488-1549-5
                                          LC 2010007510

Presents a general guide to the Pilates exercise system using a sequence of stop-action images and text instructions to illustrate some of the most common movements.

Includes bibliographical references

Atha, Antony

Fitness for young people; step-by-step. [by] Antony Atha and Simon Frost. Rosen Central 2010 93p il (Skills in motion) lib bdg $31.95

Grades: 5 6 7 8   613.7

1. Physical fitness
ISBN 978-1-4358-3364-7; 1-4358-3364-3
                                          LC 2009-13245

Describes how to maintain physical fitness for youth, providing exercises that are both effective and fun.

"Colorful photographs show the entire movement of each skill presented, giving new meaning to the term 'step-by-step.' Progression borders at the bottom of the pages highlight the salient points to notice in performing each skill from beginning to end." SLJ

Includes bibliographical references

Bellenir, Elizabeth

Fitness Information for Teens; Health Tips About Exercise & Active Lifestyles. edited by Elizabeth Bellenir. 3rd ed. Omnigraphics 2012 xiii, 387 p.p ill. (Teen health series) (hardcover : alk. paper) $69.00

Grades: 7 8 9 10 11 12   613.7

1. Physical fitness 2. Teenagers -- Health and hygiene 3. Physical fitness for youth
ISBN 9780780812673; 0780812670
                                          LC 2012024737

This book is "earmarked to provide the tools and information needed for teens to engage in a healthier lifestyle before entering adulthood. . . . Seven main sections cover information on the human body, personal fitness plans, exercise fundamentals, team activities, sports safety, obstacles to finding fitness, and resources." (Booklist)

"In this thorough, easy-to-follow single volume, seven main sections cover information on the human body, personal fitness plans, exercise fundamentals, team activities,

sports safety, obstacles to finding fitness, and resources... Highly recommended." Booklist

Includes bibliographical references and index

Birkemoe, Karen

★ **Strike** a pose; the Planet Girl guide to yoga. written by Karen Birkemoe; illustrated by Heather Collett. Kids Can Press 2007 96p il (Planet girl) spiral $12.95

Grades: 5 6 7 8   613.7

1. Yoga 2. Girls -- Health and hygiene
ISBN 978-1-55337-004-8

"This compact book offers a well-rounded overview of Hatha yoga. Using an easy conversational tone, Birkemoe relates the general practice and specific poses to reader's lives. The simple line drawings and color illustrations partner effectively with text to explain each move." SLJ

Includes glossary

Dicker, Katie

Exercise. Amicus 2010 46p il (Healthy lifestyles) lib bdg $32.80

Grades: 7 8 9 10   613.7

1. Exercise 2. Physical fitness
ISBN 978-1-60753-086-2; 1-60753-086-4
                                          LC 2009-47566

This book is "well-written and satisfyingly informative. . . . [The] magazine-like format includes numerous sidebars, color photos, and charts." SLJ

"Discusses in-depth the benefits of exercise for teenagers, including how to make exercise fun and safe and develop it into a lifelong habit." Publisher's note

Includes glossary

Eason, Sarah

Free running; by Paul Mason and Sarah Eason. Lerner Publications 2011 il (On the radar: sports)

Grades: 5 6 7 8   613.7

1. Running 2. Parkour
ISBN 076137759X; 9780761377597
                                          LC 2011000467

"Free running, also known as parkour, is a combination of speed running, gymnastics, and, in some cases, sheer fearlessness. Lovers of the sport launch over walls, clear fences in a single bound, and somersault down stairwells. This . . . captures the adrenaline-fueled energy of runners, using bold graphics, bright colors, and short interviews to showcase professionals, demonstrate moves, and trace the origins of free running." Booklist

Frederick, Shane

Strength training for teen athletes; exercises to take your game to the next level. by Karen Latchana Kenney. Capstone Press 2012 48 p. col. ill. (paperback) $7.95; (library binding) $31.32

Grades: 6 7 8 9   613.7

1. Athletes 2. Exercise 3. Weight lifting 4. Teenagers -- Health and hygiene 5. Muscle strength 6. Teenage

athletes -- Training of
ISBN 1429676809; 9781429680028; 1429680024;
9781429676809

LC 2011033561

Author Karen Latchana Kenney provides a guide for teenage athletes on how to improve their performance with strength training. "With . . . strength building exercises and tips, you'll notice a big improvement in your game. Build the power behind your baseball or softball swing, soccer kick, or swimming stroke." (Publisher's note)

Includes bibliographical references and index.

Gedatus, Gus

Exercise for weight management. LifeMatters 2001 64p il (Nutrition and fitness) lib bdg $23.93
Grades: 7 8 9 10　　　　　　　　　　　　　613.7
1. Exercise 2. Physical fitness
ISBN 9780736807067; 0-7368-0706-3

LC 00-34899

This offers information on physical fitness and setting up a healthy exercise plan

"This brief, well-designed title delivers informative and relevant material for the serious teen reader." Sci Books Films

Includes glossary and bibliographical references

Jennings, Madeleine

Tai chi step-by-step; [by] Madeleine Jennings and James Drewe. Rosen Central 2011 93p il (Skills in motion) lib bdg $31.95
Grades: 5 6 7 8　　　　　　　　　　　　　613.7
1. Tai chi
ISBN 978-1-4488-1551-7; 1-4488-1551-7

LC 2010008411

This book introduces both basic and higher level techniques of tai chi, with step-by-step instructions, illustrated by stop-motion sequential photography.

Includes bibliographical references

Kuskowski, Alex

Cool relaxing; healthy & fun ways to chill out! Alex Kuskowski. ABDO Pub. Co. 2012 32 p. col. ill. (Cool health and fitness) (library) $28.50
Grades: 4 5 6　　　　　　　　　　　　　613.7
1. Creative activities 2. Rest 3. Relaxation
ISBN 1617834289; 9781617834288

LC 2012010345

This nonfiction children's book by Alex Kuskowski presents a "hodgepodge of activities and techniques to achieve zen calm. The suggestions in this 'Cool Health and Fitness' title are all over the place--cooking, running, reading, baths, even cleaning--but that's the unspoken truth: whatever pleasantly distracts you does the trick. Eight activities are given step-by-step attention, including yoga, stretching, making a lavender pillow, and meditation." (Booklist)

Mason, Paul, 1967-

Improving endurance. PowerKids Press 2011 32p il (Training for sports) lib bdg $25.25

Grades: 5 6 7 8　　　　　　　　　　　　　613.7
1. Sports 2. Exercise
ISBN 978-1-4488-3300-9; 1-4488-3300-0

LC 2010024356

This offers "detailed tips on improving . . . endurance. All-around athletes will love this and so will kids who just want to work on getting fit." Booklist

Improving flexibility. PowerKids Press 2011 32p il (Training for sports) lib bdg $25.25
Grades: 5 6 7 8　　　　　　　　　　　　　613.7
1. Sports 2. Exercise
ISBN 978-1-4488-3299-6; 1-4488-3299-3

LC 2010024359

This offers tips on improving flexibility for sports.

"All-around athletes will love this and so will kids who just want to work on getting fit." Booklist

Improving speed. PowerKids Press 2011 32p il (Training for sports) lib bdg $25.25
Grades: 5 6 7 8　　　　　　　　　　　　　613.7
1. Speed 2. Sports 3. Exercise
ISBN 978-1-4488-3302-3; 1-4488-3302-3

LC 2010024354

This offers "detailed tips on improving speed. . . . All-around athletes will love this and so will kids who just want to work on getting fit." Booklist

Improving strength & power. PowerKids Press 2011 32p il (Training for sports) lib bdg $25.25
Grades: 5 6 7 8　　　　　　　　　　　　　613.7
1. Exercise 2. Physical fitness
ISBN 978-1-4488-3301-6; 1-4488-3301-6

LC 2010024425

This offers tips on improving strength and power for sports.

"All-around athletes will love this and so will kids who just want to work on getting fit." Booklist

Purperhart, Helen

Yoga exercises for teens; developing a calmer mind and a stronger body. Hunter House Publishers 2008 160p il pa $14.95
Grades: 7 8 9 10　　　　　　　　　　　　　613.7
1. Yoga 2. Physical fitness 3. Teenagers -- Health and hygiene
ISBN 978-0-8979-3503-6; 0-8979-3503-9

LC 2008-24262

This book about yoga "includes the eight yoga rules for life, the five precepts, and the five yoga abstinences." Publisher's note

Includes bibliographical references

Spilling, Michael

Yoga step-by-step; [by] Michael Spilling and Liz Lark. Rosen Central 2011 95p il (Skills in motion) lib bdg $31.95
Grades: 5 6 7 8　　　　　　　　　　　　　613.7
1. Yoga
ISBN 978-1-4488-1550-0; 1-4488-1550-9

LC 2010008665

Readers are introduced to basic yoga techniques through step-by-step instructions, depicted with numerous photographs.

Includes bibliographical references

613.8 Substance abuse (Drug abuse)

★ **Drug** information for teens; health tips about the physical and mental effects of substance abuse. edited by Elizabeth Magill. 3rd ed. Omnigraphics 2011 xiv, 490 p.p ill. (hardcover) $69

Grades: 7 8 9 10 11 12　　　　　**613.8**

1. Teenagers -- Drug use 2. Teenagers -- Health and hygiene 3. Drug abuse 4. Drugs -- Physiological effect 5. Teenagers -- Drug use -- United States 6. Alcoholism -- United States -- Prevention 7. Drug abuse -- United States -- Prevention 8. Teenagers -- Alcohol use -- United States 9. Teenagers -- Health and hygiene -- United States

ISBN 0780811542; 9780780811546

LC 2010048932

This book "provides updated facts about drug use, abuse, and addiction. It describes the physical and psychological effects of alcohol, marijuana, prescription drugs, inhalants, club drugs, stimulants, and many other commonly abused drugs and chemicals. It includes information about drug-related health concerns. . . . A section on substance abuse treatment describes care options and provides resources for addiction recovery." (Publisher's note)

613.81 Alcohol

★ **Alcohol** information for teens; health tips about alcohol use, abuse & dependence including facts about alcohol's effects on mental and physical health, the consequences of underage drinking & understanding alcoholic family members. edited by Karen Bellenir. 3rd ed. Omnigraphics, Inc. 2013 371 p. ill (Teen health series) (hardcover) $69

Grades: 7 8 9 10 11 12　　　　　**613.81**

1. Alcoholism 2. Teenagers -- Alcohol use 3. Drinking of alcoholic beverages

ISBN 0780813138; 9780780813137

LC 2013000216

This book "provides updated information about the use and misuse of alcohol. It describes ways alcohol can affect mental and physical health. It discusses the special vulnerabilities of the teen brain and the changes in brain functioning that lead to dependency. A section on treatment and recovery discusses achieving and maintaining sobriety, and a section on alcohol abuse in the family addresses the special concerns of teens who live with an alcoholic relative." (Publisher's note)

Includes bibliographical references and index

613.9 Birth control, reproductive technology, sex hygiene, sexual techniques

Bell, Ruth

Changing bodies, changing lives; a book for teens on sex and relationships. [by] Ruth Bell and other co-authors of Our bodies, ourselves and Ourselves and our children, together with members of the Teen Book Project. expanded 3rd ed; Times Bks. 1998 411p il pa $24.95

Grades: 7 8 9 10 11 12　　　　　**613.9**

1. Sex education

ISBN 0-8129-2990-X

LC 97-29249

First published 1980

This is a "book on sex, physical and emotional health, and personal relationships. . . . Readers . . . will find emotional support as well as specific answers to most of their questions in this nonjudgmental resource." Booklist

Bringle, Jennifer

Reproductive rights; making the right choices. Rosen Pub. 2010 112p il (A young woman's guide to contemporary issues) lib bdg $31.95

Grades: 7 8 9 10　　　　　**613.9**

1. Pregnancy 2. Birth control 3. Teenage mothers

ISBN 978-1-4358-3542-9; 1-4358-3542-5

LC 2009-13721

"Facts are shared in a conversational tone, creating the sense of a chat with a big sister. . . . [Though] designed for personal reading and browsing, the data provided are accurate and also lend themselves to use in reports." SLJ

Includes glossary and bibliographical references

Cole, Joanna

Asking about sex & growing up; a question-and-answer book for kids. illustrated by Bill Thomas. rev ed.; Collins 2009 89p il $15.99; pa $6.99

Grades: 4 5 6　　　　　**613.9**

1. Sex education

ISBN 978-0-06-142987-3; 0-06-142987-2; 978-0-06-142986-6 pa; 0-06-142986-4 pa

LC 2008022710

First published 1988 by Morrow Junior Books

This book "offers straightforward information about topics such as physical changes in puberty, masturbation, birth control, pregnancy, homosexuality, and STDs. . . . Libraries . . . should consider adding it as a source of basic information for curious preteens." SLJ

Harris, Ashley Rae

★ **Do** you love me? making healthy dating decisions. content consultant: Dr. Robyn J.A. Silverman. ABDO Pub. Company 2009 112p il (Essential health: strong beautiful girls) lib bdg $32.79

Grades: 6 7 8 9　　　　　**613.9**

1. Dating (Social customs) 2. Interpersonal relations 3. Sexual behavior 4. Girls -- Psychology

ISBN 978-1-60453-749-9 lib bdg; 1-60453-749-3 lib bdg

LC 2009002131

"The topics are well selected, the design is attractive, and the stories feature girls from a variety of cultures." Booklist

Harris, Robie H.

★ It's perfectly normal; changing bodies, growing up, sex and sexual health. Robie H. Harris ; illustrated by Michael Emberley. 4th edition Candlewick Press 2014 98 p. color illustrations (reinforced) $22.99; (pbk) $12.99

Grades: 4 5 6 7   613.9

1. Puberty 2. Sex education
ISBN 0763668710; 0763668729; 9780763668716; 9780763668723

This provides information about sex, puberty, family relationships and reproduction, sexual decision-making and birth control, abortion laws, sexual abuse, sexual health, sexually transmitted diseases, and internet safety.

"This edition has been revised for a new generation, including updates in scientific and medical information about reproduction, birth control, abortion, sexual abuse, and sexually transmitted diseases." SLJ

Murray, Craig

Sexpectations; Sex Stuff Straight Up. Allen & Unwin 2012 111 p. $19.95

Grades: 7 8 9 10 11 12   613.9

1. Sex education 2. Sexual hygiene 3. Teenagers -- Sexual behavior
ISBN 1741751438; 9781741751437

Includes bibliographical references.

This book, by Craig Murray and Leissa Pitts, offers a "teenage-friendly sex education and sexual health guide book, for both boys and girls, in one . . . volume. Designed to help teens make healthy, positive choices, . . . It takes teens through knowing themselves and their bodies, keeping safe, protecting themselves, thinking through pregnancy, knowing about relationships, and tapping into their personal power to make positive choices." (Publisher's note)

Pardes, Bronwen

Doing it right; making smart, safe, and satisfying choices about sex. by Bronwen Pardes. Simon Pulse 2013 146 p. il $17.99

Grades: 7 8 9 10 11 12   613.9

1. Sex education
ISBN 1442483709; 9781442483705

LC 2006-928450

This book, by Bronwen Pardes, presents sex education for teenagers. "Chapters, which often use a question-and-answer format based on teens' actual queries, delve into sexual anatomy, questions to consider before sex, contraception, safe-sex practices, homosexuality, masturbation, and sexual violence. Throughout, Pardes avoids a heterosexual bias, and her discussion of sexual activity is explicit and inclusive." (Publisher's note)

The author "tackles the tough questions about sexual orientation, size, abuse, orgasm, pregnancy, STDs, and masturbation among others." Voice Youth Advocates

Includes bibliographical references

★ Sexual health information for teens; edited by Sandra Augustyn Lawton. 2nd ed.; Omnigraphics 2008 430p il (Teen health series) $69

Grades: 7 8 9 10 11 12   613.9

1. Sex education 2. Teenagers -- Health and hygiene
ISBN 978-0-7808-1010-5; 0-7808-1010-4

LC 2007052454

First published 2003

"This offering represents the most up-to-date information available on an array of topics. . . . The range of coverage . . . is thorough and extensive. Each chapter includes a bibliographic citation, and the three back sections containing additional resources, further reading, and the index are all first-rate. The few illustrations and diagrams range in quality from good to excellent." SLJ

Includes bibliographical references

614   Forensic medicine; incidence of injuries, wounds, disease; public preventive medicine

Spilsbury, Richard

Bones speak! solving crimes from the past. Enslow Publishers 2009 48p il (Solve that crime!) lib bdg $23.93

Grades: 5 6 7 8   614

1. Forensic sciences 2. Forensic anthropology
ISBN 978-0-7660-3377-1 lib bdg; 0-7660-3377-5 lib bdg

LC 2008-33309

This "title boasts in-depth information, sidebars detailing events of true crime, and activities that will increase understanding. . . . Photographs are colorful, well-captioned, and related to the text." SLJ

"Learn how forensics helps solve old crimes and mysteries." Publisher's note

Includes glossary and bibliographical references

Stefoff, Rebecca

Forensics and medicine. Marshall Cavendish Benchmark 2011 95p il (Forensic science investigated) $23.95

Grades: 6 7 8 9   614

1. Forensic sciences 2. Medical jurisprudence
ISBN 978-0-7614-4143-4; 0-7614-4143-3

LC 2010010526

"Numerous color photos and digital illustrations . . . add further interest." Booklist

"Investigates how law enforcement, public health workers, doctors, and scientists contribute to the fight against medical crime." Publisher's note

Includes bibliographical references

Walker, Sally M.

★ Written in bone; buried lives of Jamestown and Colonial Maryland. Carolrhoda Books 2009 144p il map $22.95

Grades: 6 7 8 9 10   614

1. Forensic sciences 2. Maryland -- History 3. Jamestown (Va.) -- History 4. Excavations (Archeology) -- United States 5. United States -- History -- 1600-

1775, Colonial period
ISBN 978-0-8225-7135-3; 0-8225-7135-8

LC 2007-10768

"Walker takes readers on an archaeological investigation of human and material remains from 17th- and 18th-century Jamestown and colonial Maryland, while addressing relevant topics in forensic anthropology, history, and archaeology. . . . . The text succinctly explains complex forensic concepts. . . . Captioned, full-color photographs of skeletal, dental, and artifactual remains shed light on colonial life. Historical documents, illustrated maps, and anatomical drawings complement images of various specialists at work in the field. Photographs of reenactors performing period tasks . . . provide insight into the daily life of the recovered individuals." SLJ

Includes bibliographical references

614.4 Incidence of and public measures to prevent disease

Barnard, Bryn

★ **Outbreak**; plagues that changed history. written and illustrated by Bryn Barnard. Crown Publishers 2005 47p il maps $17.95

Grades: 5 6 7 8 **614.4**
1. Diseases 2. Epidemics
ISBN 0-375-82986-5

LC 2005-15086

This "volume explores specific plagues that have impacted society. Barnard begins with an introduction to microbes and the positive and negative effects that they can have on humans. A history of the study of microorganisms follows. The bulk of the book then focuses on specific plagues with a chapter devoted to each, including the Black Death, smallpox, yellow fever, cholera, tuberculosis, and influenza. The final chapter discusses the modern struggle against disease. . . . The evocative paintings help to clarify the text. Browsers and report writers alike will find this to be a fascinating and informative resource." SLJ

Brownlee, Christen

Cute, furry, and deadly; diseases you can catch from your pet! [by] Christen Brownlee. Franklin Watts 2008 64p il map (24/7, science behind the scenes) lib bdg $26

Grades: 6 7 8 9 10 **614.4**
1. Communicable diseases 2. Pets -- Health and hygiene
ISBN 0-531-12072-4 lib bdg; 978-0-531-12072-9 lib bdg

LC 2006-21230

Hopefully, the worst thing your pet ever comes home with is bad breath. But some furry friends can carry nasty germs, and that's where zoonotic disease researchers come in and investigate and stop animal diseases before they get you!

"This series is a great pick for reluctant readers, busy teens, and anyone looking for a fun (if somewhat frightening) nonfiction read." Voice Youth Advocates

Includes glossary and bibliographical references

Epidemics: opposing viewpoints; David Haugen and Susan Musser, book editors. Greenhaven Press 2011 273p (Opposing viewpoints series) lib bdg $39.70; pa $26.50

Grades: 8 9 10 11 12 **614.4**
1. Epidemics 2. Vaccination 3. Communicable diseases
ISBN 978-0-7377-5219-9; 0-7377-5219-X; 978-0-7377-5220-5 pa; 0-7377-5220-3 pa

LC 2010052249

Articles in this anthology present opposing viewpoints on the subject of epidemics.

Includes bibliographical references

Farrell, Jeanette

Invisible enemies; stories of infectious diseases. 2nd ed; Farrar, Straus & Giroux 2005 272p il $18

Grades: 7 8 9 10 **614.4**
1. Communicable diseases
ISBN 9780374336073; 0-374-33607-5

LC 2004-57668

First published 1998

The author "focuses on seven dreaded human diseases: smallpox, leprosy, plague, tuberculosis, malaria, cholera, and AIDS. Each chapter provides a description of the physical and psychological effects of the disease on its victims, early theories about its causes, and efforts made to avoid or cure it. Then the methods of research that revealed its cause and developed the means to control its spread are explained in fascinating detail. . . . If every science book for nonspecialists were written with such flair and attention to detail, science would soon become every student's favorite subject." SLJ

Includes glossary and bibliographical references

Fox, Nancy

Hide and Seek; No Ticks Please. by Nancy Fox and illustrated by Daniel Seward. Morgan James Pub 2014 42 p. $9.95

Grades: 2 3 4 5 **614.4**
1. Lyme disease 2. Tick-borne diseases
ISBN 9781614487050; 1614487057

This children's book by Nancy Fox "teaches strategies for preventing Lyme disease and tick-borne diseases. Through the story of Alex and José, children will learn about José's discovery of a hidden danger (a tick) and how their activities may put them at risk of getting a tick bite." (Publisher's note)

Friedlander, Mark P.

★ **Outbreak**; disease detectives at work. by Mark P. Friedlander Jr. [Updated and rev. ed.]; Twenty-First Century Books 2009 128p il lib bdg $31.93

Grades: 6 7 8 9 **614.4**
1. Diseases 2. Epidemiology
ISBN 978-0-8225-9039-2; 0-8225-9039-5

LC 2008025277

First published 2000

Describes the field of epidemiology and its history, presenting historical and modern case studies and biological explanations of some diseases and a discussion of the microbes most likely to be used by bioterrorists.

"This is a readable, intriguing overview of the destructive power of epidemics and the critical work of public health professionals." SLJ [review of 2003 edition]

Includes bibliographical references

Gleason, Carrie

Feasting bedbugs, mites, and ticks. Crabtree Pub. Co. 2010 32p il (Creepy crawlies) lib bdg $26.60; pa $8.95

Grades: 4 5 6 7   614.4

1. Mites 2. Ticks 3. Bedbugs

ISBN 978-0-7787-2500-8 lib bdg; 0-7787-2500-6 lib bdg; 978-0-7787-2507-7 pa; 0-7787-2507-3 pa

LC 2010009552

"The informational yet easy-to-read text in double-page spreads explains the classification, anatomy, life cycles, and ideal feeding and living conditions for mites, ticks, and bedbugs as well as the differences among them. . . . Children will be most interested in the long history, myths, and lore associated with these pests as well as the eye-catching layout, with numerous color photographs. . . . [This is an] equally repulsive and fascinating book." Booklist

Includes glossary and bibliographical references

Goldsmith, Connie

★ Invisible invaders; new and dangerous infectious diseases. Twenty-First Century Books 2006 111p il (Discovery!) lib bdg $29.27

Grades: 7 8 9 10   614.4

1. Communicable diseases

ISBN 978-0-8225-3416-7; 0-8225-3416-9

LC 2005-17271

"This title is a thorough, understandable, and accessible source of current information and medical definitions, and a trail to further research." SLJ

Includes bibliographical references

Grady, Denise

★ Deadly invaders; virus outbreaks around the world, from Marburg fever to avian flu. Kingfisher 2006 128p il map $16.95

Grades: 7 8 9 10   614.4

1. Viruses 2. Marburg virus 3. Communicable diseases

ISBN 978-0-7534-5995-9; 0-7534-5995-7

LC 2006004441

The "writing is informative and compelling. . . . The layout is appealing and includes good-quality, full-color, relevant photographs on almost every spread. . . . A fast-paced, timely, and important book." SLJ

"In the first half of the book . . . Grady discusses the Marburg virus, the incurable disease it causes, and its effects on individuals and communities, as seen through the lens of her personal experiences in Angola. . . . Next she offers a short . . . chapter on each of seven deadly diseases: Marburg fever, avian flu, HIV/AIDS, Hantavirus pulmonary syndrome, West Nile disease, SARS, and monkeypox." Booklist

Includes bibliographical references

Miller, Debra A.

Pandemics; [by] Debra A. Miller. Lucent Books 2006 un (Hot topics) $32.45

Grades: 7 8 9 10   614.4

1. Epidemics 2. Communicable diseases

ISBN 9781420502589; 1-59018-965-5; 978-1-59018-965-8

LC 2006007057

"This comprehensive and well-organized book covers potential threats; the control and prevention of pandemics; and factors that may facilitate the outbreak and transmission of diseases, such as pollution, poverty, overpopulation, and globalization. Teens will appreciate the interesting sidebars, quotations, diagrams, and full-color photos that are integrated throughout the text and will find the annotated lists of organizations and further-reading suggestions useful." SLJ

Includes bibliographical references

Piddock, Charles

★ Outbreak; science seeks safeguards for global health. [Caryn Oryniak, consultant] National Geographic 2008 64p il (National Geographic investigates) $17.95; lib bdg $27.90

Grades: 4 5 6 7   614.4

1. Diseases 2. Epidemics 3. Medicine -- Research

ISBN 978-1-4263-0357-9; 1-4263-0357-2; 978-1-4263-0263-3 lib bdg; 1-4263-0263-0 lib bdg

LC 2009-275290

This is an "introduction to the fight against infectious diseases, including scientists who discovered various viruses and bacteria. The text outlines how we have learned to fight nature's harmful strains and to use others to our advantage; it also provides the latest findings on bird flu and SARS, Ebola and AIDS, and highly resistant strains of tuberculosis." Publisher's note

Tilden, Thomasine E. Lewis

Help! What's eating my flesh? runaway staph and strep infections! [by] Thomasine E. Lewis Tilden. Franklin Watts 2008 64p il map (24/7, science behind the scenes) lib bdg $26

Grades: 6 7 8 9 10   614.4

1. Communicable diseases

ISBN 0-531-12073-2; 978-0-531-12073-6

LC 2006-5871

"A splashy tabloid-style presentation, including gross and disgusting photographs, will attract curious young teens who will be unable to resist. . . . [This] book also includes career information, resources (including Web sites and books), a historical section with key dates, and an author's note." Voice Youth Advoctaes

Includes glossary and bibliographical references

Walker, Richard, 1951-

Epidemics & plagues; foreword by Denise Grady. Kingfisher 2006 63p il (Kingfisher knowledge) hardcover o.p. $12.95

Grades: 4 5 6 7   614.4

1. Diseases 2. Epidemics

ISBN 978-0-7534-6035-1; 0-7534-6035-1; 978-0-7534-6161-7 pa; 0-7534-6161-7 pa

Discusses the spread of infectious diseases and their impact on human populations, from the Black Death in medieval Europe to such modern diseases as AIDS and West Nile virus, as well as efforts to stop the spread of these diseases.

Includes glossary

Willett, Edward

Disease -hunting scientist; careers hunting deadly diseases. Enslow Publishers 2009 112p il (Wild science careers) lib bdg $31.93

Grades: 5 6 7 8   **614.4**

1. Epidemiology 2. Vocational guidance

ISBN 978-0-7660-3052-7 lib bdg; 0-7660-3052-0 lib bdg

LC 2008-4674

"Full-color photographs show the scientists in action and a chart with career information including salary potentials wraps up . . . [this] book." SLJ

Includes glossary and bibliographical references

614.5 Incidence of and public measures to prevent specific diseases and kinds of diseases

Ballard, Carol

AIDS and other epidemics. Gareth Stevens Pub. 2008 48p il map (What if we do nothing?) lib bdg $31

Grades: 5 6 7 8   **614.5**

1. Epidemics 2. AIDS (Disease) 3. Communicable diseases

ISBN 978-1-4339-0085-3 lib bdg; 1-4339-0085-8 lib bdg

LC 2008029189

"Using intelligent, focused text; an open design; vivid photos; and excellent maps, [this] book demands attention." Booklist

"This book looks at the causes of major infectious diseases, how they spread, and how they can be treated. It also discusses different steps that governments and health organizations can take to handle and prevent epidemics and pandemics." Publisher's note

Includes bibliographical references

Cunningham, Kevin

The **bubonic** plague. ABDO Pub. Co. 2011 112p il map (Essential events) lib bdg $23.95

Grades: 7 8 9 10 11 12   **614.5**

1. Plague 2. Epidemics

ISBN 978-1-61714-762-3; 1-61714-762-1

LC 2010043852

A history of the plague which caused one of the most catastrophic losses of life in history.

"The spacious . . . design is inviting, with many color illustrations and screens, and the extensive back matter includes a detailed time line, glossary, bibliography and source notes." Booklist

Includes glossary and bibliographical references

Flu. Morgan Reynolds Pub. 2009 176p il (Diseases in history) lib bdg $28.95

Grades: 8 9 10 11 12   **614.5**

1. Influenza

ISBN 978-1-59935-105-6; 1-59935-105-6

LC 2008-51620

"This informative title reveals the continued concerns surrounding this killer disease and the possibility of a future pandemic. The text, though somewhat scientific, will help students to better understand the history of the virus, how it has mutated and jumped from animals to humans, and new concerns regarding more dangerous forms. . . . Color and black-and-white archival photos, as well as reproduction of a three-dimensional rendering of the flu virus, enhance the text." SLJ

Includes glossary and bibliographical references

Malaria. Morgan Reynolds Pub. 2009 144p il (Diseases in history) lib bdg $28.95

Grades: 8 9 10 11 12   **614.5**

1. Malaria

ISBN 978-1-59935-103-2; 1-59935-103-X

LC 2008-51619

"Provides fascinating information about an ongoing scourge. . . . Here readers have an accessible, well presented account of the continuing struggle against a deadly disease." Voice Youth Advocates

Includes glossary and bibliographical references

Plague. Morgan Reynolds Pub. 2009 144p il (Diseases in history) lib bdg $28.95

Grades: 8 9 10 11 12   **614.5**

1. Plague

ISBN 978-1-59935-102-5; 1-59935-102-1

LC 2008-51618

"Chapters based upon plagues include one on Justinian's Plague, the Black Death, The Dreadful Pestilence, the Great Plague of London, and the current H1N1 swine flu pandemic. This detailed overview . . . will appeal to more advanced students. The research is thorough and the writing is insightful, thought provoking, and accessible." Voice Youth Advocates

Includes glossary and bibliographical references

Currie, Stephen

★ The **black** death; by Stephen Currie. ReferencePoint Press, Inc. 2013 94 p. (Understanding world history series) (hardcover) $27.95

Grades: 7 8 9 10   **614.5**

1. Plague -- History 3. Black Death -- History

ISBN 1601524803; 9781601524805

LC 2012021114

This book on the Black Death by Stephen Currie is part of the "Understanding World History" series. "Readers learn the surprising benefits of depopulation and how technology, medicine, and even religion changed as a result of this tragic epidemic. . . . While it briefly covers the beginnings of the plague in Asia and the many people killed there, the bulk of the book is about the impact of the disease on Europe." (School Library Journal)

Includes bibliographical references and index.

Currie-McGhee, L. K.

Sexually transmitted diseases; [by] Leanne Currie-McGhee. ReferencePoint Press 2009 104p il map (Compact research. Diseases and disorders) lib bdg $25.95

Grades: 8 9 10   614.5

1. Sexually transmitted diseases

ISBN 978-1-60152-045-6; 1-60152-045-X

LC 2008-12554

Presents information on sexually transmitted diseases through essays, quotations, statistics, and suggestions for further research.

"Sobering, enlightening, and up-to-date, this title . . . . uses an effective blend of primary sources, diagrams, and thorough text to bring the latest facts about STDs to young readers. . . . A time line and lists of key advocacy groups and further reading close this valuable resource for teens." Booklist

Includes bibliographical references

Goldsmith, Connie

Influenza : the next pandemic? Twenty-First Century Books 2007 112p il (Twenty-first century medical library) lib bdg $27.93

Grades: 6 7 8 9 10   614.5

1. Influenza

ISBN 978-0-7613-9457-0; 0-7613-9457-5

LC 2005-23588

The author "traces the history of the flu, giving attention to past outbreaks and epidemics. She also describes flu viruses of today, explains treatments, and details health officials' concerns about bird flu. . . . Good for reports, and a worthy source to update collections." SLJ

Includes bibliographical references

Jarrow, Gail

Fatal fever; tracking down Typhoid Mary. Gail Jarrow. Calkins Creek 2015 192 p. illustrations (some color) $16.95

Grades: 6 7 8 9 10   614.5

1. Typhoid fever

ISBN 1620915979; 9781620915974

LC 2014948476

This children's book by Gail Jarrow "tells the true story of [Typhoid Mary,] the woman who unwittingly spread deadly bacteria, the epidemiologist who discovered her trail of infection, and the health department that decided her fate. This gripping story follows this tragic disease as it shatters lives from the early twentieth century to today." (Publisher's note)

"In the second book by Jarrow about a deadly disease -- Red Madness was the first -- she takes on typhoid. At the turn of the twentieth century, typhoid was still very much a mystery...Jarrow has written a suspenseful medical mystery for inquisitive readers. Timeline, glossary, author's note, source notes, bibliography, and index are included among the extensive back matter." Horn Book

Jurmain, Suzanne

★ The **secret** of the yellow death; a true story of medical sleuthing. Houghton Mifflin Books for Children 2009 104p il $19

Grades: 6 7 8 9 10   614.5

1. Epidemics 2. Physicians 3. Yellow fever 4. Army officers 5. Cuba -- History 6. Microbiologists 7. Writers on medicine 8. Medicine -- Research

ISBN 978-0-618-96581-6; 0-618-96581-5

LC 2009-22499

"This medical mystery is extremely interesting, easy to read, and well illustrated with period photos." SLJ

"Jurmain recounts the six months in 1900 when Dr. Walter Reed and his team of doctors in Cuba determined that mosquitoes carry yellow fever." Kirkus

Includes glossary and bibliographical references

Kupperberg, Paul

The **influenza** pandemic of 1918-1919. Chelsea House 2008 120p il map (Great historic disasters) $35

Grades: 7 8 9 10   614.5

1. Epidemics 2. Influenza

ISBN 978-0-7910-9640-6; 0-7910-9640-8

This is "well written and informative. . . . The inclusion of black-and-white and color photographs and drawings and sidebars help to make [this book] first-rate for reports and general browsing." SLJ

This "covers the history of the influenza outbreak and medical advances made over the last century to prevent future pandemics." Horn Book Guide

Murphy, Jim

★ An **American** plague; the true and terrifying story of the yellow fever epidemic of 1793. Clarion Bks. 2003 165p il map $18

Grades: 5 6 7 8   614.5

1. Yellow fever 2. Philadelphia (Pa.) -- History

ISBN 0-395-77608-2

LC 2002-151355

A Newbery Medal honor book, 2004

"Murphy culls from a number of historical records the story of the yellow fever epidemic that swept Philadelphia in 1793, skillfully drawing out from these sources the fear and drama of the time and making them immediate to modern readers. . . . Thoroughly documented, with an annotated source list, the work is both rigorous and inviting." Horn Book

Nardo, Don

The **Black** Death. Lucent Books 2011 96p il (World history) lib bdg $33.45

Grades: 6 7 8 9   614.5

1. Plague 2. Medieval civilization

ISBN 978-1-4205-0348-7; 1-4205-0348-0

LC 2010043804

This examines the 14th-century plague from such perspectives as epidemiology, the death toll, the medical response, social controls, the flagellants, the impact on economics and the population, education, agriculture, architecture, and the church.

"Students are given a clear explanation of the disease and how it may have spread and some coverage of its social, economic, and cultural repercussions. The essays each speak to a specific issue. An appendix that includes 16 primary documents, a concise chronology, lists for further reading divided by content, and an index complete this valuable research tool." SLJ

Includes bibliographical references

Person, Stephen

Bubonic plague; the Black Death! Bearport Pub. 2010 32p il map (Nightmare plagues) lib bdg $25.27

Grades: 4 5 6 7   614.5
1. Plague
ISBN 978-1-936088-03-4; 1-936088-03-7

This describes what causes bubonic plague and how it affects the body.

"The writing is accessible and interspersed with interesting photographs and fact boxes. . . . [The book relies] on an honest discussion of [bubonic plague and is an] . . . effective, easily navigated [introduction]." SLJ

Includes glossary and bibliographical references

Malaria; super killer! Bearport Pub. 2011 32p il map (Nightmare plagues) lib bdg $25.27

Grades: 4 5 6 7   614.5
1. Malaria
ISBN 978-1-936088-07-2 lib bdg; 1-936088-07-X lib bdg

LC 2010012018

Discover what causes malaria and how it affects the body.

"The writing is accessible and interspersed with interesting photographs and fact boxes. . . . [The book relies] on an honest discussion of [malaria and is an] . . . effective, easily navigated [introduction]." SLJ

Includes glossary and bibliographical references

Peters, Stephanie True

★ **Smallpox** in the new world. Benchmark Books 2004 69p il (Epidemic!) lib bdg $32.79

Grades: 4 5 6 7 8   614.5
1. Smallpox
ISBN 0-7614-1637-4; 9780761416371

LC 2003-2646

Describes the history of smallpox in the Americas, covering the arrival of the Spanish as carriers, its spread throughout the New World, the development of the smallpox vaccine, the elimination of the disease, and its potential use as a terrorist weapon.

Includes glossary and bibliographical references

Reingold, Adam

Smallpox; is it over? Bearport Pub. 2010 32p il map (Nightmare plagues) lib bdg $25.27

Grades: 4 5 6 7   614.5
1. Smallpox
ISBN 978-1-936088-02-7; 1-936088-02-9

LC 2010009371

Discover what causes smallpox and how it affects the body.

"The writing is accessible and interspersed with interesting photographs and fact boxes. . . . [The book relies] on an honest discussion of [smallpox and is an] . . . effective, easily navigated [introduction]." SLJ

Includes glossary and bibliographical references

Rudolph, Jessica

The **flu** of 1918; millions dead worldwide! Bearport Pub. 2011 32p il map (Nightmare plagues) lib bdg $25.27

Grades: 4 5 6 7   614.5
1. Influenza
ISBN 978-1-936088-05-8 lib bdg; 1-936088-05-3 lib bdg

LC 2010004684

Discover what caused the Influenza epidemic of 1918 and how it affected the body.

"The writing is accessible and interspersed with interesting photographs and fact boxes. . . . [The book relies] on an honest discussion of [Influenza epidemic of 1918 and is an] . . . effective, easily navigated [introduction]." SLJ

Includes glossary and bibliographical references

Slavicek, Louise Chipley

The **Black** Death. Chelsea House Publishers 2008 127p il (Great historic disasters) lib bdg $35

Grades: 6 7 8 9 10   614.5
1. Plague 2. Middle Ages
ISBN 978-0-7910-9649-9; 0-7910-9649-1; 9781438118154

LC 2008004887

This describes the Plague epidemic and it's effects on Europe in the Middle Ages

Includes glossary and bibliographical references

Smith, Tara C.

Ebola and Marburg viruses; 2nd ed.; Chelsea House Publishers 2011 104p il (Deadly diseases and epidemics) lib bdg $34.95

Grades: 8 9 10 11 12   614.5
1. Ebola virus 2. Marburg virus
ISBN 978-1-60413-252-6; 1-60413-252-3

LC 2010032999

First published 2005

This describes the outbreaks of Marburg and Ebola viruses, their characteristics and ecology, detection and treatment, developing a vaccine, and other hemorrhagic fevers.

Includes glossary and bibliographical references

Zahler, Diane

The **Black** Death. Twenty-First Century Books 2009 160p il map (Pivotal moments in history) lib bdg $38.60

Grades: 7 8 9 10   614.5
1. Plague 2. Middle Ages
ISBN 978-0-8225-9076-7; 0-8225-9076-X

LC 2008-26878

This book discusses the pivotal moment in history when one out of three people died and changed the course of world history, the Black Death.

"This is a well-written and well-researched volume. Full-color illustrations, a note explaining the value of primary sources, a who's who, and careful source notes make this book a valuable addition to history collections." SLJ

Includes glossary and bibliographical references

615 Pharmacology and therapeutics

Allman, Toney

Vaccine research. ReferencePoint Press 2010 96p il (Inside science) lib bdg $26.95

Grades: 7 8 9 10   **615**

1. Vaccination 2. Medicine -- Research
ISBN 978-1-60152-131-6; 1-60152-131-6

LC 2010-20635

This book "offers the necessary information for stellar reports. Politics, debates, and ethical concerns are briefly and fairly mentioned, but the . . . [book concentrates] on consistent, documented, and well-balanced scientific coverage. The human stories sprinkled throughout will help kids identify with both scientists and patients." SLJ

Includes bibliographical references

Bjornlund, Lydia

Oxycodone; by Lydia Bjornlund. ReferencePoint Press 2012 96 p. (Compact research series)

Grades: 7 8 9 10 11 12   **615**

1. Narcotics 2. Analgesics 3. Drug abuse 4. Drug education 5. Drugs -- Law and legislation -- United States 6. Oxycodone 7. Oxycodone abuse
ISBN 1601521618; 9781601521613

LC 2011020202

This book on oxycodone is a part of the Compact Research: Drugs series and "focus[es] on three types of information: "objective single-author narratives, opinion-based primary source quotations, and facts and statistics." What this translates to on the page is an overview of the topic and an in-depth chapter-by chapter discussion of the points raised in the overview." Lydia Bjornlund "discuss[es] . . . the health dangers of the drug and its legitimacy in medical use, government regulation of the drug, and how oxycodone abuse can be prevented." (Booklist)

Includes bibliographical references and index

Goldsmith, Connie

★ **Superbugs** strike back; when antibiotics fail. Twenty-First Century Books 2007 112p il (Discovery!) lib bdg $29.27

Grades: 7 8 9 10   **615**

1. Bacteria 2. Antibiotics 3. Drug resistance
ISBN 978-0-8225-6607-6; 0-8225-6607-9

LC 2006-10726

"The emergence of 'superbugs'—antibiotic resistant bacteria—and the threat they pose to public health are examined in this detailed introduction. . . . Full-color tables, sidebars, diagrams, and good-quality photos and micrographs are interspersed throughout. The text is meticulous without being tedious." SLJ

Includes glossary and bibliographical references

Hyde, Natalie

What is germ theory? Crabtree Pub. Co. 2011 64p il (Shaping modern science) lib bdg $30.60; pa $10.95

Grades: 5 6 7 8   **615**

1. Chemists 2. Germ theory of disease 3. Microbiologists 4. Writers on science
ISBN 978-0-7787-7201-9 lib bdg; 0-7787-7201-9 lib bdg; 978-0-7787-7208-8 pa; 0-7787-7208-X pa

LC 2010052631

This title is "not only written and organized well, but [it is] also gorgeous in design. Full-color photographs and illustrations are set over colorful backgrounds that add depth but not distraction. [The title] includes thought-provoking quotes from famous authors and scientists and some eyebrow-raising 'Quick Facts' throughout." SLJ

Includes glossary and bibliographical references

Kidd, J. S.

★ **Potent** natural medicines; Mother Nature's pharmacy. [by] J.S. Kidd and Renee A. Kidd. rev ed.; Chelsea House 2006 212p il (Science and society) lib bdg $35

Grades: 7 8 9 10   **615**

1. Pharmacology 2. Medical botany
ISBN 9781438122946; 0-8160-5607-2

LC 2005041741

This introduces "plants' medicinal properties, pioneers who hunted for sources of and applications for botanical treatments, and the ways phytochemical nutrients prevent disease. . . . [Also included] are chapters about recent research, including investigation into animal sources for medicine; the impact of field research on native peoples; and the federal regulation of herb and plant supplements. . . . This [is] a good choice to support research and debate projects." Booklist

Includes bibliographical references

Klosterman, Lorrie

The **facts** about depressants; [by] Lorrie Klosterman. Marshall Cavendish Benchmark 2005 96p il (Drugs) lib bdg $42.79; pa $6.99

Grades: 7 8 9 10   **615**

1. Drug abuse 2. Tranquilizing drugs
ISBN 0-7614-1976-4 lib bdg; 0-7614-1976-4 lib bdg; 978-0-7614-3594-5 pa; 0-7614-3594-8 pa

LC 2005001729

This "useful [volume is] attractively packaged and will be of interest to report writers and general readers. [Text] and photos do an excellent job of showing how [this] group of drugs affects the body." SLJ

Includes glossary and bibliographical references

The **facts** about drugs and the body. Marshall Cavendish Benchmark 2006 143p il (Drugs) lib bdg $42.79

Grades: 7 8 9 10 11 12   **615**

1. Drugs
ISBN 978-0-7614-2675-2; 0-7614-2675-2

LC 2007-2260

This discusses the effects of various drugs on the nervous, cardiovascular, respiratory, digestive, and reproductive systems of the body.

"Klosterman has done an excellent job of demonstrating how drugs affect the body functions. The illustrations and captions enhance the information to make it more understandable." SLJ

Includes glossary and bibliographical references

Knowles, Jo

Over -the-counter drugs. Chelsea House 2008 106p il (Junior drug awareness) lib bdg $30
Grades: 6 7 8 9   615
1. Drug abuse 2. Nonprescription drugs
ISBN 978-0-7910-9759-5 lib bdg; 0-7910-9759-5 lib bdg; 9781438118253
LC 2007-43665
This describes the uses and abuses of such over-the-counter drugs as cough medicines, diet pills, sleep aids, bodybuilding supplements, motion sickness medications, and caffeine

"The content is reliable and comprehensive." Horn Book Guide
Includes glossary and bibliographical references

Koellhoffer, Tara

Prozac and other antidepressants. Chelsea House 2008 120p il (Junior drug awareness) lib bdg $30
Grades: 6 7 8 9   615
1. Antidepressants 2. Depression (Psychology)
ISBN 978-0-7910-9747-2 lib bdg; 0-7910-9747-1 lib bdg; 9781438118260
LC 2007-43663
This "examines antidepressant therapies available today and explains how they affect the bodies and minds of people who are treated with them." Publisher's note
Includes glossary and bibliographical references

LeVert, Suzanne

The **facts** about antidepressants; [by] Suzanne LeVert. Marshall Cavendish Benchmark 2007 112p il (Drugs) lib bdg $42.79
Grades: 6 7 8 9   615
1. Antidepressants
ISBN 978-0-7614-2241-9 lib bdg; 0-7614-2241-2 lib bdg
LC 2006002403
This describes the benefits and risks of antidepressant drugs in the treatment of depression
Includes glossary and bibliographical references

Merino, Noel

Vaccines; Noel Merino, book editor. Greenhaven Press 2011 129p il (Introducing issues with opposing viewpoints) $35.75
Grades: 7 8 9 10   615
1. Vaccination
ISBN 978-0-7377-5204-5; 0-7377-5204-1
LC 2010040832
This is an "excellent [resource] both for student research and for personal interest. . . . Vaccines . . . discusses the pos-

sible connection between inoculations and autism, as well as the question of the state mandating vaccination and possible problems with giving multiple vaccines at the same time." Booklist
Includes bibliographical references

Miller, Malinda

The **pharmaceutical** industry; better medicine for the 21st century. Mason Crest Publishers 2011 64p il (New careers for the 21st century: finding your role in the global renewal) lib bdg $22.95
Grades: 7 8 9 10   615
1. Pharmacy 2. Drug industry 3. Vocational guidance
ISBN 978-1-4222-1819-8 lib bdg; 1-4222-1819-8 lib bdg
LC 2010020682
"Chapters identify and emphasize specific careers–important strengths, necessary aptitudes and interests, education and training, projected earnings, closely related occupations, type of work environment, and predictions for the future of the field. . . . Color photos have a small role amid the many statistics, figures, graphs and charts that support and supplement the . . . [text]." SLJ
Includes bibliographical references

Peterson, Judy Monroe

Frequently asked questions about antidepressants. Rosen Pub. 2010 64p il (FAQ: teen life) lib bdg $29.95
Grades: 7 8 9 10   615
1. Antidepressants 2. Depression (Psychology)
ISBN 978-1-4358-3547-4 lib bdg; 1-4358-3547-6 lib bdg
LC 2009-18962
"Defines 'antidepressants' and 'depression' in an easy-to-understand language, using words and illustrations to show the science of how these drugs work and the warning signs of different types of depression. . . . This is a good resource for teens struggling to understand what is happening to themselves or to their friends." Voice Youth Advocates
Includes glossary and bibliographical references

Rooney, Anne

Dealing with drugs. Amicus 2010 46p il (Healthy lifestyles) lib bdg $32.80
Grades: 7 8 9 10   615
1. Drugs
ISBN 978-1-60753-084-8; 1-60753-084-8
This book is "well-written and satisfyingly informative. . . . [The] magazine-like format includes numerous sidebars, color photos, and charts." SLJ
"Discusses the risks and realities of teenage drug use and abuse, including alcohol, marijuana, tobacco, prescription drugs, steroids, inhalants, party drugs such as ecstasy, and more." Publisher's note
Includes glossary

Winner, Cherie

★ **Circulating** life; blood transfusion from ancient superstition to modern medicine. Twenty-First Century Books 2007 112p il (Discovery!) $30.60

Grades: 6 7 8 9 10   **615**

  1. Blood -- Transfusion

  ISBN 978-0-8225-6606-9; 0-8225-6606-0

                         LC 2006-29921

This is a study of how bloodletting was replaced by blood transfusion as a medical therapy. Index. "Grades seven to twelve." (Sci Books Films)

This "compendium is both a history of the art of transfusions and a scientific discourse on the chemistry of blood. From early 'bleeding treatments' to the discovery of the circulatory system; from the earliest attempts at transfusions to Charles Drew's heroic work with plasma in World War II, Winner's clear text takes readers on an epic trip." SLJ

Includes bibliographical references

615.7 Pharmacokinetics

Karson, Jill

  Is medical marijuana necessary? by Bonnie Szumski and Jill Karson. ReferencePoint Press, Inc. 2013 96 p. (In controversy) (hardcover) $27.95

Grades: 7 8 9 10   **615.7**

  1. Marijuana 2. Medical botany 3. Marijuana -- Therapeutic use -- United States 4. Marijuana -- Law and legislation -- United States

  ISBN 1601524587; 9781601524584

                         LC 2012011561

This book is part of the In Controversy series and focuses on medical marijuana. "Each book explores one aspect of a debate; for instance, instead of discussing marijuana in general, the series entry focuses on medical marijuana." It notes that "most of the medical problems marijuana helps with arise later in life." (Booklist)

Includes bibliographical references and index.

Parks, Peggy J.

  Diet drugs; by Peggy J. Parks. Referencepoint Press 2013 96 p. (Compact research) (hardback) $28.95

Grades: 8 9 10 11 12   **615.7**

  1. Drugs 2. Weight loss 3. Appetite depressants -- Miscellanea 4. Weight loss preparations industry -- Miscellanea 5. Weight loss preparations -- Side effects -- Miscellanea

  ISBN 1601525184; 9781601525185

                         LC 2013021407

This book, by author Peggy J. Parks, "gives a history of early weight-loss drugs in the U.S. and their increasing popularity with the rise of obesity. It also relates the controversial effectiveness of diet drugs and the problem of diet-drug fraud. Additional back matter comprises lists of key people, advocacy groups, and related organizations." (Publisher's note)

"Backed by current facts, statistics, and first-person experiences, every chapter includes further documentation with concluding "Primary Source Quotes," from former addicts and law enforcement to health care workers and government officials. In this visual, by-the-numbers era, the series responds with end-of-chapter charts and graphs that display drug-related information." (Booklist)

Includes bibliographical references and index

Szumski, Bonnie

  Thinking critically; Medical marijuana. by Bonnie Szumski and Jill Karson. ReferencePoint Press, Inc. 2013 80 p. color illustrations & maps (hardback) $28.95

Grades: 7 8 9 10 11 12   **615.7**

  1. Marijuana 2. Marijuana -- United States 3. Marijuana -- Therapeutic use 4. Marijuana -- Law and legislation -- United States

  ISBN 1601525826; 9781601525826

                         LC 2012047796

This book, by Bonnie Szumski and Jill Karson, is a "well-researched examination" of medical marijuana. "The first page of each chapter, 'The Debate at a Glance,' offers bullet points that summarize common arguments pro and con. The design is spare, with understated graphics; bright, compelling photos; and text boxes that pull out interesting quotes. Easy-to-read graphs and charts add another layer of visual information." (School Library Journal)

"Diagrams and sidebars (and one photo per volume) support these well-organized models for classroom discourse. First chapters provide an overview of the debates surrounding medical marijuana and stem cell research; subsequent chapters present pro and con responses to four key questions. Despite lots of graphic elements, the text-heavy pages may be off-putting. Two pages of facts and lists of related organizations are appended. Reading list, websites." Horn Book

Includes bibliographical references and index

615.8 Specific therapies and kinds of therapies

Marcovitz, Hal

  Gene therapy research. ReferencePoint Press 2010 96p il (Inside science) lib bdg $26.95

Grades: 7 8 9 10 11 12   **615.8**

  1. Gene therapy 2. Medicine -- Research

  ISBN 978-1-60152-108-8; 1-60152-108-1

                         LC 2009-41686

"Opening with an account of successful gene therapy for a rare eye disease, this introduction to the research goes on to speculate about future applications for other inherited diseases. Beginning with basic definitions of such terms as gene, human genome, and DNA, the well-organized narrative explains the impact of viruses, drugs, cloning, and stem cells on gene therapy and describes recent research." Booklist

615.9 Toxicology

Karson, Jill

  Are cell phones dangerous? by Bonnie Szumski and Jill Karson. ReferencePoint Press, Inc. 2012 96 p. col. ill. (hardcover) $27.95

Grades: 7 8 9 10   **615.9**

  1. Cellular telephones -- Health aspects 2. Cellular telephones -- Social aspects 3. Cell phones -- Health aspects

  ISBN 1601522320; 9781601522320

                         LC 2011034063

This book on safety issues related to cell phones "begins with a brief history of this now ubiquitous technology and then analyzes the risks of cell phone usage in three main areas. It draws on numerous studies to report suspected links to cancer, a decline in male fertility, and other health-related problems as well as accidents and deaths related to texting while driving. The authors also look at such negative impacts on youth culture as addiction, bullying, and sexting." (Booklist)

Includes bibliographical references and index.

Landau, Elaine

Food poisoning and foodborne diseases. Twenty-First Century Books 2010 128p il (USA Today health reports: diseases and disorders) lib bdg $34.60

Grades: 7 8 9 10 11 12   **615.9**

1. Food poisoning 2. Communicable diseases

ISBN 978-0-8225-7290-9; 0-8225-7290-7

LC 2009-20325

This book "will drawn an audience with its everyday examples of food risks as well as instructions about how to buy, prepare, cook, and store food. . . . Also included are warnings about how to keep hands and kitchen surfaces clean and what to watch out for in cafeteria and fast-food outlets. . . . [The] accessible design extends the impressive educational data." Booklist

Includes bibliographical references

616   Diseases

Calamandrei, Camilla

★ **Fever**. Marshall Cavendish Benchmark 2009 64p il (Health alert) $22.95

Grades: 4 5 6 7   **616**

1. Fever

ISBN 978-0-7614-2915-9; 0-7614-2915-8

LC 2007-26002

This "title features a handsome format, with well-chosen illustrations, a substantial amount of information, and some practical insights." Booklist

"Provides comprehensive information on the causes, treatment, and history of fever." Publisher's note

Includes glossary

Dendy, Leslie A.

★ **Guinea** pig scientists; bold self-experimenters in science and medicine. [by] Leslie Dendy and Mel Boring; with illustrations by C. B. Mordan. Henry Holt & Co. 2005 213p il $19.95

Grades: 5 6 7 8   **616**

1. Scientists 2. Medicine -- Research

ISBN 9780805073164; 0-8050-7316-7

LC 2004-52364

This is a collection of "stories of human 'guinea pigs' who have tested the limits of the human body for the sake of science. Starting with Sir Charles Blagden, M.D., and his heat experiments, the stories are chronologically ordered from the 1770s to 1989. Included are descriptions of experiments dealing with digestion, laughing gas, vaccinations,

mosquitoes as vectors of yellow fever, radioactivity, [and] G-forces." (Sci Books Films) Index.

"The authors offer 10 . . . case studies of scientists from the past several centuries who became their own test subjects. . . . The accounts are lively, compelling, and not always for the squeamish. . . . The authors cogently discuss each experiment's significance in advancing our understanding of science and medicine. Illustrated with a mix of period black-and-white photos and Mordan's nineteenth-century-style portraits . . . the episodes make riveting reading." Booklist

Includes bibliographical references

Evans, Michael

The **adventures** of Medical Man; kids' illnesses and injuries explained. by Michael Evans & David Wichman; illustrated by Gareth Williams. Annick 2010 72p il $21.95; pa $12.95

Grades: 5 6 7 8   **616**

1. Diseases 2. Wounds and injuries

ISBN 978-1-55451-263-8; 1-55451-263-8; 978-1-55451-262-1 pa; 1-55451-262-X pa

"Using tangible experiences that kids can relate to, this book does a fantastic job of explaining common medical issues in an accessible way. A variety of heroic characters explain otherwise complicated and seemingly scary conditions and occurrences. Through the use of science fiction, adventure, and comics, the book covers nut allergies, concussions, broken bones, strep throat, ear infections, and asthma. . . . The extensive glossary is straightforward and user-friendly. The pumped-up graphic illustrations are extremely engaging and further bring these otherwise abstract concepts to life." SLJ

Herbst, Judith

Germ theory. Twenty-First Century Books 2008 80p il (Great ideas of science) lib bdg $27.93

Grades: 5 6 7 8   **616**

1. Germ theory of disease 2. Life -- Origin

ISBN 978-0-8225-2909-5 lib bdg; 0-8225-2909-2 lib bdg

LC 2005-08809

Discusses how the germ theory of disease came about, how it was applied to various illnesses throughout the years, and why this theory has become so important in the field of medicine

Includes glossary and bibliographical references

Marcovitz, Hal

Stem cell research. ReferencePoint Press 2011 96p il (Inside science) lib bdg $26.95

Grades: 7 8 9 10   **616**

1. Stem cell research

ISBN 978-1-60152-130-9; 1-60152-130-8

LC 2010-4128

Discusses the science behind stem cell research and the ways in which stem cells can be used in treatment of disease.

This book "offers the necessary information for stellar reports. Politics, debates, and ethical concerns are briefly and fairly mentioned, but the . . . [book concentrates] on consistent, documented, and well-balanced scientific coverage. The human stories sprinkled throughout will help kids identify with both scientists and patients." SLJ

Includes bibliographical references

Nardo, Don

Cure quest; the science of stem cell research. by Don Nardo. Compass Point Books 2009 48p il (Headline science) lib bdg $27.93; pa $7.95

Grades: 5 6 7   **616**

1. Stem cell research

ISBN 978-0-7565-3371-7 lib bdg; 0-7565-3371-6 lib bdg; 978-0-7565-3374-8 pa; 0-7565-3374-0 pa

LC 2008-5738

Explains the science behind stem cell research.

"Color photos and graphics provide visual information; a timeline is helpful to find fast facts, and the Facthound Web site provides student with additional information." Libr Media Connect

Includes glossary and bibliographical references

Skloot, Rebecca

The **immortal** life of Henrietta Lacks; by Rebecca Skloot. 1st paperback ed. Crown Publishers 2010 x, 369 p., [8] p. of plates p ill. (some col.) (hardcover) $26.00; (paperback) $16.00

Grades: 6 7 8 9   **616**

1. Cancer 2. Homemakers 3. Medical ethics 4. Human experimentation in medicine 5. African American women -- Biography

ISBN 1400052173; 9781400052172; 9781400052189

LC 200931785

Here, Rebecca Skloot tells the story of Henrietta Lacks, an African American Virginia tobacco farmer who died of cervical cancer in 1951. Unbeknownst to Mrs. Lacks and her family, scientists harvested her cells to create a human cell line known as HeLa, from the first two letters of her first and last names, "that has been kept alive indefinitely, enabling discoveries in such areas as cancer research, in vitro fertilization and gene mapping." (Publisher's note)

Includes bibliographical references and index.

Stoyles, Pennie

The **A** -Z of health. Black Rabbit/Smart Apple 2010 6v il set $119.70

Grades: 5 6 7 8   **616**

1. Health 2. Reference books 3. Medicine -- Encyclopedias

ISBN 978-1-59920-654-7; 1-59920-654-4

"This reference set provides a simple, brief, and easy-to-read introduction to key aspects of physical and mental health, including various body processes and diseases as well as information on treatments and preventative measures. . . . The explanations are concise, clear, and easy to understand. In addition to the abundance of images, the large type and white space that is prevalent on every page will make this set accessible to a broad array of young readers." Booklist

616.027   Experimental medicine

Barber, Nicola

Cloning and genetic engineering; Nicola Barber. Rosen Pub.'s Rosen Central 2013 48 p. (Both sides of the story) (library binding) $29.25

Grades: 5 6 7 8   **616.027**

1. Cloning 2. Genetic engineering

ISBN 1448871875; 9781448871872

LC 2012013797

Author Nicola Barber's book focuses on cloning and genetic engineering. The book "offers arguments for both sides of the cloning and genetic engineering debate. Among the subjects examined are the human genome, transgenics, reproductive cloning, research cloning, stem cell therapy, genetic disease and testing, gene therapy, plant and animal pharming, genetically modified animals and crops, and gene doping." (Publisher's note)

Includes bibliographical references (p. 46) and index

Green, Caroline

Stem cells. Newforest Press 2010 64p il (Cutting-edge science) lib bdg $34.25

Grades: 7 8 9 10   **616.02**

1. Stem cell research

ISBN 978-1-84898-325-0; 1-84898-325-5

This addresses the topic of stem cell research, "touching on both scientific and societal issues . . . The underlying science is addressed, as well as the current state of scientific and ethical thinking. Stock color photographs and diagrams accompany the [text]. Sidebars provide biographical information on contemporary scientists as well as highlights of their research methods and studies." Horn Book Guide

Includes glossary and bibliographical references

616.07   Pathology

Murray, Elizabeth A.

Death; corpses, cadavers, and other grave matters. Twenty-First Century Books 2010 112p il (Discovery!) lib bdg $31.93

Grades: 7 8 9 10   **616.07**

1. Death 2. Forensic sciences

ISBN 978-0-7613-3851-2; 0-7613-3851-9

LC 2009-17436

The author "has written a book that deals with the scientific aspect of life and death. Her experience as a teacher of anatomy and physiology comes through as she explains the living body, what happens when systems shut down, and how postmortem remains can give evidence to solve crimes and the mysteries of diseases. . . . First-person accounts of terminally ill patients and those working in the fields of pathology, hospice, and anatomy clarify subjects presented in the chapters. Color photographs are included throughout, some of which are potentially disturbing. The glossary and bibliography are extensive and helpful. This book provides information for those who are curious about a subject that is not easy to discuss." SLJ

Includes glossary and bibliographical references

Sherrow, Victoria

Medical imaging; [by] Victoria Sherrow. Marshall Cavendish Benchmark 2007 127p il (Great inventions) lib bdg $39.93

Grades: 7 8 9 10 **616.07**

1. Diagnostic imaging

ISBN 978-0-7614-2231-0; 0-7614-2231-5

LC 2006003229

"An examination of the origins, history, development, and societal impact of various medical-imaging devices, from X-rays to the MRI" Publisher's note

Includes glossary and bibliographical references

616.1 Specific diseases

Jones, Phill

Sickle cell disease; [by] Phill Jones. Chelsea House Pubs. 2008 143p il (Genes & disease) $35

Grades: 7 8 9 10 **616.1**

1. Sickle cell anemia

ISBN 978-0-7910-9587-4; 0-7910-9587-8

LC 2008-4959

Opens "with accounts of people who have [Sickle cell] disease . . . followed by information on history, symptoms, variations, diagnosis, treatments, and research. . . . Chapters devoted to current genetic research and therapies can become dense as they introduce complex topics but photos, diagrams and charts help to clarify the details. . . . Controversial issues . . . are introduced fairly." SLJ

Includes glossary and bibliographical references

Raabe, Michelle

Hemophilia. Chelsea House Publishers 2008 133p il (Genes & disease) lib bdg $35

Grades: 7 8 9 10 **616.1**

1. Hemophilia

ISBN 978-0-7910-9648-2 lib bdg; 0-7910-9648-3 lib bdg

LC 2008-4897

This book opens "with accounts of people who have [Hemophilia] . . . followed by information on history, symptoms, variations, diagnosis, treatments, and research. . . . Chapters devoted to current genetic research and therapies can become dense as they introduce complex topics but photos, diagrams and charts help to clarify the details. . . . Controversial issues . . . are introduced fairly." SLJ

Includes glossary and bibliographical references

Silverstein, Alvin

★ **Heart** disease; [by] Alvin & Virginia Silverstein & Laura Silverstein Nunn. Twenty-First Century Books 2006 112p il (Twenty-first century medical library) lib bdg $27.93

Grades: 8 9 10 11 12 **616.1**

1. Heart diseases

ISBN 0-7613-3420-3

LC 2005-04161

"The authors explain the causes, methods of prevention, and treatment of heart disease in an accessible and interesting way. Terms and procedures are clearly explained. Vari-

ous chapters deal effectively with everything from how the heart works to current repairs for broken hearts to the future of cardiology." SLJ

Includes bibliographical references

616.2 Diseases of respiratory system

★ **Asthma** information for teens; health tips about managing asthma and related concerns including facts about asthma causes, triggers and symptoms, diagnosis, and treatment. edited by Kim Wohlenhaus. 2nd ed.; Omnigraphics 2010 427p il (Teen health series) $69

Grades: 7 8 9 10 11 12 **616.2**

1. Asthma

ISBN 978-0-7808-1086-0; 0-7808-1086-4

LC 2009048694

First published 2005 under the editorship of Karen Bellenir

"Provides basic consumer health information for teens about asthma causes and treatments, controlling triggers, and coping with asthma at home and school. Includes index, resource information and recommendations for further reading." Publisher's note

Includes bibliographical references

Berger, William E.

Living with asthma. Facts on File 2007 183p (Teen's guides) lib bdg $34.95

Grades: 7 8 9 10 11 **616.2**

1. Asthma

ISBN 978-0-8160-6483-0 lib bdg; 0-8160-6483-0 lib bdg; 0-8160-7560-3 pa; 9781438121055

LC 2007003664

Examines asthma and provides teens with the information they need to understand it.

"There is a great directory of referral and online resources in the appendix. Although there are no illustrations, the text is appealing, well-organized, and accessible for the teen reader." Voice Youth Advocates

Includes glossary

Bjorklund, Ruth

★ **Asthma**. Benchmark Books 2005 64p il (Health alert) $28.50

Grades: 4 5 6 7 **616.2**

1. Asthma

ISBN 0-7614-1803-2

LC 2004-5976

The author explains "the causes, physiology, treatments, and complications associated with [asthma]. The [book is] well organized. . . . The photos are colorful and . . . some are startling." SLJ

Includes bibliographical references

Giddings, Sharon

Cystic fibrosis. Chelsea House 2009 128p il (Genes & disease) lib bdg $35

Grades: 7 8 9 10 **616.2**
1. Cystic fibrosis
ISBN 978-0-7910-9694-9; 0-7910-9694-7
LC 2008-44771

"Cystic fibrosis is one of the most widespread fatal genetic diseases in the United States. . . . [This book] discusses this genetic disease, its history, current treatments, and how scientists are searching for a cure." Publisher's note

Includes glossary and bibliographical references

Goldsmith, Connie
Influenza. Twenty-First Century Books 2010 128p il (USA Today health reports: diseases and disorders) lib bdg $34.60
Grades: 7 8 9 10 11 12 **616.2**
1. Influenza
ISBN 9780761363767; 978-0-7613-5881-7; 0-7613-5881-1
LC 2010-01030

"This book provides information about flu, how it spreads, and how it is prevented and treated." (Introduction) Glossary. Bibliography. Index. "Grades seven to twelve." (Sci Books Films)

This book "talks about the science behind the highly contagious disease, how it has spread to millions, and how to prevent and treat it. . . . [The] accessible design extends the impressive educational data." Booklist

Includes bibliographical references

Hoffmann, Gretchen
★ The **flu**. Marshall Cavendish Benchmark 2007 64p il (Health alert) lib bdg $31.36
Grades: 4 5 6 7 **616.2**
1. Influenza
ISBN 978-0-7614-2208-2; 0-7614-2208-0 \
LC 2006011980

This "title features a handsome format, with well-chosen illustrations, a substantial amount of information, and some practical insights." Booklist

Includes glossary and bibliographical references

Kelly, Evelyn B.
Investigating influenza and bird flu; real facts for real lives. [by] Evelyn B. Kelly and Claire Wilson. Enslow Publishers 2010 160p il (Investigating diseases) lib bdg $34.60
Grades: 6 7 8 9 10 **616.2**
1. Influenza 2. Avian influenza
ISBN 978-0-7660-3341-2; 0-7660-3341-4
LC 2009-14802

"The authors have explained the difficult problems in a clear, readable manner with lots of added pictures. . . . [Recommended] . . . for junior and senior high school students and for the general public." Sci Books Films

Includes glossary and bibliographical references

Marcovitz, Hal
Asthma. ReferencePoint Press 2010 96p il (Compact research: diseases and disorders) lib bdg $25.95

Grades: 7 8 9 10 **616.2**
1. Asthma
ISBN 978-1-60152-104-0 lib bdg; 1-60152-104-9 lib bdg
LC 2009036844

This "title begins with an overview of [asthma], followed by chapters that define the condition, explain its causes, and discuss possible treatments. . . . The last chapter . . . is about how to live with the condition. Chapters present material in accessible language, provide report-ready, primary-source quotes from experts, and end with a Facts and Illustrations section in which information is summarized in bullet points and accompanied by colorful graphs and charts that will appeal to visual learners." SLJ

Includes bibliographical references

Parks, Peggy J., 1951-
Influenza. ReferencePoint Press 2011 96p il map (Compact research: diseases and disorders) lib bdg $26.95
Grades: 7 8 9 10 11 12 **616.2**
1. Influenza 2. Swine influenza
ISBN 978-1-60152-118-7; 1-60152-118-9
LC 2010-26063

This book about influenza "begins with a general overview followed by a focus on statistics, causes, symptoms, treatments, and prevention. [The book] discusses the virus that causes the disease; presents information on prevention through proper hygiene as well as vaccination, especially during epidemics; and warns against public apathy. . . . The readable page design features pull quotes and subtitles, with occasional photos throughout." Booklist

Includes bibliographical references

Royston, Angela
Explaining asthma. Smart Apple Media 2010 45p il (Explaining) lib bdg $34.25
Grades: 5 6 7 8 **616.2**
1. Asthma
ISBN 978-1-59920-315-7 lib bdg; 1-59920-315-4 lib bdg
LC 2008-49284

Describes what living with asthma is like, discussing symptoms, triggers, treatments, and lifestyle changes that may be necessary to prevent asthma attacks

The book provides a "basic [overview] of the health concerns related to the disease; information on diagnosis and treatment; and a discussion of the challenges or complications experienced by the affected person and their family/friends, and how to manage those problems. . . . The incorporation of quotes and personal accounts in 'Case Notes' sidebars adds to the sensitive tone found throughout [the title]." SLJ

Includes glossary

Smith, Terry L.
Asthma; [by] Terry L. Smith. Chelsea House 2008 128p il (Genes & disease) lib bdg $35

Grades: 7 8 9 10 **616.2**
1. Asthma
ISBN 978-0-7910-9663-5 lib bdg; 0-7910-9663-7
lib bdg
LC 2008-44774

This book opens "with accounts of people who have
[asthma] . . . followed by information on history, symptoms,
variations, diagnosis, treatments, and research. . . . Chapters devoted to current genetic research and therapies can
become dense as they introduce complex topics but photos,
diagrams and charts help to clarify the details. . . . Controversial issues . . . are introduced fairly." SLJ
Includes glossary and bibliographical references

Yancey, Diane
Tuberculosis; rev ed; Twenty-First Century
Books 2008 128p il (Twenty-first century medical
library) lib bdg $30.60
Grades: 8 9 10 11 12 **616.2**
1. Tuberculosis
ISBN 978-0-8225-9190-0 lib bdg; 0-8225-9190-1
lib bdg
LC 2007-30486

The author begins this book with a history of tuberculosis, "tracing evidence of it back to the Neolithic Age and
then explores the variety of treatments used to combat it. .
. . The three personal cases related are from three different
socioeconomic situations. Good-quality, black-and-white
photos appear throughout." SLJ [review of 2001 edition]
Includes bibliographical references

616.3 Diseases of digestive system

Allman, Toney
Obesity. Cherry Lake Pub. 2009 32p il (Health
at risk) lib bdg $27.07
Grades: 4 5 6 7 **616.3**
1. Obesity
ISBN 978-1-60279-285-2 lib bdg; 1-60279-285-2
lib bdg
LC 2008017499

This describes the causes and dangers of obesity and the
many efforts being made to help people control their weight.
"Great for reports or reluctant readers." Booklist
Includes bibliographical references

Bjorklund, Ruth
★ Cystic fibrosis. Marshall Cavendish Bench-
mark 2009 64p il (Health alert) $22.95
Grades: 4 5 6 7 **616.3**
1. Cystic fibrosis
ISBN 978-0-7614-2912-8; 0-7614-2912-3
LC 2007-46674

This "title features a handsome format, with well-chosen
illustrations, a substantial amount of information, and some
practical insights." Booklist
"Provides comprehensive information on the causes,
treatment, and history of cystic fibrosis." Publisher's note

Fredericks, Carrie
Obesity. Reference Point Press 2008 104p il
map (Compact research. Current issues) lib bdg
$24.95
Grades: 8 9 10 11 12 **616.3**
1. Obesity
ISBN 978-1-60152-040-1; 1-60152-040-9
LC 2007-42183

Examines the topic of obesity in a format with objective overviews, primary source quotes, illustrated facts,
and statistics.
"Both general readers and serious researchers will find
something useful in this volume. It facilitates research for
less-motivated students and supplies excellent information
for better researchers." SLJ
Includes bibliographical references

Goldsmith, Connie
Hepatitis. Twenty-First Century Books 2010
128p il (USA Today health reports: diseases and dis-
orders) lib bdg $34.60
Grades: 7 8 9 10 11 12 **616.3**
1. Liver -- Diseases
ISBN 978-0-8225-6787-5; 0-8225-6787-3
LC 2009-20720

This "reveals that an estimated five million Americans
have viral Hepatitis A, B, and C, making it a major public
health problem. . . . The detailed information is combined
with photos and diagrams portraying transmission, vaccines,
and effective treatment. . . . [The] accessible design extends
the impressive educational data." Booklist
Includes bibliographical references

Hicks, Terry Allan
★ Obesity. Marshall Cavendish Benchmark
2009 63p il (Health alert) $22.95
Grades: 4 5 6 7 **616.3**
1. Obesity
ISBN 978-0-7614-2911-1; 0-7614-2911-5
LC 2007-31246

This "title features a handsome format, with well-chosen
illustrations, a substantial amount of information, and some
practical insights." Booklist
"Provides comprehensive information on the causes,
treatment, and history of obesity." Publisher's note
Includes glossary

Marcovitz, Hal
Hepatitis. ReferencePoint Press 2009 112p il
(Compact research. Diseases and disorders) lib bdg
$25.95
Grades: 8 9 10 11 12 **616.3**
1. Liver -- Diseases
ISBN 978-1-60152-039-5 lib bdg; 1-60152-039-5
lib bdg
LC 2007-38874

Presents information on hepatitis through essays, quotations, statistics, and suggestions for further research
"The coverage is succinct . . . [and] includes colorful
illustrations and figures, chronologies, related organizations,

advocacy groups and sources for additional research." Libr Media Connect

Includes bibliographical references

Obesity; Tom and Gena Metcalf, editors. Thomson / Gale 2008 136p il (Perspectives on diseases and disorders) lib bdg $34.95

Grades: 7 8 9 10   **616.3**

1. Obesity

ISBN 978-0-7377-3873-5; 0-7377-3873-1

LC 2007-37470

"This book explains what obesity is, provides insight into its causes, and takes a serious look at why it's becoming such an epidemic. Accounts by people who have firsthand experience dealing with being overweight add value to the book." SLJ

Includes glossary and bibliographical references

Powell, Jillian

Explaining cystic fibrosis. Smart Apple Media 2010 45p il (Explaining) lib bdg $34.25

Grades: 5 6 7 8   **616.3**

1. Cystic fibrosis

ISBN 978-1-59920-312-6 lib bdg; 1-59920-312-X lib bdg

LC 2008-49288

Describes the illness, including its causes, how it is diagnosed, current treatments for the illness, and how those with cystic fibrosis lead everyday lives

The book provides a "basic [overview] of the health concerns related to the disease; information on diagnosis and treatment; and a discussion of the challenges or complications experienced by the affected person and their family/friends, and how to manage those problems. . . . The incorporation of quotes and personal accounts in 'Case Notes' sidebars adds to the sensitive tone found throughout [the title]." SLJ

Includes glossary and bibliographical references

616.39   Nutritional and metabolic diseases

Jarrow, Gail

Red madness; how a medical mystery changed what we eat. Gail Jarrow. Calkins Creek 2014 192 p. $16.95

Grades: 5 6 7 8 9   **616.39**

1. Diseases 2. Malnutrition 3. Pellagra -- History 4. Epidemics -- United States -- History 5. United States. Public Health Service -- History

ISBN 1590787323; 9781590787328

LC 2008049497

In this book, author Gail Jarrow "tracks [a] disease, commonly known as pellagra, and highlights how doctors, scientists, and public health officials finally defeated it. Illustrated with 100 archival photographs, [it] includes stories about real-life pellagra victims and accounts of scientific investigations. It concludes with a glossary, timeline, further resources, author's note, bibliography, and index." (Publisher's note)

"In 1902, a young man in Georgia displayed symptoms of a disease believed to be nonexistent in the U.S.: pella-

gra, a deficiency disease. Jarrow unfolds the suspenseful search for a cause of the South's epidemic, as corn fungus, insect- and bird-born parasites, and more were all blamed and rejected. Plentiful archival photos, many of victims, add emotional heft. Reading list, timeline, websites. Bib., glos., ind." Horn Book

616.4   Diseases of endocrine, hematopoietic, lymphatic, glandular systems; diseases of male breast

Allman, Toney

Diabetes. Chelsea House 2008 136p il (Genes & disease) lib bdg $35

Grades: 7 8 9 10   **616.4**

1. Diabetes

ISBN 978-0-7910-9585-0; 0-7910-9585-1

LC 2008-1195

This "well-written book . . . [discusses] diabetes, its treatments, genetic variations contributing to the disease, and the prospects for a cure. The narrative starts with the diagnosis of diabetes and follows with seven chapters." Sci Books Films

Includes glossary and bibliographical references

Ambrose, Marylou

Investigating diabetes; real facts for real lives. Enslow Publishers 2010 160p il (Investigating diseases) lib bdg $34.60

Grades: 6 7 8 9 10   **616.4**

1. Diabetes

ISBN 978-0-7660-3338-2; 0-7660-3338-4

LC 2008-30778

"The book is a comprehensive primer that can well serve patients with newly diagnosed diabetes and their families with its detailed account of diabetes, the causes of the disease, and its potential consequences." Sci Books Films

Includes glossary and bibliographical references

Brill, Marlene Targ, 1945-

Diabetes. Twenty-First Century Books 2011 128p il (USA Today health reports: diseases and disorders) lib bdg $34.60

Grades: 7 8 9 10 11 12   **616.4**

1. Diabetes

ISBN 978-0-7613-6085-8; 0-7613-6085-9

LC 2010049454

This volume explores the history of diabetes, and explains the various treatments that are available today.

"This is an important endeavor from the author [that] will be very helpful for patients and others who are looking for basic information about diabetes. The author has done a good job of helping readers understand how their bodies function and the underlying mechanism of diabetes." Sci Books Films

Includes glossary and bibliographical references

Loughrey, Anita

Explaining diabetes. Smart Apple Media 2010 45p il (Explaining) lib bdg $34.25

Grades: 5 6 7 8 **616.4**

1. Diabetes

ISBN 978-1-59920-314-0 lib bdg; 1-59920-314-6 lib bdg

LC 2008-49290

Provides an overview of Type 1 and Type 2 diabetes, discussing causes and symptoms, recommended and required lifestyle changes, how the disease is managed, and possible complications that may occur

The book provides a "basic [overview] of the health concerns related to the disease; information on diagnosis and treatment; and a discussion of the challenges or complications experienced by the affected person and their family/friends, and how to manage those problems. . . . The incorporation of quotes and personal accounts in 'Case Notes' sidebars adds to the sensitive tone found throughout [the title]." SLJ

Includes glossary and bibliographical references

Yuwiler, Janice

Diabetes. ReferencePoint Press 2009 96p il (Compact research. Diseases and disorders) lib bdg $25.95

Grades: 7 8 9 10 **616.4**

1. Diabetes

ISBN 978-1-60152-076-0; 1-60152-076-X

LC 2009-6173

"Yuwiler discusses type 1 diabetes and its management, type 2 diabetes and its prevention, metabolic syndrome, and medical advances. . . . Subtopics are delineated by brightly colored burgundy headings; blocks of orange-colored sidebars with bright-red print and relevant color photos and illustrations appear throughout. Each chapter ends with several pages of primary-source quotes and facts and illustrations that offer greater clarity to the text." SLJ

Includes bibliographical references

616.5 Diseases of integument

Faulk, Michelle

The **case** of the flesh-eating bacteria; Annie Biotica solves skin disease crimes. by Michelle Faulk. Lake Book Manufacturing, Inc. 2013 48 p. (Body system disease investigations) (library) $23.93

Grades: 5 6 7 8 **616.5**

1. Picture books for children 2. Skin -- Diseases 3. Virus diseases 4. Skin -- Infections

ISBN 0766039455; 9780766039452

LC 2011023985

This book by Michelle Faulk "from the Body System Disease Investigations series introduces Agent Annie Biotica, a 'Disease Scene Investigator with the Major Health Crimes Unit'. This cartoon-style heroine is called in to solve a series of skin-related medical cases . . . caused by flesh-eating bacteria, pinkeye, ringworm, chicken pox, [and] measles." (Booklist)

Includes bibliographical references (p. 47) and index

Juettner, Bonnie

Acne. Lucent Books 2010 104p il (Diseases and disorders series) lib bdg $33.45

Grades: 7 8 9 10 **616.5**

1. Acne

ISBN 978-1-4205-0215-2; 1-4205-0215-8

LC 2009-33484

First published 2004

"Well-organized chapters present clear information on the causes of acne, types of self-treatment, medical and 'alternative' paths to a cure, the future of treatment, and the psychological ramifications for an affected person. . . . This title will be useful for reports and is a solid addition to health and/or disease collections." SLJ

Includes bibliographical references

Lew, Kristi

Itch & ooze; gross stuff on your skin. illustrations by Michael Slack. Millbrook Press 2010 48p il (Gross body science) lib bdg $29.27

Grades: 4 5 6 **616.5**

1. Skin 2. Skin -- Diseases

ISBN 978-0-8225-8963-1 lib bdg; 0-8225-8963-X lib bdg

LC 2008-45591

Presents disgusting facts about human skin, the diseases and parasites that can cause problems with it, and how it functions to protect the body and itself.

"Solid information layered between sarcastic comments and kid-friendly terminology like fart, poop, barf, and puke will keep readers engaged. . . . Labeled, captioned (and graphic) photographs, cartoon-style illustrations, and micrographs add information." SLJ

Includes glossary and bibliographical references

Skin health information for teens; health tips about dermatological disorders and activities that affect the skin, hair, and nails. edited by Lisa Esposito. 3rd ed. Omnigraphics, Inc. 2013 424 p. (hardcover) $69.00

Grades: 7 8 9 10 **616.5**

1. Skin -- Care 2. Skin -- Diseases 3. Teenagers -- Health and hygiene 4. Beauty, Personal 5. Skin -- Care and hygiene

ISBN 0780813170; 9780780813175

LC 2013009908

This book "provides updated information about the skin, hair, and nails. It explains how the skin and its related structures grow and how to keep them healthy. Common ailments, including acne, eczema, impetigo, psoriasis, vitiligo, and warts are explained, and a section on skin cancer provides information about cancer risks, prevention strategies, warning signs, and treatments. The care of skin injuries, including cuts, scrapes, burns, bites, and stings, is also discussed." (Publisher's note)

Includes bibliographical references and index.

616.6   Diseases of urogenital system

The **kidneys** and the renal system; edited by Kara
Rogers. Britannica Educational Pub. in association with Rosen Educational Services 2012 xvii,
174 p.p col. ill.
Grades: 7 8 9 10 11 12   616.6
1. Kidneys 2. Human anatomy 3. Urinary organs 4.
Kidneys -- Diseases
ISBN 161530679X; 9781615306794
                                 LC 2011026615
This biology reference work, edited by Kara Rogers,
describes the Human waste system. "Responsible for managing the body's waste and regulating the balance of water
and electrolytes, the kidneys and renal system, in a sense,
make up the body's plumbing network. . . . This volume
examines the various components of the renal, or urinary,
system, and the consequences of dysfunction and disease."
(Publisher's note)
Includes bibliographical references and index

616.7   Diseases of musculoskeletal system

Gray, Susan Heinrichs
Living with juvenile rheumatoid arthritis. Child's
World 2003 32p il (Living well) lib bdg $25.64
Grades: 4 5 6   616.7
1. Arthritis
ISBN 1-56766-104-1
                                  LC 2002-2870
This title "leads off with an introduction to a young
person who has [juvenile rheumatoid arthritis]. Subsequent
chapters explain the physiology of the illness, what causes
it, and what it's like to live with it. [The concluding section
looks] at possible treatments and potential cures. [The text
is] clear and simple, double spaced, and punctuated by colorful exemplary photos of kids dealing with the disease." SLJ
Includes glossary and bibliographical references

Hoffmann, Gretchen
★ **Osteoporosis**. Marshall Cavendish Bench-
mark 2007 64p il (Health alert) lib bdg $21.95
Grades: 4 5 6 7   616.7
1. Osteoporosis
ISBN 978-0-7614-2702-5; 0-7614-2702-3
                                 LC 2007008787
This describes what it is like to have osteoporosis, what
it is, its history and its diagnosis and treatment
This "title features a handsome format, with well-chosen
illustrations, a substantial amount of information, and some
practical insights." Booklist
Includes glossary and bibliographical references

616.8   Diseases of nervous system and mental disorders

Bender, Lionel
Explaining epilepsy. Smart Apple Media 2010
45p il (Explaining) lib bdg $34.25

Grades: 5 6 7 8   616.8
1. Epilepsy
ISBN 978-1-59920-309-6 lib bdg; 1-59920-309-X
lib bdg
                                 LC 2008-49292
Describes the nature, symptoms, and possible causes
of epilepsy, gives a history of its study, and discusses
its treatment
The book provides a "basic [overview] of the health concerns related to the disease; information on diagnosis and
treatment; and a discussion of the challenges or complications experienced by the affected person and their family/
friends, and how to manage those problems. . . . The incorporation of quotes and personal accounts in 'Case Notes'
sidebars adds to the sensitive tone found throughout [the
title]." SLJ
Includes glossary and bibliographical references

Bjorklund, Ruth
★ **Cerebral** palsy. Marshall Cavendish Bench-
mark 2007 64p il (Health alert) lib bdg $31.36
Grades: 4 5 6 7   616.8
1. Cerebral palsy
ISBN 978-0-7614-2209-9; 0-7614-2209-9
                                 LC 2006-15818
This "title features a handsome format, with well-chosen
illustrations, a substantial amount of information, and some
practical insights." Booklist
"Explores the history, causes, symptoms, treatments, and
future of cerebral palsy." Publisher's note
Includes glossary and bibliographical references

★ **Epilepsy**. Marshall Cavendish Benchmark
2007 63p il (Health alert) lib bdg $21.95
Grades: 4 5 6 7   616.8
1. Epilepsy
ISBN 978-0-7614-2206-8; 0-7614-2206-4
                                 LC 2006-15816
This "title features a handsome format, with well-chosen
illustrations, a substantial amount of information, and some
practical insights." Booklist
"Explores the history, causes, symptoms, treatments, and
future of epilepsy and seizure disorders." Publisher's note
Includes glossary and bibliographical references

Brill, Marlene Targ
Alzheimer's disease. Benchmark Books 2005
64p il (Health alert) $28.50
Grades: 4 5 6 7   616.8
1. Alzheimer's disease
ISBN 0-7614-1799-0
                                 LC 2004-6528
The author explains "the causes, physiology, treatments,
and complications associated with [Alzheimer's disease].
The [book is] well organized. . . . The photos are colorful
and . . . some are startling, including the brain scans of a
patient with Alzheimer's." SLJ
Includes bibliographical references

Colligan, L. H.
★ **Sleep** disorders. Marshall Cavendish Benchmark 2009 64p il (Health alert) $22.95

Grades: 4 5 6 7   **616.8**

1. Sleep disorders

ISBN 978-0-7614-2913-5; 0-7614-2913-1

This "title features a handsome format, with well-chosen illustrations, a substantial amount of information, and some practical insights." Booklist

"Provides comprehensive information on the causes, treatment, and history of sleep disorders." Publisher's note

Includes glossary

Dittmer, Lori

Parkinson's disease. Creative Education 2011 il (Living with disease) $23.95

Grades: 6 7 8 9   **616.8**

1. Parkinson's disease

ISBN 978-1-60818-076-9; 1-60818-076-X

LC 2010030366

A look at Parkinson's disease, examining the ways in which it develops, its symptoms and diagnosis, the effects it has on a person's daily life, and research toward finding better treatments.

"The text is clearly written. . . . The book's design is simple and bold. . . . A brief but informative introduction to Parkinson's disease." Booklist

Includes glossary and bibliographical references

Dougherty, Terri

Epilepsy. Lucent Books 2010 104p il (Diseases and disorders series) lib bdg $33.45

Grades: 7 8 9 10 11 12   **616.8**

1. Epilepsy

ISBN 978-1-4205-0218-3; 1-4205-0218-2

LC 2009-33344

This "offers a thorough explanation of [epilepsy], giving a basic definition; a discussion of the causes, symptoms, and treatments; a description of living with the disease; and ideas of future treatment and diagnoses. The color photographs and sidebars help to make the information in the dense text more easily understood, and personal stories provide insight into how individuals deal with their disease. . . . Different types of seizures and the varied triggers are explained." Voice Youth Advocates

Includes bibliographical references

Esherick, Joan

The **journey** toward recovery; youth with brain injury. Mason Crest Publishers 2004 127p il (Youth with special needs) hardcover o.p. pa $14.95

Grades: 7 8 9 10   **616.8**

1. Brain damaged children

ISBN 1-59084-734-2; 1-4222-0425-1 pa

LC 2003-18640

Through the story of Jerome, a teenager who suffers a traumatic brain injury from a bike accident, this book discusses different "forms of brain injury; how these injuries affect people's lives; and how schools, doctors, and lawmakers are helping youth with this form of special need." Publisher's note

Includes glossary and bibliographical references

Freedman, Jeri

Tay -Sachs disease. Chelsea House 2009 128p il (Genes & disease) lib bdg $35

Grades: 7 8 9 10   **616.8**

1. Tay-Sachs disease

ISBN 978-0-7910-9634-5; 0-7910-9634-3

LC 2008-44770

This book "discusses the nature of the disease, why it affects certain groups of people more often than others, how genetic screening can help detect carriers of the Tay-Sachs gene, and what options genetic testing and counseling provide for having children." Publisher's note

Includes glossary and bibliographical references

Goldstein, Natalie

Parkinson's disease. Chelsea House 2008 128p il (Genes & disease) lib bdg $35

Grades: 7 8 9 10   **616.8**

1. Parkinson's disease

ISBN 978-0-7910-9584-3; 0-7910-9584-3

LC 2008-10494

This book opens "with accounts of people who have [Parkinson's] disease . . . followed by information on history, symptoms, variations, diagnosis, treatments, and research. . . . Chapters devoted to current genetic research and therapies can become dense as they introduce complex topics but photos, diagrams and charts help to clarify the details. . . . [Controversial issues] are introduced fairly." SLJ

Includes glossary and bibliographical references

Klosterman, Lorrie

★ **Meningitis**. Marshall Cavendish Benchmark 2007 64p il (Health alert) lib bdg $31.36

Grades: 4 5 6 7   **616.8**

1. Meningitis

ISBN 978-0-7614-2211-2; 0-7614-2211-0

LC 2006015819

This "title features a handsome format, with well-chosen illustrations, a substantial amount of information, and some practical insights." Booklist

"Explores the history, causes, symptoms, treatments, and future of different types of meningitis." Publisher's note

Includes glossary and bibliographical references

Levete, Sarah

Explaining cerebral palsy. Smart Apple Media 2010 45p il (Explaining) lib bdg $34.25

Grades: 5 6 7 8   **616.8**

1. Cerebral palsy

ISBN 978-1-59920-311-9 lib bdg; 1-59920-311-1 lib bdg

LC 2008-49287

Describes the illness, including its causes, how it is diagnosed, current treatment methods, and how those with cerebral palsy live everyday lives

The book provides a "basic [overview] of the health concerns related to the disease; information on diagnosis and treatment; and a discussion of the challenges or complications experienced by the affected person and their family/friends, and how to manage those problems. . . . The incorporation of quotes and personal accounts in 'Case Notes' sidebars adds to the sensitive tone found throughout [the title]." SLJ

Includes glossary and bibliographical references

Marcovitz, Hal

Meningitis. ReferencePoint Press 2009 112p il (Compact research. Diseases and disorders) lib bdg $25.95

Grades: 7 8 9 10 **616.8**

1. Meningitis

ISBN 978-1-60152-043-2 lib bdg; 1-60152-043-3 lib bdg

LC 2007-45213

Presents an overview of meningitis and discusses symptoms, disease contraction, social impacts, and prevention

"The coverage is succinct . . . [and] includes colorful illustrations and figures, chronologies, related organizations, advocacy groups, and sources for additional research." Libr Media Connect

Includes bibliographical references

Sleep disorders. ReferencePoint Press 2009 104p il (Compact research. Diseases and disorders) lib bdg $25.95

Grades: 7 8 9 10 11 12 **616.8**

1. Sleep disorders

ISBN 978-1-60152-071-5; 1-60152-071-9

LC 2008-46115

"Marcovitz's coverage ranges from insomnia to potential medical conditions that can lead to death, such as sleep apnea and narcolepsy. This book is a comprehensive overview of an often misunderstood subject." SLJ

Includes bibliographical references

616.85 Miscellaneous diseases of nervous system and mental disorders

Ambrose, Marylou

Investigating eating disorders (anorexia, bulimia, and binge eating) real facts for real lives. [by] Marylou Ambrose and Veronica Deisler. Enslow Publishers 2011 160p il (Investigating diseases) lib bdg $34.60

Grades: 6 7 8 9 10 **616.85**

1. Eating disorders

ISBN 978-0-7660-3339-9; 0-7660-3339-2

LC 2009-6492

"This book is a well-organized, clear, succinct, and attractive presentation on anorexia, bulimia, and binge eating. In it, the authors have gathered helpful definitions, early religious history, international viewpoints, statistics, family issues, medical and psychological assessments, treatments, medications, and legislation to present information on the future outlook of, and research into, these eating disorders." Sci Books Films

Includes glossary and bibliographical references

Autism; Carrie Fredericks, book editor. Greenhaven Press 2008 168p il (Perspectives on diseases and disorders) $34.95

Grades: 7 8 9 10 **616.85**

1. Autism

ISBN 978-0-7377-3869-8

LC 2007-37472

"Explores the symptoms, causes and treatment of this lifelong disease that profoundly affects social functioning, language and behavior." Publisher's note

Includes glossary and bibliographical references

Baish, Vanessa

Self -image and eating disorders; by Rita Smith ... [et al.] 1st ed. Rosen Pub. 2013 48 p. col. ill. (Teen mental health) (library) $29.25

Grades: 6 7 8 9 **616.85**

1. Body image 2. Eating disorders 3. Body image in adolescence 4. Eating disorders in adolescence -- Treatment 5. Eating disorders in adolescence -- Psychological aspects

ISBN 1448868947; 9781448868940

LC 2012003030

This book on self-image and eating disorders by Rita Smith is part of the "Teen Mental Health" series. It "addresses self-esteem and negative body image. Eating disorders include anorexia nervosa, bulimia nervosa, binge eating, orthorexia nervosa, and compulsive exercise, along with related health and emotional problems. The books discuss techniques for coping and encourage teens to seek out available resources such as professional help, support groups, or school programs." (School Library Journal)

Includes bibliographical references (p. 43-46) and index.

Barbour, Scott

Post -traumatic stress disorder. ReferencePoint Press 2009 104p (Compact research: diseases and disorders) lib bdg $25.95

Grades: 7 8 9 10 **616.85**

1. Post-traumatic stress disorder

ISBN 978-1-60152-101-9 lib bdg; 1-60152-101-4 lib bdg

LC 2009033216

This "title begins with an overview of [post-traumatic stress disorder], followed by chapters that define the condition, explain its causes, and discuss possible treatments. . . . The final chapter discusses how society should help soldiers with the problem. . . . Chapters present material in accessible language, provide report-ready, primary-source quotes from experts, and end with a Facts and Illustrations section in which information is summarized in bullet points and accompanied by colorful graphs and charts that will appeal to visual learners." SLJ

Includes bibliographical references

Bingham, Jane

Eating disorders; by Jane Bingham. Gareth Stevens Pub. 2009 48p il (Emotional health issues) lib bdg $31

Grades: 6 7 8 9   **616.85**
1. Eating disorders
ISBN 978-0-8368-9200-0; 0-8368-9200-3
LC 2008-825
First published 2008 in the United Kingdom
This book about eating disorders has "clear language and explanations. . . . [It is] suitable for fact-finding missions, but the abundant graphics and case studies are likely to draw in browsers as well. Throughout, unfamiliar vocabulary is highlighted in bold and explained in context and in the glossary. . . . Fact boxes and case study sidebars add information." SLJ
Includes glossary and bibliographical references

Stress and depression; [by] Jane Bingham. Gareth Stevens 2009 48p il (Emotional health issues) lib bdg $31
Grades: 6 7 8 9   **616.85**
1. Stress (Psychology) 2. Depression (Psychology)
ISBN 978-0-8368-9203-1 lib bdg; 0-8368-9203-8 lib bdg
LC 2008-5237
First published 2008 in the United Kingdom
This book about stress and depression has "clear language and explanations. . . . [It is] suitable for fact-finding missions, but the abundant graphics and case studies are likely to draw in browsers as well. Throughout, unfamiliar vocabulary is highlighted in bold and explained in context and in the glossary. . . . Fact boxes and case study sidebars add information." SLJ
Includes glossary and bibliographical references

Bjornlund, Lydia D.
Personality disorders; by Lydia Bjornlund. ReferencePoint Press 2011 96p il (Compact research: diseases and disorders) lib bdg $26.95
Grades: 7 8 9 10   **616.85**
1. Personality disorders
ISBN 978-1-60152-139-2; 1-60152-139-1
LC 2010031384
This title provides "a systematic and focused look at [personality disorders]. . . . [It] covers 10 types, including paranoid and schizoid disorders. . . . [It explores] causes and the ways these conditions impact patients' lives and ultimately [addresses] whether sufferers can overcome them. Short sections containing primary-source quotes and bulleted facts and charts that highlight important information are appended to each chapter." SLJ
Includes bibliographical references

Brill, Marlene Targ
★ **Down** syndrome. Marshall Cavendish Benchmark 2007 64p il (Health alert) lib bdg $31.36
Grades: 4 5 6 7   **616.85**
1. Down syndrome
ISBN 978-0-7614-2207-5 lib bdg; 0-7614-2207-2 lib bdg
LC 2006-15817
This "title features a handsome format, with well-chosen illustrations, a substantial amount of information, and some practical insights." Booklist

"Explores the history, causes, symptoms, treatments, and future of Down syndrome." Publisher's note
Includes glossary and bibliographical references

Capaccio, George
★ **ADD** and ADHD. Marshall Cavendish Benchmark 2007 64p il (Health alert) lib bdg $21.95
Grades: 4 5 6 7   **616.85**
1. Attention deficit disorder
ISBN 978-0-7614-2705-6; 0-7614-2705-8
LC 2007008790
This describes what it is like to have Attention Deficit Disorder or Attention Deficit Hyperactivity Disorder, what they are, their history, and living with the disorders.
This "title features a handsome format, with well-chosen illustrations, a substantial amount of information, and some practical insights." Booklist
Includes glossary and bibliographical references

Christopherson, Sara Cohen
Living with epilepsy; by Sara Cohen Christopherson. ABDO Pub. Co. 2012 112 p. col. ill. (library) $34.22
Grades: 6 7 8   **616.85**
1. Epilepsy 2. Teenagers -- Health and hygiene
ISBN 1617831271; 9781617831270
LC 2011033155
This book "features fictional narratives paired with firsthand advice from a medical expert to help preteens and teenagers feel prepared for dealing with epilepsy during adolescence. Topics include causes, risk factors, and prevention, diagnosis, types of seizures, treatment, managing epilepsy, and dealing with social issues." (Publisher's note)
Includes bibliographical references (p. 104, 106-109) and index.

Cobain, Bev
When nothing matters anymore; a survival guide for depressed teens. edited by Elizabeth Verdick. rev and updated ed.; Free Spirit Pub. 2007 146p il pa $14.95
Grades: 7 8 9 10   **616.85**
1. Depression (Psychology)
ISBN 978-1-57542-235-0; 1-57542-235-2
LC 2006-36325
First published 1998
This book written for teens defines depression, describes the symptoms, and explains that depression is treatable
"This practical, reassuring book should be made available to all teens." Voice Youth Advocates
Includes bibliographical references

Currie-McGhee, L. K.
Exercise addiction; by Leanne Currie-McGhee. Lucent Books 2011 96p il (Diseases & disorders) lib bdg $33.45
Grades: 7 8 9 10   **616.85**
1. Exercise addiction
ISBN 978-1-4205-0551-1; 1-4205-0551-3
LC 2010039535

"Extremely readable, with helpful illustrations and sidebars, this book includes a definition of exercise addiction (with symptoms), describes how it may be related to other psychological disorders, profiles the types of people most at risk for developing it, discusses psychological and physiological dangers, and offers treatment options. . . . Personal stories appear throughout, and there is a helpful list of questions for readers to ask themselves. This volume is interesting enough to read even if not required for an assignment." SLJ

Includes bibliographical references

Denkmire, Heather

★ The **truth** about anxiety and depression; Heather Denkmire, principal author; John Perritano, contributing author; Robert N. Golden, general editor, Fred L. Peterson, general editor. 2nd ed.; Facts on File 2010 199p il (Truth about series) $35

Grades: 7 8 9 10   616.85

1. Anxiety 2. Depression (Psychology)
ISBN 978-0-8160-7643-7; 0-8160-7643-X

LC 2010005461

First published 2004 with title: The truth about fear and depression

Presents information on anxiety and depression, including the genetics of mood and anxiety disorders, gender and depression, types of treatments available, related disorders, and more.

Includes glossary and bibliographical references

Depression; Emma Carlson Berne, book editor. Greenhaven 2007 184p (Contemporary issues companion) $36.20; pa $24.95

Grades: 8 9 10 11 12   616.85

1. Depression (Psychology)
ISBN 978-0-7377-3645-8; 0-7377-3645-3; 978-0-7377-2451-6 pa; 0-7377-2451-X pa

LC 2007-19643

First published 1999 under the editorship of Henny H. Kim

"Eighteen field specialists have each contributed an essay on topics as diverse as deep brain stimulation and alternative therapies. A chapter on antidepressants and their heavily debated effects concludes the book. Thoughtfully composed, this excellent introduction to a widely recognized condition contains an extensive bibliography and support organization contact list." Libr J

Includes bibliographical references

Donovan, Sandra, 1967-

Keep your cool! what you should know about stress. illustrations by Jack Desrocher. Lerner Publications Co. 2009 64p il (Health zone) lib bdg $30.60

Grades: 4 5 6 7   616.85

1. Stress (Psychology)
ISBN 978-0-8225-7555-9; 0-8225-7555-8

LC 2007038858

This describes what causes stress and what you can do to relieve it.

"The format is beyond lively, with lots of color, cartoons, and an informal writing style, but it manages to present sometimes frightening material in a non-threatening and browsable way." Booklist

Includes glossary and bibliographical references

★ **Eating** disorders information for teens; health tips about anorexia, bulimia, binge eating, and body image disorders, including information about risk factors, prevention, diagnosis, treatment, health consequences, and other related issues. edited by Elizabeth Bellenir. 3rd ed. Omnigraphics, Inc. 2013 xiii, 380 p.p ill. (hardcover) $69

Grades: 7 8 9 10 11 12   616.85

1. Eating disorders 2. Teenagers -- Health and hygiene 3. Eating disorders in adolescence
ISBN 0780812697; 9780780812697

LC 2012036612

This book "provides information about a wide range of eating and body image disorders. The volume is broken into six parts covering general information about eating disorders; specific disorders such as anorexia nervosa, bulimia nervosa, and others; the heath consequences of eating disorders; prevention, diagnosis, and treatment; healthy eating and exercise; and additional reading, research studies, and organizations." (Voice of Youth Advocates)

Includes bibliographical references and index.

Evans-Martin, Fay

Down syndrome; [by] F. Fay Evans-Martin. Chelsea House 2008 128p il (Genes & disease) lib bdg $35

Grades: 7 8 9 10   616.85

1. Down syndrome
ISBN 978-0-7910-9644-4; 0-7910-9644-0

LC 2008-44773

"Down syndrome is a developmental disorder caused by the presence of an extra copy of chromosome 21. . . . [This book] explains this genetic disease, its history and characteristics, and what scientists are doing to study it." Publisher's note

Includes glossary and bibliographical references

Farrar, Amy

ADHD. Twenty-First Century Books 2010 112p il (USA Today health reports: diseases and disorders) lib bdg $34.60

Grades: 7 8 9 10 11 12   616.85

1. Attention deficit disorder
ISBN 978-0-7613-5455-0; 0-7613-5455-7

LC 2010-870

This book describes attention deficit-hyperactivity disorder, its causes and treatments.

This is "liberally sprinkled with relevant articles and 'snapshots' (graphs showing statistical breakdowns of the topic at hand) from the newspaper, providing a competent introduction to primary-source material." SLJ

Includes glossary and bibliographical references

Ford, Emily

★ **What** you must think of me; a firsthand account of one teenager's experience with social anxiety disorder. by Emily Ford with Michael R. Liebowitz and Linda Wasmer Andrews. Oxford University Press 2007 xxi, 152p (Annenberg Foundation Trust at Sunnylands' adolescent mental health initiative) $30; pa $9.95

Grades: 7 8 9 10 11 12 **616.85**
  1. Social phobia
  ISBN 978-0-19-531302-4; 0-19-531302-X; 978-0-19-531303-1 pa; 0-19-531303-8 pa

                   LC 2006102285

"A professor of clinical psychiatry and a woman whose life has been adversely impacted by social anxiety disorder provide a unique view of the condition and its treatment in this slim volume. . . . Readers will find helpful charts throughout the book and an appendix loaded with further reading and contact information for advocacy groups. Thanks to its informative guide to diagnosis, suggestions for treatment and tips on dealing with the health care system, this is a must read for anyone who suffers from the disorder." Publ Wkly

Includes bibliographical references

Hallowell, Edward M.

  ★ **Positively** ADD; real success stories to inspire your dreams. [by] Catherine A. Corman and Edward M. Hallowell. Walker 2006 172p il $16.95; lib bdg $17.85

Grades: 8 9 10 11 12 **616.85**
  1. Attention deficit disorder
  ISBN 978-0-8027-8988-4; 0-8027-8988-9; 978-0-8027-8071-3 lib bdg; 0-8027-8071-7 lib bdg

                   LC 2005037184

This "profiles 17 adults who began dealing with attention deficit disorder in childhood. Along with political strategist [James] Carville, subjects include a Pulitzer Prize-winning photographer, a major league pitcher, and a young Rhodes scholar. . . . [This is] an encouraging, helpful book for teens with ADD as well as for their parents, teachers, and friends." Booklist

Includes bibliographical references

Hidalgo-Robert, Alberto, 1992-

  Fat no more; a teenager's victory over obesity. by Alberto Hidalgo-Robert. Pinata Books 2012 184 p.

Grades: 7 8 9 10 11 12 **616.85**
  1. Obesity 2. Lifestyles 3. Teenagers -- Health and hygiene 4. Weight loss -- Personal narratives
  ISBN 1558857451; 9781558857452

                   LC 2012003177

This book is a "weight-loss memoir. . . . [Alberto] Hidalgo-Robert . . . weighed 230 pounds at 14. The memoir opens with a lengthy indictment of not only himself for years of junk-food addiction, but also his family for being too indulgent and the pediatricians in his native El Salvador for pushing weight-loss diets. . . . 'Read the following words carefully and engrave them on your brain: DIETS DO NOT WORK! Diets suck. Diets are unhealthy. . . .' What does work for him is . . . focusing less on weight loss than lifestyle changes. Aside from cutting out TV . . . those changes all seem to involve categorizing foods and limiting the intake of certain kinds. . . . Five years after starting, he's 69 pounds

lighter. . . . [H]e demonstrates that the approach can lead to long-term weight loss." (Kirkus)

Honos-Webb, Lara

  The **ADHD** workbook for teens; activities to help you gain motivation and confidence. Lara Honos-Webb. Instant Help Books 2010 vi, 132 p.p (pbk. : alk. paper) $15.95

Grades: 7 8 9 10 11 12 **616.85**
  1. Adolescent psychology 2. Attention deficit disorder 3. Attention-deficit disorder in adolescence -- Popular works
  ISBN 1572248653; 9781572248656

                   LC 2010040282

According to this workbook by Lara Honos-Webb, "Symptoms of attention deficit/hyperactivity disorder, or ADHD, can strike at any time-during class, when you're listening to a friend's story, while doing homework, and did we mention during class? You might find it difficult to pay attention and sit still when your impulses are constantly tempting you to do the opposite." (Publisher's note)

This book helps ADHD-affected teens "learn simple skills [they] can use to confidently handle school, make and keep friends, and organize and finish every project [they] start." Publisher's note

Hyde, Margaret Oldroyd

  Stress 101; an overview for teens. by Margaret O. Hyde and Elizabeth H. Forsyth. TwentyFirst Century Books 2008 120p il (Teen overviews) lib bdg $26.60

Grades: 8 9 10 11 12 **616.85**
  1. Stress (Psychology)
  ISBN 978-0-82256-788-2 lib bdg; 0-82256-788-1 lib bdg

                   LC 2007027631

"Beginning with a brief history of stress from the time it was first identified, Hyde and Forsyth detail its effects on a young person's brain, heart, and immune system. . . . The writing is clear and informative. Interspersed with personal vignettes, the factual information is well organized and presented in small increments." SLJ

Includes bibliographical references

It's raining cats and dogs; an autism spectrum guide to the confusing world of idioms, metaphors, and everyday expressions. Michael Barton ; foreword, Delia Barton ; illustrator, Michael Barton. Jessica Kingsley Publishers 2012 95 p. (alk. paper) $15.95

Grades: 3 4 5 6 **616.85**
  1. Autism 2. Metaphor 3. Figures of speech 4. English language -- Idioms 5. Autistic people -- Language 6. Autism spectrum disorders -- Patients -- Language
  ISBN 1849052832; 9781849052832

                   LC 2011039514

This book offers "insight into the mind of someone with an ASD [autism spectrum disorder]. It . . . illustrates why people with ASDs have problems understanding common phrases and idioms that others accept unquestioningly as part of everyday speech. The . . . drawings" are meant to "entertain and inspire those on the spectrum, giving them the confidence to recognise figures of speech, feel less alienated and even use idioms themselves. The drawings" are designed to "form instantly memorable references for those with ASDs to recall whenever they need to and" should "be helpful for anyone curious to understand the ASD way of thinking." (Publisher's note)

Kramer, Gerri Freid

★ The **truth** about eating disorders; Robert N. Golden, Fred L. Peterson general editors; Gerri Freid Kramer, principal author. 2nd ed.; Facts on File 2009 208p (Truth about series) $35
Grades: 7 8 9 10   616.85
  1. Eating disorders
  ISBN 978-0-8160-7633-8; 0-8160-7633-2
                                    LC 2008-44036
  First published 2004

This discusses anorexia, bulimia, fad diets, and laxative abuse, the causes of eating disorders, how to recognize the disorders, the portrayal of eating disorders in the media, and obesity and weight control

This title does "an excellent job of providing accurate information for teens. For reports or for self-help, [it belongs] in any library serving young adults." SLJ [review of 2004 edition]

Includes glossary and bibliographical references

Levin, Judith

Anxiety and panic attacks; [by] Judith Levin. Rosen Pub. 2008 48p il (Teen mental health) lib bdg $19.95
Grades: 7 8 9 10   616.85
  1. Anxiety 2. Panic disorders
  ISBN 9781435848450; 978-1-4042-1797-3; 1-4042-1797-5
                                    LC 2008-7144

This "volume offers a succinct discussion of mental disorders related to anxiety. . . . A vivid description of the causes and symptoms of panic attacks is followed up with a chapter suggesting ways to deal with these troubling events. . . . Color photos brighten this clearly written presentation." Booklist

Includes glossary and bibliographical references

Levy, Joel

Phobiapedia; all the things we fear the most! Scholastic 2011 80p il pa $8.99
Grades: 4 5 6 7   616.85
  1. Phobias
  ISBN 978-0-545-34929-1; 0-545-34929-X

This briefly describes over 50 phobias.

"With an appealing layout, plenty of color, and enough germs, snakes, and bats to get the heart racing, this title has kid written all over it." Booklist

Lucas, Eileen

More than the blues? understanding and dealing with depression. Enslow Publishers 2009 112p il (Issues in focus today) lib bdg $31.93

Grades: 7 8 9 10   616.85
  1. Depression (Psychology)
  ISBN 978-0-7660-3065-7 lib bdg; 0-7660-3065-2 lib bdg
                                    LC 2008-39144

"Examines depression and mood disorders, including the causes of depression, a history of the illness, the various types of mood disorders, and treatment methods." Publisher's note

Includes glossary and bibliographical references

Marcovitz, Hal

Phobias. ReferencePoint Press 2009 112p il (Compact research. Diseases and disorders) lib bdg $25.95
Grades: 7 8 9 10   616.85
  1. Phobias
  ISBN 978-1-60152-044-9 lib bdg; 1-60152-044-1 lib bdg
                                    LC 2008-10894

Through overviews, primary sources, and full color illustrations this title examines phobias

"The coverage is succinct . . . [and] includes colorful illustrations and figures, chronologies, related organizations, advocacy groups, and sources for additional research." Libr Media Connect

Includes bibliographical references

Miller, Allen R.

Living with depression. Facts on File 2007 202p (Teen's guides) $34.95
Grades: 7 8 9 10   616.85
  1. Depression (Psychology)
  ISBN 9781438121079; 978-0-8160-6345-1; 0-8160-6345-1; 0-8160-7562-X pa
                                    LC 2007-554

This "offers young adults concise information about depression and its treatments. . . . Chapters on treatments offer detailed information on psychotherapy, antidepressants, and self-help approaches such as diet, exercise, and stress management. . . . This book is a timely, useful resource." Booklist

Mooney, Carla

Mood disorders. ReferencePoint Press 2010 96p il (Compact research: diseases and disorders) lib bdg $26.95
Grades: 8 9 10 11 12   616.85
  1. Depression (Psychology) 2. Manic-depressive illness
  ISBN 978-1-60152-119-4; 1-60152-119-7
                                    LC 2010-5868

This book about mood disorders "begins with a general overview followed by focus on statistics, causes, symptoms, treatments, and prevention. . . . [The book] discusses the two main categories [of mood disorders]: unipolar (if untreated the number-one risk for suicide) and bipolar (which swings between depression and mania.) . . . The readable page design features pull quotes and subtitles, with occasional photos throughout." Booklist

Includes bibliographical references

Moragne, Wendy

Depression. Twenty-First Century Books 2011 128p (USA Today health reports: diseases and disorders) lib bdg $34.60

Grades: 8 9 10 11 12   **616.85**

1. Depression (Psychology)

ISBN 978-0-7613-5882-4; 0-7613-5882-X

LC 2010034122

This book about depression will serve as "solid report fodder. . . . [The] volume has an introduction, a description of the condition, chapters on what it is like to live with it, and material on research and treatments. A healthy smattering of statistics and personal stories appear throughout." SLJ

Includes bibliographical references

Parks, Peggy J.

Online addiction; by Peggy J. Parks. ReferencePoint Press, Inc. 2013 96 p. (hardcover) $27.95

Grades: 7 8 9 10 11 12   **616.85**

1. Internet 2. Internet gambling 3. Addiction 4. Internet addiction -- Popular works

ISBN 1601522703; 9781601522702

LC 2012014191

In this book about online addiction, Peggy J. Parks "addresses four basic questions: Is online addiction real? Can people get addicted to social networking? How serious of a problem is compulsive online gaming and gambling? Can people recover from online addiction? . . . Parks addresses each of her four questions in separate sections of her book." (Booklist)

Includes bibliographical references and index.

Parks, Peggy J., 1951-

Anorexia. ReferencePoint Press 2009 104p il (Compact research. Diseases and disorders) lib bdg $25.95

Grades: 7 8 9 10   **616.85**

1. Anorexia nervosa

ISBN 978-1-60152-042-5; 1-60152-042-5

LC 2008-4238

Presents information on anorexia, including its causes, its effect on health, and the possiblity of curing it, through essays, quotations, statistics, and suggestions for further research.

"[This] quality [source] could be used in a variety of different ways–: straight reporting for speech or debate ideas, or as a springboard for further research." SLJ

Includes bibliographical references

Anxiety disorders. ReferencePoint Press 2011 96p il (Compact research: diseases and disorders) lib bdg $26.95

Grades: 7 8 9 10   **616.85**

1. Anxiety 2. Panic disorders 3. Obsessive-compulsive disorder

ISBN 978-1-60152-137-8; 1-60152-137-5

LC 2010031813

This title provides "a systematic and focused look at [anxiety disorders]. . . . [It] covers six main types, including panic and obsessive-compulsive disorder. . . . [This title is] useful for reports as well as general interest." SLJ

Includes bibliographical references

Down syndrome. ReferencePoint Press 2009 104p il (Compact research. Diseases and disorders) $25.95

Grades: 7 8 9 10 11 12   **616.85**

1. Down syndrome

ISBN 978-1-60152-065-4; 1-60152-065-4

LC 2008-36644

"This up-to-date, excellent overview of Down syndrome addresses controversies and ethical issues associated with this genetic disorder. Parks also reports on current and potential scientific advances that may prevent it in the future and offer a better quality of life and opportunities for those born with it." SLJ

Includes bibliographical references

Obsessive -compulsive disorder. ReferencePoint Press 2010 96p il (Compact research: diseases and disorders) lib bdg $26.95

Grades: 8 9 10 11 12   **616.85**

1. Obsessive-compulsive disorder

ISBN 978-1-60152-120-0; 1-60152-120-0

LC 2010-5872

This book about obsessive-compulsive disorder is written "with objectivity and depth. . . . [It] begins with a general overview followed by a focus on statistics, treatments, and prevention. . . . [The book] shows that the irrational fears of OCD affect males and females across race and class. . . . The readable page design features pull quotes and subtitles, with occasional photos throughout." Booklist

Includes bibliographical references

Self -injury disorder. ReferencePoint Press 2011 96p il (Compact research: diseases and disorders) lib bdg $26.95

Grades: 8 9 10 11 12   **616.85**

1. Self-mutilation

ISBN 978-1-60152-112-5; 1-60152-112-X

LC 2009-50483

This book about self-injury disorder "begins with a general overview followed by a focus on statistics, causes, symptoms, treatments, and prevention. . . . [The book] states that the main cause of self-inflicted injury is to gain relief from unbearable emotional pain, and it also covers methods of treatment and prevention. The readable page design features pull quotes and subtitles, with occasional photos throughout." Booklist

Includes bibliographical references

Powell, Jillian

Self -harm and suicide; by Jillian Powell. Gareth Stevens 2009 48p il (Emotional health issues) lib bdg $31

Grades: 6 7 8 9   **616.85**

1. Suicide 2. Self-mutilation

ISBN 978-0-8368-9202-4; 0-8368-9202-X

LC 2008-4276

First published 2008 in the United Kingdom

This book about self-destructive behavior has "clear language and explanations. . . . [It is] suitable for fact-finding missions, but the abundant graphics and case studies are likely to draw in browsers as well. Throughout, unfamiliar vocabulary is highlighted in bold and explained in context and in the glossary. . . . Fact boxes and case study sidebars add information." SLJ

Includes glossary and bibliographical references

Price, Janet

Take control of Asperger's syndrome; the official strategy guide for teens with Asperger's syndrome and nonverbal learning disorder. [by] Janet Price and Jennifer Engel Fisher. Prufrock Press 2010 168p pa $16.95

Grades: 6 7 8 9 10   **616.85**
1. Asperger's syndrome
ISBN 978-1-59363-405-6; 1-59363-405-6

LC 2009-50852

"Directly addressing teens diagnosed with Asperger's Syndrome or Nonverbal Learning Disorder, two educational consultants experienced in special-needs issues lay out feasible strategies for success in school and in social interactions." Booklist

Includes bibliographical references

Quinn, Patricia O.

Attention, girls! a guide to learn all about your AD/HD. illustrated by Carl Pearce. Magination Press 2009 119p il $16.95; pa $12.95

Grades: 4 5 6 7   **616.85**
1. Attention deficit disorder
ISBN 978-1-4338-0447-2; 1-4338-0447-6; 978-1-4338-0448-9 pa; 1-4338-0448-4 pa

LC 2008054524

"Quinn has attention deficit hyperactivity disorder and is a medical doctor; she addresses the types of AD/HD; who can help; differences between girls and boys with AD/HD; making friends; talking with adults about the condition; relaxation techniques; and medication. Her aim is to give girls a variety of ways to manage their disorders. . . . The book is attractive and inviting with colorful cartoon illustrations, sidebars, and highlighted reminders." SLJ

Rodriguez, Ana Maria

Autism spectrum disorders; the complete guide to understanding autism, Asperger's syndrome, pervasive developmental disorder, and other ASDs. Chantal Sicile-Kira. Berkeley Pub. Group 2004 xxi, 360 p.p il (USA Today health reports: diseases and disorders) $17

Grades: 8 9 10 11 12   **616.85**
1. Autism 2. Autistic children 3. Asperger's syndrome
ISBN 0399166637; 0399530479; 9780399166631

LC 2004052935

This book on autism spectrum disorders, by Chantal Sicile-Kira, "explains all aspects of the condition, and is written for parents, educators, caregivers, and others looking for accurate information and expert insight. Newly updated to reflect the latest research, treatment methods, and DSM-V criteria." (Publisher's note)

This book about autism spectrum disorders will serve as "solid report fodder. . . . [The] volume has an introduction, a description of the condition, chapters on what it is like to live with it, and material on research and treatments. A healthy smattering of statistics and personal stories appear throughout." SLJ

Includes bibliographical references (p. [337]-350) and index

Royston, Angela

Explaining down syndrome. Smart Apple Media 2010 45p il (Explaining) lib bdg $34.25

Grades: 5 6 7 8   **616.85**
1. Down syndrome
ISBN 978-1-59920-308-9 lib bdg; 1-59920-308-1 lib bdg

LC 2008-49291

This book about down syndrome provides a "basic [overview] of the health concerns related to the disease; information on diagnosis and treatment; and a discussion of the challenges or complications experienced by the affected person and their family/friends, and how to manage those problems. . . . The incorporation of quotes and personal accounts in 'Case Notes' sidebars adds to the sensitive tone found throughout [the title]." SLJ

Includes glossary

Scowen, Kate

My kind of sad; what it's like to be young and depressed. [by] Kate Scowen; art by Jeff Szuc. Annick Press 2006 168p il $19.95; pa $10.95

Grades: 7 8 9 10   **616.85**
1. Depression (Psychology)
ISBN 1-55037-941-0; 1-55037-940-2 pa

"The book discusses the history of depression, adolescence and depression, and treatment options. Scowen's focus is on understanding the difference between simply being sad and suffering from depression. Topics such as bipolar disorder, self-mutilation, anorexia, and suicide are also discussed. . . . Scowen's book is well-written, easy to read and use, and quite informative." Voice Youth Advocates

Includes bibliographical references

Silverstein, Alvin

★ The **ADHD** update; understanding attention-deficit/hyperactivity disorder. [by] Alvin and Virginia Silverstein and Laura Silverstein Nunn. Enslow Publishers 2008 112p il (Disease update) lib bdg $31.93

Grades: 5 6 7 8   **616.85**
1. Attention deficit disorder
ISBN 978-0-7660-2800-5 lib bdg; 0-7660-2800-3 lib bdg

LC 2007-13853

This describes Attention-deficit hyperactivity disorder (ADHD) and its history, diagnosis and treatment, living with it, and its future

"This book is an excellent primer on AD/HD." Sci Books Films

Includes glossary and bibliographical references

★ The **eating** disorders update; understanding anorexia, bulimia, and binge eating. [by] Alvin and Virginia Silverstein and Laura Silverstein Nunn. Enslow Publishers 2008 128p il (Disease update) lib bdg $31.93

Grades: 5 6 7 8 **616.85**

1. Bulimia 2. Anorexia nervosa 3. Eating disorders
ISBN 978-0-7660-2802-9 lib bdg; 0-7660-2802-X lib bdg

LC 2007013985

"An introduction to the history and most up-to-date research and treatment of eating disorders." Publisher's note
Includes glossary and bibliographical references

Skotko, Brian

Fasten your seatbelt; a crash course on Down syndrome for brothers and sisters. [by] Brian G. Skotko and Susan P. Levine. Woodbine House 2009 191p il pa $18.95

Grades: 4 5 6 7 **616.85**

1. Siblings 2. Down syndrome
ISBN 978-1-890627-86-7 pa; 1-890627-86-0 pa

LC 2008049753

"Skotko and Levine address preteens and teenagers who have a sibling with Down syndrome, answering questions that have been generated through their work with this population. . . . With a wealth of information, numerous resources, and the reassurance that all siblings of people with disabilities sometimes go through periods of contradictory feelings, this is an excellent guide for young people who are trying to figure out how to negotiate an often-confusing relationship." SLJ

Includes bibliographical references

Snedden, Robert

Explaining autism. Smart Apple Media 2010 45p il (Explaining) lib bdg $34.25

Grades: 5 6 7 8 **616.85**

1. Autism 2. Asperger's syndrome
ISBN 978-1-59920-307-2 lib bdg; 1-59920-307-3 lib bdg

LC 2008-49285

Describes the illness, including its symptoms, how it affects physical and mental health, current treatments, and how people with autism live everyday lives

"The incorporation of quotes and personal accounts in 'Case Notes' sidebars adds to the sensitive tone found throughout [the title]." SLJ

Includes glossary and bibliographical references

Sonenklar, Carol

Anorexia and bulimia. Twenty-First Century Books 2010 128p il (USA Today health reports: diseases and disorders) lib bdg $34.60

Grades: 7 8 9 10 11 12 **616.85**

1. Bulimia 2. Anorexia nervosa
ISBN 978-0-8225-6786-8; 0-8225-6786-5

This describes the symptoms and treatment of anorexia and bulimia.

This book "stands out for the substantial amount of information conveyed in a lively writing style. . . . Graphs,

sidebars, diagrams, and other illustrations [are] used judiciously." Booklist

Stefanski, Daniel, 1997-

★ **How** to talk to an autistic kid; illustrated by Hazel Mitchell. Free Spirit 2011 43p il $12.99

Grades: 3 4 5 6 **616.85**

1. Autism
ISBN 978-1-57542-365-4; 1-57542-365-0

"Stefanski provides clear, sometimes blunt, often humorous advice for readers on how to interact with autistic classmates. An authority on this topic—he is a 14-year-old boy with autism—he begins by describing autism. . . . He describes, using a brief paragraph or two per page, some of the traits many autistic people share. . . . For each trait, he offers down-to-earth suggestions for resolving problems. . . . His insightful, matter-of-fact presentation demystifies behaviors that might confuse or disturb non-autistic classmates. Simple cartoon illustrations in black, gray and two shades of turquoise accompany the text. . . . A thought-provoking introduction to autism . . . and an essential purchase for every primary and middle-school classroom." Kirkus

Stewart, Gail

Anorexia; [by] Gail B. Stewart. Cherry Lake Pub. 2009 32p il (Health at risk) lib bdg $27.07

Grades: 4 5 6 7 **616.85**

1. Anorexia nervosa
ISBN 978-1-60279-281-4 lib bdg; 1-60279-281-X lib bdg

LC 2008017496

This explains why anorexics feel the need to keep losing weight, what can happen to them as a result of their desperate struggle to be thin, and how they can get help.

"Great for reports or reluctant readers." Booklist
Includes bibliographical references

Bulimia; [by] Gail B. Stewart. Cherry Lake Pub. 2009 32p il (Health at risk) lib bdg $27.07

Grades: 4 5 6 7 **616.85**

1. Bulimia
ISBN 978-1-60279-282-1 lib bdg; 1-60279-282-8 lib bdg

LC 2008-17497

This describes the health risks of bulimia and what can be done to help people fight this disease.

"Great for reports or reluctant readers." Booklist
Includes bibliographical references

Tompkins, Michael A.

My anxious mind; a teen's guide to managing anxiety and panic. by Michael A. Tompkins and Katherine A. Martinez; illustrated by Michael Sloan. Magination Press 2009 196p il pa $14.95

Grades: 7 8 9 10 11 12 **616.85**

1. Anxiety 2. Panic disorders
ISBN 978-1-4338-0450-2 pa; 1-4338-0450-6 pa

LC 2009011442

"Tompkins and Martinez directly address their readers: 'If you have an anxious mind,' giving teens the sense of a caring adult speaking to them. . . . Following the first chapters on definitions and how to seek help, there are several chapters with increasingly more complicated aids that teens can implement. . . . The final chapters stress the importance of proper nutrition, exercise, and sleep, and the possible need for medication. Throughout the book, first-person vignettes describe specific anxieties or phobias and how they were dealt with using the strategies outlined in the middle chapters. . . . They serve the purpose, along with the appealing line drawings, of catching readers' interest and enlivening the text." SLJ

Zucker, Bonnie

Take control of OCD; the ultimate guide for kids with OCD. Prufrock Press 2010 179p il pa $16.95

Grades: 6 7 8 9 10   **616.85**

1. Obsessive-compulsive disorder
ISBN 978-1-59363-429-2; 1-59363-429-3
LC 2010-34863

The author "addresses affected young readers directly and offers a structured set of self-help strategies for coping with diagnosed obsessive-compulsive behavior. Suggesting that the chapters be read in order for best results, she opens with a nontechnical explanation of the disorder's genetic and neurological roots, then goes on to discuss creating written behavioral 'ladders,' using relaxation techniques effectively, building self-awareness, handling uncertainty, and managing stress." Booklist

Includes bibliographical references

Zucker, Faye

Beating depression; teens find light at the end of the tunnel. by Faye Zucker & Joan E. Huebl. Franklin Watts 2007 112p il (Scholastic choices) lib bdg $27; pa $8.95

Grades: 6 7 8 9   **616.85**

1. Depression (Psychology)
ISBN 978-0-531-12462-8 lib bdg; 0-531-12462-2 lib bdg; 978-0-531-17729-7 pa; 0-531-17729-7 pa
LC 2006006779

Discusses the prevalence of depression among teenagers, and examines its causes and treatment options.

Includes bibliographical references

616.86   Substance abuse (Drug abuse)

Allman, Toney

Drugs. Cherry Lake Pub. 2009 32p il (Health at risk) lib bdg $27.07

Grades: 4 5 6 7   **616.86**

1. Drug abuse
ISBN 978-1-60279-283-8 lib bdg; 1-60279-283-6 lib bdg
LC 2008017503

This describes the dangers of drug abuse, the programs that help people get off drugs, and how to avoid drug use.

"Great for reports or reluctant readers." Booklist

Includes bibliographical references

Esherick, Joan

No more butts; kicking the tobacco habit. Mason Crest 2009 112p il (Tobacco: the deadly drug) lib bdg $26.95

Grades: 6 7 8 9   **616.86**

1. Smoking cessation programs
ISBN 978-1-4222-0236-4 lib bdg; 1-4222-0236-4 lib bdg
LC 2008-13215

Explains how difficult smoking cessation can be and offers tips on how to quit for good.

"The writing is professional but not at a level that causes readers to struggle. The information is made relevant to the everyday reader . . . [and] . . . it would be a strong addition to the nonfiction section of any library and is appropriate for a broad age level." Voice Youth Advocates

Includes glossary and bibliographical references

Hunter, David

Born to smoke; nicotine and genetics. Mason Crest 2009 112p il (Tobacco: the deadly drug) lib bdg $26.95

Grades: 6 7 8 9   **616.86**

1. Smoking 2. Tobacco habit 3. Behavior genetics
ISBN 978-1-4222-0243-2; 1-4222-0243-7
LC 2008-13218

Explains how genetics may affect an individual's susceptibility to nicotine addiction, and discusses the debate over genetic predisposition to nicotine addiction versus a person's upbringing.

"The writing is professional but not at a level that causes readers to struggle. The information is made relevant to the everyday reader . . . [and] . . . it would be a strong addition to the nonfiction section of any library and is appropriate for a broad age level." Voice Youth Advocates

Includes glossary and bibliographical references

Hyde, Margaret Oldroyd

★ **Smoking** 101; an overview for teens. [by] Margaret O. Hyde, John F. Setaro. Twenty-First Century Books 2006 128p il lib bdg $26.60

Grades: 8 9 10 11 12   **616.86**

1. Smoking 2. Tobacco
ISBN 0-7613-2835-1
LC 2004-22757

"The message is clear, the facts are well-presented, and the tone is insightful. These authors understand the teen audience and how to reach it." SLJ

Includes bibliographical references

Miller, Heather

Smoking. Cherry Lake Pub. 2009 32p il (Health at risk) lib bdg $27.07

Grades: 4 5 6 7   **616.86**

1. Smoking 2. Tobacco habit
ISBN 978-1-60279-286-9 lib bdg; 1-60279-286-0 lib bdg
LC 2008017501

This describes why smoking is dangerous, how difficult it is to stop once you start, and what efforts are underway to put the brakes on this habit.

"Great for reports or reluctant readers." Booklist

Includes bibliographical references

Price, Sean

Nicotine; [by] Sean Price. Chelsea House 2008 120p il (Junior drug awareness) lib bdg $30

Grades: 6 7 8 9 **616.86**

1. Smoking 2. Tobacco habit

ISBN 9781438118185; 978-0-7910-9696-3 lib bdg; 0-7910-9696-3 lib bdg

LC 2007024829

This "provides the facts about tobacco use among teenagers and offers young readers the facts about one of the most prevalent and addictive drugs in the United States." Publisher's note

Includes glossary and bibliographical references

616.89 Mental disorders

Bellenir, Karen

★ **Mental** health information for teens; health tips about mental wellness and mental illness: including facts about mental and emotional health, depression and other mood disorders, anxiety disorders, behavior disorders, self-injury... edited by Karen Bellenir. 3rd ed.; Omnigraphics 2010 443p (Teen health series) $62

Grades: 7 8 9 10 11 12 **616.89**

1. Mental health 2. Reference books 3. Adolescent psychology 4. Teenagers -- Health and hygiene

ISBN 978-0-7808-1087-7

LC 2010-806

First published 2001

"Provides basic consumer health information for teens about mental illness and treatment, along with tips for maintaining mental and emotional health. Includes index, resource information and recommendations for further reading." Publisher's note

Includes bibliographical references

Kent, Deborah

★ **Snake** pits, talking cures, & magic bullets; a history of mental illness. 21st Cent. Bks. (Brookfield) 2003 160p il lib bdg $26.90

Grades: 6 7 8 9 **616.89**

1. Mental illness

ISBN 0-7613-2704-5

LC 2002-11208

Looks at how the mentally ill have been treated throughout history, focusing on advances made in the 19th and 20th centuries regarding mental hospitals, medications, and social acceptance

"An excellent history peppered with fascinating accounts. . . . Black-and-white archival photographs and reproductions appear throughout. . . . This is a fine treatment of a topic not heavily covered for this audience." SLJ

Includes glossary and bibliographical references

Meisel, Abigail

Investigating depression and bipolar disorder; real facts for real lives. Enslow Publishers 2010 160p il (Investigating diseases) lib bdg $34.60

Grades: 6 7 8 9 10 **616.89**

1. Depression (Psychology) 2. Manic-depressive illness

ISBN 978-0-7660-3340-5; 0-7660-3340-6

LC 2008-50060

"Meisel discusses the history, science, diagnosis, and treatment of depression and bipolar disorder. In addition, she shows how these illnesses affect not just the patients, but their families, peers, and friends. She explains the science behind the two conditions, their possible causes, and the varying nature of the illnesses themselves. . . . This is an excellent book for persons from high school age to adults to read and become familiar with these important illnesses." Sci Books Films

Includes glossary and bibliographical references

Parks, Peggy J., 1951-

Schizophrenia. ReferencePoint Press 2011 96p il (Compact research: diseases and disorders) $26.95

Grades: 7 8 9 10 11 12 **616.89**

1. Schizophrenia

ISBN 978-1-60152-140-8; 1-60152-140-5

LC 2010037253

"Fortified with contemporary individual case studies of both teens and adults [this] title . . . discusses variations of [schizophrenia], as well as the prevalence, symptoms, causes, effects, diagnoses, and treatment, drawing upon media interviews and commentary as well as clinical reports and research studies. . . . The clear design includes recent graphs and tables, color photos and diagrams, and lots of carefully documented primary-source quotes from patients, researchers, and scientists." Booklist

Includes bibliographical references

Silverstein, Alvin

★ The **depression** and bipolar disorder update; [by] Alvin and Virginia Silverstein and Laura Silverstein Nunn. Enslow Publishers 2008 128p il (Disease update) $31.93

Grades: 6 7 8 9 **616.89**

1. Depression (Psychology) 2. Manic-depressive illness

ISBN 978-0-7660-2801-2; 0-7660-2801-1

LC 2007-13854

"An introduction to the history . . . research and treatment of depression and bipolar disorder." Publisher's note

Includes bibliographical references

616.9 Other diseases

Allman, Toney

Infectious disease research; by Toney Allman. ReferencePoint Press 2012 96 p. (Inside science series) (hardback) $27.95

Grades: 6 7 8 9 10 11 12 **616.9**

1. Communicable diseases 2. Communicable diseases

-- Encyclopedias
ISBN 1601521774; 9781601521774

LC 2011007745

This book, by Toney Allman, presents a research guide to infectious disease research. "Infectious diseases are responsible for untold global suffering and the loss of millions of human lives each year. This knowledge drives the research toward a fuller understanding of infectious microbial agents and the development of new treatment and prevention methods for infectious diseases." (Publisher's note)

Includes bibliographical references and index

Aronin, Miriam

    Tuberculosis; the white plague! Bearport Pub. 2011 32p il map (Nightmare plagues) lib bdg $25.27

Grades: 4 5 6 7   616.9
    1. Tuberculosis
    ISBN 978-1-936088-06-5; 1-936088-06-1

LC 2010010679

Discover what causes tuberculosis and how it affects the body.

"The writing is accessible and interspersed with interesting photographs and fact boxes. . . . [The book relies] on an honest discussion of [tuberculosis and is an] . . . effective, easily navigated [introduction]." SLJ

Includes glossary and bibliographical references

Blank, Alison

    Invincible microbe; tuberculosis and the never-ending search for a cure. Jim Murphy, Alison Blank. Clarion Books 2012 149 p. (hardback) $18.99

Grades: 5 6 7 8 9   616.9
    1. Tuberculosis 2. Lungs -- Diseases 3. Communicable diseases -- Treatment 4. Microorganisms
    ISBN 0618535748; 9780618535743

LC 2011025951

This book looks at tuberculosis. It "starts with archeologists finding evidence of tuberculosis in a 500,000 year old skull and continues through to the present day. Various 'cures' such as the medieval 'king's touch' . . . , bloodletting of the 19th century, twentieth century sanatoriums and modern day drug cocktails are all discussed." Also "covered is the socioeconomic side of the disease, with a discussion of how treatment often varied depending on the race and economic status of the patient." (Children's Literature)

Includes bibliographical references

Colligan, L. H.

    ★ Tick -borne illnesses. Marshall Cavendish Benchmark 2009 64p il (Health alert) $22.95

Grades: 4 5 6 7   616.9
    1. Tick-borne diseases
    ISBN 978-0-7614-2914-2; 0-7614-2914-X

LC 2007-38517

This "title features a handsome format, with well-chosen illustrations, a substantial amount of information, and some practical insights." Booklist

Includes glossary

Duke, Shirley Smith

    Infections, infestations, and disease; [by] Shirley Duke. Rourke Pub. 2010 48p il (Let's explore science) $32.79

Grades: 4 5 6 7   616.9
    1. Communicable diseases
    ISBN 978-1-61590-321-4; 1-61590-321-6

LC 2010009908

This describes communicable diseases.

Includes bibliographical references

Emmeluth, Donald

    Botulism; consulting editor, Hilary Babcock; foreword by David L. Heymann. 2nd ed.; Chelsea House 2010 144p il map (Deadly diseases and epidemics) $34.95

Grades: 7 8 9 10   616.9
    1. Botulism
    ISBN 978-1-60413-235-9; 1-60413-235-3

LC 2010-8111

First published 2005

This book contains "information on this disease, exploring its history, causes, statistics, and . . . diagnostic and treatment breakthroughs. It also includes accounts of numerous recent outbreaks." Publisher's note

Includes glossary and bibliographical references

Green, Caroline

    Drug resistance. New Forest Press 2010 64p il (Cutting-edge science) lib bdg $34.25

Grades: 7 8 9 10   616.9
    1. Drug resistance
    ISBN 978-1-84898-323-6; 1-84898-323-9

This addresses the topic of drug resistance, "touching on both scientific and societal issues . . . The underlying science is addressed, as well as the current state of scientific and ethical thinking. Stock color photographs and diagrams accompany the [text]. Sidebars provide biographical information on contemporary scientists as well as highlights of their research methods and studies." Horn Book Guide

Includes glossary and bibliographical references

Hoffmann, Gretchen

    ★ Chicken pox. Marshall Cavendish Benchmark 2009 62p il (Health alert) $22.95

Grades: 4 5 6 7   616.9
    1. Chickenpox
    ISBN 978-0-7614-2916-6; 0-7614-2916-6

This "title features a handsome format, with well-chosen illustrations, a substantial amount of information, and some practical insights." Booklist

Includes glossary

Kelly, Evelyn B.

    Investigating tuberculosis and superbugs; real facts for real lives. [by] Evelyn B. Kelly, Ian Wilker, and Marylou Ambrose. Enslow Publishers 2010 160p il (Investigating diseases) lib bdg $34.60

Grades: 7 8 9 10 **616.9**
1. Tuberculosis 2. Drug resistance
ISBN 978-0-7660-3343-6; 0-7660-3343-0

LC 2009-37811

This "methodically presents medical and statistical information about major kinds of tuberculosis, malaria, AIDS/HIV, and other persistent bacterial, viral, and parasitic pandemics worldwide that are becoming ominously resistant to once-effective treatments.... [This is] massively documented with endnotes; supplemented by sidebar insertions, accounts of specific cases, and small color photos; and rounded off with digestible lists of relevant further sources." Booklist

Includes bibliographical references

Sheen, Barbara

MRSA. Lucent Books 2010 104p il (Diseases and disorders series) $33.45
Grades: 7 8 9 10 **616.9**
1. Methicillin-Resistant Staphylococcus aureus
ISBN 978-1-4205-0144-5; 1-4205-0144-5

LC 2009-32644

This "offers a thorough explanation of [MRSA] giving a basic definition; a discussion of the causes, symptoms, and treatments; a description of living with the disease; and ideas of future treatment and diagnoses. Each volume lists source notes and organizations to contact. A glossary, index, and ideas for further reading are also included. The color photographs and sidebars help to make the information in the dense text more easily understood, and personal stories provide insight into how individuals deal with their disease." Voice Youth Advocates

Includes glossary and bibliographical references

Shmaefsky, Brian

Toxic shock syndrome; [by] Brian R. Shmaefsky; consulting editor, Hilary Babcock; foreword by David L. Heymann. 2nd ed.; Chelsea House 2010 127p il (Deadly diseases and epidemics) $34.95
Grades: 8 9 10 11 12 **616.9**
1. Toxic shock syndrome
ISBN 978-1-60413-243-4; 1-60413-243-4

LC 2010029222

First published 2003

This describes types of toxic shock syndrome, its causes, diagnosis and treatment.

Includes glossary and bibliographical references

Stress information for teens; health tips about the mental and physical consequences of stress. edited by Sandra Augustyn Lawton. 1st ed. Omnigraphics, Inc. 2008 viii, 392 p.p ill. (hardcover) $69.00
Grades: 7 8 9 10 **616.9**
1. Stress (Psychology) 2. Teenagers -- Health and hygiene 3. Stress management for teenagers
ISBN 0780810120; 9780780810129

LC 2008015151

This book, a "toolkit for coping with stress[,] discusses the causes of stress, the effects of stress on the body and mind, and managing stress while including specific problems at school and with family or peer relationships.... Techniques for managing stress include controlling anger,

engaging in mind-body therapies, and building self-esteem." (Voice of Youth Advocates)

Includes bibliographical references and index.

616.95 Sexually transmitted diseases, zoonoses

Collins, Nicholas

Frequently asked questions about STDs; by Nicholas Collins and Samuel G. Woods. Rosen Pub. 2012 64 p. col. ill. (library) $31.95
Grades: 7 8 9 10 **616.95**
1. Teenagers -- Sexual behavior 2. Sexually transmitted diseases 3. Sexually transmitted diseases -- Miscellanea
ISBN 1448846307; 9781448846306

LC 2011000303

This book by Nicholas Collins looks at STDs. "Sexually transmitted diseases are clinically explained, including how they affect the body, how to recognize symptoms of infection, and how teens can protect themselves and their partner against, not only STDs, but HIV and AIDS as well." (Voice of Youth Advocates)

Includes bibliographical references (p. 83) and index.

Cozic, Charles P.

Herpes. ReferencePoint Press 2011 96p il (Compact research: diseases and disorders) $23.95
Grades: 7 8 9 10 11 12 **616.95**
1. Herpesvirus diseases
ISBN 978-1-60152-117-0; 1-60152-117-0

LC 2010030634

Introduces herpes and discusses the symptoms, possible health effects, and treatments for the virus.

Includes bibliographical references

Dougherty, Terri

Sexually transmitted diseases. Lucent Books 2010 96p il (Diseases and disorders series) $32.45
Grades: 7 8 9 10 **616.95**
1. Sexually transmitted diseases
ISBN 978-1-4205-0220-6

LC 2009-39583

"This book discusses the most common afflictions, diseases that are usually found in combinations, medical advances, and how the outlook for STDs is complicated by new trends such as drug-resistant strains. Information is also supplied about causes, prevention, diagnosis, and treatment. ... A number of the photos show some of the horrific physical manifestations in individuals, including infants.... [This book] should be considered for first purchase." SLJ

Includes bibliographical references

Yancey, Diane

STDs. Twenty-First Century Books 2012 128p il (USA today health reports: diseases and disorders)
Grades: 7 8 9 10 11 12 **616.95**
1. Sexually transmitted diseases
ISBN 0-7613-5456-5; 978-0-7613-5456-7

LC 2010036514

"Yancey writes in a straightforward manner about sexually transmitted diseases, opening with the profiles of several teens coping with an STD. . . . The causes, symptoms, and treatments of the main STDs, . . . are thoroughly covered, from the emotional side effects of genital herpes to the dangers of ordering an HIV home sample collection kit online. . . . Students, teachers, and librarians looking to supplement health textbooks with current information will find this . . . valuable." Voice Youth Advocates

Includes bibliographical references

616.97   Diseases of immune system

Aldridge, Susan

AIDS. New Forest Press 2010 64p il map (Cutting-edge science) lib bdg $34.25

Grades: 7 8 9 10   616.97

1. AIDS (Disease)

ISBN 978-1-84898-324-3; 1-84898-324-7

This addresses the topic of AIDS, "touching on both scientific and societal issues . . . The underlying science is addressed, as well as the current state of scientific and ethical thinking. Stock color photographs and diagrams accompany the [text]. Sidebars provide biographical information on contemporary scientists as well as highlights of their research methods and studies." Horn Book Guide

Ballard, Carol

Explaining food allergies. Smart Apple Media 2010 45p il (Explaining) $23.95

Grades: 5 6 7 8   616.97

1. Food allergy

ISBN 978-1-59920-316-4; 1-59920-316-2

LC 2008049936

This "does an excellent job of discussing complex clinical science while showing what daily life is like for kids living with food allergies, from the signs and symptoms to the tests and treatments. . . . This blend of the technical and the personal will have wide appeal." Booklist

Cunningham, Kevin

HIV /AIDS. Morgan Reynolds Pub. 2009 144p il (Diseases in history) lib bdg $28.95

Grades: 8 9 10 11 12   616.97

1. AIDS (Disease)

ISBN 978-1-59935-104-9; 1-59935-104-8

LC 2008-51616

"Explores the origin of the two types of HIV viruses and the reasons why poverty, promiscuity, and the common use of world blood supplies enable its horrible and devastatingly rapid spread. . . . This detailed overview . . . will appeal to more advanced students. The research is thorough and the writing is insightful, thought provoking, and accessible." Voice Youth Advocates

Includes glossary and bibliographical references

Ehrlich, Paul

Living with allergies; [by] Paul M. Ehrlich, with Elizabeth Shimer Bowers. Facts On File 2009 168p (Teen's guides) $34.95; pa $14.95

Grades: 7 8 9 10 11 12   616.97

1. Allergy

ISBN 9781438129976; 978-0-8160-7327-6; 0-8160-7327-9; 0-8160-7742-8 pa

LC 2008-34352

This "book addresses allergy triggers, preventing allergic reactions, what to expect from treatment, paying for care, and how to help yourself, friends, or family members who may have allergies." Publisher's note

Includes glossary and bibliographical references

Gordon, Sherri Mabry

★ Peanut butter, milk, and other deadly threats; what you should know about food allergies. Enslow Publishers 2006 112p il (Issues in focus today) $31.93

Grades: 8 9 10 11 12   616.97

1. Food allergy

ISBN 0-7660-2529-2

LC 2005-29219

Discusses what it is like to live with food allergies, how teens and their families cope with them, the causes of food allergies, and the research being done to prevent and control them

"The format is open, with plenty of white space, making the book accessible to reluctant readers. Full-color photos, helpful case studies, and a list of reputable organizations to contact for further information are included." SLJ

Includes glossary and bibliographical references

Hillstrom, Kevin

Food allergies; by Kevin Hillstrom. Lucent Books 2012 96 p. col. ill. (Nutrition and health) (hardcover) $30.95

Grades: 7 8 9 10 11 12   616.97

1. Food allergy

ISBN 1420507206; 9781420507201

LC 2012002945

This book on food allergies by Kevin Hillstrom is part of the "Nutrition and Health" book series. It "discusses the rising numbers of allergic young people, the physiology of the symptoms (with a clear diagram of an anaphylactic reaction), the search for a cure, and the social stigma." (Booklist) "Doctors, researchers, and people living with food allergies are quoted throughout the text." (Publisher's note)

Includes bibliographical references (p. 81-84) and index.

James, Otto

AIDS. Smart Apple Media 2010 46p il (Voices) lib bdg $34.95

Grades: 7 8 9 10 11 12   616.97

1. AIDS (Disease)

ISBN 978-1-59920-282-2; 1-59920-282-4

LC 2009-5417

"AIDS looks at causes, prevention, treatment, and the chances of a cure and also discusses abstinence, safe sex, the cost of AIDS drugs, and much more. . . . [The] blend of current political debate with witnesses' close-up experiences told through photos, narratives, and quotes will draw browsers, and many will go on to find out more." Booklist

Includes glossary and bibliographical references

Marsico, Katie

HIV /AIDS. ABDO Pub. Co. 2010 112p il (Essential issues) lib bdg $22.95

Grades: 7 8 9 10   **616.97**

1. AIDS (Disease)

ISBN 978-1-60453-955-4; 1-60453-955-0

LC 2009-29954

This is "well-written, providing examples that put a human face to each problem. Quotes and facts are clearly attributed, and their sources are noted in the extensive back matter. . . . Sidebars provide further information, or, more compellingly, offer stories about those touched by the topic. . . . [This] will be of great assistance to students writing reports." SLJ

Includes glossary and bibliographical references

★ **Quicksand;** HIV/AIDS in our world. by Anonymous. Candlewick Press 2009 103p $15.99

Grades: 6 7 8 9 10   **616.97**

1. AIDS (Disease)

ISBN 978-0-7636-1589-5; 0-7636-1589-7

LC 2009-7761

"The anonymous author explains her motivation for writing this book by telling readers that ten years ago, when HIV/AIDS was still considered a taboo subject, her brother-in-law was diagnosed with the disease. She writes in a truthful, open manner, addressing common questions about HIV/AIDS and providing easy-to-understand and honest advice. . . . The author's personal insight is what makes this book an important addition. Topics address everything from the history of HIV/AIDS to how to protect oneself from the disease. She also provides suggestions on how to cope with hearing that a family or friend has HIV/AIDS. . . . The author's focus on how the disease affects all people, whether they have contracted HIV/AIDS or not, makes this book a must-have for all teen collections." Voice Youth Advocates

Includes glossary and bibliographical references

Sonenklar, Carol

AIDS. Twenty-First Century Books 2011 128p il (USA Today health reports: diseases and disorders) lib bdg $34.60

Grades: 8 9 10 11 12   **616.97**

1. AIDS (Disease)

ISBN 978-0-8225-8581-7 lib bdg; 0-8225-8581-2 lib bdg

LC 2010-37633

This book about AIDS will serve as "solid report fodder. . . . [The] volume has an introduction, a description of the condition, chapters on what it is like to live with it, and material on research and treatments. A healthy smattering of statistics and personal stories appear throughout." SLJ

Includes glossary and bibliographical references

Yount, Lisa

Luc Montagnier; identifying the AIDS virus. by Lisa Yount. Chelsea House 2011 xix, 123 p.p col. ill. (library) $35

Grades: 7 8 9 10 11 12   **616.97**

1. AIDS (Disease) 2. HIV (Viruses)

ISBN 1604136618; 9781604136616

LC 2010047006

This book by Lisa Yount is part of the Trailblazers in Science and Technology series and looks at Luc Montagnier. It "recounts the life and career of the Nobel Prize-winning French virologist whose contributions to the understanding of the nature of viruses led to a significant advance in cancer research and in discovering the HIV virus that causes AIDS." (Publisher's note)

Includes bibliographical references and index.

616.99   Tumors and miscellaneous communicable diseases

Cancer information for teens; edited by Lisa Bakewell and Karen Bellenir. 2nd ed.; Omnigraphics 2010 445p il (Teen health series) $69

Grades: 8 9 10 11 12   **616.99**

1. Cancer

ISBN 978-0-7808-1085-3; 0-7808-1085-6

LC 2009-28456

First published 2004

"Written specifically for teens or their family members who have cancer, this volume will be a helpful, authoritative resource that should lead readers to further information about it. . . . It offers information that is current, accurate, and accessible." SLJ

Includes bibliographical references

Casil, Amy Sterling

Pancreatic cancer; current and emerging trends in detection and treatment. Rosen Pub. 2009 64p il (Cancer and modern science) lib bdg $29.25

Grades: 7 8 9 10 11 12   **616.99**

1. Pancreas -- Cancer

ISBN 9781435856998; 978-1-4358-5008-8; 1-4358-5008-4

LC 2008-25132

This book describes pancreatic cancer and its treatment.

"Clearly aimed at teens who have cancer or know someone who does, . . . [this title combines] lots of technical detail about anatomy, physiology, and pathology with a personal, interactive style. . . . With a highly readable design, including crisp color photos and anatomical diagrams, the [book] will also serve the needs of student researchers. Also features excellent, extensive back matter." Booklist

Includes glossary and bibliographical references

Freedman, Jeri

Brain cancer; current and emerging trends in detection and treatment. Rosen Pub. 2009 63p il (Cancer and modern science) lib bdg $29.25

Grades: 7 8 9 10 11 12   **616.99**

1. Brain -- Cancer

ISBN 9781435857025; 978-1-4358-5011-8; 1-4358-5011-4

LC 2008-22086

This book combines "lots of technical detail about anatomy, physiology, and pathology with a personal, interactive style. . . . Brain Cancer includes a section on Coping with School and Community that speaks directly to students with the disease and encourages them to stay active and involved. It also looks in detail at different types of brain cancer, detection and diagnosis, and present and future treatments." Booklist

Includes glossary and bibliographical references

Goldsmith, Connie

Skin cancer. Twenty-First Century Books 2010 128p il (USA Today health reports: diseases and disorders) lib bdg $34.60

Grades: 7 8 9 10 11 12   **616.99**

1. Cancer 2. Skin -- Diseases

ISBN 978-0-7613-5469-7; 0-7613-5469-7

LC 2010-10003

This describes causes, prevention, and treatments of skin cancer.

This is "liberally sprinkled with relevant articles and 'snapshots' (graphs showing statistical breakdowns of the topic at hand) from the newspaper, providing a competent introduction to primary-source material." SLJ

Includes glossary and bibliographical references

Lew, Kristi

The **truth** about cancer; understanding and fighting a deadly disease. Enslow Publishers 2009 104p il (Issues in focus today) lib bdg $31.93

Grades: 7 8 9 10   **616.99**

1. Cancer

ISBN 978-0-7660-3068-8 lib bdg; 0-7660-3068-7 lib bdg

LC 2008-32026

"Examines the deadly disease cancer, including a history of the disease, diagnosis and treatment, coping with cancer, and the fight against it around the world." Publisher's note

Includes glossary and bibliographical references

Markle, Sandra

Leukemia; true survival stories. Lerner Publications 2010 48p il (Powerful medicine) lib bdg $27.93

Grades: 5 6 7 8   **616.99**

1. Leukemia

ISBN 978-0-8225-8700-2 lib bdg; 0-8225-8700-9 lib bdg

LC 2009-34441

This book about leukemia "will grab the attention of middle school readers. . . . The illustrations and photos are stunning with medically accurate captions. Real-life patients, whose photos are included in the text, are highlighted, with updates on their progress at the end of . . . . [the] book. . . . This . . . fills the need for up-to-date books on medical topics using vocabulary that a young teenager can understand." Voice Youth Advocates

Includes glossary and bibliographical references

Parks, Peggy J., 1951-

Brain tumors. ReferencePoint Press 2011 96p il (Compact research: diseases and disorders) $26.95

Grades: 7 8 9 10 11 12   **616.99**

1. Brain -- Tumors

ISBN 978-1-60152-138-5; 1-60152-138-3

LC 2010040107

"Fortified with contemporary individual case studies of both teens and adults [this] title . . . . discusses variations of [brain tumors], as well as the prevalence, symptoms, causes, effects, diagnoses, and treatment, drawing upon media interviews and commentary as well as clinical reports and research studies. . . . The clear design includes recent graphs and tables, color photos and diagrams, and lots of carefully documented primary-source quotes from patients, researchers, and scientists." Booklist

Includes bibliographical references

Sheen, Barbara

Prostate cancer; Barbara Sheen. Lucent Books 2008 104 p. col. ill. (hardcover) $34.95

Grades: 7 8 9 10   **616.99**

1. Prostate gland -- Cancer 2. Cancer 3. Prostate -- Cancer

ISBN 1590185935; 9781590185933

LC 2008003808

This book is part of the Diseases & Disorders series and looks at prostate cancer. The series "offers young readers and researchers a means of understanding ailments and their ramifications. Clear, careful explanations offer insight into what these conditions are, what causes them, how people live with them, and the latest information about treatment and prevention." (Publisher's note)

Includes bibliographical references (p. 85-90, 96-97) and index.

Silver, Marc

My parent has cancer and it really sucks; Marc Silver, Maya Silver. Sourcebooks Fire 2013 272 p. $14.99

Grades: 6 7 8 9 10 11 12   **616.99**

1. Cancer -- Psychological aspects 2. Children of cancer patients

ISBN 9781402273070; 140227307X

LC 2012039095

This handbook "aims to guide teens through the experience of having an ill parent. . . . Short chapters include 'Let's Talk: How to Keep Your Family Communication Lines Wide Open,' 'How Things Will Change During Cancer,' 'Dealing with Stress,' 'The Power (and the Limits) of Optimism and Faith,' 'Seeking Support,' 'Facing a Dire Prognosis,' and 'Losing a Parent to Cancer.'" (School Library Journal)

"Drawing on their experiences, the Silvers offer advice for finding solace in people who have been there and who have found ways to cope... It's admirable that the authors don't sugarcoat the realities of cancer and will speak with an honesty that teens will identify with and find comfort in." Booklist

Silverstein, Alvin

★ The **breast** cancer update; [by] Alvin and Virginia Silverstein and Laura Silverstein Nunn. Enslow Publishers 2008 128p il (Disease update) lib bdg $31.93

Grades: 5 6 7 8   **616.99**

1. Breast cancer

ISBN 978-0-7660-2747-3 lib bdg; 0-7660-2747-3 lib bdg

LC 2006-32821

This offers a history of breast cancer, a definition of it, and describes its diagnosis and treatment, prevention, and future

Includes glossary and bibliographical references

Stokes, Mark

Colon cancer; current and emerging trends in detection and treatment. [by] Mark Stokes. 1st ed.; Rosen Pub. Group 2006 64p il (Cancer and modern science) lib bdg $29.25

Grades: 7 8 9 10 **616.99**

1. Colon cancer
ISBN 1-4042-0387-7
LC 2005003626

"Photographs, diagrams, multihued headings, and spotlighted insets are plentiful. . . . [This is a] solid [overview] of the current understanding of [this condition]." SLJ

Includes bibliographical references

Prostate cancer; current and emerging trends in detection and treatment. [by] Mark Stokes. 1st ed.; Rosen Pub. Group 2006 64p il (Cancer and modern science) lib bdg $29.25

Grades: 7 8 9 10 **616.99**

1. Prostate gland -- Cancer
ISBN 1-4042-0391-5
LC 2005003628

"Photographs, diagrams, multihued headings, and spotlighted insets are plentiful. . . . [This is a] solid [overview] of the current understanding of [this condition]." SLJ

Includes bibliographical references

Thornton, Denise

Living with cancer; the ultimate teen guide. Scarecrow Press 2011 il (It happened to me) $40

Grades: 7 8 9 10 **616.99**

1. Cancer
ISBN 978-0-8108-7277-6
LC 2010044140

"Written primarily for teens surviving cancer, this guide is chock-full of advice, tips, and firsthand accounts. The views of teens with a sibling or a parent battling the disease are also presented. Honest and heart-wrenching, this title doesn't shy away from the brutal realities of the disease. . . . This is a valuable resource, reminding those affected that they are not alone." SLJ

Includes glossary and bibliographical references

617 Surgery, regional medicine, dentistry, ophthalmology, otology, audiology

Markle, Sandra

Wounded brains; true survival stories. Lerner Publications 2011 48p il (Powerful medicine) lib bdg $27.93

Grades: 5 6 7 8 **617**

1. Brain -- Wounds and injuries
ISBN 978-0-8225-8704-0 lib bdg; 0-8225-8704-1 lib bdg
LC 2009034440

Describes several true cases of traumatic brain injury and the medical treatment that followed.

This narrative reads "like information from the Discovery Health channel, for kids: part fascinating science, part human interest story, and part 'Eew, gross!'. . . Clear, straightforward prose is supplemented by definitions and explanations of medical techniques and jargon. The numerous color photos and medical images will satisfy readers' curiosity." SLJ

Includes glossary and bibliographical references

Mullins, Matt

Surgical technologist. Cherry Lake Pub. 2010 32p il (Cool careers: career and technical education) lib bdg $27.07

Grades: 4 5 6 7 **617**

1. Surgery 2. Vocational guidance 3. Medical technologists
ISBN 978-1-60279-939-4 lib bdg; 1-60279-939-3 lib bdg
LC 2010001437

This "provides an overview of the duties performed by these allied health professionals, requirements and training for the job, and the anticipated future of this occupation. . . . Full color, captioned photographs . . . appear on most spreads, clarifying the text. . . . This will make a useful addition to the career shelf." Booklist

Includes bibliographical references

Townsend, John

★ Scalpels, stitches & scars; a history of surgery. Raintree 2005 56p il (Painful history of medicine) lib bdg $32.86; pa $9.90

Grades: 6 7 8 9 **617**

1. Surgery
ISBN 1-4109-1332-5 lib bdg; 1-4109-1337-6 pa
LC 2004-14248

A history of surgery from ancient times to the present

This is "packed with grisly facts and gory images. . . . But the science is accurate, and many readers will be intrigued by the medical drama. . . . The design, with lots of color pictures, captions, and boxes, will grab browsers, and the cover art is a thrilling story in itself." Booklist

Includes glossary and bibliographical references

Woog, Adam

The bionic hand. Norwood House Press 2009 48p il lib bdg $25.27

Grades: 3 4 5 6 **617**

1. Bionics 2. Artificial limbs
ISBN 978-1-59953-341-4 lib bdg; 1-59953-341-3 lib bdg
LC 2009-15640

"Explores the development and creation of the i-LIMB which is the first commercially available bionic hand." Publisher's note

617.1   Injuries and wounds

Lew, Kristi

Clot & scab; gross stuff about your scrapes, bumps, and bruises. illustrations by Michael Slack. Millbrook Press 2010 48p il (Gross body science) lib bdg $29.27

Grades: 4 5 6   **617.1**

1. Wounds and injuries

ISBN 978-0-8225-8965-5 lib bdg; 0-8225-8965-6 lib bdg

           LC 2008-45626

"Solid information layered between sarcastic comments and kid-friendly terminology like fart, poop, barf, and puke will keep readers engaged. . . . Labeled, captioned (and graphic) photographs, cartoon-style illustrations, and micrographs add information." SLJ

Includes glossary and bibliographical references

Markle, Sandra

Bad burns; true survival stories. Lerner Publications 2010 48p il (Powerful medicine) lib bdg $27.93

Grades: 5 6 7 8   **617.1**

1. Burns and scalds

ISBN 978-0-8225-8702-6 lib bdg; 0-8225-8702-5 lib bdg

           LC 2009034439

Explores how advancements in medicine and technology have helped victims of severe skin burns, and includes real-life stories of burn survivors and tips on burn prevention and treatment.

This narrative reads "like information from the Discovery Health channel, for kids: part fascinating science, part human interest story, and part 'Eew, gross!'. . . Clear, straightforward prose is supplemented by definitions and explanations of medical techniques and jargon. The numerous color photos and medical images will satisfy readers' curiosity." SLJ

Includes glossary and bibliographical references

Shattered bones; true survival stories. Lerner Publications 2010 48p il (Powerful medicine) lib bdg $27.93

Grades: 5 6 7 8   **617.1**

1. Bones 2. Fractures

ISBN 978-0-8225-8703-3 lib bdg; 0-8225-8703-3 lib bdg

           LC 2009034442

Offers true stories of people who suffered broken bones, along with information on the skeleton, its structure and function, and the treatments doctors use for injuries.

This narrative reads "like information from the Discovery Health channel, for kids: part fascinating science, part human interest story, and part 'Eew, gross!'. . . Clear, straightforward prose is supplemented by definitions and explanations of medical techniques and jargon. The numerous color photos and medical images will satisfy readers' curiosity." SLJ

Includes glossary and bibliographical references

Nagle, Jeanne

Frequently asked questions about Wii and video game injuries and fitness. Rosen Pub. 2009 64p il (FAQ: teen life) lib bdg $29.25

Grades: 6 7 8 9   **617.1**

1. Exercise 2. Video games 3. Physical fitness 4. Wounds and injuries

ISBN 978-1-4358-5329-4 lib bdg; 1-4358-5329-6 lib bdg

           LC 2009001046

"While conversational, [this volume is] surprisingly helpful—and even emotive. . . . [This book] will delight anyone who has given themselves carpal tunnel playing Wii sports. Nagle's conclusion is that 'exergames' at the very least reinforce healthy behavior." Booklist

Includes glossary and bibliographical references

★ Sports injuries information for teens; health tips about acute, traumatic, and chronic injuries in adolescent athletes. edited by Zachary Klimecki and Elizabeth Bellenir. 3rd ed. Omnigraphics, Inc. 2012 xiii, 401 p.p (hardcover) $69

Grades: 7 8 9 10 11 12   **617.1**

1. Athletes -- Wounds and injuries 2. Teenagers -- Health and hygiene 3. Sports injuries 4. Wounds and injuries 5. Teenagers -- Wounds and injuries -- Prevention

ISBN 0780812654; 9780780812659

           LC 2012018884

This book offers teens a "guide to being a healthy athlete. It includes guidelines for participating safely in sports and avoiding injury. It also discusses how to deal with injuries when they do occur. It explains diagnostic and treatment procedures and discusses issues related to rehabilitation, including suggestions for making decisions about returning to play. The book concludes with directories of resources for more information about sports-related injuries and fitness." (Publisher's note)

Includes bibliographical references and index.

617.4   Surgery by systems and regions

Goldsmith, Connie

Traumatic brain injury; from concussion to coma. Connie Goldsmith. Twenty-First Century Books 2014 88 p. illustrations (lib. bdg. : alk. paper) $34.60

Grades: 6 7 8 9 10 11   **617.4**

1. Nervous system 2. Brain -- Wounds and injuries

ISBN 1467713481; 9781467713481

           LC 2013001346

This juvenile nonfiction book, by Connie Goldsmith, explores traumatic brain injury, including "the different types of TBIs, what causes them, and how they are diagnosed and treated. . . . [It also profiles] National Hockey League player Derek Boogaard and U.S. Representative Gabby Giffords, both of whom sustained TBIs, with dramatically different outcomes. . . . [Finally, it previews] medical technologies that help victims recover and promise hope for the future." (Publisher's note)

"Photographs, charts, and statistics are included, which expand the information. Appended are source notes, a glossary, a bibliography, and a list of websites and resources. The currency of this topic and its potential impact on teens make this a smart choice for school and public libraries." - Booklist

Includes bibliographical references and index

McClafferty, Carla Killough

Fourth down and inches; concussions and football's make-or-break moment. by Carla Killough McClafferty. Carolrhoda Books 2013 96 p. (lib. bdg. : alk. paper) $20.95

Grades: 6 7 8 9 10 11 12   **617.4**

1. Brain -- Concussion 2. Football players -- Wounds and injuries 3. Football injuries 4. Brain -- Concussion 5. Head -- Wounds and injuries 6. Football players -- Health and hygiene

ISBN 1467710679; 9781467710671

LC 2013004192

This book by Carla Killough McClafferty presents a "warning about the dangers of playing football, especially at the youth level. . . . The author . . . presents story after poignant story of high school and professional players who suffered brain damage or worse. Among their profiles are details of research studies, photos of MRI images and damaged brain tissue, and explanations of chronic traumatic encephalopathy (CTE) and second-impact syndrome." (Publishers Weekly)

Includes bibliographical references and index

Yount, Lisa

Alfred Blalock, Helen Taussig, and Vivien Thomas; mending children's hearts. by Lisa Yount. Chelsea House 2012 xviii, 127 p.p col. ill. (Trailblazers in science and technology) (library) $35

Grades: 7 8 9 10 11 12   **617.4**

1. Heart -- Surgery 2. Surgeons 3. Pediatric cardiology -- History 4. Heart surgeons -- United States -- Biography

ISBN 1604136588; 9781604136586

LC 2010035656

This book, part of the Trailblazers in Science and Technology series, focuses on medical professionals Alfred Blalock, Helen Taussig, and Vivien Thomas. The book "recounts the lives and careers of three medical pioneers—a white male surgeon (Blalock), a white female cardiologist (Taussig), and an African-American male laboratory technician (Thomas)—who combined their skills in 1944 to create a groundbreaking operation" for pediatric cardiology. (Publisher's note)

"Sidebars and captioned color and archival photographs round out the dense, though clearly written, texts." SLJ

Includes bibliographical references and index.

617.5   Regional medicine

Ear, nose, and throat; edited by Kara Rogers. Britannica Educational Pub. in association with Rosen Educational Services 2012 xvii, 186 p.p col. ill.

Grades: 7 8 9 10 11 12   **617.5**

1. Ear 2. Nose 3. Throat 4. Otolaryngology

ISBN 1615306579; 9781615306572

LC 2011013432

Editor Kara Rogers presents a book on otolaryngology. "The interconnectedness of the ear, nose, and throat is evident when you consider how the smell . . . can affect your perception of their taste, or how a runny nose and scratchy throat can lead to an ear infection. In addition to enabling sensory perception, the ear, nose, and throat perform a number of vital functions in the human body. This incisive volume examines the structure of each in turn and in concert with the other, also exploring the diseases and disorders that sometimes afflict them." (Publisher's note)

Includes bibliographical references (p. 170-171) and index

617.7   Ophthalmology

Bender, Lionel

Explaining blindness. Smart Apple Media 2010 45p il (Explaining) lib bdg $34.25

Grades: 5 6 7 8   **617.7**

1. Blind

ISBN 978-1-59920-310-2 lib bdg; 1-59920-310-3 lib bdg

LC 2008-49286

Describes blindness, including its possible causes, the different types of visual impairment, current treatments and cures, and how blind and visually impaired people live everyday lives

"The incorporation of quotes and personal accounts in 'Case Notes' sidebars adds to the sensitive tone found throughout [the title]." SLJ

Includes glossary

Markle, Sandra

Lost sight; true survival stories. Lerner Publications 2010 48p il (Powerful medicine) lib bdg $27.93

Grades: 5 6 7 8   **617.7**

1. Eye 2. Blind 3. Vision

ISBN 978-0-8225-8701-9 lib bdg; 0-8225-8701-7 lib bdg

LC 2009-34443

This book about vision loss "will grab the attention of middle school readers. . . . The illustrations and photos are stunning with medically accurate captions. Real-life patients, whose photos are included in the text, are highlighted, with updates on their progress at the end of . . . [the] book." Voice Youth Advocates

Includes glossary and bibliographical references

617.8 Otology and audiology

Levete, Sarah

Explaining deafness. Smart Apple Media 2010 45p il (Explaining) lib bdg $34.25

Grades: 5 6 7 8 **617.8**

1. Deafness

ISBN 978-1-59920-313-3 lib bdg; 1-59920-313-8 lib bdg

LC 2008-49289

Discusses the history, diagnosis, and treatment of deafness, including ways to cope with living with the condition

"The incorporation of quotes and personal accounts in 'Case Notes' sidebars adds to the sensitive tone found throughout [the title]." SLJ

Includes glossary, bibliographical references and filmography

617.9 Operative surgery and special fields of surgery

Campbell, Andrew

Cosmetic surgery. Smart Apple Media 2010 44p il (Science in the news) lib bdg $34.25

Grades: 6 7 8 9 **617.9**

1. Plastic surgery

ISBN 978-1-59920-322-5 lib bdg; 1-59920-322-7 lib bdg

LC 2008-49274

This book about cosmetic surgery "move[s] smoothly, occasionally pausing for the definition of a term. [The title] boast[s] plenty of attractive photos, and a clean layout allows the information to be easily consumed. . . . Provides the information that younger teens need." SLJ

Includes glossary

Organ transplants. Smart Apple Media 2010 45p il (Science in the news) lib bdg $34.25

Grades: 6 7 8 9 **617.9**

1. Transplantation of organs, tissues, etc.

ISBN 978-1-59920-321-8 lib bdg; 1-59920-321-9 lib bdg

LC 2008-41436

"Discusses current practices of organ transplants, developments in science that make transplants possible, and the history of organ transplants as well as issues surrounding organ shortage and organ selling." Publisher's note

Includes glossary

Foran, Racquel

★ **Organ** transplants; Racquel Foran. Abdo Pub. Co. 2013 112 p. illustrations (chiefly color) $34.22

Grades: 6 7 8 9 10 **617.9**

1. Medical technology 2. Transplantation of organs, tissues, etc.

ISBN 1617839043; 9781617839047

LC 2013932976

Written by Racquel Foran and part of the Medical Marvels series, "This title follows the development of organ transplants, including early attempts at transplantation, groundbreaking discoveries and the doctors who made them, and where the science is heading in the future. . . . Sidebars, full-color photos, a glossary, and well-placed graphs, charts, and maps, enhance this . . . title." (Publisher's note)

"The book is handsomely designed, with interesting full-bleed photographs often facing a page of text. Sidebars, highlighted in yellow, pertain to the topic and never feel intrusive. Source notes and a bibliography . . . add to the title's usefulness for researchers." Booklist

Includes bibliographical references and index

Fullick, Ann

Rebuilding the body; organ transplantation. Ann Fullick. Rev. and updated Heinemann Library 2002 64 p. col. ill. (library) $34.29; (library) $35

Grades: 5 6 7 8 **617.9**

1. Medicine 2. Medical ethics 3. Transplantation of organs, tissues, etc.

ISBN 9781588107008 out of print; 1432924524; 9781432924522

LC 2001006082

This book is part of the Science at the Edge series and looks at organ transplantation. It "begins with a survey of the major human body organs. . . . This is followed by a description of the failure of major organs, infections that occur within them, and gradual damage and deterioration. This leads to a discussion about organ transplants . . . . The challenges of organ transplantation, pitfalls of rejection, and ethics of transplantation from the dead are all touched upon." (NSTA Recommends)

Includes bibliographical references (p. 63) and index

Jango-Cohen, Judith

Bionics; [by] Judith Jango-Cohen. Lerner Publications Co. 2007 48p il (Cool science) lib bdg $26.60

Grades: 4 5 6 7 **617.9**

1. Bionics 2. Artificial organs

ISBN 978-0-8225-5937-5 lib bdg; 0-8225-5937-4 lib bdg

LC 2005032221

This "introduction to the field of bionics is divided into four chapters: 'Replacing Parts,' 'Fixing Malfunctions,' 'Assisting the Senses,' and 'Facing the Future.' Jango-Cohen uses a number of personal stories and references to pop culture to engage readers. . . . The explanations are clearly written and easily understood. Colorful photographs and illustrations are featured throughout the text." SLJ

Includes bibliographical references

Schwartz, Tina P.

Organ transplants; a survival guide for the entire family: the ultimate teen guide. Scarecrow Press 2005 243p il (It happened to me) $36.50

Grades: 7 8 9 10 **617.9**

1. Transplantation of organs, tissues, etc.

ISBN 0-8108-4924-0

LC 2004-21563

"The 13 chapters, written in a question-and-answer format, detail the steps involved from diagnosis and being placed on a waiting list to pre and post-surgery. . . .The well-written text is complemented by a comprehensive section of suggestions for additional information. . . . Texts with this breadth of coverage are rare." SLJ

Includes bibliographical references

618.1 Gynecology and obstetrics

Fullick, Ann

Test tube babies; in-vitro fertilization. Ann Fullick. Rev. and updated Heinemann Library 2002 64 p. col. ill. (library) $34.29 (USD); (library) $35
Grades: 7 8 9 10   618.1
1. Fertilization in vitro 2. Reproductive technology 3. Infertility 4. Reproduction 5. Test tube babies 6. Fertilization in vitro, Human
ISBN 1432924532; 1588107035 out of print; 9781432924539
                                    LC 2001006080
This book by Ann Fullick is part of the Science at the Edge series and looks at in vitro fertilization. It "begins with a discussion of the causes of infertility, the biology of reproduction, and the development of a human embryo from conception to birth. The choice between the use of infertility drugs or in-vitro fertilization is mentioned." An "explanation of in-vitro fertilization follows, with some . . . illustrations, taking readers stepwise through the process." (NSTA Recommends)

Includes bibliographical references (p. 63) and index.

Vaughan, Jenny

Making new life. Smart Apple Media 2010 45p il (Science in the news) lib bdg $34.25
Grades: 6 7 8 9   618.1
1. Reproductive technology
ISBN 978-1-59920-318-8 lib bdg; 1-59920-318-9 lib bdg
                                    LC 2008-49276
This book about reproductive technologies "move[s] smoothly, occasionally pausing for the definition of a term. [The title] boast[s] plenty of attractive photos, and a clean layout allows the information to be easily consumed. . . . Provides the information that younger teens need." SLJ

Includes glossary

Waters, Sophie

Seeing the gynecologist. Rosen Pub. Group 2007 47p il (Girls' health) $19.95
Grades: 7 8 9 10 11 12   618.1
1. Girls -- Health and hygiene 2. Women -- Health and hygiene
ISBN 978-1-4042-1948-9; 1-4042-1948-X
                                    LC 2007-1633
"Introductory chapters include a brief introduction to the physiology of women's reproduction and menstruation, but the majority of the book covers the specifics of a gynecological visit, from choosing a doctor and insurance concerns to what happens during a pelvic exam. . . . The accessible text is informative and supportive." Booklist

Includes bibliographical references

Winkler, Kathleen

★ High -tech babies; the debate over assisted reproductive technology. [by] Kathleen Winkler. Enslow Publishers 2006 58p il (Issues in focus today) lib bdg $31.93
Grades: 7 8 9 10 11 12   618.1
1. Infertility 2. Medical ethics 3. Fertilization in vitro
ISBN 0-7660-2528-4
                                    LC 2005-34656
This discusses infertility and how it is diagnosed, assisted reproductive technologies such as intrauterine insemination (IUI) and in vitro fertilization (IVF), and the ethics of those technologies.

Includes glossary and bibliographical references

618.2 Obstetrics

★ Pregnancy information for teens; health tips about teen pregnancy and teen parenting. edited by Elizabeth Magill. 2nd ed. Omnigraphics 2012 xiii, 396 p.p ill. (hardcover) $69.00
Grades: 7 8 9 10   618.2
1. Teenage pregnancy 2. Teenagers -- Health and hygiene 3. Teenage parents
ISBN 0780812204; 9780780812208
                                    LC 2011042323
This book uses "articles reprinted with permission from sources such as the March of Dimes and The National Campaign to Prevent Teen Pregnancy." This "second edition gives updated information on unplanned pregnancies. While part one features aspects of the phenomenon as a social issue, the rest of the book provides health tips and options for teens who are pregnant." (School Library Journal)

Includes bibliographical references and index.

618.92 Pediatrics

★ Allergy information for teens; health tips about allergic reactions to food, pollen, mold, and other substances, including facts about diagnosing, treating, and preventing allergic responses and complications. edited by Karen Bellenir. 2nd ed. Omnigraphics, Inc. 2013 xiii, 388 p.p ill. (hardcover) $69
Grades: 8 9 10 11 12   618.92
1. Allergy -- Encyclopedias 2. Teenagers -- Health and hygiene 3. Allergy 4. Food allergy 5. Insect allergy 6. Allergy in children
ISBN 0780812883; 9780780812888
                                    LC 2012038514
This book is a "51-chapter resource for reliable information about the many kinds of allergic reactions, triggers, symptoms, tests, treatments, and management strategies. Each chapter presents topics in short sections, using a handy question-and-answer format interwoven with many diagrams and sidebars. The volume concludes with lists of 19 additional titles, 10 cookbooks, and 24 articles, many with 2005 publication dates." (School Library Journal)

Includes bibliographical references and index.

Chesner, Jonathan

ADHD in HD; brains gone wild. by Jonathan Chesner. Free Spirit Pub. 2012 145 p. ill. (some col.) (pbk.) $14.99

Grades: 6 7 8 9   **618.92**

1. Attention deficit disorder 2. Teenagers -- Conduct of life 3. Abnormal psychology 4. Anxiety in adolescence
ISBN 1575423863; 9781575423869; 9781575426716
LC 2011047036

This book, by actor Jonathan Chesner, "is a kinetic collection of frank personal stories of failure and success, hilarious anecdotes, wild ideas, and point-blank advice that will resonate with teens and young adults. . . . The book addresses the four main characteristics of ADHD: hyperactivity, impulsivity, inattention, and indecisiveness. It provides positive advice about school, family life, social life, dating, careers, medicine, and how to be like Mr. T." (Publisher's note)

"With much practical advice (for example, taking "baby steps" when trying to establish eating habits), this packs in plenty of valuable content—and is pretty enjoyable, too." Booklist

Currie-McGhee, Leanne K.

Childhood obesity; by Leanne K. Currie-McGhee. Lucent Books 2012 104 p. ill. (some col.) (Nutrition and health) (hardcover) $30.95

Grades: 7 8 9 10 11 12   **618.92**

1. Obesity in children
ISBN 1420507230; 9781420507232
LC 2012002939

This book by Leanne K. Currie-McGhee, part of the "Nutrition & Health" series, "explores global issue of childhood obesity. Causes of and proposed solutions to this public health issue are explored, and the findings of current studies are detailed. The text features comments from scientists and researchers, but also includes first-hand accounts from children and teens who have struggled with obesity." (Publisher's note)

Includes bibliographical references (p. 90-93) and index.

Grossberg, Blythe

★ **Asperger's** rules! how to make sense of school and friends. by Blythe Grossberg. Magination Press 2012 127 p. col. ill. (paperback) $9.95; (hardcover) $14.95

Grades: 5 6 7 8   **618.92**

1. Life skills 2. Social skills 3. Asperger's syndrome 4. Autism in children 5. Autistic children -- Education 6. Asperger's syndrome -- Social aspects
ISBN 1433811286; 9781433811272; 9781433811289
LC 2011053483

This book by Blythe Grossberg presents a "guide for readers with Asperger's, covering feelings and emotions, teachers, asking for help, and dealing with bullies. Quizzes let readers reflect on their own approaches to situations like interacting with kids at school, and Grossberg also includes tips on how to interpret social situations. . . . Flowcharts illustrate how various conversations might progress, and other sections focus on dressing properly and eating healthful meals." (Publishers Weekly)

Reeve, Elizabeth

The **survival** guide for kids with autism spectrum disorders (and their parents) by Elizabeth Verdick & Elizabeth Reeve ; illustrated by Nick Kobyluch. Free Spirit Pub. 2012 234 p. col. ill. (pbk.) $16.99

Grades: 5 6 7 8 Adult   **618.92**

1. Autism 2. Autistic children 3. Parents of autistic children
ISBN 1575423855; 9781575423852; 9781575426747
LC 2011046520

This book "offers kids with autism spectrum disorders (ASDs) their own comprehensive resource for both understanding their condition and finding tools to cope with the challenges they face every day . . . with an emphasis on helping children gain new self-understanding and self-acceptance. Meant to be read with a parent, the book addresses questions . . . and provides strategies for communicating, making and keeping friends, and succeeding in school." (Publisher's note)

"This volume could become a treasured resource for families looking for help in successfully working through some of the problems faced by higher-functioning children with ASD." SLJ

618.927   Pediatric musculoskeletal diseases

Skrypuch, Marsha Forchuk

One Step at a Time; A Vietnamese Child Finds Her Way. by Marsha Forchuk Skrypuch. Pajama Press 2013 vii, 93 p.p (hardcover) $17.95

Grades: 6 7 8   **618.927**

1. Orphans 2. Poliomyelitis
ISBN 1927485010; 9781927485019

In this true story, Marsha Forchuk Skrypuch "continues the story of Tuyet, an eight-year-old Vietnamese refugee and polio survivor with a damaged leg, whose rescue she narrated in 'Last Airlift: A Vietnamese Orphan's Rescue from War.' Adopted by an unconditionally loving and supportive Canadian family, unable to understand or express much in English, Tuyet begins a difficult journey through surgeries and arduous physical therapy to repair her leg." (Publishers Weekly)

620   Engineering and allied operations

Johnson, Rebecca L.

Nanotechnology. Lerner Publications 2006 48p il (Cool science) lib bdg $25.26

Grades: 4 5 6   **620**

1. Nanotechnology
ISBN 978-0-8225-2111-2 lib bdg; 0-8225-2111-3 lib bdg
LC 2005008791

"From clear sunscreen to space elevators, nanotechnology promises big changes in our daily lives. . . . Pointing to recent advances in sports equipment, stain resistant fabrics and moving parts for dolls that are but harbingers of revolutionary new developments in science, medicine and the whole approach to manufacturing things. In a final chapter,

'Nanobots and Beyond,' [the author] considers the potential—and . . . the dangers—of submicroscopic self-replicating machines." Kirkus

Includes glossary and bibliographical references

620.1 Engineering mechanics and materials

Finkelstein, Norman H.

Plastics; [by] Norman H. Finkelstein. Marshall Cavendish Benchmark 2007 144p il (Great inventions) lib bdg $27.95

Grades: 7 8 9 10   **620.1**

1. Plastics

ISBN 978-0-7614-2600-4

LC 2006020909

"An examination of the origin, history, development, and societal impact of the development of plastics." Publisher's note

Includes glossary and bibliographical references

Kassinger, Ruth

Glass; from Cinderella's slippers to fiber optics. [by] Ruth G. Kassinger. Twenty-First Century Bks. 2003 80p il lib bdg $25.90

Grades: 7 8 9 10   **620.1**

1. Glass

ISBN 0-7613-2109-8

LC 2002-5329

Describes the physical composition and characteristics of glass, and presents glassmaking techniques and the various uses made of glass throughout history

This "will catch the interest of a wide variety of readers. The color photographs are clear, interesting, and self-explanatory." Libr Media Connect

Includes bibliographical references

Knapp, Brian J.

Materials science. Grolier 2003 9v il set$319

Grades: 7 8 9 10   **620.1**

1. Materials

ISBN 0-7172-5697-9

LC 2002-44537

Presents the main scientific properties of materials and how they are determined, as well as how substances can be manipulated or modified to produce a wide array of materials with an equally wide array of applications

"The volumes are generously enhanced with photographs and appropriate illustrative figures. . . . The written presentations are all brief, but clear and understandable for anyone who has had a general science background." Sci Books Films

Morris, Neil

Glass. Amicus 2010 48p il (Materials that matter) lib bdg $28.50

Grades: 4 5 6 7   **620.1**

1. Glass

ISBN 978-1-60753-065-7 lib bdg; 1-60753-065-1 lib bdg

LC 2009029796

"The clean layout includes photographs and occasional charts, graphs, and technical illustrations against a range of pastel backgrounds. Inset boxes provide further detail, interesting extras, and recycling information. . . . [This book offers] easily accessible background information for report writers." SLJ

Includes glossary and bibliographical references

Metals. Amicus 2010 48p il (Materials that matter) lib bdg $28.50

Grades: 4 5 6 7   **620.1**

1. Metals

ISBN 978-1-60753-066-4 lib bdg; 1-60753-066-X lib bdg

LC 2009029797

"The clean layout includes photographs and occasional charts, graphs, and technical illustrations against a range of pastel backgrounds. Inset boxes provide further detail, interesting extras, and recycling information. . . . [This book offers] easily accessible background information for report writers." SLJ

Includes glossary and bibliographical references

Ward, David J.

Materials science; by D. J. Ward. Lerner Publications 2009 47p il (Cool science) lib bdg $26.60

Grades: 4 5 6   **620.1**

1. Materials

ISBN 978-0-8225-7588-7 lib bdg; 0-8225-7588-4 lib bdg

LC 2007042176

This describes how scientists study the microscopic parts of materials such as plastic, glass, or stainless steel, how they learn how each part makes something hard or soft, strong or weak, or good or bad at carrying heat, and how they use that knowledge to create supermaterials to help make better sports equipment, tinier computer chips, and more.

Includes glossary and bibliographical references

620.2 Sound and related vibrations

Claybourne, Anna

Ear -splitting sounds and other vile noises; by Anna Claybourne. Crabtree Pub Co 2013 32 p. (reinforced library binding : alk. paper) $27.60

Grades: 4 5 6   **620.2**

1. Noise 2. Sound 3. Science 4. Sounds

ISBN 0778709256; 9780778709251; 9780778709510

LC 2012043526

This book, by Anna Claybourne, part of the "disgusting and dreadful science" series, "features a look at the weird, revolting and shocking aspects of science for children at KS2." This volume focuses on sound and noise. "The books offer . . . fascinating facts, fun examples and true-life stories to provide ways in to understanding solid scientific principles." (Publisher's note)

"These brief and lively introductions provide a plethora of fun and gross facts. Sounds explains the science behind sound, how ears work, ultrasound, and more. It also includes

a scientific explanation of how whoopee cushions work..."
SLJ

Includes bibliographical references and index
Other titles in the series include:
Electric shocks and other energy evils (2013)
Glaring light and other eye-burning rays (2013)
Gut-wrenching gravity and other fatal forces (2013)

Rooney, Anne

Audio engineering and the science of sound-waves; Anne Rooney. Crabtree Publishing 2014 32 p. (Engineering in action) (reinforced library binding) $27.60

Grades: 5 6 7 8   **620.2**
1. Sound 2. Sound -- Recording and reproducing 3. Acoustical engineering 4. Sound -- Recording and reproducing
ISBN 077871196X; 9780778711964; 9780778712299
LC 2013035439

"From sound effects in video games and movies to surround-sound theatres, this fact-filled book [by Anne Rooney] explores the many ways audio engineers apply the science of sound. Readers will explore how sound travels and the characteristics of sound waves. Readers will also learn how to combine their understanding of sound science and the engineering design process to tackle a design challenge of their own." (Publisher's note)

"Books in the Engineering in Action series provide broad introductions to their respective fields in a colorfully illustrated, large-format package...Audio tackles the science of sound and hearing, the differences between analog and digital signals, and the varied work of audio engineers. Solid information for engineering-minded students." Booklist

Includes index
Other titles in the series include:
Aerospace engineering and the principles of flight (2013)
Chemical engineering and chain reactions (2014)
Civil engineering and the science of structures (2013)
Electrical engineering and the science of circuits (2013)
Environmental engineering and the science of sustainability (2014)
Mechanical engineering and simple machines (2013)
Optical engineering and the science of light (2014)

621 Applied physics

Silverstein, Alvin

Energy; [by] Alvin Silverstein, Virginia Silverstein, Laura Silverstein Nunn. rev ed.; Twenty-First Century Books 2008 128p il (Science concepts, second series) lib bdg $31.93

Grades: 6 7 8 9   **621**
1. Energy resources
ISBN 978-0-8225-8655-5 lib bdg; 0-8225-8655-X lib bdg
LC 2007049535

First published 1998

Discusses the sources and uses of different types of energy, both natural and manmade, including electrical, magnetic, light, heat, sound, and nuclear energy

Includes glossary and bibliographical references

Sobey, Ed

Electric motor experiments. Enslow Publishers 2011 128p il (Cool science projects with technology) lib bdg $31.93

Grades: 6 7 8 9   **621**
1. Electric motors 2. Science -- Experiments
ISBN 978-0-7660-3306-1; 0-7660-3306-6

This explains how motors work and includes experiments in how to build and use a motor.

Includes glossary and bibliographical references

621.1 Fluid-power technologies

Collier, James Lincoln

★ The steam engine. Marshall Cavendish Benchmark 2006 112p il (Great inventions) lib bdg $37.07

Grades: 7 8 9 10   **621.1**
1. Steam engines
ISBN 0-7614-1880-6

This is a history of the steam engine and its influence on American history and culture.

This is presented "thoughfully yet conversationally. . . . [It] will reward steady reading." Horn Book Guide

Includes glossary and bibliographical references

O'Neal, Claire

How to use waste energy to heat and light your home. Mitchell Lane Publishers 2009 47p il (Tell your parents) lib bdg $21.50

Grades: 4 5 6 7   **621.1**
1. Recycling 2. Waste products as fuel
ISBN 978-1-58415-765-6 lib bdg; 1-58415-765-8 lib bdg
LC 2009-4483

Explores how to reduce the amount of trash produced and stored by reusing items and recycling materials, and describes how these efforts can help protect the environment

This title "offers numerous facts and statistics, all of which are cited. . . . Chapters cover present-day issues and . . . are interspersed with full-color photographs and short 'Did You Know' trivia boxes. . . . Back matter includes detailed resource lists and 'Try This!' experiments." SLJ

Includes glossary and bibliographical references

621.3092 Electrical engineers

Yount, Lisa

Nikola Tesla; harnessing electricity. by Lisa Yount. Chelsea House 2012 xviii, 128 p.p col. ill. (Trailblazers in science and technology) (library) $35

Grades: 7 8 9 10 11 12   **621.3092**
1. Electricity 2. Tesla, Nikola, 1856-1943 3. Inventors -- United States -- Biography 4. Electrical engineers -- United States -- Biography
ISBN 1604136707; 9781604136708
LC 2010052627

This book by Lisa Yount is part of the Trailblazers in Science and Technology series and looks at Nikola Tesla. He "saw his fortunes reverse as many times." He "drew the attention of businessman George Westinghouse with his alternating current (AC), a method of delivering electricity more efficiently and over greater distances than Edison's direct current (DC). With Westinghouse's support, Tesla's method soon became dominant in the industry." (Publisher's note)

Includes bibliographical references and index.

621.31 Generation, modification, storage, transmission of electric power

Lew, Kristi

Goodbye, gasoline; the science of fuel cells. Compass Point Books 2009 48p il (Headline science) lib bdg $27.93

Grades: 5 6 7 8   **621.31**

1. Fuel cells
ISBN 978-0-7565-3521-6 lib bdg; 0-7565-3521-2 lib bdg

LC 2008011729

This "clearly examines the history and technology of hydrogen fuel cells, including the various types such as proton exchange membrane and alkaline cells. An excellent description of how the technology works gives readers an understanding of both the successes and problems relating to these promising energy sources. . . . The color illustrations and charts . . . are clear and helpful, and the text, although information rich, is not overly difficult." SLJ

O'Neal, Claire

How to use wind power to light and heat your home. Mitchell Lane Publishers 2009 47p il map (Tell your parents) lib bdg $21.50

Grades: 4 5 6 7   **621.31**

1. Wind power 2. Renewable energy resources
ISBN 978-1-58415-762-5 lib bdg; 1-58415-762-3 lib bdg

LC 2009-4530

Introduces wind power, including the history of harnessing the wind for work, how modern wind power generates electricity, and how to install a turbine to a home

This book "offers numerous facts and statistics, all of which are cited. . . . Chapters cover present-day issues and . . . are interspersed with full-color photographs and short 'Did You Know' trivia boxes. . . . Back matter includes detailed resource lists and 'Try This!' experiments." SLJ

Includes glossary and bibliographical references

Rusch, Elizabeth

★ The **next** wave; the quest to harness the power of the oceans. by Elizabeth Rusch. Houghton Mifflin Harcourt 2014 80 p. color illustrations (Scientists in the field) $18.99

Grades: 5 6 7 8 9   **621.31**

1. Ocean 2. Ocean energy resources 3. Renewable energy resources 4. Tidal power 5. Renewable energy

sources
ISBN 0544099990; 9780544099999

LC 2013050150

In this book, by Elizabeth Rusch, part of the Scientists in the Field series, readers "journey to the wave-battered coast of the Pacific Northwest to meet some of the engineers and scientists working to harness the punishing force of our oceans. . . . With an array of amazing devices that cling to the bottom of the sea floor and surf on the crests of waves, these explorers are using a combination of science, imagination, and innovation to try to capture wave energy." (Publisher's note)

"Transferring ocean wave action into electricity (without damaging collection equipment or harming marine life) is a significant engineering challenge with a potentially big financial payoff. Rusch captures the determined, entrepreneurial spirit of the profiled engineers as well as the need for creative problem-solving and ingenuity. Photographs and illustrations feature prototypes in both small-scale laboratory and full-ocean tests. Reading list, websites. Bib., glos., ind." Horn Book

Includes bibliographical references and index

621.32 Lighting

Collier, James Lincoln

★ **Electricity** and the light bulb; [by] James Lincoln Collier. Marshall Cavendish Benchmark 2006 112p il (Great inventions) lib bdg $37.07

Grades: 7 8 9 10   **621.32**

1. Electric power 2. Electric lighting
ISBN 0-7614-1878-4

LC 2004-21623

This is a history of electric power and the invention of the light bulb and their influence on American history and culture.

This is presented "thoughfully yet conversationally. . . . [It] will reward steady reading." Horn Book Guide

Includes glossary and bibliographical references

Sonneborn, Liz

The **electric** light; Thomas Edison's illuminating invention. Chelsea House 2007 120p il (Milestones in American history) lib bdg $35

Grades: 7 8 9 10   **621.32**

1. Inventors 2. Electric lighting
ISBN 978-0-7910-9350-4 lib bdg; 0-7910-9350-6 lib bdg

LC 2006-34432

This "accessible [volume captures] the hard work, perseverance, and natural talent of Edison. . . . The [text explores] the [man's life] along with providing information about the genesis and development of [electric light]. Many photographs, reproductions, and sidebars contribute to a clean design and help clarify topics." Horn Book Guide

Includes bibliographical references

621.38   Electronics, communications engineering

Gregory, Josh

From butterfly wings to display technology; by Josh Gregory. Cherry Lake Publishing 2014 32 p. color illustrations (Innovations from Nature) (lib. bdg.) $28.50

Grades: 6 7 8 9 10   **621.38**

1. Biomimicry 2. Inventions 3. Butterflies 4. Inventions 5. Flat panel displays

ISBN 1624317545; 9781624317545; 9781624317606

LC 2013030377

This book, by Josh Gregory, part of the Innovations from Nature series, "explores how researchers take ideas from plants and animals and turn them into projects with practical applications. . . . [It] explains the concept of structural color, such as the iridescent colors formed by the ridged scales on a butterfly's wings. This concept has led to the development of IMOD display screens for electronic devices." (Booklist)

"These creative books use a pleasantly unusual angle to show how aspects of nature can inspire scientists and engineers. For instance, some scientists, inspired by the way a gecko's feet allow it to stick to surfaces, are attempting to create an adhesive tape using the structure of the lizard's foot. High-resolution photographs and a dark black and purple layout give the books a slick, stylish look, while the narrative is both fascinating and informative. Intriguing additions to science collections." SLJ

Includes bibliographical references and index

Other titles in the series include:

From African Plants to Vaccine Preservation (2014)

From Bats to Radar (2013)

From Birds to Aircraft (2013)

From Cats' Eyes to Reflectors (2013)

From Gecko Feet to Adhesive Tape (2014)

From Kingfishers to Bullet Trains (2013)

From Locusts to Automobile Anti-Collision Systems (2013)

From Sharks to Swimsuits (2013)

From Termite Den to Office Building (2014)

From Thistle Burrs to Velcro (2013)

From Woodpeckers to Helmets (2013)

621.381   Electronics

Electronics; edited by Sherman Hollar. Britannica Educational Pub. in association with Rosen Educational Services 2012 80 p. (Introduction to physics) (library binding) $31.70

Grades: 7 8 9 10 11 12   **621.381**

1. Electronics

ISBN 9781615306640; 1615306641

LC 2011017100

This book, edited by Sherman Hollar, is part of the Introduction to Physics series. It "examines various components, such as electron tubes and semiconductors, that have been essential to electronics over the years, as well as the history of the field in general and its applications in everyday life." (Publisher's note)

Includes bibliographical references and index

621.383   Specific communications systems

Coe, Lewis

The telegraph; a history of Morse's invention and its predecessors in the United States. McFarland & Co. 1993 184p il hardcover o.p. pa $29.95

Grades: 7 8 9 10   **621.383**

1. Artists 2. Painters 3. Inventors 4. Telegraph

ISBN 0-7864-1808-7 pa

LC 92-53597

This study of the development of the telegraph includes brief biographical sketches of Samuel Morse and other inventors

Includes bibliographical references

621.384   Radio and radar

Firestone, Mary

Wireless technology. Lerner Publications 2009 48p il (Cool science) lib bdg $27.93

Grades: 4 5 6   **621.384**

1. Wireless communication systems

ISBN 978-0-8225-7590-0 lib bdg; 0-8225-7590-6 lib bdg

LC 2007041102

This describes "how cutting-edge science helps people communicate better, live healthier, and have more fun!" Publisher's note

Includes glossary and bibliographical references

Kling, Andrew A.

Cell phones. Lucent Books 2010 112p il (Technology 360) $33.45

Grades: 8 9 10 11 12   **621.384**

1. Cellular telephones

ISBN 978-1-4205-0164-3; 1-4205-0164-X

LC 2009-6249

This book explores "the early development and advances of [cell phone] technology, its impact on society both positive and negative, and the importance it plays in our lives. . . . The history . . . progresses from the telegraph to the invention of the telephone, the merging of radio and telephone, and the implementation of computers to replace humans, eventually leading to wireless phones. Issues in regard to texting, the addition of cameras, video capabilities, disposal, safety, multimedia, and numerous other advances are addressed. . . . numerous color photos, diagrams, 'Bits & Bytes' boxes as well as many other additional text boxes create appeal and provide beneficial informative and complementary material to aid in understanding the technical details of the [text]." SLJ

Includes glossary and bibliographical references

Sequeira, Michele

Cell phone science; what happens when you call and why. [by] Michele Sequeira, Michael Westphal. University of New Mexico Press 2010 174p il (Barbara Guth worlds of wonder science series for young readers) $24.95

Grades: 6 7 8 9 **621.384**
1. Cellular telephones 2. Wireless communication systems
ISBN 978-0-8263-4968-2; 0-8263-4968-4
LC 2010028600

"The book sets out to help readers understand the complex science behind . . . [cell phones]. . . . The book features clear explanations, easy-to-read text, and colorful photographs and illustrations on almost every page. Boxed areas and information in the margins supplement the text. Students interested in learning the story of the science behind their cell phone will be well rewarded with this title." SLJ

Includes glossary and bibliographical references

621.385 Telephony

Spilsbury, Richard
The **telephone**; [by] Richard and Louise Spilsbury. Heinemann Library 2011 32p il (Tales of invention) lib bdg $29; pa $7.99
Grades: 4 5 6 7 **621.385**
1. Telephone 2. Cellular telephones
ISBN 978-1-4329-3826-0 lib bdg; 1-4329-3826-6 lib bdg; 978-1-4329-3833-8 pa; 1-4329-3833-9 pa
LC 2009049027

"Beginning with the first telegraph, the book discusses how sound travels, how speech is transmitted by wire, and how Alexander Graham Bell's first telephones worked. Then the text quickly traces later technological developments, from transatlantic cables to early cell phones to the small, light, versatile models available today. . . . The many photographs and other illustrations include excellent labeled diagrams." Booklist

Includes bibliographical references

Stefoff, Rebecca
★ The **telephone**; by Rebecca Stefoff. Marshall Cavendish Benchmark 2006 127p il (Great inventions) lib bdg $37.07
Grades: 7 8 9 10 **621.385**
1. Telephone
ISBN 0-7614-1879-2
LC 2004-22108

This is a history of the telephone, from Alexander Graham Bell to today's cell phones.

This is presented "thoughtfully yet conversationally. . . . [It] will reward steady reading." Horn Book Guide

Includes glossary and bibliographical references

621.388 Television

Grabowski, John
Television. Lucent Books 2011 112p il (Technology 360) $33.45
Grades: 7 8 9 10 **621.388**
1. Television
ISBN 978-1-4205-0169-8; 1-4205-0169-0
LC 2010033525

This book offers "clean design with clear explanations of sometimes-complicated scientific subjects. . . . This brings the information [about television] up to date with flat screens and 3-D. . . . A strong [title] for report writers and students with a serious interest in technology and its inventions." Booklist

Includes bibliographical references

Otfinoski, Steven
Television; [by] Steven Otfinoski. 1st ed.; Marshall Cavendish Benchmark 2007 111p il (Great inventions) lib bdg $42.79
Grades: 7 8 9 10 **621.388**
1. Television
ISBN 978-0-7614-2228-0 lib bdg; 0-7614-2228-5 lib bdg
LC 2005026787

"An examination of the origin, history, development, and societal impact of television." Publisher's note

Includes glossary and bibliographical references

621.4 Prime movers and heat engineering

Woelfle, Gretchen
The **wind** at work; an activity guide to windmills. Gretchen Woelfle. 2nd ed. Chicago Review Press 2013 vii, 145 p.p ill. (paperback) $16.95
Grades: 4 5 6 **621.4**
1. Windmills 2. Wind power
ISBN 1613741006; 9781613741009
LC 2012046319

This introduction to windmills "discusses their history and function through modern times. . . . About one-third of the book is devoted to activities illustrating the properties of wind and the jobs performed by windmills. . . . The concluding chapters focus on windmills as a source of energy and suggest how to chart household energy use." (Booklist) Index. "Grades four to eight." (SLJ)

"The historical information is excellent, and includes Persian windmills of 1000 years ago, Dutch windmills of the 17th century, and modern wind turbines. Amusing anecdotes and intriguing facts are woven into the text, keeping it lively. . . . Black-and-white historical prints, photographs, and diagrams appear throughout." SLJ

Includes bibliographical references (pages 133-135) and index

621.43 Internal-combustion engines

Miller, Ron
Rockets. Lerner 2008 112p il (Space innovations) lib bdg $31.93
Grades: 7 8 9 10 **621.43**
1. Rocketry 2. Rockets (Aeronautics)
ISBN 978-0-8225-7153-7; 0-8225-7153-6
LC 2006-21220

The author "describes the history of rocket science, beginning in ancient China, where saltpeter, sulfur, and charcoal were first combined to create gunpowder. . . . The stories of the development of rockets through time are complemented by short biographies of important scientists such as Robert Goddard, stories of young model rocket makers, and sidebars explaining the science that makes rockets work. . . . It is a good choice for high school libraries, as well as for boys who are interested in science and nonfiction." Voice Youth Advocates

Includes bibliographical references

Otfinoski, Steven

Rockets; [by] Steven Otfinoski. Marshall Cavendish Benchmark 2007 111p il (Great inventions) lib bdg $42.79

Grades: 7 8 9 10 **621.43**

1. Rocketry 2. Rockets (Aeronautics)
ISBN 978-0-7614-2232-7 lib bdg; 0-7614-2232-3 lib bdg

LC 2005034205

"An examination of the origins, history, development, and impact of rockets and rocketry science." Publisher's note

Includes glossary and bibliographical references

621.44 Geothermal engineering

Boyle, Jordan

Examining geothermal energy; Jordan Boyle. Clara House Books 2013 48 p. (Examining energy) (alk. paper) $24.95

Grades: 5 6 7 **621.44**

1. Geothermal resources 2. Geothermal engineering
ISBN 1934545414; 9781934545416

LC 2012035244

"This entry in the Examining Energy series presents . . . [an] overview of the advantages as well as past and present uses of geothermal energy. There are also glimpses of current research on future means of producing this energy in locales where no heat sources are conveniently near the earth's surface." It is "framed as a series of first-person conversations between a fictional student named Derek and likewise fictional scientists or tour guides at seven actual sites." (Booklist)

Includes bibliographical references and index

621.46 Electric and related motors

Gabrielson, Curt

Kinetic contraptions; build a hovercraft, airboat, and more with a hobby motor. Chicago Review Press 2010 176p il pa $16.95

Grades: 7 8 9 10 **621.46**

1. Airplanes -- Models 2. Motorboats -- Models 3. Automobiles -- Models
ISBN 978-1-55652-957-3; 1-55652-957-0

LC 2009-25695

The author "describes projects intended to foster in students a passion for electrical experimentation as they construct more than 20 motor-powered devices. With sections dedicated to creating machines that run on land, water, and air, as well as spinning machines (such as a snow globe) and bizarre machines (such as a bubble maker), the book has projects designed to appeal to everyone." Education Digest

621.47 Solar-energy engineering

Bearce, Stephanie

How to harness solar power for your home. Mitchell Lane Publishers 2009 47p il map (Tell your parents) lib bdg $21.50

Grades: 4 5 6 7 **621.47**

1. Solar energy
ISBN 978-1-58415-761-8 lib bdg; 1-58415-761-5 lib bdg

LC 2009-4529

This title about solar power "offers numerous facts and statistics, all of which are cited. . . . Chapters cover present-day issues and . . . are interspersed with full-color photographs and short 'Did You Know' trivia boxes. . . . Back matter includes detailed resource lists and 'Try This!' experiments." SLJ

Includes glossary and bibliographical references

Bright, Sandra

Examining solar energy; by Sandra Bright. Clara House Books 2013 48 p. (hardcover : alk. paper) $24.95

Grades: 5 6 7 8 **621.47**

1. Solar energy 2. Energy resources
ISBN 1934545457; 9781934545454

LC 2012035316

This book, by Sandra Bright, looks at solar energy through "fictitious research journals that examine the history, science, and future outlook of [energy resources]. Additional historical information, better scientific explanations, and extended future outlooks round-out the content." (Publisher's note)

Includes bibliographical references (pages 46-47) and index

Walker, Niki

Harnessing power from the sun; [by] Niki Walker. Crabtree Pub. Co. 2007 32p il map (Energy revolution) lib bdg $23.93; pa $8.95

Grades: 5 6 7 8 **621.47**

1. Solar energy
ISBN 978-0-7787-2912-9 lib bdg; 0-7787-2912-5 lib bdg; 978-0-7787-2926-6 pa; 0-7787-2926-5 pa

LC 2006014368

This describes various ways of gathering and distributing solar energy, and includes a brief history of solar power, and tips on energy conservation

"Vivid color photographs with informative captions extend the [text], showing diverse people and applications." SLJ

Includes glossary

621.48 Nuclear engineering

Kidd, J. S.

★ **Nuclear** power; the study of quarks and sparks. [by] J.S. Kidd and Renee A. Kidd. rev ed.; Chelsea House 2006 208p il (Science and society) $35

Grades: 7 8 9 10   **621.48**

1. Nuclear energy
ISBN 978-0-8160-5606-4; 0-8160-5606-4

LC 2005-52872

First published 1999 with title: Quarks and sparks: the story of nuclear power

Examines the people, events, and motivations leading up to modern-day discoveries and advances in nuclear physics

"Extensive scientific explanations are kept manageable, thanks to consistent references to their historical context; and descriptions of the nuclear race during the Second World War are especially riveting." Booklist [review of 1999 edition]

Includes bibliographical references

Mahaffey, James A.

Fusion; James A. Mahaffey. Facts on File 2012 x, 142 p.p (ebook) $45.00; (hardcover) $45.00

Grades: 7 8 9 10 11 12   **621.48**

1. Sun 2. Nuclear fusion 3. Big bang theory 4. Nuclear reactors 5. Fusion -- Popular works
ISBN 9781438138435; 0816076537; 9780816076536

LC 2011012505

This book, by author James A. Mahaffey, "deliver[s] complex information including background on the theories, applications, devices, and future of fusion. [Topics include] . . . hydrogen fusion in the Sun . . . the big bang nucleosynthesis . . . [and] the International Tokamak Experimental Reactor and the Demonstration Power Plant." (School Library Journal)

Includes bibliographical references and index.

Oxlade, Chris

Nuclear power. Smart Apple Media 2010 44p il map (Science in the news) lib bdg $34.25

Grades: 6 7 8 9   **621.48**

1. Nuclear energy 2. Nuclear engineering
ISBN 978-1-59920-320-1 lib bdg; 1-59920-320-0 lib bdg

LC 2008-49277

This book about nuclear power "move[s] smoothly, occasionally pausing for the definition of a term. [The title] boast[s] plenty of attractive photos, and a clean layout allows the information to be easily consumed. . . . Provides the information that younger teens need." SLJ

Includes glossary

621.5 Pneumatic, vacuum, low-temperature technologies

Pringle, Laurence

Ice! the amazing history of the ice business. Laurence Pringle. Calkins Creek 2012 74 p. $17.95

Grades: 4 5 6 7 8   **621.5**

1. Ice 2. Refrigeration 3. Food -- Preservation
ISBN 159078801X; 9781590788011

LC 2012937320

This book looks at "iceboxes, icehouses, icemen, and . . . more about the history of the harvesting, storage, and delivery of ice." Author Laurence Pringle "briefly covers early food preservation . . . before delving into the rise of the ice industry in the early 1800s, and, in particular, the harvesting of the frozen stuff at pristine Rockland Lake in New York." (School Library Journal)

Includes bibliographical references and index.

621.9 Tools

Tomecek, Steve

Tools and machines; by Stephen M. Tomecek. Chelsea House Publishers 2010 182p il (Experimenting with everyday science) $35

Grades: 5 6 7 8   **621.9**

1. Tools 2. Machinery 3. Science -- Experiments
ISBN 978-1-60413-171-0; 1-60413-171-3

LC 2009-22332

This "offers 25 easy-to-perform activities that illuminate scientific principles. . . . [This] discusses levers, pulleys, and meters and explains how people use them in their daily lives. . . . Following each experiment are additional comments on the science behind the experiment and link to the one that follows. Photographs, simple diagrams and illustrations, and sample data tables appear throughout, and the [layout is] clear and colorful." SLJ

Includes bibliographical references

622 Mining and related operations

Squire, Ann O.

Hydrofracking; the process that has changed America's energy needs. by Ann O. Squire. Children's Press, an imprint of Scholastic Inc. 2013 64 p. (Cornerstones of freedom) (library binding) $30

Grades: 4 5 6   **622**

1. Hydraulic fracturing 2. Shale gas 3. Gas well drilling
ISBN 0531236048; 9780531219621; 9780531236048

LC 2012034322

This book by Ann O. Squire is part of the "Cornerstones of Freedom" series, which provides "overviews of important national and global issues and their effects on current world development, especially in the United States." It "discusses the advantages and disadvantages of this method of extracting petroleum and natural gas, by pumping water and chemicals deep below the Earth's surface. Renewable energy sources are discussed as alternatives to this practice." (School Library Journal)

Includes bibliographical references (page 61) and index

623.4   Ordnance

Boos, Ben

Swords; an artist's devotion. written & illustrated by Ben Boos. Candlewick Press 2008 82p il $24.99; pa $12.99

Grades: 6 7 8 9   **623.4**
1. Swords
ISBN 978-0-7636-3148-2; 0-7636-3148-5; 978-0-7636-5098-8 pa

LC 2007-52333

"This absorbing, large-format collection of sketches, paintings, and historical notes on sword craft is not called an artist's devotion for nothing. Boos's treatment of his subject is reverential and his artwork is outstanding, combining meticulous attention to detail and a designer's sense for layout. The spare text provides just enough information but generally allows the illustrations to speak for themselves." SLJ

Includes bibliographical references

Collier, James Lincoln

★ **Gunpowder** and weaponry. Benchmark Bks. 2004 124p il (Great inventions) lib bdg $37.07

Grades: 6 7 8 9   **623.4**
1. Guns 2. Gunpowder 3. Military art and science 4. Firearms
ISBN 0-7614-1540-8

LC 2002-156289

This is a history of warfare and weaponry with emphasis on the significance of the invention of gunpowder

Includes bibliographical references

Diagram Group

The **new** weapons of the world encyclopedia; an international encyclopedia from 5000 B.C. to the 21st century. [by] the Diagram Group. rev ed.; St Martin's Press 2007 368p il pa $24.95

Grades: 8 9 10 11 12 Adult   **623.4**
1. Reference books 2. Weapons -- History
ISBN 978-0-312-36832-6 pa; 0-312-36832-1 pa

First published 1980 with title: Weapons: an international encyclopedia from 5000 B.C. to 2000 A.D

This "guide covers the entire history of weapons, from the earliest, most primitive instruments up to remarkable advances in modern defense and warfare.... Includes weapons used in Kosovo, Afghanistan, Iraq and the Israel-Lebanon conflict. . . . [This book is] illustrated, with hundreds of color diagrams, charts [and] photographs." Publisher's note

Includes bibliographical references

Gurstelle, William

The **art** of the catapult; build Greek ballistae, Roman onagers, English trebuchets, and more ancient artillery. Chicago Review Press 2004 172p il map $16.95

Grades: 5 6 7 8   **623.4**
1. Catapult
ISBN 1-55652-526-5

"This collection of 10 working catapult projects offers a fascinating look at world history, military strategy, and physics, related with an engaging yet lighthearted touch. . . . Instructions are clear, with full materials lists, helpful diagrams, and no skipped steps. . . . There's excellent booktalk potential here, and lively reading even for those who never get around to constructing a catapult." SLJ

Includes bibliographical references

Sheinkin, Steve

★ **Bomb**; the race to build and steal the world's most dangerous weapon. Steve Sheinkin. Roaring Brook Press 2012 266 p. ill. (hc) $19.99

Grades: 5 6 7 8 9 10 11 12 Adult   **623.4**
1. Nuclear warfare 2. Nuclear weapons 3. World War, 1914-1918 -- Chemical warfare 4. Atomic bomb -- History 5. Operation Freshman, 1942 6. Atomic bomb -- Germany -- History 7. World War, 1939-1945 -- Secret service -- Soviet Union 8. World War, 1939-1945 -- Secret service -- Great Britain 9. World War, 1939-1945 -- Commando operations -- Norway -- Vemork
ISBN 1596434872; 9781596434875

LC 2011044096

YALSA Award for Excellence in Nonfiction for Young Adults (2013)

John Newbery Honor Book (2013)

Robert F. Sibert Informational Book Medal (2013)

Author Steve Sheinkin's "story unfolds in three parts, covering American attempts to build the [atomic] bomb, how the Soviets tried to steal American designs and how the Americans tried to keep the Germans from building a bomb. It was the eve of World War II, and the fate of the world was at stake . . . all along the way spies in the United States were feeding sensitive information to the KGB." (Kirkus Reviews)

Includes bibliographical references (p. [243]-259) and index

Trueit, Trudi Strain

Gunpowder. Franklin Watts 2005 80p il (Inventions that shaped the world) $30.50

Grades: 6 7 8 9   **623.4**
1. Gunpowder
ISBN 978-0-531-12371-3; 0-531-12371-5

LC 2004030437

Describes the invention of gunpowder, the impact it has had on modern culture, and patterns of change that resulted from its use

Includes bibliographical references

623.7 Communications, vehicles, sanitation, related topics

101 great tanks; edited by Robert Jackson. Rosen Pub. 2010 112p il (The 101 greatest weapons of all times) lib bdg $31.95

Grades: 7 8 9 10   **623.7**
1. Military tanks
ISBN 978-1-4358-3595-5 lib bdg; 1-4358-3595-6 lib bdg

LC 2009-32880

Presents photographs and detailed information about 101 great tanks, from the very first British tank to ultramodern armored fighting vehicles.

Describes "why and when the type of vehicle was created, its advantages and disadvantages, when and where it served, countries that may have purchased or license-built it, and when it was removed from service. . . . Contains a detailed two-dimensional color drawing and black-and-white or color photo of the featured vehicle. . . . Back matter includes a listing of memorials and museums and an excellent further-reading list. A first purchase where the subject is popular." SLJ

Includes glossary

Mooney, Carla
  Pilotless planes. Norwood House Press 2010 48p il (A great idea) lib bdg $25.27
  Grades: 3 4 5 6   **623.7**
    1. Drone aircraft 2. Military aeronautics
    ISBN 978-1-59953-381-0 lib bdg; 1-59953-381-2 lib bdg
                                          LC 2010008500
  This "discusses the development and use of unmanned aerial vehicles, also called UAVs or drones, such as the Predator planes currently used by the U.S. Air Force. Looking beyond military uses, the last chapter also considers future public safety, environmental, and commercial applications. . . . Presenting specific, current information, [this book] will appeal to young people intrigued by inventions." Booklist
  Includes glossary and bibliographical references

623.74   Vehicles

101 great bombers; Robert Jackson, editor. Rosen Pub. 2010 112p il (The 101 greatest weapons of all times) lib bdg $31.95
  Grades: 7 8 9 10   **623.74**
    1. Bombers
    ISBN 978-1-4358-3594-8 lib bdg; 1-4358-3594-8 lib bdg
                                          LC 2009-32090
  Presents photographs and detailed information about 101 great bombers, from the early twentieth-century biplanes to ultramodern stealth bombers.
  Describes "why and when the type of vehicle was created, its advantages and disadvantages, when and where it served, countries that may have purchased or license-built it, and when it was removed from service. . . . Contains a detailed two-dimensional color drawing and black-and-white or color photo of the featured vehicle. . . . Back matter includes a listing of memorials and museums and an excellent further-reading list. A first purchase where the subject is popular." SLJ
  Includes glossary

101 great fighters; edited by Robert Jackson. Rosen Pub. 2010 112p il (The 101 greatest weapons of all times) lib bdg $31.95
  Grades: 7 8 9 10   **623.74**
    1. Fighter planes
    ISBN 978-1-4358-3597-9 lib bdg; 1-4358-3597-2 lib bdg
                                          LC 2009-32122

Presents photographs and detailed information about 101 great fighter planes, from the early twentieth-century biplanes to ultramodern jet fighters.
  Describes "why and when the type of vehicle was created, its advantages and disadvantages, when and where it served, countries that may have purchased or license-built it, and when it was removed from service. . . . Contains a detailed two-dimensional color drawing and black-and-white or color photo of the featured vehicle. . . . Back matter includes a listing of memorials and museums and an excellent further-reading list. A first purchase where the subject is popular." SLJ
  Includes glossary

623.82   Nautical craft

101 great warships; Robert Jackson, editor. Rosen Pub. 2010 112p il (The 101 greatest weapons of all times) lib bdg $31.95
  Grades: 7 8 9 10   **623.82**
    1. Warships
    ISBN 978-1-4358-3596-2 lib bdg; 1-4358-3596-4 lib bdg
                                          LC 2009-32929
  Presents photographs and detailed information about 101 great warship, from the early twentieth-century battleships to ultramodern aircraft carriers.
  Describes "why and when the type of vehicle was created, its advantages and disadvantages, when and where it served, countries that may have purchased or license-built it, and when it was removed from service. . . . Contains a detailed two-dimensional color drawing and black-and-white or color photo of the featured vehicle. . . . Back matter includes a listing of memorials and museums and an excellent further-reading list. A first purchase where the subject is popular." SLJ
  Includes glossary

Stefoff, Rebecca
  Submarines; [by] Rebecca Stefoff. Marshall Cavendish Benchmark 2006 127p il (Great inventions) lib bdg $39.93
  Grades: 7 8 9 10   **623.82**
    1. Submarines
    ISBN 978-0-7614-2229-7 lib bdg; 0-7614-2229-3 lib bdg
                                          LC 2005033984
  "An examination of the origin, history, development, and impact of the submarine and related underwater exploration and transport technology." Publisher's note
  Includes glossary and bibliographical references

623.89   Navigation

Morrison, Taylor
  The **coast** mappers. Houghton Mifflin Co. 2004 45p il map $16
  Grades: 5 6 7 8   **623.89**
    1. Maps 2. Surveying 3. Astronomers 4. Geographers

5. Cartographers 6. College teachers 7. Pacific Coast (North America)
ISBN 0-618-25408-0

LC 2003-13534

Chronicles the difficulties encountered by George Davidson and others as they attempted to create nautical charts to complete the U.S. Coast Survey of the West Coast in the mid-nineteenth century

"Cartographic methods are clearly explained through both the carefully researched text and the precise illustrations. . . . The artwork clarifies the text, depicts the breathtaking beauty of the coastline, and adds a sense of adventure." SLJ

Includes glossary and bibliographical references

Williams, Linda D.

Navigational aids; [by] Linda Williams. Marshall Cavendish Benchmark 2007 128p il (Great inventions) lib bdg $27.95

Grades: 6 7 8 9   623.89
1. Navigation 2. Aids to navigation.
ISBN 978-0-7614-2599-1

LC 2006028959

"An examination of the origins, history, development, and impact of the various navigational aids humans have used through the centuries." Publisher's note

Includes glossary and bibliographical references

Young, Karen Romano

Across the wide ocean; the why, how, and where of navigation for humans and animals at sea. Greenwillow Books 2007 78p il $18.99; lib bdg $19.89

Grades: 4 5 6 7   623.89
1. Ocean 2. Navigation 3. Marine animals
ISBN 978-0-06-009086-9; 0-06-009086-3; 978-0-06-009087-6 lib bdg; 0-06-009087-1 lib bdg

LC 2005-46146

"Readers follow such disparate entities as a loggerhead sea turtle, a nuclear submarine, and a sailboat crew seeking scientific sightings of North Atlantic right whales as Young explores the concept of navigation. . . . Larded with photos, diagrams, and maps. . . . Deceptively simple in appearance, the informative text can push some intense mental activity." SLJ

624   Civil engineering

Aaseng, Nathan

Construction : building the impossible. Oliver Press (Minneapolis) 2000 144p il (Innovators) $21.95

Grades: 6 7 8 9   624
1. Generals 2. Pyramids 3. Inventors 4. Architects 5. Physicians 6. Panama Canal 7. Civil engineering 8. Hoover Dam (Ariz. and Nev.) 9. Civil engineers 10. Bridge engineers 11. Mechanical engineers 12. Structural engineers 13. Brooklyn Bridge (New York, N.Y.)
ISBN 1-88150-859-5

LC 98-51815

Profiles eight builders and their famous construction projects, including Imhotep and the Step Pyramid, Alexandre Eiffel and the Eiffel Tower, and William Lamb and the Empire State Building

"The prose is clear and engaging, with a layperson's approach to technical information. Sidebars feature related anecdotes, fun facts, and word definitions. Historical photos, drawings, and diagrams are fascinating and well chosen." Booklist

Includes glossary and bibliographical references

Caney, Steven

★ **Steven** Caney's ultimate building book. Running Press 2006 596p il $29.95

Grades: 4 5 6 7 8   624
1. Building 2. Civil engineering
ISBN 0-7624-0409-4

"Caney examines 'building' in its broadest sense, encompassing everything from skyscrapers and bridges to bird feeders and peanut-shell 'bricks.' Opening sections investigate the history and techniques of construction, with clearly written explanations supported by black-and-white photographs and diagrams. . . . The author reinforces important concepts of design in a way that is fascinating and effective." SLJ

Fantastic feats and failures; by the editors of YES magazine. Kids Can Press 2004 52p il hardcover o.p. pa $7.95

Grades: 4 5 6 7   624
1. Civil engineering
ISBN 1-55337-633-1; 1-55337-634-X pa

This "book spotlights 20 notable highs and lows in engineering. The 'feats' celebrated include the Sydney Opera House, the Brooklyn Bridge, and Canadarm (a huge, Canadian-built robotic arm used for repairs in space). Among the 'failures' are the space shuttle Challenger, the Tacoma Narrows Bridge, and the Chernobyl nuclear power plant. . . . Well organized and engagingly written. . . . Excellent photos . . . illustrate the places and events discussed, while colorful drawings visually represent concepts." Booklist

Levy, Matthys

Engineering the city; how infrastructure works: projects and principles for beginners. [by] Matthys Levy and Richard Panchyk. Chicago Review Press 2000 129p pa $14.95

Grades: 6 7 8 9   624
1. Civil engineering 2. Municipal engineering
ISBN 1-55652-419-6

LC 00-31774

"Combining a study of urban infrastructure with the history of human development, the authors examine the topics of water, transportation, waste and garbage disposal, and pollution. A wide variety of projects include scientific experiments and extension activities. . . . Containing scientific and historical information, this book will serve as a springboard for cross-curricular projects in history and science, with connections to math and language arts." Book Rep

Includes glossary and bibliographical references

Macaulay, David

★ **Underground**. Houghton Mifflin 1976 109p il hardcover o.p. pa $9.95

Grades: 5 6 7 8 9   **624**

1. Subways 2. Building 3. Sewerage 4. Electric lines 5. Public utilities 6. Civil engineering

ISBN 0-395-24739-X; 0-395-34065-9 pa

"Introduced by a visual index—a bird's eye view of a busy, hypothetical intersection with colored indicators marking the specific locations analyzed in subsequent pages—detailed illustrations are combined with a clear, precise narrative to make the subject comprehenssible and fascinating." Horn Book

Includes glossary

Reeves, Diane Lindsey

Career ideas for teens in architecture and construction; [by] Diane Lindsey Reeves with Gail Karlitz and Don Rauf. Ferguson 2005 170p il (Career ideas for teens) $40

Grades: 7 8 9 10   **624**

1. Building 2. Engineering 3. Architecture 4. Vocational guidance

ISBN 0-8160-5289-1

LC 2004-20030

The careers described in this book include architect, carpenter, electrician, interior designer, and urban planner

Sullivan, George

★ **Built** to last; building America's amazing bridges, dams, tunnels, and skyscrapers. Scholastic Nonfiction 2005 128p il map $18.99

Grades: 5 6 7 8   **624**

1. Civil engineering

ISBN 0-439-51737-0

LC 2004-60996

This is a "survey of American building—from the Erie Canal to Boston's current 'Big Dig.' Chronological chapters describe the historical forces that helped drive each project as well as the specific technological feats linked to each pioneering structure. . . . The wide selection of captivating illustrations includes archival photos and engravings, architectural drawings, and color photos. . . . Sullivan's skillful integration of social and economic history distinguishes this clear, well-designed title." Booklist

624.1 Structural engineering and underground construction

Graham, Ian

Tremendous tunnels. Amicus 2010 32p il (Superstructures) lib bdg $28.50

Grades: 5 6 7 8   **624.1**

1. Tunnels

ISBN 978-1-60753-134-0; 1-60753-134-8

LC 2009030865

"The vivid illustrations often help clarify points made in the text. . . . [This] colorful, informative [book offers] intriguing glimpses of notable engineering feats." Booklist

"Describes some of the longest and most famous tunnels ever built. Includes information on the tunnel designers, the challenges they faced, and statistics of the finished tunnels." Publisher's note

Includes glossary and bibliographical references

624.2 Bridges

Graham, Ian

Fabulous bridges. Amicus 2010 32p il (Superstructures) lib bdg $28.50

Grades: 5 6 7 8   **624.2**

1. Bridges

ISBN 978-1-60753-132-6; 1-60753-132-1

LC 2009030864

"The vivid illustrations often help clarify points made in the text. . . . [This] colorful, informative [book offers] intriguing glimpses of notable engineering feats." Booklist

"Describes some of the longest and most famous bridges ever built. Includes information on the bridge designers, the challenges they faced, and statistics of the finished bridges." Publisher's note

Includes glossary and bibliographical references

Prentzas, G. S.

The **Brooklyn** Bridge. Chelsea House Publishers 2009 120p il (Building America: then and now) lib bdg $35

Grades: 6 7 8 9   **624.2**

1. Bridges 2. Brooklyn Bridge (New York, N.Y.)

ISBN 978-1-60413-073-7 lib bdg; 1-60413-073-3 lib bdg

LC 2008-25543

This describes the construction and impact of the Brooklyn Bridge

Includes glossary and bibliographical references

627 Hydraulic engineering

Aldridge, Rebecca

The **Hoover** Dam. Chelsea House 2009 119p il (Building America: then and now) lib bdg $35

Grades: 6 7 8 9   **627**

1. Dams 2. Hoover Dam (Ariz. and Nev.)

ISBN 978-1-60413-069-0 lib bdg; 1-60413-069-5 lib bdg

LC 2008-25545

This describes the history and impact of Hoover Dam

"Photos, maps, and informative sidebars supplement the densely detailed writing. American history buffs will find [this volume] useful for doing research." Horn Book Guide

Includes bibliographical references

Mann, Elizabeth

Hoover Dam; with illustrations by Alan Witschonke. Mikaya Press 2001 44p il (Wonders of the world) $19.95; pa $9.95

Grades: 4 5 6 7 **627**
1. Hoover Dam (Ariz. and Nev.)
ISBN 978-1-931414-02-9; 1-931414-02-5; 978-1-931414-13-5 pa; 1-931414-13-0 pa
LC 2001-34520
Describes the engineering, construction, and social and historical contexts of the Hoover Dam
"A wonderfully readable, well-organized book filled with fascinating detail." SLJ

627.13 Canals

Latham, Donna
Canals and dams; investigate feats of engineering. Nomad Press 2013 122 p. $21.95
Grades: 5 6 7 8 **627.13**
1. Dams 2. Canals
ISBN 1619301695; 9781619301696
This book "opens with an explanation of engineering, introduces the different types of engineers, and describes the problem-solving process they use. Canals and dams are given center stage as their structures and the scientific principles behind them are explained, history and examples are given, and disasters caused by or resulting from their construction or aging are shared." (School Library Journal)

628 Sanitary engineering

Harmon, Dan
Jobs in environmental cleanup and emergency hazmat response; [by] Daniel E. Harmon. Rosen Pub. 2010 80p il (Green careers) lib bdg $30.60
Grades: 7 8 9 **628**
1. Hazardous wastes 2. Vocational guidance 3. Environmental sciences
ISBN 978-1-4358-3570-2; 1-4358-3570-0
LC 2009-14946
"Written in clear, concise language, . . . [this] features color pictures and boxes with supplementary information. Chapters and sections are broken into reasonable lengths suitable for reluctant readers, but interesting enough for advanced students." Libr Media Connect
Includes glossary and bibliographical references

Horn, Geoffrey
Environmental engineer; by Geoffrey M. Horn. Gareth Stevens Pub. 2010 32p il (Cool careers: cutting edge) lib bdg $26; pa $8.95
Grades: 4 5 6 **628**
1. Vocational guidance 2. Sanitary engineering 3. Environmental protection
ISBN 978-1-4339-1956-5 lib bdg; 1-4339-1956-7 lib bdg; 978-1-4339-2155-1 pa; 1-4339-2155-3 pa
LC 2009004746
This introduction to environmental engineering careers offers "clear, solid information in a large font. . . . [This] short [book is] packed with relevant, current material." SLJ
Includes glossary and bibliographical references

628.4 Waste technology, public toilets, street cleaning

Gardner, Robert
Recycle; green science projects for a sustainable planet. Enslow Publishers 2011 128p il (Team Green science projects) lib bdg $31.93
Grades: 6 7 8 9 10 **628.4**
1. Recycling 2. Science projects 3. Science -- Experiments
ISBN 978-0-7660-3648-2; 0-7660-3648-0
LC 2009-37903
This describes science projects about recycling, including experiments and information about plastics, solid waste and decomposition, composting, aluminum, and paper.
"Gardner provides plenty of information, well-designed experiments, and demonstrations, and then shares brief science-fair ideas. . . . Experiments and demonstrations are presented with clear step-by-step instructions and occasional illustrations and represent a wide range of complexity." SLJ
Includes glossary and bibliographical references

629 Other branches of engineering

Richie, Jason
Space flight; crossing the last frontier. Oliver Press (Minneapolis) 2002 144p il (Innovators) lib bdg $21.95
Grades: 5 6 7 8 **629**
1. Physicists 2. Scientists 3. Space flight 4. Aerospace engineers 5. NASA officials 6. Electrical engineers 7. Aeronautical engineers 8. Aerospace industry executives
ISBN 1-881508-77-3
LC 2001-36507
Profiles seven engineers and scientists who made space flight possible, including Robert Goddard, Sergei Korolev, and Wernher von Braun
"The biographies are readable, entertaining, and informative." SLJ
Includes glossary and bibliographical references

629.1 Aerospace engineering

Hickam, Homer H.
★ **Rocket** boys; a memoir. [by] Homer H. Hickam, Jr. Delacorte Press 1998 368p $25.95; pa $14
Grades: 7 8 9 10 11 12 Adult **629.1**
1. Authors 2. Novelists 3. Aerospace engineers 4. Memoirists 5. West Virginia 6. Authors, American 7. Writers on science
ISBN 0-385-33320-X; 0-385-33321-8 pa
LC 98-19304
"Even if Hickam stretched the strict truth to metamorphose his memories into Stand By Me-like material for Hollywood . . . the embellishing only converts what is a good story into an absorbing, rapidly readable one that is unsentimental but artful about adolescence, high school, and family life." Booklist

Rooney, Anne

Aerospace engineering and the principles of flight; Anne Rooney. Crabtree Publishing Company 2013 32 p. (Engineering in action) (pbk. : alk. paper) $9.95

Grades: 5 6 7 8 **629.1**

1. Aeronautics 2. Aerospace engineering 3. Airplanes -- Design and construction 4. Flight

ISBN 0778775003; 9780778774952; 9780778775003

LC 2012040538

This book, "part of the Engineering in Action series, presents a "glimpse at the basics of flight and what aerospace engineers do. The initial sections are about the history of flight, including information about how engineers use flight dynamics for their designs. The following sections lead readers through the design process from brainstorming to the actual aircraft testing. Two simple activities are included." (Booklist)

Includes bibliographical references and index

629.13 Aeronautics

Carson, Mary Kay

★ The **Wright** Brothers for kids; how they invented the airplane: 21 activities exploring the science and history of flight. illustrations by Laura D'Argo. Chicago Review Press 2003 146p il pa $14.95

Grades: 4 5 6 7 **629.13**

1. Inventors 2. Aeronautics -- History 3. Science -- Experiments 4. Aircraft industry executives

ISBN 1-55652-477-3

LC 2002-155449

This account of the Wright brothers' invention of the airplane, explains the forces of flight-lift, thrust, gravity, and drag and includes such activities as making a Chinese flying top, building a kite, bird watching, making a paper glider and a rubber-band-powered flyer

"A treasure trove of activities awaits readers of this wonderfully executed survey of the Wright brothers and their invention. The narrative flows easily and is complemented by numerous photographs that give a sense of history and this event. . . . This is a valuable resource for student reports and projects, and for classroom units." SLJ

Includes glossary and bibliographical references

Finkelstein, Norman H.

Three across; the great transatlantic air race of 1927. [by] Norman H. Finkelstein. Calkins Creek 2008 134p il $17.95

Grades: 5 6 7 8 **629.13**

1. Admirals 2. Generals 3. Explorers 4. Air pilots 5. Memoirists 6. Travel writers 7. Air force officers 8. Aeronautics -- History 9. Metal industry executives 10. Aircraft industry executives

ISBN 978-1-59078-462-4; 1-59078-462-6

LC 2007-18345

"Framing the story in way that should enthrall any aviation fan, Finklestein traces the rise of aviation from Kitty Hawk to the 1927 Orteig Prize, a $25,000 award for the first person to fly nonstop across the Atlantic. This book focuses on the first three flights to pull it off: the Spirit of St. Louis, piloted by Charles Lindbergh; the Columbia, led by ambitious shyster Charles A. Levine; and the America, boasting Arctic explorer Richard E. Byrd at the controls." Booklist

Includes bibliographical references

★ **Flight** and motion; the history and science of flying. M.E. Sharpe 2008 5v il set $325

Grades: 6 7 8 9 10 **629.13**

1. Reference books 2. Flight -- Encyclopedias 3. Aeronautics -- Encyclopedias

ISBN 978-0-7656-8100-3 set; 0-7656-8100-5 set

LC 2007030815

"Report writers as well as those simply interested in browsing will find much to hold their interest in this set, which provides comprehensive coverage of the history of aviation, including spaceflight, as well as the science and technology on which it depends." Booklist

Includes bibliographical references

Giblin, James

★ **Charles** A. Lindbergh; a human hero. [by] James Cross Giblin. Clarion Bks. 1997 212p il $22

Grades: 6 7 8 9 **629.13**

1. Generals 2. Air pilots 3. Memoirists 4. Air force officers

ISBN 0-395-63389-3

LC 96-9501

A biography of the pilot whose life was full of controversy and tragedy, but also fulfilling achievements

"This sympathetic and informed account (beautifully illustrated with contemporary photographs) is an excellent introduction to Lindbergh and also to the early years of the celebrity society in which we live now." N Y Times Book Rev

Includes bibliographical references

Hardesty, Von

Epic flights. Kingfisher 2011 il (Epic adventure) $19.99

Grades: 5 6 7 8 **629.13**

1. Aeronautics -- History

ISBN 978-0-7534-6669-8; 0-7534-6669-4

LC 2011041637

This describes Charles Lindbergh's transatlantic flight; the Breitling Orbiter 3 which set a record for non-stop around the world flight by balloon; the Apollo 11 flight to the moon; Amy Johnson's solo flight from England to Australia in a small bi-plane; and the Voyager, which set a record by flying non-stop around the world without refueling.

"The graphics will grab readers in [this] exciting, extra-large-size [title] . . . packed with high-quality color photos on every double-page spread. Just as gripping are the narratives, captions, and technical details of exploration, adventure, and survival." Booklist

Includes glossary

Hense, Mary

How fighter pilots use math; math curriculum consultant: Rhea A. Stewart. Chelsea Clubhouse 2010 32p il (Math in the real world) lib bdg $28

Grades: 4 5 6 **629.13**

1. Air pilots 2. Aeronautics 3. Mathematics 4.

Vocational guidance
ISBN 978-1-60413-605-0 lib bdg; 1-60413-605-7
lib bdg

LC 2009-20242

This describes how fighter pilots use math to judge speed, attain altitude, and maintain safety, and includes relevant math problems and information about how to become a fighter pilot

Includes glossary and bibliographical references

629.130   Biography of flight

Brown, Jeremy K.

Amelia Earhart; by Jeremy K. Brown. Chelsea House 2011 132p ill. (hardcover : acid-free paper) $35.00

Grades: 6 7 8 9   629.130

1. Biography 2. Women air pilots 3. Air pilots -- United States -- Biography 4. Women air pilots -- United States -- Biography 5. Cross-country flying -- History -- 20th century 6. Flights around the world -- History -- 20th century

ISBN 9781604139105

LC 2011000037

This book chronicles the life of female aviator Amelia Earhart. "From her . . . beginnings in a small Kansas town to her . . . solo flight across the Atlantic, Earhart defied expectations and rose to become the most famous female pilot of all time. Despite the restrictions placed on women of her era, she broke through barriers and refused to allow society to label her. As a result, she made history through her daring flights all over the world. In 1937, she disappeared without a trace while on a solo flight around the world." (Kids' Catalog Web)

Includes bibliographical references (p. 124-125) and index

629.133   Aircraft types

Faber, Harold

★ The airplane; [by] Harold Faber. Marshall Cavendish Benchmark 2006 128p il (Great inventions) lib bdg $37.07

Grades: 7 8 9 10   629.133

1. Airplanes 2. Aeronautics -- History
ISBN 0-7614-1876-8

LC 2004-22107

This is history of aviation and its influence on American history and culture.

This is presented "thoughtfully yet conversationally. . . . [It] will reward steady reading." Horn Book Guide

Includes glossary and bibliographical references

Greger, Margaret

Kites for everyone; how to make and fly them. diagrams by Del Greger. 3rd ed.; Dover Publications 2006 121p il pa $9.95

Grades: 7 8 9 10 11 12 Adult   629.133

1. Kites
ISBN 978-0-4864-5295-1 pa; 0-4864-5295-6 pa

LC 2006048453

First published 1984 by Richland, WA

This is a "guide with . . . illustrated instructions for creating more than 50 . . . airborne objects—everything from simple bag kites to Vietnamese, Snake, Dutch, Dragon, Bullet, Delta, and Flowform flyers." Publisher's note

Includes bibliographical references

Nahum, Andrew

Flying machine; written by Andrew Nahum. rev ed; DK Pub. 2004 72p il (DK eyewitness books) $15.99; lib bdg $19.99

Grades: 4 5 6 7   629.133

1. Aeronautics -- History
ISBN 0-7566-0680-2; 0-7566-0679-9 lib bdg
First published 1990 by Knopf

A photo essay tracing the history and development of aircraft from hot-air balloons to jetliners. Includes information on the principles of flight and the inner workings of various flying machines.

Oxlade, Chris

Airplanes; uncovering technology. Firefly Books 2006 52p il $16.95

Grades: 4 5 6 7   629.133

1. Airplanes
ISBN 1-55407-134-8

This offers "appealing visuals and plenty of well-chosen facts." SLJ

This "book covers civilian and military airplanes and helicopters as well as the pilots and engineers that put them in the air. . . . [The] book contains four acetate overlays, used in some cases to show changes over time, in others to show a cutaway interior." Publisher's note

629.2   Motor land vehicles, cycles

Mara, Wil

From locusts to...automobile anti-collision systems; by Wil Mara. Cherry Lake Pub. 2012 32 p. col. ill. (Innovations from nature) (library) $28.50; (e-book) $28.50; (paperback) $14.21

Grades: 4 5 6 7   629.2

1. Automobiles -- Collision avoidance systems 2. Locusts 3. Biomimicry
ISBN 1610805011; 9781610805018; 9781610805889; 9781610806756

LC 2012011856

"This . . . entry in the '21st Century Skills Innovation Library: Innovations from Nature' series explores how automobile manufacturers and scientists are trying to develop . . . collision avoidance systems based on the instincts of the humble locust, which has the ability to avoid oncoming objects while in a swarm. . . . [Wil] Mara describes the science of biomimicry, or 'the practice of copying nature--plants and animals--to build or improve something.'" (Booklist)

Includes bibliographical references (p. 31) and index.

Smith, Miranda

Speed machines; and other record-breaking vehicles. Kingfisher 2009 63p il (Kingfisher knowledge) $12.95

Grades: 5 6 7 8   **629.2**

1. Speed 2. Vehicles

ISBN 978-0-7534-6287-4; 0-7534-6287-7

"This well-organized, full-color book is packed with facts, photos, and history. It covers all aspects in history dealing with humankind's quest for speed, including land, water and air. . . . There are short blocks of main text and sidebars or blurbs to add additional information. Besides the usual suspects in books that cover this topic—cars, motorcycles, and planes—this book includes boats, gliders, hot air balloons, trains, and windsurfing among other speed machines. . . . It is an essential purchase, especially where books about racing, cars, planes, trucks, motorcycles, etc. are popular." Voice Youth Advocates

629.22 Types of vehicles

Balmer, Alden J.

Doc Fizzix mousetrap racers; the complete builder's manual. [by] Alden J. Balmer; [illustrations by Mike Harnisch] Fox Chapel 2008 142p il pa $14.95

Grades: 6 7 8 9   **629.22**

1. Physics 2. Automobiles -- Models

ISBN 978-1-56523-359-1; 1-56523-359-X

"Building a mousetrap-powered model racer is more complex than it first appears, and Balmer uses this project as a springboard for teaching principles of physics such as energy, forces, torque, friction, and traction. . . . The author's enthusiasm for the topic and for teaching are apparent throughout, and his focus on safety is consistent. The thorough instructions are complemented by clear, captioned, full-color photos and line drawings and diagrams that illustrate each step of the construction process." SLJ

Mackay, Jenny

Electric cars. Lucent Books 2011 104p il (Technology 360) $33.45

Grades: 7 8 9 10   **629.22**

1. Electric automobiles

ISBN 978-1-4205-0612-9; 1-4205-0612-9

LC 2011016597

This book describes the technology of electric cars.

Includes bibliographical references

629.222 Gasoline-powered, oil-powered, man-powered vehicles

Bearce, Stephanie

All about electric and hybrid cars; and who's driving them. Mitchell Lane Publishers 2009 47p il (Tell your parents) lib bdg $21.50

Grades: 4 5 6 7   **629.222**

1. Electric automobiles

ISBN 978-1-58415-763-2 lib bdg; 1-58415-763-1 lib bdg

LC 2009004528

This describes how hybrid and electric cars work and new inventions in the automotive industry, including vehicles powered by hydrogen and solar powered cars

Includes bibliographical references

Collier, James Lincoln

★ The automobile; by James Lincoln Collier. Marshall Cavendish Benchmark 2005 112p il (Great inventions) lib bdg $37.07

Grades: 7 8 9 10   **629.222**

1. Automobiles

ISBN 0-7614-1877-6

LC 2004-22109

This is a history of the automobile and its affects on American culture.

This is presented "thoughtfully yet conversationally. . . . [It] will reward steady reading." Horn Book Guide

Includes glossary and bibliographical references

Harmon, Dan

First car smarts; by Daniel E. Harmon. Rosen Pub. 2010 64p il (Get smart with your money) lib bdg $29.95; pa $12.95

Grades: 7 8 9 10 11 12   **629.222**

1. Automobiles

ISBN 978-1-4358-5269-3 lib bdg; 1-4358-5269-9 lib bdg; 978-1-4358-5544-1 pa; 1-4358-5544-2 pa

This is a guide to buying your first car and the costs of car ownership including maintanence and insurance.

This offers "practical information and advice. . . . The writing is accessible. . . . The [book is] heavily illustrated with large, clear, up-to-date photographs of teens." SLJ

Includes glossary and bibliographical references

Williams, Brian

Who invented the automobile? Arcturus Pub. 2010 46p il (Breakthroughs in science and technology) lib bdg $32.80

Grades: 5 6 7 8   **629.222**

1. Engines 2. Automobiles

ISBN 978-1-84837-681-6; 1-84837-681-2

LC 2010011019

Examines the history of the automobile.

This book is "divided into easy to read short chapters with large, colorful photographs and graphics on every page. . . . The added inserts provide additional information to engage readers and help them connect with the scientific details." Libr Media Connect

Woods, Bob

Hottest muscle cars; by Bob Woods. Enslow Publishers 2008 48p il (Wild wheels!) lib bdg $23.93; pa $7.95

Grades: 4 5 6 7 **629.222**

1. Automobiles

ISBN 978-0-7660-2872-2 lib bdg; 0-7660-2872-0 lib bdg; 978-0-7660-3611-6 pa; 0-7660-3611-1 pa

LC 2007007423

This focuses on "the beginning of America's love for muscle cars, and see why they are still loved today." Publisher's note

Includes glossary and bibliographical references

Hottest sports cars; by Bob Woods. Enslow Publishers 2008 48p il (Wild wheels!) lib bdg $23.93; pa $7.95

Grades: 4 5 6 7 **629.222**

1. Automobiles

ISBN 978-0-7660-2873-9 lib bdg; 0-7660-2873-9 lib bdg; 978-0-7660-3609-3 pa; 0-7660-3909-X pa

LC 2007007428

This focuses on "some of the world's most famous sports cars; how they began, and where they are going in the future." Publisher's note

Includes glossary and bibliographical references

629.227 Cycles

Haduch, Bill

★ **Go** fly a bike! the ultimate book about bicycle fun, freedom & science. illustrated by Chris Murphy. Dutton Children's Books 2004 83p il $16.99

Grades: 4 5 6 7 **629.227**

1. Cycling 2. Bicycles

ISBN 0-525-47024-7

Gives the history, science, types of cycles, safety and the basics and maintenance of bicycles

"Halftone cartoonlike illustrations are scattered throughout, and a funny fact or joke appears in an inset on most pages. . . . This is a versatile, fact-packed book that can work for both research and recreational reading." Booklist

Smedman, Lisa

From boneshakers to choppers; the rip-roaring history of motorcycles. Annick Press 2007 120p il $24.95; pa $14.95

Grades: 5 6 7 8 **629.227**

1. Motorcycles

ISBN 978-1-55451-016-0; 1-55451-016-3; 978-1-55451-015-3 pa; 1-55451-015-5 pa

"Smedman defines 'motorcycles' broadly enough to include everything from Harleys to Vespas, and even bicycles, in this lively, wide-ranging history. . . . Illustrated with a generous array of action photos, historical shots, and period advertisements." Booklist

Includes bibliographical references

Woods, Bob

Hottest motorcycles; by Bob Woods. Enslow Publishers 2008 48p il (Wild wheels!) lib bdg $23.93; pa $7.95

Grades: 4 5 6 7 **629.227**

1. Motorcycles

ISBN 978-0-7660-2874-6 lib bdg; 0-7660-2874-7 lib bdg; 978-0-7660-3608-6 pa; 0-7660-3608-1 pa

LC 2007007425

This focuses on "the motorcycle's beginning, the chopper phenomenon, and motorcycle racing." Publisher's note

Includes bibliographical references

629.28 Tests, driving, maintenance, repair

Miller, Malinda

Modern mechanics; maintaining tomorrow's green vehicles. Mason Crest Publishers 2011 64p il (New careers for the 21st century: finding your role in the global renewal) lib bdg $22.95

Grades: 7 8 9 10 **629.28**

1. Machinery 2. Mechanics (Persons) 3. Vocational guidance

ISBN 978-1-4222-1818-1 lib bdg; 1-4222-1818-X lib bdg

LC 2010016870

"Chapters identify and emphasize specific careers-important strengths, necessary aptitudes and interests, education and training, projected earnings, closely related occupations, type of work environment, and predictions for the future of the field. . . . Color photos have a small role amid the many statistics, figures, graphs and charts that support and supplement the . . . [text]." SLJ

Includes bibliographical references

629.4 Astronautics

Benoit, Peter

The **space** race; by Peter Benoit. Children's Press 2012 64 p. ill. (some col.) (library) $30.00; (paperback) $8.95

Grades: 4 5 6 **629.4**

1. Space flight 2. Astronautics -- Soviet Union -- History 3. Astronautics -- United States -- History 4. Space race -- History 5. Space flight -- History

ISBN 0531281655; 9780531230657; 9780531281659

LC 2011031454

This book by Peter Benoit is part of the "Cornerstones of Freedom" series. It "attempts to provide an historical overview of the race between the United States and Soviet Union to explore space. . . . The book ends with a map . . . a . . . list of influential individuals, a timeline, and a glossary." (Children's Literature)

Includes bibliographical references (p. 60-61) and index.

Bortz, Alfred B.

Seven wonders of space technology; by Fred Bortz. Twenty-First Century Books 2011 80p il (Seven wonders) lib bdg $33.26; ebook $24.95

Grades: 5 6 7 8 **629.4**

1. Astronautics 2. Space vehicles 3. Outer space --

Exploration
ISBN 978-0-7613-5453-6 lib bdg; 0-7613-5453-0 lib bdg; 9780761372806

LC 2010-23996

This book examines the science involved in the Great Observatories, the International Space Station, New Horizons, Moon bases and lunar water, Mars rovers, rocketry, and weather satellites. Glossary. Index. "Grades seven to twelve." (Sci Books Films)

"Highlights some of astronomy's greatest technical advancements, from land observatories to spinning satellites to moon bases. . . . [This] volume makes basic concepts clear in lively, energetic language that, along with the mesmerizing color photos and artists' renderings of space, will easily captivate a young audience, while up-to-date examples, including discoveries made in the last five years, will only increase the sense of immediacy and excitement." Booklist

Includes glossary and bibliographical references

Carlisle, Rodney P.

Exploring space; rev ed.; Chelsea House 2010 120p il (Discovery and exploration) lib bdg $35
Grades: 7 8 9 10   **629.4**
    1. Astronautics 2. Outer space -- Exploration
    ISBN 978-1-60413-188-8; 1-60413-188-8

LC 2009-25585

First published 2005 by Facts on File

This describes the history of space exploration, from early astronomers to first steps into space by Germans, Soviets, and Americans, space flight to the Moon, space stations, space shuttles, unmanned space exploration, the Hubble space telescope, radio telescopes, and possible future explorations

Includes glossary and bibliographical references

Chaikin, Andrew

★ **Space**; a history of space exploration in photographs. [by] Andrew Chaikin; foreword by James A. Lovell. Firefly Books 2004 249p il pa $24.95
Grades: 6 7 8 9   **629.4**
    1. Outer space -- Exploration
    ISBN 1-55297-987-3

First published 2002 in the United Kingdom

This is a "collection of more than 300 images that pay tribute to and trace the history of space exploration." Publisher's note

Crompton, Samuel

Sputnik /Explorer 1; the race to conquer space. [by] Samuel Willard Crompton. Chelsea House 2007 106p il (Milestones in American history) lib bdg $35
Grades: 7 8 9 10   **629.4**
    1. Astronautics 2. Space flight
    ISBN 0-7910-9357-3 lib bdg; 978-0-7910-9357-3 lib bdg

LC 2006034127

"This book begins in 1957 with Russia's successful launch of the first artificial sattelite. With the Cold War as a backdrop, the text goes on to describe the space race between the United States and Russia. . . . Many photographs,

quotations, and sidebars detail the roles played by key figures." Horn Book Guide

Includes bibliographical references

Harris, Joseph

Space exploration; impact of science and technology. Gareth Stevens Pub. 2010 64p il map (Pros and cons) lib bdg $35
Grades: 5 6 7 8   **629.4**
    1. Astronautics 2. Outer space -- Exploration
    ISBN 978-1-4339-1989-3 lib bdg; 1-4339-1989-3 lib bdg

LC 2009-12436

An "active layout that features color photographs, maps, graphs or charts on every spread, this . . . [book] has much to offer. . . . It conveniently outlines the range of views . . . helping students to learn how to view both sides of [the] issue[s]." SLJ

Includes glossary and bibliographical references

Jedicke, Peter

Great moments in space exploration. Chelsea House 2007 72p il (Scientific American) $30
Grades: 5 6 7 8   **629.4**
    1. Astronautics 2. Outer space -- Exploration
    ISBN 978-0-7910-9046-6; 0-7910-9046-9

LC 2006-14774

This "introduction to the history of space exploration is well illustrated with numerous photos, many from NASA. The history is well told, with the achievements of the Soviet Union, in particular, covered quite nicely." Sci Books Films

Includes glossary and bibliographical references

Miller, Ron

Space exploration. Twenty-First Century Books 2008 112p il (Space innovations) lib bdg $31.93
Grades: 4 5 6 7   **629.4**
    1. Astronautics 2. Outer space -- Exploration
    ISBN 978-0-8225-7155-1; 0-8225-7155-2

LC 2007002863

"Busy pages include text, photographs, sidebars, and diagrams. . . . The information . . . is accurate and focused." Horn Book Guide

"Ron Miller describes the long, hard trek from the first tentative attempts to fly rocket-powered vehicles, to the first humans to brave traveling beyond Earth's atmosphere, to the explorers who left their footprints in the soil of the Moon." Publisher's note

Includes glossary and bibliographical references

Nagel, Rob

Space exploration, Almanac; [by] Rob Nagel; Sarah Hermsen, project editor. U.X.L., Thomson Gale 2005 2v il (Space exploration reference library) set$115
Grades: 7 8 9 10   **629.4**
    1. Astronautics 2. Outer space -- Exploration
    ISBN 0-7876-9209-3

LC 2004-15823

Presenting key developments, discussion ranges from ancient views of a sun-centered universe to current understanding of planetary motion and gravity

Includes bibliographical references

Saari, Peggy

Space exploration. Primary sources; [by] Peggy Saari. U.X.L, Thomson Gale 2005 203p il (Space exploration reference library) $63

Grades: 7 8 9 10   **629.4**
1. Astronautics
ISBN 0-7876-9213-1

LC 2004-15879

This volume contains excerpts from 17 documents and speeches, beginning with a chapter from a Jules Verne book and ending with remarks made in early 2004 by George W. Bush on a new vision for space exploration. Each selection is introduced with material on the context, key points, and information on the author

Includes glossary and bibliographical references

Skurzynski, Gloria

★ **This** is rocket science; true stories of the risk-taking scientists who figure out ways to explore beyond Earth. National Geographic 2010 80p il $18.95; lib bdg $28.90

Grades: 5 6 7 8   **629.4**
1. Rocketry 2. Aeronautics 3. Aerospace engineers
ISBN 978-1-4263-0597-9; 1-4263-0597-4; 978-1-4263-0598-6 lib bdg; 1-4263-0598-2 lib bdg
LC 2009-20386

"This concise book provides a historical, as well as contemporary, introduction to the field of aeronautical engineering with a decidedly human interest perspective. . . . This text will be a great introduction to many of the significant contributors to the field of rocket science." Sci Books Films

Includes glossary and bibliographical references

Stott, Carole

Space exploration; written by Carole Stott; photographed by Steve Gorton. Dorling Kindersley 2009 71p il (DK eyewitness books) $16.99

Grades: 4 5 6 7   **629.4**
1. Astronautics 2. Outer space -- Exploration
ISBN 978-0-7566-5828-1; 0-7566-5828-4
First published 1997 by Knopf

Describes rockets, exploratory vehicles, and other technological aspects of space exploration, satellites, space stations, and the life and work of astronauts.

629.4092   Astronautical engineers

Waxman, Laura Hamilton

Aerospace engineer Aprille Ericsson; by Laura Hamilton Waxman. Lerner Publications 2015 32 p. color illustrations (STEM trailblazer bios) (lib. bdg. : alk. paper) $26.60

Grades: 4 5 6 7   **629.4092**
1. Women engineers 2. Aerospace engineers -- United States -- Biography 3. African American women

aerospace engineers -- United States -- Biography
ISBN 1467757934; 9781467757935; 9781467761185
LC 2014013767

In this biography by Laura Hamilton Waxman, readers learn how "Aprille Ericsson's passion for science has helped her pave the way for future engineers. Ericsson was one of the few girls in her middle school who loved math and science. Years later, she became the first woman to receive a PhD in mechanical engineering from Howard University. At NASA, she's helped build spacecraft that can map the moon, monitor climate change, or even bring soil and rocks back from Mars." (Publisher's note)

"Highly recommended, especially where current biographies, particularly of those involved in STEM careers, are needed and requested; strong supplemental reading for science classes, too." SLJ

Includes bibliographical references and index

629.43   Unmanned space flight

Kerrod, Robin

★ **Space** probes; [by] Robin Kerrod. World Almanac Library 2005 48p il (History of space exploration) hardcover o.p. lib bdg $30

Grades: 5 6 7 8   **629.43**
1. Space probes
ISBN 0-8368-5708-9 lib bdg; 0-8368-5715-1 pa
LC 2004-48207

Discusses how technology has changed the way we look at the celestial bodies of our Solar System, and examines how the space probes have helped discover black holes, star clusters, and nebulae

This "is profusely illustrated with sharply reproduced space photos and artists' conceptions. . . . [This] makes an important addition for any collection supporting avid young scientists or strong science curricula." SLJ

Includes bibliographical references

Miller, Ron

Robot explorers. Twenty-First Century Books 2007 112p il (Space innovations) lib bdg $31.93

Grades: 4 5 6   **629.43**
1. Robots 2. Space probes
ISBN 978-0-8225-7152-0 lib bdg; 0-8225-7152-8 lib bdg

LC 2007002864

This describes how robots are used for space exploration

Includes bibliographical references

Siy, Alexandra

★ **Cars** on Mars; roving the red planet. Charlesbridge 2009 57p il $18.95

Grades: 5 6 7 8   **629.43**
1. Space vehicles 2. Mars (Planet) -- Exploration
ISBN 978-1-57091-462-1; 1-57091-462-1
LC 2008-40751

Presents an introduction to the Mars Exploration Rovers (MERS), 'Spirit' and 'Opportunity,' with photographs of the Mars landscape taken over a five-year period as the rovers searched for water on the red planet

"This title will sweep readers up in an exploratory mission that has come closer than any other so far to finding sure signs of extraterrestrial life." SLJ

Includes glossary and bibliographical references

629.44 Auxiliary spacecraft

Cole, Michael D.

The **Columbia** space shuttle disaster; from first liftoff to tragic final flight. Enslow Pubs. 2003 48p il (Countdown to space) lib bdg $18.95

Grades: 4 5 6   629.44

1. Space vehicle accidents 2. Columbia (Space shuttle)
ISBN 0-7660-2295-1

LC 2003-4823

First published 1995 with title: Columbia

Details the first flight of the space shuttle Columbia, as well as its tragic final flight

"The account offers a lot of information, helping to make sense of a highly complicated subject. . . . The color and b&w photographs complement the story." Libr Media Connect

Includes glossary and bibliographical references

Holden, Henry M.

The **coolest** job in the universe; working aboard the International Space Station. Henry M. Holden. Enslow 2013 48 p. (American space missions, astronauts, exploration, and discovery) (hbk.) $23.93

Grades: 4 5 6 7 8   629.44

1. International Space Station 2. Space flight 3. Space sciences 4. Manned space flight 5. Space sciences -- Research
ISBN 0766040747; 9780766040748

LC 2012002222

This book, by Henry M. Holden, is part of the "American Space Missions: Astronauts, Exploration, and Discovery" series. In it the daily life of astronauts working on the International Space Station is explored. This book "focuses on the construction of the ISS, what life is like onboard, and the importance of the research projects conducted. . . . Throughout, the courage, dedication, and sacrifice of the astronauts are emphasized." (School Library Journal)

Includes bibliographical references (p. 43-45, 47) and index

Kerrod, Robin

Space shuttles; [by] Robin Kerrod. World Almanac Library 2005 48p il (History of space exploration) hardcover o.p. lib bdg $30

Grades: 5 6 7 8   629.44

1. Space shuttles
ISBN 0-8368-5709-7 lib bdg; 0-8368-5716-X pa

LC 2004-49217

Explores the successes of the shuttle program, including the daring recovery and repair of satellites by space-walking astronauts, and examines the human and technological costs of its tragic failures, such as the losses the Challenger and Columbia

This "is profusely illustrated with sharply reproduced space photos and artists' conceptions. . . . [This] makes an

important addition for any collection supporting avid young scientists or strong science curricula." SLJ

Includes bibliographical references

Space stations; [by] Robin Kerrod. World Almanac Library 2005 48p il (History of space exploration) hardcover o.p. lib bdg $30

Grades: 5 6 7 8   629.44

1. Space stations
ISBN 0-8368-5710-0 lib bdg; 0-8368-5717-8 pa

LC 2004-49071

Explores the history of space homes such as the Soviet's Salyut 1, Mir, the United States's Skylab, and the International Space Station, a truly international venture between several countries and scheduled for completion in 2008

This "is profusely illustrated with sharply reproduced space photos and artists' conceptions. . . . [This] makes an important addition for any collection supporting avid young scientists or strong science curricula." SLJ

Includes bibliographical references

Miller, Ron

Satellites; by Ron Miller. Twenty-First Century Books 2007 112p il (Space innovations) lib bdg $31.93

Grades: 7 8 9 10   629.44

1. Artificial satellites
ISBN 978-0-8225-7154-4

LC 2007001075

This "begins with the science of Newton, the history of rockets, and the vivid imaginations of nineteenth-century science-fiction writers. It traces the historical development of man-made satellites from Sputnik 1 to the Earth orbiters currently transmitting everything from Earth-based communications signals to images of the universe. . . . Illustrations include many small color photos and some paintings, diagrams, satellite images, and black-and-white photos. . . . Miller synthesizes his evident research into a well-organized discussion." Booklist

Includes bibliographical references

629.45 Manned space flight

Bodden, Valerie

Man walks on the Moon. Creative Education 2009 48p il map (Days of change) $32.80

Grades: 5 6 7 8   629.45

1. Space flight to the moon 2. Project Apollo
ISBN 978-1-58341-735-5; 1-58341-735-4

LC 2008009166

"With elegant design and mature prose, the Days of Change series is an ideal starting point for all manner of school projects. . . . The very first page of Man Walks on the Moon questions whether or not the feat was worth the resources, before reveling in the tech-heavy details of spaceflight and offering up some telling photos." Booklist

Includes bibliographical references

To the moon; by Valerie Bodden. Creative Education 2011 48 p. col. ill. (Great expeditions) (paperback) $12.00; (hardcover) $34.25

Grades: 5 6 7 8   **629.45**

1. Apollo project 2. Space flight to the moon -- History 3. Project Apollo (U.S.) -- History

ISBN 1608180689; 9780898126662; 9781608180684

LC 2010033549

This book by Valerie Bodden on the 1969 moon landing is part of the "Great Expeditions" series. "This factual account is . . . accompanied with both black and white and color photographs. Profiles of four of the astronauts, reproductions of some of their significant journal entries, and inset boxes of supplemental information aid in understanding. Includes a table of contents, a timeline, end notes, a bibliography, and an index." (Children's Literature)

Includes bibliographical references (p. 46-47) and index.

Chaikin, Andrew

★ **Mission** control, this is Apollo; the story of the first voyages to the moon. [by] Andrew Chaikin, with Victoria Kohl; [with paintings by] Alan Bean. Penguin Group 2009 114p il $23.99

Grades: 5 6 7 8 9   **629.45**

1. Astronautics 2. Space flight to the moon 3. Project Apollo

ISBN 978-0-670-01156-8; 0-670-01156-8

LC 2009000833

"Based on interviews with 28 astronauts, this history of the Apollo program masterfully describes the missions and personalizes them with astronauts' own words. Chaikin starts with a brief overview of its origins and of the Mercury and Gemini missions. He then highlights the significance of each manned Apollo mission in chronological chapters, with full-page sidebars on such topics as food, TV coverage, space sickness and going to the bathroom in space. The handsome design has many photographs, diagrams of the rockets and modules and more than 30 well-reproduced paintings by Apollo 12 astronaut Bean." Kirkus

Includes bibliographical references

Collins, Michael

Flying to the moon; an astronaut's story. 2nd ed, with a preface & a revised final chapter; Farrar, Straus & Giroux 1994 162p il pa $6.95

Grades: 5 6 7 8   **629.45**

1. Astronauts 2. Space flight to the moon

ISBN 0-374-42356-3

LC 93-42001

First published 1976 with title: Flying to the moon, and other strange places

The author recounts his early days as an Air Force test pilot, his NASA training and his experiences aboard Gemini 10 and the Apollo 11 mission to the moon. Collins also advocates continued exploration of the universe

"A well told tale, which includes a lot of easily explained science." BAYA Book Rev

Dell, Pamela

Man on the moon; how a photograph made anything seem possible. Compass Point Books 2011 64p il (Captured history) lib bdg $33.99

Grades: 6 7 8 9   **629.45**

1. Astronauts 2. Documentary photography 3. Space flight to the moon 4. Project Apollo 5. Air force officers 6. Nonfiction writers

ISBN 978-0-7565-4396-9; 0-7565-4396-7

LC 2010038577

This book about the iconic photograph of Neil Armstrong walking on the moon, taken by fellow astronaut Buzz Aldrin, places the photo "in historical context, profiles the photographer, describes the conditions under which it was taken, and analyzes both its immediate and its continuing impact. The [text includes] ample background information and details and [is] enhanced by large photos and sidebars." SLJ

Includes glossary and bibliographical references

Dyson, Marianne J.

Home on the moon; living on a space frontier. National Geographic Soc. 2003 64p il $18.95

Grades: 4 5 6 7   **629.45**

1. Moon

ISBN 0-7922-7193-9

LC 2002-5280

Considers the moon as a frontier that has been only partially explored, looking at its history, geography, and weather, as well as what people would require to live and work there. Includes activities

"Clear writing, vivid images, interesting details, and quotes from astronauts and scientists make this a lively, fact-filled introduction." Booklist

Includes glossary and bibliographical references

Godwin, Robert

Project Apollo; exploring the Moon. Apogee Books 2006 49p il (Pocket space guide) pa $9.95

Grades: 7 8 9 10 11 12   **629.45**

1. Space flight to the moon 2. Project Apollo 3. Moon -- Exploration

ISBN 978-1-894959-37-7 pa; 1-894959-37-X pa

LC 2007-5457

"Facts and images for Apollo missions 12 through 17 are covered in this concise guide to the program's essentials— mission objectives, dates, flight plans, astronauts, space suits, and vehicles—for collectors, educators, space enthusiasts, and those just discovering the history of the space program." Publisher's note

Goodman, Susan

Ultimate field trip 5; blasting off to Space Academy. by Susan E. Goodman; photographs by Michael J. Doolittle. Atheneum Bks. for Young Readers 2001 41p il hardcover o.p. $17

Grades: 4 5 6 7   **629.45**

1. Astronauts 2. Space flight 3. U.S. Space Camp (Huntsville, Ala.)

ISBN 0-689-83044-0; 0-689-84863-3 pa

LC 00-38082

"This book follows student trainees through a weeklong session at the U.S. Space Academy in Huntsville, AL, as they are exposed to what it takes to become an astronaut and to the inner workings of the entire space program. . . . Varied-colored pages, replete with outstanding full-color, captioned photos, are artistically appealing as well as informative." SLJ

Includes glossary and bibliographical references

Goodman, Susan E.

How do you burp in space? and other tips every space tourist needs to know. by Susan Goodman ; illustrated by Michael Slack. Bloomsbury Pub."||"Distributed by Macmillan Publishers 2013 80 p. (hardback) $16.99

Grades: 4 5 6   **629.45**
1. Space flight 2. Interplanetary voyages 3. Space tourism 4. Manned space flight
ISBN 1599900688; 9781599900681; 9781599909349
    LC 2011035303

In this children's book, author Susan E. Goodman "gives readers who will be the first generation of true space tourists general advice about how to prepare for the trip, what to pack, what food and accommodations will be like, and recreational opportunities both in Earth's orbit and on the moon. She also highlights some hazards, such as drinking carbonated drinks: Burping in microgravity brings up more than just CO2." (Kirkus Reviews)

Green, Carl R.

Spacewalk; the astounding Gemini 4 mission. Carl R. Green. Enslow Publishers 2013 48 p. $23.93

Grades: 4 5 6 7 8   **629.45**
1. Gemini project 2. Outer space 3. Space flight 4. Project Gemini (U.S.) -- History
ISBN 0766040755; 9780766040755
    LC 2011030869

This children's book, by Carl R. Green, "explores the astounding GEMINI 4 mission. . . . Pilot Ed White could see Hawaii, California, Texas, and Florida . . . while walking in space! . . . The first American spacewalk was a monumental achievement, and it helped push the space program toward its ultimate goal of landing men on the Moon." (Publisher's note)

Includes bibliographical references and index

Hartman, Eve

Mission to Mars; [by] Eve Hartman and Wendy Meshbesher. Raintree 2010 56p il (Science missions) lib bdg $33.50; pa $9.49

Grades: 5 6 7 8   **629.45**
1. Space flight to Mars 2. Mars (Planet)
ISBN 9781-4109-3821-3 lib bdg; 1-4109-3821-2 lib bdg; 978-1-4109-3996-8 pa; 1-4109-3996-0 pa
    LC 2009-53209

"Excellent black-and-white and color photos throughout are matched perfectly to the texts and well captioned. Good choices for reports and debates." SLJ

"Will human beings ever explore Mars? Can it be colonized? Find out in this fascinating book on Martian exploration." (Publisher's note)

Includes glossary and bibliographical references

Hense, Mary

How astronauts use math; math curriculum consultant: Rhea A. Stewart. Chelsea Clubhouse 2010 32p il (Math in the real world) lib bdg $28

Grades: 4 5 6   **629.45**
1. Astronauts 2. Mathematics 3. Astronautics 4. Vocational guidance
ISBN 978-1-60413-610-4 lib bdg; 1-60413-610-3 lib bdg
    LC 2009-23926

This describes how astronauts use math for such tasks as calculating distance, speed, and velocity, and includes relevant math problems and information about how to become an astronaut

Includes glossary and bibliographical references

Holden, Henry M.

Danger in space; surviving the Apollo 13 disaster. Henry M. Holden. Enslow Publishers 2013 48 p. $23.93

Grades: 4 5 6 7 8   **629.45**
1. Apollo project 2. Picture books for children 3. Apollo 13 (Spacecraft) 4. Project Apollo (U.S.) 5. Space vehicle accidents -- United States
ISBN 0766040720; 9780766040724
    LC 2011037734

This children's picture book tells the story of the U.S. National Aerospace and Space Administration's Apollo 13 mission. "Soaring through space at twenty-five thousand miles per hour, Apollo 13 was on course for the Moon. Suddenly, the three astronauts aboard the spacecraft heard a loud bang. A strong vibration rumbled through the crew cabin. There had been an explosion in the oxygen tank! More than two hundred thousand miles from Earth, Apollo 13 was in grave danger." (Publisher's note)

Includes bibliographical references and index

Kuhn, Betsy

★ The race for space; the United States and Soviet Union compete for the new frontier. Lerner 2006 112p il (People's history) lib bdg $31.93

Grades: 6 7 8 9   **629.45**
1. Astronautics
ISBN 978-0-8225-5984-9 lib bdg; 0-8225-5984-6 lib bdg

"Kuhn has seamlessly woven the history into a compelling story." Booklist

Includes bibliographical references

Ottaviani, Jim

T -Minus: the race to the moon; [illustrated by] Zander Cannon, Kevin Cannon. Aladdin 2009 124p il $21.99; pa $12.99

Grades: 4 5 6 7 8 9 10 11 12 Adult   **629.45**
1. Graphic novels 2. Apollo project -- Graphic novels 3. Gemini project -- Graphic novels 4. Space flight to the moon -- Graphic novels
ISBN 978-1-4169-8682-9; 1-4169-8682-0; 978-1-4169-4960-2 pa; 1-4169-4960-7 pa
    LC 2009-920999

Ottaviani, Zander Cannon, and Kevin Cannon show what happened when the U.S. and the U.S.S.R. started the space race in the 1950s, and how it progressed to the NASA Apollo 11 mission which landed two men on the moon in July of 1969.

"Organized as a countdown, making the outcome seem inevitable, the frequent, prominent sidebars list a type of rocket, the duration of its flight, and whether the mission was a success or a failure. There are more than 30 attempts chronicled, and the shift between Soviet and U.S. successes creates an interesting balance in the narrative. . . . Ottaviani is particular with facts and eager to inspire readers with regard to the scientific process." SLJ

Platt, Richard

★ **Moon** landing; a pop-up celebration of Apollo 11. by Richard Platt; paper engineering by David Hawcock. Candlewick Press 2008 un il $29.99

Grades: 4 5 6 7   **629.45**

1. Space flight to the moon 2. Pop-up books 3. Apollo 11 (Spacecraft)

ISBN 978-0-7636-4046-0; 0-7636-4046-8

"This is a handsome, carefully engineered compendium. The text begins with the so-called space race between the United States and the Soviet Union in the 1950s and '60s and then offers brief descriptions of the 17 flights that made up the Apollo program. Here the emphasis is on the famous landing of the Eagle on the Moon in July 1969. The pop-ups and foldout pages on sturdy, shiny paper demonstrate the mechanical aspects of the spacecraft and offer a bold sense of both the rocketry and the trip. Small photographs and drawings surround the larger views." SLJ

Ross, Stewart

Moon : science, history, and mystery. Scholastic 2009 128p il lib bdg $18.99

Grades: 4 5 6   **629.45**

1. Astronautics 2. Space flight to the moon 3. Project Apollo 4. Moon -- Exploration

ISBN 978-0-545-12732-5 lib bdg; 0-545-12732-7 lib bdg

"Jam-packed with information, this colorful oversize volume chronicles the race to land a person on the Moon. Alternating chapters describe Moon mythologies and superstitions, the history of astronomical study, and the efforts involved in launching a lunar expedition. . . . The photographs pop with color and action. . . . The invaluable contribution of Muslim scientists is included. . . . [The book's] multicultural history will expand any collection." SLJ

Includes glossary

Saari, Peggy

Space exploration, Biographies; [by] Peggy Saar; Lawrence W. Baker, Sarah Hermsen, and Deborah J. Baker, project editors. U.X.L, Thomson Gale 2005 219p il (Space exploration reference library) $63

Grades: 7 8 9 10   **629.45**

1. Astronauts 2. Outer space -- Exploration

ISBN 0-7876-9212-3

LC 2004-15822

This volume profiles 25 astronauts, scientists, theorists, and writers involved in space exploration, including Sally

Ride, Yuri A. Gagarin, Neil Armstrong, John H. Glenn, Jr., Ellen Ochoa, Hermann Oberth and others

Includes bibliographical references

Solway, Andrew

Can we travel to the stars? space flight and space exploration. Heinemann Library 2006 48p il (Stargazers guides) lib bdg $31.43; pa $8.99

Grades: 4 5 6   **629.45**

1. Astronautics 2. Space flight 3. Interplanetary voyages 4. Outer space -- Exploration

ISBN 978-1-4034-7711-8 lib bdg; 1-4034-7711-6 lib bdg; 978-1-4034-7718-7 pa; 1-4034-7718-3 pa

LC 2005-29086

Realistically explores the possibility of mankind ever achieving the goal of traveling to the planets and to other stars

This book "is clearly written and engaging . . . . with just the right level of information and explanation." Horn Book Guide

Includes glossary and bibliographical references

Stone, Tanya Lee

★ **Almost** astronauts; 13 women who dared to dream. Candlewick Press 2008 133p il $24.99; pa $17.99

Grades: 5 6 7 8 9 10   **629.45**

1. Women astronauts 2. Sex discrimination 3. Project Mercury -- History 8. Sex discrimination against women

ISBN 0-7636-3611-8; 0-7636-4502-8 pa; 978-0-7636-3611-1; 978-0-7636-4502-1 pa

LC 2008-17487

Boston Globe-Horn Book Award honor book: Nonfiction (2009)

This book "explores the little known experiences of 13 brave, inspiring women who dreamed of becoming astronauts in the very early days of NASA's training program and submitted themselves to many of the tests undertaken by their male counterparts, the Mercury 7." Tanya Lee Stone "brings together a variety of primary and secondary sources, including her interviews with some of the women involved, to provide a unique view of the challenges faced by the female pilots of the day." (School Library Journal)

"In 1960, thirteen American women passed the physical exams required to become astronauts as surely as any of the men already involved in NASA's early space flight endeavors, but they were disqualified solely because of their gender. This book is their story. . . . Any girl with an interest in space flight or the history of women's rights will enjoy this account and applaud these courageous pioneers." Voice Youth Advocates

Includes bibliographical references

Thimmesh, Catherine

★ **Team** moon; how 400,000 people landed Apollo 11 on the moon. Houghton Mifflin Company 2006 80p il $19.95

Grades: 5 6 7 8   **629.45**

1. Space flight to the moon 2. Apollo 11 (Spacecraft)

ISBN 0-618-50757-4

LC 2005-10755

"Thimmesh retraces the course of the space mission that landed an actual man, on the actual Moon. It's an oft-told tale, but the author tells it from the point of view not of astronauts or general observers, but of some of the 17,000 behind-the-scenes workers at Kennedy Space Center, the 7500 Grumman employees who built the lunar module, the 500 designers and seamstresses who actually constructed the space suits, and other low-profile contributors who made the historic flight possible. . . . This dramatic account will mesmerize even readers already familiar with the event. . . . This stirring, authoritative tribute to the collective effort . . . belongs in every collection." SLJ

Includes glossary and bibliographical references

629.46   Engineering of unmanned spacecraft

Johnson, Rebecca L.
Satellites. Lerner Publications Co. 2006 48p il (Cool science) lib bdg $25.26
Grades: 4 5 6   629.46
    1. Artificial satellites
    ISBN 978-0-8225-2908-8 lib bdg; 0-8225-2908-4 lib bdg
                                        LC 2004-30298
This book has "an attractive, colorful layout that will appeal to readers. Each spread includes captioned, color photographs and/or illustrations; text boxes; and, often, a 'fun fact.' . . . [This] title explains what a satellite is and discusses many aspects of satellites, including how they pertain to television broadcasts, weather forecasting, and locating black holes. Numerous amazing facts are included to pique readers' interest." SLJ

Includes bibliographical references

629.8   Automatic control engineering

Chaffee, Joel
How to build a prize-winning robot. Rosen Central 2011 48p il (Robotics) lib bdg $26.50; pa $11.75
Grades: 5 6 7 8   629.8
    1. Robots
    ISBN 978-1-4488-1238-7 lib bdg; 1-4488-1238-0 lib bdg; 978-1-4488-2252-2 pa; 1-4488-2252-1 pa
                                        LC 2010025748
"Kids who are fascinated with robots will want [this title] available." SLJ

"This book explains how to build a competitive robot and it encourages readers to take a try at this thrilling pastime." Publisher's note

Includes glossary and bibliographical references

Freedman, Jeri
Robots through history. Rosen Central 2011 48p il (Robotics) lib bdg $26.50; pa $11.75

Grades: 5 6 7 8   629.8
    1. Robots
    ISBN 978-1-4488-1236-3 lib bdg; 1-4488-1236-4 lib bdg; 978-1-4488-2250-8 pa; 1-4488-2250-5 pa
                                        LC 2010024139
"Kids who are fascinated with robots will want [this title] available." SLJ

"This book shows the fascinating development of robots through the ages. Readers will learn about the invention of the earliest robotlike mechanical devices, the advent of electronics, the first instances of robot automation, and the development of artificial intelligence." Publisher's note

Includes glossary and bibliographical references

Graham, Ian
Robot technology. Smart Apple Media 2012 il (New technology)
Grades: 4 5 6 7   629.8
    1. Robots
    ISBN 1-599-20533-5; 978-1-599-20533-5
                                        LC 2010044240
Describes current robotics technology, including the applications of robots in space, in the military, in industry, and around the house. Discusses the pros and cons of creating fully autonomous robots.

This "offers a fine overview for reports, and its attractive design may also entice middle-grade readers to learn more." Booklist

Mackay, Jenny
Robots. Lucent Books 2010 104p il (Technology 360) $32.45
Grades: 8 9 10 11 12   629.8
    1. Robots
    ISBN 978-1-4205-0168-1; 1-4205-0168-2
                                        LC 2009045634
This book explores "the early development and advances of [robotics], its impact on society both positive and negative, and the importance it plays in our lives. . . . [It] describes the technical aspects of movement, artificial intelligence, and robots of the future. . . . Numerous color photos, diagrams, 'Bits & Bytes' boxes as well as many other additional text boxes create appeal and provide beneficial informative and complementary material to aid in understanding the technical details of the [text]." SLJ

Includes glossary and bibliographical references

Mercer, Bobby
The **Robot** book; build and control 20 electric gizmos, machines, and hacked toys. Bobby Mercer. Chicago Review Press Inc. 2014 208 p. illustrations (Science in motion) (trade paper) $14.95
Grades: 4 5 6   629.8
    1. Machinery 2. Robots 3. Robotics 4. Personal robotics
    ISBN 1556524072; 9781556524073
                                        LC 2014015327
In this book author "Bobby Mercer will show you how to turn common household objects and repurposed materials into 20 easy-to-build robots for little or no cost. Every hands-on project contains a materials list and detailed step-by-step instructions with photos for easy assembly. Mercer

also explains the science and technology behind each robot, including concepts such as friction, weight and mass, [and] center of gravity." (Publisher's note)

"A solid starting point for readers with an interest in circuitry or engineering—or who simply like to take things apart to see how they work." Publishers Weekly

Payment, Simone

Robotics careers; preparing for the future. Rosen Central 2011 48p il (Robotics) lib bdg $26.50; pa $11.75

Grades: 5 6 7 8   **629.8**
    1. Robots 2. Vocational guidance
    ISBN 978-1-4488-1239-4 lib bdg; 1-4488-1239-9 lib bdg; 978-1-4488-2253-9 pa; 1-4488-2253-X pa
                 LC 2010024134

"Kids who are fascinated with robots will want [this title] available." SLJ

Includes glossary and bibliographical references

Shea, Therese

The **robotics** club; teaming up to build robots. Rosen Central 2011 48p il (Robotics) lib bdg $26.50; pa $11.75

Grades: 5 6 7 8   **629.8**
    1. Clubs 2. Robots
    ISBN 978-1-4488-1237-0 lib bdg; 1-4488-1237-2 lib bdg; 978-1-4488-2251-5 pa; 1-4488-2251-3 pa

This title "will provide students with the information necessary to form a club and compete at making and using robots. Kids who are fascinated with robots will want [this title] available." SLJ

Sobey, Ed

Robot experiments. Enslow Publishers 2011 128p il (Cool science projects with technology) lib bdg $31.93

Grades: 6 7 8 9   **629.8**
    1. Robots 2. Science projects 3. Science -- Experiments
    ISBN 978-0-7660-3303-0; 0-7660-3303-1
                 LC 2009037897

While this book "includes some suggestions for science-fair projects and a few experiments throughout, it also provides a detailed description of each component and step-by-step instruction for building a robot. This highly complicated process is explained using understandable terms and in a well-organized manner and includes information as detailed as computer-programming codes." SLJ

Includes glossary and bibliographical references

Stefoff, Rebecca

Robots. Marshall Cavendish Benchmark 2007 144p il (Great inventions) lib bdg $27.95

Grades: 6 7 8 9   **629.8**
    1. Robots
    ISBN 978-0-7614-2601-1

This is a history of robots in the imagination, from ancient myths to motion pictures, and in reality, including toy robots and robots in medicine, manufacturing, the military, science, and space exploration

Includes glossary and bibliographical references

VanVoorst, Jennifer

Rise of the thinking machines; the science of robots. Compass Point Books 2009 48p il (Headline science) lib bdg $27.93; pa $7.95

Grades: 5 6 7   **629.8**
    1. Robots
    ISBN 978-0-7565-3377-9 lib bdg; 0-7565-3377-5 lib bdg; 978-0-7565-3518-6 pa; 0-7565-3518-2 pa
                 LC 2008-05732

"Describes various types of robots and their functions, discusses technological advancements in the field of robotics, and considers the ethical issues surrounding autonomous robots." Publisher's note

Includes glossary and bibliographical references

Woog, Adam

SCRATCHbot. Norwood House Press 2010 48p il (A great idea) lib bdg $25.27

Grades: 3 4 5 6   **629.8**
    1. Robots
    ISBN 978-1-59953-380-3 lib bdg; 1-59953-380-4 lib bdg
                 LC 2010008502

"Woog introduces a small, rolling robot with prominent whiskers, used to mimic a rodent's ability to sense its surroundings through touch. Discussions include how inventors are inspired by nature and how this appealing robot might be useful. Presenting specific, current information, [this book] will appeal to young people intrigued by inventions." Booklist

Includes glossary and bibliographical references

630 Agriculture and related technologies

Apte, Sunita

Eating green. Bearport Pub. 2009 32p il map (Going green) lib bdg $25.27

Grades: 4 5 6 7   **630**
    1. Natural foods 2. Sustainable agriculture
    ISBN 978-1-59716-965-3 lib bdg; 1-59716-965-X lib bdg
                 LC 2009-19183

"Color photographs (most full page) and a few diagrams accompany the informative text. . . . Overall, the [book] . . . is user-friendly and covers topics that are not easily found elsewhere." SLJ

Includes glossary and bibliographical references

Bailey, Gerry

Farming for the future. Gareth Stevens Pub. 2011 48p il (Planet SOS) lib bdg $31.95; pa $14.05

Grades: 4 5 6   **630**
    1. Agriculture 2. Food supply
    ISBN 978-1-4339-4966-1 lib bdg; 1-4339-4966-0 lib bdg; 978-1-4339-4967-8 pa; 1-4339-4967-9 pa
                 LC 2010032887

This well-designed book presents farming methods "and how they affect human beings. . . . [It] includes a chapter on new types of farms and foods. . . . The many large, colorful photos will engage readers and assist them in understanding the important concepts introduced." SLJ

Includes glossary

Casper, Julie Kerr

Agriculture; the food we grow and animals we raise. Chelsea House 2007 210p il (Natural resources) $39.50

Grades: 8 9 10 11 12   630

1. Agriculture

ISBN 978-0-8160-6352-9; 0-8160-6352-4

LC 2006027454

This "explores why managing the land, water, and soil is a balancing act and why recycling, reducing, and reusing are concepts that affect everyone—now and in the future." Publisher's note

Includes bibliographical references

Hopkins, William G.

Plant biotechnology. Chelsea House 2006 143p il (The green world) lib bdg $37.50

Grades: 7 8 9 10   630

1. Plants 2. Biotechnology 3. Food -- Biotechnology

ISBN 0-7910-8964-9

"This is a highly accurate, very well written book about both the history of and current innovations in, plant biotechnology. The illustrative pictures are clear and attractive." Sci Books Films

Includes bibliographical references

Johanson, Paula

Jobs in sustainable agriculture. Rosen Pub. 2010 80p il (Green careers) lib bdg $30.60

Grades: 7 8 9 10   630

1. Vocational guidance 2. Sustainable agriculture

ISBN 978-1-4358-3568-9 lib bdg; 1-4358-3568-9 lib bdg

LC 2009014426

In this book "only one chapter is devoted to farm-based employment; work in a slaughterhouse, a recycling plant, in transportation, and in restaurant management are given equal space. Careers in research or legislative work are also considered. . . . [This] slim [title is] well organized and [contains] informatively captioned color photos." SLJ

Includes glossary and bibliographical references

Parker, Steve, 1952-

Food and farming. QEB Pub. 2010 32p il (QEB changes in . . .) lib bdg $28.50

Grades: 3 4 5 6   630

1. Farms 2. Agriculture 3. Food supply

ISBN 978-1-59566-775-5 lib bdg; 1-59566-775-X lib bdg

LC 2008-56069

"The information is presented in brief paragraphs and sidebars. Suggestions for kids to help improve the planet are sprinkled throughout. . . . Students will enjoy this appealing layout and the information can spark further research on the topic. . . . Either digitally or on paper, students could make fantastic presentations using a similar design." Libr Media Connect

Includes glossary

Rosen, Michael J.

★ **Our** farm; four seasons with five kids on one family's farm. written and photographed by Michael J. Rosen. Darby Creek Pub. 2008 144p il $18.95

Grades: 4 5 6 7 8   630

1. Family life 2. Ohio 3. Farm life -- United States

ISBN 978-1-58196-067-9; 1-58196-067-0

A journal of one year on the Bennett farm in central Ohio. Shows how one family, with the help of relatives and friends, creates a life and livelihood on a 150-acre farm.

"This engaging book is an unsentimental, appreciative look into the world of one farm family." SLJ

Rothman, Julia

Farm anatomy; the curious parts & pieces of country life. Julia Rothman. Storey Pub. 2011 223 p. col. ill., col. maps

Grades: 7 8 9 10 11 12   630

1. Barns 2. Farms 3. Farm life 4. Farm produce 5. Domestic animals 6. Farm life -- Miscellanea 7. Farm life -- Pictorial works

ISBN 1603429816; 9781603429818

LC 2012360929

This book explains the "difference between a weanling and a yearling, or a farrow and a barrow . . . [in this] guide to the curious parts and pieces of rural living. Dissecting everything from tractors and pigs to fences, hay bales, crop rotation patterns, and farm tools, [Julia] Rothman gives a . . . tour of the quirky details of country life. From the shapes of squash varieties to the parts of a goat; from how a barn is constructed to what makes up a beehive, every corner of the barnyard is uncovered and celebrated." (Publisher's note)

Includes bibliographical references (p. 220-222).

630.9   Agriculture - History

Richardson, Gillian

10 plants that shook the world; Gillian Richardson ; illustrated by Kim Rosen. Annick Press 2013 132 p. (hardcover) $24.95

Grades: 4 5 6 7 8   630.9

1. Plants 2. Agriculture -- History

ISBN 1554514452; 9781554514458

This book, by Gillian Richardson, illustrated by Kim Rosen, profiles ten plants with significant histories. It describes how "countries went to war to control trade centers for pepper . . . , a grass called papyrus became the first effective tool for sharing knowledge through writing . . . , Europeans in the 1600s cut down rainforests to grow sugar, contributing to soil erosion . . . [and] dependence on the potato caused one of the greatest tragedies in history." (Publisher's note)

"With bold, lively caricatures from Rosen throughout, it's an intriguing and well-designed study of the ways plants have helped start wars, cure diseases, and advance technology." Pub Wkly

633.1　Cereals

Sobol, Richard

The **life** of rice; from seedling to supper. Candlewick Press 2010 36p il map (Traveling photographer) $17.99

Grades: 3 4 5 6　　　　　　　　　　**633.1**

1. Rice 2. Thailand

ISBN 978-0-7636-3252-6; 0-7636-3252-X

LC 2009-15138

"Turning his lens to the rice fields of Thailand, Sobol begins this affectionate account with a description of the Royal Plowing Ceremony that kicks off the planting season and continues through cultivation and into the harvest. Brief explanations of the growing stages of rice are accompanied by beautiful color photographs of the fields in their various phases. . . . Sobol offers an interesting look at a country and its people, and their relationship to the land. The writing is accessible and lively, providing a unique, specific look at one of the world's most important staples." SLJ

633.5　Fiber crops

Meltzer, Milton

★ The **cotton** gin. Benchmark Bks. 2003 123p il (Great inventions) lib bdg $25.95

Grades: 6 7 8 9　　　　　　　　　　**633.5**

1. Cotton

ISBN 0-7614-1537-8

LC 2002-15308

The author describes the invention of the cotton gin and its effects on history including "the influence of mechanized cotton processing on the growth of slavery in the United States and the increase in textile mills. . . . The author expertly describes a setting that is ripe for invention. Powerful photographs . . . historical artwork, and personal narratives make the times real and relevant to readers." SLJ

Includes bibliographical references

634.9　Forestry

Morris, Neil

Wood. Amicus 2011 48p il map (Materials that matter) lib bdg $28.50

Grades: 4 5 6 7　　　　　　　　　　**634.9**

1. Wood

ISBN 978-1-60753-070-1 lib bdg; 1-60753-070-8 lib bdg

LC 2010001621

"The clean layout includes photographs and occasional charts, graphs, and technical illustrations against a range of pastel backgrounds. Inset boxes provide further detail, interesting extras, and recycling information. . . . [This book offers] easily accessible background information for report writers." SLJ

Includes glossary and bibliographical references

Silverstein, Alvin

Wildfires; the science behind raging infernos. [by] Alvin and Virginia Silverstein and Laura Silverstein Nunn. Enslow Publishers 2010 48p il map (The science behind natural disasters) lib bdg $23.93

Grades: 4 5 6　　　　　　　　　　**634.9**

1. Wildfires

ISBN 978-0-7660-2973-6 lib bdg; 0-7660-2973-5 lib bdg

LC 2008-48025

"Scientific explanations are accompanied by plentiful color diagrams that will help students to grasp causes and effects. . . . Photos . . . are effective, and are sometimes turned into helpful, lively diagrams by the addition of such features as wind-direction arrows." SLJ

Includes glossary and bibliographical references

Trammel, Howard K.

Wildfires; by Howard K. Trammel. Children's Press 2009 48 p. col. ill. (A true book) (library) $29

Grades: 4 5 6　　　　　　　　　　**634.9**

1. Wildfires 2. Natural disasters

ISBN 0531168875; 9780531168875

LC 2008014796

This book by Howard K. Trammel is part of the True Books: Earth Science series and looks at wildfires. The series answers questions such as "what makes the earth quake, rivers flood, and volcanoes blow their tops? How do natural forces become natural disasters?" (Publisher's note)

635　Garden crops (Horticulture)

Cohen, Whitney

The **book** of gardening projects for kids; 101 ways to get kids outside, dirty, and having fun. Whitney Cohen and John Fisher. 1st ed. Timber Press 2012 264 p. col. ill. $29.95

Grades: Adult　　　　　　　　　　**635**

1. Gardening 2. Gardens -- Guidebooks 3. Gardens -- Activity projects 4. Gardening for children

ISBN 1604693738; 9781604692457

LC 2011036778

In this book, "Whitney Cohen and John Fisher draw on years of experience in the Life Lab Garden Classroom and gardening with their own children to teach parents how to integrate the garden into their family life, no matter its scope or scale. The book features . . . gardening advice, including how to design a play-friendly garden, ideas for fun-filled theme gardens, and how to cook and preserve the garden's bounty. 101 . . . garden activities are also featured." (Publisher's note)

Morris, Karyn

★ The **Kids** Can Press jumbo book of gardening; written by Karyn Morris; illustrated by Jane Kurisu. Kids Can Press 2000 240p il pa $14.95

Grades: 4 5 6 7　　　　　　　　　　**635**

1. Gardening

ISBN 1-55074-690-1

"Sections cover general information; fruit, vegetable, and flower gardens; noninvasive native plants; gardens that attract wildlife; and group projects. Projects range from a few annuals in a container and thickets designed with native wildlife in mind to community gardens. Directions are clear, with plenty of diagrams and illustrations." Booklist

635.9   Flowers and ornamental plants

Rice, Barry A.

Growing carnivorous plants; [by] Barry A. Rice. Timber 2006 224p il $39.95

Grades: 7 8 9   **635.9**

   1. Carnivorous plants

   ISBN 978-0-8819-2807-5; 0-8819-2807-0

                         LC 2007295063

A "guide to identifying and cultivating [carnivorous plants]. . . . This book will help readers select the best plants to grow on a windowsill, in a terrarium or greenhouse. Information on how to feed carnivorous plants [is included]." Publisher's note

Includes bibliographical references

636   Animal husbandry

Keenan, Sheila

   ★ **Animals** in the house; a history of pets and people. Scholastic Nonfiction 2007 112p il $17.99

Grades: 4 5 6   **636**

   1. Pets

   ISBN 978-0-439-69286-1; 0-439-69286-5

"Keenan provides an overview of pets and their people. Beginning with statistics about pet ownership, the text goes on to describe how animals and humans came together . . . and discusses how this relationship has changed and deepened. . . . Eye-catchingly designed, the format uses Photoshop to best advantage, providing interesting graphics, popping borders, and plenty of pictures featuring adorable animals." Booklist

Includes bibliographical references

Martin, Claudia

   Farming. Marshall Cavendish Benchmark 2010 64p il (Working animals) $28.50

Grades: 4 5 6 7   **636**

   1. Agriculture 2. Domestic animals

   ISBN 978-1-60870-162-9; 1-60870-162-X

                         LC 2010006895

"Attractively designed and packed with information. . . . The composition of each page is attractively set up with well-selected and reproduced stock and historical photos." SLJ

McAlpine, Margaret

   Working with animals. Gareth Stevens Pub. 2005 64p il (My future career) lib bdg $24

Grades: 6 7 8 9   **636**

   1. Animals 2. Vocational guidance

   ISBN 0-8368-4240-5

                         LC 2004-45229

This describes seven occupations related to animals, such as animal groomer and zookeeper, including the responsibilities, qualifications, and best personality type for each one

"The writing is clear and interesting, and the [book is] visually well organized." SLJ

Includes bibliographical references

Montgomery, Sy

   Temple Grandin; how the girl who loved cows embraced autism and changed the world. by Sy Montgomery. Houghton Mifflin Harcourt 2012 147 p. col. ill. $17.99

Grades: 4 5 6 7 8   **636**

   1. Autism 2. Cattle 3. Biography 4. Women scientists -- Biography 5. Animal welfare -- United States 6. Livestock -- Housing -- United States 7. Livestock -- Handling -- United States 8. Autistic people -- United States -- Biography

   ISBN 0547443153; 9780547443157

                         LC 2011039911

AAAS/Subaru SB&F Prize for Excellence in Science Books: Middle Grade Science Book (2013)

This book by Sy Montgomery presents a biography of autistic animal scientist Temple Grandin. Sy Montgomery argues that "though one never outgrows autism, it doesn't condemn those who have it to unproductive lives, and an appendix, 'Temple's Advice for Kids on the Spectrum,' provides first-hand wisdom. Photos and diagrams depict Grandin's work as well as documenting her early life and career." (Kirkus Reviews)

Includes bibliographical references and index.

Steele, Christy

   Cattle ranching in the American West; by Christy Steele. World Almanac Library 2005 48p il map (America's westward expansion) lib bdg $30; pa $11.95

Grades: 5 6 7 8   **636**

   1. Cattle 2. Ranch life 3. West (U.S.) -- History

   ISBN 0-8368-5787-9 lib bdg; 0-8368-5794-1 pa

                         LC 2004-56769

This volume describing Western cattle ranching is "richly illustrated with historical photographs, illustrations, maps, and quotes from primary sources presented in sidebars." SLJ

Includes bibliographical references

636.088   Animals for specific purposes

Grayson, Robert

   Transportation. Marshall Cavendish Benchmark 2010 64p il (Working animals) $28.50

Grades: 4 5 6 7   **636.088**

   1. Pack animals (Transportation)

   ISBN 978-1-60870-167-4; 1-60870-167-0

                         LC 2010006899

"Describes animals that people all over the world use to transport people and goods, such as elephants, horses, yaks, water buffalo, and dogs." Publisher's note

Includes glossary and bibliographical references

Halls, Kelly Milner

Saving the Baghdad Zoo; a true story of hope and heroes. by Kelly Milner Halls, with William Sumner. Greenwillow Books 2010 64p il map $17.99

Grades: 4 5 6 7   **636.088**

1. Zoos 2. Wildlife conservation 3. Baghdad (Iraq) 4. Baghdad Zoo (Iraq)

ISBN 978-0-06-177202-3; 0-06-177202-X

LC 2008-52820

"This eye-opening tale of compassion and cooperation chronicles the mission of an international team of military personnel, zoo staffers, veterinarians, and relief workers to rescue neglected animals in Baghdad. . . . Sobering and up-lifting photographs—many taken by Sumner—underscore both the direness of the situation and the spirit of hope that drove the project." Publ Wkly

Includes bibliographical references

Kent, Deborah

Animal helpers for the disabled. Watts 2003 63p il (Watts library) hardcover o.p. $25.50

Grades: 4 5 6 7   **636.088**

1. Guide dogs 2. Animals and people with disabilities 3. Animals -- Training

ISBN 0-531-12017-1; 0-531-16663-5 pa

LC 2002-8885

Explores the history of guide dogs, service animals, and assistance dogs, and discusses the process of training them to help people who have physical disabilities

This is an "informative, often inspirational and thought-provoking [book]." Booklist

Includes bibliographical references

Laidlaw, Rob

Wild animals in captivity; [by] Rob Laidlaw. Fitzhenry & Whiteside 2008 48p il $19.95

Grades: 4 5 6 7 8   **636.088**

1. Zoos 2. Animal welfare

ISBN 978-1-55455-025-8; 1-55455-025-4

"A passionate, well-written, and well-researched argu-ment against the practices of most zoos around the world. . . . Describes the damage done when animals are unnaturally confined and moved to inhospitable climates, and compares the wild and captive lives of polar bears, orcas, elephants, and great apes—the four species most harmed by captivity. . . . The issues raised in this important and powerful book will resonate with young and old." SLJ

Markle, Sandra

Animal heroes; true rescue stories. by Sandra Markle. Millbrook Press 2009 64p il lib bdg $29.27

Grades: 4 5 6 7   **636.088**

1. Pets 2. Animals 3. Rescue work

ISBN 978-0-8225-7884-0 lib bdg; 0-8225-7884-0 lib bdg

LC 2007-50435

"Nine stories, based on interviews with the grateful survivors, describe how brave animals rescued people in catastrophic circumstances. Each edgy retelling reveals details that only the participants could know, including sounds, smells, sights, and the knowledge that at any mo-ment they could die, deepening the tension. Mixed in are

Markle's broad and perfectly attuned insights about animal behavior." SLJ

Includes glossary and bibliographical references

636.089   Veterinary medicine

Jackson, Donna M.

★ **ER** vets; life in an animal emergency room. Houghton Mifflin 2005 88p il $17

Grades: 5 6 7 8   **636.089**

1. Veterinary medicine

ISBN 0-618-43663-4

"With plentiful, excellent-quality photographs, this highly visual book offers a behind-the-scenes look at an emergency animal hospital in Colorado. . . . A section on grief counseling for families with critically ill pets and a spread on how to put together a pet first-aid kit are included. Well-researched and well-written, ER Vets is an engaging book on a hot topic." SLJ

636.1   Horses

Bowers, Nathan

4 -H guide to training horses. Voyageur Press 2009 176p il $18.99

Grades: 5 6 7 8   **636.1**

1. Horses -- Training

ISBN 978-0-7603-3627-4; 0-7603-3627-X

LC 2009015299

This provides "sound and comprehensive information. [The book] covers basic training techniques and riding skills such as mounting, saddling, reining, stopping and starting, and posture among other topics. The training techniques offer insight into equine behavior based on their history as prey animals. The authors also emphasize that horse owners' success will be determined by how much effort they are will-ing to expend on their relationship with their animals. The many color photographs clearly depict the methods and ac-tivities that are taking place, and the accompanying images further clarify what is happening and its significance." SLJ

Includes glossary

Clutton-Brock, Juliet

Horse; written by Juliet Clutton-Brock. DK Pub. 2008 72p il (DK eyewitness books) $15.99

Grades: 4 5 6 7   **636.1**

1. Horses

ISBN 978-0-7566-3775-0; 0-7566-3775-9

LC 2008276033

First published 2003 in the United Kingdom

Examines the anatomy, history, and breeds of horses, and discusses the different ways horses have been used throughout history

Crosby, Jeff

Harness horses, bucking broncos & pit ponies; a history of horse breeds. written and illustrated by Jeff Crosby and Shelley Ann Jackson. Tundra Books 2011 69p il map $21.99

Grades: 4 5 6 7 **636.1**

1. Horses

ISBN 978-0-88776-986-3; 0-88776-986-1

"After a brief introduction, the animals are grouped by the roles they have played in relation to people: 'Rapid Transit,' 'Military Advantage,' 'Horsepower,' 'Equine Entertainment,' and 'Feral Horses.' The concise and interesting information on each of the 43 breeds is accompanied by an illustration of the type as well as one of the horse in action and often includes a small map showing its origins. The excellent painterly pictures clearly capture the unique life of each horse." SLJ

Includes bibliographical references

Ransford, Sandy

★ The **Kingfisher** illustrated horse & pony encyclopedia; written by Sandy Ransford; photographed by Bob Langrish. Kingfisher 2004 224p il $24.95

Grades: 4 5 6 7 **636.1**

1. Horses 2. Horsemanship

ISBN 0-7534-5781-4

LC 2003-27293

"The first part of the book covers the life cycle, domestication, and types of horses and ponies. . . . The second part deals with how to care for these animals and discusses horsemanship from taking riding lessons to training and driving a horse. . . . Filled with appealing photos of young people interacting with their four-legged friends, this title is an extremely useful addition to any collection." SLJ

Wilsdon, Christina

For horse-crazy girls only; everything you want to know about horses. illustrated by Alecia Underhill. Feiwel and Friends 2010 150p il $14.99

Grades: 4 5 6 7 **636.1**

1. Horses

ISBN 978-0-312-60323-6; 0-312-60323-1

LC 2010015677

"Filled with quizzes, trivia, top 10 lists, and information about equine behavior, history, sports, and more, this guidebook aims straight at the hearts of horse-loving tweens. . . . The book runs the gamut from how to pick a horse's name to horses in popular culture, the evolution of the species, and horse-related events nationwide. The many sidebars, tidbits, and anecdotes encourage casual browsing-horse lovers will be in heaven." Publ Wkly

636.2 Cattle and related animals

Freedman, Russell

★ **In** the days of the vaqueros; America's first true cowboys. Clarion Bks. 2001 70p il $18; pa $9.99

Grades: 4 5 6 7 **636.2**

1. Cowhands 2. Ranch life 3. Mexican Americans 4. Southwestern States

ISBN 0-395-96788-0; 978-0-395-96788-1; 978-0-547-13365-2 pa; 0-547-13365-0 pa

LC 2001-17357

The author "tells the story with depth, clarity, and a vigor that conveys the thrilling excitement of the work and the macho swagger of the culture. . . . The book's design is beautiful, with spacious type on thick paper, and the dazzling illustrations—prints, paintings, and photos on almost every page." Booklist

Includes glossary and bibliographical references

636.5 Chickens and other kinds of domestic birds

Kindschi, Tara

4 -H guide to raising chickens. Voyageur Press 2010 176p il pa $18.99

Grades: 5 6 7 8 **636.5**

1. Chickens

ISBN 978-0-7603-3628-1 pa; 0-7603-3628-8 pa

LC 2009015300

"This title has everything one ever wanted to know about chickens but didn't know enough to ask. Eight chapters divide the text into broad topics such as getting started, choosing a breed, housing equipment, and exhibiting chickens. . . . Line drawings and charts give additional information, and the excellent color photography is profuse." SLJ

Includes glossary and bibliographical references

636.7 Dogs

American Kennel Club

The **complete** dog book; American Kennel Club. 20th ed.; Ballantine Books 2006 xxi, 858p il $35

Grades: 7 8 9 10 11 12 Adult **636.7**

1. Dogs

ISBN 0-345-47626-3; 978-0-345-47626-5

LC 2005-48263

First published 1935. Periodically revised

"The official guide to 124 AKC registered breeds and their history, appearance, selection, training, care and feeding, and first aid. Some color plates." N Y Public Libr. Ref Books for Child Collect. 2d edition

★ The **Complete** dog book for kids; official publication of the American Kennel Club. Howell Book House 1996 274p il maps hardcover o.p. pa $22.95

Grades: 4 5 6 7 **636.7**

1. Dogs

ISBN 0-87605-458-0; 0-87605-460-2 pa

LC 96-29228

This "begins with a general section that advises readers on buying a dog, responsibilities, rewards, and how to match a dog with one's situation. . . . More than 100 dogs are profiled, with information on history, appearance, health, and 'fun facts.' Crisp color photographs accompany each article. . . . A final section gives good advice about nutrition and health issues." Booklist

Bial, Raymond

　Rescuing Rover; saving America's dogs. Houghton Mifflin 2011 80p il

Grades: 4 5 6 7　　　　　　　　　　**636.7**

　1. Dogs 2. Animal welfare

　ISBN 0-547-34125-3; 978-0-547-34125-5

　　　　　　　　　　　　LC 2010025123

"This accessible, amply illustrated title offers and informative introduction to canine-rescue endeavors. After recounting his own moving story of adopting a rescue dog, Bial provides a history of human-dog relationships. . . . Bial also explores rescue organizations, such as the ASPCA. . . . Bial frankly discusses the abuse many dogs experience . . . as well as euthanasia. . . . Historical and contemporary photos; extensive book lists . . .; websites; and detailed index complete this well-presented resource." Booklist

　Includes bibliographical references

Biniok, Janice

　The **miniature** schnauzer. Eldorado Ink 2010 112p il (Our best friends) lib bdg $34.95

Grades: 4 5 6 7　　　　　　　　　　**636.7**

　1. Dogs

　ISBN 978-1-932904-61-1 lib bdg; 1-932904-61-1 lib bdg

"The Our Best Friends series continues to be an ideal resource for those kids (or even adults) looking for a cradle-to-grave primer on responsible pet ownership. . . . These [books] offer far more than the customary cursory enticements and warnings usually aimed at first-time animal caregivers, with in-depth information on health issues and extensive explanations of the various types of species. . . . This is required (if sobering) reading for the serious pet owner." Booklist

　Includes bibliographical references

　The **rottweiler**. Eldorado Ink 2010 112p il (Our best friends) lib bdg $34.95

Grades: 4 5 6 7　　　　　　　　　　**636.7**

　1. Dogs

　ISBN 978-1-932904-64-2 lib bdg; 1-932904-64-6 lib bdg

"The Our Best Friends series continues to be an ideal resource for those kids (or even adults) looking for a cradle-to-grave primer on responsible pet ownership. . . . These [books] offer far more than the customary cursory enticements and warnings usually aimed at first-time animal caregivers, with in-depth information on health issues and extensive explanations of the various types of species. . . . This is required (if sobering) reading for the serious pet owner." Booklist

　Includes bibliographical references

Bolan, Sandra

　Caring for your mutt; [by] Sandra Bolan. El-Dorado Ink 2008 128p (Our best friends) lib bdg $25.95

Grades: 4 5 6 7　　　　　　　　　　**636.7**

　1. Dogs

　ISBN 978-1-932904-20-8; 1-932904-20-4

　　　　　　　　　　　　LC 2007051607

"Although Bolan's excellent advice on selection, training, and care applies to nearly all canines, she makes it plain that mixed breeds can be a 'challenging guessing game' when it comes to predicting size, temperment, and overall health. All the expected information is here, clearly presented and quite thorough." Booklist

　Includes bibliographical references

Castaldo, Nancy F.

　Sniffer dogs; how dogs (and their noses) save the world. Nancy F. Castaldo. Houghton Mifflin Harcourt 2014 160 p. color illustrations $16.99

Grades: 4 5 6 7 8　　　　　　　　　　**636.7**

　1. Rescue dogs 2. Search dogs 3. Smell 4. Detector dogs 5. Dogs -- Sense organs

　ISBN 054408893X; 9780544088931

　　　　　　　　　　　　LC 2013017612

This middle grade book by Nancy F. Castaldo describes how "some dogs work with police officers, soldiers and even scientists to put their 'sniffers' to work. Sniffer dogs make use of the amazing biology behind their noses to protect people from bombs, catch criminals smuggling drugs, or help researchers locate a hard to find snail in a forest." (Publisher's note)

"The attractive color photos that capture many of these canines in action and the accessible tone of the text make this an appealing read. A well-organized, thoughtfully written title that celebrates the achievements of these great dogs." SLJ

　Includes bibliographical references and index

Gewirtz, Elaine Waldorf

　The **bulldog**. Eldorado Ink 2010 112p il (Our best friends) lib bdg $34.95

Grades: 4 5 6 7　　　　　　　　　　**636.7**

　1. Dogs

　ISBN 978-1-932904-58-1 lib bdg; 1-932904-58-1 lib bdg

"The Our Best Friends series continues to be an ideal resource for those kids (or even adults) looking for a cradle-to-grave primer on responsible pet ownership. These [books] offer far more than the customary cursory enticements and warnings usually aimed at first-time animal caregivers, with in-depth information on health issues and extensive explanations of the various types of species. . . . This is required (if sobering) reading for the serious pet owner." Booklist

　Includes bibliographical references

　Fetch this book. Eldorado Ink 2010 112p il (Our best friends) lib bdg $34.95

Grades: 4 5 6 7　　　　　　　　　　**636.7**

　1. Dogs -- Training

　ISBN 978-1-932904-60-4 lib bdg; 1-932904-60-3 lib bdg

This "is a dog-training manual, with pet-care advice only in reference to training. [This] well-written [book provides] examples to support [its] points and solid online and text resources and feature [a] clean, uncluttered [layout]. . . . There is plenty of practical information that motivated readers can glean from [this title]." SLJ

　Includes bibliographical references

Gorrell, Gena K.

Working like a dog; the story of working dogs through history. Tundra 2003 156p il pa $16.95

Grades: 4 5 6 7   **636.7**

1. Working dogs

ISBN 0-88776-589-0

"Gorrell begins by tracing the evolution of 'household canids' from the wild into the civilized world. Other chapters delve into the many ways in which these animals have been viewed throughout history, what makes particular breeds right for certain jobs, dogs at war, famous pooches, etc. . . . The well-captioned, black-and-white photographs and reproductions add greatly to a narrative that's packed with intriguing details." SLJ

Includes bibliographical references

Houston, Dick

Bulu, African wonder dog. Random House 2010 323p il $15.99; lib bdg $18.99

Grades: 5 6 7 8   **636.7**

1. Dogs 2. Wildlife conservation 3. Zambia

ISBN 978-0-375-84723-3; 0-375-84723-5; 978-0-375-94720-9 lib bdg; 0-375-94720-5 lib bdg

LC 2009015804

"In the Nyanja language, bulu means 'wild dog,' and that's what Steve and Anna Tolan named the beloved little Jack Russell mix they adopted. Disregarding warnings about the dangers of raising a dog in the bush, the Tolans moved from England to rural Zambia to fulfill their lifelong dream of setting up an animal rescue and conservation center. . . . Bulu's energy, high spirits, and loyalty to his masters make the book read like a praise song to dogs. Houston's account is an animal-lover's delight, complete with the action-adventure of surviving the bush, fighting poachers, and spreading a message of conservation." Booklist

Laidlaw, Rob

No shelter here; Making the world a kinder place for dogs. Rob Laidlaw. Pajama Press 2012 63 p.

Grades: 3 4 5 6 7 8   **636.7**

1. Dogs 2. Animal rights 3. Animal welfare

ISBN 0986949558; 9780986949555

This book provides an "informative and visually varied introduction to problems affecting dogs worldwide. In a short, colorful volume with sidebars and photographs on nearly every page, professional dog advocate [Rob] Laidlaw . . . presents facts about how dogs live, provides an overview of the cruelty dogs face at the hands of humans and offers profiles of young activists who are working to better dogs' lives. . . . A list of animal welfare websites points interested readers toward further information." (Kirkus)

Includes bibliographical references and index.

Mehus-Roe, Kristin

Dogs for kids! everything you need to know about dogs. by Kristin Mehus-Roe. BowTie Press 2007 384p il pa $14.95

Grades: 4 5 6 7   **636.7**

1. Dogs

ISBN 978-1-931993-83-8 pa; 1-931993-83-1 pa

LC 2006035434

"If you are looking for a book about canines that is entertaining as well as immensely informative, this is it. In a lively, conversational tone, Mehus-Roe offers a vast amount of material, from the history of dogs to vacationing with a pet, and provides practical and upbeat explanations, ideas, offbeat tidbits, and pertinent details." SLJ

Includes bibliographical references

Morn, September B.

The **pug.** Eldorado Ink 2010 112p il (Our best friends) lib bdg $34.95

Grades: 4 5 6 7   **636.7**

1. Dogs

ISBN 978-1-932904-63-5 lib bdg; 1-932904-63-8 lib bdg

"The Our Best Friends series continues to be an ideal resource for those kids (or even adults) looking for a cradle-to-grave primer on responsible pet ownership. . . . These [books] offer far more than the customary cursory enticements and warnings usually aimed at first-time animal caregivers, with in-depth information on health issues and extensive explanations of the various types of species. . . . This is required (if sobering) reading for the serious pet owner." Booklist

Includes bibliographical references

Rogers, Tammie

4 -H guide to dog training and dog tricks. Voyageur Press 2009 176p il pa $18.99

Grades: 5 6 7 8 9 10   **636.7**

1. Dogs -- Training

ISBN 978-0-7603-3629-8; 0-7603-3629-6

LC 2009-17040

"This is not simply a how-to-train book; it is also a guide to cultivating a respectful relationship with your dog. The excellent information is comprehensive, and it is presented in a clear and detailed style. The author covers different training methods, discussing the tools needed from food to collar selection. Using this manual, dog owners can move through the basics (sit, down, etc.) to obedience competition and fun tricks and activities." SLJ

Includes bibliographical references

Schweitzer, Karen

The **beagle.** Eldorado Ink 2010 112p il (Our best friends) lib bdg $34.95

Grades: 4 5 6 7   **636.7**

1. Dogs

ISBN 978-1-932904-57-4 lib bdg; 1-932904-57-3 lib bdg

"The Our Best Friends series continues to be an ideal resource for those kids (or even adults) looking for a cradle-to-grave primer on responsible pet ownership. . . . These [books] offer far more than the customary cursory enticements and warnings usually aimed at first-time animal caregivers, with in-depth information on health issues and extensive explanations of the various types of species. . . . This is required (if sobering) reading for the serious pet owner." Booklist

Includes bibliographical references

The **dachshund**. Eldorado Ink 2010 112p il (Our best friends) lib bdg $34.95

Grades: 4 5 6 7   636.7

1. Dogs

ISBN 978-1-932904-59-8 lib bdg; 1-932904-59-X lib bdg

"The Our Best Friends series continues to be an ideal resource for those kids (or even adults) looking for a cradle-to-grave primer on responsible pet ownership. . . . These [books] offer far more than the customary cursory enticements and warnings usually aimed at first-time animal caregivers, with in-depth information on health issues and extensive explanations of the various types of species. . . . This is required (if sobering) reading for the serious pet owner." Booklist

Includes bibliographical references

Whitehead, Sarah

How to speak dog. Scholastic Reference 2008 96p il pa $6.99

Grades: 4 5 6 7 8   636.7

1. Dogs

ISBN 978-0-545-02078-7 pa; 0-545-02078-6 pa

Explains how to read a dog's body language and vocalizations and presents step-by-step instructions for training, housebreaking, teaching tricks, and playing several types of games.

This is "well-organized and interesting. . . . Whitehead discusses, and clearly shows in good-quality, full-color photographs, various canine emotions." SLJ

636.8 Cats

Bidner, Jenni

Is my cat a tiger? how your cat compares to its wild cousins. Lark Books 2006 64p il $9.95

Grades: 3 4 5 6   636.8

1. Cats 2. Wild cats

ISBN 1-57990-815-2

LC 2006023356

"This book shows how domestic cats compare with their wild cousins. Specifically, it addresses what domestic behavior reveals about wild roots. . . . The color photographs are fantastic. . . . This is a fascinating volume." SLJ

Biniok, Janice

Mixed breed cats. Eldorado Ink 2010 112p il (Our best friends) lib bdg $34.95

Grades: 4 5 6 7   636.8

1. Cats

ISBN 978-1-932904-62-8 lib bdg; 1-932904-62-X lib bdg

This "is a cradle-to-grave overview of a cat's life. . . . [This] well-written [book provides] examples to support [its] points and solid online and text resources and feature [a] clean, uncluttered [layout]. . . . There is plenty of practical information that motivated readers can glean from [this title]. [It] debunks some presumptions about domesticated

felines, commenting that the 'finicky eater' tag is unwarranted, and that cats are easier to train than people think." SLJ

Includes bibliographical references

Edney, A. T. B.

ASPCA complete cat care manual; [by] Andrew Edney; foreword by Roger Caras. Dorling Kindersley 1992 192p il hardcover o.p. pa $14.95

Grades: 8 9 10 11 12 Adult   636.8

1. Cats

ISBN 1-56458-064-4; 0-7566-1742-1 pa

LC 92-52783

"Cat care is made easy through step-by-step photographs that illustrate grooming, handling, detecting illness, first aid, and other concerns. Difficult-to-explain procedures, such as how to administer medication or transport an injured cat, are clearly understandable." Libr J

Includes bibliographical references

Laidlaw, Rob

★ **Cat** champions; caring for our feline friends. By Rob Laidlaw. Orca Book Pub 2014 64 p. illustrations (chiefly color) $19.95

Grades: 4 5 6 7 8   636.8

1. Cats 2. Animal welfare 3. Voluntarism 4. Cats -- Health 5. Animal shelters

ISBN 1927485312; 9781927485316

In this book, readers "meet kids who are helping at shelters, fostering kittens, volunteering with sterilization programs and caring for abandoned cats. Animal advocate Rob Laidlaw brings readers a hopeful, inspiring look at the issues facing domesticated and feral cats, and the cat champions who are working to help them." (Publisher's note)

"Here's a book for cat lovers and those who want to know more about caring for furry friends...The format is busy, but cat lovers probably won't mind so many photos, and the sidebars are all informative. The list of organizations where kids can learn about ways they can help is extensive and useful." Booklist

Myron, Vicki

Dewey the library cat; a true story. [by] Vicki Myron with Bret Witter. Little, Brown 2010 214p $16.99

Grades: 4 5 6 7 8   636.8

1. Cats 2. Libraries

ISBN 978-0-316-06871-0; 0-316-06871-3

Adapted from: Dewey: the small town library cat who touched the world, published 2008 by Grand Central Publisher for adults

"From the opening chapter, when librarian Vicki Myron finds a fragile, freezing kitten in the book return, children will be hooked on her heartwarming story about Dewey Readmore Books. . . . Anecdotes such as Dewey's fascination with rubber bands, his bizarre behavior during a bat invasion, and his finicky eating habits are ideal booktalk material. So are descriptions of Dewey's tender, intuitive interactions with people of all ages and backgrounds." Booklist

Stefoff, Rebecca

Cats. Benchmark Bks. 2004 112p il (Animalways) $34.21

Grades: 6 7 8 9   **636.8**

1. Cats

ISBN 0-7614-1577-7

LC 2002-155247

This introduction to cat biology, life cycle, behavior, and relationship to people offers "a strong combination of text and illustration." SLJ

Includes bibliographical references

Whitehead, Sarah

How to speak cat. Scholastic 2009 96p il pa $6.99

Grades: 4 5 6 7 8   **636.8**

1. Cats

ISBN 978-0-545-02079-4 pa; 0-545-02079-4 pa

"This pet-care book focuses on developing a relationship with a pet. The author states that the communication process is a two-way street, and she describes how readers can translate a cat's body language and vocalizations. . . . the bright color photographs of children with their cats on every page will appeal greatly to readers. This is a fun book that offers a good understanding of its audience and subject." SLJ

636.9   Other mammals

McNicholas, June

Rats. Heinemann Lib. 2003 48p il (Keeping unusual pets) $24.22

Grades: 4 5 6 7   **636.9**

1. Rats

ISBN 1-4034-0283-3

LC 2002-3164

Describes how to select a pet rat, what to feed it, and when to take it to the vet, as well as how to keep a pet scrapbook

"A valuable, accessible resource." Booklist

Includes bibliographical references

Sullivant, Holly J.

Hamsters. ElDorado Ink 2009 il (Our best friends) $26.95

Grades: 7 8 9 10 11 12   **636.9**

1. Hamsters

ISBN 978-1-93290430-7

LC 2008040365

This is a guide to caring for a pet hamster.

"An ideal resource for those kids (or even adults) looking for a cradle-to-grave primer on responsible pet ownership. . . . Well formatted and broken up with vivid photographs and fascinating 'Fast Facts.'" Booklist

636.935   Rodents – animal husbandry

Boruchowitz, David E.

Sugar gliders; David E. Boruchowitz ; [editor, Thomas Mazorlig] T.F.H. 2012 111 p. (Animal planet. Pet care library) (pbk. : alk. paper) $10.95

Grades: 4 5 6 7   **636.935**

1. Sugar glider 2. Sugar gliders as pets

ISBN 0793837111; 9780793837113

LC 2011049947

This book on sugar gliders by David E. Boruchowitz is part of the "Animal Planet Pet Care Library" series. "According to Boruchowitz, they make excellent house pets due to their affinity for cuddling in tiny places. . . . Every aspect of ownership is covered, from basic dietary requirements to grooming and socialization." (Booklist)

Includes bibliographical references and index

638   Insect culture

Buchmann, Stephen

Honey bees; letters from the hive. Delacorte Press 2010 212p il $16.99; lib bdg $19.99

Grades: 7 8 9 10   **638**

1. Bees 2. Honey

ISBN 978-0-385-73770-8; 0-385-73770-X; 978-0-385-90683-8 lib bdg; 0-385-90683-8 lib bdg

LC 2010-6093

Based on the adult book, Letters from the hive: an intimate history of bees, honey, and humankind published by Delacorte Press in 2005

"This sweeping survey engagingly discusses bee biology and behavior and examines humanity's relationship with bees, from prehistoric times to the present, through their significant roles in art, religion, literature and medicine. Buchmann, a beekeeper and entomologist, also offers a great deal of information about honey. . . . The text is illustrated with black-and-white photographs and documented with source notes." Kirkus

Burns, Loree Griffin

The hive detectives; chronicle of a honey bee catastrophe. by Loree Griffin Burns with photographs by Ellen Harasimowicz. HMH Books for Young Readers 2010 80 p. il (Scientists in the field) $18.99

Grades: 5 6 7 8 9 10   **638**

1. Bees 2. Beekeeping 3. Insects -- Behavior 4. Honeybee 5. Bee culture

ISBN 0547152310; 9780547152318

LC 2009045249

In this book, author Loree Griffin Burns "profiles bee wranglers and bee scientists who have been working to understand colony collapse disorder, or CCD. In this dramatic and enlightening story, readers explore the lives of the fuzzy, buzzy insects and learn what might happen to us if they were gone." (Publisher's note)

"Not long after beekeepers encountered a devastating new problem in their hives in 2006, a team of bee scientists began working to discover the causes of colony collapse disorder (CCD), now attributed to a combination of factors possibly including pesticides, nutrition, mites and viruses. . . . Mock notebook pages break up the narrative with biographies of the individual scientists, information about who and what can be found inside the hive and the features of bee bodies. An appendix adds varied fascinating facts about bees—again using the format of an illustrated research journal. Harasimowicz's clear, beautifully reproduced photographs support and extend the text." Kirkus

Includes bibliographical references (p. 65) and index

Harkins, Susan Sales

Design your own butterfly garden; by Susan Sales Harkins and William H. Harkins. Mitchell Lane Publishers 2008 48p il (Gardening for kids) lib bdg $29.95

Grades: 3 4 5 6   **638**

1. Butterfly gardens

ISBN 978-1-58415-638-3 lib bdg; 1-58415-638-4 lib bdg

LC 2008-2245

Introduces the principles of butterfly gardening, discussing how to plan the garden, what flowers to plant there, and how to maintain it in all seasons

"All the tasks delineated are well within the scope of children's abilities, and the items needed to complete them are not hard to find. . . . [The book has] excellent full-color photography and include[s] charts and diagrams to assist in the completion of the projects." SLJ

Includes bibliographical references

639.2   Commercial fishing, whaling, sealing

Foster, Mark

★ **Whale** port; a history of Tuckanucket. written by Mark Foster; illustrated by Gerald Foster. Houghton Mifflin Company 2007 64p il $18

Grades: 4 5 6 7   **639.2**

1. Whaling

ISBN 978-0-618-54722-7; 0-618-54722-3

LC 2006018772

This describes the history of whaling in New England through the fictional village of Tuckanucket and Zachariah Taber, his family and neighbors.

The village is "depicted in precisely detailed ink and crayon pictures. . . . The Fosters . . . have elegantly synthesized a tremendous amount of information into a beguiling format." Horn Book

McKissack, Patricia C.

★ **Black** hands, white sails; the story of African-American whalers. [by] Patricia C. McKissack & Fredrick L. McKissack. Scholastic Press 1999 xxiv, 152p il $17.95

Grades: 5 6 7 8   **639.2**

1. Whaling 2. Abolitionists 3. African Americans

ISBN 0-590-48313-7

LC 99-11439

A Coretta Scott King honor book for text, 2000

A history of African-American whalers between 1730 and 1880, describing their contributions to the whaling industry and their role in the abolitionist movement

"A well-researched and detailed book." SLJ

Includes bibliographical references

Sandler, Martin W.

Trapped in ice! an amazing true whaling adventure. Scholastic Nonfiction 2006 168p il $16.99

Grades: 5 6 7 8   **639.2**

1. Whaling

ISBN 0-439-74363-X

LC 2005-42644

"In 1871, people aboard 32 whaling ships discovered just how dangerous Arctic waters could be after they ignored warnings of an early winter. As conditions worsened, the ships were trapped by ice, forcing the 1,219 people to abandon the vessels or die. Sandler's account of this true story is both informative and absorbing. . . . Well-chosen illustrations and side notes on such topics as life aboard ship and women at sea extend readers' understanding." Booklist

Includes glossary and bibliographical references

Somervill, Barbara A.

Commercial fisher. Cherry Lake Pub. 2011 32p il (Cool careers) lib bdg $27.07

Grades: 4 5 6 7   **639.2**

1. Commercial fishing 2. Vocational guidance

ISBN 978-1-60279-986-8; 1-60279-986-5

LC 2010029123

This book begins "with a personal story of a teen and then [segues] into the occupation [of commercial fisher]. . . . [It covers] the necessary training and skills for the job (and options for obtaining them), a typical day, salary expectations, and well-known professionals in the field. The [text is] accessible and clearly written. . . . The [volume has] a generous number of clear color photographs that depict people at work." SLJ

Includes glossary and bibliographical references

639.3   Culture of cold-blooded vertebrates

Bartlett, Richard D.

Aquatic turtles; sliders, cooters, painted, and map turtles. [by] R.D. Bartlett, Patricia Bartlett. Barron's Educational Series 2003 46p il (Reptile keeper's guides) pa $7.99

Grades: 6 7 8 9   **639.3**

1. Turtles

ISBN 978-0-7641-2278-1 pa; 0-7641-2278-9 pa

LC 2002-26264

"This guide offers . . . advice on the maintenance and care of [aquatic turtles]. . . . Readers . . . get advice on selecting a good specimen, determining sex, and providing proper housing, feeding, and health care." Publisher's note

Geckos; everything about housing, health, nutrition, and breeding. [by] R.D. Bartlett and Patricia P. Bartlett. Barron's 2006 95p il (A Complete pet owner's manual) pa $8.99

Grades: 6 7 8 9   **639.3**

1. Geckos

ISBN 978-0-7641-2855-4 pa; 0-7641-2855-8 pa

LC 2005-50024

First published 1995

"Advice on purchasing geckos, as well as feeding, breeding, and health care." Publisher's note

Includes glossary and bibligrapical references

Turtles and tortoises; everything about selection, care, nutrition, housing, and behavior. [by] R.D. Bartlett and Patricia P. Bartlett; with full-color photographs; illustrations by Michele Earl-Bridges. Barron's 2006 111p il (A complete pet owner's manual) pa $8.99

Grades: 6 7 8 9   **639.3**

1. Turtles

ISBN 978-0-7641-3400-5; 0-7641-3400-0

LC 2006-40101

"Information on both land and water species, with specifics on determining sex, life expectancy, housing, feeding, and health care." Publisher's note

Includes bibliographical references

Coates, Jennifer

Lizards. ElDorado Ink 2008 il (Our best friends) $26.95

Grades: 7 8 9 10 11 12   **639.3**

1. Lizards

ISBN 978-1-93290-431-4

LC 2008033060

This is a guide to caring for lizards as pets.

"An ideal resource for those kids (or even adults) looking for a cradle-to-grave primer on responsible pet ownership. . . . Well formatted and broken up with vivid photographs and fascinating 'Fast Facts.'" Booklist

639.34 Fish culture in aquariums

Indiviglio, Frank

The **everything** aquarium book; all you need to build the aquarium of your dreams. Adams Media 2007 287p il (Everything series) pa $14.95

Grades: 7 8 9 10   **639.34**

1. Aquariums

ISBN 978-1-59337-715-1; 1-59337-715-0

LC 2006-28187

This book about aquariums includes information about "proper fish selection, marine plants and understanding fish behavior." Publisher's note

Includes bibliographical references

Mills, Dick

Aquarium fish. DK 2004 72p il (101 essential tips) pa $5

Grades: 7 8 9 10 11 12 Adult   **639.34**

1. Fishes 2. Aquariums

ISBN 0-7566-0611-X; 978-0-7566-0611-4

LC 2004-303366

Reprint of paperback printed by DK Pub. in 1996

This book offers advice on choosing fish for aquariums, aquarium equipment, decoration, feeding, and health care, and describes various species of tropical, coldwater, freshwater, and marine fishes.

"Accurate, clear, and concise writing is enhanced with wonderful color photographs on each page." Voice Youth Advocates [review of 1996 edition]

Wood, Kathleen

The **101** best tropical fishes; how to choose & keep hardy, brilliant, fascinating species that will thrive in your home aquarium. by Kathleen Wood; with Mary E. Sweeney and Scott W. Michael. T.F.H. Publications 2007 192p il (Adventurous aquarist guide) $18.95

Grades: 6 7 8 9   **639.34**

1. Aquariums 2. Tropical fish

ISBN 978-1-8900-8793-7; 1-8900-8793-9

LC 2008-28294

"Presents 101 full-page species accounts of fishes that not only have high survival rates in captivity but also are appealing in appearance and behave well in community tanks. Also included are 33 species to avoid—fishes that most commonly wreak havoc in home aquariums because of their size or aggressiveness, or that tend to perish in the hands of inexperienced aquarists." Publisher's note

Includes bibliographical references

639.9 Conservation of biological resources

George, Jean Craighead

A **tarantula** in my purse; and 172 other wild pets. written and illustrated by Jean Craighead George. HarperCollins Pubs. 1996 134p il hardcover o.p. pa $5.99

Grades: 4 5 6   **639.9**

1. Pets 2. Artists 3. Authors 4. Naturalists 5. Illustrators 6. Women authors 7. Authors, American 8. Children's authors

ISBN 0-06-023626-4; 0-06-446201-3 pa

LC 95-54151

"Brief, engaging stories about the many wild animals that lived in and around the author's home over the years are filled with humor, affection, and just enough drama." Horn Book

"George tells of the many wild pets that lived with her family, particularly while her children were growing up. Each chapter describes a different animal or incident." Booklist

Montgomery, Sy

★ **Kakapo** rescue; saving the world's strangest parrot. text by Sy Montgomery; photographs by Nic Bishop. Houghton Mifflin 2010 73p il map (Scientists in the field) $18

Grades: 4 5 6 7   **639.9**

1. Parrots 2. Endangered species 3. Wildlife conservation 4. New Zealand

ISBN 978-0-618-49417-0; 0-618-49417-0

LC 2009-45250

Awarded the Robert F. Sibert Medal, 2011

Montgomery and Bishop head "to a remote island off the southern tip of New Zealand, where they join a local government-sponsored research team that is working to save the Kakapo parrot from extinction. . . . Montgomery's delight in her subject is contagious, and throughout her enthusiastic text, she nimbly blends scientific and historical facts with immediate, sensory descriptions of fieldwork. Young readers will be fascinated. . . . Bishop's photos of the creatures and their habitat are stunning." Booklist

640   Home and family management

Walsh, Peter

It's all too much, so get it together; with illustrations by John Hendrix. Simon & Schuster BFYR 2009 278p il pa $12.99

Grades: 7 8 9 10   **640**

1. House cleaning 2. Conduct of life 3. Storage in the home

ISBN 978-1-4169-9549-4 pa; 1-4169-9549-8 pa

This book suggests ways for teens to get rid of clutter and lead more organized, less stressful lives.

This is "is fun and light in tone. . . . For teens who are as overwhelmed by their lives as they are by their stuff, the quizzes and fictional scenarios will be right on point and may help them approach what they own and why in a new way. In addition to the suggestions for managing clutter (physical and mental), Walsh also offers tips for clutter-free friendships, jobs, studying, and even family fights." Voice Youth Advocates

641.3   Food

Chapman, Garry

Coffee; by Garry Chapman and Gary Hodges. Black Rabbit 2010 32p il (World commodities) lib bdg $28.50

Grades: 5 6 7 8   **641.3**

1. Coffee

ISBN 978-1-59920-584-7 lib bdg; 1-59920-584-X lib bdg

"The first part of the book discusses how coffee beans are grown, treated, prepared, and enjoyed around the world. . . . The second section offers an opportunity to use the commodity of coffee to understand such economics concepts as supply and demand or futures trading. . . . Finally, the book spins through a look at fair trade practices; political, environmental, and social issues surrounding coffee trade; and the sustainability and outlook of the global coffee industry. In all, the book gleans a pretty impressive and diverse array of accessible information from such a small bean." Booklist

Includes glossary

Jango-Cohen, Judith

The **history** of food; [by] Judith Jango-Cohen. Twenty-First Century Books 2006 56p il (Major inventions through history) lib bdg $26.60

Grades: 5 6 7 8   **641.3**

1. Food -- History

ISBN 0-8225-2484-8

LC 2004-23022

This history of food "discusses canning, pasteurization, refrigeration, supermarkets, and genetically modified foods.

. . . The text . . . is breezy but informative; unfamiliar terms are defined. Illustrations are a mixture of period black-and-white and color photos." SLJ

Includes bibliographical references

Llewellyn, Claire

Cooking with fruits and vegetables; by Claire Llewellyn with recipes by Clare O'Shea. Rosen Central 2011 48p il (Cooking healthy) lib bdg $27.95

Grades: 5 6 7 8   **641.3**

1. Fruit 2. Cooking 3. Vegetables

ISBN 978-1-4488-4844-7; 1-4488-4844-X

LC 2010039333

This book pairs "facts about [fruits and vegetables], including where it is eaten, with eye-catching photos. . . . Each course (section) has an overview of the vegetable group . . . . followed by recipes from all over the world. They vary in difficulty. . . . The cooking directions are clear and straightforward. . . . [The book is] profusely illustrated with full-color photos. Students who are learning to cook will appreciate [this] excellently organized [read]." SLJ

Includes bibliographical references

Menzel, Peter

★ **What** the world eats; photographed by Peter Menzel; written by Faith D'Aluisio. Tricycle Press 2008 160p il map $22.99

Grades: 4 5 6 7 8   **641.3**

1. Diet 2. Eating customs 3. Food -- Pictorial works

ISBN 978-1-58246-246-2; 1-58246-246-1

LC 2007-41439

An adaptation of Hungry Planet, published 2005 by Ten Speed Press for adults

"Stunning color photographs of mealtimes and daily activities illustrate the warm, informative, anecdotal narratives. . . . This is a fascinating, sobering, and instructive look at daily life around the world." Booklist

Includes bibliographical references

Miller, Debra A.

Organic foods; by Debra A. Miller. Thomson/ Gale 2008 111p il (Hot topics) lib bdg $32.45

Grades: 6 7 8 9   **641.3**

1. Natural foods 2. Natural foods industry

ISBN 978-1-59018-994-8 lib bdg; 1-59018-994-9 lib bdg

LC 2007-35909

"This title about organic foods gives a concise but thorough overview of a complex issue. . . . Sidebars, study questions, ample photos, and comprehensive chapter notes complete this on-target resource." Booklist

Includes bibliographical references

Miller, Jeanne

Food science. Lerner Publications 2009 48p il (Cool science) lib bdg $27.93

Grades: 4 5 6   **641.3**

1. Food

ISBN 978-0-8225-7589-4 lib bdg; 0-8225-7589-2 lib bdg

This describes how food scientists "explore how cooking changes food, create dishes that surprise the senses, and help farmers grow food in healthier ways." Publisher's note

Includes glossary and bibliographical references

Organic food and farming; Lauri S. Friedman, book editor. Greenhaven Press 2009 138p il (Introducing issues with opposing viewpoints) $34.70

Grades: 6 7 8 9 10   **641.3**

1. Natural foods 2. Organic farming

ISBN 978-0-7377-4483-5; 0-7377-4483-9

LC 2009-36912

"This title first examines the difference between organic and conventional food in terms of human health. The articles have been successfully edited for brevity and clarity. Whether organic farming can improve the world is discussed in the second . . . section of the book. . . . The bulk of the final section discusses the future of organic food and looks at the debate within the organic community on the direction of sustainable agriculture and the label organic. . . . With its colorful graphs and photographs nicely breaking up the text, this . . . book will provide a starting point for assignments." SLJ

Includes bibliographical references

Reilly, Kathleen M.

Food; 25 amazing projects investigate the history and science of what we eat. illustrated by Farah Rizvi. Nomad Press 2010 124p il (Build it yourself) pa $15.95

Grades: 4 5 6   **641.3**

1. Food

ISBN 978-1-934670-59-0; 1-934670-59-6

"This broad overview of food touches on its history and future, production and packaging, social and cultural practices, and health and safety concerns. . . . The information presented and questions posed on food packaging, megafarming, locally grown vs. commercially grown foods, free-range grazing, and healthy food choices make this a particularly up-to-date survey. . . . Every chapter concludes with two to three hands-on activities that range from cooking to science and art projects. . . . This soup-to-nuts look at the business and consumption of food will make a good addition to most collections." SLJ

Includes glossary and bibliographical references

Thornhill, Jan

Who wants pizza? the kids' guide to the history, science & culture of food. Maple Tree Press 2010 64p il $22.95; pa $10.95

Grades: 4 5 6   **641.3**

1. Food 2. Agriculture

ISBN 978-1-897349-96-0; 1-897349-96-3; 978-1-897349-97-7 pa; 1-897349-97-1 pa

This discusses "where food comes from and if there's enough to go around. Amid color photographs and sidebars, Thornhill writes concisely about hunter-gatherers, agriculture, processed foods, globalization, and poverty, among numerous other topics, providing a straightforward and balanced overview of the modern food industry, and the choices readers have when it comes to their own meals." Publ Wkly

641.5   Cooking

Arroyo, Sheri L.

How chefs use math; math curriculum consultant, Rhea A. Stewart. Chelsea Clubhouse 2010 32p il (Math in the real world) lib bdg $28

Grades: 4 5 6   **641.5**

1. Cooks 2. Cooking 3. Mathematics 4. Vocational guidance

ISBN 978-1-60413-608-1 lib bdg; 1-60413-608-1 lib bdg

LC 2009-14180

This describes how chefs use math for such tasks as measuring ingredients, watching temperatures, buying food, setting menu prices, and managing restaurant and catering businesses, and includes relevant math problems and information about how to become a chef

Includes glossary and bibliographical references

Batmanglij, Najmieh

Happy Nowruz; cooking with children to celebrate the Persian New Year. [by] Najmieh Batmanglij. Mage Publishers 2008 119p il $40

Grades: 4 5 6 7 8   **641.5**

1. New Year 2. Eating customs 3. Middle Eastern cooking 4. Iran -- Social life and customs

ISBN 1-933823-16-X; 978-1-933823-16-4

LC 2007-036047

"Combining a cookbook format with straightforward, informational text, this amply illustrated title offers a detailed introduction to the history and customs surrounding Nowruz, the Persian New Year. . . . The covered spiral binding allows pages to remain open while cooking, and the uncluttered, attractive format, featuring color photos of kids in the kitchen and whimsical illustrations, will attract interested browsers." Booklist

Bloomfield, Jill

Jewish holidays cookbook; by Jill Colella Bloomfield; Janet Ozur Bass, consultant; photography by Angela Coppola. DK Pub. 2008 128p il spiral bdg $19.99

Grades: 4 5 6 7   **641.5**

1. Jewish cooking 2. Jewish holidays

ISBN 978-0-7566-4089-7 spiral bdg; 0-7566-4089-X spiral bdg

"More than 40 recipes are included for celebrations from Shabbat to Lag B'Omer. Several introductions explain cooking tools, kitchen safety, and the general principles of keeping kosher, and brief background information is given for each holiday. Simple step-by-step instructions make the recipes easy. . . . Beautiful color photographs, both full page and spot, whet the appetite." SLJ

Carle, Megan

Teens cook; how to make what you want to eat. [by] Megan and Jill Carle with Judi Carle. Ten Speed Press 2004 146p il pa $19.95

Grades: 7 8 9 10   **641.5**

1. Cooking

ISBN 1-58008-584-9

This cookbook features "recipes for a variety of dishes including chocolate chip scones, potato skins, broccoli cheese soup, steak fajitas, baked macaroni and cheese, and toffee bars. Because Megan is a vegetarian, there are several vegetarian recipes or vegetarian substitutes. . . . Attractive, engaging, and told from a teen perspective, this cookbook will make an excellent addition to any nonfiction collection." Voice Youth Advocates

D'Amico, Joan

★ The **coming** to America cookbook; delicious recipes and fascinating stories from America's many cultures. [by] Joan D'Amico, Karen Eich Drummond. Wiley 2005 180p il pa $14.95

Grades: 5 6 7 8   641.5

1. Cooking 2. United States -- Immigration and emigration

ISBN 0-471-48335-4

LC 2004-14947

The authors "provide information about American immigrants from 18 nations as well as recipes representing each group. . . . Accompanied by line drawings of ethnic families choosing, preparing, and eating food, . . . chapters discuss each country's climate, history, major waves of emigration, and traditional foods. Typically, three recipes follow. . . . Teachers and students looking for recipes from American immigrant cultures will make good use of this handy resource." Booklist

Ejaz, Khadija

Recipe and craft guide to India. Mitchell Lane Publishers 2010 63p il map (World crafts and recipes) lib bdg $33.95

Grades: 4 5 6 7 8   641.5

1. Handicraft 2. Indic cooking

ISBN 978-1-58415-938-4 lib bdg; 1-58415-938-3 lib bdg

LC 2010008950

Provides recipes for several popular Indian dishes and includes instructions on creating colorful and traditional Indian crafts.

This provides "plenty of ideas for adding tasty treats and impressive visual aids to cultural reports or presentations." SLJ

Includes glossary and bibliographical references

Gold, Rozanne

★ **Eat** fresh food; awesome recipes for teen chefs. by Rozanne Gold and her all-star team; photographs by Phil Mansfield. Bloomsbury Children's Books 2009 160p il $21.99; pa $17.99

Grades: 6 7 8 9 10   641.5

1. Cooking

ISBN 978-1-59990-282-1; 1-59990-282-6; 978-1-59990-445-0 pa; 1-59990-445-4 pa

LC 2008-42443

"This joyful recipe book features fresh, healthful ingredients and encourages ambitious young chefs to collaborate on such mature dishes as Grape-and-Pignoli Breakfast Cake, Crunchy Wasabi-Lime Salmon with red cabbage and sugar snaps and orange-ginger sweet potato puree. . . . A prime pick for adventurous eaters and a potential catalyst for those in a junk food rut." Publ Wkly

The **green** teen cookbook; [edited by] Laurane Marchive, Pam McElroy. Zest Books 2014 144 p. $14.99

Grades: 6 7 8 9 10   641.5

1. Cookbooks 2. Vegetarian cooking 3. Nutrition 4. Low-budget cooking

ISBN 1936976587; 9781936976584

LC 2013951195

Edited by Laurane Marchive and Pam McElroy, this book "cuts through the chaos and shows teens how to shop smarter, cook more consciously, and eat a healthier diet. . . . In addition to the 70+ . . . recipes . . . , the book also includes illuminating essays about freeganism, flexitarians, vegetarianism, and more; tips about how to shop on a budget and get the most out of what you already have in your pantry; a seasonal key that ensures the freshness of the recipes (and a minimal carbon footprint). (Publisher's note)

"Originally published in the U.K., Marchive and McElroy's cookbook gives teenage home cooks ideas for every meal of the day, including snacks and desserts, with an eye toward healthy, seasonal options (brief essays explore organic and fair-trade food, vegetarianism, and other topics)... Color photos, clear instructions, and quotes from the teens providing the recipes should help bolster the confidence of young cooks." PW

Gregory, Josh

Chef. Cherry Lake Pub. 2011 32p il (Cool careers) lib bdg $27.07

Grades: 4 5 6 7   641.5

1. Cooks 2. Cooking 3. Vocational guidance

ISBN 978-1-60279-985-1; 1-60279-985-7

LC 2010029085

This book begins "with a personal story of a teen and then [segues] into the occupation [of chef]. . . . [It covers] the necessary training and skills for the job (and options for obtaining them), a typical day, salary expectations, and well-known professionals in the field. The [text is] accessible and clearly written. . . . The [volume has] a generous number of clear color photographs that depict people at work." SLJ

Includes glossary and bibliographical references

Hengel, Katherine

Garden to table; a kid's guide to planting, growing, and preparing food. by Katherine Hengel. Scarletta Junior Readers, an imprint of Scarletta 2014 144 p. (pbk.) $15.95

Grades: 5 6 7   641.5

1. Cooking 2. Vegetable gardening

ISBN 1938063422; 9781938063428

LC 2013037309

This book, by Katherine Hengel, "instructs readers in the cultivation of basil, carrots, green beans, lettuce, potatoes, and tomatoes. Instructions for growing the produce have been given with container gardening in mind, offering a practical alternative for readers with limited space, but they could easily be adapted for those with garden plots. . . . Photographs accompany every cooking term, ingredient, and kitchen tool as well as . . . each step of the growing process and recipes." (School Library Journal)

"The recipes are perfect for budding chefs, offering a succinct list of extra ingredients and cooking tools, along with warnings about potentially dangerous steps, and definitions of unfamiliar culinary terms. Each recipe is illustrated with clear step-by-step photographs, and the finished dishes look appetizing." Booklist

Includes bibliographical references and index

How to cook; delicious dishes perfect for teen cooks.
DK Pub. 2011 127p il $17.99
Grades: 7 8 9 10   **641.5**
1. Cooking
ISBN 978-0-7566-7214-0; 0-7566-7214-7

"This attractive book has dozens of recipes with an international flair. Some spreads feature a single dish, like lamb tagine, while others focus on several recipes using a single ingredient or technique. Experimentation is encouraged, and developing confidence is an unstated but obvious goal. This book is not for beginners, but teens with a bit of experience will enjoy trying the many tasty-sounding recipes for everything from jambalaya to macaroons. Vegetarian options are included throughout. Bright color photos show the finished dishes, and the pages are embellished with simple drawings showing processes and ingredients." SLJ

Includes glossary

Jacob, Jeanne

The **world** cookbook for students; [by] Jeanne Jacob, Michael Ashkenazi. Greenwood Press 2007 5v il map set $225
Grades: 7 8 9 10 11 12   **641.5**
1. Cooking 2. Eating customs
ISBN 0-313-33454-4; 978-0-313-33454-2
LC 2006-26184

"The volumes are organized alphabetically by country or group name. Each entry includes a brief introduction to the land and people and their cuisine and then an overview of the foodstuffs, typical dishes, and styles of eating in simple bulleted lists. Approximately 5 recipes are provided per country/ethnic group of typical dishes and holiday fare, for a total of 1,198." Publisher's note

Includes bibliographical references

LaRoche, Amelia

Recipe and craft guide to France. Mitchell Lane Publishers 2010 63p il map (World crafts and recipes) lib bdg $33.95
Grades: 4 5 6 7 8   **641.5**
1. Handicraft 2. French cooking
ISBN 978-1-58415-936-0 lib bdg; 1-58415-936-7 lib bdg
LC 2010008949

Provides recipes for several popular French dishes and includes instructions on creating crafts using household items.

This provides "plenty of ideas for adding tasty treats and impressive visual aids to cultural reports or presentations." SLJ

Includes glossary and bibliographical references

Lee, Frances

Fun with Chinese cooking. PowerKids Press 2009 32p il (Let's get cooking!) lib bdg $18.95; pa $11.75
Grades: 4 5 6 7   **641.5**
1. Chinese cooking
ISBN 978-1-4358-3453-8 lib bdg; 1-4358-3453-4 lib bdg; 978-1-4358-3475-0 pa; 1-4358-3475-5 pa
LC 2009010337

This includes recipes for such Chinese dishes as spring rolls and braised mushrooms, and highlights the history and dishes that surround the Chinese New Year.

"The photography is exceptional, with children engaged in the cooking process. . . . Children, and the adults who assist them, will spend hours together mastering the techniques." SLJ

Locricchio, Matthew

The **2nd** international cookbook for kids; photographs by Jack McConnell. Marshall Cavendish 2008 176p il $18.99
Grades: 5 6 7 8   **641.5**
1. Cooking
ISBN 978-0-7614-5513-4
LC 2008003178

The recipes are "presented in a challenging yet teen-friendly step-by-step sequence. The book is best for patient chefs with kitchen experience and adventurous appetites. Informative sidebars provide facts about the recipes and cultures." Horn Book Guide

The **international** cookbook for kids; by Matthew Locricchio; photographs by Jack McConnell. Reprint Marshall Cavendish 2012 175p il $12.99
Grades: 5 6 7 8   **641.5**
1. Cooking
ISBN 9780761463139
LC 2004-5894

This includes "60 classic recipes from Italy, France, China, and Mexico, . . . chef's tips discussing ingredients, nutrition, and technique, safety section discussing basic kitchen precautions, cooking terms and definitions." Publisher's note

Teen cuisine; illustrated by Janet Hamlin; photographs by James Peterson. Marshall Cavendish Children 2010 207p il $22.95
Grades: 6 7 8 9 10   **641.5**
1. Cooking
ISBN 978-0-7614-5715-2; 0-7614-5715-1
LC 2009-46847

"This contemporary collection of recipes will appeal to teen cooks and would make a great gift or an excellent addition to a library's cookbook collection." Voice Youth Advocates

Mattern, Joanne

Recipe and craft guide to China. Mitchell Lane Publishers 2010 63p il map (World crafts and recipes) lib bdg $33.95

Grades: 4 5 6 7 8   **641.5**
  1. Handicraft 2. Chinese cooking
ISBN 978-1-58415-937-7 lib bdg; 1-58415-937-5
lib bdg

LC 2010009242

Provides recipes for several popular Chinese dishes and includes instructions on creating crafts using household items.

This provides "plenty of ideas for adding tasty treats and impressive visual aids to cultural reports or presentations." SLJ

Includes glossary and bibliographical references

Mofford, Juliet Haines

Recipe and craft guide to Japan. Mitchell Lane Publishers 2010 63p il map (World crafts and recipes) lib bdg $33.95
Grades: 4 5 6 7 8   **641.5**
  1. Handicraft 2. Japanese cooking
ISBN 978-1-58415-933-9 lib bdg; 1-58415-933-2
lib bdg

LC 2010008951

Provides recipes for several popular Japanese dishes and includes instructions on creating traditional Japanese crafts using household items.

This provides "plenty of ideas for adding tasty treats and impressive visual aids to cultural reports or presentations." SLJ

Includes glossary and bibliographical references

Recipe and craft guide to the Caribbean. Mitchell Lane Publishers 2010 64p il map (World crafts and recipes) lib bdg $33.95
Grades: 4 5 6 7 8   **641.5**
  1. Handicraft 2. Caribbean cooking
ISBN 978-1-58415-935-3 lib bdg; 1-58415-935-9
lib bdg

LC 2010009240

Provides recipes for several popular Caribbean dishes and includes instructions on creating traditional Caribbean crafts using household items.

This provides "plenty of ideas for adding tasty treats and impressive visual aids to cultural reports or presentations." SLJ

Includes glossary and bibliographical references

Rau, Dana Meachen

Teen guide to breakfast on the go. Compass Point Books 2011 64p il (Teen cookbooks) lib bdg $33.99
Grades: 6 7 8 9   **641.5**
  1. Cooking 2. Breakfasts
ISBN 978-0-7565-4407-2; 0-7565-4407-6

LC 2010038580

Information and recipes help readers create quick, healthy, and tasty breakfasts.

An overview "about produce, packaged foods, organics, and kitchen and food safety [sets] the tone for the rest of the content, which encourages kids to hit the kitchen and helps them to make good nutritional choices. . . . Suggestions for vegetarian options, prep time, and substitute ingredients pop up periodically. . . . [The] full-page color photographs make

even a simple rice cake topped with cheese and a few apple slices look delectable." SLJ

Includes glossary and bibliographical references

Teen guide to creative, delightful dinners. Compass Point Books 2011 64p il (Teen cookbooks) lib bdg $33.99
Grades: 6 7 8 9   **641.5**
  1. Dining 2. Cooking
ISBN 978-0-7565-4408-9; 0-7565-4408-4

LC 2010040682

Information and recipes help readers create quick, healthy, and tasty dinners.

An overview "about produce, packaged foods, organics, and kitchen and food safety [sets] the tone for the rest of the content, which encourages kids to hit the kitchen and helps them to make good nutritional choices. . . . Suggestions for vegetarian options, prep time, and substitute ingredients pop up periodically. . . . [The] full-page color photographs make even a simple rice cake topped with cheese and a few apple slices look delectable." SLJ

Includes glossary and bibliographical references

Teen guide to fast, delicious lunches. Compass Point Books 2011 64p il (Teen cookbooks) lib bdg $33.99
Grades: 6 7 8 9   **641.5**
  1. Cooking 2. Luncheons
ISBN 978-0-7565-4405-8; 0-7565-4405-X

LC 2010040680

Information and recipes help readers create quick, healthy, and tasty lunches.

An overview "about produce, packaged foods, organics, and kitchen and food safety [sets] the tone for the rest of the content, which encourages kids to hit the kitchen and helps them to make good nutritional choices. . . . Suggestions for vegetarian options, prep time, and substitute ingredients pop up periodically. . . . [The] full-page color photographs make even a simple rice cake topped with cheese and a few apple slices look delectable." SLJ

Includes glossary and bibliographical references

Teen guide to quick, healthy snacks. Compass Point Books 2011 64p il (Teen cookbooks) lib bdg $33.99
Grades: 6 7 8 9   **641.5**
  1. Cooking 2. Snack foods
ISBN 978-0-7565-4406-5; 0-7565-4406-8

LC 2010040681

Information and recipes help readers create quick, healthy, and tasty snacks.

An overview "about produce, packaged foods, organics, and kitchen and food safety [sets] the tone for the rest of the content, which encourages kids to hit the kitchen and helps them to make good nutritional choices. . . . Suggestions for vegetarian options, prep time, and substitute ingredients pop up periodically. . . . [The] full-page color photographs make even a simple rice cake topped with cheese and a few apple slices look delectable." SLJ

Reusser, Kayleen

Recipe and craft guide to Indonesia. Mitchell Lane Publishers 2010 64p il map (World crafts and recipes) lib bdg $33.95

Grades: 4 5 6 7 8   **641.5**

1. Handicraft 2. Indonesian cooking
ISBN 978-1-58415-934-6 lib bdg; 1-58415-934-0 lib bdg

LC 2010009243

Provides recipes for several popular Indonesian dishes and includes instructions on creating crafts using household items.

This provides "plenty of ideas for adding tasty treats and impressive visual aids to cultural reports or presentations." SLJ

Includes glossary and bibliographical references

Sheen, Barbara

Foods of Chile. KidHaven Press 2011 64p il map (A taste of culture) $28.75

Grades: 4 5 6   **641.5**

1. Chilean cooking 2. Chile -- Social life and customs
ISBN 978-0-7377-5421-6; 0-7377-5421-4

LC 2010035995

"Demonstrating that a nation's cuisine springs from its geography, history, and traditions, [this volume explores Chile's background], the availability of fresh ingredients, and recipes that followed. . . . Culturally specific foods are described alongside some accompanying recipes and photos of people enjoying the dishes." Horn Book Guide

Includes glossary and bibliographical references

Foods of Cuba. KidHaven Press 2011 64p il map (A taste of culture) $28.75

Grades: 4 5 6   **641.5**

1. Cuban cooking 2. Cuba -- Social life and customs
ISBN 978-0-7377-5113-0; 0-7377-5113-4

LC 2010030795

"Demonstrating that a nation's cuisine springs from its geography, history, and traditions, [this volume explores Cuba's background], the availability of fresh ingredients, and recipes that followed. . . . Culturally specific foods are described alongside some accompanying recipes and photos of people enjoying the dishes." Horn Book Guide

Includes glossary and bibliographical references

Foods of Egypt. KidHaven Press 2010 64p il map (A taste of culture) $28.75

Grades: 4 5 6   **641.5**

1. Egyptian cooking 2. Egypt -- Social life and customs
ISBN 978-0-7377-4843-7; 0-7377-4843-5

LC 2009038461

"Sheen explores how different native dishes and types of local celebrations emerge from [Egypt's] culture and surroundings. [An] introductory [map] with a [key] to areas of food production illuminate the country's cuisine by identifying geographical landforms and climate. Traditions and tastes are described in accessible detail; key recipes are included and unfamiliar foods are pictured." Horn Book Guide

Includes glossary and bibliographical references

Foods of Ireland. KidHaven Press 2011 64p il map (A taste of culture) $28.75

Grades: 4 5 6   **641.5**

1. Irish cooking 2. Ireland -- Social life and customs
ISBN 978-0-7377-5114-7; 0-7377-5114-2

LC 2010018791

"Sheen explores how different native dishes and types of local celebrations emerge from [Ireland's] culture and surroundings. [An] introductory [map] with a [key] to areas of food production illuminate the country's cuisine by identifying geographical landforms and climate. Traditions and tastes are described in accessible detail; key recipes are included and unfamiliar foods are pictured." Horn Book Guide

Includes glossary and bibliographical references

Foods of Kenya. KidHaven Press 2010 64p il map (A taste of culture) $28.75

Grades: 4 5 6   **641.5**

1. African cooking 2. Kenyan cooking 3. Kenya -- Social life and customs
ISBN 978-0-7377-4813-0; 0-7377-4813-3

LC 2009048378

"Sheen explores how different native dishes and types of local celebrations emerge from [Kenya's] culture and surroundings. [An] introductory [map] with a [key] to areas of food production illuminate the country's cuisine by identifying geographical landforms and climate. Traditions and tastes are described in accessible detail; key recipes are included and unfamiliar foods are pictured." Horn Book Guide

Includes glossary and bibliographical references

Foods of Korea. KidHaven Press 2011 64p il map (A taste of culture) $26.75

Grades: 4 5 6   **641.5**

1. Korean cooking 2. Korea -- Social life and customs
ISBN 978-0-7377-5115-4; 0-7377-5115-0

LC 2010018789

"Demonstrating that a nation's cuisine springs from its geography, history, and traditions, [this volume explores Korea's background], the availability of fresh ingredients, and recipes that followed. . . . Culturally specific foods are described alongside some accompanying recipes and photos of people enjoying the dishes." Horn Book Guide

Includes glossary and bibliographical references

Foods of Peru. KidHaven Press 2011 64p il map (A taste of culture) $28.75

Grades: 4 5 6   **641.5**

1. Peruvian cooking 2. Peru -- Social life and customs
ISBN 978-0-7377-5346-2; 0-7377-5346-3

LC 2010032959

"Demonstrating that a nation's cuisine springs from its geography, history, and traditions, [this volume explores Peru's background], the availability of fresh ingredients, and recipes that followed. . . . Culturally specific foods are described alongside some accompanying recipes and photos of people enjoying the dishes." Horn Book Guide

Includes glossary and bibliographical references

Smart, Denise

The **cookbook** for girls; written by Denise Smart; photography by Howard Shooter. DK Pub. 2009 128p il $17.99

Grades: 4 5 6   **641.5**

1. Cooking

ISBN 978-0-7566-4500-7; 0-7566-4500-X

"The photos alone make this attractive cookbook worth the price of admission. . . . Most of these dishes will appeal to adventurous eaters and their foodie parents." SLJ

Includes "more than fifty dishes for making with friends, serving at parties, and learning all about the kitchen, and includes craft projects designed to help young hostesses serve up their culinary achievements." Publisher's note

Stern, Sam

Real food, real fast; [by] Sam Stern & Susan Stern. Candlewick Press 2008 128p il $16.99

Grades: 6 7 8 9   **641.5**

1. Cooking

ISBN 978-0-7636-3533-6; 0-7636-3533-2

LC 2007025635

"This book is full of time-management advice, recipes, and tips for combining dishes. Cross-references enable novices to put together full meals, and the index encourages browsing by ingredient or type of recipe. . . . Each recipe includes serving sizes, variations to adapt the recipes to one's own taste, pictures of the author and friends, and often pictures of the finished product. The directions are easy. . . . A teen-friendly guide to healthy eating, featuring foods that are fast and easy to make." SLJ

Sam Stern's get cooking. Candlewick Press 2009 144p $17.99

Grades: 6 7 8 9   **641.5**

1. Cooking

ISBN 978-0-7636-3926-6; 0-7636-3926-5

British teenage cook Sam Stern presents over 100 new recipes based on his own favorite ingredient, chocolate, and the favorite ingredients of seven of his friends.

"Stern does an excellent job of introducing teens to the kitchen. . . . Every page boasts bright colors and pictures with large print and a user-friendly ingredients list in sidebar format. The recipes run from very easy to a bit challenging, but the step-by-step directions will help even the most challenged cook find a way around the kitchen." Voice of Youth Advocates

Tuminelly, Nancy

Cool meat-free recipes; delicious & fun foods without meat. Nancy Tuminelly. ABDO Pub. Co. 2013 32 p. (Checkerboard how-to library. Cool recipes for your health) $28.50

Grades: 3 4 5 6 7 8   **641.5**

1. Cooking 2. Vegetarian cooking

ISBN 161783582X; 9781617835827

LC 2012023989

Author Nancy Tuminelly's book "gives young readers the tools to make healthy, tasty--and safe--dishes for anybody, anytime. This book has kid-tested, easy meat-free recipes, perfect for those who follow a vegetarian or vegan diet. Basic baking techniques, tools, and ingredients are illustrated so kids can quickly prepare each recipe, such as Breakfast Bars and Sloppy Joes." (Publisher's note)

Includes bibliographical references and index

Warren, Rachel Meltzer

The **smart** girl's guide to going vegetarian; how to look great, feel fabulous, and be a better you. Rachel Meltzer Warren, MS, RDN. Sourcebooks Fire 2014 240 p. (alk. paper) $12.99

Grades: 7 8 9 10 11 12   **641.5**

1. Veganism 2. Eating habits 3. Vegetarianism 4. Vegetarian cooking 5. Teenagers -- Nutrition

ISBN 1402284918; 9781402284915

LC 2013023334

In this book, author Rachel Meltzer Warren "encourages readers who are considering changing their diet to begin by participating in Meatless Mondays. Chapters include information on nutrients that are crucial to a healthy diet and what foods they can be found in for all types of diets (vegan, lacto-ovo, pescetarian). The book also includes types of restaurants with vegetarian-friendly options and an explanation of how to use the choosemyplate.gov resource to practice planning a healthy meal." (Publisher's note)

"A vegetarian herself since age 12, Warren knows the questions that teen girls ask and the arguments their parents raise when kids want to experience vegetarianism or veganism. Here, she offers sound advice for girls who are considering being or have chosen to go vegetarian or vegan and for those who waver about where they stand on the topic...The catchy, accessible text is broken up by generous topic headings and questions. Overall, a sound guide for any teenager, really, and her or his parents." (Booklist)

Includes bibliographical references and index

Webb, Lois Sinaiko

Holidays of the world cookbook for students; [by] Lois Sinaiko Webb and Lindsay Grace Roten. updated and rev.; Greenwood 2011 442p il map $95; pa $32.95

Grades: 5 6 7 8 9 10   **641.5**

1. Cooking 2. Holidays

ISBN 978-0-313-38393-9; 0-313-38393-6; 978-0-313-39790-5 pa; 0-313-39790-2 pa; 978-0-313-38394-6 ebook

LC 2011-8458

First published 1995 by Oryx Press

"The recipes appear with each country entry, and the countries are arranged in alphabetical order within each region: Africa, Asia and the South Pacific, the Caribbean, Europe, Latin America, the Middle East, and North America." Publisher's note

The **multicultural** cookbook for students; [by] Lois Sinaiko Webb and Lindsay Grace Roten. Updated & rev.; Greenwood Press 2009 354p map $85

Grades: 7 8 9 10   **641.5**

1. Cooking

ISBN 978-0-313-37558-3; 0-313-37558-5

LC 2009-26718

First published 1993 under the authorship of Carole Lisa Albyn

"This highly informative cookbook includes not only recipes, but also information on the country, its food staples, and ethnic and cultural divisions. Recipes are divided into seven sections according to geography: Africa, Asia and South Pacific, The Caribbean, Europe, Latin America, The Middle East, and North America. . . . Recipes are then divided by country with a description of the country concentrating on culinary information. A minimum of two recipes per country are also annotated with information about the ingredients or why the dish was important to the area. . . . This book is a great resource for cultural research even if the actual recipes will not be prepared. There is a comprehensive index by recipe name, country, and ingredients." Libr Media Connect

Includes glossary and bibliographical references

641.509 Cooking -- History, geographic treatment, biography

Abrams, Dennis

Julia Child, Chef; by Dennis Abrams. Chelsea House 2011 134 p. ill. (some col.) (Women of achievement) lib bdg $35

Grades: 6 7 8 9 **641.509**
1. Cooks 2. Television personalities 3. Cookbook writers 4. Cooks -- United States -- Biography
ISBN 1604139129; 9781604139129
LC 2011000039

'This book offers a biography of chef "Julia Child . . . [who] started a cooking revolution when she burst onto television screens in the 1960s. Before long, Americans inspired by her example began cooking French food at home in droves and truly appreciating the pleasure that preparing good food can provide. Yet Child did not grow up knowing how to cook or even with an interest in fine cuisine. Her story is one of an American woman's quest to find herself, to find her passion, and then to find a way to share that passion with the world. It is the story of how Julia McWilliams of Pasadena, California, transformed herself into Julia Child, 'The French Chef.'" (Publisher's note)

This "provides an engaging introduction to the chef as a privileged but the individualistic woman who took some time to find her way in life but eventually shared her passion for French cooking with the world. . . . Solid fare for the biography collection." Booklist

Includes bibliographical references and index

641.59 Cooking characteristic of specific geographic environments, ethnic cooking

Blaxland, Wendy

Chinese food; by Wendy Blaxland. Smart Apple Media 2012 32 p. (library binding) $28.50

Grades: 4 5 6 7 **641.59**
1. Cooking, Chinese
ISBN 1599206714; 9781599206714
LC 2011005448

Author Wendy Blaxland's book "offers them the tastes of foreign or favorite cuisine. Beginning with a discussion about this area's culinary roots, it shows the growing of favorite foods are grown, its purchase and preparation. Step-by-step illustrated instructions for recipes are included along with nutritional data, safety and hygiene information." (Wheelers)

Mexican food; by Wendy Blaxland. Smart Apple Media 2012 32 p. (I can cook!) (library binding) $28.50

Grades: 4 5 6 7 **641.59**
1. Cookbooks 2. Mexican cooking 3. Food -- Mexico -- History
ISBN 1599206684; 9781599206684
LC 2011005444

This book, by Wendy Blaxland, "presents a good amount of information on the geography, food staples, and even culture of [Mexico]. 'Mexican Food' finds a balance of spicy and sweet flavors in dishes from huevos rancheros to pan de muertos. Each recipe features helpful digital step-by-step illustrations and ideas for variations, underlining the fact that cooking is a creative process." (Booklist)

D'Amico, Joan

The **United** States cookbook; fabulous foods and fascinating facts from all 50 states. [by] Joan D'Amico and Karen Eich Drummond; illustrations by Jeff Cline and Tina Cash-Walsh. Wiley 2000 186p il pa $12.95

Grades: 5 6 7 8 **641.59**
1. Cooking
ISBN 0-471-35839-8
LC 99-39548

Provides information about the fifty states along with a recipe native to each of them, such as Boston baked beans from Massachusetts, crab cakes from Maryland, Key lime pie from Florida, corn dogs from Iowa, and taco soup from New Mexico

"There are helpful sections on the use of equipment; cooking skills, such as cutting, measuring, and mixing, and safety rules." SLJ

Locricchio, Matthew

The **cooking** of Brazil; Matthew Locricchio; with photos by Jack McConnell. 2nd ed. Marshall Cavendish Benchmark 2012 96 p. ill. (library) $35.64; (ebook) $35.64

Grades: 7 8 9 10 11 12 **641.59**
1. Cookbooks 2. Brazilian cooking 3. Food -- Brazil
ISBN 1608705498; 9781608705498; 9781608707379
LC 2011004948

This book, by Matthew Locricchio, "invites . . . readers to the kitchen to experience the satisfaction of preparing authentic [Brazilian] recipes." The book "opens with a . . . look at the . . . country and their culinary traditions and contributions to international cuisine. This cultural introduction is followed with an overview of kitchen safety, food handling, and common sense nutrition, then on to a wide variety of recipes that range from soups and salads to main entrees and desserts." (Publisher's note)

Includes bibliographical references and index.

The **cooking** of France; by Matthew Locricchio. Benchmark Books 2011 96 p. (Superchef) (print) $35.64

Grades: 4 5 6 7 8   641.59

1. Cookbooks 2. French cooking 3. Food habits -- France
ISBN 160870551X; 9781608705511; 9781608707393
LC 2010052549

Author Matthew Locricchio presents a book on French cooking. "After a shared introduction about safety, [it] introduces . . . regional cuisines, mentioning festivals, traditions, and music to give readers a broader cultural view of [France]. Recipes, divided into categories such as soups and salads, main courses, and so on, make up the bulk of [the] book." (Booklist)

Includes bibliographical references and index

The **cooking** of Greece; Matthew Locricchio. Marshall Cavendish Benchmark 2011 96 p. (print) $35.64

Grades: 4 5 6 7 8   641.59

1. Cookbooks 2. Greek cooking 3. Food habits -- Greece 4. Cooking, Mediterranean
ISBN 1608705528; 9781608705528; 9781608707409
LC 2010052548

In this book, author Matthew Locricchio "begins with a region-by-region overview of Greece, highlighting the natural produce of each area and the resulting cuisine, then groups his recipes by type–'Pies & Pitas,' 'Entrées,' etc. A section on kitchen safety . . . gives particulars on using knives. Fresh, healthful ingredients are emphasized, and suggestions are offered for adapting the recipes for vegetarians." (School Library Journal)

Includes bibliographical references and index

The **cooking** of Italy; by Matthew Locricchio. Marshall Cavendish Benchmark 2011 96 p. (print) $35.64

Grades: 4 5 6 7 8   641.59

1. Cookbooks 2. Italian cooking 3. Food habits -- Italy
ISBN 1608705544; 9781608705542; 9781608707423
LC 2010051849

In this book, by Matthew Locricchio, Italian cooking recipes are presented. It also "discusses general safety rules in the kitchen as well as specific rules for using knives. Regions of Italy . . . are defined along with a description of how geography influences crops, celebrations, and traditions that flourish within each area. Cooking terms are [also] explained." (Publisher's note)

Includes bibliographical references and index

Mendez, Sean

One world kids cookbook; easy, healthy and affordable family meals. by Sean Mendez. Interlink 2011 96 p. $20

Grades: 5 6 7 8   641.59

1. Diet 2. Cookbooks 3. Eating habits
ISBN 1566568668; 9781566568661

Author Sean Mendez presents a cookbook "aimed at encouraging young people to think about what they eat through emphasizing the importance of a balanced diet. It contains

kitchen tips and suggests vegetarian substitutes to the meat recipes. One World Kids Cookbook aims to instill a passion for good, wholesome, healthy food as well as a passion for life." (Publisher's note)

Sheen, Barbara

Foods of Australia; by Barbara Sheen. KidHaven Press 2010 64 p. (hardcover) $31.95

Grades: 4 5 6   641.59

1. Australian cooking 2. Australia -- Social life and customs 3. Cooking, Australian
ISBN 0737748125; 9780737748123
LC 2009032643

This book, by Barbara Sheen, "explores the foods, cooking traditions, customs, eating habits, and food sources of [Australia]. [It discusses] ingredients that form the staples of cooking . . ., the favorite dishes, the snacks and sweets, the traditional holiday meals, and the preparations and traditions associated with these foods." (Publisher's note)

Includes bibliographical references and index

641.5944   Cooking – French

Wagner, Lisa

Cool French cooking; fun and tasty recipes for kids. by Lisa Wagner. Checkerboard Library 2011 32 p. $28.50

Grades: 3 4 5 6   641.5944

1. French cooking
ISBN 1617146609; 9781617146602
LC 2010022192

This book, by Lisa Wagner, "introduces readers to world geography and authentic, easy-to-make recipes [for French cuisine]. Cooking teaches kids about food, math and measuring, and following directions. Each kid-tested recipe includes step-by-step instructions and how-to photos. Tools and ingredients lists are also provided, as well as pronunciation guides when needed." (Publisher's note)

641.5945   Cooking – Italian

Cool Italian cooking; fun and tasty recipes for kids. by Lisa Wagner. Checkerboard Library 2011 32 p. $28.50

Grades: 3 4 5 6   641.5945

1. Italian cooking
ISBN 1617146617; 9781617146619
LC 2010022193

This book, by Lisa Wagner, "introduces readers to world geography and authentic, easy-to-make recipes [for Italian cuisine}. Cooking teaches kids about food, math and measuring, and following directions. Each kid-tested recipe includes step-by-step instructions and how-to photos. Tools and ingredients lists are also provided, as well as pronunciation guides when needed." (Publisher's note)

641.595   Cooking – Asia

Wagner, Lisa

Cool Chinese and Japanese cooking; fun and tasty recipes for kids. by Lisa Wagner. ABDO Pub. 2011 32 p. (Cool world cooking) $28.50

Grades: 3 4 5 6   **641.595**
1. Chinese cooking 2. Japanese cooking
ISBN 1617146595; 9781617146596

LC 2010022191

This book, by Lisa Wagner, "introduces readers to world geography and authentic, easy-to-make recipes [for Chinese and Japanese cuisine]. Cooking teaches kids about food, math and measuring, and following directions. Each kid-tested recipe includes step-by-step instructions and how-to photos. Tools and ingredients lists are also provided, as well as pronunciation guides when needed." (Publisher's note)

641.5972   Cooking – Mexican

Wagner, Lisa

Cool Mexican cooking; fun and tasty recipes for kids. by Lisa Wagner. Checkerboard Library 2011 32 p. (Cool world cooking) $28.50

Grades: 3 4 5 6   **641.5972**
1. Mexican cooking
ISBN 1617146625; 9781617146626

LC 2010022194

This book, by Lisa Wagner, "introduces readers to world geography and authentic, easy-to-make recipes [for Mexican cuisine]. Cooking teaches kids about food, math and measuring, and following directions. Each kid-tested recipe includes step-by-step instructions and how-to photos. Tools and ingredients lists are also provided, as well as pronunciation guides when needed." (Publisher's note)

641.6   Cooking specific materials

Llewellyn, Claire

Cooking with meat and fish; [by] Claire Llewellyn, Clare O'Shea. Rosen Central 2011 48p il map (Cooking healthy) lib bdg $27.95

Grades: 5 6 7 8   **641.6**
1. Meat 2. Cooking 3. Seafood
ISBN 978-1-4488-4845-4; 1-4488-4845-8

LC 2010039337

A description of each type of meat and fish, how to cook them in a healthy manner, and recipe examples of each.

This book pairs "facts about [meat and fish], including where it is eaten, with eye-catching photos. . . . Each course (section) has an overview of the . . . [meat] followed by recipes from all over the world. They vary in difficulty. . . . The cooking directions are clear and straightforward. . . . [The book is] profusely illustrated with full-color photos. Students who are learning to cook will appreciate [this] excellently organized [read]." SLJ

Includes glossary and bibliographical references

641.8   Cooking specific kinds of dishes and preparing beverages

Carle, Megan

Teens cook dessert; [by] Megan and Jill Carle, with Judi Carle. Ten Speed Press 2006 158p pa $19.95

Grades: 6 7 8 9 10   **641.8**
1. Cooking 2. Desserts
ISBN 978-1-58008-752-0; 1-58008-752-3

LC 2005-24343

The authors "start out with the all-around favorites, like classic chocolate chip cookies. There are holiday recipes for Halloween dirt pie, complete with cookie tombstones and gummy worms that seem to crawl out of the chocolate 'earth.' The final chapter has fancy foods like vanilla soufflt with chocolate sauce or fresh raspberry napoleons. . . . Not only do the recipes sound delicious, they look delicious in glossy color pictures. . . . The instructions are easy to understand." Voice Youth Advocates

Love, Ann

Sweet! the delicious story of candy. [by] Ann Love & Jane Drake; illustrated by Claudia Dávila. Tundra Books 2007 64p il map $19.95

Grades: 4 5 6 7   **641.8**
1. Candy
ISBN 978-0-88776-752-4

"This history of things sweet and sugary is a yummy feast. The prose is chatty and inviting. Color cartoon illustrations show multiethnic people in the process of making or enjoying everything from honey to ice cream to cotton candy (called candy floss here) to jelly beans and chocolate." SLJ

644.6   Plumbing

DiPiazza, Francesca Davis

Remaking the john; the invention and reinvention of the toilet. Francesca Davis DiPiazza. Twenty-First Century Books 2015 64 p. color illustrations (lib. bdg. : alk. paper) $34.60

Grades: 6 7 8 9   **644.6**
1. Toilets 2. Sewage disposal 3. Toilets -- History
ISBN 1467726451; 9781467726450

LC 2013040138

Readers of this book by Francesca Davis Dipiazza will "explore the many ways people across the globe and through the ages have invented--and reinvented--the toilet. You will learn about everything from ancient Roman sewers to the world's first flush toilets. You'll also find out about the twenty-first-century Reinvent the Toilet Challenge--an engineering contest designed to spur creation of an ecologically friendly, water-saving, inexpensive, and sanitary toilet." (Publisher's note)

"This honest, fact-filled little book should attract readers and researchers (who may even begin celebrating World Toilet Day every November 19)." SLJ

Includes bibliographical references (pages 58-59) and index

646.2   Sewing and related operations

Plumley, Amie Petronis

Sewing school; 21 sewing projects kids will love to make. [by] Amie Petronis Plumley & Andria Lisle; photography by Justin Fox Burks. Storey Pub. 2010 143p il $16.95

Grades: 3 4 5 6   **646.2**

1. Sewing

ISBN 978-1-60342-578-0; 1-60342-578-0

LC 2010022154

"This large-format book offers appealing projects illustrated with color photos of step-by-step directions as well as kids engaged in sewing and showing off work. The opening 12 lessons begin with topics such as threading a needle, knotting the thread, and making a basic running stitch. After covering basic knowledge and skills, the presentation moves on to instructions for fun easy projects." Booklist

646.4   Clothing and accessories construction

Zent, Sheila

Sew teen; make your own cool clothes. Sterling 2006 160p il pa $17.95

Grades: 7 8 9 10   **646.4**

1. Sewing 2. Clothing and dress

ISBN 1-931543-90-9

"Zent presents 21 projects and accessory designs that will appeal to budding seamstresses and novice stitchers alike, although teens should know the basics of using a sewing machine or have assistance. . . . The step-by-step instructions include drawn renderings to assist with the construction and full-color photographs of teen models wearing each garment or accessory." SLJ

646.7   Management of personal and family life

Bergamotto, Lori

Skin; the bare facts. Zest Books 2009 97p il pa $18.95

Grades: 6 7 8 9 10   **646.7**

1. Skin -- Care 2. Teenagers -- Health and hygiene

ISBN 978-0-9800732-5-6; 0-9800732-5-1

Presents an overview on skin types, methods for treating common problems, and tips for skin care and makeup application.

"There's something for every girl here, whether she's just had her first breakout or needs a refresher on which sunscreen to use and when to reapply." SLJ

Buchanan, Andrea J.

The daring book for girls; Andrea Buchanan, Miriam Peskowitz ; illustrated by Alexis Seabrook. 1st ed. Collins 2007 viii, 279 p.p ill. (some col.), col. map (hardcover) $26.95

Grades: 4 5 6 7 8 9   **646.7**

1. Girls 2. Amusements 3. Recreation 4. Curiosities and wonders 5. Girls in literature 6. Girls -- Conduct of life 7. Girls -- Life skills guides

ISBN 0061472573; 9780061472572

LC 2007031986

This book is "filled with interesting activities to try and important facts [girls] may not know, but are sure to keep them busy for hours. The authors cover everything from making a lemon-powered clock to the history of writing and cursive, from how to paddle a canoe to the Periodic Table of the Elements." (School Library Journal)

Includes bibliographical references (p. 274-276).

Buchholz, Rachel

How to survive anything; shark attack, quicksand, embarrassing parents, pop quizzes, and other perilous situations. illustrations by Chris Philpot. National Geographic 2011 176p il (National geographic kids) pa $12.95

Grades: 5 6 7 8   **646.7**

1. Life skills 2. Survival skills

ISBN 978-1-4263-0774-4; 1-4263-0774-8

LC 2010028045

"Buchholz doles out hilarious and handy advice for suffering though both natural and manmade catastrophes. Part survival guide and part self-help book, it provides honest, tongue-in-cheek answers to questions teens may be reluctant to ask out loud, in addition to imparting disaster preparedness strategies. It's a clever, winning combination. Superb full-color digital illustrations and photographs and a lively, conversational tone will catch and keep readers' attention, and the list-heavy layout is fun to read and easy to understand." SLJ

Ehrman, M. K.

★ Taking a stand; being a leader & helping others. ABDO Pub. Co. 2009 112p il (Essential health: strong beautiful girls) lib bdg $22.95

Grades: 6 7 8 9   **646.7**

1. Leadership 2. Life skills 3. Attitude (Psychology)

ISBN 978-1-60453-105-3 lib bdg; 1-60453-105-3 lib bdg

LC 2008-15211

This features fictional narratives paired with firsthand advice from a licensed psychologist to help preteen and teen girls evaluate success and build leadership skills. Topics include the challenges of competition, and taking on too much.

"The topics are well selected, the design is attractive, and the stories feature girls from a variety of cultures." Booklist

Includes glossary and bibliographical references

Fonseca, Christine

The girl guide; finding your place in a mixed-up world. by Christine Fonseca. Prufrock Press 2013 228 p. $14.95

Grades: 6 7 8 9   **646.7**

1. Girls 2. Teenagers

ISBN 1618210270; 9781618210272

This book, by Christine Fonseca, is designed "for girls in grades 6-8 as they enter the tumultuous world of adolescence. Worksheets and quizzes, as well as stories from older girls and women, [cover] everything a teenage girl needs to know on the journey toward her own identity. Proven strategies for dealing with stress management, confronting relational aggression, being safe online, navigating the changing mother-daughter relationship, and more make this [a] guide for any girl to get through the teen years." (Publisher's note)

"—Sporting a sassy, appealing cover, The Girl Guide elbows its way into the already-crowded market of self-help and self-esteem-building books...There's a bit of genius at play here as the author gives the gift of time to her readers-time for reflection and for de-stressing through the act of creating. Teens should not rush through this book. No quick fixes are offered, just reasonable suggestions for maintaining true north through the turbulent teen years.—" (School Library Journal)

Fornay, Alfred

Born beautiful; the African American teenager's complete beauty guide. John Wiley & Sons 2002 166p il pa $14.95

Grades: 8 9 10 11 12   **646.7**
    1. Personal grooming 2. Personal appearance 3. Teenagers -- Health and hygiene 4. African American women -- Health and hygiene
    ISBN 0-471-40275-3
                LC 2002-18131

This book on beauty and grooming for African American teenage girls includes information on makeup, hairstyles, nail and skin care, diet, and clothing.

Harris, Ashley Rae

★ **Is** this really my family? relating to your relatives. ABDO Pub. Co. 2009 112p il (Essential health: strong, beautiful girls) lib bdg $22.95

Grades: 6 7 8 9   **646.7**
    1. Family 2. Parent-child relationship
    ISBN 978-1-60453-101-5 lib bdg; 1-60453-101-0 lib bdg
                LC 2008-12105

Presents character narratives and discussion questions to help teenage girls develop positive ways to build healthy relationships with members of their immediate family.

"The topics are well selected, the design is attractive, and the stories feature girls from a variety of cultures." Booklist

Includes glossary and bibliographical references

Heos, Bridget

A **career** as a hairstylist. Rosen 2010 80p il (Essential careers) lib bdg $30.60

Grades: 7 8 9 10 11 12   **646.7**
    1. Hairstylists 2. Vocational guidance
    ISBN 978-1-4358-9474-7 lib bdg; 1-4358-9474-X lib bdg

This title "is so informative it could be subtitled 'Everything You Want to Know about Becoming a Hair Stylist.'... After the basics, Heos discusses the nitty-gritty of finding a job, keeping it, and running one's own business. The history of hair-cutting careers follows, and there are even ethical discussions. . . . A must for career shelves." Booklist

Jeffrie, Sally

The **girls'** book of glamour; a guide to being a goddess. 1st American ed.; Scholastic, Inc. 2009 126p il $9.99

Grades: 6 7 8 9 10   **646.7**
    1. Girls 2. Etiquette 3. Life skills
    ISBN 978-0-545-08537-3; 0-545-08537-3
                LC 2008-17119
    First published 2008 in the United Kingdom

This is "focused on lifestyle, health, and beauty. Each entry has simple instructions accompanied by entertaining illustrations. This upbeat and amusing style guide adopts a hip tone for the tween and young-teen set. . . . Jeffrie's snappy writing and Ryan's great line drawings and stylish design make [this] an easy, breezy read." SLJ

Morgenstern, Julie

★ **Organizing** from the inside out for teens; the foolproof system for organizing your room, your time, and your life. [by] Julie Morgenstern and Jessi Morgenstern-Colón; illustrations by Janet Pedersen. Holt & Co. 2002 238p il pa $15

Grades: 7 8 9 10   **646.7**
    1. Life skills 2. Time management
    ISBN 0-8050-6470-2
                LC 2002-68552

The authors "offer practical advice to teenagers who want to get organized. After considering what might be holding them back and the three steps to success (analyze, strategize, attack), the discussion shifts to the two major areas of concern: managing space and managing time. . . . Useful advice in an accessible paperback format." Booklist

Rosenwald, Laurie

★ **All** the wrong people have self esteem; an inappropriate book for young ladies (or, frankly, anybody else) Bloomsbury Children's Books 2008 un il $16.99

Grades: 6 7 8 9   **646.7**
    1. Life skills 2. Conduct of life
    ISBN 978-1-59990-240-1; 1-59990-240-0
                LC 2008-14386

Rosenwald "tackles political correctness, the follies of prevailing wisdom and her favorite peeves using all the tools in her arsenal: her spread-size collages feature fonts on sterioids, magazine cut-outs, photos and cartoons paired with witty diatribes confessions. . . . Funny, fresh and impossible not to read cover to cover." Publ Wkly

Shoket, Ann

Seventeen ultimate guide to beauty; the best hair, skin, nails & makeup ideas for you. Ann Shoket & the editors of Seventeen Magazine. Running Press 2012 191 p.

Grades: 7 8 9 10   **646.7**
    1. Hair 2. Cosmetics 3. Personal appearance 4. Beauty, Personal 5. Skin -- Care and hygiene
    ISBN 0762445246; 9780762445240
                LC 2012935723

This book, by Ann Shoket and the editors of "Seventeen" magazine, "is a girl's handbook to celebrating her natural beauty. It's packed with clear, customized service that helps make the most of her skin tone, her face shape, her hair texture, and her style! Each chapter is filled with detailed how-tos, amazing inspiration, and awesome advice from 'Seventeen's' editors." (Publisher's note)

"illed with great fashion photography featuring the Beauty Smarties, this guide highlights real girls' personal styles... The detailed photographs and step-by-step instructions will have readers practicing braids, up-dos, and smoky eye makeup for hours. A fine addition to the 646.7 shelves." (School Library Journal)

647.95 Eating and drinking places

Food. Ferguson's 2011 122 p. (Discovering careers series) (hardcover : alk. paper) $30

Grades: 7 8 9 10   **647.95**
1. Food service -- Vocational guidance 2. Food industry and trade -- Vocational guidance
ISBN 0816080577; 9780816080571

LC 2011022916

"Each volume breaks down broad career umbrellas into 20 specific subsets and examines them from the vantage point of "Education and Training," "Outlook," "Earnings," and so on. A clean design, sidebars, and the occasional on-the-job action photo add to the appeal. Food moves from the ground (farmers and fishers) to the plate (personal chefs)... both younger and older kids will find tempting—perhaps before unheard-of—career options to get them thinking about down the road." (Booklist)

Includes bibliographical references and index

649 Child rearing; home care of people with disabilities and illnesses

Buckley, Annie

Be a better babysitter; by Annie Buckley. Child's World 2007 32p il (Girls rock!) lib bdg $24.21

Grades: 5 6 7 8   **649**
1. Babysitting
ISBN 1-59296-740-X

LC 2006001639

This "describes what babysitting entails, examines pros and cons, discusses safety issues, offers tips for doing a good job, and suggests saving as much as half of any money earned. . . . [This] realistic [title is] well written and [provides] excellent information." SLJ

Includes bibliographical references

Chasse, Jill D.

The **babysitter's** survival guide; fun games, cool crafts, and how to be the best babysitter in town. illustrated by Jessica Secheret. Sterling Pub. Co. 2010 107p il $12.95

Grades: 5 6 7 8   **649**
1. Babysitting
ISBN 978-1-4027-4654-3; 1-4027-4654-7

LC 2009-2538

"This useful, up-to-date handbook offers plenty of practical advice with a wise emphasis on safety, which makes it a good choice for new sitters as well as those with experience. Chassé starts with information on starting a business, includ-

ing references, advertising, and interviewing. Child development is a main focus; suggested activities and tips on interaction with children at different developmental stages will be appreciated by sitters and parents alike. . . . Occasional two-color cartoons feature diverse children and sitters." SLJ

Includes bibliographical references

Crissey, Pat

Personal hygiene? What's that got to do with me? Jessica Kingsley 2005 94p il pa $19.95

Grades: 5 6 7   **649**
1. Autism 2. Hygiene 3. Asperger's syndrome
ISBN 978-1-8431-0796-5; 1-8431-0796-1

LC 2004-24966

Explains the importance of personal hygiene to children with autism and asperger's syndrome.

649.1 Child rearing

Bondy, Halley

Don't sit on the baby; the ultimate guide to sane, skilled, and safe babysitting. Halley Bondy. Zest Books 2012 127 p. (pbk.) $12.99

Grades: 7 8 9 10 11 12   **649.1**
1. Child care 2. Babysitting 3. Infants -- Care
ISBN 0982732236; 9780982732236

LC 2011942757

This book is a "how to guide [that] covers everything . . . that a teen might need to know to become a babysitter. The first section covers topics such as . . . what to expect from kids ages newborn to ten. Section two covers essential skills such as feeding, dressing, playing, bathing, bedtime, and keeping kids healthy. The final section includes tips on how to get a job, how to interview, how much to charge, and even how to quit a job." (Children's Literature)

Includes web resources and index.

650 Management and auxiliary services

Trueit, Trudi Strain

Animal trainer; Trudi Strain Trueit. Cavendish Square 2014 64 p. color illustrations $34.21

Grades: 6 7 8 9 10   **650**
1. Animal trainers 2. Vocational guidance 3. Animal trainers -- literature 4. Animal training -- Vocational guidance -- literature
ISBN 1627124616; 9780761480754; 9780761480822; 9781627124614

LC 2012027729

This late-juvenile book, by Trudi Strain Trueit, focuses on "professionals engaged in a wide range of careers with animals and . . . [describes] their daily work to bring to life numerous options for animal trainers and wildlife conservationists. After a general introduction to animal training, . . . [the author] includes focus chapters for those working with dogs, horses, and marine mammals." (School Library Journal)

"The books include color pictures and a section with more resources. There is enough information in each book to give students an idea of the working conditions and job requirements for each career." Lib Med Con

Includes bibliographical references and index

Wildlife Conservationist; Trudy Strain Trueit. Cavendish Square 2014 64 p. color illustrations (Careers with Animals) $34.21

Grades: 6 7 8 9 10 **650**

1. Vocational guidance 2. Wildlife conservation 3. Wildlife conservation -- Vocational guidance 4. Environmental protection -- Vocational guidance

ISBN 1627124675; 9781627124676

This children's book by Trudi Strain Trueit, part of the Careers with Animals series, discusses career options in the field of wildlife conservation. It aims to help readers to "Explore the job duties, career specialties, educational requirements, and job outlook in this growing field." (Publisher's note)

"While offering encouragement to animal lovers, Trueit does not minimize hard work and long hours involved, sometimes in adverse conditions. A list of relevant websites provides additional resources to expand the information supplied in these readable and realistic career overviews." SLJ

650.1 Personal success in business

Fischer, James

Earning money; jobs. Mason Crest Publishers 2011 64p il (Junior library of money) $22.95

Grades: 6 7 8 9 **650.1**

1. Work 2. Employment 3. Job hunting

ISBN 978-1-4222-1763-4; 1-4222-1763-9

LC 2010-28156

"Teens learn why working is important and how to find the right job, including what steps to take in preparation and what is expected of them once they have a job. . . . This . . . is stunning, with vivid color illustrations on every page. Each subtopic is covered in a two-page spread that features bold graphics and bright colors. This succinct and visually appealing coverage is sure to fit the attention span of students." Voice Youth Advocates

Includes glossary and bibliographical references

Harmon, Dan

First job smarts; by Daniel E. Harmon. Rosen Pub. 2010 64p il (Get smart with your money) lib bdg $29.95; pa $12.95

Grades: 7 8 9 10 11 12 **650.1**

1. Personal finance 2. Part-time employment 3. Teenagers -- Employment

ISBN 978-1-4358-5268-6 lib bdg; 1-4358-5268-0 lib bdg; 978-1-4358-5542-7 pa; 1-4358-5542-6 pa

LC 2008-42892

This offers information on topics such as income tax and saving and investing.

This offers "practical information and advice. The writing is accessible. . . . [The book is] heavily illustrated with large, clear, up-to-date photographs of teens." SLJ

Includes glossary and bibliographical references

652 Processes of written communication

Bell-Rehwoldt, Sheri

Speaking secret codes. Capstone Press 2010 32p il (Edge books: making and breaking codes) lib bdg $26.65

Grades: 4 5 6 7 **652**

1. Ciphers 2. Cryptography

ISBN 978-1-4296-4569-0 lib bdg; 1-4296-4569-5 lib bdg

LC 2010004163

"Spoken codes in history, including the Underground Railroad and POWs during the Vietnam War, are introduced by using various examples of word substitutions. Educators will appreciate the concise information provided by codes that have shaped world history. . . . Historical photographs, highlighted vocabulary words and definitions, and do-it-yourself suggestions will keep readers interested." SLJ

Includes glossary and bibliographical references

Blackwood, Gary L.

Mysterious messages; a history of codes and ciphers. [by] Gary Blackwood; designed and illustrated by Jason Henry. Dutton Children's Books 2009 170p il $16.99

Grades: 5 6 7 8 **652**

1. Ciphers 2. Cryptography

ISBN 978-0-525-47960-4; 0-525-47960-0

LC 2008-48970

"This well-written history of cryptography begins with a pottery-glaze formula encrypted in cuneiform on a clay tablet (1500 BCE) and traces the uses of secret messages in statecraft, espionage, warfare, crime, literature, and business up to the present. Along the way, Blackwood . . . discusses the historical development of coding and encryption and tells many good stories of messages ciphered and deciphered. . . . The many sidebars and illustrations, including photos, reproductions of artworks and artifacts, and the pictures demonstrating the codes themselves, contribute to the book's approachable look." Booklist

Gregory, Jillian

Breaking secret codes. Capstone Press 2010 32p il (Edge books: making and breaking codes) lib bdg $26.65

Grades: 4 5 6 7 **652**

1. Ciphers 2. Cryptography

ISBN 978-1-4296-4568-3 lib bdg; 1-4296-4568-7 lib bdg

LC 2010004162

"Educators will appreciate the concise information provided by codes that have shaped world history. Sample cryptographs are scattered throughout the pages, along with other noteworthy facts. Historical photographs, highlighted vocabulary words and definitions, and do-it-yourself suggestions will keep readers interested." SLJ

Includes glossary and bibliographical references

Making secret codes. Capstone Press 2010 32p il (Edge books: making and breaking codes) lib bdg $26.65

Grades: 4 5 6 7   **652**
1. Ciphers 2. Cryptography
ISBN 978-1-4296-4567-6 lib bdg; 1-4296-4567-9
lib bdg

LC 2010004161

"Educators will appreciate the concise information provided by codes that have shaped world history. Sample cryptographs are scattered throughout the pages, along with other noteworthy facts. Historical photographs, highlighted vocabulary words and definitions, and do-it-yourself suggestions will keep readers interested." SLJ
Includes glossary and bibliographical references

Mitchell, Susan K.
Spy codes and ciphers. Enslow Publishers 2011 48p il (The secret world of spies) lib bdg $23.93
Grades: 4 5 6   **652**
1. Spies 2. Ciphers 3. Espionage 4. Cryptography
ISBN 978-0-7660-3709-0

LC 2010006176

Discusses different methods of secret communications used by spies, such as Morse code, the Enigma machine, the Najavo language, and digital steganography, and includes career information.
Includes glossary and bibliographical references

Pincock, Stephen
★ **Codebreaker**; the history of codes and ciphers, from the ancient pharaohs to quantum cryptography. 1st U.S. ed; Walker 2006 176p il $19.95
Grades: 6 7 8 9   **652**
1. Ciphers 2. Cryptography
ISBN 978-0-8027-1547-0; 0-8027-1547-8

LC 2007310362

"Pincock's fascinating book reveals to the reader that codes and ciphers have been used by pharaohs, queens, generals, politicians, and lovers for at least 4,000 years. . . Beautifully written, entertaining but never shallow, and replete with fascinating insights into the arcane world of cryptography, Codebreaker is that rare work—a nonfiction title that is as appealing as a fast-paced thriller. It should be an essential purchase for libraries serving young adults." Voice Youth Advocates
Includes bibliographical references

658   General management

Andrews, David
Business without borders; globalization. Heinemann Library 2010 56p il map (The global marketplace) lib bdg $33.50
Grades: 6 7 8 9   **658**
1. Globalization 2. International trade
ISBN 978-1-4329-3933-5 lib bdg; 1-4329-3933-5
lib bdg

LC 2010004097

This title covers "a wealth of material in concise paragraphs with pertinent subheadings. . . . [It has] clearly written, accessible content. It touches on currency, global trade,

and purchasing power, and stresses that globalization is 'a process that is still going on today.'" SLJ
Includes glossary and bibliographical references

Bochner, Arthur Berg
The **new** totally awesome business book for kids (and their parents) with twenty super businesses you can start right now! [by] Arthur Bochner & Rose Bochner; foreword by Andriane G. Berg. rev and updated 3rd ed.; Newmarket Press 2007 188p il pa $9.95
Grades: 4 5 6 7   **658**
1. Small business 2. Money-making projects for children
ISBN 978-1-55704-757-1 pa; 1-55704-757-X pa

LC 2007002637

First published 1995 with title: The totally awesome business book for kids
A comprehensive look at the basic financial and management aspects of moneymaking businesses for children
"This book can certainly be thought provoking for young people with an entrepreneurial spirit. . . . The illustrations are lively and engaging, and the text non-threatening." Voice Youth Advocates
Includes bibliographical references

658.1   Organization and financial management

Bielagus, Peter G.
Quick cash for teens; be your own boss and make big bucks. Sterling Pub. 2009 249p pa $12.95
Grades: 7 8 9 10 11 12   **658.1**
1. Small business 2. Entrepreneurship 3. Money-making projects for children
ISBN 978-1-4027-6038-9; 1-4027-6038-8

LC 2008-42793

"Young entrepreneurs wanting to own and operate their own businesses will find this practical, introductory guide an excellent source of advice. . . . Bielagus' conversational style and the frequent insertion of anecdotes from successful teen entrepreneurs make the text accessible." Booklist

658.8   Management of marketing

Weinick, Suzanne
Increasing your tweets, likes, and ratings; marketing your digital business. Suzanne Weinick. 1st ed. Rosen Pub. 2013 64 p. col. ill. (Digital entrepreneurship in the age of apps, the web, and mobile devices) (library) $31.95; (paperback) $12.95
Grades: 8 9 10 11 12   **658.8**
1. Marketing 2. Social media 3. Internet marketing 4. Electronic commerce -- Marketing
ISBN 1448869285; 9781448869282; 9781448869763; 9781448869770

LC 2012006836

This "entry in the . . . Digital Entrepreneurship in the Age of Apps, the Web, and Mobile Devices series . . . focuses on marketing minutiae, including giving your app a savvy name, choosing a useful Twitter image, monitoring your Facebook page, vlogging, and knowing your SEO [search engine optimization] from your PPC [pay per click] and CPM [cost per impression]." (Booklist)

Includes bibliographical references (p. 57-62) and index.

659.1   Advertising

Beker, Jeanne

Strutting it! the grit behind the glamour. Tundra Books 2011 78p il pa $17.95

Grades: 6 7 8 9   659.1

1. Fashion models 2. Vocational guidance 3. Modeling

ISBN 978-1-77049-224-0 pa; 1-77049-224-0 pa

"Beker—for 25 years a host of Canada's Fashion Television—distills the essence of her many years of experience as a model-watcher into this slim but engaging combination of advice, history and truth-telling. Each chapter showcases a different aspect of a model's career development. . . . Blessedly responsible and sane, a worthy title for any career collection for teens and a must for aspiring models." Kirkus

660.6   Biotechnology

Aldridge, Susan

Cloning. New Forest Press 2010 64p il (Cutting-edge science) $34.25

Grades: 7 8 9 10   660.6

1. Cloning

ISBN 978-1-84898-326-7; 1-84898-326-3

"Beginning with a description of cell division and cloning in nature, [this book] continues with the differences between cloning plants and more complex animals. . . . In a balanced treatment of the topic, Aldridge explains both the ethical debate surrounding stem cell research and human cloning and the possibilities of stem cell therapy to treat degenerative diseases. . . . The presentation is effective, with an attractive and colorful layout featuring photographs of various cells, chromosomes, and actual cloned animals. . . . Equally enticing and informational." Booklist

Biotechnology: changing life through science; [by] K. Lee Lerner and Brenda Wilmoth Lerner, editors. Thomson/Gale 2007 3v il set $196

Grades: 8 9 10 11 12   660.6

1. Biotechnology 2. Reference books

ISBN 978-1-4144-0151-5

"This set introduces students to the science of biotechnology, the issues pertaining to biotechnology, and how the issues impact society. . . . The clean layout features more than 150 color photographs as well as many diagrams and boxed areas. . . . The articles contain more than enough information to meet the needs of younger students as well as general readers." Booklist

George, Charles

Biotech research; by Charles and Linda George. ReferencePoint Press 2012 96 p. (Inside science) (hardback) $27.95

Grades: 6 7 8 9 10 11 12   660.6

1. Discoveries in science 2. Biotechnology

ISBN 1601521766; 9781601521767

LC 2011007744

This juvenile academic book, by Charles George and Linda George, presents an overview of bio-technological research in the 21st century. "Biotech research has expanded exponentially since the mapping of the Human Genome. This knowledge drives the research toward finding genetic causes and cures for thousands of human conditions and diseases, and toward enhancing agricultural products, improving industrial processes, and toward environmental reclamation and conservation." (Publisher's note)

Includes bibliographical references and index

Hartman, Eve

What are the issues with genetic technology? by Eve Hartman and Wendy Meshbesher. Raintree 2012 48 p. (Sci-hi: science issues) (pb) $8.99

Grades: 6 7 8 9 10   660.6

1. Genetic engineering 2. Genetics 3. DNA 4. Genes

ISBN 1410944719; 9781410944641; 9781410944719

LC 2011015013

This book, written by authors Eve Hartman and Wendy Meshbesher, "explains what genetic technology is, what can be done with it, what will be possible in the future, and what the ethical concerns are regarding this evolving technology." (Publisher's note)

"Tackling intriguing and sometimes controversial topics, these hi/lo titles provide a thorough, yet approachable exploration of their subjects...Readers are encouraged to think critically and actively engage in the scientific and ethical debates. Suitable for reports or simply to satisfy readers' curiosity." (School Library Journal)

Includes bibliographical references and index

664   Food technology

Aronson, Marc

★ **Sugar** changed the world; a story of magic, spice, slavery, freedom, and science. by Marc Aronson and Marina Budhos. Clarion Books 2010 166p il map

Grades: 7 8 9 10 11 12   664

1. Slavery 2. World history 3. Sugar -- History

ISBN 0618574921; 9780618574926

LC 2009033579

The book discusses the history of sweet substances. "Sugar was the substance that drove the bloody slave trade and caused the loss of countless lives but it also planted the seeds of revolution that led to freedom in the American colonies, Haiti, and France." (Publisher's note) Chronology. Bibliography. Index. "Grades seven to twelve." (Bull Cent Child Books)

"From 1600 to the 1800s, sugar drove the economies of Europe, the Americas, Asia and Africa and did more 'to reshape the world than any ruler, empire, or war had ever done.' Millions of people were taken from Africa and enslaved to work the sugar plantations throughout the Caribbean, worked to death to supply the demand for sugar in Europe. . . . Maps, photographs and archival illustrations, all with captions that are informative in their own right, richly complement the text, and superb documentation and an essay addressed to teachers round out the fascinating volume." Kirkus

Includes bibliographical references

Gardner, Robert

Ace your food science project; great science fair ideas. [by] Robert Gardner, Salvatore Tocci, and Thomas R. Rybolt. Enslow Publishers 2009 128p il (Ace your science project) lib bdg $31.93

Grades: 5 6 7 8   **664**

1. Food 2. Science projects 3. Science -- Experiments

ISBN 978-0-7660-3228-6 lib bdg; 0-7660-3228-0 lib bdg

LC 2008-49780

"Presents several science experiments and project ideas using food." Publisher's note

Includes bibliographical references

665   Technology of industrial oils, fats, waxes, gases

Walker, Niki

Hydrogen; running on water. [by] Niki Walker. Crabtree Pub. 2007 32p il (Energy revolution) lib bdg $25.20; pa $8.95

Grades: 5 6 7 8   **665**

1. Hydrogen as fuel

ISBN 978-0-7787-2915-0 lib bdg; 0-7787-2915-X lib bdg; 978-0-7787-2929-7 pa; 0-7787-2929-X pa

LC 2006014369

This describes various sources of hydrogen power, including natural gas, gasified coal, fuel from water, and biomass gas, and how it is stored and distributed, and offers energy conservation tips.

Includes glossary

668.4   Plastics

Morris, Neil

Plastics. Amicus 2010 48p il (Materials that matter) lib bdg $28.50

Grades: 4 5 6 7   **668.4**

1. Plastics

ISBN 978-1-60753-068-8 lib bdg; 1-60753-068-6 lib bdg

LC 2009051435

"The clean layout includes photographs and occasional charts, graphs, and technical illustrations against a range of pastel backgrounds. Inset boxes provide further detail, interesting extras, and recycling information. . . . [This book offers] easily accessible background information for report writers." SLJ

Includes glossary and bibliographical references

670   Manufacturing

Slavin, Bill

Transformed; how everyday things are made. written by Bill Slavin with Jim Slavin; illustrated by Bill Slavin. Kids Can Press 2005 160p il $24.95

Grades: 4 5 6 7   **670**

1. Manufactures

ISBN 1-55337-179-8

This describes the manufacture of such items "as baseballs, plastic dinosaurs, toothpaste, cereal, paper, and bricks. Each two-page spread covers the making of one of the 69 items in numbered paragraphs. The pictures are the best part—clear watercolor and ink images, made all the more engaging by folks in overalls directing the action." Booklist

Includes glossary and bibliographical references

671.5   Joining and cutting of metals

Nelson, David Erik

Soldering; by David Erik Nelson. Cherry Lake Publishing 2015 32 p. color illustrations (21st Century skills innovation library. Makers as innovators) (lib. bdg.) $28.50

Grades: 4 5 6 7 8   **671.5**

1. Soldering 2. Metal-work 3. Solder and soldering

ISBN 1631377744; 9781631377747; 9781631377945

LC 2014005538

This juvenile manual, by David Erik Nelson, part of the "21st Century Skills Innovation Library: Makers As Innovators" series, teaches "how to solder electronic components together and build your own devices. Readers will learn basic soldering skills, which will be useful in pursuing a variety of engineering projects." (Publisher's note)

"Though not the most obvious fit into the 21st Century Skills Innovation Library series, this introduction to soldering provides DIYers with basic guidelines to a skill still useful for a variety of projects, from jewelry making and plumbing to creating or repairing electronic circuits. ..Color photos depict gear, a soldered electronic board, and a young solderer at work. This quick but utilitarian guide closes with leads to several more detailed print and online resources." Booklist

Includes bibliographical references and index

Other titles in the series include:

3D Modeling (2015)

3D Printing (2014)

Arduino (2014)

Digital Badges (2013)

E-textiles (2013)

Game Design (2014)

Maker Faire (2014)

Makerspaces (2014)

Raspberry Pi (2014)

Squishy Circuits (2014)

Web Design with HTML5 (2015)

676 Pulp and paper technology

Morris, Neil

Paper. Amicus 2010 48p il (Materials that matter) lib bdg $28.50

Grades: 4 5 6 7   **676**

1. Paper

ISBN 978-1-60753-067-1 lib bdg; 1-60753-067-8 lib bdg

LC 2009051436

"The clean layout includes photographs and occasional charts, graphs, and technical illustrations against a range of pastel backgrounds. Inset boxes provide further detail, interesting extras, and recycling information. . . . [This book offers] easily accessible background information for report writers." SLJ

Includes glossary and bibliographical references

677 Textiles

Morris, Neil

Textiles. Amicus 2010 48p il (Materials that matter) lib bdg $28.50

Grades: 4 5 6 7   **677**

1. Fabrics

ISBN 978-1-60753-069-5 lib bdg; 1-60753-069-4 lib bdg

LC 2009051434

"The clean layout includes photographs and occasional charts, graphs, and technical illustrations against a range of pastel backgrounds. Inset boxes provide further detail, interesting extras, and recycling information. . . . [This book offers] easily accessible background information for report writers." SLJ

Includes glossary and bibliographical references

682 Small forge work (Blacksmithing)

Weitzman, David

★ **Skywalkers**; Mohawk ironworkers build the city. Roaring Brook Press/Flash Point 2010 124p il $19.99

Grades: 8 9 10 11 12 Adult   **682**

1. Bridges 2. Building 3. Skyscrapers 4. Mohawk Indians 5. Steel construction

ISBN 1-59643-162-8; 978-1-59643-162-1

Weitzman relates the history of Mohawks from Kahnawàke, Québec, known for their ability to navigate heights, who worked on the construction of bridges and tall buildings in Canada and New York City. "Intermediate, middle school." (Horn Book)

"Stunning photographs complement Weitzman's comprehensive research and clear text in this memorable tribute to Mohawk ironworkers. . . . Weitzman wisely intersperses passages of construction history and technical technique with numerous personal stories. . . . Plentiful black and white archival photographs . . . are chilling or breathtaking.

Throughout, Weitzman's admiration and respect for the Mohawk people shine through." Voice Youth Advocates

Includes glossary and bibliographical references

685 Leather and fur goods, and related products

Blaxland, Wendy

Sneakers. Marshall Cavendish Benchmark 2009 32p il (How are they made?) $19.95

Grades: 4 5 6   **685**

1. Sneakers

ISBN 978-0-7614-3810-6; 0-7614-3810-6

LC 2008026211

This is an "introduction to athletic shoes and the global trade involved in their manufacture and marketing. . . . A typical page offers a paragraph or more of informative text as well as a color photo and, perhaps, a small sidebar." Booklist

688.7 Recreational equipment

Bedford, Allan

The **unofficial** LEGO builder's guide; by Allan Bedford. No Starch Press 2005 xviii, 319 p.p $24.95

Grades: 4 5 6 7 8   **688.7**

1. LEGO toys

ISBN 1593270542; 1593274416; 9781593274412

LC 2005013747

This is a handbook about building LEGO structures. "Starting with the basic structure, anatomy, and flexibility of the Lego system, readers are taught different building techniques to add stability and ideas to their creations. Much of the book is devoted to the kinds of scale used in the Lego world and provides mathematical explanations for one's work. Chapters on sculpting and mosaic-making are also" offered. (School Library Journal)

Fridell, Ron

Sports technology. Lerner Publications 2009 48p il (Cool science) lib bdg $27.93

Grades: 4 5 6   **688.7**

1. Sports 2. Technology

ISBN 978-0-8225-7587-0 lib bdg; 0-8225-7587-6 lib bdg

LC 2007050905

This describes "how science helps athletes stay safer, perform better, and have more fun." Publisher's notes

Includes glossary and bibliographical references

Oxlade, Chris

Gadgets and games; Chris Oxlade. Capstone Heinemann Library 2013 56 p. col. ill. (Design and engineering for STEM) (library) $33.50; (paperback) $9.49

Grades: 5 6 7   **688.7**

1. Electronics 2. Industrial design 3. Product life cycle 4. Toys -- Design and construction 5. Household appliances -- Design and construction 6. Electronic

apparatus and appliances -- Design and construction
ISBN 1432970364; 9781432970314; 9781432970369

LC 2012013468

This book, part of the Design and Engineering for STEM series, looks at electronic devices and mobile games. It looks at the life cycle of these items, or "the stages from their design, manufacture, and sale to their use, maintenance, and disposal." Topics include "prototyping, the sourcing of components, the production process, the decisions made by designers and engineers, and recycling." (Publisher's note)

Includes bibliographical references (p. 54) and index.

Ross, Stewart

Sports technology. Smart Apple Media 2011 il (New technology)

Grades: 4 5 6 7   **688.7**

1. Sports

ISBN 1-599-20534-3; 978-1-599-20534-2

LC 2010044241

Describes the technological advances in the sports industry, including the technology used to create better equipment, sports wear, judging tools, and playing surfaces.

This "offers a fine overview for reports, and its attractive design may also entice middle-grade readers to learn more." Booklist

Stone, Tanya Lee

★ The **good,** the bad, and the Barbie; a doll's history and her impact on us. Viking 2010 130p il $19.99

Grades: 6 7 8 9 10   **688.7**

1. Barbie dolls 2. Mattel Inc. 3. Toy industry executives

ISBN 978-0-670-01187-2; 0-670-01187-8

LC 2010-7507

"Stone tantalizes with her brief and intriguing survey of Barbie. She begins with the history of Mattel, started by self-made businesswoman Ruth Handler in the 1940s, and moves onto materialism, body image, portrayals of ethnicity, nudity, taboo and art." Kirkus

Includes bibliographical references

Wulffson, Don L.

Toys! amazing stories behind some great inventions. [by] Don Wulffson; with illustrations by Laurie Keller. Holt & Co. 2000 137p il $16.95

Grades: 4 5 6 7   **688.7**

1. Toys 2. Inventions

ISBN 0-8050-6196-7

LC 99-58440

Describes the creation of a variety of toys and games, from seesaws to Silly Putty and toy soldiers to Trivial Pursuit

"Each of the 25 chapters is illustrated with small, humorous drawings and discusses a particular toy or game's origin and development. The book ends with a bibliography and a list of Web sites. Good, readable fare for browsing or light research." Booklist

Includes bibliographical references

688.72 Toys

Rothrock, Megan

The **LEGO** adventure book; cars, castles, dinosaurs & more! Megan Rothrock. No Starch Press 2013 199 p. [Vol. 1] $24.95

Grades: 4 5 6 7 8 9   **688.72**

1. LEGO toys 2. Models and modelmaking

ISBN 1593274424; 9781593274429

LC 2012033902

This book on LEGO building, by Megan Rothrock, "is filled with bright visuals, step-by-step breakdowns of 25 models, and nearly 200 example models from the world's best builders. Learn to build robots, trains, medieval villages, spaceships, airplanes, and much more." (Publisher's note)

"—LEGO enthusiast Megs builds an Idea Lab for creating projects and, with its completion, travels by Transport-O-lux to see what others are inspired to make...This one certainly won't sit on shelves. A fun read for LEGO fans of all ages." SLJ

Cars, castles, dinosaurs & more!

Cars, castles, dinosaurs and more!

Schwartz, Jordan

The **art** of LEGO design; creative ways to build amazing models. Jordan Schwartz. No Starch Press 2014 267 p. (pbk.) $24.95

Grades: 4 5 6 7 8 9   **688.72**

1. LEGO toys 2. LEGO toys -- Design and construction

ISBN 1593275536; 9781593275532

LC 2013048974

This book, by Jordan Schwartz, "explores LEGO as an artistic medium. This wide-ranging collection of creative techniques will help you craft your own amazing models as you learn to see the world through the eyes of some of the greatest LEGO builders. Each concept is presented with a collection of impressive models to spark your imagination, like fantastic dragons, futuristic spaceships, expressive characters, and elaborate dioramas." (Publisher's note)

"Part inspirational guide and part project design manual, the book encourages creativity and ingenuity while educating builders about the customs of the LEGO community (e.g., never paint LEGOs). There are helpful sections designed for novices that suggest how to organize workspace, find inspiration, select tools, and prepare for projects, while more advanced builders might embrace sections about developing personal style, sharing models publicly, and using feedback to enhance skills...The creative thinking process conveyed in the book is fascinating and could inspire non-LEGO builders (e.g., writers and painters) in their innovative efforts." VOYA

690 Construction of buildings

Byers, Ann

Jobs as green builders and planners. Rosen Pub. 2010 80p il (Green careers) lib bdg $30.60

Grades: 5 6 7 8   **690**

1. Building 2. Vocational guidance 3. Environmental

science
ISBN 978-1-4358-3566-5 lib bdg; 1-4358-3566-2
lib bdg

LC 2009015517

This "well-conceived [introduction focuses] on various jobs in [building and construction planning], the education and experience required, and expected earnings. The [book is] well organized, making it easy to gain an overview of the major aspects of the work. . . . [This book] will make [a] good [addition] to career collections. Photographs from the field and website and contact information for professional organizations add value." SLJ

Includes glossary and bibliographical references

Dillon, Patrick

The **Story** of buildings; from the pyramids to the Sydney Opera House and beyond. Patrick Dillon, illustrated by Stephen Biesty. Candlewick Press 2014 96 p. $19.99

Grades: 5 6 7 8   690
1. Building 2. Buildings 3. Architecture 4. Architecture -- History
ISBN 0763669903; 9780763669904

LC 2013943096

This book, by Patrick Dillon and illustrated by Stephen Biesty, is a "narrative history of buildings. . . . Why and how did people start making buildings? How did they learn to make them stronger, bigger, and more comfortable? Why did they start to decorate them in different ways? . . . Dillon's stories of remarkable buildings—and the remarkable people who made them—celebrates the ingenuity of human creation." (Publisher's note)

"This large, handsome volume combines broad discussions of architectural history with exceptional drawings of significant buildings from ancient to modern times... Through his signature cross sections, details of interiors and construction can be seen as well. While the text, illustrations, and captions all provide information, it's the drawings of buildings that make this a valuable resource. " Booklist

Macaulay, David

★ **Unbuilding**. Houghton Mifflin 1980 78p il $18; pa $9.95

Grades: 4 5 6 7 8 9   690
1. Building 2. Skyscrapers 3. Empire State Building (New York, N.Y.)
ISBN 0-395-29457-6; 0-395-45425-5 pa

LC 80-15491

This fictional account of the dismantling and removal of the Empire State Building describes the structure of a skyscraper and explains how such an edifice would be demolished

"Save for the fact that one particularly stunning double-page spread is marred by tight binding, the book is a joy: accurate, informative, handsome, and eminently readable." Bull Cent Child Books

Miller, Malinda

Green construction; creating energy-efficient, low-impact buildings. Mason Crest Publishers 2010 64p il (New careers for the 21st century: finding your role in the global renewal) lib bdg $22.95

Grades: 7 8 9 10   690
1. Vocational guidance 2. Sustainable architecture
ISBN 978-1-4222-1815-0 lib bdg; 1-4222-1815-5 lib bdg

LC 2010010013

"Chapters identify and emphasize specific careers—important strengths, necessary aptitudes and interests, education and training, projected earnings, closely related occupations, type of work environment, and predictions for the future of the field. . . . Color photos have a small role amid the many statistics, figures, graphs and charts that support and supplement the . . . [text]." SLJ

Includes bibliographical references

Somervill, Barbara A.

Green general contractor. Cherry Lake Pub. 2011 32p il (Cool careers) lib bdg $27.07

Grades: 4 5 6 7   690
1. Building 2. Vocational guidance 3. Sustainable architecture
ISBN 978-1-60279-987-5; 1-60279-987-3

LC 2010029535

This book begins "with a personal story of a teen and then [segues] into the occupation [of general contractor]. . . . [It covers] the necessary training and skills for the job (and options for obtaining them), a typical day, salary expectations, and well-known professionals in the field. The [text is] accessible and clearly written. . . . The [volume has] a generous number of clear color photographs that depict people at work." SLJ

Includes glossary and bibliographical references

Woolf, Alex

Buildings; by Alex Woolf. Heinemann Library 2013 56 p. ill. (chiefly col.) (library) $33.50; (paperback) $9.49

Grades: 6 7 8 9   690
1. Building 2. Architecture
ISBN 1432970291; 9781432970291; 9781432970345

LC 2012013465

This book by Alex Woolf examines the life cycle of a building, covering "the stages from its design, construction, and opening to its use, maintenance, and demolition and disposal at the end of its useful life. This book explains what happens during these stages, such as planning, the sourcing of materials, the construction process, the decisions made by designers and engineers, and refurbishing and recycling." (Publisher's note)

"Books in the Design and Engineering for STEM series offer an up-to-date introduction to an industry in a time of change..Buildings emphasizes the impact of architecture, construction, and demolition on the environment and shows how that impact can be minimized at different stages. Appearing on nearly every page, illustrations include many color photos and the occasional graph, digital drawing, or map. This attractive, informative series tackles meaningful topics and doesn't talk down to readers." (Booklist)

Includes bibliographical references (page 55) and index.

696   Utilities

Gregory, Josh

Plumber. Cherry Lake Pub. 2011 32p il (Cool careers) lib bdg $27.07

Grades: 4 5 6 7   **696**

1. Plumbing 2. Vocational guidance

ISBN 978-1-60279-984-4; 1-60279-984-9

LC 2010029538

This book begins "with a personal story of a teen and then [segues] into the occupation [of plumber]. . . . [It covers] the necessary training and skills for the job (and options for obtaining them), a typical day, salary expectations, and wellknown professionals in the field. The [text is] accessible and clearly written. . . . The [volume has] a generous number of clear color photographs that depict people at work." SLJ

Includes glossary and bibliographical references

700   ARTS

700   The arts

Makosz, Rory

Latino arts and their influence on the United States; songs, dreams, and dances. Mason Crest Publishers 2005 112p il (Hispanic heritage) $22.95

Grades: 7 8 9 10   **700**

1. Latin American art 2. Arts -- United States

ISBN 1-59084-938-8

LC 2004022968

This "book begins with a general discussion of the ways in which cultures express themselves through their arts. It goes on to discuss the arts of Latin American cultures and their growing prominence in the United States, with emphasis on dance and music. Writing, painting, theater arts, and holidays are also included. . . . [This is] an excellent resource both for students researching Latino arts for reports and for general readers." SLJ

Includes bibliographical references

Robson, David

The **Black** arts movement. Lucent Books 2009 104p il (Lucent Library of Black History) $32.45

Grades: 7 8 9 10   **700**

1. African American arts 2. Arts -- United States

ISBN 978-1-4205-0053-0; 1-4205-0053-8

LC 2008016446

This focuses on African American literature, music, and art.

This is "highly accessible and [provides] cultural context to help readers understand [the] topic. . . . [The] book includes captioned color and black-and-white photographs and reproductions on every spread. Well-organized and clearly written." SLJ

Includes bibliographical references

700.9   History, geographic treatment, biography of the arts

Flatt, Lizann

Arts and culture in the early Islamic world; Lizann Flatt. Crabtree Pub. Company 2012 48 p. col. ill., col. map (Life in the early Islamic world) (reinforced library binding : alk. paper) $30.60

Grades: 5 6 7   **700.9**

1. Islamic art 2. Islamic civilization

ISBN 0778721671; 9780778721673; 9780778721741; 9781427195609; 9781427198372

LC 2012000074

This book by Lizann Flatt is part of the "Life in the Early Islamic World" series. It "introduces the important roles that many of the arts, but especially calligraphy, architecture, and the decorative arts, have had in Islamic culture, in which art is meant to be 'useful as well as beautiful.'" (Booklist) "The main texts are supplemented with blue boxes of information, subsections, and many high-quality reproductions, maps, and paintings." (School Library Journal)

701   Philosophy and theory of fine and decorative arts

Dickins, Rosie

The **Usborne** art treasury; pictures, paintings, and projects. [by] Rosie Dickins; designed by Nicola Butler. Usborne 2007 94p il $19.99

Grades: 4 5 6 7   **701**

1. Painting 2. Art appreciation

ISBN 978-0-7945-1452-5

"Each project in this colorful, attractive compendium of art projects begins with a particular work of art. . . . Throughout the book, the excellent presentation of the projects makes them seem not only possible to complete but also worth doing. Illustrated step-by-step, the instructions are clearly written and practical." Booklist

Hensley, Laura

Art for all; what is public art? Raintree 2010 32p il (Culture in action) $29

Grades: 5 6 7 8   **701**

1. Art

ISBN 978-1-4109-3923-4; 1-4109-3923-5

LC 2009051126

This "briefly surveys public art, from murals and graffiti to obelisks and religious statues. . . . A world map shows the locations of 16 public artworks mentioned in the text. . . . The quality of the illustrations is fine. . . . Given the book's broad scope and few pages, it accomplishes a good deal. Three activities, a time line, a glossary, and a brief bibliography round out this attractive presentation." Booklist

Includes glossary and bibliographical references

Tomecek, Steve

Art & architecture; by Stephen M. Tomecek. Chelsea House Publishers 2010 174p il (Experimenting with everyday science) $35

Grades: 4 5 6 7 **701**
1. Architecture 2. Art and science 3. Science -- Experiments 4. Art -- Study and teaching
ISBN 978-1-60413-168-0; 1-60413-168-3
LC 2009030195

"This fun and informative book features 25 simple experiments using common household items and foods such as blueberries, colored cellophane, food coloring, Magic Markers, miniature marshmallows, and wooden toothpicks to demonstrate principles and inspire creative thought about the intersection of science with the visual and mechanical arts. The six chapters include activities that illuminate certain scientific aspects of each respective subject. . . . Accessible for independent reading by children with a scientific bent or curiosity about how the world works, these experiments would also be useful for scout projects or science clubs." SLJ

Includes bibliographical references

702.8 Auxiliary techniques and procedures; apparatus, equipment, materials

Luxbacher, Irene

★ The **jumbo** book of art; written and illustrated by Irene Luxbacher. Kids Can Press 2003 208p il pa $14.95
Grades: 4 5 6 7 **702.8**
1. Color 2. Drawing 3. Painting 4. Sculpture 5. Art -- Study and teaching
ISBN 1-55074-762-2

"Each of the four chapters is devoted to instructing readers in the basics of one technique—drawing, creating with color, sculpture, and mixed-media projects, respectively—and then inspires those readers to let loose and have fun making something beautiful. . . . The book features clear layouts, well-written definitions of terms, full-color illustrations, and more than 90 projects. . . . This practical, lively, and smart package is a must-have for every art and elementary school classroom, and a welcome addition to most library collections." SLJ

Includes glossary

704 Special topics in fine and decorative arts

Bolden, Tonya

Wake up our souls; a celebration of Black American artists. Published in association with Smithsonian American Art Museum. Harry N. Abrams 2004 128p il $24.95
Grades: 6 7 8 9 10 **704**
1. African American art
ISBN 0-8109-4527-4

Presents a history of African American visual arts and artists from the days of slavery to the present

"Bolden's writing is rich and lyrical. She smoothly incorporates the historical context, explaining pivotal events and relevant artistic movements clearly and succinctly." SLJ

Brooks, Susie

Get into Art! Enjoy Great Art--then Create Your Own! by Susie Brooks. Kingfisher 2013 31 p. col. ill. (hardcover) $14.99
Grades: 3 4 5 6 7 **704**
1. Art 2. Art -- Guidebooks 3. Picture books for children
ISBN 0753470586; 9780753470589

For this book, Susie Brooks' "goal is to convince her readers that art is not just something one observes, but rather something that one does. Using a topic beloved by many kids—animals—she presents 13 works by famous artists, each of which incorporates animals into its subject and theme. Each reproduced masterpiece occupies its own two-page spread, and Brooks explores one major art technique for each." (Bookstlist)

January, Brendan

★ **Native** American art & culture; [by] Brendan January. Raintree 2005 56p il map (World art & culture) lib bdg $23; pa $9.99
Grades: 5 6 7 8 **704**
1. Native Americans 2. Native American art
ISBN 978-1-4109-1108-7 lib bdg; 1-4109-1108-X lib bdg; 978-1-4109-2118-5 pa; 1-4109-2118-2 pa
LC 2004-8072

"January investigates the many art forms of the Native American tribes. . . . Chapters are dedicated to pottery, textiles, carving, and painting as well as body art, architecture, ceremonies, songs, and dances. . . . Numerous color photographs of both ancient and modern artwork are included on each spread, and they are exceptional. . . . This fresh look at Native American culture through its artwork will be a welcome alternative for reports and classroom discussion, and the popularity of the subject matter and appealing design will attract readers outside the classroom environment." SLJ

Includes bibliographical references

Raczka, Bob

Before they were famous; how seven artists got their start. Millbrook Press 2010 32p il (Art adventures) $25.26
Grades: 4 5 6 7 **704**
1. Artists 2. Creative ability
ISBN 978-0-7613-6077-3; 0-7613-6077-8
LC 2009049596

"Short biographies written in conversational, jargon-free text introduce seven great artists, as young beginners and then as creators of famous works. From Dürer and Michelangelo to Picasso and Dali, the featured artists are presented chronologically on uncluttered, open spreads that include beautiful full-page reproductions. . . . Great preparation for a gallery visit, this will appeal to older readers, too, for its exciting, never-condescending talk about the pictures and the artists who created them." Booklist

704.03 Ethnic and national groups

★ **Dreaming** in Indian; Contemporary Native American Voices. edited by Lisa Charleyboy and

Mary Leatherdale. Firefly Books Ltd 2014 128 p. color illustrations $19.95

Grades: PreK 7 8 9 10 11 12   **704.03**

1. Native Americans 2. Indian artists -- United States -- Biography

ISBN 1554516870; 9781554516872

LC 2014045769

This book, edited by Lisa Charleyboy and Mary Leatherdale, is an "anthology from some of the most groundbreaking Native artists working in North America today. . . . Emerging and established Native artists, including acclaimed author Joseph Boyden, renowned visual artist Bunky Echo Hawk, and stand-up comedian Ryan McMahon, contribute thoughtful and heartfelt pieces on their experiences growing up Indigenous." (Publisher's note)

"Original and accessible, both an exuberant work of art and a uniquely valuable resource." Kirkus

704.9   Iconography

Stieff, Barbara

Earth, sea, sun, and sky; art in nature. translated from German by Cynthia Hall; illustrated by Michael Schmölzl. Prestel 2011 88p il lib bdg $14.95

Grades: 6 7 8 9   **704.9**

1. Art 2. Nature 3. Aesthetics

ISBN 978-3-7913-7048-4; 3-7913-7048-0

"A conversational writing style combines with many color photographs and drawings to convey information about art inspired by nature. In the beginning, Stieff describes the historical development of gardens and how they are an art form. She moves on to provide many examples of how art is found on land, in water, and in the air. The photographs, which range in size, further illuminate the text. Throughout the work, references are made to activities detailed in the final section. These projects, which include making daisy soup, learning some water games, forming seed balls, and creating pictures in water, encourage readers to look at or create art." SLJ

708   Galleries, museums, private collections of fine and decorative arts

An eye for art; focusing on great artists and their work. National Gallery of Art with Chicago Review Press, Incorporated 2013 180 p. (pbk.) $19.95

Grades: 4 5 6 7 8 9 10 11 12   **708**

1. Art 2. Art appreciation 3. National Gallery of Art (U.S.)

ISBN 1613748973; 9781613748978

LC 2013009403

This book is an "introduction to the works collected in the National Gallery of Art. More than 50 great artists are highlighted, from the 13th to the 21st centuries. The artists and their works and techniques are . . . arranged stylistically in categories that include 'Studying Nature,' 'Observing Everyday Life,' 'Exploring Places,' and 'Telling Stories.'" (School Library Journal)

709   Arts -- History, geographic treatment, biography

Ayres, Charlie

Lives of the great artists. Thames & Hudson 2008 96p il $19.95

Grades: 5 6 7 8   **709**

1. Artists 2. Art -- History

ISBN 978-0-500-23853-0; 0-500-23853-7

LC 2008-91000

Presents illustrated and age-appropriate imaginary tours of the studios of famous artists from Leonardo da Vinci and Michelangelo to Monet and van Gogh, in an anecdotal reference that is complemented by reproductions of famous works and introductory portraits

This is "brightly written and augmented with activities, Web resources, and fun facts. . . . The works of art chosen to represent each artist are heavy on the drama and detail, resulting in high kid appeal and interesting captions. . . . The layout is clean and clear." SLJ

Children's book of art; an introduction to the world's most amazing paintings and sculptures. DK Pub. 2009 139p il $24.99

Grades: 4 5 6 7   **709**

1. Art appreciation 2. Art -- History

ISBN 978-0-7566-5511-2; 0-7566-5511-0

"From prehistoric to modern times, this expertly designed survey delivers a wealth of information. Much more than a mere time line, the focus shifts from artist to movement to medium with fluidity. Gallery pages examine how particular subjects are depicted in art from a variety of cultures and time periods. Hundreds of color reproductions are sure to hold readers' interest. . . . The vast amount of information presented is neither overwhelming nor superficial." SLJ

Finger, Brad

13 American artists children should know. Prestel 2010 46p il $14.95

Grades: 4 5 6   **709**

1. American art 2. Art appreciation 3. Artists -- United States

ISBN 978-3-7913-7036-1; 3-7913-7036-7

"Beginning with Winslow Homer and ending with Andy Warhol and Jasper Johns, this picture-book overview introduces 13 well-known American artists. On each double-page spread, short biographies combine with richly reproduced images of the artists' famous works. . . . Finger . . . writes with clarity and enthusiasm." Booklist

Includes glossary

Raczka, Bob

★ **Name** that style; all about isms in art. by Bob Raczka. Millbrook Press 2008 32p il (Art adventures) lib bdg $25.26; pa $9.95

Grades: 5 6 7 8   **709**

1. Art -- History

ISBN 978-0-8225-7586-3 lib bdg; 0-8225-7586-8 lib bdg; 978-1-58013-824-6 pa; 1-58013-824-1 pa

LC 2008000312

"Beginning with naturalism and ending with photorealism, with many stops along the way, this compact overview documents the shifts, both in terms of technique as well as subject matter, that differentiate each style from its predecessors. Each 'ism' gets a two-page spread, with a beautifully reproduced example. . . . This is . . . indispensible for any middle-grade classrooms introducing art history." Booklist

Schumann, Bettina

13 women artists children should know; [by] Bettina Schumann; [translated from German by Jane Michael] Prestel 2009 46p il $14.95

Grades: 5 6 7 8 **709**

1. Women artists 2. Art appreciation
ISBN 978-3-7913-4333-4; 3-7913-4333-5

This is profiles women artists such as Sofonisba Anguissola, Maria Sybilla Merian, Mary Cassatt, Georgia O'Keeffe, Frida Kahlo, Louise Bourgeois, and Cindy Sherma

This "large-format, brightly colored [survey proves a] solid, even inspiring [introduction] to the art world. . . . Leading questions encourage budding artists to use the featured subjects and artworks as inspiration." Horn Book Guide

Includes glossary

Wenzel, Angela

13 artists children should know; [translation by Jane Michael] Prestel 2010 46p il $14.95

Grades: 4 5 6 **709**

1. Artists 2. Art appreciation 3. Art -- History
ISBN 978-3-7913-4173-6; 3-7913-4173-1

This profiles 13 artists such as Leonardo da Vinci, Vincent Van Gogh, Vermeer, and Henri Matisse

This "large-format, brightly colored [survey provides a] solid, even inspiring [introduction] to the art world. . . . Leading questions encourage budding artists to use the featured subjects and artworks as inspiration." Horn Book Guide

Includes glossary

709.03 Modern period, 1500-

Gunderson, Jessica

Impressionism; by Jessica Gunderson. Creative Education 2008 48p il (Movements in art) lib bdg $32.80

Grades: 6 7 8 9 **709.03**

1. Impressionism (Art)
ISBN 978-1-58341-611-2 lib bdg; 1-58341-611-0 lib bdg

LC 2007008493

This "discusses the leading Impressionist artists, their subjects, and their techniques. Quality reproductions of many paintings and occasional sepia photos of the painters and their settings illustrate the detailed, informative overview." Booklist

Includes glossary and bibliographical references

Realism; by Jessica Gunderson. 1st ed.; Creative Education 2009 48p il (Movements in art) lib bdg $32.80

Grades: 6 7 8 9 **709.03**

1. Realism in art
ISBN 978-1-58341-612-9 lib bdg; 1-58341-612-9 lib bdg

LC 2007008494

"Gunderson describes how art trends, politics, and inventions informed the work that was produced during [the Realism] movement. . . . [The] book provides an overview of the movement and its key players in continuous prose that is broken up by an occasional highlighted section of text. The color photographs, illustrations, and reproductions, many of them full page, are relevant and of high quality. . . . The [text delivers a] well-rounded [account] that students will find accessible." SLJ

Includes glossary and bibliographical references

Romanticism; [by] Jessica Gunderson. Creative Education 2009 48p il (Movements in art) lib bdg $32.80

Grades: 6 7 8 9 **709.03**

1. Romanticism in art
ISBN 978-1-58341-613-6; 1-58341-613-7

LC 2007008495

"Gunderson describes how art trends, politics, and inventions informed the work that was produced during [the Romantic] movement. . . . [The] book provides an overview of the movement and its key players in continuous prose that is broken up by an occasional highlighted section of text. The color photographs, illustrations, and reproductions, many of them full page, are relevant and of high quality. . . . The [text delivers a] well-rounded [account] that students will find accessible." SLJ

Includes glossary and bibliographical references

709.04 Arts -- 20th century, 1900-1999

Claybourne, Anna

Surrealism. Heinemann Library 2009 48p il (Art on the wall) lib bdg $32.86

Grades: 5 6 7 8 9 10 **709.04**

1. Surrealism 2. Modern art
ISBN 978-1-4329-1367-0; 1-4329-1367-0

LC 2008020316

This title succeeds "in presenting a bird's-eye view of [Surrealism] without oversimplification. Information on individual artists is included in the broader context of the movement. Visually exciting, with plenty of color, [the layout is] hip and should appeal to the target audience." SLJ

Includes glossary and bibliographical references

Spilsbury, Richard

Pop art. Heinemann Library 2009 48p il (Art on the wall) lib bdg $23

Grades: 5 6 7 8 9 10 **709.04**

1. Pop art
ISBN 978-1-4329-1368-7 lib bdg; 1-4329-1368-9 lib bdg

LC 2008020358

This describes how Pop art began, some of the movement's artists, and the influence of Pop art

This title succeeds "in presenting a bird's-eye view of [Pop art] without oversimplification. Information on individual artists is included in the broader context of the movement. Visually exciting, with plenty of color, [the layout is] hip and should appeal to the target audience." SLJ

Includes glossary and bibliographical references

Yancey, Diane

Art deco. Lucent Books 2010 112p il (Eye on art) $33.45

Grades: 7 8 9 10	**709.04**

1. Art deco

ISBN 978-1-4205-0340-1; 1-4205-0340-5

LC 2010032961

"Presents an in-depth look at the art deco movement and its lasting legacy. . . . [It provides] a great deal of information, so middle school readers may not read them cover to cover; however, ample cover photos and quotes from artists will make this . . . appealing to students interested in art." Voice Youth Advocates

Includes glossary and bibliographical references

709.2 Arts -- Biography

Amado, Elisa

High riders, saints and death cars; a life saved by art. as told to Elisa Amado; photos by John T. Denne. Groundwood Books/House of Anansi Press 2011 55p il

Grades: 9 10 11 12	**709.2**

1. Motorcycles 2. Art and religion 3. American folk art 4. Hispanic American artists -- Biography 5. Sculptors -- United States -- Biography 6. Artists 7. Sculptors 8. Artists -- United States 9. Hispanic Americans -- Biography

ISBN 0888998546; 9780888998545

In "New Mexican folk artist [Nicholas] Herrera's autobiography (told to and written by [Elisa] Amado) . . . even Herrera's mother wasn't sure he would survive his wild and self-destructive teenage years during the 1960s. . . . Herrera does make it--barely. After emerging from a coma following an alcohol-related car accident, Herrera devotes his life to creating art, following in the footsteps of his great-uncle, a "santero" who created statues of saints. Herrera's folk art sculptures are all his own, however, blending religious iconography with imagery from contemporary Hispanic and biker culture, as well as social and political commentary (the . . . The Three Kings shows the Holy Family fleeing Herod on an eight-cylinder "trike" motorcycle)." (Publishers Weekly)

"The subtitle of New Mexican folk artist Herrera's autobiography (told to and written by Amado) isn't hyperbole: even Herrera's mother wasn't sure he would survive his wild and self-destructive teenage years during the 1960s. . . . After emerging from a coma following an alcohol-related car accident, Herrera devotes his life to creating art. . . . Herrera's folk art sculptures . . . [blend] religious iconography with imagery from contemporary Hispanic and biker culture, as well as social and political commentary. . . . Never minimizing the gravity of Herrera's struggles, the book makes clear the concrete impact that art can have." Publ Wkly

Bernier-Grand, Carmen T.

Pablo Picasso; I the king, yo el rey. by Carmen T. Bernier-Grand ; illustrated by David Diaz. 1st ed. Marshall Cavendish 2012 64 p. ill. (hardcover) $19.99

Grades: 5 6 7	**709.2**

1. Art -- History

ISBN 0761461779; 9780761461777

LC 2011032177

This biography of painter Pablo Picasso is written "in free-verse style. . . . The artist's strong will and drive are demonstrated in his decision to wander Madrid with sketchbook in lieu of attending art school; by his insistent attempts to develop his own style (e.g., his Blue Period; his fascination with masklike faces; his creation of Cubism); by his move to Paris; and his insatiable desire for women." (School Library Journal)

Spence, David

Michelangelo; written by David Spence; editor, Guy Croton. North American ed. New Forest Press 2010 48 p. col. ill. (Great artists and their world) (library) $32.80

Grades: 6 7 8 9	**709.2**

1. Artists 2. Painters 3. Sculptors 4. Architects 5. Artists, Italian 6. Art, Renaissance -- Italy 7. Art -- 15th and 16th centuries

ISBN 1848983093; 9781848983090

"Offers biographical information [of Michelangelo Buonarroti] . . . interspersed with art history and criticism in an eye-catching format. . . . [Includes] a long introductory paragraph and four-to-six images with explanatory notes. . . . Spence . . . does a good job of explaining why art that might seem ordinary today was revolutionary at the time of its creation." SLJ

Includes bibliographical references and index.

709.3 Specific continents, countries, localities

Langley, Andrew

★ Ancient Greece. Raintree 2005 48p il (History in art) lib bdg $31.43; pa $8.99

Grades: 4 5 6 7	**709.3**

1. Greek art 2. Greece -- Civilization

ISBN 978-1-4109-0517-8 lib bdg; 1-4109-0517-9 lib bdg; 978-1-4109-2035-5 pa; 1-4109-2035-6 pa

LC 2004-7523

The author shows "how art provides primary-source information about everyday and family life, beliefs and religion, and philosophy and mythology in . . . ancient [Greece]. . . . The [book follows] a well-organized format that makes the history accessible for reports, but the [author takes the book] beyond a reports-only status. Captions for the two or three illustrations per spread are clear." SLJ

Includes glossary and bibliographical references

711   Area planning (Civic art)

Macaulay, David

★ **City** : a story of Roman planning and construction. Houghton Mifflin 1974 112p il $18; pa $10.99

Grades: 4 5 6 7 8 9 10 **711**

1. Civil engineering 2. Roman architecture 3. City planning -- Rome

ISBN 0-395-19492-X; 0-395-34922-2 pa

LC 74-4280

"By following the inception, construction, and development of an imaginary Roman city, the account traces the evolution of Verbonia from the selection of its site under religious auspices in 26 B.C. to its completion in 100 A.D." Horn Book

Includes glossary

720   Architecture

Barker, Geoff P.

Incredible skyscrapers. Amicus 2011 32p il (Superstructures) lib bdg $28.50

Grades: 5 6 7 8 **720**

1. Skyscrapers

ISBN 978-1-6075-3133-3; 1-6075-3133-X

LC 2009044044

"The vivid illustrations often help clarify points made in the text. . . . [This] colorful, informative [book offers] intriguing glimpses of notable engineering feats." Booklist

Includes bibliographical references

Hosack, Karen

Buildings; [by] Karen Hosack. Raintree 2009 32p il map (What is art?) lib bdg $27.50

Grades: 5 6 7 8 **720**

1. Buildings 2. Architecture

ISBN 978-1-4109-3165-8 lib bdg; 1-4109-3165-X lib bdg

LC 2008-9700

This "features public spaces and private residences created from a variety of materials. Every page includes a paragraph about the structure with glossary terms in bold type. . . . [Title is] consistent in quality of design and content." SLJ

Includes glossary and bibliographical references

Macaulay, David

★ **Building** big. Houghton Mifflin 2000 192p il $30; pa $12.95

Grades: 5 6 7 8 9 10 **720**

1. Dams 2. Bridges 3. Tunnels 4. Engineering 5. Skyscrapers 6. Architecture

ISBN 0-395-96331-1; 0-618-46527-8 pa

LC 00-28116

"Macaulay combines his detailed yet vaguely whimsical illustrations with simple, straightforward prose that breaks down complex architectural and engineering accomplishments into easily digestible tidbits that don't insult the intelligence of the reader of any age." N Y Times Book Rev

Includes glossary

Paxmann, Christine

From mud huts to skyscrapers; architecture for children. by Christine Paxmann ; illustrated by Anne Ibelings. Prestel Pub. Random House 2012 64 p. ill. (hardcover) $19.95

Grades: 4 5 6 **720**

1. Picture books for children 2. Architecture

ISBN 3791371134; 9783791371139

LC 2012939038

This book "takes readers on a journey through time, exploring well-known structures such as the pyramids, Hagia Sophia, Versailles, and the Guggenheim Museum. Each spread is dedicated to a single building; in addition to a detailed illustration of the structure, it also includes information about the architect, the architectural style, and/or definitions of particular details." (School Library Journal)

Roeder, Annette

13 buildings children should know; [translator, Jane Michael] Prestel 2009 46p il $14.95

Grades: 5 6 7 8 **720**

1. Architecture

ISBN 978-3-7913-4171-2; 3-7913-4171-5

"The famous buildings featured in this pictorial collection include Notre Dame cathedral in Paris, Neuschwanstein Castle in Germany, New York City's Guggenheim Museum and the Beijing National Stadium (built for the 2008 Olympics), each pictured in color photographs, cross-sections and/or ground plans, with time lines tracing the buildings' developments and changes over time. . . . A sound introduction to some impressive structures." Publ Wkly

Stern, Steven L.

Building greenscrapers; consultant, Frank Robbins. Bearport Pub. 2009 32p il (Going green) lib bdg $25.27

Grades: 4 5 6 7 **720**

1. Skyscrapers 2. Sustainable architecture

ISBN 978-1-59716-962-2 lib bdg; 1-59716-962-5 lib bdg

LC 2009-12494

"Color photographs (most full page) and a few diagrams accompany the informative text. . . . Overall, the [book] . . . is user-friendly and covers topics that are not easily found elsewhere." SLJ

Includes glossary and bibliographical references

720.9   History, geographic treatment, biography

Clements, Gillian

A **picture** history of great buildings. Frances Lincoln Children's 2007 61p il map $19.95

Grades: 7 8 9 10 **720.9**

1. Buildings 2. Architecture -- History

ISBN 978-1-84507-488-3; 1-84507-488-2

An illustrated history of over 9,000 years of great buildings around the world from the tombs of ancient Egypt to the modern skyscrapers of today.

This is "an excellent resource, jam-packed with information for anyone interested in a basic study of architecture throughout the ages." Libr Media Connect

Includes glossary

726   Buildings for religious and related purposes

Macaulay, David

★ **Mosque**. Houghton Mifflin 2003 96p il $18
Grades: 4 5 6 7 8 9 10   **726**

1. Mosques -- Design and construction
ISBN 0-618-24034-9

LC 2003-177

"Once again Macaulay uses clear words and exemplary drawings to explore a majestic structure's design and construction. . . . In his respectful, straightforward explanation of the mosque's design, Macaulay offers an unusual, inspiring perspective into Islamic society." Booklist

Includes glossary

★ **Pyramid**. Houghton Mifflin 1975 80p il $20; pa $9.95
Grades: 4 5 6 7 8 9 10   **726**

1. Pyramids 2. Egypt -- Civilization
ISBN 0-395-21407-6; 0-395-32121-2 pa

LC 75-9964

The construction of a pyramid in 25th century B.C. Egypt is described. "Information about selection of the site, drawing of the plans, calculating compass directions, clearing and leveling the ground, and quarrying and hauling the tremendous blocks of granite and limestone is conveyed as much by pictures as by text." Horn Book

Includes glossary

Mann, Elizabeth

The **Parthenon**; illustrations by Yuan Lee. Mikaya Press 2006 47p il (Wonders of the world) $22.95
Grades: 4 5 6 7   **726**

1. Athens (Greece) -- History 2. Greece -- Civilization 3. Parthenon (Athens, Greece)
ISBN 1-931414-15-7

This "volume introduces the history of ancient Athens culminating in the building of the Parthenon. . . . [The text is] well-researched and clearly written. . . . The color illustrations include an excellent map of Greece, photos of artifacts and sculptures, and many clearly deliniated, large-scale paintings." Booklist

726.6   Cathedrals

Macaulay, David

Building the book Cathedral. Houghton Mifflin 1999 112p il $29.95
Grades: 4 5 6 7 8 9   **726.6**

1. Cathedrals 2. Gothic architecture
ISBN 0-395-92147-3

LC 99-17975

"On its twenty-fifth anniversary, the author recounts the origins of his first book and suggests revisions he'd make in light of what he's learned. . . . Most of the original Cathedral: the story of it's construction is reproduced in this oversized celebratory volume, along with lots of preliminary sketches, new commentary, and revised, or newly deployed, art. . . . Touches of informal humor further enliven a book that's already mesmerizing for both its original content and its insights into this author-illustrator's incisive, ebulliently creative mind." Horn Book

728.8   Large and elaborate private dwellings

Humphrey, Paul

Building a castle; by Paul Humphrey. Arcturus Pub. 2012 32 p. col. ill. (library) $28.50
Grades: 4 5 6   **728.8**

1. Castles -- Design and construction 2. Castles -- Europe -- Design and construction
ISBN 1848585594; 9781848585591

LC 2011051450

This book by Paul Humphrey "takes readers on a journey from the very beginnings of castles as fortresses to the lavish tourist destinations of today." The text, along with "contextual photographs, staged reenactments, and detailed diagrams offers . . . [an] overview of how an architectural structure reveals the culture, class system, and daily life of the Middle Ages. Castles from the Czech Republic, Scotland, England, Turkey, and Holland are highlighted." (Children's Literature)

729   Design and decoration of structures and accessories

Macaulay, David

★ **Built** to last. Houghton Mifflin Harcourt 2010 272p il $24.99
Grades: 4 5 6 7 8 9 10   **729**

1. Castles 2. Cathedrals 3. Architecture 4. Mosques -- Design and construction
ISBN 978-0-547-34240-5; 0-547-34240-3

"Significantly updating the Caldecott Honor-winning Castle (1977) and Cathedral (1973) with new text and full-color illustrations, this hefty volume combines them with a very lightly revised Mosque (2003) for a three-in-one architectural spree. No mere colorization of the black-and-white originals of the first two books, . . . the all-new, often breathtaking images have been drawn by hand and then digitally colored to harmonize, beautifully with the look of Mosque. . . . Take a moment to mourn the originals, then celebrate this entirely worthy revision." Kirkus

731   Sculpture

Wenzel, Angela

13 sculptures children should know. Prestel 2010 il $14.95

Grades: 4 5 6 **731**

1. Sculpture 2. Art appreciation

ISBN 978-3-7913-7010-1; 3-7913-7010-3

This "large-format, brightly colored [survey provides a] well-oranized [introduction] to the . . . world [of sculpture]. [It] highlights a variety of works from antiquity to modern times. . . . Leading questions encourage budding artists to use the featured subjects and artworks as inspiration." Horn Book Guide

Includes glossary

736   Other plastic arts

Boursin, Didier

★ **Easy** origami. Firefly 2005 64p il $19.95; pa $9.95

Grades: 4 5 6 7 **736**

1. Origami

ISBN 1-55297-928-8; 1-55297-939-3 pa

This guide provides step-by-step instructions for 24 origami projects, ranked as very easy, easy, and detailed, and the book includes tips for best results

"Paper-folding novices in particular may be drawn to this collection by its unusually clean design and bright, inviting colors." SLJ

Nguyen, Duy

Zombigami; paper folding for the living dead. Sterling 2011 il pa $9.95

Grades: 5 6 7 8 **736**

1. Origami 2. Zombies

ISBN 978-1-4027-8646-4; 1-4027-8646-8

"Featuring both a detachable photo gallery of folded ghouls placed in atmospheric settings and a package of origami paper in suitably ominous colors and patterns, this collection of 13 undead figures may not survive intact for long but offers experienced paper folders hours of creepy fun. Nguyen opens with a tutorial of creases and folding symbology then . . . goes on to show how each figure is folded with plenty of carefully drawn and clearly labeled step diagrams. Nonetheless, most of these models are challenging projects." SLJ

Stern, Joel

Jewish holiday origami; photographs by David Greenfield. Dover Publications 2006 64p il pa $5.95

Grades: 8 9 10 11 12 Adult **736**

1. Origami 2. Jewish holidays

ISBN 0-486-45076-7; 978-0-486-45076-6

LC 2005-56934

This book contains a "year's worth of holiday projects—from Chanukah dreidels and a menorah with candles, to Passover pyramids and an image of the Red Sea parting." Publisher's note

Temko, Florence

Origami holiday decorations for Christmas, Hanukkah, and Kwanzaa. Tuttle Pub. 2003 63p il pa $8.95

Grades: 5 6 7 8 **736**

1. Origami 2. Holiday decorations

ISBN 0-8048-3477-6 pa; 978-0-8048-3477-3 pa

LC 2002075060

"Among the 25 original projects are a Holiday Calendar, Jewish Star, Kwanzaa Bowl, and Santa Claus Table Decoration." Publisher's note

739.27   Jewelry

Macfarlane, Katherine

The **jeweler's** art; by Katherine Nell Macfarlane. Lucent Books 2007 112p il (Eye on art) lib bdg $32.45

Grades: 7 8 9 10 11 12 **739.27**

1. Jewelry

ISBN 978-1-59018-984-9

LC 2007-7804

A look at jewelry through the ages.

This "title is thoroughly researched and fully referenced, and contains quotations from artists and art historians. The writing is generally clear and fluid. . . . Many of the pages have good-quality photos of artwork and artists." SLJ

Includes bibliographical references

740   Graphic arts

Kidd, Chip

Go; a Kidd's guide to graphic design. Chip Kidd. Workman Publishing Company, Inc. 2013 160 p. (alk. paper) $17.95

Grades: 5 6 7 8 9 10 11 12 **740**

1. Graphic design 2. Children and design 3. Graphic arts -- Technique

ISBN 076117219X; 9780761172192

LC 2013032394

YALSA Award for Excellence in Nonfiction for Young Adults: Finalist (2014)

This book is an introduction to graphic design for children. It introduces "the aspiring designer to the thought processes behind typography and visual organization. Among the topics are color, juxtaposition, typography, design history, and the use of design to convey concepts such as irony and metaphor." (Library Journal)

Includes bibliographical references and index

741   Drawing and drawings

Ames, Lee J.

Draw 50 animal 'toons; [by] Lee J. Ames and Bob Singer. Doubleday 2000 un il (Draw 50) hardcover o.p. pa $8.95

Grades: 4 5 6 7 **741**

1. Animals in art 2. Cartooning -- Technique

ISBN 978-0-385-49142-6; 0-385-49142-5; 978-0-767-90544-2 pa; 0-767-90544-X pa

LC 00020750

"Step-by-step method shows how to draw cartoon animals, including dogs, mice, and a skateboarding crocodile." Publisher's note

741.2 Techniques, procedures, apparatus, equipment, materials

Ames, Lee J.

Drawing with Lee Ames; from the bestselling, award-winning creator of the Draw 50 series, a proven step-by-step guide to the fundamentals of drawing for all ages. Doubleday 1990 262p il pa $21

Grades: 6 7 8 9   **741.2**

1. Drawing
ISBN 0-385-23701-4

LC 90-31436

The author "offers a compendium of samples for beginning artists. Ames explains his approach to beginning art instruction as a form of mimicry, where students copy samples in order to get a feel for the process of drawing. . . . This is definitely for the beginning student who possesses very little to no drawing experience. . . . Ames's approach offers a good base from which students can then move on to more in-depth instruction." Voice Youth Advocates

Includes bibliographical references

McMillan, Sue

How to improve at drawing. Crabtree Pub. Co. 2010 48p il (How to improve at) lib bdg $29.27; pa $9.95

Grades: 7 8 9 10   **741.2**

1. Drawing -- Technique
ISBN 978-0-7787-3576-2 lib bdg; 0-7787-3576-1 lib bdg; 978-0-7787-3598-4 pa; 0-7787-3598-2 pa

"McMillan begins [this] book with a spread each on the history of drawing, equipment, perspective, color and textures, and composition. . . . [The] book has step-by-step instructions for a variety of attractive projects. The . . . book has, for each project, a series of four to six preliminary sketches that show the progression from first line to complete outline, but it is left to the artist to add the final shading." SLJ

Includes glossary

Scott, Damion

★ **How** to draw hip-hop; [by] Damion Scott and Kris Ex. Watson-Guptill 2006 144p il pa $19.95

Grades: 7 8 9 10   **741.2**

1. Drawing 2. Hip-hop
ISBN 0-8230-1446-0

LC 2005-29156

"This book combines the bold and energetic lines of graffiti art with the bright colors of cel-shaded video games and an obvious Japanese manga influence. . . . [It discusses] genre-specific concepts like wild style lettering [and] hip-hop clothing. . . . There is no other book of this kind on the market, making it a necessary and relevant purchase." SLJ

Temple, Kathryn

★ **Drawing**; the only drawing book you'll ever need to be the artist you've always wanted to be. [by] Kathryn Temple. Lark Books 2005 112p il (Art for kids) $17.95

Grades: 5 6 7 8   **741.2**

1. Drawing
ISBN 1-57990-587-0

LC 2004-17909

This "introduction to essential drawing techniques builds from the starting points of lines and simple shapes. . . . Eight concise chapters explore seeing with artist's eyes, line drawing, light and shadow, proportion and scale, perspective, drawing faces, drawing bodies, and using imagination. The succinct text reads smoothly and is written in a clear, understandable style. Sample sketches and crisp, color photographs extend the text." SLJ

Drawing in color. Lark Books 2009 112p il (Art for kids) $17.95

Grades: 5 6 7 8   **741.2**

1. Color 2. Drawing
ISBN 978-1-57990-821-8; 1-57990-821-7

LC 2008050618

"This heavily illustrated guide encourages budding artists to learn some basic skills and decide what works for them. Before jumping into project ideas, Temple explains some drawing tools and the basics of color theory. She provides clear, step-by-step instructions while reminding children that there is no right or wrong way to draw. Then, in nine chapters that each cover a particular technique or type of subject. . . . Projects use a variety of mediums, including colored pencils, markers, and oil pastels. The balance of detailed text and color images is visually appealing. Children will enjoy honing their observation skills as they practice using color in new ways." SLJ

741.5 Cartoons, graphic novels, caricatures, comics

Abadzis, Nick

★ **Laika.** First Second Books 2007 205p il

Grades: 5 6 7 8 9 10 11 12 Adult   **741.5**

1. Graphic novels 2. Space flight -- Graphic novels 3. Soviet Union -- History -- 1953-1991 -- Graphic novels
ISBN 1-59643-101-6; 978-1-59643-101-0

LC 2006-51907

Laika was the abandoned puppy destined to become Earth's first space traveler. This is her journey. Along with Laika, there is Korolev, once a political prisoner and now a driven engineer at the top of the Soviet space program, and Yelena, the lab technician responsible for Laika's health and life. The book depicts the dedication and struggles of the scientists and technicians who worked in the Soviet space program, based on research Abadzis did before writing this book. The book includes a bibliography of books and websites.

"Abadzis's tear-inducing and solidly researched graphic novel treatment of Laika's surpassingly tragic story is a standout." Publ Wkly

Akira, Shouko

Monkey High!: vol. 1; story and art by Shouko Akira; [translation and adaptation, Mai Ihara] Viz Media 2008 il pa $8.99

Grades: 7 8 9 10 11 12   **741.5**

1. Anime 2. Graphic novels 3. Romance -- Graphic novels 4. High school students -- Graphic novels

ISBN 978-1-4215-1518-2 pa; 1-4215-1518-0 pa

"Haruna sees the students in her new school . . . as acting ike monkeys. . . . She wants to keep to herself, but because she's beautiful, the boys start vying for her attention and the girls are getting jealous. . . . The artwork is lively and bright. . . . Readers who get caught up in the couple's first fight, first hand-holding, and first kiss will wait breathlessly for the other volumes in this series." SLJ

Volume 1 of an 8 volume series

Anderson, Eric A.

PX! Book one: a girl and her panda; written by Eric A. Anderson and Manny Trembley ; illustrated by Manny Trembley. Image Comics 2007 un il $16.99

Grades: 6 7 8 9 10 11 12 Adult   **741.5**

1. Graphic novels 2. Humorous graphic novels 3. Adventure graphic novels 4. Science fiction graphic novels

ISBN 978-1-58240-820-0; 1-58240-820-3

A young girl named Dahlia and her trusty (robot) panda sidekick set off on a journey around the world to save her missing scientist father, who has been kidnapped by Pollo, an evil goat mastermind who wants to take over the world (and yes, people keep telling him his name means chicken" in Spanish). Along the way, Dahlia meets Weatherby Ian Poppington III, a Victorian English secret agent also known as Double Aught Seven," and Wikkity Jones, a rollerskating swordsman who talks like a hillbilly and stands ready to fight ninja any time. The absurd humor is punctuated by moments of intense violent action, especially in the side story about fighting zombies. This book collects the webcomic.

Followed by: PX! v.2: in the service of the Queen (2009)

Appignanesi, Richard

As you like it; by William Shakespeare; illustrated by Chie Kutsuwada; adapted by Richard Appignanesi. Amulet Books 2009 207p (Manga Shakespeare) pa $10.95

Grades: 7 8 9 10   **741.5**

1. Poets 2. Authors 3. Dramatists 4. Graphic novels

ISBN 978-0-8109-8351-9; 0-8109-8351-6

LC 2008-45920

Banished to the Forest of Arden, Rosalind, disguised as a boy, reunites with true love Orlando.

"While maintaining considerable Shakespearian language, the plot is staged in a thoroughly manga manner, with Japanese settings, hairstyles, and posturing readily recognizable to the contemporary teen manga fan. . . . This is an excellent choice not only as curriculum support but also for manga readers." Booklist

Hamlet; [Richard Appignanesi, text adaptor]; illustrated by Emma Vieceli. Harry N. Abrams/Amulet Books 2007 195p (Manga Shakespeare) pa $9.95

Grades: 8 9 10 11 12 Adult   **741.5**

1. Poets 2. Authors 3. Dramatists 4. Graphic novels

ISBN 978-0-8109-9324-2; 0-8109-9324-4

Shakespeare's classic play of murder and revenge is here adapted into a manga-style graphic novel. It's now set in 2107, after global climate change has devastated the Earth. Appignanesi uses the text of the play and abridges it to fit the pages, while Vieceli's art vigorously carries the story along. The book includes a summary of the plot and a brief biography of Shakespeare.

A **midsummer** night's dream; illustrated by Kate Brown. Abrams 2008 207p (Manga Shakespeare) pa $9.95

Grades: 7 8 9 10   **741.5**

1. Poets 2. Authors 3. Dramatists 4. Graphic novels

ISBN 978-0-8109-9475-1; 0-8109-9475-5

Shakespeare's comedy of romance, Faerie, and shenanigans in the forest is adapted into a manga-style graphic novel. Hermia is in love with Lysander, while Demetrius is in love with Hermia, and Helen loves Demetrius. When mischievous fairy Puck decides to have some fun with the powerful love potion he has fetched for Fairy King Oberon, chaos reigns. While the human foursome needs to sort itself out, Oberon seeks revenge against his wife, Queen Titania, by having Puck use the love potion on her so she falls in love with the first creature she sees—who happens to be a yokel to whom Puck gave a donkey's head. The text takes dialog from the original play. The book includes a plot summary and a brief biography of Shakespeare.

Romeo and Juliet; by William Shakespeare; adapted by Richard Appignanesi; illustrated by Sonia Leong. Amulet Books 2007 195p (Manga Shakespeare) pa $9.95

Grades: 8 9 10 11 12   **741.5**

1. Poets 2. Authors 3. Dramatists 4. Graphic novels

ISBN 978-0-8109-9325-9; 0-8109-9325-2

LC 2006-100362

First published in the United Kingdom

Shakespeare's classic play of star-crossed young lovers gets the manga treatment. The book is set in modern Tokyo with rival yakuza gangs and uses somewhat abridged text from the play for the dialogue.

"Although the richness of the language may be lost, the script keeps the spirit of the story intact, hitting all the major speeches." Booklist

The **tempest**; illustrated by Paul Duffield; [adaptor, Richard Appignanesi] Abrams 2008 207p il (Manga Shakespeare) pa $9.95

Grades: 7 8 9 10   **741.5**

1. Poets 2. Authors 3. Dramatists 4. Graphic novels

ISBN 978-0-8109-9476-8

Prospero and his daughter Miranda have lived on an isolated island for twelve years, after he had been deposed from his rule as Duke of Naples and cast out to sea to die. A powerful magician, Prospero has caused the survivors of a shipwreck to land on his island, in order to get his revenge, for these survivors are his enemies. Problems arise when Miranda falls in love with Ferdinand, the monster Caliban tries to use the survivors to kill Prospero, and Ariel the sprite is trying to set things right while still obeying Prospero. The book includes a plot summary and a brief biography of Shakespeare

"This adaptation would be useful both as an introduction to the play and as a companion piece for classroom study of it, using images to illuminate the Bard's eloquent poetry." SLJ

Arai, Kiyoko

Beauty Pop, Vol. 1; story and art by Kiyoko Arai. Viz Media/Shojo Beat 2006 194p il pa $8.99

Grades: 7 8 9 10 11 12   **741.5**

1. Manga 2. Shojo manga 3. Graphic novels 4. Hair -- Graphic novels

ISBN 978-1-4215-0575-6

At Kiri Koshiba's high school, three popular upper classmen do occasional "Scissors Projects," working makeovers on specially selected girls. Narumi Shogo, who cuts hair, wants to become the best beautician in Japan and has won every youth competition - except one, years ago, that a younger girl won. When girls who aren't already pretty ask Narumi for a makeover, he tells them they're too ugly. Kiri helps two of the girls, working a stylist's magic that makes the girls glow; she's not interested in competition, even though her family owns a salon. Narumi wants to know who dares to be the upstart and challenge him, and he sets up the school's cultural festival to be a haircutting duel. Will Kiri even bother to compete?

Other titles in this series are:

Beauty pop, Vol. 2 (2006) (978-1-4215-0576-6)
Beauty pop, Vol. 3 (2007) (978-1-4215-1009-5)
Beauty pop, Vol. 4 (2007) (978-1-4215-1010-1)
Beauty pop, Vol. 5 (2007) (978-1-4215-1011-8)
Beauty pop, Vol. 6 (2007) (978-1-4215-1323-2)
Beauty pop, Vol. 7 (2008) (978-1-4215-1784-1)
Beauty pop, Vol. 8 (2008) (978-1-4215-2310-1)
Beauty pop, Vol. 9 (2008) (978-1-4215-2310-1)
Beauty pop, Vol. 10 (2009) (978-1-4215-2594-5)

Aristophane

The **Zabime** sisters; translation & afterword by Matt Madden; lettering by Nicholas Breutzman. First Second 2010 80p il pa $16.99

Grades: 7 8 9 10   **741.5**

1. Graphic novels 2. Sisters -- Graphic novels 3. Caribbean region -- Fiction

ISBN 978-1-59643-638-1; 1-59643-638-7

LC 2010-33986

On the first day of summer vacation, teenaged sisters M'Rose, Elle, and Celina step out into the tropical heat of their island home of Guadaloupe and encounter boys, schoolyard fights, petty thievery, and even illicit alcohol.

"The text is coupled with expressive images that offer glimpses into the personality of each character and allow the story to slowly unfold. The interplay among the siblings and each girl's singular response to events allow readers to establish a personal connection with each sister. The artist's dry brush technique and controlled use of line, mastery of

light and shadow, interesting and unusual framing, and expressive facial close-ups are compelling." SLJ

Arni, Samhita

★ **Sita's** Ramayana; Moyna Chitrakar, illustrator. Groundwood Books 2011 il $24.95

Grades: 5 6 7 8   **741.5**

1. Graphic novels 2. Ramayana 3. Hindu mythology -- Graphic novels

ISBN 978-1-55498-145-8; 1-55498-145-X

"The Ramayana is the story of the exiled prince Rama and his beautiful wife, Sita. When she is kidnapped by a love-struck demon king, her husband's efforts to rescue her result in a war that eventually involves not only demons and mortals, but also gods, monsters, and even animals. . . . Here, a Patua scroll painter has adapted it as a fast-paced, brilliantly bold graphic novel. All of the suspense, treachery, sorcery, and pathos of this epic is depicted in homemade natural dyes layered onto paper in energetic lines, rhythmic patterns, and fields of hot, bright colors. . . . This book would be a must-purchase based on the strength of its dramatic story and arresting art, enhanced by superior design and high-quality production. Brilliant and fresh." SLJ

Atangan, Patrick

The **yellow** jar; two tales from Japanese tradition. NBM 2003 48p il (Songs of our ancestors) $12.92

Grades: 5 6 7 8 9 10 11 12   **741.5**

1. Graphic novels 2. Folklore -- Japan -- Graphic novels

ISBN 1-56163-331-3

LC 2002-32132

"To render two magical Japanese legends, one about a fisherman who discovers a fair maiden in a big pot, the other about a monk whose fastidiously kept garden is invaded by two chrysanthemums, Atangan charmingly adopts the sharp outlines, boldly juxtaposed color fields, and striking compositions of eighteenth-century Japanese woodblock prints." Booklist

Other titles in this series are:

Silk tapestry and other Chinese folktales (2004)
Tree of love (2005)

Baker, Kyle

How to draw stupid and other essentials of cartooning. Watson-Guptill 2008 110p il pa $16.95

Grades: 8 9 10 11 12 Adult   **741.5**

1. Cartooning -- Technique 2. Graphic novels -- Drawing

ISBN 978-0-8230-0143-9

LC 2008-922161

"Baker, an award-winning cartoonist and graphic-novel illustrator, gives aspiring cartoonists irreverent advice about how to succeed in their chosen field. He offers instruction in basic drawing techniques such as choosing the right tools and discusses the importance of learning to draw shapes, exaggerating, and using references. But the author's most inspiring advice focuses on how to succeed as a cartoonist." SLJ

Bannister (Person)

The **shadow** door; art by Bannister; story by Nykko; [colors by Jaffre; translation by Carol Klio

Burrell] Graphic Universe 2009 46p il (The Elsewhere chronicles) lib bdg $27.93; pa $6.95

Grades: 4 5 6 7   **741.5**

1. Graphic novels 2. Horror graphic novels
ISBN 978-0-7613-4459-9 lib bdg; 0-7613-4459-4 lib bdg; 978-0-7613-3963-2 pa; 0-7613-3963-9 pa
LC 2008-39442

Four friends discover a movie projector that opens a passageway into a world threatened by creatures of shadow, where their only weapon is light

"This is an undeniably attractive offering, as the artwork, with deep darks and effervescent lights splayed across large, glossy pages, is strikingly rendered. . . . [This] should have no problem gaining an appreciative readership." Booklist

Other titles in this series are:
The shadow spies (2009)
The master of shadows (2009)
The calling (2010)
The parting (2011)
The tower of shadows (2013)

Beagle, Peter S.

The **last** unicorn; original story by Peter S. Beagle; adaptation by Peter B. Gillis; art by Renae De Liz. IDW 2011 167p il rpt $16.00; $24.99

Grades: 6 7 8 9 10   **741.5**

1. Graphic novels 2. Unicorns -- Fiction
ISBN 9780451450524 rpt; 978-1-60010-851-8; 1-60010-851-2

Presents a graphic novel adaptation of the famous novel, in which a unicorn, alone in an enchanted wood, discovers she might be the last of her kind and sets out on a journey to find others like her.

"A beloved story is now a graphic novel in this excellent adaptation. . . . Much of the original novel's lyrical language has been included, and readers will be eager to find out if the unicorn will give up her quest for love, or if any of Schmendrick's spells will ever turn out right. . . . The illustrations are graceful and detailed, and inked in warm, glowing colors. This is a worthy successor to the classic novel and film." SLJ

Bell, Cece

★ **El** deafo; Cece Bell; color by David Lasky. Abrams Books 2014 233 p. color illustrations $21.95

Grades: 3 4 5 6 7   **741.5**

1. Deaf children 2. Autobiographical graphic novels 3. Schools 4. Friendship 5. Hearing aids for children
ISBN 1419710206; 9781419710209
LC 2013955590

Eisner Award: Best Publication for Kids (2015)
Newbery Honor Book (2015)

"In this . . . graphic novel memoir, author/illustrator Cece Bell chronicles her hearing loss at a young age and her subsequent experiences with the Phonic Ear, a very powerful--and very awkward--hearing aid. The Phonic Ear gives Cece the ability to hear--sometimes things she shouldn't--but also isolates her from her classmates." (Publisher's note)

"Bell's bold and blocky full-color cartoons perfectly complement her childhood stories--she often struggles to fit in and sometimes experiences bullying, but the cheerful illustrations promise a sunny future." Booklist

Bendis, Brian Michael

Takio; vol. 2 Brian Michael Bendis, illustrated by Michael Avon Oeming. Marvel Enterprises 2013 96 p. col. ill. hbk $16.99

Grades: 5 6 7 8   **741.5**

1. Graphic novels 2. Sisters -- Fiction
ISBN 0785165533; 9780785165538

"Taki and Olivia are sisters with super-powers! In fact, they are the only ones in the world with super-powers! So obviously, they have to become super heroes! But is the world ready for real-life super heroes? Are the girls ready for the challenge? And will the accident that made them who they are reveal secrets that will change their lives forever?" (Publisher's note)

"Taki and Olivia face down danger in this bright, colorful, action-heavy series, which is unconventionally (and refreshingly) girl-focused." Booklist

Takio, vol. 1. Marvel Icon 2011 un il $9.95

Grades: 5 6 7 8   **741.5**

1. Graphic novels 2. Superhero graphic novels 3. Sisters -- Graphic novels
ISBN 978-0-7851-5326-9; 0-7851-5326-8

"This entertaining graphic novel features a crunchy and kinetic art style, quick pacing, realistic dialogue, and enough action to appeal to most middle-school readers." Booklist

Benjamin, P

Hulk : misunderstood monster; Writer, Paul Benjamin; illustrated by David Nakayama and Juan Santacruz. Marvel 2007 v1 il (Marvel adventures Hulk) $6.99

Grades: 5 6 7 8 9   **741.5**

1. Graphic novels 2. Superhero graphic novels 3. The Hulk (Fictional character)
ISBN 978-0-7851-2642-3; 0-7851-2642-2

Caught in the explosion of a gamma bomb, brilliant scientist Bruce Banner was transformed into a hulking beast. With no control over the transformations, Banner lives on the run, helping those less fortunate than he, hoping to one day find a cure to rid himself of the rampaging Hulk.

Other titles in this series are:
Hulk: defenders (2007)
Hulk: strongest one there is (2008)
Hulk: tales to astonish (2008)

Black, Holly

The **Good** Neighbors; book one: Kin. Graphix 2008 117p (The Good Neighbors) $16.99

Grades: 7 8 9 10 11 12   **741.5**

1. Graphic novels 2. Fantasy graphic novels 3. Fairies -- Graphic novels
ISBN 978-0-439-85562-4; 0-439-85562-4
LC 2007-49008

Sixteen-year-old Rue has grown up in a world much like ours, except that the human world and the world of faerie have co-existed, as good neighbors, for a long time. When Rue's mother disappears and her professor father becomes the main suspect in the murder of a young woman, Rue's life turns strange. As she digs for information to figure out what is happening in her life, Rue discovers that her mother is a faerie and has returned to that realm because of a broken promise.

"This sophisticated tale is well served by Naifeh's stylish, angular illustrations." SLJ

Other titles in this series are:

Kith (2009)

Kind (2010)

Bohl, Al

Guide to cartooning. Pelican 1997 176p il hardcover o.p. pa $14.95

Grades: 8 9 10 11 12   **741.5**

1. Cartooning

ISBN 1-56554-367-X; 1-56554-177-4 pa

LC 96-44340

This guide to the art of cartooning includes "history, the fundamentals of the craft, and discussions of various modes, including political panels, strips, greeting cards, comic books, and animation. Bohl ends with an . . . appendix of related schools, books, videos, biographies, and periodicals." (Libr J)

This "is so chockablock with information that any teen interested in cartooning will come away with a multitude of tips and tricks." Booklist

Includes bibliographical references

Bouchard, Hervé

Harvey; how I became invisible. [by] Hervé Bouchard and Janice Nadeau; translated by Helen Mixter. Groundwood Books/House of Anansi Press 2010 un il $19.95

Grades: 5 6 7 8   **741.5**

1. Graphic novels 2. Death -- Fiction 3. Fathers -- Fiction 4. Bereavement -- Fiction 5. Family life -- Fiction

ISBN 978-1-55498-075-8; 1-55498-075-5

Original French edition 2009

"This open-ended book is deserving of discussion, difficult though it may be." Booklist

Bowers, Rick

Superman versus the Ku Klux Klan; the true story of how the iconic superhero battled the men of hate. by Rick Bowers. National Geographic 2012 160 p.

Grades: 7 8 9 10 11 12   **741.5**

1. Ku Klux Klan 2. Comic books, strips, etc. -- History and criticism 3. United States -- Social life and customs -- History 4. Ku Klux Klan (1915-) 5. Superman (Comic strip) 6. Superman (Fictitious character) 7. Comic books, strips, etc. -- Social aspects

ISBN 1426309155; 1426309163; 9781426309151; 9781426309168

LC 2011024660

This book by Richard Bowers relates how "In 1946 . . . the powers behind the Superman franchise decided to use the superhero (in his radio incarnation) to take on a growing concern: the reemergence of the Ku Klux Klan . . . [Rick] Bowers begins with the story of Superman's creators, two Jewish kids who grew up in Cleveland. In alternating sections, he also follows the evolution of the Klan, from its beginnings after the Civil War to its renaissance . . . in the

1920s and beyond. A dual biography of both the hero and the hate group, this book also chronicles the early years of comics . . . and discusses how both Superman and the Klan came with values they wanted to impress upon young people." (Booklist)

Includes bibliographical references and index.

Bronte, Charlotte

Jane Eyre; the graphic novel. [by] Charlotte Bronte; original script by Amy Corzine. Lucent 2010 160p il (Classic graphic novel collection) $32.45

Grades: 7 8 9 10   **741.5**

1. Graphic novels 2. Orphans -- Graphic novels

ISBN 978-1-4205-0375-3; 1-4205-0375-8

LC 2010924004

In graphic novel format, presents an adaptation of Bronté's story about an orphaned young English woman who accepts employment as a governess at Thornfield Hall, a country estate owned by the mysterious and remote Mr. Rochester.

"The entire [story is] told through speech balloons. . . . This format offers readers an experience closer to a theatrical performance than a prose condensation of the plot. . . . Excellent graphics bring the [story] to life and set the mood. Lush art in jewel tones heightens interest. [The title is] replete with support materials beginning with an illustrated cast of characters and an introduction or plot summary and concluding with back matter." SLJ

Brosgol, Vera

★ **Anya's** ghost. First Second 2011 221p il $19.99; pa $15.99

Grades: 6 7 8 9 10   **741.5**

1. Graphic novels 2. Ghosts -- Graphic novels 3. School stories -- Graphic novels

ISBN 978-1-59643-713-5; 1-59643-713-8; 978-1-59643-552-0 pa; 1-59643-552-6 pa

LC 2010036251

"A deliciously creepy page-turning gem from first-time writer and illustrator Brosgol. . . . A moodily atmospheric spectrum of grays washes over the clean, tidy panels, setting a distinct stage before the first words appear. . . . In addition to the supernatural elements, Brosgol interweaves some savvy insights about the illusion of perfection and outward appearance. . . . A book sure to haunt its reader long after the last page is turned—exquisitely eerie." Kirkus

Brown, Jeffrey

★ **Star** Wars; Jedi Academy. Jeffrey Brown ; [edited by] Rex Ogle. Scholastic, Inc 2013 160 p. illustrations (Star Wars: Jedi Academy) (paper over board) $12.99

Grades: 3 4 5 6 7   **741.5**

1. Outer space -- Fiction 2. Middle schools -- Fiction 3. Star Wars -- Comic books, strips, etc.

ISBN 0545505178; 9780545505178; 9780545609999

LC 2013931939

In this book, by Jeffrey Brown, "Roan Novachez thought he was destined to attend Pilot Academy Middle School, just as his older brother and father did. His dreams are crushed when he is rejected by Pilot Academy and accepted into a sketchy new school called Coruscant Jedi Academy.

Confused and struggling to keep up, Roan tries to fly under the radar and passes the time drawing comics of his daily life at his strange boarding school." (Booklist)

"While it might be disappointing for those familiar with this world to see scant representation of beloved characters, it makes the book an easy starting point for new fans. There are plenty of references to other elements (the T-16 Skyhopper and Jedi training remotes, for example) for diehards to get excited about." SLJ

Followed by: Return of the Padawan (2014)

Brubaker, Jason

ReMIND. Coffee Table Comics 2011 il $24.95
Grades: 7 8 9 10   **741.5**
1. Fantasy graphic novels 2. Cats -- Graphic novels
ISBN 978-0-9831149-0-1; 0-9831149-0-0

"Sonia and her cat live in the quiet coastal town of Cripple Peaks, which is most famous for being the home of the 'lizard man,' a legendary creature that her father claimed to have seen in 1974. . . . . One day Victuals disappears, and as the days pass Sonia loses hope for his return. Then a week later the feline suddenly comes back, but with two alarming changes: there are stitches in his head, and now he can talk. Brubaker's artwork will definitely pull readers into this unusual story and keep them there. The illustrations are colorful and expressive, combining cartoon line drawings with jewel-toned paintings. . . . [This] is sure to capture readers' imaginations and keep them turning the pages." SLJ

Campbell, Ross

★ Shadoweyes; written and illustrated by Ross Campbell. SLG Publishing 2010 un il pa $14.95
Grades: 8 9 10 11 12   **741.5**
1. Graphic novels 2. Superhero graphic novels 3. Science fiction graphic novels 4. Crime -- Graphic novels
ISBN 978-1-59362-189-6; 1-59362-189-2

"Most convincing is the sharp dialogue, which speaks with such familiar rhythms and sentiment that teens will swear it came out of their own mouths. The art, too, balances a sleek manga technique, credible future looks and grunge fashions, the grotesquerie of zombie flesh, and inventive page composition." Booklist

Camper, Cathy

Lowriders in space; book 1 by Cathy Camper ; illustrated by Raul Gonzalez III. Chronicle Books 2014 112 p. chiefly color illustrations (Lowriders) hc $22.99
Grades: 4 5 6 7 8   **741.5**
1. Space vehicles 2. Mechanics (Persons) 3. Automobiles -- Fiction 4. Graphic novels 5. Lowriders -- Fiction 6. Friendship -- Fiction 7. Mexican Americans -- Fiction 8. Competition (Psychology) -- Fiction 9. Lowriders -- Comic books, strips, etc
ISBN 9781452121550; 1452121559
LC 2013040709

Cathy Camper "introduces readers to Lupe Impala, Flapjack Octopus, and Elirio Malaria, three friends who love working with cars and dream of having their own garage shop. One day they see an opportunity to achieve their goal--a car competition. When they start working on a lowrider to

prepare it for the competition, an out-of-this world journey begins." (School Library Journal)

"Raúl's snazzy panels--impressively drawn in only red, blue, and black ballpoint pen on tea-stained paper--resemble an amped-up Mighty Mouse cartoon rendered in anarchic yet skillful doodles. It's a joyfully explosive style, and it perfectly matches the Latino characters and barrio setting." Booklist

Card, Orson Scott

Laddertop. Tor 2011 un il pa $10.99
Grades: 6 7 8 9 10   **741.5**
1. Graphic novels 2. Science fiction graphic novels
ISBN 978-0-7653-2460-3; 0-7653-2460-1

"Preteens Robbi and Azure are best friends, though the girls couldn't be more opposite: Robbi is a sensitive dreamer, while Azure is a driven go-getter with a short temper. Azure's biggest dream is to be picked for Laddertop. This is a program of the Givers, aliens who claim to help conserve Earth's resources by building power-providing space stations 36,000 feet above the Earth; these are reached by giant ladders. . . . The main characters in this volume are largely female, strong and intelligent, a wonderful departure from male-dominated extraterrestrial offerings. Ibardolaza's muscular art blends manga and Western aesthetics." Kirkus

Carey, Mike

★ Re -Gifters; written by Mike Carey; art by Sonny Liew and Marc Hempel. DC Comics/Minx 2007 148p il pa $9.99
Grades: 7 8 9 10 11 12   **741.5**
1. Graphic novels 2. Romance graphic novels 3. Martial arts -- Graphic novels 4. School stories -- Graphic novels 5. High school students -- Graphic novels
ISBN 978-1-4012-0371-9 pa; 1-4109-0371-X pa

"Jen Dik Seong, or Dixie, is having trouble getting her ki focused. Normally an outstanding hapkido student, she finds that her crush on classmate Adam is affecting her ability to fight. This is not good, as the national competition is fast approaching, and her parents expect her to do well. . . . Dixie makes a series of poor choices. She decides to spend the entry fee . . . on an elaborate birthday present for Adam. . . . This is a terrific read that features complex characters dealing with internal and external conflicts that make them believable and endearing. Lively black-and-white illustrations bring action and emotion to the story." SLJ

Carroll, Emily

★ Through the woods; Emily Carroll. 1st ed Margaret K. McElderry Books 2014 208 p. chiefly color illustrations (trade paper) $14.99; (hardcover) $21.99
Grades: 8 9 10 11 12 Adult   **741.5**
1. Horror fiction 2. Comic books, strips, etc. 3. Short stories 4. Graphic novels
ISBN 9781442465961; 9781442465954
LC 2013030969

Eisner Award: Best Graphic Album--Reprint (2015)

In this book, Emily Carroll "crafts five unsettling tales in graphic-novel format inspired by common folkloric themes--from wolves in the woods to peculiar visitors to dark possessions. In 'Our Neighbor's House,' three sisters who find themselves alone in a cabin are taken, one by one, in the middle of the night by a smiling stranger. . . . 'The Nesting Place' focus on malevolent spirit possession." (Horn Book Magazine)

"All the tales in Carroll's debut graphic novel are fairly standard ghost stories, but it is her eerie illustrations--popping with bold color on black, glossy pages--that masterfully build terrifying tension and a keep-the-lights-on atmosphere." Booklist

Castellucci, Cecil

Janes in love; by Cecil Castellucci and Jim Rugg; with lettering by Rob Clark Jr. and gray tones by Jasen Lex. DC Comics/Minx 2008 176p il (Plain Janes) pa $9.99

Grades: 7 8 9 10 11 12   **741.5**
1. Graphic novels 2. Romance graphic novels 3. Art -- Graphic novels 4. Friendship -- Graphic novels 5. School stories -- Graphic novels 6. High school students -- Graphic novels

ISBN 978-1-4012-1387-9 pa; 1-4012-1387-1 pa

"Castellucci deftly deals with a number of serious issues, including anxiety and depression, mortality, body image, gay relationships, and community activism. Fortunately, they never weigh down the narrative: this is a sweet, quirky story with some uplifting (though never pedantic) messages. Rugg's clean, crisp illustrations are the perfect accompaniment." SLJ

★ The **Plain** Janes; [illustrated by] Jim Rugg. DC Comics/Minx 2007 un il pa $9.99

Grades: 7 8 9 10 11 12   **741.5**
1. Graphic novels 2. Art -- Graphic novels 3. Friendship -- Graphic novels 4. School stories -- Graphic novels 5. High school students -- Graphic novels

ISBN 978-1-4012-1115-8

After a bomb attack in Metro City, Jane's parents move to suburban Kent Waters, where Jane feels lost. Then she meets three other Janes at the "reject" table in the high school lunch room, and she convinces them to help her form their own secret club: P.L.A.I.N.—People Loving Art in Neighborhoods. However, their "art attacks" cause the authorities to think that P.L.A.I.N. is a terrorist group.

"The art, inspired by Dan Clowes' work, is absolutely engaging. Packaged like manga this is a fresh, exciting use of the graphic-novel format." Booklist

Another title about the Janes is:
Janes in love (2008)

Christmas classics; edited by Tom Pomplun. Eureka 2010 144p il (Graphic classics) $17.95
Grades: 7 8 9 10 11 12   **741.5**
1. Graphic novels 2. Christmas -- Fiction
ISBN 978-0-9825630-1-4; 0-9825630-1-9

This is a collection of graphic adaptations of Christmas classics including Charles Dickens' "A Christmas Carol," an early F. Scott Fitzgerald tale, an O. Henry western, a fairy tale by Willa Cather, and a Christmas horror story by Fitz-James O'Brien, a seasonal Sherlock Holmes adventure by Arthur Conan Doyle, Clement C. Moore's classic poem "A

Visit from St. Nicholas," and a letter from Santa Claus to Mark Twain's daughter.

"The variety of art styles and solid selection choices make this . . . essential for collections that include holiday books for teens and adults." Booklist

Chwast, Seymour

★ The **odyssey**; [Homer] ; adapted by Seymour Chwast. 1st U.S. ed. Bloomsbury 2012 128 p. ill. (All-action classics) (hardcover) $20.00
Grades: Adult   **741.5**
1. Epic literature 2. Adventure graphic novels 3. Odysseus (Greek mythology) 4. Graphic novels
ISBN 9781608194865

LC 2012010047

In this graphic retelling of Homer's "The Odyssey," "Odysseus faces storm and shipwreck, a terrifying man-eating Cyclops, the alluring but deadly Sirens, and the fury of the sea-god Poseidon as he makes his ten-year journey home from the Trojan War. While Odysseus struggles to make it home, his wife, Penelope, fights a different kind of battle as her palace is invaded by forceful, greedy men who tell her that Odysseus is dead and she must choose a new husband." (Publisher's note)

This graphic novel adaptation of Homer's classic epic is "a crackling adventure that also penetrates the recessess of the human heart. . . . Caldwell's art has the force and vibrant life of a Samurai Jack cartoon." Booklist

Colfer, Eoin

Artemis Fowl: the graphic novel; adapted by Eoin Colfer and Andrew Donkin; art by Giovanni Rigano; color by Paolo Lammana. Hyperion Books for Children 2007 un il $18.99; pa $9.99
Grades: 4 5 6 7 8 9   **741.5**
1. Graphic novels 2. Fantasy graphic novels 3. Adventure graphic novels
ISBN 978-0-7868-4881-2; 0-7868-4881-2; 978-0-7868-4882-9 pa; 0-7868-4882-0 pa

Twelve-year-old genius and criminal mastermind Artemis Fowl runs his missing father's crime empire and gets his hands on a book that will give him access to the underground fairy world. This graphic novel adaptation gives the book a European look and color palette

"Excellent use of color and shading gives the panels a tremendous sense of light with enchanting effect. Characters are expressively brought to life with fun, exaggerated style." SLJ

Other Artemis Fowl graphic novels are:
Artemis Fowl: the Arctic incident (2009)
Artemis Fowl: the eternity code (2013)
Artemis Fowl: the opal deception (2014)

Crilley, Mark

Miki Falls, Book One: Spring. HarperCollins/HarperTeen 2007 176p il pa $7.99
Grades: 7 8 9 10 11 12   **741.5**
1. Graphic novels 2. Friendship -- Graphic novels 3. School stories -- Graphic novels 4. High school students -- Graphic novels
ISBN 978-0-06-084616-9

"Crilley uses mystery to drive the narrative and creates characters that the reader will care about. The black-and-white, manga-style art is beautiful." Voice Youth Advocates

Other titles in this series are:

Miki Falls, Book Two: Summer
Miki Falls, Book Three: Autumn
Miki Falls, Book Four: Winter

Dawson, Willow

Lila & Ecco's do-it-yourself comics club. Kids Can Press 2010 112p il $16.95

Grades: 4 5 6 7   **741.5**

1. Graphic novels 2. Cartoons and caricatures

ISBN 978-1-55453-438-8; 1-55453-438-0

Twelve-year-olds Lila and Ecco are obsessed with comics. Every summer, they dress up as their favorite characters to attend the local comic book convention. This year, after they stumble into a workshop of comics creators, Lila and Ecco come to an exciting realization they can make their very own comic books!.

"Is it a story of two friends creating a comic, or a step-by-step guide to making comics? Why, it's both, actually. And what's most surprising is not that the guide is so comprehensive and easy to follow but that the framing story not only couches the lessons in comfortable language but is also diverting in its own right. . . . Dawson's savvy, sassy black-and-white art gives the static idea of instructions some pep, and the information is quite complete." Booklist

Deas, Mike

Dalen & Gole; scandal in Port Angus. Orca Book Publishers 2011 123p il pa $9.95

Grades: 4 5 6 7   **741.5**

1. Graphic novels 2. Science fiction graphic novels 3. Extraterrestrial beings -- Graphic novels

ISBN 978-1-55469-800-4; 1-55469-800-6

Dalen and Gole, refugees on Earth from the distant planet of Budap, must solve the mystery of diminishing fish stocks and save their home planet from an evil plot.

Deas "provides solid graphics, pacing, dialogue, and humor. . . . A fun mystery-adventure that's just right for young space cases." Booklist

Dezago, Todd

Spider -man: Spidey strikes back Vol. 1 digest. Marvel Comics 2005 96p il pa $5.99

Grades: 4 5 6 7 8 9   **741.5**

1. Graphic novels 2. Superhero graphic novels 3. Spider-Man (Fictional character)

ISBN 0-7851-1632-X

Tired of saving the day and getting no respect, Spider-Man considers taking a break from his superhero duties, which leaves the city wide open for the likes of the Sandman and the Enforcers. Will Spidey let it all go to pot, or will he step up to the plate and take one for the team? This volume collects Marvel Age Spider-Man issues 17-20. Previous volumes were published under the series title Marvel Age Spider-Man. The Marvel Age titles are being collected and published in the digest size, similar to manga, and at an affordable price. The Marvel Age series are aimed at younger audiences than the other superhero titles from Marvel.

Emerson, Sharon

Zebrafish; written by Sharon Emerson; drawn by Renee Kurilla. Atheneum Books for Young Readers 2010 119p il $16.99

Grades: 4 5 6 7   **741.5**

1. Graphic novels 2. Rock music -- Graphic novels

ISBN 978-1-4169-9525-8; 1-4169-9525-0

LC 2009-41683

When their rock band becomes popular, five middle schoolers use their new fame to generate awareness (and donations) for an important cause.

Explorer; the mystery boxes. Kazu Kibuishi. Abrams Books 2012 126 p. (Explorer) (pbk.) $10.95; (hardcover with jacket) $19.95

Grades: 4 5 6 7 8   **741.5**

1. Short stories 2. Graphic novels 3. Boxes -- Fiction 4. Mystery graphic novels 5. Boxes

ISBN 1419700103; 9781419700095; 9781419700101

LC 2011025343

This collection of short stories offers "[s]even . . . stories [which] answer one simple question: what's in the box? . . . [E]ach of these . . . illustrated short graphic works revolves around a central theme: a mysterious box and the marvels--or mayhem--inside. Artists include . . . Kazu Kibuishi, Raina Telgemeier ('Smile'), and Dave Roman ('Astronaut Academy'), as well as Jason Caffoe, Stuart Livingston, Johane Matte, Rad Sechrist (all contributors to the . . . comics anthology series 'Flight'), and . . . artist Emily Carroll." (Publisher's note)

Fairfield, Lesley

★ Tyranny. Tundra Books 2009 114p il pa $10.95

Grades: 8 9 10 11 12   **741.5**

1. Graphic novels 2. Eating disorders -- Graphic novels

ISBN 0-88776-903-9; 978-0-88776-903-0

This graphic novel portrays teenager Anna's struggle with anorexia, "personified as her tormentor, Tyranny." (Publisher's note) "Age eleven and up." (Quill Quire)

"This is one of the most moving and important graphic novels to come along in years. Many stories have been written about teens who try to change what they see in the mirror through anorexia and bulimia, but this one features a girl who is driven by her own personal demon. That demon is called Tyranny, and it is represented by an angry and chaotic swirl of lines that form the shape of a person. . . . Fairfield treats this important subject with intelligence and empathy. . . . The simple yet powerful black-and-white drawings do wonders in bringing the book's message to its readers." SLJ

Fajardo, Alexis E.

Kid Beowulf and the blood-bound oath. Bowler Hat 2008 il pa $14.95

Grades: 6 7 8 9   **741.5**

1. Graphic novels 2. Beowulf -- Graphic novels 3. Monsters -- Graphic novels

ISBN 978-0-9801419-1-7 pa; 0-9801419-1-5 pa

"In the standard Beowulf story, the character appears as a full-fledged hero, with little concept of how he actually became one. Fajardo tells the backstory, using a blend of humor and soap-opera plot twists. . . . The cartoon-style illustrations are lively and contain lots of visual humor." SLJ

Fisch, Sholly

Super friends: for justice! Sholly Fisch writer; Dario Brizuela ... [et. al] artists. DC Comics 2009 un il $12.99

Grades: 5 6 7 8 9   **741.5**

1. Graphic novels 2. Superhero graphic novels 3. Batman (Fictional character) 4. Superman (Fictional character) 5. Wonder Woman (Fictional character)

ISBN 978-1-4012-2156-0; 1-4012-2156-4

"This volume features the JLA facing off with some of their biggest foes including the power-stealing android Amazo and the super-ape known as Gorilla Grodd." Publisher's note

Flight explorer; edited by Kazu Kibuiski. Villard 2008 112p il pa $10

Grades: 4 5 6 7   **741.5**

1. Graphic novels 2. Fantasy graphic novels 3. Humorous graphic novels 4. Adventure graphic novels 5. Science fiction graphic novels

ISBN 978-0-345-50313-8 pa; 0-345-50313-9 pa

This anthology includes stories that Kibuishi kept from Flight Volume 4 because they had all-ages appeal, as well as stories submitted especially for this volume. Kibuishi's own Copper and his talking dog cross a deep canyon by leaping onto mushrooms, only to discover the vegetation is intelligent. Kean Soo's Jellaby and his human friends frolic in the snow. Missile Mouse by Jake Parker defends a village on another planet, only to discover his coming was prophesied (this story includes two uses of the word "crap"). The other stories will appeal to younger readers, while some of the humor will also appeal to older readers. Other than the one bad word in "Missile Mouse" (noted above), there shouldn't be any other content that would keep this book out of most elementary and middle schools.

"Every story has a layout that promotes an acute sense of pacing and showcases the crisp, defined, full-color art." SLJ

Foley, Ryan

Stolen hearts; the love of Eros and Psyche. illustrated by Sankha Banerjee. Campfire 2011 84p il (Campfire mythology) pa $11.99

Grades: 6 7 8 9   **741.5**

1. Graphic novels 2. Love -- Graphic novels 3. Greek mythology -- Graphic novels

ISBN 978-93-80028-48-4; 93-80028-48-2

Aphrodite, the Greek goddess of beauty, has grown jealous of a young girl named Psyche. The goddess decides to dispatch her mischievous son Eros, the god of love, to perform a nasty trick. When the trick goes awry, Eros finds himself falling in love with Psyche.

"Foley retells one of the most famous love stories of all time, and it is certainly beautiful to behold. Banerjee's lovely, jewel-toned paintings will keep readers' eyes glued to the page. . . . This is a good adaptation of an old story, and one that will entice today's readers." SLJ

Ford, Christopher

Stickman Odyssey; an epic doodle. Philomel Books 2011 200p il $12.99

Grades: 5 6 7 8   **741.5**

1. Graphic novels 2. Humorous graphic novels 3. Adventure graphic novels 4. Greek mythology -- Graphic novels

ISBN 978-0-399-25426-0; 0-399-25426-9

LC 2010-36900

In this humorous take on the Odyssey, Zozimos, banished from his country by his evil stepmother, has many adventures as he prepares to return home to reclaim the throne that is rightfully his.

"The black-and-white illustrations are occasionally simple to the point of hilarity. . . . There is subtlety and depth here, however, and the contrast between the intentionally plain characters and their seemingly larger-than-life (but ultimately universal) quests . . . makes the final product both the promised Greek epic tale and an examination of the ways in which modern humans are isolated and lost. . . . Ford balances allegory and madcap quest so perfectly that the book inspires reflection even while it is clearly a quick-reading, ridiculous, often gross adventure." Bull Cent Child Books

★ **Fractured** fables; edited by Jim Valentino and Kristen K. Simon; book design by Jim Valentino; cover illustration by Michael and Laura Allred from a sketch by Jim Valentino; cover design and graphics by Tim Daniel. Image Comics 2010 159p il $29.99

Grades: 6 7 8 9   **741.5**

1. Graphic novels 2. Literature -- Collections

ISBN 978-1-60706-269-1; 1-60706-269-0

LC 2010014838

Presents, in comic book format, thirty familiar fairy tales, songs, fables, and stories as retold by such acclaimed authors and illustrators as Ben Templesmith, Jim Di Bartolo, Scott Morse, and May Ann Licudine.

"This is a great adaptation highly worth reading or just browsing the artwork and illustrations." Voice Youth Advocates

Friesen, Ray

A **cheese** related mishap and other stories. Don't Eat Any Bugs 92p il (LOOKIT! comedy and mayhem) pa $8.95

Grades: 3 4 5 6   **741.5**

ISBN 0-9728177-6-X pa

"Held together by dueling narrators, this volume features Mellville the penguin and a cast of several as they struggle to save exploding cheese from a horde of evil chicken ninjas! Interspersed are stories of Captain Cautious, the timid super hero, and Tbyrd Fearlessness, the inept ostrich outlaw." (Publisher's note)

Other titles in this series are:

Yarg! and other stories (2007)

Cupcakes of doom! (2009)

Piranha pancakes (2011)

Gaiman, Neil, 1960-

★ The **graveyard** book graphic novel Volume 1; based on the novel by Neil Gaiman ; adapted by P. Craig Russell ; illustrated by Kevin Nowlan, P. Craig Russell, Tony Harris, Scott Hampton, Galen Showman, Jill Thompson, Stephen B. Scott ; colorist, Lovern Kindzierski ; letterer, Rick Parker. HarperCollins 2014 188 p. color illustrations $19.99

Grades: 5 6 7 8 9 10   **741.5**
    1. Graphic novels 2. Orphans -- Fiction 3. Cemeteries -- Fiction
    ISBN 9780062194817; 006219481X
                     LC 2013953799

This graphic novel is an adaptation of the "Newbery Medal-winning novel, [where] Bod is an unusual boy . . . , the only living resident of a graveyard. Raised from infancy by the ghosts, werewolves, and other cemetery denizens, Bod has learned the antiquated customs of his guardians' time as well as their ghostly teachings." (Publisher's note)

"Russell brings his decades of comics know-how to this lovely, lyrical adaptation of [Gaiman's] well-loved, Newbery Medal--winning book. Not content to rely exclusively on his own distinctive talents, Russell has enlisted some of the industry's greatest contemporary illustrators as contributors, who fill the panels with appropriately gothic tones. In order to give ample room to the novel's twists and turns, the adaptation has been divided into two parts." Booklist

★ The **graveyard** book graphic novel Volume 2; based on the novel by Neil Gaiman ; adapted by P. Craig Russell ; illustrated by David LaFuente, Scott Hampton, P. Craig Russell, Kevin Nowlan, Galen Showman ; colorist, Lovern Kindzierski ; letterer, Rick Parker. HarperCollins 2014 188 p. color illustrations (hardcover) $19.99

Grades: 5 6 7 8 9 10   **741.5**
    1. Dead -- Fiction 2. Orphans -- Fiction 3. Cemeteries -- Fiction 4. Supernatural graphic novels 5. Graphic novels 6. Supernatural -- Fiction
    ISBN 0062194836; 9780062194831
                     LC 2013497350

"Russell concludes the two-part adaptation of Gaiman's Newbery Medal winner, encompassing the final three chapters of the novel. Bod, raised by the ghostly denizens of a graveyard, is a young adult now, yearning for knowledge of the world of the living. After a showdown with a pair of school bullies . . . Bod finally confronts the ancient order who murdered his family and overcomes them with his supernatural know-how and his innate courage and cleverness." (Booklist)

"Russell and his team of illustrators continue to do this amazing story justice with images that lead readers down a path into Bod's dark and magical graveyard world. Gaiman has the ability to weave beauty and intrigue into a story that has a strong potential to frighten." VOYA

Hansel & Gretel; a Toon graphic. Neil Gaiman, Lorenzo Mattotti. Toon Books 2014 56 p. black and white illustrations hbk $16.95

Grades: 2 3 4 5 6   **741.5**
    1. Folklore -- Germany 2. Fairy tales -- Graphic novels

3. Fairy tales 4. Graphic novels
    ISBN 9781935179627; 1935179624
                     LC 2014000694

This graphic novel offers a retelling of the Germanic folk tale of Hansel and Gretel. "Hansel overhears his mother presenting her logical argument to abandon the children in the forest so that she and her husband might have some hope of surviving the famine caused by the war. He reluctantly agrees, but he is happy when the children outsmart the plan. However, as conditions worsen, their mother persuades their father to abandon them a second time." (Bulletin of the Center for Children's Books)

"Mattotti contributes elegant b&w ink spreads that alternate with spreads of text. His artistry flows from the movement of his brush and the play of light and shadow. . . . Gaiman makes the story's horrors feel very real and very human, and Mattotti's artwork is genuinely chilling." Pub Wkly

Includes bibliographical references

Geary, Rick

Great expectations; adapted by Rick Geary. rev ed; Papercutz 2008 56p il (Classics illustrated) $9.95

Grades: 4 5 6 7 8 9   **741.5**
    1. Graphic novels 2. Orphans -- Graphic novels 3. Great Britain -- History -- 19th century -- Graphic novels
    ISBN 978-1-59707-097-3; 1-59707-097-1

After harsh early years, Pip, an orphan growing up in Victorian England, is given the means to become a gentleman by an unknown benefactor and learns that outward appearances can be deceiving. Presented in comic book format.

"This pleasant graphic interpretation can serve as an introduction to Dickens for younger readers and perhaps eventually steer them to the wider world of the source material and beyond." Publ Wkly

Glass, Bryan J. L.

The **mice** templar, volume one: the prophecy; created by Bryan J.L. Glass & Michael Avon Oeming. Image Comics 2008 256p il $29.99

Grades: 6 7 8 9 10 11 12 Adult   **741.5**
    1. Graphic novels 2. Fantasy graphic novels 3. Adventure graphic novels 4. Mice -- Graphic novels
    ISBN 978-1-58240-871-2; 1-58240-871-8

In a land populated by animals, the Mice Templar used to protect the people of the mouse kingdom, but a civil war destroyed them; the king now employs rat soldiers, and they prey upon the mouse villages. Young Karic still idolizes the Mice Templar, but everything he knows and believes is shattered when his village is raided by rats, burned, and his family captured as slaves. He survives, saved by a mysterious mouse named Pilot, who says he was once a Templar and offers to train Karic. The salmon in the river say that Karic is the one prophesied to restore the Templar, but can he truly be the one? The book includes considerable battle violence.

"Equal parts Norse myth, Arthurian legend, and Mrs. Frisby and the Rats of N.I.M.H., The Mice Templar series re-imagines the warrior animal tale with just enough of its own spin to make it well worth adding to the collection." Voice Youth Advocates

Other titles in this series are:

Destiny Part One (2010)
Destiny Part Two (2010)
Legend (2013)
A Midwinter Night's Dream (2012)

Gorman, Michele

★ **Getting** graphic! using graphic novels to promote literacy with preteens and teens. with a foreword by Jeff Smith. Linworth Pub. 2003 100p il pa $36.95

Grades: Adult Professional   **741.5**
1. Graphic novels -- Administration
ISBN 1-58683-089-9

LC 2003-13199

"A must-have first resource for school and public libraries that are considering adding graphic novels to their collections but are unsure how to proceed." Booklist

"This title serves as an introduction to the world of fiction and nonfiction comics. Collection-development policies are addressed as well as cataloging, shelving, and maintaining these . . . books. Gorman provides ideas for the genre's integration into classroom curriculum and suggests promotional activities for school and public libraries." SLJ

Includes bibliographical references

Gownley, Jimmy

Amelia rules!: the whole world's crazy! Renaissance Press 2003 176p $24.95; pa $14.95

Grades: 3 4 5 6   **741.5**
1. Graphic novels 2. Humorous graphic novels 3. Friendship -- Graphic novels 4. Family life -- Graphic novels
ISBN 0-9712169-3-2; 0-9712169-2-4 pa

"Amelia . . . is getting used to life with her newly divorced mom and her hip, young aunt Tanner; settling in at a strange new school; and finding a group of friends. Amelia is no sweet innocent, nor are her three G.A.S.P (Gathering of Awesome Superpals) buddies: Reggie, superhero in the making; Rhonda, Amelia's tough bete noire with a fourth-grade 'thing' for Reggie; and quiet, mysterious Pajamaman. Jealousy, meanness, sadness, and confusion, as well as surprising generosity, and love crisscross the pages in energetic, freewheeling, full-color cartoon art that unwraps a kid's-eye view of life honestly, poignantly, and with a hefty dollop of melodrama." Booklist

Other titles in this series are:

Amelia rules!: What makes you happy? (2004)
Amelia rules! Superheroes (2005)
Amelia rules! a very ninja Christmas (2009)
Amelia rules! When the past is a present (2010)
Amelia rules! The tweenage guide to not being unpopular (2010)
Amelia rules! True things (adults don't want kids to know (2010)
Amelia rules! The meaning of life. . . and other stuff (2011)
Amelia rules! Her permanent record (2012)

The **dumbest** idea ever! by Jimmy Gownley. Graphix / Scholastic 2014 240 p. color illustrations $24.99

Grades: 5 6 7   **741.5**
1. High school -- Graphic novels 2. Autobiographical graphic novels
ISBN 0545453461; 9780545453462; 9780545453479

LC 2013939128

In this graphic memoir by Jimmy Gownley, "at thirteen, Jimmy was popular, at the top of his class, and the leading scorer on his basketball team. But . . . when chicken pox forced him to miss the championship game . . . , he got pneumonia and missed . . . school. Before Jimmy knew it, his grades were sinking and nothing seemed to be going right. How would Jimmy turn things around, get back on top at school, and maybe even get a date with the cutest girl in school?" (Publisher's note)

"[Gownley] recounts his beginnings as a cartoonist. . . . Humble, endearing and utterly easy to relate to." Kirkus

Grant, Alan

Robert Louis Stevenson's Kidnapped; adaptation by Alan Grant; illustrator, Cam Kennedy. Tundra Books 2007 un il pa $11.95

Grades: 6 7 8 9 10   **741.5**
1. Graphic novels 2. Adventure graphic novels
ISBN 978-0-88776-843-9 pa; 0-88776-843-1 pa

LC 2007921350

Kidnapped is set in 1751, during the time of the Jacobite rebellion — a tumultuous and tragic period in Scottish history. When David Balfour sets out to find his uncle, he never dreamed that he would be kidnapped — but saved from a life of slavery — and thrown from one escapade to another in the company of the fugitive, masterful swordsman Alan Breck Stewart.

"This is an engaging adaptation, aided by Kennedy's vibrant illustrations in a palette dominated by blues, greens, and sepia tones. The action scenes are exciting." SLJ

Robert Louis Stevenson's Strange case of Dr. Jekyll and Mr. Hyde; adapted by Alan Grant; illustrated by Cam Kennedy; colored and lettered by Jamie Grant. Tundra Books 2008 40p il pa $11.95

Grades: 6 7 8 9 10   **741.5**
1. Graphic novels
ISBN 978-0-88776-882-8 pa; 0-88776-882-2 pa

"Stevenson's classic tale takes on a new format in a vivid graphic novel. This mysterious story of the struggle between good and evil is one that has been popular since its publication and continues to hold its appeal. Much about this adaptation honors the original version of the story—the language of the period remains true, and the drawings of 1880s London and the furnishings and fashion within it are realistic as well." Voice Youth Advocates

★ **Graphic** novels and comic books; edited by Kat Kan. The H.W. Wilson Co. 2010 195p il (Reference shelf) pa $35

Grades: Adult Professional   **741.5**
1. Graphic novels -- History and criticism
ISBN 978-0-8242-1100-4; 0-8242-1100-6

LC 2010-34209

"This collection of articles from scholarly journals, newspapers, and blogs gives a well-rounded overview of graphic novels, as well as a strong argument for their place in schools and libraries. The first section chronicles the growing mainstream acceptance of graphic novels in the United States. . . . . Susequent sections look at these books as complex works of literature, as education and literacy aids, and as significant additions to library collections, with advice for librarians on how to purchase, catalog, file, and promote them. In the final section, readers hear from writers and artists . . . who clearly convey the joy they get from this medium. This is both an entertaining and highly practical read." SLJ

Includes bibliographical references

Grayson, Devin

Uglies; Shay's story. created by Scott Westerfeld ; written by Scott Westerfeld and Devin Grayson ; illustrations by Steven Cummings. Del Rey 2012 160 p. chiefly ill. (prebind) $22.10; (paperback) $10.99

Grades: 7 8 9 10   **741.5**

1. Dystopian graphic novels 2. Conformity -- Graphic novels 3. Plastic surgery -- Graphic novels 4. Graphic Novels 5. Science fiction 6. Friendship -- Fiction 7. Beauty, Personal -- Fiction

ISBN 9780606264754; 0345527224; 9780345527226

LC 2012374898

This young adult graphic novel retells the story of author Scott Westerfeld's dystopia "Uglies" from "the point of view of recurring frenemy Shay." It is "set in a . . . future time when discord is suppressed through ruthlessly enforced conformity and obligatory plastic surgery at age 16. . . . Shay yearns for freedom. An encounter with the flawed and alluring David, a covert envoy from the Smoke, a secret community of nonconformists, may offer Shay the escape she craves." (Publishers Weekly)

Followed by:
Uglies: Cutters (2012);

Gulledge, Laura Lee

Page by Paige. Amulet Books 2011 un il $18.95; pa $9.95

Grades: 7 8 9 10 11 12   **741.5**

1. Graphic novels 2. Humorous graphic novels 3. Artists -- Graphic novels 4. Friendship -- Graphic novels 6. New York (N.Y.) -- Graphic novels

ISBN 0-8109-9721-5; 0-8109-9722-3 pa; 978-0-8109-9721-9; 978-0-8109-9722-6 pa

Teenage Paige Turner (blame her writer parents) moves to New York City from Virginia, and she finds the big city rather overwhelming. She decides to buy a sketchbook and sort out her thoughts and feelings in drawings. Soon she does make some friends, and she explores more of the city, but as she begins to feel happier, she clashes with her parents. All of this goes into her sketchbook journal, which she starts to show to her new friends—Jules, Longo, and Gabe. The book is organized by Paige's "rules," which she uses to try to change herself, such as "Rule #2: Draw what you know. If you feel it or see it . . . DRAW IT!"

"Gulledge's b&w illustrations are simple but well-suited to their subject matter; the work as a whole is a good-natured, optimistic portrait of a young woman evolving toward adulthood." Publ Wkly

Will & whit; Laura Lee Gulledge. Abrams Book 2013 192 p. ill. (paperback) $12.95

Grades: 7 8 9 10   **741.5**

1. Grief -- Graphic novels 2. Fear of the dark -- Graphic novels

ISBN 1419705466; 9781419705465

LC 2012955192

In this graphic novel, by Laura Lee Gulledge, "Wilhelmina 'Will' Huxstep is a creative soul struggling to come to terms with a family tragedy. She crafts whimsical lamps, in part to deal with her fear of the dark. . . . She longs for unplugged adventures with her fellow creative friends, Autumn, Noel, and Reese. Little does she know that she will get her wish in the form of an arts carnival and a blackout . . . which forces Will to face her fear of darkness." (Publisher's note)

Hale, Dean

★ **Rapunzel's** revenge; [by] Shannon and Dean Hale; illustrated by Nathan Hale. Bloomsbury 2008 144p il map $18.99; pa $14.99

Grades: 5 6 7 8   **741.5**

1. Graphic novels 2. Fantasy graphic novels 3. Humorous graphic novels 4. Fairy tales -- Graphic novels

ISBN 1-59990-070-X; 1-59990-288-5 pa; 978-1-59990-070-4; 978-1-59990-288-3 pa

LC 2007-37670

In this graphic novel, Rapunzel escapes "from the enchanted tree where Mother Gothel imprisoned her. Rapunzel sets off alone through the ghost towns and Badlands of Gothel's Reach. She is determined to find Gothel's Villa and teach Mother Gothel a long-overdue lesson for her years of treachery and lies, and help her real mother get out of the mine camps where Mother Gothel has kept her enslaved." (Publisher's note)

"The dialogue is witty, the story is an enticing departure from the original, and the illustrations are magically fun and expressive." SLJ

Another title about these characters is:
Calamity Jack (2009)

Hale, Shannon

Calamity Jack; [by] Shannon Hale, Dean Hale, and Nathan Hale. Bloomsbury 2010 144p il $19.99; pa $14.99

Grades: 5 6 7 8   **741.5**

1. Graphic novels 2. Fairy tales -- Graphic novels

ISBN 978-1-59990-076-6; 1-59900-076-9; 978-1-59990-373-6 pa; 1-59990-373-3 pa

LC 2008-41332

In this graphic novel interpretation of "Jack and the beanstalk," Jack is a born schemer who climbs a magical beanstalk in the hope of exacting justice from a mean giant and gaining a fortune for his widowed mother, aided by some friends.

"The urban setting suits this retelling of the familiar beanstalk tale; Nathan Hale's art gives it a steampunk twist, and the addition of fairy-tale creatures like giants and pixies is natural and convincing." Booklist

Harrell, Rob

Monster on the Hill; by Rob Harrell. Top Shelf Productions 2013 192 p. color illustrations pbk $19.95

Grades: 4 5 6 7 8   **741.5**
   1. Monsters -- Graphic novels 2. Friendship -- Graphic novels

ISBN 1603090754; 9781603090759

This graphic novel by Rob Harrell is set in "1860s England [where] every . . . township is terrorized by a . . . monster - much to the townsfolk's delight! Each town's . . . monster is a source of local pride [and] tourism. Unfortunately, for . . . Stoker-on-Avon, their monster isn't quite as impressive. Can the morose Rayburn get a monstrous makeover and become a proper horror? It's up to the eccentric Dr. Charles Wilkie and plucky street urchin Timothy to get him up to snuff." (Publisher's note)

Hart, Christopher

Drawing the new adventure cartoons; cool spies, evil guys and action heroes. Sixth & Spring Books 2008 126p il pa $19.95

Grades: 4 5 6 7   **741.5**
   1. Drawing 2. Cartoons and caricatures

ISBN 978-1-933027-60-9 pa; 1-933027-60-6 pa

"This fun guide works best for those with some previous figure-drawing experience. . . . Sections on 'Drawing the Head,' 'Drawing the Teen Action Body,' and 'Using Body Language to Convey Emotion' offer detailed and, for the most part, step-by-step instructions. Subsequent sections . . . provide examples of unique and zany aspects of adventure-style characters. . . . Throughout the book, Hart also includes useful tip boxes, often demonstrating how not to draw a character. These suggestions are invaluable, providing insight into creating kinetic and expressive cartoons." SLJ

How to draw comic book bad guys and gals. Watson-Guptill 1998 64p il pa $10.95

Grades: 6 7 8 9 10 11 12   **741.5**
   1. Drawing 2. Cartoons and caricatures 3. Comic books, strips, etc.

ISBN 0-8230-2372-9

LC 98-6411

This guide to drawing comic book villains covers such topics as head tilts, facial expressions, hands and muscle groups, the body in action, using light and shadow, composition, and storytelling

"Not for beginners, but for those who already have some knowledge of drawing and ability. . . . Boldly colored illustrations combined with the line drawings add to the professional look of the book." Voice Youth Advocates

Manga for the beginner; everything you need to start drawing right away! Watson-Guptill Publications 2008 192p il $21.95

Grades: 5 6 7 8 9 10   **741.5**
   1. Manga -- Drawing 2. Graphic novels -- Drawing

ISBN 978-0-8230-3083-5; 0-8230-3083-0

LC 2007-40490

"Hart's latest drawing book . . . contains detailed and easy-to-follow instructions for drawing types of shojo man-

ga (aimed at girls) and shonen manga (aimed at boys). . . . He describes in concise language and through clear illustrations how to use lettering, lighting effects, and other techniques to achieve a certain mood to advance a plot. . . . Anyone even slightly interested in drawing manga will find it appealing." Voice Youth Advocates

Manga mania romance; drawing shojo girls and bishie boys. [by] Chris Hart. Chris Hart Books 2008 147p il pa $19.95

Grades: 6 7 8 9 10   **741.5**
   1. Drawing 2. Manga -- Drawing 3. Cartooning -- Technique

ISBN 978-1-933027-43-2; 1-933027-43-6

LC 2007-907250

"This crisply illustrated work aims to give aspiring cartoonists the basics of drawing. . . . A wonderful introduction to the shojo style. A great first choice for creating a cartooning/drawing collection." SLJ

Mecha mania; how to draw the battling robots, cool spaceships, and military vehicles of Japanese comics. Watson-Guptill 2002 128p il pa $19.95

Grades: 5 6 7 8   **741.5**
   1. Drawing 2. Cartoons and caricatures

ISBN 0-8230-3056-3

LC 2002-6402

"Hart offers budding cartoonists a mix of basic instructions and savvy technical advice for creating a wide variety of generic giant robots, robotlike craft, cyborgs of both sexes, and bad-guy types . . . then posing them for maximum visual effect. . . . His 'can-do!' tone and cogent instructions, as well as the gallery of chiseled, heavily armed, hypercomplicated machines, will make this volume appealing to both casual browsers and serious young artists." SLJ

Helfand, Lewis

Conquering Everest; the lives of Edmund Hillary and Tenzing Norgay. illustrated by Amit Tayal. Kalyani Navyug Media 2011 91p il (Campfire Graphic Novels Series) pa $12.99

Grades: 5 6 7 8   **741.5**
   1. Mountaineering 2. Mountaineers 3. Nonfiction writers

ISBN 978-93-80741-24-6; 93-80741-24-3

LC 2011321480

"The exploits of two young men mad for climbing mountains are retold in graphic panels. . . . Tayal captures their likeness in flurries of small but visually varied cartoon scenes, often placing figures in front of reworked photos of forbidding ice fields and peaks. Helfand fills the dialogue-heavy narrative with specific biographical details amd exciting accounts of some of the great triumphs and tragedies of Himalayan mountaineering. . . . A vivid double character portrait, enhanced by equally sharp glimpses of climbing techniques, strategies and hazards." Kirkus

Kim; [by] Rudyard Kipling; [adapted by Lewis Helfand; illustrated by Rakesh Kumar] Kalyani Navyug Media 2011 68p il pa $9.99

Grades: 6 7 8 9 **741.5**

1. Graphic novels 2. Adventure graphic novels 3. India -- Fiction

ISBN 978-8-1907326-3-5; 8-1907326-3-3

LC 2010319053

"Rudyard Kipling's adventure novel is luminously visualized in this adaptation. The story line remains true to the original and follows Kim as he departs from his boyhood home with a Buddhist lama and embarks on adventures as a boy spy. Kumar's watercolor scenes and expressions lend authentic views of Kim's moods as well as his surroundings." Booklist

They Changed the World; Bell, Edison and Tesla. Random House Inc 2014 96 p. $12.99

Grades: 7 8 9 10 **741.5**

1. Inventors -- Biography 2. Graphic novels 3. Inventors -- United States -- Biography -- Comic books, strips, etc.

ISBN 9380741871; 9789380741871

In this young adult book by Lewis Helfand, illustrated by Naresh Kumar, part of the Campfire Graphic Novels series, readers will "Find out how Alexander Graham Bell, Thomas Edison and Nicola Tesla changed the world we live in forever! Three men, three great minds and three completely different approaches to science." (Publisher's note)

"Once again, Helfand and Kumar bring their graphic-novel talents to bear on a complex subject to make it accessible, engaging, concise, and sure to whet the reader's interest...Kumar shows not only the fundamental intelligence but also the hard work and productive attitudes these three geniuses brought to their work. Helfand's solid research is a great jumping-off point for student researchers, and the inclusion of a DIY project—building a rudimentary phone—adds to the appeal." Booklist

Heuvel, Eric

★ A **family** secret; [English translation, Lorraine T. Miller] Farrar, Straus and Giroux 2009 62p il pa $9.99; $18.99

Grades: 7 8 9 10 11 12 **741.5**

1. Graphic novels 2. Jews -- Graphic novels 3. Grandmothers -- Graphic novels 4. Holocaust, 1933-1945 -- Graphic novels

ISBN 0-374-32271-6; 978-0-374-42265-3 pa; 0-374-42265-6 pa; 978-0-374-32271-7

LC 2009-13943

Original Dutch edition, 2003

While searching his Dutch grandmother's attic for yard sale items, Jeroen finds a scrapbook which leads Gran to tell of her experiences as a girl living in Amsterdam during the Holocaust, when her father was a Nazi sympathizer and Esther, her Jewish best friend, disappeared

This is a "moving graphic novel.... The art is in ink and watercolor, with very clear, highly detailed panels.... [A] gripping story." Booklist

Hicks, Faith Erin

Friends with boys; Faith Erin Hicks. First Second 2012 un chiefly ill $16.99

Grades: 6 7 8 9 10 **741.5**

1. Ghost stories 2. Graphic novels 3. Teenagers --

Fiction

ISBN 9781596435568

LC 2011030470

In this graphic novel, "[the] youngest of four siblings and the only girl, Maggie is both excited and worried about starting high school after being home-schooled her whole life. . . . As Maggie makes friends with a perky indie girl named Lucy and her mysterious brother, Alistair, she broods over the loss of her mother, who recently left the family without much of an explanation, and tries to figure out what the ghost wants from her." (Bulletin of the Center for Children's Books)

The **war** at Ellsmere. Slave Labor Graphics 2008 156p il pa $12.95

Grades: 6 7 8 9 10 11 **741.5**

1. Graphic novels 2. Humorous graphic novels 3. Friendship -- Graphic novels 4. School stories -- Graphic novels

ISBN 1-59362-140-X; 978-1-59362-140-7

Juniper is the newest scholarship student at the prestigious Ellsmere Academy; she wanted to attend there in order to increase her chances of getting into a good medical school. She's on scholarship because her mom has had to raise her alone since her father died when she was young. Jun makes one friend at Ellsmere, Cassie, who calls herself the cliche of the poor little rich girl. Wealthy Emily calls Cassie "Orphan" because her parents ignore her, and chooses to call Jun "Project," as in Headmistress Ms. Bishop's latest project. Emily is also determined to get rid of Jun, especially when Jun encourages Cassie to work harder and even win the extra credit essay contest. Now it's war, or as Jun puts it, "It's like Upstairs Downstairs meets Lord of the Flies. In plaid skirts. And sweater vests." There's one incident when Jun punches Emily in the face.

"Hicks gives readers enough tension and quirky turns to satisfy and pleasantly surprise." Booklist

Hinds, Gareth

★ **Beowulf**; adapted and illustrated by Gareth Hinds. Candlewick Press 2007 un il $21.99; pa $9.99

Grades: 8 9 10 11 12 Adult **741.5**

1. Graphic novels 2. Adventure graphic novels 3. Beowulf -- Graphic novels 4. Monsters -- Graphic novels

ISBN 978-0-7636-3022-5; 0-7636-3022-5; 978-0-7636-3023-2 pa; 0-7636-3023-3 pa

LC 2006-49023

Graphic novel adaptation of the Old English epic poem, Beowulf

"For fantasy fans both young and old, this makes an ideal introduction to a story without which the entire fantasy genre would look very different; many scenes may be too intense for very young readers." Publ Wkly

★ **King** Lear; a play by William Shakespeare; adapted and illustrated by Gareth Hinds. Candlewick Press 2009 123p il $22.99; pa $11.99

Grades: 7 8 9 10 11 12   741.5
1. Poets 2. Authors 3. Dramatists 4. Graphic novels
ISBN 978-0-7636-4343-0; 0-7636-4343-2; 978-0-
7636-4344-7 pa; 0-7636-4344-0 pa
A reissue of the title first published 2007 by Thecomic.
com
This graphic novel adaptation of Shakespeare's King
Lear is "an excellent rendition of one the bard's great tragedies. Using splash pages that open up the settings, washes
of otherworldly colors, grotesquely expressive faces . .
. and figural work . . . Hinds occasionally attains a visual
poetry." Booklist

The **merchant** of Venice; a play. by William
Shakespeare; adapted and illustrated by Gareth Hinds.
Candlewick Press 2008 68p il $21.99; pa $11.99
Grades: 8 9 10 11 12 Adult   741.5
1. Poets 2. Authors 3. Dramatists 4. Graphic novels
ISBN 978-0-7636-3024-9; 978-0-7636-3025-6 pa
LC 2007-938349
Hinds uses a sketchy art style and blue and gray tones to
illustrate his graphic adaptation of Shakespeare's controversial play. He sets the play in modern Venice and uses more
modern language, including prose, at the beginning of the
play and then gradually returns to Shakespeare's original
language for the courtroom scenes. The play tells the story
of a debt owed to a Jewish merchant of Venice, of a strong-
willed young woman who is determined to choose her own
husband, and of the quest to save a young man from the fate
of having a pound of flesh cut from him.
"Fans of the play will find this an intriguing adaptation."
Publ Wkly

★ The **Odyssey**. Candlewick Press 2010 248p
il $24.99; pa $14.99
Grades: 7 8 9 10 11 12   741.5
1. Poets 2. Authors 3. Graphic novels 4. Greek
mythology -- Graphic novels
ISBN 978-0-7636-4266-2; 0-7636-4266-5; 978-0-
7636-4268-6 pa; 0-7636-4268-1 pa
This is "the most lavish retelling of Homer yet. . . . Hinds
lets the epic story take its time, with a slow build and pages
that aren't afraid to alternate packed dialogue with titanic
action. The sumptuous art, produced with grain, texture, and
hue, evokes a time long past while detailing every line and
drop of sweat on Odysseus' face and conveying the sheer
grandeur of seeing a god rise out of the ocean." Booklist

Hitch, Bryan

Bryan Hitch's Ultimate Comics Studio. Impact
2010 128p il pa $24.99
Grades: 7 8 9 10   741.5
1. Comic books, strips, etc.
ISBN 978-1-6006-1327-2; 1-6006-1327-6
"Well-known illustrator of Marvel classics such as Fantastic Four and Captain America, Hitch has a passion for
comics and comic art that is evident in this well-designed
volume. The book is a skillful blend of text, photos of the
artist at work, annotated sketches, and finished illustrations. .
. . Filled with sound advice, the book is useful to both comic
artists and those desiring a deeper understanding of comic
art." SLJ

Hoena, B. A.

Perseus and Medusa; by Blake A. Hoena; illustrated by Daniel Perez. Stone Arch Books 2009 72p
il (Graphic revolve) lib bdg $23.93; pa $6.95
Grades: 4 5 6 7 8 9   741.5
1. Graphic novels 2. Monsters -- Graphic novels 3.
Greek mythology -- Graphic novels
ISBN 978-1-4342-1170-5 lib bdg; 1-4342-1170-3 lib
bdg; 978-1-4342-1394-5 pa; 1-4342-1386-2 pa
LC 2008-32065
Perseus is the son of Danae, daughter of the King of Ar-
gos, and of Zeus; due to a prophecy that Perseus would cause
his death, the King puts his daughter and grandson into a
wooden chest and has it cast out to sea. A fisherman rescues
them, and Perseus grows up unaware of his royal lineage.
King Polydectes wants Danae for himself and sends Perseus
on what should be an impossible task that will kill him he
wants Perseus to bring him the head of Medusa, whose gaze
turns anyone into stone. Perseus enjoys the guidance and advice of gods and goddesses to accomplish his task
This title has a "solid awareness of how to balance visual depiction and expository captions, evident right from
the striking prologue. While the artwork is cartoony and the
dialogue deliberately casual and modern, the style doesn't
prevent the artist from providing heroic vistas, or the author
from slipping in a couple of humorous moments, and the
action is sufficiently thrilling." SLJ

Horowitz, Anthony

Stormbreaker : the graphic novel; [by] Anthony
Horowitz; adapted Antony Johnston; illustrated by
Kanako Damerum & Yusuru Takasaki. Philomel
Books 2006 un il (Alex Rider) pa $14.99
Grades: 5 6 7 8   741.5
1. Graphic novels 2. Spies -- Graphic novels
ISBN 0-399-24633-9
In this graphic novel version on Horowitz's novel, four-
teen-year-old Alex Rider is coerced into continuing his un-
cle's dangerous work for Britain's intelligence agency, MI6.
"If it's possible, this is even more rapidly paced than the
novel. Alex remains an appealing hero here, and the idea of
a heroic teen up against insidious adults continues to be an
extremely powerful draw for readers." Booklist
Other graphic novel adaptations in this series are:
Point blank (2007)
Skeleton key (2009)
Eagle strike (2012)

Hosler, Jay

Clan Apis. Active Synapse 2000 158p il pa
$15
Grades: 4 5 6 7 8 9 10 11 12   741.5
1. Graphic novels 2. Bees -- Graphic novels 3. Science
-- Graphic novels
ISBN 0-9677255-0-X
"Opening with a creation myth . . . and working through
the biological, sociological, and ecological changes affecting the life of Nyuki the bee, the text is a combination of
authoritative science; appealing, detailed black-and-white
drawings; and dialogue replete with humor, pubescent angst,
political sloganeering, and more. Nyuki's colony undertakes migration to a new hive, is beset by a woodpecker,

and hibernates through a winter that yields to a revitalizing spring." Booklist

Hotta, Yumi

Hikaru No Go, Volume 1; [by] Yumi Hotta and Takeshi Obata. Viz Media, LLC 2004 192p il pa $7.95

Grades: 5 6 7 8 9 10 11 12   **741.5**

1. Manga 2. Shonen manga 3. Graphic novels 4. Board games -- Graphic novels

ISBN 1-59116-222-X

Sixth-grader Hikaru Shindo is not interested in intellectual pursuits, but by a twist of fate, the spirit of Fujiwara no Sai, the ghost of an ancient Go master, manages to bond with Hikaru. Now, suddenly, Hikaru can play Go, a complex board game of strategy, better than almost anyone under 18 and most adults, too. Akira, who has been raised by his Go master father, needs to know more about the upstart Hikaru, who beats him and yet seems so casual about the game. This is the first volume of an ongoing series.

Volume 1 of a 23 volume series

Hunter, Erin

The **lost** warrior; created by Erin Hunter; written by Dan Jolley; art by James L. Barry. Tokyopop/ HarperCollins Publishers 2007 96p il (Warriors) $6.99

Grades: 4 5 6 7   **741.5**

1. Graphic novels 2. Adventure graphic novels 3. Cats -- Graphic novels

ISBN 978-0-06-124020-1; 0-06-124020-6

LC 2006-30426

Thunderclan warrior Greystripe helps clan members escape when the twolegs destroy their forest home and capture many of them, but he himself gets captured. Now he's a kittypet and desperate to return home to his clan. He meets Millie, another kittypet who wants to learn how to become a warrior, but can Greystripe find his way out of the twolegs' land?

Other titles in this series are:
Warrior's refuge (2008)
Warrior's return (2008)
The rise of the scourge (2008)

Warriors: Tigerstar & Sasha #1: into the woods; created by Erin Hunter; written by Dan Jolley; art by Don Hudson. HarperCollins/Tokyopop 2008 108p il $6.99

Grades: 3 4 5 6 7 8 9   **741.5**

1. Graphic novels 2. Adventure graphic novels 3. Cats -- Graphic novels

ISBN 978-0-06-154792-8; 0-06-154792-1

Sasha was a loved, pampered kittypet, but when one of the housefolk dies and the other moves away, they leave her behind. She had always explored the woods at night, but now she has to survive on her own. Then she meets Tigerstar, leader of ShadowClan, and they spend a lot of time together as he teaches her how to improve her hunting. He even offers her membership in the clan, but he has secrets, and when Sasha discovers one of them, she has to decide if she can trust him. There are scenes of cats hunting prey such as mice and squirrels, and fighting with foxes.

Other titles in this series are:
Escape from the forest (2008)
Return to the clans (2009)

Igarashi, Daisuke

★ **Children** of the sea, vol. 1. Viz Media/Viz Signature 2009 320p il pa $14.99

Grades: 7 8 9 10 11 12   **741.5**

1. Manga 2. Graphic novels 3. Fantasy graphic novels 4. Mystery graphic novels 5. Adventure graphic novels 6. Ocean -- Graphic novels

ISBN 978-1-4215-2914-1; 1-4215-2914-9

"Igarashi's storytelling is quiet, thoughtful, and thought provoking, but it is his drawings that make this manga so amazing. Extremely detailed settings turn panels into minimasterpieces." Booklist

Volume 1 of a 5-volume series

Inzana, Ryan

Ichiro; written & illustrated by Ryan Inzana. Houghton Mifflin/Houghton Mifflin Harcourt 2012 288 p. ill. (chiefly col.)

Grades: 7 8 9 10   **741.5**

1. Fantasy graphic novels 2. Supernatural graphic novels 3. Japan -- History -- Graphic novels 4. Folklore -- Japan -- Graphic novels 5. Japanese Americans -- Graphic novels 6. Graphic novels 7. Japan -- Fiction 8. Monsters -- Fiction 9. Grandfathers -- Fiction 10. Supernatural -- Fiction 11. Gods and goddesses -- Fiction

ISBN 0547252692; 9780547252698

LC 2011277558

This graphic novel depicts the story of Ichiro, "a young American teen, son of a Japanese immigrant and an American soldier killed in combat, [who] goes to Japan with his mother for an extended visit and begins to grapple with sophisticated cultural complexities. . . . After his mother and Japanese grandfather tell him stories of Japanese history and folklore, Ichiro has a fantastical adventure involving the Japanese myth of the shape-shifting tanuki spirit." (Kirkus Reviews)

Irwin, Jane

Vogelein; clockwork faerie. [by] Jane Irwin with Jeff Berndt; foreword by Jennifer M. Contino. Fiery Studios 2003 167p il pa $12.95

Grades: 6 7 8 9 10 11 12   **741.5**

1. Graphic novels 2. Fantasy graphic novels 3. Fairies -- Graphic novels

ISBN 0-9743110-06

This is a "graphic novel about Vogelein, a beautiful mechanical fairy created in the seventeenth century. Although she is immortal, she must be wound every 36 hours. After her old friend and caretaker dies, she must find someone new to take care of her. . . . This modern fable is a rare treasure that weaves fanciful imagination into themes of individuality, diversity, and independence. The art is beautifully shaded black and white, and it carries the narrative impeccably." Booklist

Ita, Sam

★ The **Odyssey**; a pop-up book. Sterling 2011
il $26.95

Grades: 4 5 6 7   **741.5**

1. Graphic novels 2. Adventure graphic novels 3. Pop-
up books

ISBN 978-1-4027-5867-6; 1-4027-5867-7

"A highlight-reel version of Odysseus' journey home,
framed as a graphic novel and plastered with fantastically
dramatic pop-ups and other special effects. Opening with
Penelope working on a tapestry that transforms into an entirely different scene with the drop of a step-flap, the tale
plunges on into the many escapes of Odysseus and his crew.
. . . Ita . . . tells the tale in balloons of colloquial dialogue. . .
. Even newbies will be riveted by this nonstop, high-energy
retelling. Homer himself would be agog." Kirkus

Jablonski, Carla

Defiance; written by Carla Jablonski; art by Leland Purvis; color by Hilary Sycamore. First Second
2011 126p il (Resistance) $16.99

Grades: 7 8 9 10 11 12   **741.5**

1. Graphic novels 2. World War, 1939-1945 -- Fiction
3. World War, 1939-1945 -- Underground movements
-- Fiction 4. France -- History -- 1940-1945, German
occupation -- Graphic novels

ISBN 978-1-59643-292-5; 1-59643-292-6

LC 2010036253

Sequel to: Resistance, book 1 (2010)

In 1943, as the German occupation of France continues,
the Tessier siblings increase their involvement in the Resistance while staying out of the way of the Millice, the Vichy
military police. Includes facts about Charles De Gaulle and
his support of resistance movements.

"The graphic novel format effectively portrays the layers
of story and emotion, words and visual elements working
in tandem to bring a complicated story to life. . . . As in the
first volume, historical notes at the beginning and end are
essential for placing the story in the larger context of World
War II." Horn Book

Resistance, book 1; art by Leland Purvis; color
by Hilary Sycamore. First Second Books 2010 121p
il (Resistance) pa $16.99

Grades: 6 7 8 9 10 11 12   **741.5**

1. Graphic novels 2. Adventure graphic novels 3.
World War, 1939-1945 -- Jews -- Rescue -- Graphic
novels 4. World War, 1939-1945 -- Underground
movements -- Graphic novels 5. France -- History --
1940-1945, German occupation -- Graphic novels

ISBN 978-1-59643-291-8; 1-59643-291-8

Paul and his younger sister Marie live in a small village in Vichy France during World War II. Thus far, the war
hasn't really touched them, but now Nazi soldiers come, and
Paul's friend, Henri, and his parents are Jews and therefore
in danger. When Paul and Marie try to protect Henri, their
secret leaks out to members of the Resistance. Although
they are young, they soon become recruits in the Resistance.
Paul's incessant sketching in his book turns out to be a valuable talent, but he and Marie, and then their older sister, Sylvie, don't quite realize just how dangerous things can get.
The cover is very striking, with Paul aiming a slingshot at a

Nazi soldier. The Author's Note at the end of the book talks
about history, the Resistance, and why the events in France
during World War II should not be depicted as black and
white, heroic Resistance versus villainous Vichy.

Followed by: Defiance (2011)

Victory; written by Carla Jablonski ; art by Leland Purvis ; color by Hilary Sycamore. First Second
2012 123 p. col. ill.

Grades: 6 7 8 9 10 11 12   **741.5**

1. France -- History -- Graphic novels 2. Resistance
to government -- Fiction 3. World War, 1939-1945
-- Underground movements -- France -- Fiction 4.
Graphic novels 5. World War, 1939-1945 -- France
-- Fiction 6. France -- History -- German occupation,
1940-1945 -- Fiction

ISBN 1596432934; 9781596432932

LC 2011030504

"In this third volume in the graphic novel trilogy about
the Tessier family," set during the French Resistance, "Sylvie relays information she gathers from her unwitting German boyfriend, Marie hides a man she discovers after a
plane crash in the woods, and Paul is the ears of the Resistance in town. . . . At the end of the book, Paul travels to
Paris to pass along information. He's on the scene for the
city's liberation." (Horn Book Magazine)

"The storyline is brisk and edgy, complementing the
worn nerves of people who have lived through war... Fans
of graphic art and WWII will appreciate this book, as
well as reluctant readers who are interested in historical
fiction." VOYA

Jacques, Brian

Redwall : the graphic novel; by Brian Jacques;
illustrated by Bret Blevins; adapted by Stuart Moore;
lettering by Richard Starkings. Philomel Books 2007
143p il pa $12.99

Grades: 4 5 6 7 8 9   **741.5**

1. Graphic novels 2. Fantasy graphic novels 3.
Adventure graphic novels 4. Mice -- Graphic novels

ISBN 978-0-399-24481-0; 0-399-24481-6

When Cluny the rat's army attacks Redwall Abbey,
young Matthias the mouse follows in the footsteps of the
long-ago hero Martin the Warrior to defend his home

"The story is a page-turner, and the detailed black-and-
white drawings capture both the passion and the pathos." SLJ

Jaffe, Michele

Bad kitty volume 1: catnipped. HarperCollins/
Tokyopop 2008 176p il $9.99

Grades: 7 8 9 10 11 12   **741.5**

1. Graphic novels 2. Mystery graphic novels 3.
Humorous graphic novels

ISBN 978-0-06-135162-4; 0-06-135162-8

Teenage aspiring detective Jasmine Callihan just wants
to hang out with her boyfriend, rock star Jack, but while
they're at the mall, trouble strikes. First, Jas finds a schoolmate's purse, then there's a jewelry store heist and the cops
arrest the store owner whom she believes is innocent, then
she says exactly the wrong thing to Jack, and her cousin
Alyson with her Evil Hench Twin Veronique decided to join
the investigation along with Jas and her best friends Roxy,

Polly, and Tom. This global manga is an original story using the same characters as Jaffe's prose teen novels Bad Kitty and Kitty Kitty.

"Catnipped will be especially appreciated by fans of Jaffe's novels, but it is not necessary to have read them to enjoy this rollicking, fast-paced, and funny mystery." SLJ

Jamieson, Victoria

★ **Roller** girl; by Victoria Jamieson. Dial Books 2015 240 p. chiefly color illustrations (paperback) $12.99

Grades: 4 5 6 7 8   **741.5**
1. Graphic novels 2. Friendship -- Fiction 3. Roller derby -- Fiction 4. Roller skating -- Fiction
ISBN 0803740166; 9780803740167
     LC 2014011310

This graphic novel, by Victoria Jamieson, is "about friendship and surviving junior high through the power of roller derby. For most of her twelve years, Astrid has done everything with her best friend Nicole. But after Astrid falls in love with roller derby and signs up for derby camp, Nicole decides to go to dance camp instead. And so begins the most difficult summer of Astrid's life as she struggles to keep up with the older girls at camp." (Publisher's note)

"Jamieson captures this snapshot of preteen angst with a keenly decisive eye, brilliantly juxtaposing the nuances of roller derby with the twists and turns of adolescent girls' friendships." Kirkus

Jolley, Dan

My boyfriend bites; illustrated by Alitha E. Martinez. Graphic Universe 2011 126p il (My boyfriend is a monster) lib bdg $29.27; pa $9.95; e-book $21.95

Grades: 7 8 9 10 11 12   **741.5**
1. Graphic novels 2. Horror graphic novels 3. New Mexico -- Fiction 4. Vampires -- Graphic novels
ISBN 978-0-7613-5599-1 lib bdg; 0-7613-5599-5 lib bdg; 978-0-7613-7078-9 pa; 0-7613-7078-1 pa; 978-0-7613-7187-8 e-book
     LC 2010028723

Seventeen-year-old New Mexico high school senior Vanessa Shingle learns that she destined to be a monster-hunter like her Van Helsing ancestor, and that the gorgeous janitor she is dating, Jean-Paul, is there to help although he, himself, is a vampire.

"Hip, steamy fun." Kirkus

Wrapped up in you; by Dan Jolley ; illustrated by Natalie Nourigat. Graphic Universe 2012 127 p. (lib. bdg.) $29.27

Grades: 6 7 8 9 10 11 12   **741.5**
1. Horror graphic novels 2. Mummies -- Graphic novels 3. Supernatural graphic novels 4. Love stories -- Graphic novels 5. Graphic novels 6. Horror stories 7. Mummies -- Fiction 8. Witches -- Fiction 9. North Carolina -- Fiction
ISBN 0761368566; 9780761368564
     LC 2011044655

This graphic novel, by Dan Jolley, illustrated by Natalie Nourigat, is book 6 in the "My Boyfriend Is a Monster" se-

ries. "Prince Pachacutec--or 'Chuck'--is a man with a past. He died tragically five hundred years ago, but that's all ancient history as far as Staci is concerned. He is everything she could want. . . . But the witches aren't willing to live and let live. Will Staci fight for Chuck? Or do the witches have a point when they say reanimated corpses make bad boyfriends?" (Publisher's note)

Keenan, Sheila

Dogs of war; by Sheila Keenan and illustrated by Nathan Fox. Graphix 2013 208 p. (hardcover) $22.99

Grades: 4 5 6 7   **741.5**
1. Dogs -- Fiction 2. War -- Graphic novels 3. Graphic novels 4. Dogs -- War use -- Fiction 5. World War, 1914-1918 -- Fiction 6. World War, 1939-1945 -- Fiction 7. Vietnam War, 1961-1975 -- Fiction
ISBN 0545128870; 9780545128872; 9780545128889
     LC 2011006735

This graphic novel, by Sheila Keenan, "tells the stories of the canine military heroes of World War I, World War II, and the Vietnam War. This collection of three fictional stories was inspired by historic battles and real military practice. Each story tells the remarkable adventures of a soldier and his service dog . . . bringing to life the faithful dogs who braved bombs, barrages, and battles to save the lives of countless soldiers." (Publisher's note)

Includes bibliographical references

Kibuishi, Kazu

★ **Amulet,** book one: The Stonekeeper. Graphix 2008 185p $21.99; pa $9.99

Grades: 3 4 5 6 7 8   **741.5**
1. Graphic novels 2. Fantasy graphic novels 3. Mystery graphic novels 4. Adventure graphic novels
ISBN 978-0-439-84680-6; 0-439-84680-3; 978-0-439-84681-3 pa; 0-439-84681-1 pa

After a family tragedy, Emily, Navin, and their mother move to an ancestral home to start a new life. When their mother is kidnapped by a tentacled creature, Em and Navin have to figure out how to set things straight and save their mother's life.

"Filled with excitement, monsters, robots, and mysteries, this fantasy adventure will appeal to many readers." SLJ

Other titles in this series are:
The Stonekeeper's curse (2009)
The Cloud Searchers (2010)
The Last Council (2011)
Prince of the elves (2012)
Escape from Lucien (2014)

Copper. Graphix/Scholastic 2010 94p il $21.99; pa $12.99

Grades: 5 6 7 8   **741.5**
1. Graphic novels 2. Adventure graphic novels 3. Science fiction graphic novels 4. Dogs -- Graphic novels
ISBN 978-0-545-09892-2; 0-545-09892-0; 978-0-545-09893-9 pa; 0-545-09893-9 pa

A collection of graphic novel adventures about a boy named Copper and his dog, Fred, including "navigating a dangerous forest of giant mushrooms, [and] surviving a crash landing in a homemade airplane—that run from lyrical to the downright apocalyptic. Illustrated in a deceptively simple style, its solemn tenor and deep strangeness . . . will likely inspire heavy investment from those who prefer a somewhat off-kilter read." Booklist

Kim, Derek Kirk

★ **Good** as Lily; written by Derek Kirk Kim; illustrated by Jesse Hamm; lettering by Jared K. Fletcher. DC Comics/Minx 2007 un il pa $9.99
Grades: 7 8 9 10 11 12   **741.5**
1. Graphic novels 2. Fantasy graphic novels 3. Humorous graphic novels
ISBN 978-1-4012-1381-7

"On her eighteenth birthday, Korean American Grace suddenly finds herself surrounded by three very corporeal essences of herself: as a small child, as a 30-year-old woman, and as 'a cranky old fart.' Each of these incarnations is at an emotional precipice, which teenage Grace helps resolve, allowing the other self to quietly disappear. . . . Kim's pacing and plotting are excellent, and Hamm's black, white, and gray artwork is lively, witty, and full of appropriate comedy and melodrama." Booklist

Kim, Susan

★ **City** of spies; [by] Susan Kim [and] Laurence Klavan; illustrated by Pascal Dizin. First Second 2010 172p il pa $17
Grades: 4 5 6 7   **741.5**
1. Graphic novels 2. Adventure graphic novels 3. Spies -- Graphic novels 4. World War, 1939-1945 -- Graphic novels
ISBN 1-59643-262-4 pa; 978-1-59643-262-8 pa

This graphic novel, set in New York City during World War II, tells the story of Kim and Klavan, who are hunting for Nazi spies. (Bull Cent Child Books)

"With her mother gone and a father who has better things to do than be bothered raising a daughter, Evelyn is sent to live with her unconventional Aunt Lia in the bohemian art world of 1942 New York City. . . . Evelyn spends much of her time in the company of imaginary superheroes, fouling up the plans of Nazi spies. Before long she finds an unlikely friend in the building superintendent's son, Tony. Together, they . . . stumble upon an actual Nazi plot. With stupefying precision, Dizin's art channels Hergé's Tintin in tone, palette, and with the remarkable expressiveness of the clean, flexible figures. . . . With villains and danger that just border on the genuinely scary, the tale is filled not only with a thrilling sense of excitement but also with a child's longing for a grown-up to believe in." Booklist

Kitoh, Mohiro

Bokurano : Ours. Viz Media 2010 198p il pa $12.99
Grades: 6 7 8 9   **741.5**
1. Science fiction graphic novels 2. Robots -- Graphic novels
ISBN 978-1-4215-3361-2 pa; 1-4215-3361-8 pa

"After wandering into a cave by the sea, 15 kids meet Kokopelli, who invites them to play a video game that involves piloting a giant robot. They are asked to sign a contract, not knowing the deadly repercussions or that they will

have to protect the planet. The cockpit consists of designated, floating chairs for each one while at the controls of the robot designed to defeat alien invaders. . . . Sound effects and large frames help create action and edginess on the pages. This story will intrigue readers." SLJ
Volume 1 of 11

Klimowski, Andrzej

Dr. Jekyll and Mr. Hyde; a graphic novel. illustrated and adapted by Andrzej Klimowski and Danusia Schejbal. Sterling 2009 122p il (Illustrated classics) pa $14.95
Grades: 6 7 8 9   **741.5**
1. Graphic novels 2. Horror graphic novels
ISBN 978-1-4114-1595-9 pa; 1-4114-1595-7 pa

"Klimowski captures a . . . formal air with a literal but still quick-moving adaptation, and Schejbal's grainy art displays a Richard Sala-like sense of both grit and unease. . . . Overall, this will have the most appeal for readers with an eye for the moody and strange." Booklist

Konomi, Takeshi

The **Prince** of Tennis, Vol. 1. Viz Media, LLC 2004 192p il pa $7.95
Grades: 6 7 8 9 10   **741.5**
1. Manga 2. Shonen manga 3. Graphic novels 4. Tennis -- Graphic novels
ISBN 1-59116-435-4

"Ryoma is a former U.S. junior tennis champion who attends a Japanese academy, where his skill and natural talent make him nearly unbeatable. The younger students are inspired by him, but he's ruffling the feathers of the older tennis team members. Then the journalists appear, trying to discover the next champion, adding to the pressure. There's lots of tennis action, dramatically illustrated, and the characters, already pretty boys, are made even more attractive with their intensity." Publ Wkly
Volume 1 of 42

Kovac, Tommy

Wonderland; written by Tommy Kovac; illustrated by Sonny Liew. Disney Press 2008 159p il $19.99
Grades: 4 5 6 7 8   **741.5**
1. Graphic novels 2. Fantasy graphic novels
ISBN 978-1-4231-0451-3; 1-4231-0451-X

First published as single-issue comics by SLG Publishing

"Ever wonder what happened in Wonderland after Alice left? Follow the quirky tale of Mary Ann, the meticulous and dutiful housekeeper for the White Rabbit, as she continues the tale. Her boss is now wanted for treason by the Queen of Hearts for allowing the Alice Monster to enter the kingdom—off with his head! On the run and fearing for their lives, Mary Ann and White Rabbit encounter the meddlesome Cheshire Cat, the ever-contentious troublemaker, sending the White Rabbit straight into the clutches of the queen and poor Mary Ann tumbling into the Treacle Well. . . . This is a terrific look at a great classic. The energetic, action-packed illustrations complement the story in Disney-cartoon style, making for a great read for all ages" SLJ

Kreisberg, Andrew

Green Arrow and Black Canary: five stages; [by] Andrew Kreisberg, J.T. Krul, writers; Mike Norton, Renato Guedes, Diogenes Neves, pencillers; Bill Sienkiewicz . . . [et al.], inkers. DC Comics 2010 un pa $17.99

Grades: 7 8 9 10 **741.5**

1. Graphic novels 2. Superhero graphic novels 3. Green Arrow (Fictional character) 4. Black Canary (Fictional character)

ISBN 978-1-4012-2898-9; 1-4012-2898-4

"Oliver Queen, a spoiled rich playboy who eventually becomes the heroic Green Arrow, has recently married his longtime girlfriend Dinah Lance, the Black Canary. The emerald archer's latest adventure pits him against the murderous Cupid, a female soldier twisted to darkness during an experimental drug trial. . . . The gritty, urban artwork includes muted colors that add to the militaristic and ultimately sadistic feel of the antagonist Cupid, whose origin story is revealed in this volume. Perfect for readers looking to break into superhero comics." SLJ

Krensky, Stephen

Comic book century; the history of American comic books. Twenty-First Century Books 2007 112p il lib bdg $30.60

Grades: 5 6 7 8 9 10 **741.5**

1. Cartoons and caricatures 2. Comic books, strips, etc.

ISBN 978-0-8225-6654-0; 0-8225-6654-0

LC 2006-20795

Provides a history of comic books in America during the twentieth century, showing how it has influenced and been influenced by American culture. Includes an epilogue about comics in the early twenty-first century

"Frequent full-color comic-book representations and black-and-white photographs, . . . flashy sidebars, and a striking blue background combine well with the accessible text, making this . . . visually appealing as well as highly entertaining." Bull Cent Child Books

Includes bibliographical references

L'Engle, Madeleine, 1918-2007

A wrinkle in time; the graphic novel. Madeleine L'Engle ; adapted and illustrated by Hope Larson. Farrar Straus Giroux 2012 392 p. $19.99

Grades: 4 5 6 7 **741.5**

1. Time travel -- Fiction 2. Space and time -- Fiction 3. Graphic novels 4. Science fiction

ISBN 0374386153; 9780374386153

LC 2010044120

Hope Larson presents a graphic novel adaptation of Madeleine L'Engle's "allegorical fantasy in which a group of young people are guided through the universe by Mrs. Who, Mrs. Which and Mrs. What -- women who possess supernatural powers. They traverse fictitious regions, meet and face evil and demonstrate courage at the right moment. Religious allusions are secondary to the philosophical struggle designed to yield the meaning of life and one's place on earth." (Kirkus Reviews)

Lagos, Alexander

The sons of liberty; created and written by Alexander Lagos and Joseph Lagos; art by Steve Walker; color by Oren Kramek; letters by Chris Dickey. Random House 2010 un il $18.99; lib bdg $21.99; pa $12.99

Grades: 6 7 8 9 10 11 12 **741.5**

1. Graphic novels 2. Adventure graphic novels 3. Superhero graphic novels 4. African Americans -- Graphic novels 5. United States -- History -- 1600-1775, Colonial period -- Graphic novels

ISBN 978-0-375-85670-9; 0-375-85670-6; 978-0-375-95667-6 lib bdg; 0-375-95667-6 lib bdg; 978-0-375-85667-9 pa; 0-375-85667-9 pa

In the mid-eighteenth century American colonies, Graham and Brody work as slaves on a tobacco plantation not far from Philadelphia. When they run away after injuring the plantation owner's son for threatening another slave, they seek Benjamin Lay, an eccentric abolitionist who might give them shelter. Instead, William Franklin, son of Benjamin Franklin, finds them and conducts unknown experiments on them.

"History offers few villains as vile as slaveholders, but this graphic novel is far from being a simple revenge thriller. The use of historical figures and well-researched (but embellished) history, and a willingness to flesh out characters and set up situations to pay off in future installments, makes for an uncommonly complex, literate, and satisfying adventure." Booklist

The sons of liberty 2; death and taxes. created and written by Alexander Lagos and Joseph Lagos; art by Steve Walker; color by Oren Kramek; letters by Chris Dickey. Random House Children's Books 2011 un il $18.99; pa $12.99

Grades: 6 7 8 9 10 11 12 **741.5**

1. Scientists 2. Graphic novels 3. Adventure graphic novels 4. Superhero graphic novels 5. African Americans -- Graphic novels 6. United States -- History -- 1600-1775, Colonial period -- Graphic novels

ISBN 978-0-375-85671-6; 978-0-375-85668-6 pa

"Graham and Brody, escaped slaves gifted with superpowers, remain at the center of this continuing pre-Revolutionary War saga of political intrigue and reimagined history. As Benjamin Franklin seeks to stop the stamp tax from falling on the colonies and enemies attack his good name, Graham attempts to arrange an escape back to Africa along with his love, the slave girl Isabel. . . . The embellishments, literate dialogue, and several historical truths—effectively counterpointed with glossy contemporary art—keep things fun and suspenseful." Booklist

Langridge, Roger

★ Thor, the mighty avenger, v.1. Marvel 2011 un il pa $14.99

Grades: 8 9 10 11 12 **741.5**

1. Graphic novels 2. Greek mythology -- Graphic novels

ISBN 978-0-7851-4121-1; 0-7851-4121-9

"Readers meet the mysterious blond-haired God of Thunder with no memory when historian Jane Foster watches him get tossed out of a Norse exhibition one day. After the gallant fellow helps her out and she takes him in, an utterly charming romance ensues. . . . Langridge deserves top marks for taking a character whose story possibilities might seem limited and imbuing him with a fresh and highly entertaining life. . . . Samnee's art grounds the vigorous superhero action with expressive faces, subtle lighting tones, and an individual style that makes the drama sing." Booklist

Larson, Hope

Chiggers; [by] Hope Larson; lettered by Jason Azzopardi. Atheneum Books for Young Readers 2008 170p il $17.99; pa $9.99

Grades: 5 6 7 8 9   741.5

1. Graphic novels 2. Camps -- Fiction 3. Friendship -- Graphic novels

ISBN 978-1-4169-3584-1; 978-1-4169-3587-2 pa

LC 2008-09557

When Abby returns to the same summer camp she always goes to, she is dismayed to find that her old friends have changed, and the only person who wants to be her friend is the strange new girl, Shasta.

"Chiggers provides a ticket to summer fun. Larson delicately handles both the usual middle-school angst and the additional pressures that come with being somewhat different. . . . The content is perfect for upper elementary and middle school students." SLJ

★ **Mercury**. Atheneum Books for Young Readers 2010 234p il $19.99; pa $9.99

Grades: 8 9 10 11 12   741.5

1. Graphic novels 2. Supernatural graphic novels 3. Nova Scotia -- Graphic novels

ISBN 978-1-4169-3585-8; 1-4169-3585-1; 978-1-4169-3588-9 pa; 1-4169-3588-6 pa

LC 2009-903638

This book, "relates two coming-of-age stories in tandem, showing how the past interweaves with the present. In the present, Tara and her mother have lost their old farmhouse in a fire, and Tara's mother is struggling to support them from far away while Tara lives with relatives. . . . In 1859, Josey, Tara's ancestor, falls in love with a gold dowser who has convinced her father to open a mine. Her mother, who has supernatural sight, is sure that the dowser means no good." (School Library Journal)

"The storytelling, both in words and pictures, brilliantly offers details from Canadian history and modern life. The dialogue varies from funny to poignant. An excellent graphic novel." SLJ

Lat

★ **Kampung** boy. First Second 2006 141p il pa $16.95

Grades: 7 8 9 10 11 12 Adult   741.5

1. Graphic novels 2. Muslims -- Graphic novels 3. Malaysia -- Graphic novels 4. Family life -- Graphic novels

ISBN 1-59643-121-0

LC 2005-34135

First published 1979 in Malaysia with title: Lat, the kampung boy

"Malaysian cartoonist Lat uses the graphic novel format to share the story of his childhood in a small village, or kampung. From his birth and adventures as a toddler to the enlargement of his world as he attends classes in the village, makes friends, and, finally, departs for a prestigious city boarding school, this autobiography is warm, authentic, and wholly engaging." Booklist

★ **Town** boy. First Second Books 2007 191p il pa $16.95

Grades: 7 8 9 10 11 12 Adult   741.5

1. Graphic novels 2. Humorous graphic novels 3. Malaysia -- Graphic novels 4. Bildungsromans -- Graphic novels

ISBN 978-1-59643-331-1; 1-59643-331-0

LC 2006-102857

In this sequel to Kampung Boy, it's the late 1960s and Mat is now a teenager attending a boarding school in the town of Ipoh, far from his kampung. He discovers bustling streets, hip music, heady literature, budding romance, and through it all his growing passion for art.

Lee, Tony

Excalibur; the legend of King Arthur, a graphic novel. written by Tony Lee; illustrated, colored, and lettered by Sam Hart. Candlewick Press 2011 un il

Grades: 7 8 9 10   741.5

1. Graphic novels 2. Fantasy graphic novels 3. Kings 4. Middle Ages -- Graphic novels 5. Kings and rulers -- Graphic novels 6. Knights and knighthood -- Graphic novels 7. Merlin (Legendary character) -- Graphic novels 8. Great Britain -- History -- 0-1066 -- Graphic novels

ISBN 0-7636-4643-1 pa; 0-7636-4644-X; 978-0-7636-4643-1 pa; 978-0-7636-4644-8

LC 2010-39163

Retells, in graphic novel form, the tale of Arthur Pendragon who, raised in obscurity, draws a legendary sword from a stone and begins the life he was born to lead, guided by the elusive wizard Merlin.

The author is "a master of graphic-novel adaptations. Teaming up with illustrator and colorist Hart, . . . Lee negotiates the terrain of medieval legend with finesse, rendering it easily accessible for a new generation of readers." Kirkus

★ **Outlaw** : the legend of Robin Hood; a graphic novel. written by Tony Lee; illustrated by Sam Hart; colored by Artur Fujita. Candlewick Press 2009 un il $21.99; pa $11.99

Grades: 7 8 9 10 11 12   741.5

1. Graphic novels 2. Adventure graphic novels 3. Robin Hood (Legendary character) 5. Great Britain -- History -- 1154-1399, Plantagenets -- Graphic novels

ISBN 978-0-7636-4399-7; 0-7636-4399-8; 978-0-7636-4400-0 pa; 0-7636-4400-5 pa

LC 2008-943331

In this retelling of the Robin Hood legend, it's the year 1192, and Robin of Loxley has returned home from the Crusades after receiving news of his father's death. The Sheriff of Nottingham and Sir Guy of Gisburn govern Nottingham at the pleasure of Prince John. When Gisburn treacherously stabs Robin in a murder attempt, Robin escapes to Sherwood Forest, where the outlaws befriend him. With the help of such men as Little John and Friar Tuck, he organizes the outlaws and they start hurting Prince John where it matters– in his moneybags.

"Lee's excellent rendition of the famed selfless hero goes hand-in-hand with Hart's expressive illustrations, featuring lots of closeups and dramatic lighting and a beautiful jewel-toned palette. Teens will get caught up in this exciting page-turner." SLJ

Li, Nana

Twelfth night; adapted by Richard Appignanesi; illustrated by Nana Li. Amulet Books 2011 207p il (Manga Shakespeare) pa $10.95

Grades: 7 8 9 10 **741.5**

1. Poets 2. Authors 3. Dramatists 4. Graphic novels
ISBN 978-0-8109-9718-9; 0-8109-9718-5

LC 2010024429

Retells, in comic book format, Shakespeare's comedy about Viola who, upon finding herself shipwrecked, pretends to be a servant but finds herself falling in love with Duke Orsino.

"Since plays are written to be performed, to be seen, a manga adaptation is a very satisfying way to enjoy Shakespeare. . . . Fans of the Bard should be delighted to experience his works through comics, while manga fans can be exposed to Shakespeare in a familiar way." Voice Youth Advocates

Liu, Na

★ **Little** White Duck; a childhood in China. by Andrés Vera Martínez and Na Liu ; illustrated by Andrés Vera Martínez. Graphic Universe 2012 96 p. col. ill. (lib. bdg. : alk. paper) $29.27; (pbk.) $9.95

Grades: 4 5 6 **741.5**

1. China -- History -- 1976- 2. Biographical graphic novels 3. Graphic novels
ISBN 0761365877; 9780761365877; 9780761381150; 0761381155

LC 2011005347

This graphic novel provides a "glimpse into Chinese girlhood during the 1970s and '80s." It begins with the 3-year-old narrator trying to understand the death of Chairman Mao. "From there, her life unfolds in short sketches. . . . She explains about the four pests that plague China . . . and her stomach-turning school assignment to catch rats and deliver the severed tails to her teacher . . . [as well as] the origins of Chinese New Year, her favorite holiday." (Kirkus Reviews)

"This picturesque treasure introduces Chinese culture through a personal perspective that is both delightful and thought-provoking." SLJ

Lutes, Jason

★ **Houdini** : the handcuff king. Hyperion Books for Children/Jump at the Sun 2007 90p il (Center for Cartoon Studies presents) $16.99; pa $9.99

Grades: 4 5 6 7 8 9 10 **741.5**

1. Magicians 2. Graphic novels 3. Biographical graphic novels 4. Nonfiction writers 5. Magicians -- Graphic novels
ISBN 978-0-7868-3902-5; 978-0-7868-3903-2 pa

On May 1, 1908, magician Harry Houdini performed one of his famous handcuff escapes, this time in handcuffs and leg irons, while jumping off the Cambridge Bridge in Massachusetts into the frigid Boston River. This graphic novel takes the reader through Houdini's day, from 5:00 a.m. as he makes his preparations, makes a practice jump, coaches his wife Bess on how she's to help him, and then makes the jump.

This is a "fascinating graphic novel. . . . The format will instantly draw a lot of attention from readers and then hold on to it. Lutes and Bertozzi use grayscale comic panels to share their story about the life of Harry Houdini in a unique way. . . . The book resembles a hybrid between fiction and nonfiction, and the ingenious choice of format will appeal to a broad age range of readers." Voice Youth Advocates

Lyga, Barry

Mangaman; illustrated by Colleen Doran. Houghton Mifflin 2011 il $18.99

Grades: 7 8 9 10 **741.5**

1. Graphic novels 2. School stories
ISBN 978-0-547-42315-9; 0-547-42315-2

LC 2011403000

"Ryoko, a manga character, falls through a mysterious hole in the space-time continuum to enter the real world of high-schooler Marissa Montaigne. Ryoko--literally a manga character come to life, with the requisite tropes like androgynous looks, huge eyes, and features that distort wildly when he emotes--freaks out all the "normal" inhabitants of Castleton, U.S.A., except for the former teen-queen Marissa. As they get to know each other better, Ryoko starts to reveal more and more of his reality to her, including life beyond the edges of a panel." (Booklist)

"A daring piece of graphic-novel meta-fiction. . . . In complement to Lyga's clever meta tone is Doran's highly stylized black-and-white art, seamlessly melding both the Western and Japanese comics aesthetics." Kirkus

Wolverine : worst day ever; by Barry Lyga; artist, Todd Nauck. Marvel Publishing 2009 184p il $14.99

Grades: 5 6 7 8 9 **741.5**

1. Graphic novels 2. Humorous graphic novels 3. Superhero graphic novels 4. Wolverine (Fictional character)
ISBN 978-0-7851-3757-3; 0-7851-3757-2

Teenager Eric Mattias has just recently discovered he has mutant powers. Very sucky mutant powers: suddenly no one notices him even when he's in the same room. He's not invisible, but he might as well be, and people don't even notice him when he speaks. Eric decides to follow Wolverine around and see if he can't pick up a few pointers about living a loner-type life, as the adamantium-clawed mutant tends to do. Only when they end up in a remote forested area does Eric realize he may not have made the smartest move, because someone else has come, someone who is as strong as Wolverine, and maybe meaner: Sabretooth.

"It's a coming-of-age tale with bursts of action that's sure to appeal to its large, built-in audience." Booklist

MacHale, D. J.

Pendragon book one: the merchant of death graphic novel; adapted and illustrated by Carla Speed McNeil. Aladdin Paperbacks 2008 172p il $9.99

Grades: 5 6 7 8 9 10   **741.5**
1. Graphic novels 2. Fantasy graphic novels 3.
Adventure graphic novels
ISBN 978-1-4169-5080-6; 1-4169-5080-X
LC 2007-937920

Fourteen-year-old Bobby Pendragon has had a good life
with a loving family, friends, and sports, but it all changes
the night his Uncle Press takes him into New York City, to a
deserted subway station that contains a gate that leads them
to another world. On Denduron, a peaceful tribe called the
Milago face annihilation from the Bedowan, and Uncle Press
expects Bobby to help him stop it. Press is what he calls a
Traveler, and he says Bobby is one, too, and they have a job
to do. Bobby is able to write journals and send them home to
his best friends Mark and Courtney. Meanwhile, he needs to
learn so much, can he do it in time to help—and stay alive?

"This graphic-format adaptation streamlines the already
fast-moving experience, providing satisfying interpretations
of favorite characters and situations." Booklist

Macherot, R.

Sibyl -Anne vs. Ratticus; translated from the
French by Kim Thompson. Fantagraphics 2011 64p
il $16.99
Grades: 5 6 7 8   **741.5**
1. Graphic novels 2. Mice -- Graphic novels
ISBN 978-1-60699-452-8; 1-60699-452-2

"This collection of comics, originally published in Spir-
ou magazine in 1966 and 1967, contains several stories in
which the mouse Sibyl-Anne and her friends fight back the
greedy villain Ratticus. This is the first time that American
audiences will be able to appreciate this story arc from the
golden age of Franco-Belgian comics. . . . [The stories] are
lighthearted and sometimes surreal adventures that use an
artistic style reminiscent of classic comics such as Blondie
or Pogo. The colors are bright and the creatures are adorable.
. . . An enjoyable read for kids, teens, and even adults." SLJ

Manning, Matthew K.

Wolverine; inside the world of the living weapon.
written by Matthew K. Manning. DK 2009 199p il
$24.95
Grades: 6 7 8 9   **741.5**
1. Wolverine (Fictional character)
ISBN 978-0-7566-4547-2; 0-7566-4547-6
LC 2009284799

Presents a chiefly illustrated a look at Wolverine's history, a summation of Logan's rather extensive past, and his
alternate futures.

"Decades of information merge seamlessly in a beautifully illustrated package. Practically every nook and cranny
of the character's history gets attention, from a long line
of love interests to his mortal enemies. . . . The book is no
doubt of greatest interest to diehard fans, if readers have
ever opened an issue of X-Men, even with vague interest,
chances are there is something here for them. If not, odds
are good that the book will do a good job of convincing one
to do so. Even those who remain steadfast in their dislike
for comic books will find something of value here." Voice
Youth Advocates

Martin, Ann M.

The **Baby** -sitter's Club: Kristy's great idea; a
graphic novel. [text by Ann M. Martin; art] by Raina
Telgemeier. Scholastic Graphix 2006 192p il
$16.99; pa $8.99
Grades: 3 4 5 6   **741.5**
1. Graphic novels 2. Friendship -- Graphic novels 3.
Babysitting -- Graphic novels
ISBN 0-439-80241-5; 0-439-73933-0 pa
LC 2005-37749

McAdoo, David

★ **Red** moon. Cossack Comics 2010 un il
$19.99
Grades: 7 8 9 10   **741.5**
1. Graphic novels 2. Fantasy graphic novels 3. Dogs
-- Graphic novels 4. Crows -- Graphic novels
ISBN 978-0-615-35324-1; 0-615-35324-X

"This graphic novel is told entirely from the point of
view of a small dog. After Mox runs away from his family,
he starts having visions of an ominous red moon heralding
destruction and runs afoul of a pack of crows determined
to bring a new world order where birds, not humans, reign
supreme. . . . The . . . characters are carefully constructed,
with clear, ringing voices that will linger in readers' minds.
McAdoo's highly detailed style . . . adds gripping tension to
every panel. . . . [An] action-packed, beautifully illustrated
tale." Booklist

McCann, Jim

★ **Return** of the Dapper Men; written by Jim
McCann; art by Janet Lee; lettered by Dave Lan-
phear; edited by Stephen Christy. Archaia Comics
2010 un il $24.95
Grades: 4 5 6 7 8   **741.5**
1. Graphic novels 2. Science fiction graphic novels 3.
Robots -- Graphic novels
ISBN 978-1-932386-90-5; 1-932386-90-4

"In the dreamy land of Anorev, children, all under age 11,
live underground among intricate gear-work mechanisms,
while elegant robots live in abandoned houses aboveground.
. . . All are perpetually stuck in the same day, and time has,
essentially, ceased to mean anything—until 314 Dapper
Men rain from the sky and set in motion the impetus for
change. . . . Where this book truly stands out is how well the
story works in concert with Lee's stunning artwork, which
employs an art nouveau sheen. . . . A true dazzler that speaks
on multiple levels for both child and adult readers and one
that gets richer with each read." Booklist

Mechner, Jordan

Solomon's thieves; artwork by LeUyen Pham
& Alex Puvilland. First Second 2010 139p il pa
$12.99
Grades: 6 7 8 9 10   **741.5**
1. Graphic novels 2. Middle Ages -- Graphic novels
3. Knights and knighthood -- Graphic novels 4. France
-- History -- 0-1328 -- Graphic novels
ISBN 978-1-59643-391-5; 1-59643-391-4
LC 2010-282641

Life as a Templar Knight returning from the Crusades is dull— bread, beans, and lots and lots of walking. But after Martin stumbles upon his lost love (now married—to some-one else), things begin to get more interesting very quickly. There's a vast conspiracy afoot to destroy the Templar Order and steal their treasure. Soon, Martin finds himself one of the only Templars out of prison—and out for revenge!

"Pham and Puvilland . . . are again in top form, balancing grainy, hatched textures and clean spaces to lend a weighty historical feel as a vibrant sense of kineticism brings the ac-tion sequences to life." Booklist

Includes bibliographical references

Medley, Linda

★ **Castle** waiting. Fantagraphics 2006 456p il $29.95

Grades: 5 6 7 8 9 10 11 12   **741.5**
1. Graphic novels 2. Fantasy graphic novels 3. Fairy tales -- Graphic novels
ISBN 1-56097-747-7

All of Medley's previously self-published comics are collected here in one volume for the first time. The titular castle was the home of Sleeping Beauty, whose story is re-told from the viewpoint of the flibbertigibbet ladies in wait-ing. After the flighty princess awakens with the kiss of a handsome but not too bright prince, the castle becomes a sanctuary for various misfits. Readers will find references to many fairy tales, folk tales, and nursery rhymes in Medley's book, and her clean, clear black-and-white art reflects the works of classic illustrators such as Arthur Rackham.

Momo no Tane

Shugo chara! Peach-Pit; translated by June Kato; adapted by David Walsh; lettered by North Market Street Graphics. Del Rey/Ballantine Books 2007 v1-v6 il v1 $10.95

Grades: 5 6 7 8 9   **741.5**
1. Graphic novels
ISBN 978-0-345-49745-1 v1

LC 2007296632

"Readers should revel in the lightly romantic and come-dic plot and delight in the adorably stylized characters, from brooding mysterious cat-eared boys to small, sweet doll-like girls. Fans of CLAMP's Cardcaptor Sakura (Tokyopop) will enjoy these adventures of another plucky fourth grader un-covering magical secrets and learning of her wondrous fan-tasy world. Sheer bubblegum fun." SLJ

Volume 1 of 12

Mouly, Francoise

★ The **TOON** treasury of classic children's com-ics; selected and edited by Art Spiegelman and Fran-coise Mouly; introduction by Jon Scieszka. Abrams ComicArts 2009 350p il $40

Grades: 3 4 5 6   **741.5**
1. Comic books, strips, etc.
ISBN 978-0-8109-5730-5; 0-8109-5730-2

LC 2009009830

"These stories are terrifically funny, joltingly exuberant, bafflingly bizarre, and best of all, compiled into one hearty, hefty, handsome volume." Booklist

Nagatomo, Haruno

Draw your own Manga; beyond the basics. translated by Francoise White. Kodansha Interna-tional 2005 111p il pa $19.95

Grades: 7 8 9 10 11 12   **741.5**
1. Manga -- Drawing 2. Graphic novels -- Drawing
ISBN 4-7700-2304-9; 978-4-7700-2304-9

"This advanced manual looks at how to enhance manga with a range of special effects as well as how to use vari-ous types of color ink, markers, and airbrushes to reach more creative levels. Supplemented by an interview with the immensely popular Japanese sports manga artist Shinji Mizushima, this book is recommended for any cartoon or animation library." Libr J

Nakajo, Hisaya

Sugar Princess volume 1: skating to win; story & art by Hisaya Nakajo. Viz Media/Shojo Beat 2008 184p il $8.99

Grades: 7 8 9 10 11 12   **741.5**
1. Manga 2. Shojo manga 3. Graphic novels 4. Romance graphic novels 5. Ice skating -- Graphic novels
ISBN 978-1-4215-1930-2; 1-4215-1930-5
Orginal Japanese editon, 2005

Maya Kurinoko takes her little brother to the local ice-skating rink with free tickets, but he won't skate unless she does a jump just like they saw on television the night before. So, she attempts a double axel, and lands it. Skating coach Eishi Todo sees her make the jump and scouts her as an ice skater. He wants famous skater Shun Kano (who attends Maya's high school she's in junior high) to coach and then partner with her, but Shun doesn't want it. However, Maya loves ice skating and realizes it may be the one thing she can be good at doing, and she's willing to persevere.

Followed by: Sugar pincess. Vol. 2 : skating to win (2008)

Neri, Greg

★ **Yummy**; the last days of a Southside Shorty. by G. Neri; illustrated by Randy DuBurke. Lee & Low Books 2010 94p il pa $16.95

Grades: 8 9 10 11 12   **741.5**
1. Children 2. Graphic novels 3. Biographical graphic novels 4. Gang members 5. Murder victims 6. Gangs -- Graphic novels 7. Violence -- Graphic novels 8. Chicago (Ill.) -- Graphic novels 9. African Americans -- Graphic novels
ISBN 978-1-58430-267-4 pa; 1-58430-267-4 pa

LC 2006-17771

Coretta Scott King Author Award honor book, 2011

"Neri's straightforward, unadorned prose is the perfect complement to DuBurke's stark black-and-white inks; great slabs of shadow and masterfully rendered faces breathe real, tragic life into the players." Publ Wkly

Nobleman, Marc Tyler

★ **Boys** of Steel; The Creators of Superman. Random House Childrens Books 2013 40 p. (li-brary) $19.99; (paperback) $7.99

Grades: 4 5 6 7   **741.5**

1. Superhero comic books, strips, etc.

ISBN 9780375938023; 0449810631; 9780449810637

This book by Marc Tyler Nobleman and illustrated by Ross MacDonald "tells how writer Jerry Siegel and artist Joe Shuster, two misfit teens in Depression-era Cleveland who were more like Clark Kent than his alter ego, created this superhero [Superman] and published his adventures in comic-book format." (Publishers Weekly)

O'Connor, George

★ **Zeus**; king of the gods. Roaring Brook Press 2010 76p il (Olympians) $16.99; pa $9.99

Grades: 5 6 7 8   **741.5**

1. Graphic novels 2. Classical mythology 3. Zeus (Greek deity)

ISBN 978-1-59643-431-8; 1-59643-625-5; 978-1-59643-432-5 pa; 1-59643-431-7 pa

Retells in graphic novel format stories from Greek mythology about the exploits of the young Zeus and how he rallied an army and overthrew his father, Kronos, to become king of the gods

"It's [the] balance between respect for myth and adherence to comic-book form that works so wonderfully well here." Bull Cent Child Books

Other titles in this series are:

Athena: grey-eyed goddess (2010)

Hera: the goddess and her glory (2011)

Hades: lord of the dead (2012)

Poseidon: earth shaker (2013)

Aphrodite: goddess of love (2013)

Ares: bringer of war (2015)

O'Donnell, Liam

Media meltdown: a graphic guide adventure; written by Liam O'Donnell; illustrated by Mike Deas. Orca Book Publishers 2009 un il pa $9.95

Grades: 6 7 8 9 10   **741.5**

1. Graphic novels 2. Mystery graphic novels 3. Media literacy -- Graphic novels

ISBN 978-1-55469-065-7 pa; 1-55469-065-X pa

LC 2009-927573

Pema and Bounce find a new housing development going up in the middle of what used to be their favorite biking trail, and then they learn that the developer is trying to force Jagroop's farmer father to sell his land. Pema's older sister Nima has been working as an intern at the local TV station, and she tries to help the teens put together a news story about what's happening. Then they learn that the developer buys a lot of advertising on the station, and he gets the station owner to pressure the producer to kill their story. They need to get their story out, but since traditional media won't help them, they turn to alternate media on the internet and a little guerilla newscasting by Nima to stop the developer and preserve their land.

This "is an excellent choice for developing media literacy. . . . The design and layout are colorful and fast paced. The text is well written and paired with useful imagery." SLJ

Ottaviani, Jim

Levitation : physics and psychology in the service of deception; [by] Jim Ottaviani and Janine Johnston; lettering by Tom Orzechowski. G. T. Labs 2007 71p il pa $12.95

Grades: 6 7 8 9 10 11 12 Adult   **741.5**

1. Graphic novels 2. Magic tricks -- Graphic novels

ISBN 978-0-9788037-0-4

This book tells the story of how John Neville Maskelyne developed the stage magic trick of levitation, of the American Harry Kellar, who acquired the trick through devious means, of the old school engineer Guy Jarrett, who perfected the magicians' tricks, and of stage performer Howard Thurston, who inherited the levitation trick from Kellar and ruined it. Or did he? The book includes notes and reprints of old posters and other information on the magicians.

Includes bibliographical references

Parker, Jeff

The **avengers** : heroes assembled; artist, Manuel Garcia. Marvel 2006 v1 il (Marvel adventures: the avengers) pa $6.99

Grades: 5 6 7 8 9   **741.5**

1. Graphic novels 2. Superhero graphic novels

ISBN 978-0-7851-2306-4; 0-7851-2306-7

Presents adventures in which various superheroes, including Captain America, Storm, Wolverine, and Spider-Man battle numerous foes. Publisher's note

Other titles in the series about the Avengers are:

The avengers v2: mischief (2007)

The avengers v3: bizarre adventures (2007)

The avengers v4: dream team (2007)

The avengers v5: some assembling required (2008)

The avengers v6: mighty marvels (2008)

The avengers v7: weirder and wilder (2008)

The avengers v8: the new recruits (2009)

Pearson, Luke

Hilda and the troll; Flying Eye Books 2013 40 p. chiefly color illustrations (Hildafolk) $18.95

Grades: 3 4 5 6   **741.5**

1. Adventure fiction 2. Trolls -- Fiction 3. Explorers -- Fiction

ISBN 1909263141; 9781909263147

Originally appearing in print in 2010 as Hildafolk

This book, by Luke Pearson, is "about an adventurous little girl and her habit of befriending anything, no matter how curious it might seem. While on an expedition to illustrate the magical creatures of the mountains around her home, Hilda spots a mountain troll. As the blue-haired explorer sits and sketches, she slowly starts to nod off. By the time she wakes up, the troll has totally disappeared and, even worse, Hilda is lost in a snowstorm." (Publisher's note)

"The art is as whimsical as the protagonist, and the bright colors enhance this comic book's magical-realistic effect." Horn Book

Other titles about Hilda are:

Hilda and the Midnight Giant (2012)

Hilda and the Bird Parade (2013)

Hilda and the Black Hound (2014)

Petersen, David

★ **Mouse** Guard: Fall 1152. Archaia Studios Press 2007 un il $24.95

Grades: 5 6 7 8   **741.5**

1. Graphic novels 2. Fantasy graphic novels 3. Mice
-- Graphic novels
ISBN 978-1-932386-57-8; 1-932386-57-2
Eisner Award: Best Publication for Kids (2008)

In a medieval world populated by animals, mice have their own civilization but live in constant peril from predators. They live in hidden towns protected by the Guard, who also escort travelers between towns. Three young members of the Guard, Lieam, Saxon, and Kenzie, go in search of a missing grain merchant. They find him dead in the belly of a snake who tried to eat them; but they also find evidence that the dead merchant is a traitor. Now they need to find out to whom he was betraying the Guard and why. While this story features animals and is suitable for most readers who can handle some fighting action, there's nothing cute or Disney-esque in the art. Characters die, this is a serious story, but readers who have read Bone or the Harry Potter series can handle the action in this book. This is the first in a series.

Followed by: Mouse Guard: Winter 1152 (2009)

Mouse Guard: Winter 1152; story & art by David Petersen. Archaia Studios Press 2009 un il $24.95
Grades: 5 6 7 8   **741.5**

1. Graphic novels 2. Fantasy graphic novels 3. Mice
-- Graphic novels
ISBN 978-1-932386-74-5; 1-932386-74-2
Sequel to: Mouse Guard: Fall 1152 (2007)

"Picking up where Fall 1152 . . . left off, Winter 1152 follows the darkening adventures of the brave troops of the Mouse Guard as they battle the elements, predators, and even other mice in order to secure their way of life. The high-quality artwork found in the first volume carries over into this one. The narrative . . . is fast paced and compelling. . . . Combining a tale of action, romance, comedy, and tragedy with the graphic-novel format results in a topnotch work with wide appeal." SLJ

Followed by: Mouse Guard: The black axe (2013)

Mouse guard; volume 1 legends of the guard. Jeremy Bastian, Ted Naifeh, Alex Sheikman, et al. Archaia Entertainment 2010 144 p. col. ill. hbk $19.95
Grades: 5 6 7 8   **741.5**

1. Mice -- Fiction 2. Adventure fiction 3. Short stories
-- Collections
ISBN 1932386947; 9781932386943
Eisner Award: Best Anthology (2011)

"Petersen turns to the tested and reliable bar story as a framing device to allow other writers and artists to play in his Mouse Guard universe, where heroic mice heroes are set in a world of epic fantasy. . . . One night barkeep June . . . stages a story-telling contest. What follows are thirteen tales of danger and adventure, as protagonists contend against the predators around them and the flaws that divide mouse from mouse." (Publisher's note)

"More than just supplemental material, this book broadens Petersen's magnificently imagined miniature world and is a welcome addition for any collection that values quality, all-ages graphic novels." Booklist

Phelan, Matt

★ **Around** the world. Candlewick Press 2011 240p il $24.99
Grades: 4 5 6 7   **741.5**

1. Graphic novels 2. Voyages and travels
ISBN 978-0-7636-3619-7; 0-7636-3619-3
LC 2010043153

"Phelan presents three true stories of around-the-world adventures inspired by Jules Verne's Around the World in Eighty Days that, even though they were undertaken in the late 1800s, would be hardly less arduous today. Thomas Stevens, Joshua Slocum, and Nellie Bly saw the world from the seat of a bicycle, aboard a 36-foot sloop, and via trains and ships, respectively. The small, specific pleasures of Phelan's work . . . are showcased in panels laid out in horizontal bands, reinforcing the linear, ever-onward nature of each narrative. The use of limited color palettes enhances the artist's characteristic delicate, expressive pen-and-ink drawings without overpowering them, allowing each traveler's character to be the dominant story element. . . . Design elements such as borders and frames lend a jaunty festivity to a graphic novel that will appeal to aficionados of the form and any reader in search of engrossing true journeys." SLJ

★ The **storm** in the barn. Candlewick Press 2009 201p il $24.99; pa $14.99
Grades: 4 5 6 7 8 9   **741.5**

1. Graphic novels 2. Adventure graphic novels 3. Kansas -- Graphic novels 4. Monsters -- Graphic novels 5. Dust storms -- Graphic novels 6. United States -- History -- 1933-1945 -- Graphic novels
ISBN 978-0-7636-3618-0; 0-7636-3618-5; 978-0-7636-5290-6 pa; 0-7636-5290-3 pa

In Kansas of 1937, the land has been in the grip of the Dust Bowl for four years, and eleven-year-old Jack Carter has seen his family worn down by it. But the day Jack outruns a dust storm all the way home from town, he glimpses something odd in the abandoned Talbot barn, and he tries to find the courage to go into the barn and confront what is there.

"Children can read this as a work of historical fiction, a piece of folklore, a scary story, a graphic novel, or all four. Written with simple, direct language, it's an almost wordless book: the illustrations' shadowy grays and blurry lines eloquently depict the haze of the dust. A complex but accessible and fascinating book." SLJ

Prince, Liz

Tomboy; A Graphic Memoir. by Liz Prince. Zest Books 2014 256 p. illustrations $15.99
Grades: 7 8 9 10 11 12 Adult   **741.5**

1. Gender role 2. Sex differences (Psychology) 3. Stereotype (Social psychology) 4. Sex role 5. Graphic novels 6. Gender identity 7. Cartoonists -- Caricatures and cartoons 8. Cartoonists -- United States -- Biography
ISBN 1936976552; 9781936976553
LC 2014034070
Rainbow List (2015)

This memoir, by Liz Prince, "is a graphic novel about refusing gender boundaries, yet unwittingly embracing gender stereotypes at the same time, and realizing later in life that you can be just as much of a girl in jeans and a T-shirt as you can in a pink tutu." (Publisher's note)

"Prince's honest voice and self-deprecating humor help make young Liz a sympathetic and relatable character. The simply rendered black-and-white panel drawings have an unpretentious quality, in keeping with the narrative tone." Horn Book

Pyle, Kevin C.

Katman. Henry Holt and Co. 2009 un il pa $12.99

Grades: 7 8 9 10 11 12   **741.5**
1. Graphic novels 2. Cats -- Graphic novels 3. Friendship -- Graphic novels
ISBN 978-0-8050-8285-2; 0-8050-8285-9
LC 2008-937398

Kit is a bored sixteen-year-old with nothing to do one summer when he starts feeding stray cats. He loves it when cool, artistic Jess helps him out, even though he has to endure constant taunting by her disaffected metalhead friends. They make fun of him for being like the local cat lady, but Kit doesn't care—especially after Jess draws him an anime-style avatar named Katman.

"Beautifully simple and straightforward." Voice Youth Advocates

Raven, Nicky

Bram Stoker's Dracula; adapted by Nicky Raven; illustrated by Anne Yvonne Gilbert. Candlewick Press 2010 96p il $19.99

Grades: 7 8 9 10   **741.5**
1. Graphic novels 2. Horror graphic novels 3. Vampires -- Graphic novels
ISBN 978-0-7636-4793-3; 0-7636-4793-4
LC 2009-22116

A modern, illustrated retelling of the Bram Stoker classic, in which young Jonathan Harker first meets and then must destroy the vampire, Count Dracula, in order to save those closest to him.

Raven "successfully abridges a vaunted classic. . . . Raven does a great job fleshing out characters that even in Stoker's original felt bloodless. . . . Gilbert's gothic drawings, the crosshatches of which often conceal layers of spooky elements, are a perfect fit for the somber tone." Booklist

Reed, Gary

Mary Shelley's Frankenstein: the graphic novel. Puffin Graphics 2005 176p il pa $9.99

Grades: 5 6 7 8 9 10 11 12   **741.5**
1. Authors 2. Novelists 3. Graphic novels 4. Horror graphic novels
ISBN 0-14-240407-1

Scientist Victor Frankenstein decided to create a man, only to create something he deemed a monster.

"Reed concentrates on the emotional anguish of the story, ably capturing the rage, the hurt, and the guilt of both monster and creator. Irving . . . creates a hazy, suitably murky black-and-white backdrop, never exploiting the violence inherent in the monster's quest for vengeance." Booklist

Reed, M. K.

Americus; written by MK Reed; art by Jonathan Hill. First Second 2011 215p il pa $14.99

Grades: 8 9 10 11 12   **741.5**
1. Graphic novels 2. Libraries -- Fiction 3. Censorship -- Fiction 4. Books and reading -- Fiction 5. Christian fundamentalism -- Fiction
ISBN 978-1-59643-601-5; 1-59643-601-8
LC 2010051586

"Neil Barton finds the transition from middle school to high school to be challenging. He finds solace reading and listening to music, and working at the library. A censorship challenge by a fundamentalist Christian group forces him to courageously stand up before the public library board." (Library Media Connection)

"The clever mix of fantasy and realistic fiction, thoughtful pacing, authentic dialogue, and expressive art perfectly captures the angst of a nerdy teen who is at first ostracized but then finds his niche as he finds his voice." Booklist

Renier, Aaron

★ The **Unsinkable** Walker Bean; written and illustrated by Aaron Renier; colored by Alec Longstreth. First Second 2010 191p il pa $13.99

Grades: 5 6 7 8   **741.5**
1. Graphic novels 2. Adventure graphic novels
ISBN 978-1-59643-453-0 pa; 1-59643-453-8 pa

The story "centers around a cursed skull stolen from the lair of two deep-sea crustacean witches. Like all who look upon the skull, Walker's beloved grandpa falls deathly ill when he finds it, and the boy sets out to return the skull from whence it came. . . . The generous page size lets [the] reader dive into Renier's quavery and painstakingly detailed cartooning, and he really shows off his stuff with a bounty of full-splash dazzlers. . . . Exciting, deep, funny, and scary, with tremendous villains and valor galore." Booklist

Riordan, Richard

The **red** pyramid; the graphic novel. Rick Riordan ; adapted by Orpheus Collar ; lettered by Jared Fletcher. Disney/Hyperion Books 2012 un chiefly color illustrations (The Kane chronicles) pbk $12.99; hbk $21.99

Grades: 4 5 6 7 8 9   **741.5**
1. Magic -- Fiction 2. Egyptian mythology -- Fiction 3. Brothers and sisters -- Fiction
ISBN 1423150694 ; 1423150686 ; 9781423150695 ; 9781423150688
LC 2012007905

"Since their mother's death, Sadie and Carter have become near-strangers. While Sadie has lived with her grandparents in London, Carter has traveled the world with their father, the famed Egyptologist Dr. Julius Kane. One night, Dr. Kane brings the siblings to the British Museum, where he hopes to set things right for his family. Instead, he unleashes the Egyptian god Set, who banishes him to oblivion and forces the children to flee for their lives." (Publisher's note)

"Out of necessity, much of the dialogue is dedicated to explaining actions and events, but a constant stream of humor prevents the reader from getting bogged down by logistics. The colorful artwork has an almost painting-like quality, . . . and some clever visual jokes and thoughtful use of panels make good use of the format." VOYA

Robbins, Trina

The **drained** brains caper; [by] Trina Robbins and Tyler Page. Graphic Universe 2010 64p il (Chicagoland Detective Agency) lib bdg $27.97; pa $6.95

Grades: 4 5 6 7   **741.5**

  1. Graphic novels 2. Mystery graphic novels 3. Humorous graphic novels 4. Brainwashing -- Fiction 5. Schools -- Graphic novels 6. Japanese Americans -- Graphic novels

  ISBN 978-0-7613-4601-2 lib bdg; 0-7613-4601-5 lib bdg; 978-0-7613-5635-6 pa; 0-7613-5635-5 pa

LC 2009-32620

Required to attend summer school after moving to Chicagoland, thirteen-year-old manga-love Megan Yamamura needs help from twelve-year-old computer genius Raf Hernandez to escape the maniacal principal's mind control experiment.

This tells "an entertaining story. . . . Page's black-and-white cartooning has a loose manga slant, with peppy goofiness popping out from stippled screen tones." Booklist

  Other titles in this series are:

  The Maltese mummy (2011)

  Night of the living dogs (2012)

  The big flush (2012)

  The bark in space (2013)

  A midterm night's scheme (2014)

Go girl!. Vol. 1, The time team; story, Trina Robbins, art , Anne Timmons. Dark Horse Comics 2004 95p il pa $5.95

Grades: 3 4 5 6 7 8   **741.5**

  1. Graphic novels 2. Adventure graphic novels 3. Superhero graphic novels 4. Go Girl (Fictional character) -- Graphic novels

  ISBN 1-59307-230-9

"Robbins, who has made a name for herself as a feminist in the comics world, creates a story about three stereotypical high school girls--the dismissive cheerleader, the misunderstood brain, and the daughter of a 1970s-era superheroine--who become stranded in prehistory. The girls are quick-witted, the dinosaurs are cartoony, and a late appearance by Vikings offers readers a taste of what Nordic women might have been like in a confrontation. This isn't high concept, but it's definitely good, clean fun." Booklist

  Followed by:

  Vol. 2: Robots gone wild

Roche, Art

Comic strips; create your own comic strips from start to finish. Lark 2007 112p il (Art for kids) $17.95

Grades: 4 5 6 7   **741.5**

  1. Drawing 2. Cartoons and caricatures

  ISBN 978-1-57990-788-4; 1-57990-788-1

Explains the process of drawing comic strips and makes suggestions for developing a style all one's own

"The bright, dynamic layout includes full-color illustrations. The writing is clear and concise so that after complet-

ing the book, readers will feel confident to branch out on their own." SLJ

Roman, Dave

Astronaut Academy: Zero gravity. First Second Books 2011 185p il pa $9.99; $16.99

Grades: 4 5 6 7 8   **741.5**

  1. Graphic novels 2. Humorous graphic novels 3. Science fiction graphic novels 4. School life -- Graphic novels

  ISBN 9781596436206; 9781596437562

LC 2010-941434

Hakata Soy has been the leader of a futuristic superhero team, but he has given that up and just wants to be a normal student at Astronaut Academy, a school on a space station, where students take such courses as anti-gravity gymnastics and fire-throwing. Other students include Doug Hiro, who always wears his space helmet, rich girl Maribelle Mellonbelly, Miyumi San (Maribelle's rival), and egotistical Billy Lee. Hakata Soy has some trouble adjusting to school life, and things get much worse when the villainous Gotcha Birds steal a robotic twin to Hakata Soy and reprogram it to kill him.

"Students like the introspective Hakata Soy, the space-gymnastics-obsessed Doug Hiro, and the snooty rich girl Mirabelle Mellonbelly meet up at Astronaut Academy, a middle school where the zany mixes with the postmodern. . . . Silliness is high on the agenda, aided by minimal, cartoonish art that plays on manga tropes but also manages to build character into the simple lines of a face. . . . This is one for readers looking for more involved and complex comedy than a cursory glance at the images might lead one to expect." Booklist

  Followed by: Astronaut academy: Re-entry (2013)

Rosinsky, Natalie M.

Graphic content! the culture of comic books. Compass Point Books 2010 64p il (Pop culture revolutions) lib bdg $31.99

Grades: 5 6 7 8 9 10   **741.5**

  1. Comic books, strips, etc. -- History and criticism

  ISBN 978-0-7565-4241-2 lib bdg; 0-7565-4241-3 lib bdg

Traces the origins of comic books and discusses the emergence of superheroes, censorship issues, their depiction of increased social diversity, and their impact on society

"This slim and splashily designed book . . . does an admirable job of keeping things succinct yet thorough. . . . [The author] maintains a nice international scope throughout. . . . This is a super resource to have on hand to give a broader context of the medium and its fascinating history." Booklist

Ruiz, Emilio

Waluk; by Emilio Ruiz ; illustrated by Ana Miralles ; translated and adapted by Dan Oliverio. Graphic Universe 2013 52 p. (lib. bdg. : alk. paper) $26.60; $7.95

Grades: 3 4 5 6   **741.5**

  1. Friendship -- Fiction 2. Polar bear -- Fiction 3.

Graphic novels 4. Bears -- Fiction 5. Tundras -- Fiction
ISBN 1467715980; 1467716065; 9781467715980;
9781467716062

LC 2012047787

"Young Waluk is all alone. His mother has abandoned
him, as is the way of polar bears, and now he must fend for
himself. But he doesn't know much about the world--and
unfortunately, his Arctic world is changing quickly. The ice
is melting, and food is hard to find." (Publisher's note)

"Marrying exemplary sequential storytelling, mythology, and science and enhanced through respectful anthro-
pomorphizing, Waluk takes readers into a realistic world of
polar bears endangered by climate change." Booklist

Russell, P. Craig

★ **Coraline**; based on the novel by Neil Gaiman;
adapted and illustrated by P. Craig Russell; colorist,
Lovern Kindzierski; letterer, Todd Klein. HarperCol-
lins 2008 186p il $18.99; lib bdg $19.89
Grades: 4 5 6 7   **741.5**
1. Graphic novels 2. Horror graphic novels
ISBN 978-0-06-082543-0; 978-0-06-082544-7 lib bdg
LC 2007-930658

"An adaptation of Gaiman's 2002 novel Coraline, . . . a
tale of childhood nightmares. As in the original story, Coraline wanders around her new house and discovers a door
leading into a mirror place, where she finds her button-eyed
'other mother,' who is determined to secure Coraline's love
one way or another. This version is a virtuoso adaptation. .
. . A master of fantastical landscapes, Russell sharpens the
realism of his imagery, perserving the humanity of the characters and heightening the horror." Booklist

Sakura, Kenichi

Dragon drive. Vol. 1, D-break; story & art by
Ken-ichi Sakura. Viz Media/Shonen Jump 2007
195p il $7.99
Grades: 6 7 8 9 10   **741.5**
1. Manga 2. Shonen manga 3. Graphic novels 4.
Video games -- Graphic novels
ISBN 978-1-4215-1187-0; 1-4215-1187-8

Reiji Ozora knows that he's no good at anything, people
keep telling him that. Then best friend Maiko takes him
to a secret center where people play a virtual reality game,
Dragon Drive. Reiji signs up and finds that, despite the fact
that his virtual dragon, Chibi, is small and weak, together
they have more power than meets the eye. While they play
the game, they're in a world called Rikyu, where everything
feels all too real; can Reiji, Chibi, and their friends be in
real danger?

Other titles in the Dragon Drive series are:
Dragon drive. Vol. 2 : another world (2007)
Dragon drive. Vol. 3: believe (2007)
Dragon drive. Vol. 4: hero (2007)
Dragon drive. Vol. 5: mission (2007)
Dragon drive. Vol. 6: hope (2008)
Dragon drive. Vol. 7: decisive battle (2008)
Dragon drive. Vol. 8: excitement (2008)
Dragon drive. Vol. 9: reshuffle (2008)
Dragon drive. Vol. 10: departure (2008)
Dragon drive. Vol. 11: trust (2008)
Dragon drive. Vol. 12: promise (2009)

Dragon drive. Vol. 13: reunion (2009)
Dragon drive. Vol. 14: wait (2009)

Sala, Richard

Cat burglar black. First Second 2009 126p il
pa $16.99
Grades: 5 6 7 8 9 10   **741.5**
1. Graphic novels 2. Mystery graphic novels 3.
Orphans -- Graphic novels
ISBN 978-1-59643-144-7; 1-59643-144-X

K.'s aunt, who works at the Bellsong Academy for Girls,
has invited K. to attend the school. But as soon as she arrives, K. notices some strange goings-on: her aunt has suddenly taken ill; there are only three other students and no
regular classes; and a statue speaks to K. when no one else
is around.

"The story is structured like a lighthearted cross between
a fable and a horror film, but only ever teetering on the edge
of horror without depicting it. This could have resulted in a
mishmash, but Sala elegantly dances through the creepy and
the sweet." SLJ

Schweizer, Chris

Crogan's march. Oni Press 2009 212p il $14.95
Grades: 8 9 10 11 12 Adult   **741.5**
1. Graphic novels 2. Adventure graphic novels 3.
Imperialism -- Graphic novels 4. North Africa -- World
history -- 20th century -- Graphic novels
ISBN 978-1-934964-24-8
Sequel to: Crogan's vengeance (2008)

When brothers Eric and Cory squabble at the dinner
table, their father tells them the story of Peter Crogan, one
of their ancestors, who fought in the French Foreign Legion
in 1912. Crogan's five-year term of service is one month
from completion when he's asked to stay and become an officer. His unit is stationed in North Africa, where the French
hold territory and depend on the French Foreign Legion to
police the territory, putting down the rebellious attacks of
the Tuaregs. He finds himself torn between the heroic Captain Poitelet (who tends to be the sole survivor of various
battles) and the grizzled sergeant who actually cares about
the people the Legion polices. When Crogan's unit escorts
a caravan that endures an attack by Tuaregs, the captain's
reckless actions endanger everyone, and Crogan must find
help. Schweizer's story includes the kind of violence military actions cause, but very little in the way of bad language.
Some may wince at the heavily French-accented English of
some of the characters ("zee Daughters of France send zem
out to all of zee units," etc.). This action-packed historical
fiction graphic novel will appeal to teens, but adults who remember such novels as Beau Geste by Percival Christopher
Wren (and the movies, of course) will also enjoy reading
Schweizer's tale.

Serling, Rod

The **Twilight** Zone: the after hours; adaptation by Mark Kneece; illustrated by Rebekah Isaacs.
Walker & Company 2008 un il $16.99; pa $9.99
Grades: 5 6 7 8 9 10   **741.5**
1. Graphic novels 2. Supernatural graphic novels 3.

Twilight zone (Television program) -- Graphic novels
ISBN 978-0-8027-9716-2; 978-0-8027-9717-9 pa
LC 2008-4310

Marsha White visits a department store to buy an advertised gold thimble, is taken by elevator to a floor with empty display cases except for one, which has the thimble, and she deals with an odd saleswoman who knows her name. When Marsha is in the elevator, she discovers the thimble is defective and tries to complain, but the manager insists there is no eighteenth floor, the store has no elevator, and the store has never carried gold thimbles. As she begins to leave, Marsha faints at the sight of a mannequin that looks exactly like the strange saleswoman, and she's put into a back room to recover. When she wakes up, the store has been closed and she's locked in. This is an actual episode of the old Twilight Zone television show.

"Kneece's adaptation is quick and enjoyable and introduces a classic TV series to a new generation of readers. Isaacs's illustrations are clean, distinct and cinematic in scope, employing an interesting variety of angles." Kirkus

The **Twilight** Zone: walking distance; adaptation from Rod Serling's original script by Mark Kneece; illustrated by Dove McHargue. Walker & Company 2008 un il $16.99; pa $9.99

Grades: 5 6 7 8 9 10 **741.5**
1. Graphic novels 2. Supernatural graphic novels 3. Twilight zone (Television program) -- Graphic novels
ISBN 978-0-8027-9714-8; 978-0-8027-9715-5 pa
LC 2008-4273

Thirty-nine-year-old businessman Martin Sloan's car blows a tire as he's driving, and he realizes he is within walking distance of his hometown. Leaving his car to be repaired, he decides to walk there. However, when he reaches town, he has also gone back in time. Can he find his boyhood self and give his younger self advice? Or will everyone think he's just crazy? This is an actual episode of the old Twilight Zone television show.

The story is "exceptionally well told and . . . [is] brilliantly adapted to a new medium." SLJ

Sfar, Joann

★ The **little** prince; adapted from the book by Antoine de Saint-Exupéry; translated by Sarah Ardizzone; colour by Brigitte Findakly. Houghton Mifflin Harcourt 2010 110p il $19.99

Grades: 5 6 7 8 9 **741.5**
1. Graphic novels 2. Fantasy graphic novels 3. Extraterrestrial beings -- Graphic novels
ISBN 978-0-547-33802-6; 0-547-33802-3

"On the surface, this is a straight graphic-novel retelling of the narrator pilot getting stranded in the desert, where he meets a curious little boy who claims to be from a wee planet very far away. . . . The ultimately tricky task is to honor the source but not sound like an adaptation (otherwise, why not just read the original?) and Sfar nails it on both counts. . . . Everything is handled with both reverence and ingenuity." Booklist

Shakespeare, William, 1564-1616

Macbeth; the graphic novel. [by] William Shakespeare; script by John McDonald; adapted by Brigit

Viney. Lucent Books 2010 144p il (Classic graphic novel collection) $34.10

Grades: 7 8 9 10 **741.5**
1. Poets 2. Authors 3. Dramatists 4. Graphic novels
ISBN 978-1-4205-0373-9; 1-4205-0373-1
First published 2008 in the United Kingdom

In graphic novel format, presents an adaptation of Shakespeare's classic tale about a man who kills his king after hearing the prophesies of three witches.

"The entire [story is] told through speech balloons. . . . This format offers readers an experience closer to a theatrical performance than a prose condensation of the plot. . . . Excellent graphics bring the [story] to life and set the mood. Lush art in jewel tones heightens interest. . . . Macbeth . . . includes a wealth of additional resources such as a main-character summary, family tree, link map of characters, and listing of famous quotations." SLJ

Includes glossary

The **merchant** of Venice; adapted by Richard Appignanesi; illustrated by Faye Yong. Amulet Books 2011 207p il (Manga Shakespeare) pa $10.95

Grades: 7 8 9 10 **741.5**
1. Poets 2. Authors 3. Dramatists 4. Graphic novels
ISBN 978-0-8109-9717-2; 0-8109-9717-7
LC 2010021938

In sixteenth-century Venice, when a merchant must default on a large loan from an abused Jewish moneylender for a friend with romantic ambitions, the bitterly vengeful creditor demands a gruesome payment instead. Presented in comic book format.

"Since plays are written to be performed, to be seen, a manga adaptation is a very satisfying way to enjoy Shakespeare. . . . Fans of the Bard should be delighted to experience his works through comics, while manga fans can be exposed to Shakespeare in a familiar way." Voice Youth Advocates

The **most** excellent and lamentable tragedy of Romeo & Juliet; a play by William Shakespeare. by William Shakespeare, adapted and illustrated by Gareth Hinds. Candlewick Press 2013 128 p. (hardcover) $21.99; (pbk.) $12.99

Grades: 7 8 9 10 **741.5**
1. Graphic novels
ISBN 0763659487; 0763668079; 9780763659486; 9780763668075
LC 2012950561

This book by Gareth Hinds presents a graphic novel adaptation of William Shakespeare's play "Romeo and Juliet." "The most notable change between this story and Shakespeare's original is the creative license that Hinds takes with ethnicity--he makes the characters of African, Indian, and Caucasian descent in order to promote the universality of the story. The Shakespearean language is abridged but not adapted into contemporary English." (School Library Journal)

"Cleaving to Shakespeare's words and dramatic arc, Hinds (The Merchant of Venice) creates another splendid graphic novel, tracing each scene in taut, coherent dialogue. The characters, in period dress modified by a few more contemporary touches, are poignantly specific yet universal. Hinds delivers the play's essence and beauty, its glorious language, furious conflict, yearning love, and wrenching tragedy." (Horn Book)

Shelley, Mary Wollstonecraft, 1797-1851

Gris Grimly's Frankenstein, or, The modern Prometheus; assembled from the original text by Mary Shelley in three volumes. Balzer + Bray 2013 208 p. (trade bdg.) $24.99

Grades: 8 9 10 11 12   741.5

1. Horror graphic novels 2. Monsters -- Graphic novels 3. Graphic novels 4. Horror stories 5. Monsters -- Fiction

ISBN 0061862975; 9780061862977

LC 2010046237

This is a graphic novel version of Mary Shelley's "Frankenstein" by Gris Grimly. "Spidery ink lines and a palette of jaundiced yellows and faded sepias plumb the darkness of the writer's imaginings. Frankenstein's bone-embellished military jacket and pop-star shock of hair turn him into a sort of anachronistic punk scientist." Focus is given to "the monster's self-loathing and Frankenstein's ruin." (Publishers Weekly)

"This graphic novel adaptation abridges Shelley's tale while staying true to its spirit. The inventive illustrations, in a muted palette punctuated by black, pinks, purples, and bilious green, are a mix of modern, nineteenth-century, and steampunk sensibilities. Grimly makes excellent use of format with dynamic shapes, sizes, and pacing of panels; the epistolary sections have an elegant (if difficult to read) handwritten look." (Horn Book)

Shiga, Jason

★ **Meanwhile**. Abrams/Amulet 2010 un il $15.95

Grades: 4 5 6 7 8 9   741.5

1. Graphic novels 2. Science fiction graphic novels

ISBN 0-8109-8423-7; 978-0-8109-8423-3

LC 2009-39844

In this choose-your-own adventure graphic novel, a boy stumbles on the laboratory of a mad scientist who asks him to choose between testing a mind-reading device, a time machine, and a doomsday machine. (Bull Cent Child Books)

"In this graphic novel mind boggler . . . readers play the role of little Jimmy and on the first page make the seemingly innocuous decision of ordering a vanilla or chocolate ice-cream cone. Tubes connect panels in all directions and veer off into tabs to other pages, creating a head-spinningly tangled web of story. . . . The crux is that Jimmy stumbles into the lab of an affable mad scientist and is allowed to tinker with three inventions: a mind reader, a time machine, and the Killitron, which obliterates all life on earth aside from the user's. . . . It's maddening and challenging, all right, but that's precisely what makes it so crazy fun." Booklist

Siddell, Thomas

★ **Gunnerkrigg** Court: orientation; [by] Tom Siddell. Archaia Studios Press 2009 296p il $26.95

Grades: 6 7 8 9 10 11 12   741.5

1. Graphic novels 2. Fantasy graphic novels

ISBN 978-1-932386-34-9; 1-932386-34-3

"The first 14 chapters of Siddell's popular webcomic are collected here in an alluring hardcover. The premise, best described as science-fantasy, involves a young girl named Antimony plopped into a strange boarding-school/industrial-complex which . . . she knows nothing about. Discrete chapters . . . all feature varying levels of jaw-dropping peculiarity, devilish bursts of humor, and sublime creativity that lurk at the ends of the school's corridors. The darkly hued artwork is deceptively simplistic and displays a flair for the crucial details of setting and atmosphere." Booklist

Other titles in this series are:

Vol. 2: Research (2009)

Vol. 3: Reason (2011)

Vol. 4: Materia (2013)

Vol. 5: Refine (2015)

Sizer, Paul

Little White Mouse collection 1; Dream of the ghost. Café Digital Comics 2004 144p ill. (paperback) $14.95

Grades: 7 8 9 10   741.5

1. Graphic novels

ISBN 9781888429077

In a future universe, sixteen-year-old Loo is shipwrecked on a remote, automated mining satellite when the space liner on which she and her sister were traveling was destroyed. Considered an intruder by the satellite's computer, she must survive, build a robot body for her dead sister's preserved memory, and find a way home before the satellite's life support system shuts down. Creator Sizer is now self-publishing this series of four volumes and selling it at his website, www.paulsizer.com.

Slate, Barbara

You can do a graphic novel. Alpha Books 2010 187p il pa $19.95

Grades: 7 8 9 10   741.5

1. Graphic novels -- Authorship

ISBN 978-1-59257-955-6; 1-59257-955-8

LC 2009-930703

"This is a practical book for those who aspire to create their own graphic novels. Slate . . . is fair handed with the advice she gives to writers as well as artists. . . . The instructions and illustrations are easy to follow, and the format is colorful and eye-catching." SLJ

Smith, Jeff

Bone : out from Boneville. Scholastic Graphix 2005 144p il $18.95; pa $9.99

Grades: 4 5 6 7 8 9 10 11 12   741.5

1. Graphic novels 2. Fantasy graphic novels 3. Adventure graphic novels

ISBN 0-439-70623-8; 0-439-70640-8 pa

"The story follows three cousins who have been thrown out of their town for cheating the citizens. Shortly thereafter, they are separated. Each Bone stumbles into a mysterious valley full of odd creatures that reveal strange happenings. The story is well paced with smooth transitions. It is dark, witty, mysterious, and exciting. The full-color art reflects that of classic comic books." SLJ

Other titles in this series are:

Bone: the great cow race (vol. 2)

Bone: eyes of the storm (vol. 3)

Bone: the dragonslayer (vol. 4)

Bone: Rock Jaw: Master the Eastern Border (vol. 5)
Bone: old man's cave (vol. 6)
Bone: ghost circles (vol. 7)
Bone: treasure hunters (vol. 8)
Bone: crown of horns (vol. 9)

Bone : Rose; with illustrations by Charles Vess. Scholastic Graphix 2009 138p il $21.99; pa $10.99
Grades: 4 5 6 7 8   **741.5**
1. Graphic novels 2. Fantasy graphic novels 3. Adventure graphic novels
ISBN 978-0-545-13542-9; 0-545-13542-7; 978-0-545-13543-6 pa; 0-545-13543-5 pa
"When a terrifying dragon attacks the small towns of the Northern Valley, a young Princess Rose (known later as Gran'ma Ben) must defeat it. The beast is actually the ancient evil, the Lord of the Locusts, and while Rose faces danger with honor, her elder sister, Princess Briar, follows a more sinister path." Publisher's note

Bone : tall tales; by Jeff Smith with Tom Sniegoski; color by Steve Hamaker. Graphix 2010 108p il $21.99; pa $10.99
Grades: 4 5 6 7 8   **741.5**
1. Graphic novels 2. Fantasy graphic novels 3. Adventure graphic novels
ISBN 978-0-545-14095-9; 0-545-14095-1; 978-0-545-14096-6 pa; 0-545-14096-X pa
This "introduces Big Johnson Bone, the explorer who founded Boneville. A fearless Davey Crockett-like character, he defeats a cave bear when just a baby and grows up to best all manner of beasts, including a pack of ratlike creatures intent on taking over the forest. Big Johnson's recklessness in the face of danger results in much humor, as does the commentary of his terrified, sarcastic monkey companion. Smith's quick wit shines through in the exchanges between Johnson and his companions. The colorful art is jam-packed with action, and the characters are enhanced with exaggerated features and movements." SLJ

Soo, Kean
Jellaby; Volume 1 the lost monster. by Kean Soo. Stone Arch Books 2014 160 p. color illustrations (Jellaby) (pbk.) $12.95; (library binding) $19.99
Grades: 4 5 6 7 8 9   **741.5**
1. Monsters -- Fiction 2. Friendship -- Fiction 3. Extraterrestrial beings -- Fiction 4. Human-alien encounters -- Comic books, strips, etc
ISBN 1434291952; 9781434264206; 9781434291950
LC 2013037026
First published 2008
"Portia has just moved to a new neighborhood with her mom. Adjusting to life without a father is hard enough, but school is boring and her classmates are standoffish. . . . But things start to get better when Portia mounts a midnight excursion into the woods behind her house where she discovers a shy and sweet purple monster. Life with Jellaby is exciting, but Portia's purple friend has secrets of his own." (Publisher's note)
"Soo grounds the story in a fairly gritty contemporary reality, where kids deal with bullies and well-meaning adults

try to help. Clear, clean lines and easy-to-follow panel layouts round out the package." Booklist

Jellaby : monster in the city. Hyperion Books 2009 172p il pa $9.99
Grades: 4 5 6 7 8 9   **741.5**
1. Graphic novels 2. Fantasy graphic novels 3. Monsters -- Graphic novels 4. Friendship -- Graphic novels
ISBN 1-4231-0565-6 pa; 978-1-4231-0565-7 pa
Beginning right where the first book ended, Portia, Jason, and Jellaby continue on their way to Toronto, walking after Portia panicked and they got off the train. They're searching for a way home for Jellaby, and they think a door somewhere in Exhibition Place, where the Canadian National Exhibition is taking place, holds a clue. Portia feels torn between wanting to help her friend yet not wanting to say goodbye forever, and her ambivalence causes a rift between her and Jason. When she doesn't want to trust a masked magician who seems to know too much about them and Jellaby, Portia leaves Jason. They all end up in the Automotive Building, where the masked man leads Jason and Jellaby down below the building, while Portia seems to find her long lost father. But is he really her father, and just what is waiting for Jason and Jellaby under the Automotive Building? Soo again uses a mostly purple color palette.

Stevenson, Noelle
Lumberjanes 1; Beware the kitten holy. by Noelle Stevenson, Grace Ellis, Brooke Allen, and Shannon Watters. Simon & Schuster 2015 128 p. ill. (chiefly col.) (Lumberjanes) pbk $14.99
Grades: 6 7 8 9 10 11 12 Adult   **741.5**
1. Camps -- Fiction 2. Adventure fiction 3. Summer -- Fiction 4. Monsters -- Fiction 5. Female friendship -- Graphic novels
ISBN 1608866874; 9781608866878
Eisner Award: Best New Series (2015)
Eisner Award: Best Publication for Teens (2015)
"[This] graphic novel begins mid-adventure as five campers are out after hours investigating a strange event that they all witnessed: a woman turning into a giant bear. This is just the first of many odd occurrences that Jo, April, Molly, Mal, and Ripley encounter at the summer camp for 'Hardcore Lady Types.' The Lumberjanes, as the scouts are called, band together to solve puzzles, defeat three-eyed creatures, and escape the ire of their watchful counselor Jen." (School Library Journal)
"Humorously riffing on everything from scout badges to the X-Men to feminist heroes . . ., it's a sharp, smart, and most of all fun celebration of sisterhood." Pub Wkly
Volume 1 of an ongoing series

★ **Nimona**; by Noelle Stevenson. HarperCollins Childrens Books 2015 272 p. $17.99
Grades: 7 8 9 10 11 12   **741.5**
1. Fantasy graphic novels 2. Magic -- Graphic novels 3. Good and evil -- Fiction 4. Heroes and heroines -- Graphic novels 5. Shapeshifting -- Comic books, strips, etc.
ISBN 0062278231; 9780062278234
Eisner Nominee: Best Digital/Web Comic (2015)

In this graphic novel, by Noelle Stevenson, "Nimona is an impulsive young shapeshifter with a knack for villainy. Lord Ballister Blackheart is a villain with a vendetta. As sidekick and supervillain, Nimona and Lord Blackheart are about to wreak some serious havoc. Their mission: prove to the kingdom that Sir Ambrosius Goldenloin and his buddies at the Institution of Law Enforcement and Heroics aren't the heroes everyone thinks they are." (Publisher's note)

"This celebrated webcomic, a mash-up of medieval culture with modern science and technology, is now available in print. . . . Action scenes dominate as Nimona shifts with Hulk-like ferocity from frightful creatures such as a fire-breathing dragon to a docile cat or a timid child. Dialogue is fresh and witty with an abundance of clever lines." SLJ

Stolarz, Laurie Faria

Black is for beginnings; adaptation by Barbara Randall Kesel; artwork by Janina Gørrissen. Llewellyn Publications/Flux 2009 160p il pa $9.95
Grades: 8 9 10 11 12   **741.5**
1. Graphic novels 2. Romance graphic novels 3. Supernatural graphic novels 4. Dreams -- Graphic novels
ISBN 978-0-7387-1438-7; 0-7387-1438-0

When Stacey, a college student and hereditary witch, again begins to have disturbing dreams about her former boyfriend and a little girl who was murdered years earlier, she knows that the dreams are trying to tell her something important, but she does not know what

"The story's weirdo flashes of humor make the darkness bearable, as do the everyday settings of a pizza parlor and dorm room. A unique and somewhat unhinged blend of realism and fantasy." Booklist

Storrie, Paul D.

Made for each other; or I made my prom date of Hunkenstein or love in stitches or our love's aliiiiive!! illustrated by Eldon Cowgur. Graphic Universe 2011 127p il (My boyfriend is a monster) lib bdg $29.27; pa $9.95
Grades: 7 8 9 10   **741.5**
1. Graphic novels 2. Romance graphic novels 3. Monsters -- Graphic novels
ISBN 978-0-7613-5601-1 lib bdg; 0-7613-5601-0 lib bdg; 978-0-7613-7077-2 pa; 0-7613-7077-3 pa
     LC 2010028722

"Maria falls for the new guy in school, Tom, and he likes her, too. The problem is that the recent mysterious rash of deaths in their town might have something to do with his strange family. Will Maria be able to save the guy she loves, or will monstrous history repeat itself? . . . The black-and-white art brings the wilds of both high school and Alaska to life . . . The romance and scares are real, but light, and make for a thoroughly enjoyable read." Booklist

Stroud, Jonathan

The **Amulet** of Samarkand; a Bartimaeus graphic novel. adapted by Jonathan Stroud and Andrew Donkin; art by Lee Sullivan; color by Nicolas Chapuis; lettering by Chris Dickey. Disney/Hyperion Books 2010 un il $19.99

Grades: 7 8 9 10   **741.5**
1. Graphic novels 2. Magic -- Graphic novels
ISBN 978-1-4231-1146-7; 1-4231-1146-X
     LC 2010-35513

Nathaniel, a magician's apprentice, summons up the djinni Bartimaeus and instructs him to steal the Amulet of Samarkand from the powerful magician Simon Lovelace.

"The artwork is lively, atmospheric, and exciting. . . . The depth of Stroud's alternate London, some complex political machinations, and the large cast of human and demon characters are all well realized here." Booklist

★ **Stuck** in the middle; seventeen comics from an unpleasant age. edited by Ariel Schrag. Viking 2007 210p il $18.99
Grades: 7 8 9 10   **741.5**
1. Graphic novels
ISBN 978-0-670-06221-8
     LC 2006-52581

This graphic novel collects seventeen short stories about the perils of middle school, each by independent comics creators, including editor Schrag, her younger sister Tania Schrag, Aaron Renier, Daniel Clowes, Gabrielle Bell, and others.

"Highly recommended for junior high graphic novel collections on up; but please keep in mind that this graphic novel does contain some strong material, including obscenities . . . and sexual material." Kliatt

Sturm, James

★ **Satchel** Paige; striking out Jim Crow. by James Sturm & Rich Tommaso; with an introduction by Gerald Early. Jump at the Sun 2007 89p il $16.99; pa $9.99
Grades: 6 7 8 9 10 11 12   **741.5**
1. Graphic novels 2. Baseball players 3. Baseball -- Graphic novels
ISBN 0-7868-3900-7; 0-7868-3901-5 pa
     LC 2007-61362

This graphic novel is "about fictional Emmet Wilson, a black farmer whose moment of glory as a player in the Negro Leagues came when he scored a run off the great pitcher, Satchel Paige. . . . This visually powerful, suspenseful, even profound story makes an excellent choice for readers interested in baseball or in the history of race relations." Booklist

Tamaki, Mariko

★ **Emiko** superstar; written by Mariko Tamaki; illustrated by Steve Rolston. DC Comics/Minx 2008 149p il pa $9.99
Grades: 7 8 9 10 11 12   **741.5**
1. Graphic novels 2. Performance art -- Graphic novels 3. Racially mixed people -- Graphic novels
ISBN 978-1-4012-1536-1

"Emiko, a half-Japanese, half-Caucasian Canadian, is a self-described geek facing a summer of babysitting and isolation. Things change when she stumbles upon an underground performing art scene inspired by Andy Warhol's Factory. She eventually takes to the stage . . . and achieves minor celebrity. Soon, though, Emiko must face the troubling complexities in the lives of her new friends and the consequences of her own questionable actions. . . . Rolston's playful, vibrant b&w illustrations bring the characters to life." Publ Wkly

Skim; words by Mariko Tamaki; drawings by Jillian Tamaki. Groundwood Books 2008 144p il $18.95

Grades: 7 8 9 10 11 12   **741.5**

1. Graphic novels 2. Humorous graphic novels 3. Friendship -- Graphic novels 4. School stories -- Graphic novels

ISBN 978-0-88899-753-1; 0-88899-753-1

Skim is Kimberly Keiko Cameron, a not-slim half-Japanese would-be Wiccan goth who attends a private school. When classmate Katie Matthews' ex-boyfriend commits suicide, concerned guidance counselors descend upon the school because so many of the student body goes into mourning overdrive. The popular clique starts a new club, Girls Celebrate Life, and make Katie their project, especially after she falls off her roof and breaks both arms. Kim and her best friend Lisa observe all this, but counselors target Kim for her goth tendencies and are convinced she'll become suicidal any moment. All she is, is in love with her English teacher, Ms. Archer, who seems to reciprocate and then leaves the school. As Lisa starts to get sucked into the GLC, Kim and Katie tentatively begin a new friendship. There is only one rather chaste kiss between Kim and Ms. Archer. Artist Jillian Tamaki draws Kim to look like a classical Heian period Japanese woman.

★ **This** One Summer; Mariko Tamaki, Jillian Tamaki. First Second 2014 320 p. chiefly ill. $21.99

Grades: 7 8 9 10 11 12 Adult   **741.5**

1. Graphic novels 2. Vacations -- Fiction 3. Friendship -- Fiction

ISBN 1626720940; 9781626720947

Eisner Award: Best Graphic Album--New (2015)

Caldecott Honor Book (2015)

Printz Honor Book (2015)

In this young adult graphic novel written by Mariko Tamaki and illustrated by Jillian Tamaki, "Every summer, Rose goes with her mom and dad to a lake house in Awago Beach. . . . Rosie's friend Windy is always there, too, like the little sister she never had. But this summer is different. . . . It's a summer of secrets, and sorrow, and growing up, and it's a good thing Rose and Windy have each other." (Publisher's note)

"This captivating graphic novel presents a fully realized picture of a particular time in a young girl's life, an in-between summer filled with yearning and a sense of ephemerality." SLJ

Tan, Shaun

★ The **arrival**. Arthur A. Levine Books 2007 un il $19.99

Grades: 6 7 8 9 10   **741.5**

1. Graphic novels 2. Stories without words 3. Immigrants -- Graphic novels

ISBN 0-439-89529-4

LC 2006-21706

Boston Globe-Horn Book Award special citation (2008)

In this wordless graphic novel, a man leaves his homeland and sets off for a new country, where he must build a new life for himself and his family.

"Young readers will be fascinated by the strange new world the artist creates. . . . They will linger over the details in the beautiful sepia pictures and will likely pick up the book to pore over it again and again." SLJ

Telgemeier, Raina

★ **Drama**; Raina Telgemeier ; with color by Gurihiru. 1st ed. Graphix 2012 233 p. chiefly ill. $23.99

Grades: 5 6 7 8   **741.5**

1. Graphic novels 2. School stories 3. Middle schools -- Fiction 4. Children's plays -- Fiction 5. Schools -- Fiction 6. Theater -- Fiction 7. Interpersonal relations -- Fiction

ISBN 0545326982; 0545326990; 9780545326988; 9780545326995

LC 2011040748

Stonewall Honor Book (2013)

Author Raina Telgemeier's book focuses on a middle school drama production. "Callie loves theater . . . [S]he's the set designer for the stage crew, and this year she's determined to create a set worthy of Broadway on a middle-school budget. But how can she, when she doesn't know much about carpentry, ticket sales are down, and the crew members are having trouble working together?" (Publisher's note)

"In this realistic and sympathetic story, feelings and thoughts leap off the page, revealing Telgemeier's keen eye for young teen life." Booklist

Includes bibliographical references

★ **Sisters**; Raina Telgemeier; with color by Braden Lamb. First edition Graphix 2014 197 p. chiefly color illustrations hbk $24.99; pbk $10.99

Grades: 5 6 7 8   **741.5**

1. Siblings 2. Family life 3. Autobiographical graphic novels 4. Interpersonal relations

ISBN 9780545540599; 9780545540605

LC 2013008700

"Raina can't wait to be a big sister. But once Amara is born, things aren't quite how she expected them to be. . . . They are sisters, after all. Raina uses her signature humor . . . in both present-day narrative and perfectly placed flashbacks to tell the story of her relationship with her sister, which unfolds during the course of a road trip from their home in San Francisco to a family reunion in Colorado." (Publisher's note)

"The author's narrative style is fresh and sharp, and the combination of well-paced and well-placed flashbacks pull the plot together, moving the story forward and helping readers understand the characters' point of view. The volume captures preadolescence in an effortless and uncanny way and turns tough subjects, such as parental marriage problems, into experiences with which readers can identify." (School Library Journal)

★ **Smile**. Scholastic/Graphix 2010 213p il $21.99; pa $10.99

Grades: 5 6 7 8   **741.5**
1. Graphic novels 2. Autobiographical graphic novels
3. Dentistry -- Graphic novels 4. Friendship -- Graphic
novels 5. Personal appearance -- Graphic novels
ISBN 978-0-545-13205-3; 0-545-13205-3; 978-0-545-
13206-0 pa; 0-545-13206-1 pa

LC 2008-51782

Eisner Award: Best Publication for Teens (2011)
Boston Globe-Horn Book Honor: Nonfiction (2010)

Sixth grader Raina just wants to be normal, but when she
falls down going home from a Girl Scout meeting, she severely injures her two front teeth, and this starts her down a
long road with braces, surgery, retainers, embarrassing headgear—all sure to make her stand out from her middle school
classmates for all the wrong reasons. There's also a major
earthquake, then boy confusion, friends who turn out not to
be good friends, sibling jealousy, all the stuff that makes life
interesting, if not fun. Telgemeier wrote and drew the autobiographical Smile as a webcomic; this volume collects the
story in color.

"The dental case that Telgemeier documents in this
graphic memoir was extreme: a random accident led to front
tooth loss when she was 12, and over the next several years,
she suffered through surgery, implants, headgear, false teeth,
and a rearrangement of her remaining incisors. . . . Both
adults and kids . . . are vividly and rapidly portrayed. . . . Telgemeier's storytelling and full-color cartoony images form a
story that will cheer and inspire any middle-schooler dealing
with orthodontia." Booklist

TenNapel, Douglas R.

Bad Island; created, written, and drawn by Doug
TenNapel. Graphix 2011 218p il $24.99
Grades: 6 7 8 9 10   **741.5**
1. Adventure graphic novels 2. Family life -- Graphic
novels 3. Extraterrestrial beings -- Graphic novels 4.
Father-son relationship -- Graphic novels 5. Survival
after airplane accidents, shipwrecks, etc. -- Graphic
novels
ISBN 0545314798; 0545314801 pa; 9780545314794;
9780545314800 pa

LC 2011276008

"Dad has decided to take Reese, who is too cool for family outings, and his sister, Janine, on a fishing trip. The vacation takes an unexpected turn when their boat capsizes during a storm and they find themselves marooned on a strange
island. To their horror, the family slowly realizes that the island is the submerged body of a giant creature, escaped from
another world. The story alternates between the shipwreck
survivors and the faraway world that created this "island."
Both stories feature conflict between an adolescent son and
his father. . . . Ultimately, both rebellious adolescents grow
up and find their place as young men." (School Libr J)

"Though father, mother, teenage son, and tween daughter face the various dangers like a gang of Indiana Joneses,
their family stresses are believable. . . . A clever, old-fashioned adventure with some modern twists and a lighthearted
tone." Booklist

Flink. Image Comics 2007 122p il $13.99
Grades: 6 7 8 9 10 11 12 Adult   **741.5**
1. Graphic novels 2. Adventure graphic novels 3.

Sasquatch -- Graphic novels
ISBN 978-1-58240-891-0; 1-58240-891-2

Conrad is flying with his father on his first hunting trip
when the plane crashes in the wilderness. When Conrad
comes to after the crash, he's completely alone, with only the
clothes on his back, a handheld game player, and a pocket-
knife his father had just given him. When he wakes up from
a sleep, he finds a deerskin wrapped around him and follows
a trail of berries; a Bigfoot named Flink has saved him. Now
they have to deal with a rabid she-bear that injures Flink;
he needs his brother's medicine to heal, but the Bigfoot
community hates humans who hunt them. How can Flink
convince them that Conrad is harmless? The book includes
some violence and one scene where Conrad pees on a tree.

Ghostopolis; created, written, and drawn by
Doug TenNapel. Graphix 2010 266 p. il pa $12.99;
$24.99
Grades: 7 8 9 10   **741.5**
1. Graphic novels 2. Ghosts -- Graphic novels
ISBN 9780545210287; 9780545210270; 0545210275

LC 20090942984

This graphic novel tells the story of an "agent for the
Supernatural Immigration Task Force, . . . Frank Gallows[,
whose] . . . job [is] to catch ghosts on Earth and send them
back to the afterlife. However, during one particularly tricky
deportation, he accidentally zaps a young—living—boy.
Garth Hale suddenly finds himself surrounded by mummies
and goblins in a crumbling, ghastly city, with a skeleton
horse and his long-departed grandfather as his only friends.
Gallows comes crashing into the afterlife, as well, on a daring rescue mission. As this bumbling team tries to find a
way home, they end up face to face with the evil ruler of
Ghostopolis, who doesn't look too kindly upon mortals in
his city." (Kirkus)

"When readers first meet Garth Hale, he is about to receive the fifth diagnosis that his disease is incurable. How
fitting, then, that a boy who thinks about death more than
other kids his age should be accidentally zapped into the
afterlife. When washed-up ghost wrangler Frank Gallows
realizes that he accidentally sent Garth through to the other
side, he does everything in his power to rescue him. Meanwhile, Garth explores the spirit world. . . . TenNapel mixes
emotional epiphanies with humor in a way that will appeal
to a broad audience. Characters experience personal growth
and learn lessons about themselves throughout the course of
this book. . . . TenNapel's colorful illustrations are filled with
energy and life, and they use shade and silhouettes to great
advantage." SLJ

Tommysaurus Rex. Image Comics 2005 110p
il pa $11.95
Grades: 5 6 7 8 9 10 11 12   **741.5**
1. Graphic novels 2. Dinosaurs -- Graphic novels
ISBN 1-58240-395-3

When Ely loses his dog, Tommy, in a car accident, his
parents send him to Grandpa Joe's farm for the summer.
He discovers a live, 40-foot Tyrannosaurus Rex in a cave
on the farm, and soon the boy and his pet dinosaur cause
a big ruckus in town. Ely promises to train the dinosaur he
names Tommysaurus, but not if the town's bully, Randy, has
his way.

Toriyama, Akira

Cowa! story and art by Akira Toriyama; translation & English adaptation Alexander O. Smith, et. al. Viz Media/Shonen Jump 2008 208p il $7.99

Grades: 5 6 7 8 9 10 11 12   **741.5**

  1. Manga 2. Graphic novels 3. Humorous graphic novels 4. Monsters -- Graphic novels

  ISBN 978-1-4215-1805-3; 1-4215-1805-8

  Original Japanese edition, 1997

Mischievous Paifu is half-vampire and half-werekoala, and he's usually getting into lots of trouble with his best buddy, Jose the ghost. When the Monster Flu sweeps through town, the doctor says that without medicine, everyone will die. The only person who makes the medicine is the witch who lives hundreds of miles away, and all the adults except for the doctor are ill. Paifu and Jose team up with grumpy ex-sumo wrestler Maruyama to make the journey; will they make it before they get sick? The book includes some potty humor (Jose farts a lot) and lots of fighting scenes (Toriyama created Dragon Ball Z).

Torres, J.

Lola : a ghost story; [by] J. Torres & [illustrated by] Elbert Or. Oni Press 2009 102p il $14.95

Grades: 4 5 6 7 8   **741.5**

  1. Graphic novels 2. Ghosts -- Graphic novels 3. Family life -- Graphic novels 4. Philippines -- Graphic novels

  ISBN 978-1-934964-33-0; 1-934964-33-6

"Lola ('grandmother' in Tagalog) has just died, and Jesse is reluctant to visit her home in the Philippines. He was afraid of her because she was rumored to have magical abilities, and because he thinks she tried to drown him when he was a baby. Jesse listens to family members tell stories about her as he tries to adjust to their strange mix of superstitions and religion. . . . Jesse is an unusually nuanced character. . . When he sees something extraordinary, it's unclear if he is dreaming, hallucinating, or if he has inherited his grandmother's abilities. Torres's gradual revelation of details will keep readers hanging until they learn the truth. Or's artwork uses sepia tones and smooth lines, and features characters with cute button eyes. But the sweet images can quickly turn horrific when Jesse has his visions." SLJ

Trondheim, Lewis

Tiny Tyrant; by Lewis Trondheim; translated from the French by Alexis Siegel; illustrated by Fabrice Parme. First Second Books 2007 124p il $12.95

Grades: 4 5 6 7 8 9 10 11 12 Adult   **741.5**

  1. Graphic novels 2. Humorous graphic novels

  ISBN 978-1-59643-094-5

               LC 2006021479

"Tiny child-king Ethelbert is spoiled and difficult, expecting to have his every whim fulfilled-or else. . . . In the end, though, he becomes a hero. The dynamic cartoons are filled with details and riddled with humor; most pages have between six and eight small pictures. . . . This title will have wide appeal. It's young and accessible enough for elementary-grade kids, but teens will also be charmed by the rascally king." SLJ

Tsang, Evonne

I love him to pieces; or my date is dead weight or he only loves me for my brains. illustrated by Janina Gorrissen. Graphic Universe 2011 123p il (My boyfriend is a monster) lib bdg $29.27; pa $9.95

Grades: 6 7 8 9 10 11 12   **741.5**

  1. Graphic novels 2. Horror graphic novels 3. Romance graphic novels 4. Humorous graphic novels 5. Zombies -- Graphic novels

  ISBN 978-0-7613-6004-9 lib bdg; 0-7613-6004-2 lib bdg; 978-0-7613-7079-6 pa; 0-7613-7079-X pa

               LC 2010-30774

Dicey Bell, star of her high school baseball team in St. Petersburg, Florida, falls for Jack Chen, the star of the science program, and she wangles her way into partnering with Jack on a school project. They work together well, like each other a lot, and things look good for a romance, when a weird infection hits the city. The infection attacks the brain and turns the infected people into human flesh-craving monsters. Dicey and Jack try to get to safety, but find themselves surrounded by zombie-like monsters. This story combines romance with zombie fighting in a story that works like a lighter version of The Walking Dead; the extra subtitles on the title page indicate the humor: "My Date is Dead Weight, or He Only Loves Me For My Brains." Gorrissen's black and white art makes the teens look like teens, and the zombies look yucky and scary without being too icky for most teen readers. This is the first volume in a series of standalone stories, each taking on a different kind of monster.

Van Meter, Jen

Hopeless Savages; greatest hits, 2000-2010. Oni 2010 391p pa $19.99

Grades: 7 8 9 10   **741.5**

  1. Graphic novels

  ISBN 978-1-934964-48-4; 1-934964-48-4

Follows the Hopeless Savages, the first family of punk, as they navigate through kidnapping plots, first love, and international intrigue.

"The characters are richly developed; the plots in each chapter are engaging and fast moving, and the stylized black-and-white illustrations will keep readers engaged and begging for more. . . . This collection of stories can serve as an appealing entree into the world of graphic novels." Voice Youth Advocates

Venditti, Robert

★ The lightning thief: the graphic novel; by Rick Riordan; adapted by Robert Venditti; art by Attila Futaki; color by Jose Villarrubia; layouts by Orpheus Collar; lettering by Chris Dickey. Disney/Hyperion Books 2010 un il (Percy Jackson and the Olympians) $19.99; pa $9.99

Grades: 5 6 7 8   **741.5**

  1. Graphic novels 2. Greek mythology -- Graphic novels

  ISBN 978-1-4231-1696-7; 1-4231-1696-8; 978-1-4231-1710-0 pa; 1-4231-1710-7 pa

               LC 2010035512

After learning that he is the son of a mortal woman and Poseidon, god of the sea, twelve-year-old Percy is sent to a summer camp for demigods like himself, and joins his new friends on a quest to prevent a war between the gods.

This graphic novel adaptation of Rick Riordan's novel "succeeds in spectacular fashion. . . . The book retains the excellent pacing of the original and gives a face to Riordan's vision of the mythological made modern. Futaki's artwork is exemplary but what leaves such a lasting impression is Villarrubia's coloring, which reveals both subtlety and spectacle when needed." Publ Wkly

Other graphic adaptations in this series are:

The sea of monsters (2013)

The Titan's curse (2013)

Viney, Brigit

Frankenstein; [by] Mary Shelley; [adapted and illustrated by Brigit Viney] Lucent 2010 144p il (Classic comics) $32.45

Grades: 6 7 8 9   741.5

1. Graphic novels 2. Horror graphic novels

ISBN 978-1-4205-0374-6; 1-4205-0374-X

"Much of the power of Viney's adaptation of Mary Shelley's horror classic lies within the artwork. Action sequences jump off the page, while portraits of each character provide nuance and depth to the text. . . . This . . . wins points for a masterful rendition that adds much value to the original." Kirkus

Vollmar, Rob

★ The **castaways**; illustrated by Pablo G. Callejo. NBM/ComicsLit 2007 64p il pa $17.95

Grades: 6 7 8 9 10 11 12   741.5

1. Graphic novels 2. United States -- History -- 1919-1933 -- Graphic novels

ISBN 978-1-56163-492-7

An expanded and newly illustrated edition of the title first published 2002 by Absence of Ink Comic Press

"Afraid that he's just a burden on his family, 13-year-old Tucker Freeman lets himself be driven away from home and jumps on a freight train heading west. His inexperience makes him vulnerable to all the angry, desperate people looking for any way they can survive during America's economic collapse, but fortunately he's taken under the wing of Elijah Hopkins, an elderly colored man who introduces him to the cooperative hobo subculture. . . . Vollmar's script, based on family reminiscences, rings true; his dialogue has the vocabulary and the rhythms of real people talking. . . . Callejo's art creates a solid setting in which Tucker's experience can reveal squalor or grace." Publ Wkly

Walker, Landry Q.

The **super** scary monster show, featuring Little Gloomy; written by Landry Walker; drawn by Eric Jones; tones by Rikki Simons. Amaze Ink/SLG Publishing 2008 un il $9.95

Grades: 3 4 5 6 7 8 9   741.5

1. Graphic novels 2. Horror graphic novels 3. Humorous graphic novels

ISBN 978-1-59362-103-2; 1-59362-103-5

This book collects the three issues (so far) of The Super Scary Monster Show comics. Little Gloomy, her friends, and her enemies, live in the world called Frightsylvania. Gloomy deals with an alien who crashlands in her backyard

and wants to take over the world (she has plenty of "pet" monsters in her house who take care of her problem). Carl the squid lies to his parents about taking over the world and enslaving all its creatures, then they come for a visit. . . . Gloomy buys a golden scorpion as a gift for her friend the Mummy, but it turns out to be cursed, and everyone around her suffers accidents. The witch Evey has come up with a new spell to torment Gloomy, but it hits werewolf buddy Larry instead and shrinks him. There are plenty more stories, all written with tongue-in-cheek humor and just a touch of horror for younger readers. Gloomy does not suffer fools gladly, so the invading alien gets eaten (off page), and other inimical creatures suffer similar fates, so this book shouldn't be given to younger readers who are sensitive and don't like any violence. There is little in the way of any gore or overt violence, except for poor Frank, whose body parts often come apart.

Watson, Andi

Princess at midnight. Image Comics 2008 un il $5.99

Grades: 4 5 6 7 8 9 10   741.5

1. Graphic novels 2. Fantasy graphic novels 3. War -- Graphic novels 4. Princesses -- Graphic novels

ISBN 978-1-58240-928-3; 1-58240-928-5

Holly Crescent and her twin brother Henry lead sheltered lives as home-schooled children by day; their parents don't want any harm to come to their children after they were born prematurely and their early lives were so worrisome. At night, however, Holly becomes Princess of Castle Waxing, where life is good until the Horrible Horde takes over one of her favorite picnic spots. All too soon, her nights are spent in warfare against the Horde, and her days in reading books on war strategy. And when she wins, she's not satisfied with winning, she must pursue more warfare against the Horde, even as her dragon Chancellor warns her of overspending and the consequences of war on her people.

Weiner, Stephen

101 outstanding graphic novels; Stephen Weiner; [edited by] Daniel J. Fingeroth. 3rd edition NBM Pub. 2015 80 p. (hardcover) $15.99

Grades: Adult Professional   741.5

1. Graphic novels

ISBN 1561639443; 9781561639441

LC 2014958652

Previously called 101 Best Graphic Novels

"The popular primer on the best graphic novels, initially called The 101 Best Graphic Novels, is back in its third updated edition. Expert librarian Stephen Weiner--with the crowdsourcing help of professionals in the field, from artists to critics to leading comic store owners--has sifted through the bewildering thousands of graphic novels now available to come up with an outstanding, not-to-be-missed 101." (Publisher's note)

Weing, Drew

★ **Set** to sea. Fantagraphics 2010 un il $16.99

Grades: 8 9 10 11 12   741.5

1. Graphic novels 2. Poets -- Graphic novels 3. Sea stories -- Graphic novels 4. Seafaring life -- Graphic

novels

ISBN 978-1-60699-368-2; 1-60699-368-2

The author "has produced a beautiful gem here, with minimal dialogue, one jolting battle scene, and each small page owned by a single panel filled with art whose figures have a comfortable roundness dredged up from the cartoon landscapes of our childhood unconscious, even as the intensely crosshatched shadings suggest the darkness that sometimes traces the edges of our lives. . . . [This book] is playful, atmospheric, dark, wistful, and wise." Booklist

Weinstein, Lauren

★ **Girl** stories; by Lauren R. Weinstein. Henry Holt 2006 237p il pa $16.95

Grades: 7 8 9 10 11 12 Adult   **741.5**

1. Graphic novels 2. Humorous graphic novels 3. Girls -- Graphic novels 4. Friendship -- Graphic novels

ISBN 978-0-8050-7863-3; 0-8050-7863-0

LC 2005-46205

"Smart, creative Lauren sheds her geeky rep in high school in Weinstein's collection of comic strips, which have to intimacy of a teen's diary. The color-washed sketches have an edgy quality." Booklist

White, Tracy

How I made it to eighteen; a mostly true story. Roaring Brook 2010 151p il $16.99

Grades: 8 9 10 11 12   **741.5**

1. Graphic novels 2. Autobiographical graphic novels 3. Mental illness -- Graphic novels

ISBN 978-1-59643-454-7; 1-59643-454-6

"White's story of a 17-year-old girl's ordeals with depression, addiction, and body image issues is all the more powerful because of its basis in truth. The story follows Stacy Black, whose nervous breakdown leads to her decision to check into the Golden Meadows Hospital for mental health. . . . White's very simple hand-drawn, b&w artistic style enhances the personal touch of the work, creating the effect of an illustrated diary. While text-heavy, the narration is clear-eyed and affecting." Publ Wkly

Wilson, Tom

Ziggy goes for broke; a cartoon collection. Andrews McMeel Publisher 2010 128p il pa $12.99

Grades: 7 8 9 10   **741.5**

1. Graphic novels

ISBN 978-0-7407-9153-6; 0-7407-9153-2

LC 2010481277

"Ziggy brings to life both the simplicities and complexities of daily life. His struggles with lost luggage, insurance, finances, dating, and customer service are sure to hit home with many adults. Teens will find humor in his interactions with his pets and the pigeons in the park. Ziggy's experiences can evoke a contemplative mood or an inspiring and uplifting change of heart. The humor in the one-liners goes hand-in-hand with Wilson's simple yet effective rendering of the little bald man who rarely wears pants." SLJ

Wood, Don

★ **Into** the volcano; a graphic novel. Blue Sky Press 2008 174p il map $18.99

Grades: 2 3 4 5 6 7 8   **741.5**

1. Graphic novels 2. Adventure graphic novels 3. Brothers -- Graphic novels

ISBN 978-0-439-72671-9; 0-439-72671-9

LC 2007-51084

While their parents are away doing research, brothers Duffy and Sumo Pugg go with their cousin, Mister Come-and-Go, to Kokalaha Island, where they meet Aunt Lulu and become trapped in an erupting volcano.

"The visual format combined with nonstop action will keep reluctant readers and adventure fans turning pages to the very end." Voice Youth Advocates

Yakin, Boaz

Marathon; by Boaz Yakin ; [illustrations by Joe Infurnari] First Second 2012 186 p. $16.99

Grades: 6 7 8 9   **741.5**

1. Adventure graphic novels 2. Greece -- History -- Graphic novels 3. Marathon, Battle of, 490 B.C. -- Graphic novels 4. Graphic novels 5. Greece -- History -- Persian Wars, 500-449 B.C. -- Fiction 6. Greece -- History -- Persian Wars, 500-449 B.C. -- Fiction

ISBN 9781596436800; 1596436808

LC 2011030472

This book is a graphical "account of the battle of Marathon" in which "Hippias, former king of Athens, is on his way back with a huge army of Persians to reclaim the throne and crush Athenian democracy. . . . Eucles, Athens' best runner, is charged to race the 153 miles to Sparta in hopes of finding an ally, . . . [returning] with the dismaying news that the Spartans will not be coming in time. He joins the savage fight and then runs 26 more miles over rugged mountains to Athens . . . warning of an impending surprise attack by sea." (Kirkus Reviews)

Yang, Gene Luen, 1973-

★ **American** born Chinese; color by Lark Pien. First Second 2006 233p il pa $16.95

Grades: 7 8 9 10 11 12   **741.5**

1. Graphic novels 2. Chinese Americans -- Graphic novels

ISBN 1-59643-152-0; 978-1-59643-152-2

LC 2005-58105

Michael L. Printz Award, 2007

In this graphic novel by Gene Luen Yang, "Jin Wang is the only Asian American boy in his new school; Danny is a young man deeply embarrassed by his visiting Chinese cousin, portrayed deliberately by the author as an ethnic cliché; and the Monkey King, a figure from Chinese lore, is desperate to be treated like a god. This . . . story relates how three characters overcome hurdles to find satisfaction within themselves." (Library Journal)

"True to its origin as a Web comic, this story's clear, concise lines and expert coloring are deceptively simple yet expressive. Even when Yang slips in an occasional Chinese ideogram or myth, the sentiments he's depicting need no translation. Yang accomplishes the remarkable feat of practicing what he preaches with this book: accept who you are and you'll already have reached out to others." Publ Wkly

★ **Boxers**; Gene Luen Yang ; color by Lark Pien. First Second 2013 328 p. (pbk.) $18.99

Grades: 7 8 9 10 11 12 Adult   **741.5**
1. Historical fiction 2. China -- History -- Boxer
Rebellion, 1899-1901 -- Graphic novels
ISBN 1596433590; 9781596433595

LC 2013947229
National Book Award for Young People's Literature: Fi-
nalist (2013)
Boston Globe-Horn Book Honor: Fiction (2014)

"Life in Little Bao's peaceful rural village is disrupted
when . . . a priest and his phalanx of soldiers . . . arrive."
They start "smashing the village god, appropriating property, and administering vicious beatings for no reason. Little
Bao and his older brothers train in kung fu and swordplay." .
. . Little Bao "becomes the leader of a peasant army, eventually marching to Beijing." (School Library Journal)

"China's Boxer Rebellion is the unlikely backdrop for
this graphic treatment of young villagers on the opposite
sides of history. Bao wants to drive out the white devils that
poison his country with opium and Christianity. Four-Girl is
an unwanted daughter who finds purpose in the missionary
life. Their stories collide in a moment of grace that could
only be penned by the Printz Award-winning author of
'American Born Chinese.'" LJ

★ **Saints**; by Gene Luen Yang and Lark Pien.
First Second 2013 170 p. (pbk.) $15.99
Grades: 7 8 9 10 11 12 Adult   **741.5**
1. Historical fiction 2. China -- History -- Boxer
Rebellion, 1899-1901 -- Graphic novels
ISBN 1596436891; 9781596436893

LC 2013947228
Boston Globe-Horn Book Honor: Fiction (2014)
National Book Award for Young People's Literature: Fi-
nalist (2013)

This graphic novel, by Gene Luen Yang and Lark Pien,
"follows a lonely girl . . . . Unwanted by her family, Four-
Girl isn't even given a proper name until she converts to
Catholicism and is baptized by the very same priest who
bullies Little Bao's village. Four-Girl, now known as Vibiana, leaves home and finds fulfillment in service to the
Church, while Little Bao roams the countryside committing acts of increasing violence as his army grows." (School
Library Journal)

"Yang presents a 'diptych' of graphic novels set during China's Boxer Rebellion. Boxers follows Little Bao,
who learns to harness the power of ancient gods to fight the
spread of Christianity; Saints centers on Four-Girl, who sits
squarely on the other side of the rebellion. Yang's characteristic infusions of magical realism, bursts of humor, and
distinctively drawn characters make for a compelling read."
(Horn Book)

The **Shadow** Hero; Gene Luen Yang. First Sec-
ond 2014 176 p. chiefly color illustrations $17.99
Grades: 6 7 8 9 10   **741.5**
1. Superheroes -- Fiction 2. Comic books, strips, etc. 3.
Chinese Americans -- Fiction
ISBN 1596436972; 9781596436978

This book, by Gene Luen Yang, is about "Green Turtle,
a 1940s comic book hero. . . . The Green Turtle is cast as
an unlikely 19-year-old young man, Hank, the son of Chinese immigrants who own a grocery store in 1940s America.
When his mother is rescued by a superhero, the loving but

overbearing woman decides that it's Hank's fate to become
a hero himself, and she does everything in her power to push
her son in that direction." (School Library Journal)

"Yang and Liew have crafted an origin story for the
Green Turtle, a little-known . . . World War II-era comic
superhero created by cartoonist Chu Hing in 1944. Much
about the series remains a mystery, as Yang shares in an author's note, but according to rumors Hing wanted his star to
be Chinese, and, not surprisingly for the era, his publishers
balked at the idea. Now seventy years later, Yang and Liew
vindicate the cartoonist by imagining the Green Turtle as
'perhaps...the first Asian American superhero.'" Horn Book

Yolen, Jane
Foiled; written by Jane Yolen; artwork by Mike
Cavallaro. First Second 2010 160p il pa $15.99
Grades: 7 8 9 10   **741.5**
1. Graphic novels 2. Fantasy graphic novels 3. Fencing
-- Graphic novels
ISBN 978-1-59643-279-6; 1-59643-279-9

"Besting competitors twice her age in tournaments, and
keeping a strict routine of fencing practice, homework, and
role-playing games, Aliera is a loner and likes it that way—
until she becomes lab partners with the cutest boy in school.
. . . Turns out her new ruby-handled foil is the key to his
interest in her, and to the yet-unseen magical dimension she
must keep in balance. . . . [Yolen] has created a strong, conflicted, and relatable girl hero. . . . Cavallaro's artwork suits
Aliera's monochrome existence, but burst into life when
she finally sees (in color!) the faerie beasties cheering her
on." Booklist

Zornow, Jeff
The **legend** of Sleepy Hollow; adapted and illustrated by Jeff Zornow; based upon the works of Washington Irving. Magic Wagon 2007 un il (Graphic
horror) $18.95
Grades: 5 6 7 8 9 10 11 12   **741.5**
1. New York (State) -- Graphic novels
ISBN 978-1-60270-060-4; 1-60270-060-5

LC 2007-9615
This "is an entertaining and faithful, if much adapted
version of Irving's classic story. Zornow's illustrations are
the highlight of the work, successfully bringing the characters of the story to life." Booklist

**741.6   Graphic design, illustration, commercial
art**

★ **Artist** to artist; 23 major illustrators talk to children about their art. Philomel Books 2007 105p
il $30
Grades: 4 5 6 7   **741.6**
1. Illustrators 2. Illustration of books 3. Picture books
for children
ISBN 978-0-399-24600-5

"This anthology celebrates and elucidates contemporary
picture-book art. . . . Ashley Bryan, Quentin Blake, Leo Li-
onni, Alice Provensen, and Gennady Spirin are among the
contributors, whose comments are formatted as signed let-

ters illustrated with childhood photographs. . . . Each artist includes glorious self-portraits and a gatefold page that reveals a marvelous array of sketches, color mixes, and studio scenes. All readers will find something that piques curiosity or provides insight." Booklist

Ellabbad, Mohieddine

The **illustrator's** notebook; [translated from the Arabic by Sarah Quinn] Groundwood Books/House of Anansi Press 2006 30p il $16.95

Grades: 5 6 7 8   **741.6**

1. Illustrators 2. Illustration of books

ISBN 0-88899-700-0

"Part children's book, part autobiography, part design treatise, this hard-to-categorize Egyptian import is full of wonders from start to finish. Ellabbad uses excerpts from his notebooks to discuss ways of seeing art from an artist's perspective and as someone from an Arabic culture. Printed like the Egyptian edition—read right to left—the pages are magnificently and surprisingly illustrated, juxtaposing Arabic script (English translations appear in the margins), watercolor paintings, pasted-in photos and pictures from comic books, and all manner of characters from Eastern and Western cultures." SLJ

Flath, Camden

Media in the 21st century; artists, animators, and graphic designers. Mason Crest Publishers 2010 64p il (New careers for the 21st century: finding your role in the global renewal) lib bdg $22.95; pa $9.95

Grades: 7 8 9 10   **741.6**

1. Artists 2. Vocational guidance

ISBN 978-1-4222-1816-7 lib bdg; 1-4222-1816-3 lib bdg; 978-1-4222-2037-5 pa; 1-4222-2037-0 pa

LC 2010014935

"Chapters identify and emphasize specific careers—important strengths, necessary aptitudes and interests, education and training, projected earnings, closely related occupations, type of work environment, and predictions for the future of the field. . . . Color photos have a small role amid the many statistics, figures, graphs and charts that support and supplement the . . . [text]." SLJ

Includes bibliographical references

Marcus, Leonard S., 1950-

Randolph Caldecott; the man who could not stop drawing. Leonard S. Marcus. Farrar, Straus & Giroux (BYR) 2013 64 p. (hardcover) $24.99

Grades: 5 6 7 8   **741.6**

1. Picture books for children 2. Illustrators -- England -- Biography

ISBN 0374310254; 9780374310257

LC 2012050406

This book is a biography of Randolph Caldecott, "the illustrator for whom the Caldecott Medal is named." Leonard S. Marcus begins by "describing the changes wrought in 19th-century Great Britain by the steam engine, which eased travel and greatly expanded distribution of media. He details Caldecott's early days clerking in a bank and his search for freelance illustration work, then describes how diligence and charm lead to his first book-illustrating assignment" and then to a career in illustration. (Publishers Weekly)

Neuburger, Emily K.

A **Caldecott** celebration; seven artists and their paths to the Caldecott medal. rev ed.; Walker & Co. 2008 55p il $19.95; lib bdg $20.85

Grades: Adult Professional   **741.6**

1. Illustrators 2. Caldecott Medal 3. Illustration of books

ISBN 978-0-8027-9703-2; 0-8027-9703-2; 978-0-8027-9704-9 lib bdg; 0-8027-9704-0 lib bdg

LC 2007-23132

First published 1998

Profiles seven Caldecott award winning books and their authors, including Robert McCloskey's "Make Way for Ducklings," Marcia Brown's "Cinderella," Maurice Sendak's "Where the Wild Things Are," William Steig's "Sylvester and the Magic Pebble," Chris Van Allsburg's "Jumanji," David Wiesner's "Tuesday," and Mordicai Gerstein's "The Man Who Walked Between the Towers"

"The value of this volume is that Marcus makes these exceptional author/illustrators, and the processes by which they created their award-winning picture books, accessible to children and to adults who value children's literature." SLJ

Tan, Shaun

★ The **bird** king; an artist's notebook. Shaun Tan. Arthur A. Levine Books 2013 128 p. (hardcover : alk. paper) $19.99

Grades: 3 4 5 6 7   **741.6**

1. Artists' notebooks

ISBN 0545465133; 9780545465137

LC 2012016625

This book by author and illustrator Shaun Tan "is a collection of sketches, random jottings, preliminary designs for book, film and theatre projects, sketchbook pages and drawings from life. Each of these represent some aspect of a working process, whereby stories generally evolve from visual research and free-wheeling doodles. They are also 'unfinished' pieces created in a single sitting, not originally intended for publication." (Publisher's note)

741.9 Collections of drawings

Volavkova, Hana

--I never saw another butterfly-- children's drawings and poems from Terezin concentration camp, 1942-1944. edited by Hana Volavková; foreword by Chaim Potok; afterword by Vaclav Havel. expanded 2nd ed; Schocken Bks. 1993 xxii,106p il hardcover o.p. pa $17.50

Grades: 4 5 6 7   **741.9**

1. Child artists 2. Children's writings 3. Holocaust, 1933-1945 4. Terezin (Czechoslovakia: Concentration camp)

ISBN 0-8052-1015-6 pa

LC 92-50477

Original Czech edition, 1959; first American edition published 1964 by McGraw-Hill

"Of the the 15,000 children who passed through Terezin before going to Auschwitz, only 100 lived. This book is a collection of poems and drawings by some of them. . . . This touching book adds another facet to library collections on the Holocaust." SLJ

742   Perspective in drawing

DuBosque, Doug

★ **Draw** 3-D; a step-by-step guide to perspective drawing. Peel Productions 1999 63p il pa $8.99
Grades: 6 7 8 9 10   **742**
  1. Drawing 2. Perspective
  ISBN 0-939217-14-7

                    LC 98-42174

"Using easy-to-follow, step-by-step sketches, DuBosque introduces readers to the techniques of three-dimensional drawing. Beginning with such elementary concepts as depth, he progresses logically through shading, reflections, and multiple vanishing points. The supportive tone encourages novices to keep trying and not become discouraged." SLJ

743   Drawing and drawings by subject

Ames, Lee J.

Draw 50 aliens, UFO's galaxy ghouls, milky way marauders, and other extra terrestrial creatures; [by] Lee J. Ames with Ric Estrada. Doubleday 1998 un il (Draw 50) hardcover o.p. pa $8.95
Grades: 4 5 6 7   **743**
  1. Drawing
  ISBN 978-0-385-49144-0; 0-385-49144-1; 978-0-385-49145-7 pa; 0-385-49145-X pa

                    LC 98-20077

A step-by-step guide to drawing outer space creatures

Draw 50 animals. Doubleday 1974 un il (Draw 50) hardcover o.p. pa $8.95
Grades: 4 5 6 7   **743**
  1. Drawing 2. Animal painting and illustration
  ISBN 978-0-385-07712-5; 0-385-07712-2; 978-0-385-19519-5 pa; 0-385-19519-2 pa

                    LC 73-13083

This book provides step-by-step instructions for drawing animals ranging from penguins and seals to elephants and monkeys

Draw 50 athletes. Doubleday 1985 un il (Draw 50) hardcover o.p. pa $8.95
Grades: 4 5 6 7   **743**
  1. Drawing 2. Athletes in art
  ISBN 978-0-385-19055-8; 0-385-19055-7; 978-0-385-24638-5 pa; 0-385-24638-2 pa

                    LC 83-45569

This book "consists of single-page spreads, each devoted to one athlete. Each figure is drawn in a series of six or more steps, starting with a basic shape and ending with a stylish, somewhat detailed india ink drawing." Booklist

Draw 50 baby animals; the step-by-step way to draw kittens, lambs, chicks, and other adorable off-spring. Broadway Books 2003 un il (Draw 50) hardcover o.p. pa $8.95
Grades: 4 5 6 7   **743**
  1. Drawing 2. Animals in art
  ISBN 978-0-767-91283-9; 0-767-91283-7; 978-0-767-91284-6 pa; 0-767-91284-5 pa

                    LC 2002-33247

Step-by-step instructions for drawing fifty baby animals.

Draw 50 beasties and yugglies and turnover ug-lies and things that go bump in the night. Doubleday 1988 il (Draw 50) hardcover o.p. pa $8.95
Grades: 4 5 6 7   **743**
  1. Drawing 2. Monsters in art
  ISBN 978-0-385-24625-5; 0-385-24625-0; 978-0-385-26767-0 pa; 0-385-26767-3 pa

                    LC 88-16143

Provides step-by-step instructions for drawing monsters, goons, and gruesome beasts

Ames "encourages readers to take plenty of time and suggests very lightly sketching out the step-by-step draw-ings so that mistakes may be rectified. This one, with its popular subject of imaginative monsters and other night-mare inhabitants, will be a sure-fire circulator." SLJ

Draw 50 birds; [by] Lee J. Ames with Tony D'Adamo. Doubleday 1996 un il (Draw 50) hard-cover o.p. pa $8.95
Grades: 4 5 6 7   **743**
  1. Drawing 2. Birds in art
  ISBN 978-0-385-47006-3; 0-385-47006-1; 978-0-385-47163-3 pa; 0-385-47163-7 pa

                    LC 96-27621

Draw 50 boats, ships, trucks & trains. Doubleday 1976 un il (Draw 50) hardcover o.p. pa $8.95
Grades: 4 5 6 7   **743**
  1. Drawing 2. Vehicles in art
  ISBN 978-0-385-08903-6; 0-385-08903-1; 978-0-385-23630-0 pa; 0-385-23630-1 pa

                    LC 75-19011

Step-by-step instructions for drawing fifty different ships, boats, trucks, and trains

Draw 50 buildings and other structures. Double-day 1980 un il (Draw 50) hardcover o.p. pa $8.95
Grades: 4 5 6 7   **743**
  1. Drawing 2. Buildings in art
  ISBN 978-0-385-14401-8; 0-385-14401-6; 978-0-385-41777-8 pa; 0-385-41777-2 pa

                    LC 79-7483

This is similar in format to the author's other books. Step by step procedures enable the reader to draw houses from the U.S. and Ireland, bridges and even a torii (a Japanese gateway)

Draw 50 cats. Doubleday 1986 un il (Draw 50) hardcover o.p. pa $8.95
Grades: 4 5 6 7   **743**
  1. Drawing 2. Cats in art 3. Animal painting and

illustration
ISBN 978-0-385-23484-9; 0-385-23484-8; 978-0-385-24640-8 pa; 0-385-24640-4 pa

LC 86-8964

Step-by-step instructions on how to draw a variety of cats, including domestic breeds, wild cats, cuddly kittens, and celebrity cats

Draw 50 dinosaurs and other prehistoric animals; with a foreword by George Zappler. Doubleday 1977 un il (Draw 50) hardcover o.p. pa $8.95
Grades: 4 5 6 7   **743**
1. Drawing 2. Dinosaurs in art 3. Animal painting and illustration
ISBN 978-0-385-11134-8; 0-385-11134-7; 978-0-385-19520-1 pa; 0-385-19520-6 pa

LC 76-7285

Step-by-step instructions for drawing a variety of dinosaurs and other prehistoric animals

Draw 50 dogs. Doubleday 1981 un il (Draw 50) hardcover o.p. pa $8.95
Grades: 4 5 6 7   **743**
1. Drawing 2. Dogs in art 3. Animal painting and illustration
ISBN 978-0-385-15686-8; 0-385-15686-3; 978-0-385-23431-3 pa; 0-385-23431-7 pa

LC 79-6853

"Ames' six-step drawings guide youngsters along toward fashioning their own canine figures. Each species starts out with an ultrasimple shape; ovals, circles, or rectangular extensions suggest developing proportions that lead to the completed sketch." Booklist

Draw 50 endangered animals; [by] Lee J. Ames with Warren Budd. Doubleday 1992 un il (Draw 50) hardcover o.p. pa $8.95
Grades: 4 5 6 7   **743**
1. Drawing 2. Animals in art 3. Animal painting and illustration
ISBN 978-0-385-41191-2; 0-385-41191-X; 978-0-385-46985-2 pa; 0-385-46985-3 pa

LC 92-23092

Step-by-step instructions on how to draw a variety of threatened species from all over the world

Draw 50 famous faces. Doubleday 1978 un il (Draw 50) hardcover o.p. pa $8.95
Grades: 4 5 6 7   **743**
1. Drawing 2. Portraits
ISBN 978-0-385-13217-6; 0-385-13217-4; 978-0-385-23432-0 pa; 0-385-23432-5 pa

LC 77-15878

Step-by-step instructions for drawing historical figures, statesmen, sports, stars, and entertainers

Draw 50 flowers, trees, and other plants. Doubleday 1994 un il (Draw 50) hardcover o.p. pa $8.95
Grades: 4 5 6 7   **743**
1. Drawing 2. Plants in art 3. Flowers in art 4.

Botanical illustration
ISBN 978-0-385-47004-9; 0-385-47004-5; 978-0-385-47150-3 pa; 0-385-47150-5 pa

LC 94-7192

Draw 50 holiday decorations; [by] Lee J. Ames with Ray Burns. Doubleday 1987 un il (Draw 50) hardcover o.p. pa $8.95
Grades: 4 5 6 7   **743**
1. Drawing 2. Holiday decorations
ISBN 978-0-385-19057-2; 0-385-19057-3; 978-0-385-26770-0 pa; 0-385-26770-3 pa

LC 87-15581

Step-by-step instructions for drawing a variety of holiday subjects such as Baby New Year, Cupid and his arrow, July 4th rockets, turkey, pumpkin, Easter basket, Santa Claus, and a menorah

Draw 50 horses. Doubleday 1984 un il (Draw 50) hardcover o.p. pa $8.95
Grades: 4 5 6 7   **743**
1. Horses in art 2. Animal painting and illustration 3. Drawing -- Technique
ISBN 978-0-385-17640-8; 0-385-17640-6; 978-0-385-17642-2 pa; 0-385-17642-2 pa

LC 81-43646

Step-by-step instructions for drawing different breeds of horses in a variety of poses

Draw 50 monsters, creeps, superheroes, demons, dragons, nerds, dirts, ghouls, giants, vampires, zombies, and other curiosa. Doubleday 1983 un il (Draw 50) hardcover o.p. pa $8.95
Grades: 4 5 6 7   **743**
1. Drawing 2. Monsters in art
ISBN 978-0-385-17637-8; 0-385-17637-6; 978-0-385-17639-2 pa; 0-385-17639-2 pa

LC 80-3006

A "demonstration of how to draw a lengthy lineup of cartoon superheroes and assorted creeps, villains, monsters, and miscellaneous odd creatures. Each page features step-by-step directions, beginning with a simple basic shape that becomes ever more elaborate until the final version sits triumphantly at the bottom right corner of each page." Booklist

Draw 50 people; [by] Lee J. Ames with Creig Flessel. Doubleday 1993 un il (Draw 50) hardcover o.p. pa $8.95
Grades: 4 5 6 7   **743**
1. Portraits 2. Drawing -- Technique
ISBN 978-0-385-41193-6; 0-385-41193-6; 978-0-385-41194-3 pa; 0-385-41194-4 pa

LC 93-20631

[Draw 50 series] Doubleday 1974 21v
Grades: 4 5 6 7   **743**
1. Drawing
Each volume presents step-by-step instructions for drawing a variety of animals, people, or objects

Bergin, Mark

How to draw pets. PowerKids Press 2011 32p il (How to draw) lib bdg $25.25; pa $11.75

Grades: 4 5 6 7   **743**

1. Animals in art 2. Drawing -- Technique
ISBN 978-1-4488-4511-8 lib bdg; 978-1-4488-4517-0 pa

LC 2010049184

"The cover features sketches of a cat, dog, and rabbit, allowing children to see both structure as well as finished product. Inside, the book starts by showing pictures of animals drawn with different materials such as pencils, ink, charcoals, and pastels, and explains what each medium accomplishes. Next comes an introduction to perspective and looks at different parts of animals. The familiar circle method then gets kids drawing pets from head to tails. . . . The amount of information throughout is just right: thorough but not overwhelming." Booklist

Includes glossary

Butkus, Mike

How to draw zombies; discover the secrets to drawing, painting, and illustrating the undead. by Mike Butkus and Merrie Destefano. Walter Foster 2011 128p il map $48.95

Grades: 8 9 10 11 12   **743**

1. Zombies 2. Monsters in art 3. Drawing -- Technique
ISBN 978-1-936309-63-4; 1-936309-63-7

LC 2010052983

"For young artists fascinated by the living dead, this sophisticated drawing book gives step-by-step instructions for creating a variety of unexpected characters. . . . Most of the drawings are done in pencil, but acrylic paints are also occasionally featured. An added bonus is the instructions for giving a final digital touch to the drawings on the computer. . . . Extra bits of zombie lore are added. Fans of the truly terrifying will appreciate the fact that the featured pictures attain a high level of creepiness. . . . Those looking for a zombie drawing book with added bite will find hours of fun with this one." Booklist

Hodges, Jared

Draw furries; how to create anthropomorphic and fantasy animals. by Jared Hodges and Lindsay Cibos. IMPACT Books 2009 127p il pa $22.99

Grades: 7 8 9 10   **743**

1. Animals in art 2. Fantasy in art 3. Drawing -- Technique
ISBN 978-1-60061-417-0 pa; 1-60061-417-5 pa

LC 2009019609

"Hodges and Cibos have created a thorough guide. Describing creatures in terms of a sliding scale from human to animal, they begin with some tips on basic anatomy and style. . . . The instruction is grouped by the kind of animal portrayed. . . . Full-color spreads throughout show what can be achieved with practice, and the book concludes with chapters on color and perspective." SLJ

Masiello, Ralph

Ralph Masiello's ancient Egypt drawing book. Charlesbridge 2008 un $16.95; pa $7.95

Grades: 4 5 6 7   **743**

1. Drawing 2. Egypt -- Civilization
ISBN 978-1-57091-533-8; 978-1-57091-534-5 pa

LC 2007027023

"Masiello starts by showing readers how to draw the Great Pyramid of Khafre using simple shapes and lines. His easy-to-follow instructions gradually build in complexity, as he moves to ancient symbols, then Egyptian gods, Queen Nefertiti, and King Tutankhamen. The finished pictures are colored with mixed media. Concise paragraphs tell more about each subject, including historical context." Horn Book Guide

Includes bibliographical references

Miller, Steve

Dinosaurs : how to draw thunder lizards and other prehistoric beasts; [by] Steve Miller. Watson-Guptill Publications 2008 144p il pa $19.95

Grades: 8 9 10 11 12 Adult   **743**

1. Drawing 2. Dinosaurs in art
ISBN 978-0-8230-9919-1 pa; 0-8230-9919-9 pa

LC 2008531195

First published 2005 with title: Thunder lizards; how to draw fantastic dinosaurs

This offers instruction in drawing dinosaurs based on scientific research and includes examples of the work of such artists as Arthur Adams, Bryan Baugh, Brett Booth, Scott Harman, Gregory S. Paul, and Bernie Wrightson

Includes bibliographical references

Peffer, Jessica

DragonArt; how to draw fantastic dragons and fantasy creatures. Impact Books 2005 127p il pa $19.99

Grades: 5 6 7 8   **743**

1. Dragons 2. Drawing 3. Mythical animals
ISBN 1-58180-657-4

LC 2005013013

This is a guide to drawing dragons and other mythical beasts such as griffins, guardian gargoyles, and deadly basilisks.

"This book has great writing and superb illustrations and manages to do everything right from the front cover to the index." SLJ

Stephens, Jay

Heroes! draw your own superheroes, gadget geeks & other do-gooders. [by] Jay Stephens. Lark Books 2007 64p il $12.95; pa $5.95

Grades: 4 5 6 7   **743**

1. Drawing 2. Superheroes 3. Cartoons and caricatures
ISBN 978-1-57990-934-5; 1-57990-934-5; 978-1-60059-179-2 pa; 1-60059-179-5 pa

LC 2006101661

"Stephens shows just how to draw [superheroes]. . . . Stephens does a good job organizing his material, beginning with a bit of history, then moving quickly to hero heads, . . . and on to masks, disguises, physical features, power effects, and action moves. The brightly colored illustrations offer plenty of how-to info and lots of great heroes, male and female, to use as models." Booklist

745 Decorative arts

Govenar, Alan B.

★ **Extraordinary** ordinary people; five American masters of traditional arts. Candlewick Press 2006 85p il $22.99

Grades: 6 7 8 9   **745**

1. Folk art 2. Handicraft
ISBN 0-7636-2047-5

LC 2005-44864

"The featured artists all live in the United States but come from a variety of cultural backgrounds. The art forms they practice include singing with the Bejing Opera, boat building, waxflower making, weaving, and performing at Mardi Gras. Govenar's interviews with them not only explore their art, but also their history. . . . High-quality color and black-and-white photographs appear throughout." SLJ

Includes bibliographical references

Major, John S.

★ **Caravan** to America; living arts of the Silk Road. [by] John S. Major and Betty J. Belanus. Cricket Bks. 2002 130p il map hardcover o.p. pa $15.95

Grades: 4 5 6 7   **745**

1. Arts 2. Cookbook writers 3. Cooking teachers
ISBN 0-8126-2666-4; 0-8126-2677-X pa

LC 2002-5477

Profiles eight artists and artisans now living in America who are originally from the "Silk Road," an ancient network of caravan trails through which trade goods, ideas, and arts pass between Asia and the Mediterranean

"Full of colorful and informative archival and contemporary photographs and drawings. . . . Each person's story is told in an interesting manner, and information about their specialty and its history is woven throughout the text. . . . Not only is the work informative, but it is handsome as well." SLJ

Includes glossary and bibliographical references

Panchyk, Richard

American folk art for kids; with 21 activities. Chicago Review Press 2004 118p il $16.95

Grades: 4 5 6 7   **745**

1. Handicraft 2. American folk art
ISBN 1-55652-499-4

LC 2004-4879

"Panchyk begins with a general introduction to folk art, and then explicates the main categories of these traditional crafts. He covers a variety of decorative arts, including painting, fabric work, woodworking, and found objects. Each chapter contains several related projects ranging from reverse painting on glass to quilting, stenciling, and tin-can sculpture. . . . Many quality, full-color photos are included." SLJ

Includes bibliographical references

Tejubehan (Singer)

★ **Drawing** from the City; Teju Behan. Pgw 2012 28 p. $35.95

Grades: 3 4 5 6 7 8   **745**

1. India 2. Artists 3. Poverty
ISBN 9380340176; 9789380340173

This "autobiographical art book recounts self-taught artist Teju Behan's journey from an impoverished childhood in rural India, through her family's efforts to improve their lot in a tent city in Mumbai, and into her adulthood, when she lived as a singer and artist with her husband. . . . Hand-screen-printed illustrations comprised of intricate linework and patterns of dots underscore elements of the text." (Kirkus)

745.2 Industrial art and design

Arato, Rona

Design it! the ordinary things we use every day and the not-so-ordinary ways they came to be. illustrations by Claudia Newell. Tundra Books 2010 71p il pa $20.95

Grades: 4 5 6 7   **745.2**

1. Industrial design 2. Inventors 3. Inventions
ISBN 978-0-88776-846-0 pa; 0-88776-846-6 pa

"This book opens with an explanation of what industrial designers do and with whom they work to make better products. Brief chapters then cover such topics as home, communications, lighting, and toy design and include a good-design checklist that takes function, usability, ergonomics, aesthetics, and greenness into consideration. The language is chatty and inviting, and the pages are full of cartoon illustrations and text superimposed on colorful geometric backgrounds. Sidebars offer a wealth of further information." SLJ

Welsbacher, Anne

Earth -friendly design; by Anne Welsbacher. Lerner Publications Company 2009 72p il (Saving our living Earth) lib bdg $30.60

Grades: 5 6 7 8   **745.2**

1. Industrial design 2. Environmental protection
ISBN 978-0-8225-7564-1 lib bdg; 0-8225-7564-7 lib bdg

LC 2007-35925

"Provides a thorough, interesting discussion of multiple aspects of [Earth-friendly design], including historical origins, the current situation, and potential solutions. . . . Photos from around the world accompany discussions. . . . [This is a] solid choice to replace outdated books." SLJ

Includes glossary and bibliographical references

745.5 Handicrafts

Bell-Rehwoldt, Sheri

The **kids'** guide to building cool stuff; by Sheri Bell-Rehwoldt. Capstone Press 2009 32p il (Kids' guides) lib bdg $23.99

Grades: 4 5 6 7   **745.5**

1. Amusements 2. Handicraft 3. Science -- Experiments
ISBN 978-1-4296-2276-9 lib bdg; 1-4296-2276-8 lib bdg

LC 2008-29687

This provides instructions for building such items as a kite, a balloon rocket, a paper boat, a milk carton bird feeder, and a plastic plate hovercraft

Includes glossary and bibliographical references

Blake, Susannah

Crafts for pampering yourself; Susannah Blake. Enslow Publishers, Inc. 2013 32 p. color illustrations (Eco chic) $22.60

Grades: 4 5 6 7 8   **745.5**

1. Cosmetics 2. Handicraft 3. Green products

ISBN 0766043142; 9780766043145

LC 2012045280

In this book, author Susannah Blake offers suggestions on how readers can "have an eco-friendly pampering party with these . . . craft ideas. From lip balm to bath infusion, this book offers easy step-by-step instructions to upcycle, customise and add sparkle to your bathroom routines." (Publisher's note)

"Numbered step-by-step illustrations; a fresh, tween-friendly design; explanations of basic craft skills; and instructions for throwing a 'pamper party' round out the beauty-meets-responsibility fun."

Dobson, Jolie

The **duct** tape book; 25 Projects to Make With Duct Tape. Firefly Books Ltd 2012 144 p. (paperback) $14.95

Grades: 7 8 9 10 11 12   **745.5**

1. Duct tape 2. Handicraft

ISBN 1770850988; 9781770850989

This book by Jolie Dobson on crafting with duct tape "contains 25 . . . projects" with "instructions and color photographs." The projects include a "bike pannier . . . vest . . . purse . . . piggy bank . . . wallet . . . bow ties . . . picture frames . . . knapsack . . . skirt and chaps . . . [and] tissue box." (Publisher's note)

Martin, Laura C.

Nature's art box; from t-shirts to twig baskets: 65 cool projects for crafty kids to make with natural materials you can find anywhere. written by Laura C. Martin; with drawings by David Cain. Storey Bks. 2003 215p il hardcover o.p. pa $16.95

Grades: 4 5 6 7   **745.5**

1. Nature craft

ISBN 1-58017-503-1; 1-58017-490-6 pa

LC 2002-154374

"Each chapter includes information about historical and ethnic uses for the natural substances. Activities are rated by level of difficulty; all have easy-to-follow instructions. Projects range from baskets, picture frames, wreaths, necklaces, and gift wrap to body paint, amulet bags, and painted stones. . . . The projects display a respect for nature and art, and a simple, subtle beauty." SLJ

Includes bibliographical references

Ross, Kathy

Earth -friendly crafts; clever ways to reuse everyday items. [by] Kathy Ross; illustrated by Celine

Malepart. Millbrook Press 2009 48p il lib bdg $26.60

Grades: 3 4 5 6   **745.5**

1. Recycling 2. Handicraft

ISBN 978-0-8225-9099-6 lib bdg; 0-8225-9099-9 lib bdg

LC 2008025481

"This clear, colorful title offers a selection of environmentally focused projects that encourage kids to reduce, reuse, and recycle. Both practical and eye-catching, the projects, from pencil cups to decorative pins, rely on everyday discarded items that many kids will find around their homes. . . . [The crafts] are presented in line drawings that demonstrate the construction step by step along with color photos of the finished product." Booklist

Torres, Laura

Best friends forever! 199 crafts to make and share. Workman Pub. 2004 148p il pa $13.95

Grades: 5 6 7 8   **745.5**

1. Handicraft

ISBN 0-7611-3274-0

LC 2004-45635

"These projects are organized into seven categories: 'Photo Fun,' 'Cool Notes,' 'Gifts to Make Together,' 'Home and School,' 'Fashions,' 'Fun and Games,' and 'Jewelry.' . . . Using clear language, detailed directions, and bright color photos of the finished products, Torres has pulled together a wealth of craft ideas." SLJ

Warwick, Ellen

Everywear; written by Ellen Warwick; illustrated by Bernice Lum. Kids Can Press 2008 80p il (Planet girl) $14.95

Grades: 5 6 7 8   **745.5**

1. Handicraft 2. Fashion accessories 3. Dress accessories

ISBN 978-1-55337-799-3; 1-55337-799-0

"After several opening pages that introduce supplies, . . . very basic stitching skills, and terminology, girls turn to the . . . issue of hair: woven-ribbon bands, jazzed-up chopsticks; fabric-flower-bedecked combs; reversible ponytail wraps. Next come body adornments . . . followed by stuff to stow it in, of clutched, dangled, and toted varieties. Each project features a list of supplies, . . . clearly numbered steps with cartoon-styled illustrations . . . and full-color photograph of the finished item. . . . [This has] genuine sleepover appeal." Bull Cent Child Books

Wolf, Laurie Goldrich

Recyclo -gami; 40 crafts to make your friends green with envy! Running Press Teens 2010 112p il $14.95

Grades: 4 5 6 7   **745.5**

1. Recycling 2. Handicraft

ISBN 978-0-7624-4052-8; 0-7624-4052-X

"Wolf's fun, resourceful projects offer straightforward ways to reuse common materials to make accessories, jewelry, household decorations, games, and gifts. Leftover tissue or wrapping paper can be used to create decoupage plates; old crayons are melted and baked into molds to make multicolored crayons; and unused CDs and DVDs are transformed into funky, freeform bowls when melted in the oven. . . . The ease of most of the activities should inspire readers to see the recycling bin as a potential treasure trove." Publ Wkly

Wolfe, Brian

Extreme face painting; 50 friendly & fiendish demos. [by] Brian and Nick Wolfe. IMPACT Books 2010 127p il pa $24.99

Grades: 6 7 8 9 10 11 12 Adult   **745.5**

1. Face painting

ISBN 978-1-4403-0270-1; 1-4403-0270-7

LC 2010-17861

"This is a guide for experienced artists ready to take their craft to the next level. . . . These instructions show how to use shading and highlights to shape a variety of frightening and whimsical forms. The authors open the book with basic information about materials, colors, and techniques. Then they demonstrate different projects. . . . Each entry has a full-page color photograph of the final product and smaller photos of each step in the painting process. Clearly written instructions appear below each photo. . . . Some of the fiendish visages are quite frightening. The book comes with an informative DVD where the authors demonstrate two of the face paintings from the book. . . . This is a great resource." SLJ

745.54   Papers

Diehn, Gwen

★ **Making** books that fly, fold, wrap, hide, pop up, twist, and turn; books for kids to make. Lark Bks. 1998 96p il hardcover o.p. pa $12.95

Grades: 4 5 6 7   **745.54**

1. Handicraft 2. Paper crafts

ISBN 1-57990-023-2; 978-1-57990-326-8 pa; 1-57990-326-6 pa

LC 97-41037

Presents instructions for making various kinds of books including those that carry messages across space and time as well as those that save words, ideas, and pictures

"Clear directions and diagrams and attractive full-color photographs of completed projects will make it easy for readers to duplicate 18 different folded, wrapped, and pop-up books." Booklist

Includes glossary

Latno, Mark

The **paper** boomerang book; build them, throw them, and get them to return every time. Chicago Review Press 2010 245p il pa $12.95

Grades: 5 6 7 8   **745.54**

1. Boomerangs 2. Paper crafts

ISBN 978-1-56976-282-0 pa; 1-56976-282-1 pa

LC 2010007251

"In a unique . . . guide Latno . . . [explains] how to make, fine-tune, and decorate a type of paper boomerang that can be constructed with commonly available materials and thrown with (relative) safety indoors. The instructions and simply drawn diagrams are embedded in a history of boo-

merangs and throwing sticks, a challenging technical discussion of the physics of boomerangs and gyroscopes, and very detailed descriptions of the characteristics of railroad board (Latno's preferred paper) and alternatives, plus art-and-craft materials that can be used to dress up finished models." SLJ

Includes glossary and bibliographical references

Phillips, Jennifer

Paper artist; creations kids can fold, tear, wear, or share. by Gail D. Green, Kara L. Laughlin, and Jennifer Phillips. Capstone 2013 112 p. col. ill. (pbk.) $12.95

Grades: 4 5 6 7 8   **745.54**

1. Paper crafts 2. Paper work

ISBN 1623700043; 9781623700041

LC 2012032454

"From the garland wind chimes on the front cover to the picture frame on the back cover, the book is filled with easy, creative paper projects set within a clear, mature, magazine design." (Booklist)

"The well-organized layout is stunning, with beautiful photographs and step-by-step instructions that are appealing and simple to follow. Useful extra tips are added if needed." SLJ

745.592   Toys, models, miniatures, related objects

Aranzi Aronzo Inc.

Cute dolls; by Aranzi Aronzo! Vertical Inc. 2007 79p il (Let's make cute stuff) pa $14.95

Grades: 6 7 8 9 10   **745.592**

1. Dolls 2. Handicraft

ISBN 978-1-932234-78-7 pa; 1-932234-78-0 pa

Original Japanese edition 2002

"Familiarity with Japan's Aranzi Aronzo brand . . . won't be necessary to muster an audience for this doll-making book. The felt-trimmed, jersey-cloth, self-consciously cute 'mascots' will be an instant draw for manga-loving teens. . . . Those who attempt one of the 21 rag dolls, for which a sewing machine is recommended, will find the techniques well explained, as well as supported by and entertainingly extended by photographs and small cartoon representations of the doll characters." Booklist

Castleforte, Brian

Papertoy monsters; 50 cool papertoys you can make yourself! Workman Pub. Co. 2010 233p il pa $16.95

Grades: 4 5 6 7   **745.592**

1. Paper crafts 2. Monsters in art

ISBN 978-0-7611-5882-0 pa; 0-7611-5882-0 pa

"Twenty-five 'papertoy' artists contribute 50 original monster designs made of colorful cardstock that can be punched out and glued together to form three dimensional cartoon characters, each with its own quirky backstory. The menagerie includes the tentacled OctoPup, who devours small boats; Yucky Chuck, a serrated-toothed 'mutant lunchbox monster'; and Lester Rottenbottom, a teacher-turned-mad-scientist. The designers' enthusiasm for their subjects should inspire readers to invent their own monsters on the blank templates provided." Publ Wkly

Harbo, Christopher L.

The **kids'** guide to paper airplanes. Capstone Press 2009 32p il (Kids' guides) $23.93

Grades: 4 5 6 7   **745.592**

1. Paper crafts 2. Airplanes -- Models
ISBN 978-1-4296-2274-5; 1-4296-2274-1

LC 2008029688

"Using colorful, vivid, and clear step-by-step illustrations, Harbo demonstrates how to construct everything from the classic Dart to the circular Space Ring to the 18-step Silent Huntress." Booklist

Includes glossary and bibliographical references

Paper airplanes: Captain, level 4. Capstone Press 2010 32p il (Edge books. Paper airplanes) lib bdg $26.65

Grades: 3 4 5 6   **745.592**

1. Paper crafts 2. Airplanes -- Models
ISBN 978-1-4296-4744-1 lib bdg; 1-4296-4744-2 lib bdg

LC 2010001003

This "includes a list of basic materials and an overview of folding instructions and techniques. . . . Along with hints on how to hold the plane for take-off to maximize strengths are suggestions on conducting friendly competitions with the finished products. Sure to keep readers busy for hours." SLJ

Includes bibliographical references

Paper airplanes: Copilot, level 2. Capstone Press 2010 32p il (Edge books. Paper airplanes) lib bdg $26.65

Grades: 3 4 5 6   **745.592**

1. Paper crafts 2. Airplanes -- Models
ISBN 978-1-4296-4742-7 lib bdg; 1-4296-4742-6 lib bdg

LC 2010001004

This "includes a list of basic materials and an overview of folding instructions and techniques. . . . Along with hints on how to hold the plane for takeoff to maximize strengths are suggestions on conducting friendly competitions with the finished products. Sure to keep readers busy for hours." SLJ

Includes bibliographical references

Paper airplanes: Flight school, level 1. Capstone Press 2010 32p il (Edge books. Paper airplanes) lib bdg $26.65

Grades: 3 4 5 6   **745.592**

1. Paper crafts 2. Airplanes -- Models
ISBN 978-1-4296-4741-0 lib bdg; 1-4296-4741-8 lib bdg

LC 2010001005

This "includes a list of basic materials and an overview of folding instructions and techniques. . . . Along with hints on how to hold the plane for takeoff to maximize strengths are suggestions on conducting friendly competitions with the finished products. Sure to keep readers busy for hours." SLJ

Includes bibliographical references

Paper airplanes: Pilot, level 3. Capstone Press 2010 32p il (Edge books. Paper airplanes) lib bdg $26.65

Grades: 3 4 5 6   **745.592**

1. Paper crafts 2. Airplanes -- Models
ISBN 978-1-4296-4743-4 lib bdg; 1-4296-4743-4 lib bdg

LC 2010001006

This "includes a list of basic materials and an overview of folding instructions and techniques. . . . Along with hints on how to hold the plane for takeoff to maximize strengths are suggestions on conducting friendly competitions with the finished products. Sure to keep readers busy for hours." SLJ

Includes bibliographical references

Mercer, Bobby

The **flying** machine book; build and launch 35 rockets, gliders, helicopters, boomerangs, and more. Bobby Mercer. Chicago Review Press 2012 ix, 197 p.p ill. (pbk.) $14.95

Grades: 4 5 6   **745.592**

1. Flight 2. Aeronautics 3. Airplanes -- Models 4. Models and modelmaking 5. Paper airplanes 6. Flying-machines -- Models
ISBN 9781613740866

LC 2011041174

This book provides "step-by-step instructions for 35 aerodynamic projects . . . Physics teacher [Bobby] Mercer . . . here provides . . . directions for building a variety of flying machines including rockets, gliders, helicopters, boomerangs and assorted launchers. An opening chapter called 'Flight School' introduces the Bernoulli principle and four forces: lift, thrust, drag and weight. . . . Each subsequent chapter begins with more flight school, repeating the relevant principles and applying them to the different forms of flying machines described. Many of the constructions use similar techniques and most are not difficult. The models are made of common materials: card stock and old folders, drinking straws, rubber bands and duct tape." (Kirkus Reviews)

Rigsby, Mike

Amazing rubber band cars; easy-to-build wind-up racers, models, and toys. [by] Mike Rigsby. Chicago Review Press 2007 121p il lib bdg $12.95

Grades: 4 5 6 7   **745.592**

1. Toys 2. Handicraft 3. Automobiles -- Models
ISBN 978-1-55652-736-4 lib bdg; 1-55652-736-5 lib bdg

LC 2007013969

This offers instructions for making toy and model cars "using mostly cardboard, glue, pencils, rubber bands, and a few other easily obtainable materials. . . . Readers will learn about corrugated and flat cardboard, and how to use glue and work with templates. Excellent instructions are accompanied by black-and-white photos every step of the way. . . . These projects are fun to construct, and inquisitive minds will be fascinated by the moving cars." SLJ

745.594 Decorative objects

Trusty, Brad

The **kids'** guide to balloon twisting; by Brad and Cindy Trusty. Capstone Press 2011 32p il (Kids' guides) lib bdg $26.65

Grades: 4 5 6 7 **745.594**

1. Balloons 2. Handicraft

ISBN 978-1-4296-5444-9; 1-4296-5444-9

LC 2010036470

Gives kids step-by-step instructions about how to twist balloon animals and other shapes.

"Rare is the kid not dazzled by the squeaking, twisting balloon maestros out there, and this brightly illustrated, step-by-step guide makes it easy—well, easy-ish." Booklist

Includes bibliographical references

745.6 Calligraphy, heraldic design, illumination

Winters, Eleanor

★ **Calligraphy** for kids. Sterling Pub. Co. 2004 128p il $14.95

Grades: 6 7 8 9 **745.6**

1. Calligraphy

ISBN 1-4027-0664-2

LC 2003-23438

This "guide to calligraphy begins with a survey of materials, a glossary, and suggestions on posture and pen and paper positions. Succinct chapters showing how to create a variety of alphabets follow. Winters . . . folds fascinating history into her expert instructions. Her clean layouts showcase beautifully rendered examples and practical exercises." Booklist

746.43 Knitting, crocheting, tatting

Bradberry, Sarah

★ **Kids** knit! simple steps to nifty projects. [by] Sarah Bradberry. Sterling Pub. Co. 2004 96p il hardcover o.p. pa $9.95

Grades: 5 6 7 8 **746.43**

1. Knitting

ISBN 0-8069-7733-7; 978-1-4027-4057-2 pa; 1-4027-4057-3 pa

LC 2004-19375

Presents basic knitting techniques and instructions for making a backpack, pillow, doll, and other simple projects

This "book works equally well for beginners and experienced knitters. . . . Besides the requisite information on knitting and purling, there are invaluable tips about finishing garments, fixing mistakes, and adding embellishments. The projects have been chosen with an eye toward simplicity, yet they have real appeal." Booklist

Haden, Christen

Creepy cute crochet; zombies, ninjas, robots, and more! Quirk Books 2008 96p il $14.95

Grades: 7 8 9 10 11 12 Adult **746.43**

1. Toys 2. Crocheting

ISBN 978-1-5947-4232-3; 1-5947-4232-4

"Japanese-inspired amigurumi (literal translation: 'knitted stuffed toy') is one of the latest crafting crazes, and Haden's first book puts a unique spin on amigurumi by focusing on the creepy side of crocheted creatures. . . . There are . . . crocheted ninjas, a Grim Reaper, Day of the Dead figures, and vampires, all lovingly rendered. Although some beginner information is provided, a basic knowledge of crochet stitches and techniques is assumed." Libr J

Rimoli, Ana Paula

Amigurumi world; seriously cute crochet. Martingale & Co. 2008 80p il $18.95

Grades: 7 8 9 10 11 12 Adult **746.43**

1. Toys 2. Crocheting

ISBN 978-1-5647-7847-5; 1-5647-7847-9

LC 2007041240

This offers instructions for crocheting toy animals such as baby monkeys, bears, owls, hedgehogs, and elephants.

Snow, Tamie

Tiny yarn animals; amigurumi friends to make and enjoy. Home 2008 61p il $12.95

Grades: 8 9 10 11 12 Adult **746.43**

1. Toys 2. Crocheting

ISBN 978-1-55788-530-2; 1-55788-530-3

LC 2008-013935

This is a "book of crocheted animal patterns. The 20 toys in the collection range from the expected (pig, lamb, and mouse) to the quirky (beaver, lemur, and hedgehog) and they are all cheery, colorful, and cute. A beginners' tutorial provides full-color photographic illustrations of basic crochet stitches, and the directions are clear enough for first-time crocheters to understand." Libr J

Turner, Sharon

Find your style and knit it too; by Sharon Turner. Wiley 2007 165p il pa $14.99

Grades: 6 7 8 9 **746.43**

1. Knitting

ISBN 978-0-470-13987-5 pa; 0-470-13987-0 pa

LC 2007028419

This is a "full-service knit book for teens and pre-teens. . . . The book works on every level. Beginning with knitting basics, Turner explains everything from choosing materials to fundamental how-tos . . . to fixing mistakes. . . . [This offers] easy-to-follow patterns, each illustrated by a crisp color photograph." Booklist

746.9 Other textile products

Bertoletti, John C.

How fashion designers use math; math curriculum consultant: Rhea A. Stewart. Chelsea Clubhouse 2010 32p il (Math in the real world) lib bdg $28

Grades: 4 5 6 **746.9**

1. Mathematics 2. Fashion design 3. Fashion --

Vocational guidance
ISBN 978-1-60413-606-7 lib bdg; 1-60413-606-5
lib bdg

LC 2009-22683

This describes how designers use math to measure, create, and produce their fashions, and includes problems to solve and information about how to become a fashion designer

"Color photos of designers in action combine with diagrams that further clarify the easily digestible text." Booklist

Includes glossary and bibliographical references

Spilsbury, Richard

Hi -tech clothes; Richard Spilsbury. Capstone Heinemann Library 2013 56 p. (Design and engineering for STEM) (hb) $33.50

Grades: 5 6 7   746.9

1. Fashion 2. Clothing and dress 3. Fashion design 4. Product life cycle 5. Clothing factories -- Technological innovations

ISBN 1432970321; 9781432970321; 9781432970376

LC 2012013469

This book by Richard Spilsbury focuses on clothes, discussing "design, manufacture, and sale to their use, cleaning, and repair, and eventually their disposal. This book explains what happens during these stages, such as prototyping, the sourcing of materials and components, the manufacturing process, the decisions made by designers, and recycling." (Publisher's note)

Includes bibliographical references and index

★ The **teen** vogue handbook; an insider's guide to careers in fashion. Razorbill 2009 276p il pa $24.95

Grades: 7 8 9 10 11 12   746.9

1. Clothing industry 2. Fashion -- Vocational guidance
ISBN 978-1-59514-261-0; 1-59514-261-4

LC 2009-10626

"Any teen interested in a career in fashion should read this handbook. It is filled with advice from top designers, photographers, models, stylists, makeup artists, writers, and their interns and assistants. They share how they got started and give tips to those interested in a fashion career. This book looks and reads like a magazine on glossy pages filled with photographs and sidebars, but the interviews give pertinent information on every aspect of work in fashion." Voice Youth Advocates

Includes bibliographical references

Vendittelli, Marie

The **Fashion** Book; written by Marie Vendittelli ; illustrated by Sophie Griotto ; translated by Annie Barton ; edited by Jen Wainwright ; concept and design by Laëtitia Robaeys ; cover design by Barbara Ward. Trafalgar Square Books 2013 128 p. $15.99

Grades: 6 7 8 9 10   746.9

1. Fashion design 2. Fashion designers
ISBN 1780551134; 9781780551135

This book is a guide to becoming a confident fashion designer. Marie Vendittelli and Sophie Griotto offer "numerous ideas and tips for drawing, working with color and fabric, designing with the seasons in mind, and accessorizing.

. . . There are brief profiles of famed designers, including Coco Chanel, Yves St. Laurent, and Alexander McQueen." (Publishers Weekly)

Wooster, Patricia

So, you want to work in fashion? how to break into the world of fashion and design. Patricia Wooster. Aladdin 2014 192 p. illustrations (Be what you want series) (hardcover) $19.99

Grades: 4 5 6 7 8   746.9

1. Clothing industry 2. Fashion -- Vocational guidance
ISBN 1582704538; 9781582704524; 9781582704531

LC 2014005268

"In addition to tips and interviews from a variety of fashion professionals, 'So, You Want to Work in Fashion?' includes inspiring stories from young people who are in the industry right now, as well as activities, a glossary, and resources to help you on your way to a successful career in fashion." (Publisher's note)

"A wonderfully comprehensive, accessible and realistic entree into the dynamic world of fashion." Kirkus

Includes bibliographical references

747   Interior decoration

Weaver, Janice

★ It's your room; a decorating guide for real kids. [by] Janice Weaver and Frieda Wishinsky; illustrated by Claudia Dávila. Tundra Books 2006 63p il pa $14.95

Grades: 5 6 7 8   747

1. Interior design
ISBN 0-88776-711-7

"Budding interior designers and readers who want to personalize their rooms will appreciate this title. It is filled with step-by-step guidelines for creating a budget, selecting paint colors and fabrics, organizing closets and desks, laying everything out, and adding finishing touches. The illustrations will be a hit with first-time decorators just starting to develop their own color sense." SLJ

748.2   Blown, cast, decorated, fashioned, molded, pressed glass

Emert, Phyllis Raybin

Art in glass. Lucent Books 2007 112p il map (Eye on art) $32.45

Grades: 7 8 9 10 11 12   748.2

1. Glassware
ISBN 978-1-59018-983-2; 1-59018-983-3

LC 2007-10118

This is an introduction to the history of glassmaking, including its ancient origins, Roman glass, Middle Eastern and Venetian glass, European and American glass, and contemporary glass.

This "title is thoroughly researched and fully referenced, and contains quotations from artists and art historians. The writing is generally clear and fluid. . . . Many of the pages have good-quality photos of artwork and artists." SLJ

Includes bibliographical references

750 Painting and paintings

Raczka, Bob

Unlikely pairs; fun with famous works of art. [by] Bob Raczka. Millbrook Press 2006 31p il lib bdg $23.93; pa $9.95

Grades: 4 5 6 7   **750**

1. Painting 2. Art appreciation
ISBN 0-7613-2936-6 lib bdg; 0-7613-2378-3 pa
LC 2003-14078

Invites the reader to discover fourteen funny stories produced by pairing twenty-eight paintings from different eras and styles

"Raczka deserves an A+ for cleverness. . . . Rodin's The Thinker is juxtaposed with Klee's modernistic painting of a chessboard so that the statue looks as if it is contemplating the next move. Siméon-Chardin's picture of a boy blowing soap bubbles seems to be creating Kandinsky's Several Circles. Each selection takes up a page and is reproduced in crisp color. . . . This book is an amusing way to introduce children to famous works of art." SLJ

751.4 Techniques and procedures

Peot, Margaret

★ **Inkblot**; drip, splat, and squish your way to creativity. Boyds Mills Press 2011 56p il $19.95

Grades: 4 5 6 7   **751.4**

1. Ink painting 3. Art -- Technique 4. Painting -- Technique
ISBN 1-59078-720-X; 978-1-59078-720-5
LC 22010-929541

This describes how to make inkblots and use them in art and as inspiration for writing and other forms of creativity.

"Peot's own entrancing inkblots . . . plus a few guest blots, illustrate every step, showing how the pure blot becomes a final artwork. . . . Readers get clear directions and lively encouragement." Kirkus

Includes bibliographical references

Self, Caroline

Chinese brush painting; [by] Caroline Self and Susan Self. 1st ed.; Tuttle 2007 64p il $16.95

Grades: 7 8 9 10 11 12   **751.4**

1. Calligraphy 2. Ink painting 3. Chinese painting
ISBN 978-0-8048-3877-1; 0-8048-3877-1
LC 2006037838

This "introduces readers to the art of Chinese calligraphy and brush painting. The text is fluid and graceful . . . and the authors wrap succinct accounts of Chinese history and lore around their clear, step-by-step, illustrated instructions." Booklist

Includes bibliographical references

751.7 Specific forms

Bingham, Jane

Graffiti. Raintree 2009 32p il (Culture in action) $28.21; pa $7.99

Grades: 5 6 7 8   **751.7**

1. Graffiti 2. Mural painting and decoration
ISBN 978-1-4109-3401-7; 1-4109-3401-2; 978-1-4109-3418-5 pa; 1-4109-3418-7 pa
LC 2008054323

"According to the time line in the . . . book, graffiti can be traced back to 60,000 BCE and paintings on cave walls. A note on the contents page states that it is illegal to draw on other people's property without permission. The different types of graffiti described are interesting, and some of the artwork is beautiful. A section on problems talks about ugly tags (short nicknames), the expense of cleanup, and how some cities have legal graffiti walls. . . . Well organized and with bright, colorful photography, [this] introductory [title gives] readers good basic knowledge." SLJ

Includes glossary and bibliographical references

Uschan, Michael V., 1948-

Graffiti. Lucent Books 2010 112p il (Eye on art) $33.45

Grades: 7 8 9 10   **751.7**

1. Graffiti
ISBN 978-1-4205-0324-1; 1-4205-0324-3
LC 2010028699

Looks at the history of painted graffiti and explores the work of early artists as well as current ones.

This provides "a great deal of information, so middle school readers may not read them cover to cover; however, ample color photos and quotes from artists will make this . . . appealing to students interested in art." Voice Youth Advocates

Includes glossary and bibliographical references

758 Nature, architectural subjects and cityscapes, other specific subjects

Lanza, Barbara

Enchanting elves; paint elven worlds and fantasy characters. IMPACT Books 2009 128p il pa $22.99

Grades: 7 8 9 10   **758**

1. Fantasy in art 2. Watercolor painting -- Technique
ISBN 978-1-60061-307-4; 1-60061-307-1
LC 2009014745

"Lanza includes watercolors of elves and similar creatures such as sprites, gnomes, and dwarves. Materials and basic skills are explained before moving on to chapters that explore faces, figures, and settings. This approach makes the projects accessible to artists who may not have worked with watercolor before. . . . Useful coloring instructions specify brush and color choices." SLJ

759　Painting -- History, geographic treatment, biography

Serres, Alain

★ **And** Picasso painted Guernica; written and designed by Alain Serres; translated by Rosalind Price. Allen & Unwin Children's 2010 51p il $24.99

Grades: 5 6 7 8　　　　　　　　　　　**759**

1. Artists 2. Painters 3. War in art 4. Spain -- History -- 1936-1939, Civil War

ISBN 978-1-74175-994-5; 1-74175-994-3

Original French edition, 2007

"Serres explains the mechanics of cubism . . . , tells the story of the horrifying German bombing of the civilians of Guernica and Picasso's reaction to it . . . , and finishes by tracing the rest of Picasso's career as he paints 'all the beauty of the world and its monstrous face as well.' The oversize pages are packed with period photographs and color reproductions of Picasso's sketches and paintings, each captioned in detail, with a double gatefold of Guernica at the center. . . . A passionate and intelligent tribute to the transformative power of art." Publ Wkly

759.03　Painting 1400-1599

D'Elia, Una Roman

Painting in the Renaissance; [by] Una D'Elia. Crabtree Pub. Co. 2009 32p il pa $8.95; lib bdg $26.60

Grades: 6 7 8 9　　　　　　　　　　　**759.03**

1. Art -- 15th and 16th centuries

ISBN 978-0-7787-4612-6; 978-0-7787-4592-1

LC 2008-52600

"--Ideal introductions to concepts, people, and events of the Renaissance... succinct and thorough." SLJ

759.05　Painting 1800-1899

Bingham, Jane

Impressionism. Heinemann Library 2008 48p il (Art on the wall) lib bdg $32.86

Grades: 5 6 7 8 9 10　　　　　　　　　**759.05**

1. French painting 2. Impressionism (Art)

ISBN 978-1-4329-1371-7; 1-4329-1371-9

LC 2008020468

This title succeeds "in presenting a bird's-eye view of [Impressionism] without oversimplification. Information on individual artists is included in the broader context of the movement. Visually exciting, with plenty of color, [the layout is] hip and should appeal to the target audience." SLJ

Includes glossary and bibliographical references

Post -Impressionism. Heinemann Library 2009 48p il (Art on the wall) lib bdg $32.86

Grades: 5 6 7 8 9 10　　　　　　　　　**759.05**

1. French painting 2. Postimpressionism (Art)

ISBN 978-1-4329-1369-4; 1-4329-1369-7

LC 2008020464

This book "discusses how Post-Impresssionism developed, examines the distinctive styles of individual Post-Impressionist artists, and looks at how the Post-Impressionists used colour, shape, and composition." Publisher's note

Includes glossary and bibliographical references

Sabbeth, Carol

★ **Monet** and the impressionists for kids; their lives and ideas, 21 activities. Chicago Review Press 2002 140p il pa $17.95

Grades: 5 6 7 8　　　　　　　　　　　**759.05**

1. Art appreciation 2. Impressionism (Art)

ISBN 1-55652-397-1

LC 2001-47191

Discusses the nineteenth-century French art movement known as Impressionism, focusing on the works of Monet, Renoir, Degas, Cassatt, Cezanne, Gauguin, and Seurat

"A beautifully designed introduction to Impressionism. . . . Sabbeth also includes 21 appealing extension activities such as recipes, crafts, games, and writing suggestions. Quality color reproductions on glossy pages, and varied, attractive layouts add to the book." SLJ

Includes glossary and bibliographical references

Van Gogh and the Post-Impressionists for kids; their lives and ideas, 21 activities. Chicago Review Press 2011 160p il pa $17.95

Grades: 4 5 6 7　　　　　　　　　　　**759.05**

1. Artists 2. Painters 3. Art appreciation 4. Postimpressionism (Art)

ISBN 1-56976-275-9; 978-1-56976-275-2

LC 2010053908

"The bulk of this wonderfully thorough study of Post-Impressionist artists focuses on van Gogh, with smaller sections devoted to Paul Gauguin, Henri de Toulouse-Lautrec, Paul Signac, and Emile Bernard. The highly engaging text follows the artists' lives with crisp writing and vivid detail, delving into their family backgrounds and relationships, and doesn't sugarcoat dark and gritty incidents such as van Gogh's self-inflicted ear amputation. Information is well organized. . . . Full-color reproductions of paintings discussed in the text add visual interest, and educational sidebars expound on topics mentioned in the main narrative. . . . With its creative, hands-on ideas for teaching art technique and history, this book is an excellent resource for students and teachers." SLJ

Includes glossary and bibliographical references

759.06　Painting 1900-1999

Barsony, Piotr

The **stories** of the Mona Lisa; an imaginary museum tale about the history of modern art. Piotr Barsony ; translated from the French by Joanna Oseman. Skyhorse Publishing 2012 55 p. (hardcover : alk. paper) $19.95

Grades: 5 6 7 8　　　　　　　　　　　**759.06**

1. Art -- History 2. Mona Lisa (Painting) 3. Art

movements 4. Painting, Modern
ISBN 1620872285; 9781620872284

LC 2012015603

"As [this book by Pietr Barsony] begins, a little girl asks: 'Dad, will you tell me a story?' The story her painter father tells is a history of art with the Mona Lisa as its central character. . . . He takes daughter and readers both on a journey of discovery through an imaginary museum. . . . Each painting is of only the Mona Lisa. . . . They are his own responses to and interpretations of Leonardo's masterpiece as filtered through the vision of other artists and movements." (Kirkus Reviews)

759.13   Painting - United States

Duggleby, John
★ **Story** painter: the life of Jacob Lawrence. Chronicle Bks. 1998 55p il $16.95
Grades: 4 5 6 7   **759.13**
1. Artists 2. Painters 3. Illustrators 4. African American artists 5. African American painters -- Biography 6. African Americans in art
ISBN 0-8118-2082-3

LC 98-4513

This is a biography of the twentieth-century African American painter. Bibliography. "Grades four to eight." (SLJ)

"Lawrence's expressionistic, stark paintings, in excellent full-page color reproduction . . . nicely complement Duggleby's measured account of a materially poor but culturally rich childhood and Lawrence's subsequent struggles and successes." Publ Wkly
Includes bibliographical references

Gherman, Beverly
Norman Rockwell; storyteller with a brush. Atheneum Bks. for Young Readers 2000 57p il $19.95
Grades: 4 5 6 7   **759.13**
1. Artists 2. Painters 3. Illustrators 4. Artists -- United States
ISBN 0-689-82001-1

LC 98-36546

Describes the life and work of the popular American artist who depicted both traditional and contemporary subjects, including children, family scenes, astronauts, and the poor

"The format of the biography is appealing and attractive. The pages are replete with color reproductions of Rockwell's paintings as well as photographs of the man and his family. The text is well researched and authentic; the writing style is free-flowing and the words capture the naturalness of Rockwell's paintings." SLJ
Includes bibliographical references

Lawrence, Jacob
The **great** migration; an American story. paintings by Jacob Lawrence; with a poem in appreciation by Walter Dean Myers. HarperCollins Pubs. 1993 un il hardcover o.p. pa $8.99

Grades: 4 5 6 7   **759.13**
1. African Americans in art
ISBN 0-06-023037-1; 0-06-443428-1 pa

LC 93-16788

"Lawrence is a storyteller with words as well as pictures: his captions and his own 1992 introduction to this book are the best commentary on his work." Booklist

759.9494   Swiss painting

Vry, Silke
Paul Klee for children; Silke Vry ; [translation, Jane Michael] Prestel 2011 95 p. $14.95
Grades: 4 5 6   **759.9494**
1. Art -- Technique 2. Art appreciation
ISBN 3791370774; 9783791370774

LC 2011937220

This book, by Silke Vry, is about the art work of Paul Klee. "Paul Klee's playful paintings are a natural introduction for children to the world of creativity and art. . . . The German artist was fascinated by children's drawings, and incorporated their energy and simplicity into his own work. This . . . introduction to Klee's paintings focuses on the artist's love of color and symbols, his lighthearted technique, and his belief that music and painting were inextricably linked." (Publisher's note)

759.972   Mexican painting

Rubin, Susan Goldman
★ **Diego** Rivera; an artist for the people. by Susan Goldman Rubin. Abrams Books for Young Readers 2013 56 p. (reinforced) $21.95
Grades: 5 6 7 8   **759.972**
1. Mural painting and decoration 2. Painters -- Mexico -- Biography
ISBN 0810984113; 9780810984110

LC 2012010022

This book, by Susan Goldman Rubin, "offers young readers . . . insight into the life and artwork of the famous Mexican painter and muralist [Diego Rivera]. The book follows Rivera's career, looking at his influences and tracing the evolution of his style. His work often called attention to the culture and struggles of the Mexican working class. . . . The book contains a list of museums where you can see Rivera's art, a historical note, a glossary, and a bibliography." (Publisher's note)
Includes bibliographical references and index

761   Printmaking

Boonyadhistarn, Thiranut
Stamping art; imprint your designs. by Thiranut Boonyadhistarn. Capstone Press 2007 31p il $25.26

Grades: 4 5 6 7   **761**
1. Handicraft 2. Rubber stamp printing
ISBN 978-0-7368-6477-0; 0-7368-6477-6
LC 2006004077
This "describes how to make stamps from common household objects, create 'embossed' cards, make a 'stained glass' lampshade, and more." SLJ
Includes bibliographical references

769.56 Postage stamps and related devices

Postal Service guide to U.S. stamps. U.S. Postal Service il
Grades: 8 9 10 11 12 Adult   **769.56**
1. Reference books 2. Postage stamps -- Catalogs
First published 1974 with title: United States stamps and stories. Revised annually
Contains reproductions and histories of U.S. postage stamps

770 Photography, computer art, cinematography, videography

Finger, Brad
13 photos children should know. Prestel 2011
45p il lib bdg $14.95
Grades: 4 5 6   **770**
1. Modern history 2. Documentary photography
ISBN 978-3-7913-7047-7; 3-7913-7047-2
Examines the history behind thirteen popular photographs, including the moon landing, the fall of the Berlin Wall, and the wedding of Prince Charles and Princess Diana.

Kallen, Stuart A.
Photography. Lucent Books 2007 112p il (Eye on art) $32.45
Grades: 7 8 9 10 11 12   **770**
1. Photography -- History
ISBN 978-1-59018-986-3
LC 2007015978
"This volume surveys the history of photography, from the ancient camera obscura to the digital camera. . . . This title offers a clear overview of an art form that many teens both practice and appreciate." Booklist
Includes bibliographical references

770.9 Photography -- History, geographical treatment, biography

Sandler, Martin W.
★ **America** through the lens; photographers who changed the nation. Henry Holt and Co. 2005
182p il $19.95
Grades: 6 7 8 9   **770.9**
1. Photography 2. Photographers
ISBN 0-8050-7367-1
"The photographs are stunning." SLJ

This is a "collective biography of influential photographers whose work made a lasting impact on American society and the world. The chapter-length profiles begin with Civil War photographer Matthew Brady and move forward through sections on Jacob Riis, Edward Curtis, and James Van der Zee, among others. The final chapter celebrates NASA's photographs of space." Booklist
Includes bibliographical references

775 Digital photography

Johnson, Daniel
4 -H guide to digital photography. Voyageur Press 2009 176p $18.99
Grades: 5 6 7 8   **775**
1. Digital photography
ISBN 978-0-7603-3652-6; 0-7603-3652-0
LC 2009014679
This guide to digital photography offers "sound and comprehensive information. . . . [It] features numerous excellent photos that support the text. It explores types of digital cameras, how to take good photos, the complexities of lighting, managing images . . . and the importance of just enjoying this activity. Types of photography such as landscape and macro are explained. The author does an excellent job of discussing the importance of both technological details and artistic creativity." SLJ
Includes glossary

Rabbat, Suzy
Using digital images. Cherry Lake Pub. 2010
32p il (Super smart information strategies) lib bdg $27.07
Grades: 3 4 5 6   **775**
1. Digital photography
ISBN 978-1-60279-954-7 lib bdg; 1-60279-954-7 lib bdg
LC 2010018941
"The information on deciding between file formats and resolutions in Using Digital Images will be tremendously helpful, and some beginner techniques on taking and editing effective photos are a nice bonus." Booklist
Includes bibliographical references

778.5 Cinematography and videography

Green, Julie
Shooting video to make learning fun. Cherry Lake Pub. 2010 32p il (Super smart information strategies) lib bdg $27.07
Grades: 3 4 5 6   **778.5**
1. Digital video recording 2. Motion pictures -- Production and direction
ISBN 978-1-60279-955-4 lib bdg; 1-60279-955-5 lib bdg
LC 2010002022
"This books helps students learn how to harness the power of video to inform and entertain. Includes back-

ground information and practical hands on activities." Publisher's note

Includes bibliographical references

Miller, Ron

★ **Special** effects; an introduction to movie magic. [by] Ron Miller. Twenty-first Century Books 2006 128p il lib bdg $26.60

Grades: 7 8 9 10 **778.5**

1. Cinematography

ISBN 978-0-7613-2918-3 lib bdg; 0-7613-2918-8 lib bdg

LC 2005013123

"An excellent mix of photographs, including stills of special-effects triumphs ranging from the original King Kong to The Matrix and closeups of experts at work, will easily pull browsers and researchers alike to this comprehensive title." Booklist

Includes bibliographical references

779 Photographic images

Delannoy, Isabelle

★ **Our** living Earth; a story of people, ecology, and preservation. by Isabelle Delannoy; photographs by Yann Arthus-Bertrand. Harry N. Abrams 2008 157p il $24.95

Grades: 5 6 7 8 **779**

1. Human geography 2. Aerial photography

ISBN 978-0-8109-7132-5; 0-8109-7132-1

LC 2008010324

"Wrapped around Arthus-Bertrand's magnificent aerial photographs from around the world, Delannoy's text is organized thematically, covering fresh water, biodiversity, oceans, land, cities, people, food, and climate. . . . Readers will find surprising information and images to ponder. Almost every page supports the overarching theme that social justice and environmental protection are inextricably related. . . . This volume raises awareness, and the striking images, astonishing statistics, and brief explanations will stimulate readers to investigate further and possibly to take action." SLJ

780 Music

Bourne, Joyce

The **concise** Oxford dictionary of music; [by] Michael Kennedy and Joyce Bourne Kennedy. 5th ed.; Oxford University Press 2007 839p il (Oxford paperback reference) pa $17.99

Grades: 8 9 10 11 12 Adult **780**

1. Reference books 2. Music -- Dictionaries 3. Musicians -- Dictionaries

ISBN 978-0-19-920383-3 pa; 0-19-920383-0 pa

LC 2007008461

First published 1952 as a condensation of the Oxford companion to music

This music "dictionary includes over 14,000 entries on terms from 'allegro' to 'zingaro,' and on works from 'Aida' to 'Tosca,' as well as instruments and their history, compos-

ers, librettists, musicians, singers, and orchestras. It also [includes] comprehensive works lists for major composers." Publisher's note

McAlpine, Margaret

Working in music and dance; [by] Margaret McAlpine. Gareth Stevens Pub. 2006 54p il (My future career) lib bdg $26

Grades: 6 7 8 9 **780**

1. Dance 2. Music 3. Vocational guidance

ISBN 0-8368-4777-6

LC 2005042522

This is "well organized, full of beautiful photography, and [presents] honest snapshots of the featured professions. . . . Attractive, informative, and interesting." SLJ

Includes bibliographical references

Nathan, Amy

Meet the musicians; from prodigy (or not) to pro. Henry Holt and Co. 2006 168p il $17.95

Grades: 5 6 7 8 **780**

1. Music 2. Musicians

ISBN 978-0-8050-7743-8; 0-8050-7743-X

LC 2005026508

The author "interviewed 13 of the New York Philharmonic's members, representing 11 different instruments, and spun their articulate comments into brief, readable profiles, supplemented by various sidebars—among them, an invaluable feature outlining pros and cons of individual instruments. . . . The practical advice mixed with inspirational words strikes just the right note for children at many different stages in their musical education." Booklist

Includes bibliographical references

780.89 Music - Ethnic and national groups

Tsoukanelis, Erika Alexia

The **Latin** music scene; the stars, the fans, the music. Enslow Publishers 2009 48p il (The music scene) lib bdg $23.93

Grades: 6 7 8 9 **780.89**

1. Music -- Latin America

ISBN 978-0-7660-3399-3 lib bdg; 0-7660-3399-6 lib bdg

LC 2008-48013

This describes the music, stars, clothes, contracts, and world of Latin music

Includes glossary and bibliographical references

780.9 Music -- History, geographic treatment, biography

Solway, Andrew

Africa; [by] Andrew Solway. Heinemann Library 2008 48p il (World of music) lib bdg $22

Grades: 5 6 7 8　　　　　　　　　　**780.9**
　1. African music
　ISBN 978-1-4034-9891-5 lib bdg; 1-4034-9891-1
　lib bdg

　　　　　　　　　　　　LC 2006100578
This introduction to African music discusses "instruments, dance, and vocal styles. The photographs presented are wonderfully colorful in quality and narrative. Topics covered include history, famous players, current styles, pop-culture, politics, world-wide connections." Libr Media Connect
　Includes glossary and bibliographical references

　Latin America and the Caribbean; [by] Andrew Solway. Heinemann Library 2008 48p il (World of music) lib bdg $22
Grades: 5 6 7 8　　　　　　　　　　**780.9**
　1. Music -- Latin America 2. Music -- Caribbean region
　ISBN 978-1-4034-9889-2 lib bdg; 1-4034-9889-X
　lib bdg

　　　　　　　　　　　　LC 2006100579
This introduction to music of Latin America and the Caribbean discusses "instruments, dance, and vocal styles. The photographs presented are wonderfully colorful in quality and narrative. Topics covered include history, famous players, current styles, pop-culture, politics, and world-wide connections." Libr Media Connect
　Includes glossary and bibliographical references

Underwood, Deborah
　Australia, Hawaii, and the Pacific; [by] Deborah Underwood. Heinemann Library 2008 48p il (World of music) lib bdg $22
Grades: 5 6 7 8　　　　　　　　　　**780.9**
　1. Music -- Hawaii 2. Music -- Oceania 3. Music -- Australia
　ISBN 978-1-4034-9894-6 lib bdg; 1-4034-9894-6
　lib bdg

　　　　　　　　　　　　LC 2006100576
This introduction to the music of Australia, Hawaii, and the Pacific discusses "instruments, dance, and vocal styles. The photographs presented are wonderfully colorful in quality and narrative. Topics covered include history, famous players, current styles, pop-culture, politics, and world-wide connections." Libr Media Connect
　Includes glossary and bibliographical references

780.92　Music -- Biography

Earls, Irene
　Young musicians in world history. Greenwood Press 2002 139p il $44.95
Grades: 8 9 10 11 12　　　　　　　　**780.92**
　1. Musicians
　ISBN 0-313-31442-X

　　　　　　　　　　　　LC 2001-40559
Profiles thirteen musicians who achieved high honors and fame before the age of twenty-five, representing many different time periods and musical styles
　"A useful introduction to some of the musical giants of the last four centuries." SLJ
　Includes glossary and bibliographical references

Roberts, Russell, 1953-
　★ **Scott** Joplin; by Russell Roberts. Mitchell Lane Publishers 2012 47 p. ill. (chiefly col.) (library) $29.95
Grades: 6 7 8 9　　　　　　　　　　**780.92**
　1. Jazz music 2. Composers -- United States -- Biography
　ISBN 1612282733; 9781612282732

　　　　　　　　　　　　LC 2012008633
This book by Russ Roberts is part of the American Jazz series and looks at musician Scott Joplin. Within each entry, "information about the subjects' childhoods and preparation for their musical careers is included, as are the positive and negative aspects of their adult lives. Their contributions to the world of jazz are . . . explored." (School Library Journal)
　Includes bibliographical references (pages 44-45), chronology (pages 40-41) and index.

780.94　Music of Europe

Allen, Patrick
　Europe; [by] Patrick Allen. Heinemann Library 2008 48p il (World of music) lib bdg $22
Grades: 5 6 7 8　　　　　　　　　　**780.94**
　1. Music -- Europe
　ISBN 978-1-4034-9890-8 lib bdg; 1-4034-9890-3
　lib bdg

　　　　　　　　　　　　LC 2006100580
This introduction to European music discusses "instruments, dance, and vocal styles. The photographs presented are wonderfully colorful in quality and narrative. Topics covered include history, famous players, current styles, pop-culture, politics, and world-wide connections." Libr Media Connect
　Includes glossary and bibliographical references

781.2　Elements of music

Tomecek, Steve
　Music; [by] Stephen M. Tomecek. Chelsea House 2010 165p il (Experimenting with everyday science) $35
Grades: 5 6 7 8　　　　　　　　　　**781.2**
　1. Musical instruments 2. Science -- Experiments 3. Music -- Acoustics and physics
　ISBN 978-1-60413-169-7; 1-60413-169-1

　　　　　　　　　　　　LC 2009-22333
This "offers 25 easy-to-perform activities that illuminate scientific principles. . . . Topics . . . include the history of music, various instruments, and how scientific principles explain the creation of sounds. . . . Following each experiment are additional comments on the science behind the experiment and link to the one that follows. Photographs, simple diagrams and illustrations, and sample data tables appear throughout, and the [layout is] clear and colorful." SLJ
　Includes bibliographical references

781.6 Traditions of music

Kallen, Stuart A.

The **history** of classical music. Lucent Bks. 2002 112p il (Music library) $28.70

Grades: 6 7 8 9   **781.6**

1. Music -- History and criticism

ISBN 978-1-59018-123-2; 1-59018-123-9

LC 2002-3815

This follows classical music "from Medieval times into the present, closing with a description of avant-garde composer John Cage's 4′33″—4 minutes and 33 seconds of silence. . . . [The volume is] greatly enhanced by fascinating excerpts from primary material, including articles, letters, and diaries, often in the words of the composer or musician. . . . Students reading for reports or for personal interest will find much useful information." Booklist

Includes bibliographical references

781.62 Folk music

Handyside, Chris

★ **Folk.** Heinemann Library 2006 48p il (A history of American music) lib bdg $31.43

Grades: 5 6 7 8   **781.62**

1. Folk music

ISBN 1-4034-8150-4

This history of folk music is an "excellent, clear [introduction]. . . . [It] starts with the post-Civil War era, when folklorists gathered slave songs. It describes the music's commercial success beginning with early recordings of the Carter family and Jimmie Rodgers in the 1920s and continuing with Leadbelly, Woody Guthrie, Pete Seeger, and the many musicians who became popular during the folk revival of the late 50s and early 60s. . . . It concludes with sections on folk rock, punk rock, and the future of folk music." SLJ

Includes bibliographical references

781.642 Country music

Bertholf, Bret

★ **Long** gone lonesome history of country music; by Bret Bertholf. Little, Brown 2007 un il $18.99

Grades: 4 5 6   **781.642**

1. Country music

ISBN 978-0-316-52393-6; 0-316-52393-3

LC 2005016036

"This tongue-in-cheek overview features a folksy narrative of how and why country music developed in the barns and back roads of rural America. The text . . . covers instruments, early recordings, yodeling, . . . the Great Depression, gospel, movie cowboys, a 'paper-doll' spoof of singers' costumes, hillbilly jazz, World War II, . . . and much more. While poking fun at itself . . . the book offers a vast amount of historical fact amid a multitude of caricatures of country stars. . . . The ever-changing backgrounds and fonts with colored-pencil and crayon illustrations carry an amazing variation of detail." SLJ

Kallen, Stuart A.

The **history** of country music. Lucent Bks. 2002 112p il (Music library) $28.70

Grades: 6 7 8 9   **781.642**

1. Country music

ISBN 1-59018-124-7

LC 2002-664

A history of country music which discusses its roots, influences, and various types including bluegrass, honky tonk, cowboy music, western swing, and rockabilly

Includes bibliographical references

781.643 Blues

Handyside, Chris

★ **Blues**; [by] Christopher Handyside. Heinemann Library 2006 48p il (A history of American music) lib bdg $31.43

Grades: 5 6 7 8   **781.643**

1. Blues music

ISBN 1-4034-8148-2

LC 2005019280

"This book charts the development of this uniquely American Music form from the 1600s through to the present. It also shows how social, economic, and regional factors have all helped to shape the blues over time and, in turn, how this music has gone on to influence other genres." Publisher's note

Includes glossary and bibliographical references

781.644 Soul

Handyside, Chris

★ **Soul** and R&B; [by] Christopher Handyside. Heinemann Library 2006 48p il (A history of American music) lib bdg $31.43

Grades: 5 6 7 8   **781.644**

1. Soul music 2. Rhythm and blues music

ISBN 1-4034-8153-9

LC 2005019324

"This book charts the development of this uniquely American music form from the 1800s through to the present. It also shows how social, economic, and regional factors have all helped to shape soul and R&B over time and, in turn, how this music has gone on to influence other genres." Publisher's note

Includes glossary and bibliographical references

Mendelson, Aaron A

★ **American** R & B; Gospel grooves, funky drummers, and soul power. Aaron Mendelson. Twenty-First Century Books 2013 64 p. (lib. bdg. : alk. paper) $30.60

Grades: 7 8 9 10 11 12   **781.644**

1. Blues music 2. American songs 3. African American music 4. Soul music -- History and criticism 5. Rhythm and blues music -- History and criticism

ISBN 0761345019; 9780761345015

LC 2011045636

Author Aaron Mendelson's book focuses on R&B music. "Rhythm and blues music evolved from all sorts of sounds: swinging jazz, gritty blues, and African American spiritual songs. The music's smooth mix of styles made it unique, and its passionate performers made it a sensation. Ever since Ray Charles hit the charts in the 1950s, R & B fans have held it down on dance floors. And R & B singers have belted out messages of love and calls for social change." (Publisher's note)

Includes bibliographical references and index.

781.646 Reggae

Neely, Daniel T.

The **reggae** scene; the stars, the fans, the music. [by] Peter Manuel and Daniel T. Neely. Enslow Publishers 2009 48p il (The music scene) lib bdg $23.93

Grades: 6 7 8 9 **781.646**

1. Reggae music

ISBN 978-0-7660-3400-6 lib bdg; 0-7660-3400-3 lib bdg

LC 2008-48014

This describes the music, stars, clothes, contracts, and world of reggae music

This "is clearly written, well organized, and copiously illustrated with full-color photographs of noted performers." SLJ

Includes glossary and bibliographical references

781.65 Jazz

Handyside, Chris

★ **Jazz**; [by] Christopher Handyside. Heinemann Library 2006 48p il (A history of American music) lib bdg $31.43

Grades: 5 6 7 8 **781.65**

1. Jazz music

ISBN 1-4034-8149-0

LC 2005019305

"This book charts the development of this uniquely American Music form from the 1600s through to the present. It also shows how social, economic, and regional factors have all helped to shape Jazz over time and, in turn, how this music has gone on to influence other genres." Publisher's note

Includes glossary and bibliographical references

Kallen, Stuart A.

The **history** of jazz. Lucent Bks. 2003 112p il (Music library) lib bdg $21.96

Grades: 6 7 8 9 **781.65**

1. Jazz music

ISBN 1-59018-125-5

LC 2002-2220

This follows jazz music's "evolution from its African roots through contemporary forms. [The volume is] greatly enhanced by fascinating excerpts from primary material, including articles, letters, and diaries, often in the words of the composer or musician. . . . Students reading

for reports or for personal interest will find much useful information." Booklist

Includes bibliographical references

Marsalis, Wynton

★ **Jazz** A-B-Z; [by] Wynton Marsalis and Paul Rogers; with biographical sketches by Phil Schaap. Candlewick Press 2005 un il $24.99

Grades: 5 6 7 8 9 10 **781.65**

1. Jazz music 2. Jazz musicians

ISBN 978-0-7636-3434-6

LC 2005-48448

This is an illustrated alphabetically arranged introduction to jazz musicians.

This is a "witty, stunningly designed alphabet catalog. . . . The biographical sketches and notes on poetic forms by Phil Schaap are concise and genuinely informative. . . . Rogers's pastiche full-page portraits, his use of expressive typography and the smaller vignettes he sprinkles throughout are bound to heighten any reader's appreciation of both the musicians and the music. . . . [Marsalis offers] clever . . . poems, wordplays, odes and limericks." N Y Times Book Rev

781.66 Rock (Rock 'n' roll)

Aberback, Brian

Black Sabbath; pioneers of heavy metal. Enslow Publishers 2010 112p il (Rebels of rock) lib bdg $31.93

Grades: 6 7 8 9 10 **781.66**

1. Rock musicians 2. Black Sabbath (Musical group)

ISBN 978-0-7660-3379-5 lib bdg; 0-7660-3379-1 lib bdg

LC 2009012295

"Refreshingly levelheaded and loaded with sourced quotes, [this is] that rare middle-grade biography . . . that is able to trace a band's history, revel in its rock awesomeness, and be blunt about such things as drug abuse, all the while keeping things at an age-appropriate keel. . . . Packed with pics, it's all here." Booklist

Includes bibliographical references

Bowe, Brian J.

The **Ramones**; American Punk Rock Band. Enslow Publishers 2010 128p il (Rebels of rock) lib bdg $31.93

Grades: 6 7 8 9 10 **781.66**

1. Rock musicians 2. Ramones (Musical group)

ISBN 978-0-7660-3233-0; 0-7660-3233-7

LC 2008040362

"Avid fans of rock music will find [this title] appealing, entertaining, and enlightening. [The] book begins with a brief introduction to the band through an account of a major musical event. Subsequent chapters include short biographies of the various band members. . . . Direct quotes add life to the well-written and lively [narrative]. . . . Descriptions and analyses of the music and albums offer insight into the impact [the] band had on today's rock music." SLJ

Includes bibliographical references

Burlingame, Jeff

Aerosmith; hard rock superstars. Enslow Publishers 2010 112p il (Rebels of rock) lib bdg $31.93
Grades: 6 7 8 9 10 **781.66**
    1. Rock musicians 2. Aerosmith (Musical group)
    ISBN 978-0-7660-3236-1; 0-7660-3236-1
                        LC 2009006469
  "Avid fans of rock music will find [this title] appealing, entertaining, and enlightening. [The] book begins with a brief introduction to the band through an account of a major musical event. Subsequent chapters include short biographies of the various band members. . . . Direct quotes add life to the well-written and lively [narrative]. . . . Descriptions and analyses of the music and albums offer insight into the impact [the] band had on today's rock music." SLJ
  Includes bibliographical references

George-Warren, Holly

Shake, rattle, & roll; the founders of rock & roll. words by Holly George-Warren; pictures by Laura Levine. Houghton Mifflin 2001 un il hardcover o.p. pa $5.95
Grades: 3 4 5 6 **781.66**
    1. Musicians 2. Rock music
    ISBN 0-618-05540-1; 0-618-43229-9 pa
                        LC 00-33480
  "A wonderfully entertaining browsing book that will also fill a gap in most music collections." SLJ
  "Brief profiles of 15 men and women whose music 'created a sound that changed our culture forever,' including Bill Haley, Fats Domino, Little Richard, Elvis Presley, Carl Perkins, Wanda Jackson and Ritchie Valens." N Y Times Book Rev

Goodmark, Robyn

Girls rock; how to get your group together and make some noise. [by] Robyn Goodmark; illustrated by Adrienne Yan. Billboard Books 2008 178p il pa $13.95
Grades: 6 7 8 9 10 **781.66**
    1. Rock music 2. Bands (Music) 3. Women musicians
    ISBN 978-0-8230-9948-1; 0-8230-9948-2
                      LC 2008007386
  This "shows the ins, outs, and good and bad things that come with starting a band and making it successful. . . . The conversational tone and quizzes throughout give the presentation the feel of a teen magazine. . . . Clever cartoon illustrations appear throughout. . . . Not only does this book provide the technical assistance newbie musicians might need, but it also provides advice on choosing a band name and more emotional topics like how to find creative inspiration. This is a wonderful guide for any girl who wants to start a band." SLJ

Guillain, Charlotte

Punk; music, fashion, attitude! Raintree 2011 32p il (Culture in action) lib bdg $29
Grades: 5 6 7 8 **781.66**
    1. Punk rock music
    ISBN 978-1-4109-3916-6; 1-4109-3916-2
                      LC 2009052585

  "Guillain delves into the history of punk and follows its influence on modern art, fashion, and politics. . . . [This volume is] quick, interesting, up-to-date . . . with plenty of supportive, captioned, full-color photographs. [It] also [provides] related project suggestions." SLJ
  Includes glossary and bibliographical references

Handyside, Chris

★ Rock. Heinemann Library 2006 48p il (A history of American music) lib bdg $31.43
Grades: 5 6 7 8 **781.66**
    1. Rock music
    ISBN 1-4034-8150-4
  This history of rock music is an "excellent, clear [introduction]. . . . [It] opens with the mid-1950s advent of rock n roll and continues with surf music, girl groups, the British invasion, psychedelic rock, heavy metal, punk, and grunge. Featured musicians range from Elvis Presley to Kurt Cobain." SLJ
  Includes bibliographical references

Kallen, Stuart A.

The history of rock and roll. Lucent Bks. 2003 128p il (Music library) lib bdg $21.96
Grades: 6 7 8 9 **781.66**
    1. Rock music
    ISBN 1-59018-126-3
                      LC 2002-3923
  "Kallen traces the history of rock and roll from its early 1950s beginnings through its most significant developments to date." Publisher's note
  Includes bibliographical references

Mead, Wendy

The alternative rock scene; the stars, the fans, the music. [by] Wendy S. Mead. Enslow Publishers 2009 48p il (The music scene) lib bdg $23.93
Grades: 6 7 8 9 **781.66**
    1. Rock music
    ISBN 978-0-7660-3401-3 lib bdg; 0-7660-3401-1 lib bdg
                      LC 2008-48015
  This describes the music, stars, clothes, contracts, and world of alternative rock music
  This "is clearly written, well organized, and copiously illustrated with full-color photographs of noted performers." SLJ
  Includes glossary and bibliographical references

Moore, Sarah W.

The rap scene; the stars, the fans, the music. Enslow Publishers 2009 48p il (The music scene) lib bdg $23.95
Grades: 6 7 8 9 **781.66**
    1. Rap music
    ISBN 978-0-7660-3397-9 lib bdg; 0-7660-3397-X lib bdg
                      LC 2008048011
  This is about the music, stars, clothes, contracts, and world of rap music
  Includes glossary and bibliographical references

Nichols, Travis

★ **Punk** rock etiquette; the ultimate how-to guide for punk, underground, DIY, and indie bands. Roaring Brook Press 2008 128p il pa $10.95

Grades: 7 8 9 10 11 12   **781.66**

1. Punk rock music 2. Music industry -- Vocational guidance

ISBN 978-1-59643-415-8; 1-59643-415-5

LC 2008-11706

"Lively, knowledgeable, witty, and wise, this title offers a sound foundation in the social economics of indie rock. . . . From how to put together a band that functions rather than fights, to designing and creating appealing merchandise and running a successful tour, this heavily illustrated guide covers every aspect of how to be a bona fide DIY rock star for the twenty-first century." Voice Youth Advocates

Roberts, Jeremy

The **Beatles**; music revolutionaries. Twenty-First Century Books 2011 112p il (USA Today lifeline biographies) lib bdg $33.26

Grades: 6 7 8 9 10   **781.66**

1. Rock musicians 2. Beatles

ISBN 978-0-7613-6421-4; 0-7613-6421-8

LC 2010031041

This "takes readers on an accessible tour of the band's rollicking run from Liverpool's underground scene to its nearly decade-long perch atop the charts. Written in a straightforward, reportorial style, . . . the book offers a fine dissection of the Beatle phenomenon. . . . As easy on the eyes as it is fun to read." Booklist

Includes   discography,   filmography,   and bibliographical references

The **Rolling** Stone encyclopedia of rock & roll; edited by Holly George-Warren and Patricia Romanowski; consulting editor, Jon Pareles. rev and updated for the 21st century; Fireside 2001 1114p il $27

Grades: 7 8 9 10 11 12 Adult   **781.66**

1. Reference books 2. Rock music -- Encyclopedias

ISBN 0-7432-0120-5

LC 2001-40285

"The scope is excellent: few works can compete in terms of blanket coverage of the major rock'n'roll players." Libr J

Includes discographies

Sanna, Ellyn

Hip -hop: a short history; [by] Rosa Waters. Mason Crest Publishers 2007 64p il (Hip-hop) lib bdg $22.95; pa $7.95

Grades: 4 5 6 7   **781.66**

1. Hip-hop 2. Rap music

ISBN 1-4222-0109-0 lib bdg; 978-1-4222-0109-1 lib bdg; 1-4222-0261-5 pa; 978-1-4222-0261-6 pa

LC 2006004320

"The book begins with a visually eye-popping time line, then moves quickly through the roots of hip-hop—through slavery, the civil rights movement, and the black church. Musical influences included gospel, blues, jazz, funk, and rock. . . . A wide-awake design, full-color photos, and a winning writing style put a positive spin on this musical phenomenon." Booklist

Includes glossary and bibliographical references

Tanner, Mike

Flat -out rock; ten great bands of the '60s. Annick Press 2006 158p $24.95; pa $12.95

Grades: 7 8 9 10   **781.66**

1. Rock music

ISBN 1-55451-036-8; 1-55451-035-X pa

"Ten of the great bands in the forefront of the music scene from 1964 to 1974 are highlighted here. Tanner offers a description of how each group came together and how its distinctive style developed. The discussion includes the social and political history of the period and shows how the musicians were impacted by broader events. . . . The narrative style will hold readers' attention. . . . This book would be a helpful resource." SLJ

Witmer, Scott

Bookings & gigs. ABDO 2009 32p il (Rock band) lib bdg $27.07

Grades: 6 7 8 9   **781.66**

1. Rock music 2. Music industry -- Vocational guidance

ISBN 978-1-60453-689-8 lib bdg; 1-60453-689-6 lib bdg

LC 2009-6606

This offers advice to rock bands on how to find places to perform

"Copious examples and photos of bands drawn from a wide chronological and stylistic range ensure that every reader, from metalheads (Metallica) to Linkin Park fans will find something of interest here." SLJ

Includes glossary

History of rock bands. ABDO 2010 32p il (Rock band) lib bdg $27.07

Grades: 6 7 8 9   **781.66**

1. Rock music -- History and criticism

ISBN 978-1-60453-692-8 lib bdg; 1-60453-692-6 lib bdg

LC 2009-6609

This is a history of rock music

"Copious examples and photos of bands drawn from a wide chronological and stylistic range ensure that every reader, from metalheads (Metallica) to Linkin Park fans will find something of interest here." SLJ

Includes glossary

Managing your band. ABDO 2010 32p il (Rock band) lib bdg $27.07

Grades: 6 7 8 9   **781.66**

1. Rock music 2. Music industry -- Vocational guidance

ISBN 978-1-60453-693-5 lib bdg; 1-60453-693-4 lib bdg

LC 2009-6610

This offers information and advice about managing a rock music band

"Copious examples and photos of bands drawn from a wide chronological and stylistic range ensure that every reader, from metalheads (Metallica) to Linkin Park fans will find something of interest here." SLJ

Includes glossary

Recording. ABDO 2010 32p il (Rock band) lib bdg $27.07

Grades: 6 7 8 9   781.66

1. Rock music 2. Sound recordings 3. Music industry -- Vocational guidance

ISBN 978-1-60453-694-2 lib bdg; 1-60453-694-2 lib bdg

LC 2009-6611

This offers information and advice on recording for rock bands

"Copious examples and photos of bands drawn from a wide chronological and stylistic range ensure that every reader, from metalheads (Metallica) to Linkin Park fans will find something of interest here." SLJ

Includes glossary

The **show**. ABDO 2010 32p il (Rock band) lib bdg $27.07

Grades: 6 7 8 9   781.66

1. Rock music 2. Music industry -- Vocational guidance

ISBN 978-1-60453-695-9 lib bdg; 1-60453-695-0 lib bdg

LC 2009-6612

This offers information and advice about performing for rock bands

"Copious examples and photos of bands drawn from a wide chronological and stylistic range ensure that every reader, from metalheads (Metallica) to Linkin Park fans will find something of interest here." SLJ

Includes glossary

782.1   Vocal forms

Siberell, Anne

★ **Bravo!** brava! a night at the opera; behind the scenes with composers, cast, and crew. introduction by Frederica von Stade. Oxford Univ. Press 2001 64p il $19.95

Grades: 4 5 6 7   782.1

1. Opera

ISBN 0-19-513966-6

LC 2001-21206

"An excellent resource for reports, this unusual book has an exceptional range of topics for younger students and is an essential purchase for upper elementary and middle school music programs." SLJ

Includes glossary and bibliographical references

782.25   Small-scale vocal forms

Cooper, Michael L.

★ **Slave** spirituals and the Jubilee Singers. Clarion Bks. 2001 86p il music $16

Grades: 7 8 9 10   782.25

1. Spirituals (Songs) 2. African American music 3.

Jubilee Singers (Musical group)

ISBN 0-395-97829-7

LC 00-65854

"The first half of this book traces the development of spirituals from African musical traditions and discusses the place of religion in the lives of the slaves. The second half focuses on Fisk University's Jubilee Singers. . . . Illustrated with many archival prints and photographs, the book includes extensive annotated source notes and the words and music to seven of the spirituals popularized by the Jubilee Singers." SLJ

Includes bibliographical references

Giovanni, Nikki

★ **On** my journey now; looking at African-American history through the spirituals. [by] Nikki Giovanni; foreword by Arthur C. Jones. 1st ed.; Candlewick Press 2007 116p $18.99; pa $8.99

Grades: 7 8 9 10   782.25

1. Spirituals (Songs) 2. African Americans -- History

ISBN 978-0-7636-2885-7; 0-7636-2885-9; 978-0-7636-4380-5 pa; 0-7636-4380-7 pa

LC 2006051695

"Personal and passionate, Giovanni's short narrative talks about the sacred songs first sung by slaves, tracing how the people in bondage created the great spirituals to tell their stories, and what the songs still mean to us today." Booklist

782.42   Songs

Crossingham, John

★ **Learn** to speak music; a guide to creating, performing, and promoting your songs. written by John Crossingham; illustrated by Jeff Kulak. Owl-Kids 2009 96p il $27.95; pa $17.95

Grades: 6 7 8 9   782.42

1. Songwriters and songwriting 2. Music industry -- Vocational guidance

ISBN 978-1-897349-64-9; 1-897349-64-5; 978-1-897349-65-6 pa; 1-897349-65-3 pa

This is an "incredibly readable book. Crossingham uses a comfortable, conversational tone with a sensibility that will appeal to teens and preteens alike. . . . The exceptional graphic design and illustrations . . . enhance and broaden the musical themes addressed with humor, wit, and style." SLJ

Guerinot, Jim

Legends, icons & rebels; music that changed the world. by Robbie Robertson, Jim Guerinot, Sebastian Robertson, and Jared Levine. Tundra Books 2013 128 p. (hardcover) $29

Grades: 6 7 8 9 10 11 12   782.42

1. Musicians 2. Music -- History and criticism

ISBN 1770495711; 9781770495715; 9781770495739

LC 2013931040

Authors Robbie Robertson, Jim Guerinot, Jared Levine, and Sebastian Robertson discuss "twenty-seven musical legends. Short profiles chronicle personal stories and achievements of extraordinarily talented artists whose innovations changed the landscape of music for generations to come.

Carefully compiled like any great playlist, the line-up features . . . Ray Charles to Johnny Cash, Chuck Berry to Bob Dylan." (Publisher's note)

"In this oversize, weighty volume, music-industry-veteran authors offer collected anecdotal sketches, including personal memories, of twenty-seven music "risk-takers" such as Aretha Franklin, the Beatles, and Bob Dylan. Their meteoric careers, many touched by tragedy, are justly celebrated. A timeline of these artists' first recordings (1925-1968) ends the book; includes two CDs of sparkling audio quality with one iconic song by each." (Horn Book)

★ **National** anthems of the world; edited by Michael Jamieson Bristow. 11th ed.; Weidenfeld & Nicolson 2006 629p $90

Grades: 5 6 7 8 9 10 11 12 Adult   **782.42**
1. National songs
ISBN 0-304-36826-1

First published 1943 in the United Kingdom with title: National anthems of the United Nations and France

This volume contains national anthems of about 198 nations, including melody and accompaniment. Words are presented in the native language with transliteration provided where necessary. English translations follow. Brief historical notes on the adoption of each anthem are included

"An essential reference resource for all libraries." Libr J

Silverman, Jerry

Songs and stories of the Civil War. 21st Cent. Bks. (Brookfield) 2002 96p il lib bdg $30.60

Grades: 5 6 7 8   **782.42**
1. United States -- History -- 1861-1865, Civil War -- Songs
ISBN 0-7613-2305-8

LC 2001-35795

Provides a history of the music and lyrics of a dozen Civil War songs, describing the circumstances under which they were created and performed

"Black-and-white reproductions of period photos, engravings, paintings, and drawings illustrate the text. A good resource offering an interesting sidelight on the times." Booklist

Includes discography and bibliographical references

Stotts, Stuart

★ **We** shall overcome; a song that changed the world. by Stuart Stotts; foreword by Pete Seeger; with illustrations by Terrance Cummings. Clarion Books 2009 72p il $18

Grades: 5 6 7 8   **782.42**
1. African Americans -- Civil rights -- Songs
ISBN 978-0-547-18210-0; 0-547-18210-4

LC 2009022578

"This smart, effective telling has few missteps. From the informative black-and-white photographs to the solid back matter to the CD sung by Pete Seeger, it is a complete package." Booklist

Witmer, Scott

Songwriting. ABDO 2010 32p il (Rock band) lib bdg $27.07

Grades: 6 7 8 9   **782.42**
1. Rock music 2. Vocational guidance 3. Songwriters and songwriting
ISBN 978-1-60453-696-6 lib bdg; 1-60453-696-9 lib bdg

LC 2009-6613

This offers advice on songwriting for rock bands

"Copious examples and photos of bands drawn from a wide chronological and stylistic range ensure that every reader, from metalheads (Metallica) to Linkin Park fans will find something of interest here." SLJ

Includes glossary

Yolen, Jane

★ **Apple** for the teacher; thirty songs for singing while you work. collected and introduced by Jane Yolen; music arranged by Adam Stemple; art edited by Eileen Michaelis Smiles. Harry N. Abrams 2005 117p il $24.95

Grades: 4 5 6 7   **782.42**
1. Songs 2. Work -- Songs
ISBN 0-8109-4825-7

LC 2004-24404

"Yolen has brought together a collection of 30 work songs . . . which represent a wide variety of occupations. . . . She introduces each job, explaining unusual vocabulary and references in the songs. . . . The artwork . . . is elegant. Ranging from sculpture to paintings to needlework, each selection of Americana has been carefully matched to the occupation, beautifully reproduced on high-quality paper, and meticulously identified." Booklist

782.42166   Rock (Rock 'n' roll) songs

Behnke, Alison Marie

Death of a dreamer; the assassination of John Lennon. Alison Marie Behnke. Twenty-First Century Books 2012 96 p.

Grades: 5 6 7 8   **782.42166**
1. Assassination 2. Rock musicians -- Political activity 3. Rock musicians -- England -- Biography 4. Rock musicians 5. Murder -- New York (State) -- New York 6. Rock musicians -- England -- Biography 7. Murderers -- New York (State) -- Biography
ISBN 0822590360; 9780822590361

LC 2010005550

In this young adult book, "[t]win narratives converge in New York City on December 8, 1980, when John Lennon was murdered by Mark David Chapman. [Alison Marie] Behnke calls the murder an assassination, and by the general definition of the word--'to murder (a usually prominent person) by sudden or secret attack, often for political reasons'--the murder of John Lennon might qualify. Lennon was political by the end of his life, writing 'Give Peace a Chance,' which became the anthem of the peace movement, but he was hardly a revolutionary, as Behnke terms him. Chapman was not especially political, and he didn't really seem to know why he attacked Lennon; it was certainly not from any well-thought-out political motives, as the author herself describes." (Kirkus)

Includes bibliographical references (p. 92), discography

(p. 93), filmography (p. 93), and index

783 Music for single voices

Fishkin, Rebecca Love

Singing; a practical guide to pursuing the art. Compass Point Books 2010 48p il (Performing arts) lib bdg $28.65

Grades: 5 6 7 8   **783**

1. Singing 2. Vocational guidance

ISBN 978-0-7565-4362-4 lib bdg; 0-7565-4362-2 lib bdg

LC 2010012607

This guide on a singing career includes tips on education, technique, and more.

"Meant for students contemplating a career in the field . . . [this book goes] beyond basic introductions and into more detail about what it takes to make it as a professional. . . . [The author maintains] . . . a frank, realistic tone, stressing the importance of hard work and dedication. Great [resource] . . . for those wanting to make their passions more than just a hobby." SLJ

Includes glossary and bibliographical references

Landau, Elaine

Is singing for you? Lerner Publications 2011 40p il (Ready to make music) lib bdg $27.93

Grades: 4 5 6 7   **783**

1. Singing

ISBN 978-0-7613-5427-7 lib bdg; 0-7613-5427-1 lib bdg

LC 2009052350

Helps readers explore the art of singing. This book covers the basics, including tips for getting started and info on vocal technique.

"Landau covers all the bases so that prospective musicians have the information they need. . . . Kids thinking about taking up an instrument will find . . . [this book] helpful in their decision-making process." SLJ

Includes glossary and bibliographical references

784.19 Instruments

Baines, Anthony

The **Oxford** companion to musical instruments; written and edited by Anthony Baines. Oxford University Press 1992 404p il $85

Grades: 8 9 10 11 12 Adult   **784.19**

1. Reference books 2. Musical instruments -- Dictionaries

ISBN 0-19-311334-1

LC 92-8635

Based on The New Oxford companion to music (1983)

This volume presents alphabetically arranged entries for musical instruments. "The individual entries cover specific instruments and families thereof (e.g., Wind Instruments) as well as their representation in different countries (e.g., Africa) and time periods (e.g., Baroque). . . . Playing tech-

niques, a brief history, and a list of the major repertory are [discussed]." Booklist

Helsby, Genevieve

★ **Those** amazing musical instruments; [by] Genevieve Helsby; with Marin Alsop as your guide. Sourcebooks Jabberwocky 2007 176p il $19.95

Grades: 4 5 6 7 8 9   **784.19**

1. Musical instruments

ISBN 978-1-4022-0825-6; 1-4022-0825-1

LC 2007013821

This is "a guide to instruments commonly found in an orchestra. . . . Utilizing large print; ample, colorful illustrations; and an open format, the book is logically organized into chapters about each of the musical instrument families, including keyboards, the voice, and modern electronic instruments. Throughout, readers are prompted to listen to the accompanying CD-ROM, which features more than 100 musical samples. Information is clearly presented, and the author's enthusiasm for her subject is contagious." SLJ

Kallen, Stuart A.

The **instruments** of music. Lucent Bks. 2003 112p il (Music library) lib bdg $27.45

Grades: 6 7 8 9   **784.19**

1. Musical instruments

ISBN 1-59018-127-1

LC 2001-6609

This volume "includes history, cultural background, and the place of individual instruments in music from classical orchestra to rock and roll." Publisher's note

Includes bibliographical references

VanHecke, Susan

★ **Raggin'**, jazzin', rockin' a history of American musical instrument makers. Boyds Mills Press 2011 136p il $17.95

Grades: 5 6 7 8 9   **784.19**

1. Musical instruments 2. C. G. Conn Ltd. 3. C. F. Martin & Co. 4. Manufacturing executives 5. Musical instrument makers

ISBN 1-59078-574-6; 978-1-59078-574-4

LC 2010-04877

This is a history of American musical instrument making, including the stories of the Zildjian family's cymbals, Steinway's pianos, Charles Gerard Conn's brass instruments, C. F. Martin's guitars, William F. Ludwig's drums, Hammond keyboards, Fender electric guitars, and Moog synthesizers.

"Musicians and music lovers look no further. [This] is a book for everyone. . . . This is an interesting book." Voice Youth Advocates

Includes bibliographical references

784.192 Techniques and procedures for instruments themselves

Pagliaro, Michael

The **musical** instrument desk reference; a guide to how band and orchestral instruments work. Michael J. Pagliaro. Scarecrow Press 2012 189 p. (cloth : alk. paper) $65

Grades: Adult Professional   **784.192**

1. Musical instruments 2. Wind instruments -- Construction 3. Bowed stringed instruments -- Construction

ISBN 0810882701; 9780810882706; 9780810882713

LC 2012007244

This book "begins with an 'easy-reference quick start' section on woodwinds, followed by more in-depth chapters on the flute, clarinet, saxophone, oboe, and the bassoon. For the brass instruments, there are fingering charts, an expanded in-depth study chapter, and a chapter on functioning. Nonfretted string instruments . . . are also given a chapter on producing sound and an expanded in-depth study chapter. The final chapter consists of an overview of percussion instruments." (Booklist)

784.2   Full orchestra (Symphony orchestra)

Ganeri, Anita

★ The **young** person's guide to the orchestra; Benjamin Britten's composition on CD narrated by Ben Kingsley. book written by Anita Ganeri. Harcourt Brace & Co. 1996 56p il $25

Grades: 4 5 6 7   **784.2**

1. Orchestra 2. Music appreciation 3. Musical instruments

ISBN 0-15-201304-0

LC 95-41478

"Accompanying this book on orchestral music is a CD featuring Britten's A Young Person's Guide to the Orchestra . . . as well as Dukas' The Sorcerer's Apprentice. The book begins with an overview of the orchestra and then introduces around groups of instruments, explaining a bit of their history and their sound's distinctive quality. . . . The book also introduces eight famous composers, world music, Benjamin Britten, and the background of The YoungPerson's Guide to the Orchestra. . . . Handsome and useful." Booklist

Includes glossary

784.4   Light orchestra

Bolden, Tonya

Take -off! American all-girl bands during WW II. Alfred A. Knopf 2007 76p il $18.99; lib bdg $21.99

Grades: 6 7 8 9   **784.4**

1. Jazz musicians 2. Women musicians

ISBN 978-0-375-82797-6; 0-375-82797-8; 978-0-375-92797-3 lib bdg; 0-375-92797-2 lib bdg

LC 2006-24523

"To appreciate this book, readers need at least a nodding acquaintance with swing music. The accompanying CD will help, and Bolden's introduction, which features opinions from Benny Goodman, Ella Fitzgerald, and others, gets things off to a good start. Then, using fascinating archival material . . . she goes on to discuss pioneering female jazz

bands. . . . Bolden [uses] a fresh style of writing, as bouncy as the music." Booklist

Includes glossary and bibliographical references

785   Ensembles with only one instrument per part

Marx, Trish

Steel drumming at the Apollo; the road to Super Top Dog. by Trish Marx; photographs by Ellen B. Senisi. Lee & Low Books 2007 56p il $22

Grades: 4 5 6 7   **785**

1. Musicians 2. Bands (Music) 3. Steel drum (Musical instrument) 4. Apollo Theatre (New York, N.Y.)

ISBN 978-1-60060-124-8; 1-60060-124-3

LC 2007008947

"Marx traces the band's progress through the tiers of competition in clear evocative prose depicting the visceral experience of performing as well as the hard work of practice and composition. Senisi's color photographs enliven every page." SLJ

786   Specific instruments and their music

Witmer, Scott

Drums, keyboards, and other instruments. ABDO 2009 32p il (Rock band) lib bdg $27.07

Grades: 6 7 8 9   **786**

1. Drums 2. Rock music 3. Musical instruments 4. Keyboards (Electronics)

ISBN 978-1-60453-690-4 lib bdg; 1-60453-690-X lib bdg

LC 2009-6607

This offers information for rock bands about keyboards, drums, and other instruments

"Copious examples and photos of bands drawn from a wide chronological and stylistic range ensure that every reader, from metalheads (Metallica) to Linkin Park fans will find something of interest here." SLJ

Includes glossary

786.2   Keyboard instruments

Batten, Jack

Oscar Peterson; the man and his jazz. Jack Batten. Tundra Books of Northern New York 2012 165 p. (hardcover) $19.95

Grades: 6 7 8   **786.2**

1. Jazz music -- History and criticism

ISBN 1770492690; 9781770492691

LC 2011940582

This children's book, by Jack Batten, is a biography of the Jazz pianist Oscar Peterson. "Oscar Peterson released over 200 recordings, won seven Grammy Awards, received the Order of Canada and is considered to have been one of the greatest jazz pianists of all time. This new biography . . . is the story of a black kid from a Montreal ghetto who reached acclaim in the great music halls of the world." (Publisher's note)

Reich, Susanna

★ **Clara** Schumann; piano virtuoso. Clarion Bks. 1999 118p il $18; pa $9.95

Grades: 5 6 7 8 **786.2**

1. Pianists 2. Women composers
ISBN 0-395-89119-1; 0-618-55160-3 pa

LC 98-24510

Describes the life of the German pianist and composer who made her professional debut at age nine and who devoted her life to music and to her family

"This thoroughly researched book draws on primary sources, both Clara's own diaries and her voluminous correspondence with her husband. . . . Reich's lucid, quietly passionate biography is liberally illustrated with photographs and reproductions." Horn Book Guide

786.9 Drums and devices used for percussive effects

Landau, Elaine

Are the drums for you? Lerner Publications 2011 40p il (Ready to make music) lib bdg $27.93

Grades: 4 5 6 7 **786.9**

1. Drums 2. Percussion instruments
ISBN 978-0-7613-5426-0 lib bdg; 0-7613-5426-3 lib bdg

LC 2009-48971

Hear what professional drummers like about their instrument, and learn what skills a good drummer needs.

"Landau covers all the bases so that prospective musicians have the information they need. . . . Kids thinking about taking up an instrument will find . . . [this book] helpful in their decision-making process." SLJ

Includes glossary and bibliographical references

787 Stringed instruments (Chordophones)

Ganeri, Anita

Stringed instruments. Smart Apple Media 2011 32p il (How the world makes music) lib bdg $28.50

Grades: 4 5 6 **787**

1. Stringed instruments
ISBN 978-1-599-20480-2

LC 2010042418

Describes various stringed instruments from around the world including familiar instruments such as the guitar and violin, along with other traditional instruments such as the Japanese Koto and Indian lutes.

787.2 Violins

Landau, Elaine

Is the violin for you? Lerner Publications 2011 40p il (Ready to make music) lib bdg $27.93

Grades: 4 5 6 7 **787.2**

1. Violins
ISBN 978-0-7613-5423-9 lib bdg; 0-7613-5423-9 lib bdg

LC 2009045609

Hear what professional violinists like about their instrument, and learn what skills a good violinist needs.

"Landau covers all the bases so that prospective musicians have the information they need. . . . Kids thinking about taking up an instrument will find . . . [this book] helpful in their decision-making process." SLJ

Includes glossary and bibliographical references

787.8 Plectral lute family

Ellis, Rex M.

With a banjo on my knee; a musical journey from slavery to freedom. Watts 2001 160p il lib bdg $28

Grades: 7 8 9 10 **787.8**

1. Banjos 2. African American music
ISBN 0-531-11747-2 lib bdg; 978-0-531-11747-7 lib bdg

LC 00-33035

This is a "well-written, attractive work, which unveils a segment of social history both powerful and far reaching." Booklist

Includes glossary, discography and bibliographical references

787.87 Guitars

Landau, Elaine

Is the guitar for you? Lerner Publications 2011 40p il (Ready to make music) lib bdg $27.93

Grades: 4 5 6 7 **787.87**

1. Guitars
ISBN 978-0-7613-5424-6 lib bdg; 0-7613-5424-7 lib bdg

LC 2009-48750

Hear what professional guitarists like about their instrument, and learn what skills a good guitarist needs.

"Landau covers all the bases so that prospective musicians have the information they need. . . . Kids thinking about taking up an instrument will find . . . [this book] helpful in their decision-making process." SLJ

Includes glossary and bibliographical references

Witmer, Scott

Guitars & bass. ABDO 2010 32p il (Rock band) lib bdg $27.07

Grades: 6 7 8 9 **787.87**

1. Guitars 2. Rock music
ISBN 978-1-60453-691-1 lib bdg; 1-60453-691-8 lib bdg

LC 2009-6608

This offers information about guitars and basses for rock bands

"Copious examples and photos of bands drawn from a wide chronological and stylistic range ensure that every reader, from metalheads (Metallica) to Linkin Park fans will find something of interest here." SLJ

Includes glossary

788   Wind instruments (Aerophones)

Landau, Elaine

Is the flute for you? Lerner Publications 2011 40p il (Ready to make music) lib bdg $27.93
Grades: 4 5 6 7   **788**
1. Flutes
ISBN 978-0-7613-5420-8 lib bdg; 0-7613-5420-4 lib bdg

LC 2009048970

Hear what professional flutists like about their instrument, and learn what skills a good flutist needs.

"Landau covers all the bases so that prospective musicians have the information they need. . . . Kids thinking about taking up an instrument will find . . . [this book] helpful in their decision-making process." SLJ

Includes glossary and bibliographical references

Is the trumpet for you? Lerner Publications 2011 40p il (Ready to make music) lib bdg $27.93
Grades: 4 5 6 7   **788**
1. Trumpet
ISBN 978-0-7613-5422-2 lib bdg; 0-7613-5422-0 lib bdg

LC 2009048280

Hear what professional trumpeters like about their instrument, and learn what skills a good trumpeter needs.

"Landau covers all the bases so that prospective musicians have the information they need. . . . Kids thinking about taking up an instrument will find . . . [this book] helpful in their decision-making process." SLJ

Includes glossary and bibliographical references

788.7   Saxophones

Golio, Gary

Spirit seeker; John Coltrane's musical journey. by Gary Golio ; paintings by Rudy Gutierrez. Clarion Books 2012 48 p. (hardcover) $17.99
Grades: 3 4 5 6 7   **788.7**
1. Music and religion 2. Creation (Literary, artistic, etc.) 3. Saxophonists -- United States -- Biography 4. Jazz musicians -- United States -- Biography
ISBN 0547239947; 9780547239941

LC 2011045948

Includes bibliographical references and discography.

This book, by Gary Golio, illustrated by Rudy Gutierrez, explores the musical career of Jazz saxophonist John Coltrane. "Growing up, John was a seeker. He wondered about spirit, and the meaning of life. And whether music could be a key to unlocking those mysteries. . . . This is the story of a shy, curious boy from a deeply religious family who grew up to find solace and inspiration in his own unique approach to both spirituality and music." (Publisher's note)

Rice, Earle

★ Charlie Parker; by Earle Rice Jr. Mitchell Lane Publishers 2012 47 p. ill. (library) $29.95
Grades: 6 7 8 9   **788.7**
1. Jazz musicians -- Biography 2. African American musicians -- Biography 3. Jazz musicians -- United States -- Biography
ISBN 1612282660; 9781612282664

LC 2012008628

This biography of musician Charlie Parker, part of the American Jazz series, presents an "account of Parker's drug-abuse-shortened life and stellar career--along with a . . . technical, specific analysis of his musical education and innovations." It includes "period photos of 'Bird' and his bandmates, plus a time line, a discography, and . . . sets of print and web resources for children and adults alike." (Booklist)

Includes discography (p. [41]), bibliographical references (p. 44), and index.

788.9   Brass instruments (Lip-reed instruments)

Boone, Mary

★ Dizzy Gillespie; by Mary Boone. Mitchell Lane Publishers 2013 47 p. ill. (some col.) (library) $29.95
Grades: 6 7 8 9   **788.9**
1. Jazz musicians -- Biography 2. Gillespie, Dizzy, 1917-1993 3. Bop (Music) -- History and criticism 4. Jazz musicians -- United States -- Biography
ISBN 9781612282725

LC 2012008630

This book by Mary Boone, part of the "American Jazz" series, presents a "biography of Jazz great Dizzy Gillespie written for intermediate through middle school age readers. . . . Gillespie owed much of his success to an elementary school teacher who worked to harness his energy and anger by recruiting him for the school band. . . . In the 1940s, the trumpet virtuoso and respected improviser teamed up with musician Charlie Parker to lay the foundations for bebop." (Publisher's note)

Includes discography (p. 42), bibliographical references (p. 44-45), and index.

Orr, Tamra

★ Miles Davis; by Tamra Orr. Mitchell Lane Publishers 2012 47 p. ill. (library) $29.95
Grades: 6 7 8 9   **788.9**
1. Picture books for children 2. Jazz musicians -- United States
ISBN 1612282652; 9781612282657

LC 2012008632

This book by Tamra Orr is part of the American Jazz series and looks at Miles Davis. "Known to jazz lovers around the world as the Prince of Darkness, Miles Davis lived a roller-coaster life of highs and lows. . . . You can follow his lows of grappling with the power of drug and alcohol addiction and racial prejudice to his highs of achieving world fame and appreciation, plus becoming a husband, father, and grandfather." (Publisher's note)

Includes discography (pages 41-42), bibliographical references (pages 44-45), and index.

790   Recreational and performing arts

Glenn, Joshua

Unbored; the essential field guide to serious fun. [compiled by] Joshua Glenn & Elizabeth Foy Larsen ; design by Tony Leone. Bloomsbury USA 2012 352 p. (hardback) $25

Grades: 5 6 7   **790**

1. Games 2. Amusements 3. Handicraft 4. Recreation
ISBN 1608196410; 9781608196418

LC 2012012368

This activity book by Elizabeth Foy Larsen and Joshua Glen, illustrated by Heather Kasunick and Mister Reusch, "provides kids with information to round out their world view and inspire them to learn more. From how-tos on using the library or writing your representative to a graphic history of video games, the book isn't shy about teaching. Yet the bulk of the 350-page mega-resource presents hands-on activities." (Publisher's note)

790.1   General kinds of recreational activities

Ball, Jacqueline A.

Traveling green. Bearport Pub. 2009 32p il (Going green) lib bdg $25.27

Grades: 4 5 6 7   **790.1**

1. Travel -- Environmental aspects
ISBN 978-1-59716-964-6 lib bdg; 1-59716-964-1 lib bdg

LC 2009-19836

"Color photographs (most full page) and a few diagrams accompany the informative text[s]. . . . . Overall, the [book] . . . is user-friendly and covers topics that are not easily found elsewhere." SLJ

Includes glossary and bibliographical references

Ferrer, J. J.

The art of stone skipping and other fun old-time games; stoopball, jacks, string games, coin flipping, line baseball, jump rope, and more. by J.J. Ferrer ; illustrated by Todd Dakins. Charlesbridge Pub., Inc. 2012 192 p. (paperback) $14.95

Grades: K 1 2 3 4 5 6 7 8 9 10 11 12 Adult   **790.1**

1. Games
ISBN 1936140748; 9781936140749

LC 2012015052

This book, by J. J. Ferrer, offers a "collection of timeless games that guarantees kids a good time- by themselves, with a group of friends, or with family. Includes ball games . . . , card games . . . , sack races, and old favorites such as Duck, Duck, Goose and Red Rover. There is also a chapter for car games. Simple instructions explain the rules, how many people can play, the object of the game, and what you need." (Publisher's note)

Includes bibliographical references and index.

Hines-Stephens, Sarah

Show off; how to do absolutely everything one step at a time. [by] Sarah Hines Stephens and Bethany Mann. Candlewick Press 2009 224p il $18.99

Grades: 5 6 7 8   **790.1**

1. Amusements 2. Handicraft 3. Recreation
ISBN 978-0-7636-4599-1; 0-7636-4599-0

LC 2009015847

"This lively illustrated activity book delivers concise instructions for a variety of indoor and outdoor activities. Projects include crafts, pranks and magic tricks; ideas for nature exploration; and other purely entertaining feats. . . . The instructions are heavy on graphics and light on detail, making for an eye-catching but potentially frustrating experience. But readers should enjoy the irreverence and variety." Publ Wkly

Rowell, Victoria

Tag, toss & run; 40 classic lawn games. Paul Tukey & Victoria Rowell. Storey Pub. 2012 207 p. (pbk. : alk. paper) $14.95

Grades: Adult Professional   **790.1**

1. Games 2. Outdoor recreation
ISBN 1603425608; 9781603425605

LC 2011049410

This book on "family lawn games" presents a "guide to 40 time-tested favorites -- from classics like capture the flag, croquet, badminton, and bocce to the lesser-known Cherokee marbles, cornhole, and Kubb. The authors offer a quick overview of the basic structure of each game, as well as strategies for playing and tips for creating fun variations." (Publisher's note)

Includes bibliographical references and index.

791   Public performances

Lusted, Marcia Amidon

Entertainment. ABDO Pub. Company 2011 112p il (Inside the industry) $23.95

Grades: 5 6 7 8   **791**

1. Performing arts -- Vocational guidance
ISBN 978-1-61714-799-9; 1-61714-799-0

LC 2010041255

This "well-designed [book describes] a variety of careers in [entertainment]. Because [it helps] readers assess if these positions are suitable for their personality types and backgrounds, the [title is a] good [choice] for career exploration and self-discovery. [It is] also useful for research and reports. . . . Sidebars and full-color photos appear throughout." SLJ

Includes bibliographical references

791.4   Motion pictures, radio, television

Gilbert, Sara D., 1943-

The story of Pixar; Sara Gilbert. Creative Education 2014 46 p. illustrations (chiefly color) (Built for success) (hardcover : alkaline paper) $37.10

Grades: 6 7 8 9   **791.4**

1. Animated films 2. Computer animation 3. Pixar (Firm) 4. Animated films -- United States 5. Computer animation -- United States
ISBN 1608183963; 9781608183968

LC 2013029615

This book, by Sara Gilbert, presents a "look at the origins, leaders, growth, and innovations of Pixar, the movie studio founded in 1986, which is one of the most successful producers of computer-animated films today." (Publisher's note)

"This series that profiles well-known businesses (previous books include The Story of Google, The Story of Microsoft, The Story of Amazon, and The Story of Nike, which SLJ called "interesting and well written") continues with some more winners. Though books on corporate America sound like a hard sell, the large, attractive photos and beautiful design will pull in readers, and these companies—focusing on music, movies, and social media—have a fairly high "cool" quotient. Well written and well organized, the text flows smoothly, providing comprehensive coverage." SLJ

Includes bibliographical references and index

Other titles in this series include:

The Story of Amazon.com (2013)
The Story of Apple (2012)
The Story of CNN (2013)
The Story of Coca-Cola (2009)
The Story of Disney (2009)
The Story of eBay (2012)
The Story of Facebook (2012)
The Story of Ford (2009)
The Story of Google (2009)
The Story of McDonald's (2009)
The Story of Microsoft (2009)
The Story of MTV (2015)
The Story of Nike (2009)
The Story of Starbucks (2008)
The Story of Target (2015)
The Story of the NFL (2012)
The Story of Twitter (2015)
The Story of Wal-Mart (2011)

791.43　Motion pictures

Baker, Frank W.

Coming distractions; questioning movies. by Frank W. Baker. Fact Finders 2007 32p (Media literacy) lib bdg $22.60; pa $7.95

Grades: 4 5 6 7　　　　　**791.43**
1. Motion pictures
ISBN 978-0-7368-6766-5 lib bdg; 0-7368-6766-X lib bdg; 978-0-7368-7862-3 pa; 0-7368-7862-9 pa
LC 2006021441

This is a "solid title. . . . The book's punchy headlines, sound-bite-style text, and bold design will help hold readers' attention." Booklist

"These titles are designed to help children critique the media and understand the motives behind the production of popular entertainment. Each one makes it clear that producers create movies, magazines, TV programs, and online sites with particular audiences in mind, and that they target them by showing these specific population groups what they want to see. . . . Overall, these are useful and attractive books that encourage children to begin thinking about media with necessary skepticism." SLJ

Includes bibliographical references

Bliss, John

Art that moves; animation around the world. Raintree 2011 32p il (Culture in action) lib bdg $29

Grades: 5 6 7 8　　　　　**791.43**
1. Animated films
ISBN 978-1-4109-3922-7; 1-4109-3922-7
LC 2009051125

This "is a good choice for children interested in animated movies. Bliss looks at techniques from the early beginnings to modern times and mentions recent film releases such as Cars (2006) and Where the Wild Things Are (2010). . . . [This volume is] quick, interesting, up-to-date . . . with plenty of supportive, captioned, full-color photographs. [It] also [provides] related project suggestions." SLJ

Includes bibliographical references

Cohn, Jessica

Animator. Gareth Stevens Pub. 2010 32p il (Cool careers: cutting edge) lib bdg $26; pa $8.95

Grades: 4 5 6　　　　　**791.43**
1. Vocational guidance 2. Animation (Cinematography)
ISBN 978-1-4339-1953-4 lib bdg; 1-4339-1953-2 lib bdg; 978-1-4339-2152-0 pa; 1-4339-2152-9 pa
LC 2009002006

Describes the work of an animator.

This title offers "clear, solid information in a large font. . . . [This] short [book is] packed with relevant, current material." SLJ

Includes glossary and bibliographical references

Finch, Christopher

The **art** of Walt Disney; from Mickey Mouse to the Magic Kingdoms. rev and expanded ed; Harry N. Abrams 2004 504p il $60

Grades: 7 8 9 10　　　　　**791.43**
1. Animators 2. Walt Disney Company 3. Motion picture producers 4. Motion picture executives
ISBN 0-8109-4964-4
LC 2004-10016

First published 1973

This is the "story of Walt Disney and the company he built, from Mickey Mouse to animated feature films to theme parks. The text is illustrated with more than 800 illustrations." Publisher's note

Hill, Z. B.

Filmmaking & documentaries; Z.B. Hill. Mason Crest, an imprint of National Highlights 2014 64 p. (Art today!) (hardback) $23.95

Grades: 5 6 7 8　　　　　**791.43**
1. Vocational guidance 2. Motion pictures -- Production and direction 3. Documentary films -- Production and direction
ISBN 1422231712; 9781422231678; 9781422231715; 9781422287088
LC 2014011828

In this book, by Z. B. Hill, "[d]iscover the world of filmmaking, including the business behind both Hollywood hits and small films. Learn how you can get started on a career behind the camera!" (Publisher's note)

"This entry in the Art Today! series provides students interested in filmmaking with a solid introductory survey, including basic definitions of jobs and elements of the industry, a brief history of filmmaking and documentaries, the all-important business of profitability and funding, and realistic ways to get involved at a beginner's level...Though this offers more of a broad overview than detailed instruction, tweens who want to know where to start with filmmaking will find enough direction here. A "Find Out More" section, further reading, and a glossary append the text." Booklist

Filmmaking and documentaries

Indovino, Shaina Carmel

Dracula and beyond; famous vampires & werewolves in literature and film. Mason Crest Publishers 2011 63p il (The making of a monster: vampires & werewolves) lib bdg $22.95; pa $9.95

Grades: 7 8 9 10 **791.43**

1. Vampires 2. Werewolves 3. Vampires in literature 4. Horror fiction -- History and criticism
ISBN 978-1-4222-1803-7 lib bdg; 1-4222-1803-1 lib bdg; 978-1-4222-1956-0 pa; 1-4222-1956-9 pa
LC 2010020684

Explores portrayals of vampires and werewolves in literature and movies.

"The writing is engaging and accessible, and peppered easily with teen vernacular. . . . Large, clear photographs and period and contemporary drawings appear on every other page or so. . . . First-rate entertainment." SLJ

Includes glossary and bibliographical references

O'Brien, Lisa

Lights, camera, action! making movies and TV from the inside out. [by] Lisa O'Brien; illustrated by Stephen MacEachern. 2nd ed.; Maple Tree Press 2007 64p il $21.95; pa $12.95

Grades: 4 5 6 7 **791.43**

1. Acting 2. Motion pictures -- Production and direction
ISBN 978-1-897066-88-1; 1-897066-88-0; 978-1-897066-89-8 pa; 1-897066-89-9 pa
First published 1998 by Firefly Books

This book "follows Johnny, a young aspiring actor, as he auditions for and gets a part in a new movie called The Mists of Time. Author Lisa O'Brien examines the development and production of movies from early concept through final production. Along the way, readers get a guided tour of the world of acting, from finding an agent, through to 'acting' an audition, to handling the media." Publisher's note

Reynolds, David West

Star Wars: the complete visual dictionary; written by David West Reynolds (episodes I, II and IV-VI) and James Luceno (episode III); updates and new material by Ryder Windham; special fabrications by Robert E. Barnes . . . [et. al.]; new photography by Alex Ivanov. 1st American ed.; DK Pub. 2006 270p il $40

Grades: 6 7 8 9 10 11 12 Adult **791.43**

1. Star Wars films
ISBN 0-7566-2238-7; 978-0-7566-2238-1
LC 2006298949

Material in this book was originally published in various DK Pub. publications, 1998-2005

"Star Wars Complete Visual Dictionary brings together all four . . . titles from The Visual Dictionary series (Episode I-III and the Trilogy) in one volume. . . . This book is [a] comprehensive visual guide to every character, weapon, starship, droid, creature and alien in the Star Wars universe." Publisher's note

Seba, Jaime

Gay characters in theatre, movies, and television: new roles, new attitudes; by Jaime A. Seba. Mason Crest Publishers 2011 64p il (Gallup's guide to modern gay, lesbian, and transgender lifestyle) lib bdg $22.95; pa $9.95

Grades: 8 9 10 11 12 **791.43**

1. Gay men 2. Lesbians 3. Homosexuality in literature 4. Homosexuality on television 5. Homosexuality in motion pictures
ISBN 978-1-4222-2012-2 lib bdg; 1-4222-2012-5 lib bdg; 978-1-4222-2013-9 pa; 1-4222-2013-3 pa
LC 2010017051

"This slender, accessible overview uses numerous examples, past and present, to show how the depiction of gay, lesbian, bisexual, and transgender (GLBT) characters in the entertainment industry affects popular culture and has helped push growing acceptance into the mainstream. . . . The book features an open, inviting format, and portraits, reproduced posters, and short profiles of GLTB stars . . . add to the title's browsability." Booklist

Includes bibliographical references

Woog, Adam

Vampires in the movies. ReferencePoint Press, Inc. 2010 80p il (The vampire library) $26.95

Grades: 7 8 9 10 **791.43**

1. Vampires 2. Motion pictures -- History and criticism
ISBN 978-1-60152-135-4; 1-60152-135-9
LC 2010017982

Examines different ways vampires have been presented throughout history in films, from the early-twentieth century for Lugosi films to the present-day mania for Twilight and other modern takes.

"Energetic and suprisingly educational, this lively [book] seizes upon a zietgeist topic and takes it as far as possible." Booklist

Includes bibliographical references

791.5 Puppetry and toy theaters

Kennedy, John E.

★ **Puppet** planet. North Light Books 2006 79p il $16.99

Grades: 4 5 6 7 **791.5**

1. Puppets and puppet plays
ISBN 978-1-58180-794-3; 1-58180-794-5
LC 2005033711

This book offers twelve "puppet projects, each using a variety of techniques, [and] features 'action panels' so readers can see how each puppet comes to life. [It also] Includes staging ideas to play up each project's uniqueness." Publisher's note

791.8 Animal performances

Collard III, Sneed B.

The **world** famous Miles City Bucking Horse Sale. Bucking Horse Books 2010 64p il $18

Grades: 5 6 7 8   791.8

1. Horses 2. Rodeos 3. Montana
ISBN 0984446001; 9780984446001; 978-0-9844460-0-1; 0-9844460-0-1

"Collard takes readers inside the Miles City [Montana] Bucking Horse Sale, a four-day event that draws visitors from across the country. Started in 1951 as a sale of wild horses, it's evolved into a jamboree of music, rodeo, food, contests, and a parade.... Plenty of action-filled color photographs break up the narrative.... Handsomely designed, ... this is a fascinating look at a fresh topic." Booklist
Includes glossary

Grayson, Robert

Performers. Marshall Cavendish Benchmark 2010 64p il (Working animals) lib bdg $28.50

Grades: 4 5 6 7   791.8

1. Animals in entertainment
ISBN 978-1-60870-165-0 lib bdg; 1-60870-165-4 lib bdg

LC 2010006893

"Describes the role of animals in movies, sporting events, and various competitions." Publisher's note
Includes glossary and bibliographical references

Laidlaw, Rob

On parade; the hidden world of animals in entertainment. Fitzhenry & Whiteside 2010 55p il $19.95

Grades: 4 5 6   791.8

1. Zoos 2. Circus 3. Animal welfare 4. Animals in entertainment
ISBN 978-1-55455-143-9; 1-55455-143-9

This book examines animals at the zoo and circus, animals working in movies and television, violence in the world of performing animals and offers ways to improve conditions and prevent animal abuse.

The author's "clearly argued text; crisp, captioned color photos; and appended list of organizations make this an important source for animal advocates." Booklist

792 Stage presentations

Becker, Helaine

Funny business; clowning around, practical jokes, cool comedy, cartooning, and more ... illustrated by Claudia Dávila. Maple Tree 2005 160p il $21.95; pa $9.95

Grades: 5 6 7 8   792

1. Clowns 2. Cartooning 3. Wit and humor
ISBN 1-897066-40-6; 1-897066-41-4 pa

"Becker offers funny facts, an informative diagram showing what goes on in the body when you laugh, brief discussions of different types of humor (situation comedy, parody, farce, riddles, puns), a How Funny Are You? quiz, tips and timing for standup routines, body lingo, props, six improvisation games, clowning material, and more. For kids who want to learn how to juggle, tell jokes, or use sight-gag items, it's all here. Cartooning is explained as well." SLJ

Belli, Mary Lou

Acting for young actors; the ultimate teen guide. [by] Mary Lou Belli & Dinah Lenney. Back Stage Books 2006 205p il pa $16.96

Grades: 7 8 9 10 11 12   792

1. Acting
ISBN 978-0-8230-4947-9 pa; 0-8230-4947-7 pa

LC 2006007265

"Belli and Lenney, an Emmy-winning director of Girl-friends and a Yale-educated ER actress offer stagestruck teens trunks-full of sound advice packaged with a conversational tone and grounded experience.... The authors offer a series of questions for character analysis; suggested readings and viewings abound.... The handbook succeeds at communicating clearly without talking down to readers; engaging prose makes it an ideal text for classes and teens who want commonsense career prep and insight." Voice Youth Advocates

Includes bibliographical references

Lamedman, Debbie

The **ultimate** audition book for teens; 111 one-minute monologues. Smith & Kraus (Young actor series)

Grades: 7 8 9 10 11 12   792

A series of collections of 111 original monologues, all about one minute long, to be used by male and female teen-age actors in auditions.

"Some suggestive sexual situations described here will not be acceptable in some classrooms. Drama teachers may, however, welcome some of this material for beginning acting students." Book Rep [review of volume one]

Millennium monologs; 95 contemporary characterizations for young actors. edited by Gerald Lee Ratliff. Meriwether 2002 261p pa $15.95

Grades: 8 9 10 11 12   792

1. Acting 2. Monologues 3. American drama -- Collections
ISBN 1-56608-082-7

LC 2002-13009

An anthology of monologues by contemporary writers, divided into four categories: "Hope and Longing," "Spirit and Soul," "Fun and Fantasy," and "Doubt and Despair." Includes audition techniques

"This fine collection of American monologues is notable for its diversity as well as for the high quality of the material." Booklist

Rogers, Barb

Costumes, accessories, props, and stage illusions made easy. Meriwether Pub. 2005 205p il pa $19.95

Grades: 8 9 10 11 12 **792**

1. Costume 2. Theater -- Production and direction
ISBN 978-1-56608-103-0; 1-56608-103-3

LC 2005-4359

This book details ways to make theater "costumes with simple tools such as scissors, glue guns, and paint. In addition, there are chapters on how to make hats, gloves, armor, and animal heads, as well as other props and accessories from rummage-sale finds and a little imagination. . . . This is a useful volume for schools and community theaters with little or no budgets for costumes and props." SLJ

Includes bibliographical references

Schumacher, Thomas L.

How does the show go on? an introduction to the theater. by Thomas Schumacher with Jeff Kurtti. 2nd ed; Disney 2008 128p il $22.95

Grades: 4 5 6 7 **792**

1. Theater
ISBN 978-1-4231-2031-5; 1-4231-2031-0

"Filled with lavish color photos of Disney theater productions, this eye-catching volume has clever chapter titles, beginning with 'Overture,' which tells about 'styles of theaters' and 'kinds of shows.' In 'Act One' and 'Act Two,' aspects of the front and back of the house are discussed, including the marquee, the box office, props, special effects, and so on. Interspersed throughout the facts and photos are 'Stage Notes,' where bits of trivia are doled out." SLJ

Skog, Jason

Acting; a practical guide to pursuing the art. Compass Point Books 2010 48p il (Performing arts) lib bdg $28.65

Grades: 5 6 7 8 **792**

1. Acting 2. Vocational guidance
ISBN 978-0-7565-4364-8 lib bdg; 0-7565-4364-9 lib bdg

LC 2010012604

A guide for those interested in a career in acting, and includes tips on education, technique, and more.

"Meant for students contemplating a career in the field . . . [this book goes] beyond basic introductions and into more detail about what it takes to make it as a professional. . . . [The author maintains] . . . a frank, realistic tone, stressing the importance of hard work and dedication. Great [resource] . . . for those wanting to make their passions more than just a hobby." SLJ

Includes glossary and bibliographical references

Underwood, Deborah

Staging a play. Raintree 2009 32p il (Culture in action) $28.21; pa $7.99

Grades: 5 6 7 8 **792**

1. Theater -- Production and direction
ISBN 978-1-4109-3396-6; 1-4109-3396-2; 978-1-4109-3413-0 pa; 1-4109-3413-6 pa

LC 2009000417

This "discusses the various professionals involved in a production, such as actors, costume designers, prop masters, and stage handlers. Well organized and with bright, colorful photography, [this] introductory [title gives] readers good basic knowledge." SLJ

Includes glossary and bibliographical references

792.09 Stage presentations -- History, geographic treatment, biography

Aliki

★ **William** Shakespeare & the Globe; written & illustrated by Aliki. HarperCollins Pubs. 1999 48p il hardcover o.p. pa $6.99

Grades: 4 5 6 7 8 9 **792.09**

1. Poets 2. Authors 3. Dramatists 4. Globe Theatre (London, England) 5. Shakespeare's Globe (London, England)
ISBN 0-06-027820-X; 0-06-443722-1 pa

LC 98-7903

"A logically organized and engaging text, plenty of detailed illustrations with informative captions, and a clean design provide a fine introduction to both bard and theater." Horn Book Guide

Currie, Stephen

An **actor** on the Elizabethan stage. Lucent Bks. 2003 96p il maps (Working life) $27.45

Grades: 6 7 8 9 **792.09**

1. Theater -- History 2. Great Britain -- History -- 1485-1603, Tudors
ISBN 1-59018-174-3

LC 2002-9460

Discusses various aspects of theatrical life, including staging and performance, financing, types of acting troupes, and social and economic influences

This is "well written and the [author draws on quotes] from many primary sources." Libr Media Connect

Includes bibliographical references

792.6 Musical plays

Amendola, Dana

★ A **day** at the New Amsterdam Theatre; photos by Gino Domenico; written by Dana Amendola. Disney Editions 2004 125p il $24.95

Grades: 4 5 6 7 **792.6**

1. Theater 2. New Amsterdam Theatre (New York, N.Y.)
ISBN 0-7868-5438-3

"This title covers a day in the life of Disney's The Lion King, the long-running Broadway musical. . . . A clock in a corner of each spread guides readers through the day as box-office personnel, makeup designers, dancers, actors, cleaning staff, and others do their jobs. Each spread includes several full-color photos that are often gritty, sometimes glamorous. . . . This unique volume provides an honest, realistic, eye-opening look at the behind-the-scenes work that goes into the running of a Broadway show." SLJ

Bezdecheck, Bethany

Directing. Rosen Pub. 2009 64p il (High school musicals) lib bdg $21.95

Grades: 7 8 9 10   **792.6**

1. Musicals -- Production and direction

ISBN 978-1-4358-5259-4 lib bdg; 1-4358-5259-1 lib bdg

LC 2008041598

"Bezdecheck lays out the process of directing a musical production, from play selection to auditions to dress rehearsals. . . . There's some good, practical advice here." Booklist

Includes bibliographical references

Michael, Ted

So you wanna be a superstar? the ultimate audition guide. by Ted Michael ; with contributions by Nic Cory & Mara Jill Herman ; introduction by Lea Salonga ; edited by Lisa Cheng. RP Kids 2012 151 p. (paperback: consumable) $10.95; (paperback) $10.95; (ebook) $10.95

Grades: 4 5 6 7 8   **792.6**

1. Auditions 2. Voice culture

ISBN 0762446102; 9780762446100; 9780762447015 pdf

LC 2012932845

This book by Ted Michael presents a guide for " hopeful musical theater, show choir, a cappella, and glee club singers" with advice designed to help readers "train [their] vocal cords, pick the right audition material, and become comfortable with the spotlight. Interactive quizzes . . . and words of advice from industry professionals" are also included. (Publisher's note)

792.8   Ballet and modern dance

Augustyn, Frank

★ **Footnotes**; dancing the world's best-loved ballets. [by] Frank Augustyn and Shelley Tanaka. Millbrook Press 2001 94p il $17.95

Grades: 5 6 7 8   **792.8**

1. Ballet

ISBN 0-7613-1646-9

LC 00-50075

"Fine photographs, most in color, add enormously to the book's appeal. A well-crafted, readable volume." Booklist

Balanchine, George

101 stories of the great ballets; George Balanchine and Francis Mason. First edition Dolphin Books 1975 xiv, 541 p.p $18.95

Grades: 5 6 7 8 9 10 11 12 Adult   **792.8**

1. Ballet -- Stories, plots, etc. 2. Ballets -- Stories, plots, etc

ISBN 0385033982; 9780385033985

LC 73009140

This book, by George Balanchine and Francis Mason, "includes scene-by-scene retellings of the most popular classic and contemporary ballets, as performed by the world's leading dance companies. Certain to delight long-time fans

as well as those just discovering the beauty and drama of ballet." (Publisher's note)

"Accessible books on ballet are few and far between . . . [but] George Balanchine and Francis Mason's 101 Stories of the Great Ballets is considered the bible of ballet librettos." Christian Science Monitor

Freedman, Russell

★ **Martha** Graham, a dancer's life. Clarion Bks. 1998 175p il $18

Grades: 7 8 9 10   **792.8**

1. Dancers 2. Modern dance 3. Choreographers 4. Dance teachers

ISBN 0-395-74655-8

LC 97-15832

A photo-biography of the American dancer, teacher, and choreographer who was born in Pittsburgh in 1895 and who became a leading figure in the world of modern dance

"A showstopping biography that captures its dynamic subject's personality, vision, and artistry." SLJ

Includes bibliographical references

Froman, Kyle

In the wings; behind the scenes at the New York City Ballet. Kyle Froman. John Wiley & Sons 2007 ix, 118 p.p ill. (some col.) ;

Grades: 6 7 8 9 10 11 12 Adult   **792.8**

1. Ballet 2. Anecdotes 3. New York City Ballet -- Anecdotes. 4. New York City Ballet -- Pictorial works.

ISBN 9780470173435 (cloth)

LC 2007024556

"Here is New York City Ballet as it really is- the good, the not so good, and the majestically beautiful. It's a true story, and it's told by someone who can honestly claim that he was there." (Publisher's Note)

"An 11-year veteran dancer for the New York City Ballet, Froman here documents life in the corps de ballet in a photo-album and diarylike format. Presenting a day in the life of the dancers, he takes readers through the stages of warming up, class, physical therapy, rehearsals, preparation, and, of course, the show. . . . An engaging point of view and an attractive layout make this an entertaining read. YAs may also find it a good introduction to the dance world as a possible career. Recommended for all libraries." LJ

Kupesic, Rajka

The white ballets. Tundra Books 2011 40p il $19.95

Grades: 4 5 6 7   **792.8**

1. Ballet -- Stories, plots, etc.

ISBN 978-0-88776-923-8; 0-88776-923-3

This retells the stories of Swan Lake, Giselle, and La Bayadère and includes information and comments on the three ballets.

"The tales are well told, and the author, a former ballerina, provides information on the history of the ballet. Each painting in gold leaf and oil represents a scene from one of the ballets. The richly colored illustrations are very stylized with graceful figures dressed in flowing, romantic costumes, and Kupesic elaborates on the details, symbols, and characters in her artwork. . . . For ballet enthusiasts this is a unique look at these classics." SLJ

Lee, Laura

A **child's** introduction to ballet; the stories, music and magic of classical dance. [by] Laura Lee; illustrated by Meredith Hamilton. Black Dog & Leventhal Publishers 2007 96p il $19.95

Grades: 4 5 6 7 8   **792.8**

1. Ballet

ISBN 978-1-57912-699-5; 1-57912-699-5

LC 2006048867

"This lively and attractive volume delves into the history of ballet from its beginnings in Italy through the 20th century. . . . Detailed and well-written descriptions of 25 of the most famous and influential ballets are provided along with colorful illustrations of scenes. A CD presents excerpts from them and the author poses some questions and gives some insights to think about as one listens to the music." SLJ

Marsico, Katie

Choreographer. Cherry Lake Pub. 2011 32p il (Cool arts careers) lib bdg $18.95

Grades: 4 5 6 7   **792.8**

1. Dance 2. Choreographers 3. Vocational guidance

ISBN 978-1-61080-136-2; 1-61080-136-9

LC 2011001170

"Illustrated with color photos of the famous, the young, and the fabulously festooned, this is a sturdy presentation of facts and case studies that will bring the process of professional choreography home to those students considering such a competitive and demanding career." Booklist

Includes bibliographical references

Miles, Lisa

Ballet spectacular; a young ballet lover's guide and an insight into a magical world. Lisa Miles. Barrons Educational Series, Inc. 2014 80 p. color illustrations $18.99

Grades: 4 5 6 7 8   **792.8**

1. Ballet 2. Ballet dancers 3. Royal Ballet

ISBN 0764167456; 9780764167454

LC 2014940905

Author Lisa Miles presents this "reference volume for children who love ballet. Featuring stunning full-color photos from The Royal Ballet's own collections and informative, fact-filled entries, it covers all things dance. Most intriguing to passionate young lovers of dance will be the exploration of a day in the life of a professional ballet dancer, images of beloved performers such as Margot Fonteyn, Darcey Bussell, and Carlos Acosta, detailed close-ups of costumes, and photos." (Publisher's note)

"Combining aspects of a coffee-table book and an introductory handbook, it provides a hodgepodge of basic information about ballet history, famous ballets, life in a major company, and the elements involved in a performance, such as choreography, music, sets, and costumes, while Britain's Royal Ballet Company and School are referenced throughout the book." Booklist

Minden, Eliza Gaynor

The **ballet** companion; a dancer's guide to the technique, traditions, and joys of ballet. Eliza Gaynor Minden. Touchstone Books 2005 xv, 331 p.p illustrations (some color) $29.95

Grades: 6 7 8 9 10 11 12 Adult   **792.8**

1. Ballet 2. Ballet dancers 3. Ballet dancing -- Handbooks, manuals, etc

ISBN 9780743264075; 074326407X

LC 2005044102

This book, by Eliza Gaynor Minden "is a fresh, comprehensive, and thoroughly up-to-date reference book for the dancer. With 150 stunning photographs of ballet stars Maria Riccetto and Benjamin Millepied demonstrating perfect execution of positions and steps, this elegant volume brims with everything today's dance student needs" (Publisher's note)

"[The Author's] explanation of the differences between the six major ballet styles, along with the superb glossaries of terms and dance history timeline, make this book a valuable resource for dance studios and a great primer for dancers in the early stages of training." Publishers Weekly

Includes bibliographical references (p. [316]-317) and index

Schorer, Suki

Put your best foot forward; a young dancer's guide to life. by Suki Schorer and the School of American Ballet; illustrations by Donna Ingemanson. Workman Publishing 2005 96p il pa $9.95

Grades: 4 5 6 7   **792.8**

1. Ballet

ISBN 978-0-7611-3795-5 pa; 0-7611-3795-5 pa

LC 2005051428

"The words of counsel proffered by the author, who was a principal dancer for the New York City Ballet and is a teacher at the School of American Ballet, are engaging, imaginative, and right on target. . . . Practical tips such as essentials that need to be in your bag and behavioral advice such as being grateful for criticism are nicely woven into the book. The photographs, mainly of female dancers, are clear and colorful. These words of wisdom will keep dancers on their toes and stretching their minds and hearts." SLJ

792.802   Specific aspects of ballet and modern dance

Bernstein, Richard

A **girl** named Faithful Plum; Richard Bernstein. Alfred A. Knopf Books for Young Readers 2011 270p. ill. $15.99; lib bdg $18.99

Grades: 7 8 9 10 11 12   **792.802**

1. Dancers 2. Arts -- China 3. Dance directors 4. China -- Biography

ISBN 978-0-375-86960-0; 0-375-86960-3; 978-0-375-96960-7 lib bdg; 0-375-96960-8 lib bdg

LC 2010048722

This book tells the childhood story of dancer "Zhongmei . . . [who] is a young Chinese girl from a rural family so poor that though they raise chickens, she herself is allowed only one boiled egg a year. At the age of 11, she hears the Beijing Dance Academy is holding open auditions for the first time since the Cultural Revolution. Without any connections to the Communist Party or even money for the train ride,

Zhongmei's parents at first refuse to let her audition. But after Zhongmei stages a hunger strike, her parents borrow money to send her on the grueling trip to Beijing. There, Zhongmei endures an even more demanding seven-stage audition and beats out over 20,000 girls to enter the school. Soon she discovers that was the easy part." (N Y Times)

"In 1978, an 11-year-old girl fights poverty and prejudice with gutsy perseverance and talent to fulfill her dream of studying at the Beijing Dance Academy. . . . Faithful Plum, or Zhongmei, lives in a remote area of China near Siberia. . . . She loves to dance, though, and upon hearing that the Academy is holding national auditions she sets her mind on going. . . . After a horrific three-day journey by trains and buses, Zhongmei comes through the difficult audition only to face an extreme daily regimen of exercise and instruction, an appallingly rigid dormitory supervisor and a ballet teacher scarred by the Cultural Revolution. . . . The conversations ring true, albeit 'imagined,' and events have been compressed to keep the pace flowing. A fascinating and memorable account of a life and times difficult to imagine today." Kirkus

792.9   Stage productions

Cox, Carole
Shakespeare kids; performing his plays, speaking his words. Libraries Unlimited 2010 xx, 126p il pa $30

Grades: Adult Professional   **792.9**
   1. Poets 2. Authors 3. Dramatists 4. Theater -- Production and direction
   ISBN 978-1-59158-838-2 pa; 1-59158-838-3 pa
                   LC 2009041731

This is a "a practical guide for performing Shakespeare's plays, albeit in condensed form, without changing his poetic dialogue. . . . Cox gears her work to teachers of students in grades 3-8, librarians, or adults leading recreational programs, providing precise, detailed instructions on all facets of youth-oriented Shakespearean play production. . . . The text is clear and concise . . . Black-and-white photos capture specific moments that illustrate the performers' enthusiasm." SLJ

Includes bibliographical references

793.3   Social, folk, national dancing

Ancona, George
★ **Ole!** Flamenco. Lee & Low 2010 un il map $19.95

Grades: 5 6 7 8   **793.3**
   1. Flamenco
   ISBN 978-1-60060-361-7; 1-60060-361-0
                   LC 2010-22272

Ancona tells "the story of flamenco, an art form that's more than dancing and has been around for hundreds of years. He begins with a short introduction that chronicles his visit to Spain. . . . He then returns readers to Santa Fe, New Mexico, where a group of young people are learning flamenco. A helpful map traces the art form's roots, while the text explains both the history of the Gypsies and flamenco. Full-

color photographs capture the excitement and dazzle. . . . All aspects of flamenco are explored, including movements, facial expressions, and sound effects." Booklist

Includes glossary and bibliographical references

Fishkin, Rebecca Love
Dance; a practical guide to pursuing the art. content adviser, Hannah Seidel and Chris Ferris and dancers; reading adviser, Alexa L. Sandmann. Compass Point Books 2011 48p il (Performing arts) lib bdg $28.65

Grades: 5 6 7 8   **793.3**
   1. Dance 2. Vocational guidance
   ISBN 978-0-7565-4363-1 lib bdg; 0-7565-4363-0 lib bdg
                   LC 2010012605

This guide about a career in dance includes tips on education, technique, and more.

"Meant for students contemplating a career in the field . . . [this book goes] beyond basic introductions and into more detail about what it takes to make it as a professional. . . . [The author maintains] . . . a frank, realistic tone, stressing the importance of hard work and dedication. Great [resource] . . . for those wanting to make their passions more than just a hobby." SLJ

Includes glossary and bibliographical references

Garofoli, Wendy
Hip -hop dancing. Capstone Press 2011 4v il lib bdg ea $30.65

Grades: 4 5 6   **793.3**
   1. Dance 2. Hip-hop
   ISBN 978-1-4296-5484-5 v1; 1-4296-5484-5 v1; 978-1-4296-5485-2 v2; 1-4296-5485-6 v2; 978-1-4296-5486-9 v3; 1-4296-5486-9 v3; 978-1-4296-5487-6 v4; 1-4296-5487-2 v4
                   LC 2010030394

Provides instructions for joining or starting a hip-hop dance crew, and includes information about real-life crews.

"These volumes cover the basic moves as well as more detailed movements often seen on television programs. . . . Everything about the set is jazzy and current. Sentences are short and direct, with a small-sized font detailing step-by-step instructions and fact boxes extending the information." Booklist

Includes bibliographical references

Haney, Johannah
Capoeira. Marshall Cavendish Benchmark 2011 47p il (Martial arts in action) $29.93

Grades: 4 5 6 7   **793.3**
   1. Capoeira (Dance)
   ISBN 978-0-7614-4932-4; 978-1-6087-0362-3 e-book
                   LC 2010013829

This describes the history, equipment, and technique of capoeira.

This treats "martial arts with the dignity that serious enthusiasts bring to the sport. . . . Illustrations include not only photos of modern gear and from films but also historical images." Booklist

Smith, Karen Lynn

Popular dance; from ballroom to hip-hop. consulting editor, Elizabeth A. Hanley; foreword by Jacques D'Amboisse. Chelsea House Publishers 2010 165p il (World of dance) lib bdg $35

Grades: 6 7 8 9   **793.3**

1. Dance

ISBN 978-1-60413-484-1; 1-60413-484-4

LC 2009053491

"Students who want a deeper and more comprehensive understanding of the origins and present status of various styles [of popular dance] will find this volume useful. It takes readers from the saltarello and galliard of the Renaissance to present-day hip-hop and zumba. . . . It has an encyclopedic approach as it identifies and defines the dances and touches on their cultural influences. . . . This volume would be a valuable resource for research and casual browsing." SLJ

Includes glossary and bibliographical references

793.73   Puzzles and puzzle games

Moscovich, Ivan

Big book of brain games; 1000 playthinks of art, mathematics & science. by Ivan Moscovich; foreword by Ian Stewart; illustrated by Tim Robinson. Workman Pub. 2006 420p il pa $22.95

Grades: 7 8 9 10   **793.73**

1. Scientific recreations

ISBN 0-7611-3466-2 pa; 978-0-7611-3466-4 pa

LC 2006299017

First published 2001 with title: 1000 playthinks: puzzles, paradoxes, illusions & games

This is a "collection of 1,000 challenges, puzzles, riddles, illusions. . . . Twelve basic categories include Geometry, Patterns, Numbers, Logic and Probability, and Perception. [A] key at the top of each game ranks its difficulty on a scale of 1 to 10, while indices in the back cross-reference the puzzles." Publisher's note

Includes bibliographical references

793.74   Mathematical games and recreations

Ball, Johnny

Go figure! DK Pub. 2005 96p il map $15.99

Grades: 4 5 6 7   **793.74**

1. Mathematics 2. Mathematical recreations

ISBN 0-7566-1374-4

A collection of math activities that include brainteasers, magic tricks, and mind-reading games

"A dynamic book. . . . Blocks of color, diagrams, and photo collages contribute to the exciting layout. . . . A fun romp for number and puzzle lovers." SLJ

793.8   Magic and related activities

Jennings, Madeleine

Magic step-by-step; [by] Madeleine Jennings and Colin Francome. Rosen Central 2010 89p il (Skills in motion) lib bdg $31.95

Grades: 5 6 7 8   **793.8**

1. Magic tricks

ISBN 978-1-4358-3363-0; 1-4358-3363-5

LC 2009-13221

Presents step-by-step instructions on performing magic tricks, including card tricks, rope tricks, and sleight of hand.

"Colorful photographs show the entire movement of each skill presented, giving new meaning to the term 'step-by-step.' Progression borders at the bottom of the pages highlight the salient points to notice in performing each skill from beginning to end." SLJ

Includes bibliographical references

794.1   Chess

Basman, Michael

Chess for kids; written by Michael Basman. Dorling Kindersley 2001 45p il $12.99; pa $6.99

Grades: 4 5 6 7   **794.1**

1. Chess

ISBN 0-7894-6540-X; 0-7566-1807-X pa

LC 00-59018

This guide to chess explains the rudiments of the game, techniques and winning strategies

"A solid introduction for novices and good for skilled players wanting to develop their strategies and find out about chess clubs and tournaments." Booklist

King, Daniel

★ Chess; from first moves to checkmate. New ed.; Kingfisher 2010 64p il pa $8.99

Grades: 5 6 7 8 9 10 11 12   **794.1**

1. Chess

ISBN 978-0-7534-1930-4

First published 2000

Introduces the rules and strategies of chess, as well as its history and some of the great players and matches.

794.8   Electronic games

Adams, Suellen S.

Crash course in gaming; Suellen S. Adams. Libraries Unlimited, an imprint of ABC-CLIO, LLC 2014 xi, 125 p.p (Libraries unlimited crash course series) (pbk.) $45

Grades: Adult Professional   **794.8**

1. Video games

ISBN 161069046X; 9781610690461

LC 2013031465

This book, by Suellen S. Adams, "discusses the pros and cons of gaming, the types of games and game systems, circulating collections, and game programs. It explains how a library's video game program can—and should—do much more than simply draw younger users to the library, providing examples of how everyone from parents to senior citizens can benefit from a patron-oriented computer gaming program." (Publisher's note)

"Librarians who are considering adding a circulating video-game collection will find guidance in this volume. It provides readers with information on evaluating video games, building a strong circulating collection, creating programming for all ages around that collection, and engaging children and teens with related literature...Libraries looking for guidance on building, maintaining, and growing a successful circulating collection for gamers will find this book invaluable, as will libraries with a need to overhaul their collections."

Includes bibliographical references (pages 121-122) and index

Egan, Jill

How video game designers use math; math curriculum consultant: Rhea A. Stewart. Chelsea Clubhouse 2010 32p il (Math in the real world) lib bdg $28

Grades: 4 5 6   **794.8**

    1. Mathematics 2. Video games 3. Computer games 4. Computer animation 5. Vocational guidance
    ISBN 978-1-60413-603-6 lib bdg; 1-60413-603-0 lib bdg

                    LC 2009-24173

This describes how video game designers use math to create and produce their games and includes relevant math problems and information about how to become a video game designer

Includes glossary and bibliographical references

Haugen, Hayley Mitchell

Video games; by Hayley Mitchell Haugen. Norwood HousePress 2015 64 p. (Matters of Opinion) (library edition : alk. paper) $27.93

Grades: 5 6 7 8 9   **794.8**

    1. Video games -- Social aspects
    ISBN 1599536013; 9781599536019

                    LC 2014003798

This book, by Hayley Mitchell Haugen, "explores the pros and cons of several issues related to video games, including whether video games cause violence, discourage exercise, and proper regulation." (Publisher's note)

"Students will be interested in debating issues surrounding video games: whether the games lead to violence, health risks, and whether there should be regulation. In addition to pros and cons of each and a final writing assignment, three debate techniques--the author's credibility, deceptive arguments, and logical fallacies--are also analyzed. Sidebars and captioned photos support the choppy text. Reading list, timeline, websites. Glos., ind." Horn Book

Includes bibliographical references (page 60) and index

Jozefowicz, Chris

Video game developer. Gareth Stevens Pub. 2010 32p il (Cool careers: cutting edge) lib bdg $26; pa $8.95

Grades: 4 5 6   **794.8**

    1. Video games 2. Computer games 3. Vocational

guidance
    ISBN 978-1-4339-1958-9 lib bdg; 1-4339-1958-3 lib bdg; 978-1-4339-2157-5 pa; 1-4339-2157-X pa

                    LC 2008053549

This introduction to video game developer careers offers "clear, solid information in a large font. . . . [This] short [book is] packed with relevant, current material." SLJ

Includes glossary and bibliographical references

Oxlade, Chris

Gaming technology. Smart Apple Media 2011 46p il (New technology) lib bdg $34.25

Grades: 4 5 6 7   **794.8**

    1. Video games 2. Computer games
    ISBN 9781599205311

                    LC 2010044239

Describes the technology used for creating and playing video games. Includes information on how different platforms work and the direction video game technology may be going.

This "offers a fine overview for reports, and its attractive design may also entice middle-grade readers to learn more." Booklist

Includes glossary and bibliographical references

Parks, Peggy J., 1951-

Video games. ReferencePoint Press 2008 104p il map (Compact research. Current issues) $25.95

Grades: 8 9 10 11 12   **794.8**

    1. Video games
    ISBN 978-1-60152-053-1; 1-60152-053-0

                    LC 2007-49886

This "book opens with descriptions of the growing popularity of video games and the regulation and legislation of content and sales; ratings; connections with violent crime; and health effects, including addiction. An overview provides further background and context to these issues, and . . . chapters follow addressing related questions and providing other related material." SLJ

Includes bibliographical references

Rauf, Don

Computer game designer; [by] Don Rauf and Monique Vescia. Ferguson 2007 un il (Virtual apprentice) lib bdg $29.95; pa $9.95

Grades: 6 7 8 9   **794.8**

    1. Computer games 2. Vocational guidance
    ISBN 978-0-8160-6754-1 lib bdg; 0-8160-6754-6 lib bdg; 0-8160-7550-6 pa; 978-0-8160-7550-8 pa

                    LC 2006036565

"This in-depth introduction to the field of computer-game design offers specific practical advice. . . . Following a basic history of computer games and information about game types and rating levels, chapters, which are illustrated with many color photos, profile contemporary professionals and delve into current trends and the day-to-day work of game creators." Booklist

796 Athletic and outdoor sports and games

Berman, Len

The **greatest** moments in sports; upsets and underdogs. Len Berman. Sourcebooks Jabberwocky 2012 iv, 124 p.p ill. (hardcover) $19.99

Grades: 5 6 7 8   796

1. Sports upsets -- History

ISBN 140227226X; 9781402272264

In this sports book, "[Len] Berman offers his take on 25 of the most unexpected victories. . . . Youngsters learn about Billy Mills's surprise win of Olympic Gold for the 10,000 meter run in 1964, and Mexico's Little League World Series win of 1957. Text boxes . . . [present] biographical information and quick glimpses into the records of the 'champions' versus the 'underdogs.' The accompanying CD offers additional insight from Berman on 10 of the upsets." (School Library Journal)

Blumenthal, Karen

★ **Let** me play; the story of Title IX, the law that changed the future of girls in America. Atheneum Books for Young Readers 2005 152p il $19.95

Grades: 6 7 8 9 10   796

1. Women athletes 2. Sex discrimination 4. Education Amendments of 1972 -- Title IX

ISBN 0-689-85957-0

LC 2004-1450

Title IX legislation assured "that 'no one could be closed out of any educational program or activity receiving federal money simply because of sex.' After explaining the genesis of the legislation, . . . Blumenthal discusses how evolving guidelines and interpretations brought girls' school athletic programs into its purview. [Bibliography. Index.] Grades nine to twelve." (Bull Cent Child Books)

"The author looks at American women's evolving rights by focusing on the history and future of Title IX, which bans sex discrimination in U.S. education. . . . The images are . . . gripping, and relevant political cartoons and fact boxes add further interest. Few books cover the last few decades of American women's history with such clarity and detail." Booklist

Includes bibliographical references

Fay, Gail

Sports; the ultimate teen guide. by Gail Fay. Scarecrow Press, Inc. 2012 338 p. (It happened to me) (cloth : alk. paper) $50

Grades: 7 8 9 10 11 12   796

1. Teenagers 2. School sports 3. Teenage athletes -- Training of 4. High school athletes -- Training of

ISBN 0810882175; 9780810882171; 9780810882188

LC 2012028320

This book, by Gail Fay, is "for high school athletes of all levels [and] provides up-to-date information on sports-related issues, practical tips, and valuable resources. Each chapter features quotes from current and former high school athletes who share their experiences related to the given topic. Issues discussed include choosing a sport to play, balancing all aspects of life as a student-athlete, [and] dealing with the pressures of competition." (Publisher's note)

Includes bibliographical references and index

Gifford, Clive

Sports. Amicus 2010 46p il (Healthy lifestyles) lib bdg $32.80

Grades: 7 8 9 10   796

1. Sports 2. Physical fitness

ISBN 978-1-60753-088-6; 1-60753-088-0

LC 2009-47567

This book is "well-written and satisfyingly informative. . . . [The] magazine-like format includes numerous sidebars, color photos, and charts." SLJ

Includes glossary and bibliographical references

Hile, Lori

Surviving extreme sports. Raintree 2011 56p il (Extreme survival) lib bdg $33.50

Grades: 4 5 6 7   796

1. Extreme sports 2. Wilderness survival

ISBN 978-1-4109-3968-5; 1-4109-3968-5

LC 2010028689

This book is "fun and informative. [This] well-organized title starts with an overview [of extreme sports], offers some specific examples, and includes additional facts or tips and resources. . . . [It features] dramatic archival and full-color photos on nearly every page. . . . [This is a book] that youngsters will enjoy and talk about." SLJ

Includes glossary and bibliographical references

Howell, Brian

Sports. ABDO Pub. Co. 2011 112p il (Inside the industry) lib bdg $23.95

Grades: 5 6 7 8   796

1. Sports -- Vocational guidance

ISBN 978-1-61714-804-0; 1-61714-804-0

LC 2010042558

This " well-designed [book describes] a variety of careers in [sports]. Because [it helps] readers assess if these positions are suitable for their personality types and backgrounds, the [title is a] good [choice] for career exploration and self-discovery. [It is] also useful for research and reports. . . . Sidebars and full-color photos appear throughout." SLJ

Includes bibliographical references

Mattern, Joanne

So, you want to work in sports? the ultimate guide to exploring the sports industry. Joanne Mattern. Aladdin/Beyond Words 2014 224 p. illustrations (Be what you want) (paperback) $9.99; (hardback) $18.99

Grades: 4 5 6 7 8   796

1. Sports 2. Vocational guidance

ISBN 1582704481; 158270449X; 9781582704487; 9781582704494

LC 2013025469

This book, by Joanne Mattern, is a "guide that can help you score a career in the sports industry. . . . From the popular careers of professional athlete, coach, sports broadcaster, and photographer, to the lesser-known professions of sports agent, statistician, sports therapist, and scout, [this book] delves into a wide variety of possible futures that are exciting and rewarding." (Publisher's note)

"Information is presented dynamically, with numerous sidebars ("Did you know "), graphs, lists, a career quiz, and hand-drawn illustrations. There are no photos. One of the book's strongest assets is its excellent resource section, including a six-page list of websites for professional organizations . . . and two pages of books and online documents." SLJ

Includes bibliographical references and index

Ralston, Birgitta

Snow play; how to make forts & slides & winter campfires plus the coolest Loch Ness monster and 23 other brrrilliant [i.e. brilliant] project in the snow. Artisan 2010 111p il $14.95

Grades: 4 5 6 7 8 9 10 11 12 Adult   796
1. Snow 2. Outdoor recreation
ISBN 978-1-57965-405-4; 1-57965-405-3

"Opening with explanations of different types of snow and the various tools needed to work with it, this how-to book describes more than two dozen projects, most of which will require adult help and supervision. . . . Ratings of difficulty, the number of people and tools needed, the type of snow required, and the time frame are included with each project. Short snow-related facts appear throughout. . . . A brief listing of worldwide snow festivals, snow hotels and igloos, and an ice museum completes the package. While kids can certainly use this book to inspire ideas for winter fun, adults will find it equally useful, especially for generating ideas for family projects." SLJ

Rand, Casey

Graphing sports. Heinemann Library 2009 32p il (Real world data) $28.21; pa $7.99

Grades: 5 6 7 8   796
1. Graphic methods 2. Sports -- Statistics
ISBN 978-1-4329-2621-2; 1-4329-2621-7; 978-1-4329-2630-4 pa; 1-4329-2630-6 pa
LC 2009001189

This explains sports related concepts through charts and graphs.

"The writing is spot-on for the audience. Most importantly, the statistics used are well chosen and instantly understandable, and the text clearly explains how each type of graph can be used to best display different types of data." SLJ

Includes glossary and bibliographical references

Sports illustrated 2011 almanac; by the editors of Sports illustrated. Time Home Entertainment 2010 559p il pa $14.99

Grades: 7 8 9 10 11 12 Adult   796
1. Sports 2. Reference books
ISBN 978-1-60320-863-5

Annual. First published 1991 with title: Sports illustrated . . . sports almanac

"Provides team and individual records and highlights for all major sports. . . . A brief essay opens the section on each sport, followed by page upon page of records, both current and retrospective. Interspersed throughout . . . are black-and-white and color photographs and notable quotations by sports figures." Am Ref Books Annu, 1993

Strother, Scott

The adventurous book of outdoor games; classic fun for daring boys and girls. [by] Scott Strother. Sourcebooks 2008 293p il pa $14.99

Grades: 4 5 6 7 Adult Professional   796
1. Games
ISBN 978-1-4022-1443-1 pa; 1-4022-1443-X pa

This book "outlines more than 100 games, each at different activity levels set by the amount of physical exertion required. . . . Each game discusses the number of players, ages, time allotted, and type of playing field, followed by a brief description of equipment, startup, object of the game, and how to play. . . . The easy-to-read, easy-to-follow format will provide hours of imaginative play for all of those who are willing to try. An excellent resource for parents, teachers, and activity directors and even for children themselves." SLJ

796.1   Miscellaneous games

Birmingham, Maria

Weird zone; sports. Maria Birmingham. Owlkids Books Inc. 2013 128 p. (Weird zone) $22.95

Grades: 4 5 6 7   796.1
1. Sports
ISBN 1926973607; 9781926973609
LC 2012948714

This book on unusual sports by Maria Birmingham is part of the "Weird Zone" book series. It includes such sports as "rolling down a hill in a plastic ball (aka 'zorbing') . . . professional-grade pillow fighting . . . lawn-mower racing . . . [and] extreme ironing. . . . Each sport gets a two-page spread." (Kirkus Reviews)

Sobey, Ed

Radio -controlled car experiments. Enslow Publishers 2011 128p il (Cool science projects with technology) lib bdg $31.93

Grades: 6 7 8 9   796.1
1. Science projects 2. Automobiles -- Models 3. Science -- Experiments
ISBN 978-0-7660-3304-7; 0-7660-3304-X

This explains how and why radio-controlled cars work, and offers experiments.

This book "is bursting with fast-paced experiments that have easy-to-follow instructions and are sure to interest young car enthusiasts." SLJ

Includes glossary and bibliographical references

796.2   Activities and games requiring equipment

Bell-Rehwoldt, Sheri

The kids' guide to jumping rope. Capstone Press 2011 32p il (Kids' guides) lib bdg $26.65

Grades: 4 5 6 7   796.2
1. Rope skipping
ISBN 978-1-4296-5443-2; 1-4296-5443-0
LC 2010035018

Describes the sport of jumping rope, including how-to information on jumps and tricks.

This includes "plentiful photos of giddy girls (and a few guys) madly skipping rope. . . . This makes jumping rope look like the best time in the world." Booklist

Includes bibliographical references

796.22 Skateboarding

Fitzpatrick, Jim

Skateboarding. Cherry Lake Pub. 2009 32p il (Innovation in sports) lib bdg $27.07

Grades: 4 5 6 7 **796.22**

1. Skateboarding

ISBN 978-1-60279-259-3 lib bdg; 1-60279-259-3 lib bdg

LC 2008007548

This describes skateboarding history, equipment, safety, and health benefits

This "stands out by emphasizing monumental shifts and advances in the events themselves. . . . Concise and occasionally revelatory." Booklist

Includes glossary and bibliographical references

Powell, Ben

Skateboarding skills; the rider's guide. Firefly Books 2008 128p il pa $16.95

Grades: 7 8 9 10 11 12 Adult **796.22**

1. Skateboarding

ISBN 978-1-55407-360-3; 1-55407-360-X

LC 2008-275044

The author "offers a colorful and useful manual for mastering numerous skateboard tricks. Intended for riders of all ages, the book presents step-by-step breakdowns of skills illustrated with photographs of children around age 12; each step of a trick features a picture and a written description." Libr J

Stock, Charlotte

Skateboarding step-by-step; [by] Charlotte Stock and Ben Powell. Rosen Central 2010 91p il (Skills in motion) lib bdg $31.95

Grades: 5 6 7 8 **796.22**

1. Skateboarding

ISBN 978-1-4358-3365-4; 1-4358-3365-1

LC 2009-11414

Presents instructions on skateboarding from learning to skateboard to executing jumps, flips, and tricks.

"Colorful photographs show the entire movement of each skill presented, giving new meaning to the term 'step-by-step.' Progression borders at the bottom of the pages highlight the salient points to notice in performing each skill from beginning to end." SLJ

Includes bibliographical references

796.3 Ball games

Chetwynd, Josh

The **secret** history of balls; Josh Chetwynd ; Illustrations by Emily Stackhouse. Perigee Trade 2011 xiv, 221p ill.

Grades: 7 8 9 10 11 12 Adult **796.3**

1. Ball games 2. Sporting goods 3. Sports -- History

ISBN 9780399536748

LC 2010054221

This book "mines the stories and lore of sports and recreation to offer insight into 60 balls - whether they're hollow, solid, full of air, or stuffed with twine or made of leather, metal, rubber, plastic, or polyurethane - that give us joy on playing fields and in every arena from backyards to stadiums around the globe." (Publishers' note)

796.323 Basketball

Burns, Brian

Basketball step-by-step; [by] Brian Burns and Mark Dunning. Rosen Central 2010 95p il (Skills in motion) lib bdg $31.95

Grades: 5 6 7 8 **796.323**

1. Basketball

ISBN 978-1-4358-3360-9; 1-4358-3360-0

LC 2009-14417

An introduction to the skills needed to play basketball uses a sequence of stop-action images and text instructions to illustrate such offensive and defensive moves as inside pivot and shoot, blocking out, and overhead pass.

"Colorful photographs show the entire movement of each skill presented, giving new meaning to the term 'step-by-step.' Progression borders at the bottom of the pages highlight the salient points to notice in performing each skill from beginning to end." SLJ

Includes bibliographical references

Coy, John

Hoop genius; how a desperate teacher and a rowdy gym class invented basketball. by John Coy ; illustrated by Joe Morse. Carolrhoda Books 2013 32 p. (reinforced) $16.95

Grades: 2 3 4 5 6 **796.323**

1. Basketball 2. Picture books for children 3. Basketball -- United States -- History

ISBN 0761366172; 9780761366171

LC 2011021235

This children's picture book looks at the invention of basketball. "In 1891, a teacher named James Naismith invented a game that was destined to become a national sensation. The boys' gym class at his school was particularly rowdy. He needed to find an indoor activity for the energetic lads that was fun, but not too rough. Inspired by a favorite childhood game, he stayed up late one night typing the rules of his new game." The class was captivated and the game's popularity spread. (School Library Journal)

Doeden, Matt

The **greatest** basketball records; by Matt Doeden. Capstone Press 2009 32p il (Sports records) lib bdg $17.95

Grades: 4 5 6 7 8   **796.323**
1. Basketball 2. National Basketball Association
ISBN 978-1-4296-2006-2 lib bdg; 1-4296-2006-4
lib bdg

LC 2008-2033

This "has enough historical insight and trivia to remain appealing over time. . . . Brief, lively sentences sum up individual feats and set them in context. . . . [This] should appeal to a wide audience." SLJ

Includes glossary and bibliographical references

Gifford, Clive
Basketball; [by] Clive Gifford. PowerKids Press 2009 32p il (Personal best) lib bdg $25.25
Grades: 4 5 6 7 8   **796.323**
1. Basketball
ISBN 978-1-4042-4444-3 lib bdg; 1-4042-4444-1
lib bdg

LC 2007-42989

This guide to basketball "offers well-organized and easy-to-follow instructions, focusing on rules, clothing, specific skills, and competitions. . . . Informative, readable." SLJ

Includes bibliographical references

Labrecque, Ellen
Basketball; by Ellen Labrecque. Cherry Lake Pub. 2009 32p il (Innovation in sports) lib bdg $27.07
Grades: 4 5 6 7   **796.323**
1. Basketball
ISBN 978-1-60279-256-2 lib bdg; 1-60279-256-9
lib bdg

LC 2008002044

This describes basketball history, rules, equipment, training, and great players

This "stands out by emphasizing monumental shifts and advances in the events themselves. . . . Concise and occasionally revelatory." Booklist

Includes glossary and bibliographical references

Robinson, Tom
Basketball. Norwood House Press 2010 64p il (Girls play to win) lib bdg $26.60
Grades: 4 5 6 7   **796.323**
1. Basketball
ISBN 978-1-59953-388-9; 1-59953-388-X

LC 2010009814

Covers the history, rules, fundamentals and significant personalities of the sport of women's basketball. Topics include: techniques, strategies, competitive events, and equipment

"With an easy design and format, the [text is] highly accessible to even the most reluctant readers and [provides] great exposure and insight into the world of female professional sports." Horn Book Guide

Includes glossary and bibliographical references

Slade, Suzanne
Basketball; how it works. Capstone Press 2010 48p il (Science of sports) lib bdg $29.32; pa $7.95

Grades: 4 5 6 7   **796.323**
1. Basketball
ISBN 978-1-4296-4021-3 lib bdg; 1-4296-4021-9 lib bdg; 978-1-4296-4873-8 pa; 1-4296-4873-2 pa

The book's "photograph-heavy design works to engage its audience, while the easy-to-read [text explains] the science." Horn Book Guide

Includes glossary

Stewart, Mark
Swish; the quest for basketball's perfect shot. by Mark Stewart and Mike Kennedy. Millbrook Press 2009 64p il lib bdg $25.26
Grades: 5 6 7 8   **796.323**
1. Basketball
ISBN 978-0-8225-8752-1 lib bdg; 0-8225-8752-1
lib bdg

LC 2008-24958

"The wide pages offer plenty of room for well-spaced text, sidebars, and illustrations. Each page has at least one picture, with mostly color photos, and the many action shots make the book more exciting. With information on women's and men's basketball at both collegiate and professional levels, this is a nice addition to sports collections." Booklist

Includes bibliographical references

Thornley, Stew
Kevin Garnett; champion basketball star. by Stew Thornley. Enslow Publishers 2013 48 p. col. ill. (library) $23.93
Grades: 4 5 6 7   **796.323**
1. Picture books for children 2. Basketball players -- United States -- Biography
ISBN 0766040283; 9780766040281

LC 2011031517

This book by Stew Thornley is a children's picture book biography of professional basketball player Kevin Garnett. In his "career, Garnett has won MVP trophies and other individual awards, but his NBA championship ring is most important to him. The team has always come first for KG." (Publisher's note)

Includes bibliographical references (p. 47) and index.

Kobe Bryant; champion basketball star. by Stew Thornley. Enslow Publishers 2013 48 p. col. ill. (library) $23.93
Grades: 4 5 6 7   **796.323**
1. Picture books for children 2. Bryant, Kobe, 1978- 3. Basketball players -- United States -- Biography
ISBN 0766040291; 9780766040298

LC 2011038174

This picture book by Stew Thornley is a biography of professional basketball player Kobe Bryant. "He can swish shots from long range or drive to the basket for a vicious dunk. Bryant once scored 81 points in a single game! He can also dish it to his teammates and play lockdown defense. . . . The Los Angeles Lakers superstar has won five NBA titles since coming out of high school, and he has earned many individual awards." (Publisher's note)

Tim Duncan; champion basketball star. by Stew Thornley. Enslow Publishers 2013 48 p. col. ill. (Sports Star Champions) (library) $23.93

Grades: 4 5 6 7 **796.323**

1. Basketball players -- United States -- Biography

ISBN 0766040305; 9780766040304

LC 2011050440

This book by Stew Thornley is part of the Sports Star Champions series and looks at basketball player Tim Duncan. The texts "focus on the athletes' professional careers, with very little information about their personal lives. . . . Each book ends with career statistics, the player's address, and a brief list for further reading." (School Library Journal)

Includes bibliographical references (p. 47) and index.

Yancey, Diane

Basketball. Lucent Books 2011 112p il (Science behind sports) lib bdg $33.45

Grades: 5 6 7 8 **796.323**

1. Basketball

ISBN 978-1-4205-0293-0; 1-4205-0293-X

LC 2010035239

This "explores the scientific principles such as momentum, gravity, friction, and aerodynamics, plus many more, behind [basketball]. . . . [The author discusses the sport's] origins, history, and changes, . . . the biomechanics and physiology of playing, related health and medical concerns, and the causes and treatment of sports-related injuries. Additional information tells how exercise, diet and nutrition, warming up, and training relate to peak performance and enjoyment of the sport. . . . [The book] has features on possible side effects of anabolic steroid use; how MRIs work; and how various improvements to the courts, basketballs, shoes, and uniforms have affected the game. The action photography . . . is fantastic. . . . [A must-have] for sports fans, athletes, science students, and even anyone considering a career in sports-related medicine, coaching, or other connected fields." SLJ

Includes glossary and bibliographical references

796.325 Volleyball

Crisfield, Deborah

Winning volleyball for girls; [by] Deborah W. Crisfield, John Monteleone; foreword by Maria Nolan. 3rd ed.; Chelsea House 2009 189p il (Winning sports for girls) lib bdg $44.95; pa $11.96

Grades: 7 8 9 10 11 12 **796.325**

1. Volleyball

ISBN 978-0-8160-7720-5 lib bdg; 0-8160-7720-7 lib bdg; 978-0-8160-7721-2 pa; 0-8160-7721-5 pa

LC 2009-5733

First published 1995 by Facts on File

This includes a brief history of volleyball followed by descriptions of the rules, court and equipment, training, techniques such as the spike, the serve, the block, and the pass, offensive and defensive play, putting a team together, and game strategies.

Includes glossary and bibliographical references

McDougall, Chros

Volleyball. Norwood House Press 2010 64p il (Girls play to win) lib bdg $26.60

Grades: 4 5 6 7 **796.325**

1. Volleyball

ISBN 978-1-59953-392-6; 1-59953-392-8

LC 2010009810

Covers the history, rules, fundamentals and significant personalities of the sport of women's volleyball. Topics include: techniques, strategies, competitive events, and equipment.

"With an easy design and format, the [text is] highly accessible to even the most reluctant readers and [provides] great exposure and insight into the world of female professional sports." Horn Book Guide

Includes glossary and bibliographical references

796.332 American football

Buckley, James

Ultimate guide to football; by James Buckley, Jr. Franklin Watts 2010 160p il $30; pa $7.99

Grades: 4 5 6 7 **796.332**

1. Football

ISBN 978-0-531-20752-9; 0-531-20752-8; 978-0-531-21023-9 pa; 0-531-21023-5 pa

LC 2009011003

This guide to football covers "historical highlights and delectable ephemera . . . with spreads covering each NFL team interspersed among chatty tales. . . . The highlighter-green color scheme matches the loud, vibrant layout and heightens the contrasting black-and-white player photos, while sporadic cartoons add some pep to the presentation." Booklist

Includes bibliographical references

Dougherty, Terri

The **greatest** football records; by Terri Dougherty. Capstone Press 2009 32p il (Sports records) lib bdg $17.95

Grades: 4 5 6 7 8 **796.332**

1. Football 2. National Football League

ISBN 978-1-4296-2007-9 lib bdg; 1-4296-2007-2 lib bdg

LC 2008-2035

This "has enough historical insight and trivia to remain appealing over time. . . . Brief, lively sentences sum up individual feats and set them in context. . . . [This] should appeal to a wide audience." SLJ

Includes glossary and bibliographical references

Frederick, Shane

Football; the math of the game. Capstone Press 2011 il (Sports math) lib bdg $30.65; pa $7.95

Grades: 6 7 8 9 **796.332**

1. Football 2. Mathematics

ISBN 978-1-4296-6567-4 lib bdg; 1-4296-6567-X lib bdg; 978-1-4296-7319-8 pa; 1-4296-7319-2 pa

LC 2011007864

Presents the mathematical concepts involved with the sport of football.

This offers a "dazzling layout, which includes countless vivid photographs and overlays of facts and figures. . . . This takes its concept and runs all the way to the end zone with it—dense and heavy, but undoubtedly impressive." Booklist

Includes bibliographical references

Gigliotti, Jim

  Football. Cherry Lake Pub. 2009 32p il (Innovation in sports) lib bdg $27.07

Grades: 4 5 6 7   **796.332**

  1. Football

  ISBN 978-1-60279-257-9 lib bdg; 1-60279-257-7 lib bdg

                       LC 2008002305

This describes football history, rules, equipment, training and strategy, and innovators

This "stands out by emphasizing monumental shifts and advances in the events themselves. . . . Concise and occasionally revelatory." Booklist

Includes glossary and bibliographical references

Gilbert, Sara

  The **story** of the NFL. Creative Education 2011 un il (Built for success) $23.95

Grades: 6 7 8 9   **796.332**

  1. Football 2. National Football League

  ISBN 978-1-60818-063-9; 1-60818-063-8

                       LC 2010031224

  A look at the origins, leaders, growth, and management of the NFL, the professional football league that was formed in 1920 and today governs 32 teams throughout the United States.

This book is "written in a lively style, yet with a minimum of fuss. . . . The slim, gleaming format, well-chosen photos, and the effort to explore what makes a company successful today [makes this title] unique." Booklist

Includes bibliographical references

Rappoport, Ken

  Peyton Manning; champion football star. by Ken Rappoport. Enslow Publishers 2013 48 p. col. ill. (Sports Star Champions) (library) $23.93

Grades: 4 5 6 7   **796.332**

  1. Quarterbacks (Football) 2. Football players -- United States -- Biography

  ISBN 0766040275; 9780766040274

                       LC 2011052759

This book is part of the Sports Star Champion series and looks at quarterback Peyton Manning. The "texts focus on the athletes' professional careers, with very little information about their personal lives. Occasional sidebars add additional interest, and each book ends with career statistics, the player's address, and a brief list for further reading." (School Library Journal)

Includes bibliographical references (p. 47) and index.

Stewart, Mark

  Touchdown; the power and precision of football's perfect play. by Mark Stewart and Mike Kennedy. Millbrook Press 2009 64p il lib bdg $27.93

Grades: 5 6 7 8   **796.332**

  1. Football

  ISBN 978-0-8225-8751-4 lib bdg; 0-8225-8751-3 lib bdg

                       LC 2008044295

"This attractive book opens with an intriguing history of American football. . . . Next, 10 double-page spreads feature 'Ten Unforgettable Touchdowns' in both professional and collegiate games from 1913 to 2006. After a chapter on 'touchdown makers,' spotlighting outstanding players . . . comes a short section on notable touchdown bloopers and another on trick plays and the element of surprise. . . . Photos, period prints, and reproductions of trading cards illustrate the text while adding color to the pages. . . . This nicely designed book provides plenty of on-the-field drama as well as pertinent information in a smoothly written overview of the touchdown." Booklist

796.334   Soccer (Association football)

Bazemore, Suzanne

  Soccer : how it works. Capstone Press 2010 48p il (Science of sports) lib bdg $29.32; pa $7.95

Grades: 4 5 6 7   **796.334**

  1. Soccer

  ISBN 978-1-4296-4025-1 lib bdg; 1-4296-4025-1 lib bdg; 978-1-4296-4876-9 pa; 1-4296-4876-7 pa

  The book's "photography-heavy design works to engage its audience, while the easy-to-read [text explains] the science." Horn Book Guide

  Includes glossary

Crisfield, Deborah

  Winning soccer for girls; [by] Deborah W. Crisfield; foreword by Bill Hawkey and Patrick Murphy. 3rd ed.; Chelsea House 2010 164p il (Winning sports for girls) lib bdg $39.50; pa $14.95

Grades: 7 8 9 10   **796.334**

  1. Soccer

  ISBN 978-0-8160-7714-4 lib bdg; 0-8160-7714-2 lib bdg; 978-0-8160-7715-1 pa; 0-8160-7715-0 pa

                       LC 2008-50595

  First published 1996 by Facts on File

  This soccer guidebook contains "material on developing agility, power, and strength and improving ball control and handling. The history and rules of the game are also examined, and a glossary lists soccer terms." Publisher's note

  Includes glossary and bibliographical references

Gifford, Clive

  The **Kingfisher** soccer encyclopedia. Kingfisher 2010 144p il $19.99

Grades: 5 6 7 8   **796.334**

  1. Reference books 2. Soccer -- Encyclopedias

  ISBN 978-0-7534-6397-0; 0-7534-6397-0

  First published 2006

  "Gifford does an excellent job of covering most aspects of the game from its history of a hundred-plus years to its current rules and tactics, teams, competitions, and famous players. Each section is clearly identified and provides additional information about the game. . . . Students involved in the sport or interested in specific teams or players will appreciate this book." Voice Youth Advocates

Includes glossary and bibliographical references

Hornby, Hugh

Soccer; written by Hugh Hornby; photographed by Andy Crawford. DK Pub. 2008 70p il (DK eyewitness books) $15.99

Grades: 4 5 6 7 **796.334**
1. Soccer
ISBN 978-0-7566-3779-8; 0-7566-3779-1
LC 2008276290

First published 2000

Examines all aspects of the game of soccer: its history, rules, techniques, tactics, equipment, playing fields, competitive play, and more.

Jennings, Madeleine

Soccer step-by-step; [by] Madeleine Jennings and Ian Howe. Rosen Central 2010 95p il (Skills in motion) lib bdg $31.95

Grades: 5 6 7 8 **796.334**
1. Soccer
ISBN 978-1-4358-3362-3; 1-4358-3362-7
LC 2009-12538

Presents instructions on the basic movements of soccer, including passing, shooting, and goalkeeping.

"Colorful photographs show the entire movement of each skill presented, giving new meaning to the term 'step-by-step.' Progression borders at the bottom of the pages highlight the salient points to notice in performing each skill from beginning to end." SLJ

Includes bibliographical references

Kassouf, Jeff

Soccer. Norwood House Press 2011 64p il (Girls play to win) lib bdg $26.60

Grades: 4 5 6 7 **796.334**
1. Soccer
ISBN 978-1-59953-464-0; 1-59953-464-9
LC 2011011037

Covers the history, rules, fundamentals, and significant personalities of the sport of women's soccer. Topics include: techniques, strategies, competitive events, and equipment.

Includes glossary and bibliographical references

St. John, Warren

Outcasts united; the story of a refugee soccer team that changed a town. Warren St. John. Delacorte Press 2012 226 p. (trade hardcover) $16.99

Grades: 6 7 8 **796.334**
1. Refugees 2. Soccer teams 3. Soccer coaches 4. Refugees -- Africa 5. Refugee children -- Georgia -- Clarkston 6. Soccer coaches -- Georgia -- Clarkston -- Biography
ISBN 0385741944; 9780375988806; 9780375990335; 9780385741941
LC 2012001412

This book by Warren St. John "is the story of a refugee soccer team, a remarkable woman coach and a small

southern town turned upside down by the process of refugee resettlement. It's a tale about resilience, the power of one person to make a difference and the daunting challenge of creating community in a place where people seem to have little in common." (Publisher's note)

Stewart, Mark

★ Goal! : the fire and fury of soccer's greatest moment; [by] Mark Stewart and Mike Kennedy. Millbrook Press 2010 64p il lib bdg $27.93

Grades: 5 6 7 8 **796.334**
1. Soccer
ISBN 978-0-8225-8754-5 lib bdg; 0-8225-8754-8 lib bdg
LC 2009014098

"This well-written book explores the nuances of scoring in the world's most popular sport. A quick history of the game lays the groundwork with details that may be new to even hard-core fans. The second chapter jumps right into the good stuff with descriptions of 10 of the most famous goals. . . . Also included is a rundown of the best male and female scorers from the early twentieth century to the present and weird anomalies and amusing anecdotes from soccer lore." Booklist

796.34 Racket games

Smolka, Bo

Lacrosse. Norwood House Press 2011 64p il (Girls play to win) lib bdg $26.60

Grades: 4 5 6 7 **796.34**
1. Lacrosse
ISBN 978-1-59953-463-3; 1-59953-463-0
LC 2011011050

Covers the history, rules, fundamentals, and significant personalities of the sport of women's lacrosse. Topics include: techniques, strategies, competitive events, and equipment.

Includes glossary and bibliographical references

Swissler, Becky

Winning lacrosse for girls; foreword by Katie Bergstrom. 2nd ed.; Chelsea House 2010 212p il (Winning sports for girls) lib bdg $44.95; pa $14.95

Grades: 7 8 9 10 **796.34**
1. Lacrosse
ISBN 978-0-8160-7712-0 lib bdg; 0-8160-7712-6 lib bdg; 978-0-8160-7713-7 pa; 0-8160-7713-4 pa
LC 2008-51346

First published 2004 by Facts on File

This lacrosse guidebook "teaches the game's basic skills, strategies, and drills and how to master them. Chapters cover the history of the game, the basics of stick handling, the rules of play, passing and receiving, offense and defense, key strategies, skills and tactics, conditioning, and . . . more." Publisher's note

Includes bibliographical references

796.342   Tennis (Lawn tennis)

Gifford, Clive

Tennis; [by] Clive Gifford. Sea-to-Sea Publications 2009 30p il (Know your sport) lib bdg $27.10

Grades: 5 6 7 8   **796.342**

1. Tennis

ISBN 978-1-59771-153-1 lib bdg; 1-59771-153-5 lib bdg

LC 2008-7322

"Describes the equipment, courts, training, moves, and competitions of tennis. Includes step-by-step descriptions of moves." Publisher's note

Includes glossary

796.352   Golf

Gifford, Clive

Golf : from tee to green; the essential guide for young golfers. Sea-to-Sea Publications 2010 64p il (Know your sport) $16.99

Grades: 5 6 7 8   **796.352**

1. Golf

ISBN 978-1-59771-217-0; 1-59771-217-5

LC 2008045861

Presents an instructional guide to the sport of golf, with information on different aspects of play and the equipment used.

"This book will be welcomed by young golf enthusiasts, whether they're beginners or experienced players.... A useful and attractive guide." Horn Book Guide

Includes bibliographical references

Kelley, K. C.

Golf. Cherry Lake Pub. 2009 32p il (Innovation in sports) lib bdg $27.07

Grades: 4 5 6 7   **796.352**

1. Golf

ISBN 978-1-60279-262-3 lib bdg; 1-60279-262-3 lib bdg

LC 2008002045

This describes golf history, rules, balls, and club technology, and innovators

This "stands out by emphasizing monumental shifts and advances in the events themselves.... Concise and occasionally revelatory." Booklist

Includes bibliographical references

796.357   Baseball

Adamson, Thomas K.

Baseball; the math of the game. Capstone Sports 2012 48p il (Sports math) lib bdg $30.65

Grades: 6 7 8 9   **796.357**

1. Baseball 2. Mathematics

ISBN 978-1-4296-6569-8

LC 2011004483

"Overall these books will appeal to serious sports fans who want to learn more about the numbers of the game." SLJ

Includes bibliographical references

Bertoletti, John C.

How baseball managers use math; math curriculum consultant: Rhea A. Stewart. Chelsea Clubhouse 2010 32p il (Math in the real world) lib bdg $28

Grades: 4 5 6   **796.357**

1. Baseball 2. Mathematics 3. Vocational guidance

ISBN 978-1-60413-604-3 lib bdg; 1-60413-604-9 lib bdg

LC 2009-16265

"The layout for [this] slim [title] is bright and colorful with a photograph and a 'You Do the Math' problem to solve and large, easy-to-read text on every spread. An answer key is included in the back matter, along with a page detailing the career choices and the educational requirements. . . . [It] includes such topics as how managers rely on player statistics to make decisions and why the pitch count is important to monitor. [This title] would be useful to supplement lessons on mathematics. [It] will also appeal to students wanting to learn more about math as it relates to specific careers." SLJ

Includes glossary and bibliographical references

Bryant, Howard

★ Legends; the best players, games, and teams in baseball. Howard Bryant. Philomel Books 2015 240 p. (Legends) $16.99

Grades: 6 7 8 9   **796.357**

1. Baseball 2. Baseball players 3. Baseball -- United States -- History 4. Baseball players -- United States -- Biography

ISBN 0399169032; 9780399169038

LC 2014031744

This book, by Howard Bryant, "is no traditional almanac of mundane statistics, but rather a storyteller's journey through baseball's storied game. . . . This collection covers some of the greatest players from Babe Ruth to Hank Aaron; the greatest teams to take the field and swing the bats; . . . the greatest playoff rivalries, including the 2004 showdown between the Red Sox and Yankees that turned into an instant classic; and . . . edge-of-your-seat World Series moments." (Publisher's note)

"Baseball fans are known for their mental repositories of statistics, facts, and figures, and this book will attract all manner of analysis and discussion among lovers of America's favorite pastime...Fans of other sports will cheer: this is only the first in a series devoted to sports legends, and a second volume, about football, will come out this fall."

Buckley, James

Ultimate guide to baseball. Shoreline Pub. 2010 160p il $30; pa $7.99

Grades: 4 5 6 7   **796.357**

1. Baseball

ISBN 978-0-531-20750-5; 0-531-20750-1; 978-0-531-21021-5 pa; 0-531-21021-9 pa

LC 2009043684

"This is a wide-ranging, brisk overview of the game. Sections briefly skim baseball history, hitting, pitching, defense and baserunning, and the World Series. Each major league team is introduced in a thumbnail sketch. . . . Other topics include baseball slang and nicknames, the 11 ways to get on base, and the author's choices for the best defensive players of all time. . . . Buckley writes with a lightly humorous touch that should appeal to fans and browsers." SLJ

Includes bibliographical references

Doeden, Matt

The **World** Series; baseball's biggest stage. by Matt Doeden. Millbrook Press, A division of Lerner Publishing Group, Inc. 2014 64 p. (lib. bdg. : alk. paper) $33.27

Grades: 4 5 6 7   **796.357**

1. Baseball 2. World Series (Baseball) 3. World Series (Baseball) -- History

ISBN 1467718963; 9781467718967

LC 2013018082

This book describes how "when the top teams face off in the World Series each season, team legacies and fans' hearts are on the line. Author Matt Doeden covers the century-long history of the World Series, from its humble beginnings to becoming a worldwide sensation. Discover the drama behind the statistics and record books that keeps the crowd enthralled!" (Publisher's note)

"This valentine to the Fall Classic opens with a quick history—though only through the 2012 series—then goes on in separate chapters to highlight renowned games, awesome individual performances, and memorable plays or incidents...The color photos on every spread are almost all action shots and capture the excitement of each feat or moment. An adequate set of recommended print and web resources follows a closing won-lost chart. A fine commemoration of the World Series' first century." Booklist

Includes bibliographical references (p. 62) and index

Dreier, David

Baseball; how it works. Capstone Press 2010 48p il (Science of sports) lib bdg $29.32; pa $7.95

Grades: 4 5 6 7   **796.357**

1. Baseball

ISBN 978-1-4296-4020-6 lib bdg; 1-4296-4020-0 lib bdg; 978-1-4296-4872-1 pa; 1-4296-4872-4 pa

"The well-designed layout, featuring glossy color visuals, is stimulating, and the concepts are further reinforced in brief definitions that appear at the bottom of many pages and in an appended glossary. . . . The clever approach will help draw interest and build understanding." Booklist

Includes glossary

Frager, Ray

Baltimore Orioles. ABDO Pub. Co. 2011 48p il (Inside MLB) $31.35

Grades: 4 5 6   **796.357**

1. Baseball 2. Baltimore Orioles (Baseball team)

ISBN 978-1-61714-036-5; 1-61714-036-8

LC 2010036557

"Written by [a] professional [sportswriter], peppered with well-chosen quotations and illustrated with photos on every page turn, this [book about the Baltimore Orioles] will interest die-hard baseball fans and is likely to engage reluctant readers." Horn Book Guide

Includes glossary and bibliographical references

Freedman, Lew

Boston Red Sox. ABDO Pub. Co. 2011 48p il (Inside MLB) $31.35

Grades: 4 5 6   **796.357**

1. Baseball 2. Boston Red Sox (Baseball team)

ISBN 9781617140372; 1617140376

LC 2010036554

"Written by [a] professional [sportswriter], peppered with well-chosen quotations and illustrated with photos on every page turn, this [book about the Boston Red Sox] will interest diehard baseball fans and is likely to engage reluctant readers." Horn Book Guide

Includes glossary and bibliographical references

Gitlin, Marty

Softball. Norwood House Press 2011 64p il (Girls play to win) lib bdg $26.60

Grades: 4 5 6 7   **796.357**

1. Softball

ISBN 978-1-59953-465-7; 1-59953-465-7

LC 2011011051

Covers the history, rules, fundamentals, and significant personalities of the sport of women's softball. Topics include: techniques, strategies, competitive events, and equipment.

Includes glossary and bibliographical references

Gola, Mark

Winning softball for girls; foreword by Gretchen Cammiso. 2nd ed.; Chelsea House 2009 220p il (Winning sports for girls) pa $14.95; lib bdg $44.95

Grades: 7 8 9 10   **796.357**

1. Softball

ISBN 0-8160-7716-9 lib bdg; 978-0-8160-7717-5 pa; 0-8160-7717-7 pa; 978-0-8160-7716-8 lib bdg

LC 2008-54453

First published 2002 by Facts on File

"Gola covers the history, rules of the game, and necessary equipment as well as tips for hitting, pitching, and base running. The fundamentals of defense and offense are covered, along with a number of drills in each area. In addition, the author details the various positions and gives advice on conditioning. . . . This title could prove useful in balancing baseball-laden collections." SLJ

Includes bibliographical references

Jennings, Madeleine

Baseball step-by-step; [by] Madeleine Jennings, Alan Smith, and Alan Bloomfield. Rosen Central 2009 95p il (Skills in motion) lib bdg $31.95

Grades: 5 6 7 8   **796.357**

1. Baseball

ISBN 978-1-4358-3361-6; 1-4358-3361-9

LC 2009-13246

An introduction to the skills needed to play baseball uses a sequence of stop-action images and text instructions to illustrate the moves needed to pitch, catch, field, hit, and run bases.

"Colorful photographs show the entire movement of each skill presented, giving new meaning to the term 'step-by-step.' Progression borders at the bottom of the pages highlight the salient points to notice in performing each skill from beginning to end." SLJ

Includes bibliographical references

Lipsyte, Robert

Heroes of baseball; the men who made it America's favorite game. [by] Robert Lipsyte. Atheneum Books for Young Readers 2006 92p il $19.95

Grades: 4 5 6 7   796.357

1. Baseball -- Biography

ISBN 0-689-86741-7; 978-0-689-86741-5

LC 2005010841

"Using as a focus some of baseball's greats—Big Al Spalding, Babe Ruth, Mickey Mantle, Jackie Robinson, Curt Flood . . . —Lipsyte offers a strong history of the game and its place in American culture. . . . Although much of this material, including the pictures, might be familiar to young readers already absorbed in the game, it is nicely laid out and colorfully formatted. Lipsyte has a clear, vivid style." Booklist

Includes glossary and bibliographical references

Rappoport, Ken

Alex Rodriguez; champion baseball star. by Ken Rappoport. Enslow Publishers 2013 48 p. col. ill. (Sports star champions) (library) $23.93

Grades: 4 5 6 7   796.357

1. Baseball players -- Biography 2. Baseball players -- United States -- Biography

ISBN 0766040267; 9780766040267

LC 2011043754

"Of the forty-three glossy story pages in the book, fifteen describe . . . [baseball player Alex Rodriguez's] career from 2004 forward. A Career Statistics Chart follows his performance through 2011. Color photos include A-Rod's early baseball career through 2011. Many of his impressive stats are discussed, including being the only major league player to hit thirty home runs and drive in one hundred runs in thirteen consecutive seasons." (Children's Literature)

Derek Jeter; champion baseball star. by Ken Rappoport. Enslow Publishers 2013 48 p. col. ill. (Sports star champions) (library) $23.93

Grades: 4 5 6 7   796.357

1. Baseball players -- Biography

ISBN 0766040259; 9780766040250

LC 2011033514

This book by Ken Rappoport, part of the Sports Star Champions series, presents a biography of "New York Yankees shortstop" Derek Jeter, who "has led the Yankees to five World Series titles and has won several individual awards." (Publisher's note) The "book ends with career statistics, the player's address, and a brief list for further reading." (School Library Journal)

Thorn, John

First pitch; how baseball began. Beach Ball Books 2011 40p il pa $14.99

Grades: 4 5 6 7   796.357

1. Baseball -- History

ISBN 978-1-936310-04-3; 1-936310-04-X

"Packed with vintage images and photographs, this history of baseball takes readers from the origins of the sport to the present day. . . . Thorn . . . writes clearly and eloquently. . . . Fans who think they know baseball may discover they have much to learn." Publ Wkly

Wong, Stephen

Baseball treasures; by Stephen Wong; photographs by Susan Einstein. Collins 2007 58p il $16.99; lib bdg $17.89

Grades: 5 6 7 8   796.357

1. Baseball -- History 2. Baseball -- Collectibles

ISBN 978-0-06-114464-6; 0-06-114464-9; 978-0-06-114473-8 lib bdg; 0-06-114473-8 lib bdg

LC 2006036069

This describes collectibles connected with the history of baseball, including balls, gloves and bats, jerseys, baseball cards, World Series memorabilia, and trophies.

This is "a well-designed, well-illustrated book for kids. . . . The text manages to impart the essential information without becoming bogged down in too much detail." Booklist

796.4 Weight lifting, track and field, gymnastics

Bobrick, Benson

A passion for victory: the story of the Olympics in ancient and early modern times; the story of the Olympics in ancient and early modern times. Benson Bobrick. Alfred A. Knopf 2012 xvi, 143 p.p ill. (hardback) $19.99

Grades: 4 5 6 7   796.4

1. Olympic games 2. Sports tournaments

ISBN 9780375868696; 9780375968693

LC 2011016036

The book offers an "account of the Olympic Games and their place in history. . . . [Athletes] Milo of Croton, Jim Thorpe, Johnny Weissmuller and Jesse Owens are given their due here. The photo-essay format conveys their stories . . . as well as the glory, shenanigans and pettiness of the Olympics throughout history. Almost every full-page spread includes at least one photograph, and the text . . . addresses the cultural context of the games." (Kirkus Reviews)

Includes bibliographical references.

Schwartz, Heather E.

Gymnastics. Lucent Books 2011 96p il (Science behind sports) lib bdg $33.45

Grades: 5 6 7 8   796.4

1. Gymnastics

ISBN 978-1-4205-0277-0; 1-4205-0277-8

LC 2010033544

This "explores the scientific principles such as momentum, gravity, friction, and aerodynamics, plus many more, behind [gymnastics]. . . . [The author discusses the sport's] origins, history, and changes, . . . the biomechanics and physiology of playing, related health and medical concerns, and the causes and treatment of sports-related injuries. Additional information tells how exercise, diet and nutrition, warming up, and training relate to peak performance and enjoyment of the sport. . . . One of the most interesting chapters .... is 'The Psychology of Gymnastics,' which discusses fears, force of will, honing the competitive edge, and the pressure to succeed. . . . [This volume is] jam-packed full of information. [A must-have] for sports fans, athletes, science students, and even anyone considering a career in sports-related medicine, coaching, or other connected fields." SLJ

Includes glossary and bibliographical references

796.42　Track and field

Cantor, George

Usain Bolt; by George Cantor. Lucent Books 2011 96 p. col. ill. (People in the News) (hardcover) $33.95

Grades: 6 7 8 9 **796.42**

1. Sprinters 2. Olympic athletes 3. Track and field athletes -- Jamaica -- Biography

ISBN 1420503413; 9781420503418

LC 2011006980

This book offers a biography of Olympic sprinter Usain Bolt, a Jamaican athlete who set several world records, by author George Cantor. It is part of the "People in the News" series, which "profiles the lives and careers of some of today's most prominent newsmakers. Whether covering contributions and achievements or notorious deeds, books in this series examine why these well-known individuals garnered public attention." (Publisher's note)

Includes bibliographical references and index

Gifford, Clive

Track and field; [by] Clive Gifford. PowerKids Press 2009 32p il (Personal best) lib bdg $25.25

Grades: 4 5 6 7 8 **796.42**

1. Track athletics

ISBN 978-1-4042-4442-9 lib bdg; 1-4042-4442-5 lib bdg

LC 2007-42984

This guide to track and field "offers well-organized and easy-to-follow instructions, focusing on rules, clothing, specific skills, and competitions. . . . Informative, readable." SLJ

Includes bibliographical references

Track athletics; [by] Clive Gifford. Sea-to-Sea Publications 2009 30p il (Know your sport) lib bdg $27.10

Grades: 5 6 7 8 **796.42**

1. Track athletics

ISBN 978-1-59771-154-8 lib bdg; 1-59771-154-3 lib bdg

LC 2008-7323

"Describes the equipment, training, moves, and running events of track competitions. Includes step-by-step descriptions of moves." Publisher's note

Includes glossary

Housewright, Ed

Winning track and field for girls; foreword by Jason-Lamont Jackson. 2nd ed.; Chelsea House 2009 194p il (Winning sports for girls) lib bdg $44.95; pa $11.96

Grades: 7 8 9 10 11 12 **796.42**

1. Track athletics

ISBN 978-0-8160-7718-2 lib bdg; 0-8160-7718-5 lib bdg; 978-0-8160-7719-9 pa; 0-8160-7719-3 pa

LC 2009-9019

First published 2004 by Facts on File

This includes a brief history of women's track, followed by topics including sprints, hurdles, middle and long distances, relays, jumping events, throwing events, the heptathlon, cross-country, and the triathlon, mental preparations and nutrition, stetches and weight lifting.

Includes bibliographical references

McDougall, Chros

Track & field. Norwood House Press 2011 64p il (Girls play to win) lib bdg $26.60

Grades: 4 5 6 7 **796.42**

1. Track athletics

ISBN 978-1-59953-467-1; 1-59953-467-3

LC 2011011053

Covers the history, rules, fundamentals, and significant personalities of the sport of women's track and field. Topics include: techniques, strategies, competitive events, and equipment.

Includes glossary and bibliographical references

796.48　Olympic games

Butterfield, Moira

Events. Sea-to-Sea Publications 2011 32p il (The Olympics) lib bdg $19.95

Grades: 4 5 6 7 **796.48**

1. Olympic games

ISBN 978-1-5977-1321-4; 1-5977-1321-X

LC 2011006465

This describes events of the Olympics.

Includes glossary and bibliographical references

History. Sea-to-Sea Publications 2011 32p il (The Olympics) lib bdg $28.50

Grades: 4 5 6 7 **796.48**

1. Olympic games

ISBN 978-1-5977-1319-1; 1-5977-1319-8

LC 2011006470

This is a history of the Olympics.

Includes glossary and bibliographical references

Scandals. Sea-to-Sea Publications 2011 32p il (The Olympics) lib bdg $28.50

Grades: 4 5 6 7 **796.48**

1. Olympic games 2. Sports -- Corrupt practices

ISBN 978-1-5977-1320-7; 1-5977-1320-1

LC 2011006473

"The book is divided into chapters that cover such topics as bribes, doping, and political problems. Along with famous events, such as the tragedy at the Munich Olympics, in which Israeli athletes were murdered, and the Marion Jones running scandal, in which she was stripped of her medals, there are other shocking and suprising moments. . . . This . . .

. volume, full of historical and contemporary photos, gives readers a lot to think about." Booklist

Other titles in the series are:

Events (2012)

History (2012)

Records (2012)

Farrell, Courtney

Terror at the Munich Olympics. ABDO 2010 112p il map (Essential events) $22.95

Grades: 6 7 8 9   **796.48**

1. Terrorism 2. Olympic games, 1972 (Munich, Ger.)

ISBN 978-1-60453-945-5; 1-60453-945-3

LC 2009-30426

This offers "vivid detail as well as historical and political context. . . . Farrell starts with the Munich Olympics but quickly backtracks to offer an explanation of the conflicts in the Middle East surrounding the creation of the State of Israel, and the rise of terrorism in response to these conflicts. The kidnapping and murder of the Israeli athletes is then described, along with the apparent bungling of rescue efforts. The book concludes with chapters on the response to the killings by Israel, as well as attempts at brokering peace in the region among the various countries in conflict. . . . [This title has] pertinent sidebars with primary source material. Archival photos add to the dramatic [narrative]." SLJ

Includes bibliographical references

Hotchkiss, Ron

The **matchless** six; the story of Canada's first women's Olympic team. Tundra Books 2006 194p il pa $16.95

Grades: 7 8 9 10   **796.48**

1. Olympic games 2. Women athletes 3. Track athletics

ISBN 0-88776-738-9; 978-0-88776-738-8

"Hotchkiss provides detailed information on the six Canadian athletes who won the track-and-field event in 1928, the first Olympics that included women. The personalities and accomplishments of Jane Bell, Myrtle Cook, Bobbie Rosenfeld, Ethel Smith, Ethel Catherwood, and Jean Thompson are highlighted with biographical information. . . . Accuracy is supported by quotes from newspapers, sports writers, coaches, and managers. . . . Anyone interested in the history of the Olympics, the history of women in the Games, or of track and field will find the book worth reading." SLJ

Macy, Sue

★ **Swifter,** higher, stronger; a photographic history of the Summer Olympics. by Sue Macy; foreword by Bob Costas. updated for the 2008 Summer Olympics; National Geographic 2008 96p il $18.95; lib bdg $27.90

Grades: 4 5 6 7   **796.48**

1. Olympic games

ISBN 978-1-4263-0290-9; 1-4263-0290-8; 978-1-4263-0302-9 lib bdg; 1-4263-0302-5 lib bdg

First published 2004

A detailed look at the history of the Olympic Games, from their origins in Ancient Greece, through their rebirth in nineteenth century France, to the present, highlighting the contributions of individuals to the Games' success and popularity.

"While other books on the topic go into more depth on specific sports, athletes, or historical events, none are as enthusiastically broad or as enjoyable to read as this one. And, it's superbly illustrated with colorful, well-chosen, and enticing photographs." SLJ [review of 2004 ed.]

Includes bibliographical references

796.5   Outdoor life

George, Jean Craighead

★ **Pocket** guide to the outdoors; [by] Jean Craighead George; with Twig C. George . . . [et al.] Dutton Children's Books 2009 138p il pa $9.99

Grades: 5 6 7 8   **796.5**

1. Camping 2. Outdoor life 3. Wilderness survival

ISBN 978-0-525-42163-4 pa; 0-525-42163-7 pa

"This survival guide is the book to read before a wilderness adventure. In short, clearly written chapters, it provides practical tips about ways to enjoy nature and includes information about building shelters, starting fires, making a fishing line and cleaning a fish, outdoor cooking, identifying animal tracks and edible and poisonous plants, and the basics of orienteering. Safety is always considered. Drawings and clearly labeled sketches help with identification." SLJ

Includes bibliographical references

Paulsen, Gary

★ **Woodsong**. Bradbury Press 1990 132p map hardcover o.p. pa $6.99

Grades: 7 8 9 10   **796.5**

1. Outdoor life 2. Sled dog racing 3. Minnesota

ISBN 0-02-770221-9; 1-4169-3939-3 pa

LC 89-70835

ALA YALSA Margaret A. Edwards Award (1997)

For the author and his family, life in northern Minnesota is a wild experience involving wolves, deer, and the sled dogs that make their way of life possible. Includes an account of Paulsen's first Iditarod, a dogsled race across Alaska

"The book is packed with vignettes that range among various shades of terror and lyrical beauty." Voice Youth Advocates

Schofield, Jo

Make it wild; 101 things to make and do outdoors. [by] Jo Schofield and Fiona Danks. Frances Lincoln 2010 159p il pa $24.95

Grades: 4 5 6 7 8   **796.5**

1. Nature craft 2. Outdoor life

ISBN 978-0-7112-2885-6; 0-7112-2885-X

"Using the raw materials nature has to offer, the authors offer clear, concise instructions on how to create ephemeral art, outdoor toys, jewelry, sculptures, and dozens of other things using materials like clay, ice, leaves, sand, and wood. The instructions offer good guidance but also encourage children to use their own creativity and imagination to craft the final product. The projects range in level of difficulty and, depending on the age of the child, can be done individually or in collaboration with siblings, peers, or parents. The authors include safety instructions and recommendations for further resources on outdoor creative exercises. The activities will teach problem solving and commonsense, useful skills; instill a deeper appreciation of nature; and encourage creativity and ingenuity. An excellent choice for any library collection." Booklist

796.51   Walking

Hart, John

Walking softly in the wilderness; the Sierra Club guide to backpacking. 4th ed, complete rev and updated; Sierra Club Books 2005 508p il map (Sierra Club outdoor adventure guide) pa $16.95

Grades: 8 9 10 11 12 Adult   796.51

1. Backpacking 2. Wilderness areas
ISBN 1-57805-123-1

LC 2004-56554

First published 1977

This guide for both the novice and experienced hiker reflects the environmental concerns of the Sierra Club. Among topics covered are: clothing and equipment; making and breaking camp; problem animals and plants; hiking and camping with kids. Listings of conservation and wilderness travel organizations, map and equipment sources, land management agencies, and Internet contacts are appended.

Includes bibliographical references

796.52   Walking and exploring by kind of terrain

Bodden, Valerie

To the top of Mount Everest; by Valerie Bodden. 1st ed. Creative Education 2012 48 p. ill. (some col.) (Great Expeditions) (paperback) $12.00; (library) $34.25

Grades: 5 6 7 8   796.52

1. Exploration 2. Mount Everest (China and Nepal) 3. Mountaineering -- Everest, Mount (China and Nepal) -- History 4. Mountaineers -- Everest, Mount (China and Nepal) -- Biography
ISBN 1608180700; 9780898126686; 9781608180707

LC 2010033553

This book by Valerie Bodden is part of the Great Expeditions series and looks at expeditions to the top of Mount Everest. "Bodden includes brief biographies of major people involved in each expedition, interspersed with the text. There are also numerous photographs or reproductions of paintings and woodcuts from the time of the expeditions." (Library Media Connection)

Includes bibliographical references and index.

Brennan, Kristine

Sir Edmund Hillary, modern day explorer. Chelsea House 2001 63p il (Explorers of new worlds) hardcover o.p. lib bdg $21.85

Grades: 4 5 6 7   796.52

1. Mountaineering 2. Mountaineers 3. Nonfiction writers 4. Mount Everest (China and Nepal)
ISBN 0-7910-5953-7 lib bdg; 0-7910-6163-9 pa

LC 00-43077

A biography of the New Zealander who, with his Sherpa climbing partner Tenzing Norgay, first reached the Summit of Mount Everest in 1953

"Accessible and well organized. . . . Fresh, appealing, and well written." SLJ

Includes glossary and bibliographical references

Cleare, John

Epic climbs. Kingfisher 2011 64p il (Epic adventure) $19.95

Grades: 5 6 7 8   796.52

1. Mountaineering
ISBN 978-0-7534-6573-8; 0-7534-6573-6

"Cleare gives the history of five of the most famous and dangerous mountains to climb: Eiger, K2, Everest, McKinley, and Matterhorn. Each section has a short, easy-to-read summary that gives the history of climbers who have conquered these peaks. Full-color photos include the view from the top and historical and contemporary climbing equipment." SLJ

Skreslet, Laurie

To the top of Everest; [by] Laurie Skreslet with Elizabeth MacLeod. Kids Can Press 2001 56p il hardcover o.p. pa $9.95

Grades: 4 5 6 7   796.52

1. Mountaineering 2. Mount Everest (China and Nepal)
ISBN 1-55074-721-5; 1-55074-814-9 pa

This is an account of Skreslet's "1982 trek up Everest when he became one of the first Canadians to make it to the top. Skreslet takes readers through every exciting, excruciating element of the climb. Beautiful color photographs abound." Booklist

Includes glossary

Wurdinger, Scott D.

Rock climbing; [by] Scott Wurdinger and Leslie Rapparlie. Creative Education 2007 48p il (Adventure sports) $31.35

Grades: 6 7 8 9   796.52

1. Mountaineering
ISBN 978-1-58341-394-4; 1-58341-394-4

LC 2005051785

This outlines "the history, gear, safety equipment, and competitions for [rock climbing]. . . . Large, full-color glossy photos . . . include action shots, closeup views of equipment and techniques, and pictures of exotic landscapes." SLJ

Includes bibliographical references

796.522   Mountains, hills, rocks

Athans, Sandra K.

Secrets of the sky caves; danger and discovery on Nepal's Mustang Cliffs. Sandra K. Athans. Millbrook Press 2014 64 p. color illustrations (lib. bdg. : alk. paper) $33.27

Grades: 4 5 6 7   796.522

1. Mountaineering 2. Nepal -- Description and travel 3. Caves -- Nepal -- Mustang (District) 4. Mustang (Nepal : District) -- Antiquities 5. Mountaineering -- Nepal

-- Mustang (District) 6. Mustang (Nepal : District) --
Discovery and exploration
ISBN 1467700169; 9781467700160

LC 2013017736

"What's more dangerous than scaling Mount Everest? For mountaineer Pete Athans, the answer lies in the ancient kingdom of Mustang, a remote part of the Asian nation of Nepal. . . From 2007 to 2012, Pete explored Mustang's sky caves with a team that included scientists, mountain climbers, and even two children. They found mummies, murals, manuscripts, and other priceless artifacts." (Publisher's note)

"The author, sister of expedition leader Pete Athans, offers a wealth of information about this little-known archaeological wonder. Color photographs provide stunning visuals. Reading list, timeline, websites. Bib., glos., ind." Horn

Includes bibliographical references (pages 61-62) and index

Berne, Emma Carlson

Summiting Everest; how a photograph celebrates teamwork at the top of the world. by Emma Carlson Berne. Capstone Compass Point Books 2014 64 p. (Compass point books. Captured history.) (library binding) $33.99

Grades: 5 6 7 8 9   **796.522**

1. Mountaineering 2. Mount Everest (China and Nepal) 3. Portrait photography -- Everest, Mount (China and Nepal) 4. Mountaineering expeditions -- Everest, Mount (China and Nepal) -- Pictorial works

ISBN 0756547342; 9780756547349; 9780756547905

LC 2013027843

This middle grades book by Emma Carlson Berne describes how "Not far from the top, before their final hours of climbing, team photographer Alfred Gregory snapped a picture of [Edmund] Hillary and [Tenzing] Norgay, with the imposing Himalayas spread out behind them. It was the highest photograph anyone in human history had ever taken. With a click of his camera shutter in May 1953, Gregory opened up a hidden world for the rest of humanity to share." (Publisher's note)

"—This outstanding follow-up to Capstone's "Captured History" series continues the same format, focusing on a single, emblematic photograph that defines an era or event... This set will show students how a single image can "capture" history and influence the perceptions and actions of those who see it. The books will certainly draw a large readership and are must-buys for all middle-level and secondary collections." SLJ

Includes bibliographical references and index

Other titles in the series include:

Assassination and its Aftermath (2014)
The Blue Marble (2014)
Breaker Boys (2012)
Civil War Witness (2014)
Hitler in Paris (2014)
Little Rock Girl 1957 (2012)
Man on the Moon (2011)
Migrant Mother (2011)
Raising the Flag (2011)
Tank Man (2014)

796.54 Camping

Champion, Neil

Fire and cooking. Amicus 2010 32p il (Survive alive) lib bdg $19.95

Grades: 4 5 6 7   **796.54**

1. Fires 2. Camping 3. Wilderness survival

ISBN 978-1-60753-039-8 lib bdg; 1-60753-039-2 lib bdg

LC 2010001626

This offers survival tips for building a fire and cooking in the wild, including information on different kinds of fires. Also discusses how to know what to cook and utensils to use.

This "colorful [book contains] numerous photos and illustrations that effectively break the [text] into small, readable chucks. There's lots of practical, everyday information here. . . . Brief yet gripping real-life survival stories are interspersed throughout the [book]." SLJ

796.6 Cycling and related activities

Macy, Sue, 1954-

★ **Wheels** of change; how women rode the bicycle to freedom (with a few flat tires along the way) National Geographic 2011 96p il map $18.95; lib bdg $27.90

Grades: 4 5 6 7 8   **796.6**

1. Cycling 2. Bicycles 3. Gender role 4. Women athletes 5. Sex role 6. Feminism

ISBN 978-1-4263-0761-4; 1-4263-0761-6; 978-1-4263-0762-1 lib bdg; 1-4263-0762-4 lib bdg

LC 2010-27141

This is an "engaging look at the emancipating impact that bikes had on late-nineteenth-century U.S. women. The eye-catching chapters, filled with archival images . . . zero in on the profound ways that bicycles subverted traditional notions of femininity. . . . Macy seamlessly weaves together research, direct quotes . . . and historical overviews that put the facts into context, while sidebars expand on related topics. . . . A strong, high-interest choice for both classroom and personal reading." Booklist

Includes bibliographical references

Robinson, Laura

★ **Cyclist** bikelist; a book for every rider. illustrated by Ramón K. Pérez. Tundra Books 2010 55p il pa $17.95

Grades: 4 5 6 7   **796.6**

1. Cycling 2. Bicycles

ISBN 978-0-88776-784-5; 0-88776-784-2

The author "covers a broad range of topics, from choosing and caring for a bike to differences in tires, how gear ratios work, and even proper dress and nutrition. She also provides a quick overview of the bicycle's history and inspiring sketches of several renowned racers. . . . Supplemented by photos of different types of bikes, Pérez's bright, cartoon-style pictures add both humor and . . . sharply drawn details. A first-rate guide." Booklist

796.72 Automobile racing

Arroyo, Sheri L.

How race car drivers use math; math curriculum consultant: Rhea A. Stewart. Chelsea Clubhouse 2010 32p il (Math in the real world) lib bdg $28

Grades: 4 5 6   **796.72**

1. Mathematics 2. Automobile racing 3. Vocational guidance

ISBN 978-1-60413-609-8 lib bdg; 1-60413-609-X lib bdg

LC 2009-21476

"The layout for [this slim [title] is bright and colorful with a photograph and a 'You Do the Math' problem to solve and large, easy-to-read text on every spread. An answer key is included in the back matter, along with a page detailing the career choices and the educational requirements. . . . In [this title], readers learn about qualifying times, track designs, and tracking fuel. . . . [This title] would be useful to supplement lessons on mathematics. [It] will also appeal to students wanting to learn more about math as it relates to specific careers." SLJ

Includes glossary and bibliographical references

Blackwood, Gary L.

The **Great** Race; the amazing round-the-world auto race of 1908. [by] Gary Blackwood. Abrams Books for Young Readers 2008 141p il $19.95

Grades: 6 7 8 9   **796.72**

1. Automobile racing 2. Voyages around the world

ISBN 978-0-8109-9489-8; 0-8109-9489-5

LC 2007-22414

"In 1908, several car manufacturers sponsored a global race that was routed across America, then across Siberia and Europe, ending in Paris. . . . Blackwood presents an extremely well-researched and detailed account of this large-scale publicity stunt. . . . There's enough sheer adventure here, carried out by some eccentric characters, to attract almost every reader. Helping things along are the photographs from the event. . . . A fascinating account." Booklist

Eagen, Rachel

NASCAR; written by Rachel Eagen. Crabtree Pub. Co. 2007 32p il (Automania!) lib bdg $25.20; pa $8.95

Grades: 4 5 6   **796.72**

1. Automobile racing 2. National Association for Stock Car Auto Racing

ISBN 978-0-7787-3007-1 lib bdg; 0-7787-3007-7 lib bdg; 978-0-7787-3029-3 pa; 0-7787-3029-8 pa

LC 2006012406

"Eagen has done an excellent job explaining the National Association of Stock Car Automobile Racing—the history, the modification of the cars, the drivers, and the competitions—while conveying a sense of the magnitude of the sport's current fan base. Her lucid, interesting text gets a lift from plenty of high-energy photos." Booklist

Kelley, K. C.

Hottest NASCAR machines; by K. C. Kelley. Enslow Publishers 2008 48p il (Wild wheels!) lib bdg $23.93

Grades: 4 5 6 7   **796.72**

1. Automobile racing 2. National Association for Stock Car Auto Racing

ISBN 978-0-7660-2869-2 lib bdg; 0-7660-2869-0 lib bdg

LC 2007007426

"Experience the thrill of a NASCAR race, and learn about the cars, personalities, and races associated with this sport." Publisher's note

"These books provide insight into the high-speed world of car racing. Types, styles, characteristics, and capabilities of the various racing machines are presented, along with the sport's history, statistics, and notable personalities in the field. Racing enthusiasts will appreciate the photographs and text boxes that expand the simple but informative text." Horn Book

Includes glossary and bibliographical references

Morganelli, Adrianna

Formula One. Crabtree Pub. 2007 32p il (Automania!) lib bdg $25.20; pa $8.95

Grades: 4 5 6   **796.72**

1. Automobile racing

ISBN 978-0-7787-3009-5 lib bdg; 0-7787-3009-3 lib bdg; 978-0-7787-3031-6 pa; 0-7787-3031-X pa

LC 2006-14362

This book "traces the history of Grand Prix racing, the development of the cars and their equipment, qualifying and racing, the tracks, safety measures, racing teams, and dominant drivers, with a sidebar on women in F1 racing. . . . Morganelli's writing is . . . organized and . . . readable. . . . [This] book is an attractive introduction." SLJ

Includes glossary

Pimm, Nancy Roe

The **Daytona** 500; the thrill and thunder of the great American race. Milbrook Press 2011 64p il (Spectacular sports) lib bdg $29.27

Grades: 5 6 7 8   **796.72**

1. Automobile racing

ISBN 978-0-7613-6677-5; 0-7613-6677-6

LC 2010027263

"Pimm, who worked in the pit box during her husband Ed Pimm's NASCAR racing days, offers an informative introduction to the Daytona 500. Beginning in 1903 . . . this traces the event's history and discusses the cars, drivers, strategies, and memorable moments. Colorful photos illustrate the clear text, while the many sidebars spotlight related facts." Booklist

Includes bibliographical references

796.8 Combat sports

Bjorklund, Ruth

Aikido. Marshall Cavendish Benchmark 2011 47p il (Martial arts in action) $29.93

Grades: 4 5 6 7 **796.8**
  1. Aikido
  ISBN 978-0-7614-4931-7; 978-1-6087-0361-6 e-book
  LC 2010013820
  This describes the history, equipment, and technique of aikido.
  This treats "martial arts with the dignity that serious enthusiasts bring to the sport. . . . Illustrations include not only photos of modern gear and from films but also historical images." Booklist

Ellis, Carol
  Judo and jujitsu. Marshall Cavendish Benchmark 2011 47p il (Martial arts in action) $29.93
  Grades: 4 5 6 7 **796.8**
  1. Judo 2. Jiu-jitsu
  ISBN 978-0-7614-4933-1; 978-1-6087-0363-0 e-book
  LC 2010013821
  This describes the history, equipment, and technique of judo and jujitsu.
  This treats "martial arts with the dignity that serious enthusiasts bring to the sport. . . . Illustrations include not only photos of modern gear and from films but also historical images." Booklist

  Kendo. Marshall Cavendish Benchmark 2010 47p il (Martial arts in action) $29.93
  Grades: 4 5 6 7 **796.8**
  1. Kendo
  ISBN 978-0-7614-4935-5; 0-7614-4935-3
  LC 2010013827
  This book about kendo offers "an introduction, a brief history, and expectations for students who begin taking classes. . . . [This title is] outstanding, using an approachable voice without fictionalizing and presenting the history of [kendo] in a way that makes it feel relevant." SLJ
  Includes glossary and bibliographical references

  Wrestling. Marshall Cavendish Benchmark 2010 47p il (Martial arts in action) $29.93
  Grades: 4 5 6 7 **796.8**
  1. Wrestling
  ISBN 978-0-7614-4941-6; 0-7614-4941-8
  LC 2010013819
  This book about wrestling offers "an introduction, a brief history, and expectations for students who begin taking classes. . . . [This title is] outstanding, using an approachable voice without fictionalizing and presenting the history of [wrestling] in a way that makes it feel relevant." SLJ
  Includes glossary and bibliographical references

Haney-Withrow, Anna
  Tae kwon do. Marshall Cavendish Benchmark 2011 47p il (Martial arts in action) $29.93
  Grades: 4 5 6 7 **796.8**
  1. Tae kwon do
  ISBN 978-0-7614-4940-9; 978-1-6087-0368-5 e-book
  LC 2010013828
  This describes the history, equipment, and technique of tae kwon do.
  This treats "martial arts with the dignity that serious enthusiasts bring to the sport. . . . Illustrations include not

only photos of modern gear and from films but also historical images." Booklist

Inman, Roy
  The **judo** handbook; [by] Roy Inman. North American ed.; Rosen Pub. 2008 256p il (Martial arts) lib bdg $39.95
  Grades: 7 8 9 10 11 12 **796.8**
  1. Judo
  ISBN 978-1-4042-1393-7; 1-4042-1393-7
  LC 2007-37742
  This features "step-by-step descriptions of various moves, accompanied by detailed, full-color photographs. [This] volume offers a background on the history of the art and its use as a sport as well as a system for self-defense. [The] handbook features a concise description of the judo fundamentals, then begins describing the techniques: throwing techniques, combination and counter-techniques, ground techniques, and combination and counter-techniques against them. The book makes good use of the Japanese terms used in judo study, integrating their meanings seamlessly into the text." SLJ
  Includes bibliographical references

Mack, Gail
  Kickboxing. Marshall Cavendish Benchmark 2011 47p il lib bdg $29.93
  Grades: 4 5 6 7 **796.8**
  1. Kickboxing
  ISBN 978-0-7614-4936-2; 978-1-6087-0366-1 e-book
  LC 2010014798
  This describes the history, equipment, and technique of kickboxing.
  This treats "martial arts with the dignity that serious enthusiasts bring to the sport. . . . Illustrations include not only photos of modern gear and from films but also historical images." Booklist

Mason, Paul, 1967-
  Boxing. Sea-to-Sea Publications 2011 32p il (Combat sports) lib bdg $28.50
  Grades: 4 5 6 **796.8**
  1. Boxing
  ISBN 978-1-59771-273-6; 1-59771-273-6
  "...[Provides] an inviting look for students who are learning about techniques and for examining records and statistics... Use to refresh an older collection." SLJ
  Includes glossary and bibliographical references

Pawlett, Mark
  The **tae** kwon do handbook; [by] Mark and Ray Pawlett. Rosen Pub. 2008 256p il (Martial arts) lib bdg $39.95
  Grades: 7 8 9 10 11 12 **796.8**
  1. Tae kwon do
  ISBN 978-1-4042-1396-8; 1-4042-1396-1
  LC 2007-31559
  This features "step-by-step descriptions of various moves, accompanied by detailed, full-color photographs. [The] volume offers a background on the history of the art and its use as a sport as well as a system for self-defense. .

. . [The book] spends about 150 pages on techniques, and also covers dietary recommendations, a history of Korea, a description of the I Ching, and other concepts. . . . It [includes] an excellent section on strength training . . . and the text devoted to basic fundamentals of the sport, such as stances and stepping, gives those building blocks appropriate importance." SLJ

Includes bibliographical references

Pawlett, Raymond

The **karate** handbook; [by] Ray Pawlett. Rosen Pub. Group 2008 256p il (Martial arts) $39.95

Grades: 7 8 9 10 11 12   **796.8**

1. Karate

ISBN 978-1-4042-1394-4; 1-4042-1394-5

LC 2007-32795

This "offers a thorough introduction to karate that covers both the underlying philosophy and the physical practice. A thoughtful, sophisticated history opens the book and discusses karate's roots in Zen Buddhism, the styles of karate, and dojo etiquette. Later spreads feature lucid, step-by-step instructions." Booklist

Includes bibliographical references

Ritschel, John

The **kickboxing** handbook; [by] John Ritschel. Rosen Pub. 2008 256p il (Martial arts) lib bdg $39.95

Grades: 7 8 9 10 11 12   **796.8**

1. Martial arts

ISBN 978-1-4042-1395-1; 1-4042-1395-3

LC 2007-37746

"This volume features step-by-step descriptions of various moves and strength-building exercises, accompanied by detailed, full-color photographs. . . . [This book] does emphasize safety, showing the correct way to punch in order to avoid injuring one's hand and displaying clear photographs on striking areas of the foot in order to perform kicks properly." SLJ

Whiting, Jim

Blood and guts; the basics of mixed martial arts. Capstone Press 2010 48p il (Velocity. the world of mixed martial arts) lib bdg $27.99

Grades: 5 6 7 8   **796.8**

1. Martial arts

ISBN 978-1-4296-3428-1 lib bdg; 1-4296-3428-6 lib bdg

LC 2009-7346

"Whiting provides information in fact boxes and in short bursts of text. Dramatic camera angles show sweating, bloody kickboxers, and cagefighters from just outside the ring. . . . The author also discusses how politics has entered into the viewing of competitions on network and pay-per-view television. Fans of the sport will be mesmerized." SLJ

Includes glossary and bibliographical references

Inside the cage; the greatest fights of mixed martial arts. Capstone Press 2010 48p il (Velocity. the world of mixed martial arts) lib bdg $27.99

Grades: 5 6 7 8   **796.8**

1. Martial arts

ISBN 978-1-4296-3426-7 lib bdg; 1-4296-3426-X lib bdg

LC 2009-7344

"Whiting provides information in fact boxes and in short bursts of text. Dramatic camera angles show sweating, bloody kickboxers, and cagefighters from just outside the ring. . . . The author also discusses how politics has entered into the viewing of competitions on network and pay-per-view television. Fans of the sport will be mesmerized." SLJ

Includes glossary and bibliographical references

A **new** generation of warriors; the history of mixed martial arts. Capstone Press 2010 48p il (Velocity. The world of mixed martial arts) lib bdg $27.99

Grades: 5 6 7 8   **796.8**

1. Martial arts

ISBN 978-1-4296-3427-4 lib bdg; 1-4296-3427-8 lib bdg

LC 2009-7339

"Whiting provides information in fact boxes and in short bursts of text. Dramatic camera angles show sweating, bloody kickboxers, and cagefighters from just outside the ring. . . . The author also discusses how politics has entered into the viewing of competitions on network and pay-per-view television. Fans of the sport will be mesmerized." SLJ

Includes glossary and bibliographical references

Striking, grappling, and ground fighting; the skills behind mixed martial arts. Capstone Press 2010 48p il (Velocity. the world of mixed martial arts) lib bdg $27.99

Grades: 5 6 7 8   **796.8**

1. Martial arts

ISBN 978-1-4296-3425-0 lib bdg; 1-4296-3425-1 lib bdg

LC 2009-7337

"Whiting provides information in fact boxes and in short bursts of text. Dramatic camera angles show sweating, bloody kickboxers, and cagefighters from just outside the ring. . . . The author also discusses how politics has entered into the viewing of competitions on network and pay-per-view television. Fans of the sport will be mesmerized." SLJ

Includes glossary and bibliographical references

796.815   Oriental martial arts forms

Mason, Paul, 1967-

Judo; [by] Paul Mason. Sea-to-Sea Publications 2009 30 p. col. ill. (Know your sport) (library) $27.10

Grades: 5 6 7 8   **796.815**

1. Judo

ISBN 978-1-59771-151-7; 1-59771-151-9

LC 2008007318

"Describes the equipment, training, moves, and competitions of judo. Includes step-by-step descriptions of moves." Publisher's note

Includes index.

796.91   Ice skating

McDougall, Chros

Figure skating. Norwood House Press 2010 64p il (Girls play to win) lib bdg $26.60

Grades: 4 5 6 7   **796.91**

1. Ice skating

ISBN 978-1-59953-389-6; 1-59953-389-8

LC 2010009809

"This begins with a look back at the origin of [figure skating] and the traces the young women who played a role in skating from the olden days to today. The first of six chapters describes skating basics . . . and then the progression of stars begins. . . . Color photos, sidebars, and boxed explanations break up the text. . . . A nicely compact history." Booklist

Includes glossary and bibliographical references

Uschan, Michael V., 1948-

Apolo Anton Ohno; by Michael V. Uschan. Lucent Books 2011 104 p. (People in the News) (hbk.) $33.95

Grades: 7 8 9 10   **796.91**

1. Speed skating 2. Olympic athletes 3. Speed skaters -- United States 4. Speed skaters -- United States -- Biography

ISBN 142050603X; 9781420506037

LC 2011003418

This book offers a biography of Olympic speed skater Apolo Anton Ohno, an athlete who has won eight Olympic medals as of 2012, by author Michael V. Uschan. It is part of the "People in the News" series, which "profiles the lives and careers of some of today's most prominent newsmakers. Whether covering contributions and achievements or notorious deeds, books in this series examine why these well-known individuals garnered public attention." (Publisher's note)

Includes bibliographical references and index.

796.93   Skiing and snowboarding

Kenney, Karen Latchana

Skiing & snowboarding. Norwood House Press 2010 64p il (Girls play to win) lib bdg $26.60

Grades: 4 5 6 7   **796.93**

1. Skiing 2. Snowboarding

ISBN 978-1-59953-391-9; 1-59953-391-X

LC 2010009808

Covers the history, rules, fundamentals and significant personalities of the sports of women's skiing and snowboarding. Topics include: techniques, strategies, competitive events, and equipment.

"With an easy design and format, the [text is] highly accessible to even the most reluctant readers and [provides]

great exposure and insight into the world of female professional sports." Horn Book Guide

Includes glossary and bibliographical references

Schwartz, Heather E.

Snowboarding. Lucent Books 2011 104p il (Science behind sports) $33.45

Grades: 5 6 7 8   **796.93**

1. Snowboarding

ISBN 978-1-4205-0322-7; 1-4205-0322-7

LC 2010033274

This "explores the scientific principles such as momentum, gravity, friction, and aerodynamics, plus many more, behind [snowbarding]. . . . [The author discusses the sport's] origins, history, and changes, . . . the biomechanics and physiology of playing, related health and medical concerns, and the causes and treatment of sports-related injuries. Additional information tells how exercise, diet and nutrition, warming up, and training relate to peak performance and enjoyment of the sport. . . . The action photography . . . is fantastic. . . . [This volume is] jam-packed full of information. [A must-have] for sports fans, athletes, science students, and even anyone considering a career in sports-related medicine, coaching, or other connected fields." SLJ

Includes glossary and bibliographical references

796.94   Snowmobiling

Woods, Bob

Snowmobile racers. Enslow Publishers 2010 48p il (Kid racers) lib bdg $23.93

Grades: 5 6 7 8   **796.94**

1. Snowmobiles

ISBN 978-0-7660-3487-7 lib bdg; 0-7660-3487-9 lib bdg

LC 2009020784

This describes snowmobiles and races for kids, discussing which snowmobiles qualify, how they are built and raced, who the best drivers are, what to look for in a snowmobile, safety, good sportsmanship, and how racing activities can be a good part of family life.

"The easily digestible text gets more visual weight on the page, but there are plenty of captioned color photos depicting different sorts of races as well as recreational snowmobiling." Booklist

Includes glossary and bibliographical references

796.962   Ice hockey

Adams, Carly

Queens of the ice; they were fast, they were fierce, they were teenage girls. Lorimer 2011 131p il (Record books) $16.95; pa $9.95

Grades: 5 6 7 8   **796.962**

1. Hockey 2. Women athletes

ISBN 978-1-55277-721-3; 1-55277-721-9; 978-1-55277-720-6 pa; 1-55277-720-0 pa

"Filled with exciting action, this . . . title . . . showcases the history of the Preston Rivulettes, a Canadian hockey team of teenage girls who played together for 10 seasons, from 1931 until 1940, without losing a game and at a time when many believed that girls could not play the sport and needed chaperones. . . . Adams deepens the story with the historical background of the Great Depression and the team's struggle to find money. Occasional archival photos and boxed inserts add to the clear, readable account." Booklist

Johnstone, Robb

Hockey; rev ed.; Weigl Publishers 2009 24p il (In the zone) $24.45; pa $8.95

Grades: 4 5 6 7   **796.962**

1. Hockey

ISBN 978-1-6059-6130-9; 1-6059-6130-2; 978-1-6059-6131-6 pa; 1-6059-6131-0 pa

LC 2009005607

First published 2001

"Colorful, informative. . . . For those just showing an interest in the bone-crushing sport, [this is] an excellent place to get their bearings. Using short, mostly two-page chapters, Johnstone explains the genesis of the sport, the gear needed, the rules, the positions, and the leagues, before concluding with biographies of eight legendary NHL players." Booklist

McKinley, Michael

Ice time; the story of hockey. Tundra Books 2006 80p il $18.95

Grades: 5 6 7 8   **796.962**

1. Hockey

ISBN 978-0-88776-762-3; 0-88776-762-1

"This straightforward history of hockey emphasizes the professional game and Canadian players. . . . Hockey enthusiasts will find this a welcome arrival." Booklist

"This book traces the sport from its modern beginning in 1875 to the present, crediting indoor rinks introduced in Canada during the late 1800s for the game's popularity. Historic personalities, athletes, and promoters are featured throughout in photos, sidebars, and vignettes. Although the book is written from a Canadian perspective, hockey enthusiasts of any nationality will appreciate the informative text and engaging photographs." Horn Book

McMahon, Dave

Hockey. Norwood House Press 2010 64p il (Girls play to win) lib bdg $26.60

Grades: 4 5 6 7   **796.962**

1. Hockey

ISBN 978-1-59953-390-2; 1-59953-390-1

LC 2010009811

Covers the history, rules, fundamentals and significant personalities of the sport of women's hockey. Topics include: techniques, strategies, competitive events, and equipment.

"With an easy design and format, the [text is] highly accessible to even the most reluctant readers and [provides] great exposure and insight into the world of female professional sports." Horn Book Guide

Includes glossary and bibliographical references

Sharp, Anne Wallace

Ice hockey. Lucent Books 2011 112p il map (Science behind sports) lib bdg $33.45

Grades: 5 6 7 8   **796.962**

1. Hockey

ISBN 978-1-4205-0281-7; 1-4205-0281-6

LC 2010025670

This book about ice hockey highlights "performance; chapter headings include topics such as 'Training and Nutrition,' 'High-Tech Equipment,' and 'Injuries and Treatments.' Physics, biology, and psychology concepts related to the [sport] are . . . wrapped into technical discussions of moves and techniques. Many photographs of pros and novices in action add interest." Horn Book Guide

Includes glossary and bibliographical references

Stewart, Mark

Score! the action and artistry of hockey's magnificent moment. Millbrook Press 2010 64p il $29.27

Grades: 5 6 7 8   **796.962**

1. Hockey

ISBN 978-0-8225-8753-8; 0-8225-8753-X

"Stewart and Kennedy take readers on a chatty, photo-studded tour of the art of scoring in the rink. This intermediate-level hockey book definitely isn't for beginners. . . . What savvy readers will get, however, is a bounty of information on the game's defining goals, goal scorers, and goal-scoring techniques. . . . This makes a worthy addition to any sports shelf." Booklist

797.1 Aquatic sports

Storey, Rita

Sailing. Sea-to-Sea Publications 2011 30p il (Know your sport) lib bdg $28.50

Grades: 4 5 6   **797.1**

1. Sailing

ISBN 978-1-59771-286-6

LC 2010003439

This "volume provides an introduction to the equipment, techniques, and safety measures for [sailing]. . . . Instructive photographs help illustrate such concepts as [tacking a sailboat], . . . while engaging stock images capture the excitement on the water. The [volume concludes] with racing information, profiling top racers, rules, and tactics." Horn Book Guide

Includes glossary

Thorpe, Yvonne

Canoeing and kayaking. Sea-to-Sea Publications 2011 30p il (Know your sport) $28.50

Grades: 4 5 6   **797.1**

1. Canoes and canoeing 2. Kayaks and kayaking

ISBN 9781597712859

LC 2010003438

This "volume provides an introduction to the equipment, techniques, and safety measures for [canoeing and kayaking]. . . . Instructive photographs help illustrate such concepts as . . . paddling a kayak, while engaging stock images capture the excitement on the water. The [volume concludes] with racing information, profiling top racers, rules, and tactics." Horn Book Guide

Includes glossary

Wurdinger, Scott D.

Kayaking; by Scott Wurdinger and Leslie Rapparlie. Creative Education 2006 48p il (Adventure sports) $21.95

Grades: 5 6 7 8   **797.1**

1. Kayaks and kayaking
ISBN 978-1-58341-397-5

LC 2005051057

"Strong, full-page color photographs illustrate this overview of kayaking. . . . Tracing the use of kayaks back thousands of years, the authors touch on the history of the boats before moving on to contemporary usage for sports and recreation. . . . The exciting views . . . will instantly draw browsers and serious readers alike." Booklist

Includes bibliographical references

797.2   Swimming and diving

Arroyo, Sheri L.

How deep sea divers use math; math curriculum consultant: Rhea A. Stewart. Chelsea Clubhouse 2010 32p il (Math in the real world) lib bdg $28

Grades: 4 5 6   **797.2**

1. Mathematics 2. Scuba diving 3. Vocational guidance
ISBN 978-1-60413-611-1 lib bdg; 1-60413-611-1 lib bdg

LC 2009-18413

"The layout for [this] slim [title] is bright and colorful with a photograph and a 'You Do the Math' problem to solve and large, easy-to-read text on every spread. An answer key is included in the back matter, along with a page detailing the career choices and the educational requirements. . . . [It] discusses how divers use math to determine how much air they will need in their tanks and use grids to map underwater shipwrecks. The mathematical topics covered include measurement, estimation, data analysis, and problem solving. . . . [This title] would be useful to supplement lessons on mathematics. [It] will also appeal to students wanting to learn more about math as it relates to specific careers." SLJ

Includes glossary and bibliographical references

Gifford, Clive

Swimming; [by] Clive Gifford. PowerKids Press 2009 32p il (Personal best) lib bdg $25.25

Grades: 4 5 6 7 8   **797.2**

1. Swimming
ISBN 978-1-4042-4443-6 lib bdg; 1-4042-4443-3 lib bdg

LC 2007-43003

This guide to swimming "offers well-organized and easy-to-follow instructions, focusing on rules, clothing, specific skills, and competitions. . . . Informative, readable." SLJ

Hoblin, Paul

Swimming & diving. Norwood House Press 2011 64p il (Girls play to win) lib bdg $26.60

Grades: 4 5 6 7   **797.2**

1. Diving 2. Swimming
ISBN 978-1-59953-466-4; 1-59953-466-5

LC 2011011038

Covers the history, rules, fundamentals, and significant personalities of the sport of women's swimming and diving. Topics include: techniques, strategies, competitive events, and equipment.

Includes glossary and bibliographical references

797.5   Air sports

Blair, Margaret Whitman

The roaring 20; the first cross-country air race for women. National Geographic 2006 128p il map $21.95

Grades: 6 7 8 9   **797.5**

1. Airplane racing 2. Women air pilots
ISBN 0-7922-5389-2

LC 2005-05472

"This book offers a detailed look at the first 'Powder Puff Derby' run in the summer of 1929. . . . Starting in Santa Monica, California, and ending in Cleveland, Ohio, the women flew over deserts and mountains. . . . It was an all-star event with racers including Amelia Earhart, 'Pancho' Barnes, and Louise Thaden. . . . The photos of flyers, landscapes, and memorabilia bring the story to life. This book is a welcome addition." Voice Youth Advocates

Includes bibliographical references

798.4   Horse racing

Scanlan, Lawrence

The big red horse; the story of Secretariat and the loyal groom who loved him. with photos by Raymond Woolfe. Harper Trophy 2011 166p il pa $7.99

Grades: 4 5 6 7   **798.4**

1. Horse racing 2. Stablehands
ISBN 978-0-06-202669-9; 0-06-202669-0

"This biography of the legendary racehorse provides many intimate details about his daily life and incredible prowess. . . . His good looks and tremendous athletic ability enabled him to win the Triple Crown at a record-breaking pace and the hearts of the American people. Scanlan focuses on the special relationship between Secretariat and his groom, Eddie Sweat. . . . Black-and-white photos are scattered throughout. . . . This solid book will have special appeal for horse lovers." SLJ

Tate, Nikki

Behind the scenes: the racehorse. Fitzhenry & Whiteside 2008 72p il $22.95; pa $18.95

Grades: 5 6 7 8   **798.4**

1. Horse racing
ISBN 978-1-55455-018-0; 1-55455-018-1; 978-1-55455-032-6 pa; 1-55455-032-7 pa

"A short history of horse racing opens this attractive and informative book. Tate discusses the breeding, training, and care of the horses but devotes plenty of space to the people who are involved in the sport. . . . The many color photos . . . are quite clear and well matched to the text." Booklist

799.2 Hunting

Peterson, Judy Monroe

Big game hunting. Rosen Central 2011 64p il map (Hunting: pursuing wild game!)) lib bdg $29.25; pa $12.95

Grades: 5 6 7 8   **799.2**
1. Hunting
ISBN 978-1-4488-1240-0 lib bdg; 1-4488-1240-2 lib bdg; 978-1-4488-2270-6 pa; 1-4488-2270-X pa
LC 2010006859

In this introduction to big game hunting "Peterson displays an impressive grasp of the pastime by throwing in almost everything: types of guns and bows, safety laws, licenses, land access, animal behavior, clothing, methods of hunting, and preparing harvested meat. . . . [The book] is jam-packed with info. . . . A green-heavy design, bright photoss of hunters . . . and prey, and above average back matter close out this solid entry." Booklist

Includes bibliographical references

Wolny, Philip

Waterfowl. Rosen Central 2011 64p il (Hunting: pursuing wild game!) lib bdg $29.25; pa $12.95

Grades: 4 5 6 7   **799.2**
1. Hunting 2. Water birds
ISBN 978-1-4488-1243-1 lib bdg; 1-4488-1243-7 lib bdg; 978-1-4488-2273-7 pa; 1-4488-2273-4 pa
LC 2010017396

This guide to waterfowl hunting covers what to wear and pack, shooting strategies, the construction of duck blinds, gun safety, hunting permits and licenses, and other laws relating to hunting limits, seasons, and private and public property.

Includes bibliographical references

800 LITERATURE, RHETORIC & CRITICISM

803 Dictionaries, encyclopedias, concordances

Benet's reader's encyclopedia; edited by Bruce F. Murphy. 5th ed.; Collins 2008 1210p $60

Grades: 8 9 10 11 12 Adult   **803**
1. Reference books 2. Literature -- Dictionaries
ISBN 978-0-06-089016-2
LC 2008-31430

First published 1948 under the editorship of William Rose Benet

This encyclopedia contains over 10,000 entries and covers world literature from early times to the present. Includes entries on authors, literary movements, principal characters, plot synopses, terms, awards, myths and legends, etc.

This is "an edifying staple for any literary library." Libr J

Dictionary of phrase and fable

Brewer's dictionary of phrase & fable; edited by Camilla Rockwood. 18th ed.; Brewer's 2009 xxv, 1460p il $49.95

Grades: 5 6 7 8 9 10 11 12 Adult   **803**
1. Allusions 2. Reference books 3. Mythology -- Dictionaries 4. Literature -- Dictionaries 5. English language -- Terms and phrases
ISBN 978-0-550-10411-3
LC 2009-379960

First published 1870 under the editorship of Ebenezer Cobham Brewer

"Over 15,000 brief entries give the meanings and origins of a broad range of terms, expressions, and names of real, fictitious and mythical characters from world history, science, the arts and literature." N Y Public Libr. Ref Books for Child Collect. 2d edition

Lewis, Catherine

★ **Thrice** told tales; Catherine Lewis. Atheneum Books for Young Readers 2013 144 p. (hardcover) $16.99

Grades: 7 8 9 10   **803**
1. Literary style 2. Authorship -- Handbooks, manuals, etc. 3. Literature -- Terminology
ISBN 1416957847; 9781416957843; 9781442460768
LC 2012010644

In this book, Catherine Lewis makes "use of the 'Three Blind Mice' nursery rhyme to illustrate nearly 100 elements of writing and literature—plot, dialogue, flashbacks, coincidence, and more. . . . Lewis expands on each term in brief 'Snip of the Tale' summaries and an extensive appendix." (Publishers Weekly)

"Three blind mice. See how they run—and how they take your writing to a new level. This clever review of literary terms will delight students and experts looking for a concise way to understand exposition and point-of-view or discern an epic from a bildungsroman." (Library Journal)

808 Rhetoric and collections of literary texts from more than two literatures

Bauer, Marion Dane

A **writer's** story; from life to fiction. Clarion Bks. 1995 134p $14.95; pa $6.95

Grades: 7 8 9 10   **808**
1. Authors 2. Women authors 3. Authors, American 4. Children's authors
ISBN 0-395-72094-X; 0-395-75053-9 pa
LC 94-48800

"Drawing on her own experiences, the novelist examines the origins of inspiration and the subconscious drives that compel authors to write. She points out that many components of fiction—characters, settings, plot details—need not be autobiographical, yet the text does suggest that a story's meaning is directly linked to the unique experiences of its creator. . . . Bauer provides invaluable information for both writers and readers of fiction." Publ Wkly

Cornwall, Phyllis

Put it all together. Cherry Lake Pub. 2010 32p il (Super smart information strategies) lib bdg $27.97

Grades: 3 4 5 6   **808**
  1. Report writing
  ISBN 978-1-60279-643-0 lib bdg; 1-60279-643-2
  lib bdg
                          LC 2009027806

"The appealing layout includes manageable paragraphs, a variety of engaging illustrations, and examples that clearly guide readers through each topic. In [this book], strategies include gathering resources, organizing information, and ways of presenting discoveries." SLJ

Includes glossary and bibliographical references

Dunn, Jessica

★ A **teen's** guide to getting published; publishing for profit, recognition, and academic success. [by] Jessica Dunn & Danielle Dunn. 2nd ed.; Prufrock Press 2006 249p pa $14.95

Grades: 7 8 9 10 11 12   **808**
  1. Authorship 2. Publishers and publishing
  ISBN 1-59363-182-0
                          LC 2006005109
First published 1997

"In addition to standard advice on publishers and agents, the authors give practical suggestions for finding a writing environment that is accessible to teens, such as school publication staffs and local newspaper internships. . . . Annotated appendixes list Web sites, books, journals, and contests. Also provided is information on mentors, writing camps, and courses catering to young authors, and a valuable list of mainstream publishers who have expressed openness to submissions from teens. This compact, sensible book discusses all kinds of writing." SLJ

Flath, Camden

Freelance and technical writers; words for sale. Mason Crest Publishers 2010 64p il (New careers for the 21st century: finding your role in the global renewal) $22.95

Grades: 7 8 9 10   **808**
  1. Authorship 2. Technical writing 3. Vocational
  guidance
  ISBN 1-4222-1814-7; 978-1-4222-1814-3
                          LC 2010011419

"Each chapter divides information between general freelance writing and technical writing, with the latter painted as the way of the future. . . . Flath carefully details the highs and lows of self-employment, keeping readers abreast of freelancers' special concerns, including taxes, time management, networking, and health insurance. He also highlights which personality types might enjoy writing projects. . . . Overall, the information is helpful for anxious students concerned about job prospects." Booklist

Fletcher, Ralph

How to write your life story; [by] Ralph Fletcher. Collins 2007 102p $15.99; pa $5.99

Grades: 5 6 7 8   **808**
  1. Authorship 2. Autobiography -- Authorship
  ISBN 978-0-06-050770-1; 978-0-06-050769-5 pa
                        LC 2007010990
A guide to help write an autobiography

"Fletcher gives readers and educators many practical and supportive tips. . . . Interspersed within the text are interviews with Jack Gantos, Kathi Appelt, and Jerry Spinelli, along with passages from the author's own memoir." SLJ

How writers work; finding a process that works for you. HarperTrophy 2000 114p pa $4.99

Grades: 4 5 6 7   **808**
  1. Authorship 2. Creative writing
  ISBN 0-380-79702-X
                        LC 00-27573

Focuses on the skills and techniques necessary for good writing, with excerpts from established writers and samples of young people's work as examples

"The book makes youngsters feel good about their writing without making light of the work involved. . . . This is a useful resource." SLJ

Includes bibliographical references

Gaines, Ann

★ **Don't** steal copyrighted stuff! avoiding plagiarism and illegal internet downloading. [by] Ann Graham Gaines. Enslow Publishers 2008 192p il (Prime) $38.60

Grades: 7 8 9 10   **808**
  1. Copyright 2. Plagiarism 3. Bibliographical citations
  ISBN 978-0-7660-2861-6; 0-7660-2861-5
                        LC 2007-8370

"The first three chapters explain just what plagiarism is, the types of plagiarism, and what copyright and fair use are. Two chapters explain how to find sources, take notes properly, and construct a project or paper using proper citations in MLA format. . . . Every student should be required to read this. . . . Librarians and teachers who are looking for explanations of copyright and plagiarism and illustrative examples will find this book to be a good resource." Libr Media Connect

Includes bibliographical references

Gilbert, Sara D., 1943-

Write your own article; newspaper, magazine, online. by Sara Gilbert. Compass Point Books 2009 64p il (Write your own) lib bdg $33.26; pa $5.95

Grades: 6 7 8 9   **808**
  1. Authorship 2. Journalism
  ISBN 0-7565-3855-6 lib bdg; 0-7565-3945-5 pa;
  978-0-7565-3855-2 lib bdg; 978-0-7565-3945-0 pa
                        LC 2008-13342

"There is much useful information provided. . . . [The book has] full-color photos, graphics, and tinted text boxes on nearly every page. [This is a solid selection] for aspiring writers." SLJ

Includes glossary and bibliographical references

Harper, Elizabeth

Your name in print; a teen's guide to publishing for fun, profit, and academic success. [by] Elizabeth Harper and Timothy Harper. St. Martin's Griffin 2005 186p pa $13.95

Grades: 7 8 9 10   **808**
1. Authorship 2. Publishers and publishing
ISBN 0-312-33759-0
LC 2004-24675
The authors "offer chapters and features on a variety of subjects: writing outlets (such as local papers and blogs); article topics; workspaces; book publishing and agents; tips from pros; sample columns; [and] 'glances' at current teen writers. . . . This book will be a useful addition for most libraries." Voice Youth Advocates
Includes bibliographical references

Janeczko, Paul B.
★ **Writing** winning reports and essays. Scholastic Reference 2003 224p (Scholastic guides) lib bdg $16.95; pa $7.95
Grades: 5 6 7 8   **808**
1. Authorship 2. Report writing
ISBN 0-439-28717-0 lib bdg; 0-439-28718-9 pa
LC 2002-30543
Provides strategies for writing successful research reports and essays, including social studies reports, book reports, persuasive essays, personal essays, and descriptive essays
"A solid and useful resource." SLJ

Mack, James
Journals and blogging; [by] Jim Mack. Raintree 2009 32p il (Culture in action) $28.21; pa $7.99
Grades: 5 6 7 8   **808**
1. Diaries 2. Weblogs
ISBN 978-1-4109-3406-2; 1-4109-3406-3; 978-1-4109-3423-9 pa; 1-4109-3423-3 pa
LC 2009000490
This "encourages readers to write as a way to express their feelings. It describes different types of journals and blogs. A page on Internet safety and the danger of downloading material encourages adult supervision. . . . Well organized and with bright, colorful photography, [this] introductory [title gives] readers good basic knowledge." SLJ
Includes glossary and bibliographical references

Miles, Liz
Writing a screenplay. Raintree 2009 32p il (Culture in action) $28.21; pa $7.99
Grades: 5 6 7 8   **808**
1. Drama -- Technique
ISBN 978-1-4109-3407-9; 1-4109-3407-1; 978-1-4109-3424-6 pa; 1-4109-3424-1 pa
This covers writing for "film and television. Plot, location, characters, dialogue, and mood are a few of the components discussed. . . . Well organized and with bright, colorful photography, [this] introductory [title gives] readers good basic knowledge." SLJ
Includes glossary and bibliographical references

Nobleman, Marc Tyler
★ **Extraordinary** e-mails, letters, and resumes; by Marc Tyler Nobleman. Watts 2005 128p il (F. W. Prep) $30.50
Grades: 7 8 9 10   **808**
1. E-mail 2. Letter writing 3. Résumés (Employment)

4. Electronic mail systems
ISBN 0-531-16759-3
This "builds a resume step-by-step, shows examples of different types of business letters, and addresses basic and not-so-basic netiquette. . . . [It is] laid out clearly and attractively, using bulleted lists, sample writings, and tables comparing examples of outstanding versus dull writing. The language is easy to follow, and the graphics and coloring enhances the books' readability." Voice Youth Advocates

Nuwer, Hank
To the young writer; nine writers talk about their craft. Watts 2002 111p il lib bdg $23 **808**
1. Authorship 2. Authors, American
ISBN 0-531-11591-7
LC 2001-24895
Nine writers, including a Hollywood screenwriter, a novelist, and a sportswriter, talk about their craft
"A concise, practical, and accessible guide. . . . A range of topics is discussed including the thrill of reporting, editing, storytelling, and writing for student publications, different audiences, and from personal experience. Also included are tips for aspiring writers. . . . This inspiring book offers a number of options for those considering the field." SLJ
Includes bibliographical references

Rosinsky, Natalie M.
Write your own biography; by Natalie M. Rosinsky. Compass Point Books 2008 64p il (Write your own) lib bdg $31.93
Grades: 5 6 7 8   **808**
1. Biography -- Authorship
ISBN 978-0-7565-3366-3 lib bdg; 0-7565-3366-X lib bdg
LC 2007011471
"Rosinsky adroitly leads readers through the challenging process of researching and writing a biography. Chapters include helpful suggestions, excerpts from published works, and writing exercises. Full-color photos, charts, and graphics break up the text." SLJ
Includes glossary and bibliographical references

Tadjo, Veronique
★ **Talking** drums; a selection of poems from Africa south of the Sahara. edited and illustrated by Véronique Tadjo. Bloomsbury Children's Books 2003 96p il map $15.95
Grades: 5 6 7 8   **808**
1. African poetry -- Collections
ISBN 1-58234-813-8
LC 2003-52173
A collection of traditional and twentieth-century poems from sub-Saharan Africa, written in or translated into English, that expresses the spirit and history of this region
"The contemporary and the traditional are both well represented in this lively anthology. . . . Illustrated with small, black-and-white folk-art drawings, the collection ranges widely, including poems of love, sorrow, and pride. . . . This [is a] fine resource for social studies and literature classes, which will also be great for reading aloud." Booklist
Includes glossary

Writing and publishing; the librarian's handbook. edited by Carol Smallwood. American Library Association 2010 189p (ALA guides for the busy librarian) pa $65

Grades: Adult Professional   **808**

1. Authorship 2. Library science

ISBN 978-0-8389-0996-6; 0-8389-0996-5

LC 2009-25047

"This important writer's guide is readable from cover to cover or by bits and pieces and is a helpful and handy read for every librarian." Libr Media Connect

Includes bibliographical references

808.02   Authorship techniques, plagiarism, editorial techniques

Levine, Gail Carson, 1947-

Writer to writer; from think to ink. Gail Carson Levine. HarperCollins 2014 304 p. (hardback) $16.99

Grades: 5 6 7 8   **808.02**

1. Authorship 2. Creative writing

ISBN 0062275305; 9780062275301

LC 2014005858

In this book, author Gail Carson Levine "offers a behind-the-scenes take on writing and teaches you how to become a world-class author. Drawing from her popular blog, Gail answers readers' fiction- and poetry-writing questions and dives into how to make a story come alive. If you're interested in writing prose and poetry or just want to be a better and more rounded writer, this book will help you on your creative journey." (Publisher's note)

"Ella Enchanted author Levine offers writing advice and prompts, primarily for fiction writers. The chapters, mostly expanded from her blog, look in-depth at aspects of writing including large-scale character and plot concerns and more specific matters of style. A lengthy section focuses on poetry and its role in fiction. Levine's second book on writing (Writing Magic) takes budding authors' craft questions seriously." Horn Book

Myers, Walter Dean, 1937-2014

Just write; here's how. Walter Dean Myers. 1st ed. Collins 2012 161 p. (lib. bdg.) $17.99; (trade paperback) $7.99

Grades: 7 8 9   **808.02**

1. Authorship 2. Fiction -- Technique 3. Creative writing 4. Authorship -- Miscellanea

ISBN 0062203894; 9780062203892; 9780062203908

LC 2012931468

In this book, "[t]he third National Ambassador for Young People's Literature offers a how-to guide for young writing enthusiasts. . . . [Walter Dean] Myers tells about his own life and how he became a writer before moving on to the craft itself, offering advice on structuring fiction using a six-box outline and nonfiction with a four-box outline. Excerpts from his own notebooks and commentaries on his work with teen writer Ross Workman" are also presented. (Kirkus Reviews)

808.042   Rhetoric in English

Gutman, Dan

My weird writing tips; by Dan Gutman and illustrated by Jim Paillot. HarperCollins Publishers 2013 160 p. $5.99

Grades: 3 4 5 6 7   **808.042**

1. Language arts 2. English language -- Composition and exercises

ISBN 0062091069; 9780062091062; 9780062091079

LC 2012029985

This book by Dan Gutman "offers tricks for spelling hard words, understanding the difference between similar words like "its" and "it's," and conquering grammar stumbling blocks like commas and apostrophes. He also teaches readers how to write an engaging story, in line with the grades 2–5 Common Core goals for writing a narrative." (Publisher's note)

808.1   Rhetoric in specific literary forms

Fandel, Jennifer

Puns, allusions, and other word secrets; [by] Jennifer Fandel. Creative Education 2005 48p il (Understanding poetry) $21.95

Grades: 7 8 9 10   **808.1**

1. Poetics

ISBN 1-58341-341-3

LC 2004058229

This "deals with the importance of choosing the right word, the opportunity to create new words or strange combinations, point of view, and hidden meanings. An excellent choice of poems . . . enhances the discussion of these aspects of poetry. The text asks readers questions about their impressions and reactions to the various verses." SLJ

Includes bibliographical references

Rhyme, meter, and other word music; [by] Jennifer Fandel. Creative Education 2005 48p il (Understanding poetry) $21.95

Grades: 7 8 9 10   **808.1**

1. Poetics

ISBN 1-58341-342-1

LC 2004058230

This "title offers clear explanations and examples of perfect, slant, and internal rhymes. The various forms a poem can take, including haiku, limerick, and sonnet, are also described. . . . The selections will increase young peoples understanding and appreciation of this word music." SLJ

Includes bibliographical references

Fletcher, Ralph

Poetry matters; writing a poem from the inside out. HarperCollins Pubs. 2002 142p hardcover o.p. pa $4.99

Grades: 4 5 6 7   **808.1**

1. Poetics

ISBN 0-06-623599-5 lib bdg; 0-380-79703-8 pa

LC 2001-24640

"Chapters deal with images; creating 'music,' or sounds and rhythms; how to generate ideas for poems; the construction of the words on the page; and more. Tips on fine-tuning are also given.... Major poetic forms are defined, including haiku, ode, and free verse, and there is a section on ways to share your work. Interspersed are Fletcher's personal insights and interviews with three poets—Kristine O'Connell George, Janet S. Wong, and J. Patrick Lewis.... Since this thought-provoking book covers more of the internal, less-tangible aspects of poetry, it may be more suited for readers who have some experience with the genre." SLJ

Includes bibliographical references

The **Poetry** Friday Anthology for Middle School; Poems for the School Year with Connections to the Common Core State Standards (CCSS) for English Language Arts (ELA) Edited by Sylvia M. Vardell and Janet S. Wong. Pomelo Books 2013 284 p. $26.98

Grades: Professional   808.1
1. Children's poetry 2. Common Core State Standards 3. Poetry -- study and teaching (elementary)
ISBN 193705778X; 9781937057787

Edited by Sylvia Vardell and Janet S. Wong, "The Poetry Friday Anthology is a series for K-5 and Middle School (6-8) designed to help teachers meet the Common Core State Standards (CCSS) in the English Language Arts (ELA)... . Teaching tips for each poem provide step-by-step poetry lessons that address curriculum requirements. The poems .. . include examples of ... metaphor and simile; personification; onomatopoeia; hyperbole; dramatic irony; and different forms." (Publisher's note)

Prelutsky, Jack
★ **Pizza,** pigs, and poetry; how to write a poem. Greenwillow Books 2008 191p il $16.99; pa $5.99
Grades: 4 5 6   808.1
1. Poetics
ISBN 978-0-06-143449-5; 0-06-143449-3; 978-0-06-143448-8 pa; 0-06-143448-5 pa
                                            LC 2007-36738
"Along with easy-to-follow tips for creating verse, haiku, and concrete poetry, the reigning Children's Poet Laureate offers insights into his own thought processes, . . . glimpses of his childhood, and personal anecdotes. . . . Prelutsky tucks in more than a dozen examples of his own work, plus 10 two-and-part-of-a-third line 'poem starts.'" Booklist

Seeing the blue between; advice and inspiration for young poets. compiled by Paul B. Janeczko. Candlewick Press 2002 132p $18.99; pa $7.99
Grades: 7 8 9 10   808.1
1. Poetics 2. American poetry -- Collections
ISBN 0-7636-0881-5; 0-7636-2909-X pa
                                            LC 2001-25882
"The letters are personal, friendly, and supportive. . . . A valuable addition to public and school libraries, with the potential for much classroom and personal use." SLJ

"Thirty-two established poets share their writing secrets in short letters addressed directly to readers. Accompanying poems may connect directly to a letter's content, give a representative sample of an individual's body of work, or

impart advice. This examination of individual style and fascination with the art of writing offers respect for both a craft and the readers interested in it." Horn Book

Wolf, Allan
Immersed in verse; an informative, slightly irreverent & totally tremendous guide to living the poet's life. [by] Allan Wolf; illustrated by Tuesday Mourning. Lark Books 2006 112p il $14.95
Grades: 5 6 7 8   808.1
1. Poetics
ISBN 1-57990-628-1
                                            LC 2005024825
Contains advice, ideas, writing activities, and encouragement from a working poet for aspiring poets. Includes poems by a variety of poets from the unknown to the famous, including Langston Hughes, E.E. Cummings, Eve Merriam, and more

"This how-to guide—chock-full of examples—is sure to inspire and nurture young poets. The information is intensive without being overwhelming, wise without being didactic. Wolf's love of language is evident throughout." SLJ

Includes glossary and bibliographical references

808.2   Rhetoric of drama

Elish, Dan
Screenplays. Marshall Cavendish 2011 95p il (Craft of writing) $34.21
Grades: 7 8 9 10   808.2
1. Motion picture plays -- Technique
ISBN 1-6087-0501-3; 978-1-6087-0501-6
This "deftly explores the essentials of the form and function of storytelling for a visual medium. Beginning with an extensive history of filmmaking . . . young writers get a glimpse of the evolution of the writer's role. . . . Snippets of scripts and full-page film stills used to illustrate various stages of writing reinforce the thrilling idea that your work could come to life onscreen. . . . Writing exercises and a further-reading section are included." Booklist

Includes bibliographical references

Lawrence, Colton
Big fat paycheck; a young person's guide to writing for the movies. Bantam Bks. 2004 269p il hardcover o.p. $11.99
Grades: 7 8 9 10   808.2
1. Motion picture plays -- Technique
ISBN 0-553-13122-2; 0-553-13122-2 pa
"A lively, compelling, and concisely concrete guide for creative kids with big-screen dreams." SLJ

808.3   Rhetoric of fiction

Bodden, Valerie
Creating the character; dialogue and characterization. [by] Valerie Bodden. Creative Education 2009 48p il (The art of creative prose) lib bdg $22.95

Grades: 6 7 8 9   **808.3**

1. Authorship 2. Creative writing 3. Characters and characteristics in literature 4. Fiction -- Technique
ISBN 978-1-58341-622-8 lib bdg; 1-58341-622-6 lib bdg

LC 2007-19611

"Young authors learn the importance of showing, rather than telling, when developing a character, as well as creating well-developed protagonists and antagonists, memorable minor characters, and natural-sounding dialogue. . . . Young writers who pick [this] up . . . will find valuable guidance." SLJ

Includes glossary and bibliographical references

Painting the picture; imagery and description. by Valerie Bodden. Creative Education 2009 48p il (The art of creative prose) lib bdg $22.95

Grades: 6 7 8 9   **808.3**

1. Authorship 2. Creative writing 3. Fiction -- Technique
ISBN 978-1-58341-623-5 lib bdg; 1-58341-623-4 lib bdg

LC 2007-18964

"Highlights the use of images that appeal to the senses, word choice, and figurative language. . . . Concludes with several suggested exercises. . . . Young writers who pick [this] up . . . will find valuable guidance." SLJ

Includes glossary and bibliographical references

Setting the style; wording and tone. [by] Valerie Bodden. Creative Education 2009 48p il (The art of creative prose) lib bdg $22.95

Grades: 6 7 8 9   **808.3**

1. Authorship 2. Creative writing 3. Fiction -- Technique
ISBN 978-1-58341-625-9 lib bdg; 1-58341-625-0 lib bdg

LC 2007-19609

"Encourages authors to find their own voice, explaining the difference between literary and direct styles and detailing the importance of rhythm, tone, and atmosphere in fiction writing. . . . Young writers who pick [this] up . . . will find valuable guidance." SLJ

Includes glossary and bibliographical references

Telling the tale; narration and point of view. [by] Valerie Bodden. Creative Education 2009 48p il (The art of creative prose) lib bdg $22.95

Grades: 6 7 8 9   **808.3**

1. Authorship 2. Creative writing 3. Fiction -- Technique
ISBN 978-1-58341-624-2 lib bdg; 1-58341-624-2 lib bdg

LC 2007-4198

"Covers the choice of a narrator and viewpoint, including multiple and unreliable narrators. . . . Young writers who pick [this] up . . . will find valuable guidance." SLJ

Includes glossary and bibliographical references

Farrell, Tish

Write your own fantasy story; by Tish Farrell. Compass Point Books 2006 64p il $31.93; pa $6.95

Grades: 4 5 6 7   **808.3**

1. Creative writing 2. Fantasy fiction -- Authorship
ISBN 0-7565-1639-0; 0-7565-1814-8 pa

LC 2005033654

"Full-color photographs, movie stills, and fun graphics enliven the [presentation]. . . . It's hard to think of a better way to hook emerging writers up with good advice about honing their skills." SLJ

Includes bibliographical references

Write your own mystery story; by Tish Farrell. Compass Point Books 2006 64p il $31.93; pa $6.95

Grades: 4 5 6 7   **808.3**

1. Creative writing 2. Mystery fiction -- Authorship
ISBN 0-7565-1641-2; 0-7565-1816-4 pa

LC 2005030730

"Full-color photographs, movie stills, and fun graphics enliven the [presentation]. . . . It's hard to think of a better way to hook emerging writers up with good advice about honing their skills." SLJ

Includes bibliographical references

Write your own science fiction story; by Tish Farrell. Compass Point Books 2006 64p il $31.93; pa $6.95

Grades: 4 5 6 7   **808.3**

1. Creative writing 2. Science fiction -- Authorship
ISBN 0-7565-1643-9; 0-7565-1818-0 pa

LC 2005030732

"Full-color photographs, movie stills, and fun graphics enliven the [presentation]. . . . It's hard to think of a better way to hook emerging writers up with good advice about honing their skills." SLJ

Includes bibliographical references

Hanley, Victoria

★ **Seize** the story; a handbook for teens who like to write. [by] Victoria Hanley. Cottonwood Press 2008 213p il pa $15.95

Grades: 7 8 9 10   **808.3**

1. Authorship 2. Creative writing 3. Fiction -- Technique
ISBN 978-1-877673-81-8 pa; 1-877673-81-1 pa

A guide to fiction writing for teenagers with advice on approaching the young-adult market, and discusses dialogue, plot, and other related topics; and presents interviews with established authors such as T. A. Barron, Joan Bauer, and Chris Crutcher.

"Hanley uses examples from familiar novels and authors such as 'Harry Potter' and Stephenie Meyer's Twilight . . . to illustrate elements of writing. . . . This book is an excellent resource for creative writing classes as well as individuals." SLJ

Includes bibliographical references

Levine, Gail Carson

★ **Writing** magic; creating stories that fly. Collins 2006 167p $16.99; pa $5.99

Grades: 5 6 7 8   **808.3**

1. Authorship 2. Creative writing 3. Fiction --

Technique

ISBN 978-0-06-051961-2; 0-06-051969-4; 978-0-06-051960-5 pa; 0-06-051960-6 pa

LC 2006-00481

"Levine, best known for Ella Enchanted (1997), offers middle-graders ideas about making their own writing take flight. . . . Among the topics she covers are shaping character, beginnings and endings, revising, and finding ideas. . . . Each chapter concludes with writing exercises. . . . A terrific item to have on hand for writing groups or for individual young writers who want to improve." Booklist

Litwin, Laura Baskes

Write horror fiction in 5 simple steps; Laura Baskes Litwin. Enslow Publishers 2013 48 p. (Creative Writing in 5 Simple Steps) $23.93

Grades: 4 5 6   **808.3**

1. Horror fiction -- Authorship 2. Horror tales -- Technique 3. Horror tales -- Authorship

ISBN 076603836X; 9780766038363

LC 2010038776

This book by Laura Baskes Litwin, part of the Creative Writing in 5 Simple Steps series, "shows aspiring writers how to write a terrifying tale of horror. . . . A good horror story is like a good ride at an amusement park. Feeling scared without having to face real danger is exhilarating. The story builds with tantalizing ideas. The reader inches out on the coaster track, knowing the precarious drop is seconds away." (Publisher's note)

Includes bibliographical references, filmography and index

Mazer, Anne

★ Spilling ink; a young writer's handbook. by Anne Mazer and Ellen Potter; illustrated by Matt Phelan. Flash Point 2010 275p il $17.99; pa $9.99

Grades: 5 6 7 8   **808.3**

1. Authorship 2. Creative writing 3. Fiction -- Technique

ISBN 978-1-59643-514-8; 1-59643-514-3; 978-1-59643-628-2 pa; 1-59643-628-X pa

"Two fine writers put their heads together and come up with an equally fine guide to their craft for beginners. . . . Mazer speaks to beginnings . . . while Potter tackles endings; and both have diverting things to say about everything that happens in between, whether it's the narrative voice or (eek) writer's block. [They are] always agreeable, practical, and commonsensical in their approach. . . . Their text is enlivened with sidebar features, personal anecdotes, and suggestions to readers for exercising their new skills. . . . Such devices, along with the authors' unfailing good humor, will go a long way to convincing their audience that writing can actually be fun! A notion that is nicely underscored by Phelan's engaging and always appealing illustrations." Booklist

Mlynowski, Sarah

See Jane write; a girl's guide to writing chick lit. by Sarah Mlynowski and Farrin Jacobs. Quirk Books 2006 191p il pa $14.95

Grades: 8 9 10 11 12   **808.3**

1. Authorship 2. Creative writing 3. Publishers and publishing 4. Fiction -- Technique

ISBN 1-59474-115-8

"Fun, inspiring, and organized in a clear and encouraging style, this book covers topics from what chick lit is to how to create believable characters, develop a plot, and set a tone. The authors discuss seeing a project through to the finish and getting it published. The writing style is quirky and the advice is sound." SLJ

Otfinoski, Steven

★ Extraordinary short story writing; by Steven Otfinoski. Franklin Watts 2005 128p il (F.W. prep) lib bdg $30.50; pa $9.95

Grades: 5 6 7 8   **808.3**

1. Authorship 2. Short story 3. Creative writing 4. Fiction -- Technique

ISBN 0-531-16760-7 lib bdg; 0-531-17578-2 pa

LC 2005006650

"In this excellent resource, specific ways to write different types of stories, project ideas, and resources are presented in such a way as to make short story assignments enjoyable. Readers are given many tips and practice activities in chapters that progress from gathering ideas to the final revision. Each section includes quotes from wellknown authors such as Edgar Allan Poe, Richard Peck, and Louis Sachar." SLJ

Includes bibliographical references

Rosinsky, Natalie M.

Write your own fairy tale; by Natalie M. Rosinsky. Compass Point Books 2008 64p il (Write your own) lib bdg $33.26; pa $6.95

Grades: 5 6 7 8   **808.3**

1. Creative writing 2. Fairy tales -- Authorship

ISBN 978-0-7565-3369-4 lib bdg; 0-7565-3369-4 lib bdg; 978-0-7565-3370-0 pa; 0-7565-3370-8 pa

LC 2007015720

This offers suggestions on how to write fairy tales, discussing settings, characters, viewpoint, plots, and style

Includes glossary and bibliographical references

Write your own myth; by Natalie M. Rosinsky. Compass Point Books 2008 64p il (Write your own) lib bdg $33.26; pa $6.95

Grades: 5 6 7 8   **808.3**

1. Creative writing 2. Authorship -- Myths

ISBN 978-0-7565-3372-4 lib bdg; 0-7565-3372-4 lib bdg; 978-0-7565-3373-1 pa; 0-7565-3373-2 pa

LC 2007011472

This offers suggestions for writing myths, discussing setting, characters, viewpoint, plots and style

Includes bibliographical references

Write your own tall tale; by Natalie M. Rosinsky. Compass Point Books 2008 64p il (Write your own) pa $6.95; lib bdg $33.26

Grades: 5 6 7 8   **808.3**

1. Creative writing 2. Tall tales -- Authorship

ISBN 978-0-7565-3376-2 pa; 0-7565-3376-7 pa; 978-0-7565-3375-5 lib bdg; 0-7565-3375-9 lib bdg

LC 2007012462

This offers suggestions for writing tall tales, discussing settings, characters, viewpoint, plots, and style

Includes glossary and bibliographical references

808.4   Rhetoric of essays

Orr, Tamra

★ **Extraordinary** essays. Franklin Watts 2005 128p il (F. W. Prep) $31; pa $9.95

Grades: 7 8 9 10   **808.4**

1. Essay 2. Authorship

ISBN 0-531-16761-5; 0-531-17576-6 pa

"This concise, appealingly designed writing guide offers practical advice to students on how to successfully complete essay assignments. Topics covered include choosing a topic, brainstorming, researching, crafting and defending a thesis statement, and revising." Booklist

Includes bibliographical references

808.5   Rhetoric of speech

Ryan, Margaret

★ **Extraordinary** oral presentations. Franklin Watts 2005 128p il (F. W. Prep) $31; pa $9.95

Grades: 7 8 9 10   **808.5**

1. Public speaking

ISBN 0-531-16758-5; 0-531-17577-4 pa

This offers advice on preparing oral presentations

This book provides "good, practical ideas for students." SLJ

Includes bibliographical references

808.8   Collections of literary texts from more than two literatures

Beware! R.L. Stine picks his favorite scary stories. HarperCollins Pubs. 2002 214p il $16.99; pa $5.99

Grades: 4 5 6 7   **808.8**

1. Horror fiction 2. Literature -- Collections

ISBN 0-06-623842-0; 0-06-055547-5 pa

LC 2002-18938

Stine "brings together 19 brief stories, folktales, poems, and cartoons from the likes of Ray Bradbury, William Sleator, Robert W. Service . . . Gahan Wilson, and Alvin Schwartz. . . . There's something in this diverse literary buffet for every taste—including enough genuine eeriness to make it a discomfiting choice for under-the-covers reading." Booklist

Classic horse stories; compiled by Christina Rossetti Darling and Blue Lantern Studio. Chronicle Books 2010 144p $19.99

Grades: 4 5 6   **808.8**

1. Horses 2. Literature -- Collections

ISBN 978-0-8118-6569-2; 0-8118-6569-X

LC 2010008550

"This compilation of stories, poems, and artwork celebrates the relationship between horses and their devotees. Darling pulls from a wide range of familiar, beloved material: excerpts from Steinbeck's The Red Pony, Farley's The Black Stallion, and Lewis's The Horse and His Boy join poetry from Shakespeare, Farjeon, and Stevenson. Varied paintings and illustrations from throughout the 20th century underscore the point that the book offers something for all tastes." Publ Wkly

Classic western stories; the most beloved stories. compiled by Cooper Edens. Chronicle Books 2009 140p il $19.99

Grades: 5 6 7 8   **808.8**

1. West (U.S.) 2. American literature -- Collections

ISBN 978-0-8118-6325-4

LC 2008009819

Stories, folktales, and poems with a western setting, including stories of Paul Bunyan, Pecos Bill, Indian legends, and tales of Lewis and Clark, among others.

"Colorful, often full-page, exquisitely produced illustrations by artists such as Frederic Remington, N. C. Wyeth, and Winslow Homer bring the words to life. Overall a visual delight, this stunning book is an excellent addition to art and literature collections." SLJ

The **Coyote** Road; trickster tales. edited by Ellen Datlow and Terri Windling; introduction by Terri Windling; decorations by Charles Vess. Viking Childrens Books 2007 523p il $19.99; pa $10.99

Grades: 7 8 9 10 11 12   **808.8**

1. Short stories 2. Literature -- Collections

ISBN 978-0-670-06194-5; 0-670-06194-8; 978-0-14-241300-5 pa; 0-14-241300-3 pa

LC 2007-12414

A collection of stories and poems about tricksters in all parts of the world by a variety of authors.

"This excellent collection is bound to find an audience among experienced readers of the genre but is attractive to less-able readers, as well, for the short, punchy stories and an always-engaging trickster character." SLJ

First kiss (then tell) [edited by] Cylin Busby. Bloomsbury Children's Books 2008 212p il $15.95; pa $8.95

Grades: 7 8 9 10   **808.8**

1. Kissing 2. Literature -- Collections

ISBN 978-1-59990-199-2; 978-1-59990-241-8 pa

LC 2007-42365

Twenty-five best-selling young adult authors share stories about their first kiss. Includes quotations, facts, advice, and illustrations.

This is an "entertaining collection. . . . These authors treat their own stories with the same freshness and respect with which they approach their YA novels. . . . Some stories are poems, one is a play, and a few are in comic form. . . . This is a good collection for browsing." Booklist

Flake, Sharon G.

You don't even know me; stories and poems about boys. Hyperion/Jump at the Sun 2010 195p $16.99

Grades: 7 8 9 10 **808.8**

1. Short stories 2. Boys -- Poetry 3. Boys -- Fiction 4. African Americans -- Poetry 5. African Americans -- Fiction

ISBN 978-1-4231-0014-0; 1-4231-0014-X

"This memorable collection of short stories and poems offers a glimpse into the urban lives of several African American boys. . . . Flake offers a vivid, unforgettable collection. . . . The voices ring true. . . . The stories and poetry are quite thought provoking." Voice Youth Advocates

Hip deep; opinions, essays, and vision from American teenagers. edited by Abe Louise Young. Next Generation Press 2006 164p pa $12.95 **808.8**

1. Teenagers' writings 2. American literature -- Collections

ISBN 0-9762706-2-5

"This collection of essays and poems by teens should inspire even the most reluctant writer to press on. By writing about their feelings on subjects ranging from frustration and anger to determination and renewal, these young people expose themselves from the inside out and launch themselves onto new paths." Voice Youth Advocates

I can't keep my own secrets; six-word memoirs by teens famous & obscure: from Smith magazine. edited by Rachel Fershleiser and Larry Smith. HarperTeen 2009 184p il pa $8.99

Grades: 7 8 9 10 **808.8**

1. Autobiographies 2. Teenagers' writings

ISBN 978-0-06-172684-2; 0-06-172684-2

LC 2009-14584

"The ruminations span from the haunting . . . to the funny . . . to the inspirational. . . . A razor focus is put on issues that hit youths the hardest. . . . It has just the right proportion of humor and heartbreak." Booklist

"Almost 800 authors, ranging in age from 13 to 19, contributed to this thought-provoking collection of individual memoirs. Based on the interest resulting from the publication of Not Quite What I Was Planning (HarperCollins, 2008), the editors of SMITH Magazine decided to challenge teens to write the story of their lives in a few brief words. . . . English teachers, theater teachers, and student book-club sponsors will revel in the instructional possibilities that could spring from this anthology. It may require some initial hand selling, but ultimately this book will find broad appeal in most collections." SLJ

Jocelyn, Marthe

Scribbling women; true tales from astonishing lives. Tundra Books 2011 197p il $19.95

Grades: 6 7 8 9 10 **808.8**

1. Literature -- Biography 2. Literature -- Women authors

ISBN 978-0-88776-952-8; 0-88776-952-7

Profiles women authors who have defied something that would have held others back, from societal convention to

oppression, including Nellie Bly, Daisy Ashford, and Dang Thuy Tram.

"Liberally using each writer's own words, Jocelyn's lyrical prose takes us deep into their lives, but mostly into their spirits and courageous souls. Young readers can share the obstacles, joys, and/or sorrows each women faced," Kirkus

Includes bibliographical references

★ **Leaving** home: stories; selected by Hazel Rochman and Darlene Z. McCampbell. HarperCollins Pubs. 1997 231p hardcover o.p. pa $11.99

Grades: 6 7 8 9 10 **808.8**

1. Short stories 2. Youth -- Fiction

ISBN 0-06-440706-3

LC 96-28979

An international anthology that reflects the thoughts and feelings of young people as they make their way into the world. Authors represented include Amy Tan, Sandra Cisneros, Tim Wynne-Jones, and Toni Morrison

"The editors have varied the tones, the music, the voices, and the meanings of the pieces, which provide both humorous and heartbreaking stories of the meaning of adolescence." ALAN

Read all about it! great read-aloud stories, poems, and newspaper pieces for preteens and teens. edited by Jim Trelease. Penguin Bks. 1993 489p il pa $13.95

Grades: 8 9 10 11 12 **808.8**

1. Authors 2. Literature -- Collections

ISBN 0-14-014655-5

LC 93-21781

This is a collection of 52 selections of fiction, poetry, and nonfiction from newspapers, magazines, and books by such authors as Cynthia Rylant, Jerry Spinelli, Howard Pyle, Rudyard Kipling, Robert W. Service, Maya Angelou, Moss Hart, Pete Hamill, and Leon Garfield. Includes biographical information about the authors

Spinelli, Eileen

Today I will; a year of quotes, notes, and promises to myself. [by] Eileen & Jerry Spinelli; illustrated by Julia Rothman. Alfred A. Knopf 2009 un il $15.99; lib bdg $18.99

Grades: 5 6 7 8 **808.8**

1. Quotations 2. Conduct of life 3. American literature -- Collections

ISBN 978-0-375-84057-9; 0-375-84057-5; 978-0-375-96230-1 lib bdg; 0-375-96230-1 lib bdg

LC 2008047869

"The Spinellis turn their skills to inspiring readers with quotes and promises for every day of the year. There is a single-page entry for each day, and each one begins with a quote from children's literature. . . . Each quote is followed by an explanatory note. Each note is then summarized into a short promise on which readers can reflect. . . . The book covers a vast array of topics and themes, from serious to silly, and is inspiring and helpful." SLJ

808.81   Collections in specific forms

★ **Crush:** love poems. Word of Mouth Books/KA
Productions 2007 72p pa $10
Grades: 8 9 10 11 12   **808.81**
1. Love poetry 2. Poetry -- Collections
ISBN 978-1-88801-840-0

"Alexander offers a cosmopolitan menu of tanka, haiku,
long titles that lead into short first lines, verbal formulas that
lead to sung discoveries, French phrases, prose poems, and
poems written in Spanglish. The book is divided into three
sections with various speakers, and a fourth section that
includes poems by Sherman Alexie, Pablo Neruda, Nikki
Giovanni, and the title poem, 'Crush' by Naomi Shihab Nye.
. . . This well-crafted anthology will capture the interest of
teens." SLJ

★ The **Death** of the Hat; A Brief History of Poetry in 50 Objects. selected by Paul B. Janeczko
; illustrated by Chris Raschka. Candlewick Press
2015 80 p. color illustrations $17.99
Grades: 3 4 5 6 7   **808.81**
1. Poetry -- Collections 2. Creation (Literary, artistic, etc.)
ISBN 0763669636; 9780763669638
LC 2013957308

This children's book, by Paul B. Janeczko, illustrated by
Chris Raschka, focuses on "poems through history inspired
by objects. . . . A book-eating moth in the early Middle Ages.
A peach blossom during the Renaissance. A haunted palace
in the Victorian era. A lament for the hat in contemporary
times. Poetry has been a living form of artistic expression
for thousands of years, and throughout that time poets have
found inspiration in everything." (Publisher's note)

"Janeczko and Raschka's stellar fourth poetry collaboration, following A Poke in the I and other acclaimed titles,
presents a chronological 'history' of the development of poetry, from the Middle Ages to the present. The highlighted
poems are, ostensibly, about objects, but a cigar is rarely
just a cigar. . . . Janeczko's substantial introduction gives an
overview of poetry's evolution over the centuries, yet works
like Lord Byron's 'A Riddle, on the Letter E' resonate powerfully on their own." Pub Wkly

★ A **foot** in the mouth; poems to speak, sing, and
shout. [edited by Paul B. Janeczko; illustrated by
Chris Raschka] Candlewick Press 2009 64p il
$17.99
Grades: 4 5 6 7   **808.81**
1. Poetry -- Collections
ISBN 978-0-7636-0663-3; 0-7636-0663-4
LC 2008-935581

"The poems in Janeczko and Raschka's collection . . .
are not complacent, although plenty are funny and some are
familiar. . . . Punchy collages flutter across airy white pages
in loose visual arrangements; torn scraps of origami paper
layer with fluid lines in tart color. Janeczko introduces the
collection with the idea that 'Poetry is sound,' a pleasure to
vocalize and memorize. . . . Readers will be emboldened to
join in the 'song.'" Publ Wkly

Greenberg, Jan

★ **Side** by side; new poetry inspired by art
from around our world. collected by Jan Greenberg.
Abrams Books for Young Readers 2008 88p il
$19.95
Grades: 8 9 10 11 12   **808.81**
1. Art -- Poetry 2. Poetry -- Collections
ISBN 978-0-8109-9471-3; 0-8109-9471-2
LC 2007-11973

This is an "anthology of accomplished poems inspired
by artworks. . . . [Greenberg brings] together the work of
poets and artists from around the globe. . . . The poems are
grouped loosely into categories, defined in Greenberg's inspirational introduction. . . . Each spread features a poem in
its original language, the English translation, and an artwork,
usually from the same country or culture as the poem. With
a few exceptions, the reproductions of the art, which ranges
from ancient to contemporary work, are sharp and clear, and
the moving, often startling poems invite readers to savor the
words and then look closely at each image." Booklist

★ **I** feel a little jumpy around you; a book of her
poems & his poems collected in pairs. [by] Naomi Shihab Nye and Paul B. Janeczko. Simon &
Schuster Bks. for Young Readers 1996 256p
hardcover o.p. pa $10
Grades: 7 8 9 10   **808.81**
1. Poetry -- Collections
ISBN 0-689-81341-4
LC 95-44904

A collection of poems, by male and female authors,
presented in pairings that offer insight into how men and
women look at the world, both separately and together

"Though the gender counterpoint really plays little part
in the juxtaposition, the pairings are piquant and provide a
manageable way to start talking about a very large collection
of poetry. An engaging marginal dialogue, taken from Nye's
and Janeczko's collaborative fax correspondence, appears
alongside the appendix and permits a revealing peek behind
the scences. Highly readable notes from contributors are
included, as is an index of poems and a gender-segregated
index of poets." Bull Cent Child Books

★ **It's** a woman's world; a century of women's
voices in poetry. edited by Neil Philip. Dutton
Children's Bks. 2000 93p il $17.99
Grades: 7 8 9 10   **808.81**
1. Women poets 2. Poetry -- Collections
ISBN 0-525-46328-3
LC 99-88363

An anthology of poetry by twentieth-century women
from around the world including, Sylvia Plath, Nigar Hanim,
Sonia Sanchez, and Nellie Wong

"Beautifully reproduced black-and-white photos introduce each section. Overall, this book is dense, challenging,
and provocative." SLJ

Light-gathering poems; edited by Liz Rosenberg. Holt & Co. 2000 146p $15.95

Grades: 7 8 9 10 **808.81**

1. Poetry -- Collections

ISBN 0-8050-6223-8

LC 99-49231

Companion volume to Earth-shattering poems (1997)

"Poems were chosen for their ability to 'gather light,' some representing beauty, some joy, some fascinating imagery, and some the illusive light at the end of a dark tunnel.... Notable writers such as Robert Frost, Walt Whitman, Langston Hughes, Edna St. Vincent Millay, Emily Dickinson, and Allen Ginsberg share the spotlight with contemporaries such as Gary Soto, Kate Schmitt, Mary Oliver, Steven Dauer, and Henry M. Seiden." Voice Youth Advocates

Includes bibliographical references

Nye, Naomi Shihab

★ **What** have you lost? poems. selected by Naomi Shihab Nye; photographs by Michael Nye. Greenwillow Bks. 1999 206p hardcover o.p. pa $9.99

Grades: 7 8 9 10 **808.81**

1. Loss (Psychology) 2. Poetry -- Collections

ISBN 0-380-73307-2

LC 98-26674

The topic of loss is "explored by the one hundred and forty poets whose work is collected here in twenty-two unlabeled, thematically arranged sections. The poems focus on specific losses, including those we experience as we grow up, leave home or homeland, fall in love, grow old; what we suffer when someone dies suddenly—or slowly; what we're deprived of by acts of violence and anger; and losses accrued through travel and distance. The poets are all contemporary. {Index.} Young adult." (Horn Book)

In her "introduction, the anthologist-poet considers loss—its certainty, scope, and effect, and its ability to give rise to art. The topic is thoroughly explored by the one hundred and forty poets whose work is collected here in twenty-two unlabeled, thematically arranged sections.... The poets are all contemporary, with a dozen or so hailing from outside the United States." Horn Book

The **Oxford** book of story poems; [compiled by] Michael Harrison and Christopher Stuart-Clark. Oxford University Press 2006 175p il pa $18.95

Grades: 5 6 7 8 **808.81**

1. Poetry -- Collections

ISBN 978-0-19-276344-0 pa; 0-19-276344-X pa

LC 2007282711

First published 1990

This anthology contains "narrative verse by British and American poets, from traditional ballads such as 'Sir Patrick Spens' to contemporary poems such as Judith Nicholls' 'Storytime.'... The poets include Carroll, Keats, de la Mare, Kennedy, Lear, Lindsay, Longfellow, Noyes, Poe, Southey, and Tolkien.... A handy collection of story poems for reading aloud or alone." Booklist [review of 1990 edition]

The **Oxford** book of war poetry; chosen and edited by Jon Stallworthy. Oxford University Press 2008 xxxi, 358 p.p (paperback) $19.95

Grades: 8 9 10 11 12 Adult **808.81**

1. War poetry 2. Poetry -- Collections 3. War poetry/Collections

ISBN 0199554536; 9780199554539

LC 8319303

This book is a collection of war poetry, arranged chronologically by conflict. The "250 poems in John Stallworthy's ... anthology span centuries of human experience of war, from David's 'Lament for Saul and Jonathan,' and Homer's 'Iliad,' to the finest poems of the First and Second World Wars, and beyond." (Publisher's note)

Includes bibliographical references and indexes.

★ **Poetry** speaks: who I am; poems of discovery, inspiration, independence, and everything else. Sourcebooks Jabberwocky 2010 136p $19.99

Grades: 5 6 7 8 9 10 **808.81**

1. Poetry -- Collections

ISBN 978-1-4022-1074-7; 1-4022-1074-4

This collection "aims at middle-grade readers with more than 100 strikingly diverse poems by writers including Poe, Frost, Nikki Giovanni, and Sandra Cisneros. The works are slotted together in mindful thematic order, beside occasional spot art.... Pairing a contemporary poem like Toi Derricotte's 'Fears of the Eighth Grade' alongside Keats's 'When I Have Fears That I May Cease to Be,' results in a refreshing lack of literary hierarchy that enables disparate works to build and reflect upon one another. An accompanying CD features recordings of 44 of the poems.... A sound and rewarding introduction to the joys of poetry." Publ Wkly

★ **River** of words; young poets and artists on the nature of things. edited by Pamela Michael; introduced by Robert Hass. Milkweed Editions 2008 298p il hardcover o.p. pa $18

Grades: 4 5 6 7 8 9 **808.81**

1. Nature poetry 2. Children's art 3. Children's writings 4. Teenagers' writings 5. Poetry -- Collections

ISBN 978-1-57131-685-1; 1-57131-685-X; 978-1-57131-680-6 pa; 1-57131-680-9 pa

"In 1995 Michael and Hass ... cofounded the River of Words project, designed to connect students' art and poetry education to the natural world immediately around them.... The poems and pictures in this handsomely designed volume have been culled from yearly contests.... The works are startling, many of them dislocating and highly complex." Publ Wkly

Step lightly; poems for the journey. collected by Nancy Willard. Harcourt Brace & Co. 1998 99p hardcover o.p. pa $12

Grades: 7 8 9 10 **808.81**

1. Poetry -- Collections

ISBN 0-15-202052-7

LC 98-5228

A collection of poems celebrating the ordinary in an unordinary way, by such authors as Emily Dickinson, Theodore Roethke, and D. H. Lawrence

"Willard weaves an anthology in which readers can find happiness, insight, inspiration, and wisdom." SLJ

The **tree** that time built; a celebration of nature, science, and imagination. selected by Mary Ann Hoberman and Linda Winston; [illustrations by Barbara Fortin] Sourcebooks Jabberwocky 2009 209p il $19.99

Grades: 5 6 7 8　　　　　　　　　**808.81**

1. Nature poetry 2. Science -- Poetry 3. Poetry -- Collections

ISBN 978-1-4022-2517-8; 1-4022-2517-2

LC 2009032608

An anthology of more than 100 poems celebrating the wonders of the natural world and encouraging environmental awareness. Includes an audio CD that comprises readings of 44 of the poems, many performed by the poets themselves.

"Classic works by Walt Whitman, Emily Dickinson, Christina Rossetti, and the like, and selections from contemporary poets are included. . . . This handsome collection is especially appropriate for classroom use and instruction. . . . From the playful to the profound, the poems invite reflection and inspire further investigation." SLJ

Includes glossary and bibliographical references

★ **War** and the pity of war; edited by Neil Philip; illustrated by Michael McCurdy. Clarion Bks. 1998 96p il $20

Grades: 5 6 7 8 9 10　　　　　　**808.81**

1. War poetry 2. Poetry -- Collections

ISBN 0-395-84982-9

LC 97-32897

"The selections, covering conflicts from ancient Persia to modern-day Bosnia, are by a wide variety of poets, from the well known (Tennyson, Whitman, Sandburg, Auden), to the obscure (Anakreon from ancient Greece and 11th-century Chinese poet Bunno). . . . The stark and simple scratchboard drawings are reminiscent of the Ernie Pyle illustrations from World War II and are as memorable as the best propaganda." SLJ

808.82　Collections of drama

Actor's choice; monologues for teens. edited by Erin Detrick. Playscripts 2008 131p pa $14.95

Grades: 6 7 8 9 10　　　　　　　**808.82**

1. Acting 2. Monologues 3. Drama -- Collections

ISBN 978-0-9709046-6-9; 0-9709046-6-5

LC 2007-50166

"This volume of highly entertaining monologues is gleaned from one-act and full-length plays published by Playscripts, Inc. . . . This is an excellent volume to help students prepare for competitions as well as to use in drama, speech, or English classes." SLJ

The **Book** of monologues for aspiring actors; [edited by] Marsh Cassady. NTC Pub. Group 1995 212p il pa $23.96

Grades: 7 8 9 10　　　　　　　　**808.82**

1. Acting 2. Monologues 3. Drama -- Collections

ISBN 0-8442-5771-0

LC 94-66239

"The selections range from the classical Greeks to Sam Shepard and Oscar Wilde; they give YA's the opportunity to develop characters of like ages in many different settings. Several questions to probe the actors' imaginations appear at the end of each monologue." SLJ

Great monologues for young actors; Craig Slaight, Jack Sharrar, editors. Smith & Kraus 1992 3v v1 pa $11.95; v2-v3 pa ea $14.95

Grades: 8 9 10 11 12　　　　　　**808.82**

1. Acting 2. Monologues 3. Drama -- Collections

ISBN 1-880399-03-2 v1; 0-57525-106-X v2; 1-57525-408-1 v3

These volumes provide an introduction and acting notes for monologues for men and women drawn from contemporary and classic works

★ **Great** scenes for young actors from the stage; Craig Slaight, Jack Sharrar, editors. Smith & Kraus 1991 256p 2v v1 pa $11.95; v2 pa $14.95

Grades: 7 8 9 10　　　　　　　　**808.82**

1. Acting 2. Drama -- Collections

ISBN 0-9622722-6-4 v1; 1-57525-107-8 v2

Contains scenes from classic and contemporary plays. The selections, graded according to ability level, include a range of roles for men, women, and groups. Includes a brief synopsis of each play along with special notes

New audition scenes and monologs from contemporary playwrights; the best new cuttings from around the world. edited by Roger Ellis. Meriwether Pub. 2005 177p pa $15.95

Grades: 6 7 8 9　　　　　　　　　**808.82**

1. Acting 2. Monologues 3. Drama -- Collections

ISBN 1-56608-105-X

"This work presents a wide variety of scenes selected especially for performers aged 12 to 24. . . . Introductions to each scene are informative and were reviewed and approved with some reshaping by the authors. . . . A good choice for students who seek new ideas for drama, forensic, and writing classes." SLJ

Surface, Mary Hall

★ **More** short scenes and monologues for middle school students; inspired by literature, social studies, and real life. by Mary Hall Surface. 1st ed.; Smith and Kraus 2007 207p (Young actors series) pa $11.95

Grades: 6 7 8 9　　　　　　　　　**808.82**

1. Acting 2. Monologues 3. Drama -- Collections

ISBN 978-1-57525-560-6 pa; 1-57525-560-X pa

LC 2007281299

A collection of original scenes and monologues written especially for middle-school actors

"This volume stands out for its distinct voices, multicultural characters, and engaging scenes. The book is well organized. . . . This excellent book would be useful in a variety of classrooms including speech/communication, drama, English, and social studies." SLJ

Includes bibliographical references

★ **Short** scenes and monologues for middle school actors. Smith & Kraus 1999 183p (Young actors series) pa $11.95

Grades: 6 7 8 9   **808.82**

1. Acting 2. Monologues 3. Drama -- Collections
ISBN 1-57525-179-5

LC 99-52457

A collection of original scenes and monologues written especially for middle-school actors

"A welcome find for young actors in search of material for auditions." SLJ

Includes bibliographical references

808.83   Collections of fiction

Hague, Michael

The **Book** of dragons; selected and illustrated by Michael Hague. Morrow 1995 146p il hardcover o.p. pa $10.99

Grades: 5 6 7 8   **808.83**

1. Short stories 2. Fantasy fiction 3. Dragons -- Fiction
ISBN 0-688-10879-2; 0-06-075968-2 pa

LC 94-42958

This collection comprises an anonymous poem, "The Dragon of Wantley," and sixteen literary fairy tales and retellings of folktales and legends about dragons. The tales include "Kenneth Grahame's 'Reluctant Dragon,' Kan Pao's 'Li Chi Slays the Serpent,' J.R.R. Tolkien's 'Bilbo Baggins and Smaug,' the Grimms' 'Devil and His Grandmother,' and William H.H. Kingston's 'St. George and the Dragon.'" (Booklist) "Grades three to six." (SLJ)

"Excerpts from classic novels such as J. R. R. Tolkien's The Hobbit, C. S. Lewis's Voyage of the Dawn Treader, and short stories such as Kenneth Grahame's 'The Reluctant Dragon' are included. In addition, there are folktales from China, Italy, and Germany. Most of the heroes are men, but occasionally children are the only ones who can outsmart the dragon. . . . Hague's beautiful full-page watercolors reflect the different moods of the stories and the temperaments of the dragons depicted." SLJ

808.85   Collections of speeches

Lend me your ears; great speeches in history. selected and introduced by William Safire. Updated and expanded; W.W. Norton 2004 1157p $39.95

Grades: 8 9 10 11 12 Adult   **808.85**

1. Speeches
ISBN 978-0-393-05931-1; 0-393-05931-6

LC 2004-13625

First published 1992

This "is a good addition for those . . . in need of modern speeches. With an excellent index." Libr J

"The third edition of this comprehensive collection of oratory through the ages is appropriately edited by former presidential speechwriter Safire—a man who knows firsthand the importance of putting together the right words for the right moment. . . . This is an invaluable reference for writers and speakers, students of history and those who simply appreciate great oratory." PW

808.88   Collections of miscellaneous writings

Alcorn, Stephen

A **gift** of days; the greatest words to live by. Atheneum Books for Young Readers 2009 115p il $21.99

Grades: 5 6 7 8   **808.88**

1. Quotations 2. Celebrities
ISBN 978-1-4169-6776-7; 1-4169-6776-1

LC 2007-48766

"Beautifully designed and imaginatively conceptualized, this volume presents 366 days and 366 quotations from famous people, tagged to the days they were born. Alcorn lays this out on each double-page spread with a stunning polychrome-relief block-print bordered with pattern on one leaf and, facing, a week of birthdays and quotes. These images are often brilliantly inventive. . . . Librarians, educators and historically minded kids will take much pleasure from looking up birthdays to see the associated wisdom from women and men across the ages." Kirkus

O'Brien, Geoffrey

Bartlett's familiar quotations; a collection of passages, phrases, and proverbs traced to their sources in ancient and modern literature. by John Bartlett ; Geoffrey O'Brien, general editor. 18th ed. Little, Brown, and Co. 2012 lxi, 1438 p.p (hardcover) $50.00

Grades: 8 9 10 11 12 Adult   **808.88**

1. Quotations 2. Quotations, English
ISBN 0316017590; 9780316017596

LC 2012019870

This book, in its 18th edition, presents a collection of quotations "from the times of ancient Egyptians to the present day." (Publisher's note) It "includes 2500 new quotes and more than 800 newcomers, from Julia Child to David Foster Wallace. Quotes have been culled to bring in more foreigners and women and more material from fiction and poetry." (Library Journal)

809   History, description, critical appraisal of more than two literatures

Bookmarked; teen essays on life and literature from Tolkien to Twilight. edited by Ann Camacho. Free Spirit Pub. 2012 215 p. $15.99

Grades: 6 7 8   **809**

1. Essays 2. Teenagers -- Conduct of life 3. Literature

-- History and criticism 4. Life in literature 5. Literature and morals 6. Literature -- Appreciation 7. Teenagers -- Books and reading
ISBN 1575423960; 9781575423968

LC 2011043942

Edited by Ann Camacho, the book offers 50 essays in which "young people from a wide range of backgrounds reflect on how words from literature connect with and influence their lives, goals, and personal philosophies. Essays explore character building topics including suffering the death of a parent, facing a life-threatening illness, letting go of perfectionism, making friends, reaching goals, and grappling with questions of identity." (Publisher's note)

Campbell, Kimberly

Less is more; teaching literature with short texts, grades 6-12. [by] Kimberly Hill Campbell. Stenhouse Publishers 2007 222p il pa $18.50
Grades: Adult Professional   **809**
1. Literature -- Study and teaching
ISBN 978-1-57110-710-7; 1-57110-710-X

LC 2007019310

"Campbell's book makes a very good case for teaching with short texts. Through chapters on short stories, essays, memoirs, poetry, picture books, and graphic novels, she shows how all aspects of literature can be taught using a variety of short pieces. She suggests structures for the classroom and strategies for eliciting both written and oral responses to these texts. She ties reading short texts to ways of looking at student writing in similar genres. . . . This book will be valuable for beginning and veteran teachers because of the lists of short texts." Voice Youth Advocates

Includes bibliographical references

Campbell, Patricia J.

Campbell's scoop; reflections on young adult literature. [by] Patty Campbell. Scarecrow Press 2010 245p (Scarecrow studies in young adult literature) $40
Grades: Adult Professional   **809**
1. Teenagers -- Books and reading 2. Young adult literature -- History and criticism
ISBN 978-0-8108-7293-6; 0-8108-7293-5

LC 2009-45563

"This resource represents the accumulated wisdom of a veteran librarian, author, speaker, critic, and pioneer of young adult services. Selected from several sources over many years, these essays and articles present a broad collection of critical writing. The articles are grouped into categories that include 'How We Got Here,' 'Trends and Tendencies,' 'Defining YA,' and 'Censorship Near and Far.' . . . Campbell's Scoop is a solidly useful professional title that weighs in on a diversity of topics. Unlike professional books that discuss and recommend specific YA titles, Campbell's Scoop is timeless. The information will not become dated and the breadth of the articles makes the collection relevant to a wide audience." Voice Youth Advocates

Includes bibliographical references

Hirschmann, Kris

Vampires in literature. ReferencePoint Press 2010 80p il (The vampire library) lib bdg $26.95

Grades: 7 8 9 10   **809**
1. Vampires in literature
ISBN 978-1-60152-134-7; 1-60152-134-0

LC 2010010104

Examines different ways vampires have been presented in literature from the first vampire novel in 1819 to the present-day.

"Energetic and surprisingly educational, this lively [book] seizes upon a zietgeist and takes it as far as possible." Booklist

Sutton, Roger

A **family** of readers; the book lover's guide to children's and young adult literature. [by] Roger Sutton and Martha V. Parravano; foreword by Gregory Maguire. Candlewick Press 2010 350p il $22; pa $14.99
Grades: Adult Professional   **809**
1. Children -- Books and reading 2. Teenagers -- Books and reading 3. Children's literature -- History and criticism
ISBN 978-0-7636-3280-9; 0-7636-3280-5; 978-0-7636-5755-0 pa; 0-7636-5755-7 pa

"This collection of essays from editors, reviewers, and authors emanates enthusiasm for books and reading. . . . Each section begins with an overview, followed by a selection of essays. The first chapter addresses the very smallest book lovers, and the last tackles the needs of young adults. Each chapter is followed by an annotated list of books. A complete bibliography and biographical sketches of the contributors are included in the end. . . . It should be required reading for every youth services librarian." Voice Youth Advocates

809.1   Literature in specific forms other than miscellaneous writings

Bodden, Valerie

Concrete poetry. Creative Education 2010 32p il (Poetry basics) $28.50
Grades: 5 6 7 8   **809.1**
1. Poetry -- History and criticism
ISBN 978-1-58341-775-1; 1-58341-775-3

LC 2008009156

This book describes concrete poetry's "history, characteristics, and variations. Many examples are provided as well as ideas for how children can write their own pieces. The information is accessible, and the writing is sufficiently lively to engage readers. The well-designed pages feature a variety of art reproductions from different literary eras and some photographs." Horn Book Guide

Includes glossary and bibliographical references

Haiku. Creative Education 2010 32p il (Poetry basics) $19.95
Grades: 5 6 7 8   **809.1**
1. Haiku
ISBN 978-1-58341-776-8; 1-58341-776-1

LC 2008-9158

Presents history and examples of the Japanese form of poetry called haiku.

"The information is accessible, and the writing is sufficiently lively to engage readers. The well-designed pages feature a variety of art reproductions from different literary eras and some photographs." Horn Book Guide

Includes glossary and bibliographical references

Limericks. Creative Education 2010 32p il (Poetry basics) $19.95
Grades: 5 6 7 8   **809.1**
  1. Limericks
  ISBN 978-1-58341-777-5; 1-58341-777-X
                                          LC 2008-9159

This describes limericks' "history, characteristics, and variations. Many examples are provided as well as ideas for how children can write their own pieces. The information is accessible, and the writing is sufficiently lively to engage readers. The well-designed pages feature a variety of art reproductions from different literary eras and some photographs." Horn Book Guide

Includes glossary and bibliographical references

810   Literatures of specific languages and language families

911: the book of help; edited by Michael Cart; with Marianne Carus and Marc Aronson. Cricket Bks. 2002 178p $17.95; pa $9.95
Grades: 8 9 10 11 12   **810**
  1. Terrorism 2. September 11 terrorist attacks, 2001 3. American literature -- Collections
  ISBN 0-8126-2659-1; 0-8126-2676-1 pa
                                          LC 2002-4707

A collection of essays, poems, and short fiction, created in response to the terrorist attacks of September 11, 2001. Contributors include Katherine Paterson, Joan Bauer, Walter Dean Myers, Nikki Giovanni, Arnold Adoff, and Russell Freedman

This "stands out for its rich prose, its unusual reporting, its search for context, its reminder of wonders." NY Times Book Rev

Amend, Allison
  Hispanic -American writers. Chelsea House 2010 128p il (Multicultural voices) $35
Grades: 7 8 9 10 11 12   **810**
  1. Latino authors 2. Hispanic American authors 3. American literature -- Hispanic American authors -- History and criticism
  ISBN 978-1-60413-312-7; 1-60413-312-0
                                          LC 2009-46535

Profiles notable Hispanic Americans and their work in the field of literature, including Sandra Cisneros, Julia Alvarez, and Junot Diaz.

"This volume opens with a succinct yet thorough introduction to the historical and cultural context of eight authors. The overview explains the origins and uses of the terms Chicano, Hispanic, and Latino and sketches the histories of the nations where most Hispanic-Americans have their roots. Amend also identifies common themes in Hispanic-American literature such as language and family; however, she also notes each community's unique concerns. . . . Amend

also suggests books by other Latino writers for further reading." SLJ

Includes bibliographical references

Aronson, Marc
  Beyond the pale; new essays for a new era. Scarecrow Press 2003 145p (Scarecrow studies in young adult literature) $37.50
Grades: Adult Professional   **810**
  1. Books and reading 2. Young adult literature -- History and criticism
  ISBN 0-8108-4638-1; 978-0-8108-4638-8
                                          LC 2002-151299

"Teachers, librarians, and students of children's and young adult literature will appreciate the breadth and clarity of this book, as well as the impressive bibliographies of fantasy and of professional reading on it." SLJ

Includes bibliographical references

Crowe, Chris
  More than a game; sports literature for young adults. [by] Chris Crowe. Scarecrow Press 2004 171p (Scarecrow studies in young adult literature) $45
Grades: Adult Professional   **810**
  1. Sports in literature 2. Young adult literature -- History and criticism
  ISBN 0-8108-4900-3; 978-0-8108-4900-6
                                          LC 2003-13561

"Readable and fascinating. . . . Categorizing and listing every sports-related book with teen appeal is an impossible feat, but the appendixes earn a medal for their impressive range. If only all professional reading could be so brainy and muscular." Voice Youth Advocates

Includes bibliographical references

Dude! stories and stuff for boys. edited by Sandy Asher and David Harrison. Dutton Childrens Books 2006 258p il $17.99
Grades: 4 5 6 7   **810**
  1. Boys 2. American literature -- Collections
  ISBN 0-525-47684-9
                                          LC 2005025060

"These 18 original stories, plays, and poems by prize-winning writers range from entertaining to challenging and offer an array of characters and experiences. In Bill C. Davis' intimate, thought-provoking 'Family Meeting,' a boy whose stepbrother committed suicide discovers the value of life. Jamie Adoff's 'Twelve' is a rap poem about experiencing violence but still retaining hope. Jose Cruz Gonzalez's play Watermelon Kisses is an amusing, credible portrayal of brotherly love and squabbles. The selections, which include many well-written gems, will resonate with and also amuse middle-grade boys." Booklist

★ **Girls** got game; sports stories and poems. edited by Sue Macy. Holt & Co. 2001 152p $17.95
Grades: 6 7 8 9   **810**
  1. Sports 2. Women athletes 3. American literature

-- Collections
ISBN 0-8050-6568-7

LC 00-47297

A collection of short stories and poems written by and about young women in sports

"The lineup of authors includes heavy hitters such as Virginia Euwer Wolff and Jacqueline Woodson as well as some lesser-known talents. . . . This earnest and high-minded anthology can be dipped into or devoured in one sitting; however it is read, it should empower girls and guide them along their paths toward becoming strong, independent women." SLJ

★ **Growing** up Latino; memoirs and stories. edited with an introduction by Harold Augenbraum and Ilan Stavans; foreword by Ilan Stavans. Houghton Mifflin 1993 xxix, 344p hardcover o.p. pa $15

Grades: 6 7 8 9 10   810

1. American literature -- Hispanic American authors -- Collections
ISBN 0-395-66124-2

LC 92-32624

A collection of short stories and excerpts from novels and memoirs written by twenty-five Latino authors. Among the contributors are Julia Alvarez, Oscar Hijuelos, Denise Chávez, Rolando Hinojosa, and Sandra Cisneros.

Includes bibliographical references

★ **Guys** write for Guys Read; edited by Jon Scieszka. Viking 2005 272p il $16.99; pa $11.99

Grades: 6 7 8 9 10   810

1. American literature -- Collections
ISBN 0-670-06007-0; 0-670-01144-4 pa

LC 2004-28984

This is a collection of short stories, essays, columns, cartoons, anecdotes, and artwork by such writers and illustrators as Brian Jacques, Jerry Spinelli, Chris Crutcher, Mo Willems, Chris Van Allsburg, Matt Groening, and Neil Gaiman, selected by voters at the Guys Read web site.

This is "a diverse and fast-paced anthology . . . that deserves a permanent place in any collection . . . . There's something undeniably grand about this collective celebration of the intellectual life of the common boy." SLJ

Hill, Laban Carrick

★ **Harlem** stomp! a cultural history of the Harlem Renaissance. Little, Brown 2004 151p il hardcover o.p. pa $12.99

Grades: 7 8 9 10   810

1. Harlem Renaissance 2. African American arts 3. African Americans -- Intellectual life
ISBN 0-316-81411-3; 0-316-03424-X pa

LC 2002-73067

"The vibrancy, energy, and color of the Harlem Renaissance come to life in this gem of a book packed with poetry, prose, song lyrics, art, and photography created by some of the period's most influential figures. . . . Informative and highly entertaining, it deserves to be shelved in any library." Voice Youth Advocates

Includes bibliographical references

Hillstrom, Kevin

The **Harlem** Renaissance. Omnigraphics 2008 228p il map (Defining moments) $49

Grades: 7 8 9 10   810

1. Harlem Renaissance 2. African American arts
ISBN 978-0-7808-1027-3; 0-7808-1027-9

LC 2007-51132

"This an insightful, highly accessible subject primer for general collections." Libr J

Includes glossary and bibliographical references

Otfinoski, Steven

Native American writers. Chelsea House 2010 126p il (Multicultural voices) $35

Grades: 8 9 10 11 12   810

1. American literature -- Native American authors 2. Native American literature -- History and criticism
ISBN 978-1-60413-314-1; 1-60413-314-7

LC 2009-41334

"This title introduces 10 major Native American poets and writers, such as N. Scott Momaday, Louise Erdrich, James Welch, and Sherman Alexie. An overview preceding the author entries explains the impact of white settlers on the culture of Native Americans, as well as the utilization of Native American storytelling and traditions in their literature and development of their writings. . . . The easily accessible information and fascinating details of the lives and writings of these authors make this a useful resource for both informative reading and research." SLJ

Includes bibliographical references

Things I have to tell you; poems and writing by teenage girls. edited by Betsy Franco; photographs by Nina Nickles. Candlewick Press 2001 63p il hardcover o.p. pa $8.99

Grades: 7 8 9 10   810

1. Girls 2. Teenagers' writings 3. American literature -- Collections
ISBN 0-7636-0905-6; 0-7636-1035-6 pa

LC 99-46884

A collection of poems, stories, and essays written by girls twelve to eighteen years of age and revealing the secrets which enabled them to overcome the challenges they faced

"Several striking entries in this compilation of poems and prose lift it above the majority of such offerings; all of these writers take on issues of family, love, body image, drugs, and sexuality with clarity and insight. The black-and-white photographs are neither literal illustrations of the pieces nor portraits of the writers; they reflect the emotional currents of the writing and provide further expression of a diverse group of young women." Horn Book

Wachale! poetry and prose on growing up Latino in America; edited by Ilan Stavans. Cricket Publs. 2001 146p $16.95

Grades: 5 6 7 8   810

1. Latinos (U.S.) 2. Hispanic Americans 3. Bilingual books -- English-Spanish 4. American literature -- Hispanic American authors -- Collections
ISBN 0-8126-4750-5

LC 2001-47189

A bilingual collection of poems, stories, and other writings which celebrates diversity among Latinos.

"This collection would make a fine classroom text, great for reading aloud and for stimulating students from everywhere to write about their roots and celebrate their shifting places across borders." Booklist

Includes glossary and bibliographical references

Walking on earth and touching the sky; poetry and prose by Lakota youth at Red Cloud Indian School. edited by Timothy P. McLaughlin ; illustrations by S.D. Nelson ; with a foreword by Joseph M. Marshall III. Abrams Books for Young Readers 2012 80 p. $19.95

Grades: 6 7 8   810

1. Children's writings 2. Native American children 3. Poor children -- United States 4. Indian children's writings 5. American literature -- Indian authors 6. Teton Indians -- Literary collections

ISBN 1419701797; 9781419701795

LC 2011036454

This book is an "anthology of work by children in grades five through eight." Poet "and teacher [Timothy P.] McLaughlin, after gradually connecting with his students at Red Cloud Indian School, provided them with creative-writing prompts that yielded sometimes-magical outcomes." The students, living in "the second-poorest county in the country," wrote on themes like the :Natural World" and "Family, Youth, and Dreams." (Kirkus)

Wilkin, Binnie Tate

African and African American images in Newbery Award winning titles; progress in portrayals. Scarecrow Press 2009 195p pa $40

Grades: Adult Professional   810

1. Newbery Medal 2. African Americans in literature 3. Children's literature -- History and criticism

ISBN 978-0-8108-6959-2 pa; 0-8108-6959-4 pa

LC 2009017726

"The author has exhaustively examined all books that have won the Newbery Medal and been cited as honor books since the award's creation in 1922. Her purpose is to evaluate the representation of Africans and African Americans, and to describe how these groups are portrayed in each title's historical context. . . . Books with the most positive images are awarded three pluses, while books with marginal African-American characters are indicated with an 'M.' . . . An essential volume for scholars, teachers, and librarians." SLJ

Includes bibliographical references

WritersCorps

City of one; young writers speak to the world. from WritersCorps; foreword by Isabel Allende; edited by Collete DeDonato. Aunt Lute Books 2004 239p pa $10.95

Grades: 7 8 9 10   810

1. Teenagers' writings

ISBN 1-87996-069-9

LC 2004-45089

"This anthology celebrates the 10th anniversary of WritersCorps workshops, which bring creative-writing instruc-

tion to low-income kids from public schools, youth detention centers, halfway houses, and afterschool programs. More than 150 young people ranging in age from 9 to 23 write about their lives and the state of the world. . . . Poems about family, freedom, inner peace, self-identity, and the writing process round out this remarkable anthology." SLJ

810.9 American literature (English) - history and criticism

Student's encyclopedia of great American writers; edited by Patricia Gantt and Robert Evan. 1st ed. Facts On File, Inc. 2009 2576p 3 5 v. $425.00

Grades: 8 9 10 11 12   810.9

1. American authors -- Encyclopedias 2. American literature -- Encyclopedias 3. American literature -- Encyclopedias, Juvenile 4. Authors, American -- Biography -- Encyclopedias, Juvenile

ISBN 0816060878; 9780816060870

This book is part of the Student's Encyclopedia of Great American Writers series. "More than 180 writers currently studied are profiled in this set. Arranged chronologically, the volumes begin with colonists . . . . Subsequent volumes feature both canonical figures identified with America's literary movements and lesser-known writers gaining public and scholarly interest." (School Library Journal)

Includes bibliographical references and index

811 American poetry

Adoff, Jaime

The **song** shoots out of my mouth; illustrated by Martin French. Dutton Children's Bks. 2002 48p il $17.99

Grades: 7 8 9   811

1. Music -- Poetry 2. Poetry -- By individual authors

ISBN 0-525-46949-4

LC 2002-284232

This is a "collection of 24 poems. Though free in form and diverse in mood and tone, all are about music, from Hip Hop to classical and from reggae to gospel. Another common element is the energy underscoring Adoff's language, which invites readers to move to the rhythm of the words. . . . All shine with the poet's obvious love of music and musicians." Booklist

Includes glossary and discography

African American Poetry; edited by Arnold Rampersad and Marcellus Blount ; illustrated by Karen Barbour. Sterling Pub Co Inc. 2013 48 p. ill. (hardcover) $14.95

Grades: 3 4 5 6 7   811

1. American poetry -- Asian American authors

ISBN 1402716893; 9781402716898

This book of poetry by African American authors"introduces 27 poets from the days of Phillis Wheatley to well-established poets writing in the 21st century. A four-page introduction outlines historical periods and influences. Presented chronologically, the entries begin with a paragraph describing the poet's life and work. Paul Laurence Dunbar, Countee Cullen, Langston Hughes, Lucille Clifton, Maya Angelou, and others are joined by George Moses Horton . . .and others." (School Library Journal)

Alexander, Elizabeth

Miss Crandall's School for Young Ladies and Little Misses of Color; poems. by Elizabeth Alexander and Marilyn Nelson; pictures by Floyd Cooper. Wordsong 2007 47p il $17.95

Grades: 7 8 9 10 **811**
1. Teachers 2. Abolitionists 3. Schools -- Poetry 4. African Americans -- Poetry 5. Poetry -- By individual authors

ISBN 978-1-59078-456-3; 1-59078-456-1

LC 2006-38985

"Twenty-four sonnets tell the story of Prudence Crandall and her efforts to educate young African-American women in Canterbury, CT, 1833-1834. . . . The sonnet format is challenging but compelling. . . . There are empty spaces in the pictures just as the language of the poetry leaves openness for readers' interpretation. A heartfelt, unusual presentation." SLJ

★ **America** at war; poems. selected by Lee Bennett Hopkins; illlustrated by Stephen Alcorn. Margaret K. McElderry Books 2008 84p il $21.99

Grades: 5 6 7 8 **811**
1. War poetry 2. American poetry -- Collections 3. United States -- History -- Poetry

ISBN 978-1-4169-1832-5; 1-4169-1832-9

LC 2006-08723

"This handsome anthology, expressing Americans' varied experience during wartime, is a fine selection of poems accessible to children. . . . The poems will touch readers with their sharp poignancy and undeniable power. Throughout the well-designed book, the expressive watercolor artwork enhances the poetry." Booklist

Angelou, Maya

★ **Maya** Angelou; edited by Edwin Graves Wilson; illustrated by Jerome Lagarrigue. Sterling Pub. 2007 48 p. col. ill. (Poetry for young people) (hardcover) $14.95

Grades: 4 5 6 7 **811**
1. African American women 2. Poets, American 3. African Americans -- Poetry 4. Poetry -- By individual authors

ISBN 9781402720239; 1402720238

LC 2006013803

"Wilson's introduction . . . addresses how Angelou's life has informed her imagination. . . . Twenty-five poems show her concern with the African-American experience. . . . Dignity, pride, and resiliancy are at this collection's core. . . . Footnotes offer definitions of colloquialisms and difficult words. Lagarrigue's painterly artwork uses golds, greens, and violets to capture the luminescent quality of the poems. . . . This [is a] distinguished work." SLJ

Atkins, Jeannine

★ **Borrowed** names; poems about Laura Ingalls Wilder, Madam C. J. Walker, Marie Curie, and their daughters. Henry Holt & Co. 2010 209p il $16.99

Grades: 6 7 8 9 10 **811**
1. Authors 2. Chemists 3. Novelists 4. Physicists 5. Entrepreneurs 6. Philanthropists 7. Cosmeticians 8. Western writers 9. College teachers 10. Children's authors 11. Nonfiction writers 12. Patrons of the arts 13. Young adult authors 14. Nobel laureates for physics 15. Cosmetics industry executives 16. Nobel laureates for chemistry 17. Poetry -- By individual authors 18. Mother-daughter relationship -- Poetry

ISBN 978-0-8050-8934-9; 0-8050-8934-9

LC 2009-23446

"In 1867, three women who achieved great success were born: writer Laura Ingalls Wilder, entrepreneur Madam C. J. Walker, and scientist Marie Curie. All three had complicated relationships with their daughters, relationships that Atkins explores in this unusual volume of poetry. . . . In vivid scenes written with keen insight and subtle imagery, the poems offer a strong sense of each daughter's personality as well as the tensions and ties they shared with their notable mothers." Booklist

Bernier-Grand, Carmen T.

★ **Diego**; bigger than life. illustrated by David Diaz. Marshall Cavendish Children 2009 64p il $18.99

Grades: 8 9 10 11 12 **811**
1. Artists 2. Painters 3. Poetry -- By individual authors

ISBN 978-0-7614-5383-3; 0-7614-5383-0

LC 2007-13761

ALA ALSC Belpre Illustrator Medal Honor Book (2010)

This is a "well written and beautifully illustrated volume. . . . Almost all written in first-person from the artist's point of view, the poems convey information succinctly within a context of colorful narrative and clearly expressed emotion. . . . Apart from four reproductions of Rivera's paintings and one photo of the artist, the illustrations are mixed-media pictures by Diaz. Depicting Rivera and his world, these iconic images glow with warmth, light, and color." Booklist

Includes bibliographical references

★ **Frida**; viva la vida = long live life. by Carmen T. Bernier-Grand. Marshall Cavendish Children 2007 64 p. ill. $14.24

Grades: 8 9 10 11 12 **811**
1. Artists 2. Painters 3. Poetry -- By individual authors 4. Painters -- Mexico -- Biography

ISBN 9780761453369

LC 2006014479

In this book, "Frida Kahlo, a native of Mexico, is described . . . in biographical poems accompanied by her own artwork. Both text and images reveal the anguish and joy of her two marriages to muralist Diego Rivera, her life-long suffering from a crippling bus accident, and her thirst for life, even as she tasted death. . . . Back matter includes excerpts from Frida's diary and letters, a prose biography, a chronology of the artist's life, a glossary of Spanish words, sources, and notes." (Publisher's note)

"Bernier-Grand introduces a famous life with lyrical free-verse poems. Nearly every double-page spread pairs a well-reproduced painting by Frida Kahlo with an original poem that defines turning points in the artist's life. Bernier-Grand's words expertly extend the autobiographical imagery so evident in the art." Booklist

Includes bibliographical references (p. 61).

Borus, Audrey

A **student's** guide to Emily Dickinson. Enslow Publishers 2005 152p il (Understanding literature) $27.93

Grades: 7 8 9 10   **811**

1. Poets 2. Authors

ISBN 0-7660-2285-4

LC 2004-18098

"A short discussion of Dickinson's life and times is followed by a chapter on how to read and analyze her poems, which would be particularly useful for students reading her work for the first time. Subsequent chapters focus on particular themes in the poems such as death and eternity, truth, faith and reality, the natural world, and the influence of the Civil War." SLJ

Includes bibliographical references

Bryan, Ashley

Ashley Bryan's Puppets; Making Something from Everything. Ashley Bryan. Simon & Schuster 2014 80 p. $19.99

Grades: PreK K 1 2 3 4 5 6   **811**

1. Poetry 2. Waste products 3. Puppets and puppet plays 4. Children's poetry 5. Puppets -- Poetry 6. Found objects -- Poetry

ISBN 1442487283; 9781442487284

In this book, "storyteller and creator Ashley Bryan reveals the vibrant spirit of found objects in this . . . treasury of poetry and puppets. . . . For decades, Ashley has walked up and down the beach, stopping to pick up sea glass, weathered bones, a tangle of fishing net, an empty bottle, a doorknob. Treasure. And then, with glue and thread and paint and a sprinkling of African folklore, Ashley breathes new life into these materials." (Publisher's note)

"—Award-winning author and illustrator Bryan has combined his love of art and poetry in this captivating and beautifully designed book...Traditional African themes abound as the characters introduce themselves through their poems, and readers are invited into the world of puppets and poetry. Bryan has truly created a book for all to treasure.—" SLJ

Bulion, Leslie

At the sea floor cafe; odd ocean critter poems. written by Leslie Bulion; illustrated by Leslie Evans. Peachtree Publishers 2011 45p il $14.95

Grades: 5 6 7 8   **811**

1. Marine animals -- Poetry 2. Poetry -- By individual authors

ISBN 978-1-56145-565-2; 1-56145-565-2

LC 2010026691

"Using complex poetry forms and cleverly constructed lines, Bulion plays tribute to sea creatures. . . . Evans's spare,

well-placed hand-colored linoleum block prints hold their own without overwhelming the text." Horn Book Guide

Burleigh, Robert

★ **Hoops**; illustrated by Stephen T. Johnson. Harcourt Brace & Co. 1997 un il hardcover o.p. pa $6

Grades: 6 7 8 9   **811**

1. Basketball -- Poetry 2. Poetry -- By individual authors

ISBN 0-15-201450-0; 0-15-216380-8 pa

LC 96-18440

Illustrations and poetic text describe the movement and feel of the game of basketball

"Burleigh's staccato text is well matched by Johnson's dynamic pastels. Muted colors and a strong sense of motion as bodies leap and lift, pounce and poke, aptly complement the words." SLJ

★ **Cool** salsa; bilingual poems on growing up Latino in the United States. edited by Lori M. Carlson; introduction by Oscar Hijuelos. Holt & Co. 1994 xx, 123p il hardcover o.p. pa $6.99

Grades: 5 6 7 8 9 10   **811**

1. Bilingual books -- English-Spanish 2. American poetry -- Hispanic American authors -- Collections

ISBN 0-8050-3135-9; 978-0-449-70436-3 pa; 0-449-70436-X pa

LC 93-45798

"This collection presents poems by 29 Mexican-American, Cuban-American, Puerto Rican, and other Central and South American poets, including Sandra Cisneros, Luis J. Rodriguez, Pat Mora, Gary Soto, Ana Castillo, Oscar Hijuelos, Ed J. Vega, Judith Ortiz-Cofer, and other Latino writers both contemporary and historical. Brief biographical notes on the authors are provided. All the poems deal with experiences of teenagers." Book Rep

Crisler, Curtis L.

★ **Tough** boy sonatas; illustrations by Floyd Cooper. Wordsong 2007 86p il $19.95

Grades: 8 9 10 11 12   **811**

1. Indiana -- Poetry 2. African Americans -- Poetry 3. City and town life -- Poetry 4. Poetry -- By individual authors

ISBN 978-1-932425-77-2; 1-932425-77-2

LC 2006-11836

"Crisler presents a collection of potent, hard-hitting poems about growing up in Gary, Indiana. Written mostly in voices of young African American males, the poems evoke the grit and ash of crumbling, burned-out streets as well as the realities of hardscrabble life. . . . Written with skillful manipulation of sound, rhythm, and form, the poems are filled with sophisticated imagery and graphic words . . . and Cooper's illustrations extend . . . the poems' impact. Created in sooty black and gray, the powerful drawings are mostly portraits of anguished young men." Booklist

Dickinson, Emily, 1830-1886

My letter to the world and other poems; with illustrations by Isabelle Arsenault. KCP Poetry 2008 un il (Visions in poetry) $17.95; pa $9.95

Grades: 7 8 9 10 11 12   **811**

1. Poets 2. Authors 3. Children's poetry 4. Poetry -- By individual authors

ISBN 1-55453-103-9; 1-55453-339-2 pa; 978-1-55453-103-5; 978-1-55453-339-8 pa

This is an illustrated edition of seven Emily Dickinson poems. "Age ten and up." (N Y Times Book Rev)

"The long final biographical note about the introvert and recluse who gloried in being 'Nobody' will take readers back to the poetry, which speaks as a 'letter to the world,' as will the clear analysis of the mixed-media illustrations, in which Arsenault links the poet's repeated images of isolation with her intense connections to nature. . . . Dickinson's exploration of the difference between loneliness and rich solitude will resonate with teens." Booklist

Engle, Margarita

★ The **surrender** tree; poems of Cuba's struggle for freedom. Henry Holt and Co. 2008 169p $17.95

Grades: 7 8 9 10 11 12   **811**

1. Novels in verse 2. Cuba -- Fiction

ISBN 978-0-8050-8674-4; 0-8050-8674-9

LC 2007-27591

A Newbery Medal honor book, 2009

Pura Belpre Author Award, 2009

This "book is written in clear, short lines of stirring free verse. . . . [The author] draws on her own Cuban American roots . . . to describe those who fought in the nineteenth-century Cuban struggle for independence. At the center is Rosa, a traditional healer, who nurses runaway slaves and deserters in caves and other secret hideaways. . . . Many readers will be caught by the compelling narrative voices and want to pursue the historical accounts in Engle's bibliography." Booklist

Fields, Terri

After the death of Anna Gonzales. Holt & Co. 2002 100p $16.95

Grades: 7 8 9 10   **811**

1. Suicide -- Poetry 2. Poetry -- By individual authors

ISBN 0-8050-7127-X

LC 2002-24074

Poems written in the voices of forty-seven people, including students, teachers, and other school staff, record the aftermath of a high school student's suicide and the preoccupations of teen life

"A short book, easily read, which should generate serious thought and discussion." BAYA Book Rev

Fleischman, Paul

★ **Big** talk; poems for four voices. illustrated by Beppe Giacobbe. Candlewick Press 2000 44p il $17.99; pa $7.99

Grades: 4 5 6 7   **811**

1. Poetry -- By individual authors

ISBN 0-7636-0636-7; 0-7636-3805-6 pa

LC 99-46882

A collection of poems to be read aloud by four people, with color-coded text to indicate which lines are read by which readers

"Each poem is more demanding, and more rewarding, than the last. Giacobbe highlights the humor in strips of vignettes that run along the bottom of the page. This is 'toe-tapping, tongue-flapping fun.'" Horn Book Guide

★ **I** am phoenix: poems for two voices; illustrated by Ken Nutt. Harper & Row 1985 51p il hardcover o.p. pa $5.99

Grades: 4 5 6 7   **811**

1. Birds -- Poetry 2. Poetry -- By individual authors

ISBN 0-06-446092-4 pa

LC 85-42615

A collection of poems about birds to be read aloud by two voices

"Devotés of the almost lost art of choral reading should be among the first to appreciate this collection. . . . Printed in script form, the selections . . . have a cadenced pace and dignified flow; their combination of imaginative imagery and realistic detail is echoed by the combination of stylized fantasy and representational drawings in the black and white pictures, all soft line and strong nuance." Bull Cent Child Books

★ **Joyful** noise: poems for two voices; illustrated by Eric Beddows. Harper & Row 1988 44p il $15.99; lib bdg $16.89; pa $5.99

Grades: 4 5 6 7   **811**

1. Insects -- Poetry 2. Poetry -- By individual authors

ISBN 0-06-021852-5; 0-06-021853-3 lib bdg; 0-06-446093-2 pa

LC 87-45280

Awarded the Newbery Medal, 1989

"There are fourteen poems in the handsomely designed volume, with stylish endpapers and wonderfully interpretive black-and-white illustrations. Each selection is a gem, polished perfection." Horn Book

Forbes, Robert L.

Beast Friends Forever; by Robert L. Forbes ; illustrated by Ronald Searle. Penguin Group USA 2013 80 p. (hardcover) $19.95

Grades: 4 5 6 7   **811**

1. Animal courtship 2. Animals -- Poetry 3. Animals

ISBN 1590208080; 9781590208083

In this book of children's poetry by Robert Forbes, "animal courtship is infused with quirky human characteristics and some sneaky social commentary. Readers meet Lancelot the Ocelot, doing time for 'his romance turned to tragedy, ending in a crime.' And Babette the Skunk, having studied with 'Parisian perfumers,' has fashioned a new scent, 'packaged in black and called "In-d-scent,"/It's sure to enflame any white-striped gent.'" (School Library Journal)

Forler, Nan

Winterberries and apple blossoms; reflections and flavors of a Mennonite year. paintings by Peter Etril Snyder. Tundra Books 2011 39p il $22.95

Grades: 4 5 6 7   **811**
1. Cooking 2. Months -- Poetry 3. Mennonites --
Poetry 4. Poetry -- By individual authors
ISBN 978-1-77049-254-7; 1-77049-254-2

With a poem for every month of the year, young Naomi
introduces us to her family and hosts a journey through the
seasonal rhythms of her rural Mennonite community. Includes a recipe for each month of the year.

This includes "12 evocative poems. . . . Snyder . . . contributes smudgy, sunlit acrylic scenes that convey a close-
knit family that works, plays, and prays together. Along with
Forler's graceful verse, and recipes for every season, it all
adds up to a warm portrait of a community seldom found in
the spotlight." Publ Wkly

Frost, Robert
★ **Robert** Frost; edited by Gary D. Schmidt;
illustrated by Henri Sorensen. Sterling 1994 48p il
(Poetry for young people) $14.95; pa $6.95
Grades: 4 5 6 7   **811**
1. Poetry -- By individual authors
ISBN 0-8069-0633-2; 1-4027-5475-2 pa
                                                                            LC 94-11161

This volume "contains a three-page overview of the poet's life, 29 poems selected and arranged around the seasons
of the year, brief and apt commentaries on each, and a useful
index of titles and subject matter. The realistic watercolor
illustrations capture the delicate beauty of a New England
spring and the glory of fall while still suggesting the around-
the-corner chill of winter, a disquiet echoing throughout
much of Frost's poetry." SLJ

George, Kristine O'Connell
★ **Swimming** upstream; middle school poems.
illustrated by Debbie Tilley. Clarion Bks. 2002 79p
il $14
Grades: 5 6 7 8   **811**
1. Schools -- Poetry 2. Poetry -- By individual authors
ISBN 0-618-15250-4
                                                                            LC 2002-2746

A collection of poems capture the feelings and experiences of a girl in middle school

"Students will relate to this voice 'navigating upstream,'
while they try to find their own place in the middle-school
wilderness." SLJ

Giovanni, Nikki
Ego -tripping and other poems for young people;
illustrations by George Ford; foreword by Virginia
Hamilton. 2nd ed; Hill Bks. 1993 52p il hardcover
o.p. pa $10.95
Grades: 5 6 7 8   **811**
1. African Americans -- Poetry 2. Poetry -- By
individual authors
ISBN 1-55652-189-8; 1-55652-188-X pa
                                                                            LC 93-29578

First published 1974
Giovanni has added 10 new poems to her earlier "collection of 23 poems for young people. Ford's illustrations in
sepia shades are bold and full of character and dreaming. As
Virginia Hamilton says in her foreword, Giovanni's voice
is personal and warm, she 'celebrates ordinary folks' and

writes of struggle and liberation. She's upbeat and celebratory without minimizing hard times." Booklist

Grandits, John
★ **Blue** lipstick; concrete poems. Clarion Books
2007 un il $15; pa $5.95
Grades: 5 6 7 8 9 10   **811**
1. Poetry -- By individual authors
ISBN 978-0-618-56860-4; 0-618-56860-3; 978-0-618-
85132-4 pa; 0-618-85132-1 pa
                                                                            LC 2006-23332

"This selection introduces readers to Jessie, who impulsively purchases blue lipstick, but later, regretfully decides
to give it 'the kiss-off.' Jessie is big sister to Robert, who
was featured in Grandits's Technically, It's Not My Fault
(Clarion, 2004). As he did in that terrific collection, the author uses artful arrangements of text on the page, along with
54 different typefaces, to bring his images and ideas to life.
. . . This irreverent, witty collection should resonate with a
wide audience." SLJ

★ **Technically,** it's not my fault; concrete poems. by John Grandits. Clarion Books 2004 un il
$15; pa $5.95
Grades: 5 6 7 8   **811**
1. Poetry -- By individual authors
ISBN 0-618-42833-X; 0-618-50361-7 pa
                                                                            LC 2004-231

A collection of concrete poems on such topics as roller
coasters, linguini, basketball, and sisters

"Grandits combines technical brilliance and goofy good
humor to provide an accessible, fun-filled collection of poems, dramatically brought to life through a brilliant book
design." SLJ

Grimes, Nikki
At Jerusalem's gate; poems of Easter. with
woodcuts by David Frampton. Eerdmans Books for
Young Readers 2005 un il $20
Grades: 5 6 7 8   **811**
1. American poetry 2. Easter -- Poetry 3. Children's
poetry, American 4. Poetry -- By individual authors
ISBN 0-8028-5183-5
                                                                            LC 2003-1089

"Twenty-two poems trace the events celebrated by
Christians as Easter Week, from Jesus' entry into Jerusalem
through his appearance to disciples after the Resurrection. . .
. Grades five to eight." (Bull Cent Child Books)

"Each poem is preceded by a brief synopsis of the event,
often accompanied by the author's own musings and queries, which prompt readers to think and ask questions of their
own. . . . Bold, handsome woodcuts reinforce the powerful
drama depicted in poetry. An outstanding effort." SLJ

A **dime** a dozen; pictures by Angelo. Dial Bks.
for Young Readers 1998 54p il $17.99
Grades: 5 6 7 8   **811**
1. African Americans -- Poetry 2. Poetry -- By
individual authors
ISBN 0-8037-2227-3
                                                                            LC 97-5798

A collection of poems about an African-American girl growing up in New York

"Free-flowing and very accessible, the poetry may inspire readers to distill their own life experiences into precise, imaginative words and phrases." Booklist

Grover, Lorie Ann

Loose threads. Margaret K. McElderry Bks. 2002 296p $16.95 **811**

1. Breast cancer -- Poetry 2. Poetry -- By individual authors

ISBN 0-689-84419-0

LC 2001-44724

A series of poems describes how seventh-grader Kay Garber faces her grandmother's battle with breast cancer while living with her mother and great-grandmother and dealing with everyday junior high school concerns

"The poetic, spare language, written in Kay's self-possessed, first-person voice, is refreshingly frank about the disease. . . . Grover's book balances vivid emotional scenes with plenty of space between the words." Booklist

Includes bibliographical references

Harley, Avis

★ **African** acrostics; a word in edgeways. poems by Avis Harley; photographs by Deborah Noyes. Candlewick Press 2009 un il $17.99; pa $6.99

Grades: 4 5 6 7 **811**

1. Acrostics 2. Children's poetry 3. Animals -- Africa 4. Animals -- Poetry 5. Poetry -- By individual authors

ISBN 978-0-7636-3621-0; 0-7636-3621-5; 978-0-7636-5818-2 pa

LC 2008017916

This volume depicts "such wild animals as giraffes, zebras, and lions, in poems written to contain acrostics, in which beginning or ending letters from the poetry lines can be used to spell other words." (Publisher's note) "Grades four to six." (Bull Cent Child Books)

"Harley has written 18 poems, each one featuring a different animal. All are written as acrostics, with most of them based on the first letter of each line, but several with more unusual patterns. . . . Much of Harley's poetry consists of carefully crafted descriptive word imagery that is right on target. . . . Most of the full-page, full-color photos of the animals are perfect companions to the facing selections." SLJ

Haskins-Bookser, Laura

The **softer** side of hip-hop; poetic reflections on love, family, and relationships. by Laura Haskins-Bookser; illustrated by Jami Moffett. Morning Glory Press 2008 il pa $9.95

Grades: 8 9 10 11 12 **811**

1. Teenage mothers -- Poetry 2. Poetry -- By individual authors

ISBN 978-1-932538-83-0 pa; 1-932538-83-6 pa

"Haskins-Bookser brings her hip-hop sensibility to a genre—poetry—that is really at the heart and soul of both hip-hop and rap. She voices the hopes, fears, and joys of a single teen mother. . . . Her poems are at once cautionary, but are tales of hope and transcendence as well. Each poem is heartfelt and well crafted. This is a lovely treasure,

enhanced by Moffett's beautifully executed drawings and quotes from teen mothers." SLJ

★ **Heart** to heart; new poems inspired by twentieth-century American art. edited by Jan Greenberg. Abrams 2001 80p il map $19.95

Grades: 5 6 7 8 9 10 **811**

1. American art 2. Art -- 20th century 3. American poetry -- Collections

ISBN 0-8109-4386-7

LC 99-462335

Michael L. Printz Award honor book, 2002

A compilation of poems by Americans writing about American art in the twentieth century, including such writers as Nancy Willard, Jane Yolen, and X. J. Kennedy.

"From a tight diamante and pantoum to lyrical free verse, the range of poetic styles will speak to a wide age group. . . . Concluding with biographical notes on each poet and artist, this rich resource is an obvious choice for teachers, and the exciting interplay between art and the written word will encourage many readers to return again and again to the book." Booklist

Hemphill, Stephanie

Your own, Sylvia; a verse portrait of Sylvia Plath. Alfred A. Knopf 2007 261p $15.99; lib bdg $18.99

Grades: 8 9 10 11 12 **811**

1. Poets 2. Authors 3. Novelists 4. Poetry -- By individual authors

ISBN 978-0-375-83799-9; 978-0-375-93799-6 lib bdg

LC 2006-07253

Michael L. Printz Award honor book, 2008

The author interprets the people, events, influences and art that made up the brief life of Sylvia Plath.

"Hemphill's verse, like Plath's, is completely compelling: every word, every line, worth reading." Horn Book

Includes bibliographical references

Herrera, Juan Felipe

★ **Laughing** out loud, I fly; poems in English and Spanish. drawings by Karen Barbour. HarperCollins Pubs. 1998 un il $15.99

Grades: 6 7 8 9 **811**

1. Mexican Americans -- Poetry 2. Poetry -- By individual authors 3. Bilingual books -- English-Spanish

ISBN 0-06-027604-5

LC 96-45476

A collection of poems in Spanish and English about childhood, place, and identity

"Barbour's black-and-white drawings accompany each poem, delicately underlining its images but allowing the strong sensuality of the words to seep into readers' minds." SLJ

Holbrook, Sara

More than friends; poems from him and her. [by] Sara Holbrook and Allan Wolf. Wordsong 2008 64p il $16.95

Grades: 6 7 8 9 10 **811**
1. Love poetry 2. Poetry -- By individual authors
ISBN 978-1-59078-587-4; 1-59078-587-8
LC 2007-50282

"In these parallel poems, a boy and a girl describe their progression from friendship to romance. . . . The simple language expresses strong feelings in a variety of poetic forms. . . . Small black-and-white photos never get in the way of the words, which tell the edgy truth of romance in all its joy and confusion." Booklist

Hopkins, Lee Bennett
Been to yesterdays: poems of a life; illustrations by Charlene Rendeiro. Wordsong 1995 64p il $15.95; pa $9.95
Grades: 4 5 6 7 **811**
1. Poetry -- By individual authors
ISBN 1-56397-467-3; 1-56397-808-3 pa
LC 94-73320

"Hopkins distills the experience of his middle-grade years into 28 poems of poignant clarity. . . . Good reading and an excellent, unconventional choice for teachers doing units on poetry and autobiography." Booklist

Hovey, Kate
★ **Ancient** voices; written by Kate Hovey; with illustrations by Murray Kimber. Margaret McElderry Books 2004 un il $18.95
Grades: 6 7 8 9 **811**
1. Classical mythology -- Poetry 2. Poetry -- By individual authors
ISBN 0-689-83342-3
LC 00-28359

Twenty-three poems give voice to a variety of goddesses, gods, and mortals from Greek and Roman mythology

"These lyrical poems and dramatic picture-book-size illustrations humanize the Greek myths with flashes of contemporary realism. . . . The poetry here is both intense and accessible, with unobtrusive rhyme that adds to the music of the lines." Booklist

Hughes, Langston
★ The **dream** keeper and other poems; including seven additional poems. [by] Langston Hughes; illustrated by Brian Pinkney. 75th anniversary ed.; Alfred A. Knopf 2007 83p il $16.99
Grades: 4 5 6 7 **811**
1. African Americans -- Poetry 2. Poetry -- By individual authors
ISBN 978-0-679-84421-1

First published 1932; this is a reissue of the 1994 edition
A collection of sixty-six poems, selected by the author for young readers, including lyrical poems, songs, and blues, many exploring the black experience

"Black-and-white scratchboard illustrations in Pinkney's signature style express the emotion and beat of the poetry. . . . The poems are . . . colloquial and direct yet mysterious and complex." Booklist

★ **Langston** Hughes; edited by Arnold Rampersad & David Roessel; illustrations by Benny An-

drews. Sterling Pub. 2006 48p il (Poetry for young people) $14.95
Grades: 5 6 7 8 **811**
1. African Americans -- Poetry 2. Poetry -- By individual authors
ISBN 1-4027-1845-4; 978-1-4027-1845-8
LC 2005025369

A brief profile of African American poet Langston Hughes accompanies some of his better known poems for children.

"This charming collection of 26 poems is vibrantly illustrated with depictions of African Americans in varied settings. . . . This will be a welcome introduction to Hughes's poetry for elementary students, and it includes sufficient detail to make it useful and enjoyable for older students." SLJ

★ **I** am the darker brother; an anthology of modern poems by African Americans. edited and with an afterword by Arnold Adoff; drawings by Benny Andrews; introduction by Rudine Sims Bishop; foreword by Nikki Giovanni. rev ed; Simon & Schuster Bks. for Young Readers 1997 208p il hardcover o.p. $5.99
Grades: 6 7 8 9 10 **811**
1. American poetry -- African American authors -- Collections
ISBN 0-689-81241-8; 0-689-80869-0 pa
LC 97-144181

First published 1968
This anthology presents "the African-American experience through poetry that speaks for itself. . . . Because of the historical context of many of the poems, the book will be much in demand during Black History Month, but it should be used and treasured as part of the larger canon of literature to be enjoyed by all Americans at all times of the year. An indispensable addition to library collections." SLJ

★ **I**, too, sing America; three centuries of African American poetry. [selected and annotated by] Catherine Clinton; illustrated by Stephen Alcorn. Houghton Mifflin 1998 128p il $21
Grades: 6 7 8 9 **811**
1. African Americans -- Poetry 2. American poetry -- African American authors -- Collections
ISBN 0-395-89599-5
LC 97-46137

"For each poet, Clinton provides a biography and a brief, insightful commentary on the poem(s) she has chosen, including a discussion of political as well as literary connections. Alcorn's dramatic, full-page, full-color illustrations opposite each poem evoke the quiltlike patterns and rhythmic figures of folk art." Booklist

Indivisible; poems for social justice. edited by Gail Bush & Randy Meyer ; foreword by Common. Norwood House Press 2013 94 p. (pbk. : alk. paper) $14.60
Grades: 7 8 9 10 11 12 **811**
1. Poetry 2. Social justice 3. Social problems 4.

Social justice -- Poetry 5. Social problems -- Poetry
ISBN 9781603574174

LC 2012021600

In this book of poetry, editors Gail Bush and Randy
Meyer "have selected 54 previously published works by
twentieth-century poets. The work represents a broad variety
of races, cultures, and ethnicities and deals with such issues
as bigotry and injustice, as well as with freedom, equality,
and comity. Divided into five sections, the poems essentially
chart a course from outside our culture to an inside where we
can celebrate common dreams." (Booklist)

"From Langston Hughes and Amiri Baraka to Joy Harjo
and Toi Derricotte, the poets discuss perspective, misguided
pity, stereotyping, patriarchy, and thousands of other sticky
issues. This carefully selected collection is not only poetically breathtaking, but will undoubtedly prove useful time
and again as we seek to provide resources for educating empathetic global citizens.—" (School Library Journal)

Includes bibliographical references and index.

The **Invisible** ladder; an anthology of contemporary
American poems for young readers with the po-
ets' own photos and commentary. edited by Liz
Rosenberg. Holt & Co. 1996 210p il $21.95
Grades: 7 8 9 10   811
1. Poets, American 2. American poetry -- Collections
ISBN 0-8050-3836-1

LC 96-12361

Features such poets as Robert Bly, Allen Ginsberg, Nikki
Giovanni, and Galway Kinnell by including photos, selections of their work, and comments on their poetry

Rosenberg "introduces many exciting new adult voices
to young people. Some of the poets' commentaries are sophisticated, some are pretentious; but most are immediate
and extraordinarily moving, nearly as powerful as the poetry
they lead into." Booklist

Janeczko, Paul B., 1945-

Requiem; poems of the Terezin ghetto. Candle-
wick Press 2011 112p $16.99
Grades: 7 8 9 10   811
1. Children's poetry 2. Holocaust, 1933-1945 --
Poetry 3. Poetry -- By individual authors 4. Terezin
(Czechoslovakia: Concentration camp) -- Poetry
ISBN 978-0-7636-4727-8; 0-7636-4727-6

LC 2010-38882

"Janeczko reflects on Terezin through thirty-five compact free-verse poems, most written in the voice of named
(and numbered) inhabitants and guards, almost all fictional,
of the camp. . . . The verses are spare and accessible, filled
with crushing historical weight; the first-person approach
will make the entries particularly compelling as readers theater or readalouds." Bull Cent Child Books

Johnston, Tony

Voice from afar; poems of peace. by Tony Johnston; paintings by Susan Guevara. Holiday House
2008 32p il $16.95
Grades: 5 6 7 8   811
1. War poetry 2. Poetry -- By individual authors
ISBN 978-0-8234-2012-4; 0-8234-2012-4

LC 2007031434

"Johnston offers thoughtful responses to war's senseless
violence. Her free-verse word pictures call to mind scenes
of terrible devastation. . . . Yet Johnston finds cause for hope
amid the grimness. . . . Johnston adds her own voice, the
sympathetic observer from afar, sending prayers for peace.
Guevara's paintings, crafted with acrylic and oil paint with
collage on textured canvas, feature subdued, neutral colors
and haunting images." SLJ

Katz, Bobbi

Trailblazers; poems of exploration. by Bobbi
Katz; illustrations by Carin Berger. Greenwillow
Books 2007 208p il $18.99; lib bdg $19.89
Grades: 5 6 7 8   811
1. Explorers -- Poetry 2. Poetry -- By individual authors
ISBN 978-0-688-16533-8; 0-688-16533-8; 978-0-688-
16534-5 lib bdg; 0-688-16534-6 lib bdg

LC 2006016696

This is a collection of poems about "the lives of more
than 120 explorers, from ancient times to the present. . . .
Katz challenges readers to consider not only the courage of
these individuals, but also to broaden their horizons in terms
of the definition of exploration and the motivations behind it.
. . . All the selections encourage reading aloud, especially the
poems for two voices. The few black-and-white illustrations
scattered throughout are small and iconic." SLJ

Includes bibliographical references

★ A **kick** in the head; selected by Paul B. Janeczko;
illustrated by Chris Raschka. Candlewick Press
2005 61p il $17.99; pa $9.99
Grades: 4 5 6 7   811
1. American poetry -- Collections
ISBN 978-0-7636-0662-6; 0-7636-0662-6; 978-0-
7636-4132-0 pa; 0-7636-4132-4 pa

LC 2004-48508

"Raschka's high-spirited, spare torn-paper-and-paint
collages ingeniously broaden the poems' wide-ranging
emotional tones. . . . Clear, very brief explanations of poetic
forms . . . accompany each entry; a fine introduction and
appended notes offer further information. . . . This is the introduction that will ignite enthusiasm." Booklist

Kirk, Connie Ann

A **student's** guide to Robert Frost. Enslow Pubs.
2006 160p il (Understanding literature) $27.93
Grades: 7 8 9 10   811
1. Poets 2. Authors
ISBN 0-7660-2434-2

LC 2005-13392

In this book, "the career of this literary giant is examined. . . . Poems are put into historical and biographical
context, with special emphasis placed on curriculum-related
works, including 'Stopping by Woods on a Snowy Evening,'
'The Road Not Taken,' 'The Gift Outright,' and 'Fire and
Ice.'" Publisher's note

Lawson, JonArno

Black stars in a white night sky; [by] JonArno
Lawson; illustrated by Sherwin Tjia. Wordsong 2008
118p il $16.95

Grades: 4 5 6 7 **811**

1. Humorous poetry 2. Poetry -- By individual authors
ISBN 978-1-59078-521-8

LC 2007018927

First published 2006 in Canada

"This uproarious collection blends slapstick, puns, parodies, and sheer absurdity with lots of wry ideas. . . . Tjia's surreal art, in black-and-white silhouettes, is as rhythmic and absurd as the verse, which is perfect for reading aloud." Booklist

Think again; written by JonArno Lawson; illustrated by Julie Morstad. Kids Can Press 2010 62p il $16.95

Grades: 6 7 8 9 **811**

1. Children's poetry 2. Poetry -- By individual authors 3. Interpersonal relations -- Poetry
ISBN 978-1-55453-423-4; 1-55453-423-2

"More than 40 introspective poems and accompanying illustrations explore the complexity of close relationships. . . . Ever playful, the poet's pithy quatrains distill relational truths to their essence. . . . The illustrator's spare grayscale drawings . . . effectively amplify the tension they masterfully depict. An entirely rewarding combination." Kirkus

Levy, Debbie

★ The **year** of goodbyes; a true story of friendship, family and farewells. Disney-Hyperion Books 2010 136p il $16.99

Grades: 5 6 7 8 **811**

1. Jews -- Poetry 2. Holocaust, 1933-1945 -- Poetry 3. Poetry -- By individual authors
ISBN 1-4231-2901-6; 978-1-4231-2901-1

LC 2009-18671

"In 1930s Germany, it was common for young girls to keep poesiealbums, or autograph books, in which friends could write poems, draw pictures, or offer wishes to the owner. Levy has based this novel in verse on the actual poesiealbum kept by her mother, Jutta Salzberg, when she was twelve years old. . . . Grades four to seven." (Bull Cent Child Books)

"Artfully weaving together her mother's poesiealbum (autograph/poetry album), diary, and her own verse, Levy crafts a poignant portrait of her Jewish mother's life in 1938 Nazi Germany that crackles with adolescent vitality." Publ Wkly

Lewis, J. Patrick

★ **Black** cat bone; [by] J. Patrick Lewis; illustrations by Gary Kelley. Creative Editions 2006 48p il $19.95

Grades: 6 7 8 9 10 **811**

1. Singers 2. Guitarists 3. Blues musicians 4. Songwriters 5. Blues music -- Poetry 6. Mississippi -- Poetry 7. Poetry -- By individual authors 8. African American musicians -- Poetry
ISBN 978-1-56846-194-6

LC 2005-52298

"Robert Johnson, the celebrated blues musician, is said to have sold his soul to the devil for his skills on the guitar. . . . Lewis's verse echoes Johnson's music. . . . A single line of text parades ghostlike across the bottom of each page,

explaining the aspect of the man's life that the poem sings of, and becoming a cumulative mini-bio in itself. A couple of Johnson's own lyrics appear with the sequence of Lewis's poems where they add to the narrative tension. Kelley's mixed-media illustrations in blues and browns add to the mood and enliven the layout." SLJ

★ The **brothers'** war; Civil War voices in verse. including photographs by Civil War photographers. National Geographic 2007 31p il $17.95; lib bdg $20.90

Grades: 5 6 7 8 9 10 **811**

1. Poetry -- By individual authors 2. United States -- History -- 1861-1865, Civil War -- Poetry
ISBN 978-1-4263-0036-3; 978-1-4263-0037-0 lib bdg

LC 2006-103275

"This heartrending collection of original poems paired with photographs by Civil War photographers makes real what statistics about war cannot—that the casualties of any war have human faces. Lewis . . . writes poignantly and lyrically. . . . An elegant design of gold, silver and black handsomely frames the text and photographs." Publ Wkly

Countdown to summer; a poems for every day of the school year. illustrations by Ethan Long. Little, Brown and Co. 2009 un il $15.99

Grades: 4 5 6 **811**

1. Schools -- Poetry 2. Poetry -- By individual authors
ISBN 978-0-316-02089-3; 0-316-02089-3

LC 2008016772

"180 poems are here gathered to be enjoyed on a vitamin-like one-a-day basis. . . . Some verses are long, some short, some thought-provoking, some laugh-provoking. Long's penciled spot art provides an agreeable visual accompaniment." Kirkus

The **house**; illustrated by Roberto Innocenti. Creative Editions 2009 un il $19.95

Grades: 4 5 6 7 **811**

1. Houses -- Poetry 2. Poetry -- By individual authors
ISBN 978-1-56846-201-1; 1-56846-201-8

"The walls in a stone farmhouse literally talk in this first-person narrative that deals with the ravages of time and their effects on the structure and its inhabitants. After a brief history, the house (constructed in 1656, 'a plague year') fast forwards to the dawn of the 20th century, when children discover its ruins. The quatrains, one to a spread, alternate between an AABB and ABBA rhyme scheme, thus avoiding singsong predictability. . . . Children will pore over Innocenti's marvelously detailed spreads, composed in an oversize, vertical format and set in an Italian hill town. . . . In the subset of books dealing intelligently with the effects of time on a single location, this is a provocative choice." SLJ

★ **Monumental** verses. National Geographic 2005 31p il $16.95; lib bdg $25.90

Grades: 5 6 7 8 **811**

1. Monuments -- Poetry 2. Poetry -- By individual authors
ISBN 0-7922-7135-1; 0-7922-7139-4 lib bdg

"Lewis offers 14 poems celebrating monumental structures. From the remnants of civilizations at Stonehenge, Easter Island, and Machu Picchu to the more modern achievements of the Taj Mahal, the Eiffel Tower, and the Statue of Liberty, the subjects are varied and the accompanying photos are striking." Booklist

★ **Self** -portrait with seven fingers; the life of Marc Chagall in verse. [by] J. Patrick Lewis & Jane Yolen. Creative Editions 2011 38p il $18.99
Grades: 5 6 7 8   811
 1. Artists 2. Painters 3. Jews -- Poetry 4. Artists -- Poetry 5. Jews -- Biography
 ISBN 978-1-56846-211-0; 1-56846-211-5
          LC 2009034767
"Lewis and Yolen pair 14 poems about Marc Chagall (1887–1985) with reproductions of more than a dozen of his paintings (as well as vintage photographs) in this moving account of the artist's Jewish upbringing in what is now Belarus, . . . his ascent in the art world, and his loves and losses, including arrest by the Nazis while living in Paris. . . . The duo's emphatic and empathetic verse is put into context by informative biographical sidebars that appear beneath each poem. A study in resilience, dedication, and wide-ranging talent." Publ Wkly
 Includes bibliographical references

★ **Lives:** poems about famous Americans; selected by Lee Bennett Hopkins; illustrated by Leslie Staub. HarperCollins Pubs. 1999 31p il $15.99
Grades: 4 5 6 7   811
 1. American poetry -- Collections 2. United States -- Biography -- Poetry
 ISBN 0-06-027767-X; 0-06-027768-8 lib bdg
          LC 98-29851
A collection of poetic portraits of sixteen famous Americans from Paul Revere to Neil Armstrong, by such authors as Jane Yolen, Nikki Grimes, and X. J. Kennedy
"Hopkins's eloquent introduction praises the power of poetry. Concluding 'Notes on the Lives' give readers useful biographical information. Full-page portraits feature Staub's distinctive, flat, primitive style, and their backgrounds have details particular to the subject. . . . A winning combination of poems and illustrations." SLJ

Longfellow, Henry Wadsworth
 ★ **Henry** Wadsworth Longfellow; edited by Frances Schoonmaker; illustrated by Chad Wallace. Sterling 1998 48p il (Poetry for young people) $14.95
Grades: 4 5 6 7   811
 1. Children's poetry, American 2. Poetry -- By individual authors
 ISBN 0-8069-9417-7
          LC 98-14833
A collection of 27 poems, "among them, 'The Village Blacksmith,' 'The Wreck of the Hesperus,' 'The Children's Hour,' 'Paul Revere's Ride,' and 'Hiawatha's Childhood' from 'The Song of Hiawatha.' A several-page introduction to Longfellow's life also includes some of the stories behind the poems." Booklist

Hiawatha and Megissogwon; illustrated by Jeffrey Thompson; afterword by Joseph Bruchac. National Geographic Soc. 2001 un il $16.95
Grades: 5 6 7 8   811
 1. Native Americans -- Poetry 2. Poetry -- By individual authors
 ISBN 0-7922-6676-5
          LC 00-12719
"Readers who persevere through the no-longer-familiar poem will be rewarded for their efforts by Hiawatha's exciting adventures, ferocious battles, and victorious homecoming. The text has been capably illustrated in a complex process utilizing original drawings, black-and-white scratchboard, and a computer program for color." SLJ

Maddox, Marjorie
 Rules of the game; baseball poems. illustrated by John Sandford. Wordsong 2009 32p il $16.95
Grades: 5 6 7 8   811
 1. Baseball -- Poetry 2. Poetry -- By individual authors
 ISBN 978-1-59078-603-1; 1-59078-603-3
          LC 2008-19018
"Sports fans will find themselves nodding in recognition of Maddox's sophisticated grasp of the game's intricacies, while language mavens will appreciate her joyous wordplay and dead-on command of poetic devices. . . . Sandford's charcoal pencil drawings, backed by sepia-toned pages . . . impart a classy timelessness to the book that's a nice match to its subject." Booklist

Meltzer, Milton
 ★ **Walt** Whitman; a biography. 21st Cent. Bks. (Brookfield) 2002 160p il lib bdg $31.90
Grades: 7 8 9 10   811
 1. Poets 2. Authors 3. Essayists 4. Poets, American
 ISBN 0-7613-2272-8
          LC 2001-27798
"The book honestly explores Whitman's character and actions, including his racial prejudice and his tendency to write anonymous (and effective) praises of his own writing. Ultimately, this has a definite edge and relevance that gives it more resonance than blander overviews of the poet. . . . Photographs of Whitman and his family, images of his work, and reproductions of period illustrations . . . liven up the formatting." Bull Cent Child Books
 Includes bibliographical references

Mora, Pat
 Dizzy in your eyes; poems about love. Alfred A. Knopf 2010 165p il $15.99; lib bdg $18.99
Grades: 7 8 9 10   811
 1. Love poetry 2. Poetry -- By individual authors
 ISBN 978-0-375-84375-4; 0-375-84375-2; 978-0-375-94565-6 lib bdg; 0-375-94565-2 lib bdg
          LC 2009-04300
"From family and school to dating and being dumped, the subjects in these 50 poems cover teens' experiences of love in many voices and situations. . . . Mora writes in free verse, as well as a variety of classic poetic forms—including haiku, clerihew, sonnet, cinquain, and blank verse—and for each form there is an unobtrusive explanatory note on the facing page. The tight structures intensify the strong feelings

in the poems, which teens will enjoy reading on their own or hearing aloud in the classroom." Booklist

★ **My** America; a poetry atlas of the United States. selected by Lee Bennett Hopkins; illustrated by Stephen Alcorn. Simon & Schuster Bks. for Young Readers 2000 83p il $21.95

Grades: 4 5 6 7 **811**

1. United States -- Poetry 2. American poetry -- Collections

ISBN 0-689-81247-7

LC 98-47402

A collection of poems evocative of seven geographical regions of the United States, including the Northeast, Southeast, Great Lakes, Plains, Mountain, Southwest, and Pacific Coast States.

"Some poems are purposive, but the best . . . capture places and people in all their diversity. Stephen Alcorn's handsome, multi-textured pictures . . . avoid literal interpretation and capture the sweep of the land and the rhythm of the words." Booklist

My black me; a beginning book of black poetry. edited by Arnold Adoff. [rev ed.]; Dutton Children's Bks. 1994 83p hardcover o.p. pa $6.99

Grades: 5 6 7 8 **811**

1. African Americans -- Poetry 2. American poetry -- African American authors -- Collections

ISBN 0-525-45216-8; 0-14-037443-4 pa

First published 1974

A compilation of poems reflecting thoughts on being black by such authors as Langston Hughes, Lucille Clifton, Nikki Giovanni, and Imamu Amiri Baraka

Myers, Walter Dean, 1937-2014

★ **Harlem**; a poem. pictures by Christopher Myers. Scholastic 1997 un il $16.95

Grades: 5 6 7 8 9 10 **811**

1. African Americans -- Poetry 2. Poetry -- By individual authors 3. Harlem (New York, N.Y.) -- Poetry

ISBN 0-590-54340-7

LC 96-8108

A Caldecott Medal honor book, 1998

A poem celebrating the people, sights, and sounds of Harlem

"Myers's paean to Harlem sings, dances, and swaggers across the pages, conveying the myriad sounds on the streets. . . . Christopher Myers's collages add an edge to his father's words, vividly bringing to life the sights and scenes of Lenox Avenue." Horn Book Guide

Here in Harlem; poems in many voices. written by Walter Dean Myers. Holiday House 2004 88p il $16.95

Grades: 7 8 9 10 **811**

1. African Americans -- Poetry 2. Poetry -- By individual authors 3. Harlem (New York, N.Y.) -- Poetry

ISBN 0-8234-1853-7

LC 2003-67605

"In each poem here, a resident of Harlem speaks in a distinctive voice, offering a story, a thought, a reflection, or a memory. The poetic forms are varied and well chosen. . .

. Expressive period photos from Myers' collection accompany the text of this handsome book." Booklist

National Council of Teachers of English

A **Jar** of tiny stars: poems by NCTE award-winning poets; Bernice E. Cullinan, editor; illustrations by Andi MacLeod; portraits by Marc Nadel. Wordsong 1996 94p il $17.95

Grades: 4 5 6 7 **811**

1. American poetry -- Collections

ISBN 1-56397-087-2

LC 93-60466

"Each poet who has won the NCTE Poetry Award—David McCord, Aileen Fisher, Karla Kuskin, Myra Cohn Livingston, Eve Merriam, John Ciardi, Lilian Moore, Arnold Adoff, Valerie Worth, and Barbara Esbensen—is pictured at the beginning of a section that includes several representative poems and a significant quote. The portraits are watercolor renditions from photographs, with cheerful pen-and-ink sketches accompanying the verse; all are in black and white." Bull Cent Child Books

Nelson, Marilyn, 1946-

Carver, a life in poems. Front St. 2001 103p il $16.95

Grades: 7 8 9 10 **811**

1. Botanists 2. Poetry -- By individual authors

ISBN 1-88691-053-7

LC 00-63624

A Newbery Medal honor book, 2002

"A series of fifty-nine poems portrays George Washington Carver as a private, scholarly man of great personal faith and social purpose. Nelson fills in the trajectory of Carver's life with details of the cultural and political contexts that shaped him even as he shaped history. As individual works, each poem stands as a finely wrought whole of . . . high caliber." Horn Book Guide

★ **Fortune's** bones; the manumission requiem. Front Street 2004 32p il $16.95

Grades: 7 8 9 10 **811**

1. Slavery -- Poetry 2. African Americans -- Poetry 3. Poetry -- By individual authors

ISBN 1-932425-12-8

LC 2004-46917

"This requiem honors a slave who died in Connecticut in 1798. His owner, a doctor, dissected his body, boiling down his bones to preserve them for anatomy studies. The skeleton . . . hung in a local museum until 1970. . . . The museum . . . uncovered the skeleton's provenance, created a new exhibit, and led to the commissioning of these six poems. The selections . . . arc from grief to triumph. . . . The facts inform the verse and open up a full appreciation of its rich imagery and rhythmic, lyrical language." SLJ

Includes bibliographical references

★ The **freedom** business; including a narrative of the life & adventures of Venture, a native of Africa. Wordsong 2008 72p il $18.95

Grades: 8 9 10 11 12 **811**

1. Slavery -- Poetry 2. Connecticut -- Poetry 3. African

Americans -- Poetry
ISBN 978-1-932425-57-4; 1-932425-57-8

LC 2008-04437

"Venture Smith, born Broteer Furro in Guinea, was captured and enslaved at the age of six and brought to America in 1738. . . . His narrative, published in 1798, appears continuously on the left-hand page of each spread; Nelson's luminous poems appear on the right. Both are thrown into relief by Dancy's mixed-media artwork, which includes images of birds, ropes, chains and blood to heighten the visceral emotions of both texts. . . . Tragic, important, breathtaking." Kirkus

★ **How** I discovered poetry; by Marilyn Nelson and illustrated by Hadley Hooper. Dial Books 2014 112 p. (hardcover : alk. paper) $17.99

Grades: 7 8 9 10 11 12   **811**

1. American poets 2. Civil rights -- United States -- History 3. Authorship -- Poetry 4. Poetry -- Authorship
ISBN 0803733046; 9780803733046

LC 2013005289

Coretta Scott King Author Award Honor Book (2015)

In this memoir, author Marilyn Nelson "tells the story of her development as an artist and young woman through fifty eye-opening poems. Readers are given an intimate portrait of her growing self-awareness and artistic inspiration along with a larger view of the world around her: racial tensions, the Cold War era, and the first stirrings of the feminist movement." (Publisher's note)

"In this fictionalized memoir in verse, renowned poet Nelson lyrically recounts her passage from ages 4 to 14, from numerous military base homes; through friends, schools, and dogs; and from developmental stages of initiative through industry to identity..Hooper's line-and-shade illustrations, along with Nelson's family photos, set a quiet and respectful tone and offer readers the feeling of taking an unsolicited peek behind a heavy curtain. For fans of Nelson's impressive body of children's and adult poetry, including the brilliant A Wreath for Emmett Till (2005), this insight into her modulated memories gratifies that heartfelt belief that here writes a woman of great substance." (Booklist)

★ **Sweethearts** of rhythm; the story of the greatest all-girl swing band in the world. written by Marilyn Nelson; illustrated by Jerry Pinkney. Dial Books 2009 un il $21.99

Grades: 4 5 6 7   **811**

1. Women musicians 2. Jazz music -- Poetry 3. Jazz 4. Poetry -- By individual authors 5. International Sweethearts of Rhythm
ISBN 0-8037-3187-6; 978-0-8037-3187-5

LC 2008-46255

This is a study of the racially mixed group the International Sweethearts of Rhythm. Bibliography. "Grades six to nine." (Bull Cent Child Books)

"On all fronts, a resonant performance." Publ Wkly

★ A **wreath** for Emmett Till; illustrated by Philippe Lardy. Houghton Mifflin 2005 un il $17

Grades: 8 9 10 11 12   **811**

1. Children 2. Murder victims 3. Lynching -- Poetry 4. Mississippi -- Poetry 5. African Americans -- Poetry

6. Poetry -- By individual authors
ISBN 0-618-39752-3

LC 2004-9205

Michael L. Printz Award honor book, 2006

This is a "poetry collection about Till's brutal, racially motivated murder. The poems form a heroic crown of sonnets—a sequence in which the last line of one poem becomes the first line of the next. . . . The rigid form distills the words' overwhelming emotion into potent, heart-stopping lines that speak from changing perspectives. . . . When matched with Lardy's gripping, spare, symbolic paintings of tree trunks, blood-red roots, and wreaths of thorns, these poems are a powerful achievement that teens and adults will want to discuss together." Booklist

Nye, Naomi Shihab

★ **19** varieties of gazelle; poems of the Middle East. Greenwillow Bks. 2002 142p $16.95; pa $6.99

Grades: 7 8 9 10   **811**

1. Middle East -- Poetry 2. Poetry -- By individual authors
ISBN 0-06-009765-5; 0-06-050404-8 pa

LC 2002-771

In this "volume, Nye collects her poems about growing up as an Arab American (her ancestry is Palestinian), including previously published poems and newly written pieces. This rich and varied volume offers insights into the experience of childhood in two very different worlds. . . . This volume will fill a need for classroom use, for young people seeking a more personal understanding of the Middle East, and for readers seeking a connection with their own Middle Eastern background." Bull Cent Child Books

★ **Honeybee**; poems & short prose. Greenwillow Books 2008 164p $16.99; lib bdg $17.89

Grades: 8 9 10 11 12   **811**

1. Poetry -- By individual authors
ISBN 978-0-06-085390-7; 0-06-085390-5; 978-0-06-085391-4 lib bdg; 0-06-085391-3 lib bdg

LC 2007-36742

This poetry "anthology is a rallying cry, a call for us to rediscover such beelike traits as interconnectedness, strong community, and honest communication. . . . Teens at the very start of their questioning years will recognize their own angst in Nye's sense of irony, their idealistic optimism in her simple wonder." SLJ

A **maze** me; poems for girls. pictures by Terre Maher. 1st ed; Greenwillow Books 2005 118p il $16.99; lib bdg $17.89

Grades: 7 8 9 10   **811**

1. Girls -- Poetry 2. Poetry -- By individual authors
ISBN 0-06-058189-1; 0-06-058190-5 lib bdg

LC 2004-3283

These "poems draw from Nye's observations about nature, home, school, and neighborhood to make connections to a girl's inner world. . . . Most poems . . . speak with a powerful immediacy. . . . A wide age range will respond to these deeply felt poems about everyday experiences." Booklist

Salting the ocean; 100 poems by young poets. selected by Naomi Shihab Nye; pictures by Ashley Bryan. Greenwillow Bks. 2000 111p il $16.99

Grades: 4 5 6 7   **811**

1. Children's writings 2. American poetry -- Collections

ISBN 0-688-16193-6

LC 99-30590

"While working within various school systems during the 1970s, Nye collected and saved these poems written by students in grades 1-12. . . . The collection is divided into four sections, each of which has approximately 25 poems. . . . In 'The Self and the Inner World,' the young poets express their thoughts about growing up, how they feel about their bodies . . . and make observations about people and events that surround them. 'Where We Live' looks at the trees, birds, sounds, and other aspects of the community in which the children live. 'Anybody's Family' includes poems about ethnicity, members of the students' households, and their feelings toward family members. In 'The Wide Imagination,' the poets . . . write about such topics as mirrors, history, time, words, and love." (SLJ) Index. "Grades four to twelve." (Booklist)

"These poems are divided into four topics: The Self and the Inner World, Where We Live, Anybody's Family, and the Wide Imagination." Horn Book Guide

Includes bibliographical references

The **Oxford** book of American poetry; chosen and edited by David Lehman; associate editor, John Brehm. Oxford University Press 2006 lvii, 1132p $35

Grades: 8 9 10 11 12 Adult   **811**

1. American poetry -- Collections

ISBN 0-19-516251-X; 978-0-19-516251-6

LC 2005-36590

First published 1950 with title: The Oxford book of American verse

"The book is not only a sound historical survey, but also gives the reader a powerful taste of poetry's impact upon the wider world." Economist

Includes bibliographical references

The **Oxford** book of children's verse in America; edited by Donald Hall. Oxford University Press 1985 xxxviii, 319p $39.95; pa $19.95

Grades: 5 6 7 8 9 10 11 12 Adult   **811**

1. American poetry -- Collections

ISBN 0-19-503539-9; 0-19-506761-4 pa

LC 84-20755

"A fine and carefully winnowed collection of American poetry is gathered in a book that will interest students of children's literature and young people who simply enjoy browsing." Horn Book

★ The **Place** my words are looking for; what poets say about and through their work. selected by

Paul B. Janeczko. Bradbury Press 1990 150p il $17.95

Grades: 4 5 6 7   **811**

1. Poetics 2. American poetry -- Collections

ISBN 0-02-747671-5

LC 89-39331

"More than forty contemporary poets are included: Eve Merriam, X. J. Kennedy, Felice Holman, Gary Soto, Mark Vinz, Karla Kuskin, and John Updike, among others. Their contributions vary widely in theme and mood and style, though the preponderance of the pieces are written in modern idiom and unrhymed meter. The accompanying comments frequently are as insightful and eloquent as the poems themselves." Horn Book

Poe, Edgar Allan

The **raven**; with illustrations by Ryan Price. KCP Poetry 2006 un il (Visions in poetry) $17.95

Grades: 7 8 9 10   **811**

1. Poetry -- By individual authors

ISBN 978-1-55337-473-2; 1-55337-473-8

This poem originally published by Poe in 1845 is presented with illustrations by Price that "suggest a background story shaped by the narrator's guilt, embodied in the terrifying figure of the raven. . . . Ages ten and up." (Publisher's note)

"Originally published in 1845, the poem is narrated by a melancholy scholar brooding over Lenore, a woman he loved who is now lost to him. One bleak December at midnight, a raven with fiery eyes visits the scholar and perches above his chamber door. Struggling to understand the meaning of the word his winged visitant repeats 'Nevermore!' the narrator descends by stages into madness." Publisher's note

★ A **Poem** of her own; voices of American women yesterday and today. edited by Catherine Clinton; illustrated by Stephen Alcorn. Abrams 2003 79p il $17.95

Grades: 6 7 8 9   **811**

1. American poetry -- Women authors -- Collections

ISBN 0-8109-4240-2

LC 2002-12851

Presents a collection of more than twenty poems by American women published between 1678 and 2001. Includes poems by Phillis Wheatley, Gertrude Stein, Lucille Clifton, Sandra Cisneros, and Naomi Shihab Nye

"The intelligent selection is matched by the fresh, open design, highlighted by Alcorn's exciting paintings, executed in light-fast casein paint." Booklist

Poetry from the masters: the pioneers; edited by Wade Hudson; illustrated by Stephan J. Hudson. Just Us Books 2003 88p il pa $9.95

Grades: 7 8 9 10   **811**

1. African American authors 2. American poetry -- African American authors -- Collections

ISBN 0-940975-96-3

This book "focuses on a particular group of black poets, 'trailblazers' who forged a path by overcoming 'almost impossible obstacles.' Hudson puts these writers in perspective and provides a social and literary context. Eleven poets are profiled, starting with Phillis Wheatley and ending with

Gwendolyn Brooks. . . . Each writer is introduced with a brief biographical sketch that highlights his or her literary significance and contributions, followed by the full text of two or more poems. . . . This is an excellent resource for students seeking research materials or just looking for wonderful examples of poetry to read." SLJ

Includes bibliographical references

★ A **Poke** in the I; [selected by] Paul Janeczko; illustrated by Chris Raschka. Candlewick Press 2001 35p il hardcover o.p. pa $7.99

Grades: 4 5 6 7 8 9 10   **811**

1. American poetry -- Collections

ISBN 0-7636-0661-8; 0-7636-2376-8 pa

LC 00-33675

"Thirty concrete poems of all shapes and sizes are carefully laid on large white spreads, extended by Raschka's quirky watercolor and paper-collage illustrations. . . . Beautiful and playful, this title should find use in storytimes, in the classroom, and just for pleasure anywhere." SLJ

★ The **Random** House book of poetry for children; selected and introduced by Jack Prelutsky; illustrated by Arnold Lobel. Random House 1983 248p il $19.95; lib bdg $21.99

Grades: 3 4 5 6   **811**

1. English poetry -- Collections 2. American poetry -- Collections

ISBN 0-394-85010-6; 0-394-95010-0 lib bdg

LC 83-2990

In this anthology emphasis "is placed on humor and light verse; but serious and thoughtful poems are also included. . . . Approximately two thirds of the selections were written within the past forty years—the splendid contributions of such writers as John Ciardi, Aileen Fisher, Dennis Lee, Myra Cohn Livingston, David McCord, Eve Merriam, and Lilian Moore. [There are] . . . samplings of earlier poets from Shakespeare and Blake to Emily Dickinson and Walter de la Mare." Horn Book

★ **Reflections** on a gift of watermelon pickle--and other modern verse; [compiled by] Stephen Dunning, Edward Lueders, Hugh Smith. Lothrop, Lee & Shepard Bks. 1967 139p il $19.99

Grades: 6 7 8 9 10   **811**

1. American poetry -- Collections

ISBN 0-688-41231-9

First published 1966 by Scott, Foresman in a text edition

"Although some of the [114] selections are by recognized modern writers, many are by minor or unknown poets, and few will be familiar to the reader. Nearly all are fresh in approach and contemporary in expression. . . . Striking photographs complementing or illuminating many of the poems enhance the attractiveness of the volume." Booklist

Rylant, Cynthia

Something permanent; photographs by Walker Evans; poetry by Cynthia Rylant. Harcourt Brace & Co. 1994 61p il $18

Grades: 7 8 9 10   **811**

1. Poetry -- By individual authors

ISBN 0-15-277090-9

LC 93-3861

"For students in junior high and high school, the juxtaposition of Evans' photos and Rylant's poems will demonstrate how emotions can be rooted in objects and how, to dig them out, you need to use strong, sturdy words." Booklist

Sendak, Maurice, 1928-2012

★ **My** brother's book; Maurice Sendak ; [edited by] Michael di Capua. HarperCollins 2013 32 p. (hardcover bdg.) $18.95

Grades: 4 5 6 7 8   **811**

1. Poetry -- Collections

ISBN 0062234897; 9780062234896

LC 2012942549

In this book, "with influences from Shakespeare and William Blake, [Maurice] Sendak pays homage to his late brother, Jack, whom he credited for his passion for writing and drawing. Pairing Sendak's . . . poetry with his . . . artwork, . . . Sendak's tribute to his brother is an expression of both grief and love. . . . Pulitzer Prize--winning literary critic and Shakespearean scholar Stephen Greenblatt contributes a[n] . . . introduction." (Publisher's note)

Service, Robert W.

★ The **cremation** of Sam McGee; by Robert W. Service; paintings by Ted Harrison; introduction by Pierre Berton. 20th anniversary ed.; Kids Can Press 2006 un il $17.95

Grades: 4 5 6 7   **811**

1. Yukon Territory -- Poetry 2. Poetry -- By individual authors

ISBN 978-1-55453-092-2; 1-55453-092-X

Text first published 1907. This is a reissue of the edition first published 1986 in Canada and 1987 in the United States by Greenwillow Bks.

This poem "has gripped readers and listeners for decades. . . . [The illustrator] obviously appreciates the humor inherent in the text. . . . As Pierre Berton observes in his introduction, [Harrison's] 'style is unique: part Oriental, part native American, part Ted Harrison.'" Horn Book

Shange, Ntozake

★ **Freedom's** a-callin' me; poems by Ntozake Shange; paintings by Rod Brown. Amistad/Collins 2012 il $16.99

Grades: 4 5 6 7   **811**

1. Slavery -- Poetry 2. African Americans -- Poetry 3. Underground railroad -- Poetry

ISBN 978-0-06-133741-3; 0-06-133741-2

LC 2010050515

The author and illustrator present "a series of poems and paintings that express the hope and frustration of enslaved people trying to navigate the Underground Railroad. Using dialect to convey a Southern cadence, Shange's poems communicate powerful emotions. . . . These poems are a cry from the heart. . . . The expressive, impressionistic paintings capture attention with their bold strokes and vivid coloring." SLJ

★ **We** troubled the waters; poems by Ntozake Shange; paintings by Rod Brown. Amistad/Collins 2009 un il $16.99; lib bdg $17.89

Grades: 4 5 6 7 8 9 10 **811**
    1. Poetry -- By individual authors 2. African Americans -- Civil rights -- Poetry
    ISBN 978-0-06-133735-2; 0-06-133735-8; 978-0-06-133737-6 lib bdg; 0-06-133737-4 lib bdg
                                        LC 2008025360

"Each spread pairs a poem with blurred, expressive acrylic paintings, and the pages feature both well-known civil rights leaders and ordinary people who endured oppression. . . . The messages are haunting. . . . The colloquial lines, indelible images, and comparisons between then and now will keep readers talking." Booklist

Shields, Carol Diggory

English, fresh squeezed! 40 thirst-for-knowledge-quenching poems. by Carol Diggory Shields; illustrations by Tony Ross. Handprint Books 2004 80p il $14.95

Grades: 4 5 6 7 **811**
    1. English language -- Poetry 2. Poetry -- By individual authors
    ISBN 1-59354-053-1
                                        LC 2004-53905

"Shields presents humorous poems both celebrating and bemoaning parts of speech, grammatical rules, and other annoyances of English class. Her rhyming verse is generally snappy and pointed. . . . Ross's spot illustrations in black and white with a blue tone add visual amusement without overwhelming." SLJ

★ **Shimmy** shimmy shimmy like my sister Kate; looking at the Harlem Renaissance through poems. [edited by] Nikki Giovanni. Holt & Co. 1995 186p $17.95

Grades: 8 9 10 11 12 **811**
    1. Harlem Renaissance 2. American poetry -- African American authors -- Collections
    ISBN 0-8050-3494-3
                                        LC 95-38617

This anthology includes poems by such authors as Paul Laurence Dunbar, Langston Hughes, Countee Cullen, Gwendolyn Brooks, and Amiri Baraka. Commentary and a discussion of the development of African American arts known as the Harlem Renaissance is provided by editor Giovanni

Includes bibliographical references

Sidman, Joyce

★ **What** the Heart Knows; chants, charms, and blessings. written by Joyce Sidman and illustrated by Pamela Zagarenski. Houghton Mifflin Harcourt 2013 80 p. $16.99

Grades: 6 7 8 9 10 11 12 **811**
    1. Children's poetry 2. Blessing and cursing 3. Children's poetry, American
    ISBN 0544106164; 9780544106161
                                        LC 2012047836

This book, by Joyce Sidman and illustrated by Pamela Zagarenski, "is a collection of poems to provide comfort, courage, and humor at difficult or daunting moments in life. It conjures forth laments, spells, invocations, chants, blessings, promises, songs, and charms. Here are pleas on how to repair a friendship, wishes to transform one's life or to slow down time, charms to face the shame of a disapproving crowd, invocations to ask for forgiveness, [and] to understand the mysteries of happiness." (Publisher's note)

"Sidman and Zagarenski present "Chants & Charms," "Spells & Invocations," "Laments & Remembrances," and "Praise Songs & Blessings" in a variety of poetic forms. Each poem speaks directly from Sidman's heart to the reader's, addressing subjects of deep importance: forgiveness, friendship, bravery, death, illness, moving. Zagarenski's illustrations beautifully extend the poems with her dreamy style and deft use of white space, symbolism, and images." (Horn Book)

Silverstein, Shel

★ **Every** thing on it; poems and drawings by Shel Silverstein. Harper 2011 194p il $19.99; lib bdg $20.89

Grades: 3 4 5 6 **811**
    1. Humorous poetry 2. Nonsense verses 3. Poetry -- By individual authors
    ISBN 978-0-06-199816-4; 0-06-199816-8; 978-0-06-199817-1 lib bdg; 0-06-199817-6 lib bdg

The second original book to be published since Silverstein's passing in 1999, this poetry collection includes more than one hundred and thirty never-before-seen poems and drawings completed by the cherished American artist and selected by his family from his archives.

"Silverstein's inspired word play and impish sense of humor are in abundant evidence. His signature line drawings accompany many of the poems and complete the jokes of some. . . . Adults who grew up with Uncle Shelby will find themselves wiping their eyes by the time they get to the end of this collection; children new to the master will find themselves hooked." Kirkus

Falling up; poems and drawings by Shel Silverstein. HarperCollins Pubs. 1996 171p il $17.99; lib bdg $18.89

Grades: 3 4 5 6 **811**
    1. Humorous poetry 2. Nonsense verses 3. Poetry -- By individual authors
    ISBN 0-06-024802-5; 0-06-024803-3 lib bdg
                                        LC 96-75736

This "collection includes more than 150 poems. . . . As always, Silverstein has a direct line to what kids like, and he gives them poems celebrating the gross, the scary, the absurd, and the comical. The drawings are much more than decoration. They often extend a poem's meaning and, in many cases, add some great comedy." Booklist

★ **A light** in the attic; Special edition; Harper 2009 185p il $18.99

Grades: 3 4 5 6 **811**
    1. Humorous poetry 2. Nonsense verses 3. Poetry -- By individual authors
    ISBN 978-0-06-190585-8; 0-06-190585-2
    First published 1981

This collection of more than one hundred poems "will delight lovers of Silverstein's raucous, rollicking verse and his often tender, whimsical, philosophical advice. . . . The poems are tuned in to kids' most hidden feelings, dark wishes and enjoyment of the silly. . . . The witty line drawings are a full half of the treat of this wholly satisfying anthology by the modern successor to Edward Lear and Hilaire Belloc." SLJ [review of 1981 edition]

★ **Where** the sidewalk ends; the poems & drawings of Shel Silverstein. 30th anniversary special ed; HarperCollins 2004 183p il $17.99; lib bdg $18.89
Grades: 3 4 5 6 7 8 9 10   **811**
1. Humorous poetry 2. Nonsense verses 3. Poetry -- By individual authors
ISBN 0-06-057234-5; 0-06-058653-2 lib bdg
LC 2004-269335
First published 1974

"There are skillful, sometimes grotesque line drawings with each of the 127 poems, which run in length from a few lines to a couple of pages. The poems are tender, funny, sentimental, philosophical, and ridiculous in turn, and they're for all ages." Sat Rev

Singer, Marilyn
★ **Central** heating; poems about fire and warmth. illustrated by Meilo So. Alfred A. Knopf 2005 41p il $15.95; lib bdg $17.99
Grades: 4 5 6 7   **811**
1. Fire -- Poetry 2. Heat -- Poetry 3. Poetry -- By individual authors
ISBN 0-375-82912-1; 0-375-92912-6 lib bdg
LC 2004-4274

"The complicated nature of fire is explored in Singer's energetic short poems and So's deceptively simple single-color illustrations. . . . This title . . . belongs on library shelves everywhere." SLJ

Smith, Charles R., 1969-
★ **Hoop** queens; poems. Candlewick Press 2003 35p il hardcover o.p. pa $5.99
Grades: 4 5 6 7   **811**
1. Basketball -- Poetry 2. Women athletes -- Poetry 3. Poetry -- By individual authors
ISBN 0-7636-1422-X; 0-7636-3561-8 pa
LC 2002-41111

A collection of twelve poems that celebrate contemporary women basketball stars, including Yolanda Griffith, Chamique Holdsclaw, and Natalie Williams

"Action photos of the athletes are pasted large on colorful, dynamic backgrounds that barely hold the motion-filled poems to the page. Notes about each player and poem communicate the joy Smith finds both in watching the game and writing poetry. Pure pleasure for basketball fans and inspiration for kids who doubted poetry was alive." SLJ

Smith, Hope Anita
★ **Mother** poems; words and pictures by Hope Anita Smith. Henry Holt and Co. 2009 72p il $16.95

Grades: 4 5 6 7   **811**
1. Death -- Poetry 2. Mothers -- Poetry 3. Bereavement -- Poetry 4. African Americans -- Poetry 5. Poetry -- By individual authors
ISBN 978-0-8050-8231-9; 0-8050-8231-X
LC 2008-18342

"Smith writes about an African American child's grief at the sudden death of her mother. . . . Like the poetry, Smith's simple, torn-paper collages in a folk-art style show the close embraces and vignettes without overwhelming the words." Booklist

Soto, Gary
Canto familiar; [illustrated by Annika Nelson] Harcourt Brace & Co. 1995 79p il $18; pa $5.95
Grades: 4 5 6   **811**
1. Mexican Americans -- Poetry 2. Poetry -- By individual authors
ISBN 978-0-15-200067-7; 0-15-200067-4; 978-0-15-205885-2 pa; 0-15-205885-0 pa
LC 94-24218

"This collection of simple free verse captures common childhood moments at home, at school, and in the street. Many of the experiences are Mexican American . . . and occasional Spanish words are part of the easy, colloquial, short lines. . . . The occasional full-page, richly colored woodcuts by Annika Nelson capture the child's imaginative take on ordinary things." Booklist

★ **A fire** in my hands; poems by Gary Soto. rev and expanded ed.; Harcourt 2006 74p $16
Grades: 6 7 8 9   **811**
1. Mexican Americans -- Poetry 2. Poetry -- By individual authors
ISBN 0-15-205564-9
LC 2005024610
First published 1991 by Scholastic

"Half the poems are new to this expanded edition of a collection first published 15 years ago, including some great ones from Soto's adult books that speak about feeling stuck at home and growing up poor, Catholic, and Mexican American. Soto's chatty introduction about writing poetry that celebrates small, common things will appeal to both readers and writers, as will the informal questions and answers at the back of the book and the brief autobiographical notes Soto includes with each poem." Booklist

A **natural** man. Chronicle Bks. 2000 71p pa $13.95
Grades: 7 8 9 10   **811**
1. Mexican Americans -- Poetry 2. Poetry -- By individual authors
ISBN 0-8118-2518-3
LC 99-18353

"This poetry anthology offers a photographic glimpse into the lives of California's Chicanos. But although the titles and use of Spanish words create a very particular setting, the characters, stories, and truths of these selections have a universal resonance." SLJ

★ **Neighborhood** odes; illustrated by David Diaz. Harcourt Brace Jovanovich 1992 68p il hardcover o.p. pa $5.95

Grades: 4 5 6 **811**

1. Hispanic Americans -- Poetry 2. Poetry -- By individual authors

ISBN 0-15-256879-4; 0-15-205364-6 pa

LC 91-20710

"Twenty-one poems, all odes, celebrate life in a Hispanic neighborhood. Other than the small details of daily life— peoples' names or the foods they eat—these poems could be about any neighborhood. With humor, sensitivity, and insight, Soto explores the lives of children. . . . David Diaz's contemporary black-and-white illustrations, which often resemble cut paper, effortlessly capture the varied moods— happiness, fear, longing, shame, and greed—of this remarkable collection. With a glossary of thirty Spanish words and phrases." Horn Book

Partly cloudy; poems of love and longing. Harcourt 2009 100p $16

Grades: 7 8 9 10 **811**

1. Love poetry 2. Poetry -- By individual authors

ISBN 978-0-15-206301-6; 0-15-206301-3

LC 2008-22267

Poet Gary Soto captures the voices of young people as they venture toward their first kiss, brood over bruised hearts, and feel the thrill of first love.

"Soto's new book of verse about adolescent love is remarkable. . . . The language of the poems is spare but evocative, with not one word wasted. . . . Teens will find these poems very engaging and will relate to how the emotion of love is expressed in everyday moments." Voice Youth Advocates

★ **Soul** looks back in wonder; [illustrated by] Tom Feelings. Dial Bks. 1993 un il hardcover o.p. pa $7.99

Grades: 4 5 6 7 **811**

1. African Americans -- Poetry 2. American poetry -- African American authors -- Collections

ISBN 0-8037-1001-1; 0-14-056501-9 pa

LC 93-824

Coretta Scott King Award for illustration

Artwork and poems by such writers as Maya Angelou, Langston Hughes, and Askia Toure portray the creativity, strength, and beauty of their African American heritage

"This thoughtful collection of poetry is unique. . . . Feelings selected sketches done while he was in West Africa, South America, and at home in America. The original drawings were enhanced with colored pencils, colored papers, stencil cut-outs, and other techniques to give a collage effect. Marbled textures bring vibrancy to the work." Horn Book

Spires, Elizabeth

★ **I** heard God talking to me; William Edmondson and his stone carvings. Farrar, Straus and Giroux 2009 56p il $17.95

Grades: 8 9 10 11 12 Adult **811**

1. Artists 2. Sculptors 3. Religious poetry 4. Artists -- Poetry 5. Sculpture -- Poetry 6. African Americans -- Poetry 7. Poetry -- By individual authors

ISBN 978-0-374-33528-1; 0-374-33528-1

LC 2008-02343

"Moved by a religious vision at age 57, Nashville janitor William Edmondson began carving tombstones and whimsical figures out of stone in 1931 and went on to attract the attention of international collectors, eventually becoming the first African American artist to have a solo show at the Museum of Modern Art in New York. This handsome picture-book-sized poetry collection pairs full-page, black-and-white photos of Edmondson and his works with poems inspired by the images. . . . Supported by an appended prose biography, these playful, thought-provoking poems introduce a fascinating artist." Booklist

Tell the world; teen poems from WritersCorps. HarperTeen 2008 116p $16.99; pa $8.99

Grades: 7 8 9 10 11 12 **811**

1. Teenagers' writings 2. American poetry -- Collections

ISBN 978-0-06-134505-0; 0-06-134505-9; 978-0-06-134504-3 pa; 0-06-134504-0 pa

LC 2007-49577

"This worthy collection of brief poems offers an array of teen voices. . . . An essay by WritersCorps teacher Michelle Matz adds a vivid picture of her students and their lives. This fine collection should inspire creativity and resonate with teens who find their own hopes, fears, and dreams eloquently voiced in the works of these young poets." SLJ

Testa, Maria

Something about America. Candlewick Press 2005 84p $14.99

Grades: 6 7 8 9 **811**

1. Immigrants -- Poetry 2. Burns and scalds -- Poetry 3. Serbian Americans -- Poetry 4. Poetry -- By individual authors

ISBN 0-7636-2528-0

LC 2005-47064

"Testa's distilled poetry never seems forced, and her stirring words enhance a sense of the characters' experiences and emotions. . . . Based on an actual incident, this is an excellent choice for readers' theater and classroom discussion." Booklist

Thayer, Ernest Lawrence

Casey at the bat; written by Ernest L. Thayer; with illustrations by Joe Morse. Kids Can Press 2006 un il (Visions in poetry) $16.95

Grades: 5 6 7 8 **811**

1. Baseball -- Poetry 2. Poetry -- By individual authors

ISBN 1-55337-827-X; 978-1-55337-827-3

"Morse updates Thayer's baseball classic to a modern, urban setting with a multiracial cast filling the familiar roles. As tall buildings loom above them, metallic fences confine the players who seem pensive and watchful. The figures are strikingly rendered in oils and acrylics, their features sharply limned in thick black lines and smudges of neutral color." SLJ

★ **Time** you let me in; 25 poets under 25. selected by Naomi Shihab Nye. Greenwillow Books 2010 236p $16.99; lib bdg $17.89

Grades: 8 9 10 11 12   **811**

1. American poetry -- Collections

ISBN 978-0-06-189637-8; 0-06-189637-3; 978-0-06-189638-5 lib bdg; 0-06-189638-1 lib bdg

LC 2009-19387

"This lively collection by young contemporary writers is rooted in the strong, emotional particulars of family, friendship, childhood memories, school, dislocation, war, and more. . . . Teens will connect with the passionate, unmoderated feelings that are given clarity and shape in each poem." Booklist

Includes bibliographical references

Weatherford, Carole Boston

Remember the bridge; poems of a people. designed by Semador Megged. Philomel Bks. 2002 53p il $17.99

Grades: 5 6 7 8   **811**

1. African Americans -- Poetry 2. Poetry -- By individual authors

ISBN 0-399-23726-7

LC 2001-36161

"The author evokes imagined and actual individual experiences of the people . . . in the historical black-and-white photos, drawings, and etchings. . . . This celebratory, visually striking book will be appreciated in most collections." SLJ

Whipple, Laura

If the shoe fits; voices from Cinderella. illustrations by Laura Beingessner. Margaret K. McElderry Bks. 2002 67p il $17.95

Grades: 5 6 7 8   **811**

1. Cinderella -- Poetry 2. Fairy tales -- Poetry 3. Poetry -- By individual authors

ISBN 0-689-84070-5

LC 2001-30778

In this version of the fairy tale "the characters tell the story in blank verses. . . . The story unfolds just as it always does, but the multiple points of view—from Cinderella's to the prince's to the rat's to the queen's—enlarge and enrich the familiar tale to win a more sophisticated audience. . . . Paintings by Beingessner achieve just the right mixture of sorrow, beauty, and humor." Booklist

Whisper and shout; poems to memorize. edited by Patrice Vecchione. Cricket Bks. 2002 120p $16.95

Grades: 4 5 6 7   **811**

1. American poetry -- Collections

ISBN 0-8126-2656-7

LC 2002-591

A collection of poems on different subjects and in different styles, that lend themselves to memorization. Among the poets represented are Jack Prelutsky, Edward Lear, Ogden Nash, T. S. Eliot, Edna St. Vincent Millay, Christina Rossetti, and Lewis Carroll

"With a lengthy, enthusiastic introduction and a generous final section of resources and biographies, this anthology will get as much use in the classroom as with individual readers." Booklist

Includes bibliographical references

Whitman, Walt

★ **Walt** Whitman; edited by Jonathan Levin; illustrated by Jim Burke. Sterling 1997 48p il (Poetry for young people) $14.95; pa $6.95

Grades: 5 6 7 8 9   **811**

1. Children's poetry, American 2. Poetry -- By individual authors

ISBN 0-8069-9530-0; 1-4027-5477-9 pa

LC 97-433

An illustrated collection of twenty-six poems and excerpts from longer poems by the renowned nineteenth-century poet

"An outstanding introduction to Whitman's life and work. . . . This superb volume can be used to teach literature or to show a variety of poetic devices and style." SLJ

Wicked poems; edited by Roger McGough; illustrated by Neal Layton. Bloomsbury Children's Books 2004 208p il $15

Grades: 4 5 6 7   **811**

1. Good and evil -- Poetry 2. American poetry -- Collections

ISBN 1-58234-854-5

LC 2002-38551

"The 134 poems in this . . . collection focus on people exhibiting various degrees of wickedness. The book includes works from well-known poets . . . and children's authors such as Shel Silverstein, Eve Merriam, Myra Cohn Livingston, and Jack Prelutsky. . . . Childlike, black-and-white cartoons are laugh-out-loud funny. . . . A perfect choice for reading aloud as well as independent browsing." SLJ

Williams, William Carlos

William Carlos Williams; edited by Christopher MacGowan; illustrated by Robert Crockett. Sterling Pub. Co. 2004 48p il (Poetry for young people) $14.95

Grades: 7 8 9 10   **811**

1. Poetry -- By individual authors

ISBN 1-4027-0006-7

LC 2003-6885

A collection of thirty poems with illustrations and brief introductory remarks

"The introduction and commentary that MacGowan . . . provides not only fills in biographical details but expertly illuminates the craft and sensibility behind these 31 deceptively simple imagist poems . . . Despite its simple language and clear imagery, Williams' poetry is not widely available to young readers. This gathering should help to remedy that." Booklist

Words with wings; a treasury of African-American poetry and art. selected by Belinda Rochelle. HarperCollins Pubs. 2001 un il lib bdg $18.99

Grades: 4 5 6 7   **811**

1. African Americans in art 2. African Americans -- Poetry 3. American poetry -- African American authors

-- Collections
ISBN 0-688-16415-3

LC 00-26864

Pairs twenty works of art by African-American artists such as Horace Pippin and Jacob Lawrence with twenty poems by African-American poets such as Langston Hughes, Countee Cullen, and Lucille Clifton

"Most of the combinations are stunning. . . . Short biographical paragraphs on each poet and artist round out this moving presentation." SLJ

Worth, Valerie

Pug and other animal poems; Valerie Worth ; pictures by Steve Jenkins. Margaret Ferguson Books, Farrar Straus Giroux 2012 40 p. $16.99

Grades: 2 3 4 5   **811**

1. Animals -- Poetry 2. Children's poetry 4. Children's poetry, American

ISBN 0374350248; 9780374350246

LC 2010034300

This juvenile poetry collection, by Valerie Worth, illustrated by Steve Jenkins, "examines a wide range of animal behavior, from the fleetingness of a fly sipping spilled milk to the constant steely presence of a powerful bull; the greedy meal of a street rat to a cat's quiet gift of a dead mouse on the doorstep." (Publisher's note)

WritersCorps

Paint me like I am; teen poems from WritersCorps. HarperTempest 2003 128p hardcover o.p. pa $6.99

Grades: 7 8 9 10   **811**

1. Teenagers' writings 2. American poetry -- Collections

ISBN 0-06-029288-1; 0-06-447264-7 pa

LC 2002-5942

"The teen voices in these poems, collected from the WritersCorps youth program, are LOUD—raging, defiant, giddy, lusty, and hopeful. Grouped into arbitrary categories, the poems explore identity, creative expressions, family, neighborhood, drugs, and relationships. . . . A foreword from Nikki Giovanni rounds out this moving collection, which also includes a few thoughtful writing exercises." Booklist

Yolen, Jane

The **Emily** sonnets; the life of Emily Dickinson. by Jane Yolen ; illustrations by Gary Kelley. 1st ed. Creative Editions 2012 40 p. col. ill. (reinforced) $19.99

Grades: 5 6 7   **811**

1. Dickinson, Emily, 1830-1886 -- Poetry

ISBN 1568462158; 9781568462158

LC 2011040841

This book by Jane Yolen presents 15 sonnets about poet Emily Dickinson. "The selections are constructed in various voices. . . . In the first five pieces, Emily speaks of the family's brick house, her close relationship with her sister Vinnie, her schooling, her variance with her family's religious beliefs, and the companionship of her dog. . . . The other speakers . . . tell of her always dressing in white, her life as a recluse, and her work." (School Library Journal)

★ **Sacred** places; illustrated by David Shannon. Harcourt Brace & Co. 1996 38p il $16

Grades: 4 5 6 7   **811**

1. Religious poetry 2. Poetry -- By individual authors

ISBN 0-15-269953-8

LC 92-30323

"The hazy moodiness of Shannon's paintings capture the mystery Yolen explores in her text, while his dense figures and literal interpretations of a passage from each poem draw Yolen's mystical flights back down to solid ground. Appended notes offer historical information on each sacred place." Bull Cent Child Books

Young, Ed

Beyond the great mountains; a visual poem about China. Chronicle Books 2005 32p il $17.95

Grades: 4 5 6 7   **811**

1. China -- Poetry 2. Poetry -- By individual authors

ISBN 0-8118-4343-2

"The book is comprised of 14 lines, each of which is accompanied by its own double-page illustration, done in cut and torn-paper collage. Young also provides the ancient characters for the images he presents. . . . Designed to be read vertically, each page is flipped up to reveal the accompanying illustration. In this way, the entire book becomes a piece of art, a visual treat of sublime colors and textures that joins with text and characters to describe the vastness and beauty of China." SLJ

812   American drama in English

Acting out; six one-act plays!: six Newbery stars! edited by Justin Chanda; featuring the playwrights, Avi . . . [et. al.] Atheneum Books for Young Readers 2008 175p il $16.99

Grades: 5 6 7 8 9   **812**

1. One act plays 2. American drama -- Collections

ISBN 978-1-4169-3848-4; 1-4169-3848-6

Contains six original one-act plays by Newbery Award-winning children's authors, including Sharon Creech, Susan Cooper, Avi, Patricia Maclachlan, Katherine Paterson, and Richard Peck

"Each play was inspired by a theater-improv game in which the authors started with the selection of a single word. The pieces all include the following words: 'dollop,' 'hoodwink,' 'Justin,' 'knuckleball,' 'panhandle,' and 'raven.'. . . An engaging choice for literature and acting classes as well as general reading." SLJ

Includes bibliographical references

Black, Ann N.

Readers theatre for middle school boys; investigating the strange and mysterious. illustrated by Cody Rust. Teachers Idea Press 2008 190p il (Readers theatre) pa $30

Grades: Adult Professional   **812**

1. Readers' theater 2. Drama -- Collections

ISBN 978-1-59158-535-0 pa; 1-59158-535-X pa

LC 2007034923

"This book provides solid offerings of Readers Theater scripts for educators working with middle school boys. Selections include adaptations of such creepy classics as 'The Legend of Sleepy Hollow,' 'The Masque of the Red Death,' . . . and 'The Monkey's Paw.' The scripts have a new, fresh feel, and contain plenty of elements to capture and maintain adolescent males' attention." Libr Media Connect

Includes bibliographical references

Children's Theatre Company (Minneapolis, Minn.)

Fierce & true; plays for teen audiences. Peter & Elissa Adams, editors; The Children's Theatre Company. University of Minnesota Press 2010 219p il pa $17.95

Grades: 7 8 9 10 11 12   812

1. Drama -- Collections

ISBN 978-0-8166-7311-7; 0-8166-7311-X

The Children's Theatre Company "located in Minneapolis, wanted to broaden its audience, so it commissioned four playwrights to create works with young people (ages 12-18) specifically in mind. The results are the full-length plays in this anthology. . . . 'Anon(ymous)' is a contemporary retelling of Homer's Odyssey, set in a dirty North American city, and 'Five Fingers of Funk' is a mature musical celebrating the roots of hip-hop while dealing with issues of poverty and drugs. In 'The Lost Boys of Sudan,' three Dinka refugees flee the horrors of war and begin a harrowing yet humorous journey that takes them to Fargo, ND. And 'Prom' is played out as a frenetic battle between students and chaperones. Each of these selections has a distinctive voice, honoring adolescents as both actor and audience capable of understanding and engaging in today's complex issues." SLJ

Dunkleberger, Amy

A **student's** guide to Arthur Miller. Enslow Publs. 2005 160p il (Understanding literature) lib bdg $27.93

Grades: 7 8 9 10   812

1. Authors 2. Dramatists 3. Screenwriters

ISBN 0-7660-2432-6

This discusses the life of Arthur Miller and his works All My Sons, Death of a Salesman, The Crucible, A View From the Bridge, After the Fall, Incident at Vichy, and The Price

"Engaging and informative. . . . The very accessible format and the solid information make [this book] useful to students, and the engaging style should interest casual readers." SLJ

Includes glossary and bibliographical references

Hermann, Spring

A **student's** guide to Eugene O'Neill. Enslow Publishers 2009 176p il (Understanding literature) lib bdg $27.93

Grades: 7 8 9 10   812

1. Authors 2. Dramatists 3. Nobel laureates for literature

ISBN 978-0-7660-2886-9; 0-7660-2886-0

LC 2008-14599

"An introduction to the work of Eugene O'Neill for . . . students, which includes relevant biographical background on the author, explanations of various literary devices and

techniques, and literary criticism for the novice reader." Publisher's note

Includes glossary and bibliographical references

Levine, Karen

★ **Hana's** suitcase on stage; original story by Karen Levine; play by Emil Sher. Second Story 2007 171p il (Holocaust remembrance book for young readers) pa $18.95

Grades: 5 6 7 8   812

1. Holocaust victims 2. Holocaust, 1933-1945 -- Drama

ISBN 978-1-89718-705-0 pa; 1-89718-705-X pa

"Set in the Tokyo Holocaust Center, the two-act play opens with the woman and two of her student helpers questioning and searching for answers to the suitcase's history. . . . Act II blends characters of Ishioka and her students with Hana and her family, each group individually recounting their stories in alternating voices. As with the original book, this title succeeds in recreating a striking representation of one child's tragic and beautiful life in a terrifying world of hate and prejudice. This volume will serve as one of the most effective teaching models for Holocaust curriculums available. Photographs and facsimiles of Nazi documents are included." SLJ

Loos, Pamela

A **reader's** guide to Lorraine Hansberry's A raisin in the sun. Enslow Publishers 2008 128p il (Multicultural literature) lib bdg $31.93

Grades: 7 8 9 10   812

1. Authors 2. Dramatists 3. African Americans in literature 4. Essayists 5. Newspaper editors 6. Nonfiction writers 7. American drama -- History and criticism

ISBN 978-0-7660-2830-2; 0-7660-2830-5

LC 2006-17900

"A Raisin in the Sun has become part of the literary canon and is required reading for many students. This guide is intended to help them better appreciate the social milieu out of which this play emerged . . . making this volume a fine resource." SLJ

Includes bibliographical references

Soto, Gary

★ **Novio** boy; a play. Harcourt 2006 78p pa $5.95

Grades: 7 8 9 10   812

1. Mexican Americans -- Drama 2. Dating (Social customs) -- Drama

ISBN 978-0-15-205863-0; 0-15-205863-X

LC 2007-271308

First published 1997

Rudy anxiously prepares for and then goes out on a first date with an attractive girl who is older than he is.

Stuyvesant High School (New York, N.Y.)

With their eyes; September 11th: the view from a high school at ground zero. edited by Annie Thoms; created by Taresh Batra [et. al.]; photos by Ethan Moses. HarperTempest 2002 228p il hardcover o.p. pa $6.99

Grades: 7 8 9 10 **812**
1. Teenagers' writings 2. American drama -- Collections
3. Stuyvesant High School (New York, N.Y.) 4.
September 11 terrorist attacks, 2001 -- Drama
ISBN 0-06-051806-5; 0-06-051718-2 pa

LC 2002-4552

"The speakers reveal their emotions with painful honesty.
. . . The book is an obvious choice for reader's theater and for
use across the curriculum; its deeply affecting contents will
also make compelling personal-interest reading." Booklist

Theatre for young audiences; 20 great plays for children. edited by Coleman A. Jennings; foreword
by Maurice Sendak. St. Martin's Press 1998
604p il $35; pa $19.95 **812**
1. Drama -- Collections
ISBN 0-312-18194-9; 0-312-33714-0 pa

LC 97-36542

A collection of plays, many of which are based on fa-
vorite children's tales, including such titles as: "Charlotte's
Web," "Really Rosie," "Wiley and the Hairy Man," "Wise
Men of Chelm," and "The Crane Wife"

"Highly recommended for school and public libraries
and anyone interested in a substantial collection of plays for
children." Booklist

813 American fiction in English

Blasingame, James B.
Gary Paulsen. Greenwood Press 2007 164p
(Teen reads: student companions to young adult lit-
erature) $45
Grades: 7 8 9 10 11 12 **813**
1. Authors 2. Sled dog racers 3. Children's authors 4.
Short story writers 5. Young adult authors
ISBN 978-0-313-33532-7; 0-313-33532-X

LC 2007-21446

"This volume examines a sample of . . . books by
Paulsen. A biographical chapter demonstrates how Paulsen's
life experiences, notably the Iditarod, have influenced his
writing. Each book is analyzed for plot, characterization,
setting, and themes." Publisher's note
Includes bibliographical references

Bodart, Joni Richards
They suck, they bite, they eat, they kill; the
psychological meaning of supernatural monsters in
young adult fiction. Joni Richards Bodart. Scarecrow Press 2012 xxxi, 268 p.p (Scarecrow studies
in young adult literature) $45
Grades: Adult Professional **813**
1. Folklore in literature 2. Monsters in literature 3.
Supernatural in literature 4. Literature -- Psychological
aspects 5. Young adult literature -- History and criticism
ISBN 9780810882270

LC 2011029544

This book examines the "rise of paranormal young adult
fiction" and "focuses on popular contemporary titles lightly
contextualized in a historical frame. . . . The book is divided
into four sections: 'Vampires: The Aristocratic Monster';

'Shapeshifters: The Transforming Monster'; 'Zombies:
The Reanimated, Resurrected Monster'; and 'Angels, Unicorns, Demons: The Unexpectedly Deadly Monsters.' Each
section opens with an overview of the literary and, when
applicable, folkloric history of each supernatural being."
(School Libr J) "Chapters focusing on individual authors
follow . . . . [T]he chapters serve both as a tour through each
invented universe and as a study of the author's relationship
to the books, drawn mostly through existing interviews."
(Booklist)
Includes bibliographical references

Cammarano, Rita
Betsy Byars. Chelsea House 2002 106p il (Who
wrote that?) lib bdg $30
Grades: 4 5 6 7 **813**
1. Authors 2. Women authors 3. Authors, American 4.
Children's authors 5. Young adult authors
ISBN 0-7910-6720-3

LC 2001-8337

Describes the personal life and successful writing career
of the Newbery Award-winning author, whose memorable
characters include Bingo Brown, Herculeah Jones, and the
Golly sisters
"An excellent resource for author studies and creative
writing classes." Book Rep
Includes bibliographical references

Carroll, Pamela S.
Sharon Creech; [by] Pamela Sissi Carroll.
Greenwood Press 2007 195p (Teen reads: student
companions to young adult literature) lib bdg $45
Grades: 7 8 9 10 11 12 **813**
1. Authors 2. Novelists 3. Authors, American 4.
Children's authors 5. Young adult authors 6. Young
adult literature -- History and criticism
ISBN 978-0-313-33598-3 lib bdg; 0-313-33598-2
lib bdg

LC 2007-21470

This focuses on Sharon Creech's "work as a teacher and
shows how she uses the practice of journal-keeping to create
an emotional experience for both character and reader. Of
special interest are the chapters on Creech's life and those
that discuss Absolutely Normal Chaos, Bloomability, and
The Wanderer." Voice Youth Advocates
Includes bibliographical references

Cart, Michael
The **heart** has its reasons; young adult literature with gay/lesbian/queer content, 1969-2004. [by]
Michael Cart [and] Christine A. Jenkins. Scarecrow
Press 2006 207p (Scarecrow studies in young adult
literature) $42
Grades: Adult Professional **813**
1. Homosexuality in literature 2. Teenagers -- Books
and reading 3. Young adult literature -- History and
criticism
ISBN 0-8108-5071-0

LC 2005-31320

"Both a comprehensive overview and a lively, detailed
discussion of individual landmark books, this highly readable title . . . discusses 35 years of YA books with gay, lesbi-

an, bisexual, transgender, and queer/questioning (GLBTQ) content. . . . With fully annotated bibliographies, including a chronological list, this is a valuable YA and adult resource, sure to be in great demand for personal reference and group discussion." Booklist

Includes bibliographical references

Cook, Judy

Natural writer: a story about Marjorie Kinnan Rawlings; by Judy Cook and Laura Lee Smith; illustrated by Laurie Harden. Carolrhoda Bks. 2001 64p il (Creative minds biography) lib bdg $21.27

Grades: 4 5 6   **813**

1. Authors 2. Novelists 3. Women authors 4. Frontier and pioneer life 5. Authors, American 6. Children's authors 7. Short story writers

ISBN 1-57505-468-X

LC 00-9657

"This biography begins with Rawling's childhood in the early 1900s and shows her development as a writer through her death. . . . This easy-to-read biography has an attractive cover and a full-page charcoal illustration in each chapter." SLJ

Includes bibliographical references

Crayton, Lisa A.

A **student's** guide to Toni Morrison. Enslow Publs. 2006 160p il (Understanding literature) lib bdg $27.93

Grades: 7 8 9 10   **813**

1. Authors 2. Novelists 3. Dramatists 4. Essayists 5. College teachers 6. Literary critics 7. Nobel laureates for literature

ISBN 0-7660-2436-9

LC 2005-19069

"Each work is placed in historical and biographical context, with special emphasis placed on curriculum-related material, including The Bluest Eye, Song of Solomon, and Beloved, along with several other noteworthy works." Publisher's note

Includes glossary and bibliographical references

Dean, Tanya

Theodor Geisel. Chelsea House 2002 112p il (Who wrote that?) $22.95

Grades: 4 5 6 7   **813**

1. Artists 2. Authors 3. Humorists 4. Illustrators 5. Authors, American 6. Children's authors

ISBN 0-7910-6724-6

LC 2002-166

Describes the life and career of the author and illustrator known as Dr. Seuss who created such popular children's picture books as The cat in the hat, How the Grinch stole Christmas, and Horton hears a Who

"Well organized and clearly written." Booklist

Includes bibliographical references

Diorio, Mary Ann L.

A **student's** guide to Herman Melville. Enslow Publs. 2006 160p il (Understanding literature) lib bdg $27.93

Grades: 7 8 9 10   **813**

1. Authors 2. Novelists

ISBN 0-7660-2435-0

LC 2005-10159

"Each work is placed in historical and biographical context, with special emphasis placed on curriculum-related works, including his masterpiece, Moby Dick, along with Billy Budd, several of his short stories, including 'Bartleby the Scrivener,' and several of his poetic works." Publisher's note

Includes glossary and bibliographical references

A **student's** guide to Mark Twain; [by] Mary Ann L. Diorio. Enslow Publishers 2007 160p il (Understanding literature) $27.93

Grades: 7 8 9 10   **813**

1. Authors 2. Humorists 3. Novelists 4. Essayists 5. Satirists 6. Memoirists 7. Travel writers 8. Short story writers

ISBN 978-0-7660-2438-0; 0-7660-2438-5

LC 2006005888

"After a brief account of the writer's life, Diorio discusses 11 of his major works in chronological order, starting with 'The Jumping Frog' and ending with The Tragedy of Pudd'nhead Wilson. For each highlighted selection, she gives a bare-bones plot summary and a brief discussion of major themes, characters, and literary devices. . . . The book is nicely formatted, with readable font on uncluttered pages. There are a few black-and-white photographs of Twain and some relevant reproductions." SLJ

Includes bibliographical references

Don, Katherine

Real courage; the story of Harper Lee. by Katherine Don. Morgan Reynolds Pub. 2013 128 p. ill. (some col.) $28.95

Grades: 7 8 9 10   **813**

1. Women -- Biography 2. American authors -- Biography 3. Authors, American -- 20th century -- Biography

ISBN 9781599353487; 9781599353494

LC 2012016871

This book examines author Nelle Harper Lee and "the publication and film adaptation of her novel 'To Kill a Mockingbird.'" The book looks at "the turbulent 1960's civil rights movement and how Lee's book, which spoke of racial injustice, struck a nerve with the public. Lee grew up in a small Mississippi town that experienced segregation, which she later used as the fictional setting for 'Mockingbird.' The biography describes Lee's rise to fame and the legacy she left." (Voice of Youth Advocates)

"Students and teachers looking for a solid, accessible biography will find this to be a fine choice as the writing is straightforward and engaging." SLJ

Includes bibliographical references and index

Experiencing America's story through fiction; historical novels for grades 7-12. Hilary Crew. ALA Editions, An imprint of the American Library Association 2014 xii, 193 p.p (paper) $57

Grades: Professional   **813**

1. American fiction -- Bibliography 2. Historical fiction

-- Bibliography 3. Historical fiction, American 4. Historical fiction, American -- Bibliography 5. Young adult fiction, American -- Bibliography 6. United States -- In literature -- Bibliography 7. Teenagers -- Books and reading -- United States 8. United States -- History -- Fiction -- Bibliography

ISBN 0838912257; 9780838912256

LC 2014008471

This annotated bibliography by Hillary Susan Crew "highlights more than 150 titles of historical fiction published since 2000 appropriate for seventh to twelfth graders." (Publisher's note)

"Historical fiction is a popular and effective way to connect literature to curriculum. Although the new Common Core Curriculum emphasizes informational texts, fiction can introduce different viewpoints and provide unique opportunities for evaluation and critical thinking. This book seeks to help history teachers and school and public librarians discover new historical fiction (most of the titles included were published between 2000 and 2013) and find ways to effectively use these titles to support their curriculum...The selection of books embodies a multitude of perspectives and truly represents the diversity of the United States. This outstanding bibliography is perfect for teachers, librarians, or history fans searching for just the right book." Horn Book

Includes bibliographical references (pages 183-185) and index

Fleischman, Sid

★ The **abracadabra** kid; a writer's life. Greenwillow Bks. 1996 198p il hardcover o.p. $16.99

Grades: 5 6 7 8   813

1. Authors 2. Magicians 3. Magazine editors 4. Authors, American 5. Children's authors 6. Young adult authors

ISBN 0-688-14859-X; 0-688-15855-2 pa

LC 95-47382

This autobiography, "turns real life into a story complete with cliffhangers. And it's a classic boy's story, from card tricks and traveling magic shows to World War II naval experiences and screen-writing gigs for John Wayne movies. En route, we learn how Fleischman learned the craft of writing." Bull Cent Child Books

Includes bibliographical references

Fradin, Dennis Brindell

★ **Zora!** the life of Zora Neal Hurston. Judith Bloom Fradin and Dennis Brindell Fradin. Clarion Books 2012 xi, 180 p.p ill. $17.99

Grades: 5 6 7 8   813

1. African American authors -- Biography 2. African American women -- Biography 3. Folklorists -- United States -- Biography 4. Authors, American -- 20th century -- Biography

ISBN 0547006950; 9780547006956

LC 2011025949

This book by Dennis Brindell Fradin and Judith Bloom Fradin presents a "biography of . . . African-American author . . . [Zora Neale] Hurston. . . . Beginning with a . . . scene of the 59-year-old Hurston, already a well-known author, working as a white family's domestic helper because she needed a paycheck, the Fradins . . . establish the complexities of

Zora's inner and external worlds, before offering highlights of her life in chronological order." (Publishers Weekly)

Includes bibliographical references and index.

Fritz, Jean

★ **Harriet** Beecher Stowe and the Beecher preachers. Putnam 1994 144p il $15.99; pa $5.99

Grades: 5 6 7 8   813

1. Authors 2. Novelists 3. Abolitionists 4. Women authors 5. Authors, American 6. Children's authors 7. Nonfiction writers 8. Short story writers

ISBN 0-399-22666-4; 0-698-11660-7 pa

LC 93-6408

This is a biography of the abolitionist author of "Uncle Tom's Cabin" with an emphasis on the influence of her preacher father and her family on her life and work.

"Written with vivacity and insight, this readable and engrossing biography is an important contribution to women's history as well as to the history of American letters." Horn Book

Includes bibliographical references

Gallo, Donald R.

Richard Peck; the past is paramount. [by] Donald R. Gallo, Wendy J. Glenn. Scarecrow Press 2009 208p (Scarecrow studies in young adult literature) $35

Grades: 7 8 9 10 Adult Professional   813

1. Authors 2. Novelists 3. Children's authors 4. Young adult authors

ISBN 978-0-8108-5848-0; 0-8108-5848-7

LC 2008036524

"Gallo and Wendy J. Glenn recount the highlights of Peck's life, focusing on his world travels, his accomplishments as a teacher and his renowned writing career. Gallo and Glenn examine Peck's 30 novels, as well as his short stories and children's books, poems, essays and other nonfiction." Publisher's note

Includes bibliographical references

Gantos, Jack

★ **Hole** in my life. Farrar, Straus & Giroux 2002 199p il $16; pa $8

Grades: 7 8 9 10   813

1. Authors 2. College teachers 3. Authors, American 4. Children's authors

ISBN 0-374-39988-3; 0-374-43089-6 pa

LC 2001-40957

Michael L. Printz Award honor book, 2003

The author relates how, as a young adult, he became a drug user and smuggler, was arrested, did time in prison, and eventually got out and went to college, all the while hoping to become a writer

"Gantos' spare narrative style and straightforward revelation of the truth have, together, a cumulative power that will capture not only a reader's attention but also empathy and imagination." Booklist

The **girl** who was on fire; your favorite authors on Suzanne Collins' Hunger games trilogy. edited by

Leah Wilson. BenBella Books 2011 211p pa
$12.95

Grades: Adult Professional   **813**

1. Authors 2. Novelists 3. Fantasy writers 4. Young
adult authors

ISBN 978-1-935618-04-1; 1-935618-04-0

LC 2011007180

"Fans of the trilogy will undoubtedly enjoy exploring
elements of the series through the eyes of the author's contemporaries, each with a different expertise. The selections
address the deeper social and political issues as well as the
development of multilayered characters through witty and
sometimes raw essays that ask readers to look deeper. . . .
Essays explore . . . subjects from within Katniss's world of
Panem with humor, irreverence, and social understanding.
This thought-provoking text will be especially useful for
educators or librarians utilizing the multidiscplinary themes
in this trilogy with their students." SLJ

Includes bibliographical references

Glenn, Wendy J.

Sarah Dessen; from burritos to box office.
[by] Wendy J. Glenn. Scarecrow Press 2005 147p
(Scarecrow studies in young adult literature) $45

Grades: 7 8 9 10 Adult Professional   **813**

1. Authors 2. Novelists 3. Young adult authors

ISBN 0-8108-5325-6; 978-0-8108-5325-6

LC 2004016058

This offers literary criticism of the works of Sarah Dessen, author of such young adult novels as The Truth About
Forever, and Lock and Key

"Glenn's book is an excellent example of the kind of
meaning-making exploration that students can examine in
a work of literature written for adolescents. . . . Informative
and lively." Voice Youth Advocates

Includes bibliographical references

Hamilton, Virginia

★ **Virginia** Hamilton: speeches, essays, and conversations; edited by Arnold Adoff & Kacy Cook.
Blue Sky Press 2010 368p $29.99

Grades: 8 9 10 11 12 Adult Professional   **813**

1. Authorship 2. Children's literature -- History and
criticism

ISBN 978-0-439-27193-6; 0-439-27193-2

LC 2009031676

"A groundbreaking writer of children's fiction, folktales,
biography, and picture books, Hamilton won every major
award, and much of this book is made up of her acceptance
speeches, including those for the Newbery, Hans Christian
Andersen, and Coretta Scott King awards, as well as her
Arbuthnot and Zena Sutherland lectures. Aimed at a general audience, the book employs a tone both scholarly and
informal, as Hamilton talks about her career as a woman
and a black writer in America and about the form and content of her work in general and with particular titles. . . .
Many speeches include introductions by children's literature
scholars and editors, who add perspective on Hamilton's
lasting influence, while family members fill in biographical details. A must for YAs who love her books, this will

also appeal to librarians, teachers, and children's literature
students." Booklist

Includes bibliographical references

Hickam, Homer H.

The **Coalwood** way; by Homer H. Hickam, Jr.
Delacorte Press 2000 318p hardcover o.p. pa $6.99

Grades: 7 8 9 10 11 12 Adult   **813**

1. Authors 2. Novelists 3. Aerospace engineers 4.
Memoirists 5. West Virginia 6. Authors, American 7.
Writers on science

ISBN 0-440-23716-5

LC 00-35884

This sequel to Rocket boys "continues the author's life
story with his senior year in high school, 1959, in the declining West Virginia mining town of Coalwood. The rocket
club, featured in the last book, is pushed to the periphery,
and the focus shifts to Hickam's teenage problems, which
include his parents, girls, and a sadness whose cause he cannot divine." Booklist

Hinds, Maurene J.

A **reader's** guide to Richard Wright's Black boy.
Enslow Publishers 2010 128p il (Multicultural literature) lib bdg $31.93

Grades: 6 7 8 9   **813**

1. Authors 2. Novelists 3. Dramatists 4. Essayists 5.
Nonfiction writers 6. Short story writers 7. American
literature -- African American authors

ISBN 978-0-7660-3165-4 lib bdg; 0-7660-3165-9
lib bdg

LC 2008-36473

"An introduction to Richard Wright's novel Black Boy . .
. which includes relevant biographical background on the author, explanations of various literary devices and techniques,
and literary criticism for the novice reader." Publisher's note

Includes glossary and bibliographical references

Hinton, KaaVonia

Angela Johnson; poetic prose. [by] KaaVonia
Hinton. Scarecrow Press 2006 107p (Scarecrow
studies in young adult literature) $35

Grades: 7 8 9 10 Adult Professional   **813**

1. Poets 2. Authors 3. Novelists 4. Children's authors
5. Short story writers 6. Young adult authors

ISBN 978-0-8108-5092-7; 0-8108-5092-3

LC 2006001893

The examines the life and works of Angela Johnson, author of such novels as Toning the Sweep and A
Cool Moonlight

"This book is a well-researched biography suitable for
reports or even thoughtful fans. Certainly teachers seeking
to use Johnson's books in their classes should find the literary criticism very useful." Voice Youth Advocates

Includes bibliographical references

Sharon M. Draper; embracing literacy. [by]
KaaVonia Hinton. Scarecrow Press 2009 131p
(Scarecrow studies in young adult literature) $35

Grades: 7 8 9 10 Adult Professional   **813**

1. Authors 2. Teachers 3. Novelists 4. Children's

authors 5. Young adult authors

ISBN 978-0-8108-5985-2; 0-8108-5985-8

LC 2008036695

"Author KaaVonia Hinton reveals how Draper became an exceptional teacher and writer, and how she uses her writing to urge young people to embrace literacy. Hinton also explores how Draper has made a lasting contribution to the field of young adult literature. This book-length study examines both her life and work." Publisher's note

Includes bibliographical references

Hirschmann, Kris

Frankenstein. ReferencePoint Press 2011 80p il (Monsters and mythical creatures) $27.95

Grades: 6 7 8 9   813

1. Authors 2. Novelists 3. Monsters in literature

ISBN 978-1-60152-180-4; 1-60152-180-4

LC 2011002145

This is "an ideal starting point for young researchers interested in the weird, mysterious, and paranormal. Using fleet, descriptive prose to communicate the impressively researched (and sourced) information, [this] medium-length [work manages] to rope in just about everything, from folklore to history to pop culture. The bulk of Frankenstein focuses upon Mary Shelley's masterpiece, not just the infamous contest for which it was written but also the reception and critical analysis, both then and now. . . . The illustrations are fine and varied, the sidebars always illuminating, and the back matter robust." Booklist

Includes bibliographical references

Hogan, Walter

★ **Humor** in young adult literature; a time to laugh. Scarecrow Press 2005 223p (Scarecrow studies in young adult literature) $40

Grades: Adult Professional   813

1. Teenagers -- Books and reading 2. Wit and humor -- History and criticism

ISBN 0-8108-5072-9

LC 2004-18903

"As a reader's advisory tool, this book is invaluable, paving the way for many laughter-filled hours to come." Voice Youth Advocates

"Hogan, author of a book about funny-man Daniel Pinkwater and a perennial reviewer for Voice of Youth Advocates, has ably taken on the formidable task of writing the first book-length exploration of humor in YA fiction. . . . The book is especially helpful for looking at Joan Bauer, Eoin Colfer, Diana Wynne Jones, Ron Koertge, and Gordon Korman. It will be welcomed by juvenile librarians, teachers of YA literature, and possibly by librarians who will use it as a selection tool for their YA collections." Booklist

Includes bibliographical references

Jones, Jen

A **reader's** guide to Gary Soto's Taking sides. Enslow Publishers 2010 127p il (Multicultural literature) lib bdg $31.93

Grades: 8 9 10 11 12   813

1. Poets 2. Authors 3. Novelists 4. Hispanic Americans in literature 5. Essayists 6. College teachers

7. Children's authors 8. Young adult authors

ISBN 978-0-7660-3168-5 lib bdg; 0-7660-3168-3 lib bdg

LC 2008-38587

An introduction to Gary Soto's novel Taking sides for high school students, which includes biographical background on the author, explanations of various literary devices and techniques, and literary criticism for the novice reader.

Includes glossary and bibliographical references

Juster, Norton

The **annotated** Phantom tollbooth; by Norton Juster; illustrations by Jules Feiffer; introduction and notes by Leonard Marcus. Alfred A. Knopf 2011 284p il $29.99; lib bdg $32.22

Grades: Adult Professional   813

1. Authors 2. Architects 3. Children's authors

ISBN 978-0-375-85715-7; 0-375-85715-X; 978-0-375-95715-4 lib bdg; 0-375-95715-4 lib bdg

LC 2011013174

"Still ferrying dazzled readers to Dictionopolis and beyond 50 years after his first appearance, young Milo is accompanied this time through by encyclopedic commentary from our generation's leading (and most readable) expert on the history of children's literature and publishing. . . . Leonard opens with typically lucid and well-organized pictures of both Juster's and Feiffer's formative years and later careers, interwoven with accounts of the book's conception, publication and critical response. In notes running alongside the ensuing facsimile, he puts on an intellectual show. . . . he delivers notes on topics as diverse as the etymological origins of "BALDERDASH!" and mimetic architecture to textual parallels with the Wizard of Oz and echoes of Winsor McKay and George Grosz in the art. Family photos, scrawled notes and images of handwritten and typescript manuscript pages further gloss a work that never ages nor fails to astonish." Kirkus

Kramer, Barbara

Toni Morrison; a biography of a nobel prize-winning writer. by Barbara Kramer. Enslow Publishers 2012 104 p. (library) $26.60

Grades: 7 8 9 10   813

1. Morrison, Toni 2. African American novelists -- Biography 3. Novelists, American -- 20th century -- Biography

ISBN 0766039897; 9780766039896

LC 2011024344

In this biography of African American author Toni Morrison, "Barbara Kramer explores the life and career of this talented writer. From her childhood in Lorain, Ohio, to her creative expressions of African-American culture, Morrison has always remembered her past. She has taught at several universities, as well as being the author of novels, short stories essays, and a play." (Publisher's note)

Includes bibliographical references (p. 88-99) and index.

Lazo, Caroline Evensen

F. Scott Fitzgerald; voice of the Jazz Age. {by} Caroline Lazo. Lerner Publs. 2003 128p il (Lerner long biographies) lib bdg $25.26 813

1. Authors 2. Novelists 3. Screenwriters 4. Authors,

American 5. Short story writers
ISBN 0-8225-0074-4

LC 2001-7210

"This well-documented book offers a fascinating glimpse into the acclaimed author's early years, unremarkable academic record, extravagant lifestyle, and work." SLJ

Includes bibliographical references

Litwin, Laura Baskes

A **reader's** guide to Zora Neale Hurston's Their eyes were watching god. Enslow Publishers 2010 128p il (Multicultural literature) lib bdg $31.93

Grades: 8 9 10 11 12   813

1. Authors 2. Novelists 3. Dramatists 4. African Americans in literature 5. Memoirists 6. Folklorists 7. Short story writers

ISBN 978-0-7660-3164-7; 0-7660-3164-0

LC 2008-38524

An introduction to Zora Neale Hurston's novel Their eyes were watching God for high school students, which includes biographical background on the author, explanations of various literary devices and techniques, and literary criticism for the novice reader.

Includes glossary and bibliographical references

Loos, Pamela

A **reader's** guide to Amy Tan's The joy luck club. Enslow Publishers 2008 112p il (Multicultural literature) $31.93

Grades: 6 7 8 9   813

1. Authors 2. Novelists 3. Mother-daughter relationships in literature 4. Essayists 5. Children's authors 6. Short story writers 7. Literature -- Women authors 8. American literature -- Asian American authors

ISBN 978-0-7660-2832-6; 0-7660-2832-1

LC 2006102440

The book is "an excellent resource for the student wanting to do more in depth research. . . . [The] photos . . . chosen are of good quality. . . . The [volume is] well organized, clearly written, and simple to understand." Voice Youth Advocates

Includes bibliographical references

Lowry, Lois

★ **Looking** back; a book of memories. Houghton Mifflin 1998 181p il $17

Grades: 5 6 7 8   813

1. Authors 2. Novelists 3. Women authors 4. Authors, American 5. Young adult authors

ISBN 0-395-89543-X

LC 98-11376

Using family photographs and quotes from her books, the author provides glimpses into her life

"A compelling and inspirational portrait of the author emerges from these vivid snapshots of life's joyful, sad and surprising moments." Publ Wkly

Lukes, Bonnie L.

Soldier's courage: the story of Stephen Crane. Morgan Reynolds 2002 144p il lib bdg $21.95

Grades: 7 8 9 10   813

1. Authors 2. Novelists 3. Authors, American

ISBN 1-88384-694-3

LC 2002-5095

"Lukes's gift for storytelling and her stirring prose result in a thoroughly readable and informative volume." SLJ

"The author of "The Red Badge of Courage", as well as short stories and poems, compressed into his short life adventurous experiences and a rich literary output against seemingly constant personal bankruptcy. Illustrated with black-and-white photos, Lukes's biography uses primary sources to dramatically and sympathetically retell Crane's amazing life." Horn Book

Includes bibliographical references

Marler, Myrna Dee

Walter Dean Myers. Greenwood Press 2008 198p (Teen reads: student companions to young adult literature) $45

Grades: 8 9 10 11 12 Adult Professional   813

1. Poets 2. Authors 3. Novelists 4. Editors 5. Children's authors 6. Young adult authors

ISBN 978-0-313-33628-7; 0-313-33628-8

LC 2008010070

"Marler analyzes the life and works of the accomplished author. The first two chapters are devoted to a brief biography and the historical and cultural influences on Myers's writing. The remainder of the volume looks at his books, including comparisons of plots and characters as well as thematic development within each novel." SLJ

Includes bibliographical references

McArthur, Debra

A **student's** guide to Edgar Allan Poe. Enslow Publishers 2006 160p il por (Understanding literature) lib bdg $27.93

Grades: 7 8 9 10   813

1. Poets 2. Authors 3. Essayists 4. Short story writers

ISBN 0-7660-2437-7

LC 2005024273

This examines the life and career of Edgar Allan Poe, discussing such works as The Raven, The Fall of the House of Usher, and The Tell-TaleHeart.

Includes glossary and bibliographical references

A **student's** guide to William Faulkner; [by] Debra A. McArthur. Enslow Publishers 2009 160p il (Understanding literature) lib bdg $27.93

Grades: 7 8 9 10   813

1. Authors 2. Novelists 3. Screenwriters 4. Short story writers 5. Nobel laureates for literature

ISBN 978-0-7660-2885-2; 0-7660-2885-2

LC 2008-3010

"An introduction to the work of William Faulkner for . . . students, which includes relevant biographical background on the author, explanations of various literary devices and techniques, and literary criticism for the novice reader." Publisher's note

Includes glossary and bibliographical references

McClellan, Marilyn

Madeleine L'Engle; banned, challenged, and censored. Enslow Publishers 2008 160p il (Authors of banned books) $25.95

Grades: 8 9 10 11 12   **813**

1. Authors 2. Novelists 3. Essayists 4. Memoirists 5. Mystery writers 6. Children's authors 7. Books -- Censorship 8. Short story writers 9. Writers on religion 10. Young adult authors 11. Science fiction writers
ISBN 978-0-7660-2708-4; 0-7660-2708-2

LC 2007015134

This "uses the attacks on one classic yet frequently challenged book, L'Engle's 1963 Newbery Medal winner, A Wrinkle in Time, to draw teens into a dynamic discussion of general censorship history and issues. McClellan describes the objections, frequently Christian fundamentalists citing the book's 'satanic content,' and counters them with comments from the other side. . . . Readers will also find a succinct biography of L'Engle. . . . occasional photos, a chapter of literary analysis, and summaries of both Wrinkle and L'Engle's Many Waters (1986)." Booklist

Includes bibliographical references

Myers, Walter Dean, 1937-2014

★ **Bad** boy; a memoir. HarperCollins Pubs. 2001 214p $15.95; pa $6.99

Grades: 7 8 9 10   **813**

1. Poets 2. Authors 3. Novelists 4. African American authors 5. Editors 6. Authors, American 7. Children's authors 8. Young adult authors
ISBN 0-06-029523-6; 0-06-447288-4 pa

LC 00-52978

This "is a story full of funny anecdotes, lofty ideals, and tender moments." SLJ

"I didn't want to be defiant. I wanted to be in the system that I was walking away from, but I didn't know how to get in." Many teens will see themselves in Myers' account of his troubled coming-of-age, especially since he offers no pat solutions. He doesn't analyze or laugh at his youth from an adult perspective, and he doesn't overdramatize his childhood self. . . . The most beautiful writing is about Mama: how she taught him to read, sharing True Romance magazines. He still feels ashamed about how he hurt her: "Later when I had learned to use words better, I lost my ability to speak so freely with Mama." The aching truth is that although books saved him and helped him become a famous writer, they moved him away from the adoptive parents he loved." Booklist

Napoli, Donna Jo

Zel. Dutton Children's Bks. 1996 227p hardcover o.p. pa $5.99

Grades: 7 8 9 10   **813**

1. Fairy tales 2. Mother-daughter relationship -- Fiction
ISBN 0-525-45612-0; 0-14-130116-3 pa

LC 96-15135

Based on the fairy tale Rapunzel, the story is told in alternating chapters from the point of view of Zel, her mother, and the prince, and delves into the psychological motivations of the characters

"This version, with its Faustian overtones, will challenge readers to think about this old story on a deeper level. It begs for discussion in literature classes." SLJ

Nilsen, Alleen Pace

Names and naming in young adult literature; [by] Alleen Pace Nilsen, Don L. F. Nilsen. Scarecrow Press 2007 173p (Scarecrow studies in young adult literature) $45

Grades: Adult Professional   **813**

1. Personal names in literature 2. Characters and characteristics in literature 3. Young adult literature -- History and criticism
ISBN 978-0-8108-5808-4; 0-8108-5808-8

LC 2007-11281

This "book consists of an introduction about the role of names in young adult literature, eight essay chapters, a bibliography, and an index. . . . The authors do a good job in writing engaging content. . . . School, public, and academic libraries will find this title an asset." Booklist

Includes bibliographical references

Paulsen, Gary

★ **Guts**; the true stories behind Hatchet and the Brian books. Delacorte Press 2001 148p hardcover o.p. pa $5.50

Grades: 6 7 8 9   **813**

1. Authors 2. Hunting 3. Wilderness survival 4. Sled dog racers 5. Authors, American 6. Children's authors 7. Short story writers 8. Young adult authors 9. Children's stories -- Authorship 10. Authors, American -- 20th century -- Biography
ISBN 0385326505; 0440407125

LC 00-34061

The author relates incidents in his life and how they inspired parts of his books about the character, Brian Robeson

"Readers squeamish about hunting or the death of animals will find many of the stories disturbing . . . but those who embrace the sport or have enjoyed the novels will see in Paulsen a responsible role model—a man who respects life and death as equal partners." Booklist

★ **How** Angel Peterson got his name; and other outrageous tales about extreme sports. Wendy Lamb Bks. 2003 111p hardcover o.p. pa $5.99

Grades: 5 6 7 8   **813**

1. Authors 2. Sled dog racers 3. Authors, American 4. Children's authors 5. Short story writers 6. Young adult authors
ISBN 0-385-72949-9; 0-385-90090-2 lib bdg; 978-0-440-22935-3 pa; 0-440-22935-9 pa

LC 2002-7668

Author Gary Paulsen relates tales from his youth in a small town in northwestern Minnesota in the late 1940s and early 1950s, such as skiing behind a souped-up car and imitating daredevil Evel Knievel

"Writing with humor and sensitivity, Paulsen shows boys moving into adolescence believing they can do anything. . . . None of them dies (amazingly), and even if Paulsen exaggerates the teensiest bit, his tales are side-splittingly funny and more than a little frightening." Booklist

★ **My** life in dog years; with drawings by Ruth Wright Paulsen. Delacorte Press 1998 137p il $15.95; pa $6.50

Grades: 4 5 6 7　　　**813**

1. Dogs 2. Authors 3. Sled dog racers 4. Authors, American 5. Children's authors 6. Short story writers 7. Young adult authors

ISBN 0-385-32570-3; 0-440-41471-7 pa

LC 97-40254

The author describes some of the dogs that have had special places in his life, including his first dog, Snowball, in the Philippines; Dirk, who protected him from bullies; and Cookie, who saved his life

"Paulsen differentiates his canine friends beautifully, as only a keen observer and lover of dogs can. At the same time, he presents an intimate glimpse of himself, a lonely child of alcoholic parents, who drew strength and solace from his four-legged companions and a love of the great outdoors. Poignant but never saccharine, honest, and open." Booklist

Peet, Bill

★ **Bill** Peet: an autobiography. Houghton Mifflin 1989 190p il hardcover o.p. pa $15

Grades: 4 5 6 7　　　**813**

1. Artists 2. Authors 3. Illustrators 4. Authors, American 5. Children's authors 6. Walt Disney Productions

ISBN 0-395-50932-7; 0-395-68982-1 pa

LC 88-37067

A Caldecott Medal honor book, 1990

"Every page of this oversized book is illustrated with Peet's unmistakable black-and-white drawings of himself and the people, places, and events described in the text. Familiar characters from his books and movies appear often." SLJ

Pingelton, Timothy J.

A **student's** guide to Ernest Hemingway. Enslow Publishers 2005 160p il map (Understanding literature) lib bdg $27.93

Grades: 7 8 9 10　　　**813**

1. Poets 2. Authors 3. Novelists 4. Short story writers 5. Nobel laureates for literature

ISBN 0-7660-2431-8

This discusses Hemingway's life and his novels In Our Time, The Sun Also Rises, A Farewell to Arms, and The Old Man and the Sea

"Engaging and informative. . . . The very accessible format and the solid information make [this book] useful to students, and the engaging style should interest casual readers." SLJ

Includes glossary and bibliographical references

Reef, Catherine

★ **John** Steinbeck. Clarion Bks. 1996 163p il $17.95; pa $8.95

Grades: 7 8 9 10　　　**813**

1. Authors 2. Novelists 3. Screenwriters 4. Authors, American 5. Nobel laureates for literature

ISBN 0-395-71278-5; 0-618-43244-2 pa

LC 95-11500

"The book traces Steinbeck's life from his childhood in California, to his burgeoning writing career and his passion for social justice, to his worldwide recognition. Reef does an excellent job of synthesizing Steinbeck's work, his private life, and his politics and philosophy." Bull Cent Child Books

Includes bibliographical references

Reid, Suzanne Elizabeth

Virginia Euwer Wolff; capturing the music of young voices. [by] Suzanne Elizabeth Reid. Scarecrow Press 2003 137p il (Scarecrow studies in young adult literature) $49

Grades: 8 9 10 11 12 Adult Professional　　　**813**

1. Authors 2. Children's authors 3. Young adult authors

ISBN 978-0-8108-4858-0; 0-8108-4858-9

LC 2003-10897

"In five short chapters, Reid provides an intriguing exploration of this popular author's personal life along with an in-depth summary and analysis of five of her young adult novels." Voice Youth Advocates

Includes bibliographical references

Ross-Stroud, Catherine

Janet McDonald; the original project girl. [by] Catherine Ross-Stroud. Scarecrow Press 2009 137p il (Scarecrow studies in young adult literature) $35

Grades: 7 8 9 10 Adult Professional　　　**813**

1. Authors 2. Lawyers 3. Novelists 4. Young adult authors

ISBN 978-0-8108-5802-2; 0-8108-5802-9

LC 2008030712

This "is a bio-critical study of McDonald and her work as it relates to the contributions she has made to the genre of teen fiction." Publisher's note

Includes bibliographical references

Schroeder, Heather Lee

A **reader's** guide to Marjane Satrapi's Persepolis. Enslow Publishers 2010 152p il map (Multicultural literature) lib bdg $34.60

Grades: 8 9 10 11 12　　　**813**

1. Artists 2. Authors 3. Novelists 4. Cartoonists 5. Memoirists

ISBN 978-0-7660-3166-1; 0-7660-3166-7

LC 2008-51820

An introduction to Marjane Satrapi's graphic novel Persepolis for high school students, which includes biographical background on the author, explanations of various literary devices and techniques, and literary criticism for the novice reader.

Includes glossary and bibliographical references

Spinelli, Jerry

★ **Knots** in my yo-yo string; the autobiography of a kid. Knopf 1998 148p il hardcover o.p. pa $10.95

Grades: 4 5 6 7　　　**813**

1. Authors 2. Magazine editors 3. Authors, American 4. Children's authors

ISBN 0-679-98791-6; 0-679-88791-1 pa

LC 97-30827

This Italian-American Newbery Medalist presents a humorous account of his childhood and youth in Norristown, Pennsylvania

"There is an 'everyboy' universality to Spinelli's experiences, but his keen powers of observation and recall turn the story into a richly rewarding personal history." Horn Book Guide

Stefoff, Rebecca

Jack London; an American original. Oxford Univ. Press 2002 127p il maps (Oxford portraits) lib bdg $28

Grades: 7 8 9 10   **813**
1. Authors 2. Novelists 3. Authors, American 4. Short story writers
ISBN 0-19-512223-2

LC 2001-53087

"This volume does an excellent job of illuminating London's extraordinary life and career. The narrative is exciting and accessible. . . . The text is supplemented by interesting and informative illustrations, and includes excerpts from primary-source material." SLJ

Includes bibliographical references

Stover, Lois T.

Jacqueline Woodson; the real thing. [by] Lois Thomas Stover. Scarecrow Press 2003 189p (Scarecrow studies in young adult literature) $49

Grades: 8 9 10 11 12 Adult Professional   **813**
1. Authors 2. Novelists 3. College teachers 4. Children's authors 5. Young adult authors
ISBN 978-0-8108-4857-3; 0-8108-4857-0

LC 2003-9881

"Students who are interested in learning more about this particular author will find plenty of information that will illuminate second and deeper readings of her works. Teachers searching for ways to help make connections among the books will find Stover's work of great value." Voice Youth Advocates

Includes bibliographical references

Tighe, Mary Ann

Sharon Creech; the words we choose to say. Scarecrow Press 2006 123p (Scarecrow studies in young adult literature) $35

Grades: 7 8 9 10   **813**
1. Authors 2. Novelists 3. Children's authors 4. Young adult authors
ISBN 978-0-8108-5086-6; 0-8108-5086-9

LC 2005037615

"Tighe bills her resource as a 'biocritical volume' on Sharon Creech, beginning with a chronology of her life before continuing with a more complete look, as well as the influence of her life experiences on her writing. . . . Tighe does an admirable and complete job of examining Creech's body of work." Voice Youth Advocates

Includes bibliographical references

Tyson, Edith S.

Orson Scott Card; writer of the terrible choice. Scarecrow Press 2003 xxv, 187p (Scarecrow studies in young adult literature) $40

Grades: 8 9 10 11 12 Adult Professional   **813**
1. Authors 2. Novelists 3. Editors 4. Fantasy writers 5. Short story writers 6. Science fiction writers
ISBN 0-8108-4790-6

LC 2003-5730

"Tyson begins her book with a . . . preface gleaned from Card's own explanation of the purpose of his writing, followed by a light biographical skimming of his life and development as a writer. The best features of the book are Tyson's excellent analyses of Card's books. Each book is summarized . . . and then enriched with different perspectives on the meaning, or some relevant background information, or something that Card himself wrote about that particular book. The sequence and interrelatedness of his books are also well documented. This book is a must-have for both professional and circulating collections." Voice Youth Advocates

Includes bibliographical references

★ The **wand** in the word; conversations with writers of fantasy. compiled and edited by Leonard S. Marcus. Candlewick Press 2006 202p il $19.99

Grades: 6 7 8 9   **813**
1. Authors, English 2. Authors, American 3. Fantasy fiction -- History and criticism
ISBN 0-7636-2625-2

LC 2005-46913

"Marcus presents interviews with 13 fantasy luminaries, including Lloyd Alexander, Susan Cooper, Nancy Farmer, Brian Jacques, Garth Nix, Tamora Pierce, and Philip Pullman. The writers' distinct personalities and career paths emerge, as do intriguing similarities. . . . Each profile includes a black-and-white author's photo, a reading list, and a bit of ephemera, often a handwritten manuscript page. . . . [This is] a rich resource that will be consulted as frequently by children's literature professionals as by genre fans themselves." Booklist

813.009   American fiction--History and criticism

★ **Brave** new words; the Oxford dictionary of science fiction. edited by Jeffrey Prucher; introduction by Gene Wolfe. Oxford University Press 2007 xxxi, 342p $29.95

Grades: 7 8 9 10 11 12 Adult   **813.009**
1. Reference books 2. Science fiction -- Dictionaries
ISBN 978-0-19-530567-8; 0-19-530567-1

LC 2006-37280

This is a "dictionary of the language of science fiction based on historical principles. . . . Entries include part of speech, etymology, definition with cross references to related terms, usage status (e.g., historical, jocular, derogatory, obsolete), variant forms, and . . . dated citations and quotations illustrating the usage of the word over time." Libr J

Includes bibliographical references

814   American essays in English

Kirk, Andrew

Understanding Thoreau's Civil disobedience. Rosen Pub. 2010 128p il (Words that changed the world) lib bdg $31.95

Grades: 7 8 9 10   **814**

1. Authors 2. Naturalists 3. Resistance to government 4. Essayists 5. Pacifists 6. Writers on nature 7. Nonfiction writers

ISBN 978-1-4488-1671-2; 1-4488-1671-8

LC 2010-10221

First published 2004 by Barrons with title: Civil disobedience

This considers Thoreau's Civil Disobedience, including its "'Context and Creator,' 'Immediate Impact,' 'Legacy,' and 'Aftermath.' . . . [Exploring] the historical context of transcendentalism and resistance to big government. . . . [The] author provides a balance of deep context, expressive writing, and pertinent information." SLJ

Includes glossary and bibliographical references

Red; the next generation of American writers--teenage girls--on what fires up their lives today. edited by Amy Goldwasser. Hudson Street Press 2007 267p $21.95

Grades: 8 9 10 11 12 Adult   **814**

1. Girls 2. Essays 3. Teenagers' writings

ISBN 978-1-59463-040-8; 1-59463-040-2

LC 2007027247

"The authors are complicated and real, with interests and concerns of immense scope. . . . It will be a surefire hit for girls." Voice Youth Advocates

"Hoping to "explode the puffy pink stereotype of the American teenage girl," writer and editor Goldwasser invited young women between the ages of 13 and 18 to submit personal essays. . . . the honesty is powerful, as is the girls' determination to claim and shape their futures: "I am going to be one of the anonymous extraordinary women who inspire so many people, " says a 13-year-old. A corresponding Web site continues the girls' memorable stories." Booklist

815   American speeches in English

★ **American** Heritage book of great American speeches for young people; edited by Suzanne McIntire. Wiley 2001 292p il pa $14.95

Grades: 7 8 9 10   **815**

1. American speeches

ISBN 0-471-38942-0

LC 00-43749

This is a "compendium of more than 100 speeches that span nearly 400 years of American history, from Powhatan (1609) to Senator Charles Robb (2000). Prominent orators include Patrick Henry, Thomas Jefferson, John Kennedy, Richard Nixon, Martin Luther King, Jr., and Malcolm X. . . . The speeches inform readers and provide examples of how the spoken word has affected Americans throughout our past." SLJ

★ **U-X-L** Asian American voices; edited by Deborah Gillan Straub. 2nd ed; U.X.L 2004 xxv, 315p il $58

Grades: 7 8 9 10 11 12   **815**

1. Asian Americans 2. American speeches

ISBN 0-7876-7600-4

LC 2003-110048

First published 1997 with title: Asian American voices

This "reference presents full or excerpted speeches, sermons, orations, poems, testimony and other notable spoken words of Asian Americans. Each entry is accompanied by an introduction and boxes explaining terms and events to which the speech refers. The volume is illustrated with photographs and drawings." Publisher's note

817   American humor and satire in English

Cleary, Brian P.

The **laugh** stand; adventures in humor. by Brian P. Cleary; illustrated by J.P. Sandy. Millbrook Press 2008 48p il lib bdg $16.95

Grades: 4 5 6   **817**

1. Word games 2. Wit and humor

ISBN 978-0-8225-7849-9

LC 2007021889

Cleary "promotes fun with words in 13 small sections that toy with puns, anagrams, daffynitions, Tom Swifties, and more. . . . Sandy's ideally matched cartoons are a google-eyed cast that includes humans, animals, food items with faces, and societal icons. This team marries humor with sublime learning." SLJ

Includes bibliographical references

818   American miscellaneous writings in English

★ **Guys** read; true stories. edited and with an introduction by Jon Scieszka ; stories by Candace Fleming, Douglas Florian, Nathan Hale, Thanhha Lai, Sy Montgomery, Jim Murphy, T. Edward Nickens, Elizabeth Partridge, Steve Sheinkin, and James Sturm ; with illustrations by Brian Floca. Walden Pond Press 2014 272 p. (Guys read) (hardback) $16.99

Grades: 4 5 6 7 8   **818**

1. Essays 2. Short stories 3. American prose literature 4. American prose literature -- 21st century

ISBN 0061963828; 9780061963810; 9780061963827

LC 2014010024

Part of the Guys Read series, edited by Jon Scieszka, this book "features ten stories that are 100% amazing, 100% adventurous, 100% unbelievable--and 100% true. A starstudded group of award-winning nonfiction authors and journalists provides something for every reader, all aligned with the Common Core State Standards." (Publisher's note)

"Ten terrifically told true stories demonstrate the wide range of subjects and formats available for young readers of nonfiction. This fifth anthology in the Guys Read series stars some of the best-known names in informational writing today. . . . Selected, edited, and neatly introduced by Scieszka, National Ambassador for Young People's Literature emeritus, these appetite-whetting accounts are accompanied by occasional illustrations by Floca (not seen). You certainly don't have to be a guy to appreciate these morsels of fact-based storytelling and then beg for more." Booklist

Hargrave, John

Sir John Hargrave's mischief maker's manual; by Sir John Hargrave. Grosset & Dunlap 2009 270p il $15.99

Grades: 7 8 9 10 **818**

1. Practical jokes

ISBN 978-0-448-44982-1; 0-448-44982-X

LC 2008-34518

Presents a definitive guide to pulling off such perfect pranks as making crank calls and freezing worms inside ice cubes, divided into five specific sections.

"Pranks include making a 'Screaming Cabinet' (using the device from musical greeting cards), creating the 'World's Largest Butt Photo' and faking an alien landing. What's most appealing, however, is the emphasis on being clever, creative and funny while making mischief." Publ Wkly

Mark Twain; Todd Howard, book editor. Greenhaven Press 2002 190p il (People who made history) lib bdg $34.95; pa $23.70 **818**

1. Authors 2. Humorists 3. Novelists 4. Essayists 5. Satirists 6. Memoirists 7. Travel writers 8. Authors, American 9. Short story writers

ISBN 0-7377-0897-2 lib bdg; 0-7377-0896-4 pa

LC 2001-28923

A collection of essays about the American author and humorist with primary source documents

Includes bibliographical references

McCurdy, Michael

Walden then & now; an alphabetical tour of Henry Thoreau's pond. Charlesbridge 2010 un il lib bdg $16.95

Grades: 4 5 6 7 **818**

1. Authors 2. Alphabet 3. Naturalists 4. Essayists 5. Pacifists 6. Writers on nature 7. Nonfiction writers 8. Natural history -- Massachusetts

ISBN 978-1-58089-253-7 lib bdg; 1-58089-253-1 lib bdg

LC 2009-26645

"Elegiac woodcarvings evoke the setting of Henry Thoreau's Walden Pond as the text weaves past and present in this lengthy alphabet poem. On each spread, consecutive letters face one another, making a couplet of the lines. A dark, but not somber, woodcarving illustrates each letter, and an explanatory paragraph expands upon the information in the verse. . . . The book ends with entries from Thoreau's diary and McCurdy's inspiration and starting point for this book. Purchase as an introduction to Thoreau and for poetry shelves." SLJ

Paulsen, Gary

★ **Caught** by the sea; my life on boats. Delacorte Press 2001 103p maps $15.95; pa $5.50

Grades: 5 6 7 8 **818**

1. Authors 2. Ocean travel 3. Boats and boating 4.

Sled dog racers 5. Authors, American 6. Children's authors 7. Short story writers 8. Young adult authors

ISBN 0-385-32645-9; 0-440-40716-8 pa

LC 2001-17336

"Paulsen traces his life at sea, from buying his first sailboat to getting lost in the Pacific to encountering sharks. . . . His sometimes comic, sometimes near-fatal sea-going errors make for absorbing, captivating reading." Booklist

821 English poetry

Blake, William

William Blake; edited by John Maynard; illustrated by Alessandra Cimatoribus. Sterling Pub. 2006 48p il (Poetry for young people) $14.95

Grades: 5 6 7 8 **821**

1. Children's poetry, English. 2. Poetry -- By individual authors

ISBN 978-0-8069-3647-5; 0-8069-3647-9

LC 2006013858

"The book begins with a heroic attempt to explain some of [Blake's] themes and philosophy in a four-page introduction. Maynard speaks of the poet with insight, eloquence, and obvious admiration. . . . He prefaces each poem with explanatory comments that are also thought-provoking and illuminating. . . . The artwork is well matched to the tone of the poems. Cimatoribus's illustrations are at the same time childlike and surreal." SLJ

Carroll, Lewis, 1832-1898

★ **Jabberwocky**; the classic poem from Lewis Carroll's Through the looking glass, and what Alice found there. reimagined and illustrated by Chistopher Myers. 1st ed. Jump at the Sun/Hyperion Books for Children 2007 1 v. (unpaged) col. ill. $15.99

Grades: 4 5 6 7 **821**

1. Nonsense verses 2. Poetry -- By individual authors

ISBN 978-1-4231-0372-1; 1-4231-0372-6

LC 2007018337

This reinterpretation of Lewis Carroll's poem about the Jabberwock uses a basketball court as setting. "Ages five to nine." (N Y Times Book Rev)

"Myers cleverly translates Carroll's nonsense poem into a contemporary tale through sports imagery. . . . The spectacular paintings have silhouetted figures on vibrant backgrounds. . . . The jaunty text is in capital letters in an extra-large black font, with some words highlighted in color." SLJ

Classic poetry; an illustrated collection. selected by Michael Rosen; pictures by Paul Howard. Candlewick Press 1998 160p il $21.99; pa $12.99

Grades: 7 8 9 10 **821**

1. Poetry -- Collections

ISBN 978-1-56402-890-7; 1-56402-890-9; 978-0-7636-4210-5 pa; 0-7636-4210-X pa

LC 98-18282

A collection of favorite poems by such writers as William Shakespeare, Emily Dickinson, Edward Lear, Walt Whitman, and Langston Hughes, with portraits of the poets, brief biographical background, and illustrations

"This handsome edition introduces major poets through works accessible to young people. Each section begins with a portrait of the author and a short summary of his or her life, followed by one or two poems or parts of poems. Each spread includes at least one illustration evocative of the tone of the poetry as well as the times of the poet. . . . Illustrator Paul Howard's gifts are not diminished by the smaller size of some pictures, for some of his best work here is in miniature. . . . Few anthologies for this age group include such a fine selection of works from beyond the childhood classics, introduce the poets so vividly, or provide such a rich collection of haunting illustrations." Booklist

Cohen, Barbara

★ **Canterbury** tales; [by] Geoffrey Chaucer; selected, translated, and adapted by Barbara Cohen; illustrated by Trina Schart Hyman. Lothrop, Lee & Shepard Bks. 1988 87p il $24.99

Grades: 4 5 6 7   **821**
1. Poets 2. Authors 3. Middle Ages 4. Poetry -- By individual authors
ISBN 0-688-06201-6
LC 86-21045

"Cohen's evident love and respect for Chaucer's writing keep her close to the text. Her writing retains the flavor of the times and the spirit of Chaucer's words while her prose retelling, enriched by Hyman's lively full-color paintings, enhances the book's appeal to young people. . . . An excellent introduction to The Canterbury Tales for young readers." Booklist

Coleridge, Samuel Taylor

Samuel Taylor Coleridge; edited by James Engell; illustrated by Harvey Chan. Sterling 2003 48p il (Poetry for young people) $14.95

Grades: 7 8 9 10   **821**
1. Poetry -- By individual authors
ISBN 0-8069-6951-2
LC 2003-6549

Introduces the life of author Samuel Taylor Coleridge and presents a sample of his poetry, including complete works and excerpts, with a brief, explanatory introduction to each

"Chan's enchanting paintings embellish the text and do a nice job of capturing the mood of the poetry without dominating it. . . . A useful purchase for any collection." SLJ

The **Kingfisher** book of funny poems; selected by Roger McGough; illustrated by Caroline Holden. Kingfisher (NY) 2002 256p il $18.95

Grades: 4 5 6 7   **821**
1. Humorous poetry 2. English poetry -- Collections 3. American poetry -- Collections
ISBN 0-7534-5480-7
LC 2001-38942

A collection of over 200 poems, limericks, and verses from such authors as Emily Dickinson, Lewis Carroll, and Shel Silverstein

"This collection is chock-full of wacky, witty, and whimsical poems that will hook readers from the first stanza to the last. . . . What really brings out the humor are the equally zany black-and-white drawings that appear on almost every page." SLJ

Kipling, Rudyard, 1865-1936

If; a father's advice to his son. [by] Rudyard Kipling; photographs by Charles R. Smith. Atheneum Books for Young Readers 2007 un il $14.99

Grades: 4 5 6   **821**
1. Poetry -- By individual authors
ISBN 978-0-689-87799-5; 0-689-87799-4
LC 2006005312

"Kipling's powerful poem comes to life for a contemporary audience in atmospheric photographs that use the metaphor of sports. A lovely shot of a boy heading a soccer ball accompanies the opening couplet: 'If you can keep your head/when all about you/are losing theirs/and blaming it on you.' The mood and actions in most of the illustrations clearly invoke the verse." SLJ

Lear, Edward

The **owl** and the pussycat; illustrations by Stephane Jorisch. KCP Poetry 2007 un il (Visions in poetry) $16.95; pa $9.95

Grades: 5 6 7 8   **821**
1. Nonsense verses 2. Cats -- Poetry 3. Owls -- Poetry 4. Poetry -- By individual authors
ISBN 978-1-55337-828-0; 1-55337-828-8; 978-1-55453-232-2 pa; 1-55453-232-9 pa

"This striking entry in an aptly named series envisions a darker subtext to Lear's well-known poem. Jorisch consulted Lear's own drawings when preparing his winsome watercolor and ink illustrations, noting the melancholy quality of the title characters. The light verse is transformed by the artist's vision into a mismatched couple seeking a place of acceptance. . . . For older readers, this book shows true artistic vision and a great example of the power of personal interpretation and inspiration." SLJ

Love and longing; a collection of classic poetry and prose. introduced by Jacqueline Wilson; edited by Kate Agnew. Totem 2011 128p pa $9.95

Grades: 8 9 10 11 12   **821**
1. Love poetry 2. English poetry -- Collections
ISBN 978-1-840-46523-5; 1-840-46523-9
First published 2004 in the United Kingdom

This collection "features love poems and prose excerpts by writers including Sappho, Shakespeare, Milton, the Brontës, and Wordsworth. Works are loosely arranged according to chapter headings drawn from particular poems. . . . creating an engaging interchange of images and ideas. . . . This is a resonant sampling of both standards and lesser-known gems." Publ Wkly

Noyes, Alfred

The **highwayman**; [by] Alfred Noyes; with illustrations by Murray Kimber. Kids Can Press 2005 un il (Visions in poetry) $17.95

Grades: 7 8 9 10   **821**
1. Thieves -- Poetry 2. Poetry -- By individual authors
ISBN 978-1-55337-425-1; 1-55337-425-8

"Painting in an art deco style and film noir palette, Kimber casts a motorcycle-riding rebel as the highwayman; a curvaceous glamour girl as Bess; and tommy-gun toting cops as the soldiers who intrude upon the lovers' tryst. . . . The dramatic artwork plays up the elements teens will find most rewarding—particularly the protagonists' defiance of authority and the unblushingly melodramatic conclusion." Booklist

Tennyson, Alfred Tennyson

The **Lady** of Shalott; illustrated by Geneviève Côté. Kids Can Press 2005 un il (Visions in poetry) $16.95

Grades: 7 8 9 10   **821**

1. Arthurian romances 2. Poetry -- By individual authors

ISBN 978-1-55337-874-7; 1-55337-874-1

"The pictures in this small book bring an early-twentieth-century urban setting to Tennyson's classic Arthurian poem, written in 1842, about a young woman imprisoned in a tower, endlessly weaving what she sees in the mirror, until she dares to break free and look outside. . . . Cote's quiet line-and-watercolor and pastel artwork opens up the story, preserving the romance and mystery without filling in too much." Booklist

Williams, Marcia

★ **Chaucer's** Canterbury Tales; retold and illustrated by Marcia Williams. Candlewick Press 2007 45p il $16.99

Grades: 4 5 6 7   **821**

1. Poets 2. Authors 3. Middle Ages 4. Poetry -- By individual authors

ISBN 978-0-7636-3197-0; 0-7636-3197-3

A retelling in comic strip form of Geoffrey Chaucer's famous work in which a group of pilgrims in fourteenth-century England tell each other stories as they travel on a pilgrimage to the cathedral at Canterbury

"Chaucer's pilgrims come to life in the energetic retelling of nine tales. . . . The watercolor-and-ink cartoon-art displayed in a comic-book format is a perfect match for the raucous and sometimes-raw humor." SLJ

Wordsworth, William

William Wordsworth; edited by Alan Liu; illustrated by James Muir. Sterling 2003 48p il (Poetry for young people) $14.95

Grades: 7 8 9 10   **821**

1. Poetry -- By individual authors

ISBN 0-8069-8277-2

LC 2003-6163

An illustrated collection of nineteen popular poems by William Wordsworth, who was the poet laureate of England in the mid-nineteenth century. Includes an introduction to the poet's life and work

The editor has "chosen well, bringing together about 20 of [the] great poet's most accessible, compelling poems. . . . The full color paintings on each page are beautiful." Booklist

821.008   English poetry -- collections

Poems to learn by heart; [selected by] Caroline Kennedy ; paintings by Jon J Muth. Disney Hyperion Books 2012 192 p. (hardcover) $19.99

Grades: 2 3 4 5 6 7 8   **821.008**

1. Poetry -- Collections 2. English poetry 3. American poetry

ISBN 1423108051; 9781423108054

LC 2011022651

This anthology, by Caroline Kennedy, illustrated by John J. Muth, offers "more than a hundred poems that speak to all of us: the young and young at heart, readers new to poetry and devoted fans. These poems explore deep emotions, as well as ordinary experiences. They cover the range of human experience and imagination. Divided into sections about nature, sports, monsters and fairies, friendship and family." (Publisher's note)

822   English drama

Christie, Agatha

The **mousetrap** and other plays. New American Library 2000 742p hardcover o.p. pa $7.99

Grades: 7 8 9 10 11 12 Adult   **822**

1. English drama -- Collections

ISBN 0-451-20118-3; 0-451-20114-0 pa

LC 00-64727

First published 1978 by Dodd, Mead

"The noted mystery writer composed adaptations of seven novels and stories into arresting plays as well as creating one original theater piece ('Verdict'). . . . All are as delightful to read for pleasure as Christie's mystery novels, especially since some that earlier appeared in the latter form have been intriguingly altered." Booklist

822.3   Drama of Elizabethan period, 1558-1625

Coville, Bruce

William Shakespeare's A midsummer night's dream. Dial Bks. 1996 un $17.95; pa $7.99

Grades: 5 6 7 8 9   **822.3**

1. Poets 2. Authors 3. Audiobooks 4. Dramatists

ISBN 0-8037-1784-9; 0-14-250168-9 pa

LC 94-12600

A simplified prose retelling of Shakespeare's play about the strange events that take place in a forest inhabited by fairies who magically transform the romantic fate of two young couples.

"Coville introduces the story and also conveys something of the poetry and drama. Nolan's framed graphite and watercolor paintings express the dreaminess and absurdity of the play, and the pictures have a theatrical flair." Booklist

William Shakespeare's Romeo and Juliet; retold by Bruce Coville; pictures by Dennis Nolan. Dial Bks. 1999 un il $16.99

Grades: 5 6 7 8 9   **822.3**
1. Poets 2. Authors 3. Dramatists
ISBN 0-8037-2462-4

LC 98-36178

A simplified prose retelling of Shakespeare's play about two young people who defy their warring families' prejudices and dare to fall in love

"Coville's treatment is generally faithful to the original and is nicely enhanced by Dennis Nolan's lushly romantic illustrations. . . . This is an accessible and enticing introduction to one of Shakespeare's most popular works." Booklist

Krueger, Susan Heidi

The **tempest**; [by] Susan H. Krueger; introduction by Joseph Sobran. Marshall Cavendish Benchmark 2009 127p il (Shakespeare explained) lib bdg $29.93
Grades: 7 8 9 10 11 12   **822.3**
1. Poets 2. Authors 3. Dramatists
ISBN 978-0-7614-3423-8; 0-7614-3423-2

LC 2009-2587

This book offers an "engaging [introduction] to the Bard's work. . . . Krueger's lively, opinionated, and knowledgeable analysis of the complex play . . . will easily draw students into further discussion." Booklist

Includes glossary and bibliographical references

McDermott, Kristen

William Shakespeare; his life and times. [by] Kristen McDermott, and Ari Berk; including extracts from the works of William Shakespeare. Candlewick Press 2010 un il $19.99
Grades: 6 7 8 9   **822.3**
1. Poets 2. Authors 3. Dramatists
ISBN 978-0-7636-4794-0; 0-7636-4794-2

"This fictionalized amalgamation of original and secondary source materials is presented with panache. . . . The authors succinctly sum up Shakespeare's life and works with the help of snippets from his plays. Contemporaneous images and literary excerpts, in addition to pop-ups, foldouts, and removable letters, help set the scene for readers." Horn Book Guide

McKeown, Adam

Julius Caesar; a retelling by Adam McKeown; illustrated by Janet Hamlin. Sterling Pub. Co. 2008 80p il (Young reader's Shakespeare) $14.95
Grades: 6 7 8 9   **822.3**
1. Poets 2. Authors 3. Statesmen 4. Dramatists 5. Historians 6. Rome -- History -- Fiction
ISBN 978-1-4027-3579-0; 1-4027-3579-0

LC 2007030733

"This handsomely illustrated retelling . . . stays true both to the rousing action of [Shakespeare's] play and to the characters' inner conflicts. McKeown's clear, stimulating introduction raises the complex moral issues. . . . Hamlin's dramatic, full-color art . . . ably captures the personal torment as well as the dynamics of the battlefield." Booklist

Mussari, Mark

Othello; [by] Mark Mussari; introduction by Joseph Sobran. Marshall Cavendish Benchmark 2009 111p il (Shakespeare explained) lib bdg $29.95
Grades: 7 8 9 10 11 12   **822.3**
1. Poets 2. Authors 3. Dramatists
ISBN 978-0-7614-3422-1; 0-7614-3422-4

LC 2008-37506

"A literary analysis of the play Othello. Includes information on the history and culture of Elizabethan England." Publisher's note

Includes glossary and bibliographical references

Nettleton, Pamela Hill

William Shakespeare; playwright and poet. by Pamela Hill Nettleton. Compass Point Books 2005 112p il map (Signature lives) lib bdg $30.60
Grades: 5 6 7 8   **822.3**
1. Poets 2. Authors 3. Dramatists
ISBN 0-7565-0816-9

LC 2004-23081

Profiles the life and work of William Shakespeare

"This biography is one of the best available for younger students. Nettleton supplements what little is actually known about the bard's life with detailed and accurate information about everyday life in England during the period, the theater, and publishing practices of the time. The text is enhanced by full-color illustrations and black-and-white reproductions." SLJ

Includes bibliographical references

Packer, Tina

★ **Tales** from Shakespeare; retold by Tina Packer; illustrated by Gail de Marcken . . . [et al.] Scholastic Press 2004 192p il $24.95
Grades: 5 6 7 8   **822.3**
1. Poets 2. Authors 3. Dramatists
ISBN 0-439-32107-7

LC 2003-42710

Tina Packer retells ten of Shakespeare's plays. The stories are illustrated by various artists: Macbeth by Barry Moser, The Tempest by Mark Teague, Othello by Kadir Nelson, Twelfth Night by Chesley McLaren, Romeo and Juliet by David Shannon, Much Ado About Nothing by Mary Grand-Pre, King Lear by Leo and Diane Dillon, As You Like It by Barbara McClintock, A Midsummer Night's Dream by Gail De Marcken, and Hamlet by P.J. Lynch

This is "a treasure trove of well-told tales. In these adaptations, Packer captures the essence of the playwright's words and ideas, placing them in concise and clearly told stories. . . . Each illustrator sets the appropriate tone for and conveys the mood of the tale, and the breadth of artistic interpretations gives the book appeal to a wide audience." SLJ

Raum, Elizabeth

Twenty -first-century Shakespeare. Raintree 2011 32p il (Culture in action) lib bdg $29
Grades: 5 6 7 8   **822.3**
1. Poets 2. Authors 3. Dramatists 4. Dramatists,

English 5. Authors, English

ISBN 978-1-4109-3920-3; 1-4109-3920-0

LC 2009050693

This "discusses modern adaptations of the Bard's classic works; teachers may find this a useful resource to help students see how Shakespeare remains a part of today's culture. [This volume is] quick, interesting, up-to-date . . . with plenty of supportive, captioned, full-color photographs. [It] also [provides] related project suggestions." SLJ

Includes glossary and bibliographical references

Shakespeare, William, 1564-1616

One hundred and eleven Shakespeare monologues; the ultimate audition book for teens. edited by Lisa Bansavage and L. E. McCullough; introduction by Jill K. Swanson. Smith & Kraus 2003 176p (Young actors series) pa $11.95

Grades: 7 8 9 10 11 12   **822.3**

1. Acting 2. Monologues

ISBN 1-57525-356-9

"These monologues are divided into three sections: those for female actors, male actors, or either. They are further subdivided into comedies, histories, and tragedies. . . . The genius of this book is in the introduction, which offers a wealth of information for teens who have never encountered Shakespeare." SLJ

Sobran, Joseph

A **midsummer** night's dream; Joseph Sobran. Marshall Cavendish Benchmark 2008 111p. ill. (some col.) lib bdg $29.95

Grades: 7 8 9 10 11 12   **822.3**

1. Poets 2. Authors 3. Dramatists

ISBN 978-0-7614-3030-8; 0-7614-3030-X

LC 2008007079

"A literary analysis of the play A Midsummer Night's Dream. Includes information on the history and culture of Elizabethan England." Publisher's note

"[This book] provides practical information, skillfully presented, making the complexities of Shakespearean theater accessible to present-day students. [The] author's contagious enthusiasm and attractive presentation make [it] imminently useful for high school and public libraries.—" VOYA

Includes glossary and bibliographical references

Stanley, Diane

★ **Bard** of Avon: the story of William Shakespeare; by Diane Stanley and Peter Vennema; illustrated by Diane Stanley. Morrow Junior Bks. 1992 un il hardcover o.p. pa $6.99

Grades: 4 5 6 7   **822.3**

1. Poets 2. Authors 3. Dramatists

ISBN 0-688-09108-3; 0-688-09109-1 lib bdg; 0-688-16294-0 pa

LC 90-46564

A brief biography of the world's most famous playwright, using only historically correct information

"A remarkably rounded picture of Shakespeare's life and the period in which he lived is presented . . . together with a thoughtful attempt to relate circumstances in his personal life to the content of his plays. . . . The text is splendidly

supported by the illustrations, which are stylized, yet recognizable, and present a clear view of life in the late sixteenth century. A discerning, knowledgeable biography, rising far above the ordinary." Horn Book

Includes bibliographical references

823   English fiction

Colbert, David

The **magical** worlds of Harry Potter; David Colbert. Updated and complete ed. Berkley Books 2008 xi, 209 p.p ill. (paperback) $14.00

Grades: 5 6 7 8   **823**

1. Authors 2. Novelists 3. Fantasy writers 4. Children's authors 5. Young adult authors 6. Fantasy fiction -- History and criticism

ISBN 0425223183; 9780425223185

LC 2008274096

First published 2001 in the United Kingdom; first United States edition 2002

Explores the sources and meanings of aspects of the literary world of Harry Potter within myths, legends, and history.

"Long after the enthusiasm for Harry and friends has abated, this small volume will serve as a resource to answer questions that may result from reading other stories in the genre." SLJ [review of 2002 edition]

Includes bibliographical references (p. 317-318) and index.

Cooling, Wendy

D is for Dahl; a gloriumptious A-Z guide to the world of Roald Dahl. illustrations by Quentin Blake; compiled by Wendy Cooling. Viking 2005 149p il hardcover o.p. pa $5.99

Grades: 4 5 6 7   **823**

1. Authors 2. Children's authors 3. Short story writers

ISBN 0-670-06023-2; 0-14-240934-0 pa

This is an alphabetically arranged collection of facts about the life and work of the popular author of children's books

"This dictionary-of-sorts is entertaining, insightful, and of particular interest to Dahl's fans. . . . The writing is clear, wicked, and fun. An occasional black-and-white photograph complements Blake's illustrations." SLJ

Gribbin, Mary

The **science** of Philip Pullman's His Dark Materials; [by] Mary and John Gribbon; with an introduction by Philip Pullman. Knopf 2005 203p il $15.95; lib bdg $17.99; pa $5.99

Grades: 6 7 8 9   **823**

1. Authors 2. Science 3. Novelists 4. Fantasy writers 5. Young adult authors

ISBN 0-375-83144-4; 0-375-93144-9 lib bdg; 0-375-83146-0 pa

LC 2004-57731

"The Gribbins show how concepts are the real magic of Pullman's trilogy. Each chapter begins with a quote drawn from the books, which leads to an elegantly written explanation of the science. . . . The authors do an amazing job teasing an introduction to string theory from Will's 'subtle knife.' . . . Naturally, fans of the series will be the best audience, but the book offers much to readers simply interested in the advanced sciences, who then may be led back to His Dark Materials." Booklist

Jones, Diana Wynne, 1934-2011

Reflections; on the magic of writing. by Diana Wynne Jones. Greenwillow Books 2012 368 p. (hardback) $24.99

Grades: 7 8 9 10 11 12   **823**

1. Fantasy fiction -- Authorship 2. Children's stories -- Authorship

ISBN 0062219898; 9780062219893

LC 2012018080

This book, by Diana Wynne Jones, was arranged "after being informed that she had terminal cancer in 2010." It "pull[s] together" a "group of essays, lectures, and articles . . . about writing fantasy for children. . . . The selected pieces are thematically arranged, beginning with . . . a contemplative piece about watching children at play that sets the stage for her subsequent arguments regarding the importance of imagination and creativity." (Bulletin of the Center for Children's Books)

Includes bibliographical references and index

Latham, Don

David Almond; memory and magic. Scarecrow Press 2006 151p (Scarecrow studies in young adult literature) $40

Grades: 7 8 9 10 11 12 Adult Professional   **823**

1. Authors 2. Novelists 3. Short story writers 4. Young adult authors

ISBN 978-0-8108-5500-7; 0-8108-5500-3

LC 2006002300

This "explores the writings of the critically acclaimed YA author best known for Skellig . . . and Kit's Wilderness. . . . After a brief biography and thematic overview, Latham addresses Almond's published works one by one. . . . Weaving his explorations almost as seamlessly as Almond wove the original stories, Latham clearly illustrates the novels' inherent depth and teachability." Voice Youth Advocates

Includes bibliographical references

Nardo, Don

Understanding Frankenstein. Lucent Bks. 2003 128p il (Understanding great literature) lib bdg $27.45

Grades: 7 8 9 10   **823**

1. Authors 2. Novelists

ISBN 1-59018-147-6

LC 2002-12560

Discusses Mary Shelley's sources of ideas for the compelling plot, well-developed characters, and universal themes of "Frankenstein" which have led to its enduring popularity.

"The text is easy to understand. A solid introduction for middle school students." SLJ

Includes bibliographical references

Pascal, Janet B.

Arthur Conan Doyle; beyond Baker Street. Oxford Univ. Press 1999 158p il (Oxford portraits) $28

Grades: 7 8 9 10   **823**

1. Authors 2. Novelists 3. Authors, Scottish 4. Mystery writers

ISBN 0-19-512262-3

LC 99-36643

"Pascal does a fine job of conveying the era in which her object lived." SLJ

Includes bibliographical references (p. 151-154) and index

Reef, Catherine

★ The **Bronte** sisters; the brief lives of Charlotte, Emily and Anne. by Catherine Reef. Clarion Books 2012 240 p. ill. (hardcover) $18.99

Grades: 7 8 9 10   **823**

1. Bronte family 2. Women authors -- Biography 3. Women authors, English -- Biography 4. Sisters -- England -- Yorkshire -- Biography 5. Authors, English -- 19th century -- Biography

ISBN 0547579667; 9780547579665

LC 2011043559

"This collective biography of the Bronte family fills in . . . detail of their personal and public lives: what they wrote, their family stories as a minister's unmarried daughters, how they published under men's names, and how their groundbreaking novels were received at a time when women were expected to 'stay home and be quiet.'" (Booklist)

"A solid and captivating look at these remarkable pioneers of modern fiction." Kirkus

Includes bibliographical references (p. 212-217) and index.

Shea, George

A **reader's** guide to Chinua Achebe's Things fall apart; [by] George Shea. Enslow Publishers 2008 128p il (Multicultural literature) lib bdg $31.93

Grades: 7 8 9 10   **823**

1. Poets 2. Authors 3. Novelists 4. Essayists 5. Short story writers

ISBN 978-0-7660-2831-9 lib bdg; 0-7660-2831-3 lib bdg

LC 2006038486

"Shea explores why many consider the book to be the greatest African novel ever written. . . . Extensive back matter includes a chronology, glossary, chapter notes, and a bibliography of books and Web sites." Booklist

Includes glossary and bibliographical references

Wells-Cole, Catherine

Charles Dickens; England's most captivating storyteller. written by Catherine Wells-Cole ; including extracts from the works of Charles Dickens. 1st U.S. ed. Candlewick/Templar Books 2011 28 p. ill., maps (some col.) (Historical notebook) (hardcover) $19.99

Grades: 7 8 9 10 11 12   **823**

1. Authors 2. Novelists 3. Authors, English 4. London

(England) -- Social life and customs -- 19th century
ISBN 0763655678; 9780763655679

LC 2011013677

This book by Catherine Wells-Cole "provides a . . . glimpse into the life" of author Charles Dickens. "Like a scrapbook, the book includes excerpts from Dickens' personal letters, illustrations from his original books, family photos, and other images from the Victorian age. . . . Double-page spreads focus on Dickens' childhood, family life, and fame. Other spreads focus on topics that influenced his writing, including schools, prisons, and workhouses." (Library Media Connection)

"In this scrapbook homage to Dickens, each page teems with images and reproductions, from letters to book excerpts to maps, all pertaining to a different area of Dickens's life and work. The topics range widely, skimming the surface of both the esteemed author's life and the subjects that interested him most. . . . The gorgeous, high-quality reproductions make a strong visual impact, and while the flaps, folds, and envelopes make readers work to uncover information, most will be quickly drawn into the hunt for more treasured tidbits about Dickens and his time." SLJ

828   English miscellaneous writings

Jones, Diana Wynne
★ The **tough** guide to Fantasyland; rev and updated ed.; Firebird 2006 234p pa $9.99
Grades: 8 9 10 11 12   **828**
1. Fantasy fiction
ISBN 0-14-240722-4

LC 2006041153

First published 1996

This "book contains alphabetic entries for people, places, and events in a fantasy world and information on how travelers can best find their way to the epic final battle. Icons conveniently identify lodging, food, and other necessary elements that travelers will need in their journey. . . . This brilliantly written satire perfectly celebrates and skewers the clichés of the fantasy genre." Voice Youth Advocates

Means, A. L.
A **student's** guide to George Orwell. Enslow Pubs. 2005 176p il (Understanding literature) lib bdg $27.93
Grades: 7 8 9 10   **828**
1. Authors 2. Novelists 3. Essayists
ISBN 0-7660-2433-4
An introduction to the life and work of the author of 1984, Animal Farm and other works
Includes glossary and bibliographical references

Neimark, Anne E.
Myth maker: J.R.R. Tolkien; illustrated by Brad Weinman. Harcourt Brace & Co. 1996 118p il rpt $12.99 **828**
1. Authors 2. Novelists 3. Linguists 4. Philologists 5. Fantasy writers 6. Authors, English 7. Children's authors
ISBN 0-15-298847-5; 9780547997346 rpt

LC 96-4196

Follows the life and work of the renowned fantasy writer, creator of hobbits and Middle Earth and "The Lord of the Rings."

843   French fiction

Schoell, William
Remarkable journeys: the story of Jules Verne. Morgan Reynolds 2002 112p il (World writers) lib bdg $21.95 **843**
1. Authors 2. Novelists 3. Authors, French 4. Children's authors 5. Science fiction writers
ISBN 1-88384-692-7

LC 2002-2016

A biography of the nineteenth-century Frenchman whose childhood love of literature, science, and adventure, along with his vivid imagination, led him to become a highly successful science fiction author

"Thanks to Schoell's smooth, crisp writing, this fascinating, approachable biography, which lends insight into Verne's eccentric characters and relatives, proves nearly as exciting as the writer's best stories." Booklist
Includes bibliographical references

860   Literatures of Spanish, Portuguese, Galician languages

Ortiz Cofer, Judith
Riding low on the streets of gold; Latino literature for young adults. edited, with an introduction, by Judith Ortiz Cofer. Arte Publico Press 2003 p. cm
Grades: 7 8 9 10 11 12   **860**
ISBN 1-558-85380-4 (alk. paper)

LC 2003-61231

"These 11 poems and 12 stories explore growing up, recognizing one's place in the world, and living the bilingual immigrant experience. The collection blends works of familiar authors, including José Martí, Tomás Rivera, Victor Villaseñor, and Pat Mora, with the writings of newcomers. Mike Padilla's 'Carrying Sergei' relates the story of a Mexican girl who befriends a Russian immigrant boy after pushing him down a flight of stairs and breaking his leg. Through visits to his home, she discovers much about him and even more about herself. Friendship is also the theme of Daniel Chacón's 'Too White,' in which the protagonist faces the decision of admitting his friendship with a white boy or choosing to be part of the local Mexican gang. In Jesús Salvador Treviño's 'The Fabulous Sinkhole,' the personalities of an entire neighborhood are revealed as various individuals react to the emergence of a giant hole in Mrs. Romero's front yard. The poems are well chosen and blend well with the prose. The stories could be a starting point for interesting discussion topics, but the gritty language in a few of them may keep the book from being an assigned text. A photograph and brief biography of the author precede each work. Several poems in Spanish are accompanied by the English translation. Unfortunately, there are a handful of Spanish terms that are not defined within the text and there is no glossary. However, this is a minor detraction from this solid introduction to Latino literature." SLJ

"In this vibrant collection, Cofer collects memoir, poetry, and fiction by Latino writers who muse on las luchas, or struggles, of young people's daily lives: the universal coming-of-age experiences and the specific issues of Latino youth. Set in diverse locations . . . Teens of all cultural backgrounds will find much to connect with and contemplate in these rich offerings." Booklist

★ The **Tree** is older than you are; a bilingual gathering of poems & stories from Mexico with paintings by Mexican artists. selected by Naomi Shihab Nye. Simon & Schuster Bks. for Young Readers 1995 111p il hardcover o.p. pa $13.95
Grades: 7 8 9 10   860
1. Mexican literature -- Collections 2. Bilingual books -- English-Spanish
ISBN 0-689-82097-8; 0-689-82087-9 pa
LC 95-1565
"This bilingual anthology of poems, stories, and paintings by Mexican writers and artists brims over with a sense of wonder and playful exuberance, its themes as varied and inventive as a child's imagination." Voice Youth Advocates

883   Classical Greek epic poetry and fiction

Homer
The **Iliad**; translated by Robert Fagles; introduction and notes by Bernard Knox. Viking 1990 683p $40; pa $15.95
Grades: 8 9 10 11 12 Adult   883
1. Poetry -- By individual authors
ISBN 978-0-670-83510-2; 978-0-14-027536-0 pa
LC 89-70695
Homer's epic of the Trojan War.
"Fagles gives us a stark and terrible poem, an Iliad about, as its first word announces, rage. He conveys, far better than either Lattimore or Fitzgerald, the psychological experience of combat and war." Classical World

Landmann, Bimba
★ The **fate** of Achilles. Getty 2011 36p il $19.95
Grades: 4 5 6 7   883
1. Poets 2. Authors
ISBN 978-1-60606-085-8; 1-60606-085-6
"Landmann (The Incredible Voyage of Ulysses) continues her retelling of Homer's epics with this haunting version of the Iliad. Ghostly, Giacometti-style figures accompany the story of Achilles's life, from his baptism in the river Styx . . . to his departure for Troy, . . . the death of his dearest friend, . . . and his reconciliation with the father of the enemy he has slain. . . . Readers with the patience to sit through saga-length narratives will be fascinated by her prose, which moves easily through the sprawling epic without feeling ponderous or hurried. These kinds of retellings are few and far between, and hers are magic." Publ Wkly

The **incredible** voyage of Ulysses; text and illustrations by Bimba Landmann. Getty Publications 2010 un il $19.95

Grades: 4 5 6 7   883
1. Poets 2. Authors
ISBN 978-1-60606-012-4; 1-60606-012-0
"With narrative restraint and illustrative power, Landmann's . . . retelling of Homer's Odyssey follows Ulysses as he battles frightening creatures and endures the treachery of the gods while sailing home to Ithaca. . . . The paintings, worked with swift, bold strokes, combine the solemn stiffness of Greek statuary with the prophetic sweep of William Blake's imaginings." Publ Wkly

Lister, Robin
The **odyssey**; retold by Robin Lister; illustrated by Alan Baker. reformatted ed.; Kingfisher 2004 175p il (Kingfisher epics) pa $7.95
Grades: 5 6 7 8   883
1. Poets 2. Authors 3. Odysseus (Greek mythology)
ISBN 0-7534-5723-7
First published 1988
A retelling of Homer's epic poem that describes the wanderings of Odysseus after the fall of Troy.

Odyssey
The **Odyssey**; translated by Robert Fagles; introduction and notes by Bernard Knox. Viking 1996 541p $35; pa $16
Grades: 8 9 10 11 12 Adult   883
1. Poetry -- By individual authors
ISBN 978-0-670-82162-4; 978-0-14-026886-7 pa
LC 96-17280
This is a verse translation of Homer's epic poem
"Fagles' Odyssey is the one to put into the hands of younger, first-time readers, not least because of its paucity of notes, which, though sometimes frustrating, is a sign that translation has been used to do the work of explanation. Altogether, an outstanding piece of work." Booklist
Includes bibliographical references

Osborne, Mary Pope
The **gray** -eyed goddess; with artwork by Troy Howell. Hyperion Bks. for Children 2003 120p il (Mary Pope Osborne's Tales from the Odyssey) hardcover o.p. pa $4.99
Grades: 4 5 6 7   883
1. Poets 2. Authors 3. Odysseus (Greek mythology)
ISBN 0-7868-0773-3; 0-7868-0931-0 pa
Retells a part of the Odyssey in which Odysseus' wife, Penelope, and their son, Telemachus, are desperately warding off the men who want to marry her. Then a visit from a mysterious stranger gives Telemachus the courage to confront the suitors, and to search for his long-lost father

The **land** of the dead; illustrated by Troy Howell. Hyperion Bks. for Children 2002 105p il (Mary Pope Osborne's Tales from the Odyssey) $9.99; pa $4.99
Grades: 4 5 6 7   883
1. Poets 2. Authors 3. Odysseus (Greek mythology)
ISBN 0-7868-0771-7; 0-7868-0929-9 pa
LC 2002-69078

A retelling of part of the Odyssey in which Odysseus and his fleet continue their journey and encounter giant cannibals, a beautiful witch, and the Land of the Dead

"Osborne's simple, engaging narrative will surely capture interest as it presents a great hero in bold, yet human, dimensions." Booklist

The **one** -eyed giant; with artwork by Troy Howell. Hyperion Bks. for Children 2002 105p il (Mary Pope Osborne's Tales from the Odyssey) hardcover o.p. pa $4.99

Grades: 4 5 6 7 **883**

1. Poets 2. Authors 3. Odysseus (Greek mythology)
ISBN 0-7868-0770-9; 0-7868-0928-0 pa

LC 2002-68539

Retells a part of the Odyssey in which King Odysseus fights the cyclops

"In brief chapters and concise sentences, Osborne pares down . . . . [this adventure] into easily absorbed, swiftly paced episodes." Publ Wkly

Return to Ithaca; with artwork by Troy Howell. Hyperion Books for Children 2004 105p (Mary Pope Osborne's Tales from the Odyssey) $9.99

Grades: 4 5 6 7 **883**

1. Poets 2. Authors 3. Odysseus (Greek mythology)
ISBN 0-7868-0774-1

LC 2003-60355

Retells part of Homer's Odyssey in which Odysseus, with the help of the goddess Athena, plans to get revenge on those who have plagued his wife and son during his absence

895.1   Chinese literature

Liu Siyu

★ A **thousand** peaks; poems from China. [by] Siyu Liu and Orel Protopopescu; illustrated by Siyu Liu. Pacific View Press 2002 52p il $19.95

Grades: 5 6 7 8 9 10 **895.1**

1. Chinese poetry 2. Bilingual books -- English-Chinese
ISBN 1-88189-624-2

LC 2001-34008

A collection of thirty-five poems spanning nineteen centuries, representing both famous and lesser-known poets, including both the Chinese text and a literal translation.

This "is an anthology of considerable fascination and broad utility. . . . The layout is neat, tidily fitting each poem's material on a single page and adding a line drawing featuring a relevant Chinese character. The wealth of material here provides a more stimulating entree to Chinese history than any dry textbook." Bull Cent Child Books

Includes bibliographical references

897   Literatures of North American native languages

★ **Dancing** teepees: poems of American Indian youth; selected by Virginia Driving Hawk Sneve,

with art by Stephen Gammell. Holiday House 1989 32p il $17.95; pa $8.95

Grades: 4 5 6 **897**

1. Native Americans -- Poetry
ISBN 0-8234-0724-1; 0-8234-0879-5 pa

LC 88-11075

An illustrated collection of poems from the oral tradition of Native Americans

This is an "eclectic collection, drawn from a variety of tribal traditions. Printed on heavy paper, the book is illustrated with a catalogue of marvelously rendered designs and motifs, ranging from those of the Northwest Coast to the intricate beadwork patterns of the Great Lakes and the zigzag geometric borders of Southwestern pottery." N Y Times Book Rev

900   HISTORY

901   Philosophy and theory of history

Beller, Susan Provost

★ The **history** puzzle; how we know what we know about the past. [by] Susan Provost Beller. Twenty-First Century Books 2006 128p il lib bdg $26.60

Grades: 7 8 9 10 **901**

1. History -- Philosophy
ISBN 978-0-7613-2877-3; 0-7613-2877-7

LC 2005017745

"Beller looks at more than 20 historical sites or archaeological excavations . . . in order to present the varying interpretations of history and how they have been colored by tradition, socioeconomic factors, and religious beliefs. . . . . Frequent, well-placed sepia-toned photographs and period reproductions serve to enhance the text, and the source notes, further reading, and list of Web sites give students an ample list of resources for further study." SLJ

Includes bibliographical references

902   Miscellany of history

Hughes, Susan

Case closed? nine mysteries unlocked by modern science. written by Susan Hughes; illustrated by Michael Wandelmaier. Kids Can Press 2010 88p il map $17.95

Grades: 6 7 8 9 **902**

1. Archeology 2. Technological innovations 3. History -- Miscellanea
ISBN 978-1-55453-362-6; 1-55453-362-7

Examines how developments in modern science, such as DNA analysis and spectroscopy, have helped to re-open archaeological mysteries about ancient cities, Egypt's first female pharaoh, a missing expedition to find the Northwest Passage, and more.

"The writing is clear and engaging. The full-color illustrations are a mix of photographs, maps, and flat, animation-style art." SLJ

Includes glossary

904 Collected accounts of events

Beyer, Rick

The **greatest** stories never told; 100 tales from history to astonish, bewilder, & stupefy. HarperResource 2003 214p il $17.95

Grades: 7 8 9 10   904

1. History -- Miscellanea
ISBN 0-06-001401-6

LC 2004-296419

"Beginning with the year 46 B.C. and ending in 1990, Beyer presents a chronological account of one hundred unknown, partially known, and familar tales about an array of people and events that have shaped the world. . . . They range from the mundane to the fantastic. . . . Extensive research went into the production of this charming work. Primary documents in the form of letters, laws, illustrations, and photographs bring to life these unique and incredible anecdotes." Voice Youth Advocates

Includes bibliographical references

Blackwood, Gary L.

Enigmatic events. Marshall Cavendish Benchmark 2005 72p il (Unsolved history) lib bdg $29.93

Grades: 4 5 6 7   904

1. Disasters 2. Curiosities and wonders 3. History -- Miscellanea
ISBN 0-7614-1889-X

LC 2004-23755

Explores several events that have baffled scientists and historians for years, such as the demise of the dinosaurs, the "lost colony" of Roanoke, the sinking of the Main, and the Hindenberg disaster

This collection of "tidbits about lingering mysteries of the past . . . [offers] more substance than most. . . . [This offers] a full-page illustration opening each chapter; reproductions, many in color; and a generously spaced format." SLJ

Includes glossary and bibliographical references

Guiberson, Brenda Z.

★ **Disasters**; natural and man-made catastrophes through the centuries. Henry Holt and Company 2010 228p il $18.99

Grades: 5 6 7 8 9   904

1. Disasters 2. Natural disasters
ISBN 978-0-8050-8170-1; 0-8050-8170-4

LC 2009018908

"The subtitle provides an accurate outline of the contents of this lively treatment of disasters from smallpox to Hurricane Katrina. In each chapter, Guiberson outlines the sources of the disaster, the results, and means of obviating the problems that caused these tragedies. For example, the chapter on the Great Chicago Fire begins with the construction of the city over unstable marshland. . . . This kind of exhaustive background serves to create an understanding of the contributory issues and demonstrates possible preventive

steps. Guiberson's compellingly written exegesis is equally good in the other nine chapters. Well-placed, black-and-white reproductions and photos extend the text. A perfect example of solid historical research coupled with engaging writing." SLJ

Includes bibliographical references

Meissner, David

Call of the Klondike; a true gold rush adventure. by David Meissner and Kim Richardson. Calkins Creek 2013 168 p. (reinforced) $16.95

Grades: 6 7 8   904

1. Alaska -- Gold discoveries 2. Klondike River valley (Yukon) -- Gold discoveries
ISBN 1590788230; 9781590788233

LC 2013931060

Here, the authors share the experience of two 20-something Yale graduates from 1897, Stanley Pearce and Marshall Bond, who participated in the Klondike gold rush. Their letters are offered along with "diary entries, telegrams and Pearce's articles for the Denver Republican." The book also incorporates "pull-out quotes, maps, posters, documents and many . . . captioned photographs, including one of Jack London, who camped near Pearce and Bond's cabin." (Kirkus Reviews)

909 World history

Adams, Simon

★ The **Kingfisher** atlas of world history; a pictorial guide to the world's people and events, 10,000 BCE-present. Kingfisher 2010 181p il map $24.99

Grades: 4 5 6 7   909

1. World history 2. Historical geography
ISBN 978-0-7534-6388-8; 0-7534-6388-1

"This colorful and fact-packed book is not only informative but well organized. Sections cover 'The Ancient World,' 'The Medieval World,' 'Exploration and Empire,' and 'The Modern World,' and each section contains 15 or 16 thematic maps presented in chronological order. . . . It is very useful and entertaining as well as data-filled." Booklist

Badcott, Nicholas

Pocket timeline of Islamic civilizations. Interlink 2009 32p il $13.95

Grades: 7 8 9 10   909

1. Reference books 2. Islamic civilization -- Chronology
ISBN 978-1-56656-758-9; 1-56656-758-0

"Badcott takes readers on a colorful and captivating tour of Islamic civilizations from the 7th to the 20th century. He discusses the rise and fall of dynasties, along with their achievements and contributions in art, medicine, architecture, commerce, and science. . . . The writing style is easy to read. . . . Attractive color photographs of buildings, pottery, jewelry, art, and inventions help maintain readers' interest throughout." SLJ

Includes bibliographical references

Chrisp, Peter

History year by year; written by Peter Chrisp, Joe Fullman, and Susan Kennedy ; consultant, Philip Parker. DK Publishing 2013 320 p. col. ill., col. maps $24.99

Grades: 4 5 6 7 8 9   909

1. Anthropology 2. World history 3. Chronology, Historical

ISBN 1465414185; 9781465414182

LC 2012286068

Learning Magazine Teacher's Choice Awards for the Classroom (2015)

This book "presents the world through a detailed timeline, letting children follow the influences, patterns, and connections between historical events.Beginning with prehistory and running up to the Arab Spring, budding historians will learn about the history of humans across the world. Spreads highlight major historical eras . . . while quotations from primary and secondary sources alongside insight from experts give proper historical context." (Publisher's note)

"...Every few pages, a particular subtopic gets extra attention. For instance, in the "700 BCE-500 CE" section, there is a two-page discussion, replete with a color picture of Chinese emperor Qin Shi Huangdi's terra-cotta army. Features such as these make this an excellent browsing book, but students can still pull information from the text. A brief history of both the United States and Canada is appended. A good addition to most collections, both for the information it offers and for its appealing format.—" SLJ

Smithsonian history year by year

Eamer, Claire

Traitors' Gate and other doorways to the past. Annick Press 2008 154p il $24.95; pa $12.95

Grades: 6 7 8 9   909

1. Doorways 2. World history

ISBN 978-1-55451-145-7; 1-55451-145-3; 978-1-55451-144-0 pa; 1-55451-144-5 pa

"Eamer uses the concrete image of doorways to introduce famous (and not-so-famous) structures. She begins with perhaps the most amazing one, located in Petra, Jordan. Al-Khazner is hidden in a sandstone cliff. . . . Among the other structures discussed are Cape Coast Castle in Ghana, through whose doorway Africans were led to slave ships; the six doors of the Kremlin's Holy Antechamber; . . . and Spruce Tree House, an ancient cliff house in Colorado. . . . The many photographs are nicely reproduced, and Eamer's text is always solid and sometimes soars." Booklist

Includes bibliographical references

Hinds, Kathryn, 1962-

★ The city; by Kathryn Hinds. Marshall Cavendish Benchmark 2008 96 p. col. ill., maps (library) $8.66

Grades: 6 7 8 9 10   909

1. Middle Ages 2. City and town life 3. Medieval civilization 4. Islamic countries

ISBN 076143089X; 9780761430896

LC 2008019432

"A social history of the Islamic world from the eighth through the mid-thirteenth century, with a focus on life in the cities" Publisher's note

Includes bibliographical references and index.

★ The countryside; by Kathryn Hinds. Marshall Cavendish Benchmark 2008 95 p. col. ill. (library) $8.66

Grades: 6 7 8 9 10   909

1. Deserts 2. Middle Ages 3. Country life 4. Medieval civilization 5. Islamic countries

ISBN 0761430911; 9780761430919

LC 2008019266

"Presents a social history of the Islamic world from the eighth through the mid-thirteenth century, with a focus on life in the desert and countryside." Publisher's note

Includes bibliographical references and index.

Hussain, Saima S.

The Arab world thought of it; inventions, innovations, and amazing facts. Saima S. Hussain. Annick Press 2013 48 p. $21.95

Grades: 6 7 8   909

1. Arab civilization 2. Arab countries -- History

ISBN 1554514770; 9781554514779

This book is an "introduction to the Arab world through the arts and sciences developed in the many countries of the Middle East and North Africa and other regions where Arab culture flourished." Topics include "education, astronomy, weaponry, architecture, food, medical discoveries, arts and crafts, religion, and everyday inventions such as mattresses and hard soap." (Kirkus Reviews)

Moore, Christopher, 1957-

From then to now; a short history of the world. illustrated by Andrej Krystoforski. Tundra Books 2011 188p il map $25.95

Grades: 7 8 9 10   909

1. World history 2. Civilization -- History

ISBN 978-0-88776-540-7; 0-88776-540-8

"Capably told and uniquely illustrated, From Then to Now explains how imaginative human cultures have produced an intellectually and socially dynamic world. The work follows the course of human history from hunter-gatherer beginnings, through expansion and contact, to a modern, tightly interconnected global world. Along the way, Moore tackles how humanity, through agricultural and industrial innovations, has shaped and been shaped by environmental obstacles. Full-color spot art appears occasionally, and color sidebars provide information on a number of subjects. . . . This exceptional history of humanity is a breath of fresh air." SLJ

Morris, Neil

Beyond Europe; [by] Neil Morris and John Malam. Zak Books 2009 48p il map (History of the world) lib bdg $34.25

Grades: 7 8 9 10   **909**
1. Middle Ages 2. Medieval civilization
ISBN 978-88-6098-151-6 lib bdg; 88-6098-151-4
lib bdg

LC 2008-8406

The "effectiveness lies in the combination of lush illustrations, well-chosen, captioned photographs of contemporary artifacts, and . . . [a] reasoned, concise [narrative].
Succinct time lines border most pages, and . . . the proper
amount of white space, and clear dark print maintain organization and clarity. A superior choice." SLJ

Includes glossary

Smith, Tom

Discovery of the Americas, 1492-1800; rev ed.;
Chelsea House 2010 134p il map (Discovery and
exploration) lib bdg $35

Grades: 7 8 9 10 11   **909**
1. Explorers 2. America -- Exploration
ISBN 978-1-60413-195-6; 1-60413-195-0

LC 2009-22330

First published 2005

"The chapters are well-illustrated with color and black
and white historic photos, illustrations and maps. Chapter layout is clearly organized with helpful subtitles; sidebars develop related themes in eye-catching colors." Libr
Media Connect

Includes glossary and bibliographical references

Technology in world history; W. Bernard Carlson,
editor. Oxford University Press 2005 7v il maps
set $299

Grades: 7 8 9 10   **909**
1. Reference books 2. Technology and civilization
ISBN 0-19-521820-5; 978-0-19-521820-6

LC 2003-55300

"Seeking to explore how people have used technology
to shape societies, Carlson and 10 other scholars examine
the distinctive development and effects of technology in 18
cultures—defined either geographically (Pacific Peoples,
Sub-Saharan Africa) or by historical period (Stone Age, The
World Since 1970)." SLJ

Includes bibliographical references

909.07   General historical periods

Currie, Stephen

The **Medieval** crusades; by Stephen Currie. Lucent Books 2009 96 p. ill. (chiefly col.), col. map
(library) $34.95

Grades: 6 7 8 9   **909.07**
1. Crusades 2. Middle Ages 3. Civilization, Medieval
ISBN 1420500627; 9781420500622

LC 2008046532

This book by Stephen Currie is part of the World History series and looks at the medieval crusades. It "begins
with an explanation of early Christendom and Islam and
the schisms that existed within each religion. . . . The focus
of the book falls on the long-term effects of the Crusades,
creating European awareness of other countries and cultures

that led to increased commerce and trade, which in turn led
to the Age of Exploration and the Renaissance." (Voice of
Youth Advocates)

Includes bibliographical references and index.

Hinds, Kathryn, 1962-

★ The **palace**; [by] Kathryn Hinds. Marshall
Cavendish Benchmark 2008 96p il map (Life in the
Medieval Muslim world) lib bdg $23.95

Grades: 6 7 8 9 10   **909.07**
1. Middle Ages 2. Medieval civilization 3. Elite
(Social sciences) 4. Islamic countries
ISBN 978-0-7614-3088-9 lib bdg; 0-7614-3088-1
lib bdg

LC 2008010734

"Richly illustrated with art reproductions, maps, photos,
and ornate Islamic border designs, [this] . . . will entice visual learners." Libr Media Connect

Includes glossary and bibliographical references

Knight, Judson

Middle ages: almanac; edited by Judy Galens.
U.X.L 2001 lxv, 226p il map (Middle Ages reference library) $60

Grades: 8 9 10 11 12   **909.07**
1. Middle Ages 2. World history 3. Reference books
4. Medieval civilization
ISBN 0-7876-4856-6

LC 00-59442

This reference's 19 chapters review world history from
the fall of the Roman Empire in 500 A.D. to the beginning of
the Renaissance in 1500 A.D.

"The volume's strength is its broad coverage; it includes
material on India, Southeast Asia, China, Japan, the Americas, and Africa as well as Europe and the Middle East, making it unique among other books for this age group." SLJ

Includes bibliographical references

Middle ages: primary sources; [compiled by] Judson
Knight; Judy Galens, editor. U.X.L 2000 xxxiv,
161p il (Middle Ages reference library) $60

Grades: 8 9 10 11 12   **909.07**
1. Middle Ages
ISBN 0-7876-4860-4

LC 00-59441

This volume contains "19 full or excerpted documents
written during this period, including the work of celebrated
writers such as St. Augustine, Marco Polo, and Dante as
well as less familiar individuals such as Anna Comnena and
Lo Kuan-chung. Each selection is placed in its historical
context and followed by a section entitled 'What happened
next'. . . . Unfamiliar words or terms are defined in sidebars.
Each entry has a box profiling the author of the documents
and at least two illustrations." Booklist

Includes bibliographical references

909.08   Modern history, 1450/1500-

Huff, Toby E.

★ An **age** of science and revolutions, 1600-1800; [by] Toby Huff. Oxford University Press 2005 173p il map (Medieval & early modern world) lib bdg $32.95

Grades: 7 8 9 10   **909.08**

1. Europe -- Civilization 2. World history -- 17th century 3. World history -- 18th century
ISBN 0-19-517724-X

LC 2004-21612

This volume "looks at 200 years of world history. . . . [It includes] overview chapters on China, India, and the Middle East . . . [and] discusses the Enlightenment in Europe in some depth. . . . [This is a] useful book, which may spark discussion about current controversies about connections between science and religion." Booklist

Includes bibliographical references

Wiesner, Merry E.

★ An **age** of voyages, 1350-1600; [by] Merry E. Wiesner-Hanks. Oxford University Press 2005 189p il map (Medieval & early modern world) $32.95

Grades: 7 8 9 10   **909.08**

1. Middle Ages 2. World history -- 16th century
ISBN 0-19-517672-3; 978-0-19-517672-8

LC 2004021178

"In accessible language supported by prolific illustrations and primary sources, [this volume describes an era] that transformed the world." SLJ

Includes bibliographical references

909.8   World history--1800-

Winkler, Allan M.

The **Cold** War; a history in documents. by Allan M. Winkler. 2nd ed. Oxford University Press 2011 ix, 160 p.p ill., maps (Pages from History) (paperback) $34.95; (hardcover) $42.95

Grades: 8 9 10 11 12   **909.8**

1. Cold War 2. United States -- Foreign relations -- Soviet Union 3. Cold War -- Sources 4. World politics -- 1945-1989 -- Sources 5. Russia -- Foreign relations -- United States -- Sources 6. United States -- Foreign relations -- Russia -- Sources
ISBN 0199765995; 9780199765980; 9780199765997

LC 2010049111

This book by Allan M. Winkler is part of the Pages from History series and "traces the evolution of the Cold War . . . . By addressing the key issues of the Cold War via documents, the author provides a . . . look into a time that set the table for the modern era. Topics such as nuclear proliferation, McCarthyism, censorship, the Vietnam War and the Civil Rights Movement are all" addressed. (Children's Literature)

Includes bibliographical references and index.

909.82   World history--20th century, 1900-1999

Grant, R. G.

The **Cold** War. Arcturus Pub. 2011 46p il (Secret history) lib bdg $32.80 **909.82**

1. Cold war
ISBN 978-1-84837-696-0; 1-84837-696-0

LC 2010011765

This book explores the secrets of the Cold War. The superpowers never fought openly on a battlefield. Instead, they attacked one another by underhand means-spying, propaganda, secret operations, and guerrilla wars.

"The title of the Secret History series will grab readers, even reluctant ones, and they won't be disappointed by the intriguing info regarding codes and code breakers, spies, terrorists, and double agents, with profiles of heroes and traitors on all sides. . . . The readable design, with clear type on thick, high-quality paper, includes lots of sidebars, photos, screens, and quotes." Booklist

Includes bibliographical references

Harrison, Paul

Why did the Cold War happen? Gareth Stevens Pub. 2011 48p il map (Moments in history) lib bdg $31.95; pa $14.05

Grades: 6 7 8 9   **909.82**

1. Cold war 2. World politics -- 1945-1991
ISBN 978-1-4339-4166-5 lib bdg; 1-4339-4166-X lib bdg; 978-1-4339-4167-2 pa; 1-4339-4167-8 pa

LC 2010012456

"Examines the events that served as . . . [precursors to the Cold War]. . . . Brightly colored pullout boxes highlight important turning points, the perspective of the everyday man, and further information on why specific events occurred. Numerous photographs help readers visualize concepts more fully. . . . Students should be able to easily use this resource." Libr Media Connect

Includes glossary and bibliographical references

Kaufman, Michael T.

★ **1968**. Roaring Brook Press 2009 148p il $22.95

Grades: 7 8 9 10 11 12   **909.82**

1. World history -- 20th century
ISBN 978-1-59643-428-8; 1-59643-428-7

LC 2008-15471

Kaufman "expertly draws young readers into the worldwide events of a single, watershed year: 1968. . . . Each chapter focuses on a different hot spot around the globe, beginning with the Tet Offensive and the Vietnam War and moving through uprisings in New York, Paris, Prague, Chicago, and Mexico City, as well as the assassinations of Martin Luther King Jr. and Robert F. Kennedy. . . . The images, drawn from the [New York] Times archives, are riveting and will easily draw young people into the fascinating, often horrifying events." Booklist

909.83   World history--21st century, 2000-2099

Lace, William W.

The **Indian** Ocean tsunami of 2004. Chelsea House 2008 127p il map (Great historic disasters) $35

Grades: 7 8 9 10   909.83

1. Indian Ocean earthquake and tsunami, 2004
ISBN 978-0-7910-9642-0; 0-7910-9642-4

LC 2007-36950

"The author explains in detail the seismic activities that caused the 2004 Indian Ocean tsunami, as well as the lack of systems in place to quickly notify those in danger. Also included are many well-captioned photos .... and short but interesting personal stories of both survivors and victims." Horn Book Guide

Includes glossary and bibliographical references

Torres, John Albert

Disaster in the Indian Ocean, Tsunami 2004; [by] John A. Torres. Mitchell Lane 2005 48p il map (Monumental milestones) lib bdg $19.95

Grades: 5 6 7 8   909.83

1. Indian Ocean earthquake and tsunami, 2004
ISBN 1-58415-344-X

This "emerges from the author's personal trip to Indonesia after the December 26, 2004, catastrophe. . . . Primary-source accounts, many taken from Torres' own interviews, chillingly recreate the tsunami's initial strike, its chaotic aftermath, and the challenges of recovery." Booklist

Includes bibliographical references

910   Geography and travel

Belmont, Helen

★ **Looking** at aerial photographs; [by] Helen Belmont. Smart Apple Media 2008 46p il map (Geography skills) $22.95

Grades: 6 7 8 9   910

1. Geography 2. Aerial photography
ISBN 978-1-59920-048-4; 1-59920-048-1

LC 2006036139

"The text is easy to follow. . . . The examples given in the text that involve places are almost always accompanied by excellent photographs. . . . Maps, block diagrams, tables, and graphs are clearly presented and easy to interpret." Sci Books Films

Includes glossary and bibliographical references

Dumont-Le Cornec, Elisabeth

Wonders of the world; natural and man-made majesties. by Elisabeth Dumont-Le Cornec; illustrated by Laureen Topalian and Kristel Riethmuller. Abrams Books for Young Readers 2007 151p il $24.95

Grades: 6 7 8 9   910

1. Antiquities 2. Civilization 3. Historic sites 4. Natural monuments 5. Curiosities and wonders
ISBN 978-0-8109-9417-1; 0-8109-9417-8

LC 2007016198

This "volume features 71 natural and man-made wonders selected from sites on the UNESCO World Heritage list. . . . This visually stunning book presents each selected site on a double-page spread. Most of the spread is devoted to an excellent color photo reproduced on heavy, glossy paper and accompanied by several paragraphs of explanatory text, good captions, and a small washed drawing. . . . A rich visual experience." Booklist

Elliott, Lynne

Exploration in the Renaissance; [by] Lynne Elliott. Crabtree 2009 32p il pa $8.95; lib bdg $26.60

Grades: 6 7 8 9   910

1. Renaissance 2. America -- Exploration 3. Discoveries in geography -- European
ISBN 978-0-7787-4613-3 pa; 978-0-7787-4593-8 lib bdg

LC 2008-52601

"Ideal introductions to concepts, people, and events of the Renaissance... succinct and thorough." SLJ

Goodman, Joan E.

A **long** and uncertain journey: the 27,000 mile voyage of Vasco da Gama; by Joan Elizabeth Goodman; illustrated by Tom McNeely. Mikaya Press 2001 47p il map (Great explorers book) $22.95

Grades: 4 5 6 7   910

1. Explorers
ISBN 0-9650493-7-X

LC 00-63795

"McNeely's full-page illustrations, which vibrate with life and action, lighten the format, and quotations from the diary of an anonymous sailor on the voyage add fascinating detail and vivid description. . . . A good resource for reports, but the book is also intelligently written and exciting." Booklist

Jennings, Ken

Maps and geography; by Ken Jennings ; illustrated by TK. Little Simon, an imprint of Simon & Schuster Children's Pub. Division 2014 160 p. (The junior genius guide) $18.99

Grades: 3 4 5 6   910

1. Maps 2. Geography
ISBN 144249848X; 9781442473287; 9781442498488

LC 2012050862

This book, by Ken Jennings and illustrated by Mike Lowery, is part of the "Junior Genius Guides" series. "With this . . . guide to maps and geography, you'll become an expert and wow your friends and teachers with clever facts. . . . With great illustrations, cool trivia, and fun quizzes to test your knowledge, this guide will have you on your way to whiz-kid status in no time!" (Publisher's note)

"The new line of Junior Genius Guide books kicks off with a stellar collection of facts about climate, national flags, maps, and more, all in an engaging, arch tone. Jeopardy! champ and author Jennings, making his first foray into books for children, arranges the trivia in chapters that lightly satirize a school-day schedule, including a lunch period offering an ingenious and easy recipe for an edible map, a craft project in art class, and an official certification exam before the dismissal bell... Lowery's black-and-white spot illustrations help explain concepts, such as cartographic projections, and add the overall levity, making this a successful nonfiction package as well as pure reading fun. Published simultaneously with the second in the series, Greek Mythology." Booklist

Includes bibliographical references and index

Other titles include:

Greek Mythology

Outer Space

U.S. Presidents

Kerley, Barbara

★ The **world** is waiting for you; by Barbara Kerley. National Geographic 2013 48 p. (hardcover : alk. paper) $17.95

Grades: 1 2 3 4 5 6   **910**

1. Vocational guidance 2. Discoveries in geography
ISBN 1426311141; 9781426311147; 9781426311154
LC 2012026526

This book, by Barbara Kerley, "shows kids a pathway from their current interests and talents to a future career or interest. And in so doing, it also encourages adventure, exploration, and discovery, three core principles of National Geographic's mission. Selected photos make the connections compelling and the future real for kids, then rich back matter brings the message home with inspirational quotes from the real-life adventurers pictured in the images." (Publisher's note)

Richards, Jon

Planet Earth; by Jon Richards and illustrated by Ed Simkins. Owl Kids 2013 32 p. $15.95

Grades: 3 4 5 6   **910**

1. Graphic design 2. Signs and symbols
ISBN 1926973755; 9781926973753

In this book by Jon Richards "explores planet Earth using a wide variety of icons, graphics, and pictograms." Readers can "compare the tallest mountains from each continent, see the entire volume of water on the Earth poured into one glass, stack up Eiffel Towers and compare the height of the world's tallest waterfall." (Publisher's note)

Wojtanik, Andrew, 1989-

The **National** Geographic Bee ultimate fact book; countries A to Z. Andrew Wojtanik. National Geographic 2012 384 p. maps (pbk.) $21.90; (reinforced library binding) $21.90

Grades: 5 6 7 8 9 10   **910**

1. Atlases 2. Nations 3. Geography -- Encyclopedias
ISBN 1426309473; 1426309635; 9781426309472; 9781426309632
LC 2011282873

This book "provides statistical information for the world's 195 countries at a glance. The book starts off with a world map and full-page continental maps. Individual entries for countries are listed alphabetically. . . . A glossary explains terms that may be unfamiliar to students . . . . Each country entry includes a map with longitude and latitude and basic facts: continent, size, population, and capital." (Voice of Youth Advocates)

Includes bibliographical references (p. 382)

910.2   Geography--Miscellany; world travel guides

Ching, Jacqueline

Jobs in green travel and tourism. Rosen Pub. 2010 80p il (Green careers) lib bdg $30.60

Grades: 5 6 7 8   **910.2**

1. Tourist trade 2. Vocational guidance 3. Environmental movement 4. Environmental protection 5. Travel -- Environmental aspects
ISBN 978-1-4358-3571-9 lib bdg; 1-4358-3571-9 lib bdg
LC 2009016587

This "well-conceived [introduction focuses] on various jobs in [travel and tourism], the education and experience required, and expected earnings. The [book is] well organized, making it easy to gain an overview of the major aspects of the work. . . . [This book] will make [a] good [addition] to career collections. Photographs from the field and website and contact information for professional organizations add value." SLJ

Includes glossary and bibliographical references

910.3   Geography--Dictionaries, encyclopedias, concordances, gazetteers

Gifford, Clive

The **Kingfisher** geography encyclopedia; 2nd ed., rev. and updated ed.; Kingfisher 2011 487p il map $34.99

Grades: 4 5 6 7   **910.3**

1. Reference books 2. Geography -- Encyclopedias
ISBN 978-0-7534-6575-2; 0-7534-6575-2

Statistics, text, and color maps reveal the physical geography, peoples, politics, governments, languages, religions, and currencies of each nation of the world.

"The geographical descriptions are well written and include striking photos. The text is large and easy to read. . . . It is a great book to keep around the library for students to browse and dream about their next journey." Voice Youth Advocates

★ **Junior** worldmark encyclopedia of the nations; Timothy L. Gall, Susan Bevan Gall, and Derek M. Gleason, editors. 6th ed; Gale, Cengage Learning 2012 3200 p. 10v col. ill. (set : alk. paper) $677

Grades: 5 6 7 8   **910.3**

1. Geography -- Encyclopedias 2. World history -- Encyclopedias 3. Political science -- Encyclopedias 4. History -- Encyclopedias, Juvenile
ISBN 1414463138; 9781414463131; 9781414463148; 9781414463155; 9781414463162; 9781414463179; 9781414463186; 9781414463193; 9781414463209; 9781414463216; 9781414463223; 9781414463230; 9781414490861
LC 2011050016

First published 1996

This book series, edited by Timothy L. Gall, Susan Bevan Gall, and Derek M. Gleason, is a juvenile national encyclopedia. "Each volume . . . starts with a table of contents for the specific volume and a guide to country articles. Each country profile, organized alphabetically, begins with . . . capital, flag, anthem, monetary unit, weights and measures. . . . . Thirty-five color-coded subheadings and their corresponding numbers, as well as geographical profiles, complete each section." (Booklist)

"This new edition contains 196 countries of the world and the Palestinian Territories. Color maps... photos, and charts enhance the overall attractiveness of this updated set... This well-written encyclopedia would be a valuable resource for elementary, middle-school, and public libraries." Booklist

Includes bibliographical references and index

910.4 Accounts of travel and facilities for travelers

Anderson, Harry S.

Exploring the polar regions; rev ed.; Chelsea House 2010 116p il map (Discovery and exploration) lib bdg $35

Grades: 7 8 9 10   910.4
1. Polar regions -- Exploration
ISBN 978-1-60413-190-1; 1-60413-190-X
LC 2009-22863

First published 2004 by Facts on File

Covers exploration and discovery of the Arctic and Antarctic regions.

"The chapters are well-illustrated with color and black and white historic photos, illustrations and maps. Chapter layout is clearly organized with helpful subtitles; sidebars develop related themes in eye-catching colors. . . . [This book] attractively and effectively surveys an important . . . area in world studies." Libr Media Connect

Includes glossary and bibliographical references

Aronson, Marc

★ The **world** made new; why the Age of Exploration happened & how it changed the world. [by] Marc Aronson & John W. Glenn. National Geographic 2007 64p il map $17.95; lib bdg $27.90

Grades: 4 5 6 7   910.4
1. Explorers 2. Exploration
ISBN 978-0-7922-6454-5; 978-0-7922-6978-6 lib bdg
LC 2006022091

"This highly pictorial, readable overview provides significant depth of coverage. . . . The illustrations, most in full color, make ample and appropriate use of period prints as well as contemporary illustrations and photographs. The result is a visual feast that fleshes out the . . . remarkably evenhanded narrative." SLJ

Includes glossary and bibliographical references

Baker, Julie

The **great** whaleship disaster of 1871; [by] Julie Baker. Morgan Reynolds Pub. 2007 144p $27.95

Grades: 6 7 8 9   910.4
1. Whaling 2. Survival after airplane accidents, shipwrecks, etc.
ISBN 978-1-59935-043-1; 1-59935-043-2
LC 2007002807

"A compelling tale of survival. In 1871, at the peak of whale hunting, a fleet of 32 ships was trapped in Arctic ice, and the 1200 men, women, and children onboard faced a long winter with limited supplies. . . . Readers are given a picture of the hazards of whaling and the endurance required in the best of conditions. In the final chapters, the events leading up to the disaster are described. . . . The account is presented in an easy-to-follow, attractive format with concise chapters and ample diagrams, full-color reproductions, illustrations, and maps." SLJ

Includes bibliographical references

Bristow, David

★ **Sky** sailors; true stories of the balloon era. [by] David L. Bristow. Farrar Straus Giroux 2010 134p il $18.99

Grades: 4 5 6 7   910.4
1. Balloons
ISBN 978-0-374-37014-5; 0-374-37014-1
LC 2009037285

"This lively look at escapades of daring men—and a surprising number of women—who risked their lives flying in balloons will appeal to adventure, history and science buffs—and perhaps steampunk fans as well. Each of the nine chapters, which are chronologically arranged, focuses on an exciting story, starting with the first confirmed human balloon flight in 1783 . . . and ending with Dolly Shepherd, a young British woman in the early 1900s who parachuted out of balloons, hanging onto a trapeze. . . . Useful captions accompany many full-color illustrations of artwork and photographs." Kirkus

Includes bibliographical references

Burlingame, Jeff

The **Titanic** tragedy. Marshall Cavendish Benchmark 2011 111p il (Perspectives on) lib bdg $33.93

Grades: 8 9 10 11 12   910.4
1. Shipwrecks 2. Titanic (Steamship)
ISBN 978-1-60870-450-7 lib bdg; 1-60870-450-5 lib bdg; 978-1-60870-722-5 ebook
LC 2010041560

This title offers "excellent, thorough, and accurate information for reports or for general reading. [It] examines safety issues in the shipping industry in relation to the importance of profit, the historical background of the Gilded Age, the effects of privilege on the survivors of the disaster, the economic impact on those less well off, and the way the disaster affected future regulation of the shipping industry." SLJ

Includes bibliographical references

Cerullo, Mary M.

Shipwrecks; exploring sunken cities beneath the sea. [by] Mary M. Cerullo. Dutton Children's Books 2009 64p il $18.99

Grades: 5 6 7 8   910.4
1. Shipwrecks 2. Portland (Steamer) 3. Henrietta Marie (Ship)
ISBN 978-0-525-47968-0; 0-525-47968-6
LC 2008-48967

This focuses "on two wrecks: the Henrietta Marie, sunk in 1700 near the Florida Keys, and the Portland, sunk in

1898 off the coast of Massachusetts. The book makes the convincing case that these wrecks are important not only for historical reasons but also for the underwater ecosystems their structures now host. . . . This delivers both education and shivers." Booklist

Clifford, Barry

Real pirates; the untold story of the Whydah from slave ship to pirate ship. by Barry Clifford and Kenneth J. Kinkor with Sharon Simpson; photography by Kenneth Garrett. National Geographic 2008 175p il map $16.95

Grades: 4 5 6 7   **910.4**
1. Pirates 2. Archeology 3. Shipwrecks 4. Slave trade 5. Whidah (Ship) 6. Cape Cod (Mass.)
ISBN 978-1-4263-0279-4; 1-4263-0279-7
                   LC 2008299778

"Clifford, an underwater archaeological explorer, used research and the artifacts recovered from the Whydah to tell the story of its life as a slave galley and pirate ship. In the process, he dispels many myths about buccaneers. . . . Photographs of artifacts . . . and the recovery crew at work combine with large visually appealing paintings of dramatic battle, storm, and courtroom scenes. . . . The book is a fascinating blend of history, ocean-diving recovery, and archaeology, and demonstrates archaeology in action and the role artifacts play in informing us about the past." SLJ

Includes bibliographical references

Denenberg, Barry

★ **Titanic** sinks! Viking 2011 72p il $19.99

Grades: 5 6 7 8   **910.4**
1. Shipwrecks 2. Titanic (Steamship)
ISBN 0670012432; 9780670012435
                   LC 2011012040

This is a "gripping recounting of the Titanic's doomed maiden voyage, chronicled in the tabloid-style pages of a fictional magazine. . . . Melding fact and fiction, the book compiles dramatic headlines, articles that range from news bulletins about the building of the ship to a chatty tour of its lavish interior, and an array of stunning period photographs." Publ Wkly

Gilkerson, William

A **thousand** years of pirates. Tundra Books 2009 96p il map $32.95

Grades: 6 7 8 9 10   **910.4**
1. Pirates
ISBN 978-0-88776-924-5; 0-88776-924-1

"Pirates are given scholarly scrutiny in this handsome and invigorating overview. Short but dense chapters introduce the major factions, characters, and incidents that connect the scattered history of seagoing bandits. . . . Gilkerson's grasp of the politics surrounding each nation's pirates . . . is most impressive." Booklist

Includes bibliographical references

Grove, Tim

First flight around the world; the adventures of the American fliers who won the race. by Tim Grove. Abrams Books for Young Readers, in assoc. w/Smith-

sonian Ntl. Air & Space Museum 2015 96 p. col. ill.; maps (hardcover) $21.95

Grades: 5 6 7 8   **910.4**
1. Aeronautics -- Flights 2. Voyages around the world 3. World records 4. Flights around the world 5. United States. Army. Air Corps
ISBN 1419714821; 9781419714825
                   LC 2014024665

This children's book, by Tim Grove, "documents the exciting journey of four American planes--the Chicago, Boston, New Orleans, and Seattle--and their crews on a race around the world. The trip held many challenges: extreme weather, tricky navigation, unfamiliar cultures, fragile planes, and few airfields. The world fliers risked their lives for the sake of national pride." (Publisher's note)

"This gripping, well-designed title details the United States' 1924 successful attempt to become the first nation to circumnavigate the globe by flight...Offering a look at a lesser-known historical event, this beautiful, well-written book is an essential addition for all collections." SLJ

Includes bibliographical references

Hagglund, Betty

Epic treks. Kingfisher 2011 64p il (Epic adventure) $19.99

Grades: 5 6 7 8   **910.4**
1. Explorers 2. Voyages and travels
ISBN 978-0-7534-6668-1; 0-7534-6668-6
                   LC 2011041638

"The graphics will grab readers in [this] exciting, extra-large-size [title] . . . packed with high-quality color photos on every double-page spread. Just as gripping are the narratives, captions, and technical details of exploration, adventure, and survival. . . . Epic Treks covers Lewis and Clark, Livingston and Stanley, Burk and Wells, and Amundsen and Scott, each journey an exciting adventure filled with details about what they endured and what they found, as well as their failures and shortcomings." Booklist

Includes glossary

Hanel, Rachael

Pirates; [by] Rachael Hanel. Creative Education 2008 48p il map (Fearsome fighters) $31.35

Grades: 4 5 6   **910.4**
1. Pirates
ISBN 978-1-58341-537-5; 1-58341-537-8
                   LC 2006021844

"This book explores 'the golden age of piracy' from the sixteenth through the nineteenth centuries. Hanel discusses battles, types of ships and weapons, and attire and behavior. Vignettes of well-known male and female pirates are included. Archival reproductions and sidebars provide additional information." Horn Book Guide

Includes glossary and bibliographical references

Hopkinson, Deborah

★ **Titanic**; voices from the disaster. by Deborah Hopkinson. Scholastic Press 2012 289 p. (hardcover) $17.99

Grades: 5 6 7 8   **910.4**
1. Titanic (Steamship) 2. Shipwrecks
ISBN 0545116740; 9780545116749

LC 2011006695

Robert F. Sibert Honor Book (2013)

YALSA Award for Excellence in Nonfiction for Young
Adults Finalist (2013)

In this book about the sinking of the Titanic, author Deborah "Hopkinson begins with a description of the ship . . .
and introduces some of the passengers who embarked on its
maiden voyage. The narrative shifts . . . to the disaster itself
with a litany of things gone wrong. . . . [M]emoirs . . . are
interlaced throughout the text, as survivors testified . . . on
the relative chaos or calm, heroism or cowardice, of passengers and crew." (Bulletin of the Center for Children's Books)

Includes bibliographical references

Hunter, Nick

Pirate treasure; by Nick Hunter. Raintree 2013
48 p. (hb) $29.33

Grades: 5 6 7 8   **910.4**
1. Pirates 2. Buried treasure 3. Treasure troves
ISBN 1410949532; 9781410949530; 9781410949608

LC 2012012890

This book, by Nick Hunter, "examines the hunt for treasures lost or hidden by pirates, and examines whether any of
the legends of buried treasure could really be true. Part of the
Treasure Hunters series, 'Pirate Treasure' offers a crosscurricular mix of science & technology and history & civilizations. Pirate treasures covered in the book include those of
the famous Blackbeard and Captain Kidd, the pirate shipwreck the Whydah, and the mysterious Oak Island Money
Pit." (Publisher's note)

Includes bibliographical references and index

Lavery, Brian

The **conquest** of the ocean; the illustrated history
of seafaring. Brian Lavery. Dk Pub 2013 400 p. $30

Grades: 8 9 10 11 12   **910.4**
1. Seafaring life 2. Maritime history
ISBN 146540841X; 9781465408419

This book offers a "survey of humanity's history on
the seas." It "begins about 30,000 years ago with Polyne-
sian seafarers' colonization of Pacific islands and continues
through to address harrowing accounts of modern-day piracy. Ports of call between these distant coasts include the
treasure voyages of Ming official Zheng He, the discovery of
the New World, the invention of the Fresnel lens, the Battle
of Midway, and many others." (Publishers Weekly)

Lawlor, Laurie

Magnificent voyage; an American adventurer
on Captain James Cook's final expedition. Holiday
House 2002 236p il maps $22.95

Grades: 7 8 9 10   **910.4**
1. Explorers 2. Oceania 3. Naval officers 4. Travel
writers 5. Resolution (Ship)
ISBN 0-8234-1575-9

LC 2002-17148

Based on the writings of John Ledyard, an American
cook on the ship Resolution, tells of explorer James Cook's

final voyage in search of the Northwest Passage, discovery
of the Hawaiian Islands, and murder

"The author's detailed picture of the voyage, and of Ledyard's relatively brief career, makes engrossing, if gloomy,
reading." Booklist

Includes glossary and bibliographical references

Marschall, Ken

Inside the Titanic; illustrated by Ken Marschall;
text by Hugh Brewster. Little, Brown 1997 32p il
$19.95

Grades: 4 5 6 7   **910.4**
1. Shipwrecks 2. Titanic (Steamship)
ISBN 0-316-55716-1

LC 97-382

"Color cutaway paintings of the Titanic in this oversize
book allow readers to view every deck as they follow two
12-year-old boys exploring the vessel, and to see how the
liner struck the iceberg and sank." Booklist

Includes glossary and bibliographical references

McPherson, Stephanie Sammartino

★ **Iceberg** right ahead! the tragedy of the Titanic. Twenty-First Century Books 2011 112p il lib
bdg $33.26

Grades: 4 5 6 7 8   **910.4**
1. Shipwrecks 2. Titanic (Steamship)
ISBN 9780761367567

LC 2011002352

"With innumerable books, movies, documentaries, novels, and biographies all telling versions of the Titanic story,
it would seem that there is little more to learn, yet by providing more details and some of the most up-to-date research,
McPherson's compelling, thoughtful narrative proves otherwise. . . . The layout includes plenty of period photographs,
diagrams, artwork, and sidebars with interesting tangential
tidbits, making for a thorough resource. . . . A comprehensive, well-written, thoroughly researched title." SLJ

Includes bibliographical references

Morris, Neil

Voyages of discovery. Zak Books 2009 48p il
map (History of the world) lib bdg $34.25

Grades: 7 8 9 10   **910.4**
1. Explorers 2. Exploration
ISBN 978-88-6098-154-7 lib bdg; 88-6098-154-9
lib bdg

LC 2008-8409

The "effectiveness lies in the combination of lush illustrations, well-chosen, captioned photographs of contemporary artifacts, and . . . [a] reasoned, concise [narrative].
Succinct time lines border most pages, and . . . the proper
amount of white space, and clear dark print maintain organization and clarity. A superior choice." SLJ

Includes glossary

Mundy, Robyn

Epic voyages. Kingfisher 2011 64p il (Epic
adventure) $19.99

Grades: 5 6 7 8   **910.4**
    1. Explorers
    ISBN 978-0-7534-6574-5; 0-7534-6574-4

"The graphics will grab readers in [this] exciting, extra-large-size [title] . . . packed with high-quality color photos on every double-page spread. Just as gripping are the narratives, captions, and technical details of exploration, adventure, and survival. . . . [This] book covers Magellan, Cook, Shackleton, Heyedahl and also Chichester, who, in 1966, sailed alone around the world." Booklist

Nardo, Don
    Polar explorations; by Don Nardo. Lucent Books 2011 104 p. ill., col. maps, photographs (library) $34.95
Grades: 6 7 8 9   **910.4**
    1. Polar regions -- Exploration 2. Exploration 3. Explorers -- Polar regions -- Biography 4. Polar regions -- Discovery and exploration
    ISBN 142050360X; 9781420503609
                                    LC 2010039667
This book by Don Nardo is part of the World History series and looks at polar explorations. The series "examines the eras, events, civilizations, and movements that have shaped human history, providing readers with insight into the past and its many legacies. Vivid writing, full-color photographs and extensive use of fully cited primary and secondary source quotations provide a sense of immediacy." (Publisher's note)
    Includes bibliographical references and (p. 95-97) index.

Philbrick, Nathaniel
    ★ **Revenge** of the whale; the true story of the whaleship Essex. Putnam 2002 164p il maps $16.99; pa $7.99
Grades: 7 8 9 10   **910.4**
    1. Whaling 2. Shipwrecks 3. Essex (Whaleship)
    ISBN 0-399-23795-X; 0-14-240068-8 pa
                                    LC 2002-667
Recounts the 1820 sinking of the whaleship "Essex" by an enraged sperm whale and how the crew of young men survived against impossible odds. Based on the author's adult book "In the heart of the sea"
    "The story of the Essex crew is a compelling saga of desperation and survival that will appeal to young people. The grisly details of cannibalism necessary to the telling of the story may provoke shivers but should not give anyone nightmares." SLJ
    Includes bibliographical references

Rose, Jamaica
    The **book** of pirates; a guide to plundering, pillaging, and other pursuits. [by] Jamaica Rose & Michael MacLeod. Gibbs Smith 2010 224p il map $12.99
Grades: 6 7 8 9 10   **910.4**
    1. Pirates
    ISBN 978-1-4236-0670-3; 1-4236-0670-1
                                    LC 2010009086
    "This delightful book, written partly in pirate dialect, is full of creative activities, interspersed with plenty of fascinating historical facts. . . . The introduction defines piracy.

The opening chapter is a true-or-false account of some of the many well-known myths about pirates. . . . The authors discuss the origins and history of these rogues, the lives of famous pirates (including females), rules and codes and behavior, and present-day piracy. Those planning to attend an event as a pirate can follow the instructions for proper attire, along with diagrams and directions for makeup and the construction of a foam cutlass. . . . Jokes, games, songs, and a recipe for making cannonballs (from peanut butter) add to the fun." SLJ
    Includes glossary

Ross, Stewart
    ★ **Into** the unknown; how great explorers found their way by land, sea, and air. Candlewick Press 2011 un il map $19.99
Grades: 4 5 6 7   **910.4**
    1. Explorers 2. Discoveries in geography
    ISBN 978-0-7636-4948-7; 0-7636-4948-1
                                    LC 2010038720
    "Biesty's trademark amusing, informatively detailed illustrations are a highlight of this entertaining examination of several voyages of exploration. . . . Chapters cover an impressive range of exploration. In addition to the usual suspects, they include a 340 B.C.E. Greek voyage to the Arctic Circle; Chinese Admiral Zheng He to India; [and] David Livingston and Mary Kingsley into the African interior. . . . Each chapter includes a fold-out section of illustrations with a map of the journey and a cross-section of the method of transportation. . . . An altogether agreeable package for armchair explorers." Kirkus

Vail, Martha
    Exploring the Pacific; [by] Martha Vail; John S. Bowman and Maurice Isserman, general editors. rev ed.; Chelsea House 2010 120p il map (Discovery and exploration) $35
Grades: 7 8 9 10   **910.4**
    1. Explorers 2. Pacific Ocean
    ISBN 978-1-60413-197-0; 1-60413-197-7
                                    LC 2009-22106
    First published 2005 by Facts on File
    "The chapters are well-illustrated with color and black and white historic photos, illustrations, and maps. Chapter layout is clearly organized with helpful subtitles; sidebars develop related themes in catching colors." Libr Media Connect
    Includes glossary and bibliographical references

Weatherly, Myra
    Women of the sea; ten pirate stories. Morgan Reynolds 2006 160p il map lib bdg $26.95
Grades: 7 8 9 10   **910.4**
    1. Women pirates
    ISBN 1-931798-80-X
    A revised edition of Women pirates: eight stories of adventure (1998)
    This is a collective biography of such women pirates as Lady Killigrew, Lai Choi San, and Maria Cobham
    Includes glossary and bibliographical references

White, Pamela

Exploration in the world of the Middle Ages, 500-1500; Pamela White, John S. Bowman, and Maurice Isserman, general editors. Rev. ed.; Chelsea House 2010 132p il map (Discovery and exploration) $35

Grades: 7 8 9 10   **910.4**

1. Explorers 2. Exploration 3. Middle Ages

ISBN 978-1-60413-193-2; 1-60413-193-4

LC 2009-30202

First published 2005 by Facts On File

This describes world exploration in the Middle Ages by pilgrims and missionaries, the Vikings, Muslim travelers, Europeans seeking Asia, Marco Polo, and Portuguese sailors, and describes Medieval legends of mythical monsters and lands

Includes glossary and bibliographical references

910.452   Shipwrecks

Sherman, Casey

The **finest** hours; the true story of a heroic sea rescue. Michael J. Tougias and Casey Sherman. Christy Ottaviano Books 2014 176 p. illustrations (hardback) $17.99

Grades: 4 5 6 7 8   **910.452**

1. Shipwrecks 2. Survival after airplane accidents, shipwrecks, etc. 3. CG36500 (Lifeboat) 4. Pendleton (Tanker) 5. Shipwrecks -- Massachusetts 6. Shipwreck survival -- History

ISBN 0805097643; 9780805097641; 9781250044235

LC 2013030661

This book by Michael J. Tougias and Casey Sherman "tells the story of a harrowing Coast Guard rescue when four men in a tiny lifeboat overcame insurmountable odds and saved more than 30 stranded sailors." In this book, the events of the February 18, 1952 wreck of two oil tankers near Cape Cod are adapted for middle-grade readers. (Publisher's note)

"The accounts of each rescue's logistics—for example, sailors trying to time their leaps from their destroyed tanker to the rescue boat amid rocking waves—are nail-biting, and they are relayed by the authors with an effectively sober, just-the-facts terseness." Booklist

Includes bibliographical references

910.92   Geographers, travelers, explorers regardless of country of origin

Fritz, Jean

Around the world in a hundred years; from Henry the Navigator to Magellan. illustrated by Anthony Bacon Venti. Putnam 1994 128p il map hardcover o.p. pa $8.99

Grades: 4 5 6 7   **910.92**

1. Princes 2. Explorers 3. Colonial administrators

ISBN 0-399-22527-7; 0-698-11638-0 pa

LC 92-27042

"Fritz examines the voyages of ten explorers, acknowledging that their contributions, though deserving of recognition, were dearly bought. Opening and closing chapters summarize the fourteenth-century world view and indicate later expansion of geographic understanding. As always, Fritz tempers scholarship with humor in this brief volume—illustrated with drawings in pencil—which reads like an adventure story." Horn Book Guide

Includes bibliographical references

911   Historical geography

Chrisp, Peter

Atlas of ancient worlds; author, Peter Chrisp; consultant, Philip Parker. DK Pub. 2009 96p il map $21.99

Grades: 4 5 6 7 8   **911**

1. Reference books 2. Historical atlases 3. Ancient civilization

ISBN 978-0-7566-4512-0; 0-7566-4512-3

This atlas consists "of maps and illustrations accompanied by extensive captions outlining the cultures of many civilizations. Each section begins with a map of a continent and a table of contents detailing which peoples will be discussed in it. Each civilization is covered in a chapter spread that includes a small map of the extent of each empire and many photos, pictures, and captioned drawings. . . . The accompanying clip art CD contains images of many of the artifacts as well as of the maps found in the book. . . . This atlas offers a wonderful introduction to [ancient civilizations] as well as solid geography basics." SLJ

Includes glossary

Leacock, Elspeth

Places in time; a new atlas of American history. [by] Elspeth Leacock and Susan Buckley; illustrations by Randy Jones. Houghton Mifflin 2001 48p il $15; pa $6.95

Grades: 4 5 6 7   **911**

1. Reference books 2. United States -- Historical geography

ISBN 0-395-97958-7; 0-618-3113-0 pa

LC 00-59741

This book presents "20 sites in American history at the moment of their historical significance, beginning in 1200 (Cahokia) and ending in 1953. Places and times include New Plymouth—1627, Charlestown—1739, Saratoga—1777, Philadelphia—1787, Abilene—1871, and Chicago—1893. The detailed cutaway views of homes, forts, and mills are impressive enough to keep readers looking again and again. These fascinating slices of life stir the imagination and lead to questions and further research." SLJ

Includes bibliographical references

Todras, Ellen H.

Explorers, trappers, and pioneers; by Ellen H. Todras. Kingfisher 2012 32 p. ill. (All About America) (paperback) $9.99

Grades: 4 5 6   **911**

1. America -- Exploration 2. Frontier and pioneer life

-- United States
ISBN 0753465159; 9780753465158

This book by Ellen H. Todras is part of the "All About America" series. It "begins with the Vikings landing in Newfoundland 1,000 years ago and concludes with the Oklahoma Land Rush in 1889." It "offers 13 highly illustrated double-page spreads that present topics using a few paragraphs of information, related text boxes, and several color illustrations and five or more captioned illustrations." (Booklist)

912   Graphic representations of surface of earth and of extraterrestrial worlds

Facts on File, Inc.

Maps on file. Facts on File 2v maps
Grades: Adult Professional   912
1. Atlases 2. Reference books
First published 1981. Frequently revised

A collection of approximately 500 black-and-white maps covering countries, every U.S. state, Canadian provinces, oceans, and continents

Hollingum, Ben

Maps and mapping the world; [Ben Hollingum, editor] Gareth Stevens Pub. 2010 48p il map (Understanding maps of our world) lib bdg $31; pa $14.95
Grades: 6 7 8 9   912
1. Maps
ISBN 978-1-4339-3498-8 lib bdg; 1-4339-3498-1 lib bdg; 978-1-4339-3501-5 pa; 1-4339-3501-5 pa
LC 2009-37275

"These fascinating books open with an identical whirlwind time line of cartographic history, beginning with a map of the world as 15th-century Europeans knew it and ending with the first photos of Earth taken from space...Related events and topics also spring up... The books' further-reading lists, which include print and Web materials, are particularly extensive. Wonderful resources." SLJ

Includes glossary and bibliographical references

Travel maps; [Ben Hollingum, editor] Gareth Stevens Pub. 2010 48p il map (Understanding maps of our world) lib bdg $31; pa $14.95
Grades: 6 7 8 9   912
1. Maps
ISBN 978-1-4339-3506-0 lib bdg; 1-4339-3506-6 lib bdg; 978-1-4339-3507-7 pa; 1-4339-3507-4 pa
LC 2009-37277

"These fascinating books open with an identical whirlwind time line of cartographic history...descriptions of cartographic challenges, old and new, result in a lot of valuable extras. Wonderful resources." SLJ

Includes glossary and bibliographical references

★ National Geographic atlas of the world; 9th ed.; National Geographic Society 2010 153p il $175
Grades: 5 6 7 8 9 10   912
1. Atlases 2. Reference books
ISBN 978-1-4262-0634-4

First published 1963

"The National Geographic Society presents more than 80 large-format color maps grouped by continent portraying the world with detailed, digitally painted terrain modeling. Each continent is introduced by satellite, political, and physical maps. Political maps for regions and specific countries follow." Libr J

National Geographic student atlas of the world; 3rd ed; National Geographic 2009 143p il map pa $12.95
Grades: 6 7 8 9   912
1. Atlases 2. Reference books
ISBN 978-1-4263-0446-0 pa; 1-4263-0446-3 pa; 978-1-4263-0458-3 lib bdg; 1-4263-0458-7 lib bdg; 978-1-4263-0445-3; 1-4263-0445-5
LC 2009-583028

First published 2001

This volume juxtaposes maps and text on adjoining pages. Glossary. Indexes. "Grades seven to twelve." (Sci Books Films)

This offers information "about maps and how to read them. Then [it describes] the world's physical and human systems, including Earth's geologic history, natural vegetation, and world cultures. A . . . view from space introduces each continent, and full-page, full-color maps represent its physical and political makeup, its climate and precipitation, and its population and predominant economies. A . . . photo essay highlights an issue relevant to each continent, such as the European Union, or deforestation in the Amazon." Publisher's note

★ National Geographic United States atlas for young explorers; 3rd ed.; National Geographic 2008 175p il map $24.95
Grades: 4 5 6 7   912
1. Atlases 2. Reference books 3. United States -- Maps
ISBN 978-1-4263-0255-8; 1-4263-0255-X
First published 1999

This atlas offers maps of each of the states in the United States, divided into five geographical regions, plus U.S. territories. Each state map indicates physical features such as mountains and rivers, national forests, cities, major interstate roads, and industries, and is accompanied by color photos and facts about the state. An introductory section describes how to use the companion web site for more information, maps of the United States biomes, climates, natural hazards, political states, population, ethnic diversity, and energy use.

★ Oxford Atlas of the world; [cartography by Philip's] 19th ed. Oxford University Press 2012 448 p. il map (hardcover) $89.95
Grades: 7 8 9 10 11 12 Adult   912
1. Atlases 2. Earth -- Maps 3. Physical geography 4. Reference books
ISBN 0199937826; 9780199937820
LC 20100594813

First published 1992. Frequently revised. Variant title: Atlas of the world

This world atlas offers "new census information, dozens of city maps . . . satellite images of Earth, and a geographical glossary." It " provides details on such topics as climate, the greenhouse effect, employment and industry, standards of living, agriculture, population and migration, and global conflicts." (Publisher's note)

"...[U]pdated annually, this large-format resource continues to earn pride of place on the atlas case's top shelf for its combination of currency and eye-widening graphics. The physical, political, and country and regional maps that make up the volume's core are works of art-brilliantly designed for easy comprehension, rendered in bright colors and sharp detail... Atlases are among the quickest reference sources to age, so for classroom or library collections in which students search in vain...this makes a first-rate replacement." SLJ

Oxford new concise world atlas; [cartography by Philip's; text, Keith Lye]. 3rd ed; Oxford University Press 2010 1 atlas (224 p.) col. ill., col. maps $39.95

Grades: 6 7 8 9 10 11 12 Adult   912
1. Atlases 2. Reference books
ISBN 0195393295; 9780195393293

LC 2009292676

Containing over 100 pages of the most up-to-date topographic and political maps, the New Concise World Atlas also features a unique overview of the planet's human and natural processes in photographs, accessible text, and thematic maps. (Publisher's note)

"This update of the 2006 edition contains 128 pages of full-color, computer-generated maps by Philip's, a division of Octopus Publishing, with detailed and dramatic terrain modeling... This condensed and abridged version of the premium Oxford Atlas of the World offers all libraries outstanding value in an up-to-date, medium-sized atlas for an amazingly low price.—" LJ

Includes index.

Panchyk, Richard

Charting the world; geography and maps from cave paintings to GPS with 21 activities. by Richard Panchyk. Chicago Review Press 2011 xi, 132 p.p ill., maps (some col.) (paperback) $18.95

Grades: 7 8 9 10   912
1. Maps 2. Cartography -- Maps 3. Map reading 4. Maps -- History
ISBN 1569763445; 9781569763445

LC 2011019317

Author "[Richard] Panchyk's book helps explain why maps are exciting, how they expand our world, and have done so for generations. . . . Maps document the lay of the land, the placement of cities, and the height of mountains, among many other things. Panchyk walks us through these mapmaking skills, offering activities along the way. . . .Panchyk also provides sidebars about such notable explorers as Amerigo Vespucci, for whom America was named." (Children's Literature)

Includes bibliographical references (p. 126-127) and index.

Rand McNally Goodes World Atlas; edited by Howard Veregin. Rand McNally 2009 400 p. $45

Grades: 4 5 6 7 8 9 10 11 12 Adult   912
1. Maps 2. Atlases
ISBN 0528877542; 9780528877544

This book, edited by Howard Veregin, "features over 250 pages of maps, from definitive physical and political maps to important thematic maps that illustrate the spatial aspects of many important topics. [It] includes 160 pages of new, digitally produced reference maps, as well as new thematic maps on global climate change, sea level rise, CO2 emissions, polar ice fluctuations, deforestation, extreme weather events, infectious diseases, water resources, and energy production." (Publisher's note)

Ross, Val

The **road** to there; mapmakers and their stories. Tundra Books 2003 146p il map $22.95; pa $15.95

Grades: 6 7 8 9   912
1. Maps
ISBN 0-88776-621-8; 0-88776-933-0 pa

"Ross presents an intriguing look at several mapmakers and the way that their work reflected not only physical boundaries, but also important aspects of their lives and the times in which they lived. . . . The tone of the text is chatty, sometimes humorous, and never dry. . . . Filled with details and insights and written with a storyteller's touch, this book will simultaneously inform and fascinate readers." SLJ

Student atlas; Dorling Kindersley, Inc. 6th ed. DK Pub. 2013 176 p. ill. (hardcover) $14.99

Grades: 5 6 7 8   912
1. Atlases 2. Geography
ISBN 0756663199; 9780756663193

This book from DK Publishing is part of the Student Atlas series. It is a "single-volume guide to the nations of the world. [It's] fully revised and updated, and packed with clear, detailed maps highlighting landscape, industry, land use, population, climate and environmental issues." (Publisher's note)

Taylor, Barbara

★ **Looking** at maps; [by] Barbara Taylor. Smart Apple Media 2008 46p il map (Geography skills) $22.95

Grades: 6 7 8 9   912
1. Maps
ISBN 1-59920-050-3; 978-1-59920-050-7

LC 2006100224

"The text is easy to follow. . . . The examples given in the text that involve places are almost always accompanied by excellent photographs. . . . Maps, block diagrams, tables, and graphs are clearly presented and easy to interpret." Sci Books Films

Includes glossary and bibliographical references

916   Geography of and travel in Africa

Bodden, Valerie

To the heart of Africa; by Valerie Bodden. Creative Education 2011 48 p. col. ill. (Great Expeditions) (library) $34.25

Grades: 5 6 7 8   916
1. Exploration 2. Africa -- Exploration 3. Explorers -- Scotland -- Biography 4. Explorers -- Africa, Southern

-- Biography 5. Africa, Sub-Saharan -- Discovery and exploration 6. Missionaries, Medical -- Africa, Southern -- Biography
ISBN 1608180662; 9781608180660

LC 2010033414

This book by Valerie Bodden is part of the Great Expeditions series and looks at expeditions into Africa. "Bodden includes brief biographies of major people involved in each expedition, interspersed with the text. There are also numerous photographs or reproductions of paintings and woodcuts from the time of the expeditions." (Library Media Connection)

Includes bibliographical references (p. 46-47) and index.

917   Geography of and travel in North America

Butts, Edward

Shipwrecks, monsters, and mysteries of the Great Lakes; [by] Ed Butts. Tundra Books 2010 80p il pa $14.95

Grades: 4 5 6 7   **917**

1. Shipwrecks 2. Great Lakes
ISBN 978-1-77049-206-6 pa; 1-77049-206-2 pa

"In 1679, a French ship called the Griffon left Green Bay on Lake Michigan, bound for Niagara with a cargo of furs. Neither the Griffon nor the five-man crew was ever seen again. . . . Its disappearance was probably the result of the first shipwreck on a Great Lake. Since then, more than six thousand vessels, large and small, have met tragic ends. . . . Shoals and reefs, uncharted rocks, and sandbars could snare a ship or rip open a hull. Unpredictable winds could capsize a vessel at any moment. . . . The wreckage of ships and the bones of the people who sail them litter the bottoms of the five lakes: Ontario, Erie, Huron, Michigan, and Superior. Ed Butts has gathered stories and lake lore in this [volume]." (Publisher's note) "Ages nine to twelve." (Quill Quire)

Includes bibliographical references

Clark, William

Off the map; the journals of Lewis and Clark. edited by Peter and Connie Roop; illustrations by Tim Tanner. Walker & Co. 1993 40p il hardcover o.p. pa $8.95

Grades: 5 6 7 8   **917**

1. Lewis and Clark Expedition (1804-1806) 2. West (U.S.) -- Exploration
ISBN 0-8027-7546-2

LC 92-18340

A compilation of entries and excerpts from the journals of William Clark and Meriwether Lewis, describing their historic expedition

"The full-color illustrations, mainly in warm earth tones, give the pages an attractive look, but the most vivid pictures come from the journals themselves. . . . This vivid source material would be a welcome part of any classroom study of the subject." Booklist

Hirschfelder, Arlene B.

Photo odyssey: Solomon Carvalho's remarkable Western adventure, 1853-54. Clarion Bks. 2000 118p il $18

Grades: 6 7 8 9   **917**

1. Artists 2. Painters 3. Photographers 4. West (U.S.) -- Exploration
ISBN 0-395-89123-X

LC 99-42201

Describes the life of Carvalho, a Jewish photographer who accompanied John Charles Fremont on his last expedition to the West

"Through the author's historically accurate, vivid descriptions of the various stages of this journey, the reader gains incredible insight into the rigors endured by those who explored the vastness of our country during the 19th century." Book Rep

Includes bibliographical references

917.804   West (U.S.) -- travel

Bodden, Valerie

Through the American West; by Valerie Bodden. Creative Education 2011 48 p. col. ill. (Great Expeditions) (library) $34.25

Grades: 5 6 7 8   **917.804**

1. Lewis and Clark Expedition (1804-1806) 2. West (U.S.) -- Discovery and exploration
ISBN 1608180654; 9781608180653

LC 2010033413

This book by Valerie Bodden is part of the "Great Expeditions" series. It describes an expedition "led by William Clark and Meriwether Lewis to explore the wilderness to the west and look for an all water route to the Pacific Ocean. They were aided by Sacagawea, a Shoshone Indian. The adventures and hardships of the arduous three-year journey include both the achievements and the disappointments encountered along the way". (Children's Literature)

Includes bibliographical references (p. 46-47) and index.

Stille, Darlene R., 1942-

The journals of Lewis and Clark; by Darlene R. Stille. Heinemann Library 2012 48 p. ill. (some col.), col. map (Documenting U.S. History) (library) $32; (paperback) $8.99

Grades: 4 5 6   **917.804**

1. United States -- History -- Sources 2. Lewis and Clark Expedition (1804-1806) 3. Explorers -- West (U.S.) -- Diaries
ISBN 1432967541; 9781432967543; 9781432967635

LC 2011037783

This book on the journals of Meriwether Lewis and William Clark by Darlene R. Stille is part of the "Documenting U.S. History" series. It answers such questions as "What writing materials did Lewis and Clark take on their expedition? What types of plants and animals did Lewis and Clark describe in their journals? [and] where can the journals be seen and read today?" (Publisher's note)

Includes bibliographical references and index

919   Geography of and travel in Australasia, Pacific Ocean islands, Atlantic Ocean islands, Arctic islands, Antarctica and on extraterrestrial worlds

Armstrong, Jennifer

★ **Shipwreck** at the bottom of the world; the extraordinary true story of Shackleton and the Endurance. Crown 1998 134p il maps pbk $12.95

Grades: 7 8 9 10 11 12   **919**

1. Explorers 2. Endurance (Ship) 3. Imperial Trans-Antarctic Expedition (1914-1917) 1914-1917:
ISBN 0-517-80014-4; 9780375810497

LC 97-52063

This book describes the events of the 1914 Shackleton Antarctic expedition when, after being trapped in a frozen sea for nine months, their ship, Endurance, was finally crushed, forcing Shackleton and his men to make a very long and perilous journey across ice and stormy seas to reach inhabited land. (Booklist)

A book that will capture the attention and imagination of any reader." SLJ

Includes bibliographical references and index

919.89   Antarctica - Geography

Bertozzi, Nick

Shackleton; Antarctic odyssey. Nick Bertozzi. First edition First Second 2014 128 p. illustrations, maps $16.99

Grades: 5 6 7 8 9 10   **919.89**

1. Antarctica -- Exploration 2. Graphic novels 3. Explorers -- Great Britain -- Biography 4. Antarctica -- Discovery and exploration -- British
ISBN 1596434511; 9781596434516

This book by Nick Bertozzi describes how "Ernest Shackleton was one of the last great Antarctic explorers, and he led one of the most ambitious Antarctic expeditions ever undertaken. This is his story, and the story of the dozens of men who threw in their lot with him--many of whom nearly died in the unimaginably harsh conditions of the journey." (Publisher's note)

"Bertozzi eschews all narrative explanation, relying solely on dialogue among the crew and the detailed black-and-white panels to tell the story. The snow- and ice-bound journey is the perfect match for Bertozzi's minimal style--vast stretches of white become gasp-worthy, desolate vistas." Booklist

Bodden, Valerie

To the South Pole; by Valerie Bodden. Creative Education 2011 48 p. col. ill. (Great Expeditions) (library) $34.25

Grades: 5 6 7 8   **919.89**

1. South Pole -- Exploration 2. Amundsen, Roald, 1872-1928 3. Explorers -- Norway -- Biography 4. South Pole -- Discovery and exploration
ISBN 1608180697; 9781608180691

LC 2010033552

This book by Valerie Bodden, part of the "Great Expeditions" series, presents "a history of Roald Amundsen's . . . 1911 trip to the South Pole, detailing the challenges encountered, the individuals involved, the discoveries made, and how the expedition left its mark upon the world." (Publisher's note) . Major historical milestones and details about the search for the southernmost tip of the world are related in" addition to "profiles of four of the major explorers". (Children's Literature)

Includes bibliographical references (p. 46-47) and index.

92   Biography

Abbott, Berenice, 1898-1991

★ Sullivan, George. **Berenice** Abbott, photographer; an independent vision. Clarion Books 2006 170p il $20

Grades: 7 8 9 10   **92**

1. Photographers 2. Women photographers
ISBN 978-0-618-44026-9; 0-618-44026-7

LC 2005-30736

A biography of Berenice Abbott, who was a pioneer in the field of professional photography and is particularly acclaimed for her photographs of the streets and buildings of New York City before they were replaced by skyscrapers during a building boom in the 1920s and early 1930s.

"Sullivan brings together an enormous amount of information about Abbott and presents it in a clear, thoughtful manner. . . . Large, clear reproductions of Abbott's photos appear throughout the book." Booklist

Includes bibliographical references

Abu al-Qasim Khalafibn Abbas al-Zahrawi, d. 1013?

Ramen, Fred. **Albucasis** (Abu al-Qasim al-Zahrawi) renowned Muslim surgeon of the Tenth Century. [by] Fred Ramen. Rosen Pub. Group 2006 112p il map (Great Muslim philosophers and scientists of the Middle Ages) lib bdg $33.25

Grades: 5 6 7 8   **92**

1. Arabs 2. Surgeons 3. Physicians 4. Medieval civilization 5. Spain -- History 6. Writers on medicine
ISBN 1-4042-0510-1

LC 2005015786

"Acknowledging the skimpy historical record on his subject, Ramen fleshes out this profile of an influential Spanish physician with sweeping histories of ancient Mediterranean civilizations, early medicine, the rise of Islam, and the rise and fall of Muslim culture in Spain. Readers will come away impressed by the surgeon's contributions to medicine, which ranged from an encyclopedic surgical text to the invention of the forceps to the pioneering use of sutures. The information is buttressed by color photos of architectural remains and manuscript pages." Booklist

Includes glossary and bibliographical references

Adams, Ansel, 1902-1984

West, Krista. **Ansel** Adams. Chelsea House 2011 124p il map (Conservation heroes) lib bdg $35

Grades: 6 7 8 9   92
1. Photographers
ISBN 978-1-60413-946-4; 1-60413-946-3
LC 2010030591
This is a biography of the American photographer and environmentalist, best known for his black-and-white photographs of the American West,

"Captivating, richly informative. . . . The scope of [this book] is comprehensive. . . . [The book is] engaging as [it is] educational and will be ideal for research and reports." SLJ

Includes glossary and bibliographical references

Adams, John, 1735-1826

Adams, John. **John** Adams the writer; a treasury of letters, diaries, and public documents. compiled and edited by Carolyn P. Yoder. 1st ed.; Calkins Creek 2007 144p il $16.95
Grades: 8 9 10 11 12   92
1. Presidents 2. Vice-presidents 3. Presidents -- United States
ISBN 978-1-59078-247-7; 1-59078-247-X
LC 2006101748
"Yoder's succinct introductions provide ample context for each selection, and the diverse writings give a sense of the man's intelligence, resolve, and dedication to the ideals that created America. . . . Numerous black-and-white illustrations and a list of historic sites round out the title. . . . Those who seek an easily digestible overview of the second president's life and times will find this book both informative and appealing." SLJ

Includes bibliographical references

Addams, Jane, 1860-1935

★ Caravantes, Peggy. **Waging** peace; the story of Jane Addams. [by] Peggy Caravantes. rev ed; Morgan Reynolds Publishing 2004 144p il lib bdg $23.95
Grades: 5 6 7 8   92
1. Authors 2. Philanthropists 3. Essayists 4. Pacifists 5. Social welfare leaders 6. Nobel laureates for peace
ISBN 1-93179-840-0
LC 2004-8357
This is a "biography of the social reformer, humanitarian, and winner of the 1931 Nobel Peace Prize. . . . Archival black-and-white photos . . . grace the book. This is a solid addition to women's history collections." SLJ

Includes bibliographical references

Fradin, Judith Bloom. **Jane** Addams; champion of democracy. by Judith Bloom Fradin and Dennis Brindell Fradin. Clarion Books 2006 216p il $21
Grades: 7 8 9 10   92
1. Authors 2. Philanthropists 3. Hull House (Chicago, Ill.) 4. Essayists 5. Pacifists 6. Social welfare leaders 7. Nobel laureates for peace 8. Chicago (Ill.) -- Social conditions
ISBN 0-618-50436-1
A biography of the social activist, pacifist, author, founder of Hull House in Chicago, and winner of the Nobel Peace Prize.

"A fascinating and rich life is related in strong, unfussy prose." Booklist

Includes bibliographical references

Aguirre, Hank, 1932-1994

Copley, Bob. The **tall** Mexican: the life of Hank Aguirre, all-star pitcher, businessman, humanitarian; with a foreword by Jose F. Niño. Piñata Bks. 1998 159p il hardcover o.p. pa $9.95
Grades: 7 8 9 10   92
1. Businesspeople 2. Baseball players 3. Automobile executives 4. Baseball -- Biography
ISBN 1-55885-294-8
LC 98-3185
A biography of the All-Star major-league pitcher whose commitment to his Hispanic heritage led him to found Mexican Industries to help provide economic opportunities to the inner-city Detroit community

"Myriad reminiscences from friends, family, employees, colleagues, and fellow athletes provide readers with the sense of true admiration felt for the subject." SLJ

Alcott, Louisa May, 1832-1888

Meigs, Cornelia Lynde. **Invincible** Louisa; the story of the author of Little Women. with a new introduction by the author. Little, Brown 1995 210p il pa $9.00
                                                   92
1. Authors 2. Novelists 3. Women authors 4. Authors, American 5. Young adult authors
ISBN 9780316565943
First published 1933
Awarded the Newbery Medal, 1934
This biography "is to be praised still for its straightforward account of a life of struggle and success. . . . If you want to know about Louisa's external life, and trace there the events which gave rise to the internal urges and passions that produced 'Little Women,' this book will serve well." N Y Times Book Rev

Silverthorne, Elizabeth. **Louisa** May Alcott; foreword by Kyle Zimmer. 2nd ed; Chelsea House 2011 117p il (Who wrote that?) lib bdg $35
Grades: 6 7 8 9   92
1. Authors 2. Novelists 3. Women authors 4. Authors, American 5. Young adult authors
ISBN 978-1-60413-760-6; 1-60413-760-6
First published 2002
"Silverthorne covers Alcott's life from her birth in 1832 to her death in 1888, with information about her writing life and major titles. The author creates a clear picture of the period and of a determined, diligent, and loyal woman who was shocked at the popularity of her most famous work." SLJ [review of 2002 edition]

Includes bibliographical references

Alexander, the Great, 356-323 B.C.

★ Adams, Simon. **Alexander**; the boy soldier who conquered the world. National Geographic 2005 64p il map (World history biographies) $17.95; lib bdg $27.90

Grades: 4 5 6 7　　　　　　　　　　**92**
1. Ancient civilization 2. Kings
ISBN 0-7922-3660-2; 0-7922-3661-0 lib bdg
This describes the life and times of Alexander the Great.
This is a "handsomely designed [book]. . . . illustrated
with maps and many color photographs of art and sculpture
that give substance to [the era]. . . . Adams does not down-
play Alexander's brutality or all-consuming ambition and
includes examples of both." SLJ
Includes bibliographical references

Behnke, Alison. The **conquests** of Alexander
the Great; by Alison Behnke. Twenty-First Century
Books 2008 159p il map (Pivotal moments in history) lib bdg $38.60
Grades: 6 7 8 9　　　　　　　　　　**92**
1. Kings and rulers 2. Kings 3. Greece -- History
-- 323-1453
ISBN 978-0-8225-5920-7 lib bdg; 0-8225-5920-X
lib bdg
　　　　　　　　　　　　　　　LC 2006-11824
Presents a profile of the young military leader and king
of ancient Macedonia, who conquered most of the known
world of his era, before his untimely death at the age of
thirty-three.
This is a "very thorough account. . . . Behnke gives
enough background information about Greece and the world
in which Alexander was raised to bring him to life for readers. . . . Helpful maps of the route through the Middle East
and Asia and interesting sidebars and illustrations of Alexander and his contemporaries appear throughout." SLJ
Includes bibliographical references

Alhazen, 965-1039
Steffens, Bradley. **Ibn** al-Haytham; first scientist. Morgan Reynolds Pub. 2007 128p il (Profiles
in science) lib bdg $27.95
Grades: 7 8 9 10　　　　　　　　　**92**
1. Physicists 2. Scientists 3. Mathematicians
ISBN 978-1-59935-024-0; 1-59935-024-6
　　　　　　　　　　　　　　　LC 2006-23970
The author "has organized what is known of his subject's
life and work into a coherent narrative. . . . Like the history
of mathematics, the history of science is incomplete without
an acknowledgment of early scholars in the Middle East.
This clearly written introduction to al-Haytham, his society,
and his contributions does that." Booklist
Includes bibliographical references

Ali, Muhammad, 1942-
Micklos, John. **Muhammad** Ali; I am the great-
est. [by] John Micklos, Jr. Enslow Publishers 2010
160p il (American rebels) lib bdg $34.60
Grades: 6 7 8 9 10　　　　　　　　**92**
1. African American athletes 2. Boxers (Persons) 3.
Boxing -- Biography
ISBN 978-0-7660-3381-8; 0-7660-3381-3
　　　　　　　　　　　　　　　LC 2009-17593
"This biography of the three-time heavyweight world
champion, Vietnam War protester, and Nobel Peace Prize
nominee includes useful context-setting background; Mick-

los's play-by-play descriptions of Ali's bouts provide just
enough detail for boxing fans." Horn Book Guide
Includes bibliographical references

Myers, Walter Dean, 1937-2014 The **greatest**:
Muhammad Ali. Scholastic 2001 172p il hardcover
o.p. pa $4.99
Grades: 7 8 9 10　　　　　　　　　**92**
1. African American athletes 2. Boxers (Persons) 3.
Boxing -- Biography
ISBN 0-590-54342-3; 0-590-54343-1 pa
This is a biography of the boxer. Bibliography. Index.
"Middle school." (Horn Book)
In this biography Myers combines "reportage of Ali's
major fights (especially against Sonny Liston, Joe Frazier,
and George Foreman) with his own reflections about the
sport's destructiveness and about Ali's unpopular views."
Horn Book

★ Smith, Charles R., 1969- **Twelve** rounds to
glory: the story of Muhammad Ali; illustrated by
Bryan Collier. Candlewick Press 2007 80p il $19.99
Grades: 5 6 7 8　　　　　　　　　**92**
1. African American athletes 2. Boxers (Persons) 3.
Boxing -- Biography
ISBN 978-0-7636-1692-2; 0-7636-1692-3
　　　　　　　　　　　　　　　LC 2007-25998
"Rap-style cadences perfectly capture the drama that has
always surrounded the boxer's life. . . . Collier's compelling
watercolor collages with their brown overtones beautifully
portray Ali's determination and strength." SLJ

Ali, Rubina
Ali, Rubina. **Slumgirl** dreaming; Rubina's jour-
ney to the stars. [by] Rubina Ali in collaboration with
Anne Berthod and Divya Dugar. Delacorte Press
2009 187p il pa $9.99
Grades: 5 6 7 8　　　　　　　　　**92**
1. Actors 2. Children 3. India 4. Slumdog millionaire
(Motion picture)
ISBN 978-0-385-73908-5 pa; 0-385-73908-7 pa
　　　　　　　　　　　　　　　LC 2009029305
The young actress describes her life growing up in the
slums of Mumbai, her experiences on the set of the film
"Slumdog Millionaire," and how her life has changed as a
result of her role in the film
"The writing here has a journalistic feel. It is not poetic or especially nuanced. But in a sea of cookie-cutter
biography series, this book stands out. It has heart, and is
aimed at an age group that will identify with Ali in essential
ways." SLJ

Allende, Isabel
Axelrod-Contrada, Joan. **Isabel** Allende. Marshall Cavendish Benchmark 2010 159p il (Today's
writers and their works) $42.79
Grades: 8 9 10 11 12　　　　　　　**92**
1. Authors 2. Novelists 3. Dramatists 4. Journalists
5. Women authors 6. Authors, Chilean 7. Children's
authors
ISBN 978-0-7614-4116-8; 0-7614-4116-6

This biography of Isabel Allende places the author in the context of her times and discusses her work.

This book provides "excellent information for reports. . . . [The text is] organized well, lending [itself] to be read in [its] entirety or used as needed for research, and [includes] full-color photos and illustrations." SLJ

Includes bibliographical references

Alonso, Alicia

★ Bernier-Grand, Carmen T. **Alicia** Alonso; prima ballerina. illustrated by Raúl Colón. Marshall Cavendish Children's 2011 64p il $19.99

Grades: 4 5 6 7   **92**

1. Cubans 2. Ballet dancers 3. Choreographers 4. Dance directors

ISBN 978-0-7614-5562-2; 0-7614-5562-0

LC 2010018269

"An informative, beautifully illustrated introduction to the world-renowned dancer. Alonso's focused life and illustrious career are made even more remarkable by the fact that she lost her peripheral vision at age 19 and had to learn to visualize both the stage set and the dance itself in order to execute spins and lifts, and to choreograph ballets. Each one is presented as a titled one-page piece in abbreviated poetic prose; many face full-page textured paintings rendered in Colón's distinctive mix of watercolor, colored, and lithograph pencils." SLJ

Includes bibliographical references

Alvarez, Julia, 1950-

Aykroyd, Clarissa. **Julia** Alvarez; novelist and poet. by Clarissa Aykroyd. Lucent Books 2008 104p il (The twentieth century's most influential Hispanics) $32.45

Grades: 7 8 9 10   **92**

1. Poets 2. Authors 3. Novelists 4. Women authors 5. Hispanic American women 6. Essayists 7. Poets, American 8. College teachers 9. Children's authors

ISBN 978-1-4205-0022-6; 1-4205-0022-8

LC 2007025974

"This introduction to author Alvarez gives a comprehensive look at the Dominican American writer's life and literary career. The lively writing . . . is supported by numerous quotes from Alvarez and details . . . that will pique kids' interest." Booklist

Includes bibliographical references

Andersen, Hans Christian, 1805-1875

★ Varmer, Hjordis. **Hans** Christian Andersen; his fairy tale life. illustrated by Lilian Brogger; translated by Tiina Nunnally. Groundwood Books 2005 111p il $19.95

Grades: 5 6 7 8   **92**

1. Authors 2. Novelists 3. Dramatists 4. Authors, Danish 5. Children's authors 6. Short story writers

ISBN 0-88899-690-X

"Most of this book describes Andersen's childhood and belated schooling, showing his poverty and the grief he experienced over the death of his beloved father, as well as several horrifying events such as being forced by a teacher to witness the beheading of three young people. . . . The biography is divided into 11 chapters, set up as if they were stories.

. . . The writing flows smoothly, with many details provided to help students picture the places and events. Brøgger's haunting, mixed-media illustrations add to the somber and at times surreal feeling of the text." SLJ

Anderson, Laurie Halse, 1961-

Glenn, Wendy J. **Laurie** Halse Anderson; speaking in tongues. Scarecrow Press 2010 169p (Scarecrow studies in young adult literature) $40

Grades: 8 9 10 11 12   **92**

1. Authors 2. Novelists 3. Women authors 4. Authors, American 5. Young adult authors

ISBN 978-0-8108-7281-3

LC 2009-30545

"This book is a comprehensive look at the life, work, and thoughts of Laurie Halse Anderson. . . . Any teen with a research paper on Laurie Halse Anderson who is lucky enough to have access to this title will walk away with a high mark." Voice Youth Advocates

Includes bibliographical references

Anderson, Marian, 1897-1993

★ Freedman, Russell. The **voice** that challenged a nation; Marian Anderson and the struggle for equal rights. Clarion Books 2004 114p il $18

Grades: 5 6 7 8   **92**

1. African American singers 2. Opera singers 3. African Americans -- Civil rights 4. African American women -- Biography

ISBN 0-618-15976-2

LC 2003-19558

A Newbery Medal honor book, 2005

In the mid-1930s, Marian Anderson was a famed vocalist who had been applauded by European royalty and welcomed at the White House. But, because of her race, she was denied the right to sing at Constitution Hall in Washington, D.C. This is the story of her resulting involvement in the civil rights movement of the time.

"In his signature prose, plain yet eloquent, Freedman tells Anderson's triumphant story, with numerous black-and-white photos and prints that convey her personal struggle, professional artistry, and landmark civil rights role." Booklist

Includes bibliographical references

Jones, Victoria Garrett. **Marian** Anderson; a voice uplifted. [by] Victoria Garrett Jones. Sterling Pub. 2007 124p il (Sterling biographies) $12.95

Grades: 6 7 8 9   **92**

1. African American singers 2. Opera singers 3. African American women -- Biography

ISBN 978-1-4027-4239-2; 1-4027-4239-8

LC 2007019268

"Filled with archival photographs and quotes, this stirring biography of Anderson gives a concise, yet thorough introduction to the famous contralto's life." Booklist

"The authors present their subjects from early childhood and follow them chronologically as their life achievements unfold. Each chapter begins with an appropriate quote that sets the stage for the content within. Informational sidebars help flesh out the story by providing a picture of the larger historical context such as a description of the northern migration of blacks after the Civil War or musicians' lives during the Great Depression. . . . They highlight the inspiring lives of important African Americans who, through their courage and conviction, fought against injustice and made significant contributions to society." SLJ

Includes bibligraphical references

Andrews, Roy Chapman, 1884-1960

★ Bausum, Ann. **Dragon** bones and dinosaur eggs: a photobiography of Roy Chapman Andrews. National Geographic Soc. 2000 64p il map $17.95

Grades: 5 6 7 8   92

1. Fossils 2. Dinosaurs 3. Explorers 4. Zoologists 5. Naturalists 6. Travel writers 7. Writers on nature 8. Writers on science 9. Museum administrators

ISBN 0-7922-7123-8

LC 99-38363

A biography of the great explorer-adventurer, who discovered huge finds of dinosaur bones in Mongolia, pioneered modern paleontology field research, and became the director of the American Museum of Natural History

"Bausum's account reads smoothly, and a layout dense with captioned sepia photographs and quotes from Andrews provides plenty of oases for readers as they follow him through the desert." Bull Cent Child Books

Includes bibliographical references

Anthony, Susan B., 1820-1906

Colman, Penny. **Elizabeth** Cady Stanton and Susan B. Anthony; a friendship that changed the world. Henry Holt and Company 2011 256p il $18.99

Grades: 7 8 9 10   92

1. Feminism 2. Suffragists 3. Women -- Suffrage 4. Biography, Individual

ISBN 978-0-8050-8293-7; 0-8050-8293-X

LC 2010-39762

"Elizabeth Cady Stanton, a married mother of four boys at the time they met, and Susan B. Anthony, an unmarried schoolteacher, formed a friendship that lasted until Elizabeth's death more than 50 years later. Their tireless work, including advocacy, speeches, organizing and writing, placed them at the center of tumultuous events in the middle of the 19th century. . . . This [is a] lively, very readable narrative. . . . This thoughtful portrayal to two complex women is . . . enhanced by comprehensive backmatter, making this an invaluable addition to the literature of suffrage." Kirkus

Includes bibliographical references

Todd, Anne M. **Susan** B. Anthony; activist. Chelsea House Publishers 2009 128p bibl il por (Women of achievement) $30

Grades: 6 7 8 9   92

1. Feminism 2. Suffragists 3. Abolitionists

ISBN 978-1-60413-087-4; 1-60413-087-3

LC 2008034641

A biography of the women's rights activist.

The book is "well written; sidebars supplement the [narrative] with interesting facts." Horn Book Guide

Includes bibliographical references

Appleseed, Johnny, 1774-1845

Worth, Richard. **Johnny** Appleseed; select good seeds and plant them in good ground. Enslow Publishers 2010 128p il map (Americans: the spirit of a nation) $23.95

Grades: 4 5 6 7   92

1. Apples 2. Frontier and pioneer life 3. Pioneers 4. Fruit growers

ISBN 978-0-7660-3352-8; 0-7660-3352-X

LC 2008048701

"This nicely illustrated and sourced [biography] . . . includes full-page sidebars." Booklist

"From heroes and heroines to bandits and beloved American icons, these balanced titles consistently sort fact from fiction and confirm each figure's place in history. First chapters successfully introduce the subjects and draw readers in by describing dynamic events. Archival photographs, maps, primary sources, and sidebars combine with dry but informative texts to complete these well-documented biographies." Horn Book

Includes glossary and bibliographical references

Archimedes, ca. 287-212 B.C.

Hightower, Paul. The **greatest** mathematician; Archimedes and his eureka! moment. Enslow Publishers 2010 128p il (Great minds of ancient science and math) lib bdg $31.93

Grades: 5 6 7 8   92

1. Mathematicians 2. Greece -- History 3. Writers on science

ISBN 978-0-7660-3408-2 lib bdg; 0-7660-3408-9 lib bdg

LC 2008051818

This biography is a "solid [choice], as . . . [it provides] a good overview of the cultural and political landscape of the times, as well as pictures." SLJ

Includes glossary and bibliographical references

Aristotle, 384-322 B.C.

Gow, Mary. The **great** thinker: Aristotle and the foundations of science. Enslow Publishers 2010 128p il (Great minds of ancient science and math) lib bdg $31.93

Grades: 6 7 8 9   92

1. Philosophy 2. Scientists 3. Philosophers 4. Writers on science

ISBN 978-0-7660-3121-0; 0-7660-3121-7

LC 2009023813

"Presents a biography of the fourth-century B.C.E. Greek philosopher and scientist Aristotle, whose writings on logic, metaphysics, ethics, politics, and literary criticism influenced Western thought for hundreds of years. . . . [This] colorful, attractive book includes simple, straightforward text with nice illustrations and appendixes of suggested activities, a supplemental chronology, chapter notes, and glossary." Voice Youth Advocates

Includes glossary and bibliographical references

Katz Cooper, Sharon. **Aristotle**; philosopher, teacher, and scientist. Compass Point Books 2006 112p il (Signature lives) $31.93

Grades: 6 7 8 9   **92**

1. Philosophers 2. Writers on science

ISBN 978-0-7565-1873-8; 0-7565-1873-3

LC 2006005403

Includes glossary and bibliographical references

Armstrong, John Barclay, 1850-1913

Alter, Judy. **John** Barclay Armstrong; Texas Ranger. by Judy Alter. Bright Sky Press 2007 59p il $14.95

Grades: 4 5 6 7   **92**

1. Sheriffs 2. Texas Rangers 3. West (U.S.) -- History

ISBN 978-1-931721-86-8

"Born in 1850 and raised in Tennessee, Armstrong went west to seek his fortune. At 25, he joined the Texas Rangers and soon came to embody the legendary qualities of these remarkable lawmen. He is an interesting character, and the author aptly tells his tale. The archival black-and-white photos add authenticity and help bring the man to life." SLJ

Armstrong, Louis, 1900-1971

★ Orr, Tamra. **Louis** Armstrong; by Tamra Orr. Mitchell Lane Publishers 2012 47 p. ill. (chiefly col.) (library) $29.95

Grades: 6 7 8 9   **92**

1. Jazz musicians -- United States -- Biography

ISBN 1612282644; 9781612282640

LC 2012008631

This book by Tamra Orr is part of the American Jazz series and looks at musician Louis Armstrong. Within each entry, "information about the subjects' childhoods and preparation for their musical careers is included, as are the positive and negative aspects of their adult lives. Their contributions to the world of jazz are . . . explored." (School Library Journal)

Includes bibliographical references (pages 44-45) and index.

Partridge, Kenneth. **Louis** Armstrong; musician. Chelsea House 2011 110p il (Black Americans of achievement) lib bdg $35

Grades: 6 7 8 9   **92**

1. Singers 2. Jazz musicians 3. African American musicians 4. Band leaders 5. Trumpet players

ISBN 978-1-60413-833-7; 1-60413-833-5

This "is a sweet, touching biography that looks at the extraordinary life of a musical genius. The writing is clear and engaging, with a light, humorous touch. . . . Readers are treated to an overview of a unique personality." SLJ

Includes bibliographical references

Arnold, Benedict, 1741-1801

Fritz, Jean. **Traitor** : the case of Benedict Arnold. Putnam 1981 191p il hardcover o.p. pa $5.99

Grades: 5 6 7 8   **92**

1. Spies 2. Generals 3. Army officers 4. United States -- History -- 1775-1783, Revolution

ISBN 0-399-20834-8; 0-698-11553-8 pa

LC 81-10584

"The writing is smooth, the material carefully organized and used in the best of biographical style—that is, Arnold

is presented accurately and the reader is left to judge the strength and weaknesses of his character rather than being told by the author." Bull Cent Child Books

Includes bibliographical references

★ Murphy, Jim. The **real** Benedict Arnold. Clarion Books 2007 264p il map $20

Grades: 7 8 9 10   **92**

1. Spies 2. Generals 3. Army officers 4. United States -- History -- 1775-1783, Revolution

ISBN 978-0-395-77609-4; 0-395-77609-0

LC 2007-5700

"Using Arnold's surviving military journals and political documents, Murphy carefully contrasts popular myth with historical fact. . . . As far as possible, he meticulously traces Arnold's life, revealing a complex man who was actually as much admired as he was loathed." Booklist

Includes bibliographical references

★ Sheinkin, Steve. The **notorious** Benedict Arnold; a true story of adventure, heroism, & treachery. Steve Sheinkin. Roaring Brook Press 2010 337p. ill. $19.99

Grades: 7 8 9 10   **92**

1. Spies 2. Generals 3. American Loyalists 4. Army officers 5. United States -- Continental Army 6. Biography, Individual 7. United States -- History -- 1775-1783, Revolution 8. United States -- History -- Revolution, 1775-1783

ISBN 1-59643-486-4; 978-1-59643-486-8

LC 201034797

Boston Globe-Horn Book Awards: Nonfiction (2012)

YALSA Award for Excellence in Nonfiction for Young Adults (2012)

This is a biography of the Continental Army officer who won battles for the Americans during the Revolutionary War but felt ill-used and unappreciated by the Continental Congress. He obtained command of the fort at West Point, New York, and plotted to surrender it to the British. After the plot was exposed in September 1780, he was commissioned into the British Army. Bibliography. Index. "Middle school, high school." (Horn Book)

"Sheinkin sees Arnold as America's 'original action hero' and succeeds in writing a brilliant, fast-paced biography that reads like an adventure novel. . . . The author's obvious mastery of his material, lively prose and abundant use of eyewitness accounts make this one of the most exciting biographies young readers will find." Kirkus

Includes bibliographical references

Asimov, Isaac, 1920-1992

Hoppa, Jocelyn. **Isaac** Asimov; science fiction trailblazer. [by] Jocelyn Hoppa. Enslow Publishers 2009 104p il (Authors teens love) lib bdg $31.93

Grades: 6 7 8 9   **92**

1. Authors 2. Novelists 3. Biochemists 4. Authors, American 5. Children's authors 6. Writers on science 7. Short story writers 8. Young adult authors 9. Science fiction writers

ISBN 978-0-7660-2961-3; 0-7660-2961-1

LC 2008-12299

"A biography of Russian-American science-fiction author Isaac Asimov." Publisher's note

"This series focuses on writers who are popular with teen readers, and although several authors contribute, the entries are extremely consistent in format. Each book has a comparable number of pages and features a time line, suggestions for further reading, and words to know. . . . Each volume provides young readers with information on its subject in a highly readable format. They would be a good choice for middle school and junior high school libraries." VOYA

Includes bibliographical references

Attila, King of the Huns, d. 453

★ Price, Sean. **Attila** the Hun; leader of the barbarian hordes. [by] Sean Stewart Price. Franklin Watts 2009 128p il (A wicked history) $30; pa $5.95

Grades: 6 7 8 9   92

1. Huns 2. Kings and rulers 3. Tribal leaders
ISBN 978-0-531-21801-3; 0-531-21801-5; 978-0-531-20737-6 pa; 0-531-20737-4 pa

LC 2008040520

"In fascinating detail, the book not only introduces Attila, but gives the backstory on what made the rise of the Huns possible. The exciting yet concise writing brings readers close to the battlefield, but the fighting and intrigue are neatly set against the sweep of history." Booklist

Includes bibliographical references

Audubon, John James, 1785-1851

Plain, Nancy. **This** strange wilderness; the life and art of John James Audubon. Nancy Plain. University of Nebraska Press 2015 136 p. illustrations (chiefly color) (pbk. : alk. paper) $19.95

Grades: 4 5 6 7 8   92

1. Bird watching 2. Naturalists -- Biography 3. Naturalists -- United States -- Biography 4. Ornithologists -- United States -- Biography
ISBN 0803248849; 9780803248847; 9780803284012; 9780803284029; 9780803284036

LC 2014020552

This book, by Nancy Plain, focuses on the founder of modern ornithology John James Audubon. "His masterpiece, 'The Birds of America' depicts almost five hundred North American bird species, each image - lifelike and life size - rendered in vibrant color. . . . Plain brings together the amazing story of this American icon's career and the beautiful images that are his legacy." (Publisher's note)

"In this insightful biography, Plain demonstrates how naturalist and artist John James Audubon's groundbreaking The Birds of America, published in England in 1827, rocked the art and science worlds through its depictions of birds in naturalistic poses and in their own habitats...This narrative of the life of a dedicated and hard-working figure is the story of an amazing individual and a glimpse into the natural history of the early United States. An excellent addition to science and biography collections." SLJ

Includes bibliographical references and index
Life and art of John James Audubon

Sherman, Pat. **John** James Audubon. Chelsea House 2010 152p il map (Conservation heroes) lib bdg $35

Grades: 6 7 8 9 10   92

1. Artists 2. Painters 3. Naturalists 4. Ornithologists 5. Writers on science 6. Birds -- United States 7. Artists -- United States
ISBN 978-1-60413-953-2; 1-60413-953-6

LC 2010026480

A biography of the French American ornithologist and artist famous for his paintings and study of American birds.

"Captivating, richly informative. . . . The scope of [this book] is comprehensive. . . . [The book is] engaging as [it is] educational and will be ideal for research and reports." SLJ

Includes glossary and bibliographical references

Aung San Suu Kyi

O'Keefe, Sherry. **Champion** of freedom; Aung San Suu Kyi. Sherry O'Keefe. Morgan Reynolds Pub. 2011 160 p. ill. (some col.), col. maps $28.95

Grades: 7 8 9 10 11 12   92

1. Myanmar 2. Political activists 3. Democracy -- Burma 4. Burma -- Politics and government -- 1988- 5. Women Nobel Prize winners -- Burma -- Biography 6. Women political activists -- Burma -- Biography 7. Women political prisoners -- Burma -- Biography
ISBN 1599351684; 9781599351681; 9781599353142

LC 2011035740

Author Sherry O'Keefe tells the story of politician Aung San Suu Kyi. "Knowing that the military regime will not allow her to return if she leaves, the Nobel Peace Prize laureate has remained in Burma, enduring extreme isolation, the threat of death, and personal pain and sacrifice, including the chance to see her dying husband one last time. . . . [Suu Kyi] remains as determined as ever to see Burma emerge from its isolation and join the family of democratic nations in the world." (Publisher's note)

Includes bibliographical references and index.

Rose, Simon. **Aung** San Suu Kyi. 2011 24p il por (Remarkable people) $27.13; pa $12.95

Grades: 4 5 6 7   92

1. Political prisoners 2. Women political activists 3. Dissenters 4. Political leaders 5. Nonfiction writers 6. Human rights activists 7. Nobel laureates for peace 8. Myanmar -- Politics and government
ISBN 978-1-61690-833-1; 1-61690-833-5; 978-1-61690-834-8 pa; 1-61690-834-3 pa

LC 2011011584

This looks at Aung San Suu Kyi's "life, accomplishments, and challenges while including a page of quotes, an annotated list of contemporaries and influences, starter suggestions for writing a paper, and a time line and glossary. [The book] looks into the Nobel Peace Prize–winning Myanmar activist, whose struggle for democracy has landed her under house arrest multiple times." Booklist

Austen, Jane, 1775-1817

Locke, Juliane Poirier. **England's** Jane; the story of Jane Austen. [by] Juliane Locke. Morgan Reynolds Pub. 2006 144p il lib bdg $26.95

Grades: 7 8 9 10   **92**

1. Authors 2. Novelists 3. Women authors 4. Authors, English

ISBN 978-1-931798-82-2 lib bdg; 1-931798-82-6 (lib. bdg.)

LC 2005026279

"Drawing on letters, biographical works, archival pictures, and Austens novels, Locke offers a readable biography for students who cant manage a larger work. The language is uncomplicated and the topics are aimed at helping readers better understand Pride and Prejudice, Emma, and Austen's other writings." SLJ

Includes bibliographical references

★ Reef, Catherine. **Jane** Austen; a life revealed. Clarion Books 2011 192p il $18.99

Grades: 6 7 8 9 10   **92**

1. Authors 2. Novelists 3. Women authors 4. Novelists, English 5. Biography, Individual

ISBN 0-547-37021-0; 978-0-547-37021-7

LC 2011008146

In this biography of the English novelist, Reef "combines firsthand accounts of Austen written by relatives and friends, historical information about Britain in the late 1700s, the basic facts of Austen's life, . . . and Austen's own novels and surviving letters. . . . A family tree, notes, a selected bibliography, a list of Austen's work, and an index are appended. . . . Middle school, high school." (Horn Book)

Reef "combines firsthand accounts of Austen written by relatives and friends, historical information about Britain in the late 1700s, the basic facts of Austen's life that are readily known, and Austen's own novels and surviving letters, presented in a chronological format. . . . Reef's account also focuses on Austen's large family and many friends, highlighting the connections between Austen's novels and her life. . . . For devout Janeites it's fascinating to see all this information combined, and for others it's a worthwhile introduction to a masterful writer's life." Horn Book

Includes bibliographical references

Babbage, Charles, 1791-1871

Collier, Bruce. **Charles** Babbage and the engines of perfection; [by] Bruce Collier and James MacLachlan. Oxford Univ. Press 1998 123p il (Oxford portraits in science) $28

Grades: 7 8 9 10   **92**

1. Mathematicians 2. Writers on science 3. Computers -- History

ISBN 0-19-508997-9

LC 98-17054

"This book tells the story of the mathematician's conception of and work on the first computers. Collier and MacLachlan discuss their subject's upbringing, education, and marriage as backdrops to his work. {Chronology. Bibliography. Index.} Grade seven and up." (SLJ)

"This is a fascinating portrait of Charles Babbage. . . . Generous b&w illustrations enliven the work." Book Rep

Includes bibliographical references

Baker, Ella, 1903-1986

Bohannon, Lisa Frederiksen. **Freedom** cannot rest; Ella Baker and the civil rights movement. [by]

Lisa Frederiksen Bohannon. 1st ed; Morgan Reynolds Pub. 2005 176p il map (Portraits of Black Americans) lib bdg $26.95

Grades: 7 8 9 10   **92**

1. Essayists 2. Political leaders 3. Civil rights activists 4. African Americans -- Civil rights

ISBN 978-1-931798-71-6; 1-931798-71-0

LC 2005007156

"Baker was a major player in the Civil Rights movement of the 1960s. She was the principal organizer of SNCC, the Student Nonviolent Coordinating Committee. . . . Bohannon . . . makes good use of vintage photographs, artwork, and text boxes that further explain historical events. . . . Her biography might be a good place to start to get a good overview of Baker's life and the times in which she lived." SLJ

Includes bibliographical references

Barakat, Ibtisam

★ Barakat, Ibtisam. **Tasting** the sky; a Palestinian childhood. Farrar, Straus & Giroux 2007 176p $16

Grades: 6 7 8 9 10   **92**

1. Poets 2. Authors 3. Palestinian Arabs 4. Israel-Arab conflicts 5. Memoirists 6. College teachers 7. Young adult authors

ISBN 0-374-35733-1; 978-0-374-35733-7

LC 2006-41265

"In 1981 the author, then in high school, boarded a bus bound for Ramallah. The bus was detained by Israeli soldiers at a checkpoint on the West Bank, and she was taken to a detention center before being released. The episode triggers sometimes heart-wrenching memories of herself as a young child, at the start of the 1967 Six Days' War, as Israeli soldiers conducted raids, their planes bombed her home, and she fled with her family across the border to Jordan. . . . What makes the memoir so compelling is the immediacy of the child's viewpoint, which depicts both conflict and daily life without exploitation or sentimentality." Booklist

Barnum, P. T. (Phineas Taylor), 1810-1891

★ Fleming, Candace. The **great** and only Barnum; the tremendous, stupendous life of showman P.T. Barnum. illustrated by Ray Fenwick. Schwartz & Wade Books 2009 151p il $18.99; lib bdg $21.99

Grades: 5 6 7 8   **92**

1. Circus 2. Circus executives

ISBN 978-0-375-84197-2; 0-375-84197-0; 978-0-375-94597-7 lib bdg; 0-375-94597-0 lib bdg

LC 2008-45847

"In this sweeping yet cohesive biography, Fleming so finely tunes Barnum's legendary ballyhoo that you can practically hear the hucksterism and smell the sawdust. . . . The material is inherently juicy, but credit Fleming's vivacious prose, bountiful period illustrations, and copious source notes for fashioning a full picture on one of the forebearers of modern celebrity." Booklist

Includes bibliographical references

Barton, Clara, 1821-1912

Hamen, Susan E. **Clara** Barton; Civil War hero & American Red Cross founder. ABDO Pub. 2010 112p il map (Military heroes) lib bdg $22.95

Grades: 7 8 9   92

1. Nurses 2. American Red Cross 3. Red Cross officials 4. Social welfare leaders

ISBN 978-1-60453-960-8; 1-60453-960-7

LC 2009-32363

"The rush of literary adrenalin will hook readers immediately and keep them enthralled until the end. . . . Given the dynamic topic [and] . . . appealing layout . . . [this is] likely to attract reluctant readers. In addition, sources are plentiful and well documented." SLJ

Includes glossary and bibliographical references

Krensky, Stephen. **Clara** Barton. DK Pub. 2011 128p il (DK biography) $14.99; pa $5.99

Grades: 5 6 7 8   92

1. Nurses 2. American Red Cross 3. Red Cross officials 4. Social welfare leaders

ISBN 978-0-7566-7279-9; 0-7566-7279-1; 978-0-7566-7278-2 pa; 0-7566-7278-3 pa

Describes the life and accomplishments of Clara Barton, a teacher who organized efforts to bring nursing care to wounded soldiers during the Civil War and who went on to become the founder of the American Red Cross.

"Barton is placed in historical context, and key concepts, such as the causes of the Civil War, the struggle for women's suffrage, and the importance of the Geneva Convention, are explained. Compact in form, the text is complemented by full-color and archival photographs and reproductions on every spread. . . . An excellent resource for reports that will also appeal to fans of biography." SLJ

Includes bibliographical references

Beck, Glenn

Novak, Amy. **Glenn** Beck; by Amy Novak. Lucent Books 2011 112 p. col. ill. (hbk.) $33.95; (hbk.) $33.95

Grades: 6 7 8 9   92

1. Radio broadcasting 2. Conservatism -- United States 3. Conservatives -- United States -- Biography 4. Radio personalities -- United States -- Biography 5. Television personalities -- United States -- Biography

ISBN 1420506056; 9781420506051

LC 2011005084

This book offers a biography of Conservative radio and television personality Glenn Beck by author Amy Novak. It is part of the "People in the News" series, which "profiles the lives and careers of some of today's most prominent newsmakers. Whether covering contributions and achievements or notorious deeds, books in this series examine why these well-known individuals garnered public attention." (Publisher's note)

Includes bibliographical references (p. 103-105) and index

Beethoven, Ludwig van, 1770-1827

Bauer, Helen. **Beethoven** for kids; his life and music with 21 activities. Chicago Review Press 2011 129p il pa $16.95

Grades: 4 5 6 7   92

1. Composers 2. Composers, Austrian

ISBN 1-56976-711-4; 978-1-56976-711-5

LC 2011018131

"This introduction to the towering classical composer sets the story of his life and work in the context of the revolutionary events of early-19th-century Europe. . . . The author's own extensive musical experience contributes to the breadth of this title. Sidebars and historical prints add further information about musical forms and instruments, historical events and people mentioned. . . . This will be particularly useful for parents and classroom teachers hoping to make the study of great music more interesting." Kirkus

Includes bibliographical references

Martin, Russell. The **mysteries** of Beethoven's hair; [by Russell Martin and Lydia Nibley] Charlesbridge 2009 120p il lib bdg $15.95

Grades: 5 6 7 8   92

1. Composers

ISBN 978-1-57091-714-1 lib bdg; 1-57091-714-0 lib bdg

LC 2008-07257

"Based on Martin's adult book Beethoven's Hair: An Extraordinary Historical Odyssey and Scientific Mystery Solved (Broadway, 2000), this reworking for a young audience presents an intriguing interdisciplinary story. Martin and Nibley trace the labyrinthine journey of a lock of Beethoven's hair encased in a glass and wooden locket from the 18th century to the present. . . . This is a most unusual, thoroughly researched detective story written in a clearly accessible and lively tone. Black-and-white photos and reproductions appear throughout. . . . It is . . . an incredibly readable and absorbing selection that demonstrates the multidimensional nature of true scholarship." SLJ

Viegas, Jennifer. **Beethoven's** world; [by] Jennifer Viegas. Rosen Pub. Group 2008 64p il (Music throughout history) lib bdg $29.25

Grades: 5 6 7 8   92

1. Composers

ISBN 1-4042-0724-4 lib bdg; 978-1-4042-0724-0 lib bdg

LC 2005028917

This "book begins with an introduction briefly addressing social issues of the day, historical background, or other significant information. . . . Successive chapters discuss the [man's] early [life], family background, social status, personality characteristics, musical training and education, obstacles or challenges, and influences. A chapter . . . focuses on the musician's well-known compositions, describing through lively and colorful language some of the musical elements employed . . . The format and layout are appealing and uncluttered." SLJ

Includes glossary and bibliographical references

Bell, Alexander Graham, 1847-1922

Carson, Mary Kay. **Alexander** Graham Bell; giving voice to the world. [by] Mary Kay Carson. Sterling 2007 124p il (Sterling biographies) lib bdg $12.95; pa $5.95

Grades: 6 7 8 9   **92**

1. Inventors 2. Teachers of the deaf 3. Telecommunications executives

ISBN 978-1-4027-4951-3 lib bdg; 1-4027-4951-1 lib bdg; 1-4027-3230-9 pa; 978-1-4027-3230-0 pa

LC 2007003502

"Carson introduces Bell's life, giving readers an excellent picture of why this man became so famous. . . . [The book provides] clear, concise information in an easy-to-follow format with captioned photographs and illustrations on most pages." SLJ

Includes glossary and bibliographical references

Bell, Cool Papa, 1903-1991

McCormack, Shaun. **Cool** Papa Bell. Rosen Pub. Group 2002 112p il (Baseball Hall of Famers of the Negro leagues) lib bdg $29.25

Grades: 5 6 7 8   **92**

1. Baseball players 2. African American athletes 3. Baseball -- Biography

ISBN 0-8239-3474-8

LC 2001-3121

This is a biography of the African American who played in the Negro Leagues and was elected to the Baseball Hall of Fame in 1974

This "title presents an unvarnished picture of the racism in this country and how it impacted amateur and professional baseball from 1868 onward. . . . The layout . . . is attractive, the style . . . is engaging, and the b&w photographs enhance the narrative." Book Rep

Includes glossary and bibliographical references

Bernstein, Leonard, 1918-1990

★ Rubin, Susan Goldman. **Music** was IT: young Leonard Bernstein. Charlesbridge 2011 178p il lib bdg $19.95

Grades: 5 6 7 8   **92**

1. Composers 2. Conductors (Music) 3. Jews -- Biography 4. Biography, Individual

ISBN 1-58089-344-9 lib bdg; 978-1-58089-344-2 lib bdg; 978-1-60734-276-2 e-book

LC 2010-07584

This is a biography of composer and conductor Leonard Bernstein. Bibliography. Index. "Grades five to nine." (Bull Cent Child Books)

"An impeccably researched and told biography of Leonard Bernstein's musical apprenticeship, from toddlerhood to his conducting debut with the New York Philharmonic at age 25. . . . Drawn from interviews, family memoirs and other print resources, quotations are well-integrated and assiduously attributed. Photos, concert programs, early doodles and letters, excerpts from musical scores and other primary documentation enhance the text. Excellent bookmaking— from type to trim size—complements a remarkable celebration of a uniquely American musical genius." Kirkus

Bezos, Jeffrey, 1964-

Robinson, Tom. **Jeff** Bezos; Amazon.com architect. ABDO Pub. Co. 2010 112p il (Publishing pioneers) $22.95

Grades: 5 6 7 8   **92**

1. Businessmen 2. Internet marketing 3. Booksellers and bookselling 4. Amazon.com Inc. 5. Retail executives 6. Internet executives

ISBN 978-1-60453-759-8; 1-60453-759-0

LC 2009015989

In this biography of Amazon.com executive Jeff Bezos "the research is solid and there are extensive source notes. . . . With marbled borders and an array of photographs, maps, diagrams, and document reproductions, [this book has] an engaging and pleasing design. " SLJ

Includes glossary and bibliographical references

Scally, Robert. **Jeff** Bezos; founder of Amazon and the Kindle. by Robert D. Scally. Morgan Reynolds Pub. 2011 112p il (Business leaders) $28.95

Grades: 7 8 9 10 11 12   **92**

1. Businessmen 2. Amazon.com Inc. 3. Retail executives 4. Internet executives

ISBN 978-1-59935-178-0; 1-59935-178-1; 978-1-59935-214-5 e-book

LC 2011015611

This biography of Jeff Bezos, founder of Amazon and Kindle, "will grab YAs. . . . The design is browsable, with clear type and lots of color screens and informal photos of young people at work." Booklist

Includes bibliographical references

Bhutto, Benazir

Naden, Corinne J. **Benazir** Bhutto. Marshall Cavendish Benchmark 2010 96p il (Leading women) $39.93

Grades: 5 6 7 8   **92**

1. Prime ministers 2. Women politicians 3. Political leaders 4. Pakistan -- Politics and government

ISBN 978-0-7614-4952-2; 0-7614-4952-3

In this biography "readers learn about Bhutto's student years at Radcliffe College and her rise to prime minister of Pakistan, the first woman to lead a Muslim state. . . . The [woman's life is] revealed within the political and historical context of [her] times and [includes] quotes from autobiographical material. . . . Color and black-and-white photos are included. . . . The compact size, chronological organization, and accessible writing [style makes this biography a] good [resource] for reports." SLJ

Includes bibliographical references

★ Price, Sean. **Benazir** Bhutto. Heinemann Library 2009 112p il map (Front-page lives) $38.93

Grades: 6 7 8 9 10   **92**

1. Prime ministers 2. Political leaders 3. Women -- Pakistan 4. Prime ministers -- Pakistan 5. Pakistan -- Politics and government

ISBN 978-1-43293-222-0; 1-43293-222-5

LC 2009018315

"This volume, on the assassinated leader of Pakistan, is particularly well done, thanks to Price's clear and compelling text. . . . The many color photographs are particularly crisp and colorful, and the sidebars briefly but effectively deal with important topics." Booklist

Includes bibliographical references

Bieber, Justin, 1994-

Bieber, Justin. **Justin** Bieber: first step 2 forever; my story. HarperCollins Children's Books 2010 236p il $21.99

Grades: 4 5 6 7   92

1. Singers 2. Pop musicians

ISBN 978-0-06-203974-3; 0-06-203974-1

"Bieber, the platinum-selling singer/songwriter . . . debuts with an account of his 16-year-old life that's cheeky yet entirely in line with his safe and wholesome image. . . . The book covers his upbringing in Ontario, his early introduction to music, YouTube stardom, his love of pranks, and the stratospheric success he now enjoys—all interspersed with lyrics, tweets, and numerous full-bleed photographs of Bieber." Publ Wkly

Binstock, Melissa

Binstock, Melissa. **Nourishment**; feeding my starving soul when my mind and body betrayed me. Health Communications 2011 276p pa $14.95

Grades: 7 8 9 10   92

1. Students 2. Mentally ill 3. Tourette syndrome 4. Learning disabilities 5. Attention deficit disorder 6. Obsessive-compulsive disorder 7. Memoirists 8. Anorexia nervosa -- Personal narratives

ISBN 978-0-7573-1542-8 pa; 0-7573-1542-9 pa; 978-0-7573-9193-4 ebook; 0-7573-9193-1 ebook

LC 2010039690

"This unforgettable memoir chronicles the torment and challenges that plague the author. She is diagnosed with various psychological and neurological disorders by the young age of eleven years. . . . Melissa becomes acquainted with a new-type of therapy through her equestrian accomplishments. Soon however, . . . Melissa's fragile system, sends Melissa into a serious bout of mental illness and anorexia nervosa. . . . Once inside this facility, Melissa generously allows readers to eavesdrop into the day-to-day world of those who suffer from this plight. . . . This is a great read for teenagers who suffer from mental illness, peer acceptance issues, and eating disorders." Voice Youth Advocates

Black Elk, 1863-1950

★ Nelson, S. D. **Black** Elk's vision; a Lakota story. Abrams Books for Young Readers 2010 47p il $19.95

Grades: 5 6 7 8   92

1. Shamans 2. Oglala Indians 3. Indian leaders 4. Native Americans -- Biography

ISBN 978-0-8109-8399-1; 0-8109-8399-0

LC 2009-9392

"This handsomely designed, large-format book tells the story of Black Elk (1863-1950), a Lakota man who saw many changes come to his people. . . . Often quoting from Black Elk Speaks (1932), Nelson makes vivid the painful ways life changed for the Lakotain in the 1800s. . . . Colorful, imaginative artwork, created using pencils and acrylic paints, is interspersed with nineteenth-century photos, un-

derscoring that this dramatic account reflects the experiences of a man who witnessed history." Booklist

Blake, William, 1757-1827

Bedard, Michael. **William** Blake; the gates of paradise. Tundra Books 2006 192p il $28.99

Grades: 8 9 10 11 12   92

1. Poets 2. Artists 3. Authors 4. Engravers 5. Illustrators 6. Poets, English

ISBN 978-0-88776-763-0; 0-88776-763-X

"Bedard provides a satisfying biography of English artist, poet, and visionary William Blake. . . . Illustrated with drawings, paintings, engravings, and photos of sites and artifacts, the book is handsomely produced. . . . Bedard writes with precision, simplicity, and grace." Booklist

Includes bibliographical references

Bly, Nellie, 1864-1922

Bankston, John. **Nellie** Bly; journalist. John Bankston. Chelsea House 2011 155 p. ill. (hc) $35.00

Grades: 7 8 9 10   92

1. Women journalists 2. Journalists -- United States -- Biography 3. Women journalists -- United States -- Biography

ISBN 1604139080; 9781604139082

LC 2011000040

This book offers a biography journalist Elizabeth Cochrane, better known as Nellie Bly. An angry letter she wrote in response to a newspaper article about the role of women "earned her a job and a new name: Nellie Bly. As her alter ego, she gave a voice to women who worked in factories and were being treated in asylums. And she would travel around the world faster than anyone ever had. By the time she was 25, Nellie Bly was the most famous reporter in the world." (Google Books)

Includes bibliographical references (p. 144-147) and index

★ Macy, Sue. **Bylines** : a photobiography of Nellie Bly; foreword by Linda Ellerbee. National Geographic 2009 64p il map $19.95; lib bdg $28.90

Grades: 5 6 7 8   92

1. Authors 2. Journalists 3. Women journalists 4. Nonfiction writers

ISBN 978-1-4263-0513-9; 1-4263-0513-3; 978-1-4263-0514-6 lib bdg; 1-4263-0514-1 lib bdg

LC 2008-52329

This is a biography of the American reporter. Index. "Grades five to nine." (Bull Cent Child Books)

"This detailed biography of the trailblazing 19th-century journalist incorporates photographs of Bly and her subjects. The extensive text explores the details of a life spent seeking justice. . . . A thorough introduction to the life of a fascinating figure." Publ Wkly

Bohr, Niels

Spangenburg, Ray. **Niels** Bohr; atomic theorist. [by] Ray Spangenburg and Diane Kit Moser. Rev ed; Chelsea House 2008 141p bibl il (Makers of modern science) $35

Grades: 7 8 9 10 11 12   **92**
1. Scientists
ISBN 978-0-8160-6178-5; 0-8160-6178-5
LC 2008-1196

"Spangenburg and Moser delve into Bohr's background and present him as a loving, talkative, and inquisitive person who liked soccer. He was also concerned about the consequences of his work with nuclear weapons and was involved in many humanitarian efforts... New content includes informational sidebars and a discussion of string theory." SLJ

Includes bibliographical references

Bolívar, Simón, 1783-1830

Reis, Ronald A. **Simon** Bolivar. Chelsea House 2010 120p il (The great Hispanic heritage) $30
Grades: 6 7 8 9   **92**
1. Generals 2. Statesmen 3. Revolutionaries 4. South America -- History
ISBN 978-1-60413-731-6; 1-60413-731-2
LC 2010-9485

This "offers a balanced view of El Liberator, who shed his privileged youth in a wealthy Creole Venezuelan family and became a military strategist determined to create independent Latin American states. . . . A selection of well-chosen images, a chronology, chapter notes, and [a] suggested reading [list] round out [this] engaging [title] in a sure-to-be popular [book] for reports and personal interest." Booklist

Includes bibliographical references

Bonhoeffer, Dietrich, 1906-1945

Martin, Michael J. **Champion** of freedom; Dietrich Bonhoeffer. by Michael Martin. Morgan Reynolds Pub. 2012 144 p. ill. (some col.) (hbk.) $28.95
Grades: 7 8 9 10 11 12   **92**
1. Clergy 2. Theologians
ISBN 1599351692; 9781599351698
LC 2010049095

This book looks at "Dietrich Bonhoeffer [who in 1943] was arrested and imprisoned by the Gestapo for crimes [against] the government. . . . [This] German Lutheran Pastor was integrally involved in the plot to assassinate Adolf Hitler. During his two years of imprisonment, Bonhoeffer manages extreme circumstances, including interrogation and isolation, but is able to protect both himself and his co-conspirators through careful rhetorical practices. How does a pastor and a loyal German justify his involvement in the plot? . . . How could a pastor who penned a book titled Ethics, ethically justify his actions? This book considers some of those questions and is for theologians, ethicists, and rhetoricians as it examines the intersection of faith, politics, and classic rhetorical theory. (Amazon.com)

Includes bibliographical references (p. 140) and index.

Borges, Jorge Luis, 1899-1986

McNeese, Tim. **Jorge** Luis Borges; [by] Tim McNeese. Chelsea House 2008 119p il (The great Hispanic heritage) $30
Grades: 6 7 8 9   **92**
1. Poets 2. Authors 3. Novelists 4. Authors, Argentine 5. Essayists 6. Translators 7. Literary critics 8. Short

story writers
ISBN 978-0-7910-9665-9; 0-7910-9665-3
LC 2007032008

This biography provides a "substantive [portrait], including background information and historical context, of . . . beloved writer Borges. . . . The well-documented [text] effectively [combines] anecdotes, quotations, and historical details. Many photographs and sidebars are also included." Horn Book Guide

Includes bibliographical references

Bourgeois, Louise, 1911-2010

★ Greenberg, Jan. **Runaway** girl: the artist Louise Bourgeois; [by] Jan Greenberg and Sandra Jordan. Abrams 2003 80p il $19.95
Grades: 7 8 9 10   **92**
1. Artists 2. Sculptors 3. Women artists 4. Artists -- United States
ISBN 0-8109-4237-2
LC 2002-11922

Introduces the life of renowned modern artist Louise Bourgeois, who is known primarily for her sculptures

"In clear, elegant prose, bolstered with numerous quotes from the artist, the authors seamlessly juxtapose stories of Bourgeois' life with relevant artworks. . . . Beautifully reproduced photographs, printed on well-designed pages, offer an excellent mix of the artist's personal life and her art." Booklist

Includes bibliographical references

Boyle, Robert, 1627-1691

Baxter, Roberta. **Skeptical** chemist; the story of Robert Boyle. Morgan Reynolds Pub. 2006 128p il (Profiles in science) lib bdg $27.95
Grades: 7 8 9 10   **92**
1. Chemists 2. Physicists 3. Scientists 4. Nonfiction writers 5. Writers on science
ISBN 978-1-59935-025-7; 1-59935-025-4
LC 2006-23969

The author makes a "case for Boyle's significance as a key figure in the field of scientific experimentation as well as his contributions to modern chemistry and physics. Well organized and clearly written, her book offers a good view of changes in science and society at this pivotal time and presents a well-rounded view of Boyle, whose interests extended beyond scientific inquiry and discussion." Booklist

Includes bibliographical references

Bradbury, Ray, 1920-2012

Bankston, John. **Ray** Bradbury; foreword by Kyle Zimmer. Chelsea House 2011 140p il (Who wrote that?) lib bdg $35.00
Grades: 6 7 8 9 10   **92**
1. Authors 2. Novelists 3. Screenwriters 4. Authors, American 5. Children's authors 6. Short story writers 7. Science fiction writers
ISBN 1-60413-778-9; 978-1-60413-778-1

This discusses the life and work of author Ray Bradbury.
Includes bibliographical references

Brahe, Tycho, 1546-1601

Nardo, Don. **Tycho** Brahe; pioneer of astronomy. by Don Nardo. Compass Point Books 2008 112p il (Signature lives) lib bdg $23.95

Grades: 6 7 8 9   92

1. Poets 2. Authors 3. Astronomers
ISBN 978-0-7565-3309-0 lib bdg; 0-7565-3309-0 lib bdg

LC 2007004608

A biography of the sixteenth-century Danish astronomer Tycho Brahe.

"Nardo brings his lively, informative approach to this stanout biography." Booklist

Includes bibliographical references

Braille, Louis, 1809-1852

★ Freedman, Russell. **Out** of darkness: the story of Louis Braille; illustrated by Kate Kiesler. Clarion Bks. 1997 81p il $16.95; pa $7.95

Grades: 4 5 6 7   92

1. Blind 2. Inventors 3. Teachers of the blind 4. Blind -- Books and reading
ISBN 0-395-77516-7; 0-395-96888-7 pa

LC 95-52353

"Without melodrama, Freedman tells the momentous story in quiet chapters in his best plain style, making the facts immediate and personal. . . . A diagram explains how the Braille alphabet works, and Kate Kessler's full-page shaded pencil illustrations are part of the understated poignant drama." Booklist

Brave Bird, Mary

Brave Bird, Mary. **Lakota** woman; by Mary Crow Dog and Richard Erdoes. 1st HarperPerennial ed; HarperPerennial 1991 263p il rpt $14.95

Grades: 8 9 10 11 12 Adult   92

1. Dakota Indians 2. Political activists 3. Memoirists 4. Indian leaders 5. American Indian Movement 6. Native Americans -- Biography
ISBN 0-06-097389-7; 9780802145420 rpt

LC 90-55980

First published 1990 by Grove Weidenfeld

"Born in 1955 and raised in poverty on the Rosebud Reservation, Mary Crow Dog escaped an oppressive Catholic boarding school but fell into a marginal life of urban shoplifting and barhopping. A 1971 encounter with AIM (the American Indian Movement), participation in the 1972 Trail of Broken Treaties march on Washington, and giving birth to her first child while under fire at the 1973 siege of Wounded Knee radicalized her." Libr J

Breckinridge, Mary, 1881-1965

★ Wells, Rosemary. **Mary** on horseback; three mountain stories. pictures by Peter McCarty. Dial Bks. for Young Readers 1998 53p il $16.99; pa $4.99

Grades: 4 5 6 7   92

1. Nurses 2. Midwives
ISBN 0-670-88923-7; 0-14-130815-X pa

LC 97-43409

Tells the stories of three families who were helped by the work of Mary Breckinridge, the first nurse to go into the Appalachian Mountains and give medical care to the isolated inhabitants. Includes an afterword with facts about Breckinridge and the Frontier Nursing Service she founded

"These beautifully written stories will remain with the reader long after the book is closed." Booklist

Bridgman, Laura Dewey, 1829-1889

Alexander, Sally Hobart. **She** touched the world: Laura Bridgman, deaf-blind pioneer; by Sally Hobart Alexander and Robert Alexander. Clarion Books 2008 100p il $18

Grades: 5 6 7 8   92

1. Deaf 2. Blind 3. Students 4. Physicians 5. Philanthropists 6. Humanitarians 7. Teachers of the blind
ISBN 978-0-618-85299-4; 0-618-85299-9

"At the age of three, in 1832, Laura Bridgman contracted scarlet fever and lost her sight, her hearing, her sense of smell, and much of her sense of taste. Her family sent her to Dr. Samuel [Gridley] Howe at the New England Institute for the Education of the Blind, and by the age of 10, Laura was world-famous for her accomplishments. . . . Alexander . . . presents a well-written and thoroughly researched biography of this remarkable woman, with numerous black-and-white photos." Booklist

Includes bibliographical references

Brin, Sergey

Sapet, Kerrily. **Google** founders: Larry Page and Sergey Brin. Morgan Reynolds Pub. 2011 112p il (Business leaders) $28.95

Grades: 7 8 9 10 11 12   92

1. Businesspeople 2. Web search engines 3. Computer scientists 4. Google, Inc. 5. Internet executives 6. Information technology executives
ISBN 978-1-59935-177-3; 1-59935-177-3; 978-1-59935-213-8 e-book

LC 2011014665

This biography of Google founders Larry Page and Sergey Bring "will grab YAs. . . . The design is browsable, with clear type and lots of color screens and informal photos of young people at work." Booklist

Includes bibliographical references

Brown, John, 1800-1859

★ Hendrix, John. **John** Brown; his fight for freedom. written and illustrated by John Hendrix. Abrams Books for Young Readers 2009 39p il $18.95

Grades: 4 5 6 7   92

1. Abolitionists 2. Slavery -- United States
ISBN 978-0-8109-3798-7; 0-8109-3798-0

LC 2008-45969

The author "traces how John Brown went from conducting slaves along the Underground Railroad to espousing violent insurrection as a means to end slavery. . . . Reinforcing Brown as a larger-than-life folk hero, the pictures are exhilarating. . . . By embracing Brown's complexity, especially in the well-argued afterword, Hendrix sows acres of fertile ground for discussion." Booklist

Marrin, Albert, 1936- A **volcano** beneath the snow; John Brown's war against slavery. Albert Marrin. Alfred A. Knopf 2014 256 p. illustrations, maps (trade) $19.99

Grades: 8 9 10 11 12   92

1. United States -- Biography 2. Abolitionists -- United States 3. Harpers Ferry (W. Va.) -- History -- John Brown's Raid, 1859 4. Abolitionists -- United States -- Biography

ISBN 0307981525; 9780307981523; 9780307981530

LC 2012043231

This book, by Albert Marrin, focuses on John Brown. "Deeply religious, Brown believed that God had chosen him to right the wrong of slavery. He was willing to kill and die for something modern Americans unanimously agree was a just cause. And yet he was a religious fanatic and a staunch believer in 'righteous violence,' an unapologetic committer of domestic terrorism." (Publisher's note)

"Chapters present the history of the 'peculiar institution' (slavery) both here and abroad, details of Brown's life and family, his relationship with the abolitionists, his radicalization leading to the killings at Pottawatomie, Kansas, and, eventually, the uprising at Harper's Ferry and his trial and hanging. . . . black-and-white illustrations include period photos, portraits, artwork, maps, fliers, and posters. Extensive notes and further-reading suggestions are included. This will be an excellent resource for U.S. history collections." SLJ

Includes bibliographical references

Sterngass, Jon. **John** Brown. Chelsea House 2009 144p il (Leaders of the Civil War era) lib bdg $30

Grades: 7 8 9 10   92

1. Abolitionists

ISBN 978-1-60413-305-9; 1-60413-305-8

LC 2008-44622

This is a biography of the abolitionist, John Brown.

This is an "even-keeled and well-written account of the man's life and times. . . . Sterngass displays a sharp awareness that what makes the man so controversial is also what makes him so fascinating. . . . [This book] should add depth to Civil War studies." Booklist

Includes glossary and bibliographical references

Bruchac, Joseph, 1942-

★ Bruchac, Joseph. **Bowman's** store; a journey to myself. 1st Lee & Low ed; Lee & Low Books 2001 315p il pa $9.95

Grades: 7 8 9 10   92

1. Poets 2. Authors 3. Abnaki Indians 4. Storytellers 5. College teachers 6. Magazine editors 7. Authors, American 8. Children's authors 9. Nonfiction writers 10. Native Americans -- Biography

ISBN 1-58430-027-2; 978-1-58430-027-4

LC 2001-16435

A reissue of the title first published 1997 by Dial Books

"Each episode is constructed with a true storyteller's attention to language and plot development. Students of modern Native American cultures will find plenty of food for thought." Booklist

Buchanan, James, 1791-1868

Burgan, Michael. **James** Buchanan. Marshall Cavendish Benchmark 2011 112p il (Presidents and their times) lib bdg $23.95

Grades: 5 6 7 8   92

1. Presidents 2. Senators 3. Members of Congress 4. Secretaries of state 5. Presidents -- United States

ISBN 978-0-7614-4810-5; 0-7614-4810-1

LC 2009025933

This offers information on President James Buchanan and places him within his historical and cultural context. Also explored are the formative events of his times and how he responded.

"The abundant sidebars provide a good deal of background information that will be helpful to students. . . . Attractive . . . as well as useful." Booklist

Includes glossary and bibliographical references

Buffett, Warren E.

Johnson, Anne Janette. **Warren** Buffett; [by] Anne Janette Johnson. Morgan Reynolds Pub. 2008 128p il (Business leaders) $28.95

Grades: 7 8 9 10   92

1. Capitalists and financiers 2. Financiers

ISBN 978-1-59935-080-6; 1-59935-080-7

LC 2007045963

"This book answers many questions about the unassuming billionaire from Omaha. Buffett's life . . . is detailed on both personal and professional levels. . . . Anecdotes make the book accessible and demystify the sometimes-confusing world of stocks and investments. . . . A fair number of color photos is included." SLJ

Includes bibliographical references

Bullard, Eugene Jacques, 1894-1961

Greenly, Larry. **Eugene** Bullard; world's first Black fighter pilot. Larry W. Greenly. Junebug Books 2012 160 p. illustrations $19.95

Grades: 8 9 10 11 12   92

1. Fighter pilots -- France -- Biography 2. African American fighter pilots -- Biography 3. World War, 1914-1918 -- Aerial operations, French 4. World War, 1939-1945 -- Aerial operations, French 5. African American fighter pilots -- France -- Biography 6. Race discrimination -- United States -- History -- 20th century

ISBN 158838280X; 9781588382801

LC 2012036425

This book, by Larry Greenly, "tells the story of pioneering black aviator Eugene Bullard from his birth in 1895 to his combat experiences in both World War I and II and, finally, his return to America. . . . He ran away from home at twelve and eventually made his way to France, where he joined the French Foreign Legion and later the Lafayette Flying Corps, to become the world's first black fighter pilot." (Publisher's note)

"The incredible story of Eugene Bullard—an African American honored by the French, yet shunned by the Americans—is one too long neglected. . . . Though his heroic deeds brought recognition from the French, a white American doctor in Paris became a constant stumbling block for further progress in Eugene's life and career. . . . Using Bullard's memoirs and other sparse information about him, Greenly crafts a moving, novelistic biography that portrays Bullard's courage throughout his life. Meanwhile, the black-and-white photos, of everything from a teenage Bullard boxing to wartime aircrafts, add plenty of historical flavor." Booklist

Includes bibliographical references

Burns, Anthony, 1834-1862

★ Hamilton, Virginia. **Anthony** Burns: the defeat and triumph of a fugitive slave. Knopf 1988 193p hardcover o.p. pa $5.50

Grades: 5 6 7 8   92

1. Slaves 2. Slavery -- United States 3. African Americans -- Biography

ISBN 0-679-83997-6 pa

LC 87-38063

A biography of the slave who escaped to Boston in 1854, was arrested at the instigation of his owner, and whose trial caused a furor between abolitionists and those determined to enforce the Fugitive Slave Act

"This book does exactly what good biography for children ought to do: takes readers directly into the life of the subject and makes them feel what it was like to be that person in those times." Horn Book

Includes bibliographical references

Burr, Aaron, 1756-1836

★ St. George, Judith. The **duel** : the parallel lives of Alexander Hamilton and Aaron Burr. Viking 2009 97p il $16.99

Grades: 6 7 8 9 10   92

1. Statesmen 2. Vice-presidents 3. Secretaries of the treasury 4. Politicians -- United States

ISBN 978-0-670-01124-7; 0-670-01124-X

LC 2009-5660

"After a prologue following the steps of Alexander Hamilton and Aaron Burr on the morning of their famous duel, St. George backtracks to trace the 'parallel lives' mentioned in the subtitle. . . . Well researched and organized, the book offers insights into the personalities, lives, and times of Burr and Hamilton." Booklist

Burton, Richard Francis Sir, 1821-1890

Young, Serinity. **Richard** Francis Burton; explorer, scholar, spy. [by] Serinity Young. Marshall Cavendish Benchmark 2006 80p il map (Great explorations) lib bdg $32.79

Grades: 5 6 7 8   92

1. Explorers 2. Travel writers 3. Asian studies specialists 4. Middle Eastern studies specialists

ISBN 978-0-7614-2222-8 lib bdg; 0-7614-2222-6 lib bdg

LC 2005027932

A biography of the 19th century English explorer of Asia and Africa

Includes bibliographical references

Busby, Cylin, 1970-

★ Busby, Cylin. The **year** we disappeared; a father-daughter memoir. [by] Cylin Busby & John Busby. Bloomsbury 2008 329p $16.99

Grades: 8 9 10 11 12   92

1. Police 2. Authors 3. Violence 4. Father-daughter relationship 5. Magazine editors 6. Children's authors

ISBN 978-1-59990-141-1; 1-59990-141-2

LC 2008017215

"No one with even a marginal interest in true crime writing should miss this page-turner, by turns shocking and almost unbearably sad. In 1979, in an underworld-style hit, a gunman shot John Busby, a policeman in Cape Cod; a fluke saved John's life, but he was permanently disfigured and disabled, and the family placed under 24-hour protection. Eventually the family went into hiding in Tennessee, but arguably their 'disappearance' takes place long before they move—as John and his daughter, Cylin, alternately narrate, readers can see how the shooting erased the family's sense of themselves. . . . Where John's chapters provide the grim facts, it is Cylin's authentically childlike perspective that, in revealing the cost to her innocence, renders the tragic experience most searingly." Publ Wkly

Includes bibliographical references

Busby, John, 1942-

★ Busby, Cylin. The **year** we disappeared; a father-daughter memoir. [by] Cylin Busby & John Busby. Bloomsbury 2008 329p $16.99

Grades: 8 9 10 11 12   92

1. Police 2. Authors 3. Violence 4. Father-daughter relationship 5. Magazine editors 6. Children's authors

ISBN 978-1-59990-141-1; 1-59990-141-2

LC 2008017215

"No one with even a marginal interest in true crime writing should miss this page-turner, by turns shocking and almost unbearably sad. In 1979, in an underworld-style hit, a gunman shot John Busby, a policeman in Cape Cod; a fluke saved John's life, but he was permanently disfigured and disabled, and the family placed under 24-hour protection. Eventually the family went into hiding in Tennessee, but arguably their 'disappearance' takes place long before they move—as John and his daughter, Cylin, alternately narrate, readers can see how the shooting erased the family's sense of themselves. . . . Where John's chapters provide the grim facts, it is Cylin's authentically childlike perspective that, in revealing the cost to her innocence, renders the tragic experience most searingly." Publ Wkly

Includes bibliographical references

Caesar, Julius, 100-44 B.C.

Galford, Ellen. **Julius** Caesar; the boy who conquered an empire. [by] Ellen Galford. National Geographic 2007 64p il map (World history biographies) $17.95; lib bdg $27.90

Grades: 5 6 7 8   92

1. Statesmen 2. Historians 3. Rome -- History 4. Emperors -- Rome

ISBN 978-1-4263-0064-6; 978-1-4263-0065-3 lib bdg

LC 2006020777

A biography of the Roman emperor

This "visually appealing [title is] packed with excellent photographs and reproductions, interesting sidebars, and [has] a time line running along the bottom of every page. . . . [This book is] useful, well-written." SLJ

Includes glossary and bibliographical references

Calcines, Eduardo F., 1955-

★ Calcines, Eduardo F. **Leaving** Glorytown; one boy's struggle under Castro. Farrar, Straus & Giroux 2009 221p il $17.95

Grades: 7 8 9 10   **92**

1. Businesspeople 2. Cuban refugees 3. Memoirists 4. Cuba -- History -- 1959-

ISBN 978-0-374-34394-1; 0-374-34394-2

LC 2008-7506

"Calcines's spirited memoir captures the political tension, economic hardship, family stress, and personal anxiety of growing up during the early years of the Castro regime in Cuba. . . . The author shares startling, clear memories about his life in the Glorytown barrio of Cienfuegos. . . . Calcines writes about Cuba with immediacy, nostalgia, and passion. This personal account will acquaint readers with the oppressive and ironic effects of communism." SLJ

Callwood, June, 1924-2007

Dublin, Anne. **June** Callwood; a life of action. Second Story Press 2007 140p il pa $14.95

Grades: 7 8 9 10 11 12   **92**

1. Canadians 2. Journalists 3. Social action 4. Women journalists 5. Feminists 6. Social activists

ISBN 978-1-89718-714-2

"This biography of the Canadian journalist and social activist chronicles Callwood's long life with loving care and places her activism within the cultural and historical context of pre and postwar Canada. . . . This is a well-told life story, with many black-and-white photographs that infuse the subject with personality." SLJ

Canaletto, 1697-1768

Rice, Earle. **Canaletto**; by Earle Rice Jr. Mitchell Lane Publishers 2007 48p il (Art profiles for kids) lib bdg $29.95

Grades: 7 8 9 10   **92**

1. Artists 2. Painters 3. Artists, Italian

ISBN 978-1-58415-561-4 lib bdg; 1-58415-561-2 lib bdg

LC 2007023412

This offers "well-documented information for teens doing reports. [The] volume covers the painter's childhood, training, travels, influences, and historical context. The chronological chapters build a survey of the [artist's] oeuvres, including the style and subject matter of [his] works and past and present critical reaction." SLJ

Includes glossary and bibliographical references

Carnegie, Andrew, 1835-1919

Edge, Laura Bufano. **Andrew** Carnegie; industrial philanthropist. [by] Laura B. Edge. Lerner Publications Co. 2004 128p il (Lerner biography) lib bdg $27.93

Grades: 6 7 8 9   **92**

1. Steel industry 2. Philanthropists 3. Capitalists and financiers 4. Metal industry executives

ISBN 0-8225-4965-4

LC 2002-152936

Chronicles the rags-to-riches tale of a Scottish immigrant who used most of the millions he earned as a steel tycoon to set up a fund for the advancement of science, education, and peace.

"Children will come away with a good sense of a man driven by contradictory impulses." Booklist

Includes bibliographical references

Carr, Emily, 1871-1945

★ Debon, Nicolas. **Four** pictures by Emily Carr. Douglas & McIntyre 2003 un il $15.95

Grades: 4 5 6 7   **92**

1. Artists 2. Painters 3. Women artists 4. Artists, Canadian 5. Diarists 6. Memoirists

ISBN 0-88899-532-6

"Debon has distilled four periods in the Canadian artist's life (1871-1945) into enticing vignettes that illuminate her passions, determination, health problems, relationships with fellow Group of Seven artists, and, most of all, her dramatic progression as a painter. . . . Engaging artwork and brisk storytelling make this a consideration for most libraries." SLJ

Carroll, Lewis, 1832-1898

Carpenter, Angelica Shirley. **Lewis** Carroll; through the looking glass. Lerner Publs. 2003 128p il map (Lerner biography) lib bdg $27.93

Grades: 7 8 9 10   **92**

1. Authors 2. Novelists 3. Mathematicians 4. Authors, English 5. Children's authors 6. Writers on science

ISBN 0-8225-0073-6

LC 2002-3266

A biography of the mathematician, teacher, photographer, and author who wrote "Alice in Wonderland"

"An accessible, well-documented portrait." SLJ

Includes bibliographical references

Rubin, C. M. The **real** Alice in Wonderland; a role model for the ages. [by] C.M. Rubin with Gabriella Rose Rubin. AuthorHouse 2010 134p il $29.95

Grades: 7 8 9 10   **92**

1. Authors 2. Children 3. Novelists 4. Mathematicians 5. Characters and characteristics in literature 6. Children's authors 7. Writers on science

ISBN 978-1-4490-8131-7; 1-4490-8131-2

LC 2010-901865

"Readers will follow this title down the rabbit hole to discover the world of the real Alice who inspired Lewis Carroll's Alice in Wonderland. The book moves seamlessly through the life of Alice Pleasance Liddell. . . . This offering paints a full picture of Alice, not only as a child who has captivated literature but also as a woman who was truly ahead of her time. This is a purchase that will do well with a range of people and should be offered as a standard accompaniment to Alice in Wonderland. The illustrations and pictures will make it quite popular in a public library." Voice Youth Advocates

Includes bibliographical references

Carson, Rachel, 1907-1964

Piddock, Charles. **Rachel** Carson; a voice for the natural world. Gareth Stevens Pub. 2009 112p il map (Life portraits) lib bdg $34

Grades: 7 8 9 10   **92**
     1. Authors 2. Biologists 3. Conservationists 4. Women scientists 5. Environmentalists 6. College teachers 7. Marine biologists 8. Writers on nature 9. Writers on science
ISBN 978-1-4339-0058-7 lib bdg; 1-4339-0058-0 lib bdg

                 LC 2008-31544
     "Readers learn not only about . . . [Carson's] successful writing career but also about the sacrifices she made for her family and the injustices she sometimes suffered, both as a woman scientist and as someone who fought against chemical companies long before today's environmental movement. . . . Many photos, images, and sidebars . . . inform without being didactic and educate without preaching." Voice Youth Advocates

Includes glossary and bibliographical references

Scherer, Glenn. **Who** on earth is Rachel Carson? mother of the environmental movement. [by] Glenn Scherer and Marty Fletcher. Enslow Publishers 2009 112p il (Scientists saving the earth) lib bdg $31.93
Grades: 5 6 7 8   **92**
     1. Authors 2. Biologists 3. Conservationists 4. Women scientists 5. Environmentalists 6. College teachers 7. Marine biologists 8. Writers on nature 9. Writers on science
ISBN 978-1-59845-116-0 lib bdg; 1-59845-116-2 lib bdg

                 LC 2008028498
     "The writing is clear and informative. . . . Color photographs are relevant and of good quality." SLJ
Includes bibliographical references

Cartier, Jacques, 1491-1557

Woog, Adam. **Jacques** Cartier. Chelsea House 2009 109p bibl il map (Great explorers) lib bdg $30
Grades: 6 7 8 9   **92**
     1. Explorers
ISBN 978-1-60413-430-8 lib bdg; 1-60413-430-5 lib bdg

                 LC 2009-16267
Biography of the explorer Jacques Cartier
     "The information . . . is presented in such a way as to attract and maintain readers' interest. . . . With a full complement of maps, photographs (where available), illustrations, time lines, and document reproductions, a full story is told. Well-written and thoroughly researched, this . . . will make a solid addition." SLJ

Includes glossary and bibliographical references

Carver, George Washington, 1864?-1943

Abrams, Dennis. **George** Washington Carver; scientist and educator. [by] Dennis Abrams. Chelsea House 2008 119p il (Black Americans of achievement) $30
Grades: 6 7 8 9   **92**
     1. Botanists 2. Scientists 3. African Americans -- Biography
ISBN 978-0-7910-9717-5; 0-7910-9717-X

                 LC 2007035677

This biography details the African American scientist's "rise from adversity to . . . recognition. The [book goes] beyond the typical personal information to provide some social history relevant to the subject's time. Captioned photographs and boxed inserts enhance the conversational [text]." Horn Book Guide
Includes bibliographical references

Harness, Cheryl. The **groundbreaking,** chance-taking life of George Washington Carver and science & invention in America; by Cheryl Harness. National Geographic 2008 143p il map (Cherly Harness histories) $16.95; lib bdg $25.90
Grades: 4 5 6 7   **92**
     1. Botanists 2. Scientists 3. African Americans -- Biography
ISBN 978-1-4263-0196-4; 1-4263-0196-0; 978-1-4263-0197-1 lib bdg; 1-4263-0197-9 lib bdg

                 LC 2007029316
     "Harness presents Carver as a man who, regardless of constant hardship and racial prejudice, persevered to become a beloved teacher and devoted scientist. . . . The author raises challenging questions throughout. . . . The lively prose style conveys his sense of passion and adventure about the man and his intellectual pursuits, and the simple black-and-white drawings add a further sense of drama." SLJ

Includes bibliographical references

★ MacLeod, Elizabeth. **George** Washington Carver; an innovative life. written by Elizabeth MacLeod. Kids Can Press 2007 32p il $14.95
Grades: 4 5 6 7   **92**
     1. Botanists 2. Scientists 3. African Americans -- Biography
ISBN 978-1-55337-906-5; 1-55337-906-3
     "MacLeod chronicles Carver's life from childhood to the end of his career, and the recognition he received posthumously. Each spread has a page of text with a quote from Carver in the margin and a page filled with many graphics in black and white and color, including photographs, illustrations, and reproductions of artifacts, all with captions. . . . With the richness of detail presented, even reluctant readers will find something of interest about this exceptional individual." SLJ

Cash, Johnny

Willett, Edward. **Johnny** Cash; the man in black. Enslow Publishers 2010 160p il (American rebels) lib bdg $34.60
Grades: 6 7 8 9   **92**
     1. Singers 2. Country music 3. Country musicians 4. Songwriters
ISBN 978-0-7660-3386-3 lib bdg; 0-7660-3386-4 lib bdg

                 LC 2009017346
     This "fascinating, well-organized [portrait of the country music singer] . . . opens with the infamous 1968 live-album recording at California's Folsom State Prison. . . . Skillfully chosen photos, chapter notes, and [a] suggested-reading [list completes this] well-researched, wholly engaging [introduction]." Booklist
Includes bibliographical references

Cather, Willa, 1873-1947

Meltzer, Milton. **Willa** Cather; a biography. Twenty-First Century Books 2008 160p il (Literary greats) $33.26

Grades: 7 8 9 10 11 12   92

1. Authors 2. Novelists 3. Women authors 4. Western writers 5. Authors, American 6. Short story writers

ISBN 978-0-8225-7604-4; 0-8225-7604-X

LC 2007-25629

A biography of the author of such novels as O Pioneers! and My Antonia.

"With signature clarity, Meltzer's . . . biography . . . sets his detailed discussion of Cather's life and work against the larger backdrop of her times. . . . The book's handsome, inviting design includes photos on almost every spread." Booklist

Includes bibliographical references

Catherine II, the Great, Empress of Russia, 1729-1796

★ Vincent, Zu. **Catherine** the Great; Empress of Russia. Franklin Watts 2009 128p il map (A wicked history) $30; pa $5.95

Grades: 6 7 8 9   92

1. Empresses 2. Russia -- History 3. Russia -- Kings and rulers

ISBN 978-0-531-21802-0 lib bdg; 0-531-21802-3 lib bdg; 978-0-531-20738-3 pa; 0-531-20738-2 pa

LC 2008041543

"Catherine the Great might be . . . known as a cruel dictator with lots of lovers, but author Vincent shows how the Empress of Russia actually took on her position (well, after she had her husband murdered) with some good intentions. . . . Young readers will find the manipulation of Catherine's early days particularly interesting." Booklist

Includes bibliographical references

Catherine, Duchess of Cambridge, 1982-

Doeden, Matt. **Prince** William & Kate; a royal romance. Lerner Publications 2011 48p il lib bdg $26.60

Grades: 5 6 7 8   92

1. Princes 2. Princesses

ISBN 978-0-7613-8029-0; 0-7613-8029-9

LC 2011003413

"This short and sweet volume accents what down-to-earth and normal newlyweds Prince William and Kate Middleton are really like. After a brief recap of the couple's engagement interview, the book goes on to profile the pair individually and then as a duo. . . . This is an upbeat, readable narrative about a handsome, appealing couple. The color photographs are well chosen." Booklist

Includes glossary and bibliographical references

Catlin, George, 1796-1872

★ Reich, Susanna. **Painting** the wild frontier: the art and adventures of George Catlin. Clarion Books 2008 160p il map $21

Grades: 7 8 9 10 11 12   92

1. Artists 2. Painters 3. West (U.S.) in art 4. Native Americans in art 5. Artists -- United States

ISBN 978-0-618-71470-4; 0-618-71470-7

LC 2007-38847

This is a "biography of nineteenth-century painter George Catlin, famous for his portraits of Native American life. . . . A great introduction to Catlin's work as well as an excellent title to use in social studies, history, and art classes." Booklist

Includes bibliographical references

Worth, Richard. **George** Catlin; painter of Indian life. Sharpe Focus 2009 80p il (Show me America) $32.95

Grades: 6 7 8 9   92

1. Artists 2. Painters 3. West (U.S.) 4. Artists -- United States

ISBN 978-0-7656-8152-2; 0-7656-8152-8

LC 2007040694

"This is an attractive book with an engaging text that relates the remarkable story of an early American artist who is best remembered for his lifelike depictions of Native Americans. The book incorporates outstanding full-color reproductions of his sketches and paintings, with explanations of their context." SLJ

Includes bibliographical references

Cavell, Edith, 1865-1915

Batten, Jack. **Silent** in an evil time: the brave war of Edith Cavell. Tundra Books 2007 135p il pa $16.95

Grades: 7 8 9 10   92

1. Nurses 2. World War, 1914-1918

ISBN 978-0-88776-737-1

A biography of the British nurse who was executed by the Germans for sheltering British and French soldiers in Brussels during World War I

"This exceptional biography reads like an adventure novel. . . . The historical facts are well explained and Cavell is placed clearly in context." SLJ

Cezanne, Paul, 1839-1906

Burleigh, Robert. **Paul** Cezanne; a painter's journey. H.N. Abrams 2006 31p il $17.95

Grades: 4 5 6 7   92

1. Artists 2. Painters 3. Artists, French

ISBN 0-8109-5784-1

LC 2005011779

"Burleigh offers brief insights into Cézanne's personal life, such as his relationship with his father, who did not support his sons interest in art. However, the emphasis is on interpreting some individual paintings and understanding the artist's various styles, including the impact of the Impressionists and his evolution to a freer and simpler manner of expression in his later years. . . . The high-quality reproductions demonstrate Burleigh's points. . . . A solid, lively introduction." SLJ

Chaplin, Charlie, 1889-1977

★ Fleischman, Sid. **Sir** Charlie; Chaplin, the funniest man in the world. Greenwillow Books 2010 268p il $19.99; lib bdg $20.89

Grades: 5 6 7 8 9   **92**
1. Actors 2. Comedians 3. Motion pictures 4. Motion picture directors 5. Motion picture producers 6. Biography, Individual
ISBN 0-06-189640-3; 0-06-189641-1 lib bdg; 978-0-06-189640-8; 978-0-06-189641-5 lib bdg
LC 2009019689
This is a biography of the actor and director who starred in such films as City Lights (1931), Modern Times (1940), The Great Dictator (1947) and Limelight (1952). Chronology. Bibliography. Index. "Grades six to ten." (Bull Cent Child Books)

"This lively and engaging account of a poor Cockney boy who became the world's greatest silent-movie comedian is a must for biography collections. . . . Brief, easily digestible chapters, an extensive time line, and plenty of photos make the book's well-researched content accessible and appealing." SLJ

Charles, Ray

Duggleby, John. **Uh** huh!: the story of Ray Charles. Morgan Reynolds Pub. 2005 160p il $26.95

Grades: 7 8 9 10   **92**
1. Blind 2. Singers 3. Pianists 4. Blues musicians 5. African American singers
ISBN 1-931798-65-6
LC 2005-1287
The author "traces Charles' long career and displays a sensitivity to the events surrounding his life (including his bitter battles with heroin and alcohol addiction), as well as a genuine understanding of his music and the breadth of his musical influence. Sidebars on 'race' music, Braille, the Grammys, soul, and rock and roll enrich the narrative." Booklist

Includes bibliographical references

★ Woog, Adam. **Ray** Charles and the birth of soul; [by] Adam Woog. Lucent Books 2006 112p il (Lucent library of Black history) lib bdg $28.70

Grades: 7 8 9 10   **92**
1. Blind 2. Singers 3. Pianists 4. Soul music 5. Blues musicians 6. African American singers
ISBN 1-59018-844-6
LC 2005022586
"Woog does an excellent job of describing Charles's rare talent and the trajectory of his long and legendary career. . . . The text is clearly written and well organized. Black-and-white photographs illustrate and inform." SLJ

Includes bibliographical references

Chaucer, Geoffrey

Hubbard-Brown, Janet. **Chaucer**; celebrated poet and author. Chelsea House 2005 p. cm. (Makers of the Middle Ages and Renaissance)

Grades: 6 7 8 9   **92**
1. Poets, English -- Middle English, 1100-1500 -- Biography
ISBN 0-7910-8635-6 (hardcover)
LC 2005004784
"Profiles of two of the most important writers of the Middle Ages, each of whom was heavily influenced by the

religious and political situations of his respective country and who reflected these influences in his writing. Dante's Divine Comedy is dark and brutally moral, while Chaucer's Canterbury Tales is humorous and satirical. Both books provide information to help students better understand all of the works of these two prominent men. Each title describes its subject's childhood and background as well as his influences, career, and writing. The colorful illustrations, many from illuminated manuscripts, short chapters, simple vocabulary, and large print present an attractive format. Sidebars and captions contain additional information." SLJ Reviews

"Well-documented and illustrated with color photographs of period art and artifacts, these volumes describe and thoughtfully contextualize their subjects' lives, accomplishments, and contemporaries. Chapters include sidebars of related material and end with five multiple-choice questions. Though details occasionally overwhelm major trajectories, the books offer responsible historical interpretations." Horn Book

Includes bibliographical references

Chavez, Cesar, 1927-1993

Haugen, Brenda. **Cesar** Chavez; crusader for social change. by Brenda Haugen. Compass Point Books 2008 112p il map $35.32

Grades: 6 7 8 9   **92**
1. Labor leaders. 2. Mexican Americans -- Biography. 3. Mexican American migrant agricultural laborers. 4. Labor leaders -- United States -- Biography. 5. Mexican American migrant agricultural laborers -- Biography
ISBN 978-0-7565-3321-2 (lib bdg); 0-7565-3321-X (lib bdg)
LC 2007003939
Profiles the Mexican American who helped create a union to protect the rights of migrant agricultural laborers. (Publisher's note)

"Provides solid basic information... attractively packaged with many photos, interesting sidebars, and reader-friendly text arrangement." VOYA

Includes bibliographical references

Stavans, Ilan, 1961- **Cesar** Chavez; a photographic essay. Cinco Puntos Press 2010 91p il pa $13.95

Grades: 7 8 9 10   **92**
1. Agricultural laborers 2. Migrant agricultural laborers 3. Labor leaders 4. Mexican Americans -- Biography
ISBN 1-933693-22-3; 978-1-933693-22-4
LC 2009044179
"Chavez secured better working conditions for thousands with his 1970 victory for the United Farm Workers Union by bargaining with the table-grape growers. This photo-biography covers the high points of his career, including ample and pointed quotes by him and touching on his global recognition and interactions with activist Fred Ross Jr., Dolores Huerta, Pope Paul VI, and Senator Robert F. Kennedy. The full-page black-and-white photos give a sense of the man at various ages, of the migrant workers' lives, and of being on the road demonstrating and striking. The book also includes a comprehensive time line. It is an excellent introduction to social activism from the 1950s through the 1980s." SLJ

Child, Lydia Maria Francis, 1802-1880

Kenschaft, Lori. **Lydia** Maria Child; the quest for racial justice. Oxford Univ. Press 2002 126p il (Oxford portraits) lib bdg $24

Grades: 7 8 9 10   **92**

1. Authors 2. Novelists 3. Suffragists 4. Abolitionists 5. Women authors 6. Essayists 7. Authors, American

ISBN 0-19-513257-2

LC 2001-52339

A biography of the popular writer who, in the mid-nineteenth century, gave up her literary success to fight for the abolition of slavery, for women's rights, and for the fair treatment of American Indians

"This well-done book will give young people an opportunity to learn more about one woman and the ideals for which she stood," SLJ

Includes bibliographical references

Chisholm, Shirley, 1924-2005

Raatma, Lucia. **Shirley** Chisholm. Marshall Cavendish Benchmark 2010 96p il (Leading women) $39.93

Grades: 4 5 6 7   **92**

1. Women politicians 2. Members of Congress 3. Presidential candidates 4. African American women -- Biography

ISBN 978-0-7614-4953-9; 0-7614-4953-1

"The arresting portrait on the cover will guide readers right into this well-written [biography of] . . . the first African American woman to enter Congress. . . . Raatma vividly explains what was happening in the country at the time and uses those events effectively as a backdrop. The many photos, both black and white and color, are good choices for the well-designed book." Booklist

Includes bibliographical references

Cho, Margaret, 1968-

Tiger, Caroline. **Margaret** Cho. Chelsea House 2007 111p bibl il por (Asian Americans of achievement) lib bdg $30

Grades: 7 8 9 10   **92**

1. Comedians 2. Korean Americans -- Biography

ISBN 0-7910-9275-5; 978-0-7910-9275-0

LC 2006028385

This is "a lively introduction to the comedian, from her rebellious childhood and teen years to her current successes. . . . The frequent quotes from Cho's funny insightful material will guide readers to seek out her performances." Booklist

Includes glossary and bibliographical references

Choo, Jimmy, 1961-

Sapet, Kerrily. **Jimmy** Choo. Morgan Reynolds Pub. 2010 112p il (Profiles in fashion) $28.95

Grades: 7 8 9 10   **92**

1. Shoemakers 2. Fashion designers 3. Shoe designers

ISBN 978-1-59935-151-3; 1-59935-151-X

LC 2010018813

"Malaysian-born Choo has shod some of the most famous feet in the world. . . . Sapet provides insider details about Choo's remarkable career. . . . Explanations of shoe-biz terms, as well as Asian concepts such as feng shui, en-liven the text, and the eye-catching design includes many color photos of both the shoes and their celebrity fans. . . . This [is an] engrossing introduction to both an exemplary designer and to the fashion business." Booklist

Includes bibliographical references

Chopin, Frédéric, 1810-1849

Malaspina, Ann. **Chopin's** world; [by] Ann Malaspina. Rosen Pub. Group 2008 64p il (Music throughout history) lib bdg $29.25

Grades: 5 6 7 8   **92**

1. Pianists 2. Composers 3. Classical musicians

ISBN 978-1-4042-0723-3 lib bdg; 1-4042-0723-6 lib bdg

LC 2005031281

This "book begins with an introduction briefly addressing social issues of the day, historical background, or other significant information. . . . Successive chapters discuss the [man's] early [life], family background, social status, personality characteristics, musical training and education, obstacles or challenges, and influences. A chapter . . . focuses on the musician's well-known compositions, describing through lively and colorful language some of the musical elements employed. . . . The format and layout are appealing and uncluttered." SLJ

Includes glossary and bibliographical references

Christo, 1935-

★ Greenberg, Jan. **Christo** & Jeanne-Claude; through the Gates and beyond. [by] Jan Greenberg and Sandra Jordan. Roaring Brook Press 2008 50p il $19.95

Grades: 6 7 8 9   **92**

1. Artists 2. Artists -- Biography 3. Gates: Project for Central Park, New York

ISBN 978-1-59643-071-6; 1-59643-071-0

LC 2007-19951

"In 2005, the dull gray of a New York City winter was interrupted when two indomitable artists, Christo and his partner, Jeanne-Claude, brought Central Park brilliantly to life with their outdoor work The Gates. . . . This book, chronicling both The Gates as well as the artists' other projects, is as thoughtful, eye-opening, and meticulous as the work it celebrates." Booklist

Includes bibliographical references

Christo, Jeanne-Claude, 1935-2009

★ Greenberg, Jan. **Christo** & Jeanne-Claude; through the Gates and beyond. [by] Jan Greenberg and Sandra Jordan. Roaring Brook Press 2008 50p il $19.95

Grades: 6 7 8 9   **92**

1. Artists 2. Artists -- Biography 3. Gates: Project for Central Park, New York

ISBN 978-1-59643-071-6; 1-59643-071-0

LC 2007-19951

"In 2005, the dull gray of a New York City winter was interrupted when two indomitable artists, Christo and his partner, Jeanne-Claude, brought Central Park brilliantly to life with their outdoor work The Gates. . . . This book, chronicling both The Gates as well as the artists' other projects, is as thoughtful, eye-opening, and meticulous as the work it celebrates." Booklist

Includes bibliographical references

Churchill, Winston Sir, 1874-1965

★ Severance, John B. **Winston** Churchill; soldier, statesman, artist. Clarion Bks. 1996 144p il map $17.95

Grades: 5 6 7 8   **92**

1. Statesmen 2. Historians 3. Prime ministers 4. Memoirists 5. Cabinet members 6. Members of Parliament 7. Nobel laureates for literature 8. Prime ministers -- Great Britain 9. Great Britain -- Politics and government -- 20th century
ISBN 0-395-69853-7

LC 94-25129

This is a biography of the British "Prime Minister. Although Severance focuses on Churchill's contributions during World War II, he also describes the statesman's boyhood, Boer War adventures, and political ascendancy." (SLJ) Bibliography. Index. "Grades five to eight." (Booklist)

This "biography presents an affectionate portrait of Britain's renowned Prime Minister. Although Severance focuses on Churchill's contributions during World War II, he also describes the statesman's boyhood, Boer War adventures, and political ascendancy." SLJ

Includes bibliographical references

Cisneros, Sandra

Warrick, Karen Clemens. **Sandra** Cisneros; inspiring Latina author. Enslow Publishers 2009 128p il (Latino biography library) $31.93

Grades: 6 7 8 9   **92**

1. Poets 2. Authors 3. Novelists 4. Women authors 5. Mexican American authors 6. Essayists 7. Authors, American 8. Short story writers
ISBN 978-0-7660-3162-3; 0-7660-3162-4

LC 2008041798

Discusses the life of Latina author Sandra Cisneros, including her childhood in Chicago, her path to becoming an accomplished author, and her work in the Latino community.

"Warrick brings originality to Cisnero's story by explaining how the facts of the novelist's life provide a foundation for her advocacy on behalf of others. . . . The text is well documented. . . . This straightforward, thorough biography is a solid addition to most collections." SLJ

Includes bibliographical references

Clark, William, 1770-1838

Crompton, Samuel. **Lewis** and Clark; [by] Samuel Willard Crompton. Chelsea House 2009 116p il map (Great explorers) lib bdg $30

Grades: 6 7 8 9   **92**

1. Explorers 2. Lewis and Clark Expedition (1804-1806) 3. West (U.S.) 4. Territorial governors
ISBN 978-1-60413-418-6 lib bdg; 1-60413-418-6 lib bdg

LC 2009-8687

Biography of the explorers Lewis and Clark

"The information . . . is presented in such a way as to attract and maintain readers' interest. . . . With a full complement of maps, photographs (where available), illustrations,

time lines, and document reproductions, a full story is told. Well-written and throughly researched, this . . . will make a solid addition." SLJ

Includes glossary and bibliographical references

Cleary, Beverly

Cleary, Beverly. A **girl** from Yamhill: a memoir. Morrow 1988 279p il hardcover o.p. pa $12.99

Grades: 6 7 8 9   **92**

1. Authors 2. Women authors 3. Authors, American 4. Children's authors
ISBN 0-688-07800-1; 0-380-72740-4 pa

LC 87-31554

Follows the popular children's author from her childhood years in Oregon through high school and into young adulthood, highlighting her family life and her growing interest in writing

"The author sees her child self with the same clarity and objectivity as she has seen her fictional characters, and her reminiscences have a resultant integrity and candor." Bull Cent Child Books

Clemente, Roberto, 1934-1972

Freedman, Lew. **Roberto** Clemente; baseball star & humanitarian. ABDO Pub. Co. 2011 112p il (Legendary athletes) lib bdg $34.22

Grades: 6 7 8 9   **92**

1. Baseball players 2. Baseball -- Biography 3. Puerto Ricans -- Biography
ISBN 978-1-61714-754-8; 1-61714-754-0

LC 2010041161

This biography of baseball star Roberto Clemente "goes beyond merely discussing [his] accomplishments. . . . [It] also [explores] the social and political [influence he] had on society as a whole. In addition, [it introduces] historical events in the context of [his life]. . . . This . . . is teeming with information and is a must-purchase for sports fans and readers interested in social activism." SLJ

Includes glossary and bibliographical references

Marquez, Heron. **Roberto** Clemente; baseball's humanitarian hero. by Herón Márquez. Carolrhoda Books 2005 112p il (Trailblazer biography) lib bdg $27.93

Grades: 4 5 6 7   **92**

1. Baseball players 2. Baseball -- Biography 3. Puerto Ricans -- Biography
ISBN 1-57505-767-0

LC 2004-2319

"This excellent biography is well organized and enlivened with interesting details and anecdotes. . . . Balancing facts with insightful perspective, this is a readable, well-rounded portrait." SLJ

Includes bibliographical references

Cleopatra, Queen of Egypt, d. 30 B.C.

Blackaby, Susan. **Cleopatra**; Egypt's last and greatest queen. Sterling Pub. 2009 124p il (Sterling biographies) $12.95; pa $5.95

Grades: 5 6 7 8   92

1. Queens 2. Egypt -- History
ISBN 978-1-4027-6540-7; 1-4027-6540-1; 978-1-
4027-5710-5 pa; 1-4027-5710-7 pa

LC 2008030146

"Villainess or goddess, a great queen or a selfish and
overly ambitious woman—readers get to decide. They will
be drawn into this biography by a description of a legendary
magnificent banquet given by Mark Antony for Cleopatra.
The lively narrative maintains interest from her birth in 69
BCE to her death in 31 BCE. . . . Sidebars, color photographs, and reproductions appear throughout. . . . This book
leaves readers fascinated and eager to learn more about her
time in history." SLJ

Includes glossary and bibliographical references

Shecter, Vicky Alvear. **Cleopatra** rules! the
amazing life of the original teen queen. Boyds Mills
Press 2010 128p il map $17.95

Grades: 5 6 7 8   92

1. Queens 2. Egypt -- History 3. Biography, Individual
ISBN 1590787188; 9781590787182

LC 2009-26737

This is a biography of "Cleopatra VII, the last pharaoh of
Egypt." (Publisher's note) Bibliography. Index. "Grades six
to ten." (Bull Cent Child Books)

"This attractive book presents Cleopatra's story through
an unusual text, informative sidebars, and excellent color
illustrations. . . . Calling attention to the writing as much
as its story, the text includes puns, informal language, and
contemporary metaphors. . . . Shecter's solid research is
evident." Booklist

Includes glossary and bibliographical references

Clinton, Hillary Rodham, 1947-

Abrams, Dennis. **Hillary** Rodham Clinton;
politician. Chelsea House Publishers 2009 144p il
(Women of achievement) lib bdg $30

Grades: 6 7 8 9   92

1. Lawyers 2. Women politicians 3. Senators 4.
Secretaries of state 5. Spouses of presidents 6.
Presidential candidates 7. Presidents' spouses -- United
States
ISBN 978-1-60413-077-5; 1-60413-077-6

LC 2008-34639

A biography of the Secretary of State, former presidential candidate, and former First Lady.

"This series contextualizes its subjects' lives and accomplishments in politics, culture, and/or history. The books,
though dense and lengthy, are well written; sidebars supplement the narratives with interesting facts (e.g., women in the
1920s used radium to curl their hair; both Hillary and Bill
Clinton have won Grammy awards). Photographs and reproductions illustrate the texts." Horn Book

Includes bibliographical references

Blashfield, Jean F. **Hillary** Clinton. Marshall
Cavendish Benchmark 2010 112p il (Leading
women) $39.93

Grades: 4 5 6 7   92

1. Lawyers 2. Women politicians 3. Senators 4.
Secretaries of state 5. Spouses of presidents 6.

Presidential candidates 7. Presidents' spouses -- United
States
ISBN 978-0-7614-4954-6; 0-7614-4954-X

A biography of the Secretary of State and former Senator, presidential candidate, and First Lady.

"This information-rich series profiles women of cultural
importance in a clear and engaging manner. Shining a light
on a diverse group of history makers who do not necessarily get a lot of mainstream attention, the books detail their
subjects' childhoods, education, accomplishments, honors,
etc., while also giving historical context. . . . While the text-
dense series might not be ideal for reluctant readers, students
who doing reports will benefit from having access to it." SLJ

Includes bibliographical references

Tracy, Kathleen. The **Clinton** view; the historic
fight for the 2008 Democratic presidential nomination. Mitchell Lane Publishers 2009 48p il (Monumental milestones) lib bdg $29.95

Grades: 6 7 8 9   92

1. Lawyers 2. Women politicians 3. Senators 4.
Secretaries of state 5. Spouses of presidents 6.
Presidential candidates 7. Presidents' spouses -- United
States 8. Presidents -- United States -- Election -- 2008
ISBN 978-1-58415-731-1; 1-58415-731-3

LC 2008053545

This looks at the 2008 presidential campaign from the
point of view of candidate Hillary Clinton

This "begins with the Iowa caucus, the effect the loss
had on front-runner Clinton, and how her win in New Hampshire made her the second Clinton 'comeback kid.' Then,
the book goes back to Clinton's early years, her academic
successes, and her tenures as First Lady and senator. Tracy captures some of the excitement of the campaign. . . .
The design is lively and colorful, and the photos will draw
readers." Booklist

Includes bibliographical references

Cobain, Kurt, 1967-1994

Burlingame, Jeff. **Kurt** Cobain; oh well, whatever, nevermind. Enslow Publishers 2006 160p il
(American rebels) lib bdg $27.93

Grades: 6 7 8 9   92

1. Singers 2. Guitarists 3. Rock musicians
ISBN 0-7660-2426-1

LC 2006001742

A biography of the Rock musician belonging to the
group Nirvana

This "is an unusually intimate account of the rock
legend. A resident of Cobain's hometown, Burlingame
supports his well-researched portrait with personal interviews with Cobain's family, friends, and other local
acquaintances." Booklist

Includes glossary and bibliographical references

Collins, Michael, 1930-

Schyffert, Bea Uusma. The **man** who went to the
far side of the moon: the story of Apollo 11 astronaut
Michael Collins. Chronicle 2003 77p il $14.95

Grades: 5 6 7 8   92

1. Astronauts 2. Space flight 3. Aerospace consultants

4. Museum administrators
ISBN 0-8118-4007-7

A biography of the astronaut, Michael Collins, who circled the moon in the Apollo 12 space capsule while his colleagues Neil Armstrong and Buzz Aldrin landed the lunar module and walked on the moon.

"This excellent book—illustrated scrapbook-style with a cleverly presented mix of photographs, illustrations, and charts—communicates the excitement of space travel." Booklist

Columbus, Christopher

Feinstein, Stephen. **Columbus**; opening up the new world. Enslow Publishers 2009 112p il (Great explorers of the world) lib bdg $31.93

Grades: 6 7 8 9   **92**

1. Explorers 2. America -- Exploration
ISBN 978-1-59845-101-6 lib bdg; 1-59845-101-4 lib bdg

LC 2008-38633

This "balances the explorer's achievements with his inhumane treatment of Indians. The last chapter offers an unusually good summary of how the world changed as different cultures encountered the others' foods, products, diseases, and social ideologies." Booklist

Includes glossary and bibliographical references

Colvin, Claudette

★ Hoose, Phillip. **Claudette** Colvin; twice toward justice. by Phillip Hoose. Melanie Kroupa Books 2009 133p il $19.95

Grades: 6 7 8 9 10   **92**

1. Civil rights activists 2. African Americans -- Civil rights 3. African American women -- Biography 4. Biography, Individual 5. Civil rights movements 6. African Americans -- Civil rights -- History
ISBN 978-0-374-31322-7; 0-374-31322-9

LC 2008-05435

ALA ALSC Newbery Medal Honor Book (2010)

"Teenager Claudette Colvin's significant contribution to the struggle for equal accommodation is presented in this biography that smoothly weaves excerpts from Hoose's extensive interviews with Colvin and his own supplementary commentary. . . . [Readers learn] why her arrest for refusing to give up her bus seat to a white passenger never became the crucial incident to spark the Montgomery Bus Boycott. . . . Plenty of black-and-white photographs and well-deployed sidebars enhance the text." Bull Cent Child Books

Includes bibliographical references

Cone, Claribel, 1864-1929

★ Fillion, Susan. **Miss** Etta and Dr. Claribel; Bringing Matisse to America. David R. Godine 2011 83p il $18.95

Grades: 4 5 6 7   **92**

1. Artists 2. Painters 3. Physicians 4. Art collectors 5. Art -- Collectors and collecting
ISBN 978-1-56792-434-3; 1-56792-434-4

LC 2010048937

"An affectionate, lively examination of the reciprocal relationship between a great artist and two great art lovers. Etta and Claribel Cone, unmarried sisters from a wealthy Baltimore family . . . [were] discerning collectors of modern art, particularly that of Henri Matisse. . . . Their account is lavishly illustrated in full color by reproductions from the Cone Collection at the Baltimore Museum of Art and Matisse-inflected paintings by the author, who drew extensively on the Cone archive that is also housed at the museum. . . . This appealing work stands as both a portrait of two unconventional women and a celebration of the possibilities of arts patronage." Kirkus

Cone, Etta, 1870-1949

★ Fillion, Susan. **Miss** Etta and Dr. Claribel; Bringing Matisse to America. David R. Godine 2011 83p il $18.95

Grades: 4 5 6 7   **92**

1. Artists 2. Painters 3. Physicians 4. Art collectors 5. Art -- Collectors and collecting
ISBN 978-1-56792-434-3; 1-56792-434-4

LC 2010048937

"An affectionate, lively examination of the reciprocal relationship between a great artist and two great art lovers. Etta and Claribel Cone, unmarried sisters from a wealthy Baltimore family . . . [were] discerning collectors of modern art, particularly that of Henri Matisse. . . . Their account is lavishly illustrated in full color by reproductions from the Cone Collection at the Baltimore Museum of Art and Matisse-inflected paintings by the author, who drew extensively on the Cone archive that is also housed at the museum. . . . This appealing work stands as both a portrait of two unconventional women and a celebration of the possibilities of arts patronage." Kirkus

Cook, James, 1728-1779

Feinstein, Stephen. **Captain** Cook; great explorer of the Pacific. Enslow 2010 112p il (Great explorers of the world) lib bdg $31.93

Grades: 6 7 8 9   **92**

1. Explorers 2. Voyages around the world 3. Naval officers 4. Travel writers 5. Oceania -- Exploration
ISBN 978-1-59845-102-3; 1-59845-102-2

LC 2009006503

Examines the life of Captain James Cook, a British explorer and scientist, including his early life, his many Pacific voyages, and his death and legacy

This "provides a harrowing and enlightening account of Cook's discoveries. . . . Cook is portrayed as an intelligent and thoughtful man who regretted some of these negative impacts. Each volume is well organized, with text that is easy to read. . . . This . . . would serve as a useful resource for middle and elementary school students and may inspire them to read further." Voice Youth Advocates

Includes glossary and bibliographical references

Lace, William W. **Captain** James Cook. Chelsea House Publishers 2009 112p il (Great explorers) lib bdg $30

Grades: 6 7 8 9   **92**

1. Explorers 2. Voyages around the world 3. Naval officers 4. Travel writers
ISBN 978-1-60413-416-2 lib bdg; 1-60413-416-X lib bdg

LC 2009-9891

Biography of the explorer Captain James Cook.

"The information ... is presented in such a way as to attract and maintain readers' interest. ... With a full complement of maps, photographs (where available), illustrations, time lines, and document reproductions, a full story is told. Well-written and thoroughly researched, this ... will make a solid addition." SLJ

Includes glossary and bibliographical references

Copernicus, Nicolaus, 1473-1543

Andronik, Catherine M. **Copernicus**; founder of modern astronomy. rev ed; Enslow Publishers 2009 128p bibl il (Great minds of science) lib bdg $31.93

Grades: 5 6 7 8   **92**

1. Astronomers

ISBN 978-0-7660-3013-8 lib bdg; 0-7660-3013-X lib bdg

LC 2008-23940

First published 2002

"A highly readable book that presents a good balance between the biographical information needed to understand Copernicus as a man and the scientific explanations necessary to understand his work. ... Good-quality, black-and-white reproductions, illustrations, and photographs add interest to the clearly written text." SLJ [review of 2002 edition]

Includes glossary and bibliographical references

Sakolsky, Josh. **Copernicus** and modern astronomy. Rosen Pub. Group 2005 64p il (Primary sources of revolutionary scientific discoveries and theories) $29.25

Grades: 6 7 8 9   **92**

1. Astronomy 2. Astronomers

ISBN 1-4042-0305-2; 978-1-4042-0305-1

LC 2004011296

An introduction to the life and work of the pioneering astronomer who proved that the earth revolved around the sun

Includes bibliographical references

Cormier, Robert

Beckman, Wendy Hart. **Robert** Cormier; banned, challenged, and censored. Enslow Publishers 2008 160p bibl il por (Authors of banned books) lib bdg $34.60

Grades: 6 7 8 9 10   **92**

1. Authors 2. Novelists 3. Censorship 4. Authors, American 5. Young adult authors

ISBN 978-0-7660-2691-9; 0-7660-2691-4

LC 2007-28003

"Cormier is generally cited as one of the finest and most challenged writers for teens. This combination of biography and literary criticism explains his appeal to readers as well as the most common objections to his works from parents and school districts. A history of other censorship, including several recent court cases involving the First Amendment, and a biographical sketch of Cormier precede the discussion of The Chocolate War (1974), I Am the Cheese (1977), and After the First Death (1979, all Knopf). ... A helpful overview of the works of a major YA author." SLJ

Includes glossary and bibliographical references

Cortés, Hernán, 1485-1547

Wagner, Heather Lehr. **Hernan** Cortes. Chelsea House 2009 119p il map (Great explorers) lib bdg $30

Grades: 6 7 8 9   **92**

1. Explorers 2. Mexico -- History 3. Colonial administrators

ISBN 978-1-60413-424-7 lib bdg; 1-60413-424-0 lib bdg

LC 2009-14165

Biography of the explorer Hernan Cortes

"The information ... is presented in such a way as to attract and maintain readers' interest. ... With a full complement of maps, photographs (where available), illustrations, time lines, and document reproductions, a full story is told. Well-written and thoroughly researched, this ... will make a solid addition." SLJ

Includes glossary and bibliographical references

Corwin, Jeff

Corwin, Jeff. **Jeff** Corwin: a wild life; the authorized biography. Penguin Group 2009 100p il pa $6.99

Grades: 4 5 6 7   **92**

1. Biologists 2. Naturalists 3. Conservationists 4. Television personalities

ISBN 978-0-14-241403-3 pa; 0-14-241403-4 pa

LC 2009008092

"The host of Animal Planet ... and other popular TV programs blends his exciting adventure in the wild with his passionate call for conservation. ... An insert of beautifully reproduced color photos from his global travels show him with a giraffe in Kenya, a moose in Alaska, and more. ... The adventures are thrilling, and the messages are urgent." Booklist

Cosgrove, Miranda, 1993-

Yasuda, Anita. **Miranda** Cosgrove. Weigl 2011 24p il (Remarkable people) $27.13; pa $12.95

Grades: 4 5 6 7   **92**

1. Actors 2. Singers

ISBN 978-1-6169-0668-9; 1-6169-0668-5; 978-1-6169-0673-3 pa; 1-6169-0673-1 pa

LC 2010051144

A biography of actress and singer Miranda Cosgrove

Cousteau, Jacques Yves, 1910-1997

Knowles, Jo. **Jacques** Cousteau. Chelsea House 2011 117p il (Conservation heroes) lib bdg $35

Grades: 6 7 8 9 10   **92**

1. Ocean 2. Authors 3. Scientists 4. Skin diving 5. Divers 6. Naval officers 7. Oceanographers 8. Nonfiction writers

ISBN 978-1-60413-947-1; 1-60413-947-1

LC 2010030584

A biography of the French undersea explorer and conservationist.

"Captivating, richly informative. . . . The scope of [this book] is comprehensive, . . . [The book is] engaging as [it is] educational and will be ideal for research and reports." SLJ

Includes glossary and bibliographical references

Olmstead, Kathleen A. **Jacques** Cousteau; a life under the sea. [by] Kathleen Olmstead. Sterling Pub. Co. 2008 124p il (Sterling biographies) pa $5.99

Grades: 7 8 9 10   92

1. Ocean 2. Authors 3. Scientists 4. Oceanography 5. Divers 6. Naval officers 7. Oceanographers 8. Nonfiction writers

ISBN 978-1-4027-4440-2; 1-4027-4440-4

LC 2007048195

"Most of the text . . . is concerned with Cousteau's evolving inventions for breathing and exploring underwater. Olmstead describes how his films and television specials opened a new world to viewers, and how he became a leading advocate for the oceans. She also makes mention of Cousteau's secret second family and his dispute with his son Jean-Michel over using the family name for an ecotourist resort. . . . [This] attractively formatted [title has] black-and-white and full-color photographs or reproductions as well as sidebars. [A] solid [addition] to biography shelves." SLJ

Includes glossary and bibliographical references

Coville, Bruce

Marcovitz, Hal. **Bruce** Coville. Chelsea House 2006 124p bibl il por (Who wrote that?) $30

Grades: 6 7 8 9   92

1. Authors 2. Authors, American 3. Children's authors

ISBN 0-7910-8656-9

LC 2005008182

A biography of the popular author of children's and young adult fantasy and science fiction books.

Includes bibliographical references

Crandall, Prudence, 1803-1890

★ Jurmain, Suzanne. The **forbidden** schoolhouse; the true and dramatic story of Prudence Crandall and her students. Houghton Mifflin 2005 150p il $18

Grades: 5 6 7 8   92

1. Teachers 2. Educators 3. Abolitionists 4. African Americans -- Education

ISBN 0-618-47302-5

This is the story of Prudence Crandall, who, in 1831, opened a school for African American girls in Canterbury, Connecticut.

"A compelling, highly readable book. . . . Writing with a sense of drama that propels readers forward . . . Jurmain makes painfully clear what Crandall and her students faced. . . . Including a number of sepia-toned and color photographs as well as historical engravings, the book's look will draw in readers." Booklist

Includes bibliographical references

Creech, Sharon

Baptiste, Tracey. **Sharon** Creech; foreword by Kyle Zimmer. Chelsea House 2011 118p il (Who wrote that?) lib bdg $35

Grades: 6 7 8 9   92

1. Authors 2. Novelists 3. Women authors 4. Authors, American 5. Children's authors 6. Young adult authors

ISBN 978-1-60413-774-3; 1-60413-774-6

LC 2010030595

A biography of the author of Walk Two Moons and Absolutely Normal Chaos.

Includes bibliographical references

Cromwell, Oliver, 1599-1658

Aronson, Marc. **John** Winthrop, Oliver Cromwell, and the Land of Promise. Clarion Books 2004 205p il map $20

Grades: 7 8 9 10   92

1. Clergy 2. Puritans 3. Heads of state 4. Revolutionaries 5. Government officials 6. Colonial administrators 7. Great Britain -- History -- 1603-1714, Stuarts 8. Massachusetts -- History -- 1600-1775, Colonial period

ISBN 0-618-18177-6

LC 2003-16418

"The accessible text is accompanied by excerpts from primary source documents and vivid illustrations. The author's passion for the period comes across in his writing. Aronson provides an excellent source for historical and biographical data." Voice Youth Advocates

Includes bibliographical references

Crutcher, Chris, 1946-

★ Crutcher, Chris. **King** of the mild frontier: an ill-advised autobiography. Greenwillow Bks. 2003 260p il $16.99; pa $6.99

Grades: 8 9 10 11 12   92

1. Authors 2. Novelists 3. Authors, American 4. Young adult authors

ISBN 0-06-050249-5; 0-06-050251-7 pa

LC 2002-11224

Chris Crutcher, author of young adult novels such as "Ironman" and "Whale Talk," as well as short stories, tells of growing up in Cascade, Idaho, and becoming a writer

"Like his novels, Crutcher's autobiography is full of heartbreak, poignancy, and hilarity. . . . This honest, insightful, revealing autobiography is a joy to read." Booklist

Sommers, Michael A. **Chris** Crutcher; Michael A. Sommers. 1st ed; Rosen Pub. Group 2005 112p il (Library of author biographies) lib bdg $26.50

Grades: 5 6 7 8   92

1. Authors 2. Novelists 3. Authors, American 4. Young adult authors

ISBN 1-4042-0325-7

LC 2004-13100

"Sommers describes Crutcher as an author who writes from his experience as a teacher, therapist, and writer. . . . Selections of book reviews of [his] work are included. . . . [This is] well-written." SLJ

Includes bibliographical references

Cruz, Celia, 1929-2003

Cartlidge, Cherese. **Celia** Cruz. Chelsea House Publishers 2010 112p il (The great Hispanic heritage) lib bdg $30

Grades: 6 7 8 9   92

1. Singers 2. Salsa musicians
ISBN 978-1-60413-771-2; 1-60413-771-1

LC 2010007809

This "delves frankly into the Cuban-born singer-songwriter's life, including her blatant rejection of Fidel Castro and her subsequent immigration to the U.S., where President Clinton eventually honored her with a Presidential Medal. . . . A selection of well-chosen images, a chronology, chapter notes, and [a] suggested reading [list] round out [this] engaging and sure-to-be-popular [book] for reports and personal interest." Booklist

Cummings, E. E. (Edward Estlin), 1894-1962

Reef, Catherine. **E.** E. Cummings. Clarion Books 2006 149p il $21

Grades: 7 8 9 10 11 12   92

1. Poets 2. Authors 3. Poets, American
ISBN 978-0-618-56849-9; 0-618-56849-2

LC 2006-10453

"Reef explores the interaction of events and poetry to portray a man whose story would not be complete without an understanding of both. She makes clear that the king of experimental poetry was deeply grounded in the very structure he subverted. Black-and-white photographs vivify the facts, while the spacious format gives Cummings's words room to spread out. List of major works, source notes. Bib., glos., ind." (Horn Book)

Includes bibliographical references

Curie, Marie, 1867-1934

Borzendowski, Janice. **Marie** Curie; mother of modern physics. Sterling Pub 2009 124p il map (Sterling biographies) $12.95; pa $5.95

Grades: 7 8 9 10   92

1. Chemists 2. Physicists 3. Women scientists 4. Nobel laureates for physics
ISBN 978-1-4027-6543-8; 1-4027-6543-6; 978-1-4027-5318-3 pa; 1-4027-5318-7 pa

LC 2008-30701

"This interesting, informative biography of the scientist and Nobel Prize winner explores both Curie's personal and professional life. It includes numerous archival and modern photos and reproductions. . . . The book is far more thorough and satisfying than most biographies of Curie for teens." SLJ

Includes bibliographical references

Cregan, Elizabeth R. **Marie** Curie; pioneering physicist. Compass Point Books 2009 40p il map (Mission: Science) lib bdg $26.60

Grades: 4 5 6   92

1. Chemists 2. Physicists 3. Women scientists 4. Nobel laureates for physics
ISBN 978-0-7565-3960-3

This biography of the discoverer of radium "does a good job of connecting the scientist's work to our lives today. . . . [The] book has a variety of graphics including diagrams, photos, and reproductions of paintings and sketches. [This volume is] a definite plus for a school library or the juvenile collection in a public library." Libr Media Connect

Koestler-Grack, Rachel A. **Marie** Curie; scientist. Chelsea House 2009 136p bibl il por (Women of achievement) $30

Grades: 6 7 8 9   92

1. Chemists 2. Physicists 3. Women scientists 4. Nobel laureates for physics
ISBN 978-1-60413-086-7; 1-60413-086-5

LC 2008034999

A biography of the scientist who, with her husband, Pierre Curie, discovered the phenomenon of radioactivity.

The book is "well written; sidebars supplement the [narrative] with interesting facts." Horn Book Guide

Includes bibliographical references

★ Krull, Kathleen. **Marie** Curie; [illustrations by] Boris Kulikov. Viking 2007 128p il (Giants of science) $15.99

Grades: 5 6 7 8   92

1. Chemists 2. Physicists 3. Women scientists 4. Nobel laureates for physics
ISBN 978-0-670-05894-5; 0-670-05894-7

LC 2007-24251

"The compelling and conversational narrative (ably assisted by Kulikov's black-and-white drawings) portrays a brilliant . . . woman with plenty of idiosyncrasies, and the story of her discovery of radium . . . is as engaging as any of her personal dramas and challenges." Horn Book

MacLeod, Elizabeth. **Marie** Curie; a brilliant life. written by Elizabeth MacLeod. Kids Can Press 2004 32p il $14.95; pa $6.95

Grades: 5 6 7 8   92

1. Chemists 2. Physicists 3. Women scientists 4. Nobel laureates for physics
ISBN 1-55337-570-X; 1-55337-571-8 pa

"The drive and self-sacrifice that enabled Marie Curie to win two Nobel Prizes and become the most acclaimed female scientist to date are explored in this accessible biography, which covers Curie's personal and professional lives. Illustrated with well-chosen archival photos." Horn Book Guide

Cézanne, Paul, 1839-1906

Spence, David. **Cezanne**. New Forest Press 2010 48p il (Great artists and their world) lib bdg $32.80

Grades: 6 7 8 9   92

1. Artists 2. Painters 3. Artists, French
ISBN 978-1-84898-315-1; 1-84898-315-8

"Offers biographical information [of Paul Cezanne] . . . interspersed with art history and criticism in an eye-catching format. . . . [Includes] a long introductory paragraph and four-to-six images with explanatory notes. . . . Spence . . . does a good job of explaining why art that might seem ordinary today was revolutionary at the time of its creation." SLJ

Includes glossary

Dahl, Roald

★ Dahl, Roald. **Boy** : tales of childhood. Farrar, Straus & Giroux 1984 160p il hardcover o.p. rpt $6.99

Grades: 6 7 8 9   **92**

1. Authors 2. Authors, English 3. Children's authors 4. Short story writers

ISBN 0-14-130305-0; 9780142413814 rpt

LC 84-48462

"In these memoirs, Dahl reminisces about growing up in a large Norwegian family living in Wales during the 1920s and 1930s. The text is illustrated with sketches, old photographs and excerpts of letters he wrote as a boy." SLJ

Dahl, Roald. **More** about Boy; Roald Dahl's tales from childhood. Farrar, Straus, and Giroux 2009 229p il $16.99

Grades: 5 6 7 8   **92**

1. Authors 2. Authors, English 3. Children's authors 4. Short story writers

ISBN 978-0-374-35055-0; 0-374-35055-8

LC 2009016118

First published 2008 in the United Kingdom

"Containing the entire text and artwork from Dahl's 1984 autobiography Boy, this reworked and expanded version also incorporates previously unpublished materials from the Roald Dahl Museum and Story Centre in England, as well as excerpts that have appeared in earlier books. . . . Dahl's revealing writing, open and full of wicked humor, is certain to endear the beloved writer . . . to a new generation." Publ Wkly

Dalai Lama XIV, 1935-

Kimmel, Elizabeth Cody. **Boy** on the lion throne; the childhood of the 14th Dalai Lama. with a foreword by His Holiness the Dalai Lama. Roaring Brook Press 2009 146p il map $18.95

Grades: 4 5 6 7   **92**

1. Buddhism 2. Tibet (China) 3. Buddhist leaders 4. Political leaders 5. Nobel laureates for peace

ISBN 978-1-59643-394-6; 1-59643-394-9

Follows the childhood of Lhamo Thondup, who was identified at the age of two as the fourteenth reincarnation of the Dalai Lama, describing the humble life he was born into and how his life changed after he was recognized

"Kimmel is reverent without being adulatory, and her explanation of the Dalai Lama's relationship with Maoist China is presented in simple, clear language. This is a strange and fascinating story told in an engaging style, and young readers will find lots to keep them turning the pages." Bull Cent Child Books

Includes bibliographical references

Dalí, Salvador, 1904-1989

McNeese, Tim. **Salvador** Dali; [by] Tim McNeese. Chelsea House Publishers 2006 122p il (Great Hispanic heritage) lib bdg $30

Grades: 7 8 9 10   **92**

1. Artists 2. Painters 3. Artists, Spanish

ISBN 0-7910-8837-5

LC 2005025998

A biography of the 20th century surrealist painter.

"McNeese does a wonderful job of describing [this man's life] and, more importantly, the times in which [he] lived. . . . [The book is] expertly researched." SLJ

Includes bibliographical references

Dandridge, Dorothy

Herringshaw, DeAnn. **Dorothy** Dandridge; singer & actress. ABDO Pub. Co. 2011 112p il (Essential lives) $23.95

Grades: 6 7 8 9 10   **92**

1. Actors 2. Singers 3. African American actors

ISBN 978-1-61714-779-1; 1-61714-779-6

LC 2010042150

"This volume profiles the life of . . . actress Dorothy Dandridge . . . Dandridge's life reads much like a screenplay. . . . Students will be captivated by Dandridge's guts and by the naked hypocrisy of the racisim that she faced even as a movie star." Booklist

Includes bibliographical references

Dante Alighieri, 1265-1321

Davenport, John. **Dante**; poet, author, and proud Florentine. [by] John Davenport. Chelsea House 2006 140p il (Makers of the Middle Ages and Renaissance) lib bdg $30

Grades: 6 7 8 9   **92**

1. Poets 2. Authors 3. Authors, Italian

ISBN 0-7910-8634-8

LC 2005007492

This biography of the Italian Renaissance author of The Divine Comedy describes his "childhood and background as well as his influences, career, and writing. The colorful illustrations, many from illuminated manuscripts, short chapters, simple vocabulary, and large print present an attractive format. Sidebars and captions contain additional information." SLJ

Includes bibliographical references

Darwin, Charles, 1809-1882

Ashby, Ruth. **Young** Charles Darwin and the voyage of the Beagle; written by Ruth Ashby. Peachtree 2009 116p il map $12.95

Grades: 4 5 6   **92**

1. Evolution 2. Naturalists 3. Travel writers 4. Writers on science 5. Beagle Expedition (1831-1836)

ISBN 978-1-56145-478-5; 1-56145-478-8

LC 2008-36747

"Beginning with the letter inviting him to sail aboard the Beagle, this traditional biography relates Darwin's life with an emphasis on the trip that led him to forge his theory about natural selection. Ashby makes good use of Darwin's own writing, sprinkling quotes throughout the text, which allow his adventures and opinions to come to life. . . . This biography will work well for book reports . . . providing accurate and readable information about the scientist and his journey." Booklist

Includes bibliographical references

★ Eldredge, Niles. **Charles** Darwin and the mystery of mysteries; by Niles Eldredge and Susan

Pearson. Rb Flash Point 2010 135p il map lib bdg $19.99

Grades: 7 8 9 10   **92**

1. Naturalists 2. Travel writers 3. Writers on science 4. Beagle Expedition (1831-1836)

ISBN 978-1-59643-374-8; 1-59643-374-4

Follows Charles Darwin on his journey aboard the HMS Beagle and presents the thinking that led him to the theory of evolution and the writing of The origin of the species. Includes historical photographs and passages from Darwin's personal diary.

"Numerous quotations from Darwin's works and correspondence bring his voice to readers. . . . Eldredge and Pearson have done a fine job of summarizing both Darwin's life and work." SLJ

★ Heiligman, Deborah. **Charles** and Emma; the Darwins' leap of faith. Henry Holt and Company 2009 268p il $18.95

Grades: 7 8 9 10 11 12   **92**

1. Naturalists 2. Travel writers 3. Writers on science 4. Spouses of prominent persons

ISBN 978-0-8050-8721-5; 0-8050-8721-4

LC 2008-26091

ALA YALSA Printz Award Honor Book (2010)

ALA Excellence in Nonfiction Award (2010)

"This rewarding biography of Charles Darwin investigates his marriage to his cousin Emma Wedgwood. . . . Embracing the paradoxes in her subjects' personalities, the author unfolds a sympathetic and illuminating account, bolstered by quotations from their personal writings as well as significant research into the historical context." Publ Wkly

Includes bibliographical references

★ Krull, Kathleen. **Charles** Darwin; illustrated by Boris Kulikov. Viking 2010 144p il (Giants of science) $15.99

Grades: 5 6 7 8   **92**

1. Evolution 2. Naturalists 3. Travel writers 4. Writers on science

ISBN 978-0-670-06335-2; 0-670-06335-5

LC 2010-07315

"Krull once again offers an illuminating, humanizing portrait of a famous scientist. . . . Krull . . . writes in easily paced, lively, conversational prose, knitting together interesting facts, anecdotes, and historical overviews into a fascinating whole. She offers clear definitions of not only Darwin's theories but also how his discoveries built on previous scientists' work. . . . Kulikov's whimsical ink drawings and well-culled list of resources round out this strong entry in the series." Booklist

Schanzer, Rosalyn. **What** Darwin saw; the journey that changed the world. National Geographic 2009 47p il map $17.95; lib bdg $26.90

Grades: 3 4 5 6   **92**

1. Evolution 2. Naturalists 3. Travel writers 4. Writers on science 5. Beagle Expedition (1831-1836)

ISBN 978-1-4263-0396-8; 1-4263-0396-3; 978-1-4263-0397-5 lib bdg; 1-4263-0397-1 lib bdg

LC 2008-39809

"Schanzer uses Darwin's own words, taken from his journals, books, and letters, in the speech balloons of her graphic depiction of the voyage of the Beagle. This is not a full biography, but begins with Darwin's acceptance of the offer to sail on the expedition and ends with the presentation of his theory of evolution in 1860. Bright, watercolor cartoons accurately portray landscapes and specimens while also creating a vivid sense of adventure." SLJ

Includes bibligraphical references

Darwin, Emma Wedgwood, 1808-1896

★ Heiligman, Deborah. **Charles** and Emma; the Darwins' leap of faith. Henry Holt and Company 2009 268p il $18.95

Grades: 7 8 9 10 11 12   **92**

1. Naturalists 2. Travel writers 3. Writers on science 4. Spouses of prominent persons

ISBN 978-0-8050-8721-5; 0-8050-8721-4

LC 2008-26091

ALA YALSA Printz Award Honor Book (2010)

ALA Excellence in Nonfiction Award (2010)

"This rewarding biography of Charles Darwin investigates his marriage to his cousin Emma Wedgwood. . . . Embracing the paradoxes in her subjects' personalities, the author unfolds a sympathetic and illuminating account, bolstered by quotations from their personal writings as well as significant research into the historical context." Publ Wkly

Includes bibliographical references

Dave, fl. 1834-1864

Cheng, Andrea. **Etched** in clay; the life of Dave, enslaved potter and poet. Andrea Cheng ; with woodcuts by the author. Lee & Low Books 2012 144 p. (hardcover : alk. paper) $17.95

Grades: 4 5 6   **92**

1. Slaves 2. Potters 3. African American poets 4. African American potters 5. Slaves -- South Carolina

ISBN 160060451X; 9781600604515; 9781600608933

LC 2012027280

In this children's biography in verse, Caldecott Honor-winner Andrea Cheng looks at the "life of the enslaved potter Dave," who wrote poetry. "Records indicate Dave, who was born in the United States in 1801, was most likely purchased at a slave auction at age 17 by Harvey Drake, who, with his uncles, held the Pottersville Stoneware Manufactory in South Carolina. Dave took to the wheel within weeks and went on to become one of the most accomplished potters in the region." (Kirkus Reviews)

Davis, Benjamin O., Jr.

★ Earl, Sari. **Benjamin** O. Davis, Jr. Air Force general & Tuskegee Airmen leader. ABDO Pub. Co. 2010 111p il map (Military heroes) lib bdg $22.95

Grades: 7 8 9   **92**

1. Generals 2. Air force officers 3. United States -- Air Force

ISBN 978-1-60453-961-5; 1-60453-961-5

LC 2009-32339

Biography of Benjamin O. Davis Jr.

"The rush of literary adrenalin will hook readers immediately and keep them enthralled until the end. . . . Given the dynamic topic [and] . . . appealing layout . . . [this is] likely to attract reluctant readers. In addition, sources are plentiful and well documented." SLJ

Includes glossary and bibliographical references

De la Renta, Oscar

Darraj, Susan Muaddi. **Oscar** de la Renta. Chelsea House 2010 116p il (The great Hispanic heritage) lib bdg $30

Grades: 6 7 8 9   **92**

1. Fashion designers
ISBN 978-1-60413-733-0; 1-60413-733-9

LC 2010009488

This "presents a warm, almost fawning account of the wildly successful fashion designer, who maintains a home in and close ties to his native Dominican Republic. . . . A selection of well-chosen images, a chronology, chapter notes, and [a] suggested reading [list] round out [this] engaging [title] in a sure-to-be-popular [book] for reports and personal interest." Booklist

Includes bibliographical references

DeGeneres, Ellen

Paprocki, Sherry Beck. **Ellen** Degeneres; entertainer. Sherry Beck Paprocki. Chelsea House Publishers 2009 136p bibl il por (Women of achievement) $30

Grades: 6 7 8 9   **92**

1. Actors 2. Comedians 3. Entertainers 4. Television personalities 5. Talk show hosts
ISBN 978-1-60413-082-9; 1-60413-082-2

LC 2008034638

A biography of comedian, actress, and TV talk show host Ellen Degeneres.

"This series contextualizes its subjects' lives and accomplishments in politics, culture, and/or history. The books, though dense and lengthy, are well written; sidebars supplement the narratives with interesting facts (e.g., women in the 1920s used radium to curl their hair; both Hillary and Bill Clinton have won Grammy awards). Photographs and reproductions illustrate the texts." Horn Book

Includes bibliographical references

Degas, Edgar, 1834-1917

Spence, David. **Degas**. New Forest Press 2010 48p il (Great artists and their world) lib bdg $32.80

Grades: 6 7 8 9   **92**

1. Artists 2. Painters 3. Artists, French
ISBN 978-1-84898-318-2; 1-84898-318-2

"Offers biographical information [of Edgar Degas] . . . interspersed with art history and criticism in an eye-catching format. . . . [Includes] a long introductory paragraph and four-to-six images with explanatory notes. . . . Spence . . . does a good job of explaining why art that might seem ordinary today was revolutionary at the time of its creation." SLJ

Includes glossary

Democritus

Macfarlane, Katherine. The **father** of the atom; Democritus and the nature of matter. Enslow Publishers 2010 112p il map (Great minds of ancient science and math) lib bdg $31.93

Grades: 5 6 7 8   **92**

1. Atoms 2. Matter 3. Mathematics 4. Philosophers 5. Writers on science
ISBN 978-0-7660-3410-5 lib bdg; 0-7660-3410-0 lib bdg

LC 2008-46265

This biography is a "solid [choice], as . . . . [it provides] a good overview of the cultural and political landscape of the times, as well as pictures." SLJ

Includes glossary and bibliographical references

Diana, Princess of Wales, 1961-1997

Paprocki, Sherry Beck. **Diana,** Princess of Wales; humanitarian. Chelsea House 2009 136p il (Women of achievement) $30

Grades: 6 7 8 9   **92**

1. Princesses
ISBN 978-1-60413-463-6; 1-60413-463-1

LC 2009008690

A biography of Lady Diana Spencer who became Princess of Wales when she married Prince Charles in 1981, and who became known as The People's Princess for her charitable works.

Includes bibliographical references

Dickens, Charles, 1812-1870

Caravantes, Peggy. **Best** of times: the story of Charles Dickens. Morgan Reynolds Pub. 2005 160p il (World writers) $26.95

Grades: 7 8 9 10   **92**

1. Authors 2. Novelists 3. Authors, English
ISBN 1-931798-68-0

LC 2005-8405

"Beginning with Dickens' childhood trauma (his father was put in debtors' prison, and Charles, 12, had to work in a blacking factory), this highly readable [book] . . . relates the extraordinary writer's stories to his life and times. . . . [It includes] many interesting quotes, color prints, and photos." Booklist

Includes bibliographical references

★ Rosen, Michael, 1946- **Dickens**; his work and his world. illustrated by Robert Ingpen. Candlewick Press 2005 95p il $19.99

Grades: 5 6 7 8   **92**

1. Authors 2. Novelists 3. Authors, English 4. Biography, Individual
ISBN 0-7636-2752-6

LC 2004-61847

"The art adds to the richness of a volume designed and written with care." Booklist

★ Warren, Andrea. **Charles** Dickens and the street children of London. Houghton Mifflin Books for Children/Houghton Mifflin Harcourt 2011 144p il $18.99

Grades: 6 7 8 9 10   **92**

1. Authors 2. Novelists 3. Children in literature 4. Authors, English 5. London (England) 6. Poor -- Great

Britain 7. Great Britain -- History -- 19th century
ISBN 978-0-547-39574-6; 0-547-39574-4

LC 2011003450

"This absorbing book introduces Dickens within the context of his times. . . . Chapters about his life and his novels alternate with related chapters describing the plight of the poor (especially children) in Victorian England (especially London). . . . Glimpses of his world are offered in reproductions of illustrations from Dickens' novels as well as period portraits and photos of people and places that appear throughout the book. . . . Warren writes in a clear, direct, vivid manner that brings it all to life." Booklist

Dickinson, Emily, 1830-1886

★ Meltzer, Milton. **Emily** Dickinson; a biography. Twenty-first Century Books 2006 128p il (American literary greats) lib bdg $31.93
Grades: 7 8 9 10   92
1. Women poets 2. Poets, American
ISBN 0-7613-2949-8; 978-0-7613-2949-7

LC 2003-22978

Examines the life of the reclusive nineteenth-century Massachusetts poet whose posthumously published poetry brought her the public attention she had carefully avoided during her lifetime.

"This introduction to an important American literary figure is notable for its clear and succinct writing. . . . Excerpts from her letters and poems appear throughout. A worthwhile book for students who might have difficulty with more scholarly works." SLJ

Includes bibliographical references

Dorsey, Jack

Smith, Chris. **Twitter**; Jack Dorsey, Biz Stone and Evan Williams. [by] Chris Smith and Marci McGrath. Morgan Reynolds Pub. 2011 112p il (Business leaders) $28.95
Grades: 7 8 9 10 11 12   92
1. Online social networks 2. Twitter, Inc. 3. Internet executives 4. Computer programmers 5. Computer software executives
ISBN 978-1-59935-179-7; 1-59935-179-X; 978-1-59935-216-9 e-book

LC 2011024699

This biography of the founders of Twitter "will grab YAs. . . . The design is browsable, with clear type and lots of color screens and informal photos of young people at work." Booklist

Includes bibliographical references

Douglass, Frederick, 1817?-1895

★ Adler, David A. **Frederick** Douglass; a noble life. Holiday House 2010 138p il $18.95
Grades: 7 8 9 10   92
1. Slaves 2. Authors 3. Abolitionists 4. Memoirists 5. African Americans -- Biography
ISBN 978-0-8234-2056-8; 0-8234-2056-6

LC 2009-29970

A biography of Frederick Douglass, who was born into slavery in 1818 and raised on a Maryland plantation under brutal conditions and who grew up to become a famous orator, journalist, author, and adviser to U.S. presidents.

This is "a thoroughly researched, lucidly written biography. . . . Adler does an excellent job of exploring the atrocities and dehumanizing indignities . . . visited on those who lived in slavery." Booklist

Includes bibliographical references

Cline-Ransome, Lesa. **Words** set me free; the story of young Frederick Douglass. Lesa Cline-Ransome; illustrated by James E. Ransome. Simon & Schuster Books for Young Readers 2012 32 p. (hardback) $17.99
Grades: 6 7 8   92
1. Abolitionists 2. Slaves -- Emancipation 3. African Americans -- Biography 4. Slaves -- United States -- Biography 5. Abolitionists -- United States -- Biography 6. African American abolitionists -- Biography
ISBN 9781416959038

LC 2011013323

In this book, the historical character Frederick Douglass "relates his early years, from first vague memories of his mother . . . through his childhood, with his service leased to the Auld family of Baltimore; to his first attempt to make an escape from Talbot County, Maryland. The narration is . . . focused on the way learning to read both inspired and enabled young Frederick to plan for a life of freedom in the North . . . This chapter in Douglass' story concludes with his forgery of a pass, written 'in a firm and steady hand,' which would allow him to 'walk right out of Talbot County and into freedom up north.'" (Bulletin of the Center for Children's Books)

Includes bibliographical references and index

Esty, Amos. **Unbound** and unbroken: the story of Frederick Douglass. Morgan Reynolds Pub. 2010 143p il map (Civil rights leaders) lib bdg $28.95
Grades: 7 8 9 10   92
1. Slaves 2. Authors 3. Abolitionists 4. Memoirists 5. African Americans -- Biography
ISBN 978-1-59935-136-0; 1-59935-136-6

LC 2009-54287

Traces the life and historical impact of the noted abolitionist, detailing his birth into slavery and harsh upbringing, his subsequent escape, and his emergence as a leader.

"Multiple biographies have been written about Douglass; however, few capture the depth of his intellect as an orator and writer. Through interwoven quotes from his autobiography, speeches, and pictures, this story also serves as prime research material. Douglass's ingenious case for the Constitution and fifth of July speech make the biography accessible from cover to cover." Voice Youth Advocates

Includes bibliographical references

Schuman, Michael. **Frederick** Douglass; truth is of no color. [by] Michael A. Schuman. Enslow Publishers 2009 128p il map (Americans: the spirit of a nation) lib bdg $31.93
Grades: 6 7 8 9   92
1. Slaves 2. Authors 3. Abolitionists 4. Memoirists 5. African Americans -- Biography
ISBN 978-0-7660-3025-1 lib bdg; 0-7660-3025-3 lib bdg

LC 2008-29634

This "is an engaging introduction to famous abolitionist. Well-sourced excerpts, including many passages from Douglass' own writings, and vivid description enliven the text. . . . The visuals ably support the writing, with a strong mix of engravings, maps, and photos." Booklist

Includes glossary and bibliographical references

Douglas, Gabrielle

Buford, Michael. **Grace,** gold and glory; my leap of faith : the Gabrielle Douglas story. by Gabrielle Douglas ; with Michelle Burford. Zondervan 2012 222 p. ill. (hardcover) $24.99

Grades: 4 5 6 7 8   **92**
   1. Gymnastics 2. Olympic athletes 3. Women gymnasts -- United States -- Biography 4. Women Olympic athletes -- United States -- Biography
ISBN 0310740614; 9780310740612

                    LC 2012042389

This book is a "first-person account of 2012 Olympic gold medalist [Gabrielle] Douglas's life from birth to the Olympics written in collaboration with [Michelle] Burford. . . . Douglas mentions the lows—her family lived in their van for months when she was an infant—and bullying, but never dwells on them. . . . Supported by her mother and siblings, and by her strong faith in God, she sees herself as capable of achieving greatness 'because God has equipped me with all I need to succeed.'" (Publishers Weekly)

Drake, Francis Sir, 1540?-1596

Lace, William W. **Sir** Francis Drake. Chelsea House 2009 112p il map (Great explorers) lib bdg $30

Grades: 6 7 8 9   **92**
   1. Admirals 2. Explorers 3. Voyages around the world
ISBN 978-1-60413-417-9 lib bdg; 1-60413-417-8 lib bdg

                    LC 2009-15017

Biography of the explorer Sir Francis Drake

"The information . . . is presented in such a way as to attract and maintain readers' interest. . . . With a full complement of maps, photographs (where available), illustrations, time lines, and document reproductions, a full story is told. Well-written and thoroughly researched, this . . . will make a solid addition." SLJ

Includes glossary and bibliographical references

Du Bois, W. E. B. (William Edward Burghardt), 1868-1963

Bolden, Tonya. **W.E.B.** Du Bois; a twentieth-century life. Viking Children's Books 2008 224p il (Up close) $16.99

Grades: 7 8 9 10   **92**
   1. Authors 2. Novelists 3. Historians 4. Editors 5. Essayists 6. Sociologists 7. Nonfiction writers 8. Civil rights activists 9. African Americans -- Biography 10. African Americans -- Civil rights
ISBN 978-0-670-06302-4; 0-670-06302-9

                    LC 2007-52380

"The author covers her subject's life, which spanned 95 years, from Reconstruction to the modern Civil Rights Movement. . . . This balanced, lively account records his many contributions as a teacher, speaker, Civil Rights activ-

ist, sociologist, writer, and cofounder of several organizations, including the NAACP, as well as his failings." SLJ

Includes bibliographical references

Hinman, Bonnie. A **stranger** in my own house; the story of W.E.B. Du Bois. Morgan Reynolds Pub. 2005 176p il map $26.95

Grades: 7 8 9 10   **92**
   1. Authors 2. Novelists 3. Historians 4. Editors 5. Essayists 6. Sociologists 7. Nonfiction writers 8. Civil rights activists 9. African Americans -- Biography 10. African Americans -- Civil rights
ISBN 1-931798-45-1

                    LC 2004-26460

"The long, complex life of this scholar and controversial civil rights leader is examined in this . . . biography. Hinman offers insights into the background, beliefs, and conflicts that shaped and defined Du Bois. . . . The engaging, informative, balanced text is enhanced with documentary photographs and illustrations." SLJ

Includes bibliographical references

Whiting, Jim. **W.E.B.** Du Bois; civil rights activist, author, historian. Mason Crest Publishers 2010 64p il (Transcending race in America: biographies of biracial achievers) $22.95; pa $9.95

Grades: 5 6 7 8   **92**
   1. Authors 2. Novelists 3. Historians 4. Editors 5. Essayists 6. Sociologists 7. Nonfiction writers 8. Civil rights activists 9. African Americans -- Biography 10. African Americans -- Civil rights
ISBN 978-1-4222-1618-7; 1-4222-1618-7; 978-1-4222-1632-3 pa; 1-4222-1632-2 pa

                    LC 2009022049

"The author openly discusses Du Bois' political and ideological struggles, which concluded with his move to Ghana and admittance into the Communist Party. . . . The book . . . provides solid information about Du Bois." Booklist

Includes glossary and bibliographical references

Duncan, Lois, 1934-

Campbell, Kimberly Edwina. **Lois** Duncan; author of I know what you did last summer. [by] Kimberly Campbell. Enslow Publishers 2009 104p bibl il por (Authors teens love) lib bdg $31.93

Grades: 6 7 8 9   **92**
   1. Authors 2. Novelists 3. Women authors 4. Authors, American 5. Young adult authors
ISBN 978-0-7660-2963-7 lib bdg; 0-7660-2963-8 lib bdg

                    LC 2008013874

This discusses the life and work of author Lois Duncan

Includes glossary and bibliographical references

Dvořák, Antonín, 1841-1904

Horowitz, Joseph. **Dvorak** in America; in search of the New World. Cricket Bks. 2003 158p il $17.95

Grades: 7 8 9 10   **92**
   1. Composers
ISBN 0-8126-2681-8

                    LC 2002-151456

An account of Antonin Dvorak's 1890s stay in America, where he took the essences of Indian drums, slave spirituals, and other musical forms and created from them a distinctly new music

"A welcome addition to music and biography collections." SLJ

Includes bibliographical references

Délano, Poli, 1936-

Delano, Poli. **When** I was a boy Neruda called me Policarpo; illustrated by Manuel Monroy. Groundwood Books/House of Anansi Press 2006 84p il $15.95

Grades: 5 6 7 8   92

1. Poets 2. Authors 3. Diplomats 4. Novelists 5. Poets, Chilean 6. Mexico 7. Memoirists 8. Short story writers 9. Nobel laureates for peace 10. Nobel laureates for literature
ISBN 0-88899-726-4

In this book, the author "offers seven vignettes, interspersed with six of Neruda's . . . . poems and biographical information, to give middle-grade readers a sense of what it was like to grow up in the constant presence of a kindly, though spoiled and eccentric, celebrity. . . . Grades four to six." (MultiCult Rev)

"Based on the author's childhood remembrances of when he and his diplomat parents lived with Tío Pablo [Neruda] in Mexico, these seven chapters reveal both the genius and the eccentricities of the Nobel Prize-winning Chilean poet. . . . The chapters are short, well written, and filled with interesting details that will open up a new and exotic world. . . . Monroy's pen-and-sepia-toned drawings are . . . at times humorous, at times dramatic, but always enticing." SLJ

Earhart, Amelia, 1898-1937

Brown, Jeremy K. **Amelia** Earhart. Chelsea House 2011 132p il lib bdg $35

Grades: 6 7 8   92

1. Air pilots 2. Missing persons 3. Women air pilots 4. Memoirists
ISBN 978-1-60413-910-5; 1-60413-910-2

This "supplies an evenhanded account of Earhart's personal life, her challenges as a woman in aviation, and her many achievements in flight. . . . Solid fare for the biography collection." Booklist

★ Fleming, Candace. **Amelia** lost: the life and disappearance of Amelia Earhart. Schwartz & Wade Books 2011 118p il map

Grades: 4 5 6 7   92

1. Air pilots 2. Missing persons 3. Women air pilots 4. Memoirists 5. Biography, Individual
ISBN 0-375-84198-9; 0-375-94598-9 lib bdg; 978-0-375-84198-9; 978-0-375-94598-4 lib bdg

LC 2010-05279

Fleming "offers a fresh look at this famous aviatrix. Employing dual narratives—straightforward biographical chapters alternating with a chilling recounting of Earhart's final flight and the search that followed—Fleming seeks to uncover the 'history of the hype,' pointing out numerous examples in which Earhart took an active role in mythologizing her own life. . . . Frequent sidebars, well-chosen maps, archi-

val documents, and photos further clarify textual references without disturbing the overall narrative flow." Booklist

★ Micklos, John. **Unsolved** : what really happened to Amelia Earhart? [by] John Micklos, Jr. Enslow Publishers 2006 144p bibl il map por lib bdg $31.93

Grades: 5 6 7 8   92

1. Air pilots 2. Missing persons 3. Women air pilots 4. Memoirists
ISBN 0-7660-2365-6

LC 2005020875

"Micklos discusses the pilot's childhood, including what made her tick and what made her fly. However, the book's real focus is on the events of her fateful round-the-world adventure. . . . There are several theories about what happened to her and her copilot, Fred Noonan, on July 2, 1937. . . . As the plane and remains have never been found and identified, no one really knows. Fully half of this book is devoted to the famous flight and the possible explanations for what occurred. Chock-full of photos . . . Unsolved captures the imagination." SLJ

Includes glossary and bibliographical references

Tanaka, Shelley. **Amelia** Earhart; the legend of the lost aviator. by Shelley Tanaka; illustrated by David Craig. Abrams Books for Young Readers 2008 48p il map $18.95

Grades: 3 4 5 6   92

1. Air pilots 2. Missing persons 3. Women air pilots 4. Memoirists
ISBN 978-0-8109-7095-3; 0-8109-7095-3

LC 2007-39749

NCTE Orbis Pictus Award (2009)

This is an account of the life of aviator Amelia Earhart from her childhood up to the time she disappeared on a flight in 1937.

"This title is notable . . . for its smooth, powerful storytelling, ample gallery of well-chosen photographs, and nicely placed sidebar information on such topics as flight delays, navigation, and around-the-world flight records." Bull Cent Child Books

Includes bibliographical references

Earle, Sylvia A., 1935-

Reichard, Susan E. **Who** on earth is Sylvia Earle? undersea explorer of the ocean. Enslow Publishers 2009 112p il (Scientists saving the earth) lib bdg $31.93

Grades: 5 6 7 8   92

1. Botanists 2. Marine biology 3. Women scientists 4. Underwater exploration 5. Divers 6. Marine biologists
ISBN 978-1-59845-118-4 lib bdg; 1-59845-118-9 lib bdg

LC 2008032014

"The writing is clear and informative. . . . Color photographs are relevant and of good quality." SLJ

"Details Sylvia Earle's life, with chapters devoted to her early years, life, work, writings, and legacy" Publisher's note

Includes glossary and bibliographical references

Edison, Thomas A. (Thomas Alva), 1847-1931

Baxter, Roberta. **Illuminated** progress; the story of Thomas Edison. [by] Roberta Baxter. Morgan Reynolds Pub. 2009 144p il (Profiles in science) lib bdg $27.95

Grades: 6 7 8 9   **92**
   1. Inventors
   ISBN 978-1-59935-085-1 lib bdg; 1-59935-085-8 lib bdg
                                        LC 2008007411

This title "offers a concise, informative overview of the inventor who ushered in the world the Age of Electricity. . . . This well-documented biography is illustrated throughout with photographs." Booklist

Includes bibliographical references

★ Carlson, Laurie M. **Thomas** Edison for kids; his life and ideas: 21 activities. [by] Laurie Carlson. Chicago Review Press 2006 147p il $14.95

Grades: 5 6 7 8   **92**
   1. Inventors 2. Science -- Experiments
   ISBN 1-55652-584-2
                                        LC 2005025659

"Part biography, part science activity book, this resource will appeal to casual researchers and novice inventors. It contains a wealth of full-page primary source archival photographs, sidebars, and short biographical profiles of Edison's contemporaries, in addition to short and straightforward experiments." Voice Youth Advocates

Includes bibliographical references

Woodside, Martin. **Thomas** A. Edison; the man who lit up the world. [by] Martin Woodside. Sterling 2007 124p (Sterling biographies) lib bdg $12.95; pa $5.95

Grades: 5 6 7 8   **92**
   1. Inventors
   ISBN 978-1-4027-4955-1 lib bdg; 1-4027-4955-4 lib bdg; 978-1-4027-3229-4 pa; 1-4027-3229-5 pa
                                        LC 2007003509

"Woodside presents the life, struggles, failures, and successes of a man whose motto was 'the most important way to succeed is always to try one more time.' [The book provides] clear, concise information in an easy-to-read format with captioned photographs and illustrations on most pages." SLJ

Includes glossary and bibliographical references

Einstein, Albert, 1879-1955

★ Delano, Marfe Ferguson. **Genius**; a photobiography of Albert Einstein. National Geographic 2005 64p il $17.95; lib bdg $27.90; pa $7.95

Grades: 5 6 7 8   **92**
   1. Physicists 2. Nobel laureates for physics
   ISBN 0-7922-9544-7; 0-7922-9545-5 lib bdg; 1-4263-0294-0 pa
                                        LC 2004-15001

A biography of the German American physicist.

This "combines a solid text with a particularly attractive format. . . . Delano offers just enough information about Einstein's theories to give a sense of his work. . . . Oversize

and filled with well-selected photographs, the book is very handsome." Booklist

★ Krull, Kathleen. **Albert** Einstein; illustrated by Boris Kulikov. Viking 2009 141p il (Giants of science) $15.99

Grades: 5 6 7 8   **92**
   1. Physicists 2. Nobel laureates for physics
   ISBN 978-0-670-06332-1; 0-670-06332-0
                                        LC 2009-16037

"Krull delivers a splendidly humane biography of that gold standard of brilliance, Albert Einstein. . . . Drawing extensively on Einstein's writings, she presents a fully rounded portrait of a man whose genius combined with a bad temper and arrogance, to the detriment of his own professional advancement, not to mention his relationships with women and his children. Using concrete examples, the author brings such mind-bending notions as his General Theory of Relativity within the grasp of child readers." Kirkus

Eisenhower, Dwight D. (Dwight David), 1890-1969

Mara, Wil. **Dwight** Eisenhower. Marshall Cavendish Benchmark 2011 112p il (Presidents and their times) lib bdg $34.21

Grades: 5 6 7 8   **92**
   1. Generals 2. Presidents 3. College presidents 4. Presidents -- United States
   ISBN 978-0-7614-4812-9; 0-7614-4812-8
                                        LC 2009033042

"The size makes it ideal for that one-hundred page biography assignment; the readability makes the titles accessible to reluctant readers in high school; the succinct, well-presented information makes the volumes fitting for initial research at both the middle and high school level." Voice Youth Advocates

Includes glossary and bibliographical references

Eisner, Will, 1917-2005

Greenberger, Robert. **Will** Eisner; [by] Robert Greenberger. Rosen Pub. Group 2005 112p il (Library of graphic novelists) lib bdg $31.95

Grades: 6 7 8 9   **92**
   1. Authors 2. Cartoonists 3. Cartoons and caricatures 4. Comic book writers 5. Publishing executives
   ISBN 1-4042-0286-2
                                        LC 2004-16656

This "book focuses on the artist's work rather than on his life. It sketches in major events, . . . but dwells heavily on the characters he created and his influence on the graphic-novel format. This is a well-organized and easy-to-read volume." SLJ

Includes bibliographical references

Eleanor, of Aquitaine, Queen, consort of Henry II, King of England, 1122?-1204

★ Kramer, Ann. **Eleanor** of Aquitaine; the queen who rode off to battle. National Geographic 2006 64p il map (World history biographies) $17.95; lib bdg $27.90

Grades: 5 6 7 8   **92**
   1. Queens 2. France -- History -- 0-1328 3. Great

Britain -- History -- 1154-1399, Plantagenets
ISBN 0-7922-5895-9; 0-7922-5896-7 lib bdg

An illustrated biography of the medieval queen who traveled to the Crusades with her first husband King Louis VII of France and later married King Henry II of England.

Includes glossary and bibliographical references

Elizabeth I, Queen of England, 1533-1603

★ Adams, Simon. **Elizabeth** I; the outcast who became England's queen. [by] Simon Adams. National Geographic 2005 64p il map (World history biographies) $17.95; lib bdg $27.90

Grades: 4 5 6 7   92

1. Queens 2. Great Britain -- Kings and rulers 3. Great Britain -- History -- 1485-1603, Tudors
ISBN 0-7922-3649-1; 0-7922-3654-8 lib bdg

LC 2005001359

An illustrated introduction to the life and times of the 16th century queen of England

"Accomplishments and hardships are clearly explained with supporting quotes and facts. . . . Beautifully illustrated and visually appealing." SLJ

Includes glossary and bibliographical references

Stanley, Diane. **Good** Queen Bess: the story of Elizabeth I of England; by Diane Stanley and Peter Vennema; illustrated by Diane Stanley. HarperCollins Pubs. 2001 un il $16.99

Grades: 4 5 6 7   92

1. Queens 2. Great Britain -- Kings and rulers 3. Great Britain -- History -- 1485-1603, Tudors
ISBN 0-688-17961-4

LC 00-47267

A reissue of the title first published 1990 by Four Winds Press

Follows the life of the strong-willed queen who ruled England in the time of Shakespeare and the defeat of the Spanish Armada

"The handsome illustrations . . . are worthy of their subject. Although the format suggests a picture-book audience, this biography needs to be introduced to older readers who have the background to appreciate and understand this woman who dominated and named an age." SLJ

Includes bibliographical references

Weatherly, Myra. **Elizabeth** I; Queen of Tudor England. by Myra Weatherly. Compass Point Books 2006 112p il (Signature lives) $30

Grades: 6 7 8 9   92

1. Queens 2. Great Britain -- Kings and rulers 3. Great Britain -- History -- 1485-1603, Tudors
ISBN 0-7565-0988-2

LC 2005002790

"This engaging biography brings the monarch's complicated and fascinating life to light. . . . The text is clearly written and highly readable." SLJ

Includes bibliographical references

Ellington, Duke, 1899-1974

Stein, Stephanie. **Duke** Ellington; his life in jazz with 21 activities. [by] Stephanie Stein Crease. Chi-

cago Review Press 2009 148p il (For kids) pa $16.95

Grades: 5 6 7 8   92

1. Composers 2. Jazz musicians 3. Band leaders
ISBN 978-1-55652-724-1; 1-55652-724-1

LC 2008-23742

"This large-format book combines an illustrated biography of Duke Ellington with activities designed to offer insights into Ellington s era and his music. An informative account in an attractive...format." Booklist

Includes bibliographical references, discography, and filmography

Stein, Stephanie. **Duke** Ellington; his life in jazz with 21 activities. [by] Stephanie Stein Crease. Chicago Review Press 2009 148p il $16.95

Grades: 4 5 6 7 8   92

1. Composers 2. Jazz musicians 3. African American musicians 4. Band leaders
ISBN 978-1-55652-724-1; 1-55652-724-1

LC 2008023742

"This biography begins with a brief discussion of the lives of Ellington's parents and his childhood introduction to music and instruments. As each chapter introduces separate highlights of the man's life and musical growth, sidebar articles emphasize historical milestones in music . . . and the impact of individuals or events on his life. The book also features 21 interactive activities, each of which is positioned to provide a greater understanding of an instrument, performance, or music theory in jazz style. . . . Illustrations include performance photographs and portraits of notable names from the Big Band era." SLJ

Emerson, Ralph Waldo, 1803-1882

Caravantes, Peggy. **Self** -reliance: the story of Ralph Waldo Emerson. Morgan Reynolds Pub. 2010 143p il map (World writers) lib bdg $28.95

Grades: 7 8 9 10   92

1. Poets 2. Authors 3. Philosophers 4. Essayists 5. Authors, American
ISBN 978-1-59935-124-7; 1-59935-124-2

LC 2010-8143

Presents the life and career of the eighteenth century New England essayist, poet, and lecturer who advocated a philosophy of self-reliance and individualism and was an important figure in the American Transcendental Movement.

This volume treats "young adult readers with respect and . . . [works] to ease them into scholarly research and writing in an engaging manner." Voice Youth Advocates

Includes bibliographical references

Eratosthenes, 3rd cent. B.C.

Gow, Mary. **Measuring** the Earth; Eratosthenes and his celestial geometry. Enslow 2010 128p il (Great minds of ancient science and math) lib bdg $31.93

Grades: 5 6 7 8   92

1. Astronomers 2. Mathematicians 3. Geographers 4.

Writers on science
ISBN 978-0-7660-3120-3 lib bdg; 0-7660-3120-9
lib bdg

LC 2008-38523

This biography is a "solid [choice], as . . . [it provides] a good overview of the cultural and political landscape of the times, as well as pictures." SLJ

Includes glossary and bibliographical references

Euclid

Hightower, Paul. The **father** of geometry: Euclid and his 3D world. Enslow Publishers 2010 112p il (Great minds of ancient science and math) lib bdg $31.93

Grades: 6 7 8 9 **92**

1. Geometry 2. Mathematicians 3. Writers on science
ISBN 978-0-7660-3409-9 lib bdg; 0-7660-3409-7
lib bdg

LC 2009-23814

"Describes the life of another fourth-century B.C.E. man who would ultimately become known as the 'father of geometry.' He was not famous like the philosophers of his time, but his book The Elements totally revised what was known of mathematics at the time. . . . Includes simple, straightforward text with nice illustrations and appendixes of suggested activities, a supplemental chronology, chapter notes, and glossary." Voice Youth Advocates

Includes glossary and bibliographical references

Farmer, Paul, 1959-

★ Kidder, Tracy. **Mountains** beyond mountains; the quest of Dr. Paul Farmer, a man who would cure the world. by Tracy Kidder ; adapted for young people by Michael French. Delacorte Press 2013 288 p. hardcover o.p. (hardcover trade) $16.99

Grades: 7 8 9 10 11 12 Adult **92**

1. Physicians 2. Access to health care 3. Human rights 4. Right to health 5. Poor -- Medical care 6. Physicians -- Biography 7. Missionaries, Medical -- Biography
ISBN 0385743181; 9780307980885; 9780375990991; 9780385743181

LC 2012024905

This book is a study of Paul Farmer, an American doctor who opened a healthcare center for the poor in Haiti. "By Farmer's decree, no patient can be turned away. But medical aid alone is not enough. He also emphasizes the need to eliminate problems that contribute to illness: dirty water, inadequate nutrition, poor sanitation, illiteracy. . . . Encouraged by the success of his clinic, Farmer wants to replicate it as 'a laboratory for the world.'" (Christian Science Monitor)

This is a "portrait of Paul Farmer (MacArthur 'genius' grant, 1993), a driven, dedicated, rigidly idealistic doctor who commutes between Harvard and Haiti, where he works . . . to relieve the suffering of some of the poorest people on earth." N Y Times Book Rev

Includes bibliographical references

Fermi, Enrico, 1901-1954

Cooper, Dan. **Enrico** Fermi and the revolutions in modern physics. Oxford Univ. Press 1999 117p il (Oxford portraits in science) lib bdg $28

Grades: 7 8 9 10 **92**

1. Physicists 2. College teachers 3. Nobel laureates for physics
ISBN 0-19-511762-X

LC 98-34471

A biography of the Nobel Prize-winning physicist whose work led to the discovery of nuclear fission, the basis of nuclear power and the atom bomb

"This book will be useful for reports. . . . The extensive list for further reading includes biographies of Fermi, books on both scientific and political aspects of the atomic-bomb project, and information on tours of laboratories involved in nuclear research today." SLJ

Ferrera, America, 1984-

Abrams, Dennis. **America** Ferrera. Chelsea House Publishers 2010 107p il (The great Hispanic heritage) lib bdg $30

Grades: 6 7 8 9 **92**

1. Actors
ISBN 978-1-60413-967-9; 1-60413-967-6

LC 2010009481

A biography of the actress best known for her roles in television's Ugly Betty and in films such as Real Women Have Curves and The Sisterhood of the Traveling Pants.

Fey, Tina, 1970-

Friedman, Lauri S. **Tina** Fey. Lucent Books 2010 96p il (People in the news) $33.45

Grades: 7 8 9 10 **92**

1. Actors 2. Comedians 3. Screenwriters 4. Television scriptwriters
ISBN 978-1-4205-0238-1; 1-4205-0238-7

LC 2009039362

A biography of writer, producer and Saturday Night Live funnygirl Tina Fey.

"With color photos of the actress at work throughout, this . . . does an excellent job of contexualizing Fey's comedy in the stream of current events. . . . This offers plenty of insight and inspiration for budding comedians, actors, and writers as well as researchers." Booklist

Includes bibliographical references

Feynman, Richard Phillips, 1918-1988

★ Henderson, Harry. **Richard** Feynman; quarks, bombs, and bongos. Chelsea House 2010 138p il (Makers of modern science) $35

Grades: 7 8 9 10 **92**

1. Authors 2. Physicists 3. Writers on science 4. Nobel laureates for physics
ISBN 978-0-8160-6176-1; 0-8160-6176-9

A biography of physicist Richard Feyman.

"The mark of a good biography is when it makes people you may never have heard of, in fields you might not be interested in, fascinating. [This book] does this with [a] well-chosen [subject], engaging writing, plenty of sidebars that take the text in new directions, and perhaps most importantly, the determination to present a fully-rounded person, not just a scientist." Booklist

LeVine, Harry. The **great** explainer; the story of Richard Feynman. by Harry LeVine, III. Morgan Reynolds Pub. 2009 144p il $28.95

Grades: 6 7 8 9   **92**

1. Physicists 2. Writers on science 3. Nobel laureates for physics

ISBN 978-1-59935-113-1; 1-59935-113-7

LC 2009006677

"Feynman was a particularly fascinating fellow who was involved in everything from building the atomic bomb at Los Alamos to constructing the first computers to figuring out why the Space Shuttle Challenger crashed. Children who might have trouble with the specifics of physics will be drawn in by Feynman's personal story. . . . Throughout there is a very personal feel, and when the science becomes difficult to understand, readers will still want to learn more about Feynman and his restless, sometimes chaotic search for knowledge." Booklist

Includes bibliographical references

Filipovic, Zlata

Filipovic, Zlata. **Zlata's** diary; a child's life in Sarajevo. with an introduction by Janine Di Giovanni; translated with notes by Christina Pribichevich-Zoric. Penguin Books 2006 195p il pa $13

Grades: 6 7 8 9   **92**

1. Children 2. Diarists 3. Sarajevo (Bosnia and Hercegovina)

ISBN 0-14-303687-4

A reissue with a new preface of the title first published 1994 by Viking

"Filipovic's diary personalizes the tragedy in war-torn Sarajevo." Booklist

"In September 1991, at the beginning of a new school year and while war was already as close as Croatia, Filipovic, a ten-year-old girl in Sarajevo began keeping a diary about her school friends, her classes, and her after-school activities. The following spring that childhood world disappeared when the war moved to Sarajevo." Libr J

Fillmore, Millard, 1800-1874

Gottfried, Ted. **Millard** Fillmore; by Ted Gottfried. Marshall Cavendish Benchmark 2007 96p il (Presidents and their times) lib bdg $22.95

Grades: 5 6 7 8   **92**

1. Vice-presidents 2. Presidents -- United States

ISBN 978-0-7614-2431-4

LC 2006019707

"Primary-source materials and quotes, helpful insets, and carefully selected . . . reproductions bring history to life and help make [this] clearly written [biography] highly readable." SLJ

Includes glossary and bibliographical references

Fitzgerald, Ella

★ Stone, Tanya Lee. **Ella** Fitzgerald. Viking 2008 203p il (Up close) $16.99

Grades: 7 8 9 10   **92**

1. Singers 2. African American singers 3. Pop musicians 4. African American women -- Biography

ISBN 978-0-670-06149-5; 0-670-06149-2

LC 2007-23117

This is a "strong biography [of the African American singer]. . . . Stone's smooth, straightforward narrative draws from authoritative sources. . . . The abundant quotes from Fitzgerald and her musician peers greatly develop the narrative." Booklist

Includes bibliographical references

Fleischman, Sid, 1920-2010

Freedman, Jeri. **Sid** Fleischman; [by] Jeri Freedman. Rosen Pub. Group 2004 112p (Library of author biographies) lib bdg $31.95

Grades: 5 6 7 8   **92**

1. Authors 2. Magicians 3. Authorship 4. Magazine editors 5. Authors, American 6. Children's authors 7. Young adult authors

ISBN 0-8239-4019-5

LC 2003-5203

Discusses the life and work of this popular author, including his writing process and methods, inspirations, a critical discussion of his books, biographical timeline, and awards

"Libraries looking to expand their biography section will be well served by [this] informative [title]." SLJ

Includes bibliographical references

Ford, Henry, 1863-1947

Mitchell, Don. **Driven**; a photobiography of Henry Ford. foreword by Lee Iacocca. National Geographic 2010 64p il map $18.95; lib bdg $27.90

Grades: 5 6 7 8   **92**

1. Businessmen 2. Philanthropists 3. Automobile industry 4. Automobile executives

ISBN 978-1-4263-0155-1; 1-4263-0155-3; 978-1-4263-0156-8 lib bdg; 1-4263-0156-1 lib bdg

LC 2009-07136

"Mitchell introduces readers to the founder of the auto company. . . . Thoughts, feelings, and quotes abound, and they are well sourced. . . . The writing is clear, and the organization is chronological. . . . Driven combines fine photography and an inviting text to depict Ford's life and his impact on the world." SLJ

Includes bibliographical references

Fossey, Dian

Kushner, Jill Menkes. **Who** on earth is Dian Fossey? defender of the mountain gorillas. Enslow Publishers 2009 112p il (Scientists saving the earth) lib bdg $31.93

Grades: 5 6 7 8   **92**

1. Authors 2. Gorillas 3. Women scientists 4. Murder victims 5. Primatologists 6. Writers on science

ISBN 1-59845-117-0 lib bdg; 978-1-59845-117-7 lib bdg

LC 2008029376

"The book is filled with factual information, yet is written in a manner that makes both Fossey and her gorillas come to life for the reader." Sci Books Films

Includes glossary and bibliographical references

Fox, Paula

Daniel, Susanna. **Paula** Fox; [by] Susanna Daniel. 1st ed; Rosen Central 2004 112p il (Library of author biographies) lib bdg $26.50

Grades: 7 8 9 10　　　　　　　　　　　　**92**

1. Novelists 2. Women authors 3. Authors, American 4. Children's authors 5. Young adult authors

ISBN 0-8239-4525-1

LC 2003-9176

Discusses the life and work of this award-winning author, including her writing process and methods, inspirations, a critical discussion of her books, biographical timeline, and awards.

Includes bibliographical references

France, Diane L.

★ Hopping, Lorraine Jean. **Bone** detective; the story of forensic anthropologist Diane France. Franklin Watts 2005 118p il (Women's adventures in science) lib bdg $31.50

Grades: 7 8 9 10　　　　　　　　　　　　**92**

1. Anthropologists 2. Women scientists 3. Forensic anthropology 4. Forensic scientists 5. Forensic sciences 6. Biography, Individual

ISBN 0-531-16776-3

LC 2005-0784

This book by Lorraine Jean Hopping is part of the Women's Adventures in Science series. It presents a biography of forensic anthropologist Diane France. "The book describes her marriages and divorce, a battle with cancer, experiences with sexism on the job, working at the World Trade Center site, and how one must learn to put personal feelings 'in a box' when working on forensic cases." (SB&F: Your Guide to Science Resources for All Ages)

This "introduces the life and work of a contemporary forensic anthropologist, from her rural childhood to her work identifying the victims of the 9/11 tragedies. . . . The extensive detail gives readers a vivid sense of the daily work of a 'bone detective,' and clear explanations of the science will intrigue and inspire readers." Booklist

Includes glossary and bibliographical references

Frank, Anne, 1929-1945

Frank, Anne. The **diary** of a young girl: the definitive edition; edited by Otto H. Frank and Mirjam Pressler; translated by Susan Massotty. Doubleday 1995 340p $29.95; pa $6.99

Grades: 6 7 8 9　　　　　　　　　　　　**92**

1. Children 2. Diarists 3. Holocaust victims 4. Jews -- Netherlands 5. Holocaust, 1933-1945 6. World War, 1939-1945 -- Jews 7. Netherlands -- History -- 1940-1945, German occupation

ISBN 0-385-47378-8; 0-553-57712-3 pa

LC 94-41379

"This new translation of Frank's famous diary includes material about her emerging sexuality and her relationship with her mother that was originally excised by Frank's father, the only family member to survive the Holocaust." Libr J

★ Metselaar, Menno. **Anne** Frank: her life in words and pictures; from the archives of The Anne Frank House. [by] Menno Metselaar and Ruud van der Rol; translated by Arnold J. Pomerans. Roaring Brook Press 2009 215p il map pa $12.99

Grades: 5 6 7 8　　　　　　　　　　　　**92**

1. Children 2. Diarists 3. Holocaust victims 4. Jews -- Netherlands 5. Holocaust, 1933-1945 6. World War, 1939-1945 -- Jews 7. Netherlands -- History -- 1940-1945, German occupation

ISBN 978-1-59643-546-9; 1-59643-546-1; 978-1-59643-547-6 pa; 1-59643-547-X pa

First published 2004 in the Netherlands with title: The story of Anne Frank

Boston Globe-Horn Book Award honor book: Nonfiction (2010)

"Beginning with a single photograph of the cover of Anne Frank's diary and the quote, 'One of my nicest presents,' this small, beautifully formatted book is accessible, compelling, and richly pictorial. . . . The book immediately immerses readers in the girl's life via a series of family photographs, many previously unpublished. Divided chronologically, the accompanying text is enhanced by diary entries, resulting in a historically succinct yet descriptive presentation. . . . Even for those collections where Anne Frank is well represented, this is a moving and valuable book." SLJ

Müller, Melissa, 1967- **Anne** Frank; the biography. by Melissa Muller ; translated by Rita and Robert Kimber. 2nd U.S. ed. Metropolitan Books/ Henry Holt and Company 2013 480 p. hardcover o.p. (hardcover) $35

Grades: 7 8 9 10 11 12 Adult　　　　　　　**92**

1. Children 2. Amsterdam (Netherlands) -- Biography 3. Jewish children in the Holocaust -- Biography 4. Jews -- Netherlands -- Amsterdam -- Biography 5. Holocaust, Jewish (1939-1945) -- Netherlands -- Amsterdam -- Biography

ISBN 0805087311; 9780805087314

LC 2013000297

This biography of Anne Frank "was originally published in 1998, but this expanded edition takes into account diary entries that had previously been redacted by Anne's father [Otto], as well as recently discovered letters from Otto to relatives in the United States and unpublished documents provided to [Melissa] Müller during interviews with those who knew Anne and her family." (Publishers Weekly)

"Müller includes a family tree; a family history; and considerable insight into the character, personality, and quality of life of Anne's parents, relatives, and friends. Interviews with many of these surviving people give a clearer idea of the situation and Anne's reactions to it." SLJ

Franklin, Benjamin, 1706-1790

★ Dash, Joan. A **dangerous** engine; Benjamin Franklin, from scientist to diplomat. pictures by Dusan Petricic. Frances Foster Books 2006 246p il $17

Grades: 7 8 9 10　　　　　　　　　　　　**92**

1. Authors 2. Diplomats 3. Inventors 4. Statesmen 5. Scientists 6. Writers on science 7. Members of

Congress 8. Statesmen -- United States
ISBN 0-374-30669-9

                         LC 2004-63204

"Franklin's long, productive, and interesting life is vividly recounted in a lively manner. Familiar aspects are covered, from his days as a printer in Philadelphia to his diplomatic service and his role in the development of the fledgling United States democracy. What may be new to some readers is Franklin's dedication to, and life-long love of, science and invention. . . . Witty pen-and-ink illustrations appear throughout." SLJ

   ★ Fleming, Candace. **Ben** Franklin's almanac; being a true account of the good gentleman's life. Atheneum Bks. for Young Readers 2003 120p il $19.95

Grades: 5 6 7 8   **92**
   1. Authors 2. Diplomats 3. Inventors 4. Statesmen 5. Scientists 6. Writers on science 7. Members of Congress 8. Statesmen -- United States
   ISBN 0-689-83549-3

                         LC 2002-6136

Brings together eighteenth century etchings, artifacts, and quotations to create the effect of a scrapbook of the life of Benjamin Franklin

"An authoritative work of depth, humor, and interest, presenting Franklin in all his complexity, ranging from the heroic to the vulgar, the saintly to the callous." SLJ

   ★ Freedman, Russell, 1929- **Becoming** Ben Franklin; how a candle-maker's son helped light the flame of liberty. Russell Freedman. 1st ed. Holiday House 2013 86 p. col. ill. (hardcover) $24.95

Grades: 5 6 7 8   **92**
   1. Franklin, Benjamin, 1706-1790 2. Founding Fathers of the United States 3. Printers -- United States -- Biography 4. Inventors -- United States -- Biography 5. Statesmen -- United States -- Biography 6. Scientists -- United States -- Biography
   ISBN 0823423743; 9780823423743

                      LC 2012002971

This book is a biography of Ben Franklin. Russell Freedman "chose episodes that reflect how the young man, disgruntled with being his brother's apprentice, made a life for himself . . . . By describing the obstacles Franklin overcame in establishing his print shop in Philadelphia, Freedman delineates a . . . path between his subject's early ambition and his ease with people to his success in business and then to his later roles as a diplomat, revolutionary, and public servant." (School Library Journal)

   Includes bibliographical references (p. 78-82) and index.

   Krull, Kathleen. **Benjamin** Franklin; by Kathleen Krull ; illustrated by Boris Kulikov. Viking 2013 121 p. (Giants of science) (hardcover) $15.99

Grades: 5 6 7 8   **92**
   1. Inventors 2. Scientists 3. Franklin, Benjamin, 1706-1790 4. Inventors -- United States -- Biography 5. Scientists -- United States -- Biography
   ISBN 0670012874; 9780670012879

                      LC 2013018404

This book, by Kathleen Krull, part of the Giants of Science series, "explains the many ways that Franklin was the American manifestation of the European Enlightenment, putting his discoveries in clear historical context. Known as 'natural philosophers' in the eighteenth century, scientists like Franklin specialized in the kind of theoretical thinking that could result in inventions to make life better, from lightning rods to efficient heating stoves." (Booklist)

"The majority of this helpful book deals with Franklin's innovative scientific processes and his reasoning behind such inventions as the Franklin stove and the lightning rod; he coined words (still in use today) with definitions specific to the field, such as positive, negative, and charge. Kulikov's occasional black-and-white illustrations add sly humor to the account." (Horn Book)

   Includes bibliographical references and index

   Miller, Brandon Marie. **Benjamin** Franklin, American genius; his life and ideas, with 21 activities. Chicago Review Press 2009 125p il pa $16.95

Grades: 4 5 6 7   **92**
   1. Authors 2. Diplomats 3. Inventors 4. Statesmen 5. Scientists 6. Writers on science 7. Members of Congress
   ISBN 978-1-55652-757-9 pa; 1-55652-757-8 pa

                      LC 2009012456

"Miller does an excellent job of presenting a synopsis of Franklin's life in a highly readable manner. . . . Imbedded in each chapter are asides that further elaborate on Franklin's life and times and activities that coordinate with the text or the historical facts presented. The directions are easy to follow and enhance the overall presentation, especially in terms of classroom connections. Illustrations accompany each project and reproductions of primary documents, renderings, and paintings provide added value." SLJ

   Includes glossary and bibliographical references

Franklin, Rosalind, 1920-1958

   Polcovar, Jane. **Rosalind** Franklin and the structure of life. Morgan Reynolds 2006 144p il lib bdg $26.95

Grades: 7 8 9 10   **92**
   1. DNA 2. Chemists 3. Biologists 4. Women scientists 5. Geochemists
   ISBN 978-1-59935-022-6; 1-59935-022-X

                      LC 2006-16864

A biography of the scientist whose unpublished research led to the discovery of the structure of DNA

"Polcovar writes a rattling good story on two fronts: a woman becoming a scientist in an age when that was still unusual and the complex dynamics of personalities in a field sometimes thought of as impersonal." Booklist

   Includes bibliographical references

Friedman, Cory

   Patterson, James. **Med** head; my knock-down, drag-out, drugged-up battle with my brain. as told by James Patterson & Hal Friedman. Little Brown & Co. 2010 302p il pa $8.99

Grades: 6 7 8 9 10   **92**
   1. Mentally ill 2. Tourette syndrome 3. Obsessive-

compulsive disorder

ISBN 978-0-316-076173 pa; 0-316-07617-1 pa

The story of Cory Friedman and his family's decades-long struggle to determine the cause of Cory's neurological disease.

"Based on detailed notes on medications, physician appointments, and school visits, this is a page-turning examination of what could have been a wasted, despairing life. . . . While nonfiction resources can provide the facts on mental disorders, this excellent biography puts them into a context that promotes compassion. " Voice Youth Advocates

Friedman, Milton, 1912-2006

Crain, Cynthia D. **Milton** Friedman; by Cynthia D. Crain and Dwight R. Lee. Morgan Reynolds Pub. 2009 144p il (Profiles in economics) lib bdg $28.95
Grades: 8 9 10 11 12   **92**

1. Economists 2. College teachers 3. Nobel laureates for economic sciences

ISBN 978-1-59935-108-7 lib bdg; 1-59935-108-0 lib bdg

LC 2009-169

Biography of the economist Milton Friedman

"Relationships, education, early influences, and family life are all described . . . [and] economic theory is closely tied to cultural and political events. . . . The writing is straightforward, the . . . [author] assume[s] a certain level of knowledge about world events." SLJ

Includes bibliographical references

Fritz, Jean

★ Fritz, Jean. **Homesick** : my own story; illustrated with drawings by Margot Tomes and photographs. Putnam 1982 163p il $16.99; pa $5.99
Grades: 5 6 7 8   **92**

1. Authors 2. Women authors 3. China 4. Children's authors

ISBN 0-399-20933-6; 0-698-11782-4 pa

LC 82-7646

Companion volume to China homecoming

A Newbery Medal honor book, 1983

"The descriptions of places and the times are vivid in a book that brings to the reader, with sharp clarity and candor, the yearnings and fears and ambivalent loyalties of a young girl." Bull Cent Child Books

Frost, Robert, 1874-1963

★ Caravantes, Peggy. **Deep** woods; the story of Robert Frost. Morgan Reynolds 2006 176p il (World writers) lib bdg $27.95
Grades: 7 8 9 10   **92**

1. Poets, American

ISBN 978-1-931798-92-1; 1-931798-92-3

LC 2005037514

This "introduces poet Robert Frost. . . . Though focused on the man, Caravantes' presentation includes a few short selections from Frost's verse and, in sidebars, a bit of information about poetic forms. . . . Well organized and clearly written, the book offers a very readable account of Frost's often troubled life as an individual, a family man, a poet, and a public figure." Booklist

Includes bibliographical references

Wooten, Sara McIntosh. **Robert** Frost; the life of America's poet. Enslow Publishers 2006 128p (People to know today) lib bdg $31.93
Grades: 6 7 8 9   **92**

1. Poets 2. Authors 3. Poets, American

ISBN 0-7660-2627-2 lib bdg; 978-0-7660-2627-8 lib bdg

LC 2005034882

"In this insightful biography, Wooten recounts Frost's difficult life from his childhood with an abusive, alcoholic father, through his many financial challenges as he tried to establish a career, to his constant struggle with shyness and depression. . . . Her book is thoroughly researched." SLJ

Includes bibliographical references

Fry, Varian, 1907-1967

★ McClafferty, Carla Killough. **In** defiance of Hitler; the secret mission of Varian Fry. Farrar, Straus & Giroux 2008 196p il $19.95
Grades: 7 8 9 10 11 12   **92**

1. Journalists 2. Editors 3. Classicists 4. Humanitarians 5. Holocaust, 1933-1945 6. World War, 1939-1945 -- France 7. World War, 1939-1945 -- Jews -- Rescue

ISBN 978-0-374-38204-9; 0-374-38204-2

LC 2007-33271

"This stirring account of a young New York City journalist who secretly helped more than 2,000 refugees escape Nazi-occupied France blends exciting adventure with the grim history. . . : The author begins with a brief overview of Hitler's rise and the threat to the Jews, and then draws heavily on Fry's autobiography and his letters home." Booklist

Fulton, Robert, 1765-1815

Herweck, Don. **Robert** Fulton; engineer of the steamboat. Compass Point Books 2009 40p il (Mission: Science) lib bdg $26.60
Grades: 4 5 6 7   **92**

1. Engineers 2. Inventors 3. Steamboats

ISBN 978-0-7565-3961-0 lib bdg; 0-7565-3961-7 lib bdg

LC 2008007728

Covers the life and accomplishments of American inventor and mechanic, Robert Fulton, who is best known for building the first successful steamboat

Gaines, Ernest J., 1933-

Abrams, Dennis. **Ernest** J. Gaines. Chelsea House 2010 120p il (Who wrote that?) lib bdg $30
Grades: 6 7 8 9   **92**

1. Authors 2. Novelists 3. African American authors 4. Authors, American 5. Children's authors 6. Short story writers

ISBN 978-1-60413-683-8; 1-60413-683-9

LC 2009022340

This discusses the life and work of author Ernest J. Gaines.

Includes bibliographical references

Galen, ca. 129-ca. 200

Yount, Lisa. The **father** of anatomy; Galen and his dissections. Enslow Publishers 2010 128p il (Great minds of ancient science and math) lib bdg $31.93

Grades: 6 7 8 9   92

1. Physicians 2. Human anatomy 3. Writers on medicine

ISBN 978-0-7660-3380-1; 0-7660-3380-5

LC 2008-29633

"A biography of ancient Greek physician Galen, whose dissections of animals led to discoveries about human anatomy. He was the authority on medical knowledge in the Western world for more than fifteen hundred years." Publisher's note

Includes glossary and bibliographical references

Galilei, Galileo, 1564-1642

Hightower, Paul. **Galileo**; astronomer and physicist. rev ed; Enslow Publishers 2008 128p il (Great minds of science) lib bdg $31.93

Grades: 5 6 7 8   92

1. Astronomers 2. Writers on science

ISBN 978-0-7660-3008-4 lib bdg; 0-7660-3008-3 lib bdg

LC 2007020302

First published 1997

"A biography of the seventeenth-century Italian astronomer and physicist Galileo and includes related activities for readers." Publisher's note

Includes glossary and bibliographical references

★ Panchyk, Richard. **Galileo** for kids; his life and ideas: 25 activities. foreword by Buzz Aldrin. Chicago Review Press 2005 166p il map pa $16.95

Grades: 5 6 7 8   92

1. Astronomers 2. Writers on science

ISBN 1-55652-566-4

LC 2004-22936

A biography of the Renaissance scientist and his times with related activities

"Clear . . . writing places Galileo squarely within the historical context of the turbulent Italian Renaissance. . . . Panchyk's title is a good choice for those interested in integrating history and science curriculums." SLJ

Includes bibliographical references

★ Steele, Philip. **Galileo**; the genius who faced the Inquisition. National Geographic 2005 64p il (World history biographies) $17.95; lib bdg $27.90

Grades: 4 5 6 7   92

1. Astronomers 2. Writers on science

ISBN 0-7922-3656-4; 0-7922-3657-2 lib bdg

LC 2005-01357

An illustrated introduction to the 16th century astronomer and his times

"Accompliments and hardships are clearly explained with supporting quotes and facts. . . . Beautifully illustrated and visually appealing." SLJ

Gama, Vasco da, 1469-1524

★ Calvert, Patricia. **Vasco** da Gama; so strong a spirit. [by] Patricia Calvert. Benchmark Books 2005 96p il map (Great explorations) lib bdg $29.93

Grades: 5 6 7 8   92

1. Explorers

ISBN 0-7614-1611-0

LC 2003-22946

Recounts the voyages undertaken by fifteenth-century Portuguese explorer Vasco da Gama to strengthen his nation's power by establishing a sea trade route to India.

Includes bibliographical references

Gandhi, Indira

Schupach, Sara. **Indira** Gandhi; by Sara Schupack. Marshall Cavendish Benchmark 2012 96 p. (print) $39.93

Grades: 6 7 8 9   92

1. Prime ministers -- India 2. Prime ministers -- India -- Biography 3. Women prime ministers -- India -- Biography 4. India -- Politics and government -- 20th century

ISBN 0761449558; 9780761449553; 9781608707126

LC 2011009224

Author Sara Schupack presents a biography of former Indian Prime Minister Indira Ghandi. Part of the "Leading Women series [which] focus on the background and political achievements of twentieth-century women, . . . [it] also include[s] helpful sidebars that provide context on related people, organizations, and events mentioned in the text." (Booklist)

Includes bibliographical references and index

Gandhi, Mahatma, 1869-1948

De Lambilly, Elisabeth. **Gandhi**; his life, his struggles, his words. written by Elisabeth de Lambilly; illustrated by Severine Cordier; [translated by Robert Brent] Enchanted Lion Books 2010 67p il (Great spiritual leaders of modern times)

Grades: 6 7 8 9   92

1. Authors 2. Pacifism 3. Journalists 4. Nonviolence 5. Resistance to government 6. Essayists 7. Pacifists 8. Memoirists 9. Political leaders 10. Statesmen -- India 11. Writers on politics 12. India -- Politics and government

ISBN 1-59270-094-2; 978-1-59270-094-3

LC 2010025235

Original French edition, 2007

"The historical facts are as compelling as the biographical story, and the message of nonviolence will spark intense debate about political action, then and now." Booklist

Includes bibliographical references

Ebine, Kazuki. **Gandhi** : a manga biography. Penguin 2011 192p il pa $15

Grades: 7 8 9 10   92

1. Manga 2. Authors 3. Journalists 4. Graphic novels 5. Essayists 6. Pacifists 7. Memoirists 8. Political leaders 9. Statesmen -- India 10. Writers on politics 11. India -- Politics and government

ISBN 978-0-14-312024-7; 0-14-312024-7

"Ebine's nicely drawn manga biography is a clear and concise introduction to Gandhi's life. The biography not only touches upon Gandhi's major accomplishments . . . but also humanizes Gandhi by showing his struggles with insecurity as a young man. . . . This title is a great addition to social studies curricula, and it will have special appeal to budding young activists and idealists." Booklist

Sawyer, Kem Knapp. **Mohandas** Gandhi. Morgan Reynolds Pub. 2011 144p il (Champion of freedom) lib bdg $28.95
Grades: 6 7 8 9 10   92
1. Authors 2. Journalists 3. Essayists 4. Pacifists 5. Memoirists 6. Political leaders 7. Statesmen -- India 8. Writers on politics 9. India -- Politics and government
ISBN 978-1-59935-166-7; 1-59935-166-8
LC 2010047904
This title "starts with an overview of the British Raj at the time of Mohandas Gandhi's birth and what life was like for those living under it. The thorough biography then goes on to trace the key events, philosophical influences, and personal relationships that shaped the life of a man who spread the doctrine of nonviolence. Interesting anecdotes, explanations of Indian culture, and an engaging, well-organized narrative make this a solid resource." Booklist
Includes bibliographical references

★ Wilkinson, Philip. **Gandhi**; the young protester who founded a nation. National Geographic 2005 64p il (World history biographies) $17.95; lib bdg $27.90
Grades: 4 5 6 7   92
1. Authors 2. Journalists 3. Passive resistance 4. Essayists 5. Pacifists 6. Memoirists 7. Political leaders 8. Writers on politics 9. India -- Politics and government
ISBN 0-7922-3647-5; 0-7922-3648-3 lib bdg
"Double-page spreads describe phases in Gandhi's life, from childhood to his tragic death, detailed in Wilkinson's straightforward, succinct language and in anecdotes, which will capture young people's attention and also humanize the great leader." Booklist
Includes glossary and bibliographical references

García Márquez, Gabriel, 1928-
Darraj, Susan Muaddi. **Gabriel** Garcia Marquez. Chelsea House 2006 112p bibl il por (Great Hispanic heritage) lib bdg $30
Grades: 6 7 8 9   92
1. Journalists 2. Authors, Colombian 3. Short story writers 4. Nobel laureates for literature
ISBN 0-7910-8839-1
LC 2006010615
A biography of the Colombian novelist who won the Nobel Prize for Literature in 1982
"A great deal of biographical information and some historical context is imparted in [this volume]. . . . Scattered throughout are many photographs and helpful boxed historical asides." Horn Book Guide
Includes bibliographical references

Garrison, William Lloyd, 1805-1879
Esty, Amos. The **liberator** : the story of William Lloyd Garrison. Morgan Reynolds Pub. 2010 144p il (Civil rights leaders) lib bdg $28.95
Grades: 7 8 9 10   92
1. Abolitionists 2. Newspaper editors 3. Slavery -- United States
ISBN 978-1-59935-137-7; 1-59935-137-4
LC 2009-54290
This biography of abolitionist William Lloyd Garrison "will hook readers with discussions of the larger political issues as well as [Garrison's] personal struggles. . . . The design . . . is readable, with spacious type and many kinds of illustrations, including color and sepia photos, paintings, and reproductions of famous documents." Booklist
Includes bibliographical references

Garvey, Marcus, 1887-1940
Kallen, Stuart A. **Marcus** Garvey and the Back to Africa Movement. Lucent Books 2006 112p il map (Lucent library of Black history) $32.45
Grades: 7 8 9 10   92
1. Writers on politics 2. Civil rights activists 3. African Americans -- Civil rights
ISBN 1-59018-838-1
LC 2005027286
"Kallen seeks . . . to discuss and expand on [Garvey's] contributions to Black Nationalism, and to place his particular movement within the context of his times. Here, Garvey emerges as a man who anticipated those later movements that centered on black pride and black power. In an exceptionally evenhanded manner, the author also shows Garvey to have been naive, unrealistic, and lacking in management skills. A superb speechmaker, a charismatic leader, and an excellent propagandist, he seemed ill prepared to deal with the powerful enemies he made. . . . Kallen describes this all in clear, well-written prose. Archival photographs are placed throughout to good advantage." SLJ
Includes bibliographical references

Gates, Bill, 1955-
★ Aronson, Marc. **Bill** Gates; a twentieth-century life. Penguin Group 2008 192p il (Up close) $16.99
Grades: 7 8 9 10   92
1. Businesspeople 2. Computer software industry 3. Microsoft Corporation 4. Computer software executives
ISBN 978-0-670-06348-2; 0-670-06348-7
LC 2008-15552
This is a biography of the businessman who cofounded Microsoft.
"Well researched, thought-provoking, and up-to-date, this biography . . . offers insights into Gates' character as well as an engaging account of his life." Booklist

Isaacs, Sally Senzell. **Bill** and Melinda Gates; [by] Sally Isaacs. Heinemann Library 2010 112p il (Front-page lives) $38.93
Grades: 6 7 8 9 10   92
1. Businesspeople 2. Philanthropists 3. Computer industry 4. Foundation officials 5. Computer software

executives 6. Spouses of prominent persons 7. Microsoft Corporation -- History 8. Bill and Melinda Gates Foundation
ISBN 978-1-4329-3220-6; 1-4329-3220-9

LC 2009-18180

A biography of Microsoft founder and billionaire Bill Gates and his wife, Melinda who, through the Bill and Melinda Gates Foundation, have helped people around the world by donating billions of dollars to solve global health problems and other issues.

"The subjects' lives are presented with depth and breadth and in such a way as to make clear how their actions impacted the world and why they are or were so important. . . The writing is accessible and engaging, with color and black-and-white photographs." SLJ

Includes glossary and bibliographical references

Lesinski, Jeanne M. **Bill** Gates; entrepreneur and philanthropist. rev ed; Twenty-First Century Books 2009 112p il (Lifeline biographies) lib bdg $33.26
Grades: 6 7 8 9   92
1. Businesspeople 2. Computer software industry 3. Microsoft Corporation 4. Computer software executives
ISBN 978-1-58013-570-2; 1-58013-570-6

LC 2008008565

A revised edition of the title first published 2000

This biography "boasts lively, credible writing and a compelling layout. Particularly interesting are the reprints of USA Today articles found throughout, which flesh out the [narrative] in a unique and appealing manner. . . . Full-color and black-and-white photos appear on almost every spread." SLJ

Includes bibliographical references

Gates, Melinda French

Isaacs, Sally Senzell. **Bill** and Melinda Gates; [by] Sally Isaacs. Heinemann Library 2010 112p il (Front-page lives) $38.93
Grades: 6 7 8 9 10   92
1. Businesspeople 2. Philanthropists 3. Computer industry 4. Foundation officials 5. Computer software executives 6. Spouses of prominent persons 7. Microsoft Corporation -- History 8. Bill and Melinda Gates Foundation
ISBN 978-1-4329-3220-6; 1-4329-3220-9

LC 2009-18180

A biography of Microsoft founder and billionaire Bill Gates and his wife, Melinda who, through the Bill and Melinda Gates Foundation, have helped people around the world by donating billions of dollars to solve global health problems and other issues.

"The subjects' lives are presented with depth and breadth and in such a way as to make clear how their actions impacted the world and why they are or were so important. . . The writing is accessible and engaging, with color and black-and-white photographs." SLJ

Includes glossary and bibliographical references

Gauguin, Paul, 1848-1903

Spence, David. **Gauguin.** New Forest Press 2010 48p il map (Great artists and their world) lib bdg $32.80

Grades: 6 7 8 9   92
1. Artists 2. Painters 3. Artists, French
ISBN 978-1-84898-316-8; 1-84898-316-6

"Offers biographical information [of Paul Gauguin] . . . interspersed with art history and criticism in an eye-catching format. . . . [Includes] a long introductory paragraph and four-to-six images with explanatory notes. . . . Spence . . . does a good job of explaining why art that might seem ordinary today was revolutionary at the time of its creation." SLJ

Includes glossary

Gehrig, Lou, 1903-1941

Buckley, James. **Lou** Gehrig; Iron Horse of baseball. Sterling 2010 124p il (Sterling biographies) pa $5.95
Grades: 6 7 8 9   92
1. Baseball players 2. Baseball -- Biography
ISBN 978-1-4027-7151-4 pa; 1-4027-7151-7 pa

This biography of Lou Gehrig is "studded with quotes and illustrated with photos. . . . Lou Gehrig is today inextricably linked with ALS, the progressive nerve disease that ended his baseball career and ultimately his life, but he is also remembered as the Iron Horse of baseball, the legendary slugger who played a phenomenal 2,130 consecutive games for the Yankees. Written in a straightforward, journalistic style, [this biography presents a] very readable [account] of the [life] of [an athlete] who made [his mark] on American culture." Booklist

Includes glossary and bibliographical references

Gehry, Frank

Bodden, Valerie. **Frank** Gehry. Creative Education 2009 48p il (Xtraordinary artists) lib bdg $32.80
Grades: 4 5 6 7   92
1. Architects
ISBN 978-1-58341-662-4 lib bdg; 1-58341-662-5 lib bdg

LC 2007004201

This is a biography of architect Frank Gehry

This offers an "interesting [layout]; big, high-quality reproductions and photographs on heavy paper; insightful quotes from diverse sources; and . . . an excerpt from an essay about [Gehry] at the end of the book. Readers get a strong sense of [the] artist's personality along with an excellent survey of his work." SLJ

Includes bibliographical references

Geronimo, Apache Chief, 1829-1909

Sullivan, George. **Geronimo**; Apache renegade. Sterling 2010 124p il map (Sterling biographies) lib bdg $12.95; pa $5.95
Grades: 7 8 9 10   92
1. Apache Indians 2. Indian chiefs 3. Native Americans -- Biography
ISBN 978-1-4027-6843-9 lib bdg; 1-4027-6843-5 lib bdg; 978-1-4027-6279-6 pa; 1-4027-6279-8 pa

LC 2009-24135

"Geronmino describes how the Apache leader was feared and hated as he led violent clashes with whites, pursuing bloody vengeance for the massacre of his family and all that his people had lost, an identity far from the romanticized image that glorified him. . . . [The] spacious design is highly scannable, with color background screens, photos, maps, and historic prints throughout." Booklist

Includes glossary and bibliographical references

Gibson, Josh, 1911-1947

Twemlow, Nick. **Josh** Gibson. Rosen Pub. Group 2002 112p il (Baseball Hall of Famers of the Negro leagues) lib bdg $29.25

Grades: 5 6 7 8   **92**

1. Baseball players 2. African American athletes 3. Baseball -- Biography
ISBN 0-8239-3475-6

LC 2001-4143

Presents a biography of the powerful home run hitter and chronicles the history of African American participation in organized baseball, the formation of the Negro leagues, and racial politics in America

Includes glossary and bibliographical references

Giff, Patricia Reilly

Giff, Patricia Reilly. **Don't** tell the girls; a family memoir. by Patricia Reilly Giff. Holiday House 2005 131p il $16.95

Grades: 4 5 6 7   **92**

1. Teachers 2. Women authors 3. Authors, American 4. Children's authors
ISBN 0-8234-1813-8

LC 2004-47452

"Giff reflects on her childhood and her family, going back through several generations. Spotlighting her two grandmothers, she lovingly relates remembered conversations and incidents involving the one she knew well before turning to the other grandmother, whom she never met. . . . This little book has much to offer thoughtful children. . . . With . . . sharply reproduced family photos and documents, this handsome book's small format reflects its intimate, conversational style." Booklist

Ginsberg, Blaze

Ginsberg, Blaze. **Episodes**; my life as I see it. Roaring Brook Press 2009 274p $16.99

Grades: 6 7 8 9 10   **92**

1. Autism 2. Teenagers' writings 3. Memoirists
ISBN 978-1-59643-461-5; 1-59643-461-9

"The high-functioning spectrum-disorder child portrayed in his mother Debra's Raising Blaze (2002) steps up to offer his own views of high school and after. He structures his memoir . . . as thumbnail summaries of concurrent or successive TV series. . . . He writes in a distant but often humorous voice about feelings, fixations, and the seemingly aimless way people move in and out of his life. . . . This book provides memorable insight into the author's distinctive mind and spirit." Booklist

Glenn, John, 1921-

Mitchell, Don. **Liftoff**; a photobiography of John Glenn. National Geographic Society 2006 64p il $17.95; lib bdg $27.90

Grades: 5 6 7 8   **92**

1. Astronauts 2. Senators 3. Statesmen -- United States
ISBN 0-7922-5899-1; 0-7922-5900-9 lib bdg

LC 2005-30916

This is a biography of the American astronaut, pilot, and U.S. Senator from Ohio.

This is "well-written and well-illustrated." Sci Books Films

Includes bibliographical references

Goeppert-Mayer, Maria, 1906-1972

Ferry, Joseph. **Maria** Goeppert Mayer; [by] Joseph P. Ferry. Chelsea House 2003 110p il (Women in science) lib bdg $22.95

Grades: 7 8 9 10   **92**

1. Physicists 2. Women scientists 3. College teachers 4. Nobel laureates for physics
ISBN 0-7910-7247-9

LC 2002-15580

A biography of Maria Goeppert-Mayer, a physicist who contributed to the development of the atomic bomb and who, in 1963, was cowinner of the Nobel Prize in Physics for her work on the nuclear shell model theory

This is "well written and well organized." SLJ

Includes bibliographical references

Gogh, Vincent van, 1853-1890

Bodden, Valerie. **Vincent** van Gogh. Creative Education 2009 48p il (Xtraordinary artists) lib bdg $32.80

Grades: 4 5 6 7   **92**

1. Artists 2. Painters 3. Artists, Dutch
ISBN 978-1-58341-663-1 lib bdg; 1-58341-663-3 lib bdg

LC 2007002118

This biography of the artist offers an "interesting [layout]; big, high-quality reproductions and photographs on heavy paper; insightful quotes from diverse sources; and meaty selections of the artist's own writing . . . at the end of the book. Readers get a strong sense of [the] artist's personality along with an excellent survey of his work." SLJ

Includes bibliographical references

Crispino, Enrica. **Van** Gogh; illustrated by Simone Boni . . . [et. al.]; [English translation, Susan Ashley] Oliver Press 2008 64p il (Art masters) $27.95

Grades: 6 7 8 9 10   **92**

1. Artists 2. Painters 3. Artists, Dutch
ISBN 978-1-934545-05-8; 1-934545-05-8

"Using generous, colorful, and cleanly designed two-page spreads, Crispino situates Van Gogh among other artists within certain time periods and locations, portraying his work and life as a counterpoint to various traditions and trends. Most topics are centered by an original drawing that is surrounded by photographs, paintings, artifacts, and descriptions. . . . Consider this volume the equivalent of an unusually insightful museum tour guide." Booklist

Whiting, Jim. **Vincent** Van Gogh; by Jim Whiting. Mitchell Lane 2007 48p il (Art profiles for kids) lib bdg $29.95

Grades: 7 8 9 10   **92**
1. Artists 2. Painters 3. Artists, Dutch
ISBN 978-1-58415-564-5 lib bdg; 1-58415-564-7
lib bdg

LC 2007000662

This offers "well-documented information for teens doing reports. [The] volume covers the painter's childhood, training, travels, influences, and historical context. The chronological chapters build a survey of the [artist's] oeuvres, including the style and subject matter of [his] works and past and present critical reaction." SLJ

Includes glossary and bibliographical references

Goh, Chan Hon, 1969-
Goh, Chan Hon. **Beyond** the dance; a ballerina's life. [by] Chan Hon Goh with Cary Fagan. Tundra Bks. 2002 151p lib bdg $15.95
Grades: 6 7 8 9   **92**
1. Ballet 2. Authors 3. Ballet dancers 4. Children's authors
ISBN 0-88776-596-3

LC 2002-101724

This "autobiography introduces a prima ballerina with the National Ballet of Canada. Goh was born in Beijing but raised in Vancouver by her dancer parents. She discusses the events in her homeland that led her family to emigrate, their adjustment to life in Vancouver, and her parents' struggles to build the Goh Ballet Company. . . . The book is lavishly illustrated with black-and-white photographs, and balletomanes will enjoy poring over every detail." SLJ

Goodall, Jane, 1934-
Bardhan-Quallen, Sudipta. **Jane** Goodall; a twentieth-century life. Penguin Group 2008 218p (Up close) $16.99
Grades: 7 8 9 10   **92**
1. Women scientists 2. Primatologists 3. Writers on nature 4. Nonfiction writers
ISBN 978-0-670-06263-8; 0-670-06263-4

LC 2007-38206

"This profile of the renowned primatologist highlights her independent spirit and deep love of animals as well as the significant roles Goodall's long-lived mother, Vanne, and the scientist Louis B. Leakey . . . played in shaping her character and career. . . . Readers will be inspired by this account." Booklist

Silvey, Anita. Untamed; the wild life of **Jane** Goodall. Anita Silvey; foreword by Jane Goodall. National Geographic Books 2015 96 p. col. illustrations, col. maps (library binding : alk. paper) $28.90
Grades: 4 5 6 7 8   **92**
1. Primates -- Behavior 2. Primatology 3. Chimpanzees -- Behavior 4. Primatologists -- England -- Biography 5. Women primatologists -- England -- Biography
ISBN 1426315198; 9781426315183; 9781426315190

LC 2014017715

This children's book by Anita Silvey profiles "Jane Goodall, one of the most recognized scientists in the Western world, [who] became internationally famous because of her ability to observe and connect with another species. She began tirelessly fighting to protect the environment so that

chimpanzees and other animals will continue have a place and a future on our planet." (Publisher's note)

"Silvey (The Plant Hunters) adeptly chronicles the life of Goodall from her childhood fascination with animal behavior to her groundbreaking field research of chimpanzees in Africa and her work to preserve endangered animals' habitats." Publishers Weekly

Wild life of Jane Goodall

Welty, Tara. **Jane** Goodall. Chelsea House 2011 124p il (Conservation heroes) lib bdg $35
Grades: 6 7 8 9   **92**
1. Chimpanzees 2. Women scientists 3. Primatologists 4. Writers on nature 5. Nonfiction writers
ISBN 978-1-60413-952-5; 1-60413-952-8

LC 2010030583

This is a biography of primatologist and conservationist Jane Goodall, who studied the chimpanzees of Tanzania.

"Captivating, richly informative. . . . The scope of [this book] is comprehensive. . . . [The book is] engaging as [it is] educational and will be ideal for research and reports." SLJ

Includes glossary and bibliographical references

Goodman, Benny, 1909-1986
★ Mattern, Joanne. **Benny** Goodman; by Joanne Mattern. Mitchell Lane Publishers 2013 47 p. ill. (some col.) (library) $29.95
Grades: 6 7 8 9   **92**
1. Jazz musicians 2. Clarinetists -- United States -- Biography 3. Jazz musicians -- United States -- Biography
ISBN 1612282695; 9781612282695

LC 2012008483

This book by Joanne Mattern is part of the American Jazz series and looks at musician Benny Goodman. Within each entry, "information about the subjects' childhoods and preparation for their musical careers is included, as are the positive and negative aspects of their adult lives. Their contributions to the world of jazz are . . . explored." (School Library Journal)

Includes bibliographical references (p. 44-45) and index.

Gore, Al, 1948-
Baptiste, Tracey. **Al** Gore. Chelsea House 2011 119p il (Conservation heroes) lib bdg $35
Grades: 6 7 8 9   **92**
1. Vice-presidents 2. Conservationists 3. Environmentalists 4. Senators 5. Members of Congress 6. Presidential candidates 7. Nobel laureates for peace 8. Vice-presidents -- United States
ISBN 978-1-60413-949-5; 1-60413-949-8

LC 2010030592

A biography of the environmentalist and former vice-president.

"Captivating, richly informative. . . . The scope of [this book] is comprehensive. . . . [The book is] engaging as [it is] educational and will be ideal for research and reports." SLJ

Includes glossary and bibliographical references

Greenberg, Hank, 1911-1986

Sommer, Shelley. **Hammerin'** Hank Greenberg; baseball pioneer. Calkins Creek 2011 135p il $17.95

Grades: 5 6 7 8   **92**

1. Baseball players 2. Jews -- Biography 3. Baseball -- Biography

ISBN 1-59078-452-9; 978-1-59078-452-5

"Greenberg grew up in an Orthodox Jewish family in New York and went on to be a Hall-of-Fame first baseman and left fielder, playing most of his career with the Detroit Tigers in the 1930s and 1940s. . . . Sommer presents a fast-moving, straightforward biography. . . . Numerous black-and-white photos enhance the text. . . . An excellent choice for kids who enjoy delving into baseball history." Booklist

Greene, Nathanael, 1742-1786

Mierka, Gregg A. **Nathanael** Greene; the general who saved the Revolution. [by] Gregg A. Mierka. OTTN Pub. 2007 88p il map (Forgotten heroes of the American Revolution) $23.95; pa $12.95

Grades: 5 6 7 8   **92**

1. Generals 2. Society of Friends 3. United States -- History -- 1775-1783, Revolution

ISBN 978-1-59556-012-4; 1-59556-012-2; 978-1-59556-017-9 pa; 1-59556-017-3 pa

LC 2006021044

"This lively profile combines an engrossing account of the Revolutionary War with healthy measures of images and passages drawn from primary—and sometimes previously unpublished—sources." Booklist

Includes bibliographical references

Grimberg, Tina

Grimberg, Tina. **Out** of line; growing up Soviet. Tundra Books 2007 117p il $22.95

Grades: 7 8 9 10   **92**

1. Rabbis 2. Memoirists 3. Soviet Union 4. Jews -- Russia 5. Jews -- Biography 6. Children's authors

ISBN 978-0-88776-803-3; 0-88776-803-2

"In this warm memoir, Grimberg recalls her childhood in Kiev during the '60s and '70s. She shares the difficulties of Soviet life and explains how members of her family coped with challenges such as shortages. . . . Interwoven with her own experience of growing up in a Jewish family are the stories of her maternal and paternal grandparents. . . . The book is an exemplar of clear, graceful writing and fine storytelling skills." SLJ

Gross, Elly Berkovits, 1929-

Gross, Elly Berkovits. **Elly**; my true story of the Holocaust. [by] Elly Berkovits Gross. Scholastic Press 2009 125p il $14.99

Grades: 4 5 6 7   **92**

1. Poets 2. Authors 3. Holocaust survivors 4. Memoirists 5. Jews -- Romania 6. Holocaust, 1933-1945 -- Personal narratives

ISBN 978-0-545-07494-0; 0-545-07494-0

Relates how the author was torn from her happy home and sent to Birkenau by the Nazis, describing how she worked long hours and fought for survival before being set free at the end of the war and beginning a new life in America.

"As a powerful reminder of man's capacity for inhumanity, this memoir is essential reading." Booklist

Guevara, Ernesto, 1928-1967

Abrams, Dennis. **Ernesto** Che Guevara. Chelsea House Publishers 2010 128p il (The great Hispanic heritage) lib bdg $30

Grades: 6 7 8 9   **92**

1. Guerrillas 2. Physicians 3. Revolutionaries 4. Cuba -- History -- 1959-

ISBN 978-1-60413-732-3; 1-60413-732-0

This "begins with Guevara's childhood as the son of Argentinean aristocrats and gives a balanced portrait of the controversial figure, from his famous worldwide revolutionary efforts to his assassination at the age of 39. . . . A selection of well-chosen images, a chronology, chapter notes, and [a] suggested reading [list] round out [this] engaging [title] in a sure-to-be popular [book] for reports and personal interest." Booklist

Includes bibliographical references

Kallen, Stuart A. **Che** Guevara; by Stuart A. Kallen. Twenty-First Century Books 2013 88 p. (lib. bdg. : alk. paper) $33.27

Grades: 8 9 10 11 12   **92**

1. Cuba -- History -- 1958-1959, Revolution 2. Cuba -- History -- 1959-1990 3. Revolutionaries -- Cuba -- Biography 4. Latin America -- History -- 1948-1980 5. Guerrillas -- Latin America -- Biography

ISBN 0822590352; 9780822590354

LC 2011045480

In author Stuart A. Kallen's book on Che Guevara, "the charismatic Argentinian revolutionary had been leading guerilla fighters in the jungles of Bolivia and was captured by the Bolivian army. Mario Terán, a sergeant in the Bolivian army, volunteered to execute the prisoner. He carried out the bloody assignment with nine point-blank shots to Guevara's body . . . In this chronicle of an assassination, find out what inspired the myth of Che Guevara and what brought him to this bloody crossroads of history." (Publisher's note)

Includes bibliographical references and index.

★ Miller, Calvin Craig. **Che** Guevara; in search of revolution. Morgan Reynolds Pub. 2006 192p il map (World leaders) lib bdg $27.95

Grades: 7 8 9 10   **92**

1. Guerrillas 2. Physicians 3. Revolutionaries 4. Cuba -- History -- 1959-

ISBN 978-1-931798-93-8; 1-931798-93-1

LC 2006-5975

This biography of the guerilla leader is "woven into . . . [an] account of the global politics of his day, including his role in the Cuban revolution and the showdown with the U.S. The design is appealing, with clear type, occasional photos, and maps, and teens will be drawn to the account of the young leader who made a difference in spite of an inglorious defeat." Booklist

Includes bibliographical references

Gunther, John, 1929-1947

Gunther, John. **Death** be not proud; a memoir. Harper & Row 1949 261p il hardcover o.p. pa $13.95

Grades: 7 8 9 10   **92**

1. Sick 2. Cancer 3. Brain -- Tumors
ISBN 0-06-123097-9

A memoir of John Gunther's seventeen-year-old son, who died after a series of operations for a brain tumor. Not only a tribute to a remarkable boy but an account of a brave fight against disease

Guthrie, Woody, 1912-1967

★ Partridge, Elizabeth. **This** land was made for you and me; the life and songs of Woody Guthrie. Viking 2002 217p il $21.99

Grades: 7 8 9 10   **92**

1. Singers 2. Folk musicians 3. Memoirists 4. Songwriters
ISBN 0-670-03535-1

LC 2001-46770

A biography of Woody Guthrie, a singer who wrote over 3,000 folk songs and ballads as he traveled around the United States, including "This Land is Your Land" and "So Long It's Been Good to Know Yuh"

This "presents an unflinchingly accurate portrait of a rambling and unpredictable man.... In addition to a panoply of archival photographs, which add realism to this engrossing story of a life, the book includes carefully selected quotes from songs, acquaintances, and documents to punctuate the story with authenticating detail without detracting from the momentum of the narrative." Bull Cent Child Books

Includes bibliographical references

Halley, Edmond, 1656-1742

Fox, Mary Virginia. **Scheduling** the heavens; the story of Edmond Halley. [by] Mary Virginia Fox. Morgan Reynolds Pub. 2007 128p il map por (Profiles in science) lib bdg $27.95

Grades: 6 7 8 9   **92**

1. Astronomers
ISBN 978-1-59935-021-9 lib bdg; 1-59935-021-1 lib bdg

LC 2006031269

"Though best known for calculating the orbit and predicting the return on a regular schedule of the eponymous comet, the brilliant scientist Halley excelled in many other fields besides astronomy.... Fox conveys Halley's life and times, and his lasting contributions to science, in vivid detail. The informative text is supported with maps and portraits."

Includes bibliographical references

Halvorsen, Gail

★ Tunnell, Michael. **Candy** bomber; the story of the Berlin airlift's chocolate pilot. Charlesbridge 2010 110p il $18.95; pa $9.95

Grades: 4 5 6 7   **92**

1. Air pilots 2. Air force officers 3. Biography, Individual 4. Berlin (Germany) -- History -- Blockade,

1948-1949
ISBN 1-58089-336-8; 1-58089-337-6 pa; 978-1-58089-336-7; 978-1-58089-337-4 pa

This book takes place "[i]n 1948, after World War II, [in] Berlin, . . . [where Michael] Tunnell tells us that pilot Gail Halvorsen spent a night in the city, noticing kids behind a fence watching the planes land. He offered sticks of Doublemint gum to two of the kids, who passed them around so their pals could get a whiff. . . . Soon people all over began sending candy-and-handkerchief parachutes to Halvorsen and other pilots to drop over Berlin." (School Library Journal)

"Curious about the city into which he ferried goods during the Berlin Airlift in 1948, pilot Gail Halvorsen stayed over to visit, met some children, and offered to drop candy and gum when he next flew over. This simple idea grew into a massive project with reverberations today. Tunnell tell this appealing story . . . clearly and chronologically, weaving just enough background for twenty-first century readers and illustrating almost every page with black-and-white photographs, many from Halvorsen's own collection." Booklist

Includes bibliographical references

Hamilton, Alexander, 1757-1804

★ Fritz, Jean. **Alexander** Hamilton; the outsider. illustrations by Ian Schoenherr. G.P. Putnam's Sons 2011 144p il $16.99

Grades: 5 6 7 8   **92**

1. Statesmen 2. Statesmen -- United States 3. Secretaries of the treasury 4. United States -- History -- 1775-1783, Revolution 5. United States -- Politics and government -- 1783-1809
ISBN 039925546X; 9780399255465

LC 2010006008

Fritz "provides a brisk, well-written account introducing Founding Father Alexander Hamilton as an outsider to America. . . . Fast moving and engaging, this straightforward biography acknowledges Hamilton's flaws while portraying him as an intelligent, energetic man who rose to the challenge of his times. . . . In addition to the black-and-white reproductions of period paintings and prints that illustrate the text, Schoenherr's striking, engraving-like images of Hamilton as scholar, soldier, aide-decamp, statesman, and duelist introduce each section." Booklist

Includes bibliographical references

★ St. George, Judith. The **duel** : the parallel lives of Alexander Hamilton and Aaron Burr. Viking 2009 97p il $16.99

Grades: 6 7 8 9 10   **92**

1. Statesmen 2. Vice-presidents 3. Secretaries of the treasury 4. Politicians -- United States
ISBN 978-0-670-01124-7; 0-670-01124-X

LC 2009-5660

"After a prologue following the steps of Alexander Hamilton and Aaron Burr on the morning of their famous duel, St. George backtracks to trace the 'parallel lives' mentioned in the subtitle. . . . Well researched and organized, the book offers insights into the personalities, lives, and times of Burr and Hamilton." Booklist

Hammel, Heidi B.

★ Bortz, Fred. **Beyond** Jupiter; the story of planetary astronomer Heidi Hammel. [by] Fred Bortz. Franklin Watts 2005 110p il (Women's adventures in science) lib bdg $31.50

Grades: 7 8 9 10   **92**

1. Astronomers 2. Women astronomers 3. College teachers 4. Biography, Individual
ISBN 0-531-16775-5

LC 2005-0778

This book by Fred Bortz is part of the Women's Adventures in Science series. It profiles "Heidi Hammel . . . a planetary astronomer, a scientist who uses the world's most powerful telescopes to learn about planets. By making remarkable discoveries in the farthest reaches of our solar system, Heidi also helps us better understand the planet we call home. The giant planets Neptune and Uranus are Heidi's specialties." (Publisher's note)

The author "has captured some of the engaging qualities of Heidi Hammel's personality through extensive work with her and with the cooperation of her friends and family." Sci Books Films

Includes glossary and bibliographical references

Handel, George Frideric, 1685-1759

Getzinger, Donna. **George** Frideric Handel and music for voices; [by] Donna Getzinger and Daniel Felsenfeld. Morgan Reynolds Pub. 2004 144p il (Classical composers) lib bdg $28.95

Grades: 7 8 9 10   **92**

1. Composers
ISBN 1-931798-23-0

LC 2003-26729

"Handel's importance in the field of music is described in this carefully researched and highly detailed biography. The authors explain how the composer's focus on music began at an early age and how he managed to pursue his interests despite his father's belief that music was not an acceptable profession. A social history of the time underscores the details of Handel's career. Black-and-white and full-color reproductions appear throughout." SLJ

Includes bibliographical references

Lee, Lavina. **Handel's** world; [by] Lavina Lee. Rosen Pub. Group 2008 64p il (Music throughout history) lib bdg $29.25

Grades: 5 6 7 8   **92**

1. Composers
ISBN 978-1-4042-0726-4 lib bdg; 1-4042-0726-0 lib bdg

LC 2005030127

This "book begins with an introduction briefly addressing social issues of the day, historical background, or other significant information. . . . Successive chapters discuss the [man's] early [life], family background, social status, personality characteristics, musical training and education, obstacles or challenges, and influences. A chapter . . . focuses on the musician's well-known compositions, describing through lively and colorful language some of the musical elements employed." SLJ

Includes glossary and bibliographical references

Hannibal, 247-183 B.C.

Mills, Cliff. **Hannibal**; [by] Cliff Mills. Chelsea House 2008 120p bibl il map (Ancient world leaders) lib bdg $30

Grades: 6 7 8 9   **92**

1. Generals 2. Rome -- History
ISBN 978-0-7910-9580-5 lib bdg; 0-7910-9580-0 lib bdg

LC 2007-50493

"Mills's informative biography starts with Hannibal preparing to attack the Romans and then goes back in time to explain the founding of Carthage and the history of its conflict with Rome, mainly focusing on the Second Punic War and the subject's journey and battles during that time. . . . Frequent inserts add extra information . . . , without distracting readers from the narrative. Colorful reproductions are also interspersed throughout. . . . [This offers] clear, descriptive writing." SLJ

Includes bibliographical references

Hargreaves, Alice Pleasance Liddell, 1852-1934

Rubin, C. M. The **real** Alice in Wonderland; a role model for the ages. [by] C.M. Rubin with Gabriella Rose Rubin. AuthorHouse 2010 134p il $29.95

Grades: 7 8 9 10   **92**

1. Authors 2. Children 3. Novelists 4. Mathematicians 5. Characters and characteristics in literature 6. Children's authors 7. Writers on science
ISBN 978-1-4490-8131-7; 1-4490-8131-2

LC 2010-901865

"Readers will follow this title down the rabbit hole to discover the world of the real Alice who inspired Lewis Carroll's Alice in Wonderland. The book moves seamlessly through the life of Alice Pleasance Liddell. . . . This offering paints a full picture of Alice, not only as a child who has captivated literature but also as a woman who was truly ahead of her time. This is a purchase that will do well with a range of people and should be offered as a standard accompaniment to Alice in Wonderland. The illustrations and pictures will make it quite popular in a public library." Voice Youth Advocates

Includes bibliographical references

Harvey, William, 1578-1657

Yount, Lisa. **William** Harvey; discoverer of how blood circulates. [by] Lisa Yount. rev ed.; Enslow Publishers 2008 128p il map (Great minds of science) lib bdg $31.93

Grades: 5 6 7 8   **92**

1. Biologists 2. Physicians 3. Physiologists 4. Writers on science 5. Writers on medicine 6. Blood -- Circulation
ISBN 978-0-7660-3010-7 lib bdg; 0-7660-3010-5 lib bdg

LC 2007020301

First published 1994

"A biography of the seventeenth-century English physician William Harvey and includes related activities for readers." Publisher's note

Includes glossary and bibliographical references

Hatshepsut, Queen of Egypt

Dell, Pamela. **Hatshepsut**; Egypt's first female pharaoh. Compass Point Books 2009 112p il map (Signature lives) lib bdg $34.60

Grades: 6 7 8 9   92

1. Queens 2. Kings and rulers 3. Egypt -- History 4. Egypt -- Civilization

ISBN 978-0-7565-3835-4 lib bdg; 0-7565-3835-1 lib bdg

LC 2008005721

This biography of the Egypt's first female pharaoh offers "details about the history and daily life of Egypt's New Kingdom era. . . . It also discusses . . . topics concerning women, such as giving birth and the role of female royalty. The book expects some sophistication from its readers. . . . [The text is] accompanied by high-quality photographs of artifacts, maps, and floor plans. [The] book's detailed time line, comparing events in Egypt to those throughout the world, is helpful for placing the lives of the pharaohs in context." SLJ

Includes glossary and bibliographical references

★ Galford, Ellen. **Hatshepsut**; the princess who became king. National Geographic 2005 64p il map (World history biographies) $17.95; lib bdg $27.90

Grades: 4 5 6 7   92

1. Queens 2. Kings and rulers 3. Egypt -- History 4. Egypt -- Civilization

ISBN 0-7922-3645-9; 0-7922-3646-7 lib bdg

This "presents the life of Queen Hatshepsut, who ruled Egypt as pharaoh during the New Kingdom, around 3500 years ago. Illustrated with clear, color photos of artifacts and sites as well as colorful maps, the text discusses aspects of Egyptian life such as education and religion in Hatshepsut's life. . . . With a clearly written text and many handsome photos, this provides an accessible introduction to Hatshepsut and her times." Booklist

Hawking, Stephen W., 1942-

★ Bankston, John. **Stephen** Hawking; breaking the boundaries of time and space. [by] John Bankston. Enslow Publishers 2005 128p il (Great minds of science) $26.60

Grades: 5 6 7 8   92

1. Physicists 2. People with disabilities 3. People with physical disabilities 4. College teachers 5. Writers on science

ISBN 0-7660-2281-1

LC 2004-9193

This biography of the English physicist, who suffers from amyotrophic lateral sclerosis, includes explanations of his theories and experiments

"This excellent book features large font size and double spacing that makes it easy for any one to read. . . . The activities part of the book is outstanding." Sci Books Films

Includes glossary and bibliographical references

Hawthorne, Nathaniel, 1804-1864

Meltzer, Milton. **Nathaniel** Hawthorne; a biography. Twenty-First Century Books 2007 160p il (American literary greats) lib bdg $31.93

Grades: 7 8 9 10   92

1. Authors 2. Novelists 3. Authors, American 4. Short story writers

ISBN 978-0-7613-3459-0 lib bdg; 0-7613-3459-9 lib bdg

LC 2005000018

"The legendary novelist's life is portrayed as being as dramatic as the plotlines of his novels, and readers will be captivated by the detailed accounts of the family tragedies that made up his childhood and the financial and literary vicissitudes of his adult life. Meltzer provides sufficient background about New England at the time as well as accounts of the historical events that were shaping the country." SLJ

Includes bibliographical references

Hemingway, Ernest, 1899-1961

★ Reef, Catherine. **Ernest** Hemingway; a writer's life. Clarion Books 2009 183p il $20

Grades: 8 9 10 11 12   92

1. Poets 2. Authors 3. Novelists 4. Authors, American 5. Short story writers 6. Nobel laureates for literature

ISBN 978-0-618-98705-4; 0-618-98705-3

LC 2008-32885

"Reef creates a memorable portrait of the writer and his times, and even readers too young for most of Hemingway's oeuvre will enjoy armchair traveling to the bullfights in Spain, fishing expeditions to the Dry Tortugas and the Marquesas Keys, big-game hunting on the Serengeti and covering the Spanish Civil War. Along the way, they will gain a sense of the writer and his times and will even pick up some writing tips." Kirkus

Includes bibliographical references

Whiting, Jim. **Ernest** Hemingway. Mitchell Lane 2005 48p il (Classic storytellers) lib bdg $19.95

Grades: 7 8 9 10   92

1. Poets 2. Authors 3. Novelists 4. Authors, American 5. Short story writers 6. Nobel laureates for literature

ISBN 1-58415-376-8

A biography of the American author.

"A brief, accessible introduction to this classic writer. Whiting balances the extremes in Hemingway's life, from his literary successes to his risky stunts, drinking, and bullying. . . . The book's design is attractive, with good use of color and photos." SLJ

Hendrix, Jimi

Gelfand, Dale Evva. **Jimi** Hendrix; musician. [by] Dale Evva Gelfand. Legacy ed; Chelsea House 2006 120p bibl il por (Black Americans of achievement) lib bdg $30

Grades: 6 7 8 9   92

1. Singers 2. Guitarists 3. Rock musicians 4. African American musicians

ISBN 0-7910-9214-3

LC 2006004574

A biography of the rock musician

This book goes "beyond the typical personal information to provide some social history relevant to the subject's

time. Captioned photographs and boxed inserts enhance the conversational [text]." Horn Book Guide
Includes bibliographical references

Willett, Edward. **Jimi** Hendrix; kiss the sky. Enslow Publishers 2006 160p bibl por (American rebels) lib bdg $27.93
Grades: 7 8 9 10   **92**
1. Singers 2. Guitarists 3. Rock musicians 4. African American musicians
ISBN 0-7660-2449-0
LC 2005033751
"This biography introduces electric-guitar virtuouso Jimi Hendrix. . . . [This is a] good, basic introduction to Hendrix's life and the reasons for his enduring fame." Booklist
Includes bibliographical references

Henry, John William, 1847?-ca. 1875
★ Nelson, Scott Reynolds. **Ain't** nothing but a man; my quest to find the real John Henry. [by] Scott Reynolds Nelson with Marc Aronson. National Geographic 2008 64p il $18.95; lib bdg $27.90
Grades: 4 5 6 7 8   **92**
1. John Henry (Legendary character) 2. Railroad workers 3. Railroads -- History 4. African Americans -- Biography
ISBN 978-1-4263-0000-4; 1-4263-0000-X; 978-1-4263-0001-1 lib bdg; 1-4263-0001-8 lib bdg
LC 2007-12446
This describes the author's research to find the real man who inspired the songs and legends about the African American steel-driving hero.
"The layout is attractive, with a sepia and beige background for the text and sepia-toned photographs. . . . This is an excellent example of how much detective work is needed for original research." SLJ
Includes bibliographical references

Henry, O., 1862-1910
Caravantes, Peggy. **Writing** is my business; the story of O. Henry. Morgan Reynolds Pub. 2006 160p il map (World writers) lib bdg $27.95
Grades: 7 8 9 10   **92**
1. Authors 2. Authors, American 3. Short story writers
ISBN 978-1-59935-031-8; 1-59935-031-9
LC 2006-16126
This is a biography of the short story writer
"This title grabs readers' attention and never lets go." SLJ
Includes bibliographical references

Henson, Matthew Alexander, 1866-1955
★ Johnson, Dolores. **Onward**; a photobiography of African-American polar explorer Matthew Henson. National Geographic 2006 64p il $17.95
Grades: 5 6 7 8   **92**
1. Explorers 2. North Pole 3. African Americans -- Biography
ISBN 0-7922-7914-X
LC 2005-05837
"The quest to be the first to reach the North Pole is an exciting adventure story, and Henson got there first, as part

of the ninth expedition led by Robert Peary in 1909. But Henson was African American, labeled as Peary's 'Negro manservant,' and he did not get full recognition until 2001. This . . . focuses on the physical details of the dangerous Arctic journeys . . . the repeated failures and the teamwork, as well as Henson's skills, stamina, and essential role in forging relationships with the Inuit. . . . The book design is beautiful: thick paper, spacious type, and stirring photos that capture the icy storms as well as the people involved in the history." Booklist

Olmstead, Kathleen A. **Matthew** Henson; the quest for the North Pole. [by] Kathleen Olmstead. Sterling Pub. Co. 2008 124p il (Sterling biographies) pa $5.95
Grades: 7 8 9 10   **92**
1. Explorers 2. North Pole 3. African Americans -- Biography
ISBN 978-1-4027-4441-9 pa; 1-4027-4441-2 pa
LC 2007048106
"Henson's own contradictory and partially fabricated writing about his effort to reach the North Pole with Robert Peary presented some challenges to the biographer, but she gamely sorts out the most likely version of the story, letting readers know what is unsubstantiated and what is corroborated fact. . . . [This] attractively formatted [title has] black-and-white and full-color photographs or reproductions as well as sidebars. [A] solid [addition] to biography shelves." SLJ
Includes glossary and bibliographical references

★ Prins, Marcel. **Hidden** like Anne Frank; fourteen true stories of survival. Marcel Prins and Peter Henk Steenhuis ; translated by Laura Watkinson. Arthur A. Levine Books, An Imprint of Scholastic Inc. 2014 256 p. illustrations, maps (hardback) $16.99
Grades: 7 8 9 10 11 12   **92**
1. Holocaust, 1939-1945 2. Hidden children (Holocaust) 3. Jewish children in the Holocaust 4. World War, 1939-1945 -- Children 5. Netherlands -- Biography 6. Hidden children (Holocaust) -- Netherlands -- Biography 7. World War, 1939-1945 -- Netherlands -- Personal narratives 8. Jewish children in the Holocaust -- Netherlands -- Biography 9. Holocaust, Jewish (1939-1945) -- Netherlands -- Personal narratives
ISBN 0545543622; 9780545543620; 9780545543637; 9780545543644
LC 2013040908
This book, by Marcel Prins and Peter Henk Steenhuis, presents "fourteen . . . true stories of children hidden away during World War II. . . . Some children were only three or four years old when they were hidden; some were teenagers. Some hid with neighbors or family, while many were with complete strangers. But all know the pain of losing their homes, their families, even their own names. They describe the secret network of brave people who kept them safe." (Publisher's note)
"This volume includes compelling first-person accounts of survival during the Holocaust and WWII in Holland, including coauthor Prins's mother's experience. Readers will encounter incredible acts of courage, both from the subjects

themselves and the Resistance fighters and ordinary people willing to risk their lives. Family photos and archival images appear throughout; a glossary and pictures of the survivors today are appended." Horn Book

Hillary, Edmund Sir

Crompton, Samuel. **Sir** Edmund Hillary; [by] Samuel Willard Crompton. Chelsea House 2009 112p il map (Great explorers) lib bdg $30

Grades: 6 7 8 9 10 11 12   **92**

1. Mountaineering 2. Mountaineers 3. Nonfiction writers 4. Mount Everest (China and Nepal)
ISBN 978-1-60413-420-9 lib bdg; 1-60413-420-8 lib bdg

LC 2009-8688

Biography of the explorer Sir Edmund Hillary

"The information . . . is presented in such a way as to attract and maintain readers' interest. . . . With a full complement of maps, photographs (where available), illustrations, time lines, and document reproductions, a full story is told. Well-written and thoroughly researched, this . . . will make a solid addition." SLJ

Includes glossary and bibliographical references

★ Elish, Dan. **Edmund** Hillary; first to the top. [by] Dan Elish. Marshall Cavendish Benchmark 2007 80p il map (Great explorations) lib bdg $32.79

Grades: 5 6 7 8   **92**

1. Mountaineering 2. Mountaineers 3. Nonfiction writers 4. Mount Everest (China and Nepal)
ISBN 978-0-7614-2224-2 lib bdg; 0-7614-2224-2 lib bdg

LC 2005027929

This "appealing [title features] readable [text], solid research, and variety of color illustrations." SLJ

"An examination of the life and accomplishments of the famed explorer from New Zealand who was one of the first to scale Mount Everest." Publisher's note

Includes bibliographical references

Hinton, S. E.

★ Kjelle, Marylou Morano. **S.E.** Hinton; author of The outsiders. Enslow Publishers 2007 112p bibl il por (Authors teens love) lib bdg $31.93

Grades: 6 7 8 9   **92**

1. Authors 2. Novelists 3. Women authors 4. Authors, American 5. Children's authors 6. Young adult authors
ISBN 978-0-7660-2720-6 lib bdg; 0-7660-2720-1 lib bdg

LC 2006036820

"This well-written and informative biography weaves facts about Hinton's life with analyses of and reflections on her novels." SLJ

Includes glossary and bibliographical references

Hippocrates

Gow, Mary. The **greatest** doctor of ancient times: Hippocrates and his oath. Enslow Publishers 2009 128p il map (Great minds of ancient science and math) lib bdg $31.93

Grades: 5 6 7 8   **92**

1. Physicians 2. Medicine -- History 3. Writers on medicine 4. Greece -- Civilization
ISBN 978-0-7660-3118-0 lib bdg; 0-7660-3118-7 lib bdg

LC 2008029630

"This interesting take on medicine concludes with several activities. . . . Photographs on sepia-colored pages are a good match for the subject." Booklist

Includes glossary and bibliographical references

Hitler, Adolf, 1889-1945

Rice, Earle. **Adolf** Hitler and Nazi Germany. Morgan Reynolds 2005 176p il map lib bdg $28.95

Grades: 7 8 9 10   **92**

1. Dictators 2. Heads of state 3. National socialism 4. Nazi leaders 5. Germany -- Politics and government -- 1933-1945
ISBN 978-1-931798-78-5; 1-931798-78-8

LC 2005-17825

"Clear, concise writing coupled with impressive illustrations that include black-and-white and color photos of cityscapes and individuals make this book a useful resource." SLJ

Hodgman, Ann

Hodgman, Ann. **How** to die of embarrassment every day. Henry Holt and Co. 2011 208p il $16.99

Grades: 5 6 7 8   **92**

1. Authors 2. Women authors 3. Cookbook writers 4. Authors, American 5. Children's authors
ISBN 978-0-8050-8705-5; 0-8050-8705-2

LC 2010-49004

Hodgman offers a "chatty personal narrative . . . focusing on her childhood years and her tendency to land herself into humiliating situations. . . . The generous supply of spot art and relevant images from Hodgman's childhood adds to the browsibility. . . . There's . . . plenty of humor . . . but more importantly there's a tacit message about the survivability of embarrassment and the fact that we all, even seemingly perfect and polished adults, spend our lives goofing up." Bull Cent Child Books

Hopper, Edward, 1882-1967

★ Rubin, Susan Goldman. **Edward** Hopper; painter of light and shadow. Abrams Books for Young Readers 2007 47p il $18.95

Grades: 5 6 7 8   **92**

1. Artists 2. Painters 3. Artists -- United States
ISBN 978-0-8109-9347-1; 0-8109-9347-3

LC 2006-31978

"On every page of this beautifully designed biography, readers will find a reproduction of Hopper's work, matched to clear, eloquent commentary. . . . Readers . . . will come back to read about the man and look at his art again and again." Booklist

Includes bibliographical references

Horowitz, Anthony, 1955-

Abrams, Dennis. **Anthony** Horowitz; [by] Dennis Abrams; foreword by Kyle Zimmer. Chelsea

House Publishers 2006 123p il map (Who wrote that?) lib bdg $30

Grades: 6 7 8 9   **92**

1. Authors 2. Novelists 3. Authors, English 4. Short story writers 5. Young adult authors

ISBN 0-7910-8968-1

LC 2005030090

A biography of the author of the popular Alex Rider series

"Even teens who don't know Horowitz's books will enjoy reading this frank account that describes how his unhappy childhood . . . influenced his books. . . . Just as compelling are Horowitz's perspectives on what makes good horror and spy fiction." Booklist

Includes bibliographical references

Houdini, Harry, 1874-1926

Biskup, Agnieszka. **Houdini**; the life of the great escape artist. illustrated by Pat Kinsella. Capstone Press 2011 32p il (Graphic library: American graphic) lib bdg $29.32; pa $7.95

Grades: 4 5 6 7   **92**

1. Magicians 2. Biographical graphic novels 3. Nonfiction writers

ISBN 978-1-4296-5474-6 lib bdg; 1-4296-5474-0 lib bdg; 978-1-4296-6268-0 pa; 1-4296-6268-9 pa

LC 2010024848

In graphic novel format, explores the life of Harry Houdini and describes some of his most daring escapes.

"The illustrations are eye-catching and the narration is presented simply, yet compellingly. . . . Fact-filled, entertaining, and accessible." SLJ

Includes bibliographical references

Carlson, Laurie M. **Harry** Houdini for kids; his life and adventures with 21 magic tricks and illusions. Chicago Review Press 2009 136p il pa $16.95

Grades: 4 5 6 7   **92**

1. Magicians 2. Magic tricks 3. Nonfiction writers

ISBN 978-1-55652-782-1 pa; 1-55652-782-9 pa

LC 2008021404

"Reluctant readers (as well as budding troublemakers) will flock to this biography/handbook hybrid about one of the most famous magicians who ever lived. Even for those familiar with Houdini's fascinating story, Carlson's snappy writing gives it new life. . . . Nearly every page is enlivened with period photographs, boxed sections containing biographies and definitions, and, most important, 21 magic tricks that will have readers breaking out their deck of cards and practicing their sleight of hand." Booklist

★ Fleischman, Sid. **Escape!** the story of the great Houdini. Greenwillow Books 2006 210p il $18.99; lib bdg $19.89

Grades: 5 6 7 8   **92**

1. Magicians 2. Nonfiction writers

ISBN 978-0-06-085094-4; 0-06-085094-9; 978-0-06-085095-1 lib bdg; 0-06-0850957-1 lib bdg

LC 2005052631

"Fleischman looks at Houdini's life through his own eyes, as a fellow magician. . . . Fleischman's tone is lively and he develops a relationship with readers by revealing just

enough truth behind Houdini's razzle-dazzle to keep the legend alive. . . . Engaging and fascinating." SLJ

Includes bibliographical references

Houston, Samuel, 1793-1863

Bodden, Valerie. **Samuel** Houston; Army leader & historic politician. ABDO Pub. Co. 2010 112p il map (Military heroes) lib bdg $22.95

Grades: 7 8 9   **92**

1. Governors 2. Statesmen 3. Senators 4. Army officers 5. Texas -- History 6. Politicians -- United States

ISBN 978-1-60453-962-2; 1-60453-962-3

LC 2009-32373

Biography of Samuel Houston.

"The rush of literary adrenalin will hook readers immediately and keep them enthralled until the end. . . . Given the dynamic topic [and] . . . appealing layout . . . [this is] likely to attract reluctant readers. In addition, sources are plentiful and well documented." SLJ

Includes glossary and bibliographical references

Howe, Samuel Gridley, 1801-1876

Alexander, Sally Hobart. **She** touched the world: Laura Bridgman, deaf-blind pioneer; by Sally Hobart Alexander and Robert Alexander. Clarion Books 2008 100p il $18

Grades: 5 6 7 8   **92**

1. Deaf 2. Blind 3. Students 4. Physicians 5. Philanthropists 6. Humanitarians 7. Teachers of the blind

ISBN 978-0-618-85299-4; 0-618-85299-9

"At the age of three, in 1832, Laura Bridgman contracted scarlet fever and lost her sight, her hearing, her sense of smell, and much of her sense of taste. Her family sent her to Dr. Samuel [Gridley] Howe at the New England Institute for the Education of the Blind, and by the age of 10, Laura was world-famous for her accomplishments. . . . Alexander . . . presents a well-written and thoroughly researched biography of this remarkable woman, with numerous black-and-white photos." Booklist

Includes bibliographical references

Hubble, Edwin Powell, 1889-1953

Datnow, Claire L. **Edwin** Hubble; discoverer of galaxies. rev ed; Enslow Publishers 2007 128p il (Great minds of science) lib bdg $31.93

Grades: 5 6 7 8   **92**

1. Astronomers

ISBN 978-0-7660-2791-6 lib bdg; 0-7660-2791-0 lib bdg

LC 2006-20111

First published 1997

Traces the life and work of the man whose study of galaxies led to a new understanding of the universe

Includes glossary and bibliographical references

Hudson, Henry, d. 1611

★ Otfinoski, Steven. **Henry** Hudson; in search of the Northwest Passage. [by] Steven Otfinoski.

Marshall Cavendish Benchmark 2006 80p il map (Great explorations) lib bdg $32.79
Grades: 5 6 7 8   **92**
    1. Explorers 2. America -- Exploration
    ISBN 978-0-7614-2225-9 lib bdg; 0-7614-2225-0 lib bdg
"An examination of the life and accomplishments of the famed explorer who lent his name to several geographic locations in North America" Publisher's note
    Includes bibliographical references

★ Weaver, Janice. **Hudson**; written by Janice Weaver; illustrated by David Craig. Tundra Books 2010 47p il map $22.95
Grades: 3 4 5 6   **92**
    1. Explorers 2. Biography, Individual 3. America -- Exploration 4. Canada -- Discovery and exploration -- British 5. America -- Discovery and exploration
    ISBN 978-0-88776-814-9; 0-88776-814-8
This is a biography of the explorer. "The grandson of a trader, Hudson sailed under both British and Dutch flags, looking for a northern route to China. Although none of his voyages led to the discovery of a northwest passage, he did explore what is now Hudson's Bay and what is now New York City." (Publisher's note) Index. "Ages eight to twelve." (Quill Quire)
    "This dramatic picture-book biography about Henry Hudson, who discovered neither the new land nor the passage to Asia he sought, makes the explorer's lack of success a gripping read. . . . Weaver is clear about what is fact and what is supposition, and the tumultuous early-seventeenth-century history is meticulously documented. . . . Craig's glowing period portraits, landscapes, and watercolors of the ship in dangerous seas intensify the drama, and archival prints and maps add interest." Booklist
    Includes bibliographical references

Young, Jeff C. **Henry** Hudson; discoverer of the Hudson River. Enslow Publishers 2009 112p il map (Great explorers of the world) lib bdg $31.93
Grades: 6 7 8 9   **92**
    1. Explorers 2. America -- Exploration
    ISBN 978-1-59845-123-8 lib bdg; 1-59845-123-5 lib bdg
                       LC 2008-30752
"Examines the life of explorer Henry Hudson, including his quest for the elusive Northeast passage, his discovery of the Hudson River, and his mysterious death." Publisher's note
    Includes glossary and bibliographical references

Hudson, Jennifer, 1981-

Cartlidge, Cherese. **Jennifer** Hudson; by Cherese Cartlidge. Lucent Books 2011 96 p. ill. (hardcover) $33.95
Grades: 6 7 8 9   **92**
    1. Actresses 2. African American singers 3. Singers -- United States -- Biography 4. Motion picture actors and actresses -- United States -- Biography
    ISBN 1420506072; 9781420506075
                       LC 2011006366

This book offers a biography of actress Jennifer Hudson by author Cherese Cartlidge. It is part of the "People in the News" series, which "profiles the lives and careers of some of today's most prominent newsmakers. Whether covering contributions and achievements or notorious deeds, books in this series examine why these well-known individuals garnered public attention." (Publisher's note)
    Includes bibliographical references and index

Hunter, Clementine, 1886?-1988

Whitehead, Kathy. **Art** from her heart: folk artist Clementine Hunter; [illustrated by] Shane Evans. G.P. Putnam's Sons 2008 un il $16.99
Grades: 4 5 6 7   **92**
    1. Artists 2. Folk art 3. Painters 4. Women artists 5. African American artists 6. Centenarians 7. Biography, Individual
    ISBN 0-399-24219-8; 978-0-399-24219-9
                       LC 2006-34458
This is a biography of Louisiana artist Clementine Hunter, who depicted life on a plantation. Bibliography. "Ages five to eight." (Bull Cent Child Books) "In the 1950s, segregation laws denied artist Clementine Hunter admission to the gallery that exhibited her work. . . . Hunter was not stopped by self-pity, and she did not wait for 'the perfect time to paint.' She had no canvas, so she made art with whatever she could find--window shades, glass bottles, old boards." (Booklist)
    "Whitehead's lyrical text speaks of Hunter's perseverance and talent as well as of the simplicity, love of nature, and caring of friends and family that informed her work. Evans bolsters Whitehead's words with bold mixed-media illustrations that portray Hunter in hard times and in good." SLJ

Hunter-Gault, Charlayne, 1942-

To the mountaintop! Charlayne Hunter-Gault. Roaring Brook Press 2012 v, 198 p.p ill.
Grades: 6 7 8 9 10 11 12   **92**
    1. Colleges and universities 2. Women political activists 3. African Americans -- Civil rights 4. Southern States -- Race relations 5. African American journalists -- Biography 6. Journalists -- United States -- Biography 7. Civil rights movements -- Southern States -- History -- 20th century 8. African Americans -- Civil rights -- Southern States -- History -- 20th century
    ISBN 9781596436053
                       LC 2011020894
This book is written by Charlayne "Hunter-Gault . . . [who along with her] classmate Hamilton Holmes . . . [was one of] the first African Americans to be admitted to the University of Georgia, Athens. . . . [It] recalls the turbulent years from 1959, when she was first approached to challenge the system by seeking admission, through two years of legal battles for her admission to be finalized, through the campus protests and challenges unleashed by her actual enrollment, to graduation and her full-time position in 1965 at the 'New Yorker.' Organized by year, Hunter-Gault's personal experiences are set within the context of the larger civil rights movement." (Bulletin of the Center for Children's Books)
    Includes bibliographical references and index

Hurston, Zora Neale, 1891-1960

★ Litwin, Laura Baskes. **Zora** Neale Hurston; I have been in sorrow's kitchen. Enslow Publishers 2007 128p bibl il por (African-American biography library) lib bdg $23.95

Grades: 7 8 9 10   **92**

1. Authors 2. Novelists 3. Dramatists 4. Women authors 5. African American authors 6. Memoirists 7. Folklorists 8. Short story writers
ISBN 978-0-7660-2536-5 lib bdg; 0-7660-2536-5 lib bdg

LC 2005034881

Litwin "offers an engaging portrait of legendary author and folklorist Zora Neale Hurston. . . . Well-paced . . . chapters follow Hurston through her remarkable career. . . . Generously sprinkled with excerpts from Hurston's own works and illustrated with numerous black-and-white portraits of Hurston and her prominent friends and collaborators." Booklist

Includes bibliographical references

★ Lyons, Mary E. **Sorrow's** kitchen; the life and folklore of Zora Neale Hurston. 1st Collier Books ed; Collier Books 1993 144p il (Great achievers) pa $7.99

Grades: 7 8 9 10   **92**

1. Authors 2. Novelists 3. Dramatists 4. Women authors 5. African American authors 6. Memoirists 7. Folklorists 8. Short story writers
ISBN 0-02-044445-1

LC 92-30600

First published 1990 by Scribner

This biography details "Hurston's migration from Florida to Baltimore, Washington, D.C., and finally Harlem as well as her travels through the West Indies to collect folklore. The text contains eleven excerpts from Hurston's books. . . . Lyons has created a prime example of biography—fascinating, enlightening, stimulating, and satisfying." Horn Book

Includes bibliographical references

Sapet, Kerrily. **Rhythm** and folklore; the story of Zora Neale Hurston. Morgan Reynolds Pub. 2008 160p il lib bdg $27.95

Grades: 7 8 9 10 11 12   **92**

1. Authors 2. Novelists 3. Dramatists 4. Women authors 5. African American authors 6. Memoirists 7. Folklorists 8. Short story writers
ISBN 978-1-59935-067-7; 1-59935-067-X

LC 2008-844

A biography of the African American author and folklorist

"With lots of personal quotes, this lively biography stays true to Hurston's defiant, independent spirit. . . . Sapet give a strong sense of the times, including the Harlem Renaissance. . . . With lots of full-page photos, this biography will encourage teens to read and discuss Hurston's work." Booklist

Includes bibliographical references

Hutchinson, Anne Marbury, 1591-1643

Stille, Darlene R. **Anne** Hutchinson; Puritan protester. by Darlene R. Stille. Compass Point Books 2006 112p il map (Signature lives) lib bdg $31.93

Grades: 6 7 8 9   **92**

1. Puritans 2. Colonists 3. Dissenters 4. Religious leaders 5. Massachusetts -- History -- 1600-1775, Colonial period
ISBN 978-07565-1577-5 lib bdg; 0-7565-1577-7 lib bdg

LC 2005025093

A biography of Anne Hutchinson, who was put on trial in colonial Massachusetts for challenging Puritan beliefs

This is an "excellent biography. . . . Stille neither glorifies nor condemns her but rather reveals her strength of character in the context of her historical era, enhancing the interesting, accessible narrative with numerous full-color illustrations." Booklist

Includes bibliographical references

Inouye, Daniel K.

Slavicek, Louise Chipley. **Daniel** Inouye. Chelsea House 2007 128p bibl il por (Asian Americans of achievement) lib bdg $30

Grades: 6 7 8 9   **92**

1. Lawyers 2. Senators 3. State legislators 4. District attorneys 5. Members of Congress 6. Statesmen -- United States 7. Asian Americans -- Biography
ISBN 978-0-7910-9271-2 lib bdg; 0-7910-9271-2 lib bdg

LC 2006026062

A biography of the Senator from Hawaii

This is "well-researched . . . attractive . . . solid." SLJ

Includes glossary and bibliographical references

IraqiGirl

IraqiGirl. **IraqiGirl;** diary of a teenage girl in Iraq. Haymarket 2009 205p pa $13

Grades: 6 7 8 9 10   **92**

1. Weblogs 2. Bloggers 3. Iraq War, 2003- -- Personal narratives
ISBN 978-1-931859-73-8; 1-931859-73-6

"In 2004 in Mosul (the third largest city in Iraq), a 15-year-old girl started a blog detailing her life in the midst of the Iraq War. Her journal encompasses the day-to-day trauma the American invasion has caused her city, her family and friends. . . . [The author's] authentically teenage voice, emotional struggles and concerns make her story all the more resonant." Publ Wkly

Irwin, Bindi, 1998-

Breguet, Amy. **Steve** and Bindi Irwin. Chelsea House 2011 140p il map (Conservation heroes) lib bdg $35

Grades: 6 7 8 9   **92**

1. Conservationists 2. Wildlife conservation 3. Television personalities 4. Zoo directors 5. Herpetologists 6. Children of prominent persons
ISBN 978-1-60413-957-0; 1-60413-957-9

A biography of Steve Irwin, Australian star of The Crocodile Hunter, who died in 2006, and his daughter, Bindi.

"Captivating, richly informative. . . . The scope of [this book] is comprehensive. . . . [The book is] engaging as [it is] educational and will be ideal for research and reports." SLJ

Irwin, Steve, 1962-2006

Breguet, Amy. **Steve** and Bindi Irwin. Chelsea House 2011 140p il map (Conservation heroes) lib bdg $35

Grades: 6 7 8 9   92

1. Conservationists 2. Wildlife conservation 3. Television personalities 4. Zoo directors 5. Herpetologists 6. Children of prominent persons

ISBN 978-1-60413-957-0; 1-60413-957-9

A biography of Steve Irwin, Australian star of The Crocodile Hunter, who died in 2006, and his daughter, Bindi.

"Captivating, richly informative. . . . The scope of [this book] is comprehensive. . . . [The book is] engaging as [it is] educational and will be ideal for research and reports." SLJ

Jackson, Michael, 1958-2009

Pratt, Mary. **Michael** Jackson; king of pop. ABDO Pub. Co. 2010 112p il (Lives cut short) lib bdg $32.79

Grades: 5 6 7 8   92

1. Singers 2. Rock musicians 3. African American musicians 4. Songwriters 5. Pop musicians

ISBN 978-1-60453-788-8 lib bdg; 1-60453-788-4 lib bdg

This discusses Michael Jackson's "early life, providing details that give insight into later success and troubles and maintaining a laudatory tone that focuses on the individual's artistic achievements and hard work to achieve fame. Details [such as] explaining . . . that young Michael Jackson never got to play with his peers . . . are bound to resonate with readers. Numerous photos and sidebars appear throughout. [A] worthwhile [resource] for reports as well as popular reading." SLJ

Includes glossary and bibliographical references

Jackson, Robert Houghwout, 1892-1954

Jarrow, Gail. **Robert** H. Jackson; New Deal lawyer, Supreme Court Justice, Nuremberg prosecutor. Calkins Creek 2008 128p il $18.95

Grades: 7 8 9 10   92

1. Judges 2. Lawyers 3. Nuremberg Trial of Major German War Criminals, 1945-1946 4. Attorneys general 5. Government officials 6. Supreme Court justices

ISBN 978-1-59078-511-9

LC 2007-18858

"Framed by Jackson's famous speech as chief American prosecutor at the 1945 international Nuremberg trial of Nazi war criminals, this detailed biography sets his law career within the history and politics of his time and raises essential issues of human rights." Booklist

Includes bibliographical references

Jacobs, Jane, 1916-2006

Lang, Glenna. **Genius** of common sense; Jane Jacobs and the story of The death and life of great American cities. [by] Glenna Lang & Marjory Wunsch. David R. Godine 2009 127p il map $17.95

Grades: 7 8 9 10 11 12   92

1. Authors 2. City planning 3. Urban sociology 4. Urban planners 5. Nonfiction writers 6. New York

(State) -- History

ISBN 978-1-56792-384-1; 1-56792-384-4

LC 2009-08304

"This is the story of a remarkable woman, brought up during the Depression and with no college education, who single-handedly changed the way America viewed its cities. . . . At 18, she moved to New York to pursue her career as a writer and fell in love with the city. It was there that she had her infamous battles with Robert Moses over urban renewal and did the research for her most famous book, The Death and Life of Great American Cities. Black-and-white photographs, maps, and political cartoons and other reproductions appear on most pages. . . . Lang and Wunsch are to be commended for introducing a fascinating female role model." SLJ

Includes bibliographical references

Jacobs, Marc, 1963-

Branscomb, Leslie Wolf. **Marc** Jacobs. Morgan Reynolds Pub. 2011 112p il (Profiles in fashion) $28.95

Grades: 7 8 9 10   92

1. Fashion designers

ISBN 978-1-59935-153-7; 1-59935-153-6

LC 2010022226

This biography of Marc Jacobs describes "the personal [life] and economic details of the multimillion-dollar business of [this] high-profile [designer]. [It discusses] the designer's cultural background, childhood, family, work history and education. The . . . [author describes] the early influences that inspired the [designer] to pursue this career and [provides] details of the philosophy [the] designer uses to make [his] clothing unique. . . . The writing is clear and well organized. Color photos are included and give readers a feel for the time period and the types of clothing and accessories the [designer] created." Voice Youth Advocates

Includes bibliographical references

Jalāl al-Dīn Rūmī, Maulana

★ Demi. **Rumi**; whirling dervish. written and illustrated by Demi. Marshall Cavendish Children 2009 31p il $19.99

Grades: 4 5 6 7   92

1. Poets 2. Persian poetry

ISBN 978-0-7614-5527-1; 0-7614-5527-2

LC 2008012920

"Demi presents this picture-book introduction to the thirteenth-century mystical poet. . . . Demi condenses her famous subject's life into a brief but substantive text. . . . She adds frequent excerpts from Rumi's poems and writings. . . . In an introductory note, Demi cites Turkish miniatures as her inspiration for the small-scale, elaborately patterned pictures, rendered in Turkish and Chinese inks with gold overlay. . . . The gilded, celebratory pictures create shimmering beauty from the smallest details." Booklist

James, LeBron

Yasuda, Anita. **Lebron** James. 2011 24p il (Remarkable people) $27.13; pa $12.95

Grades: 4 5 6 7   **92**

1. Basketball players 2. Basketball -- Biography
ISBN 978-1-6169-0669-6; 1-6169-0669-3; 978-1-6169-0674-0 pa; 1-6169-0674-X pa

LC 2010051003

This looks at Lebron James' "life, accomplishments, and challenges while including a page of quotes, an annotated list of contemporaries and influences, starter suggestions for writing a paper, and a time line and glossary. . . . [This book] follows basketball's 'King James' from his early life with a single teen mother to his splashy entry into the NBA at age 19." Booklist

Jay-Z, 1969-

Spilsbury, Richard. **Jay** -Z; Richard Spilsbury. Heinemann Library 2013 48 p. (Titans of business) (pbk.) $8.99

Grades: 4 5 6 7   **92**

1. Businessmen 2. Rap musicians 3. Success in business 4. Rap musicians -- United States -- Biography
ISBN 1432964305; 1432964372; 9781432964306; 9781432964375

LC 2011050758

This book, part of the Titans of Business series, looks at rapper and entrepreneur Jay-Z. "Starting with Jay-Z's early life as Shawn Corey Carter in a poor Brooklyn neighborhood, the biography recounts how he overcame his difficult adolescence as a drug dealer with his desire to be a musician." (Booklist)

Includes bibliographical references and index

Jefferson, Thomas, 1743-1826

Miller, Brandon Marie. **Thomas** Jefferson for kids; his life and times, with 21 activities. Chicago Review Press 2011 ix, 132p il $16.95

Grades: 4 5 6 7   **92**

1. Architects 2. Presidents 3. Vice-presidents 4. Essayists 5. Presidents -- United States
ISBN 978-1-56976-348-3; 1-56976-348-8

LC 2011019318

"Miller offers a thorough and methodical overview of Jefferson's life and political career. . . . The presentation is expecially forthright about Jefferson's ownership of slaves and his fathering of children with Sally Hemmings. . . . The volume offers the chance to delve into Jefferson's life and be inspired by the range of his interests." Kirkus

Includes bibliographical references

Jemison, Mae C.

Jemison, Mae C. **Find** where the wind goes; moments from my life. [by] Mae Jemison. Scholastic Press 2001 196p il hardcover o.p. $16.95

Grades: 5 6 7 8   **92**

1. Astronauts 2. Physicians 3. African American women -- Biography
ISBN 0-439-13195-2; 0-439-13196-0 pa

LC 00-41008

"Mae Jemsion, doctor, scientist, astronaut, and professor, here tells of the formative incidents of her life. . . . The author discusses her youth—her days in the South, her family's move to Chicago's South Side, school experiences, and growing up—as well as her later life and her place in

the space program. . . . Grades five to eight." (Bull Cent Child Books)

"Dr. Jemison, the first woman of color to travel in space, shares her life story in this autobiographical selection." Book Rep

Jobs, Steve, 1955-2011

Blumenthal, Karen. **Steve** Jobs; the man who thought different ; a biography. by Karen Blumenthal. Feiwel and Friends 2012 310 p. ill., ports.

Grades: 7 8 9 10   **92**

1. Apple Computer, Inc. 2. Inventors -- United States -- Biography 3. Businesspeople -- United States -- Biography 4. Computer industry -- United States -- History
ISBN 125001445X; 125001557X; 9781250014450; 9781250015570

LC 2012376637

YALSA Award for Excellence in Nonfiction for Young Adults Finalist (2013)

This book is a biography of technology executive Steve Jobs. "[Karen] Blumenthal weaves her portrait on the thematic frame used by Jobs himself in his autobiographical 2005 Stanford commencement address." She chronicles "his adoption as an infant through his 'phone phreaking' days to a spectacular rise and just as meteoric fall from corporate grace in the 1980s. Following a decade of diminished fortunes and largely self-inflicted complications in personal relationships, he returned to Apple." (Kirkus)

Includes bibliographical references (p. [278]-283) and index

Goldsworthy, Steve. **Steve** Jobs. Weigl 2011 24p il (Remarkable people) $27.13; pa $12.95 **92**

1. Entrepreneurs 2. Businesspeople 3. Computer industry 4. Computer scientists 5. Apple Computer Inc. 6. Computer industry executives 7. Electronics industry executives
ISBN 978-1-6169-0670-2; 1-6169-0670-7; 978-1-6169-0675-7 pa; 1-6169-0675-8 pa

LC 2010050999

This looks at Steve Jobs' "life, accomplishments, and challenges while including a page of quotes, an annotated list of contemporaries and influences, starter suggestions for writing a paper, and a time line and glossary. . . . [This book] kicks off as current as possible with a picture of the bearded Apple CEO displaying an iPad, before getting into the ups (he became a multimillionaire in just two years) and downs (his struggle with cancer)." Booklist

Quinn, Jason. **Steve** Jobs; genius by design. by Jason Quinn ; illustrated by Amit Tayal. Random House Inc 2012 104 p. ill. (chiefly col.) $12.99

Grades: 7 8 9 10 11 12 Adult   **92**

1. Computer industry 2. Biographical graphic novels
ISBN 9380028768; 9789380028767

This graphic novel, by Jason Quinn, illustrated by Amit Tayal, presents a biography of the 20th-century technology entrepreneur and Apple Inc. founder Steve Jobs. "Steve Jobs and his inventions changed the world we live in." The book ranges "from his birth and his adoption, through the advent of the computer age and on into the digital age. Forced out of the company he created, his indomitable vision allowed him to change the world of computers, movies, music and telecommunications." (Publisher's note)

"This cleverly designed volume provides a concise but well-balanced view of Steve Jobs the wunderkind, including his difficult personality and complex genius." Booklist

Johansson, Scarlett, 1984-

Schuman, Michael. **Scarlet** Johansson; hollywood superstar. [by] Michael A. Schuman. Enslow Publishers 2011 112p il (People to know today) lib bdg $31.93

Grades: 6 7 8 9   92

1. Actors

ISBN 978-0-7660-3556-0; 0-7660-3556-5

This "title is an enjoyable introduction to Johansson that avoids a gossipy, tabloid tone. After general background on family and childhood, . . . the chapters detail Johansson's progress from stage to screen. . . . Her experiences afford an interesting glimpse into Hollywood and the film industry." Booklist

John Paul II, Pope, 1920-2005

Renehan, Edward J. **Pope** John Paul II; [by] Edward J. Renehan, Jr. Chelsea House 2007 109p il (Modern world leaders) lib bdg $30

Grades: 7 8 9 10 11 12   92

1. Popes

ISBN 978-0-7910-9227-9 lib bdg; 0-7910-9227-5 lib bdg

LC 2006-10612

This "biography follows the arch of the pontiff's life in the context of world politics." Publisher's note

Includes bibliographical references

Johnson, Earvin, 1959-

Roselius, J Chris. **Magic** Johnson; basketball star and entrepreneur. ABDO Pub. Co. 2011 112p il (Legendary athletes) lib bdg $34.22

Grades: 6 7 8 9   92

1. African American athletes 2. Basketball coaches 3. Basketball players 4. Real estate developers 5. Basketball -- Biography

ISBN 978-1-61714-756-2; 1-61714-756-7

LC 2010046696

This biography of basketball star Magic Johnson "goes beyond merely discussing [his] accomplishments. . . . [It] also [explores] the social and political [influence he] had on society as a whole. In addition, [it introduces] historical events in the context of [his life]. . . . This . . . is teeming with information and is a must-purchase for sports fans and readers interested in social activism." SLJ

Includes glossary and bibliographical references

Johnson, Lyndon B. (Lyndon Baines), 1908-1973

Gold, Susan Dudley. **Lyndon** B. Johnson. Marshall Cavendish Benchmark 2009 112p il (Presidents and their times) lib bdg $34.21

Grades: 5 6 7 8   92

1. Presidents 2. Vice-presidents 3. Senators 4.

Members of Congress 5. Presidents -- United States

ISBN 978-0-7614-2837-4 lib bdg; 0-7614-2837-2 lib bdg

LC 2007038518

A biography of the thirty-sixth president of the United States discusses his personal life, education, and political career and covers the formative events of his time

Includes glossary and bibliographical references

Johnson, Mamie, 1935-

★ Green, Michelle Y. A **strong** right arm: the story of Mamie Peanut Johnson; introduction by Mamie Johnson. Dial Bks. for Young Readers 2002 111p il $15.99; pa $5.99

Grades: 4 5 6 7   92

1. Women athletes 2. Baseball players 3. African American athletes 4. Collectibles dealers 5. Baseball -- Biography

ISBN 0-8037-2661-9; 0-14-240072-6 pa

LC 2001-28616

"Johnson was a pitcher with the Negro Leagues' Indianapolis Clowns from 1953 to 1955. In the introduction, Johnson speaks directly and movingly to the reader about her meeting with author Green, who then lets the famous ballplayer tell her own story in a lively first-person narrative. Johnson's ebullient personality and determination fairly leap off the page." Booklist

Includes bibliographical references

Jolie, Angelina

Abrams, Dennis. **Angelina** Jolie; actress and activist. Chelsea House 2011 146p il (Women of achievement) $35

Grades: 6 7 8 9   92

1. Actors

ISBN 978-1-60413-909-9; 1-60413-909-9

This "focuses on the superstar's troubled youth, her award-winning performances as an actress, and her work on behalf of refugees around the world. Abrams is frank in discussing Jolie's fascination, in her younger years, with knives, cutting, and blood. . . . Solid fare for the biography collection." Booklist

Jones, John Paul, 1747-1792

Brager, Bruce L., 1949- **John** Paul Jones; America's sailor. Morgan Reynolds Pub. 2006 160p il map lib bdg $26.95

Grades: 7 8 9 10   92

1. Admirals 2. Naval officers

ISBN 978-1-931798-84-6; 1-931798-84-2

LC 2005-30443

The author "begins with Jones's Scottish childhood, where he developed a bitter resentment of the British class system. He then traces the man's career as a commercial seaman, privateer, naval commander, and soldier of fortune. . . . This often-unflattering portrait of Jones will require readers who can place his good and bad traits in perspective and judge his place in history, making it a good choice for mature students." SLJ

Includes bibliographical references

Cooper, Michael L. **Hero** of the high seas; John Paul Jones and the American Revolution. National Geographic 2006 128p il map $21.95; lib bdg $32.90

Grades: 5 6 7 8   **92**

1. Admirals 2. Naval officers 3. United States -- History -- 1775-1783, Revolution

ISBN 0-7922-5547-X; 0-7922-5548-8 lib bdg

LC 2005-36256

"Cooper charts his subject's life from a scandal-ridden Scottish captain on a trading ship to a man of self-invention who came to the American colonies to start a new life and became a naval hero. Jones is presented as a loyal captain, an arrogant leader, a determined sailor, and a flagrant social climber. The narrative style will appeal to reluctant readers, for it reads like a chronicle of thrilling naval adventures.... The text is clear and understandable." SLJ

Includes bibliographical references

Jordan, Barbara

Raatma, Lucia. **Barbara** Jordan; Lucia Raatma. Marshall Cavendish 2012 96 p. (Leading women) (print) $39.93

Grades: 7 8 9   **92**

1. Women political activists 2. Civil rights -- United States 3. Legislators -- United States -- Biography 4. Texas -- Politics and government -- 1951- 5. United States. Congress. House -- Biography 6. African American women legislators -- Texas -- Biography 7. African American women legislators -- United States -- Biography

ISBN 0761449566; 9780761449560; 9781608707133

LC 2011003470

This biography of Barbara Jordan by Lucia Raatma is part of the Leading Women series. The books "focus on the background and political achievements of twentieth-century women, including those well known in America and those lesser known, too. Each woman's story is told in a narrative, chronological style, illustrated by photographs.... Barbara Jordan's connection to the civil rights movement" is noted. (Booklist)

Includes bibliographical references and index

Joseph, Nez Percé Chief, 1840-1904

Biskup, Agnieszka. **Thunder** rolling down the mountain; the story of Chief Joseph and the Nez Perce. illustrated by Rusty Zimmerman. Capstone Press 2011 32p il (Graphic library: American graphic) lib bdg $29.32; pa $7.95

Grades: 4 5 6 7   **92**

1. Biographical graphic novels 2. Indian chiefs 3. Nez Percé Indians

ISBN 978-1-4296-5472-2 lib bdg; 1-4296-5472-4 lib bdg; 978-1-4296-6270-3 pa; 1-4296-6270-0 pa

LC 2010027914

In graphic novel format, explores the battles and hardships faced by Chief Joseph and the Nez Perce when they were forced to leave their homelands.

"The illustrations are eye-catching and the narration is presented simply, yet compellingly.... Fact-filled, entertaining, and accessible." SLJ

Includes bibliographical references

Hopping, Lorraine Jean. **Chief** Joseph; the voice for peace. Sterling 2010 124p il map (Sterling biographies) lib bdg $12.95

Grades: 7 8 9 10   **92**

1. Indian chiefs 2. Nez Percé Indians 3. Native Americans -- Biography

ISBN 978-1-4027-6842-2; 1-4027-6842-7

LC 2009-24132

This biography is "packed with fast action and detailed analysis.... Hopping tells of Joseph's painful decision to leave his land to save Nez Percé lives, choosing peace because he knew they could not win against the U.S.... [The] spacious design is highly scannable, with color background screens, photos, maps, and historic prints throughout." Booklist

Includes glossary and bibliographical references

Julian, Percy L., 1899-1975

Stille, Darlene R. **Percy** Lavon Julian; pioneering chemist. Compass Point Books 2009 112p il map (Signature lives) lib bdg $34.65

Grades: 6 7 8 9 10   **92**

1. Chemists 2. Pharmaceutical executives

ISBN 978-0-7565-4089-0; 0-7565-4089-5

LC 2008-38462

Details the life of chemist Percy Lavon Julian and his accomplishments

The "inviting page design features photos and boxed screens on each spread, and ... includes a detailed bibliography, source notes, time line and glossary." Booklist

Includes glossary and bibliographical references

Juárez, Benito, 1806-1872

Stein, R. Conrad. **Benito** Juarez and the French intervention; [by] R. Conrad Stein. Morgan Reynolds Pub. 2008 160p il map (The story of Mexico) lib bdg $27.95

Grades: 6 7 8 9   **92**

1. Presidents 2. Mexico -- History

ISBN 978-1-59935-052-3 lib bdg; 1-59935-052-1 lib bdg

LC 2007016005

The book provides "detailed information in a readable format, and [a] lively writing style.... Colorful reproductions and photographs help to maintain interest. [This] title tells the story of Juárez, a Zapotec Indian, and his rise to political leadership. Born into poverty in 1806, he became Mexico's first Indian president, presiding over a country in turmoil." SLJ

Includes glossary and bibliographical references

Kahlo, Frida, 1907-1954

Hillstrom, Laurie. **Frida** Kahlo; painter. by Laurie Collier Hillstrom. Lucent Books 2008 104p il (The twentieth century's most influential Hispanics) lib bdg $32.45

Grades: 6 7 8 9 10   **92**
1. Artists 2. Painters 3. Women artists 4. Artists, Mexican
ISBN 978-1-4205-0019-6 lib bdg; 1-4205-0019-8 lib bdg

LC 2007-32106

"Kahlo's life . . . is chronicled as are the influences of her marriage to Rivera and her physical pain on on her art. . . . The layout draws the eye with colorful chapter headings and highlighted quotes." Lib Media Connect

Includes bibliographical references

Kamkwamba, William, 1987-
Kamkwamba, William. The **boy** who harnessed the wind; Creating Currents of Electricity and Hope. William Kamkwamba and Bryan Mealer ; pictures by Elizabeth Zunon. Dial Press 2012 32 p. illustrations (chiefly color) $17.99; $16.99
Grades: 4 5 6 7 8 9 10   **92**
1. Malawi 2. Windmills 3. Irrigation 4. Electric power 5. Mechanical engineering 6. Irrigation -- Malawi 7. Windmills -- Malawi 8. Electric power production -- Malawi 9. Mechanical engineers -- Malawi -- Biography
ISBN 0803735111; 0803740808; 9780803735118; 9780803740808

LC 2011021536

In this memoir, "when fourteen-year-old William Kamkwamba's Malawi village was hit by a drought, everyone's crops began to fail. Without enough money for food, let alone school, William spent his days in the library . . . and figured out how to bring electricity to his village. Persevering against the odds, William built a functioning windmill out of junkyard scraps, and thus became the local hero who harnessed the wind." (Publisher's note)

"This youth edition of the original adult book of the same title has been skillfully adapted for middle grade readers. Kamkwamba recounts a period from his childhood living in a small Malawi village. His family was poor, but they got by working as farmers. Kamkwamba was in elementary school, about to graduate to secondary school, when the drought and famine of the mid-2000s upset the patterns of local life...This is a fascinating, well-told account that will intrigue curious minds, even the somewhat anticlimactic closing chapters describing Kamkwamba's education. There is also a picture book version of this tale (Dial, 2012), making it of interest to all-school reading programs. An inspiring, incredible story." SLJ

Kazerooni, Abbas. **On** two feet and wings; Abbas Kazerooni. Skyscape 2014 199 p. (trade pbk : alk. paper) $16.99
Grades: 5 6 7 8   **92**
1. Refugees 2. Children and war 3. Iran-Iraq War, 1980-1988
ISBN 1477847839; 9781477847831

LC 2014933778

This book, by Abbas Kazerooni is set when "the Iran-Iraq war is at its bloodiest, and the Ayatollahs who rule Iran have reduced the recruitment age for the army. If Abbas doesn't escape, it's almost certain that he will be drafted and die fighting for a regime that has stripped his family of all

they have. On his own in the strange, often frightening city of Istanbul, Abbas grows up fast." (Publisher's note)

"Since the overthrow of the shah, Abbas Kazerooni's once wealthy and influential family has had to sell most of their valuables and negotiate the new regime with trepidation. Iran is at war with Iraq, and when the draft age is reduced to eight, Abbas' father sends nine-year-old Abbas and his mother to safety, first to Turkey and then on to England... Still, young readers will understand his overwhelming loneliness and fear as well as his satisfaction at managing on his own. With child immigrants so much in the news, Kazerooni's unusual, compelling story is especially timely." Booklist

Keat, Nawuth, 1964-
Keat, Nawuth. **Alive** in the killing fields; surviving the Khmer Rouge genocide. by Nawuth Keat with Martha E. Kendall. National Geographic 2009 127p il map $15.95; lib bdg $23.90
Grades: 7 8 9 10 11   **92**
1. Authors 2. Cambodian refugees 3. Political refugees 4. Young adult authors
ISBN 978-1-4263-0515-3; 1-4263-0515-X; 978-1-4263-0516-0 lib bdg; 1-4263-0516-8 lib bdg

LC 2008-39805

"Told with stark simplicity, Nawuth's narrative is memorable yet accessible to young readers." Voice Youth Advocates

"At age nine, Keat was rousted from his bed by Khmer Rouge soldiers. After savagely murdering most of his family, they shot him three times and left him for dead. Miraculously, he survived, only to spend the next few years fighting for his life and running from the Khmer Rouge along with his remaining family members." SLJ

Includes bibliographical references

Keckley, Elizabeth, ca. 1818-1907
Jones, Lynda. **Mrs.** Lincoln's dressmaker: the unlikely friendship of Elizabeth Keckley and Mary Todd Lincoln; by Lynda D. Jones. National Geographic 2009 80p il $18.95; lib bdg $27.90
Grades: 5 6 7 8   **92**
1. Memoirists 2. Dressmakers 3. Spouses of presidents 4. Slavery -- United States 5. United States -- Race relations 6. African American women -- Biography 7. Presidents' spouses -- United States 8. Washington (D.C.) -- Social life and customs
ISBN 978-1-4263-0377-7; 1-4263-0377-7; 978-1-4263-0378-4 lib bdg; 1-4263-0378-5 lib bdg

LC 2008-29314

"Readers may be familiar with the ups and downs of Lincoln's life, but details of Keckley's story . . . will give them new insights into the life of a slave, in this case, one who was educated and had a profession." Booklist

Includes bibliographical references

Kellar, Harry
★ Jarrow, Gail. G. The **amazing** Harry Kellar; great American magician. Gail G. Jarrow. Calkins Creek 2012 96 p. col. ill. $17.95

Grades: 3 4 5 6 7 8   **92**
  1. Magicians 2. Optical illusions
  ISBN 1590788656; 9781590788653

LC 2011940465

This book is a biography of Harry Keller (later Kellar), "the first dean of the Society of American Magicians, a man [magician Harry] Houdini regarded as a mentor. . . . Few secrets of the illusions are revealed here, but [Gail] Jarrow makes it clear that it was Kellar's art that made them seem like real magic." The book also includes "[d]ozens of . . . Kellar posters" and a "timeline, bibliography, [and] annotated sources." (Kirkus)

Keller, Helen, 1880-1968

Delano, Marfe Ferguson. **Helen's** eyes; a photobiography of Annie Sullivan, Helen Keller's teacher. [foreword by Keller Johnson Thompson] National Geographic 2008 63p il map $17.95; lib bdg $27.90

Grades: 4 5 6 7   **92**
  1. Deaf 2. Blind 3. Authors 4. Teachers 5. Memoirists 6. Humanitarians 7. Teachers of the deaf 8. Inspirational writers 9. Teachers of the blind 10. Social welfare leaders
  ISBN 978-1-4263-02-9-1; 1-4263-0209-6; 978-1-4263-0210-7 lib bdg; 1-4263-0210-X lib bdg

"There are many biographies of Helen Keller and Annie Sullivan, but this one is very nicely done. . . . The book is honest in its portrayals, especially of Sullivan. . . . What makes this oversize book so appealing is the clean design, with large typeface. The many fascinating photographs are sometimes placed over historical documents." Booklist

  Includes bibliographical references

★ Keller, Helen. The **story** of my life; edited and with a preface by James Berger. The restored ed.; Modern Library 2003 xlvi, 343p il hardcover o.p. pa $9.95

Grades: 8 9 10 11 12 Adult   **92**
  1. Deaf 2. Blind 3. Authors 4. Memoirists 5. Humanitarians 6. Inspirational writers 7. Social welfare leaders
  ISBN 0-679-64287-0; 0-8129-6886-7 pa

LC 2002-40971

First published 1903

This biography of the inspirational Keller contains accounts of her home life and her relationship with her devoted teacher Anne Sullivan.

  Includes bibliographical references

Lawlor, Laurie. **Helen** Keller: rebellious spirit. Holiday House 2001 168p il $22.95

Grades: 5 6 7 8   **92**
  1. Deaf 2. Blind 3. Authors 4. Memoirists 5. Humanitarians 6. Inspirational writers 7. Social welfare leaders
  ISBN 0-8234-1588-0

LC 00-36950

A "biography of the most famous deaf and blind person in history. Drawing on social and scientific studies of deafness and blindness as well as on American history texts, Lawlor puts Keller's experiences in context. . . . At the same

time, readers get a strong feel for Keller's personality and for the personalities of Annie Sullivan, Alexander Graham Bell, and other major figures in her life. Aided by numerous well-chosen photographs and excerpts from Keller's writings." Horn Book

  Includes bibliographical references

Sullivan, George. **Helen** Keller; her life in pictures. foreword by Keller Johnson Thompson. Scholastic Nonfiction 2007 80p il $17.99

Grades: 4 5 6 7   **92**
  1. Deaf 2. Blind 3. Authors 4. Memoirists 5. Humanitarians 6. Inspirational writers 7. Social welfare leaders
  ISBN 0-439-91815-4; 978-0-439-91815-2

LC 2006-51401

"Accompanied by brief, simply phrased commentary from Sullivan, this suite of photos portrays Keller from early childhood into her 80s. . . . This profile will serve equally well as an introduction, or as supplementary reading for confirmed admirers." Booklist

  Includes bibliographical references

Kennally, James

Sheinkin, Steve. **Lincoln's** Grave Robbers. Scholastic 2013 224 p. $16.99

Grades: 5 6 7 8   **92**
  1. Grave robbing 2. Counterfeits and counterfeiting
  ISBN 0545405726; 9780545405720

This book is an "account of the attempted heist of Abraham Lincoln's body in 1876." Steve Sheinkin first "delv[es] into the history of counterfeiting. . . . James Kennally, leader of one of the largest counterfeiting rings in the Midwest, masterminded the plot to steal the late president's body from the Lincoln Monument," intending "to ransom the purloined corpse" and extort "the government for a tidy sum of money and the freedom of his jailed, top-notch engraver." (Publishers Weekly)

Kennedy, John F. (John Fitzgerald), 1917-1963

★ Heiligman, Deborah. **High** hopes; a photobiography of John F. Kennedy. National Geographic 2003 63p il map $17.95

Grades: 4 5 6 7   **92**
  1. Presidents 2. Senators 3. Members of Congress 4. Presidents -- United States
  ISBN 0-7922-6141-0

LC 2003-7819

Photographs and text trace the life of President John F. Kennedy.

The text "successfully captures the spirit that makes Kennedy an enduring figure in our history. . . . This well-designed book features large, well-chosen, black-and-white photographs." SLJ

  Includes bibliographical references

Sandler, Martin W. **Kennedy** through the lens; how photography and television revealed and shaped an extraordinary leader. Walker & Co. 2011 96p il

Grades: 6 7 8 9 10   **92**
  1. Presidents 2. Senators 3. Members of Congress 4.

Presidents -- United States 5. United States -- History -- 1961-1974 -- Pictorial works
ISBN 0802721605; 0802721613; 9780802721600; 9780802721617

LC 2010-11103

This book describes how John F. Kennedy used the medium of television and advances in photography to mold his image and further his political agenda. Index. "Grades five to nine." (Bull Cent Child Books)

"Sandler offers a fascinating photo-essay examining how images shaped public perceptions of John F. Kennedy. . . . The book begins with an overview of Kennedy's life and the role photography and television played in his career. Subsequent spreads are chronological, covering Kennedy's life from childhood through assassination. . . . Kennedy's life and administration were documented with a groundbreaking intimacy the public had never known before, making this an accessible, insightful perspective on one of America's most famous presidents." Kirkus

Kennedy, Robert F., 1925-1968

Aronson, Marc. **Robert** F. Kennedy; a twentieth-century life. Viking 2007 204p il (Up close) $15.99
Grades: 8 9 10 11 12   92
1. Senators 2. Attorneys general 3. Siblings of presidents 4. Presidential candidates 5. Politicians -- United States
ISBN 978-0-670-06066-5; 0-670-06066-6

LC 2006-102150

Explores Robert F. Kennedy's life from his childhood to his adult years as Attorney General, New York state senator, and candidate for the presidency of the United States.

"Aronson draws on a wide variety of sources and is very honest in examining his subject as a complete human being, warts and all. . . . This text stands as an unbiased and illuminating resource." SLJ
Includes bibliographical references

Kepler, Johannes, 1571-1630

Hasan, Heather. **Kepler** and the laws of planetary motion. Rosen Pub. Group 2005 64p il (Primary sources of revolutionary scientific discoveries and theories) lib bdg $29.25
Grades: 6 7 8 9   92
1. Astronomers 2. Mathematicians
ISBN 1-40420-308-7

LC 2004007794

"Using primary sources, this book illustrates the timeline of Kepler's discovery of planetary motion. . . . Also included are Kepler's notes and manuscripts as well as reproductions of some of the tools he used." Publisher's note
Includes bibliographical references

Keynes, John Maynard, 1883-1946

Crain, Cynthia D. **John** Maynard Keynes; by Cynthia D. Crain and Dwight R. Lee. Morgan Reynolds Pub. 2009 144p il (Profiles in economics) lib bdg $28.95

Grades: 8 9 10 11 12   92
1. Economists 2. Patrons of the arts
ISBN 978-1-59935-109-4 lib bdg; 1-59935-109-9 lib bdg

LC 2009-168

Biography of the economist John Maynard Keynes

"Relationships, education, early influences, and family life are all described . . . [and] economic theory is closely tied to cultural and political events. . . . The writing is straightforward, the . . . [author] assume[s] a certain level of knowledge about world events." SLJ
Includes bibliographical references

Kim, Jong Il, 1942-2011

Wyborny, Sheila. **Kim** Jong Il; by Sheila Wyborny. Lucent Books 2009 104 p. ill. (some col.), map (People in the News) (library) $35.95
Grades: 6 7 8 9   92
ISBN 9781420500912; 1420500910

LC 2008049567

This book by Sheila Wyborny is part of the People in the News series and focuses on late North Korean leader Kim Jong Il. The series "profiles the lives and careers of some of today's most prominent newsmakers. Whether covering contributions and achievements or notorious deeds, books in this series examine why these well-known people garner public attention." (Publisher's note)
Includes bibliographical references (p. 90-91) and index.

King, Billie Jean

Gitlin, Marty. **Billie** Jean King; tennis star and social activist. ABDO Pub. Co. 2011 112p il (Legendary athletes) lib bdg $34.22
Grades: 6 7 8 9   92
1. Women athletes 2. Sportscasters 3. Tennis players 4. Tennis -- Biography
ISBN 978-1-61714-757-9; 1-61714-757-5

LC 2010046584

This biography of tennis champion Billie Jean King "goes beyond merely discussing [her] accomplishments. . . . [It] also [explores] the social and political [influence she] had on society as a whole. In addition, [it introduces] historical events in the context of [her life]. . . . This . . . is teeming with information and is a must-purchase for sports fans and readers interested in social activism." SLJ
Includes glossary and bibliographical references

King, Coretta Scott, 1927-2006

Gelfand, Dale Evva. **Coretta** Scott King; civil rights activist. Legacy ed; Chelsea House 2006 137p bibl il por (Black Americans of achievement) lib bdg $30
Grades: 7 8 9 10   92
1. African Americans -- Civil rights
ISBN 0-7910-9522-3

LC 2006022651

First published 1997 under the authorship of Lisa Renee Rhodes

A biography of the civil rights activist and widow of Martin Luther King
Includes bibliographical references

King, Martin Luther, Jr., 1929-1968

★ Aretha, David. **Martin** Luther King Jr. and the 1963 March on Washington; by David Aretha. Morgan Reynolds Pub. 2014 112 p. illustrations (some color) $28.95

Grades: 7 8 9 10 11 12   92

1. African Americans -- Civil rights 2. March on Washington for Jobs and Freedom (1963 : Washington, D.C.) 3. Civil rights demonstrations -- Washington (D.C.) -- History -- 20th century

ISBN 1599353725; 9781599353722

LC 2012035355

In this book, author David "Aretha begins his look at the historic 1963 March on Washington with a review of Jim Crow in the American South and the early days of the modern Civil Rights Movement. . . . Aretha offers considerable detail about the march, including the peaceful, racially integrated crowd and the rousing speeches, which culminated with Dr. King's 'Dream' speech." (Publisher's note)

"Black-and-white archival photographs, boxed quotes, and excerpts from notable speeches enhance this series documenting pivotal laws and incidents of the civil rights movement. Each title builds up to the featured event, though Brown more successfully sets the stage with historical context and what follows. Both are well researched additions to library collections. Timeline, websites. Bib., ind." (Horn Book)

Includes bibliographical references

★ Bolden, Tonya. **M.L.K.** journey of a King. photography editor, Bob Adelman. Abrams Books for Young Readers 2006 128p il $19.95

Grades: 7 8 9 10   92

1. Clergy 2. Nonfiction writers 3. Civil rights activists 4. Nobel laureates for peace 5. African Americans -- Biography 6. African Americans -- Civil rights

ISBN 978-0-8109-5476-2; 0-8109-5476-1

LC 2006-13332

"Do libraries need another biography of King? Yes, if it's as good as this one, which will reach a wide audience. . . . Stirring, beautifully reproduced, well-captioned photos . . . accompany the text." Booklist

King, Stephen, 1947-

Stefoff, Rebecca, 1951- **Stephen** King. Marshall Cavendish Benchmark 2010 175p il (Today's writers and their works) lib bdg $42.79

Grades: 8 9 10 11 12   92

1. Authors 2. Novelists 3. Authors, American 4. Short story writers 5. Science fiction writers

ISBN 0-7614-4122-0; 978-0-7614-4122-9

This biography of Stephen King places the author in the context of his times and discusses his work.

This book provides "excellent information for reports." SLJ

Includes bibliographical references

Whitelaw, Nancy. **Dark** dreams; the story of Stephen King. Morgan Reynolds 2005 128p il map (World writers) $26.95

Grades: 7 8 9 10   92

1. Authors 2. Novelists 3. Authors, American 4. Short story writers 5. Science fiction writers 6. Horror fiction -- Authorship

ISBN 1-931798-77-X

LC 2005-20112

"This well-documented look at King's life introduces the man who has become a legend for reinventing and legitimizing horror. Whitelaw has put together a seamless synthesis of interviews, biographies, and King's own writing, pared down for younger readers and illustrated with plenty of full-color photographs." Booklist

Koehl, Mimi, 1948-

Parks, Deborah. **Nature's** machines; the story of biomechanist Mimi Koehl. by Deborah Amel Parks. Joseph Henry Press 2005 118p il (Women's adventures in science) lib bdg $31; pa $9.95

Grades: 7 8 9 10   92

1. Biologists 2. Ergonomics 3. Women scientists 4. Bioengineers 5. College teachers 6. Human engineering

ISBN 0-531-16780-1 lib bdg; 0-309-09559-X pa

LC 2005-10201

Mimi Koehl "wanted to know more about sea anemones, particularly how they survive the turbulent surf on rocky beaches. Her inquiries and experiments led to discoveries in a new field, biomechanics, in which scientists examine how form determines movement and function in the animal kingdom. . . . This [book] should spark the curiosity of any reader." Voice Youth Advocates

Includes bibliographical references

Kor, Eva Mozes, 1935-

Kor, Eva Mozes. **Surviving** the Angel of Death; the story of a Mengele twin in Auschwitz. [by] Eva Mozes Kor and Lisa Rojany Buccieri. Tanglewood Pub. 2009 141p il map $14.95

Grades: 7 8 9 10   92

1. Twins 2. Holocaust survivors 3. Jews -- Hungary 4. Jews -- Persecutions 5. Holocaust, 1933-1945 -- Personal narratives

ISBN 978-1-933718-28-6; 1-933718-28-5

LC 2009-9494

"Born in 1934, Eva and her identical twin, Miriam, were loved and doted over. They lived a comfortable and happy life on their family's farm in Transylvania until the summer of 1940, when their family was herded onto a train with the other Jews in their town and transported to Auschwitz supposedly for their 'protection.' . . . They soon joined a large group of other twins who were under the care of Dr. Josef Mengele, otherwise known as the Angel of Death. . . . Eva's story will have the reader hooked until the very end. . . . This book is an essential purchase for libraries with a Holocaust collection, but it would also be a valuable addition to any library with young impressionable readers." Voice Youth Advocates

Kwan, Michelle

Koestler-Grack, Rachel A. **Michelle** Kwan. Chelsea House 2007 127p bibl por (Asian Americans of achievement) lib bdg $30

Grades: 7 8 9 10   **92**
1. Ice skaters 2. Olympic athletes 3. Ice skating --
Biography 4. Asian Americans -- Biography
ISBN 0-7910-9273-9 lib bdg; 978-0-7910-9273-6
lib bdg

LC 2006026069

Profiles the life and career of figure skating champion
Michelle Kwan.

"With clear, full-color photos and lots of detail about
training and competition, this lively biography . . . will grab
fans." Booklist

Includes bibliographical references

La Salle, Robert Cavelier, sieur de, 1643-1687
Crompton, Samuel. **Robert** de La Salle; [by]
Samuel Willard Crompton. Chelsea House 2009
110p il map (Great explorers) lib bdg $30
Grades: 6 7 8 9   **92**
1. Explorers
ISBN 978-1-60413-419-3 lib bdg; 1-60413-419-4
lib bdg

LC 2009014166

Biography of the explorer Robert de La Salle

"The information . . . is presented in such a way as to
attract and maintain readers' interest. . . . With a full complement of maps, photographs (where available), illustrations,
time lines, and document reproductions, a full story is told.
Well-written and throughly researched, this . . . . will make a
solid addition." SLJ

Includes glossary and bibliographical references

Goodman, Joan E. **Despite** all obstacles: La Salle
and the conquest of the Mississippi; by Joan Elizabeth Goodman; illustrated by Tom McNeely. Mikaya Press 2001 47p il map (Great explorers book)
$19.95
Grades: 4 5 6 7   **92**
1. Explorers 2. Mississippi River valley
ISBN 1-931414-01-7

LC 2001-31732

A biography of the man who explored the St. Lawrence,
Ohio, Illinois, and Mississippi rivers, and who claimed
America's heartland for King Louis XIV and France

"Vivid color illustrations and Goodman's exciting writing style will attract both researchers and pleasure readers."
Voice Youth Advocates

**Lafayette, Marie Joseph Paul Yves Roch Gilbert
du Motier, marquis de, 1757-1834**
★ Freedman, Russell. **Lafayette** and the American Revolution. Holiday House 2010 88p il $24.95
Grades: 6 7 8 9   **92**
1. Generals 2. Statesmen 3. United States -- History
-- 1775-1783, Revolution
ISBN 978-0-8234-2182-4; 0-8234-2182-1

LC 2009052342

A Robert F. Sibert Medal honor book, 2011

A biography of the French general who fought Cornwal-
lis' troops at Yorktown in the American Revolution.

"In this solidly researched and smoothly written biography, Freeman creates a vivid portrait of Lafayette. . . . Hand-

somely designed with a spacious format and good use of
color, the book includes many clearly reproduced paintings
and prints." Booklist

Includes bibliographical references

Lang, Lang, 1982-
★ Lang, Lang. **Lang** Lang; playing with flying
keys. by Lang Lang with Michael French; introduction by Daniel Barenboim. Delacorte Press 2008
215p il $16.99; lib bdg $19.99
Grades: 7 8 9 10   **92**
1. Pianists 2. China 3. Classical musicians
ISBN 978-0-385-73578-0; 0-385-73578-2; 978-0-385-
90564-0 lib bdg; 0-385-90564-5 lib bdg

LC 2007-51597

"Although he is only 26, Chinese-born Lang is recognized as one of the world's most accomplished classical pianists. This smoothly paced, often rivetingly candid autobiography . . . follows the musician through his first encounters
with the keyboard and grueling training to his triumphant
debut concerts with the Chicago Symphony." Booklist

"Provides an-depth look at the life, struggles, training,
and major accomplishments of this noted pianist through his
opinions of the differences between the cultures of the East
and West, the great changes in his homeland of China, and
his personal feelings on classical music." (Publisher's Note)

Lauren, Ralph
Mattern, Joanne. **Ralph** Lauren. Chelsea House
2011 101p il (Famous fashion designers) lib bdg
$35
Grades: 6 7 8 9 10   **92**
1. Fashion designers
ISBN 978-1-60413-978-5; 1-60413-978-1

LC 2010036192

This is a biography of fashion designer Ralph Lauren.

"Biography collections in need of a bit of sprucing up
should find these titles helpful. Although the books do not
follow a direct path from early years to current careers, the
personal and professional lives of these fashion idols are
covered equally. The volumes are fairly dense with information, so readers may have to use the indexes to find particular
facts. . . ." SLJ

Includes glossary and bibliographical references

Lavoisier, Antoine Laurent, 1743-1794
Van Gorp, Lynn. **Antoine** Lavoisier; and his
impact on modern chemistry. Compass Point Books
2009 40p il (Mission: Science) lib bdg $26.60
Grades: 4 5 6 7   **92**
1. Chemists 2. Scientists
ISBN 978-0-7565-3959-7 lib bdg; 0-7565-3959-5
lib bdg

LC 2008007283

Profiles the life and career of the Frenchman who is considered the founder of chemistry

"Color photographs, reproductions, diagrams, and maps
are liberally sprinkled throughout [this] attractive [book].
Numerous sidebars offer tangential information." SLJ

Layson, Annelex Hofstra

Layson, Annelex Hofstra. **Lost** childhood; my life in a Japanese prison camp during World War II. [by] Annelex Hofstra Layson; with Herman Viola. National Geographic 2008 111p il $15.95; lib bdg $23.90

Grades: 5 6 7 8 9   **92**

1. Prisoners of war 2. Memoirists 3. World War, 1939-1945 -- Personal narratives 4. World War, 1939-1945 -- Prisoners and prisons

ISBN 978-1-4263-0321-0; 1-4263-0321-1; 978-1-4263-0322-7 lib bdg; 1-4263-0322-X lib bdg

LC 2008-11671

In a shockingly honest narrative, a former prisoner-of-war tells how her family, along with ten thousand other Dutch residents living in the Dutch East Indies were shipped off to interment camps where food rationing, terrible sanitary conditions, and an uncertain future were the norms for more than three years

The author's narrative is warm and enthralling. . . . Layson's voice captivates and engages. Libr Media Connect

Includes bibliographical references

Le Guin, Ursula K., 1929-

Brown, Jeremy K. **Ursula** K. Le Guin; foreword by Kyle Zimmer. Chelsea House Publishers 2010 128p il (Who wrote that?) lib bdg $35

Grades: 6 7 8 9 10   **92**

1. Authors 2. Novelists 3. Women authors 4. Fantasy writers 5. College teachers 6. Authors, American 7. Children's authors 8. Short story writers 9. Science fiction writers

ISBN 978-1-60413-724-8; 1-60413-724-X

LC 2010006600

"Le Guin's work raises questions about identity and morality, and Brown explores her treatment of these themes in a way that readers, whether they're reading for pleasure or for reports, will appreciate. . . . This title does a fine job of conveying both the story of an author's long career and the vision that fuels it." SLJ

Includes bibliographical references

Ledger, Heath, 1979-2008

Watson, Stephanie. **Heath** Ledger; talented actor. ABDO Pub. Company 2010 112p il (Lives cut short) lib bdg $32.79

Grades: 5 6 7 8   **92**

1. Actors

ISBN 978-1-60453-789-5 lib bdg; 1-60453-789-2 lib bdg

LC 2009034353

This discusses Heath Ledger's "early life, providing details that give insight into later success and troubles and maintaining a laudatory tone that focuses on the individual's artistic achievements and hard work to achieve fame. Details [such as] explaining that Jack Nicholson warned Heath Ledger about the Joker role . . . are bound to resonate with readers. Numerous photos and sidebars appear throughout. [A] worthwhile [resource] for reports as well as popular reading." SLJ

Includes bibliographical references

Lee, Harper, 1926-

★ Madden, Kerry. **Harper** Lee; a twentieth-century life. Viking Children's Books 2009 223p il map (Up close) $16.99

Grades: 7 8 9 10   **92**

1. Authors 2. Novelists 3. Women authors 4. Essayists 5. Authors, American 6. Short story writers

ISBN 978-0-670-01095-0; 0-670-01095-2

LC 2008-53911

"A narrative both well paced and richly detailed . . . this biography will appeal to fans of the novel and to newcomers. . . . Extensive source notes and an excellent bibliography round out this superb biography." Kirkus

Includes bibliographical references

Shields, Charles J. **I** am Scout: the biography of Harper Lee. Henry Holt & Co. 2008 245p il $18.95

Grades: 7 8 9 10   **92**

1. Authors 2. Novelists 3. Women authors 4. Essayists 5. Authors, American 6. Short story writers

ISBN 978-0-8050-8334-7; 0-8050-8334-0

LC 2007-27572

A biography of the author of To Kill a Mockingbird

Shields "offers a fascinating look at the unconventional Lee, which captures his elusive subject and her lifelong friend, Truman Capote. . . . Shields' formidable research . . . will impress any student who has ever written a term paper." Booklist

Includes bibliographical references

Lee, Robert E. (Robert Edward), 1807-1870

Robertson, James I. **Robert** E. Lee; Virginian soldier, American citizen. [by] James I. Robertson, Jr. Atheneum Books for Young Readers 2005 159p il maps $21.95

Grades: 7 8 9 10   **92**

1. Generals 2. College presidents 3. United States -- History -- 1861-1865, Civil War

ISBN 0-689-85731-4

LC 2003-22108

This portrait of the Confederate general "puts particular emphasis on his life during the Civil War years but provides plenty of information on his youth, his early military career, and his postwar years. . . . Useful for reports and interesting in its own right, this well-researched biography will be a solid addition to library collections." Booklist

Includes bibliographical references

Leeuwenhoek, Antoni van, 1632-1723

Yount, Lisa. **Antoni** van Leeuwenhoek; first to see microscopic life. [by] Lisa Yount. rev ed.; Enslow Publishers 2008 128p il map (Great minds of science) lib bdg $31.93

Grades: 5 6 7 8   **92**

1. Biologists 2. Microscopes 3. Microscopists

ISBN 978-0-7660-3012-1 lib bdg; 0-7660-3012-1 lib bdg

LC 2007020300

First published 1996

This biography of seventeenth-century Dutch scientist Antoni van Leeuwenhoek includes related activities

Includes glossary and bibliographical references

Leif Eriksson, fl. 1000

DeFries, Cheryl L. **Leif** Eriksson; Viking explorer of the New World. Enslow Publishers 2010 112p il map (Great explorers of the world) lib bdg $31.93

Grades: 6 7 8 9   92

1. Vikings 2. Explorers 3. America -- Exploration
ISBN 978-1-59845-126-9; 1-59845-126-X

This "provides some interesting stories from the Vikings' family history. Readers will be intrigued by the folklore and legends. The mystery behind [Ericksson's] discovery of America is explored briefly, as well as his impact on navigation, law, and culture. Photographs of Viking artifacts bring provide an interesting glimpse into the past. . . . This . . . would serve as a useful resource for middle and elementary school students and may inspire them to read further." Voice Youth Advocates

Includes glossary and bibliographical references

Lennon, John, 1940-1980

Burlingame, Jeff. **John** Lennon; Imagine. Enslow Publishers 2010 160p il (American rebels) lib bdg $34.60

Grades: 6 7 8 9   92

1. Singers 2. Rock musicians 3. Beatles 4. Songwriters
ISBN 978-0-7660-3675-8 lib bdg; 0-7660-3675-8 lib bdg

LC 2009040045

A biography of the rock musician and peace-activist John Lennon.

"This attractive biography includes sidebars, wide margins, large type, and many photographs throughout. Burlingame maintains readers' interest." SLJ

Includes bibliographical references

★ Partridge, Elizabeth. **John** Lennon; all I want is the truth. a photographic biography by Elizabeth Partridge. Viking 2005 232p il $24.99

Grades: 8 9 10 11 12   92

1. Singers 2. Rock musicians 3. Beatles 4. Songwriters
ISBN 0-670-05954-4

LC 2005-11850

Michael L. Printz Award honor book, 2006

"This handsome book will be eagerly received by both Beatles fans, who are legion, and their elders, who will enjoy reliving the glory days of the Fab Four and exploring the inner workings of a creative talent." SLJ

Includes bibliographical references

★ Rappaport, Doreen. **John's** secret dreams; the life of John Lennon. written by Doreen Rappaport; illustrated by Bryan Collier. Hyperion Books for Children 2004 un il $16.99

Grades: 4 5 6 7   92

1. Singers 2. Rock musicians 3. Beatles 4. Songwriters
ISBN 0-7868-0817-9

LC 2003-57116

"Using a combination of simple prose, song lyrics, and illustration, this heartfelt picture-book biography traces Lennon's life from his childhood to his death. Striking in both its simplicity and complexity, it captures this enigmatic singer, artist, songwriter, and folk hero in a way that will move and fascinate those too young to remember the man but are surrounded by his music and myth." SLJ

Leonard, Buck, 1907-1997

Payment, Simone. **Buck** Leonard. Rosen Pub. Group 2002 112p il (Baseball Hall of Famers of the Negro leagues) lib bdg $29.25

Grades: 5 6 7 8   92

1. Baseball players 2. African American athletes 3. Baseball -- Biography
ISBN 0-8239-3473-X

LC 2001-3151

A biography of first-baseman who played in the Negro Leagues and was inducted into the Baseball Hall of Fame in 1972

This "title presents an unvarnished picture of the racism in this country and how it impacted amateur and professional baseball from 1868 onward. . . . The layout . . . is attractive, the style . . . is engaging." Book Rep

Includes glossary and bibliographical references

Leonardo, da Vinci, 1452-1519

Anderson, Maxine. **Amazing** Leonardo da Vinci inventions you can build yourself. Nomad Press 2006 122p il map (Learn some hands-on history) pa $14.95

Grades: 5 6 7 8   92

1. Artists 2. Painters 3. Handicraft 4. Inventions 5. Scientists 6. Renaissance 7. Artists, Italian 8. Writers on science
ISBN 0-9749344-2-9

"Anderson has combined biography with doable activities that mirror ideas found in Leonardo's notebooks. Using common household objects (duct tape, foil, cereal boxes, paper-towel tubes, etc.), readers can make a parachute, hydrometer, invisible ink, walk-on-water shoes, etc. Anderson introduces each project with an explanation of why Leonardo came up with the idea and whether he created just the sketch or the sketch and the object. Detailed steps and illustrations provide clarity." SLJ

★ Krull, Kathleen. **Leonardo** da Vinci; illustrated by Boris Kulikov. Viking 2005 128p il (Giants of science) $15.99

Grades: 5 6 7 8   92

1. Artists 2. Painters 3. Scientists 4. Renaissance 5. Artists, Italian 6. Writers on science
ISBN 0-670-05920-X

This is a "biography of Leonardo da Vinci that highlights his scientific approach to understanding the physical world. The first half of the book describes Leonardo's apprenticeship and his work as an artist in Milan. The second half relates events in his later life, emphasizing his observation and investigation of the human body and nature. . . . Six excellent ink drawings illustrate this attractive volume. A very readable, vivid portrait set against the backdrop of remarkable times." Booklist

Includes bibliographical references

Phillips, John. **Leonardo** da Vinci; the genius who defined the Renaissance. National Geographic 2006 64p bibl il (World history biographies) $17.95; lib bdg $27.90; pa $6.95

Grades: 5 6 7 8   **92**

1. Artists 2. Painters 3. Scientists 4. Renaissance 5. Artists, Italian 6. Writers on science

ISBN 978-0-7922-5385-3; 0-7922-5385-X; 978-0-7922-5386-0 lib bdg; 0-7922-5386-8 lib bdg; 978-1-4263-0248-0 pa; 1-4263-0249-7 pa

Examines the life of Renaissance genius Leonardo da Vinci, discussing his inquiries and accomplishments in art and various fields of science

Includes bibliographical references

Levine, Gail Carson, 1947-

Abrams, Dennis. **Gail** Carson Levine; [by] Dennis Abrams; foreword by Kyle Zimmer. Chelsea House 2007 120p bibl il por (Who wrote that?) $30

Grades: 6 7 8 9   **92**

1. Authors 2. Women authors 3. Authors, American 4. Children's authors

ISBN 978-0-7910-8970-5; 0-7910-8970-3

LC 2007019449

This biography examines the "writer's life, including the inspiration behind some of [her] works. [The] volume includes photographs and quotations from interviews, as well as descriptions of main characters and annotated lists of books and awards. Useful for aspiring authors as well as book report writers." Horn Book Guide

Includes bibliographical references

Lewis, C. S. (Clive Staples), 1898-1963

Hamilton, Janet. **C.** S. Lewis; twentieth century pilgrim. Morgan Reynolds Pub. 2010 128p il (World writers) lib bdg $28.95

Grades: 7 8 9 10   **92**

1. Authors 2. Novelists 3. Theologians 4. Essayists 5. Satirists 6. Authors, English 7. Literary critics 8. Children's authors

ISBN 978-1-59935-112-4; 1-59935-112-9

LC 2009-7134

In this biography of the British author, "Lewis' childhood is well-documented, as is his love of literature as an escape from the real world. Hamilton clearly shows the importance religion played in Lewis's life. The impact that war, and the resulting loss of the imaginative worlds he could find in literature, and his struggle with religious belief are tied directly to his writing." Voice Youth Advocates

Includes bibliographical references

Lewis, John, 1940-

★ Lewis, John R., 1940- **March**; Book One. John Lewis ; [co-written by] Andrew Aydin ; [art by] Nate Powell. Top Shelf Productions 2013 121 p. chiefly ill. (acid-free paper) $14.95

Grades: 8 9 10 11 12 Adult   **92**

1. African Americans -- Civil rights -- Graphic novels 2. Civil rights movements -- United States -- Comic books, strips, etc

ISBN 9781603093002

LC 2013218903

Coretta Scott King (Author) Honor Book (2014)

This graphic novel, by U.S. congressman John Lewis, "in collaboration with co-writer Andrew Aydin and New York Times best-selling artist Nate Powell . . . spans John Lewis' youth in rural Alabama, his life-changing meeting with Martin Luther King, Jr., the birth of the Nashville Student Movement, and their battle to tear down segregation through nonviolent lunch counter sit-ins, building to a . . . climax on the steps of City Hall." (Publisher's note)

"This is superb visual storytelling that establishes a convincing, definitive record of a key eyewitness to significant social change." SLJ

★ Lewis, John. **March** Book Two; by Andrew Aydin; illustrated by Nate Powell. Top Shelf Productions 2015 192 p. chiefly ill. (pbk) $19.95

Grades: 8 9 10 11 12 Adult   **92**

1. African Americans -- Civil rights -- Graphic novels 2. Civil rights movements 3. African American legislators 4. Legislators -- United States 5. African Americans -- Civil rights 6. African American civil rights workers 7. Civil rights workers -- United States 8. Autobiographical comic books, strips, etc.

ISBN 9781603094009; 1603094008

LC bl2015004150

This graphic novel, by John Lewis and Andrew Aydin, illustrated by Nate Powell, "takes us behind the scenes of some of the most pivotal moments of the Civil Rights Movement. . . . After the success of the Nashville sit-in campaign, John Lewis is more committed than ever to changing the world through nonviolence -- but as he and his fellow Freedom Riders board a bus into the vicious heart of the deep south, they will be tested like never before." (Publisher's note)

"Heroism and steadiness of purpose continue to light up Lewis' frank, harrowing account of the civil rights movement's climactic days. . . . The contrast between the dignified marchers and the vicious, hate-filled actions and expressions of their tormentors will leave a deep impression on readers." Kirkus

Sapet, Kerrily. **John Lewis**. Morgan Reynolds Pub. 2009 128p il (Political profiles) lib bdg $28.95

Grades: 6 7 8 9   **92**

1. Members of Congress 2. Civil rights activists 3. African Americans -- Civil rights 4. Southern States -- Race relations

ISBN 978-1-59935-130-8 lib bdg; 1-59935-130-7 lib bdg

LC 2009027748

A biography of African American civil rights activist John Lewis

This is "solid, evenhanded, and wonderfully helpful. . . . Particularly interesting is the section of the book that describes Lewis' congressional race against fellow civil rights activist Julian Bond. . . . Unusually well-chosen photos, fine notes, and [a list] of further sources add to the usefulness and appeal of this [book]." Booklist

Includes bibliographical references

Lewis, Meriwether, 1774-1809

Crompton, Samuel. **Lewis** and Clark; [by] Samuel Willard Crompton. Chelsea House 2009 116p il map (Great explorers) lib bdg $30

Grades: 6 7 8 9 **92**

1. Explorers 2. Lewis and Clark Expedition (1804-1806) 3. West (U.S.) 4. Territorial governors

ISBN 978-1-60413-418-6 lib bdg; 1-60413-418-6 lib bdg

LC 2009-8687

Biography of the explorers Lewis and Clark

"The information . . . is presented in such a way as to attract and maintain readers' interest. . . . With a full complement of maps, photographs (where available), illustrations, time lines, and document reproductions, a full story is told. Well-written and throughly researched, this . . . will make a solid addition." SLJ

Includes glossary and bibliographical references

Leyson, Leon, 1929-2013

★ Leyson, Leon, 1929-2013. The **boy** on the wooden box; Leon Leyson ; with Marilyn J Harran and Elisabeth B Leyson. Atheneum Books for Young Readers 2013 240 p. (hardcover) $16.99

Grades: 6 7 8 9 **92**

1. Holocaust survivors 2. World War, 1939-1945 -- Jews -- Rescue 3. Narewka (Poland) -- Biography 4. Jews -- Poland -- Narewka -- Biography 5. Płaszów (Concentration camp) 6. Concentration camp inmates -- Poland -- Płaszów -- Biography 7. Jewish children in the Holocaust -- Poland -- Kraków -- Biography 8. Holocaust, Jewish (1939-1945) -- Poland -- Kraków -- Personal narratives

ISBN 1442497815; 9781442497818; 9781442497832

LC 2013017987

In this book, "Leon Leyson (born Leib Lezjon) was only ten years old when the Nazis invaded Poland and his family was forced to relocate to the Krakow ghetto. With incredible luck, perseverance, and grit, Leyson was able to survive the sadism of the Nazis, including that of the demonic Amon Goeth, commandant of Plaszow, the concentration camp outside Krakow. Ultimately, it was the generosity and cunning of one man, a man named Oskar Schindler, who saved Leon Leyson's life, and the lives of his mother, his father, and two of his four siblings, by adding their names to his list of workers in his factory—a list that became world renowned: Schindler's List." (Publisher's Note)

"This powerful memoir of one of the youngest boys on Schindler's list deserves to be shared...This memoir is a natural curriculum addition to WWII units for upper-elementary- and middle-school readers. Be sure to have additional materials on hand about Oskar Schindler, as readers will want to do more research into Leyson's story." (Booklist)

Li Cunxin

Li Cunxin. **Mao's** last dancer; [by] Li Cunxin. Young readers' ed.; Walker & Co. 2008 290p il map $16.99

Grades: 6 7 8 9 **92**

1. Defectors 2. Ballet dancers 3. Securities brokers 4. China -- History -- 1949-1976

ISBN 978-0-8027-9779-7; 0-8027-9779-2

LC 2008-6104

An adaptation of the title published 2003 by Putnam for adults

Chosen from millions of children to serve in Mao's cultural revolution by studying at the Beijing Dance Academy, Li knew ballet would be his family's best opportunity to escape the bitter poverty in his rural China home. From one hardship to another, Li persevered, never forgetting the family he left behind.

"Cunxin's tale is a wonderfully crafted coming-of-age story. . . . He paints a clear picture of harsh realities of life in communist China but does so without being overly negative. . . . Photographs provide readers with a glimpse of varying aspects of Cunxin's life, a short note on the history of China, and a time line of China in the twentieth century." Voice Youth Advocates

Li, Moying, 1954-

★ Moying Li. **Snow** falling in spring; coming of age in China during the cultural revolution. Farrar, Straus and Giroux 2008 176p $16

Grades: 7 8 9 10 11 12 **92**

1. Memoirists 2. Financial consultants 3. Biography, Individual 4. China -- History -- 1949-1976 -- Personal narratives

ISBN 978-0-374-39922-1; 0-374-39922-0

LC 2006-38356

"This memoir . . . offers a highly personal look at China's Cultural Revolution. The author is four years old when Mao initiates the Great Leap Forward in 1958. . . . Li effectively builds the climate of fear that accompanies the rise of the Red Guard, while accounts of her headmaster's suicide and the pulping of her father's book collection give a harrowing, closeup view of the persecution. Sketches about her grandparents root the narrative within a broader context of Chinese traditions as well as her own family's values." Publ Wkly

Lichtenstein, Roy, 1923-1997

★ Rubin, Susan Goldman. **Whaam!** : the art & life of Roy Lichtenstein. Abrams 2008 47p il $18.95

Grades: 4 5 6 7 **92**

1. Artists 2. Pop art 3. Painters 4. Sculptors 5. Printmakers 6. Artists -- United States

ISBN 978-0-8109-9492-8; 0-8109-9492-5

LC 2007-42048

"Rubin presents an overview of a modern master with clear writing and an abundance of his eye-popping works, all framed on pages that mirror the artist's signature use of primary colors and Benday dots." Booklist

"Rubin begins in 1961 with a glimpse at Lichtenstein's first foray into cartoon art reproduction, "]Look Mickey", the painting that launched his fame. Showing pivotal pieces of Lichtenstein's art, Rubin also manages to include related images that help explain each piece's predecessors. The book's design pops without overshadowing its material, and back matter is impressive in its completeness." Horn Book

Lin, Maya Ying

Lashnits, Tom. **Maya** Lin; [by] Tom Lashnits. Chelsea House 2007 128p il (Asian Americans of achievement) lib bdg $30

Grades: 7 8 9 10   **92**

1. Artists 2. Sculptors 3. Architects 4. Women architects 5. Vietnam Veterans Memorial (Washington, D.C.) 6. Asian Americans -- Biography

ISBN 978-0-7910-9268-2 lib bdg; 0-7910-9268-2 lib bdg

LC 2006026064

A biography of the architect who designed the Vietnam Veterans' Memorial in Washington D.C.

This is "well-researched . . . attractive . . . solid." SLJ

Includes glossary and bibliographical references

Lincoln family

★ Holzer, Harold. **Father** Abraham; Lincoln and his sons. Calkins Creek 2011 231p il $17.95

Grades: 6 7 8 9   **92**

1. Lawyers 2. Presidents 3. Pioneers 4. State legislators 5. Members of Congress 6. Presidents -- United States 7. Biography, Individual

ISBN 1590783034; 9781590783030

This biography "looks at the lives of Abraham Lincoln and his family, including the relationship between the president and his sons." (Publisher's note) Bibliography. Index. "Middle school, high school." (Horn Book)

"This profile of 'the clan that might have become America's royal family but instead became America's cursed family' offers both a wagonload of fascinating period photos and a case study in domestic tragedy and dysfunction. . . . If the author sometimes hobbles his narrative with fussy details, he also tucks in such intimate touches as samples of homely verse from both parents and children and finishes off with quick looks at all of the direct descendants." Kirkus

Lincoln, Abraham, 1809-1865

Aronson, Billy. **Abraham** Lincoln. Marshall Cavendish Benchmark 2009 112p il (Presidents and their times) lib bdg $23.95

Grades: 5 6 7 8   **92**

1. Lawyers 2. Presidents 3. State legislators 4. Members of Congress 5. Presidents -- United States 6. United States -- History -- 1861-1865, Civil War

ISBN 978-0-7614-2839-8 lib bdg; 0-7614-2839-9 lib bdg

LC 2007019190

This provides "information on President Abraham Lincoln and places him within his historical and cultural context. Also explored are the formative events of his times and how he responded." Publisher's note

Includes glossary and bibliographical references

★ Denenberg, Barry. **Lincoln** shot! a president's life remembered. chief writer, Barry Denenberg; artist, Christopher Bing. Feiwel and Friends 2008 40p il $24.95

Grades: 5 6 7 8   **92**

1. Lawyers 2. Presidents 3. State legislators 4. Members of Congress 5. Presidents -- United States 6.

United States -- History -- 1861-1865, Civil War

ISBN 978-0-312-37013-8; 0-312-37013-X

LC 2007-48851

"The concept is that this is a commemorative edition of 'The National News' published one year after Lincoln's death . . . Also included is an engaging, readable yet detailed account of Lincoln's life. . . . [This book] is an example of how high-quality bookmaking can turn a history lesson into an authentic experience." Booklist

★ Fleming, Candace. The **Lincolns**; a scrapbook look at Abraham and Mary. Schwartz & Wade Books 2008 177p il map $24.99; lib bdg $28.99

Grades: 7 8 9 10 11 12   **92**

1. Lawyers 2. Presidents 3. State legislators 4. Members of Congress 5. Spouses of presidents 6. Presidents -- United States 7. Presidents' spouses -- United States 8. United States -- History -- 1861-1865, Civil War

ISBN 978-0-375-83618-3; 0-375-83618-7; 978-0-375-93618-0 lib bdg; 0-375-93618-1 lib bdg

LC 2007-44113

Boston Globe-Horn Book Award: Nonfiction (2009)

Fleming twines "accounts of two lives—Abraham and Mary Todd Lincoln—into one fascinating whole. On spreads that combine well-chosen visuals with blocks of headlined text, Fleming gives a full, birth-to-death view of the 'inextricably bound' Lincolns." Booklist

★ Freedman, Russell. **Abraham** Lincoln and Frederick Douglass; the story behind an American friendship. by Russell Freedman. Houghton Mifflin Harcourt 2012 119 p. $18.99

Grades: 4 5 6 7 8   **92**

1. Friendship 2. Abolitionists -- United States 3. United States -- History -- 1861-1865, Civil War -- Biography 4. Friendship -- United States 5. Presidents -- United States -- Biography 6. African American abolitionists -- Biography

ISBN 9780547385624

LC 2011025953

This book tells the story of Abraham Lincoln, "the 16th president, . . . [along] with his friend and ally, abolitionist Frederick Douglass. The story opens with Douglass anxiously waiting to meet Lincoln for the first time to air grievances about the treatment of African-American soldiers during the Civil War. . . . Subsequent chapters detail the leaders' often parallel biographies. Both were self-made and shared a passion for reading, rising from poverty to prominence." (Publishers Weekly)

Includes bibliographical references (p. [108]-109) and index

★ Freedman, Russell. **Lincoln** : a photobiography. Clarion Bks. 1987 149p il $18; pa $7.95

Grades: 5 6 7 8 9 10   **92**

1. Lawyers 2. Presidents 3. State legislators 4. Members of Congress 5. Presidents -- United States 6. United States -- History -- 1861-1865, Civil War

ISBN 0-89919-380-3; 0-395-51848-2 pa

LC 86-33379

Awarded the Newbery Medal, 1988

This is "a balanced work, elegantly designed and enhanced by dozens of period photographs and drawings, some familiar, some refreshingly unfamiliar." Publ Wkly

Includes bibliographical references

Giblin, James. **Good** brother, bad brother; the story of Edwin Booth and John Wilkes Booth. Clarion Books 2005 244p il $22

Grades: 5 6 7 8   92

1. United States -- History -- 1861-1865, Civil War
ISBN 0-618-09642-6

LC 2004-21260

This is a dual biography of John Wilkes Booth, who assassinated Abraham Lincoln, and his brother, Edwin, an actor. (Horn Book)

Giblin "frames the intertwined tale of two brothers with accounts of their families, friends, the Civil War, and nineteenth-century theater. . . . Alcoholism and depression afflicted the family, but Giblin is brilliant at showing that darkness was only one part of a life. . . . Giblin's book will engross readers until the very last footnote." Booklist

Includes bibliographical references

★ Holzer, Harold. **Father** Abraham; Lincoln and his sons. Calkins Creek 2011 231p il $17.95

Grades: 6 7 8 9   92

1. Lawyers 2. Presidents 3. Pioneers 4. State legislators 5. Members of Congress 6. Presidents -- United States 7. Biography, Individual
ISBN 1590783034; 9781590783030

This biography "looks at the lives of Abraham Lincoln and his family, including the relationship between the president and his sons." (Publisher's note) Bibliography. Index. "Middle school, high school." (Horn Book)

"This profile of 'the clan that might have become America's royal family but instead became America's cursed family' offers both a wagonload of fascinating period photos and a case study in domestic tragedy and dysfunction. . . . If the author sometimes hobbles his narrative with fussy details, he also tucks in such intimate touches as samples of homely verse from both parents and children and finishes off with quick looks at all of the direct descendants." Kirkus

Lincoln, Abraham. **Abraham** Lincoln the writer; a treasury of his greatest speeches and letters. compiled and edited by Harold Holzer. Boyds Mills Press 2000 106p il lib bdg $15.95

Grades: 7 8 9 10   92

1. Lawyers 2. Presidents 3. State legislators 4. Members of Congress 5. Presidents -- United States 6. United States -- History -- 1861-1865, Civil War
ISBN 1-56397-772-9

LC 99-66551

"Lincoln's writings include personal letters, notes on the law, excerpts from speeches, debates, and inaugural addresses, letters to parents of fallen soldiers, and telegrams to his family. Reproductions of period photos, portraits, and documents illustrate the text effectively. . . . Highly interesting and a fine resource for students seeking quotations or for those wanting to meet Lincoln through his own words." Booklist

★ Sandler, Martin W. **Lincoln** through the lens; how photography revealed and shaped an extraordinary life. Walker Pub. Co. 2008 97p il $19.99; lib bdg $20.89

Grades: 6 7 8 9 10   92

1. Lawyers 2. Presidents 3. State legislators 4. Members of Congress 5. Photography -- History 6. Presidents -- United States 7. United States -- History -- 1861-1865, Civil War -- Pictorial works
ISBN 978-0-8027-9666-0; 0-8027-9666-4; 978-0-8027-9667-7 lib bdg; 0-8027-9667-2 lib bdg

LC 2008-0219

"When Lincoln became president, photography was new and he joined the 'very first generation of human beings ever to be photographed.' . . . This extraordinary book is a tribute to the way contemporary and future generations came to view Lincoln. . . . Part biography, part history of of the Civil War, the book touches on many interesting topics. . . . Every step of the way there are fascinating photographs. . . . Although it's the pictures that provide the 'wow factor,' Sandler's perceptive words have their own elegance." Booklist

Waldman, Neil. **Voyages**; reminiscences of young Abe Lincoln. Calkins Creek 2009 32p $16.95

Grades: 4 5 6 7   92

1. Lawyers 2. Presidents 3. Mississippi River 4. State legislators 5. Members of Congress 6. Slavery -- United States 7. Presidents -- United States
ISBN 978-1-59078-471-6

LC 2008024022

This "volume integrates some of Lincoln's own words with an imagined narrative based on documented accounts of river voyages he took between the ages of 18 and 22. . . . The two narratives blend fairly smoothly, and the book offers both a quick read and extensive opportunities for study and discussion. . . . The nostalgic design, featuring a distressed sepia-toned appearance and the author's own illustrations, further adds to the book's appeal." Booklist

Includes bibliographical references

★ Zeller, Bob. **Lincoln** in 3-D; by Bob Zeller and John Richter. Chronicle Books 2010 223p il $35

Grades: 6 7 8 9   92

1. Lawyers 2. Presidents 3. Three-dimensional photography 4. State legislators 5. Members of Congress 6. Three dimensional photography 7. United States -- History -- 1861-1865, Civil War -- Pictorial works
ISBN 978-0-8118-7231-7; 0-8118-7231-9

LC 2010013792

"This visually striking volume is built around 185 stereoscopic photographs from the Civil War era. Glasses included in the back give the full three-dimensional effect. . . . The introduction offers fascinating background on stereoscopic pictures, followed by a narrative text tracing Lincoln's life and the stages of the war. All of the photos include informative captions that give context even for images not mentioned in the text. . . . The striking images make this a powerful visual depiction of Lincoln and his times." SLJ

Includes bibliographical references

Lincoln, Mary Todd, 1818-1882

Jones, Lynda. **Mrs.** Lincoln's dressmaker: the unlikely friendship of Elizabeth Keckley and Mary Todd Lincoln; by Lynda D. Jones. National Geographic 2009 80p il $18.95; lib bdg $27.90

Grades: 5 6 7 8   **92**

1. Memoirists 2. Dressmakers 3. Spouses of presidents 4. Slavery -- United States 5. United States -- Race relations 6. African American women -- Biography 7. Presidents' spouses -- United States 8. Washington (D.C.) -- Social life and customs

ISBN 978-1-4263-0377-7; 1-4263-0377-7; 978-1-4263-0378-4 lib bdg; 1-4263-0378-5 lib bdg

LC 2008-29314

"Readers may be familiar with the ups and downs of Lincoln's life, but details of Keckley's story . . . will give them new insights into the life of a slave, in this case, one who was educated and had a profession." Booklist

Includes bibliographical references

Lindbergh, Anne Morrow, 1906-2001

Gherman, Beverly. **Anne** Morrow Lindbergh; between the sea and the stars. [by] Beverly Gherman. Twenty-first Century Books 2008 160p (Lerner biography) lib bdg $27.93

Grades: 6 7 8 9   **92**

1. Poets 2. Authors 3. Generals 4. Novelists 5. Air pilots 6. Women air pilots 7. Diarists 8. Essayists 9. Memoirists 10. Air force officers 11. Spouses of prominent persons

ISBN 978-0-8225-5970-2 lib bdg; 0-8225-5970-6 lib bdg

LC 2005022498

Explores the life and career of Anne Morrow Lindbergh, including her marriage to Charles Lindbergh, flying experiences, and success as an author.

"Clearly written and illustrated with frequent, clear black-and-white photos, the book is strongest in demonstrating Gherman's thorough understanding of Anne's emotional core. . . . A solid resource for reports as well as a fascinating portrait for biography fans." Booklist

Includes bibliographical references

Lindbergh, Charles, 1902-1974

Gherman, Beverly. **Anne** Morrow Lindbergh; between the sea and the stars. [by] Beverly Gherman. Twenty-first Century Books 2008 160p (Lerner biography) lib bdg $27.93

Grades: 6 7 8 9   **92**

1. Poets 2. Authors 3. Generals 4. Novelists 5. Air pilots 6. Women air pilots 7. Diarists 8. Essayists 9. Memoirists 10. Air force officers 11. Spouses of prominent persons

ISBN 978-0-8225-5970-2 lib bdg; 0-8225-5970-6 lib bdg

LC 2005022498

Explores the life and career of Anne Morrow Lindbergh, including her marriage to Charles Lindbergh, flying experiences, and success as an author.

"Clearly written and illustrated with frequent, clear black-and-white photos, the book is strongest in demonstrating Gherman's thorough understanding of Anne's emotional core. . . . A solid resource for reports as well as a fascinating portrait for biography fans." Booklist

Includes bibliographical references

Linné, Carl von, 1707-1778

Anderson, Margaret Jean. **Carl** Linnaeus; father of classification. [by] Margaret J. Anderson. rev ed; Enslow Publishers 2009 128p il (Great minds of science) lib bdg $31.93

Grades: 5 6 7 8 9   **92**

1. Botanists 2. Naturalists 3. Writers on science

ISBN 978-0-7660-3009-1 lib bdg; 0-7660-3009-1 lib bdg

LC 2008-23941

First published 1997

"Budding scientists will surely draw inspiration from this biography of Linnaeus. . . . Anderson creates a dramatic narrative fully capable of keeping readers enthralled." Kirkus

Includes glossary and bibliographical references

Lockwood, Belva Ann, 1830-1917

Norgren, Jill. **Belva** Lockwood; equal rights pioneer. by Jill Norgren. Twenty-First Century Books 2009 112p il (Trailblazer biography) lib bdg $31.93

Grades: 6 7 8 9   **92**

1. Lawyers 2. Suffragists 3. Women lawyers 4. Women's rights 5. Lecturers 6. Presidential candidates

ISBN 978-0-8225-9068-2 lib bdg; 0-8225-9068-9 lib bdg

LC 2007-50265

First published 2007 by New York University Press with title: Belva Lockwood: the woman who would be president

"Through a clear and engaging text, this biography shows how Lockwood, a relatively unknown historical figure, was an inspiring pioneer of the equal-rights movement." SLJ

Includes bibliographical references

Louis, Joe, 1914-1981

Sullivan, George. **Knockout!** : a photobiography of boxer Joe Louis. National Geographic 2008 64p il $17.95; lib bdg $27.90

Grades: 6 7 8 9   **92**

1. Soldiers 2. African American athletes 3. Boxers (Persons) 4. Boxing -- Biography

ISBN 978-1-4263-0328-9; 1-4263-0328-9; 978-1-4263-0329-6 lib bdg; 1-4263-0329-7 lib bdg

LC 2008-25036

"This oversize biography of Joe Louis is just the thing for getting the blood of reluctant readers and sports fans pumping. Using copious period photographs . . . and full-color reproductions of fight posters and memoriblia, Sullivan relays in straightforward language the rags-to-riches saga of the 'Brown Bomber,' and sets the story against the rampant racism of 1920s America. . . . Sullivan's fight recaps are clear and vivid." Booklist

Includes bibliographical references

Love, Nat, 1854-1921

Bloom, Barbara Lee. **Nat** Love. Chelsea House 2010 102p il (Legends of the Wild West) lib bdg $35

Grades: 6 7 8 9   **92**

1. Cowhands 2. Cowboys 3. Porters 4. West (U.S.) -- History 5. African Americans -- Biography
ISBN 978-1-60413-599-2; 1-60413-599-9

A biography of Nat Love, who was born in a log cabin in Tennessee in 1854 as the slave of Robert Love and who, in 1869, four years after the slaves had been freed, moved out West to find work as a cowhand.

Bloom "does a fine job chronicling [Love's] exploits as a black cowboy and beyond. . . . Weaving historical context throughout in related sidebars and lengthy captions, the book features black-and-white and color photos, paintings, and other illustrations." Booklist

Includes glossary and bibliographical references

Lowry, Lois

Albert, Lisa Rondinelli. **Lois** Lowry; the giver of stories and memories. Enslow Publishers 2008 128p il (Authors teens love) lib bdg $31.93

Grades: 5 6 7 8   **92**

1. Authors 2. Novelists 3. Women authors 4. Authors, American 5. Young adult authors
ISBN 978-0-7660-2722-0 lib bdg; 0-7660-2722-8 lib bdg

LC 2006034045

A biography of the author of the Anastasia Krupnik series, as well as the Newbery Medal winning novels The giver and Number the Stars

Includes bibliographical references

Bankston, John. **Lois** Lowry; [by] John Bankston. Chelsea House 2009 127p bibl il (Who wrote that?) lib bdg $30

Grades: 6 7 8 9   **92**

1. Authors 2. Novelists 3. Women authors 4. Authors, American 5. Young adult authors
ISBN 978-1-6041-3335-6 lib bdg; 1-6041-3335-X lib bdg

LC 2008035039

This examines the life and work of the popular author for children and young adults

"Lowry's road to publication was a winding one, with her first novel, A Summer to Die (1977), published at age 40. She went on to become the two-time Newbery Medal winner—Number the Stars (1989) and The Giver (1993)—that most kids remember from classroom encounters. This generous entry into the Who Wrote That? series answers not only the series title but also how Lowry wrote and why it matters. . . . Among the highlights is the focus on Lowry's willingness to broach controversial topics, which make her a perennial on ALA's challenged-books list. This is a welcome addition to a rather small pool of biographies on this prolific author." Booklist

Includes bibliographical references

Lugovskaia, Nina, 1918-1993

Lugovskaia, Nina. **I** want to live; the diary of a young girl in Stalin's Russia. translated by Andrew Bromfield. Houghton Mifflin 2006 280p il $17.99

Grades: 7 8 9 10 11 12   **92**

1. Artists 2. Painters 3. Persecution 4. Diarists 5. Soviet Union -- Politics and government
ISBN 978-0-618-60575-0; 0-618-60575-4
Original Russian edition, 2003

Reveals the life of a teenage girl in Stalin's Russia, where fear of arrest was a fact of daily life.

"Lugovskaya's diary, which was found in the NKVD archives, stands as a compelling historical artifact and Nina's story gives a moving—if relentlessly melancholy—personal account of life in Communist Russia." Publ Wkly

Includes bibliographical references

Lyons, Maritcha Rémond, 1848-1929

★ Bolden, Tonya. **Maritcha**; a nineteenth-century American girl. Abrams 2005 47p il $17.95

Grades: 4 5 6 7 8 9 10   **92**

1. Teachers 2. Civic leaders 3. New York (N.Y.) -- Race relations 4. African American women -- Biography 5. African Americans -- New York (N.Y.)
ISBN 0-8109-5045-6

LC 2004-05849

"The high quality of writing and the excellent documentation make this a first choice for all collections." SLJ

Ma, Yo-Yo, 1955-

Worth, Richard. **Yo** -Yo Ma. Chelsea House 2006 119p bibl il por (Asian Americans of achievement) lib bdg $30

Grades: 7 8 9 10   **92**

1. Chinese Americans 2. Cellists 3. Violoncellists 4. Classical musicians
ISBN 978-0-7910-9270-5 lib bdg; 0-7910-9270-4 lib bdg

LC 2006026335

"World-famous cellist Ma was born in Paris to a family originally from China. He was taught the cello at the age of four by his father, and early on it became obvious that he was a musical genius. The book has information about Ma's teachers, influences, and favorite composers." (School Library Journal)

Includes glossary and bibliographical references

MacMillan, Donald, 1874-1970

Cowan, Mary Morton. **Captain** Mac: the life of Donald Baxter MacMillan, Arctic explorer. Calkins Creek 2010 208p il $17.95

Grades: 6 7 8 9   **92**

1. Explorers 2. Arctic regions
ISBN 978-1-59078-709-0; 1-59078-709-9

LC 2009-36113

"This biography, written with obvious respect and admiration, covers the life and achievements of the Arctic explorer. . . . The author skillfully weaves primary-source quotes with short, action-oriented sentences. . . . This engaging biography is also a solid overview of an era of exploration that still captivates adventurous youths." SLJ

Includes bibliographical references

Magellan, Ferdinand, 1480?-1521

Aretha, David. **Magellan**; first to circle the globe. Enslow Publishers 2009 112p il map (Great explorers of the world) lib bdg $31.93

Grades: 6 7 8 9   **92**

1. Explorers
ISBN 978-1-59845-097-2 lib bdg; 1-59845-097-2 lib bdg

LC 2008-13550

This "biography of Magellan reads like an adventure, detailing his life, while intriguing the reader with the danger and adversity surrounding his career. . . . Antique and current maps punctuate the text together with modern photographs and historic illustrations. The monumental implications of Magellan's life and voyage make this true adventure a winner." Libr Media Connect

Includes glosaary and bibliographical references

Koestler-Grack, Rachel A. **Ferdinand** Magellan. Chelsea House 2009 112p il map (Great explorers) lib bdg $30

Grades: 6 7 8 9   **92**

1. Explorers 2. Voyages around the world
ISBN 978-1-60413-422-3 lib bdg; 1-60413-422-4 lib bdg

LC 2009011587

Biography of the explorer Ferdinand Magellan

"The information . . . is presented in such a way as to attract and maintain readers' interest. . . . With a full complement of maps, photographs (where available), illustrations, time lines, and document reproductions, a full story is told. Well-written and throughly researched, this . . . will make a solid addition." SLJ

Includes glossary and bibliographical references

Malcolm X, 1925-1965

Burlingame, Jeff. **Malcolm** X. Enslow Publishers 2010 160p il lib bdg $34.60

Grades: 6 7 8 9   **92**

1. Black Muslims 2. Black Muslim leaders 3. Civil rights activists 4. African Americans -- Biography 5. African Americans -- Civil rights
ISBN 978-0-7660-3384-9; 0-7660-3384-8

LC 2009017597

In this biography the life of Malcolm X is "effectively explored to provide an understanding of [the] man's ideals, values, and perspectives on society as well as his reactions to pivotal events. . . . [The book] highlights the development of the human-rights activist's philosophy by exploring the impact of several childhood tragedies, causing him to question authority and to encourage others to do so as well. . . . [This title is] clear and concise and [includes] many images and descriptions of important events and people that [Malcolm X] interacted with and [was] impacted by." SLJ

Gunderson, Jessica. **X** : the biography of Malcolm X; illustrated by Seitu Hayden. Graphic Library

2011 32p il (Graphic library: American graphic) lib bdg $29.32; pa $7.95

Grades: 4 5 6 7   **92**

1. Black Muslims 2. Biographical graphic novels 3. Black Muslim leaders 4. Civil rights activists 5. African Americans -- Biography
ISBN 978-1-4296-5471-5 lib bdg; 1-4296-5471-6 lib bdg; 978-1-4296-6267-3 pa; 1-4296-6267-0 pa

LC 2010037029

In graphic novel format, explores the life and death of Malcolm X.

"The illustrations are eye-catching and the narration is presented simply, yet compellingly. . . . Fact-filled, entertaining, and accessible." SLJ

Includes glossary and bibliographical references

★ Sharp, Anne Wallace. **Malcolm** X and Black pride. Lucent Books 2010 104p il (Lucent library of black history) $32.45

Grades: 6 7 8 9   **92**

1. Black Muslims 2. Black Muslim leaders 3. Civil rights activists 4. African Americans -- Biography 5. African Americans -- Civil rights
ISBN 978-1-4205-0123-0; 1-4205-0123-2

LC 2009038463

This book takes "a frank, balanced, and compelling look at the man who was born Malcolm Little and whose furious insistence on equality for African Americans continues to both inspire and provoke controversy. . . . Supported by well-selected photos, extensive chapter notes, and further-reading suggestions, this is a strong choice for student research." Booklist

Includes bibliographical references

Mandela, Nelson

Catel, Patrick. **Nelson** Mandela. Heinemann Library 2010 112p il map (Front-page lives) $38.93

Grades: 6 7 8 9 10   **92**

1. Presidents 2. Political prisoners 3. Political leaders 4. Human rights activists 5. Nobel laureates for peace 6. South Africa -- Politics and government
ISBN 978-1-4329-3219-0; 1-4329-3219-5

LC 2009-18178

The life of South African President Nelson Mandela is "presented with depth and breadth. . . . The writing is accessible and engaging, with color and black-and-white photographs and . . . color maps complementing the text." SLJ

Includes glossary and bibliographical references

Gormley, Beatrice. **Nelson** Mandela; South African revolutionary. by Beatrice Gormley. Aladdin 2014 256 p. illustrations (Real-life story) (hardback) $17.99

Grades: 5 6 7 8   **92**

1. Presidents -- South Africa -- Biography
ISBN 1481420593; 9781481420594; 9781481420600

LC 2014019020

This book, by Beatrice Gormley, is a "comprehensive biography that tells the complete life story of internationally renowned peacemaker Nelson Mandela. . . . Born in 1918 in South Africa, he grew up in a culture of government-enforced racism and became involved in the anti-apartheid movement at a young age. Deeply committed to nonviolent activism, Mandela directed a peaceful campaign against the racist policies of his South African government, and spent 27 years in prison as a result." (Publisher's note)

"More than a year after his death, the influence of Nelson Mandela is still felt keenly by people around the world. This timely biography provides a complete picture of a complex man...This book is an understandable and multifaceted tribute to an icon of defiance and optimism in the face of tribulation." Booklist

Includes bibliographical references and index

Keller, Bill. **Tree** shaker; the story of Nelson Mandela. Kingfisher 2008 128p il $17.95
Grades: 8 9 10 11 12   92
1. Presidents 2. Political prisoners 3. Political leaders 4. Human rights activists 5. Nobel laureates for peace 6. South Africa -- Race relations 7. South Africa -- Politics and government
ISBN 978-0-7534-5992-8; 0-7534-5992-2
                                              LC 2007-03559
The author "offers a balanced, thoughtful account of Mandela's political activism and accomplishments and his pivotal role in South Africa's modern history. . . . [The book is] packed with dramatic photos, swathes of paint, handprints and images of the African continent." Publ Wkly
Includes bibliographical references

Manet, Édouard, 1832-1883

Spence, David. **Manet**. New Forest Press 2010 48p il (Great artists and their world) lib bdg $32.80
Grades: 6 7 8 9   92
1. Artists 2. Painters 3. Artists, French
ISBN 978-1-84898-313-7; 1-84898-313-1
"Offers biographical information [of Edouard Manet] . . . interspersed with art history and criticism in an eye-catching format. . . . [Includes] a long introductory paragraph and four-to-six images with explanatory notes. . . . Spence . . . does a good job of explaining why art that might seem ordinary today was revolutionary at the time of its creation." SLJ
Includes glossary

Mankiller, Wilma

Sonneborn, Liz. **Wilma** Mankiller. Marshall Cavendish Benchmark 2010 112p il (Leading women) $39.93
Grades: 5 6 7 8   92
1. Cherokee Indians 2. Indian chiefs
ISBN 978-0-7614-4959-1; 0-7614-4959-0
                                              LC 2009029399
"The story of Mankiller's lifelong work for the Cherokee Nation and her role as its first female principal chief will absorb readers. The [woman's life is] revealed within the political and historical context of [her] times and [includes] quotes from autobiographical material. . . . Color and black-and-white photos are included. . . . The compact size, chronological organization, and accessible writing [style makes this biography a] good [resource] for reports." SLJ

Manzano, Juan Francisco, 1797-1854

Engle, Margarita. The **poet** slave of Cuba: a biography of Juan Francisco Manzano; art by Sean Qualls. Henry Holt 2006 183p il $16.95
Grades: 7 8 9 10   92
1. Poets 2. Slaves 3. Authors 4. Slavery -- Cuba 5. Biography, Individual
ISBN 0-8050-7706-5; 978-0-8050-7706-3
                                              LC 2005-46200
Awarded the Pura Belpré Author Award, 2008
This is a "biography of a Cuban slave who escaped to become a celebrated poet." (Publisher's note) "Grades seven to twelve." (Bull Cent Child Books)
"This is a book that should be read by young and old, black and white, Anglo and Latino." SLJ

Mao Zedong, 1893-1976

Heuston, Kimberley Burton. **Mao** Zedong; [by] Kimberley Heuston. Franklin Watts 2010 128p il map (Wicked history) lib bdg $30
Grades: 5 6 7 8   92
1. Heads of state 2. Communist leaders 3. Political leaders 4. China -- History -- 1949-1976
ISBN 978-0-531-20756-7; 0-531-20756-0
                                              LC 2009034157
"...short enough not to intimidate yet long enough to impart the enormity of the tyrant's atrocities. Opening with a description of Zedong's ruthlessness as an early revolutionary, Heuston follows him through the 82 years of his life, describing his devastating impact on China. Black-and-white photos, maps of Uganda and of China, time lines of the men's lives, and labeled webs showing their allies and enemies... make the books accessible." SLJ
Includes glossary and bibliographical references

Naden, Corinne J. **Mao** Zedong and the Chinese Revolution. Morgan Reynolds Pub. 2009 144p il map (World leaders) lib bdg $28.95
Grades: 7 8 9 10 11 12   92
1. Heads of state 2. Communist leaders 3. Political leaders 4. China -- History -- 1949-1976
ISBN 978-1-59935-100-1; 1-59935-100-5
                                              LC 2008-27829
This "discusses Chariman Mao Zedong's rise to power and his crucial role in national and international history. . . . Naden's analysis of the significant role of young people will draw YA readers for reports and for personal interest. The readable design, with clear type and lots of historic color photos as well as screens and detailed maps, includes spacious back matter." Booklist
Includes bibliographical references

Slavicek, Louise Chipley. **Mao** Zedong. Chelsea House 2004 116p il (Great military leaders of the 20th century) lib bdg $23.95
Grades: 6 7 8 9   92
1. Heads of state 2. Communist leaders 3. Political leaders 4. China -- History -- 1949-1976
ISBN 0-7910-7407-2
                                              LC 2003-6929

A biography of Chinese leader Mao Zedong, discussing the battles that helped shape him and reasons behind his popularity among his countrymen

"Slavicek blends personal, philosophical, and historical information to trace Mao's journey to power. Clear accounts of the communist movement, the Long March, and the eventual battle with the Nationalists and Japanese are included." SLJ

Includes bibliographical references

Marley, Bob

★ Medina, Tony. **I** and I; Bob Marley. illustrated by Jesse Joshua Watson. Lee & Low Books 2009 un il $19.95

Grades: 4 5 6   **92**

1. Singers 2. Jamaica 3. Reggae musicians

ISBN 978-1-60060-257-3; 1-60060-257-6

LC 2008-33485

"In the words and rhythms of Jamaican patois, Medina's lyrical, direct lines make the most sense when read in tandem with the extensive appended notes. . . . Like the words, Watson's beautifully expressive acrylic paintings evoke a strong sense of Marley's remarkable life and his Caribbean homeland." Booklist

Includes bibliographical references

Miller, Calvin Craig. **Reggae** poet: the story of Bob Marley. Morgan Reynolds Pub. 2007 128p il $27.95

Grades: 7 8 9 10   **92**

1. Singers 2. Musicians 3. Reggae music 4. Reggae musicians

ISBN 978-1-59935-071-4; 1-59935-071-8

LC 2007-27476

In this biography of the Jamaican musician "Miller does a fine job showing the effect the music and the politics had on each other. He also skillfully weaves in the complicated topic of the Rastaferian religion and the part ganja (marijuana) plays in it, and he doesn't hesitate when explaining Marley's complicated romantic life. The . . . photos are well chosen." Booklist

Includes bibliographical references

Paprocki, Sherry Beck. **Bob** Marley; musician. [by] Sherry Beck Paprocki. legacy ed.; Chelsea House 2006 111p bibl il por (Black Americans of achievement) lib bdg $30

Grades: 6 7 8 9   **92**

1. Singers 2. Musicians 3. Reggae music 4. Reggae musicians

ISBN 0-7910-9213-5

LC 2006004578

A biography of the Jamaican reggae musician.

The book goes "beyond the typical personal information to provide some social history revelant to the subject's time. Captioned photographs and boxed inserts enhance the conversational [text]." Horn Book Guide

Includes bibliographical references

Marshall, Thurgood, 1908-1993

Crowe, Chris. **Thurgood** Marshall; a twentieth-century life. Viking 2008 248p il (Up close) $16.99

Grades: 6 7 8 9 10   **92**

1. Judges 2. Lawyers 3. Solicitors general 4. Civil rights activists 5. Supreme Court justices 6. African Americans -- Biography 7. United States -- Supreme Court

ISBN 978-0-670-06228-7; 0-670-06228-6

LC 2007-042794

"This is a captivating portrait of a heroic champion of justice that also offers great insight into the most pivotal moments of the Civil Rights Movement." Kirkus

"Marshall served 24 years as the first African American judge on the U.S. Supreme Court, but this biography . . . focuses on his pioneer work as a lawyer and civil rights activist and on the landmark cases in which he fought segregation in public education and elsewhere." Booklist

Marx, Karl, 1818-1883

Rossig, Wolfgang. **Karl** Marx. Morgan Reynolds 2009 112p il (Profiles in economics) lib bdg $28.95

Grades: 8 9 10   **92**

1. Philosophers 2. Writers on politics 3. Political and social philosophers

ISBN 978-1-59935-132-2; 1-59935-132-3

LC 2009-29563

"This book presents the life of Karl Marx and places his social and economic theories within the useful context of his youth in a prosperous German family. . . . [The author] provides a well-researched account of Marx's life and his work." Booklist

Includes bibliographical references

Matisse, Henri

★ Fillion, Susan. **Miss** Etta and Dr. Claribel; Bringing Matisse to America. David R. Godine 2011 83p il $18.95

Grades: 4 5 6 7   **92**

1. Artists 2. Painters 3. Physicians 4. Art collectors 5. Art -- Collectors and collecting

ISBN 978-1-56792-434-3; 1-56792-434-4

LC 2010048937

"An affectionate, lively examination of the reciprocal relationship between a great artist and two great art lovers. Etta and Claribel Cone, unmarried sisters from a wealthy Baltimore family . . . [were] discerning collectors of modern art, particularly that of Henri Matisse. . . . Their account is lavishly illustrated in full color by reproductions from the Cone Collection at the Baltimore Museum of Art and Matisse-inflected paintings by the author, who drew extensively on the Cone archive that is also housed at the museum. . . . This appealing work stands as both a portrait of two unconventional women and a celebration of the possibilties of arts patronage." Kirkus

Welton, Jude. **Henri** Matisse. Watts 2002 46p il (Artists in their time) $22; pa $6.95

Grades: 5 6 7 8   **92**
1. Artists 2. Painters 3. Artists, French
ISBN 0-531-12228-X; 0-531-16621-X pa
LC 2002-69106

Discusses the life and career of this French artist, describing and giving examples of his work

This offers a "clear and lively [text]. . . . Captioned, full-color and black-and-white photographs and art reproductions are liberally scattered throughout." SLJ

Mawson, Douglas Sir, 1882-1958

Bredeson, Carmen. **After** the last dog died; the true-life, hair-raising adventure of Douglas Mawson and his 1912 Antarctic Expedition. National Geographic 2003 63p il map $18.95
Grades: 5 6 7 8   **92**
1. Explorers 2. Geologists 3. Mountaineers 4. Antarctica -- Exploration
ISBN 0-7922-6140-2
LC 2003-0756

Describes the life and career of the Australian explorer, Sir Douglas Mawson, focusing on his 1912 scientific expedition to Antarctica

"Bredson's compelling story of courage and survival draws heavily on quotes from Mawson and other primary source documents; there are also charts, maps, and many photographs." Booklist

McCain, John S., 1936-

Robinson, Tom. **John** McCain; POW & statesman. ABDO Pub. 2010 112p il map (Military heroes) lib bdg $22.95
Grades: 7 8 9   **92**
1. Prisoners of war 2. Senators 3. Members of Congress 4. Presidential candidates 5. Politicians -- United States 6. United States -- Congress -- Senate
ISBN 978-1-60453-963-9; 1-60453-963-1
LC 2009-32369

"The rush of literary adrenalin will hook readers immediately and keep them enthralled until the end. . . . Given the dynamic topic [and] . . . appealing layout . . . [this is] likely to attract reluctant readers. In addition, sources are plentiful and well documented." SLJ

Includes glossary and bibliographical references

McCarthy, Joseph, 1908-1957

★ Giblin, James Cross, 1933- The **rise** and fall of Senator Joe McCarthy; [by] James Cross Giblin. Clarion Books 2009 294p il $22.00
Grades: 8 9 10 11 12   **92**
1. Anticommunist movements 2. Senators 3. United States -- History -- 1953-1961 4. Biography, Individual
ISBN 0-618-61058-8; 978-0-618-61058-7
LC 2009015005

Giblin examines the life of Joseph Mccarthy, the junior senator from Wisconsin. The book "discusses the Cold War tensions that shaped his beliefs and the unconstitutional methods he used to further his ends." (Publisher's note)

"YAs will see the contemporary parallels in this biography of the anti-Communist crusader who rose to power over 50 years ago. . . . Giblin's title, formatted with an open, photo-filled design and written in easy, direct style,

makes no superficial connections, and the afterword, 'Another McCarthy?' will prompt discussion about the accusations of terrorism in the aftermath of 9/11. Just as memorable is the scathing commentary from famous journalist Edward Murrow about the differences between dissent and disloyalty." Booklist

Includes bibliographical references

McCartney, Stella

Aldridge, Rebecca. **Stella** McCartney. Chelsea House 2011 112p il (Famous fashion designers) lib bdg $35
Grades: 6 7 8 9 10   **92**
1. Fashion designers
ISBN 978-1-60413-982-2; 1-60413-982-X
LC 2010033972

A biography of fashion designer Stella McCartney.

"Biography collections in need of a bit of sprucing up should find [this title] helpful." SLJ

Includes glossary and bibliographical references

McClintock, Barbara

Spangenburg, Ray. **Barbara** McClintock; pioneering geneticist. by Ray Spangenburg and Diane Kit Moser. Chelsea House 2008 xxi, 136p il (Makers of modern science) $29.95
Grades: 8 9 10 11 12   **92**
1. Genetics 2. Women scientists 3. Geneticists 4. Nobel laureates for physiology or medicine
ISBN 978-0-8160-6172-3; 0-8160-6172-6
LC 2006032356

A biography of the Nobel Prize winning geneticist.

"These in-depth accounts detail the accomplishments of two pioneering scientists as well as the research fields (immunology and virology, genetics) to which they made major contributions. The texts are dense, but, notably, the books reveal the inner workings of academic science in the twentieth century, where both intense competition and collaboration aided the quest for knowledge. Black-and-white illustrations and photographs are included." Horn Book

Includes glossary and bibliographical references

McMullan, James

McMullan, James. **Leaving** China; an artist paints his World War II childhood. James McMullan. Algonquin Young Readers 2014 128 p. color illustrations (alk. paper) $19.95
Grades: 7 8 9 10 11 12   **92**
1. Artists 2. World War, 1939-1945 -- Art and the war 3. China -- History -- 1937-1945 -- Anecdotes 4. Illustrators -- United States -- Biography 5. Children of missionaries -- China -- Biography 6. World War, 1939-1945 -- Personal narratives, American
ISBN 1616202556; 9781616202552
LC 2013035241

"A memoir of celebrated artist McMullan's early years, from age 2 to 11. His was a hopscotch childhood, thanks to WWII. Born in 1934 in Tsingtao, China, he subsequently lived in Shanghai, Canada, India, then China and Canada again and, finally, in the U.S. 'My mother and I were now wanderers,' he writes. 'Not yet attached to any particular place.' His life was not always a happy story; his mother was a deep depressive who abused alcohol, and his strict, British military-officer father died in a plane wreck. Moreover, he had a self-described nervous, timid, introspective personality, but he found much comfort in the intelligence of his visual surroundings, and, accordingly, his story is informed by a keen sense of place. The book consists of 54 chronologically arranged full-page illustrations, each accompanied by a facing page of text. The exquisite full-color pictures are filled with air and space, reminiscent of the Chinese scrolls that fascinated McMullan as a child. These pictures and the evocative text are a happy exercise in harmony. A fascinating, seamless portrait of a young life and the wartime world that will have appeal not only to young readers but to adults as well." Booklist

Includes bibliographical references and index

Meir, Golda, 1898-1978

Blashfield, Jean F. **Golda** Meir. Marshall Cavendish Benchmark 2010 112p il (Leading women) $39.93

Grades: 5 6 7 8   92

1. Diplomats 2. Prime ministers 3. Women politicians 4. Cabinet members 5. Israel -- History 6. Jews -- Biography

ISBN 978-0-7614-4960-7; 0-7614-4960-4

"Meir survived pogroms in Russia as a child and became prime minister of Israel. . . . The [woman's life is] revealed within the political and historical context of [her] times and [includes] quotes from autobiographical material. . . . Color and black-and-white photos are included. . . . The compact size, chronological organization, and accessible writing [style makes this biography a] good [resource] for reports." SLJ

Includes bibliographical references

Meltzer, Milton, 1915-2009

★ Meltzer, Milton. **Milton** Meltzer; writing matters. Franklin Watts 2004 160p il lib bdg $29

Grades: 7 8 9 10   92

1. Authors 2. Historians 3. Biographers 4. Authors, American 5. Children's authors 6. Nonfiction writers

ISBN 0-531-12257-3

LC 2004-2947

"The author includes clear, interesting explanations about the American historical and economic events that influenced his life. While this book is a pleasure to read for general interest, it would also supplement units on American history." SLJ

Includes bibliographical references

Menchú, Rigoberta

Kallen, Stuart A. **Rigoberta** Menchu, Indian rights activist; by Stuart A. Kallen. Lucent Books 2007 104p il (The 20th century's most influential Hispanics) $31.20

Grades: 6 7 8 9   92

1. Mayas 2. Guatemala 3. Memoirists 4. Indian leaders 5. Human rights activists 6. Nobel laureates for peace 7. Native Americans -- Civil rights

ISBN 1-59018-975-2

LC 2006025690

Presents the life and accomplishments of the human rights activist who won the Noble Peace Prize in 1992 for her work to stop the oppression of her people, the Mayas of Guatemala.

This is a "stirring biography. . . . The selection of photos and captions enhance the text." SLJ

Includes bibliographical references

Mendel, Gregor, 1822-1884

Van Gorp, Lynn. **Gregor** Mendel; genetics pioneer. science contributor, Sally Ride Science. Compass Point Books 2008 40p il (Mission: Science) lib bdg $26.60

Grades: 4 5 6   92

1. Genetics 2. Scientists 3. Geneticists

ISBN 978-0-7565-3963-4 lib bdg; 0-7565-3963-3 lib bdg

LC 2008-07725

A biography of scientist Gregor Mendel, with an introduction to the principles of genetics

This "will entice students to become excited about an assignment or just satisfy their own curiosity. . . . The text . . . does a good job of connecting the scientist's work to our lives today. . . . [The] book has a variety of graphics including diagrams, [and] photos." Libr Media Connect

Mendes, Chico

Murphy, Alexa Gordon. **Chico** Mendes. Chelsea House 2011 126p il (Conservation heroes) lib bdg $35

Grades: 6 7 8 9   92

1. Rubber 2. Rain forests 3. Conservationists 4. Social activists 5. Amazon River valley

ISBN 978-1-60413-951-8; 1-60413-951-X

LC 2010030590

A biography of the Brazilian rubber tapper, trade union leader and environmentalist who fought to preserve the Amazon rainforest

"Captivating, richly informative. . . . The scope of [this book] is comprehensive. . . . [The book is] engaging as [it is] educational and will be ideal for research and reports." SLJ

Includes glossary and bibliographical references

Mercator, Gerardus, 1512-1594

Heinrichs, Ann. **Gerardus** Mercator; father of modern mapmaking. by Ann Heinrichs. Compass Point Books 2008 112p il map (Signature lives) lib bdg $31.93

Grades: 6 7 8 9   92

1. Maps 2. Cartographers

ISBN 978-0-7565-3312-0 lib bdg; 0-7565-3312-0 lib bdg

LC 2007004902

A biography of the sixteenth-century geographer who created a world map in 1569 which introduced a new way of showing the spherical earth on a flat sheet of paper.

"Clear explanations of scientific thought and fact are presented in conversational tones and illuminated by easily grasped examples. . . . [The book includes] sidebars, maps, and well-captioned illustrations." SLJ

Includes glossary and bibliographical references

Mexia, Ynes, 1870-1938

Anema, Durlynn. **Ynes** Mexia, botanist and adventurer; [by] Durlynn Anema. 1st ed; Morgan Reynolds Pub. 2005 144p il (Women adventurers) lib bdg $26.95

Grades: 6 7 8 9   92

1. Botanists 2. Explorers 3. Women scientists 4. Mexican Americans -- Biography

ISBN 1-931798-67-2; 978-1-931798-67-9

LC 2005010694

A biography of the botanist who traveled on expeditions throughout South America and Mexico during the 1920s and collected over 500 new plant species.

"An interesting and colorful look at a Mexican-American scientist. The easy-to-read narrative draws on the woman's correspondences." SLJ

Includes bibliographical references

Michelangelo Buonarroti, 1475-1564

Spence, David. **Michelangelo**; [written by David Spence]; editor Guy Croton. North American ed.; New Forest Press 2010 48p il map (Great artists & their world) lib bdg $32.80

Grades: 6 7 8 9   92

1. Artists 2. Painters 3. Sculptors 4. Architects 5. Artists, Italian 6. Art -- 15th and 16th centuries

ISBN 978-1-84898-309-0; 1-84898-309-3

LC 2010925210

Explores the world, art, and life of the great Italian artist. Includes glossary and bibliographical references

Milk, Harvey

Aretha, David. **No** compromise: the story of Harvey Milk. Morgan Reynolds 2010 128p il (Civil rights leaders) lib bdg $28.95

Grades: 7 8 9 10 11 12   92

1. Gay rights activists 2. Gay men -- Civil rights 3. Local government officials

ISBN 1-59935-129-3; 978-1-59935-129-2

LC 2009-25708

This is a biography of the gay-rights activist and San Francisco politician who was killed in 1973.

This is written "with simple and engaging prose. . . . Full-color and black-and-white photos are interspersed thoughout, giving a sense of the time period." SLJ

Miller, Arthur, 1915-2005

Andersen, Richard. **Arthur** Miller. Marshall Cavendish Benchmark 2005 144p il (Writers and their works) lib bdg $25.95

Grades: 7 8 9 10   92

1. Authors 2. Dramatists 3. Screenwriters 4. Authors, American

ISBN 0-7614-1946-2

This "attractive, well-organized [book fills] a gap in literary criticism for intermediate readers. Heavily illustrated with color and black-and-white photographs, [it] will appeal to students who might be intimidated by longer or more scholarly titles." SLJ

Mitchell, Maria, 1818-1889

Anderson, Dale. **Maria** Mitchell, astronomer. Chelsea House 2003 110p il (Women in science) $22.95

Grades: 7 8 9 10   92

1. Astronomers 2. Women astronomers 3. College teachers

ISBN 0-7910-7249-5

LC 2002-13738

Profiles a Vassar professor who was one of the most famous astronomers in the United States at the end of the nineteenth century and whose central message to her students was never cease to wonder

"Color prints or photographs with brief descriptions are interspersed throughout and add considerably to the [text]." Libr Media Connect

Includes bibliographical references

Gormley, Beatrice. **Maria** Mitchell; the soul of an astronomer. [by] Beatrice Gormley. Eerdmans Books for Young Readers 2004 137p il pa $12

Grades: 7 8 9 10   92

1. Astronomers 2. Women astronomers 3. College teachers

ISBN 978-0-8028-5264-9 pa; 0-8028-5264-5 pa

First published 1995

A biography of the first female science professor at Vassar College and the first American woman astronomer

"With a smoothly flowing and lively style, this biography introduces readers to the 19th-century astronomer. Well-chosen, primary-source quotations and quality black-and-white photos add authenticity to the text, and contribute greatly to the author's objective and comprehensive description of Mitchell's accomplishments." SLJ [review of 1995 edition]

Includes bibliographical references

Mizrahi, Isaac

Petrillo, Lisa. **Isaac** Mizrahi. Morgan Reynolds Pub. 2011 111p il $28.95

Grades: 7 8 9 10   92

1. Fashion designers 2. Television personalities 3. Talk show hosts

ISBN 978-1-59935-152-0; 1-59935-152-8

LC 2010018312

This biography of Isaac Mizrahi discusses "the designer's cultural background, childhood, family, work history and education. The [author describes] the early influences that inspired the [designer] to pursue this career and [provides] details of the philosophy [the] designer uses to make [his] clothing unique. . . . The writing is clear and well organized. Color photos are included and give readers a feel for the time period and the types of clothing and accessories the [designer] created." Voice Youth Advocates

Includes bibliographical references

Mohapatra, Jyotirmayee, 1978-

Woog, Adam. **Jyotirmayee** Mohapatra; by Adam Woog. KidHaven Press 2006 48p il $24.95

Grades: 4 5 6 7   92

1. Social action 2. Feminists 3. Women -- India 4.

Children's rights advocates
ISBN 0-7377-3611-9

LC 2006009121

"Mohapatra grew up in a rural village in India and became a leader in the fight for the rights of girls and women. . . . The power of one individual to inspire others to action is clearly expressed in this well-written profile. Full-color photos and a map enhance the presentation." SLJ

Includes bibliographical references

Molnar, Haya Leah

Molnar, Haya Leah. **Under** a red sky; memoir of a childhood in Communist Romania. Farrar Straus Giroux 2010 302p il $17.99

Grades: 6 7 8 9 10   92

1. Copywriters 2. Jews -- Romania 3. Advertising executives
ISBN 978-0-374-31840-6; 0-374-31840-9

LC 2008055562

"Molnar began life as Eva Zimmerman . . . in Bucharest, Romania. . . . It came as a huge shock to Molnar when she learned in 1958 that her entire family had applied to emigrate to Israel and that she was Jewish. . . . As Eva pieces together her family's history, a vivid story emerges, ranging from funny, tender moments of family life to the horrific revelations of the Romanian holocaust. . . . Black-and-white family photos illustrate this poignant, memorable offering." Booklist

Monaque, Mathilde

Monaque, Mathilde. **Trouble** in my head; a young girl's fight with depression. translated by Lorenza Garcia. Trafalgar Square 2009 167p pa $15.95

Grades: 7 8 9 10   92

1. Depression (Psychology)
ISBN 978-0-09-191723-4 pa; 0-09-191723-9 pa

"Monaque tells her own story of depression, which began at age 14. Recounting her experience from memory, the teen attempts to discern what caused the illness as well as to explain the process she went through to overcome it. . . . She is bright and articulate and paints a vivid picture of what depression feels like from the inside." SLJ

Monet, Claude, 1840-1926

Kallen, Stuart A. **Claude** Monet. Lucent Books 2009 112p il (Eye on art) lib bdg $32.45

Grades: 7 8 9 10   92

1. Artists 2. Painters 3. Artists, French 4. Impressionism (Art)
ISBN 978-1-4205-0074-5; 1-4205-0074-0

LC 2008-20640

An introduction to the life and career of the artist Claude Monet, and how he painted his way into history.

"This biography paints a clear picture of the artist's life, work, and legacy. . . . The accompanying color reproductions of the artworks and black-and-white photographs of Monet contribute to the book's clean and attractive design. . . . This work stands out as a balanced description of the man's legacy and an enjoyable read." SLJ

Includes glossary and bibliographical references

Spence, David. **Monet**. New Forest Press 2010 48p il (Great artists and their world) lib bdg $32.80

Grades: 6 7 8 9   92

1. Artists 2. Painters 3. Artists, French
ISBN 978-1-848983-12-0; 1-848983-12-3

"This slender title offers a thorough introduction to Oscar Claude Monet, who, before helping to found the French Impressionist movement, was known for his sharp-eyed, witty caricature drawings. . . . The spreads cover a wide range of topics, all presented in short paragraphs and long captions that accompany the multiple, mostly well-reproduced artwork and archival photos on every page." Booklist

Monroe, James, 1758-1831

Naden, Corinne J. **James** Monroe; [by] Corinne J. Naden and Rose Blue. Marshall Cavendish Benchmark 2009 96p il map (Presidents and their times) lib bdg $34.21

Grades: 5 6 7 8   92

1. Presidents 2. Secretaries of state 3. Presidents -- United States
ISBN 978-0-7614-2838-1 lib bdg; 0-7614-2838-0 lib bdg

LC 2007-29480

"Provides comprehensive information on President James Monroe and places him within his historical and cultural context. Also explored are the formative events of his times and how he responded." Publisher's note

Includes glossary and bibliographical references

Mora, Pat

Marcovitz, Hal. **Pat** Mora; [by] Hal Marcovitz; forward by Kyle Zimmer. Chelsea House 2008 134p il (Who wrote that?) $30

Grades: 6 7 8 9   92

1. Poets 2. Authors 3. Women authors 4. Mexican American authors 5. Essayists 6. Poets, American 7. College teachers 8. Children's authors 9. Young adult authors 10. Museum administrators 11. College administrators 12. Mexican Americans -- Biography
ISBN 978-0-7910-9528-7; 0-7910-9528-2

LC 2007019452

This biography examines the "writer's life, including the inspiration behind some of [her] works. [The] volume includes photographs and quotations from interviews, as well as descriptions of main characters and annotated lists of books and awards. Useful for aspiring authors as well as book report writers." Horn Book Guide

Includes bibliographical references

Mozart, Wolfgang Amadeus, 1756-1791

Riggs, Kate. **Wolfgang** Amadeus Mozart. Creative Education 2009 48p il (Xtraordinary artists) lib bdg $32.80

Grades: 4 5 6 7   92

1. Composers
ISBN 978-1-58341-664-8 lib bdg; 1-58341-664-1 lib bdg

LC 2007008963

This biography of the composer offers an "interesting [layout]; big, high-quality reproductions and photographs on heavy paper; insightful quotes from diverse sources; and meaty selections of the artist's own writing . . . at the end of the book. Readers get a strong sense of [Mozart's] personality along with an excellent survey of his work." SLJ

Includes bibliographical references

Weeks, Marcus. **Mozart**; the boy who changed the world with his music. [by] Marcus Weeks. National Geographic 2007 64p il map (World history biographies) $17.95; lib bdg $27.90

Grades: 5 6 7 8   **92**

1. Composers

ISBN 978-1-4263-0002-8; 1-4263-0002-6; 978-1-4263-0003-5 lib bdg; 1-4263-0003-4 lib bdg

          LC 2006020783

An introduction to the life and music of the composer and musician Mozart.

This "visually appealing [title is] packed with excellent photographs and reproductions, interesting sidebars, and have a time line running along the bottom of every page. . . . [The book is] useful, well-written." SLJ

Includes bibliographical references

Mozes, Miriam, 1935-1993

Kor, Eva Mozes. **Surviving** the Angel of Death; the story of a Mengele twin in Auschwitz. [by] Eva Mozes Kor and Lisa Rojany Buccieri. Tanglewood Pub. 2009 141p il map $14.95

Grades: 7 8 9 10   **92**

1. Twins 2. Holocaust survivors 3. Jews -- Hungary 4. Jews -- Persecutions 5. Holocaust, 1933-1945 -- Personal narratives

ISBN 978-1-933718-28-6; 1-933718-28-5

          LC 2009-9494

"Born in 1934, Eva and her identical twin, Miriam, were loved and doted over. They lived a comfortable and happy life on their family's farm in Transylvania until the summer of 1940, when their family was herded onto a train with the other Jews in their town and transported to Auschwitz supposedly for their 'protection.' . . . They soon joined a large group of other twins who were under the care of Dr. Josef Mengele, otherwise known as the Angel of Death. . . . Eva's story will have the reader hooked until the very end. . . . This book is an essential purchase for libraries with a Holocaust collection, but it would also be a valuable addition to any library with young impressionable readers." Voice Youth Advocates

Muir, John, 1838-1914

Goldstein, Natalie. **John** Muir. Chelsea House 2011 139p il (Conservation heroes) lib bdg $35

Grades: 6 7 8 9   **92**

1. Authors 2. Naturalists 3. Conservationists 4. Nature conservation 5. Writers on nature

ISBN 978-1-60413-945-7; 1-60413-945-5

          LC 2010030582

This is a biography of naturalist John Muir, who founded the Sierra Club and helped save forest areas in the American West.

"Captivating, richly informative. . . . The scope of [this book] is comprehensive. . . . [The book is] engaging as [it is] educational and will be ideal for research and reports." SLJ

Includes glossary and bibliographical references

Naden, Corinne J. **John** Muir; saving the wilderness. [by] Corinne J. Naden and Rose Blue. Millbrook Press 1992 48p il (Gateway biography) hardcover o.p. pa $9.95

Grades: 4 5 6 7   **92**

1. Authors 2. Naturalists 3. Nature conservation 4. Writers on nature

ISBN 1-56294-797-4 pa

          LC 91-18106

This book profiles the life and times of naturalist John Muir

"Attractively designed with clear framed text and lots of photographs. . . . Kids will be intrigued by Muir's work for conservation, especially his role in founding the national parks." Booklist

Includes bibliographical references

Munch, Edvard, 1863-1944

Whiting, Jim. **Edvard** Munch; by Jim Whiting. Mitchell Lane 2009 48p il (Art profiles for kids) lib bdg $20.95

Grades: 7 8 9 10   **92**

1. Artists 2. Painters 3. Artists, Norwegian

ISBN 978-1-58415-712-0; 1-58415-712-7

          LC 2008-2250

"The profile of Munch explains how the artist attempted to convey his deep feelings of anxiety in his paintings. . . . [Goes] beyond basic facts, providing historical context and significance of the art and the artist. . . . Provide[s] plenty of information for reports in a reader-friendly format." SLJ

Includes glossary and bibliographical references

Murakami, Haruki, 1949-

Mussari, Mark. **Haruki** Murakami. Marshall Cavendish Benchmark 2010 127p il (Today's writers and their works) lib bdg $42.79

Grades: 8 9 10 11 12   **92**

1. Authors 2. Novelists 3. Authors, Japanese 4. Nonfiction writers 5. Short story writers

ISBN 978-0-7614-4124-3; 0-7614-4124-7

This biography of Haruki Murakami places the author in the context of his times and discusses his work.

"High-school students who need an analysis of a literary work or writer may want to check out the Today's Writers and Their Works series. This group is particularly multicultural: a white American man, a Mexican American woman, a Chinese man, and a British biracial woman. Each book begins with a biography of the author and then discusses major works with plot summaries and analysis of main characters." Horn Book

Includes bibliographical references

Myers, Walter Dean, 1937-2014

Sickels, Amy. **Walter** Dean Myers; [by] Amy Sickels. Chelsea House 2008 128p il (Who wrote that?) $30

Grades: 6 7 8 9   92
1. Poets 2. Authors 3. Novelists 4. African American authors 5. Editors 6. Authors, American 7. Children's authors 8. Young adult authors
ISBN 978-0-7910-9524-9; 0-7910-9524-X
LC 2007045507
This biography examines the "writer's life, including the inspiration behind some if [his] works. [The] volume includes photographs and quotations from interviews, as well as descriptions of main characters and annotated lists of books and awards. Useful for aspiring authors as well as book report writers." Horn Book Guide
Includes bibliographical references

Nakahama, Manjirō, 1827-1898

★ Blumberg, Rhoda. **Shipwrecked!** : the true adventures of a Japanese boy. HarperCollins Pubs. 2000 80p il map hardcover o.p. pa $7.99
Grades: 5 6 7 8   92
1. Survival after airplane accidents, shipwrecks, etc. 2. Interpreters 3. Japan -- History 4. Japan -- Foreign relations -- United States 5. United States -- Foreign relations -- Japan
ISBN 0-688-17484-1; 0-688-17485-X pa
LC 99-86664
In 1841, rescued by an American whaler after a terrible shipwreck leaves him and his four companions castaways on a remote island, fourteen-year-old Manjiro learns new laws and customs as he becomes the first Japanese person to set foot in the United States
"Exemplary in both her research and writing, Blumberg hooks readers with anecdotes that astonish without sensationalizing, and she uses language that's elegant and challenging, yet always clear. Particularly notable is the well-chosen reproductions of original artwork." Booklist
Includes bibliographical references

Napoleon I, Emperor of the French, 1769-1821

Burleigh, Robert. **Napoleon**; the story of the little corporal. Abrams Books for Young Readers 2007 43p il map $18.95
Grades: 4 5 6 7   92
1. Emperors 2. France -- Kings and rulers 3. France -- History -- 1799-1815
ISBN 978-0-8109-1378-3; 0-8109-1378-X
LC 2006-23610
"Burleigh's straightforward style and clear focus make accessible this account of the rapid rise and fall of the skilled military leader and emperor of France. The period artwork, accompanied by helpful captions, enhances the cleanly designed presentation." Horn Book Guide

Nefertiti, Queen, consort of Akhenaton, King of Egypt, 14th cent. B.C.

Lange, Brenda. **Nefertiti**. Chelsea House Publishers 2009 108p bibl il (Ancient world leaders) lib bdg $30
Grades: 6 7 8 9   92
1. Queens 2. Egypt -- History
ISBN 978-0-7910-9581-2 lib bdg; 0-7910-9581-9 lib bdg
LC 2008004869

This biography of Nefertiti "deals less with the specifics of the [ancient Egyptian queen] and more with [her world] and times, including religious and political issues. The [author uses] speculation, derived from both tradition and scholarship, as to who [this] ancient [leader] may have been and how [she] might have governed." SLJ
Includes bibliographical references

Neruda, Pablo, 1904-1973

Delano, Poli. **When** I was a boy Neruda called me Policarpo; illustrated by Manuel Monroy. Groundwood Books/House of Anansi Press 2006 84p il $15.95
Grades: 5 6 7 8   92
1. Poets 2. Authors 3. Diplomats 4. Novelists 5. Poets, Chilean 6. Mexico 7. Memoirists 8. Short story writers 9. Nobel laureates for peace 10. Nobel laureates for literature
ISBN 0-88899-726-4
In this book, the author "offers seven vignettes, interspersed with six of Neruda's . . . poems and biographical information, to give middle-grade readers a sense of what it was like to grow up in the constant presence of a kindly, though spoiled and eccentric, celebrity. . . . Grades four to six." (MultiCult Rev)
"Based on the author's childhood remembrances of when he and his diplomat parents lived with Tío Pablo [Neruda] in Mexico, these seven chapters reveal both the genius and the eccentricities of the Nobel Prize-winning Chilean poet. . . . The chapters are short, well written, and filled with interesting details that will open up a new and exotic world. . . . Monroy's pen-and-sepia-toned drawings are . . . . at times humorous, at times dramatic, but always enticing." SLJ

Shull, Jodie A. **Pablo** Neruda; passion, poetry, politics. [by] Jodie A. Shull. Enslow Publishers 2009 128p bibl il por (Latino biography library) lib bdg $31.93
Grades: 6 7 8 9   92
1. Authors 2. Diplomats 3. Novelists 4. Poets, Chilean 5. Nobel laureates for peace 6. Nobel laureates for literature
ISBN 978-0-7660-2966-8; 0-7660-2966-2
LC 2008008698
This book contains information about Pablo Neruda: "After openly denouncing the president of Chile in 1948, Pablo Neruda was declared an enemy of his own country. Despite being forced into exile for three years, Neruda maintained his political views. Nothing could deter Neruda from these beliefs or his most celebrated passion-poetry. Author Jodie A. Shull explores the life of this talented writer from his childhood in the Chilean rainforests to winning the Nobel Prize for Literature." Publisher's note.
Includes bibliographical references

Newton, Isaac Sir, 1642-1727

Hollihan, Kerrie Logan. **Isaac** Newton and physics for kids; his life and ideas with 21 activities. Chicago Review Press 2009 131p il map pa $16.95
Grades: 4 5 6 7   92
1. Physicists 2. Scientists 3. Mathematicians 4.

Writers on science
ISBN 978-1-55652-778-4 pa; 1-55652-778-0 pa
LC 2008048635

"Hollihan introduces readers to the scientific brilliance, as well as the social isolation, of this giant figure, blending a readable narrative with an attractive format that incorporates maps, diagrams, historical photographs, and physics activities." Booklist

Includes bibliographical references

★ Krull, Kathleen. **Isaac** Newton; illustrated by Boris Kulikov. Viking 2006 126p il (Giants of science) $15.99
Grades: 5 6 7 8   **92**
1. Physicists 2. Scientists 3. Mathematicians 4. Writers on science
ISBN 0-670-05921-8
LC 2005017741

This "profiles Sir Isaac Newton, the secretive, obsessive, and brilliant English scientist who invented calculus, built the first reflecting telescope, developed the modern scientific method, and discerned many of our laws of physics and optics. . . . The lively, conversational style will appeal to readers. . . . Kulikov's humorous pen-and-ink drawings complement the lighthearted text of this fascinating introduction." Booklist

Steele, Philip. **Isaac** Newton; the scientist who changed everything. [by] Philip Steele. National Geographic Society 2007 64p il map (World history biographies) $17.95; lib bdg $27.90
Grades: 4 5 6 7   **92**
1. Physicists 2. Scientists 3. Mathematicians 4. Writers on science
ISBN 978-1-4263-0114-8; 978-1-4263-0115-5 lib bdg
LC 2006020772

"The cradle-to-grave text includes vivid descriptions of Newton's youth. . . . The dynamic format is a draw; numerous mostly archival images . . . and a time-line border add interest and cultural context on each spacious page." Booklist

Includes bibliographical references

Nezahualcóyotl, King of Texcoco, 1402-1472
★ Serrano, Francisco. The **poet** king of Texcoco; a great leader of Ancient Mexico. illustrated by Pablo Serrano; biography translated and adapted by Trudy Balch; poetry translated by Jo Anne Engelbert. Groundwood Books/House of Anansi Press 2007 35p il $18.95
Grades: 4 5 6 7   **92**
1. Aztecs 2. Kings 3. Mexico -- History
ISBN 978-0-88899-787-6; 0-88899-787-6

"In the fifteenth century, the land where Mexico City now sprawls was a vast, green kingdom called Tezcoco. This . . . introduces one of Tezcoco's greatest rulers, a Toltec royal named Nezahualcoyotl. . . . The folk-art inspired illustrations echo the area's artistic traditions with beautiful patterning and symbolic imagery and flat , simplified characters reminiscent of hieroglyphics. Groundbreaking in its coverage of exciting history, this book offers details that are rarely presented to young people." Booklist

Nixon, Richard M. (Richard Milhous), 1913-1994
★ Aronson, Billy. **Richard** M. Nixon; [by] Billy Aronson. Marshall Cavendish Benchmark 2007 96p il (Presidents and their times) lib bdg $22.95
Grades: 5 6 7 8   **92**
1. Presidents 2. Vice-presidents 3. Senators 4. Nonfiction writers 5. Members of Congress 6. Presidents -- United States
ISBN 978-0-7614-2428-4
LC 2006013839

Aronson "is able to paint a picture so full that readers will come away feeling that they know the man and understand at least some of the forces that shaped him. . . . The narrative moves chronologically, marching through the war years, Nixon's tenure in Congress and as vice-president, his presidential loss to JFK, his successful efforts to remake himself as a politician, and his years as president. . . . The typeface is clear, the photographs are well chosen." Booklist

Includes glossary and bibliographical references

Noguchi, Isamu, 1904-1988
Tiger, Caroline. **Isamu** Noguchi. Chelsea House 2007 112p bibl il por (Asian Americans of achievement) lib bdg $30
Grades: 6 7 8 9   **92**
1. Artists 2. Sculptors 3. Industrial designers 4. Japanese Americans -- Biography
ISBN 0-7910-9276-3 lib bdg; 978-0-7910-9276-7 lib bdg
LC 2006026230

A biography of the artist, born in 1904 to an American mother and a Japanese poet father, who created sculpture, furniture, stage sets, and public gardens.

"This engaging account of the prolific and diverse artist will add depth to any biography collection." SLJ

Includes bibliographical references

Nuñez Cabeza de Vaca, Alvar, 16th cent.
Childress, Diana. **Barefoot** conquistador; Cabeza de Vaca and the struggle for Native American rights. Twenty-First Century Books 2008 160p il map lib bdg $30.60
Grades: 7 8 9 10   **92**
1. Explorers 2. Historians 3. Travel writers 4. Government officials 5. America -- Exploration 6. Colonial administrators
ISBN 978-0-8225-7517-7; 0-8225-7517-5
LC 2007-22059

"This clearly written biography introduces a 16th-century Spanish explorer who made two expeditions to North and South America and eventually became a champion for Native Americans. . . . Childress's well-researched, lively text will fascinate readers. . . . The pages are sprinkled with period illustrations and maps." SLJ

Includes bibliographical references

Lourie, Peter. **On** the Texas trail of Cabeza de Vaca; 1st ed.; Boyds Mills Press 2008 48p il map $17.95
Grades: 4 5 6 7   **92**
1. Explorers 2. Historians 3. Travel writers 4. Texas

-- History 5. Mexico -- History 6. Government officials
7. America -- Exploration 8. Colonial administrators
ISBN 978-1-59078-492-1; 1-59078-492-8

LC 2007049180

"In 1527, Governor Pánfilo de Narváez sailed westward from Spain to explore the land that stretched between present-day Florida and Mexico, colonizing and conquering. With him, as his treasurer and sheriff, was Cabeza de Vaca. . . . He [returned] with a wealth of information, codified in La Relación , his account of his experience. Then, 475 years later, Lourie set out to follow Cabeza de Vaca's trail through Texas. . . . This well-researched, beautifully composed book is the result. Using primary sources and period reproductions as well as the author's experiences and contemporary pictures, it highlights historical information within the context of current circumstances. Beautifully placed photos, reproductions, maps, and sidebars enhance the fluid text." SLJ

Includes bibliographical references

Nye, Naomi Shihab, 1952-

Nye, Naomi Shihab. **I'll** ask you three times, are you ok? tales of driving and being driven. Greenwillow Books 2007 242p $15.99; lib bdg $16.89

Grades: 7 8 9 10 11 12   **92**

1. Poets 2. Authors 3. Voyages and travels 4. Editors 5. Essayists 6. Children's authors
ISBN 978-0-06-085392-1; 978-0-06-085393-8 lib bdg

LC 2006-36548

The author "writes about sudden intimate connections with strangers, especially taxi drivers, who often yield glimpses of family and exile that can sometimes change us. . . . The prose is chatty, fast, and unpretentious, and teens will enjoy the driving stuff and the idea of her kissing in the backseat, and they'll feel her sense of control when she is behind the wheel herself." Booklist

O'Connor, Sandra Day

Abrams, Dennis. **Sandra** Day O'Connor; U.S. Supreme Court Justice. Chelsea House 2009 136p il (Women of achievement) $30

Grades: 6 7 8 9   **92**

1. Judges 2. Supreme Court justices
ISBN 978-1-60413-337-0; 1-60413-337-6

LC 2008055367

A biography of the first woman U. S. Supreme Court Justice.

Includes bibliographical references

O'Dell, Scott, 1898-1989

Marcovitz, Hal. **Scott** O'Dell; [by] Hal Marcovitz; foreword by Kyle Zimmer. Chelsea House 2008 128p il (Who wrote that?) lib bdg $30

Grades: 6 7 8 9   **92**

1. Authors 2. Novelists 3. Authors, American 4. Children's authors 5. Nonfiction writers 6. Short story writers 7. Young adult authors
ISBN 978-0-7910-9526-3 lib bdg; 0-7910-9526-6 lib bdg

LC 2007019577

This biography examines the "writer's life, including the inspiration behind some of [his] works. [The] volume includes photographs and quotations from interviews, as well as descriptions of main characters and annotated lists of books and awards. Useful for aspiring authors as well as book report writers." Horn Book Guide

Includes bibliographical references

O'Keeffe, Georgia, 1887-1986

Rubin, Susan Goldman. **Wideness** and wonder: the life and art of Georgia O'Keeffe. Chronicle Books 2011 117p il $16.99

Grades: 6 7 8 9   **92**

1. Artists 2. Painters 3. Women artists 4. Artists -- United States 5. Biography, Individual
ISBN 0-8118-6983-0; 978-0-8118-6983-6

LC 2010008256

This is a biography of the American artist and a study of her work. Index. "Intermediate, middle school." (Horn Book)

Rubin "here looks at the life and work of Georgia O'Keeffe. Nicely illustrated with family photos, portrait photos by Stieglitz, and many reproductions of the artist's drawings and paintings, the book builds a convincing portrayal of O'Keeffe from her student days to her ultimate recognition as an important American artist. The book's design is striking." Booklist

Includes bibliographical references

Oakley, Annie, 1860-1926

Koestler-Grack, Rachel A. **Annie** Oakley. Chelsea House 2010 102p bibl il por (Legends of the wild west) lib bdg $30

Grades: 6 7 8 9   **92**

1. Entertainers 2. Marksmen 3. West (U.S.) -- History
ISBN 978-1-60413-594-7; 1-60413-594-8

LC 2009041338

"Compelling, sometimes controversial, the lives of these high-profile figures have been wellsprings for speculation and rumor. Here, extensive and thoroughly documented research dispels the myths. Each of the 10- to 12-page chronologically arranged chapters contains a few smaller, boldly captioned sections, such as "In Search of a Wife" and "Deceived Again" in the "Courtin' and Marriage" chapter of Davy Crockett. Though the volumes have several authors, a fluid, straightforward writing style is a series mainstay that makes the figures and the era come alive. The sepia-toned illustrations, most of which are period photographs, corroborate the texts effectively. This is top-notch nonfiction." SLJ

Includes glossary and bibliographical references

Wills, Charles A. **Annie** Oakley: a photographic story of a life; [by] Chuck Wills. DK Pub. 2007 128p il (DK biography) $14.99

Grades: 4 5 6 7   **92**

1. Entertainers 2. Marksmen
ISBN 978-0-7566-2986-1

A biography of the sharp-shooter in Buffalo Bill's Wild West Show, from her humble Quaker heritage, her childhood filled with poverty and abuse, to her rise to international fame.

"This highly readable book has a rich layout of photographs and illustrations on every spread." SLJ

Obama, Barack, 1961-

Abramson, Jill. **Obama**; the historic journey. Young reader's ed.; Callaway 2009 94p il map $24.95

Grades: 5 6 7 8   **92**

1. Lawyers 2. Presidents 3. Racially mixed people 4. Senators 5. State legislators 6. Nobel laureates for peace 7. Presidents -- United States 8. African Americans -- Biography

ISBN 978-0-670-01208-4; 0-670-01208-4

LC 2009-5051

"This scaled down, teen-friendly version of The New York Times's adult biography is geared for middle school students. Containing many of the same photos, it provides a brief overview of the President's life, information that has been revealed over the election year and during his administration. . . . Its allure is in the many photographs with captions, sidebars, speech quotes, and charts. The book is nicely organized. The writing is direct and simple, explaining things such as convention delegates. . . . The book should entice young readers to explore his life further." Voice Youth Advocates

Burgan, Michael. **Barack** Obama. Heinemann Library 2010 112p il (Front-page lives) $38.93

Grades: 6 7 8 9 10   **92**

1. Lawyers 2. Presidents 3. Racially mixed people 4. Senators 5. State legislators 6. Nobel laureates for peace 7. Presidents -- United States 8. African Americans -- Biography

ISBN 978-1-4329-3218-3; 1-4329-3218-7

LC 2009-18176

President Obama's life is "presented with depth and breadth. . . . The writing is accessible and engaging, with color and black-and-white photographs." SLJ

"Focusing on headline makers from the past 20 years or so, this series does not shy away from the controversial topics that are part of what make this grouping of people noteworthy. . . . The writing is accessible and engaging, with color and black-and-white photographs and (except in Obama and Gates) color maps complementing the text." SLJ

Includes glossary and bibliographical references

Gibson, Karen Bush. The **Obama** view; the historic fight for the 2008 Democratic presidential nomination. Mitchell Lane Publishers 2009 il (Monumental milestones) lib bdg $20.95

Grades: 6 7 8 9   **92**

1. Lawyers 2. Presidents 3. Racially mixed people 4. Senators 5. State legislators 6. Nobel laureates for peace 7. African Americans -- Biography 8. Presidents -- United States -- Election -- 2008

ISBN 978-1-5841-5732-8; 1-5841-5732-1

LC 2008053464

This book is "clearly and crisply written. Starting with Obama's career in Illinois politics, the book then details his unlikely journey to the presidency, starting with his childhood in Hawaii and Indonesia. The final chapter deals with the presidential election and doesn't shy away from such issues as the way race was an election subtext. . . .

The design is lively and colorful, and the photos will draw readers." Booklist

Includes bibliographical references

Krensky, Stephen. **Barack** Obama. DK Pub. 2010 128p il map (DK biography) $14.99; pa $5.99

Grades: 6 7 8 9   **92**

1. Lawyers 2. Presidents 3. Racially mixed people 4. Senators 5. State legislators 6. Nobel laureates for peace 7. Presidents -- United States 8. African Americans -- Biography

ISBN 978-0-7566-5804-5; 0-7566-5804-7; 978-0-7566-5805-2 pa; 0-7566-5805-5 pa

LC 2010277785

Presents the life of Barack Obama, including his childhood in the United States and abroad, careers as a community organizer and lawyer, and his election as the forty-fourth president.

"Krensky excels at providing context not only for Obama's election, but also for his unlikely rise to prominence. . . . DK's powerful photographic format and the usual blurbs and sidebars work well at keeping this age group's interest." SLJ

Includes bibliographical references

Obama, Barack. **Dreams** from my father; a story of race and inheritance. Crown Publishers 2007 442p $25.95

Grades: 7 8 9 10 11 12 Adult   **92**

1. Lawyers 2. Presidents 3. Racially mixed people 4. Senators 5. State legislators 6. Nobel laureates for peace 7. Presidents -- United States 8. African Americans -- Biography

ISBN 978-0-307-38341-9

LC 2007-271892

First published 1995 by Times Books

This is the autobiography of the Illinois senator who would later become the 44th president of the United States.

The author "offers an account of his life's journey that reflects brilliantly on the power of race consciousness in America. . . . Obama writes well; his account is sensitive, probing, and compelling." Choice [review of 1995 edition]

Thomas, Garen Eileen. **Yes** we can: a biography of Barack Obama. Feiwel and Friends 2009 236p il map pa $6.99

Grades: 6 7 8 9   **92**

1. Lawyers 2. Presidents 3. Racially mixed people 4. Senators 5. State legislators 6. Nobel laureates for peace 7. Presidents -- United States 8. African Americans -- Biography

ISBN 978-0-312-58639-3 pa; 0-312-58639-6 pa

"The updated edition of this bestselling biography of Barack Obama covers his life from birth through the 2008 Presidential election. . . . [This] is a nice, fast introduction to the nation's current president for those who want more than an encyclopedia article and less then the autobiographical volumes and speeches." Voice Youth Advocates

Includes bibliographical references

Obama, Michelle

Brophy, David. **Michelle** Obama; meet the First Lady. by David Bergen Brophy. HarperCollins 2009 114p il $16.99; pa $6.99

Grades: 5 6 7 8   **92**

1. Lawyers 2. Spouses of presidents 3. Hospital administrators 4. African American women -- Biography 5. Presidents' spouses -- United States
ISBN 978-0-06-177991-6; 0-06-177991-1; 978-0-06-177990-9 pa; 0-06-177990-3 pa

A brief biography of Michelle Obama, wife of President Barack Obama

"The author . . . mixes personal data with information about the political process that brought the Obamas to the White House. . . . This biography is a must-have for all school libraries." Voice Youth Advocates

Includes glossary

Colbert, David. **Michelle** Obama; an American story. Houghton Mifflin Harcourt 2009 151p il $16

Grades: 5 6 7 8   **92**

1. Lawyers 2. Spouses of presidents 3. Hospital administrators 4. African American women -- Biography 5. Presidents' spouses -- United States
ISBN 978-0-547-24941-4; 0-547-24941-1

This biography delves into "the subject of The First Lady's family roots. . . . It offers a strong sense of who Obama was as a child, her solid upbringing, and her adult choices, all bolstered with numerous quotes from Obama and those who know her best. . . . Two sections of color photos and appended source notes for direct quotes complete this timely, highly readable biography." Booklist

Uschan, Michael V., 1948- **Michelle** Obama. Lucent Books 2010 112p il (People in the news) $32.45

Grades: 8 9 10 11 12   **92**

1. Lawyers 2. Spouses of presidents 3. Hospital administrators 4. African American women -- Biography 5. Presidents' spouses -- United States
ISBN 978-1-4205-0209-1; 1-4205-0209-3

LC 2009036557

"This biography is enjoyable reading for those writing reports and for those who simply want to learn more about the First Lady. As well as covering her life with Barack Obama and in the White House, Uschan discusses her family life, education, and early career and includes sidebars on such topics as her experience as a black student at mostly white Ivy League schools. Quotes from interviews with Obama reveal her intelligence, humor, and down-to-earth sensibility." SLJ

Includes bibliographical references

Ocampo, Adriana C., 1955-

Hopping, Lorraine Jean. **Space** rocks; the story of planetary geologist Adriana Ocampo. Franklin Watts 2005 118p il (Women's adventures in science) $9.95

Grades: 7 8 9 10   **92**

1. Geologists 2. Women scientists
ISBN 0-531-16783-6

LC 2005006644

"Adriana Ocampo grew up in Argentina. . . . When her father moved the family to the United States. . . . her enthusiasm for satellite design and interest in geology eventually led to a job [with NASA]. First helping to design a Mars rover, she then got involved in the search for a crater created by a massive asteroid collision that evidently caused mass extinctions in the age of dinosaurs. She now examines photos of distant planets taken by 'flyby' space probes and [plans] new geological expeditions." Voice Youth Advocates

Includes bibliographical references

Ochoa, Ellen, 1958-

Schraff, Anne E. **Ellen** Ochoa; astronaut and inventor. [by] Anne Schraff. Enslow Publishers 2010 128p il (Latino biography library) lib bdg $31.93

Grades: 6 7 8 9   **92**

1. Inventors 2. Astronauts 3. Women inventors 4. Women astronauts 5. NASA officials 6. Hispanic Americans -- Biography
ISBN 978-0-7660-3163-0; 0-7660-3163-2

LC 2008-40349

"Explores the life of Ellen Ochoa, including her childhood in California, her rise through the ranks in NASA, several space shuttle missions, and becoming the first Latino woman in space." Publisher's note

Includes bibliographical references

Ohr, George E.

Greenberg, Jan. The **mad** potter; George E. Ohr, eccentric genius. Jan Greenberg and Sandra Jordan. Roaring Brook Press 2013 56 p. (hardcover : alk. paper) $17.99

Grades: 4 5 6 7 8   **92**

1. American pottery 2. Potters -- United States -- Biography
ISBN 159643810X; 9781596438101

LC 2012047601

Robert F. Sibert Honor Book (2014)

This children's book is a biography of American potter George E. Ohr. "Ohr's eccentricities and his penchant for self-promotion are clearly presented. . . . What makes a George E. Ohr vase sell at auction nowadays for $84,000, and is he really America's greatest art potter? Certainly his work is whimsical . . . vases tilting like leaning towers, a teapot with a spout like an open-mouthed serpent, and all manner of wrinkled, twisted and squashed vessels." (Kirkus Reviews)

Includes bibliographical references and index

Osceola, Seminole chief, 1804-1838

Sanford, William R. **Seminole** chief Osceola; by William R. Sanford. Enslow Publishers 2013 48 p. (library) $21.26

Grades: 6 7 8 9   **92**

1. Native Americans -- United States 2. Seminole Indians -- Kings and rulers -- Biography
ISBN 0766041174; 9780766041172

LC 2011050996

This book is part of the Native American Chiefs and Warriors series and looks at Seminole Chief Osceola. "Osceola led his people, the Seminoles, in one of the longest struggles of the Indian Wars. In a game of hide and seek in the Florida wetlands, the Seminoles struck deadly blows to the U.S. Army. Osceoloa was never defeated, but was finally double-crossed and captured." (Publisher's note)

Includes bibliographical references and index.

Owens, Jesse, 1913-1980

Burlingame, Jeff. **Jesse** Owens; I always loved running. Enslow Publishers 2011 128p il (African-American biography library) lib bdg $31.93
Grades: 6 7 8 9   92
1. Track athletics 2. African American athletes 3. Olympic athletes 4. Runners (Athletes)
ISBN 978-0-7660-3497-6; 0-7660-3497-6
LC 2010015697

"This book opens with Jesse Owens' celebrated victory in the 1936 Olympics in Berlin, when he triumphed in the 100-meter dash and Hitler refused to congratulate him. In a more nuanced historical account than many books offer, Burlingame looks at different interpretations of the day's events and comments on how Owens' own account changed over time. . . . After the dramatic opening chapter, the book offers a chronological account of Owens' life. . . . On every page, color brightens the headings, backgrounds, bordered photos, sidebars, and boxed quotes." Booklist

Includes bibliographical references

Gigliotti, Jim. **Jesse** Owens; gold medal hero. Sterling 2010 124p il $12.95; pa $5.95
Grades: 6 7 8 9   92
1. Track athletics 2. African American athletes 3. Olympic athletes 4. Runners (Athletes)
ISBN 978-1-4027-7149-1; 1-4027-7149-5; 978-1-4027-6361-8 pa; 1-4027-6361-1 pa
LC 2009024221

A biography of African-American runner Jesse Owens, whose success in the 1936 Berlin Olympic games was a victory for equality and an affront to Nazi leader Adolf Hitler's view of Aryan supremacy.

"Opinionated yet informative, . . . [this blends] anecdotes, quotations, and facts to create [an] engaging [portrait]. . . . Photographs and sidebars are incorporated into [a] reader-friendly [design]." Horn Book Guide

Includes glossary and bibliographical references

McDougall, Chros. **Jesse** Owens; trailblazing sprinter. ABDO Pub. Co. 2011 112p il (Legendary athletes) lib bdg $34.22
Grades: 6 7 8 9   92
1. Track athletics 2. African American athletes 3. Olympic athletes 4. Runners (Athletes)
ISBN 978-1-61714-758-6; 1-61714-758-3
LC 2010046697

This biography of track star Jesse Owens "goes beyond merely discussing [his] accomplishments. . . . [It] also [explores] the social and political [influence he] had on society as a whole. In addition, [it introduces] historical events in the context of [his life]. . . . This . . . is teeming with information

and is a must-purchase for sports fans and readers interested in social activism." SLJ

Includes glossary and bibliographical references

Page, Larry

Sapet, Kerrily. **Google** founders: Larry Page and Sergey Brin. Morgan Reynolds Pub. 2011 112p il (Business leaders) $28.95
Grades: 7 8 9 10 11 12   92
1. Businesspeople 2. Web search engines 3. Computer scientists 4. Google, Inc. 5. Internet executives 6. Information technology executives
ISBN 978-1-59935-177-3; 1-59935-177-3; 978-1-59935-213-8 e-book
LC 2011014665

This biography of Google founders Larry Page and Sergey Bring "will grab YAs. . . . The design is browsable, with clear type and lots of color screens and informal photos of young people at work." Booklist

Includes bibliographical references

Palin, Sarah, 1964-

Petrillo, Lisa. **Sarah** Palin. Morgan Reynolds 2009 112p il (Political profiles) lib bdg $28.95
Grades: 6 7 8 9   92
1. Mayors 2. Governors 3. Women politicians
ISBN 978-1-59935-133-9 lib bdg; 1-59935-133-1 lib bdg
LC 2009040834

A biography of the former governor of Alaska, and former vice-presidential candidate

This is "solid, evenhanded, and wonderfully helpful. . . . Unusually well-chosen photos, fine notes, and [a list] of further sources add to the usefulness and appeal of this [book]." Booklist

Paolini, Christopher

Bankston, John. **Christopher** Paolini; foreword by Kyle Zimmer. Chelsea House Publishers 2010 132p il (Who wrote that?) lib bdg $35
Grades: 6 7 8 9 10   92
1. Authors 2. Novelists 3. Fantasy writers 4. Authors, American 5. Young adult authors
ISBN 978-1-60413-727-9; 1-60413-727-4
LC 2010001366

This discusses the life and work of author Christopher Paolini.

Includes bibliographical references

Parks, Rosa, 1913-2005

Tracy, Kathleen. The **life** and times of Rosa Parks. Mitchell Lane Publishers 2009 48p il (Profiles in American history) lib bdg $29.95
Grades: 6 7 8 9   92
1. Civil rights activists 2. African Americans -- Civil rights 3. African American women -- Biography 4. Montgomery (Ala.) -- Race relations
ISBN 978-1-58415-666-6 lib bdg; 1-58415-666-X lib bdg
LC 2008020927

This a biography of the American American seamstress who refused to give up her seat on a Montgomery, Albama, city bus to a white passenger, which led to challenging the constitutionality of Montgomery's bus segregation laws

This offers "a wealth of concise and well-organized information. . . . [The] book is fair and balanced and includes viewpoints from those who opposed or disagreed with [Parks'] accomplishments. The design is crisp and colorful without overwhelming the words on the page." SLJ

Includes glossary and bibliographical references

Pasteur, Louis, 1822-1895

Zamosky, Lisa. **Louis** Pasteur; founder of microbiology. Compass Point Books 2009 40p il map (Mission: Science) lib bdg $26.60

Grades: 4 5 6   92

1. Chemists 2. Scientists 3. Microbiologists 4. Writers on science

ISBN 978-0-7565-3962-7

LC 2008007726

This biography of the father of microbiology "does a good job of connecting the scientist's work to our lives today. . . . [The] book has a variety of graphics including diagrams, photos, and reproductions of paintings and sketches. [This volume is] a definite plus for a school library or the juvenile collection in a public library." Libr Media Connect

Includes glossary and bibliographical references

Paterson, Katherine

Bankston, John. **Katherine** Paterson. Chelsea House 2010 128p il (Who wrote that?) lib bdg $30

Grades: 6 7 8 9   92

1. Authors 2. Novelists 3. Women authors 4. Authors, American 5. Young adult authors

ISBN 978-1-60413-499-5; 1-60413-499-2

LC 2009022345

This discusses the life and work of author Katherine Paterson.

Includes bibliographical references

McGinty, Alice B. **Katherine** Paterson; [by] Alice B. McGinty. 1st ed; Rosen Publishing Group 2005 112p il (Library of author biographies) lib bdg $26.50

Grades: 5 6 7 8   92

1. Authors 2. Novelists 3. Women authors 4. Young adult authors

ISBN 1-4042-0328-1

LC 2004-11420

This biography of the Newbery award-winning author "explains that Paterson's experiences growing up as the daughter of missionaries shaped her commitment to reflect the realistic feelings of children in her literature. . . . [This is] well-written." SLJ

Includes bibliographical references

Patrick, Danica, 1982-

★ Sirvaitis, Karen. **Danica** Patrick; racing's trailblazer. Twenty-First Century Books 2010 112p il (USA Today: lifeline biographies) lib bdg $33.26

Grades: 7 8 9 10 11 12   92

1. Women athletes 2. Automobile racing 3. Automobile racing drivers

ISBN 978-0-7613-5222-8; 0-7613-5222-8

LC 2009-45846

This biography is "both informative and eye-catching. . . . Even young readers with little interest in car racing will be caught up in the story behind Danica Patrick. . . . This involving story does more than recount the high times. Teammates are killed, loyalties switch, and personal criticism is a fact of life in the limelight." Booklist

Patton, George S. (George Smith), 1885-1945

Gitlin, Marty. **George** S. Patton; World War II general & military innovator. ABDO Pub. Co. 2010 112p il (Military heroes) lib bdg $22.95

Grades: 7 8 9 10   92

1. Generals 2. Army officers 3. World War, 1939-1945 -- Campaigns

ISBN 978-1-60453-964-6; 1-60453-964-X

LC 2009032371

This volume "offers a solid introduction to the controversial World War II commander, chronicling Patton's life from his childhood through his untimely death from injuries suffered in an automobile accident. . . . Quoting primary sources, Gitlin effectively portrays Patton as an aggressive, ambitious, courageous, often reckless, and occasionally visionary military commander. The volume is illustrated throughout with black-and-white photographs." Booklist

Includes bibliographical references

Pavlov, Ivan Petrovich, 1849-1936

Saunders, Barbara R. **Ivan** Pavlov; exploring the mysteries of behavior. Enslow Publishers 2006 112p il por (Great minds of science) lib bdg $31.93

Grades: 5 6 7 8   92

1. Scientists 2. Behaviorism 3. Physiologists 4. Writers on medicine 5. Nobel laureates for physiology or medicine

ISBN 0-7660-2506-3

LC 2005031648

This is a biography of Russian scientist Ivan Pavlov, best known for his experiments with dogs, which were key to the development of behaviorism, and who won the 1904 Nobel Prize for his research on digestion

"The accessible [text has] an inviting, open format and [offers] many anecdotes. . . . Good-quality photos and illustrations complement the [narrative]." SLJ

Includes glossary and bibliographical references

Peary, Marie Ahnighito, 1893-1978

Kirkpatrick, Katherine A. **Snow** baby; the Arctic childhood of Admiral Robert E. Peary's daring daughter. [by] Katherine Kirkpatrick. Holiday House 2007 50p il map $16.95

Grades: 5 6 7 8   92

1. Admirals 2. Explorers 3. Arctic regions 4. Children of prominent persons 5. Biography, Individual

ISBN 0-8234-1973-8; 978-0-8234-1973-9

LC 2006-02016

This is a biography of Marie Peary, the daughter of the discoverer of the North Pole. Chronology. Bibliography. Index. "Grades four to seven." (Bull Cent Child Books)

"Born north of the Arctic Circle in 1893, Marie Ahnighito Peary published her own version of her youth in 1934 (The Snowbaby's Own Story), on which this book is based. Kirkpatrick's engaging text captures the girl's adventurous spirit and the opportunities that her father's life as an explorer presented, as well as her love of the North and her Inuit friends." SLJ

Peary, Robert Edwin, 1856-1920

Kirkpatrick, Katherine A. **Snow** baby; the Arctic childhood of Admiral Robert E. Peary's daring daughter. [by] Katherine Kirkpatrick. Holiday House 2007 50p il map $16.95

Grades: 5 6 7 8   92

1. Admirals 2. Explorers 3. Arctic regions 4. Children of prominent persons 5. Biography, Individual
ISBN 0-8234-1973-8; 978-0-8234-1973-9

LC 2006-02016

This is a biography of Marie Peary, the daughter of the discoverer of the North Pole. Chronology. Bibliography. Index. "Grades four to seven." (Bull Cent Child Books)

"Born north of the Arctic Circle in 1893, Marie Ahnighito Peary published her own version of her youth in 1934 (The Snowbaby's Own Story), on which this book is based. Kirkpatrick's engaging text captures the girl's adventurous spirit and the opportunities that her father's life as an explorer presented, as well as her love of the North and her Inuit friends." SLJ

Peck, Richard, 1934-

Campbell, Kimberly. **Richard** Peck; a spellbinding storyteller. Enslow Publishers 2008 112p bibl por (Authors teens love) lib bdg $31.93

Grades: 6 7 8 9   92

1. Authors 2. Novelists 3. Authors, American 4. Children's authors 5. Young adult authors
ISBN 978-0-7660-2723-7 lib bdg; 0-7660-2723-6 lib bdg

LC 2006034069

A biography of the 2001 Newbery-winning book, A Year Down Yonder

Includes bibliographical references

Sickels, Amy. **Richard** Peck. Chelsea House 2009 124p il (Who wrote that?) lib bdg $30

Grades: 6 7 8 9   92

1. Authors 2. Novelists 3. Authors, American 4. Children's authors 5. Young adult authors
ISBN 978-0-7910-9530-0 lib bdg; 0-7910-9530-4 lib bdg

LC 2008-35035

A biography of the author of such young adult novels as Are You in the House Alone? and A Long Way from Chicago.

Includes bibliographical references

Pei, I. M., 1917-

★ Rubalcaba, Jill. **I.M.** Pei; architect of time, place, and purpose. Marshall Cavendish 2011 92p il map $23.99; ebook $23.99

Grades: 6 7 8 9 10 11 12   92

1. Architects 2. Chinese Americans
ISBN 978-0-7614-5973-6; 0-7614-5973-1; 978-0-7614-6081-7 ebook; 0-7614-6081-0 ebook

LC 2011001910

"An exquisite package, much like one of Pei's buildings." Kirkus

Includes bibliographical references

Slavicek, Louise Chipley. **I.M.** Pei. Chelsea House 2009 120p bibl il por (Asian Americans of achievement) lib bdg $30

Grades: 6 7 8 9   92

1. Architects 2. Chinese Americans
ISBN 978-1-60413-567-1; 1-60413-567-0

LC 2009014609

"A fascinating look at the world-renowned architect. . . . Slavecek deftly covers Pei's life, including his childhood and political events that were going on in China at the time. . . . The narrative is easy to read, the sidebars are informative, and the chronology and glossary are very helpful. A solid choice for most libraries." SLJ

Includes glossary and bibliographical references

Pelosi, Nancy, 1940-

Marcovitz, Hal. **Nancy** Pelosi; politician. Chelsea House Publishers 2009 144p il (Women of achievement) lib bdg $30

Grades: 7 8 9 10   92

1. Women politicians 2. Members of Congress 3. Speakers of the House
ISBN 978-1-60413-075-1 lib bdg; 1-60413-075-X lib bdg

LC 2008-34674

This is a biography of the first woman to serve as speaker of the U.S. House of Representatives

Includes bibliographical references

Pelé, 1940-

Buckley, James. **Pele**. DK Pub. 2007 128p il (DK biography) $14.99; pa $4.99

Grades: 6 7 8 9   92

1. Soccer players 2. Soccer -- Biography
ISBN 978-0-7566-2996-0; 978-0-7566-2987-8 pa

This "introduces Edson Arantes do Nascimento, known to the world as soccer legend Pelé. The chapters stretch from Pelé's Brazilian youth . . . through is astonishing career and his current retirement. . . . Buckley grounds his enthusiasm with well-integrated facts and quotes. . . . Crisply reproduced photographs appear on every page." Booklist

Includes bibliographical references

Perkins, Frances, 1882-1965

Keller, Emily. **Frances** Perkins; first woman cabinet member. Morgan Reynolds Pub. 2006 160p il lib bdg $27.95

Grades: 8 9 10 11 12   **92**
1. Cabinet officers 2. Women politicians 3. College teachers 4. Secretaries of labor 5. State government officials
ISBN 978-1-931798-91-4 lib bdg; 1-931798-91-5 lib bdg

LC 2006023971

"This clearly written title highlights the groundbreaking accomplishments of the woman who served under Franklin D. Roosevelt as the U.S. Secretary of Labor. . . . The narrative is well researched and includes numerous quotes that are cited in a source notes section. Good-quality photographs depict many of the individuals mentioned in the text and illustrate the historical period." SLJ

Includes bibliographical references

Perón, Eva, 1919-1952
Favor, Lesli J. **Eva** Peron. Marshall Cavendish Benchmark 2010 112p il (Leading women) $39.93
Grades: 5 6 7 8   **92**
1. Women politicians 2. Argentina -- History 3. Spouses of presidents
ISBN 978-0-7614-4962-1; 0-7614-4962-0

A biography of the influential and admired First Lady of Argentina.

Includes bibliographical references

Picasso, Pablo, 1881-1973
Kallen, Stuart A. **Pablo** Picasso. Lucent Books 2009 104p il (Eye on art) lib bdg $32.45
Grades: 7 8 9 10   **92**
1. Cubism 2. Artists 3. Painters 4. Artists, French
ISBN 978-1-4205-0045-5; 1-4205-0045-7

LC 2008-13338

"Kallen tackles the complicated man that was Pablo Picasso and gives readers a look at both his genius and his eccentricities. . . . Visually, this is supported by the many photos of Picasso's art that appear throughout. Excellent sidebars offer solid information on such topics as communism or the influence of the Impressionists. This is just the kind of book that engages enough to become a gateway." Booklist

Includes bibliographical references

Spence, David. **Picasso**. New Forest Press 2010 48p il (Great artists and their world) lib bdg $32.80
Grades: 6 7 8 9   **92**
1. Cubism 2. Artists 3. Painters 4. Artists, French
ISBN 978-1-848983-14-4; 1-848983-14-X

"Offers biographical information [of Pablo Picasso] . . . interspersed with art history and criticism in an eye-catching format. . . . [Includes] a long introductory paragraph and four-to-six images with explanatory notes. . . . Spence . . . does a good job of explaining why art that might seem ordinary today was revolutionary at the time of its creation." SLJ

Includes glossary

Pierce, Tamora, 1954-
Dailey, Donna. **Tamora** Pierce; foreword by Kyle Zimmer. Chelsea House Publishers 2006 146p bibl il por (Who wrote that?) lib bdg $30
Grades: 6 7 8 9   **92**
1. Authors 2. Novelists 3. Women authors 4. Fantasy

writers 5. College teachers 6. Authors, American 7. Children's authors
ISBN 978-0-7910-8795-4 lib bdg; 0-7910-8795-6 lib bdg

LC 2005025041

This biography, which examines the "writer's personal life and writing career, [is] ideal for fans. . . . The synopses of most popular books, and lists of works, well-known characters, and major awards may help report writers." Horn Book Guide

Includes bibliographical references

Planck, Max, 1858-1947
Weir, Jane. **Max** Planck; revolutionary physicist. Compass Point Books 2009 40p il (Mission: science) lib bdg $26.60
Grades: 4 5 6   **92**
1. Physicists 2. Nobel laureates for physics
ISBN 978-0-7565-4073-9 lib bdg; 0-7565-4073-9 lib bdg

LC 2008-37622

Biography of the physicist Max Planck

Includes glossary and bibliographical references

Pocahontas, d. 1617
Jones, Victoria Garrett. **Pocahontas**; a life in two worlds. Sterling 2010 124p il map (Sterling biographies) lib bdg $12.95; pa $9.95
Grades: 7 8 9 10   **92**
1. Powhatan Indians 2. Indian leaders 3. Jamestown (Va.) -- History 5. Native Americans -- Biography
ISBN 978-1-4027-6844-6 lib bdg; 1-4027-6844-3 lib bdg; 978-1-4027-5158-5 pa; 1-4027-5158-3 pa

LC 2009-24136

A biography of the daughter of Chief Powhatan and her friendship with the colonists of the Jamestown settlement.

Includes glossary and bibliographical references

Poe, Edgar Allan, 1809-1849
Lange, Karen E. **Nevermore**; a photobiography of Edgar Allan Poe. National Geographic 2009 64p il $19.95; lib bdg $28.90
Grades: 6 7 8 9   **92**
1. Poets 2. Authors 3. Essayists 4. Authors, American 5. Short story writers 6. Biography, Individual
ISBN 978-1-4263-0398-2; 1-4263-0398-X; 978-1-4263-0399-9 lib bdg; 1-4263-0399-8 lib bdg

LC 2008-39833

In text and photographs, this volume depicts the life of the poet and short story writer. Chronology. Index. "Grades five to nine." (Bull Cent Child Books)

"The drama of Poe's tortured life unfolds in accessible prose. Textual information is interspersed with photos, artistic interpretations, and revealing quotations presented in script. . . . This volume offers a fairly complete and thoroughly readable description of Poe's life and his importance to literature." SLJ

Includes bibliographical references

★ Meltzer, Milton. **Edgar** Allan Poe; a biography. Twenty-First Century Books 2003 144p $31.90

Grades: 7 8 9 10 **92**
1. Poets 2. Authors 3. Essayists 4. Authors, American
5. Short story writers
ISBN 0-7613-2910-2

LC 2002-155802

"More than most other biographers for young people, Meltzer places his subject within the framework of his society. Readers will come away not only with greater knowledge of Poe's life and accomplishments but also a clearer picture of American life in the first half of the nineteenth century." Booklist

Includes bibliographical references

Polo, Marco, 1254-1323?

Childress, Diana. **Marco** Polo's journey to China; [by] Diana Childress. Twenty-First Century Books 2008 160p (Pivotal moments in history) lib bdg $38.60

Grades: 7 8 9 10 11 12 **92**
1. Travelers 2. Voyages and travels 3. Travel writers
4. China -- Description and travel
ISBN 978-0-8225-5903-0 lib bdg; 0-8225-5903-X lib bdg

LC 2005024003

This details the travels of the medieval explorer through Asia.

"Sure to satisfy history buffs, [the book] not only [relates] facts about the . . . [topic] but also [delves] into the events leading up to [the journey] as well as exploring [its] effects throughout history. Numerous sidebars, illustrations, maps, and art reproductions provide additional information." Horn Book Guide

Includes glossary and bibliographical references

Demi. **Marco** Polo; written and illustrated by Demi. Marshall Cavendish 2008 un il map $19.99

Grades: 4 5 6 7 **92**
1. Explorers 2. Travelers 3. Voyages and travels 4. Travel writers
ISBN 978-0-7614-5433-5; 0-7614-5433-0

"This elegant, scholarly picture-book biography brings the explorer's fantastic journey to life. . . . Demi weaves her subject's own accounts into a seamless tale of wonder. . . . The delicately rendered illustrations, painted with Chinese inks and gold overlays . . . capture the exotic beauty of 13th-century China." SLJ

Feinstein, Stephen. **Marco** Polo; amazing adventures in China. Enslow Publishers 2009 112p il (Great explorers of the world) lib bdg $31.93

Grades: 6 7 8 9 **92**
1. Explorers 2. Travelers 3. Voyages and travels 4. Travel writers
ISBN 978-1-59845-103-0 lib bdg; 1-59845-103-0 lib bdg

LC 2008-40344

"Examines the life of Italian explorer Marco Polo, including a childhood in Venice, his travels in China and the Mongol empire, his service to Kublai Khan, and his imprisonment in Genoa." Publisher's note

Includes glossary and bibliographical references

Twist, Clint. **Marco** Polo; history's great adventurer. Candlewick Press 2011 un il (Historical notebooks) $19.99

Grades: 5 6 7 8 **92**
1. Explorers 2. Travelers 3. Voyages and travels 4. Travel writers
ISBN 978-0-7636-5286-9; 0-7636-5286-5

LC 2010040131

First published 2010 in the United Kingdom with title: Marco Polo; geographer of distant lands

"In this sumptuous scrapbook, excerpts from Marco Polo's own account of his travels are paired with beautiful maps, drawings, and illustrations. . . . This volume is well suited to browsing, and many readers will want to spend time poring over the many details." SLJ

Powell, Barbara Johns, 1935-1991

Kanefield, Teri, 1960- The **girl** from the tar paper school; Barbara Rose Johns and the advent of the civil rights movement. by Teri Kanefield. Abrams Books for Young Readers 2013 56 p. (alk. paper) $19.95

Grades: 5 6 7 8 **92**
1. Segregation in education 2. African Americans -- Civil rights 3. Civil rights -- United States -- History 4. Civil rights workers -- United States -- Biography 5. Virginia -- Race relations -- History -- 20th century 6. Women civil rights workers -- United States -- Biography 7. Segregation in education -- Virginia -- History -- 20th century 8. Civil rights movements -- United States -- History -- 20th century
ISBN 1419707965; 9781419707964

LC 2012040990

This book, by Teri Kanefield, focuses on "Barbara Rose Johns. . . . In 1951, witnessing the unfair conditions in her racially segregated high school, Barbara Johns led a walkout . . . jumpstarting the American civil rights movement. Ridiculed by the white superintendent and school board . . . Barbara and her classmates held firm and did not give up. Her school's case went all the way to the Supreme Court and helped end segregation as part of Brown v. Board of Education." (Publisher's note)

"A heartfelt tribute to Barbara Rose Johns, a lesser-known heroine of the early civil rights movement. In 1951 Virginia, black Robert R. Moton High School and white Farmville High were separate but definitely not equal, and quiet Barbara and her classmates decided to strike. Profuse details, some extraneous, threaten to overtake the inspiring story of bravery." (Horn Book)

Includes bibliographical references and index

Powell, Colin L., 1937-

Shichtman, Sandra H. **Colin** Powell; Have a vision. Be demanding. [by] Sandra H. Shichtman. Enslow 2005 128p il lib bdg $31.93

Grades: 5 6 7 8 **92**
1. Generals 2. Secretaries of state 3. Statesmen -- United States 4. African Americans -- Biography
ISBN 0-7660-2464-4

LC 2004-16799

This is "clearly written. . . . The captioned color photos add to the visual appeal." SLJ

Vander Hook, Sue. **Colin** Powell; general & statesman. ABDO Pub. Co. 2010 112p il (Military heroes) lib bdg $22.95

Grades: 7 8 9 10   **92**

1. Generals 2. Statesmen 3. Secretaries of state 4. African Americans -- Biography

ISBN 978-1-60453-965-3; 1-60453-965-8

LC 2009032364

This biography of Colin Powell covers Powell's service in the Vietnam War, his role as a White House fellow, a four-star general, and commander-in-chief of Forces Command and Powell's service to the U.S. presidents as the chairman of the Joint Chiefs of Staff and the secretary of state.

"The rush of literary adrenalin will hook readers immediately and keep them enthralled until the end. . . . Given the dynamic topic . . . [and] appealing layout [this book is] likely to appeal to reluctant readers. In addition, sources are plentiful and well-documented, making the [title] suitable for research projects." SLJ

Includes bibliographical references

Presley, Elvis, 1935-1977

Collins, Terry. **Elvis**; a graphic novel. illustrated by Michele Melcher. Capstone Press 2011 32p il (Graphic library: American graphic) lib bdg $29.32; pa $7.95

Grades: 4 5 6 7   **92**

1. Actors 2. Singers 3. Rock musicians 4. Biographical graphic novels

ISBN 978-1-4296-5476-0 lib bdg; 1-4296-5476-7 lib bdg; 978-1-4296-6266-6 pa; 1-4296-6266-2 pa

LC 2010024847

In graphic novel format, explores the life of Elvis Presley and describes his return to stardom through his '68 Comeback Special.

"The illustrations are eye-catching and the narration is presented simply, yet compellingly. . . . Fact-filled, entertaining, and accessible." SLJ

Includes glossary and bibliographical references

Hampton, Wilborn. **Elvis** Presley; a twentieth century life. Viking 2007 197p il (Up close) $15.99

Grades: 7 8 9 10   **92**

1. Actors 2. Singers 3. Rock musicians

ISBN 978-0-670-06166-2

LC 2006029074

A biography of the legendary "King of rock and roll."

The author's "enthusiasm and passion for his subject are evident throughout this appealing biography, yet he remains objective about the performer's virtues as well as his tragic flaws. The striking cover photograph complements the lively and accessible text that delves not only into Elvis's life but also his impact on music and American culture." SLJ

Micklos, John. **Elvis** Presley; I want to entertain people. [by] John Micklos, Jr. Enslow Publishers 2010 160p il (American rebels) lib bdg $34.60

Grades: 6 7 8 9   **92**

1. Actors 2. Singers 3. Rock musicians

ISBN 978-0-7660-3382-5 lib bdg; 0-7660-3382-1 lib bdg

LC 2009017595

The first chapter of this "fascinating, well-organized [portrait of the the rock musician] . . . describes the King's 1956 Ed Sullivan Show appearance, which was watched by a screaming audience of 60 million home viewers. . . . Skillfully chosen photos, chapter notes, and [a] suggested-reading [list completes this] well-researched, wholly engaging [introduction]." Booklist

Includes bibliographical references

Priestley, Joseph, 1733-1804

Conley, Kate A. **Joseph** Priestley and the discovery of oxygen. Mitchell Lane 2006 48p il (Uncharted, unexplored, and unexplained) $19.95

Grades: 6 7 8 9   **92**

1. Oxygen 2. Chemists 3. Writers on science

ISBN 1-58415-367-9

"This introductory title follows the scientist from his childhood in Fieldhead, England, to his death in Northumberland, PA. . . . Color photographs and illustrations are featured throughout. The attractive, open layout makes this title especially appealing to reluctant readers." SLJ

Puente, Tito, 1923-2000

McNeese, Tim. **Tito** Puente; [by] Tim McNeese. Chelsea House 2008 118p il (The great Hispanic heritage) lib bdg $30

Grades: 6 7 8 9   **92**

1. Composers 2. Musicians 3. Band leaders 4. Percussionists 5. Music arrangers 6. Puerto Ricans -- Biography

ISBN 978-0-7910-9666-6 lib bdg; 0-7910-9666-1 lib bdg

LC 2007031984

This biography provides a "substantive [portrait], including background information and historical context of . . . charismatic band leader Puente. . . . The well-documented [text] effectively [combines] anecdotes, quotations, and historical details. Many photographs and sidebars are also included." Horn Book Guide

Includes bibliographical references

Pujols, Albert, 1980-

Needham, Tom. **Albert** Pujols; MVP on and off the field. Enslow Publishers 2007 128p bibl por (Sports stars with heart) lib bdg $23.95

Grades: 4 5 6 7   **92**

1. Baseball players 2. Baseball -- Biography

ISBN 978-0-7660-2866-1 lib bdg; 0-7660-2866-6 lib bdg

LC 2006031843

"Baseball fans know Pujols from his outstanding record: Rookie of the Year, a National League MVP, a team leader helping the St. Louis Cardinals win the World Series in 2006. However, with its combination of sharp writing, eye-catching design, and well-chosen photos, this . . . is so pleasing that even those who don't follow baseball will enjoy learning about Pujols." Booklist

Includes bibliographical references

Pullman, Philip, 1946-

Speaker-Yuan, Margaret. **Philip** Pullman. Chelsea House 2006 118p il (Who wrote that?) lib bdg $30

Grades: 6 7 8 9   **92**

1. Authors 2. Novelists 3. Fantasy writers 4. Authors, English 5. Young adult authors

ISBN 0-7910-8658-5

LC 2005-8184

This "draws upon an impressive array of sources—particularly Pullman's own writings—to present the groundbreaking author's life and work. . . . What may thrill readers most . . . are the insights into the writing process." Booklist

Includes bibliographical references

Putin, Vladimir

Shields, Charles J. **Vladimir** Putin; 2nd ed.; Chelsea House 2007 120p il (Modern world leaders) lib bdg $30

Grades: 7 8 9 10   **92**

1. Presidents 2. Prime ministers 3. Russia (Federation) -- Politics and government

ISBN 0-7910-9215-1

LC 2006013657

First published 2003

A biography of the Russian president.

Includes bibliographical references

Ramirez, Manny, 1972-

Friedman, Ian C. **Manny** Ramirez. Chelsea House Publishers 2010 111p il (The great Hispanic heritage) lib bdg $30

Grades: 6 7 8 9   **92**

1. Baseball players 2. Baseball -- Biography

ISBN 978-1-60413-730-9; 1-60413-730-4

LC 2010007813

A biography of the baseball player.

Includes bibliographical references

Ramses II, King of Egypt

Fitzgerald, Stephanie J. **Ramses** II; Egyptian pharaoh, warrior, and builder. Compass Point Books 2009 112p il map (Signature lives) lib bdg $34.60

Grades: 6 7 8 9   **92**

1. Kings and rulers 2. Kings 3. Egypt -- History 4. Egypt -- Civilization

ISBN 978-0-7565-3836-1 lib bdg; 0-7565-3836-X lib bdg

LC 2008005726

This biography of the pharaoh Ramses II offers "details about the history and daily life of Egypt's New Kingdom era. . . . [The texts is] accompanied by high-quality photographs of artifacts, maps, and floor plans. [The] book's detailed time line, comparing events in Egypt to those throughout the world, is helpful for placing the lives of the pharaohs in context." SLJ

Includes glossary and bibliographical references

Randolph, Asa Philip, 1889-1979

Miller, Calvin Craig. **A.** Philip Randolph and the African American labor movement. Morgan Reynolds 2005 160p il (Portraits of Black Americans) $24.95

Grades: 8 9 10 11 12   **92**

1. Labor unions 2. Labor leaders 3. Civil rights activists 4. African Americans -- Biography 5. African Americans -- Civil rights

ISBN 1-931798-50-8

LC 2004-23706

A biography of the African American leader

"Miller lucidly traces Randolph's spectacular career while presenting a case study in the effective use of hard-nosed rhetoric and nonviolent tactics to achieve breakthroughs in the fight against segregation. Profusely illustrated with photographs, sometimes in color, and capped by resource lists." Booklist

Includes bibliographical references

Rankin, Jeannette, 1880-1973

Naden, Corinne J. **Jeanette** Rankin; Corinne J. Naden. Marshall Cavendish Benchmark 2012 96 p. (print) $39.93

Grades: 2   **92**

1. Legislators 2. Suffragists -- Montana -- Biography 3. Women pacifists -- United States -- Biography 4. Women legislators -- United States -- Biography

ISBN 0761449639; 9780761449638; 9781608707171

LC 2010047559

This biography of Jeannette Rankin by Corinne J. Naden is part of the Leading Women series. The books' "focus on the background and political achievements of twentieth-century women, including those well known in America and those lesser known, too. Each woman's story is told in a narrative, chronological style, illustrated by photographs." (Booklist)

Includes bibliographical references and index

Rasputin, Grigoriĭ Efimovich, 1871-1916

Goldberg, Enid A. **Grigory** Rasputin; holy man or mad monk? [by] Enid A. Goldberg & Norman Itzkowitz. Scholastic 2008 128p il map (Wicked history) lib bdg $30

Grades: 6 7 8 9   **92**

1. Monks 2. Courtiers 3. Russia -- History

ISBN 978-0-531-12594-6 lib bdg; 0-531-12594-7 lib bdg

LC 2007001692

"This engaging, thought-provoking book provides a chronological account of Rasputin's life as well as the historical background necessary to understand it in context. Was Rasputin a holy man, or was he simply a philandering charlatan who rose to power because of his unique relationship with Tsar Nicholas and Tsarina Alexandra? . . . Captioned, black-and-white period photographs enhance the text. Recommended for both curricular pursuits and pleasure reading." SLJ

Includes glossary and bibliographical references

Ray, Rachael

★ Abrams, Dennis. **Rachael** Ray; food entrepreneur. Chelsea House Publishers 2009 128p bibl il por (Women of achievement) lib bdg $30

Grades: 6 7 8 9   **92**

1. Cooks 2. Television personalities 3. Talk show hosts 4. Cookbook writers

ISBN 978-1-60413-078-2 lib bdg; 1-60413-078-4 lib bdg

LC 2008034642

"Rachael Ray will be familiar to kids for her talk show and other television appearances, and that will draw them in. But once there, they'll respond to the story of Ray. . . . As a cook who never went to culinary school, Ray knows that her career is an unlikely one. Abrams does a particularly good job of capturing that unpredictability as well as Ray's uniquely exuberant personality. . . . Enjoyable and useful." Booklist

Includes bibliographical references

Reagan, Ronald, 1911-2004

Burgan, Michael. **Ronald** Reagan; a photographic story of a life. DK Pub. 2011 128p il (DK biography) $14.99; pa $5.99

Grades: 5 6 7 8   **92**

1. Actors 2. Governors 3. Presidents 4. Presidents -- United States

ISBN 978-0-7566-7075-7; 0-7566-7075-6; 978-0-7566-7074-0 pa; 0-7566-7074-8 pa

"Burgan's survey covers the basic facts in a positive but not propagandistic introduction. . . . Featuring small but clear photos or boxed commentary on every page and capped with a substantial . . . multimedia resource list, this compact volume . . . gives readers a broad picture of his achievements and a sense of his compelling personal style." Booklist

Includes bibliographical references

Marsico, Katie. **Ronald** Reagan. Marshall Cavendish Benchmark 2011 112p il (Presidents and their times) lib bdg $23.95

Grades: 5 6 7 8   **92**

1. Actors 2. Governors 3. Presidents 4. Presidents -- United States

ISBN 978-0-7614-4814-3; 0-7614-4814-4

LC 2009044590

This offers information on President Ronald Reagan and places him within his historical and cultural context. Also explored are the formative events of his times and how he responded.

"The abundant sidebars provide a good deal of background information that will be helpful to students. . . . Attractive . . . as well as useful." Booklist

Includes glossary and bibliographical references

Reiss, Johanna

Reiss, Johanna. The **journey** back. Crowell 1976 212p hardcover o.p. pa $17.95

Grades: 5 6 7 8 9 10   **92**

1. Authors 2. Holocaust survivors 3. Children's authors 4. Jews -- Netherlands

ISBN 978-0-690-01252-1; 978-0-59543-050-5 pa

Sequel to The upstairs room

"The journey is the return home in the spring of 1945 for thirteen-year-old Annie and her older sister Sini. . . . The background of the early years is recapitulated. . . . The book offers an intensely provocative story, recalling many personal crises and tests of human nature cruelly beset by the dangers and deprivations of war." Horn Book

★ Reiss, Johanna. The **upstairs** room. Crowell 1972 273p hardcover o.p. pa $5.99

Grades: 5 6 7 8 9 10   **92**

1. Authors 2. Holocaust survivors 3. Children's authors 4. Jews -- Netherlands 5. World War, 1939-1945 -- Jews 6. Holocaust, 1933-1945 -- Personal narratives 7. Netherlands -- History -- 1940-1945, German occupation

ISBN 0-690-85127-8; 0-06-440370-X pa

A Newbery Medal honor book, 1973

"In a vital, moving account the author recalls her experiences as a Jewish child hiding from the Germans occupying her native Holland during World War II. . . . Ten-year-old Annie and her twenty-year-old sister Sini, . . . are taken in by a Dutch farmer, his wife, and mother who hide the girls in an upstairs room of the farm house. Written from the perspective of a child the story affords a child's-eye-view of the war." Booklist

Followed by The journey back

Rembrandt Harmenszoon van Rijn, 1606-1669

Roberts, Russell. **Rembrandt;** [by] Russell Roberts. Mitchell Lane 2009 48p il (Art profiles for kids) lib bdg $20.95

Grades: 7 8 9 10   **92**

1. Artists 2. Etchers 3. Painters 4. Artists, Dutch 5. Drafters

ISBN 978-1-58415-710-6 lib bdg; 1-58415-710-0 lib bdg

LC 2008-2241

"Tracks the artist's rise to fame and the bitter years and bankruptcy that followed. . . . [Goes] beyond basic facts, providing historical context and significance of the art and the artist. . . . Provide[s] plenty of information for reports in a reader-friendly format." SLJ

Includes glossary and bibliographical references

Renoir, Auguste, 1841-1919

Somervill, Barbara A. **Pierre** -Auguste Renoir; [by] Barbara Somervill. Mitchell Lane 2007 48p il (Art profiles for kids) lib bdg $29.95

Grades: 5 6 7 8   **92**

1. Artists 2. Painters 3. Artists, French

ISBN 978-1-58415-566-9 lib bdg; 1-58415-566-3 lib bdg

LC 2007000661

Profiles the famous French artist best known for his portraits and his paintings such as "The Luncheon of the Boating Party" that depict people enjoying themselves

"The glossy pages allow for good reproductions of paintings as well as a few photos. . . . Back matter includes a glossary, chronology, chapter notes for quotes, lists of books and

Internet sites, and a Timeline in History . . . offers a concise, readable account of the artist's life." Booklist

Includes glossary and bibliographical references

Spence, David. **Renoir**. New Forest Press 2010 48p il (Great artists and their world) lib bdg $32.80
Grades: 6 7 8 9   92
1. Artists 2. Painters 3. Artists, French 4. Impressionism (Art)
ISBN 978-1-848983-15-5; 1-848983-17-4

"Offers biographical information [of Auguste Renoir] . . . interspersed with art history and criticism in an eye-catching format. . . . [Includes] a long introductory paragraph and four-to-six images with explanatory notes. . . . Spence . . . does a good job of explaining why art that might seem ordinary today was revolutionary at the time of its creation." SLJ

Includes glossary

Revere, Paul, 1735-1818
★ Giblin, James. The **many** rides of Paul Revere; by James Cross Giblin. Scholastic Press 2007 85p il map $17.99
Grades: 4 5 6 7   92
1. Artisans 2. Metalworkers 3. Revolutionaries 4. United States -- History -- 1775-1783, Revolution
ISBN 978-0-439-57290-3; 0-439-57290-8
LC 2006-38369

"This well-organized biography presents a lucid account of Revere's childhood, his limited education, his training in his father's workshop, his brief military career, and his adult life as a silversmith, family man, and Revolutionary War leader. . . . Giblin presents salient facts and intriguing details to create a well-rounded and credible image of the man. Among the many illustrations are period portraits, narrative paintings, engravings, drawings, and maps as well as photos of significant sites and artifacts." Booklist

Includes bibliographical references

Rhodes-Courter, Ashley Marie
Rhodes-Courter, Ashley Marie. **Three** little words; a memoir. Atheneum Books for Young Readers 2008 304p il $17.99; pa $9.99
Grades: 8 9 10 11 12 Adult   92
1. Foster children 2. Adopted children 3. Foster home care 4. Memoirists 5. Child benefactors
ISBN 978-1-4169-4806-3; 1-4169-4806-6; 978-1-4169-4807-0 pa; 1-4169-4807-4 pa
LC 2007-21629

"This memoir lends a powerful voice to thousands of 'boomerang kids' who repeatedly wind up back in foster care." SLJ

Rector, Sarah
Bolden, Tonya. **Searching** for Sarah Rector; the richest black girl in America. Tonya Bolden. Abrams Books for Young Readers 2014 80 p. $21.95
Grades: 4 5 6 7 8   92
1. Rich 2. African American women 3. Creek County (Okla.) -- Biography 4. Creek Indians -- Oklahoma -- Creek County -- Biography 5. Women millionaires -- Oklahoma -- Creek County -- Biography 6. Petroleum industry and trade -- Oklahoma -- History -- 20th century 7. African American women -- Oklahoma -- Creek County -- Biography
ISBN 1419708465; 9781419708466
LC 2012039254

Author Tonya Bolden presents a biography of Sarah Rector, who "turned 18 in 1920, [and] the young black woman had amassed a fortune estimated at $1 million. In telling her story, Bolden makes a largely unknown portion of American history accessible to young readers. Rector and her family were 'Creek freedmen,' black citizens of the Creek Indian nation." (School Library Journal)

Includes bibliographical references and index

Rice, Condoleezza, 1954-
Hubbard-Brown, Janet. **Condoleezza** Rice; stateswoman. Chelsea House Publishers 2008 113p il (Black Americans of achievement) lib bdg $30
Grades: 6 7 8 9   92
1. Women politicians 2. College teachers 3. Government officials 4. Political scientists 5. Secretaries of state 6. Presidential advisers 7. College administrators 8. African American women -- Biography
ISBN 978-0-7910-9715-1; 0-7910-9715-3
LC 2007035678

This biography details the African American stateswoman's "rise from adversity to . . . recognition. The [book goes] beyond the typical personal information to provide some social history relevant to the subject's time. Captioned photographs and boxed inserts enhance the conversational [text]." Horn Book Guide

Includes bibliographical references

Ride, Sally
Macy, Sue, 1954- **Sally** Ride; life on a mission. by Sue Macy. Aladdin 2014 160 p. illustrations (Real-life story) (hardback) $17.99
Grades: 4 5 6 7 8   92
1. Astronauts 2. Women astronauts 3. Physicists
ISBN 1442488549; 9781442488540; 9781442488557
LC 2014016685

"Sally Ride was more than the first woman in space--she was a real-life explorer and adventurer whose life story is a true inspiration for all those who dream big. . . . She was also a nationally ranked tennis player, a physicist who enjoyed reading Shakespeare, a university professor, the founder of a company that helped inspire girls . . . , and a recipient of the Presidential Medal of Freedom." (Publisher's note)

"The extensive backmatter provides scholarly data, while the writing imparts the drive and character of this famous woman. Macy's slim, empathetic account makes readers see the woman behind the achievement." Kirkus

Includes bibliographical references and index

Rivera, Diego, 1886-1957
Hillstrom, Kevin. **Diego** Rivera; muralist. by Kevin Hillstrom. Lucent Books 2008 104p il (The twentieth century's most influential Hispanics) lib bdg $32.45

Grades: 6 7 8 9 10   **92**

1. Artists 2. Painters 3. Artists, Mexican
ISBN 978-1-4205-0018-9 lib bdg; 1-4205-0018-X
lib bdg

LC 2007-32104

"Rivera's life, beginnning with his childhood, is placed
in the context of the artistic, political, and economic influences on family and his career. . . . The layout draws the
eye with colorful headings and highlighted quotes." Libr
Media Connect

Includes bibliographical references

Rizal, José, 1861-1896

Arruda, Suzanne Middendorf. **Freedom's** mar-
tyr; the story of Jose Rizal, national hero of the Phil-
lipines. [by] Suzanne Middendorf Arruda. Avisson
Press 2003 106p il (Avisson young adult series)
pa $19.95

Grades: 7 8 9 10   **92**

1. Authors 2. Novelists 3. Physicians 4. Philippines
5. Revolutionaries 6. Political leaders
ISBN 1-88810-555-0

LC 2003-45320

"Born in the Philippines on June 19, 1861, Rizal was
executed by the Spanish for treason on December 30, 1896.
. . . Rizal wanted representation for native peoples in the
Spanish government and wrote three novels and several poems detailing their plight. . . . This well-written, readable
biography will prove useful for reports and background information on the history of the Philippines." SLJ

Includes bibliographical references

Robeson, Paul, 1898-1976

Slavicek, Louise Chipley. **Paul** Robeson; entertainer and activist. Chelsea House 2011 112p il
(Black Americans of achievement) lib bdg $35

Grades: 6 7 8 9 10   **92**

1. Actors 2. Singers 3. Football players 4. African
American actors 5. African American singers 6. Civil
rights activists 7. African Americans -- Biography
ISBN 978-1-60413-843-6; 1-60413-843-2

This biography of the African American singer, actor,
and activist "chronicles Robeson's struggles to overcome
racial prejudice, leading to his staunch support of communism—a stand that caused him to lose favor in Hollywood
and contributed to his eventual reclusion. Slavicek delves
deeply into Robeson's story, giving readers a strong sense of
the challenges Robeson faced, as well as the complex, courageous individual behind the legend. Archival black-and-
white photos further lend a sense of intimacy, while 'did you
know' sidebars expand on related topics." Booklist

Includes bibliographical references

Robinson, Jackie, 1919-1972

★ Robinson, Sharon. **Promises** to keep: how
Jackie Robinson changed America. Scholastic 2004
64p il $16.95

Grades: 4 5 6 7   **92**

1. Baseball players 2. African American athletes 3.

Army officers 4. Baseball -- Biography
ISBN 0-439-42592-1

LC 2003-42709

"Robinson's daughter, Sharon, describes her father's
youth, his rise to become major-league baseball's first African American player, and his involvement in the civil rights
movement. . . . Her private view of her father's accomplishments, placed within the context of American sports and
social history, makes for absorbing reading. An excellent selection of family and team photographs and other materials .
. . illustrate this fine tribute." Booklist

Wukovits, John F. **Jackie** Robinson and the integration of baseball; [by] John F. Wukovits. Lucent
Books 2007 104p il (Lucent library of Black history) $28.70

Grades: 7 8 9 10   **92**

1. Baseball players 2. African American athletes 3.
Army officers 4. Baseball -- Biography
ISBN 1-59018-913-2; 978-1-59018-913-9

LC 2006010831

"Wukovits does a credible job of adding historical perspective to a straightforward account of Robinson's life and
accomplishments. He sets the stage by focusing on baseball's
history of racial exclusion, and on the discrimination faced
by the athlete and his family. He covers Robinson's military career and his brief stint in the Negro Leagues before he
signed with the Brooklyn Dodgers. Robinson's triumphant
career in the major leagues and his later life are detailed as
well. This is a well-researched and concise account." SLJ

Includes bibliographical references

Roosevelt, Eleanor, 1884-1962

★ Fleming, Candace. **Our** Eleanor; a scrapbook
look at Eleanor Roosevelt's remarkable life. Atheneum Books for Young Readers 2005 176p il $19.95

Grades: 5 6 7 8   **92**

1. Diplomats 2. Columnists 3. Humanitarians 4.
Social activists 5. Spouses of presidents 6. United
Nations officials 7. Presidents' spouses -- United States
ISBN 0-689-86544-9

LC 2004-22825

Told in scrapbook style, this biography looks behind
the politics to present First Lady Eleanor Roosevelt in her
many roles: wife and mother, United Nations delegate,
popular columnist, civil rights crusader, and champion of
the underprivileged.

"Each of the seven chapters leads readers through the
subject's busy life with short sections of text filled with
well-documented first-person accounts and direct quotes. .
. . Not a spread goes by without incredible archival photographs or reproductions, newspaper and magazine clippings,
handwritten letters, and diary entries. . . . They all provide
relevant and fascinating insight." SLJ

MacLeod, Elizabeth. **Eleanor** Roosevelt; an inspiring life. written by Elizabeth MacLeod. Kids Can
Press 2006 32p il (Snapshots) $14.95; pa $6.95

Grades: 4 5 6   **92**

1. Diplomats 2. Columnists 3. Humanitarians 4.
Social activists 5. Spouses of presidents 6. United

Nations officials 7. Presidents' spouses -- United States
ISBN 978-1-55337-778-8; 1-55337-778-8; 978-1-
55337-811-2 pa; 1-55337-811-3 pa

"Fourteen short chapters take readers from Roosevelt's
privileged but sad childhood through her marriage, political and family life, and post-FDR humanitarian work. . . .
The period photographs . . . [are] plentiful and engrossing.
. . . This attractive title will appeal to browsers and report
writers." SLJ

Roosevelt, Franklin D. (Franklin Delano), 1882-1945

Panchyk, Richard. **Franklin** Delano Roosevelt
for kids; his life and times with 21 activities. [by]
Richard Panchyk. Chicago Review Press 2007 147p
il pa $14.95

Grades: 4 5 6 7   **92**
1. Governors 2. Presidents 3. People with disabilities
4. Presidents -- United States 5. United States -- Politics
and government -- 1933-1945
ISBN 978-1-55652-657-2 pa; 1-55652-657-1 pa
LC 2007003484

"There are many interesting photos . . . , and they are all
sufficiently captioned. . . . Information about the Roosevelts
[is] presented in a lively, engaging manner." SLJ

Includes bibliographical references

Roosevelt, Theodore, 1858-1919

★ Cooper, Michael L. **Theodore** Roosevelt; a
twentieth-century life. Viking 2009 208p il (Up
close) $16.99

Grades: 7 8 9 10   **92**
1. Governors 2. Presidents 3. Vice-presidents 4.
Nobel laureates for peace 5. Presidents -- United States
ISBN 978-0-670-01134-6; 0-670-01134-7
LC 2010-279534

"This biography presents an evenhanded account of
the life and presidency of Theodore Roosevelt. . . . This
clearly written biography includes many anecdotes and
well-chosen quotes that help bring Roosevelt to life. . . .
Cooper offers a solid portrayal of this noteworthy American
president." Booklist

Includes biblographical references

Fitzpatrick, Brad. **Theodore** Roosevelt. Chelsea
House 2011 142p il (Conservation heroes) lib bdg
$35

Grades: 6 7 8 9 10   **92**
1. Governors 2. Presidents 3. Vice-presidents 4.
Nobel laureates for peace 5. Presidents -- United States
ISBN 978-1-60413-948-8; 1-60413-948-X
LC 2010026475

A biography of President Theodore Roosevelt which concentrates on his contributions to environmental conservation.

"Captivating, richly informative. . . . The scope of [this
book] is comprehensive. . . . [The book is] engaging as [it is]
educational and will be ideal for research and reports." SLJ

Includes glossary and bibliographical references

★ Fritz, Jean. **Bully** for you, Teddy Roosevelt!
illustrations by Mike Wimmer. Putnam 1991 127p
il hardcover o.p. pa $5.99

Grades: 5 6 7 8   **92**
1. Governors 2. Presidents 3. Vice-presidents 4.
Nobel laureates for peace 5. Presidents -- United States
ISBN 0-399-21769-X; 0-698-11609-7 pa
LC 90-8142

Follows the life of the twenty-sixth president, discussing
his conservation work, hunting expeditions, family life, and
political career

"Jean Fritz gives a rounded picture of her subject and
deftly blends the story of a person and a picture of an era."
Bull Cent Child Books

Includes bibliographical references

Hollihan, Kerrie Logan. **Theodore** Roosevelt for
kids; his life and times + 21 activities. Chicago Review Press 2010 133p il pa $16.95

Grades: 5 6 7 8   **92**
1. Governors 2. Handicraft 3. Presidents 4. Vice-
presidents 5. Nobel laureates for peace 6. Presidents
-- United States 7. United States -- Politics and
government -- 1898-1919
ISBN 978-1-55652-955-9 pa; 1-55652-955-4 pa

"What stands out in this volume is the writing, which
presents history as an engaging and informative story.
. . . The projects are interesting and accessible. . . . Both
useful and entertaining, this is a worthy addition to most
collections." SLJ

Rappaport, Doreen, 1939- **To** dare mighty things;
the life of Theodore Roosevelt. written by Doreen
Rappaport ; illustrated by C. F. Payne. Disney-Hyperion 2013 48 p. (hardback) $17.99

Grades: 2 3 4 5 6   **92**
1. Presidents -- United States 2. Presidents -- United
States -- Biography
ISBN 142312488X; 9781423124887
LC 2013010691

This picture book, by Doreen Rappaport and illustrated
by C. F. Payne, is a biography of American president Theodore Roosevelt. "As an American president, he left [a] . . .
mark upon his country. He promised a 'square deal' to all
citizens, he tamed big businesses, and protected the nation's
wildlife and natural beauty. His . . . leadership assured that
he would always be remembered." (Publisher's note).

Rowling, J. K.

Peterson-Hilleque, Victoria. **J.K.** Rowling, extraordinary author. ABDO Pub. Company 2010
112p il (Essential lives) $32.79

Grades: 5 6 7 8   **92**
1. Authors 2. Novelists 3. Women authors 4. Fantasy
writers 5. Authors, English 6. Children's authors 7.
Young adult authors
ISBN 978-1-61613-517-1; 1-61613-517-4
LC 2010000503

This biography of author J. K. Rowling "toggles between the subject's personal and professional life. . . . [The
book] offers sidebar . . . definitions of particular characters

or events in the 'Harry Potter' series. The writing is accessible, the format is open, and full-color photos appear throughout." SLJ

Includes glossary and bibliographical references

Sickels, Amy. **Mythmaker** : the story of J.K. Rowling; foreword by Kyle Zimmer. 2nd ed; Chelsea House Pubs. 2008 136p bibl il por (Who wrote that?) lib bdg $30
Grades: 5 6 7 8   **92**
1. Authors 2. Novelists 3. Women authors 4. Fantasy writers 5. Authors, English 6. Children's authors 7. Young adult authors
ISBN 978-0-7910-9632-1 lib bdg; 0-7910-9632-7 lib bdg

LC 2008001202

A revised edition of Mythmaker by Charles J. Shields published 2002
"Useful for report writers and aspiring authors." Horn Book Guide

Includes bibliographical references

Rudolph, Wilma, 1940-1994
Anderson, Jennifer Joline. **Wilma** Rudolph; track and field inspiration. ABDO Pub. Co. 2011 112p il (Legendary athletes) lib bdg $34.22
Grades: 6 7 8 9   **92**
1. Women athletes 2. Track athletics 3. Olympic athletes 4. Runners (Athletes)
ISBN 978-1-61714-759-3; 1-61714-759-1

LC 2010046698

This biography of track star Wilma Rudolph "goes beyond merely discussing [her] accomplishments. . . . [It] also [explores] the social and political [influence she] had on society as a whole. In addition, [it introduces] historical events in the context of [her life]. . . . This . . . is teeming with information and is a must-purchase for sports fans and readers interested in social activism." SLJ

Includes glossary and bibliographical references

Runyon, Brent
Runyon, Brent. The **burn** journals. Alfred A. Knopf 2004 373p hardcover o.p. pa $13.95
Grades: 7 8 9 10   **92**
1. Authors 2. Suicide 3. Burns and scalds 4. Essayists 5. Memoirists
ISBN 0-375-82621-1; 1-4000-9642-1 pa

LC 2004-5643

"One February day in 1991, Runyon came home from eighth grade . . . and set himself on fire. . . . The dialogue between Runyon and his nurses, parents, and especially his hapless psychotherapists is natural and believable, and his inner dialogue is flip, often funny, and sometimes raw. . . . The authentically adolescent voice of the journals will engage even those reluctant to read such a dark story." SLJ

Rustin, Bayard, 1910-1987
★ Brimner, Larry Dane. **We** are one: the story of Bayard Rustin. Calkins Creek 2007 48p il $17.95
Grades: 5 6 7 8   **92**
1. Civil rights activists 2. African Americans --

Biography 3. African Americans -- Civil rights
ISBN 1-59078-498-7
"Brimner sets Rustin's personal story against the history of segregation in his time and focuses on his leadership role . . . in the struggle for civil rights. On each page, the clearly written, informal text is accompanied by eloquently captioned archival photos." Booklist

Includes bibliographical references

★ Miller, Calvin Craig. **No** easy answers; Bayard Rustin and the civil rights movement. Morgan Reynolds Pub. 2005 160p il lib bdg $24.95
Grades: 7 8 9 10   **92**
1. Civil rights activists 2. African Americans -- Biography 3. African Americans -- Civil rights
ISBN 1-931798-43-5

LC 2004-18518

"Miller combines the life story of a great social activist with the history of the struggle for civil rights in the U.S. The politics are exciting, with details of the radical campaigns in the 1940s and 1950s, Rustin's impassioned call for nonviolent protest, and his role in organizing both the Montgomery Bus Boycott and the 1963 March on Washington." Booklist

Includes bibliographical references

Ruth, Babe, 1895-1948
Hampton, Wilborn. **Babe** Ruth; a twentieth-century life. Viking 2009 203p il (Up close) $16.99
Grades: 6 7 8 9 10   **92**
1. Baseball players 2. Baseball -- Biography
ISBN 978-0-670-06305-5; 0-670-06305-3

LC 2008-21550

"Hampton announces early in this biography of Babe Ruth that his emphasis is on separating fact from legend, and he is not afraid to dig up some of the more tawdry aspects of the slugger's life. . . . The focus here is on Ruth's sad early life and his career as a pitcher with the Boston Red Sox. Throughout, an attempt is made to give some sense of the grace, power, and skill of Ruth on the field. . . . [This title,] illustrated with a nice selection of photos, has the advantage of telling the complete, unvarnished story in a snappy, concise style." Booklist

Includes bibliographical references

Yomtov, Nelson. The **Bambino** : the story of Babe Ruth's legendary 1927 season; illustrated by Tim Foley. Capstone Press 2011 32p il (Graphic library: American graphic) lib bdg $29.32; pa $7.95
Grades: 4 5 6 7   **92**
1. Baseball players 2. Biographical graphic novels 3. Baseball -- Biography
ISBN 978-1-4296-5473-9 lib bdg; 1-4296-5473-2 lib bdg; 978-1-4296-6265-9 pa; 1-4296-6265-4 pa

LC 2010024764

In graphic novel format, follows Babe Ruth through the 1927 season and describes his attempt to break his own home run record.
"The illustrations are eye-catching and the narration is presented simply, yet compellingly. . . . Fact-filled, entertaining, and accessible." SLJ

Includes glossary and bibliographical references

Sís, Peter, 1949-

★ Sis, Peter, 1949- The **wall**; growing up behind the Iron Curtain. Farrar, Straus and Giroux 2007 un il $18

Grades: 4 5 6 7 8 9 10 **92**

1. Artists 2. Authors 3. Cold war 4. Animators 5. Illustrators 6. Set designers 7. Children's authors 8. Prague (Czech Republic) 9. Biography, Individual

ISBN 978-0-374-34701-7; 0-374-34701-8

LC 2006-49149

Boston Globe-Horn Book Award: Nonfiction (2008)

"The author pairs his remarkable artistry with journal entries, historical context and period photography to create a powerful account of his childhood in Cold War-era Prague." Publ Wkly

Sacagawea, b. 1786

Berne, Emma Carlson. **Sacagawea**; crossing the continent with Lewis & Clark. Sterling 2010 124p il map (Sterling biographies) lib bdg $12.95; pa $5.95

Grades: 7 8 9 10 **92**

1. Shoshoni Indians 2. Lewis and Clark Expedition (1804-1806) 3. Interpreters 4. Guides (Persons) 5. Shoshone Indians 6. West (U.S.) -- Exploration 7. Native Americans -- Biography

ISBN 978-1-4027-6845-3 lib bdg; 1-4027-6845-1 lib bdg; 978-1-4027-5738-9 pa; 1-4027-5738-7 pa

LC 2009-24139

"Contrary to myth, Sacagawea explains that the Shoshone teen was not a princess, her relationship with Clark was platonic, and she was a peace symbol rather than a guide until they finally reached the Shoshone tribe. . . . [The] spacious design is highly scannable, with color background screens, photos, maps, and historic prints throughout." Booklist

Includes glossary and bibliographical references

Crosby, Michael T. **Sacagawea**; Shoshone explorer. OTTN Pub. 2008 144p il map (Shapers of America) lib bdg $25.95

Grades: 6 7 8 9 10 **92**

1. Shoshoni Indians 2. Lewis and Clark Expedition (1804-1806) 3. Interpreters 4. Guides (Persons) 5. West (U.S.) -- Exploration 6. Native Americans -- Biography

ISBN 978-1-59556-026-1 lib bdg; 1-59556-026-2 lib bdg

LC 2007-24698

"This attractive title introduces the young Shoshone woman who accompanied the Lewis and Clark Expedition. . . . Full of clear maps, historical paintings, reproductions of period documents (including journals), and color photographs of landmarks along the route, this is a visually attractive package. . . . Detailed endnotes show the depth of the author's research, and the suggested reading includes books for both younger and older students and Internet sources." SLJ

Includes glossary and bibliographical references

Saint-Georges, Joseph Boulogne, chevalier de,

1745-1799

Brewster, Hugh. The **other** Mozart; the life of the famous Chevalier de Saint George. [by] Hugh Brewster; illustrated by Eric Velasquez. Abrams Books for Young Readers 2007 48p il $18.95

Grades: 4 5 6 7 **92**

1. Nobility 2. Composers 3. Violinists 4. Racially mixed people

ISBN 978-0-8109-5720-6; 0-8109-5720-5

LC 2006-07488

"Born to a white plantation owner and a black slave in eighteenth-century Guadeloupe, Joseph Bologne grew up to become the Chevalier de Saint-George, one of France's most accomplished composers. In this picture-book biography for middle-graders, Brewster introduces his subject's fascinating life. . . . Archival images and Velasquez's arresting full-page portraits will captivate many young readers." Booklist

Salisbury, Graham, 1944-

★ Gill, David Macinnis. **Graham** Salisbury; island boy. David Macinnis Gill. Scarecrow Press 2005 109p (Scarecrow studies in young adult literature) $35

Grades: 7 8 9 10 **92**

1. Authors 2. Novelists 3. Authors, American 4. Children's authors 5. Short story writers

ISBN 0-8108-5338-8

LC 2004031042

"Part literary analysis and part biography, this is a well-balanced look at an unusual talent, a writer who has an eye for the frailties of life and the rites of adolescence. Gill discusses how growing up in Hawaii in the '50s influenced Salisbury's writing and does a fine job of showing the complexity of his work." SLJ

Includes bibliographical references

Salk, Jonas, 1914-1995

Sherrow, Victoria. **Jonas** Salk; beyond the microscope. 2nd rev ed; Chelsea House 2008 146p il (Makers of modern science) $35

Grades: 7 8 9 10 **92**

1. Physicians 2. Scientists 3. Poliomyelitis vaccine 4. Microbiologists 5. Writers on medicine

ISBN 978-0-8160-6180-8; 0-8160-6180-7

LC 2006-33429

First published 1993 by Facts on File

This biography of Jonas Salk "describes this respected immunologist's medical research and his lifelong efforts to promote scientific and human progress on a global scale." Publisher's note

Includes glossary and bibliographical references

Santa Anna, Antonio López de, 1794?-1876

Lange, Brenda. **Antonio** Lopez de Santa Anna. Chelsea House Publishers 2010 102p il map (The great Hispanic heritage) lib bdg $30

Grades: 6 7 8 9 **92**

1. Generals 2. Presidents 3. Texas -- History 4. Mexico -- History

ISBN 978-1-60413-734-7; 1-60413-734-7

LC 2010007515

A biography the Mexican general and president who is well-known for his part in the Battle of the Alamo during the U.S. Mexican War.

Includes bibliographical references

Santana, Carlos, 1947-

Slavicek, Louise Chipley. **Carlos** Santana. Chelsea House Publishers 2006 120p il (Great Hispanic heritage) lib bdg $30

Grades: 6 7 8 9   92

1. Guitarists 2. Rock musicians 3. Band leaders 4. Mexican Americans -- Biography

ISBN 978-0-7910-8844-9 lib bdg; 0-7910-8844-8 lib bdg

LC 2005026000

This biography of rock musician Santana is filled "with excellent details—music and familial [history sheds] light on the man's roots and focus strongly on his humanitarian efforts. . . . Color photos and sidebars add interest, and quotes from magazines, newspapers, and interviews are meticulously cited in the endnotes." SLJ

Includes bibliographical references

Sarkozy, Nicolas, 1955-

Abrams, Dennis. **Nicolas** Sarkozy. Chelsea House 2009 136p il (Modern world leaders) lib bdg $30

Grades: 6 7 8 9   92

1. Mayors 2. Lawyers 3. Presidents 4. Cabinet members 5. Members of Parliament 6. France -- Politics and government

ISBN 978-1-60413-081-2 lib bdg; 1-60413-081-4 lib bdg

LC 2008-26567

"Abrams deftly explores both the personal and public spheres of this 'most untraditional politician.' . . . Probing, evenhanded." Booklist

"Examines the life and career of the president of France." Publisher's note

Includes bibliographical references

Schaller, George B.

★ Turner, Pamela S. A **life** in the wild; George Schaller's struggle to save the last great beasts. Farrar, Straus and Giroux 2008 103p il map $21.95

Grades: 5 6 7 8   92

1. Zoologists 2. Wildlife conservation 3. Nonfiction writers

ISBN 978-0-374-34578-5; 0-374-34578-3

LC 2007-42844

"The author interviewed Schaller and had access to his photos, which allowed her to capture beautifully the spirit of Schaller's work. The book is organized chronologically, and each chapter covers a geographic area and the principal animals that Schaller studied there. . . . Animal lovers and conservation-minded students will enjoy this excellent introduction to Schaller and his ideals." Voice Youth Advocates

Includes bibliographical references

Schindler, Oskar, 1908-1974

★ Leyson, Leon, 1929-2013. The **boy** on the wooden box; Leon Leyson ; with Marilyn J Harran and Elisabeth B Leyson. Atheneum Books for Young Readers 2013 240 p. (hardcover) $16.99

Grades: 6 7 8 9   92

1. Holocaust survivors 2. World War, 1939-1945 -- Jews -- Rescue 3. Narewka (Poland) -- Biography 4. Jews -- Poland -- Narewka -- Biography 5. Płaszów (Concentration camp) 6. Concentration camp inmates -- Poland -- Płaszów -- Biography 7. Jewish children in the Holocaust -- Poland -- Kraków -- Biography 8. Holocaust, Jewish (1939-1945) -- Poland -- Kraków -- Personal narratives

ISBN 1442497815; 9781442497818; 9781442497832

LC 2013017987

In this book, "Leon Leyson (born Leib Lezjon) was only ten years old when the Nazis invaded Poland and his family was forced to relocate to the Krakow ghetto. With incredible luck, perseverance, and grit, Leyson was able to survive the sadism of the Nazis, including that of the demonic Amon Goeth, commandant of Plaszow, the concentration camp outside Krakow. Ultimately, it was the generosity and cunning of one man, a man named Oskar Schindler, who saved Leon Leyson's life, and the lives of his mother, his father, and two of his four siblings, by adding their names to his list of workers in his factory—a list that became world renowned: Schindler's List." (Publisher's Note)

"This powerful memoir of one of the youngest boys on Schindler's list deserves to be shared...This memoir is a natural curriculum addition to WWII units for upper-elementary- and middle-school readers. Be sure to have additional materials on hand about Oskar Schindler, as readers will want to do more research into Leyson's story." (Booklist)

Schliemann, Heinrich, 1822-1890

★ Schlitz, Laura Amy. The **hero** Schliemann; the dreamer who dug for Troy. illustrated by Robert Byrd. Candlewick Press 2006 72p il $12.23

Grades: 4 5 6   92

1. Archeologists 2. Excavations (Archeology) 3. Archaeologists 4. Troy (Extinct city)

ISBN 0-7636-2283-4

LC 2005046916

This is a biography of the archaeologist who rediscovered ancient Troy. "Intermediate." (Horn Book)

"In this slim biography, Schlitz introduces Heinrich Schliemann, a nineteenth-century 'storyteller, archaeologist, and crook,' who led a search for the lost cities of Homer's epic poems." Booklist

Schloss, Eva

Schloss, Eva. **Eva's** story; a survivor's tale by the stepsister of Anne Frank. [by] Eva Schloss with Evelyn Julia Kent. W.B. Eerdmans Pub. Co. 2010 226p il map pa $14.99

Grades: 7 8 9 10   92

1. Jewish refugees 2. Holocaust survivors 3. Jews -- Netherlands 4. Auschwitz (Poland: Concentration

camp) 5. Holocaust, 1933-1945 -- Personal narratives
ISBN 978-0-8028-6495-6; 0-8028-6495-3

LC 2009-51022

Schulke, Flip

Schulke, Flip. **Witness** to our times; my life as a photojournalist. [by] Flip Schulke; in association with Matt Schudel. Cricket Books 2003 112p il $19.95

Grades: 8 9 10 11 12   92
1. Photographers 2. Documentary photography 3. Photojournalists
ISBN 0-8126-2682-6

LC 2002-151457

An autobiography of a man whose documentary photographs in American magazines helped to shape public opinion on such issues as the civil rights movement and the space race

"Photojournalist Schulke shot some of the most important photographs of the twentieth century, and the passion, concentration, and sensitivity that characterize his photos come across as powerfully in his prose. . . . His black-and-white photos make up most of the book, and they express such strong emotion that readers will feel the depth of his passion even on pages without a word of text." Booklist

Includes bibliographical references

Schulz, Charles M.

★ Gherman, Beverly. **Sparky** : the life and art of Charles Schulz. Chronicle Books 2010 125p il $16.99

Grades: 5 6 7 8   92
1. Cartoonists
ISBN 978-0-8118-6790-0; 0-8118-6790-0

A look at the life and influences of Charles Schulz, creator of the beloved comic strip Peanuts.

"Gherman's clear and direct prose is just right for portraying the life of the famous cartoonist for young readers. The splashy, bright design, with multicolored pages and several of Schulz's cartoons included, makes this a cheery read that may well introduce the Peanuts comic strip to a new generation, who likely know Charlie Brown mostly through the holiday TV specials. An informative yet lighthearted look at the life of an American icon." Kirkus

Schumann, Clara, 1819-1896

Shichtman, Sandra H. The **joy** of creation; the story of Clara Schumann. by Sandra Shichtman and Dorothy Indenbaum. Morgan Reynolds 2011 159p il (Classical composers) lib bdg $28.95

Grades: 6 7 8 9 10   92
1. Pianists 2. Composers
ISBN 978-1-59935-123-0; 1-59935-123-4

LC 2009054289

This title "provides a detailed account of the acclaimed nineteenth-century German pianist and composer Clara Schumann. . . . Adundant quotes, many from Schumann's diary, add intimacy to the straightforward, sometimes dense narrative, which also provides historical context and background to her notable life and legacy. The attractively

designed volume intersperses color and black-and-white illustrations." Booklist

Includes bibliographical references

Schutz, Samantha, 1978-

Schutz, Samantha. **I** don't want to be crazy; a memoir of anxiety disorder. PUSH Books 2006 280p $16.99

Grades: 8 9 10 11 12   92
1. Anxiety 2. Panic disorders 3. Editors 4. Memoirists
ISBN 0-439-80518-X

LC 2005028964

"In this moving memoir, Schutz details her struggle with anxiety disorder. . . . Written in verse, this memoir successfully conveys what it is like to suffer from panic attacks." Voice Youth Advocates

Scieszka, Jon, 1954-

Scieszka, Jon. **Knucklehead**; tall tales and mostly true stories of growing up Scieszka. Viking 2008 106p il $16.99; pa $12.99

Grades: 4 5 6 7   92
1. Authors 2. Authors, American 3. Children's authors
ISBN 978-0-670-01106-3; 0-670-01106-1; 978-0-670-01138-4 pa; 0-670-01138-X pa

LC 2008-16870

"Scieszka . . . has written an autobiography about boys, for boys and anyone else interested in baseball, fire and peeing on stuff. . . . The text is divided into two- to three-page nonsequential chapters and peppered with scrapbook snapshots and comic-book-ad reproductions. . . . By themselves, the chapters entertain with abrupt, vulgar fun. Taken together, they offer a look at the makings of one very funny author." Booklist

Selkirk, Alexander, 1676-1721

Kraske, Robert. **Marooned**; the strange but true adventures of Alexander Selkirk, the real Robinson Crusoe. illustrated by Robert Andrew Parker. Clarion Books 2005 120p il map $15

Grades: 5 6 7 8   92
1. Sailors 2. Survival after airplane accidents, shipwrecks, etc.
ISBN 0-618-56843-3

LC 2004-28769

"In 1704, English sailing master Alexander Selkirk was marooned on Juan Fernandez, an isolated Pacific island. . . . In 1709, two English ships rescued him, hired him as a second mate, and later captured a Spanish treasure ship. . . . Kraske offers a well-focused look at life in several quite different settings during the early eighteenth century as well as an absorbing telling of Selkirk's story." Booklist

Includes glossary and bibliographical references

Seuss, Dr.

Anderson, Tanya. **Dr.** Seuss (Theodor Geisel) foreword by Kyle Zimmer. 2nd ed; Chelsea House 2011 128p il (Who wrote that?) lib bdg $35

Grades: 6 7 8 9   92
1. Artists 2. Authors 3. Humorists 4. Illustrators 5.

Authors, American 6. Children's authors
ISBN 978-1-60413-750-7; 1-60413-750-9

LC 2010030589

This discusses the life and work of author Theodor Geisel, known as Dr. Seuss.

Includes bibliographical references

Sewall, May Wright, 1844-1920

Boomhower, Ray E. **Fighting** for equality; a life of May Wright Sewall. [by] Ray E. Boomhower. Indiana Historical Society Press 2007 160p il $17.95

Grades: 4 5 6   92

1. Feminism 2. Educators 3. Reformers 4. Suffragists 5. Lecturers 6. Pacifists

ISBN 978-0-87195-253-0; 0-87195-253-X

LC 2007008517

"This accessible volume tells of the life and work of suffragist and educator [May] Wright Sewall. . . . Archival black-and-white photos enhance the text." Horn Book Guide

Includes bibliographical references

Shackleton, Ernest Henry Sir, 1874-1922

Johnson, Rebecca L. **Ernest** Shackleton; gripped by the Antarctic. Carolrhoda Bks. 2003 112p il map (Trailblazer biography) lib bdg $25.26

Grades: 6 7 8 9   92

1. Explorers 2. Endurance (Ship) 3. Antarctica -- Exploration 4. Imperial Trans-Antarctic Expedition (1914-1917)

ISBN 0-87614-920-4

LC 2002-6816

A biography of Sir Ernest Shackleton, the daring, charismatic Antarctic explorer who fell short of his goal of crossing Antarctica, but accomplished a far greater feat by bringing every member of his crew back alive

"The writing is lively and clear and the story is compelling. A useful title for reports and recreational reading." SLJ

Includes bibliographical references

Koestler-Grack, Rachel A. **Sir** Ernest Shackleton; [by] Linda Davis. Chelsea House 2009 143p il (Great explorers) lib bdg $30

Grades: 6 7 8 9   92

1. Explorers 2. Antarctica -- Exploration

ISBN 978-1-60413-421-6 lib bdg; 1-60413-421-6 lib bdg

LC 2009-14164

Biography of Sir Ernest Shackleton

"The information . . . is presented in such a way as to attract and maintain readers' interest. . . . With a full complement of maps, photographs (where available), illustrations, time lines, and document reproductions, a full story is told. Well-written and throughly researched, this . . . will make a solid addition." SLJ

Includes glossary and bibliographical references

Shakur, Tupac

★ Golus, Carrie. **Tupac** Shakur; hip-hop idol. Twenty-First Century Books 2010 112p il (USA Today: lifeline biographies) lib bdg $33.26

Grades: 7 8 9 10 11 12   92

1. Poets 2. Actors 3. Rap music 4. African American musicians 5. Rap musicians

ISBN 978-0-7613-5473-4; 0-7613-5473-5

LC 2009-38127

"The story told in Tupac Shakur will be inspirational for some and a cautionary tale for others. Born into poverty, Shakur became one of hip-hop's biggest stars. But even as he climbed up the ladder of success, drugs and violence were always there to pull him back down." Booklist

Includes bibliographical references

Harris, Ashley Rae. **Tupac** Shakur; multi-platinum rapper. ABDO Pub. Co. 2010 112p il (Lives cut short) lib bdg $32.79

Grades: 5 6 7 8   92

1. Poets 2. Actors 3. Hip-hop 4. Rap music 5. African American musicians 6. Rap musicians

ISBN 978-1-60453-791-8; 1-60453-791-4

This discusses Tupac Shakur's early life, "providing details that give insight into later success and troubles and maintaining a laudatory tone that focuses on the individual's artistic achievements and hard work to achieve fame. Details [such as] explaining . . . that Tupac Shakur was a standout student in high school are bound to resonate with readers. Numerous photos and sidebars appear throughout. [A] worthwhile [resource] for reports as well as popular reading." SLJ

Sheba, Queen of

Lucks, Naomi. **Queen** of Sheba. Chelsea House Publishers 2009 112p il (Ancient world leaders) lib bdg $30

Grades: 6 7 8 9   92

1. Queens 2. Biblical characters

ISBN 978-0-7910-9579-9 lib bdg; 0-7910-9579-9 lib bdg

LC 2008004872

This biography of the Queen of Sheba "references various oral traditions from Europe, the Middle East, and Ethiopia to reveal aspects of the woman's personality. Classical paintings and full-color photographs of sculptures, landscapes, and archaeological finds complement the text. . . . The [text is] easily digestible and appropriate for the intended age group." SLJ

Includes glossary and bibliographical references

Shelley, Mary Wollstonecraft, 1797-1851

Wells, Catherine. **Strange** creatures: the story of Mary Shelley. Morgan Reynolds 2009 160p il (World writers) $28.95

Grades: 7 8 9 10   92

1. Authors 2. Novelists 3. Women authors 4. Authors, English

ISBN 978-1-59935-092-9; 1-59935-092-0

LC 2008039042

"This engaging biography limns [Mary Shelley's] unconventional life, focusing on her love affair (and later marriage) with poet Percy Bysshe Shelley, the writing of Frankenstein when she was still a teenager, and the novel's infamy and lasting influence. Period illustrations and photographs appear throughout." Horn Book Guide

Includes bibliographical references

Shiner, Michael

Capital days; Michael Shiner's journal and the growth of our nation's capital. by Tonya Bolden. Abrams Books for Young Readers 2015 90 p. (hardback) $21.95

Grades: 4 5 6   **92**

1. Washington (D.C.) -- History 2. African Americans -- Biography 3. Washington (D.C.) -- Biography 4. Slaves -- Maryland -- Biography 5. Freedmen -- Washington (D.C.) -- Biography 6. Washington (D.C.) -- History -- 19th century 7. African Americans -- Washington (D.C.) -- Biography 8. Washington (D.C.) -- Race relations -- History -- 19th century

ISBN 1419707337; 9781419707339

LC 2014024668

This book, by Tonya Bolden, "introduces young readers to Washington, D.C., during the early to mid-19th century. Spanning more than 60 years, the story of Michael Shiner (c. 1804–1880) highlights a period of immense change in our country and its capital." Topics include the burning of the city during the War of 1812, the rebuilding of the Capitol and White House, the raising of the Washington Monument . . . the Civil War, [and] the end of slavery." (Publisher's note)

Includes bibliographical references and index

Shivack, Nadia

Shivack, Nadia. **Inside** out; portrait of an eating disorder. written and illustrated by Nadia Shivack. Atheneum Books for Young Readers 2007 un il $17.99

Grades: 6 7 8 9   **92**

1. Graphic novels 2. Memoirists 3. Bulimia -- Graphic novels

ISBN 0-689-85216-9; 978-0-689-85216-9

LC 2004016096

"In this heartfelt, honest memoir, the author uses a graphic novel format to reveal her anguished, ongoing struggle with bulimia. . . . Though intensely personal and—perhaps of necessity—repetitious, this harrowing chronicle may well provide support and solace to teens facing a similar crisis." Publ Wkly

Siegal, Aranka

Siegal, Aranka. **Memories** of Babi; stories. Farrar, Straus & Giroux 2008 116p $16

Grades: 4 5 6 7   **92**

1. Authors 2. Farm life 3. Grandmothers 4. Holocaust survivors 5. Ukraine 6. Jews -- Biography 7. Children's authors

ISBN 978-0-374-39978-8; 0-374-39978-6

LC 2007007002

Siegal's "Upon the Head of the Goat (1981) is about her childhood in Hungary as Hitler comes to power. In this follow-up, written in nine wry sketches, she remembers the years before that—especially her close relationship with her Jewish grandmother, who lived on a small farm just across the Hungarian border in Ukraine." Booklist

★ Siegal, Aranka. **Upon** the head of the goat: a childhood in Hungary, 1939-1944. Farrar, Straus & Giroux 1981 213p hardcover o.p. pa $5.95

Grades: 6 7 8 9   **92**

1. Authors 2. Holocaust survivors 3. Jews -- Hungary 4. Children's authors 5. World War, 1939-1945 -- Jews 6. Holocaust, 1933-1945 -- Personal narratives

ISBN 0-374-38059-7; 0-374-48079-6 pa

LC 81-12642

A Newbery Medal honor book, 1982

"The story is familiar . . . but a few pages into Aranka Siegal's fine memoir . . . you feel the power and interest of her particular experience and remember that this story cannot be told too often." Newsweek

Silverstein, Shel

Baughan, Michael Gray. **Shel** Silverstein; [by] Michael Gray Baughan. Chelsea House 2008 120p il (Who wrote that?) lib bdg $30

Grades: 6 7 8 9   **92**

1. Poets 2. Authors 3. Singers 4. Cartoonists 5. Songwriters 6. Authors, American 7. Children's authors

ISBN 978-0-7910-9676-5 lib bdg; 0-7910-9676-9 lib bdg

LC 2007045336

This biography of the popular author of Where the Sidewalk Ends examines the writer's "life, including the inspiration behind some of [his] works. [The] volume includes photographs and quotations from interviews, as well as descriptions of main characters and annotations lists of books and awards. Useful for aspiring authors as well as book report writers." Horn Book Guide

Includes bibliographical references

Simmons, Russell, 1957-

Baughan, Brian. **Russell** Simmons; [by] Brian Baughan. Morgan Reynolds 2009 112p il (Business leaders) lib bdg $27.95

Grades: 6 7 8 9   **92**

1. Record producers 2. Broadcasting executives 3. Motion picture executives 4. Recording industry executives

ISBN 978-1-59935-075-2 lib bdg; 1-59935-075-0 lib bdg

LC 2007-37797

"Baughan describes Simmons's childhood in Queens, NY, his college days as a rap promoter, his teen years when he was involved with drugs, his early efforts as a music producer, business collaborations, and media empire. . . . Contain[s] full-color photos that add visual appeal, sidebars about related topics, and helpful time lines." SLJ

Includes bibliographical references

Lommel, Cookie. **Russell** Simmons. Chelsea House 2007 104p bibl il por (Hip-hop stars) lib bdg $30

Grades: 7 8 9 10   **92**

1. Record producers 2. Broadcasting executives 3. Motion picture executives 4. Recording industry

executives
ISBN 978-0-7910-9467-9 lib bdg; 0-7910-9467-7
lib bdg

LC 2007001463

This "weaves a concise history of hip-hop music and
culture into a solid biography of one of its originators, Def
Jam Records founder Russell Simmons. . . . [This is an] inspiring title that's sure to find wide circulation among hip-
hop fans." Booklist

Includes glossary and bibliographical references

Sitting Bull, Dakota Chief, 1831-1890

Stanley, George Edward. **Sitting** Bull; great
Sioux hero. Sterling 2010 124p il map (Sterling
biographies) lib bdg $12.95

Grades: 7 8 9 10   **92**

1. Dakota Indians 2. Indian chiefs 3. Native Americans
-- Biography
ISBN 978-1-4027-6846-0 lib bdg; 1-4027-6846-X
lib bdg

LC 2009-24141

This is a biography of the Sioux Indian chief.

"Each title opens with an introduction that arouses
compassion and interest for the featured subject. Succeeding chapters present chronological biographies, with vivid
portrayals of daily life, culture, and the impact an expanding
America had on the individual and his or her people. Paintings, drawings, and occasional photographs combine with
detail-rich sidebars and maps to provide a cumulatively engaging, accessible history lesson." Horn Book

Includes glossary and bibliographical references

Smith, Adam, 1723-1790

Crain, Cynthia D. **Adam** Smith; by Cynthia D.
Crain and Dwight R. Lee. Morgan Reynolds Pub.
2009 160p il map (Profiles in economics) lib bdg
$28.95

Grades: 8 9 10 11 12   **92**

1. Economists 2. Nonfiction writers
ISBN 978-1-59935-107-0 lib bdg; 1-59935-107-2
lib bdg

LC 2009-138

Biography of the economist Adam Smith

"Relationships, education, early influences, and family
life are all described . . . . [and] economic theory is closely tied to cultural and political events. . . . The writing is
straightforward, the . . . [author] assume[s] a certain level of
knowledge about world events." SLJ

Includes bibliographical references

Snicket, Lemony, 1970-

Abrams, Dennis. **Lemony** Snicket (Daniel Handler) foreword by Kyle Zimmer. Chelsea House Publishers 2010 117p il (Who wrote that?) lib bdg $35

Grades: 6 7 8 9 10   **92**

1. Authors 2. Novelists 3. Authors, American 4.
Children's authors
ISBN 978-1-60413-726-2; 1-60413-726-6

LC 2010006599

A biography of the author of the A Series of Unfortunate
Events series.

"Abrams delivers a witty account of his subject. . . . He
presents a substantive look at Snicket/Handler, including
synopses of and reactions to his adult books, his major influences, and musical interests. Abundant secondary-source
quotes, full-color photos and film stills, and a chapter devoted to the series that made him famous will appeal to many
readers. This lively biography will not disappoint." SLJ

Includes bibliographical references

Snyder, Grace, 1882-1982

Warren, Andrea. **Pioneer** girl; a true story of
growing up on the prairie. with a new afterword by
the author. University of Nebraska Press 2009 104p
il map pa $14.95

Grades: 5 6 7 8   **92**

1. Frontier and pioneer life 2. Quiltmakers 3.
Centenarians
ISBN 978-0-8032-2526-8 pa; 0-8032-2526-1 pa

LC 2009-20883

First published 1998 by Morrow Junior Books

Biography of Nebraska homesteader, Grace
McCance Snyder

"This new edition offers an afterword that includes information about black homesteaders, Native Americans,
and the specific tasks of women, especially quilting. . . . Although it is written for younger readers than a teen audience,
readability and intense subject matter should make the book
popular with those readers." Voice Youth Advocates

Includes bibliographical references

Soto, Gary

Abrams, Dennis. **Gary** Soto; foreword by Kyle
Zimmer. Chelsea House Pubs. 2008 120p bibl il por
(Who wrote that?) $30

Grades: 5 6 7 8   **92**

1. Poets 2. Authors 3. Novelists 4. Mexican American
authors 5. Essayists 6. College teachers 7. Authors,
American 8. Children's authors 9. Young adult authors
10. Mexican Americans -- Biography
ISBN 978-0-7910-9529-4; 0-7910-9529-0

LC 2007045509

A biography of the popular Mexican American author
for children and young adults.

Includes bibliographical references

Soto, Hernando de, ca. 1500-1542

Young, Jeff C. **Hernando** de Soto; Spanish conquistador in the Americas. Enslow Publishers 2009
112p il (Great explorers of the world) lib bdg $31.93

Grades: 6 7 8 9   **92**

1. Explorers 2. America -- Exploration 3. Colonial
administrators 4. Mississippi River valley
ISBN 978-1-59845-104-7 lib bdg; 1-59845-104-9
lib bdg

LC 2008-30753

"Discusses the life of Spanish explorer Hernando de
Soto, including his travels in the Americas, the claim of
Florida for Spain, and his eventual discovery of the Missis-
sippi River." Publisher's note

Includes glossary and bibliographical references

Sotomayor, Sonia, 1954-

Gitlin, Marty. **Sonia** Sotomayor; Supreme Court justice. by Martin Gitlin. ABDO Pub. Co. 2011 112p il (Essential lives) $32.79

Grades: 5 6 7 8   92
1. Judges 2. Women judges 3. District attorneys 4. Supreme Court justices 5. Hispanic Americans -- Biography
ISBN 978-1-61613-518-8; 1-61613-518-2
LC 2010000499

This biography of Supreme Court Justice Sonia Sotomayor "toggles between the subject's personal and professional life; [it] offers sidebar explanations of legal issues. . . . The writing is accessible, the format is open, and full-color photos appear throughout." SLJ

Includes glossary and bibliographical references

McElroy, Lisa Tucker. **Sonia** Sotomayor; first Hispanic U.S. Supreme Court justice. Lerner Publications 2010 48p il lib bdg $26.60

Grades: 5 6 7 8   92
1. Judges 2. Women judges 3. District attorneys 4. Supreme Court justices 5. Hispanic Americans -- Biography
ISBN 978-0-7613-5861-9 lib bdg; 0-7613-5861-7 lib bdg
LC 2009037703

"Well organized and straightforward, this biography is appealing with its bright photographs and bold, easy-to-read font. Starting with Sotomayor's childhood in the Bronx, the author covers the justice's life and career up to her nomination to the Supreme Court. . . . An informative, interesting, and, most of all, inspiring read." SLJ

Includes bibliographical references

Spade, Kate

Freistadt, Margo. **Kate** Spade. Morgan Reynolds Pub. 2011 112p il (Profiles in fashion) $28.95

Grades: 7 8 9 10   92
1. Fashion designers
ISBN 978-1-59935-154-4; 1-59935-154-4
LC 2010022227

A biography of Kate Spade, designer of handbags, luggage, stationery, shoes, eyeglasses, homewares and other products.

Includes bibliographical references

Standish, Myles, 1584?-1656

Harness, Cheryl. The **adventurous** life of Myles Standish; and the amazing-but-true survival story of Plymouth Colony. painstakingly written and illustrated by Cheryl Harness. National Geographic 2006 144p il map (Cheryl Harness history) $16.95; lib bdg $25.90

Grades: 4 5 6 7   92
1. Pilgrims (New England colonists) 2. Colonists 3. Pilgrim fathers 4. Colonial leaders 5. Massachusetts -- History -- 1600-1775, Colonial period
ISBN 978-0-7922-5918-3; 0-7922-5918-1; 978-0-7922-5919-0 lib bdg; 0-7922-5919-X lib bdg

"Harness chronicles the history of the Plymouth Pilgrims from their troubles in England to their first years in North America, with the focus on Standish. Separating documented history from speculation, the narrative explains religious movements, introduces key figures, and gives a balanced account of Pilgrim-Indian relationships. . . . The tone is casual. . . . A reader-friendly approach to history." Booklist

Includes bibliographical references

Stanton, Elizabeth Cady, 1815-1902

Colman, Penny. **Elizabeth** Cady Stanton and Susan B. Anthony; a friendship that changed the world. Henry Holt and Company 2011 256p il $18.99

Grades: 7 8 9 10   92
1. Feminism 2. Suffragists 3. Women -- Suffrage 4. Biography, Individual
ISBN 978-0-8050-8293-7; 0-8050-8293-X
LC 2010-39762

"Elizabeth Cady Stanton, a married mother of four boys at the time they met, and Susan B. Anthony, an unmarried schoolteacher, formed a friendship that lasted until Elizabeth's death more than 50 years later. Their tireless work, including advocacy, speeches, organizing and writing, placed them at the center of tumultuous events in the middle of the 19th century. . . . This [is a] lively, very readable narrative. . . . This thoughtful portrayal to two complex women is . . . enhanced by comprehensive backmatter, making this an invaluable addition to the literature of suffrage." Kirkus

Includes bibliographical references

Sigerman, Harriet. **Elizabeth** Cady Stanton; the right is ours. Oxford Univ. Press 2001 143p il (Oxford portraits) $28

Grades: 7 8 9 10   92
1. Feminism 2. Suffragists 3. Women -- Suffrage
ISBN 0-19-511969-X
LC 2001-31404

A biography of one of the first leaders of the women's rights movement, whose work led to women's right to vote

"This inspiring biography . . . is both interestingly written and easy to follow. . . . Black-and-white photographs and original documents add greatly to the appeal of this resource." SLJ

Includes bibliographical references

Steiner, Matt

Warren, Andrea. **Escape** from Saigon; how a Vietnam War orphan became an American boy. Farrar, Straus and Giroux 2004 110p il map hardcover o.p. pa $9.95

Grades: 6 7 8 9 10   92
1. Refugees 2. Physicians 3. Interracial adoption 4. Vietnamese Americans 5. Racially mixed people 6. Vietnam War, 1961-1975
ISBN 978-0-374-32224-3; 0-374-32224-4; 978-0-374-40023-1 pa; 0-374-40023-7 pa
LC 2003-60672

Chronicles the experiences of Matt Steiner, an orphaned Amerasian boy, from his birth and early childhood in Saigon through his departure from Vietnam in the 1975 Operation Babylift and his subsequent life as the adopted son of an American family in Ohio.

"The child-at-war story and the facts about the Operation Babylift rescue are tense and exciting. Just as gripping is the boy's personal conflict." Booklist

Steller, Georg Wilhelm, 1700-1746

Arnold, Ann. **Sea** cows, shamans, and scurvy: Alaska's first naturalist: Georg Wilhelm Steller. Farrar, Straus & Giroux 2008 227p il map $21

Grades: 6 7 8 9   92

1. Explorers 2. Naturalists 3. Alaska
ISBN 978-0-374-39947-4; 0-374-39947-6
                                          LC 2006037400

"This is a detailed and lavishly illustrated biography of Georg Wilhelm Steller (1707-1746), Alaska's first naturalist. . . . He is the only scientist ever to describe, dissect, and eat the flightless spectacled cormorant. Species bear his name, including Steller's albatross, eider, jay, sculpin, sea cow, sea eagle, and sea lion. Arnold's exciting, harrowing account is personalized by excerpts from Steller's journal." KLIATT

Includes bibliographical references

Stine, R. L., 1943-

Marcovitz, Hal. **R.L.** Stine; foreword by Kyle Zimmer. Chelsea House Publishers 2006 134p bibl il por (Who wrote that?) lib bdg $30

Grades: 6 7 8 9   92

1. Authors 2. Magazine editors 3. Authors, American 4. Children's authors
ISBN 0-7910-8659-3
                                          LC 2005008186

A biography of the popular author of Goosebumps and other children's horror stories.

Includes bibliographical references

Stone, Biz

Smith, Chris. **Twitter**; Jack Dorsey, Biz Stone and Evan Williams. [by] Chris Smith and Marci McGrath. Morgan Reynolds Pub. 2011 112p il (Business leaders) $28.95

Grades: 7 8 9 10 11 12   92

1. Online social networks 2. Twitter, Inc. 3. Internet executives 4. Computer programmers 5. Computer software executives
ISBN 978-1-59935-179-7; 1-59935-179-X; 978-1-59935-216-9 e-book
                                          LC 2011024699

This biography of the founders of Twitter "will grab YAs. . . . The design is browsable, with clear type and lots of color screens and informal photos of young people at work." Booklist

Includes bibliographical references

Su, Shih, 1036 or 7-1101

Demi. **Su** Dongpo; Chinese genius. Lee & Low Books 2006 un il map $24

Grades: 4 5 6 7   92

1. Poets 2. Authors 3. Authors, Chinese 4. Calligraphers
ISBN 978-1-58430-256-8; 1-58430-256-9
                                          LC 2005030437

"In reverent tribute to a 'statesman, philosopher, poet, painter, engineer, architect, and humanitarian' born nearly ten centuries ago, Demi offers a text in which quoted passages of poetry and references to 'mystical painting skills' mingle with biographical detail. She pairs this with her trademark scenes of dignified, finely detailed figures floating through luminescent clouds in traditional dress. Though she sounds a false note near the end with a dismissive description of Hainan Island as 'a place inhabited only by natives,' this portrait of a 'knight-errant,' who shone brightly in both the literary and political arenas while surviving several severe reversals of fortune, presents an exemplary role model. In the author's view, he still stands at the 'heart and soul of Chinese culture.'" Kirkus

"This handsome volume introduces Su Dongpo (1036–1101), an intriguing figure in Chinese history who will likely be unknown to many readers. Offering examples of his writing and calling his accomplishments "almost superhuman," Demi describes him as "a statesman, philosopher, poet, painter, engineer, architect, and humanitarian." The striking illustrations combine small, meticulous figures with spacious, misty backgrounds and touches of gold." Horn Book

Sui, Anna

Darraj, Susan Muaddi. **Anna** Sui. Chelsea House Publishers 2009 120p il (Asian Americans of achievement) $30

Grades: 7 8 9 10   92

1. Fashion designers
ISBN 978-1-60413-570-1; 1-60413-570-0
                                          LC 2009-14608

"Anna Sui is known for her youthful 'baby doll' designs and extravagant combinations inspired by the hippie and rock-'n'-roll fashions of the '60s and early '70s. Readers learn about the setbacks and hard work required to become successful. . . . The quality of research and in-depth coverage broadens [the book's] usefulness. . . . [This book is] inspiring." SLJ

Includes glossary and bibliographical references

Sullivan, Anne, 1866-1936

Delano, Marfe Ferguson. **Helen's** eyes; a photobiography of Annie Sullivan, Helen Keller's teacher. [foreword by Keller Johnson Thompson] National Geographic 2008 63p il map $17.95; lib bdg $27.90

Grades: 4 5 6 7   92

1. Deaf 2. Blind 3. Authors 4. Teachers 5. Memoirists 6. Humanitarians 7. Teachers of the deaf 8. Inspirational writers 9. Teachers of the blind 10. Social welfare leaders
ISBN 978-1-4263-02-9-1; 1-4263-0209-6; 978-1-4263-0210-7 lib bdg; 1-4263-0210-X lib bdg

"There are many biographies of Helen Keller and Annie Sullivan, but this one is very nicely done. . . . The book is honest in its portrayals, especially of Sullivan. . . . What makes this oversize book so appealing is the clean design, with large typeface. The many fascinating photographs are sometimes placed over historical documents." Booklist

Includes bibliographical references

Tan, Amy

Mussari, Mark. **Amy** Tan. Marshall Cavendish Benchmark 2010 125p il (Today's writers and their works) lib bdg $42.79

Grades: 8 9 10 11 12   **92**

1. Authors 2. Novelists 3. Women authors 4. Essayists 5. Authors, American 6. Children's authors 7. Short story writers 8. Chinese Americans -- Biography

ISBN 978-0-7614-4127-4; 0-7614-4127-1

This biography of Amy Tan places the author in the context of her times and discusses her work.

Includes bibliographical references

O'Keefe, Sherry. **From** China to America; the story of Amy Tan. Morgan Reynolds Pub. 2011 112p il lib bdg $28.95

Grades: 7 8 9 10   **92**

1. Authors 2. Novelists 3. Women authors 4. Essayists 5. Authors, American 6. Children's authors 7. Short story writers 8. Chinese Americans -- Biography

ISBN 978-1-59935-138-4; 1-59935-138-2

LC 2010-7594

"Born in California, the daughter of Chinese immigrants, Tan grew up as an American on the outside and Chinese on the inside. . . . Growing up, Tan faced the loss of her brother and father and the morbid outlook of her mother. Their tumultuous relationship led her to write stories about mother-and-daughter conflict, which later became the basis for The Joy Luck Club. This book gives readers a brief overview of the novelist's life and a greater understanding of the inspiration behind her novels." SLJ

Includes bibliographical references

Tarbell, Ida M. (Ida Minerva), 1857-1944

McCully, Emily Arnold, 1939- **Ida** M. Tarbell; the woman who challenged big business--and won! by Emily Arnold McCully. Clarion Books/Houghton Mifflin Harcourt 2014 288 p. illustrations (hardcover) $18.99

Grades: 7 8 9 10 11 12   **92**

1. Women journalists 2. Journalists -- Biography 3. Journalists 4. Women -- Biography 5. Journalists -- United States -- Biography

ISBN 0547290926; 9780547290928

LC 2012039650

YALSA Award for Excellence in Nonfiction for Young Adults: Finalist (2015)

"Born in 1857 and raised in oil country, Ida M. Tarbell was one of the first investigative journalists and probably the most influential in her time. Her series of articles on the Standard Oil Trust, a complicated business empire run by John D. Rockefeller, revealed to readers the underhanded, even illegal practices that had led to Rockefeller's success." (Publisher's note)

"McCully expertly brings to life the story of a unique and determined woman in this well-written and thoroughly researched biography, filled with numerous and pertinent photographs." SLJ

Includes bibliographical references and index

Taylor, Major, 1878-1932

Brill, Marlene Targ. **Marshall** Major Taylor; world champion bicyclist, 1899-1901. by Marlene Targ Brill. Twenty-First Century Books 2008 112p il (Trailblazer biography) lib bdg $31.93

Grades: 5 6 7 8   **92**

1. Bicycle racing 2. African American athletes 3. Cyclists

ISBN 978-0-8225-6610-6 lib bdg; 0-8225-6610-9 lib bdg

LC 2006003883

"Marshall Taylor, an African American bicyclist who, despite facing prejudice in racing and in life, achieved world renown at the turn of the last century. . . . Brill's accessible, personable prose vividly relates Taylor's experiences." Booklist

Includes bibliographical references

Tecumseh, Shawnee Chief, 1768-1813

Zimmerman, Dwight Jon. **Tecumseh**; shooting star of the Shawnee. Sterling 2010 124p il map (Sterling biographies) lib bdg $12.95

Grades: 7 8 9 10   **92**

1. Shawnee Indians 2. Indian chiefs 3. Native Americans -- Biography

ISBN 978-1-4027-6847-7; 1-4027-6847-8

LC 2009-24142

"Lots of detailed physical battles dominate Tecumseh, with a strong focus on the Shawnee's brutal displacement by white settlers and the Indians caught up in the tensions between the U.S. and Great Britain. . . . [The] spacious design is highly scannable, with color background screens, photos, maps, and historic prints throughout." Booklist

Includes glossary and bibliographical references

Teresa, Mother, 1910-1997

Slavicek, Louise Chipley. **Mother** Teresa; caring for the world's poor. Chelsea House 2007 113p bibl il por (Modern peacemakers) lib bdg $30

Grades: 7 8 9 10   **92**

1. Nuns 2. Missionaries 3. Nobel laureates for peace

ISBN 0-7910-9433-2 lib bdg; 978-0-7910-9433-4 lib bdg

LC 2006028383

A biography of the nun who won the Nobel Peace Prize for her work with the poor of India

This "book is well organized and well written, and reads like a story. It is balanced in that it points out the critics of Mother Teresa's selection for the Nobel Peace Prize . . . as well as her admirers." SLJ

Includes bibliographical references

Tesla, Nikola, 1856-1943

Burgan, Michael. **Nikola** Tesla; physicist, inventor, electrical engineer. Compass Point Books 2009 112p il map (Signature lives) lib bdg $34.65

Grades: 6 7 8 9 10   **92**

1. Inventors 2. Electrical engineers

ISBN 978-0-7565-4086-9; 0-7565-4086-0

LC 2008-35725

A biography of Nikola Tesla, physicist, inventor, and electrical engineer

The "inviting page design features photos and boxed screens on each spread, and . . . includes a detailed bibliography, source notes, time line and glossary." Booklist

Includes glossary and bibliographical references

Thoreau, Henry David, 1817-1862

★ Meltzer, Milton. **Henry** David Thoreau; a biography. Twenty-First Century Books 2007 160p il lib bdg $31.93

Grades: 7 8 9 10 11 12   **92**

1. Authors 2. Naturalists 3. Essayists 4. Pacifists 5. Authors, American 6. Writers on nature 7. Nonfiction writers

ISBN 978-0-8225-5893-4 lib bdg; 0-8225-5893-9 lib bdg

LC 2006013747

In this biography "readers see Thoreau through a variety of lenses—brother, friend, pencil maker, abolitionist, naturalist, and transcendentalist—to name only a few. Meltzer's clear and succinct writing style is punctuated with well-chosen and good-quality photographs and reproductions. . . . A first-rate choice for any student seeking a well-organized introduction to the life of the author and philosopher." SLJ

Includes bibliographical references

Thorpe, Jim, 1888-1953

Bruchac, Joseph. **Jim** Thorpe; original All-American. Dial Books/Walden Media 2006 277p il $16.99

Grades: 6 7 8 9   **92**

1. Athletes 2. Decathletes 3. Pentathletes 4. Olympic athletes 5. Native Americans -- Biography

ISBN 0-8037-3118-3

LC 2005-32173

A biography of Native American athlete Jim Thorpe, focusing on his early athletic career.

"Bruchac relates the story in first person as if the reader is listening to Thorpe tell about his early life. . . . This conceit is extremely effective, and combined with Bruchac's excellently written first-person reminiscences of key football plays and Olympic competition, will make the book appeal to reluctant readers who might otherwise not read biographies." Voice Youth Advocates

Includes bibliographical references

Labrecque, Ellen. **Jim** Thorpe; an athlete for the ages. Sterling 2010 124p il (Sterling biographies) $12.95

Grades: 7 8 9 10   **92**

1. Athletes 2. Decathletes 3. Pentathletes 4. Olympic athletes 5. Native Americans -- Biography

ISBN 978-1-4027-7150-7; 1-4027-7150-9

This biography of Native American athlete Jim Thorpe is "studded with quotes and illustrated with photos. . . . [It] details his taking of Olympic gold in the 1912 decathlon and pentathlon events, though he was forced to return the medals the following year amid charges of professionalism, a matter resolved in his favor 70 years later. Written in a straightforward, journalistic style, [this biography presents a] very

readable [account] of the [life] of [an athlete] who made [his mark] on American culture." Booklist

Schuman, Michael. **Jim** Thorpe; There's no such thing as 'can't' [by] Michael A. Schuman. Enslow Publishers 2009 128p il map (Americans: the spirit of a nation) lib bdg $31.93

Grades: 6 7 8 9   **92**

1. Athletes 2. Decathletes 3. Pentathletes 4. Olympic athletes 5. Native Americans -- Biography

ISBN 978-0-7660-3021-3 lib bdg; 0-7660-3021-0 lib bdg

LC 2008-21486

This "describes the Native American baseball player's birth in the Indian Territory of Oklahoma, his education at the repressive Indian schools, and his groundbreaking career as one of the most well-rounded and talented athletes of the 20th century." SLJ

Includes glossary and bibliographical references

Tillage, Leon, 1936-

★ Tillage, Leon. **Leon's** story; [by] Leon Walter Tillage; collage art by Susan L. Roth. Farrar, Straus & Giroux 1997 107p il hardcover o.p. pa $6.95

Grades: 4 5 6 7 8 9 10   **92**

1. African Americans -- Biography 2. North Carolina -- Race relations

ISBN 0-374-34379-9; 0-374-44330-0 pa

LC 96-43544

The son of a North Carolina sharecropper recalls the hard times faced by his family and other African Americans in the first half of the twentieth century and the changes that the civil rights movement helped bring about

The author's "voice is direct, the words are simple. There is no rhetoric, no commentary, no bitterness. . . . This quiet drama will move readers of all ages . . . and may encourage them to record their own family stories." Booklist

Tolkien, J. R. R. (John Ronald Reuel), 1892-1973

Willett, Edward. **J.R.R.** Tolkien; master of imaginary worlds. Enslow Publishers 2004 128p il (Authors teens love) lib bdg $26.60

Grades: 6 7 8 9   **92**

1. Authors 2. Novelists 3. Linguists 4. Philologists 5. Fantasy writers 6. Authors, English 7. Children's authors

ISBN 0-7660-2246-3

LC 2003-15657

Examines the personal life and literary career of the author of the Lord of the Rings trilogy

This "clearly goes a step beyond the typical series book, offering a more perceptive and more detailed, satisfying portrayal of its subject. . . . [The] volume includes a great deal of back matter: a time line, a list of selected works, a glossary, detailed chapter notes, and lists of recommended books and Internet sites." Booklist

Includes bibliographical references

Tom Thumb, 1838-1883

★ Sullivan, George. **Tom** Thumb; the remarkable true story of a man in miniature. Clarion Books 2010 200p il $20

Grades: 6 7 8 9   92

1. Circus 2. Dwarfs 3. Little people 4. Circus performers 5. Biography, Individual
ISBN 0-547-18203-1; 978-0-547-18203-2

LC 2009-52910

This is a biography of the circus performer who was part of the P.T. Barnum troupe. Index. "Grades five to eight." (Bull Cent Child Books)

"Insets on dwarfism appear early in the text, elucidating Tom Thumb's condition for readers without seriously interrupting to genial flow of the narration. Generous leading and a large stock of photographs and period reproductions will entice readers who shy away from longer works of nonfiction." Bull Cent Child Books

Toussaint Louverture, 1743?-1803

★ Rockwell, Anne F. **Open** the door to liberty!: a biography of Toussaint L'Ouverture; illustrated by R. Gregory Christie. Houghton Mifflin Books for Children 2009 64p il $18

Grades: 5 6 7 8   92

1. Generals 2. Revolutionaries 3. Haiti -- History 4. Blacks -- Biography 5. Slavery -- West Indies
ISBN 978-0-618-60570-5; 0-618-60570-3

LC 2007-25746

"In this eye-opening biography, Rockwell makes a strong case that Toussaint L'Ouverture is one of the most overlooked heroes of the eighteenth century. A freed slave of the French colony of St. Domingue (what we now know as Haiti), L'Ouverture was 48 when he was so inspired by his people's uprising against the French that he joined them and, through his oratory and strategical skills, became their leader. In 1793, he led history's first triumphant slave rebellion, but the resulting freedom would not last long. . . . Evocative paintings in primary colors help tell the story." Booklist

Includes bibliographical references

Truth, Sojourner, d. 1883

Butler, Mary G. **Sojourner** Truth; from slave to activist for freedom. PowerPlus Bks. 2003 112p il map (Library of American lives and times) lib bdg $31.95

Grades: 5 6 7 8   92

1. Feminism 2. Abolitionists 3. Memoirists 4. African American women -- Biography
ISBN 0-8239-5736-5

LC 2001-6169

A biography of the former slave who became an abolitionist and advocate for women's rights

"The text is well documented, and the numerous illustrations, photos, and reproductions, both in color and in black and white, are authoritative and informative." SLJ

Includes glossary and bibliographical references

Tubman, Harriet, 1820?-1913

★ Allen, Thomas B. **Harriet** Tubman, secret agent; how daring slaves and free Blacks spied for the Union during the Civil War. featuring illustrations by Carla Bauer. National Geographic Society 2006 191p il map $16.95; lib bdg $25.90

Grades: 6 7 8 9   92

1. Abolitionists 2. Underground railroad 3. Slavery -- United States 4. African American women -- Biography
ISBN 0-7922-7889-5; 0-7922-7890-9 lib bdg

LC 2005030927

"Allen brings readers much more than the usual biography of the brave rescuer on the Underground Railroad. This small, packed volume tells of Harriet Tubman's astonishing roles as spy, secret agent, and military leader, and it combines her personal story with a history of the abolitionist movement and the Civil War, focusing on how ex-slaves and free blacks served the Union cause. . . . The dense history is illustrated with numerous archival images, maps, and woodcuts, and the documentation is meticulous." Booklist

Includes bibliographical references

Sawyer, Kem Knapp. **Harriet** Tubman. DK Publishing 2010 128p il (DK biography) pa $5.99

Grades: 6 7 8 9   92

1. Abolitionists 2. Underground railroad 3. Slavery -- United States 4. African American women -- Biography
ISBN 978-0-7566-5806-9; 0-7566-5806-3

An illustrated exploration of the life of Harriet Tubman that covers her childhood, experiences as a slave, escape to freedom, work on the Underground Railroad, antislavery activism, and other topics.

"Meticulous about what is known and what is 'not confirmed,' the simple prose is eloquent in describing how Tubman started as a passenger on the Underground Railroad and went on to become one of its most famous conductors. . . . Highly readable, the series design, with highly legible type on thick paper, includes color photographs and prints on every spread." Booklist

Includes bibliographical references

Turing, Alan Mathison, 1912-1954

Corrigan, Jim. **Alan** Turing. Morgan Reynolds Pub. 2008 112p il (Profiles in mathematics) lib bdg $27.95

Grades: 7 8 9 10   92

1. Mathematicians
ISBN 978-1-59935-064-6; 1-59935-064-5

LC 2007-11704

"Corrigan's descriptions of English mathematician Turing as sporting 'ragged, wrinkled clothes' and few social graces will fit many readers' mental image of a numbers genius. But other aspects of this portrait push against stereotypes. . . . Throughout, candid mentions of Turing's homosexuality help readers contextualize the scandal he endured after running afoul of the era's discriminatory legislation. Equal sensitivity distinguishes Corringan's handling of Turing's death, officially (but not decisively) a suicide." Booklist

Includes bibliographical references

★ Henderson, Harry. **Alan** Turing; computing genius and wartime code breaker. Chelsea House 2011 133p il (Makers of modern science) $35

Grades: 7 8 9 10   **92**
  1. Mathematicians
  ISBN 978-0-8160-6175-4; 0-8160-6175-0
                         LC 2010-15798

A biography of code breaker and computer pioneer Alan Turing.

"The mark of a good biography is when it makes people you may never have heard of, in fields you might not be interested in, fascinating. [This book] does this with [a] well-chosen [subject], engaging writing, plenty of sidebars that take the text in new directions, and perhaps most importantly, the determination to present a fully-rounded person, not just a scientist." Booklist

Includes bibliographical references

Tutankhamen, King of Egypt

★ Demi. **Tutankhamun**; written and illustrated by Demi. Marshall Cavendish Children 2009 un il map $19.99

Grades: 4 5 6 7   **92**
  1. Kings and rulers 2. Kings 3. Egypt -- History
  ISBN 978-0-7614-5558-5; 0-7614-5558-2
                         LC 2008029313

"The unmistakable designs and opulent glitter of ancient Egyptian art gleam on every page of Demi's picture-book introduction to Tutankhamun. Beginning with King Tut's great-grandfather, Demi presents the broad historical context surrounding the young monarch's reign.... Demi's language, organized into brief but pithy paragraphs, is clear. . . . It's the beautiful illustrations that will attract and hold a young audience most, and as usual, Demi incorporates artistic motifs and materials appropriate to her subject." Booklist

Twain, Mark, 1835-1910

Caravantes, Peggy. A **great** and sublime fool; the story of Mark Twain. Morgan Reynolds Pub. 2009 176p il map (World writers) lib bdg $28.95

Grades: 7 8 9 10   **92**
  1. Authors 2. Humorists 3. Novelists 4. Essayists 5. Satirists 6. Memoirists 7. Travel writers 8. Authors, American 9. Short story writers
  ISBN 978-1-599-35088-2; 1-599-35088-2
                         LC 2008-34139

This "offers a workmanlike but readable account of one of America's first great writers.... A nice selection of photographs and artwork complement the narrative.... Detailed source notes and an in-depth time line round out this even and reliable . . . biography." Booklist

Includes bibliographical references

★ Fleischman, Sid. The **trouble** begins at 8; a life of Mark Twain in the wild, wild West. Greenwillow Books 2008 224p il $18.99; lib bdg $19.89

Grades: 5 6 7 8   **92**
  1. Authors 2. Humorists 3. Novelists 4. Essayists 5. Satirists 6. Memoirists 7. Travel writers 8. Authors, American 9. Short story writers 10. Biography, Individual
  ISBN 0-06-134431-1; 0-06-134432-X lib bdg; 978-0-06-134431-2; 978-0-06-134432-9 lib bdg
                         LC 2007-37891

This biography of Mark Twain focuses on his travels. Chronology. Index. "Grades five to nine." (Bull Cent Child Books)

"Fleischman writes a charming biography of Samuel Clemens before he became Mark Twain, the great American novelist.... Written with a sense of humor and wit that honors Twain, this book is sprinkled with famous Twain quotes, excerpts of his writing, and pictures of Twain and other primary documents from the era Clemens spent both on the Mississippi River and in the West." Voice Youth Advocates

Includes bibliographical references

Houle, Michelle M. **Mark** Twain; banned, challenged, and censored. Enslow Publishers 2008 160p il (Authors of banned books) lib bdg $34.60

Grades: 8 9 10 11 12   **92**
  1. Authors 2. Humorists 3. Novelists 4. Censorship 5. Essayists 6. Satirists 7. Memoirists 8. Travel writers 9. Authors, American 10. Short story writers
  ISBN 978-0-7660-2689-6 lib bdg; 0-7660-2689-2 lib bdg
                         LC 2007-22362

"This book combines biography, criticism, and an exploration of the role of censorship in literature and education. .... Houle offers a brief history of censorship in literature in order to place Twain's case in context, and a history of the challenges and defenses of the author's work from his contemporaries and modern critics. Illustrations include color photographs of related modern scenes (such as one that shows book burning), reproductions of artwork from early editions of Twain's works, and period cartoons and photographs." SLJ

Includes glossary and bibliographical references

Sonneborn, Liz. **Mark** Twain; foreword by Kyle Zimmer. Chelsea House Publishers 2010 125p il (Who wrote that?) lib bdg $35

Grades: 6 7 8 9 10   **92**
  1. Authors 2. Humorists 3. Novelists 4. Essayists 5. Satirists 6. Memoirists 7. Travel writers 8. Authors, American 9. Short story writers
  ISBN 978-1-60413-728-6; 1-60413-728-2
                         LC 2010006601

This biography of Mark Twain "begins with the writer's memorable visit to his Missouri hometown in 1902, then tracks back to his early days and his well-known transformation from Sam Clemens to Mark Twain. Sonneborn deals with her material well, hitting all the highlights and keeping the narrative moving along. Good use of details adds interest.... A solid purchase." SLJ

Includes bibliographical references

Valentino

Reis, Ronald A. **Valentino**. Chelsea House 2011 119p il (Famous fashion designers) lib bdg $35

Grades: 6 7 8 9 10   **92**
  1. Fashion designers
  ISBN 978-1-60413-983-9; 1-60413-983-8
                         LC 2010034101

This is a biography of fashion designer Valentino.
Includes glossary and bibliographical references

Vedder, Amy

Ebersole, Rene. **Gorilla** mountain; the story of wildlife biologist, Amy Vedder. [by] Rene Ebersole. F. Watts 2005 118p il (Women's adventures in science) lib bdg $31

Grades: 7 8 9 10   92

1. Gorillas 2. Conservationists 3. Women scientists

ISBN 0-531-16779-8

LC 2005-00823

A biography of wildlife biologist Amy Vedder

This is "interesting, substantive, and eminently readable." SLJ

Includes bibliographical references

Versace, Gianni, 1946-1997

Davis, Daniel K. **Versace**. Chelsea House 2011 116p il (Famous fashion designers) lib bdg $35

Grades: 6 7 8 9 10   92

1. Fashion designers

ISBN 978-1-60413-980-8; 1-60413-980-3

LC 2010034103

This is a biography of fashion designer Gianni Versace.

"Biography collections in need of a bit of sprucing up should find [this title] helpful." SLJ

Includes glossary and bibliographical references

Vincent, Erin

Vincent, Erin. **Grief** girl; my true story. Delacorte Press 2007 306p $15.99; lib bdg $18.99

Grades: 8 9 10 11 12   92

1. Authors 2. Bereavement 3. Memoirists

ISBN 978-0-385-73353-3; 0-385-73353-4; 978-0-385-90368-4 lib bdg; 0-385-90368-5 lib bdg

LC 2006-11650

"In 1983, Vincent, then 14, lost both her parents in a road accident. In this poignant memoir, she chronicles her rocky journey through adolescence as she, her 17-year-old sister, Tracy, and their brother, Trent, learn to cope on their own." Booklist

Wague Diakite, Baba

A **gift** from childhood; memories of an African boyhood. Groundwood Books 2010 134p il $18.95

Grades: 5 6 7 8   92

1. Artists 2. Authors 3. Illustrators 4. Mali 5. Children's authors 6. Africa 7. Biography, Individual

ISBN 0-88899-931-3; 978-0-88899-931-3

This is a memoir about growing up in a small village in Mali. "Age ten and up." (N Y Times Book Rev)

"Diakite's . . . illustrated memoir focuses on his childhood in a small Malian village. . . . Interspersed with Diakite's recounting of his youth . . . are stories about his grandfather's brokering peaceful relations with the French, a blacksmith who stymies Death, and others. . . . Diakite's precise language and vibrant illustrations, created on earthenware tiles, form an engrossing story of community life. Studded with Malian proverbs, metaphors, and morals . . . it's a memoir alive with far more voices than just that of the author." Publ Wkly

Waldman, Neil, 1947-

★ Waldman, Neil. **Out** of the shadows; an artist's journey. Boyds Mills Press 2006 144p il $21.95

Grades: 5 6 7 8   92

1. Artists 2. Authors 3. Illustrators 4. Jews -- Biography 5. Children's authors 6. Artists -- United States

ISBN 1-59078-411-1

Neil Waldman reveals how his passion for art emerged in the kitchen of his family's apartment, where he discovered the work of Vincent Van Gogh and the ability to use illustration as a means to escape the sadness that plagued his home.

"Young artists, as well as readers who wonder about the person behind the pictures they have seen, will appreciate every element of this book: well-constructed story, visual richness, and uncompromising honesty." Booklist

Walker, C. J., Madame, 1867-1919

Bundles, A'Lelia P. **Madam** C.J. Walker; entrepreneur. [by] A'Lelia Bundles. Legacy ed; Chelsea House Publishers 2008 103p (Black Americans of achievement) lib bdg $30

Grades: 6 7 8 9   92

1. Philanthropists 2. African American businesspeople 3. Cosmeticians 4. Cosmetics industry executives 5. African American women -- Biography

ISBN 978-1-60413-072-0 lib bdg; 1-60413-072-5 lib bdg

LC 2008008429

First published 1991

A biography of the African American businesswoman whose invention of facial creams and other cosmetics led to great financial success

The book goes "beyond the typical personal information to provide some social history relevant to the subject's time. Captioned photographs and boxed inserts enhance the conversational [text]." Horn Book Guide

Includes bibliographical references

Walker, Maggie Lena, 1867-1934

Ransom, Candice F. **Maggie** L. Walker; pioneering banker and community leader. Twenty-First Century Books 2009 112p il (Trailblazer biographies) lib bdg $31.93

Grades: 6 7 8 9   92

1. African American businesspeople 2. Bankers 3. African American women -- Biography

ISBN 978-0-8225-6611-3 lib bdg; 0-8225-6611-7 lib bdg

LC 2007-42906

Retells the life and career of Maggie L. Walker, who founded the St. Luke Penny Savings Bank, the first bank established specifically for African Americans.

"The text is thoroughly researched and well organized. . . . Good-quality archival photographs add interest and clarity. A solid selection for report writers." SLJ

Includes bibliographical references

Walker, Mary Edwards, 1832-1919

Goldsmith, Bonnie Zucker. **Dr.** Mary Edwards Walker; Civil War surgeon & medal of honor recipient. [by] Bonnie Z. Goldsmith. ABDO Pub. 2010 112p il (Military heroes) lib bdg $22.65

Grades: 7 8 9   **92**

1. Physicians 2. Suffragists 3. Women physicians 4. Feminists 5. United States -- History -- 1861-1865, Civil War -- Women 6. United States -- History -- 1861-1865, Civil War -- Medical care

ISBN 978-1-60453-966-0; 1-60453-966-6

LC 2009-32367

Biography of suffragist and physician, Dr. Mary Edwards Walker.

"The rush of literary adrenalin will hook readers immediately and keep them enthralled until the end. . . . Given the dynamic topic [and] . . . appealing layout . . . [this is] likely to attract reluctant readers. In addition, sources are plentiful and well documented." SLJ

Includes glossary and bibliographical references

Wallenberg, Raoul

★ Borden, Louise, 1949- **His** name was Raoul Wallenberg. Houghton Mifflin 2012 135p il $18.99

Grades: 7 8 9 10 11 12   **92**

1. Diplomats 2. Missing persons 3. Political prisoners 4. Humanitarians 5. Holocaust, 1933-1945 6. World War, 1939-1945 -- Jews -- Rescue

ISBN 0-618-50755-8; 978-0-618-50755-9

This book offers a "biography . . . of Raoul Wallenberg, a Swedish businessman who dedicated the latter part of his life to helping Hungarian Jews escape from Budapest at the end of the Second World War. . . . Wallenberg's business dealings in Hungary made him an ideal candidate when the American-based War Refugee Board came to Sweden seeking someone for a mission to Hungary, to provide assistance to Jews who were being deported to Auschwitz by the trainload. Upon arrival in Budapest, Wallenberg invented the 'schutzpasse' system, wherein falsified documents connected Hungarian Jews to neutral Sweden and subsequently saved the lives of thousands." (Bulletin of the Center for Children's Books)

"Based on Borden's years of intensive personal research, including interviews and archival sources, this account written in rapid-reading free verse . . . is presented in a spacious, accessible format that includes lots of historic and personal photos, documents, and profiles of victims and heroes. Borden skillfully places the biographical story in historical context. . . . This is an important addition to the Holocaust curriculum." Booklist

Walton, Sam

Blumenthal, Karen. **Mr.** Sam; how Sam Walton built Wal-Mart and became America's richest man. Penguin Group 2011 183p il $17.99

Grades: 5 6 7 8   **92**

1. Businessmen 2. Discount stores 3. Retail executives 4. Wal-Mart Stores, Inc. 5. Biography, Individual

ISBN 978-0-670-01177-3; 0-670-01177-0

LC 2010049520

"This spectacular success story tracks Walton's rise from lower-middle-class origins to, by the mid-1980s, the top of the 'America's Richest' list. . . . Written in a fluid, journalistic style and enhanced by photos, boxed-out 'Sam stories,' charts tracking changes in Americans' spending habits, and a lavish source list, this account of the man who created what is today the world's largest company makes compelling reading." Booklist

Wang, Vera

Krohn, Katherine E. **Vera** Wang; enduring style. by Katherine Krohn. Twenty-First Century Books 2009 112p il (Lifeline biographies) lib bdg $33.26

Grades: 6 7 8 9   **92**

1. Fashion designers 2. Magazine editors

ISBN 978-1-58013-572-6 lib bdg; 1-58013-572-2 lib bdg

LC 2008009198

This biography "boasts lively, credible writing and a compelling layout. Particularly interesting are the reprints of USA Today articles found throughout, which flesh out the [narrative] in a unique and appealing manner. . . . Full-color and black-and-white photos appear on almost every spread." SLJ

Includes bibliographical references

Petrillo, Lisa. **Vera** Wang. Morgan Reynolds 2010 112p il (Profiles in fashion) $28.95

Grades: 7 8 9 10   **92**

1. Fashion designers 2. Magazine editors

ISBN 978-159935-150-6; 1-59935-150-1

This discusses the fashion "designer's cultural background, childhood, family, work history and education. . . . The writing is clear and well organized. Color photos are included and give readers a feel for the time period and the types of clothing and accessories the [designer] created." Voice Youth Advocates

Todd, Anne M. **Vera** Wang; [by] Anne M. Todd. Chelsea House 2007 120p bibl il por (Asian Americans of achievement) lib bdg $30

Grades: 7 8 9 10   **92**

1. Fashion designers 2. Magazine editors

ISBN 978-0-7910-9272-9 lib bdg; 0-7910-9272-0 lib bdg

LC 2006028386

A biography of the fashion designer

This is "well-researched . . . attractive . . . solid." SLJ

Warhol, Andy, 1928?-1987

★ Rubin, Susan Goldman. **Andy** Warhol; pop art painter. H.N. Abrams 2006 48p il $18.95

Grades: 4 5 6 7   **92**

1. Artists 2. Pop art 3. Artists -- United States 4. Motion picture directors

ISBN 0-8109-5477-X

LC 2005-13238

"Andy Warhol was a colorful figure who revolutionized how the world looks at art. Rubin's coherent and interesting narrative is filled with quotes by the artist and people who knew him. . . . Excellent-quality black-and-white and full-color photographs of Warhol and his family and reproductions of his paintings and those of others who influenced him appear throughout." SLJ

Willett, Edward. **Andy** Warhol; everyone will be famous for 15 minutes. Enslow Publishers 2010 160p il (American rebels) lib bdg $34.60

Grades: 6 7 8 9   **92**
1. Artists 2. Pop art 3. Artists -- United States 4. Motion picture directors
ISBN 978-0-7660-3385-6 lib bdg; 0-7660-3385-6 lib bdg

LC 2009017596

This "fascinating, well organized [portrait] . . . starts with the 1962 L.A. art exhibition at which the artist first presented his iconic paintings of Campbell Soup cans that kicked off the pop-art movement into high gear. . . . Skillfully chosen photos, chapter notes, and [a] suggested-reading [list completes this] well-researched, wholly engaging [introduction]." Booklist

Includes bibliographical references

Warren, Earl, 1891-1974

Branscomb, Leslie Wolf. **Earl** Warren. Morgan Reynolds Pub. 2011 112p il (Supreme Court justices) lib bdg $28.95

Grades: 7 8 9 10   **92**
1. Judges 2. Governors 3. Supreme Court justices
ISBN 978-1-59935158-2; 1-59935158-7

LC 2010020403

This "offers a balanced look at the life and career of Earl Warren. . . . He was appointed chief justice of the U.S. Supreme Court in 1953. Branscomb includes Warren's mistakes but portrays him as a fair-minded man who led the court ably through a series of controversial and significant decisions. . . . Well-chosen boxed quotes and period photos appear throughout the book, with color used sparingly but effectively. This well-researched and clearly written volume offers a good introduction to Warren." Booklist

Includes bibliographical references

Wasdin, Howard E.

★ Wasdin, Howard E. **I** am a SEAL Team Six warrior; memoirs of an American soldier. Howard E. Wasdin and Stephen Templin. 1st ed. St. Martin's Griffin 2012 vi, 182 p.p ill. (paperback) $7.99

Grades: 8 9 10 11 12   **92**
1. Snipers -- United States -- Biography 2. United States. Navy. SEALs -- Biography 3. United States. Navy -- Commando troops -- Biography
ISBN 1250016436; 9781250016430

LC 2012376658

This book offers an "[a]bridged, . . . young-readers version of an ex-SEAL sniper's account ('SEAL Team Six,' 2011) of his training and combat experiences in Operation Desert Storm and the first Battle of Mogadishu. . . . In later chapters he retraces his long, difficult physical and emotional recovery from serious wounds received during the 'Black Hawk Down' operation, his increasing focus on faith and family after divorce and remarriage and his second career as a chiropractor." (Kirkus Reviews)

Includes bibliographical references (p. [181]-182).

Washington, Booker T., 1856-1915

★ Washington, Booker T. **Up** from slavery; edited with an introduction and notes by William L. Andrews. Oxford University Press 2008 xxvii, 196p (Oxford world's classics) pa $9.95

Grades: 7 8 9 10 11 12 Adult   **92**
1. Slaves 2. Authors 3. Educators 4. African American educators 5. Memoirists 6. Nonfiction writers 7. Tuskegee Institute 8. Civil rights activists 9. African Americans -- Biography
ISBN 978-0-19-955239-9

LC 2008-279129

First published 1901

"The classic autobiography of the man who, though born in slavery, educated himself and went on to found Tuskegee Institute." N Y Public Libr

Includes bibliographical references

Washington, George, 1732-1799

Allen, Thomas B. **George** Washington, spymaster; how America outspied the British and won the Revolutionary War. featuring illustrations by Cheryl Harness. National Geographic 2004 184p il $16.95

Grades: 6 7 8 9   **92**
ISBN 0-7922-5126-1

LC 2003-6019

Dolan, Edward F. **George** Washington; [by] Edward F. Dolan. Marshall Cavendish Benchmark 2008 96p il (Presidents and their times) lib bdg $32.79

Grades: 5 6 7 8   **92**
1. Generals 2. Presidents 3. Presidents -- United States
ISBN 978-0-7614-2427-7 lib bdg; 0-7614-2427-X lib bdg

LC 2006037802

This biography of the first president of the United States "is illustrated with color photos and contains boxed descriptions of key historical events, artwork, and political concepts experienced during the time period. . . . This . . . will be of great use both for biographical research and for enriching the curriculum." Libr Media Connect

Includes glossary and bibliographical references

Earl, Sari. **George** Washington; revolutionary leader & founding father. by Sari K. Earl. ABDO Pub. 2010 112p il map (Military heroes) lib bdg $22.95

Grades: 7 8 9   **92**
1. Generals 2. Presidents 3. Presidents -- United States 4. United States -- Continental Army
ISBN 978-1-60453-967-7; 1-60453-967-4

LC 2009-32372

"The rush of literary adrenalin will hook readers immediately and keep them enthralled until the end. . . . Given the dynamic topic [and] . . . appealing layout . . . [this is] likely to attract reluctant readers. In addition, sources are plentiful and well documented." SLJ

Includes glossary and bibliographical references

★ McClafferty, Carla Killough. The **many** faces of George Washington; remaking a presidential icon. Carolrhoda Books 2011 120p il lib bdg $20.95

Grades: 6 7 8 9   92

1. Generals 2. Presidents 3. Presidents -- United States 4. Biography, Individual

ISBN 978-0-7613-5608-0; 0-7613-5608-8

LC 2010-28178

"With the goal of boosting interest in George Washington, in 2005 Mount Vernon commissioned three life-size reproductions of him at ages 19, 45 and 57. Enthusiastic prose and informative photographs convey in considerable detail the work on this project by a variety of experts, including sculptors, archaeologists, historians, dentists, painters, taxidermists and more. . . . Quotations from Washington and his contemporaries add a personal note, while reproductions of portraits, statues and artifacts supply visual interest. Color photographs show some of the steps in the reconstruction." Kirkus

Includes bibliographical references

Mooney, Carla. **George** Washington; 25 great projects you can build yourself. illustrated by Samuel Carbaugh. Nomad 2011 121p il (Build it yourself) $21.95; pa $15.95

Grades: 4 5 6 7   92

1. Generals 2. Handicraft 3. Presidents 4. Presidents -- United States

ISBN 978-1-934670-64-4; 1-934670-64-2; 978-1-934670-63-7 pa pa; 1-934670-63-4 pa

"The life of George Washington lends itself remarkably well to a variety of kid-friendly crafts that don't require old-fashioned materials or 18th-century skills. . . . The projects separate biographical chapters that are thorough and clear. . . . Sidebars with vocabulary words, quotes, interesting facts about the man and his time, and 'What if?' questions regarding pivotal moments in Washington's life add to the text. These sidebars, as well as amusing cartoon illustrations, make the subject light and approachable." SLJ

Includes glossary and bibliographical references

Weber, EdNah New Rider

Weber, EdNah New Rider. **Rattlesnake** Mesa; stories from a native American childhood. by EdNah New Rider Weber; photographs by Richela Renkun. Lee & Low Books 2004 132p il $18.95

Grades: 4 5 6 7   92

1. Artisans 2. Memoirists 3. Storytellers 4. Native Americans -- Biography

ISBN 1-58430-231-3

LC 2004-2385

"Weber describes her experiences with warmth and affection in this unusually compelling memoir. Striking black-and-white photos . . . add to the book's appeal." Horn Book Guide

Wells, H. G. (Herbert George), 1866-1946

Abrams, Dennis. **H.G.** Wells; foreword by Kyle Zimmer. Chelsea House 2011 128p il (Who wrote that?) lib bdg $35

Grades: 6 7 8 9 10   92

1. Authors 2. Novelists 3. Historians 4. Authors, English 5. Writers on science 6. Writers on politics 7. Science fiction writers

ISBN 978-1-60413-770-5; 1-60413-770-3

LC 2010030588

This discusses the life and work of author H. G. Wells. Includes bibliographical references

Wells-Barnett, Ida B., 1862-1931

Hinman, Bonnie. **Eternal** vigilance: the story of Ida B. Wells-Barnett. Morgan Reynolds Pub. 2010 128p il (Civil rights leaders) $28.95

Grades: 7 8 9 10   92

1. Authors 2. Lynching 3. Journalists 4. Women journalists 5. African American educators 6. Essayists 7. Nonfiction writers 8. Newspaper executives 9. Civil rights activists 10. United States -- Race relations 11. African Americans -- Civil rights 12. African American women -- Biography 13. African Americans -- Social conditions

ISBN 978-1-59935-111-7; 1-59935-111-0

LC 2010-8144

"Hinman tells of Wells-Barnett's tireless efforts as an antilynching crusader and civil rights advocate. . . . Hinman paints an engaging portrait of the activist who was instrumental in the formation of the NAACP. Each stage of Wells-Barnett's life is placed in historical context, providing students with a better understanding of the world in which she lived. Well-chosen black-and-white photographs and other period materials are included throughout the text." SLJ

Includes bibliographical references

Schraff, Anne E. **Ida** B. Wells-Barnett; strike a blow against a glaring evil; [by] Anne Schraff. Enslow Publishers 2008 128p il map (African-American biography library) lib bdg $23.95

Grades: 6 7 8 9 10   92

1. Authors 2. Journalists 3. Essayists 4. Nonfiction writers 5. Newspaper executives 6. Civil rights activists 7. United States -- Race relations 8. African Americans -- Civil rights 9. African American women -- Biography

ISBN 978-0-7660-2704-6 lib bdg; 0-7660-2704-X lib bdg

LC 2007016051

"Short chapters, succinct text, frequent sidebars, and numerous period photographs keep the narrative from becoming overwhelming. . . . This will . . . aid report writers." Booklist

Includes bibliographical references

Wharton, Edith, 1862-1937

★ Wooldridge, Connie Nordhielm. The **brave** escape of Edith Wharton; a biography. Clarion Books 2010 184p il $20

Grades: 7 8 9 10   92

1. Authors 2. Novelists 3. Women authors 4. Authors, American 5. Nonfiction writers 6. Short story writers

ISBN 978-0-547-23630-8; 0-547-23630-1

LC 2009-33574

"In this thoroughly researched, humanizing biography, Wooldridge writes with lively specifics about both the author and her time. . . . Frequent, well-woven quotes from Wharton's family and friends contribute to a strong sense of an energetic, groundbreaking, and ferociously intelligent writer, but it's the many quotes in Wharton's own voice that leave the most indelible impact." Booklist

Whitfield, Simon, 1975-

Whitfield, Simon. **Simon** says gold: Simon Whitfield's pursuit of athletic excellence; by Simon Whitfield with Cleve Dheensaw. Orca Publishers 2009 118p il pa $14

Grades: 5 6 7 8   92

1. Athletes 2. Track athletics 3. Triathletes
ISBN 978-1-55469-141-8 pa; 1-55469-141-9 pa
"In 2000, Whitfield won a gold medal in the inaugural triathlon race held in the Sydney Summer Olympics. . . . He tells his story with candor, and he sheds light on the dark side of early success and the pressures athletes face. Sidebars offer more information on the sport of triathlon, and scrapbook-style color photographs enliven the tale." SLJ

Whitman, Narcissa Prentiss, 1808-1847

Harness, Cheryl. The **tragic** tale of Narcissa Whitman and a faithful history of the Oregon Trail; written and illustrated by Cheryl Harness. National Geographic Society 2006 144p il map (Cheryl Harness history) $16.95; lib bdg $25.90

Grades: 4 5 6 7   92

1. Frontier and pioneer life 2. Overland journeys to the Pacific 3. Pioneers 4. Missionaries
ISBN 0-7922-5920-3; 0-7922-7890-9 lib bdg
LC 2005-30930
This "introduces a nineteenth-century pioneer and missionary. . . . [She and her husband Marcus Whitman] journeyed along the Oregon Trail to the Waiilatpu Mission, where they ministered to the Cayuse. . . . Harness' chatty, conversational style makes the pair accessible to modern readers, and frequent quotes from Narcissa's diaries and letters and a time line help to frame the story in light of world and national events. Harness' black-line illustrations . . . help to break up the text for younger readers." Booklist
Includes bibliographical references

Whitman, Walt, 1819-1892

Kerley, Barbara. **Walt** Whitman; words for America, illustrated by Brian Selznick. Scholastic Press 2004 un il $16.95

Grades: 4 5 6 7   92

1. Poets 2. Authors 3. Essayists 4. Poets, American
ISBN 0-439-35791-8
LC 2003-20085
A biography of the American poet whose compassion led him to nurse soldiers during the Civil War, to give voice to the nation's grief at Lincoln's assassination, and to capture the true American spirit in verse
"Delightfully old-fashioned in design, [the book's] oversized pages are replete with graceful illustrations and snippets of poetry. The brilliantly inventive paintings add vibrant testimonial to the nuanced text." SLJ

Wiesel, Elie, 1928-

Koestler-Grack, Rachel A. **Elie** Wiesel; witness for humanity. by Rachel Koestler-Grack. Gareth Stevens Pub. 2009 112p il map (Life portraits) lib bdg $34

Grades: 7 8 9 10   92

1. Authors 2. Novelists 3. Journalists 4. Holocaust survivors 5. Jews -- Romania 6. Holocaust, 1933-1945 7. Human rights activists 8. Nobel laureates for peace
ISBN 978-1-4339-0054-9 lib bdg; 1-4339-0054-8 lib bdg
LC 2008-31630
"Recounts the struggles . . . [Wiesel] experienced as a Holocaust survivor and as someone who still works to end all violence against humanity. . . . Many photos, images, and sidebars, as well as the expected back matter contribute . . . without being didactic and educate without preaching." Voice Youth Advocates
Includes glossary and bibliographical references

Wiesenthal, Simon

★ Rubin, Susan Goldman. The **Anne** Frank Case: Simon Wiesenthal's search for the truth; illustrated by Bill Farnsworth. Holiday House 2009 40p il $18.95

Grades: 4 5 6 7   92

1. Authors 2. Architects 3. Holocaust survivors 4. Essayists 5. Memoirists 6. Nazi hunters 7. Jewish leaders 8. Jews -- Biography 9. Holocaust, 1933-1945
ISBN 978-0-8234-2109-1; 0-8234-2109-0
LC 2007-28396
"Even those who have heard of Wiesenthal will be thrilled by this account. . . . Farnsworth's stirring full-page oil paintings are filled with emotion." Booklist
Includes glossary and bibliographical references

Wilder, Laura Ingalls, 1867-1957

Berne, Emma Carlson. **Laura** Ingalls Wilder; by Emma Carlson Berne. ABDO Pub. 2008 112p il map $22.95

Grades: 4 5 6 7   92

1. Authors 2. Novelists 3. Women authors 4. Frontier and pioneer life 5. Western writers 6. Authors, American 7. Children's authors 8. Young adult authors
ISBN 978-1-59928-843-7; 1-59928-843-5
LC 2007012513
"Beginning in 1929 with the events that led up to the publication of Little House in the Big Woods , this readable biography further amplifies Wilder's life and correlates it with her books. . . . This volume is packed with relevant material, a time line, archival photographs, quotes from primary sources, and an official Web site." SLJ
Includes glossary and bibliographical references

Sickels, Amy. **Laura** Ingalls Wilder; [by] Amy Sickels. Chelsea House 2007 125p il (Who wrote that?) lib bdg $30

Grades: 6 7 8 9   92

1. Authors 2. Novelists 3. Women authors 4. Frontier and pioneer life 5. Western writers 6. Authors,

American 7. Children's authors 8. Young adult authors
ISBN 978-0-7910-9525-6 lib bdg; 0-7910-9525-8
lib bdg

LC 2007019615

This biography examines the "writer's life, including
the inspiration behind some of [her] works. [The] volume
includes photographs and quotations from interviews, as
well as descriptions of main characters and annotated lists
of books and awards. Useful for aspiring writers as well as
book report writers." Horn Book Guide

Includes bibliographical references

Wilder, Laura Ingalls. A **Little** House traveler;
writings from Laura Ingalls Wilder's journeys across
America. by Laura Ingalls Wilder. HarperCollins
2006 344p il $16.99; pa $7.99

Grades: 5 6 7 8   92

1. Authors 2. Novelists 3. Women authors 4. Western
writers 5. Authors, American 6. Children's authors
7. Young adult authors 8. United States -- Description
and travel

ISBN 978-0-06-072491-7; 0-06-072491-9; 978-0-06-
072492-4 pa; 0-06-072492-7 pa

LC 2005014975

"This volume combines three Wilder travel diaries: On
the Way Home, recounting the 1894 trip from South Dakota
to Missouri, with husband Almanzo and daughter Rose;
West from Home, featuring letters written by Laura to Almanzo during her 1915 solo visit to Rose in San Francisco;
and The Road Back, highlighting Laura's previously unpublished record of a 1931 trip with Almanzo to De Smet, South
Dakota, and the Black Hills. . . . This offers an amazing look
at a beloved author, as well as a fascinating account of travel
before interstate highways and air-conditioning." Booklist

William, Prince, Duke of Cambridge, 1982-

Doeden, Matt. **Prince** William & Kate; a royal
romance. Lerner Publications 2011 48p il lib bdg
$26.60

Grades: 5 6 7 8   92

1. Princes 2. Princesses
ISBN 978-0-7613-8029-0; 0-7613-8029-9

LC 2011003413

"This short and sweet volume accents what down-
to-earth and normal newlyweds Prince William and Kate
Middleton are really like. After a brief recap of the couple's
engagement interview, the book goes on to profile the pair
individually and then as a duo. . . . This is an upbeat, readable narrative about a handsome, appealing couple. The
color photographs are well chosen." Booklist

Includes glossary and bibliographical references

Williams, Evan

Smith, Chris. **Twitter**; Jack Dorsey, Biz Stone
and Evan Williams. [by] Chris Smith and Marci Mc-
Grath. Morgan Reynolds Pub. 2011 112p il (Business leaders) $28.95

Grades: 7 8 9 10 11 12   92

1. Online social networks 2. Twitter, Inc. 3. Internet
executives 4. Computer programmers 5. Computer

software executives
ISBN 978-1-59935-179-7; 1-59935-179-X; 978-1-
59935-216-9 e-book

LC 2011024699

This biography of the founders of Twitter "will grab
YAs. . . . The design is browsable, with clear type and lots
of color screens and informal photos of young people at
work." Booklist

Includes bibliographical references

Williams, Lindsey, 1987-

Houle, Michelle E. **Lindsey** Williams; gardening for impoverished families. [by] Michelle Houle.
KidHaven Press 2008 48p il (Young heroes) lib
bdg $27.45

Grades: 4 5 6 7   92

1. Gardening 2. Food relief 3. Social action 4.
Gardeners 5. Humanitarians

ISBN 978-0-7377-3867-4 lib bdg; 0-7377-3867-7
lib bdg

LC 2007022923

This "introduces 20-year-old Lindsey Williams, who has
won numerous awards, including the International Eco-Hero
Award, for her groundbreaking work with agriculture and
hunger issues. . . . Williams has developed growing techniques that produce more food using fewer natural resources. . . . The straightforward text, with many quotes from Williams, will draw children into the science and environmental
issues." Booklist

Includes glossary and bibliographical references

Williams, Serena, 1981-

Williams, Venus. **Venus** & Serena; serving from
the hip, ten rules for living, loving, and winning.
[by] Venus and Serena Williams with Hilary Beard.
Houghton Mifflin 2005 133p il pa $14

Grades: 7 8 9 10   92

1. Women athletes 2. African American athletes 3.
Tennis players 4. Tennis -- Biography
ISBN 0-618-57653-3

LC 2004-13204

"The sisters and tennis players . . . give teens advice
on everyday living, showing them how to aim high and
reach their goals. The 10 rules for success include building
a 'dream team' (people who support your goals), doing well
in school, learning self-respect, valuing friendships, taking
care of yourself emotionally and physically, obtaining financial security, and overcoming setbacks. The final chapter
discusses the virtues of volunteerism and charity. . . . Never
preachy and always practical, this is a welcome addition to
most collections." SLJ

Williams, Venus, 1980-

Williams, Venus. **Venus** & Serena; serving from
the hip, ten rules for living, loving, and winning.
[by] Venus and Serena Williams with Hilary Beard.
Houghton Mifflin 2005 133p il pa $14

Grades: 7 8 9 10   92

1. Women athletes 2. African American athletes 3.

Tennis players 4. Tennis -- Biography
ISBN 0-618-57653-3

LC 2004-13204

"The sisters and tennis players . . . give teens advice on everyday living, showing them how to aim high and reach their goals. The 10 rules for success include building a 'dream team' (people who support your goals), doing well in school, learning self-respect, valuing friendships, taking care of yourself emotionally and physically, obtaining financial security, and overcoming setbacks. The final chapter discusses the virtues of volunteerism and charity. . . . Never preachy and always practical, this is a welcome addition to most collections." SLJ

Wilson, Jacqueline

Bankston, John. **Jacqueline** Wilson. Chelsea House 2011 128p il (Who wrote that?) lib bdg $35
Grades: 6 7 8 9 10   92

1. Authors 2. Novelists 3. Women authors 4. Authors, American 5. Young adult authors
ISBN 978-1-60413-773-6; 1-60413-773-8

LC 2010047679

"Wilson knew from an early age that writing was her calling. Growing up in a turbulent home and dropping out of school at 16 pushed her to start writing for Jackie, a magazine for teenage girls. This well-written biography includes a quick-paced, fact-filled synopsis of her life." SLJ

Includes bibliographical references

Wilson, Woodrow, 1856-1924

Marsico, Katie. **Woodrow** Wilson. Marshall Cavendish Benchmark 2011 112p il (Presidents and their times) $23.95
Grades: 5 6 7 8   92

1. Governors 2. Presidents 3. College presidents 4. Nobel laureates for peace 5. Presidents -- United States
ISBN 978-0-7614-4815-0; 0-7614-4815-2

LC 2009041116

This offers information on President Woodrow Wilson and places him within his historical and cultural context. Also explored are the formative events of his times and how he responded.

"The abundant sidebars provide a good deal of background information that will be helpful to students. . . . Attractive . . . as well as useful." Booklist

Includes glossary and bibliographical references

Winfrey, Oprah

★ Cooper, Ilene. **Oprah** Winfrey. Viking 2007 204p il (Up close) $15.99
Grades: 7 8 9 10   92

1. Philanthropists 2. African American actors 3. Television personalities 4. Talk show hosts 5. Television producers 6. African American women -- Biography
ISBN 978-0-670-06162-4

LC 2006-9805

"Cooper discusses her subject's early traumatic and dramatic experiences. She shows how a poor, abused, bright child from Mississippi overcame her past, becoming perhaps the most influential woman in America. Much of the book focuses on Winfrey's work and philanthropy. . . . This well-

documented, easy-to-read biography is a good resource for reports." SLJ

Krohn, Katherine E. **Oprah** Winfrey; global media leader. by Katherine Krohn. rev ed; Twenty-First Century Books 2009 112p il (Lifeline biographies) lib bdg $33.26
Grades: 6 7 8 9   92

1. Philanthropists 2. African American actors 3. Television personalities 4. Talk show hosts 5. Television producers 6. African American women -- Biography
ISBN 978-1-58013-571-9 lib bdg; 1-58013-571-4 lib bdg

LC 2008016951

First published 2002 by Lerner Publications

This biography "boasts lively, credible writing and a compelling layout. Particularly interesting are the reprints of USA Today articles found throughout, which flesh out the [narrative] in a unique and appealing manner. . . . Full-color and black-and-white photos appear on almost every spread." SLJ

Includes bibliographical references

Winthrop, John, 1588-1649

Aronson, Marc. **John** Winthrop, Oliver Cromwell, and the Land of Promise. Clarion Books 2004 205p il map $20
Grades: 7 8 9 10   92

1. Clergy 2. Puritans 3. Heads of state 4. Revolutionaries 5. Government officials 6. Colonial administrators 7. Great Britain -- History -- 1603-1714, Stuarts 8. Massachusetts -- History -- 1600-1775, Colonial period
ISBN 0-618-18177-6

LC 2003-16418

"The accessible text is accompanied by excerpts from primary source documents and vivid illustrations. The author's passion for the period comes across in his writing. Aronson provides an excellent source for historical and biographical data." Voice Youth Advocates

Includes bibliographical references

Woodhull, Victoria C., 1838-1927

Havelin, Kate. **Victoria** Woodhull. Twenty-First Century Books 2007 112p (Trailblazer biography) lib bdg $30.60
Grades: 7 8 9 10   92

1. Feminism 2. Suffragists 3. Feminists 4. Presidential candidates
ISBN 978-0-8225-5986-3 lib bdg; 0-8225-5986-2 lib bdg

LC 2005022824

A biography of the nineteenth century feminist who became the first woman to run for president of the U.S.

"A well-researched, well-organized biography. . . . [Woodhull's] fascinating and full life is expertly detailed in this narrative." SLJ

Includes bibliographical references

Woods, Tiger, 1975-

Roberts, Jeremy. **Tiger** Woods; golf's master. by Jeremy Roberts. Twenty-First Century Books 2009 112p il (Lifeline biographies) lib bdg $33.26

Grades: 6 7 8 9   **92**

1. Golf 2. Golfers

ISBN 978-1-58013-569-6 lib bdg; 1-58013-569-2 lib bdg

LC 2008-3098

"There are a number of biographies about the world's best golfer, but this one is particularly good. Not only does it chronicle the life of Woods but it offers a solid look at family influences, various tournaments, and personal relationships. . . . Color photographs are well chosen." Booklist

Includes bibliographical references

Woodson, Jacqueline

Hinton, KaaVonia. **Jacqueline** Woodson; by KaaVonia Hinton. Mitchell Lane Publishers 2008 48p il (Classic storytellers) lib bdg $29.95

Grades: 5 6 7 8   **92**

1. Authors 2. Novelists 3. Women authors 4. African American authors 5. College teachers 6. Children's authors 7. Young adult authors

ISBN 978-1-58415-533-1 lib bdg; 1-58415-533-7 lib bdg

LC 2007-669

"This biography details the life of a popular African-American author. It covers her childhood, the challenges she faced growing up during the height of the Civil Rights Movement, what inspired her to begin to write, and her many literary successes. The book is filled with photos of the writer at various stages of her life and the covers of some of her books. Young people should find inspiration in Woodson's story." SLJ

Includes glossary and bibliographical references

★ Woodson, Jacqueline. **Brown** girl dreaming; Jacqueline Woodson. Nancy Paulsen Books 2014 336 p. illustrations, photographs (hardback) $16.99

Grades: 4 5 6 7 8   **92**

1. African American women -- Biography 2. American poetry -- African American authors 3. African American women authors -- Biography -- Poetry 4. Authors, American -- 20th century -- Biography -- Poetry

ISBN 0399252517; 9780399252518

LC 2014021346

Newbery Honor Book (2015)

Boston Globe-Horn Book Honor: Nonfiction (2015)

National Book Award: Young People's Literature (2014)

Coretta Scott King Author Award (2015)

Robert F. Sibert Honor Book (2015)

"Raised in South Carolina and New York, [author Jacqueline] Woodson always felt halfway home in each place. In vivid poems, she shares what it was like to grow up as an African American in the 1960s and 1970s, living with the remnants of Jim Crow and her growing awareness of the Civil Rights movement." (Publisher's note)

"Here is a memoir-in-verse so immediate that readers will feel they are experiencing the author's childhood right along with her." Horn Book

Wright, Orville, 1871-1948

★ Collins, Mary. **Airborne** : a photobiography of Wilbur and Orville Wright. National Geographic Soc. 2003 63p il maps $18.95

Grades: 4 5 6 7   **92**

1. Inventors 2. Aeronautics -- History 3. Aircraft industry executives

ISBN 0-7922-6957-8

LC 2002-5279

Examines the lives of the Wright brothers and discusses their experiments and triumphs in the field of flight

"The well-chosen photos give readers a feel for Kitty Hawk—windy, sandy, solitary. This is an exceptionally well-informed picture of the Wright brothers and what their 100-year-old achievement really meant." SLJ

Crompton, Samuel. The **Wright** brothers; first in flight. [by] Samuel Willard Crompton. Chelsea House 2007 110p il (Milestones in American history) lib bdg $35

Grades: 7 8 9 10   **92**

1. Inventors 2. Aeronautics -- History 3. Aircraft industry executives

ISBN 978-0-7910-9356-6 lib bdg; 0-7910-9356-5

LC 2006034131

Describes the careers and achievements of the Wright Brothers, who are credited with the invention of the airplane in 1903.

An "interesting and factual account of the Wright brothers. . . . [This book has] well-reproduced archival photos and drawings with explanatory captions . . . [and an] open layout and lively [text]." SLJ

Includes bibliographical references

★ Freedman, Russell. The **Wright** brothers: how they invented the airplane; with original photographs by Wilbur and Orville Wright. Holiday House 1991 129p il hardcover o.p, pa $14.95

Grades: 5 6 7 8 9 10   **92**

1. Inventors 2. Aeronautics -- History 3. Aircraft industry executives

ISBN 0-8234-0875-2; 0-8234-1082-X pa

LC 90-48440

A Newbery Medal honor book, 1992

In this "combination of photography and text, Freedman reveals the frustrating, exciting, and ultimately successful journey of these two brothers from their bicycle shop in Dayton, Ohio, to their Kitty Hawk flights and beyond. . . . An essential purchase for younger YAs." Voice Youth Advocates

Includes bibliographical references

Wright, Richard, 1908-1960

Hart, Joyce. **Native** son: the story of Richard Wright. Morgan Reynolds 2002 128p il (World writers) lib bdg $21.95

Grades: 7 8 9 10   **92**

1. Authors 2. Novelists 3. Dramatists 4. African American authors 5. Essayists 6. Authors, American 7. Nonfiction writers 8. Short story writers

ISBN 1-931798-06-0

LC 2002-13686

"The writing is accessible and flows smoothly." SLJ
Includes bibliographical references

Levy, Debbie. **Richard** Wright. Twenty-First Century Books 2008 160p (Literary greats) $33.26
Grades: 7 8 9 10 11 12   **92**
1. Authors 2. Novelists 3. Dramatists 4. African American authors 5. Essayists 6. Nonfiction writers 7. Short story writers
ISBN 978-0-8225-6793-6

LC 2006-101189
A biography of the African American author of Native Son and Black Boy
This "absorbing biography . . . does a fine job of placing Wright's personal life in the context of black history. . . . Cleanly designed and featuring a small photo on every double-page spread." Booklist
Includes bibliographical references

Wright, Wilbur, 1867-1912

★ Collins, Mary. **Airborne** : a photobiography of Wilbur and Orville Wright. National Geographic Soc. 2003 63p il maps $18.95
Grades: 4 5 6 7   **92**
1. Inventors 2. Aeronautics -- History 3. Aircraft industry executives
ISBN 0-7922-6957-8

LC 2002-5279
Examines the lives of the Wright brothers and discusses their experiments and triumphs in the field of flight
"The well-chosen photos give readers a feel for Kitty Hawk—windy, sandy, solitary. This is an exceptionally well-informed picture of the Wright brothers and what their 100-year-old achievement really meant." SLJ

Crompton, Samuel. The **Wright** brothers; first in flight. [by] Samuel Willard Crompton. Chelsea House 2007 110p il (Milestones in American history) lib bdg $35
Grades: 7 8 9 10   **92**
1. Inventors 2. Aeronautics -- History 3. Aircraft industry executives
ISBN 978-0-7910-9356-6 lib bdg; 0-7910-9356-5

LC 2006034131
Describes the careers and achievements of the Wright Brothers, who are credited with the invention of the airplane in 1903.
An "interesting and factual account of the Wright brothers. . . . [This book has] well-reproduced archival photos and drawings with explanatory captions . . . [and an] open layout and lively [text]." SLJ
Includes bibliographical references

★ Freedman, Russell. The **Wright** brothers: how they invented the airplane; with original photographs by Wilbur and Orville Wright. Holiday House 1991 129p il hardcover o.p. pa $14.95
Grades: 5 6 7 8 9 10   **92**
1. Inventors 2. Aeronautics -- History 3. Aircraft

industry executives
ISBN 0-8234-0875-2; 0-8234-1082-X pa

LC 90-48440
A Newbery Medal honor book, 1992
In this "combination of photography and text, Freedman reveals the frustrating, exciting, and ultimately successful journey of these two brothers from their bicycle shop in Dayton, Ohio, to their Kitty Hawk flights and beyond. . . . An essential purchase for younger YAs." Voice Youth Advocates
Includes bibliographical references

Yep, Laurence

Marcovitz, Hal. **Laurence** Yep; [by] Hal Marcovitz. Chelsea House 2008 136p il (Who wrote that?) $30
Grades: 6 7 8 9   **92**
1. Authors 2. Novelists 3. College teachers 4. Authors, American 5. Children's authors 6. Young adult authors 7. Chinese Americans -- Biography
ISBN 978-0-7910-9527-0; 0-7910-9527-4

LC 2007045508
This biography of the Chinese American author examines the "writer's life, including the inspiration behind some of [his] works. [The] volume includes photographs and quotations from interviews, as well as descriptions of main characters and annotated lists of books and awards. Useful for aspiring authors as well as book report writers." Horn Book Guide
Includes bibliographical references

Yolen, Jane

Carpan, Carolyn. **Jane** Yolen; [by] Carolyn Carpan. Chelsea House 2006 128p bibl il (Who wrote that?) lib bdg $30
Grades: 6 7 8 9   **92**
1. Authors 2. Novelists 3. Women authors 4. Editors 5. Fantasy writers 6. Authors, American 7. Children's authors 8. Science fiction writers
ISBN 978-0-7910-8660-5 lib bdg; 0-7910-8660-7 lib bdg

LC 2005007828
This describes the life and work of author Jane Yolen
"The photographs that illustrate the text show places from the author's life or period photos. . . . The extensive quotes from Yolen share her feelings as she wrote full time and published more than 250 books while raising a family. . . . [The book includes] extensive notes, a chronology, works by the author listed by publication date, major awards, and most wellknown characters." Voice Youth Advocates
Includes bibliographical references

Yousafzai, Malala, 1997-

Aretha, David. **Malala** Yousafzai and the girls of Pakistan; by David Aretha. Morgan Reynolds Publishing 2014 64 p. (Out in front) $27.45
Grades: 5 6 7 8   **92**
1. Women political activists 2. Taliban 3. Girls -- Education -- Pakistan 4. Political activists -- Pakistan 5. Women social reformers -- Pakistan 6. Girls -- Violence against -- Pakistan 7. Sex discrimination in education

-- Pakistan
ISBN 1599354543; 9781599354545
LC 2013044510

This book, by David Aretha, offers "the story of Malala Yousafzai's life.... By the time she was 11, she wrote candidly about the Taliban and their efforts to block girls' access to schools. Two years later, she was nominated for the International Children's Peace Prize but less than a year after that she was shot in the face by a Taliban assassin.... Yousafzai's eventual recovery and continued activism is a demonstration of bravery and conviction." (School Library Journal)

"This biography of the Pakistani girl who survived an assassination attempt by the Taliban provides geographical, historical, and sociopolitical context for Yousafzai's dedication to education activism. Captioned color photographs pair well with the concise and factual text. Important quotes are printed in red, which is difficult to read on some backgrounds. Significant terms are defined in the text. Websites. Bib., ind." Horn Book

Includes bibliographical references and index

Yousafzai, Malala. **I** am Malala; how one girl stood up for education and changed the world. Malala Yousafzai with Patricia McCormick. Young readers edition Little Brown & Co 2014 230 p. illustrations, map (hardback) $17

Grades: 5 6 7 8   **92**
   1. Women -- Education 2. Children's rights -- Pakistan
   3. Young women -- Education -- Pakistan -- Biography
   ISBN 031632793X; 9780316327930
LC 2014015881

"Malala Yousafzai was only ten years old when the Taliban took control of her region.... They said girls couldn't go to school. Raised in a once-peaceful area of Pakistan transformed by terrorism, Malala was taught to stand up for what she believes. So she fought for her right to be educated." (Publisher's note)

"Young education activist and Taliban victim Malala Yousafzai recounts her Pakistani childhood in this deftly adapted memoir. Domestic and academic tales illustrate her unusual maturity and resilience in the face of increasing Taliban threats. Yousafzai's moving narrative and engaging, sincere voice may provide an entryway to international awareness for middle-grade readers; a map and a thorough timeline provide additional political context." Horn Book

Zaharias, Babe Didrikson, 1911-1956

Lobby, Mackenzie. **Babe** Didrikson Zaharias; groundbreaking all-around athlete. ABDO Pub. Co. 2011 112p il (Legendary athletes) lib bdg $34.22
Grades: 6 7 8 9   **92**
   1. Women athletes 2. Golfers 3. Hurdlers 4. High jumpers 5. Javelin throwers 6. Olympic athletes
   ISBN 978-1-61714-755-5; 1-61714-755-9
LC 2010041158

This biography of athlete Babe Didrikson Zaharias "goes beyond merely discussing [her] accomplishments.... [It] also [explores] the social and political [influence she] had on society as a whole. In addition, [it introduces] historical events in the context of [her life].... This ... is teeming

with information and is a must-purchase for sports fans and readers interested in social activism." SLJ

Includes glossary and bibliographical references

Van Natta, Don, 1964- **Wonder** girl; the magnificent sporting life of Babe Didrikson Zaharias. Little, Brown and Co. 2011 403p il $27.99
Grades: 5 6 7 8   **92**
   1. Women athletes 2. Golfers 3. Hurdlers 4. High jumpers 5. Javelin throwers 6. Olympic athletes
   ISBN 978-0-316-05699-1; 0-316-05699-5
LC 2010041794

Describes the life and times of LPGA founder Babe Didrikson, the Texas woman who achieved All-American status in basketball, won gold medals in track and field in the 1932 Olympics, and became the first woman to play against men in a PGA tournament.

This is an "engaging biography.... Van Natta marvelously narrates the forgotten life of the 'greatest all-around athlete of all time,' a story that every American sport fan should relish." Publ Wkly

Includes bibliographical references

Wallace, Rich. **Babe** conquers the world; the legendary life of Babe Didrikson Zaharias. Rich Wallace, Sandra Neil Wallace. Calkins Creek 2014 272 p. (Includes bibliographical references (page 266-268) and index.) $16.95
Grades: 4 5 6 7 8   **92**
   1. Women athletes -- Biography
   ISBN 1590789814; 9781590789810
LC 2013953471

This book, by Rich Wallace and Sandra Neil Wallace, is a biography of Babe Didrikson Zaharias. "A champion basketball player, an Olympic track-and-field star, and a career golfer, Babe didn't let obstacles stand in the way of her success. The authors detail her trajectory from the daughter of a Norwegian immigrant born in a working-class Texas neighborhood to record wins at the 1932 Olympics (still not broken to this day) to her last days as she fought cancer." (School Library Journal)

"Babe Didrikson Zaharias is perhaps the most accomplished athlete that young people have never heard of. She was an Olympic track star in the 1932 games, a noted professional basketball player, and a formative member of the LPGA...This is part sports journalism, part narrative nonfiction, and part proof that professional athletes can be exemplary role models for young people." Booklist

Zapata, Emiliano, 1879-1919

Stein, R. Conrad. **Emiliano** Zapata and the Mexican Revolution. Morgan Reynolds Pub. 2011 144p il map (The story of Mexico) $28.95
Grades: 6 7 8 9   **92**
   1. Generals 2. Revolutionaries 3. Mexico -- History -- Revolution, 1910-1920
   ISBN 978-1-5993-5163-6; 1-5993-5163-3
LC 2010041616

This traces the life and impact of Zapata and his revolutionary movement on the history of Mexico.

"Stein organizes and clearly presents a great deal of information.... The ... format features a chronological text supplemented with useful sidebars and brightened with color illustrations, including many photos, artifacts, and period artworks." Booklist

Includes bibliographical references

Zenatti, Valérie, 1970-

Zenatti, Valerie. **When** I was a soldier; a memoir. translated by Adriana Hunter. Bloomsbury Children's Books 2005 235p $16.95

Grades: 7 8 9 10   **92**

1. Authors 2. Soldiers 3. Novelists 4. Women soldiers 5. Israel 6. Memoirists 7. Translators 8. Children's authors

ISBN 1-58234-978-9

A "fast, wry, present-tense memoir. . . . Readers on all sides of the war-peace continuum, here and there, will find much to talk about." Booklist

In this "memoir, Zenatti, first among her group of friends to be called for compulsory military service, chronicles two years of growing up in the Israeli army between 1988 and 1990." SLJ

Zindel, Paul

Daniel, Susanna. **Paul** Zindel. Rosen Publishing Group 2004 112p il (Library of author biographies) lib bdg $26.50

Grades: 5 6 7 8   **92**

1. Authors 2. Novelists 3. Dramatists 4. Authors, American 5. Children's authors

ISBN 0-8239-4524-3

Discusses the life and work of this popular author, including his writing process and methods, inspirations, a critical discussion of his books, biographical timeline, and awards.

Includes bibliographical references

Zuckerberg, Mark

Hasday, Judy L. **Facebook** and Mark Zuckerberg. Morgan Reynolds Pub. 2011 112p il (Business leaders) $28.95

Grades: 7 8 9 10 11 12   **92**

1. Businessmen 2. Online social networks 3. Facebook Inc. 4. Internet executives

ISBN 978-1-59935-176-6; 1-59935-176-5; 978-1-59935-215-2 e-book

LC 2011023210

This biography of Mark Zuckerberg and how he started Facebook "will grab YAs. . . . The design is browsable, with clear type and lots of color screens and informal photos of young people at work." Booklist

Includes bibliographical references

Woog, Adam. **Mark** Zuckerberg, Facebook creator. KidHaven Press 2009 48p il map (Innovators) $28.25

Grades: 4 5 6 7   **92**

1. Businesspeople 2. Facebook Inc. 3. Internet executives

ISBN 978-0-7377-4566-5; 0-7377-4566-5

LC 2009013458

"This brisk, readable [biography the creator of Facebook] . . . presents an appealing picture of the shy, lonely future billionaire . . . This is fascinating and relevant stuff." Booklist

Includes bibliographical references

920   Biography, genealogy, insignia

Aaseng, Nathan

Business builders in sweets and treats; [by] Nathan Aaseng. Oliver Press 2005 160p il (Business builders) $24.95

Grades: 5 6 7 8   **920**

1. Food industry 2. Businesspeople

ISBN 1-881508-84-6

LC 2003-64984

This is a "study of Hershey and chocolate, Wrigley and chewing gum, Ben and Jerry and ice cream, and others who make things we love to eat. . . . A few well-chosen sidebars document sweets that don't get a whole chapter. Excellent sources and citations, boxed facts, a lively style, and sometimes mouthwatering pictures finish the package." Booklist

Includes bibliographical references

Almanac of Famous People; A Comprehensive Reference Guide to More Than 40,000 Famous and Infamous Newsmakers from Biblical Times to the Present. edited by Kristin Mallegg. 10th ed. Gale / Cengage Learning 2011 2887 p. (hardcover) $280

Grades: 7 8 9 10 11 12 Adult   **920**

1. Celebrities -- Encyclopedias

ISBN 1414445482; 9781414445489

This reference book offers "biographical information on more than 30,000 famous individuals and groups." Entries provide the "subject's best-known name, complete name, nickname, [and] name of group," "dates and places of birth and death," and "nationality and occupation. Most entries include citations to sources that provide additional biographical information." (Publisher's note)

Armstrong, Mabel

Women astronomers; reaching for the stars. Stone Pine Press 2008 179p il (Discovering women in science series) pa $16.95

Grades: 7 8 9 10   **920**

1. Women astronomers

ISBN 978-0-972892-95-7 pa; 0-972892-95-8 pa

LC 2007-22318

This introduces 21 women astronomers, from ancient times to the present.

"A worthy addition to science collections, this well-documented collective biography not only fills gaps in existing books on astronomers, but also offers engaging accounts of the women's careers as well as unusually clear explanations of what they achieved and why each discovery was important." Booklist

Includes bibliographical references

Baker, Rosalie F.

Ancient Egyptians; people of the pyramids. [by] Rosalie F. and Charles F. Baker. Oxford Univ. Press 2001 189p il maps (Oxford profiles) $50

Grades: 7 8 9 10   **920**

1. Egypt -- Biography 2. Egypt -- Civilization

ISBN 0-19-512221-6

LC 2001-21209

"Divided into five periods from the Old Kingdom, about 2686 B.C., to the declining New Kingdom, about 245 B.C., this book profiles some 30 Egyptian leaders, devoting a three- to seven-page chapter to each one. . . . The entries are well written and researched. . . . A useful addition for report writers and subject enthusiasts." SLJ

Includes glossary and bibliographical references

Bausum, Ann

★ **Our** country's first ladies; [by] Ann Bausum; with a foreword by First Lady Laura Bush. National Geographic 2007 127p il $19.95; lib bdg $28.90

Grades: 5 6 7 8   **920**

1. Presidents' spouses -- United States

ISBN 978-1-4263-0006-6; 978-1-4263-0007-3 lib bdg

LC 2006021284

"A well-researched, thoughtfully written, attractive account. Fact boxes provide basic information such as birth and death dates, marriage dates, and children's names; a 'Did You Know' section shares interesting personal tidbits. Periodic time lines help to place the women's lives within the broader events of history. There is enough information here for simple reports. Interesting facts and anecdotes will hold readers' attention. . . . An excellent layout and clear, colorful photographs and reproductions will further entice readers." SLJ

Includes bibliographical references

Beccia, Carlyn

The **raucous** royals; test your royal wits: crack codes, solve mysteries, and deduce which royal rumors are true. Houghton Mifflin 2008 64p il $17

Grades: 4 5 6 7   **920**

1. Nobility 2. Historiography 3. Kings and rulers

ISBN 978-0-618-89130-6; 0-618-89130-7

LC 2008-298419

"Thirteen beliefs about rulers receive an acerbic and irreverent interrogation in this blend of royal-watching and skeptical investigation. The royal rumors, arranged chronologically, start with the real story behind Prince Dracula and Richard III's murderous ways, stopping en route at Napoleon's short stature and Marie Antoinette's 'let them eat cake' utterance, and finish up with Catherine the Great's death and King George's madness. . . . The energy and gleefully gossipy nature makes this a fine companion for Krull's Lives of . . . series, while its verve particularly recommends it as an entreé into historiography and critical thinking." Bull Cent Child Books

Includes bibliographical references

Benjamin, Michelle

Nobel's women of peace; by Michelle Benjamin and Maggie Mooney. Second Story Press 2008 146p il (Women's Hall of fame) pa $10.95

Grades: 6 7 8 9   **920**

1. Nobel Prizes 2. Women -- Biography

ISBN 978-1-897187-38-8; 1-897187-38-6 pa

Profiles the twelve female recipients of the Nobel Peace Prize since its creation, including how they became activists for peace and their accomplishments before and after winning the prestigious award.

"Substantive enough to support basic reports, the profiles include many women who are rarely featured in books for youth. . . . The international stories of individuals dedicating their lives to humanitarian efforts will inspire young activists, who will want to move on to the extensive list of appended resources." Booklist

Includes bibliographical references

Benson, Sonia

Korean War: biographies; [by] Sonia G. Benson; Gerda-Ann Raffaelle, editor. U.X.L 2002 xxx, 268p il pa $60

Grades: 7 8 9 10   **920**

1. Korean War, 1950-1953 -- Biography

ISBN 0-7876-5692-5

LC 2001-44241

Presents biographies of twenty-six men and women who participated in or were affected by the Korean War, including politicians, military leaders, journalists, and nurses

"An excellent starting point for researching the . . . people of the Korean War." Booklist

Includes bibliographical references

Bolden, Tonya

Portraits of African-American heroes; paintings by Ansel Pitcairn. Dutton Children's Books 2003 88p il $18.99; pa $11.99

Grades: 4 5 6 7   **920**

1. African Americans -- Biography

ISBN 0-525-47043-3; 0-14-240473-X pa

LC 2002-75911

"Each profile lists expected biographical information, but offers even more by way of keen insights into a subject's personality based on interviews and information drawn from personal memoirs. . . . Pitcairn's beautifully rendered sepia-toned portraits make each subject jump from the page, beckoning children to come ever closer and learn." Booklist

Bragg, Georgia

How they choked; failures, flops, and flaws of the awfully famous. by Georgia Bragg ; illustrated by Kevin O'Malley. Bloomsbury/Walker 2014 208 p. (pbk.) $18.89

Grades: 5 6 7 8   **920**

1. Inventions 2. Celebrities 3. Decision making 4. Celebrities -- Conduct of life 5. History -- Errors, inventions, etc.

ISBN 0802734898; 9780802734884; 9780802734891

LC 2013039127

This book, by Georgia Bragg, "knocks fourteen famous achievers off their pedestals to reveal the human side of history. Successful 'failures' include: Marco Polo, Queen Isabella of Spain, Montezuma II, Ferdinand Magellan, Anne Boleyn, Isaac Newton, Benedict Arnold, Susan B. Anthony, George Armstrong Custer, Thomas Alva Edison, Vincent Van Gogh, J. Bruce Ismay, 'Shoeless Joe' Jackson, [and] Amelia M. Earhart." (Publisher's note)

"On the heels of How They Croaked: The Awful Ends of the Awfully Famous (2011), Bragg seeks to reconcile what she sees as a major flaw of the biography genre—that authors ignore the human potential for error. Her compendium is unapologetically full of bad news, criticism, and belly flops...The snarkily entertaining narratives are illustrated with caricatures of each subject. For better or worse, subjects are rarely as one-dimensional as most biographies paint them, and this book proves that nobody is perfect." Booklist

★ **How** they croaked; the awful ends of the awfully famous. Walker & Co. 2011 178p il $17.99; lib bdg $18.89
Grades: 5 6 7 8   920
1. Death 2. Biography 4. Celebrities -- Death 5. Biography, Collective
ISBN 978-0-8027-9817-6; 0-8027-9817-9; 978-0-8027-9818-3 lib bdg; 0-8027-9818-7 lib bdg
LC 2010-08659

"Bragg chronicles with ghoulish glee the chronic or fatal maladies that afflicted 19 historical figures. Nonsqueamish readers will by entranced by her riveting descriptions. . . . The author tucks quick notes on at least marginally relevant topics, such as leeching, scurvy, presidential assassins, and mummy eyes . . . between the chapters. . . . O'Malley's cartoon portraits and spot art add just the right notes of humor to keep the contents from becoming too gross." Booklist

Butts, Edward
She dared; true stories of heroines, scoundrels, and renegades. [by] Ed Butts; illustrated by Heather Collins. Tundra Bks. 2005 121p il pa $8.95
Grades: 6 7 8 9 10   920
1. Women -- Biography 2. Canada -- Biography
ISBN 0-88776-718-4

This "details the lives of some of Canada's most famous and infamous women. The stories showcase explorers, spies, criminals, and pioneers in a variety of career fields. Organized chronologically from the 16th to the mid-20th century, this 12-chapter offering is historically sound and well researched." SLJ

Castro, Ivan A.
★ **100** hispanics you should know. Libraries Unlimited 2007 303p bibl il $55
Grades: 6 7 8 9   920
1. Hispanic Americans -- Biography
ISBN 1-59158-327-6

"This eye-opening and valuable reference is one of the few biographical compilations for young people that address the achievements of Spanish-speaking individuals across the world and throughout history, especially in the sciences, arts, politics, and military. The alphabetically arranged entries begin with key information about the individuals, such

as birthplaces, birth and death dates, career highlights, and b&w portraits; then continue with important contributions; and end with bibliographies." Libr Media Connect

Chemistry, Earth, and space sciences; edited by Derek Hall. Brown Bear Books 2010 64p il (Facts at your fingertips) lib bdg $35.65
Grades: 8 9 10 11   920
1. Chemists 2. Scientists 3. Astronomers 4. Space sciences 5. Science -- History 6. Chemistry -- History
ISBN 978-1-933834-47-4 lib bdg; 1-933834-47-1 lib bdg
LC 2009-13342

Profiles the lives and work of nine scientists and chemists who have made significant contributions to modern science, including Nicolaus Copernicus, Antoine Lavoisier, Dmitri Mendeleev, and Stephen Hawking

This provides "explanations about important discoveries, related work, and social and political influences that impacted the subjects' work. . . . The approximately six-to-eight page entries include important dates, photographs, diagrams, and sidebars on relevant scientists. The writing is often highly technical and some knowledge of the basics is assumed." SLJ

Includes glossary and bibliographical references

Chin-Lee, Cynthia
★ **Amelia** to Zora; twenty-six women who changed the world. illustrated by Megan Halsey and Sean Addy. Charlesbridge 2005 32p il $15.95
Grades: 4 5 6 7   920
1. Women -- Biography
ISBN 1-57091-522-9

"The illustrations are done in a remarkable mix of media. . . . The text portions are short . . . but they are enticing. By choosing her subjects from every culture, the author introduces children to the scope of the struggles and achievements of women from many times and many places." Booklist

Cotter, Charis
Born to write; the remarkable lives of six famous authors. Annick Press 2009 167p il $24.95; pa $14.95
Grades: 5 6 7 8   920
1. Authors
ISBN 978-1-55451-192-1; 1-55451-192-5; 978-1-55451-191-4 pa; 1-55451-191-7 pa

A collective biography of authors Lucy Maud Montgomery, Christopher Paul Curtis, C. S. Lewis, E.B. White, Madeleine L'Engle, and Philip Pullman

"Younger readers will find the presentation of the book appealing, with many colorful photographs and illustrations; however, more mature readers will gain the most enjoyment as they discover the backgrounds and inspirations of some of their favorite writers. . . . An excellent resource for reports and pleasure reading." SLJ

Kids who rule; the remarkable lives of five child monarchs. Annick Press 2007 120p il map $24.95; pa $14.95

Grades: 5 6 7 8   920
1. Queens 2. Emperors 3. Kings and rulers 4. Kings
5. Buddhist leaders 6. Political leaders 7. Nobel
laureates for peace
ISBN 978-1-55451-062-7; 1-55451-062-7; 978-1-
55451-061-0 pa; 1-55451-061-9 pa
This "book discusses five people who became monarchs
as children: Tutankhamen of Egypt, Mary Queen of Scots,
Queen Christina of Sweden, China's Emperor Puyi, and the
fourteenth Dalai Lama. . . . The illustrations, many in color,
include portrait paintings, engravings, and maps as well as
photos of people, places, and artifacts. . . . This appealing
collective biography presents five unusual children whose
stories are well worth reading." Booklist

D'Agnese, Joseph
Signing their rights away; the fame and misfor-
tune of the men who signed the United States Con-
stitution. by Denise Kiernan & Joseph D'Agnese.
Quirk Books 2011 254p il $19.95
Grades: 8 9 10 11 12 Adult   920
1. Statesmen -- United States 2. Presidents -- United
States 3. United States -- Constitution 4. United States
-- History -- 1775-1783, Revolution -- Biography 5.
United States -- Politics and government -- 1775-1783,
Revolution
ISBN 978-1-59474-520-1
Presents the lives, deaths, and scandals involving the
thirty-nine signers of the United States Constitution, in-
cluding Benjamin Franklin, Alexander Hamilton, and
James McHenry.
"For readers of American history, this is both education-
al and entertaining." Booklist
Includes bibliographical references

Drucker, Malka
Portraits of Jewish American heroes; by Malka
Drucker; illustrated by Elizabeth Rosen. Dutton Chil-
dren's Books 2008 96p il $22.99
Grades: 4 5 6   920
1. Jews -- United States -- Biography
ISBN 978-0-525-47771-6; 0-525-47771-3
                                     LC 2007-028481
"From Albert Einstein and Bella Abzug to Ruth Bader
Ginsburg, Hank Greenberg, and Steven Spielberg, this invit-
ingly illustrated collective biography celebrates 20 Jewish
American heroes in all their diversity. . . . The nicely designed volume includes full-page portraits of the subjects in
various media. . . . Drucker's eloquent, chatty style opens up
big issues about Judaism as a source of idealism and for a
just, compassionate society." Booklist
Includes bibliographical references

Dublin, Anne
Dynamic women dancers. Second Story Press
2009 128p il (The women's hall of fame) pa $10.95
Grades: 6 7 8 9   920
1. Dancers
ISBN 978-1-897187-56-2 pa; 1-897187-56-4 pa
"Profiles ten dancers, each from different countries and
backgrounds. Most of the dancers performed ballet or modern dance, but a flamenco dancer and a South Indian classi-

cal dancer are also included. Entries are brief, detailing their
backgrounds, studies, and the challenges each woman faced.
. . . Black-and-white pictures help break up the text, and a
few inset boxes offer supplemental quotes or information. . .
. Present[s] information well, and the lives profiled are both
interesting and inspirational." Voice Youth Advocates
Includes glossary and bibliographical references

Fortey, Jacqueline
Great scientists; written by Jacqueline Fortey.
DK Pub. 2007 72p il map (DK eyewitness books)
$15.99
Grades: 5 6 7 8   920
1. Scientists
ISBN 978-0-7566-2974-8; 0-7566-2974-8
                                     LC 2007-298205
This introduces readers to the great scientists and their
discoveries from ancient history to modern times.
"An accompanying CD provides clip art taken from the
book; this art can prove invaluable to both teachers and stu-
dents. . . . A very fine book for elementary and middle school
students and those who teach them." Sci Books and Films

Fradin, Dennis B.
★ The **founders**; the 39 stories behind the U.S.
Constitution. [by] Dennis Brindell Fradin; illustrated
by Michael McCurdy. Walker & Co. 2005 162p il
map $22.95; lib bdg $23.95
Grades: 4 5 6 7   920
1. Statesmen -- United States 2. United States --
Constitution 3. United States -- Politics and government
-- 1783-1809
ISBN 0-8027-8972-2; 0-8027-8973-0 lib bdg
"The makers of the U.S. Constitution are profiled in
two or three pages each, in sections introduced by a brief
note about their home states. McCurdy's black-and-white
scratchboard illustrations are properly stately and engaging.
Readers will find great nuggets of fact." Booklist
Includes bibliographical references

★ **Funny** business; conversations with writers of
comedy. compiled and edited by Leonard S. Marcus. Candlewick Press 2009 214p il $21.99
Grades: 5 6 7 8 9 10   920
1. Authors 2. Authorship 3. Wit and humor
ISBN 978-0-7636-3254-0; 0-7636-3254-6
This book comprises interviews with writers of humorous books for young people: Judy Blume, Beverly Cleary,
Sharon Creech, Christopher Paul Curtis, Anne Fine, Daniel
Handler, Carl Hiaasen, Norton Juster, Dick King-Smith, Hilary McKay, Daniel Pinkwater, Louis Sachar, and Jon Scieszka. Index. "Intermediate, middle school." (Horn Book)
"In 12 entertaining interviews . . . Marcus's compilation
explores the childhoods, writing processes and senses of
humor of well-known writers for children, including Judy
Blume, Beverly Cleary, Daniel Handler, Norton Juster and
Jon Scieszka. Marcus's evident knowledge of his subjects'
writing makes for some intriguing questions and answers.
. . . Photographs, manuscript pages and even e-mail chains
between the writers and their editors add fascinating tidbits."
Publ Wkly

Gifford, Clive

10 inventors who changed the world; written by Clive Gifford; illustrated by David Cousens. Kingfisher 2009 63p il $14.99

Grades: 4 5 6 7 **920**

1. Inventors 2. Inventions

ISBN 978-0-7534-6259-1; 0-7534-6259-1

"The innovative efforts of nine men and one woman are presented here. Some of the names will be familiar (Galileo, Franklin, Edison, Curie) while others will prove less so (Isambard Kindgom Brunel, Glenn Curtiss, Sergei Korolev). Starting in ancient times with Archimedes, the chronology ends in modern times with Korolev, a Soviet-era rocket designer. Each section offers a succinct yet thorough biography of the inventors. Striking graphic-novel-style art is a visual aid to draw readers into each setting and era." SLJ

10 kings & queens who changed the world; written by Clive Gifford; illustrated by David Cousens. Kingfisher 2009 63p il map $14.99

Grades: 4 5 6 7 **920**

1. Kings and rulers

ISBN 978-0-7534-6252-2; 0-7534-6252-4

"Cousens' bright graphic novel-style artwork is the grabber here; he uses theatrical angles to portray each historical figure as a chiseled or beautiful adventurer. . . . The writing is clear, packed with information, and presented in agile paragraphs that twist around the scenes of war, plotting, and murder." Booklist

Gourse, Leslie

Sophisticated ladies; the great women of jazz. illustrated by Martin French. Dutton Children's Books/Penguin Young Readers Group 2007 64p il $19.99

Grades: 7 8 9 10 11 12 **920**

1. Singers 2. Jazz music 3. Women -- Biography

ISBN 978-0-525-47198-1; 0-525-47198-7

LC 2006-14852

"This lively collective biography of 14 singers begins in the 1920s with Bessie Smith and Ethel Waters and moves on through current performers Cassandra Wilson and Diana Krall. A vibrant, full-page portrait opens each chapter, depicting the performer with bold vitality, in a style suggestive of a theater poster." SLJ

Includes discography and bibliographical references

Graham, Amy

Astonishing ancient world scientists; 8 great brains. MyReportLinks.com Books 2010 128p il (Great scientists and famous inventors) $33.27

Grades: 6 7 8 9 **920**

1. Scientists 2. Mathematicians 3. Science -- History 4. Mathematics -- History

ISBN 978-1-59845-079-8; 1-59845-079-4

LC 2008-53925

This is a collective biography of ancient scientists and mathematicians: Pythagoras, Hippocrates, Aristotle, Archimedes, Galen, Ptolemy, Zhang Heng, and al-Khwarizmi.

"An interesting and sometimes amusing book. . . . The illustrations are captivating and will appeal to students, as will some of the anecdotes about scientists." Sci Books Films

Includes glossary and bibliographical references

Greathouse, Lisa E.

Skygazers; from Hypatia to Faber. Compass Point Books 2009 40p il (Mission: science) lib bdg $26.60

Grades: 4 5 6 **920**

1. Stars 2. Astronomy 3. Astronomers

ISBN 978-0-7565-4075-3 lib bdg; 0-7565-4075-5 lib bdg

LC 2008-35734

Brief lives of outstanding astronomers through the ages, beginning with the first notable woman astronomer, Hypatia of Alexandria

Includes glossary and bibliographical references

Haskins, James

African American religious leaders; [by] Jim Haskins and Kathleen Benson. Wiley 2008 162p il (Black stars) lib bdg $24.95

Grades: 6 7 8 9 10 11 12 Adult **920**

1. African Americans -- Religion 2. African Americans -- Biography

ISBN 978-0-471-73632-5; 0-471-73632-5

LC 2007-27347

"It's great to have all these figures between two covers, and even a sampling of the entries captures the importance of religion, and its leaders, in African American life." Booklist

Includes bibliographical references

Henderson, Harry

Larry Page and Sergey Brin; information at your fingertips. author, Harry Henderson. Chelsea House 2012 134 p. (Trailblazers in science and technology) (library) $35

Grades: 7 8 9 10 11 12 **920**

1. Google 2. Web search engines 3. Webmasters -- United States -- Biography 4. Businesspeople -- United States -- Biography

ISBN 1604136766; 9781604136760

LC 2011032584

This book, by Harry Henderson, is a biography of the founders of the Internet company Google Inc. as part of the "Trailblaizers in Science and Technology" series. "When . . . Larry Page and Sergey Brin collaborated on the search engine Google, they didn't realize that their invention would soon become so ingrained in Web culture that its name would be used as a verb." (Publisher's note)

Includes bibliographical references and index

Herrera, Juan Felipe, 1948-

Portraits of Hispanic American heroes; by Juan Felipe Herrera; pictures by Raul Colon. Dial Books for Young Readers 2014 96 p. color illustrations (hardback) $19.99

Grades: 4 5 6 7 8   **920**
1. Biography 2. Latinos (U.S.)
ISBN 0803738099; 9780803738096
              LC 2013044661
Pura Belpré (Author) Honor Book (2015)

This book by Juan Felipe Herrera "showcases twenty Hispanic and Latino American men and women who have made outstanding contributions to the arts, politics, science, humanitarianism, and athletics. Biographies of Cesar Chavez, Sonia Sotomayor, Ellen Ochoa, Roberto Clemente, and many more [are included]." (Publisher's note)

"Herrera packs relevant info and kid-appropriate details . . . without overwhelming the work, infusing the narratives with engaging text. Colon's portraits are luminous." SLJ
Includes bibliographical references

Hodgkins, Fran

Champions of the ocean; illustrations by Cris Arbo. Dawn Publications 2009 144p il (Earth heroes) pa $11.95
Grades: 5 6 7 8   **920**
1. Scientists 2. Oceanography 3. Environmentalists
ISBN 978-1-58469-119-8 pa; 1-58469-119-0 pa
              LC 2009-17926

This is a collective biography of oceanographers William Beebe, Archie Carr, Jacques-Yves Cousteau, Margaret Wentworth Owings, Eugenie Clark, Roger Payne, Sylvia Earle, and Tierney Thys.

This is illustrated with "black-and-white photographs and illustrations. [The book] provides young readers with fascinating facts and insights. . . . This volume is an excellent introduction to the biography genre, as well as a terrific research book." Sci Books Films
Includes bibliographical references

Housel, Debra J.

Ecologists; from Woodward to Miranda. Compass Point Books 2009 40p il (Mission: science) lib bdg $26.60
Grades: 4 5 6   **920**
1. Ecology 2. Environmentalists
ISBN 978-0-7565-4076-0 lib bdg; 0-7565-4076-3 lib bdg
              LC 2008-35733

Profiles ecologists John Woodward, Aldo Leopold, Rachel Carson, Ruth Patrick, Eugene Odum, Lan Lubchenco, and Neo Martinez
Includes glossary and bibliographical references

Jankowski, Connie

Astronomers; from Copernicus to Crisp. Compass Point Books 2009 40p il (Mission: science) lib bdg $26.60
Grades: 4 5 6   **920**
1. Astronomers
ISBN 978-0-7565-3965-8 lib bdg; 0-7565-3965-X lib bdg
              LC 2008-8325

Explores the lives and discoveries of noted astronomers from the fifteenth to the twenty-first century.
Includes glossary and bibliographical references

Jokulsson, Illugi

Stars of the World Cup; Illugi Jökulsson. Abbeville Kids 2014 63 p. (World soccer legends) (hardback) $12.95
Grades: 5 6 7 8   **920**
1. Soccer 2. Soccer teams 3. World Cup (Soccer) 4. Soccer players -- Biography
ISBN 0789212110; 9780789212115
              LC 2014014490

In this book, by Illugi Jokulsson, "learn all about twenty-eight of the best players competing for the 2014 FIFA World Cup, from unstoppable scorers like Messi and Ronaldo to crafty playmakers like Iniesta and Modric, and ironclad defenders like Philipp Lahm and Thiago Silva." (Publisher's note)

"Young soccer fans will find plenty to enjoy in this visually dynamic introduction to 28 world-class soccer players... Readers will enjoy the information-packed text, but it's the eye-catching color photos (usually action shots) that will draw them to this attractive sports book." Booklist
Includes bibliographical references and index

Kane, Joseph Nathan

★ **Facts** about the presidents; a compilation of biographical and historical information. Joseph Nathan Kane, Janet Podell [editors] 8th ed; Wilson, H.W. 2009 720p $150
Grades: 8 9 10 11 12 Adult   **920**
1. Reference books 2. Presidents -- United States
ISBN 9780824210878
              LC 2008056016
First published 1959

The main part of this work provides an individual chapter on each President, from Washington through Barack Obama, presenting such information as family, education, election, Vice President, main events and accomplishments of his administration, and First Lady. Part two contains tables and lists presenting comparative data on all the Presidents

Kennedy, John F.

Profiles in courage. HarperCollins Pubs. 2003 xxii, 245p $19.95; pa $13.95
Grades: 7 8 9 10 11 12 Adult   **920**
1. Judges 2. Courage 3. Lawyers 4. Governors 5. Statesmen 6. Presidents 7. Senators 8. Army officers 9. Political leaders 10. State legislators 11. Members of Congress 12. Newspaper executives 13. Secretaries of state 14. Territorial governors 15. Supreme Court justices 16. Presidential candidates 17. Secretaries of the interior 18. Politicians -- United States
ISBN 0-06-053062-6; 0-06-085493-6 pa
              LC 2003-40676
A reissue of the title first published 1956

This series of profiles of Americans who took courageous stands at crucial moments in public life includes John Quincy Adams, Daniel Webster, Thomas Hart Benton, Sam Houston, Edmund G. Ross, Lucius Q. C. Lamar, George Norris, Robert A. Taft and others.
Includes bibliographical references

Kennedy, Kerry

Speak truth to power; human rights defenders who are changing our world. photographs by Eddie Adams; edited by Nan Richardson. Crown 2000 256p il hardcover o.p. pa $34.95

Grades: 7 8 9 10 **920**
1. Human rights
ISBN 0-8129-3062-2; 1-88416-733-0 pa

LC 00-34557

This book "is composed of fifty three-page interviews with people who have made strides in the global fight to ensure basic human rights for everyone. . . . The Dalai Lama, Desmond Tutu, and Elie Wiesel are included, but most subjects are everyday people who have survived imprisonment, death threats, and torture to bring about change. . . . Their reports are sad but inspiring. . . . The haunting photographs and stories are gripping." Voice Youth Advocates

Kiernan, Denise

★ **Signing** our lives away; the fame and misfortune of the men who signed the Declaration of Independence. by Denise Kiernan & Joseph D'Agnese. Quirk 2009 255p $19.95

Grades: 5 6 7 8 **920**
1. Statesmen -- United States 2. United States -- Declaration of Independence 3. United States -- Politics and government -- 1775-1783, Revolution
ISBN 978-1-59474-330-6; 1-59474-330-4

"Kiernan and D'Agnese present readers with astonishing individual portraits of all the signers [of the Declaration of Independence] in an attempt both to dispel some of the mythology surrounding the document as well as to establish a place in the historical discourse for those men not named Jefferson, Hancock, Franklin, or Adams. The marvelously arranged work lends itself to either straightforward reading or skipping around. . . . An entertaining and effective narrative of about three to five pages per individual is presented." SLJ

Includes bibliographical references

Killam, G. D.

Student encyclopedia of African literature; [by] Douglas Killam and Alicia L. Kerfoot. Greenwood Press 2008 xxiii, 339p $85

Grades: 8 9 10 11 12 **920**
1. Reference books 2. African literature -- Encyclopedias
ISBN 978-0-313-33580-8; 0-313-33580-X

LC 2007-35356

"Killam, professor emeritus of Commonwealth literature at the University of Guelph, has published extensively on the subject of African literature. In the current work, Killam and Kerfoot, a Ph.D. candidate in the Department of English and Cultural Studies at McMaster University, include 598 entries on authors, works, and subjects related to all genres as well as literature of the diaspora (African-American literature, African-British literature). The preface explains that the goal is to provide guidance rather than critical commentary for students of African literature. Entries are arranged alphabetically. Those on works are short and provide only the date published, author, and a synopsis. Entries on writers range from a paragraph to more than a page. All writer entries

contain biographical data and information on works. Some entries, such as that for Chinua Achebe, also discuss the writer's influence. Subject entries generally run to several pages, and some (for example, Censorship) are divided into regional subtopics. Writer and subject entries frequently include lists of further reading. The A–Z portion of the volume is followed by a selected bibliography containing additional references. Access is provided through several means. The beginning of the book contains a complete alphabetic list of entries. This is followed by a subject-based list called 'Guide to Related Topics.' Additional aids are cross-references and a comprehensive index. The Student Encyclopedia of African Literature is similar in structure and content to The Companion to African Literatures, which Killam coedited in 2000 for Indiana University Press. For this reason, libraries that already own the latter may consider this a replacement. This is a useful resource, especially for libraries serving undergraduates or the general public." Booklist

"This alphabetically arranged volume provides brief information about authors, individual works, and issues related to the literature of the African continent, and a few themed articles that cover the literature of its diaspora. The articles are concise, if academic, and the coverage reasonably comprehensive. . . . Despite the somewhat confusing heading fonts, this will be a welcome contribution to reference collections." SLJ Reviews

Kimmel, Elizabeth Cody

Ladies first; 40 daring American women who were second to none. [by] Elizabeth Cody Kimmel; foreword by Stacy Allison. National Geographic 2006 192p il $18.95

Grades: 5 6 7 8 **920**
1. Women -- Biography 2. United States -- Biography
ISBN 0-7922-5393-0

LC 2005005113

This offers "introductions to forty of America's most brilliant and courageous women. Each essay is three pages in length and includes a fourth full-page portrait of the woman being introduced. . . . The women chosen achieved greatness in a wide range of endeavors, from athletics to the arts to politics. . . . Students will find these excellent essays useful as an introduction to the women portrayed and as a good jumping off point for further research." Voice Youth Advocates

Includes bibliographical references

The **look** -it-up book of explorers. Random House 2004 128p il map hardcover o.p. pa $19.99

Grades: 5 6 7 8 **920**
1. Explorers 2. Exploration
ISBN 0-375-92478-7; 0-375-82478-2 pa

"Beginning with Leif Ericksson and his trip to Greenland and the Americas to Robert Ballard's 1985 expedition to search for the Titanic , the chronologically arranged spreads give readers a better understanding of how the world was explored. . . . Informative black-and-white photos and reproductions appear throughout. . . . This is an excellent quick resource that will appeal to researchers and general readers alike." SLJ

Krull, Kathleen

Lives of the explorers; discoveries, disasters (and what the neighbors thought) Kathleen Krull ; illustrated by Kathryn Hewitt. HMH Books for Young Readers 2014 96 p. col. ill., col. maps (hardback) $20.99

Grades: 4 5 6 7   **920**

1. Explorers 2. Exploration 3. United States -- Exploration 4. Discoveries in geography 5. Adventure and adventurers

ISBN 0152059105; 9780152059101

LC 2013037697

"Krull introduces middle-grade readers to a diverse cast of 17 explorers in this latest offering from her series. A short, two-to five page chapter is devoted to each explorer, incorporating a biographical sketch and a short discussion of the explorer's contributions. The subjects are presented chronologically, beginning in the medieval period with the Norseman Leif Ericson and finishing with the astronaut Sally Ride." (School Library Journal)

"The straightforward, accessible prose makes for fast reading, and Krull doesn't shy away from some deplorable, stomach-turning facts, which kids will devour and use to spice up staid homework assignments." Kirkus

Includes bibliographical references

★ Lives of the presidents; fame, shame (and what the neighbors thought) written by Kathleen Krull; illustrated by Kathryn Hewitt. updated ed.; Harcourt Children's Books 2011 104p il $21

Grades: 4 5 6 7   **920**

1. Presidents -- United States

ISBN 978-0-547-49809-6; 0-547-49809-8

First published 1998

"This new edition is sure to be even more popular than the original title (Harcourt, 1998) as it includes Presidents George W. Bush and Barack Obama, who are given the same cheeky-but-respectful treatment as their predecessors. . . . [Krull] provides further information on ex-Presidential activity since 1998, such as Jimmy Carter's Nobel Prize, Ronald Reagan's passing, and the Clintons' post-White House work. All other entries and art are virtually unaltered. Guaranteed to inject some levity into the ubiquitous presidential biography assignment, the 2011 Lives of the Presidents is a must-have for elementary schools and public libraries." SLJ

Includes bibliographical references

Langley, Wanda

Women of the wind; early women aviators. [by] Wanda Langley. Morgan Reynolds Pub. 2006 160p il map lib bdg $26.95

Grades: 6 7 8 9   **920**

1. Women air pilots

ISBN 978-1-931798-81-5; 1-931798-81-8

LC 2005022951

"This collective biography celebrates the accomplishments of nine American women who pioneered in the field of aviation: Harriet Quimby, Katherine Stinson, Ruth Law, Bessie Coleman, Amelia Earhart, Ruth Nichols, Louise Thaden, Anne Morrow Lindbergh, and Jacqueline Cochran. . . . Well reproduced and often in color, the illustrations include a great many photos, as well as maps and period advertisements. . . . Langley . . . offers information, anecdotes, and inspiring stories." Booklist

Includes bibliographical references

Life sciences; edited by Derek Hall. Brown Bear Books 2010 64p il (Facts at your fingertips) lib bdg $35.65

Grades: 8 9 10 11   **920**

1. Scientists 2. Life sciences

ISBN 978-1-933834-45-0 lib bdg; 1-933834-45-5 lib bdg

LC 2009-13343

Profiles the lives and work of famous life scientists, including Charles Darwin, Louis Pasteur, and Alexander Fleming

This provides "explanations about important discoveries, related work, and social and political influences that impacted the subjects' work. . . . The approximately six-to-eight page entries include important dates, photographs, diagrams, and sidebars on relevant scientists. The writing is often highly technical and some knowledge of the basics is assumed." SLJ

Includes glossary and bibliographical references

Malnor, Bruce

Champions of the wilderness; by Bruce and Carol L. Malnor; illustrated by Anisa Claire Hovemann. Dawn Publications 2009 143p il (Earth heroes) pa $11.95

Grades: 5 6 7 8   **920**

1. Environmentalists

ISBN 978-1-58469-116-7 pa; 1-58469-116-6 pa

LC 2008-53670

"This is a short gem of a book that includes short biographies of eight 'heroes' who have championed the preservation and/or conservation of wilderness areas around the world over the past two centuries. Henry David Thoreau, John Muir, Teddy Roosevelt, Aldo Leopold, Richard St. Barbe Baker, Mardy Murie, David Suzuki, and Wangari Maathai are the heroes in question. The storytelling is fluent and engaging." Sci Books Films

Includes bibliographical references

Malnor, Carol

Champions of wild animals; by Carol L. and Bruce Malnor; illustrations by Anisa Claire Hovemann. Dawn Publications 2010 144p il (Earth heroes) pa $11.95

Grades: 5 6 7 8   **920**

1. Naturalists 2. Endangered species 3. Wildlife conservation

ISBN 978-1-58469-123-5 pa; 1-58469-123-9 pa

LC 2010-16030

This describes "the youth and careers of eight of the world's greatest environmentalists who championed the protection of wildlife, including William Hornaday (saved the bison from extinction), Ding Darling (A Duck's Best Friend), Rachel Carson (author of Silent Spring), Roger Tory Peterson (Inventor of the Modern Field Guide), R.D. Lawrence (Storyteller for Wolves), E.O. Wilson (Lord of the Ants), Jane Goodall (Champion for Chimps), and Ian and

Saba Douglas-Hamilton (Saving the Elephants)." Publisher's note

Includes bibliographical references

Mattern, Joanne

Mystics and psychics. Morgan Reynolds Pub. 2011 128p il (World religions and beliefs) $28.95

Grades: 6 7 8 9   **920**

1. Mysticism 2. Extrasensory perception

ISBN 978-1-59935-148-3; 1-59935-148-X

LC 2010008690

"Mattern offers an evenhanded look at some of the most famous (and controversial) of those with otherworldly powers. The mystics are Hildegard of Bingen, a twelfth-century German anchoress, and Padre Pio, and Italian monk who died in 1968. . . . Others profiled include Nostradamus; Edgar Cayce . . . ; Jeanne Dixon . . . ; and Peter Hurkos. . . . The profiles are interspersed with comments from skeptics and other reasons for visions. . . . Good illustrations and excellent back matter extend the well-written text." Booklist

Includes bibliographical references

Maydell, Natalie

★ **Extraordinary** women from the Muslim world. Global Content Publishing 2008 117p il map $16.95

Grades: 5 6 7 8   **920**

1. Muslim women 2. Women -- Biography

ISBN 978-0-97999-010-6; 0-97999-010-6

This "is an illustrative introduction to 13 Muslim women in history who have lived extraordinary lives and influenced their communities in a positive way, often overcoming extreme hardship and inaccurate stereotypes that have been placed on the role of women in Islam." Publisher's note

Nathan, Amy

Meet the dancers; from ballet, broadway, and beyond. Henry Holt 2008 231p il $18.95

Grades: 5 6 7 8   **920**

1. Dance 2. Dancers

ISBN 978-0-8050-8071-1; 0-8050-8071-6

LC 2007-27589

"This collective biography reveals the paths that 16 diverse dancers followed to become professionals and to join prestigious companies. . . . The tone of the text is conversational. . . . The pictures dramatically capture how talented these performers are. Anyone, whether considering a career in dance or not, will be inspired and educated by these up-close-and-personal accounts." SLJ

Open the unusual door; true life stories of challenge, adventure, and success by black Americans. edited and with an introduction by Barbara Summers. Graphia 2005 206p pa $7.99

Grades: 7 8 9 10   **920**

1. African Americans -- Biography

ISBN 0-618-58531-1

"A wonderful cross section of excerpts from published autobiographies. The 16 stories tell of challenges met and opportunities recognized and realized. Colin Powell's recollection of his introduction to the military life at City Col-

lege in New York City stands alongside Russell Simmons's retelling of the turning point in his life when, at 16 years of age, he shot at and missed a fellow drug dealer. . . . This little gem of a book should be a first purchase for public and school libraries." SLJ

Orgill, Roxane

★ **Shout,** sister, shout! the girl singers who shaped a century. Margaret K. McElderry Bks. 2001 148p il hardcover o.p. pa $12.95

Grades: 6 7 8 9   **920**

1. Actors 2. Singers 3. Popular music 4. Folk musicians 5. Jazz musicians 6. Blues musicians 7. Songwriters 8. Pop musicians 9. Children's authors 10. Women -- Biography

ISBN 0-689-81991-9; 978-1-4169-6391-2 pa; 1-4169-6391-X pa

LC 99-54374

"The lives of ten 'girl singers,' representing different genres of popular music, from vaudeville to blues to jazz to country, are arranged by decade. Profiles of Sophie Tucker, Ma Rainey, Bessie Smith, Ethel Merman, Judy Garland, Anita O'Day, Joan Baez, Bette Midler, Madonna, and Lucinda Williams are included." Voice Youth Advocates

Includes discography and bibliographical references

Ottaviani, Jim

★ **Dignifying** science; stories about women scientists. written by Jim Ottaviani and illustrated by Donna Barr . . . [et al.] 3rd ed; G.T. Labs 2009 142p il pa $16.95

Grades: 6 7 8 9 10 11 12   **920**

1. Graphic novels 2. Biographical graphic novels 3. Women scientists -- Graphic novels

ISBN 978-0-9788037-3-5; 0-9788037-3-5

First published 1999

Ottaviani provides biographical sketches of women scientists such as Lise Meitner, Rosalind Franklin, Barbara McClintock, and Hedy Lamarr (yes, the actress was also an inventor); all the stories are illustrated by women comics artists, including Lea Hernandez, Linda Medley, Anne Timmons, and others.

★ **Philosophy,** invention, and engineering; edited by Derek Hall. Brown Bear Books 2009 64p il (Facts at your fingertips) lib bdg $35.65

Grades: 8 9 10 11 12   **920**

1. Inventors 2. Inventions 3. Scientists 4. Philosophers

ISBN 978-1-93383-448-1 lib bdg; 1-93383-448-X lib bdg

LC 2009013344

"The book provides a multitude of facts—and fairly deep content—about Aristotle, James Watt, Charles Babbage and Ada Lovelace, Turing, and Jonas Salk. . . . Rich in synthesized information, this book encompasses a wealth of knowledge and gives a clear overall picture of the world at the time of each scientist's life." Booklist

Physical sciences; edited by Derek Hall. Brown Bear Books 2010 64p il (Facts at your fingertips) lib bdg $35.65

Grades: 8 9 10 11   **920**

1. Chemists 2. Physicists 3. Scientists
ISBN 978-1-933834-46-7; 1-933834-46-3

LC 2009-13345

Profiles the lives and work of people who have made significant contributions in physical sciences, including Isaac Newton, Marie and Pierre Curie, Albert Einstein and Richard Feynman.

This provides "explanations about important discoveries, related work, and social and political influences that impacted the subjects' work. . . . The approximately six-to-eight page entries include important dates, photographs, diagrams, and sidebars on relevant scientists. The writing is often highly technical and some knowledge of the basics is assumed." SLJ

Includes glossary and bibliographical references

Pinkney, Andrea Davis

★ **Let** it shine; stories of Black women freedom fighters. illustrated by Stephen Alcorn. Harcourt 2000 107p il $20

Grades: 4 5 6 7   **920**

1. United States -- Race relations 2. African Americans -- Civil rights 3. African American women -- Biography 4. African Americans -- Civil rights -- History 5. African American women civil rights workers -- Biography
ISBN 0-15-201005-X

LC 99-42806

This is a collection of "sketches celebrating the contributions of 10 women who moved forward the cause of civil rights in America. . . . They include Harriet Tubman, Mary McLeod Bethune and Rosa Parks, as well as Biddy Mason, Ida B. Wells-Barnett, Ella Josephine Baker, Dorothy Irene Height and Fannie Lou Hamer." (SLJ) Bibliography. "Grades three to six." (Bull Cent Child Books)

This "collective biography tells of 10 extraordinary black women. From Sojourner Truth to Shirley Chisholm, this is also a view of African American history through individual lives. . . . Stephen Alcorn's allegorical oil portraits are dramatic and beautiful. . . . The immediacy of the text and the spacious design of the large volume make this a natural for reading aloud." Booklist

Includes bibliographical references

Pouy, Jean-Bernard

The **big** book of dummies, rebels and other geniuses; [by] Jean-Bernard Pouy & Serge Bloch; Anne Blanchard. 1st American ed.; Enchanted Lion Books 2008 123p il $19.95

Grades: 6 7 8 9   **920**

1. Celebrities 2. Reference books 3. Biography -- Dictionaries
ISBN 978-1-59270-103-2; 1-59270-103-5

LC 2008-12278

Original French edition, 2006

"Pouy offers a wide variety of biographical sketches of famous names . . . from Charlie Chaplin to Louis Armstrong and Albert Einstein. The author nicely makes sure to include

little-known details. . . . [This book] will sell itself." Voice Youth Advocates

Includes bibliographical references

Reed, Jennifer

The **Saudi** royal family; [by] Jennifer Bond Reed. Chelsea House Publishers 2007 120p il (Modern world leaders) lib bdg $30

Grades: 6 7 8 9 10   **920**

1. Saudi Arabia -- Kings and rulers
ISBN 978-0-7910-9218-7; 0-7910-9218-6

LC 2006-10613

First published 2003 by Chelsea House in the series: Major world leaders

This book "deciphers the nuances of Islamic law, an integral part of the Arabian peninsula's history. Tumultuous and violent times are recorded, and democratic-like changes are chronicled as well. The result is as neutral and evenhanded an approach as a Westerner can use to describe this succession of Arab leaders." Libr Media Connect

Includes bibliographical references

Reef, Catherine

Frida & Diego; art, love, life. Catherine Reef. Houghton Mifflin Harcourt 2014 176 p. illustrations (some color) (hardcover) $18.99

Grades: 7 8 9 10   **920**

1. Artists -- Biography 2. Painters -- Mexico -- Biography 3. Artist couples -- Mexico -- Biography
ISBN 0547821840; 9780547821849

LC 2013021340

"Nontraditional, controversial, rebellious, and politically volatile, the Mexican artists Frida Kahlo and Diego Rivera are remembered for their provocative paintings as well as for their deep love for each other. Their marriage was one of the most tumultuous and infamous in history--filled with passion, pain, betrayal, revolution, and, above all, art that helped define the twentieth century." (Publisher's note)

"Reef points out each individual's artistic development and unique qualities as a painter. Archival photos and color reproductions of artworks further enhance the narrative. Writing a dual biography is challenging, but in this case, the portrayal of each person would seem incomplete without an understanding of the other." Booklist

Includes bibliographical references and index

Roberts, Cokie

Founding mothers; remembering the ladies. by Cokie Roberts and illustrated by Diane Goode and edited by Alyson Day. HarperCollins 2014 40 p. (hardcover bdg.) $17.99

Grades: 3 4 5 6 7   **920**

1. Women -- United States -- History 2. United States -- History -- 1775-1783, Revolution
ISBN 0060780029; 9780060780029; 9780060780036

LC 2013936887

This book, by Cokie Roberts and illustrated by Diane Goode, "reveals the incredible accomplishments of the women who orchestrated the American Revolution behind the scenes. Roberts traces the stories of heroic, patriotic women such as Abigail Adams, Martha Washington, Phillis Wheatley, Mercy Otis Warren, Sarah Livingston Jay, and others. Details are gleaned from their letters, private journals, lists, and ledgers." (Publisher's note)

"Most children know that the "Founding Fathers" are the men who helped the 13 colonies develop into the United States. What about the women of the time period?...Grammarians may not appreciate the author's colloquial style, but the conversational tone is appealing. Beautifully intricate illustrations, rendered with antique pens, sepia ink, and watercolors, suit the text well. Thoughtful design, well-chosen facts, and an approachable format combine to make a book readers will enjoy and appreciate.—" (SLJ)

Rosenberg, Aaron

The **Civil** War; one event, six people. Scholastic 2011 160p il map (Profiles) $14.99

Grades: 5 6 7 8   **920**

1. Nurses 2. Slaves 3. Authors 4. Lawyers 5. Generals 6. Presidents 7. Abolitionists 8. Photographers 9. Memoirists 10. Police officials 11. State legislators 12. College presidents 13. Members of Congress 14. Red Cross officials 15. Social welfare leaders 16. United States -- History -- 1861-1865, Civil War -- Biography
ISBN 978-0-545-28926-9; 0-545-28926-2

"This collective biography . . . introduces Abraham Lincoln, Frederick Douglass, Clara Barton, George McClellan, Robert E. Lee, and Matthew Brady. Single paragraph summaries of each subject's historical relevance are followed by resumes of their lives that focus on how each affected and was affected by the Civil War and that point out connections between them all. . . . Archival photographs are instuctive." Booklist

Includes bibliographical references

Rubin, Susan Goldman

Everybody paints! the lives and art of the Wyeth family. by Susan Goldman Rubin. Chronicle Books 2013 105 p. illustrations (chiefly color) (alk. paper) $16.99

Grades: 6 7 8 9 10   **920**

1. American painting 2. Artists -- United States -- Biography 3. Wyeth family
ISBN 0811869849; 9780811869843

LC 2013006595

Author Susan Goldman Rubin "shares the . . . story of the Wyeths--N.C., Andrew, and Jamie--three generations of painters and arguably the First Family of American Art. The . . . text traces the events that shaped their art and the ways their art influenced them in return, while the . . . design showcases . . . reproductions of the works that have made the Wyeth family legendary." (Publisher's note)

"This small-trim book celebrates the artistic Wyeth family, mostly the work of revered illustrator N. C. Wyeth; his son Andrew, popular modern realist best-known for Christina's World; and grandson Jamie, an acclaimed painter working today. Rubin's prose is fluid, and seamlessly worked-in quotes from her subjects add to the narrative's personal feel. The handsome, clean design showcases the excellent reproductions." Horn Book

Schatz, Kate

Rad American women A-Z; written by Kate Schatz; illustrated by Miriam Klein Stahl. City

Lights Books 2015 64 p. color illustrations, portraits $14.95

Grades: 6 7 8 9   **920**

1. Women -- United States -- Biography
ISBN 0872866831; 9780872866836

LC 2014037930

This book on American women, written by Kate Schatz and illustrated by Miriam Klein Stahl, features "26 diverse individuals. There are artists and abolitionists, scientists and suffragettes, rock stars and rabble-rousers, and agents of change of all kinds. The book includes an introduction that discusses what it means to be 'rad' and 'radical,' an afterword with 26 suggestions for how you can be 'rad,' and a Resource Guide with ideas for further learning and reading." (Publisher's note)

"Colorful and hip potraitures create a visual sensation that immediately draws in readers. Profiled are 26 American women from the 18th through 21st centuries, who have made—or are still making—history as artists, writers, teachers, lawyers, or athletes...Classes across the curriculum can utilize this informative book." SLJ

Simoni, Suzanne

Fantastic women filmmakers. Second Story Press 2008 122p il (Women's hall of fame) pa $10.95

Grades: 7 8 9 10   **920**

1. Women in the motion picture industry 2. Motion picture producers and directors -- Biography
ISBN 978-1-897187-36-4 pa; 1-897187-36-X pa

"Includes profiles of earlier filmmakers such as Nell Shipman and Ida Lupiano as well as contemporary directors like Deepa Mehta, Patricia Rozema, and Mira Nair. The author includes filmmakers who found varied and unique ways to navigate the industry. . . . The profiles . . . are revealing, inspiring, and insightful." Voice Youth Advocates

Includes glossary and bibliographical references

Spitz, Bob

Yeah! yeah! yeah! the Beatles, Beatlemania, and the music that changed the world. Little, Brown 2007 234p il $18.99

Grades: 7 8 9 10   **920**

1. Rock musicians 2. Beatles
ISBN 978-0-316-11555-1; 0-316-11555-X

LC 2006-39575

Based on the author's title for adults: The Beatles (2005)

This is "packed with all the fun and fabulousness that were the Beatles. The book begins at the church festival where John and Paul met as teens, and ends with Paul's formal declaration to leave the group. . . . [This is] comprehensive, sensitive to its subjects, and told with a flow that carries readers along. Many smartly chosen black-and-white photographs help re-create the times." Booklist

Stout, Glenn

Yes she can! women's sports pioneers. Houghton Mifflin Harcourt 2011 117p il (Good sports) pa $5.99

Grades: 4 5 6 7   **920**
1. Women athletes
ISBN 978-0-547-41725-7; 0-547-41725-X

"In chapters devoted to swimmer Trudy Ederle, runners Louise Stokes and Tidye Pickett, jockey Julie Krone, and Indy car driver Danica Patrick, Stout covers each woman's hard work, setbacks, and triumphs without minimizing the challenges and disappointments along the way. . . . Accessible and inspirational." Publ Wkly

Sullivan, Otha Richard

African American millionaires. John Wiley & Sons 2004 158p il (Black stars) $24.95
Grades: 6 7 8 9   **920**
1. African Americans -- Biography
ISBN 0-471-46928-9

LC 2004-14694

This profiles 25 African American millionaires

"Sullivan offers an exemplary compilation of a relatively unexplored subject area. . . . The book is well organized, highly readable, and inspiring." SLJ

Includes bibliographical references

Tate, Eleanora E.

★ **African** American musicians; Jim Haskins, general editor. Wiley 2000 70p il (Black stars) $24.95
Grades: 6 7 8 9   **920**
1. African American musicians
ISBN 0-471-25356-1

LC 99-51360

"Many genres and skills are represented from spirituals, gospel, ragtime, blues, jazz, and soul. Scott Joplin, Marian Anderson, Duke Ellington, and Aretha Franklin are here as well as Michael Jackson and a few lesser-known individuals. Each entry includes a black-and-white photo or reproduction and sidebars on pertinent topics." SLJ

Includes bibliographical references

Thimmesh, Catherine

★ **Girls** think of everything; illustrated by Melissa Sweet. Houghton Mifflin 2000 57p $16; pa $6.95
Grades: 5 6 7 8   **920**
1. Admirals 2. Chemists 3. Students 4. Inventors 5. Inventions 6. Physicists 7. Women inventors 8. Computer scientists 9. Home economists 10. Clothing industry executives 11. Office supply industry executives
ISBN 0-395-93744-2; 0-618-19563-7 pa

LC 99-36270

"Ten women and two girls are given a few pages each. Included are Mary Anderson, who invented the windshield wiper (after she was told it wouldn't work); Ruth Wakefield, who, by throwing chunks of chocolate in her cookie batter, gave Toll House cookies to the world; and young Becky Schroeder, who invented Glo-paper because she wanted to write in the dark. The text is written in a fresh, breezy manner, but it is the artwork that is really outstanding." Booklist

Walters, Eric

When elephants fight; written by Eric Walters and Adrian Bradbury. Orca Book Publishers 2008 89p il $19.95
Grades: 7 8 9 10   **920**
1. Children and war
ISBN 978-1-55143-900-6; 1-55143-900-X

"The authors detail the lives of children growing up in . . . [war torn nations]. They provide rich, detailed histories of each nation, and explain the current conflicts which have led to the destruction of families and normal childhood. . . . This would be an excellent supplemental text for a high school geography or world civilization program." Libr Media Connect

Winter, Jonah

Peaceful heroes; illustrated by Sean Addy. Arthur A. Levine Books 2009 56p il $17.99
Grades: 4 5 6 7   **920**
1. Peace 2. Heroes and heroines
ISBN 978-0-439-62307-0; 0-439-62307-3

LC 2008-48311

"Starting off with Jesus, Gandhi, King, and Sojourner Truth, this collective biography goes on to profile many less well-known peace activists across the world. . . . The detailed portraits never deny the horrifying realities that the peace-seeking leaders are fighting against. With the chatty interactive text, there are handsome full-page pictures of each activist, rendered in oil, acrylic, and collage in shades of red and brown." Booklist

Ying, Chris

109 forgotten American heroes; created by Chris Ying and Brian McMullen. DK Publishing 2009 175p il $19.99
Grades: 6 7 8   **920**
1. Heroes and heroines 2. United States -- Biography
ISBN 978-0-7566-5405-4; 0-7566-5405-X

Photographs, graphics, and text bring to life the contributions, inventions, wisdom, savvy, and courage of 109 American originals, including Frank Epperson, the inventor of the popsicle, cereal creator John Harvey Kellogg, and Shamu, the killer whale who began her stay at the San Diego Sea World in 1965.

"Reading this book is a rip-roaring, entertaining experience with a lot of American history woven through its pages. Some articles might inspire further research and report topics." Voice Youth Advocates

Yolen, Jane

Sea queens; women pirates around the world. illustrated by Christine Joy Pratt. Charlesbridge 2008 103p il $18.95
Grades: 4 5 6 7   **920**
1. Women pirates 2. Women -- Biography
ISBN 978-1-58089-131-8; 1-58089-131-4

LC 2007026983

This offers "12 portraits of sword-swinging, seafaring women throughout history, from Artemisia, in 500 B.C.E. Persia, to Madame Ching, an early nineteenth-century Chinese woman and named here as 'the most successful pirate in the world.' . . . The scratchboard illustrations work well as portraits. . . . The book is filled with fascinating, dramatically told stories and sidebars." Booklist

Includes bibliographical references

Young, Jeff C.

Brilliant African-American scientists; 9 exceptional lives. MyReportLinks.com Books 2009 128p il (Great scientists and famous inventors) lib bdg $33.27

Grades: 5 6 7 8 **920**

1. Scientists 2. African Americans -- Biography
ISBN 978-1-59845-083-5 lib bdg; 1-59845-083-2 lib bdg

LC 2008053924

"Each chapter provides a graphic time line of the milestones in each of the scientists' lives and relates details on their early life, education, research and accomplishments. Several disciplines and science-related careers are highlighted. . . . Each of the chapters contains an inset that provides a link to a website for information on the scientist. A listing of Internet sites and brief descriptions of them are included, as are a glossary, chapter notes, and suggestions for further reading." Sci Books Films

Includes glossary and bibliographical references

Inspiring African-American inventors; 9 extraordinary lives. Enslow Publishers 2009 128p il (Great scientists and famous inventors) lib bdg $33.27

Grades: 5 6 7 **920**

1. African American inventors
ISBN 978-1-59845-080-4 lib bdg; 1-59845-080-8 lib bdg

LC 2007-22937

"This collective biography . . . profiles nine African American inventors: Lewis Howard Latimer, Jan E. Matziliger, Granville T. Woods, George Washington Carver, Madam C. J. Walker, Garrett A. Morgan, Percy Lavon Julian, Patricia Era Bath, and Lonnie G. Johnson. . . . Clearly written and logically organized, this volume provides a useful guide to the subject." Booklist

Includes glossary and bibliographical references

920.003 Dictionaries, encyclopedias, concordances of biography as a discipline

American Indian biographies; edited by Carole Barrett, Harvey Markowitz, project editor, R. Kent Rasmussen. rev ed.; Salem Press 2005 623p il map (Magill's choice) $62

Grades: 8 9 10 11 12 Adult **920.003**

1. Reference books 2. Native Americans -- Biography
ISBN 1-58765-233-1; 978-1-58765-233-2

LC 2004-28872

First published 1999; some essays originally appeared in Dictionary of world biography, Great lives from history: the Renaissance & early modern era, 1454-1600 (2005), and American ethnic writers (2000)

"The book contains essays on religious, social, and political leaders; warriors; and reformers from the past as well as modern activists, writers, artists, entertainers, scientists, and athletes. . . . A great bargain and an asset in any library that supports an American history curriculum." Booklist

Includes bibliographical references

★ **Great** athletes; edited by The Editors of Salem Press; special consultant Rafer Johnson. Salem Press 2010 13v il set $1,020

Grades: 7 8 9 10 11 12 **920.003**

1. Reference books 2. Athletes -- Dictionaries
ISBN 978-1-58765-473-2; 1-58765-473-3

LC 2009-21905

"This massive undertaking totals 1,470 entries covering athletes in baseball, basketball, boxing, football, golf, auto racing, soccer, tennis, and Olympic sports. Additionally, well-known athletes in other, less recognized sports—such as cycling, skateboarding, stunt riding, martial-arts and chess—are included. . . . Overall, this is a well-put-together and wide-ranging set." Booklist

Includes bibliographical references

Lifelines in world history; general editor, Mounir A. Farah. Sharpe Reference 2009 4v il map set $299

Grades: 6 7 8 9 10 11 12 **920.003**

1. World history 2. Reference books 3. Civilization -- History 4. Biography -- Dictionaries
ISBN 978-0-7656-8125-6; 0-7656-8125-0

LC 2008-16288

"This set provides profiles of influential world leaders. Each volume contains 15 to 20 sketches that include basic biographical information, an overview of the subject's achievements, and analysis of the 'interplay' between the person and the 'political, economic, and social circumstances' in which he or she lived. . . . Entries range in length from five to eight pages and offer well-captioned color reproductions, photos, and maps. . . . This attractive set provides well-illustrated, objective information in a global context." SLJ

Includes bibliographical references

Rich, Mari

World authors, 2000-2005; editors, Jennifer Curry, David Ramm, Mari Rich, Albert Rolls. Wilson, H. W. 2007 800p il (Authors series) $170

Grades: 11 12 Adult **920.003**

1. Reference books 2. Authors -- Dictionaries 3. Literature -- Bio-bibliography
ISBN 978-0-8242-1077-9

This book "covers some 300 novelists, poets, dramatists, essayists, scientists, biographers, and other authors whose books [were] published 2000 through 2005." Publisher's note

Riley, Sam G.

African Americans in the media today; an encyclopedia. [by] Sam G. Riley. Greenwood Press 2007 581p 2v set $175

Grades: 7 8 9 10 11 12 **920.003**

1. Mass media 2. Reference books 3. African

Americans in television broadcasting 4. African Americans -- Biography -- Dictionaries
ISBN 978-0-313-33679-9; 0-313-33679-2 set; 978-0-313-33680-5 v1; 0-313-33680-6 v1; 978-0-313-33681-2 v2; 0-313-33681-4 v2

LC 2007008192

"This concise, alphabetically arranged work describes hundreds of people . . . in various fields of communications. It includes, for example, reporters, anchormen and women, talk-show hosts, and television producers. . . . Each of the mostly one to two-page entries includes biographical information, . . . work experience, awards, and, in some cases, includes anecdotes or articles by or about the individual. . . . A worthwhile resource for biography or communications projects." SLJ

Includes bibliographical references

Rockman, Connie C.

Tenth book of junior authors and illustrators; edited by Connie C. Rockman. Wilson, H.W. 2008 803p autog il por (Junior authors & illustrators series) hardcover o.p. $120

Grades: Adult Professional   **920.003**

1. Reference books 2. Authors -- Dictionaries 3. Illustrators -- Dictionaries 4. Children's literature -- Bio-bibliography
ISBN 978-0-8242-1066-3; 0-8242-1066-2

LC 2008043312

This volume covers some 200 authors and illustrators of books for children and young adults including David Almond, Blue Balliett, Terry Pratchett, and Laura Vaccaro Seeger. For 17 authors and artists whose careers include significant new works and honors since their profile in earlier editions of the series, newly written entries are featured

"Standard resource for libraries serving young readers and students studying children's and young adult literature." Booklist

Includes bibliographical references

Something about the author; facts and pictures about authors and illustrators of books for young people. Gale Res. il

Grades: Adult Professional   **920.003**

1. Reference books 2. Authors -- Dictionaries 3. Illustrators -- Dictionaries 4. Children's literature -- Bio-bibliography
First published 1971. Frequency varies

"This important series gives comprehensive coverage of the individuals who write and illustrate books for children. Each new volume adds about 100 profiles. Entries include career and personal data, a bibliography of the author's works, information on works in progress and references to further information." Safford. Guide to Ref Materials for Sch Libr Media Cent. 5th edition

Something about the author: autobiography series. Gale Res. il

Grades: Adult Professional   **920.003**

1. Reference books 2. Authors -- Dictionaries 3. Illustrators -- Dictionaries 4. Children's literature -- Bio-bibliography
First published 1986

An "ongoing series in which juvenile authors discuss their lives, careers, and published works. Each volume contains essays by 20 established writers or illustrators (e.g., Evaline Ness, Nonny Hogrogian, Betsy Byars, Jean Fritz) who represent all types of literature, preschool to young adult. . . . Some articles focus on biographical information, while others emphasize the writing career. Most, however, address young readers and provide family background, discuss the writing experience, and cite some factors that influenced it. Illustrations include portraits of the authors as children and more recent action pictures and portraits. There are cumulative indexes by authors, important published works, and geographical locations mentioned in the essays." Safford. Guide to Ref Books for Sch Libr Media Cent. 5th edition

Sonneborn, Liz

★ **A to Z of American Indian women**; rev ed; Facts on File 2007 320p il map (Facts on File library of American history) $60

Grades: 8 9 10 11 12   **920.003**

1. Reference books 2. Native American women -- Dictionaries
ISBN 978-0-8160-6694-0

LC 2007-8162

First published 1998 with title: A to Z of Native American women

"This resource is of exceptionally high quality." SLJ

Includes bibliographical references

Yount, Lisa

A to Z of women in science and math; rev ed; Facts on File 2007 368p il (Facts on File library of world history) $60

Grades: 8 9 10 11 12   **920.003**

1. Reference books 2. Women scientists -- Dictionaries 3. Women mathematicians -- Dictionaries
ISBN 978-0-8160-6695-7; 0-8160-6695-7

LC 2007-23966

First published 1999

"More than 195 alphabetically arranged articles detail the lives of women from antiquity through modern day, including well-known scientists and mathematicians and less well-documented individuals. . . . The usefulness of this resource lies not only in the balanced group of profiles that have been assembled, providing a valuable tool for teachers and curriculum developers, but also in the readable and engaging entries themselves." Booklist

Includes bibliographical references

920.02   General collections of biography

Donovan, Sandy

Lethal leaders and military madmen; by Sandy Donovan. Lerner Publications Company 2013 32 p. col. ill. (library) $26.60

Grades: 5 6 7 8   **920.02**

1. Picture books for children 2. Kings and rulers 3.

Dictators 4. Dictatorship 5. Military government
ISBN 1467706094; 9781467706094

LC 2012018444

This book by Sandy Donovan is part of the Shockzone Villains series and looks at political and military leaders. "Some of history's most ruthless leaders are headed your way. Some of these rulers schemed their way to the top. Others just conquered everything around them." (Publisher's note)

920.72 Women -- Collective biography

Branzei, Sylvia

Adventurers; Sylvia Branzei ; illustrated by Melissa Sweet. Running Press 2011 96 p. ill., maps (ebook) $10.95; (paperback) $10.95

Grades: 3 4 5 6 7   **920.72**

1. Women 2. Adventure and adventurers 3. Women -- Biography 4. Women adventurers -- Biography 5. Adventure and adventurers -- Biography

ISBN 9780762443857; 0762436964; 9780762436965

LC 2009923889

This book "provides 6- to 8-page biographical sketches of 12 women who are 'the stuff of legends.' Each one is identified with a character trait, e.g. balloonist Sophie Blanchard is 'Intrepid' and Margaret Bourke-White is 'Relentless,' although most of the adjectives could apply to every subject, as [Sylvia] Branzei makes plain." Among those included are Amelia Earhart, Nellie Bly, Susan Butcher, and Kit Deslauriers. (School Library Journal)

Cowgirls; by Sylvia Branzei ; illustratrated by Melissa Sweet. Running Press Kids 2011 96 p. ill. (some col.), map (paperback) $10.95

Grades: 3 4 5 6 7   **920.72**

1. Picture books for children 2. Cowgirls 3. Ranch life -- West (U.S.) 4. Cowgirls -- West (U.S.) -- History 5. Cowgirls -- West (U.S.) -- Biography

ISBN 0762436956; 9780762436958

LC 2009923890

This book "profiles 12 sketches of working cowgirls and rodeo riders from the 19th century through the present day. The term 'cowgirl' also covers other Western types: stagecoach driver Mary Fields is here, along with outlaw Sally Skull and 'Little Sure-Shot' Annie Oakley. 'Lady cowboy poet' Georgie Sicking will probably be new to most readers; one of her poems is included." (School Library Journal)

Includes bibliographical references (p. 92-96)

León, Vicki

★ **Outrageous** women of the Middle Ages; by Vicki Leon. Wiley 1998 ix, 118 p.p ill., maps hardcover o.p. (paperback) $14.95; (prebind) $23.95

Grades: 4 5 6 7 8   **920.72**

1. Middle Ages 2. Women -- History 3. Women -- Biography 4. Women -- History -- Middle Ages, 500-1500 5. Civilization, Medieval 6. Biography -- Middle Ages, 500-1500

ISBN 9780471170044; 9781435280090

LC 97030307

In this book, Vicki Leon looks at women of the Middle Ages. She "tells of a Viking killed by a severed head, a queen who knew the meaning of congregating frogs, and much more. The stories and sidebars provide a detailed picture of the times. . . . The women profiled lived in the 6th through 14th centuries in Europe, Asia, and Africa. Their spheres included everything from astronomy to warfare. They were nomads and empresses." (School Library Journal)

Includes bibliographical references (p. 115-117).

McCann, Michelle Roehm

Girls who rocked the world; heroines from Sacagawea to Natalie Portman. Michelle Roehm McCann and Amelie Welden. Simon & Schuster 2012 p. cm. (hardcover : alk. paper) $18.99

Grades: 5 6 7 8   **920.72**

1. Feminism 2. Women -- History 3. Women -- Biography 4. Girls -- Biography 5. Heros -- Biography 6. Women heros -- Biography

ISBN 9781582703022; 9781582703619

LC 2011050502

Author Michelle Roehm McCann presents "examples of strong, independent female role models, all of whom first impacted the world as teenagers or younger." The book "spans a variety of achievements, interests, and backgrounds, from Harriet Tubman and Coco Chanel to S.E. Hinton and Maya Lin--each with her own incredible story of how she created life-changing opportunities for herself and the world." (Publisher's note)

Includes bibliographical references and index.

929   Genealogy, names, insignia

Ollhoff, Jim

Beginning genealogy; expert tips to help you trace your own ancestors. ABDO Pub. Co. 2011 32p il (Your family tree) $18.95

Grades: 4 5 6 7   **929**

1. Research 2. Genealogy

ISBN 978-1-61613-460-0; 1-61613-460-7

LC 2009050812

This is "great . . . for kids interested in genealogy. . . . [It does] a wonderful job of presenting the fundamentals of genealogical research in a clear and exciting manner. . . . Understanding and properly using primary documents is stressed throughout. . . . [An] attractive, spacious [layout]; full-color, sharp images; clearly labeled diagrams; and scattered maps add information and appeal." SLJ

Includes glossary

Collecting primary records. ABDO Pub. Co. 2011 32p il (Your family tree) $18.95

Grades: 4 5 6 7   **929**

1. Research 2. Genealogy

ISBN 978-1-61613-461-7; 1-61613-461-5

LC 2009050811

This describes how to collect primary records for geneological research.

This is "great . . . for kids interested in genealogy. . . . [It does] a wonderful job of presenting the fundamentals of genealogical research in a clear and exciting manner. . . .

. Understanding and properly using primary documents is stressed throughout. . . . [An] attractive, spacious [layout]; full-color, sharp images; clearly labeled diagrams; and scattered maps add information and appeal." SLJ

Includes glossary

DNA; window to the past: how science can help untangle your family roots. ABDO Pub. Co. 2011 32p il map (Your family tree) $18.95

Grades: 4 5 6 7   **929**

1. Genetics 2. Genealogy

ISBN 978-1-61613-462-4; 1-61613-462-3

LC 2009050808

This explains how DNA is used in geneology.

This is "great . . . for kids interested in genealogy. . . . [It does] a wonderful job of presenting the fundamentals of genealogical research in a clear and exciting manner. . . . Understanding and properly using primary documents is stressed throughout. . . . [An] attractive, spacious [layout]; full-color, sharp images; clearly labeled diagrams; and scattered maps add information and appeal." SLJ

Includes glossary

Filling the family tree. ABDO Pub. Co. 2011 32p il (Your family tree) lib bdg $18.95

Grades: 4 5 6 7   **929**

1. Research 2. Genealogy

ISBN 978-1-61613-464-8; 1-61613-464-X

LC 2009050806

This is "great . . . for kids interested in genealogy. . . . [It does] a wonderful job of presenting the fundamentals of genealogical research in a clear and exciting manner. . . . Understanding and properly using primary documents is stressed throughout. . . . [An] attractive, spacious [layout]; full-color, sharp images; clearly labeled diagrams; and scattered maps add information and appeal." SLJ

Using your research; how to check your facts and use your information. ABDO Pub. Co. 2011 32p il (Your family tree) lib bdg $18.95

Grades: 4 5 6 7   **929**

1. Research 2. Genealogy

ISBN 978-1-61613-465-5; 1-61613-465-8

LC 2009050805

Presents a brief guide on how to check facts and use other information in genealogical research.

This is "great . . . for kids interested in genealogy. . . . [It does] a wonderful job of presenting the fundamentals of genealogical research in a clear and exciting manner. . . . Understanding and properly using primary documents is stressed throughout. . . . [An] attractive, spacious [layout]; full-color, sharp images; clearly labeled diagrams; and scattered maps add information and appeal." SLJ

Includes glossary

929.9   Forms of insignia and identification

Bateman, Teresa

Red, white, blue, and Uncle who? the stories behind some of America's patriotic symbols. illus-

trated by John O'Brien. Holiday House 2001 64p il $16.95; pa $6.95

Grades: 4 5 6 7   **929.9**

1. National emblems 2. National monuments

ISBN 0-8234-1285-7; 0-8234-1784-0 pa

LC 00-57258

This "volume presents 17 'patriotic symbols,' an umbrella term that encompasses everything from the flag to Uncle Sam, from Mount Rushmore to the Korean War Memorial. Bateman finds plenty of interesting information to share about each symbol or site, and browsers will be entertained by the many stories of origination, construction, and history." Booklist

Includes bibliographical references

Jackson, Donna M.

The **name** game; a look behind the labels. illustrated by Ted Stearn. Viking 2009 64p il $16.99

Grades: 4 5 6 7 8   **929.9**

1. Names

ISBN 978-0-670-01197-1; 0-670-01197-5

LC 2008-37705

"All kinds of entertaining and random facts are found in this quirky book. Tips for naming pets and companies are given, in a chapter each, along with hints for remembering people's names, explanations of conventions in other countries, and the system of choosing hurricane monikers. Sports, people, and geographic locations all have different sections. Black-and-white cartoons add a bit of humor. Students will navigate this book with ease." SLJ

Shearer, Benjamin F.

State names, seals, flags, and symbols; a historical guide. [by] Benjamin F. Shearer and Barbara S. Shearer. 3rd ed, rev and expanded; Greenwood Press 2001 495p il $73.95

Grades: 8 9 10 11 12 Adult   **929.9**

1. Reference books 2. Seals (Numismatics) 3. Flags -- United States 4. Geographic names -- United States

ISBN 0-313-31534-5

LC 2001-23525

First published 1987

"Chapters on mottoes, flowers, trees, birds, songs, holidays, and license plates are just a sampling of what is covered, and the format is such that the concisely written material can be found as expeditiously as possible. Even though the book is touted predominantly as a reference tool, the information provided makes fascinating and enlightening reading." Libr J [review of 1994 edition]

Includes bibliographical references

Znamierowski, Alfred, 1940-

The **World** Encyclopedia of Flags; The definitive guide to international, flags, banners, standards and ensigns, with over 1400 illustration. by Alfred Znamierowski. Lorenz Books 2013 256 p. $16.99

Grades: 5 6 7 8 9 10 11 12 Adult   **929.9**

1. Flags

ISBN 0754826295; 9780754826293

This book, by Alred Znamierowski, presents "a directory of flags and a fascinating history of their development and usage, featuring over 600 flags including military signs, royal standards, civic flags, ensigns and national flags, expertly illustrated throughout." (Publisher's note)

930 History of ancient world (to ca. 499)

Adams, Simon

The **Kingfisher** atlas of the ancient world; illustrated by Katherine Baxter. Kingfisher 2006 44p il $15.95

Grades: 4 5 6 7 930

1. Reference books 2. Ancient civilization 3. Historical geography

ISBN 978-0-7534-5914-0; 0-7534-5914-0

"Featuring seventeen . . . hand-illustrated maps and . . . with . . . information about ancient civilizations and peoples, this is [a] . . . pictorial guide to what the world was like between 10,000 B.C. and A.D. 1000. Each . . . map shows the major sites from a particular civilization or group of civilizations. . . . Feature spreads use photographs of cultural and architectural artifacts, as well as additional information, to focus in greater depth on the key cultures of Egypt, Greece, and Rome." Publisher's note

Morris, Neil

Prehistory. Zak Books 2009 48p il map (History of the world) lib bdg $34.25

Grades: 7 8 9 10 930

1. History 2. Prehistoric peoples

ISBN 978-88-6098-156-1 lib bdg; 88-6098-156-5 lib bdg

LC 2008-8399

The "effectiveness lies in the combination of lush illustrations, well-chosen, captioned photographs of contemporary artifacts, and . . . [a] reasoned, concise [narrative]. Succinct time lines border most pages, . . . the proper amount of white space, and clear dark print maintain organization and clarity. A superior choice." SLJ

Includes glossary

The **world** in ancient times; primary sources and reference volume. Ronald Mellor & Amanda Podany, general editors. Oxford University Press 2005 188p il map (World in ancient times) $32.95

Grades: 7 8 9 10 930

1. Ancient history 2. Reference books 3. Ancient civilization

ISBN 978-0-19-522220-3; 0-19-522220-2

LC 2004026578

"An excellent introduction to the use of primary resources in historical research. The 76 selections include poems, letters, inscriptions, and other contemporary accounts from antiquity as well as more modern descriptions and excerpts. Materials from Asia, Europe, and the Americas are highlighted." SLJ

Includes bibliograghical references

930.1 Archaeology

Barber, Nicola

Lost cities; by Nicola Barber. Capstone Raintree 2013 48 p. col. ill. (Treasure hunters) (hardcover) $29.33; (paperback) $8.99

Grades: 5 6 7 8 930.1

1. Picture books for children 2. Extinct cities 3. Legends 4. Civilization, Ancient 5. Archaeology -- History

ISBN 1410949524; 1410949591; 9781410949523; 9781410949592

LC 2012012891

This book by Nicola Barber is part of the Treasure Hunters series and looks at lost cities. This entry "examines the search for lost cities and the important artefacts within them that can offer us an extraordinary window on to the past. . . . Cities covered in the book include Pompeii, Troy, the desert city of Ubar, and the Inca city of Machu Picchu." (Publisher's note)

Includes bibliographical references (p. 46-47) and index.

Tomb explorers; by Nicola Barber. Capstone Raintree 2013 48 p. ill. (mostly col.) (Treasure hunters) (library) $29.33; (paperback) $8.99

Grades: 5 6 7 8 930.1

1. Tombs 2. Archeology 3. Antiquities 4. Treasure troves 5. Civilization, Ancient 6. Archaeology -- History

ISBN 1410949559; 9781410949554; 9781410949622

LC 2012012894

This book by Nicola Barber "examines the hunt for and discovery of ancient tombs, and the valuable treasures they hold. . . . Part of the Treasure Hunters series, 'Tomb Explorers' offers a crosscurricular mix of science & technology and history & civilizations. . . . Tombs covered in the book include that of Tutankhamun, the Sumerian royal tombs of Ur, the Terracotta Army of ancient China, and the Mayan tombs of Palanque in the Mexican Rainforest, and the Oseberg ship burial." (Publisher's note)

Includes bibliographical references and index.

Compoint, Stephane

Buried treasures; uncovering secrets of the past. Abrams Books for Young Readers 2011 72p il $19.95

Grades: 5 6 7 8 930.1

1. Archeology 2. Antiquities 3. Ancient civilization

ISBN 978-0-8109-9781-3; 0-8109-9781-9

LC 2010021626

"Showcasing the work of a specialist in archaeological photography, this loosely themed album offers a broad range of eye candy for fans of ancient artifacts, fossils, remote natural locales, and rare animals. . . . Confined to captions and a few introductory paragraphs, the text supplies useful background. . . . The photos are . . . dramatically lit, sharply reproduced, and tellingly angled. . . . Casual browsers will consider this book a real find." Booklist

Croy, Anita

Exploring the past. Marshall Cavendish Benchmark 2010 48p il (Invisible worlds) $28.50
Grades: 4 5 6 7   **930.1**
1. Fossils 2. Archeology 3. Human origins 4. Prehistoric peoples 5. Ancient civilization
ISBN 978-0-7614-4194-6; 0-7614-4194-8

The narrative is "clear, well written, broken down into manageable pieces, and peppered with eye-opening facts. The numerous photographs are so phenomenal that they will inspire kids to read the text . . . so that they can wrap their minds around what they see." SLJ

Includes glossary and bibliographical references

Hunter, Nick

Ancient treasures; by Nick Hunter ; edited by Laura Knowles ... [et al.] ; illustrated by Martin Bustamante. Raintree 2013 48 p. col. ill., col. maps (Treasure hunters) (hardcover) $29.33; (paperback) $8.99
Grades: 5 6 7 8   **930.1**
1. Archeology 2. Buried treasure 3. Ancient civilization 4. Treasure troves 5. Civilization, Ancient 6. Archaeology -- History
ISBN 1410949508; 9781410949509; 9781410949578
LC 2012012757

"Part of the Treasure Hunters series, 'Ancient Treasures' offers a crosscurricular mix of science & technology and history. . . .Treasures covered in the book include the Roman Hoxne Hoard, the Anglo-Saxon Staffordshire Hoard, the extraordinary discoveries of the Rosetta Stone and Dead Sea Scrolls, and the South American treasures of Lake Guatavita. The book also looks at the motives for these searches, and the importance of responsible archaeology." (Publisher's note)

Includes bibliographical references (p. 46-47) and index.

Matthews, Rupert

Ancient mysteries. QEB Pub. 2011 32p il (Unexplained) lib bdg $28.50
Grades: 4 5 6 7   **930.1**
1. Legends 2. Ancient civilization 3. Curiosities and wonders
ISBN 978-1-59566-854-7; 1-59566-854-3
LC 2010014189

This discusses mysteries in the ancient world.

"This well-written and thoughtfully designed [book] features [an] engrossing [topic]. . . . Though the pages are profusely illustrated with large, well-reproduced photographs and drawings, the layout is not cluttered. This [book] just might inspire kids to seek out more in-depth materials." SLJ

Rubalcaba, Jill

Every bone tells a story; hominid discoveries, deductions, and debates. [by] Jill Rubalcaba and Peter Robertshaw. Charlesbridge 2010 185p il map lib bdg $18.95
Grades: 8 9 10 11 12   **930.1**
1. Archeology 2. Fossil hominids 3. Prehistoric

peoples 4. Excavations (Archeology)
ISBN 978-1-58089-164-6; 1-58089-164-0
LC 2008-26961

"Archaeology and paleontology are the exciting focus in this accessible account of four hominins who lived long before recorded history. . . . The informal style never oversimplifies the engaging science and technology, and the authors raise as many questions as they answer in the detailed chapters." Booklist

931   China to 420

Ball, Jacqueline A.

★ **Ancient** China; archaeology unlocks the secrets of China's past. by Jacqueline Ball and Richard Levey, Robert Murowchick, consultant. National Geographic 2006 64p il (National Geographic investigates) hardcover o.p. lib bdg $27.90; $17.95
Grades: 5 6 7 8   **931**
1. China -- Antiquities 2. China -- Civilization
ISBN 9780792278566 lib bdg; 9780792277835

"This volume spotlights archaeological finds from Ancient China. . . . While the discussions of archaeology will hold readers' interest, the accompanying illustrations steal the show." Booklist

Kleeman, Terry F.

The **ancient** Chinese world; [by] Terry Kleeman & Tracy Barrett. Oxford University Press 2005 174p il map (World in ancient times) $32.95
Grades: 7 8 9 10   **931**
1. China -- History
ISBN 0-19-517102-0
LC 2004-14408

"Readers seriously interested in history, in archaeology—or in China—will be well served by this engrossing book." SLJ

Includes bibliographical references

Liu-Perkins, Christine

At home in her tomb; Lady Dai and the ancient Chinese treasures of Mawangdui. Christine Liu-Perkins ; illustrated by Sarah Brannen. Charlesbridge 2013 80 p. (reinforced for library use) $19.95
Grades: 5 6 7 8   **931**
1. Tombs 2. Excavations (Archeology) -- China 3. China -- History -- Han dynasty, 202 B.C.-220 A.D. 4. Treasure troves -- China -- Changsha (Hunan Sheng) 5. Material culture -- China -- Changsha (Hunan Sheng)
ISBN 1580893708; 9781580893701; 9781607346159
LC 2012024630

This book, by Christine Liu-Perkins, "unearths the mysteries of the Mawangdui tombs, one of China's top archaeological finds of the last century. Miniature servants, mysterious silk paintings, scrolls of long-lost secrets, and the best preserved mummy in the world (the body of Lady Dai) are just some of the artifacts that shed light upon life in China during the Han dynasty." (Publisher's note)

"In 1971, the tomb of "Lady Dai" was discovered, virtually intact and of enormous archaeological significance.

Here, buried in 158 BCE, was her still-soft body and more than a thousand artifacts. Liu-Perkins describes the discovery in fascinating detail; brief imagined scenes supplement the evidence. Illustrative materials include maps and well-captioned photos as well as Brannen's watercolors of the fictionalized scenes. Timeline. Bib., glos., ind." Horn Book

Includes bibliographical references and index

O'Connor, Jane

★ The **emperor's** silent army; terracotta warriors of Ancient China. Viking 2002 48p il $17.99

Grades: 4 5 6 7   **931**

1. Emperors 2. China -- Antiquities

ISBN 0-670-03512-2

LC 2001-46900

Describes the archaeological discovery of thousands of life-sized terracotta warrior statues in northern China in 1974, and discusses the emperor who had them created and placed near his tomb

"This intriguing book is enhanced by beautiful illustrations—pictures of stone engravings, colorful paintings, drawings, and maps—while numerous photographs show the clay soldiers from different perspectives. . . . The author's writing style is entertaining, yet informative." Book Rep

Includes bibliographical references

Rosinsky, Natalie M.

Ancient China; by Natalie M. Rosinsky. Compass Point Books 2013 48 p. col. ill., col. maps (Exploring the ancient world) (library) $28.65; (paperback) $8.95

Grades: 6 7 8   **931**

1. China -- History 2. Ancient civilization 3. China -- Civilization

ISBN 0756545684; 9780756545680; 9780756545789

LC 2012001965

This book is part of the Exploring the Ancient World series and focuses on Ancient China. Topics include "advancements in science and knowledge, the arts, social structures, religious practices, and the causes for the civilization's eventual demise." This entry "covers the dynasties beginning with Xia and ending with Qing. . . . Each title includes maps, a table listing periods or rulers, and well-chosen photographs and art reproductions." (School Library Journal)

Includes bibliographical references (p. 46-47) and index.

Shaughnessy, Edward L.

Exploring the life, myth, and art of ancient China. Rosen 2009 144p il map (Civilizations of the world) lib bdg $29.95

Grades: 7 8 9 10 11 12   **931**

1. Chinese mythology 2. Arts -- China 3. China -- Civilization

ISBN 978-1-4358-5617-2; 1-4358-5617-1

LC 2009-10290

This is an introduction to ancient Chinese civilization

"This beautifully illustrated and well-written [title] . . . is perfect for those assignments where students must look at the culture of a civilization. Artwork and pictures blend seamlessly with the information and the reader is taken on a journey of discovery. Myths are used as the story of how the people view themselves, blended with the discussion of

the reality of life. Everyday life is tied to the belief systems and is explained in light of those beliefs. The pictures are beautifully done and there is almost as much information in the captions as there is in the text." Libr Media Connect

Includes glossary and bibliographical references

Shuter, Jane

Ancient China; [by] Jane Shuter. Raintree 2007 64p il map (Time travel guide) lib bdg $34.29; pa $9.99

Grades: 6 7 8 9   **931**

1. China -- Civilization

ISBN 978-1-4109-2729-3 lib bdg; 1-4109-2729-6 lib bdg; 978-1-4109-2736-1 pa; 1-4109-2736-9 pa

LC 2006033868

This describes life in Ancient China in the form of a travel guide.

Includes glossary and bibliographical references

932   Egypt to 640

Ancient Egypt; edited by Sherman Hollar. Britannica Educational Pub. in association with Rosen Educational Services 2011 87p il map (Ancient civilizations) lib bdg $31.70

Grades: 5 6 7 8   **932**

1. Egypt -- History 2. Egypt -- Civilization

ISBN 978-1-61530-523-0; 1-61530-523-8

LC 2011004714

This book provides "enough information about the development, way of life, accomplishments, and decline of [Ancient Egypt] without overwhelming readers. Maps; full-color illustrations and photographs, many full page; and sidebars provide additional focus. . . . The use of the Nile and its influence on the development of this civilization is emphasized. . . . The building of the great pyramids and the art of mummification are also mentioned. A detailed discussion of the everyday lives of the rich and the poor provide valuable insight." SLJ

Includes glossary and bibliographical references

Berger, Melvin

★ **Mummies** of the pharaohs; exploring the Valley of the Kings. [by] Melvin Berger & Gilda Berger. National Geographic Soc. 2001 64p il $17.95

Grades: 4 5 6 7   **932**

1. Mummies 2. Egypt -- Antiquities

ISBN 0-7922-7223-4

LC 00-55411

This offers "stunning photographs and clear, compelling text. . . . A fascinating historical resource that kids will read straight through for pleasure and also find useful for report writing." Booklist

Fletcher, Joann

Exploring the life, myth, and art of ancient Egypt. Rosen Pub. 2009 144p il map (Civilizations of the world) $29.95

Grades: 7 8 9 10 11 12 **932**

1. Egypt -- Antiquities 2. Egypt -- Civilization
ISBN 978-1-4358-5616-5; 1-4358-5616-3

LC 2009-8792

"This attractively designed and handsomely illustrated book offers a rich and informative introduction to ancient Egyptian culture. Abundantly illustrated with beautifully rendered color representations of architecture, works of art, and other artifacts, the book offers insight into the beliefs and rituals, economy, and social organization of ancient Egyptian civilization." Booklist

Includes glossary and bibliographical references

George, Charles, 1949-

★ The **pyramids** of Giza; by Charles and Linda George. ReferencePoint Press 2012 80 p. (Ancient Egyptian wonders) (hardcover) $28.95

Grades: 8 9 10 11 12 **932**

1. Pyramids 2. Egypt -- Antiquities 3. Pyramids of Giza (Egypt)
ISBN 1601522584; 9781601522580

LC 2012000282

This book by Charles George is part of the Ancient Egyptian Wonders series and looks at the pyramids of Giza. "Three of the grandest of all the pyramids built by the pharaohs of Egypt still stand on the Giza Plateau. These monuments serve as reminders of their builders but also of the glory and grandeur that was ancient Egypt." (Publisher's note)

Includes bibliographical references and index.

Grant, Neil

Ancient Egypt and Greece. Zak Books 2009 48p il map (History of the world) lib bdg $34.25

Grades: 7 8 9 10 **932**

1. Egypt -- Civilization 2. Greece -- Civilization
ISBN 978-88-6098-158-5 lib bdg; 88-6098-158-1 lib bdg

LC 2008-8401

The "effectiveness lies in the combination of lush illustrations, well-chosen, captioned photographs of contemporary artifacts, and [a] reasoned, concise [narrative]. . . . A superior choice." SLJ

Includes glossary

Kerrigan, Michael

Egyptians. Marshall Cavendish Benchmark 2010 64p il (Ancients in their own words) $32.79

Grades: 5 6 7 8 **932**

1. Egypt -- Civilization
ISBN 978-1-60870-064-6; 1-60870-064-X

Features "Numerous photographs provide visual interest, with text describing the images to give details and background. Translations of the writings offer primary sources to accompany the secondary material presented. . . . The text is interesting enough to read cover to cover while the table of contents' descriptive chapter titles and the comprehensive index enable the . . . [book] to be used for specific research." Libr Media Connect

Includes bibliographical references

Lace, William

★ **King** Tut's curse; by William W. Lace. ReferencePoint Press 2012 80 p. ill. (Ancient Egyptian wonders series.) (hardcover) $27.95

Grades: 8 9 10 11 12 **932**

1. Egypt -- Antiquities 2. Tutankhamen, King of Egypt -- Tombs 3. Valley of the Kings (Egypt) -- Antiquities 4. Excavations (Archaeology) -- Egypt -- Valley of the Kings
ISBN 1601522509; 9781601522504

LC 2011048987

This book by William W. Lace is part of the Ancient Egyptian Wonders series and looks at King Tut's curse. Topics include "its origin, how it spread, and the remaining mysteries and search for answers. The title opens with Lord Carnarvon's 1923 death . . . and continues on to discuss Tutankhamen's life, rule, and death (including recent DNA testing, which indicates he had malaria) as well as the endeavors of those involved in the tomb's discovery." (Booklist)

This "explores Egyptian history, mummy making, the discovery and opening of the tomb of Tutankhamen in 1922, and the events that happened after that. Much of the book is based on archaeologist Howard Carter's diaries and letters, and on period newspaper articles. The color photographs in [this attractive [book] are excellent, and the readable [text is] interesting." SLJ

★ **Mummification** and death rituals of ancient Egypt; by William W. Lace. ReferencePoint Press, Inc. 2013 80 p. (Ancient Egyptian wonders) (hardcover) $27.95

Grades: 8 9 10 11 12 **932**

1. Egypt -- Antiquities 2. Ancient civilization 3. Mummies -- Egypt 4. Egypt -- Civilization -- 332-30 B.C. 5. Funeral rites and ceremonies -- Egypt -- History
ISBN 1601522541; 9781601522542

LC 2012011481

This book is part of the Ancient Egyptian Wonders series and focuses on mummification and death rituals of ancient Egypt. "Each book contains a timeline, important facts highlighted in sidebars, and websites." Each book "includes quotes from experts and ancient texts." (Library Media Connection)

Includes bibliographical references and index.

Netzley, Patricia D.

The **Greenhaven** encyclopedia of ancient Egypt. Greenhaven Press 2003 336p (Greenhaven encyclopedia of) $74.95

Grades: 8 9 10 11 12 **932**

1. Reference books 2. Egypt -- Antiquities -- Encyclopedias
ISBN 0-7377-1150-7

LC 2002-6965

"Alphabetical entries range from prehistory to the time of Greco-Roman domination and are generally between a paragraph and a page in length. Coverage includes individual pharaohs, places, practices, trades, beliefs, artwork, and aspects of daily and family life with entries such as 'furniture,' 'children,' and 'entertaining guests.' Important individuals such as archaeologist Howard Carter are also included." SLJ

Includes bibliographical references

The **new** cultural atlas of Egypt; edited by Leon Gray. Marshall Cavendish References 2010 192p il map lib bdg $99.93

Grades: 7 8 9 10   **932**

1. Atlases 2. Egypt -- History 3. Egypt -- Antiquities 4. Egypt -- Civilization

ISBN 978-0-7614-7877-5; 0-7614-7877-9

This title offers "students a wealth of information on all aspects of [Ancient Egyptian civilization]. . . . Packed with well-chosen, pertinent photos and artwork that add stunning detail to the study of [this culture] . . . [this book stands] out with excellent maps inserted within lucid, relevant text." SLJ

Includes glossary and bibliographical references

Rubalcaba, Jill

★ **Ancient** Egypt; archaeology unlocks the secrets of Egypt's past. by Jill Rubalcaba. National Geographic 2007 64p il map (National Geographic investigates) $17.95; lib bdg $27.90

Grades: 5 6 7 8   **932**

1. Egypt -- Antiquities 2. Egypt -- Civilization 3. Excavations (Archeology) -- Egypt

ISBN 0-7922-7784-8; 978-0-7922-7784-2; 0-7922-7857-7 lib bdg; 978-0-7922-7857-3 lib bdg

LC 2006032111

This describes how archeologists have learned about Ancient Egypt.

This offers "the beautiful photography and illustrations characteristic of the National Geographic Society, [a] well-written [text] and sidebars, and information on recent archaeological finds." SLJ

Includes bibliographical references

Smith, Miranda

Ancient Egypt. Kingfisher 2010 48p (Navigators) $12.99

Grades: 4 5 6 7   **932**

1. Egypt -- Civilization

ISBN 978-0-7534-6429-8; 0-7534-6429-2

"Ancient Egypt opens with prominent pharaohs and continues with life at home, within a palace, and amidst the construction of a pyramid. Although it includes such typical subjects as religion, mummification, and tomb raiders, it also comprises female rulers, taxes, and extensive trading expeditions... a good first stop in the research process." Booklist

Weitzman, David L.

★ **Pharaoh's** boat; written and illustrated by David Weitzman. Houghton Mifflin Harcourt 2009 un il map $17

Grades: 4 5 6 7   **932**

1. Ships 2. Kings 3. Egypt -- Civilization

ISBN 978-0-547-05341-7; 0-547-05341-X

LC 2008036081

"Weitzman recounts the construction of a boat made for the Pharaoh Cheops and discusses its rediscovery and restoration in the 20th century. He weaves the history, texts,

mythology, and customs of ancient Egypt into an effective narrative. . . . The volume's stylized illustrations are inspired by the two-dimensional depictions from ancient Egyptian art. The paintings' earth tones, accentuated by bright greens and blues, are both appropriate for the subject matter and pleasing to the eye." SLJ

932.01   Egypt--Early history to 332 B.C.

Kallen, Stuart A.

★ **Pharaohs** of Egypt; by Stuart A Kallen. ReferencePoint Press, Inc. 2013 80 p. (Ancient Egyptian wonders series) (hardcover) $27.95

Grades: 8 9 10 11 12   **932.01**

1. Egypt -- Civilization 2. Pharaohs -- History 3. Egypt -- Antiquities 4. Egypt -- Civilization -- To 332 B.C 5. Egypt -- Politics and government -- To 332 B.C

ISBN 1601522568; 9781601522566

LC 2012000360

This book is part of the Ancient Egyptian Wonders series and looks at the pharaohs of Egypt. The series provides an "overview of ancient Egyptian civilization. . . . Each book contains a timeline, important facts highlighted in sidebars, and websites." Photographs and artwork are included. (Library Media Connection)

Includes bibliographical references and index

Whiting, Jim

★ **Life** along the ancient Nile; by Jim Whiting. ReferencePoint Press, Inc. 2013 80 p. (Ancient Egyptian wonders series.) (hardcover) $27.95

Grades: 8 9 10 11 12   **932.01**

1. Egypt -- History 2. Ancient civilization 3. Nile River Valley -- Civilization 4. Egypt -- Civilization -- To 332 B.C

ISBN 1601522525; 9781601522528

LC 2012000358

This book is part of the Ancient Egyptian Wonders series and focuses on life along the ancient Nile. It offers "coverage of marriage, fashion, medicine, and social classes" as well as dental procedures and wild parties. "Each book contains a timeline, important facts highlighted in sidebars, and websites." (Library Media Connection)

Includes bibliographical references and index.

935   Mesopotamia to 637 and Iranian Plateau to 637

Ancient Mesopotamia; edited by Anita Dalal. Brown Bear Books 2010 64p il map (Facts at your fingertips) lib bdg $35.65

Grades: 6 7 8 9   **935**

1. Iraq -- Civilization

ISBN 978-1-933834-57-3 lib bdg; 1-933834-57-9 lib bdg

LC 2009-16804

Presents the history of ancient Mesopotamia, describing the succession of civilizations that existed there and the agriculture, trade, religion, art, writing, and warfare practices of each one

This begins "with an introduction accompanied by a striking full-page photo, followed by a two-page time line, and a two-paged spread for each topic. This format makes information easily accessible. Beautiful color photos of ancient ruins, drawings, maps, diagrams, and re-creations create appeal and enhance the information. . . . Whether for recreational browsing or serious research, this . . . will certainly prove useful for students." Libr Media Connect

Includes glossary and bibliographical references

Gruber, Beth

★ **Ancient** Iraq; archaeology unlocks the secrets of Iraq's past. by Beth Gruber; Tony Wilkinson, consultant. National Geographic 2007 64p il map (National Geographic investigates) $17.95; lib bdg $27.90

Grades: 5 6 7 8   **935**

1. Iraq -- Antiquities   2. Iraq -- Civilization   3. Excavations (Archeology) -- Iraq
ISBN 978-0-7922-5382-2; 978-0-7922-5383-9 lib bdg
LC 2006032109

This explores the "world of ancient Iraq, in the region once known as Mesopotamia, the cradle of civilization. Join scientists as they study the Citadel in northern Iraq; explore the ancient city of Nineveh; and see how ancient treasures help scientists reassemble the mosaic-like puzzle of Iraq's past." Publisher's note

Includes bibliographical references

Kerrigan, Michael

Mesopotamians. Marshall Cavendish Benchmark 2010 64p il (Ancients in their own words) lib bdg $32.79

Grades: 5 6 7 8   **935**

1. Iraq -- Civilization
ISBN 978-1-60870-066-0; 1-60870-066-6

"Numerous photographs provide visual interest, with text describing the images to give details and background. Translations of the writings offer primary sources to accompany the secondary material presented. . . . The text is interesting enough to read cover to cover while the table of contents' descriptive chapter titles and the comprehensive index enable the . . . [book] to be used for specific research." Libr Media Connect

Includes bibliographical references

Morris, Neil

Mesopotamia and the Bible lands. Zak Books 2009 48p il map (History of the world) lib bdg $34.25

Grades: 7 8 9 10   **935**

1. Iraq -- History 2. Middle East -- History
ISBN 978-88-6098-157-8 lib bdg; 88-6098-157-3 lib bdg
LC 2008-8400

The "effectiveness lies in the combination of lush illustrations, well-chosen, captioned photographs of contemporary artifacts, and . . . [a] reasoned, concise [narrative]. Succinct time lines border most pages, and . . . the proper

amount of white space, and clear dark print maintain organization and clarity. A superior choice." SLJ

Includes glossary

Schomp, Virginia

The **ancient** Mesopotamians; [by] Virginia Schomp. Marshall Cavendish Benchmark 2008 94p il map (Myths of the world) lib bdg $23.95

Grades: 6 7 8 9   **935**

1. Iraq -- Civilization
ISBN 978-0-7614-3095-7 lib bdg; 0-7614-3095-4 lib bdg
LC 2008007052

"A retelling of several major ancient Mesopotamian myths, with background information describing the history, geography, belief systems, and customs of Mesopotamia" Publisher's note

Includes glossary and bibliographical references

936   Europe north and west of Italian Peninsula to ca. 499

Aronson, Marc

★ **If** stones could speak; unlocking the secrets of Stonehenge. by Marc Aronson; with Mike Parker Pearson and the Riverside Project. National Geographic 2010 64p il map $17.95; lib bdg $26.90

Grades: 4 5 6 7   **936**

1. Archeology 2. Archaeologists 3. College teachers 4. Stonehenge (England) 5. Excavations (Archeology) -- England
ISBN 978-1-4263-0599-3; 1-4263-0599-0; 978-1-4263-0600-6 lib bdg; 1-4263-0600-8 lib bdg

"Aronson investigates the work of archaeologist Mike Parker Pearson and his controversial theory that Stonehenge is but one end of a memorial ritual pathway that would have had an equivalent wood structure at the other end. . . . Time lines, resource lists, and photos of researchers at work add even more value to this informative, thought-provoking study. A uniquely perceptive look at how real science works." Booklist

Includes bibliographical references

Green, Jen

★ **Ancient** Celts; archaeology unlocks the secrets of the Celts' past. by Jen Green; Bettina Arnold, consultant. National Geographic 2008 64p il map (National Geographic investigates) $17.95; lib bdg $27.90

Grades: 4 5 6 7   **936**

1. Celts 2. Celtic civilization 3. Ireland -- Antiquities 4. Great Britain -- Antiquities 5. Excavations (Archeology) -- Europe
ISBN 978-1-4263-0225-1; 1-4263-0225-8; 978-1-4263-0226-8 lib bdg; 1-4263-0226-6 lib bdg
LC 2007047836

This describes ancient Celtic civilization and how archeologists have found out about it.

"With excellent-quality photographs and a well-written text, this is a thorough presentation of the most up-to-date knowledge about this ancient European culture." SLJ

Includes glossary and bibliographical references

Hinds, Kathryn, 1962-

Ancient Celts. Marshall Cavendish Benchmark 2009 79p il map (Barbarians!) lib bdg $35.64

Grades: 6 7 8 9   **936**

1. Celts

ISBN 978-0-7614-4062-8 lib bdg; 0-7614-4062-3 lib bdg

LC 2008-35976

This book has "wonderful photographs of contemporaneous and more recent artwork and sculpture, which bring the . . . [Ancient Celts] to life for the modern reader." Voice Youth Advocates

Includes glossary and bibliographical references

Early Germans. Marshall Cavendish Benchmark 2009 80p il (Barbarians!) lib bdg $35.64

Grades: 6 7 8 9   **936**

1. Germanic peoples 2. Rome -- History 3. Germany -- History

ISBN 978-0-7614-4064-2 lib bdg; 0-7614-4064-X lib bdg

LC 2008055789

"This . . . devotes excellent coverage and exposure to the emergence, development, and legacy of [the early Germans]." Libr Media Connect

Includes glossary and bibliographical references

Goths. Marshall Cavendish Benchmark 2009 80p il (Barbarians!) lib bdg $35.64

Grades: 6 7 8 9   **936**

1. Goths 2. Rome -- History

ISBN 978-07614-4065-9 lib bdg; 0-7614-4065-8 lib bdg

LC 2009014114

This has "wonderful photographs of contemporaneous and more recent artwork and sculpture, which bring the . . . [Goths] to life for the modern reader." Voice Youth Advocates

Includes glossary and bibliographical references

Huns. Marshall Cavendish Benchmark 2009 80p il (Barbarians!) lib bdg $35.64

Grades: 6 7 8 9   **936**

1. Huns 2. Nomads 3. Tribal leaders 4. Asia -- History 5. Europe -- History

ISBN 978-0-7614-4066-6 lib bdg; 0-7614-4066-6 lib bdg

LC 2008054828

"This . . . devotes excellent coverage and exposure to the emergence, development, and legacy of [the Huns]." Libr Media Connect

Includes glossary and bibliographical references

Millard, Anne

A **street** through time; written by Anne Millard; illustrated by Steve Noon. Revised ed. DK Pub. 2012 32p col il $17.99

Grades: 4 5 6 7   **936**

1. Cities and towns

ISBN 0-7894-3426-1

LC 98-3226

Traces the development of one street from the Stone Age to the present day, from dirt track to the rebuilding of inns as wine bars, showing how people lived and what they did all day

"The time-line construct is a useful demonstration for children, and the busy vistas would make a fine spring-board for encouraging students to create scenes of local history." Horn Book Guide

Includes glossary

937   Italian Peninsula to 476 and adjacent territories to 476

Allan, Tony

Exploring the life, myth, and art of ancient Rome; Tony Allan. Rosen Pub. 2012 144 p. (lib. bdg.) $39.95

Grades: 7 8 9 10 11   **937**

1. Roman art 2. Roman mythology 3. Rome -- History 4. Rome -- Civilization 5. Art, Roman 6. Mythology, Roman

ISBN 9781448848317

LC 2011009799

This book on Ancient Rome "offers an informative overview of . . . political and social history as well as its art, architecture, and mythology, all bolstered with plenty of . . . details and narratives. . . . [T]he illustrations include artworks, documents, and handsome maps as well as photos of significant sites and artifacts. . . . Besides showing how the great city rose to domination, 'Ancient Rome' looks at how it changed and was changed by the civilizations it housed." (Booklist)

The book "put[s] the art . . . in context, explaining how a society's religious beliefs, legends, and cultural traditions manifest themselves through images and iconography. The . . . layout features full-color photographs of architecture, sculpture, and painting on every page, accompanied by informative captions." (School Libr J)

Includes bibliographical references (p. 138-139) and index

The **Roman** world. Zak Books 2009 48p il map (History of the world) lib bdg $34.25

Grades: 7 8 9 10   **937**

1. Ancient civilization 2. Rome -- History 3. Rome -- Civilization

ISBN 978-88-6098-159-2 lib bdg; 88-6098-159-X lib bdg

LC 2008-8402

The "effectiveness lies in the combination of lush illustrations, well-chosen, captioned photographs of contemporary artifacts, and [a] reasoned, concise [narrative]. Succinct time lines border most pages, and [a] . . . clear dark print maintain organization and clarity. A superior choice." SLJ

Includes glossary

Ancient Rome; edited by Michael Anderson. Britannica Educational Pub. in association with Rosen Educational Services 2011 88p il map (Ancient civilizations) lib bdg $31.70

Grades: 5 6 7 8   937

1. Rome -- History 2. Rome -- Civilization

ISBN 978-1-61530-522-3; 1-61530-522-X

LC 2011004749

This book provides "enough information about the development, way of life, accomplishments, and decline of [Ancient Rome] without overwhelming readers. Maps; full-color illustrations and photographs, many full page; and sidebars provide additional focus. . . . [The book] discusses the military expertise of Caesar and Pompey and the winning of the Punic Wars that led to world domination. The Romans' genius in engineering is highlighted." SLJ

Includes glossary and bibliographical references

Beller, Susan Provost

Roman legions on the march; soldiering in the ancient Roman Army. by Susan Provost Beller. Twenty-First Century Books 2008 112p il map (Soldiers on the battlefront) lib bdg $33.26

Grades: 5 6 7 8   937

1. Soldiers -- Rome 2. Rome -- Civilization

ISBN 978-0-8225-6781-3

LC 2006037829

"The format is inviting with a variety of fonts at the beginning of each chapter, quotations, and a multitude of illustrations. . . . The text is clear and to the point, and chapters are divided into short topics." SLJ

Includes bibliographical references

Deckker, Zilah

★ **Ancient** Rome; archaeology unlocks the secrets of Rome's past. by Zilah Deckker; Robert Lindley Vann, Consultant. National Geographic 2007 64p il map (National Geographic investigates) $17.95; lib bdg $27.90

Grades: 4 5 6 7   937

1. Archeology 2. Rome -- Antiquities 3. Rome -- Civilization

ISBN 978-1-4263-0128-5; 978-1-4263-0129-2 lib bdg

LC 2007024795

This describes what archeologists have learned about Ancient Rome

Includes glossary and bibliographical references

Deem, James M.

★ **Bodies** from the ash. Houghton Mifflin 2005 50p il $16

Grades: 4 5 6 7   937

1. Pompeii (Extinct city)

ISBN 0-618-47308-4

LC 2004-26553

"On August 24, 79 C.E., the long-silent Mt. Vesuvius erupted, and volcanic ash rained down on the 20,000 residents of Pompeii. This photo-essay explains what happened when the volcano exploded—and how the results of this disaster were discovered hundreds of years later. . . . [This offers an] enormous amount of information. . . . But the jewels here are the numerous . . . photographs, especially those featuring the plaster casts and skeletons of people in their death throes. . . . Excellent for browsers as well as researchers." Booklist

Hanel, Rachael

Gladiators. Creative Education 2008 48p il (Fearsome fighters) lib bdg $31.35

Grades: 4 5 6   937

1. Gladiators 2. Rome -- Civilization

ISBN 978-1-58341-535-1 lib bdg; 1-58341-535-1 lib bdg

LC 2006021842

This "recounts the brutality and cruelty of fighting for sport celebrated during Roman times. . . . [The book does] an adequate job of covering fighting techniques, weapons, and history. Photographs and archival reproductions enhance the [presentation]; sidebars provide additional information." Horn Book Guide

Includes glossary and bibliographical references

Hinds, Kathryn, 1962-

★ **Everyday** life in the Roman Empire. Marshall Cavendish Benchmark 2010 320p il lib bdg $42.79

Grades: 7 8 9 10   937

1. Rome -- History

ISBN 978-0-7614-4484-8; 0-7614-4484-X

LC 2009-5913

A compilation of four titles in the Everyday Life in the Roman Empire series, published 2004: The city; The countryside; The Patricians; Religion

This book combines "clear, bold text with vivid reproductions of period paintings, frescoes, and sculptures, making for [a] stunning [presentation]." SLJ

Includes glossary and bibliographical references

James, Simon

Ancient Rome; written by Simon James. rev ed.; DK Pub. 2008 72p il map (DK eyewitness books) $15.99

Grades: 4 5 6 7   937

1. Rome -- Antiquities 2. Rome -- Civilization

ISBN 978-0-7566-3766-8; 0-7566-3766-X

LC 2008-276034

First published 1990 by Knopf

A photo essay documenting ancient Rome and the people who lived there as revealed through the many artifacts they left behind, including shields, swords, tools, toys, cosmetics, and jewelry

Includes glossary

Kerrigan, Michael

Romans. Marshall Cavendish Benchmark 2010 64p il (Ancients in their own words) lib bdg $32.79

Grades: 5 6 7 8   937

1. Rome -- Civilization

ISBN 978-1-60870-067-7; 1-60870-067-4

"Numerous photographs provide visual interest, with text describing the images to give details and background. Translations of the writings offer primary sources to accompany the secondary material presented. . . . The text is interesting enough to read cover to cover while the table of contents' descriptive chapter titles and the comprehensive index enable the . . . [book] to be used for specific research." Libr Media Connect

Includes bibliographical references

Lassieur, Allison

★ The **ancient** Romans; written by Allison Lassieur. Franklin Watts 2004 112p il map (People of the ancient world) lib bdg $30.50; pa $9.95

Grades: 5 6 7 8   **937**

1. Rome -- Civilization

ISBN 0-531-12338-3 lib bdg; 0-531-16742-9 pa

LC 2004-1955

"This attractive, thorough, and comprehensible book . . . offers a stellar introduction to life in ancient Rome." Booklist

Includes bibliographical references

Mann, Elizabeth

The **Roman** Colosseum; with illustrations by Michael Racz. Mikaya Press 1998 45p il (Wonders of the world) $19.95

Grades: 4 5 6   **937**

1. Rome -- Antiquities 2. Colosseum (Rome, Italy)

ISBN 0-9650493-3-7

LC 98-20060

Describes the building of the Colosseum in ancient Rome, and tells how it was used

This offers "a clear, well-written text and full-color drawings and paintings." SLJ

Includes glossary

Markel, Rita J.

The **fall** of the Roman Empire; by Rita J. Markel. Twenty-First Century Books 2008 160p il map (Pivotal moments in history) lib bdg $38.60

Grades: 7 8 9 10 11 12   **937**

1. Rome -- History 2. Rome -- Civilization

ISBN 978-0-8225-5919-1 lib bdg; 0-8225-5919-6 lib bdg

LC 2006100918

This offers a brief history of the rise of the Roman Empire and explores the factors that contributed to its decline.

"Sure to satisfy history buffs. . . . Numerous sidebars, illustrations, maps, and art reproductions provide additional information." Horn Book Guide

Includes glossary and bibliographical references

Moser, Barry

Ashen sky; the letters of Pliny the Younger on the eruption of Vesuvius. illustrated by Barry Moser; written and translated by Benedicte Gilman. The J. Paul Getty Museum 2007 39p il map $19.95

Grades: 7 8 9 10 11 12 Adult   **937**

1. Pompeii (Extinct city)

ISBN 978-0-89236-900-3; 0-89236-900-0

LC 2007-2781

This is a "handsome volume. Using an advanced vocabulary and sophisticated sentence structure, the text sets the event in historical context and gives brief biographical information about the elder and younger Pliny and Tacitus.

. . . Moser's engravings reflect the darkness described in the text as day was turned to night by clouds of ash." SLJ

Includes bibliographical references

Nardo, Don

Classical civilization; by Don Nardo. Morgan Reynolds Pub. 2011 128 p. col. ill., maps (World history) (library) $28.95

Grades: 6 7 8 9   **937**

1. Rome -- History 2. Rome -- Civilization

ISBN 1599351749; 9781599351742

LC 2011005672

This book by Don Nardo on ancient Rome is part of the World History series. "Nardo provides a framework of history, then discusses aspects of the culture with far-reaching effects, such as its government, laws, architecture, roads, and language. The section called 'The First Urban Civilization' reveals surprising similarities between ancient Roman cities and their modern counterparts." (Booklist)

Includes bibliographical references (p. 120-121) and index.

Words of the ancient Romans; primary sources. Don Nardo, editor. Lucent Books 2003 128p il (The Lucent library of historical eras, Ancient Rome) $27.45

Grades: 6 7 8 9   **937**

1. Rome -- History 2. Rome -- History -- Sources

ISBN 1-59018-318-5

LC 2003-1645

"Excerpts from historians such as Plutarch, Livy, and Suetonius, as well as the satires of Juvenal and poetry of Ovid, are included in this history of ancient Rome as told through the words of those who lived at the time. Various chapters cover the founding of the city, Julius Caesar's life, the reign of Augustus, home and family life, entertainment, leisure, and religion. . . . Each chapter . . . [begins] with an introduction that helps to put the subject in perspective for modern readers." SLJ

Park, Louise

The **Roman** gladiators; by Louise Park and Timothy Love. Marshall Cavendish Benchmark 2009 32p il (Ancient and medieval people) $19.95

Grades: 4 5 6   **937**

1. Gladiators 2. Rome -- History 3. Rome -- Social life and customs

ISBN 978-0-7614-4443-5; 0-7614-4443-2

This title has "a simple and elegant design with the proper balance of quality writing and quantity of information. . . . Handy time lines, well-chosen photos of ruins and artifacts, quality illustrations, inset 'Quick Facts,' and 'What You Should Know About' features will grab reluctant readers and captivate even those with short attention spans." SLJ

Includes glossary

Sonneborn, Liz

Pompeii; by Liz Sonneborn. Twenty-First Century Books 2008 80p il map (Unearthing ancient worlds) lib bdg $30.60

Grades: 5 6 7 8   **937**
  1. Pompeii (Extinct city) 2. Rome (Italy) -- Antiquities
  3. Excavations (Archeology) -- Italy
  ISBN 978-0-8225-7505-4 lib bdg; 0-8225-7505-1
lib bdg
                       LC 2007022058

This describes the excavation of the Roman city buried
in lava and ash when the volcano Mount Vesuvius erupted
in A.D. 79.

This "clearly written [title is] illustrated with large photographs and period artwork, and the pages are broken up with
text boxes featuring quotes and interesting anecdotes." SLJ

Includes glossary and bibliographical references

938   Greece to 323

Ancient Greece; edited by Michael Anderson. Britannica Educational Pub. in association with
  Rosen Educational Services 2012 88p il (Ancient civilizations) lib bdg $31.70
Grades: 5 6 7 8   **938**
  1. Greece -- Civilization
  ISBN 978-1-61530-513-1; 1-61530-513-0
                       LC 2011000086

This book provides "enough information about the development, way of life, accomplishments, and decline of
[Ancient Greece] without overwhelming readers. Maps;
full-color illustrations and photographs, many full page; and
sidebars provide additional focus. . . . The system of city-
states is explained. Literature, art, and architecture and their
lasting influence are described in detail." SLJ

Includes glossary and bibliographical references

Kerrigan, Michael
  Greeks. Marshall Cavendish Benchmark 2010
64p il (Ancients in their own words) lib bdg $32.79
Grades: 5 6 7 8   **938**
  1. Greece -- Civilization
  ISBN 978-1-60870-065-3; 1-60870-065-8

"Numerous photographs provide visual interest, with
text describing the images to give details and background.
Translations of the writings offer primary sources to accompany the secondary material presented. . . . The text is
interesting enough to read cover to cover while the table of
contents' descriptive chapter titles and the comprehensive
index enable the . . . [book] to be used for specific research."
Libr Media Connect

Includes bibliographical references

Marcovitz, Hal
  ★ **Ancient** Greece; by Hal Marcovitz. Refer-
encePoint Press 2012 96 p. (Understanding world
history) (hardcover) $27.95
Grades: 7 8 9 10   **938**
  1. Greece -- History 2. Greece -- Civilization 3.
Greece -- Civilization -- To 146 B.C.
  ISBN 9781601522849; 1601522843
                      LC 2011048991

This book on ancient Greece by Hal Marcovitz is part of
"Understanding World History, a series that surveys the po-

litical, social, and cultural trends of major periods and events
in world history."(Publisher's note) It "combines mythology,
history, and politics and provides an enlightening perspective on the treatment of women in the cultures of Athens and
Sparta." (Booklist)

Includes bibliographical references and index.

McGee, Marni
  ★ **Ancient** Greece; archaeology unlocks the
secrets of Greece's past. by Marni McGee; Michael
Shanks, consultant. National Geographic 2007 64p
il map (National Geographic investigates) $17.95;
lib bdg $27.90
Grades: 5 6 7 8   **938**
  1. Greece -- Antiquities 2. Greece -- Civilization 3.
Excavations (Archeology) -- Greece
  ISBN 978-0-7922-7826-9; 0-7922-7826-7; 978-0-
7922-7872-6 lib bdg; 0-7922-7872-0 lib bdg
                      LC 2006032108

This describes how archeologists have found out about
Ancient Greek civilization

This offers "the beautiful photography and illustrations
characteristic of the National Geographic Society, [a] well-
written [text] and sidebars, and information on recent archaeological finds." SLJ

Includes bibliographical references

Nardo, Don
  Classical civilization; by Don Nardo. Morgan
Reynolds Pub. 2011 112 p. ill. (some col.), col. map
(World history) (library) $28.95
Grades: 6 7 8 9   **938**
  1. Greece -- History 2. Greece -- Civilization 3. Greece
-- History -- To 146 B.C. 4. Greece -- Civilization -- To
146 B.C.
  ISBN 1599351730; 9781599351735
                      LC 2011000235

This book by Don Nardo on ancient Greece is part of the
World History series. It "encompasses not only political history but also influential developments in political thinking,
philosophy, science, literature, architecture, sports, and the
military. The section on the Olympics debunks the notion
that early Olympic athletes were amateurs without financial
backing." (Booklist)

Includes bibliographical references and index.

The **new** cultural atlas of the Greek world; edited by
  Tim Cooke. Marshall Cavendish Reference 2010
  192p il map lib bdg $99.93
Grades: 7 8 9 10   **938**
  1. Atlases 2. Greece -- History 3. Greece -- Antiquities
4. Greece -- Civilization
  ISBN 978-0-7614-7878-2; 0-7614-7878-7

This offers "students a wealth of information on all aspects of . . . ancient [Greek civilization]. . . . Packed with
well-chosen, pertinent photos and artwork that add stunning
detail to the study of [this culture] . . . . [this book stands] out
with excellent maps inserted within lucid, relevant text." SLJ

Includes glossary and bibliographical references

Park, Louise

The **Spartan** hoplites; by Louise Park and Timothy Love. Marshall Cavendish Benchmark 2009 32p il map (Ancient and medieval people) $19.95

Grades: 4 5 6   **938**

1. Soldiers 2. Sparta (Extinct city) 3. Athens (Greece) -- History

ISBN 978-0-7614-4449-7; 0-7614-4449-1

LC 2008-55779

This title has "a simple and elegant design with the proper balance of quality writing and quantity of information. . . . Handy time lines, well-chosen photos of ruins and artifacts, quality illustrations, inset 'Quick Facts', and 'What You Should Know About' features will grab reluctant readers and captivate even those with short attention spans." SLJ

Includes glossary

Powell, Anton

Ancient Greece; 3rd ed.; Chelsea House 2007 96p il map (Cultural atlas for young people) $35

Grades: 5 6 7 8   **938**

1. Greece -- Civilization 2. Greece -- History -- 0-323

ISBN 978-0-8160-6821-0; 0-8160-6821-6

First published 1989

Maps, charts, illustrations, and text trace the history and culture of ancient Greece.

"Filled with excellent captioned, color maps, photographs, and illustrations of primary source materials. There are sidebars, gazetteers, and timelines of events in politics, war, art, technology, etc." Libr Media Connect

Includes glossary and bibliographical references

Roberts, Jennifer Tolbert

The **ancient** Greek world. Oxford University Press 2004 190p il map $32.95

Grades: 7 8 9 10   **938**

1. Greece -- Civilization 2. Greece -- History -- 0-323

ISBN 0-19-515696-X

Introduces the history, culture, and people of ancient Greece and examines its many contributions to the development of Western society

"A thoroughly researched political and cultural history. . . . Extensive quotes from primary sources, attractive page layouts, numerous good-quality color photographs of ruins and artifacts, plus the infusion of humor make for a palatable, solid resource for any collection." SLJ

Stafford, Emma, 1968-

Exploring the life, myth, and art of ancient Greece; Emma J. Stafford. Rosen Pub. 2012 144 p. (lib. bdg.) $42.60

Grades: 7 8 9 10 11   **938**

1. Greek art 2. Greek mythology 3. Greece -- Religion 4. Greece -- Civilization 5. Greece -- History -- 0-323 6. Greece -- Civilization -- To 146 B.C.

ISBN 9781448848300

LC 2011009898

This book on Ancient Greece "offers an informative overview of . . . political and social history as well as its art, architecture, and mythology, all bolstered with plenty of . . . details and narratives. . . . [T]he illustrations include

artworks, documents, and handsome maps as well as photos of significant sites and artifacts. "Ancient Greece" traces the development of Greek society and its expression through mythology and the arts." (Booklist) The book "put[s] the art . . . in context, explaining how a society's religious beliefs, legends, and cultural traditions manifest themselves through images and iconography. The . . . layout features full-color photographs of architecture, sculpture, and painting on every page, accompanied by informative captions." (School Libr J)

Includes bibliographical references (p. 137) and index

Steele, Phillip

Ancient Greece; by Philip Steele. Kingfisher 2011 48 p. ill. (hardcover) $12.99

Grades: 4 5 6 7   **938**

1. Greece -- History 2. Greece -- Civilization

ISBN 0753465795; 9780753465790

In this "look at ancient Greece," author Philip Steele "offers young readers insight into the origins of all things Greek. Two page spreads cover Minoan civilization, the rise of the Mycenaean, war with Troy, the establishment of city-states, and the spread of the Hellenistic empire in a somewhat chronological order. Digital illustrations merge with historical artifacts, maps, works of art, and photographs." (Children's Literature)

Villing, Alexandra

The **ancient** Greeks; their lives and their world. J. Paul Getty Museum 2010 80p il $17.95

Grades: 7 8 9 10   **938**

1. Greece -- Civilization

ISBN 978-0-89236-985-0; 0-89236-985-X

"This volume provides a colorful overview of life in ancient Greece. Each chapter covers a different topic and, though short, contains lots of information. Numerous photographs of art and artifacts, along with accompanying captions, illustrate the bygone culture." Horn Book Guide

939   Other parts of ancient world

Cline, Eric H., 1960-

★ **Digging** for Troy; from Homer to Hisarlik. [by] Jill Rubalcaba and Eric H. Cline; with illustrations by Sarah S. Brannen. Charlesbridge 2011 74p il map $17.95; pa $9.95

Grades: 5 6 7 8   **939**

1. Trojan War 2. Troy (Extinct city) 3. Greece -- Civilization 6. Excavations (Archaeology) -- Turkey 7. Archaeologists

ISBN 978-1-58089-326-8; 1-58089-326-0; 978-1-58089-327-5 pa; 1-58089-327-9 pa

LC 2010-07586

"Rubalcaba teams up with a noted archaeologist to make sense of the complicated, controversial, contradictory history and remains of the Turkish site called Hisarlik, better known as Troy. . . . The book begins with a brief but exciting retelling of the Trojan War . . . and goes on to profile Heinrich Schliemann. . . . After Schliemann, generations of archaeologists have excavated Hisarlik: along with the history of the excavations, readers are given an overview of technological developments in the field. . . . Source notes and an impressive bibliography attest to meticulous research and guide readers to journal articles, books, and online museum exhibits. Elegant illustrations mimicking Greek red-figure pottery are lovely and appropriate. Extraordinarily readable, gracefully laid out, and speckled with lines from The Iliad, this book will inspire young people interested in solving the mysteries of the past." SLJ

Includes bibliographical references

Hinds, Kathryn, 1962-

Scythians and Sarmatians. Marshall Cavendish Benchmark 2009 80p il map (Barbarians!) lib bdg $35.64

Grades: 6 7 8 9   **939**

1. Horses 2. Nomads 3. Scythians 4. Sarmatians
ISBN 978-0-7614-4072-7 lib bdg; 0-7614-4072-0 lib bdg

LC 2009016496

"This . . . devotes excellent coverage and exposure to the emergence, development, and legacy of [the Scythians and Sarmatians]." Libr Media Connect

Includes glossary and bibliographical references

Podany, Amanda H.

The **ancient** Near Eastern world; [by] Amanda H. Podany & Marni McGee. Oxford University Press 2005 174p il map (World in ancient times) $32.95

Grades: 7 8 9 10   **939**

1. Middle East -- Antiquities 2. Middle East -- Civilization
ISBN 0-19-516159-9

LC 2004-13622

This "traces the history of the Fertile Crescent until Alexander the Great's conquest in 330 B.C.E. . . . The text is matched with a great deal of supporting matter including time lines, maps, dramatis personae, high-quality photos, and artists' renderings. [This] fine [volume is a] worthy [addition] to most libraries." SLJ

Includes bibliographical references

Sherrow, Victoria

Ancient Africa; archaeology unlocks the secrets of Africa's past. by Victoria Sherrow; James Denbow, consultant. National Geographic Society 2007 64p il map (National Geographic investigates) $17.95

Grades: 4 5 6 7   **939**

1. Africa -- Antiquities 2. Africa -- Civilization
ISBN 978-0-7922-5384-6; 0-7922-5384-1

LC 2007277594

This describes archeological discoveries about ancient peoples of Africa including the Dogon people of Mali, the ancient city of Jenne-jeno, and the Kushite temples at Jebel Barkal.

Includes bibliographical references

940   History of Europe

Feed the children first; Irish memories of the Great Hunger. edited by Mary E. Lyons. Atheneum Bks. for Young Readers 2002 43p il pbk. $22.99

Grades: 5 6 7 8   **940**

1. Famines 2. Ireland -- History
ISBN 9781442482920

LC 00-49606

The editor presents extracts from memoirs of the Irish famine period. Bibliography. "Intermediate, middle school." (Horn Book)

Lyons "compiles quotations from Irish citizens on the devastating effects of the potato famine that ravaged Ireland between 1845 and 1852." Publ Wkly

Includes bibliographical references

940.1   Europe--Early history to 1453

Corbishley, Mike

The **Middle** Ages; 3rd ed.; Chelsea House 2007 96p il map (Cultural atlas for young people) $35

Grades: 5 6 7 8   **940.1**

1. Middle Ages 2. Medieval civilization
ISBN 978-0-8160-6825-8; 0-8160-6825-9

First published 1989

Maps, charts, illustrations, and text explore the history and culture of the Middle Ages.

"The maps are excellent, precise, clear, and easy to read and understand, and the illustrations, particularly those of works of art, are wonderful. . . . This attractive volume provides an intriguing cross-cultural look at the medieval world. An excellent addition." SLJ

Includes glossary and bibliographical references

Durman, Laura

Castle life; by Laura Durman. Arcturus Pub. 2013 32 p. col. ill. (library) $28.50

Grades: 4 5 6   **940.1**

1. Castles 2. Medieval civilization
ISBN 1848585608; 9781848585607

LC 2011051440

In this book, author "[Laura] Durman presents young readers with a . . . view of what life was really like for everyday people in the Middle Ages. Bound by the strict societal system known as feudalism, peasants, knights, and nobles shared space . . . in castles. Readers take a room by room tour, learning how castles functioned both day-to-day, when under siege, and at times of feasting and banqueting." (Children's Literature)

Knights; by Laura Durman. Arcturus Pub. 2012 32 p. col. ill. (Knights and castles) (library) $28.50

Grades: 4 5 6   **940.1**

1. Picture books for children 2. Knights and knighthood 3. Civilization, Medieval
ISBN 1848585616; 9781848585614

LC 2011051452

This book by Laura Durman is part of the Knights and Castles series and looks at knights. The "books cover a wide range of topics such as weapons, castle construction, food, religion, and the structure and hierarchy of society." Full-color photographs and illustrations are included. (School Library Journal)

Includes bibliographical references (p. 31) and index.

Helget, Nicole

Barbarians; Nicole Helget. Creative Education 2012 48 p. (alk. paper) $35.65

Grades: 5 6 7 8   **940.1**

1. Huns 2. Nomads 3. Vikings 4. Teutonic peoples 5. Classical civilization 6. Middle Ages 7. Migrations of nations 8. Europe -- History -- 392-814

ISBN 1608181820; 9781608181827

LC 2011035798

This book by Nicole Lea Helget "focuses on the transient, adaptable Gelts, Franks, Goths, Huns, and Vikings, collectively known as 'barbarians,' and their differing warring skills against the Greek and Roman Empires." (Booklist) "Viewed as threats by the Romans in particular, the barbarian people were often co-opted or conquered and then integrated into the Empire. Eventually, as the Roman Empire waned, the pressure of nomadic barbarians proved too much to withstand and Rome fell." (Children's Literature)

Includes bibliographical references and index

Hinds, Kathryn, 1962-

★ Everyday life in medieval Europe. Marshall Cavendish Benchmark 2009 285p il lib bdg $42.79

Grades: 6 7 8 9   **940.1**

1. Middle Ages 2. Medieval civilization 3. Europe -- Social conditions 4. Europe -- Economic conditions 5. Europe -- History -- 476-1492 6. Europe -- Social life and customs

ISBN 978-0-7614-3927-1; 0-7614-3927-7

LC 2008012748

"Fluid, approachable, beautifully illustrated, and fascinatingly detailed." Booklist

Includes glossary and bibliographical references

Langley, Andrew

Medieval life; written by Andrew Langley; photographed by Geoff Brightling. rev ed; DK Pub. 2011 72p il (DK eyewitness books) lib bdg $19.99

Grades: 4 5 6 7   **940.1**

1. Medieval civilization

ISBN 9780756682828 lib bdg

First published 1996 by Knopf

An illustrated look at various aspects of life in medieval Europe, covering everyday life, religion, royalty, and more.

Malam, John

Early medieval times. Zak Books 2009 48p il map (History of the world) lib bdg $34.25

Grades: 7 8 9 10   **940.1**

1. Middle Ages 2. Medieval civilization 3. Europe -- History -- 476-1492

ISBN 978-88-6098-150-9 lib bdg; 88-6098-150-6 lib bdg

LC 2008-8405

The "effectiveness lies in the combination of lush illustrations, well-chosen, captioned photographs of contem-

porary artifacts, and . . . [a] reasoned, concise [narrative]. Succinct time lines border most pages, and . . . the proper amount of white space, and clear dark print maintain organization and clarity. A superior choice." SLJ

Includes glossary

Morris, Neil

Late medieval Europe. Zak Books 2009 48p il map (History of the world) lib bdg $34.25

Grades: 7 8 9 10   **940.1**

1. Middle Ages 2. Medieval civilization 3. Europe -- History -- 476-1492

ISBN 978-88-6098-152-3 lib bdg; 88-6098-152-2 lib bdg

LC 2008-8407

The "effectiveness lies in the combination of lush illustrations, well-chosen, captioned photographs of contemporary artifacts, and . . . [a] reasoned, concise [narrative]. Succinct time lines border most pages, and . . . the proper amount of white space, and clear dark print maintain organization and clarity. A superior choice." SLJ

Includes glossary

Nardo, Don

Medieval Europe; by Don Nardo. 1st ed. Morgan Reynolds Pub. 2011 128 p. col. ill., maps (World history) (library) $28.95

Grades: 6 7 8 9   **940.1**

1. Middle Ages 2. Great Britain -- History -- 1066-1485, Medieval period 3. Civilization, Medieval 4. Europe -- History -- 476-1492 5. Europe -- Social life and customs

ISBN 1599351722; 9781599351728

LC 2010054477

This book by Don Nardo, part of the World History series, focuses on Medieval Europe. Medieval Europe "was the bridge that led from the ancient world to the modern one." Topics include the Roman Catholic Church, the stone castles built by kings and nobles, the Crusades, and the Renaissance. (Publisher's note)

Includes bibliographical references (p. 120-121) and index.

Park, Louise

The medieval knights; by Louise Park and Timothy Love. Marshall Cavendish Benchmark 2009 32p il map (Ancient and medieval people) $19.95

Grades: 4 5 6   **940.1**

1. Medieval civilization 2. Knights and knighthood

ISBN 978-0-7614-4444-2; 0-7614-4444-0

LC 2008-55777

This title has "a simple and elegant design with the proper balance of quality writing and quantity of information. . . . Handy time lines, well-chosen photos of ruins and artifacts, quality illustrations, inset 'Quick Facts', and 'What You Should Know About' features will grab reluctant readers and captivate even those with short attention spans." SLJ

Includes glossary

Schlitz, Laura Amy

★ Good masters! Sweet ladies! voices from a medieval village. [by] Laura Amy Schlitz; illustrated by Robert Byrd. Candlewick Press 2007 85p il $19.99; pa $9.99

Grades: 5 6 7 8   **940.1**

1. Monologues 2. Middle Ages -- Drama
ISBN 978-0-7636-1578-9; 0-7636-1578-1; 978-0-7636-4332-4 pa; 0-7636-4332-7 pa
Awarded the Newbery Medal, 2008

A collection of short one-person plays featuring characters, between ten and fifteen years old, who live in or near a thirteenth-century English manor

"Designed for performance and excellent for use in interdisciplinary history classrooms, the book offers students an incredibly approachable format for learning about the Middle Ages that makes the period both realistic and relevant. . . . Byrd's illustrations evoke the era and give dramatists ideas for appropriate costuming and props." SLJ

940.2   Europe--1453-

Claybourne, Anna

The **Renaissance**; [by] Anna Claybourne. Raintree 2008 64p il map (Time travel guide) lib bdg $34.29; pa $9.99

Grades: 6 7 8 9   **940.2**

1. Renaissance
ISBN 978-1-4109-2910-5 lib bdg; 978-1-4109-2916-7 pa

     LC 2007006027

This describes life in 15th and 16th century Europe in the form of travel guide.

The book "is chock-full of color photographs and reproductions, maps, sidebars, and age-appropriate humor. . . . The [author has] done a commendable job of writing [text] that [measures] up to the rich visual layout." SLJ

Includes bibliographical references

Currie, Stephen

★ The **Renaissance**; by Stephen Currie. ReferencePoint Press, Inc. 2012 96 p. (hardcover) $27.95

Grades: 7 8 9 10   **940.2**

1. Renaissance
ISBN 1601521898; 9781601521897

     LC 2011048993

This book by Stephen Currie is part of the "Understanding World History" series. It "opens with an . . . overview of the circumstances that came together to inspire a Renaissance." (School Library Journal) It profiles "artists and philosophers . . . along with scientists like [Isaac] Newton. Also discussed is the tension between religion and humanism." (Booklist)

Includes bibliographical references and index.

Elliott, Lynne

The **Renaissance** in Europe; [by] Lynne Elliott. Crabtree Pub. Co. 2009 32p il lib bdg $26.60; pa $8.95

Grades: 6 7 8 9   **940.2**

1. Renaissance 2. Europe -- Civilization
ISBN 978-0-7787-4591-4 lib bdg; 0-7787-4591-0 lib bdg; 978-0-7787-4611-9 pa; 0-7787-4611-9 pa

     LC 2008-52410

"Ideal introductions to concepts, people, and events of the Renaissance... succinct and thorough. "SLJ

Encyclopedia of women in the Renaissance; Italy, France, and England. Diana Robin, Anne R. Larsen, Carole Levin, editors. ABC-CLIO 2007 xx, 459p il $95

Grades: 7 8 9 10 11 12   **940.2**

1. Renaissance 2. Women -- Europe 3. Women -- History
ISBN 1-85109-772-4; 978-1-85109-772-2

     LC 2006038854

"This work covers how women of the [Renaissance] lived; how they were treated and viewed; and literary, artistic musical, social, political, scientific, and religious contributions they made. Most of the roughly 150 entries are biographies. . . . Each of the alphabetically arranged essays is about one-half to two pages long, and is signed, concise, and well written. . . . An excellent addition." SLJ

Includes bibliographical references

Grant, Neil

Renaissance Europe. Zak Books 2009 48p il map (History of the world) lib bdg $34.25

Grades: 7 8 9 10   **940.2**

1. Renaissance 2. Medieval civilization 3. Europe -- History -- 476-1492 4. Europe -- History -- 1492-1789
ISBN 978-88-6098-153-0 lib bdg; 88-6098-153-0 lib bdg

     LC 2008-8408

The "effectiveness lies in the combination of lush illustrations, well-chosen, captioned photographs of contemporary artifacts, and . . . [a] reasoned, concise [narrative]. Succinct time lines border most pages, and . . . clear dark print maintain organization and clarity. A superior choice." SLJ

Includes glossary

Hinds, Kathryn, 1962-

★ **Everyday** life in the Renaissance. Marshall Cavendish Benchmark 2010 327p il lib bdg $42.79

Grades: 7 8 9 10   **940.2**

1. Renaissance 2. Europe -- Civilization
ISBN 978-0-7614-4483-1; 0-7614-4483-1

     LC 2008-54829

A compilation of four titles in the Everyday Life in the Renaissance series, published 2004: The church; The city; The countryside; The court

This book combines "clear, bold text with vivid reproductions of period paintings, frescoes, and sculptures, making for [a] stunning [presentation]." SLJ

Includes glossary and bibliographical references

Malam, John

The **birth** of modern nations. Zak Books 2009 48p il map (History of the world) lib bdg $34.25

Grades: 7 8 9 10 **940.2**
1. Europe -- History -- 17th century
ISBN 978-88-6098-155-4 lib bdg; 88-6098-155-7
lib bdg
LC 2008-8570

The "effectiveness lies in the combination of lush illustrations, well-chosen, captioned photographs of contemporary artifacts, and . . . [a] reasoned, concise [narrative]. Succinct time lines border most pages, and . . . the proper amount of white space, and clear dark print maintain organization and clarity. A superior choice." SLJ

Includes glossary

940.3   World War I, 1914-1918

Adams, Simon
World War I; written by Simon Adams ; photographed by Andy Crawford. DK Publishing 2014 72 p. color illustrations, color map (paperback) $9.99
Grades: 4 5 6 7 **940.3**
1. World War, 1914-1918
ISBN 1465420584; 9781465420589; 9781465421005
LC 2013362556

This book, by Simon Adams, part of the Eyewitness series, "provides a quick, informative overview of WWI: how it started; who fought and why; the equipment used; what it was like in the trenches and at home; the horrific final cost. . . . It's the dramatic photos (many from London's Imperial War Museum) that will make readers pause and bring them close to the soldiers' experiences." (Booklist)

"The DK Eyewitness series exemplifies what the publisher does best: taking a broad topic and slicing it into two-page chapters that, while they contain no narrative thread, make for excellent museum-type browsing... Each book rounds out the guided tour with an FAQ of sorts, profiles, and plenty of places for interested readers to keep looking. Just the thing to whet appetites before trucking down to the local real-life museum." Booklist

World War One
Part of the "Eyewitness" series

Barber, Nicola
World War I; by Nicola Barber. Heinemann Library 2012 80 p. ill. (some col.), col. maps (Living through) (library) $36.50; (paperback) $10.99
Grades: 6 7 8 9 **940.3**
1. World War, 1914-1918
ISBN 1432960105; 9781432960018; 9781432960100
LC 2011015931

In this book on World War I, part of the "Living Through" series, "[Nicola] Barber explains the European political powder keg of the late 1800s and the turn of the last century before telling of the assassination of Archduke Franz Ferdinand." (VOYA) Other topics include " the role of women in the war, propaganda, and the misalignment of the Peace Treaty of Versailles." (Children's Literature)

Includes bibliographical references (p. 76-78) and index.

Batten, Jack
The **war** to end all wars; the story of World War I. Tundra Books 2009 154p il $22.95

Grades: 7 8 9 10 11 12 **940.3**
1. World War, 1914-1918
ISBN 978-0-88776-879-8; 0-88776-879-2

"More than six million soldiers perished in World War I . . . and this beautifully designed, highly readable photo-essay combines a few of their personal stories with the larger picture of politics and military strategies on all sides. . . . Young people with a particular interest in the war will be enthralled." Booklist

Bausum, Ann
★ **Unraveling** freedom; the battle for democracy on the home front during World War I. National Geographic 2010 88p il $19.95; lib bdg $28.90
Grades: 7 8 9 10 **940.3**
1. Civil rights 2. German Americans 3. World War, 1914-1918 -- United States 4. United States -- Politics and government -- 1898-1919
ISBN 978-1-4263-0702-7; 1-4263-0702-0; 978-1-4263-0703-4 lib bdg; 1-4263-0703-9 lib bdg
LC 2010-10631

"Bausum describes the events that would eventually lead the U.S. into the European conflict that ultimately led to World War I. She then turns her attention to describing the destruction of civil liberties by President Wilson, Congress, and those in control of political power during the country's campaign to 'make the world safe for democracy.' . . . Black-and-white archival photos and political cartoons are arranged in an artistic manner with informative captions. Appropriate quotations by various people of the time are displayed in elegant fonts. Make this unique and timely offering a definite first purchase." SLJ

Includes bibliographical references

Carlisle, Rodney P.
World War I. Facts on File 2006 454p il map (Eyewitness history) $75
Grades: 8 9 10 11 12 **940.3**
1. World War, 1914-1918 -- Personal narratives
ISBN 0-8160-6061-4; 978-0-8160-6061-0
LC 2005-27236

First published 1992 under the authorship of Joe H. Kirchberger with title: The First World War

This book "provides hundreds of firsthand accounts—from diary entries, letters, speeches, and newspaper accounts—that focus on different warfare issues and on the social and cultural impacts of the war on Europe and the United States. . . . This volume also includes critical documents related to this topic, as well as capsule biographies of key figures, narrative sections, eyewitness testimonies, 102 black-and-white photographs, maps and graphs, a bibliography, notes, a glossary, chronologies, appendixes, and an index." Publisher's note

Includes bibliographical references

Coetzee, Marilyn Shevin
★ **World** War I; a history in documents. [by] Marilyn Shevin-Coetzee and Frans Coetzee. 2nd ed; Oxford University Press 2011 182p il (Pages from history) $39.95; pa $24.95

Grades: 7 8 9 10　　　　　　　　　940.3
　　1. World War, 1914-1918 -- Sources
　　ISBN 978-0-19-973151-0; 978-0-19-973152-7 pa
　　　　　　　　　　　　　　LC 2009049519
　　First published 2002 with authors' names in reverse order
　　Offering an "account of the war as more than a purely military phenomenon, . . . [this book] also addresses its profound social, cultural, and economic implications. Authors Marilyn Shevin-Coetzee and Frans Coetzee use editorials, memoirs, newspaper articles, poems, and letters to recreate the many facets of the war." Publisher's note
　　Includes bibliographical references

Freedman, Russell
　　★ The **war** to end all wars; World War I. Clarion Books 2010 176p il map $22
Grades: 6 7 8 9 10　　　　　　　　940.3
　　1. World War, 1914-1918
　　ISBN 978-0-547-02686-2; 0-547-02686-2
　　　　　　　　　　　　　　LC 2009-28971
　　"In his signature lucid style, Freedman offers a photo-essay that examines World War I, the first global war in which modern weapons inflicted mass slaughter and an estimated 20 million people were killed. Interwoven into the big picture of the war's causes and consequences are unforgettable vignettes of German and Allied soldiers, drawn from reports, letters, and diaries, and the personal details are heartbreaking." Booklist

Grant, R. G.
　　Why did World War I happen? Gareth Stevens Pub. 2011 48p il map (Moments in history) lib bdg $31.95; pa $14.05
Grades: 6 7 8 9　　　　　　　　　940.3
　　1. World War, 1914-1918
　　ISBN 978-1-4339-4181-8 lib bdg; 1-4339-4181-3 lib bdg; 978-1-4339-4182-5 pa; 1-4339-4182-1 pa
　　　　　　　　　　　　　　LC 2010012459
　　"Examines the events that served as . . . . [precursors to World War I]. . . . Brightly colored pull-out boxes highlight important turning points, the perspective of the everyday man, and further information on why specific events occurred. Numerous photographs help readers visualize concepts more fully. . . . Students should be able to easily use this resource." Libr Media Connect
　　Includes glossary and bibliographical references

Swain, Gwenyth
　　World War I; an interactive history adventure. by Gwenyth Swain ; consultant: Timothy Solie. Capstone Press 2012 112 p. ill. (some col.) (library) $31.32; (paperback) $6.95
Grades: 3 4 5 6　　　　　　　　　940.3
　　1. World War, 1914-1918
　　ISBN 1429679972; 9781429660204; 9781429679978
　　　　　　　　　　　　　　LC 2011033624
　　This book by Gwenyth Swain is part of the You Choose series. "At the bottom of many pages, you are asked to make a decision about what to do or where to go. Subsequent decisions take you to the adventure's end, at which point readers may choose to go back and begin again and find out where an alternate path might have led. . . . [In] Belgium . . . student

nurses must decide whether to stay at their hospital or flee. Later, a British teen has to choose whether to enlist or wait." (Booklist)
　　Includes bibliographical references (p. 111) and index.

940.4　Military history of World War I

Bausum, Ann
　　Stubby the War Dog; The True Story of World War I's Bravest Dog. by Ann Bausum. Natl Geographic Soc Childrens books 2014 80 p. $26.90
Grades: 4 5 6 7　　　　　　　　　940.4
　　1. Dogs -- War use 2. World War, 1914-1918 -- United States 3. Stubby (Dog) 4. Dogs -- War use -- United States 5. United States. Army. Infantry Regiment, 102nd -- Mascots
　　ISBN 1426314868; 1426314876; 9781426314865; 9781426314872
　　This book, by Ann Bausum, is the story of "Stubby, a terrier of unknown origin, [who] found his way to the training grounds in New Haven, CT, as recruits were preparing to ship off to . . . World War I. . . . He attached himself to J. Robert Conroy, one of the recruits, and they became an inseparable team for the rest of Stubby's life. . . . [T]he dog lived the life of any soldier: sleeping in trenches, dodging bullets in the heat of battle, and ferreting out enemy combatants." (School Library Journal)
　　"The popularity of tales about dogs in war stems from the inherent poignancy—sweet, loyal, sad-eyed canines entered into the mad chaos of man-made destruction. But enter they occasionally do, and none more famously than Stubby... The speedy story is surrounded by evocative period photos, including plenty of the goofy-faced Stubby, and leads up to his later careers as a vaudeville star and a football mascot, and his eventual taxidermied inclusion in the Smithsonian. A triumph on three fronts: educational, emotional, and inspirational. For older teens, suggest Bausman's adult title, Sergeant Stubby." Booklist

Beller, Susan Provost
　　The **doughboys** over there; soldiering in World War I. by Susan Provost Beller. Twenty-First Century Books 2008 112p il map (Soldiers on the battlefront) lib bdg $33.26
Grades: 5 6 7 8　　　　　　　　　940.4
　　1. World War, 1914-1918 2. Soldiers -- United States
　　ISBN 978-0-8225-6295-5 lib bdg; 0-8225-6295-2 lib bdg
　　　　　　　　　　　　　　LC 2006026249
　　The is an account of the U.S. soldiers who fought in Europe in the First World War.
　　"The format is inviting with a variety of fonts at the beginning of each chapter, quotations, and a multitude of illustrations. . . . The text is clear and to the point, and chapters are divided into short topics." SLJ
　　Includes bibliographical references

Murphy, Jim
　　★ **Truce**; the day the soldiers stopped fighting. Scholastic Press 2009 116p il map $19.99

Grades: 5 6 7 8   **940.4**
  1. World War, 1914-1918
  ISBN 978-0-545-13049-3; 0-545-13049-2
                    LC 2008-40500

"By December 1918, the western front of World War I featured two parallel trenches stretching from the North Sea to the Alps. . . . On Christmas Day, an informal peace broke out in many locations along the front. . . . Murphy's excellent telling of this unusual war story begins with an account of the events that led to WWI and follows the shift in the soldiers' mind-sets. . . . Printed in tones of sepia, the illustrations in this handsome volume include many period photos as well as paintings and maps. . . . Well organized and clearly written, this presentation vividly portrays the context and events of the Christmas Truce." Booklist

Includes bibliographical references

Oxlade, Chris

World War I. Arcturus Pub. 2011 46p il (Secret history) lib bdg $32.80

Grades: 7 8 9 10   **940.4**
  1. World War, 1914-1918
  ISBN 978-1-84837-700-4; 1-84837-700-2
                    LC 2010011012

This book explores the secrets of World War I. As in all wars, each side needed to keep secrets from the enemy. At the same time, they tried to discover the enemy's secrets, using spies and code-breakers.

"The title of the Secret History series will grab readers, even reluctant ones, and they won't be disappointed by the intriguing info regarding codes and code breakers, spies, terrorists, and double agents, with profiles of heroes and traitors on all sides. . . . The readable design, with clear type on thick, high-quality paper, includes lots of sidebars, photos, screens, and quotes." Booklist

Includes bibliographical references

940.53   World War II, 1939-1945

Adams, Simon

World War II; written by Simon Adams; photographed by Andy Crawford. rev ed.; DK Pub. 2007 72p il (DK eyewitness books) $16.99

Grades: 4 5 6 7   **940.53**
  1. World War, 1939-1945
  ISBN 978-0-7566-3008-9; 0-7566-3008-8
                    LC 2008273315

First published 2000

Provides a concise history of World War II including information about the Holocaust, the code-breaking Enigma, and the deadly V2 rocket

Alma, Ann

Brave deeds; how one family saved many from the Nazis. Groundwood Books 2008 95p il map $17.95

Grades: 4 5 6 7   **940.53**
  1. Holocaust, 1933-1945 2. World War, 1939-1945 -- Netherlands 3. World War, 1939-1945 -- Jews -- Rescue
  ISBN 978-0-88899-791-3; 0-88899-791-4

This recounts "how the Braal family, living in Holland near the end of World War II, set up a hideout on the island of Voorne and rescued many from the Nazis. . . . What will excite kids are the facts, full explained in a long historical note, accompanied by a map, and the many archival black-and-white photos." Booklist

Includes glossary

Altman, Linda Jacobs

Escape --teens on the run; primary sources from the Holocaust. Holocaust research by Margaret Shannon. Enslow Publishers 2010 128p il map (True stories of teens in the Holocaust) lib bdg $31.93

Grades: 7 8 9 10 11 12   **940.53**
  1. Holocaust, 1933-1945 2. World War, 1939-1945 -- Children 3. World War, 1939-1945 -- Refugees
  ISBN 978-0-7660-3270-5 lib bdg; 0-7660-3270-1 lib bdg
                    LC 2009021378

Discusses children and teens on the run during the Holocaust in Europe, including the different ways young people escaped the Nazis, places of refuge in Europe, and hiding and resistance.

The "book provides historical background, but the narratives rest upon the recollections, making the material immediate and horrifyingly real." SLJ

Includes glossary and bibliographical references

Hidden teens, hidden lives; primary sources from the Holocaust. Enslow Publishers 2010 128p il (True stories of teens in the Holocaust) lib bdg $31.93

Grades: 8 9 10 11 12   **940.53**
  1. Holocaust survivors 2. Holocaust, 1933-1945 3. World War, 1939-1945 -- Children 4. World War, 1939-1945 -- Personal narratives
  ISBN 978-0-7660-3271-2; 0-7660-3271-X
                    LC 2009-6504

"Explores the lives of children and teens who went into hiding during the Holocaust; looks at various places used as hiding spots, such as barns and attics, and different ways to hide, like assuming false identities, and how these were used as a tool to survive." Publisher's note

Includes bibliographical references

Shattered youth in Nazi Germany; primary sources from the Holocaust. Holocaust research by Margaret Shannon. Enslow Publishers 2010 128p il map (True stories of teens in the Holocaust) lib bdg $31.93

Grades: 8 9 10 11 12   **940.53**
  1. National socialism 2. Hitler-Jugend 3. Holocaust, 1933-1945 4. Germany -- Politics and government -- 1933-1945
  ISBN 978-0-7660-3268-2 lib bdg; 0-7660-3268-X lib bdg
                    LC 2008048002

Examines the lives of children and teens living in Germany before and during the Holocaust, including the rise of Nazism, growing persecution of Jews, and the Hitler Youth

The "book provides historical background, but the narratives rest upon the recollections, making the material immediate and horrifyingly real." SLJ

Includes glossary and bibliographical references

The **Warsaw** Ghetto Uprising; striking a blow against the Nazis. Enslow 2011 128p il map (The Holocaust through primary sources) lib bdg $31.93

Grades: 7 8 9 10 11 12 **940.53**

1. Jews -- Poland 2. Holocaust, 1933-1945 3. Warsaw (Poland) -- History -- Uprising of 1943

ISBN 978-0-7660-3320-7; 0-7660-3320-1

LC 2010021596

Examines the Warsaw ghetto uprising, including the roots of the resistance in the Warsaw ghetto, stories from the participants in the uprising, how the battle ended, and how the small group of fighters became heroes during the Holocaust

Includes glossary and bibliographical references

Ambrose, Stephen E.

★ The **good** fight; how World War II was won. Atheneum Bks. for Young Readers 2001 96p il maps $19.95

Grades: 5 6 7 8 **940.53**

1. World War, 1939-1945

ISBN 0-689-84361-5

LC 00-49600

"An excellent balance between the big picture and the humanizing details, well supported by fact boxes, tinted photographs, and battlefield maps that are both simple and clear. . . . Ambrose's style is authoritative and warm." Booklist

Includes glossary and bibliographical references

Bitton-Jackson, Livia

★ **I** have lived a thousand years; growing up in the Holocaust. by Livia E. Bitton-Jackson. Simon & Schuster Bks. for Young Readers 1997 224p hardcover o.p. pa $5.99

Grades: 7 8 9 10 **940.53**

1. Jews -- Hungary 2. Holocaust, 1933-1945 -- Personal narratives

ISBN 0-689-81022-9; 0-689-82395-9 pa

LC 96-19971

Based on the author's book for adults, Elli: coming of age in the Holocaust (1980)

"This is a memorable addition to the searing accounts of Holocaust survivors." Horn Book

Includes glossary

My bridges of hope; searching for life and love after Auschwitz. Simon & Schuster Bks. for Young Readers 1999 258p hardcover o.p. pa $4.99

Grades: 7 8 9 10 **940.53**

1. Holocaust survivors 2. Hebraists 3. Memoirists 4. College teachers

ISBN 0-689-84898-6 pa

LC 98-8046

In 1945, after surviving a harrowing year in Auschwitz, fourteen-year-old Elli returns, along with her mother and

brother, to the family home, now part of Slovakia, where they try to find a way to rebuild their shattered lives

The author's "story is utterly involving, and adds an important chapter to the ongoing attempt to understand the Holocaust and its consequences." Publ Wkly

Includes glossary

Byers, Ann

Courageous teen resisters; primary sources from the Holocaust. Holocaust research by Margaret Shannon. Enslow Publishers 2010 128p il map (True stories of teens in the Holocaust) lib bdg $31.93

Grades: 8 9 10 11 12 **940.53**

1. Holocaust, 1933-1945 2. Jews -- Persecutions 3. World War, 1939-1945 -- Jews 4. World War, 1939-1945 -- Children 5. Holocaust, 1933-1945 -- Personal narratives

ISBN 978-0-7660-3269-9; 0-7660-3269-8

LC 2009-1374

This is an "interesting and revealing collection of personal accounts. . . . Lively writing, which connects paragraphs, brings the events and actions alive with each personal account flowing smoothly. Black and white photos provide an even more personal connection to the teens and the horrific events." Libr Media Connect

Includes glossary and bibliographical references

Rescuing the Danish Jews; a heroic story from the Holocaust. Enslow Publishers 2011 128p il map (The Holocaust through primary sources) lib bdg $31.95

Grades: 7 8 9 10 11 12 **940.53**

1. Denmark -- History 2. Holocaust, 1933-1945 3. Jews -- Persecutions 4. World War, 1939-1945 -- Jews -- Rescue

ISBN 978-0-7660-3321-4; 0-7660-3321-X

LC 2009053595

Examines the rescue of the Danish Jews during World War II, including background on Denmark and the Holocaust, firsthand accounts from the many people involved, and how thousands of Jews were saved from the Nazis.

Includes glossary and bibliographical references

Saving children from the Holocaust; the Kindertransport. Enslow Publishers 2011 128p il (The Holocaust through primary sources) lib bdg $31.93

Grades: 7 8 9 10 11 12 **940.53**

1. Holocaust, 1933-1945 2. World War, 1939-1945 -- Jews -- Rescue

ISBN 978-0-7660-3323-8; 0-7660-3323-6

LC 2010014215

Discusses the Kindertransport, including the people who organized the operation, how the transports worked, the children's lives who escaped on a transport, and how ten thousand children were saved from the Holocaust.

Includes glossary and bibliographical references

Trapped --youth in the Nazi ghettos; primary sources from the Holocaust. Holocaust research by Margaret Shannon. Enslow Publishers 2010 128p il (True stories of teens in the Holocaust) lib bdg $31.95

Grades: 8 9 10 11 12   **940.53**

1. Holocaust, 1933-1945 2. World War, 1939-1945 -- Children 3. World War, 1939-1945 -- Personal narratives

ISBN 978-0-7660-3272-9; 0-7660-3272-8

LC 2009013475

Examines the lives of Jewish children and teens in the ghettos during the Holocaust, including the formation of the ghettos, the miserable conditions, hard labor, and the deportations to camps.

The "book provides historical background, but the narratives rest upon the recollections, making the material immediate and horrifyingly real." SLJ

Includes glossary and bibliographical references

Youth destroyed--the Nazi camps; primary sources from the Holocaust. Holocaust research by Margaret Shannon. Enslow Publishers 2010 128p il map (True stories of teens in the Holocaust) lib bdg $31.93

Grades: 7 8 9 10 11 12   **940.53**

1. Concentration camps 2. Holocaust, 1933-1945

ISBN 978-0-7660-3273-6; 0-7660-3273-6

Discusses the experiences of children and teens in concentration camps during the Holocaust, including the first camps in Germany, the forced labor camps, the six death camps, and the aftermath

The "book provides historical background, but the narratives rest upon the recollections, making the material immediate and horrifyingly real." SLJ

Includes glossary and bibliographical references

Callery, Sean

★ **World** War II; Visual history of the world's darkest days. by Sean Callery. 1st ed. Scholastic 2013 105 p. ill. (some col.), col. maps (paperback) $15.99

Grades: 5 6 7 8   **940.53**

1. Military history 2. World War, 1939-1945

ISBN 0545479754; 9780545479752

LC 2012285678

This book presents "World War II in a nutshell. The text is divided into five chapters: 'The Path to War,' 'Europe & the Atlantic War,' the Pacific theater, Africa & the Middle East, and the end of the war. Each section is divided into several two-page topics. The title page of each chapter asks three questions that are answered in the text. It is followed by a two-page time line with boxed information and vintage photos." (School Library Journal)

Davenport, John

The **internment** of Japanese Americans during World War II; detention of American citizens. [by] John C. Davenport. Chelsea House Publishers 2010 122p il (Milestones in American history) lib bdg $35

Grades: 6 7 8 9 10   **940.53**

1. Japanese Americans -- Evacuation and relocation,

1942-1945

ISBN 978-1-60413-681-4; 1-60413-681-2

LC 2009-29613

The "chapters outline the impact of the bombing [of Pearl Harbor], the history of Japanese immigrants and citizens in the United States, Executive Order 9066 (permitting evacuation and internment of Japanese citizens on the West coast), Japanese American participation in the armed forces, reparations, and the legacy left by the internment. . . . A sound reference and research work." SLJ

Includes bibliographical references

Deem, James M.

Auschwitz; voices from the death camp. Enslow Publishers 2011 128p il map (The Holocaust through primary sources) lib bdg $31.93

Grades: 7 8 9 10 11 12   **940.53**

1. Holocaust, 1933-1945 2. Jews -- Persecutions 3. Auschwitz (Poland: Concentration camp)

ISBN 978-0-7660-3322-1; 0-7660-3322-8

LC 2010003064

Examines Auschwitz, a death camp during the Holocaust, including its construction and daily workings, true accounts from prisoners of the camp and Nazi perpetrators, and how more than 1 million people were murdered there.

Includes glossary and bibliographical references

Kristallnacht; the Nazi terror that began the Holocaust. Enslow Publishers 2011 128p il (The Holocaust through primary sources) lib bdg $31.93

Grades: 7 8 9 10 11 12   **940.53**

1. Kristallnacht, 1938 2. Jews -- Germany 3. Holocaust, 1933-1945 4. Jews -- Persecutions

ISBN 978-0-7660-3324-5; 0-7660-3324-4

LC 2010015696

Discusses Kristallnacht, a four-day pogrom instigated by the Nazis against Germany's Jews, including stories from the victims, witnesses and perpetrators of the attack, and how it marked the beginning of the Holocaust.

"Personal testimony is a powerful way to tell history. . . . These accounts . . . are tightly edited, drawing on the memories of victims, perpetrators, and witnesses. . . . Each chapter blends an individual's testimony with historical background and commentary as well as photos of the witness and of the brutal events." Booklist

Includes glossary and bibliographical references

DeSaix, Debbi Durland

Hidden on the mountain; stories of children sheltered from the Nazis in Le Chambon. [by] Deborah Durland DeSaix [and] Karen Gray Ruelle. Holiday House 2007 275p il map $24.95

Grades: 7 8 9 10   **940.53**

1. Holocaust, 1933-1945 2. World War, 1939-1945 -- France 3. World War, 1939-1945 -- Jews -- Rescue

ISBN 978-0-8234-1928-9; 0-8234-1928-2

LC 2006-02033

This is the "story of the thousands of children who were sheltered in the tiny mountainous French village of Le Chambon-sur-Lignon during the Holocaust. The first chapters provide readers with an introduction to World War II, the Vichy government, and the region in southern France of La Montange Protestante. Subsequent chapters contain first-person accounts by individuals who, as children, were hidden on the mountain, along with black-and-white photographs and an epilogue detailing their lives after the war. . . . The book is an invaluable resource for Holocaust educators, and many of the children's narratives would read beautifully out loud." SLJ

Includes glossary and bibliographical references

Downing, David

★ The **origins** of the Holocaust; [by] David Downing. World Almanac Library 2006 48p il map (World Almanac Library of the Holocaust) lib bdg $30

Grades: 7 8 9 10   **940.53**
1. Antisemitism 2. Holocaust, 1933-1945
ISBN 0-8368-5943-X

LC 2005042114

This "adds essential background history to the many accounts of the Nazi genocide. Downing goes back nearly 2,000 years to show the roots of antiSemitism and the long persecution of the Jews. . . . The clear overview connects that history with the rise of the Nazi Party and Hitler's vision of the Aryan master race. . . . The book design is spacious, with many photos, clear maps, and boxed insets." Booklist

Includes glossary and bibliographical references

Fishkin, Rebecca Love

Heroes of the Holocaust. Compass Point Books 2011 64p il (The holocaust) lib bdg $33.32; pa $8.95

Grades: 6 7 8 9   **940.53**
1. Holocaust, 1933-1945 2. World War, 1939-1945 -- Jews -- Rescue 3. World War, 1939-1945 -- Underground movements
ISBN 978-0-7565-4391-4 lib bdg; 0-7565-4391-6 lib bdg; 978-0-7565-4443-0 pa; 0-7565-4443-2 pa

LC 2010026492

This book tells the stories of those who defied and resisted the Nazis. Some helped one person or family, some saved dozens, and others organized efforts that helped thousands.

This volume "succeeds in outlining a horrific chapter in history without oversimplifying. . . . [This] book features multiple quotes from survivors about their wartime experiences, providing voices with which young people can identify." SLJ

Includes glossary and bibliographical references

Fitzgerald, Stephanie

Children of the Holocaust. Compass Point Books 2011 64p il (The holocaust) lib bdg $33.32; pa $8.95

Grades: 6 7 8 9   **940.53**
1. Holocaust survivors 2. Holocaust, 1933-1945 3. World War, 1939-1945 -- Children
ISBN 978-0-7565-4390-7 lib bdg; 0-7565-4390-8 lib bdg; 978-0-7565-4442-3 pa; 0-7565-4442-4 pa

LC 2010019975

At the start of World War II, there were about 1.6 million Jewish children living in Europe. Fewer than one in 10 of those children survived German leader Adolf Hitlers reign of terror. More than 100,000 Jewish children did survive, how-

ever through a combination of strength, cleverness, the help of others, and, more often than not, simple good luck. Children of the Holocaust tells the stories of these young people.

This volume "succeeds in outlining a horrific chapter in history without oversimplifying. . . . [This] book features multiple quotes from survivors about their wartime experiences, providing voices with which young people can identify." SLJ

Includes glossary and bibliographical references

Kristallnacht, the night of broken glass; igniting the Nazi War against Jews. by Stephanie Fitzgerald. Compass Point Books 2008 96p il map (Snapshots in history) lib bdg $33.26

Grades: 6 7 8 9   **940.53**
1. Kristallnacht, 1938 2. Jews -- Germany 3. Holocaust, 1933-1945
ISBN 978-0-7565-3489-9; 0-7565-3489-5

LC 2007-32701

"Opening with an overview of November 9, 1938, Kristallnacht goes on to provide background on anti-Semitism, the rise of the Nazis, . . . the impact of Herschel Grynszpan's shooting of Ernst vom Rath . . . and its aftermath. . . . Abundant archival photographs (some full color), quotes from eyewitnesses, and accessible maps enhance chapter content. An excellent time line and information on related historic sites further enrich the [work]." SLJ

Includes bibliographical references

Fox, Anne L.

Ten thousand children; true stories told by children who escaped the Holocaust on the Kindertransport. by Anne L. Fox and Eva Abraham-Podietz. Behrman House 1998 128p il pa $11.75

Grades: 5 6 7 8   **940.53**
1. Jewish refugees 2. Holocaust, 1933-1945 -- Personal narratives
ISBN 0-87441-648-5

LC 98-33600

Tells the true stories of children who escaped Nazi Germany on the Kindertransport, a rescue mission led by concerned British to save Jewish children from the Holocaust

"The design is like an open scrapbook, with different size typefaces, snapshots, news photos, and marginal notes; and the combination of the general overview with personal memories will bring readers, from middle grades through adult, close to the experience." Booklist

Friedman, Ina R.

★ The **other** victims; first-person stories of non-Jews persecuted by the Nazis. Houghton Mifflin 1990 214p hardcover o.p. pa $6.95

Grades: 6 7 8 9   **940.53**
1. Holocaust survivors 2. Holocaust, 1933-1945 -- Personal narratives
ISBN 0-395-74515-2 pa

LC 89-27036

Personal narratives of Christians, Gypsies, deaf people, homosexuals, and blacks who suffered at the hands of the Nazis before and during World War II.

"Well organized and edited, the tales are harrowing, though they all end happily, often with escape or immigration to America and highly successful careers. Friedman points out that these were the lucky ones, and her book serves as a much-needed reminder that the Nazi nightmare extended far beyond Europe's Jewish population." Bull Cent Child Books

Includes bibliographical references

Heinrichs, Ann

The **Japanese** American internment; innocence, guilt, and wartime justice. Marshall Cavendish Benchmark 2010 112p il (Perspectives on) $39.93
Grades: 7 8 9 10   **940.53**
1. Japanese Americans -- Evacuation and relocation, 1942-1945
ISBN 978-0-7614-4983-6; 0-7614-4983-3

"A solid resource for school reports, this straightforward account includes an overview of the events that led up to the signing of Executive Order 9066, which authorized the relocation of Japanese Americans; details about life in the internment camps; and an examination of the long-term ramifications for the Japanese-American community. Information is accompanied by photographs and illustrations in color and black-and-white. A balanced view of the internment is presented." SLJ

Hillman, Laura

I will plant you a lilac tree; a memoir of a Schindler's list survivor. Atheneum Books for Young Readers 2005 243p il map $16.95
Grades: 7 8 9 10   **940.53**
1. Jews -- Germany 2. Holocaust, 1933-1945 -- Personal narratives
ISBN 0-689-86980-0

LC 2004-10534

"In 1942 Berlin, Hannelore, 16, bravely volunteers to be deported with her mother and two younger brothers to Poland. . . . They are soon separated, and during the next three years Hannelore is moved through eight concentration camps. In clipped, first-person narrative, she remembers the worst. . . . She tells it as she endured it, quietly relaying the facts without sensationalism or sentimentality." Booklist

Hodge, Deborah

Rescuing the children; the story of the kindertransport. Deborah Hodge. Tundra Books of Northern New York 2012 60 p. (hardcover) $17.95
Grades: 4 5 6   **940.53**
1. Holocaust, 1939-1945 2. Jewish children in the Holocaust 3. World War, 1939-1945 -- Children 4. World War, 1939-1945 -- Refugees 5. Child refugees -- Great Britain -- History
ISBN 1770492569; 9781770492561

LC 2011938776

This children's book, by Deborah Hodge, "tells the story of how ten thousand Jewish children were rescued out of Nazi Europe just before the outbreak of World War 2. They were saved by the Kindertransport--a rescue mission that transported the children (or Kinder) from Nazi-ruled countries to safety in Britain. The book includes real-life accounts of the children and is illustrated with archival photographs . . . and original art by the Kinder commemorating their rescue." (Publisher's note)

Hoffman, Betty N.

Liberation; stories of survival from the Holocaust. Enslow Publishers 2011 128p il map (The Holocaust through primary sources) lib bdg $31.93
Grades: 7 8 9 10 11 12   **940.53**
1. Immigrants 2. Jewish refugees 3. Holocaust survivors 4. Jews -- Europe 5. Holocaust, 1933-1945 6. World War, 1939-1945 -- Europe 7. World War, 1939-1945 -- Refugees
ISBN 978-0-7660-3319-1; 0-7660-3319-8

LC 2010007234

Discusses the liberation of Europe and the aftermath of the Holocaust, including the displaced persons camps, primary source accounts from Holocaust survivors, and how those survivors started new lives in new countries

Includes glossary and bibliographical references

Hoose, Phillip

★ The **boys** who challenged Hitler; Knud Pedersen and the Churchill Club. Phillip Hoose. First edition Farrar, Straus, Giroux 2015 208 p. illustrations (hardback) $19.99
Grades: 7 8 9 10 11 12   **940.53**
1. Resistance to government 2. World War, 1939-1945 -- Underground movements 3. Heroes -- Denmark -- Biography 4. Sabotage -- Denmark -- History -- 20th century
ISBN 0374300224; 9780374300227

LC 2014026101

This book, by Phillip Hoose, describes how "at the outset of World War II, Denmark did not resist German occupation. Deeply ashamed of his nation's leaders, fifteen-year-old Knud Pedersen resolved with his brother and a handful of schoolmates to take action against the Nazis if the adults would not. . . . The boys' exploits and eventual imprisonment helped spark a full-blown Danish resistance." (Publisher's note)

"Hoose brilliantly weaves Pedersen's own words into the larger narrative of Denmark's stormy social and political wartime climate, showing how the astonishing bravery of otherwise ordinary Danish teens started something extraordinary." Horn Book

Includes bibliographical references and index

Houston, Jeanne Wakatsuki

★ **Farewell** to Manzanar; a true story of Japanese American experience during and after the World War II internment. [by] Jeanne Wakatsuki Houston and James D. Houston. Houghton Mifflin 2002 188p $15
Grades: 7 8 9 10   **940.53**
1. Manzanar War Relocation Center 2. World War, 1939-1945 -- United States 3. Japanese Americans -- Evacuation and relocation, 1942-1945
ISBN 0-618-21620-0

LC 2002-727748

A reissue with a new afterword of the title first published 1973

"The author tells of the three years she and her family spent at Manzanar, a Japanese internment camp. . . . The last part of the book deals with her postwar adolescence and reentry into American life." Libr J

"A spare, powerful memoir." Rochman. Against borders

Isserman, Maurice

★ **World** War II; John S. Bowman, general editor. rev ed; Chelsea House 2010 256p il map (America at war) lib bdg $45

Grades: 8 9 10 11 12   **940.53**

1. United States -- History -- 1933-1945 2. World War, 1939-1945 -- United States

ISBN 978-0-8160-8185-1; 0-8160-8185-9

LC 2009-52541

First published 1991

This book describes and interprets the role of the United States in World War II.

Includes glossary and bibliographical references

Kacer, Kathy

Hiding Edith; a true story. Second Story 2006 120p (Holocaust remembrance book for young readers) pa $10.95

Grades: 4 5 6 7   **940.53**

1. Holocaust survivors 2. Jews -- France 3. Holocaust, 1933-1945

ISBN 1-897187-06-8

"Kacer recounts some extraordinary history: in Moissac, France, under Nazi occupation, a French Jewish couple hid 100 Jewish refugee children—with the support of the townspeople. Kacer, who based her account on interviews, tells the story of one child, Edith Schwalb. Captioned black-and-white photos on almost every page show Edith at home in Vienna before the war, then in Belgium, and then, separated from her parents, living with the rescuers." Booklist

We Are Their Voice; Young People Respond to the Holocaust. created and edited by Kathy Kacer with Karen Krasny ... [et al.] Orca Book Pub 2012 232 p. ill. (paperback) $16.95

Grades: 7 8 9 10 11 12   **940.53**

1. Children's writings 2. Holocaust, 1939-1945

ISBN 1926920775; 9781926920771

"This volume is a compilation of present-day students' responses to the Holocaust. It includes imagined diary entries, reflections on archival photographs, artwork by students, letters to relevant figures such as Anne Frank, and, finally, the retelling of stories told by Holocaust survivors. These original student works are organized by topic, such as Hope." (School Library Journal)

Kent, Deborah

The **tragic** history of the Japanese-American internment camps; [by] Deborah Kent. Enslow Pub. 2007 128p il (From many cultures, one history) lib bdg $31.93

Grades: 6 7 8 9   **940.53**

1. World War, 1939-1945 -- United States 2. Japanese Americans -- Evacuation and relocation, 1942-1945

ISBN 978-0-7660-2797-8 lib bdg; 0-7660-2797-X lib bdg

LC 2007015125

This "will provide clear, easy-to-understand facts with critical analysis and will be useful for reports." Libr Media Connect

"Examines the sad history of the Japanese-American internment camps, including adapting to the American lifestyle before Pearl Harbor, life and the conditions inside the camps, and creating a new life after leaving the camps." Publisher's note

Includes glossary and bibliographical references

Kris, 1972-

A **bag** of marbles; based on the memoir by Joseph Joffo; adapted by Kris; illustrated by Vincent Bailly; translated by Edward Gauvin. Graphic Universe 2013 126 p. color illustrations (pbk) $9.95

Grades: 6 7 8 9 10   **940.53**

1. Holocaust, 1939-1945 2. Children and war -- Fiction 3. World War, 1939-1945 -- France 4. Graphic novels 5. Jews -- France -- Fiction 6. World War, 1939-1945 -- France -- Fiction 7. Holocaust, Jewish (1939-1945) -- France -- Fiction

ISBN 1467715166; 9781467707008; 9781467715164; 9781467716512

LC 2013002284

In this book by Joseph Joffo, set "in 1941 in occupied Paris, brothers Maurice and Joseph play a last game of marbles before running home to their father's barbershop. With the German occupation threatening their family's safety, the boys' parents decide Maurice and Joseph must disguise themselves and flee to their older brothers in the free zone. Surviving the long journey will take every scrap of ingenuity and courage they can muster. And if they hope to elude the Nazis, they must never, under any circumstances, admit to being Jewish."

"This graphic-novel adaptation of Joffo's 1973 memoir of the same name succeeds in melding sensitive and accurate imagery with the original narrative flow of a young secular Jewish boy's experiences in occupied France." Booklist

Langley, Andrew

World War II; by Andrew Langley. Heinemann Library 2012 80 p. ill. (some col.), col. maps (Living through) (library) $36.50; (paperback) $10.99

Grades: 6 7 8 9   **940.53**

1. Picture books for children 2. World War, 1939-1945

ISBN 1432960024; 9781432960025; 9781432960117

LC 2011016056

This book by Andrew Langley is part of the Living Through series and looks at World War II. It answers questions including "why was World War II so devastating, and how had the world become so divided into armed camps? How did the war affect people on both sides of the conflict, and why are its consequences still felt today?" (Publisher's note)

Includes bibliographical references (p. 76-78) and index.

Laskier, Rutka

Rutka's notebook; a voice from the Holocaust. Time Books 2008 90p il map $19.95

Grades: 7 8 9 10 11 12   **940.53**

1. Jews -- Poland 2. Holocaust, 1933-1945 -- Personal

narratives
ISBN 978-1-60320-019-6; 1-60320-019-3

"Rutka Laskier was a Jewish teenager in Poland during World War II. For a few short months, before being deported to a concentration camp, she kept a diary describing her experiences. It was kept safe by a non-Jewish friend for 60 years following the war, and was finally published in Poland and Israel. This is the first U.S. edition. The diary itself is a combination of wartime horrors, social gossip, and teen angst. Photos and editorial notes clarify the situations that Laskier describes. . . . A must-have for Holocaust collections, and a solid purchase for general YA collections." SLJ

Lee, Carol Ann

Anne Frank and the children of the Holocaust. Viking 2006 242p il map $16.99

Grades: 6 7 8 9 10 **940.53**
1. Children 2. Diarists 3. Holocaust victims 4. Holocaust, 1933-1945
ISBN 0-670-06107-7

"This book will still serve as an excellent overview in the classroom and for personal reading." Booklist

"Lee provides an overview that broadens the story that Anne Frank started in her diary. She details the girl's life before her family went into hiding and places Anne in context with other persecuted children and their attempts to survive." SLJ

Includes bibliographical references

Levine, Karen

Hana's suitcase; a true story. Whitman, A. 2003 111p il lib bdg $15.95

Grades: 4 5 6 7 **940.53**
1. Holocaust victims 2. Holocaust, 1933-1945
ISBN 0-8075-3148-0

LC 2002-27439

First published 2002 in Canada

A biography of a Czech girl who died in the Holocaust, told in alternating chapters with an account of how the curator of a Japanese Holocaust center learned about her life after Hana's suitcase was sent to her

"The account, based on a radio documentary Levine did in Canada . . . is part history, part suspenseful mystery, and always anguished family drama, with an incredible climactic revelation." Booklist

Meltzer, Milton

★ **Never** to forget: the Jews of the Holocaust. Harper & Row 1976 217p maps hardcover o.p. pa $9.99

Grades: 6 7 8 9 **940.53**
1. Holocaust, 1933-1945
ISBN 0-06-446118-1 pa

"The mass murder of six million Jews by the Nazis during World War II is the subject of this compelling history. Interweaving background information, chilling statistics, individual accounts and newspaper reports, it provides an excellent introduction to its subject." Interracial Books Child Bull

Includes bibliographical references

★ **Rescue** : the story of how Gentiles saved Jews in the Holocaust. Harper & Row 1988 168p maps hardcover o.p. pa $9.99

Grades: 6 7 8 9 **940.53**
1. Holocaust, 1933-1945 2. World War, 1939-1945 -- Jews -- Rescue
ISBN 0-06-024210-8; 0-06-446117-3 pa

LC 87-47816

A recounting drawn from historic source material of the many individual acts of heroism performed by righteous gentiles who sought to thwart the extermination of the Jews during the Holocaust

"This is an excellent portrayal of a difficult topic. Meltzer manages to both explain without accusing, and to laud without glorifying. . . . The discussion of the complicated relations between countries are clear, but not simplistic. An impressive aspect of this book is its lack of didacticism." Voice Youth Advocates

Includes bibliographical references

Mullenbach, Cheryl

★ **Double** victory; how African American women broke race and gender barriers to help win World War II. Cheryl Mullenbach. Chicago Review Press 2012 272 p. (Women of action) (hardcover) $19.95

Grades: 7 8 9 10 11 12 **940.53**
1. World War, 1939-1945 -- Women 2. African American women -- Biography 3. United States -- Race relations -- History 4. African Americans -- Employment 5. African Americans -- Civil rights 6. World War, 1939-1945 -- African Americans 7. World War, 1939-1945 -- Women -- United States 8. African American women -- History -- 20th century 9. United States -- Race relations -- History -- 20th century 10. African American women -- Employment -- History -- 20th century 11. African American women -- Civil rights -- History -- 20th century
ISBN 1569768080; 9781569768082

LC 2012021343

This book, by Cheryl Mullenbach, is part of the "Women of Action" series. "African American women . . . did extraordinary things to help their country during World War II. In these pages young readers meet a range of remarkable women: war workers, political activists, military women, volunteers, and entertainers. . . . But many others fought discrimination at home and abroad in order to contribute to the war effort." (Publisher's note)

Includes bibliographical references and index

Nolan, Cathal J.

The **concise** encyclopedia of World War II. Greenwood Press 2010 2v set $195

Grades: 7 8 9 10 11 12 Adult **940.53**
1. World War, 1939-1945 -- Encyclopedias
ISBN 978-0-313-33050-6 set; 0-313-33050-6 set; 978-0-313-36527-0 set: ebook; 0-313-36527-X set: ebook

LC 2009036965

"This rigorous A-Z set will be valuable for defining vocabulary such as 'friendly fire' or 'leaflet bombing,' and identifying people, places, tactics, and campaigns. Included are numerous Russian, Japanese, and German terms. . . . Entries vary in length, from mere definitions to 17 pages (on Adolf Hitler), and are often followed up with 'see' or 'see-also' references and additional reading suggestions. . . . A first stop for researchers." SLJ

Includes bibliographical references

Opdyke, Irene Gut

In my hands; memories of a Holocaust rescuer. [by] Irene Gut Opdyke with Jennifer Armstrong. Knopf 1999 276p il hardcover o.p. pa $12

Grades: 7 8 9 10   **940.53**

1. World War, 1939-1945 -- Poland 2. World War, 1939-1945 -- Jews -- Rescue 3. Holocaust, 1933-1945 -- Personal narratives 4. World War, 1939-1945 -- Personal narratives

ISBN 0-679-89181-1; 0-385-72032-7 pa

LC 98-54095

Recounts the experiences of the author who, as a young Polish girl, hid and saved Jews during the Holocaust

"No matter how many Holocaust stories one has read, this one is a must, for its impact is so powerful. . . . Opdyke's remarkable story is simply told, with clarity and feeling." SLJ

Oppenheim, Joanne

★ Dear Miss Breed; true stories of the Japanese American incarceration during World War II and a librarian who made a difference. foreword by Elizabeth Kikuchi Yamada; afterword by Snowden Becker. Scholastic 2006 287p il $22.99

Grades: 7 8 9 10   **940.53**

1. Librarians 2. World War, 1939-1945 -- United States 3. Japanese Americans -- Evacuation and relocation, 1942-1945

ISBN 0-439-56992-3; 978-0-439-56992-7

LC 2004-59009

This "account focuses on Clara Breed, a children's librarian at the San Diego Public Library, and the Japanese-American children she served prior to World War II and whom she continued to serve after their families were sent to an Arizona internment camp. . . . Illustrated with numerous photographs . . . and incorporating copious letters and documents, the book is . . . compelling." Horn Book

Includes bibliographical references

Perl, Lila

Four perfect pebbles; a Holocaust story. by Lila Perl and Marion Blumenthal Lazan. Greenwillow Bks. 1996 130p il $16.99; pa $5.99

Grades: 6 7 8 9   **940.53**

1. Jews -- Germany 2. Holocaust, 1933-1945 -- Personal narratives

ISBN 0-688-14294-X; 0-380-73188-6 pa

LC 95-9752

"This book warrants attention both for the uncommon experiences it records and for the fullness of that record. . . . Quotes from Lazan's 87-year-old mother are invaluable—her memories of the family's experiences afford Marion's story a precision and wholeness rarely available to child survivors." Publ Wkly

Includes bibliographical references

Rappaport, Doreen, 1939-

★ Beyond courage; the untold story of Jewish resistance during the Holocaust. by Doreen Rappaport. 1st ed. Candlewick Press 2012 228 p. ill., maps (hardcover) $22.99

Grades: 6 7 8 9 10 11 12   **940.53**

1. Biography 2. Jews -- History 3. Resistance to government 4. Holocaust, Jewish (1939-1945) 5. Righteous Gentiles in the Holocaust 6. World War, 1939-1945 -- Jews -- Rescue 7. World War, 1939-1945 -- Jewish resistance

ISBN 0763629766; 9780763629762

LC 2011048116

In this book, Doreen Rappaport offers "more than 20 stories of Jewish resistance to the Holocaust, some never before told. From all corners of Nazi-occupied Europe, these harrowing accounts . . . pay tribute to the brave thousands who defied their oppressors in ways large and small. In one, 12-year-old Mordechai Shlayan . . . blows up a hotel where German officers are dining. In another, 22-year-old Marianne Cohn is caught smuggling children into Switzerland." (Publishers Weekly)

Includes bibliographical references (p. 209-221) and index.

Robbins, Trina

Lily Renée, escape artist; illustrated by Anne Timmons and Mo Oh. Graphic Universe 2011 96p. chiefly col. ill. $7.95

Grades: 4 5 6 7 8   **940.53**

1. Artists 2. Illustrators 3. Graphic novels 4. Jews -- Biography 5. Holocaust, 1933-1945 -- Graphic novels

ISBN 978-0-7613-6010-0; 0-7613-6010-7

LC 2011001084

Presents the story of Lily Renée Wilhelm, the Jewish girl who escaped from the Nazis through the Kindertransport operation, leaving her parents behind and traveling alone to England, later becoming a comic book artist in New York.

"This comic-book biography of a Jewish girl's life under the Nazi jackboot and then as a refugee is low key and that much more profound for it. The panels are brightly lit, and the narrative is crisp, both of which serve to chillingly amplify the everyday banality of evil. . . . A fitting tribute." Kirkus

Rol, Ruud van der

★ Anne Frank, beyond the diary; a photographic remembrance. by Ruud van der Rol and Rian Verhoeven; in association with the Anne Frank House; translated by Tony Langham and Plym Peters; with an introduction by Anna Quindlen. Viking 1993 113p il map hardcover o.p. pa $10.99

Grades: 5 6 7 8   **940.53**

1. Children 2. Diarists 3. Holocaust victims 4. Jews -- Netherlands 5. Holocaust, 1933-1945 6. World War, 1939-1945 -- Jews 7. Netherlands -- History -- 1940-1945, German occupation

ISBN 0-670-84932-4; 0-14-036926-0 pa

LC 92-41528

Original Dutch edition, 1992

Photographs, illustrations, and maps accompany historical essays, diary excerpts, and interviews, providing an insight to Anne Frank and the massive upheaval which tore apart her world

"Readers will become absorbed in the richness of the detail and careful explanation which revisit and expand the familiar, well-loved story." Horn Book

Samuels, Charlie

Home front; by Charlie Samuels. Brown Bear Books 2012 48 p. ill. (some col.) (World War II sourcebook) (library) $35.65

Grades: 5 6 7 8   **940.53**

1. Military history 2. World War, 1939-1945 3. World War, 1939-1945 -- Social aspects 4. World War, 1939-1945 -- Economic aspects

ISBN 1936333228; 9781936333226

LC 2011007054

This book by Charlie Samuels is part of the World War II Sourcebook series and focuses on the home front. "Each page is illustrated. Little-known facts and, sometimes, direct narratives are presented with the information given to the reader. . . . Each book has the same timeline of World War II, maps of both the European and Pacific theaters, interesting biographical snapshots of people involved, and a list of websites that students may use to further explore World War II." (Library Media Connection)

Life under occupation; by Charlie Samuels. Brown Bear Books 2011 48 p. ill. (chiefly col.), col. maps (World War II sourcebook) (library) $35.65

Grades: 5 6 7 8   **940.53**

1. World War, 1939-1945 2. World War, 1939-1945 -- Occupied territories 3. World War, 1939-1945 -- Europe 4. World War, 1939-1945 -- Atrocities 5. World War, 1939-1945 -- Pacific Area 6. World War, 1939-1945 -- Occupied territories

ISBN 1936333260; 9781936333264

LC 2011007055

This book by Charlie Samuels, part of the World War II Sourcebook series, and focuses on life under occupation. "Each page is illustrated. Little-known facts and, sometimes, direct narratives are presented with the information given to the reader. . . . Each book has the same timeline of World War II, maps of both the European and Pacific theaters, . . . biographical snapshots of people involved, and a list of websites." (Library Media Connection)

Includes bibliographical references and index.

Sanders, Ronald

Storming the tulips; by Ronald Sanders; translated and revised by Hannie J. Voyles. StoneBrook 2011 164p il map pa $14.00

Grades: 7 8 9 10   **940.53**

1. World War, 1939-1945 -- Netherlands 2. Holocaust, 1933-1945 -- Personal narratives 3. World War, 1939-1945 -- Underground movements

ISBN 978-0-9830800-0-8; 0-9830800-0-3

"The tragic story of the Netherlands under Nazi occupation resounds dramatically through the words of 20 survivors from the first Montessori school in Amsterdam. Contemporaries of Anne Frank, they were interviewed by Ron-

ald Sanders, now a teacher at the school. Though the book focuses on this small group, it presents a well-documented history of the country during World War II. In addition to the essays, descriptions of unusual heroes from the Resistance help to round out the picture." SLJ

Sandler, Martin W.

Imprisoned; the betrayal of Japanese Americans during World War II. by Martin W. Sandler. Walker Books For Young Readers 2013 176 p. (hardcover) $22.99; (library) $23.89

Grades: 7 8 9 10   **940.53**

1. World War, 1939-1945 2. Japanese Americans -- Evacuation and relocation, 1942-1945 3. World War, 1939-1945 -- Japanese Americans 4. Japanese Americans -- History -- 20th century

ISBN 0802722776; 0802722784; 9780802722775; 9780802722782

LC 2012032295

YALSA Award for Excellence in Nonfiction for Young Adults: Finalist (2014)

This book offers a "survey of Executive Order 9066 and its aftermath. The order authorized the U.S. military to relocate over 100,000 Japanese-Americans--many were U.S. citizens--from their homes in Washington, Oregon and California to detention camps. . . . A few government officials did object to the order, questioning its constitutionality." (Kirkus Reviews)

"Sandler's earnest telling is complemented by well-chosen primary sources, not just the words . . . but also the black-and-white photographs that present striking images." Horn Book

Sender, Ruth Minsky

The cage. Macmillan 1986 245p hardcover o.p. pa $5.99

Grades: 7 8 9 10   **940.53**

1. Jews -- Poland 2. Holocaust, 1933-1945 -- Personal narratives

ISBN 0-02-781830-6; 0-689-81321-X pa

LC 86-8562

This "Holocaust memoir presents a series of brief scenes from 1939, when the author was 12 and Hitler invaded Poland, through the Russian liberation of the Mitelsteine labor camp in 1945. . . . Older students with previous knowledge of the subject will find Sender's narrative moving and thought provoking." SLJ

Senker, Cath

Why did World War II happen? Gareth Stevens Pub. 2011 48p il map (Moments in history) lib bdg $31.95; pa $14.05

Grades: 6 7 8 9   **940.53**

1. World War, 1939-1945

ISBN 978-1-4339-4184-9 lib bdg; 1-4339-4184-8 lib bdg; 978-1-4339-4185-6 pa; 1-4339-4185-6 pa

LC 2010015834

"Examines the events that served as . . . [precursors to World War II]. . . . Brightly colored pull-out boxes highlight important turning points, the perspective of the everyday man, and further information on why specific events occurred. Numerous photographs help readers visualize concepts more fully. . . . Students should be able to easily use this resource." Libr Media Connect

Includes glossary and bibliographical references

Sheehan, Sean

Auschwitz. Arcturus Pub. 2011 46p il map (A place in history) lib bdg $34.25

Grades: 7 8 9 10   **940.53**

1. Holocaust, 1933-1945   2. Auschwitz (Poland: Concentration camp)

ISBN 978-1-84837-672-4; 1-84837-672-3

LC 2010014147

This book begins with the Auschwitz concentration camp as a landmark and broadens "outward, describing the political and economic situations that led up to notable events there. The approach works beautifully. Quotes from participants are a highlight of the [book], and all the maps and photos are clear and informative. [This] will be [a] useful [supplement] to history classes, but [is] accessible enough to appeal as extracurricular material for students already interested in the [topic]." SLJ

Includes glossary and bibliographical references

Why did the Holocaust happen? Gareth Stevens 2010 48p il map (Moments in history) lib bdg $31.95; pa $14.05

Grades: 6 7 8 9   **940.53**

1. Holocaust, 1933-1945

ISBN 978-1-4339-4172-6 lib bdg; 1-4339-4172-4; 978-1-4339-4173-3 pa; 1-4339-4173-2 pa

LC 2010015833

This "explains the before, during, and after of [the Holocaust] in a clear, unbiased manner. . . . Sidebars include meticulously cited eyewitness quotes or extra insight on particularly important events. Even more information is contained in the maps, period photographs, and well-placed captions that grace every page." SLJ

Includes glossary and bibliographical references

Skog, Jason

The **legacy** of the Holocaust. Compass Point Books 2011 64p il (The holocaust) lib bdg $33.32; pa $8.95

Grades: 6 7 8 9   **940.53**

1. Holocaust, 1933-1945

ISBN 978-0-7565-4393-8 lib bdg; 0-7565-4393-2 lib bdg; 978-0-7565-4444-7 pa; 0-7565-4444-0 pa

LC 2010026494

This discusses the lasting impact of the Holocaust, including its effects on people and families and entire cities and countries, and its influence on popular culture, art, music, and international law.

This volume "succeeds in outlining a horrific chapter in history without oversimplifying. . . . [This] book features multiple quotes from survivors about their wartime experiences, providing voices with which young people can identify." SLJ

Includes glossary and bibliographical references

Spiegelman, Art

★ **Maus**; a survivor's tale. Art Spiegelman. 25th anniversary ed. Pantheon Bks. 1996 295 p. 2v in 1 ill., maps (some col.) $35

Grades: 7 8 9 10 11 12 Adult   **940.53**

1. Graphic novels 2. Biographical graphic novels 3. Holocaust, 1933-1945 -- Graphic novels

ISBN 0-679-40641-7

LC 96-32796

A combined edition of Maus I : My father bleeds history (1986) and Maus II : And here my troubles began (1991)

Awards: 1992 Pulitzer Prize Special Award; Eisner Award for Best Graphic Album: Reprint for Maus II; Harvey Award for Best Graphic Album of Previously Published Work (for Maus II); 1993 Los Angeles Times Book Prize for Fiction (for Maus II)

"An undisputed classic and award-winning title (including a Pulitzer Prize in 1992) in which renowned cartoonist Spiegelman depicts his father's experiences as a World War II Nazi concentration camp survivor. The memoir is also a chronicle of Spiegelman's relationship with his father as we witness their visits and disagreements. The black-and-white drawings are straightforward, but with an interesting twist: all of the Jews are depicted as mice and the Nazis as cats." LJ

Stille, Darlene R.

Architects of the Holocaust. Compass Point Books 2010 64p il (The holocaust) lib bdg $33.32; pa $8.95

Grades: 6 7 8 9   **940.53**

1. Holocaust, 1933-1945 2. Germany -- Politics and government -- 1933-1945

ISBN 978-0-7565-4392-1 lib bdg; 0-7565-4392-4 lib bdg; 978-0-7565-4441-6 pa; 0-7565-4441-6 pa

LC 2010026493

While this book "covers the rise of Hitler and spends some time discussing others who organized the atrocities, its latter half discusses concentration and extermination camps and the Nuremberg trials. . . . [This volume] succeeds in outlining a horrific chapter in history without oversimplifying. . . . [This] book features multiple quotes from survivors about their wartime experiences, providing voices with which young people can identify." SLJ

Includes glossary and bibliographical references

Taylor, Peter Lane

★ The **secret** of Priest's Grotto; a Holocaust survival story. [by] Peter Lane Taylor with Christos Nicola. Kar-Ben Pub. 2007 64p il map lib bdg $10.95; pa $8.95

Grades: 5 6 7 8 9 10 11 12   **940.53**

1. Caves 2. Jews -- Ukraine 3. Holocaust, 1933-1945

ISBN 978-1-58013-260-2 lib bdg; 1-58013-260-X lib bdg; 978-1-58013-261-9 pa; 1-58013-261-8 pa

LC 2006-21709

"This volume relays the tale of 38 Ukrainian Jews who sought refuge in a local cave to escape the invading Nazis in fall of 1942 and remained there for 344 days. . . . At once sobering and uplifting, this is an astounding story of survival, powerfully told." Publ Wkly

Thomson, Ruth

★ **Terezin**; voices from the Holocaust. Candlewick Press 2011 64p il $18.99

Grades: 5 6 7 8   **940.53**

1. Jews -- Czechoslovakia 2. Holocaust, 1933-1945 3. Holocaust, Jewish (1939-1945) 4. Terezin (Czech Republic: Concentration camp)

ISBN 0-7636-4963-5; 978-0-7636-4963-0

         LC 2010-39164

"Between 1941 and 1945, Nazi Germany turned the small town of Terezín, Czechoslovakia, into a ghetto, and then into a transit camp for thousands of Jewish people. It was a 'show' camp, where inmates were forced to use their artistic talents to fool the world about the truth of gas chambers and horrific living conditions for imprisoned Jews. Here is their story, told through the firsthand accounts of those who were there." (Publisher's note) Index. "Grades five to eight." (Bull Cent Child Books)

"Two years after the Nazi invasion of Czechoslovakia, the small fortress village of Terezin was converted into a Jewish ghetto, and over the next four years, ten of thousands of Jews were transported there while in transit to death camps in the east. The history of Terezin is fascinating: the camp housed many noted artists. . . . Much of the art created at Terezin survived the Holocaust, and a generous sampling is included in this volume. Thomson opts to tell the story of Terezin almost entirely in the voices of those who lived there. . . . This is an accessible, carefully researched work that effectively uses primary-source material to make the experience of the Jews of Terezin come alive for today's students." Bull Cent Child Books

Includes glossary and bibliographical references

Warren, Andrea

Surviving Hitler; a boy in the Nazi death camps. HarperCollins Pubs. 2001 146p il hardcover o.p. pa $6.99

Grades: 5 6 7 8   **940.53**

1. Holocaust, 1933-1945

ISBN 0-688-17497-3; 0-06-029218-0 lib bdg; 0-06-000767-2 pa

        LC 00-38899

"Simply told, Warren's powerful story blends the personal testimony of Holocaust survivor Jack Mandelbaum with the history of his time, documented by stirring photos from the archives of the U.S. Holocaust Memorial Museum. . . . An excellent introduction for readers who don't know much about the history." Booklist

Includes bibliographical references

940.54 Military history of World War II

Allen, Thomas B.

★ **Remember** Pearl Harbor; American and Japanese survivors tell their stories. foreword by Robert D. Ballard. National Geographic Soc. 2001 57p il maps $17.95

Grades: 5 6 7 8   **940.54**

1. Pearl Harbor (Oahu, Hawaii), Attack on, 1941 2.

World War, 1939-1945 -- Personal narratives

ISBN 0-7922-6690-0

        LC 2001-796

Personal accounts of the Japanese attack on Pearl Harbor, with background information.

"Eyewitness testimony of Japanese and American men and women from various backgrounds enriches this balanced treatment of World War II. . . . The first-person voices along with dozens of black-and-white photos and several full-color maps make this a draw for both browsers and World War II buffs." Booklist

Includes bibliographical references

Allport, Alan

The **Battle** of Britain; by Alan Allport. Chelsea House 2012 128 p. (Milestones in modern world history) (hardcover) $35

Grades: 7 8 9 10 11 12   **940.54**

1. Britain, Battle of, 1940 2. World War, 1939-1945 -- Aerial operations

ISBN 160413920X; 9781604139204

        LC 2011023053

This book, part of the Milestones in Modern World History series, "describes the air campaign waged by the Luftwaffe (German air force) against England's Royal Air Force during WWII. It starts with a look at [Adolph] Hitler's rise to power and continues with such pivotal conflicts as the Blitz. The author also notes how important the burgeoning radar technology of the time aided England's defense." (Booklist)

Includes bibliographical references and index

Atkinson, Rick

D -Day; the invasion of Normandy, 1944. Rick Atkinson with Kate Waters. Henry Holt & Co. 2014 224 p. (hardcover) $18.99

Grades: 6 7 8 9 10 11 12   **940.54**

1. World War, 1939-1945 2. Normandy (France), Attack on, 1944 3. World War, 1939-1945 -- Campaigns -- France -- Normandy

ISBN 1627791116; 9781627791113; 9781627791120

        LC 2014005162

Written by Rick Atkinson, "Adapted for young readers from . . . 'The Guns at Last Light,' 'D-Day' captures the events and the spirit of that day--June 6, 1944--the day that led to the liberation of western Europe from Nazi Germany's control. They came by sea and by sky to reclaim freedom from the occupying Germans, turning the tide of World War II." (Publisher's note)

"With Kate Waters. Adapted from Atkinson's adult book The Guns at Last Light, this young readers' edition focuses, effectively and excitingly, on the invasion of Normandy but provides enough context for WWII both before and after June 6, 1944. Copious photographs and a vibrant design will invite war buffs in; appended lists of interesting facts add appeal. Reading list, timeline, websites. Bib., glos., ind." Horn Book

Includes bibliographical references and index

The **attack** on Pearl Harbor; David Haugen and Susan Musser, book editors. Greenhaven Press

2011 204p il map (Perspectives on modern world history) lib bdg $39.70

Grades: 8 9 10 11 12   **940.54**

1. Pearl Harbor (Oahu, Hawaii), Attack on, 1941
ISBN 978-0-7377-5004-1; 0-7377-5004-9

LC 2010033590

In "discussing the events of December 7, 1941. . . [this] well-organized [volume presents] a wealth of clearly written analyses from a rich variety of viewpoints. With the inclusion of historical background, firsthand experiences, and discussions of particular points of controversy, [it helps] to familiarize readers with the [attack on Pearl Harbor] and [serves] as [an exercise] in the development of analytical thinking skills." SLJ

Includes bibliographical references

Atwood, Kathryn

Women heroes of World War II; 26 stories of espionage, sabotage, resistance, and rescue. Chicago Review Press 2011 266p il map $19.95

Grades: 7 8 9 10   **940.54**

1. World War, 1939-1945 -- Women 2. World War, 1939-1945 -- Underground movements
ISBN 978-1-55652-961-0; 1-55652-961-9

LC 2010-41830

"The 26 women profiled in this collective biography served on the front lines and behind enemy lines in Europe as correspondents, couriers, propagandists, Resistance fighters, saboteurs and spies. . . . Atwood's admiration and enthusiasm for her subjects is apparent in these engaging profiles, and readers will likely be inspired to investigate these fascinating women further." Kirkus

Includes glossary and bibliographical references

Bradley, James

Flags of our fathers; heroes of Iwo Jima. [by] James Bradley with Ron Powers; adapted for young people by Michael French. Delacorte Press 2001 211p il $15.95; pa $8.95

Grades: 7 8 9 10   **940.54**

1. Iwo Jima, Battle of, 1945 2. Photojournalists 3. United States -- Marine Corps
ISBN 0-385-72932-4; 0-385-73064-0 pa

LC 00-50914

"A journalistic, accessible adaptation of the earlier book for adult readers, this account by a survivor's son centers on [Rosenthal's] famous photo of six Marines raising a U.S. flag on Iwo Jima. The accurate, engaging text provides the men's pre-war backgrounds, their war service to that time, what they actually did on the island and afterward, and the consequences of the famous photo." Horn Book Guide

Includes bibliographical references

Burgan, Michael

Hiroshima; birth of the nuclear age. Marshall Cavendish Benchmark 2009 128p il (Perspectives on) lib bdg $27.95

Grades: 8 9 10 11 12   **940.54**

1. Atomic bomb 2. Hiroshima (Japan) -- Bombardment,

1945
ISBN 978-0-7614-4023-9; 0-7614-4023-2

LC 2008-29249

This provides information on the Manhattan Project, the bombing of Hiroshima, and its legacy.

"Utilizing an unbiased and chronological narrative, [the author delves] deeply into the [topic], providing an overall representation as well as a substantial degree of insight. . . . The potency of [this title] lies in the excellent arrangement of numerous well-chosen sidebars and photos, and fluent, concise prose." SLJ

Includes bibliographical references

Raising the flag; how a photograph gave a nation hope in wartime. Compass Point Books 2011 64p il (Captured history) lib bdg $33.99; pa $8.95

Grades: 6 7 8 9   **940.54**

1. World War, 1939-1945 2. Documentary photography 3. Iwo Jima, Battle of, 1945 4. Photojournalists
ISBN 978-0-7565-4395-2; 0-7565-4395-9; 978-0-7565-4449-2 pa; 0-7565-4449-1 pa

LC 2010038572

This book about the iconic Joe Rosenthal photograph of American soldiers raising the flag at Iwo Jima places the photo "in historical context, profiles the photographer, describes the conditions under which it was taken, and analyzes both its immediate and its continuing impact. The [text includes] ample background information and details and [is] enhanced by large photos and sidebars." SLJ

Includes glossary and bibliographical references

Chrisp, Peter

World War II: fighting for freedom; the story of the conflict that changed the world 1939-1945. Scholastic 2010 63p il map $12.99

Grades: 4 5 6 7   **940.54**

1. World War, 1939-1945
ISBN 978-0-545-24984-3; 0-545-24984-8

Provides information and facts on events leading up to the war, important battles and campaigns, political and military leaders, and life on the home fronts.

"Fascinating photographs dominate each spread, but there are also maps, quotations, diagrams, and interesting text box features. . . . This book provides a solid overview of World War II, but it is the visual aspect that makes it stand out." Libr Media Connect

Includes glossary

Cornioley, Pearl Witherington

Code name Pauline; memoirs of a World War II special agent. Pearl Witherington Cornioley with Hervé Larroque ; edited by Kathryn J. Atwood. Chicago Review Press 2013 208 p. (Women of action) (hardback) $19.95

Grades: 8 9 10 11 12   **940.54**

1. World War, 1939-1945 -- Secret service 2. World War, 1939-1945 -- Underground movements -- France
ISBN 1613744870; 9781613744871

LC 2013008734

In this memoir, "one of the most celebrated female World War II resistance fighters shares . . . her experiences as a special agent for the British Special Operations Executive.

French-born British citizen [Pearl Witherington] Cornioley tells her story through a series of reminiscences, including . . . her recruitment and training as a special agent, and parachuting into a remote, rural area of occupied France." (Kirkus Reviews)

"Cornioley's detailed account of her time as a British special agent in Nazi-occupied France is suited for readers already familiar with the basic events of World War II. She narrates with short sentences and a matter-of-fact tone that keeps readers at a distance from her story, but the material is well documented and thorough. Appropriate for students needing primary source material. " (Horn Book)

Includes bibliographical references and index

De Capua, Sarah

The **Tuskegee** airmen; by Sarah E. De Capua. Child's World 2009 32p il map (Journey to freedom) lib bdg $28.50

Grades: 4 5 6 **940.54**

1. African American pilots 2. World War, 1939-1945 -- Aerial operations
ISBN 978-1-60253-138-3 lib bdg; 1-60253-138-2 lib bdg

LC 2008031939

Tuskegee "Airmen celebrates the pilots' extraordinary achievements by placing them within the context of their time, when segregation was common. . . . Personal accounts, historical photographs of training, news stories about the men's fighting ability, and records of successful missions help to explain the squadron's determination not only to fly but also to prove its proficiency and bravery. . . . The [book is] concise and direct, yet the writing remains sophisticated. Vibrant personal stories accompanied by striking photographs of historical figures and artifacts provide a sense of the subjects' hopes and dreams." SLJ

Includes glossary and bibliographical references

DeMallie, H. R.

Behind enemy lines; a young pilot's story. [by] Howard R. DeMallie. Updated ed; Sterling Pub. 2007 178p il map $12.95; pa $6.95

Grades: 6 7 8 9 **940.54**

1. World War, 1939-1945 -- Personal narratives
ISBN 978-1-4027-4517-1; 1-4027-4517-6; 978-1-4027-4137-1 pa; 1-4027-4137-5 pa

LC 2006032134

First published 2000 by Dry Bones Press with title: Beyond the dikes

"The story follows the 22-year-old American Air Force officer who was forced to bail out of his B-17 in 1944, highlighting his hiding out in the Netherlands, imprisonment in a German POW camp, and liberation by Russian soldiers. There are vivid recollections of hunger, loneliness, and uncertainty. . . . This a a good choice for nonfiction enthusiasts." SLJ

Dougherty, Steve

Pearl Harbor; the U.S. enters World War II. Franklin Watts 2010 64p il map (24/7 goes to war) lib bdg $27; pa $7.95

Grades: 6 7 8 9 **940.54**

1. Pearl Harbor (Oahu, Hawaii), Attack on, 1941 2.

World War, 1939-1945 -- Causes 3. Japan -- Foreign relations -- United States 4. United States -- Foreign relations -- Japan
ISBN 978-0-531-25525-4 lib bdg; 0-531-25525-5 lib bdg; 978-0-531-25450-9 pa; 0-531-25450-X pa

LC 2009-20143

Describes the Japanese surprise attack on the United States naval base at Pearl Harbor, which resulted in the deaths of more than 2,000 American officers and servicemen and an immediate declaration of war on Japan.

This "will appeal to these readers, because . . . [it tells] a story while presenting the facts. . . . The first chapter gives the historic details concerning the war up to the particular battle, with the story of the battle told from a first-person perspective. A mixture of news photos and photos taken by the men involved appear throughout the book." Libr Media Connect

Includes glossary and bibliographical references

Drez, Ronald J.

★ **Remember** D-day; the plan, the invasion, survivor stories. National Geographic Books 2004 61p il map $17.95; lib bdg $27.90

Grades: 5 6 7 8 **940.54**

1. World War, 1939-1945 -- Campaigns -- France
ISBN 0-7922-6666-8; 0-7922-6965-9 lib bdg

LC 2003-17733

Discusses the events and personalities involved in the momentous Allied invasion of France on June 6, 1944

"This well-organized, clearly written account provides a solid overview for readers unfamiliar with the subject. A first-rate purchase." SLJ

Includes bibliographical references

Farrell, Mary Cronk

Pure grit; how American World War II nurses survived battle and prison camp in the Pacific. by Mary Cronk Farrell. Abrams Books for Young Readers 2014 160 p. illustrations, color maps (hardcover : alk. paper) $24.95

Grades: 7 8 9 10 11 12 **940.54**

1. Nurses 2. Military medicine 3. World War, 1939-1945 -- Medical care 4. World War, 1939-1945 -- Prisoners and prisons 5. Prisoners of war -- Philippines 6. Prisoners of war -- United States 7. Military nursing -- United States -- History 8. World War, 1939-1945 -- Campaigns -- Philippines 9. Nurses -- United States -- History -- 20th century 10. World War, 1939-1945 -- Medical care -- United States 11. World War, 1939-1945 -- Prisoners and prisons, Japanese
ISBN 1419710281; 9781419710285

LC 2013017134

This book, by Mary Cronk Farrell, focuses on American World War II Navy and Army nurses who were stationed in the Pacific. "Nurses, deeply engaged in caring for desperately wounded soldiers, were sent to Bataan. After living on near-starvation rations, the nurses on Bataan were evacuated to Corregidor. . . . A few were rescued from Corregidor before it too fell to enemy forces. . . . The remaining nurses were then imprisoned . . . and not released until late winter of 1945." (Kirkus Reviews)

"Using historical interviews and modern correspondence with the subjects' relatives, Farrell presents a fascinating account of the more than one hundred army and navy nurses who served in the South Pacific in WWII. Through every battle and retreat, and even in POW camps, these nurses cared for the injured under the most primitive of conditions. The book's utilitarian design features archival photographs." Horn Book

Includes bibliographical references and index

Grant, R. G.

Why did Hiroshima happen? Gareth Stevens Pub. 2010 48p il map (Moments in history) lib bdg $31.95; pa $14.05

Grades: 6 7 8 9   **940.54**

1. Atomic bomb 2. World War, 1939-1945 -- Japan 3. World War, 1939-1945 -- United States 4. Hiroshima (Japan) -- Bombardment, 1945
ISBN 978-1-4339-4163-4 lib bdg; 1-4339-4163-5 lib bdg; 978-1-4339-4164-1 pa; 1-4339-4164-3 pa
LC 2010012464

This "explains the before, during, and after of [the bombing of Hiroshima]. . . . Sidebars include meticulously cited eyewitness quotes or extra insight on particularly important events. Even more information is contained in the maps, period photographs, and well-placed captions that grace every page." SLJ

Includes glossary and bibliographical references

Hama, Larry

★ The **battle** of Iwo Jima; guerilla warfare in the Pacific. by Larry Hama; illustrated by Anthony Williams. Rosen Pub. 2007 48p il map (Graphic battles of World War II) lib bdg $29.25

Grades: 5 6 7 8 9   **940.54**

1. Graphic novels 2. World War, 1939-1945 -- Graphic novels 3. Iwo Jima, Battle of, 1945 -- Graphic novels
ISBN 978-1-4042-0781-3 lib bdg; 1-4042-0781-3 lib bdg
LC 2006007645

"Using a graphic novel to introduce the battle for Iwo Jima makes it very accessible. Before the graphic-novel section of the book begins, Hama provides a short, informative background piece describing the run-up to World War II, the significance of the Japanese war machine, and the importance of the tiny island of Iwo Jima. Then the graphic novel, illustrated by Williams in camouflage colors, does a terrific job of examining the ups and downs of the battle as well as the horror of so many losses—on both sides." Booklist

Includes bibliographical references

Hillstrom, Laurie

The **attack** on Pearl Harbor; [by] Laurie Collier Hillstrom. Omnigraphics 2009 237p il (Defining moments) $49

Grades: 7 8 9 10 11 12   **940.54**

1. Reference books 2. Pearl Harbor (Oahu, Hawaii), Attack on, 1941
ISBN 978-0-7808-1069-3; 0-7808-1069-4
LC 2009-4236

"This book is divided into three well-organized sections. Part one provides a narrative overview detailing the events

leading up to the attack, the attack itself, and the aftermath, including the U.S. victory in the Pacific as well as the occupation and reconstruction of Japan after World War II. Part two is composed of eight two to three-page biographies of the important figures such as Yamamoto, Roosevelt, and Doris Miller, the first African-American to receive the Navy Cross. A final section of primary documents from the Japanese attack plan to Truman's announcement of the end of the war provides insight into the war in the Pacific. . . . This work is a must-have for reports and assignments." SLJ

Includes glossary and bibliographical references

Holm, Tom

Code talkers and warriors; Native Americans and World War II. Chelsea House 2007 168p il map (Landmark events in Native American history) $35

Grades: 7 8 9 10   **940.54**

1. World War, 1939-1945 -- Native Americans
ISBN 978-0-7910-9340-5; 0-7910-9340-9
LC 2006102263

"In this title about Native Americans in World War II, Holm . . . expands considerably on his specific topic to highlight significant miliary roles played by Native Americans in conflicts dating back to the sixteenth century. . . . [This is] outstanding. . . . [A] valuable resource." Booklist

Includes bibliographical references

Kuhn, Betsy

Angels of mercy; the Army nurses of World War II. Atheneum Bks. for Young Readers 1999 114p il map $18

Grades: 5 6 7 8   **940.54**

1. Women in the armed forces 2. World War, 1939-1945 -- Women 3. United States -- Army Nurse Corps
ISBN 0-689-82044-5
LC 98-36610

Relates the experiences of World War II Army nurses, who brought medical skills, courage, and cheer to hospitals throughout Europe, North Africa, and the Pacific

"Excellent reproductions, maps and a time line accompany the clear, well-written text." SLJ

Includes bibliographical references

Lawton, Clive

★ **Hiroshima**; the story of the first atom bomb. [by] Clive A. Lawton. Candlewick Press 2004 48p il map $18.99

Grades: 5 6 7 8   **940.54**

1. Atomic bomb 2. World War, 1939-1945 -- Japan 3. Hiroshima (Japan) -- Bombardment, 1945
ISBN 0-7636-2271-0
LC 2004-45166

"Engaging text and powerful photographs are intricately woven together to make a long-lasting impact on readers." Libr Media Connect

Miller, Terry

D -Day; the Allies strike back during World War II. Franklin Watts 2009 64p il map (24/7 goes to war) lib bdg $27; pa $7.95

Grades: 4 5 6   **940.54**
1. World War, 1939-1945 -- Campaigns -- France
ISBN 978-0-531-25527-8 lib bdg; 0-531-25527-1 lib
bdg; 978-0-531-25452-3 pa; 0-531-25452-6 pa
LC 2009016544

The author has "done a remarkable job of discussing and
describing [the World War II D-Day invasion] in a limited
number of pages. . . . The [book provides a] solid [introduc-
tion], followed by three chapters, one of which is based on
the personal experiences of a named soldier, and the other
two covering broader historical details and strategies of the
battle. . . . Excellent maps and plenty of paintings and vintage photos enhance the [text]." SLJ

Includes bibliographical references

Moore, Kate
★ The **Battle** of Britain. Osprey 2010 200p il
map $29.95

Grades: 7 8 9 10   **940.54**
1. Britain, Battle of, 1940 2. World War, 1939-1945
-- Great Britain
ISBN 978-1-84603-474-9; 1-84603-474-4

"In the summer and autumn of 1940, Britain faced an
unparalleled challenge. Forced to beat a quick retreat from
Dunkirk with the German Luftwaffe in hot pursuit, the British dug in for what was to be one of the most remarkable
feats in the history of human endurance. In this spectacular
oversize volume, Moore recounts with notable lucidity and
depth the events and characters from both the British and
German home fronts during this critical moment in world
history and offers an excellent analysis of prewar preparations by both sides. The most outstanding feature of the
work is without a doubt the stunning visuals. The book is
packed with a fantastic range of archival photos, maps, and
war posters." SLJ

Nathan, Amy
Yankee doodle gals; women pilots of World War
II. foreword by Eileen Collins. National Geographic
Soc. 2001 86p il maps $21

Grades: 6 7 8 9   **940.54**
1. Women air pilots 2. World War, 1939-1945 -- Aerial
operations
ISBN 0-7922-8216-7
LC 2001-560

This describes the Women's Air Force Service Pilots of
World War II

"There's plenty of action to involve readers, and the
women's perseverance in the face of obstacles is inspiring.
Wonderful black-and-white photos extend the text." Booklist
Includes bibliographical references

Nelson, Pete
Left for dead; a young man's search for justice
for the USS Indianapolis. [by] Peter Nelson; with a
preface by Hunter Scott. Delacorte Press 2002 xx,
201p il hardcover o.p. pa $8.95

Grades: 7 8 9 10   **940.54**
1. Children 2. Students 3. Naval officers 4.
Indianapolis (Cruiser) 5. World War, 1939-1945 --

Naval operations
ISBN 0-385-72959-6; 0-385-73091-8 pa
LC 2001-53774

Recalls the sinking of the U.S.S. Indianapolis at the end
of World War II, the navy cover-up and unfair court martial
of the ship's captain, and how a young boy helped the survivors set the record straight fifty-five years later.

"Written in simple chronological order, it tells a powerful story." Book Rep
Includes bibliographical references

Ross, Stewart
Hiroshima. Arcturus Pub. 2011 46p il map (A
place in history) lib bdg $34.25

Grades: 7 8 9 10   **940.54**
1. Atomic bomb 2. Hiroshima (Japan) -- Bombardment,
1945
ISBN 978-1-84837-674-8; 1-84837-674-X
LC 2010014149

This describes the city of Hiroshima and broadens "outward, describing the political and economic situations that
led up to notable events there. The approach works beautifully. Quotes from participants are a highlight of the [book],
and all the maps and photos are clear and informative. [This]
will be [a] useful [supplement] to history classes, but [is]
accessible enough to appeal as extracurricular material for
students already interested in the [topic]." SLJ

Includes glossary and bibliographical references

Pearl Harbor; [by] Stewart Ross and Joe Woodward. Arcturus Pub. 2010 46p il map (A place in
history) lib bdg $34.25

Grades: 7 8 9 10   **940.54**
1. World War, 1939-1945 2. Pearl Harbor (Oahu,
Hawaii), Attack on, 1941 3. Japan -- Foreign relations
-- United States 4. United States -- Foreign relations
-- Japan
ISBN 978-1-84837-676-2; 1-84837-676-6
LC 2010017108

This book describes Pearl Harbor and broadens "outward, describing the political and economic situations that
led up to notable events there. The approach works beautifully. Quotes from participants are a highlight of the [book],
and all the maps and photos are clear and informative. [This]
will be [a] useful [supplement] to history classes, but [is]
accessible enough to appeal as extracurricular material for
students already interested in the [topic]." SLJ

Includes glossary and bibliographical references

Samuels, Charlie
Propaganda; by Charlie Samuels. Brown Bear
Books 2011 48 p. ill. (chiefly col.), col. maps (World
War II sourcebook) (library) $35.65

Grades: 5 6 7 8   **940.54**
1. World War, 1939-1945 -- Propaganda
ISBN 1936333236; 9781936333233
LC 2011010241

This book by Charlie Samuels on propaganda is part of
the World War II Sourcebook series. "Each page is illustrated. Little-known facts and, sometimes, direct narratives are
presented with the information given to the reader. . . . Each
book has the same timeline of World War II, maps of both

the European and Pacific theaters, interesting biographical snapshots of people involved, and a list of websites that students may use to further explore World War II." (Library Media Connection)

Includes bibliographical references and index.

Soldiers; [Charlie Samuels] Brown Bear Books 2011 48 p. ill. (some col.), maps (col.) (World War II sourcebook) (library binding) $35.65

Grades: 5 6 7 8   **940.54**

1. World War, 1939-1945 2. Soldiers -- History -- 20th century

ISBN 1936333244; 9781936333240

LC 2011007057

This book by Charlie Samuels, part of the World War II Sourcebook series, "Describes the life of a soldier in World War II, from recruitment efforts around the world, to the daily life during the fighting." (Publisher's note)

Includes bibliographical references (p. 47) and index

Spying and security; by Charlie Samuels. Brown Bear Books 2012 48 p. ill. (some col.) (World War II Sourcebook) (library binding) $35.65

Grades: 5 6 7 8   **940.54**

1. Police -- History -- 20th century 2. World War, 1939-1945 -- Secret service 3. Spies -- History -- 20th century 4. Espionage -- History -- 20th century 5. World War, 1939-1945 -- Cryptography

ISBN 1936333252; 9781936333257

LC 2011007058

This book by Charlie Samuels, part of the World War II Sourcebook, provides a history of spying and security for young readers. It "Describes the role spies and police played around the world during World War II, from controlling riots to gathering intelligence from the enemy." (Publisher's note)

Seiple, Samantha

Ghosts in the fog; the untold story of Alaska's WWII invasion. Scholastic 2011 221p il map $16.99

Grades: 5 6 7 8   **940.54**

1. Alaska 2. World War, 1939-1945 -- Campaigns 3. Japan. -- Kaigun -- History -- World War, 1939-1945

ISBN 978-0-545-29654-0; 0-545-29654-4

LC 2011027821

"A little-known story from World War II shows the unique role played by a small group of military personal and native civilians in a remote region of the county. The role of Alaska in World War II following the attack on Pearl Harbor is not often told. . . . The story illuminates the cultural differences between the American and Japanese cultures at that time as well as the reluctance of the U.S. government to treat the native Alaskans as full citizens. The narrative is full of details, and . . . the text is supported by many photographs of those involved. Maps, including a strategic military map, increase the level of specificity." Kirkus

Includes bibliographical references

Sheinkin, Steve

★ The **Port** Chicago 50; disaster, mutiny, and the fight for civil rights. Steve Sheinkin. Roaring Brook Press 2014 208 p. illustrations (hardcover : alk. paper) $19.99

Grades: 5 6 7 8 9   **940.54**

1. United States. Navy 2. African American sailors 3. African Americans -- Civil rights 4. World War, 1939-1945 5. Port Chicago Mutiny, Port Chicago, Calif., 1944

ISBN 1596437960; 9781596437968

LC 2013013452

National Book Award Shortlist: Young People's Literature (2014)

YALSA Award for Excellence in Nonfiction for Young Adults: Finalist (2015)

Boston Globe-Horn Book Award: Nonfiction (2014)

Author Steve Sheinkin tells how "on July 17, 1944, a massive explosion rocked the segregated Navy base at Port Chicago, California. On August 9th, 244 men refused to go back to work until unsafe and unfair conditions at the docks were addressed. Fifty were charged with mutiny." (Publisher's note)

"An unusual entry point for the study of WWII and the nascent civil rights movement. Photographs are helpful, and documentation is thorough." (Horn Book)

Includes bibliographical references and index

Stone, Tanya Lee

★ **Courage** has no color, the true story of the Triple Nickles; America's first black paratroopers. Tanya Lee Stone. Candlewick Press 2013 160 p. $24.99

Grades: 5 6 7 8   **940.54**

1. Parachute troops 2. United States. Army 3. World War, 1939-1945 4. African American soldiers

ISBN 0763651176; 9780763651176

LC 2012942315

YALSA Award for Excellence in Nonfiction for Young Adults: Finalist (2014)

Orbis Pictus Awards Honor Book (2014)

This book tells the "untold story of the 555th Parachute Infantry Battalion, America's first black paratroopers." Enlisted black men "faced the tyranny of racial discrimination on the homefront. . . . When 1st Sgt. Walter Morris, whose men served as guards at The Parachute School at Fort Benning, saw white soldiers training to be paratroopers, he knew his men would have to train and act like them to be treated like soldiers." (Kirkus Reviews)

Torres, John Albert

The **Battle** of Midway; by John A. Torres. Mitchell Lane Publishers 2011 48p il map (Technologies and strategies in battle) lib bdg $29.95

Grades: 6 7 8 9   **940.54**

1. Midway, Battle of, 1942 2. World War, 1939-1945 -- Campaigns

ISBN 978-1-61228-078-3; 1-61228-078-1

LC 2011002746

This "is an in-depth account of the 1942 Battle of Midway, detailing how it was fought by sea and air by the U.S. and Japan. . . . This useful research source packs a wealth of information into its straightforward narrative. This colorful layout intersperses abundant visuals, including maps and archival photos as well as sidebars." Booklist

Includes glossary and bibliographical references

Townsend, John

World War II. Arcturus Pub. 2011 46p il (Secret history) lib bdg $32.80

Grades: 7 8 9 10   **940.54**

1. World War, 1939-1945

ISBN 978-1-84837-701-1; 1-84837-701-0

LC 2010012017

This book explores the secrets of World War II. Throughout the war, both sides made great efforts to uncover enemy plans and keep their own secrets hidden. They engaged in secret operations, plots, and missions, always attempting to wrongfoot the enemy or take them by surprise.

"The title of the Secret History series will grab readers, even reluctant ones, and they won't be disappointed by the intriguing info regarding codes and code breakers, spies, terrorists, and double agents, with profiles of heroes and traitors on all sides. . . . The readable design, with clear type on thick, high-quality paper, includes lots of sidebars, photos, screens, and quotes." Booklist

Includes bibliographical references

Williams, Brian

The Normandy beaches. Arcturus Pub. 2011 46p il map (A place in history) lib bdg $34.25

Grades: 7 8 9 10   **940.54**

1. Normandy (France), Attack on, 1944 2. World War, 1939-1945 -- Campaigns -- France

ISBN 978-1-84837-675-5; 1-84837-675-8

LC 2010014194

This book begins with describing the Normandy beaches and broadens "outward, describing the political and economic situations that led up to notable events there. The approach works beautifully. Quotes from participants are a highlight of the [book], and all the maps and photos are clear and informative. [This] will be [a] useful [supplement] to history classes, but [is] accessible enough to appeal as extracurricular material for students already interested in the [topic]." SLJ

Includes glossary and bibliographical references

Wukovits, John F., 1944-

The bombing of Pearl Harbor; by John F. Wukovits. Lucent Books 2011 112 p. ill. (some col.), photographs (World history) (library) $34.95

Grades: 6 7 8 9   **940.54**

1. World War, 1939-1945 -- Causes 2. Pearl Harbor (Oahu, Hawaii), Attack on, 1941

ISBN 1420503308; 9781420503302

LC 2010035993

This book by John Wukovits is part of the World History series and looks at the bombing of Pearl Harbor. Each book in the series offers an "overview of an important historical event or period. The series is designed both to acquaint readers with the basics of history and to make them aware that their lives and their own historical era are an intimate part of the ongoing human saga." (Publisher's note)

Includes bibliographical references (p. 97-100) and index.

Zaloga, Steven J.

The most daring raid of World War II; D-Day--Pointe-du-Hoc. Rosen Pub. 2011 64p il map (The most daring raids in history) lib bdg $29.25

Grades: 7 8 9 10   **940.54**

1. Normandy (France), Attack on, 1944 2. World War, 1939-1945 -- Campaigns -- France 3. United States -- Army -- Ranger Battalion, 2nd

ISBN 978-1-4488-1867-9; 1-4488-1867-2

LC 2010030631

This describes the U.S. Army Rangers' attack on the German gun battery on Pointe-du-Hoc in Normandy on D-day in 1944.

This book is "packed with facts, covering the details of the action, the people involved, and the tools used, in engaging prose. The authors cite their sources thoroughly. . . . Diagrams, photos, . . . and maps make the action easy to follow and provide visual context for the raids. . . . This . . . is sure to find a large readership." SLJ

Includes glossary and bibliographical references

941   British Isles

Dillon, Patrick

The story of Britain from the Norman Conquest to the European Union; illustrated by P.J. Lynch. Candlewick Press 2011 341p il map $21.99

Grades: 5 6 7 8   **941**

1. Great Britain -- History

ISBN 978-0-7636-5122-0; 0-7636-5122-2

LC 2010038883

"This well-written, thoughtfully illustrated volume [is] an indispensible tool for European history buffs." Horn Book Guide

Indovino, Shaina C.

United Kingdom; by Rae Simons and Shaina C. Indovino. Mason Crest Publishers 2012 64 p. col. ill., col. maps (library) $22.95

Grades: 5 6 7 8   **941**

1. Great Britain 2. Northern Ireland 3. European Union -- Great Britain 4. European Union -- Northern Ireland

ISBN 1422222616; 9781422222614; 9781422222928

LC 2010051852

This book on the United Kingdom by Rae Simons and Shaina Carmel Indovino "covers Modern Issues, History and Government, The Economy, People and Culture, and Looking to the Future. . . Identical information on "The Formation of the European Union" appears in every book" in the series. (Library Media Connection) Also covered are "issues like immigration and the global financial crisis". (Publisher's note)

Includes bibliographical references (p. 60) and index.

941.081   British Isles--Reign of Victoria, 1837-1901

Schomp, Virginia

   Victoria and her court. Marshall Cavendish Benchmark 2010 80p il (Life in Victorian England) lib bdg $34.21

Grades: 6 7 8 9   **941.081**

   1. Queens 2. Courts and courtiers 3. Great Britain -- History -- 19th century

   ISBN 978-1-60870-028-8 lib bdg; 1-60870-028-3 lib bdg

   A social history of Victorian England, focusing on the upper echelons of society during the reign of Queen Victoria (1837-1901)

   This "is clearly written, thorough, and informative. The visually rich layout includes photographs and paintings from the time period, full-page illustrations, and attention-grabbing sidebars. Most appealing are the primary source quotations, which are plentiful and relevant.." Libr Media Connect

   Includes glossary and bibliographical references

941.1   Scotland

Waldron, Melanie

   Scotland; by Melanie Waldron. Heinemann Library 2012 48 p. col. ill., col. maps (Countries around the world) (library) $32.65; (paperback) $8.99

Grades: 6 7 8 9   **941.1**

   1. Scotland

   ISBN 1432952161; 9781432952167; 9781432952419

                 LC 2010044776

   This book by Melanie Waldron is part of the Countries Around the World series and looks at Scotland. This entry "offers complete coverage of this . . . country, including sections on history, geography, wildlife, infrastructure and government, and culture. It also includes a detailed fact file, maps and charts, and a traceable flag." (Publisher's note)

   Includes bibliographical references (p. 44) and index.

941.5   Ireland

McQuinn, Colm

   ★ **Ireland**; [by] Anna and Colm McQuinn; Elizabeth Malcolm and John McDonagh, consultants. National Geographic 2008 64p il map (Countries of the world) lib bdg $27.90

Grades: 4 5 6 7   **941.5**

   1. Ireland

   ISBN 978-1-4263-0299-2 lib bdg; 1-4263-0299-1 lib bdg

   This describes the geography, nature, history, people and culture, government, and economy of Ireland.

   "This book provides basic information for elementary school research assignments. The photographs (especially those of the countryside) and maps are nicely reproduced and are larger and clearer than in most reference books. The text is succinct but gives an adequate overview of major

historical events, economic trends, geography, ecology, and other topics." Horn Book

   Includes glossary and bibliographical references

941.508   Ireland 1800-1899

Bartoletti, Susan Campbell

   ★ **Black** potatoes; the story of the great Irish famine, 1845-1850. Houghton Mifflin 2001 184p il hardcover o.p. pa $9.95

Grades: 7 8 9 10   **941.508**

   1. Famines 2. Ireland -- History -- Famine, 1845-1852

   ISBN 0-618-00271-5; 0-618-54883-1 pa

                 LC 2001-24156

   Bartoletti discusses "the potato blight, its . . . causes, and the societal attitudes and political legacies that exacerbated the famine. {Chronology. Annotated bibliography. Index.} Grades five to ten." (Bull Cent Child Books)

   "The bibliography (also narrative) provides some of the most fascinating historical reading in the book. Overall, a useful addition to collections, for both personal and research uses." SLJ

   Includes bibliographical references

Fradin, Dennis Brindell

   The **Irish** potato famine; by Dennis Fradin. Marshall Cavendish Benchmark 2012 32 p. (Great escapes) (library) $34.21

Grades: 5 6 7 8   **941.508**

   1. Famines 2. Ireland -- History -- Famine, 1845-1852 3. Ireland -- History -- Famine, 1845-1852 4. Escapes -- Ireland -- History -- 19th century 5. Irish -- Migrations -- History -- 19th century 6. Disaster victims -- Ireland -- History -- 19th century 7. Ireland -- Emigration and immigration -- History -- 19th century

   ISBN 1608704734; 9781608704736

                 LC 2010018788

   This book, part of the Great Escapes series, focuses on the Irish Potato Famine. "Each book begins with an introduction to an individual who escaped, followed by the history of the precipitating events, the escape itself, and a follow-up on what happened after the escape. Each title includes a timeline, notes, and additional information on the topic." (Library Media Connection)

   Includes bibliographical references and index.

941.7   Republic of Ireland

Blashfield, Jean F.

   Ireland; Enchantment of the World. by Jean F. Blashfield. Children's Press ; an imprint of Scholastic Inc. 2014 144 p. (Enchantment of the world--second series) (library binding) $40

Grades: 5 6 7 8   **941.7**

   1. Ireland

   ISBN 0531236765; 9780531236765

                 LC 2013002015

   This book, by Jean F. Blashfield, focuses on Ireland. The book focuses on "country's culture, history, and geography are explored in detail. . . . Sidebars highlight especially interesting people, places, and events. . . . Recipes give readers the opportunity to experience foreign cuisine." (Publisher's note)

"Many students turn to the Internet for writing reports, but for reliably accurate, attractively presented and well-calibrated information, the long-standing Enchantment of the World series remains a superior choice. Each volume has been completely rewritten from a previous edition—in many cases to startling effect given recent political events. Although the basic structure holds true to past versions, the updated photographs are truly eye-popping and take care to portray the countries as modern often opting for showing, say, a surgeon at work rather than a rural farmer. It might not be necessary for libraries to replace Ireland, since it hasn't changed radically, but this is a solid offering with updated statistics. Each volume in this reliable series includes extensive back matter with a detailed index." Booklist.

Includes bibliographical references and index

942 England and Wales

Banting, Erinn

England; by Erinn Banting ; edited by Sarah Cairns ; illustrated by Jeff Crosby, Dianne Eastman, and David Wysotski. Revised ed. Crabtree Pub. Co. 2012 32 p. ill. (some col.) (Lands, peoples, and cultures) (library) $26.60; (paperback) $8.95; (ebook) $26.60

Grades: 4 5 6   **942**
   1. England -- Civilization 2. England -- Social life and customs
   ISBN 0778798283; 9780778798286; 9780778798316; 9781427180056 pdf

LC 2012013776

This book by Erinn Banting is part of the Lands, Peoples and Cultural Series and looks at the culture of England. The books offer information about "folktales, sports, and history." Also included are "a table of contents, short glossary (words highlighted in test) and index." (Catholic Library World)

Includes index

Blashfield, Jean F.

England; by Jean F. Blashfield. Children's Press 2013 144 p. ill. (some col.), col. maps (Enchantment of the world) (library) $40.00

Grades: 4 5 6 7   **942**
   1. England
   ISBN 9780531275429

LC 2012000503

This book by Jean F. Blashfield, part of the "Enchantment of the World" series, "describes the geography, history, economy, language, religions, culture, people, plants, and animals of England." (Publisher's note) It includes "topics as recent as the 2012 Olympics and 2012 Grammy winners, as well as the latest royal wedding." (Children's Literature)

Includes bibliographical references (p. 134-135) and index.

942.02 England--Norman period, 1066-1154

Hamilton, Janice

The **Norman** conquest of England; by Janice Hamilton. Twenty-First Century Books 2008 un il map (Pivotal moments in history) lib bdg $38.60

Grades: 7 8 9 10   **942.02**
   1. Normans 2. Kings 3. Great Britain -- History -- 1066-1154, Norman period
   ISBN 978-0-8225-5902-3

LC 2006102629

This is an account of the invasion and conquest of England by the Normans in 1066 and its consequences.

This is "clearly written and interesting enough for browsers as well as report writers. Maps, full-color and black-and-white photos, and reproductions of manuscripts contribute to the attractive format and make the subject matter come alive." SLJ

Includes glossary and bibliographical references

942.03 England--Period of House of Plantagenet, 1154-1399

Brooks, Polly Schoyer

Queen Eleanor, Independent Spirit of the Medieval World; A Biography of Eleanor of Aquitaine. 1st ed. Houghton Mifflin 1999 vii, 183 p.p ill. (paperback) $8.95

Grades: 7 8 9   **942.03**
   1. Queens
   ISBN 0395981395; 9780395981399

LC 82048776

This is a biography of Eleanor of Aquitaine, the twelfth-century queen, first of France, then of England, who was the wife of Henry II and mother of several notable sons, including Richard the Lionhearted. "Born in 1122, Eleanor refused to be confined by the traditional gender roles of her time. She became well educated, gaining political and governing know-how from her father, William X, duke of Aquitaine." (Publisher's note)

Includes bibliography (p. 171-172) and index.

Levy, Debbie

The **signing** of the Magna Carta. Twenty-First Century Books 2008 160p il map (Pivotal moments in history) lib bdg $38.60

Grades: 7 8 9 10 11 12   **942.03**
   1. Magna Carta 2. Great Britain -- History -- 1154-1399, Plantagenets
   ISBN 978-0-8225-5917-7 lib bdg; 0-8225-5917-X lib bdg

LC 2005-20971

This "research source explains the intent of the treaty of 1215 that became the Magna Carta, the factors that produced it, as well as its evolution, historical significance, and relevance today. . . . The clear explanation of the 'Great Charter's' historical context accompanied by informative inserts and beautiful, relevant illustrations make this a book to dip into as well as to read through." Voice Youth Advocates

Includes glossary and bibliographical references

942.05 England--Period of House of Tudor, 1485-1603

Aronson, Marc

★ **Sir** Walter Ralegh and the quest for El Dorado. Clarion Bks. 2000 222p il map $20

Grades: 7 8 9 10   **942.05**

1. Poets 2. Authors 3. Explorers 4. Historians 5. Courtiers 6. Travel writers

ISBN 0-395-84827-X

LC 99-43096

"Incorporating critical examinations of period art and poetry as well as standard historical documentary evidence and pausing frequently to review and explicitly support its thesis, this title is at once lively, accessible, and challenging. Period illustrations, an index, and fastidiously annotated endnotes and bibliography are included." Bull Cent Child Books

Includes bibliographical references

Hollihan, Kerrie Logan

Elizabeth I--the people's queen; her life and times: 21 activities. Chicago Review Press 2011 129p il (For kids) pa $16.95

Grades: 4 5 6 7 8   **942.05**

1. Queens 2. Great Britain -- History -- 1485-1603, Tudors

ISBN 978-1-56976-349-0; 1-56976-349-6

LC 2010047647

This is an interactive biography of Queen Elizabeth I.

"The writing is clear and suited to readers with no previous knowledge of the topic. The activities vary in difficulty, from reading The Faerie Queen, to creating a family coat of arms, to growing a knot garden. The book is well illustrated with black-and-white reproductions of portraits, engravings, and paintings depicting major events in the Tudors' lives. . . . This well-organized book succeeds at being interesting and scholarly at the same time." SLJ

Includes bibliographical references

Kallen, Stuart A.

★ **Elizabethan** England; by Stuart A. Kallen. ReferencePoint Press 2013 96 p. (Understanding world history series) (hardcover) $27.95

Grades: 7 8 9 10   **942.05**

1. Great Britain -- History -- 1558-1603, Elizabeth 2. England -- Civilization -- 16th century 3. England -- Social conditions -- 16th century 4. Great Britain -- History -- Elizabeth, 1558-1603

ISBN 1601524846; 9781601524843

LC 2012026174

This book, part of the Understanding World History series, looks at Elizabethan England. It "relates Queen Elizabeth I's advance to power and considers the hardships of life in London, the rise of the arts during the Renaissance, and Elizabeth's role as 'pirate queen,' endorsing privateering, slave trading, and the defeat of the Spanish Armanda." (Booklist)

Includes bibliographical references and index

942.9 Wales

Hestler, Anna

Wales; [by] Anna Hestler and Jo-Ann Spilling. 2nd ed.; Marshall Cavendish Benchmark 2011 144p il map (Cultures of the world) lib bdg $42.79

Grades: 5 6 7 8   **942.9**

1. Wales

ISBN 978-1-6087-0457-6; 1-6087-0457-2

LC 2010030339

First published 2001

Provides information on the geography, history, wildlife, governmental structure, economy, cultural diversity, peoples, religion, and culture of Wales.

"Plentiful color photographs accompany substantial amounts of information." Booklist

Includes glossary and bibliographical references

943 Germany and neighboring central European countries

Burgan, Michael

The **Berlin** airlift; by Michael Burgan. Compass Point Books 2007 48 p. ill. (some col.) (We the people) (paperback) $7.95; (library) $27.99

Grades: 4 5 6 7   **943**

1. Berlin (Germany) -- History -- Blockade, 1948-1949

ISBN 9780756520366; 0756520363; 075652024X; 9780756520243

LC 2006006766

Examines the joint effort of the United States and Great Britain who flew in around the clock to deliver supplies to Berlin during the Soviet blockade of 1948-49.

"The writing is clear and concise and the vocabulary is age-appropriate. [This] title contains excellent contemporary photographs." SLJ

Includes bibliographical references (p. 46-47) and index.

Indovino, Shaina C.

Germany; by Ida Walker and Shaina C. Indovino. Mason Crest Publishers 2013 64 p. ill. (some col.), col. maps (Major European nations) (library) $22.95

Grades: 5 6 7 8   **943**

1. Germany 2. Germany -- Politics and government 3. Germany -- History 4. European Union -- Germany 5. German -- Description and travel 6. Germany -- Social life and customs

ISBN 1422222438; 9781422222430

LC 2010051291

This book on Germany by Ida Walker and Shaina Carmel Indovino is part of the "Major European Nations" series, which "stresses the modern relationships, goals, and problems of the European Union. . . . Chapters begin with 'Modern Issues' and a brief summary of the country's history and government, followed by chapters on economy, people and culture, and 'Looking to the Future.' In addition, there is a time line and a few suggestions for finding out more." (School Library Journal)

Nardo, Don

Hitler in Paris; how a photograph shocked a world at war. by Don Nardo. Compass Point Books 2014 64 p. (library binding) $33.99

Grades: 6 7 8 9   **943**

1. World War, 1939-1945 -- France -- Paris 2. France -- History -- 1940-1945, German occupation 3. Photographs -- Political aspects

ISBN 0756547334; 9780756547332; 9780756547899

LC 2013030415

This book, by Don Nardo, focuses on a photograph of dictator Adolf Hitler in Paris, France during World War II. "Only days before, on June 14, 1940, German soldiers had overrun the city, shocking the world. . . . He posed for a photo in front of the Eiffel Tower, the beloved symbol of France and the country's free, democratic people. The photo, taken by his personal photographer, Heinrich Hoffmann, would show the world that Nazi Germany had triumphed over its bitter enemy." (Publisher's note)

"Analyzing visual images and setting them in a larger historical and cultural context is an important skill. This volume uses Heinrich Hoffmann's 1940 photograph of Hitler in front of the Eiffel Tower to discuss the dictator's rise to power and Hoffmann's image-crafting of his subject. A spacious page design, which includes plenty of photos, enhances the presentation. Reading list, timeline. Bib., glos., ind." Horn Book

Includes bibliographical references (page 63) and index

Other titles in the series include:

Assassination and its Aftermath (2014)

The Blue Marble (2014)

Breaker Boys (2012)

Civil War Witness (2014)

Little Rock Girl 1957 (2012)

Man on the Moon (2011)

Migrant Mother (2011)

Raising the Flag (2011)

Summiting Everest (2014)

Tank Man (2014)

Rooney, Anne

The **Berlin** Wall. Arcturus Pub. 2011 46p il (A place in history) lib bdg $34.25

Grades: 7 8 9 10   **943**

1. Cold war 2. Berlin Wall (1961-1989) 3. Germany -- History -- 1945-1990

ISBN 978-1-84837-673-1; 1-84837-673-1

LC 2010014193

This book begins with The Berlin Wall as a landmark and broadens "outward, describing the political and economic situations that led up to notable events there. The approach works beautifully. Quotes from participants are a highlight of the [book], and all the maps and photos are clear and informative. [This] will be [a] useful [supplement] to history classes, but [is] accessible enough to appeal as extracurricular material for students already interested in the [topic]." SLJ

Includes glossary and bibliographical references

Russell, Henry

★ **Germany**; [by] Henry Russell; Benedict Kork and Antje Schlottmann, consultants. National Geographic 2007 64p il map (Countries of the world) lib bdg $27.90

Grades: 4 5 6 7   **943**

1. Germany

ISBN 978-1-4263-0059-2

LC 2007024677

Describes the geography, nature, history, people and culture, government and economy of Germany.

This "appealing [title has] wonderful photographs and maps. . . . The [book offers] reliable sources for country research, and the interesting and current material holds browsing potential as well." SLJ

Includes glossary and bibliographical references

943.085   Period of Weimar Republic, 1918-1933

Freeman, Charles

Why did the rise of the Nazis happen? Gareth Stevens Pub. 2011 48p il map (Moments in history) lib bdg $31.75; pa $14.05

Grades: 6 7 8 9   **943.085**

1. Heads of state 2. National socialism 3. Nazi leaders 4. Germany -- Politics and government -- 1918-1933

ISBN 978-1-4339-4175-7 lib bdg; 1-4339-4175-9 lib bdg; 978-1-4339-4176-4 pa; 1-4339-4176-7 pa

LC 2010017229

"Examines the events that served as . . . [precursors to the rise of the Nazis]. . . . Brightly colored pullout boxes highlight important turning points, the perspective of the everyday man, and further information on why specific events occurred. Numerous photographs help readers visualize concepts more fully. . . . Students should be able to easily use this resource." Libr Media Connect

Includes glossary and bibliographical references

943.086   Germany--Period of Third Reich, 1933-1945

Bartoletti, Susan Campbell

★ **Hitler** Youth; growing up in Hitler's shadow. Scholastic Nonfiction 2005 176p il map $19.95

Grades: 7 8 9 10   **943.086**

1. National socialism 2. Holocaust, 1933-1945 3. Germany -- History -- 1933-1945

ISBN 0-439-35379-3

LC 2004-51040

A Newbery Medal honor book, 2006

"Bartoletti draws on oral histories, diaries, letters, and her own extensive interviews with Holocaust survivors, Hitler Youth, resisters, and bystanders to tell the history from the viewpoints of people who were there. . . . The stirring photos tell more of the story. . . . The extensive back matter is a part of the gripping narrative." Booklist

Includes bibliographical references

Living in Nazi Germany; Elaine Halleck, book editor. Greenhaven Press 2004 158p il map (Exploring cultural history) $29.95; pa $21.20

Grades: 7 8 9 10 **943.086**

1. National socialism 2. Germany -- Politics and government -- 1933-1945

ISBN 0-7377-1731-9; 0-7377-1732-7 pa

LC 2003-57961

This includes "eyewitness accounts from victims of Hitler's brutality as well as from those who found places in the Nazi machine. . . . Most of the accounts are from less well known sources, and many are compelling. Excerpts from a few familiar volumes, such as Albert Speer's memoirs and the wartime diaries of Joseph Goebbels, also appear. . . . An effective, insightful look at aspects of the Nazi system." Booklist

Includes bibliographical references

Shuter, Jane

Resistance to the Nazis. Heinemann Lib. 2003 56p il map (Holocaust) lib bdg $28.50; pa $8.95

Grades: 7 8 9 10 **943.086**

1. Holocaust, 1933-1945 2. Germany -- History -- 1933-1945 3. World War, 1939-1945 -- Underground movements

ISBN 1-4034-0814-9 lib bdg; 1-4034-3206-6 pa

LC 2002-6853

This is "an excellent blend of overview and personal stories." SLJ

"Describes how certain people, both Jews and Gentiles, were brave enough to stand up to the Nazis during the Holocaust despite the price they would pay if caught." Publisher's Note

Includes glossary and bibliographical references

943.6 Austria and Liechtenstein

Indovino, Shaina C.

Austria; by Jeanine Sanna and Shaina C. Indovino. Mason Crest Publishers 2012 64 p. col. ill., col. maps (library) $22.95

Grades: 5 6 7 8 **943.6**

1. Austria -- History 2. European Union -- Austria

ISBN 1422222322; 9781422222324

LC 2010051075

This book, part of the Major European Union Nations series, focuses on Austria. In "addition to history, the book details government, economy, culture, and prospects for the future. There is a glossary and an index and a nice chronology in the back of the book as well as a brief bibliography and a list of photo credits." (Children's Literature)

Includes bibliographical references (p. 57) and index.

943.7 Czech Republic and Slovakia

Sioras, Efstathia

Czech Republic; [by] Efstathia Sioras and Michael Spilling. Marshall Cavendish Benchmark 2010 144p il map (Cultures of the world) lib bdg $42.79

Grades: 5 6 7 8 **943.7**

1. Czech Republic

ISBN 978-0-7614-4476-3 lib bdg; 0-7614-4476-9 lib bdg

LC 2009003185

This describes the geography, history, wildlife, governmental structure, economy, cultural diversity, peoples, religion, and culture of the Czech Republic

Includes glossary and bibliographical references

943.710 Czech Republic -- Period of Republic, 1993-

Docalavich, Heather

Czech Republic; by Heather Docalavich and Shaina C. Indovino. Mason Crest Publishers 2013 64 p. col. ill, col. maps (library) $22.95; (ebook) $28.95

Grades: 5 6 7 8 **943.710**

1. Czech Republic 2. European Union -- Czech Republic

ISBN 1422222373; 9781422222379; 9781422222683; 9781422292648

LC 2010051083

This book by Heather Docalavich is part of the Major European Union Nations series and focuses on the Czech Republic. "The Czech Republic is one of the newest countries in the world. It's also new to the EU—it joined in 2004. People have lived in what we now call the Czech Republic for thousands of years, however. This land has a long history and is moving forward while dealing with challenges like the recent global recession." (Publisher's note)

Includes bibliographical references (p. 57-58, 63) and index.

943.8 Poland

Deckker, Zilah

★ **Poland**; [by] Zilah Deckker; Richard Butterwick and Iwona Sagan, consultants. National Geographic 2008 64p il map (Countries of the world) lib bdg $27.90

Grades: 4 5 6 7 **943.8**

1. Poland

ISBN 978-1-4263-0201-5

LC 2007047823

This describes the geography, nature, history, people and culture, government, and economy of Poland.

Includes glossary and bibliographical references

Docalavich, Heather

Poland; by Healther Docalavich and Shaina C. Indovino. Mason Crest Publishers 2013 64 p. col. ill., col. maps (library) $22.95

Grades: 5 6 7 8 **943.8**

1. Poland 2. European Union -- Poland

ISBN 1422222543; 9781422222546

LC 2010051465

This book by Heather Docalavich and Shaina C. Indovino is part of the Major European Union Nations series and looks at Poland. "It joined the EU in 2004 . . . . For long time, Poland has been home to scientific thinkers, artists, and musicians. Today, it is one of the countries that have weathered the global recession the best, proving this nation's strength." (Publisher's note)

Includes bibliographical references and index

Kadziolka, Jan

Poland; [by] Jan Kadziolka, Tadeusz Wojciechowski. Oliver Press 2011 48p il map (Looking at Europe) lib bdg $24.95

Grades: 7 8 9 10   **943.8**

1. Poland

ISBN 978-1-881508-89-2; 1-881508-89-7

LC 2009035350

This describes Poland today, its history, cities, transportation, culture, education, economy, cuisine, tourism, and natural environment.

This will "best suit students with good vocabularies and some knowledge of European history. . . . [It is] clearly written and well organized. . . . [It includes] many clear photos as well as colorful sidebars. . . . Attractive, informative." Booklist

Includes glossary and bibliographical references

Mara, Wil

Poland; by Wil Mara. Children's Press, an imprint of Scholastic Inc. 2014 144 p. illustrations and maps (library binding) $40

Grades: 5 6 7 8   **943.8**

1. Poland

ISBN 0531220168; 9780531220160

LC 2013026061

This book, by Wil Mara, focuses on Poland. The book discusses the "country's culture, history, and geography are explored in detail, allowing readers a chance to see how people live. . . . Sidebars highlight especially interesting people, places, and events . . . [and] easy recipes give readers the opportunity to experience foreign cuisine first-hand." (Publisher's note)

Includes bibliographical references and index

943.9 Hungary

Lang, Stephan

Hungary. Oliver Press 2011 48p il map (Looking at Europe) lib bdg $24.95

Grades: 7 8 9 10   **943.9**

1. Hungary

ISBN 978-1-881508-88-5; 1-881508-88-9

LC 2009033276

This describes Hungary today, its history, cities, transportation, culture, education, economy, cuisine, tourism, and natural environment.

This will "best suit students with good vocabularies and some knowledge of European history. . . . [It is] clearly written and well organized. . . . [It includes] many

clear photos as well as colorful sidebars. . . . Attractive, informative." Booklist

Includes glossary and bibliographical references

944   France and Monaco

Indovino, Shaina C.

France; by Jeanine Sanna and Shaina C. Indovino. Mason Crest Publishers 2013 64 p. col. ill., col. maps (hardcover) $22.95

Grades: 5 6 7 8   **944**

1. France

ISBN 142222242X; 9781422222423

LC 2010051290

This book by Liz Sonneborn is part of the Enchantment of the World series and looks at France. It covers "history, government, geography, natural resources, economics, the arts, and culture. . . . Maps, charts, sidebars highlighting items of interest, a time line, and a 'Fast Facts' section add to the presentation." (School Library Journal)

Includes bibliographical references (p. 59) and index.

King, David C.

★ Monaco; [by] David C. King. Marshall Cavendish Benchmark 2008 144p il map (Cultures of the world) lib bdg $42.79

Grades: 5 6 7 8   **944**

1. Monaco

ISBN 978-0-7614-2567-0

LC 2006030238

This describes the geography, history, government, economy, environment, people, and culture of Monaco

Includes glossary and bibliographical references

Sonneborn, Liz

France; by Liz Sonneborn. Children's Press 2013 144 p. ill., maps (library) $40

Grades: 5 6 7 8   **944**

1. France

ISBN 0531256006; 9780531256008

LC 2012047113

"Sonneborn updates Don Nardo's 2007 edition. She follows the same outline and covers similar material-history, government, geography, natural resources, economics, the arts, and culture. . . . Maps, charts, sidebars highlighting items of interest, a time line, and a "Fast Facts" section add to the presentation. The book is physically attractive and simple to use, and has far-ranging appeal; it's ideal for middle-grade reports but will inform teens and adults who want to learn the basics in a format that's easily read and understood." SLJ

Includes bibliographical references (page 134) and index

944.04   France since 1789

Riggs, Kate

The French Revolution. Creative Education 2009 48p il map (Days of change) lib bdg $32.80

Grades: 5 6 7 8   **944.04**
1. France -- History -- 1789-1799, Revolution
ISBN 978-1-58341-734-8 lib bdg; 1-58341-734-6
lib bdg

              LC 2008009728

"With elegant design and mature prose, the Days of Change series is an ideal starting point for all manner of school projects. . . . The political pressures at the center of The French Revolution are difficult to dramatize, but Riggs carefully lays out the factions and civil disobedience that led to the Declaration of the Rights of Man and of The Citizen—and then the emperor's reign that overthrew everything." Booklist

Includes bibliographical references

945   Italy, San Marino, Vatican City, Malta

Blashfield, Jean F.
     Italy; by Jean F. Blashfield. Children's Press, an imprint of Scholastic Inc. 2014 144 p. (library binding) \$40
Grades: 5 6 7 8   **945**
1. Italy
ISBN 0531236773; 9780531236772

              LC 2013000087

This book, by Jean F. Blashfield, focuses on Italy. The book discusses the "country's culture, history, and geography are explored in detail, allowing readers a chance to see how people live. . . . Sidebars highlight especially interesting people, places, and events . . . [and] recipes give readers the opportunity to experience foreign cuisine firsthand." (Publisher's note)

"Many students turn to the Internet for writing reports, but for reliably accurate, attractively presented and well-calibrated information, the long-standing Enchantment of the World series remains a superior choice. Each volume has been completely rewritten from a previous edition—in many cases to startling effect given recent political events. Although the basic structure holds true to past versions, the updated photographs are truly eye-popping and take care to portray the countries as modern often opting for showing, say, a surgeon at work rather than a rural farmer. It might not be necessary for libraries to replace [this title], since it hasn't changed radically, but this is a solid offering with updated statistics. Each volume in this reliable series includes extensive back matter with a detailed index." Booklist

Includes bibliographical references and index

Indovino, Shaina C.
     Italy; by Ademola O. Sadik and Shaina C. Indovino. Mason Crest Publishers 2013 64 p. ill. (col. ill.), maps (library) \$22.95
Grades: 5 6 7 8   **945**
1. Italy 2. European Union -- Italy
ISBN 1422222489; 9781422222485

              LC 2010051333

This book by Ademola O. Sadek and Shaina C. Indovino is part of the Major European Nations series and looks at Italy. "Chapters begin with "Modern Issues" and a brief summary of the country's history and government, followed by chapters on economy, people and culture, and 'Look-

ing to the Future.'" The texts "liken Italy's treatment of the "Roma" (Gypsies) to the U.S. treatment of the American Indian; the social standing of Italy's women is examined." (School Library Journal)

945.8   Sicily and adjacent islands

Sheehan, Sean
     Malta; by Sean Sheehan and Yong Jui Lin. 2nd ed. Marshall Cavendish Benchmark 2010 144 p. col. ill. (library) \$47.07
Grades: 5 6 7 8   **945.8**
1. Malta 2. Culture 3. Malta -- Social life and customs
ISBN 1608700240; 9781608700240

              LC 2010000733

This book by Sean Sheehan is part of the Cultures of the World series and looks at Malta. The books in the series provide "broad overviews of each country's culture, geography, and history. The . . . texts discuss government, economy, people, lifestyles, religion, language, arts and leisure, festivals, and food." (School Library Journal)

Includes bibliographical references (p. 142) and index.

946   Spain, Andorra, Gibraltar, Portugal

Augustin, Byron
     Andorra; by Byron D. Augustin. Marshall Cavendish Benchmark 2009 144p il map (Cultures of the world) lib bdg \$42.79
Grades: 5 6 7 8   **946**
1. Andorra
ISBN 978-0-7614-3122-0 lib bdg; 0-7614-3122-5 lib bdg

              LC 2007040356

"Provides comprehensive information on the geography, history, governmental structure, economy, cultural diversity, peoples, religion, and culture of Andorra." Publisher's note

Includes glossary and bibliographical references

Croy, Anita
     Spain. National Geographic 2010 64p il map (Countries of the world) lib bdg \$27.90
Grades: 4 5 6 7   **946**
1. Spain
ISBN 978-1-4263-0633-4 lib bdg; 1-4263-0633-4 lib bdg

This describes the geography, nature, history, people and culture, government and economy of Spain

"The information is substantial but not overwhelming. The [text is] clear, and the discussion points are well chosen. . . . [The text is] complemented with stunning photographs." SLJ

Includes glossary and bibliographical references

Hanks, Reuel R.
     Spain; by Zoran Pavlovic and Reuel Hanks. Chelsea House 2006 104 p. col. ill., col. maps (library) \$35.00; (hardcover) \$35

Grades: 5 6 7 8 **946**
1. Spain
ISBN 9780791066973 out of print; 1617530476;
9781617530470

LC 2006002218

This book by Zoran Pavlovic is part of the Modern World Nations series and looks at Spain. "Although Spain is now part of a unified Europe, . . . it is also a land divided by a combination of its own history, ethnicity, and geography." This entry "offers readers a wealth of information about this nation, touching on a variety of topics such as Spanish geography, history, political evolution, and ethnic issues." (Publisher's note)

Includes bibliographical references (p. 96) and index.

Indovino, Shaina C.
Spain; by Rae Simons and Shaina C. Indovino. Mason Crest Publishers 2013 64 p. col. ill., col. maps (library) $22.95
Grades: 5 6 7 8 **946**
1. Spain 2. European Union -- Spain
ISBN 9781422222904; 1422222594; 9781422222591

LC 2010051847

This book by Rae Simons is part of the Major European Union Nations series and looks at Spain. "Spain has it all: beaches, modern cities, soaring architecture, mountains, and more. It has been a member of the EU since 1986. From the ancient Celts to the Moors to the Christian kings and queens, many people have influenced Spain. It has recently taken a step back in the current financial crisis, but this proud nation is slowly getting back on its feet." (Publisher's note)

946.9 Portugal

Deckker, Zilah
★ **Portugal**. National Geographic 2009 64p il map (Countries of the world) lib bdg $27.90
Grades: 4 5 6 7 **946.9**
1. Portugal
ISBN 978-1-4263-0390-6 lib bdg; 1-4263-0390-4 lib bdg

LC 2009275584

This describes the geography, nature, history, people and culture, government and economy of Portugal
Includes glossary and bibliographical references

Etingoff, Kim
Portugal; by Kim Etingoff and Shaina C. Indovino. Mason Crest Publishers 2013 64 p. col. ill. (library) $22.95
Grades: 5 6 7 8 **946.9**
1. Portugal
ISBN 1422222551; 9781422222553

LC 2010051466

This book by Kim Etingoff and Shaina C. Indovino is part of the Major European Union Nations series and looks at Portugal. "Long ago, Portugal was one of the world's most powerful countries, as it explored and conquered places far from home. Today, it is a nation that has had some economic

and social struggles, but also some triumphs. It joined the EU in 1986." (Publisher's note)

947 Russia and neighboring east European countries

Gottfried, Ted
The **road** to Communism; illustrated by Melanie Reim. 21st Cent. Bks. (Brookfield) 2002 144p il lib bdg $28.90
Grades: 8 9 10 11 12 **947**
1. Soviet Union -- History -- 1917-1921, Revolution
ISBN 0-7613-2557-3

LC 2001-52252

Chronicles the Czarist Russian Empire in the 1800s, the birth of Bolshevism, events leading to the Russian Revolution of 1917, and the development of new political structures in its aftermath

"Gottfried writes with clarity and distance even as he narrates the dramatic details of the political conflict and the emotion of the 'dream that failed.'" Booklist

Includes glossary and bibliographical references

Yomtov, Nel
Russia; by Nel Yomtov. Children's Press 2012 144 p. col. ill., col. maps (library) $40
Grades: 5 6 7 8 **947**
1. Russia 2. Russia (Federation)
ISBN 0531275450; 9780531275450

LC 2012000520

This children's book, by Nel Yomtov, describes the geography and culture of Russia as part of the "Enchantment of the World" series. The book includes "colourful photos . . . [with] views of foreign cities and landscapes," facts and statistics on "interesting people, places, and events" in Russian history, and "delicious, easy recipes [to] give readers the opportunity to experience foreign cuisine firsthand." (Publisher's note)

Includes bibliographical references and index

947.08 Russia since 1855

Fleming, Candace
★ The **family** Romanov; murder, rebellion, and the fall of imperial Russia. Candace Fleming. Schwartz & Wade Books 2014 304 p. il, maps, genealogical table $18.99
Grades: 7 8 9 10 11 12 **947.08**
1. Russia -- History -- 1917-1921, Revolution 2. Russia -- History -- Nicholas II, 1894-1917 3. Soviet Union -- History -- Revolution, 1917-1921
ISBN 0375867821; 9780375867828; 9780375967825

LC 2013037904

Robert F. Sibert Honor Book (2015)
YALSA Award for Excellence in Nonfiction for Young Adults: Finalist (2015)
Boston Globe-Horn Book Award: Nonfiction (2015)
This book, by Candace Fleming, describes how "when Russia's last tsar, Nicholas II, inherited the throne in 1894,

he was unprepared to do so. With their four daughters (including Anastasia) and only son, a hemophiliac, Nicholas and his reclusive wife, Alexandra, buried their heads in the sand, living a life of opulence as World War I raged outside their door and political unrest grew into the Russian Revolution." (Publisher's note)

"Fleming crafts an exciting narrative from this complicated history and its intriguing personalities. It is full of rich details about the Romanovs, insights into figures such as Vladimir Lenin and firsthand accounts from ordinary Russians affected by the tumultuous events. A variety of photographs adds a solid visual dimension." Kirkus

Includes bibliographical references and index

947.084   Russia (Soviet Union)--1917-1991

Gay, Kathlyn

The **aftermath** of the Russian Revolution. Twenty-First Century Books 2009 160p il (Aftermath of history) lib bdg $38.60

Grades: 8 9 10 11 12   947.084

1. Soviet Union -- History

ISBN 978-0-8225-9092-7; 0-8225-9092-1

LC 2008-25276

This book "begins with an overview of the Czar's Russia and the political machinations that brought about revolution. The disputes between different revolutionary groups led to the eventual triumph of the Bolsheviks and the reigns of Lenin and Stalin. Stalin's brutality in particular receives a lot of attention. The final chapters cover the transition to a more open society, the fall of the Soviet Union, and the age of Putin." SLJ

Includes glossary and bibliographical references

The **Rise** of the Soviet Union; Tom Streissguth, book editor. Greenhaven Press 2002 256p (Turning points in world history) hardcover o.p. pa $23.70

Grades: 7 8 9 10   947.084

1. Soviet Union -- History

ISBN 0-7377-0929-4; 0-7377-0928-6 pa

LC 2001-40866

A collection of essays concerning the social, economic and political issues in the history of the Soviet Union

Includes bibliographical references

947.085   Russia (Soviet Union)--1953-1991

Langley, Andrew

The **collapse** of the Soviet Union; the end of an empire. Compass Point Books 2006 96p il map (Snapshots in history) lib bdg $31.93

Grades: 7 8 9 10   947.085

1. Soviet Union -- History

ISBN 978-0-7565-2009-0; 0-7565-2009-6

LC 2006003003

This "describes leaders, their plans, and their ultimate downfalls, from the removal of Tsar Nicholas II to the prob-

lems of present-day Russia. [This book is] great for research . . . brief but comprehensive." SLJ

Includes glossary and bibliographical references

947.5   Caucasus

Dhilawala, Sakina

★ **Armenia**; [by] Sakina Dhilawala. 2nd ed.; Marshall Cavendish Benchmark 2008 144p il map (Cultures of the world) lib bdg $39.93

Grades: 5 6 7 8   947.5

1. Armenia

ISBN 978-0-7614-2029-3

LC 2007014890

First published 1997

"Provides comprehensive information on the geography, history, wildlife, governmental structure, economy, cultural diversity, peoples, religion, and culture of Armenia." Publisher's note

Includes glossary and bibliographical references

947.7   Ukraine

Bassis, Volodymyr

★ **Ukraine**; [by] Volodymyr Bassis & Sakina Dhilawala. 2nd ed.; Marshall Cavendish Benchmark 2008 144p il map (Cultures of the world) lib bdg $42.79

Grades: 5 6 7 8   947.7

1. Ukraine

ISBN 978-0-7614-2090-3

LC 2007019179

First published 1997

"Provides comprehensive information on the geography, history, wildlife, governmental structure, economy, cultural diversity, peoples, religion, and culture of Ukraine." Publisher's note

Includes glossary and bibliographical references

Cooper, Catherine W.

Ukraine; [by] Catherine W. Cooper; with additional text by Zoran Pavlovic. 2nd ed.; Chelsea House 2006 120p il map (Modern world nations) lib bdg $30

Grades: 7 8 9 10   947.7

1. Ukraine

ISBN 0-7910-9207-0

LC 2006015643

First published 2003

This describes the geography, history, people, and culture of Ukraine.

Includes bibliographical references

947.93 Lithuania

Kagda, Sakina
★ **Lithuania**; [by] Sakina Kagda & Zawiah Abdul Latif. 2nd ed.; Marshall Cavendish Benchmark 2008 144p il map (Cultures of the world) lib bdg $42.79
Grades: 5 6 7 8   **947.93**
1. Lithuania
ISBN 978-0-7614-2087-3
LC 2007016290
First published 1997
"Provides comprehensive information on the geography, history, wildlife, governmental structure, economy, cultural diversity, peoples, religion, and culture of Lithuania." Publisher's note
Includes glossary and bibliographical references

947.98 Estonia

Spilling, Michael
Estonia; 2nd ed.; Marshall Cavendish Benchmark 2010 142p il map (Cultures of the world) lib bdg $42.79
Grades: 5 6 7 8   **947.98**
1. Estonia
ISBN 978-0-7614-4846-4 lib bdg; 0-7614-4846-2 lib bdg
LC 2009021201
First published 1999
This describes the geography, history, wildlife, governmental structure, economy, cultural diversity, peoples, religion, and culture of Estonia
Includes glossary and bibliographical references

948 Scandinavia

Allan, Tony
Exploring the life, myth, and art of the Vikings; Tony Allan. Rosen Pub. 2012 144 p. (Civilizations of the world)
Grades: 7 8 9 10 11   **948**
1. Vikings 2. Viking art 3. Norse mythology 4. Viking civilization 5. Art, Viking 6. Mythology, Norse 7. Civilization, Viking
ISBN 9781448848331
LC 2011008856
This book on the Vikings "offers an informative overview of . . . political and social history as well as its art, architecture, and mythology, all bolstered with plenty of . . . details and narratives. . . . [T]he illustrations include artworks, documents, and handsome maps as well as photos of significant sites and artifacts. . . . 'Vikings' explores heritage that the Norse people shared and their history as traders, raiders, and settlers in other lands." (Booklist) The book "put[s] the art . . . in context, explaining how a society's religious beliefs, legends, and cultural traditions manifest themselves through images and iconography. The . . . layout features full-color photographs of architecture, sculpture,

and painting on every page, accompanied by informative captions." (School Libr J)
Includes bibliographical references (p. 136-137) and index

Hinds, Kathryn, 1962-
Vikings; masters of the sea. Marshall Cavendish Benchmark 2009 79p il (Barbarians!) lib bdg $24.95
Grades: 6 7 8 9   **948**
1. Vikings
ISBN 978-0-7614-4074-1 lib bdg; 0-7614-4074-7 lib bdg
LC 2008039052
"This . . . devotes excellent coverage and exposure to the emergence, development, and legacy of [the Vikings]." Libr Media Connect
"A history of the Viking Age, from about 793 to 1066." Publisher's note
Includes glossary and bibliographical references

Nardo, Don
The **Vikings**. Lucent Books 2010 112p il (World history) lib bdg $33.45
Grades: 6 7 8 9   **948**
1. Vikings
ISBN 978-1-4205-0316-6; 1-4205-0316-2
LC 2010010500
This is an introduction to Viking civilization.
This "shines as it provides a contemporaneous writing as well as work by scholars that offer plenty of drama—and lots of facts too. . . . [It also] provides a solid time line, plenty of photographs, sourced quotes, and a list of books and websites for further investigation. Excellent for reports and research." Booklist
Includes bibliographical references

Park, Louise
The **Scandinavian** Vikings; by Louise Park and Timothy Love. Marshall Cavendish Benchmark 2009 32p il map (Ancient and medieval people) $19.95
Grades: 4 5 6   **948**
1. Vikings 2. Scandinavia -- Civilization
ISBN 978-0-7614-4445-9; 0-7614-4445-9
This title has "a simple and elegant design with the proper balance of quality writing and quantity of information. . . . Handy time lines, well-chosen photos of ruins and artifacts, quality illustrations, inset 'Quick Facts', and 'What You Should Know About' features will grab reluctant readers and captivate even those with short attention spans." SLJ
Includes glossary

948.5 Sweden

Docalavich, Heather
Sweden; by Heather Docalavich and Shaina C. Indovino. Mason Crest Publishers 2013 64 p. col. ill., col. maps (library) $22.95

Grades: 5 6 7 8   **948.5**

1. Sweden 2. European Union -- Sweden
ISBN 1422222608; 9781422222607; 9781422222911

    LC 2010051848

This book by Heather Docalavich is part of the Major European Union Nations series and looks at Sweden. "A member of the EU since 1995, Sweden is one of the most stable and [peaceful] countries in the world. It takes caring for its people and the environment very seriously." The 2008-2009 financial crisis is discussed. (Publisher's note)

Includes bibliographical references (p. 57-58) and index

Heinrichs, Ann

Sweden; by Ann Heinrichs. Children's Press, an Imprint of Scholastic Inc. 2014 144 p. color illustrations (library binding) $40

Grades: 5 6 7 8   **948.5**

1. Sweden
ISBN 0531220176; 9780531220177

    LC 2013022562

This book, by Ann Heinrichs, focuses on Sweden. The "country's culture, history, and geography are explored in detail, allowing readers a chance to see how people live. . . . Sidebars highlight especially interesting people, places, and events [and] recipes give readers the opportunity to experience foreign cuisine first-hand." (Publisher's note)

"Introduces Sweden, describing its geography, history, animals, government, economy, food, religion, cities, culture, and family life." Baker & Taylor

Includes bibliographical references and index

Phillips, Charles

★ **Sweden**; [by] Charles Phillips; Susan C. Brantly and Eric Clark consultants. National Geographic 2009 64p il map (Countries of the world) lib bdg $27.90

Grades: 4 5 6 7   **948.5**

1. Sweden
ISBN 978-1-4263-0389-0 lib bdg; 1-4263-0389-0 lib bdg

    LC 2009275585

This describes the geography, nature, history, people & culture, and government & economy of Sweden

Includes glossary and bibliographical references

948.9   Denmark and Finland

Docalavich, Heather

Denmark; by Heather Docalavich and Shaina C. Indovino. Mason Crest Publishers 2013 64 p. col. ill., col. maps (hardcover) $22.95

Grades: 5 6 7 8   **948.9**

1. Denmark 2. European Union -- Denmark
ISBN 1422222381; 9781422222386

    LC 2010051090

This book by Heather Docalavich and Shaina Carmel Indovino is part of the Major European Union Nations series and focuses on Denmark. "Denmark is a peaceful northern country that joined the EU in 1973. From the Vikings to the modern day, Denmark has a long [history]. Today, Denmark

is a very environmentally conscious nation with a lot going on. It also must figure out how to deal with issues of immigration and the global recession as it looks to the future." (Publisher's note)

Includes bibliographical references (p. 57) and index

948.97   Finland

Skog, Jason

Teens in Finland. Compass Point Books 2008 96p il map (Global connections) lib bdg $31.93

Grades: 7 8 9 10   **948.97**

1. Teenagers 2. Finland
ISBN 978-0-7565-3405-9 lib bdg; 0-7565-3405-4 lib bdg

    LC 2007032691

Uncovers the challenges, pastimes, customs and culture of teens in Finland

"Informaion is solid, giving readers an informed and realistic view of life in that country. A historical timeline is included, and suggestions for other nonfiction and fiction titles for further reading." Youth Voice Advocate

Includes glossary and bibliographical references

Tan, Chung Lee

★ **Finland**; [by] Tan Chung Lee. 2nd ed.; Marshall Cavendish Benchmark 2007 144p il map (Cultures of the world) lib bdg $39.93

Grades: 5 6 7 8   **948.97**

1. Finland
ISBN 978-0-7614-2073-6 lib bdg; 0-7614-2073-8 lib bdg

    LC 2006015897

First published 1996

This provides "information on the geography, history, governmental structure, economy, cultural diversity, peoples, religion, and culture of Finland." Publisher's note

Includes glossary and bibliographical references

949.12   Iceland

Somervill, Barbara A.

Iceland; by Barbara A. Somervill. Children's Press 2013 144 p. ill., maps (library) $40

Grades: 5 6 7 8   **949.12**

1. Iceland 2. Icelandic language
ISBN 0531256022; 9780531256022

    LC 2012047117

This book by Barbara A. Somervill is part of the Enchantment of the World series and looks at Iceland. A discussion is offered of "how this land near the Arctic Circle came to be. . . . Maps and illustrations show the variety in the terrain and the areas of major geological activity. . . . Chapters [are] devoted to history, the economy, the government and the flora and fauna." (Children's Literature)

Includes bibliographical references (page 134) and index.

949.2   Netherlands

Docalavich, Heather

The **Netherlands**; by Heather Docalavich and Shaina Carmel Indovino. Mason Crest Publishers 2013 64 p. col. ill. (library) $22.95; (ebook) $28.95

Grades: 5 6 7 8 **949.2**

1. Netherlands
ISBN 9781422222539; 9781422222843; 9781422292716

LC 2010051464

This book on the Netherlands by Heather Docalvich and Shaina Carmel Indovino is part of the "Major European Union Nations" series. It presents an "overview of some of the successes and challenges that the Netherlands has faced and continues to face." Topics include "history, one on government, the economy, people and culture, and . . . global climate change." (Children's Literature)

Includes bibliographical references (p. 57-58, 63) and index.

949.304   Belgium 1909-

Indovino, Shaina C.

Belgium; by Ida Walker and Shaina C. Indovino. Mason Crest Publishers 2012 64 p. col. ill., col. maps (library) $22.95

Grades: 5 6 7 8 **949.304**

1. Belgium 2. European Union -- Belgium
ISBN 1422222330; 9781422222331

LC 2010051078

This book, "part of the 'Modern World Nations' series, is an . . . introduction to the kingdom of Belgium. For middle school and high school readers, the chapters are descriptive of the physical features, the history, people, government, and economy. There is a chapter about the future of the nation as well as a description of life in the country today." (Children's Literature)

Includes bibliographical references and index.

949.35   Luxembourg

Sheehan, Patricia

★ **Luxembourg**; by Patricia Sheehan & Sakina Dhilawala. 2nd ed.; Marshall Cavendish Benchmark 2008 144p il map (Cultures of the world) lib bdg $42.79

Grades: 5 6 7 8 **949.35**

1. Luxembourg
ISBN 978-0-7614-2088-0

LC 2007014891

First published 1997

Discusses the geography, history, government, economy, and customs of the smallest of the Benelux countries

Includes glossary and bibliographical references

949.5   Greece

Etingoff, Kim

Greece; by Kim Etingoff and Shaina C. Indovino. Mason Crest Publishers 2013 64 p. ill. (library) $22.95

Grades: 5 6 7 8 **949.5**

1. Greece
ISBN 1422222446; 9781422222447; 9781422222751

LC 2010051304

This book by Kim Etingoff and Shaina C. Indovino is part of the Major European Union Nations series and looks at Greece. The series "stresses the modern relationships, goals, and problems of the European Union. . . . Chapters begin with 'Modem Issues' and a brief summary of the country's history and government, followed by chapters on economy, people and culture, and 'Looking to the Future.'" (School Library Journal)

Feldman, Ruth Tenzer

The **fall** of Constantinople. Twenty-First Century Books 2008 160p il map (Pivotal moments in history) lib bdg $38.60

Grades: 7 8 9 10 **949.5**

1. Byzantine Empire 2. Istanbul (Turkey) -- History -- Siege, 1453
ISBN 978-0-8225-5918-4 lib bdg; 0-8225-5918-8 lib bdg

LC 2006037501

"This volume examines the fall of Constantinople, marking the end of the Middle Ages. Sure to satisfy history buffs, the book not only relates military facts but also delves into the events leading up to Constantinople's defeat as well as exploring its effects throughout history. Numerous sidebars, illustrations, maps, and art reproductions provide additional information." Horn Book Guide

Includes glossary and bibliographical references

Green, Jen

★ **Greece**; [by] Greg Anderson and Kostas Vlassopoulos, consultants. National Geographic 2009 64p il map (Countries of the world) lib bdg $27.90

Grades: 4 5 6 7 **949.5**

1. Greece
ISBN 978-1-4263-0470-5 lib bdg; 1-4263-0470-6 lib bdg

This describes the geography, nature, history, people and culture, government and economy of Greece

Includes glossary and bibliographical references

Heinrichs, Ann

Greece; by Ann Heinrichs. Children's Press 2012 144 p. col. ill., col. maps (library) $40

Grades: 5 6 7 8 **949.5**

1. Greece -- History 2. Greece -- Civilization 3. Greece
ISBN 0531275434; 9780531275436

LC 2012000519

This book, part of the Enchantment of the World series, focuses on Greece. The books in the series each feature 10 "chapters, several maps, a fast-facts section, and a few references to other sources, including a referral to a Scholastic website . . . . The chapters cover geography, natural environment, history, politics, people and culture." (School Library Journal)

Includes bibliographical references and index.

Vanvoorst, Jennifer Fretland

The **Byzantine** Empire; by Jenny Fretland VanVoorst. Compass Point Books 2013 48 p. ill. (chiefly col.), col. map (library) $28.65; (paperback) $8.95

Grades: 6 7 8   **949.5**

1. Byzantine Empire -- Civilization

ISBN 075654565X; 0756545862; 9780756545659; 9780756545864

LC 2012001994

This children's nonfiction book, by Jennifer Fretland VanVoorst, profiles the Byzantine Empire as part of the "Exploring the Ancient World" series. "The Byzantine Empire, which thrived from 395 to 1453, was a fascinating place. Its people thought of themselves as Romans, spoke Greek, and hailed from all across Europe and Asia. . . . It was a Christian empire that preserved and developed Europe's intellectual heritage at a time when western Europe was in decline." (Publisher's note)

Includes bibliographical references (p. 46-47) and index.

949.65 Albania

Knowlton, MaryLee

★ **Albania**; by MaryLee Knowlton. Marshall Cavendish Benchmark 2005 144p il map (Cultures of the world) lib bdg $42.79

Grades: 5 6 7 8   **949.65**

1. Albania

ISBN 0-7614-1852-0

LC 2004-22236

An overview of the history, culture, peoples, religion, government, and geography of Albania

Includes glossary and bibliographical references

949.7 Serbia, Croatia, Slovenia, Bosnia and Hercegovina, Montenegro, Macedonia

Cooper, Robert

Croatia; [by] Robert Cooper and Michael Spilling. 2nd ed; Marshall Cavendish Benchmark 2011 144p il map (Cultures of the world) lib bdg $42.79

Grades: 5 6 7 8   **949.7**

1. Croatia

ISBN 978-1-6087-0215-2; 1-6087-0215-4

LC 2010019626

First published 2001

Provides information on the geography, history, wildlife, governmental structure, economy, cultural diversity, peoples, religion, and culture of Croatia.

"Plentiful color photographs accompany substantial amounts of information." SLJ

Includes glossary and bibliographical references

Halilbegovich, Nadja

My childhood under fire; a Sarajevo diary. Kids Can Press 2006 120p il $14.95

Grades: 5 6 7 8   **949.7**

1. Yugoslav War, 1991-1995 2. Sarajevo (Bosnia and Hercegovina)

ISBN 1-55337-797-4

"In 1992, when the bombing started in Sarajevo, Halilbegovich, 12, kept a diary of her terrifying daily life under siege. Her terse vignettes replay the horror of her comfortable home torn apart." Booklist

"Twelve-year-old Nadja describes living in Sarajevo during the Yugoslav War. Nadja tells of the daily struggles for food, heat, and water and her intense fear and feelings of being deserted by the world. She also adds new details and reflections in "Looking Back" passages. Though she gives little context for the conflict, this is a readable adolescent's experience of war." Horn Book

Knowlton, MaryLee

★ **Macedonia**; by MaryLee Knowlton. Benchmark Books 2005 144p il map (Cultures of the world) lib bdg $42.79

Grades: 5 6 7 8   **949.7**

1. Macedonia (Republic)

ISBN 0-7614-1854-7

LC 2004-22735

Describes the geography, history, government, economy, people, and culture of Macedonia

Includes glossary and bibliographical references

949.8 Romania

Bos, Jan-Willem

Romania. Oliver Press 2011 48p il map (Looking at Europe) lib bdg $24.95

Grades: 7 8 9 10   **949.8**

1. Romania

ISBN 978-1-881508-86-1; 1-881508-86-2

LC 2009034604

This describes Romania today, its history, cities, transportation, culture, education, economy, cuisine, tourism, and natural environment.

This will "best suit students with good vocabularies and some knowledge of European history. . . . [It is] clearly written and well organized. . . . [It includes] many clear photos as well as colorful sidebars. . . . Attractive, informative." Booklist

Includes glossary and bibliographical references

949.9 Bulgaria

Prazdny, Bronja

Bulgaria. Oliver Press 2011 48p il map (Looking at Europe) lib bdg $24.95

Grades: 7 8 9 10   **949.9**

1. Bulgaria

ISBN 978-1-881508-85-4; 1-881508-85-4

LC 2009032670

This describes Bulgaria today, its history, cities, transportation, culture, education, economy, cuisine, tourism, and natural environment.

This will "best suit students with good vocabularies and some knowledge of European history. . . . [It is] clearly written and well organized. . . . [It includes] many clear photos as well as colorful sidebars. . . . Attractive, informative." Booklist

Includes glossary and bibliographical references

950 History of Asia

Campbell, Rusty

Atlas of Asia; [by] Rusty Campbell, Malcolm Porter, and Keith Lye. Rosen Central 2010 il map lib bdg $26.50; pa $11.75

Grades: 4 5 6 7   950

1. Asia

ISBN 978-1-4358-8455-7 lib bdg; 1-4358-8455-8 lib bdg; 978-1-4358-9112-8 pa; 1-4358-9112-0 pa

"Most of the spreads cover a region or one of the continent's bigger countries and provide large, clear maps and columns of almanac data surrounded by short chapters on famous people, animals, industries, cities, sports, and more, all accompanied by color illustrations or photographs and informative sidebars... with guidance [children] will encounter some absorbing and informative material." SLJ

Galloway, Priscilla

★ Adventures on the ancient Silk Road; [by] Priscilla Galloway with Dawn Hunter. Annick Press 2009 164p il $24.95; pa $14.95

Grades: 6 7 8 9   950

1. Explorers 2. Travelers 3. Voyages and travels 4. Kings 5. Buddhist monks 6. Travel writers 7. Asia -- Description and travel

ISBN 978-1-55451-198-3; 1-55451-198-4; 978-1-55451-197-6 pa; 1-55451-197-6 pa

"The monk Xuanzang, the conqueror Genghis Khan, and the merchant Marco Polo each traveled the Silk Road, years apart. Their journeys, by different routes and for different motives, are gripping historical narratives, sensitively and excitingly fictionalized here, in language that is lively and descriptive, clear but not oversimplified. Vibrant reproductions of art and photos of artifacts leap off every colorful page." SLJ

Helget, Nicole

Mongols; Nicole Helget. Creative Education 2013 48 p. (Fearsome fighters) (alk. paper) $35.65

Grades: 5 6 7 8   950

1. Mongols 2. Asia -- History 3. Military art and science -- History 4. Mongols -- History 5. Mongols -- Warfare

ISBN 1608181847; 9781608181841

LC 2011035800

Author Nicole Helget presents a book on the history of the people of Mongolia, their influence on world culture, and their impact on society. The book presents a "look at the Mongols, including how they built the most widespread empire in history, their lifestyle, their weapons, and how they

remain a part of today's culture through books and film." (Publisher's note)

Includes bibliographical references (p. 48) and index

Morris, Neil

Asian civilizations. Zak Books 2009 48p il map (History of the world) lib bdg $34.25

Grades: 7 8 9 10   950

1. Ancient civilization 2. Asia -- History 3. Asia -- Civilization

ISBN 978-88-6098-160-8 lib bdg; 88-6098-160-3 lib bdg

LC 2008-8403

The "effectiveness lies in the combination of lush illustrations, well-chosen, captioned photographs of contemporary artifacts, and . . . . [a] reasoned, concise [narrative]. Succinct time lines border most pages, and . . . the proper amount of white space, and clear dark print maintain organization and clarity. A superior choice." SLJ

Includes glossary

Nardo, Don

Genghis Khan and the Mongol Empire. Lucent Books 2011 96p il map (World history) $33.45

Grades: 5 6 7 8 9   950

1. Mongols

ISBN 978-1-4205-0326-5; 1-4205-0326-X

LC 2010032960

"Using new scholarship, Nardo paints a more nuanced and sophisticated picture of a man who united several nomadic clans and then went on to found history's largest empire. Starting with his early childhood and ending with the death of his grandson, Kublai Khan, the book focuses on Genghis Khan's empire building and leadership, including his code of laws and justice. The book features several color photographs of present-day Mongolia period reenactments, as well as artistic representations from the era. . . . Nardo includes quotations from several scholars while still keeping the book engaging and accessible for a wide variety of readers." SLJ

Includes glossary and bibliographical references

Woods, Michael

Seven wonders of Ancient Asia; by Michael Woods and Mary B. Woods. Twenty-First Century Books 2008 80p il map (Seven wonders) lib bdg $33.26

Grades: 6 7 8 9   950

1. Asian architecture 2. Asia -- History

ISBN 978-0-8225-7569-6 lib bdg; 0-8225-7569-8 lib bdg

LC 2007-40824

"This handsome volume presents seven notable 'wonders' of ancient Asia: the Great Wall of China, Mahabodhi Temple in India, Angkor Wat in Cambodia, Todaiji Temple in Japan, Pha That Luang in Laos, Borobudur Temple on Java in Indonesia, and the Banaue Rice Terraces of the Philippines. . . . With good writing and a nice design, this book offers a fine introduction to some historically significant places." Booklist

Includes glossary and bibliographical references

951 China and adjacent areas

Langley, Andrew

Cultural Revolution; years of chaos in China. by Andrew Langley. Compass Point Books 2008 96p il map (Snapshots in history) lib bdg $33.26

Grades: 6 7 8 9 **951**

1. China -- History -- 1949-1976

ISBN 978-0-7565-3483-7 lib bdg; 0-7565-3483-6 lib bdg

LC 2007032699

This book "provides more than just a 'snapshot' of China's violent Cultural Revolution . . . The inviting layout has a photo and boxed data on almost every double-page spread, and the main account is buoyed by extensive back matter, including chapter notes for quotations." Booklist

Includes bibliographical references

Levy, Patricia

★ Tibet; [by] Patricia Levy & Don Bosco. 2nd ed.; Marshall Cavendish Benchmark 2007 144p il map (Cultures of the world) lib bdg $42.79

Grades: 5 6 7 8 **951**

1. Tibet (China)

ISBN 978-0-7614-2076-7 lib bdg; 0-7614-2076-2 lib bdg

LC 2006015826

First published 1996

This provides "information on the geography, history, wildlife, governmental structure, economy, diversity, peoples, religion, and culture of Tibet." Publisher's note

Includes glossary and bibliographical references

Mara, Wil

People's Republic of China; by Wil Mara. Children's Press 2012 144 p. ill., maps (library) $40

Grades: 5 6 7 8 **951**

1. China -- Economic conditions

ISBN 053125352X; 9780531253526

LC 2011011308

This book, part of the Enchantment of the World, offers an "introduction to China. The book covers geography, climate, history, language, different ethnic groups, religion, government structure, and the arts. Frequent text boxes and large, bright photographs add extra information and deeper context. There is a heavy focus on the Chinese economy and recent strides made in human rights." (School Library Journal)

Includes bibliographical references and index.

Marx, Trish

Elephants and golden thrones; inside China's Forbidden City. written by Trish Marx; photographs and photograph selection by Ellen B. Senisi; foreword by Li Ji. Abrams Books for Young Readers 2008 48p il $18.95

Grades: 4 5 6 7 **951**

1. Forbidden City (Beijing, China)

ISBN 978-0-8109-9485-0; 0-8109-9485-2

LC 2007-022413

Introduces Beijing's Forbidden City, recounting some of the most famous incidents from its past, and describing its rooms, their function, and some of the daily rituals of palace life.

The author "brings the Forbidden City to life by telling stories about six different royal inhabitants from Zhengde, 'one of the worst emperors in Chinese history,' to Puyi, who became a pawn of the invading Japanese. . . . Beautiful drawings and photographs, some provided by the Palace Museum and some taken for this book, lend color and provide additional information. Of particular note are the photos of the interiors of buildings, a number of which are not regularly open to the public." Booklist

Includes bibliographical references

Pelleschi, Andrea

China. ABDO 2012 144p. il (Countries of the world) lib bdg $35.64

Grades: 6 7 8 9 **951**

1. China

ISBN 978-1-61783-107-2

LC 2011019959

" Chapters then cover all the expected details for reportwriters... Vivid photographs and useful maps in an eye-pleasing design enliven the presentation." Horn Book

Includes glossary and bibliographical references

Sis, Peter

★ Tibet; through the red box. Farrar, Straus & Giroux 1998 un il maps $25

Grades: 4 5 6 7 **951**

1. Tibet (China)

ISBN 0-374-37552-6

LC 97-50175

A Caldecott Medal honor book, 1999

"When Sis opens the red lacquered box that has sat on his father's table for decades, he finds the diary his father kept when he was lost in Tibet in the mid-1950s. The text replicates the diary's spidery handwriting, while the illustrations depict elaborate mazes and mandalas, along with dreamlike spreads that are filled with fragmented details of the father's and son's lives. . . . Impeccably designed and beautifully made, the book has a dreamlike quality that will keep readers of many ages coming back to find more in its pages." Booklist

Ting, Renee

Chinese history stories; edited by Renee Ting; translated from Chinese by Qian Jifang. Shens Books 2009 2v il ea $19.95

Grades: 6 7 8 9 **951**

1. China -- History

ISBN 978-1-885008-37-4 v1; 1-885008-37-6 v1; 978-1885008-38-1 v2; 1-885008-38-4 v2

LC 2009027288

"These first two entries in a planned series of 12 volumes offer gripping introductions to China's cultural narratives. From the initial two-page condensation of 3000 years of history to the suggestions to 'Learn More' after (often more useful to read before), the well-told stories and the attractively varied illustrations are riveting. . . . Multiple illustrators provide changing art styles and historical allusions, but all are detailed, lively, and colorful." SLJ

951.04 China--Period of Republic, 1912-1949

Gay, Kathlyn

The **aftermath** of the Chinese nationalist revolution. Twenty-First Century Books 2008 160p il (Aftermath of history) lib bdg $38.60

Grades: 7 8 9 10 **951.04**
   1. China -- History -- 1912-1949
   ISBN 978-0-8225-7601-3; 0-8225-7601-5
                 LC 2007-15082

This book "offers a lucid account of the civil turmoil that began in China with the successful revolution led by Dr. Sun Yat-sen in 1911, and culminated in the establishment of the People's Republic in 1949." Booklist

Includes bibliographical references

951.05 China--Period of People's Republic, 1949-

Burgan, Michael

Tank man; how a photograph defined China's protest movement. by Michael Burgan. Compass Point Books 2014 64 p. (Captured history) (library binding) $33.99

Grades: 6 7 8 9 **951.05**
   1. Demonstrations 2. Tiananmen Square Incident, Beijing (China), 1989 3. Photojournalism -- China 4. China -- History -- Tiananmen Square Incident, 1989 -- Pictorial works
   ISBN 0756547318; 9780756547318; 9780756547875
                 LC 2013031196

"This middle grades book by Michael Burgan describes how "For almost two months in spring 1989, Beijing's Tiananmen Square had been the site of growing protests against China's hardline communist government. In early June, China's leaders had had enough. In a matter of days soldiers cleared the square. . . . As tanks rumbled through the streets near Tiananmen Square, a man in a white shirt came suddenly into view. He held up his right hand." (Publisher's note)

"Analyzing visual images and setting them in a larger historical and cultural context is an important skill. In this volume Burgan uses the iconic photograph of a Tiananmen Square protester facing down a tank to discuss the 1989 student protest in China and the Communist government's violent retaliation. A spacious page design, which includes plenty of photos, enhances the presentation. Reading list, timeline. Bib., glos., ind." Horn Book

   Includes bibliographical references (page 63) and index
   Other titles in the series include:
   Assassination and its Aftermath (2014)
   The Blue Marble (2014)
   Breaker Boys (2012)
   Civil War Witness (2014)
   Hitler in Paris (2014)
   Little Rock Girl 1957 (2012)

   Man on the Moon (2012)
   Migrant Mother (2011)
   Raising the Flag (2011)
   Summiting Everest (2014)

Jiang, Ji-li

   ★ **Red** scarf girl; a memoir of the Cultural Revolution. foreword by David Henry Hwang. HarperCollins Pubs. 1997 285p $16.99; pa $6.99

Grades: 6 7 8 9 10 **951.05**
   1. Communism -- China 2. China -- History -- 1949-1976 -- Personal narratives
   ISBN 0-06-027585-5; 0-06-446208-0 pa
                 LC 97-5089

"This is an autobiographical account of growing up during Mao's Cultural Revolution in China in 1966. . . . Jiang describes in terrifying detail the ordeals of her family and those like them, including unauthorized search and seizure, persecution, arrest and torture, hunger, and public humiliation. . . . Her voice is that of an intelligent, confused adolescent, and her focus is on the effects of the revolution on herself, her family, and her friends provides an emotional focal point for the book, and will allow even those with limited knowledge of Chinese history to access the text." Bull Cent Child Books

Ma Yan

The **diary** of Ma Yan; the struggles and hopes of a Chinese schoolgirl. edited and introduced by Pierre Haski; translated from the French by Lisa Appignanesi. HarperCollins 2005 166p $15.99; lib bdg $16.89

Grades: 5 6 7 8 **951.05**
   1. China 2. Diarists 3. Students
   ISBN 0-06-076496-1; 0-06-076497-X lib bdg
                 LC 2004-16136

   Original French edition, 2002

This book, edited by Pierre Haski offers "Ma Yan's . . . diary chronicles her struggle to escape hardship and bring prosperity to her family through her persistent, sometimes desperate, attempts to continue her schooling." The book discusses her efforts to continue schooling despite the hunger and poverty she endures in rural China. (Publisher's note)

"In 2001, while a French journalist was visiting remote Ningxia province in northwest China, a Muslim woman wearing the white headscarf of the Hui people thrust the diaries of her daughter into his hands. The three small notebooks described the girl's struggle to get an education despite extreme poverty. . . . The girl's feelings for her mother were powerful and complex, and she alternated between overwhelming love and rage at the injustices she suffered." SLJ

Slavicek, Louise Chipley

The **Chinese** Cultural Revolution. Chelsea House Publishers 2010 128p il (Milestones in modern world history) lib bdg $35

Grades: 8 9 10 11 12 **951.05**
   1. China -- History -- 1949-1976
   ISBN 978-1-60413-278-6; 1-60413-278-7
                 LC 2008-54885

"From the cover photo onward, young people are front and center in [this book,] . . . which focuses on the Red

Guards who heard the anti-establishment call of their leader, Mao Zedong, in 1966. This political upheaval led to the deaths of up to four million Chinese over 10 years." Booklist

Includes bibliographical references

The **Tiananmen** Square protests of 1989; Jeff Hay, editor. Greenhaven Press 2010 177p il map (Perspectives on modern world history) lib bdg $39.70

Grades: 7 8 9 10   **951.05**

1. Tiananmen Square Incident, Beijing (China), 1989

ISBN 978-0-7377-4796-6; 0-7377-4796-X

LC 2009041850

Offers basic historical information about the Tiananmen Square protests of 1989, examining the controversies surrounding this event and providing first-person narratives from people who lived through or were impacted by it.

"The book has numerous full-color photographs, sidebars to enhance the text, and illustrations. This is a highly readable book and would be a good addition to the library's world history collection." Libr Media Connect

Includes glossary and bibliographical references

Uschan, Michael V., 1948-

China since World War II; by Michael V. Uschan. Lucent Books 2008 104 p. ill. (some col.), col. map (library) $34.95

Grades: 6 7 8 9   **951.05**

1. China -- History -- 1949-

ISBN 142050097X; 9781420500974

LC 2008014727

This book by Michael V. Uschan looks at the history of China since World War II. "Mao [Zedong] naturally dominates, the focus of five chapters. . . . One of the remaining two chapters is devoted to Deng Xiaoping, and the other to the Chinese economy. . . . There is no mention of the environmental consequences of China's prosperity, the human costs of the disappearance of social security . . . or the widespread corruption reflected in such recent events as collapsing schools." (School Library Journal)

Includes bibliographical references and index.

Yu Chun

Little Green; growing up during the Chinese Cultural Revolution. [by] Chun Yu. Simon & Schuster Books for Young Readers 2005 112p il $15.95

Grades: 6 7 8 9   **951.05**

1. China -- History -- 1949-1976

ISBN 0-689-86943-6

LC 2003-27433

"Chun Yu was born in China in 1966, the year the Great Cultural Revolution began, and in spare poetry she remembers the first 10 years of her life. True to a child's bewildered viewpoint and augmented by occasional, small black-and-white family photos, Yu gets across the grief at home and the school indoctrination." Booklist

951.25   Hong Kong

Kagda, Falaq

★ **Hong** Kong; [by] Falaq Kagda & Magdalene Koh. 2nd ed.; Marshall Cavendish Benchmark 2008 144p il map (Cultures of the world) lib bdg $42.79

Grades: 5 6 7 8   **951.25**

1. Hong Kong (China)

ISBN 978-0-7614-3034-6 lib bdg; 0-7614-3034-2 lib bdg

LC 2007048285

First published 1998

Surveys the geography, history, government, economy, and culture of Hong Kong

Includes glossary and bibliographical references

951.7   Mongolia

Pang, Guek-Cheng, 1950-

Mongolia; Pang Guek Cheng. Marshall Cavendish Benchmark 2010 144 p. col. ill., col. maps (Cultures of the world) (library) $42.79

Grades: 5 6 7 8   **951.7**

1. Mongolia

ISBN 9780761448495; 0761448497

LC 2009022643

This describes the geography, history, wildlife, governmental structure, economy, cultural diversity, peoples, religion, and culture of Mongolia

Includes bibliographical references and index.

951.9   Korea

Bowler, Ann Martin

All about Korea; stories, songs, crafts, and more. illustrated by Soosoonam Barg. Periplus Editions 2011 64p il $16.95

Grades: 3 4 5 6   **951.9**

1. Korea

ISBN 978-0-8048-4012-5; 0-8048-4012-1 (hardcover)

LC 2010040845

Reece, Richard

The **Korean** War. ABDO Pub. 2011 112p il map (Essential events) lib bdg $23.95

Grades: 7 8 9 10 11 12   **951.9**

1. Korean War, 1950-1953

ISBN 978-1-61714-766-1; 1-61714-766-4

LC 2010044661

This describes the Korean War and discusses the political and social issues pertaining to it.

Includes glossary and bibliographical references

Santella, Andrew

The **Korean** War; by Andrew Santella. Compass Point Books 2007 48p il map (We the people) lib bdg $25.26; pa $8.95

Grades: 4 5 6 7   **951.9**
1. Korean War, 1950-1953
ISBN 978-0-7565-2027-4 lib bdg; 0-7565-2027-4 lib
bdg; 978-0-7565-2039-7 pa; 0-7565-2039-8 pa
LC 2006006767

This "begins by explaining how North and South Korea
became divided; the involvement of the United Nations and
the United States; conflict between President Harry Truman
and General Douglas MacArthur; eventual peace talks; and
the division still occurring today. Accessible and straightforward, this book is an excellent one for the intended
audience." SLJ

Includes bibliographical references

Senker, Cath
★ **North** Korea and South Korea; by Cath Sen-
ker. 1st ed. Rosen Pub. 2013 48 p. col. ill. (library)
$29.25
Grades: 6 7 8   **951.9**
1. Korea (North) 2. Korea (South) 3. Korea (North) --
History 4. Korea (South) -- History 5. Korea (North) --
Social conditions 6. Korea (South) -- Social conditions
ISBN 1448860296; 9781448860296
LC 2012010617

This book by Cath Senker is part of the Our World Divided series and looks at North Korea and South Korea.
"Each of these volumes begins with a recent news event pertaining to the featured conflict and then looks back at the origin and milestones of the discord. . . . 'Viewpoints' sidebars
are . . . supplementary features. They showcase quotations
about a specific matter from individuals on opposing sides."
(School Library Journal)

Includes bibliographical references (p. 46) and index.

951.93   North Korea (People's Democratic Republic of Korea)

Kummer, Patricia K.
North Korea; by Patricia K. Kummer. Children's Press 2008 144p il map (Enchantment of the
world, second series) lib bdg $38
Grades: 5 6 7 8 9   **951.93**
1. Korea (North)
ISBN 978-0-531-18485-1 lib bdg; 0-531-18485-4
lib bdg
LC 2007025693

In this introduction to North Korea "geography is the
focus, but Kummer also discusses ancient and recent history, . . . the economy, religion, sports, education, and more.
Without discounting the rich culture, the book doesn't shy
away from more sensitive issues. . . . The open design will
draw readers, with clear type on thick, high-quality paper;
numerous maps and color photos and spacious back matter
are also included." Booklist

Includes bibliographical references

Sonneborn, Liz
North Korea; by Liz Sonneborn. Children's
Press ; an imprint of Scholastic Inc. 2014 144 p. il-

lustrations. maps (Enchantment of the world. Second
series) (library binding) $40
Grades: 5 6 7 8   **951.93**
1. Korea (North)
ISBN 0531236781; 9780531236789
LC 2013003650

This book, by Liz Sonneborn, is part of the Enchantment
of the World Series. "Each volume has been completely rewritten from a previous edition. . . . 'North Korea' has a new
author and a strong political focus, discussing life under the
new leader, Kim Jong-un. . . . Each volume in this . . . series includes extensive back matter with a detailed index."
(Booklist)

Includes bibliographical references and index

952   Japan

Blumberg, Rhoda
★ **Commodore** Perry in the land of the Shogun.
Lothrop, Lee & Shepard Bks. 1985 144p il map
$21.99; pa $8.99
Grades: 5 6 7 8   **952**
1. Naval officers 2. Japan -- History 3. Japan -- Foreign
relations -- United States 4. United States -- Foreign
relations -- Japan 5. United States Naval Expedition to
Japan (1852-1854)
ISBN 0-688-03723-2; 0-06-008625-4 pa
LC 84-21800

A Newbery Medal honor book, 1986

This "is a well-written story of Matthew Perry's expedition to open Japan to American trade and whaling ports.
The account is sensitive to the extreme cultural differences
that both the Japanese and Americans had to overcome. Especially good are the chapters and paragraphs explaining
Japanese feudal society and culture. The text is marvelously
complemented by the illustrations, almost all reproductions
of contemporary Japanese art." SLJ

Includes bibliographical references

Moore, Willamarie
All about Japan; stories, songs, crafts, and more.
illustrated by Kazumi Wilds. Tuttle Pub. 2011 63p
il $16.95
Grades: 3 4 5 6   **952**
1. Japan
ISBN 978-4-8053-1077-9; 4-8053-1077-4
LC 2010040843

"In this treasure-trove of information, two children, one
a Tokyo urbanite and the other from a rural village, introduce
readers to their country and its culture, including geography,
language, traditional arts, costume, etiquette, sports, and
festivals. The dual narrators' conversational descriptions of
their homes and daily routines will engage young readers
while highlighting the differences between the Westernized
big-city existence and the traditional way of life in Japan's
countryside, deftly demonstrating the rich variety of lifestyles within this island nation. The scope of this book is remarkably comprehensive, covering almost anything a child
would want to know." SLJ

Niz, Xavier

Samurai; a guide to the feudal knights. by Xavier W. Niz. Capstone Press 2012 48p il map (History's greatest warriors) lib bdg $30.65

Grades: 6 7 8   **952**

1. Samurai

ISBN 978-1-4296-6601-5 lib bdg; 1-4296-6601-3 lib bdg

LC 2011004956

"...Focuses [more] on relaying facts about the four groups of exceptional fighters than on a narrative... [and has] extensive modern cultural references to which students will relate." SLJ

Includes bibliographical references

Somervill, Barbara A.

Japan; by Barbara A. Somervill. Children's Press 2012 144 p. ill., maps (library) $40

Grades: 5 6 7 8   **952**

1. Japan 2. Japan -- Social life and customs

ISBN 0531253546; 9780531253540

LC 2011009503

This book is part of the Enchantment of the World series and focuses on Japan. "Topics such as climate, wildlife, history, government, pop culture, and the arts are all addressed, providing a . . . look at Japan's past and present. With content revised considerably from previous editions, this book goes beyond facts and statistics to give readers an intimate glimpse at typical Japanese youth through fictionalized anecdotes detailing moments in their daily lives." (School Library Journal)

Includes bibliographical references and index.

Turnbull, Stephen R.

The **most** daring raid of the samurai. Rosen Pub. 2011 64p il map (The most daring raids in history) lib bdg $29.25

Grades: 7 8 9 10   **952**

1. Samurai 2. Japan -- History

ISBN 978-1-4488-1872-3; 1-4488-1872-9

LC 2010030843

First published 2009 in the United Kingdom with title: The samurai capture a king

In 1609, the Samurai from the Shimazu clan of Satsuma took control of the independent kingdom of Ryukyu. This audacious military campaign brought an end to centuries of warfare between the Shimazu clan and the king of Ryukyu.

This book is "packed with facts, covering the details of the action, the people involved, and the tools used, in engaging prose. The authors cite their sources thoroughly. . . . Diagrams, . . . and maps make the action easy to follow and provide visual context for the raids. . . . This . . . . is sure to find a large readership." SLJ

Includes glossary and bibliographical references

953   Arabian Peninsula and adjacent areas

King, David C.

★ The **United** Arab Emirates; [by] David C. King. 2nd ed; Marshall Cavendish Benchmark 2008 144p il map (Cultures of the world) lib bdg $42.79

Grades: 5 6 7 8   **953**

1. United Arab Emirates

ISBN 978-0-7614-2565-6

LC 2006030237

This describes the geography, history, government, economy, environment, people, and culture of the United Arab Emirates.

Includes glossary and bibliographical references

953.3   Yemen (Republic)

Hestler, Anna

Yemen; by Anna Hestler and Jo-Ann Spilling. 2nd ed.; Marshall Cavendish Benchmark 2010 144p il map (Cultures of the world) lib bdg $42.79

Grades: 5 6 7 8   **953.3**

1. Yemen

ISBN 978-0-7614-4850-1 lib bdg; 0-7614-4850-0 lib bdg

LC 2009021200

First published 1999

This describes the geography, history, wildlife, governmental structure, economy, cultural diversity, peoples, religion, and culture of Yemen

Includes glossary and bibliographical references

O'Neal, Claire

We visit Yemen; by Claire O'Neal. Mitchell Lane Publishers 2012 63 p. ill. (chiefly col.), col. maps (library) $33.95; (ebook) $33.95

Grades: 4 5 6 7 8   **953.3**

1. Yemen -- Description and travel 2. Yemen (Republic) 3. Yemen (Republic)

ISBN 1584159618; 1612281060; 9781584159612; 9781612281063

LC 2011016773

This book on Yemen by Claire O'Neal is part of the "Your Land and My Land: The Middle East" series, which "provides an . . . introduction to the history and geography of several Middle Eastern and Southeast Asian countries from a tourist's perspective." Also included are a "recipe and a . . . craft project representing the country." (Booklist)

Includes bibliographical references and index.

953.53   Oman

Ejaz, Khadija

We visit Oman; by Khadija Ejaz. Mitchell Lane Publishers 2012 63 p. col. ill., col. maps (library) $33.95; (ebook) $33.95

Grades: 4 5 6 7 8   **953.53**
1. Oman -- Description and travel 2. Oman
ISBN 1584159626; 1612281044; 9781584159629;
9781612281049

LC 2011000724

This book on Oman by Khadija Ejaz is part of the "Your Land and My Land: The Middle East" series, which "provides an . . . introduction to the history and geography of several Middle Eastern and Southeast Asian countries from a tourist's perspective." Also included are a "recipe and a . . . craft project representing the country." (Booklist)

Includes bibliographical references (p. 59-61) and index.

953.6   Persian Gulf States

Cooper, Robert
Bahrain; [by] Robert Cooper and Jo-Ann Spilling. 2nd ed.; Marshall Cavendish Benchmark 2011 144p il map (Cultures of the world) lib bdg $42.79
Grades: 5 6 7 8   **953.6**
1. Bahrain
ISBN 978-1-6087-0213-8; 1-6087-0213-8

LC 2010019621

First published 2000

Provides information on the geography, history, wildlife, governmental structure, economy, cultural diversity, peoples, religion, and culture of Bahrain.

Includes glossary and bibliographical references

Orr, Tamra
★ **Qatar**; [by] Tamra Orr. Marshall Cavendish Benchmark 2008 144p il map (Cultures of the world) lib bdg $42.79
Grades: 5 6 7 8   **953.6**
1. Qatar
ISBN 978-0-7614-2566-3; 0-7614-2566-7

LC 2006033626

This describes the geography, history, government, economy, environment, people, and culture of Qatar

Includes glossary and bibliographical references

953.67   Kuwait

O'Shea, Maria
Kuwait; by Maria O'Shea and Michael Spilling. 2nd ed.; Marshall Cavendish Benchmark 2010 144p il map (Cultures of the world) lib bdg $42.79
Grades: 5 6 7 8   **953.67**
1. Kuwait
ISBN 978-0-7614-4479-4 lib bdg; 0-7614-4479-3 lib bdg

LC 2009007069

First published 1999

Provides information on the geography, history, wildlife, governmental structure, economy, cultural diversity, peoples, religion, and culture of Kuwait

Includes glossary and bibliographical references

Sonneborn, Liz
Kuwait; Enchantment of the World. by Liz Sonneborn. Children's Press, an imprint of Scholastic Inc. 2014 144 p. ill., maps. (library binding) $40
Grades: 5 6 7 8   **953.67**
1. Kuwait
ISBN 053122015X; 9780531220153

LC 2013026062

This book, by Liz Sonneborn, focuses on Kuwait. The book discusses the "country's culture, history, and geography are explored in detail, allowing readers a chance to see how people live. . . . Sidebars highlight especially interesting people, places, and events . . . [and] easy recipes give readers the opportunity to experience foreign cuisine first-hand." (Publisher's note)

"Many students turn to the Internet for writing reports, but for reliably accurate, attractively presented and well-calibrated information, the long-standing Enchantment of the World series remains a superior choice. Each volume has been completely rewritten from a previous edition—in many cases to startling effect given recent political events. Although the basic structure holds true to past versions, the updated photographs are truly eye-popping and take care to portray the countries as modern often opting for showing, say, a surgeon at work rather than a rural farmer. It might not be necessary for libraries to replace [this title], since it hasn't changed radically, but this is a solid offering with updated statistics. Each volume in this reliable series includes extensive back matter with a detailed index." Booklist

Includes bibliographical references and index

Tracy, Kathleen
We visit Kuwait; by Kathleen Tracy. Mitchell Lane Publishers 2012 63 p. ill. (chiefly col.), col. maps (Your land and my land. The Middle East) (library bound) $33.95; (ebook) $33.95
Grades: 4 5 6 7 8   **953.67**
1. Kuwait -- Description and travel 2. Kuwait
ISBN 1584159588; 1612281001; 9781584159582;
9781612281001

LC 2011002756

This book on Kuwait by Kathleen Tracy is part of the "Your Land and My Land: The Middle East" series, which "provides an . . . introduction to the history and geography of several Middle Eastern and Southeast Asian countries from a tourist's perspective." Also included are a "recipe and a . . . craft project representing the country." (Booklist)

Includes bibliographical references (p. 58-61) and index.

953.8   Saudi Arabia

Tracy, Kathleen
We visit Saudi Arabia; by Kathleen Tracy. Mitchell Lane Publishers 2011 63 p. col. ill., map (library) $33.95
Grades: 4 5 6 7 8   **953.8**
1. Persian Gulf region 2. Saudi Arabia
ISBN 1584159634; 9781584159636

LC 2011000728

This book by Kathleen Tracy is part of the Social Studies series and looks at Saudi Arabia. "One of the most socially conservative countries on earth, Saudi Arabia is defined by Islam and ancient traditions. At the same time, its vast oil fields have helped build glistening, modern cities filled with world-class restaurants and designer shops." (Publisher's note)

Includes bibliographical references and index.

954   India and neighboring south Asian countries

Arnold, Caroline

★ **Taj** Mahal; by Caroline Arnold and Madeleine Comora; illustrated by Rahul Bhushan. Carolrhoda Books 2007 un il lib bdg $17.95

Grades: 4 5 6 7   **954**
1. Mogul Empire 2. Taj Mahal (Agra, India)
ISBN 978-0-7613-2609-0 lib bdg; 0-7613-2609-X lib bdg

LC 2001006685

Recounts the love story behind the building of the Taj Mahal in India, discussing how it was constructed and providing information on Indian culture.

"The small, detailed paintings are . . . set on beautifully constructed pages resembling those of illuminated manuscripts. . . . The book is sumptuous in appearance and presents a bit of history not often told for children." SLJ

Mann, Elizabeth

★ **Taj** Mahal; a story of love and empire. by Elizabeth Mann; with illustrations by Alan Witschonke. Mikaya 2008 47p il (Wonders of the world) $22.95

Grades: 4 5 6 7   **954**
1. Mogul Empire 2. Taj Mahal (Agra, India)
ISBN 1-931414-20-3; 978-1-931414-20-3

LC 2008060054

This is a "dramatic retelling of the construction of the Taj Mahal. Mann begins with two pages of prose that relay the commonly told legend, but then proceeds to explode that legend with descriptive writing, colorful illustrations, ancient paintings, maps, and photographs." Booklist

Includes bibliographical references

Ram-Prasad, Chakravarthi

Exploring the life, myth, and art of India. Rosen 2009 144p il map (Civilizations of the world) lib bdg $29.95

Grades: 7 8 9 10 11 12   **954**
1. Indic mythology 2. Indic art 3. India -- Civilization
ISBN 978-1-4358-5615-8; 1-4358-5615-5

LC 2009-9274

This describes the civilization, mythology and art of ancient India

"This beautifully illustrated and well-written [title] . . . is perfect for those assignments where students must look at the culture of a civilization. Artwork and pictures blend seamlessly with the information and the reader is taken on a journey of discovery. Myths are used as the story of how

the people view themselves, blended with the discussion of the reality of life. Everyday life is tied to the belief systems and is explained in light of those beliefs. The pictures are beautifully done and there is almost as much information in the captions as there is in the text." Libr Media Connect

Includes glossary and bibliographical references

954.9   Other jurisdictions

NgCheong-Lum, Roseline, 1962-

Maldives; 2nd ed.; Marshall Cavendish Benchmark 2011 144p il map (Cultures of the world) lib bdg $42.79

Grades: 5 6 7 8   **954.9**
1. Maldives
ISBN 978-1-6087-0217-6; 1-6087-0217-0

LC 2010019746

First published 2001

Provides information on the geography, history, wildlife, governmental structure, economy, cultural diversity, peoples, religion, and culture of Maldives.

Includes glossary and bibliographical references

Taylor-Butler, Christine

Sacred mountain; Everest. Lee & Low Books 2009 48p il $19.95

Grades: 5 6 7 8   **954.9**
1. Mount Everest (China and Nepal)
ISBN 978-1-60060-255-9; 1-60060-255-X

LC 2008-30423

"The informative text is amply illustrated with well-chosen black-and-white and color photographs." SLJ

Includes glossary

Yackley-Franken, Nicki

Teens in Nepal; by Nicki Yackley-Franken. Compass Point Books 2008 96p map (Global connections) lib bdg $31.93

Grades: 7 8 9 10   **954.9**
1. Teenagers 2. Nepal
ISBN 978-0-7565-3411-0 lib bdg; 0-7565-3411-9 lib bdg

LC 2007-32693

Uncovers the challenges, pastimes, customs and cultures of teens in Nepal.

"Information is solid, giving readers an informed and realistic view of life in that country. A historical time line is included, and suggestions for other nonfiction and fiction titles for further reading." Voice Youth Advocates

Includes glossary and bibliographical references

954.91   Pakistan

Hinman, Bonnie

We visit Pakistan; by Bonnie Hinman. Mitchell Lane Publishers 2012 63 p. ill. (chiefly col.), col. maps (Your land and my land. The Middle East) (library) $33.95

Grades: 4 5 6 7 8 **954.91**
1. Pakistan
ISBN 158415960X; 9781584159605

LC 2011030763

This book on Pakistan by Bonnie Hinman is part of the "Your Land and My Land: The Middle East" series, which "provides an . . . introduction to the history and geography of several Middle Eastern and Southeast Asian countries from a tourist's perspective." Topics such as "terrorism and al-Qaeda" are covered along with "descriptions of the country's history and attractions." Also included are a "recipe and a . . . craft project representing the country." (Booklist)

Includes bibliographical references (p. 59-61) and index.

Morgan, Sally

Focus on Pakistan; [by] Sally Morgan. World Almanac Library 2007 64p il map (World in focus) lib bdg $33.27; pa $11.95

Grades: 6 7 8 9 **954.91**
1. Pakistan
ISBN 978-0-8368-6752-7 lib bdg; 978-0-8368-6759-6 pa

LC 2007022011

This describes the history, landscape and climate, population and settlements, government and politics, energy and resources, economy and income, global connections, transportation and communications, education and health, culture and religion, leisure and tourism, environment and conservation, and future challenges of Pakistan.

"Attractive color photographs, graphs, and charts illustrate [this] volume. . . . [This book presents] current, accurate information in a way that is not too dry or overwhelming for the intended age group." SLJ

Includes glossary and bibliographical references

Sonneborn, Liz

Pakistan; by Liz Sonneborn. Children's Press 2013 144 p. ill. (mostly col.), col. maps. (Enchantment of the world, second series) (library) $40

Grades: 5 6 7 8 **954.91**
1. Pakistan 2. Pakistan -- Description and travel
ISBN 0531275442; 9780531275443

LC 2012000505

This book, by Liz Sonneborn, is part of the "Enchantment of the World" series. In it the author provides information and photographs showcasing the people, places and events surrounding the South Asian country of Pakistan. Contents include photographs of Pakistani cities and landscapes, statistics describing the nation's features, and traditional Pakistani recipes.

Includes bibliographical references and index

954.92 Bangladesh

Phillips, Douglas A.

Bangladesh; [by] Douglas A. Phillips and Charles F. Gritzner. Chelsea House 2007 107p il map (Modern world nations) lib bdg $30

Grades: 7 8 9 10 **954.92**
1. Bangladesh
ISBN 0-7910-9251-8 lib bdg; 978-0-7910-9251-4 lib bdg

LC 2006032006

Describes the geography, history, people, culture, economy, and government of Bangladesh

Includes bibliographical references

955 Iran

DiPrimio, Pete

We visit Iran; by Pete DiPrimio. Mitchell Lane Publishers 2012 63 p. col. ill., maps (library) $33.95

Grades: 4 5 6 7 8 **955**
1. Iran -- History 2. Iran
ISBN 1584159545; 9781584159544

LC 2011016765

This book by Pete DiPrimio looks at Iran. "It is a Middle Eastern country with European (not Arabian) founders. It was the home of one of the ancient world's greatest empires, the Persian Empire. Its many ancient ruins include the palace complex of Persepolis, which was so big it took 150 years to finish. While the nation develops nuclear technology, its government—called an Islamic Republic—dictates people's lives, from the clothing they wear to the news they hear." (Publisher's note)

Includes bibliographical references and index.

Seidman, David

Teens in Iran; by David Seidman. Compass Point Books 2008 96p il map (Global connections) lib bdg $31.93

Grades: 7 8 9 10 **955**
1. Youth -- Iran
ISBN 978-0-7565-3300-7 lib bdg; 0-7565-3300-7 lib bdg

LC 2007-5411

Explores the daily lives and customs of Iranian teenagers, discussing holidays, education, religion, employment, and culture.

"The information is solid, giving readers an informed and realistic view of life in that country. A historical time line is included, and suggestions for other nonfiction and fiction titles for further reading. Readers are directed to a Web site, where Internet links and a list of additional nonfiction titles are provided." Voice Youth Advocates

Shapera, Paul M.

Iran's religious leaders. Rosen Pub. 2009 80p il (Understanding Iran) lib bdg $22.95

Grades: 6 7 8 9 **955**
1. Islam 2. Religion and politics 3. Iran -- Assembly of Experts 4. Iran -- Politics and government
ISBN 978-1-4358-5283-9 lib bdg; 1-4358-5283-4 lib bdg

LC 2008047709

"The book begins with an introduction to Islam, including differences between the Sunni and Shi'a branches. There's also a history lesson. . . . The book [describes] . . . religious leaders and how the Iranian government is organized.

. . . [The book offers] an accessible format and a layout filled with many interesting color photographs. . . . An extremely helpful book for report writers, this also works for anyone who wants to understand how and why Iran functions the way it does." Booklist

Includes glossary and bibliographical references

Wagner, Heather Lehr

The **Iranian** Revolution. Chelsea House 2010 111p il (Milestones in modern world history) lib bdg $35

Grades: 7 8 9 10 11 12   **955**

1. Iran -- History -- 1941-1979
ISBN 978-1-60413-490-2; 1-60413-490-9

LC 2009-22336

"Chapters cover the origin of the Pahlavi dynasty, [Ayatollah] Khomeini's early life and how he came to symbolize opposition to the shah's regime, and the shah's aggressive campaigns of reform and Westernization. . . . A solid addition to the series." SLJ

Includes bibliographical references

955.06   Iran - 2005 -

Steele, Philip

★ **Iran** and the West; by Philip Steele. 1st ed. Rosen Pub. 2013 48 p. col. ill. (library) $29.25

Grades: 6 7 8   **955.06**

1. Iran -- Foreign relations 2. Iran 3. Iran -- History
ISBN 1448860318; 9781448860319

LC 2012010613

In this book, readers "explore the long history and culture of Iran—the rise of the Ayatollah, the election of current president Mahmoud Ahmadinejad, diplomatic relations with countries in Europe and the United States, and the importance of Iran in the global economy." Photographs, illustrations, maps, and further reading are included. (Publisher's note)

Includes bibliographical references (p. 46) and index.

956   Middle East (Near East)

Abbott, David

Conflict in the Middle East. Arcturus Pub. 2011 46p il (Secret history) lib bdg $32.80

Grades: 7 8 9 10   **956**

1. Spies 2. Espionage 3. Israel-Arab conflicts 4. Middle East -- Politics and government
ISBN 978-1-8483-7697-7; 1-8483-7697-9

LC 2010011001

This book explores the secrets of the Arab-Israeli conflict. Both sides in this war have made use of spies, surveillance, special operations, and secret weapons. Even the peace talks have their own secret history.

"The title of the Secret History series will grab readers, even reluctant ones, and they won't be disappointed by the intriguing info regarding codes and code breakers, spies, terrorists, and double agents, with profiles of heroes and traitors on all sides. . . . The readable design, with clear type on

thick, high-quality paper, includes lots of sidebars, photos, screens, and quotes." Booklist

Includes bibliographical references

Crompton, Samuel

The **Third** Crusade; Richard the Lionhearted vs. Saladin. [by] Samuel Willard Crompton. Chelsea House 2003 114p il map (Great battles through the ages) $22.95

Grades: 7 8 9 10   **956**

1. Crusades 2. Kings 3. Sultans 4. Islamic leaders
ISBN 0-7910-7437-4

LC 2003-4593

"In 1187 King Richard I sought control of the Holy Land. This text details the Third Crusade in which the king of England lead an army of Christians to sieze the Holy Land from the Muslims." Publisher's note

Includes bibliographical references

Gritzner, Jeffrey A.

North Africa and the Middle East; [by] Jeffrey A. Gritzner and Charles F. Gritzner. Chelsea House 2006 120p il map (Modern world cultures) lib bdg $30

Grades: 7 8 9 10   **956**

1. Middle East 2. North Africa
ISBN 0-7910-8145-1

LC 2006011649

Describes the history, culture, peoples, and physical geography of North Africa and the Middle East.

Includes bibliographical references

January, Brendan

The **Arab** Conquests of the Middle East. Twenty First Century Books 2009 160p il (Pivotal moments in history) $38.60

Grades: 8 9 10 11 12   **956**

1. Islam -- History 2. Middle East -- History
ISBN 978-0-8225-8744-6; 0-8225-8744-0

"One hundred years after the death of Muhammad, Muslim armies had conquered most of North Africa, the Middle East, and parts of Spain and were fighting as far north as modern France. This attractively illustrated history begins with Muhammad's life and revelations and covers the early period of the Muslim community first as it struggled to survive and then as it gradually assumed dominance over the Arabian peninsula. . . . A section on primary-source research will intrigue historically minded readers, and a who's who and lists of further reading make this volume highly useful for reports." SLJ

Includes bibliographical references

Kort, Michael

The **handbook** of the Middle East; by Michael G. Kort. rev ed.; Twenty-First Century Books 2008 320p il map lib bdg $39.95

Grades: 8 9 10 11 12   **956**

1. Middle East
ISBN 978-0-8225-7143-8; 0-8225-7143-9

LC 2006-34917

First published 2002

Examines the past, present, and future of all the countries in the Middle East, discussing their history and culture
Includes bibliographical references

The **Middle** East: opposing viewpoints; David M. Haugen, Susan Musser and Kacy Lovelace, book editors. Greenhaven Press 2009 261p il map (Opposing viewpoints series) lib bdg $38.50; pa $26.75

Grades: 8 9 10 11 12 **956**
1. Middle East -- Politics and government 2. Middle East -- Foreign relations -- United States 3. United States -- Foreign relations -- Middle East
ISBN 978-0-7377-4532-0 lib bdg; 0-7377-4532-0 lib bdg; 978-0-7377-4533-7 pa; 0-7377-4533-9 pa
LC 2008-55848
The articles in this anthology cover such topics as U.S. relations with Middle Eastern nations, the Israeli/Palestinian conflict, whether Iran is a threat to the United States, and counterterrorism efforts in Middle Eastern nations.
Includes bibliographical references

956.04   Middle East--1945-1980

Hampton, Wilborn
★ **War** in the Middle East; a reporter's story. Candlewick Press 2007 112p il map $19.99

Grades: 6 7 8 9 10 11 12 **956.04**
1. Israel-Arab War, 1973 2. Middle East -- History
ISBN 978-0-7636-2493-4; 0-7636-2493-4
LC 2006-51694
"Recalling experiences as a reporter assigned to cover the 1970 Jordanian civil conflict dubbed Black September, and the Yom Kippur War that began in October 1973, Hampton not only presents a clear summary of the issues that provoked each outbreak of violence but also provides both personal slant and a sense of immediacy to his account of events." Booklist
Includes bibliographical references

Senker, Cath
The **Arab** -Israeli conflict; [by] Cath Senker. new ed.; Arcturus Pub. 2008 48p il map (Timelines) lib bdg $32.80

Grades: 5 6 7 8 **956.04**
1. Israel-Arab conflicts
ISBN 978-1-84193-725-0 lib bdg; 1-84193-725-8 lib bdg
LC 2007-7547
First published 2005 by Smart Apple Media
This describes current conditions in Israel and the occupied territories and includes a history of major events and political developments.
"A complex situation is clearly explained. . . . [This is] well-illustrated. . . . Throughout, the tone is nonjudgmental." SLJ [review of 2005 edition]
Includes bibliographical references

Woolf, Alex
The **Arab** -Israeli War since 1948; by Alex Woolf. 1st ed. Heinemann Library 2011 80 p. ill. (some col.), col. maps (library) $36.50; (paperback) $10.99

Grades: 6 7 8 9 **956.04**
1. Israel-Arab conflicts 2. Arab-Israeli conflict
ISBN 1432959956; 9781432959951; 9781432960049
LC 2011015920
"In this volume of the illustrated 'Living Through' series, readers are given a . . . summary of the critical events that shaped what we now think of as the Arab-Israeli Wars. . . . Readers will encounter some of the individuals, causes, and ongoing contradictions that make this international issue so seemingly unsolvable." (Children's Literature)
Includes bibliographical references (p. 76-78) and index.

956.1   Turkey

Lace, William W.
★ The **unholy** crusade; the ransacking of medieval Constantinople. [by] William W. Lace. Lucent Books 2007 104p il map (Lucent library of historical eras, Middle Ages) lib bdg $32.45

Grades: 6 7 8 9 **956.1**
1. Crusades 2. Middle Ages 3. Istanbul (Turkey)
ISBN 978-1-59018-846-0 lib bdg; 1-59018-846-2 lib bdg
LC 2006002572
"Lace gives equal attention to the events leading up to the destruction of Constantinople and traces the planning and plotting of the Crusades. . . . [The book has] numerous color reproductions. Clear, concise writing makes [it] highly readable, while the scholarship makes [it a] valuable [resource]." SLJ
Includes bibliographical references

LaRoche, Amelia
We visit Turkey; by Amelia LaRoche. Mitchell Lane Publishers 2012 63 p. ill. (chiefly col.), col. maps (library) $33.95

Grades: 4 5 6 7 8 **956.1**
1. Turkey -- Description and travel 2. Turkey
ISBN 1584159561; 9781584159568
LC 2011030765
This book on Turkey by Amelia Laroche is part of the "Your Land and My Land: The Middle East" series, which "provides an . . . introduction to the history and geography of several Middle Eastern and Southeast Asian countries from a tourist's perspective." It "similarly mentions but does not dwell upon the rise of Islam and the hijab controversy." Also included are a "recipe and a . . . craft project representing the country." (Booklist)
Includes bibliographical references (p. 59-61) and index.

Shields, Sarah D.
★ **Turkey**; [by] Sarah Shields. National Geographic 2009 64p il map (Countries of the world) lib bdg $27.90

Grades: 4 5 6 7   **956.1**
1. Turkey
ISBN 978-1-4263-0387-6 lib bdg; 1-4263-0387-4
lib bdg
LC 2009275583

This describes the geography, nature, history, people and
culture, government and economy of Turkey
Includes glossary and bibliographical references

956.7 Iraq

Adams, Simon

The **Iraq** War. Arcturus Pub. 2011 46p il map
(Secret history) lib bdg $32.80
Grades: 7 8 9 10   **956.7**
1. Iraq War, 2003-2011
ISBN 978-1-84837-698-4; 1-84837-698-7
LC 2010011764

This examines the Iraq War, including "from propaganda
and intelligence to technology and sacrifice. . . . Archival
photographs combine with a busy but well-organized design
to present an engaging perspective. . . . Both reluctant readers and history buffs in need of a fresh approach to events
will appreciate this [book]." Horn Book Guide
Includes bibliographical references

Ellis, Deborah

★ **Children** of war; voices of Iraqi refugees.
Groundwood Books 2009 128p il $15.95; pa $9.95
Grades: 7 8 9 10 11 12   **956.7**
1. Refugees 2. Children and war 3. Iraq War, 2003-
2011
ISBN 978-0-88899-907-8; 0-88899-907-0; 978-0-
88899-908-5 pa; 0-88899-908-9 pa

Ellis "interviews child refugees from Iraq, now living in
Jordan, and a few who have made it to Canada. . . . Accompanying each of the . . . interviews with young people
is a brief introduction and a photo. . . . What is haunting
are their graphic recent memories of what they witnessed.
. . . An important, current title that will have lasting
significance." Booklist
Includes glossary

Mason, Paul, 1967-

The **Iraq** War. Arcturus Pub. 2011 48p il map
(Secret history) lib bdg $32.80
Grades: 7 8 9 10   **956.7**
1. Iraq War, 2003-2011 2. Iraq -- Politics and
government
ISBN 978-1-84837-639-4; 1-84837-639-1
LC 2009051266

"The title of the Secret History series will grab readers,
even reluctant ones, and they won't be disappointed by the
intriguing info regarding codes and code breakers, spies, terrorists, and double agents, with profiles of heroes and traitors on all sides. . . . The readable design, with clear type on
thick, high-quality paper, includes lots of sidebars, photos,
screens, and quotes." Booklist
Includes bibliographical references

O'Neal, Claire

We visit Iraq; by Claire O'Neal. Mitchell Lane
Publishers 2012 63 p. ill. (chiefly col.), col. maps
(library bound) $33.95
Grades: 4 5 6 7 8   **956.7**
1. Persian Gulf region 2. Iraq
ISBN 1584159553; 9781584159551
LC 2011016771

This book by Claire O'Neal is part of the Social Studies
series and looks at Iraq. "Iraq's Tigris and Euphrates rivers turned this Middle Eastern desert into the world's first
farmland. Over six millenia, Iraq's civilizations have laid
foundations for the rest of the world. They built great stone
ziggurats and soaring mosques. They invented the wheel, the
calendar, and the written word. With their riches, they also
attracted war." (Publisher's note)
Includes bibliographical references (p. 59-61) and index.

Samuels, Charlie

★ **Iraq**; [by] Charlie Samuels; Sarah Shields and
Shakir Mustafa, consultants. National Geographic
2007 64p il map (Countries of the world) lib bdg
$27.90
Grades: 4 5 6 7   **956.7**
1. Iraq
ISBN 978-1-4263-0061-5
LC 2007024675

This describes the geography, nature, history, people and
culture, government and economy of Iraq.
Includes glossary and bibliographical references

Smithson, Ryan

Ghosts of war; my tour of duty. HarperTeen
2009 321p il $16.99; lib bdg $17.89
Grades: 8 9 10 11 12   **956.7**
1. Soldiers -- United States 2. Iraq War, 2003- --
Personal narratives
ISBN 978-0-06-166468-7; 0-06-166468-5; 978-0-06-
166470-0 lib bdg; 0-06-166470-7 lib bdg
LC 2008-35420

"Ryan Smithson was a typical 16-year-old high-school
student until 9/11. . . . Smithson enlisted in the Army Reserve the following year and, a year into the Iraq war, was
deployed to an Army engineer unit as a heavy-equipment
operator. His poignant, often harrowing account, especially
vivid in sensory details, chronicles his experiences in basic
training and in Iraq. . . . This memoir is a remarkable, deeply
penetrating read that will compel teens to reflect on their
own thoughts about duty, patriotism and sacrifice." Kirkus
Includes glossary and bibliographical references

Wilkes, Sybella

Out of Iraq; refugees' stories in words, paintings
and music. Evans 2010 70p il map $17.99
Grades: 4 5 6 7   **956.7**
1. Refugees 2. Iraq
ISBN 978-0-237-53930-6; 0-237-53930-6

"Provides an concise overview of events before and
during the invasion, interspersed with first-person narratives of Iraqi refugees, gathered while Wilkes worked with
the United Nations Refugee Agency in Syria. . . . Moving

photographs and artwork, quotations from political figures, and accessible language form a harrowing window into lives rarely paid witness." Publ Wkly

Zeinert, Karen

The **brave** women of the Gulf Wars; Operation Desert Storm and Operation Iraqi Freedom. [by] Karen Zeinert & Mary Miller. 21st Century Bks. 2006 112p il $30.60

Grades: 7 8 9 10   **956.7**

1. Iraq War, 2003 2. Women in the armed forces 3. Persian Gulf War, 1991 -- Women

ISBN 0-7613-2705-3

"Zeinert and Miller reinforce the argument that women do, indeed, belong in the U.S. military by highlighting their contributions in Operations Desert Storm (Kuwait) and Iraqi Freedom. . . . The narrative paints a picture of consistent courage under fire and, one terse mention of the abuses at Abu Ghraib Prison aside, of professional conduct. The authors extend their purview with a chapter on women journalists in the campaigns, and while thoroughly villainizing Saddam Hussein, they also indicate that the official justifications for the war in Iraq turned out to be weak at best. A utilitarian but cogent assessment of the topic, well supported by notes and sources." Booklist

Includes bibliographical references

956.704   Iraq--1979-

Bingham, Jane

The **Gulf** wars with Iraq; by Jane Bingham. Heinemann Library 2012 80 p. ill., maps (library) $36.50; (paperback) $10.99

Grades: 6 7 8 9   **956.704**

1. Iraq War, 2003-2011 2. Persian Gulf War, 1991

ISBN 1432959972; 9781432959975; 9781432960063

LC 2011015922

This book by Jane Bingham is part of the Living Through series and looks at the U.S. Gulf Wars with Iraq. Here, "Bingham takes her readers back through the twists and turns of fact and fiction that are part and parcel of these connected conflicts." Topics include "the falsification of intelligence linked to Saddam Hussein's weapons program, the ruthless nature of the Iraqi dictator and his family, and the human cost of these two wars." (Children's Literature)

Includes bibliographical references (p. 77-78) and index.

956.91   Syria

Gelfand, Dale Evva

Syria; by Dale Evva Gelfand. ABDO Pub. Co. 2013 144 p. (library) $35.64

Grades: 8 9 10 11 12   **956.91**

1. Syria

ISBN 1617836397; 9781617836398

LC 2012946084

This book by Dale Evva Gelfant is part of the Countries of the World series and looks at Syria. It "introduces Syria's history, geography, culture, climate, government, economy,

and other significant features. Sidebars, maps, fact pages, a glossary, a timeline, historic images and full-color photos" are included. (Publisher's note)

Yomtov, Nel

Syria; Nel Yomtov. Children's Press, an imprint of Scholastic Inc. 2013 144 p. color illustrations (library binding) $40

Grades: 5 6 7 8   **956.91**

1. Syria

ISBN 053123679X; 9780531236796

LC 2013000088

This book, by Nel Yomtov, focuses on Syria. The "country's culture, history, and geography are explored in detail, allowing readers a chance to see how people live. . . . Sidebars highlight especially interesting people, places, and events [and] recipes give readers the opportunity to experience foreign cuisine first-hand." (Publisher's note)

"Many students turn to the Internet for writing reports, but for reliably accurate, attractively presented and well-calibrated information, the long-standing Enchantment of the World series remains a superior choice. Each volume has been completely rewritten from a previous edition—in many cases to startling effect given recent political events. Although the basic structure holds true to past versions, the updated photographs are truly eye-popping and take care to portray the countries as modern—often opting for showing, say, a surgeon at work rather than a rural farmer. Syria obviously can't be completely up-to-date because of the ongoing rebellion, but it does a good job of explaining the roots of the unrest, along with the usual topics of food, religion, and customs. Each volume in this reliable series includes extensive back matter with a detailed index." Booklist

Includes bibliographical references and index

956.92   Lebanon

Sheehan, Sean

Lebanon; [by] Sean Sheehan & Zawiah Abdul Latif. 2nd ed.; Marshall Cavendish Benchmark 2008 144p il map (Cultures of the world) lib bdg $42.79

Grades: 5 6 7 8   **956.92**

1. Lebanon

ISBN 978-0-7614-2081-1 lib bdg; 0-7614-2081-9 lib bdg

LC 2006101735

First published 1997

"Provides comprehensive information on the geography, history, wildlife, governmental structure, economy, cultural diversity, peoples, religion, and culture of Lebanon." Publisher's note

Includes bibliographical references

956.93   Cyprus

Spilling, Michael

Cyprus; [by] Michael Spilling and Jo-Ann Spilling. 2nd ed.; Marshall Cavendish Benchmark 2010 144p il map (Cultures of the world) lib bdg $42.79

Grades: 5 6 7 8   **956.93**
1. Cyprus
ISBN 978-0-7614-4855-6 lib bdg; 0-7614-4855-1
lib bdg

LC 2009045689

First published 2000
This offers information on the geography, history, wildlife, governmental structure, economy, cultural diversity,
peoples, religion, and culture of Cyprus
Includes glossary and bibliographical references

956.94   Palestine; Israel

Ellis, Deborah
★ **Three** wishes; Palestinian and Israeli children
speak. Groundwood Bks. 2004 110p il map hardcover o.p. pa $9.99
Grades: 5 6 7 8   **956.94**
1. Palestinian Arabs 2. Israel-Arab conflicts
ISBN 0-88899-608-X; 0-88899-645-4 pa
"An excellent presentation of a confusing historic
struggle, told within a palpable, perceptive and empathetic
format." SLJ
Includes bibliographical references

Frank, Mitch
Understanding the Holy Land; answering questions about the Israeli-Palestinian Conflict. Viking
2005 152p il map (paperback) $8.99
Grades: 6 7 8 9 10   **956.94**
1. Israel-Arab conflicts
ISBN 0670060437; 9780670060436

LC 2004014973

The author "tackles the complex subject of the Israeli-
Palestinian conflict, making it comprehensible, if not any
less horrific. . . . He uses a simple yet wonderfully effective
technique to present the information: questions and answers.
. . . Evenhanded and honest." Booklist
Includes bibliographical references

Israel: opposing viewpoints; Myra Immell, book
editor. Greenhaven Press 2011 193p map (Opposing viewpoints series) $41.70; pa $28.90
Grades: 8 9 10 11 12   **956.94**
1. Israel-Arab conflicts
ISBN 978-0-7377-4974-8; 0-7377-4974-1; 978-0-
7377-4975-5 pa; 0-7377-4975-X pa

LC 2010022999

Articles in this anthology discuss Israel's right to exist,
key issues in the conflict between Israel and Palestine, and
what U.S. policy should be regarding Israel.
Includes bibliographical references

Owings, Lisa
Israel; by Lisa Owings. ABDO Pub. Co. 2013
144 p. (library) $35.64
Grades: 8 9 10 11 12   **956.94**
1. Israel
ISBN 1617836303; 9781617836305

LC 2012946075

This book by Lisa Owings is part of the Countries of
the World series and looks at Israel. It "introduces Israel's
history, geography, culture, climate, government, economy,
and other significant features. Sidebars, maps, fact pages, a
glossary, a timeline, historic images and full-color photos,
and well-placed graphs and charts" are included. (Publisher's note)

Saul, Laya
We visit Israel; by Laya Saul. Mitchell Lane
Publishers 2012 63 p. ill., maps (library) $33.95
Grades: 4 5 6 7 8   **956.94**
1. Israel -- Description and travel 2. Israel
ISBN 158415957X; 9781584159575

LC 2011024706

This book on Israel by Laya Saul is part of the "Your
Land and My Land: The Middle East" series, which "provides an . . . introduction to the history and geography of
several Middle Eastern and Southeast Asian countries from
a tourist's perspective. . . . 'We Visit Israel' is clearly written
from a Jewish Israeli perspective, but Saul makes sure to
mention areas of conflict and controversy." Also included
are a "recipe and a . . . craft project representing the country." (Booklist)
Includes bibliographical references (p. 60-61) and index.

Young, Emma
★ **Israel;** [by] Emma Young; Zvi Ben-Dor
Benite, George Kanazi, and Aviva Halamish, consul-
tants. National Geographic 2008 64p il map (Coun-
tries of the world) lib bdg $27.90
Grades: 4 5 6 7   **956.94**
1. Israel
ISBN 978-1-4263-0258-9 lib bdg; 1-4263-0258-4
lib bdg
This describes the geography, nature, history, people and
culture, government, and economy of Israel.
Includes glossary and bibliographical references

Zeigler, Donald J.
Israel; [by] Donald J. Zeigler. 2nd ed.; Chelsea
House 2007 120p il map (Modern world nations)
lib bdg $30
Grades: 7 8 9 10   **956.94**
1. Israel
ISBN 0-7910-9210-0

LC 2006014242

First published 2002
Describes the geography, history, people and culture,
politics, and economy of Israel
Includes bibliographical references

956.95 Jordan and West Bank

Understanding Jordan today; by Laura Perdew. Mitchell Lane Publishers 2014 63 p. (A kid's guide to the Middle East) $33.95

Grades: 4 5 6 7   956.95

1. Jordan

ISBN 1612286542; 9781612286549

LC 2014020462

This children's book, by Laura Perdew, part of the "Kid's Guide to the Middle East" series, "is an accurate and contemporary presentation that explores the Middle Eastern nation of Jordan with a focus on the country as it is today: current issues, culture, and lifestyle. The book is written in an easy-to-read enjoyable narrative form for elementary readers grades 3-6." (Publisher's note)

"Trying to sort through the Middle East can be difficult for even the most educated adults, but the titles in A Kid's Guide to the Middle East series breaks down the culture and ongoing conflict into manageable portions...Extensive back matter includes a recipe, craft, time line, glossary, and area facts. An essential series to help children appreciate and understand the rich diversity of this region." Booklist

Includes bibliographical references and index

Other recommended titles in the series are:
Understanding Afghanistan Today (2014)
Understanding Iran Today (2014)
Understanding Iraq Today (2014)
Understanding Israel Today (2014)
Understanding Lebanon Today (2015)
Understanding Palestine Today (2015)
Understanding Saudi Arabia Today (2014)
Understanding Syria Today (2014)
Understanding Turkey Today (2015)

Wingate, Katherine

The **Intifadas**; by Katherine Wingate. Rosen Pub. Group 2004 64p il map (War and conflict in the Middle East) lib bdg $26.50

Grades: 5 6 7 8   956.95

1. Israel-Arab conflicts 2. Palestine

ISBN 0-8239-4546-4

LC 2003-12562

"Wingate focuses on how the Palestinians lost their land and how the Palestinians in occupied territories retaliated. . . . Wingate sees hope in the peace organizations that work with young people. The series design is spacious, with clear type, lots of well-captioned news photos, up-to-date statistics, maps, and occasional boxed profiles of important leaders. . . . There's a lot to spark discussion." Booklist

Includes glossary and bibliographical references

958.1 Afghanistan

Ali, Sharifah Enayat

★ **Afghanistan**; by Sharifah Enayat Ali. 2nd ed.; Marshall Cavendish Benchmark 2006 144p il map (Cultures of the world) lib bdg $42.79

Grades: 5 6 7 8   958.1

1. Afghanistan

ISBN 978-0-7614-2064-4 lib bdg; 0-7614-2064-9 lib bdg

LC 2005034789

First published 1995

This is "well organized, informative, and entertaining. . . . Excellent-quality full-color photographs and reproductions show the people, landforms, buildings, and everyday activities of [Afghanistan]." SLJ [review of 1995 edtion]

Includes glossary and bibliographical references

Behnke, Alison

Afghanistan in pictures; rev and expanded; Lerner Publs. 2003 80p il map (Visual geography series) lib bdg $31.93

Grades: 5 6 7 8   958.1

1. Afghanistan

ISBN 0-8225-4683-3

LC 2002-13613

An introduction to the geography, history, government, people, and economy of this landlocked country with a long history of warfare and conquest

Includes glossary and bibliographical references

Bjorklund, Ruth

Afghanistan; by Ruth Bjorklund. Children's Press 2012 144 p. col. ill., col. maps (library) $40

Grades: 5 6 7 8   958.1

1. Afghanistan 2. Afghanistan -- Description and travel

ISBN 0531253503; 9780531253502

LC 2011013627

This book by Ruth Bjorklund is part of the Enchantment of the World series and looks at Afghanistan. In each book, "colourful photos provide . . . views of foreign cities and landscapes," "sidebars highlight especially interesting people, places, and events," and "recipes give readers the opportunity to experience foreign cuisine firsthand." (Publisher's note)

Includes bibliographical references (p. 134-135) and index.

Hunter, Dawn

Beyond bullets; a photo journal of Afghanistan. by Rafal Gerszak, with Dawn Hunter; photographs by Rafal Gerszak. Annick Press 2011 127p il $19.95

Grades: 7 8 9 10 11 12   958.1

1. Photographers 2. Photojournalism 3. Afghan War, 2001- 4. Afghanistan

ISBN 978-1-55451-293-5; 1-55451-293-X

"Photographer Rafal Gerszak spent a year embedded with the American military in Afghanistan, where he used his camera to document everyday life in the wartorn country. While there, he developed a deep affection for the land and its people, and he later returned on his own. Framed by journal entries that relate his experiences on two levels—as a foreigner looking for a deeper connection to a country that has stirred him and as a journalist looking for another side to the story—Beyond Bullets addresses the volatile situation in Afghanistan." (Publisher's note) "Age twelve and up." (Quill Quire)

"Author/photographer Gerszak first went to Afghanistan to spend a year embedded with an American military unit documenting house searches, disputes with village elders and the aftermath of battles. He returned as an unaffiliated photographer without a military escort, determined to document civilian life. This 'photo journal' features images from both trips to Afghanistan, accompanied by diary-like accounts of his travels. Gerszak's frank and descriptive observations effectively convey the ugliness, monotony and tragedy of war." Kirkus

Lusted, Marcia Amidon

The **capture** and killing of Osama bin Laden. ABDO Pub. Co. 2012 112p il (Essential events) lib bdg $23.95

Grades: 6 7 8   **958.1**
1. Terrorism 2. Terrorists 3. Al Qaeda (Organization)
ISBN 978-1-61783-180-5; 1-61783-180-8
           LC 2011025479

"Lusted explores Osama bin Laden's early life and the influences leading to his radicalization...The hunt for and eventual killing of bin Laden are not sensationalized." Horn Book

Includes glossary and bibliographical references

Steele, Philip

★ **Afghanistan**; from war to peace? by Philip Steele. 1st ed. Rosen Central 2012 48 p. col. ill., col. maps (library) $29.25

Grades: 6 7 8   **958.1**
1. Afghanistan -- History 2. Afghanistan -- Foreign relations 3. Afghanistan -- Politics and government 4. Afghanistan
ISBN 9781448860302
           LC 2012010616

This book by Philip Steele " examine[s] the history of Afghanistan, including its wars with the British Empire through its present-day occupation by American and NATO forces. Issues explored include the rise of the Taliban, the 9/11 attacks and the subsequent U.S. military ouster of the Taliban, the war of insurgency, and the plan for military withdrawal." (Publisher's note)

Includes bibliographical references and index.

Whitehead, Kim

Afghanistan; Revised ed. Mason Crest 2009 112 p. il map (Major Muslim Nations) lib bdg $25.95

Grades: 7 8 9 10   **958.1**
1. Islam 2. Taliban 3. Afghanistan
ISBN 9781422214039

This examines the ways Islam has influenced the culture and politics of Afghanistan, including how the Taliban came to power.

This "presents a cogent overview of [Afghanistan]. Excellent-quality photos and reproductions appear throughout." SLJ

Includes bibliographical references

Whitfield, Susan

★ **Afghanistan**; [by] Susan Whitfield; Thomas Barfield and Maliha Zulfacar, consultants. National

Geographic 2008 64p il map (Countries of the world) lib bdg $27.90

Grades: 4 5 6 7   **958.1**
1. Afghanistan
ISBN 978-1-4263-0256-5 lib bdg; 1-4263-0256-8 lib bdg

This describes the geography, nature, history, people and culture, government, and economy of Afghanistan.

Includes glossary and bibliographical references

958.104   Afghanistan--1919-

Lunis, Natalie

The **takedown** of Osama bin Laden; by Natalie Lunis. Bearport Publishing 2012 32 p. (Special ops) (lib. bdg.) $25.27

Grades: 4 5 6 7   **958.104**
1. United States. Navy 2. Terrorism 3. Terrorists -- Biography 4. United States. Navy. SEALs
ISBN 1617724599; 9781617724596
           LC 2011040472

In this book by Natalie Lunis on U.S. Navy SEALs "young readers will follow this elite group of soldiers on their raid and explore the context for their mission, from the 9/11 attacks by Al Qaeda to the war against terrorists in Afghanistan. Large, full-color photos, grade-appropriate text, and a narrative format [are designed to] keep kids turning the pages as they learn about [the U.S.] military." (Publisher's note)

Includes bibliographical references (p. 31) and index

958.4   Turkestan

King, David C.

Kyrgyzstan; [by] David C. King. Marshall Cavendish Benchmark 2005 144p il map (Cultures of the world) lib bdg $42.79

Grades: 5 6 7 8   **958.4**
1. Kyrgyzstan
ISBN 0-7614-2013-4
           LC 2005001314

Describes the geography, history, government, economy, people, and culture of Kyrgyzstan

Includes glossary and bibliographical references

Pang, Guek-Cheng, 1950-

Kazakhstan; 2nd ed.; Marshall Cavendish Benchmark 2011 144p il map (Cultures of the world) lib bdg $42.79

Grades: 5 6 7 8   **958.4**
1. Kazakhstan
ISBN 978-1-6087-0455-2; 1-6087-0455-6
First published 2001

This offers information on the geography, history, wildlife, governmental structure, economy, cultural diversity, peoples, religion, and culture of Kazakhstan.

958.5 Turkmenistan

Knowlton, MaryLee

Turkmenistan; [by] MaryLee Knowlton. Marshall Cavendish Benchmark 2006 144p il map (Cultures of the world) lib bdg $42.79

Grades: 5 6 7 8 **958.5**
1. Turkmenistan
ISBN 0-7614-2014-2

LC 2005006455

Describes the geography, history, government, economy, people, and culture of Turkmenistan

Includes glossary and bibliographical references

958.6 Tajikistan

Abazov, Rafis

Tajikistan; [by] Rafis Abazov. Marshall Cavendish Benchmark 2006 144p il map (Cultures of the world) lib bdg $42.79

Grades: 5 6 7 8 **958.6**
1. Tajikistan
ISBN 0-7614-2012-6

LC 2005001166

Describes the geography, history, government, economy, people, and culture of the former Soviet republic of Tajikistan

Includes glossary and bibliographical references

959 Southeast Asia

Phillips, Douglas A.

Southeast Asia; series consulting editor Charles F. Gritzner. Chelsea House Publishers 2006 129p (Modern world cultures) lib bdg $30

Grades: 7 8 9 10 **959**
1. Southeast Asia
ISBN 0-7910-8149-4

This describes the geography, history, people and cultures, politics, economics, and possible future of Southeast Asia.

This "accessible [title is] generously illustrated with colorful photos, maps, and clear charts, graphs, and other statistical data. . . . Phillips does an excellent job of organizing each topic by providing clear and outlined information. The research is well done, and information and statistics are up to date." SLJ

959.3 Thailand

Phillips, Douglas A.

Thailand. Chelsea House 2007 108p il map (Modern world nations) lib bdg $30

Grades: 7 8 9 10 **959.3**
1. Thailand
ISBN 978-0-7910-9250-7 lib bdg; 0-7910-9250-X lib bdg

LC 2006032009

Describes the geography, history, people, culture, economy, and government of Thailand

Includes bibliographical references

959.4 Laos

Dalal, A. Kamala

★ Laos; [by] A. Kamala Dalal. National Geographic 2009 64p il (Countries of the world) lib bdg $27.90

Grades: 4 5 6 7 **959.4**
1. Laos
ISBN 978-1-4263-0388-3 lib bdg; 1-4263-0388-2 lib bdg

This describes the geography, nature, history, people and culture, and govenment and economy of Laos

Includes glossary and bibliographical references

959.5 Malaysia, Brunei, Singapore

Foo Yuk Yee

Malaysia; by Heidi Munan, Foo Yuk Yee, and Jo-Ann Spilling. 3rd ed. Marshall Cavendish Benchmark 2012 144 p. col. ill., col. maps (library) $47.07

Grades: 5 6 7 8 **959.5**
1. Culture 2. Malaysia
ISBN 1608707857; 9781608707850

LC 2011004468

This book by Heidi Munan is part of the Cultures of the World series and looks at Malaysia. The "geography, history, economy and culture are all covered . . . . An entire chapter is devoted to the festivals, which are many because of the ethnic diversity of Malaysia. This is also made apparent in the section about food and manners, as the Muslims do not eat pork and the Hindus and Sikhs cannot eat beef, making it necessary to prepare various dishes for parties." (Children's Literature)

Includes bibliographical references and index.

959.57 Singapore

Layton, Leslie

Singapore; by Lesley Layton, Pang Guek Cheng,and Jo-Ann Spilling. 3rd ed. Marshall Cavendish Benchmark 2012 144 p. (library) $47.07

Grades: 5 6 7 8 **959.57**
1. Singapore
ISBN 1608707873; 9781608707874

LC 2011004479

This book is part of the Cultures of the World series and looks at Singapore. "Singapore is a small but mighty nation. Thanks to its strategic position and the energy of its people—the Malays, and migrant Chinese, Indians, and

Eurasians—it is now the world's number one airport and sea port, a regional financial center, a telecommunications hub, and a favored tourist destination." (Publisher's note)

Includes bibliographical references and index.

959.604   Cambodia 1949-

Sonneborn, Liz

The **Khmer** Rouge; by Liz Sonneborn. Marshall Cavendish Benchmark 2012 80 p. ill. (some col.), col. map (library) $34.21; (ebook) $34.21

Grades: 5 6 7 8   **959.604**
    1. Dith Pran, 1942-2008 2. Genocide -- Cambodia 3. Cambodia -- History -- 1975- 4. Parti communiste du Kampuchea 5. Cambodia -- History -- 1975-1979 6. Political atrocities -- Cambodia 7. Journalists -- Cambodia -- Biography 8. Political refugees -- Cambodia -- Biography
    ISBN 1608704742; 9781608704743; 9781608706952 pdf
                                          LC 2011005595

This book "tells the story of Dith Pran, a Cambodian journalist and translator who provided support to Sydney Schanberg, a New York Times correspondent. . . . Sadly, when Schanberg evacuated, Pran was forced to remain behind where he fell into captivity. Over a three year time period Dith Pran survived horrendous conditions but ultimately escaped and fled to Thailand. There, in a refugee camp, Pran was rescued by Schanberg and relocated to the United States." (Children's Literature)

Includes bibliographical references and index.

959.7   Vietnam

Green, Jen

★ **Vietnam**; [by] Jen Green. National Geographic 2008 64p il map (Countries of the world) lib bdg $27.90

Grades: 4 5 6 7   **959.7**
    1. Vietnam
    ISBN 978-1-4263-0202-2
                                          LC 2007047832

This describes the geography, nature, history, people and culture, government, and economy of Vietnam.

Includes glossary and bibliographical references

959.704   Vietnam--1945-

Caputo, Philip

★ **10,000** days of thunder; a history of the Vietnam War. [by] Philip Caputo. 1st ed; Atheneum Books for Young Readers 2005 128p il $22.95

Grades: 6 7 8 9   **959.704**
    1. Vietnam War, 1961-1975
    ISBN 0-689-86231-8
                                          LC 2004-15468

In this history of the Vietnam War "Caputo has produced what is at once an overview and a sensitive, resonant picture of the war as seen and experienced by American soldiers, the Viet Cong, North Vietnamese guerrillas, and the citizens of both South Vietnam and the United States. . . . Caputo's prose is clear and direct, and the award-winning photos . . . add an immediacy that sets this title apart from more conventional treatments." SLJ

Includes glossary and bibliographical references

DiConsiglio, John

Vietnam; the bloodbath at Hamburger Hill. Franklin Watts 2010 64p il map (24/7: goes to war) lib bdg $27; pa $7.95

Grades: 6 7 8 9   **959.704**
    1. Hamburger Hill, Battle of, Vietnam, 1969
    ISBN 978-0-531-25526-1 lib bdg; 0-531-25526-3 lib bdg; 978-0-531-25451-6 pa; 0-531-25451-8 pa
                                          LC 2009-14912

Describes the eight-day battle in May 1969 where American forces struggled to capture a tiny piece of the Vietnam countryside, considered a watershed turning point in the Vietnam War

This "will appeal to these readers, because . . . . [it tells] a story while presenting the facts. . . . The first chapter gives the historic details concerning the war up to the particular battle, with the story of the battle told from a first-person perspective. A mixture of news photos and photos taken by the men involved appear throughout the book." Libr Media Connect

Includes glossary and bibliographical references

Gifford, Clive

Why did the Vietnam War happen? Gareth Stevens 2011 48p il map (Moments in history) lib bdg $31.95; pa $14.05

Grades: 6 7 8 9   **959.704**
    1. Vietnam War, 1961-1975
    ISBN 978-1-4339-4178-8 lib bdg; 1-4339-4178-3 lib bdg; 978-1-4339-4179-5 pa; 1-4339-4179-1 pa
                                          LC 2010015835

This book looks at the causes of the Vietnam War and surrounding controversies.

"Brightly colored pull-out boxes highlight important turning points, the perspective of the everyday man, and further information on why specific events occurred. Numerous photographs help readers visualize concepts more fully. . . . Students should be able to easily use this resource." Libr Media Connect

Includes glossary and bibliographical references

Gitlin, Marty

U.S. involvement in Vietnam; by Martin Gitlin; content consultant Clarence R. Wyatt. ABDO Pub. Co. 2010 112p il map (Essential events) lib bdg $32.79

Grades: 6 7 8 9   **959.704**
    1. Vietnam War, 1961-1975 2. United States -- History -- 1961-1974
    ISBN 978-1-60453-949-3; 1-60453-949-6
                                          LC 2009-31071

This title examines an important historic event, the U.S. involvement in Vietnam. Readers will learn about the events leading up to this, including Communist North Vietnam taking military action over South Vietnam, the United States sending aid to South Vietnam.

"The writing is accessible and is richer than a lot of history writing, allowing the reader to become engaged in the text as a story, and the layout provides enought white space to allow lower level readers to feel confident." Libr Media Connect

Includes glossary and bibliographical references

Senker, Cath

The **Vietnam** War; by Cath Senker. Heinemann Library 2012 80 p. ill. (some col.), col. maps (Living through) (library) $36.50; (paperback) $10.99
Grades: 6 7 8 9 **959.704**
   1. Vietnam War, 1961-1975
   ISBN 1432960008; 9781432960001; 9781432960094
                     LC 2011015928

In this book on the Vietnam War, part of the "Living Through" series, author "[Cath] Senker begins her story with the French colonization of Southeast Asia and ends it with an analysis of why the war ended the way it did. In between, Senker takes her readers back to a time in American history when policies went awry and the nation imposed terrible destruction on foreign lands and its own people." (Children's Literature)

Includes bibliographical references (p. 76-77) and index

Skrypuch, Marsha Forchuk

Last airlift; a Vietnamese orphan's rescue from war. Marsha Forchuk Skrypuch. Pajama Press 2012 120 p. $17.95
Grades: 3 4 5 6 **959.704**
   1. Orphans 2. Aeronautics -- Flights 3. International adoption 4. Evacuation of civilians -- Vietnam 5. Vietnam War, 1961-1975 -- Children
   ISBN 098694954X; 9780986949548

This book "tells the story of the last Canadian airlift [from Vietnam] through the memories of one child, Son Thi Anh Tuyet. Nearly 8 years old, the sad-eyed girl . . . had lived nearly all her life in a Catholic orphanage." When "she and a number of the institution babies were taken away, placed on an airplane and flown to a new world. . . . she assumed that John and Dorothy Morris had chosen her to help with their three children; instead, she had acquired a family." (Kirkus Reviews)

Young, Marilyn Blatt

The **Vietnam** War: a history in documents; [by] Marilyn B. Young, John J. Fitzgerald, A. Tom Grunfeld. Oxford Univ. Press 2002 175p il maps (Pages from history) lib bdg $32.95; pa $19.95
Grades: 7 8 9 10 **959.704**
   1. Vietnam War, 1961-1975
   ISBN 0-19-512278-X lib bdg; 0-19-516635-3 pa
                     LC 2001-52338

"The documents are skillfully tied together by brief text that gives good background information. . . . The book is well balanced in showing both sides. . . . Good-quality, black-and-white photos and illustrations are plentiful and informative." SLJ

Includes glossary and bibliographical references

959.8   Indonesia and East Timor

Cooper, Robert

Indonesia; by Gouri Mirpuri and Robert Cooper. 3rd ed. Marshall Cavendish Benchmark 2012 144 p. ill., maps (library) $47.07
Grades: 5 6 7 8 **959.8**
   1. Indonesia
   ISBN 1608707830; 9781608707836
                     LC 200128607

First published 1990

This "nonfiction book in the 'Cultures of the World' series presents a . . . story of the physical, social and historical characteristics of Indonesia. . . . Throughout the book, also, there are textboxes that add . . . information to the subject matter and include . . . drawings of native musical instruments, weapons, foods and other" things. (Children's Literature)

"The pictures are lush, with captions in tiny print offering much additional information. The text is written smoothly and readably, and it contains a substantial amount of information." Booklist

Includes bibliographical references and index

959.9   Philippines

Skog, Jason

Teens in the Philippines; by Jason Skog. Compass Point Books 2009 96p il map (Global connections) lib bdg $33.26
Grades: 6 7 8 9 **959.9**
   1. Teenagers 2. Philippines
   ISBN 978-0-7565-3853-8 lib bdg; 0-7565-3853-X lib bdg
                     LC 2008-6504

Uncovers the challenges, pastimes, customs and culture of teens in the Philippines

This book is "concise and highly readable. . . . Clear, colorful photos and sidebars on a range of topics provide further context. . . . [This title] will enrich young adult collections." SLJ

Includes glossary and bibliographical references

960   History of Africa

Africa: opposing viewpoints; David M. Haugen, book editor. Gale/Cengage Learning 2008 219p (Opposing viewpoints series) lib bdg $39.70; pa $27.50
Grades: 8 9 10 11 12 **960**
   1. Africa -- Social conditions 2. Africa -- Economic conditions 3. Africa -- Politics and government
   ISBN 978-0-7377-3988-6 lib bdg; 978-0-7377-3989-3 pa
                     LC 2008-811

Articles in this anthology discuss important issues facing Africa today, foreign aid and free trade, the status of democracy and human rights in Africa, and ways the United States and other western nations can help Africa.

Includes bibliographical references

Bowden, Rob, 1973-

★ **African** culture; [by] Rob Bowden and Rosie Wilson. Heinemann Library 2009 48p il map (Africa focus) $30; pa $8.99

Grades: 4 5 6   **960**

1. Africa -- Civilization 2. Africa -- Social life and customs
ISBN 978-1-4329-2440-9; 1-4329-2440-0; 978-1-4329-2445-4 pa; 1-4329-2445-1 pa

LC 2008-48310

This book "presents a clear and timely overview of the diverse and complex continent. The full-color photographs are of exceptional quality. [The] book also includes interesting fact boxes, sidebars, maps, and a time line. [It] focuses on traditions and how they are relevant for today. Highlights include family and daily life; religion, beliefs, and customs; and the performing and visual arts." SLJ

Includes bibliographical references

★ **Ancient** Africa; [by] Rob Bowden and Rosie Wilson. Heinemann Library 2008 48p il map (Africa focus) $30; pa $8.99

Grades: 4 5 6   **960**

1. Africa -- History
ISBN 978-1-4329-2439-3; 1-4329-2439-7; 978-1-4329-2444-7 pa; 1-4329-2444-3 pa

LC 2008-48306

This book "presents a clear and timely overview of the diverse and complex continent. The full-color photographs are of exceptional quality. [The] book also includes interesting fact boxes, sidebars, maps, and a time line. . . . [It] begins with the origin of humankind and continues through the beginning of the slave trade in Europe and America. Early civilizations such as Egypt, ancient Ghana, the Mali Empire, Great Zimbabwe, and Kongo are represented. Invasions and explorations are discussed, as is slavery and colonialism." SLJ

Includes bibliographical references

★ **Changing** Africa; [by] Rob Bowden and Rosie Wilson. Heinemann Library 2009 48p il map (Africa focus) $30; pa $8.99

Grades: 4 5 6   **960**

1. Africa -- Social conditions 2. Africa -- Economic conditions
ISBN 978-1-4329-2437-9; 1-4329-2437-0; 978-1-4329-2442-3 pa; 1-4329-2442-7 pa

LC 2008-48277

This book "presents a clear and timely overview of the diverse and complex continent. The full-color photographs are of exceptional quality. [The] book also includes interesting fact boxes, sidebars, maps, and a time line. . . . [It] presents recent positive and negative changes. The rise of poverty and slums is explored, as is the lowered life expectancy due to the spread of malaria and HIV/AIDS. Positive changes include the freedom that voting has brought." SLJ

Includes bibliographical references

★ **Modern** Africa; [by] Rosie Wilson and Rob Bowden. Heinemann Library 2009 48p il map (Africa focus) $30; pa $8.99

Grades: 4 5 6   **960**

1. Africa
ISBN 978-1-4329-2438-6; 1-4329-2438-9; 978-1-4329-2443-0 pa; 1-4329-2443-5 pa

This book "presents a clear and timely overview of the diverse and complex continent. The full-color photographs are of exceptional quality. [The] book also includes interesting fact boxes, sidebars, maps, and a time line. . . . [It] chronicles the history of colonial Africa to independence, and the changes that have arisen and continue to manifest themselves. Topics include apartheid and recent and ongoing violence in Rwanda, Darfur, and the Congo. While corrupt leaders continue to hamper Africa's attempts at advancement, the exportation of oil as well as aid from missionaries and international organizations are presented as hopes for the future." SLJ

Diagram Group

African history on file; rev ed; Facts on File 2003 various paging il maps loose-leaf $185

Grades: Adult Professional   **960**

1. Africa -- History
ISBN 0-8160-5139-9

LC 2002-192848

First published 1994

More than 500 "reproducible maps, charts, timelines, and drawings visually detail the broad range of human experience in Africa, from prehistory to the present." Publisher's note

Includes bibliographical references

Habeeb, William Mark

Africa; Facts and Figures. by William Mark Habeeb. Mason Crest Publishers 2012 87 p. ill. (chiefly col.), col. map (The Evolution of Africa's Major Nations) (library) $22.95

Grades: 7 8 9 10   **960**

1. Africa -- History 2. Africa -- Social conditions 3. Africa -- Politics and government 4. Africa
ISBN 1422221768; 9781422221761

LC 2010048000

This book is "[t]he first of a new series, 'Continent in the Balance: Africa,' . . . introduces the continent in all its geographical and cultural diversity. . . . [H]istorian [William Mark] Habeeb discusses the huge contemporary problems in many countries, including poverty and AIDS, and examines how colonialism carved up the continent with arbitrary borders that have resulted in devastating ethnic and religious conflicts that exist even today." (Booklist)

This is an "excellent, detailed overview. . . . The attractive, open design, with clear type, beautiful photos, maps, and lots of extras in lists and insets, manages to pack in an extraordinary amount of information." Booklist

Includes bibliographical references (p. 82-83) and index.

Middleton, John

Africa : an encyclopedia for students; John Middleton, editor. Scribner 2002 4v il maps set $395

Grades: 7 8 9 10 **960**

1. Reference books 2. Africa -- Encyclopedias
ISBN 0-684-80650-9

LC 2001-49348

A comprehensive look at the continent of Africa and the countries that comprise it, including peoples and cultures, the land and its history, art and architecture, and daily life

Mooney, Carla

Amazing Africa; projects you can build yourself. illustrated by Megan Stearns. Nomad Press 2010 122p il (Build it yourself) pa $15.95

Grades: 4 5 6 7 **960**

1. Handicraft 2. Africa
ISBN 978-1-934670-41-5; 1-934670-41-3

"Casual and informative, this large, attractive, browsable paperback . . . offers a view of contemporary African life that reaches far beyond the usual scenery-and-wildlife tourists' perspective. Blending history, culture, and tradition with politics and life in both cities and rural areas, the chapters begin with a look at natural wonders and dangerous wildlife that will grab readers, then move on to historical discussions of humankind's birthplace and early civilizations. . . . The open design includes sketches on every page. . . . The craft projects [include making] your own Maasai beaded necklace, kente cloth, woven basket, galimoto doll, and . . . . more." Booklist

Murray, Jocelyn

Africa; updated by Brian A. Stewart. 3rd ed.; Chelsea House 2007 96p il map (Cultural atlas for young people) $35

Grades: 5 6 7 8 **960**

1. Africa -- History 2. Africa -- Civilization
ISBN 978-0-8160-6826-5; 0-8160-6826-7

First published 1990

Presents information on the history and various regions and cultures of Africa.

Includes glossary and bibliographical references

Nardo, Don

The **European** colonization of Africa. Morgan Reynolds 2010 112p il (World history) lib bdg $28.95

Grades: 7 8 9 10 11 12 **960**

1. Africa -- History 2. Europe -- Colonies -- Africa
ISBN 978-1-59935-142-1 lib bdg; 1-59935-142-0 lib bdg

"Drawing on some of the best scholarship, this compelling account of Europeans' colonization of Africa begins with Greco-Roman and early medieval times. Then, with the horiffic facts of the slave trade, Nardo goes on to discuss the greed and brutality of the mad 'scramble' for African land by those who saw themselves as chosen people of God. . . . With period illustrations, the design . . . is clear and open, and the excellent back matter . . . will spark further research." Booklist

Includes bibliographical references (p. 98-106)

Peoples and cultures of Africa; edited by Peter Mitchell. Chelsea House 2006 6v il map set $234

Grades: 5 6 7 8 **960**

1. Reference books 2. Ethnology -- Africa 3. Africa -- Civilization
ISBN 0-8160-6260-9 set; 978-0-8160-6261-4 v1; 978-0-8160-6262-1 v2; 978-0-8160-6263-8 v3; 978-0-8160-6264-5 v4; 978-0-8160-6265-2 v5; 978-0-8160-6266-9 v6

LC 2006040011

"This attractive and informative set provides well-written, well-researched introductory information about African geography and culture. Each of the first five volumes covers a region within the continent . . . and opens with introductory information on that area's physical features, biomes, religions, languages, and cultures, and includes an extensive time line. It is followed by color-coded, alphabetically arranged entries examining the region's tribal and ethnic groups; art, sculpture, and textiles; performing arts and literature; and religion and individual cultures in further detail. . . . The final volume is devoted to single-page geographic and economic profiles of Africa's nations. . . . This quality set will give report writers a solid introduction to the diversity of Africa." SLJ

Includes bibliographical references

961.1 Tunisia

Brown, Roslind Varghese

Tunisia; [by] Roslind Varghese Brown & Michael Spilling. 2nd ed.; Marshall Cavendish Benchmark 2008 144p il map (Cultures of the world) lib bdg $42.79

Grades: 5 6 7 8 **961.1**

1. Tunisia
ISBN 978-0-7614-3037-7 lib bdg; 0-7614-3037-7 lib bdg

LC 2007050798

First published 1998

"Provides comprehensive information on the geography, history, wildlife, governmental structure, economy, cultural diversity, peoples, religion, and culture of Tunisia." Publisher note

Includes glossary and bibliographical references

962 Egypt, Sudan, South Sudan

Heinrichs, Ann

The **Nile**. Marshall Cavendish Benchmark 2008 96p il map (Nature's wonders) lib bdg $24.95

Grades: 5 6 7 8 **962**

1. Nile River 2. Nile River valley
ISBN 978-0-7614-2854-1

LC 2007019187

"It's tough to make a river interesting, but this . . . does an admirable job of it. . . . Crisp, full-color photos and original artwork decorate nearly every page. . . . [This is a] well-thought-out natural history." Booklist

Includes glossary and bibliographical references

Zuehlke, Jeffrey

   Egypt in pictures. Lerner Publs. 2003 80p il map (Visual geography series) lib bdg $31.93

Grades: 5 6 7 8   **962**

   1. Egypt

   ISBN 0-8225-0367-0

                     LC 2001-6613

   Discusses the physical features, history, government, people, culture, and economy of Egypt

   Includes bibliographical references

962.4   Sudan and South Sudan

Brownlie, Ali

   Sudan in our world; by Ali Brownlie Bojang. Smart Apple Media 2010 32p il (Countries in our world) lib bdg $28.50

Grades: 5 6 7 8   **962.4**

   1. Sudan

   ISBN 978-1-59920-434-5 lib bdg; 1-59920-434-7 lib bdg

                   LC 2009052421

   "Issues such as Civil War, fighting in Darfur, the government, and millions of displaced refugees continue to cripple the country and impede its advancement. While Sudan is rich in resources, its future remains uncertain. [This title] will appeal to children interested in learning more about Africa and those needing factual information for reports." SLJ

   Includes glossary and bibliographical references

   The **crisis** in Darfur; Jeff Hay, book editor. Greenhaven Press 2011 165p il map (Perspectives on modern world history) $39.70

      Grades: 8 9 10 11 12   **962.4**

      1. Sudan -- History -- Darfur conflict, 2003-

      ISBN 978-0-7377-5257-1; 0-7377-5257-2

                  LC 2010033168

   In discussing "the continuing human tragedy in Darfur, [this] well-organized [volume presents] a wealth of clearly written analyses from a rich variety of viewpoints. With the inclusion of historical background, firsthand experiences, and discussions of particular points of controversy, [it helps] to familiarize readers with the [topic] . . . and [serves] as [an exercise] in the development of analytical thinking skills." SLJ

   Includes bibliographical references

Dau, John Bul

   Lost boy, lost girl; escaping civil war in Sudan. by John Bul Dau and Martha Arual Akech; with Michael Sweeney and K. M. Kostyal. National Geographic 2010 159p il map $15.95; lib bdg $23.90

Grades: 7 8 9 10   **962.4**

   1. Refugees 2. Sudan -- History -- Civil War, 1983-

2005

   ISBN 978-1-4263-0708-9; 1-4263-0708-X; 978-1-4263-0709-6 lib bdg; 1-4263-0709-8 lib bdg

                  LC 2010-17960

   "The tragic story of Sudan's Lost Boys and Lost [Girls] is told in simple language by two survivors. . . . In 1987, when Dau was 13 and Akech was 6, war came to their village. Both traveled hundreds of miles to a UN refugee camp in Ethiopia. After a few years of safety, the refugees were forced to move again. . . . Teens who know little about Sudan and its problems will be drawn into this moving, inspiration story." SLJ

Levy, Patricia

   Sudan; [by] Patricia Levy and Zawiah Abdul Latif. 2nd ed.; Marshall Cavendish Benchmark 2008 144p il map (Cultures of the world) lib bdg $42.79

Grades: 5 6 7 8   **962.4**

   1. Sudan

   ISBN 978-0-7614-2083-5 lib bdg; 0-7614-2083-5 lib bdg

                  LC 2006101725

   Describes the geography, history, government, economy, people, lifestyle, religion, language, arts, leisure, festivals, and food of Sudan

   Includes bibliographical references

Steele, Philip

   ★ **Sudan,** Darfur and the nomadic conflicts; by Philip Steele. 1st ed. Rosen Pub. 2013 48 p. col. ill. (library) $29.25

Grades: 6 7 8   **962.4**

   1. Current events 2. Sudan -- History -- Darfur conflict, 2003- 3. Sudan -- History 4. Sudan -- Ethnic relations

   ISBN 1448860288; 9781448860289

                  LC 2012010639

   This book by Philip Steele is part of the Our World Divided series and looks at Sudan, Darfur, and the nomadic conflicts. "Each of these volumes begins with a recent news event pertaining to the featured conflict and then looks back at the origin and milestones of the discord. . . . 'Viewpoints' sidebars . . . showcase quotations about a specific matter from individuals on opposing sides." (School Library Journal)

   Includes bibliographical references (p. 46) and index.

Xavier, John

   ★ **Darfur**; African genocide. [by] John Xavier. 1st ed.; Rosen Pub. Group 2008 64p il map (In the news) $29.95

Grades: 6 7 8 9   **962.4**

   1. Genocide 2. Sudan -- History -- Darfur conflict, 2003-

   ISBN 978-1-4042-1912-0; 1-4042-1912-9

                  LC 2007002909

   An overview of the crisis in Darfur, its history and why it matters.

   "Informative reflection of today's headlines. . . . In-depth exploration of the crisis in Darfur, the history of the conflict, and why it matters to the rest of the world. . . . The glossaries and Web sites at the end of each are most helpful." Voice Youth Advocates

   Includes glossary and bibliographical references

963   Ethiopia and Eritrea

Gish, Steven

★ **Ethiopia**; [by] Steven Gish & Winnie Thay & Zawiah Abdul Latif. 2nd ed.; Marshall Cavendish Benchmark 2007 144p il map (Cultures of the world) lib bdg $42.79

Grades: 5 6 7 8   963

1. Ethiopia

ISBN 978-0-7614-2025-5 lib bdg; 0-7614-2025-8 lib bdg

LC 2006020819

First published 1996

This provides "information on the geography, history, governmental structure, economy, cultural diversity, peoples, religion, and culture of Ethiopia." Publisher's note

Includes glossary and bibliographical references

963.5   Eritrea

NgCheong-Lum, Roseline, 1962-

Eritrea; 2nd ed.; Marshall Cavendish Benchmark 2011 144p il map (Cultures of the world) lib bdg $42.79

Grades: 5 6 7 8   963.5

1. Eritrea

ISBN 978-1-6087-0454-5; 1-6087-0454-8

LC 2010035973

First published 2001

Provides information on the geography, history, wildlife, governmental structure, economy, cultural diversity, peoples, religion, and culture of Eritea.

"Plentiful color photographs accompany substantial amounts of information." SLJ

Includes glossary and bibliographical references

964   Morocco, Ceuta, Melilla, Western Sahara, Canary Islands

Seward, Pat

Morocco; [by] Pat Seward & Orin Hargraves. 2nd ed.; Marshall Cavendish Benchmark 2006 144p il map (Cultures of the world) lib bdg $42.79

Grades: 5 6 7 8   964

1. Morocco

ISBN 0-7614-2051-7

LC 2005020782

First published 1995

Describes the geography, history, government, economy, people, and culture of Morocco

Includes glossary and bibliographical references

965   Algeria

Kagda, Falaq

Algeria; [by] Falaq Kagda & Zawiah Abdul Latif. 2nd ed.; Marshall Cavendish Benchmark 2008 144p il map (Cultures of the world) lib bdg $42.79

Grades: 5 6 7 8   965

1. Algeria

ISBN 978-0-7614-2085-9 lib bdg; 0-7614-2085-1 lib bdg

LC 2007014888

First published 1997

"Provides comprehensive information on the geography, history, wildlife, governmental structure, economy, cultural diversity, peoples, religion, and culture of Algeria." Publisher's note

Includes glossary and bibliographical references

Wagner, Heather Lehr

The **Algerian** war; by Heather Lehr Wagner. Chelsea House 2012 120 p. (Milestones in modern world history) (hardcover) $35

Grades: 7 8 9 10 11 12   965

1. France -- Foreign relations -- Algeria 2. Algeria -- History -- 1954-1962, Revolution 3. France -- Colonies -- Africa -- History 4. National liberation movements -- Algeria 5. Algeria -- History -- Revolution, 1954-1962

ISBN 1604139234; 9781604139235

LC 2011023060

This book, part of the Milestones in Modern World History series, "opens with a triumphant France celebrating its freedom at the end of WWII while citizens of its colony, Algeria, were denied their own equality and freedom. Following an overview of Algerian possession, the text outlines French injustices toward Algeria, most notably discrimination of its Muslim population and the rise of revolution." (Booklist)

Includes bibliographical references and index

966   West Africa and offshore islands

Haywood, John

West African kingdoms; [by] John Haywood. Raintree 2008 64p il map (Time travel guide) lib bdg $34.29; pa $9.99

Grades: 6 7 8 9   966

1. West Africa 2. Ghana Empire 3. Songhai Empire 4. Mali -- History

ISBN 978-1-4109-2912-9 lib bdg; 978-1-4109-2918-1 pa

LC 2007006053

This describes life in West Africa between 1200 and 1600 AD, including the kingdoms of Mali, Songhai, and Benin, in the form of a travel guide.

Includes glossary and bibliographical references

Heinrichs, Ann

The **Sahara**; [by] Ann Heinrichs. Marshall Cavendish Benchmark 2009 96p il map (Nature's wonders) lib bdg $24.95

Grades: 5 6 7 8   **966**

1. Sahara Desert

ISBN 978-0-7614-2855-8 lib bdg; 0-7614-2855-0 lib bdg

          LC 2007-20326

This book is "full of interesting information and feature[s] a format that enables students to quickly find specific information." Voice Youth Advocates

Includes glossary and bibliographical references

966.1   Mauritania

Blauer, Ettagale

Mauritania; [by] Ettagale Blauer & Jason Lauré. Marshall Cavendish Benchmark 2009 144p il map (Cultures of the world) lib bdg $42.79

Grades: 5 6 7 8   **966.1**

1. Mauritania

ISBN 978-0-7614-3116-9

This describes the geography, history, government, economy, environment, people, and culture of Mauritania

966.2   Mali, Burkina Faso, Niger

Blauer, Ettagale

Mali; [by] Ettagale Blauer & Jason Lauré. 2nd ed.; Marshall Cavendish Benchmark 2008 144p il map (Cultures of the world) lib bdg $42.79

Grades: 5 6 7 8   **966.2**

1. Mali

ISBN 978-0-7614-2568-7

First published 1997

This describes the geography, history, government, economy, environment, people, and culture of Mali

Includes glossary and bibliographical references

McKissack, Patricia C.

The **royal** kingdoms of Ghana, Mali, and Songhay; life in medieval Africa. [by] Patricia and Fredrick McKissack. Holt & Co. 1993 142p il maps hardcover o.p. pa $12.99

Grades: 5 6 7 8   **966.2**

1. Ghana Empire 2. Songhai Empire 3. Mali -- History

ISBN 0-8050-4259-8 pa

          LC 93-4838

Examines the civilizations of the Western Sudan which flourished from 700 to 1700 A.D., acquiring such vast wealth that they became centers of trade and culture for a continent

"The McKissacks are careful to distinguish what is known from what is surmised; they draw on the oral tradition, eyewitness accounts, and contemporary scholarship; and chapter source notes discuss various conflicting views of events." Booklist

Includes bibliographical references

966.3   Senegal

Berg, Elizabeth

Senegal; by Elizabeth L. Berg and Ruth Lau. 2nd ed.; Marshall Cavendish Benchmark 2009 144p il map (Cultures of the world) lib bdg $42.79

Grades: 5 6 7 8   **966.3**

1. Senegal

ISBN 978-0-7614-4481-7 lib bdg; 0-7614-4481-5 lib bdg

          LC 2009007067

First published 1999

Describes the geography, history, wildlife, governmental structure, economy, cultural diversity, peoples, religion, and culture of Senegal

Includes glossary and bibliographical references

Mulroy, Tanya

Senegal; [by] Tanya Mulroy. Mason Crest Publishers 2008 79p il map (Africa: continent in the balance) lib bdg $21.95

Grades: 5 6 7 8   **966.3**

1. Senegal

ISBN 978-1-4222-0091-9 lib bdg; 1-4222-0091-4 lib bdg

          LC 2006-17341

This book is "clear and concise, and the authors' easy-to-read texts impart a good deal of up-to-date information. . . . Chapters . . . cover the . . . country's history; politics and government; economy; and people, including discussions of family life, education, ethnic groups, health care, sports, and the arts, with the focus being on the largest cities." SLJ

Includes glossary and bibliographical references

966.4   Sierra Leone

Fowler, Will

Counterterrorism in West Africa; the most dangerous SAS assault. Rosen Pub. 2011 64p il map (The most daring raids in history) lib bdg $29.25

Grades: 7 8 9 10   **966.4**

1. Rescue work 2. Sierra Leone -- History -- Civil War, 1991- 3. Great Britain -- Army -- Special Air Service Regiment

ISBN 978-1-4488-1871-6; 1-4488-1871-0

          LC 2010029621

This book offers a scene-by-scene account of the SAS (Special Air Service) and Operation Barras in Sierra Leone in 2000.

This book is "packed with facts, covering the details of the action, the people involved, and the tools used, in engaging prose. The authors cite their sources thoroughly. . . . Diagrams, photos, . . . and maps make the action easy to follow and provide visual context for the raids. . . . This . . . is sure to find a large readership." SLJ

Includes glossary and bibliographical references

Hasday, Judy L.

Sierra Leone; [by] Judy Hasday. Mason Crest Publishers 2008 79p il map (Africa: continent in the balance) lib bdg $21.95

Grades: 5 6 7 8 **966.4**

1. Sierra Leone

ISBN 978-1-4222-0092-6; 1-4222-0092-2

LC 2006-17342

This book features the country's "history; politics and government; economy; and people, including discussions of family life, education, ethnic groups, health care, sports, and the arts, with the focus being on the largest cities. . . . Interspersed throughout are numerous color and some black-and-white photographs, with descriptive captions, as well as 'Quick Facts' regarding geography, the economy, and the people. . . . The information is presented in an engaging manner." SLJ

Includes glossary and bibliographical references

LeVert, Suzanne

★ **Sierra** Leone; [by] Suzanne LeVert. Marshall Cavendish Benchmark 2007 144p il map (Cultures of the world) lib bdg $42.79

Grades: 5 6 7 8 **966.4**

1. Sierra Leone

ISBN 978-0-7614-2334-8 lib bdg; 0-7614-2334-6 lib bdg

LC 2005035964

This provides "information on the geography, history, governmental structure, economy, cultural diversity, peoples, religion, and culture of Sierra Leone." Publisher's note

Includes glossary and bibliographical references

966.62 Liberia

Reef, Catherine

★ **This** our dark country; the American settlers of Liberia. Clarion Bks. 2002 136p il maps $17

Grades: 7 8 9 10 **966.62**

1. Liberia -- History 2. Slavery -- United States 3. African Americans -- History 4. American Colonization Society

ISBN 0-618-14785-3

LC 2002-3966

Explores the history of the colony, later the independent nation of Liberia, which was established on the west coast of Africa in 1822 as a haven for free African Americans

"This photo-essay is a grim, disturbing history of Liberia. . . . Reef tells it in clear, plain style, always showing the connections between the two homelands. The handsome, very spacious design . . . makes the hard facts accessible. . . . A must for history collections." Booklist

Includes bibliographical references

966.68 Cote d'Ivoire (Ivory Coast)

Sheehan, Patricia

Cote d'Ivoire; [by] Patricia Sheehan and Jacqueline Ong. 2nd ed.; Marshall Cavendish Benchmark

2010 144p il map (Cultures of the world) lib bdg $42.79

Grades: 5 6 7 8 **966.68**

1. Ivory Coast

ISBN 978-0-7614-4854-9 lib bdg; 0-7614-4854-3 lib bdg

LC 2009045688

First published 2000

This offers information on the geography, history, wildlife, governmental structure, economy, cultural diversity, peoples, religion, and culture of Cote d'Ivoire

Includes glossary and bibliographical references

966.7 Ghana

Levy, Patricia

Ghana; [by] Patricia Levy and Winnie Wong. 2nd ed.; Marshall Cavendish Benchmark 2010 144p il map (Cultures of the world) lib bdg $42.79

Grades: 5 6 7 8 **966.7**

1. Ghana

ISBN 978-0-7614-4847-1 lib bdg; 0-7614-4847-0 lib bdg

First published 1999

Introduces the geography, history, government, economy, culture, and people of Ghana

Includes glossary and bibliographical references

Weatherly, Myra

Teens in Ghana. Compass Point Books 2008 96p il map (Global connections) lib bdg $33.26

Grades: 7 8 9 10 **966.7**

1. Teenagers 2. Ghana

ISBN 978-0-7565-3417-2; 0-7565-3417-8

LC 2007-33086

Uncovers the challenges, pastimes, customs and culture of teens in Ghana

"Color photographs of native teens enliven the text and help reinforce the connection between reader and subject matter. . . . Religion is discussed, as well as technology, government, and social roles and expectations. . . . [This] would be a wonderful addition to any library." Voice Youth Advocates

Includes bibliographical references

966.9 Nigeria

Giles, Bridget

★ **Nigeria**; [by] Bridget Giles. National Geographic 2007 64p il map (Countries of the world) lib bdg $27.90

Grades: 4 5 6 7 **966.9**

1. Nigeria

ISBN 978-1-4263-0124-7

LC 2007024729

This describes the geography, nature, history, people and culture, government, and economy of Nigeria

"What helps [this book] stand out from the pack is [its] high-quality, rich photography. . . . The photos provide as much information as the [text]. . . . The writing is straight-forward and solid." SLJ

Includes glossary and bibliographical references

Walker, Ida

★ **Nigeria**; Ida Walker. Mason Crest Publishers 2013 79 p. (hardcover : alk. paper) $22.95

Grades: 5 6 7 8 9 10 11   **966.9**

1. Nigeria

ISBN 1422222004; 9781422222003; 9781422222287; 9781422294406

LC 2010047767

This book, by Ida Walker, focuses on the country of Nigeria. "With a population of more than 133 million people, Nigeria is Africa's most populous country. Military leaders have ruled Nigeria for much of its history as an independent country, and it was not until 1999 that a civilian government was restored. However, this has not ensured peace. . . . Although Nigeria controls great reserves of oil, and is one of the largest exporters of oil to the United States, most Nigerians are very poor." (Publisher's note)

"This series is a needed collection for high school media centers. It fills a void by supplying up-to-date books on African countries that incorporates both an historical and modern perspective. Each book covers the land, government, economy, culture, people, religion, holidays, and festivals... These books will be useful for researchers and browsers alike." (Library Media Connection)

Includes bibliographical references and index

967 Central Africa and offshore islands

Oppong, Joseph R.

Africa South of the Sahara; series consulting editor Charles F. Gritzner. Chelsea House Publishers 2006 124p il map (Modern world cultures) lib bdg $30

Grades: 6 7 8 9 10   **967**

1. Sub-Saharan Africa

ISBN 0-7910-8146-X

This describes the physical and historical geography, population and settlement, cultures, politics, and economy of sub-Saharan Africa.

This "accessible [title is] generously illustrated with colorful photos, maps, and clear charts, graphs, and other statistical data." SLJ

967.11 Cameroon

Sheehan, Sean

Cameroon; [by] Sean Sheehan and Josie Elias. 2nd ed.; Marshall Cavendish Benchmark 2011 144p il map (Cultures of the world) lib bdg $42.79

Grades: 5 6 7 8   **967.11**

1. Cameroon

ISBN 978-1-6087-0214-5; 1-6087-0214-6

LC 2010019623

First published 2001

Provides information on the geography, history, wildlife, governmental structure, economy, cultural diversity, peoples, religion, and culture of Cameroon.

Includes glossary and bibliographical references

967.3 Angola

Sheehan, Sean

Angola; [by] Sean Sheehan and Jui Lin Yong. 2nd ed.; Marshall Cavendish Benchmark 2010 144p il map (Cultures of the world) lib bdg $42.79

Grades: 5 6 7 8   **967.3**

1. Angola

ISBN 978-0-7614-4845-7 lib bdg; 0-7614-4845-4 lib bdg

LC 2009021203

"Provides comprehensive information on the geography, history, wildlife, governmental structure, economy, cultural diversity, peoples, religion, and culture of Angola." Publisher's note

Includes glossary and bibliographical references

967.43 Chad

Kneib, Martha

Chad; [by] Martha Kneib. Marshall Cavendish Benchmark 2007 144p il map (Cultures of the world) lib bdg $42.79

Grades: 5 6 7 8   **967.43**

1. Chad

ISBN 978-0-7614-2327-0 lib bdg; 0-7614-2327-3 lib bdg

LC 2005027079

This provides "information on the geography, history, governmental structure, economy, cultural diversity, peoples, religion, and culture of Chad." Publisher's note

Includes glossary and bibliographical references

967.51 Democratic Republic of the Congo

Heale, Jay

Democratic Republic of the Congo; by Jay Heale and Yong Jui Lin. 2nd ed.; Marshall Cavendish Benchmark 2009 144p il map (Cultures of the world) lib bdg $42.79

Grades: 5 6 7 8   **967.51**

1. Congo (Republic)

ISBN 978-0-7614-4478-7 lib bdg; 0-7614-4478-5 lib bdg

LC 2009003195

First published 1999

Describes the geography, history, government, economy, people, lifestyle, religion, languages, arts, leisure, festivals, and food of The Democratic Republic of the Congo

Includes glossary and bibliographical references

967.571 Rwanda

King, David C.

Rwanda; [by] David C. King. Marshall Cavendish Benchmark 2007 144p il map (Cultures of the world) lib bdg $42.79

Grades: 5 6 7 8   **967.571**

1. Rwanda

ISBN 978-0-7614-2333-1 lib bdg; 0-7614-2333-8 lib bdg

LC 2005031817

This provides "information on the geography, history, governmental structure, economy, cultural diversity, peoples, religion, and culture of Rwanda." Publisher's note

Includes glossary and bibliographical references

Koopmans, Andy

Rwanda; Andy Koopmans. Mason Crest 2013 87 p. color illustrations (The evolution of Africa's major nations) $22.95

Grades: 7 8 9 10   **967.571**

1. Rwanda

ISBN 9781422221839

Introduces Rwanda, describing its history, politics, religion, economy, culture, and most important cities.

Includes bibliographical references and index

Nardo, Don

The **Rwandan** genocide; by Don Nardo. Lucent Books 2011 104 p. ill. (hardcover) $34.95

Grades: 6 7 8 9   **967.571**

1. Genocide 2. Ethnic relations 3. Rwanda -- History 4. Rwanda -- History -- Civil War, 1994 5. Genocide -- Rwanda -- History -- 20th century 6. Ethnic conflict -- Rwanda -- History -- 20th century 7. Rwanda -- Ethnic relations -- History -- 20th century

ISBN 142050567X; 9781420505672

LC 2010039533

This book by Don Nardo is part of the World History series and looks at the Rwandan Genocide. The series "examines the eras, events, civilizations, and movements that have shaped human history, providing readers with insight into the past and its many legacies." Photographs, timelines, sidebars, and annotated bibliographies are included. (Publisher's note)

Includes bibliographical references and index.

967.61 Uganda

Barlas, Robert

Uganda; [by] Robert Barlas and Yong Jui Lin. 2nd ed.; Marshall Cavendish Benchmark 2010 144p il map (Cultures of the world) lib bdg $42.79

Grades: 5 6 7 8   **967.61**

1. Uganda

ISBN 978-0-7614-4859-4 lib bdg; 0-7614-4859-4 lib bdg

LC 2009046002

First published 2000

This offers information on the geography, history, wildlife, governmental structure, economy, cultural diversity, peoples, religion, and culture of Uganda

Includes glossary and bibliographical references

Dunstan, Simon

Entebbe; the most daring raid of Israel's special forces. Rosen Pub. 2011 64p il map (The most daring raids in history) lib bdg $29.25

Grades: 7 8 9 10   **967.61**

1. Israel -- History

ISBN 978-1-4488-1868-6; 1-4488-1868-0

LC 2010029622

The Israeli Forces operation at Entebbe was one of the most daring counter-terrorist assaults of all time. This book explores this important piece of history with narration and illustrations and diagrams.

This book is "packed with facts, covering the details of the action, the people involved, and the tools used, in engaging prose. The authors cite their sources thoroughly. . . . Diagrams, photos (where available), and maps make the action easy to follow and provide visual context for the raids. . . . This . . . is sure to find a large readership." SLJ

Includes glossary and bibliographical references

967.62 Kenya

Bowden, Rob, 1973-

Kenya; Rob Bowden. Facts on File 2003 61 p. ill., map (Countries of the world) (hardcover) $30

Grades: 7 8 9 10   **967.62**

1. Kenya

ISBN 9780816053841; 0816053847

This covers Kenya's "physical geography, resources, ethnic populations, tourism, and commerce. . . . It includes a detailed overview of the tensions between commercial development in an impoverished nation and the need to protect natural resources and wildlife. . . . [This title offers] a wealth of nearly up-to-date information and a realistic introduction to [its subject]. . . . [It also features] good-quality color photos of urban and rural homes and buildings and traditional and western lifestyles." Booklist

Includes bibliographical references

Broberg, Catherine

Kenya in pictures; rev and expanded; Lerner Publs. 2003 80p il map (Visual geography series) lib bdg $31.93

Grades: 5 6 7 8   **967.62**

1. Kenya

ISBN 0-8225-1957-7

LC 2001-3829

First published 1988 under the authorship of Joel Reuben

A brief overview of Kenya's land, history, government, people, and culture

The book is "visually appealing with photos and sidebars that complement the text." Libr Media Connect

Includes bibliographical references

Lekuton, Joseph

★ **Facing** the lion; growing up Maasai on the African savanna. by Joseph Lekuton with Herman Viola. National Geographic Soc. 2003 127p il map $15.95

Grades: 7 8 9 10 11 12   **967.62**

1. Masai (African people) 2. Kenya 3. Authors 4. Teachers 5. Memoirists

ISBN 0-7922-5125-3

LC 2003-750

A member of the Masai people describes his life as he grew up in a northern Kenya village, travelled to America to attend college, and became an elementary school teacher in Virginia

"Lekuton's story touches a universal chord, and shows readers the beauty of another culture from the inside. Simple and direct enough for reluctant readers, and written in a conversational and occasionally wryly humorous style, this book will be enjoyed by a wide range of readers." SLJ

Tanguay, Bridget

Kenya; Bridget Tanguay; Chege Githiora and Tabitha Otieno, consultants. National Geographic 2006 p. cm. **967.62**

1. Kenya

ISBN 978-0-7922-7628-9 (hardcover : alk. paper); 978-0-7922-7668-5 (lib bdg: alk. paper)

LC 2006029047

Includes bibliographical references

967.73   Somalia

Hassig, Susan M.

Somalia; by Susan M. Hassig & Zawiah Abdul Latif. 2nd ed.; Marshall Cavendish Benchmark 2008 144p il map (Cultures of the world) lib bdg $42.79

Grades: 5 6 7 8   **967.73**

1. Somalia

ISBN 978-0-7614-2082-8 lib bdg; 0-7614-2082-7 lib bdg

LC 2006102270

First published 1997

"Provides comprehensive information on the geography, history, wildlife, governmental structure, economy, cultural diversity, peoples, religion, and culture of Somalia." Publisher's note

Includes glossary and bibliographical references

967.8   Tanzania

Heale, Jay

Tanzania; by Jay Heale & Winnie Wong. 2nd ed.; Marshall Cavendish Benchmark 2009 144p il map (Cultures of the world) lib bdg $42.79

Grades: 5 6 7 8   **967.8**

1. Tanzania

ISBN 978-0-7614-3417-7 lib bdg; 0-7614-3417-8 lib bdg

LC 2008028802

First published 1998

"Provides comprehensive information on the geography, history, wildlife, governmental structure, economy, cultural diversity, peoples, religion, and culture of Tanzania." Publisher's note

Includes glossary and bibliographical references

MacDonald, Joan Vos

Tanzania; Joan Vos MacDonald. Mason Crest 2013 87 p. illustrations, maps (The evolution of Africa's major nations) $22.95

Grades: 7 8 9 10   **967.8**

1. Tanzania

ISBN 9781422221860

Describes the history, geography, and culture of Tanzania

Includes bibliographical references and index

967.9   Mozambique

King, David C.

Mozambique; [by] David C. King. Marshall Cavendish Benchmark 2007 144p il map (Cultures of the world) lib bdg $42.79

Grades: 5 6 7 8   **967.9**

1. Mozambique

ISBN 978-0-7614-2331-7 lib bdg; 0-7614-2331-1 lib bdg

LC 2006002302

This provides "information on the geography, history, wildlife, governmental structure, economy, cultural diversity, peoples, religion, and culture of Mozambique." Publisher's note

Includes glossary and bibliographical references

Mulroy, Tanya

Mozambique; Tanya Mulroy. Mason Crest 2013 87 p. color illustrations (The evolution of Africa's major nations) $22.95

Grades: 5 6 7 8   **967.9**

1. Mozambique

ISBN 9781422221822

This book "covers the land, government, economy, culture, people, religion, holidays, and festivals" of Mozambique. (Library Media Connection)

Includes bibliographical references and index

968   Republic of South Africa and neighboring southern African countries

Coster, Patience

The **struggle** against apartheid. Arcturus Pub. 2010 48p il (Timelines) lib bdg $34.25

Grades: 7 8 9 10   **968**

1. Apartheid 2. South Africa -- History 3. South Africa -- Race relations

ISBN 978-1-84837-640-3; 1-84837-640-5

LC 2009051269

Discusses events in South Africa that lead up to and followed the end of apartheid, beginning with the peace treaty of Vereeniging and continuing through the election of Jacob Zuma.

"Background information about major figures is appended. The many images are relevant and well-placed." Horn Book Guide

Includes glossary and bibliographical references

Downing, David

★ **Apartheid** in South Africa; [by] David Downing. Heinemann Library 2004 56p il (Witness to history) $31.36

Grades: 7 8 9 10   **968**

1. Apartheid 2. South Africa -- Race relations
ISBN 1-4034-4870-1; 9780431170619

LC 2003-18235

Examines the historical forces that led to the development of the system of apartheid, what life was like under the system for both blacks and whites, and the efforts that caused the end of this system

"This dense volume is an excellent narrative overview of the apartheid struggle, drawing extensively on primary sources that provide depth, detail, drama, and authenticity." Booklist

Mace, Virginia

★ **South** Africa; [by] Virginia Mace; Kate Rowntree and Vukile Khumalo, consultants. National Geographic 2008 64p il map (Countries of the world) lib bdg $27.90

Grades: 4 5 6 7   **968**

1. South Africa
ISBN 978-1-4263-0203-9

LC 2007047835

This describes the geography, nature, history, people and culture, government, and economy of South Africa.

"Through its numerous maps and standout photographs, this book provides a general overview of South Africa that will satisfy the basic needs of upper-elementary research paper writers." Horn Book Guide

Includes glossary and bibliographical references

Seidman, David

Teens in South Africa; by David Seidman. Compass Point Books 2009 96p il map (Global connections) lib bdg $33.26

Grades: 6 7 8 9   **968**

1. Teenagers 2. South Africa
ISBN 978-0-7565-3854-5 lib bdg; 0-7565-3854-8 lib bdg

LC 2008-9480

Uncovers the challenges, pastimes, customs and culture of teens in South Africa

This book is "concise and highly readable. . . . Clear, colorful photos and sidebars on a range of topics provide further context. . . . [This title] will enrich young adult collections." SLJ

Inlcudes glossary and bibliographical references

Weltig, Matthew Scott

The **aftermath** of the Anglo-Zulu war; by Matthew S. Weltig. Twenty-First Century Books 2008 160p il (Aftermath of history) lib bdg $38.60

Grades: 6 7 8 9 10   **968**

1. Zulu War, 1879 2. Zulu (African people) 3. South Africa -- History
ISBN 978-0-8225-7599-3; 0-8225-7599-X

LC 2007-50826

"The well–written text provides a detailed account of the devastation and ruin brought to Zululand by the British government and by Boer settlers, replete with text boxes that provide clarification and further explanation of what are often complex and confusing issues and events. Illustrations consist of both period photographs and paintings of the fierce fighting. Reckless bravery, treachery, cruelty, betrayal, and greed are all here, resulting in an absorbing, but tragic story." SLJ

Includes glossary and bibliographical references

968.06   South Africa--Period as Republic, 1961-

Beecroft, Simon

The **release** of Nelson Mandela; by Simon Beecroft. World Almanac Library 2004 48p il (Days that changed the world) lib bdg $30; pa $11.95

Grades: 5 6 7 8   **968.06**

1. Apartheid 2. Presidents 3. Political prisoners 4. Political leaders 5. Human rights activists 6. Nobel laureates for peace 7. South Africa -- Politics and government
ISBN 0-8368-5571-X lib bdg; 0-8368-5578-7 pa

LC 2003-65807

First published 2003 in the United Kingdom with title: The freeing of Nelson Mandela

A biography of the black South African leader who became a civil rights activist, political prisoner, and president of South Africa, told in the context of the history of his country

This does "a fine job of combining a closeup view of an earth-shattering event with what led up to the drama and a sense of the event's impact on the future. . . . The . . . design is ideal for browsing." Booklist

Includes bibliographical references

Brownlie, Ali

South Africa in our world; [by] Ali Brownlie Bojang. Smart Apple Media 2010 32p il (Countries in our world) lib bdg $28.50

Grades: 5 6 7 8   **968.06**

1. South Africa
ISBN 978-1-59920-444-4 lib bdg; 1-59920-444-4 lib bdg

LC 2009043163

This "contains relevant information presented in a visually appealing layout. Large colorful photographs inform readers about the past, present, and future of the country. . . . The book gives an honest view of apartheid, poverty, and government conflicts. At the same time, it is hopeful about recent changes, such as the hosting of the World Cup and the growing economy." SLJ

Includes glossary and bibliographical references

Sonneborn, Liz

★ The **end** of apartheid in South Africa. Chelsea House Publishers 2010 120p il (Milestones in modern world history) lib bdg $35

Grades: 8 9 10 11 12   **968.06**

1. Apartheid 2. Anti-apartheid movement 3. South Africa -- Race relations

ISBN 978-1-60413-409-4; 1-60413-409-7

LC 2008-54805

This is "an excellent in-depth overview, one of the best on the subject, with chapters on the early history before the establishment of the apartheid regime and with profiles of many important leaders (not just Nelson Mandela), as well as clear discussion of present-day politics, the role of the Truth and Reconciliation Commission, and the ongoing inequality. Never simplistic, it is an outstanding overview for teens new to the subject; for those who know something of the history, it fills in the big picture with depth and detail about both leaders and ordinary people, what has changed, and how much still needs to be done." Booklist

Includes bibliographical references

968.83   Botswana

Botswana; Kelly Wittmann. Mason Crest 2013 79 p. ill. (some col.), col. map $22.95

Grades: 5 6 7 8   **968.83**

1. Botswana

ISBN 9781422221938

This book "covers the land, government, economy, culture, people, religion, holidays, and festivals" of Botswana. (Library Media Connection)

Includes bibliographical references and index

968.91   Zimbabwe

Arnold, James R.

Robert Mugabe's Zimbabwe; by James R. Arnold and Roberta Wiener. Twenty-First Century Books 2008 160p (Dictatorships) lib bdg $38.60

Grades: 7 8 9 10   **968.91**

1. Presidents 2. Prime ministers 3. Zimbabwe

ISBN 978-0-8225-7283-1

LC 2006-100765

This history of Zimbabwe under the dictatorship of Robert Mugabe gives "students a glimpse into the repression and daily struggle for survival under [this] brutal [government]." SLJ

Includes glossary and bibliographical references

Hall, Martin

Great Zimbabwe; [by] Martin Hall and Rebecca Stefoff. 1st ed.; Oxford University Press 2006 47p il map (Digging for the past) $23

Grades: 7 8 9 10   **968.91**

1. Archeology 2. Shona (African people) 3. Zimbabwe

ISBN 978-0-19-515773-4; 0-19-515773-7

LC 2005014607

This "explores a ruined fourteenth-century stone city in Zimbabwe and covers controversies over its origin, its artifacts, and theories about its former inhabitants. The well-written text will spur readers' curiosity, while archival and modern photos, ancient maps, and European explorers' notes add a fascinating variety to the book's visual presentation." Horn Book Guide

Includes glossary and bibliographical references

968.94   Zambia

Holmes, Timothy

Zambia; by Timothy Holmes & Winnie Wong. rev ed.; Marshall Cavendish Benchmark 2008 144p il map (Cultures of the world) lib bdg $42.79

Grades: 5 6 7 8   **968.94**

1. Zambia

ISBN 978-0-7614-3039-1 lib bdg; 0-7614-3039-3 lib bdg

LC 2007050794

First published 1998

Describes the geography, history, government, economy, people, lifestyle, religion, language, arts, leisure, festivals, and food of Zambia

Includes glossary and bibliographical references

969.1   Madagascar

Heale, Jay

Madagascar; [by] Jay Heale & Zawiah Abdul Latif. 2nd ed.; Marshall Cavendish Benchmark 2008 144p il map (Cultures of the world) lib bdg $42.79

Grades: 5 6 7 8   **969.1**

1. Madagascar

ISBN 978-0-7614-3036-0 lib bdg; 0-7614-3036-9 lib bdg

LC 2007048288

First published 1998

"Provides comprehensive information on the geography, history, wildlife, governmental structure, economy, cultural diversity, peoples, religion, and culture of Madagascar." Publisher's note

Includes glossary and bibliographical references

970   History of North America

Bial, Raymond

The **Crow.** Marshall Cavendish Benchmark 2006 124p il map (Lifeways) lib bdg $38.50

Grades: 5 6 7 8   **970**

1. Crow Indians 2. Native Americans

ISBN 978-0-7614-1901-3; 0-7614-1901-2

LC 2004-22235

Discusses the history, culture, beliefs, changing ways, and notable people of the Crow.

Includes glossary and bibliographical references

Desaulniers, Kristi L.

Northern America; [by] Kristi L. Desaulniers and Charles F. Gritzner. Chelsea House 2006 128p il map (Modern world cultures) lib bdg $30

Grades: 7 8 9 10   **970**

1. North America
ISBN 0-7910-8141-9

LC 2005031766

This describes the geography, history, culture, population, politics, economy, regions, and possible future of The United States and Canada.

Includes bibliographical references

970.004   North American native peoples

Bial, Raymond

The **Apache**. Benchmark Books 2001 128p il map (Lifeways) lib bdg $38.50

Grades: 5 6 7 8   **970.004**

1. Apache Indians 2. Native Americans
ISBN 978-0-7614-0939-7; 0-7614-0939-4

LC 99-44717

Discusses the history, culture, beliefs, changing ways, and notable people of the Apache.

"Crisp, clear photos in full color and black and white, some taken by the author and some archival, as well as original art, appear on almost every other page. . . . It's the comprehensive content, the attractive presentation, and the varied and well-chosen illustrations that make [this book] . . . worthy of consideration." SLJ

Includes glossary and bibliographical references

The **Huron**. Benchmark Bks. 2001 128p il (Lifeways) lib bdg $38.50

Grades: 5 6 7 8   **970.004**

1. Huron Indians 2. Native Americans
ISBN 978-0-7614-0940-3; 0-7614-0940-8

LC 99-49261

Discusses the history, culture, social structure, beliefs, and customs of the Huron people, also known as the Wyandot.

Includes glossary and bibliographical references

Lifeways [series] Benchmark Books 1999 28v il map Each group set of four volumes $136.86

Grades: 5 6 7 8   **970.004**

1. Native Americans
ISBN 0-614-0800-2 Group 1; 0-7614-0860-6 Group 2; 0-7614-0936-X Group 3; 0-7614-1208-5 Group 4; 0-7614-1412-6 Group 5; 0-7614-1680-3 Group 6; 0-7614-1900-4 Group 7

"It's the comprehensive content, the attractive presentation, and the varied and well-chosen illustrations that make these books worthy of consideration." SLJ

The **Long** Walk; the story of Navajo captivity. Benchmark Bks. 2003 94p il map (Great journeys) lib bdg $31.36

Grades: 5 6 7 8   **970.004**

1. Navajo Indians 2. Scouts 3. Pioneers 4. Indian chiefs
ISBN 0-7614-1322-7

LC 2001-43969

"The book is illustrated with informative black-and-white photographs and reproductions." SLJ

Includes bibliographical references

The **Shoshone**. Benchmark Bks. 2001 128p il (Lifeways) lib bdg $38.50

Grades: 5 6 7 8   **970.004**

1. Shoshoni Indians
ISBN 978-0-7614-1211-3; 0-7614-1211-5

LC 2001-18496

This examines the origins, villages and camps, lifeways, beliefs, history, language, and social conditions of The Shoshone Indians

Includes glossary and bibliographical references

Bjornlund, Lydia D.

The **Trail** of Tears; the relocation of the Cherokee Nation. Lucent Books 2010 104p il map (American history) lib bdg $33.45

Grades: 5 6 7 8   **970.004**

1. Cherokee Indians 2. Native Americans -- Relocation
ISBN 978-1-4205-0211-4; 1-4205-0211-5

LC 2010001549

Describes the Federal government's seizure of Cherokee lands in Georgia and the forced migration of the Cherokee Nation to Oklahoma along the route that came to be known as the Trail of Tears.

This is "well written and [includes] primary sources, photographs, reproductions, and maps." SLJ

Includes bibliographical references

Brown, Dee Alexander

★ **Bury** my heart at Wounded Knee; an Indian history of the American West. [by] Dee Brown. Thirtieth anniversary ed; Holt & Co. 2001 487p il hardcover o.p. pa $16

Grades: 8 9 10 11 12 Adult   **970.004**

1. Generals 2. Indian chiefs 3. Civil engineers 4. Government officials 5. West (U.S.) -- History 6. Native Americans -- Wars 7. Native Americans -- West (U.S.)
ISBN 0-8050-6634-9; 0-8050-6669-1 pa

LC 00-40958

First published 1970

This is an account of the experience of the American Indian during the white man's expansion westward.

Includes bibliographical references

Connolly, Sean

The **Americas** and the Pacific. Zak Books 2009 48p il map (History of the world) lib bdg $34.25

Grades: 4 5 6 7 8   **970.004**

1. Maoris 2. Aboriginal Australians 3. Native

Americans -- History
ISBN 978-88-60981-61-5 lib bdg; 88-60981-61-1
lib bdg

LC 2008008404

"Artists' renderings show groups of people engaged in representative activities, but it's the reproductions of artifacts . . . that will pull readers and browsers most. . . . [This is an] engaging overview." Booklist

Includes bibliographical references

Denetdale, Jennifer

The **Long** Walk; the forced Navajo exile. [by] Jennifer Denetdale. Chelsea House 2007 143p il map (Landmark events in Native American history) lib bdg $30

Grades: 7 8 9 10   **970.004**

1. Navajo Indians
ISBN 978-0-7910-9344-3 lib bdg; 0-7910-9344-1
lib bdg

LC 2007021723

"In 1863, the Diné (Navajo) faced transformations to their way of life with the Americans' determination to first subjugate and then remove them to a reservation. . . . This book exposes the series of events that facilitated the Navajo's removal from their homeland, their experiences during the Long Walk, their time at the Bosque Redondo reservation, their return home, and the ways in which they remember the Long Walk and the Bosque Redondo." Publisher's note

Includes bibliographical references

Dolan, Edward F.

The **American** Indian wars; [by] Edward F. Dolan. Millbrook Press 2003 112p il map lib bdg $29.90

Grades: 5 6 7 8   **970.004**

1. Native Americans -- Wars
ISBN 0-7613-1968-9

LC 2002-153012

Examines the battles and treaties between native peoples and early European settlers of what was to become the United States, as conflicts arose primarily over land, but also over food and other issues

"Period drawings, paintings, and photographs effectively illustrate a text packed with history." Booklist

Includes bibliographical references

Edwards, Judith

The **history** of the American Indians and the reservation; [by] Judith Edwards. Enslow Publishers 2008 128p il map (From many cultures, one history) lib bdg $31.93

Grades: 6 7 8 9   **970.004**

1. Native Americans -- History
ISBN 978-0-7660-2798-5 lib bdg; 0-7660-2798-8
lib bdg

LC 2007028275

"Explores the difficult changes American Indians were forced to make, including moving off their land, adapting to like on reservations, and how those reservations have changed since their creation." Publisher's note

Includes glossary and bibliographical references

Ehrlich, Amy

★ **Wounded** Knee: an Indian history of the American West; adapted for young readers by Amy Ehrlich from Dee Brown's Bury my heart at Wounded Knee. Holt & Co. 1974 202p il maps hardcover o.p. pa $13.95

Grades: 6 7 8 9   **970.004**

1. Generals 2. Ghost dance 3. Apache Indians 4. Dakota Indians 5. Navajo Indians 6. Arapaho Indians 7. Cheyenne Indians 8. Sand Creek, Battle of, 1864 9. Indian chiefs 10. Civil engineers 11. Government officials 12. West (U.S.) -- History 13. Native Americans -- Wars 14. Native Americans -- West (U.S.)
ISBN 0-8050-2700-9 pa

This book traces the plight of the Navaho, Apache, Cheyenne and Sioux Indians in their struggles against the white man in the West between 1860 and 1890. It recounts battles and their causes, participants, and consequences during this era

"Some chapters [of the original] have been deleted, others condensed, and in some instances sentence structure and language have been simplified. The editing is good, and this version is interesting, readable, and smooth." SLJ

Includes bibliographical references

Elish, Dan

★ The **Trail** of Tears; the story of the Cherokee removal. Benchmark Books 2002 96p il map (Great journeys) lib bdg $32.79

Grades: 5 6 7 8   **970.004**

1. Cherokee Indians 2. Native Americans -- Relocation
ISBN 0-7614-1228-X

LC 00-52902

This "is particularly moving. Elish does a fine job introducing the Cherokee nation. . . . Filled with crisp, well-selected photographs and historical illustrations." Booklist

Includes bibliographical references

Encyclopedia of Native American wars and warfare; general editors, William B. Kessel, Robert Wooster. Facts on File 2005 398p il map $75; pa $21.95

Grades: 7 8 9 10   **970.004**

1. Reference books 2. Native Americans -- Wars -- Encyclopedias
ISBN 0-8160-3337-4; 0-8160-6430-X pa

LC 00-56200

"This encyclopedia offers readers a wide range of information about Native American history in North America after 1492." Choice

Includes bibliographical references

Freedman, Russell

★ **Indian** chiefs. Holiday House 1987 151p il $24.95; pa $14.95

Grades: 6 7 8 9 10   **970.004**

1. Kiowa Indians 2. Dakota Indians 3. Oglala Indians 4. Comanche Indians 5. Shoshoni Indians 6. Centenarians 7. Indian chiefs 8. Shoshone Indians 9.

Nez Percé Indians 10. Native Americans -- Biography
ISBN 0-8234-0625-3; 0-8234-0971-6 pa

LC 86-46198

This "book chronicles the lives of six renowned Indian chiefs, each of whom served as a leader during a critical period in his tribe's history. . . . The text relates information about the lives of each chief and aspects of Indian/white relationships that illuminate his actions. Interesting vignettes and quotations are well integrated into the narrative as are dramatic accounts of battles. While the tone of the text is nonjudgmental, an underlying sympathy for the Indians' situation is apparent." Horn Book

Includes bibliographical references

Gibson, Karen Bush

Native American history for kids; with 21 activities. Chicago Review Press 2010 127p il pa $16.95
Grades: 6 7 8 9 10   **970.004**
1. Native Americans
ISBN 978-1-56976-280-6 pa; 1-56976-280-5 pa

LC 2010005695

"This gripping, highly readable overview will draw teens and even some adults into the history of Native Americans, from early times and the arrival of European settlers up to the present. The examples of racism are horrifying. . . . Also horrifying are the accounts of forced assimilation." Booklist

Includes glossary and bibliographical references

Gitlin, Marty

Wounded Knee Massacre. Greenwood 2011 xxiii, 185p il (Landmarks of the American mosaic) $35; e-book $35
Grades: 7 8 9 10   **970.004**
1. Wounded Knee Creek, Battle of, 1890 2. Native Americans -- West (U.S.)
ISBN 978-1-59884-409-2; 1-59884-409-1; 978-1-59884-410-8 e-book; 1-59884-410-5 e-book

LC 2010035200

"This concise, chronologically arranged text places the massacre in context by concisely examining the 'seeds of conflict' into the late 1860s; the fallout from Little Big Horn; the reemergence of the Ghost Dance; and, ultimately, the worst slaughter of Native men, women, and children in American history. . . . Substantial back matter includes lucid biographies of key figures and 13 primary documents." SLJ

Includes glossary and bibliographical references

Goble, Paul

★ **All** our relatives; traditional Native American thoughts about nature. compiled and illustrated by Paul Goble. World Wisdom 2005 un il $15.95
Grades: 5 6 7 8   **970.004**
1. Native Americans 2. Philosophy of nature
ISBN 0-941532-77-1; 978-0-941532-77-8

LC 2005004285

"The pages of this book are chock-full of quotations, songs, and brief stories that exemplify Native American attitudes toward nature. . . . Black Elk, Standing Bear, Brave Buffalo, and others observe the importance of various animals and the sacred qualities of all living things. . . . The spaces between text blocks are filled with Goble's familiar

illustrations based on traditional Native American designs and colors." SLJ

Includes bibliographical references

Jastrzembski, Joseph C.

The **Apache** wars; the final resistance. Chelsea House Publishers 2007 133p il map (Landmark events in Native American history) lib bdg $35
Grades: 7 8 9 10   **970.004**
1. Apache Indians
ISBN 978-0-7910-9343-6; 0-7910-9343-3

LC 2007-990

This account features "lively writing and direct quotes, and [is] enhanced by many color and black-and-white photos, drawings, and illustrations." SLJ

Includes bibliographical references

Keoke, Emory Dean

★ **American** Indian contributions to the world; [by] Emory Dean Keoke and Kay Marie Porterfield. Facts on File 2005 5v il map set$175
Grades: 7 8 9 10   **970.004**
1. Native Americans
ISBN 0-8160-5392-8

This set "focuses on the many significant contributions that members of North, Central, and South American tribes have made to both United States and world culture. . . . The appendixes are well organized. . . . This set would be an excellent addition to any school media center's collection." Voice Youth Advocates

Includes glossary and bibliographical references

King, David C.

First people; an illustrated history of American Indians. DK Pub. 2008 192p il map $19.99
Grades: 5 6 7 8   **970.004**
1. Native Americans
ISBN 978-0-7566-4092-7; 0-7566-4092-X

"This rich pictorial work serves as an entertaining, informative, and visually appealing introduction to American Indian culture and history. Each of the seven chapters covers a different time period in chronological order. . . . The glossy photographs, colorful drawings, and easily accessible paragraphs . . . make for an easy-to-use overall package." SLJ

McNeese, Tim

The **fascinating** history of American Indians; the age before Columbus. Enslow Publishers 2009 128p il map (America's living history) lib bdg $31.93
Grades: 5 6 7 8   **970.004**
1. Native Americans
ISBN 978-0-7660-2938-5 lib bdg; 0-7660-2938-7 lib bdg

"This thorough discussion of Native American life prior to Columbus's arrival combines theories of archaeologists, anthropologists, historians, and scientists to provide an engaging portrayal of the daily experiences of regional tribes. Based mostly on archaeological discoveries, the accessible text is supported by archival photographs, maps, and sidebars." Horn Book Guide

Includes glossary and bibliographical references

Media Projects Incorporated

Student almanac of Native American history;
Media Projects, Inc. Greenwood Press 2003 2v il
map (Middle school reference) set$80

Grades: 6 7 8 9   **970.004**
1. Reference books 2. Native Americans -- History
ISBN 0-313-32599-5

LC 2002-35215

Presents an overview of the history of Native Americans
from before European contact up to the present day, including historical documents, legislation, statistics, court cases,
and timelines

"This attractive almanac provides information on topics of interest to users in middle school and up. . . . [This]
will be a welcome addition to school and public libraries
where there is a need for additional information about Native Americans." Booklist

Includes bibliographical references

Murdoch, David Hamilton

North American Indian; written by David
Murdoch; chief consultant, Stanley A. Freed; photographed by Lynton Gardiner. rev ed; DK Pubs.
2005 72p il (DK eyewitness books) $16.99; lib
bdg $19.99

Grades: 4 5 6 7   **970.004**
1. Native Americans
ISBN 0-7566-1081-8; 0-7566-1082-6 lib bdg
First published 1995 by Knopf

This is a guide to the civilizations of North American
Indians including full-color photographs of artifacts and descriptions ceremonies and customs.

National Museum of the American Indian (U.S.)

Do all Indians live in tipis? questions and answers. from the National Museum of the American
Indian; foreword by Rick West; introduction by Wilma Mankiller. Collins, in association with the National Museum of the American Indian, Smithsonian
Institution 2007 239p il pa $14.95

Grades: 8 9 10 11 12   **970.004**
1. Native Americans
ISBN 978-0-06-115301-3; 0-06-115301-X

LC 2007-60874

"This highly accessible and informative book aims to
dispel some of the major myths and stereotypes still surrounding Native people in the United States and Canada. .
. . The straightforward questions were compiled from actual phone calls, emails, letters, and in-person visits to the
George Gustav Heye Center in New York, a major branch
of the National Museum of the American Indian. The Native American writers who answered them did so concisely
with hints of humor and an abundance of research and experience. . . . This is a topnotch resource for both people
just learning about Native American cultures and those who
think they know the facts." SLJ

Philip, Neil

★ The **great** circle; a history of the First Nations. foreword by Dennis Hastings. Clarion Books
2006 153p il map $25

Grades: 7 8 9 10 11 12 Adult   **970.004**
1. Native Americans
ISBN 978-0-618-15941-3; 0-618-15941-X

LC 2005032743

"Philip takes on a huge challenge here: to present a unified narrative that explains the complex and confrontational
relationships between Native Americans and white settlers.
. . . He pulls it off, however, thanks to solid research, an
engaging writing style, and a talent for making individual
stories serve the whole. . . . Top marks, too, for the volume's
photographs and historical renderings, which so intensely illustrate the pages." Booklist

Includes bibliographical references

Schomp, Virginia

The **Native** Americans; [by] Virginia Schomp.
Marshall Cavendish Benchmark 2007 96p il map
(Myths of the world) lib bdg $34.21

Grades: 6 7 8 9   **970.004**
1. Native Americans
ISBN 978-0-7614-2550-2 lib bdg; 0-7614-2550-0
lib bdg

LC 2007013511

"With [its] beautiful illustrations, high-quality production, and focus on source material, the [book] should whet
the interest of readers." SLJ

Includes glossary and bibliographical references

Terry, Michael Bad Hand

Daily life in a Plains Indian village, 1868. Clarion Bks. 1999 48p il map hardcover o.p. pa $9.95

Grades: 4 5 6 7   **970.004**
1. Native Americans -- Great Plains
ISBN 0-395-94542-9; 0-395-97499-2 pa

LC 98-32382

Depicts the historical background, social organization,
and daily life of a Plains Indian village in 1868, presenting
interiors, landscapes, clothing, and everyday objects

"The author presents short paragraphs of fascinating information accompanied by visuals that explain even more
than the text." SLJ

Includes glossary

Vander Hook, Sue

Trail of Tears. ABDO Pub. 2010 112p il map
(Essential events) lib bdg $32.79

Grades: 6 7 8 9   **970.004**
1. Cherokee Indians 2. Native Americans -- Relocation
ISBN 978-1-60453-946-2; 1-60453-946-1

LC 2009-31066

This title examines an important historic event, the Trail
of Tears. Readers will learn the background of European
settlement in Native American lands, relations between the
groups, and how this led to the Trail of Tears.

"The writing is accessible and is richer than a lot of
history writing, allowing the reader to become engaged in
the text as a story, and the layout provides enough white
space to allow lower level readers to feel confident." Libr
Media Connect

Includes glossary and bibliographical references

Waldman, Carl

Encyclopedia of Native American tribes; 3rd rev ed; Facts on File 2006 xxiv, 360p il map (Facts on File library of American history) $75; pa $21.95

Grades: 6 7 8 9 10 11 12 Adult   **970.004**

1. Reference books 2. Native Americans -- Encyclopedias

ISBN 978-0-8160-6273-7; 0-8160-6273-0; 978-0-8160-6274-4 pa; 0-8160-6274-9 pa

LC 2006-12529

First published 1988

"This well-written and easily accessible encyclopedia of a good starting point for research on Native American tribes." Libr Media Connect

Includes bibliographical references

Yue, Charlotte

★ The **wigwam** and the longhouse; [by] Charlotte and David Yue. Houghton Mifflin 2000 118p il $15

Grades: 4 5 6 7   **970.004**

1. Woodland Indians

ISBN 0-395-84169-0

LC 98-28971

Describes the history, customs, religion, government, homes, and present-day status of the various native peoples that inhabited the eastern woodlands since before the coming of the Europeans

Includes bibliographical references

Zimmerman, Dwight Jon

Saga of the Sioux; an adaptation of Dee Brown's Bury My Heart at Wounded Knee. [adapted] by Dwight Jon Zimmerman. Henry Holt and Company 2011 208p il map $18.99

Grades: 5 6 7 8   **970.004**

1. Dakota Indians 2. West (U.S.) -- History 3. Native Americans -- Wars

ISBN 978-0-8050-9364-3; 0-8050-9364-8

LC 2011004792

"Dwight Jon Zimmerman has created a masterful adaptation of Dee Brown's Bury My Heart at Wounded Knee, presenting late nineteenth century history from a Native American viewpoint. While Brown's book traces the fates of several Native American tribes in the western United States, Zimmerman's adaptation focuses solely on the Sioux. . . . Historical figures central to the narrative, both Native American and white, are portrayed as real people, rather than caricatures. Rather than simply describing what happened, the book looks at why it happened. Individuals' motivations, strengths, and flaws are all explored in relation to how historical events unfolded. The book includes numerous photographs, illustrations, and maps that aid understanding and create visual appeal. . . . This is a must-have addition to any United States history collection serving teens." Voice Youth Advocates

Includes glossary and bibliographical references

Zimmerman, Larry J.

Exploring the life, myth, and art of Native Americans. Rosen Pub. 2009 144p il map (Civilizations of the world) lib bdg $29.95

Grades: 7 8 9 10 11 12   **970.004**

1. Native Americans -- Art 2. Native Americans -- Religion

ISBN 978-1-4358-5614-1; 1-4358-5614-7

LC 2009-9268

This book describes the cultures, myths, and art of Native Americans.

"This beautifully illustrated and well-written [title] . . . is perfect for those assignments where students must look at the culture of a civilization. Artwork and pictures blend seamlessly with the information and the reader is taken on a journey of discovery. Myths are used as the story of how the people view themselves, blended with the discussion of the reality of life. Everyday life is tied to the belief systems and is explained in light of those beliefs. The pictures are beautifully done and there is almost as much information in the captions as there is in the text." Libr Media Connect

Includes glossary and bibliographical references

970.01   North America--Early history to 1599

Berne, Emma Carlson

Christopher Columbus; the voyage that changed the world. by Emma Carlson Berne. Sterling Pub. Co. 2008 124 p. ill. (some col.) (paperback) $5.95; (hardcover) $12.95

Grades: 4 5 6 7   **970.01**

1. Exploration 2. Columbus, Christopher, 1451-1506 3. Explorers -- Spain -- Biography 4. Explorers -- America -- Biography 5. America -- Discovery and exploration -- Spanish

ISBN 1402744072; 1402760566; 9781402744075; 9781402760563

LC 2007048197

This book by Emma Carlson Berne, part of the Sterling Biographies series, looks at explorer Christopher Columbus, who "made the voyage that, for better and worse, changed history. Born in the bustling port city of Genoa, Italy, Columbus fell in love with the sea, and spent his youth learning all he could about steering and navigating a ship. Dreaming of wealth and fame, he believed he could find a new route to the Indies by sailing westward." (Publisher's note)

Includes bibliographical references (p. 119-120) and index.

Demi, 1942-

Columbus; by Demi. Marshall Cavendish 2012 64 p. ill. (hardcover) $19.99

Grades: 3 4 5 6   **970.01**

1. America -- Exploration 2. Columbus, Christopher, 1451-1506 3. Explorers -- Spain -- Biography 4. Explorers -- America -- Biography 5. America -- Discovery and exploration -- Spanish

ISBN 0761461671; 9780761461678

LC 2011036019

This book on Christopher Columbus was written and illustrated by the children's book author Demi. "From his childhood in Italy to his death in Spain, this biography presents a detailed view of the explorer's life. . . .Columbus's faults and accomplishments are both presented, acknowledging that his drive to explore furthered Europeans' knowledge of other lands, but that his mistreatment of Native peoples devastated their lives and culture." (School Library Journal)

Edwards, Judith

Henry Hudson and his voyages of exploration in world history. Enslow Pubs. 2002 128p il maps (In world history) lib bdg $26.60

Grades: 7 8 9 10   **970.01**

1. Explorers 2. America -- Exploration
ISBN 0-7660-1885-7

LC 2001-4119

Examines the life and career of Henry Hudson, tracing his voyages in the Arctic and North America and his discovery of the Hudson River and other bodies of water during his unsuccessful search for a Northwest Passage to Asia

Includes bibliographical references

Freedman, Russell

★ **Who** was first? discovering the Americas. Clarion Books 2007 88p il map $19

Grades: 6 7 8 9   **970.01**

1. Explorers 2. America -- Exploration
ISBN 978-0-618-66391-0

LC 2006-102485

This "looks at various ideas about the discovery of the Americas. . . . Beyond the very readable presentation of facts and theories, the book's main accomplishment is in showing that history is . . . an evolving process of logically interpreted evidence continually questioned, disputed, and revised. . . . The illustrations, many in color, include many excellent maps as well as reproductions of period drawings, paintings, engravings, and photos. . . . A well-researched, intelligent account." Booklist

Includes bibliographical references

Gaines, Ann

Hernando de Soto and the Spanish search for gold in world history; {by} Ann Graham Gaines. Enslow Pubs. 2002 112p il maps (In world history) lib bdg $26.60

Grades: 7 8 9 10   **970.01**

1. Explorers 2. America -- Exploration 3. Colonial administrators
ISBN 0-7660-1821-0

LC 2001-1975

In this book "about the explorer's life and adventures, Gaines also gives substantial attention to the culture and history of the various Native American groups that the Spaniard encountered on his travels. . . . This detailed book should provide much information for reports." SLJ

Includes bibliographical references

Gunderson, Jessica

Conquistadors; by Jessica Gunderson. Creative Education 2011 48 p. (alk. paper) $35.65

Grades: 5 6 7 8   **970.01**

1. United States -- History 2. Soldiers 3. Military art and science -- History 4. Soldiers -- Spain -- History 5. Military art and science -- History 6. America -- Discovery and exploration -- Spanish
ISBN 1608181839; 9781608181834

LC 2011035799

Author Jessica Gunderson's book "covers the beginnings of the people, weaponry, war tactics, and famous leaders, and examines the current perception of the group in popular culture in an appealing, detailed, and evenhanded manner. Historical reproductions, primary documents, photographs, maps, and film stills appear throughout" the "explorations of history." (Publisher's note)

Includes bibliographical references and index

Harrison, David L.

Mammoth bones and broken stones; the mystery of North America's first people. with illustrations by Richard Hilliard and archaeological photographs. Boyds Mills Press 2010 48p il map $18.95

Grades: 4 5 6 7   **970.01**

1. Prehistoric peoples 2. North America -- Antiquities
ISBN 978-1-59078-561-4; 1-59078-561-4

LC 2009020247

"How and when the Western Hemisphere . . . came to be populated continues to be both mysterious and controversial for scientists. . . . Harrison does a good job setting the issue in context. He describes the earliest efforts to identify the original inhabitants of the continents, exploring the Clovis culture. . . . After clearly explaining how scholars decided that they were the first, he then lists the arguments against this hypothesis. . . . The narrative is aided by both photographs and original illustrations that imagine scenes from both the distant past and the field experiences." Kirkus

Includes glossary and bibliographical references

Hernandez, Roger E.

Early explorations: the 1500s. Marshall Cavendish Benchmark 2009 79p il map (Hispanic America) lib bdg $34.21

Grades: 4 5 6 7   **970.01**

1. Explorers 2. Spain -- Colonies 3. America -- Exploration 4. Southern States -- History 5. Southwestern States -- History
ISBN 978-0-7614-2937-1 lib bdg; 0-7614-2937-9 lib bdg

"Provides comprehensive information on the history of Spanish exploration in the United States." Publisher's note

Includes glossary and bibliographical references

Huey, Lois Miner

American archaeology uncovers the Vikings. Marshall Cavendish Benchmark 2009 64p il map (American archaeology) lib bdg $21.95

Grades: 4 5 6 7   **970.01**

1. America -- Antiquities 2. America -- Exploration 3. Vikings -- North America 4. Excavations (Archeology) -- Canada 5. Excavations (Archeology) -- United States
ISBN 978-0-7614-4270-7 lib bdg; 0-7614-4270-7 lib bdg

LC 2008050266

This describes how archeologists have learned about the Vikings in America.

This is "both intriguing and engaging for young readers. . . . A welcomed addition to classroom and school libraries." Libr Media Connect

Includes glossary and bibliographical references

Mann, Charles C.

★ **Before** Columbus; the Americas of 1491. Atheneum Books for Young Readers 2009 117p il map $24.99

Grades: 5 6 7 8 9 10   **970.01**

1. America -- Antiquities 2. Native Americans -- Origin 3. Native Americans -- History

ISBN 978-1-4169-4900-8; 1-4169-4900-3

LC 2009007691

Adapted from 1491, published 2006 by Knopf for adults

"Mann paints a superb picture of pre-Columbian America. In the process, he overturns the misconceived image of Natives as simple, widely scattered savages with minimal impact on their surroundings. Well-chosen, vividly colored graphics and photographs of mummies, pyramids, artifacts, and landscapes as well as the author's skillful storytelling will command the attention of even the most reluctant readers." SLJ

Includes glossary and bibliographical references

Mooney, Carla

Explorers of the New World; discover the golden age of exploration; with 22 projects. illustrated by Tom Casteel. Nomad 2011 120p il map (Build it yourself) pa $15.95 **970.01**

1. Explorers 2. America -- Exploration

ISBN 978-1-936313-44-0; 1-936313-44-8

Provides twenty-two step-by-step projects to help readers learn about the explorers that discovered America and their voyages.

"This informative, entertaining activity book takes readers on a fascinating voyage of their own. . . . Each chapter concludes with 'Make Your Own' activities that bring life to the history with instructions for the construction of a logbook, clay activities, recipes, games, etc. Some may require the assistance of an adult but are not complicated or time consuming." SLJ

Includes glossary and bibliographical references

Owsley, Douglas W.

★ **Their** skeletons speak; Kennewick man and the Paleoamerican world. by Sally M. Walker and Douglas W. Owsley. Carolrhoda Books 2012 136 p. (lib. bdg. : alk. paper) $22.95

Grades: 8 9 10 11 12   **970.01**

1. Kennewick Man 2. Paleo-Indians 3. Human remains (Archeology) 4. Washington (State) -- Antiquities 5. Paleo-Indians -- Washington (State) -- Origin 6. Human remains (Archaeology) -- Washington (State) 7. Paleo-Indians -- Anthropometry -- Washington (State) 8. Indians of North America -- Washington (State) -- Antiquities

ISBN 0761374574; 9780761374572

LC 2011051329

This book by Sally M. Walker and Douglas W. Owsley presents a "detailed study of the discovery and forensic evaluation of the skeleton dubbed 'Kennewick Man.' . . . From his accidental discovery in 1996 through multiple examinations by scientists with ever-improving forensic tools . . . an actual human being emerges from a time long gone, speaking to us through his bones. . . . A final facial reconstruction leaves readers face-to-face with a real person." (School Library Journal)

Includes bibliographical references and index.

Peterson, Cris

Birchbark brigade; a fur trade history. Calkins Creek 2009 135p il $18.95

Grades: 7 8 9 10   **970.01**

1. Fur trade 2. Frontier and pioneer life 3. America -- Exploration 4. Native Americans -- History

ISBN 978-1-59078-426-6; 1-59078-426-X

LC 2008055109

"Peterson first provides a history of the military, political and economic development of the [fur] trade and then gives readers a snapshot of the lives of the Indians and voyageurs who did the actual work. She relies on a wealth of primary-source material, from archival illustrations to quotes from players both large and small. . . . The author's enthusiasm for her subject will communicate itself to readers, even those who never dreamed they'd be interested, making this the best kind of discovery." Kirkus

Includes bibliographical references

Wulffson, Don L.

Before Columbus; early voyages to the Americas. by Don Wulffson. Twenty-First Century Books 2008 128p il map lib bdg $30.60

Grades: 6 7 8 9   **970.01**

1. Explorers 2. America -- Antiquities 3. America -- Exploration

ISBN 978-0-8225-5978-8 lib bdg; 0-8225-5978-1 lib bdg

LC 2005-24487

"This engaging presentation of early exploration of the Americas offers both fact and speculation on who, when, and why voyagers came; how they traveled; and what evidence they left behind. . . . Citing legends and sagas, oral and written histories, and archaeological discoveries, Wulffson presents an intriguing array of possibilities. . . . The stories and unanswered questions about pre-Columbian voyagers will capture the imaginations of many readers, offer fascinating glimpses of different cultural groups, [and] stimulate further research." SLJ

Includes bibliographical references

970.1   North American native peoples

Ellis, Deborah

Looks Like Daylight; Voices of Indigenous Kids. by Deborah Ellis, with a foreword by Loriene Roy. Pgw 2013 256 p. $15.95

Grades: 6 7 8 9 10 11 12   **970.1**

1. Interviews 2. Native American children

ISBN 1554981204; 9781554981205

This book, by Deborah Ellis, "is a . . . collection of interviews with [native] children aged nine to eighteen. They come from all over the continent, from Iqaluit to Texas, Haida Gwaai to North Carolina. . . . Many of these children are living with the legacy of the residential schools; many have lived through the cycle of foster care. Many others have found something in their roots that sustains them, have found their place in the arts, the sciences, athletics." (Publisher's note)

"In this cultural undertaking, Ellis interviews Native American and aboriginal children and teens, ages nine to eighteen. Whether heartwrenching or uplifting, each first-person narrative is compelling, insightful, and incredibly moving. Introductory matter sheds painful light on the historically horrific treatment of North America's indigenous peoples, as well as the challenges they face still. An extensive list of charitable and informational organizations is appended." (Horn Book)

971   Canada

Baker, Stuart

In the Arctic. Marshall Cavendish Benchmark 2010 32p il map (Climate change) lib bdg $19.95

Grades: 5 6 7 8   **971**

1. Arctic regions 2. Greenhouse effect
ISBN 978-0-7614-4437-4 lib bdg; 0-7614-4437-8 lib bdg

LC 2009-5767

The book about climate change in the Arctic "is perfectly organized for students. . . . Unique layout features serve as signposts and will help focus readers' attention. . . . [The book] features an outstanding chart of possible effects of global warming on the area in question, listing 'Possible Event,' 'Predicted Result,' and 'Impact' in short, bulleted statements." SLJ

Includes glossary

Bial, Raymond

The Cree. Marshall Cavendish Benchmark 2005 128p il map (Lifeways) lib bdg $38.50

Grades: 5 6 7 8   **971**

1. Cree Indians 2. Native Americans
ISBN 978-0-7614-1902-0; 0-7614-1902-0

LC 2004-22394

Discusses the history, culture, beliefs, changing ways, and notable people of the Cree.

This books "is as attractive as it is useful. . . . The clean design includes plenty of white space and eye-catching photographs, maps, and prints." Horn Book Guide

Includes glossary and bibliographical references

Ferry, Steven

Ontario. Lucent Books 2003 112p il map (Exploring Canada) $29.95

Grades: 6 7 8 9   **971**

1. Canada 2. Ontario
ISBN 978-1-59018-050-1; 1-59018-050-X

LC 2002-14351

Examines the history, geography, climate, industries, people, and culture of what is by far the most populous of Canada's provinces

Includes bibliographical references

Quebec. Lucent Books 2003 112p il map (Exploring Canada) $29.95

Grades: 6 7 8 9   **971**

1. Canada 2. Québec (Province)
ISBN 978-1-59018-051-8; 1-59018-051-8

LC 2002-4111

Examines the history, geography, climate, industries, people, culture, and ongoing separatist struggle of Canada's largest province

Includes bibliographical references

Yukon Territory; by Steven Ferry, Blake Harris, and Liz Szynkowski. Lucent Books 2003 112p il map (Exploring Canada) $29.95

Grades: 6 7 8 9   **971**

1. Canada 2. Yukon Territory
ISBN 978-1-59018-053-2; 1-59018-053-4

LC 2002-4110

Examines the history, geography, climate, industries, people, and culture of Canada's most remote and untamed region.

Includes bibliographical references

★ **Junior** Worldmark encyclopedia of the Canadian provinces; [Timothy L. Gall and Susan Bevan Gall, editors] 5th ed.; U.X.L 2007 294p il map $70

Grades: 5 6 7 8 9 10   **971**

1. Reference books 2. Canada
ISBN 978-1-4144-1060-9; 1-4144-1060-3

LC 2007003908

First published 1997

"Arranged by 40 . . . subheadings . . . this . . . resource provides . . . information on all of Canada's provinces and territories. [It includes] details on Canada's arts, climate, government, health, languages, notable persons, ethnic groups and . . . more." Publisher's note

Includes bibliographical references

Hyde, Natalie

Cryptic Canada; unsolved mysteries from coast to coast. Natalie Hyde. Owlkids Books Inc. 2012 48 p. $16.95

Grades: 4 5 6   **971**

1. Canada -- History 2. Unsolved mysteries
ISBN 1926973380; 9781926973388

LC 2011944600

This book by Natalie Hyde explores seven of Canada's "unsolved mysteries . . . beginning with the ongoing hunt in Nova Scotia for the legendary treasure of Captain Kidd and his crew, moving to the discovery of the mummified Franklin Expedition in Nunavut by modern-day scientists, and ending with an exploration of the Great Lakes Triangle phenomenon. . . . Each chapter . . . ends with an interview with an expert in the field." (Publisher's note)

Laws, Gordon D.

Alberta; by Gordon D. Laws and Lauren M. Laws. Lucent Books 2003 112p il map (Exploring Canada) $29.95

Grades: 6 7 8 9   **971**

1. Canada 2. Alberta
ISBN 978-1-59018-045-7; 1-59018-045-3

LC 2002-9880

Explains the history, geography, climate, industry, people, and culture of Canada's princess province, having been named after the daughter of Queen Victoria.

Includes bibliographical references

Manitoba; by Gordon D. Laws and Lauren M. Laws. Lucent Books 2003 112p il map (Exploring Canada) $29.95

Grades: 6 7 8 9   **971**

1. Canada 2. Manitoba
ISBN 978-1-59018-047-1; 1-59018-047-X

LC 2002-14364

Examines the history, geography, climate, industries, people, and culture of one of the most diverse of Canada's provinces

Includes bibliographical references

The **Northwest** Territories; by Gordon Laws and Lauren M. Laws. Lucent Books 2004 112p il map (Exploring Canada) $29.95

Grades: 6 7 8 9   **971**

1. Canada 2. Northwest Territories
ISBN 978-1-59018-049-5; 1-59018-049-6

LC 2002-156055

Examines the history, geography, climate, industries, people, and culture of Canada's Northwest Territories

Includes bibliographical references

Mayell, Mark

Newfoundland. Lucent Books 2003 112p il map (Exploring Canada) $29.95

Grades: 6 7 8 9   **971**

1. Canada 2. Newfoundland
ISBN 978-1-59018-048-8; 1-59018-048-8

LC 2003-2060

Examines the history, geography, climate, industries, people, and culture of Canada's Newfoundland

Includes bibliographical references

Saskatchewan. Lucent Books 2003 128p il map (Exploring Canada) $29.95

Grades: 6 7 8 9   **971**

1. Canada 2. Saskatchewan
ISBN 978-1-59018-052-5; 1-59018-052-6

LC 2003-43346

Examines the history, geography, climate, industries, people, and culture of the central province known as Canada's breadbasket

Includes bibliographical references

Palana, Brett J.

British Columbia. Lucent Books 2003 112p il map (Exploring Canada) $29.95

Grades: 6 7 8 9   **971**

1. Canada 2. British Columbia
ISBN 978-1-59018-046-4; 1-59018-046-1

LC 2002-4112

Examines the history, geography, climate, industries, people, and culture of Canada's westernmost province

Includes bibliographical references

Shea, Kitty

Teens in Canada. Compass Point Books 2008 96p il map (Global connections) lib bdg $31.93

Grades: 7 8 9 10   **971**

1. Teenagers 2. Canada
ISBN 978-0-7565-3303-8 lib bdg; 0-7565-3303-1 lib bdg

LC 2007-4899

Explores the culture and customs of Canadian teenagers

"Information is solid, giving readers an informed and realistic view of life in that country." Voice Youth Advocates

Includes glossary and bibliographical references

Sonneborn, Liz

Canada; by Liz Sonneborn. Children's Press 2012 144 p. col. ill., col. maps (library) $40

Grades: 5 6 7 8   **971**

1. Canada 2. Canada -- Social life and customs
ISBN 0531253511; 9780531253519

LC 2011011970

This book by Liz Sonneborn is part of the Enchantment of the World series and looks at Canada. The introduction focuses on Canadian Terry Fox. Sonneborn "covers geography, natural resources, environment, history, government, diversity, religions, culture, and everyday life. She includes details like 'poutine' (fries, cheese curds, and gravy) and 'Timmies' (a coffee and doughnut chain)." (School Library Journal)

Includes bibliographical references (p. 134) and index.

Walker, Sally M.

★ **Blizzard** of glass; the Halifax explosion of 1917. Henry Holt 2011 xii, 145p il $18.99

Grades: 5 6 7 8   **971**

1. World War, 1914-1918 -- Naval operations 2. Halifax (N.S.) -- History -- Explosion, 1917
ISBN 978-0-8050-8945-5; 0-8050-8945-4

LC 2011005914

"The text reads smoothly with unfamiliar words defined in the text. Illustrations consist of two full-page maps and numerous black-and-white photos. The final chapter revisits the featured families and their descendants, thus tying up the loose ends. . . . This tragic, but well-told story belongs in most collections." SLJ

Includes bibliographical references

Wallace, Mary

Inuksuk journey; an artist at the top of the world. Maple Tree Press 2008 64p il $24.95

Grades: 5 6 7 8   **971**

1. Inuit 2. Canada 3. Arctic regions
ISBN 978-1-897349-26-7; 1-897349-26-2

"Nunavut, an Arctic territory in northern Canada, is a cold, open space where inuksuk, piles of stone in the shape of a person used to 'mark a family home, welcome guests, guide travelers, and ensure safe passage,' are commonly found. Wallace has developed a passion for these ancient messengers, and here she presents a journal of her week-long trek to Inuksugassait, a place where countless numbers of the stone markers stand. . . . Wallace includes personal photos, sketches, and comments that give readers an intimate portrait of life in this place. Over a dozen vibrant oil paintings depicting scenes from her journey are scattered throughout. . . . Readers will be fascinated by this firsthand account of true adventure." SLJ

Weaver, Janice

Mirror with a memory; a nation's story in photographs. Tundra Books 2007 159p il $29.95

Grades: 6 7 8 9 **971**

1. Canada -- History

ISBN 0-88776-747-8; 978-0-88776-747-0

"Defining moments in Canadian history are thematically presented in this photography collection. . . . In the conversational commentary that accompanies each image, Weaver provides historical context. Thought-provoking media literacy issues are also raised. . . . A great visual retrospective of a nation's people, places, and events." SLJ

Williams, Brian

★ **Canada**; [by] Brian Williams; Tom Carter and Ben Cecil, consultants. National Geographic 2007 64p il map (Countries of the world) lib bdg $27.90; pa $12.95

Grades: 4 5 6 7 **971**

1. Canada

ISBN 978-1-4263-0025-7 lib bdg; 978-1-4263-0573-3 pa

LC 2007296572

A basic overview of the history, geography, climate and culture of Canada

This "clear, succinct [overview] will support assignments without overwhelming casual readers. . . . A good selection of recent, high-quality color photographs gives the [book] visual appeal." SLJ

Includes glossary and bibliographical references

971.01 Canada -- Early history to 1763

Worth, Richard

New France, 1534-1763; featuring the region that now includes all or parts of Michigan, Minnesota, Wisconsin, Illinois, Indiana, Ohio, Pennsylvania, Vermont, Maine, and Canada from Manitoba to Newfoundland. by Richard Worth. National Geographic Society 2007 109p il map (Voices from colonial America) $21.95; lib bdg $32.90

Grades: 5 6 7 8 **971.01**

1. Mississippi River valley -- History 2. Canada -- History -- 0-1763 (New France)

ISBN 978-1-4263-0147-6; 1-4263-0147-2; 978-1-4263-0148-3 lib bdg; 1-4263-0148-0 lib bdg

LC 2007-29544

"Worth presents the history of the vast French colony known as New France. Clearly written, the book is studded with quotes from people living in the colony and illustrated with colorful paintings, prints, and maps from a variety of periods. . . . This nicely designed introduction to a historically significant area fills a gap in many colonial history series and library collections." Booklist

Includes bibliographical references

971.5 Atlantic Provinces

Laws, Gordon D.

The **Maritime** Provinces; by Gordon D. Laws and Lauren M. Laws. Lucent Books 2004 112p il map (Exploring Canada) $29.95

Grades: 6 7 8 9 **971.5**

1. Canada 2. Maritime Provinces

ISBN 978-1-59018-335-9; 1-59018-335-5

LC 2003-5440

Examines the history, geography, climate, industries, people, and culture of Canada's Maritime Provinces

Includes bibliographical references

972 Mexico, Central America, West Indies, Bermuda

Ancient Aztec and Maya; edited by Anita Croy. Brown Bear Books 2010 64p il map (Facts at your fingertips) lib bdg $35.65

Grades: 6 7 8 9 **972**

1. Mayas 2. Aztecs

ISBN 978-1-933834-58-0 lib bdg; 1-933834-58-7 lib bdg

LC 2009-17295

Examines the leading Indian civilizations of Latin America and native North Americans, discussing their history, culture, food and shelter, government and trade, and geographical information

This begins "with an introduction accompanied by a striking full-page photo, followed by a two-page time line, and a two-paged spread for each topic. This format makes information easily accessible. Beautiful color photos of ancient ruins, drawings, maps, diagrams, and re-creations create appeal and enhance the information. . . . Whether for recreational browsing or serious research, this . . . will certainly prove useful for students." Libr Media Connect

Includes glossary and bibliographical references

Bingham, Jane

The **Aztec** empire; [by] Jane Bingham. Raintree 2007 64p il map (Time travel guide) lib bdg $34.29; pa $9.99

Grades: 6 7 8 9 **972**

1. Aztecs 2. Mexico -- Civilization

ISBN 978-1-4109-2730-9 lib bdg; 1-4109-2730-X lib bdg; 978-1-4109-2737-8 pa; 1-4109-2737-7 pa

LC 2006033875

A description of life in the Aztec empire written in the form of a travel guide.

Includes glossary and bibliographical references

Cooke, Tim

★ **Ancient** Aztec; archaeology unlocks the secrets of Mexico's past. National Geographic 2007 64p il map (National Geographic investigates) $17.95; lib bdg $27.90

Grades: 4 5 6 7   972
1. Aztecs 2. Mexico -- Antiquities 3. Excavations (Archeology) -- Mexico
ISBN 978-1-4263-0072-1; 1-4263-0072-7; 978-1-4263-0073-8 lib bdg; 1-4263-0073-5 lib bdg
LC 2007024813

This describes ancient Aztec origins, technology, major archeological sites, civilization, and connections to the present

"Pithy and appealing. . . . Aerial photos, time [line], informative sidebars, an interview with an archaeologist, and excellent maps augment rigorously supported [text] that [asks] and [answers] interesting questions." SLJ

George, Charles

Maya civilization; [by] Charles and Linda George. Lucent Books 2010 96p il (World history) lib bdg $33.45

Grades: 6 7 8 9   972
1. Mayas 2. Mexico -- Civilization 3. Central America -- Civilization
ISBN 978-1-4205-0240-4; 1-4205-0240-9
LC 2009053266

This is an introduction to Mayan civilization, including research which explains some of its mysteries.

This "shines as it provides a contemporaneous writing as well as work by scholars that offer plenty of drama—and lots of facts too. . . . [It also] provides a solid time line, plenty of photographs, sourced quotes, and a list of books and websites for further investigation. Excellent for reports and research." Booklist

Includes bibliographical references

Gruber, Beth

★ **Mexico**; [by] Beth Gruber; Gary S. Elbow and Jorge Zamora, consultants. National Geographic 2007 64p il map (Countries of the world) lib bdg $27.90; pa $12.95

Grades: 4 5 6 7   972
1. Mexico
ISBN 0-7922-7669-8 lib bdg; 1-4263-0566-4 pa
LC 2004026452

"This volume introduces Mexico's geography, history, wildlife, culture, and government. The many excellent color photos and maps are a striking feature of the series. . . . This will be a useful addition to many libraries." Booklist

Includes glossary and bibliographical references

Harris, Nathaniel

★ **Ancient** Maya; archaeology unlocks the secrets to the Maya's past. by Nathaniel Harris; Elizabeth Graham, consultant. National Geographic

2008 64p il map (National Geographic investigates) $17.95; lib bdg $27.90

Grades: 4 5 6 7   972
1. Mayas 2. Mexico -- Antiquities 3. Excavations (Archeology) -- Mexico
ISBN 978-1-4263-0227-5; 1-4263-0227-4; 978-1-4263-0228-2 lib bdg; 1-4263-0228-2 lib bdg
LC 2007047837

This describes ancient Mayan civilization and how archeologists found out about it.

Includes glossary and bibliographical references

Heinrichs, Ann

The **Aztecs**; by Ann Heinrichs. Benchmark Books 2011 64 p. (Technology of the ancients) (print) $32.79

Grades: 4 5 6 7   972
1. Aztecs 2. Technological innovations -- History
ISBN 1608707652; 9781608707539; 9781608707652
LC 2011018348

This book, by Ann Heinrichs, includes "presentations of [the Aztec's] ancient cultures, emphasiz[ing] governance and material culture (clothing, crafts, architecture). The book [does] not cover the origins of the empires or try to explain how they became so powerful." (School Library Journal)

★ **Junior** Worldmark encyclopedia of the Mexican states; [Timothy L. Gall and Susan Bevan Gall, editors] 2nd ed.; U.X.L, Thomson/Gale 2007 423p il map $70

Grades: 5 6 7 8 9 10   972
1. Reference books 2. Mexico
ISBN 978-1-4144-1112-5
LC 2007003906

First published 2004

"Arranged by 28 . . . subheadings . . . Junior Worldmark Encyclopedia of the Mexican States provides . . . . information on each of Mexico's 31 states. Topics covered include climate, plants and animals, population and ethnic groups, religions, transportation, history, state and local governments, political parties, judicial system, economy, education, arts, media, tourism, sports, famous people and . . . more." Publisher's note

Includes bibliographical references

Kent, Deborah

Mexico; by Deborah Kent. Children's Press 2012 144 p. cil. ill., photographs (library) $40

Grades: 5 6 7 8   972
1. Mexico 2. Culture 3. Mexico -- History
ISBN 0531253554; 9780531253557
LC 2011010812

This book by Deborah Kent is part of the Enchantment of the World series and looks at Mexico. The books in the series offer 10 "chapters, several maps, a fast-facts section, and a few references to other sources, including a referral to a Scholastic website (new). The chapters cover geography, natural environment, history, politics, people and culture." (School Library Journal)

Includes bibliographical references and index.

Kops, Deborah

Palenque; by Deborah Kops. Twenty-First Century Books 2008 80p il (Unearthing ancient worlds) lib bdg $30.60

Grades: 5 6 7 8   **972**

1. Mayas 2. Mexico -- Antiquities 3. Palenque site (Mexico) 4. Excavations (Archeology) -- Mexico
ISBN 978-0-8225-7504-7 lib bdg; 0-8225-7504-3 lib bdg

LC 2007021323

This describes the discovery of the ancient Mayan site of Palenque in 1840 by John Stephens and Frederick Catherwood, and the mid-20th century excavations of the site by Alberto Ruz Lhuillier, who discovered the tomb of the Mayan king Pakal, who died in 683 A.D., inside a pyramid

This "clearly written [title is] illustrated with large photographs and period artwork, and the pages are broken up with text boxes featuring quotes and interesting anecdotes." SLJ

Includes glossary and bibliographical references

Lourie, Peter

★ Hidden world of the Aztec. Boyds Mills Press 2006 48p il map $17.95

Grades: 4 5 6 7   **972**

1. Aztecs 2. Excavations (Archeology) -- Mexico
ISBN 978-1-59078-069-5; 1-59078-069-8

The author takes a "look at the Aztecs from the perspective of archaeological digs at the Great Temple in modern-day Mexico City and at the Pyramid of the Moon in Teotihuacan. . . . The writing style is clear, informative, and interesting." SLJ

Includes glossary and bibliographical references

McDaniel, Melissa

New Mexico; [by] Melissa McDaniel, Ettagale Blauer, and Jason Laure. 2nd ed.; Marshall Cavendish Benchmark 2008 144p il map (Celebrate the states) lib bdg $39.93

Grades: 4 5 6 7   **972**

1. New Mexico
ISBN 978-0-7614-2719-3; 0-7614-2719-8

LC 2007-9273

First published 1999

"Provides comprehensive information on the geography, history, wildlife, governmental structure, economy, cultural diversity, peoples, religion, and landmarks of New Mexico." Publisher's note

Includes bibliographical references

Nardo, Don

Aztec civilization. Lucent Books 2010 104p il map (World history) lib bdg $33.45

Grades: 6 7 8 9   **972**

1. Aztecs
ISBN 978-1-4205-0242-8; 1-4205-0242-5

LC 2009040802

This is an introduction to Aztec civilization, including its rise and fall and the role of women.

This "shines as it provides a contemporary writing as well as work by scholars that offer plenty of drama—and lots of facts too. . . . [It also] provides a solid time line, plen-

ty of photographs, sourced quotes, and a list of books and websites for further investigation. Excellent for reports and research." Booklist

Includes bibliographical references

Schomp, Virginia

The Aztecs; [by] Virginia Schomp. Marshall Cavendish Benchmark 2009 96p il map (Myths of the world) lib bdg $23.95

Grades: 6 7 8 9   **972**

1. Aztecs
ISBN 978-0-7614-3096-4 lib bdg; 0-7614-3096-2 lib bdg

LC 2008007082

"A retelling of several key Aztec myths, with background information describing the history, geography, belief systems, and customs of the Aztecs." Publisher's note

Includes glossary and bibliographical references

Stein, R. Conrad

Cortes and the Spanish Conquest; [by] R. Conrad Stein. 1st ed.; Morgan Reynolds Pub. 2008 160p il map (The story of Mexico) lib bdg $27.95

Grades: 6 7 8 9 10   **972**

1. Aztecs 2. Explorers 3. Mexico -- History 4. Colonial administrators
ISBN 978-1-59935-053-0 lib bdg; 1-59935-053-X lib bdg

LC 2007016004

This "identifies the 'encounter' between the Spanish and Aztecs as one that 'would put the human character itself on trial.' The author provides a look at both societies, tracing the Aztecs' rise to power and the Spaniards' interest in exploration. The Spanish conquest of the Aztecs, led by Hernando Cortés, is related in great depth, and the book ends with a discussion of its legacy. [An] excellent [introduction] to Mexican history." SLJ

Includes bibliographical references

The Mexican Revolution. Morgan Reynolds Pub. 2008 160p il map (The story of Mexico) lib bdg $27.95

Grades: 6 7 8 9 10   **972**

1. Mexico -- History
ISBN 978-1-59935-051-6; 1-59935-051-3

LC 2007-22136

"Opening with Porfirio Díaz's presidency (beginning in 1876), [this book] explains how Indian land was expropriated and allotted to rich hacienda owners, describes resistance movements led by Emiliano Zapata and Pancho Villa, and details 10 years of political upheaval and violent uprisings (1910-1920), ending with Alvaro Obregó's election as president of Mexico. . . . [The book has] a lively narrative style. . . . Pertinent illustrations, including photographs, historical paintings, and maps are sprinkled throughout. . . . Well-written and well-researched." SLJ

Includes bibliographical references

The Mexican War of Independence; [by] R. Conrad Stein. Morgan Reynolds Pub. 2008 144p il map (The story of Mexico) lib bdg $27.95

Grades: 6 7 8 9 10 **972**

1. Mexico -- History
ISBN 978-1-59935-054-7 lib bdg; 1-59935-054-8
lib bdg

LC 2007022137

This "covers the years between 1521, when Hernando Cortés completed his conquest of the Aztec empire, and 1855, when Antonio Lopez Santa Anna was overthrown. The book provides excellent background information about three centuries of Spain's rule over Mexico. . . . [The book has] a lively narrative style. . . . Pertinent illustrations, including photographs, historical paintings, and maps are sprinkled throughout. . . . Well-written and well-researched." SLJ

Includes bibliographical references

Stein, R. Conrad, 1937-
Ancient Mexico. Morgan Reynolds Pub. 2011 144p il map (The story of Mexico) $28.95
Grades: 6 7 8 9 **972**

1. Mexico -- History 2. Native Americans -- Mexico
ISBN 1-59935-161-7; 978-1-59935-161-2

LC 2010041379

"Stein organizes and clearly presents a great deal of information. . . . The . . . format features a chonological text supplemented with useful sidebars and brightened with color illustrations, including many photos, artifacts, and period artworks. . . . [The book] provides a historical survey of Mexico's early inhabitants, from the arrival of Paleo-Indians through civilizations such as the Olmecs, the Maya, and Toltecs, and the Aztecs." Booklist

Includes bibliographical references

972.08   Mexico since 1867

Stein, R. Conrad
Modern Mexico. Morgan Reynolds Pub. 2011 144p il map (The story of Mexico) $28.95
Grades: 6 7 8 9 **972.08**

1. Mexico -- History 2. Mexico -- Politics and government
ISBN 978-1-5993-5162-9; 1-5993-5162-5

LC 2010053630

"Stein organizes and clearly presents a great deal of information. . . . The . . . format features a chronological text supplemented with useful sidebars and brightened with color illustrations, including many photos, artifacts, and period artworks. . . . [The book] looks at events in Mexico since 1920, focusing primarily on presidential administrations, economic problems, political unrest, and emigration." Booklist

Includes bibliographical references

972.81   Guatemala

Croy, Anita
★ **Guatemala**. National Geographic 2009 64p il map (Countries of the world) lib bdg $27.90

Grades: 4 5 6 7 **972.81**

1. Guatemala
ISBN 978-1-4263-0471-2 lib bdg; 1-4263-0471-4 lib bdg

This describes the geography, nature, history, people and culture, government and economy of Guatemala

Includes glossary and bibliographical references

Laughton, Timothy
Exploring the life, myth, and art of the Maya; Timothy Laughton. Rosen Pub. 2012 144 p. (Civilizations of the world)
Grades: 7 8 9 10 11 **972.81**

1. Mayan art 2. Mayas -- History 3. Mayas -- Folklore 4. Mayas -- Social life and customs 5. Maya art
ISBN 9781448848324

LC 2011009790

This book on the Maya "offers an informative overview of . . . political and social history as well as its art, architecture, and mythology, all bolstered with plenty of . . . details and narratives. . . . [T]he illustrations include artworks, documents, and handsome maps as well as photos of significant sites and artifacts. . . . In "Maya," [Timothy] Laughton shows how archaeology and scholarship have shifted accepted views on this culture over the last century." (Booklist) The book "put[s] the art . . . in context, explaining how a society's religious beliefs, legends, and cultural traditions manifest themselves through images and iconography. The . . . layout features full-color photographs of architecture, sculpture, and painting on every page, accompanied by informative captions." (School Libr J)

Includes bibliographical references (p. 138) and index

Mann, Elizabeth
Tikal; the center of the Maya world. with illustrations by Tom McNeely. Mikaya Press 2002 47p il map (Wonders of the world) $19.95
Grades: 4 5 6 7 **972.81**

1. Mayas -- Antiquities
ISBN 1-931414-05-X

LC 2002-29599

A history of the Maya Indians in the city of Tikal, founded in 800 B.C.

"Mann's narrative flows smoothly, and frequent, full-color illustrations . . . help to clarify the details mentioned in the text." Booklist

Includes glossary

Vanvoorst, Jennifer Fretland
The **ancient** Maya; by Jenny Fretland VanVoorst. Compass Point Books 2013 48 p. col. ill. (library) $28.65; (paperback) $8.95
Grades: 4 5 6 7 8 **972.81**

1. Mayas 2. Civilization, Ancient 3. Mexico -- Civilization 4. Central America -- Civilization 5. Mayas -- Social life and customs
ISBN 0756545641; 0756545846; 9780756545642; 9780756545840

LC 2012001966

This children's nonfiction book, by Jennifer Fretland VanVoorst, profiles the Mayan civilization as part of the "Exploring the Ancient World" series. "The civilization of the . . . Maya reached its peak about 2,000 years ago. The Maya held a complex religious view of the world. In an effort to maintain order by pleasing their many gods, they built imposing stone temples, developed a written language, and played a ball game with life-or-death consequences." (Publisher's note)

Includes bibliographical references (p. 46) and index.

972.82   Belize

Jermyn, Leslie

    Belize; [by] Leslie Jermyn and Yong Jui Lin. 2nd ed.; Marshall Cavendish Benchmark 2012 144p il map (Cultures of the world) lib bdg $42.79

Grades: 5 6 7 8   **972.82**

    1. Belize

    ISBN 978-1-60870-452-1; 1-60870-452-1

                           LC 2010035966

    Provides information on the geography, history, wildlife, governmental structure, economy, cultural diversity, peoples, religion, and culture of Belize.

    "The concise writing offers enough material for report writers without overwhelming them. Numerous full-color and black-and-white photos of interest, a clean layout, and use of pastels to highlight headings and sidebars contribute to the attractiveness of . . . [this presentation]." SLJ

    Includes glossary and bibliographical references

972.83   Honduras

Kras, Sara Louise

    Honduras; by Sara Louise Kras. Children's Press 2006 144p il map (Enchantment of the world, second series) lib bdg $37

Grades: 5 6 7 8   **972.83**

    1. Honduras

    ISBN 978-0-516-24871-4 lib bdg; 0-516-24871-5 lib bdg

                           LC 2005024240

    Describes the geography, history, culture, religion, and people of Honduras

    Includes bibliographical references

McGaffey, Leta

    Honduras; [by] Leta McGaffey and Michael Spilling. 2nd ed.; Marshall Cavendish Benchmark 2010 144p il map (Cultures of the world) lib bdg $42.79

Grades: 5 6 7 8   **972.83**

    1. Honduras

    ISBN 978-0-7614-4848-8 lib bdg; 0-7614-4848-9 lib bdg

                           LC 2009022642

    First published 1999

    "Provides comprehensive information on the geography, history, wildlife, governmental structure, economy, cultural diversity, peoples, religion, and culture of Honduras." Publisher's note

    Includes glossary and bibliographical references

Shields, Charles J.

    Honduras. Mason Crest Pubs. 2003 63p il map (Discovering Central America) lib bdg $19.95

Grades: 4 5 6 7   **972.83**

    1. Honduras

    ISBN 1-59084-096-8

                           LC 2002-9089

    This describes the history, geography, and culture of Honduras

    This is "jam-packed with useful information. . . . [It contains] straightforward writing, clearly titled chapters, high quality color, and well-captioned photographs and graphics." Libr Media Connect

    Includes glossary and bibliographical references

972.84   El Salvador

Foley, Erin

    El Salvador; [by] Erin Foley, Rafiz Hapipi. 2nd ed.; Benchmark Bks. 2005 144p il map (Cultures of the world) lib bdg $42.79

Grades: 5 6 7 8   **972.84**

    1. El Salvador

    ISBN 0-7614-1967-5

                           LC 2005009360

    First published 1994

    This describes the geography, history, government, economy, environment, people, lifestyle, religion, language, arts, leisure, festivals, and food of El Salvador

    Includes glossary and bibliographical references

972.85   Nicaragua

Kallen, Stuart A.

    The **aftermath** of the Sandinista Revolution. Twenty-First Century Books 2009 160p il (Aftermath of history) lib bdg $38.60

Grades: 8 9 10 11 12   **972.85**

    1. Nicaragua -- Politics and government

    ISBN 978-0-8225-9091-0; 0-8225-9091-3

                           LC 2008-25356

    "The 1979 overthrow of the corrupt Nicaraguan government by the Marxist Sandinistas brought change to one of the poorest countries in the Americas and instilled in the U.S. new fears about the spread of Communism. . . . Kallen offers a good overview of one of the Latin American theaters of the Cold War." SLJ

    Includes glossary and bibliographical references

Kott, Jennifer

    Nicaragua; [by] Jennifer Kott, Kristi Streiffert. 2nd ed.; Benchmark Bks. 2005 144p il map (Cultures of the world) lib bdg $42.79

Grades: 5 6 7 8   **972.85**

    1. Nicaragua

    ISBN 0-7614-1969-1

                           LC 2005009240

    First published 1994

An illustrated overview of the geography, economy, history, government, politics, and culture of Nicaragua

Includes glossary and bibliographical references

972.86   Costa Rica

Foley, Erin

Costa Rica; [by] Erin Foley and Barbara Cooke. 2nd ed.; Marshall Cavendish Benchmark 2008 144p il map (Cultures of the world) lib bdg $42.79

Grades: 5 6 7 8   **972.86**

1. Costa Rica

ISBN 978-0-7614-2079-8 lib bdg; 0-7614-2079-7 lib bdg

LC 2006101736

First published 1997

This offers "information on the geography, history, wildlife, governmental structure, economy, cultural diversity, peoples, religion, and culture of Costa Rica." Publisher's note

Includes glossary and bibliographical references

Yomtov, Nel

★ **Costa** Rica; by Nel Yomtov. Scholastic Library Pub 2014 144 p. illustrations, color maps (library binding) $40

Grades: 5 6 7 8   **972.86**

1. Costa Rica 2. Costa Rica

ISBN 0531220141; 9780531220146

LC 2013022563

This book, by Nel Yomtov, focuses on Costa Rica. The "country's culture, history, and geography are explored in detail, allowing readers a chance to see how people live in faraway nations. . . . Sidebars highlight especially interesting people, places, and events . . . [and] easy recipes give readers the opportunity to experience foreign cuisine first-hand." (Publisher's note)

Includes bibliographical references and index

972.87   Panama

DuTemple, Lesley A.

The **Panama** Canal. Lerner Publs. 2003 96p il maps (Great building feats) lib bdg $27.93

Grades: 6 7 8 9   **972.87**

1. Panama Canal

ISBN 0-8225-0079-5

LC 2001-4656

A history of the building of the Panama Canal, with emphasis on the difficulties of digging a canal where some engineers said it could not be done

"The text is peppered with quotes from letters, speeches, and diaries of those involved in the project. . . . Sidebars present interesting asides. . . . A fascinating and well-documented blend of history and engineering." SLJ

Includes bibliographical references

Hassig, Susan M.

★ **Panama**; [by] Susan Hassig & Lynette Quek. 2nd ed.; Marshall Cavendish Benchmark 2007 144p il map (Cultures of the world) lib bdg $42.79

Grades: 5 6 7 8   **972.87**

1. Panama

ISBN 978-0-7614-2028-6 lib bdg; 0-7614-2028-2 lib bdg

LC 2006020824

First published 1996

This provides "information on the geography, history, wildlife, governmental structure, economy, cultural diversity, peoples, religion, and culture of Panama." Publisher's note

Includes glossary and bibliographical references

Vander Hook, Sue

Building the Panama Canal. ABDO Pub. Co. 2010 112p il map (Essential events) lib bdg $32.79

Grades: 6 7 8 9   **972.87**

1. Panama Canal

ISBN 978-1-60453-942-4; 1-60453-942-9

LC 2009-30373

Readers will learn about the historic quests to find a pathway between the Atlantic and Pacific oceans, France's pursuit in building a canal, and the United States' first trials in building the Panama Canal.

"The writing is accessible and is richer than a lot of history writing, allowing the reader to become engaged in the text as a story, and the layout provides enough white space to allow lower level readers to feel confident." Libr Media Connect

Includes glossary and bibliographical references

972.9   West Indies (Antilles) and Bermuda

Kras, Sara Louise

Antigua and Barbuda; [by] Sara Louise Kras. Marshall Cavendish Benchmark 2008 144p il map (Cultures of the world) lib bdg $42.79

Grades: 5 6 7 8   **972.9**

1. Antigua and Barbuda

ISBN 978-0-7614-2570-0

LC 2006031537

This describes the geography, history, government, economy, environment, people, and culture of Antigua and Barbuda

Includes glossary and bibliographical references

972.91   Cuba

★ **Castro's** Cuba; Charles W. Carey Jr., book editor. Greenhaven Press 2004 205p il (History firsthand) $37.95; pa $23.70

Grades: 8 9 10 11 12   **972.91**

1. Presidents 2. Communist leaders 3. Cuba -- Politics and government

ISBN 0-7377-1654-1; 0-7377-1655-X pa

LC 2003-47286

"Through the use of interviews, articles, and first-person narratives, this book focuses on the significance of the 1959 revolution and its aftermath. An extensive introduction explaining events precipitating the rise of Fidel Castro, the revolution, and the current situation in Cuba provides readers with a necessary overview to understand the succeeding chapters." SLJ

Includes bibliographical references

Donovan, Sandra, 1967-

Teens in Cuba; by Sandy Donovan. Compass Point Books 2009 96p il (Global connections) lib bdg $33.26

Grades: 6 7 8 9   **972.91**
1. Teenagers 2. Cuba
ISBN 978-0-7565-3851-4 lib bdg; 0-7565-3851-3 lib bdg

LC 2008-6284

Uncovers the challenges, pastimes, customs and culture of teens in Cuba

This book is "concise and highly readable. . . . Clear, colorful photos and sidebars on a range of topics provide further context. . . . [This title] will enrich young adult collections." SLJ

Includes glossary and bibliographic references

Sheehan, Sean

Cuba; [by] Sean Sheehan, Leslie Jermyn. 2nd ed.; Benchmark Bks. 2005 144p il map (Cultures of the world) lib bdg $42.79

Grades: 5 6 7 8   **972.91**
1. Cuba
ISBN 0-7614-1965-9

LC 2005009362

First published 1994

This describes the geography, history, government, economy, population, lifestyle, religion, language, arts, leisure, festivals, and food of Cuba

Includes glossary and bibliographical references

Stein, R. Conrad

Cuban Missile Crisis; in the shadow of nuclear war. Enslow Publishers 2009 128p il map (America's living history) lib bdg $31.93

Grades: 5 6 7 8   **972.91**
1. Cuban Missile Crisis, 1962 2. Soviet Union -- Foreign relations -- United States 3. United States -- Foreign relations -- Soviet Union
ISBN 978-0-7660-2905-7 lib bdg; 0-7660-2905-0 lib bdg

LC 2008-4703

"This engaging account provides a thorough discussion of events. . . . Archival photographs, maps, sidebars, and many primary sources effectively depict key figures, political posturing, and the nation's anxiety." Horn Book Guide

Includes glossary and bibliographical references

Tracy, Kathleen

We visit Cuba. Mitchell Lane Publishers 2010 63p il (Your land and my land) lib bdg $33.95

Grades: 4 5 6 7   **972.91**
1. Cuba
ISBN 978-1-58415-890-5 lib bdg; 1-58415-890-5 lib bdg

LC 2010006558

"With an inviting format that includes bright color photos on every spread, this title . . . offers an appealing overview of Cuba's history, geography, culture and lifestyle, politics, economics, and more. . . . A good starting point for research as well as for personal interest." Booklist

Includes glossary and bibliographical references

Wright, David K.

Cuba; by David K. Wright. Children's Press 2009 144p il map (Enchantment of the world, second series) lib bdg $38

Grades: 5 6 7 8   **972.91**
1. Cuba
ISBN 978-0-531-12096-5 lib bdg; 0-531-12096-1 lib bdg

LC 2008008423

This describes the geography, history, culture, people, and government of Cuba

Includes bibliographical references

972.910   Cuba - 1899-

Marsico, Katie

Fidel Castro; Cuban president & revolutionary. by Katie Marsico. ABDO Pub. Co. 2009 112 p. ill. (some col.) (library) $34.22

Grades: 6 7 8   **972.910**
1. Heads of state 2. Cuba -- History -- 1959- 3. Cuba -- History -- 1959-1990 4. Heads of state -- Cuba -- Biography 5. Revolutionaries -- Cuba
ISBN 1604535229; 9781604535228

LC 2008033493

This book by Katie Marsico is part of the Essential Lives series and looks at Cuban dictator Fidel Castro. This entry "focuses as much on Cuban history and its relationship with the U.S. as it does on its former leader; details about Castro's family life, for example, often appear in sidebars." (Booklist)

Includes bibliographical references and index.

972.92   Jamaica and Cayman Islands

Green, Jen

★ Jamaica; [by] Jen Green; David J. Howard and Joel Frater, consultants. National Geographic 2008 64p il map (Countries of the world) lib bdg $27.90

Grades: 4 5 6 7   **972.92**
1. Jamaica
ISBN 978-1-4263-0300-5 lib bdg; 1-4263-0300-9 lib bdg

This describes the geography, nature, history, people and culture, government, and economy of Jamaica.

Includes glossary and bibligraphical references

Jamaica; writers, Sean Sheehan, Angela Black, Debbie Nevins. Cavendish Square 2015 144 p. ill. (chiefly col.), col maps $47.07

Grades: 5 6 7 8   **972.92**

1. Jamaica

ISBN 9781502600776

Introduces the geography, history, religion, government, economy, and culture of Jamaica.

Includes bibliographical references, discography (page 141), filmography (page 141), and index.

972.93 Dominican Republic

Foley, Erin

★ **Dominican** Republic; [by] Erin Foley & Leslie Jermyn. 2nd ed; Marshall Cavendish Benchmark 2005 144p (Cultures of the world) lib bdg $42.79

Grades: 5 6 7 8   **972.93**

1. Dominican Republic

ISBN 0-7614-1966-7

First published 1995

"The material is well organized in easily readable sections, accurately illustrated with well-placed, full-color photographs on every page." SLJ

Rogers Seavey, Lura

Dominican Republic; by Lura Rogers and Barbara Radcliffe Rogers. Children's Press 2009 144p il map (Enchantment of the world, second series) lib bdg $37

Grades: 5 6 7 8   **972.93**

1. Dominican Republic

ISBN 978-0-531-12097-2 lib bdg; 0-531-12097-X lib bdg

LC 2008000087

Describes the geography, history, culture, religion, and people of the Caribbean island nation of the Dominican Republic

Includes bibliographical references

972.94 Haiti

Aronin, Miriam

Earthquake in Haiti. Bearport Pub. 2011 32p il map (Code red) lib bdg $25.27

Grades: 4 5 6 7   **972.94**

1. Earthquakes 2. Haiti

ISBN 978-1-936088-66-9; 1-936088-66-5

LC 2010011126

Describes the devastating earthquake that occurred in Haiti on January 12, 2010.

"The text is written from the points of view of some of the people involved, including primary source direct quotes. Some of the pictures are necessarily graphic, which adds to the authenticity. . . . This title will be used for browsing as well as for reports." Libr Media Connect

Includes glossary and bibliographical references

NgCheong-Lum, Roseline, 1962-

★ **Haiti**; [by] Roseline Ng Cheong-Lum & Leslie Jermyn. 2nd ed; Marshall Cavendish Benchmark 2005 144p il map (Cultures of the world) lib bdg $42.79

Grades: 5 6 7 8   **972.94**

1. Haiti

ISBN 0-7614-1968-3

First published 1995

Describes the geography, history, government, economy, culture, peoples, and religion of Haiti

Includes glossary and bibliographical references

Yomtov, Nel

Haiti; by Nel Yomtov. Children's Press 2012 144 p. col. ill. (library) $40

Grades: 5 6 7 8   **972.94**

1. Haiti

ISBN 0531253538; 9780531253533

LC 2011010048

This book is part of the Enchantment of the World series and focuses on Haiti. This series presents "factual information against a backdrop of brightly colored pictures and maps. . . . Each book provides a timeline, Fast Facts, and embassies." The books also include "brief chapters that follow real people in their daily lives." (Library Media Connection)

Includes bibliographical references and index.

972.95 Puerto Rico

Lopez, Jose Javier

Puerto Rico; [by] José Javier López. Chelsea House Pub. 2006 108p il map (Modern world nations) lib bdg $30

Grades: 7 8 9 10   **972.95**

1. Puerto Rico

ISBN 0-7910-8798-0

LC 2005028216

Describes the geography, history, people and culture, politics, and economy of Puerto Rico

Includes bibliographical references

Puerto Rico; by Darlene R. Stille. Revised edition Children's Press 2015 144 p. illustrations, maps $40

Grades: 4 5 6 7   **972.95**

1. Puerto Rico

ISBN 9780531282908

Explores the land, people, history, economy, and travel opportunities of Puerto Rico.

Includes bibliographical references and index

Schwabacher, Martin

Puerto Rico; by Martin Schwabacher and Steve Otfinoski. 2nd ed.; Marshall Cavendish Benchmark 2010 144p il map (Celebrate the states) $42.79

Grades: 5 6 7 8　　　　　　　　　**972.95**
　　1. Puerto Rico
　　ISBN 978-0-7614-4734-4; 0-7614-4734-2
　　　　　　　　　　　　　LC 2009007066
　First published 2001
　This offers information on the geography, history, wild-
life, governmental structure, economy, cultural diversity,
peoples, religion, and landmarks of Puerto Rico.
　Includes bibliographical references

Worth, Richard
　Puerto Rico in American history. Enslow Publishers 2008 128p il map (From many cultures, one
history) lib bdg $23.95
Grades: 6 7 8 9 10　　　　　　　**972.95**
　　1. Puerto Rico
　　ISBN 978-0-7660-2836-4; 0-7660-2836-4
　　　　　　　　　　　　　LC 2006-37087
　This is a "book about the ties between Puerto Rico and
the U.S. . . . . Worth's overview will help to acclimate readers new to the island's history. . . . Writing in short, plain
sentences, the author touches upon the commonwealth's
ongoing struggle with poverty, migration, and language
and the current conflicts about statehood and independence.
The book's clean design is inviting, with lots of color-
screened boxes, full-color photos, archival artwork, and
maps." Booklist
　Includes glossary and bibliographical references

972.96　Bahama Islands

Hintz, Martin
　The **Bahamas**; by Martin Hintz. Children's
Press 2013 144 p. col. ill., col. maps (Enchantment
of the world. Second series) (library) $40
Grades: 5 6 7 8　　　　　　　　　**972.96**
　　1. Bahamas 2. Bahamas -- Description and travel
　　ISBN 0531275418; 9780531275412
　　　　　　　　　　　　　LC 2012000513
　This book, by Martin Hintz, is part of the "Enchantment
of the World" series. In it the author provides information
and photographs showcasing the people, places and events
surrounding the Caribbean island chain of the Bahamas.
Contents include photographs of Bahaman cities and landscapes, statistics describing the islands' features, and traditional Bahaman recipes.
　Includes bibliographical references and index

972.98　Windward and other southern islands

Elias, Marie Louise
　Barbados; [by] Marie Louise Elias and Josie
Elias. 2nd ed.; Marshall Cavendish Benchmark
2010 144p il map (Cultures of the world) lib bdg
$42.79

Grades: 5 6 7 8　　　　　　　　　**972.98**
　　1. Barbados
　　ISBN 978-0-7614-4853-2 lib bdg; 0-7614-4853-5
lib bdg
　　　　　　　　　　　　　LC 2009044592
　First published 2000
　This offers information on the geography, history, wild-
life, governmental structure, economy, cultural diversity,
peoples, religion, and culture of Barbados.
　Includes glossary and bibliographical references

Orr, Tamra
　Saint Lucia; [by] Tamra Orr. 2nd ed.; Marshall
Cavendish Benchmark 2008 144p il map (Cultures
of the world) lib bdg $42.79
Grades: 5 6 7 8　　　　　　　　　**972.98**
　　1. Saint Lucia
　　ISBN 978-0-7614-2569-4
　First published 1997
　This describes the geography, history, government,
economy, environment, people, and culture of Saint Lucia
　Includes glossary and bibliographical references

Pang, Guek-Cheng, 1950-
　Grenada; 2nd ed.; Marshall Cavendish Bench-
mark 2011 144p il map (Cultures of the world) lib
bdg $42.79
Grades: 5 6 7 8　　　　　　　　　**972.98**
　　1. Grenada
　　ISBN 978-1-6087-0216-9; 1-6087-0216-2
　　　　　　　　　　　　　LC 2010019807
　First published 2001
　Provides information on the geography, history, wild-
life, governmental structure, economy, cultural diversity,
peoples, religion, and culture of Grenada.
　Includes glossary and bibliographical references

972.983　Trinidad and Tobago

Sheehan, Sean
　Trinidad & Tobago. Benchmark Bks. 2001
128p il maps (Cultures of the world) lib bdg $37.07
Grades: 5 6 7 8　　　　　　　　　**972.983**
　　1. Trinidad and Tobago
　　ISBN 0-7614-1194-1
　　　　　　　　　　　　　LC 00-47457
　"The exuberance of the many different ethnic groups
shines out of the photographs." Horn Book Guide
　Includes glossary and bibliographical references

973　United States

Addasi, Maha
　A **kid's** guide to Arab American history; more
than 50 activities. by Yvonne Wakim Dennis and
Maha Addasi. 1st ed. Chicago Review Press 2013
xx, 204 p.p ill. (paperback) $16.95

Grades: 4 5 6 7   973
1. Arab Americans -- History 2. Arab Americans -- Social life and customs 3. Arab Americans -- History 4. Arab Americans -- History -- Study and teaching -- Activity programs
ISBN 1613740174; 9781613740170
LC 2012035758
This book by Yvonne Wakim Dennis and Maha Addasi "provides a contemporary as well as historical look at the people and experiences that have shaped Arab American culture. Each chapter focuses on a different group of Arab Americans including those of Lebanese, Syrian, Palestinian, Jordanian, Egyptian, Iraqi, and Yemeni descent and features more than 50 fun activities that highlight their distinct arts, games, clothing, and food." (Publisher's note)

Africa to America; from the Middle Passage through the 1930s. edited by Jeff Wallenfeldt, Manager, Geography and History. Britannica Educational Pub. 2010 268 p. (library binding) $45.00
Grades: 6 7 8   973
1. Slavery 2. Human rights 3. Harlem Renaissance 4. African Americans -- History 5. African Americans -- Biography 6. African Americans -- Intellectual life
ISBN 1615301267; 9781615301263
LC 2009054299
Editor Jeff Wallenfeldt offers a history of African Americans. "At the expense of basic human rights, dignity, and decency, Africans were torn from their native countries and first brought to the United State as slaves. Yet even in the face of injustice and hardship they have endured since then, African Americans have been bolstered by the sacrifices, leadership, and determination of courageous individuals . . . [Wallenfeldt captures] the history of African Americans . . . from origins on the African continent to the end of the Harlem Renaissance." (Barnes & Noble)
Includes bibliographical references and index

American history on file; [by] George Ochoa and Melinda Corey, editors. Facts on File 2002 un 2v il set$297
Grades: Adult Professional   973
1. United States -- History
ISBN 0-8160-4661-1
LC 2002-1673
This includes maps, timelines, illustrations and text divided into ten eras of United States history, which may be reproduced for classroom use
Includes bibliographical references

Armstrong, Jennifer
★ The **American** story; 100 true tales from American history. illustrated by Roger Roth. Alfred A. Knopf 2006 358p il map $34.95; lib bdg $39.99
Grades: 4 5 6 7   973
1. United States -- History
ISBN 0-375-81256-3; 0-375-91256-8 lib bdg
LC 2005-34822
"This large, fully illustrated compendium features 100 stories, familiar and lesser known, drawn from America's past and arranged in chronological order. . . . Thanks to writing that is consistently good and sometimes excellent, the

tales will certainly hold readers' attention, and brightening nearly every page are lively drawings enhanced by watercolor washes." Booklist
Includes bibliographical references

Benson, Sonia
★ **UXL** encyclopedia of U.S. history; [by] Sonia Benson, Daniel E. Brannen Jr., and Rebecca Valentine; Lawrence W. Baker and Sarah Hermsen, project editors. U.X.L 2008 8v il map set$485
Grades: 6 7 8 9 10 11 12   973
1. Reference books 2. United States -- History -- Encyclopedias
ISBN 978-1-4144-3043-0
LC 2008022347
"This set offers more than 700 entries addressing various cultural, political, economic, and social events, trends, movements, and developments that shaped American history. . . . Black-and-white illustrations, reproductions, archival photographs, maps, sidebars, and inserts accompany the text. . . . Most school and public library collections that serve students in grades 6 through 12 will want to have this recommended resource." Booklist
Includes bibliographical references

Bockenhauer, Mark H.
Our fifty states; by Mark H. Bockenhauer and Stephen F. Cunha; foreword by former president Jimmy Carter. National Geographic Society 2004 239p il map $25.95; lib bdg $45.90
Grades: 4 5 6 7   973
1. Reference books 2. United States
ISBN 0-7922-6402-9; 0-7922-6992-6 lib bdg
LC 2004-1190
This "book is organized by regions: the Northeast, Southeast, Midwest, Southwest, and West, with a map of each region and a short history. Four pages are devoted to each state and include basic facts and a map. The full-color photographs are outstanding. Reproductions of archival illustrations depict four important events from each state's history. The final sections offer a paragraph about each of the territories and a page of facts and figures about the United States." SLJ
Includes bibliographical references

Brownstone, David M.
The **young** nation: America 1787-1861; [by] David M. Brownstone, Irene M. Franck. Grolier Educ. 2002 10v il maps set $339
Grades: 973
1. United States -- History -- 1783-1865
ISBN 0-7172-5645-6
LC 2002-20047
This "set covers American history during the period beginning with the Constitution and ending with the Civil War. . . . A handsome layout and many excellent pictures, most in full color, give the books an inviting look. The illustrations include many period paintings and engravings as well as maps, documents, and photos of historic sites and reenactments of events." Booklist
Includes bibliographical references

Buckley, Susan

★ **Journeys** for freedom; a new look at America's story. [by] Susan Buckley and Elspeth Leacock; illustrations by Rodica Prato. Houghton Mifflin Co. 2006 48p il map $17

Grades: 4 5 6 7   **973**
1. United States -- History
ISBN 978-0-618-22323-7; 0-618-22323-1

LC 2004000974

This "history focuses on 20 individuals' quest for freedom across U.S. history. Some . . . will be familiar, but most will not. The stories, both varied and fascinating, often go beyond the personal. . . . Running along the bottom of each double-page spread is a pictorial map keyed to the text. . . . The authors make excellent use of primary sources. . . . As powerful as it is useful." Booklist

Kids make history; a new look at America's story. [by] Susan Buckley and Elspeth Leacock; Illustrations by Randy Jones. Houghton Mifflin 2006 48p il $17

Grades: 4 5 6 7   **973**
1. United States -- History
ISBN 978-0-618-22329-9; 0-618-22329-0

LC 2005036309

"This book introduces 20 children in extraordinary times, starting in 1607 with Pocahontas and ending in 2001 with 9/11 as experienced by high school senior Jukay Hsu. Laura Ingalls Wilder; John Rankin, Jr.; and Susie Baker, a young slave celebrating her independence in 1863, are among those included. The text and the highly detailed watercolor illustrations are married with numbers in small red boxes keyed to both elements for clarification. . . . A good browsing choice for children interested in American history." SLJ

Cooper, Ilene

★ **Jack**; the early years of John F. Kennedy. by Ilene Cooper. 1st ed. Penguin Group USA 2013 168 p. ill. (paperback) $12.99

Grades: 5 6 7 8 9 10 11 12   **973**
1. Catholics 2. Presidents 3. Presidents -- United States
ISBN 0147510317; 9780147510310

LC 2002075912

This book by Ilene Cooper offers a "portrait of [John F.] Kennedy's "youth and the forces that shaped it. . . . Readers discover what it was like for Jack to grow up under the paradoxical influences of privilege and prejudice. His father's wealth . . . couldn't remove the perceived taint of the family's Irish Catholic heritage . . . . To compensate, Joseph and Rose Kennedy pushed their children to excel at everything they did," leading to rivalry between Jack and his brother Joe. (Horn Book Magazine)

"Intelligent design and numerous fabulous, well-placed, and well-captioned black-and-white photographs enrich Cooper's clear prose. . . . This sensitive, well-researched biography will enhance any collection." Voice of Youth Advocates

Includes bibliographical references and index.

Croy, Elden

United States. National Geographic 2010 64p il map (Countries of the world) lib bdg $27.90

Grades: 4 5 6 7   **973**
1. United States
ISBN 978-1-4263-0632-7 lib bdg; 1-4263-0632-6 lib bdg

This describes the geography, nature, history, people and culture, government and economy of the United States.

"The information is substantial but not overwhelming. The [text is] clear, and the discussion points are well chosen. . . . [The text is] complemented with stunning photographs." SLJ

★ **Exploring** American history: from colonial times to 1877; editors, Tom Lansford, Thomas E. Woods, Jr. Marshall Cavendish Reference 2008 11v il map set$359.95

Grades: 6 7 8 9   **973**
1. Reference books 2. United States -- History -- 1775-1783, Revolution -- Encyclopedias 3. United States -- History -- 1600-1775, Colonial period -- Encyclopedias
ISBN 978-0-7614-7746-4; 0-7614-7746-2

LC 2007060896

"This set contains 219 signed articles on the nearly 250 years of American life. . . . The articles have a uniform format and are color coded to indicate broad subject areas—culture, government, laws, people, or places. . . . The articles present a solid overview of current research as well as a rich array of information. . . . The set is thoughtfully arranged, easy to use, and accessible for a wide range of students." Booklist

Includes bibliographical references

Hoose, Phillip M.

★ **We** were there, too! young people in U.S. history. [by] Phillip Hoose. Farrar, Straus & Giroux 2001 264p il $28

Grades: 5 6 7 8   **973**
1. Youth 2. Children 3. United States -- History
ISBN 0-374-38252-2

LC 99-89052

Biographies of dozens of young people who made a mark in American history, including explorers, planters, spies, cowpunchers, sweatshop workers, and civil rights workers

"A treasure chest of history come to life, this is an inspired collection. . . . Because the book is packed with historical documents, evocatively illustrated . . . and full of eyewitness quotations, it should prove valuable to young historians and researchers." SLJ

Includes bibliographical references

Johnston, Robert D.

★ **The making** of America; the history of the United States from 1492 to the present. Robert D. Johnston ; with a foreword by Douglas Brinkley. Revised ed. National Geographic 2010 240 p. ill. (chiefly col.), col. maps (hardcover) $29.95; (library) $38.90

Grades: 5 6 7 8   **973**
1. United States -- History
ISBN 9781426306631; 1426306636; 9781426306655;
1426306652
LC 2011401219
First published 2002
Includes bibliographical references (p. 226-234)
and index.

"This energetically written and profusely illustrated history remains one of the top-drawer single-volume accounts of the founding and growth of the U.S. for middle grade students. The previous edition ended with 9/11; here, into the same page count, Johnston fits Hurricane Katrina, the wars in Iraq and Afghanistan, Barack Obama's election, and other major events." Booklist

Lake, Matthew

Weird U.S. a freaky field trip through the 50 states. [by] Matt Lake and Randy Fairbanks. Sterling Pub. 2011 128p il $14.95
Grades: 6 7 8 9   **973**
1. Curiosities and wonders 2. United States -- History 3. Folklore -- United States 4. United States -- Guidebooks
ISBN 978-1-4027-5462-3; 1-4027-5462-0
LC 2010027019

"Imagine the kitsch of a field trip to the world's largest ball of twine and multiple it by about a thousand and you'll begin to appreciate the imaginative and colorful romp through the United States' weirdest roadside attractions. Each site . . . is described in detail with full-color photographs. . . . Sure to be a hit with students that pore over the Guiness Book of World Records and Ripley's Believe It or Not!." Booklist

Leacock, Elspeth

Journeys in time; a new atlas of American history. [by] Elspeth Leacock and Susan Buckley; illustrations by Rodica Prato. Houghton Mifflin 2001 48p il maps $15; pa $6.95
Grades: 4 5 6 7   **973**
1. United States -- History 2. United States -- Historical geography
ISBN 0-395-97956-0; 0-618-31114-9 pa
LC 00-40803

Each double-page spread of this book "takes an individual who was part of a historic movement (such as the Underground Railroad or immigration) and gives a brief narrative outlining his or her circumstances. Added to the text are sequential numbers that indicate major events in each of the twenty journeys. A double-page location map traces the routes each took, using illustrative vignettes marked with corresponding numbers that reference the text." Horn Book

Our country's founders; a book of advice for young people. edited with commentary by William J. Bennett. Simon & Schuster 1998 314p il hardcover o.p. pa $16.95
Grades: 7 8 9 10   **973**
1. Social ethics 2. United States -- History -- Sources
ISBN 0-689-82106-9; 0-689-84469-7 pa
LC 98-6592

A book of advice from our nation's founders on how to be a good citizen and a worthy member of civil society

Bennett "draws on a wide variety of primary, secondary, and tertiary sources, ranging from the love letters of John and Abigail Adams to Mason Weems' apocryphal tale of George Washington and the cherry tree. Few young adults are likely to pick this up on their own, but teachers will find it a valuable resource." Booklist

Includes bibliographical references

Panchyk, Richard

★ The **keys** to American history; understanding our most important historic documents. Chicago Review Press 2009 241p il map $24.95; pa $19.95
Grades: 7 8 9 10 11 12   **973**
1. United States -- History -- Sources
ISBN 978-1-55652-716-6; 1-55652-716-0; 978-1-55652-804-0 pa; 1-55652-804-3 pa

"This impressive collection is a valuable resource for gaining a greater appreciation for and understanding of our nation's dynamic history." SLJ

Includes bibliographical references

Pinkney, Andrea Davis

Hand in hand; ten Black men who changed America. by Andrea Davis Pinkney ; paintings by Brian Pinkney. Disney/Jump at the Sun 2012 243 p. $19.99
Grades: 4 5 6 7   **973**
1. Biography 2. United States -- History 3. African Americans -- Biography 4. African American men -- Biography 5. Social change -- United States -- History
ISBN 1423142578; 9781423142577
LC 2011051348

Coretta Scott King Author Book Award (2013)
Boston Globe-Horn Book Honor: Nonfiction (2013).

In this book, Andrea Davis Pinkney profiles "ten influential black men--including Frederick Douglass, W.E.B. Du Bois, Thurgood Marshall, Jackie Robinson, and Martin Luther King Jr." She presents "descriptions of each man's influence on civil rights, culture, art, or politics. . . . An examination of Barack Obama's life and presidential election carries readers into the present day, placing the achievements of those who came before him into perspective." (Publishers Weekly)

Includes bibliographical references and index.

★ **Scholastic** encyclopedia of the presidents and their times; David Rubel ; with a foreword by James M. McPherson. Updated edition Scholastic 2013 248 p. illustrations, maps $24.99
Grades: 5 6 7 8   **973**
1. United States -- History 2. Presidents -- United States
ISBN 9780545499859

This encyclopedia "documents the tenure of each of the American presidents. It also includes information about the headlines, people, and fads that defined America during each presidency." (Publisher's note)

Selzer, Adam

The **smart** aleck's guide to American history. Delacorte Press 2009 326p il lib bdg $15.99; pa $12.95

Grades: 7 8 9 10 11 12   **973**

1. United States -- History

ISBN 978-0-385-90613-5 lib bdg; 0-385-90613-7 lib bdg; 978-0-385-73650-3 pa; 0-385-73650-9 pa

LC 2009-03897

"This irreverent guide to American history takes readers from the earliest days of settlement to the presidency of Barack Obama. . . . The flippant tone, mock quiz and essay questions and silly categories of information . . . are sure to appeal to the surliest of . . . students. Numerous sidebars, reproductions of paintings, engravings and photographs and even a recipe for making mustard gas keep the text from becoming dull, and students may find that they have learned a lot of history along the way." Kirkus

Yorinks, Adrienne

Quilt of states; quilts by Adrienne Yorinks; written by Adrienne Yorinks and 50 librarians from across the nation; librarian contributions compiled and edited by Jeanette Larson. National Geographic 2005 122p il $19.95

Grades: 5 6 7 8   **973**

1. United States -- History

ISBN 0-7922-7285-4

LC 2004-17796

"The United States is stitched together chronologically in this stunning book that features a quilted spread for each state. Yorinks enlisted a librarian from each state to contribute a short entry to point up a few significant facts that add to the tapestry of the emerging nation. . . . The quilted representations are not only artistically intricate and beautiful, but also informative. A handsome book to linger over and learn from." SLJ

973.03   United States -- encyclopedias

★ **Children's** encyclopedia of American history; by David C. King. Revised and updated Dk Pub 2014 320 p. illustrations (some color) $29.99

Grades: 5 6 7 8   **973.03**

1. Reference books 2. United States -- History -- Encyclopedias

ISBN 9781465428431

Full-color maps, photographs, and paintings illustrate a comprehensive reference guide to American history.

"This revised edition takes a look at U.S. history, from the exploration of the New World in the 1400s to the present day. . . . New content includes the Boston bombing of 2013, the War on Terror, the death of Osama Bin Laden, and a focus on globalization and sports. Natural disasters, such as Hurricane Katrina, and additional environmental concerns are detailed. Presidential coverage is expanded to incorporate the election of Barack Obama, while other new topics include the growth of the Tea Party Movement and controversy regarding guns." SLJ

★ **Junior** Worldmark Encyclopedia of the States; 6th edition UXL 2013 4v illustrations $354

Grades: 5 6 7 8 9 10   **973.03**

1. Reference books 2. United States -- Encyclopedias

ISBN 9781414498645; 9781414498591

First published 1996

"The sixth edition of this series thoroughly updates each of the 50 state entries as well as entries on the District of Columbia, Puerto Rico, U.S. Caribbean dependencies, U.S. Pacific dependencies, and the United States as a whole. Entries cover the geography, history, politics, economy and other facts about each state or area profiled. Alphabetically arranged entries feature consistent subheadings for each state so students can quickly find comparative information." (Publisher's note)

973.09   Presidents--United States

Bausum, Ann

★ **Our** Country's Presidents; All You Need to Know About the Presidents, From George Washington to Barack Obama. by Ann Bausum; foreword by President Barack Obama. 4th ed. National Geographic 2013 223 p. ill., maps (hardcover) $24.95

Grades: 5 6 7 8   **973.09**

1. Presidents -- United States -- Encyclopedias

ISBN 1426310897; 9781426310898

LC 2009290293

First published 2001

This book by Ann Bausum looks at U.S. presidents. The text shares "facts about the men's personal lives, humorous incidents, political backgrounds, records, struggles, battles, successes, what they are most famous for, events that occurred during their administrations, and memorable quotes." (School Library Journal)

"This exceedingly attractive offering is . . . chock-full of information, presented . . . in such an inviting manner that children will enjoy paging through, even if there's no school report looming. . . . Full of interesting tidbits as well as solid information." Booklist

Includes bibliographical references

★ The **presidency** A to Z; Gerhard Peters, editor ; John T. Woolley, editor. 5th ed. CQ Press 2012 xix, 715 p.p ill. (hardcover) $125

Grades: 8 9 10 11 12 Adult   **973.09**

1. Presidents -- United States -- Biography 2. Presidents -- United States -- Encyclopedias

ISBN 1608719081; 9781608719082

LC 2012023290

This book, by Gerhard Peters, presents a dictionary of the U.S. presidency. The book is a "tool for understanding the presidency, both historically and today and for appraising how it and the executive branch have responded to the challenges facing the nation. It provides readers with quick information and in-depth background on the presidency through a comprehensive encyclopedia of over 300 easy-to-read entries." (Publisher's note)

"At over 700 pages and also available online, this core title. . . provid[es] a comprehensive encyclopedic treatment of the U.S. presidency. . . . A recommended purchase for all libraries and a required one for those with earlier editions, which it supplants." LJ

Includes bibliographical references (p. 684-690) and index.

Rhatigan, Joe

White House kids; the perks, pleasures, problems, and pratfalls of the Presidents' children. Joe Rhatigan ; with illustrations by Jay Shin. Charlesbridge Pub. 2012 96 p. ill. (chiefly col.) $14.95
Grades: 5 6 7 8   **973.09**
1. United States. White House Office 2. Presidents -- United States -- Family 3. Presidents -- United States -- Children 4. Children of presidents -- United States 5. Children of presidents -- United States -- Biography
ISBN 1936140802; 9781936140800
                                                    LC 2011045090
This book presents "an overview of the young occupants of the White House . . . [and] details the perks and downfalls of being a president's child. Information on pets, favorite games and activities . . . and education of presidential offspring is . . . presented. [Joe] Rhatigan explores the press's and the public's fascination with the children . . . as well as the scrutiny and negative press endured by Amy Carter and Chelsea Clinton." (School Library Journal)

"An inviting collection of insightful, interesting and often wacky and weird facts and stories about U.S. presidents and their families." Kirkus

Includes bibliographical references and index

973.1   Early history to 1607

Hernandez, Roger E.

New Spain: 1600-1760s. Marshall Cavendish Benchmark 2009 79p il map (Hispanic America) lib bdg $34.21
Grades: 4 5 6 7   **973.1**
1. Southern States -- History 2. Spaniards -- United States 3. Southwestern States -- History
ISBN 978-0-7614-2936-4 lib bdg; 0-7614-2936-0 lib bdg
"Provides comprehensive information on the history of Spanish exploration in the United States." Publisher's note
Includes glossary and bibliographical references

Stefoff, Rebecca

Exploration and settlement. M.E. Sharpe 2008 95p il map (Colonial life) $37.95
Grades: 6 7 8 9 10 11 12   **973.1**
1. Explorers 2. Frontier and pioneer life 3. America -- Exploration 4. United States -- History -- 1600-1775, Colonial period
ISBN 978-0-7656-8108-9
                                                      LC 2007-3960
This "presents a solid and highly readable overview of the theories regarding the peopling of America. Stefoff skillfully interweaves world events that led up to the European exploration race of the 15th and 16th centuries and shares illuminating biographies of the key explorers of the period.

". . . The author's conversational tone and generous use of full-color reproductions, maps, and sidebars will engage readers." SLJ

Includes glossary and bibliographical references

973.2   United States--Colonial period, 1607-1775

Cappacio, George

The Countryside in colonial America; George Capaccio. Cavendish Square Publishing 2014 80 p. (library binding) $35.64
Grades: 6 7 8   **973.2**
1. United States -- History -- 1600-1775, Colonial period 2. United States -- History -- Colonial period, ca. 1600-1775 3. Indians of North America -- History -- Colonial period, ca. 1600-1775
ISBN 1627128859; 9781627128858
                                                    LC 2014006063
This book, by George Cappacio, part of the Life in colonial America series, "describes in rich detail the lives of Native Americans, African Americans, and white settlers, including children, women, and criminals. The introductory material that prefaces each title is of particular value, as it demonstrates that the colonists were part of a larger world picture." (Publisher's note)

"Thoroughly researched and expertly executed, this series describes in rich detail the lives of Native Americans, African Americans, and white settlers, including children, women, and criminals. The introductory material that prefaces each title is of particular value, as it demonstrates that the colonists were part of a larger world picture...Content in each title incorporates quotes from period letters and journals as well as a plethora of well-chosen, colorful illustrations. Strong, attractive titles for those looking for more coverage of Colonial America." SLJ

Cooper, Michael L.

Jamestown, 1607. Holiday House 2007 98p il $18.95
Grades: 6 7 8 9   **973.2**
1. Jamestown (Va.) -- History 2. United States -- History -- 1600-1775, Colonial period
ISBN 978-0-8234-1948-7; 0-8234-1948-7
                                                    LC 2006-02018
This " book presents a history of Jamestown from late 1606, when the Discovery, the Susan Constant, and the Godspeed set sail from London to Virginia, to 1609, when John Smith's injuries forced his return to England. Based largely on the writings of those present, notably Smith, the book offers a very readable, detailed account of the settlers' exploration, deprivation, starvation, illness, and political infighting as well as their relations with Native Americans. . . . Large black-and-white reproductions of period paintings, engravings, drawings, maps, and documents illustrate the book." Booklist

Includes bibliographical references

Doherty, Kieran

To conquer is to live: the life of Captain John Smith of Jamestown. 21st Cent. Bks. (Brookfield) 2001 144p il lib bdg $23.90

Grades: 6 7 8 9   **973.2**

1. Colonists 2. Travel writers 3. Jamestown (Va.) -- History 4. United States -- History -- 1600-1775, Colonial period

ISBN 0-7613-1820-8

LC 00-44309

A biography of the English soldier and adventurer who helped establish the colony of Jamestown, Virginia

A "well-written, appealing biography. . . . This book reads much like a swashbuckling adventure and most likely will inspire further interest in the man." SLJ

Includes bibliographical references

Gray, Edward G.

Colonial America; a history in documents. 2nd ed.; Oxford University Press 2011 211p il map (Pages from history) $39.95; pa $24.95

Grades: 7 8 9 10   **973.2**

1. United States -- History -- 1600-1775, Colonial period -- Sources

ISBN 978-0-19-976594-2; 978-0-19-976595-9 pa

LC 2010038458

First published 2003

This collection of primary sources examines "the lives of the colonists through their own words—in diaries, letters, sermons, newspaper columns, and poems." Publisher's note

Includes bibliographical references

Huey, Lois Miner

American archaeology uncovers the earliest English colonies. Marshall Cavendish Benchmark 2009 64p il map (American archaeology) lib bdg $31.36

Grades: 4 5 6 7   **973.2**

1. America -- Antiquities 2. America -- Exploration 3. Jamestown (Va.) -- History 4. Roanoke Island (N.C.) -- History 5. Great Britain -- Colonies -- America 6. Excavations (Archeology) -- United States

ISBN 978-0-7614-4264-6 lib bdg; 0-7614-4264-2 lib bdg

LC 2008050259

This describes how archeologists have learned about the history of early English colonists in America at Jamestown, Popham Colony, and Roanoke

"Huey enthusiastically brings . . . [this era] to life through artifacts and field research. . . . [The volume begins with an] introduction that defines 'historical archaeology' and explains its value in terms simple enough for lower-elementary readers to comprehend, yet detailed enough for older children to enjoy, an approach followed in the remaining chapters. . . . Huey's focus on American history, which is broken down into small, manageable chunks, is sure to entice budding historians." SLJ

Includes glossary and bibliographical references

Mandell, Daniel R.

King Philip's war; the conflict over New England. Chelsea House 2007 144p il map (Landmark events in Native American history) lib bdg $35

Grades: 7 8 9 10   **973.2**

1. Wampanoag Indians 2. King Philip's War, 1675-1676 3. New England -- History -- 1600-1775, Colonial

period

ISBN 978-0-7910-9346-7; 0-7910-9346-8

LC 2006-102258

This account features "lively writing and direct quotes, and [is] enhanced by many color and black-and-white photos, drawings, and illustrations." SLJ

Includes bibliographical references

McNeese, Tim

Colonial America, 1543-1763. Chelsea House 2010 136p il map (Discovering U.S. history) $35

Grades: 5 6 7 8   **973.2**

1. United States -- History -- 1600-1775, Colonial period

ISBN 978-1-60413-349-3; 1-60413-349-X

LC 2008055170

This history of Colonial America "begins with a chapter on 'Rivals for North America' and ends with 'The Fight for the Ohio Country.' . . . [The] book has an excellent chronology; rich sidebars; and numerous well-captioned illustrations, maps, and photos that enhance the texts. [This book provides a] satisfying [introduction] to American history for students." SLJ

Includes glossary and bibliographical references

Nardo, Don

Daily life in colonial America. Lucent Books 2010 96p il (Lucent library of historical eras) $32.45

Grades: 6 7 8 9   **973.2**

1. United States -- History -- 1600-1775, Colonial period 2. United States -- Social life and customs -- 1600-1775, Colonial period

ISBN 978-1-4205-0264-0; 1-4205-0264-6

LC 2009045636

Presents an introduction to life in colonial America, discussing family and home life, occupations, education, recreation, medicine, and laws.

Includes bibliographical references

The **establishment** of the thirteen colonies. Lucent Books 2010 96p il (Lucent library of historical eras) lib bdg $32.45

Grades: 6 7 8 9   **973.2**

1. United States -- History -- 1600-1775, Colonial period

ISBN 978-1-4205-0267-1 lib bdg; 1-4205-0267-0 lib bdg

In this history of the establishment of the thirteen colonies in North America, "the detailed text is interspersed with sidebars of primary and secondary quotations and historical color illustrations that add both substance and visual interest. With its long paragraphs and dutiful citations, this is a fairy advanced take on the topic." Booklist

Includes bibliographical references

Government and social class in colonial America. Lucent Books 2010 96p il map (Lucent library of historical eras) lib bdg $32.45

Grades: 6 7 8 9   **973.2**

1. Social classes 2. United States -- History -- 1600-1775, Colonial period

ISBN 978-1-4205-0265-7; 1-4205-0265-4

LC 2009043640

"The detailed text is interspersed with sidebars of primary and secondary quotations and historical color illustrations that add both substance and visual interest. With its long paragraphs and dutiful citations, this is a fairly advanced take on the topic." Booklist

Includes bibliographical references

Pederson, Charles E.

The **French** & Indian War. ABDO Pub. Co. 2010 112p il map (Essential events) lib bdg $32.79
Grades: 6 7 8 9   973.2
    1. United States -- History -- 1755-1763, French and Indian War
    ISBN 978-1-60453-943-1; 1-60453-943-7
                                    LC 2009-30425

This title examines an important historic event, the French & Indian War. Readers will learn the background of French and British settlement on Native American land and how conflict developed as a result.

"The writing is accessible and is richer than a lot of history writing, allowing the reader to become engaged in the text as a story, and the layout provides enough white space to allow lower level readers to feel confident." Libr Media Connect

Includes glossary and bibliographical references

Philbrick, Nathaniel

★ The **Mayflower** and the Pilgrims' New World. G.P. Putnam's Sons 2008 338p il map $19.99
Grades: 7 8 9 10 11 12   973.2
    1. Farmers 2. Historians 3. Native Americans 4. Pilgrims (New England colonists) 5. Colonists 6. Carpenters 7. Army officers 8. Pilgrim fathers 9. Massachusetts -- History -- 1600-1775, Colonial period
    ISBN 978-0-399-24795-8; 0-399-24795-5
                                    LC 2007-30669

An adaptation of Mayflower: a story of community, courage, and war, published 2006 by Viking for adults

"This volume highlights both the Pilgrims' determination to find and settle a home where they could worship freely and the perilous journey that it took to make that happen. In accessible prose, the author shatters the American myth of the landing at Plymouth Rock and the first Thanksgiving. . . . The various maps, reproductions of historical documents, photographs of significant locations, and illustrations all come together with the text to help separate fact from legend and create a realistic, readable portrayal of the Pilgrims and their first 50 years in America." SLJ

Includes bibliographical references

Saari, Peggy

Colonial America: almanac. U.X.L 2000 2v (Colonial America reference library) set $110
Grades: 8 9 10 11 12   973.2
    1. Reference books 2. United States -- History -- 1600-1775, Colonial period
    ISBN 0-7876-3763-7
                                    LC 99-39081

Examines the colonial period in America, discussing both the Native American culture before the arrival of Eu-

ropeans and the exploration and settlement of different parts of the New World.

Colonial America: primary sources; Julie Carnagie, editor. U.X.L 1999 297p il (Colonial America reference library) $67
Grades: 8 9 10 11 12   973.2
    1. United States -- History -- 1600-1775, Colonial period
    ISBN 0-7876-3766-1
                                    LC 99-34460

Presents the historical events and social issues of colonial America through twenty-four primary documents, including diary entries, poems, and personal narratives

"Each chapter adds helpful material before and after the excerpt to explain its importance. Illustrations and sidebars are used in this volume also, and difficult words are defined." Booklist

Sharpe, M. E.

Cities and towns. M.E. Sharpe 2008 95p il map (Colonial life) $37.95
Grades: 5 6 7 8 9 10 11 12   973.2
    1. Cities and towns 2. United States -- History -- 1600-1775, Colonial period
    ISBN 978-0-7656-8109-6
                                    LC 2007-7843

This provides "an informative look into how the forts and fishing camps of the early Colonial period became the cities and towns of the 17th and 18th centuries, and what life was like in these developing communities. The author's conversational tone and generous use of full-color reproductions, maps, and sidebars will engage readers." SLJ

Includes glossary and bibliographical references

Stanley, George Edward

★ The **European** settlement of North America (1492-1763) by George E. Stanley. World Almanac Library 2005 48p il (Primary source history of the United States) lib bdg $31; pa $14.05
Grades: 5 6 7 8   973.2
    1. Frontier and pioneer life 2. America -- Exploration 3. United States -- History -- 1600-1775, Colonial period
    ISBN 0-8368-5824-7 lib bdg; 0-8368-5833-6 pa

"Stanley includes the efforts of Columbus to gain the support of the Spanish royals, a lithograph of Columbus and Queen Isabella, and primary-source material containing the permission for exploration. The motivation of other early explorers and their financial supporters is treated in a similar manner. Coverage of Native Americans includes text from the Constitution of the Iroquois Confederation, c. 1500, used by Benjamin Franklin during the creation of the United States Constitution. . . . Well-organized, highly attractive." SLJ

Includes bibliographical references

★ The **New** Republic (1763-1815) by George E. Stanley. World Almanac Library 2005 48p il (Primary source history of the United States) lib bdg $31; pa $14.05
Grades: 5 6 7 8   973.2
    1. United States -- History -- 1783-1865 2. United

States -- History -- 1775-1783, Revolution 3. United
States -- History -- 1600-1775, Colonial period
ISBN 0-8368-5825-5 lib bdg; 0-8368-5834-4 pa

"The series of events that lead to the American Revolution is explained, helping readers to understand the connections of events inherent in historical study. Stanley's analysis of the constitutional debates of the Federalists and Anti-
Federalists is exceptionally clear. Well-organized, highly
attractive." SLJ

Includes bibliographical references

Stefoff, Rebecca

★ **American** voices from Colonial life. Benchmark Bks. 2003 119p (American voices from--) lib
bdg $32.79

Grades: 6 7 8 9   **973.2**
    1. United States -- History -- 1600-1775, Colonial period
ISBN 0-7614-1205-0

LC 2002-3223

Presents the history of the British colonies in North
America, beginning with the Jamestown settlement, through
excerpts from letters, pamphlets, journal entries, and other
documents of the time

Includes glossary and bibliographical references

Voices from colonial America [series] National Geographic 2005 18v il map

Grades: 5 6 7 8   **973.2**
    1. United States -- History -- 1600-1775, Colonial period
Each volume in this series describes the colonial history of a state illustrated with historical maps and reprints of period artwork, and includes excerpts from first-
person accounts.

"Presented in clear, succinct text . . . this resource, containing a great deal of information, will be a welcome addition to history classes and a great source for report writers."
Booklist [review of New Jersey volume]

Includes bibliographical references

973.3   United States--Periods of Revolution and Confederation, 1775-1789

Adler, David A.

★ **B.** Franklin, printer. Holiday House 2001
126p il lib bdg $19.95

Grades: 4 5 6 7   **973.3**
    1. Authors 2. Diplomats 3. Inventors 4. Statesmen
5. Scientists 6. Writers on science 7. Members of
Congress 8. Statesmen -- United States
ISBN 0-8234-1675-5

LC 2001-24535

This "surveys Benjamin Franklin's life as a printer, a scientist, an inventor, a writer, and a statesman. . . . Throughout
the book, details, anecdotes, and quotations bring the man's
portrait into clearer focus, while period illustrations . . . help
readers envision the background of his times." Booklist

Includes bibliographical references

Allen, Thomas B.

★ **Remember** Valley Forge; patriots, Tories,
and Redcoats tell their stories. [by] Thomas B. Allen.
National Geographic 2007 61p il map $17.95; lib
bdg $27.90

Grades: 5 6 7 8   **973.3**
    1. Generals 2. Presidents 3. Valley Forge (Pa.) --
History 4. United States -- History -- 1775-1783,
Revolution
ISBN 978-1-4263-0149-0; 978-1-4263-0150-6 lib bdg

LC 2007024821

The author "recounts here the activities of Washington
and his soldiers during the winter of 1777-8, spent regroup-
ing at Valley Forge, Pennsylvania. . . . Allen's strength is his
attention to military details and strategies, but his account is
clearly presented and succinctly written as well. . . . Illustrated with reproductions of period artwork, drawings, maps,
and a few contemporary photographs." Booklist

American Revolution: primary sources; [compiled
by] Linda Schmittroth; Lawrence W. Baker and
Stacy A. McConnell, editors. U.X.L 2000 xxxiii,
264p il lib bdg $60

Grades: 8 9 10 11 12   **973.3**
    1. United States -- History -- 1775-1783, Revolution
ISBN 0-7876-3790-4

LC 99-46940

This volume "presents 32 excerpted documents, beginning with the 1765 Stamp Act and ending with Washington's
farewell address to the Continental Army in 1783. Each entry has helpful material to give the context for the document.
The adjoining margins contain definitions of terms that may
be unfamiliar. . . . [This volume] is attractive and easy to
use." Booklist

Includes bibliographical references

The **American** revolutionaries: a history in their own
words, 1750-1800; edited by Milton Meltzer.
Crowell 1987 210p il hardcover o.p. pa $8.99

Grades: 6 7 8 9   **973.3**
    1. United States -- History -- 1775-1783, Revolution 2.
United States -- History -- 1755-1763, French and Indian
War
ISBN 0-06-446145-9 pa

LC 86-47846

"Meltzer has assembled a collage of eyewitness accounts, speech and diary excerpts, letters, and other documents for a chronological account of the half century that
included the American Revolution. . . . The voices of women
who accompanied the troops and of blacks who fought with
the army are both represented." Bull Cent Child Books

Aronson, Marc

★ The **real** revolution; the global story of American independence. Clarion Books 2005 238p il
map lib bdg $21

Grades: 7 8 9 10   **973.3**
    1. United States -- History -- 1775-1783, Revolution
ISBN 0-618-18179-2

LC 2005-1088

In this "volume, Aronson investigates the origins of the American Revolution and discovers some startling global connections. The colonies' quest for independence is tied to such seemingly unrelated incidents as Robert Clive's triumph over the French in India in 1750 and John Wilkes's accusations against the king in his newspaper, The North Briton, in the 1760s. . . . This outstanding work is highly compelling reading and belongs in every library." SLJ

Includes bibliographical references

Bigelow, Barbara Carlisle

American Revolution: almanac; [by] Barbara Bigelow and Linda Schmittroth; Stacy A. McConnell, editor. U.X.L 2000 xxxiii, 188, xxxv-xlip il map lib bdg $60

Grades: 5 6 7 8   973.3
  1. Almanacs 2. Reference books 3. United States -- History -- 1775-1783, Revolution
  ISBN 0-7876-3795-5

LC 99-46939

Provides in-depth background and interpretation of the American Revolution, with short biographies of people relevant to the topics discussed in each chapter

"Illustrations, sidebars, a time line, glossary, and activity ideas enhance the value of the volume." Booklist

Includes bibliographical references

Blair, Margaret Whitman

Liberty or death; the surprising story of runaway slaves who sided with the British during the American Revolution. National Geographic 2010 64p il map lib bdg $27.90

Grades: 5 6 7 8   973.3
  1. African American soldiers 2. Slavery -- United States 3. United States -- History -- 1775-1783, Revolution
  ISBN 978-1-4263-0590-0 lib bdg; 1-4263-0590-7 lib bdg

LC 2009-26853

"Blair provides a well-researched account of slaves in Virginia who, beginning in 1775, fled to the British. . . . Though told in a matter-of-fact tone, the story is often heart-wrenching. . . . Colorful reproductions of period paintings, prints, and documents illustrate the clearly written text. . . . A fine and singular addition to American history collections." Booklist

Includes bibliographical references

Bobrick, Benson

Fight for freedom; the American Revolutionary War. Atheneum Books for Young Readers 2004 96p il map $22.95

Grades: 5 6 7 8   973.3
  1. United States -- History -- 1775-1783, Revolution
  ISBN 0-689-86422-1

LC 2003-25548

"This large-format volume profiles significant individuals and discusses the progress of the Revolutionary War. . . . Printed in color, most of the illustrations are period paintings and prints. . . . Students will find the book a well-organized and clearly written introduction to the war." Booklist

Includes glossary and bibliographical references

Driver, Stephanie Schwartz

Understanding the Declaration of Independence. Rosen Pub. 2010 128p il (Words that changed the world) lib bdg $31.95

Grades: 7 8 9 10   973.3
  1. Architects 2. Presidents 3. Vice-presidents 4. Essayists 5. United States -- Declaration of Independence 6. United States -- Politics and government -- 1775-1783, Revolution
  ISBN 978-1-4488-1669-9; 1-4488-1669-6

LC 2010-10371

This surveys The Declaration of Independence, considering the "document's 'Context and Creator,' 'Immediate Impact,' 'Legacy,' and 'Aftermath.' . . . Exploring the colonial crisis leading to America's formal separation from the British Empire, . . . [the] author provides a balance of deep context, expressive writing, and pertinent information. Scattered throughout the [text] are a good number of well-captioned, color illustrations and photos. [This book is a] valuable [resource] for teachers and students doing research projects across the curriculum." SLJ

Includes glossary and bibliographical references

Fleming, Thomas J.

★ **Everybody's** revolution; a new look at the people who won America's freedom. [by] Thomas Fleming. Scholastic Nonfiction 2006 96p il $19.99

Grades: 4 5 6 7   973.3
  1. United States -- History -- 1775-1783, Revolution
  ISBN 0-439-63404-0

LC 2005051814

A history of the American Revolution, focusing on the roles played by women, young people, and various ethnic groups.

"With an open layout and clean typeface, this clearly written title is attractive and inviting. . . . Fleming's sound offering is an excellent starting point for discussions of the implications of the Revolutionary War in terms of freedom for all people." SLJ

Includes glossary and bibliographical references

The **Founding** of America; Leora Maltz, book editor. Greenhaven Press 2002 236p il (Great speeches in history series) lib bdg $34.95; pa $23.70

Grades: 8 9 10 11 12 Adult   973.3
  1. American speeches 2. United States -- Politics and government
  ISBN 0-7377-0871-9 lib bdg; 0-7377-0870-0 pa

LC 2001-40736

This collection of American speeches from the late 18th and early 19th centuries includes an introductory essay, introductions to each speech and an appendix of biographical sketches

Includes bibliographical references

Fradin, Dennis B.

★ The **signers**; the fifty-six stories behind the Declaration of Independence. [by] Dennis Brindell Fradin; illustrations by Michael McCurdy. Walker & Co. 2002 164p il map $22.95; lib bdg $23.85

Grades: 4 5 6 7   **973.3**

1. Statesmen -- United States 2. United States -- Declaration of Independence 3. United States -- Politics and government -- 1775-1783, Revolution

ISBN 0-8027-8849-1; 0-8027-8850-5 lib bdg

LC 2002-66364

Profiles each of the fifty-six men who signed the Declaration of Independence, giving historical information about the colonies they represented. Includes the text of the Declaration and its history

"Fradin gives brief, fascinating glimpses into the people who have been overlooked as well as those with whom readers might be familiar. . . . An excellent resource for report writing." SLJ

Includes bibliographical references

Freedman, Russell, 1929-

★ **Give** me liberty! the story of the Declaration of Independence. Holiday House 2000 90p il $24.95; pa $14.95

Grades: 5 6 7 8 9 10   **973.3**

1. United States 2. United States -- Declaration of Independence 3. United States -- Politics and government -- 1775-1783, Revolution 4. United States -- Politics and government -- 1775-1783

ISBN 0-8234-1448-5; 0-8234-1753-0 pa

LC 99-57513

This book describes the events leading up to the Declaration of Independence as well as the personalities and politics behind its framing. Chronology. Annotated bibliography. Index. "Grades five to eight." (Bull Cent Child Books)

"Handsomely designed with a generous and thoughtful selection of period art, the book is dramatic and inspiring." Horn Book

Includes bibliographical references

★ **Washington** at Valley Forge. Holiday House 2008 100p il map $24.95

Grades: 5 6 7 8 9   **973.3**

1. Generals 2. Presidents 3. Pennsylvania -- History 4. Valley Forge (Pa.) -- History 5. United States -- History -- 1775-1783, Revolution

ISBN 978-0-8234-2069-8; 0-8234-2069-8

LC 2007-52467

NCTE Orbis Pictus Award honor book (2009)

"With his usual clarity of focus and keen eye for telling quotations, Freedman documents how Washington struggled to maintain morale despite hunger, near-nakedness, and freezing conditions. . . . Throughout, high-quality reproductions depict Washington among the men, and with the numerous other influential people who played crucial roles." Booklist

Hughes, Christopher

★ The **Constitutional** Convention; by Chris Hughes. Blackbirch Press 2005 48p il map (People at the center of) $23.70

Grades: 5 6 7 8   **973.3**

1. United States -- Constitutional Convention (1787) 2. United States -- Politics and government -- 1775-1783,

Revolution

ISBN 1-56711-918-2

LC 2004-17601

This profiles men who participated in the United States Constitutional Convention such as George Washington, Benjamin Franklin, James Madison, and Alexander Hamilton

"Maps, photos, drawings, and a two-page artistic rendition of the event add to the appeal of [this title]. Great for reports and as supplemental teaching [material]." SLJ

Includes bibliographical references

Irvin, Benjamin

Samuel Adams; son of liberty, father of revolution. [by] Benjamin H. Irvin. Oxford University Press 2002 176p il (Oxford portraits) $28

Grades: 7 8 9 10   **973.3**

1. Statesmen 2. Members of Congress 3. Writers on politics 4. United States -- History -- 1775-1783, Revolution

ISBN 0-19-513225-4

LC 2002-4283

Examines the life of Samuel Adams, a hero of the American Revolution who is credited by some with having fired the first shot at Lexington Green, the "shot heard 'round the world"

"Irvin's account of events is exciting and written in a compelling narrative style. He presents an unbiased assessment of Adams's actions and character." SLJ

Includes bibliographical references

Kostyal, K. M.

1776; a new look at revolutionary Williamsburg. by K.M. Kostyal with the Colonial Williamsburg Foundation; photographs by Lori Epstein. National Geographic 2009 48p il $17.95; lib bdg $27.90

Grades: 4 5 6   **973.3**

1. Colonial Williamsburg (Williamsburg, Va.) 2. United States -- History -- 1775-1783, Revolution

ISBN 978-1-4263-0517-7; 1-4263-0517-6; 978-1-4263-0518-4 lib bdg; 1-4263-0518-4 lib bdg

LC 2009-18002

"Clear, distinctive photos add visual appeal to this short history of the American Revolution, written from the point of view of those living in Williamsburg, Virginia's capital in 1776. Kostyal blends political and social history into a readable account of the period, bolstered by informative sidebars, a chronology, and a closing note about the restoration of colonial Williamsburg. . . . The increasing inclusion of nonwhite colonists in the illustrations as well as the text is a welcome trend." Booklist

Includes bibliographical references

McNeese, Tim

Revolutionary America, 1764-1789; consulting editor, Richard Jensen. Chelsea House 2010 128p il map (Discovering U.S. history) $35

Grades: 5 6 7 8   **973.3**

1. United States -- History -- 1775-1783, Revolution

ISBN 978-1-60413-350-9; 1-60413-350-3

LC 2008-55179

"The information is accurate and easy to understand. Pictures are well placed, and primary sources are included.

. . . . The maps are well done and there are sidebars with additional information. . . . [This would be good] to have on hand for reports as it is well laid out and easy to use." Libr Media Connect

Includes glossary and bibliographical references

Murphy, Jim

★ The **crossing**; how George Washington saved the American Revolution. Scholastic Press 2010 96p il map $21.99

Grades: 5 6 7 8   **973.3**

1. Generals 2. Presidents 3. Trenton (N.J.), Battle of, 1776 4. United States -- History -- 1775-1783, Revolution

ISBN 978-0-439-69186-4; 0-439-69186-9

LC 2009-11561

Murphy "again digs into the well of history, this time emerging with a well-researched, absorbing account of the early battles of the Revolutionary War with General George Washington at their center. Enhanced by numerous sepia maps of troop movements, prints, paintings, and portraits of prominent figures, the blow-by-blow narrative begins with the shots fired at Lexington and Concord in 1775 and continues until the tide-turning battles at Trenton and Princeton in early 1777." Publ Wkly

Includes bibliographical references

A **young** patriot; the American Revolution as experienced by one boy. Clarion Bks. 1996 101p il maps $16; pa $7.95

Grades: 5 6 7 8   **973.3**

1. Soldiers 2. United States -- History -- 1775-1783, Revolution

ISBN 0-395-60523-7; 0-395-90019-0 pa

LC 93-38789

"Using Joseph Plumb Martin's first person account of his participation in the Revolutionary War as primary source material, Murphy intertwines this story of one teenager's life as a soldier with broader information about the Revolution, to put Martin's story in context. The handsome, informative, and fascinating look at American history is illustrated with many period reproductions." Horn Book Guide

Includes bibliographical references

Nardo, Don

The **Civil** War. Lucent Bks. 2003 109p il maps (History of weapons and warfare) $27.45

Grades: 7 8 9 10   **973.3**

1. Military art and science 2. United States -- History -- 1861-1865, Civil War

ISBN 1-59018-068-2

LC 2002-11032

Discusses the weapons of American Civil War soldiers and different means of warfare used during that conflict.

Includes glossary and bibliographical references

Nash, Gary B.

Landmarks of the American Revolution. Oxford University Press 2003 158p il map (American landmarks) lib bdg $30

Grades: 6 7 8 9   **973.3**

1. Historic sites 2. United States -- History -- 1775-1783, Revolution

ISBN 0-19-512849-4

LC 2002-14152

"Written with the idea that historic sites can be considered primary sources, this book skillfully demonstrates the 'power of places.' Traditional documents, such as excerpts from letters, broadsides, and maps, as well as well-placed quotes, are incorporated into the text. The places include churches, halls, homes, and battlefields, covering the many facets of the Revolution: political, religious, and actual battles. . . . This well-organized book includes clear, full-color photographs or reproductions and a small inset map for each site." SLJ

Includes bibliographical references

Otfinoski, Steven

The **new** republic: 1760-1840s. Marshall Cavendish Benchmark 2009 79p il map (Hispanic America) lib bdg $23.95

Grades: 4 5 6 7   **973.3**

1. Latinos (U.S.) 2. Mexico -- History 3. Florida -- History 4. Hispanic Americans 5. Spaniards -- United States 6. United States -- History -- 1775-1783, Revolution

ISBN 978-0-7614-2938-8 lib bdg; 0-7614-2938-7 lib bdg

LC 2007-45958

"Provides comprehensive information on the history of the Spanish exploring the United States." Publisher's note

Includes glossary and bibliographical references

Renehan, Edward J.

The **Treaty** of Paris; the precursor to a new nation. [by] Edward J. Renehan, Jr. Chelsea House 2007 121p il map (Milestones in American history) lib bdg $35

Grades: 7 8 9 10   **973.3**

1. Treaty of Paris (1783) 2. United States -- History -- 1775-1783, Revolution

ISBN 0-7910-9352-2 lib bdg; 978-0-7910-9352-8 lib bdg

LC 2006034129

This describes the treaty signed in Paris in 1782 in which Benjamin Franklin, John Adams, and John Jay worked to bring about British recognition of American independence and a cessation to hostilities.

The book has "well-reproduced archival photos and drawings with explanatory captions. . . . [and an] open layout and lively [text]." SLJ

Includes bibliographical references

Sanders, Nancy I.

America's black founders; revolutionary heroes & early leaders with 21 activities. Chicago Review Press 2010 150p il $16.95

Grades: 4 5 6 7   **973.3**

1. African Americans -- History 2. United States -- History -- 1775-1783, Revolution

ISBN 978-1-55652-811-8; 1-55652-811-6

"This activity-based guide reveals how African Americans played crucial roles in helping the United States gain its independence. Sanders includes well-known figures such as Phillis Wheatley, Crispus Attucks, and James Forten in her narrative, but also enriches traditional accounts of the period by explaining the contributions of lesser-known patriots.... Most of the activities help make this period real to young people. . . . Sanders makes excellent use of primary sources." SLJ

Schanzer, Rosalyn

★ **George** vs. George; the American Revolution as seen from both sides. National Geographic 2004 60p il maps $16.95

Grades: 3 4 5 6   **973.3**

1. Generals 2. Presidents 3. Kings 4. United States -- History -- 1775-1783, Revolution 6. United States -- History -- Revolution, 1775-1783

ISBN 0-7922-7349-4

LC 2003-20843

This book explores how the characters and lives of King George III of England and George Washington affected he progress and outcome of the American Revolution. Bibliography. Index. "Grades four to six." (Bull Cent Child Books)

"A carefully researched, evenhanded narrative with well-crafted, vibrant, watercolor illustrations. . . . This is a lovely book, showing historical inquiry at its best." SLJ

Includes bibliographical references

Stewart, Gail

Life of a soldier in Washington's army; by Gail B. Stewart. Lucent Bks. 2003 112p il map (American war library, American Revolution) lib bdg $21.96

Grades: 7 8 9 10   **973.3**

1. Soldiers -- United States 2. United States -- History -- 1775-1783, Revolution

ISBN 1-59018-215-4

LC 2002-6602

Discusses the training, organization, diversity, fighting and survival skills, daily routine, diseases, fears, and morale of the first army of the United States

This volume is "thorough, but not overwhelming." SLJ
Includes bibliographical references

973.4   United States--Constitutional period, 1789-1809

Bober, Natalie

Abigail Adams; witness to a revolution. {by} Natalie S. Bober. Atheneum Bks. for Young Readers 1995 248p il maps hardcover o.p. pa $9.99

Grades: 7 8 9 10   **973.4**

1. Parents of presidents 2. Spouses of presidents 3. Presidents' spouses -- United States

ISBN 0-689-31760-3; 0-689-81916-1 pa

LC 94-19259

"By interweaving excerpts from Adams's correspondence into a coherent biography, Bober creates a vibrant, three-dimensional portrait of a fascinating person whose comments on women's place have reverberated throughout

history. This scholarly, thoroughly documented study will appeal to more mature readers, but it is more formidable in appearance than in presentation. Black-and-white reproductions are included." Horn Book Guide

Includes bibliographical references

Corrick, James A.

The **Louisiana** Purchase. Lucent Bks. 2001 108p il maps (World history series) lib bdg $27.45

Grades: 7 8 9 10   **973.4**

1. Louisiana Purchase

ISBN 1-56006-637-7

LC 00-9156

Examines the Louisiana Purchase, discussing the negotiation of the treaty with France, the formation of Louisiana, taking possession of the land, and the exploration, growth, and settlement of the territory

This overview is "well-written . . . . [and] thought-provoking." SLJ

Includes bibliographical references

Lanier, Shannon

Jefferson's children; the story of one American family. by Shannon Lanier and Jane Feldman; with photographs by Jane Feldman; and an introduction by Lucian K. Truscott IV. Random House 2000 144p il hardcover o.p. pa $16.95

Grades: 7 8 9 10   **973.4**

1. Slaves 2. Architects 3. Presidents 4. Vice-presidents 5. Racially mixed people 6. Essayists 7. Mistresses 8. African Americans -- Biography 9. United States -- Race relations

ISBN 0-375-80597-4; 0-375-82168-6 pa

LC 00-44551

This is an "anthology of personal meditations by a variety of Jefferson's living descendants. Edited by Shannon Lanier, a descendant through Sally's son Madison Hemings's line, the portraits that emerge are as generous and jumbled as America itself. The statements range from hostile to conciliatory to indifferent to eloquent." NY Times Book Rev

Includes bibliographical references

McNeese, Tim

Early national America, 1790-1850. Chelsea House 2010 136p il map (Discovering U.S. history) $35

Grades: 5 6 7 8   **973.4**

1. United States -- History -- 1783-1865

ISBN 978-1-60413-351-6; 1-60413-351-1

LC 2009003679

McNeese "discusses the people, politics, economic conditions, and foreign affairs of [the U.S. from 1790 to 1850], objectively explaining how the attitudes, perceptions, and expectations of the American people and their leaders shaped the development of the country. . . . Color period art and photos, maps, and cutaway drawings supplement the [text]." SLJ

Includes glossary and bibliographical references

Severance, John B.

Thomas Jefferson; architect of democracy. Clarion Bks. 1998 192p il map $18

Grades: 7 8 9 10   **973.4**

1. Architects 2. Presidents 3. Vice-presidents 4. Essayists 5. Presidents -- United States

ISBN 0-395-84513-0

LC 97-31010

Explores the life of the third president, from his childhood in Virginia, through his involvement in the Revolutionary War, to his years in office

"In this respectful, literate, and handsomely illustrated biography, Severance focuses equally on Jefferson's remarkable accomplishments and the beliefs behind them." Booklist

Includes bibliographical references

Stefoff, Rebecca

★ **American** voices from the new republic, 1783-1830. Benchmark Books 2004 xxiii, 116p (American voices from--) lib bdg $34.21

Grades: 6 7 8 9 10   **973.4**

1. United States -- History -- 1783-1865

ISBN 0-7614-1695-1

LC 2004-11391

Describes, through excerpts from diaries, speeches, newspaper articles, and other documents of the time, United States history from 1783 to 1830. Includes review questions.

Whitelaw, Nancy

★ **Thomas** Jefferson; philosopher and president. Morgan Reynolds 2002 144p il $21.95

Grades: 7 8 9 10   **973.4**

1. Architects 2. Presidents 3. Vice-presidents 4. Essayists 5. Presidents -- United States

ISBN 1-88384-681-1

LC 2001-44960

An account of Jefferson's life highlighting his many accomplishments as governor, architect, gardener, inventor, and president

"A clear, crisp biography. . . . A solid and practical book for reports." SLJ

Includes bibliographical references

973.5   United States--1809-1845

Bowes, John P.

Black Hawk and the War of 1832; removal in the north. [by] John P. Bowes. Chelsea House 2007 131p bibl il map (Landmark events in Native American history) lib bdg $35

Grades: 6 7 8 9   **973.5**

1. Sauk Indians 2. Black Hawk War, 1832 3. Indian chiefs 4. Native Americans -- Biography

ISBN 978-0-7910-9342-9 lib bdg; 0-7910-9342-5 lib bdg

LC 2007004927

This "provides a clear overview of early American expansion in the Northwest Territory, from the 1780s through the 1930s, detailing government actions and policies of Indian Removal and how they specifically affected the Sauks

and Mesquakies, now known as the Sac and Fox tribes. . . . The battles that ensued (both intertribal and against the U.S. forces) are described, as are the policies created during this period. . . . Attractive color paintings, maps, and photographs appear throughout." SLJ

Includes bibliographical references

Macleod, D. Peter

Four Wars of 1812; One War, Four Perspectives. by D. Peter MacLeod. Pgw 2012 95 p. ill. (paperback) $19.95

Grades: 6 7 8   **973.5**

1. War of 1812

ISBN 1771000503; 9781771000505

This book on the war of 1812 "examine[s] the viewpoints, goals, and outcomes for its four major participants: Britain, Canada, the United States, and Native American nations. . . , Its four chapters, each focused on one combatant, are made up of spreads that feature either a color photo of period artifacts and weapons or reproductions of artwork . . . on one side and a[n] . . . essay that describes how it illustrates a . . . perspective about the war on the other." (School Library Journal)

Stewart, Mark

The **Indian** Removal Act; forced relocation. Compass Point Books 2007 96p il map (Snapshots in history) $23.95

Grades: 6 7 8 9   **973.5**

1. Cherokee Indians 2. Native Americans -- Relocation

ISBN 978-0-7565-2452-4; 0-7565-2452-0

LC 2006027084

Profiles the "Trail of Tears," the forced removal of five Southeastern Native American tribes to land west of the Mississippi River during the winter of 1838 and 1839.

"The book organizes a good deal of historical information into a cogent presentation. . . . Illustrations, many in color, include photos and maps as well as period engravings, portraits, and documents." Booklist

Includes glossary and bibliographical references

Warrick, Karen Clemens

The **War** of 1812; We have met the enemy and they are ours. Enslow Pubs. 2002 128p il maps (American war series) lib bdg $26.60

Grades: 6 7 8 9   **973.5**

1. War of 1812

ISBN 0-7660-1854-7

LC 2001-4120

Traces the history of the War of 1812, examining the maritime and boundary issues that caused it and highlighting the roles of famous personalities, including Oliver Hazard Perry, Andrew Jackson, and Dolley Madison

"With a text that is less dry than many history books, this title will earn its keep as a circulating resource for assignments. . . . [This book has] numerous black-and-white illustrations, a time line, solid footnotes, and chapters that begin with relevant quotes." SLJ

Includes bibliographical references

973.6 United States--1845-1861

Carey, Charles W.

The **Mexican** War; Mr. Polk's war. [by] Charles W. Carey, Jr. Enslow Pubs. 2002 128p il (American war series) lib bdg $26.60

Grades: 6 7 8 9   **973.6**

1. Mexican War, 1846-1848

ISBN 0-7660-1853-9

LC 2001-817

This "account of the 1846-1848 war addresses the origins, strategies, battles, and people involved in the conflict. The ramifications of the war for each country are discussed in separate chapters. . . . [This volume has] numerous black-and-white illustrations, a time line, solid footnotes, and chapters that begin with relevant quotes." SLJ

Includes bibliographical references

DiConsiglio, John

The **Mexican** -American War; by John DiConsiglio. Heinemann Library 2012 80 p. ill. (some col.), col. maps (library) $36.50; (paperback) $10.99

Grades: 6 7 8 9   **973.6**

1. Mexican War, 1846-1848

ISBN 1432959980; 9781432959982; 9781432960070

LC 2011016817

This book on the Mexican-American War by John DiConsiglio is part of the "Living Through" series. It "provid[e]s . . . an overview of the causes, events, and leading personalities that shaped this 19th century conflict" as well as "snapshots of the daily life of soldiers and civilians. . . . Issues linked to the legitimacy of the American invasion of Mexico, the dictatorial leadership of Mexican commanders, and the shifting course of military fortunes all are presented." (Children's Literature)

Includes bibliographical references (p. 76-77) and index.

Stein, R. Conrad

The **Mexican** -American War. Morgan Reynolds Pub. 2011 144p il map (The story of Mexico) $28.95

Grades: 6 7 8 9   **973.6**

1. Mexican War, 1846-1848

ISBN 978-1-5993-5160-5; 1-5993-5160-9

LC 2010041378

"Stein organizes and clearly presents a great deal of information. . . . The . . . format features a chronological text supplemented with useful sidebars and brightened with color illustrations, including many photos, artifacts, and period artworks. . . . [The book] explains the war's causes, its progress, and it aftermath in both countries." Booklist

Includes bibliographical references

973.7 Administration of Abraham Lincoln, 1861-1865

Adler, David A., 1947-

Harriet Tubman and the Underground Railroad; by David A. Adler. Holiday House 2013 140 p. ill. (hardcover) $18.95

Grades: 5 6 7 8   **973.7**

1. Underground Railroad 2. African American women -- Biography 3. Slaves -- United States -- Biography

ISBN 0823423654; 9780823423651

LC 2012006582

This book, by David A. Adler, gives a biography of the ex-slave Harriet Tubman. "She escaped from her owners in Maryland on the Underground Railroad in 1849 and then fearlessly returned . . . to help guide . . . others to freedom as the most famous conductor of the Underground Railroad. . . . During and after the war, she helped hundreds of freed slaves begin new lives, and she later founded a home for elderly former slaves and became active in the women's suffrage movement." (Publisher's note)

Includes bibliographical references

Allen, Roger MacBride

★ **Mr.** Lincoln's High-Tech War; how the North used the telegraph, railroads, surveillance balloons, ironclads, high-powered weapons, and more to win the Civil War. [by] Thomas B. Allen & Roger MacBride Allen. National Geographic Society 2009 144p il $18.95; lib bdg $25.90

Grades: 5 6 7 8 9 10   **973.7**

1. Lawyers 2. Presidents 3. State legislators 4. Members of Congress 5. Technology -- History 6. United States -- History -- 1861-1865, Civil War 7. Technology -- United States -- History

ISBN 1-4263-0379-3; 1-4263-0380-7 lib bdg; 978-1-4263-0379-1; 978-1-4263-0380-7 lib bdg

LC 2008-24546

This book contends that "President Lincoln's appreciation for the power of technology played a critical role in the North's Civil War victory over the less developed South, and discusses the specific technologies used by the North in the war." (Publisher's note) Bibliography. Index. "Grades nine to twelve." (Publisher's note)

"Well researched and clearly written, the book discusses the course of the Civil War in terms of new technology, from the ironclad and the submarine to the rapid-fire, repeating rifle and the use of railroads to carry troops and supplies. . . . The many illustrations include captioned black-and-white reproductions of period prints, paintings, and photos as well as clearly labeled drawings. . . . [Readers] will gain a fascinating perspective on why the war progressed as it did and how it was ultimately won." Booklist

Includes bibliographical references

Anderson, Maxine

Great Civil War projects you can build yourself; Maxine Anderson. Sesquicentennial Edition Nomad Press 2012 120 p. illustrations, map $21.95

Grades: 7 8 9 10   **973.7**

1. Handicraft 2. United States -- History -- 1861-1865, Civil War

ISBN 9781936749461

"Detailed step-by-step instructions, diagrams, and templates for creating 25 Civil War projects, combined with historical background, facts and anecdotes, and biographies and trivia, give kids a hands-on way to experience the fascinating history of one of the most important eras in American history." (Publisher's note)

Includes bibliographical references and index

Armstrong, Jennifer

Photo by Brady; a picture of the Civil War. Atheneum Books For Young Readers 2005 160p il $18.95

Grades: 6 7 8 9 10   973.7
1. Photographers 2. Photography -- History 3. United States -- History -- 1861-1865, Civil War
ISBN 0-689-85785-3

LC 2004-8967

"Armstrong chronicles the Civil War from Lincoln's election to his death with both a storylike narrative of events and a photo-essay. . . . This book is also a look at early photographic techniques and offers a description of [Mathew] Brady's rare collection. . . . When readers remember that the pictures are more than 100 years old, they should recognize their exquisiteness, grandeur, and genius." SLJ

Includes bibliographical references

Barney, William L.

The **Civil** War and Reconstruction; a student companion. Oxford Univ. Press 2001 368p il maps (Oxford student companions to American history) $60

Grades: 7 8 9 10   973.7
1. Reconstruction (1865-1876) 2. United States -- History -- 1861-1865, Civil War
ISBN 0-19-511559-7

LC 00-57444

"The book is encyclopedic in format, with many useful access points, and bibliographic information is located both at the ends of the articles and in several appendixes that suggest books, historic sites and addresses, and Web sites." Voice Youth Advocates

Includes bibliographical references (p. 358-359) and index

Beller, Susan Provost

Billy Yank and Johnny Reb; soldiering in the Civil War. Twenty-First Century Books 2008 112p il map (Soldiers on the battlefront) lib bdg $33.26

Grades: 5 6 7 8   973.7
1. Soldiers -- United States 2. United States -- History -- 1861-1865, Civil War
ISBN 978-0-8225-6803-2 lib bdg; 0-8225-6803-9 lib bdg

LC 2006010240

First published 2000

Describes military life for the average soldier in the Civil War, including camp life, diseases, and conditions for the wounded and prisoners of war. Includes excerpts from first-person accounts, letters, and diaries

The author "presents a good deal of solid information in an interesting manner. . . . Good black-and-white reproductions, mainly of photographs from the 1860s, appear throughout the book." Booklist [review of 2000 ed]

Includes bibliographical references

Benoit, Peter

The **surrender** at Appomattox; by Peter Benoit. Children's Press 2012 64 p. chiefly col. ill., col. map (library) $30.00; (paperback) $8.95

Grades: 4 5 6   973.7
1. Appomattox Campaign, 1865 2. United States -- History -- 1861-1865, Civil War -- Peace 3. United States -- History -- Civil War, 1861-1865 -- Peace
ISBN 0531250415; 9780531250419; 9780531265666

LC 2011011967

This book by Peter Benoit, part of the "Cornerstones of Freedom" series, describes the events leading up to the end of the U.S. Civil War. It "sketches the events of the Battle of the Wilderness and the capture of Richmond as well as the meeting between [Ulysses S.] Grant and [Robert E.] Lee on April 9, 1865." (School Library Journal)

Includes bibliographical references (p. 61) and index.

Bobrick, Benson

The **Battle** of Nashville; General George H. Thomas & the most decisive battle of the Civil War. Alfred A. Knopf 2010 132p il map $19.99; lib bdg $22.99

Grades: 7 8 9 10   973.7
1. Nashville (Tenn.), Battle of, 1864 2. United States -- History -- 1861-1865, Civil War
ISBN 978-0-375-84887-2; 0-375-84887-8; 978-0-375-94887-9 lib bdg; 0-375-94887-2 lib bdg

"Background, strategies, and key individuals involved in the 1864 battle of Nashville come to life in this engaging piece of history. Starting on the eve of the fighting, the narrative then shifts back to examine the complex series of events leading to that moment, outlining the causes of the Civil War, key developments, and major figures. . . . Battle scenes are vivid, capturing the chaos and emotion involved, and military strategies, such as the innovative use of cavalry, are explained clearly. Plentiful illustrations from the period, including many portraits and several dramatic two-page paintings, help bring the period to life." SLJ

Includes bibliographical references

Bolden, Tonya

★ **Cause** : Reconstruction America, 1863-1877. Knopf 2005 138p il $19.95; lib bdg $21.99

Grades: 7 8 9 10   973.7
1. Reconstruction (1865-1876) 2. United States -- History -- 1865-1898
ISBN 0-375-82795-1; 0-375-92795-6 lib bdg

"This examination of America during Reconstruction covers Lincoln's Proclamation of Amnesty and Reconstruction, the Civil Rights Act of 1866, the troubles of freed slaves, the expansion of the nation and the plight of Native Americans, the 15th Amendment, and the women's suffrage movement. While this is well-documented nonfiction, Bolden writes in the voice of a storyteller. The excellent graphics include archival photos, political cartoons, and primary resources." SLJ

Emancipation Proclamation; Lincoln and the dawn of liberty. Tonya Bolden. Abrams Books for Young Readers 2012 128 p. (alk. paper) $24.95

Grades: 6 7 8 9   **973.7**
1. Slaves -- Emancipation 2. Emancipation
Proclamation 3. United States -- History -- 1861-1865,
Civil War 4. Slaves -- Emancipation -- United States
ISBN 1419703900; 9781419703904
LC 2012000845

This book offers a "depiction of the issues and tensions
surrounding abolition and the development of [Abraham]
Lincoln's responses to them as the United States plunged
into the Civil War. . . . The author tracks rising tides of both
rhetoric and violence, as well as the evolution of President
Abraham Lincoln's determined efforts to forge a policy that
would serve military, political and moral necessities alike."
(Kirkus Reviews)

Includes bibliographical references and index

Burgan, Michael
North over South; final victory in the Civil War.
Compass Point Books 2011 64p il map (The Civil
War) lib bdg $33.32; pa $6.95
Grades: 5 6 7 8   **973.7**
1. United States -- History -- 1861-1865, Civil War
ISBN 978-0-7565-4369-3 lib bdg; 0-7565-4369-X lib
bdg; 978-0-7565-4413-3 pa; 0-7565-4413-0 pa
LC 2010001018

Recounts the end of the Civil War with insight into the
key victories at Gettysburg and Vicksburg.

The layout is "clean and attractive, with a large font and
reproductions of period illustrations and photos. . . . This . . .
will help students understand the era's most important issues
and events. A quality choice for reports." SLJ

Includes glossary and bibliographical references

Carlisle, Rodney P.
Civil War and Reconstruction. Facts on File
2008 452p il map (Eyewitness history) $75
Grades: 7 8 9 10   **973.7**
1. Reconstruction (1865-1876) 2. United States --
History -- 1861-1865, Civil War -- Sources
ISBN 978-0-8160-6347-5
LC 2006-35425

First published 1991 under the authorship of Joe
H. Kirchberger

"This illustrated chronology of the Civil War contains
over 100 black-and-white photographs (mostly from the
Library of Congress Prints and Photographs Division), 16
maps, and biographies of 50 key figures in the era. Each
period-based chapter offers a narrative that delves into
deeper issues of the causation of war; a chronicle of events,
detailed to the week; and eyewitness testimony, including diaries, journals, correspondence, editorials, and news
accounts." Choice

Includes bibliographical references

The **Civil** War; James Tackach, book editor. Greenhaven Press 2004 186 p. ill. (Turning points)
(library) $42.15
Grades: 7 8 9 10   **973.7**
1. United States -- History -- 1861-1865, Civil War
ISBN 0737711140; 9780737711141
LC 2003064297

"Comprised of 17 essays, this book is divided into four
chapters: 'A Nation Divides: The Causes of the Civil War,'
'Early Battlefield Victories and the Prospect of European Intervention Fuel the South's Hope for Independence,' 'The
North Gains the Advantage,' and 'A Changed Nation.' Many
of the most respected Civil War historians . . . are excerpted.
. . . Outstanding features of the book are discussion questions and the appendix of documents that are sure to inspire
additional research and assist classroom teachers." SLJ

Includes bibliographical references (p. 179-181)
and index.

A **Civil** War scrapbook; I was there too! History
Colorado. Fulcrum Pub. 2012 64 p. ill. (some
col.), maps (paperback) $14.95
Grades: 4 5 6 7 8   **973.7**
1. United States -- History -- 1861-1865, Civil War
ISBN 1555916686; 9781555916688
LC 2011042043

This book is "a multicultural Civil War history for children. The book . . . feature[es] chronological information"
and "focus[es] on the different types of people and their
place in the war. This . . . book emphasizes the roles of the
children, women, minorities, and even pets that became
mascots in the war." Also included are "historical photographs, drawings, maps, games, and primary quotes from
children." (Publisher's Note)

Includes bibliographical references (p. 62-63) and index.

★ The **Civil** War: a visual history. DK Pub. 2011
360p il map $40
Grades: 5 6 7 8   **973.7**
1. United States -- History -- 1815-1861 2. United
States -- History -- 1865-1898 3. United States --
History -- 1861-1865, Civil War -- Pictorial works
ISBN 978-0-7566-7185-3; 0-7566-7185-X

"A stunning, large-format pictorial history. The seven
chapters are arranged chronologically, beginning with an
overview of slavery in the United States, 1815 to 1860, and
ending with a survey of the legacies of the conflict during
the period 1865 to 1877. . . . Chapter introductions are followed by illustrated time lines and by short topical divisions
that include biographies, maps, original documents or eyewitness accounts, illustrations, historical photographs, artifacts, and reproductions of paintings. Page layouts and the
use of color are superb, and sidebars abound, adding to this
extraordinary book." SLJ

Cooke, Tim
Weapons, tactics, and strategy; edited by Tim
Cooke. Brown Bear Books 2011 112p il (Curricu-
lum connections: Civil War) lib bdg $39.95
Grades: 7 8 9 10   **973.7**
1. Reference books 2. Military art and science 3.
United States -- History -- 1861-1865, Civil War --
Encyclopedias
ISBN 978-1-936333-46-2; 1-936333-46-5
LC 2011005412

In an alphabetical almanac format, describes the weapons used, tactics invented, and strategies employed by both
sides during the U.S. Civil War.

"Well researched and clearly written, the chapters offer informative discussions supported by sidebars, page references to related content in other chapters, and definitions of terms in the margins. . . . The many small illustrations include period photos as well as prints, drawings, and paintings. A useful addition to library collections." Booklist

DeFord, Deborah H.

African Americans during the Civil War; [by] Deborah H. DeFord. Chelsea House 2006 112p il map (Slavery in the Americas) $35

Grades: 6 7 8 9 **973.7**

1. African American soldiers 2. African Americans -- History 3. United States -- History -- 1861-1865, Civil War

ISBN 0-8160-6138-6

LC 2005021497

This "covers not only African Americans but also the forces that created the 'U.S. Colored Troops' and the spread of rights during and after the war. . . . Clearly written, accessible, and well organized, [this] volume is illustrated with black-and-white drawings, period photographs, and explanatory text boxes." SLJ

Includes bibliographical references

Golay, Michael

Civil War; rev ed.; Chelsea House 2011 266p il map (America at war) lib bdg $45

Grades: 8 9 10 11 12 **973.7**

1. United States -- History -- 1861-1865, Civil War

ISBN 978-0-8160-8190-5 lib bdg; 0-8160-8190-5 lib bdg

First published 1992

An account of the Civil War, discussing political background, military strategy, and battles.

Includes glossary and bibliographical references

Gourley, Catherine

The **horrors** of Andersonville; life and death inside a Civil War prison. Twenty-First Century Books 2010 193p il lib bdg $38.60

Grades: 8 9 10 11 12 **973.7**

1. War criminals 2. Prisoners of war 3. Army officers 4. Andersonville Prison 5. United States -- History -- 1861-1865, Civil War -- Prisoners and prisons

ISBN 978-0-7613-4212-0; 0-7613-4212-5

LC 2008-46595

"This well-researched book describes the notorious Confederate prison camp known as Andersonville, where more than 45,000 Union soldiers lived in deplorable conditions and some 13,000 died, beginning in 1864. . . . Illustrated with many captioned photos and prints and enlivened with quotes from firsthand accounts, this book provides a balanced, informative introduction to Andersonville." Booklist

Includes bibliographical references

Gregory, Josh

Gettysburg; by Josh Gregory. Children's Press 2012 64 p. chiefly col. ill. (library) $30.00; (paperback) $8.95

Grades: 4 5 6 **973.7**

1. Gettysburg (Pa.), Battle of, 1863

ISBN 0531250342; 9780531250341; 9780531265598

LC 2011010751

In this book on the 1863 Battle of Gettysburg, "[Josh] Gregory takes his readers back to the precursor events that set the stage for this meeting engagement pitting General [Robert E.] Lee's Army of Northern Virginia against General [George] Meade's oft times defeated Union Army of the Potomac. In the end the efforts of Lee's seemingly indomitable veterans were not enough to overcome the forces of fate and tactics." (Children's Literature)

Includes bibliographical references (p. 61) and index.

Hernandez, Roger E.

The **Civil** War, 1840s-1890s. Marshall Cavendish Benchmark 2008 80p il map (Hispanic America) lib bdg $34.21

Grades: 4 5 6 7 **973.7**

1. Latinos (U.S.) 2. Hispanic Americans 3. United States -- Ethnic relations 4. United States -- History -- 1861-1865, Civil War

ISBN 978-0-7614-2939-5 lib bdg; 0-7614-2939-5 lib bdg

LC 2007049525

Discusses Hispanic participation during the Civil War

Includes glossary and bibliographical references

Hillstrom, Kevin

American Civil War: almanac; [by] Kevin Hillstrom and Laurie Collier Hillstrom; Lawrence W. Baker, editor. U.X.L 2000 xlvi, 251, xlvii-lxip il $60

Grades: 8 9 10 11 12 **973.7**

1. Almanacs 2. Reference books 3. United States -- History -- 1861-1865, Civil War

ISBN 0-7876-3823-4

LC 99-46918

Describes and interprets the era of the Civil War, its events, and topics with viewpoints, definitions, report topics, chronologies, sidebars, and statistics

"Added features such as 'Words to Know' and 'People to Know' sidebars in each chapter and research and activity ideas help make the volume a good jumping-off point for research on Civil War-era events." Booklist

Includes bibliographical references

American Civil War: biographies; [by] Kevin Hillstrom and Laurie Collier Hillstrom; Lawrence W. Baker, editor. U.X.L 2000 2v il (American Civil War reference library) set $110

Grades: 8 9 10 11 12 **973.7**

1. United States -- History -- 1861-1865, Civil War -- Biography

ISBN 0-7876-3820-X

LC 99-46920

This set "chronicles the lives of 60 famous and lesser-known men and women, including abolitionists, spies, commanders, and writers." SLJ

Includes bibliographical references

American Civil War: primary sources; [by] Kevin Hillstrom and Laurie Collier Hillstrom; Lawrence W. Baker, editor. U.X.L 2000 xxxi, 176, xxxiii-xliiip il $60

Grades: 8 9 10 11 12   **973.7**

   1. United States -- History -- 1861-1865, Civil War -- Sources

   ISBN 0-7876-3824-2

                      LC 99-46919

This volume "offers 14 full or excerpted speeches and written works. Each entry provides context, telling students what to keep in mind while reading the sources, as well as 'what happened next.' The speeches and writings come from Frederick Douglass, Abraham Lincoln, William Tecumseh Sherman, and Harriet Beecher Stowe, among others." Booklist

Experiencing the American Civil War; [by] Kevin Hillstrom and Laurie Collier Hillstrom; Lawrence W. Baker, editor. U.X.L 2002 2v il maps lib bdg set$105

Grades: 8 9 10 11 12   **973.7**

   1. Reference books 2. United States -- History -- 1861-1865, Civil War

   ISBN 0-7876-5585-6

"Although most useful as a supplementary source for classroom study, this reference tool has sufficient visual and textual appeal to arouse browers' curiosity about the materials discussed." SLJ

Includes bibliographical references

Holzer, Harold

The **president** is shot! the assassination of Abraham Lincoln. Boyds Mills Press 2004 181p il $17.95

Grades: 5 6 7 8   **973.7**

   1. Lawyers 2. Presidents 3. State legislators 4. Members of Congress

   ISBN 1-56397-985-3

"A page-turner of a text, a fascinating array of photos and archival illustrations, and an event that changed the course of history: all these elements combine in this strong, highly readable book." Booklist

Includes bibliographical references

Howse, Jennifer

The **Civil** War. Weigl Publishers 2009 48p il map (African American history) lib bdg $29.05; pa $10.95

Grades: 6 7 8 9   **973.7**

   1. African American soldiers 2. African Americans -- History 3. United States -- History -- 1861-1865, Civil War 4. United States -- Army -- African American troops -- History

   ISBN 978-1-59036-876-3 lib bdg; 1-59036-876-2 lib bdg; 978-1-59036-877-0 pa; 1-59036-877-0 pa

                  LC 2008-42478

"Howse creates a broad picture of the foundations leading to war, Afican Americans' role during the war, and finally the aftermath of the war, touching upon the civil rights movement. . . . This . . . is fabulous for students interested

in or researching history. Glossy pictures, quick facts, technology links, and sidebars of information interrupt the text, giving readers interesting and important information without overwhelming them." Voice Youth Advocates

Includes glossary and bibliographical references

Huey, Lois Miner

American archaeology uncovers the Underground Railroad. Marshall Cavendish Benchmark 2009 64p il map (American archaeology) lib bdg $21.95

Grades: 4 5 6 7   **973.7**

   1. Abolitionists 2. Underground railroad 3. Slavery -- United States 4. Excavations (Archeology) -- United States

   ISBN 978-0-7614-4267-7 lib bdg; 0-7614-4267-7 lib bdg

                  LC 2009003168

This describes how archeologists have learned about the history of the Underground Railroad.

This is "both intriguing and engaging for young readers. . . . A welcomed addition to classroom and school libraries." Libr Media Connect

Includes glossary and bibliographical references

Hughes, Chris

The **Battle** of Antietam. Blackbirch Press 2001 32p il maps (Civil War) $22.45

Grades: 6 7 8 9   **973.7**

   1. Antietam (Md.), Battle of, 1862

   ISBN 1-56711-551-9

                   LC 01-1572

Describes the 1862 battle in Maryland

This offers "a readable text that makes judicious use of quotes from participants. . . . Supplemental information about notable figures, locations, and incidents is included in sidebars, while historical reproductions and occasional photographs add further accessibility." Horn Book Guide

Includes glossary and bibliographical references

Isaacs, Sally Senzell

The **Civil** War; Sally Senzell Isaacs. Kingfisher 2011 32 p. ill., map (hardcover) $19.89

Grades: 3 4 5 6   **973.7**

   1. United States -- History -- 1861-1865, Civil War

   ISBN 0753466937; 9780753466933

                 LC 2011049248

This book is part of the "All About America" series which "covers the most important periods in the history of a burgeoning nation, from Colonists and Independence to The Civil War, and from Cowboys and the Wild West to the early inhabitants, the Native Americans." In this volume, readers learn about the American Civil War. (Publisher's note)

Jarrow, Gail

Lincoln's flying spies; Thaddeus Lowe and the Civil War Balloon Corp. Calkins Creek 2010 109p il $18.95

Grades: 7 8 9 10   **973.7**

   1. Spies 2. Balloons 3. Inventors 4. United States

-- History -- 1861-1865, Civil War
ISBN 978-1-59078-719-9; 1-59078-719-6

"This well-researched volume introduces American aeronaut and showman Thaddeus Lowe, who convinced President Lincoln that hydrogen-filled balloons, rising high above the countryside, could provide Union generals with useful information about the position, strength, and movements of Confederate troops and artillery. . . . The text offers a detailed account of [Lowe's] contribution to the Union war effort. Many period photos, prints, and drawings illustrate the book in black and white. . . . Jarrow provides a solid introduction to an intriguing aspect of Civil War history." Booklist

Includes bibliographical references

Johnson, Jennifer
  Gettysburg; the bloodiest battle of the Civil War. Franklin Watts 2009 64p il map (24/7 goes to war) lib bdg $27; pa $7.95
  Grades: 4 5 6   973.7
    1. Gettysburg (Pa.), Battle of, 1863
    ISBN 978-0-531-25528-5 lib bdg; 0-531-25528-X lib bdg; 978-0-531-25453-0 pa; 0-531-25453-4 pa
                                                  LC 2009016545
  The author has done "a remarkable job of discussing and describing [the Civil War Battle of Gettysburg] in a limited number of pages. . . . The [book provides a] solid [introduction], followed by three chapters, one of which is based on the personal experiences of a named soldier, and the other two covering broader historical details and strategies of the battle. . . . Excellent maps and plenty of paintings and vintage photos enhance the [text]." SLJ

  Includes bibliographical references

Jordan, Anne Devereaux
  ★ The **Civil** War; by Anne Devereaux Jordan; with Virginia Schomp. Marshall Cavendish Benchmark 2007 72p il (Drama of African-American history) lib bdg $34.21
  Grades: 5 6 7 8   973.7
    1. African Americans -- History 2. United States -- History -- 1861-1865, Civil War
    ISBN 978-0-7614-2179-5 lib bdg; 0-7614-2179-3 lib bdg
                                                  LC 2006012472
  Describes the role of African Americans during the Civil War (1861-1865)

  Includes glossary and bibliographical references

Landau, Elaine
  ★ **Fleeing** to freedom on the Underground Railroad; the courageous slaves, agents, and conductors. Twenty-First Century Books 2006 88p il map (People's history) lib bdg $26.60
  Grades: 5 6 7 8   973.7
    1. Abolitionists 2. Underground railroad 3. Slavery -- United States
    ISBN 978-0-8225-3490-7 lib bdg; 0-8225-3490-8 lib bdg
                                                  LC 2005020358
  "Landau discusses the history of slavery in the United States, slave life, the Underground Railroad, and the leaders,

both black and white, of antislavery organizations. Three chapters outline specifics of slaves' escapes. . . . An outstanding feature of this book is the use of primary sources and quotes from former slaves, contemporary newspaper accounts, and reminiscences of escaped slaves. . . . Excellent historical photographs and illustrations enhance the text." SLJ

Includes bibliographical references

Matthews, Tom L.
  Grierson's raid; a daring cavalry strike through the heart of the Confederacy. [by] Tom Lalicki; original maps by David Cain. Farrar, Straus and Giroux 2004 200p il map $18
  Grades: 7 8 9 10   973.7
    1. United States -- History -- 1861-1865, Civil War -- Campaigns
    ISBN 0-374-32787-4
                                                  LC 2003-49253
  Describes Colonel Benjamin H. Grierson's sixteen-day raid through central Mississippi in the spring of 1863, which distracted Confederate attention while Union troops moved on Vicksburg

  "The use of firsthand accounts brings the events vividly to life in a way that makes the book read more like an adventure story than a history text. . . . Accessibly written and scrupulously researched." Booklist

  Includes glossary and bibliographical references

McNeese, Tim
  The **abolitionist** movement; ending slavery. Chelsea House 2007 142p il (Reform movements in American history) lib bdg $30
  Grades: 8 9 10 11 12   973.7
    1. Abolitionists 2. Slavery -- United States
    ISBN 978-0-7910-9502-7; 0-7910-9502-9
                                                  LC 2007-14766
  "Complex, detailed, and yet very readable, this title . . . discusses the struggles and differences within the antislavery movement as well as the fight for emancipation and its crucial role in the Civil War. . . . The book offers a sound exploration of the topic." Booklist

  Includes bibliographical references

  Civil War battles. Chelsea House Publishers 2009 140p il (Civil War: a nation divided) lib bdg $35
  Grades: 6 7 8 9   973.7
    1. United States -- History -- 1861-1865, Civil War -- Campaigns
    ISBN 978-1-60413-034-8 lib bdg; 1-60413-034-2 lib bdg
                                                  LC 2008-26561
  This describes battles of the Civil War

  Includes glossary and bibliographical references

  The **Civil** War era, 1851-1865; consulting editor, Richard Jensen. Chelsea House 2010 144p il map (Discovering U.S. history) $35

Grades: 5 6 7 8   **973.7**
  1. United States -- History -- 1861-1865, Civil War
  ISBN 978-1-60413-352-3; 1-60413-352-X

          LC 2009-3660

"The information is accurate and easy to understand. Pictures are well placed, and primary sources are included. . . . The maps are well done and there are sidebars with additional information. . . . [This would be good] to have on hand for reports as it is well laid out and easy to use." Libr Media Connect

Includes glossary and bibliographical references

Civil War leaders. Chelsea House Publishers 2009 144p il (Civil War: a nation divided) lib bdg $35

Grades: 6 7 8 9   **973.7**
  1. United States -- History -- 1861-1865, Civil War -- Biography
  ISBN 978-1-60413-033-1 lib bdg; 1-60413-033-4 lib bdg

          LC 2009-655

This "features Abraham Lincoln, Jefferson Davis, Robert E. Lee, Ulysses S. Grant, Thomas 'Stonewall' Jackson, and Frederick Douglass. A short biography is followed by a brief description of the individual's part in the Civil War. . . . [The book includes] many black-and-white and color photographs and reproductions. . . . [This] well-organized [volume is a] first-rate [introduction] for students beginning their study of the era, or for those who want a basic review." SLJ

Includes glossary and bibliographical references

McPherson, James M.

Fields of fury; the American Civil War. Atheneum Bks. for Young Readers 2002 96p il map $22.95

Grades: 5 6 7 8   **973.7**
  1. United States -- History -- 1861-1865, Civil War
  ISBN 0-689-84833-1

          LC 2001-46048

Examines the events and effects of the American Civil War

"McPherson writes with authority, offering a broad overview as well as many details and anecdotes that give his account a human dimension. . . . The many fine illustrations include period photographs, paintings, prints, some excellent maps." Booklist

Includes glossary and bibliographical references

Mountjoy, Shane

Causes of the Civil War; the differences between the North and South. Chelsea House Publishers 2009 136p il (Civil War: a nation divided) lib bdg $35

Grades: 6 7 8 9   **973.7**
  1. United States -- History -- 1861-1865, Civil War -- Causes
  ISBN 978-1-60413-036-2 lib bdg; 1-60413-036-9 lib bdg

          LC 2008-30242

Examines the sectional rivalries that surfaced in the early 19th century and intensified in the decades leading up to the war

This "is especially well written. Its eight chapters outline the economic, social, and political causes of the war.

There are careful explanations of the importance of slavery to southern states, nullification and states' rights, the controversy of slavery expanding to western territories, and the impact of Lincoln's election to the presidency in 1860. [The book includes] many black-and-white and color photographs and reproductions." SLJ

Includes glossary and bibliographical references

Technology and the Civil War. Chelsea House Publishers 2009 136p il (Civil War: a nation divided) lib bdg $35

Grades: 6 7 8 9   **973.7**
  1. Technology -- History 2. United States -- History -- 1861-1865, Civil War
  ISBN 978-1-60413-037-9 lib bdg; 1-60413-037-7 lib bdg

          LC 2008-26563

This "describes advancements sparked by the Civil War: the creation of new ships and weaponry, the use of the railroad to move troops and supplies, and of the telegraph to speed dispersal of information, and improvements in medicine and photography. The book also outlines how many of the inventions and innovations of the period laid the foundation for America's economic growth in the following decades. . . . Sidebars, quotes from primary sources, color and black-and-white illustrations, and historical photographs are scattered throughout [this] clearly written, well-organized [text]." SLJ

Includes glossary and bibliographical references

Murphy, Jim

★ The **boys'** war; Confederate and Union soldiers talk about the Civil War. Clarion Bks. 1990 110p il hardcover o.p. pa $8.95

Grades: 5 6 7 8 9 10   **973.7**
  1. United States -- History -- 1861-1865, Civil War
  ISBN 0-89919-893-7; 0-395-66412-8 pa

          LC 89-23959

This book includes diary entries, personal letters, and archival photographs to describe the experiences of boys, sixteen years old or younger, who fought in the Civil War.

"An excellent selection of more than 45 sepia-toned contemporary photographs augment the text of this informative, moving work." SLJ

Includes bibliographical references

★ The **long** road to Gettysburg. Clarion Bks. 1992 116p il maps $17; pa $7.95

Grades: 5 6 7 8 9 10   **973.7**
  1. Gettysburg (Pa.), Battle of, 1863
  ISBN 0-395-55965-0; 0-618-05157-0 pa

          LC 90-21881

Describes the events of the Battle of Gettysburg in 1863 as seen through the eyes of two actual participants, nineteen-year-old Confederate lieutenant John Dooley and seventeen-year-old Union soldier Thomas Galway. Also discusses Lincoln's famous speech delivered at the dedication of the National Cemetery at Gettysburg

The author "uses all of his fine skills as an information writer—clarity of detail, conciseness, understanding of his age group, and ability to find the drama appealing to readers—to frame a well-crafted account of a single battle in the war." Horn Book

Includes bibliographical references

★ A **savage** thunder; Antietam and the bloody road to freedom. Margaret K. McElderry Books 2009 103p il map $17.99

Grades: 5 6 7 8 9 **973.7**

1. Generals 2. Governors 3. Antietam (Md.), Battle of, 1862 4. College presidents 5. Presidential candidates 6. United States -- History -- 1861-1865, Civil War

ISBN 978-0-689-87633-2; 0-689-87633-5

LC 2008-32738

"Murphy provides readers with a lucid and compelling narrative, drawn mainly from firsthand accounts. . . . Replete with excellent-quality archival photos, reproductions, and maps, this is an outstanding account of a battle." SLJ

Includes bibliographical references

Nardo, Don

Bull Run to Gettysburg; early battles of the Civil War. Compass Point Books 2011 64p il map (The Civil War) lib bdg $33.32; pa $6.95

Grades: 5 6 7 8 **973.7**

1. United States -- History -- 1861-1865, Civil War -- Campaigns

ISBN 978-0-7565-4368-6 lib bdg; 0-7565-4368-1 lib bdg; 978-0-7565-4411-9 pa; 0-7565-4411-4 pa

LC 2010001017

Reviews the early battles of the Civil War from the attack on Fort Sumter and the battle of the ironclads to Bull Run and Gettysburg.

The layout is "clean and attractive, with a large font and reproductions of period illustrations and photos. . . . This . . . will help students understand the era's most important issues and events. A quality choice for reports." SLJ

Includes glossary and bibliographical references

A **nation** divided; the long road to the Civil War. Compass Point Books 2010 64p il map (The Civil War) lib bdg $33.32

Grades: 5 6 7 8 **973.7**

1. Southern States -- History 2. United States -- History -- 1861-1865, Civil War -- Causes

ISBN 978-0-7565-4367-9 lib bdg; 0-7565-4367-3 lib bdg

LC 2010001016

Recounts events leading up to the Civil War and provides insight into the economic, cultural, and educational differences of the Northerners and Southerners.

The layout is "clean and attractive, with a large font and reproductions of period illustrations and photos. . . . This . . . will help students understand the era's most important issues and events. A quality choice for reports." SLJ

Includes glossary and bibliographical references

Netzley, Patricia D.

Civil War. Greenhaven Press 2004 336p il (Greenhaven encyclopedia of) lib bdg $74.95

Grades: 8 9 10 11 12 **973.7**

1. Reference books 2. United States -- History -- 1861-

1865, Civil War -- Encyclopedias

ISBN 0-7377-0438-1

LC 2003-11808

An alphabetical presentation of definitions and descriptions of terms, people, and events of the Civil War

"Basic, accurate information about many aspects of the war. . . . The well-written, objective entries are cross-referenced. . . . Netzley's solid volume will be helpful to students needing introductory research material." SLJ

Includes bibliographical references

O'Connor, Jim

What was the Battle of Gettysburg? by Jim O'Connor ; illustrated by John Mantha. Grosset & Dunlap 2013 106 p. (hc) $15.99

Grades: 3 4 5 6 **973.7**

1. Gettysburg (Pa.), Battle of, 1863 2. United States -- History -- 1861-1865, Civil War

ISBN 0448465752; 9780448462868; 9780448465753

LC 2012027557

This book, by Jim O'Connor, John Mantha, and James Bennett, "offers a strongly contextualized account of the bloodiest engagement of the Civil War and a mostly chronological discussion of the battle. Chapters, each beginning with a historical date, tell the story in a narrative format, but the story is effectively broken up with boxed biographies of such figures as Mathew Brady, Jeb Stuart, and Abraham Lincoln." (Booklist)

Includes bibliographical references (p. 106)

Osborne, Linda Barrett

★ **Traveling** the freedom road; from slavery and the Civil War through Reconstruction. Abrams Books for Young Readers 2009 128p il map $24.95

Grades: 6 7 8 9 10 **973.7**

1. Reconstruction (1865-1876) 2. Slavery -- United States 3. African Americans -- History 4. United States -- History -- 1861-1865, Civil War 5. United States -- Politics and government -- 1783-1865 6. United States -- Politics and government -- 1865-1898

ISBN 978-0-8109-8338-0; 0-8109-8338-9

LC 2008-22298

"This fascinating, well-designed volume offers an essential introduction to the experiences of African Americans between 1800 and 1877. . . . Osborne moves from . . . personal stories to broader historical milestones, and in highly accessible language, she provides basic background even as she challenges readers with philosophical questions. . . . This fluid exchange between political events and intimate, human stories creates a highly absorbing whole." Booklist

Porterfield, Jason

The **Lincoln** -Douglas senatorial debates of 1858; a primary source investigation. [by] Jason Porterfield. 1st ed; Rosen Central Primary Sources 2005 64p il map (Great historic debates and speeches) lib bdg $29.25

Grades: 5 6 7 8 **973.7**

1. Lawyers 2. Presidents 3. Senators 4. Political leaders 5. State legislators 6. Members of Congress 7.

Presidential candidates
ISBN 1-4042-0153-X

LC 2003-25408

Discusses the debates between Lincoln and Douglas and how they influenced political campaigns throughout history.

This "readable [text provides a] balanced [overview]. Primary-source materials include archival maps, photos, reproductions, letters, and speeches that are examined in context." SLJ

Includes bibliographical references

Raatma, Lucia

The **Underground** Railroad; by Lucia Raatma. Children's Press 2011 64 p. col. ill. (library) $30.00; (paperback) $8.95

Grades: 4 5 6   **973.7**

1. Fugitive slaves 2. Underground Railroad 3. Fugitive slaves -- United States -- History -- 19th century 4. Antislavery movements -- United States -- History -- 19th century

ISBN 0531250431; 9780531250433; 9780531265680

LC 2011009493

This book by Lucia Raatma is part of the Cornerstones of Freedom series and looks at the Underground Railroad. The entry "explains how the system worked, the journey, and important people who guided slaves such as Harriet Tubman and Levi and Catherine White Coffin of Indiana, who helped about 2,000 slaves reach freedom." (School Library Journal)

Includes bibliographical references (p. 61) and index.

Rees, Bob

The **Civil** War; by Bob Rees. Heinemann Library 2012 80 p. ill. (some col.), col. maps (library) $36.50; (paperback) $10.99

Grades: 6 7 8 9   **973.7**

1. United States -- History -- 1861-1865, Civil War 2. United States -- History -- Civil War, 1861-1865

ISBN 1432959964; 9781432959968; 9781432960056

LC 2011018258

This book by Bob Rees is part of the Living Through . . . series and looks at the U.S. Civil War. The "set summarizes events in major conflicts using brief first-person accounts, sidebars, short biographies, color and archival photos, maps, and other graphics." The authors include "views from multiple perspectives." (School Library Journal)

Includes bibliographical references (p. 76) and index.

Reis, Ronald A.

African Americans and the Civil War. Chelsea House Publishers 2009 134p il (The Civil War: a nation divided) lib bdg $35

Grades: 6 7 8 9   **973.7**

1. African American soldiers 2. Slavery -- United States 3. United States -- History -- 1861-1865, Civil War

ISBN 978-1-60413-038-6 lib bdg; 1-60413-038-5 lib bdg

LC 2008-25665

This describes the roles African Americans played in the Civil War

Includes glossary and bibliographical references

Rottman, Gordon L.

The **most** daring raid of the Civil War; the great locomotive chase. Rosen Pub. 2011 64p il map (The most daring raids in history) lib bdg $29.25

Grades: 7 8 9 10   **973.7**

1. Chattanooga, Battle of, 1863 2. United States -- History -- 1861-1865, Civil War

ISBN 978-1-4488-1870-9; 1-4488-1870-2

LC 2010030195

In a daring attempt to cut off the supply lines of Confederate forces, Union soldiers planned to steal a train and disable the line as they traveled to Chattanooga, TN. One man's daring pursuit led to their ultimate failure. This book tells the story of how the raid was planned, and how it ultimately fell apart.

This book is "packed with facts, covering the details of the action, the people involved, and the tools used, in engaging prose. The authors cite their sources thoroughly. . . . Diagrams, . . . and maps make the action easy to follow and provide visual context for the raids. . . . This . . . is sure to find a large readership." SLJ

Includes glossary and bibliographical references

Seidman, Rachel Filene

The **Civil** war: a history in documents. Oxford University Press 2001 206p il map (Pages from history) lib bdg $39.95

Grades: 8 9 10 11 12   **973.7**

1. United States -- History -- 1861-1865, Civil War -- Sources

ISBN 978-0-19-511558-1; 0-19-511558-9

LC 00-37523

"Seidman's documents bookend the Civil War with the territorial expansion that preceded the conflict and with the Reconstruction that followed it. In this structure the documents, under the guidance of Seidman's linking narrative, all make a powerful impression of immediacy about ordinary people's experience of, and condemnation or defense of, slavery." Booklist

Includes bibliographical references

Silvey, Anita

★ **I'll** pass for your comrade; women soldiers in the Civil War. Clarion Books 2008 115p il map $17

Grades: 6 7 8 9   **973.7**

1. Women soldiers 2. United States -- History -- 1861-1865, Civil War

ISBN 978-0-618-57491-9; 0-618-57491-3

LC 2008018053

This "spotlights Union and Confederate women who fought on the battlefields. . . . Period photos, prints, drawings, and documents are among the many illustrations. . . . Well researched and clearly written, this attractive book illuminates an aspect of the Civil War that is often overlooked." Booklist

Includes bibliographical references

Slavicek, Louise Chipley

Women and the Civil War. Chelsea House Publishers 2009 128p il (The Civil War: a nation divided) lib bdg $35

Grades: 6 7 8 9   **973.7**
1. Women -- United States -- History 2. United States
-- History -- 1861-1865, Civil War -- Women
ISBN 978-1-60413-040-9 lib bdg; 1-60413-040-7
lib bdg

LC 2008-26562

"After a historical overview, six chapters . . . present information on female roles during the [Civil] war. . . . Women worked as nurses and caregivers and organized aid and relief societies. . . . Hundreds disguised themselves as men to fight and others worked as spies and saboteurs. They were forced to oversee and run family farms and plantations or to find employment in factories or government offices. A chapter on African-American women reviews how the war impacted their lives and mentions significant figures such as Harriet Tubman. Sidebars, quotes from primary sources, color and black-and-white illustrations, and historical photographs are scattered throughout [this] clearly written, well-organized [text]." SLJ

Includes glossary and bibliographical references

Stein, R. Conrad

Escaping slavery on the Underground Railroad; [by] R. Conrad Stein. Enslow Publishers 2008 128p il (From many cultures, one history) lib bdg $31.93
Grades: 6 7 8 9   **973.7**
1. Abolitionists 2. Underground railroad 3. Slavery -- United States
ISBN 978-0-7660-2799-2 lib bdg; 0-7660-2799-6 lib bdg

LC 2007015124

This is an account of American slavery, the Abolitionist movement, and escapes from slavery on the The Underground Railroad.

This "will provide clear, easy-to-understand facts with critical analysis and will be useful for reports." Libr Media Connect

Includes glossary and bibliographical references

Sullivan, George

The **Civil** War at sea. 21st Cent. Bks. (Brookfield) 2001 80p il lib bdg $27.90
Grades: 8 9 10 11 12   **973.7**
1. United States -- History -- 1861-1865, Civil War -- Naval operations
ISBN 0-7613-1553-5

LC 00-41805

"The illustrations and reproductions included here and the lively text will appeal to every Civil War buff, and will be an excellent source of information for reports." SLJ

Includes bibliographical references

Swanson, James L.

★ **Bloody** times; the funeral of Abraham Lincoln and the manhunt for Jefferson Davis. Collins 2011 196p il $16.99
Grades: 6 7 8 9   **973.7**
1. Lawyers 2. Statesmen 3. Presidents 4. Senators 5. Political leaders 6. State legislators 7. Secretaries of war 8. Members of Congress 9. United States --

History -- 1861-1865, Civil War
ISBN 978-0-06-156089-7; 0-06-156089-8

LC 2010045611

An adaptation for young people of Bloody Crimes, published 2010 by William Morrow for adults

This tells "the story of Lincoln's assassination, detailing the funeral and the return of the body for burial in Springfield, IL. Juxtaposed with this compelling drama is that of Jefferson Davis, president of the Confederate States of America, as he learned of Lee's surrender and traveled across the South trying to keep the Confederacy alive while being pursued by Federal forces bent on his arrest. . . . Lincoln's body was placed aboard a train that retraced the route taken by Lincoln as he traveled to the capital as president-elect. Readers will be fascinated by the details needed to plan this trip and the people involved. . . . Just as riveting is Davis's fruitless effort to avoid arrest. . . . A brilliant book that is sure to be a hit with history aficionados." SLJ

Includes glossary and bibliographical references

★ **Chasing** Lincoln's killer; the search for John Wilkes Booth. Scholastic Press 2009 194p il map $16.99
Grades: 7 8 9 10   **973.7**
1. Actors 2. Lawyers 3. Presidents 4. Murderers 5. State legislators 6. Members of Congress 7. United States -- History -- 1861-1865, Civil War
ISBN 978-0-439-90354-7; 0-439-90354-8

LC 2008-17994

"This volume is an adaptation of Swanson's Manhunt: The 12-Day Chase for Lincoln's Killer (HarperCollins, 2006). Divided into 14 chapters and an epilogue, the sentences are shorter and chapters are condensed from the original but the rich details and suspense are ever present. . . . Excellent black-and-white illustrations complement the text. . . . Readers will be engrossed by the almost hour-by-hour search and by the many people who encountered the killer as he tried to escape. It is a tale of intrigue and an engrossing mystery." SLJ

Trudeau, Noah Andre

Like men of war; black troops in the Civil War, 1862-1865. Little, Brown 1998 xxii, 548p il maps hardcover o.p. pa $18
Grades: 7 8 9 10   **973.7**
1. African American soldiers 2. United States -- History -- 1861-1865, Civil War
ISBN 0-316-85325-9; 0-316-85344-5 pa

LC 97-15380

A "study of the battlefield experiences of black Union regiments. Some 60 maps help the reader make sense of famous engagements (Fort Wagner and the Crater) and notorious incidents (Fort Pillow) in which black soldiers fought, as well as scores of lesser-known clashes. Rich archival research is integrated into a lively narrative that places the raising and deployment of black regiments in broader contexts. This book will become a basic source of information on the subject." Libr J

Includes bibliographical references

Uschan, Michael V., 1948-

The **cavalry** during the Civil War. Lucent Bks. 2003 112p il maps (Working life) $27.45

Grades: 6 7 8 9   973.7

1. Soldiers -- United States 2. United States -- Army -- Cavalry 3. Confederate States of America -- Army -- Cavalry 4. United States -- History -- 1861-1865, Civil War

ISBN 1-59018-175-1

LC 2002-11840

This examines the life of cavalry soldiers during the civil war

This is "well written and the authors draw on and quote from many primary sources." Libr Media Connect

Includes bibliographical references

Wagner, Heather Lehr

Spies in the Civil War. Chelsea House Publishers 2009 112p il (The Civil War: a nation divided) lib bdg $35

Grades: 6 7 8 9   973.7

1. Spies 2. United States -- History -- 1861-1865, Civil War

ISBN 978-1-60413-039-3 lib bdg; 1-60413-039-3 lib bdg

LC 2008-26568

This describes the work of Civil War spies Allan Pinkerton, Elizabeth Van Lew, Belle Boyd, and Rose O'Neal Greenhow and others

Includes glossary and bibliographical references

Walker, Sally M.

Secrets of a Civil War submarine; solving the mysteries of the H.L. Hunley. Carolrhoda Books 2005 112p il lib bdg $17.95

Grades: 7 8 9 10   973.7

1. Shipwrecks 2. Submarines 3. Underwater exploration 4. Hunley (Submarine) 5. United States -- History -- 1861-1865, Civil War -- Naval operations

ISBN 1-57505-830-8

LC 2004-19646

This discusses "the Confederate submarine H. L. Hunley. . . . Walker begins with the history of the Hunley's design and construction as well as its place in Civil War and naval history. She really hits her stride, though, in explaining the complex techniques and loving care used in raising the craft, recovering its contents, and even reconstructing models of the crewmembers' bodies. . . . Thoroughly researched, nicely designed, and well illustrated with clear, color photos." Booklist

Includes glossary and bibliographical references

Warren, Andrea

★ **Under** siege! three children at the Civil War battle for Vicksburg. Melanie Kroupa Books 2009 166p il map $21.95

Grades: 7 8 9 10   973.7

1. Vicksburg (Miss.) -- Siege, 1863 2. United States -- History -- 1861-1865, Civil War

ISBN 978-0-374-31255-8; 0-374-31255-9

LC 2008-1136

"Warren creates a compelling account of the 1863 siege at Vicksburg that follows three young people from December 1862 through the aftermath of the surrender on July 4, 1863. . . . The author uses primary sources throughout, including scores of quotes, many attributed to the children themselves, period photographs, maps, and paintings. . . . The back matter is extensive, including an annotated list of recommended Civil War books, a longer bibliography of sources, and extensive endnotes and illustration credits." Voice Youth Advocates

Includes bibliographical references and index

Watkins, Samuel R.

The **diary** of Sam Watkins, a confederate soldier; edited by Ruth Ashby; illustrations by Laszlo Kubinyi. Benchmark Bks. 2004 95p il (In my own words) lib bdg $18.95

Grades: 5 6 7 8   973.7

1. Soldiers 2. United States -- History -- 1861-1865, Civil War

ISBN 0-7614-1646-3

LC 2003-1478

Excerpts from the diary of a Confederate soldier from Tennessee, describing the battles he fought in during the Civil War

This offers "an engaging history lesson." Horn Book Guide

Includes bibliographical references

Weber, Jennifer L.

Summer's bloodiest days; the Battle of Gettysburg as told from all sides. foreword by James M. McPherson. National Geographic 2010 61p il map $17.95; lib bdg $27.90

Grades: 5 6 7 8   973.7

1. Gettysburg (Pa.), Battle of, 1863 2. United States -- History -- 1861-1865, Civil War

ISBN 978-1-4263-0706-5; 1-4263-0706-3; 978-1-4263-0707-2 lib bdg; 1-4263-0707-1 lib bdg

"This colorful book tells of the Battle of Gettysburg, a dramatic event that becomes even more compelling because the text is laced with pertinent quotes from those who were there. Weber's vivid, pithy writing packs a great deal of information and many anecdotes into a relatively short account. . . . Many battle maps, short, informative sidebars, and the use of modern realistic paintings and photos of artifacts as well as period photographs . . . illustrate the book." Booklist

Includes bibliographical references

Williams, Carla

The **Underground** Railroad. Child's World 2009 32p il (Journey to freedom) lib bdg $28.50

Grades: 4 5 6   973.7

1. Underground railroad 2. Slavery -- United States

ISBN 978-1-60253-139-0 lib bdg; 1-60253-139-0 lib bdg

LC 2008031946

"Underground Railroad describes how this secret system worked and introduces key figures. Williams discusses relevant laws and amendments as well as the advent and conclusion of the Civil War. The facts, presented through stories, historical news accounts, and biographical sketches of Harriet Tubman and Levi Weeks, capture the desperation of the enslaved as well as the abolitionists' commitment to them. The [book is] concise and direct, yet the writing remains sophisticated. Vibrant personal stories accompanied by striking photographs of historical figures and artifacts provide a sense of the subjects' hopes and dreams." SLJ

Includes glossary and bibliographical references

Woog, Adam

The **Emancipation** Proclamation; ending slavery in America. Chelsea House Publishers 2009 117p il (Milestones in American history) lib bdg $35

Grades: 6 7 8 9   **973.7**

1. Slavery -- United States   2. Emancipation Proclamation (1863)   3. United States -- History -- 1861-1865, Civil War

ISBN 978-1-60413-307-3 lib bdg; 1-60413-307-4 lib bdg

LC 2008030742

This explores Lincoln's proclamation which ended slavery during the Civil War

This offers "short, clearly written chapters. . . . [It is] amply illustrated with black-and-white and color photographs and reproductions and supported with biographical sketches and excerpts from primary documents." Horn Book Guide

Includes bibliographical references

973.8   United States--Reconstruction period, 1865-1901

Collier, Christopher

★ The **United** States enters the world stage: from the Alaska Purchase through World War I, 1867-1919; [by] Christopher Collier, James Lincoln Collier. Benchmark Bks. (Tarrytown) 2001 94p il map (Drama of American history) lib bdg $31.36

Grades: 6 7 8 9   **973.8**

1. World War, 1914-1918   2. Spanish-American War, 1898   3. United States -- Foreign relations   4. United States -- History -- 1865-1898   5. United States -- History -- 1898-1919

ISBN 0-7614-1053-8

LC 00-29483

This discusses topics in United States history and politics including Westward expansion, imperialism, the Spanish-American War, the Panama Canal, and World War I

Includes bibliographical references

Custer's last stand; Thomas Streissguth, book editor. Greenhaven Press 2003 142p il maps (At issue in history) lib bdg $21.96; pa $14.96

Grades: 7 8 9 10   **973.8**

1. Generals   2. Little Bighorn, Battle of the, 1876   3. Army officers

ISBN 0-7377-1358-5 lib bdg; 0-7377-1359-3 pa

LC 2002-27875

"Using primary and secondary sources, this volume examines the controversial history of the Battle at the Little

Bighorn in June, 1876. . . . Each of the 11 entries is preceded by a summary of the author's main points and conclusions. This excellent volume helps students understand the 'what' and 'why' of history." SLJ

Includes bibliographical references

Fitzgerald, Stephanie

Reconstruction; rebuilding America after the Civil War. Compass Point Books 2011 64p il map (The Civil War) lib bdg $33.32; pa $6.95

Grades: 5 6 7 8   **973.8**

1. Reconstruction (1865-1876)   2. United States -- History -- 1865-1898

ISBN 978-0-7565-4370-9 lib bdg; 0-7565-4370-3 lib bdg; 978-0-7565-4414-0 pa; 0-7565-4414-9 pa

LC 2010001019

Recounts the history of the Reconstruction, as the United States government and people worked to recover from the effects of the Civil War.

The layout is "clean and attractive, with a large font and reproductions of period illustrations and photos. . . . This . . . will help students understand the era's most important issues and events. A quality choice for reports." SLJ

Includes glossary and bibliographical references

The **Gilded** Age: a history in documents; [compiled by] Janette Thomas Greenwood. Oxford Univ. Press 2000 191p il map (Pages from history) $39.95; pa $24.95

Grades: 7 8 9 10   **973.8**

1. United States -- History -- 1865-1898

ISBN 978-0-19-510523-0; 0-19-510523-0; 978-0-19-516638-5 pa; 0-19-516638-8 pa

LC 99-98194

Uses a wide variety of documents to show how Americans dealt with an age of extremes from 1887 to 1900, including rapid industrialization, unemployment, unprecedented wealth, and immigration

"There's plenty to absorb and much to capture the imagination. . . . Greenwood presents the history as a seamless tapestry sewn by the people who lived it." Booklist

Includes bibliographical references

Hillstrom, Kevin

American Indian removal and the trail to Wounded Knee; [by] Kevin Hillstrom and Laurie Collier Hillstrom. Omnigraphics 2010 250p il (Defining moments) lib bdg $55

Grades: 8 9 10 11 12   **973.8**

1. Wounded Knee Creek, Battle of, 1890   2. Native Americans -- Relocation   3. Native Americans -- Great Plains

ISBN 978-0-7808-1129-4; 0-7808-1129-1

LC 2010-4676

"This well-written volume effectively explores a topic of intense historical debate. Fascinating sidebars add significantly to the text." SLJ

"Analyzes the development of Indian removal policies and the tragedy at Wounded Knee, the 1890 massacre of American Indians by U.S. Cavalry troops. Examines the wider context of Indian-white relations in America." Publisher's note

Includes glossary and bibliographical references

McNeese, Tim

The **Gilded** Age and Progressivism, 1891-1913; Tim McNeese ; consulting editor, Richard Jensen. Chelsea House 2010 136 p. ill. (some col.) (Discovering U.S. history) (library) $35.00

Grades: 5 6 7 8   973.8

1. Progressivism (United States politics) 2. -- History -- 19th century 3. United States -- History -- 1865-1921 4. United States -- Social conditions -- 1865-1918 5. United States -- Politics and government -- 1901-1953 6. Progressivism (United States politics) -- History -- 19th century 7. Progressivism (United States politics) -- History -- 20th century

ISBN 1604133554; 9781604133554

LC 2009015012

McNeese "discusses the people, politics, economic conditions, and foreign affairs of [the U.S. from 1891 to 1913], objectively explaining how the attitudes, perceptions, and expectations of the American people and their leaders shaped the development of the country. . . . Color period art and photos, maps, and cutaway drawings supplement the [text]." SLJ

Includes bibliographical references and index.

Reconstruction; life after the Civil War. Chelsea House Publishers 2009 140p il (The Civil War: a nation divided) lib bdg $35

Grades: 6 7 8 9   973.8

1. Reconstruction (1865-1876)

ISBN 978-1-60413-035-5 lib bdg; 1-60413-035-0 lib bdg

LC 2008-26564

"Reconstruction examines one of the most controversial eras in U.S. history. During Reconstruction, the nation sought to reestablish itself in the aftermath of the Civil War, to overcome regional politics, and to redefine the political, social, and economic realities of the nation's four million black citizens." Publisher's note

Includes glossary and bibliographical references

Ruggiero, Adriane

★ **American** voices from Reconstruction. Marshall Cavendish Benchmark 2006 103p il (American voices from--) lib bdg $37.07

Grades: 6 7 8 9 10 11 12   973.8

1. Reconstruction (1865-1876)

ISBN 978-0-7614-2168-9 lib bdg; 0-7614-2168-8 lib bdg

LC 2005-24949

This "does an excellent job of bringing history close. . . . The spacious design . . . is very approachable, and the combination of voices and commentary will readers think critically." Booklist

Includes glossary and bibliographical references

Sanders, Nancy I.

Frederick Douglass for kids; his life and times with 21 activities. Nancy I. Sanders. Chicago Review Press 2012 ix, 145 p.p ill. (paperback) $16.95; (ebook) $11.99; (prebind) $25.95

Grades: 5 6 7   973.8

1. Biography 2. Slavery -- History 3. African Americans -- Biography 4. Abolitionists -- United States -- Biography 5. African American abolitionists -- Biography 6. Antislavery movements -- United States -- Study and teaching -- Activity programs 7. Antislavery movements -- United States -- History -- 19th century

ISBN 1569767173; 9781569767177; 9781613743560; 9781451774788

LC 2011050092

Author Nancy I. Sanders presents information on Frederick Douglass. "Born on a plantation, he later escaped slavery and helped others to freedom via the Underground Railroad. In time he became a bestselling author, an outspoken newspaper editor, a brilliant orator, a tireless abolitionist, and a brave civil rights leader. He was famous on both sides of the Atlantic in the years leading up to the Civil War, and when war broke out, Abraham Lincoln invited him to the White House for counsel and advice." (Publisher's note)

Includes bibliographical references (p. 136-137) and index.

Stroud, Bettye

★ The **Reconstruction** era; by Bettye M. Stroud with Virginia Schomp. Marshall Cavendish Benchmark 2007 70p il (Drama of African-American history) lib bdg $34.21

Grades: 5 6 7 8   973.8

1. Reconstruction (1865-1876) 2. African Americans -- History

ISBN 978-0-7614-2181-8 lib bdg; 0-7614-2181-5 lib bdg

LC 2006012149

"Traces the history of Reconstruction, from the end of the Civil War in 1865 to 1877, when federal troops were removed from the South." Publisher's note

Includes glossary and bibliographical references

Telgen, Diane

The **Gilded** Age; Diane Telgen. Omnigraphics 2012 xvi, 252 p.p ill. (hardcover : alk. paper) $16.99

Grades: 7 8 9 10 11 12   973.8

1. United States -- History -- 1865-1898 2. United States -- History -- 1865-1921 -- Sources 3. United States -- History -- 1865-1921 4. United States -- Politics and government -- 1865-1933 -- Sources 5. United States -- History -- 1865-1921 -- Biography 6. United States -- Politics and government -- 1865-1933

ISBN 0780812387; 9780780812383

LC 2011048642

This book by Diane Telgen "surveys America's rapid economic, social, demographic, and political changes from the end of the Civil War to the dawn of the twentieth century. . . . The volume also explains how various hallmarks of this era -- including rapid industrialization and urbanization, the economic divide between rich and poor, political corruption and reform, and social and religious activism -- laid the groundwork for the United States we live in today." (Publisher's note)

Includes bibliographical references (p. 237-242) and index

Walker, Paul Robert

★ **Remember** Little Bighorn; Indians, soldiers, and scouts tell their stories. [by] Paul Robert Walker; [foreword by John A. Doerner] National Geographic Society 2006 61p il map $17.95; lib bdg $27.90

Grades: 5 6 7 8   **973.8**

1. Little Bighorn, Battle of the, 1876

ISBN 0-7922-5521-6; 0-7922-5522-4 lib bdg

LC 2005030929

This "volume gives an almost blow-by-blow account of the famous battle that came to be known as Custer's Last Stand. Walker concentrates on the battle itself, fought on the Great Plains in 1876, and the book includes diagrams of each side's tactics. . . . Walker's exhaustive research . . . [brings] together the conflicting viewpoints of the whites and the Lakota Sioux, Cheyenne, and Arapaho fighters, documenting everything in source notes. The handsome book design, with thick paper, clear type, maps, stirring photos, and archival images, will attract readers to the battle story and then start them thinking about lasting historical issues." Booklist

Includes bibliographical references

Worth, Richard

African Americans during Reconstruction; [by] Richard Worth. Chelsea House 2006 112p il map (Slavery in the Americas) $35

Grades: 6 7 8 9   **973.8**

1. Reconstruction (1865-1876) 2. African Americans -- Civil rights

ISBN 0-81606-139-4

LC 2005015720

Tells the history of African Americans from the end of the Civil War through the nation's reconstruction.

Includes bibliographical references

973.9   United States--1901-

Brill, Marlene Targ

America in the 1900s. Twenty-First Century Books 2010 144p il (The decades of twentieth-century America) lib bdg $38.60

Grades: 7 8 9 10   **973.9**

1. United States -- History -- 1898-1919

ISBN 978-0-8225-3436-5 lib bdg; 0-8225-3436-3 lib bdg

LC 2007-40983

This is an overview of the 1900's

"The text is clear but not condescending, with unfamiliar terms defined in parentheses. Frequent, mostly black-and-white photographs punctuate pages with clear print and lots of white space. Time lines recap major events, while 'To

Learn More' suggests not only books but also Web sites and films. . . . A worthwhile addition." Voice Youth Advocates

Includes bibliographical references

Sandler, Martin W.

★ The **Dust** Bowl through the lens; how photography revealed and helped remedy a national disaster. Walker & Co. 2008 96p il map $15.99; lib bdg $20.89

Grades: 5 6 7 8   **973.9**

1. Dust storms 2. Documentary photography 3. Great Plains -- History

ISBN 978-0-8027-9547-2; 0-8027-9547-1; 978-0-8027-9548-9 lib bdg; 0-8027-9548-X lib bdg

LC 2008-55979

"This excellent photo-essay traces the history of the Dust Bowl from its causes to its resolution. In tandem, Sandler treats the role of the budding field of photojournalism. Forty-four spreads feature a page of clear, direct text with a large, well-reproduced image, many of which are set on color pages. . . . Seldom has the connection between the arts and the general quality of life been made so clear. The text deals equally with those who fled the decimated Bread Basket for California and those who waited out the devastation and dust. Throughout, the use of primary sources is superb, with quotations from affected citizens, the photojournalists themselves, political and entertainment figures, and writers, giving a multifaceted picture of a seminal time in United States history." SLJ

973.91   United States--1901-1953

Allen, Michael Geoffrey

Calvin Coolidge. Enslow 2002 112p il (United States presidents) $20.95

Grades: 7 8 9 10   **973.91**

1. Governors 2. Presidents 3. Vice-presidents 4. Presidents -- United States

ISBN 0-7660-1703-6

LC 2001-4206

The author highlights President Coolidge's childhood, family influences, education, career, and journey to the White House. {The author does} an impressive job of emphasizing the strength of character of {the} president while still providing a balanced history of {his} influence on U.S. history. Booklist

Includes bibliographical references

Bingham, Jane

The **Great** Depression; the Jazz Age, Prohibition, and the Great Depression, 1921-1937. Chelsea House 2011 64p il (A cultural history of women in America) $35

Grades: 5 6 7 8   **973.91**

1. Great Depression, 1929-1939 2. Women -- United States 3. Women -- United States -- History

ISBN 978-1-60413-933-4; 1-60413-933-1

LC 2010044889

An "eye-catching [layout] with good use of color, photographs, and informative sidebars, many of which use primary-source quotations, are the highlights of [this] appealing [volume]. . . . After a succinct overview of contemporary events, the chapters describe women's lives at home, at work, in education, in politics, in the arts, and their role in the general culture. . . . [This book] surveys an era after women won the right to vote and when the nation's economic crash placed new hardships on families." SLJ

Includes glossary and bibliographical references

Brill, Marlene Targ

America in the 1910s; by Marlee Richards. Twenty-First Century Books 2010 144p il (The decades of twentieth-century America) lib bdg $38.60
Grades: 7 8 9 10   **973.91**
   1. United States -- History -- 1898-1919
   ISBN 978-0-8225-3437-2 lib bdg; 0-8225-3437-1 lib bdg
                                       LC 2007-42905
Presents the social, political, economical, and technological changes in the United States during the nineteen tens, including World War I, the Prohibition era, and the birth of the skyscraper.

The text is "enlivened with quotes and excerpts from primary sources, period photos, and two sets of sidebars. 'Profiles' provides biographical sketches of important people and 'Turning Points' explains the significance of important events. . . . A solid choice for readers and researchers." SLJ

Includes bibliographical references and filmography

Burg, David F.

The **Great** Depression; updated ed; Facts on File 2005 xx, 444p il (Eyewitness history) $75
Grades: 8 9 10 11 12   **973.91**
   1. Great Depression, 1929-1939 2. United States -- Economic conditions -- 1919-1933 3. United States -- Economic conditions -- 1933-1945
   ISBN 0-8160-5709-5; 978-0-8160-5709-2
                                       LC 2004-29126
First published 1996
"The book is divided into seven chapters, each covering a specific timeframe beginning with causative events preceding the crisis (1919-1928) and ending with the emerging Second World War (1939-1941.) Each chapter opens with a narrative summary and analysis of the period, followed by a chronological listing of significant events and then by primary-source contemporary quotations from private citizens, politicians, radio broadcasts, and more." Voice Youth Advocates

Includes bibliographical references

Collier, Christopher

★ **Progressivism,** the Great Depression, and the New Deal, 1901 to 1941; by Christopher Collier, James Lincoln Collier. Benchmark Bks. (Tarrytown) 2001 95p il map (Drama of American history) lib bdg $31.36
Grades: 6 7 8 9   **973.91**
   1. Great Depression, 1929-1939 2. United States -- History -- 20th century 3. United States -- Economic conditions -- 1933-1945
   ISBN 0-7614-1054-6
                                       LC 00-29481

This "follows events and movements during the first four decades of the twentieth century, including the growing involvement of government in reforming business practices, the impact of the Great Depression, and the social policies of Franklin D. Roosevelt's New Deal. . . . Illustrations, many in color, include period photographs and engravings as well as maps and charts. . . . Highly readable and informative." Booklist

Includes bibliographical references

Corrigan, Jim

The **1900s** decade in photos; a decade of discovery. Enslow Publishers 2010 64p il (Amazing decades in photos) lib bdg $27.93
Grades: 4 5 6 7   **973.91**
   1. United States -- History -- 20th century
   ISBN 978-0-7660-3129-6 lib bdg; 0-7660-3129-2 lib bdg
                                       LC 2008042900
This highlights the important world, national, and cultural developments of the 1900s.

This is illustrated with "large, well-chosen black-and-white and color photos. . . . Captions provide specific information about the photos and supplement, rather than repeat, information in the [narrative]. Attractive and readable, this . . . will be popular with browsers and beginning researchers." SLJ

Includes glossary and bibliographical references

The **1910s** decade in photos; a decade that shook the world. Enslow Publishers 2010 64p il (Amazing decades in photos) lib bdg $27.93
Grades: 4 5 6 7   **973.91**
   1. United States -- History -- 20th century
   ISBN 978-0-7660-3130-2 lib bdg; 0-7660-3130-6 lib bdg
                                       LC 2008042902
This highlights the important world, national, and cultural developments of the decade 1910-1919, including the sinking of the Titanic, the establishment of the Boy Scouts and Girl Scouts, immigration, income tax, Hollywood feature films, World War I, the Lusitania sinking, and more.

Includes glossary and bibliographical references

The **1920s** decade in photos; the Roaring Twenties. Enslow Publishers 2010 64p il (Amazing decades in photos) lib bdg $27.93
Grades: 4 5 6 7   **973.91**
   1. United States -- History -- 1919-1933
   ISBN 978-0-7660-3131-9 lib bdg; 0-7660-3131-4 lib bdg
                                       LC 2008042903
This highlights the important world, national, and cultural developments of the decade 1920-1929, including Prohibition, jazz music, women's suffrage, the rise of Mussolini, flappers fashions, the KKK, U.S. Presidents Harding and Coolidge, the Teapot Dome Scandal, the rise of the Nazi Party, and more.

Includes glossary and bibliographical references

Davis, Barbara J.

The **Teapot** Dome Scandal; corruption rocks 1920s America. by Barbara J. Davis. Compass Point Books 2008 96p il map (Snapshots in history) lib bdg $31.93

Grades: 6 7 8 9   **973.91**
  1. Teapot Dome Scandal, 1921-1924
  ISBN 978-0-7565-3336-6 lib bdg; 0-7565-3336-8 lib bdg

                   LC 2007004920

"Describes the signature scandal of the 1920s, through which political appointees and personal friends of President Warren G. Harding used their positions to solicit bribes from powerful oil companies in return for rich Western oil leases. . . . [This] volume includes a minimal glossary, a helpful time line, and suggestions for further reading." Voice Youth Advocates

Includes glossary

Howes, Kelly King

The **roaring** twenties almanac and primary sources; [by] Kelly King Howes; Julie L. Carnagie, project editor. U.X.L 2006 liv, 286p il (The roaring twenties reference library) $60

Grades: 7 8 9 10   **973.91**
  1. United States -- History -- 1919-1933
  ISBN 1-4144-0212-0

                   LC 2005007800

This volume begins with a timeline placing the 1920s in historical context. Illustrated entries highlight such topics as politics, economics, technological advances, women's changing roles, creationism vs. evolution, anti-immigrationism, Prohibition, and writers such as Sinclair Lewis, and Langston Hughes

Includes bibliographical references

Kraft, Betsy Harvey

Theodore Roosevelt; champion of the American spirit. Clarion Bks. 2003 180p il $19

Grades: 5 6 7 8   **973.91**
  1. Governors 2. Presidents 3. Vice-presidents 4. Nobel laureates for peace 5. Presidents -- United States
  ISBN 0-618-14264-9

                   LC 2002-152825

A biography of the energetic New Yorker who became the twenty-sixth president of the United States and who once exclaimed "No one has ever enjoyed life more than I have"

"Interwoven with the well-told story of Roosevelt's public activities is Kraft's vivid portrayal of his personal life, laced with anecdotes and quotations (mainly from letters) that help bring the famous figure to life. The spacious layout and the many black-and-white reproductions of photos, drawings, and prints add to the book's appeal." Booklist

Includes bibliographical references

Lindop, Edmund

America in the 1920s; by Edmund Lindop and Margaret J. Goldstein. Twenty-First Century Books 2010 144p il (The decades of twentieth-century America) lib bdg $38.60

Grades: 7 8 9 10   **973.91**
  1. United States -- History -- 1919-1933
  ISBN 978-0-7613-2831-5 lib bdg; 0-7613-2831-9 lib bdg

                   LC 2009-703

Outlines life in the United States in the 1920s, including Prohibition, the stock market crash, and advances in technology and entertainment such as the first radios and first talking movies

The text is "enlivened with quotes and excerpts from primary sources, period photos, and two sets of sidebars. 'Profiles' provides biographical sketches of important people and 'Turning Points' explains the significance of important events. . . . A solid choice for readers and researchers." SLJ

Includes bibliographical references

McElvaine, Robert S., 1947-

★ The **Depression** and New Deal; a history in documents. Oxford Univ. Press 2000 192p il (Pages from history) hardcover o.p. pa $19.95

Grades: 7 8 9 10   **973.91**
  1. Great Depression, 1929-1939 2. United States -- Economic conditions -- 1933-1945
  ISBN 0-19-510493-5; 0-19-516636-1 pa

                   LC 99-36644

"A vast assortment of diary entries, newspaper articles, campaign memos and speeches, political cartoons, songs, poetry, art, advertisements, photographs, and personal letters provide students with a political, economic, and social picture of this nation during the Depression. . . . [This] provides a balanced, inclusive picture of the period through the senses of the people who lived it." SLJ

Includes bibliographical references

Stanley, George Edward

An **emerging** world power (1900-1929) [by] George E. Stanley. World Almanac Library 2005 48p il (Primary source history of the United States) lib bdg $30

Grades: 5 6 7 8   **973.91**
  1. United States -- Foreign relations 2. United States -- History -- 1919-1933 3. United States -- Politics and government -- 1919-1933
  ISBN 0-8368-5828-X

                   LC 2004-61501

The author describes United States politics and foreign relations in the 1920s.

"Stanley explains and connects events utilizing clear language and a blending of text, images, and primary accounts. . . . Well-organized, highly attractive." SLJ

Includes bibliographical references

973.917 Administration of Franklin Delano Roosevelt, 1933-1945

Bolden, Tonya

★ **FDR's** alphabet soup; New Deal America, 1932-1939. Alfred A. Knopf 2010 136p il $19.99; lib bdg $22.99

Grades: 5 6 7 8 **973.917**

1. Governors 2. Presidents 3. New Deal, 1933-1939
4. People with disabilities 5. United States -- History
-- 1933-1945

ISBN 978-0-375-85214-5; 0-375-85214-X; 978-0-375-95214-2 lib bdg; 0-375-95214-4 lib bdg

LC 2009-10362

"Retracing the course of New Deal intiatives from the newly elected Roosevelt's 'famous First Hundred Days of action! action! action!' to his creation of the powerful Executive Office of the President in 1939, [Bolden] presents a coherent account of how FDR and his adminstration successfully (mostly) battled political, ideological, and legal challenges to create a sweeping recovery agenda. . . . Generally illustrated with period photos . . . this lively look back both invites and equips readers to ponder the pros and cons of 'gumptious government' in any era." Booklist

Includes glossary and bibliographical references

Cooper, Michael L.

★ **Dust** to eat; drought and depression in the 1930's. Clarion Books 2004 81p il map hardcover o.p. $15

Grades: 4 5 6 7 **973.917**

1. Droughts 2. Migrant labor 3. Great Depression, 1929-1939

ISBN 0-618-15449-3

LC 2003-17807

This book begins "with the 1929 stock market crash that ushered in the Great Depression and {continues} with the severe drought in the Midwest, known as the Dust Bowl." (Publisher's note) Index. "Grades six to nine." (Bull Cent Child Books)

This includes "lots of stunning black-and-white archival photos and a clear, spacious text that draws on eloquent eyewitness reports—including comments from John Steinbeck and Woody Guthrie. . . . This is an excellent historical account." Booklist

Includes bibliographical references

Corrigan, Jim

The **1930s** decade in photos; Depression and hope. Enslow Publishers 2010 64p il (Amazing decades in photos) lib bdg $27.93

Grades: 4 5 6 7 **973.917**

1. Great Depression, 1929-1939 2. United States -- History -- 1919-1933 3. United States -- History -- 1933-1945

ISBN 978-0-7660-3132-6 lib bdg; 0-7660-3132-2 lib bdg

LC 2008042904

This highlights the important world, national, and cultural developments of the decade 1930-1939, including the Great Depression, the Lindbergh kidnapping, the administration of FDR, the New Deal, jazz and swing music, the rise of Nazism, the repeal of Prohibition and more.

Includes glossary and bibliographical references

The **1940s** decade in photos; a world at war. Enslow Publishers 2010 64p il (Amazing decades in photos) lib bdg $27.93

Grades: 4 5 6 7 **973.917**

1. World War, 1939-1945 2. United States -- History -- 1933-1945 3. United States -- History -- 1945-1953

ISBN 978-0-7660-3133-3 lib bdg; 0-7660-3133-0 lib bdg

LC 2008042910

This covers the important world, national, and cultural developments of the decade 1940-1949, focusing on World War II.

This is illustrated with "large, well-chosen black-and-white and color photos. . . . Captions provide specific information about the photos and supplement, rather than repeat, information in the [narrative]. Attractive and readable, this . . . will be popular with browsers and beginning researchers." SLJ

Includes glossary and bibliographical references

Freedman, Russell

★ **Eleanor** Roosevelt; a life of discovery. Clarion Bks. 1993 198p il hardcover o.p. pa $11.95

Grades: 5 6 7 8 9 10 **973.917**

1. Diplomats 2. Columnists 3. Humanitarians 4. Social activists 5. Spouses of presidents 6. United Nations officials 7. Presidents' spouses -- United States

ISBN 0-89919-862-7; 0-395-84520-3 pa

LC 92-25024

A Newbery Medal honor book, 1994

"This impeccably researched, highly readable study of one of this country's greatest First Ladies is nonfiction at its best. . . . Approximately 140 well-chosen black-and-white photos amplify the text." Publ Wkly

Includes bibliographical references

★ **Franklin** Delano Roosevelt. Clarion Bks. 1990 200p il hardcover o.p. pa $9.95

Grades: 5 6 7 8 9 10 **973.917**

1. Governors 2. Presidents 3. People with disabilities 4. Presidents -- United States 5. United States -- Politics and government -- 1933-1945

ISBN 0-89919-379-X; 0-395-62978-0 pa

LC 89-34986

"The carefully researched, highly readable text and extremely effective coordination of black-and-white photographs chronicle Roosevelt's priviledged youth, his early influences, and his maturation. . . . Even students with little or no background in American history will find this an intriguing and inspirational human portrait." SLJ

Includes bibliographical references

Lindop, Edmund

America in the 1930s; [by] Edmund Lindop and Margaret J. Goldstein. Twenty-First Century Books 2010 144p il (The decades of twentieth-century America) lib bdg $38.60

Grades: 7 8 9 10 **973.917**

1. New Deal, 1933-1939 2. United States -- History -- 1933-1945

ISBN 978-0-7613-2832-2 lib bdg; 0-7613-2832-7 lib bdg

LC 2007-42902

The text is "enlivened with quotes and excerpts from primary sources, period photos, and two sets of sidebars. 'Profiles' provides biographical sketches of important people and 'Turning Points' explains the significance of important events. . . . A solid choice for readers and researchers." SLJ

Includes bibliographical references and filmography

America in the 1940s; by Edmund Lindop and Margaret J. Goldstein. Twenty-First Century Books 2010 144p il (The decades of twentieth-century America) lib bdg $38.60

Grades: 7 8 9 10   973.917

1. United States -- History -- 1933-1945 2. United States -- History -- 1945-1953

ISBN 978-0-7613-2945-9 lib bdg; 0-7613-2945-5 lib bdg

LC 2007-42904

Discusses the political, economic, social, cultural, and technology landscape of the United States in the fifth decade of the 20th century

The text is "enlivened with quotes and excerpts from primary sources, period photos, and two sets of sidebars. 'Profiles' provides biographical sketches of important people and 'Turning Points' explains the significance of important events. . . . A solid choice for readers and researchers." SLJ

Includes bibliographical references

McNeese, Tim

The **Great** Depression, 1929-1940; consulting editor Richard Jensen. Chelsea House 2010 136p il map (Discovering U.S. history) $35

Grades: 5 6 7 8   973.917

1. Economic conditions 2. Great Depression, 1929-1939 3. United States -- History -- 1933-1945

ISBN 978-1-60413-357-8; 1-60413-357-0

LC 2009-22090

"The information is accurate and easy to understand. Pictures are well placed, and primary sources are included. . . . The maps are well done and there are sidebars with additional information. . . . [This would be good] to have on hand for reports as it is well laid out and easy to use." Libr Media Connect

Includes glossary and bibliographical references

Nardo, Don

★ **Migrant** mother; how a photograph defined the Great Depression. Compass Point Books 2011 64p il (Captured history) lib bdg $33.99

Grades: 6 7 8 9   973.917

1. Photographers 2. Documentary photography 3. Great Depression, 1929-1939

ISBN 978-0-7565-4397-6; 0-7565-4397-5

LC 2010038578

This describes the significance of the iconic Dorothea Lange photograph of a migrant mother during the Great Depression and places it "in historical context, profiles the photographer, describes the conditions under which it was taken, and analyzes both its immediate and continuing impact. The [text includes] ample background information and details and [is] enhanced by large photos and sidebars." SLJ

Includes glossary and bibliographical references

Ruggiero, Adriane

★ **American** voices from The Great Depression. Benchmark Books 2004 xxi, 116p il (American voices from--) lib bdg $32.21

Grades: 6 7 8 9   973.917

1. Great Depression, 1929-1939 2. United States -- Economic conditions -- 1919-1933 3. United States -- Economic conditions -- 1933-1945

ISBN 0-7614-1696-X

LC 2004-865

Presents the history of the Great Depression through excerpts from letters, newspaper articles, speeches, and songs dating from the period. Includes review questions.

This "excellent [resource stands] out . . . because [it deals] strictly with primary sources, [contains] topnotch illustrations, and [enables] students to grasp the concepts without being overwhelmed." SLJ

Includes glossary and bibliographical references

973.92   United States--1953-2001

Brill, Marlene Targ

America in the 1970s. Lerner 2009 144p il (The decades of twentieth-century America) lib bdg $38.60

Grades: 7 8 9 10   973.92

1. United States -- Social conditions 2. United States -- History -- 1961-1974 3. United States -- History -- 1974-1989

ISBN 978-0-8225-3438-9; 0-8225-3438-X

LC 2007-38570

This is "a tightly constructed, smoothly phrased overview of the tumultuous 1970s. . . . The serviceable text is bolstered by skillful connections between events and movements, well-chosen representative quotes . . . and occasional snappy headlines . . . while sidebars profiling individuals and historical turning points . . . and a well-edited selection of photos add more interest." Booklist

America in the 1990s. Twenty-First Century Books 2010 144p il (The decades of twentieth-century America) lib bdg $38.60

Grades: 7 8 9 10   973.92

1. United States -- History -- 1989-

ISBN 978-0-8225-7603-7 lib bdg; 0-8225-7603-1 lib bdg

LC 2009-11628

Presents the social, political, economical, and technological changes in the United States during the 1990's

The text is "enlivened with quotes and excerpts from primary sources, period photos, and two sets of sidebars. 'Profiles' provides biographical sketches of important people and 'Turning Points' explains the significance of important events. . . . A solid choice for readers and researchers." SLJ

Includes bibliographical references and filmography

Campbell, Geoffrey A.

The **home** front. Lucent Bks. 2003 112p il map (American war library, Cold War) $27.45

Grades: 7 8 9 10   **973.92**
1. Cold war 2. United States -- History -- 1945- 3.
United States -- Social conditions
ISBN 1-59018-213-8

LC 2002-663

Examines how the Cold War period in America, lasting
roughly fifty years following World War II, was a contradictory time of prosperity and optimism coupled with concerns
over Soviet espionage infiltrating American institutions and
fear of nuclear apocalypse

Includes bibliographical references

Collier, Christopher
★ The **changing** face of American society:
1945-2000; [by] Christopher Collier, James Lincoln
Collier. Benchmark Bks. 2002 94p il (Drama of
American history) lib bdg $31.36
Grades: 6 7 8 9   **973.92**
1. United States -- History -- 1945- 2. United States
-- Social conditions 3. United States -- Social life and
customs
ISBN 0-7614-1319-7

LC 2001-25963

This outlines American social conditions from 1945 to
2000, including greater prosperity, the movements for African American civil rights and women's rights, the 1960s
counterculture, the Vietnam War, scientific advancements
and social changes

"Illustrations are plentiful, uniformly well chosen, and
include photographs, paintings, posters, and in some titles,
maps. . . . [This title is] easy to read and informative."
Book Rep

Includes bibliographical references

★ The **middle** road: American politics, 1945-
2000; [by] Christopher Collier. James Lincoln Collier. Benchmark Bks. 2002 95p il maps (Drama of
American history) lib bdg $31.36
Grades: 6 7 8 9   **973.92**
1. United States -- Politics and government -- 1945-
ISBN 0-7614-1318-9

LC 2001-25615

This outlines the course of American politics from the
end of World War II, through McCarthyism, the 1960s,
President Nixon and the Watergate scandal, and Presidents
Carter, Reagan, Bush, and Clinton

"Illustrations are plentiful, uniformly well chosen, and
include photographs, paintings, posters, and in some titles,
maps. . . . [This title is] easy to read and informative."
Book Rep

Includes bibliographical references

Corrigan, Jim
The **1990s** decade in photos; the rise of technology. Enslow Publishers 2010 64p il (Amazing
decades in photos) lib bdg $27.93
Grades: 4 5 6 7   **973.92**
1. World history -- 20th century 2. United States --

History -- 1989-
ISBN 978-0-7660-3138-8 lib bdg; 0-7660-3138-1
lib bdg

LC 2008054648

This highlights the important world, national, and cul-
tural developments of the decade 1990-1999, including
Operation Desert Storm in 1991, race riots in Los Angeles,
the election of President Clinton, the 1993 bombing of the
World Trade Center, the Human Genome Project, the end of
Apartheid, massacres in Bosnia and Rwanda, the Oklahoma
City bombing, the O.J. Simpson murder trial, the Columbine
High School shootings, and more

Includes glossary and bibliographical references

Lindop, Edmund
America in the 1950s; by Edmund Lindop; with
Sarah Decapua. Twenty-First Century Books 2010
144p il (The decades of twentieth-century America)
lib bdg $38.60
Grades: 7 8 9 10   **973.92**
1. United States -- History -- 1945-1953 2. United
States -- History -- 1953-1961
ISBN 978-0-8225-7642-6 lib bdg; 0-8225-7642-2
lib bdg

LC 2008-40127

Presents the social, political, economical, and technological changes in the United States during the 1950s, including
school integration, the Cold War, and the popularization of
rock and roll

The text is "enlivened with quotes and excerpts from primary sources, period photos, and two sets of sidebars. 'Profiles' provides biographical sketches of important people
and 'Turning Points' explains the significance of important
events. . . . A solid choice for readers and researchers." SLJ

Includes bibliographical references and filmography

McNeese, Tim
Modern America, 1964-present; consulting editor, Richard Jensen. Chelsea House 2010 144p il
map (Discovering U.S. history) $35
Grades: 5 6 7 8   **973.92**
1. United States -- History -- 1989- 2. United States
-- History -- 1961-1974 3. United States -- History --
1974-1989
ISBN 978-1-60413-361-5; 1-60413-361-9

"Through a good balance of social and political topics,
McNeese capably covers a diverse range of subjects in [this]
volume. . . . Modern America discusses civil rights, terrorism, and Barack Obama's first year as president. [The] book
has an excellent chronology; rich sidebars; and numerous
well-captioned illustrations, maps, and photos that enhance
the [text]. [This book provides a] satisfying [introduction] to
American history for students." SLJ

Includes glossary and bibliographical references

973.921 Administration of Dwight David Eisenhower, 1953-1961

Corrigan, Jim

The **1950s** decade in photos; the American decade. Enslow Publishers 2010 64p il (Amazing decades in photos) lib bdg $27.93

Grades: 4 5 6 7 **973.921**

1. United States -- History -- 1945-1953 2. United States -- History -- 1953-1961

ISBN 978-0-7660-3134-0 lib bdg; 0-7660-3134-9 lib bdg

LC 2008042994

This highlights the important world, national, and cultural developments of the decade 1950-1959, including the Korean War, McCarthyism, the Baby Boom generation, the execution of the Rosenbergs, the Beat Generation, the polio epidemic and vaccine, the Montgomery Bus Boycott, the Suez Crisis, the beginning of rock music, the launching of Sputnik, and the Cuban Revolution

Includes glossary and bibliographical references

Fitzgerald, Brian

McCarthyism; the red scare. Compass Point Books 2007 96p il map (Snapshots in history) lib bdg $31.93

Grades: 7 8 9 10 **973.921**

1. Cold war 2. Senators 3. Communism -- United States 4. United States -- History -- 1945-1953

ISBN 978-0-7565-2007-6 lib bdg; 0-7565-2007-X lib bdg

LC 2006003005

This "vividly portrays the fear of Communism in the U.S., beginning after the Russian Revolution. This book shows, in clear language, how McCarthy spread paranoia throughout the country and ruined many lives and careers." SLJ

Includes glossary and bibliographical references

The **McCarthy** hearings; Jesse G. Cunningham, book editor; Laura K. Egendorf, assistant book editor. Greenhaven Press 2003 144p (At issue in history) lib bdg $21.96; pa $14.96

Grades: 7 8 9 10 **973.921**

1. Senators 2. United States -- Politics and government -- 1945-1953 3. United States -- Politics and government -- 1953-1961

ISBN 0-7377-1346-1 lib bdg; 0-7377-1347-X pa

LC 2002-69323

"Because of the evenhanded presentation, the title makes a strong and lasting impression. The writings are well chosen." SLJ

Includes bibliographical references

Young, Jeff C.

Dwight D. Eisenhower; soldier and president. Morgan Reynolds 2002 128p il (Notable Americans) lib bdg $21.95

Grades: 7 8 9 10 **973.921**

1. Generals 2. Presidents 3. College presidents 4.

Presidents -- United States

ISBN 1-88384-676-5

LC 2001-30822

A biography of the World War II commander general who became the thirty-fourth President of the United States

"Young reveals Ike's story with a flair that makes both the man's questionable and admirable traits interesting. . . . There is enough drama here to make the story of the thirty-fourth president a surprisingly dynamic tale." Booklist

Includes bibliographical references

973.922 Administration of John Fitzgerald Kennedy, 1961-1963

Nardo, Don

Assassination and its aftermath; how a photograph reassured a shocked nation. by Don Nardo. Compass Point Books, a Capstone imprint 2013 64 p. (Captured history) (library binding) $33.99

Grades: 6 7 8 9 **973.922**

1. Presidents -- United States -- Pictorial works 2. Kennedy, John F. (John Fitzgerald), 1917-1963 -- Assassination 3. Photojournalists -- United States -- History -- 20th century 4. Presidents -- Succession -- United States -- History -- 20th century

ISBN 0756546923; 9780756546922; 9780756546984

LC 2012051716

In this book, by Don Nardo, "vice president, Lyndon Baines Johnson, took the presidential oath of office on Air Force One just hours after the assassination [of U.S. President John F. Kennedy] . . . Cecil Stoughton's iconic photo [of this moment] showed the world that the smooth and orderly transfer of power called for in the U.S. Constitution had occurred." According to the book, "his photo helped ease the shock, tension, and fear in an anxious country." (Publisher's note)

Includes bibliographical references and index

O'Reilly, Bill, 1949-

Kennedy's last days; the assassination that defined a generation. by Bill O'Reilly. 1st ed. Henry Holt and Co. 2013 336 p. (hardcover) $19.99

Grades: 6 7 8 9 **973.922**

1. Assassination

ISBN 080509802X; 9780805098020

LC 2013009026

This book by Bill O'Reilly "chronicles John F. Kennedy's course from PT-109 through a challenging presidency and positively harps on Lee Harvey Oswald's determined but doomed quest to become a 'great man.' . . . News photos or snapshots on nearly every page provide views of the Kennedy and Oswald families over time, as well as important figures, places and major world events." (Kirkus Reviews)

Includes bibliographical references and index.

Stockland, Patricia M.

The **assassination** of John F. Kennedy; by Patricia M. Stockland. ABDO Pub. Co. 2008 112 p. ill. (some col.), map (library) $34.22

Grades: 7 8 9 10   **973.922**
1. Kennedy, John F. (John Fitzgerald), 1917-1963 --
Assassination
ISBN 1599288486; 9781599288482
LC 2007011999
This book by Patricia Stockland is part of the Essential
Events series and looks at the assassination of former U.S.
President John F. (Fitzgerald) Kennedy. The series "explores
historic happenings around the globe and how those events
have sculpted societies, the sciences, and politics." (Pub-
lisher's note)
Includes bibliographical references (p. 102) and index.

Swanson, James L.
★ The **President** Has Been Shot! The Assassi-
nation of John F. Kennedy. James L. Swanson. Scho-
lastic Press 2013 336 p. (hbk.) $18.99
Grades: 6 7 8 9 10 11 12   **973.922**
1. Kennedy, John F. (John Fitzgerald), 1917-1963 --
Assassination
ISBN 0545490073; 9780545490078; 9780545496544
LC 2012041167
YALSA Award for Excellence in Nonfiction for Young
Adults: Finalist (2014)
This book by James L. Swanson is a "young-adult
book on the Kennedy assassination" in which the author
"transport[s] readers back to one of the most shocking, sad,
and terrifying events in American history. . . . The book [is]
illustrated with archival photos, . . . diagrams, source notes,
bibliography, places to visit, and index." (Publisher's note)
"Swanson's clear, concisely written, and riveting narrative highlights the key events of the Kennedy administration before focusing on the moment-by-moment details of
JFK's assassination. Also included are an exploration of Lee
Harvey Oswald's background, an aerial-view photograph
of Dealey Plaza in Dallas, a detailed map of the motorcade
route, and images of the Texas School Book Depository,
where Oswald perched, rifle in hand." (Horn Book)

973.923   Administration of Lyndon Baines
Johnson, 1963-1969

Corrigan, Jim
The **1960s** decade in photos; love, freedom,
and flower power. Enslow Publishers 2010 64p il
(Amazing decades in photos) lib bdg $27.93
Grades: 4 5 6 7   **973.923**
1. United States -- History -- 1961-1974
ISBN 978-0-7660-3135-7 lib bdg; 0-7660-3135-7
lib bdg
LC 2008042996
This highlights the important world, national, and cul-
tural developments of the decade 1960-1969, including the
U-2 spy plane, the election and assassination of JFK, the be-
ginnings of manned space exploration, the Bay of Pigs inva-
sion, the Vietnam War, the Cuban Missile Crisis, the British
invasion in rock music, the Civil Rights movement, the Six-
Day War in the Middle East, the assassinations of RFK and
Martin Luther King, and Hippie culture
Includes glossary and bibliographical references

Lindop, Edmund
America in the 1960s; [by] Edmund Lindop;
with Margaret J. Goldstein. Twenty-First Century
Books 2009 144p il (Decades of twentieth century
America) lib bdg $38.60
Grades: 7 8 9 10   **973.923**
1. United States -- History -- 1961-1974
ISBN 978-0-7613-3453-8 lib bdg; 0-7613-3453-X
lib bdg
LC 2007-38028
Presents the social, political, economic, and technological changes in the United States during the nineteen sixties,
including the civil rights movement, the popularization of
rock music, and the expedition to the Moon
The text is "enlivened with quotes and excerpts from primary sources, period photos, and two sets of sidebars. 'Profiles' provides biographical sketches of important people
and 'Turning Points' explains the significance of important
events. . . . A solid choice for readers and researchers." SLJ
Includes bibliographical references and filmography

973.924   Administration of Richard Milhous
Nixon, 1969-1974

Corrigan, Jim
The **1970s** decade in photos; protest and change.
Enslow Publishers 2010 64p il (Amazing decades
in photos) lib bdg $27.93
Grades: 4 5 6 7   **973.924**
1. United States -- History -- 1961-1974 2. United
States -- History -- 1974-1989
ISBN 978-0-7660-3136-4 lib bdg; 0-7660-3136-5
lib bdg
LC 2008042998
This highlights the important world, national, and cul-
tural developments of the decade 1970-1979, including pro-
tests against the Vietnam War, terrorist airplane hijackings,
the thawing of the Cold War, the deaths of rock musicians
Jimi Hendrix, Janice Joplin, and Jim Morrison, the attack
at the Munich Olympics, Watergate and the resignation of
President Nixon, Three Mile Island, and more.
Includes glossary and bibliographical references

973.927   Administration of Ronald Reagan,
1981-1989

Brill, Marlene Targ
America in the 1980s. Twenty-First Century
Books 2009 144p il (The decades of twentieth-
century America) lib bdg $38.60
Grades: 7 8 9 10   **973.927**
1. Actors 2. Governors 3. Presidents 4. United States
-- History -- 1974-1989
ISBN 978-0-8225-7602-0 lib bdg; 0-8225-7602-3
lib bdg
LC 2008-50116
Presents the social, political, economical, and techno-
logical changes in the United States during the 1980's

The text is "enlivened with quotes and excerpts from primary sources, period photos, and two sets of sidebars. 'Profiles' provides biographical sketches of important people and 'Turning Points' explains the significance of important events. . . . A solid choice for readers and researchers." SLJ

Includes bibliographical references

Corrigan, Jim

The **1980s** decade in photos; the triumph of democracy. Enslow Publishers 2010 64p il (Amazing decades in photos) lib bdg $27.93

Grades: 4 5 6 7   **973.927**

1. World history -- 20th century 2. United States -- History -- 1974-1989

ISBN 978-0-7660-3137-1 lib bdg; 0-7660-3137-3 lib bdg

LC 2008052627

This highlights the important world, national, and cultural developments of the decade 1980-1989, including the 1980 Winter Olympics, the presidency of Ronald Reagan, the Iran hostage crisis, the Space Shuttle, MTV, the War on Drugs, AIDS, the rise of the computer, fashion, the Chernobyl nuclear disaster, the Iran-Contra Affair, the massacre in Tiananmen Square, the fall of the Berlin Wall, and the U.S. invasion of Panama

Includes glossary and bibliographical references

973.93   United States--2001-

Corrigan, Jim

The **2000s** decade in photos; a new millennium. Enslow Publishers 2010 64p il (Amazing decades in photos) lib bdg $27.93

Grades: 4 5 6 7   **973.93**

1. World history -- 21st century 2. United States -- History -- 21st century

ISBN 978-0-7660-3139-5 lib bdg; 0-7660-3139-X lib bdg

LC 2008054644

This highlights the important world, national, and cultural developments of the first decade of the 21st century, including the disputed presidential election of 2000, the attacks of September 11, 2001, the Iraq War, digital technology and gadgets, the drop in stock market prices of internet companies, steroid use in sports, the Space Shuttle disaster of 2003, the tsunami of 2004, Hurricane Katrina, the massacre at Virginia Tech, the energy crisis, and the 2008 presidential election

Includes glossary and bibliographical references

Sutherland, James

The **ten** -year century; explaining the first decade of the new millennium. Viking 2010 152p il $18.99

Grades: 7 8 9 10   **973.93**

1. Modern history 2. United States -- History -- 21st century 3. United States -- Politics and government -- 2001-

ISBN 978-0-670-01223-7; 0-670-01223-8

LC 2010007314

"This overview of the first 10 years of the new millennium focuses on significant developments that have shaped

life in the United States today. . . . The lucid, balanced narration results in a nuanced representation of a rapidly changing era." Publ Wkly

Includes bibliographical references

973.931   Administration of George W. Bush, 2001-2009

Abbott, David

The **Twin** Towers. Arcturus Pub. 2011 46p il (A place in history) lib bdg $34.25

Grades: 7 8 9 10   **973.931**

1. Terrorism 2. September 11 terrorist attacks, 2001 3. World Trade Center terrorist attack, 2001

ISBN 978-1-84837-677-9; 1-84837-677-4

LC 2010014195

"A recap of American Airlines Flight 11 just before it struck the north tower of the World Trade Center opens this thorough coverage of the events leading up to the attack and its affect on the nation. Following a look at the Twin Towers, this . . . title focuses on the motivation behind the terrorist attacks by addressing the rise of Islam, anti-Americanism, and al-Qaeda. . . . Additional quotes from Osama bin Laden and individuals affected by the attacks; related facts . . .; and attention-getting photos . . . make this a solid choice for U.S. studies." Booklist

Includes bibliographical references

Benoit, Peter

September 11 we will never forget; by Peter Benoit. Children's Press 2012 64 p. col. ill., col. map (ornerstones of freedom) (library) $30.00; (paperback) $8.95

Grades: 4 5 6 7   **973.931**

1. September 11 terrorist attacks, 2001 2. Terrorism -- United States

ISBN 0531250407; 9780531250402; 9780531265659

LC 2011009586

This book presents an "overview of the events of September 11, 2001 and the impact the day continues to have on present day life. . . . Boxed text adds information about international reaction, and the life of Osama Bin Laden, and other topics throughout the book. . . . .The immediate emergency responses at each site are described as well as government actions such as immediate grounding of planes . . . and military initiatives in the Middle East." (Children's Literature)

Includes bibliographical references (p. 61) and index.

Burgan, Michael

George W. Bush; Michael Burgan. Marshall Cavendish Benchmark 2012 112 p. $34.21

Grades: 5 6 7 8   **973.931**

1. Terrorism 2. Presidents -- United States 3. Presidents -- United States -- Biography

ISBN 1608701840; 9781608701841

LC 2010014801

This book "in the 'Presidents and Their Times' series provides . . . information about George W. Bush and how he handled critical situations (e.g., domestic spying vis-a-vis telephone records to highlight the difficulty battling terror-

ism and the effect of Bush's response to Hurricane Katrina).
. . . Personal information is also provided about his early
years, including his marriage to Laura, entry into politics,
relationships with other family members, a decision to stop
drinking, and his choice to become a Christian fundamentalist." Also included are "color and older black and white
photos" and back matter such as "a timeline, chapter notes
with complete citations, a glossary, books and websites for
additional information, bibliography (books, articles, media), and index." (Children's Literature)

Includes bibliographical references and index

Frank, Mitch

Understanding September 11th; answering
questions about the attacks on America. Viking 2002
136p il maps $16.99; pa $8.99
Grades: 7 8 9 10   **973.931**
    1. Islam 2. Terrorism 3. Terrorists 4. September 11
terrorist attacks, 2001 5. Middle East
    ISBN 0-670-03582-3; 0-670-03587-4 pa
                                          LC 2002-1725
Explains the historical and religious issues that sparked
terrorists to attack America on September 11, 2001, including information on Islam, Osama bin Laden, and the
Middle East

This is written "in remarkably simple, accessible language. . . . Direct, unflinching, intelligent, and humane, this
is an invaluable resource." Booklist

Includes glossary and bibliographical references

Hillstrom, Kevin

The **September** 11 terrorist attacks; by Kevin
Hillstrom. Omnigraphics 2012 xv, 268 p.p (Defining moments) (hardcover : alk. paper) $55
Grades: 8 9 10 11 12   **973.931**
    1. Qaida (Organization) 2. September 11 terrorist
attacks, 2001 3. Terrorism -- United States
    ISBN 0780812409; 9780780812406
                                          LC 2011050673
This teen nonfiction reference book, by Kevin Hillstrom,
is part of the "Defining Moments" series. It "opens with a
lengthy overview that traces the origins and evolution of
radical Islam, the birth and growth of Al Qaeda and its early
attacks on the West, the events of September 11th, and the
lasting . . . effects of the attack. The next section provides
brief biographical sketches of eight terrorists and American .
. . officials." (School Library Journal)

Includes bibliographical references and index

Wachtel, Alan

★ **September** 11; a primary source history. Gareth Stevens Pub. 2009 48p il (In their own words)
lib bdg $27
Grades: 5 6 7 8   **973.931**
    1. Terrorism 2. September 11 terrorist attacks, 2001
    ISBN 978-1-4339-0048-8; 1-4339-0048-3
                                          LC 2008045132
"The horror of September 11 feels very immediate, and
uses both quotes from those who lived through it and stills
from the attacks. The book does a fine job of chronicling
the events, up to and including the controversies surrounding the New York memorial. The use of transcripts of phone

conversations that took place aboard the doomed planes
gives the book's beginning an almost 'you are there' effect.
Later chapters feature such diverse sources as text from the
Patriot Act and lyrics from Neil Young's song 'Let's Roll' to
amplify the mood of the country." Booklist

Includes bibliographical references

Williams, Brian

The **war** on terror. Arcturus Pub. 2011 46p il
(Secret history) lib bdg $32.80
Grades: 7 8 9 10   **973.931**
    1. Terrorism 2. September 11 terrorist attacks, 2001 3.
War on terrorism
    ISBN 978-1-84837-699-1; 1-84837-699-5
                                          LC 2010011013
This book explores the secrets of the War on Terror. It
began with the terrorist attacks of 9/11, but the War on Terror is mostly fought in secret. Its fighters are spies, analysts,
moles, and informers. Its weapons are phone taps, satellites,
and killer drones.

"The title of the Secret History series will grab readers,
even reluctant ones, and they won't be disappointed by the
intriguing info regarding codes and code breakers, spies, terrorists, and double agents, with profiles of heroes and traitors on all sides. . . . The readable design, with clear type on
thick, high-quality paper, includes lots of sidebars, photos,
screens, and quotes." Booklist

Includes bibliographical references

973.932   Administration of Barack Obama, 2009-2017

Zeiger, Jennifer

Barack Obama; by Jennifer Zeiger. Children's
Press 2012 64 p. ill. (chiefly col.), col. map (library
binding) $30.00; (paperback) $8.95
Grades: 4 5 6   **973.932**
    1. Presidents -- United States -- Biography 2. Racially
mixed people -- United States -- Biography
    ISBN 0531230503; 0531281507; 9780531230503;
9780531281505
                                          LC 2011031124
This book presents a "nonfiction account of President
[Barack]Obama's life for middle school students. . . . The
book includes many color photographs of the President as a
young boy and young adult. It gives the details of his life in
Indonesia and Hawaii and traces his career up to the 2012 re-
election campaign. His education is a focus of the biography
and there is ample discussion of his educational career and
how it has helped to shape him into the man he is today."
(Children's Literature)

Includes bibliographical references (p. 61) and index.

974   Specific states of United States

Bial, Raymond

The **Delaware**. Marshall Cavendish Benchmark
2005 127p il map (Lifeways) lib bdg $38.50

Grades: 5 6 7 8 **974**

1. Delaware Indians 2. Native Americans
ISBN 978-0-7614-1904-4; 0-7614-1904-7

LC 2004-3088

Discusses the history, culture, beliefs, changing ways, and notable people of the Delaware.

Includes glossary and bibliographical references

Johnson, Claudia D.

Daily life in colonial New England; [by] Claudia Durst Johnson. Greenwood Press 2002 xxvii, 215p (Daily life through history) $49.95

Grades: 7 8 9 10 **974**

1. New England -- History 2. United States -- Social life and customs -- 1600-1775, Colonial period
ISBN 0-313-31458-6

LC 00-61721

This description of colonial life in New England covers such topics as the clergy and the church, crime and punishment, government and law, labor, shelter and attire, food and health, marriage and sex, arts and amusements, and Native Americans and Africans in New England

"In this excellent volume, Johnson draws a remarkably clear and complete picture of the day-to-day existence of the first European settlers in New England." Voice Youth Advocates

Includes bibliographical references

Rylant, Cynthia

★ **Appalachia**; the voices of sleeping birds. illustrated by Barry Moser. Harcourt Brace Jovanovich 1991 21p il $17; pa $6

Grades: 4 5 6 7 **974**

1. Appalachian region
ISBN 0-15-201605-8; 0-15-201893-X pa

LC 90-36798

"Taking her subtitle from a passage by James Agee, the author conveys with a marvelous economy of words the essence of the very special part of America where she was raised. A poetic text projects emotion as well as information. . . . Moser's watercolors capture the scene perfectly. . . . The book is a treasure—simply a beautiful combination of text and art." Horn Book

974.1 Maine

Dornfeld, Margaret

Maine; by Margaret Dornfeld and Joyce Hart. 2nd ed.; Marshall Cavendish Benchmark 2010 144p il map (Celebrate the states) lib bdg $42.79

Grades: 5 6 7 8 **974.1**

1. Maine
ISBN 978-0-7614-4726-9; 0-7614-4726-1

LC 2009002583

This offers information on the geography, history, wildlife, governmental structure, economy, cultural diversity, peoples, religion, and landmarks of Maine.

Includes bibliographical references

Maine; by Ann Heinrichs. Revised edition Children's Press 2014 144 p. ill. (chiefly col.), col maps $40

Grades: 4 5 6 7 **974.1**

1. Maine
ISBN 9780531248874

Describes the history, geography, ecology, people, economy, cities, and sights of the state of Maine.

Includes bibliographical references and index

974.2 New Hampshire

Auden, Scott

New Hampshire, 1603-1776; [by] Scott Auden ; with Alan Taylor, consultant. National Geographic Society 2007 109p il map (Voices from colonial America) $21.95; lib bdg $32.90

Grades: 5 6 7 8 **974.2**

1. New Hampshire -- History
ISBN 978-1-4263-0034-9; 1-4263-0034-4; 978-1-4263-0035-6 lib bdg; 1-4263-0035-2 lib bdg

LC 2006-36055

Provides a look at the long and changing colonial history of the state of New Hampshire through a review of its borders, founding fathers, motto, and more, complete with archival images, period maps, and various first-person accounts.

Offers " thorough, well-documented information about the struggles and successes of early non-native settlers [in New Hampshire]. . . . Many reproductions of period illustrations (both color and sepia) and some photos of archival documents and maps enhance the text." Horn Book Guide

Includes bibliographical references

Kent, Deborah

New Hampshire; by Deborah Kent. Revised edition Children's Press 2015 144 p. ill. (chiefly col.), col maps $40

Grades: 4 5 6 7 **974.2**

1. New Hampshire
ISBN 9780531282847

Takes readers on a tour of New Hampshire, describing the state's history, culture, land, economy, government, and sights, and including unique facts, color maps and photos, the state song, suggested activities, lists of famous people, cultural institutions, and annual events, and other resources.

Includes bibliographical references and index

Otfinoski, Steven

New Hampshire; [by] Steve Otfinoski. 2nd ed.; Marshall Cavendish Benchmark 2008 144p il map (Celebrate the states) lib bdg $39.93

Grades; 4 5 6 7 **974.2**

1. New Hampshire
ISBN 978-0-7614-2718-6; 0-7614-2718-X

LC 2007-9944

First published 1999

"Provides comprehensive information on the geography, history, wildlife, governmental structure, economy, cultural diversity, peoples, religion, and landmarks of New Hampshire." Publisher's note

Includes bibliographical references

974.3 Vermont

Heinrichs, Ann

Vermont; by Ann Heinrichs. Revised edition Children's Press 2015 144 p. illustrations, maps $40

    Grades: 4 5 6 7   **974.3**

    1. Vermont

    ISBN 9780531282960

Presents an introduction to the geography, natural resources, history, economy, important sites, daily life, and people of Vermont.

Includes bibliographical references and index

974.4 Massachusetts

Doherty, Kieran

William Bradford; rock of Plymouth. 21st Cent. Bks. (Brookfield) 1999 192p il lib bdg $24.90

    Grades: 6 7 8 9   **974.4**

    1. Historians 2. Pilgrims (New England colonists)
    3. Colonists 4. Pilgrim fathers 5. Massachusetts --
    History -- 1600-1775, Colonial period
    ISBN 0-7613-1304-4

                    LC 99-10631

A biography of one of the founders of the Plymouth Colony in Massachusetts and a history of the Pilgrims' difficult times during their early years in the New World

Includes bibliographical references

Edwards, Judith

The **Plymouth** Colony and the Pilgrim adventure in American history. Enslow Pubs. 2003 128p il map (In American history) lib bdg $26.60

    Grades: 7 8 9 10   **974.4**

    1. Pilgrims (New England colonists) 2. Massachusetts
    -- History -- 1600-1775, Colonial period
    ISBN 0-7660-1989-6

                  LC 2002-12809

Traces the dangers and adventures surrounding the history of the Pilgrim settlement at Plymouth, Massachusetts, highlighting the roles played by William Brewster, Miles Standish, and other individuals

Includes bibliographical references

Erickson, Paul

Daily life in the Pilgrim colony, 1636. Clarion Bks. 2001 48p il map $20; pa $9.95

    Grades: 4 5 6 7   **974.4**

    1. Pilgrims (New England colonists) 2. Massachusetts
    -- History -- 1600-1775, Colonial period
    ISBN 0-618-05846-X; 0-395-98841-1 pa

                  LC 2001-17203

This "describes the day-to-day activities of the Prentiss family, owners of a small farm just outside the colony of Plymouth. Full-color photographs, maps, line drawings, and

detailed illustrations accompany engaging present-tense text to provide insight into Pilgrim society as a whole, and into the lives of specific family members as well." Book Rep

LeVert, Suzanne

Massachusetts; by Suzanne LeVert and Tamra B. Orr. 2nd ed.; Marshall Cavendish Benchmark 2009 144p il map (Celebrate the states) lib bdg $42.79

    Grades: 4 5 6 7   **974.4**

    1. Massachusetts
    ISBN 978-0-7614-3005-6; 0-7614-3005-9
    First published 2000

"Provides comprehensive information on the geography, history, wildlife, governmental structure, economy, cultural diversity, peoples, religion, and landmarks of Massachusetts." Publisher's note

Includes glossary and bibliographical references

Trueit, Trudi Strain

Massachusetts; by Trudi Strain Trueit. Revised edition Children's Press 2014 144 p. ill. (chiefly col.), col maps $40

    Grades: 4 5 6 7   **974.4**

    1. Massachusetts
    ISBN 9780531248898
    Revised edition

Describes the history, geography, ecology, people, economy, cities, and sights of the Bay State, Massachusetts.

Includes bibliographical references and index

974.5 Rhode Island

Klein, Ted

Rhode Island; by Ted Klein. 2nd ed.; Marshall Cavendish Benchmark 2008 144p il map (Celebrate the states) lib bdg $39.93

    Grades: 4 5 6 7   **974.5**

    1. Rhode Island
    ISBN 978-0-7614-2560-1; 0-7614-2560-8

                  LC 2006-36490

    First published 1999

"Provides comprehensive information on the geography, history, wildlife, governmental structure, economy, cultural diversity, peoples, religion, and landmarks of Rhode Island." Publisher's note

Includes bibliographical references

Rhode Island; Revised edition Children's Press 2015 144 p. illustrations, maps $40

    Grades: 4 5 6 7   **974.5**

    1. Rhode Island
    ISBN 9780531282915

Explores the land, people, history, economy, and travel opportunities of the state of Rhode Island.

Includes bibliographical references and index

974.6   Connecticut

Burgan, Michael
   Connecticut,   1614-1776.   National Geographic
Society   2007   109p   il   map   (Voices from colonial
America) $21.95;   lib bdg $32.90
   Grades: 5 6 7 8   **974.6**
      1. Connecticut -- History -- 1600-1775, Colonial period
      ISBN 978-1-4263-0068-4;   1-4263-0068-9;   978-1-
      4263-0069-1   lib bdg;   1-4263-0069-7   lib bdg
                                             LC 2007-3123
   A history of Connecticut from its beginning as an Eng-
lish colony to 1788 when it became the fifth state.
   Offers " thorough, well-documented information about
the struggles and successes of early colonial settlers and
settlements. . . . Many reproductions of period illustrations
and some photographs of period documents and maps with
relevant captions are included." Horn Book Guide
   Includes bibliographical references

Kent, Zachary
   Connecticut;   by Zachary Kent.   Revised edition
Children's Press   2014   144 p.   ill. (chiefly col.); col.
maps $40
   Grades: 4 5 6 7   **974.6**
      1. Connecticut
      ISBN 9780531248799
   Describes the history, geography, ecology, people, econ-
omy, cities, and sights of the state of Connecticut.
   Includes bibliographical references and index

974.7   New York

Bial, Raymond
   ★ **Tenement**;   immigrant life on the Lower East
Side.   Houghton Mifflin   2002   48p   il $16
   Grades: 4 5 6 7   **974.7**
      1. Poor   2. Immigrants -- United States   3. Lower East
      Side (New York, N.Y.)
      ISBN 0-618-13849-8
                                             LC 2002-00407
   Presents a view of New York City's tenements during the
peak years of foreign immigration, discussing living condi-
tions, laws pertaining to tenements, and the occupations of
their residents
   "The writing is particularly clear and sharp. Calling
upon and quoting the writing of reformer Jacob Riis (and
featuring his compelling photographs), Bial explains simply,
yet engagingly, what tenement life was like. . . . Along with
Riis' photographs, Bial provides some of his own, taken
at the Lower East Side Tenement Museum in New York
City." Booklist
   Includes bibliographical references

Burgan, Michael
   New   York, 1609-1776;   [by] Michael Burgan ;
with Timothy J. Shannon, consultant.   National Geographic Society   2006   109p   il   map   (Voices from
colonial America) $21.95;   lib bdg $32.90

   Grades: 5 6 7 8   **974.7**
      1. New York (State) -- History
      ISBN 978-0-7922-6390-6;   0-7922-6390-1;   978-0-
      7922-6860-4   lib bdg;   0-7922-6860-1   lib bdg
                                             LC 2005-22033
   Presents a brief history of colonial New York, from 1609
to 1776, and contains illustrations, historical maps, and first-
person accounts from explorers, Native Americans, and
colonists on early settlements.
   Includes bibliographical references

Getzinger, Donna
   ★ The **Triangle** Shirtwaist Factory fire.   Morgan
Reynolds Pub.   2008   128p   il   map   (American workers) $27.95
   Grades: 7 8 9 10   **974.7**
      1. New York (N.Y.) -- History   2. Labor -- Law and
      legislation   3. Triangle Shirtwaist Company, Inc.
      ISBN 978-1-59935-099-8;   1-59935-099-8
                                             LC 2008-4077
   "Beginning with a brief account of the disaster, a description of the popular shirtwaist and the fabric used to
make the blouse, the women who lost their lives, and the
impact of the lack of communication among the workers,
the first chapter is sure to hook readers. Successive chapters
look more closely at New York City's growth, the varied immigrant population at that time, overcrowded factory conditions, the failure to enforce building regulations, and the
many sweatshops developed from the desire of contractors
to make money. . . . Archival photos and diagrams with captions add to the meaning of this devastating and important
event in the history of labor." SLJ
   Includes bibliographical references

Hansen, Joyce
   ★ **Breaking** ground, breaking silence; the story
of New York's African burial ground,   by Joyce Hansen and Gary McGowan.   Holt & Co.   1998   130p   il
maps $19.95
   Grades: 8 9 10 11 12 Adult   **974.7**
      1. Cemeteries   2. Excavations (Archeology)   3. African
      Americans -- History   4. New York (N.Y.) -- Antiquities
      ISBN 0-8050-5012-4
                                             LC 97-19105
   Describes the discovery and study of the African burial
site found in Manhattan in 1991, while excavating for a new
building, and what it reveals about the lives of black people
in Colonial times
   "This book is well written and attractively designed, and
readers should have access to it in social studies classrooms
as well as in libraries. It will generate lots of class discussion
and writing projects." Voice Youth Advocates

Houle, Michelle M.
   Triangle Shirtwaist Factory fire; flames of labor
reform.   Enslow Pubs.   2002   48p   il   (American disasters)   lib bdg $23.93
   Grades: 4 5 6 7   **974.7**
      1. Factories   2. Clothing industry   3. Triangle Shirtwaist
      Company, Inc.
      ISBN 0-7660-1785-0
                                             LC 2001-7667

Discusses the 1911 fire that killed 146 New York garment factory workers, the conditions that led up to it, and some of the legislation that came about to prevent the occurrence of similar disasters

"The short chapters are enlivened with period photographs, including a horrific view of the bodies of women who had leaped to their deaths to escape the flames. Although the text is easy to read, the horror is not sugarcoated." SLJ

Includes bibliographical references

Huey, Lois Miner

American archaeology uncovers the Dutch colonies. Marshall Cavendish Benchmark 2009 64p il map (American archaeology) lib bdg $21.95

Grades: 4 5 6 7   **974.7**

1. Dutch Americans 2. America -- Antiquities 3. Netherlands -- Colonies -- America 4. Excavations (Archeology) -- United States

ISBN 978-0-7614-4263-9 lib bdg; 0-7614-4263-4 lib bdg

LC 2008050187

This describes how archeologists have learned about the history of Dutch settlers in America

"The text is quite chatty in this attractive title. . . . An inviting design with clear type includes several paintings of the period by a modern artist as well as maps and photos of excavation sites." Booklist

Includes glossary and bibliographical references

Mann, Elizabeth

Statue of Liberty; a tale of two countries. with illustrations by Alan Witschonke. Mikaya Press 2011 47p il map (Wonders of the world) $22.95

Grades: 4 5 6 7   **974.7**

1. Artists 2. Authors 3. Lawyers 4. Sculptors 5. National monuments 6. Children's authors 7. Fairy tale writers 8. Members of Parliament 9. Statue of Liberty (New York, N.Y.)

ISBN 978-1-931414-43-2; 1-931414-43-2

"The story of how Lady Liberty was conceived, constructed and bestowed makes a compelling tale. Pointing to the disparate long-term outcomes of the American and French revolutions to explain why the U.S. system of government became so admired in France, Mann takes the statue from Edouard Laboulaye's pie-in-the-sky proposal at a dinner party in 1865 to the massive opening ceremonies in 1886. . . . Witschonke supplements an array of period photos and prints with full-page or larger painted reconstructions of Bartholdi's studio and workshop, of the statue's piecemeal creation and finally of the Lady herself, properly copper colored as she initially was, presiding of New York's crowded harbor. As she still does." Kirkus

Includes bibliographical references

Marrin, Albert, 1936-

★ **Flesh** & blood so cheap; the Triangle fire and its legacy. Alfred A. Knopf 2011 182p il map $19.99; lib bdg $22.99

Grades: 5 6 7 8   **974.7**

1. Fires 2. Italian Americans 3. Jews -- United States 4. Labor -- United States 5. New York (N.Y.) -- History 6. Triangle Shirtwaist Company, Inc. 7. Industrial

safety 8. United States -- Immigration and emigration

ISBN 978-0-375-86889-4; 0-375-86889-5; 978-0-375-96889-1 lib bdg; 0-375-96889-X lib bdg

LC 2010-21533

"Published to coincide with the centennial anniversary of the 1911 fire that erupted in the Triangle Shirtwaist Factory, this powerful chronicle examines the circumstances surrounding the disaster, which resulted in the deaths of 146 workers, mostly young Italian and Jewish women. . . . B&W photographs and illustrations reveal immigrant families' impoverished living environments, while testimonials describe the 'humiliating' work rules and unsafe conditions of factories like Triangle. . . . A concluding description of a Bangladeshi garment factory fire in 2010 offers contemporary parallels. Marrin's message that protecting human dignity is our shared responsibility is vitally resonant." Publ Wkly

Includes bibliographical references

Marsico, Katie

The **Triangle** Shirtwaist Factory fire; its legacy of labor rights. Marshall Cavendish Benchmark 2010 112p il (Perspectives on) lib bdg $27.95

Grades: 7 8 9 10   **974.7**

1. Fires 2. New York (N.Y.) -- History 3. Triangle Shirtwaist Company, Inc.

ISBN 978-0-7614-4027-7; 0-7614-4027-5

LC 2008-23267

"This well-written title examines many of the details preceding the 1911 disaster, the conditions that caused it, and the impact the incident continues to have on labor and businesses today. Historical accounts of the event, told through numerous direct quotes and shown in black-and-white photos of sweatshops and descriptions of tenement living conditions, reveal that poor labor laws and factory regulations were to blame. . . . Color photos and full-page sidebars provide additional information." SLJ

Includes bibliographical references

Murphy, Jim

★ The **giant** and how he humbugged America; by Jim Murphy. Scholastic Press 2012 112 p. (hardcover : alk. paper) $19.99

Grades: 5 6 7 8   **974.7**

1. Relics 2. Sculpture 3. Impostors and imposture 4. Cardiff giant 5. Cardiff (N.Y.) -- Antiquities 6. New York (State) -- Antiquities 7. Forgery of antiquities -- New York (State) -- Cardiff

ISBN 0439691842; 9780439691840

LC 2011036798

In this book, "[Jim] Murphy traces the checkered career of the 'Cardiff Giant,' a 10-foot-long stone figure unearthed in 1869 in an upstate New York farmyard. The giant was a national sensation until its unmasking as a hoax a few months later. Almost from the outset, both educated and popular opinion was divided over whether the figure was a fossilized human or a carving, an ancient relic or a modern 'humbug.' Murphy shows how the controversy itself fueled the giant's notoriety." (Booklist)

Includes bibliographical references and index

Pellowski, Michael

The **terrorist** trial of the 1993 bombing of the World Trade Center; a headline court case. Enslow Pubs. 2003 112p il (Headline court cases) lib bdg $26.60

Grades: 6 7 8 9 **974.7**

1. Trials 2. Terrorism 3. World Trade Center Bombing, New York, N.Y., 1993

ISBN 0-7660-2045-2

LC 2002-156033

Examines the trials of Mahmoud Abouhalima, Ramzi Yousef, Mohammad Salameh, Sheik Omar Abdel-Rahman, and others for their roles in the 1993 bombing of the World Trade Center

"A well-balanced look at the events leading up to, during, and after the 1993 bombing. . . . The text is clear and succinct." SLJ

Includes glossary and bibliographical references

Platt, Richard

New York City; an illustrated history of the Big Apple. illustrated by Manuela Cappon. Kingfisher 2010 45p il map (Through time) $16.99

Grades: 4 5 6 7 **974.7**

1. New York (N.Y.) -- History

ISBN 978-0-7534-6416-8; 0-7534-6416-0

This is a history of New York City from its Native American origins to the present.

"In this magnificently illustrated work, historical happenings and intriguing offshoots are showcased like stars on Broadway. . . . A wealth of information in an engaging format." Booklist

Schomp, Virginia

New York; [by] Virginia Schomp. 2nd ed.; Benchmark Books 2006 144p il map (Celebrate the states) lib bdg $39.93

Grades: 4 5 6 7 **974.7**

1. New York (State)

ISBN 978-0-7614-1738-5; 0-7614-1738-9

LC 2004-853

First published 1997

This book about New York covers "standard facts: geography, history, government, economy, landmarks, and regions. . . . [It is] attractively illustrated with clear maps, charts, and pie graphs. Photos and reproductions of original documents add to overall effectiveness. . . . Excellent additions for reports or general interest." SLJ

Includes bibliographical references

Slavicek, Louise Chipley

New York City's Central Park. Chelsea House Publishers 2009 120p il (Building America, then and now) lib bdg $35

Grades: 6 7 8 9 **974.7**

1. Central Park (New York, N.Y.)

ISBN 978-1-60413-044-7 lib bdg; 1-60413-044-X lib bdg

LC 2008-25548

This describes the history and impact of New York City's Central Park

"Photos, maps, and informative sidebars supplement the densely detailed writing. American history buffs will find [this volume] useful for doing research." Horn Book Guide

Includes glossary and bibliographical references

Somervill, Barbara A.

New York; by Barbara A. Somervill. Revised edition Children's Press 2014 144 p. col ill, col maps $40

Grades: 4 5 6 7 **974.7**

1. New York (State)

ISBN 9780531248959

Describes the history, geography, ecology, famous people, economy, cities, and sights of the state of New York.

Includes bibliographical references and index

Talbott, Hudson

★ **River** of dreams; the story of the Hudson River. G. P. Putnam's Sons 2009 un il map $17.99

Grades: 4 5 6 7 **974.7**

1. Hudson River (N.Y. and N.J.)

ISBN 978-0-399-24521-3; 0-399-24521-9

Talbott offers a "compelling blend of political and natural history in this beautifully illustrated celebration of the Hudson River. Combining delicate watercolor-and-pencil illustrations with accessible text, the spreads move briskly through the Hudson's River's history." Booklist

974.8 Pennsylvania

Koestler-Grack, Rachel A.

The **Johnstown** flood of 1889. Chelsea House 2008 101p il (Great historic disasters) lib bdg $35

Grades: 6 7 8 9 **974.8**

1. Floods 2. Pennsylvania -- History

ISBN 978-0-7910-9763-2 lib bdg; 0-7910-9763-3 lib bdg

LC 2008-4894

This is a history of the flood of May 31, 1889 in Johnstown Pennsylvania

"Combining first-hand accounts, photographs, and other primary sources with a detailed and lively text, [this] fact-packed [resource offers] much to both report writers and history buffs." Horn Book Guide

Includes glossary and bibliographical references

Peters, Stephen

Pennsylvania; by Stephen Peters and Joyce Hart. 2nd ed.; Marshall Cavendish Benchmark 2009 144p il map (Celebrate the states) lib bdg $42.79

Grades: 4 5 6 7 **974.8**

1. Pennsylvania

ISBN 978-0-7614-3403-0; 0-7614-3403-8

LC 2008-8032

First published 2000

"Provides comprehensive information on the geography, history, wildlife, governmental structure, economy, cultural diversity, peoples, religion, and landmarks of Pennsylvania." Publisher's note

Includes bibliographical references

Somervill, Barbara A.

Pennsylvania; by Barbara A. Somervill. Revised edition Children's Press 2015 144 p. illustrations, maps $40

Grades: 4 5 6 7   **974.8**

1. Pennsylvania

ISBN 9780531282892

Presents an introduction to the geography, natural resources, history, economy, important sites, daily life, and people of Pennsylvania.

Includes bibliographical references and index

Walker, Sally M.

★ **Boundaries;** how the Mason-Dixon line settled a family feud and divided a nation. Sally M Walker. Candlewick Press 2014 208 p. ill., maps. $24.99

Grades: 7 8 9 10 11 12   **974.8**

1. Mason-Dixon Line 2. Surveying -- United States -- History -- 18th century

ISBN 0763656127; 9780763656126

LC 2013946612

This book, by Sally M. Walker, details the "Mason-Dixon Line's history, replete with property disputes, persecution, and ideological conflicts. . . . Walker traces the tale of the Mason-Dixon Line through family feuds, brave exploration, scientific excellence, and the struggle to define a cohesive country. But above all, this [is a] . . . story of surveying, marking, and respecting lines of demarcation." (Publisher's note)

"This thoroughly researched account of the Mason-Dixon Line encompasses a broad span of time and place, from sixteenth-century England to twentieth-century America... Walker's latest book offers a good deal of pertinent information on the subject at hand, as well as some interesting sidelights on American history." (Booklist)

974.9   New Jersey

Doak, Robin S.

New Jersey 1609-1776; y. [by] Robin Doak with Brendan McConville. National Geographic 2005 109p il map (Voices from colonial America) $21.95; lib bdg $32.90

Grades: 5 6 7 8   **974.9**

1. New Jersey -- History

ISBN 978-0-7922-6385-2; 0-7922-6385-5; 978-0-7922-6680-8 lib bdg; 0-7922-6680-3 lib bdg

LC 2004-26242

"This book gives detailed descriptions of family life and working in a Colonial village and the fight for independence. It also includes information about the Native people, early settlers, and first developments. . . . Paintings, maps, woodcuts, portraits, and reproductions accompany the well-written text. . . . An excellent resource." SLJ

Includes bibliographical references

Kent, Deborah

New Jersey; by Deborah Kent. Revised edition Children's Press 2014 144 p. col ill, col maps $40

Grades: 4 5 6 7   **974.9**

1. New Jersey

ISBN 9780531248942

Describes the history, geography, ecology, people, economy, cities, and sights of the state of New Jersey.

Includes bibliographical references and index

Moragne, Wendy

New Jersey; by Wendy Moragne and Tamra B. Orr. 2nd ed.; Marshall Cavendish Benchmark 2009 144p il map (Celebrate the states) lib bdg $39.93

Grades: 4 5 6 7   **974.9**

1. New Jersey

ISBN 978-0-7614-3006-3; 0-7614-3006-7

LC 2007-38642

First published 2000

"Provides comprehensive information on the geography, history, wildlife, governmental structure, economy, cultural diversity, peoples, religion, and landmarks of New Jersey." Publisher's note

Includes bibliographical references

975.1   Delaware

Price, Karen

Delaware, 1638-1776; [by] Karen Hossell, with Karin Wulf, consultant. National Geographic Society 2006 109p il map (Voices from colonial America) $21.95; lib bdg $32.90

Grades: 5 6 7 8   **975.1**

1. Delaware -- History

ISBN 978-0-7922-6408-8; 0-7922-6408-8; 978-0-7922-6864-2 lib bdg; 0-7922-6864-4 lib bdg

LC 2006-13444

"Discusses the Native American massacre of the first European settlers in the Delaware region, and follows the events that helped the area develop into a thriving colony as it changed from Swedish to Dutch to British control." Publisher's note

Includes bibliographical references

Schuman, Michael

Delaware; by Michael Schuman and Marlee Richards. 2nd ed.; Marshall Cavendish Benchmark 2009 144p il map (Celebrate the states) lib bdg $42.79

Grades: 4 5 6 7   **975.1**

1. Delaware

ISBN 978-0-7614-3399-6; 0-7614-3399-6

LC 2008-5369

First published 2000

"Provides comprehensive information on the geography, history, wildlife, governmental structure, economy, cultural diversity, peoples, religion, and landmarks of Delaware." Publisher's note

Includes bibliographical references

975.2 Maryland

Blashfield, Jean F.
Maryland; by Jean F. Blashfield. Revised edition Children's Press 2014 144 p. ill. (chiefly col.), col maps $40

Grades: 4 5 6 7 **975.2**
1. Maryland
ISBN 9780531248881
Describes the geography, history, economy, culture, and people of the state of Maryland.
Includes bibliographical references and index

Doak, Robin S.
Maryland, 1634-1776. National Geographic 2007 105p il map (Voices from colonial America) $21.95; lib bdg $32.90

Grades: 5 6 7 8 **975.2**
1. Maryland -- History
ISBN 978-1-4263-0143-8; 1-4263-0143-x; 978-1-4263-0144-5 lib bdg; 1-4263-0144-8 lib bdg
LC 2007-27886
Offers "thorough, well-documented information about the struggles and successes of early colonial settlers and settlements. . . . Many reproductions of period illustrations and some photographs of period documents and maps with relevant captions are included." Horn Book Guide
Includes bibliographical references

Moore, Wes, 1978-
Discovering Wes Moore; Wes Moore. Delacorte Press 2012 160 p. (hardcover) $15.99

Grades: 7 8 9 10 11 12 **975.2**
1. Family life 2. Conduct of life 3. Blacks -- Biography 4. Youth -- Conduct of life 5. African American men -- Biography 6. Baltimore (Maryland) -- Biography 7. Bronx (New York, N.Y.) -- Biography 8. Soldiers -- United States -- Biography 9. Criminals -- Maryland -- Baltimore -- Biography 10. African Americans -- Maryland -- Baltimore -- Social conditions -- 20th century 11. African Americans -- Bronx (New York, N.Y.) -- Social conditions -- 20th century
ISBN 0385741677; 9780375986703; 9780375990182; 9780385741675
LC 2011049135
Author Wes Moore describes his experiences growing up. "After receiving poor grades and falling in with a bad crowd, his family pooled their limited finances to send him to Valley Forge Military Academy, where he found positive role models and became a Corps commander and star athlete. After earning an undergraduate degree, Wes attended Oxford as a Rhodes Scholar. When the author read about the conviction of another Wes Moore for armed robbery and killing a police officer, he wanted to find out how two youths . . . could take such divergent paths." (Kirkus)

Pietrzyk, Leslie
Maryland; by Leslie Rauth and Martha Kneib. 2nd ed.; Marshall Cavendish Benchmark 2008 144p il map (Celebrate the states) lib bdg $39.93

Grades: 4 5 6 7 **975.2**
1. Maryland
ISBN 978-0-7614-3004-9; 0-7614-3004-0
LC 2007-29497
First published 2000
"Provides comprehensive information on the geography, history, wildlife, governmental structure, economy, cultural diversity, peoples, religion, and landmarks of Maryland." Publisher's note
Includes bibliographical references

975.3 District of Columbia (Washington)

Aretha, David
The **story** of the civil rights march on Washington for jobs and freedom in photographs; David Aretha. Enslow Publishers, Inc. 2014 48 p. illustrations (some color) (The story of the civil rights movement in photographs) library $25.27

Grades: 5 6 7 8 **975.3**
1. March on Washington for Jobs and Freedom (1963 : Washington, D.C.) 2. African Americans -- Civil rights 3. Civil rights demonstrations -- Washington (D.C.) 4. March on Washington for Jobs and Freedom (1963 : Washington, D.C.) -- Pictorial works
ISBN 0766042383; 9780766042384
LC 2013004860
Author "David Aretha explores the 'greatest demonstration for freedom' in American history. On August 28, 1963, more than 250,000 people descended on Washington, D.C. They came by bus, car, and bicycle. Some even walked hundreds of miles to be there. On that day, the massive crowd gathered to march, protest, sing, and support the Civil Rights Movement and to demonstrate that the time had come to end segregation in the South." (Publisher's note)
"This series explores key events of the Civil Rights Movement through historical primary source pictures and documents. The books dramatically carry the reader from early 1963 Birmingham to sit-ins, marches, and protests. Through dramatic photographs along with descriptive captions, the reader feels the raw emotions of the times." Lib Med Con

Elish, Dan
Washington, D.C. by Dan Elish. 2nd ed.; Marshall Cavendish Benchmark 2007 144p il map (Celebrate the states) lib bdg $39.93

Grades: 4 5 6 7 **975.3**
1. Washington (D.C.)
ISBN 978-0-7614-2352-2; 0-7614-2352-4
LC 2006-13838
First published 1998
"Provides comprehensive information on the geography, history, wildlife, governmental structure, economy, cultural diversity, peoples, religion, and landmarks of Washington, D.C." Publisher's note
Includes bibliographical references

House, Katherine L.

The **White** House for kids; a history of a home, office, and national symbol : with 21 activities. Katherine L. House. Chicago Review Press 2014 144 p. illustrations, plans (For kids series) (pbk.) $16.95

Grades: 4 5 6 7   **975.3**

    1. Presidents -- United States 2. White House (Washington, D.C.) 3. Washington (D.C.) -- Buildings, structures, etc.

    ISBN 1613744617; 9781613744611

                         LC 2013038108

This children's book, by Katherine L. House, offers an "educates young readers on the White House. Blending facts from numerous primary sources with engaging anecdotes . . . , this book provides the complete story of the presidents' home. Details on the many changes, updates, renovations, and redecorations that have occurred over the years are featured as well as a look at the daily lives of the White House's inhabitants." (Publisher's note)

"Chapter organization enhances interest by covering seven subjects and including examples from multiple historical periods. From the purposes and architecture of the building to the nature of multiple jobs performed, this book shows the varied functions of the White House." VOYA

Includes bibliographical references and index

Kent, Deborah

Washington, D.C. by Deborah Kent. Revised edition Children's Press 2015 144 p. illustrations, maps $40

    Grades: 4 5 6 7   **975.3**

    1. Washington (D.C.)

    ISBN 9780531282984

Discusses the geography, history, people, government, economy, and recreation of Washington, D.C.

    Includes bibliographical references and index

★ **Our** White House; looking in, looking out. created by The National Children's Book and Literacy Alliance; introduction by David McCullough. Candlewick Press 2008 241p il $29.99

    Grades: 5 6 7 8   **975.3**

    1. White House (Washington, D.C.) 2. Washington (D.C.) 3. Short stories -- Collections 5.

    ISBN 0-7636-2067-X; 978-0-7636-2067-7

This is a collection of essays, personal accounts, historical fiction, and poetry devoted to the history of the White House. Index. "Age ten and up." (N Y Times Book Rev)

"The White House is the focus of this handsome, large-format compendium of writings, both factual and fictional, and illustrations. . . . Poems and essays, stories and memoirs—all combine to create a mosaic of impressions of the house's residents and visitors and of the important events that occurred there. . . . The often-spectacular, beautifully reproduced on glossy paper, is particularly striking." Booklist

975.4   West Virginia

Hoffman, Nancy

West Virginia; [by] Nancy Hoffman and Joyce Hart. 2nd ed.; Marshall Cavendish Benchmark 2007 144p il map (Celebrate the states) lib bdg $39.93

Grades: 4 5 6 7   **975.4**

    1. West Virginia

    ISBN 978-0-7614-2562-5; 0-7614-2562-4

                         LC 2006-29393

    First published 1999

Relates the history and describes the geographic features, places of interest, government, industry, environmental concerns, and life of the people of West Virginia.

    Includes bibliographical references

975.5   Virginia

Kent, Deborah

Virginia; by Deborah Kent. Revised edition Children's Press 2014 144 p. illustrations, maps $40

    Grades: 4 5 6 7   **975.5**

    1. Virginia

    ISBN 9780531248997

Presents an introduction to the geography, natural resources, history, economy, important sites, daily life, and people of Virginia.

    Includes bibliographical references and index

Pobst, Sandy

Virginia, 1607-1776; [by] Sandy Pobst with Kevin D. Roberts, consultant. National Geographic Society 2005 109p il map (Voices from colonial America) $21.95; lib bdg $32.90

Grades: 5 6 7 8   **975.5**

    1. Virginia -- History

    ISBN 978-0-7922-6388-3; 0-7922-6388-X; 978-0-7922-6771-3 lib bdg; 0-7922-6771-0 lib bdg

                         LC 2005-8885

"This title discusses the colony's founding, life on the Tidewater plantations, the struggles to survive, and the desire for independence. Full of period maps; portraits; photographs; and first-person accounts from masters and slaves, explorers, Native Americans, servants, and other residents, this is narrative nonfiction at its best. . . . An excellent resource." SLJ

    Includes bibliographical references

975.6   North Carolina

Cannavale, Matthew C.

North Carolina, 1524-1776; by Matthew C. Cannavale; with Patrick Griffith, consultant. National Geographic Society 2007 109p il map (Voices from colonial America) $21.95; lib bdg $32.90

Grades: 5 6 7 8 **975.6**

1. North Carolina -- History
ISBN 978-1-4263-0032-5; 1-4263-0032-8; 978-1-4263-0033-2 lib bdg; 1-4263-0033-6 lib bdg

LC 2006-36004

A history of colonial North Carolina.
Includes bibliographical references

Heinrichs, Ann

North Carolina; by Ann Heinrichs. Revised edition Children's Press 2014 144 p. col ill, col maps $40

Grades: 4 5 6 7 **975.6**
1. North Carolina
ISBN 9780531248966

Presents an introduction to the geography, natural resources, history, economy, important sites, daily life, and people of North Carolina.

Includes bibliographical references and index

Miller, Lee

Roanoke; the mystery of the Lost Colony. Scholastic Nonfiction 2007 112p il map $18.99

Grades: 4 5 6 7 **975.6**
1. Roanoke Island (N.C.) -- History 2. United States -- History -- 1600-1775, Colonial period
ISBN 0-439-71266-1; 978-0-439-71266-8

LC 2005-51820

"Miller, author of Roanoke: solving the mystery of the Lost Colony (2001), here reprises for a young audience her historical theory that a certain man sabotaged the expedition eventually known as the Lost Colony. . . . Miller does an exceptional job of presenting the Native American culture and viewpoint. . . . This handsomely designed book features one or two illustrations on each spread, many in color, including reproductions or period drawings, paintings, and maps, as well as modern photos of sites and wildlife." Booklist

Includes bibliographical references

Reed, Jennifer

Cape Hatteras National Seashore; adventure, explore, discover. [by] Jennifer Reed. MyReportLinks.com Books 2008 128p il map (America's national parks) lib bdg $33.27

Grades: 5 6 7 8 **975.6**
1. Cape Hatteras National Seashore (N.C.) 2. National parks and reserves -- United States
ISBN 978-1-59845-086-6 lib bdg; 1-59845-086-7 lib bdg

LC 2006102321

This "informative, well-written book contains a physical description of the park; a summary of its history including the Native peoples of the area; activities such as hiking trails, campsites, and visitor centers; information about the park's plants, animals, and weather; full-color photographs; and numerous approved links available through the publisher's Web page. . . . Thorough, useful, and appealing, this . . . is a great update for collections." SLJ

Includes glossary and bibliographical references

Shirley, David

North Carolina; by David Shirley and Joyce Hart. 2nd ed.; Marshall Cavendish Benchmark 2010 144p il map (Celebrate the states) lib bdg $43.79

Grades: 5 6 7 8 **975.6**
1. North Carolina
ISBN 978-0-7614-4729-0; 0-7614-4729-6

LC 2009007139

First published 2001
This offers information on the geography, history, wildlife, governmental structure, economy, cultural diversity, peoples, religion, and landmarks of North Carolina.

Includes bibliographical references

975.7   South Carolina

Doak, Robin S.

South Carolina, 1540-1776; by Robin Doak with Robert Olwell. National Geographic Society 2007 109p il map (Voices from colonial America) $21.95; lib bdg $32.90

Grades: 5 6 7 8 **975.7**
1. South Carolina -- History
ISBN 978-1-4263-0066-0; 1-4263-0066-2; 978-1-4263-0067-7 lib bdg; 1-4263-0067-0 lib bdg

LC 2007-3120

A history of South Carolina from its beginning as an English colony to 1788 when it became the eighth state.

Offers "thorough, well-documented information about the struggles and successes of early colonial settlers and settlements. . . . Many reproductions of period illustrations and some photographs of period documents and maps with relevant captions are included" Horn Book Guide

Includes bibliographical references

Hoffman, Nancy

South Carolina; by Nancy Hoffman and Joyce Hart. 2nd ed.; Marshall Cavendish Benchmark 2010 144p il map (Celebrate the states) lib bdg $42.79

Grades: 5 6 7 8 **975.7**
1. South Carolina
ISBN 978-0-7614-4034-5; 0-7614-4034-8

LC 2008038266

First published 2001
This offers information on the geography, history, wildlife, governmental structure, economy, cultural diversity, peoples, religion, and landmarks of South Carolina.

Includes bibliographical references

Somervill, Barbara A.

South Carolina; by Barbara A. Somervill. Revised edition Children's Press 2015 144 p. illustrations, maps $40

Grades: 4 5 6 7 **975.7**
1. South Carolina
ISBN 9780531282922

Presents an introduction to the geography, natural resources, history, economy, important sites, daily life, and people of South Carolina.

Includes bibliographical references and index

975.8   Georgia

Doak, Robin S.

Georgia, 1521-1776. National Geographic Society 2006 109p il map (Voices from colonial America) $21.95; lib bdg $32.90

Grades: 5 6 7 8   **975.8**

1. Georgia -- History
ISBN 978-0-7922-6389-0; 0-7922-6389-8; 978-0-7922-6858-1 lib bdg; 0-7922-6858-X lib bdg

LC 2005-22141

Provides a history of Georgia from the arrival of European explorers in the sixteenth century to its becoming a state in 1788.

Includes bibliographical references

Otfinoski, Steven

Georgia; 2nd ed.; Marshall Cavendish Benchmark 2010 144p il map (Celebrate the states) lib bdg $42.79

Grades: 5 6 7 8   **975.8**

1. Georgia
ISBN 978-0-7614-4031-4; 0-7614-4031-3

LC 2008041711

First published 2001

This offers information on the geography, history, wildlife, governmental structure, economy, cultural diversity, peoples, religion, and landmarks of Georgia.

Includes bibliographical references

Prentzas, G. S.

Georgia; by G.S. Prentzas. Revised ed. Children's Press 2014 144 p. ill. (chiefly col.), col. maps $40

Grades: 4 5 6 7   **975.8**

1. Georgia
ISBN 9780531248812

Describes the history, geography, ecology, people, economy, cities, and sights of the state of Georgia.

Includes bibliographical references (page 138) and index

975.9   Florida

Cannavale, Matthew C.

Florida, 1513-1821; [by] Matthew C. Cannavale with Robert Olwell, consultant. National Geographic 2006 109p il map (Voices from colonial America) $21.95; lib bdg $32.90

Grades: 5 6 7 8   **975.9**

1. Florida -- History
ISBN 978-0-7922-6409-5; 0-7922-6409-6; 978-0-7922-6866-6 lib bdg; 0-7922-6866-0 lib bdg

LC 2006-20505

Offers "thorough, well-documented information about the struggles and successes of early nonnative settlers [in Florida]. . . . Many reproductions of period illustrations (both color and sepia) and some photos of archival documents and maps enhance the text." Horn Book Guide

Includes bibliographical references

Hart, Joyce

Florida; [by] Perry Chang and Joyce Hart. 2nd ed.; Marshall Cavendish Benchmark 2007 144p il map (Celebrate the states) lib bdg $39.93

Grades: 4 5 6 7   **975.9**

1. Florida
ISBN 978-0-7614-2348-5; 0-7614-2348-6

LC 2006-8174

First published 1998

"Provides comprehensive information on the geography, history, wildlife, governmental structure, economy, cultural diversity, peoples, religion, and landmarks of Florida." Publisher's note

Includes bibliographical references

Jankowski, Susan

Everglades National Park; adventure, explore, discover. [by] Susan Jankowski. MyReportLinks.com Books 2009 128p il map (America's national parks) lib bdg $33.27

Grades: 5 6 7 8   **975.9**

1. Everglades National Park (Fla.) 2. National parks and reserves -- United States
ISBN 978-1-59845-091-0 lib bdg; 1-59845-091-3 lib bdg

LC 2007-38262

This "informative, well-written book contains a physical description of the park; a summary of its history including the Native peoples of the area; activities such as hiking trails, campsites, and visitor centers; information about the park's plants, animals, and weather; full-color photographs; and numerous approved links available through the publisher's Web page. . . . Thorough, useful, and appealing, this . . . is a great update for collections." SLJ

Includes glossary and bibliographical references

Orr, Tamra B.

Florida; by Tamra B. Orr. Revised edition Children's Press 2014 144 p. ill. (chiefly col.), col. maps $40

Grades: 4 5 6 7   **975.9**

1. Florida
ISBN 9780531248805

Describes the history, geography, ecology, people, economy, cities, and sights of the state of Florida.

Includes bibliographical references (page 138) and index

Turner, Glennette Tilley

★ **Fort** Mose; and the story of the man who built the first free black settlement in Colonial America. Abrams Books for Young Readers 2010 42p il map $18.95

Grades: 5 6 7 8   **975.9**

1. Army officers 2. Florida -- History 3. Fort Mose site (Fla.) 4. Slavery -- United States 5. African Americans -- History 6. United States -- History -- 1600-1775, Colonial period
ISBN 978-0-8109-4056-7; 0-8109-4056-6

LC 2009-52205

"In the 18th century, some Africans escaped slavery in England's southern colonies to find freedom in the Spanish colony of Florida. As a leader of St. Augustine's community, African-born Francisco Menendez helped establish Fort Mose, the first free black community on North American soil. Turner does an excellent job of explaining how the residents of Fort Mose probably blended African, English, and Spanish traditions to create a unique—and uniquely American—culture." SLJ

Includes glossary and bibliographical references

976.1   Alabama

Parks, Rosa

★ **Rosa** Parks: my story; by Rosa Parks with Jim Haskins. Dial Bks. 1992 192p il $17.99; pa $6.99

Grades: 5 6 7 8   **976.1**

1. Civil rights activists 2. African Americans -- Civil rights 3. African American women -- Biography 4. Montgomery (Ala.) -- Race relations

ISBN 0-8037-0673-1; 0-14-130120-1 pa

LC 89-1124

Rosa Parks describes her early life and experiences with race discrimination, and her participation in the Montgomery bus boycott and the civil rights movement

"A remarkable story, a record of quiet bravery and modesty, a document of social significance, a taut drama told with candor." Bull Cent Child Books

Shirley, David

Alabama; by David Shirley and Joyce Hart. 2nd ed.; Marshall Cavendish Benchmark 2009 144p il map (Celebrate the states) lib bdg $39.93

Grades: 4 5 6 7   **976.1**

1. Alabama

ISBN 978-0-7614-3397-2; 0-7614-3397-X

LC 2008-4601

First published 2000

"Provides comprehensive information on the geography, history, wildlife, governmental structure, economy, cultural diversity, peoples, religion, and landmarks of Alabama." Publisher's note

Includes bibliographical references

Somervill, Barbara A.

Alabama; by Barbara A. Somervill. Revised edition Childrens Pr 2014 144 p. ill., map $40

Grades: 4 5 6 7   **976.1**

1. Alabama

ISBN 9780531248751

Describes the history, geography, ecology, people, economy, cities, and sights of the state of Alabama.

Includes bibliographical references (page 138) and index

976.2   Mississippi

Dell, Pamela

Mississippi; by Pamela Dell. Revised edition Children's Press 2014 144 p. ill. (chiefly col.), col maps $40

Grades: 4 5 6 7   **976.2**

1. Mississippi

ISBN 9780531248911

Describes the history, geography, ecology, people, economy, cities, and sights of the state of Mississippi.

Includes bibliographical references and index

Ribeiro, Myra

The **assassination** of Medgar Evers. Rosen Pub. Group 2002 64p il (Library of political assassinations) $26.50

Grades: 5 6 7 8   **976.2**

1. Civil rights activists 2. African Americans -- Civil rights

ISBN 0-8239-3544-2

LC 2001-2389

The author "does a good job of introducing the inspiring leader and the cause he fought for." Booklist

Includes glossary and bibliographical references

Shirley, David

Mississippi; [by] David Shirley and Patricia K. Kummer. Marshall Cavendish Benchmark 2008 144p il map (Celebrate the states) lib bdg $39.93

Grades: 4 5 6 7   **976.2**

1. Mississippi

ISBN 978-0-7614-2717-9; 0-7614-2717-1

LC 2007-7868

First published 1999

"Provides comprehensive information on the geography, history, wildlife, governmental structure, economy, cultural diversity, peoples, religion, and landmarks of Mississippi." Publisher's note

Includes bibliographical references

976.3   Louisiana

Lassieur, Allison

Louisiana; by Allison Lassieur. Revised edition Children's Press 2014 144 p. ill. (chiefly col.); col maps $40

Grades: 4 5 6 7   **976.3**

1. Louisiana

ISBN 9780531248867

Describes the history, geography, ecology, people, economy, cities, and sights of the state of Louisiana.

Includes bibliographical references and index

Worth, Richard

Louisiana, 1682-1803. National Geographic Society 2005 109p il map (Voices from colonial America) $21.95; lib bdg $32.90

Grades: 5 6 7 8   **976.3**

1. Louisiana -- History

ISBN 978-0-7922-6544-3; 0-7922-6544-0; 978-0-7922-6850-5 lib bdg; 0-7922-6850-4 lib bdg

LC 2005-16225

This "history of Louisiana begins in 1682 when Sieur de La Salle claimed the region for France. After that time, the region was governed under several different flags, including France, Spain, and Great Britain. . . . Thomas Jefferson purchased the land for the United States in 1803." Publisher's note

Includes bibliographical references

976.4   Texas

Chemerka, William R.

Juan Seguin; Tejano leader. William R. Chemerka ; illustrations by Don Collins. Bright Sky Press 2012 64 p. ill. $16.95

Grades: 3 4 5 6   **976.4**

1. Texas -- History 2. Political activists 3. Soldiers -- Texas -- Biography 4. Politicians -- Texas -- Biography 5. Texas -- History -- Republic, 1836-1846 6. Alamo (San Antonio, Tex.) -- Siege, 1836 7. Texas -- History -- Revolution, 1835-1836 -- Biography

ISBN 1933979798; 9781933979793

LC 2011052720

This book is a biography of Texan Juan Seguin by William R. Chemerka. Despite "having been forced to flee to Mexico and die in obscurity, Tejano Juan Seguin is recognised as a Texas hero. From his family's early support of settlers such as Stephen F. Austin to his years in the Texas Senate and as mayor of Bexar, this biography celebrates the life of Juan Seguin and his . . . efforts in securing Texas' independence." (WorldCat)

Green, Carl R.

Sam Houston; courageous Texas hero. by William R. Sanford and Carl R. Green. Enslow Publishers 2013 48 p. ill., map (library) $21.26; (paperback) $7.95

Grades: 5 6 7 8   **976.4**

1. Picture books for children 2. Governors -- Texas -- Biography 3. Legislators -- United States -- Biography 4. United States. Congress. Senate -- Biography

ISBN 0766040097; 9780766040090; 9781464400926

LC 2011051265

This book, part of the Courageous Heroes of the American West series, looks at Sam Houston. "One of the founders of Texas, Sam Houston served the state as governor and senator—but he is most remembered as an American hero" for defeating the Mexican army. "Surprising the Mexican troops with their bold attack, . . . the fiery Texans rallied to an overwhelming victory, claiming their independence." (Publisher's note)

Includes bibliographical references (p. 47) and index.

Haley, James L.

Stephen F. Austin and the founding of Texas. PowerPlus Bks. 2003 112p il map (Library of American lives and times) lib bdg $31.95 **976.4**

1. Pioneers 2. Frontier and pioneer life -- Texas

ISBN 0-8239-5738-1

LC 2001-4955

Surveys the life of Stephen Austin, an American pioneer, who later became one of the founders of Texas

"Clear and engaging.... The good-quality illustrations are almost all reproductions of period paintings, maps, and documents." SLJ

Includes glossary and bibliographical references

Levy, Janey

The **Alamo**; a primary source history of the legendary Texas mission. Rosen Central Primary Source 2003 64p il maps (Primary sources in American history) lib bdg $29.25

Grades: 7 8 9 10   **976.4**

1. Texas -- History 2. Alamo (San Antonio, Tex.)

ISBN 0-8239-3681-3

LC 2002-2368

A collection of primary source materials highlights the story behind the Alamo and its place in the history of San Antonio, Texas

This "will be extremely effective when introducing students to primary source material." Libr Media Connect

Includes bibliographical references

McNeese, Tim

The **Alamo**. Chelsea House 2003 136p il map (Sieges that changed the world) lib bdg $22.95

Grades: 5 6 7 8   **976.4**

1. Texas -- History 2. Alamo (San Antonio, Tex.)

ISBN 0-7910-7101-4

LC 2002-12914

Describes the historical background, events, and aftermath of the 1836 attack on the Alamo, in which Jim Bowie and Davy Crockett were among the many Texans killed or captured by Santa Ana's troops

The author presents "an excellent overview of Texas history in the first half of the book and details the two-week siege in the second. . . . A well-written, well-researched chronicle." SLJ

Includes bibliographical references

Newton, Michael

★ The **Texas** Rangers. Chelsea House Publishers 2011 128p il (Law enforcement agencies) lib bdg $35

Grades: 6 7 8 9   **976.4**

1. Law enforcement 2. Texas Rangers 3. Texas -- History

ISBN 978-1-60413-626-5; 1-60413-626-X

"Solidly and comprehensively researched. . . . In The Texas Rangers, a group that has long excited the country's imagination gets a full treatment, including its appearances on screen. An attractive design, plenty of photos, and solid back matter complete [the] package. Extremely useful for students and appealing for browsers." Booklist

Includes bibliographical references

Somervill, Barbara A.

Texas; Barbara A. Somervill. Revised edition Children's Press 2014 144 p. illustrations, maps $40

Grades: 4 5 6 7   **976.4**

1. Texas

ISBN 9780531248980

Presents an introduction to the geography, natural resources, history, economy, important sites, daily life, and people of Texas.

Includes bibliographical references and index

Teitelbaum, Michael

Texas, 1527-1836. National Geographic Society 2005 109p il map (Voices from colonial America) $21.95; lib bdg $32.90

Grades: 5 6 7 8   976.4

1. Texas -- History

ISBN 978-0-7922-6387-6; 0-7922-6387-1; 978-0-7922-6682-2 lib bdg; 0-7922-6682-X lib bdg

LC 2005-11450

"Presents the history of Texas, including life in Spanish Texas, the arrival of American settlers, and The Texas Republic and statehood." Publisher's note

Includes bibliographical references

Wade, Mary Dodson

Henrietta King, la patrona; by Mary Dodson Wade ; illustrated by Bill Farnsworth. Bright Sky Press 2012 23 p. $16.95

Grades: 4 5 6 7   976.4

1. Women ranchers -- Biography 2. Women philanthropists -- Biography 3. King Ranch (Tex.) 4. Texas -- Biography 5. Ranchers -- Texas -- Biography 6. Women ranchers -- Texas -- Biography 7. Philanthropists -- Texas -- Biography 8. Women philanthropists -- Texas -- Biography

ISBN 1933979631; 9781933979632

LC 2011052721

This book by Mary Dodson Wade "examines the . . . life of one of Texas's foremost frontier women and philanthropists, Henrietta Maria Morse Chamberlain King. . . . Henrietta accompanied her missionary father on his travels and later settled with her husband Richard King in the untamed frontiers of the south Texas gulf coast. . . . Under her stewardship, the family ranch went from . . . $500,000 in debt at her husband's death to a debt-free enterprise of more than one million acres." (Publisher's note)

Walker, Paul Robert

Remember the Alamo; Texians, Tejanos, and Mexicans tell their stories. by Paul Robert Walker. National Geographic 2007 61p il map $17.95; lib bdg $27.90

Grades: 5 6 7 8   976.4

1. Texas -- History 2. Alamo (San Antonio, Tex.)

ISBN 978-1-4263-0010-3; 978-1-4263-0011-0 lib bdg

LC 2006034497

"Opening with clear context about why tensions between Texas residents and the Mexican government were brought to a head, the book then chronicles events directly leading to the siege of the Alamo and its immediate aftermath, following up with an epilogue on the decisive battle of San Jacinto 10 months later. Bringing the history to life is a healthy selection of dramatic, modern paintings along with plenty of archival drawings, maps, and old photos." Booklist

Includes bibliographical references

Warrick, Karen Clemens

Alamo; victory or death on the Texas frontier. Enslow Publishers 2008 128p il map (America's living history) lib bdg $31.93

Grades: 5 6 7 8   976.4

1. Texas -- History 2. Alamo (San Antonio, Tex.)

ISBN 978-0-7660-2937-8; 0-7660-2937-9

LC 2007038458

"Archival photographs, reproductions, maps, and sidebars combine with vivid [text] to provide [a] comprehensive [introduction] to [the siege and battle of the Alamo]. . . . [This] engaging [volume] vividly [brings its] time [period] to life." Horn Book Guide

Includes glossary and bibliographical references

Worth, Richard

The **Texas** war of independence: the 1800s; by Richard Worth. Marshall Cavendish Benchmark 2009 79p il map (Hispanic America) lib bdg $23.95

Grades: 6 7 8 9   976.4

1. Mexican Americans 2. Mexican War, 1846-1848 3. Texas -- History

ISBN 978-0-7614-2934-0

LC 2007029478

This "provides a solid overview of these pivotal events in Hispanic American history. Illustrated throughout with maps and archival images." Booklist

Includes glossary and bibliographical references

976.6 Oklahoma

Baldwin, Guy

Oklahoma; by Guy Baldwin and Joyce Hart. 2nd ed.; Marshall Cavendish Benchmark 2009 144p il map (Celebrate the states) lib bdg $42.79

Grades: 5 6 7 8   976.6

1. Oklahoma

ISBN 978-0-7614-4032-1; 0-7614-4032-1

LC 2008044261

First published 2001

This offers information on the geography, history, wildlife, governmental structure, economy, cultural diversity, peoples, religion, and landmarks of Oklahoma.

Includes bibliographical references

Orr, Tamra B.

Oklahoma; by Tamra B. Orr. Revised edition Children's Press 2014 144 p. ill. (chiefly col.), col maps $40

Grades: 4 5 6 7   976.6

1. Oklahoma

ISBN 9780531248973

Describes the history, geography, ecology, people, economy, cities and sights of the state of Oklahoma.

Includes bibliographical references and index

976.7   Arkansas

Altman, Linda Jacobs

Arkansas; [by] Linda Jacobs Altman, Ettagale Blauer, and Jason Laure. 2nd ed.; Marshall Cavendish Benchmark 2009 144p il map (Celebrate the states) lib bdg $42.79

Grades: 4 5 6 7   **976.7**

1. Arkansas

ISBN 978-0-7614-3001-8; 0-7614-3001-6

First published 2000

"Provides comprehensive information on the geography, history, wildlife, governmental structure, economy, cultural diversity, peoples, religion, and landmarks of Arkansas." Publisher's note

Includes bibliographical references

976.8   Tennessee

Barrett, Tracy

Tennessee; by Tracy Barrett. 2nd ed.; Marshall Cavendish Benchmark 2006 144p il map (Celebrate the states) lib bdg $39.93

Grades: 4 5 6 7   **976.8**

1. Tennessee

ISBN 978-0-7614-2151-1; 0-7614-2151-3

LC 2005-24055

First published 1998

"Provides comprehensive information on the geography, history, wildlife, governmental structure, economy, cultural diversity, peoples, religion, and landmarks of Tennessee." Publisher's note

Includes bibliographical references

Graham, Amy

Great Smoky Mountains National Park; adventure, explore, discover. [by] Amy Graham. MyReportLinks.com Books 2009 128p il map (America's national parks) lib bdg $33.27

Grades: 5 6 7 8   **976.8**

1. Great Smoky Mountains National Park (N.C. and Tenn.) 2. National parks and reserves -- United States

ISBN 978-1-59845-093-4 lib bdg; 1-59845-093-X lib bdg

LC 2007-13456

This "informative, well-written book contains a physical description of the park; a summary of its history including the Native peoples of the area; activities such as hiking trails, campsites, and visitor centers; information about the park's plants, animals, and weather; full-color photographs; and numerous approved links available through the publisher's Web page. . . . Thorough, useful, and appealing, this . . . is a great update for collections." SLJ

Includes glossary and bibliographical references

Green, Carl R.

Davy Crockett; courageous hero of the Alamo. by William R. Sanford and Carl R. Green. Rev. ed. Enslow Publishers 2013 48 p. col. ill., map (library) $21.26; (paperback) $7.95

Grades: 5 6 7 8   **976.8**

1. Alamo (San Antonio, Tex.) -- History -- Siege, 1836 2. Pioneers -- Tennessee -- Biography 3. Legislators -- United States -- Biography 4. United States. Congress. House -- Biography

ISBN 0766040054; 9780766040052; 9781464400865

LC 2011037749

This book by William Sanford is part of the Courageous Heroes of the American West series and focuses on Davy Crockett. "The courageous Texans chose to defend the fort in San Antonio against more than two thousand Mexican soldiers. . . . Although his brave deeds at the Alamo made him legendary, Crockett had already gained fame as a hunter, soldier, and U.S. Congressman." (Publisher's note)

Includes bibliographical references (p. 47) and index.

Somervill, Barbara A.

Tennessee; by Barbara A. Somervill. Revised edition Children's Press 2015 144 p. illustrations, maps $40

Grades: 4 5 6 7   **976.8**

1. Tennessee

ISBN 9780531282946

Presents an introduction to the geography, natural resources, history, economy, important sites, daily life, and people of Tennessee.

Includes bibliographical references and index

976.9   Kentucky

Barrett, Tracy

Kentucky; [by] Tracy Barrett. 2nd ed.; Marshall Cavendish Benchmark 2008 144p il map (Celebrate the states) lib bdg $39.93

Grades: 4 5 6 7   **976.9**

1. Kentucky

ISBN 978-0-7614-2715-5; 0-7614-2715-5

LC 2007-6388

First published 1999

"Provides comprehensive information on the geography, history, wildlife, governmental structure, economy, cultural diversity, peoples, religion, and landmarks of Kentucky." Publisher's note

Includes bibliographical references

Green, Carl R.

Daniel Boone; courageous frontiersman. by William R. Sanford and Carl R. Green. Enslow Publishers 2013 48 p. col. ill., map (library) $21.26; (paperback) $7.95

Grades: 5 6 7 8   **976.9**

1. Frontier and pioneer life -- United States 2. Kentucky -- Biography 3. Pioneers -- Kentucky -- Biography 4. Frontier and pioneer life -- Kentucky

ISBN 076604002X; 9780766040021; 9781464400858; 9781464509926; 9781464609923

LC 2011037736

This book by William Sanford is part of the Courageous Heroes of the American West series and focuses on Daniel Boone. "Through the untamed wilderness, Daniel Boone marched forward. He was leading a group of workers to carve out the Wilderness Road. Over hills, through dense forests, along stony paths, and fending off American Indian attacks, Boone never quit. He opened the way for thousands of settlers to move west, establishing the settlement of Boonesborough in 1775." (Publisher's note)

Includes bibliographical references (p. 47) and index.

Santella, Andrew

Kentucky; by Andrew Santella. Revised edition Children's Press 2014 144 p. ill. (chiefly col.), col maps $40

Grades: 4 5 6 7   **976.9**
1. Kentucky
ISBN 9780531248850

Describes the history, geography, ecology, people, economy, cities, and sights of the state of Kentucky.

Includes bibliographical references and index

977   North central United States

Kummer, Patricia K.

The **Great** Lakes; [by] Patricia K. Kummer. Marshall Cavendish Benchmark 2008 96p il map (Nature's wonders) lib bdg $35.64

Grades: 5 6 7 8   **977**
1. Great Lakes
ISBN 978-0-7614-2853-4 lib bdg; 0-7614-2853-4 lib bdg

           LC 2007019728

"Provides comprehensive information on the geography, history, wildlife, peoples, and environmental issues of the Great Lakes." Publisher's note

Includes glossary and bibliographical references

977.1   Ohio

Stille, Darlene R.

Ohio; by Darlene R. Stille. Revised edition Children's Press 2015 144 p. col ill, col maps $40

Grades: 4 5 6 7   **977.1**
1. Ohio
ISBN 9780531282878

Presents an introduction to the geography, natural resources, history, economy, important sites, daily life, and people of Ohio.

Includes bibliographical references and index

Sherrow, Victoria

Ohio; [by] Victoria Sherrow. 2nd. ed.; Marshall Cavendish Benchmark 2008 144p il map (Celebrate the states) lib bdg $39.93

Grades: 4 5 6 7   **977.1**
1. Ohio
ISBN 978-0-7614-2558-8; 0-7614-2558-6

           LC 2006-34103
First published 1999

"Provides comprehensive information on the geography, history, wildlife, governmental structure, economy, cultural

diversity, peoples, religion, and landmarks of Ohio." Publisher's note

Includes bibliographical references

977.2   Indiana

Stille, Darlene R.

Indiana; by Darlene R. Stille. Revised edition Children's Press 2014 144 p. ill. (chiefly col.), col maps $40

Grades: 4 5 6 7   **977.2**
1. Indiana
ISBN 9780531248843

Presents an introduction to the geography, natural resources, history, economy, important sites, daily life, and people of Indiana.

Includes bibliographical references (page 138) and index

977.3   Illinois

Burgan, Michael

Illinois; by Michael Burgan. Revised edition Children's Press 2014 144 p. ill. (chiefly col.), col maps $40

Grades: 4 5 6 7   **977.3**
1. Illinois
ISBN 9780531248836

Describes the history, geography, ecology, people, economy, cities, and sights of the state of Illinois.

Includes bibliographical references (page 138) and index

Hurd, Owen

Chicago history for kids; triumphs and tragedies of the Windy city, includes 21 activities. [by] Owen Hurd. Chicago Review Press 2007 182p il map $14.95

Grades: 5 6 7 8   **977.3**
1. Chicago (Ill.) -- History
ISBN 978-1-55652-654-1; 1-55652-654-7

           LC 2006031807

"This attractive overview begins with geography and moves to the colorful stories that characterize the city. Hurd tapped local experts and collections, using primary and secondary sources and the responses of young readers to craft this engaging resource. . . . Excellent-quality photos, maps, illustrations, or boxed facts appear on every page." SLJ

Includes bibliographical references

Morrison, Joan Wehlen

Home front girl; a diary of love, literature, and growing up in wartime America. Joan Wehlen Morrison ; edited by Susan Signe Morrison. Chicago Review Press 2012 272 p. $19.95

Grades: 7 8 9 10 11 12   **977.3**
1. History -- Sources 2. World War, 1939-1945 -- United States 3. Chicago (Ill.) -- Biography 4. Schoolgirls -- Illinois -- Chicago -- Diaries 5. Chicago (Ill.) -- Social

life and customs -- 20th century
ISBN 1613744579; 9781613744574

LC 2012027068

This book is a "collection of journal entries, poems, clippings, and sketches by the late [Joan Wehlen] Morrison, edited by her daughter, span[ing] the tumultuous years between 1937 and 1943, which took Morrison from age 14 to 20, and took the world from the Great Depression into WWII. . . . Morrison details her school day concerns and studies, exploring the city, her crushes on boys, attending the University of Chicago, and her thoughts on religion, books, films, and more." (Publishers Weekly)

Murphy, Jim

★ The **great** fire. Scholastic 1995 144p il maps $16.95; pa $12.99

Grades: 5 6 7 8 9 10   977.3
  1. Fires -- Chicago (Ill.)
ISBN 0-590-47267-4; 0-439-20307-4 pa

LC 94-9963

Newbery honor book, 1996

"Firsthand descriptions by persons who lived through the 1871 Chicago fire are woven into a gripping account of this famous disaster. Murphy also examines the origins of the fire, the errors of judgment that delayed the effective response, the organizational problems of the city's firefighters, and the postfire efforts to rebuild the city. Newspaper lithographs and a few historical photographs convey the magnitude of human suffering and confusion." Horn Book Guide

Includes bibliographical references

977.4   Michigan

Bial, Raymond

The **Menominee.** Marshall Cavendish Benchmark 2006 127p il map (Lifeways) lib bdg $38.50

Grades: 5 6 7 8   977.4
  1. Native Americans 2. Menominee Indians
ISBN 978-0-7614-1903-7; 0-7614-1903-9

LC 2004-22392

Discusses the history, culture, beliefs, changing ways, and notable people of the Menominee.

Includes glossary and bibliographical references

Brill, Marlene Targ

Michigan; by Marlene Targ Brill. 2d ed.; Marshall Cavendish Benchmark 2007 144p il map (Celebrate the states) lib bdg $39.93

Grades: 4 5 6 7   977.4
  1. Michigan
ISBN 978-0-7614-2351-5; 0-7614-2351-6

LC 2006-8181

First published 1998

"Provides comprehensive information on the geography, history, wildlife, governmental structure, economy, cultural diversity, peoples, religion, and landmarks of Michigan." Publisher's note

Includes bibliographical references

Raatma, Luica

Michigan; by Lucia Raatma. Revised edition Children's Press 2014 144 p. ill. (chiefly col.), col maps $40

Grades: 4 5 6 7   977.4
  1. Michigan
ISBN 9780531248904

Describes the history, geography, ecology, people, economy, cities, and sights of Michigan.

Includes bibliographical references and index

977.5   Wisconsin

Blashfield, Jean F.

Wisconsin; by Jean F. Blashfield. Revised edition Children's Press 2014 144 p. illustrations, maps $40

Grades: 4 5 6 7   977.5
  1. Wisconsin
ISBN 9780531248744

Describes the history, geography, ecology, famous people, economy, cities and sights of the state of Wisconsin.

Includes bibliographical references and index

977.6   Minnesota

Schwabacher, Martin

Minnesota; [by] Martin Schwabacher and Patricia K. Kummer. 2nd ed.; Marshall Cavendish Benchmark 2008 144p il map (Celebrate the states) lib bdg $39.93

Grades: 4 5 6 7   977.6
  1. Minnesota
ISBN 978-0-7614-2716-2; 0-7614-2716-3

LC 2007-2895

First published 1999

"Provides comprehensive information on the geography, history, wildlife, governmental structure, economy, cultural diversity, peoples, religion, and landmarks of Minnesota." Publisher's note

Includes bibliographical references

977.7   Iowa

Blashfield, Jean F.

Iowa; by Jean F. Blashfield. Revised edition Children's Press 2015 144 p. ill. (chiefly col.), col maps $40

Grades: 4 5 6 7   977.7
  1. Iowa
ISBN 9780531282793

Presents an introduction to the geography, natural resources, history, economy, important sites, daily life, and people of Iowa.

Includes bibliographical references and index

Morrice, Polly Alison

Iowa; by Polly Morrice and Joyce Hart. 2nd ed.; Marshall Cavendish Benchmark 2007 144p il map (Celebrate the states) lib bdg $39.93

Grades: 4 5 6 7 **977.7**

1. Iowa

ISBN 978-0-7614-2350-8; 0-7614-2350-8

LC 2006-13620

First published 1998

"Provides comprehensive information on the geography, history, wildlife, governmental structure, economy, cultural diversity, peoples, religion, and landmarks of Iowa." Publisher's note

Includes bibliographical references

977.8 Missouri

Bennett, Michelle

Missouri; by Michelle Bennett and Joyce Hart. 2nd ed.; Marshall Cavendish Benchmark 2010 144p il map (Celebrate the states) lib bdg $42.79

Grades: **977.8**

1. Missouri

ISBN 978-0-7614-4727-6; 0-7614-4727-X

LC 2009005754

First published 2001

This offers information on the geography, history, wildlife, governmental structure, economy, cultural diversity, peoples, religion, and landmarks of Missouri.

Includes bibliographical references

Blashfield, Jean F.

Missouri; by Jean F. Blashfield. Revised edition Children's Press 2015 144 p. ill. (chiefly col.), col maps $40

Grades: 4 5 6 7 **977.8**

1. Missouri

ISBN 9780531282823

Explores the land, people, history, economy, and travel opportunities of the state of Missouri.

Includes bibliographical references and index

978 Western United States

The **American** frontier; James D. Torr, book editor. Greenhaven Press 2002 240p il (Turning points in world history) lib bdg $34.95; pa $23.70

Grades: 7 8 9 10 **978**

1. West (U.S.) -- History 2. United States -- Territorial expansion 3. Frontier and pioneer life -- West (U.S.)

ISBN 0-7377-0786-0 lib bdg; 0-7377-0785-2 pa

LC 2001-33514

This is a collection of essays about the American frontier, with an introduction and summaries

Includes bibliographical references

Bertozzi, Nick

★ **Lewis** & Clark. First Second 2011 136p il pa $16.99

Grades: 5 6 7 8 **978**

1. Explorers 2. Graphic novels 3. Lewis and Clark Expedition (1804-1806) 4. Territorial governors 5. United States -- History -- 1783-1865 -- Graphic novels

ISBN 978-1-59643-450-9 pa; 1-59643-450-3 pa

LC 2010-36255

Presents, in graphic novel format, the adventures of explorers Lewis and Clark during their journey from St. Louis to the Pacific Ocean.

Bertozzi "brings new life to the epic westward journey of explorers Lewis and Clark in this graphic novel perfect for history buffs. . . . Lewis's . . . deteriorating mental state throughout the expedition and particularly on the return trip is eloquently drawn, with Bertozzi managing to combine both history lesson and character study in strong, gripping drawings." SLJ

Brown, Don

★ The **great** American dust bowl; by Don Brown. Houghton Mifflin Harcourt 2013 80 p. $18.99

Grades: 5 6 7 8 9 **978**

1. Dust storms -- Graphic novels 2. Dust Bowl Era, 1931-1939

ISBN 0547815506; 9780547815503

Author Don Brown presents a "graphic novel of one of America's most catastrophic natural events: the Dust Bowl. On a clear, warm Sunday, April 14, 1935, a wild wind whipped up millions upon millions of these specks of dust to form a duster, a savage storm on America's high southern plains." (Publisher's note)

"In this bleak yet compelling graphic-novel-style glimpse at the Dirty Thirties, Brown crisply paces the narrative with fascinating glimpses of the sociological and geological causes of the Dust Bowl. The color brown is a recurring theme here, as Brown relies, aptly, almost entirely on shades of brown throughout. Primary source material is used liberally, as characters speak directly to the reader, documentary-style." (Horn Book)

Collier, Christopher

★ **Indians,** cowboys, and farmers and the battle for the Great Plains, 1865-1910; [by] Christopher Collier, James Lincoln Collier. Benchmark Bks. (Tarrytown) 2001 95p il map (Drama of American history) lib bdg $31.36

Grades: 6 7 8 9 **978**

1. Farmers 2. Cowhands 3. Railroads 4. Great Plains -- History 5. Native Americans -- Great Plains 6. Frontier and pioneer life -- West (U.S.)

ISBN 0-7614-1052-X

LC 00-21103

Discusses the settling of the area between the Missouri River and the Rocky Mountains and the conflicting interests of the different groups involved—the Indians, cowboys, farmers, sheepherders, and railroad barons

Includes bibliographical references

Croy, Anita

★ **Ancient** Pueblo; archaeology unlocks the secrets of America's past. by Anita Croy; J. Jefferson Reid, consultant. National Geographic 2007 64p il map (National Geographic investigates) $17.95; lib bdg $27.90

Grades: 4 5 6 7 **978**

1. Archeology 2. Pueblo Indians 3. Southwestern States -- Antiquities

ISBN 978-1-4263-0130-8; 978-1-4263-0131-5 lib bdg
LC 2007024800

This describes the prehistoric sites of the American Southwest, and what archeologists have learned from them about the lives of ancient Pueblo peoples.

Includes glossary and bibliographical references

Freedman, Russell

★ **The life** and death of Crazy Horse; drawings by Amos Bad Heart Bull. Holiday House 1996 166p il maps $22.95

Grades: 5 6 7 8 9 10 **978**

1. Oglala Indians 2. Indian chiefs 3. Native Americans -- Biography

ISBN 0-8234-1219-9
LC 95-33303

A biography of the Oglala Indian leader who relentlessly resisted the white man's attempt to take over Indian lands.

This is "a compelling biography that is based on primary source documents and illustrated with pictographs by a Sioux band historian." Voice Youth Advocates

Includes bibliographical references

George-Warren, Holly

The **cowgirl** way; hats off to America's women of the West. Houghton Mifflin Books for Children 2010 112p il $18

Grades: 4 5 6 7 **978**

1. Cowhands 2. Women -- West (U.S.)

ISBN 978-0-618-73738-3; 0-618-73738-3

"With ample dynamic photos and lively quotes throughout, George-Warren presents a thoroughly absorbing overview of the history of cowgirls up to the present. . . . Famous figures such as Belle Starr, Calamity Jane, and Annie Oakley are discussed in brief, but the real delights here are the anecdotes on lesser-known figures such as Lucille Mulhall, the first woman to be dubbed a cowgirl in print. . . . The introduction of women as rodeo and trick riders and their contributions to the sports in the 1920s and '30s are covered in fascinating detail, as are the film and singing sensations of the 1940s and '50s." SLJ

Green, Carl R.

Buffalo Bill Cody; courageous wild west showman. by William R. Sanford and Carl R. Green. Enslow Publishers 2013 48 p. ill., map (library) $21.26; (paperback) $7.95

Grades: 5 6 7 8 **978**

1. Buffalo Bill's Wild West Show 2. Frontier and pioneer life -- West (U.S.) 3. West (U.S.) -- Biography 4. Pioneers -- West (U.S.) -- Biography 5. Buffalo Bill's Wild West Show -- History 6. Entertainers --

United States -- Biography

ISBN 0766040070; 9780766040076; 9781464400902
LC 2011031052

This book by William Sanford and Carl R. Green is part of the "Courageious Heroes of the American West" series. It presents a biography of Buffalo Bill Cody, who "had many jobs--Pony Express rider, scout, soldier, buffalo hunter. But he was most famous for entertaining audiences with his Wild West show. Many Americans and others around the world could not travel to see the real Wild West, so Buffalo Bill Brought it to them." (Publisher's note)

Includes bibliographical references (p. 47) and index.

Calamity Jane; courageous wild west woman. by William R. Sanford and Carl R. Green. Enslow Publishers 2013 48 p. ill., map (library) $21.26; (paperback) $7.95

Grades: 5 6 7 8 **978**

1. Cowgirls 2. West (U.S.) -- Biography 3. Pioneers -- West (U.S.) -- Biography 4. Women pioneers -- West (U.S.) -- Biography

ISBN 0766040100; 9780766040106; 9781464400933
LC 2011033840

This book by William Sanford is part of the Courageous Heroes of the American West series and focuses on Calamity Jane. "The truth and myth are difficult to separate in the wild life of Calamity Jane. An independent spirit, she never stayed in one place for long. She worked as a gold prospector, bullwhacker, nurse, and had many other jobs, Calamity Jane refused to conform to the typical roles of a nineteenth-century woman." (Publisher's note)

Includes bibliographical references (p. 47) and index.

Zebulon Pike; courageous Rocky Mountain explorer. by William R. Sanford and Carl R. Green. Enslow Publishers 2013 48 p. ill. (library) $21.26; (paperback) $7.95

Grades: 5 6 7 8 **978**

1. Exploration 2. West (U.S.) -- Biography 3. West (U.S.) -- History -- To 1848 4. Explorers -- West (U.S.) -- Biography 5. West (U.S.) -- Discovery and exploration

ISBN 1464400954; 9780766040120; 9781464400957
LC 2011051629

This book by William R. Sanford is part of the Courageous Heroes of the American West series and looks at Zebulon Pike. "After the United States purchased the Louisiana Territory in 1803, the young nation needed brave pioneers to explore this vast uncharted land. Zebulon Pike . . . led an expedition across rolling prairies before arriving at the towering mountains" and being the first to explore the southern Rocky Mountains. (Publisher's note)

Includes bibliographical references (p. 47) and index.

Huey, Lois Miner

American archaeology uncovers the westward movement. Marshall Cavendish Benchmark 2009 64p il map (American archaeology) lib bdg $21.95

Grades: 4 5 6 7 **978**

1. Historical geography 2. West (U.S.) -- History 3. United States -- Territorial expansion 4. Frontier and pioneer life -- West (U.S.) 5. Excavations (Archeology)

-- United States
ISBN 978-0-7614-4265-3 lib bdg; 0-7614-4265-0
lib bdg

LC 2009003167

This describes how archeologists have learned about the history of the American West.

"The visually pleasing . . . [book is] replete with maps, paintings, and photographs, all appropriately placed and thoughtfully captioned. . . . Huey's focus on American history, which is broken down into small, manageable chunks, is sure to entice budding historians." SLJ

Includes glossary and bibliographical references

Marrin, Albert

★ **Years** of dust; the story of the Dust Bowl. Dutton Children's Books 2009 128p il map $22.99

Grades: 6 7 8 9 10   **978**

1. Droughts 2. Dust storms 3. Great Depression, 1929-1939 4. Great Plains -- History

ISBN 978-0-525-42077-4; 0-525-42077-0

LC 2008-13898

"The engaging narrative includes quotes from a variety of primary sources, and it is abundantly illustrated throughout with photographs and other archival material, making this a reader-friendly, insightful work of history." Kirkus

Includes glossary and bibliographical references

McKissack, Fredrick, 1939-2013

★ **Best** shot in the West; the adventures of Nat Love. by Patricia C. McKissack and Fredrick L. McKissack, Jr. ; illustrated by Randy DuBurke. Chronicle Books 2012 129 p. $19.99

Grades: 7 8 9   **978**

1. Cowhands -- Graphic novels 2. Railroads -- United States 3. West (U.S.) -- History -- Graphic novels 4. African Americans -- Biography -- Graphic novels 5. Cartoons and comics 6. West (U.S.) -- Cartoons and comics 7. Cowboys -- West (U.S.) -- Cartoons and comics 8. African American cowboys -- West (U.S.) -- Cartoons and comics 9. African Americans -- West (U.S.) -- Biography -- Cartoons and comics

ISBN 0811857492; 9780811857499

LC 2007021419

In this graphic novel, "Nat Love's cattle-driving days are long over and America is a much tamer place when the black cowboy, now a Pullman porter, runs into 'Bugler,' a man he knew back in the day. Bugler's son is a publisher . . . of . . . stories from the Wild West, and Love is persuaded to contribute his memoirs. From this . . . story, . . . [Patricia C. and Frederick L.] McKissack . . . segue into Love's adventures, based on his autobiography." (Bulletin of the Center for Children's Books)

Miller, Brandon Marie

Women of the frontier; 16 tales of trailblazing homesteaders, entrepreneurs, and rabble-rousers. Brandon Marie Miller. Chicago Review Press 2013 256 p. (hardcover) $19.95

Grades: 7 8 9 10 11 12   **978**

1. Women -- United States 2. Frontier and pioneer life -- United States 3. West (U.S.) -- History -- Biography 4.

Women pioneers -- West (U.S.) -- History -- Biography
ISBN 1883052971; 9781883052973

LC 2012035756

This book, part of the Women of Action series, is a collection of "tales of women's trials and triumphs during the years of settlement in the [U.S.] West. . . . [The section] 'Many a Weary Mile' describes the trip west by wagon; 'Oh Give Me a Home' explores early pioneering experiences. 'A Woman Can Work,' 'And Now the Fun Begins' and 'Great Expectations for the Future' all examine the careers of women who stepped out of typical female roles of the era." (Kirkus)

Includes bibliographical references and index

★ The **Old** West: history and heritage. Marshall Cavendish Reference 2009 11v il map set$359.95

Grades: 6 7 8 9   **978**

1. Reference books 2. West (U.S.) -- History -- Encyclopedias

ISBN 978-0-7614-7829-4; 0-7614-7829-9

LC 2008062302

In this set "each volume contains about 100 pages with 18 to 21 signed articles that vary in length from 3 to 10 pages and are arranged in an easy-to-use alphabetical sequence. The overall style is lively and enticing. The scope of the 193 articles includes the Canadian West and the Mexican territory and deals with the time period from 1787 to 1912. . . . The set is thoughtfully arranged and can be used by a wide range of students. The articles are interesting and enlightening." Booklist

Includes glossary and bibliographical references

Olson, Tod

How to get rich on a Texas cattle drive; afterword by Marc Aronson; illustrations by Scott Allred & Gregory Proch. National Geographic 2010 47p il map $18.95

Grades: 4 5 6 7   **978**

1. Cowhands 2. West (U.S.) -- History 3. Frontier and pioneer life -- West (U.S.)

ISBN 978-1-4263-0524-5; 1-4263-0524-9

"This book provides one of the better true-to-life insider accounts of what happens on a cattle drive: why the cattle are being driven, where they're being driven to and from, and the multitude of daily chores and unforeseen obstacles along the way. Period photos and artwork, as well as original drawings, make for a lively design, and an ongoing ledger keeps track of the main character's mostly modest finances." Booklist

★ **How** to get rich on the Oregon Trail; my adventures among cows, crooks & heroes on the road to fame and fortune. [illustrations by Scott Allred & Gregory Proch; afterword by Marc Aronson] National Geographic 2009 47p il (How to get rich) $18.95; lib bdg $27.90

Grades: 4 5 6 7   **978**

1. Oregon Trail 2. Frontier and pioneer life 3. Overland journeys to the Pacific 4. West (U.S.) -- History

ISBN 978-1-4263-0412-5; 1-4263-0412-9; 978-1-4263-0413-2 lib bdg; 1-4263-0413-7 lib bdg

"The action follows young Will Reed and his family as they set off from Illinois to find their fortune along the 2,000-mile Oregon Trail. . . . Informing Will's impish sketches and wry journal entries is a wealth of information about life along the trail. . . . An ongoing ledger calculates the family's balance as it fluctuates from $10.70 to $3,021.70, but it's clear that this journey is more about survival than riches. The illustrations, historical anecdotes, and run-ins with everyone from the Mormons to escaped slaves to Abraham Lincoln form a perfect blend of history and humbuggery." Booklist

Patent, Dorothy Hinshaw

The **horse** and the Plains indians; a powerful partnership. Dorothy Hinshaw Patent ; photographs by William Munoz. Clarion Books 2012 xiii, 98 p.p ill. (chiefly col.) $17.99

Grades: 4 5 6 7 8   978
1. Horses 2. Domestic animals 3. Native Americans -- Great Plains 4. Horses -- Great Plains -- History 5. Human-animal relationships -- Great Plains -- History 6. Indians of North America -- Domestic animals -- Great Plains
ISBN 9780547125510

LC 2011025954

This book explores the relationship between Plains Indians and horses. The "Plains Indians and the horse were not always inseparable. Once, Native Americans used dogs to help carry their goods, and even after the Spaniards introduced the horse to the Americas," the Spanish hoarded the valuable animals. But "soon horses escaped from Spanish settlements, and Native Americans quickly learned how valuable the horse could be as a hunting mount, beast of burden, and military steed." (Publisher's note)

Includes bibliographical references and index

Pendergast, Tom

Westward expansion: almanac; [by] Tom Pendergast and Sara Pendergast; Christine Slovey, editor. U.X.L 2000 xlvi, 254p il (Westward expansion reference library) $60

Grades: 8 9 10 11 12   978
1. Reference books 2. West (U.S.) -- History 3. Frontier and pioneer life -- West (U.S.)
ISBN 0-7876-4862-0

LC 00-36375

This almanac "documents the chronological events that created a romantic national mythology around the pioneers who blazed trails through the wilderness." Publisher's note

Includes bibliographical references

Westward expansion: primary sources; [by] Tom Pendergast and Sara Pendergast; Christine Slovey, editor. U.X.L 2001 xxix, 260p (Westward expansion reference library) $60

Grades: 7 8 9 10   978
1. West (U.S.) -- History 2. United States -- Territorial expansion
ISBN 0-7876-4864-7

LC 00-107861

This volume provides "full text or excerpts from diaries, books, letters and many other documents." Publisher's note

Includes bibliographical references

Reis, Ronald A.

The **Dust** Bowl. Chelsea House Publishers 2008 128p il (Great historic disasters) lib bdg $35

Grades: 6 7 8 9   978
1. Droughts 2. Dust storms 3. Great Plains -- History
ISBN 978-0-7910-9737-3 lib bdg; 0-7910-9737-4 lib bdg

LC 2008004952

This describes the conditions that led up to the disastrous dust storms of the 1930s in the American Great Plains, and their consequences

The book covers its topic "thoroughly and [includes] high-quality photographs and occasional sidebars. . . . Reis includes solid research and numerous points of view." SLJ

Includes glossary and bibliographical references

Schlissel, Lillian

Black frontiers; a history of African American heroes in the Old West. Simon & Schuster Bks. for Young Readers 1995 80p il hardcover o.p. pa $7.99

Grades: 5 6 7 8   978
1. West (U.S.) -- History 2. African Americans -- History 3. Frontier and pioneer life -- West (U.S.)
ISBN 0-689-80285-4; 0-689-83315-6 pa

LC 92-120

Focuses on the experiences of blacks as mountain men, soldiers, homesteaders, and scouts on the frontiers of the American West

"Good-quality period photos and black-and-white reproductions appear on nearly every page, adding human interest and realism to the text. An excellent addition to black history or westward movement units." Booklist

Includes bibliographical references

Sheinkin, Steve

Which way to the wild West? everything your schoolbooks didn't tell you about America's westward expansion. illustrated by Tim Robinson. Roaring Brook Press 2009 260p il map $19.95

Grades: 5 6 7 8   978
1. West (U.S.) -- History 2. United States -- Territorial expansion 3. Frontier and pioneer life -- West (U.S.)
ISBN 978-1-59643-321-2; 1-59643-321-3

Presents the greatest adventures of America's Westward expansion, from the Louisiana Purchase and the gold rush to the Indian wars and life of the cowboy, as well as the everyday happenings that defined living on the frontier

"An engaging storyteller, the author uses humor and little-known anecdotes to make such subjects as Manifest Destiny, the Mexican-American War, the Gold Rush and Custer's Last Stand entertaining for readers. His chatty, informal style . . . will appeal to young readers turned off to history by stale textbooks. Robinson's cartoons complement the text. . . . An accessible and engaging historical overview." Kirkus

Includes bibliographical references

Stefoff, Rebecca

★ **American** voices from the opening of the West. Benchmark Bks. 2002 105p (American voices from--) lib bdg $32.79

Grades: 6 7 8 9 **978**

1. West (U.S.) -- History 2. Frontier and pioneer life -- West (U.S.)

ISBN 0-7614-1201-8

LC 2001-8681

Presents the history of the westward expansion of the United States in the eighteenth and nineteenth centuries through excerpts from letters, newspaper articles, journal entries, and laws of the time

Includes glossary and bibliographical references

★ **American** voices from the Wild West. Marshall Cavendish Benchmark 2007 111p (American voices from--) lib bdg $37.07

Grades: 6 7 8 9 **978**

1. West (U.S.) -- History

ISBN 978-0-7614-2170-2 lib bdg; 0-7614-2170-X lib bdg

LC 2005028192

"Presents the history of the Wild West through a variety of primary source images and documents, such as diary entries, newspaper accounts, public speeches, popular literature, and personal letters." Publisher's note

Includes glossary and bibliographical references

Tunis, Edwin

★ **Frontier** living; written and illustrated by Edwin Tunis. Lyons Press 2000 165p il map pa $18.95

Grades: 5 6 7 8 9 10 **978**

1. West (U.S.) -- History 2. Frontier and pioneer life -- West (U.S.)

ISBN 1-58574-137-X

LC 00-710694

First published 1961 by World Publishing Company

This volume "portrays the manners and customs of the frontiersman and his family from the beginning of the westward movement through the 19th century in . . . text and more than 200 drawings." Wis Libr Bull

Vivian, R. Gwinn

Chaco Canyon; [by] R. Gwinn Vivian and Margaret Anderson. Oxford University Press 2002 47p il maps (Digging for the past) $19.95

Grades: 5 6 7 8 **978**

1. Archeology 2. Pueblo Indians 3. Cliff dwellers and cliff dwellings 4. Chaco Culture National Historical Park (N.M.)

ISBN 0-19-514280-2

LC 2001-54855

Relates the nineteenth-century discovery of cliff dwellings in the Chaco Canyon of northwest New Mexico, the excavations of the ancient ruins, and what the artifacts reveal about the civilization of the ancient Pueblo Indians

This "brings young readers up close to the field of archaeology. . . . Sharp color photos show the sites, artifacts, and the scientists at work." Booklist

Includes glossary and bibliographical references

978.004 Western United States--American native peoples

Green, Carl R.

Sacagawea; courageous American Indian guide. by William R. Sanford and Carl R. Green. Enslow Publishers 2013 48 p. ill., map (library) $21.26

Grades: 5 6 7 8 **978.004**

1. Native Americans -- United States 2. Shoshone women -- Biography 3. Shoshone Indians -- Biography

ISBN 0766040062; 9780766040069

LC 2011048291

This book, part of the Courageous Heroes of the American West series, looks at Sacagawea. "Throughout Lewis and Clark's journey in the uncharted American West, this young America Indian woman proved to be an invaluable member of the expedition. Sacagawea served as translator and guide, all while caring for her infant son." (Publisher's note)

Includes bibliographical references (p. 47) and index.

Langley, Andrew

The **Plains** Indian wars 1864-1890; by Andrew Langley. Heinemann Library 2012 80 p. ill. (some col.), col. maps (hardcover) $36.50; (paperback) $10.99

Grades: 6 7 8 9 **978.004**

1. United States -- Military history 2. Native Americans -- Wars 3. Indians of North America -- Wars -- 1866-1895 4. Indians of North America -- Wars -- Great Plains 5. Indians of North America -- Great Plains -- History -- 19th century -- Chronology

ISBN 1432959999; 9781432959999; 9781432960087

LC 2011015925

This book by Andrew Langley is part of the Living Through series and focuses on the Plains Indian Wars. "The Plains Indian Wars were not like most other wars. There were few large battles, and they took place across a huge but sparsely populated region over several decades. . . . The Living Through series relates the overall chronology of major wars and shows their impact on everyday lives." (Publisher's note)

Includes bibliographical references (p. 76-78) and index.

Sanford, William R.

Comanche Chief Quanah Parker; by William R. Sanford. Enslow Publishers 2013 48 p. ill., map (library) $21.26

Grades: 6 7 8 9 **978.004**

1. Parker, Quanah, 1845?-1911 2. Comanche Indians -- History 3. Comanche Indians -- Wars 4. Comanche Indians -- Kings and rulers -- Biography

ISBN 076604095X; 9780766040953

LC 2011048762

This book by William R. Sanford is part of the Native American Chiefs and Warriors series. It "tells how Quanah,

the last Comanche chief, at first drew controversy for surrendering to the U.S. government and agreeing to live on a
reservation. He later earned praise for effectively bridging
both cultures." (Booklist)

Includes bibliographical references and index.

Oglala Lakota Chief Red Cloud; by William R.
Sanford. Enslow Publishers 2013 48 p. (library)
$21.26

Grades: 6 7 8 9   **978.004**
1. Oglala Indians -- Wars 2. Oglala Indians -- Kings and
rulers -- Biography
ISBN 0766040968; 9780766040960

LC 2011048760

This book is part of the Native American Chiefs and
Warriors series and looks at Oglala Lakota Chief Red Cloud.
Each title "focuses on the U.S. government's infringement
upon Native American land and how these leaders responded." This entry "recounts Red Cloud's fight to prevent whites
from traveling along the Bozeman and Oregon Trails, his
meeting with President Ulysses Grant, and his band's forced
move to a reservation." (Booklist)

Includes bibliographical references and index.

Oglala Sioux Chief Crazy Horse; by William R.
Sanford. Enslow Publishers 2013 48 p. (library)
$21.26

Grades: 6 7 8 9   **978.004**
1. Little Bighorn, Battle of the, Mont., 1876 2. Oglala
Indians -- Kings and rulers -- Biography
ISBN 0766040941; 9780766040946

LC 2011048758

This book is part of the Native American Chiefs and
Warriors series and looks at Oglala Sioux Chief Crazy
Horse. Each title "focuses on the U.S. government's infringement upon Native American land and how these leaders responded." This entry "describes Crazy Horse's success
as a chief and warrior, particularly during the Battle of the
Little Bighorn, and the resulting jealousy among other Sioux
leaders that led to his contentious death." (Booklist)

Includes bibliographical references (p. 46) and index.

978.1   Kansas

Bjorklund, Ruth
Kansas; by Ruth Bjorklund and Trudi Strain
Trueit. 2nd ed.; Marshall Cavendish Benchmark
2009 144p il map (Celebrate the states) lib bdg
$42.79

Grades: 4 5 6 7   **978.1**
1. Kansas
ISBN 978-0-7614-3400-9; 0-7614-3400-3

LC 2008-5537

"Provides comprehensive information on the geography,
history, wildlife, governmental structure, economy, cultural
diversity, peoples, religion, and landmarks of Kansas." Publisher's note

Includes bibliographical references

Cannarella, Deborah
Kansas; by Deborah Cannarella. Revised edition
Children's Press 2015 144 p. ill. (chiefly col.), col
maps $40

Grades: 4 5 6 7   **978.1**
1. Kansas
ISBN 9780531282809

Presents an introduction to the geography, natural resources, history, economy, important sites, daily life, and
people of Kansas.

Includes bibliographical references and index

McArthur, Debra
The **Kansas** -Nebraska Act and Bleeding Kansas
in American history. Enslow Pubs. 2003 128p il
map (In American history) lib bdg $26.60

Grades: 6 7 8 9   **978.1**
1. Abolitionists 2. Kansas -- History 3. Slavery --
United States
ISBN 0-7660-1988-8

LC 2002-152064

Describes the violent period of Kansas Territory history, prior to statehood and the Civil War, when abolitionists and pro-slavery factions openly murdered in defense of
their cause

Includes bibliographical references

978.2   Nebraska

Bjorklund, Ruth
Nebraska; [by] Ruth Bjorklund and Marlee Richards. 2nd ed.; Marshall Cavendish Benchmark 2010
144p il map (Celebrate the states) $42.79

Grades: 5 6 7 8   **978.2**
1. Nebraska
ISBN 978-0-7614-4732-0; 0-7614-4732-6

"Every school library should purchase this." Voice
Youth Advocates

Heinrichs, Ann
Nebraska; by Ann Heinrichs. Revised edition
Children's Press 2014 144 p. color illustrations $40

Grades: 4 5 6 7   **978.2**
1. Nebraska
ISBN 9780531248928

Describes the history, geography, ecology, people, economy, cities, and sights of the state of Nebraska.

Includes bibliographical references and index

978.3   South Dakota

Burgan, Michael
South Dakota; by Michael Burgan. Revised
edition Children's Press 2015 144 p. illustrations,
maps $40

Grades: 4 5 6 7   **978.3**
1. South Dakota
ISBN 9780531282939

Takes readers on a tour of South Dakota, describing the state's history, culture, land, economy, government, and sights, and including unique facts, color maps and photos, the state song, suggested activities, lists of famous people, cultural institutions, and annual events, and other resources.

Includes bibliographical references and index

978.4   North Dakota

McDaniel, Melissa

North Dakota; by Melissa McDaniel and Sara Louise Kras. 2nd ed.; Marshall Cavendish Benchmark 2010 144p il map (Celebrate the states) lib bdg $42.79

Grades: 5 6 7 8   **978.4**

1. North Dakota
ISBN 978-0-7614-4733-7; 0-7614-4733-4

LC 2009002584

First published 2001

This offers information on the geography, history, wildlife, governmental structure, economy, cultural diversity, peoples, religion, and landmarks of North Dakota.

Includes bibliographical references

Stille, Darlene R.

North Dakota; by Darlene R. Stille. Revised edition Children's Press 2015 144 p. col ill, col maps $40

Grades: 4 5 6 7   **978.4**

1. North Dakota
ISBN 9780531282861

Presents an introduction to the geography, natural resources, history, economy, important sites, daily life, and people of North Dakota.

Includes bibliographical references and index

978.6   Montana

Bennett, Clayton

Montana; by Clayton Bennett and Wendy Mead. 2nd ed.; Marshall Cavendish Benchmark 2010 144p il map (Celebrate the states) $42.79

Grades: 5 6 7 8   **978.6**

1. Montana
ISBN 978-0-7614-4731-3; 0-7614-4731-8

LC 2009007939

First published 2001

This offers information on the geography, history, wildlife, governmental structure, economy, cultural diversity, peoples, religion, and landmarks of Montana.

Includes bibliographical references

Stein, R. Conrad

Montana; by R. Conrad Stein. Revised edition Children's Press 2015 144 p. ill. (chiefly col.), col maps $40

Grades: 4 5 6 7   **978.6**

1. Montana
ISBN 9780531282830

Explores the land, people, history, economy, and travel opportunities of the state of Montana.

Includes bibliographical references and index

978.7   Wyoming

Baldwin, Guy

Wyoming; [by] Guy Baldwin and Joyce Hart. 2nd ed.; Marshall Cavendish Benchmark 2008 144p il map (Celebrate the states) lib bdg $39.93

Grades: 4 5 6 7   **978.7**

1. Wyoming
ISBN 978-0-7614-2563-2; 0-7614-2563-2

LC 2007-19560

First published 1999

"Provides comprehensive information on the geography, history, wildlife, governmental structure, economy, cultural diversity, peoples, religion, and landmarks of Wyoming." Publisher's note

Includes bibliographical references

Prentzas, G. S.

Wyoming; by G.S. Prentzas. Revised edition Children's Press 2015 144 p. illustrations, maps $40

Grades: 4 5 6 7   **978.7**

1. Wyoming
ISBN 9780531283004

Explores the land, people, history, economy, and travel opportunities of the state of Wyoming.

Includes bibliographical references and index

978.8   Colorado

Somervill, Barbara A.

Colorado; by Barbara A. Somervill. Revised edition Children's Press 2014 144 p. ill. (chiefly col.), col. maps $40

Grades: 4 5 6 7   **978.8**

1. Colorado
ISBN 9780531248782

Describes the history, geography, ecology, people, economy, cities, and sights of the state of Colorado.

Includes bibliographical references (page 138) and index

978.9   New Mexico

Burgan, Michael

New Mexico; by Michael Burgan. Revised edition Children's Press 2015 144 p. col ill, col maps $40

Grades: 4 5 6 7   **978.9**

1. New Mexico
ISBN 9780531282854

Presents an introduction to the geography, natural resources, history, economy, important sites, daily life, and people of New Mexico.

Includes bibliographical references and index

979.1   Arizona

Somervill, Barbara A.

Arizona; by Barbara A. Somervill. Revised edition Children's Press 2015 144 p. ill. (chiefly col.), col. maps $40

   Grades: 4 5 6 7   **979.1**
   1. Arizona
   ISBN 9780531282755

Presents an introduction to the geography, natural resources, history, economy, important sites, daily life, and people of Arizona.

Includes bibliographical references and index

Hernandez, Daniel

They call me a hero; a memoir of my youth. Daniel Hernandez and Susan Goldman Rubin. Simon & Schuster Books for Young Readers 2013 240 p. (hardcover) $17.99

   Grades: 7 8 9 10 11 12   **979.1**
   1. Courage 2. Interns -- United States -- Biography 3. Heroes -- Arizona -- Tucson -- Biography 4. Tucson (Ariz.) -- History -- 21st century 5. Sexual minorities -- Civil rights -- Arizona -- Tucson 6. Tucson (Ariz.) -- Officials and employees -- Biography 7. Courage -- Arizona -- Tucson -- History -- 21st century
   ISBN 1442462280; 9781442462281; 9781442462380
                     LC 2012019829

This book, by Daniel Hernandez, with Susan Gldman Rubin, is a memoir about heroism. "Daniel Hernandez was . . . working as an intern for U.S. Representative Gabrielle Giffords. On January 8, 2011, . . . Giffords was shot. Daniel Hernandez's quick thinking saved Giffords's life. . . . But while that may have been his most well-known moment in the spotlight, Daniel Hernandez, Jr. . . . [had] already accomplished much in his young life, and is working to achieve much more." (Publisher's note)

McDaniel, Melissa

Arizona; by Melissa McDaniel and Wendy Mead. 2nd ed.; Marshall Cavendish Benchmark 2009 144p il map (Celebrate the states) lib bdg $39.93

   Grades: 4 5 6 7   **979.1**
   1. Arizona
   ISBN 978-0-7614-3398-9; 0-7614-3398-8
                     LC 2008-6212

First published 2000

"Provides comprehensive information on the geography, history, wildlife, governmental structure, economy, cultural diversity, peoples, religion, and landmarks of Arizona." Publisher's note

Includes bibliographical references

979.2   Utah

Kent, Deborah

Utah; by Deborah Kent. Revised edition Children's Press 2015 144 p. illustrations, maps $40

   Grades: 4 5 6 7   **979.2**
   1. Utah
   ISBN 9780531282953

Presents an introduction to the geography, natural resources, history, economy, important sites, daily life, and people of Utah.

Includes bibliographical references and index

Stefoff, Rebecca

Utah; by Rebecca Stefoff and Wendy Mead. 2nd ed.; Marshall Cavendish Benchmark 2010 144p il map (Celebrate the states) lib bdg $42.79

   Grades: 5 6 7 8   **979.2**
   1. Utah
   ISBN 978-0-7614-4035-2; 0-7614-4035-6
                     LC 2008040026

This offers information on the geography, history, wildlife, governmental structure, economy, cultural diversity, peoples, religion, and landmarks of Utah.

Includes bibliographical references

979.3   Nevada

Heinrichs, Ann

Nevada; by Ann Heinrichs. Revised edition Children's Press 2014 144 p. ill. (chiefly col.), col maps $40

   Grades: 4 5 6 7   **979.3**
   1. Nevada
   ISBN 9780531248935

Describes the history, geography, ecology, people, economy, cities, and sights of the state of Nevada.

Includes bibliographical references and index

Stefoff, Rebecca

Nevada; 2nd ed.; Marshall Cavendish Benchmark 2010 144p il map (Celebrate the states) lib bdg $42.79

   Grades: 5 6 7 8   **979.3**
   1. Nevada
   ISBN 978-0-7614-4728-3; 0-7614-4728-8
                     LC 2009007137

This offers information on the geography, history, wildlife, governmental structure, economy, cultural diversity, peoples, religion, and landmarks of Nevada.

Includes bibliographical references

979.4   California

Calabro, Marian

★ The **perilous** journey of the Donner Party. Clarion Bks. 1999 192p il maps $20

Grades: 5 6 7 8   **979.4**
1. Donner party 2. Overland journeys to the Pacific 3.
Frontier and pioneer life -- West (U.S.)
ISBN 0-395-86610-3
LC 98-29610
Uses materials from letters and diaries written by survivors of the Donner Party to relate the experiences of that ill-fated group as they endured horrific circumstances on their way to California in 1846-47

"Calabro's offering is a fine addition to the Donner Party canon and particularly well suited to its young audience, for whom the story of hardship and survival will be nothing short of riveting. . . . From the haunting cover with its lonely campfire to the recounting of a survivors' reunion, this is a page-turner." Booklist

Includes bibliographical references

Doak, Robin S.
California, 1542-1850; by Robin Doak; Andres Resendez, consultant. National Geographic Society 2006 109p map il (Voices from colonial America) $21.95; lib bdg $32.90
Grades: 5 6 7 8   **979.4**
1. California -- History
ISBN 978-0-7922-6391-3; 0-7922-6391-X; 978-0-7922-6861-1 lib bdg; 0-7922-6861-X lib bdg
LC 2005-30920
"Traces California's history from its origins as a sparsely populated outpost of the Spanish empire in the sixteenth century to the frenzied westward migration of the 1850s." Publisher's note

Includes bibliograhical references

Freedman, Russell, 1929-
★ **Angel** Island; gateway to Gold Mountain. Russell Freedman ; Chinese poems translated by Evans Chan. Clarion Books 2013 96 p. (hardcover) $17.99
Grades: 4 5 6 7 8   **979.4**
1. Immigrants -- United States 2. Angel Island Immigration Station (San Francisco, Calif.) 3. Angel Island (Calif.) -- History 4. Asia -- Emigration and immigration -- History 5. Angel Island Immigration Station (Calif.) -- History 6. United States -- Emigration and immigration -- History 7. San Francisco Bay Area (Calif.) -- Emigration and immigration -- History
ISBN 0547903782; 9780547903781
LC 2012036532
This book is a "history of Angel Island and its legacy in the American immigration narrative. Detailed descriptions of the island, the actual building, the events that took place there, and the people who passed through its doors are sprinkled with the emotional poems, quotes, and other writings that were discovered covering the walls of the areas where the detainees were housed." (School Library Journal)

Includes bibliographical references

Hale, Nathan
Donner dinner party; by Nathan Hale. Harry N Abrams Inc 2013 123 p. (Nathan Hale's Hazardous Tales) $12.95

Grades: 5 6 7 8   **979.4**
1. Donner party 2. Sierra Nevada Mountains
ISBN 1419708562; 9781419708565
In this graphic novel, author Nathan Hale "tells the harrowing story of the ill-fated Donner party. Beginning with their departure from Springfield, Illinois, in 1846, Hale depicts the party's progress . . . and includes lots of factual details, such as a roster of everyone in the party, how they died, and a helpful map showing just how . . . close they came to California before meeting their grisly end." (Booklist)

"This informative graphic novel capitalizes on enticingly gross history to great effect, balancing raw facts with strong storytelling." Booklist

McNeese, Tim
The **Donner** Party; a doomed journey. [by] Tim McNeese. Chelsea House 2009 146p il (Milestones in American history) lib bdg $35
Grades: 6 7 8 9 10   **979.4**
1. Donner party 2. Overland journeys to the Pacific 3. Frontier and pioneer life -- California 4. Frontier and pioneer life -- West (U.S.)
ISBN 978-1-60413-025-6 lib bdg; 1-60413-025-3 lib bdg
LC 2008-29652
"McNeese presents a thoroughly researched, clearly written account of the ill-fated Donner Party and the events and decisions that conspired against this early wagon train headed from Springfield, IL, to California. . . . Photos, reproductions, drawings, and primary-source documents as well as a detailed chronology make this an excellent resource." SLJ

Includes bibliographical references

Olson, Tod
★ **How** to get rich in the California Gold Rush; an adventurer's guide to the fabulous riches discovered in 1848 . . . illustrations by Scott Allred; afterword by Marc Aronson. National Geographic 2008 47p il map (How to get rich) $16.95; lib bdg $25.90
Grades: 4 5 6 7   **979.4**
1. Gold mines and mining 2. California -- Gold discoveries 3. Prospecting 4. Frontier and pioneer life -- California 5. California -- History
ISBN 1-4263-0315-7; 1-4263-0316-5 lib bdg; 978-1-4263-0315-9; 978-1-4263-0316-6 lib bdg
LC 2008-19601
This is a personal account of the California Gold Rush from the point-of-view of the fictitious character Thomas Hartley. "Grades four to seven." (Bull Cent Child Books)

This "deftly blends story with history to not only give readers an understanding of a gold rush but also to provide a lighthearted and engaging entry point into frontier life. . . . Period lithographs are reproduced alongside original illustrations. . . . A ledger on each page tracks the young men's finances in a genuinely exciting way, adding a sly element of math to this well-conceived and compulsively appealing book." Booklist

Includes bibliographical references

Orr, Tamra B.

California; by Tamra B. Orr. Revised edition Children's Press 2014 144 p. ill. (chiefly col.), col. maps $40

Grades: 4 5 6 7   **979.4**
1. California
ISBN 9780531248775

Describes the history, geography, ecology, people, economy, cities, and sights of the state of California.

Includes bibliographical references (page 138) and index

Slavicek, Louise Chipley

The San Francisco earthquake and fire of 1906; [by] Louise Chipley Slavicek. Chelsea House 2008 128p il (Great historic disasters) lib bdg $35

Grades: 5 6 7 8   **979.4**
1. Fires 2. Earthquakes -- California 3. San Francisco (Calif.) -- History
ISBN 978-0-7910-9650-5; 0-7910-9650-5

                 LC 2008-4896

This is a history of the 1906 earthquake and fire in San Francisco.

"Combining first-hand accounts, photographs, and other primary sources with a detailed and lively text, [this] fact-packed [resource offers] much to both report writers and history buffs." Horn Book Guide

Includes glossary and bibliographical references

Yep, Laurence, 1948-

★ The lost garden; by Laurence Yep. Messner 1991 xi, 117 p.p ill. (In my own words) (library) $14.98; (hardcover) $12.95

Grades: 6 7 8 9 10 11 12   **979.4**
1. Authors 2. Novelists 3. College teachers 4. Authors, American 5. Children's authors 6. Young adult authors 7. Chinese Americans -- Biography
ISBN 9780671741594; 9780671741600

                 LC 90040647

This is a volume in the In My Own Words series. The author of Dragonwings (BRD 1976), Child of The Owl (BRD 1977), The Rainbow People (BRD 1989), and The Star Fisher (BRD 1991) discusses his life and his writing. "Grades six to twelve." (SLJ)

"The writing is warm, wry, and humorous. . . . The Lost Garden will be welcomed as a literary autobiography for children and, more, a thoughtful probing into what it means to be an American." SLJ

979.5   Oregon

Oregon; Revised edition Children's Press 2015 144 p. illustrations, maps $40

Grades: 4 5 6 7   **979.5**
1. Oregon
ISBN 9780531282885

Presents an introduction to the geography, natural resources, history, economy, important sites, daily life, and people of Oregon.

Includes bibliographical references and index

979.6   Idaho

Kent, Deborah

Idaho; by Deborah Kent. Revised edition Children's Press 2015 144 p. ill. (chiefly col.), col maps $40

Grades: 4 5 6 7   **979.6**
1. Idaho
ISBN 9780531282786

Takes readers on a tour of Idaho, describing the state's history, culture, land, economy, government, and sights, and including unique facts, color maps and photos, the state song, suggested activities, lists of famous people, cultural institutions, and annual events, and other resources.

Includes bibliographical references (page 138) and index

Stefoff, Rebecca

Idaho; by Rebecca Stefoff. 2nd ed.; Marshall Cavendish Benchmark 2008 144p il map (Celebrate the states) lib bdg $39.93

Grades: 4 5 6 7   **979.6**
1. Idaho
ISBN 978-0-7614-3003-2; 0-7614-3003-2

                 LC 2007-29496

First published 2000

"Provides comprehensive information on the geography, history, wildlife, governmental structure, economy, cultural diversity, peoples, religion, and landmarks of Idaho." Publisher's note

Includes bibliographical references

979.7   Washington

Jankowski, Susan

Olympic National Park; adventure, explore, discover. [by] Susan Jankowski. MyReportLinks.com Books 2009 128p il map (America's national parks) lib bdg $33.27

Grades: 5 6 7 8   **979.7**
1. Olympic National Park (Wash.) 2. National parks and reserves -- United States
ISBN 978-1-59845-092-7 lib bdg; 1-59845-092-1 lib bdg

                 LC 2007-17341

This "informative, well-written book contains a physical description of the park; a summary of its history including the Native peoples of the area; activities such as hiking trails, campsites, and visitor centers; information about the park's plants, animals, and weather; full-color photographs; and numerous approved links available through the publisher's Web page. . . . Thorough, useful, and appealing, this . . . is a great update for collections." SLJ

Includes glossary and bibliographical references

Kirkpatrick, Katherine

★ Mysterious bones; the story of Kennewick Man. by Katherine Kirkpatrick; illustrated by Emma Stevenson. Holiday House 2011 60p il map $17.95

Grades: 6 7 8 9   **979.7**
1. Skeleton 2. Kennewick Man 3. Native Americans

4. Washington (State) 5. North America -- Antiquities
ISBN 978-0-8234-2187-9; 0-8234-2187-2

LC 2009025575

Kennewick Man "was found in remarkable condition near the Columbia River in Washington . . . in 1996—one of the oldest and most complete skeletons found in America. Kirkpatrick addresses the controversy surrounding the treatment of his remains. . . . Excellent illustrations accompany the story, with crisp line-drawings of tools, skeletons, maps and possible facial reconstructions." Kirkus

Includes glossary and bibliographical references

Stefoff, Rebecca

Washington; [by] Rebecca Stefoff. 2nd ed.; Marshall Cavendish Benchmark 2008 144p il map (Celebrate the states) lib bdg $39.93

Grades: 4 5 6 7   **979.7**

1. Washington (State)
ISBN 978-0-7614-2561-8; 0-7614-2561-6

LC 2006-32436

First published 1999

"Provides comprehensive information on the geography, history, wildlife, governmental structure, economy, cultural diversity, peoples, religion, and landmarks of Washington." Publisher's note

Includes bibliographical references

979.8 Alaska

Orr, Tamra B.

Alaska; Tamra B. Orr. Revised edition Children's Press 2014 144 p. ill. (chiefly col.), col. maps $40

Grades: 4 5 6 7   **979.8**

1. Alaska
ISBN 9780531248768

Describes the history, geography, ecology, people, economy, cities, and sights of the state of Alaska.

Includes bibliographical references (page 138) and index

980 History of South America

Gorrell, Gena K.

★ **In** the land of the jaguar; South America and its people. illustrated by Andrej Krystoforski. Tundra Books 2007 149p il $22.95

Grades: 5 6 7 8 9   **980**

1. South America
ISBN 978-0-88776-756-2

"This beautifully designed volume, with an engaging narrative, combines a highly informative overview of the continent with country-by-country detail. . . . The spacious design includes big maps, clear type on thick paper, and small, beautiful, fully captioned illustrations." Booklist

981 Brazil

Berkenkamp, Lauri

Discover the Amazon; the world's largest rainforest. illustrated by Blair Shedd. Nomad Press 2008 90p il map pa $16.95

Grades: 4 5 6 7   **981**

1. Amazon River valley
ISBN 978-1-9346702-7-9 pa; 1-9346702-7-8 pa

"Berkenkamp's introduction to the [Amazon] river basin incorporates maps, drawings, and photos in various shades of green and brown on recycled paper. . . . The conversational style provides a 'you are there' feeling, conveying information and anecdotes while stressing outdoor survival skills. . . . Even readers who never travel to Amazonia will appreciate the region's complexity and significance after perusing this book." SLJ

Deckker, Zilah

★ **Brazil**; [by] Zilah Deckker; David Robinson and Joao Cezar de Castro Rocha, consultants. National Geographic 2008 64p il (Countries of the world) lib bdg $27.90

Grades: 4 5 6 7   **981**

1. Brazil
ISBN 978-1-4263-0298-5 lib bdg; 1-4263-0298-3 lib bdg

This describes the geography, nature, history, people and culture, government, and economy of Brazil.

Includes glossary and bibliographical references

Heinrichs, Ann

The **Amazon** rain forest. Marshall Cavendish Benchmark 2009 96p il (Nature's wonders) lib bdg $35.64

Grades: 6 7 8 9   **981**

1. Rain forests 2. Amazon River valley
ISBN 978-0-7614-3932-5; 0-7614-3932-3

LC 2008017562

Provides information on the geography, history, wildlife, peoples, and environmental issues of the Amazon Rain Forest.

Includes glossary and bibliographical references

★ **Brazil**; by Ann Heinrichs. Children's Press, an imprint of Scholastic Inc. 2013 144 p. illustrations, color maps (library binding) $40

Grades: 5 6 7 8   **981**

1. Brazil
ISBN 0531236757; 9780531236758

LC 2013000089

This book, by Ann Heinrichs, focuses on Brazil. The "country's culture, history, and geography are explored in detail, allowing readers a chance to see how people live. . . . Sidebars highlight especially interesting people, places, and events . . . [and] recipes give readers the opportunity to experience foreign cuisine first-hand." (Publisher's note)

"Many students turn to the Internet for writing reports, but for reliably accurate, attractively presented and well-calibrated information, the long-standing Enchantment of the World series remains a superior choice...Each volume in this reliable series includes extensive back matter with a detailed index." Booklist

Includes bibliographical references (page 134), filmography (page 134), and index.

982   Argentina

Fearns, Les

    Argentina; [by] Les and Daisy Fearns. Facts on File 2005 61p il map (Countries of the world) $30

Grades: 7 8 9 10   **982**

    1. Argentina

    ISBN 0-8160-6008-8

                       LC 2005040675

    This is an introduction to Argentina's "culture, history, geography, government, and economy. [It is] competently written and [contains] current information. [The text is] clear but the level of vocabulary is quite high, which might prove challenging for less competent readers. Visually, the [book is] quite impressive, with full-color photographs, maps, tables, and graphs distributed throughout." SLJ

    Includes bibliographical references

984   Bolivia

Pateman, Robert

    Bolivia; [by] Robert Pateman & Marcus Cramer. 2nd ed.; Marshall Cavendish Benchmark 2006 144p il map (Cultures of the world) lib bdg $42.79

Grades: 5 6 7 8   **984**

    1. Bolivia

    ISBN 978-0-7614-2066-8 lib bdg; 0-7614-2066-5 lib bdg

                       LC 2006002425

    First published 1995

    This is "well organized, informative, and entertaining. . . . Excellent-quality full-color photographs and reproductions show the people, landforms, buildings, and everyday activities." SLJ

    Includes bibliographical references

985   Peru

Bingham, Jane

    The **Inca** empire; [by] Jane Bingham. Raintree 2007 64p il map (Time travel guide) lib bdg $34.29; pa $9.99

Grades: 6 7 8 9   **985**

    1. Incas 2. Peru

    ISBN 978-1-4109-2731-6 lib bdg; 1-4109-2731-8 lib bdg; 978-1-4109-2738-5 pa; 1-4109-2738-5 pa

                       LC 2006033877

    This describes life in the ancient Inca empire in the form of a travel guide.

    Includes glossary and bibliographical references

Calvert, Patricia

    ★ The **ancient** Inca; written by Patricia Calvert. Franklin Watts 2004 128p il (People of the ancient world) lib bdg $30.50; pa $9.95

Grades: 5 6 7 8   **985**

    1. Incas

    ISBN 0-531-12358-8 lib bdg; 0-531-16740-2 pa

                       LC 2004-1956

    This "well-written, attractive [title has] extensive collections of quality color photographs of ruins and artifacts." SLJ

    Includes bibliographical references

Donovan, Sandra, 1967-

    Teens in Peru; by Sandy Donovan. Compass Point Books 2009 95p il (Global connections) lib bdg $33.26

Grades: 6 7 8 9   **985**

    1. Teenagers 2. Peru

    ISBN 978-0-7565-3852-1 lib bdg; 0-7565-3852-1 lib bdg

                       LC 2008-6503

    Uncovers the challenges, pastimes, customs and culture of teens in Peru

    This book is "concise and highly readable. . . . Clear, colorful photos and sidebars on a range of topics provide further context. . . . [This title] will enrich young adult collections." SLJ

    Includes glossary and bibliographic references

Falconer, Kieran

    ★ **Peru**; [by] Kieran Falconer & Lynette Quek. 2nd ed.; Marshall Cavendish Benchmark 2006 144p il map (Cultures of the world) lib bdg $42.79

Grades: 5 6 7 8   **985**

    1. Peru

    ISBN 978-0-7614-2068-2 lib bdg; 0-7614-2068-1 lib bdg

    First published 1995

    This provides "information on the geography, history, governmental structure, economy, cultural diversity, peoples, religion, and culture of Peru." Publisher's note

    Includes glossary and bibliographical references

Gruber, Beth

    ★ **Ancient** Inca; archaeology unlocks the secrets of the Inca's past. by Beth Gruber; Johan Reinhard, consultant. National Geographic 2007 64p il map (National Geographic investigates) $17.95; lib bdg $27.90

Grades: 5 6 7 8   **985**

    1. Incas 2. Peru -- Antiquities 3. Excavations (Archeology) -- Peru

    ISBN 978-0-7922-7827-6; 978-0-7922-7873-3 lib bdg

                       LC 2006032104

    This describes how archeologists have found out about ancient Incan civilization.

    This offers "the beautiful photography and illustrations characteristic of the National Geographic Society, [a] well-written [text] and sidebars, and information on recent archaeological finds." SLJ

    Includes bibliographical references

986.1 Colombia

Croy, Anita

★ **Colombia**; [by] Anita Croy; Ulrich Oslender and Mauricio Pardo, consultants. National Geographic 2008 64p il map (Countries of the world) lib bdg $27.90

Grades: 4 5 6 7 **986.1**

1. Colombia
ISBN 978-1-4263-0257-2 lib bdg; 1-4263-0257-6 lib bdg

This describes the geography, nature, history, people and culture, government, and economy of Colombia

Includes glossary and bibliographical references

Yomtov, Nel

★ **Colombia**; by Nel Yomtov. Children's Press, an imprint of Scholastic Inc. 2014 144 p. illustrations, color maps (library binding) $40

Grades: 5 6 7 8 **986.1**

1. Colombia
ISBN 0531220133; 9780531220139

LC 2013026060

This book, by Nel Yomtov, focuses on Colombia. The "country's culture, history, and geography are explored in detail, allowing readers a chance to see how people live in faraway nations. . . . Sidebars highlight especially interesting people, places, and events . . . [and] easy recipes give readers the opportunity to experience foreign cuisine first-hand." (Publisher's note)

Includes bibliographical references and index

986.6 Ecuador

Foley, Erin

★ **Ecuador**; [by] Erin L. Foley & Leslie Jermyn. 2nd ed.; Marshall Cavendish Benchmark 2006 144p il map (Cultures of the world) lib bdg $42.79

Grades: 5 6 7 8 **986.6**

1. Ecuador
ISBN 0-7614-2050-9

LC 2005022671

First published 1995

This briefly describes Ecuador's "history, government, economy, and geography. . . . Particularly useful is the information on religion, the arts, food, leisure activities, and social roles. The [book has] great visual appeal with excellent full-color photographs on every page. [It] is especially successful in explaining social and economic hierarchies within the country." SLJ

Includes glossary and bibliographical references

Kras, Sara Louise

The **Galapagos** Islands; [by] Sara Louise Kras. Marshall Cavendish Benchmark 2008 96p il map (Nature's wonders) lib bdg $35.64

Grades: 5 6 7 8 **986.6**

1. Galapagos Islands
ISBN 978-0-7614-2856-5 lib bdg; 0-7614-2856-9 lib bdg

LC 2007020416

"Provides comprehensive information on the geography, history, wildlife, peoples, and environmental issues of the Galapagos Islands." Publisher's note

Includes glossary and bibliographical references

Lourie, Peter

★ **Lost** treasure of the Inca. Boyds Mills Press 1999 48p il map $18.95

Grades: 4 5 6 7 **986.6**

1. Incas 2. Buried treasure 3. Ecuador
ISBN 1-56397-743-5

The author describes his search in the mountains of Ecuador for gold hidden by the Incas

Lourie "succumbed to altitude sickness and had to descend without discovering a glimmer of the gold. But he did return with a ripping good yarn to tell . . . and some breathtaking photographs of the mist-shrouded volcanic peaks. This should be a hot pick for armchair travelers." Bull Cent Child Books

Includes glossary

988.1 Guyana

Jermyn, Leslie

Guyana; by Leslie Jermyn and Winnie Wong. Marshall Cavendish Benchmark 2010 144 p. col. ill., col. maps (library) $47.07

Grades: 5 6 7 8 **988.1**

1. Guyana
ISBN 1608700232; 9781608700233

LC 2010000724

This book by Leslie Jermyn is part of the Cultures of the World series and looks at the South American nation of Guyana. "Touching upon everything from its history to religion to architecture, this book . . . highlights the country's rich diversity and unique qualities. With a population that includes many different ethnic groups, the author . . . examines the contributions of each to Guyana's development and to its present culture." (Children's Literature)

Includes bibliographical references (p.142) and index.

Morrison, Marion

Guyana. Children's Press 2003 144p il map (Enchantment of the world, Second series) lib bdg $38

Grades: 5 6 7 8 **988.1**

1. Guyana
ISBN 978-0-516-22377-3 lib bdg; 0-516-22377-1 lib bdg

LC 2001-6915

Describes the geography, history, culture, religion, and people of Guyana

Includes bibliographical references

989.2   Paraguay

Jermyn, Leslie

Paraguay; [by] Leslie Jermyn and Yong Jui Lin. 2nd ed.; Marshall Cavendish Benchmark 2010 144p il map (Cultures of the world) lib bdg $42.79

Grades: 5 6 7 8   **989.2**

1. Paraguay

ISBN 978-0-7614-4858-7 lib bdg; 0-7614-4858-6 lib bdg

LC 2009046495

First published 2000

This offers information on the geography, history, wildlife, governmental structure, economy, cultural diversity, peoples, religion, and culture of Paraguay

Includes glossary and bibliographical references

989.5   Uruguay

Jermyn, Leslie

Uruguay; by Leslie Jermyn and Winnie Wong. 2nd ed.; Marshall Cavendish Benchmark 2009 144p il map (Cultures of the world) lib bdg $42.79

Grades: 5 6 7 8   **989.5**

1. Uruguay

ISBN 978-0-7614-4482-4 lib bdg; 0-7614-4482-3 lib bdg

LC 2009007127

First published 1999

Provides information on the geography, history, wildlife, governmental structure, economy, cultural diversity, peoples, religion, and culture of Uruguay

Includes glossary and bibliographical references

993   New Zealand

Gillespie, Carol Ann

New Zealand; [by] Carol Ann Gillespie. updated ed.; Chelsea House Publishers 2005 100p il map (Modern world nations) lib bdg $30

Grades: 7 8 9 10   **993**

1. New Zealand

ISBN 0-7910-8708-5

LC 2005045445

First published 1992

This describes the natural landscapes, unique plant and animal life, history, culture, people, government and politics, and future outlook of New Zealand

Includes bibliographical references

Jackson, Barbara

★ New Zealand; [by] Barbara Jackson; Vaughan Wood and Simon Milne, consultants. National Geographic 2008 64p il map (Countries of the world) lib bdg $27.90

Grades: 4 5 6 7   **993**

1. New Zealand

ISBN 978-1-4263-0301-2 lib bdg; 1-4263-0301-7 lib bdg

This describes the geography, nature, history, people and culture, government, and economy of New Zealand.

Smelt, Roselynn

New Zealand; by Roselynn Smelt. 2nd ed.; Marshall Cavendish Benchmark 2009 128p il map (Cultures of the world) lib bdg $42.79

Grades: 5 6 7 8   **993**

1. New Zealand

ISBN 978-0-7614-3415-3 lib bdg; 0-7614-3415-1 lib bdg

LC 2008028792

First published 1998

"Provides comprehensive information on the geography, history, wildlife, governmental structure, economy, cultural diversity, peoples, religion, and culture of New Zealand." Publisher's note

Includes glossary and bibliographical references

994   Australia

Arnold, Caroline

★ Uluru, Australia's Aboriginal heart; photographs by Arthur Arnold. Clarion Books 2003 64p il $16

Grades: 5 6 7 8   **994**

1. Aboriginal Australians 2. Australia 3. Uluru-Kata Tjuta National Park (Australia)

ISBN 0-618-18181-4

LC 2002-15542

Describes Uluru, formerly known as Ayers Rock, in Australia's Uluru-Kata Tjuta National Park, its plant and animal life, and the country's Aboriginal people for whom the site is sacred

"The book's greatest accomplishment . . . is to give readers a sense of the ongoing spiritual importance of Uluru to the Anangu, who have lived around it for 10,000 years. Clear, colorful photos of Uluru and its surroundings appear on nearly every page, illustrating the text with beauty and finesse." Booklist

Einfeld, Jann

Life in the Australian Outback. Lucent Bks. 2003 112p il map (Way people live) lib bdg $21.96

Grades: 6 7 8 9   **994**

1. Australia 2. Australian aborigines

ISBN 1-59018-014-3

LC 2001-7504

"An in-depth look at a unique culture that exists in Australia's remote interior. Well detailed and meticulously documented, this book does an excellent job of illustrating the diversity of the outback population as well as the challenges faced by its inhabitants." SLJ

Includes glossary and bibliographical references

Leppman, Elizabeth J.

Australia and the Pacific; series consulting editor Charles F. Gritzner. Chelsea House Pubs. 2006 118p il map (Modern world cultures) lib bdg $30

Grades: 7 8 9 10 **994**

1. Oceania 2. Australia
ISBN 0-7910-8150-8

This describes the natural landscapes, history, people, culture, geopolitics, economy, regional contrasts, and future outlook of Australia and the Pacific.

Includes bibliographical references

Turner, Kate

★ **Australia**; [by] Kate Turner; Elaine Stratford and Joseph Powell, consultants. National Geographic 2007 64p il map (Countries of the world) lib bdg $27.90

Grades: 4 5 6 7 **994**

1. Australia
ISBN 978-1-4263-0055-4

Describes the geography, nature, history, people and culture, government and economy of Australia

This "appealing [title has] wonderful photographs and maps. . . . [This book is a] reliable [source] for country research, and the interesting current material hold browsing potential as well." SLJ

Includes glossary and bibliographical references

995.3 Papua New Guinea

Gascoigne, Ingrid

Papua New Guinea; [by] Ingrid Gascoigne. 2nd ed.; Marshall Cavendish Benchmark 2009 144p il map (Cultures of the world) lib bdg $42.79

Grades: 5 6 7 8 **995.3**

1. Papua New Guinea
ISBN 978-0-7614-3416-0 lib bdg; 0-7614-3416-X lib bdg

LC 2008028794

First published 1998

"Provides comprehensive information on the geography, history, wildlife, governmental structure, economy, cultural diversity, peoples, religion, and culture of Papua New Guinea." Publisher's note

Includes glossary and bibliographical references

996 Polynesia and other Pacific Ocean islands

NgCheong-Lum, Roseline, 1962-

Tahiti; [by] Roseline NgCheong-Lum. 2nd ed.; Marshall Cavendish Benchmark 2008 144p il map (Cultures of the world) lib bdg $42.79

Grades: 5 6 7 8 **996**

1. Tahiti (French Polynesia)
ISBN 978-0-7614-2089-7

LC 2007014901

"Provides comprehensive information on the geography, history, wildlife, governmental structure, economy, cultural diversity, peoples, religion, and culture of Tahiti." Publisher's note

Includes glossary and bibliographical references

Pelta, Kathy

Rediscovering Easter Island. Lerner Publs. 2000 112p il maps (How history is invented) lib bdg $23.93

Grades: 5 6 7 8 **996**

1. Easter Island
ISBN 0-8225-4890-9

LC 00-9163

Discusses the many visits made by explorers, missionaries, businessmen, scientists, and others to Easter Island since the late 1600s and what they revealed about life on this remote Pacific island

"Coverage is serious, generally evenhanded, and smoothly presented, making this a fine foundation for readers who enjoy digging up the past." Bull Cent Child Books

Includes bibliographical references

996.9 Hawaii and neighboring north central Pacific Ocean islands

Kent, Debra

Hawai'i; by Deborah Kent. Revised edition Children's Press 2014 144 p. col ill, col maps $40

Grades: 4 5 6 7 **996.9**

1. Hawaii
ISBN 9780531248829

Includes bibliographical references (page 138) and index

Describes the history, geography, ecology, people, economy, cities, and sights of the state of Hawaii.

998 Arctic islands and Antarctica

Bledsoe, Lucy Jane

★ **How** to survive in Antarctica; written and photographed by Lucy Jane Bledsoe. Holiday House 2006 101p il map $16.95

Grades: 5 6 7 8 **998**

1. Antarctica
ISBN 0-8234-1890-1

LC 2004-60639

"Bledsoe, who made three trips to study Antarctica, bases her informal, chatty narrative on her thrilling adventure, bringing close the amazing science and geography as well as the gritty facts of human survival in the frigid environment. . . . Bledsoe's own black-and-white photos . . . will grab students across the curriculum." Booklist

Includes glossary

Latta, Sara L.

Ice scientist; careers in the frozen Antarctic. Enslow Publishers 2009 128p il (Wild science careers) lib bdg $31.93

Grades: 5 6 7 8 **998**

1. Scientists 2. Vocational guidance 3. Antarctica --

Exploration
ISBN 978-0-7660-3048-0 lib bdg; 0-7660-3048-2
lib bdg

LC 2008-4652

The book's "greatest strength is in the variety of first-hand accounts and the scientists' breadth of experience. [The book has] appealing color photographs and an attractive design." SLJ

Includes glossary and bibliographical references

Lourie, Peter

Arctic thaw; the people of the whale in a changing climate. Boyds Mills Press 2007 47p il map $17.95

Grades: 5 6 7 8   **998**

1. Inupiat 2. Whaling 3. Human ecology 4. Alaska 5. Greenhouse effect

ISBN 978-1-59078-436-5; 1-59078-436-7

LC 2006-20045

"A somewhat sobering, yet upbeat examination of the probable effects of global warming on the culture of the Iñupiaq whale hunters of Alaska's North Slope. . . . [Lourie's] lively, straightforward text describes the mixture of traditional and modern ways of the present-day Iñupiaq, as well as the work of [Paul] Shepson and his team to record weather and climate changes and to predict what effect they will have locally and globally." SLJ

Includes bibliographical references

Lynch, Wayne

Arctic; text and photographs by Wayne Lynch; assisted by Aubrey Lang. NorthWord Books for Young Readers 2007 64p il map (Our wild world: ecosystems) hardcover o.p. pa $8.95

Grades: 4 5 6 7   **998**

1. Arctic regions 2. Animals -- Arctic regions

ISBN 978-1-55971-960-5; 978-1-55971-961-2 pa

LC 2006021920

"With accessible first-person writing, Lynch describes the Arctic ecosystem, discussing both the high and low Arctic. . . . Stunning photographs include close-ups and more expansive views." Horn Book Guide

Includes bibliographical references

Myers, Walter Dean, 1937-2014

★ Antarctica; journeys to the South Pole. Scholastic Press 2004 134p il maps $18.95

Grades: 6 7 8 9   **998**

1. Antarctica

ISBN 0-439-22001-7

LC 2004-2501

This book tracks "the explorers of the South Pole—including James Cook, Ernest Shackleton, and Richard Evelyn Byrd—and the dangers they encountered there, as well as their contributions to science." (Publisher's note) Index. "Grades five to nine." (Bull Cent Child Books)

This is "a lucid, well-written text." SLJ

Includes bibliographical references

Revkin, Andrew

★ The **North** Pole was here; puzzles and perils at the top of the world. [by] Andrew C. Revkin. 1st ed.; Kingfisher 2006 128p il map $15.95

Grades: 7 8 9 10   **998**

1. North Pole 2. Arctic regions 3. Greenhouse effect

ISBN 0-7534-5993-0; 978-0-7534-5993-5

LC 2005-24307

The author "relates his journey to the top of the world in the company of scientists studying climate changes. The informative chapters weave together accounts of his experiences and observations with details about the environment, its exploration, and scientific concepts. . . . The illustrations include full-color photographs of the author's trek, archival reproductions and photos of previous excursions, original diagrams that clarify concepts, and maps. . . . The wonderfully written narrative will pull youngsters into the book and hold them there willingly until the last page." SLJ

Includes bibliographical references

Tulloch, Coral

Antarctica; the heart of the world. 1st American ed.; Enchanted Lion Books 2006 48p il map $17.95

Grades: 6 7 8 9   **998**

1. Antarctica

ISBN 1-59270-054-3

LC 2005-40162

"Tulloch writes out of her experiences as a voyager on an Antarctic resupply ship to illuminate the continent's geologic history, its flora and fauna, and its importance to the global ecosystem. She also addresses the early and continuing human explorations and their impact on the region as well as the area's rich potential and possible future problems. The writing is clear, and the science is comprehensible without the slightest sense of talking down to youthful readers." Voice Youth Advocates

Includes bibliographical references

Wade, Rosalyn

Polar worlds. Simon & Schuster Books for Young Readers 2011 64p il (Insiders) $16.99

Grades: 4 5 6 7   **998**

1. Antarctica 2. Arctic regions

ISBN 978-1-4424-3275-8; 1-4424-3275-6

This "takes a look at the nether regions of the globe in this browser-friendly resource. . . . 'Introducing' opens with a geographic look at the Arctic and Antarctic regions, then moves on to the related topics of icebergs, plant and animal life, exploration, survival measures, and environmental threats. The 'In Focus' section zeroes in on 12 specific animals found in polar regions. . . . Each spread is dominated by a sharply rendered, often dramatic digital illustration. . . . A fine introduction to the world's deep freezers." Booklist

Walker, Sally M.

★ Frozen secrets; Antarctica revealed. Carolrhoda Books 2010 104p il map $20.95

Grades: 7 8 9 10   **998**

1. Antarctica

ISBN 978-1-58013-607-5; 1-58013-607-9

LC 2009-34282

This is an "account of the rich scientific findings coming out of the planet's southernmost continent. . . . It's an excellent overview that manages to pack a lot of technical and scientific information into a small space, but it's sufficiently well structured conceptually and well laid out visually . . . that it all goes down pretty easily. The photographic images reveal the stunning beauty of the continent in shot after shot, but there are also illuminating views of the scientists at work, and diagrams and maps round out the view." Bull Cent Child Books

Fic FICTION

50 Cent (Musician), 1975-
Playground; with Aura Moser. Razorbill 2011 314p $17.99

Grades: 7 8 9 10   **Fic**
  1. Bullies -- Fiction
  ISBN 978-1-59514-434-8; 1-59514-434-X
Thirteen-year-old Butterball doesn't have much going for him. He's teased about his weight. He hates the Long Island suburb his mom moved them to so she could go to nursing school and start her life over. He wishes he still lived with his dad in New York City where there's always something happening, even if his dad doesn't have much time for him. Still, that's not why he beat up Maurice on the playground.
  "Readers who were ever confused about having a gay parent, or being overweight, or going through a parental breakup, or just wanting to fit in and be accepted by their peers, will relate to Butterball. 50 Cent's debut young adult novel is a quick read that will be great for discussions on a variety of important and timely topics." VOYA

Abbott, Ellen Jensen
Watersmeet. Marshall Cavendish 2009 341p il $16.99

Grades: 6 7 8 9 10   **Fic**
  1. Fantasy fiction
  ISBN 978-0-7614-5536-3; 0-7614-5536-1
                                          LC 2008-315
Fourteen-year-old Absina escapes the escalating violence, prejudice, and religious fervor of her home town, Vranille, and sets out with a dwarf, Haret, to seek the father she has never met in a place called Watersmeet.
  "The relationship between Abisina and Haret is warm and engaging, and the dialogue between them cleverly captures the slow development of their camaraderie. . . . Fans of Ursula Le Guin's character-driven fantasies will enjoy this story of Abisina's quest to unify both her divided country and her divided self." Bull Cent Child Books

Abbott, Tony, 1952-
The **forbidden** stone; by Tony Abbott. Katherine Tegen Books, an imprint of HarperCollinsPublishers 2014 432 p. (The Copernicus legacy) (hardback) $16.99

Grades: 4 5 6 7   **Fic**
  1. Secret societies -- Fiction 2. Antiquities -- Fiction 3. Secret societies -- Fiction 4. Voyages and travels --

Fiction 5. Adventure and adventurers -- Fiction
ISBN 006219447X; 9780062194473
                                          LC 2013038560
"Four precocious preteens and a distracted astrophysicist travel to Europe to unravel a mystery that has already claimed several lives...Filled with riddles and ciphers, this first of 12 installments will keep readers intellectually stimulated as well as entertained. The stepbrothers' bond, a budding crush and a mystery that plays off of real historical figures and facts make this more than a pedestrian whodunit. With engaging characters, a globe-trotting plot and dangerous villains, it is hard to find something not to like. Equal parts edge-of-your-seat suspense and heartfelt coming-of-age." (Kirkus)

Lunch -box dream. Farrar Straus Giroux 2011 178p $16.99

Grades: 6 7 8 9   **Fic**
  1. Family life -- Fiction 2. Segregation -- Fiction 3. Race relations -- Fiction 4. Southern States -- Fiction 5. Missing children -- Fiction 6. African Americans -- Fiction 7. Voyages and travels -- Fiction
  ISBN 978-0-374-34673-7; 0-374-34673-9
                                          LC 2010-33105
Told from multiple points of view, a white family on a 1959 road trip between Ohio and Florida, visiting Civil War battlefields along the way, crosses paths with a black family near Atlanta, where one of their children has gone missing.
  "Throughout, Abbott . . . builds an increasingly disturbing undercurrent of racial conflict, sibling distrust, and marital discord. Although beautifully crafted and written, the book's emotional complexity and unsettling tone will likely prove challenging." Publ Wkly

★ The **postcard**. Little, Brown 2008 358p il $15.99; pa $5.99

Grades: 5 6 7 8   **Fic**
  1. Mystery fiction 2. Florida -- Fiction 3. Grandmothers -- Fiction 4. Books and reading -- Fiction
  ISBN 978-0-316-01172-3; 0-316-01172-X; 978-0-316-01173-0 pa; 0-316-01173-8 pa
                                          LC 2007-31074
While in St. Petersburg, Florida, to help clean out his recently-deceased grandmother's house, thirteen-year-old Jason finds an old postcard which leads him on an adventure that blends figures from an old, unfinished detective story with his family's past.
  "Mystery fans will appreciate the depth and intrigue of the dual level mysteries, and will also enjoy the wit and banter of the main characters." Libr Media Connect

The **serpent's** curse; Tony Abbott, Bill Perkins ; [edited by] Claudia Gabel. HarperCollins 2014 496 p. illustrations (The copernicus legacy) (hardcover) $16.99

Grades: 4 5 6 7   **Fic**
  1. Curses -- Fiction 2. Relics -- Fiction 3. Kidnapping -- Fiction 4. Adventure and adventurers 5. Adventure stories 6. Antiquities -- Fiction 7. Secret societies -- Fiction 8. Voyages and travels -- Fiction
  ISBN 0062194461; 9780062194466
                                          LC 2014937634

Sequel to: The Forbidden Stone (2014)

This book, by Tony Abbott, is "a globe-trotting adventure packed with more riddles, puzzles, and secret histories. The hunt for Copernicus's first relic sent Wade, Darrell, Lily, and Becca to the far reaches of the world and put them in serious danger. But they never imagined Sara Kaplan - Darrell and Wade's mother - would be kidnapped by the conniving Galina Krause. Now they must race the evil Teutonic Order to find the Serpens relic and rescue Sara before it's too late." (Publisher's note)

"Still reeling from their last adventure in The Forbidden Stone (HarperCollins, 2014) which ended only hours before, Wade, Darrell, Becca, and Lily are nearly killed by Galina and the evil Order...Readers learn a bit more about each of the four young heroes in this second installment, but those wishing for more character development will want to read the novellas. Fans of the series will eagerly await the next entry.—"

Wade and the scorpion's claw; by Tony Abbott. Katherine Tegen Books/HarperCollins 2014 224 p. illustrations (The Copernicus archives) (paperback) $3.99

Grades: 4 5 6 7   **Fic**

1. Adventure fiction 2. Relics -- Fiction 3. Antiquities -- Fiction 4. Secret societies -- Fiction 5. Voyages and travels -- Fiction 6. Adventure and adventurers -- Fiction

ISBN 0062314726; 9780062314727

LC 2014010026

"'Wade and the Scorpion's Claw' picks up right where 'The Copernicus Legacy: The Forbidden Stone' left off, with the Kaplan family seeking the next Copernicus relic. Now Wade, the curious, analytical, yet starry-eyed member of the group, leads the chase for another relic through the busy streets of San Francisco while on the run from one of Galina Krause's most treacherous henchmen." (Publisher's note)

"This first in a string of novellas is intended to link each of the six full-length novels in the Copernicus Legacy series. . . . This fast-paced adventure features vivid settings, difficult brainteasers and likable characters." Kirkus

Abdel-Fattah, Randa

★ **Does** my head look big in this? Orchard Books 2007 360p $16.99

Grades: 7 8 9 10 11 12   **Fic**

1. School stories 2. Muslims -- Fiction 3. Australia -- Fiction 4. Clothing and dress -- Fiction

ISBN 0-439-91947-9; 978-0-439-91947-0

LC 2006-29117

Year Eleven at an exclusive prep school in the suburbs of Melbourne, Australia, would be tough enough, but it is further complicated for Amal when she decides to wear the hijab, the Muslim head scarf, full-time as a badge of her faith—without losing her identity or sense of style. "Grades seven to ten." (Bull Cent Child Books)

"While the novel deals with a number of serious issues, it is extremely funny and entertaining." SLJ

Ten things I hate about me. Orchard Books 2009 297p $16.99

Grades: 7 8 9 10   **Fic**

1. School stories 2. Muslims -- Fiction 3. Lebanese -- Fiction 4. Australia -- Fiction 5. Prejudices -- Fiction

ISBN 978-0-5450-5055-5; 0-5450-5055-3

LC 2008-13667

This novel is set in Australia. Jamilia, known in school as Jamie, tries to hide her Muslim heritage from her classmates, until her conflicted feelings become too difficult for her to bear. "Grades six to nine." (Bull Cent Child Books)

A "message of the importance of self-disclosure to maintain loving relationships of all kinds plays itself out as Jamie learns to negotiate her roles as daughter, sister, and friend. Readers will also get an enlightening look at post-9/11 racial tensions outside the U.S. and the problems they pose for Muslim teens." Bull Cent Child Books

★ **Where** the streets had a name; Randa Abdel-Fattah. Scholastic Press 2010 313p (reinforced binding) $17.99

Grades: 5 6 7 8   **Fic**

1. Jerusalem -- Fiction 2. Voyages and travels -- Fiction 3. Jewish-Arab relations -- Fiction 4. Israel -- Fiction 5. Muslims -- Fiction 6. West Bank -- Fiction 7. Family life -- Fiction 8. Palestinian Arabs -- Fiction 9. ISBN 0545172926; 9780545172929; 978-0-545-17292-9; 0-545-17292-6

LC 2009043122

This book tells the story of 13-year-old Hayaat, who "lives behind the Israeli-built Separation Wall in the West Bank City of Bethlehem. When her beloved grandmother falls ill . . . [she] decides to make her way to Jerusalem to fill an empty hummus jar with soil from the land of her grandmother's ancestral home. She is certain that this will mend her heart. Unfortunately, although Jerusalem is merely minutes away, curfews, checkpoints, and an identity card that doesn't allow her to cross the border mean that Hayaat and her soccer-loving, troublemaker friend Samy face a perilous journey." (School Lib J) "At the many checkpoints, the friends encounter soldiers, both brutal and kind, and also an Israeli peacenik couple who helps the kids get past the towering barriers." (Booklist)

"Hayaat chronicles this life-altering journey in the first-person, present tense, giving readers an intimate glimpse into the life of her warm, eccentric Muslim family, who survive despite the volatile political environment. A refreshing and hopeful teen perspective on the Israeli-Palestinian dilemma." Kirkus

Abdul-Jabbar, Kareem

Stealing the game; Kareem Abdul-Jabbar and Raymond Obstfeld. Disney-Hyperion Books 2015 304 p. (Streetball crew) hc $16.99

Grades: 4 5 6 7   **Fic**

1. Brothers -- Fiction 2. Basketball -- Fiction 3. Schools -- Fiction 4. Middle schools -- Fiction 5. African Americans -- Fiction 6. Mystery and detective stories 7. Robbers and outlaws -- Fiction 8. Criminal investigation -- Fiction

ISBN 9781423178712; 1423178718

LC 2013046413

In this book, part of the Streetball Crew series by Kareem Abdul-Jabbar, "Jax asks Chris to recruit his best middle school teammates for a pick-up basketball game. Chris doesn't think much of it until the wrong team wins and Jax goes ballistic. It turns out that Jax bet on the game, hoping to earn enough money to repay a debt. While Chris tries to walk a thin tightrope between helping his brother and staying out of trouble, his friend Theo [tries] to learn what Jax has been up to." (Publisher's note)

"The shifting structure of the story and a clever series of blind alleys keep readers on tenterhooks. A deft, understated sports thriller with a solid moral compass." Kirkus

Abela, Deborah

The **ghosts** of Gribblesea Pier. Farrar Straus Giroux 2011 232p $16.99

Grades: 4 5 6   **Fic**

1. Ghost stories 2. Circus -- Fiction 3. Family life -- Fiction 4. Great Britain -- Fiction 5. Swindlers and swindling -- Fiction 6. Eccentrics and eccentricities -- Fiction

ISBN 978-0-374-36239-3; 0-374-36239-4

LC 2010022517

Aurelie Bonhoffen, who has grown up in the circus, discovers a remarkable family secret on her twelfth birthday that may help in dealing with a sinister man who wants to take over her family's pier.

This is a "charmer of a ghostly adventure tale. . . . This fast-paced, engaging, and charming story has echoes of Jeanne Birdsall's 'Penderwicks' . . . and some Dickensian elements, but in the end this is just a finely executed story of family and friendship and the ties that bind a community." SLJ

Abrahams, Peter, 1947-

Behind the curtain; an Echo Falls mystery. 1st ed.; Laura Geringer Books 2006 346p $15.99; lib bdg $16.89

Grades: 6 7 8   **Fic**

1. Mystery fiction

ISBN 9780060737047; 0-06-073704-2; 9780060737054 lib bdg; 0-06-073705-0 lib bdg

LC 2005-17774

An avid Sherlock Holmes fan, eighth grader Ingrid Levin-Hill is kidnapped while investigating mysterious happenings in her home town. "Grades six to nine." (Bull Cent Child Books)

"This is a fast-paced mystery with well-defined characters and a plausible plotline and ending." SLJ

Down the rabbit hole; an Echo Falls mystery. Laura Geringer Books 2005 375p $15.99; lib bdg $16.89; pa $6.99

Grades: 6 7 8   **Fic**

1. Mystery fiction

ISBN 0-06-073701-8; 0-06-073702-6 lib bdg; 0-06-073703-4 pa

LC 2004-14778

"Ingrid Levin-Hill . . . has just been cast as the lead in Alice in Wonderland when she finds herself in a different role—murder detective. The corpse is that of 'Cracked-Up Katie,' whom Ingrid encountered when she attempted to get from her orthodontist to soccer practice." Publ Wkly

Into the dark; an Echo Falls mystery. Laura Geringer Books 2008 300p $15.99; lib bdg $16.89

Grades: 6 7 8   **Fic**

1. Mystery fiction

ISBN 978-0-06-073708-5; 0-06-073708-5; 978-0-06-073709-2 lib bdg; 0-06-073709-3 lib bdg

LC 2006-103018

Thirteen-year-old Sherlock Holmes aficionado Ingrid Levin-Hill tries to clear her grandfather's name when he is accused of murdering an environmental activist on his farm. "Grades five to eight." (Bull Cent Child Books)

"This third installment of the enjoyable Echo Falls mysteries reaffirms the series' quality." Voice Youth Advocates

The **outlaws** of Sherwood Street; giving to the poor. Peter Abrahams. Philomel Books 2013 304 p. (Outlaws of Sherwood Street) $16.99

Grades: 5 6 7 8   **Fic**

1. Justice -- Fiction 2. Cemeteries -- Fiction 3. Brooklyn (New York, N.Y.) -- Fiction 4. Magic -- Fiction 5. Justice -- Fiction 6. Schools -- Fiction 7. Cemeteries -- Fiction 8. Neighborhoods -- Fiction 9. Conduct of life -- Fiction 10. Brooklyn (New York, N.Y.) -- Fiction 11. Family life -- New York (State) -- New York -- Fiction 12. Indians of North America -- New York (State) -- Fiction

ISBN 0399255036; 9780399255038

LC 2012026862

In this book, "seventh-grade do-gooder Robbie Sherwood and her fellow outlaws, Silas, a homeschooled keeper of obscure knowledge; Ashanti, a fellow private-school attendee . . . and Tut Tut, a Haitian immigrant . . . get caught up in the fight against Sheldon Gunn, a gentrifying millionaire . . . attempting to build a Brooklyn high-rise that will not only block the light. . . but just happens to sit atop an ancient Native American burial ground." (School Library Journal)

Reality check. HarperTeen 2009 330p $16.99; lib bdg $17.89; pa $8.99

Grades: 7 8 9 10   **Fic**

1. School stories 2. Gambling -- Fiction 3. Social classes -- Fiction 4. Missing persons -- Fiction

ISBN 978-0-06-122766-0; 0-06-122766-8; 978-0-06-122767-7 lib bdg; 0-06-122767-6 lib bdg; 978-0-06-122768-4 pa; 0-06-122768-4 pa

LC 2008-22593

After a knee injury destroys sixteen-year-old Cody's college hopes, he drops out of high school and gets a job in his small Montana town, but when his ex-girlfriend disappears from her Vermont boarding school, Cody travels cross-country to join the search.

"Abrahams writes a fine thriller that is pitched to attract everyone from reluctant readers to sports fans to romantic idealists." Voice Youth Advocates

Robbie Forester and the outlaws of Sherwood street; magic strikes. Peter Abrahams. Philomel Books 2011 320 p. $16.99

Grades: 5 6 7 8   **Fic**

1. Occult fiction -- Fiction 2. Fantasy fiction -- Fiction 3. Magic -- Fiction 4. Justice -- Fiction 5. Schools -- Fiction 6. Neighborhoods -- Fiction 7. Conduct of

life -- Fiction 8. Brooklyn (New York, N.Y.) -- Fiction
9. Family life -- New York (State) -- New York -- Fiction
ISBN 0399255028; 9780399255021

LC 2010042330

In this book, when seventh-grader Robbie "accidentally
acquires a homeless woman's charm bracelet, she discovers it's a catalyst for magical powers that engage only when
justice is being denied. She and three friends . . . use their
unique capabilities to uncover and thwart an evil real estate
developer pushing small businesses and social services out
of the borough." (School Library Journal)

Acampora, Paul

Rachel Spinelli punched me in the face. Roaring
Brook Press 2011 168p $15.99

Grades: 5 6 7 8   **Fic**

1. Moving -- Fiction 2. Musicians -- Fiction 3.
Friendship -- Fiction 4. Connecticut -- Fiction 5.
Family life -- Fiction 6. Single parent family -- Fiction
ISBN 978-1-59643-548-3; 1-59643-548-8

LC 2010027436

When fourteen-year-old Zachary and his father move
to Falls, Connecticut, he spends a summer falling in love,
coming to terms with his mother's absence, and forming
eclectic friendships.

"Realistic dialogue and poignantly amusing situations .
. . all come together to gently flesh out a few months in the
lives of people readers will savor getting to know. . . . An
outstanding, humane coming-of-age tale of loss, yearning
and forgiveness." Kirkus

Ackley, Amy

Sign language; a novel. Viking 2011 392p
$16.99

Grades: 7 8 9 10   **Fic**

1. School stories 2. Death -- Fiction 3. Fathers --
Fiction 4. Michigan -- Fiction 5. Bereavement --
Fiction 6. Family life -- Fiction
ISBN 978-0-670-01318-0; 0-670-01318-8

LC 2011003001

Teenaged Abby must deal with her feelings about her
father's cancer and its aftermath while simultaneously navigating the difficult problems of growing up.

"This is an amazing debut novel for readers who appreciate contemporary teen fiction. It is both moving and realistic, a result of the well-crafted family relationships. The
author succeeds in creating genuine connections that manage not to feel forced or rushed, despite the pace of the story,
which spans three years." Voice Youth Advocates

Adam, Paul

Max Cassidy: escape from Shadow Island.
Walden Pond Press 2010 295p $16.99; pa $5.99

Grades: 6 7 8 9   **Fic**

1. Mystery fiction 2. Adventure fiction 3. Central
America -- Fiction 4. Missing persons -- Fiction
ISBN 978-0-06-186323-3; 0-06-186323-8; 978-0-06-
186325-7 pa; 0-06-186325-4 pa

LC 2009-12031

First published 2009 in the United Kingdom with title:
Escape from Shadow Island

British fourteen-year-old Max Cassidy calls on his skills
and training as a professional escape artist when he attempts
to clear his mother of murdering his father, who disappeared two years earlier in the Central American country of
Santo Domingo.

"With a cliffhanger ending, look for much more of this
series and be sure to hand it to your reluctant readers." Voice
Youth Advocates

Adams, Douglas

★ The **hitchhiker's** guide to the galaxy; 25th
anniversary illustrated collector's ed.; Harmony
Books 2004 271p il $35

Grades: 7 8 9 10 11 12 Adult   **Fic**

1. Science fiction
ISBN 1-4000-5293-9

LC 2004-558987

First published 1980

"Based on a BBC radio series, . . . this is the episodic
story of Arthur Dent, a contemporary Englishman who discovers first that his unpretentious house is about to be demolished to make way for a bypass, and second that a good
friend is actually an alien galactic hitchhiker who announces
that Earth itself will soon be demolished to make way for
an intergalactic speedway. A suitably bewildered Dent soon
finds himself hitching . . . rides throughout space, aided by
a . . . reference book, The Hitchhiker's Guide to the Galaxy,
a compendium of 'facts,' philosophies, and wild advice."
Libr J

Life, the universe, and everything. Harmony Bks.
1982 227p hardcover o.p. pa $12.95

Grades: 11 12 Adult   **Fic**

1. Science fiction
ISBN 0-517-54874-7; 0-345-41890-6 pa

LC 82-15470

Third volume in The hitchhiker's series

"Arthur Dent and his motley crew do tie up most of the
loose ends and manage to prevent the destruction of the universe, but the first two novels . . . 'must' be read to understand the situation, and even then it's confusing." Libr J

Followed by So long, and thanks for all the fish

Mostly harmless. Harmony Bks. 1992 277p
hardcover o.p. pa $12.95

Grades: 11 12 Adult   **Fic**

1. Science fiction
ISBN 0-517-57740-2; 0-345-37933-0 pa

LC 92-25457

"A Grebulon reconnaissance ship with faulty programming, a news reporter suffering from a bad case of missed
opportunities, a fugitive from the new 'improved' offices of
the Hitchhiker's Guide to the Galaxy, and a hitchhiker lost
in a parallel universe come together in grand style in the fifth
installment of Adams's best-selling 'trilogy.'" Libr J

The **restaurant** at the end of the universe. Harmony Bks. 1981 250p hardcover o.p. pa $12.95

Grades: 11 12 Adult   **Fic**

1. Satire 2. Wit and humor 3. Science fiction 4.

Interplanetary voyages
ISBN 0-517-54535-7; 0-345-41892-1 pa

LC 81-6563

Second volume in The hitchhiker's series

First published 1980 in the United Kingdom

"Poor uprooted Arthur Dent finds himself swept along in the wake of Zaphod Beeblebrox, former President of the Galaxy, as Zaphod searches for the man who rules the Universe. They and their companions tumble from one scrape into another, with the erratic aid of Zaphod's dead great-grandfather and Marvin, their perpetually depressed robot. Adams's lively sense of the ridiculous has concocted many hilarious episodes, though the inspired lunacy of the first book has become rather uneven here. Still, this is one of the best pieces of sf humor available." Libr J

Followed by Life, the universe, and everything

So long, and thanks for all the fish. Harmony Bks. 1985 204p hardcover o.p. pa $7.99

Grades: 11 12 Adult   **Fic**

1. Satire 2. Wit and humor 3. Science fiction 4. Interplanetary voyages
ISBN 0-517-55439-9; 0-345-39183-4 pa

LC 84-19350

Fourth volume in The hitchhiker's series

Arthur Dent "returns to a supposedly destroyed Earth to build a hyperspace bypass. The night of his return, Arthur falls in love with a sedated girl (her brother says she's 'barking mad'), only to lose her, then accidentally find her twice more. She is Fenchurch, the girl who in . . . 'Guide' . . . discovered the secret of Earth's potential happiness moments before it was demolished. Her 'madness' stems from the time when Earth should have been destroyed, and wasn't, but when all the dolphins disappeared. . . . The humor is still off-the-wall, but less forced and more gentle than the other books. . . . The series seems to be winding down, but it is still an addictive commodity to its fans." SLJ

Followed by Mostly harmless

Adams, Richard

Watership Down; Scribner classics ed.; Scribner 1996 429p $30; pa $15

Grades: 6 7 8 9 10   **Fic**

1. Allegories 2. Rabbits -- Fiction
ISBN 0-684-83605-X; 0-7432-7770-8 pa

First published 1972 in the United Kingdom; first United States edition 1974 by Macmillan

"Faced with the annihilation of its warren, a small group of male rabbits sets out across the English downs in search of a new home. Internal struggles for power surface in this intricately woven, realistically told adult adventure when the protagonists must coordinate tactics in order to defeat an enemy rabbit fortress. It is clear that the author has done research on rabbit behavior, for this tale is truly authentic." Shapiro Fic for Youth. 3d edition

Adams, S. J.

Sparks; the epic, completely true blue, (almost) holy quest of Debbie. 1; Flux 2011 256p pa $9.95

Grades: 8 9 10 11 12   **Fic**

1. Iowa -- Fiction 2. Lesbians -- Fiction 3. Religion

-- Fiction
ISBN 978-0-7387-2676-2; 0-7387-2676-1

LC 2011022913

Stonewall Honor Book (2013)

A sixteen-year-old lesbian tries to get over a crush on her religious best friend by embarking on a 'holy quest' with a couple of misfits who have invented a wacky, made-up faith called the Church of Blue.

"Adams has an easy sense of humor . . . and Debbie and her offbeat cohorts are nuanced and authentic as they follow a circuitous path to greater self-awareness and self-reliance." Publ Wkly

Adler, David A.

Don't talk to me about the war. Viking 2008 216p $15.99; pa $6.99

Grades: 4 5 6 7   **Fic**

1. Friendship -- Fiction 2. Family life -- Fiction 3. World War, 1939-1945 -- Fiction 4. Bronx (New York, N.Y.) -- Fiction
ISBN 978-0-670-06307-9; 0-670-06307-X; 978-0-14-241372-2 pa; 0-14-241372-0 pa

LC 2007-17889

In 1940, thirteen-year-old Tommy's routine of school, playing stickball in his Bronx, New York, neighborhood, talking with his friend Beth, and listening to Dodgers games on the radio changes as his mother's illness and his increasing awareness of the war in Europe transform his world.

"An engaging and very accessible historical novel." Booklist

Adler, Emily

Sweet 15; by Emily Adler and Alex Echevarria. Marshall Cavendish 2009 240p $16.99

Grades: 7 8 9 10   **Fic**

1. School stories 2. Family life -- Fiction 3. Puerto Ricans -- Fiction 4. New York (State) -- Fiction 5. Quinceañera (Social custom) -- Fiction
ISBN 978-0-7614-5584-4; 0-7614-5584-1

LC 2008-21391

Shortly before her fifteenth birthday, Destiny Lozada's traditional Puerto Rican mother and feminist older sister hijack her quinceanera, each pushing her own agenda and ignoring the possibility that Destiny, a skateboarding tomboy, might have her own ideas about the coming-of-age ritual she is about to participate in.

"Destiny's resolution, the engaging dialogue, boys, gossip, best friends, fashion, texting, the first kiss and the city of New York all play a part in this charming, fresh and funny coming-of-age novel that will entertain teen readers, especially girls." Kirkus

Adlington, L. J.

Cherry Heaven. Greenwillow Books 2008 458p $16.99; lib bdg $17.89

Grades: 7 8 9 10   **Fic**

1. Science fiction 2. Orphans -- Fiction
ISBN 978-0-06-143180-7; 0-06-143180-X; 978-0-06-143181-4 lib bdg; 0-06-143181-8 lib bdg

LC 2007-24679

Kat and Tanka J leave the wartorn city, move with their adoptive parents to the New Frontier, and are soon settled into a home called Cherry Heaven, but Luka, an escaped factory worker, confirms their suspicion that New Frontier is not the utopia it seems to be.

"In this complex, absorbing, and sometimes disquieting novel, Adlington creates a world that is distinctly different from our own, yet chillingly familiar." Booklist

★ The **diary** of Pelly D. Greenwillow Books 2005 282p hardcover o.p. pa $8.99

Grades: 7 8 9 10   **Fic**

1. Science fiction
ISBN 0-06-076615-8; 0-06-076617-4 pa
     LC 2004-52258

"On the planet Home From Home, Toni V is a brute laborer, a barely educated member of the Demolition Crew that is busy pulverizing the bombed-out remains of City Five's central plaza. Pelly D is a hip member of the swank elite who used to live in an exclusive apartment fronting the plaza. Their stories come together when Toni V uncovers Pelly D's diary in the debris. . . . Middle school, high school." (Horn Book)

"Adlington has crafted an original and disturbing dystopian fantasy told in a smart and sympathetic teen voice." Booklist

Agard, John

★ The **young** inferno; written by John Agard; illustrated by Satoshi Kitamura. Frances Lincoln Children's 2009 un il $19.95

Grades: 8 9 10 11 12   **Fic**

1. Novels in verse 2. Hell -- Fiction
ISBN 978-1-84507-769-3; 1-84507-769-5

"The narrative poems in this short book are accessible and have important things to say about the state of the human race. . . . The hoodie-wearing protagonist . . . awakens in a strange and frightening forest. A dark man appears and introduces himself as the tale-teller Aesop: he is to be the teen's escort through Hell. . . . As the pair travels through the Circles of Hell, they see the sins of mankind. . . . The scribbled, heavy-lined black ink and watercolor illustrations convey exactly the right mood for a book about a modern-day expedition into Hell. This will be a great book to pair with a discussion about Dante's Inferno and/or poetic structure." SLJ

Agell, Charlotte

Shift. Henry Holt and Co. 2008 230p $16.95

Grades: 7 8 9 10   **Fic**

1. Science fiction 2. Religion -- Fiction 3. Family life -- Fiction 4. Resistance to government -- Fiction 5. Environmental degradation -- Fiction
ISBN 978-0-8050-7810-7; 0-8050-7810-X
     LC 2007-46942

In fifteen-year-old Adrian Havoc's world, HomeState rules every aspect of society and religious education is enforced but Adrian, refusing to believe that the Apocalypse is at hand, goes north through the Deadlands and joins a group of insurgents.

"The story is made particularly compelling by the economy and lyricism of the writing style. . . . Readers seeking contemplative and lyrical science fiction will find this

a haunting exploration of government gone awry and one boy's steadfast pursuit of justice." Bull Cent Child Books

Agosín, Marjorie, 1955-

★ **I** lived on Butterfly Hill; Marjorie Agosín ; translated by E.M. O'Connor ; illustrated by Lee White. Atheneum Books for Young Readers 2014 464 p. illustrations $16.99

Grades: 5 6 7 8   **Fic**

1. Chile -- Fiction 2. Political refugees -- Fiction 3. Refugees -- Fiction 4. Separation (Psychology) -- Fiction 5. Valparaíso (Chile) -- Fiction
ISBN 1416953442; 9781416953449; 9781442494763
     LC 2013018099

Pura Belpré (Author) Award (2015)
National Jewish Book Award Finalist: Children's and Young Adult (2014)

In this novel, by Marjorie Agosin, illustrated by Lee White, "Celeste Marconi . . . lives peacefully among friends and neighbors and family in the idyllic town of Valparaiso, Chile. . . . Celeste's parents--her educated, generous, kind parents--must go into hiding. . . . To protect their daughter, they send her to America. As Celeste adapts to her new life in Maine, she never stops dreaming of Chile. But even after democracy is restored to her home country, questions remain." (Publisher's note)

"The language is poetic and full of imagery and, while the book is long, it moves at a smooth pace. Occasional illustrations reflect the mood of each phase of the story." SLJ

Aguiar, Nadia

The **lost** island of Tamarind; [by] Nadia Aguiar. Feiwel and Friends 2008 437p il map (The Book of Tamarind) $17.95

Grades: 5 6 7 8   **Fic**

1. War stories 2. Adventure fiction 3. Magic -- Fiction 4. Giants -- Fiction 5. Islands -- Fiction 6. Pirates -- Fiction 7. Siblings -- Fiction
ISBN 978-0-312-38029-8; 0-312-38029-1
     LC 2008-5623

Thirteen-year-old Maya, who has spent her life at sea with her marine biologist parents, yearns for a normal life, but when a storm washes her parents overboard, life becomes anything but normal for Maya, her younger brother and baby sister, as they land at a mysterious, uncharted island filled with danger.

"Each detail of this fantasy is crafted with care; readers will be drawn into this dangerous, magical world where anything is possible and nothing can be fully explained." SLJ

Followed by: The secrets of Tamarind (2011)

Secrets of Tamarind. Feiwel and Friends 2011 373p map (The Book of Tamarind) $16.99

Grades: 5 6 7 8   **Fic**

1. Adventure fiction 2. Magic -- Fiction 3. Islands -- Fiction 4. Siblings -- Fiction 5. Environmental degradation -- Fiction
ISBN 978-0-312-38030-4; 0-312-38030-5
     LC 2010050898

Sequel to: The lost island of Tamarind (2008)

Four years after leaving the lost island of Tamarind, Maya, Simon, and Penny Nelson return to stop the Red Coral Project, a sinister group mining the magical mineral oph-alla there and, in the process, ruining the magnificent island.

"Replete with ecological warnings applicable to real as well as fantasy worlds and glossed with lush descriptions of imaginary flora and fauna, the rapid-fire plot bristles with danger." Kirkus

Aguirre, Ann

Enclave. Feiwel & Friends 2011 262p $16.99

Grades: 8 9 10 **Fic**

1. Horror fiction 2. Fantasy fiction 3. Dystopian fiction 4. Apocalyptic fiction 5. Zombies -- Fiction

ISBN 978-0-312-65008-7; 0-312-65008-6

LC 2010031039

In a post-apocalyptic future, fifteen-year-old Deuce, a loyal Huntress, brings back meat while avoiding the Freaks outside her enclave, but when she is partnered with the mys-terious outsider, Fade, she begins to see that the strict ways of the elders may be wrong—and dangerous. "Grades six to eight." (Bull Cent Child Books)

"In this skilled though violent postapocalyptic thriller, Deuce has newly earned the rank of Huntress. . . . It's her duty to provide meat for her loveless, draconian enclave, deep beneath the streets of a ruined city, as well as to defend it against cannibalistic Freaks, who are gradually eliminat-ing the scattered human survivors of a vaguely remembered plague. . . . Aguirre . . . has created a gritty and highly com-petent heroine, an equally deadly sidekick/love interest, and a fascinating if unpleasant civilization." Publ Wkly

Horde; by Ann Aguirre. Feiwel & Friends 2013 422 p. $17.99

Grades: 8 9 10 **Fic**

1. Science fiction 2. Dystopian fiction 3. Monsters -- Fiction

ISBN 1250024633; 9781250024633

This book, by Ann Aguirre, is the conclusion to the Enclave trilogy. "Salvation is surrounded, monsters at the gates, and this time, they're not going away. When Deuce, Fade, Stalker and Tegan set out, the odds are against them. But the odds have been stacked against Deuce from the mo-ment she was born. She might not be a Huntress anymore, but she doesn't run. With her knives in hand and her com-panions at her side, she will not falter, whether fighting for her life or Fade's love." (Publisher's note)

"Deuce's skills from her Huntress days come in handy when a horde of mutant "Freaks" descends upon the humans of her post-apocalyptic world, but trusting some of the en-emy turns out to be a worthwhile risk. Relationships, includ-ing Deuce's romance with Fade, soften a bloody tale; as in previous compelling installments, readers should suspend disbelief for Deuce's background-belying vocabulary and emotional intelligence." (Horn Book)

Outpost; by Ann Aguirre. Feiwel & Friends 2012 320 p. $17.99

Grades: 8 9 10 **Fic**

1. Monsters -- Fiction 2. Teenagers -- Fiction 3. Survival skills -- Fiction 4. Science fiction 5. Survival -- Fiction 6. Teenage girls -- Fiction

ISBN 0312650094; 9780312650094

LC 2011287957

In this book by Ann Aguirre "months have passed since Deuce and her band of survivors joined Salvation, a forti-fied settlement in the middle of Freak-infested land. While Tegan, Fade, and Stalker find helpful community roles, Deuce struggles to adjust to life where, as a female, she is forbidden from fighting. When the Freaks evolve into more cunning foes, however, Deuce's superior combat skills are instrumental in establishing an outpost to protect the town." (Booklist)

"When this follow-up to Enclave (2011) begins, trained Huntress Deuce and fellow travelers Fade, Stalker and Tegan have lived two months amid the town of Salvation's affluence, strict gender roles and relative freedom from the putrid, slavering, mindless Freaks who plague their world... Overall, an engaging world and forward-moving plot with a resolution that promises new settings and challenges in Book 3." (Kirkus)

Aiken, Joan

★ The **wolves** of Willoughby Chase; illustrated by Pat Marriott. Delacorte Press 2000 181p il hard-cover o.p. pa $6.99

Grades: 5 6 7 8 **Fic**

1. Great Britain -- Fiction

ISBN 0-385-32790-0; 0-440-49603-9 pa

First published 1962 in the United Kingdom; first United States edition 1963 by Doubleday

"Plot, characterization, and background blend perfectly into an amazing whole. . . . Highly recommended." SLJ

Other titles in this series are:

Black hearts in Battersea (1964)

Cold Shoulder Road (1996)

The cuckoo tree (1971)

Dangerous games (1999)

Is underground (1993)

Midwinter nightingale (2003)

Nightbirds on Nantucket (1966)

The stolen lake (1981)

The witch of Clatteringshaws (2005)

Alban, Andrea

Anya's war. Feiwel and Friends 2011 188p $16.99

Grades: 7 8 9 10 **Fic**

1. China -- Fiction 2. Jews -- China -- Fiction 3. Jewish refugees -- Fiction 4. Shanghai (China) -- Fiction 5. Abandoned children -- Fiction 6. Sino-Japanese Conflict, 1937-1945 -- Fiction

ISBN 978-0-312-37093-0; 0-312-37093-8

LC 2010-37089

In 1937, the privileged and relatively carefee life of a fourteen-year-old Jewish girl, whose family emigrated from Odessa, Ukraine, to Shanghai, China, comes to an end when she finds an abandoned baby, her hero, Amelia Earhart, goes missing, and war breaks out with Japan. Based on the au-thor's family history.

"Most moving are the scenes with the full cast of fam-ily characters, who are irritating, irritable, funny, surprising, mean, and prejudiced. Alban also explores the complexities of Anya's Jewish community. . . . An important addition to literature about WWII refugees." Booklist

Albin, Gennifer

Crewel; Gennifer Albin. by Gennifer Albin. Farrar Straus Giroux 2012 368 p. (hardcover) $17.99

Grades: 8 9 10 11   **Fic**

1. Spiritual gifts 2. Secrecy -- Fiction 3. Psychics -- Fiction 4. Science fiction

ISBN 0374316414; 9780374316419; 9780374316440

LC 2011043930

In author Gennifer Albin's book, "sixteen year-old Adelice Lewys has a secret: she wants to fail. Gifted with the ability to weave time with matter, she's exactly what the Guild is looking for, and in the world of Arras, being chosen as a Spinster is everything a girl could want. . . . It also means the power to embroider the very fabric of life . . . [and] Adelice isn't interested. Not that her feelings matter, because she slipped and wove a moment at testing, and they're coming for her--tonight. Now she has one hour . . . to escape." (genniferalbin.com)

Alcott, Louisa May

Little women; illustrated by Scott McKowen. Sterling Pub. 2004 525p il $9.95

Grades: 5 6 7 8   **Fic**

1. Sisters -- Fiction 2. Family life -- Fiction 3. New England -- Fiction

ISBN 978-1-4027-1458-0; 1-4027-1458-0

LC 2004-15669

First published 1868

Chronicles the joys and sorrows of the four March sisters as they grow into young women in mid-nineteenth-century New England.

Other titles about members of the March family are:

Eight cousins (1875)

Jo's boys (1886)

Little men (1871)

Rose in bloom (1876)

Alegria, Malin

Estrella's quinceanera. Simon & Schuster Books for Young Readers 2006 272p $14.95

Grades: 7 8 9 10   **Fic**

1. Mexican Americans -- Fiction 2. Quinceañera (Social custom) -- Fiction

ISBN 0-689-87809-5

Estrella's mother and aunt are planning a gaudy, traditional quinceañera for her, even though it is the last thing she wants.

"Alegria writes about Mexican American culture, first love, family, and of moving between worlds with poignant, sharp-sighted humor and authentic dialogue." Booklist

Alender, Katie

Bad girls don't die. Hyperion Books 2009 352p $15.99

Grades: 7 8 9 10   **Fic**

1. School stories 2. Sisters -- Fiction 3. Demoniac possession -- Fiction

ISBN 978-1-4231-0876-4; 1-4231-0876-0

LC 2008-46179

When fifteen-year-old Lexi's younger sister Kasey begins behaving strangely and their old Victorian house seems to take on a life of its own, Lexi investigates and discov-

ers some frightening facts about previous occupants of the house, leading her to believe that many lives are in danger.

This "novel is both a mystery and a trip into the paranormal. . . . With just enough violence, suspense, and romance to keep readers turning pages, this . . . will be a popular addition to any YA collection." Booklist

Followed by: From bad to cursed (2011)

Alexander, Jill S.

Paradise. Feiwel and Friends 2011 246p $16.99

Grades: 7 8 9 10   **Fic**

1. Love stories 2. Drums -- Fiction 3. Texas -- Fiction 4. Family life -- Fiction 5. Bands (Music) -- Fiction 6. Country music -- Fiction

ISBN 0312605412; 9780312605414

LC 2010050900

Teenaged Paisley Tillery dreams a career as a professional drummer will take her out of her small Texas town, but when her country rock band gets a handsome new lead singer from Paradise, Texas, those dreams may change.

"Strong, rural Southern storytelling and mother-daughter conflict are integral parts of the plot. . . . Alexander's simmering plot is . . . driven by a complex story and multiple, complex characters." SLJ

★ The sweetheart of Prosper County. Feiwel and Friends 2009 212p $16.99

Grades: 7 8 9 10   **Fic**

1. Texas -- Fiction 2. Bullies -- Fiction 3. Bereavement -- Fiction 4. Mother-daughter relationship -- Fiction

ISBN 978-0-312-54856-8; 0-312-54856-7

LC 2008-34757

In a small East Texas town largely ruled by prejudices and bullies, fourteen-year-old Austin sets out to win a ride in the next parade and, in the process, grows in her understanding of friendship and helps her widowed mother through her mourning.

"This is a warm, humorous story. . . . A refreshing picture of teen angst, with realistic dialogue and memorable characters." SLJ

Alexander, Kwame

★ The crossover; by Kwame Alexander. Houghton Mifflin Harcourt 2014 240 p. hc $16.99

Grades: 6 7 8 9 10   **Fic**

1. Rap music 2. Brothers -- Fiction 3. Basketball -- Fiction 4. Novels in verse 5. Twins -- Fiction 6. Fathers and sons -- Fiction 7. African Americans -- Fiction

ISBN 0544107713; 9780544107717

LC 2013013810

Newbery Medal (2015)

Coretta Scott King Author Award Honor Book (2015)

In this novel, by Kwame Alexander, "12-year old Josh Bell . . . and his twin brother Jordan are awesome on the court. But Josh has more than basketball in his blood, he's got mad beats, too, that tell his family's story in verse. . . . Josh and Jordan must come to grips with growing up on and off the court to realize breaking the rules comes at a terrible price, as their story's . . . climax proves a game-changer for the entire family." (Publisher's note)

"Twins Josh and Jordan are junior high basketball stars, thanks in large part to the coaching of their dad, a former professional baller who was forced to quit playing for health reasons, and the firm, but loving support of their assistant-principal mom...Despite his immaturity, Josh is a likable, funny, and authentic character. Underscoring the sports and the fraternal tension is a portrait of a family that truly loves and supports one another. Alexander has crafted a story that vibrates with energy and heart and begs to be read aloud. A slam dunk." SLJ

Alexander, Lloyd

The **Black** Cauldron; [by] Lloyd Alexander. rev. ed.; H. Holt 1999 182p (Chronicles of Prydain) $19.95
Grades: 5 6 7 8 **Fic**
1. Fantasy fiction
ISBN 0-8050-6131-2; 978-08050-6131-4
LC 98040896
First published 1965
Taran, Assistant Pig-Keeper of Prydain, faces even more dangers as he seeks the magical black cauldron, the chief implement of the evil powers of Arawn, lord of the Land of Death.

★ The **book** of three; rev ed.; Holt & Co. 1999 190p (Chronicles of Prydain) $19.95; pa $6.99
Grades: 5 6 7 8 **Fic**
1. Fantasy fiction
ISBN 978-0-8050-6132-1; 0-8050-6132-0; 978-0-8050-8048-3 pa; 0-8050-8048-1 pa
LC 98-40901
First published 1964
"Related in a simple, direct style, this fast-paced tale of high adventure has a well-balanced blend of fantasy, realism, and humor." SLJ
Other titles about the mythical land of Prydain are:
The black cauldron (1965)
The castle of Llyr (1966)
The foundling and other tales of Prydain (1999)
The high king (1968)
Taran Wanderer (1967)

★ The **golden** dream of Carlo Chuchio. Henry Holt & Co. 2007 306p il $16.95
Grades: 5 6 7 8 9 **Fic**
1. Fantasy fiction 2. Middle East -- Fiction 3. Buried treasure -- Fiction 4. Voyages and travels -- Fiction
ISBN 978-0-8050-8333-0; 0-8050-8333-2
LC 2006-49710
Naive and bumbling Carlo, his shady camel-puller Baksheesh, and Shira, a girl determined to return home, follow a treasure map through the deserts and cities of the infamous Golden Road, as mysterious strangers try in vain to point them toward real treasures
This "is an exuberant and compassionate tale of adventure." Publ Wkly

★ The **iron** ring. Dutton Children's Bks. 1997 283p hardcover o.p. pa $5.99

Grades: 5 6 7 8 **Fic**
1. Adventure fiction 2. India -- Fiction
ISBN 0-14-130348-4 pa
LC 96-29730
"Young Tamar, ruler of a small Indian kingdom, wagers with a visiting king and loses his kingdom and his freedom. Traveling to the king's land to make good on his debt, he collects quite an entourage and eventually overcomes his enemies with his friends' help. This tale offers delightful characters, a philosophical interest in the meaning of life, a thoughtful look at the caste system, and a clever use of Indian animal folktales." Horn Book Guide

★ The **remarkable** journey of Prince Jen. Dutton Children's Bks. 1991 273p hardcover o.p. pa $6.99
Grades: 5 6 7 8 **Fic**
1. Adventure fiction 2. China -- Fiction
ISBN 0-14-240225-7 pa
LC 91-13720
Bearing six unusual gifts, young Prince Jen in Tang Dynasty China embarks on a perilous quest and emerges triumphantly into manhood
"Alexander satisfies the taste for excitement, but his vivid characters and the food for thought he offers will nourish long after the last page is turned." SLJ

★ **Westmark**. Dutton 1981 184p hardcover o.p. pa $5.99
Grades: 5 6 7 8 **Fic**
1. Adventure fiction
ISBN 0-14-131068-5
A boy fleeing from criminal charges falls in with a charlatan, his dwarf attendant, and an urchin girl, travels with them about the kingdom of Westmark, and ultimately arrives at the palace where the king is grieving over the loss of his daughter
The author "peoples his tale with a marvelous cast of individuals, and weaves an intricate story of high adventure that climaxes in a superbly conceived conclusion, which, though predictable, is reached through carefully built tension and subtly added comic relief." Booklist
Other titles in this series are:
The Beggar Queen (1984)
The Kestrel (1982)

Alexander, William

Ambassador; William Alexander. Margaret K. McElderry Books 2014 240 p. (hardcover) $16.99
Grades: 5 6 7 8 **Fic**
1. Science fiction 2. Human-alien encounters -- Fiction 3. Ambassadors -- Fiction 4. Illegal aliens -- Fiction 5. Mexican Americans -- Fiction
ISBN 1442497645; 9781442497641; 9781442497658
LC 2013037333
In this middle grade book by William Alexander, "Gabe Fuentes is reading under the covers one summer night when he is interrupted by a creature who looks like a purple sock puppet. The sock puppet introduces himself as the Envoy and asks if Gabe wants to be Earth's ambassador to the galaxy. What sane eleven-year-old could refuse?" (Publisher's note)

"A shape-shifting creature called 'the Envoy' informs eleven-year-old Gabe that it has appointed him Earth's ambassador to 'everyone else.' Gabe travels across space (while he's asleep) to the Embassy. When he wakes up back home, he discovers his father is to be deported to Mexico the next day--and one of the other ambassadors is trying to kill Gabe. A meaty and entertaining novel." Horn Book

Alexie, Sherman, 1966-

★ The **absolutely** true diary of a part-time Indian; art by Ellen Forney. Little, Brown 2007 229p il $18.99

Grades: 8 9 10   **Fic**

1. School stories 2. Friendship -- Fiction 3. Family life -- Fiction 4. Native Americans -- Fiction

ISBN 0316013684; 9780316013680

LC 2007-22799

Boston Globe-Horn Book Award: Fiction and Poetry (2008)

National Book Award for Young People's Literature (2007)

Budding cartoonist Junior leaves his troubled school on the Spokane Indian Reservation to attend an all-white farm town school where the only other Indian is the school mascot. "Grades seven to ten." (Bull Cent Child Books)

"The many characters, on and off the rez, with whom he has dealings are portrayed with compassion and verve. . . . Forney's simple pencil cartoons fit perfectly within the story and reflect the burgeoning artist within Junior." Booklist

Allison, Jennifer

★ **Gilda** Joyce, psychic investigator. Sleuth/ Dutton 2005 321p pa $6.99; $13.99

Grades: 5 6 7 8   **Fic**

1. Mystery fiction 2. Cousins -- Fiction

ISBN 0-14-240698-8 pa; 0-525-47375-0; 978-0-14-240698-4 pa; 978-0-525-47375-6

LC 2004-10834

During the summer before ninth grade, intrepid Gilda Joyce invites herself to the San Francisco mansion of distant cousin Lester Splinter and his thirteen-year-old daughter, where she uses her purported psychic abilities and detective skills to solve the mystery of the mansion's boarded-up tower.

"Allison pulls off something special here. She not only offers a credible mystery . . . but also . . . provides particularly strong characterizations." Booklist

Other titles about Gilda Joyce are:

Gilda Joyce: the Ladies of the Lake (2006)

Gilda Joyce: the ghost sonata (2007)

Gilda Joyce: the dead drop (2009)

Gilda Joyce: the bones of the holy (2011)

Gilda Joyce, psychic investigator: the bones of the holy. Dutton Children's Books 2011 286p $16.99

Grades: 5 6 7 8   **Fic**

1. Ghost stories 2. Mystery fiction 3. Florida -- Fiction 4. Remarriage -- Fiction

ISBN 978-0-525-42212-9; 0-525-42212-9

LC 2010038069

Psychic investigator Gilda Joyce is appalled that her mother plans to remarry, but while they are in St. Augustine, Florida, making wedding arrangements Gilda discovers that the city is full of ghosts and mysteries, including one involving her stepfather-to-be.

"Gilda fans will rally to her latest caper, while newcomers should revel in her ghostly escapades in old St. Augustine." Kirkus

Gilda Joyce: the dead drop. Dutton Children's Books 2009 300p $16.99

Grades: 5 6 7 8   **Fic**

1. Mystery fiction 2. Spies -- Fiction 3. International Spy Museum (Washington, D.C.) -- Fiction.

ISBN 978-0-525-47980-2; 0-525-47980-5

LC 2008036269

Almost-fifteen-year-old psychic investigator Gilda Joyce interns for the summer at the International Spy Museum in Washington, D.C., and solves a mystery involving national security.

"The humor, pacing, and story line are all topnotch, and Allison succeeds at breathing life into the entire cast." SLJ

Almond, David, 1951-

The **Boy** who swam with piranhas; David Almond, illustrated by Oliver Jeffers. Candlewick Press 2013 256 p. $15.99

Grades: 4 5 6 7   **Fic**

1. Orphans -- Fiction 2. Carnivals -- Fiction 3. Runaway children -- Fiction

ISBN 0763661694; 9780763661694

LC 2012947721

"Stanley Potts's uncle Ernie has developed an over-the-top fascination with canning fish in the house, and life at 69 Fish Quay Lane has turned barmy. But there's darkness in the madness, and when Uncle Ernie's obsession takes an unexpectedly cruel turn, Stan has no choice but to leave. As he journeys away from the life he's always known, he mingles with a carnival full of eccentric characters and meets the legendary Pancho Pirelli, the man who swims in a tank full of perilous piranhas." (Publisher's note)

"After his parents' deaths, Stanley Potts runs away with a carnival. He meets Pancho Pirelli, who performs the death-defying act of swimming with piranhas. Pirelli takes Stan under his wing, grooming him to become his sidekick and successor. Almond offers up some lighthearted fare, complete with old-fashioned intrusive narrator and numerous spot illustrations. The silliness is tempered by unsentimental, clear-eyed wisdom." Horn Book

Clay. Delacorte Press 2006 247p hardcover o.p. pa $8.99

Grades: 7 8 9 10   **Fic**

1. Horror fiction 2. Supernatural -- Fiction

ISBN 0-385-73171-X; 0-440-42013-X pa

LC 2005-22681

The developing relationship between teenager Davie and a mysterious new boy in town morphs into something darker and more sinister when Davie learns firsthand of the boy's supernatural powers.

"Rooted in the ordinariness of a community and in one boy's chance to play God, this story will grab readers with its gripping action and its important ideas." Booklist

★ The **fire** -eaters. Delacorte Press 2004 218p $15.95

Grades: 7 8 9 10   **Fic**
1. Great Britain -- Fiction
ISBN 0-385-73170-1

LC 2003-55709
First published 2003 in the United Kingdom
In 1962 England, despite observing his father's illness and the suffering of the fire-eating Mr. McNulty, as well as enduring abuse at school and the stress of the Cuban Missile Crisis, Bobby Burns and his family and friends still find reasons to rejoice in their lives and to have hope for the future.
"The author's trademark themes . . . are here in full, and resonate long after the last page is turned." SLJ

★ **Kit's** wilderness; 10th-anniversary edition; Delacorte Press 2009 229p $16.99

Grades: 6 7 8 9 10   **Fic**
1. Ghost stories 2. Great Britain -- Fiction 3. Coal mines and mining -- Fiction
ISBN 978-0-385-32665-0; 0-385-32665-3
First published 1999
Michael L. Printz Award, 2001
Thirteen-year-old Kit goes to live with his grandfather in the decaying coal mining town of Stoneygate, England, and finds both the old man and the town haunted by ghosts of the past
The author "explores the power of friendship and family, the importance of memory, and the role of magic in our lives. This is a highly satisfying literary experience." SLJ

Mouse bird snake wolf; David Almond, illustrated by David McKean. Candlewick Press 2013 80 p. (reinforced) $17.99

Grades: 4 5 6 7   **Fic**
1. Animals -- Fiction 2. Fantasy fiction -- Fiction
ISBN 0763659126; 9780763659127

LC 2012950556
In this book, "Harry, Sue, and Little Ben live in a world whose lazy gods have made creatures like whales and camels but have given up their work, leaving blank spaces . . . . The children discover that they can create animals themselves, using sticks, leaves, and clay; Little Ben makes a mouse; Sue, a bird; and Harry, a snake. But Harry and Sue aren't satisfied. They create a terrifying wolf that turns on them and eats them, and Little Ben must summon the courage to save them." (Publishers Weekly)

★ **My** name is Mina. Delacorte Press 2011 300p $15.99; lib bdg $18.99

Grades: 5 6 7 8   **Fic**
1. Authorship -- Fiction
ISBN 978-0-385-74073-9; 0-385-74073-5; 978-0-375-98964-3 lib bdg; 0-375-98964-1 lib bdg; 978-0-375-98965-0 e-book

LC 2010040143
Prequel to: Skellig

"This intimate prequel to Skellig is built around Mina McKee, the curious and brilliant home-schooled child who eventually befriends that book's protagonist, Michael. Mina, a budding writer, reveals her love of words in her journal; most of the book unfolds in a handwritten-looking font, with Mina's more emphatic entries exploding onto the pages in massive display type. Her lyrical, nonlinear prose records her reflections on her past, existential musings . . . and self-directed writing exercises. . . . Almond gives readers a vivid picture of the joyfully freeform workings of Mina's mind and her mixed emotions about being an isolated child. Her gradual emergence from the protective shell of home is beautifully portrayed. . . . This novel will inspire children to let their imaginations soar." Publ Wkly

★ **Raven** summer. Delacorte Press 2009 198p $19.99

Grades: 7 8 9 10 11 12   **Fic**
1. Orphans -- Fiction 2. Great Britain -- Fiction 3. Fate and fatalism -- Fiction
ISBN 978-0-385-73806-4; 0-385-73806-4

LC 2009-1661
Led to an abandoned baby by a raven, fourteen-year-old Liam seems fated to meet two foster children who have experienced the world's violence in very different ways as he struggles to understand war, family problems, and friends who grow apart.
"The tension builds to a shocking and totally believable ending. . . . A haunting story, perfect for group discussion." Booklist

★ The **savage**; illustrated by Dave McKean. Candlewick Press 2008 79p il $17.99

Grades: 5 6 7 8   **Fic**
1. Death -- Fiction 2. Fathers -- Fiction
ISBN 978-0-7636-3932-7; 0-7636-3932-X

LC 2008-928388
A boy tells about a story he wrote when dealing with his father's death about a savage kid living in a ruined chapel in the woods-and the tale about the savage kid coming to life in the real world.
"This illustrated novella, a graphic novel within a novel, will satisfy Almond's fans and newcomers alike. McKean's illustrations-ink and watercolor in black, blues, and greens-add an appropriately eerie touch." Horn Book Guide

★ **Skellig**; 10th anniversary ed.; Delacorte Press 2009 182p $16.99; pa $6.99

Grades: 5 6 7 8 9 10   **Fic**
1. Fantasy fiction
ISBN 978-0-385-32653-7; 0-385-32653-X; 978-0-440-41602-9 pa; 0-440-41602-7 pa
First published 1998 in the United Kingdom; first United States edition 1999
Michael L. Printz Award honor book
Unhappy about his baby sister's illness and the chaos of moving into a dilapidated old house, Michael retreats to the garage and finds a mysterious stranger who is something like a bird and something like an angel.

"The plot is beautifully paced and the characters are drawn with a graceful, careful hand. . . . A lovingly done, thought-provoking novel." SLJ

Slog's dad; illustrated by Dave McKean. Candlewick Press 2011 52p il $15.99

Grades: 5 6 7 8   **Fic**

1. Death -- Fiction 2. Future life -- Fiction 3. Great Britain -- Fiction 4. Father-son relationship -- Fiction
ISBN 978-0-7636-4940-1; 0-7636-4940-6

LC 2010-38700

When Slog's father died he promised to return for one last visit in the spring, but when Slog spots a scruffy man on a bench outside the butcher shop and identifies him as his father, his best friend Davie is skeptical.

"This grief-strafed wonder tale is brilliantly matched by some of McKean's most moving artwork yet. Text pages, featuring a voice steeped on Northern English flavor, are counterpoised against wordless illustration sequences that move readers from heaven to earth and back again, beginning with a celestial descent from the sky to a park bench by a man trailing clouds of watercolor glory." Bull Cent Child Books

Alonzo, Sandra

★ **Riding** invisible; written by Sandra Alonzo; illustrated by Nathan Huang. Hyperion 2010 234p il lib bdg $15.99

Grades: 7 8 9 10   **Fic**

1. Horses -- Fiction 2. Brothers -- Fiction 3. Family life -- Fiction 4. Personality disorders -- Fiction
ISBN 978-1-4231-1898-5; 1-4231-1898-7

LC 2010-05041

After his older brother Will attacks his horse, Shy, Yancey runs away into the desert. Follow his adventures as he returns home to face life with a brother who has "conduct disorder."

"Written in a journal style and punctuated with sketches depicting Yancy's experiences, there's a lot here to engage readers." Horn Book Guide

Alter, Stephen

Ghost letters. Bloomsbury 2008 227p $16.95

Grades: 5 6 7 8   **Fic**

1. Ghost stories 2. Letters -- Fiction 3. Grandfathers -- Fiction 4. Space and time -- Fiction
ISBN 1-58234-739-5; 978-1-58234-739-4

LC 2007-30844

While exploring the area around his grandfather's home Gil discovers a bottle that carries messages into the past, finds a genie in a letter, and three letters that were never delivered but would have changed the course of history.

"Readers will find the book scary enough to thrill and clever enough to challenge their deductive reasoning." SLJ

Alvarez, Jennifer Lynn

Starfire; by Jennifer Lynn Alvarez. HarperCollins 2014 245 p. (Guardian Herd) (hardback) $16.99

Grades: 5 6 7   **Fic**

1. Fantasy fiction 2. Adventure fiction 3. Horses -- Fiction 4. Mythical animals -- Fiction 5. Fantasy

6. Animals, Mythical -- Fiction 7. Animals -- Abnormalities -- Fiction 8. Adventure and adventurers -- Fiction
ISBN 0062286064; 9780062286062

LC 2014001890

This book, by Jennifer Lynn Alvarez, is the "first book in a . . . fantasy series about winged horses. . . . Once every hundred years, a black foal is born, prophesied to either unite or destroy the five herds of flying horses that live in Anok - fated to become the most powerful pegasus in all of the land. Star is this black foal. Even though Star has malformed wings that make him unable to fly, the leaders of each herd will take no risks and want to execute Star before his first birthday." (Publisher's note)

"Born the dark foal of Anok, Star is different from other pegasi--he can't fly, and on his first birthday the light of the Hundred Year Star will empower him to heal or destroy. Thunderwing, the herd's over-stallion, has vowed to kill him first. Scenes of adolescent pegasus bullying are overwrought, but the magical frame makes strong scaffolding for the well-executed plot." Horn Book

Alvarez, Julia

★ **Before** we were free. Knopf 2002 167p $15.95; lib bdg $17.99; pa $5.99

Grades: 7 8 9 10   **Fic**

1. Generals 2. Presidents 3. Family life -- Fiction 4. Dominican Republic -- Fiction 5. Dominican Republic -- History -- 1930-1961 -- Fiction
ISBN 0-375-81544-9; 0-375-91544-3 lib bdg; 0-440-23784-X pa

LC 2001-50520

In the early 1960s in the Dominican Republic, twelve-year-old Anita learns that her family is involved in the underground movement to end the bloody rule of the dictator, General Trujillo

This "is a realistic and compelling account of a girl growing up too quickly while coming to terms with the cost of freedom." Horn Book

★ **How** Tia Lola came to visit/stay. Knopf 2001 147p $15.95; pa $5.50

Grades: 4 5 6 7   **Fic**

1. Aunts -- Fiction 2. Divorce -- Fiction 3. Vermont -- Fiction 4. Dominican Americans -- Fiction
ISBN 0-375-80215-0; 0-440-41870-4 pa

LC 00-62932

Although ten-year-old Miguel is at first embarrassed by his colorful aunt, Tia Lola, when she comes to Vermont from the Dominican Republic to stay with his mother, his sister, and him after his parents' divorce, he learns to love her.

"Readers will enjoy the funny situations, identify with the developing relationships and conflicting feelings of the characters, and will get a spicy taste of Caribbean culture in the bargain." SLJ

Other titles about Tia Lola are:
How Tia Lola learned to teach (2010)
How Tia Lola saved the summer (2011)
How Tia Lola ended up starting over (2011)

★ **Return** to sender. Alfred A. Knopf 2009 325p $16.99; lib bdg $19.99

Grades: 4 5 6 7   **Fic**

1. Vermont -- Fiction 2. Farm life -- Fiction 3. Friendship -- Fiction 4. Migrant labor -- Fiction 5. Illegal aliens -- Fiction

ISBN 978-0-375-85838-3; 0-375-85838-5; 978-0-375-95838-0 lib bdg; 0-375-95838-X lib bdg

LC 2008-23520

Awarded the Belpre Author Medal (2010)

After his family hires migrant Mexican workers to help save their Vermont farm from foreclosure, eleven-year-old Tyler befriends the oldest daughter, but when he discovers they may not be in the country legally, he realizes that real friendship knows no borders.

"Readers will be moved by small moments. . . . A tender, well-constructed book." Publ Wkly

Amateau, Gigi

A **certain** strain of peculiar. Candlewick Press 2009 261p $16.99

Grades: 6 7 8 9   **Fic**

1. Ranch life -- Fiction 2. Grandmothers -- Fiction

ISBN 978-0-7636-3009-6; 0-7636-3009-8

Tired of the miserable life she lives, Mary Harold leaves her mother behind and moves back to Alabama and her grandmother, where she receives support and love and starts to gain confidence in herself and her abilities.

"Mary Harold is a wonderfully complex and honest character. . . . [Her] narrative is heartfelt and poignant, and the message that being 'different' is nothing to be ashamed of will resonate with readers." Voice Youth Advocates

Amato, Mary

Get happy; Mary Amato. Egmont USA 2014 256 p. (hardback) $16.99

Grades: 6 7 8 9   **Fic**

1. Family -- Fiction 2. Musicians -- Fiction 3. Friendship -- Fiction 4. Father-daughter relationship -- Fiction 5. Families -- Fiction 6. Fathers and daughters -- Fiction

ISBN 1606845225; 9781606845226

LC 2014008736

"Minerva has been raised by her single mother after her father left them both. On her 17th birthday, she is shocked to discover that he has been trying to keep in touch, but her mother has been sabotaging his attempts. Furious at her mom, she begins to investigate her dad, a famous marine biologist, only to discover that he has a new family, including a beloved, and perfect, stepdaughter--a girl Minerva already knows and despises." (Publisher's note)

"Though the book explores a heavy, fraught situation, the prose is light and the ending optimistic. Some readers may be frustrated with the lack of closure, as quite a bit is left unresolved. Overall, however, this is a moving, charged tale of family and identity." SLJ

Invisible lines; illustrations by Antonio Caparo. Egmont USA 2009 319p il $15.99; lib bdg $18.99

Grades: 6 7 8 9   **Fic**

1. School stories 2. Moving -- Fiction 3. Social classes -- Fiction 4. Washington (D.C.) -- Fiction 5. Single

parent family -- Fiction

ISBN 978-1-60684-010-8; 1-60684-010-X; 978-1-60684-043-6 lib bdg; 1-60684-043-6 lib bdg

LC 2009-14639

Coming from a poor, single-parent family, seventh-grader Trevor must rely on his intelligence, artistic ability, quick wit, and soccer prowess to win friends at his new Washington, D.C. school, but popular and rich Xander seems determined to cause him trouble.

"The author's subtle sense of humor is at work here. . . . This fresh story is enhanced by notes and drawings from Trevor's fungi notebook. With its short chapters, snappy dialogue, and scientific extras, the novel should find a wide audience." SLJ

Anderson, Jodi Lynn

May Bird among the stars; book two. [by] Jodi Lynn Anderson. 1st ed.; Atheneum Books for Young Readers 2006 260p $16.95

Grades: 5 6 7 8   **Fic**

1. Fantasy fiction

ISBN 978-0-689-86924-2; 0-689-86924-X

LC 2005028832

Sequel to May Bird and The Ever After (2005)

Still trapped in The Ever After, ten-year-old May Bird struggles to decide whether to save the world of her ghostly friends from the evil Bo Cleevil or to return to her West Virginia home.

"Anderson has clearly had a great deal of fun creating a world not so different from our own where spirits go after death, and readers will love her humorous jabs at popular culture." SLJ

Followed by May Bird, warrior princess (2007)

★ **Tiger** Lily; Jodi Lynn Anderson. HarperTeen 2012 304 p. (trade bdg.) $17.99

Grades: 8 9 10 11   **Fic**

1. Love stories 2. Jealousy -- Fiction 3. Fairy tales -- Fiction 4. Peter Pan (Fictional character) 5. Love -- Fiction 6. Magic -- Fiction 7. Fairies -- Fiction

ISBN 0062003259; 9780062003256

LC 2011032659

This is the story of Tiger Lily, the girl Peter Pan spurned for Wendy. "Told from the perspective of Tinker Bell, the novel explores how Tiger Lily meets and falls in love with Peter, despite being betrothed to another villager, a man Tiger Lily despises. Tiger Lily and Peter's complicated inner conflicts emerge as they sort out their feelings about freedom, power, loyalty, and responsibility. When a girl from England arrives, Tiger Lily" feels jealous for the first time. (Publishers Weekly)

Anderson, John David

Minion; John David Anderson. Walden Pond Press, an imprint of HarperCollins 2014 288 p. (hardback) $16.99

Grades: 4 5 6 7   **Fic**

1. Adoption -- Fiction 2. Criminals -- Fiction 3. Superheroes -- Fiction 4. Good and evil -- Fiction 5. Supervillains -- Fiction

ISBN 006213311X; 9780062133113

LC 2013043188

In this book, by John David Anderson, "Michael Morn might be a villain, but he's really not a bad guy. When you live in New Liberty, known across the country as the City without a Super, there are only two kinds of people, after all: those who turn to crime and those who suffer. Michael and his adoptive father spend their days building boxes -special devices with mysterious abilities. . . . But then a Super comes to town, and Michael's world is thrown into disarray." (Publisher's note)

"The author of Sidekicked (2013) continues to scuff up the line between heroism and villainy. Spirited from the orphanage when he was nine, Michael Marion Magdalene Morn (named by the nuns) has spent four years in hiding with kind but closemouthed Professor Edson - an eccentric inventor of small black boxes capable of all sorts of shady exploit...Michael's musing that "sometimes it's just hard to know what's right and what's best and why there even has to be a difference" provides both a specific theme for this outing and an overall one for all of the author's thought-provoking work to date." (Booklist)

★ **Sidekicked**; John David Anderson. Walden Pond Press, an imprint of HarperCollinsPublishers 2013 384 p. (hardback) $16.99

Grades: 4 5 6 7   **Fic**

1. Adolescence -- Fiction 2. Superheroes -- Fiction 3. Humorous stories 4. Ability -- Fiction 5. Schools -- Fiction 6. Identity -- Fiction 7. Middle schools -- Fiction 8. Self-confidence -- Fiction

ISBN 0062133144; 9780062133144

LC 2012025495

In this book, "the main character is a sidekick named Andrew Bean. Like the best superheroes, he's down on his luck, always forgetting his utility belt when he needs it. Andrew is part of a school environmental club, H.E.R.O., that . . . doubles as a training program for sidekicks (motto: 'WE KEEP THE TRASH OFF THE STREETS'). Andrew's mentor is the Titan, an aging hero who'd rather go out drinking than fight crime." (Kirkus Reviews)

★ **Standard** hero behavior; [by] John David Anderson. Clarion Books 2007 273p $16

Grades: 6 7 8   **Fic**

1. Fantasy fiction 2. Adventure fiction 3. Heroes and heroines -- Fiction

ISBN 0-618-75920-4; 978-0-618-75920-0

LC 2007013059

When fifteen-year-old Mason Quayle finds out that their town of Darlington is about to be attacked by orcs, goblins, ogres, and trolls, he goes in search of some heroes to save the day.

"Mason is thoroughly believable. . . . Using imaginative details, witty language with a scattering of modern idiom, and lots of allusions, Anderson manages the difficult task of constructing a satisfying story while poking large fun at all genre traditions. Fantasy fans are ensured a good laugh." Booklist

Anderson, Katie D.

Kiss & Make Up. Amazon Childrens Pub 2012 307 p. (hardcover) $16.99

Grades: 7 8 9 10   **Fic**

1. Occult fiction 2. School stories

ISBN 076146316X; 9780761463160

This book focuses on Emerson Taylor, who "has a gift—or a curse. She can read a person's mind with the lightest of kisses. When her financially strapped aunt announces that Emerson will not be attending private school the following year if her grades don't improve, Emerson initializes Operation Liplock. She will begin study sessions with the geeky Ivys—those destined to attend Ivy League colleges—where she will kiss them, allowing their knowledge to transfer to her mind." (School Library Journal)

Anderson, Laurie Halse, 1961-

★ **Chains**; seeds of America. Simon & Schuster Books for Young Readers 2008 316p $17.99

Grades: 6 7 8 9 10   **Fic**

1. Spies -- Fiction 2. Slavery -- Fiction 3. New York (N.Y.) -- Fiction 4. African Americans -- Fiction 5. United States -- History -- 1775-1783, Revolution -- Fiction

ISBN 1-4169-0585-5; 1-4169-0586-3 pa; 978-1-4169-0585-1; 978-1-4169-0586-8 pa

LC 2007-52139

After being sold to a cruel couple in New York City, a slave named Isabel spies for the rebels during the Revolutionary War. "Grades seven to ten." (Bull Cent Child Books)

"This gripping novel offers readers a startlingly provocative view of the Revolutionary War. . . . [Anderson's] solidly researched exploration of British and Patriot treatment of slaves during a war for freedom is nuanced and evenhanded, presented in service of a fast-moving, emotionally involving plot." Publ Wkly

Followed by: Forge (2010)

★ **Fever,** 1793. Simon & Schuster Bks. for Young Readers 2000 251p $17.99; pa $6.99

Grades: 5 6 7 8 9   **Fic**

1. Epidemics -- Fiction 2. Yellow fever -- Fiction 3. Philadelphia (Pa.) -- Fiction

ISBN 978-0-689-83858-3; 0-689-83858-1; 978-0-689-84891-9 pa; 0-689-84891-9 pa

LC 00-32238

ALA YALSA Margaret A. Edwards Award (2009)

In 1793 Philadelphia, sixteen-year-old Matilda Cook, separated from her sick mother, learns about perseverance and self-reliance when she is forced to cope with the horrors of a yellow fever epidemic. "Age ten and up." (N Y Times Book Rev)

"A vivid work, rich with well-drawn and believable characters. Unexpected events pepper the top-flight novel that combines accurate historical detail with a spellbinding story line." Voice Youth Advocates

★ **Forge**. Atheneum Books for Young Readers 2010 297p (Seeds of America) $16.99

Grades: 6 7 8 9 10   **Fic**

1. Slavery -- Fiction 2. Soldiers -- Fiction 3. Pennsylvania -- Fiction 4. African Americans -- Fiction 5. United States -- History -- 1775-1783, Revolution -- Fiction

ISBN 978-1-4169-6144-4; 1-4169-6144-5

LC 2010-15971

Sequel to: Chains (2008)

Separated from his friend Isabel after their daring escape from slavery, fifteen-year-old Curzon serves as a free man in the Continental Army at Valley Forge until he and Isabel are thrown together again, as slaves once more.

"Weaving a huge amount of historical detail seamlessly into the story, Anderson creates a vivid setting, believable characters both good and despicable and a clear portrayal of the moral ambiguity of the Revolutionary age. Not only can this sequel stand alone, for many readers it will be one of the best novels they have ever read." Kirkus

Speak; 10th anniversary ed.; Speak 2009 197p pa $11.99
Grades: 7 8 9 10 **Fic**
1. School stories 2. Rape -- Fiction
ISBN 978-0-14-241473-6
LC 2009-502164
First published 1999

A traumatic event near the end of the summer has a devastating effect on Melinda's freshman year in high school.

The novel is "keenly aware of the corrosive details of outsiderhood and the gap between home and daily life at high school; kids whose exclusion may have less concrete cause than Melinda's will nonetheless find the picture recognizable. This is a gripping account of personal wounding and recovery." Bull Cent Child Books

★ **Wintergirls**. Viking 2009 288p $17.99
Grades: 8 9 10 11 12 **Fic**
1. Death -- Fiction 2. Friendship -- Fiction 3. Self-mutilation -- Fiction 4. Anorexia nervosa -- Fiction 5.
ISBN 0-670-01110-X; 978-0-670-01110-0
LC 2008-37452
Eighteen-year-old Lia comes to terms with her best friend's death from anorexia as she struggles with the same disorder.

"As events play out, Lia's guilt, her need to be thin, and her fight for acceptance unravel in an almost poetic stream of consciousness in this startlingly crisp and pitch-perfect first-person narrative." SLJ

Anderson, M. T., 1968-
Burger Wuss; M.T. Anderson. Candlewick Press 1999 192p (pbk.) $7.99
Grades: 7 8 9 10 11 12 **Fic**
1. Teenagers -- Fiction 2. Conformity -- Fiction 3. Fast food restaurants -- Fiction
ISBN 0763606804 ; 9780763631789 ;
9781439530726
LC 99014257

In this book that is set "[i]n a world where every teenager works at one fast food chain or another and likes it, Anthony just doesn't fit in. His first real girlfriend has dumped him for a meathead named Turner who works at O'Dermott's, so Anthony plots revenge. He gets a job at the restaurant and embarks on a complicated plot to pit the kids from Burger Queen against the kids from O'Dermott's--and thereby draw the BQ wrath down on company-man Turner's head. . . . [T]his book is a burlesque of teenage angst and conformist

culture. . . . Anarchist vagabond Shunt is Anthony's partner in his anti-conformity crimes." (Publishers Weekly)

The **chamber** in the sky. Scholastic Press 2012 282 p. (hardcover) $17.99
Grades: 5 6 7 8 **Fic**
1. American satire 2. Fantasy fiction 3. Human-alien encounters -- Fiction
ISBN 0545334934; 9780545334938

This novel, by National Book Award and Printz Honor winner M. T. Anderson, is book four of "The Norumbegan Quartet" series. "Brian and Gregory have . . . . gone to investigate intergalactic suburban sprawl that was infringing on the Vermont forests, and landed in the empire of New Norumbega inside the huge body of an alien. They've escaped certain death . . . and wreaked small amounts of havoc of their own. And finally, they're going to make sense of all their travels and adventures." (Publisher's note)

Feed. Candlewick Press 2002 237p hardcover o.p. pa $7.99
Grades: 8 9 10 11 12 **Fic**
1. Satire 2. Science fiction
ISBN 0-7636-1726-1; 0-7636-2259-1 pa
LC 2002-23738

In a future where most people have computer implants in their heads to control their environment, a boy meets an unusual girl who is in serious trouble

"An ingenious satire of corporate America and our present-day value system." Horn Book Guide

The **Game** of Sunken Places; [by] M. T. Anderson. Scholastic Press 2004 260p (The Norumbegan quartet) $16.95; pa $5.99
Grades: 5 6 7 8 **Fic**
1. Games -- Fiction 2. Vermont -- Fiction
ISBN 0-439-41660-4; 0-439-41661-2 pa
LC 2003-20055

When two boys stay with an eccentric relative at his mansion in rural Vermont, they discover an old-fashioned board game that draws them into a mysterious adventure.

"Deliciously scary, often funny, and crowned by a pair of deeply satisfying surprises, this tour de force leaves one marveling at Anderson's ability to slip between genres as fluidly as his middle-grade heroes straddle worlds." Booklist
Other titles in this series are:
The suburb beyond the stars (2010)
The empire of gut and bone (2011)

He laughed with his other mouths; M.T. Anderson ; illustrations by Kurt Cyrus. First edition Beach Lane Books 2014 304 p. illustrations (Pals in peril) (hardcover) $17.99
Grades: 4 5 6 7 **Fic**
1. Adventure fiction 2. Outer space -- Fiction 3. Humorous stories 4. Extraterrestrial beings -- Fiction 5. Adventure and adventurers -- Fiction
ISBN 1442451106; 9781442451100; 9781442451117
LC 2013034710

"In this action-packed conclusion to the celebrated Pals in Peril series, Jasper Dash soars to unprecedented heights-

-as in, intergalactic, out-of-this-world dimensions--in order to locate the father he's never known." (Publisher's note)

"The novel doesn't transcend the wacky sci-fi of old that inspired it but rather embraces it and dissects it, celebrating it and exploring why so many people fell in love with these silly worlds and gee-whiz heroes in the first place." Kirkus

★ **Whales** on stilts; illustrations by Kurt Cyrus. Harcourt 2005 188p il (Pals in peril) $15; pa $5.95

Grades: 4 5 6 7   **Fic**

1. Science fiction

ISBN 0-15-205340-9; 0-15-205394-8 pa

LC 2004-17754

Racing against the clock, shy middle-school student Lily and her best friends, Katie and Jasper, must foil the plot of her father's conniving boss to conquer the world using an army of whales.

"A story written with the author's tongue shoved firmly into his cheek. . . . It's full of witty pokes at other series novels and Jasper's nutty inventions." SLJ

Other titles in this series are:

The clue of the linoleum lederhosen (2006)

Jasper Dash and the Flame-pits of Delaware (2009)

Agent Q., or the smell of danger! (2010)

Zombie mommy (2011)

Anderson, R. J.

Spell Hunter. HarperCollinsPublishers 2009 329p (Faery rebels) $16.99

Grades: 7 8 9 10 11 12   **Fic**

1. Fantasy fiction 2. Magic -- Fiction 3. Fairies -- Fiction

ISBN 978-0-06-155474-2; 0-06-155474-X; 978-0-06-155475-9 lib bdg; 0-06-155475-8 lib bdg

LC 2008-27469

In a dying faery realm, only the brave and rebellious faery Knife persists in trying to discover how her people's magic was lost and what is needed to restore their powers and ensure their survival, but her quest is endangered by her secret friendship with a human named Paul.

"Filled with delicate, fantastical creatures; evil and dangerous crows; and a human who believes in love, this is a highly readable, sophisticated tale of romance and self-sacrifice." Booklist

Another title in this series is:

Wayfarer (2010)

Wayfarer. HarperTeen 2010 296p (Faery rebels) $16.99

Grades: 7 8 9 10 11 12   **Fic**

1. Fantasy fiction 2. Fairies -- Fiction

ISBN 978-0-06-155477-3; 0-06-155477-4

Sequel to: Spell Hunter (2009)

"The Oak's faeries are dying out, and 15-year-old faery Linden embarks on a survival quest that takes her into the human world, including London and Wales, where she meets 15-year-old Timothy, the son of missionaries. . . . Most readers will appreciate the characters' growing understanding of personal responsibility and the importance of compassion." Booklist

Andrews, Jesse

Me & Earl & the dying girl; by Jesse Andrews. Amulet Books 2012 295 p. $16.95

Grades: 8 9 10   **Fic**

1. Leukemia -- Fiction 2. Friendship -- Fiction 3. Family life -- Fiction 4. Pittsburgh (Pa.) -- Fiction 5. High school students -- Fiction 6. Humorous stories 7. Schools -- Fiction 8. High schools -- Fiction 9. Jews -- United States -- Fiction 10. Family life -- Pennsylvania -- Fiction

ISBN 9781419701764

LC 2011031796

This book is a "confessional from a teen narrator who won't be able to convince readers he's as unlikable as he wants them to believe." It covers "[h]is filmmaking ambitions . . . his unlikely friendship with the . . . Earl of the title. And his unlikelier friendship with Rachel, the titular 'dying girl'. . . . He chronicles his senior year, in which his mother guilt-trips him into hanging out with Rachel, who has acute myelogenous leukemia." (Kirkus Reviews)

Angleberger, Tom

Emperor Pickletine rides the bus; Tom Angleberger. Amulet Books 2014 205 p. illustrations (hardback) $13.95

Grades: 4 5 6 7   **Fic**

1. School stories 2. Origami -- Fiction 3. Humorous stories 4. Bus travel -- Fiction 5. Finger puppets -- Fiction 6. Washington (D.C.) -- Fiction 7. School field trips -- Fiction 8. Interpersonal relations -- Fiction 9. Eccentrics and eccentricities -- Fiction

ISBN 141970933X; 9781419709333

LC 2014012574

Origami Yoda

This middle grade novel by Tom Angleberger is "the final Origami Yoda case file from the kids at McQuarrie Middle School! After successfully fighting to save their field trip in 'Princess Labelmaker to the Rescue!,' Tommy and the gang prepare for a well-earned day of fun and adventure in Washington, DC . . . but of course it won't be that easy! This trip to the nation's capital will be full of shifting alliances and betrayals, carsickness and sugar rushes." (Publisher's note)

"The seventh grade of McQuarrie Middle School hits Washington, D.C., in this final installment of the popular Origami Yoda series. Exciting as a field trip is, the Rebel Alliance is reeling because Principal Rabbski has banned origami for the entire trip! . . . Origami Yoda has an earth-shattering revelation or two to impart before the book's end, making for a fitting series conclusion." Booklist

Horton Halfpott; or, The fiendish mystery of Smugwick Manor, or, The loosening of M'Lady Luggertuck's corset. Tom Angleberger with illustrations by the author. Amulet Books 2011 206p il $14.95

Grades: 4 5 6 7   **Fic**

1. Mystery fiction 2. Social classes -- Fiction 3. Household employees -- Fiction 4. Eccentrics and eccentricities -- Fiction 5. Great Britain -- History -- 19th century -- Fiction

ISBN 978-0-8109-9715-8; 0-8109-9715-0

LC 2010-38096

Horton, an upstanding kitchen boy in a castle in nineteenth-century England, becomes embroiled in a mystery surrounding a series of thefts. "Grades four to six." (Bull Cent Child Books)

"Readers will enjoy Angleberger's . . . penchant for the absurd as well as his many droll asides. . . . The ending satisfies, and with Angleberger's many eclectic characters, his wild-and-witty storytelling, and a lighthearted but perplexing mystery . . . readers are in for a treat." Publ Wkly

Princess Labelmaker to the rescue! an Origami Yoda book. by Tom Angleberger. Harry N. Abrams Inc. 2014 208 p. $13.95

Grades: 4 5 6 7 **Fic**
1. School stories 2. Star Wars films 3. Origami -- Fiction 4. Schools -- Fiction 5. Finger puppets -- Fiction 6. Interpersonal relations -- Fiction 7. Eccentrics and eccentricities -- Fiction
ISBN 1419710524; 9781419710520
LC 2013047291

In this book, part of the Origami Yoda series, by Tom Angleberger, "At McQuarrie Middle School, the war against the FunTime Menace--aka test prep--wages on. . . . To defeat the Dark Standardized Testing Forces they're going to need an even bigger, even more surprising ally: Principal Rabbski. But with great forces--aka the school board--pushing her from above, will the gang's former enemy don a finger puppet and join the Rebellion--or will her transformation to Empress Rabbski, Dark Lord of the Sith, be complete?" (Publisher's note)

"The FunTime Menace (a deadly boring test prep program) is still wreaking havoc at McQuarrie Middle School in the sixth book in the series. The only way to abolish FunTime is to get Principal Rabbski on the side of the Rebellion, but the Origami Rebel Alliance will have to risk everything to win her over. Angleberger continues to develop authentic and engaging voices in these "case files."" Horn Book

Other titles include:
The surprise attack of Jabba the Puppett
Darth Paper strikes back
The strange case of Origami Yoda
Emperor Pickletine rides the bus
The secret of the Fortune Wookiee

Angus, Jennifer
In search of Goliathus hercules; by Jennifer Angus. Albert Whitman 2012 350 p. (hardcover) $17.99

Grades: 3 4 5 6 7 **Fic**
1. Fantasy fiction 2. Insects -- Fiction 3. Human-animal communication -- Fiction 4. Metamorphosis -- Fiction
ISBN 0807529907; 9780807529904
LC 2011037135

In this novel, by Jennifer Angus, "Henri Bell, . . . in 1890 . . . strikes up a conversation with a friendly fly on the windowsill and discovers he possesses the astounding ability to speak with insects. Thus commences an epic journey for Henri as he manages a flea circus, commands an army of beetles, and ultimately sets out to British Malaya to find the mythical giant insect known as Goliathus Hercules." (Publisher's note)

Angus, Sam
A **Horse** Called Hero; by Sam Angus. Feiwel & Friends 2014 304 p. $16.99

Grades: 5 6 7 8 **Fic**
1. Horses -- Fiction 2. Brothers and sisters -- Fiction 3. World War, 1939-1945 -- Children
ISBN 1250045088; 9781250045089

In this book, by Sam Angus, "on the brink of World War II, a family forced out of their London home flees to the country. Wolfie and his older sister Dodo are devastated to leave behind everything they've ever known. . . . One day, they come across an orphaned foal, which they raise as Hero, a strong and beautiful horse who lives up to his name when he saves the children from a fire. . . . One night, Hero is stolen, and the children are shattered." (Publisher's note)

"With London steeled for World War II, eight-year-old Wolfie and his older sister Dodo are sent to the countryside. It's difficult being city kids among strangers, but an orphaned foal named Hero helps the children adjust. In a parallel story line, the children's father has been accused of desertion. Angus's story is a big, satisfying tale of friendship, family, and war." Horn Book

Anthony, Joelle
Restoring harmony. G.P. Putnam's Sons 2010 307p $17.99

Grades: 6 7 8 9 **Fic**
1. Science fiction 2. Voyages and travels -- Fiction 3. Environmental degradation -- Fiction
ISBN 978-0-399-25281-5; 0-399-25281-9
LC 2009-29501

Ten years after the Great Collapse of 2031, sixteen-year-old Molly McClure, with only her fiddle for company, leaves the safety of her family's island home to travel through a dangerous and desolate wasteland on her way to Oregon to find her grandparents and persuade them to return with her to Canada.

"Adeptly combining adventure and romance, Anthony's debut is a tense and often charming tale that never lets its use of the oh-so-trendy dystopian future trope overwhelm some great characters." Publ Wkly

Antieau, Kim
Ruby's imagine; written by Kim Antieau. Houghton Mifflin Co. 2008 201p $16

Grades: 6 7 8 9 **Fic**
1. African Americans -- Fiction 2. New Orleans (La.) -- Fiction 3. Hurricane Katrina, 2005 -- Fiction
ISBN 978-0-618-99767-1; 0-618-99767-9
LC 2007047736

Tells the story of Hurricane Katrina from the point of view of Ruby, an unusually intuitive girl who lives with her grandmother in New Orleans but has powerful memories of an earlier life in the swamps.

"Antieau offers a complex, personal account of Katrina and its aftermath. . . . Ruby's atmospheric narrative is as dense and pungent as the bayou." Booklist

Appelbaum, Susannah
The **Hollow** Bettle; illustrated by Jennifer Taylor. Alfred A. Knopf 2009 399p il (The Poisons of Caux) $16.99; lib bdg $19.99

Grades: 4 5 6 7   **Fic**

1. Fantasy fiction 2. Uncles -- Fiction 3. Poisons and poisoning -- Fiction

ISBN 978-0-375-85173-5; 0-375-85173-9; 978-0-375-95173-2 lib bdg; 0-375-95173-3 lib bdg

LC 2008-22626

Eleven-year-old Ivy Manx sets out with her new friend, a young "taster," to find her missing uncle, an outlawed healer, in the dangerous kingdom of Caux where magic, herbs, and poisons rule.

This "is a deeply satisfying, humor-laced quest with elements of wizardry and herbology, deeds of a dastardly nature, and, ultimately, redemption." Booklist

Other titles in this series are:

The Taster's Guild (2010)

The Shepherd of Weeds (2011)

Appelt, Kathi

★ **Keeper**; illustrations by August Hall. Atheneum Books for Young Readers 2010 399p il $16.99

Grades: 5 6 7 8   **Fic**

1. Ocean -- Fiction 2. Sailing -- Fiction 3. Mermaids and mermen -- Fiction 4. Mother-daughter relationship -- Fiction

ISBN 978-1-4169-5060-8; 1-4169-5060-5

LC 2010000795

On the night of the blue moon when mermaids are said to gather on a sandbar in the Gulf of Mexico, ten-year-old Keeper sets out in a small boat, with her dog BD and a seagull named Captain, determined to find her mother, a mermaid, as Keeper has always believed, who left long ago to return to the sea.

"Deftly spinning together mermaid lore, local legend and natural history, this stunning tale proves 'every landscape has its magical beings,' and the most unlikely ones can form a perfect family. Hall's black-and-white illustrations lend perspective and immediacy. Beautiful and evocative—an absolute 'keeper.' " Kirkus

★ The **true** blue scouts of Sugarman Swamp; by Kathi Appelt. 1st ed. Atheneum Books for Young Readers 2013 336 p. (hardcover) $16.99

Grades: 5 6 7 8   **Fic**

1. Swamps -- Fiction 2. Raccoons -- Fiction 3. Humorous stories 4. Swamp animals -- Fiction 5. Land developers -- Fiction 6. Scouting (Youth activity) -- Fiction

ISBN 1442421053; 9781442421059; 9781442481213

LC 2012023723

This book is "told from the perspectives of animals and humans. . . .The main concern of Bingo and Jeremiah, two raccoon Swamp Scouts, is the approaching brood of feral hogs, which could destroy the precious canebrake sugar used to make fried pies at the local Paradise Pies cafe. Meanwhile, 12-year-old Chap Brayburn, the cafe proprietor's son, is worried about rich, horrible Sonny Boy Beaucoup, who wants to turn the swamp into the 'Gator World Wrestling Arena and Theme Park.' " (Publishers Weekly)

★ The **underneath**; illustrated by David Small. Atheneum Books for Young Readers 2008 313p il $16.99; pa $7.99

Grades: 3 4 5 6   **Fic**

1. Cats -- Fiction 2. Dogs -- Fiction

ISBN 978-1-4169-5058-5; 1-4169-5058-3; 978-1-4169-5059-2 pa; 1-4169-5059-1 pa

LC 2007031969

A Newbery Medal honor book, 2009

An abandoned "calico cat, about to have kittens, hears the lonely howl of [Ranger], a chained-up hound deep in the backwaters of the bayou. . . . Ranger urges the cat to hide underneath the porch, to raise her kittens there because Gar-Face, the man living inside the house, will surely use them as alligator bait should he find them." (Publisher's note) "Intemediate." (Horn Book)

"Well realized in Small's excellent full-page drawings, this fine book is most of all distinguished by the originality of the story and the fresh beauty of its author's voice." Horn Book

Applegate, Katherine

Eve & Adam; by Michael Grant and Katherine Applegate. Feiwel and Friends 2012 291p. $17.99

Grades: 7 8 9 10   **Fic**

1. Medical genetics 2. Biomedical engineering 3. Mother-daughter relationship -- Fiction

ISBN 0312583516; 9780312583514

In this book by authors Michael Grant and Katherine Applegate, "a run-in with a streetcar left Evening Spiker's body seriously mangled . . . [H]er widowed mother, Terra, insists on moving her from the hospital to . . . [the] biotech company . . . Spiker Biopharmaceuticals. . . . Eve's healing is strangely swift [and] Terra drops a project . . . in her lap: Design a virtual human being from scratch. With help from her feisty, reckless friend Aislin, Eve takes up the challenge." (Kirkus Reviews)

★ **Home** of the brave. Feiwel & Friends 2007 249p $16.95

Grades: 5 6 7 8   **Fic**

1. Novels in verse 2. Cattle -- Fiction 3. Africans -- Fiction 4. Refugees -- Fiction 5. Minnesota -- Fiction 6. Immigrants -- Fiction

ISBN 0-312-36765-1; 978-0-312-36765-7

LC 2006-32053

Kek, an African refugee, is confronted by many strange things at the Minneapolis home of his aunt and cousin, as well as in his fifth grade classroom, and longs for his missing mother, but finds comfort in the company of a cow and her owner.

"This beautiful story of hope and resilience is written in free verse." Voice Youth Advocates

★ The **one** and only Ivan; illustrated by Patricia Castelao. Harper 2012 il $16.99

Grades: 3 4 5 6   **Fic**

1. Gorillas -- Fiction 2. Elephants -- Fiction 3. Animal welfare -- Fiction

ISBN 978-0-06-199225-4; 0-06-199225-9

LC 2011010034

John Newbery Medal (2013)

"Ivan narrates his tale in short, image-rich sentences and acute, sometimes humorous, observations that are all the more heartbreaking for their simple delivery. . . . Spot art captures poignant moments throughout. Utterly believable, this bittersweet story, complete with an author's note identifying the real Ivan, will inspire a new generation of advocates." Kirkus

Arbuthnott, Gill

The **Keepers'** tattoo. Chicken House 2010 425p $17.99

Grades: 6 7 8 9   **Fic**

1. Fantasy fiction 2. Dreams -- Fiction 3. Uncles -- Fiction 4. Tattooing -- Fiction 5. Identity (Psychology) -- Fiction

ISBN 978-0-545-17166-3; 0-545-17166-0

LC 2009-26327

Months before her fifteenth birthday, Nyssa learns that she is a special member of a legendary clan, the Keepers of Knowledge, as she and her uncle try to escape from Alaric, the White Wolf, who wants to use lines tattooed on her to destroy the rest of her people.

Arbuthnott "writes with restraint and thoughtfulness, never condescending to her readers. Nyssa is a convincing mixture of ignorance, courage, and resourcefulness." Publ Wkly

Archer, E.

Geek : fantasy novel. Scholastic Press 2011 310p $17.99

Grades: 7 8 9 10   **Fic**

1. Fantasy fiction 2. Aunts -- Fiction 3. Wishes -- Fiction 4. Cousins -- Fiction 5. Great Britain -- Fiction

ISBN 978-0-545-16040-7; 0-545-16040-5

This "is a stunning, often befuddling, and wildly amusing novel that will likely confound and enchant sci-fi and fantasy fans alike." Bull Cent Child Books

Archer, Jennifer

Through her eyes. HarperTeen 2011 377p $16.99

Grades: 7 8 9 10   **Fic**

1. School stories 2. Mystery fiction 3. Texas -- Fiction 4. Moving -- Fiction 5. Family life -- Fiction 6. Grandfathers -- Fiction 7. Supernatural -- Fiction

ISBN 978-0-06-183458-5; 0-06-183458-0

LC 2010-18440

Sixteen-year-old Tansy is used to moving every time her mother starts writing a new book, but in the small Texas town where her grandfather grew up, she is lured into the world of a troubled young man whose death sixty years earlier is shrouded in mystery.

"Archer's engrossing story gracefully weaves together the contemporary and historical into an eerie mystery, while examining relationships, reality, and the power of the mind." Publ Wkly

Armistead, Cal

Being Henry David; by Cal Armistead. Albert Whitman 2013 312 p. (hardcover) $16.99

Grades: 8 9 10 11 12   **Fic**

1. Mystery fiction 2. Amnesia -- Fiction 3. Guilt -- Fiction 4. Runaways -- Fiction 5. Concord (Mass.) -- Fiction 6. Family problems -- Fiction 7. New York

(N.Y.) -- Fiction 8. Street children -- Fiction

ISBN 080750615X; 9780807506158

LC 2012017377

In this book, a "boy wakes up in Penn Station, remembering nothing. He guesses that he's about 17, he has a head injury, and he is carrying only 10 dollars. Near at hand is a copy of Walden, so for want of anything better he calls himself Henry David (Hank). He heads to Concord, Massachusetts, to find, he hopes, some clues at Walden Pond. As his memories slowly return, he remembers who he was; as he copes with the memories, he discovers who he is and can be." (School Library Journal)

Armstrong, Alan

Looking for Marco Polo; illustrated by Tim Jessell. Random House 2009 286p $16.99

Grades: 4 5 6 7   **Fic**

1. Travelers 2. Travel writers 3. Venice (Italy) -- Fiction 4. Missing persons -- Fiction

ISBN 978-0-375-83321-2; 0-375-83321-8

When they lose touch with their father's Gobi Desert expedition, eleven-year-old Mark accompanies his mother to Venice, Italy, and there, while waiting for news of his father, learns about the legendary Marco Polo and his adventures in the Far East.

"Armstrong ably conjures up the atmosphere of damp, foggy Venice in late December while blowing some dust off of the accounts of Marco Polo's travels with his lively storytelling. . . . Whether or not readers know the specifics of Marco Polo's voyages, they will enjoy this entertaining blend of contemporary and historical adventure." Booklist

Racing the moon; by Alan Armstrong ; illustrated by Tim Jessell. Random House 2012 214 p. (hc : alk. paper) $16.99

Grades: 5 6 7 8   **Fic**

1. Adventure fiction 2. Historical fiction 3. Siblings -- Fiction 4. Aeronautics -- Fiction 5. Space flight -- Fiction 6. Brothers and sisters -- Fiction 7. Rockets (Aeronautics) -- Fiction 8. Adventure and adventurers -- Fiction

ISBN 037585889X; 9780375858895; 9780375858901; 9780375893094

LC 2012016261

In this children's book by Alan Armstrong "Twelve-year-old Alex hangs out with her reckless 17-year-old brother Chuck, who's always getting them in trouble. . . . Alex wants to be another Amelia Earhart [and][m]eeting her new neighbor, Captain Ebbs, Alex finds a mentor. . . . She arranges for Alex to meet pioneer rocket scientist Wernher von Braun, organizes a sailing trip to a Chesapeake Bay island near a rocket launch and provides needed direction for the risk-taking duo." (Kirkus)

Whittington; illustrated by S. D. Schindler. Random House 2005 191p il $14.95; lib bdg $16.99; pa $6.50

Grades: 4 5 6   **Fic**

1. Cats -- Fiction 2. Domestic animals -- Fiction

ISBN 0-375-82864-8; 0-375-92864-2 lib bdg; 0-375-82865-6 pa

LC 2004-05789

A Newbery Medal honor book, 2006

"A battered cat who calls himself Whittington takes up residence in a shabby barn already inhabited by a variety of scruffy livestock, owned by Bernie. . . . Bernie offers refuge not only to his animals but also to his parentless grandchildren, Abby and Ben, who carry burdens of their own. The children [can] communicate . . . with the animals, so Abby and Ben join the audience when Whittington the cat retells the story of Dick Whittington and his cat." (Bull Cent Child Books) "Intermediate, middle school." (Horn Book)

"The story works beautifully, both as historical fiction about medieval street life and commerce and as a witty, engaging tale of barnyard camaraderie and survival." Booklist

Armstrong, Kelley

The **gathering**. Harper 2011 359p (Darkness rising) $17.99

Grades: 7 8 9 10   **Fic**

1. School stories 2. Canada -- Fiction 3. Witchcraft -- Fiction 4. Family life -- Fiction 5. Supernatural -- Fiction 6. Vancouver Island (B.C.) -- Fiction

ISBN 978-0-06-179702-6 Harper; 0-06-179702-2 Harper; 978-0-385-66851-4 Doubleday Canada

LC 2010-32229

Sixteen-year-old Maya suspects there may be a relationship between her paw-print birthmark, her connection with wild animals, and strange events occurring in her tiny Vancouver Island community, where a medical research facility harbors big secrets.

"Comfortably mixing science, myth, and mystery, Armstrong creates a vivid world highlighted by appealing characters." Publ Wkly

The **summoning**. HarperCollinsPublishers 2008 390p (Darkest powers) $17.99; lib bdg $18.89

Grades: 7 8 9 10   **Fic**

1. Ghost stories 2. Supernatural -- Fiction

ISBN 978-0-06-166269-0; 0-06-166269-0; 978-0-06-166272-0 lib bdg; 0-06-166272-0 lib bdg

LC 2008-14221

After fifteen-year-old Chloe starts seeing ghosts and is sent to Lyle House, a mysterious group home for mentally disturbed teenagers, she soon discovers that neither Lyle House nor its inhabitants are exactly what they seem, and that she and her new friends are in danger.

"Suspenseful, well-written, and engaging, this pageturning . . . [novel] will be a hit." Voice Youth Advocates

Other titles in this series are:

The awakening (2009)

The reckoning (2010)

Armstrong, William Howard

★ **Sounder**; [by] William H. Armstrong; illustrations by James Barkley. Harper & Row 1969 116p il $15.99; pa $5.99

Grades: 5 6 7 8   **Fic**

1. Dogs -- Fiction 2. Family life -- Fiction 3. African Americans -- Fiction

ISBN 0-06-020143-6; 0-06-440020-4 pa

Awarded the Newbery Medal, 1970

"Set in the South in the era of sharecropping and segregation, this succinctly told tale poignantly describes the courage of a father who steals a ham in order to feed his undernourished family; the determination of the eldest son, who searches for his father despite the apathy of prison authorities; and the devotion of a coon dog named Sounder." Shapiro. Fic for Youth. 3d edition

Arnett, Mindee

Avalon; Mindee Arnett. Balzer + Bray, an imprint of HarperCollinsPublishers 2014 432 p. (hardcover) $17.99

Grades: 8 9 10 11 12   **Fic**

1. Science fiction 2. Freedom -- Fiction 3. Outer space -- Fiction 4. Mercenary soldiers -- Fiction 5. Space ships -- Fiction 6. Brothers and sisters -- Fiction 7. Life on other planets -- Fiction

ISBN 0062235591; 9780062235596

LC 2013005155

This book, by Mindee Arnett, is "about a group of teenage mercenaries who stumble upon a conspiracy that threatens the entire galaxy. Jeth Seagrave and his crew have made their name stealing metatech: the devices that allow people to travel great distances faster than the speed of light. . . . When he finds himself in possession of information that both government and the crime bosses are willing to kill for, he's going to find there's no escaping his past anymore." (Publisher's note)

"Jeth has one last job to complete before he can buy back his parents' spaceship from a crime boss. But the ship he was sent to find carries a deadly cargo that everyone in the galaxy wants. The strong bond between Jeth and his humorously motley crew of teenage mercenaries outshines the predictable plot and will appeal to Firefly-esque space-opera fans." Horn Book

Arnold, Elana K.

The **question** of miracles; by Elana K. Arnold. Houghton Mifflin Harcourt 2015 240 p. (hardback) $16.99

Grades: 4 5 6 7   **Fic**

1. Miracles -- Fiction 2. Friendship -- Fiction 3. Grief -- Fiction 4. Corvallis (Or.) -- Fiction 5. Moving, Household -- Fiction

ISBN 0544334647; 9780544334649

LC 2014000738

In this novel by Elana K. Arnold "Iris is starting sixth grade in a new school in Oregon-new house, new people, new life. Her parents want to distract her from the recent death of her best friend in California. . . . She turns away from potential friends, seeking instead someone she can barely tolerate--so that she must only endure minimal interaction. His name is Boris, and while he is obviously an outcast, Iris prefers to be on the outskirts." (School Library Journal)

"Sixth-grader Iris hates her new home in rainy Corvallis, Oregon. The move from Southern California was ostensibly because of her mother's new job...She asks the questions that many children would ask in this circumstance, and the book puts a smart circle of caring adults to help her find answers. But it is her realistic relationship with the matter-of-fact Boris, a most unlikely miracle, that will catch readers and help pull them toward seeking answers of their own for the story's very large questions." Booklist

Arnston, Steven

★ The **Wikkeling**; illustrated by Daniela Jaglen-ka Terrazzini. Running Press Kids 2011 256p il $18

Grades: 4 5 6   **Fic**

1. Science fiction

ISBN 978-0-7624-3903-4; 0-7624-3903-3

"In Henrietta's world, every part of life is monitored and regulated by computers. House cats are considered wild and dangerous animals. Old houses and old books can make children sick. The girl's orderly and safe life is disrupted the day she discovers a secret attic above her bedroom. . . . Soon after this discovery, she starts seeing the Wikkeling, a menacing yellow creature that gives children headaches with the touch of a finger. . . . Arntson has created a detailed and fascinating dystopian world that seems eerily similar to our own, and Terrazzini's illustrations strike just the right note." SLJ

The **wrap**-up list; by Steven Arntson. Houghton Mifflin Harcourt 2013 240 p. (hardcover) $15.99

Grades: 7 8 9 10   **Fic**

1. Fantasy fiction 2. Death -- Fiction 3. Conduct of life -- Fiction 4. Hispanic Americans -- Fiction

ISBN 0547824106; 9780547824109

LC 2012014035

This paranormal young adult novel, by Steven Arntson, is set in a "modern-day suburban town, [where] one percent of all fatalities come about in the most peculiar way. Deaths . . . send a letter . . . to whomever is chosen . . . , telling them to wrap up their lives and do the things they always wanted to do before they have to 'depart.' When sixteen-year-old Gabriela receives her notice, she is, of course devastated. Will she kiss her crush Sylvester before it's too late?" (Publisher's note)

Aronson, Sarah

Beyond lucky. Dial Books for Young Readers 2011 250p $16.99

Grades: 4 5 6 7   **Fic**

1. Mystery fiction 2. Chance -- Fiction 3. Soccer -- Fiction 4. Brothers -- Fiction 5. Jews -- United States -- Fiction

ISBN 978-0-8037-3520-0; 0-8037-3520-0

LC 2010-28800

Twelve-year-old Ari Fish is sure that the rare trading card he found has changed his luck and that of his soccer team, but after the card is stolen he comes to know that we make our own luck, and that heroes can be fallible.

"Aronson skillfully dodges the predictability of sports-themed books by creating multilayered characters and an intriguing whodunit. . . . Aronson . . . includes a lot of fun on-field action, but the off-field story is just as interesting. . . Aronson's graceful storytelling will keep even nonsoccer buffs turning pages." Publ Wkly

Ashby, Amanda

Fairy bad day. Speak 2011 336p pa $7.99

Grades: 7 8 9 10 11 12   **Fic**

1. School stories 2. Fantasy fiction 3. Ability -- Fiction 4. Fairies -- Fiction 5. Supernatural -- Fiction

ISBN 978-0-14-241259-6; 0-14-241259-7

LC 2010-046286

High schooler Emma is devastated to learn that she may not follow in her mother's footsteps as a dragon slayer, but with an unlikely band of allies she discovers that she may, indeed, be more adept at slaying giant killer fairies.

"The characters are nicely developed, the dialogue is fresh and engaging, the author's irreverent take on good versus evil will hook readers, and the satisfying plot twists will keep them involved till the end." SLJ

Zombie queen of Newbury High. Speak 2009 199p pa $7.99

Grades: 7 8 9 10   **Fic**

1. School stories 2. Zombies -- Fiction

ISBN 978-0-14-241256-5; 0-14-241256-5

LC 2008-41035

While trying to cast a love spell on her date on the eve of the senior prom, Mia inadvertently infects her entire high school class with a virus that will turn them all into zombies.

"Zombie Queen is light, fast-paced, and . . . will quench the thirst of the Christopher Pike and R. L. Stine set." SLJ

Asher, Jay

★ The **future** of us; [by] Jay Asher and Carolyn Mackler. Razorbill 2011 356p $18.99

Grades: 8 9 10 11 12   **Fic**

1. School stories 2. Computers -- Fiction 3. Supernatural -- Fiction

ISBN 978-1-59514-491-1; 1-59514-491-9

In this book by Jay Asher and Carolyn Mackler, "it's 1996, before Facebook's been invented. Yet Emma's first computer leads her to her Facebook page from fifteen years in the future. She tells only her friend and would-be boy-friend Josh, and they contemplate their futures with concern. Can their current actions change who they become?" (Voice of Youth Advocates)

"It's 1996, and Emma Nelson has just received her first computer. . . . When Emma powers up the computer, she discovers her own Facebook page (even though Facebook doesn't exist yet) and herself in an unhappy marriage—15 years in the future. Alternating chapters from Josh and Emma over the course of five days propel this riveting read, as Emma discovers she can alter her future by adjusting her present actions and intentions." Booklist

Thirteen reasons why; a novel. Razorbill 2007 288p $16.99

Grades: 8 9 10 11 12   **Fic**

1. School stories 2. Suicide -- Fiction

ISBN 9781595141712

LC 2007-03097

When high school student Clay Jenkins receives a box in the mail containing thirteen cassette tapes recorded by his classmate Hannah, who committed suicide, he spends a bewildering and heartbreaking night crisscrossing their town, listening to Hannah's voice recounting the events leading up to her death.

"Clay's pain is palpable and exquisitely drawn in gripping casually poetic prose. The complex and soulful characters expose astoundingly rich and singularly teenage inner lives." SLJ

Ashton, Brodi

Everbound; an Everneath novel. Brodi Ashton. Balzer + Bray 2013 368 p. (Everneath) (hardcover bdg : alk. paper) $17.99

Grades: 7 8 9 10　　　　　　　　　　　　**Fic**
　　1. Love stories 2. Occult fiction 3. Future life -- Fiction 4. Hell -- Fiction 5. Love -- Fiction 6. Supernatural -- Fiction
　　ISBN 0062071165; 9780062071163
　　　　　　　　　　　　　　　LC 2012028327
This young adult paranormal story, by Brodi Ashton, is the sequel to "Everneath." "Nikki Beckett could only watch as . . . Jack . . . sacrificed himself to save her, taking her place in the Tunnels of the Everneath for eternity. . . . Desperate for answers, Nikki turns to Cole, the immortal bad boy who wants to make her his queen. . . . But his heart has been touched by everything about Nikki, and he agrees to help in the only way he can: by taking her to the Everneath himself." (Publisher's note)

Everneath; Brodi Ashton. 1st ed; Balzer + Bray 2012 370p. $17.99

Grades: 7 8 9 10　　　　　　　　　　　　**Fic**
　　1. Love stories 2. Occult fiction 3. Fantasy fiction
　　ISBN 9780062071132 (trade bdg.)
　　　　　　　　　　　　　　　LC 2011022892
This book tells the story of "Nikki Beckett [who] vanished, sucked into an underworld known as the Everneath. Now she's returned—to her old life, her family, her boyfriend—before she's banished back to the underworld . . . this time forever. She has six months before the Everneath comes to claim her, six months for good-byes she can't find the words for, six months to find redemption, if it exists. Nikki longs to spend these precious months forgetting the Everneath and trying to reconnect with her boyfriend, Jack, the person most devastated by her disappearance—and the one person she loves more than anything. But there's just one problem: Cole, the smoldering immortal who enticed her to the Everneath in the first place, has followed Nikki home. Cole wants to take over the throne in the underworld and is convinced Nikki is the key to making it happen." (Publisher's note)

Atkins, Catherine

Alt ed. Putnam 2003 198p $17.99; pa $6.99

Grades: 7 8 9 10　　　　　　　　　　　　**Fic**
　　1. School stories
　　ISBN 0-399-23854-9; 0-14-240235-4 pa
　　　　　　　　　　　　　　　LC 2002-16942
Participating in a special after-school counseling class with other troubled students, including a sensitive gay classmate, helps Susan, an overweight tenth grader, develop a better sense of herself

"Most of the characters . . . come to life in new and interesting ways, and Susan's story is strong, because she is reinventing family relationships as well as trying to communicate with her peers." Booklist

Atkinson, Elizabeth

From Alice to Zen and everyone in between; a novel. Carolrhoda Books 2008 247p $16.95

Grades: 5 6 7　　　　　　　　　　　　　**Fic**
　　1. School stories 2. Moving -- Fiction 3. Popularity -- Fiction 4. Family life -- Fiction 5. Massachusetts -- Fiction 6. Eccentrics and eccentricities -- Fiction
　　ISBN 978-0-8225-7271-8; 0-8225-7271-0
　　　　　　　　　　　　　　　LC 2007-9659
Upon moving from Boston to the suburbs, eleven-year-old tomboy Alice meets Zen, a very strange neighbor who is determined to help her become popular when they both begin middle school, although he himself is a loner.

"Atkinson describes Alice's ethical development credibly and engagingly." Booklist

★ **I,** Emma Freke; [by] Elizabeth Atkinson. Carolrhoda Books 2010 234p $16.95

Grades: 4 5 6 7　　　　　　　　　　　　**Fic**
　　1. Wisconsin -- Fiction 2. Family life -- Fiction 3. Massachusetts -- Fiction 4. Family reunions -- Fiction 5. Single parent family -- Fiction 6. Eccentrics and eccentricities -- Fiction
　　ISBN 978-0-7613-5604-2; 0-7613-5604-5
　　　　　　　　　　　　　　　LC 2009-38923
Growing up near Boston with her free-spirited mother and old-world grandfather, twelve-year-old Emma has always felt out of place but when she attends the family reunion her father's family holds annually in Wisconsin, she is in for some surprises.

"This rich story of self-acceptance offers readers much to think about. . . . The first-person narrative moves along briskly, with believable dialogue and plenty of humor." Booklist

Atwater-Rhodes, Amelia

Persistence of memory. Delacorte Press 2008 212p $15.99; lib bdg $18.99; pa $8.99

Grades: 8 9 10 11 12　　　　　　　　　　**Fic**
　　1. Witches -- Fiction 2. Vampires -- Fiction 3. Supernatural -- Fiction 4. Schizophrenia -- Fiction
　　ISBN 978-0-385-73437-0; 0-385-73437-9; 978-0-385-90443-8 lib bdg; 0-385-90443-6 lib bdg; 978-0-440-24004-4 pa; 0-440-24004-2 pa
　　　　　　　　　　　　　　　LC 2008-16062
Diagnosed with schizophrenia as a child, sixteen-year-old Erin has spent half of her life in therapy and on drugs, but now must face the possibility of weird things in the real world, including shapeshifting friends and her "alter," a centuries-old vampire.

"What sets this novel apart . . . are the two narrators—Erin, grown used to, and even comfortable with, the idea that she is mentally ill; and Shevaun, willing to do anything to protect the family she's cobbled together. Secondary characters are equally compelling, and the world that Atwater-Rhodes has created is believable and intriguing." SLJ

Snakecharm; [by] Amelia Atwater-Rhodes. Delacorte Press 2004 167p (The Kiesha'ra) $14.95; pa $5.99

Grades: 7 8 9 10　　　　　　　　　　　　**Fic**
　　1. Fantasy fiction
　　ISBN 0-385-73072-1; 0-385-90199-2 lib bdg; 978-0-385-73072-3; 978-0-440-23804-1 pa
　　　　　　　　　　　　　　　LC 2003-20709
Sequel to: Hawksong (2002)

The peace forged by the love between Zane and Danica, leaders of the avian and serpiente realms that had been at war for generations, is threatened by the arrival of Syfka, an ancient falcon who claims one of her people is hidden in their midst.

"There is enough suspense to keep readers interested. This book is a must-have for libraries with fans of Hawksong." SLJ

Followed by: Falcondance (2005)

Auch, Mary Jane

Ashes of roses. Holt & Co. 2002 250p $16.95; pa $6.50

Grades: 7 8 9 10 11 12 Adult   **Fic**

1. Immigrants -- Fiction 2. Irish Americans -- Fiction 3. New York (N.Y.) -- Fiction 4. Triangle Shirtwaist Company, Inc. -- Fiction

ISBN 0-8050-6686-1; 0-440-23851-X pa

LC 2001-51896

Sixteen-year-old Margaret Rose Nolan, newly arrived from Ireland, finds work at New York City's Triangle Shirtwaist Factory shortly before the 1911 fire in which 146 employees died

"Fast-paced, populated by distinctive characters, and anchored in Auch's convincing sense of time and place, this title is a good choice for readers who like historical fiction." SLJ

Guitar boy. Henry Holt 2010 260p $16.99

Grades: 6 7 8 9   **Fic**

1. Guitars -- Fiction 2. Musicians -- Fiction 3. Family life -- Fiction 4. Adirondack Mountains (N.Y.) -- Fiction

ISBN 978-0-8050-9112-0; 0-8050-9112-2

LC 2009-50782

After his mother is severely injured in an accident and his father kicks him out of the house, thirteen-year-old Travis attempts to survive on his own until he meets a guitar maker and some musicians who take him in and help him regain his confidence so that he can try to patch his family back together.

"Budding musicians will be fascinated by the details, but all readers will find their heartstrings plucked by this story." Booklist

Wing nut; [by] MJ Auch. Henry Holt & Co. 2005 231p $16.95

Grades: 4 5 6   **Fic**

1. Birds -- Fiction 2. Moving -- Fiction 3. Old age -- Fiction

ISBN 0-8050-7531-3

LC 2004-54046

When twelve-year-old Grady and his mother relocate yet again, they find work taking care of an elderly man, who teaches Grady about cars, birds, and what it means to have a home

"Auch's story . . . is engaging. . . . What will attract readers . . . is the author's careful integration of bird lore and the unusual challenges of creating and maintaining a purple martin colony." Booklist

Augarde, Steve

X -Isle. David Fickling Books 2010 476p $17.99

Grades: 7 8 9 10   **Fic**

1. Science fiction 2. Islands -- Fiction

ISBN 978-0-385-75193-3; 0-385-75193-1

LC 2010-281037

Baz and Ray, survivors of an apocalyptic flood, win places on X-Isle, an island where life is rumored to be better than on the devastated mainland, but they find the island to be a violent place ruled by religious fanatic Preacher John, and they decide they must come up with a weapon to protect themselves from impending danger.

"Augarde's near-future apocalyptic world is gruesomely hardscrabble without being overly graphic. . . . A gripping tale of fighting for the slenderest chance of hope." Publ Wkly

Austen, Catherine

All good children. Orca Book Publishers 2011 300p $19.95

Grades: 7 8 9 10 11 12   **Fic**

1. Siblings -- Fiction 2. Individualism -- Fiction 3. Totalitarianism -- Fiction

ISBN 978-1-55469-824-0; 1-55469-824-3

In the not-too-distant future, Max tries to maintain his identity in a world where the only way to survive is to conform and obey.

"Action packed, terrifying, and believable, this entertaining novel will provoke important discussions about subservience, resistance, and individual freedom." Booklist

Walking backward. Orca 2009 167p pa $9.95

Grades: 6 7 8 9   **Fic**

1. Bereavement -- Fiction

ISBN 978-1-55469-147-0 pa; 1-55469-147-8 pa

After his mother dies in a phobia-related car crash, twelve-year-old Josh tries to make sense of this grief while he looks after his little brother and watches his father retreat into a fantasy world

"In this impressive debut novel, Josh keeps a journal to chart his feelings and thoughts, allowing readers to follow his journey from sadness to acceptance and the eventual return of cohesion in his family. Given the subject matter, the story is never maudlin, and Josh's voice rings natural and true. An elegantly crafted volume of lasting power." Kirkus

Auxier, Jonathan

The **Night** Gardener; by Jonathan Auxier. Amulet Books 2014 368 p. (hardback) $16.95

Grades: 4 5 6 7   **Fic**

1. Ghost stories 2. Horror stories 3. Ghosts -- Fiction 4. Orphans -- Fiction 5. Dwellings -- Fiction 6. Storytelling -- Fiction 7. Household employees -- Fiction 8. Blessing and cursing -- Fiction 9. Brothers and sisters -- Fiction

ISBN 141971144X; 9781419711442

LC 2013047655

School Library Journal (April 1, 2014); Kirkus (March 1, 2014)

"'The Night Gardener' follows two abandoned Irish siblings who travel to work as servants at a creepy, crumbling English manor house. But the house and its family are not quite what they seem. Soon the children are confronted by a mysterious spectre and an ancient curse that threatens their very lives." (Publisher's note)

"Molly's whimsical tales illustrate life's essential lessons even as they entertain. As the characters face the unhealthy pull of the tree's allurements, they grow and change, revealing unexpected personality traits. Storytelling as a force to cope with life's challenges is subtly expressed and adds complexity to the fast-paced plot." SLJ reviews

Peter Nimble and his fantastic eyes; a story. Amulet Books 2011 381p il $16.95

Grades: 4 5 6 7   **Fic**

1. Eye -- Fiction 2. Blind -- Fiction 3. Magic -- Fiction 4. Orphans -- Fiction 5. Thieves -- Fiction

ISBN 978-1-4197-0025-5; 1-4197-0025-1

LC 2010048692

Raised to be a thief, blind orphan Peter Nimble, age ten, steals from a mysterious stranger three pairs of magical eyes, that lead him to a hidden island where he must decide to become a hero or resume his life of crime.

"The fast-paced, episodic story, accompanied by Auxier's occasional pen-and-ink drawings, is inventive, unpredictable, and—like its hero—nimble." Publ Wkly

Aveyard, Victoria

Red queen; Victoria Aveyard. First edition HarperTeen, an imprint of HarperCollins Publishers 2015 388 p. (Red queen trilogy) $17.99

Grades: 8 9 10 11   **Fic**

1. Ability -- Fiction 2. Princesses -- Fiction 3. Teenage girls -- Fiction 4. Kings and rulers -- Fiction 5. Resistance to government -- Fiction 6. Blood -- Fiction 7. Government, Resistance to -- Fiction

ISBN 0062310631; 9780062310637

LC 2014952542

This book, by Victoria Aveyard, is the "sweeping tale of seventeen-year-old Mare, a common girl whose once-latent magical power draws her into the dangerous intrigue of the king's palace. Mare Barrow's world is divided by blood-- those with common, Red blood serve the Silver- blooded elite, who are gifted with superhuman abilities. Mare is a Red, scraping by as a thief in a poor, rural village, until a twist of fate throws her in front of the Silver court." (Publisher's note)

"First-time author Aveyard has created a volatile world with a dynamic heroine, and while there are moments of romance, they refreshingly take a backseat to the action. Anticipation is already high for this debut, and with the movie rights already acquired and two sequels to come, it will likely only grow." Booklist

Avi, 1937-

The **Book** Without Words; a fable of medieval magic. Hyperion Books for Children 2005 203p hardcover o.p. pa $5.99

Grades: 5 6 7 8   **Fic**

1. Magic -- Fiction 2. Middle Ages -- Fiction 3. Supernatural -- Fiction 4. Great Britain -- History -- 0-1066 -- Fiction

ISBN 0-7868-0829-2; 0-7868-1659-7 pa

"At the dawning of the Middle Ages, Thorston, an old alchemist, works feverishly to create gold and to dose himself with a concoction that will enable him to live forever. The key to his success lies in a mysterious book with blank pages

that can only be read by desperate, green-eyed people. . . . Avi's compelling language creates a dreary foreboding. . . . Clearly this is a story with a message, a true fable. Thoughtful readers will devour its absorbing plot and humorous elements, and learn a 'useful truth' along the way." SLJ

Catch you later, traitor; a novel. by Avi. Algonquin Young Readers 2015 304 p. hbk $16.95

Grades: 4 5 6 7   **Fic**

1. Mystery fiction 2. Communism -- Fiction 3. Families -- Fiction 4. Brooklyn (New York, N.Y.) -- History -- 20th century -- Fiction

ISBN 1616203595; 9781616203597

LC 2014031983

This novel by Avi is set in 1951 Brooklyn, New York. "Pete Collison is a regular kid who loves Sam Spade detective books and radio crime dramas, but when an FBI agent shows up at Pete's doorstep accusing his father of being a Communist, Pete finds himself caught in a real-life mystery. Could there really be Commies in Pete's family? As Pete follows the quickly accumulating clues, he begins to wonder if the truth could put his family's livelihood--and even their freedom--at risk." (Publisher's note)

"Avi's tale of one Brooklyn family living in a time of intolerance effectively explores the natures of suspicion, loyalty, and freedom, following a young protagonist who comes to learn the importance of freedom of speech and 'staying true to your own thoughts.'" Horn Book

Includes bibliographical references

★ **City** of orphans; with illustrations by Greg Ruth. Atheneum Books for Young Readers 2011 350p il $16.99

Grades: 5 6 7 8   **Fic**

1. Mystery fiction 2. Gangs -- Fiction 3. Immigrants -- Fiction 4. Family life -- Fiction 5. New York (N.Y.) -- Fiction 6. Homeless persons -- Fiction 7. Waldorf-Astoria Hotel (New York, N.Y.) -- Fiction.

ISBN 978-1-4169-7102-3; 1-4169-7102-5

LC 2010049229

In 1893 New York, thirteen-year-old Maks, a newsboy, teams up with Willa, a homeless girl, to clear his older sister, Emma, from charges that she stole from the brand new Waldorf Hotel, where she works. Includes historical notes.

"Avi's vivid recreation of the sights and sounds of that time and place is spot on, masterfully weaving accurate historical details with Maks' experiences." Kirkus

Includes bibliographical references

★ **Crispin** : the cross of lead. Hyperion Bks. for Children 2002 $15.99; pa $6.99

Grades: 5 6 7 8   **Fic**

1. Orphans -- Fiction 2. Middle Ages -- Fiction 3. Great Britain -- History -- 1154-1399, Plantagenets -- Fiction

ISBN 0-7868-0828-4; 0-7868-1658-9 pa

LC 2001-51829

Awarded the Newbery Medal, 2001

Falsely accused of theft and murder, an orphaned peasant boy in fourteenth-century England flees his village and meets a larger-than-life juggler who holds a dangerous secret

This "book is a page-turner from beginning to end. . . . A meticulously crafted story, full of adventure, mystery, and action." SLJ

Other titles in this series are:
Crispin at the edge of the world (2006)
Crispin: the end of time (2010)

★ **Don't** you know there's a war on? HarperCollins Pubs. 2001 200p hardcover o.p. pa $5.99

Grades: 4 5 6 7 **Fic**

1. Teachers -- Fiction 2. World War, 1939-1945 -- Fiction 3. Brooklyn (New York, N.Y.) -- Fiction
ISBN 0-380-97863-6; 0-380-81544-3 pa

LC 00-46102

In wartime Brooklyn in 1943, eleven-year-old Howie Crispers mounts a campaign to save his favorite teacher from being fired

"The 1943 Brooklyn setting is well evoked in Howie's lively, slang-spangled narration. The novel's uncomplicated, compact structure invites reading aloud." Horn Book Guide

The **fighting** ground. Lippincott 1984 157p hardcover o.p. lib bdg $16.89; pa $5.99; rpt $5.99

Grades: 5 6 7 8 **Fic**

1. United States -- History -- 1775-1783, Revolution -- Fiction
ISBN 0-397-32073-6; 0-397-32074-4 lib bdg; 0-06-440185-5 pa; 9780064401852 rpt

LC 82-47719

"It's April 1776, and the fighting ground is both the farm country of Pennsylvania and the heart of a boy which is 'wonderful ripe for war.' Twenty-four hours transform Jonathan from a cocky 13-year-old, eager to take on the British, into a young man who now knows the horror, the pathos, the ambiguities of war." Voice Youth Advocates

★ **Iron** thunder; the battle between the Monitor and the Merrimac, a civil war novel. Hyperion 2007 205p il $15.99; pa $5.99

Grades: 4 5 6 **Fic**

1. Ships -- Fiction 2. Brooklyn (New York, N.Y.) -- Fiction 3. United States -- History -- 1861-1865, Civil War -- Fiction
ISBN 978-1-4231-0446-9; 1-4231-0446-3; 978-1-4231-0518-3 pa; 1-4231-0518-4 pa

"This fascinating adventure taken from U.S. history begins in Brooklyn in 1862, when Tom Carroll, 13, is hired at the Iron Works in Greenpoint for a secret project, derisively known around the borough as Ericsson's Folly. John Ericsson, a Swedish inventor, is trying to build an ironclad ship that can battle the Merrimac, a Confederate ship being outfitted with metal plates in Virginia. . . . Illustrated with period engravings, this is gripping historical fiction from a keenly imagined perspective." Publ Wkly

The **man** who was Poe; a novel. Orchard Bks. 1989 208p hardcover o.p. pa $5.99

Grades: 4 5 6 7 **Fic**

1. Poets 2. Authors 3. Mystery fiction 4. Essayists 5. Short story writers
ISBN 0-531-08433-7; 0-380-73022-7 pa

LC 89-42537

Edmund "finds himself alone in 1848 Providence. Both his aunt and his sister have vanished under mysterious circumstances. Through a chance encounter, Edmund enlists the help of a man he comes to know as Auguste Dupin. . . . Dupin is in fact Poe." (SLJ) "Grades six to nine." (Bull Cent Child Books)

Avi blends "drama, history, and mystery without a hint of pastiche or calculation. And, as in the best mystery stories, readers will be left in the end with both the comfort of puzzles solved and the unease of mysteries remaining." Bull Cent Child Books

Midnight magic. Scholastic Press 1999 249p hardcover o.p. pa $5.99

Grades: 5 6 7 8 **Fic**

1. Italy -- Fiction 2. Magicians -- Fiction 3. Renaissance -- Fiction
ISBN 0-590-36035-3; 0-439-24219-3 pa

LC 98-50192

In Italy in 1491, Mangus the magician and his apprentice are summoned to the castle of Duke Claudio to determine if his daughter is indeed being haunted by a ghost.

An "entertaining tale of mystery and intrigue." SLJ

Another title about Mangus and Fabrizio is:
Murder at midnight (2009)

★ **Nothing** but the truth; a documentary novel. Scholastic Inc. 2010 177p pa $6.99

Grades: 6 7 8 9 **Fic**

1. School stories
ISBN 978-0-545-17415-2
First published 1991 by Orchard Bks.
A Newbery Medal honor book, 1992

A ninth-grader's suspension for singing "The Star-Spangled Banner" during homeroom becomes a national news story.

"The book is effectively set entirely in monologue or dialogue; conversations, memos, letters, diary entries, talk-radio transcripts, and newspaper articles are all interwoven to present an uninterrupted plot. The construction is nearly flawless; the characters seem painfully human and typically ordinary. . . . A powerful, explosive novel that involves the reader from start to finish." Horn Book

★ The **seer** of shadows. HarperCollinsPublishers 2008 202p $16.99; lib bdg $17.89; pa $6.99

Grades: 4 5 6 7 **Fic**

1. Ghost stories 2. Photography -- Fiction 3. New York (N.Y.) -- Fiction 4. Swindlers and swindling -- Fiction
ISBN 978-0-06-000015-8; 0-06-000015-5; 978-0-06-000016-5 lib bdg; 0-06-000016-3 lib bdg; 978-0-06-000017-2 pa; 0-06-000017-1 pa

LC 2007-10891

In New York City in 1872, fourteen-year-old Horace, a photographer's apprentice, becomes entangled in a plot to create fraudulent spirit photographs, but when Horace accidentally frees the real ghost of a dead girl bent on revenge, his life takes a frightening turn.

"Fast-paced yet haunting. . . . This engaging novel has great immediacy and strong narrative drive." Booklist

★ **Sophia's** war; a tale of the Revolution. Avi. Beach Lane Books 2012 302 p. (hardcover) $16.99

Grades: 5 6 7 8   **Fic**

1. Traitors -- Fiction 2. Women spies -- Fiction 3. United States -- History -- 1775-1783, Revolution -- Fiction 4. Spies -- Fiction 5. United States -- History -- Revolution, 1775-1783 -- Fiction 6. New York (N.Y.) -- History -- Revolution, 1775-1783 -- Fiction 7. New York (N.Y.) -- History -- Revolution, 1775-1783 -- Fiction 8. United States -- History -- Revolution, 1775-1783 -- Prisoners and prisons -- Fiction

ISBN 1442414413; 9781442414419; 9781442414426; 9781442414433

LC 2012007962

In this novel by Avi "Sophia Calderwood witnesses the execution of Nathan Hale in New York City, which is newly occupied by the British army . . . in 1776. . . . Recruited as a spy, . . . she becomes aware that someone in the American army might be switching sides, and she uncovers a plot that will grievously damage the Americans if it succeeds. But the identity of the would-be traitor is so shocking that no one believes her, and so Sophia decides to stop the treacherous plot herself." (Publisher's note)

Includes bibliographical references

★ The **true** confessions of Charlotte Doyle; decorations by Ruth E. Murray. Orchard Bks. 1990 215p $16.95; pa $5.99; rpt $16.99

Grades: 5 6 7   **Fic**

1. Sea stories

ISBN 0-531-05893-X; 0-380-72885-0 pa; 9780545477116 rpt

LC 90-30624

A Newbery Medal honor book, 1991

"Charlotte Doyle, thirteen, returning from school in England to join her family in Rhode Island, is deposited on a seedy ship with a ruthless, mad captain and a mutinous crew. Refusing to heed warnings about Captain Jaggery's brutality, Charlotte seeks his guidance and approval only to become his victim." (SLJ)

The author has "fashioned an intriguing, suspenseful, carefully crafted tale, with nonstop action on the high seas." Booklist

Axelrod, Amy

Your friend in fashion, Abby Shapiro. Holiday House 2011 261p il $17.95

Grades: 4 5 6   **Fic**

1. Editors 2. Socialites 3. Letters -- Fiction 4. Spouses of presidents 5. Family life -- Fiction 6. Massachusetts -- Fiction 7. Fashion designers -- Fiction 9. Jews -- United States -- Fiction 10.

ISBN 978-0-8234-2340-8; 0-8234-2340-9

LC 2010-24185

Beginning in 1959, Abby, nearly eleven, writes a series of letters to Jackie Kennedy, each with sketches of outfits she has designed, as she faces family problems, concerns about neighbors, and her own desperate desire for both her first bra and a Barbie doll.

"Abby is an especially memorable protagonist, but all [Axelrod's] characters vibrate with life. . . . Funny, lively, sensitive—a real winner." Kirkus

Ayarbe, Heidi

★ **Compromised.** HarperTeen 2010 452p $16.99

Grades: 8 9 10 11 12   **Fic**

1. Foster home care -- Fiction 2. Runaway teenagers -- Fiction 3. Tourette syndrome -- Fiction 4. Voyages and travels -- Fiction

ISBN 978-0-06-172849-5; 0-06-172849-7

LC 2009-23545

With her con-man father in prison, fifteen-year-old Maya sets out from Reno, Nevada, for Boise, Idaho, hoping to stay out of foster care by finding an aunt she never knew existed, but a fellow runaway complicates all of her scientifically-devised plans.

"Ayarbe offers a gut-wrenching, terrifyingly authentic story and memorably etched, courageous characters whose influence on each other is palpable." Booklist

Ayres, Katherine

Macaroni boy. Delacorte Press 2003 182p hardcover o.p. pa $5.99

Grades: 5 6 7 8   **Fic**

1. School stories 2. Great Depression, 1929-1939 -- Fiction

ISBN 0-385-73016-0; 0-440-41884-4 pa

LC 2002-6768

In Pittsburgh in 1933, sixth-grader Mike Costa notices a connection between several strange occurrences, but the only way he can find out the truth about what's happening is to be nice to the class bully. Includes historical facts

"Actual places and events are interwoven with a heart-warming story of a close-knit family facing difficult times." Voice Youth Advocates

North by night; a story of the Underground Railroad. Delacorte Press 1998 176p hardcover o.p. pa $4.99

Grades: 6 7 8 9   **Fic**

1. Slavery -- Fiction 2. Underground railroad -- Fiction

ISBN 0-385-32564-9; 0-440-22747-x pa

LC 98-10039

Presents the journal of Lucinda, a sixteen-year-old girl whose family operates a stop on the Underground Railroad

This "is an absorbing tale. Ayres slips in a lot of evocative detail about the hard work of running a farm and a household before the Civil War, as well as some rather charming musing about kissing and its myriad effects on the psyche." Booklist

Babbitt, Natalie

The **moon** over High Street; Natalie Babbitt. Scholastic 2012 148 p. (alk. paper) $15.95

Grades: 3 4 5 6 7   **Fic**

1. Family -- Fiction 2. Friendship -- Fiction 3. Decision making -- Fiction 4. Adopted children -- Fiction

ISBN 054537636X; 9780545376365

LC 2011926886

This children's novel by Natalie Babbitt "presents 12-year-old Joe. . . . Orphaned shortly after his birth, Joe, who loves the moon, has been raised by his Gran, but after she breaks a hip, he's sent to spend some of the summer with his father's cousin. . . . In nearly idyllic Midville, . . .

he inadvertently comes to the attention of the very wealthy factory owner Mr. Boulderwall . . . who decides that he will adopt Joe and raise him to take over his company." (Kirkus)

Baccalario, Pierdomenico

Ring of fire; translated by Leah D. Janeczko; illustrations by Iacopo Bruno. Random House 2009 293p il (Century quartet) $16.99; lib bdg $19.99

Grades: 5 6 7 8   **Fic**

1. Italy -- Fiction 2. Rome (Italy) -- Fiction 3. Good and evil -- Fiction

ISBN 978-0-375-85895-6; 0-375-85895-4; 978-0-375-95895-3 lib bdg; 0-375-95895-9 lib bdg

LC 2009-08204

Original Italian edition, 2006

Four seemingly unrelated children are brought together in a Rome hotel where they discover that they are destined to become involved in a deep and ancient mystery involving a briefcase full of artifacts that expose them to great danger

"There are some genuinely exciting moments and the premise is intriguing." Publ Wkly

Other titles in this series are:

Star of Stone (2010)

City of Wind (2011)

Bacigalupi, Paolo

★ The **drowned** cities; by Paolo Bacigalupi. Little, Brown and Company 2012 448p. paperback $11.00

Grades: 9 10 11 12   **Fic**

1. Science fiction 2. Apocalyptic fiction 3. Refugees -- Fiction 4. War -- Fiction 5. Orphans -- Fiction 6. Soldiers -- Fiction 7. Survival -- Fiction 8. Conduct of life -- Fiction 9. Genetic engineering -- Fiction

ISBN 9780316056243; 9780316056229 paperback

LC 2011031762

This book takes place "[i]n a dark future America where violence, terror, and grief touch everyone, young refugees Mahlia and Mouse have managed to leave behind the war-torn lands of the Drowned Cities by escaping into the jungle outskirts. But when they discover a wounded half-man--a bioengineered war beast named Tool--who is being hunted by a vengeful band of soldiers, their fragile existence quickly collapses." (Publisher's note)

★ **Ship** Breaker; Bacigalupi, Paolo. Little, Brown and Co. 2010 326p $17.99

Grades: 8 9 10 11 12   **Fic**

1. Science fiction 2. Recycling -- Fiction

ISBN 0316056219; 9780316056212

LC 2009-34424

Michael L. Printz Award, 2011

In a futuristic world, teenaged Nailer scavenges copper wiring from grounded oil tankers for a living, but when he finds a beached clipper ship with a girl in the wreckage, he has to decide if he should strip the ship for its wealth or rescue the girl.

"Bacigalupi's cast is ethnically and morally diverse, and the book's message never overshadows the storytelling, action-packed pacing, or intricate world-building. At its core, the novel is an exploration of Nailer's discovery of the na-

ture of the world around him and his ability to transcend that world's expectations." Publ Wkly

Zombie baseball beatdown; by Paolo Bacigalupi. Little, Brown and Co. 2013 304 p. $17

Grades: 5 6 7 8   **Fic**

1. Horror fiction -- Fiction 2. Zombies -- Fiction 3. Packing-houses -- Fiction 4. Hispanic Americans -- Fiction 5. East Indian Americans -- Fiction 6. Racially mixed people -- Fiction

ISBN 0316220787; 9780316220781

LC 2012041463

In this book, middle school friends "Rabi, Miguel, and Joe literally smell trouble wafting from their small town's meatpacking plant, where they find cows living in filthy conditions and behaving oddly. Then the boys' baseball coach turns up moaning 'Brainsssss!' and tries to bite Rabi. When the children discover that meat from the sick cows is being packaged and sent to local supermarkets, they are on their own to prevent a zombie cow apocalypse because no one believes their story." (School Library Journal)

Bacon, Lee

The **nameless** hero; Lee Bacon. Delacorte Press, an imprint of Random House Children's Books, a division of Random House, Inc 2013 304 p. (Joshua Dread) (hardback) $16.99

Grades: 4 5 6 7   **Fic**

1. Superheroes 2. Fantasy fiction 3. Fame -- Fiction 4. Camps -- Fiction 5. Friendship -- Fiction 6. Superheroes -- Fiction 7. Supervillains -- Fiction

ISBN 0385741863; 9780375990281; 9780385741866

LC 2013003310

This is the second book in Lee Bacon's Joshua Dread series. Here, "Joshua Dread, secretly superpowered sixth grader (whose parents are the Dread Duo) is looking forward to a quiet summer with his normal best buddy, Milton, and their superstrong friend, Sophie. Their plans are thwarted when Joshua and Sophie receive invitations to Gyfted & Talented, a summer camp for superpowered teens. . . . Milton forges an invite." Their first mission goes horribly wrong, and things get weird. (Kirkus Reviews)

Baggott, Julianna

The **Prince** of Fenway Park. HarperCollinsPublishers 2009 322p $16.99; lib bdg $17.89

Grades: 4 5 6 7   **Fic**

1. Orphans -- Fiction 2. Baseball -- Fiction 3. Supernatural -- Fiction 4. Father-son relationship -- Fiction 5. Fenway Park (Boston, Mass.) -- Fiction 6. Boston Red Sox (Baseball team) -- Fiction

ISBN 978-0-06-087242-7; 0-06-087242-X; 978-0-06-087243-4 lib bdg; 0-06-087243-8 lib bdg

LC 2008-19666

In the fall of 2004, twelve-year-old Oscar Egg is sent to live with his father in a strange netherworld under Boston's Fenway Park, where he joins the fairies, pooka, banshee, and other beings that are trapped there, waiting for someone to break the eighty-six-year-old curse that has prevented the Boston Red Sox from winning a World Series

"Both whimsical and provocative (the 'N' word crops up in some historical references), this story will engage readers who like clever tales, and also those who enjoy chewing over controversial themes." SLJ

Bailey, Em

Shift; Em Bailey. Random House Distribution Childrens 2012 304 p. (hardcover) $16.99

Grades: 7 8 9 10 11 12   **Fic**

1. Human behavior -- Fiction 2. Female friendship -- Fiction 3. High school students -- Fiction 4. Orphans -- Fiction 5. Schools -- Fiction 6. Popularity -- Fiction 7. High schools -- Fiction 8. Mental illness -- Fiction 9. Interpersonal relations -- Fiction

ISBN 1606843583; 9781606843581; 9781606843598

LC 2011034349

Author Em Bailey's character "Olive keeps it simple: take her meds, keep a low profile at school, stay away from the ocean (with its horrible memories), and try not to cause trouble since she's pretty sure her selfish, unruly behavior is what made her father take off six months ago. But then strange and mysterious Miranda Vaile shows up at her high school, and Olive's safeguards start to crumble. Miranda begins insinuating herself into the life of Olive's former best friend, Katie." (Publishers Weekly)

Bailey, Kristin

Legacy of the clockwork key; by Kristin Bailey. Simon Pulse 2013 416 p. (alk. paper) $17.99

Grades: 7 8 9 10   **Fic**

1. Inventions 2. Love -- Fiction 3. Science fiction 4. Orphans -- Fiction 5. Secret societies -- Fiction 6. London (England) -- History -- 19th century -- Fiction 7. Great Britain -- History -- Victoria, 1837-1901 -- Fiction

ISBN 1442440260; 9781442440265

LC 2011049871

In this book, "a teen girl unravels the mysteries of a secret society and their most dangerous invention. . . . When a fire consumes Meg's home, killing her parents . . . all she has left is the tarnished pocket watch she rescued from the ashes. But this is no ordinary timepiece. The clock turns out to be a mechanical key--a key that only Meg can use--which unlocks a series of deadly secrets and intricate clues that Meg has no choice but to follow." (Publisher's note)

Other titles in the series include:

Rise of the Arcane Fire (2014)

Shadow of the War Machine (2015)

Baker, Matthew

If you find this; by Matthew Baker. Little, Brown & Co. 2015 368 p. illustrations (hardcover) $17

Grades: 4 5 6 7   **Fic**

1. Old age -- Fiction 2. Heirlooms -- Fiction 3. Friendship -- Fiction 4. Grandfathers -- Fiction 5. Lost and found possessions -- Fiction

ISBN 0316240087; 9780316240086

LC 2013044749

In this book, by Matthew Baker, "Nicholas is a math and music genius with no friends and a huge problem: His father has lost his job, and they'll have to sell their house, which holds the only memory Nicholas has of his younger brother. Just in time, Nicholas's senile grandfather arrives, filled with tales of priceless treasure he has hidden somewhere in town--but where?" (Publisher's note)

"The vivid setting, complex characters, and original writing style result in a story with lasting impact. Reminiscent of Louis Sachar's Holes (1998), this is a rich, captivating tale about family and redemption that redefines the meaning of treasure." Booklist

Baldwin, James

Go tell it on the mountain. Knopf 1953 303p $15.95; pa $6.99

Grades: 8 9 10 11 12 Adult   **Fic**

1. Family life -- Fiction 2. African Americans -- Fiction 3. Harlem (New York, N.Y.) -- Fiction

ISBN 0-679-60154-6; 0-440-33007-6 pa

This novel is an "autobiographical story of a Harlem child's relationship with his father against the background of his being saved in the pentecostal church." Benet's Reader's Ency of Am Lit

Balliett, Blue

★ Chasing Vermeer; illustrated by Brett Helquist. Scholastic Press 2004 254p il $16.95

Grades: 5 6 7 8   **Fic**

1. Artists 2. Painters 3. Mystery fiction 4. Art -- Fiction

ISBN 0-439-37294-1

LC 2002-152106

When seemingly unrelated and strange events start to happen and a precious Vermeer painting disappears, eleven-year-olds Petra and Calder combine their talents to solve an international art scandal.

Balliett's purpose "seems to be to get children to think—about relationships, connections, coincidences, and the subtle language of artwork." . . . [This is] a book that offers children something new upon each reading. . . . Helquist . . . outdoes himself here, providing an interactive mystery in his pictures." Booklist

Other titles about Petra and Calder are:

The Wright 3 (2006)

The Calder game (2008)

★ The Danger Box. Scholastic Press 2010 306p $16.99

Grades: 5 6 7 8   **Fic**

1. Naturalists 2. Travel writers 3. Diaries -- Fiction 4. Writers on science 5. Antiques -- Fiction 6. Michigan -- Fiction 7. Family life -- Fiction 8. Grandparents -- Fiction

ISBN 978-0-439-85209-8; 0-439-85209-9

LC 2010-16622

In small-town Michigan, twelve-year-old Zoomy and his new friend Lorrol investigate the journal found inside a mysterious box and find family secrets and a more valuable treasure, while a dangerous stranger watches and waits.

"This highly satisfying story will enlighten readers even as it inspires them to think about their own danger boxes." SLJ

★ Hold fast; by Blue Balliett. Scholastic Press 2013 288 p. (jacketed hardcover) $17.99

Grades: 3 4 5 6   **Fic**

1. Theft -- Fiction 2. Mystery fiction -- Fiction 3. Smuggling -- Fiction 4. Kidnapping -- Fiction 5.

Chicago (Ill.) -- Fiction 6. Missing persons -- Fiction 7. Homeless persons -- Fiction 8. Mystery and detective stories 9. Fathers and daughters -- Fiction 10. Family life -- Illinois -- Chicago -- Fiction

ISBN 0545299888; 9780545299886

LC 2012041035

This book focuses on "the Pearl family: Dash, Summer, 11-year-old Early, and the little Jubie. Do they have a lot? Well, yes, they have Dash's love of words, their devotion to each other, and their dream: to have a home. Trying to help that dream along, Dash, a page at the Chicago Public Library, makes extra money inventorying a private collection of old books. One . . . day, Dash disappears, and the family must move to a shelter after an odd robbery sees their . . . apartment destroyed." (Booklist)

Pieces and players; Blue Balliett; [edited by] David Levithan. Scholastic Press 2015 320 p. illustrations $17.99

Grades: 5 6 7 8   **Fic**

1. Mystery fiction 2. Art thefts -- Fiction 3. Art museums -- Fiction

ISBN 054529990X; 9780545299909

LC 2014947736

In this children's book, by Blue Balliett, "thirteen extremely valuable pieces of art have been stolen from one of the most secretive museums in the world. A Vermeer has vanished. A Manet is missing. And nobody has any idea where they and the other eleven artworks might be . . . . or who might have stolen them. . . . Calder, Petra, and Tommy are no strangers to heists and puzzles. Now they've been matched with two new sleuths -- Zoomy . . . . and Early." (Publisher's note)

"This time it's a small family museum and 13 missing pieces of art providing the mystery that brings back characters met in previous titles. Tommy, Petra, and Calder are joined by Early Pearl and Zoomy Chamberlain. With all five kids led by their teacher Mrs. Hussey, each of the detective's special skills add to their understanding and help them arrive at the solution. Fans of the previous books will be delighted as these characters continue with their familiar predilections such as Calder's pentominoes clacking in his pockets. . . . Fun and engaging; a fitting addition for readers addicted to these art mysteries." SLJ

Bancks, Tristan

Mac Slater hunts the cool. Simon & Schuster Books for Young Readers 2010 203p $15.99

Grades: 6 7 8 9   **Fic**

1. School stories 2. Beaches -- Fiction 3. Weblogs -- Fiction 4. Australia -- Fiction 5. Video recording -- Fiction

ISBN 978-1-4169-8574-7; 1-4169-8574-3

LC 2009-00152

Mac, an Australian youth, has one week to prove that he can be a "coolhunter," identifying emerging trends and posting images on a website, but he is competing against a classmate on whom he has a crush and dealing with resistance from his best friend and his own confusion over what "cool" means.

"Mac is a likable character who will appeal to a wide range of readers." Booklist

Followed by: Mac Slater vs. the city (2011)

Mac Slater vs. the city. Simon & Schuster Books for Young Readers 2011 184p $15.99

Grades: 6 7 8 9   **Fic**

1. Inventors -- Fiction 2. Web sites -- Fiction 3. Inventions -- Fiction 4. New York (N.Y.) -- Fiction

ISBN 1-4169-8576-X; 978-1-4169-8576-1

LC 2010006858

Sequel to: Mac Slater hunts the cool (2010)

Mac and his reluctant friend Paul head from Australia to Manhattan to continue their work for the Coolhunter website, and once there they discover a group of young inventors whose work is meant to be kept top-secret.

"The story takes twists and turns that are both surprising and rewarding. . . . An easy sell to many middle graders." SLJ

Banks, Kate

Walk softly, Rachel. Farrar, Straus & Giroux 2003 149p $16

Grades: 7 8 9 10   **Fic**

1. Death -- Fiction 2. Family life -- Fiction

ISBN 0-374-38230-1

LC 2002-26503

When fourteen-year-old Rachel reads the journal of her brother, who died when she was seven, she learns secrets that help her understand her parents and herself.

"While Banks's poetic prose may consist of simple words, its effect on the ear and heart is remarkable." SLJ

Banghart, Tracy E.

Shattered Veil; The Diatous Wars. Tracy E. Banghart. Createspace Independent Publishing Platform 2014 372 p. $15.99

Grades: 7 8 9 10 11 12   **Fic**

1. Love stories 2. Mystery fiction 3. Science fiction

ISBN 1493613200; 9781493613205

In this science fiction romance novel by Tracy E. Banghart, "War has invaded Atalanta's quiet villages and lush woodlands, igniting whispered worries in its glittering capitol. Far from the front lines, 18-year-old Aris Haan, a talented wingjet flyer, has little cause for concern. Until her beloved Calix is thrust into the fray, and a stranger makes her an impossible offer: the chance to join a secret army of women embedded within the all-male military." (Publisher's note)

"Part mystery, part romance, part sci-fi, Banghart's fast-paced exploration of loyalty, identity and commitment is entertaining and intriguing." (Kirkus)

Bao, Karen

Dove arising; Karen Bao. Viking Books for Young Readers 2015 324 p. (Dove Chronicles) hardcover $17.99

Grades: 7 8 9 10   **Fic**

1. Space colonies 2. Militia movements -- Fiction 3. Children of prisoners -- Fiction 4. Moon -- Fiction 5. Science fiction 6. Youths' writings 7. Space colonies -- Fiction 8. Government, Resistance to -- Fiction

ISBN 0451469011; 9780451469014; 9780451476289

LC 2013041198

In this novel by Karen Bao, "Phaet Theta has lived her whole life in a colony on the Moon. She's barely spoken since her father died in an accident nine years ago. She cultivates the plants in Greenhouse 22, lets her best friend talk for her, and stays off the government's radar. Then her mother is arrested. The only way to save her younger siblings from the degrading Shelter is by enlisting in the Militia, the faceless army that polices the Lunar bases and protects them from attacks by desperate Earth dwellers. Training is brutal, but it's where Phaet forms an uneasy but meaningful alliance with the preternaturally accomplished Wes, a fellow outsider. Rank high, save her siblings, free her mom: that's the plan. Until Phaet's logically ordered world begins to crumble..." (Publisher's note)

"Characters are well developed, especially strong-willed Phaet, and an even pace will keep teens turning pages. Fans of Orson Scott Card's Ender's Game (Tor, 1985), Veronica Roth's Divergent (HarperCollins, 2011) and Marie Lu's Legend (Putnam, 2011) should flock to this well-written debut effort by 19-year-old Bao." SLJ

Baratz-Logsted, Lauren

Crazy beautiful. Houghton Mifflin Harcourt 2009 191p $16

Grades: 7 8 9 10   **Fic**

1. School stories 2. Bullies -- Fiction 3. Amputees -- Fiction 4. Physically disabled -- Fiction

ISBN 978-0-547-22307-0; 0-547-22307-2

LC 2008-40463

In this contemporary retelling of "Beauty and the Beast," a teenaged boy whose hands were amputated in an explosion and a gorgeous girl whose mother has recently died form an instant connection when they meet on their first day as new students.

"This romance transcends all of its potential pitfalls to create a powerful story about recovery and friendship." Kirkus

Twin's daughter. Bloomsbury 2010 390p $16.99

Grades: 7 8 9 10   **Fic**

1. Mystery fiction 2. Aunts -- Fiction 3. Twins -- Fiction 4. Homicide -- Fiction 5. London (England) -- Fiction 6. Great Britain -- History -- 19th century -- Fiction

ISBN 978-1-59990-513-6; 1-59990-513-2

LC 2010-08234

In Victorian London, thirteen-year-old Lucy's comfortable world with her loving parents begins slowly to unravel the day that a bedraggled woman who looks exactly like her mother appears at their door.

"Baratz-Logsted's gothic murder mystery is rife with twists and moves swiftly and elegantly. . . . The ending will intrigue and delight readers." Booklist

Bardugo, Leigh

Ruin and rising; Leigh Bardugo. Henry Holt and Co. 2014 432 p. (Grisha trilogy) (hardback) $18.99

Grades: 8 9 10 11 12   **Fic**

1. Fantasy fiction 2. Princes -- Fiction 3. Love stories

ISBN 080509461X; 9780805094619

LC 2013049306

In this young adult fantasy novel by Leigh Bardugo, part of the Grisha Trilogy, "Deep in an ancient network of tun-

nels and caverns, a weakened Alina must submit to the dubious protection of the Apparat and the zealots who worship her as a Saint. Yet her plans lie elsewhere, with the hunt for the elusive firebird and the hope that an outlaw prince still survives." (Publisher's note)

"Alina and company have only one hope: if they can kill the Firebird, its magical bones can be used to break the Darkling's chokehold on Ravka. In this concluding volume, Alina must rely on her childhood friend Mal's preternatural tracking ability. Bardugo's longstanding theme of "power corrupts" is developed organically; the magic she invents will surprise and delight readers." Horn Book

Shadow and bone; Leigh Bardugo. Henry Holt 2012 358 p. (Grisha trilogy) (hc) $17.99

Grades: 8 9 10 11   **Fic**

1. Fantasy fiction 2. Magic -- Fiction 3. Folklore -- Russia 4. Monsters -- Fiction 5. Slavic mythology -- Fiction 6. Fantasy 7. Ability -- Fiction 8. Orphans -- Fiction

ISBN 0805094598; 9780805094596

LC 2011034012

In this young adult novel, "[Leigh] Bardugo draws inspiration from Russian and Slavic myth and culture to kick off her 'Grisha' trilogy. In the nation of Ravka, Alina Starkov is a junior cartographer's assistant in the army, while her best friend Mai is an expert tracker. When a perilous mission into the magically created Shadow Fold goes wrong, Mai is gravely wounded and Alina manifests the rare ability to summon light. Immediately recruited into the order of the magic-using Grisha, Alina is taken under the wing of its intimidating and powerful leader, the Darkling, and heralded as the potential destroyer of the Shadow Fold. As she navigates Grisha politics and uncovers well-hidden secrets, she realizes that the fate of the nation rests on her shoulders and she may be in grave danger." (Publishers Weekly)

Siege and storm; Leigh Bardugo. 1st ed. Henry Holt and Co. 2013 448 p. (Grisha trilogy) (hardcover) $17.99

Grades: 8 9 10 11 12   **Fic**

1. Fantasy fiction 2. Russia -- Fiction 3. Monsters -- Fiction 4. Fantasy 5. Magic -- Fiction 6. Orphans -- Fiction

ISBN 0805094601; 9780805094602

LC 2012046361

This fantasy novel, by Leigh Bardugo, is book 2 of the "Grisha Trilogy." "Alina must try to make a life with Mal in an unfamiliar land, all while keeping her identity as the Sun Summoner a secret. But she can't outrun her past or her destiny for long. The Darkling has emerged from the Shadow Fold with a terrifying new power and a dangerous plan that will test the very boundaries of the natural world." (Publisher's note)

Barker, M. P.

A **difficult** boy. Holiday House 2008 298p $16.95; pa $7.95

Grades: 5 6 7 8   **Fic**

1. Massachusetts -- Fiction 2. Contract labor -- Fiction 3. Irish Americans -- Fiction 4. Swindlers and

swindling -- Fiction
ISBN 978-0-8234-2086-5; 0-8234-2086-8; 978-0-8234-2244-9 pa; 0-8234-2244-5 pa

LC 2007-37059

In Farmington, Massachusetts, in 1839, nine-year-old Ethan experiences hardships as an indentured servant of the wealthy Lyman family alongside Daniel, a boy scorned simply for being Irish, and the boys bond as they try to right a terrible wrong.

"A memorable tale of friendship and a fascinating glimpse into mid-19th-century Massachusetts." SLJ

Barkley, Brad

Dream factory; [by] Brad Barkley + Heather Hepler. Dutton Books 2007 250p $16.99; pa $8.99
Grades: 8 9 10 11 12   **Fic**
1. Love stories 2. Summer employment -- Fiction 3. Walt Disney World (Fla.) -- Fiction
ISBN 978-0-525-47802-7; 0-525-47802-7; 978-0-14-241298-5 pa; 0-14-241298-8 pa

Alternating chapters present the view points of two teenagers who find summer employment as costumed cartoon characters at Disney World and try to resist falling in love.

"Able writing moves the story along while strong characterization makes even secondary players come alive." SLJ

Jars of glass; [by] Brad Barkley & Heather Hepler. Dutton Childrens Books 2008 246p $16.99
Grades: 7 8 9 10 11 12   **Fic**
1. Adoption -- Fiction 2. Siblings -- Fiction 3. Family life -- Fiction 4. Mental illness -- Fiction
ISBN 978-0-525-47911-6; 0-525-47911-2

LC 2007-52657

Two sisters, aged fourteen and fifteen, offer their views of events that occur during the year after their mother is diagnosed with schizophrenia and their family, including a recently adopted Russian orphan, begins to disintegrate.

"Barkley and Hepler are the masters of alternating narration, with Chloe's and Shana's voices both believable, clearly different, and usefully complementary. . . . This is an affecting story about families struggling to readjust in the face of one member's affliction." Bull Cent Child Books

Scrambled eggs at midnight; by Brad Barkley, Heather Hepler. Dutton Books 2006 262p $16.99
Grades: 7 8 9 10   **Fic**
1. Love stories 2. Fairs -- Fiction 3. North Carolina -- Fiction
ISBN 0-525-47760-8

LC 2005029187

Calliope and Eliot, two fifteen-year-olds in Asheville, North Carolina, begin to acknowledge some unpleasant truths about their parents and form their own ideas about love.

"This coauthored love story unfolds in alternating chapters narrated in Cal and Eliot's hilarious, heart-tugging voices. . . . The authors raise a potentially routine summer romance into a refreshing, poetic, memorable story." Booklist

Barnaby, Hannah

Wonder show; by Hannah Barnaby. Houghton Mifflin Books for Children 2012 viii, 274 p.p $16.99

Grades: 7 8 9 10 11 12   **Fic**
1. Carnivals -- Fiction 2. Runaway children -- Fiction 3. Fathers -- Fiction 4. Runaways -- Fiction 5. Sideshows -- Fiction 6. Orphanages -- Fiction
ISBN 0547599803; 9780547599809

LC 2011052426

William C. Morris Award Finalist (2013)

In this book by Hannah Barnaby, "Portia Remini, 13 . . . escapes . . . from the McGreavey Home for Wayward Girls to search for her father. . . . She joins a carnival. . . . On the lam from sinister 'Mister,' who runs McGreavey's, Portia learns the stories of some of the carnival's strange troupe. . . . But . . . when Mister's dragnet closes in, Portia decides that to find the answers she seeks she must return to the horror of The Home." (School Library Journal)

Barnes, Jennifer

The Squad : killer spirit; [by] Jennifer Lynn Barnes. 1st Laurel-Leaf ed.; Laurel Leaf Books 2008 324p pa $6.99
Grades: 7 8 9 10   **Fic**
1. School stories 2. Spies -- Fiction 3. Computers -- Fiction 4. Cheerleading -- Fiction
ISBN 978-0-385-73455-4

LC 2007017733

Sequel to: The Squad: perfect cover (2008)

As if it were not bad enough that sophomore computer hacker Toby Klein has to be a cheerleader to be part of the elite group of government operatives called the Squad, now she is part of the Homecoming court and has agreed to attend the dance with the most popular boy in school.

The Squad : perfect cover. Delacorte Press 2008 275p pa $6.99
Grades: 7 8 9 10   **Fic**
1. School stories 2. Spies -- Fiction 3. Computers -- Fiction 4. Cheerleading -- Fiction
ISBN 978-0-385-73454-7 pa; 0-385-73454-9 pa

LC 2007-09352

High school sophomore Toby Klein enjoys computer hacking and wearing combat boots, so she thinks it is a joke when she is invited to join the cheerleading squad but soon learns cheering is just a cover for an elite group of government operatives known as the Squad.

"In addition to offering crafty plotting and time-honored, typical teen conflicts and rivalries, Barnes maintains a sharp sense of humor in this action-adventure series." Bull Cent Child Books

Another title in this series is:
The Squad: killer spirit (2008)

Barnett, Mac

The terrible two; by Mac Barnett & Jory John; illustrated by Kevin Cornell. Harry N. Abrams 2015 224 p. illustrations (The terrible two) (hardback) $13.95
Grades: 4 5 6 7 8   **Fic**
1. School stories 2. Practical jokes 3. Humorous stories 4. Tricks -- Fiction 5. Schools -- Fiction 6. Practical jokes -- Fiction 7. Moving, Household -- Fiction
ISBN 1419714910; 9781419714917

LC 2014027503

In this book by Mac Barnett and Jory John "Miles Murphy is not happy to be moving. In his old school, everyone knew him as the town's best prankster, but Miles quickly discovers that Yawnee Valley already has a prankster, and a great one. If Miles is going to take the title from this mystery kid, he is going to have to raise his game. It's prankster against prankster in an epic war of trickery, until the two finally decide to join forces and pull off the biggest prank ever seen." (Publisher's note)

"Two rival pranksters headline this boisterous series opener set in Yawnee Valley, "the cow capital of the United States, this side of the Mississippi, excluding a couple of towns that cheat.".... Eventually, Miles finally forms a partnership with his unlikely nemesis to create a "secret society founded on mutual admiration and the joy of pranking." Cornell's (The Chicken Squad) b&w cartoons layer on the laughs, especially when portraying the megalomaniacal Principal Barkin, and Barnett and John's deadpan writing lets Yawnee Valley's absurdity shine." PW

Barnhill, Kelly Regan

★ The **mostly** true story of Jack; by Kelly Barnhill. Little, Brown 2011 323p il $16.99

Grades: 5 6 7 8   **Fic**

1. Iowa -- Fiction 2. Magic -- Fiction 3. Friendship -- Fiction 4. Family life -- Fiction
ISBN 978-0-316-05670-0; 0-316-05670-7

LC 2010044934

Jack is practically invisible at home, but when his parents send him to Hazelwood, Iowa, to spend a summer with his odd aunt and uncle, he suddenly makes friends, is beaten up by the town bully, and is plotted against by the richest man in town.

"A truly splendid amalgamation of mystery, magic and creeping horror will spellbind the middle-grade set. . . . The mystery deepens with each chapter, revealing exactly the right amount with each step. Answers are doled out so meticulously that readers will be continually intrigued rather than frustrated. The result is the ultime page-turner." Kirkus

★ The **witch's** boy; Kelly Barnhill. Algonquin Young Readers 2014 384 p. $16.95

Grades: 5 6 7 8   **Fic**

1. Fantasy fiction 2. Fantasy 3. Magic -- Fiction 4. Twins -- Fiction 5. Witches -- Fiction 6. Brothers -- Fiction 7. Friendship -- Fiction 8. Robbers and outlaws -- Fiction
ISBN 9781616203511

LC 2014014704

In this juvenile fantasy novel, by Kelly Regan Barnhill, "when Ned and his identical twin brother tumble from their raft into a raging river, only Ned survives. Villagers are convinced the wrong boy lived. But when a Bandit King comes to steal the magic Ned's mother, a witch, is meant to protect, it's Ned who safeguards the magic and summons the strength to protect his family and community." (Publisher's note)

"The story of Ned, the witch's boy, and Aine, the Bandit King's daughter, begins when Ned survives a drowning accident that kills his twin brother. Ned's mother, known as Sister Witch, binds dead Tam's soul to the living Ned. She does this to save Ned, who is ill from his experience, but the dire magic damages him in the process...The writing is beautiful and lyrical, but keeps pace with an action-packed story.

Powerful themes of grief, redemption, forgiveness, sacrifice, and generosity are all present. Recommend this title to those who like retellings and strong, narrative fantasy." (VOYA)

Barnholdt, Lauren

Girl meets ghost; by Lauren Barnholdt. Aladdin 2013 224 p. (alk. paper) $15.99

Grades: 4 5 6 7   **Fic**

1. Ghost stories -- Fiction 2. School stories -- Fiction 3. Mystery fiction -- Fiction 4. Dead -- Fiction 5. Ghosts -- Fiction 6. Schools -- Fiction 7. Middle schools -- Fiction 8. Psychic ability -- Fiction 9. Mystery and detective stories
ISBN 1442442468; 9781442442467

LC 2012032234

In this children's story, by Lauren Barnholt, "a tween girl becomes a reluctant medium. . . . There's an old saying that 'dead men tell no tales'--but that saying is definitely not true. Just ask twelve-year-old Kendall Williams, who can't get dead people to stop talking to her. . . . It's pretty frustrating being able to hear and see people that no one else can. . . . But Kendall is going to have to learn how to deal, because the only way to quiet the dead is to help them." (Publisher's note)

Sometimes it happens. Simon Pulse 2011 312p $16.99

Grades: 7 8 9 10   **Fic**

1. School stories 2. Dating (Social customs) -- Fiction
ISBN 978-1-4424-1314-6; 1-4424-1314-X

With help from her best friend Ava and Ava's boyfriend Noah, Hannah is recovering from being dumped by her boyfriend Sebastian, but on the first day of their senior year in high school, Ava learns that Hannah and Noah betrayed her while she was away.

"The writing style is smooth, featuring believable dialogue and first-person narration from Hannah's perspective. Hannah is a sympathetic character struggling with a relatable dilemma of liking your friend's significant other, yet wanting to be a faithful friend. The underlying message is captured by the title, Sometimes It Happens, as Hannah grows to understand that part of being human is hurting people without meaning to and then needing to ask for forgiveness." Voice Youth Advocates

Barnhouse, Rebecca

The **book** of the maidservant. Random House 2009 232p map $16.99; lib bdg $19.99

Grades: 7 8 9 10   **Fic**

1. Mystics 2. Memoirists 3. Writers on religion 4. Middle Ages -- Fiction 5. Religious life -- Fiction 6. Voyages and travels -- Fiction 7. Pilgrims and pilgrimages -- Fiction
ISBN 978-0-375-85856-7; 0-375-85856-3; 978-0-375-95856-4 lib bdg; 0-375-95856-8 lib bdg

LC 2008-28820

In 1413, a young maidservant accompanies her deeply religious mistress, Dame Margery Kempe, on a pilgrimage to Rome. Includes author's note on Kempe, writer of "The Book of Margery Kempe," considered by some to be the first autobiography in the English language

"Earthy, authentic, and engrossing, this fast-paced, easy read belongs on the shelf with Karen Cushman's The Midwife's Apprentice." Voice Youth Advocates

Includes bibliographical references

Barratt, Mark

Joe Rat. Eerdmans Books for Young Readers 2009 307p pa $9

Grades: 7 8 9 10   **Fic**

1. Crime -- Fiction 2. Orphans -- Fiction 3. Mental illness -- Fiction 4. London (England) -- Fiction 5. Great Britain -- History -- 19th century -- Fiction
ISBN 978-0-8028-5356-1; 0-8028-5356-0

LC 2008055972

First published 2008 in the United Kingdom

In the dark, dank sewers of Victorian London, a boy known as Joe Rat scrounges for valuables which he gives to "Mother," a criminal mastermind who considers him a favorite, but a chance meeting with a runaway girl and "the Madman" transforms all their lives.

"The unraveling of the Madman's identity is but one of the pleasures of Barratt's leisurely and convincing historical fiction." Booklist

Followed by: The wild man (2010)

The **wild** man. Eerdmans Books for Young Readers 2010 341p pa $9

Grades: 7 8 9 10   **Fic**

1. Crime -- Fiction 2. Fathers -- Fiction 3. Orphans -- Fiction 4. Social classes -- Fiction 5. London (England) -- Fiction 6. Impostors and imposture -- Fiction 7. Great Britain -- History -- 19th century -- Fiction
ISBN 978-0-8028-5377-6 pa; 0-8028-5377-3 pa

LC 2010010937

Sequel to: Joe Rat (2009)

In Victorian England, Joe Rat has escaped the clutches of the criminal mastermind, Mother, and is trying to make an honest living in a better part of London, but when a rich philanthropist tracks down a man claiming to be Joe's missing father—a British army deserter—he must determine where his loyalties lie.

"Barratt writes as if he is keeping an adjacent berth to Dickens; here's hoping scrappy Joe has a few more tricks up his ratty sleeves." Booklist

Barratt, Tracy

The **100** -year-old secret. Henry Holt and Co. 2008 157p (The Sherlock files) $15.95

Grades: 4 5 6 7   **Fic**

1. Mystery fiction 2. Siblings -- Fiction 3. Great Britain -- Fiction
ISBN 978-0-8050-8340-8; 0-8050-8340-5

LC 2007034004

Xena and Xander Holmes, an American brother and sister living in London for a year, discover that Sherlock Holmes was their great-great-great grandfather when they are inducted into the Society for the Preservation of Famous Detectives and given his unsolved casebook, from which they attempt to solve the case of a famous missing painting

"The main characters are observant, bright, and gifted with powers of deduction." SLJ

Other titles in this series are:

The beast of Blackslope (2009)
The case that time forgot (2010)
The missing heir (2011)

Dark of the moon. Harcourt 2011 310p $16.99

Grades: 7 8 9 10   **Fic**

1. Greece -- Fiction 2. Classical mythology -- Fiction 3. Theseus (Greek Mythology) -- Fiction
ISBN 978-0-547-58132-3; 0-547-58132-7

LC 2011009597

Retells the story of the minotaur through the eyes of his fifteen-year-old sister, Ariadne, a lonely girl destined to become a goddess of the moon, and her new friend, Theseus, the son of Athens' king who was sent to Crete as a sacrifice to her misshapen brother.

"This retelling of the myth of the Minotaur is deft, dark, and enthralling. Barrett spares readers none of the gore and violence of the Kretan goddess-worship, which involves both human and animal sacrifice. Ariadne's beliefs, though alien to modern readers, are given sufficient context to make them comprehensible. . . . This thoughtful, well-written reimagining of a classic myth is a welcome addition to the genre." SLJ

King of Ithaka. Henry Holt and Company 2010 261p map $16.99

Grades: 7 8 9 10   **Fic**

1. Classical mythology -- Fiction 2. Odysseus (Greek mythology) -- Fiction
ISBN 978-0-8050-8969-1; 0-8050-8969-1

LC 2009-50770

Sixteen-year-old Telemachos and his two best friends leave their life of privilege to undertake a quest to find Telemachos's father Odysseus. "Grades six to ten." (Bull Cent Child Books)

"The exotic climes and vivid descriptions . . . give the story a sense of immediacy and color." Booklist

The **Stepsister's** Tale; by Tracy Barrett. Harlequin Books 2014 272 p. $16.99

Grades: 7 8 9 10   **Fic**

1. Love stories 2. Stepsisters -- Fiction 3. Cinderella (Legendary character) -- Fiction 4. Poor 5. Fantasy 6. Stepfamilies 7. Fantasy fiction 8. Poor -- Fiction
ISBN 037321121X; 9780373211210

In this novel, by Tracy Barrett, "Jane Montjoy is tired of . . . pretending to live up to the standards of her mother's noble family--especially now that the family's wealth is gone. . . . When her stepfather suddenly dies, leaving nothing but debts and a bereaved daughter behind, it seems to Jane that her family is destined for eternal unhappiness. But a mysterious boy from the woods and an invitation to a royal ball are certain to change her fate." (Publisher's note)

"Sometimes it feels like fairy-tale retellings are a dime a dozen, and this is certainly not the first or the last account of a misunderstood antagonist. But, Barrett's comparably quiet account of a household of women working to survive together as a family, sometimes in spite of one another, shines with soft, bucolic realism...Overall, this is an enjoyable read. The inclusion of discussion questions in the back makes it a solid choice for book clubs." VOYA

Barron, T. A.

The **book** of magic; illustrated by August Hall. Philomel Books 2011 il (Merlin) $17.99 **Fic**

1. Fantasy fiction 2. Magic -- Fiction 3. Merlin (Legendary character) -- Fiction

ISBN 978-0-399-24741-5; 0-399-24741-6

LC 2011013552

A compendium of maps, character descriptions, magical terms, timelines, and other tidbits from the author's Merlin saga.

"Guides to long-running series have two important jobs. They should remind fans of all the things they particularly love about the books, and they should whet the appetites of newcomers, thus creating more fans. Barron's guide to his 12-book saga about Merlin succeeds in both objectives." SLJ

★ The **lost** years of Merlin. Philomel Bks. 1996 326p pa $7.99; $19.99

Grades: 5 6 7 8   **Fic**

1. Fantasy fiction 2. Merlin (Legendary character) -- Fiction

ISBN 9780441006687 pa; 9780399230189

LC 96-33920

"A boy, hurled on the rocks by the sea, regains consciousness unable to remember anything—not his parents, not his own name. He is sure that the secretive Branwen is not his mother, despite her claims, and that Emrys is not his real name. The two soon find themselves feared because of Branwen's healing abilities and Emrys' growing powers. . . . Barron has created not only a magical land populated by remarkable beings but also a completely magical tale, filled with ancient Celtic and Druidic lore, that will enchant readers." Booklist

Other titles in this series are:

The seven songs of Merlin (1997)

The fires of Merlin (1998)

The mirror of Merlin (1999)

The wings of Merlin (2000)

Merlin's dragon. Philomel Books 2008 305p (Merlin's dragon) $19.99

Grades: 6 7 8 9   **Fic**

1. Fantasy fiction 2. Magic -- Fiction 3. Dragons -- Fiction

ISBN 978-0-399-24750-7; 0-399-24750-5

LC 2008-2469

Basil, a small, flying lizard who is searching for others like himself, discovers that there is more to him than he knows, as he becomes engaged in Avalon's great war between the evil Rhita Gawr and the forces of good.

"Basil is an appealing, complex character. . . . This first book in a new series will captivate readers already familiar with the fantasist's Merlin chronicles." Booklist

Other titles in this series are:

Doomraga's revenge (2009)

Utlimate magic (2010)

Barrow, Randi G.

Saving Zasha; by Randi Barrow. Scholastic Press 2011 229p $16.99

Grades: 4 5 6 7   **Fic**

1. Dogs -- Fiction 2. Russia -- Fiction 3. Journalists -- Fiction 4. Single parent family -- Fiction 5. World War, 1939-1945 -- Fiction

ISBN 978-0-545-20632-7; 0-545-20632-4

LC 2010-16899

In 1945 Russia, those who own German shepherds are considered traitors, but thirteen-year-old Mikhail and his family are determined to keep the dog a dying man brought them, while his classmate Katia strives to learn his secret.

"Mikhail's sense of humor, concern for his family, and love of Zasha are all readily apparent in his narration, which smoothly incorporates background information for readers unfamiliar with 20th-century Russian life and history. . . . Barrow's novel is quick reading yet weighty, and captures the prejudices and aftereffects of war." Publ Wkly

Barry, Dave

The **bridge** to Never Land; [by] Dave Barry and Ridley Pearson. Disney/Hyperion 2011 438p $18.99

Grades: 5 6 7   **Fic**

1. Fairy tales 2. Adventure fiction

ISBN 978-1-4231-3865-5; 1-4231-3865-1

Sequel to: Peter and the Sword of Mercy

"Bringing the Starcatchers series into the twenty-first century, this novel features Sarah and her brother, Aidan, who find a cryptic note in an antique desk and follow the clues to London, Princeton, and Orlando. Along the way, they clash with evil Lord Ombra, find an ally in Molly Darling's great-great-great nephew, and discover Einstein's part in the plan. The plot is a thrill ride of action and adventure, with plenty of chase scenes and (no surprise here) a trip to Never Land." Booklist

Peter & the shadow thieves; by Dave Barry and Ridley Pearson; illustrations by Greg Call. Disney Editions/Hyperion Books for Children 2006 556p il $18.99

Grades: 5 6 7   **Fic**

1. Fairy tales 2. Adventure fiction

ISBN 0-7868-3787-X

LC 2005-56033

Sequel to Peter and the starcatchers (2004)

Realizing that Molly and the other Starcatchers are in danger when the sinister being Lord Ombra visits the island and seems to control people through their shadows, Peter and Tinker Bell travel to England to help save the stardust. "Age ten and up." (N Y Times Book Rev)

This "is filled with enough rollicking, death-defying adventure to satisfy anyone." SLJ

Followed by Peter and the secret of Rundoon (2007)

Peter and the secret of Rundoon; by Dave Barry and Ridley Pearson; illustrations by Greg Call. Disney Editions/Hyperion Books for Children 2007 482p il $18.99

Grades: 5 6 7   **Fic**

1. Fairy tales 2. Adventure fiction

ISBN 0-7868-3788-8; 978-0-7868-3788-5

LC 2007006306

Sequel to Peter and the shadow thieves (2006)

Fearing that the sinister Lord Ombra was not destroyed, Peter and Molly travel to the land of Rundoon, which is ruled by the evil King Zarboff.

"This is a fun, intense, and totally worthwhile adventure." SLJ

Followed by Peter and the Sword of Mercy (2009)

Peter and the starcatchers; by Dave Barry and Ridley Pearson; illustrations by Greg Call. Hyperion 2004 451p il $17.99; pa $7.99

Grades: 5 6 7   **Fic**
1. Fairy tales 2. Adventure fiction 3. Pirates -- Fiction
ISBN 0-7868-5445-6; 0-7868-4907-X pa

LC 2004-55275

Soon after Peter, an orphan, sets sail from England on the ship Never Land, he befriends Molly, a young Starcatcher, whose mission is to guard a trunk of magical stardust from a greedy pirate and the native inhabitants of a remote island. "Age ten and up." (N Y Times Book Rev)

"The authors plait multiple story lines together in short, fast-moving chapters. . . . Capitalizing on familiar material, this adventure is carefully crafted to set the stage for Peter's later exploits. This smoothly written page-turner just might send readers back to the original." SLJ

Peter and the Sword of Mercy; by Dave Barry and Ridley Pearson; illustrations by Greg Call. Disney/Hyperion Books 2009 515p il $18.99

Grades: 5 6 7   **Fic**
1. Fairy tales 2. Adventure fiction
ISBN 978-1-4231-2134-3; 1-4231-2134-1

Sequel to: Peter and the secret of Rundoon (2007)

James, one of Peter's original Lost Boys, is now working for Scotland Yard and suspects that the heir to England's throne, Prince Albert Edward, is under the influence of shadow creatures who are after starstuff hidden in an underground vault which has only one key: the Sword of Mercy.

"This adventure is fast and intense, and readers will feel compelled to find out what happens next." VOYA

Followed by: The bridge to Never Land (2011)

The **Worst** class trip ever; Dave Barry. First edition Disney-Hyperion Books 2015 224 p. illustrations, map $13.99

Grades: 5 6 7   **Fic**
1. Field trips -- Fiction 2. Terrorism -- Prevention -- Fiction 3. Humorous stories 4. Terrorism -- Fiction 5. Conduct of life -- Fiction 6. Washington (D.C.) -- Fiction 7. School field trips -- Fiction
ISBN 1484708490; 9781484708491

LC 2014013171

In this children's novel by Dave Barry "on a class trip to Washington, DC, eighth grader Wyatt Palmer and his best friend Matt believe that they have uncovered a terrorist plot. During a scuffle with these passengers, Matt removes an odd device from one man's backpack. This event gets Matt and Wyatt into trouble with their teacher. For the rest of their trip, Wyatt, Matt, and a few more of their classmates . . . avoid bad guys, sneak away from the rest of their class, and conceal the whole situation from their chaperones." (Publisher's note)

"With its wacky humor and mildly suspenseful scenarios, this appealing book will be a good fit for most libraries." SLJ

Bartoletti, Susan Campbell

★ The **boy** who dared. Scholastic Press 2008 202p $16.99

Grades: 5 6 7 8   **Fic**
1. Courage -- Fiction 2. Underground leaders 3. National socialism -- Fiction 4. Germany -- History -- 1933-1945 -- Fiction
ISBN 0-439-68013-1; 978-0-439-68013-4

LC 2007014166

In October, 1942, seventeen-year-old Helmuth Hübener, imprisoned for distributing anti-Nazi leaflets, recalls his past life and how he came to dedicate himself to bringing the truth about Hitler and the war to the German people.

Bartoletti "does and excellent job of conveying the political climate surrounding Hitler's ascent to power, seamlessly integrating a complex range of socioeconomic conditions into her absorbing drama." Publ Wkly

Barwin, Steven

Hardball; Steven Barwin. Orca Book Publishers 2014 192 p. (Orca sports) (pbk.) $9.95

Grades: 7 8 9 10   **Fic**
1. Cousins -- Fiction 2. Baseball -- Fiction 3. School sports -- Fiction 4. Hazing
ISBN 1459804414; 9781459804418; 9781459804425; 9781459804432

LC 2014935389

"Griffin has college in his sights and plans to land himself a baseball scholarship. His determination causes him to turn a blind eye to the hazing of new players by the team captain, Wade. But when Griffin senses that his cousin Carson is getting the brunt of Wade's aggression, Griffin finally stands up to him." (Publisher's note)

"Short, fast-paced chapters keep the narrative moving with a mix of baseball play-by-plays and sleuthing. A drug-dealing subplot adds a layer of suspense and raises the stakes well beyond troubles on the ball field. Ideal for reluctant readers, this book's gritty undertones will appeal to the intended high/low audience of sports fans." Booklist

Baskin, Nora Raleigh, 1961-

All we know of love. Candlewick Press 2008 201p $16.99

Grades: 6 7 8 9 10   **Fic**
1. Mothers -- Fiction 2. Loss (Psychology) -- Fiction 3. Voyages and travels -- Fiction
ISBN 978-0-7636-3623-4; 0-7636-3623-1

LC 2007-22396

Natalie, almost sixteen, sneaks away from her Connecticut home and takes the bus to Florida, looking for the mother who abandoned her father and her when she was ten years old.

"Baskin takes a familiar story line and examines it in a new and interesting way that will engage readers." Voice Youth Advocates

★ **Anything** but typical. Simon & Schuster Books for Young Readers 2009 195p il $15.99

Grades: 4 5 6 7　　　　　　　　　　　**Fic**
1. School stories 2. Autism -- Fiction 3. Authorship
-- Fiction 4. Family life -- Fiction
ISBN 1416963782; 9781416963783

LC 2008-20994

ALA Schneider Family Book Award Honor Book (2010)

Jason, a twelve-year-old who wants to become a writer, relates what life is like as he tries to make sense of his world. "Grades six to nine." (Bull Cent Child Books)

"This is an enormously difficult subject, but Baskin, without dramatics or sentimentality, makes it universal." Booklist

Ruby on the outside; Nora Raleigh Baskin. First edition Simon & Schuster Books for Young Readers 2015 176 p. (hardcover) $16.99
Grades: 4 5 6 7 8　　　　　　　　　　　**Fic**
1. Children of prisoners -- Fiction 3. Mother-daughter relationship -- Fiction 4. Aunts -- Fiction 5. Friendship -- Fiction 6. Best friends -- Fiction 7. Prisoners' families -- Fiction 8. Mothers and daughters -- Fiction
ISBN 1442485035; 9781442485037; 9781442485044

LC 2014018268

In this novel, by Nora Raleigh Baskin, "Ruby's mom is in prison, and to tell anyone the truth is to risk true friendship. . . . Eleven-year-old Ruby Danes is about to start middle school, and only her aunt knows her deepest, darkest, most secret secret: her mother is in prison. Then Margalit Tipps moves into Ruby's condo complex, and the two immediately hit it off. Ruby thinks she's found her first true-blue friend--but can she tell Margalit the truth about her mom?" (Publisher's note)

"This lyrical novel explores multiple aspects of the effects of incarceration on family—guilt, fear, anger, loneliness, and heavy responsibility. Baskin's plot structure, which flows from the present to periodic flashbacks, keeps the story from being unbearably dark. Margalit may be too good to be true, but she is just what the doctor ordered for Ruby's healing." Booklist

Runt; Nora Raleigh Baskin. Simon & Schuster Books for Young Readers 2013 208 p. (hardback) $15.99
Grades: 5 6 7 8　　　　　　　　　　　**Fic**
1. School stories 2. Female friendship 3. Dogs -- Fiction 4. Schools -- Fiction 5. Bullying -- Fiction 6. Popularity -- Fiction 7. Middle schools -- Fiction 8. Online social networks -- Fiction
ISBN 1442458070; 9781442458079; 9781442458086

LC 2012049461

This book shows "the day-to-day torments of students in a sixth-grade class. In a series of brief vignettes, [Nora Raleigh Baskin] moves between classmates including 'Smelly-Girl' Elizabeth, who can't shake the lingering scent (or shed hair) of her mother's dog-sitting business; Elizabeth's nemesis, Maggie, who . . . hasn't been able to repair her fallout with her artistically talented former best friend Freida; and Stewart and Matthew, two athletes whose rivalry leads to a fight." (Publishers Weekly)

★ The **summer** before boys. Simon & Schuster Books for Young Readers 2011 196p $15.99

Grades: 6 7 8　　　　　　　　　　　**Fic**
1. Girls -- Fiction 2. Friendship -- Fiction 3. Dating (Social customs) -- Fiction
ISBN 978-1-4169-8673-7; 1-4169-8673-1

LC 2010045688

Twelve-year-old best friends and relatives, Julia and Eliza are happy to spend the summer together while Julia's mother is serving in the National Guard in Iraq but when they meet a neighborhood boy, their close relationship begins to change.

"A poignant story of children on the homefront and the ways that a first love can break up longtime friendships and change things forever." Booklist

The **truth** about my Bat Mitzvah. Simon & Schuster Books for Young Readers 2008 138p $15.99; pa $5.99
Grades: 5 6 7 8　　　　　　　　　　　**Fic**
1. Jews -- Fiction 2. Bat mitzvah -- Fiction 3. Grandmothers -- Fiction
ISBN 978-1-4169-3558-2; 1-4169-3558-4; 978-1-4169-7469-7 pa; 1-4169-7469-5 pa

LC 2007-01248

After her beloved grandmother, Nana, dies, non-religious twelve-year-old Caroline becomes curious about her mother's Jewish ancestry.

"Readers will identify with Caroline and her preoccupations. . . . This quick read will be a hit with preteens contemplating their own identities." Booklist

Bass, Karen, 1962-
Graffiti knight. Orca Book Publishers 2014 272 p. $14.95
Grades: 7 8 9 10　　　　　　　　　　　**Fic**
1. Graffiti -- Fiction 2. Family life -- Fiction 3. Communist countries -- Fiction 4. Resistance to government -- Fiction
ISBN 1927485533; 9781927485538

In this book, "after a childhood cut short by war and the harsh strictures of Nazi Germany, sixteen-year-old Wilm is finally tasting freedom. . . . It's dangerous, of course, to be sneaking out at night to leave messages on police buildings. But it's exciting, too, and Wilm feels justified, considering his family's suffering. Until one mission goes too far, and Wilm finds he's endangered the very people he most wants to protect." (Publisher's note)

"Just as Ruta Sepetys revealed a different perspective of the Holocaust in Between Shades of Gray (2011), Bass introduces another view of history unknown to many American readers...This eye-opening story shows that war's end is never tidy." (Booklist)

Bassoff, Leah
★ **Lost** Girl Found; by Leah Bassoff and Laura DeLuca. Pgw 2014 192 p. maps $16.95
Grades: 6 7 8 9 10　　　　　　　　　　　**Fic**
1. Refugees -- Fiction 2. Mother-daughter relationship -- Fiction 3. Sudan -- History -- Civil War, 1983-2005 -- Fiction
ISBN 1554984165; 9781554984169

LC bl2014008921

In this book, by Leah Bassoff and Laura DeLuca, "Poni
. . . [lives in a] small village in southern Sudan. . . . Then the
war comes and there is only one thing for Poni to do. Run. . .
. [She is] driven by the sheer will to survive and the hope that
she can . . . make it to the Kakuma refugee camp in Kenya. .
. . In Kakuma she is almost overwhelmed by the misery that
surrounds her. Poni realizes that she must leave the camp at
any cost. Her destination is a compound in Nairobi." (Publisher's note)

"After her southern Sudan village is bombed, Poni arrives at a Kenyan refugee camp, where conditions are brutal.
Poni wants to finish her education, and she has a chance to
do so when she escapes the refugee camp. Poni is a fully realized and sympathetic character. This fast-paced novel covers a lot of ground and incorporates a good deal of historical
background." Horn Book

Bastedo, Jamie

On thin ice. Red Deer Press 2006 348p pa
$10.95

Grades: 8 9 10 11 12   **Fic**

1. Inuit -- Fiction 2. Polar bear -- Fiction 3. Arctic
regions -- Fiction 4. Greenhouse effect -- Fiction
ISBN 978-0-88995-337-6; 0-88995-337-6

"Set in the remote Arctic village of Nanurtalik, this novel
follows Ashley as she journeys on the shaman path chosen
for her through the Inuit line of her father. Disturbed by
haunting—sometimes frightening—dreams of a gigantic polar bear that seems bent on destroying her, Ashley furiously
draws her dreams onto paper, capturing the very essence of
the bear within. . . . This novel is told with richness of language, culture, and emotion, but its sense of place sparkles
brightest." Voice Youth Advocates

Followed by: Sila's revenge (2010)

Basye, Dale E.

Heck; where the bad kids go. by Dale E. Basye;
illustrated by Bob Dob. Random House 2008 304p
il $16.99; lib bdg $19.99

Grades: 5 6 7 8   **Fic**

1. School stories 2. Siblings -- Fiction 3. Future life
-- Fiction
ISBN 978-0-375-84075-3; 0-375-84075-3; 978-0-375-
94075-0 lib bdg; 0-375-94075-8 lib bdg

LC 2007-8379

When timid Milton and his older, scofflaw sister Marlo
die in a marshmallow bear explosion at Grizzly Mall, they
are sent to Heck, an otherworldly reform school from which
they are determined to escape.

"The author's umpteen clever allusions—characters'
eternal fates are decided by standardized 'Soul Aptitude
Tests'; Mr. R. Nixon teaches ethics to evildoers in room
1972—make this book truly sparkle." Publ Wkly

Other titles in this series are:
Rapacia: the second circle of Heck (2009)
Blimpo: the third circle of Heck (2010)
Fibble: the fourth circle of Heck (2011)

Bates, Marni

Awkward. Kensington 2012 259p pa $9.95

Grades: 7 8 9 10   **Fic**

1. School stories 2. Fame -- Fiction 3. Popularity

-- Fiction
ISBN 978-0-7582-6937-9; 0-7582-6937-4

"A brilliant but socially inept girl finds herself starring in
a YouTube video gone viral when she knocks over a football
player and tries to give him CPR. . . . Mackenzie tries to
keep her head down as the entire nation laughs at her for her
awkward video moves. . . . But her notoriety takes a positive
turn when the hottest rock group around turns her film into a
music video with a new hit song, boosting her fame even further. . . . Bates keeps her prose light, always focusing on the
comedy as she lampoons high-school popularity, and gives
narrator Mackenzie some good one-liners. . . . Very funny.
Should please lots of readers, awkward or not." Kirkus

Bateson, Catherine

★ **Being** Bee. Holiday House 2007 126p il
$16.95; pa $7.95

Grades: 4 5 6   **Fic**

1. Australia -- Fiction 2. Family life -- Fiction 3.
Guinea pigs -- Fiction 4. Father-daughter relationship
-- Fiction
ISBN 978-0-8234-2104-6; 0-8234-2104-X; 978-0-
8234-2208-1 pa; 0-8234-2208-9 pa

LC 2006-101561

Bee faces friction at home and at school when her widowed father begins seriously dating Jazzi, who seems to take
over the house and their lives, but as shared secrets and common interests finally begin to draw them together, Jazzi accidentally makes a terrible mistake.

"Bee's emotions are perspectives are honest and clearly
presented. . . . She is a likable, believable character." SLJ

Magenta McPhee. Holiday House 2010 170p
$16.95

Grades: 4 5 6 7   **Fic**

1. Australia -- Fiction 2. Authorship -- Fiction 3. Single
parent family -- Fiction 4. Dating (Social customs) --
Fiction 5. Father-daughter relationship -- Fiction
ISBN 978-0-8234-2253-1; 0-8234-2253-4

LC 2009-10854

First published 2009 in Australia

Thinking her father needs a new interest in his life after
he is laid-off of work, teenaged Magenta, who envisions herself as a future fantasy author, decides to dabble in matchmaking which brings unexpected results.

"With a personality as colorful as her name, Bateson's
. . . eponymous heroine has a narrative voice that is smart,
wry, and down-to-earth. . . . This [is a] real and ultimately
reassuring story." Publ Wkly

Baucom, Ian

Through the skylight; a Venice tale. Ian Baucom. 1st ed. Atheneum Books for Young Readers
2013 400 p. ill. (hardcover) $17.99

Grades: 5 6 7 8   **Fic**

1. Fantasy fiction 2. Time travel -- Fiction 3. Venice
(Italy) -- Fiction 4. Italy -- Fiction 5. Magic -- Fiction
6. Americans -- Italy -- Fiction 7. Mystery and detective
stories 8. Brothers and sisters -- Fiction
ISBN 1416917772; 9781416917779

LC 2012010642

In this juvenile novel, by Ian Baucom, illustrated by Justin Gerard, "when Jared, Shireen, and Miranda are each given one glittering gift from an old Venetian shopkeeper, they never fathom the powers they are now able to unleash. . . . For in another time, centuries earlier, another trio . . . have been kidnapped and, along with hundreds of other children, will be sold into child slavery. Unless, that is, they can find some way to save them all." (Publisher's note)

"Frequent black-and-white illustrations support the narrative. Baucom's familiarity with the setting and use of Italian words heighten the atmosphere. . . . The mix of protagonists' genders, historical details, and interesting magic creates a story with broad appeal and a message about the power of words. . ." SLJ

Bauer, A. C. E.

★ **Come** Fall. Random House 2010 231p $15.99; lib bdg $18.99

Grades: 4 5 6 7 **Fic**

1. School stories 2. Crows -- Fiction 3. Fairies -- Fiction 4. Friendship -- Fiction 5. Foster home care -- Fiction

ISBN 978-0-375-85825-3; 0-375-85825-3; 978-0-375-95855-7 lib bdg; 0-375-95855-X lib bdg

LC 2009-32419

Drawn together by a mentoring program and an unusual crow, middle school misfits Salman, Lu, and Blos form a strong friendship despite teasing by fellow students and the maneuverings of fairies Oberon, Titania, and Puck.

"Weaving in magic, dreams, doubles, contrasts, and other elements from the original play, Bauer spins an enticing variant." Booklist

No castles here. Random House 2007 270p $15.99; lib bdg $18.99

Grades: 4 5 6 7 **Fic**

1. Magic -- Fiction 2. New Jersey -- Fiction 3. Choirs (Music) -- Fiction 4. Books and reading -- Fiction 5. City and town life -- Fiction

ISBN 978-0-375-83921-4; 978-0-375-93921-1 lib bdg

LC 2006023601

Eleven-year-old Augie Boretski dreams of escaping his rundown Camden, New Jersey, neighborhood, but things start to turn around with help from a Big Brother, a music teacher, and a mysterious bookstore owner, so when his school is in trouble, he pulls the community together to save it

This is a "heartwarming novel." Booklist

Bauer, Joan

Almost home; by Joan Bauer. Viking 2012 264 p. (hardcover) $16.99

Grades: 5 6 7 8 **Fic**

1. Pets -- Fiction 2. Homeless persons -- Fiction 3. Mother-daughter relationship -- Fiction 4. Mothers and daughters -- Fiction

ISBN 0670012890; 9780670012893

LC 2011050483

In this book by Joan Bauer, "when twelve-year-old Sugar's grandfather dies and her gambling father takes off yet again, Sugar and her mother . . . head to Chicago for a fresh start, only to discover that fresh starts aren't so easy

to come by for the homeless. . . .With the help of a rescue dog . . . a foster family . . . and her own grace and good humor, Sugar comes to understand that while she can't control the hand life deals her, she can control how she responds." (Publisher's note)

Close to famous. Viking 2011 250p $16.99

Grades: 5 6 7 8 **Fic**

1. Baking -- Fiction 2. Literacy -- Fiction 3. Country life -- Fiction 4. West Virginia -- Fiction 5. Single parent family -- Fiction

ISBN 0-670-01282-3; 978-0-670-01282-4

LC 2010030022

Twelve-year-old Foster McFee and her mother escape from her mother's abusive boyfriend and end up in the small town of Culpepper, West Virginia, where they use their strengths and challenge themselves to build a new life, with the help of the friends they make there.

"Bauer skillfully brings readers to the heart of Culpepper with rich depictions of contemporary small town and its residents and rhythms." Publ Wkly

★ **Peeled**. G.P. Putnam's Sons 2008 256p $16.99

Grades: 6 7 8 9 10 **Fic**

1. Ghost stories 2. School stories 3. Farm life -- Fiction 4. Journalism -- Fiction 5. New York (State) -- Fiction

ISBN 978-0-399-23475-0; 0-399-23475-6

LC 2007-42835

In an upstate New York farming community, high school reporter Hildy Biddle investigates a series of strange occurrences at a house rumored to be haunted.

This is "a warm and funny story full of likable, offbeat characters led by a strongly voiced, independently minded female protagonist on her way to genuine, well-earned maturity." SLJ

★ **Squashed**; [by] Joan Bauer. 1st G.P. Putnam's Sons ed; Puffin Books 2001 194p hardcover o.p. pa $7.99

Grades: 6 7 8 9 **Fic**

1. Iowa -- Fiction 2. Country life -- Fiction

ISBN 0-399-23750-X; 0-14-240426-8 pa

LC 2001-18595

A reissue of the title first published 1992 by Delacorte Press

As sixteen-year-old Ellie pursues her two goals—growing the biggest pumpkin in Iowa and losing twenty pounds herself—she strengthens her relationship with her father and meets a young man with interests similar to her own.

"Skillful plot development and strong characterization are real stengths here. Ellie's perseptive, intelligent, and funny narrative keeps the story lively right up to its satisfying conclusion." SLJ

Stand tall. Putnam 2002 182p $16.99; pa $6.99

Grades: 5 6 7 8 **Fic**

1. Divorce -- Fiction 2. Grandfathers -- Fiction

ISBN 0-399-23473-X; 0-14-240148-X pa

LC 2002-23876

Tree, a six-foot-three-inch twelve-year-old, copes with his parents' recent divorce and his failure as an athlete by helping his grandfather, a Vietnam vet and recent amputee, and Sophie, a new girl at school

The "swiftly paced story artfully blends poignant and outright funny moments, resulting in a triumphant tale that will resonate with many young readers." Publ Wkly

Bauer, Marion Dane, 1938-

Little dog, lost; Marion Dane Bauer ; with illustrations by Jennifer Bell. Atheneum Books for Young Readers 2012 197 p. ill. (hardcover) $14.99

Grades: 4 5 6 7   **Fic**

1. Dogs -- Fiction 2. Picture books for children 3. Interpersonal relations -- Fiction 4. Novels in verse 5. Parks -- Fiction 6. Loneliness -- Fiction 7. City and town life -- Fiction

ISBN 1442434236; 9781442434233; 9781442434257

LC 2011034024

This book tells the tale of "three needy creatures." Buddy the dog is "re-homed with a clueless though kind woman" after her family moves; Mark "feels his life is empty without the dog he desperately needs but his mother won't permit"; and "Charles Larue, the aging caretaker of a nearby mansion . . . spends his lonely days waiting for something—anything—to bring meaning to his life." The story is written in "[l]ong, thin lines of free-verse text." Additionally, "black-and-white illustrations" are included. (Kirkus)

★ **On** my honor. Clarion Bks. 1986 90p $15

Grades: 4 5 6 7   **Fic**

1. Accidents -- Fiction

ISBN 0-89919-439-7

LC 86-2679

A Newbery Medal honor book, 1987

When his best friend drowns while they are both swimming in a treacherous river that they had promised never to go near, Joel is devastated and terrified at having to tell both sets of parents the terrible consequences of their disobedience

"Bauer's association of Joel's guilt with the smell of the polluted river on his skin is particularly noteworthy. Its miasma almost rises off the pages. Descriptions are vivid, characterization and dialogue natural, and the style taut but unforced. A powerful, moving book." SLJ

Beaty, Andrea

Cicada summer. Amulet Books 2008 167p $15.95

Grades: 4 5 6 7   **Fic**

1. Illinois -- Fiction 2. Siblings -- Fiction 3. Bereavement -- Fiction

ISBN 978-0-8109-9472-0; 0-8109-9472-0

LC 2007-22266

Twelve-year-old Lily mourns her brother, and has not spoken since the accident she feels she could of prevented but the summer Tinny comes to town she is the only one who realizes Lily's secret.

"This is compelling fiction that will be a hit with young readers. . . . Rich and thought-provoking and yet . . . accessible." Horn Book

Dorko the magnificent; by Andrea Beaty. Amulet Books 2013 213 p. (hardcover) $16.95

Grades: 3 4 5 6   **Fic**

1. Magicians -- Fiction 2. Grandmothers -- Fiction 3. Humorous stories 4. Family life -- Fiction 5. Magic tricks -- Fiction

ISBN 1419706381; 9781419706387

LC 2012045674

In this book by Andrea Beaty "Robbie loves magic and he's good at it—sort of. When Grandma Melvyn moves in and takes over his room, Robbie discovers that she was once an internationally renowned magician and learns about the heartache that turned her into a bitter woman. Against all odds, Robbie and Grandma Melvyn form an uneasy alliance to show the world—or at least the kids of Hobson Elementary School—that he is a true magician." (Publisher's note)

Beaufrand, Mary Jane

Primavera; by Mary Jane Beaufrand. 1st ed.; Little, Brown 2007 260p $16.99

Grades: 6 7 8 9   **Fic**

1. Artists 2. Painters 3. Artists -- Fiction 4. Renaissance -- Fiction 5. Italy -- History -- 0-1559 -- Fiction

ISBN 978-0-316-01644-5; 0-316-01644-6

LC 2006025288

Growing up in Renaissance Italy, Flora sees her family's fortunes ebb, but encounters with the artist Botticelli and the guidance of her nurse teach her to look past the material world to the beauty already in her life.

"Political, historical, and art historical details provide a canvas on which this tale of murder, intrigue, and young romance is played out, but are painted with a broad stroke." SLJ

The **river**. Little, Brown 2010 215p il $16.99

Grades: 8 9 10 11 12   **Fic**

1. Mystery fiction 2. Moving -- Fiction 3. Oregon -- Fiction 4. Hotels and motels -- Fiction

ISBN 978-0-316-04168-3; 0-316-04168-8

LC 2008-50222

Teenager Ronnie's life is transformed by the murder of a ten-year-old neighbor for whom she babysat, and who had helped Ronnie adjust to living at a country inn on the banks of the Santiam River in Hoodoo, Oregon.

"With its blend of richly realistic character and slightly uncanny ambience, this will be a favorite with fans of mysteries that tug the heartstrings." Bull Cent Child Books

Beck, Ian

Pastworld. Bloomsbury Children's Books 2009 355p $16.99

Grades: 7 8 9 10   **Fic**

1. Science fiction 2. Homicide -- Fiction 3. Amusement parks -- Fiction 4. London (England) -- Fiction 5. Genetic engineering -- Fiction

ISBN 1-59990-040-8; 978-1-59990-040-7

LC 2009-8706

In 2050, while visiting Pastworld, a Victorian London theme park, teenaged Caleb meets seventeen-year-old Eve, a Pastworld inhabitant who has no knowledge of the modern world, and both become pawns in a murderer's diabolical plan that reveals disturbing truths about the teenagers' origins.

"Suspenseful and gripping. This spellbinding page-turner will keep readers on the edge of their seats." SLJ

The **secret** history of Tom Trueheart. Greenwillow Books 2007 341p il hardcover o.p. lib bdg $17.89; pa $6.99

Grades: 4 5 6 7   **Fic**
1. Fairy tales 2. Brothers -- Fiction 3. Storytelling -- Fiction
ISBN 978-0-06-115210-8; 0-06-115210-2; 978-0-06-115211-5 lib bdg; 0-06-115211-0 lib bdg; 978-0-06-115212-2 pa; 0-06-115212-9 pa

LC 2006043362

When young Tom Trueheart's seven older brothers all go missing during their adventures in the Land of Stories, he embarks on a perilous mission to save them and to capture the rogue story-writer who wants to do away with the heroes.

This "is a charming twist on fairy tales. . . . Silhouette drawings interspersed throughout add a wonderfully nostalgic touch." SLJ

Another title about Tom Trueheart is:
Tom Trueheart and the Land of Dark Stories (2008)

Tom Trueheart and the Land of Dark Stories. Greenwillow Books 2008 369p il $16.99; lib bdg $17.89

Grades: 4 5 6 7   **Fic**
1. Fairy tales 2. Brothers -- Fiction 3. Storytelling -- Fiction
ISBN 978-0-06-115213-9; 0-06-115213-7; 978-0-06-115214-6 lib bdg; 0-06-115214-5 lib bdg

"The Land of Dark Stories is guarded by the lighthouse of doom. Wolves and goblins patrol every forest and road. Here, the most frightening tales unfold. . . . When the villain Ormestone kidnaps Tom's six older brothers and their princess brides, Tom knows he must make the journey to the dark land." Publisher's note

Becker, Tom

Darkside; [by] Tom Becker. Orchard Books 2008 294p (Darkside) $16.99

Grades: 7 8 9 10   **Fic**
1. Horror fiction 2. Supernatural -- Fiction 3. London (England) -- Fiction
ISBN 978-0-545-03739-6; 0-545-03739-5

LC 2007-23634

Jonathan Starling's father is in an asylum and his home has been attacked when, while running away from kidnappers, he stumbles upon Darkside, a terrifying and hidden part of London ruled by the descendents of Jack the Ripper, where Jonathan is in mortal danger if he cannot find the way out.

"This fast-paced, unrelentingly entertaining story has plenty of suspense and lots of scares." Booklist

Followed by: Lifeblood (2008)

Lifeblood. Orchard Books 2008 279p (Darkside) $16.99

Grades: 7 8 9 10   **Fic**
1. Horror fiction 2. Supernatural -- Fiction 3. London

(England) -- Fiction
ISBN 978-0-545-03742-6; 0-545-03742-5

LC 2007051180

Sequel to: Darkside (2008)

As Jonathan searches London's Darkside for the same murderer that his mother was seeking when she disappeared twelve years earlier, it becomes clear that it is Jonathan who is being hunted.

"Horror lovers will thrill to this gleeful gothic bloodbath." Horn Book Guide

Bedford, Martyn

★ **Flip**. Wendy Lamb Books 2011 261p $16.99; lib bdg $19.99; ebook $10.99

Grades: 8 9 10 11 12   **Fic**
1. Supernatural -- Fiction 2. Great Britain -- Fiction
ISBN 978-0-385-73990-0; 0-385-73990-7; 978-0-385-90808-5 lib bdg; 0-385-90808-3 lib bdg; 978-0-375-89855-6 ebook; 0-375-89855-7 ebook

LC 2010-13158

A teenager wakes up inside another boy's body and faces a life-or-death quest to return to his true self or be trapped forever in the wrong existence.

"Bedford packs so much exhilarating action and cleanly cut characterizations into his teen debut that readers will be catapulted head-first into Alex's strange new world." Kirkus

Beil, Michael

The **Red** Blazer Girls: the mistaken masterpiece. Alfred A. Knopf 2011 309p $16.99; lib bdg $19.99

Grades: 5 6 7 8   **Fic**
1. School stories 2. Mystery fiction 3. Puzzles -- Fiction 4. Art thefts -- Fiction
ISBN 978-0-375-86740-8; 0-375-86740-6; 978-0-375-96740-5 lib bdg; 0-375-96740-0 lib bdg

LC 2010030006

Sophie and her friends, who call themselves The Red Blazer Girls, embark on solving a case involving mistaken identities, switched paintings, and some priceless family heirlooms.

"Sophie narrates with humor and self-effacing aplomb. Visual evidence inserted in the text invites reader participation." Kirkus

Beil, Michael D.

★ The **Red** Blazer Girls: the ring of Rocamadour. Alfred A. Knopf 2009 299p $15.99; lib bdg $18.99

Grades: 5 6 7 8   **Fic**
1. School stories 2. Mystery fiction 3. Puzzles -- Fiction 4. Friendship -- Fiction
ISBN 978-0-375-84814-8; 0-375-84814-2; 978-0-375-94814-5 lib bdg; 0-375-94814-7 lib bdg

LC 2008-25254

Catholic-schooled seventh-graders Sophie, Margaret, Rebecca, and Leigh Ann help an elderly neighbor solve a puzzle her father left for her estranged daughter twenty years ago.

"The dialogue is fast and funny, the clues are often solvable." Booklist

Other titles about the Red Blazer Girls are:
The Red Blazer Girls: the vanishing violin (2010)

The Red Blazer Girls: the mistaken masterpiece (2011)

The **Red** Blazer Girls: The vanishing violin. Alfred A. Knopf 2010 329p $16.99; lib bdg $19.99
Grades: 5 6 7 8   **Fic**
1. Mystery fiction 2. Violins -- Fiction
ISBN 978-0-375-86103-1; 0-375-86103-3; 978-0-375-96103-8 lib bdg; 0-375-96103-8 lib bdg
"Sophie, Margaret, Rebecca, and Leigh Ann . . . find themselves in the midst of several interlocking mysteries, mostly involving violins. . . . Beil has lost none of his edge when it comes to setting up sleuthing scenarios and offering kids codes and clues that will intrigue (or drive them crazy). Smartly plotted, smartly played." Booklist

Bell, Braden
The **kindling**; Braden Bell. Sweetwater Books 2012 291 p. (alk. paper) $14.99
Grades: 5 6 7 8 9   **Fic**
1. Occult fiction 2. Puberty -- Fiction 3. Magic -- Fiction 4. Kidnapping -- Fiction 5. Middle schools -- Fiction
ISBN 1462110274; 9781462110278
LC 2012011285
In this book, the three pubescent main characters discover they have magic powers. "This trio, under the watchful eyes of their teachers, is 'kindling,' meaning special powers they did not know they had are igniting. They are slated to join their teachers as Magi, Warriors of the Light, and will need to learn the tricks of the trade from them to fight off the darkhands from the Otherwhere, who have been kidnapping random children." (Voice of Youth Advocates)

Bell, Cathleen Davitt
Little blog on the prairie. Bloomsbury 2010 276p $16.99
Grades: 6 7 8   **Fic**
1. Camps -- Fiction 2. Weblogs -- Fiction 3. Wyoming -- Fiction 4. Frontier and pioneer life -- Fiction
ISBN 978-1-59990-286-9; 1-59990-286-9
LC 2009-46897
Thirteen-year-old Genevieve's summer at a frontier family history camp in Laramie, Wyoming, with her parents and brother is filled with surprises, which she reports to friends back home on the cell phone she sneaked in, and which they turn into a blog.
This is a "a lively journey with empathetic characters." Publ Wkly

Slipping. Bloomsbury 2008 215p $16.95
Grades: 6 7 8 9   **Fic**
1. Ghost stories 2. Death -- Fiction 3. Grandfathers -- Fiction
ISBN 978-1-59990-258-6; 1-59990-258-3
LC 2008-04420
Thirteen-year-old Michael and an unlikely group of allies journey to the river of the dead to help Michael's grandfather release his hold on a ghostly life and, in the process, heal wounds that have kept Michael's father distant.
"The balance between the supernatural and genuine human feelings creates a compelling mix." Booklist

Bell, Hilari
Fall of a kingdom; by Hilari Bell. Simon Pulse 2005 422 p. map (Simon Pulse teen fantasy) (paperback) $6.99
Grades: 7 8 9 10   **Fic**
1. Fantasy fiction 2. Persian mythology -- Fiction
ISBN 0689854145; 9780689854149
LC 2005588003
This is the first book in Hilari Bell's Farsala trilogy. "Stories are told of a hero who will come to Farsala's aid when the need is greatest. But for thousands of years the prosperous land of Farsala has felt no such need. . . . Three young people are less sure of Farsala's invincibility. Jiaan, Soraya, and Kavi see Time's Wheel turning, with Farsala headed toward the Flames of Destruction. What they cannot see is how inextricably their lives are linked to Farsala's fate." (Publisher's note)

Forging the sword. Simon & Schuster Books for Young Readers 2006 494p (Farsala trilogy) $17.99
Grades: 7 8 9 10   **Fic**
1. Fantasy fiction
ISBN 978-0-689-85416-3; 0-689-85416-1
LC 2005017730
Farsalans, including Lady Soraya and her half-brother, Jiaan, Kavi, and others, work relentlessly and often secretly in their shared strategies regarding the ultimate defeat of the Hrum.
"Bell brings the Farsala Trilogy to a rousing conclusion. . . . The author maintains the complexity of her main characters and the intensity of the story line." Booklist

The **Goblin** Gate. HarperTeen 2010 377p map $16.99
Grades: 5 6 7 8   **Fic**
1. Fantasy fiction 2. Magic -- Fiction 3. Witches -- Fiction 5. Knights and knighthood -- Fiction
ISBN 978-0-06-165102-1; 0-06-165102-8
Sequel to: The Goblin Wood (2003)
Jeriah uncovers a web of political intrigue while trying to obtain a spell from Master Lazure that might allow him to rescue his brother Tobin from the Otherworld, where he was taken by the beguiling hedgewitch Makenna and her legion of goblins.
"Author Bell has long shown herself adept in portraying social systems and political intrigues; here that talent is married to sympathetic characters struggling through challenges both external and internal." Horn Book
Followed by: The Goblin war (2011)

The **Goblin** War. HarperTeen 2011 314p $17.99
Grades: 5 6 7 8   **Fic**
1. War stories 2. Fantasy fiction 3. Magic -- Fiction 4. Goblins -- Fiction
ISBN 978-0-06-165105-2; 0-06-165105-2; 978-0-06-165106-9 lib bdg; 0-06-165106-0 lib bdg
LC 2010040322
Sequel to: The Goblin Gate (2010)
After crossing over from the Otherworld where they have been trapped in mortal danger, Tobin and Makenna must figure out how to stop an army of barbarians from taking over their Realm.

"Picking up at the immediate end of the previous novel, Bell ratchets up the suspense immediately and makes this finale a true page turner. . . . This rewarding resolution caps off a fascinating, engaging trilogy that holds appeal for a diverse fantasy audience." Kirkus

The **Goblin** Wood. Eos/HarperCollins Pubs. 2003 294p hardcover o.p. pa $7.99

Grades: 5 6 7 8   Fic
1. Fantasy fiction
ISBN 0-06-051371-3; 0-06-51373-3 pa
      LC 2002-15281

A young Hedgewitch, an idealistic knight, and an army of clever goblins fight against the ruling hierarchy that is trying to rid the land of all magical creatures.

"Leavened by humor and a dollop of romance, this well-crafted fantasy adventure demonstrates Bell's talent for creating enduring characters and worlds." Booklist

Other titles in this trilogy are:
The Goblin Gate (2010)
The Goblin War (2011)

★ The **last** knight. Eos 2007 357p (Knight and rogue) $16.99; lib bdg $17.89

Grades: 7 8 9 10   Fic
1. Fantasy fiction 2. Knights and knighthood -- Fiction
ISBN 978-0-06-082503-4; 0-06-082503-0; 978-0-06-082504-1 lib bdg; 0-06-082504-9 lib bdg
      LC 2006-36427

In alternate chapters, eighteen-year-old Sir Michael Sevenson, an anachronistic knight errant, and seventeen-year-old Fisk, his streetwise squire, tell of their noble quest to bring Lady Ceciel to justice while trying to solve her husband's murder.

"The novel is brimming with saved-by-a-hair escapades and fast-paced realistic action. . . . This well-created fantasy is a great read with worthwhile moral issues pertinent to its intended audience." SLJ

Other titles in this series are:
Rogue's home (2008)
Player's ruse (2010)

Rise of a hero. 2005 462p (Farsala trilogy) $16.95; pa $6.99

Grades: 7 8 9 10   Fic
1. Fantasy fiction
ISBN 0-689-85415-3; 0-689-85417-X pa
      LC 2003-25164

Although the Hrum believe their war against Farsala is nearly over, Soraya has strategic information that will help if she can reach Jiaan and Kavi and their separate resistance movements, but discord and Time's Wheel seem destined to keep them apart.

"With a palpable sense of danger and an ending that promises much to be revealed, this is a sequel that will fly off the shelf." Booklist

Followed by Forging the sword (2006)

Shield of stars. Simon & Schuster Books For Young Readers 2007 267p (The shield, the sword and the crown) $16.99

Grades: 6 7 8 9   Fic
1. Fantasy fiction
ISBN 978-1-4169-0594-3; 1-4169-0594-4
      LC 2005-35571

When the Justice he works for is condemned for treason, fourteen-year-old and semi-reformed pickpocket Weasel sets out to find a notorious bandit who may be able to help save his master's life.

"Bell's trademark shades of gray help shift readers' perceptions of the characters and their motivations, adding an unusual layer of depth that moves this story beyond simple adventure. Weasel's choices are complex and believable." SLJ

Other titles in this series are:
Sword of waters (2008)
Crown of earth (2009)

Traitor's son; by Hilari Bell. Houghton 2012 250 p. (The Raven duet) $16.99

Grades: 7 8 9 10 11 12   Fic
1. Science fiction 2. Magic -- Fiction 3. Bioterrorism -- Fiction 4. Environmental degradation -- Fiction 5. Native Americans -- Alaska -- Fiction 6. Alaska -- Fiction 7. Shapeshifting -- Fiction 8. Indians of North America -- Alaska -- Fiction
ISBN 9780547196213
      LC 2011012241

This book offers a "companion to [the book] 'Trickster's Girl'" where protagonist "Raven works with a different human to try to fix the world's ecosystem." (School Libr J) Terrorists "have released a bioplague that, unchecked, will destroy the world's trees and humanity along with them. . . . Raven, the shape-shifter . . . must persuade the reluctant 16-year-old Jason to accept Atalhanes' quest or doom will follow." (Booklist) Author "[Hilari] Bell blends an advanced technological society with a traditional tribal one." (School Libr J)

Trickster's girl. Houghton Mifflin Harcourt 2011 281p (The Raven duet) $16

Grades: 7 8 9 10   Fic
1. Fantasy fiction 2. Magic -- Fiction 3. Bereavement -- Fiction 4. Environmental degradation -- Fiction
ISBN 978-0-547-19620-6; 0-547-19620-2
      LC 2010-06785

In the year 2098, grieving her father and angry with her mother, fifteen-year-old Kelsa joins the magical Raven on an epic journey from Utah to Alaska to heal the earth by restoring the flow of magic that humans have disrupted.

The "degree of nuance will sit especially well with readers who prefer their speculative fiction to be character-driven, and they'll appreciate the compelling exploration of the ways the hopeful can cope with uncertainty." Bull Cent Child Books

Bell, Joanne

Juggling fire. Orca Book Publishers 2009 171p pa $12.95

Grades: 7 8 9 10   Fic
1. Missing persons -- Fiction 2. Wilderness survival -- Fiction 3. Father-daughter relationship -- Fiction 4.

Yukon River valley (Yukon and Alaska) -- Fiction
ISBN 978-1-55469-094-7; 1-55469-094-3

"Sixteen-year-old Rachel's father disappeared years earlier from her family's home in the Yukon wilderness. . . . The teen sets off on a trek through the tundra and forest with only her dog as a companion, hoping to find clues about her father's disappearance. . . . Bell beautifully captures the natural world through descriptions of the mountainous terrain as well as nail-biting encounters with bears and wolves. Rachel is a smart, resourceful narrator." SLJ

Bell, Juliet

Kepler's dream; Juliet Bell. G. P. Putnam's Sons 2012 242 p. (hardcover) $16.99

Grades: 5 6 7 8   **Fic**
1. Mystery fiction 2. Leukemia -- Fiction 3. Dysfunctional families -- Fiction 4. Cancer -- Fiction 5. Grandmothers -- Fiction 6. Books and reading -- Fiction 7. Albuquerque (N.M.) -- Fiction 8. Mystery and detective stories 9. Swindlers and swindling -- Fiction 10. Family life -- New Mexico -- Fiction
ISBN 0399256458; 9780399256455

LC 2011024136

This book tells the story of "Ella Mackenzie, a . . . fifth-going-on-sixth grader, [who] is sent to what she calls Broken Family Camp. Ella's family is broken . . . . Her mother has leukemia . . . and is about to have a stem cell transplant. Her father, who works as a guide at an outdoor travel adventure company, has literally gone fishing, as he has for most of Ella's childhood. . . . Ella is forced to spend the summer with the paternal grandmother she has never met." (New York Times)

Bell, Ted

★ **Nick** of time. St. Martin's Griffin 2008 434p il (Nick McIver time adventure) $17.95; pa $7.99

Grades: 6 7 8   **Fic**
1. Admirals 2. Statesmen 3. Historians 4. Fantasy fiction 5. Prime ministers 6. Adventure fiction 7. Memoirists 8. Cabinet members 9. Pirates -- Fiction 10. Members of Parliament 11. Nobel laureates for literature 12. World War, 1939-1945 -- Fiction 13. France -- History -- 1799-1815 -- Fiction
ISBN 978-0-312-38068-7; 0-312-38068-2; 978-0-312-58143-5 pa; 0-312-58143-2 pa

LC 2008-13634

First published 2000 by Xlibris

This novel is set in "England, 1939, on the eve of war. [12-year-old] Nick and his younger sister, Kate, live in a lighthouse on the smallest of the Channel Islands. Nick and Kate come to the aid of their father who is engaged in a . . . war of espionage with German U-boat wolf packs." (Publisher's note) "Grades five to eight." (Bull Cent Child Books)

"This is an immensely appealing book. . . . [The book is filled] with great battle scenes; lots of nautical jargon; and themes of courage, integrity, and honor." SLJ

Bellairs, John

★ The **curse** of the blue figurine. Dial Bks. for Young Readers 1983 200p hardcover o.p. pa $5.99

Grades: 5 6 7 8   **Fic**
1. Mystery fiction
ISBN 0-8446-7138-4; 0-14-240258-3 pa

LC 82-73217

The author "intertwines real concerns with sorcery in a seamless fashion, bringing dimension to his characters and events with expert timing and sharply honed atmosphere." Booklist

Other titles about Johnny Dixon and Professor Childermass are:
The chessmen of doom (1989)
The eyes of the killer robot (1986)
The mummy, the will and the crypt (1983)
The revenge of the wizard's ghost (1985)
The secret of the underground room (1990)
The spell of the sorcerer's skull (1984)
The trolley to yesterday (1989)

Bemis, John Claude

The **nine** pound hammer. Random House 2009 357p (The clockwork dark) $16.99; lib bdg $19.99

Grades: 6 7 8 9   **Fic**
1. Fantasy fiction 2. John Henry (Legendary character) 3. Orphans -- Fiction 4. Siblings -- Fiction
ISBN 978-0-375-85564-1; 0-375-85564-5; 978-0-375-95564-8 lib bdg; 0-375-95564-X lib bdg; 978-0-375-85565-8 pa; 0-375-85565-3 pa

LC 2008-22503

Drawn by the lodestone his father gave him years before, twelve-year-old orphan Ray travels south, meeting along the way various characters from folklore who are battling against an evil industry baron known as the Gog.

"If readers still possess a twinkle of wonder for the step-right-up days of side-show hucksterism, Bemis' debut will shock and amaze them." Booklist

Other books in this series are:
The Wolf Tree (2010)
The White City (2011)

The **White** City. Random House 2011 386p (The clockwork dark) $17.99; lib bdg $20.99

Grades: 6 7 8   **Fic**
1. Fantasy fiction 2. Adventure fiction 3. World's Columbian Exposition (1893: Chicago, Ill.) -- Fiction
ISBN 978-0-375-85568-9; 0-375-85568-8; 978-0-375-95568-6 lib bdg; 0-375-95568-2 lib bdg

LC 2010014252

Sequel to: The Wolf Tree (2010)

Ray, Conker, and their Rambler friends face the Gog and his Machine in a final struggle at the 1893 Chicago Exposition.

"This third book focuses the complicated plots of the trilogy into a consistent conclusion that forces the reader to consider nature's strengths and technology's dangers. . . . [Fans] will find more than enough action and thought for their . . . tastes." Voice Youth Advocates

The **Wolf** Tree. Random House 2010 385p (The clockwork dark) $16.99

Grades: 6 7 8   **Fic**
1. Fantasy fiction 2. Orphans -- Fiction
ISBN 978-0-375-85566-5; 0-375-85566-1

Sequel to: The nine pound hammer (2009)

Ray Cobb and the rest of the Ramblers must cross into the Gloaming and destroy the Gog's machine, which has started to spread a darkness over the land.

Bennett, Holly

Shapeshifter. Orca Book Publishers 2010 244p il pa $9.95

Grades: 7 8 9 10   Fic

1. Fantasy fiction

ISBN 978-1-55469-158-6; 1-55469-158-3

In order to escape the sorceror who wants to control her gift of song, Sive must transform herself into a deer, leave the Otherworld and find refuge in Eire, the land of mortals.

This is a "rich, slightly revisionist retelling of an ancient Irish legend. Basic human emotions—fear, love, greed—move the tale along, and short first-person narratives that personalize the action are interspersed throughout." Booklist

Bennett, Olivia

The **Allegra** Biscotti collection. Sourcebooks 2010 246p pa $8.99

Grades: 5 6 7 8   Fic

1. School stories 2. Fashion -- Fiction

ISBN 978-1-4022-4391-2; 1-4022-4391-X

By day, Emma Rose is a quiet, under-the-radar student who doesn't mix with the popular set. But when school's out, she becomes Queen of the Runway—whipping up cutting-edge designs.

"Credible characterizations and dialogue keep the novel real. . . . Bennett slips in detailed descriptions of the teens' outfits and Emma's designs, which appear in spot art." Publ Wkly

Followed by: Who what wear (2011)

Who what wear; illustrated by Georgia Rucker. Sourcebooks Jabberwocky 2011 231p il (The Allegra Biscotti collection) pa $8.99

Grades: 5 6 7 8   Fic

1. Fashion designers -- Fiction

ISBN 978-1-4022-4392-9; 1-4022-4392-8

"Emma Rose, 14, is still trying to hide her identity as New York City's up-and-coming fashion designer, Allegra Biscotti, while juggling the pitfalls of friendship and middle school. . . . The novel . . . comes to a satisfying, if predictable, conclusion. Interspersed throughout are illustrations of Allegra's designs. . . . Who What Wear is a great recommendation for kids who dream of a career in fashion." SLJ

Benoit, Charles

★ **You**. HarperTeen 2010 223p $16.99

Grades: 8 9 10 11 12   Fic

1. School stories 2. Conduct of life -- Fiction

ISBN 978-0-06-194704-9; 0-06-194704-0

LC 2009-43990

Fifteen-year-old Kyle discovers the shattering ramifications of the decisions he makes, and does not make, about school, the girl he likes, and his future.

"The rapid pace is well suited to the narrative. . . . In the end, Benoit creates a fully realized world where choices have impact and the consequences of both action and inaction can be severe." SLJ

Benway, Robin

Also known as; by Robin Benway. Walker Books For Young Readers 2013 320 p. (hardcover) $16.99

Grades: 7 8 9 10   Fic

1. Spy stories -- Fiction 2. School stories -- Fiction 3. Spies -- Fiction 4. Schools -- Fiction 5. High schools -- Fiction 6. New York (N.Y.) -- Fiction 7. Adventure and adventurers -- Fiction

ISBN 0802733905; 9780802733900

LC 2012026254

In this book, "Maggie is a safecracking prodigy and the only child of parents who work as spies for an organization called the Collective. When the family relocates to New York City, 16-year-old Maggie lands her first assignment: befriending Jesse, a cute private school boy, to gain access to the e-mail belonging to his magazine editor father, who is suspected to be planning a revealing story about the Collective." (Publishers Weekly)

"While the framework requires more than a little suspension of disbelief, the absolutely delightful cast of characters and snappy dialogue transform this book into a huge success." SLJ

The **extraordinary** secrets of April, May and June. Razorbill 2010 281p $16.99

Grades: 6 7 8 9 10   Fic

1. School stories 2. Sisters -- Fiction 3. Parapsychology -- Fiction

ISBN 978-1-59514-286-3; 1-59514-286-X

LC 2010-22777

When they recover supernatural powers from their childhoods in the aftermath of their parents' divorce, three sisters use their foretelling, invisibility, and mind-reading abilities to tackle school and family challenges.

"The sisters take turns narrating, and their distinct personalities and extremely funny, often barbed dialogue will keep readers laughing as each sibling learns to trust another amazing power: the strength of sisterhood." Publ Wkly

Berk, Ari

Death watch. Simon & Schuster Books for Young Readers 2011 527p (The Undertaken trilogy) $17.99

Grades: 7 8 9 10   Fic

1. Fantasy fiction 2. Father-son relationship -- Fiction

ISBN 978-1-4169-9115-1; 1-4169-9115-8

LC 2011006332

When seventeen-year-old Silas Umber's father disappears, Silas is sure it is connected to the powerful artifact he discovers, combined with his father's hidden hometown history, which compels Silas to pursue the path leading to his destiny and ultimately, to the discovery of his father, dead or alive.

"Berk's setting is atmospheric and creepy, fleshed out with a wealth of funereal traditions and folklore." Publ Wkly

Mistle child; Ari Berk. Simon & Schuster Books for Young Readers 2013 352 p. (The Undertaken trilogy) (hardcover) $17.99

Grades: 7 8 9 10   Fic

1. Ghost stories -- Fiction 2. Occult fiction -- Fiction 3. Undertakers and undertaking -- Fiction 4. Fantasy 5.

Ghosts -- Fiction 6. Families -- Fiction
ISBN 1416991174; 9781416991175; 9781442439160
LC 2012002977

This children's fantasy story, by Ari Berk, is book 2 of the "Understaken" series. "Silas Umber makes his way to the thoroughly haunted ancestral estate of Arvale to continue his training as a psychopomp. There he meets the specters of family going back thousands of years, becomes enmeshed in their subtle intrigues and undergoes a ritual that gives him the ability to banish the restless dead from this world forever. He also inadvertently frees a mad, ancient spirit." (Kirkus Reviews)

Berk, Josh

★ The **dark** days of Hamburger Halpin. Alfred A. Knopf 2010 250p $16.99; lib bdg $19.99
Grades: 8 9 10 11 12   **Fic**
   1. School stories 2. Deaf -- Fiction
   ISBN 978-0-375-85699-0; 0-375-85699-4; 978-0-375-95699-7 lib bdg; 0-375-95699-9 lib bdg
LC 2009-3118
"A coming-of-age mash-up of satire, realistic fiction, mystery, and ill-fated teen romance, The Dark Days of Hamburger Halpin is a genre-bending breakthrough that teens are going to love." SLJ

Guy Langman, crime scene procrastinator; Josh Berk. Alfred A. Knopf 2012 230 p. (lib. bdg.) $19.99
Grades: 7 8 9 10 11 12   **Fic**
   1. Clubs -- Fiction 2. Teenagers -- Fiction 3. Bereavement -- Fiction 4. Forensic sciences -- Fiction 5. Father-son relationship -- Fiction 6. Death -- Fiction 7. Grief -- Fiction 8. Humorous stories 9. New Jersey -- Fiction 10. Fathers and sons -- Fiction 11. Mystery and detective stories
   ISBN 037585701X; 9780375857010; 9780375897757; 9780375957017
LC 2011023864
This young adult book presents "wisecracking humor, teenage insecurity, and the occasional corpse. When underachieving class clown Guy Langman joins his school's forensics club, it's both to help deal him with the death of his father and to meet girls. Unfortunately, his plan to get closer to the lovely Raquel Flores fails when she falls for his best friend, Anoop. Guy throws himself into the lesson plan, mastering the art of fingerprinting and using his knowledge to pry into the mysteries of his father's checkered past. Then, during a forensics competition, he finds a real dead body. Convinced that recent events tie into one another, Guy tries to get to the heart of the matter, with help from the rest of the club." (Publishers Weekly)

Strike three, you're dead; Josh Berk. Knopf Books for Young Readers 2013 256 p. (hardback) $16.99
Grades: 3 4 5 6 7   **Fic**
   1. Mystery fiction 2. Baseball -- Fiction 3. Friendship -- Fiction 4. Murder -- Fiction 5. Best friends -- Fiction

6. Philadelphia Phillies (Baseball team) -- Fiction
ISBN 0375870083; 9780375870088; 9780375970085; 9780375987366
LC 2012023892
Edgar Award Finalist: Best Juvenile (2014)
In this mystery, by Josh Berk, twelve-year-old "Lenny, with the help of his buddies Mike and Other Mike, enters and wins a contest to guest-announce a Philadelphia Phillies game. When the hot rookie pitcher drops dead, the kids suspect that it's more than a previously undetected heart condition. They join another local sports fan and begin investigating the crime . . . while meeting their hero, flashy catcher Ramon Famosa, and other players in the process." (Publishers Weekly)

"Baseball aficionados will appreciate all the trivia Berk works into the story, with references to famous players and Phillies history scattered throughout. The wisecracking interplay between the boys is a strong point, though the solution to the mystery is really never in doubt." Pub Wkly

Berkeley, Jon

The **lightning** key. HarperCollins Pub. 2009 399p (The Wednesday tales) $16.99
Grades: 4 5 6 7   **Fic**
   1. Adventure fiction 2. Angels -- Fiction 3. Orphans -- Fiction
   ISBN 978-0-06-075513-3; 0-06-075513-X
   Sequel to: The tiger's egg (2007)
Now that Miles Wednesday has discovered his link to a magical Tiger's Egg, he's suddenly at the wheel of a great voyage. Determined to recover the stolen stone and free the trapped soul within, Miles sets off with Little, a Song Angel, and the wisecracking blind explorer Baltinglass of Araby.

"Middle and junior high students will delight in this story, the most lyrical and sharply written of the series." Voice Youth Advocates

The **tiger's** egg; [by] Jon Berkeley; illustrated by Brandon Dorman. HarperCollinsPublishers 2007 400p il (The Wednesday tales) $16.99; lib bdg $17.89
Grades: 4 5 6 7   **Fic**
   1. Adventure fiction 2. Angels -- Fiction 3. Circus -- Fiction 4. Tigers -- Fiction 5. Orphans -- Fiction
   ISBN 978-0-06-075510-2; 0-06-075510-5; 978-0-06-075511-9 lib bdg; 0-06-075511-3 lib bdg
LC 2006039842
Sequel to: The Palace of Laughter (2006)
While working for the newly revamped circus, orphaned eleven-year-old Miles gains information about his past and sets off with his angel companion, Little, on a quest to find a mystical tiger's egg before it falls into the hands of their nemesis, Cortado.

"This novel is engaging from beginning to end. Fantasy lovers will enjoy a variety of plot twists that will surprise even the most perceptive reader." Voice Youth Advocates
Followed by: The lightning key (2009)

Berlin, Eric

The **potato** chip puzzles; Eric Berlin; [drawings by Katrina Damkoehler] G.P. Putnam's Sons 2009 244p il $16.99; pa $7.99

Grades: 4 5 6 7 **Fic**
1. Mystery fiction 2. Puzzles -- Fiction 3. Contests
-- Fiction
ISBN 978-0-399-25198-6; 0-399-25198-7; 978-0-14-
241637-2 pa; 0-14-241637-1 pa
LC 2008-33698

Sequel to: The puzzling world of Winston Breen (2007)

Winston and his friends enter an all-day puzzle contest to
win fifty-thousand dollars for their school, but they must also
figure out who is trying to keep them from winning. Puzzles
for the reader to solve are included throughout the text.

"The pace is suspenseful but allows for pauses for problem-solving. The joy for both contestants and readers of this
brain-teasing mystery will be in the process." Kirkus

★ The **puzzling** world of Winston Breen; the
secret in the box. Putnam 2007 215p il $16.99;
pa $7.99
Grades: 4 5 6 7 **Fic**
1. Mystery fiction 2. Puzzles -- Fiction 3. Siblings
-- Fiction
ISBN 978-0-399-24693-7; 0-399-24693-2; 978-0-14-
241388-3 pa; 0-14-241388-7 pa
LC 2006-20531

Puzzle-crazy, twelve-year-old Winston and his ten-year-
old sister Katie find themselves involved in a dangerous
mystery involving a hidden ring. Puzzles for the reader to
solve are included throughout the text

"A delightfully clever mystery. . . . There is plenty of
suspense to engage readers." SLJ

Followed by: The potato chip puzzles (2009)

Bernard, Romily

Find me; Romily Bernard. HarperTeen, an imprint of HarperCollinsPublishers 2013 320 p. (hardback) $17.99
Grades: 7 8 9 10 11 12 **Fic**
1. Foster children -- Fiction 2. Teenagers -- Suicide --
Fiction 3. Computer hackers -- Fiction 4. Foster home
care -- Fiction 5. Mystery and detective stories
ISBN 0062229036; 9780062229038
LC 2013021519

In this book, "Tessa Waye was Wicket Tate's best friend
until five years ago when Wick's drug-dealing father drove
them apart. When Tessa commits suicide and her diary is
left on the teen's front steps, Wick suspects there might be
a dark reason she jumped to her death. Wick and her sister,
Lily, are now free of their criminal father, living a shiny new
life on the ritzy side of town with their foster parents. But
Wick . . . fears her father will come back for them." (School
Library Journal)

Bernobich, Beth

Fox & Phoenix. Viking 2011 360p $17.99
Grades: 7 8 9 10 **Fic**
1. Fantasy fiction 2. Magic -- Fiction 3. Princesses
-- Fiction 4. Apprentices -- Fiction 5. Kings and rulers
-- Fiction
ISBN 978-0-670-01278-7; 0-670-01278-5
LC 2011009388

Sixteen-year-old Kai, a magician's apprentice and former street tough, must travel to the Phoenix Empire, where
his friend Princess Lian is studying statecraft, and help her
escape so she can return home before her father, the king,
dies.

"The characters and creatures in this book are interesting
and believable; the plot is a compelling mixture of adventure, mystery, and fantasy. The most remarkable element,
however, is the world Beth Bernobich has created." Voice
Youth Advocates

Berry, Julie

All the truth that's in me; by Julie Berry. Viking
2013 288 p. (hardcover : alk. paper) $17.99
Grades: 7 8 9 10 11 12 **Fic**
1. Truth -- Fiction 2. Kidnapping -- Fiction 3.
Community life -- Fiction 4. War -- Fiction 5. Selective
mutism -- Fiction
ISBN 0670786152; 9780670786152
LC 2012043218

In this book by Julie Berry, "sixteen-year-old Judith is
still in love with Lucas, even after his father held her prisoner for two years and violently silenced her by cutting out
part of her tongue. Another girl went missing at the same
time and her body was found washed down a stream. Only
Judith knows the truth of what happened to Lottie, but her
muteness leaves her an outcast in the village, even from
her own mother, and the truth stays bottled up inside her."
(School Library Journal)

"Berry's novel is set in a claustrophobic village that
seems to resemble an early American colonial settlement.
Readers gradually learn "all the truth" from eighteen-year-
old narrator Judith, who speaks directly (though only in her
head) to her love, Lucas. Berry keeps readers on edge, tantalizing us with pieces of the puzzle right up until the gripping
conclusion." (Horn Book)

The **Amaranth** enchantment. Bloomsbury
U.S.A. Children's Books 2009 308p $16.99
Grades: 6 7 8 9 **Fic**
1. Fantasy fiction 2. Orphans -- Fiction 3.
Extraterrestrial beings -- Fiction
ISBN 978-1-59990-334-7; 1-59990-334-2
LC 2008-22354

Orphaned at age five, Lucinda, now fifteen, stands with
courage against the man who took everything from her, aided by a thief, a clever goat, and a mysterious woman called
the Witch of Amaranth, while the prince she knew as a child
prepares to marry, unaware that he, too, is in danger.

"A lively, quick, stylish, engaging first novel with some
lovely, familiar fairy-tale elements." Publ Wkly

The **scandalous** sisterhood of Prickwillow Place;
Julie Berry. Roaring Brook Press 2014 368 p. il-
lustrations (hardback) $15.99
Grades: 6 7 8 **Fic**
1. School stories 2. Humorous fiction 3. Murder --
Fiction 4. Humorous stories 5. Schools -- Fiction 6.
Boarding schools -- Fiction 7. Mystery and detective
stories 8. Ely (England) -- History -- 19th century --
Fiction 9. Great Britain -- History -- Victoria, 1837-
1901 -- Fiction
ISBN 1596439564; 9781596439566
LC 2014003249

In this middle grades book by Julie Berry, "the students of St. Etheldreda's School for Girls face a bothersome dilemma. Their irascible headmistress, Mrs. Plackett, and her surly brother, Mr. Godding, have been most inconveniently poisoned at Sunday dinner. Now the school will almost certainly be closed and the girls sent home--unless these seven very proper young ladies can hide the murders and convince their neighbors that nothing is wrong." (Publisher's note)

"Overall, this is a well-researched, clever, and deliciously dark comedy with an emphasis on female empowerment." SLJ

Includes bibliographical references

Bertagna, Julie

★ **Exodus**; [by] Julie Bertagna. Walker 2008 345p $16.95

Grades: 6 7 8 9 10   **Fic**

1. Science fiction 2. Floods -- Fiction 3. Greenhouse effect -- Fiction 4. Voyages and travels -- Fiction
ISBN 978-0-8027-9745-2; 0-8027-9745-8

LC 2007-23116

In the year 2100, as the island of Wing is about to be covered by water, fifteen-year-old Mara discovers the existence of New World sky cities that are safe from the storms and rising waters, and convinces her people to travel to one of these cities in order to save themselves.

"Astonishing in its scope and exhilarating in both its action and its philosophical inquiry." Booklist

Followed by: Zenith (2009)

Zenith. Walker & Co. 2009 340p $16.99

Grades: 6 7 8 9 10   **Fic**

1. Science fiction 2. Floods -- Fiction 3. Greenhouse effect -- Fiction 4. Voyages and travels -- Fiction
ISBN 978-0-8027-9803-9; 0-8027-9803-9
Sequel to: Exodus (2008)

After finding that New Mungo is not the refuge they sought, Mara, leaving Fox behind, again sets out to sea with a ship full of refugees and, with the help of the "Gipsea" boy Tuck, tries to find land at the top of the world that will be safe from storms and rising water.

"This is mostly Mara's story—a plucky, imperfect heroine leading the way to an uncertain future in a hostile world." Booklist

Beyer, Kat

The **demon** catchers of Milan; by Kat Beyer. Egmont, USA 2012 288 p. (Demon catchers of Milan trilogy) (hardcover) $16.99

Grades: 7 8 9 10 11   **Fic**

1. Occult fiction 2. Italy -- Fiction 3. Demoniac possession -- Fiction 4. Demonology -- Fiction 5. Milan (Italy) -- Fiction 6. Americans -- Italy -- Fiction 7. Family life -- Italy -- Fiction
ISBN 1606843141; 9781606843147; 9781606843154

LC 2011034348

This book is "a tale of demonic possession and a centuries-old family trade in exorcism." Mia's life "is upended when a horrifying demon enters and nearly kills her. After Giuliano Della Torre and his grandson Emilio, long-estranged relatives from Milan, arrive and drive it out, they talk Mia's reluctant parents into letting her return to Italy

with them." She shows a talent for the family business of exorcism. (Kirkus Reviews)

Bick, Ilsa J.

Ashes. Egmont USA 2011 465p $17.99; ebook $9.99

Grades: 8 9 10 11 12   **Fic**

1. Science fiction 2. Zombies -- Fiction 3. Wilderness survival -- Fiction
ISBN 978-1-60684-175-4; 978-1-60684-231-7 ebook

LC 2010-51825

Alex, a resourceful seventeen-year-old running from her incurable brain tumor, Tom, who has left the war in Afghanistan, and Ellie, an angry eight-year-old, join forces after an electromagnetic pulse sweeps through the sky and kills most of the world's population, turning some of those who remain into zombies and giving the others superhuman senses.

"Bick delivers an action-packed tale of an apocalypse unfolding. . . . [She] doesn't shy away from gore—one woman's guts 'boiled out in a dusky, desiccated tangle, like limp spaghetti'—but it doesn't derail the story's progress." Publ Wkly

Bickle, Laura

The **hallowed** ones; Laura Bickle. Graphia 2012 311 p. (paperback) $8.99

Grades: 7 8 9 10 11 12   **Fic**

1. Horror stories 2. Amish -- Fiction 3. Terrorism -- Fiction 4. Family life -- Fiction 5. Bioterrorism -- Fiction 6. Coming of age -- Fiction 7. Christian life -- Fiction
ISBN 0547859260; 9780547859262

LC 2012014800

This book follows "Katie [who] is [about] to taste the freedom of rumspringa, [when] the elders close the gates of her small Amish community. . . . Katie daringly ventures Outside to find true horror: vampires have decimated a small nearby town and apparently much of the world's population. . . . Her situation is further complicated when she rescues Alex, a handsome Outsider who may or may not be a carrier of the contagion that seemingly caused the vampirism epidemic." (Bulletin of the Center for Children's Books)

The **outside**; Laura Bickle. Houghton Mifflin Harcourt 2013 320 p. (hardcover) $16.99

Grades: 7 8 9 10 11 12   **Fic**

1. Horror fiction 2. Occult fiction 3. Vampires -- Fiction 4. Horror stories 5. Amish -- Fiction 6. Coming of age -- Fiction 7. Christian life -- Fiction
ISBN 0544000137; 9780544000131

LC 2012040065

Sequel to: The hallowed ones

This book is a sequel to Laura Bickle's "The Hallowed Ones." Katie, an exile from an Amish community, travels with "Alex and Ginger, the two outsiders she's befriended, seeking other survivors of the vampire plague that's unmade their world. . . . Discovering a group that's genetically engineered with immunity to vampires raises tension between them, pitting science against religion: Are these vampires aliens or mutants spawned in labs, rather than manifestations of demonic evil?" (Kirkus Reviews)

Bigelow, Lisa Jenn

Starting from here; by Lisa Jenn Bigelow. Marshall Cavendish Children 2012 282 p. (hardcover) $16.99

Grades: 8 9 10 11 12   **Fic**
1. School stories 2. Lesbians -- Fiction 3. Self-realization -- Fiction 4. Dogs -- Fiction 5. Schools -- Fiction 6. High schools -- Fiction 7. Fathers and daughters -- Fiction 8. Dating (Social customs) -- Fiction
ISBN 0761462333; 9780761462330; 9780761462347
           LC 2011040129

In this book by Lisa Jenn Bigelow, "Colby is about ready to give up on people: her girlfriend Rachel dumps her and immediately moves onto Colby's opposite (a nice Jewish guy who does well in school), her mom is dead, and her dad is a frequently absent truck driver to whom she still hasn't come out. Only her best friend, Van, can bring her out of her shell. Then she adopts Mo, a friendly but wary stray dog, and life starts to move again." (Bulletin of the Center for Children's Books)

Billingsley, Franny

★ **Chime**. Dial Books for Young Readers 2011 361p $17.99

Grades: 7 8 9 10 11 12   **Fic**
1. Guilt -- Fiction 2. Twins -- Fiction 3. Sisters -- Fiction 4. Stepmothers -- Fiction 5. Supernatural -- Fiction
ISBN 0-8037-3552-9; 978-0-8037-3552-1
           LC 2010-12140

"Since her stepmother's recent death, 17-year-old Briony Larkin knows that if she can keep two secrets--that she is a witch and that she is responsible for the accident that left Rose, her identical twin, mentally compromised--and remember to hate herself always, no other harm will befall her family in their Swampsea parsonage at the beginning of the twentieth century. The arrival of Mr. Clayborne, a city engineer, and his university-dropout son, Eldric, makes Briony's task difficult." (Booklist)

"Filled with eccentric characters—self-hating Briony foremost—and oddly beautiful language, this is a darkly beguiling fantasy." Publ Wkly

The **Folk** Keeper. Atheneum Bks. for Young Readers 1999 162p hardcover o.p. pa $4.99; pa $5.99

Grades: 5 6 7 8   **Fic**
1. Fantasy fiction
ISBN 0-689-82876-4; 0-689-84461-1 pa; 9780689844614 pa
           LC 98-48778
Boston Globe Horn Book Winner (2000)

Orphaned Corinna disguises herself as a boy to pose as a Folk Keeper, one who keeps the supernatural Folk underground at bay. She discovers her heritage as a seal maiden when she is summoned to become the Folk Keeper for a wealthy family in their manor by the sea. "Ages ten to fourteen." (N Y Times Book Rev)

"The intricate plot, vibrant characters, dangerous intrigue, and fantastical elements combine into a truly remarkable novel steeped in atmosphere." Horn Book

Binding, Tim

★ **Sylvie** and the songman; with illustrations by Angela Barrett. Random House 2009 339p il $15.99; lib bdg $18.99

Grades: 5 6 7 8   **Fic**
1. Fantasy fiction
ISBN 978-0-385-75157-5; 0-385-75159-1; 978-0-385-75159-9 lib bdg; 0-385-75159-1 lib bdg

"Sylvie's composer father . . . goes missing and that's the first odd thing that interrupts her happy routine. Next, the animals seem to have lost their voices. The third is the arrival of the eerie, malevolent Woodpecker Man. . . . The dense narrative is packed with surreal imagery. . . . It's a testament to Binding's assured writing that the abstractions become visceral thrills, like a dream you just can't shake. . . . An unforgettable tale." Booklist

Bingham, Kelly

★ **Shark** girl. Candlewick Press 2007 276p $16.99; pa $8.99

Grades: 7 8 9 10   **Fic**
1. Novels in verse 2. Artists -- Fiction 3. Amputees -- Fiction
ISBN 978-0-7636-3207-6; 0-7636-3207-4; 978-0-7636-4627-1 pa; 0-7636-4627-X pa
           LC 2006049120

After a shark attack causes the amputation of her right arm, fifteen-year-old Jane, an aspiring artist, struggles to come to terms with her loss and the changes it imposes on her day-to-day life and her plans for the future.

"In carefully constructed, sparsely crafted free verse, Bingham's debut novel offers a strong view of a teenager struggling to survive and learn to live again." Booklist

Birdsall, Jeanne

★ The **Penderwicks**; a summer tale of four sisters, two rabbits, and a very interesting boy. Knopf 2005 262p (The Penderwicks) $15.95; lib bdg $17.77; pa $6.99

Grades: 3 4 5 6   **Fic**
1. Sisters -- Fiction 2. Single parent family -- Fiction
ISBN 0-375-83143-6; 0-375-93143-0 lib bdg; 0-440-42047-4 pa
           LC 2004-20364

"Four sisters—Rosalind, Skye, Jane, and Batty—spend a few weeks with their father and dog at a cottage on the grounds of a stately home in the Berkshires, where they complicate the lives of a handsome gardener, a lonely boy, and the boy's officious mother. . . . Grades four to seven." (Bull Cent Child Books)

"This comforting family story . . . [offers] . . . four marvelously appealing sisters, true childhood behavior . . . , and a writing style that will draw readers close." Booklist

The **Penderwicks** at Point Mouette. Alfred A. Knopf 2011 295p (The Penderwicks) $16.99

Grades: 4 5 6 7   **Fic**
1. Maine -- Fiction 2. Summer -- Fiction 3. Vacations -- Fiction 4. Family life -- Fiction
ISBN 978-0-375-85851-2; 0-375-85851-2

This is the third book about the Penderwick family, who appeared previously in The Penderwicks (2005) and The Penderwicks on Gardam Street (2008). "When summer comes around, it's off to the beach for Rosalind . . . and off to Maine with Aunt Claire for the rest of the Penderwick girls, as well as their old friend, Jeffrey. That leaves Skye as OAP (oldest available Penderwick). . . . Things look good as they settle into their cozy cottage. . . . But can Skye hold it together long enough to figure out Rosalind's directions about not letting Batty explode? Will Jane's Love Survey come to a tragic conclusion after she meets the alluring Dominic? . . . And will Jeffrey be able to keep peace between the girls?" (Publisher's note) "Intermediate." (Horn Book)

"Balancing the novel's comedy is an affecting, neatly crafted subplot that builds up to the emotionally charged revelation involving Jeffrey. From start to finish, this is a summer holiday to savor." Publ Wkly

The **Penderwicks** on Gardam Street; [illustrations by David Frankland] Alfred A. Knopf 2008 307p il $15.99; lib bdg $18.99

Grades: 3 4 5 6 7 **Fic**

1. Sisters -- Fiction 2. Family life -- Fiction 3. Massachusetts -- Fiction 4. Dating (Social customs) -- Fiction

ISBN 978-0-3758-4090-6; 978-0-375-94090-3 lib bdg

LC 2007-49232

Sequel to: The Penderwicks (2005)

The four Penderwick sisters are faced with the unimaginable prospect of their widowed father dating, and they hatch a plot to stop him.

"Laugh-out-loud moments abound and the humor comes naturally from the characters and situations. . . . This is a book to cherish." SLJ

Birdseye, Tom

Storm Mountain. Holiday House 2010 135p $16.95

Grades: 4 5 6 7 **Fic**

1. Adventure fiction 2. Cousins -- Fiction 3. Blizzards -- Fiction 4. Mountaineering -- Fiction 5. Washington (State) -- Fiction 6. Wilderness survival -- Fiction

ISBN 978-0-8234-2130-5; 0-8234-2130-9

LC 2010005768

Two thirteen-year-old cousins Cat and Ty are trapped in a blizzard on the same treacherous mountain in the Cascades that claimed the lives of their world-famous, mountain-climber, twin fathers exactly two years earlier.

"Birdseye's prose, full of careening action, melodrama and overwrought similes, reflects Ty's bulldozing personality. Add believable characters, the author's mountain-climbing expertise and a tear-jerking conclusion, and there's plenty here for young adventure enthusiasts." Kirkus

Black, Bekka

★ **IDrakula.** Sourcebooks/Fire 2010 150p pa $9.99

Grades: 7 8 9 10 **Fic**

1. Horror fiction 2. Vampires -- Fiction

ISBN 978-1-4022-4465-0 pa; 1-4022-4465-7 pa

This is a "take on Bram Stoker's Dracula—told exclusively through text messages, web browser screens, e-mails, and various photo and PDF attachments. . . . Black's story-telling instinct . . . consistently proves itself able to transcend gimmick. The format . . . actually lends the book a chilling sort of one-shock-per-page pulse. . . . Fast, inventive, creepy, and sure to be popular." Booklist

Black, Holly, 1971-

Black heart; Holly Black. Margaret K. McElderry Books 2012 296 p. (The curse workers) (hardcover) $17.99

Grades: 7 8 9 10 **Fic**

1. Love stories 2. Science fiction 3. Brothers -- Fiction 4. Organized crime -- Fiction 5. Love -- Fiction 6. Criminals -- Fiction

ISBN 9781442403468; 9781442403482

LC 2011028143

This book, the final volume of the Curse Workers trilogy, continues to follow "Cassel . . . [who has] figured out the truth about himself and signed on as a Fed-in-training, as has his charming and utterly unreliable older brother. But of course things don't go as planned; there are a lot of long cons Cassel has set in play or disrupted whose ripples are still being felt. And there's Lila, Cassel's best friend and the love of his life, who is also the rising head of a crime family" and who hates Cassel's guts." (Kirkus)

★ **Doll** bones; Holly Black. 1st ed. Margaret K. McElderry Books 2013 256 p. (hardcover) $16.99

Grades: 5 6 7 8 **Fic**

1. Ghost stories 2. Dolls -- Fiction 3. Adventure fiction 4. Ghosts -- Fiction 5. Friendship -- Fiction 6. Family problems -- Fiction 7. Adventure and adventurers -- Fiction

ISBN 1416963987; 9781416963981; 9781442474871

LC 2012018299

Newberry Honor Book (2104)

In this book, by Holly Black, illustrated by Eliza Wheeler, "a doll that may be haunted leads three friends on a thrilling adventure. . . . Zach, Poppy, and Alice have been . . . playing one continuous, ever-changing game. . . . Ruling over all is the Great Queen, . . . cursing those who displease her. . . . Zach and Alice and Poppy set off on one last adventure to lay the Queen's ghost to rest. But nothing goes according to plan, and . . . creepy things begin to happen." (Publisher's note)

"Veteran Black packs both heft and depth into a deceptively simple (and convincingly uncanny) narrative. . . . A few rich metaphors . . . are woven throughout the story, as every encounter redraws the blurry lines between childishness and maturity, truth and lies, secrecy and honesty, magic and madness. Spooky, melancholy, elegiac and ultimately hopeful; a small gem." Kirkus

The **iron** trial; Holly Black, Cassandra Clare. First edition Scholastic Press 2014 304 p. illustrations (Magisterium) (hardcover) $17.99

Grades: 4 5 6 7 8 **Fic**

1. Fantasy fiction 2. Magic -- Fiction

ISBN 0545522250; 9780545522250

LC 2014937300

In this fantasy novel by Holly Black and Cassandra Clare, part of the Magisterium series, "most kids would do anything to pass the Iron Trial. Not Callum Hunt. He wants to fail. All his life, Call has been warned by his father to stay away from magic. If he succeeds at the Iron Trial and is admitted into the Magisterium, he is sure it can only mean bad things for him." (Publisher's note)

"The third-person narration, filtered through Callum's delightfully insecure-and-overcompensating-with-snarky-bravado perspective, carries a tone that will likely have readers chortling in recognition. A promising beginning to a complex exploration of good and evil, as well as friendship's loyalty." Kirkus

Red glove. Margaret K. McElderry Books 2011 325p (The curse workers) $17.99

Grades: 7 8 9 10   **Fic**

1. Science fiction 2. Magic -- Fiction 3. Brothers -- Fiction 4. Criminals -- Fiction 6. Swindlers and swindling -- Fiction

ISBN 1-4424-0339-X; 978-1-4424-0339-0

LC 2010-31884

Sequel to: White cat (2010)

When federal agents learn that seventeen-year-old Cassel Sharpe, a powerful transformation worker, may be of use to them, they offer him a deal to join them rather than the mobsters for whom his brothers work.

This offers "a sleek a stylish blend of urban fantasy and crime noir." Booklist

★ The **white** cat. Margaret K. McElderry Books 2010 310p (The curse workers) $17.99

Grades: 7 8 9 10   **Fic**

1. Science fiction 2. Memory -- Fiction 3. Brothers -- Fiction 4. Criminals -- Fiction 5. Swindlers and swindling -- Fiction

ISBN 978-1-416-96396-7; 1-416-96396-0

LC 2009-33979

When Cassel Sharpe discovers that his older brothers have used him to carry out their criminal schemes and then stolen his memories, he figures out a way to turn their evil machinations against them.

This "starts out with spine-tingling terror, and information is initially dispensed so sparingly, readers will be hooked." Booklist

Another title in this series is:

Red glove (2011)

Black, Peter Jay

Urban outlaws; Peter Jay Black. Bloomsbury USA Childrens 2014 288 p. illustration (hardback) $16.99

Grades: 5 6 7 8   **Fic**

1. Science fiction 2. Ability -- Fiction 3. Orphans -- Fiction 4. Criminals -- Fiction 5. Adventure and adventurers 6. Computers -- Fiction 7. Adventure and adventurers -- Fiction

ISBN 1619634007; 9781619634008

LC 2014005604

In this middle-grades book, by Peter Jay Black, "deep beneath the city live five extraordinary kids: world-famous hacker Jack, gadget geek Charlie, free runner Slink, communications chief Obi, and decoy expert Wren. Orphans bonded over their shared sense of justice, the kids have formed the Urban Outlaws, a group dedicated to outsmarting criminals and handing out their stolen money through Random Acts of Kindness (R.A.K.s)." (Publisher's note)

"Five orphans—Jack, Charlie, Wren, Obi, and Slink—have made a home for themselves in a WWII bunker under the London subway. They are skilled in various ways—technological savvy, surveillance, and physical prowess in particular—and work together as the Urban Outlaws, using their knowledge to play Robin Hood against local criminals and sharing the benefits of their activities with those less fortunate than themselves...The characters are warm and well developed and will appeal to reluctant readers across middle school. This new series will be an excellent choice for younger fans of Alex Rider." Booklist

Other titles in the series are:

Blackout (2015)

Blacker, Terence

Boy2girl. Farrar, Straus and Giroux 2005 296p $16

Grades: 7 8 9 10   **Fic**

1. Cousins -- Fiction 2. Sex role -- Fiction

ISBN 0-374-30926-4

LC 2004-53268

After the death of his mother, thirteen-year-old Sam comes to live with his cousin and as a prank, he dresses up as a girl for school, but it soon gets out of hand.

"Sam's tale is told in very short chapters, each narrated by one of the many lively supporting characters who Sam meets. This unconventional technique works exceptionally well, telling the fast-paced story from different perspectives while delving into the ever-complicated world of sex roles." Booklist

Blackstone, Matt

Sorry you're lost; Matt Blackstone. Farrar Straus & Giroux 2014 312 p. (hardback) $15.99

Grades: 6 7 8 9   **Fic**

1. Grief -- Fiction 2. Middle schools -- Fiction 3. Dating (Social customs) -- Fiction 4. Children -- Conduct of life -- Fiction 5. Schools -- Fiction 6. Popularity -- Fiction 7. Conduct of life -- Fiction 8. Fathers and sons -- Fiction

ISBN 0374380651; 9780374380656

LC 2013021215

In this book, by Matt Blackstone, "Denny "Donuts" Murphy's mother dies [and] he becomes the world's biggest class clown. But deep down, Donuts just wants a normal life. . . . And so Donuts tries to get back into the groove by helping his best friend with their plan to get dates for the end-of-the-year school dance. When their scheme backfires, he learns that laughter is not the best medicine for all of his problems. Sometimes it's just as important to be true to yourself." (Publisher's note)

"Ever since his mother died, seventh grader Denny 'Donuts' Murphy has felt alone and small. So he intentionally develops a big persona, making everything into a joke. With the help of friends and a budding romance, Donuts sheds his manic showman exterior. The first-person narrative is a perfect vehicle to reveal Donuts's inner self in this story of substance and hope." Horn Book

Sorry you are lost

Blackwood, Gary

Around the world in 100 days; [by] Gary Blackwood. Dutton Children's Books 2010 358p
Grades: 6 7 8 9   **Fic**
1. Adventure fiction 2. Automobiles -- Fiction 3. Journalists -- Fiction 4. Automobile travel -- Fiction 5. Voyages around the world -- Fiction 6. Great Britain -- History -- 19th century -- Fiction
ISBN 0-525-42295-1; 978-0-525-42295-2

           LC 2009-53236
When seventeen-year-old Harry Fogg undertakes a race against time to win a wager with a member of his famous father's club, he puts to good use the recklessness and fascination with all things mechanical that have caused him trouble in Victorian England.

"The journey is fun and suspenseful." Booklist

Curiosity; by Gary Blackwood. Dial Books for Young Readers, an imprint of Penguin Group (USA) Inc. 2014 320 p. (hardcover) $16.99
Grades: 5 6 7 8   **Fic**
1. Chess -- Fiction 2. Robots -- Fiction 3. Historical fiction 4. Poverty -- Fiction 5. Apprentices -- Fiction 6. Philadelphia (Pa.) -- History -- 19th century -- Fiction
ISBN 0803739249; 9780803739246

           LC 2013013438
This novel, by Gary Blackwood, begins in "Philadelphia, PA, 1835. Rufus, a twelve-year-old chess prodigy, is recruited by a shady showman named Maelzel to secretly operate a mechanical chess player called the Turk. . . . But Rufus's job working the automaton must be kept secret, and he fears he may never be able to escape his unscrupulous master. And what has happened to the previous operators of the Turk, who seem to disappear as soon as Maelzel no longer needs them?" (Publisher's note)

"In 1835, Rufus, twelve-year-old hunchback and chess prodigy, is taken in by Johann Maelzel, owner of the Turk, a chess-playing automaton. They can't seem to escape the mysterious Woman in Black, or the attention of Edgar Allan Poe, who aims to expose their operation for the fraud it is. Blackwood excels in writing historical fiction that is as informative as it is entertaining." Horn Book

★ The **Shakespeare** stealer; [by] Gary Blackwood. Dutton Children's Bks. 1998 216p $15.99; pa $5.99
Grades: 5 6 7 8   **Fic**
1. Poets 2. Authors 3. Dramatists 4. Orphans -- Fiction 5. Theater -- Fiction 6. Great Britain -- History -- 1485-1603, Tudors -- Fiction
ISBN 0-525-45863-8; 0-14-130595-9 pa

           LC 97-42987
A young orphan boy is ordered by his master to infiltrate Shakespeare's acting troupe in order to steal the script of "Hamlet," but he discovers instead the meaning of friendship and loyalty

"Wry humor, cliffhanger chapter endings, and a plucky protagonist make this a fitting introduction to Shakespeare's world." Horn Book

Other titles in this series are:
Shakespeare's scribe (2000)

Shakespeare's spy (2003)

The **year** of the hangman; [by] Gary Blackwood. Dutton Children's Bks. 2002 261p $16.99; pa $5.99
Grades: 8 9 10 11 12   **Fic**
1. United States -- History -- 1775-1783, Revolution -- Fiction
ISBN 0-525-46921-4; 0-14-240078-5 pa

           LC 2002-67498
In 1777, having been kidnapped and taken forcibly from England to the American colonies, fifteen-year-old Creighton becomes part of developments in the political unrest there that may spell defeat for the patriots and change the course of history

"Packed with action, convincing historical speculation, and compelling portrayals of real-life and fictional characters, this page-turner will appeal to fans of both history and fantasy." SLJ

Blackwood, Sage

★ **Jinx**; Sage Blackwood. Harper 2013 368 p. (Jinx) (trade bdg.) $16.99
Grades: 4 5 6 7   **Fic**
1. Fantasy fiction 2. Magic -- Fiction 3. Voyages and travels -- Fiction 4. Fantasy
ISBN 0062129902; 9780062129901

           LC 2012005249
This fantasy book is set "in the Urwald, an enormous, sentient forest where humans exist on sufferance . . . . After Jinx's brutal stepfather decides to abandon him in the forest, the boy is saved by a crusty, morally ambiguous wizard named Simon, who takes him in as a servant, eventually teaching him some magic. Years later, a 12-year-old Jinx and two new friends set off to find another wizard, the monstrous Bonemaster, in hopes he can help them overcome their respective magical troubles." (Publishers Weekly)

Jinx's fire; Sage Blackwood. Katherine Tegen Books, an imprint of HarperCollinsPublishers 2015 400 p. map (hardback) $16.99
Grades: 4 5 6 7   **Fic**
1. Fantasy fiction 2. Wizards -- Fiction 3. Forests and forestry -- Fiction 4. Fantasy 5. Magic -- Fiction 6. Orphans -- Fiction
ISBN 0062129961; 9780062129963

           LC 2014022688
Sequel to: Jinx's magic
In this novel by Sage Blackwood, "the young wizard Jinx concludes his suspenseful and dryly humorous adventures in the magical forest of the Urwald with this third installment in the series. . . . The forest is under attack and its magic is fading. Can Jinx summon enough of his magic . . . to rescue Simon, defeat the Bonemaster, unite the Urwald, and fight off the invaders?" (Publisher's note)

"In this concluding volume of Blackwood's critically acclaimed series, Jinx is nearly 15, and he finally rescues his mentor, Simon, from the fate the evil Bonemaster wrought in Jinx's Magic (2014). . . . Series fans will be elated to have another outing with the sweetly sardonic hero, whose conscience is almost as troublesome as his grasp of spells. Fans of Cornelia Funke should add this to their stacks." Booklist

Jinx's magic; Sage Blackwood. Katherine Tegen Books 2014 400 p. (hardcover) $16.99

Grades: 4 5 6 7   **Fic**

1. Fantasy 2. Magic -- Fiction 3. Wizards -- Fiction 4. Orphans -- Fiction 5. Forests and forestry -- Fiction

ISBN 9780062129932; 0062129937

LC 2013010171

Sequel to: Jinx

"Jinx knows he can do magic. But he doesn't know why he's being stalked by a werewolf with a notebook, why the trees are starting to take back the only safe paths through the Urwald, or why the elves think Jinx and the evil Bonemaster are somehow connected." (Publisher's note)

"The plot is a little convoluted, wrapping up loose ends from the first volume and setting up elements for the next before finally establishing its own internal tension, but the unique setting, smart pace, likable characters, and sprightly voice hold the narrative together." Horn Book

Blake, Kendare

★ **Anna** Dressed in Blood. Tor 2011 320p $17.99

Grades: 8 9 10 11 12   **Fic**

1. Ghost stories 2. Horror fiction 3. Cats -- Fiction 4. Witches -- Fiction

ISBN 978-0-7653-2865-6; 0-7653-2865-8

LC 2011018985

"Blake populates the story with a nice mixture of personalities, including Anna, and spices it with plenty of gallows humor, all the while keeping the suspense pounding. . . . Abundantly original, marvelously inventive and enormous fun, this can stand alongside the best horror fiction out there. We demand sequels." Kirkus

Blakemore, Megan Frazer

The **spy** catchers of Maple Hill; by Megan Frazer Blakemore. Bloomsbury 2014 320 p. (hardback) $16.99

Grades: 4 5 6 7   **Fic**

1. Mystery fiction 2. Vermont -- Fiction 3. Country life -- Fiction 4. Spies -- Fiction 5. Cold War -- Fiction 6. Friendship -- Fiction 7. City and town life -- Vermont -- Fiction 8. Vermont -- History -- 20th century -- Fiction

ISBN 1619633485; 9781619633483

LC 2013039857

In this children's novel by Megan Frazer Blakemore, "Hazel Kaplansky is a firm believer in the pursuit of knowledge and truth--and she also happens to love a good mystery. When suspicions swirl that a Russian spy has infiltrated her small town of Maple Hill, Vermont, amidst the fervor of Cold War era McCarthyism, Hazel knows it's up to her to find a suspect starting with Mr. Jones, the quietly suspicious grave digger." (Publisher's note)

"The book does a wonderful job of displaying the way in which the fear inherent in the McCarthy era turned neighbor against neighbor. While the heart of the story lies within the issues of trust and truth, the writing is never preachy, using Hazel's innate humor to deflect moments that veer close to

saccarine or preachy. A strong work of historical fiction for mystery fans." SLJ Reviews

The **Water** Castle; by Megan Frazer Blakemore. Walker 2013 352 p. (hardback) $16.99

Grades: 3 4 5 6 7   **Fic**

1. Magic -- Fiction 2. Castles -- Fiction 3. Family secrets -- Fiction 4. Maine -- Fiction 5. Families -- Fiction 6. Dwellings -- Fiction 7. Moving, Household -- Fiction 8. Discoveries in science -- Fiction

ISBN 0802728391; 9780802728395

LC 2012016442

In this novel by Megan Frazer Blakemore "Ephraim Appledore-Smith is an ordinary boy, and up until his father's stroke he lived an ordinary life. But all that changes when his family moves to the Water Castle. . . . Mallory Green's family has always been the caretakers of the Water Castle. . . . She has been raised to protect the legendary Fountain of Youth, hidden on the estate grounds. When Ephraim learns of the Fountain, he's sure finding it can cure his dad." (Publisher's note)

Blazanin, Jan

A & L do summer. Egmont USA 2011 273p pa $8.99

Grades: 7 8 9 10   **Fic**

1. Iowa -- Fiction 2. Summer -- Fiction 3. Bullies -- Fiction 4. Friendship -- Fiction 5. Family life -- Fiction 6. Domestic animals -- Fiction

ISBN 978-1-60684-191-4 pa; 1-60684-191-2 pa; 978-1-60684-243-0 ebook

LC 2010-43616

In Iowa farm country, sixteen-year-old Aspen and her friend Laurel plan to get noticed the summer before their senior year and are unwittingly aided by pig triplets, a skunk, a chicken, bullies, a rookie policeman, and potential boyfriends.

"A series of mishaps add hilarity to the story. . . . All's well that ends well in this read perfectly suited for light refreshment on a hot summer day." Booklist

Block, Francesca Lia

The **island** of excess love; Francesca Lia Block. Henry Holt Books for Young Readers 2014 240 p. (hardback) $16.99

Grades: 8 9 10 11 12   **Fic**

1. Roman mythology 2. Adventure fiction 3. Love -- Fiction 4. Science fiction 5. Visions -- Fiction 6. Survival -- Fiction 7. Friendship -- Fiction 8. Los Angeles (Calif.) -- Fiction

ISBN 0805096310; 9780805096316

LC 2014005284

Companion to: Love in the Time of Global Warming

"Pen has lost her parents. She's lost her eye. But she has fought Kronen; she has won back her fragile friends and her beloved brother. Now Pen, Hex, Ash, Ez, and Venice are living in the pink house by the sea, getting by on hard work, companionship, and dreams. Until the day a foreboding ship appears in the harbor across from their home." (Publisher's note) The book is a companion to "Love in the Time of Global Warming."

"Just as Block's earlier novel was loosely based on The Odyssey, this is even more loosely based on The Aeneid. The result is a mesmerizing, magical, and mysterious tale of love and loss, stories and visions, and betrayal and redemption, all told in the author's signature lyrical voice." Booklist

★ **Love** in the time of global warming; Francesca Lia Block. Henry Holt and Co. 2013 240 p. (hardcover) $16.99

Grades: 8 9 10 11 12   **Fic**

1. Apocalyptic fiction 2. Voyages and travels -- Fiction 3. Love -- Fiction 4. Science fiction 5. Families -- Fiction 6. Survival -- Fiction 7. Earthquakes -- Fiction 8. Los Angeles (Calif.) -- Fiction

ISBN 0805096272; 9780805096279

LC 2012047808

Rainbow List (2014)

In this book, after "an earthquake and tidal wave destroy much of Los Angeles, Penelope—now going by Pen—sets out to find her family. In the course of a journey that explicitly parallels the one described in Homer's Odyssey, Pen navigates the blighted landscape with a crew of three other searchers. . . . Eventually they arrive in Las Vegas (the contemporary stand-in for the land of the dead) where Pen confronts the evil genius behind her world's destruction." (Publishers Weekly)

"In this Odyssey-inspired story, after the devastating Earth Shaker, Penelope sets out into the brutal Los Angeles landscape in search of her family. She meets an intriguing boy named Hex who joins her on her journey. Block's imagery is remarkable in this sophisticated melding of post-apocalyptic setting, re-imagined classic, and her signature magical realism." (Horn Book)

The **waters** & the wild. HarperTeen 2009 113p $16.99; lib bdg $17.89

Grades: 7 8 9 10   **Fic**

1. School stories 2. Fairies -- Fiction 3. Los Angeles (Calif.) -- Fiction

ISBN 978-0-06-145244-4; 0-06-145244-0; 978-0-06-145245-1 lib bdg; 0-06-145245-9 lib bdg

LC 2008031452

Thirteen-year-old Bee realizes that she is a fairy who has been switched at birth with another girl who now wants her life back.

"Fragments of poems by Yeats and Shelley are eerily apropos (and may provide an irresistible invitation for further reading). Haunting and thought provoking." Publ Wkly

Bloor, Edward

London calling; 1st ed.; Alfred A. Knopf 2006 289p $16.96; lib bdg $18.99

Grades: 6 7 8 9   **Fic**

1. School stories 2. Science fiction 3. London (England) -- Fiction 4. World War, 1939-1945 -- Fiction

ISBN 0-375-83635-7; 0-375-93635-1 lib bdg

LC 2005-33330

Seventh-grader Martin Conway believes that his life is monotonous and dull until the night the antique radio he uses as a night-light transports him to the bombing of London in 1940.

"Evocative descriptions and elegant phrasings make the writing most enjoyable, and because the author uses a first-person voice, the story seems very personal." SLJ

A **plague** year. Alfred A. Knopf 2011 305p $15.99; lib bdg $10.99

Grades: 6 7 8 9 10   **Fic**

1. School stories 2. Drug abuse -- Fiction 3. Pennsylvania -- Fiction 4. Supermarkets -- Fiction 5. Coal mines and mining -- Fiction

ISBN 978-0-375-85681-5; 0-375-85681-1; 978-0-375-95681-2 lib bdg; 0-375-95681-6 lib bdg

LC 2010050651

A ninth-grader who works with his father in the local supermarket describes the plague of meth addiction that consumes many people in his Pennsylvania coal mining town from 9/11 and the nearby crash of United Flight 93 in Shanksville to the Quecreek Mine disaster in Somerset the following summer.

"The plot is message-heavy but goes down easily because Bloor excels at writing vivid scenes. Tom is a thoroughly sympathetic narrator as he grows to realize there is value in 'blooming where you are planted.'" Publ Wkly

★ **Taken.** Alfred A. Knopf 2007 247p $17; pa $8.99

Grades: 6 7 8 9 10   **Fic**

1. Science fiction 2. Kidnapping -- Fiction 3. Social classes -- Fiction

ISBN 978-0-375-83636-7; 0-375-83636-5; 978-0-440-42128-3 pa; 0-440-42128-4 pa

LC 2006-35561

In 2036 kidnapping rich children has become an industry, but when thirteen-year-old Charity Meyers is taken and held for ransom, she soon discovers that this particular kidnapping is not what it seems.

"Deftly constructed, this is as riveting as it is thought-provoking." Publ Wkly

★ **Tangerine.** Harcourt Brace & Co. 1997 294p $17

Grades: 7 8 9 10   **Fic**

1. Soccer -- Fiction 2. Florida -- Fiction 3. Brothers -- Fiction

ISBN 0-15-201246-X

LC 96-34182

Twelve-year-old Paul, who lives in the shadow of his football hero brother Erik, fights for the right to play soccer despite his near blindness and slowly begins to remember the incident that damaged his eyesight

"Readers will cheer for this bright, funny, decent kid." Horn Book Guide

Blos, Joan W.

★ **Letters** from the corrugated castle; a novel of gold rush California, 1850-1852. Atheneum Books for Young Readers 2007 310p $17.99; pa $5.99

Grades: 5 6 7 8   **Fic**

1. California -- Fiction 2. Mexican Americans -- Fiction 3. Gold mines and mining -- Fiction 4. Frontier and pioneer life -- Fiction 5. Mother-daughter relationship

-- Fiction

ISBN 978-0-689-87077-4; 0-689-87077-9; 978-0-689-87078-1 pa; 0-689-87078-7 pa

LC 2007-02673

A series of letters and newspaper articles reveals life in California in the 1850s, especially for thirteen-year-old Eldora, who was raised in Massachusetts as an orphan only to meet her influential mother in San Francisco, and Luke, who hopes to find a fortune in gold.

"It is Blos' sturdy characters, whose experiences reveal the complexity of human relationships and wisdom about 'the salt and the sweet of life,' who will make this last." Booklist

Blubaugh, Penny

Serendipity Market. HarperTeen 2009 268p $16.99; pa $8.99

Grades: 7 8 9 10   **Fic**

1. Fairy tales 2. Magic -- Fiction 3. Storytelling -- Fiction

ISBN 978-0-06-146875-9; 0-06-146875-4; 978-0-06-146877-3 pa; 0-06-146877-0 pa

LC 2008-10187

When the world begins to seem unbalanced, Mama Inez calls ten storytellers to the Serendipity Market and, through the power of their magical tales, the balance of the world is corrected once again.

"In this debut storytelling tour de force, Blubaugh repackages familiar folk and fairy-tale themes with contemporary verve and wit." Kirkus

Blue birds; Caroline Starr Rose. G. P. Putnam's Sons, an imprint of Penguin Group (USA) 2015 400 p. map (hardcover) $16.99

Grades: 4 5 6 7   **Fic**

1. Native Americans -- Fiction 2. Roanoke Island (N.C.) -- History -- Fiction 3. Novels in verse 4. Friendship -- Fiction 5. Lumbee Indians -- Fiction 6. Roanoke Colony -- Fiction

ISBN 0399168109; 9780399168109

LC 2014012100

In this novel by Caroline Starr Rose, "it's 1587 and twelve-year-old Alis has made the long journey with her parents from England to help settle the New World. But the land, the island Roanoke, is also inhabited by the Roanoke tribe and tensions between them and the English are running high, soon turning deadly. Amid the strife, Alis meets and befriends Kimi, a Roanoke girl about her age. Though the two don't even speak the same language, these girls form a special bond." (Publisher's note)

"The use of different typefaces works well to differentiate the two voices, which occasionally appear in tandem when the girls are together. An imaginative historical novel with two sympathetic protagonists." Booklist

Includes bibliographical references

Blume, Judy, 1938-

★ **Are** you there God?, it's me, Margaret; rev format ed.; Atheneum 2001 149p hc $17.99

Grades: 4 5 6 7   **Fic**

1. Bildungsromans 2. Puberty -- Fiction 3. Religion

-- Fiction

ISBN 0-689-84158-2; 9781481413978

A reissue of the title first published 1970 by Bradbury Press

A "story about the emotional, physical, and spiritual ups and downs experienced by 12-year-old Margaret, child of a Jewish-Protestant union." Natl Counc of Teach of Engl. Adventuring with Books. 2d edition

BFF* * best friends forever; two novels. Delacorte Press 496p $18.99   **Fic**

1. Friendship -- Fiction. 2. Family problems -- Fiction. 3. Gifted children -- Fiction. 4. Brothers and sisters -- Fiction. 5. Interpersonal relations -- Fiction.

ISBN 978-0-385-73407-3

A compilation of two previously published novels: Just as long and we're together (1987) and Here's to you Rachel Robinson (1993)

Here's to you, Rachel Robinson. Orchard Bks. 1993 196p hardcover o.p. pa $5.99

Grades: 5 6 7 8   **Fic**

1. Siblings -- Fiction 2. Friendship -- Fiction 3. Gifted children -- Fiction

ISBN 0-531-06801-3; 0-440-21974-4 pa

LC 93-9631

Expelled from boarding school, Charles' presence at home proves disruptive, especially for sister Rachel, a gifted seventh grader juggling friendships and school activities

"Blume once again demonstrates her ability to shape multidimensional characters and to explore—often through very convincing dialogue—the tangled interactions of believable, complex people." Publ Wkly

Tiger eyes; a novel. Bradbury Press 1981 206p $16.95; pa $6.99

Grades: 7 8 9 10   **Fic**

1. Death -- Fiction

ISBN 0-689-85872-8; 0-440-98469-6 pa

LC 81-6152

Resettled in the "Bomb City" with her mother and brother, Davey Wexler recovers from the shock of her father's death during a holdup of his 7-Eleven store in Atlantic City

"The plot is strong, interesting and believable. . . . . The story though intense and complicated flows smoothly and easily." Voice Youth Advocates

Blume, Lesley M. M.

Julia and the art of practical travel; Lesley M.M. Blume. First edition Alfred A. Knopf 2015 192 p. illustrations $16.99

Grades: 4 5 6   **Fic**

1. Aunts -- Fiction 2. Automobile travel 3. Mother-daughter relationship -- Fiction 4. Missing persons -- Fiction 5. Automobile travel -- Fiction 6. United States -- History -- 1961-1969 -- Fiction

ISBN 0385752822; 9780385752824; 9780385752831

LC 2013044490

In this book by Lesley M. M. Blume, "after Julia's wealthy grandmother dies, and the family estate in the Hudson Valley is sold, Julia and her Aunt Constance hit the road, determined to track down Julia's mother, who disappeared three years before. In an old station wagon full of family heirlooms like a silver tea set and oriental carpets--'practical travel things,' according to Aunt Constance--they travel from New York to California." (Publishers Weekly)

"Each character is delightful and quirky, and readers will enjoy all of them. The story comes to a somewhat predictable conclusion, but it hardly matters. This book is filled with familial love and the joy of traveling, and readers will appreciate Julia's journey." SLJ

★ The **rising** star of Rusty Nail; [by] Lesley M.M. Blume. Alfred A. Knopf 2007 270p $15.99; lib bdg $18.99; pa $6.50

Grades: 4 5 6   **Fic**

1. Pianists -- Fiction 2. Minnesota -- Fiction 3. Musicians -- Fiction 4. Russian Americans -- Fiction
ISBN 978-0-375-83524-7; 978-0-375-93524-4 lib bdg; 978-0-440-42111-5 pa

LC 2006024252

In the small town of Rusty Nail, Minnesota, in the early 1950s, musically talented ten-year-old Franny wants to take advanced piano lessons from newcomer Olga Malenkov, a famous Russian musician suspected of being a communist spy by gossipy members of the community

"Blume has skillfully combined humor, history, and music to create an enjoyable novel that builds to a surprising crescendo." SLJ

Tennyson. Alfred A. Knopf 2008 288p $15.99; lib bdg $18.99; pa $6.99

Grades: 6 7 8 9 10 11 12   **Fic**

1. Family life -- Fiction 2. New Orleans (La.) -- Fiction 3. Great Depression, 1929-1939 -- Fiction
ISBN 978-0-375-84703-5; 978-0-375-94703-2 lib bdg; 978-0-440-24061-7 pa

LC 2007-25983

After their mother abandons them during the Great Depression, eleven-year-old Tennyson Fontaine and her little sister Hattie are sent to live with their eccentric Aunt Henrietta in a decaying plantation house

"Many readers will respond to this novel's Southern gothic sensibility, especially Blume's beautiful, poetic writing about how the past resonates through the generations." Booklist

Blumenthal, Deborah

Mafia girl; Deborah Blumenthal. Albert Whitman & Company 2014 256 p. (hardcover) $16.99

Grades: 8 9 10 11   **Fic**

1. Mafia -- Fiction 2. Family -- Fiction 3. Identity -- Fiction 4. Father-daughter relationship -- Fiction 5. Families -- Fiction
ISBN 0807549118; 9780807549117

LC 2013028440

In this book, by Deborah Blumenthal, "seventeen-year-old Gia is the most hated/loved girl in school. Why? Her father doesn't have a boss. He is the boss - the capo di tutti cappi, boss of all bosses. Not that Gia cares. But life gets complicated when she meets a cop she calls 'Officer Hottie' and feels a suprising chemistry. Then Vogue magazine wants to feature Gia in a fashion spread about real-life bad

girls. On top of this, she's running for class president." (Publisher's note)

"Gia, the prized daughter of a New York Mafia boss, enjoys the carefree lifestyle her father's money and connections afford her. When the feds begin to close in on the family business, Gia must find an identity outside of Don's Daughter. Gia's voice is an entertaining, effervescent stream-of-consciousness, but the book's frantic pace muddles too many competing plot lines." Horn Book

Blundell, Judy

A **city** tossed and broken; the diary of Minnie Bonner. Judy Blundell. Scholastic Inc. 2013 224 p. (paper over board) $12.99

Grades: 4 5 6 7   **Fic**

1. Historical fiction 2. San Francisco (Calif.) -- History -- Fiction 3. Diaries -- Fiction 4. Earthquakes -- Fiction 5. Household employees -- Fiction 6. Family life -- California -- Fiction 7. San Francisco Earthquake and Fire, Calif., 1906 -- Fiction 8. San Francisco (Calif.) -- History -- 20th century -- Fiction 9. Women household employees -- California -- San Francisco -- Fiction
ISBN 0545310229; 9780545310222

LC 2012014742

This novel, by Judy Blundell, presents the diary of the girl Minnie Bonner during the San Francisco, California earthquake of 1906 as part of the "Dear America" series. A "wealthy gentleman . . . offers Minnie a chance to work as a lady's maid. . . . But when a powerful earthquake strikes, Minnie finds herself the sole survivor among them. . . . Minnie has turned into an heiress overnight . . . and she is soon wrapped up in a deception that leads her down a dangerous path." (Publisher's note)

"The author deftly incorporates true events, circumstances and key historical figures into the rapidly unfolding fictional plot... Exciting, suspenseful, absorbing and informative." Kirkus

Strings attached. Scholastic Press 2011 310p $17.99

Grades: 7 8 9 10   **Fic**

1. Dance -- Fiction 2. Mafia -- Fiction 3. Homicide -- Fiction 4. New York (N.Y.) -- Fiction 5. Italian Americans -- Fiction
ISBN 978-0-545-22126-9; 0-545-22126-9

LC 2010-41078

Blundell "successfully constructs a complex web of intrigue that connects characters in unexpected ways. History and theater buffs will especially appreciate her attention to detail—Blundell again demonstrates she can turn out first-rate historical fiction." Publ Wkly

★ **What** I saw and how I lied. Scholastic Press 2008 284p $16.99

Grades: 8 9 10 11 12   **Fic**

1. Mystery fiction 2. Florida -- Fiction
ISBN 978-0-439-90346-2; 0-439-90346-7

LC 2008-08503

In 1947, with her jovial stepfather Joe back from the war and family life returning to normal, teenage Evie, smitten by the handsome young ex-GI who seems to have a secret hold on Joe, finds herself caught in a complicated web of lies whose devastating outcome change her life and that of her family forever.

"Using pitch-perfect dialogue and short sentences filled with meaning, Blundell has crafted a suspenseful, historical mystery." Booklist

Bock, Caroline

★ **LIE**. St. Martin's Griffin 2011 211p pa $9.99

Grades: 8 9 10 11 12   Fic

1. Homicide -- Fiction   2. Violence -- Fiction   3. Immigrants -- Fiction   4. Prejudices -- Fiction
ISBN 978-0-312-66832-7; 0-312-66832-5

     LC 2011019824

Seventeen-year-old Skylar Thompson is being questioned by the police. Her boyfriend, Jimmy, stands accused of brutally assaulting two young El Salvadoran immigrants from a neighboring town, and she's the prime witness.

"This effective, character-driven, episodic story examines the consequences of a hate crime on the teens involved in it. . . . Realistic and devastatingly insightful, this novel can serve as a springboard to classroom and family discussions. Unusual and important." Kirkus

Bodeen, S. A.

The **Compound**. Feiwel and Friends 2008 248p $16.95; pa $8.99

Grades: 7 8 9 10   Fic

1. Twins -- Fiction   2. Fathers -- Fiction   3. Survival after airplane accidents, shipwrecks, etc. -- Fiction
ISBN 0-312-37015-6; 0-312-57860-1 pa; 978-0-312-37015-2; 978-0-312-57860-2 pa

     LC 2007-36148

After his parents, two sisters, and he have spent six years in a vast underground compound built by his wealthy father to protect them from a nuclear holocaust, fifteen-year-old Eli, whose twin brother and grandmother were left behind, discovers that his father has perpetrated a monstrous hoax on them all.

"The audience will feel the pressure closing in on them as they, like the characters, race through hairpin turns in the plot toward a breathless climax." Publ Wkly

The **gardener**. Feiwel and Friends 2010 233p $16.99

Grades: 7 8 9 10   Fic

1. Science fiction   2. Fathers -- Fiction   3. Genetic engineering -- Fiction   4. Single parent family -- Fiction
ISBN 978-0-312-37016-9; 0-312-37016-4

     LC 2009-48802

When high school sophomore Mason finds a beautiful but catatonic girl in the nursing home where his mother works, the discovery leads him to revelations about a series of disturbing human experiments that have a connection to his own life.

"This is a fast-paced read that keeps readers guessing what the turn of a page will reveal." Voice Youth Advocates

The **raft**; S.A. Bodeen. Feiwel and Friends 2012 231 p. $16.99

Grades: 7 8 9 10   Fic

1. Survival skills -- Fiction   2. Wilderness survival -- Fiction   3. Survival after airplane accidents, shipwrecks,

etc. -- Fiction
ISBN 0312650108; 9780312650100

This novel, by S. A. Bodeen, is a plane crash survival story. "All systems are go until a storm hits during the flight. The only passenger, Robie doesn't panic until the engine suddenly cuts out and Max shouts at her to put on a life jacket. . . . And then . . . she's in the water. Fighting for her life, Max pulls her onto the raft. . . . They have no water. Their only food is a bag of Skittles. There are sharks. There is an island. But there's no sign of help on the way." (Publisher's note)

Shipwreck Island; by S. A. Bodeen. Feiwel & Friends 2014 192 p. hc $16.99

Grades: 5 6 7 8   Fic

1. Islands -- Fiction   2. Shipwrecks -- Fiction   3. Family life -- Fiction   4. Stepmothers -- Fiction
ISBN 9781250027771; 1250027772

In this book, by S. A. Bodeen, "Sarah is not happy that her dad has married again, forcing her to deal with a new stepmom and two new brothers. To help them bond, Sarah's dad and stepmom decide to take everyone on a vacation to Tahiti, rent a yacht, and cruise to their own private island. They sail right into a terrible storm, the captain is swept overboard, and the yacht runs aground on a deserted island.." (Library Media Connection)

"These very human protagonists respond in believable ways to their new family situation while encountering freakish animals, bizarrely dangerous weather, and a creepy, empty house." SLJ

Boie, Kirsten

The **princess** plot; translated by David Henry Wilson. Scholastic 2009 378p $17.99

Grades: 5 6 7 8   Fic

1. Princesses -- Fiction   2. Conspiracies -- Fiction
ISBN 978-0-545-03220-9; 0-545-03220-2

     LC 2008-24403

Original German edition, 2005

Believing that she is on a film set after auditioning and winning the role of a princess, fourteen-year-old Jenna becomes the unsuspecting pawn in a royal conspiracy

"This novel takes simple, straightforward writing and layers it with kidnappings, political intrigue, and an abundance of secret plots. Readers will enjoy leisurely uncovering the mystery of Jenna's heritage, right along with Jenna herself." Booklist

Another title about Jenna is:

The princess trap (2010)

The **princess** trap; translated by David Henry Wilson. Chicken House/Scholastic 2010 405p $17.99

Grades: 5 6 7 8   Fic

1. School stories   2. Princesses -- Fiction
ISBN 978-0-545-22261-7; 0-545-22261-3

     LC 2010010072

Sequel to: The princess plot (2009)
Original German edition, 2007

Palace rules, boarding school, and paparazzi have Jenna, princess of the newly unified kingdom of Scandia, longing for her former anonymity, but when she runs away she finds herself in grave danger—and in a position to prevent the outbreak of civil war.

Bolden, Tonya

★ **Finding** family. Bloomsbury 2010 181p il $15.99

Grades: 4 5 6 7   **Fic**

1. Aunts -- Fiction 2. Family life -- Fiction 3. Grandfathers -- Fiction 4. West Virginia -- Fiction 5. African Americans -- Fiction

ISBN 978-1-59990-318-7; 1-59990-318-0

LC 2010-00535

Raised in Charleston, West Virginia, at the turn of the twentieth century by her grandfather and aunt on off-putting tales of family members she has never met, twelve-year-old Delana is shocked when, after Aunt Tilley dies, she learns the truth about her parents and some of her other relatives.

"This richly lyrical and historically persuasive coming-of-age story explores the ties that bind, break and renew an affuent African-American family. . . . Period photographic portraits from Bolden's personal collection illustrate the book. Each carefully posed subject is a fascinating enigma." Kirkus

Boles, Philana Marie

Little divas. Amistad 2006 164p $15.99; lib bdg $16.89; pa $5.99

Grades: 5 6 7 8   **Fic**

1. Cousins -- Fiction 2. Divorce -- Fiction 3. African Americans -- Fiction 4. Father-daughter relationship -- Fiction

ISBN 0-06-073299-7; 0-06-073300-4 lib bdg; 0-06-073301-2 pa

The summer before seventh grade, Cassidy Carter must come to terms with living with her father, practically a stranger, as well as her relationships with her cousins, all amidst the overall confusion of adolescence.

"Boles portrays this variable age well, and readers will feel for Cassidy's trials." SLJ

Bond, Victoria

Zora and me; the song of Ivory. [by] Victoria Bond and T. R. Simon. Candlewick Press 2010 170p $16.99; pa $6.99

Grades: 4 5 6 7   **Fic**

1. Authors 2. Novelists 3. Dramatists 4. Memoirists 5. Folklorists 6. Short story writers 7. Race relations -- Fiction 8. African Americans -- Fiction

ISBN 978-0-7636-4300-3; 0-7636-4300-9; 978-0-7636-5814-4 pa; 0-7636-5814-6 pa

LC 2009-47410

Coretta Scott King/John Steptoe New Talent Award (Author), 2011

This is a fictionalized account of Zora Neale Hurston's childhood with her best friend Carrie, in Eatonville, Florida. Annotated bibliography. "Grades four to seven." (Bull Cent Child Books)

"The brilliance of this novel is its rendering of African-American child life during the Jim Crow era as a time of wonder and imagination, while also attending to its harsh realities. Absolutely outstanding." Kirkus

Bondoux, Anne-Laure

★ A **time** of miracles; translated from the French by Y. Maudet. Delacorte Press 2010 180p map $17.99; lib bdg $20.99

Grades: 6 7 8 9   **Fic**

1. War stories 2. Europe -- Fiction 3. Refugees -- Fiction

ISBN 978-0-385-73922-1; 0-385-73922-2; 978-0-385-90777-4 lib bdg; 0-385-90777-X lib bdg

LC 2010008539

"Readers will find themselves mesmerized not only by the eloquent language but by a plot every bit as harrowing and surprising as Koumail's cherished bedtime story." Horn Book

Boniface, William

The **hero** revealed; [by] William Boniface; illustrations by Stephen Gilpin. HarperCollins Pub. 2006 294p il (The extraordinary adventures of Ordinary Boy) $15.99; lib bdg $16.89; pa $6.99

Grades: 4 5 6 7   **Fic**

1. Superheroes -- Fiction

ISBN 978-0-06-077464-6; 0-06-077464-9; 978-0-06-077465-3 lib bdg; 0-06-077465-7 lib bdg; 978-0-06-077466-0 pa; 0-06-077466-5 pa

LC 2005018676

Ordinary Boy, the only resident of Superopolis without a superpower, uncovers and foils a sinister plot to destroy the town

"This first book in a new series is great fun. . . . Boniface wields a cynical, but definitely kid-friendly, sense of humor, and Gilpin's illustrations are sharp and witty." SLJ

Other titles in this series are:

The return of Meteor Boy? (2007)

The great powers outage (2008)

Booraem, Ellen

★ **Small** persons with wings. Dial Books for Young Readers 2011 302p $16.99

Grades: 4 5 6 7   **Fic**

1. Fantasy fiction 2. Magic -- Fiction 3. Fairies -- Fiction 4. Grandfathers -- Fiction 5. Lost and found possessions -- Fiction

ISBN 978-0-8037-3471-5; 0-8037-3471-9

LC 2010008400

When Mellie Turpin's grandfather dies and leaves her family his run-down inn and bar, she learns that for generations her family members have been fairy guardians. "Grades five to eight." (Bull Cent Child Books)

"In a fairy story that's wistful, humorous, and clever, Booraem . . . suggests that the real world—with its disappointments and failings—is still better than living with illusions. . . . The theme of making progress, rather than ignoring problems, is a strong one, gently presented." Publ Wkly

Texting the underworld; by Ellen Booraem. Dial Books for Young Readers 2013 319 p. (hardcover) $16.99

Grades: 5 6 7 8   **Fic**

1. School stories -- Fiction 2. Fantasy -- Fiction 3. Death -- Fiction 4. Humorous stories 5. Schools --

Fiction 6. Banshees -- Fiction 7. Future life -- Fiction 8. Supernatural -- Fiction 9. Middle schools -- Fiction
ISBN 0803737041; 9780803737044

LC 2012032488

In this book by Ellen Booraem, "Conor O'Neill is a smart but timid seventh-grader. . . . When a banshee straight out of his Irish-born grandfather's stories appears in Conor's room, he's terrified that someone he loves is going to die soon. The banshee, Ashling, is new at her job, and . . . she's curious about the present day, [so] she masquerades as a new student at Conor's school." (Publishers Weekly)

The **unnameables**. Harcourt 2008 317p $16
Grades: 6 7 8 9   **Fic**
1. Fantasy fiction 2. Utopias -- Fiction 3. Friendship -- Fiction
ISBN 978-0-1520-6368-9; 0-1520-6368-4

LC 2007-48844

On an island in whose strict society only useful objects are named and the unnamed are ignored or forbidden, thirteen-year-old Medford encounters an unusual and powerful creature, half-man, half-goat, and together they attempt to bring some changes to the community.

"Island, a creepy and restrictive world masquuerading as a utopia, is as memorable as the intricately developed inhabitants." Bull Cent Child Books

Boos, Ben
Fantasy : an artist's realm. Candlewick Press 2010 83p il $19.99
Grades: 6 7 8 9   **Fic**
1. Fantasy fiction
ISBN 978-0-7636-4056-9; 0-7636-4056-5

LC 2010007511

"This tour of New Perigord begins by presenting the fictional realm's geography, warriors, enemies, common weapons, and mages, including full details of their abilities and spells. . . . [Boos] reveals 'commonly encountered spirits,' such as elves, undines, and banshees. . . . The large spreads are filled with authentically ancient-looking, digitally produced pictures of the many imagined inhabitants and elements, all described in densely packed, short blocks of text. . . . This offers plenty of entertainment for even those with a more casual interest in the fantasy genre." Booklist

Bow, Erin
★ **Plain** Kate. Arthur A. Levine Books 2010 314p $17.99
Grades: 7 8 9 10   **Fic**
1. Fantasy fiction 2. Cats -- Fiction 3. Magic -- Fiction 4. Orphans -- Fiction 5. Witchcraft -- Fiction 6. Wood carving -- Fiction
ISBN 978-0-545-16664-5; 0-545-16664-0

LC 2009-32652

Plain Kate's odd appearance and expertise as a woodcarver cause some to think her a witch, but friendship with a talking cat and, later, with humans help her to survive and even thrive in a world of magic, charms, and fear.

"Despite the talking animal . . . and graceful writing . . . this is a dark and complex tale, full of violence—knives cut

a lot more than wood. . . . Kate is undeniably a sympathetic character deserving of happiness." Publ Wkly

★ **Sorrow's** knot; Erin Bow. Arthur A. Levine Books 2013 368 p. (hardcover : alk. paper) $17.99
Grades: 8 9 10 11 12   **Fic**
1. Dead -- Fiction 2. Knots and splices -- Fiction 3. Magic -- Fiction 4. Identity -- Fiction 5. Fate and fatalism -- Fiction
ISBN 0545166667; 9780545166669; 9780545166676; 9780545578004

LC 2013007855

In this book, by Erin Bow, "the dead do not rest easy. Every patch of shadow might be home to something hungry, something deadly. Most of the people of this world live on the sunlit, treeless prairies. But a few carve out an uneasy living in the forest towns, keeping the dead at bay with wards made from magically knotted cords. The women who tie these knots are called binders. And Otter's mother, Willow, is one of the greatest binders her people have ever known." (Publisher's note)

"Sorrow's Knot is a dystopian novel that does not deal with the destruction of the broader world. Rather, it delves into the mythology of a group of people and how their prejudices and resistance to change came to be. Readers of suspense will love the dark tension of the story line, an ebb and flow that carries through to the very end.—" (School Library Journal)

Bowen, Fred
Quarterback season; written by Fred Bowen. Peachtree 2011 132p pa $5.95
Grades: 4 5 6 7   **Fic**
1. Diaries -- Fiction 2. Football -- Fiction
ISBN 978-1-56145-594-2; 1-56145-594-6

LC 2011002673

As a school assignment, eighth-grader Matt Monroe keeps a journal about his team's football season.

This is "another absorbing sports tale from the prolific and dependable Bowen. . . . The author expertly balances the subplots and football action." Booklist

Bowers, Laura
Beauty shop for rent; --fully equipped, inquire within. [by] Laura Bowers. 1st ed.; Harcourt 2007 328p $17; pa $6.95
Grades: 6 7 8 9   **Fic**
1. Beauty shops -- Fiction 2. Mother-daughter relationship -- Fiction
ISBN 0-15-205764-1; 978-0-15-205764-0; 978-0-15-206385-6 pa; 0-15-206385-4 pa

LC 2006016761

Raised by a great-grandmother and a bunch of beauty shop buddies, fourteen-year-old Abbey resolves to overcome her unhappy childhood and disillusionment with the mother who deserted her.

"This deceptively simple book reveals Abbey as a wonderful character who will appeal to a broad spectrum of readers." SLJ

Bowler, Tim

Blade : out of the shadows. Philomel Books 2010 232p $16.99

Grades: 7 8 9 10   **Fic**

1. Gangs -- Fiction 2. Homicide -- Fiction 3. Violence -- Fiction 4. Great Britain -- Fiction 5. Homeless persons -- Fiction

ISBN 978-0-399-25187-0; 0-399-25187-1

LC 2009-3155

Badly injured, fourteen-year-old Blade must continue to use his exceptional "street smarts" and waning strength to outsmart dangerous thugs while he considers surrendering to the police to face the consequences of a past he has tried to forget.

"Bowler combines the slow unveiling of Blade's past with short chapters and nonstop action to create tension and suspense." Kirkus

Followed by: Fighting back (2011)

Blade : playing dead. Philomel Books 2009 231p $16.99; pa $7.99

Grades: 7 8 9 10   **Fic**

1. Gangs -- Fiction 2. Violence -- Fiction 3. Great Britain -- Fiction 4. Homeless persons -- Fiction

ISBN 978-0-399-25186-3; 0-399-25186-3; 978-0-14-241600-6 pa; 0-14-241600-2 pa

LC 2008-37813

First published 2008 in the United Kingdom

A fourteen-year-old British street person with extraordinary powers of observation and self-control must face murderous thugs connected with a past he has tried to forget, when his skills with a knife earned him the nickname, Blade.

"Bowler delivers an intense, gripping novel. . . . Readers who like their thrillers brutally realistic will find much to enjoy." Publ Wkly

Other books about Blade are:

Blade: fighting back (2011)

Blade: out of the shadows (2010)

Fighting back. Philomel Books 2011 $16.99

Grades: 7 8 9 10   **Fic**

1. Gangs -- Fiction 2. Homicide -- Fiction 3. Violence -- Fiction 4. Homeless persons -- Fiction

ISBN 978-0-399-25431-4; 0-399-25431-5

LC 2010005392

First published in the United Kingdom

When streetwise fourteen-year-old Blade returns to "the Beast," the city he left years before, to find young Jaz and bring her to safety, he is forced to confront his own demons.

Frozen fire; [by] Tim Bowler. Philomel Books 2008 328p $17.99

Grades: 7 8 9 10   **Fic**

1. Brothers -- Fiction 2. Supernatural -- Fiction 3. Missing children -- Fiction

ISBN 978-0-399-25053-8; 0-399-25053-0

LC 2007-43880

First published 2006 in the United Kingdom

Fifteen-year-old Dusty gets a mysterious call from a boy who says he is going to kill himself, and while he claims to have called her randomly, he seems to know her intimately.

"Bowler plunges readers into a mystery of psychological, supernatural, and sociological dimensions. . . . The book's wintry setting is brittle and otherworldly, and the story never lacks for tension." Horn Book Guide

Boyd, Maria

★ **Will**. Alfred A. Knopf 2010 300p $16.99; lib bdg $19.99

Grades: 8 9 10 11 12   **Fic**

1. School stories 2. Theater -- Fiction 3. Musicals -- Fiction 4. Australia -- Fiction 5. Homosexuality -- Fiction

ISBN 978-0-375-86209-0; 0-375-86209-9; 978-0-375-96209-7 lib bdg; 0-375-96209-3 lib bdg

LC 2009-39888

Seventeen-year-old Will's behavior has been getting him in trouble at his all-boys school in Sydney, Australia, but his latest punishment, playing in the band for a musical production, gives him new insights into his fellow students and helps him cope with an incident he has tried to forget.

"Readers should find it easy to sympathize with Will's vibrant, deadpan narration and his frequent use of slang, while recognizing that his jocular exterior hides a deeper vulnerability. . . . Boyd effectively handles Will's final outpouring of repressed emotions: the personal growth achieved by her realistic, likeable protagonist is abundantly clear." Publ Wkly

Bradbury, Jennifer

★ **Shift**. Atheneum Books for Young Readers 2008 245p $16.99

Grades: 7 8 9 10 11 12   **Fic**

1. Travel -- Fiction 2. Cycling -- Fiction 3. Friendship -- Fiction 4. Missing persons -- Fiction

ISBN 978-1-4169-4732-5; 1-4169-4732-9

LC 2007-23558

When best friends Chris and Win go on a cross country bicycle trek the summer after graduating and only one returns, the FBI wants to know what happened.

"Bradbury's keen details . . . add wonderful texture to this exciting [novel.] . . . Best of all is the friendship story." Booklist

Wrapped. Atheneum Books for Young Readers 2011 309p $16.99

Grades: 7 8 9 10   **Fic**

1. Mystery fiction 2. Spies -- Fiction 3. Supernatural -- Fiction 4. Great Britain -- History -- 19th century -- Fiction

ISBN 978-1-4169-9007-9; 1-4169-9007-0

"An 1815 parlor diversion leads to a fizzy, frothy caper. Agnes is a Regency debutante. . . . When she pockets the trinket she finds among the linens at her neighbor's mummy-wrapping party, she unwittingly sets off a series of catastrophes . . . that include burglaries, violent attacks and murder. . . . Bradbury weaves Egyptology, Napoleanic conquest and a flirtation with the supernatural into a spy thriller." Kirkus

Bradbury, Ray

The **Halloween** tree; [by] Ray Bradbury; illustrated by Joseph Mugnaini. Alfred A. Knopf 2007 145p il $15.99

Grades: 6 7 8 9   **Fic**

1. Fantasy fiction 2. Halloween -- Fiction
ISBN 0-394-82409-1; 978-0-394-82409-3
A reissue of the title first published 1972

A group of boys meet a spirit-being and are carried back in time to the origins of Halloween celebrations.

This is "fast-moving, genuinely eerie." Booklist

Something wicked this way comes. Avon Bks. 1999 293p $15.95; pa $7.99

Grades: 7 8 9 10   **Fic**

1. Horror fiction 2. Fantasy fiction
ISBN 0-380-97727-3; 0-380-72940-7 pa

A reissue of the title first published 1962 by Simon and Schuster

"We read here of the loss of innocence, the recognition of evil, the bond between generations, and the purely fantastic. These forces enter Green Town, Illinois, on the wheels of Cooger and Dark's Pandemonium Shadow Show. Will Halloway and Jim Nightshade, two 13-year-olds, explore the sinister carnival for excitement, which becomes desperation as the forces of the dark threaten to engulf them. Bradbury's gentle humanism and lyric style serve this fantasy well." Shapiro. Fic for Youth. 3d edition

Bradford, Chris

Young samurai: the way of the sword. Disney-Hyperion Books 2010 422p $16.99

Grades: 4 5 6 7   **Fic**

1. Adventure fiction 2. Japan -- Fiction 3. Ninja -- Fiction 4. Orphans -- Fiction 5. Samurai -- Fiction 6. Martial arts -- Fiction
ISBN 978-1-4231-2025-4; 1-4231-2025-6

           LC 2009008309

Sequel to: Young samurai: the way of the warrior (2009)

In 1611 Japan, English orphan Jack Fletcher continues his difficult training at Niten Ichi Ryu Samurai School, while also trying to get back the rutter, his father's navigational logbook, that an evil ninja wants to possess.

"With straightforward prose, [Bradford] has managed to pen lively and exciting fight sequences and is slowly beginning to develop a keen edge to his cast of characters, laying significant groundwork for future installments." Booklist

★ **Young** samurai: the way of the warrior. Hyperion Books for Children 2009 359p $16.99

Grades: 4 5 6 7   **Fic**

1. Adventure fiction 2. Japan -- Fiction 3. Samurai -- Fiction 4. Martial arts -- Fiction
ISBN 978-1-4231-1871-8; 1-4231-1871-5

           LC 2008-46180

First published 2008 in the United Kingdom

Orphaned by a ninja pirate attack off the coast of Japan in 1611, twelve-year-old English lad Jack Fletcher is determined to prove himself, despite the bullying of fellow students, when the legendary sword master who rescued him begins training him as a samurai warrior.

"Jack's story alone makes for a page-turner, but coupling it with intriguing bits of Japanese history and culture, Bradford produces an adventure novel to rank among the genre's best." Publ Wkly

Includes bibliographical references

Followed by: Young samurai: the way of the sword (2010)

Bradford, Michael

Button Hill; Michael Bradford. Orca Book Publishers 2015 264 p. (pbk.) $9.95

Grades: 6 7 8   **Fic**

1. Parapsychology -- Fiction 2. Missing children -- Fiction 3. Brothers and sisters -- Fiction
ISBN 1459807553; 9781459807556; 9781459807563; 9781459807570

           LC 2014952055

In Michael Bradford's novel "Dekker isn't happy that he and his little sister, Riley, are stuck in Button Hill with their weird old great-aunt Primrose. When he discovers an old clock in the cellar, made entirely of bones and with a skull for a face, he doesn't think much about it. But when Riley goes missing, a strange boy named Cobb appears in Button Hill. He tells Dekker that Button Hill sits on the border between Nightside and Dayside--and that Riley is in Nightside." (Publisher's note)

"Dekker discovers a mysterious clock in the cellar beneath the basement of his great aunt Primrose's old house. After twisting the skull that decorates the Nightclock and unknowingly opening the border between the living world (Dayside) and that of the dead (Nightside), mischievous Dekker inadvertently allows a sinister, pointy-toothed boy named Cobb to kidnap his sister and hide her in Nightside... An additional purchase for those who like their fantasy with plenty of skeletons (and a soft-hearted zombie)."

Bradley, Alex

24 girls in 7 days. Dutton 2005 265p $15.99

Grades: 7 8 9 10   **Fic**

1. Dating (Social customs) -- Fiction
ISBN 0-525-47369-6

"When the love of his life rejects his invitation to the senior prom, Jack Grammar's so-called best friends pose as Jack and run a personal ad in the online school newspaper soliciting a date. . . . The result is a hilarious adventure as Jack tries to speed-date 24 girls in 7 days. . . . This entertaining guy's eye view on dating, friendship, and understanding one's self is one that most libraries will want to own." SLJ

Bradley, Kimberly Brubaker

★ **Jefferson's** sons; a founding father's secret children. Dial Books for Young Readers 2011 368p $17.99

Grades: 5 6 7 8   **Fic**

1. Slaves 2. Architects 3. Presidents 4. Vice-presidents 5. Essayists 6. Mistresses 7. Slavery -- Fiction 8. Virginia -- Fiction 9. African Americans -- Fiction
ISBN 978-0-8037-3499-9; 0-8037-3499-9

           LC 2010049650

"The characters spring to life. . . . [This is a] fascinating story of an American family that represents so many of the contradictions of our history. The afterword is as fascinating as the novel." Kirkus

The **lacemaker** and the princess. Margaret K. McElderry Books 2007 199p $16.99; pa $6.99

Grades: 4 5 6 7 8   **Fic**
1. Queens 2. Friendship -- Fiction 3. Lace and lace
making -- Fiction 4. France -- History -- 1789-1799,
Revolution -- Fiction
ISBN 978-1-4169-1920-9; 1-4169-1920-1; 978-1-
4169-8583-9 pa; 1-4169-8583-2 pa

In 1788, eleven-year-old Isabelle, living with her lacemaker grandmother and mother near the palace of Versailles,
becomes close friends with Marie Antoinette's daughter,
Princess Therese, and finds their relationship complicated
not only by their different social class but by the growing
political unrest and resentment of the French people.

"Skillfully integrated historical facts frame this engrossing, believable story." Booklist

The **war** that saved my life; by Kimberly Brubaker Bradley. Dial Books for Young Readers, an imprint
of Penguin Group (USA) Inc. 2015 320 p. (hardcover) $16.99

Grades: 4 5 6 7   **Fic**
1. Brothers and sisters -- Fiction 2. People with
disabilities -- Fiction 3. Great Britain -- History --
20th century -- Fiction 4. World War, 1939-1945 --
Evacuation of civilians -- Fiction 5. Great Britain --
History -- George VI, 1936-1952 -- Fiction
ISBN 0803740816; 9780803740815

LC 2014002168

In this book, by Kimberly Brubaker Bradley, "[n]ine-
year-old Ada has never left her one-room apartment. Her
mother is too humiliated by Ada's twisted foot to let her
outside. So when her little brother Jamie is shipped out of
London to escape the war, Ada doesn't waste a minute - she
sneaks out to join him. So begins a new adventure of Ada,
and for Susan Smith, the woman who is forced to take the
two kids in." (Publisher's note)

"When word starts to spread about Germans bombing
London, Ada's mother decides to send her little brother, Jamie, to the country. Not 11-year-old Ada, though—she was
born with a crippling clubfoot, and her cruel mother treats
her like a slave...The home-front realities of WWII, as well
as Ada's realistic anger and fear, come to life in Bradley's
affecting and austerely told story, and readers will cheer for
steadfast Ada as she triumphs over despair." Booklist

Brahmachari, Sita

Jasmine Skies; by Sita Brahmachari. Albert
Whitman & Company 2012 336 p. $16.99
Grades: 6 7 8 9   **Fic**
1. India -- Fiction 2. Family secrets -- Fiction 3.
Interpersonal relations -- Fiction 4. Secrecy 5. Families
-- India 6. Voyages and travels 7. Dysfunctional
families 8. Dating (social customs)
ISBN 0807537829; 1447205189; 9780807537824;
9781447205180

LC 2014013302

"Mira Levenson is excited to visit India for the first time.
But upon arriving she is hurled into new sights, sounds,
sweltering heat and deeply buried family secrets. From the
moment Mira meets Janu she feels an instant connection to
him. Nothing is as she imagined it--and suddenly home feels
a long way away. But Mira is determined to uncover the

truth about her family, and she must also make a decision
that will break someone's heart." (Publisher's note)

"Vivid descriptions of the exotic setting, an emotionally
honest (if naive and stubborn) narrator, and a sweet romance
should captivate readers." Booklist

Mira in the present tense; Sita Brahmachari. Al-
bert Whitman & Co 2013 284 p.
Grades: 5 6 7 8   **Fic**
1. Grief -- Fiction 2. Teenage girls -- Fiction 3. Diaries
-- Fiction 4. Secrecy -- Fiction 5. Families -- Fiction
ISBN 080755149X; 9780807551493

In this middle grades book by Sita Brahmachari,
"Twelve-year-old Mira comes from a chaotic, artistic, and
outspoken family in which it's not always easy to be heard.
As her beloved Nana Josie's health declines, Mira begins to
discover the secrets of those around her and also starts to
keep some of her own. She is drawn to mysterious Jide, a
boy who is clearly hiding a troubled past." (Publisher's note)

"Mira narrates her story through a diary she receives for
her twelfth birthday. She lives in London, is half Jewish and
one-quarter Indian, and has joined a writing club at school.
A few too many events and characters crowd the otherwise
engaging story, which focuses on Mira's loving relationship
with her Nana Josie, who is dying from cancer. " Horn Book

Brande, Robin

Evolution, me, & other freaks of nature. Alfred
A. Knopf 2007 268p hardcover o.p. pa $7.99
Grades: 7 8 9 10   **Fic**
1. School stories 2. Evolution -- Fiction 3. Christian
life -- Fiction
ISBN 978-0-375-84349-5; 0-375-84349-3; 978-0-375-
94349-2 lib bdg; 0-375-94349-8 lib bdg; 978-0-440-
24030-3 pa; 0-440-24030-1 pa

LC 2006-34158

Following her conscience leads high school freshman
Mena to clash with her parents and former friends from
their conservative Christian church, but might result in better things when she stands up for a teacher who refuses to
include "Intelligent Design" in lessons on evolution.

"Readers will appreciate this vulnerable but ultimately
resilient protagonist who sees no conflict between science
and her own deeply rooted faith." Booklist

★ **Fat** Cat. Alfred A. Knopf 2009 330p $16.99;
lib bdg $19.99
Grades: 8 9 10 11 12   **Fic**
1. School stories 2. Obesity -- Fiction 3. Friendship
-- Fiction 5. Science -- Experiments -- Fiction
ISBN 0-375-84449-X; 0-375-94449-4 lib bdg; 978-0-
375-84449-2; 978-0-375-94449-9 lib bdg

LC 2008-50619

Overweight teenager Catherine embarks on a high
school science project in which she must emulate the ways
of hominids, the earliest ancestors of human beings, by eating an all-natural diet and foregoing technology. "Grades
seven to ten." (Bull Cent Child Books)

The author "offers a fresh, funny portrait of a strong-
minded young woman hurdling obstacles and fighting cravings to reach her goal." Publ Wkly

Brandeis, Gayle

My life with the Lincolns. Holt & Co. 2010
248p $16.99

Grades: 4 5 6 7   **Fic**

1. Family life -- Fiction 2. Race relations -- Fiction 3.
African Americans -- Fiction
ISBN 978-0-8050-9013-0; 0-8050-9013-4

                         LC 2009-24151

"Twelve-year-old Mina Edelman is convinced that her
family members are the Lincolns reincarnate, and she has
many coincidences to back her up. . . . The strong theme of
social justice creates a unifying thread in this informative,
clear, personal, and passionate novel." Booklist

Brashares, Ann

3 willows; the sisterhood grows. Delacorte Press
2009 318p $18.99; lib bdg $21.99

Grades: 6 7 8 9 10   **Fic**

1. Maryland -- Fiction 2. Friendship -- Fiction
ISBN 978-0-385-73676-3; 0-385-73676-2; 978-0-385-
90628-9 lib bdg; 0-385-90628-5 lib bdg

                         LC 2008-34873

Ama, Jo, and Polly, three close friends from Bethesda,
Maryland, spend the summer before ninth grade learning
about themselves, their families, and the changing nature of
their friendship.

"Brashares gets her characters' emotions and interactions just right." Publ Wkly

The **sisterhood** of the traveling pants. Delacorte
Press 2001 294p $14.95; pa $8.95; pa $9.99

Grades: 8 9 10   **Fic**

1. Friendship -- Fiction
ISBN 0-385-72933-2; 0-385-73058-6 pa;
9780385730587 pa

                         LC 2002-282046

"Four teenagers—best friends since babyhood—have
different destinations for the summer and are distressed
about disbanding. When they find a pair of 'magic pants'—
secondhand jeans that fit each girl perfectly, despite their
different body types—they take a solemn vow that the Pants
'will travel to all the places we're going, and they will keep
us together when we are apart.' . . . Middle school, high
school." (Horn Book)

"Four lifelong high-school friends and a magical pair
of jeans take summer journeys to discover love, disappointment, and self-realization." Booklist

Brauner, Barbara

The **glitter** trap; Barbara Brauner, James Iver
Mattson. 1st ed. Disney-Hyperion Books 2013 240
p. (Oh my godmother) (reinforced) $16.99

Grades: 4 5 6 7   **Fic**

1. Fairies -- Fiction 2. Middle schools -- Fiction 3.
Humorous fiction
ISBN 1423163737; 9781423163732

                         LC 2013930976

In this children's novel, by Barbara Brauner, James Iver
Mattson, and illustrated by Abigail Halpin, "middle school is
far from a fairytale for adorkable misfit Lacey Unger-Ware.
When Lacey ends up with popular girl Paige Harrington's
smart-mouthed fairy godmother, Katarina, trapped in her

hair, life gets more magical--just not in a 'prince charming'
kind of way. Katarina's wings are too damaged to continue
her fairy duties, and Lacey must take over as Paige's fairy
godmother." (Publisher's note)

The **magic** mistake; Barbara Brauner and James
Iver Mattson ; illustrated by Abigail Halpin. Disney-
Hyperion Books 2014 256 p. illustrations (Oh my
godmother) (hardback) $16.99

Grades: 4 5 6 7   **Fic**

1. School stories 2. Humorous fiction 3. Fractured
fairy tales 4. Magic -- Fiction 5. Schools -- Fiction 6.
Middle schools -- Fiction 7. Fairy godmothers -- Fiction
ISBN 142316475X; 9781423164753

                         LC 2013029798

"Twelve year old Lacey Unger-Ware . . . is invited to attend the Godmother Academy. . . . But this is an offer Lacey
can't refuse. . . . Lacey will be cursed forever if she doesn't
complete the magical test. Now Lacey must find the true
love for one special lady and arrange the perfect wedding
before time runs out." (Publisher's note)

"The real draw here is Lacey, whose relatively normal
life just happens to be touched with unexpected magic. She
is the type of character that readers will cheer for and could
see as their own best friend as well." Booklist

Bray, Libba

★ **Beauty** queens. Scholastic Press 2011 396p
$18.99

Grades: 8 9 10 11 12   **Fic**

1. Beauty contests -- Fiction 2. Survival after airplane
accidents, shipwrecks, etc. -- Fiction
ISBN 978-0-439-89597-2; 0-439-89597-9

                         LC 2011-02321

In this book by Libba Bray, "on their way to the Miss
Teen Dream competition, a planeload of beauty pageant
contestants crashes on what appears to be a deserted island.
While the surviving Teen Dreamers valiantly cope with the
basics (finding food, water, and shelter; practicing their pageant skills), they become pawns in a massive global conspiracy involving a rogue former Miss Teen Dream winner;
a megalomaniacal dictator; and a Big Brother-ish pageant
sponsor, The Corporation." (Horn Book Magazine)

"A full-scale send-up of consumer culture, beauty pageants, and reality television: . . . it makes readers really examine their own values while they are laughing, and shaking
their heads at the hyperbolic absurdity of those values gone
seriously awry." Bull Cent Child Books

Breen, M. E.

★ **Darkwood**. Bloomsbury 2009 273p il
$16.99

Grades: 5 6 7 8   **Fic**

1. Fantasy fiction 2. Adventure fiction 3. Wolves --
Fiction 4. Orphans -- Fiction 5. Sisters -- Fiction
ISBN 978-1-59990-259-3; 1-59990-259-1

                         LC 2008-44413

A clever and fearless orphan endures increasing danger
while trying to escape from greedy, lawless men and elude
the terrifying "kinderstalks"—animals who steal children—
before discovering her true destiny.

"Breen's finely tuned storytelling—pithy description, quick and keen emotion, broad trust of readers' intelligence—offers equal gratification whether readers spot clues and connections early or late. Both grounded and wondrous." Kirkus

Brenna, Beverly

Waiting for no one. Red Deer 2011 187p pa $12.95

Grades: 7 8 9 10   **Fic**

1. Asperger's syndrome -- Fiction

ISBN 978-0-88995-437-3; 0-88995-437-2

Sequel to Wild orchid (2006)

Taylor Jane Smith is "taking a biology class at college and applying for a job at a local bookstore. Her Asperger's syndrome gives her an advantage in the class, but it's making the job-application process torture. . . . Taylor, with her flinty, exasperated approach to the world, remains a fascinating character and narrator." Bull Cent Child Books

Brennan, Caitlin

House of the star. Tor 2010 282p $17.99

Grades: 7 8 9 10   **Fic**

1. Fantasy fiction 2. Magic -- Fiction 3. Horses -- Fiction 4. Arizona -- Fiction 5. Princesses -- Fiction 6. Ranch life -- Fiction

ISBN 978-0-7653-2037-7; 0-7653-2037-1

LC 2010-36678

"Princess Elen of Ymbria has always wanted to be a rider of a worldrunner—a magical horse that can travel safely on faerie roads between worlds. She is invited to Earth to stay at the House of Star, an Arizona ranch where these animals are bred. The only catch is that someone from the royal family of Caledon has been invited as well. . . . Brennan creates a magical world based around a realistic ranch setting. The two main characters are complex and avoid the common clichés about princesses. Fans of fantasy and horses will find an intriguing premise and a galloping plot." SLJ

Brennan, Herbie

The **Doomsday** Box; a Shadow Project adventure. Balzer & Bray 2011 328p $16.99

Grades: 6 7 8 9   **Fic**

1. Spies -- Fiction 2. Plague -- Fiction 3. Cold war -- Fiction 4. Time travel -- Fiction 5. Extrasensory perception -- Fiction

ISBN 978-0-06-175647-4; 0-06-175647-4

LC 2010-15947

Sequel to: The Shadow Project (2010)

Working on a highly-classified espionage project, four English teenagers go back in time to the Cold War in 1962 to prevent a global outbreak of the bubonic plague in the twenty-first century.

"Readers who enjoy their action/adventure laced with weird science and real politics will enjoy this fast-paced, exciting second in the series." Bull Cent Child Books

The **Shadow** Project. Balzer & Bray 2010 355p $16.99

Grades: 6 7 8 9   **Fic**

1. Spies -- Fiction 2. Supernatural -- Fiction 3. Great

Britain -- Fiction

ISBN 978-0-06-175642-9; 0-06-175642-3

LC 2009-14276

A young English thief stumbles on, and subsequently is recruited for, a super-secret operation that trains teenagers in remote viewing and astral projection techniques in order to engage in spying.

"The action has a ready-for-its-close-up cinematic quality, and there's a manageable blend of stock and original, fully fleshed characters to guarantee investment and relatability. This is the kind of mind candy that action/adventure junkies will gobble right up." Bull Cent Child Books

Followed by: The Doomsday Box (2011)

Brennan, J. H., 1940-

The **secret** prophecy; Herbie Brennan. Balzer + Bray 2012 322 p. (hardback) $27.95

Grades: 5 6 7 8   **Fic**

1. Murder -- Fiction 2. England -- Fiction 3. Conspiracies -- Fiction 4. Secret societies -- Fiction 5. Mystery and detective stories 6. Adventure and adventurers -- Fiction

ISBN 0691155895; 9780062071804

LC 2012024991

Brennan, Sarah Rees

Team Human; Justine Larbalestier and Sarah Rees Brennan. HarperTeen 2012 344 p. (tr. bdg.) $17.99

Grades: 8 9 10 11 12   **Fic**

1. Love stories 2. School stories 3. Vampires -- Fiction 4. Female friendship -- Fiction 5. Maine -- Fiction 6. Schools -- Fiction 7. High schools -- Fiction

ISBN 0062089641; 9780062089649

LC 2011026149

In this book, "[h]igh school senior Mel Duan is not impressed when a 150-year old vampire (who looks like a teenager and talks like a 19th-century poet) enrolls in her school. Sure, New Whitby, Maine, is known for its large vampire population, but the vamps and humans keep to their own. Mel finds Francis merely annoying until her best friend Cathy falls for him and decides to become a vampire herself, at which point Mel shifts into full-blown protective mode." (Publishers Weekly)

Unspoken; by Sarah Rees Brennan. Random House Books for Young Readers 2012 373 p. (The Lynburn legacy) (hardcover) $18.99

Grades: 7 8 9 10   **Fic**

1. Gothic novels -- Fiction 2. Fantasy fiction -- Fiction 3. Mystery fiction -- Fiction 4. Horror stories 5. Magic -- Fiction 6. England -- Fiction 7. Magicians -- Fiction

ISBN 9780375870415; 9780375970412

LC 2012001954

This juvenile gothic mystery, by Sarah Rees Brennan, starts The Lynburn Legacy series. "Kami Glass knows that she could be a great reporter. . . . The aristocratic, secretive Lynburns are coming home, . . . and Kami is determined . . . [to] get the scoop. Soon, two gorgeous, near-identical Lynburn cousins . . . join her journalistic team--not to mention Kami's imaginary best friend, . . . who turns out to be not quite so imaginary after all. And that's when the grisly murders start." (Kirkus Reviews)

Brewer, Heather

The **chronicles** of Vladimir Tod: eighth grade bites. Dutton Children's Books 2007 182p (The chronicles of Vladimir Tod) $16.99

Grades: 6 7 8 9   **Fic**
    1. School stories 2. Orphans -- Fiction 3. Vampires -- Fiction
    ISBN 978-0-525-47811-9; 0-525-47811-6
                                                    LC 2006030455

For thirteen years, Vlad, aided by his aunt and best friend, has kept secret that he is half-vampire, but when his missing teacher is replaced by a sinister substitute, he learns that there is more to being a vampire, and to his parents' deaths, than he could have guessed.

This "is an exceptional current-day vampire story. The mix of typical teen angst and dealing with growing vampiric urges make for a fast-moving, engaging story." Voice Youth Advocates

    Other in this series are:
    Ninth grade slays (2008)
    Tenth grade bleeds (2009)
    Eleventh grade burns (2010)

The **chronicles** of Vladimir Tod: ninth grade slays. Dutton Children's Books 2008 278p (The chronicles of Vladimir Tod) $17; pa $7

Grades: 6 7 8 9   **Fic**
    1. Horror fiction 2. School stories 3. Orphans -- Fiction 4. Vampires -- Fiction
    ISBN 978-0-5254-7892-8; 0-5254-7892-2; 978-0-14-241342-5 pa; 0-14-241342-9 pa
                                                    LC 007028300
    Sequel to: Eighth grade bites (2007)

While half-vampire Vlad, his best friend Henry, and Henry's cousin Joss make their way through their freshman year at Bathory High, a hired vampire slayer seeks to destroy Vlad.

"Brewer does an excellent job keeping readers on their toes with an intense plot full of many twists and turns. Her writing style is original, witty, and on target." SLJ

    Followed by: Tenth grade bleeds (2009)

Eleventh grade burns. Dutton Children's Books 2010 309p (The chronicles of Vladimir Tod) $16.99; pa $8.99

Grades: 6 7 8 9   **Fic**
    1. Horror fiction 2. School stories 3. Orphans -- Fiction 4. Vampires -- Fiction
    ISBN 978-0-525-42243-3; 0-525-42243-9; 978-0-14-241647-1 pa; 0-14-241647-9 pa

Another year at Bathory High goes bad for Vlad Tod when his former friend, now a vampire slayer, returns to town and a mysterious and powerful new vampire arrives with a thirst for Vlad's blood.

"There is enough back story provided for readers to begin with this book without being lost, but series fans will learn new aspects involving many familiar characters." Voice Youth Advocates

First kill. Dial Books for Young Readers 2011 309p il (The Slayer chronicles) $17.99

Grades: 6 7 8 9   **Fic**
    1. Horror fiction 2. Vampires -- Fiction
    ISBN 0-8037-3741-6; 978-0-8037-3741-9
                                                    LC 2011006061

The summer before ninth grade, when Joss sets off to meet his uncle and hunt down the beast that murdered his younger sister three years earlier, he learns he is destined to join the Slayer Society.

"This companion volume to Brewer's Vlad series (Twelfth Grade Kills, 2010, etc.) provides a simple entry point into the opposite side of the vampire world—those tasked with killing the undead. . . . Action flows seamlessly into drama, and a betrayal comes after a series of clever misdirections." Kirkus

Tenth grade bleeds. Dutton Children's Books 2009 292p (The chronicles of Vladimir Tod) $16.99; pa $8.99

Grades: 6 7 8 9   **Fic**
    1. Horror fiction 2. School stories 3. Orphans -- Fiction 4. Vampires -- Fiction
    ISBN 978-0-525-42135-1; 0-525-42135-1; 978-0-14-241560-3 pa; 0-14-241560-X pa
                                                    LC 2008-34213
    Sequel to: Ninth grade slays (2008)

As the evil vampire D'Ablo seeks the ritual that would steal half-vampire Vlad's powers, Vlad struggles to resist feeding on the people around him, has a conflict with his best friend Henry, and gives up all hope of a normal year at Bathory High.

"Fans will eat up this installment, but new readers will find sufficient back story to enjoy the book on its own. . . . This book will be highly anticipated by fans of the teen vampire genre." Voice Youth Advocates

Brewster, Alicia Wright

Echo; Alicia Wright Brewster. Dragonfairy Press 2013 291 p. (paperback) $14.95

Grades: 7 8 9 10 11 12   **Fic**
    1. Magic -- Fiction 2. End of the world -- Fiction
    ISBN 0985023023; 9780985023027
                                                    LC 2012951596

In this book by Alicia Wright Brewster, "Earth-Two . . . will end in 10 days. Calling up all elemental practitioners to help, the Council elders have averted catastrophe only by repeatedly rewinding time back 10 days before the end. With each rewind, they become weakened echoes of their original selves. . . . Their efforts focus on eliminating the Mages--formerly human 'ether manipulators' whose elemental energies have consumed their humanity--causing the crisis." (Kirkus Reviews)

"Fully realized characters from Asha to the walk-ons lend their intense authenticity to the plot, which straddles the line between fantasy and science fiction, and deflect attention from the rubber science. This world has depth, mirroring the memorable characters who populate it." Kirkus

Brezenoff, Steve

Brooklyn, burning. Carolrhoda Lab 2011 202p $17.95

Grades: 8 9 10 11   **Fic**
1. Musicians -- Fiction 2. Runaway teenagers -- Fiction
3. Brooklyn (New York, N.Y.) -- Fiction
ISBN 978-0-7613-7526-5

LC 2010051447

"Homelessness, queerness and the rougher sides of living on the street are handled without a whiff of sensationalism, and the moments between Kid, the first-person narrator, and Scout, addressed as 'you,' are described in language so natural and vibrant that readers may not even notice that neither character's gender is ever specified.... Overall, the tone is as raw, down-to-earth and transcendent as the music Scout and Kid ultimately make together." Kirkus

Briant, Ed
Choppy socky blues. Flux 2010 259p pa $9.95
Grades: 7 8 9 10   **Fic**
1. Karate -- Fiction 2. Great Britain -- Fiction 3. Dating (Social customs) -- Fiction 4. Father-son relationship -- Fiction
ISBN 978-0-7387-1897-2; 0-7387-1897-1

LC 2009-30491

In the South of England, fourteen-year-old Jay resumes contact with his father, a movie stuntman and karate instructor, after two years of estrangement to impress a girl who turns out to be the girlfriend of Jay's former best friend.

"Jason's insecurities, resentment toward (and gradual peacemaking with) his father, and obsession with girls are believably rendered—he's the kind of awkward hero readers will be glad to see come into his own." Publ Wkly

I am (not) the walrus; Ed Briant. 1st ed. Flux 2012 280 p. (pbk.) $9.95
Grades: 8 9 10 11   **Fic**
1. Love stories 2. Rock music -- Fiction 3. Bands (Music) -- Fiction
ISBN 073873246X; 9780738732466

LC 2012004314

This novel, by Ed Briant, describes how "Toby and Zack's first gig could make or break their Beatles cover band, the Nowhere Men. But ever since getting dumped by his girlfriend, lead singer Toby can't quite pull off the Beatles' feel-good vibe. When Toby finds a note hidden inside his brother's bass claiming the instrument was stolen, he embarks on a quest to find the true owner--and hopes a girl named Michelle will help him recover his lost mojo along the way." (Publisher's note)

Bridges, Robin
The **gathering** storm; Robin Bridges. 1st ed. Delacorte Press 2012 387 p. (Katerina trilogy) (ebook) $29.97; (hardcover) $17.99; (library) $20.99
Grades: 7 8 9 10 11 12   **Fic**
1. Supernatural -- Fiction 2. Fantasy fiction -- Fiction 3. Russia -- History -- Fiction 4. Russia -- Fiction 5. Vampires -- Fiction 6. Supernatural -- Fiction 7. Good and evil -- Fiction 8. Courts and courtiers -- Fiction
ISBN 0385740220; 0385908296; 9780375899010; 9780385740227; 9780385908290

LC 2011026175

This novel, by Robin Bridges, follows "sixteen-year-old Katerina.... [T]he Crown Prince of Montenegro has taken

an interest in Katiya; after a series of . . . encounters with dark faeries and reanimated corpses, however, Katiya realizes that the prince's attention has more to do with her . . . [being] a necromancer. . . . She soon finds herself ensnared in a political plot . . . against a legion of undead ghouls awoken by vampires." (Bulletin of the Center for Children's Books)

"The fully realized setting, a fantastical version of pre-revolutionary Russia, adds a level of believability to this [book]. . . . An atmospheric and complicated vampire tale." Kirkus

Britt, Fanny
Jane, the fox & me; [written by] Fanny Britt ; [illustrated by] Isabelle Arsenault ; translated by Christine Morelli and Susan Ouriou. Pgw 2013 101 p. $19.95
Grades: 5 6 7 8 9   **Fic**
1. Teenage girls -- Fiction 2. Alienation (Social psychology) -- Fiction
ISBN 1554983606; 9781554983605

Written by Fanny Britt, illustrated by Isabelle Arsentault, and translated by Christine Morelli and Susan Ouriou, this "graphic novel reveals the casual brutality of which children are capable, but also assures readers that redemption can be found through connecting with another, whether the other is a friend, a fictional character or even, amazingly, a fox." (Publisher's note) It "centers on Hélène, ostracized by her former friends and now a loner at school." (Horn Book Magazine)

"Britt's well-constructed narrative is achieved sensitively through Arsenault's impressionistic artwork. . . . An elegant and accessible approach to an important topic." Booklist

Brittain, Bill
The **wish** giver; three tales of Coven Tree. drawings by Andrew Glass. Harper & Row 1983 181p il $16.89; pa $5.99
Grades: 5 6 7 8   **Fic**
1. Magic -- Fiction 2. Wishes -- Fiction
ISBN 0-06-020687-X; 0-06-440168-5 pa

LC 82-48264

A Newbery Medal honor book, 1984

"Captivating, fresh, and infused with homespun humor." Horn Book

Other titles about Coven Tree are:
Dr. Dredd's wagon of wonders (1987)
Professor Popkin's prodigious polish (1990)

Broach, Elise
★ **Masterpiece**; illustrated by Kelly Murphy. Henry Holt & Co. 2008 292p il $16.95
Grades: 4 5 6 7   **Fic**
1. Mystery fiction 2. Artists -- Fiction 3. Beetles -- Fiction 4. New York (N.Y.) -- Fiction
ISBN 978-0-8050-8270-8; 0-8050-8270-0

After Marvin, a beetle, makes a miniature drawing as an eleventh birthday gift for James, a human with whom he shares a house, the two new friends work together to help recover a Durer drawing stolen from the Metropolitan Museum of Art.

Broach "packs this fast-moving story with perennially seductive themes: hidden lives and secret friendships,

miniature worlds lost to disbelievers. . . . Loosely imply-
ing rather than imitating the Old Masters they reference, the
finely hatched drawings depict the settings realistically and
the characters, especially the beetles, with joyful comic license." Publ Wkly

★ **Shakespeare's** secret; [by] Elise Broach.
Henry Holt 2005 250p il $16.95; pa $5.99
Grades: 5 6 7 8   **Fic**
  1. Mystery fiction
  ISBN 0-8050-7387-6; 0-312-37132-2 pa
                                              LC 2004-54020
  Named after a character in a Shakespeare play, misfit
sixth-grader Hero becomes interested in exploring this unusual connection because of a valuable diamond supposedly
hidden in her new house, an intriguing neighbor, and the unexpected attention of the most popular boy in school.
  "The mystery alone will engage readers. . . . The main
characters are all well developed, and the dialogue is both
realistic and well planned." SLJ

Brodien-Jones, Christine

  The **glass** puzzle; Christine Brodien-Jones.
Delacorte Press 2013 336 p. (hc) $16.99
Grades: 4 5 6 7   **Fic**
  1. Horror fiction 2. Fantasy fiction 3. Wales -- Fiction
  4. Cousins -- Fiction 5. Time travel -- Fiction 6.
  Supernatural -- Fiction 7. Tenby (Wales) -- Fiction
  8. Adventure and adventurers -- Fiction 9. Wales --
  History -- 1063-1284 -- Fiction
  ISBN 0385742975; 9780307979933; 9780375990878;
  9780385742979; 9780385742986
                                              LC 2012015999
  In this book, Zoé Badger and her cousin find an antique
glass puzzle and unwittingly release Scravens—evil creatures with a craterous third eye and massive wings—into
Tenby. The cousins, in turn, are magically transported to
Wythernsea, an island long submerged underwater, whence
the Scravens come. There they learn that Scravens are taking
over the bodies of Tenby inhabitants—as well as terrorizing
Wythernsea—and that they must save both towns from the
creatures." (Kirkus Reviews)

Brody, Jessica

  My life undecided. Farrar, Straus and Giroux
2011 299p $16.99
Grades: 6 7 8 9   **Fic**
  1. School stories 2. Weblogs -- Fiction 3. Decision
  making -- Fiction 4. Books and reading -- Fiction
  ISBN 978-0-374-39905-4; 0-374-39905-0
                                              LC 2009051277
  Fifteen-year-old Brooklyn has been making bad decisions since, at age two, she became famous for falling down
a mine shaft, and so she starts a blog to let others make every decision for her, while her community-service hours are
devoted to a woman who insists Brooklyn read her 'Choose
the Story' books.
  "Brooklyn is a sympathetic protagonist with whom
teens will identify. Her journey is fun to read, and decision-
challenged readers will learn an important lesson about self-
acceptance along the way." SLJ

Unremembered; Jessica Brody. Farrar Straus &
Giroux 2013 320 p. (hardcover) $17.99
Grades: 7 8 9 10   **Fic**
  1. Amnesia -- Fiction 2. Survival after airplane
  accidents, shipwrecks, etc. -- Fiction 3. Science fiction
  4. Space and time -- Fiction 5. Foster home care --
  Fiction 6. Aircraft accidents -- Fiction 7. Genetic
  engineering -- Fiction
  ISBN 0374379912; 9780374379919
                                              LC 2012004545
  In this young adult science fiction novel, by Jessica Brody, "when Freedom Airlines flight 121 went down . . . , the
sixteen-year-old girl discovered floating among the wreckage . . . is making headlines across the globe. . . . Her body
is miraculously unharmed and she has no memories. . . . No
one knows how she survived. No one knows why she wasn't
on the passenger manifest. And no one can explain why her
DNA and fingerprints can't be found in a single database in
the world." (Publisher's note)
  "The amnesiac sole survivor of a plane crash, Sera learns
that she's a human experiment with sinister forces tracking
her down; Zen, who tells her that he's her pre-memory-wipe
soul mate, tries to keep her safe. Sera is too much of a blank
slate to make a compelling focal point, but the fated romance
and intriguing time-travel elements will attract readers."
Horn Book

Brooks, Bruce

  All that remains. Atheneum Bks. for Young
Readers 2001 168p $16; pa $6.99
Grades: 7 8 9 10   **Fic**
  1. Death -- Fiction
  ISBN 0-689-83351-2; 0-689-83442-X pa
                                              LC 00-56912
  "All three offerings feature believable dialogue and at-
titudes true to the emotions of their young characters as well
as intriguingly offbeat events." Horn Book Guide

  The **moves** make the man; a novel. HarperCol-
lins Pubs. 1984 280p hardcover o.p. pa $6.99
Grades: 7 8 9 10 11 12   **Fic**
  1. Friendship -- Fiction 2. African Americans -- Fiction
  ISBN 0-06-020679-9; 0-06-440564-8 pa
  A Newbery Medal honor book, 1985
  This is an "excellent novel about values and the way
people relate to one another." N Y Times Book Rev

  What hearts. HarperCollins Pubs. 1992 194p
$14/Can$18.75; lib bdg $13.89; rpt $6.99
Grades: 5 6 7 8   **Fic**
  1. Remarriage -- Fiction
  ISBN 0-06-021131-8; 0-06-021132-6 lib bdg;
  9780064471275 rpt
                                              LC 92-5305
  Newbery Honor Book (1993)
  "This novel is composed of four short stories that begin
when the main character, Asa, is just graduating from the
first grade and ends when Asa is an adolescent. The stories
are about love—within a family, among friends, between
boy and girl, husband and wife. . . . Age twelve and up."
(Horn Book)

"This present-day saga traces the formative years of Asa, who has spent most of his life moving from one town to another with his emotionally fragile mother and bullying stepfather. . . . Asa takes on the role of protector as he chooses to make sacrifices in order to save his mother's marriage or prevent her from falling into a depressive state." Publ Wkly

Brooks, Laurie

Selkie girl; a novel. Alfred A. Knopf 2008 262p $15.99; lib bdg $18.99

Grades: 7 8 9 10 **Fic**

1. Fantasy fiction 2. Scotland -- Fiction 3. Seals (Animals) -- Fiction

ISBN 978-0-375-85170-4; 0-375-85170-4; 978-0-375-95170-1 lib bdg; 0-375-95170-9 lib bdg

LC 2008-03547

When sixteen-year-old Elin Jean finds a seal pelt hidden at home and realizes that her mother is actually a selkie, she returns the pelt to her mother, only to find her life taking many unexpected turns.

"An extraordinary, beautifully written tale about belonging, love, and the laws of nature. . . . Brooks's rich prose reverberates with vivid, cinematic images." SLJ

Brooks, Martha

★ **Mistik** Lake. Farrar, Straus and Giroux 2007 207p $16

Grades: 8 9 10 **Fic**

1. Mothers -- Fiction 2. Manitoba -- Fiction 3. Family life -- Fiction

ISBN 978-0-374-34985-1; 0-374-34985-1

LC 2006-37391

After Odella's mother leaves her, her sisters, and their father in Manitoba and moves to Iceland with another man, she then dies there, and the family finally learns some of the secrets that have haunted them for two generations. "Grades seven to ten." (Bull Cent Child Books)

"All of the characters seem distinct and real, thanks to the author's exceptional skill with details." Publ Wkly

★ **Queen** of hearts. Farrar Straus Giroux 2011 224p $16.99

Grades: 7 8 9 10 **Fic**

1. Sick -- Fiction 2. Manitoba -- Fiction 3. Hospitals -- Fiction 4. Family life -- Fiction 5. Tuberculosis -- Fiction

ISBN 978-0-374-34229-6; 0-374-34229-6

LC 2010-52661

Shortly after her first kiss but before her sixteenth birthday in December, 1941, Marie Claire and her younger brother and sister are sent to a tuberculosis sanatorium near their Manitoba farm.

"Readers will be held by the story's heartbreaking truths, right to the end." Booklist

Brothers, Meagan

★ **Debbie** Harry sings in French. Henry Holt 2008 232p $16.95

Grades: 8 9 10 11 12 **Fic**

1. Sex role -- Fiction 2. Rock music -- Fiction 3.

Transvestites -- Fiction

ISBN 978-0-8050-8080-3; 0-8050-8080-5

LC 2007-27322

When Johnny completes an alcohol rehabilitation program and his mother sends him to live with his uncle in North Carolina, he meets Maria, who seems to understand his fascination with the new wave band Blondie, and he learns about his deceased father's youthful forays into "glam rock," which gives him perspective on himself, his past, and his current life.

"The brisk pace and the strong-willed, empathetic narrator will keep readers fully engaged." Publ Wkly

Brouwer, Sigmund

Devil's pass; Sigmund Brouwer. Orca Book Publishers 2012 237 p. (pbk) $9.95

Grades: 6 7 8 9 10 **Fic**

1. Grandfathers -- Fiction 2. Voyages and travels -- Fiction 3. Grandparent-grandchild relationship -- Fiction 4. Canada -- Fiction 5. Street musicians -- Fiction 6. Canol Heritage Trail (N.W.T.) -- Fiction

ISBN 155469938X; 9781554699384

LC 2012938220

In author Sigmund Brouwer's book, "seventeen-year-old Webb's abusive stepfather has made it impossible for him to live at home, so Webb survives on the streets of Toronto. . . . When Webb's grandfather dies, his will stipulates that his grandsons fulfill specific requests. Webb's task takes him to the Canol Trail in Canada's Far North. . . . With a Native guide, two German tourists and his guitar for company, Webb is forced to confront terrible events in his grandfather's past and somehow deal with the pain and confusion of his own life." (Publisher's note)

Brown, Don

The **train** jumper. Roaring Brook Press 2007 122p $16.95

Grades: 6 7 8 9 **Fic**

1. Tramps -- Fiction 2. Poverty -- Fiction 3. Great Depression, 1929-1939 -- Fiction

ISBN 978-1-59643-218-5; 1-59643-218-7

LC 2007-03440

Jumping freight trains during the Great Depression leads fourteen-year-old Collie to a friendship with men and boys on their way to "somewhere else."

"The matter-of-fact dialogue is easy to follow and draws readers into an accurate picture of life on the rails during the Depression." SLJ

Brown, Skila

★ **Caminar**; Skila Brown. Candlewick Press 2014 208 p. $15.99

Grades: 6 7 8 9 **Fic**

1. War stories 2. Guatemala -- Fiction 3. Novels in verse 4. Guatemala -- History -- Civil War, 1960-1996 -- fiction

ISBN 0763665169; 9780763665166

LC 2013946611

This book, by Skila Brown, is "set in 1981 Guatemala. . . . Carlos knows that when the soldiers arrive with warnings about the Communist rebels, it is time to be a man and defend the village, keep everyone safe. But Mama tells him not yet.... Numb and alone, he must join a band of guerillas as they trek to the top of the mountain where Carlos's abuela lives. Will he be in time, and brave enough, to warn them about the soldiers? What will he do then?" (Publisher's note)

"—Unlike many novels in verse, which can read like conventional narratives with line breaks, Caminarcontributes poetry that elevates the genre. In this story of a decimated Guatemalan village in 1981, readers will encounter a range of imagery, repetition, rhythms, and visual effects that bring to life the psychological experience of Carlos, a young boy caught in the violent clash between the government's army and the people's rebels...This is a much-needed addition to Latin American-themed middle grade fiction.—" (School Library Journal)

Bruchac, Joseph

Bearwalker; [by] Joseph Bruchac; illustrations by Sally Wern Comport. HarperCollinsPublishers 2007 208p il $15.99; lib bdg $16.89; pa $5.99

Grades: 5 6 7 8   **Fic**

1. Bears -- Fiction 2. Camping -- Fiction 3. Mohawk Indians -- Fiction 4. Adirondack Mountains (N.Y.) -- Fiction

ISBN 978-0-06-112309-2; 0-06-112309-9; 978-0-06-112311-5 lib bdg; 0-06-112311-0 lib bdg; 978-0-06-112315-3 pa; 0-06-112315-3 pa

LC 2006-30420

Although the littlest student in his class, thirteen-year-old Baron Braun calls upon the strength and wisdom of his Mohawk ancestors to face both man and beast when he tries to get help for his classmates, who are being terrorized during a school field trip in the Adirondacks.

"This exciting horror story, illustrated with b/w drawings, is based on Native American folklore." Kliatt

★ **Code** talker; a novel about the Navajo Marines of World War Two. Dial 2005 240p $16.99

Grades: 6 7 8 9 10   **Fic**

1. Navajo Indians -- Fiction 2. World War, 1939-1945 -- Fiction

ISBN 0-8037-2921-9

After being taught in a boarding school run by whites that Navajo is a useless language, Ned Begay and other Navajo men are recruited by the Marines to become Code Talkers, sending messages during World War II in their native tongue.

"Bruchac's gentle prose presents a clear historical picture of young men in wartime. . . . Nonsensational and accurate, Bruchac's tale is quietly inspiring." SLJ

Includes bibliographical references

Night wings; illustrations by Sally Wern Comport. HarperCollins 2009 194p $15.99; lib bdg $16.89

Grades: 5 6 7 8   **Fic**

1. Monsters -- Fiction 2. New Hampshire -- Fiction 3. Abnaki Indians -- Fiction

ISBN 978-0-06-112318-4; 0-06-112318-8; 978-0-06-112319-1 lib bdg; 0-06-112319-6 lib bdg

LC 2008032096

After being taken captive by a band of treasure seekers, thirteen-year-old Paul and his Abnaki grandfather must

face a legendary Native American monster at the top of Mount Washington.

"The intriguing Native lore, the realistic teen narrative, and cliffhanger sentences that build suspense at the end of each chapter are signature Bruchac and will captivate readers." SLJ

★ The **winter** people. Dial Bks. 2002 168p $16.99; pa $5.99

Grades: 5 6 7 8   **Fic**

1. Abnaki Indians -- Fiction 2. United States -- History -- 1755-1763, French and Indian War -- Fiction

ISBN 0-8037-2694-5; 0-14-240229-X pa

LC 2002-338

As the French and Indian War rages in October of 1759, Saxso, a fourteen-year-old Abenaki boy, pursues the English rangers who have attacked his village and taken his mother and sisters hostage

"The narrative itself is thrilling, its spiritual aspects enlightening." Booklist

Bruchac, Joseph, 1942-

Dragon castle. Dial Books for Young Readers 2011 346p $16.99

Grades: 4 5 6 7   **Fic**

1. Fairy tales 2. Dragons -- Fiction 3. Princes -- Fiction 4. Kings and rulers -- Fiction

ISBN 978-0-8037-3376-3; 0-8037-3376-3

LC 2010028798

Young prince Rashko, aided by wise old Georgi, must channel the power of his ancestor, Pavol the great, and harness a magical dragon to face the evil Baron Temny after the foolish King and Queen go missing.

Bruchac "spins a good-natured and humorous fairy tale. . . . With its subtle focus on peaceful resistance and use of classic folk-tale elements, this story exudes a gentle sense of fun." Publ Wkly

Killer of enemies; Joseph Bruchac. Tu Books, an imprint of Lee & Low Books, Inc. 2013 400 p. (hardcover : alk. paper) $19.95

Grades: 7 8 9 10 11 12   **Fic**

1. Dystopian fiction 2. Heroes and heroines -- Fiction 3. Science fiction 4. Hunting -- Fiction 5. Hostages -- Fiction 6. Survival -- Fiction 7. Southwest, New -- Fiction 8. Chiricahua Indians -- Fiction 9. Genetic engineering -- Fiction 10. Extrasensory perception -- Fiction 11. Indians of North America -- Southwest, New -- Fiction

ISBN 1620141434; 9781620141434; 9781620141441

LC 2013023567

American Indian Youth Literature Award Winner (2014)

In this dystopian young adult novel by Joseph Bruchac, "seventeen year old Apache hunter Lozen and her family lives in a world of haves and have-nots. There were the Ones (people so augmented with technology and genetic enhancements that they were barely human) and there was everyone else who served the Ones. . . . She hunts monsters for the Ones who survived the apocalyptic events of the Cloud, which ensures the safety of her kidnapped family." (Publisher's note)

"A deadly assassin with extrasensory powers, Lozen (named for an Apache-Chiricahua warrior-woman forebear) takes out genetically modified superbeasts; her family is being held hostage to ensure her continued service. Bruchac devises ever-more-dangerous battles for his protagonist in the increasingly suspenseful story. What really makes the narrative vibrate is Lozen's sardonic voice, capturing both gallows humor and a very human vulnerability." (Horn Book)

Wolf mark. Lee & Low/Tu Books 2011 377p $17.95

Grades: 6 7 8 9 **Fic**

1. Spies -- Fiction 2. Supernatural -- Fiction 3. Native Americans -- Fiction 4. Father-son relationship -- Fiction
ISBN 1-60060-661-X; 978-1-60060-661-8; 978-1-60060-878-0 e-book

LC 2011014252

When Lucas King's covert-ops father is kidnapped and his best friend Meena is put in danger, Luke's only chance to save them—a skin that will let him walk as a wolf—is hidden away in an abandoned mansion guarded by monsters.

"Bruchac has created a tense, readable novel. He combines Native American lore, supernatural elements, genetic engineering, romance, geopolitics, and adventure in one story. . . . The mystery and edge-of-your-seat action are enough to keep readers hooked." SLJ

Bryant, Jennifer

Kaleidoscope eyes; [by] Jen Bryant. Alfred A. Knopf 2009 264p $15.99; lib bdg $18.99

Grades: 5 6 7 8 **Fic**

1. Mystery fiction 2. Novels in verse 3. New Jersey -- Fiction 4. Buried treasure -- Fiction 5. Vietnam War, 1961-1975 -- Fiction
ISBN 0-375-84048-6; 0-375-94048-0 lib bdg; 978-0-375-84048-7; 978-0-375-94048-4 lib bdg

LC 2008027345

In 1968, with the Vietnam War raging, thirteen-year-old Lyza inherits a project from her deceased grandfather, who had been using his knowledge of maps and the geography of Lyza's New Jersey hometown to locate the lost treasure of Captain Kidd.

"Bryant weaves an emotional novel in poems based on a true story of buried treasure. Tensions among families are drawn with heart-wrenching prose, and her depiction of segregation is flawless. . . . The characters are witty and well developed." Voice Youth Advocates

Pieces of Georgia; a novel. [by] Jen Bryant. Knopf 2006 166p $15.95; lib bdg $17.99

Grades: 6 7 8 9 **Fic**

1. Artists -- Fiction 2. Bereavement -- Fiction
ISBN 0-375-83259-9; 0-375-93259-3 lib bdg

LC 2005-43593

In journal entries to her mother, a gifted artist who died suddenly, thirteen-year-old Georgia McCoy reveals how her life changes after she receives an anonymous gift membership to a nearby art museum.

"This is a remarkable book. . . . [The] story is a universal one of love, friendship, and loss and will be appreciated by a wide audience." SLJ

★ **Ringside,** 1925; views from the Scopes trial, a novel. [by] Jen Bryant. Alfred A. Knopf 2008 228p $15.99; lib bdg $18.99

Grades: 8 9 10 11 12 **Fic**

1. Geologists 2. Novels in verse 3. Science teachers 4. Tennessee -- Fiction 5. Evolution -- Study and teaching -- Fiction
ISBN 978-0-375-84047-0; 0-375-84047-8; 978-0-375-94047-7 lib bdg; 0-375-94047-2 lib bdg

LC 2007-7177

Visitors, spectators, and residents of Dayton, Tennessee, in 1925 describe, in a series of free-verse poems, the Scopes 'monkey trial' and its effects on that small town and its citizens.

"Bryant offers readers a ringside seat in this compelling and well-researched novel. It is fast-paced, interesting, and relevant to many current first-amendment challenges." SLJ

Bryce, Celia

Anthem for Jackson Dawes; by Celia Bryce. Bloomsbury USA Childrens 2013 240 p. (hardback) $16.99

Grades: 7 8 9 10 **Fic**

1. Hospitals -- Fiction 2. Cancer patients -- Fiction 3. Cancer -- Fiction 4. Friendship -- Fiction 5. Family life -- Fiction 6. Medical care -- Fiction
ISBN 1599909758; 9781599909752

LC 2012024989

In this book, "after 13-year-old Megan Bright is diagnosed with a cancerous brain tumor, she's . . . determined to have everything remain as normal as possible during her time in the hospital. . . . Megan gets closer to the only other teenager there . . . and begins to acknowledge the emotions she's been keeping buried. Initially, Jackson rubs her the wrong way, but his positivity and determined interest in Megan teach her about optimism and taking control of what she can." (Publishers Weekly)

"Sensitive and honest, this novel addresses meaningful questions concerning mortality and soul searching, and its content is appropriate for younger teens." SLJ

Buckingham, Royce

Demonkeeper. G. P. Putnam's Sons 2007 216p hardcover o.p. pa $7.99

Grades: 4 5 6 7 **Fic**

1. Horror fiction 2. Supernatural -- Fiction
ISBN 978-0-399-24649-4; 0-399-24649-5; 978-0-14-241166-7 pa; 0-14-241166-3 pa

LC 2006-26541

When Nat, the weirdest boy in Seattle, leaves for a date with the plainest girl in town, chaos breaks out in the houseful of demons of which he is the sole guardian.

"This is horror on the mild side. . . . The easygoing, breezy humor adds appeal to an already engaging premise." Bull Cent Child Books

Buckingham, Royce Scott

The **terminals**; Royce Scott Buckingham. First edition Thomas Dunne Books, St. Martin's Griffin 2014 288 p. (hardback) $18.99

Grades: 7 8 9 10　　　　　　　　　　**Fic**

　　1. Spy stories 2. Adventure fiction 3. Terminally ill -- Fiction 4. Spies -- Fiction 5. Ability -- Fiction 6. Adventure and adventurers -- Fiction

　　ISBN 1250011558; 9781250011558

　　　　　　　　　　　　　　LC 2014031142

This young adult adventure novel, by Royce Scott Buckingham, "tells the . . . story of a covert team of young, terminally ill teens who spend their last year alive running dangerous missions as super-spies. . . . Cam joins this extreme spy team, and . . . as his teammates fall around him, he starts to receive cryptic messages from a haggard survivor of last year's class hiding in the forest. She reveals that the program isn't what it claims to be." (Publisher's note)

"Buckingham's above-average writing and exotic settings are plenty appealing. Fans of Robert Muchamore's Cherub series will eat up this sf-tinged espionage thriller." Booklist

Budhos, Marina

Ask me no questions; [by] Marina Budhos. Atheneum Books for Young Readers 2006 162p $16.95; pa $8.99

Grades: 7 8 9 10　　　　　　　　　　**Fic**

　　1. School stories 2. Family life -- Fiction 3. Asian Americans -- Fiction 4. New York (N.Y.) -- Fiction

　　ISBN 1-4169-0351-8; 1-4169-4920-8 pa

　　　　　　　　　　　　　　LC 2005-1831

Fourteen-year-old Nadira, her sister, and their parents leave Bangladesh for New York City, but the expiration of their visas and the events of September 11, 2001, bring frustration, sorrow, and terror for the whole family.

"Nadira and Aisha's strategies for surviving and succeeding in high school offer sharp insight into the narrow margins between belonging and not belonging." Horn Book Guide

Budhos, Marina Tamar

Tell us we're home; [by] Marina Budhos. Atheneum 2010 297p $16.95

Grades: 6 7 8 9 10　　　　　　　　　　**Fic**

　　1. Immigrants -- Fiction 2. New Jersey -- Fiction 3. Social classes -- Fiction 4. Household employees -- Fiction 5. Mother-daughter relationship -- Fiction

　　ISBN 978-1-4169-0352-9; 1-4169-0352-6

　　　　　　　　　　　　　　LC 2009-27386

Three immigrant girls from different parts of the world meet and become close friends in a small New Jersey town where their mothers have found domestic work, but their relationships are tested when one girl's mother is accused of stealing a precious heirloom.

"These fully realized heroines are full of heart, and their passionate struggles against systemic injustice only make them more inspiring. Keenly necessary." Kirkus

Buffie, Margaret

Winter shadows; a novel. Tundra Books 2010 327p $19.95

Grades: 7 8 9 10　　　　　　　　　　**Fic**

　　1. Manitoba -- Fiction 2. Prejudices -- Fiction 3. Family life -- Fiction 4. Stepmothers -- Fiction 5. Racially mixed people -- Fiction

　　ISBN 978-0-88776-968-9; 0-88776-968-3

"Hatred for their wicked stepmothers bonds two girls living in a stone house in Manitoba, Canada, more than 150 years apart. Grieving for her dead mother, high-school senior Cass is furious that she has to share a room with the daughter of her dad's new, harsh-tempered wife. Then she finds the 1836 diary of Beatrice, who is part Cree and faces vicious racism as a 'half-breed' in her mostly white community. . . . The alternating narratives are gripping, and the characters are drawn with rich complexity." Booklist

Bukiet, Melvin Jules

Undertown; Melvin Jules Bukiet. Amulet Books 2013 304 p. (hardcover) $16.95

Grades: 6 7 8　　　　　　　　　　**Fic**

　　1. Sewerage -- Fiction 2. Adventure fiction 3. Sailing -- Fiction 4. New York (N.Y.) -- Fiction 5. Homeless persons -- Fiction 6. Adventure and adventurers -- Fiction

　　ISBN 141970589X; 9781419705892

　　　　　　　　　　　　　　LC 2012039246

In this adventure novel, by Melvin Jules Bukiet, "Timothy and Jessamyn are towed through the streets of Manhattan riding in Timothy's family's sailboat, . . . The teens . . . then fall down a huge construction site hole and into the vast sewer system below. . . . The kids navigate waterfalls and rapids as they travel through the rain sewers. They meet a graffiti artist their own age, a homeless person named You, and rats the size of large dogs." (Publisher's note)

"Bukiet's first children's outing veers between language carefully designed to appeal to its intended audience and occasionally sophisticated sentence structure and subjects that should instead engage far older readers. Dramatic and imaginative, this will probably most appeal to readers with a taste for the esoteric." BookList

Bullen, Alexandra

Wish; a novel. Point 2010 323p $17.99

Grades: 8 9 10 11 12　　　　　　　　　　**Fic**

　　1. Fantasy fiction 2. Magic -- Fiction 3. Twins -- Fiction 4. Wishes -- Fiction 5. Sisters -- Fiction 6. Bereavement -- Fiction 7. San Francisco (Calif.) -- Fiction

　　ISBN 978-0-545-13905-2; 0-545-13905-8

　　　　　　　　　　　　　　LC 2009-22730

After her vivacious twin sister dies, a shy teenaged girl moves with her parents to San Francisco, where she meets a magical seamstress who grants her one wish.

"The detailed descriptions of San Francisco and above all the sisters' relationship provide solid grounding for a touching, enjoyable read." Kirkus

Followed by: Wishful thinking (2011)

Bunce, Elizabeth C.

★ A **curse** dark as gold; [by] Elizabeth C. Bunce. Arthur A. Levine Books 2008 395p $17.99

Grades: 7 8 9 10　　　　　　　　　　**Fic**

　　1. Magic -- Fiction 2. Uncles -- Fiction 3. Orphans

-- Fiction 4. Sisters -- Fiction 5. Factories -- Fiction
ISBN 978-0-439-89576-7; 0-439-89576-6

LC 2007019759

ALA YALSA Morris Award, 2009

Upon the death of her father, seventeen-year-old Charlotte struggles to keep the family's woolen mill running in the face of an overwhelming mortgage and what the local villagers believe is a curse, but when a man capable of spinning straw into gold appears on the scene she must decide if his help is worth the price.

"This is a rich, compelling story that fleshes out the fairy tale, setting it in the nonspecific past of the Industrial Revolution. Readers unfamiliar with 'Rumplestilskin' will not be at a disadvantage here." KLIATT

Liar's moon. Arthur A. Levine Books 2011 356p $17.99

Grades: 8 9 10 11 12   Fic

1. Fantasy fiction 2. Mystery fiction 3. Magic -- Fiction 4. Thieves -- Fiction 5. Homicide -- Fiction 6. Social classes -- Fiction
ISBN 978-0-545-13608-2; 0-545-13608-3

LC 2011005071

"A solid fantasy sequel embroils its irresistible heroine in mystery, intrigue and romance. . . . A darn good read." Kirkus

★ **Star** crossed. Arthur A. Levine Books 2010 359p $17.99

Grades: 8 9 10 11 12   Fic

1. Fantasy fiction 2. Magic -- Fiction 3. Thieves -- Fiction 4. Religion -- Fiction 5. Social classes -- Fiction 6. Kings and rulers -- Fiction
ISBN 978-0-545-13605-1; 0-545-13605-9

LC 2010-730

In a kingdom dominated by religious intolerance, sixteen-year-old Digger, a street thief, has always avoided attention, but when she learns that her friends are plotting against the throne she must decide whether to join them or turn them in.

"Couching her characters and setting in top-notch writing, Bunce . . . hooks readers into an intelligent page-turner with strong themes of growth, determination, and friendship." Publ Wkly

Followed by: Liar's moon (2011)

Bunting, Eve

Blackwater. HarperCollins Pubs. 1999 146p hardcover o.p. pa $5.99

Grades: 5 6 7 8   Fic

1. Death -- Fiction 2. Guilt -- Fiction
ISBN 0-06-027843-9 lib bdg; 0-06-440890-6 pa

LC 99-24895

When a boy and girl are drowned in the Blackwater River, thirteen-year-old Brodie must decide whether to confess that he may have caused the accident

"Bunting's thought-provoking theme, solid characterization and skillful juggling of suspense and pathos make this a top-notch choice." Publ Wkly

The **pirate** captain's daughter; written by Eve Bunting. Sleeping Bear Press 2011 208p $15.95; pa $8.95

Grades: 7 8 9 10   Fic

1. Pirates -- Fiction 2. Sex role -- Fiction 3. Seafaring life -- Fiction 4. Father-daughter relationship -- Fiction
ISBN 978-1-58536-526-5; 1-58536-526-2; 978-1-58536-525-8 pa; 1-58536-525-4 pa

LC 2010032409

Upon her mother's death, fifteen-year-old Catherine puts her courage and strength to the test by disguising herself as a boy to join her father, a pirate captain, on a ship whose crew includes men who are trying to steal a treasure from him.

"This is a gripping and entertaining novel that will have readers sucked in until the last page. Even teens who are not fond of historical fiction will enjoy." Voice Youth Advocates

The **summer** of Riley. HarperCollins Pubs. 2001 170p $15.95; lib bdg $16.89; pa $5.99

Grades: 4 5 6   Fic

1. Dogs -- Fiction 2. Divorce -- Fiction
ISBN 0-06-029141-9; 0-06-029142-7 lib bdg; 0-06-440927-9 pa

LC 00-63203

"William is still adjusting to his parents' separation and his father's engagement when his beloved grandfather dies. He knows his mother is letting him adopt a dog so he'll start feeling better, and Riley appears to be a perfect pet. . . . But when Riley violates a state law by chasing a neighbor's horse, William has to convince the county commissioners not to destroy his friend. . . . Bunting's story will have strong appeal for middle-graders who will relish the bittersweet but satisfying resolution." Booklist

Burg, Ann E.

★ **All** the broken pieces; a novel in verse. Scholastic Press 2009 218p $16.99

Grades: 7 8 9 10   Fic

1. Novels in verse 2. Adoption -- Fiction 3. Vietnamese Americans -- Fiction 4. Vietnam War, 1961-1975 -- Fiction
ISBN 978-0-545-08092-7; 0-545-08092-4

LC 2008-12381

Two years after being airlifted out of Vietnam in 1975, Matt Pin is haunted by the terrible secret he left behind and, now, in a loving adoptive home in the United States, a series of profound events forces him to confront his past.

This is written "in rapid, simple free verse. . . . The intensity of the simple words . . . will make readers want to rush to the end and then return to the beginning again to make connections between past and present, friends and enemies." Booklist

Serafina's promise; by Ann E. Burg. Scholastic Press 2013 304 p. (alk. paper) $16.99

Grades: 5 6 7 8   Fic

1. Girls -- Fiction 2. Floods -- Fiction 3. Haiti -- Social conditions 4. Novels in verse 5. Haiti -- Fiction 6. Earthquakes -- Fiction 7. Brothers and sisters -- Fiction 8. Family life -- Haiti -- Fiction 9. Port-au-Prince

(Haiti) -- Fiction
ISBN 0545535646; 9780545535649

LC 2012045609

Parents' Choice: Gold Medal Fiction (2013)

In this book, by Ann E. Burg, "Serafina is an 11-year-old Haitian struggling to keep her dream of becoming a doctor alive. Living in a desolate mountain village, Serafina toils at her daily chores while planning to attend school . Serafina has a warm family . . . who all come to support her vision. Then a flood washes away the family home, and the roaring stampede of an earthquake devastates the city of Port-au-Prince, where Serafina's father works." (Publisher's note)

Burg, Shana

A **thousand** never evers. Delacorte Press 2008 301p $15.99; lib bdg $18.99

Grades: 6 7 8 9   **Fic**

1. Race relations -- Fiction 2. African Americans -- Fiction

ISBN 978-0-385-73470-7; 978-0-385-90468-1 lib bdg

As the civil rights movement in the South gains momentum in 1963—and violence against African Americans intensifies—the black residents, including seventh-grader Addie Ann Pickett, in the small town of Kuckachoo, Mississippi, begin their own courageous struggle for racial justice.

This is "gripping. . . . References to significant historical events . . . add authenticity and depth, while Addie's frank, expertly modulated voice delivers an emotional wallop." Publ Wkly

Burgis, Stephanie

Kat, incorrigible. Atheneum Books for Young Readers 2011 298p (The unladylike adventures of Kat Stephenson) $16.99

Grades: 6 7 8 9 10   **Fic**

1. Magic -- Fiction 2. Sisters -- Fiction 3. Great Britain -- History -- 19th century -- Fiction

ISBN 1416994475; 9781416994473

LC 2009032543

In Regency England, when twelve-year-old Kat discovers she has magical powers, she tries to use them to rescue her sister from marrying a man she does not love.

"Regency romance and fantasy adventure all in one, this is a satisfying read and a promising beginning to a trilogy that is sure to be popular with middle school girls." SLJ

Renegade Magic. Atheneum 2012 304p (The unladylike adventures of Kat Stephenson) $16.99

Grades: 6 7 8 9 10   **Fic**

1. Magic -- Fiction 2. Sisters -- Fiction 3. Great Britain -- History -- 1714-1837 -- Fiction

ISBN 9781416994497

Twelve-year-old Kat tries to use her untrained magical powers to prevent use of the wild magic of Sulis Minerva found in Bath, England, where Stepmama has brought the family in hopes of finding Kat's sister a proper match.

"This combination of history and fantasy is sure to please." SLJ

Stolen magic; Stephanie Burgis. 1st ed. Atheneum Books for Young Readers 2013 400 p. (hardcover) $17.99

Grades: 6 7 8 9 10   **Fic**

1. Magic -- Fiction 2. Nobility -- Fiction 3. Marriage -- Fiction 4. Witchcraft -- Fiction 5. Family problems -- Fiction 6. Brothers and sisters -- Fiction 7. Great Britain -- History -- George III, 1760-1820 -- Fiction

ISBN 1416994513; 9781416994510; 9781416994527; 9781442433823

LC 2011042347

In this book by Stephanie Burgis, "[w]ith just days to go before her sister Angeline's long-delayed wedding to Frederick Carlyle, the impetuous Kat Stephenson has resigned herself to good behavior. But Kat's initiation into the magical Order of the Guardians is fast approaching, and trouble seems to follow her everywhere," including "the arrival of the mysterious Marquise de Valmont, who bears suspicious resemblance to Kat's late mother." (Publisher's note)

"Though Kat's longing for the mother she never knew sounds a note of gravitas, the now-too-familiar characters and predictable plotting call for freshening. A final plot twist that moves the series action beyond lives of the rich and titled could do the trick next time around. Kat's fans will want to hang on for Book 4." Kirkus

Burnett, Frances Hodgson

The **secret** garden; illustrated by Inga Moore. Candlewick Press 2008 278p il $21.99

Grades: 3 4 5 6   **Fic**

1. Gardens -- Fiction 2. Orphans -- Fiction 3. Great Britain -- Fiction

ISBN 0-7636-3161-2; 978-0-7636-3161-1

LC 2006051838

First published 1911

A ten-year-old orphan comes to live in a lonely house on the Yorkshire moors where she discovers an invalid cousin and the mysteries of a locked garden.

"Burnett's tale . . . is presented in an elegant, oversize volume and handsomely illustrated with Moore's detailed ink and watercolor paintings. Cleanly laid-out text pages are balanced by artwork ranging from delicate spot images to full-page renderings." SLJ

Burtenshaw, Jenna

Shadowcry. Greenwillow Books 2011 311p (The secrets of Wintercraft) $16.99

Grades: 8 9 10 11 12   **Fic**

1. Fantasy fiction 2. Dead -- Fiction

ISBN 978-0-06-202642-2; 0-06-202642-9

LC 2010025823

Pursued by two ruthless men of the High Council of Albiom, fifteen-year-old Kate Winters discovers that she is one of the Skilled, a rare person who can see through the veil between the living and the dead.

"Elegant, complex prose sweeps readers along." Horn Book

Burton, Rebecca

Leaving Jetty Road; [by] Rebecca Burton. 1st ed.; Knopf 2006 248p $15.95; lib bdg $17.99

Grades: 8 9 10 11 12   **Fic**

1. School stories 2. Australia -- Fiction 3. Friendship

-- Fiction 4. Anorexia nervosa -- Fiction
ISBN 0-375-83488-5; 0-375-93488-X lib bdg
LC 2005018140

"In their final year of high school, best friends Lise, Nat, and Sofia make a New Year's resolution to become vegetarians. . . . As they prepare for the next steps in their lives, the girls become so wrapped up in themselves that they fail to see how their friends are growing, changing, and . . . hurting. Burton does an effective job of weaving the symptoms and personality characteristics of anorexia into an absorbing story about the tug and pull of old friendships as a teen's world expands." Booklist

Butcher, Kristin

Cheat; written by Kristin Butcher. Orca Book Publishers 2010 107p (Orca currents) pa $9.95
Grades: 7 8 9 10   Fic
1. School stories 2. Cheating (Education) -- Fiction
ISBN 978-1-55469-274-3; 1-55469-274-1

Laurel investigates a cheating scam at her high school.
"This novel is a realistic portrayal of high school students' attitudes towards cheating. . . . This is a well-written narrative that will challenge readers to make a decision about what's right and what's wrong." Libr Media Connect

Butler, Dori Hillestad

The **truth** about Truman School; by Dori Hillestad Butler. Albert Whitman 2008 170p $15.95; pa $7.99
Grades: 5 6 7 8   Fic
1. School stories 2. Bullies -- Fiction 3. Journalism -- Fiction 4. Newspapers -- Fiction
ISBN 978-0-8075-8095-0; 0-8075-8095-3; 978-0-8075-8096-7 pa; 0-8075-8096-1 pa
LC 2007-29977

Tired of being told what to write by the school newspaper's advisor, Zibby and her friend Amr start an underground newspaper online where everyone is free to post anything, but things spiral out of control when a cyberbully starts using the site to harrass one popular girl.
"The story moves at a good pace and the timely subject of cyberbullying will be relevant to readers. The language is accessible and the students' voices ring true." SLJ

Buyea, Rob

★ **Because** of Mr. Terupt. Delacorte Press 2010 269p $16.99; lib bdg $19.99
Grades: 4 5 6   Fic
1. School stories 2. Teachers -- Fiction 3. Connecticut -- Fiction 4. Family life -- Fiction
ISBN 0-385-73882-X; 0-385-90749-4 lib bdg; 978-0-385-73882-8; 978-0-385-90749-1 lib bdg
LC 2010-03414

Seven fifth-graders at Snow Hill School in Connecticut relate how their lives are changed for the better by "rookie teacher" Mr. Terupt. "Grades four to six." (Bull Cent Child Books)
"Introducing characters and conflicts that will be familiar to any middle-school student, this powerful and emotional story is likely to spur discussion." Publ Wkly

Mr. Terupt falls again; Rob Buyea. Delacorte Press 2012 356 p. (hc) $16.99
Grades: 4 5 6   Fic
1. Love stories 2. School stories 3. Teacher-student relationship -- Fiction 4. Summer -- Fiction 5. Classrooms -- Fiction 6. Moving, Household -- Fiction
ISBN 0385742053; 9780375989100; 9780375990380; 9780385742054
LC 2012010897

This book is a follow-up to Rob Buyea's "Because of Mr. Terupt." Here, "looping with his students into sixth grade, Mr. Terupt continues to surprise them with challenging projects and perfect reading suggestions." For the seven students who narrate the story, "family worries go along with lingering questions about the health of their teacher. Sixth-grade relationships and a grown-up romance" are also explored. (Kirkus)

Buzbee, Lewis

The **haunting** of Charles Dickens; [illustrated by] Greg Ruth. Feiwel and Friends 2009 357p il $17.99
Grades: 5 6 7 8   Fic
1. Authors 2. Novelists 3. Mystery fiction 4. Authors -- Fiction 5. Kidnapping -- Fiction 6. Family life -- Fiction 7. Missing persons -- Fiction 8. London (England) -- Fiction 9. Great Britain -- History -- 19th century -- Fiction
ISBN 978-0-312-38256-8; 0-312-38256-1
LC 2008028553

Twelve-year-old Meg travels the rooftops and streets of 1862 London, England, in search of her missing brother, Orion, accompanied by a family friend, the famed author Charles Dickens, whose quest is to find his next novel.
"Buzbee creates solid characters . . . and an authentic flavor of Dickensian London, enhanced by Ruth's striking and evocative b&w drawings . . . , while addressing issues of feminism, the search for identity, and child abuse." Publ Wkly

Byars, Betsy Cromer

Cracker Jackson; [by] Betsy Byars. Viking Kestrel 1985 147p hardcover o.p. pa $5.99
Grades: 5 6 7 8   Fic
1. Wife abuse -- Fiction 2. Child abuse -- Fiction
ISBN 0-670-80546-7; 0-14-031881-X pa
LC 84-24684

"Suspense, danger, near-tragedy, heartbreak and tension-relieving, unwittingly comic efforts at seriously heroic action mark this as the best of middle-grade fiction to highlight the problems of wife-battering and child abuse." SLJ

★ The **dark** stairs; a Herculeah Jones mystery. by Betsy Byars. Viking 1994 130p hardcover o.p. pa $5.99
Grades: 4 5 6   Fic
1. Mystery fiction
ISBN 0-670-85487-5; 0-14-240592-2 pa
LC 94-14012

The intrepid Herculeah Jones helps her mother, a private investigator, solve a puzzling and frightening case

"There is plenty to laugh at in this book, including classic chapter headings guaranteed to cause shivers for the uninitiated; practiced mystery readers may feel that they are in on a bit of a joke and appreciate the hint of parody. This is a page-turner that is sure to entice the most reluctant readers." SLJ

Other titles about Herculeah Jones are:

Tarot says beware (1995)
Dead letter (1996)
Death's door (1997)
Disappearing acts (1998)
The black tower (2006)
King of murder (2006)

The **keeper** of the doves; by Betsy Byars. Viking 2002 121p $14.99; pa $5.99

Grades: 4 5 6 7   **Fic**

1. Sisters -- Fiction 2. Kentucky -- Fiction 3. Family life -- Fiction

ISBN 0-670-03576-9; 0-14-240063-7 pa

LC 2002-9283

In the late 1800s in Kentucky, Amie McBee and her four sisters both fear and torment the reclusive and seemingly sinister Mr. Tominski, but their father continues to provide for his needs

"This is Byars at her best—witty, appealing, thought-provoking." Horn Book

Cabot, Meg

★ **Airhead**. Scholastic/Point 2008 340p $16.99

Grades: 7 8 9 10   **Fic**

1. Fashion models -- Fiction 2. New York (N.Y.) -- Fiction 3. Transplantation of organs, tissues, etc. -- Fiction

ISBN 978-0-545-04052-5; 0-545-04052-3

LC 2007-38269

Sixteen-year-old Emerson Watts, an advanced placement student with a disdain for fashion, is the recipient of a "whole body transplant"; and finds herself transformed into one of the world's most famous teen supermodels.

"Cabot's portrayal of Emerson is brilliant. . . . Pure fun, this first series installment will leave readers clamoring for the next." Publ Wkly

Other titles in this series are:
Being Nikki (2009)
Runaway (2010)

★ **All**-American girl. HarperCollins Pubs. 2002 247p hardcover o.p. pa $7.99

Grades: 7 8 9 10   **Fic**

1. Presidents -- Fiction

ISBN 0-06-029469-8; 0-06-029470-1 lib bdg; 0-06-147989-6 pa

LC 2002-19049

A sophomore girl stops a presidential assassination attempt, is appointed Teen Ambassador to the United Nations, and catches the eye of the very cute First Son. "Grades six to ten." (Bull Cent Child Books)

There's "surprising depth in the characters and plenty of authenticity in the cultural details and the teenage

voices—particularly in Sam's poignant, laugh-out-loud narration." Booklist

From the notebooks of a middle school princess; written & illustrated by Meg Cabot. First edition Feiwel & Friends 2015 192 p. illustrations (hardback) $16.99

Grades: 4 5 6 7   **Fic**

1. Orphans -- Fiction 2. Princesses -- Fiction 3. School stories -- Fiction 4. Diaries -- Fiction 5. Schools -- Fiction 6. Families -- Fiction 7. Princesses -- Fiction 8. Middle schools -- Fiction

ISBN 1250066026; 9781250066022

LC 2014043845

In this children's novel by Meg Cabot "Olivia Grace Clarisse Mignonette Harrison is a completely average twelve-year-old. The only things about her that aren't average are her name . . . and the fact that she is a half-orphan who has never met her father. Then one completely average day, everything goes wrong . . . Until a limo containing Princess Mia Thermopolis of Genovia pulls up to invite her to New York to finally meet her father, who promptly invites her to come live with him." (Publisher's note)

"Cabot manages to combine wit and lavish details to po sitive effect, as evidenced by a royal grandmother who manages to be both familiar and surprising. While readers who already know the Princess Diaries might find this fairy tale a bit too retold, young newcomers to the Cabot magic will be charmed. A sweet fantasy, both funny and highly satisfying." Kirkus

★ The **princess** diaries. Avon Bks. 2000 238p lib bdg $15.89; pa $6.99; $15.95

Grades: 6 7 8 9   **Fic**

1. Diaries 2. Identity 3. Princesses 4. New York (N.Y.) 5. Fathers and daughters 6. Princesses -- Fiction 7. New York (N.Y.) -- Fiction

ISBN 0-06-029210-5 lib bdg; 0-380-81402-1 pa; 0-380-97848-2

LC 99-46479

Fourteen-year-old Mia, who is trying to lead a normal life as a teenage girl in New York City, is shocked to learn that her father is the Prince of Genovia, a small European principality, and that she is a princess and the heir to the throne. "Grades five to nine." (Bull Cent Child Books)

"Readers will relate to Mia's bubbly, chatty voice and enjoy the humor of this unlikely fairy tale." SLJ

Other titles about Princess Mia are:
Forever princess (2008)
Party princess (2006)
Princess in pink (2004)
Princess in the spotlight (2001)
Princess in training (2005)
Princess in waiting (2003)
The princess present (2004)
Sweet sixteen princess (2006)
Valentine princess (2006)

Cadnum, Michael

The **book** of the Lion. Viking 2000 204p hardcover o.p. pa $5.99

Grades: 7 8 9 10   **Fic**

1. Crusades -- Fiction 2. Middle Ages -- Fiction 3. Knights and knighthood -- Fiction

ISBN 0-670-88386-7; 0-14-230034-9 pa

LC 99-39370

In twelfth-century England, after his master, a maker of coins for the king, is brutally punished for alleged cheating, seventeen-year-old Edmund finds himself traveling to the Holy Land as squire to a knight crusader on his way to join the forces of Richard Lionheart

"Cadnum brilliantly captures both the grisly horror and the taut, sinewy excitement of hard travel and battle readiness. . . . There's bawdy and violent talk, but religion as part of the heart and bone of life is present, too." Booklist

Followed by: The leopard sword (2002)

Peril on the sea. Farrar, Straus and Giroux 2009 245p $16.95

Grades: 7 8 9 10   **Fic**

1. Adventure fiction 2. Pirates -- Fiction 3. Great Britain -- History -- 1485-1603, Tudors -- Fiction

ISBN 978-0-374-35823-5; 0-374-35823-0

LC 2008-5421

In the tense summer of 1588, eighteen-year-old Sherwin Morris, after nearly perishing in a shipwreck, finds himself aboard the privateer Vixen, captained by the notorious and enigmatic Brandon Fletcher who offers him adventure and riches if Sherwin would write and disseminate a flattering account of the captain's exploits.

"Cadnum's prose is vivid and evocative, brilliantly recreating life at sea in the Elizabethan era. . . . The tale is expertly paced, the varied threads of the tale elegantly woven. There's plenty here to appeal to a wide audience." Kirkus

Caine, Rachel

Prince of Shadows; a novel of Romeo and Juliet. Rachel Caine. NAL, New American Library 2014 368 p. (hardback) $17.99

Grades: 7 8 9 10 11 12   **Fic**

1. Love -- Fiction 2. Italy -- Fiction 3. Family -- Fiction 4. Vendetta -- Fiction 5. Families -- Fiction 6. Italy -- History -- 1559-1789 -- Fiction 7. Verona (Italy) -- History -- 16th century -- Fiction

ISBN 0451414411; 9780451414410

LC 2013033482

This book, by Rachel Caine, is a "retelling of the starcrossed tale of Romeo and Juliet. . . . In the Houses of Montague and Capulet, there is only one goal: power. The boys are born to fight and die for honor. . . . Benvolio Montague, cousin to Romeo, knows all this. He expects to die . . . for his house, but a spark of rebellion still lives inside him. At night, he is the Prince of Shadows, the greatest thief in Verona--and he risks all as he steals from House Capulet." (Publisher's note)

"Choosing Romeo and Juliet as her base, Caine expands the story from the viewpoint of Benvolio, Romeo's Montague cousin. While Shakespeare's plot clearly anchors Caine's, the novel focuses on providing context for the wellknown story rather than embellishing it. . . . Most impressive is the author's simulation of Shakespeare's language in her prose. Never too obscure for modern readers, it retains the flavor of Shakespearean dialogue throughout, lending an atmosphere of verisimilitude that's reinforced by the detailed city setting. Simply superb," Kirkus

Caletti, Deb

★ The **last** forever; Deb Caletti. Simon Pulse 2014 336 p. (hardback) $17.99

Grades: 8 9 10 11 12   **Fic**

1. Love -- Fiction 2. Death -- Fiction 3. Grief -- Fiction 4. Father-daughter relationship -- Fiction 5. Friendship -- Fiction

ISBN 1442450002; 9781442450004

LC 2013031010

This book, by Deb Caletti, is a "novel of love and loss. . . . Nothing lasts forever, and no one gets that more than Tessa. After her mother died, it's all she can do to keep her friends, her boyfriend, her happiness from slipping away. And then there's her dad. He's stuck in his own daze, and it's hard to feel like a family when their house no longer seems like a home. Her father's solution? An impromptu road trip that lands them in a small coastal town." (Publisher's note)

"After a trying bout with cancer, Tess's mother has died, but she's left behind a one-of-a-kind pixiebell plant. "My mother vowed that the last pixiebell would never die on her watch, and now that I have it, it isn't going to die on mine, either," Tess vows... Featuring sharp-witted first-person narration, some fascinating facts about plants and seeds, relatable characters, and evocative settings, Caletti's (The Story of Us) inspiring novel eloquently depicts the nature of mutability. As with her previous books, this love story reverberates with honesty and emotion." (Publishers Weekly)

Calkhoven, Laurie

Michael at the invasion of France, 1943; by Laurie Calkhoven. Dial Books for Young Readers 2012 231 p. (hardcover) $16.99

Grades: 4 5 6 7   **Fic**

1. Children and war -- Fiction 2. Holocaust, 1939-1945 -- Fiction 3. France -- History -- 1940-1945, German occupation -- Fiction 4. World War, 1939-1945 -- Underground movements -- France -- Fiction 5. France -- History -- German occupation, 1940-1945 -- Fiction 6. France -- History -- German occupation, 1940-1945 -- Fiction 7. World War, 1939-1945 -- Underground movements -- France -- Fiction

ISBN 0803737246; 9780803737242

LC 2011021634

In this young adult novel, a "young Parisian joins the French Resistance in this Boys of Wartime series entry. . . . Michael joins a friend in distributing taunting leaflets. His involvement in Resistance activities soon escalates into helping captured British and American airmen make their way to Spain. At first he acts only as a courier of forged identity documents, but later he helps first to slip a Jewish neighbor's child out of the city, then hides an ailing American. . . . Meanwhile, he serves as a witness to . . . wartime life under the Nazis, while seeing friends, neighbors and his own older brother taken away and ultimately earning sufficient self-esteem to lose his dependence on his father's regard." (Kirkus

Includes bibliographical references

Will at the Battle of Gettysburg, 1863. Dutton Children's Books 2011 230p (Boys of wartime) $16.99

Grades: 4 5 6 7   **Fic**

1. Gettysburg (Pa.), Battle of, 1863 -- Fiction 2. United States -- History -- 1861-1865, Civil War -- Fiction
ISBN 978-0-525-42145-0; 0-525-42145-9

       LC 2010013307

In 1863, twelve-year-old Will, who longs to be a drummer in the Union army, is stuck in his sleepy hometown of Gettysburg, Pennsylvania, but when the Union and Confederate armies meet right there in his town, he and his family are caught up in the fight. Includes historical notes, glossary, and a timeline of events.

"This solid piece of fiction will appeal to history buffs and reluctant readers alike." SLJ

Includes glossary and bibliographical references

Calloway, Cassidy

Confessions of a First Daughter. HarperTeen 2009 214p pa $8.99

Grades: 6 7 8 9 10   **Fic**

1. School stories 2. Dating (Social customs) -- Fiction 3. Presidents -- United States -- Fiction
ISBN 978-0-06-172439-8; 0-06-172439-4

       LC 2009-1402

High school senior Morgan Abbott pretends to be her mother, the President of the United States, as a decoy, while she also tries to lead the life of a normal teenager.

"This is a light and entertaining read for teens who like some politics with their romance." SLJ

Calvert, Patricia

★ **Bigger**. Scribner 1994 137p hardcover o.p. pa $4.99

Grades: 5 6 7 8   **Fic**

1. Dogs -- Fiction 2. Father-son relationship -- Fiction 3. Frontier and pioneer life -- Fiction
ISBN 0-684-19685-9; 0-689-86003-X pa

       LC 93-14415

When his father disappears near the Mexican border at the end of the Civil War, twelve-year-old Tyler decides to go after him and bring him home, acquiring on the journey a strange dog which he names Bigger

"Calvert's story has many tantalizing elements: Tyler is likable and realistically portrayed, the book raises some provocative issues, and the ending is sad but satisfying. . . . This is an entertaining story even reluctant readers will relish." Booklist

Other titles in this series are:

Betrayed! (2002)

Sooner (1998)

Cameron, Sharon

The **dark** unwinding; by Sharon Cameron. Scholastic Press 2012 318 p. (jacketed hardcover) $17.99

Grades: 6 7 8 9   **Fic**

1. Alternative histories 2. Fantasy fiction 3. Eccentrics and eccentricities -- Fiction 4. Toys -- Fiction 5. Uncles -- Fiction 6. Inventions -- Fiction 7. Inheritance and succession -- Fiction 8. Great Britain -- History --

Victoria, 1837-1901 -- Fiction
ISBN 0545327865; 9780545327862

       LC 2011044431

This steampunk novel, by Sharon Cameron, begins "when Katharine Tulman's inheritance is called into question by the rumor that her eccentric uncle is squandering away the family fortune. . . . But . . . Katharine discovers . . . [he is a] genius inventor with his own set of rules, who employs a village of . . . people rescued from the workhouses of London. Katharine is now torn between protecting her own inheritance and preserving the . . . community she grows to care for deeply." (Publisher's note)

Canales, Viola

★ The **tequila** worm. Wendy Lamb Books 2005 199p hardcover o.p. pa $7.99

Grades: 6 7 8 9 10   **Fic**

1. Texas -- Fiction 2. Mexican Americans -- Fiction
ISBN 0-375-84089-3 pa; 0-385-74674-1

       LC 2004-24533

Sofia grows up in the close-knit community of the barrio in McAllen, Texas, then finds that her experiences as a scholarship student at an Episcopal boarding school in Austin only strengthen her ties to family and her "comadres."

"The explanations of cultural traditions . . . are always rooted in immediate, authentic family emotions, and in Canales' exuberant storytelling, which . . . finds both humor and absurdity in sharply observed, painful situations." Booklist

Cantor, Jillian

The **life** of glass. HarperTeen 2010 340p $16.99

Grades: 7 8 9 10 11 12   **Fic**

1. Fathers -- Fiction 2. Bereavement -- Fiction 3. Family life -- Fiction
ISBN 978-0-06-168651-1; 0-06-168651-4

       LC 2009-1758

Throughout her freshman year of high school, fourteen-year-old Melissa struggles to hold onto memories of her deceased father, cope with her mother's return to dating, get along with her sister, and sort out her feelings about her best friend, Ryan.

"Themes of memory, beauty, and secrets come together in this thoughtful, uplifting book that skillfully avoids Cinderella-tale predictability. . . . A gentle portrait of a girl growing through her grief." Booklist

The **September** sisters. HarperTeen 2009 361p $16.99

Grades: 7 8 9 10 11 12   **Fic**

1. Sisters -- Fiction 2. Family life -- Fiction 3. Missing persons -- Fiction
ISBN 978-0-06-168648-1; 0-06-168648-4

       LC 2008-7120

A teenaged girl tries to keep her family and herself together after the disappearance of her younger sister.

"Cantor treats the shape of Abby's agony with poignant credibility. . . . This is a sensitive and perceptive account of the way tragedy unfolds both quickly and slowly and life reassembles itself around it." Bull Cent Child Books

Carbone, Elisa

Blood on the river; James Town 1607. [by] Elisa Carbone. Viking 2006 237p $16.99; pa $6.99

Grades: 5 6 7 8   **Fic**

1. Powhatan Indians -- Fiction 2. Jamestown (Va.) -- History -- Fiction 3. United States -- History -- 1600-1775, Colonial period -- Fiction

ISBN 0-670-06060-7; 0-14-240932-4 pa

LC 2005023646

Traveling to the New World in 1606 as the page to Captain John Smith, twelve-year-old orphan Samuel Collier settles in the new colony of James Town, where he must quickly learn to distinguish between friend and foe.

"A strong, visceral story of the hardship and peril settlers faced, as well as the brutal realities of colonial conquest." Booklist

★ **Jump**; [by] Elisa Carbone. Viking 2010 258p $16.99

Grades: 7 8 9 10 11 12   **Fic**

1. Mountaineering -- Fiction 2. Runaway teenagers -- Fiction

ISBN 0-670-01185-1; 978-0-670-01185-8

LC 2009-30175

In this book by Elisa Carbone, "P.K. rebels against her parents and runs away from home with Critter, a boy she's just met. Their shared love of climbing takes them to Nevada and California, pursued by police. As they get acquainted in exciting circumstances, . . . romantic tension builds." (Voice of Youth Advocates)

"Chapters range from a few sentences to a few pages, and the descriptions of the pair's climbs are riveting . . . The narrators' psychological explorations are as exhilarating as their physical exploits. . . . An incisive reflection on endurance, independence, belonging, self-knowledge, and love, this story should find a wide audience." Publ Wkly

Stealing freedom; [by] Elisa Carbone. Knopf 1998 258p hardcover o.p.

Grades: 6 7 8 9   **Fic**

1. Slavery -- Fiction 2. African Americans -- Fiction 3. Underground railroad -- Fiction

ISBN 0440417074; 0679893075

LC 98-36929

This historical novel is "based on the life of Ann Maria Weems, who was born into slavery in Maryland in the 1840s. . . . Her master's debts are many and so her beloved brothers are sold without warning. Abolitionists are able to buy the freedom of the rest of her family, but the master refuses to part with Ann Maria. . . . She surreptitiously teaches herself to read and falls in love with a neighbor's slave, Alfred. She promises never to leave without him, but there is nothing she can do when she is 'kidnapped' by abolitionists and has no way to contact him." (SLJ) "Grades seven to ten." (Booklist)

"This is a fine piece of historical fiction with a strong, appealing heroine." SLJ

Card, Orson Scott

★ **Ender's** game. TOR Bks. 1991 xxi, 226p $24.95; pa $6.99

Grades: 7 8 9 10 11 12 Adult   **Fic**

1. Science fiction 2. Interplanetary voyages -- Fiction

ISBN 0-312-93208-1; 0-8125-5070-6 pa

A reissue of the title first published 1985

ALA YALSA Margaret A. Edwards Award (2008)

"The key, of course, is Ender Wiggin himself. Mr. Card never makes the mistake of patronizing or sentimentalizing his hero. Alternately likable and insufferable, he is a convincing little Napoleon in short pants." N Y Times Book Rev

Other titles in the author's distant future series about Ender Wiggin include:

Children of the mind (1996)
Ender in exile (2008)
Ender's shadow (1999)
Shadow of the giant (2005)
Shadow of the Hegemon (2001)
Shadow of the giant (2005)
Shadow puppets (2002)
Speaker for the dead (1986)
A war of gifts (2007)
Xenocide (1991)

★ **Pathfinder**. Simon Pulse 2010 662p $18.99

Grades: 6 7 8 9 10   **Fic**

1. Science fiction 2. Time travel -- Fiction 3. Parapsychology -- Fiction 4. Space colonies -- Fiction 5. Interplanetary voyages -- Fiction

ISBN 978-1-4169-9176-2; 1-4169-9176-X

LC 2010-23243

Thirteen-year-old Rigg has a secret ability to see the paths of others' pasts, but revelations after his father's death set him on a dangerous quest that brings new threats from those who would either control his destiny or kill him.

"While Card delves deeply into his story's knotted twists and turns, readers should have no trouble following the philosophical and scientific mysteries, which the characters are parsing right along with them. An epic in the best sense, and not simply because the twin stories stretch across centuries." Publ Wkly

Ruins; by Orson Scott Card. Simon Pulse 2012 544 p. (hardback) $18.99

Grades: 7 8 9 10 11 12   **Fic**

1. Evolution -- Fiction 2. Time travel -- Fiction 3. Space colonies -- Fiction 4. Science fiction

ISBN 1416991778; 9781416991779

LC 2011052745

Sequel to: Pathfinder

In this book by Orson Scott Card, part of the Pathfinders series, "three time-shifters discover that the secrets of the past threaten their world with imminent obliteration. Rigg, his sister, Param, and best friend, Umbo, have joined their abilities to slip through time . . . circumventing the invisible Wall that divides their planet into 19 independent evolutionary experiments." (Kirkus Reviews)

Cardenas, Teresa

Letters to my mother; translated by David Unger. Groundwood Books/House of Anansi Press 2006 103p $15.95; pa $7.95

Grades: 7 8 9 10   **Fic**

1. Cuba -- Fiction 2. Blacks -- Fiction 3. Race relations

-- Fiction
ISBN 0-88899-720-5; 0-88899-721-3 pa

A young African-Cuban girl is sent to live with her aunt and cousins after the death of her mother and begins to write letters to her deceased mother telling of the misery, racial prejudice, and mistreatment at the hands of those around her.

"The main character's voice is authentic, and the other characters, sketched with spare lines, are believable and sympathetic. . . . Short chapters and lucid writing will appeal to reluctant readers." SLJ

Old dog; translated by David Unger. Groundwood Books/House of Anansi Press 2007 144p $16.95

Grades: 7 8 9 10 11 12 **Fic**
1. Cuba -- Fiction 2. Slavery -- Fiction
ISBN 978-0-88899-757-9; 0-88899-757-4

Perro Viejo, an elderly slave on a Cuban sugar plantation, "recalls his life and the endless acts of atrocity and inhumanity he has witnessed. . . . [This is a] slender but powerful story that will invite classroom discussion." Booklist

Carey, Benedict
Poison most vial; a mystery. by Benedict Carey. Amulet Books 2012 215 p. (hardcover) $16.95

Grades: 5 6 7 8 **Fic**
1. Mystery fiction 2. Forensic sciences -- Fiction 3. Murder -- Fiction 4. Neighbors -- Fiction 5. Mystery and detective stories 6. Fathers and daughters -- Fiction
ISBN 1419700316; 9781419700316

LC 2011038222

In this novel by Benedict Carey "Ruby's janitor father becomes the prime suspect in a murder . . . [of] [f]orensics expert Dr. Ramachandran . . . [and] the eighth grader decides it's up to her to clear his name. . . . [She] enlists the aid of her large, Jamaican buddy, Rex, and reclusive, retired toxicologist Clara Whitmore, who lives in Ruby's building. What with hacking into computers, evading gangs and like spy-jinx, the mystery demands a lot of brain work." (Kirkus)

★ The **unknowns**. Amulet Books 2009 259p il map $16.95

Grades: 6 7 8 9 **Fic**
1. Mystery fiction 2. Mathematics -- Fiction 3. Conspiracies -- Fiction 4. Missing persons -- Fiction
ISBN 978-0-8109-7991-8; 0-8109-7991-8

LC 2008-33914

When people start vanishing from a godforsaken trailer park next to the Folsom Energy Plant, two eleven-year-olds investigate using mathematical clues that were hastily planted by their friend Mrs. Clarke before she disappeared.

"Successfully working in the concepts of pi and the Pythagorean theorem into an adventure story is no easy task, but . . . Carey succeeds because of his lively and unique writing." Voice Youth Advocates

Carey, Edward
Heap House; The Iremonger Trilogy. by Edward Carey. Overlook Press 2014 416 p. illustrations $16.99

Grades: 5 6 7 8 9 10 **Fic**
1. Boys -- Fiction 2. Houses -- Fiction 3. London

(England) -- Fiction 4. Great Britain -- History -- Victoria, 1837-1901 -- Fiction 5. Dwellings 6. London (England) 7. Orphans -- Fiction 8. Family secrets -- Fiction
ISBN 1468309536; 9781468309539

In this book, by Edward Carey, "Clod is an Iremonger. He lives in the Heaps, a vast sea of lost and discarded items collected from all over London. At the centre is Heap House, a puzzle of houses, castles, homes and mysteries reclaimed from the city and built into a living maze of staircases and scurrying rats. The Iremongers are a mean and cruel family, robust and hardworking, but Clod has an illness. He can hear the objects whispering." (Publisher's note)

"Living among sentient trash heaps, Clod Iremonger has always been able to hear the voices of the objects that his family members carry, but the arrival of serving girl Lucy imbues the objects with a new and dangerous energy. Descriptive prose and black-and-white portraits create a unique cast of characters in a bleak, dilapidated home. Fans of Joan Aiken will flock to this dark mystery." Horn Book

Carey, Janet Lee
The **beast** of Noor. Atheneum Books for Young Readers 2006 497p $16.95

Grades: 6 7 8 9 **Fic**
1. Fantasy fiction
ISBN 978-0-689-87644-8; 0-689-87644-0

LC 2005-17731

Fifteen-year-old Miles Ferrell uses the rare and special gift he is given to break the curse of the Shriker, a murderous creature reportedly brought to Shalem Wood by his family's clan centuries

"Carey delivers an eerie, atmospheric tale, full of terror and courage, set in a convincingly realized magical realm." Booklist

Followed by: The dragons of Noor (2010)

★ **Dragon's** Keep. Harcourt 2007 302p $17

Grades: 7 8 9 10 **Fic**
1. Fantasy fiction 2. Dragons -- Fiction 3. Princesses -- Fiction 4. Mother-daughter relationship -- Fiction 5. Great Britain -- History -- 1066-1154, Norman period -- Fiction
ISBN 978-0-15-205926-2; 0-15-205926-1

LC 2006-24669

In 1145 A.D., as foretold by Merlin, fourteen-year-old Rosalind, who will be the twenty-first Pendragon Queen of Wilde Island, has much to accomplish to fulfill her destiny, while hiding from her people the dragon's claw she was born with that reflects only one of her mother's dark secrets.

This is told "in stunning, lyrical prose. . . . Carey smoothly blends many traditional fantasy tropes here, but her telling is fresh as well as thoroughly compelling." Booklist

Dragons of Noor. Egmont USA 2010 421p $17.99

Grades: 6 7 8 9 **Fic**
1. Fantasy fiction 2. Dragons -- Fiction
ISBN 978-1-60684-035-1; 1-60684-035-5

LC 2010011311

Sequel to: The beast of Noor (2007)

Seven hundred years after the days of the dragon wars, magic again is stirring and three teenagers join forces to help bind the broken kingdoms of Noor and Otherworld.

"The world building and tone are just right, and the themes of friendship, loyalty, responsibility, and protection of the planet are never intrusive. Hanna and Miles are realistic teens. . . . Most of the secondary characters are equally compelling." SLJ

Dragonswood; by Janet Lee Carey. Dial Books 2012 403p

Grades: 7 8 9 **Fic**
1. Love stories 2. Occult fiction 3. Fantasy fiction 4. Fantasy 5. Dragons -- Fiction 6. Fairies -- Fiction 7. British Isles -- History -- 12th century -- Fiction

ISBN 9780803735040

LC 2011021638

This juvenile fantasy novel tells the story of "Wilde Island [which] is not at peace. The kingdom mourns the dead Pendragon king and awaits the return of his heir; the uneasy pact between dragons, fairies, and humans is strained; and the regent is funding a bloodthirsty witch hunt, hoping to rid the island of half-fey maidens. Tess, daughter of a blacksmith, has visions of the future, but she still doesn't expect to be accused of witchcraft, forced to flee with her two best friends, or offered shelter by the handsome and enigmatic Garth Huntsman, a warden for Dragonswood. But Garth is the younger prince in disguise and Tess soon learns that her true father was fey." (Publisher's note)

★ **Stealing** death. Egmont USA 2009 354p map $16.99; lib bdg $19.99

Grades: 7 8 9 10 **Fic**
1. Fantasy fiction 2. Death -- Fiction 3. Siblings -- Fiction

ISBN 978-1-60684-009-2; 1-60684-009-6; 978-1-60684-045-0 lib bdg; 1-60684-045-2 lib bdg

LC 2009-16240

After losing his family, except for his younger sister Jilly, and their home in a tragic fire, seventeen-year-old Kipp Corwin, a poor farmer, must wrestle with death itself in order to save Jilly and the woman he loves.

"Carey's wonderful language weaves family, love, wise teachers, and petty villains together in a vast landscape. . . . This is quite simply fantasy at its best—original, beautiful, amazing, and deeply moving." SLJ

Carleson, J. C.

The **tyrant's** daughter; J.C. Carleson. Alfred A. Knopf 2014 304 p. (trade) $17.99

Grades: 8 9 10 11 12 **Fic**
1. Teenagers -- Fiction 2. Middle East -- Fiction 3. Kings and rulers -- Fiction 4. Exiles -- Fiction 5. Schools -- Fiction 6. Dictators -- Fiction 7. Immigrants -- Fiction 8. High schools -- Fiction 9. Middle East -- Politics and government -- Fiction

ISBN 0449809978; 9780449809976; 9780449809983; 9780449809990

LC 2013014783

In this book by J.C. Carleson, "when her father is killed in a coup, 15-year-old Laila flees from the war-torn middle east to a life of exile and anonymity in the U.S. She adjusts

to a new school, new friends, and a new culture, but while Laila sees opportunity . . . her mother is focused on the past. She's conspiring with CIA operatives and rebel factions to regain the throne their family lost. Laila can't bear to stand still as an international crisis takes shape around her." (Publisher's note)

"Removed from her unnamed Middle Eastern country after her father is murdered during a coup, 15-year-old Laila is now living near Washington D. C. with her mother and brother...This is more than just Laila's story; rather, it is a story of context, beautifully written (by a former undercover CIA agent), and stirring in its questions and eloquent observations about our society and that of the Middle East." (Booklist)

Carman, Patrick

The **Dark** Hills divide; [by] Patrick Carman. Orchard Books 2005 253p [The land of Elyon] $11.95

Grades: 4 5 6 7 **Fic**
1. Fantasy fiction

ISBN 0-439-70093-0

LC 2004-16312

When she finds the key to a secret passageway leading out of the walled city of Bridewell, twelve-year-old Alexa realizes her lifelong wish to explore the mysterious forests and mountains that lie beyond the wall

"Narrator Aasne Vigesaa clearly portrays Alexa's thoughtful, inquisitive nature and unsettled feelings. . . . Vigesaa's excellent use of pace, pitch, and tone help differentiate each character." SLJ

Other titles in this series are:
Beyond the Valley of Thorns (2005)
The tenth city (2006)
Into the mist (2007)
Stargazer (2008)

The **dark** planet. Little, Brown 2009 350p il (Atherton) $16.99

Grades: 5 6 7 8 **Fic**
1. Science fiction

ISBN 978-0-316-16674-4; 0-316-16674-X

LC 2008-45348

After the destruction of the planet Atherton, Edgar must journey to a dark and damaged world named Earth in order to find the secrets of his civilization's past.

"This is primarily action-driven sci-fi with unique settings populated by creative creatures. Familiar and new characters (including one very cool dragon) maintain readers' interest. . . . Once again, Carman's introduction provides background information and character biographies for readers unfamiliar with the series. . . . Pencil illustrations, many appearing like full-page notes, better explain Atherton and Dark Planet phenomena." SLJ

The **house** of power. Little, Brown & Co. 2007 330p il (Atherton) $16.99; $16.99; pa $5.99

Grades: 5 6 7 8 **Fic**
1. Science fiction 2. Orphans -- Fiction 3. Friendship -- Fiction 4. Earthquakes -- Fiction 5. Social classes

-- Fiction

ISBN 978-0-316-16670-6; 0-316-16670-7; 978-0-316-16671-3 pa; 0-316-16671-5 pa

LC 2006025976

Edgar, an eleven-year-old orphan, finds a book that reveals significant secrets about Atherton, the strictly divided world on which he lives, even as geological changes threaten to shift the power structure that allows a select few to live off the labor of others.

This "is a fast-paced novel with a unique setting, fascinating plot, and cliffhanger ending. It shines because of the author's imagination and skill." SLJ

Rivers of fire; [by] Patrick Carman. 1st ed.; Little, Brown & Co. 2008 303p il (Atherton) $16.99
Grades: 5 6 7 8   Fic
1. Science fiction 2. Monsters -- Fiction 3. Friendship -- Fiction 4. Social classes -- Fiction
ISBN 978-0-316-16672-0; 0-316-16672-3

LC 2007048366

Sequel to: The house of power (2007)

After Atherton's three-tiered world collapses, ending the geographical division of the social classes, Edgar, Samuel, and Isabel try to restore the flow of water and uncover the world's mysterious origins in the process.

"There's plenty of surface excitement in the book's giant, electric eels; carniverous centipedes; and biblically rising floodwaters." Booklist

Carmichael, Clay

★ **Wild** things; [written and illustrated by Clay Carmichael] Front Street 2009 248p il $18.95
Grades: 5 6 7 8   Fic
1. Cats -- Fiction 2. Uncles -- Fiction 3. Artists -- Fiction 4. Orphans -- Fiction 5. Family life -- Fiction
ISBN 978-1-59078-627-7; 1-59078-627-0

LC 2007-49911

Stubborn, self-reliant, eleven-year-old Zoe, recently orphaned, moves to the country to live with her prickly half-uncle, a famous doctor and sculptor, and together they learn about trust and the strength of family

"Carmichael gives a familiar plot a fresh new life in this touching story with a finely crafted sense of place." Booklist

Carriger, Gail

★ **Curtsies** & conspiracies; Gail Carriger. Little, Brown and Co. 2013 320 p. (Finishing school) $18
Grades: 7 8 9 10 11 12   Fic
1. Steampunk fiction 2. Espionage -- Fiction 3. Conspiracies -- Fiction 4. Science fiction 5. Robots -- Fiction 6. Schools -- Fiction 7. Etiquette -- Fiction 8. Boarding schools -- Fiction 9. Great Britain -- History -- George VI, 1936-1952 -- Fiction
ISBN 031619011X; 9780316190114

LC 2012048520

In this book, by Gail Carriger, "Sophronia's first year at Mademoiselle Geraldine's Finishing Academy for Young Ladies of Quality . . . is training her to be a spy. A conspiracy is afoot--one with dire implications for both supernaturals and humans. Sophronia must rely on her training to discover who is behind the dangerous plot-and survive the London Season with a full dance card." (Publisher's note)

"With the school's dirigible heading toward London for a liaison with an inventor studying aetherospheric travel, Sophronia (Etiquette & Espionage) is convinced that her professors are Up To Something. Is the academy affiliated with vampire hives, werewolf packs, the anti-supernatural Picklemen, or the Crown--all of whom would benefit from controlling aether technology? A witty and suspenseful steampunk romp." (Horn Book)

Curtsies and conspiracies

★ **Etiquette** & espionage; by Gail Carriger. Little, Brown 2013 320 p. (alk. paper) $17.99
Grades: 7 8 9 10 11 12   Fic
1. Spy stories 2. School stories 3. Assassins -- Fiction 4. Science fiction 5. Robots -- Fiction 6. Schools -- Fiction 7. Espionage -- Fiction 8. Etiquette -- Fiction 9. Boarding schools -- Fiction 10. Great Britain -- History -- George VI, 1936-1952 -- Fiction
ISBN 031619008X; 9780316190084

LC 2012005498

In this book, Sophronia's mother is "desperate for her daughter to become a proper lady. So she enrolls Sophronia in Mademoiselle Geraldine's Finishing Academy for Young Ladies of Quality. But Sophronia soon realizes the school is not quite what her mother might have hoped. At Mademoiselle Geraldine's, young ladies learn to finish . . . everything. Certainly, they learn the fine arts of dance, dress, and etiquette, but they also learn to deal out death, diversion, and espionage." (Publisher's note)

Carroll, Michael

Hunter; a Super human clash. Michael Carroll. Philomel Books, an imprint of Penguin Group (USA) 2014 360 p. hbk $16.99
Grades: 5 6 7 8 9   Fic
1. Superheroes -- Fiction 2. Supervillains -- Fiction
ISBN 0399163670; 9780399163678

LC 2013024006

"The defeat of the near-invincible villain Krodin has left a void in the superhuman hierarchy, a void that two opposing factors are trying to fill. The powerful telepath Max Dalton believes that the human race must be controlled and shepherded to a safe future, while his rival Casey Duval believes that strength can only be achieved through conflict." (Publisher's note)

"After parting ways with the superhumans, Lance relies on his persuasive skills to make his way in the world and evade mind-controlling Max Dalton. This fourth book follows Lance's journey over the years, from working in a traveling circus to running his own global organization. Series followers will appreciate con-man Lance's character development and the implications of the story's surprising conclusion." Horn Book

Other titles in this series are:
Super Human (2010)
The Ascension (2011)
Stronger (2012)

Carroll, Michael Owen, 1966-

The **ascension**; a Super human clash. Philomel Books 2011 378p (Super human) $16.99

Grades: 6 7 8 9 **Fic**
1. Superheroes -- Fiction
ISBN 978-0-399-25624-0; 0-399-25624-5
LC 2010029600
Sequel to: Super human (2010)
Teenagers with super powers must try to stop a villain who has travelled from the past in order to irreversibly alter reality.

"The characters are much less absolute in their morality than in their first outing, making the narrative even more engaging. . . . One of those rare sequels that exceed the first." Kirkus

Super human; Michael Carroll. Philomel Books 2010 325 p. ill. (hardcover) $16.99; (paperback) $8.99
Grades: 5 6 7 8 9 **Fic**
1. Superheroes -- Fiction 2. Good and evil -- Fiction
ISBN 9780399252976; 9780142419052; 0142419052; 0399252975
LC 2009-29965
A group of teenage superheroes tackle a powerful warrior who has been brought back from 4,000 years in the past to enslave the modern world. (Bull Cent Child Books)

"There is enough fighting in this book to appeal to middle school boys, and the telekinetic Roz, with a controlling superhero big brother, will appeal to girls. This title is a fast read with tension, suspense, and likeable characters." Libr Media Connect

Followed by: The ascension: a super human clash (2011)

Carson, Rae

★ The **bitter** kingdom; by Rae Carson. Greenwillow Books 2013 448 p. (hardcover) $17.99
Grades: 8 9 10 11 12 **Fic**
1. Fantasy fiction 2. Magic -- Fiction 3. Queens -- Fiction 4. Love -- Fiction 5. Prophecies -- Fiction
ISBN 0062026542; 9780062026545
LC 2013011912
Sequel to: The crown of embers
This is the final book in Rae Carson's Girl of Fire and Thorns trilogy. Here, "young Queen Elisa and her companions trek into enemy territory to rescue the man she loves, while a traitor back home attempts to overthrow her. Elisa's journeys take her to . . . Invierne, where she hopes to destroy the source of the Inviernos' magic and bargain for peace; to the Basajuan desert, where only her most audacious plans have any chance to stop the war; and home to try to regain her throne." (Publishers Weekly)

★ The **crown** of embers; by Rae Carson. Greenwillow Books 2012 410 p. (hardcover) $17.99
Grades: 8 9 10 11 12 **Fic**
1. Love -- Fiction 2. Magic -- Fiction 3. Prophecies -- Fiction
ISBN 0062026518; 9780062026514
LC 2012014125
This young adult fantasy novel, by Rae Carson, is the sequel to the Morris, Cybils, and Andre Norton Award finalist book "The Girl of Fire and Thorns." "Elisa is a hero. . . . [But] to conquer the power she bears once and for all, Elisa must follow the trail of long-forgotten--and forbidden--clues

from the deep, undiscovered catacombs of her own city to the treacherous seas. With her goes a one-eyed spy, a traitor, and the man who--despite everything--she is falling in love with." (Publisher's note)

★ The **girl** of fire and thorns. Greenwillow Books 2011 423p $17.99
Grades: 8 9 10 11 12 **Fic**
1. Fantasy fiction 2. Magic -- Fiction 3. Prophecies -- Fiction 4. Kings and rulers -- Fiction
ISBN 978-0-06-202648-4; 0-06-202648-8
LC 2010042021
Morris Award Finalist (2012)
"The first book in the acclaimed and award winning New York Times bestselling trilogy. The Girl of Fire and Thorns is a remarkable novel full of adventure, sorcery, heartbreak, and power...Once a century, one person is chosen for greatness. Elisa is the chosen one. But she is also the younger of two princesses. The one who has never done anything remarkable, and can't see how she ever will. Now, on her sixteenth birthday, she has become the secret wife of a handsome and worldly king...And he's not the only one who seeks her. Savage enemies, seething with dark magic, are hunting her. A daring, determined revolutionary thinks she could be his people's savior. Soon it is not just her life, but her very heart that is at stake." (Publisher's Note)

"This fast-moving and exciting novel is rife with political conspiracies and machinations." SLJ

Carter, Ally

Embassy row #1; all fall down. Ally Carter ; [edited by] David Levithan. Scholastic Press 2015 320 p. $17.99
Grades: 7 8 9 10 **Fic**
1. Murder -- Fiction 2. Revenge -- Fiction 3. Ambassadors -- Fiction 4. Mother-daughter relationship -- Fiction
ISBN 0545654742; 9780545654746
LC 2014947739
In this book, by Ally Carter, "Grace Blakely is absolutely certain of three things: 1. She is not crazy. 2. Her mother was murdered. 3. Someday she is going to find the killer and make him pay. As certain as Grace is about these facts, nobody else believes her -- so there's no one she can completely trust. Not her grandfather, a powerful ambassador. Not her new friends, who all live on Embassy Row. . . . But they can't control Grace." (Publisher's note)

"This exciting first book in the Embassy Row series features sixteen-year-old Grace, who has moved into the United States Embassy on the coast of Adria with her ambassador grandfather. It is the first time in three years that she has been back to Adria, since her mother's tragic death in a fire... Her quest to find the truth is one that readers will love to follow, through the twists and turns of Embassy Row and with a diverse array of characters. Some help her, and some stand in her way . . . but Grace is a fighter, and she will stop at nothing to find out what happened to her mother. Readers will love this first book in what promises to be an exciting, thrilling mystery series from best-selling author Carter." VOYA

Heist Society. Hyperion 2010 287p il map

Grades: 7 8 9 10   **Fic**
1. Thieves -- Fiction
ISBN 1-4231-1639-9; 978-1-4231-1639-4
LC 2009-40377
A group of teenagers conspire to re-steal several price-less paintings and save Kat Bishop's father from a vengeful collector who is accusing him of art theft. "Grades six to ten." (Bull Cent Child Books)
Carter "skillfully maintains suspense. . . . This is a thoroughly enjoyable, cinema-ready adventure." Booklist
Another title about Kat is:
Uncommon criminals (2011)

Perfect scoundrels; a Heist society novel. by Ally Carter. 1st ed. Disney/Hyperion Books 2013 328 p. (hardcover) $17.99
Grades: 7 8 9 10   **Fic**
1. Crime -- Fiction 2. Theft -- Fiction 3. Wealth -- Fiction 4. Detective and mystery stories 5. Dating (Social customs) -- Fiction 6. Swindlers and swindling -- Fiction 7. Inheritance and succession -- Fiction
ISBN 1423166000; 9781423166009
LC 2012032405
This book is an installment of Ally Carter's Heist Society series. "When Hale suddenly inherits his grandmother's billion-dollar company, it's pretty obvious that he and Kat can't be up to their old tricks anymore. But can Hale trust Kat not to dip her hand in the cookie jar and steal the company's fortune—even though he knows she's prepared to do the impossible?" (Dolly Magazine)

Uncommon criminals; a Heist society novel. Disney/Hyperion Books 2011 298p $16.99
Grades: 7 8 9 10   **Fic**
1. Gems -- Fiction 2. Crime -- Fiction 3. Europe -- Fiction 4. Wealth -- Fiction 5. Great Britain -- Fiction 6. New York (State) -- Fiction 7. Swindlers and swindling -- Fiction
ISBN 978-1-4231-4795-4; 1-4231-4795-2
LC 2011006793
Fifteen-year-old Kat Bishop and her fellow talented teenagers work together to find and steal the "Cleopatra Emerald" from an unscrupulous dealer and return it to its rightful owner, while a former love of her Uncle Eddie tries to get the gem for herself.
"This is an exciting, entertaining read with a fast-moving plot, a spot of romance, and a strong and smart female protagonist." SLJ

Carter, Anne
The **shepherd's** granddaughter; [by] Anne Laurel Carter. Groundwood Books 2008 224p $17.95; pa $12.95
Grades: 5 6 7 8   **Fic**
1. Palestine -- Fiction 2. Shepherds -- Fiction
ISBN 978-0-88899-902-3; 0-88899-902-X; 978-0-88899-903-0 pa; 0-88899-903-8 pa
Amani longs to be a shepherd like her grandfather, Seedo. Like many Palestinians, her family has grazed sheep above the olive groves of the family homestead for generations, and she has been steeped in Seedo's stories, especially

one about a secret meadow called the Firdoos-and the wolf that once showed him the path there.
"Carter strikes a splendid balance in character development, portraying both parties' flaws while demonstrating Palestinian sympathies. Background and cultural information are seamlessly woven into the narrative, which is written simply and clearly in a skillful depiction of sensitive situation." SLJ

Carvell, Marlene
Sweetgrass basket. Dutton Childrens Books 2005 243p $16.99
Grades: 7 8 9 10   **Fic**
1. School stories 2. Sisters -- Fiction 3. Mohawk Indians -- Fiction
ISBN 0-525-47547-8
LC 2004-24374
In alternating passages, two Mohawk sisters describe their lives at the Carlisle Indian Industrial School, established in 1879 to educate Native Americans, as they try to assimilate into white culture and one of them is falsely accused of stealing.
"Carvell has put together a compelling, authentic, and sensitive portrayal of a part of our history that is still not made accurately available to young readers." SLJ

Who will tell my brother? Hyperion Bks. for Children 2002 150p hardcover o.p. pa $5.99
Grades: 7 8 9 10   **Fic**
1. School stories 2. Mohawk Indians -- Fiction
ISBN 0-7868-0827-6; 0-7868-1657-0 pa
LC 2001-51759
During his lonely crusade to remove offensive mascots from his high school, Evan, part-Mohawk Indian, learns more about his heritage, his ancestors, and his place in the world
"The blank verse format will be appealing, especially to reluctant readers. . . . [A] lovely, heart-wrenching and profound little book." Voice Youth Advocates

Carvell, Tim
Return to Planet Tad; Tim Carvell ; illustrated by Doug Holgate. Harper, an imprint of HarperCollins Publishers 2014 240 p. (hardcover) $12.99
Grades: 4 5 6 7   **Fic**
1. Weblogs 2. Middle schools -- Fiction 3. Blogs -- Fiction 4. Humorous stories 5. Schools -- Fiction
ISBN 006226625X; 9780062266255
LC 2013043142
Sequel to: Planet Ted
In this book by Tim Carvell "Tad may have survived seventh grade, but his troubles are just getting started. From his first sort-of date (a disaster) to his first semiformal dance (a bigger disaster), all Tad wants to do is make it out of this year alive. But that's not the only reason he keeps a blog. Tad also has a lot of important thoughts he needs to get off his chest." (Publisher's note)
"Fictional blog entries (some originally appeared in Mad magazine) span Tad's year of middle-school mishaps (Planet Tad). Filled with random quips ("I bet that when elephants laugh so hard that water comes out of their nose, it's no big deal"), the book reads more like standup than story. Tad's

ungrammatical kid-speak--"There's nothing awkwarder in the world..."--is grating. Black-and-white cartoons illustrate the text." Horn Book

Cary, Kate

Bloodline; a novel. Razor Bill 2005 324p hardcover o.p. pa $9.99

Grades: 7 8 9 10   **Fic**

1. Horror fiction 2. Vampires -- Fiction 3. World War, 1914-1918 -- Fiction

ISBN 1-59514-012-3; 1-59514-078-6 pa

In this story told primarily through journal entries, a British soldier in World War I makes the horrifying discovery that his regiment commander is descended from Count Dracula.

"This story is an interesting blend of mystery, horror, and romance, and readers who love vampire novels will find it a refreshing twist to the classic story." SLJ

Followed by Bloodline: reckoning (2007)

Bloodline : reckoning. Razorbill 2007 311p (Bloodline) hardcover o.p. pa $9.99

Grades: 7 8 9 10   **Fic**

1. Horror fiction 2. Vampires -- Fiction 3. World War, 1914-1918 -- Fiction

ISBN 978-1-59514-013-5; 1-59514-013-1; 978-1-59514-179-8 pa; 1-59514-179-0 pa

LC 2006-101841

Sequel to Bloodline (2005)

In this story told primarily through journal entries, Quincey Harker, the heir to Dracula's bloodline, returns to England in 1918 to pursue Nurse Mary Seward, whose fiance has been transformed into a monstrous vampire.

"This novel about good, evil, and the gray areas in between will be a favorite with fans of the vampire genre." SLJ

Casanova, Mary

Frozen; Mary Casanova. University of Minnesota Press 2012 264 p. (hc/j : alk. paper) $16.95

Grades: 7 8 9 10   **Fic**

1. Voice -- Fiction 2. Conduct of life -- Fiction 3. Mother-daughter relationship -- Fiction 4. Memory -- Fiction 5. Families -- Fiction 6. Identity -- Fiction 7. Selective mutism -- Fiction 8. Minnesota -- History -- 20th century -- Fiction

ISBN 0816680566; 9780816680566; 9780816680573

LC 2012019376

Author Mary Casanova tells the story of a young girl's life after her mother dies. "Sixteen-year-old Sadie Rose hasn't spoken in eleven years—ever since she was found in a snowbank the night her mother died under strange circumstances . . . Like her voice, her memories of her mother and what happened that night were frozen . . . [The book] is a suspenseful, moving testimonial to the power of family and memory and the extraordinary strength of a young woman who has lost her voice in nearly every way, but is determined to find it again." (Publisher's note)

Includes bibliographical references (p.)

The **klipfish** code; by Mary Casanova. Houghton Mifflin Company 2007 227p map $16

Grades: 4 5 6 7   **Fic**

1. Norway -- Fiction 2. Family life -- Fiction 3. World War, 1939-1945 -- Norway -- Fiction 4. World War, 1939-1945 -- Underground movements -- Fiction

ISBN 978-0-618-88393-6; 0-618-88393-2

LC 2007012752

Sent with her younger brother to Godøy Island to live with her aunt and grandfather after Germans bomb Norway in 1940, ten-year-old Marit longs to join her parents in the Resistance and when her aunt, a teacher, is taken away two years later, she resents even more the Nazis' presence and her grandfather's refusal to oppose them.

"Casanova spins an adventure-filled and harrowing story." SLJ

Includes glossary and bibliographical references

Cashore, Kristin

★ **Fire**; a novel. Dial Books 2009 461p map $17.99

Grades: 9 10 11 12   **Fic**

1. Fantasy fiction

ISBN 978-0-8037-3461-6; 0-8037-3461-1

LC 2009-5187

In a kingdom called the Dells, Fire is the last human-shaped monster, with unimaginable beauty and the ability to control the minds of those around her, but even with these gifts she cannot escape the strife that overcomes her world.

"Many twists propel the action . . . [and] Cashore's conclusion satisfies, but readers will clamor for a sequel to the prequel—a book bridging the gap between this one and Graceling." Publ Wkly

★ **Graceling**. Harcourt 2008 471p map $17; pa $9.99

Grades: 8 9 10 11 12   **Fic**

1. Fantasy fiction

ISBN 978-0-15-206396-2; 0-15-206396-X; 978-0-547-25830-0 pa; 0-547-25830-5 pa

LC 2007045436

ALA YALSA Morris Award Finalist, 2009

In a world where some people are born with extreme skills called Graces, Katsa struggles for redemption from her own horrifying Grace, the Grace of killing. She teams up with another young fighter to save their land from a corrupt king. "Age fourteen and up." (N Y Times Book Rev)

"This is gorgeous storytelling: exciting, stirring, and accessible. Fantasy and romance readers will be thrilled." SLJ

Castan, Mike

Fighting for Dontae; Mike Castan. Holiday House 2012 150 p. (hardcover) $16.95

Grades: 6 7 8 9 10 11 12   **Fic**

1. Gangs -- Fiction 2. Reading -- Fiction 3. Children with disabilities -- Fiction 4. Schools -- Fiction 5. California -- Fiction 6. Middle schools -- Fiction 7. Conduct of life -- Fiction 8. Family problems -- Fiction 9. Mexican Americans -- Fiction 10. People with disabilities -- Fiction 11. People with mental disabilities -- Fiction

ISBN 0823423484; 9780823423484

LC 2011042115

This book is the story of seventh-grader Javier, who "does not really want to be in a gang," but thinks he must join the Playaz gang to be cool, which he desperately wants to be. "When he is assigned to work with the special-ed class at school, Javier knows that his days as a cool kid are officially over. He does not expect to enjoy it, but reading to Dontae, a severely disabled boy, becomes the one thing Javier looks forward to." (Children's Literature)

The **price** of loyalty. Holiday House 2011 150p
$17.95

Grades: 7 8 9 10   **Fic**
1. School stories 2. Gangs -- Fiction 3. Mexican Americans -- Fiction 4. Los Angeles (Calif.) -- Fiction
ISBN 978-0-8234-2268-5; 0-8234-2268-2
LC 2010024065
Mexican American middle-schooler Manny finds himself caught between going along with his friends who are set on forming a gang and cutting his ties to them and following his own inclination to stay out of trouble.

"Kids will recognize the peer pressure and how authorities contribute to it. . . . But the drama is never simplistic. . . . Readers will want to discuss it all." Booklist

Castellucci, Cecil

Boy proof. Candlewick Press 2005 203p
$15.99; pa $7.99
Grades: 7 8 9 10   **Fic**
1. Motion pictures -- Fiction 2. Los Angeles (Calif.) -- Fiction
ISBN 0-7636-2333-4; 0-7636-2796-6 pa
LC 2004-50256
Feeling alienated from everyone around her, Los Angeles high school senior and cinephile Victoria Denton hides behind the identity of a favorite movie character until an interesting new boy arrives at school and helps her realize that there is more to life than just the movies.

This "novel's clipped, funny, first-person, present-tense narrative will grab teens . . . with its romance and the screwball special effects, and with the story of an outsider's struggle both to belong and to be true to herself." Booklist

First day on Earth. Scholastic Press 2011 150p
$17.99
Grades: 7 8 9 10   **Fic**
1. Children of alcoholics -- Fiction 2. Extraterrestrial beings -- Fiction
ISBN 978-0-545-06082-0; 0-545-06082-6
"Mal's spare first-person narration is wistful and raw, reflecting the feelings of anyone who's ever felt misunderstood or abandoned. . . . Castellucci also creates vibrant secondary characters. . . . A simple, tender work that speaks to the alien in all of us." Kirkus

Rose sees red. Scholastic Press 2010 197p
$17.99
Grades: 7 8 9 10   **Fic**
1. School stories 2. Ballet -- Fiction 3. Russians -- Fiction 4. Friendship -- Fiction 5. New York (N.Y.) -- Fiction
ISBN 978-0-545-06079-0; 0-545-06079-6
LC 2009-36850

In the 1980s, two teenaged ballet dancers—one American, one Russian—spend an unforgettable night in New York City, forming a lasting friendship despite their cultural and political differences.

"The protagonist is a complexly layered character who suffers from crippling sensitivity, and her difficulty feeling at home in her body will resonate with teens. She is honest, funny, and completely authentic. . . . The prose is poetic and rich." SLJ

Castle Hangnail; by Ursula Vernon. Dial Books for Young Readers, an imprint of Penguin Group (USA) Inc. 2015 384 p. (hardback) $16.99
Grades: 5 6 7 8 9   **Fic**
1. Humorous fiction 2. Magic -- Fiction 3. Witches -- Fiction 4. Haunted houses -- Fiction 5. Humorous stories
ISBN 0803741294; 9780803741294
LC 2014017106
In this book, by Ursula Vernon, "Molly shows up on Castle Hangnail's doorstep to fill the vacancy for a wicked witch [and] the castle's minions are understandably dubious. After all, she is twelve years old, barely five feet tall, and quite polite. . . . But the castle desperately needs a master or else the Board of Magic will decommission it, leaving all the minions without the home they love." (Publisher's note)

"Molly, a 12-year-old witch, arrives as the new master of Castle Hangnail, despite some misgivings on the part of Majordomo, the Igor-like guardian responsible for the management of its legacy and various minion occupants.. An appealing fantasy for upper middle grade readers." SLJ

Castle, Jennifer

You look different in real life; Jennifer Castle. HarperTeen, an imprint of HarperCollinsPublishers 2013 368 p. (hardback) $17.99
Grades: 7 8 9 10   **Fic**
1. School stories 2. Documentary films -- Fiction 3. Identity -- Fiction 4. Celebrities -- Fiction 5. New York (State) -- Fiction 6. Interpersonal relations -- Fiction 7. Family life -- New York (State) -- Fiction
ISBN 0061985813; 9780061985812
LC 2012051743
This book follows five ordinary 16-year-olds who have been the subjects of two documentaries at ages 6 and 11. Now, many "changes have occurred since the last time they were filmed" so the "producers struggle to find usable footage and resort to staging some scenes, which in previous years was unnecessary." (School Library Journal)

Castor, H. M.

VIII; H.M. Castor. Simon & Schuster Books for Young Readers 2013 399 p. (hardcover) $17.99
Grades: 8 9 10 11 12   **Fic**
1. Great Britain -- History -- 1485-1603, Tudors 2. Kings, queens, rulers, etc. -- Fiction 3. Great Britain -- History -- Henry VII, 1485-1509 -- Fiction 4. Great Britain -- History -- Henry VIII, 1509-1547 -- Fiction
ISBN 1442474181; 9781442474185; 9781442474208
LC 2012021550
This book is a biography of Henry VIII of England. As a second son, Henry's youth is full of "fighting, jousting

and gambling. When his elder brother, Arthur, unexpectedly dies, Hal realizes that . . . he now has a straight line to the throne. However . . . the difficulties of producing a royal heir, together with the thwarting of his overweening military ambition against the French by Spanish Catherine's family and his own . . . advisers cause Henry to become increasingly cynical and desperate." (Kirkus Reviews)

Catanese, P. W.

Dragon games. Aladdin 2010 373p il (The books of Umber) $16.99

Grades: 5 6 7 8 **Fic**

1. Fantasy fiction 2. Adventure fiction
ISBN 1-4169-7521-7; 978-1-4169-7521-2

LC 2009018743

Sequel to: Happenstance found (2009)

This is a sequel to Happenstance Found (2009). Having learned more about his mysterious past, Happenstance accompanies Lord Umber on a journey that could affect the future of Kuraharen. "Grades seven to ten." (Bull Cent Child Books)

"The fast-paced and high-energy action of this video-game-like quest will please fantasy adventure fans." Kirkus

Happenstance found. Aladdin 2009 342p il (The books of Umber) $16.99

Grades: 5 6 7 8 **Fic**

1. Fantasy fiction 2. Adventure fiction 3. Magic -- Fiction
ISBN 978-1-4169-7519-9; 1-4169-7519-5

LC 2008-45966

A boy awakens, blindfolded, with no memory of even his name, but soon meets Lord Umber, an adventurer and inventor, who calls him Happenstance and tells him that he has a very important destiny—and a powerful enemy.

"Catanese packs a lot into the book: rich characterizations, . . . well-choreographed action sequences and genuinely surprising twists at the end." Publ Wkly

Followed by: Dragon games (2010)

Catmull, Katherine

Summer and Bird; by Katherine Catmull. Dutton Children's Books 2012 344 p. (hardback) $16.99

Grades: 5 6 7 8 **Fic**

1. Fairy tales 2. Fantasy fiction 4. Fantasy 5. Birds -- Fiction 6. Sisters -- Fiction 7. Puppeteers -- Fiction 8. Adventure and adventurers -- Fiction
ISBN 0525953469; 9780525953463

LC 2012015587

This children's book, by Katherine Catmull, is "an enchanting--and twisted--tale of two sisters' quest to find their parents. When their parents disappear in the middle of the night, young sisters Summer and Bird set off on a quest to find them. A cryptic picture message from their mother leads them to a familiar gate in the woods, but comfortable sights quickly give way to a new world entirely--Down--one inhabited by talking birds and the evil Puppeteer queen." (Publisher's note)

Cavanaugh, Nancy J.

★ **This** journal belongs to Ratchet; by Nancy J. Cavanaugh. Sourcebooks Jabberwocky 2013 320 p. (hardcover) $12.99

Grades: 4 5 6 7 **Fic**

1. Diaries -- Fiction 2. Home schooling -- Fiction 3. Father-daughter relationship -- Fiction 4. Self-acceptance -- Fiction 5. Fathers and daughters -- Fiction 6. Environmental protection -- Fiction
ISBN 1402281064; 9781402281068

LC 2012041339

This juvenile novel, by Nancy Cavanaugh, begins on "the first day of school for all the kids in the neighborhood. But not for me. I'm homeschooled. . . . The best I've got is this notebook. I'm supposed to use it for my writing assignments, but my dad never checks. Here's what I'm really going to use it for: Ratchet's Top Secret Plan . . . : turn my old, recycled, freakish, friendless, motherless life into something shiny and new." (Publisher's note)

"At first it seems artificial, with observations that are too on-the-nose. But as the novel's unexpectedly multifaceted plot comes together, it becomes increasingly compelling, suspenseful and moving. Triumphant enough to make readers cheer; touching enough to make them cry." Kirkus

Caveney, Philip

Sebastian Darke: Prince of Fools. Delacorte Press 2008 338p $15.99; lib bdg $18.99

Grades: 7 8 9 10 **Fic**

1. Fantasy fiction 2. Princesses -- Fiction 3. Fools and jesters -- Fiction
ISBN 978-0-385-73467-7; 978-0-385-90465-0 lib bdg

LC 2006-25262

First published 2007 in the United Kingdom

Accompanied by his sardonic buffalope Max, seventeen-year-old Sebastian Darke meets a spoiled princess and a diminutive soldier who aid in his quest to become court jester to the evil King Septimus.

"In a very plot-driven book, the central characters are nonetheless well developed. Max is a particularly creative invention. . . . There are enough sword fights, treachery, and wicked creatures for any adventure reader. The sense of humor . . . makes it a fun read." Voice Youth Advocates

Other titles about Sebastian Darke are:
Sebastian Darke: Prince of Pirates (2009)
Sebastian Darke: Prince of Explorers (2010)

Ceccarelli, David

The **Yawning** Rabbit River Chronicle; by Janine Layton Kimmel, David Ceccarelli. Spring Tree Press 2012 296 p. (hardcover) $17.99

Grades: 5 6 7 **Fic**

1. Fantasy fiction 2. Rivers -- Fiction 3. Forest animals -- Fiction
ISBN 0978500717; 9780978500719

In this novel, by Janine Layton Kimmel and David Ceccarelli, "the Yawning Rabbit River was returned to the forest by an act of love and sacrifice. . . . But now old enemies and old ghosts rise again to threaten its existence. . . . When young Nub meets Nil he doesn't realize the dangers that they are about to face. . . . When the truth of who they are is revealed the powers of good and evil that are swirling around

Briarwood moves them towards an ultimate confrontation."
(Publisher's note)

Cerra, Kerry O'Malley

Just a drop of water; Kerry O'Malley Cerra.
Skyhorse Publishing, Inc. 2014 320 p. (hardback)
$14.95

Grades: 5 6 7 8 9   **Fic**

1. School stories 2. Friendship -- Fiction 3. September
11 terrorist attacks, 2001 -- Fiction 4. Muslims -- Fiction
5. Best friends -- Fiction 6. Arab Americans -- Fiction
7. Family life -- Florida -- Fiction 8. September 11
Terrorist Attacks, 2001 -- Fiction

ISBN 1629146137; 9781629146133

LC 2014015987

In this novel by Kerry O'Malley Cerra's "historical
novel takes place in . . . the days leading up to and after September 11, 2001. Jake Green struggles with the knowledge
that one of the hijackers was living in his town prior to the
attacks. His best friend and neighbor, Sam Medina, an Arab
Muslim, is targeted by boys in their class. [When] Sam's
father is taken into FBI custody after the discovery that he
serviced the hijacker at the bank he worked . . . Jake soon
finds himself at odds with his immediate family." (School
Library Journal)

"The tragedy of 9/11 forces a 13-year-old Florida boy
who has always lived with a comfortable, straightforward
code of conduct to explore the issues of loyalty, patriotism
and fair play... Cerra does a good job of re-creating the
combination of fear, confusion, patriotism, prejudice and
community spirit the attack engendered, and readers should
identify with Jake's plight. A perceptive exploration of an
event its audience already sees as history." Kirkus

Cerrito, Angela

The **end** of the line. Holiday House 2011 213p
$17.95

Grades: 6 7 8 9   **Fic**

1. Ohio -- Fiction 2. Guilt -- Fiction 3. Uncles --
Fiction 4. Reformatories -- Fiction 5. Iraq War, 2003-
-- Fiction

ISBN 978-0-8234-2287-6; 0-8234-2287-9

LC 2010-23475

"In the prison-like school that is his last chance, thirteen-
year-old Robbie tries to recover from events that brought
him there, including his uncle's war injuries and the death
of [Ryan], a classmate." (Publisher's note) "Grades six to
nine." (Bull Cent Child Books)

"The author does an outstanding job of revealing compelling and complex characters through Robbie's narrative.
. . . This book would work well as a class read-aloud or a
literature circle title." Voice Youth Advocates

Cervantes, Angela

Gaby, Lost and Found. Scholastic Inc. 2013 224
p. $16.99

Grades: 5 6 7   **Fic**

1. Bullies -- Fiction 2. Immigrants -- Fiction

ISBN 0545489458; 9780545489454

In this book, Gaby's mother is deported to Honduras.
"Though she lives with her dad, Gaby basically parents herself with the help of her friend Alma's family. Her physi-

cal and emotional needs are barely met at home. Gaby's
world brightens when her class begins a long-term volunteer
project at the Furry Friends animal shelter. Like her mom,
Gaby is an animal lover, and she develops her writing talent by crafting adoption profiles for the cats and dogs."
(Kirkus Reviews)

Cervantes, Jennifer

Tortilla sun. Chronicle Books 2010 224p
$16.99

Grades: 5 6 7 8   **Fic**

1. New Mexico -- Fiction 2. Grandmothers -- Fiction
3. Father-daughter relationship -- Fiction

ISBN 978-0-8118-7015-3; 0-8118-7015-4

While spending a summer in New Mexico with her
grandmother, twelve-year-old Izzy makes new friends,
learns to cook, and for the first time hears stories about her
father, who died before she was born.

"Cervantes evokes the beauty of the setting and develops a memorable cast of characters, brought to life through
Izzy's heartfelt narration. A beautiful and engaging debut
novel." Kirkus

Chabon, Michael

Summerland. Hyperion Bks. for Children 2002
500p hardcover o.p. pa $8.95

Grades: 5 6 7 8   **Fic**

1. Fantasy fiction 2. Magic -- Fiction 3. Baseball
-- Fiction

ISBN 0-7868-0877-2; 0-7868-1615-5 pa

LC 2002-27497

Ethan Feld, the worst baseball player in the history of the
game, finds himself recruited by a 100-year-old scout to help
a band of fairies triumph over an ancient enemy

"Much of the prose is beautifully descriptive as Chabon
navigates vividly imagined other worlds and offers up some
timeless themes." Horn Book

Chadda, Sarwat

The **devil's** kiss. Disney/Hyperion Books 2009
327p $17.99

Grades: 8 9 10   **Fic**

1. Templars -- Fiction 2. Supernatural -- Fiction 3.
Good and evil -- Fiction 4. London (England) -- Fiction

ISBN 978-1-4231-1999-9; 1-4231-1999-1

LC 2009-8313

Fifteen-year-old Billi SanGreal has grown up knowing
that being a member of the Knights Templar puts her in danger, but if she is to save London from catastrophe she must
make sacrifices greater than she imagined.

"Scenes of spiritual warfare are gripping (and often
gruesome), as is the undercurrent of supernatural romance.
Chadda offers an original take on familiar creatures like
vampires, the undead and fallen angels, but it's Billi's
personality and tumult of emotions that will keep readers
hooked." Publ Wkly

Followed by Dark goddess (2010)

Chaltas, Thalia

Because I am furniture. Viking Children's Books
2009 352p $16.99

Grades: 8 9 10 11   **Fic**
1. School stories 2. Novels in verse 3. Guilt -- Fiction
4. Child abuse -- Fiction 5. Child sexual abuse -- Fiction
ISBN 978-0-670-06298-0; 0-670-06298-7

LC 2008-23235

The youngest of three siblings, fourteen-year-old Anke feels both relieved and neglected that her father abuses her brother and sister but ignores her, but when she catches him with one of her friends, she finally becomes angry enough to take action.

"Incendiary, devastating, yet—in total—offering empowerment and hope, Chaltas's poems leave an indelible mark." Publ Wkly

Chambers, Veronica

Fifteen candles. Hyperion 2010 187p (Amigas) pa $7.99

Grades: 6 7 8 9 10   **Fic**
1. Friendship -- Fiction 2. Cuban Americans -- Fiction
3. Business enterprises -- Fiction 4. Quinceañera (Social custom) -- Fiction
ISBN 978-1-4231-2362-0; 1-4231-2362-X

"It's Alicia's quince años, and even though her thoroughly modern parents took her to Spain for her quinceañera, most of her friends are having elaborate parties to celebrate their entry into womanhood. When she realizes that a fellow intern in the mayor's office needs help in planning her quince, Alicia envisions a new business venture for her and her three best friends, Amigas Inc. . . . . A warm celebration of Latin culture, especially the traditional quinceañera, this is the first in a series that is sure to draw a large audience." Booklist

Chan, Gillian

A **foreign** field. Kids Can Press 2002 184p $16.95; pa $5.95

Grades: 7 8 9 10   **Fic**
1. Love stories 2. World War, 1939-1945 -- Fiction
ISBN 1-55337-349-9; 1-55337-350-2 pa

"Fourteen-year-old Ellen, who lives near a Canadian air base that the Royal Air Force is using for training during WWII, has what she considers a tedious job as her war work: looking after her disobedient, airplane-mad younger brother, Colin. Colin introduces her to Stephen, a very young RAF trainee. . . . They find common ground and their friendship grows and deepens into love. . . . Chan beautifully captures the particular tensions and intensity of wartime relationships in this quiet, absorbing novel." Booklist

Chandler, Kristen

Girls don't fly. Viking 2011 300p $16.99

Grades: 7 8 9 10   **Fic**
1. Utah -- Fiction 2. Contests -- Fiction 3. Pregnancy -- Fiction 4. Family life -- Fiction 5. Dating (Social customs) -- Fiction
ISBN 978-0-670-01331-9; 0-670-01331-5

LC 2011010563

Myra, a high school senior, will do almost anything to win a contest and earn money for a study trip to the Galapagos Islands, which would mean getting away from her demanding family life in Utah and ex-boyfriend Erik, but Erik is set on winning the same contest.

"As Myra navigates from one trauma to the next, we know she is a princess in a scullery maid's disguise. Her cast of supporting characters is equally entertaining: sniveling Erik, sarcastic Melyssa, rough and tumble siblings, and, of course, Prince Charming, incognito as a graduate student. Funny, sensitive, loyal and endearing, Myra is a heroine to remember." Voice Youth Advocates

Wolves, boys, & other things that might kill me. Viking 2010 371p $17.99; pa $8.99

Grades: 7 8 9 10 11 12   **Fic**
1. Wolves -- Fiction 2. Yellowstone National Park -- Fiction
ISBN 978-0-670-01142-1; 0-670-01142-8; 978-0-14-241883-3 pa; 0-14-241883-8 pa

LC 2009-30179

Two teenagers become close as the citizens of their town fight over the packs of wolves that have been reintroduced into the nearby Yellowstone National Park.

This "is a lively drama, saturated with multifaceted characters and an environmental undercurrent. She writes persuasively about the great outdoors, smalltown dynamics and politics, and young love." Publ Wkly

Chapman, Fern Schumer

★ **Is** it night or day? Farrar, Straus, Giroux 2010 205p $17.99

Grades: 6 7 8 9 10   **Fic**
1. Chicago (Ill.) -- Fiction 2. Jewish refugees -- Fiction
3. Jews -- Germany -- Fiction 4. Holocaust, 1933-1945 -- Fiction 5. World War, 1939-1945 -- Fiction 6. Jews -- United States -- Fiction
ISBN 0-374-17744-9; 978-0-374-17744-7

LC 2008055602

In 1938, Edith Westerfeld, a young German Jew, is sent by her parents to Chicago, Illinois, where she lives with an aunt and uncle and tries to assimilate into American culture, while worrying about her parents and mourning the loss of everything she has ever known. Based on the author's mother's experience, includes an afterword about a little-known program that brought twelve hundred Jewish children to safety during World War II.

"In Edith's bewildered, sad, angry voice, the words are eloquent and powerful." Booklist

Chapman, Lara

Flawless. Bloomsbury 2011 258 p. $16.99; pa $9.99

Grades: 7 8 9 10   **Fic**
1. Love stories 2. School stories 3. Friendship -- Fiction 4. Personal appearance -- Fiction
ISBN 1599906317; 1599905965; 9781599906317; 9781599905969

LC 2010049102

In this modern take on the Cyrano story, brilliant and witty high school student Sarah Burke, who is cursed with an enormous nose, helps her beautiful best friend try to win the heart of a handsome and smart new student, even though Sarah wants him for herself.

"This retelling of Cyrano de Bergerac is great fun. . . . The ending is predictable but satisfying. Each chapter begins with thoughtful quotes about love. This novel will attract both reluctant readers and literature lovers." SLJ

Charbonneau, Joelle

Graduation day; Joelle Charbonneau. Houghton Mifflin Harcourt 2014 304 p. (hardback) $17.99
Grades: 7 8 9 10 11 12   **Fic**

1. Dystopian fiction 2. Love -- Fiction 3. Loyalty -- Fiction 4. Survival -- Fiction 5. Adventure and adventurers -- Fiction 6. Government, Resistance to -- Fiction
  ISBN 0547959214; 9780547959214
                LC 2013034743

In this book, by Joelle Charbonneau, "The United Commonwealth teeters on the brink of all-out civil war. The rebel resistance plots against a government that rules with cruelty and cunning. Gifted student and Testing survivor, Cia Vale, vows to fight. . . . This is the chance to lead that Cia has trained for -- but who will follow? Plunging through layers of danger and deception, Cia must risk the lives of those she loves--and gamble on the loyalty of her lethal classmates." (Publisher's note)

"Charbonneau concludes her dystopian Testing trilogy with this action-packed finale, which sees Cia Vale secretly tasked by the President of the United Commonwealth to remove the officials behind the lethal Testing process that has claimed so many young lives...As in the previous books, Charbonneau remains focused on philosophical worries and moral tests over spectacle and bloodshed, with multiple layers and twists to keep readers forever guessing. Enough potential threads are left dangling to leave room for future stories." (Publishers Weekly)

Independent study; by Joelle Charbonneau. Houghton Mifflin, Houghton Mifflin Harcourt 2014 320 p. (The testing) (hardback) $17.99
Grades: 7 8 9 10 11 12   **Fic**

1. Adventure and adventurers 2. Love -- Fiction 3. Survival -- Fiction 4. Examinations -- Fiction
  ISBN 0547959206; 9780547959207
                LC 2013004815

In this book, by Joelle Charbonneau, "sixteen-year-old Cia Vale was chosen by the United Commonwealth government as one of the best and brightest graduates of all the colonies. . . . [Now], Cia is a freshman at the University in Tosu City with her hometown sweetheart, Tomas—and though the government has tried to erase her memory of the brutal horrors of The Testing, Cia remembers. Her attempts to expose the ugly truth behind the government's murderous programs put her . . . in a world of danger." (Publisher's note)

"—In this sequel to The Testing (Houghton Harcourt, 2013), Cia is drawn deeper into the political machinations of Tosu City as she enters the University...Fans of The Testing will be thrilled with this new installment and will be anxiously waiting for the story's conclusion." (School Library Journal)

★ The **Testing**; by Joelle Charbonneau. Houghton Mifflin Harcourt 2013 344 p. (hardcover) $17.99
Grades: 7 8 9 10 11 12   **Fic**

1. Examinations -- Fiction 2. Survival skills -- Fiction 3. Schools -- Fiction 4. Missing persons -- Fiction

5. Graduation (School) -- Fiction 6. Universities and colleges -- Fiction
  ISBN 0547959109; 9780547959108
                LC 2012018090

In this book by Joelle Charbonneau, "Cia Vale is one of four teens chosen to represent her small colony at the annual Testing, an intensive mental and physical examination aimed at identifying the best and brightest, who will go on to the University and help rebuild their shattered world. Forewarned not to trust anyone, Cia nonetheless forms a tentative partnership with resourceful Tomas, with whom she shares an unexpected emotional connection." (Publishers Weekly)

Chari, Sheela

Vanished. Disney/Hyperion Books 2011 240p $16.99
Grades: 5 6 7 8   **Fic**

1. Mystery fiction 2. East Indian Americans -- Fiction 3. Lost and found possessions -- Fiction
  ISBN 978-1-4231-3163-2; 1-4231-3163-0
                LC 2010019660

Eleven-year-old Neela must solve the mystery when her beautiful, but cursed, veena, a classical Indian musical instrument, goes missing.

"Well-paced and with moments of family humor . . . the novel offers a strong cast of characters and richly-described settings; both the legend and the contemporary come alive for readers. . . . Chari . . . strikes the right note with this engaging, intricate story that spans generations and two countries." Kirkus

Includes bibliographical references

Chatterton, Martin

The **Brain** finds a leg. Peachtree Publishers 2009 212p $16.95
Grades: 4 5 6   **Fic**

1. School stories 2. Mystery fiction 3. Animals -- Fiction 4. Australia -- Fiction 5. Intellect -- Fiction 6. Inventions -- Fiction
  ISBN 978-1-56145-503-4; 1-56145-503-2
                LC 2009-00304

First published 2007 in Australia

In Farrago Bay, Australia, thirteen-year-old Sheldon is recruited by a new student, Theo Brain, to help investigate a murder, which is tied not only to bizzare animal behavior but also to a diabolical plot to alter human intelligence.

"Several deaths in the story war against the comedy but the laughs win. Readers shouldn't expect anything remotely realistic and instead surrender themselves to the industrial-strength zaniness." Kirkus

Another title about The Brain is:
The Brain full of holes (2010)

The **Brain** full of holes. Peachtree 2010 250p $16.95
Grades: 4 5 6   **Fic**

1. Mystery fiction 2. Inventions -- Fiction 3. Switzerland -- Fiction
  ISBN 978-1-56145-527-0; 1-56145-527-X

"Kid detective The Brain and his Watson are called in on a missing-person case. Their search takes them to Switzerland, home of the new super-particle accelerator, but their real adventure occurs in an alternate universe filled with zaniness. Chatterton explores speculations about physics throughout in amusing ways. . . . Those who like laughs along with a sf-influenced mystery will enjoy this." Booklist

Cheaney, J. B.

The **middle** of somewhere. Alfred A. Knopf 2007 218p $15.99; lib bdg $18.99; pa $6.50

Grades: 5 6 7 8 **Fic**

1. Kansas -- Fiction 2. Siblings -- Fiction 3. Grandfathers -- Fiction 4. Automobile travel -- Fiction 5. Attention deficit disorder -- Fiction

ISBN 978-0-375-83790-6; 978-0-375-93790-3 lib bdg; 978-0-440-42165-8 pa

LC 2006-29202

Twelve-year-old Ronnie loves organization, especially because her brother has attention-deficit hyperactivity disorder, but traveling with their grandfather who is investigating wind power in Kansas brings some pleasant, if chaotic, surprises.

"The main characters are particularly well drawn and believable, and readers will root for both children as they attempt to overcome the obstacles placed in front of them." Booklist

Chen, Justina

Return to me; by Justina Chen. Little, Brown and Co. 2013 352 p. (hardcover) $17.99

Grades: 7 8 9 10 **Fic**

1. Moving -- Fiction 2. Family life -- Fiction 3. Clairvoyance -- Fiction 4. Love -- Fiction 5. Architecture -- Fiction 6. Family problems -- Fiction 7. Moving, Household -- Fiction 8. Self-actualization (Psychology) -- Fiction

ISBN 0316102555; 9780316102551

LC 2012001549

In this book, "moving away from her Washington home seems to be a logical part of Reb's life plan; after the summer, she'll start at Columbia University, studying to be a corporate architect in the family firm, while her family moves to New Jersey for her father's new job. All that unravels upon their arrival on the East Coast, when her father announces that he's leaving the family to be with another woman, forcing Reb to question everything." (Bulletin of the Center for Children's Books)

Cheng, Andrea

Brushing Mom's hair; illustrations by Nicole Wong. Wordsong 2009 59p il $17.95

Grades: 4 5 6 7 8 **Fic**

1. Novels in verse 2. Sick -- Fiction 3. Cancer -- Fiction 4. Mother-daughter relationship -- Fiction

ISBN 978-1-59078-599-7; 1-59078-599-1

LC 2009021965

A fourteen-year-old girl, whose mother's breast cancer diagnosis and treatment have affected every aspect of their lives, finds release in ballet and art classes.

"With one or two words on each line, the poems are a fast read, but the chatty voice packs in emotion. . . . Wong's small black-and-white pencil drawings on every page extend the poetry through the characters' body language." Booklist

Where do you stay? Boyds Mills Press 2011 134p $17.95

Grades: 4 5 6 7 **Fic**

1. Aunts -- Fiction 2. Cousins -- Fiction 3. Pianists -- Fiction 4. Bereavement -- Fiction 5. Homeless persons -- Fiction

ISBN 1-59078-707-2; 978-1-59078-707-6

Jerome is staying with his Aunt Geneva and her family, now that his mother has passed away. Aunt Geneva tries to make Jerome feel welcome, but his cousins are not happy about the new "member" of their family. Though Jerome has a place to stay, he doesn't feel he has a home, until he meets Mr. Willie, who lives in a ramshackle carriage house.

"In short chapters of lyrical prose, Cheng . . . provides a moving tribute to a multigenerational community's ability to sustain and recreate itself in times of change through resilience, hard work, and a commitment to beauty and kindness." Publ Wkly

Cheva, Cherry

DupliKate; a novel. HarperTeen 2009 242p $16.99

Grades: 7 8 9 10 **Fic**

1. School stories 2. Computer games -- Fiction 3. Virtual reality -- Fiction

ISBN 978-0-06-128854-8; 0-06-128854-3

LC 2009-18292

When she wakes up one morning to find her double in her room, seventeen-year-old Kate, already at wit's end with college applications, finals, and extracurricular activities, decides to put her to work.

This is a "light and funny novel. . . . Though this is lightweight territory, there is a strong message here about being true to yourself and balancing fun and work in your life. . . . This is sure to fly off the shelves." SLJ

Chibbaro, Julie

Deadly; illustrations by Jean-Marc Superville Sovak. Atheneum Books for Young Readers 2011 293 p. $16.99

Grades: 6 7 8 9 10 **Fic**

1. Sick 2. Domestics 3. Diaries -- Fiction 4. Diaries -- Fiction 5. Sex role -- Fiction 6. Epidemiology -- Fiction 7. Typhoid fever -- Fiction 8. New York (N.Y.) -- Fiction 10. Interpersonal relations -- Fiction 11. New York (N.Y.) -- History -- 1898-1951 -- Fiction

ISBN 0689857381; 9780689857386; 978-0-689-85738-6; 0-689-85738-1

LC 2010002291

"Sixteen-year-old Prudence lives in a New York City tenement with her mother and attends a school where she feels like a misfit. Haunted by memories of her brother's painful dying and by unanswered questions about her father, who never returned from the Spanish-American War, she longs to fight death itself. Prudence takes a job with the health department, where she helps track down the source of a typhoid outbreak, a healthy carrier now remembered as Typhoid Mary." (Booklist)

"A deeply personal coming-of-age story set in an era of tumultuous social change, this is topnotch historical fiction that highlights the struggle between rational science and popular opinion as shaped by a sensational, reactionary press." SLJ

Childs, Tera Lynn

Oh. My. Gods. Dutton Books 2008 224p $16.99
Grades: 7 8 9 10   **Fic**
1. School stories 2. Running -- Fiction 3. Stepfamilies -- Fiction 4. Classical mythology -- Fiction
ISBN 978-0-525-47942-0; 0-525-47942-2
LC 2007-28294
When her mother suddenly decides to marry a near-stranger, Phoebe, whose passion is running, soon finds herself living on a remote Greek island, completing her senior year at an ancient high school where the students and teachers are all descended from gods or goddesses.

"Childs does a great job of character development and creating a fast-paced plot to keep readers engaged." Voice Youth Advocates

Sweet venom. Katherine Tegen Books 2011 345p $17.99
Grades: 7 8 9 10   **Fic**
1. Sisters -- Fiction 2. Monsters -- Fiction 3. Fate and fatalism -- Fiction 4. Classical mythology -- Fiction 5. San Francisco (Calif.) -- Fiction 6. Medusa (Greek mythology) -- Fiction
ISBN 978-0-06-200181-8; 0-06-200181-7
LC 2010050525
As monsters walk the streets of San Francisco, unseen by humans, three teenaged descendants of Medusa, the once-beautiful gorgon maligned in Greek mythology, must reunite and embrace their fates.

"Childs clearly has a sequel (or more) in mind and uses this book to ably set up an appealing conflict, introduce quite likable characters, and get readers ready for intrigue in the romance and fate-of-the-world departments." Booklist

Chima, Cinda Williams

The **Crimson** Crown; a Seven Realms novel. Cinda Williams Chima. Hyperion 2012 598 p. (hardback) $18.99
Grades: 7 8 9 10 11 12   **Fic**
1. Fantasy fiction 2. Queens -- Fiction 3. Magicians -- Fiction 4. Fantasy 5. Wizards -- Fiction
ISBN 1423144333; 9781423144335
LC 2011053079
In this fantasy novel by Cinda Williams Chima, book 4 of the Seven Realms series, "the Queendom of the Fells seems likely to shatter apart. For young queen Raisa . . . , maintaining peace even within her own castle walls is nearly impossible; tension between wizards and Clan has reached a fevered pitch. . . . Raisa's best hope is to unite her people against a common enemy. But that enemy might be the person with whom she's falling in love." (Publisher's note)

★ The **Demon** King; a Seven Realms novel. Disney Hyperion 2009 506p map (Seven Realms) $17.99
Grades: 7 8 9 10 11 12   **Fic**
1. Fantasy fiction 2. Princesses -- Fiction 3. Witchcraft

-- Fiction
ISBN 978-1-4231-1823-7; 1-4231-1823-5
LC 2008-46178
Relates the intertwining fates of former street gang leader Han Alister and headstrong Princess Raisa, as Han takes possession of an amulet that once belonged to an evil wizard and Raisa uncovers a conspiracy in the Grey Wolf Court.

"With full-blooded, endearing heroes, a well-developed supporting cast and a detail-rich setting, Chima explores the lives of two young adults, one at the top of the world and the other at the bottom, struggling to find their place and protect those they love." Publ Wkly

Other titles in this series are:
The exiled queen (2010)
The Gray Wolf Throne (2011)

★ The **warrior** heir. Hyperion Books for Children 2006 426p hardcover o.p.
Grades: 7 8 9 10 11 12   **Fic**
1. Fantasy fiction 2. Magic -- Fiction
ISBN 0-7868-3916-3; 0-7868-3917-1 pa; 978-0-7868-3916-2; 978-0-7868-3917-9 pa
LC 2005-52720
After learning about his magical ancestry and his own warrior powers, sixteen-year-old Jack embarks on a training program to fight enemy wizards. "Grades seven to ten." (Bull Cent Child Books)

"Twists and turns abound in this remarkable, nearly flawless debut novel that mixes a young man's coming-of-age with fantasy and adventure. Fast paced and brilliantly plotted." Voice Youth Advocates

Other titles in this series are:
The dragon heir (2008)
The wizard heir (2007)

The **wizard** heir. Hyperion 2007 458p hardcover o.p. pa $8.99
Grades: 7 8 9 10 11 12   **Fic**
1. Fantasy fiction 2. Magic -- Fiction
ISBN 978-1-4231-0487-2; 1-4231-0487-0; 978-1-4231-0488-9 pa; 1-4231-0488-9 pa
LC 2007-15262
Sequel to: The warrior heir
Sixteen-year-old Seph, a powerful wizard, gets caught up in a conflict between the Wizard Council, smaller groups with their own agendas, and a rogue politician—the Dragon—whose identity and whereabouts the others seek to know.

"Chima uses her pen like a wand and crafts a wonderfully rich web of magic." Voice Youth Advocates

Followed by: The dragon heir

Choat, Beth

Soccerland. Marshall Cavendish 2010 231p (The International Sports Academy) $16.99
Grades: 7 8 9 10   **Fic**
1. Soccer -- Fiction
ISBN 978-0-7614-5724-4; 0-7614-5724-0
"Flora Dupre loves soccer, and before her mom died of cancer, she made a promise that one day she was going to play for the U.S. Women's National Team. . . . Choat's background in sports journalism is obvious. While soccer

action takes precedence over any deep character development, readers will enjoy following Flora's new friendships, budding romance, and changing relationship with her father." SLJ

Choi, Sook Nyul

★ **Year** of impossible goodbyes. Houghton Mifflin 1991 171p hardcover o.p. pa $5.99

Grades: 5 6 7 8 **Fic**

1. Korea -- Fiction

ISBN 0-395-57419-6; 978-0-440-40759-1 pa

LC 91-10502

This is the story "of Sookan, a young girl living in northern Korea during the turbulent period of the Second World War. As the war rages, ten-year-old Sookan, her mother, and her younger brother courageously endure the cruelties of the Japanese military occupying Korea. Forced to work for the war effort, Sookan dreams of a time of peace and liberty for herself and her family.... With the end of the war in 1945, Sookan's hopes for freedom are dashed as she watches the superpowers divide her country and the Communist Russian troops take control of North Korea, coercing its citizens to adopt the Communist lifestyle.... Dangerous as it is, Sookan's family comes to believe that escape is their only chance for a happy future." (Publisher's note) "Grades five to nine." (Bull Cent Child Books)

"Tragedies are not masked here, but neither are they overdramatized.... The observations are honest, the details authentic, the characterizations vividly developed." Bull Cent Child Books

Choldenko, Gennifer

Al Capone does my homework; by Gennifer Choldenko. Dial Books for Young Readers 2013 224 p. (Al Capone Trilogy) (hardcover) $17.99

Grades: 5 6 7 8 **Fic**

1. Mystery fiction -- Fiction 2. Historical fiction -- Fiction 3. Fires -- Fiction 4. Autism -- Fiction 5. Brothers and sisters -- Fiction 6. Swindlers and swindling -- Fiction 7. Alcatraz Island (Calif.) -- History -- 20th century -- Fiction 8. United States Penitentiary, Alcatraz Island, California -- Fiction 9. United States Penitentiary, Alcatraz Island, California -- Fiction

ISBN 0803734727; 9780803734722

LC 2012039138

Sequel to: Al Capone shines my shoes

This book, set on Alcatraz Island in the 1930s, is the third in Gennifer Choldenko's Al Capone trilogy. Moose lives with his parents and autistic sister on the island. "When Moose's dad gets promoted to Associate Warden, . . . it's a big deal. But the cons have a point system for targeting prison employees, and his dad is now in serious danger. After a fire starts in the Flanagan's apartment, Natalie is blamed, and Moose bands with the other kids to track down the possible arsonist." (Publisher's note)

Includes bibliographical references

★ **Al** Capone does my shirts. G.P. Putnam's Sons 2004 225p il $15.99; pa $6.99

Grades: 5 6 7 8 **Fic**

1. Autism -- Fiction 2. Siblings -- Fiction 3. Alcatraz

Island (Calif.) -- Fiction

ISBN 0-399-23861-1; 0-14-240370-9 pa

LC 2002-31766

A Newbery Medal honor book, 2005

A twelve-year-old boy named Moose moves to Alcatraz Island in 1935 when guards' families were housed there, and has to contend with his extraordinary new environment in addition to life with his autistic sister.

"With its unique setting and well-developed characters, this warm, engaging coming-of-age story has plenty of appeal, and Choldenko offers some fascinating historical background on Alcatraz Island in an afterword." Booklist

Followed by: Al Capone shines my shoes (2009)

Al Capone shines my shoes. Dial Books for Young Readers 2009 274p $16.99

Grades: 5 6 7 8 **Fic**

1. Autism -- Fiction 2. Siblings -- Fiction 3. Alcatraz Island (Calif.) -- Fiction

ISBN 978-0-8037-3460-9; 0-8037-3460-3

LC 2009-04157

Sequel to: Al Capone does my shirts (2004)

Moose Flanagan, who lives on Alcatraz along with his family and the families of the other prison guards, is frightened when he discovers that noted gangster Al Capone, a prisoner there, wants a favor in return for the help that he secretly gave Moose.

"Effortless period dialogue, fully developed secondary characters and a perfectly paced plot combine to create a solid-gold sequel that will not disappoint." Kirkus

Includes bibliographical references

No passengers beyond this point. Dial Books for Young Readers 2011 244p $16.99

Grades: 5 6 7 8 **Fic**

1. Fantasy fiction 2. Siblings -- Fiction 3. Space and time -- Fiction

ISBN 978-0-8037-3534-7; 0-8037-3534-0

LC 2009-51661

With their house in foreclosure, sisters India and Mouse and brother Finn are sent to stay with an uncle in Colorado until their mother can join them, but when the plane lands, the children are welcomed by cheering crowds to a strange place where each of them has a perfect house and a clock that is ticking down the time.

"Choldenko keeps the plot moving rapidly and constantly shifts the point of view, with each chapter narrated by one of the three siblings, so that both readers and characters feel discombobulated—everything is both concrete yet dreamlike.... No one can write a hormonal teenage girl at war with her family like Choldenko, but in the end the family relationships and the determination each sibling has to protect the others is what saves them all." Horn Book

Notes from a liar and her dog. Putnam 2001 216p hardcover o.p. pa $5.99

Grades: 5 6 7 8 **Fic**

1. Family life -- Fiction 2. Truthfulness and falsehood -- Fiction

ISBN 0-399-23591-4; 0-14-250068-2 pa

LC 00-55354

Eleven-year-old Ant, stuck in a family that she does not like, copes by pretending that her "real" parents are coming to rescue her, by loving her dog Pistachio, by volunteering at the zoo, and by bending the truth and telling lies

"Choldenko's writing is snappy and tender, depicting both Ant's bravado and her isolation with sympathy." Bull Cent Child Books

The chosen prince; Diane Stanley. Harper, an imprint of HarperCollinsPublishers 2015 368 p. illustration, map $16.99

Grades: 5 6 7 8   **Fic**

1. Magic -- Fiction 2. Princes -- Fiction 3. Shipwrecks -- Fiction 4. Fate and fatalism -- Fiction

ISBN 0062248979; 9780062248978

LC 2014022042

This children's book by Diane Stanley is "based on [William] Shakespeare's 'The Tempest.' On the day of his birth, Prince Alexos is revealed to be the long-awaited champion of Athene. He grows up lonely, conscious of all that is expected of him. Alexos follows the course of his destiny through war and loss and a deadly confrontation with his enemy to its end: shipwreck on a magical, fog-shrouded island. There he meets the unforgettable Aria and faces the greatest challenge of his life." (Publisher's note)

"Stanley's newest fantasy, set in ancient Greece, is a bittersweet delight. Prince Alexos learns early that being the champion of a goddess does not make for an easy life. Alexos is destined to bring about reconciliation between battling gods, Athene and Zeus, if he can survive a childhood filled with near-impossible challenge and little joy, except for his love of running and his little brother Teo... Other characters—especially the court physician Suliman and Teo's new sister Aria—are equally well done. The language is lyrical and accessible, and the end is satisfying in the extreme." SLJ

Chotjewitz, David

Daniel half human; and the good Nazi. translated by Doris Orgel. Atheneum Books for Young Readers 2004 298p hardcover o.p. pa $6.99

Grades: 7 8 9 10   **Fic**

1. Jews -- Fiction 2. Germany -- Fiction 3. National socialism -- Fiction

ISBN 0-689-85747-0; 0-689-85748-9 pa

LC 2003-25554

In 1933, best friends Daniel and Armin admire Hitler, but as anti-Semitism buoys Hitler to power, Daniel learns he is half Jewish, threatening the friendship even as life in their beloved Hamburg, Germany, is becoming nightmarish. Also details Daniel and Armin's reunion in 1945 in interspersed chapters.

"Orgel's translation reads smoothly and movingly. An outstanding addition to the large body of World War II/Holocaust fiction." SLJ

Choyce, Lesley

Deconstructing Dylan. Boardwalk Books/Dundurn Press 2006 174p pa $12.99

Grades: 7 8 9 10 11 12   **Fic**

1. Science fiction 2. Cloning -- Fiction

ISBN 1-55002-603-8

"The year is 2014. . . . The only child of well-known genetics researchers, Dylan has always felt that he is different from his peers in some fundamental way that he cannot define. . . . [His parents] confess that Dylan is a clone of his dead brother. . . . Choyce uses a tantalizing story line to ask some difficult questions about the consequences of scientific progress. Dylan is an unforgettable character." Voice Youth Advocates

Christopher, John

The City of gold and lead; 35th anniversary ed.; Simon & Schuster Books for Young Readers 2003 180p hardcover o.p. pa $5.99

Grades: 5 6 7 8   **Fic**

1. Science fiction

ISBN 0-689-85505-2; 0-689-85666-0 pa

LC 2002026670

Sequel to: The White Mountains

A reissue of the title first published 1967

Three boys set out on a secret mission to penetrate the City of the Tripods and learn more about these strange beings that rule the earth.

Followed by: The pool of fire

The pool of fire; 35th anniversary ed.; Simon & Schuster Books for Young Readers 2003 176p hardcover o.p. pa $5.99

Grades: 5 6 7 8   **Fic**

1. Science fiction

ISBN 0-689-85506-0; 0-689-85669-5 pa

LC 2002026883

Sequel to: City of gold and lead

A reissue of the title first published 1968

Will and a small group of free people plan to destroy the three great cities of the Tripods before the arrival of a space ship destined to doom humanity.

When the Tripods came. Dutton 1988 151p hardcover o.p. pa $5.99

Grades: 5 6 7 8   **Fic**

1. Science fiction

ISBN 0-525-44397-5; 978-0-689-85762-1 pa; 0-689-85762-4 pa

LC 88-478

"A prequel to the author's well-known White Mountains trilogy . . . this relates how the Tripods came to Earth and imposed a new subservient order on its population. The protagonist is Laurie Corday, who, with his friend Andy, witnesses the first arrival of these towering metallic creatures. . . . The story's scenario exudes a chill; Laurie lives in the present, not some futuristic world, and the Tripods' insidious rise to power seems quite reasonable in the context of the story." Booklist

★ The White Mountains; 35th anniversary ed; Simon & Schuster Bks. for Young Readers 2003 164p hardcover o.p. pa $5.99

Grades: 5 6 7 8   **Fic**

1. Science fiction

ISBN 0-689-85504-4; 0-689-85672-5 pa

LC 2002-70808

A reissue of the title first published 1967 by Macmillan

Young Will Parker and his companions make a perilous journey toward an outpost of freedom where they hope to escape from the ruling Tripods, who capture mature human beings and make them docile, obedient servants

This "remarkable story . . . belongs to the school of science-fiction which puts philosophy before technology and is not afraid of telling an exciting story." Times Lit Suppl

Other titles about the Tripods are:

The city of gold and lead (2003 c1967)

The pool of fire (2003 c1968)

When the Tripods came (2003 c1988)

Christopher, Lucy

★ Flyaway; Lucy Christopher. Chicken House 2011 314p $16.99

Grades: 5 6 7 8   **Fic**

1. Sick -- Fiction 2. Swans -- Fiction 3. Hospitals -- Fiction 4. Wildlife conservation -- Fiction 5. Family life -- Fiction 6. Father-daughter relationship -- Fiction
ISBN 0545317711; 9780545317719

LC 2010051425

In this young adult novel, "when newly constructed power lines ruin the annual return of the whooping swans Isla and her father rise early to witness, the death of several of the wild creatures and her father's sudden and severe illness both confound Isla and emphasize her loneliness. At the hospital where her father awaits a heart operation, Harry, waiting there for a bone-marrow transplant, befriends Isla and points out the young swan he can see from his bed. . . . News broadcasts . . . about deadly outbreaks of bird flu contrast with the small unfolding of Isla's widowed grandfather's stiff grief as he helps her construct an art project--a harness and wings from an ancient stuffed swan--and innocent romance flutters between Isla and Harry even as the young swan regains flight and her father begins to recover." (Kirkus)

Christopher offers "readers a quiet but compelling story with several well-realized, idiosyncratic characters. She skillfully develops the novel's varied elements and weaves them into a unified narrative. . . . This sensitive novel will resonate with many readers." Booklist

Churchyard, Kathleen

Bye for now; a Wishers story. Egmont USA 2011 264p $15.99

Grades: 4 5 6   **Fic**

1. Wishes -- Fiction 2. London (England) -- Fiction
ISBN 978-1-60684-190-7; 1-60684-190-4; 978-1-60684-278-2 e-book

LC 2011005895

While blowing out the candles on her birthday cake, eleven-year-old Robin wishes she were someone else, and wakes up to find herself in the body of an eleven-year-old British actress.

"Robin's an engaging character whose lively narrative incorporates issues such as self-esteem and self-discovery." Booklist

Cisneros, Sandra

★ The **house** on Mango Street. Knopf 1994 134p $24

Grades: 7 8 9 10   **Fic**

1. Chicago (Ill.) -- Fiction 2. Mexican Americans -- Fiction
ISBN 0-679-43335-X

LC 93-43564

Originally published by Arte Público Press in 1984.

In this book by Sandra Cisneros, "Esperanza Cordero, a girl coming of age in the Hispanic quarter of Chicago, uses poems and stories to express thoughts and emotions about her . . . environment." (Publishers Weekly) It is "told in a series of vignettes--sometimes heartbreaking, sometimes deeply joyous". (Publisher's note)

This is "a composite of evocative snapshots that manages to passionately recreate the milieu of the poor quarters of Chicago." Commonweal

Clare, Cassandra

Clockwork prince; Cassandra Clare. 1st ed. Margaret K. McElderry Books 2011 528 p. (The infernal devices) (hardcover) $19.99

Grades: 6 7 8 9 10 11 12   **Fic**

1. Fantasy fiction 2. Orphans -- Fiction 3. Demonology -- Fiction 4. Supernatural -- Fiction 5. London (England) -- Fiction 6. Secret societies -- Fiction 7. Identity -- Fiction 8. London (England) -- History -- 19th century -- Fiction
ISBN 9781416975885; 9781442431348

LC 2011017869

In this book, a #1 New York Times Bestseller, set "[i]n the magical underworld of Victorian London, Tessa Gray has at last found safety with the Shadowhunters. But that safety proves fleeting when rogue forces in the Clave plot to see her protector, Charlotte, replaced as head of the Institute. If Charlotte loses her position, Tessa will be out on the street—and easy prey for the mysterious Magister, who wants to use Tessa's powers for his own dark ends. With the help of the handsome, self-destructive Will and the fiercely devoted Jem, Tessa discovers that the Magister's war on the Shadowhunters is deeply personal. . . . To unravel the secrets of the past, the trio journeys from mist-shrouded Yorkshire to a manor house that holds untold horrors, from the slums of London to an enchanted ballroom where Tessa discovers that the truth of her parentage is more sinister than she had imagined." (Publisher's note)

Clockwork princess; Cassandra Clare. 1st ed. Margaret K. McElderry Books 2013 592 p. (The infernal devices) (hardcover) $19.99

Grades: 6 7 8 9 10 11 12   **Fic**

1. Love stories 2. Fantasy fiction 3. Orphans -- Fiction 4. Demonology -- Fiction 5. Supernatural -- Fiction 6. Secret societies -- Fiction 7. London (England) -- History -- 19th century -- Fiction 8. Great Britain -- History -- Victoria, 1837-1901 -- Fiction
ISBN 141697590X; 9781416975908

LC 2012048910

This is the third installment of Cassandra Clare's The Infernal Devices trilogy. Here, "Tessa leads the fight against Mortmain (a.k.a. the Magister) and his army of clockwork automatons that threaten to wipe out the Shadowhunter race," automatons that are "reanimated with demon souls." Also of note are "Tessa's tangled relationships with her fiancé, Jem Carstairs, who has a terminal demon-related illness, and Jem's blood brother, Will Herondale, who's also in love with her." (Entertainment Weekly)

Clark, Clara Gillow

Secrets of Greymoor. Candlewick Press 2009 166p $15.99

Grades: 4 5 6 7 **Fic**

1. School stories 2. Wealth -- Fiction 3. Grandmothers -- Fiction 4. New York (State) -- Fiction

ISBN 978-0-7636-3249-6; 0-7636-3249-X

LC 2008019063

As her grandmother's financial situation worsens, Hattie is forced to attend a "common school," in late nineteenth-century Kingston, New York, where she stands up to a show-off, shares embellished stories about life as a rich girl, and tries to recover her family's wealth.

"Even readers new to Hattie's story will cheer. . . . [This is an] accessible first-person narrative." Booklist

Clark, Henry

What we found in the sofa (and how it saved the world) by Henry Clark ; illustrated by Jeremy Holmes. Little, Brown and Co. 2013 368 p. $17

Grades: 3 4 5 6 7 **Fic**

1. Fantasy fiction 2. Science fiction 3. Humorous stories 4. Adventure and adventurers -- Fiction 5. Eccentrics and eccentricities -- Fiction

ISBN 0316206660; 9780316206662

LC 2012032467

Clark, Kathy

★ **Guardian** angel house. Second Story Press 2009 225p il map (Holocaust remembrance book for young readers) pa $14.95

Grades: 6 7 8 9 10 **Fic**

1. Nuns -- Fiction 2. Jews -- Hungary -- Fiction 3. Holocaust, 1933-1945 -- Fiction

ISBN 978-1-89718-758-6; 1-89718-758-0

When Mama decides to send Susan and Vera to a Catholic convent to hide from the Nazi soldiers, Susan is shocked. Will the two Jewish girls be safe in a building full of strangers?

"Based on the experiences of her mother and aunt, Clark provides a compelling, fictionalized account documenting the courage and compassion of these nuns. . . . Black-and-white photographs and an afterword help to bring the story and history to life." SLJ

Clarke, Arthur C.

2001 : a space odyssey. New Am. Lib. 1968 221p hardcover o.p. pa $7.99

Grades: 7 8 9 10 11 12 Adult **Fic**

1. Science fiction

ISBN 0-451-45799-4 pa

Astronauts of the spaceship Discovery, aided by their computer, HAL, blast off in search of proof that extraterrestrial beings had a part in the development of intelligent life forms on Earth millions of years ago.

"By standing the universe on its head, the author makes us see the ordinary universe in a different light. . . . [This novel becomes] a complex allegory about the history of the world." New Yorker

Clarke, Judith

One whole and perfect day. Front Street 2007 250p $16.95

Grades: 7 8 9 10 **Fic**

1. Australia -- Fiction 2. Family life -- Fiction 3. Grandfathers -- Fiction

ISBN 978-1-932425-95-6; 1-932425-95-0

LC 2006-20126

Michael L. Printz Award honor book, 2008

As her irritating family prepares to celebrate her grandfather's eightieth birthday, sixteen-year-old Lily yearns for just one whole perfect day together.

The author's "sharp, poetic prose evokes each character's inner life with rich and often amusing vibrancy." Horn Book

Starry nights. Front St. 2003 148p $15.95

Grades: 6 7 8 9 **Fic**

1. Ghost stories 2. Death -- Fiction

ISBN 1-88691-082-0

LC 2002-192884

Guilty over their older brother's drowning and their mother's subsequent breakdown, fourteen-year-old Vida ventures into the occult but it is ten-year-old Jess who meets the ghost who is trying to help them

"This tantalizing ghost story . . . will keep readers on the edge of their seats. . . . A spine-tingler with staying power." Publ Wkly

Clayton, Emma

The **roar**. Chicken House/Scholastic Inc. 2009 481p $17.99

Grades: 5 6 7 8 **Fic**

1. Science fiction 2. Twins -- Fiction

ISBN 978-0-439-92593-8; 0-439-92593-2

LC 2008-8311

"Mika and Ellie live in a future behind a wall: Solid concrete topped with high-voltage razor wire and guarded by a battalion of Ghengis Borgs, it was built to keep out the animals, because animals carry the plague. At least that's what Ellie, who was kidnapped as a child, has always been taught. But when she comes to suspect the truth behind her captivity, she's ready to risk exposure to the elements and answer the call of the wild." (Publisher's note) "Grades six to nine." (Bull Cent Child Books)

"This is an unusually gripping adventure that targets a younger audience than most young adult sci-fi." Bull Cent Child Books

The **Whisper**; Clayton, Emma. Chicken House/ Scholastic 2012 309 p. $17.99

Grades: 5 6 7 8 **Fic**

1. Science fiction 2. Twins -- Fiction 3. Youth -- Fiction 4. Telepathy -- Fiction 5. Revolutions -- Fiction

ISBN 9780545433655; 0545433657; 054531772X; 9780545317726

LC 2011278492

Sequel to: The Roar (2009)

In this book, "the story opens with the mutant Chosen Ones (Mika; his twin sister, Ellie; Audrey; and four other kids who remain entirely interchangeable) making their plans to stop Gorman (who has overdosed on Everlife-9 and is now a 13-year-old himself) and his equally scary counterpart, Raphael Mose, by taking control of . . . pretty much everything. Meanwhile Kobi (maybe the last free 13-year-old in London) and his father fall in with terrorists who will stop at nothing to blow up the towers where the rich people live. . . . Mika and company, with the help of Kobi, Grace (Raphael's mutant daughter), and a few functional adults actually do exactly what they set out to do—save the world." (School Libr J)

"Clayton writes for young people, and you can tell. The dialogue is authentic, and there is not a labored sentence or abrupt transition in sight." VOYA

Cleary, Beverly

Dear Mr. Henshaw; illustrated by Paul O. Zelinsky. Morrow 1983 133p il $15.99; lib bdg $16.89; pa $5.99

Grades: 4 5 6 7   **Fic**
1. School stories 2. Divorce -- Fiction 3. Parent-child relationship -- Fiction
ISBN 0-688-02405-X; 0-688-02406-8 lib bdg; 0-380-70958-9 pa

LC 83-5372
Awarded the Newbery Medal, 1984

"Leigh Botts lives with his recently divorced mother and writes to his favorite author, Boyd Henshaw. When Henshaw answers his letters and encourages him to keep a journal, he does so, and in the process solves the mystery of who is stealing food from his lunchbox, tries to write a novel, and in the end, writes a prize-winning short story about an experience with his father. . . . Grades four to seven." (SLJ)

"Leigh Botts started writing letters to his favorite author, Boyd Henshaw, in the second grade. Now, Leigh is in the sixth grade, in a new school, and his parents are recently divorced. This year he writes many letters to Mr. Henshaw, and also keeps a journal. Through these the reader learns how Leigh adjusts to new situations, and of his triumphs." Child Book Rev Serv

Followed by: Strider (1991)

Strider; illustrated by Paul O. Zelinsky. Morrow Junior Bks. 1991 179p il hardcover o.p. lib bdg $16.89; pa $5.99

Grades: 4 5 6 7   **Fic**
1. Dogs -- Fiction 2. Divorce -- Fiction
ISBN 0-688-09900-9; 0-688-09901-7 lib bdg; 0-380-71236-9 pa

LC 90-6608
Sequel to Dear Mr. Henshaw

In a series of diary entries, Leigh tells how he comes to terms with his parents' divorce, acquires joint custody of an abandoned dog, and joins the track team at school

"The development of the narrative is vintage Beverly Cleary, an inimitable blend of comic and poignant moments." Horn Book

Cleaver, Vera

★ **Where** the lillies bloom; [by] Vera & Bill Cleaver; illustrated by Jim Spanfeller. Lippincott 1969 174p il hardcover o.p. pa $5.99

Grades: 5 6 7 8   **Fic**
1. Orphans -- Fiction 2. Siblings -- Fiction 3. Appalachian region -- Fiction
ISBN 0-397-31111-7; 0-06-447005-9 pa

"The setting is fascinating, the characterization good, and the style of the first-person story distinctive." Bull Cent Child Books

Followed by Trial Valley (1977)

Clement-Moore, Rosemary

★ **Texas** gothic. Delacorte Press 2011 406p $17.99; lib bdg $20.99

Grades: 6 7 8 9 10   **Fic**
1. Ghost stories 2. Texas -- Fiction 3. Sisters -- Fiction 4. Farm life -- Fiction 5. Witchcraft -- Fiction
ISBN 978-0-385-73693-0; 0-385-73693-2; 978-0-385-90636-4 lib bdg; 0-385-90636-6 lib bdg

LC 2010-47923

"The one person in the magic-practicing Goodnight family who strives for normality, Amy (short for Amaryllis) is happy for a summer of plain old hard work running Aunt Hyacinth's Texas ranch, leaving her sister Phin to her supernatural science experiments. She should have known better. Ghosts are nothing new for the Goodnight girls -- Hyacinth's late husband Burt has been a friendly presence for years -- but the deathly cold apparition in Amy's bedroom pulls them into a dangerous mystery." (Horn Book)

"This engaging mystery has plenty of both paranormal and romance, spiced with loving families and satisfyingly packed with self-sufficient, competent girls." Kirkus

Clements, Andrew, 1949

Extra credit; illustrations by Mark Elliott. Atheneum Books for Young Readers 2009 183p il $16.99

Grades: 4 5 6   **Fic**
1. Letters -- Fiction 2. Illinois -- Fiction 3. Afghanistan -- Fiction 4. Family life -- Fiction
ISBN 978-1-4169-4929-9; 1-4169-4929-1

LC 2008-42877

"Unless [Abby] wants to repeat the sixth grade, she'll have to meet some specific conditions, including taking on an extra-credit project: find a pen pal in a foreign country. Simple enough (even for a girl who hates homework). Abby's first letter arrives at a small school in Afghanistan, and Sadeed Bayat is chosen to be her pen pal.... Well, kind of. He is the best writer, but he is also a boy, and in his village it is not appropriate for a boy to correspond with a girl. So his younger sister dictates and signs the letter. Until Sadeed decides what his sister is telling Abby isn't what he'd like Abby to know." (Publisher's note) "Grades four to seven." (Bull Cent Child Books)

Clements "successfully bridges two cultures in this timely and insightful dual-perspective story." Publ Wkly

The **school** story; illustrated by Brian Selznick.
Simon & Schuster Bks. for Young Readers 2001
196p il $16; pa $5.99

Grades: 4 5 6 7   **Fic**
1. Authorship -- Fiction 2. Publishers and publishing
-- Fiction
ISBN 0-689-82594-3; 0-689-85186-3 pa
                                        LC 00-49683

After twelve-year-old Natalie writes a wonderful novel,
her friend Zoe helps her devise a scheme to get it accepted
at the publishing house where Natalie's mother works as
an editor

"The girls are believable characters. . . . Selznick's
black-and-white illustrations add humorous details. A comic
novel that's a sure winner." SLJ

Things not seen. Philomel Bks. 2002 251p
$15.99; pa $5.99

Grades: 7 8 9 10   **Fic**
1. Science fiction 2. Blind -- Fiction
ISBN 0-399-23626-0; 0-14-240076-9 pa
                                        LC 00-69900

When fifteen-year-old Bobby wakes up and finds himself invisible, he and his parents and his new blind friend
Alicia try to find out what caused his condition and how to
reverse it.

"The author spins a convincing and affecting story."
Publ Wkly

Other titles in this series are:
Things hoped for (2006)
Things that are (2008)

Troublemaker; Andrew Clements; illustrated by
Mark Elliott. Atheneum Books for Young Readers
2011 p. cm. $16.99

Grades: 4 5 6 7   **Fic**
1. Schools -- Fiction 2. Behavior -- Fiction 3. Brothers
-- Fiction
ISBN 978-1-4169-4930-5; 1-4169-4930-5;
1416949305; 9781416949305
                                        LC 2010045018

When his older brother gets in serious trouble, sixth-
grader Clay decides to change his own mischief-mak-
ing ways, but he cannot seem to shake his reputation as
a troublemaker.

"Clements here enters into provocative territory and
pulls it off like the pro he is. Kids will easily relate to Clay,
and the secondary characters come alive as well." Kirkus

Clifton, Lutricia

Freaky Fast Frankie Joe; Lutricia Clifton. Holiday House 2012 248 p. (hardcover) $16.95

Grades: 4 5 6   **Fic**
1. Boys -- Fiction 2. Family -- Fiction 3. Brothers
-- Fiction 4. Illinois -- Fiction 5. Stepfamilies --
Fiction 6. Mothers and sons -- Fiction 7. Delivery of
goods -- Fiction 8. Family life -- Illinois -- Fiction 9.
Community life -- Illinois -- Fiction
ISBN 0823423670; 9780823423675
                                        LC 2011019976

This is the story of Frankie Joe. While "his mom is in jail,
Frankie Joe tries to adjust to living with his newly surfaced

father, FJ, his stepmother and 'the four legitimate Huckaby
sons.' The brothers tease Frankie Joe because, academically,
he is 'freaky slow,' which is at odds with how fast he is when
he runs or bikes. . . . Frankie Joe . . . launches Frankie Joe's
Freaky Fast Delivery Service. With his income, he plans his
escape back home from Illinois to Texas. But with each day
Frankie Joe becomes more integrated into—and essential
to—the town and the family, starting with his friendship
with another town oddball, elderly Miss Peachcott. She tells
Frankie Joe his family history." (Kirkus)

Clinton, Cathryn

A **stone** in my hand. Candlewick Press 2002
191p hardcover o.p. pa $6.99

Grades: 8 9 10 11   **Fic**
1. Family life -- Fiction 2. Palestinian Arabs -- Fiction
ISBN 0-7636-1388-6; 0-7636-4772-1 pa
                                        LC 2001-58423

Eleven-year-old Malaak and her family are touched by
the violence in Gaza between Jews and Palestinians when
first her father disappears and then her older brother is drawn
to the Islamic Jihad

"With a sharp eye for nuances of culture and the political
situation in the Middle East, Clinton has created a rich, colorful cast of characters and created an emotionally charged
novel." SLJ

Coakley, Lena

★ **Witchlanders**. Atheneum Books for Young
Readers 2011 400p $16.99

Grades: 7 8 9 10 11 12   **Fic**
1. War stories 2. Fantasy fiction 3. Witches -- Fiction
ISBN 978-1-4424-2004-5; 1-4424-2004-9
                                        LC 2010051922

After the prediction of Ryder's mother, once a great
prophet and powerful witch, comes true and their village is
destroyed by a deadly assassin, Ryder embarks on a quest
that takes him into the mountains in search of the destroyer.

"Plot twists unfold at a riveting pace, the boys' characters are compellingly sketched, and Coakley explores her
subject matter masterfully without falling prey to safe plot
choices." Publ Wkly

Coats, J. Anderson

The **wicked** and the just; by Jillian Anderson
Coats. Harcourt 2012 344 p. $16.99

Grades: 7 8 9 10 11 12   **Fic**
1. Daughters -- Fiction 2. Prejudices -- Fiction 3.
Middle Ages -- Fiction 4. Wales -- History -- Fiction
5. Household employees -- Fiction 6. Wales -- History
-- 1284-1536 -- Fiction 7. Wales -- History -- 1284-
1536 -- Fiction
ISBN 0547688377; 9780547688374
                                        LC 2011027315

In this young adult historical novel, "two girls of very
different degree are brought together unwillingly by the
English conquest of Wales. Cecily is in a pet at having to
leave the home of her youth . . . and relocate to the Welsh
frontier. . . . Cecily hates Caernarvon. She hates its weather,
its primitive appointments and its natives, especially Gwin-
ny, the servant girl who doesn't obey, and the young man
who stares at her." (Kirkus Review)

Coben, Harlan

Shelter; a Mickey Bolitar novel. G. P. Putnam's Sons 2011 304p $18.99

Grades: 8 9 10 11 12   Fic

1. School stories 2. Mystery fiction 3. Moving -- Fiction 4. Uncles -- Fiction 5. Missing persons -- Fiction

ISBN 9780399256509

LC 2011009004

After tragic events tear Mickey Bolitar away from his parents, he is forced to live with his estranged Uncle Myron and switch high schools, where he finds both friends and enemies, but when his new girlfriend, Ashley, vanishes, he follows her trail into a seedy underworld that reveals she is not what she seems to be.

This is a "suspenseful, well-executed spin-off of [the author's] bestselling Myron Bolitar mystery series for adults. . . . Coben's semi-noir style translates well to YA, and the supporting cast is thoroughly entertaining." Publ Wkly

Coben, Harlan, 1962-

★ Seconds away; a Mickey Bolitar novel. Harlan Coben. G. P. Putnam's Sons 2012 352 p. (hardback) $18.99

Grades: 8 9 10 11 12   Fic

1. Mystery fiction 2. Adventure fiction 3. Murder -- Fiction 4. Uncles -- Fiction 5. Schools -- Fiction 6. High schools -- Fiction 7. Mystery and detective stories 8. Adventure and adventurers -- Fiction

ISBN 9780399256516; 0399256512

LC 2012026728

This young adult adventure novel, by Harlan Coben, is the second book in his Mickey Bolitar series. "Mickey . . . continues to hunt for clues about the Abeona Shelter and the mysterious death of his father--all while trying to navigate the challenges of a new high school. . . . Now, not only does Mickey need to keep himself and his friends safe from the Butcher of Lodz, but he needs to figure out who shot [his classmate] Rachel." (Publisher's note)

Cochrane, Mick

The girl who threw butterflies. Alfred A. Knopf 2009 177p $15.99; $18.99

Grades: 6 7 8 9   Fic

1. Baseball -- Fiction 2. Sex role -- Fiction 3. Bereavement -- Fiction 4. Mother-daughter relationship -- Fiction

ISBN 978-0-375-85682-2; 0-375-85682-X; 978-0-375-95682-9 lib bdg; 0-375-95682-4 lib bdg

LC 2008-15986

Eighth-grader Molly's ability to throw a knuckleball earns her a spot on the baseball team, which not only helps her feel connected to her recently deceased father, who loved baseball, it helps in other aspects of her life, as well.

"Cochrane crafts an awkward yet engaging heroine whose perceptions and interactions with family, friends, and supporting characters ring true. Crisply written sports action balances the internal drama." SLJ

Cody, Matthew

Powerless. Alfred A. Knopf 2009 279p $15.99; lib bdg $18.99

Grades: 5 6 7 8   Fic

1. School stories 2. Moving -- Fiction 3. Bullies -- Fiction 4. Family life -- Fiction 5. Superheroes -- Fiction 6. Pennsylvania -- Fiction 7. Supernatural -- Fiction

ISBN 978-0-375-85595-5; 0-375-85595-5; 978-0-375-95595-2 lib bdg; 0-375-95595-X lib bdg

LC 2008-40885

Soon after moving to Noble's Green, Pennsylvania, twelve-year-old Daniel learns that his new friends have super powers that they will lose when they turn thirteen, unless he can use his brain power to protect them.

"This first novel has an intriguing premise, appealing characters, and a straightforward narrative arc with plenty of action as well as some serious moments." Booklist

Super; Matthew Cody. Alfred A. Knopf 2012 298 p. (Sequel to Powerless) (trade) $16.99; (lib. bdg.) $19.99

Grades: 5 6 7 8   Fic

1. Superheroes -- Fiction 2. Pennsylvania -- Fiction 3. Supernatural -- Fiction 4. Supervillains -- Fiction

ISBN 0375968946; 9780375868948; 9780375899799; 9780375968945

LC 2012008220

In this children's novel, by Matthew Cody, "Daniel Corrigan is as regular as can be, especially when compared to the Supers: kids in his new hometown with actual powers like flight and super strength. But . . . only he was able to stop the Shroud, a supervillian bent on stealing his new-found friends' powers. . . . Now Daniel himself is starting to display powers, while . . . his friends are losing theirs. . . . Daniel worries there may be something . . . sinister at work." (Publisher's note)

Cohn, Rachel

The Steps. Simon & Schuster Bks. for Young Readers 2003 137p hardcover o.p. pa $4.99

Grades: 5 6 7 8   Fic

1. Australia -- Fiction 2. Family life -- Fiction 3. Stepfamilies -- Fiction

ISBN 978-0-689-84549-9; 0-689-84549-9; 978-0-689-87414-7 pa; 0-689-87414-6 pa

LC 2001-57566

Over Christmas vacation, Annabel goes from her home in Manhattan to visit her father, his new wife, and her half- and step-siblings in Sydney, Australia

"Packed with humorous incident, life lessons learned, Australian travel tidbits, and a litany of preteen-girl touchstones." Horn Book

Another title about this family is:
Two steps forward (2006)

★ You know where to find me. Simon & Schuster Books for Young Readers 2008 208p $15.99; pa $8.99

Grades: 8 9 10 11 12   Fic

1. Cousins -- Fiction 2. Obesity -- Fiction 3. Suicide -- Fiction 4. Drug abuse -- Fiction 5. Washington (D.C.)

-- Fiction
ISBN 978-0-689-87859-6; 0-689-87859-1; 978-0-689-87860-2 pa; 0-689-87860-5 pa

LC 20070-0851

In the wake of her cousin's suicide, overweight and introverted seventeen-year-old Miles experiences significant changes in her relationships with her mother and father, her best friend Jamal and his family, and her cousin's father, while gaining insights about herself, both positive and negative.

"Cohn once again excels at crafting a multidimensional, in-the-moment teenage world. . . . Her work is heartbreaking . . . but it rings with authenticity." Publ Wkly

Colasanti, Susane

So much closer. Viking 2011 241p $17.99

Grades: 7 8 9 10   Fic

1. School stories 2. Moving -- Fiction 3. Divorce -- Fiction 4. New York (N.Y.) -- Fiction
ISBN 978-0-670-01224-4; 0-670-01224-6

LC 2010-31962

Seventeen-year-old Brooke has a crush on Scott so big that when he heads for New York City, she moves into her estranged father's Greenwich Village apartment, but soon she begins to focus on knowing herself and finding her future path.

"Colasanti has once again formulated a teen romance that feels realistic, which will make this novel a hit with readers." SLJ

Something like fate. Viking 2010 268p il $17.99

Grades: 7 8 9 10   Fic

1. Love stories 2. School stories 3. Guilt -- Fiction 4. Friendship -- Fiction
ISBN 978-0-670-01146-9; 0-670-01146-0

Lani and Jason, who is her best friend's boyfriend, fall in love, causing Lani tremendous anguish and guilt.

"Colasanti provides credible and engaging character development for each cast member and interactions that spark just the right amount of tension to make this a romantic page-turner." Booklist

Cole, Brock

The goats; written and illustrated by Brock Cole. Farrar, Straus & Giroux 1987 184p il hardcover o.p. pa $5.99

Grades: 7 8 9 10   Fic

1. Camps -- Fiction 2. Friendship -- Fiction
ISBN 0-374-32678-9; 0-374-42575-2 pa

LC 87-45362

"This is an unflinching book, and there is a quality of raw emotion that may score some discomfort among adults. Such a first novel restores faith in the cultivation of children's literature." Bull Cent Child Books

Cole, Stephen

Thieves like us. Bloomsbury 2006 349p $16.95

Grades: 8 9 10 11 12   Fic

1. Adventure fiction
ISBN 978-1-58234-653-3; 1-58234-653-4

LC 2005030616

A mysterious benefactor hand-picks a group of teen geniuses to follow a set of clues leading to the secrets of everlasting life, secrets which they must steal and for which they risk being killed.

"This novel relies on fast action, cool gadgets, and clever problem solving." Booklist

Followed by Thieves till we die (2007)

Thieves till we die. Bloomsbury 2007 311p $16.95

Grades: 8 9 10 11 12   Fic

1. Adventure fiction
ISBN 978-1-59990-082-7; 1-59990-082-3

LC 2006-28419

Sequel to: Thieves like us (2006)

Teen geniuses Jonah, Motti, Con, Tye, and Patch, working for their mysterious benefactor, Coldhardt, are out to recover more stolen artifacts when one of their members is kidnapped, and they must add a rescue operation to the mission.

"The page-turning mystery's fun comes from the terrifying escapes, clever gadgetry and detailed Aztec lore, and, of course, the central cast of death-defying teen savants who discover that home is wherever they are, together." Booklist

Z. Raptor; [by] Steve Cole. Philomel Books 2011 265p (The hunting) $16.99

Grades: 5 6 7 8   Fic

1. Science fiction 2. Islands -- Fiction 3. Dinosaurs -- Fiction 4. Virtual reality -- Fiction 5. Father-son relationship -- Fiction
ISBN 978-0-399-25254-9; 0-399-25254-1

LC 2010041650

Sequel to: Z. Rex (2009)

In New York City to spend Christmas with his father, thirteen-year-old Adam Adlar discovers that he and his father are still targets of sinister forces and, despite his father's objections, Adam finds himself drawn back into the struggle against hyper-evolved, deadly velociraptors determined to wreak havoc and spread terror.

"A non-stop ride from beginning to end, this installment is well constructed, larded with frequent and often violent action and reads even better than the first." Kirkus

Z. Rex; [by] Steve Cole. Philomel Books 2009 245p (The hunting) $16.99; pa $7.99

Grades: 5 6 7 8   Fic

1. Science fiction 2. Scotland -- Fiction 3. Dinosaurs -- Fiction 4. New Mexico -- Fiction 5. Virtual reality -- Fiction 6. Father-son relationship -- Fiction
ISBN 978-0-399-25253-2; 0-399-25253-3; 978-0-14-241712-6 pa; 0-14-241712-2 pa

LC 2009-6637

From Santa Fe, New Mexico, to Edinburgh, Scotland, thirteen-year-old Adam Adlar must elude police while being hunted by a dinosaur come-to-life from a virtual reality game invented by his father, who has gone missing.

"Cole has created a likable character who manages to come out on top in an extraordinary situation. The science aspects offer an interesting perspective and dilemma for a discussion on genetic engineering. In addition, the adventure, video gaming, and the perilous, sometimes bloody scenes will capture reluctant readers who may not normally devour their reading materials." SLJ

Followed by: Z. Raptor (2011)

Colfer, Eoin, 1965-

★ **Airman**; [by] Eoin Colfer. Hyperion Books for Children 2008 412p $17.99; pa $7.99

Grades: 5 6 7 8 9   **Fic**

1. Adventure fiction 2. Ireland -- Fiction 3. Airplanes -- Fiction 4. Inventors -- Fiction 5. Prisoners -- Fiction
ISBN 978-1-4231-0750-7; 1-4231-0750-0; 978-1-4231-0751-4 pa; 1-4231-0751-9 pa

LC 2007-38415

In the late nineteenth century, when Conor Broekhart discovers a conspiracy to overthrow the king, he is branded a traitor, imprisoned, and forced to mine for diamonds under brutal conditions while he plans a daring escape from Little Saltee prison by way of a flying machine that he must design, build, and, hardest of all, trust to carry him to safety.

This is "polished, sophisticated storytelling. . . . A tour de force." Publ Wkly

★ **Artemis** Fowl. Hyperion Bks. for Children 2001 277p $16.95; pa $7.99

Grades: 5 6 7 8   **Fic**

1. Fantasy fiction 2. Fairies -- Fiction
ISBN 0-7868-0801-2; 1-4231-2452-9 pa

LC 2001-16632

When a twelve-year-old evil genius tries to restore his family fortune by capturing a fairy and demanding a ransom in gold, the fairies fight back with magic, technology, and a particularly nasty troll

"Colfer's antihero, techno fantasy is cleverly written and filled to the brim with action, suspense, and humor." SLJ

Other titles in this series are:

Artemis Fowl: the Arctic incident (2002)
Artemis Fowl: the Eternity code (2003)
Artemis Fowl: the Opal deception (2005)
Artemis Fowl: the lost colony (2006)
Artemis Fowl: the time paradox (2008)
Artemis Fowl: the Atlantis complex (2010)

Half -Moon investigations. Miramax Books/Hyperion Books for Children 2006 290p $16.95; pa $7.99

Grades: 4 5 6 7   **Fic**

1. Mystery fiction
ISBN 0-7868-4957-6; 0-7868-4960-6 pa

"The private-eye lingo has a great, comical grade-school snap, and . . . the kid's goofy charm and stubborn dedication to crime solving will win him a hefty, enthusiastic following." Booklist

The **hangman's** revolution; Eoin Colfer. Hyperion 2014 384 p. (W.A.R.P.) (hardback) $17.99

Grades: 5 6 7 8   **Fic**

1. Science fiction 2. Assassins -- Fiction 3. Time travel -- Fiction 4. London (England) -- Fiction 5. Great Britain -- History -- Fiction
ISBN 9781423161639; 1423161637

LC 2014001938

Sequel to: The Reluctant Assassin (2013)

In this book, "young FBI agent Chevie Savano arrives back in modern-day London after a time-trip to the Victorian age, to find the present very different from the one she left. Europe is being run by a Fascist movement known as the Boxites. . . . Chevie's memories come back to her in fragments, and just as she is learning about the WARP program from Professor Charles Smart, inventor of the time machine, he is killed by secret service police." (Publisher's note)

"Returning from her jaunt to Victorian London in The Reluctant Assassin, Chevie Savano finds that fellow time-traveler Colonel Box must have succeeded in his conquest, since she's now a cadet in the repressive Boxite Empire's military academy. Going back to the past, Chevie reunites with magician and good friend Riley to change history in this funny, high-octane adventure with thought-provoking time-travel insights." Horn Book

The **reluctant** assassin; Eoin Colfer. Hyperion Book CH 2013 352 p. (W.A.R.P.) (hardcover) $17.99

Grades: 5 6 7 8   **Fic**

1. Alternative histories -- Fiction 2. Science fiction 3. Assassins -- Fiction 4. Time travel -- Fiction 5. London (England) -- History -- 19th century -- Fiction 6. Great Britain -- History -- Victoria, 1837-1901 -- Fiction
ISBN 1423161629; 9781423161622

LC 2012048160

This is the first book in the time-travel W.A.R.R. series from Eoin Colfer. "After a bungled mission, [FBI agent] Chevie has been sent to London where she is 'baby-sitting a metal capsule,' which she learns is one end of a wormhole to the year 1898, when [young assassin] Riley (and a corpse) materialize, direct from the Victorian era." (Publishers Weekly)

Collar, Orpheus

★ The **Red** Pyramid; Rick Riordan. Hyperion 2010 516 p. (Kane chronicles) (hardback) $17.99

Grades: 4 5 6 7   **Fic**

1. Fantasy fiction 2. Brothers and sisters -- Fiction 3. Egypt -- Fiction 4. Siblings -- Fiction 5. Secret societies -- Fiction 6. Gods and goddesses -- Fiction 7. Voyages and travels -- Fiction
ISBN 1423113381; 9781423113386

LC 2010549563

This is the first installment of the Kane chronicles. "Since their mother's death, Carter and Sadie have become near strangers. While Sadie has lived with her grandparents in London, her brother has traveled the world with their father, the brilliant Egyptologist, Dr. Julius Kane. . . . [Dr. Kane] unleashes the Egyptian god Set, who banished him to oblivion and forces the children to flee for their lives." (Publisher's note)

"The first-person narrative shifts between Carter and Sadie, giving the novel an intriguing dual perspective made more complex by their biracial heritage and the tension between the siblings. . . . This fantasy adventure delivers . . . young protagonists with previously unsuspected magical powers, a riveting story marked by headlong adventure, a complex background rooted in ancient mythology, and wry, witty twenty-first-century narration." Booklist

Collard, Sneed B.

Double eagle. Peachtree 2009 245p $15.95

Grades: 4 5 6 7   **Fic**

1. Coins -- Fiction 2. Alabama -- Fiction 3. Hurricanes -- Fiction 4. Buried treasure -- Fiction

ISBN 978-1-56145-480-8; 1-56145-480-X

LC 2008036746

In 1973, Michael and Kyle's discovery of a rare Confederate coin near an old Civil War fort turns into a race against time as the boys try to find more coins before a hurricane hits Alabama's Gulf coast.

"Mike's narrative moves quickly with likable and believable characters. The story will have particular appeal to readers with an interest in historical places and artifacts." SLJ

Includes bibliographical references

Collier, James Lincoln

★ **Jump** ship to freedom; [by] James Lincoln Collier, Christopher Collier. Delacorte Press 1981 198p hardcover o.p. pa $5.99

Grades: 6 7 8 9   **Fic**

1. Slavery -- Fiction 2. African Americans -- Fiction 3. United States -- History -- 1783-1809 -- Fiction

ISBN 0-440-44323-7 pa

LC 81-65492

Companion volume to War comes to Willy Freeman and Who is Carrie?

In 1787 Dan Arabus, a fourteen-year-old slave, anxious to buy freedom for himself and his mother, escapes from his dishonest master and tries to find help in cashing the soldier's notes received by his father, Jack Arabus, for fighting in the Revolution

"The period seems well researched, and the speech has an authentic ring without trying to imitate a dialect." SLJ

★ **My** brother Sam is dead; by James Lincoln Collier and Christopher Collier. Four Winds Press 1985 216p $17.95

Grades: 6 7 8 9   **Fic**

1. United States -- History -- 1775-1783, Revolution -- Fiction

ISBN 0-02-722980-7

LC 84-28787

A reissue of the title first published 1974

A Newbery Medal honor book, 1975

"In 1775 the Meeker family lived in Redding, Connecticut, a Tory community. Sam, the eldest son, allied himself with the Patriots. The youngest son, Tim, watched a rift in the family grow because of his brother's decision. Before the war was over the Meeker family had suffered at the hands of both the British and the Patriots." Shapiro. Fic for Youth. 3d edition

★ **War** comes to Willy Freeman; [by] James Lincoln Collier, Christopher Collier. Delacorte Press 1983 178p hardcover o.p. pa $5.99

Grades: 6 7 8 9   **Fic**

1. Slavery -- Fiction 2. African Americans -- Fiction 3. United States -- History -- 1775-1783, Revolution -- Fiction

ISBN 0-440-49504-0 pa

LC 82-70317

This deals with events prior to those in Jump ship to freedom, and involves members of the same family. "Willy is thirteen when she begins her story, which takes place during the last two years of the Revolutionary War; her father, a free man, has been killed fighting against the British, her mother has disappeared. Willy makes her danger-fraught way to Fraunces Tavern in New York, her uncle, Jack Arabus, having told her that Mr. Fraunces may be able to help her. She works at the tavern until the war is over, goes to the Arabus home to find her mother dying, and participates in the trial (historically accurate save for the fictional addition of Willy) in which her uncle sues for his freedom and wins." Bull Cent Child Books

With every drop of blood; [by] James Lincoln Collier, Christopher Collier. Delacorte Press 1994 235p maps hardcover o.p. pa $6.99

Grades: 5 6 7 8   **Fic**

1. Race relations -- Fiction 2. African Americans -- Fiction 3. United States -- History -- 1861-1865, Civil War -- Fiction

ISBN 0-385-32028-0; 0-440-21983-3 pa

LC 93-37655

"The relationship of Cush and Johnny and the convincingly conversational tone of Johnny's voice make this book an effectively immediate evocation of a distant and sometimes difficult-to-understand time." Horn Book

Collins, P. J. Sarah

What happened to Serenity? Red Deer Press 2011 222p pa $12.95

Grades: 7 8 9 10   **Fic**

1. Science fiction 2. Missing persons -- Fiction

ISBN 978-0-88995-453-3; 0-88995-453-4

Katherine lives in a post-apocalyptic community completely cut off from the rest of the world and when her best friend's sister Serenity suddenly disappears, Katherine must break out of town to find her.

"The story is set in 2021 and paints a unique picture of what lack of freedom and free speech could look like if this reality existed. Collins moves beyond the basic mystery and explores the intricate workings of the mind, the body, and the power of basic knowledge. Her story will keep readers engaged from beginning to end." SLJ

Collins, Pat Lowery

Daughter of winter. Candlewick Press 2010 272p $16.99

Grades: 4 5 6 7   **Fic**

1. Winter -- Fiction 2. Massachusetts -- Fiction 3. Wampanoag Indians -- Fiction 4. Wilderness survival -- Fiction

ISBN 978-0-7636-4500-7; 0-7636-4500-1

LC 2009049099

In the mid-nineteenth-century shipbuilding town of Essex, Massachusetts, twelve-year-old Addie learns a startling secret about her past when she escapes servitude by running away to live in the snowy woods and meets an elderly Wampanoag woman.

"Collins' sense of place, incorporation of cultural and historical details, and the richly evoked winter setting make for a vividly imagined novel. An engaging survival story intertwined with a search for identity." Booklist

Hidden voices; the orphan musicians of Venice. Candlewick Press 2009 345p $17.99

Grades: 8 9 10 11 12   Fic

1. Composers 2. Violinists 3. Orphans -- Fiction 4. Musicians -- Fiction 5. Venice (Italy) -- Fiction

ISBN 978-0-7636-3917-4; 0-7636-3917-6

LC 2008-18762

Anetta, Rosalba, and Luisa, find their lives taking unexpected paths while growing up in eighteenth century Venice at the orphanage Ospedale della Pieta, where concerts are given to support the orphanage as well as expose the girls to potential suitors.

"Collins's descriptive prose makes Venice and a unique slice of history come alive as the three connecting narrative strains create a rich story of friendship and self-realization." SLJ

Collins, Suzanne, 1962-

★ **Catching** fire. Scholastic Press 2009 391p $17.99

Grades: 7 8 9 10   Fic

1. Science fiction

ISBN 978-0-439-02349-8; 0-439-02349-1

LC 2008-50493

Sequel to: Hunger Games (2008)

This dystopian young adult novel, volume 2 of the Hunger Games trilogy, takes place after a televised, state-sponsored duel known as the Hunger Games. "Katniss Everdeen has won . . . with fellow district tribute Peeta Mellark. But it was a victory won by defiance of the Capitol and their harsh rules. Katniss and Peeta should be happy. After all, they have just won for themselves and their families a life of safety and plenty. But there are rumors of rebellion among the subjects, and Katniss and Peeta, to their horror, are the faces of that rebellion." (Publisher's note)

"Beyond the expert world building, the acute social commentary and the large cast of fully realized characters, there's action, intrigue, romance and some amount of hope in a story readers will find completely engrossing." Kirkus

Followed by: Mockingjay (2010)

Gregor the Overlander. Scholastic Press 2003 311p (Underland chronicles) $16.95; pa $5.99

Grades: 4 5 6 7   Fic

1. Fantasy fiction

ISBN 0-439-43536-6; 0-439-67813-7 pa

LC 2002-155865

When eleven-year-old Gregor and his two-year-old sister are pulled into a strange underground world, they trigger an epic battle involving men, bats, rats, cockroaches, and spiders while on a quest foretold by ancient prophecy

"Collins creates a fascinating, vivid, highly original world and a superb story to go along with it." Booklist

Other titles in this series are:

Gregor and the prophecy of Bane (2004)
Gregor and the curse of the warmbloods (2005)
Gregor and the marks of secret (2006)
Gregor and the code of claw (2007)

★ The **Hunger** Games. Scholastic Press 2008 374p $17.99; pa $8.99

Grades: 7 8 9 10   Fic

1. Science fiction

ISBN 978-0-439-02348-1; 0-439-02348-3; 978-0-439-02352-8 pa; 0-439-02352-1 pa

LC 2007-39987

In this dystopian young adult novel, "in the ruins of a place once known as North America lies the nation of Panem, a shining Capitol surrounded by twelve outlaying districts. The Capitol . . . keeps the districts in line by forcing them all to send one girl and one boy between the ages of twelve and eighteen to participate in the annual Hunger Games, a fight to the death on live TV. Sixteen-year-old Katniss Everdeen , . . regards it as a death sentence when she is forced to represent her district in the Games." (Publisher's note)

"Collins's characters are completely realistic and sympathetic. . . . The plot is tense, dramatic, and engrossing." SLJ

Mockingjay. Scholastic Press 2010 390p (Hunger Games) $17.99

Grades: 7 8 9 10   Fic

1. Science fiction

ISBN 978-0-439-02351-1; 0-439-02351-3

LC 2008-50493

Sequel to: Catching fire (2009)

This dystopian novel, volume 3 of the Hunger Games trilogy, takes place after heroine Katniss Everdeen has "survived the Hunger Games twice. But now that she's made it out of the bloody arena alive, she's still not safe. . . . The Capitol wants revenge. Who do they think should pay for the unrest? Katniss. And what's worse, President Snow has made it clear that no one else is safe either. Not Katniss's family, not her friends, not the people of District 12." (Publisher's note)

"This concluding volume in Collins's Hunger Games trilogy accomplishes a rare feat, the last installment being the best yet, a beautifully orchestrated and intelligent novel that succeeds on every level." Publ Wkly

Collins, Tim

Notes from a totally lame vampire; because the undead have feelings too. written by Tim Collins; illustrated by Andrew Pinder. Aladdin 2010 328p il $12.99

Grades: 6 7 8 9   Fic

1. School stories 2. Love -- Fiction 3. Diaries -- Fiction 4. Vampires -- Fiction 5. Great Britain -- Fiction

ISBN 978-1-4424-1183-8; 1-4424-1183-X

LC 2010-10634

Published in the United Kingdom with title: Diary of a wimpy vampire

Nigel Mullet, a 100-year-old vampire doomed to spend eternity in the body of a socially awkward fifteen-year-old boy, records his attempts to impress the love of his life, Chloe, while battling an embarrassingly overwhelming desire to sink his fangs into her.

"This book has a witty, laugh-out-loud story line and cartoon illustrations that are liberally sprinkled throughout. Readers will sympathize with Nigel and his teen angst, and the great ending makes this a satisfying and entertaining read." SLJ

Collins, Yvonne

The **new** and improved Vivien Leigh Reid; diva in control. [by] Yvonne Collins and Sandy Rideout. 1st ed.; St. Martin's Griffin 2007 231p pa $9.95

Grades: 7 8 9 10   **Fic**

1. Actors -- Fiction 2. Remarriage -- Fiction 3. Hollywood (Calif.) -- Fiction 4. Mother-daughter relationship -- Fiction

ISBN 978-0-312-35828-0 pa; 0-312-35828-8 pa

LC 2006050570

Sequel to: Now starring Vivien Leigh Reid

When she arrives to spend Thanksgiving with her actress mother, sixteen-year-old Leigh is horrified to discover that her mother is planning to marry the producer who had fired Leigh the summer before and whose daughters are determined to sabotage their father's relationship as well as any hopes of reviving Leigh's budding acting career.

"Leigh is a likeable, funny, and realistic heroine" Kliatt

Now starring Vivien Leigh Reid: Diva in training; by Yvonne Collins and Sandy Rideout. Griffin 2006 242p pa $9.95

Grades: 7 8 9 10   **Fic**

1. Actors -- Fiction 2. Mother-daughter relationship -- Fiction

ISBN 0-312-33839-2

"Leigh Reid, who first appeared in Introducing Vivien Leigh Reid, ... spent the summer she was 15 with Annika Anderson, her estranged, actress mother who left the family when Leigh was just a toddler. . . . In this book, Leigh . . . is recommended for a soap-opera audition that she nails due to her varied accents and versatility. . . . This volume is pop-culture fun with a moral." SLJ

Followed by: The new and improved Vivien Leigh Reid: diva in control (2007)

Collomore, Anna

The **ruining**; Anna Collomore. Razorbill 2013 272 p. $17.99

Grades: 7 8 9 10 11 12   **Fic**

1. Nannies -- Fiction 2. Mental illness -- Fiction 3. Psychopaths -- Fiction 4. Emotional problems -- Fiction 5. Marin County (Calif.) -- Fiction

ISBN 1595144706; 9781595144706

LC 2012032007

In this novel, by Anna Collomore, "Annie Phillips is thrilled to . . . begin . . . as a nanny for the picture-perfect Cohen family. In no time at all, she falls in love with the Cohens. . . . All too soon cracks appear in Annie's . . . perfect world. She's blamed for mistakes she doesn't remember making . . . and she feels like she's always being watched. . . . Annie's fear gives way to . . . hallucinations. Is she tumbling into madness, or is something sinister at play?" (Publisher's note)

Columbus, Chris, 1958-

Battle of the beasts; Chris Columbus, Ned Vizzini, Greg Call ; [edited by] Alessandra Balzer. Balzer + Bray 2014 480 p. (House of secrets) (hardcover) $17.99

Grades: 5 6 7 8   **Fic**

1. Fantasy fiction 2. Adventure fiction 3. Witches -- Fiction 4. Brothers and sisters -- Fiction

ISBN 0062192493; 9780062192493

LC 2013956357

This book, by Chris Columbus and Ned Vizzini, is the sequel to "House of Secrets." "Since the siblings' last adventure, life in the Walker household is much improved the family is rich and the Wind Witch is banished. But no Walker will be safe until she is found, and summoning her to San Francisco brings all the danger that comes with her and puts the Walkers in the crosshairs of a mysterious journey through Denver Kristoff's books." (Publisher's note)

"An exorcism is just the beginning; the siblings also battle gladiators in ancient Rome, outwit cyborg Nazis, and face Yeti-like monsters in a Tibetan monastery in another imaginative, fast-paced adventure that is sure to please fans. Vizzini's older readers will miss his elegant and often eloquent, wry tone. Here's hoping another writer steps in to finish the planned trilogy." Booklist

House of secrets; Chris Columbus ; Ned Vizzini. 1st ed. Balzer + Bray 2013 496 p. (hardcover) $17.99

Grades: 5 6 7 8   **Fic**

1. Haunted houses -- Fiction 2. Fantasy fiction -- Fiction 3. Adventure fiction -- Fiction 4. Fantasy 5. Dwellings -- Fiction 6. Supernatural -- Fiction 7. Books and reading -- Fiction 8. Brothers and sisters -- Fiction

ISBN 0062192469; 9780062192462

LC 2012051815

In this juvenile fantasy story, by Chris Columbus and Ned Vizzini, three siblings "relocate to an old Victorian house that used to be the home of occult novelist Denver Kristoff. . . . By the time the Walkers realize that one of their neighbors has sinister plans for them, they're banished to a primeval forest way off the grid. . . . Bloodthirsty medieval warriors patrol the woods around them, supernatural pirates roam the neighboring seas, and a power-hungry queen rules the land." (Publisher's note)

Combres, Elisabeth

Broken memory; a novel of Rwanda. translated by Shelley Tanaka. Groundwood Books/House of Anansi Press 2009 139p $17.95

Grades: 6 7 8 9 10   **Fic**

1. Rwanda -- Fiction 2. Orphans -- Fiction 3. Genocide -- Fiction 4. Hutu (African people) -- Fiction 5. Tutsi (African people) -- Fiction

ISBN 978-0-88899-892-7; 0-88899-892-9

Original French edition, 2007

"This is a quiet, reflective story; neither laden with detail nor full of historical descriptions, it is simply one girl's horrific tale of personal tragedy. . . . Combres' story offers readers intimate access to this chapter of history as well as considerable potential for discussion." Bull Cent Child Books

Combs, Sarah

Breakfast served anytime; Sarah Combs. Candlewick Press 2014 272 p. $16.99

Grades: 7 8 9 10 11 12   **Fic**

1. Bildungsromans 2. Camps -- Fiction 3. Kentucky

-- Fiction 4. Gifted children -- Fiction
ISBN 0763667919; 9780763667917

LC 2013944002

In this book, by Sarah Combs, "when Gloria sets out to spend the summer before her senior year at a camp for gifted and talented students, she doesn't know quite what to expect. Fresh from the heartache of losing her grandmother and missing her best friend, Gloria resolves to make the best of her new circumstances. But some things are proving to be more challenging than she expected." (Publisher's note)

"At a summer college program in Kentucky, a classroom of gifted students studying "The Secrets of the Written Word" grapples with life's big questions. Mercurial, dreamy, and verbose, protagonist Gloria narrates with intellectual enthusiasm and attention to emotional detail. Although the plot meanders, Gloria's open, genuine voice carries this debut novel to the end of a life-changing summer." Horn Book

Comerford, Lynda B.

Rissa Bartholomew's declaration of independence. Scholastic Press 2009 250p $16.99

Grades: 4 5 6 7　　　　　　　　　　　　　**Fic**
1. School stories 2. Illinois -- Fiction 3. Friendship -- Fiction
ISBN 978-0-545-05058-6; 0-545-05058-8

LC 2008-26618

Having told off all of her old friends at her eleventh birthday party, Rissa starts middle school determined to make new friends while being herself, not simply being part of a herd.

"Rissa's troubles are ones that many middle-schoolers will identify with: new schools, shifting allegiances, new feelings, and changing bodies. First-time novelist Comerford gives her readers an appealing heroine who, despite her flaws and quirks, finds herself along the way." Booklist

Compestine, Ying Chang

Revolution is not a dinner party; a novel. Henry Holt and Company 2007 256p map $16.95; pa $7.99

Grades: 5 6 7 8　　　　　　　　　　　　　**Fic**
1. Communism -- Fiction 2. Persecution -- Fiction 3. China -- History -- 1949-1976 -- Fiction
ISBN 978-0-8050-8207-4; 0-8050-8207-7; 978-0-312-58149-7 pa; 0-312-58149-1 pa

LC 2006035465

Starting in 1972 when she is nine years old, Ling, the daughter of two doctors, struggles to make sense of the communists' Cultural Revolution, which empties stores of food, homes of appliances deemed "bourgeois," and people of laughter.

"Readers should remain rapt by Compestine's storytelling throughout this gripping account of life during China's Cultural Revolution." Publ Wkly

Condie, Ally

Crossed; Ally Condie. Dutton Books 2011 367p map $17.99

Grades: 7 8 9 10　　　　　　　　　　　　**Fic**
1. Fantasy fiction 2. Resistance to government --

Fiction
ISBN 978-0-525-42365-2; 0-525-42365-6

LC 2011016442

Sequel to: Matched (2010)

Seventeen-year-old Cassia sacrifices everything and heads to the Outer Provinces in search of Ky, where she is confronted with shocking revelations about Society and the promise of rebellion.

"Newcomers will need to read the first book for background, but vivid, poetic writing will pull fans through as Condie immerses readers in her characters' yearnings and hopes." Publ Wkly

★　**Matched**; Ally Condie. Dutton Books 2010 369p $17.99

Grades: 7 8 9 10　　　　　　　　　　　　**Fic**
1. Fantasy fiction
ISBN 978-0-525-42364-5; 0-525-42364-8

All her life, Cassia has never had a choice. The Society dictates everything: when and how to play, where to work, where to live, what to eat and wear, when to die, and most importantly to Cassia as she turns 17, who to marry. When she is Matched with her best friend Xander, things couldn't be more perfect. But why did her neighbor Ky's face show up on her match disk as well?

"Condie's enthralling and twisty dystopian plot is well served by her intriguing characters and fine writing. While the ending is unresolved . . . , Cassia's metamorphosis is gripping and satisfying." Publ Wkly

Followed by: Crossed (2011)

Reached; Ally Condie. Dutton 2012 512 p. (Matched trilogy) (hardcover) $17.99

Grades: 7 8 9 10　　　　　　　　　　　　**Fic**
1. Science fiction 2. Epidemics -- Fiction 3. Resistance to government -- Fiction 4. Fantasy 5. Government, Resistance to -- Fiction
ISBN 9780525423669; 0525423664

LC 2012031916

Sequel to: Crossed

"This final story in the 'Matched' trilogy finds Cassia, Ky, and Xander all working for the Rising, but in different locations and for different reasons. The Rising has introduced a plague into the cities for which they have the cure. They are easily able to take control as they cure people. An unexpected mutation of the illness catches the Rising off guard, and the Pilot (the Rising's leader) realizes he could quickly lose all that has been gained." (Voice of Youth Advocates)

Conly, Jane Leslie

★　**Murder** afloat. Hyperion Books for Children 2010 164p $17.99

Grades: 5 6 7 8　　　　　　　　　　　　　**Fic**
1. Adventure fiction 2. Kidnapping -- Fiction 3. Seafaring life -- Fiction
ISBN 978-1-4231-0416-2; 1-4231-0416-1

Benjamin Franklin Orville is caught up in a scuffle, kidnapped with a group of immigrants and forced to work aboard the Ella Dawn—one of the most ill-reputed oystering vessels in Baltimore.

"With compelling characters and details of the little-known process of oystering woven throughout, Conly's tale touches on the hardships of many German immigrants to the U.S., whose desperate plights offer parallels to contemporary immigration issues. Short chapters and suspenseful plot twists will keep readers turning the pages in this engaging historical adventure." Booklist

Connelly, Neil O.

★ The **miracle** stealer; [by] Neil Connelly. Arthur A. Levine Books 2010 230p $17.99

Grades: 8 9 10 11 12   **Fic**

1. Camps -- Fiction 2. Faith -- Fiction 3. Miracles -- Fiction 4. Siblings -- Fiction 5. Family life -- Fiction 6. Pennsylvania -- Fiction

ISBN 978-0-545-13195-7; 0-545-13195-2

LC 2010-727

In small-town Pennsylvania, nineteen-year-old Andi Grant will do anything to protect her six-year-old brother Daniel from those who believe he has a God-given gift as a healer—including their own mother.

"Neil Connelly has written a deeply thought provoking novel. . . . Throughout this gripping novel the climax builds from a slow burn to a tension packed conclusion." Libr Media Connect

Connor, Leslie

★ **Crunch**. Katherine Tegen Books 2010 330p $16.99; lib bdg $17.89

Grades: 5 6 7 8   **Fic**

1. Bicycles -- Fiction 2. Siblings -- Fiction 3. Family life -- Fiction 4. New England -- Fiction 5. Energy conservation -- Fiction 6. Business enterprises -- Fiction

ISBN 978-0-06-169229-1; 0-06-169229-8; 978-0-06-169233-8 lib bdg; 0-06-169233-6 lib bdg

LC 2009-24339

This novel concerns "the trials and tribulations of 14-year-old Dewey Mariss and his family. His parents are away from home, unable to return because of a gasoline shortage. Running their small family business, the Bike Barn, with his younger brother and helping older sister Lil look after the five-year-old twins keeps Dewey plenty busy. . . . Characters are colorful but believable, dialogue crisp and amusing. The New England setting is attractively realized, and the underlying energy crisis treated seriously but not sensationally." Kirkus

Dead on town line; illustrations by Gina Triplett. Dial Books 2005 131p il $15.99

Grades: 7 8 9 10   **Fic**

1. Ghost stories 2. Homicide -- Fiction

ISBN 0-8037-3021-7

LC 2004-15312

"Cassie's body lies hidden in a crevice, where she tries to figure out what happens next. She meets the ghost of Birdie, another murdered girl who was hidden in the same crevice years earlier. . . . Each verse/chapter adds a piece to the puzzle of Cassie's death until her body is found and the crime is solved. . . . This is an absorbing and moving story." SLJ

★ **Waiting** for normal. Katherine Tegen Books 2008 290p $16.99; lib bdg $17.89

Grades: 5 6 7 8   **Fic**

1. Mothers -- Fiction 2. Family life -- Fiction 3. New

York (State) -- Fiction

ISBN 978-0-06-089088-9; 0-06-089088-6; 978-0-06-089089-6 lib bdg; 0-06-089089-4 lib bdg

LC 2007-06881

Twelve-year-old Addie tries to cope with her mother's erratic behavior and being separated from her beloved stepfather and half-sisters when she and her mother go to live in a small trailer by the railroad tracks on the outskirts of Schenectady, New York.

"Connor . . . treats the subject of child neglect with honesty and grace in this poignant story. . . . Characters as persuasively optimistic as Addie are rare, and readers will gravitate to her." Publ Wkly

Conrad, Pam

★ **My** Daniel. Harper & Row 1989 137p pa $5.99

Grades: 5 6 7 8   **Fic**

1. Nebraska -- Fiction

ISBN 0-06-440309-2 pa

LC 88-19850

"Rendering scenes from both the past and the present with equal skill, Conrad is at the peak of her storytelling powers." Publ Wkly

Constable, Kate

The **singer** of all songs. Arthur A. Levine Books 2004 297p hardcover o.p. pa $6.99

Grades: 7 8 9 10   **Fic**

1. Fantasy fiction 2. Magic -- Fiction

ISBN 0-439-55478-0; 0-439-55479-9 pa

LC 2003-9034

First published 2002 in Australia

Calwyn, a young priestess of ice magic, or chantment, joins with other chanters who have different magical skills to fight a sorcerer who wants to claim all powers for his own

"An impressive debut by an author who clearly has much to contribute to the fantasy genre." Booklist

Other available titles in this series are:

The waterless sea (2005)

The tenth power (2006)

The **tenth** power. Arthur A. Levine Books 2006 306p (Chanters of Tremaris trilogy) $16.99; pa $5.99

Grades: 7 8 9 10   **Fic**

1. Fantasy fiction 2. Magic -- Fiction

ISBN 0-439-55482-9; 0-439-55483-7 pa

LC 2005018716

Having lost her magical powers of chantment, eighteen-year-old Calwyn searches for the missing half of the broken Wheel of the Tenth Power with the hope of stopping the plague and endless winter that have fallen on her world.

"The detailed descriptions of the settings and the natures of the various chantments are what give the story the richness of elaborate tapestries." SLJ

The **waterless** sea. Arthur A. Levine Books 2005 314p (Chanters of Tremaris trilogy) $16.95; pa $5.99

Grades: 7 8 9 10   **Fic**
1. Fantasy fiction 2. Magic -- Fiction
ISBN 0-439-55480-2; 0-439-55481-0 pa

LC 2004-11223

Sequel to The singer of all songs
First published 2003 in Australia

Calwyn and friends travel to the desert land of Merithuros to rescue some captive magical children, even as their friend Darrow begins a plot of his own.

This "is a well-written story and an excellent fantasy, pulling together issues of identity, belonging, equality, and the environment." SLJ

Coombs, Kate

The **runaway** dragon. Farrar, Straus and Giroux 2009 292p $16.99
Grades: 5 6 7 8   **Fic**
1. Fairy tales 2. Dragons -- Fiction 3. Princesses -- Fiction
ISBN 978-0-374-36361-1; 0-374-36361-7

LC 2008034362

Sequel to: The runaway princess (2006)

When her beloved dragon Laddy runs away from the castle, Princess Meg and some of her friends embark on a quest to find him and bring him home.

"Funny, lighthearted. . . . Enchanted forests, rampant transmogrification, evil sorceresses and giants are all fine fodder for Coombs's inventive twists on traditional fairy tales." Kirkus

★ The **runaway** princess. Farrar, Straus and Giroux 2006 279p $17
Grades: 5 6 7 8   **Fic**
1. Fairy tales 2. Dragons -- Fiction 3. Princesses -- Fiction
ISBN 0-374-35546-0

LC 2005-51225

Fifteen-year-old Princess Meg uses magic and her wits to rescue a baby dragon and escape the unwanted attentions of princes hoping to gain her hand in marriage through a contest arranged by her father, the king.

"This witty, humorous tale will be popular with fantasy buffs who enjoy takeoffs on fairy tales." Booklist

Another title about Princess Meg is:
The runaway dragon (2009)

Cooney, Caroline B., 1947-

Code orange. Delacorte 2005 200p hardcover o.p. pa $6.99
Grades: 7 8 9 10   **Fic**
1. School stories 2. Smallpox -- Fiction 3. New York (N.Y.) -- Fiction
ISBN 0-385-73260-0 pa; 0-385-90277-8

LC 2004-26422

While conducting research for a school paper on smallpox, Mitty finds an envelope containing 100-year-old smallpox scabs and fears that he has infected himself and all of New York City. "Grades six to ten." (Bull Cent Child Books)

"Readers won't soon forget either the profoundly disturbing premise of this page-turner or its likable, ultimately heroic slacker protagonist." Booklist

Diamonds in the shadow. Delacorte Press 2007 228p $15.99; pa $8.99
Grades: 7 8 9 10 11 12   **Fic**
1. Refugees -- Fiction 2. Connecticut -- Fiction 3. Family life -- Fiction 4. Africans -- United States -- Fiction
ISBN 978-0-385-73261-1; 978-0-385-73262-8 pa

LC 2006-27811

The Finches, a Connecticut family, sponsor an African refugee family of four, all of whom have been scarred by the horrors of civil war, and who inadvertently put their benefactors in harm's way.

"Tension mounts in a novel that combines thrilling suspense and a story about innocence lost." Booklist

The **face** on the milk carton. Delacorte Press 2006 184p $15.95; pa $6.99
Grades: 7 8 9 10   **Fic**
1. Kidnapping -- Fiction
ISBN 978-0-385-32328-4; 0-385-32328-X; 978-0-440-22065-7 pa; 0-440-22065-3 pa

A reissue of the title first published 1990 by Bantam Books

A photograph of a missing girl on a milk carton leads Janie on a search for her real identity.

Cooney "demonstrates an excellent ear for dialogue and a gift for portraying responsible middle-class teenagers trying to come to terms with very real concerns." SLJ

Hit the road. Delacorte Press 2006 183p $15.95; lib bdg $17.99
Grades: 6 7 8 9   **Fic**
1. Old age -- Fiction 2. Kidnapping -- Fiction 3. Grandmothers -- Fiction 4. Automobile travel -- Fiction
ISBN 0-385-72944-8; 0-385-90174-7 lib bdg

LC 2004-10106

Sixteen-year-old Brittany acts as chauffeur for her grandmother and three other eighty-plus-year-old women going to what is supposedly their college reunion, on a long drive that involves lies, theft, and kidnappings.

"Cooney masterfully combines nonstop, cleverly plotted action with heartfelt emotion." Booklist

If the witness lied. Delacorte Press 2009 213p $16.99; lib bdg $19.99
Grades: 6 7 8 9 10   **Fic**
1. Orphans -- Fiction 2. Siblings -- Fiction 3. Bereavement -- Fiction 4. Connecticut -- Fiction
ISBN 978-0-385-73448-6; 0-385-73448-4; 978-0-385-90451-3 lib bdg; 0-385-90451-7 lib bdg

LC 2008-23959

Torn apart by tragedies and the publicity they brought, siblings Smithy, Jack, and Madison, aged fourteen to sixteen, tap into their parent's courage to pull together and protect their brother Tris, nearly three, from further media exploitation and a much more sinister threat.

"The pacing here is pure gold. Rotating through various perspectives to follow several plot strands . . . Cooney draws out the action, investing it with the slow-motion feel of an impending collision. . . . This family-drama-turned-thriller will have readers racing, heart in throat, to reach the conclusion." Horn Book

Janie face to face; Caroline B. Cooney. Delacorte Press 2013 352 p. (Janie Johnson) (ebk) $20.99; (trade hardcover) $17.99

Grades: 7 8 9 10   **Fic**

1. Love stories 2. Kidnapping -- Fiction 3. Family life -- Fiction 4. Love -- Fiction 5. Identity -- Fiction 6. Authorship -- Fiction 7. New York (N.Y.) -- Fiction 8. Universities and colleges -- Fiction

ISBN 0385742061; 9780375979972; 9780375990397; 9780385742061

LC 2012006145

This book, by Caroline B. Cooney, is the conclusion to the "Janie Johnson" series which begun in 1990. "All will be revealed as readers find out if Janie and Reeve's love has endured, and whether or not the person who brought Janie and her family so much emotional pain and suffering is brought to justice." (Publisher's note)

Three black swans. Delacorte Press 2010 276p $17.99; lib bdg $20.99

Grades: 7 8 9 10   **Fic**

1. Cousins -- Fiction 2. Sisters -- Fiction 3. Adoption -- Fiction 4. Triplets -- Fiction 5. Impostors and imposture -- Fiction

ISBN 978-0-385-73867-5; 0-385-73867-6; 978-0-385-90741-5 lib bdg; 0-385-90741-9 lib bdg

LC 2009-41990

When sixteen-year-old Missy Vianello decides to try to convince her classmates that her cousin Claire is really her long-lost identical twin, she has no idea that the results of her prank will be so life-changing.

"Cooney's psychologically probing story darts among multiple characters, forming a complex web of mistrust, economic stress, and parental sins that will keep readers guessing." Booklist

The **voice** on the radio. Delacorte Press 1996 183p hardcover o.p. pa $6.99

Grades: 7 8 9 10   **Fic**

1. Radio programs -- Fiction

ISBN 0-385-32213-5; 0-440-21977-9 pa

LC 96-3688

Sequel to Whatever happened to Janie?

"Janie is a high-school junior and in love with Reeve. She finally feels that her life is somewhat normal and begins to reconcile with her biological family, but the voice on the radio destroys her trust. Cooney plots an engaging and realistic picture of betrayal, commitment, unconditional love, and forgiveness." ALAN

What Janie found. Delacorte Press 2000 181p pa $6.99

Grades: 7 8 9 10   **Fic**

1. Kidnapping -- Fiction 2. Parent-child relationship -- Fiction

ISBN 0-385-32611-4; 0-440-22772-0 pa

LC 99-37409

Sequel to: Whatever happened to Janie?

While still adjusting to the reality of having two families, her birth family and the family into which she was kid-napped as a small child, seventeen-year-old Janie makes a shocking discovery about her long-gone kidnapper

"Readers of the previous books will find this a satis-fying closure to the unsettling circumstances of Janie's life." Booklist

Whatever happened to Janie? Delacorte Press 1993 199p hardcover o.p. pa $6.99

Grades: 7 8 9 10   **Fic**

1. Kidnapping -- Fiction

ISBN 0-385-31035-8; 0-440-21924-8 pa

LC 92-32334

Sequel to The face on the milk carton

The members of two families have their lives disrupt-ed when Jane who had been kidnapped twelve years ear-lier discovers that the people who raised her are not her biological parents

"However strange the events of this book, the emotions of its characters remain excruciatingly real." Publ Wkly

Followed by The voice on the radio

Cooper, Ilene

Angel in my pocket. Feiwel and Friends 2011 278p $16.99

Grades: 4 5 6 7   **Fic**

1. School stories 2. Charms -- Fiction 3. Chicago (Ill.) -- Fiction 4. Loss (Psychology) -- Fiction

ISBN 978-0-312-37014-5; 0-312-37014-8

LC 2010-34756

When seventh-grader Bette finds an angel coin she puts it in her pocket and forgets it but soon the mysterious and kind Gabby moves into her building and helps her face her major losses, and then the coin connects her with three class-mates who all find new ways to believe in themselves.

"The characters and setting are lovingly crafted, and readers will be left contemplating the roles of luck, magic, and inner strength in the kids' transformed lives." Publ Wkly

Cooper, Michelle

★ A **brief** history of Montmaray. Alfred A. Knopf 2009 296p $16.99; lib bdg $19.99

Grades: 7 8 9 10   **Fic**

1. Europe -- Fiction 2. Diaries -- Fiction 3. Islands -- Fiction 4. Princesses -- Fiction 5. Family life -- Fiction

ISBN 0-375-85864-4; 0-375-95864-9 lib bdg; 978-0-375-85864-2; 978-0-375-95864-9 lib bdg

LC 2008-49800

This book features "Sophie FitzOsborne [who] lives in a crumbling castle in the tiny island kingdom of Montma-ray, along with her tomboy younger sister Henry, her beauti-ful, intellectual cousin Veronica, and Veronica's father, the completely mad King John. When Sophie receives a leather journal for her sixteenth birthday, she decides to write about her life on the island. But it is 1936 and bigger events are on the horizon." (Publisher's note)

"Cooper has crafted a sort of updated Gothic romance where sweeping adventure play equal with fluttering hearts." Booklist

Followed by: The FitzOsbornes in exile (2011)

The **FitzOsbornes** at war; Michelle Cooper. Al-fred A. Knopf 2012 560 p. (hardcover) $17.99

Grades: 7 8 9 10 **Fic**

1. Exiles -- Fiction 2. Diaries -- Fiction 3. Historical fiction 4. World War, 1939-1945 -- Fiction 5. War -- Fiction 6. Family life -- England -- Fiction 7. World War, 1939-1945 -- England -- Fiction 8. Great Britain -- History -- George VI, 1936-1952 -- Fiction

ISBN 0375870504; 9780307974044; 9780375870507; 9780375970504

LC 2012009094

In this historical novel, by Michelle Cooper, "Sophie Fitz Osborne and the royal family of Montmaray escaped their remote island home when the Nazis attacked. But as war breaks out in England and around the world, nowhere is safe. Sophie fills her journal with tales of a life during wartime. . . . But even as bombs rain down on London, hope springs up, and love blooms for this most endearing princess." (Publisher's note)

The **FitzOsbornes** in exile. Alfred A. Knopf 2011 457p $17.99; lib bdg $20.99

Grades: 7 8 9 10 **Fic**

1. Diaries -- Fiction 2. Princesses -- Fiction 3. Family life -- Fiction 4. Great Britain -- Fiction

ISBN 0-375-85865-2; 0-375-95865-7 lib bdg; 978-0-375-85865-9; 978-0-375-89802-0 e-book; 978-0-375-95865-6 lib bdg

LC 2010-34706

Sequel to: A brief history of Montmaray (2009)

In this second volume of the Montmaray Journals series, "forced to leave their island kingdom, Sophie FitzOsborne and her eccentric family take shelter in England. . . . Aunt Charlotte is ruthless in her quest to see Sophie and Veronica married off by the end of the Season, Toby is as charming and lazy as ever, Henry is driving her governess to the brink of madness, and the battle of wills between Simon and Veronica continues." (Publisher's note)

"Readers who enjoy their history enriched by immersion into the social milieu of the time period will find this a fascinating, utterly absorbing venture into English society of the late '30s." Bull Cent Child Books

Cooper, Susan

The **Boggart**. Margaret K. McElderry Bks. 1993 196p hardcover o.p. pa $5.99

Grades: 4 5 6 7 **Fic**

1. Canada -- Fiction 2. Scotland -- Fiction 3. Supernatural -- Fiction

ISBN 0-689-50576-0; 0-689-86930-4 pa

LC 92-15527

After visiting the castle in Scotland which her family has inherited and returning home to Canada, twelve-year-old Emily finds that she has accidentally brought back with her a boggart, an invisible and mischievous spirit with a fondness for practical jokes

"Using both electronics and theater as metaphors for magic, Cooper has extended the world of high fantasy into contemporary children's lives through scenes superimposing the ordinary and the extraordinary." Bull Cent Child Books

Another title about the Boggart is:
The Boggart and the monster (1997)

The **Boggart** and the monster. Margaret K. McElderry Bks. 1997 185p $17.99; pa $5.99 **Fic**

1. Supernatural -- Fiction

ISBN 0-689-81330-9; 0-689-86931-2 pa

LC 96-42389

The Boggart, the invisible and mischievous spirit living in the Scottish Castle Keep, sets out to help save Nessie the Loch Ness Monster, one of its few remaining cousins

"Cooper adroitly incorporates ancient lore into a contemporary setting while producing an imaginative and compelling tale." Publ Wkly

★ **King** of shadows. Margaret K. McElderry Bks. 1999 186p $16; pa $4.99; pa $6.99

Grades: 5 6 7 8 **Fic**

1. Poets 2. Authors 3. Dramatists 4. Actors -- Fiction 5. Globe Theatre (London, England) -- Fiction

ISBN 0-689-82817-9; 0-689-84445-X pa; 9780689844454 pa

LC 98-51127

Boston Globe Horn Book Honor Book (2000)

"Nat Field is thrilled when theater director Richard Babbage chooses him to become a player in the Company of Boys, an American summer drama troupe that will appear in Shakespeare's A Midsummer Night's Dream at the new replica of the Globe Theater in London. Shortly after his arrival in England, though, Nat feels ill and falls into a troubled sleep. To the doctor's astonishment, he seems to be suffering from the effects of the bubonic plague. He awakens in 1599 as another Nat Field, a child actor from St. Paul's School who is about to go to the Globe to rehearse A Midsummer Night's Dream in the role of Puck." (Booklist) "Grades six to nine." (Bull Cent Child Books)

"Cleverly explicating old and new acting and performance techniques, Susan Cooper entertains her contemporary readers while giving them a first-rate theatrical education." N Y Times Book Rev

★ **Over** sea, under stone; illustrated by Margery Gill. Harcourt Brace Jovanovich 1966 252p il $19; pa $5.99

Grades: 5 6 7 8 **Fic**

1. Fantasy fiction 2. Good and evil -- Fiction 3. Great Britain -- Fiction

ISBN 0-15-259034-X; 0-689-84035-7 pa

First published 1965 in the United Kingdom

Three children on a holiday in Cornwall find an ancient manuscript which sends them on a dangerous quest for a grail that would reveal the true story of King Arthur and that entraps them in the eternal battle between the forces of the Light and the forces of the Dark.

"The air of mysticism and the allegorical quality of the continual contest between good and evil add much value to a fine plot, setting, and characterization." Horn Book

Other titles in this series are:
The dark is rising (1973)
Greenwitch (1974)
The grey king (1975)
Silver on the tree (1977)

Cooper, Susan, 1935-

★ **Ghost** Hawk; by Susan Cooper. 1st ed. Margaret K. McElderry Books 2013 328 p. map (hardcover) $16.99

Grades: 5 6 7 8　　　　　　　　　　　　　　**Fic**

1. Friendship -- Fiction 2. Native Americans -- North America 3. Native Americans -- Relations with early settlers 4. Ghosts -- Fiction 5. Survival -- Fiction 6. Coming of age -- Fiction 7. Wampanoag Indians -- Fiction 8. Massachusetts -- History -- New Plymouth, 1620-1691 -- Fiction

ISBN 1442481412; 9781442481411; 9781442481435
　　　　　　　　　　　　　　　　　LC 2012039892

Parents' Choice: Gold Medal Fiction (2013)

This novel is "a story of adventure and friendship between a young Native American and a colonial New England settler. Little Hawk is sent into the woods alone [and] if [he] survives three moons by himself, he will be a man. John Wakely is only ten when his father dies. . . . John sees how quickly the relationships between settlers and natives are deteriorating. His friendship with Little Hawk will put both boys in grave danger." (Publisher's note)

Cooper, T.

Changers book one; drew. T Cooper, Allison Glock. Akashic Books 2014 288 p. illustrations (Black sheep) (trade pbk.) $11.95

Grades: 7 8 9 10 11 12　　　　　　　　　　　**Fic**

1. Fantasy fiction 2. High school students 3. Identity (Psychology) 4. Science fiction

ISBN 1617751952; 9781617751950; 9781617752070; 9781617752117
　　　　　　　　　　　　　　　　　LC 2013938807

This book, by T Cooper and Allison Glock, "opens on the eve of Ethan Miller's freshman year of high school in a brand-new town. . . . everything is looking up in life. Until the next morning. When Ethan awakens as a girl. Ethan is a Changer, a little-known, ancient race of humans who live out each of their four years of high school as a different person. After graduation, Changers choose which version of themselves they will be forever." (Publisher's note)

"Ethan wakes up on his first day of high school to discover that he is no longer the same person he was when he went to sleep—overnight he was transformed into a beautiful girl. His parents inform him that his father was a Changer and that this is the first of four transformations. He will experience each year of high school in a new body, and at the end of his senior year, he will get to choose which body he will live in for the rest of his life...By the end of this book, readers will be invested in this character and will want to know what Ethan's future holds and how he will physically and emotionally transform over the next installments." SLJ

Corbett, Sue

Free baseball; [by] Sue Corbett. Dutton Children's Books 2006 152p $15.99; pa $5.99

Grades: 5 6 7 8　　　　　　　　　　　　　　**Fic**

1. Florida -- Fiction 2. Baseball -- Fiction 3. Cuban Americans -- Fiction

ISBN 0-525-47120-0; 0-14-241080-2 pa
　　　　　　　　　　　　　　　　　LC 2005004792

Angry with his mother for having too little time for him, eleven-year-old Felix takes advantage of an opportunity to become bat boy for a minor league baseball team, hoping to someday be like his father, a famous Cuban outfielder. Includes glossaries of baseball terms and Spanish words and phrases

"An engaging, well-written story with a satisfying ending." SLJ

The **last** newspaper boy in America. Dutton Childrens Books 2009 199p $16.99

Grades: 4 5 6 7　　　　　　　　　　　　　　**Fic**

1. Mystery fiction 2. Newspaper carriers -- Fiction

ISBN 978-0-525-42205-1; 0-525-42205-6

When the newspaper company cancels his route, Wil David is prepared to fight to get his job back, but his focus changes when he stumbles upon a carnival mystery and a plot by a con man that could destroy the town.

"Corbett's graceful dialogue, lovingly drawn characters and clever plot form a timely and refreshing tale." Publ Wkly

Cormier, Robert

★ **After** the first death. Dell Publishing 1991 233p pa $6.50

Grades: 7 8 9 10　　　　　　　　　　　　　　**Fic**

1. Terrorism -- Fiction

ISBN 0-440-20835-1

First published 1979 by Pantheon Bks.

ALA YALSA Margaret A. Edwards Award (1991)

"A busload of children is hijacked by a band of terrorists whose demands include the exposure of a military brainwashing project. The narrative line moves from the teenage terrorist Milo to Kate the bus driver and the involvement of Ben, whose father is the head of the military operation, in this confrontation. The conclusion has a shocking twist." Shapiro. Fic for Youth. 2d edition

Beyond the chocolate war; a novel. Dell 1986 278p pa $6.99

Grades: 9 10 11 12　　　　　　　　　　　　　**Fic**

1. School stories

ISBN 0-440-90580-X

First published 1985

Dark deeds continue at Trinity High School, climaxing in a public demonstration of one student's homemade guillotine. Sequel to "The Chocolate War."

★ The **chocolate** war; a novel. Pantheon Bks. 1974 253p rpt $8.99; $19.95

Grades: 7 8 9 10　　　　　　　　　　　　　　**Fic**

1. School stories

ISBN 9780375829871 rpt; 0-394-82805-4

ALA YALSA Margaret A. Edwards Award (1991)

"In the Trinity School for Boys the environment is completely dominated by an underground gang, the Vigils. During a chocolate candy sale Brother Leon, the acting headmaster of the school, defers to the Vigils, who reign with terror in the school. Jerry Renault is first a pawn for the Vigils' evil deeds and finally their victim." Shapiro. Fic for Youth. 3d edition

Followed by Beyond the chocolate war (1985)

★ **I** am the cheese; a novel. Pantheon Bks. 1977 233p hardcover o.p. pa $6.50

Grades: 7 8 9 10 11 12 Adult **Fic**

1. Intelligence service -- Fiction

ISBN 0-394-83462-3; 0-440-94060-5 pa

LC 76-55948

ALA YALSA Margaret A. Edwards Award (1991)

"The suspense builds relentlessly to an ending that, although shocking, is entirely plausible." Booklist

Cornish, D. M.

Factotum. Putnam Pub. 2010 684p (Monster blood tattoo) $19.99

Grades: 8 9 10 11 12 **Fic**

1. Fantasy fiction 2. Orphans -- Fiction 3. Monsters -- Fiction 4. Tattooing -- Fiction

ISBN 978-0-399-24640-1; 0-399-24640-1

Sequel to: Lamplighter (2008)

Accused of being a monster instead of human, Rossamünd Bookchild looks to monster-hunter Branden Rose for help, but powerful forces are after them both, believing that Rossamünd holds the secret to perpetual youth.

"Along with many splendid names . . . and linguistic fancies . . . the author laces his rococo but fluent narrative with moral and ethical conundrums, twists both terrible and tongue in cheek, startling revelations about humans and 'monsters' alike and sturdy themes of loyalty, courage and self-realization. Readers new to the series should start with the first volume; fans will be more than satisfied." Kirkus

Cornwell, Autumn

★ **Carpe** diem. Feiwel & Friends 2007 360p $16.95; pa $8.99

Grades: 7 8 9 10 **Fic**

1. Artists -- Fiction 2. Authorship -- Fiction 3. Grandmothers -- Fiction 4. Southeast Asia -- Fiction

ISBN 0-312-36792-9; 978-0-312-36792-3; 978-0-312-56129-1 pa; 0-312-56129-6 pa

LC 2006-32054

Sixteen-year-old Vassar Spore's detailed plans for the next twenty years of her life are derailed when her bohemian grandmother insists that she join her in Southeast Asia for the summer, but as she writes a novel about her experiences, Vassar discovers new possibilities.

"Suspenseful and wonderfully detailed, the well-crafted story maintains its page-turning pace while adding small doses of insight and humor." SLJ

Cornwell, Betsy

Tides; by Betsy Cornwell. Clarion Books 2013 304 p. (hardcover) $16.99

Grades: 7 8 9 10 11 12 **Fic**

1. Love stories 2. Selkies -- Fiction 3. Internship programs -- Fiction 4. Love -- Fiction 5. Isles of Shoals (Me. and N.H.) -- Fiction

ISBN 054792772X; 9780547927725

LC 2012022415

In this teen novel, by Betsy Cornwell, "high school senior Noah Gallagher and his adopted teenage sister, Lo, go to live with their grandmother in her island cottage for the summer. . . . Noah has landed a marine biology internship, and Lo wants to draw and paint, perhaps even to vanquish her struggles with bulimia. But then things take a dramatic turn for them both when Noah mistakenly tries to save a mysterious girl from drowning." (Publisher's note)

Correa, Shan

Gaff; written by Shan Correa. Peachtree 2010 212p $15.95

Grades: 4 5 6 7 **Fic**

1. Hawaii -- Fiction 2. Roosters -- Fiction 3. Animal welfare -- Fiction

ISBN 978-1-56145-526-3; 1-56145-526-1

In Hawaii, thirteen-year-old Paul Silva is determined to find a way to get his family out of the illegal cockfighting business.

"Correa's debut evokes the lush melange of sights, sounds and smells in 13-year-old Paulie's multicultural neighborhood in Hawaii. . . . Also woven into this ethical debate, rooted in economics and traditions, is Hawaiian pidgin English, which may challenge even experienced readers. . . . A fascinating look at the United States most mainlanders have never seen." Kirkus

Corrigan, Eireann

★ **Accomplice**. Scholastic Press 2010 296p $17.99

Grades: 7 8 9 10 **Fic**

1. School stories 2. Fraud -- Fiction 3. Friendship -- Fiction 4. New Jersey -- Fiction

ISBN 978-0-545-05236-8; 0-545-05236-X

LC 2009-53869

High school juniors and best friends Finn and Chloe hatch a daring plot to fake Chloe's disappearance from their rural New Jersey town in order to have something compelling to put on their college applications, but unforeseen events complicate matters.

"Corrigan has crafted a complex, heart-wrenchingly plausible YA thriller. . . . A fascinating character study of individuals and an entire town, this tension-filled story will entice readers with a single booktalk." Booklist

Cotler, Steve

Cheesie Mack is cool in a duel; Steve Cotler ; illustrated by Adam McCauley. Random House 2012 229 p. (hardcover library binding) $18.99

Grades: 4 5 6 **Fic**

1. Camps -- Fiction 2. Siblings -- Fiction 3. Interpersonal relations -- Fiction 4. Maine -- Fiction 5. Contests -- Fiction

ISBN 9780375864384; 9780375895715; 9780375964381

LC 2011016921

This book is the second in the Cheesie Mack series. "Ronald 'Cheesie' Mack and his best friend Georgie secured the funds to go to summer camp on Bufflehead Lake in Maine. Days later, the duo climbs aboard a bus and head off to Camp Windward. Unfortunately Cheesie's older sister, June . . . will be none too far away at Camp Leeward. . . . T late registration results in both boys being stuck in a cabin with the older guys including Kevin, [June's] boyfriend. When Kevin gives Cheesie a hard time once too often, Cheesie suggests a Cool Duel. Each night the boys in the cabin will vote on who did the coolest thing; in a week, the loser will have to embarrass himself in front of the whole camp by bowing to the winner. Can Cheesie prevail and still have fun at the camp he worked so hard to attend?" (Kirkus Reviews)

Cheesie Mack is not a genius or anything; illustrated by Adam McCauley. Random House 2011 229p il $15.99; lib bdg $18.99

Grades: 4 5 6   **Fic**
1. Mystery fiction 2. Summer -- Fiction 3. Friendship -- Fiction
ISBN 978-0-375-86437-7; 0-375-86437-7; 978-0-375-96437-4 lib bdg; 0-375-96437-1 lib bdg; 978-0-375-89570-8 e-book

LC 2009-33329

Ronald, aka Cheesie, Mack and his best friend Georgie find opportunies for summertime mischief "when Georgie finds a nearly century-old letter containing a worn penny and a locket, a mystery that eventually leads the pals to the Haunted Toad, a local rundown mansion. . . . Cheesie's . . . easygoing, accessible voice will certainly appeal to middle-grade readers. . . . The action . . . is all fun and games. . . . A light-hearted and fast-moving read for kids looking for middle-school shenanigans." Bull Cent Child Books

Cheesie Mack is running like crazy! by Steve Cotler ; illustrated by Douglas Holgate. 1st ed. Random House Inc. 2013 256 p. ill. (hardcover) $15.99; (library) $18.99; (ebook) $47.97; (paperback) $6.99

Grades: 4 5 6   **Fic**
1. Schools -- Fiction 2. Elections -- Fiction 3. Friendship -- Fiction 4. Best friends -- Fiction 5. Middle schools -- Fiction 6. Track and field -- Fiction 7. Brothers and sisters -- Fiction
ISBN 0307977145; 9780307977137; 9780307977144; 9780307977151; 9780307977168

LC 2012017978

In this book by Steve Colter, "Cheesie and his best friend, Georgie, are off to the middle school, where there will be lots of new kids and new teachers. Cheesie has a terrific idea--what better way to meet all the new kids than to run for class president? Plus, if he wins, it'll drive his evil older sister nuts! Then Cheesie gets bad news. One of his friends from his old school is also running for president." (Publisher's note

Cottrell Boyce, Frank
★ **Cosmic**. Walden Pond Press 2010 311p $16.99; lib bdg $17.89

Grades: 4 5 6 7   **Fic**
1. Size -- Fiction 2. Outer space -- Exploration -- Fiction
ISBN 978-0-06-183683-1; 0-06-183683-4; 978-0-06-183686-2 lib bdg; 0-06-183686-9 lib bdg

LC 2008277816

Boyce "knows how to tell a compellingly good story. But in his latest extravagantly imaginative and marvelously good-natured novel he has also written one that is bound to win readers' hearts." Booklist

Framed. HarperCollins 2006 306p $16.99; lib bdg $17.89; pa $6.99

Grades: 5 6 7 8   **Fic**
1. Art -- Fiction 2. Wales -- Fiction 3. Automobiles -- Fiction 4. Family life -- Fiction 5. Business enterprises -- Fiction
ISBN 0-06-073402-7; 0-06-073403-5 lib bdg; 0-06-073404-3 pa

LC 2006-00557

Dylan and his sisters have some ideas about how to make Snowdonia Oasis Auto Marvel into a more profitable business, but it is not until some strange men arrive in their small town of Manod, Wales with valuable paintings, and their father disappears, that they consider turning to crime.

"The colorful characters steal the show—even the secondary players are cleverly drawn. But it is Dylan's narrative voice . . . that is truly a masterpiece." SLJ

★ The **un** -forgotten coat. Candlewick Press 2011 92p il $15.99

Grades: 5 6 7 8 9   **Fic**
1. Refugees -- Fiction 2. Immigrants -- Fiction 3. Great Britain -- Fiction
ISBN 978-0-7636-5729-1; 0-7636-5729-8

LC 2010048224

"Funny, sad, haunting and original, Cottrell Boyce's story leaves important elements unexpressed. . . . To complete the narrative, readers must actively participate. They'll find myriad paths to follow—immigration, demons, social networking, the mystery of cultural difference and the nature of enchantment. A tricky, magical delight." Kirkus

Couloumbis, Audrey
★ **Love** me tender. Random House 2008 209p $16.99; lib bdg $19.99; pa $6.50

Grades: 5 6 7 8   **Fic**
1. Pregnancy -- Fiction 2. Family life -- Fiction 3. Grandmothers -- Fiction 4. Memphis (Tenn.) -- Fiction
ISBN 978-0-375-83839-2; 0-375-83839-2; 978-0-375-93839-9 lib bdg; 0-375-93839-7 lib bdg; 978-0-375-83840-8 pa; 0-375-83840-6 pa

LC 2006033162

Thirteen-year-old Elvira worries about her future when, after a fight, her father heads to Las Vegas for an Elvis impersonator competition and her pregnant mother takes her and her younger sister to Memphis to visit a grandmother the girls have never met.

"Tart characterizations, lively dialogue and Elvira's frank narration keep this perceptive novel both credible and buoyant." Publ Wkly

Maude March on the run! or, Trouble is her middle name. Random House 2007 309p $15.99; lib bdg $17.99

Grades: 4 5 6 7   **Fic**
1. Adventure fiction 2. Orphans -- Fiction 3. Frontier and pioneer life -- Fiction
ISBN 978-0-375-83246-8; 978-0-375-93246-5 lib bdg; 978-0-375-83248-2 pa

LC 2005036133

Due to a misunderstanding over her involvement in a botched robbery, Maude, with younger sister Sallie, hides out at the home of an uncle, but when she is discovered and arrested, the orphaned sisters flee, trying to clear Maude's name.

"The excitement of the Wild West comes to life in this action-packed sequel to The Misadventures of Maude March." SLJ

★ The **misadventures** of Maude March; or, Trouble rides a fast horse. [by] Audrey Couloumbis. Random House 2005 295p hardcover o.p. lib bdg $17.99; pa $7.50

Grades: 4 5 6 7   **Fic**

1. Adventure fiction 2. Orphans -- Fiction 3. Frontier and pioneer life -- Fiction

ISBN 0-375-83245-9; 0-375-93245-3 lib bdg; 0-375-83247-5 pa

       LC 2004-16464

After the death of the stern aunt who raised them since they were orphaned, eleven-year-old Sallie and her fifteen-year-old sister escape their self-serving guardians and begin an adventure resembling those in the dime novels Sallie loves to read. "Grades six to ten." (Bull Cent Child Books)

"Sallie's narration is delightful, with understatements that are laugh-out-loud hilarious. . . . Hard to put down, and a fun read-aloud." SLJ

★ **War** games; a novel based on a true story. [by] Audrey Couloumbis & Akila Couloumbis. Random House Children's Books 2009 232p $16.99; lib bdg $19.99

Grades: 5 6 7 8   **Fic**

1. Greece -- Fiction 2. Cousins -- Fiction 3. Brothers -- Fiction 4. World War, 1939-1945 -- Underground movements -- Fiction

ISBN 978-0-375-85628-0; 0-375-85628-5; 978-0-375-95628-7 lib bdg; 0-375-95628-X lib bdg

       LC 2008-46784

"For 12-year-old Petros, World War II feels unreal and far away. . . . But when the Germans invade Greece, the war suddenly comes impossibly close. Overnight, neighbors become enemies. People begin to keep secrets (Petros's family most of all). And for the first time, Petros has the chance to show Zola that he's not just a little brother but that he can truly be counted on." (Publisher's note) "Grades six to nine."(Bull Cent Child Books)

"The climactic violence is believable, and the resolution—though it takes place offstage—is deeply satisfying. Memorable." SLJ

Cousins, Dave

Waiting for Gonzo; Dave Cousins. First U.S. edition Flux 2015 288 p. $9.99

Grades: 7 8 9 10   **Fic**

1. Moving -- Fiction 2. Family life -- Fiction 3. High schools -- Fiction 4. Practical jokes -- Fiction 5. Brothers and sisters -- Fiction 6. England -- Fiction 7. Schools -- Fiction 8. Pregnancy -- Fiction 9. Moving, Household -- Fiction 10. Family life -- England -- Fiction

ISBN 073874199X; 9780738741994

       LC 2014031277

In this book, by Dave Cousins, "[t]hings could be going better for Oz. He's just moved miles from all his friends. A prank at his new school puts him in the crosshairs of 'Psycho' Isobel Skinner, a bully who also happens to be his mum's new best friend. And he's driven off the only other kid who will have anything to do with him: a Tolkien-obsessed boy in desperate need of a decent playlist." (Publisher's note)

"In a darkly comic story written as Marcus's monologue to his unborn nephew (whom he nicknames Gonzo), Cousins (15 Days Without a Head) offers a vibrant, highly visual account of teen angst and backfiring schemes. Marcus makes more than a few mistakes at school and at home, but readers will never doubt that his heart is in the right place." Publishers Weekly

Coutts, Alexandra

Tumble & fall; Alexandra Coutts. Farrar Straus & Giroux (BYR) 2013 384 p. (hardback) $17.99

Grades: 8 9 10 11 12   **Fic**

1. Love stories 2. Apocalyptic fiction 3. Science fiction 4. Family life -- Fiction 5. Conduct of life -- Fiction 6. Interpersonal relations -- Fiction 7. Islands of the Atlantic -- Fiction 8. Asteroids -- Collisions with Earth -- Fiction

ISBN 0374378614; 9780374378615

       LC 2013012969

In this book, as "the world faces a catastrophic collision with a giant asteroid, three teenagers spending the summer on Martha's Vineyard discover that their last week on Earth may be life-changing in good ways as well." Sienna "tries to relearn how to trust and love with help from a childhood friend; Zan wonders whether the dead boyfriend she has grieved for was faithful to her . . . ; and Caden has to decide whether he can forgive two parents who have abandoned him." (Publishers Weekly)

Couvillon, Jacques

The **chicken** dance; [by] Jacques Couvillon. 1st U.S. ed.; Bloomsbury Children's Books 2007 326p $16.95

Grades: 6 7 8 9   **Fic**

1. Chickens -- Fiction 2. Louisiana -- Fiction 3. Family life -- Fiction 4. Country life -- Fiction

ISBN 978-1-59990-043-8; 1-59990-043-2

       LC 2006102093

When eleven-year-old Don Schmidt wins a chicken-judging contest in his small town of Horse Island, Louisiana and goes from outcast to instant celebrity, even his neglectful mother occasionally takes notice of him and eventually he discovers some shocking family secrets.

"A funny, sometimes poignant novel. . . . [This offers] strong characters, interesting concepts, and a deft comedic touch." SLJ

Coventry, Susan

The **queen's** daughter. Henry Holt and Company 2010 373p map $16.99

Grades: 8 9 10 11 12   **Fic**

1. Queens 2. Princesses -- Fiction 3. Middle Ages -- Fiction 4. Sicily (Italy) -- Fiction 5. Great Britain

-- History -- 1154-1399, Plantagenets -- Fiction
ISBN 978-0-8050-8992-9; 0-8050-8992-6

LC 2009-24154

A fictionalized biography of Joan of England, the youngest child of King Henry II of England and his queen consort, Eleanor of Aquitaine, chronicling her complicated relationships with her warring parents and many siblings, particularly with her favorite brother Richard the Lionheart, her years as Queen consort of Sicily, and her second marriage to Raymond VI, Count of Toulouse.

"Fans of historical fiction, and especially historical romance, will devour this volume." SLJ

Coville, Bruce

★ **Aliens** ate my homework; illustrated by Katherine Coville. Pocket Bks. 1993 179p il hardcover o.p. pa $5.99

Grades: 4 5 6 **Fic**
1. Science fiction 2. Extraterrestrial beings -- Fiction
ISBN 1-4169-3883-4 pa

LC 93-3945

Rod is surprised when a miniature spaceship lands in his school science project and reveals five tiny aliens, who ask his help in apprehending an interstellar criminal

"A funny and suspenseful romp, with appealing illustrations throughout." Horn Book Guide

Other titles in this series are:
Aliens stole my body (1998)
I left my sneakers in dimension X (1994)
The search for Snout (1995)

★ **Juliet** Dove, Queen of Love; a magic shop book. Harcourt 2003 190p $17; pa $5.95

Grades: 4 5 6 **Fic**
1. Magic -- Fiction 2. Classical mythology -- Fiction
ISBN 0-15-204561-9; 0-15-205217-8 pa

LC 2003-11846

A shy twelve-year-old girl must solve a puzzle involving characters from Greek mythology to free herself from a spell which makes her irresistible to boys

"Although humorous, the story has surprising depth. . . . Coville capably interweaves mythological characters with realistic modern ones, keeping readers truly absorbed." SLJ

The **monster's** ring; by Bruce Coville ; illustrated by Katherine Coville. Harcourt Brace & Co. 2002 105 p. ill. (reinforced) $16

Grades: 4 5 6 **Fic**
1. Fantasy fiction 2. Magic -- Fiction 3. Bullies -- Fiction 4. Schools -- Fiction 5. Monsters -- Fiction 6. Halloween -- Fiction
ISBN 0152046186; 9780152046187

LC 2002003537

In this book by Bruce Coville, "Russell, the main character, has problems with the class bully. But then Russell gets a magic ring from a mysterious magic shop. He isn't careful with the ring's directions, and this leads to big problems." Namely, Russell begins turning into a monster. (Scholastic News)

The **monsters** of Morley Manor. Harcourt 2001 224p $16; pa $5.95

Grades: 4 5 6 **Fic**
1. Monsters -- Fiction 2. Extraterrestrial beings -- Fiction
ISBN 0-15-216382-4; 0-15-204705-0 pa

LC 00-12912

Anthony and his younger sister discover that the monster figures he got in an unusual box at an estate sale are alive, but they have no way of knowing that the "monsters" will lead them on fantastical adventures to other worlds in an effort to try to save Earth

"Coville's rollicking tale has an unbelievable plot and exaggerated characters, but this is exactly what makes it so entertaining." Horn Book Guide

★ The **skull** of truth; a magic shop book. illustrated by Gary A. Lippincott. Harcourt Brace & Co. 1997 195p il $17

Grades: 4 5 6 7 **Fic**
1. Fantasy fiction 2. Truthfulness and falsehood -- Fiction
ISBN 0-15-275457-1

LC 97-9264

Charlie, a sixth-grader with a compulsion to tell lies, acquires a mysterious skull that forces its owner to tell only the truth, causing some awkward moments before he understands its power

"Coville has structured the story very carefully, with a great deal of sensitivity to children's thought processes and emotions. The mood shifts from scary to funny to serious are fused with understandable language and sentence structures." SLJ

Cowing, Sue

You will call me Drog. Carolrhoda Books 2011 281p $16.95

Grades: 4 5 6 7 **Fic**
1. Aikido -- Fiction 2. Divorce -- Fiction 3. Illinois -- Fiction 4. Supernatural -- Fiction 5. Puppets and puppet plays -- Fiction
ISBN 978-0-7613-6076-6; 0-7613-6076-X

LC 2010050891

Unless eleven-year-old Parker can find a way to remove the sinister puppet that refuses to leave his hand, he will wind up in military school or worse but first he must stand up for himself to his best friend Wren, his mother, and his nearly-absent father.

"There is nothing else out there quite like this, and Cowing shifts fluidly from sensitive drama to startling violence to high comedy. . . . A unique look at speaking your mind." Booklist

Cox, Suzy

The **Dead** Girls Detective Agency; Suzy Cox. Harper 2012 355 p. (trade bdg.) $9.99

Grades: 7 8 9 10 **Fic**
1. Future life -- Fiction 2. Ghost stories -- Fiction 3. Mystery fiction 4. Dead -- Fiction 5. Murder -- Fiction 6. New York (N.Y.) -- Fiction 7. Mystery and detective stories
ISBN 0-06-202064-1; 9780062020642

LC 2012006567

This novel, by Suzy Cox, follows the ghost of a teenager seeking to solve her own murder. "Meet the Dead Girls Detective Agency: Nancy, Lorna, and Tess--not to mention Edison, the really cute if slightly hostile dead boy. Apparently, the only way out of this limbo is to figure out who killed me, or I'll have to spend eternity playing Nancy Drew. Considering I was fairly invisible in life, who could hate me enough to want me dead? And what if my murderer is someone I never would have suspected?" (Publisher's note)

Coy, John

★ **Box** out. Scholastic Press 2008 276p $16.99

Grades: 6 7 8 9 10   **Fic**

1. School stories 2. Prayer -- Fiction 3. Basketball -- Fiction

ISBN 978-0-439-87032-0; 0-439-87032-1

LC 2007-45354

High school sophomore Liam jeopardizes his new position on the varsity basketball team when he decides to take a stand against his coach who is leading prayers before games and enforcing teamwide participation.

"Plainly acquainted with teenagers and well as b-ball play and lingo, Coy adds subplots and supporting characters to give Liam's life dimension, but he weaves plenty of breathlessly compelling game action too." Booklist

★ **Crackback**. Scholastic 2005 201p $16.99

Grades: 7 8 9 10   **Fic**

1. School stories 2. Football -- Fiction 3. Drug abuse -- Fiction 4. Father-son relationship -- Fiction

ISBN 0-439-69733-6

LC 2004-30972

Miles barely recalls when football was fun after being sidelined by a new coach, constantly criticized by his father, and pressured by his best friend to take performance-enhancing drugs. "Grades seven to ten." (Bull Cent Child Books)

The author "writes a moving, nuanced portrait of a teen struggling with adults who demand, but don't always deserve, respect." Booklist

Love of the game. Feiwel and Friends 2011 182p $16.99

Grades: 4 5 6 7   **Fic**

1. School stories 2. Football -- Fiction 3. Family life -- Fiction

ISBN 978-0-312-37331-3; 0-312-37331-7

LC 2010050897

Sixth-grader Jackson has a rough start in middle school, with bullies on the bus, few classes with his friends, and changes at home but some good teachers, meeting a girl, joining a club, and playing football soon turn things around.

"Realistic characters, believable dialogue and a genuine feel for the rhythms and issues of middle-schoolers make this a satisfying addition to a solid middle-grade set." Kirkus

Craig, Colleen

★ **Afrika**. Tundra Books 2008 233p pa $9.95

Grades: 7 8 9 10   **Fic**

1. Fathers -- Fiction 2. Mothers -- Fiction 3. South Africa -- Fiction

ISBN 978-0-88776-807-1; 0-88776-807-5

"Growing up in Canada with her white South African mother, Kim van der Merwe does not know who her father is. Now, at 13, she goes to Cape Town for the first time, shortly after independence in the mid-1990s, because her mother, a journalist, is going to report on the Truth and Reconciliation Commission. . . . Visiting and meeting her family for the first time, she decides that her mission will be to discover her father's identity. . . . . The realities of the society are carefully and skillfully portrayed, so that Kim's story is truly the emotional heart of the book, and not a vehicle for ideas." SLJ

Crane, Dede

Poster boy. Groundwood Books 2009 214p $18.95

Grades: 8 9 10 11   **Fic**

1. Cancer -- Fiction 2. Siblings -- Fiction 3. Family life -- Fiction

ISBN 978-0-88899-855-2; 0-88899-855-4

"Cruising along on the fringes of stoner life is cool with 16-year-old Gray Fallon. . . . Life's all good until Gray's younger sister, 12-year-old Maggie, begins to complain about aches in her legs and arms. It's a rare form of terminal cancer. . . . Crane effectively shows a family unraveling, and Gray's authentic teen narration springs from the pages." Kirkus

Crane, E. M.

Skin deep; [by] E. M. Crane. Delacorte Press 2008 273p $16.99; lib bdg $19.99

Grades: 7 8 9 10 11 12   **Fic**

1. Dogs -- Fiction 2. Death -- Fiction 3. Friendship -- Fiction

ISBN 978-0-385-73479-0; 0-385-73479-4; 978-0-385-90477-3 lib bdg; 0-385-90477-0 lib bdg

When sixteen-year-old Andrea Anderson begins caring for a sick neighbor's dog, she learns a lot about life, death, pottery, friendship, hope, and love.

"Teenage girls who can empathize with Andrea's journey of self-discovery and its triumphs and losses will find a well-written story, with lyrical explorations of nature, and memorable characters." Voice Youth Advocates

Crawford, Brent

★ **Carter** finally gets it. Disney Hyperion Books 2009 300p $15.99; pa $8.99

Grades: 7 8 9 10   **Fic**

1. School stories

ISBN 978-1-4231-1246-4; 1-4231-1246-6; 978-1-4231-1247-1 pa; 1-4231-1247-4 pa

LC 2008-46541

Awkward freshman Will Carter endures many painful moments during his first year of high school before realizing that nothing good comes easily, focus is everything, and the payoff is usually incredible.

"Crawford expertly channels his inner 14-year-old for this pitch-perfect comedy. . . . His stream-consciousness, first-person narrative flails around in an excellent imitation of a freshman." Booklist

Followed by Carter's big break (2010)

Carter's big break. Hyperion 2010 231p
$15.99; pa $8.99

Grades: 8 9 10 11 12   **Fic**

1. Actors -- Fiction 2. Drug abuse -- Fiction 3. Self-
perception -- Fiction 4. Motion pictures -- Production
and direction -- Fiction

ISBN 978-1-4231-1243-3; 1-4231-1243-3; 978-1-
4231-1244-0 pa; 1-4231-1244-X pa

LC 2010-5040

Sequel to Carter finally gets it (2009)

Fourteen-year-old Will Carter's summer gets off to a bad
start when his girlfriend leaves him, but then he is cast opposite a major star, Hilary Idaho, in a small movie being filmed
in his town and things start looking up.

"This fast and fun read will definitely appeal to reluctant readers who want to see the underdog succeed in life
and love. A must-have, especially where the first book is
popular." SLJ

Carter's unfocused, one-track mind; a novel. by
Brent Crawford. Hyperion 2012 296 p. (Carter)
(hardback) $16.99

Grades: 7 8 9 10   **Fic**

1. High school students -- Fiction 2. School stories
-- Fiction 3. Dating (Social customs) -- Fiction 4.
Schools -- Fiction 5. High schools -- Fiction 6. Self-
perception -- Fiction 7. Dating (Social customs) --
Fiction 8. Interpersonal relations -- Fiction

ISBN 1423144457; 9781423144458

LC 2012001231

This young adult novel, by Brent Crawford, is the third
book in the author's "Carter" series. "After an eventful freshman year and disastrous summer, fifteen-year-old Will Carter
returns to Merrian High none the wiser. His sophomore year
will present a host of new problems. . . . When Abby announces that she might be transferring to a New York arts school,
Carter's world is turned upside down and he'll be forced to
make the biggest decision of his life." (Publisher's note)

Creech, Sharon

Absolutely normal chaos. HarperCollins Pubs.
1995 230p $16.99; pa $5.99

Grades: 5 6 7 8   **Fic**

1. Family life -- Fiction

ISBN 0-06-026989-8; 0-06-440632-6 pa

LC 95-22448

First published 1990 in the United Kingdom

"Those in search of a light, humorous read will find
it; those in search of something a little deeper will also be
rewarded." SLJ

Bloomability. HarperCollins Pubs. 1998 273p
hardcover o.p. pa $5.99

Grades: 5 6 7 8   **Fic**

1. School stories 2. Switzerland -- Fiction

ISBN 0-06-026993-6; 0-06-440823-X pa

LC 98-14601

When her aunt and uncle take her from New Mexico to
Lugano, Switzerland, to attend an international school, thirteen-year-old Dinnie discovers her world expanding

"As if fresh, smart characters in a picturesque setting
weren't engaging enough, Creech also poses an array of

knotty questions, both personal and philosophical. . . . A
story to stimulate both head and heart." Booklist

The **Castle** Corona; illuminated by David Diaz.
Joanna Cotler Books 2007 320p il $18.99; lib bdg
$19.89; pa $7.99

Grades: 4 5 6 7   **Fic**

1. Italy -- Fiction 2. Orphans -- Fiction 3. Siblings
-- Fiction 4. Kings and rulers -- Fiction

ISBN 978-0-06-084621-3; 0-06-084621-6; 978-0-06-
084622-0 lib bdg; 0-06-084622-4 lib bdg; 978-0-06-
084623-7 pa; 0-06-084623-2 pa

LC 2006-32004

Two orphaned peasant children discover a mysterious
pouch, the contents of which lead them to the majestic Castle Corona, where their lives may be transformed forever.

"The engaging, puzzle-like plot will attract readers,
as the novel's heady themes, from wisdom to empathy to
the fate-changing power of story, prompt them to deeper
thought. Diaz's full-color chapter-heading artwork and or-
namental flourishes lend the novel substantial aesthetic
appeal." Booklist

The **great** unexpected; Sharon Creech ; edited
by Alyson Day. HarperCollins 2012 240 p. (lib.
bdg.) $17.89

Grades: 4 5 6 7   **Fic**

1. Ireland -- Fiction 2. Orphans -- Fiction 3. Friendship
-- Fiction

ISBN 0061892335; 9780061892325; 9780061892332

LC 2012942431

In this book by Sharon Creech, "best friends and orphans
Naomi Deane and Lizzie Scattering are surprised when a
strange boy falls out of a tree in their little town of Blackbird
Tree, USA. His name is Finn, and Naomi falls immediately
under his spell. . . . Meanwhile, in Ireland, an old woman
and her companion talk of murder and revenge." (Horn
Book Magazine)

Hate that cat. Joanna Cotler Books 2008 153p
$15.99; lib bdg $16.89

Grades: 4 5 6 7   **Fic**

1. School stories 2. Novels in verse 3. Poetry -- Fiction

ISBN 978-0-06-143092-3; 978-0-06-143093-0 lib bdg

LC 2007044182

Jack is studying poetry again in school, and he continues
to write poems reflecting his understanding of famous poems and how they relate to his life.

"Creech employs sensitivity and spare verse to carve an
indelible portrait of a boy who discovers the power of self-
expression." Booklist

Love that dog. HarperCollins Pubs. 2001 86p
$15.99; lib bdg $14.89; pa $5.99

Grades: 4 5 6 7   **Fic**

1. School stories 2. Poetry 3. Poetry -- Fiction

ISBN 0-06-029287-3; 0-06-029289-X lib bdg; 0-06-
440959-7 pa

LC 00-54233

"Jack thinks that boys don't write poetry. . . . The trouble
is that his teacher, Ms. Stretchberry, keeps insisting that he
read more and more poetry. Worse, she keeps insisting that

he write poems, as well! . . . This book comes to us in the form of journal entries in Jack's own freeverse." (Christ Sci Monit) "Ages eight to twelve." (N Y Times Book Rev)

"Creech has created a poignant, funny picture of a child's encounter with the power of poetry. . . . This book is a tiny treasure." SLJ

Another title about Jack is:
Hate that cat (2008)

Replay; a new book. Joanna Cotler Books 2005 180; 31 $15.99; pa $5.99

Grades: 5 6 7 8   **Fic**
1. Theater -- Fiction 2. Family life -- Fiction 3. Italian Americans -- Fiction
ISBN 0-06-054019-2; 0-06-054021-4 pa

While preparing for a role in the school play, twelve-year-old Leo finds an autobiography that his father wrote as a teenager and ponders the ways people change as they grow up. Includes the text for the play, "Rumpopo's Porch."

"Both uproarious and tender, this story . . . . captures [Leo's] big, noisy, extended Italian family with pitch-perfect dialogue that will sweep readers right to the end of the story." Booklist

★ The **unfinished** angel. Joanna Cotler Books 2009 164p

Grades: 4 5 6   **Fic**
1. Angels -- Fiction 2. Orphans -- Fiction 3. Villages -- Fiction 4. Switzerland -- Fiction
ISBN 0-06-143095-1; 0-06-143096-X lib bdg; 0-06-143097-8 pa; 978-0-06-143095-4; 978-0-06-143096-1 lib bdg; 978-0-06-143097-8 pa
LC 2009-02796

In a tiny village in the Swiss Alps, an angel meets an American girl named Zola who has come with her father to open a school, and together Zola and the angel rescue a group of homeless orphans. "Ages eight to twelve." (Publisher's note)

"Some books are absolute magic, and this is one of them. . . . Creech's protagonist is hugely likable. . . . Creech's offering deserves to be read out loud and more than once to truly enjoy the angel's hilarious malapropisms and outright invented words, and to appreciate the book's tender, comical celebration of the human spirit." SLJ

★ **Walk** two moons. HarperCollins Pubs. 1994 280p $16.99; lib bdg $17.89; pa $6.99

Grades: 6 7 8 9   **Fic**
1. Death -- Fiction 2. Friendship -- Fiction 3. Family life -- Fiction 4. Grandparents -- Fiction
ISBN 0-06-023334-6; 0-06-023337-0 lib bdg; 0-06-440517-6 pa
LC 93-31277

Awarded the Newbery Medal, 1995
After her mother leaves home suddenly, thirteen-year-old Sal and her grandparents take a car trip retracing her mother's route. Along the way, Sal recounts the story of her friend Phoebe, whose mother also left

"An engaging story of love and loss, told with humor and suspense. . . . A richly layered novel about real and metaphorical journeys." SLJ

Cremer, Andrea
Invisibility; Andrea Cremer and David Levithan. Philomel Books 2013 320 p. (hardcover) $18.99

Grades: 7 8 9 10 11 12   **Fic**
1. Love -- Fiction 2. Invisibility -- Fiction 3. Magic -- Fiction 4. Charms -- Fiction 5. Friendship -- Fiction 6. Family problems -- Fiction 7. New York (N.Y.) -- Fiction
ISBN 0399257608; 9780399257605
LC 2012024514

This book by Andrea Cremer and David Levithan chronicles the "romance between a boy cursed with invisibility and the one girl who can see him. . . . Stephen is used to invisibility. He was born that way. . . . Elizabeth sometimes wishes for invisibility. . . . To Stephen's amazement, she can see him. And to Elizabeth's amazement, she wants him to be able to see her--all of her. But as the two become closer, an invisible world gets in their way." (Publisher's note)

"hough it begins as a stumbling, near-coming-out story (for Stephen), the novel deftly switches gears to a fast-paced supernatural thriller that will surely leave readers wanting more." Kirkus

Crewe, Megan
Give up the ghost. Henry Holt and Co. 2009 244p $17.99

Grades: 7 8 9 10   **Fic**
1. Ghost stories 2. School stories 3. Sisters -- Fiction 4. Bereavement -- Fiction
ISBN 978-0-8050-8930-1; 0-8050-8930-6
LC 2008-50274

Sixteen-year-old Cass's only friends are her dead sister and the school ghosts who feed her gossip that she uses to make students face up to their bad behavior, but when a popular boy asks for her help, she begins to reach out to the living again.

The story "provides page-turning action. . . . Mysterious plot elements and the budding relationship between Cass and the VP will quickly engage reluctant readers." Publ Wkly

The **lives** we lost; a Way we fall novel. Megan Crewe. Hyperion 2013 288 p. (The fallen world) (alk. paper) $16.99

Grades: 7 8 9 10 11 12   **Fic**
1. Science fiction 2. Epidemics -- Fiction 3. Survival skills -- Fiction 4. Survival -- Fiction 5. Virus diseases -- Fiction
ISBN 1423146174; 9781423146179
LC 2012032510

This novel, by Megan Crewe, is book two of "The Fallen World Trilogy." "A deadly virus has destroyed Kaelyn's small island community and spread beyond the quarantine. No one is safe. But when Kaelyn finds samples of a vaccine in her father's abandoned lab, she knows there must be someone, somewhere, who can replicate it. . . . How much will Kaelyn risk for an unproven cure, when the search could either destroy those she loves or save the human race?" (Publisher's note)

Crichton, Michael
Jurassic Park; a novel. Knopf 1990 399p $28.95; pa $7.99

Grades: 7 8 9 10 11 12 Adult   **Fic**
  1. Science fiction 2. Dinosaurs -- Fiction 3. Genetic engineering -- Fiction
ISBN 0-394-58816-9; 0-345-37077-5 pa
                  LC 90-52960
"Crichton is a master at blending technology with fiction. . . . Suspense, excitement, and good adventure pervade this book." SLJ
Followed by The lost world (1995)

Crocker, Nancy
  ★ **Billie** Standish was here. Simon & Schuster Books for Young Readers 2007 281p $16.99
Grades: 7 8 9 10   **Fic**
  1. Rape -- Fiction 2. Missouri -- Fiction 3. Friendship -- Fiction 4. Child abuse -- Fiction
ISBN 978-1-4169-2423-4; 1-4169-2423-X
                LC 2006-32688
When the river jeopardizes the levee and most of the town leaves, Miss Lydia, an elderly neighbor, and Billie form a friendship that withstands tragedy and time.
  "This story is beautiful, painful, and complex, and the descriptions of people, events, and emotions are graphic and tangible. The rape scene is described but not sensationalized." SLJ

Crockett, S. D.
  After the snow; S. D. Crockett. Feiwel & Friends 2012 304 p. (hardback) $22.55
Grades: 6 7 8 9 10 11 12   **Fic**
  1. Science fiction 2. Adventure fiction 3. Winter -- Fiction 4. Missing persons -- Fiction 5. Children and war -- Fiction 6. Survival -- Fiction 7. Voyages and travels -- Fiction 8. Adventure and adventurers -- Fiction
ISBN 9780312641696
                LC 2011036122
William C. Morris Award Finalist (2013)
In this book, "Willo's father can still remember what life was like in Great Britain before the country entered a new ice age. . . . When his father and the rest of his family mysteriously disappear, Willo leaves the scant safety of home to search for them. . . . [He] saves a . . . girl he encounters along the way, and together they find their way into the city, in which a long-dormant resistance movement is preparing for a final desperate exodus." (Bulletin of the Center for Children's Books)

  One Crow Alone; by S.D. Crockett. Feiwel & Friends 2013 320 p. $16.99
Grades: 6 7 8 9 10 11 12   **Fic**
  1. Evacuation of civilians 2. Mother-daughter relationship -- Fiction
ISBN 1250024250; 9781250024251
In this book, by S.D. Crockett, "living in an isolated Polish village with her grandmother, fifteen-year-old Magda Krol has no idea of the troubles sweeping across the planet. But when her village is evacuated without her, Magda must make her way alone across the frozen wilderness to Krakow, and then on to London, where she dreams of finding warmth and safety with her long-lost mother." (Publisher's note)

Cross, Gillian, 1945-
  Where I belong. Holiday House 2011 245p $17.95
Grades: 7 8 9 10   **Fic**
  1. Somalia -- Fiction 2. Refugees -- Fiction 3. Kidnapping -- Fiction 4. London (England) -- Fiction 5. Fashion designers -- Fiction
ISBN 978-0-8234-2332-3; 0-8234-2332-8
                LC 2010-23671
This is a "fast-paced adventure. . . . The fashion element will engage readers who would otherwise not read this genre. . . . This broadly appealing title has an engaging cover and is a worthy addition to any collection." SLJ

Cross, Julie
  Tempest; Julie Cross. St. Martin's Griffin 2012 339p. (hardback) $17.99
Grades: 8 9 10 11 12   **Fic**
  1. Love stories 2. Science fiction 3. Suspense fiction 4. Young men -- Fiction 5. Time travel -- Fiction 6. Spies -- Fiction
ISBN 9780312568894
                LC 2011032799
This novel follows "[n]ineteen-year-old Jackson Meyer . . . [who is] able to jump a couple of hours back in time . . . [and decides to] keep his . . . skill set a secret from his overprotective father and his beloved girlfriend Holly. When two armed men attempt to kidnap Jackson, shooting and most likely killing Holly in the process, Jackson time-jumps in a panic and inexplicably finds himself in 2007, where he is stuck until he can figure out how to get back to the future and save Holly. In the meantime, Jackson discovers that the man he has called Dad all these years is not in fact his father but rather a CIA agent and part of a shadowy government experiment called Tempest—an experiment that includes Jackson as one of its results." (Bulletin of the Center for Children's Books)

Cross, Sarah
  Dull boy. Dutton Childrens Books 2009 308p $17.99
Grades: 7 8 9 10   **Fic**
  1. Science fiction 2. Superheroes -- Fiction 3. Supernatural -- Fiction
ISBN 978-0-525-42133-7; 0-525-42133-5
                LC 2008-34208
Avery, a teenaged boy with frightening super powers that he is trying to hide, discovers other teenagers who also have strange powers and who are being sought by the icy and seductive Cherchette, but they do not know what she wants with them.
  "Avery's narration, generously peppered with swear words, is hip, witty, funny, and sarcastic." SLJ

Crossan, Sarah
  Breathe; Sarah Crossan. Greenwillow Books 2012 373 p. (hardback) $17.99
Grades: 7 8 9 10 11 12   **Fic**
  1. Friendship -- Fiction 2. Dystopian Fiction 3. Science fiction 4. Survival -- Fiction 5. Insurgency -- Fiction
ISBN 0062118692; 9780062118691
                LC 2012017496

In author Sarah Crossan's book, "Alina has been stealing for a long time . . . Quinn should be worried about Alina and a bit afraid for himself, too, but . . . it isn't every day that the girl of your dreams asks you to rescue her. Bea wants to tell him that none of this is fair; they'd planned a trip together, the two of them, and she'd hoped he'd discover her out here, not another girl. And as they walk into the Outlands with two days' worth of oxygen in their tanks, everything they believe will be shattered. Will they be able to make it back? Will they want to?" (Publisher's note)

★ The **Weight** of Water; by Sarah Crossan. Bloomsbury USA 2013 224 p. $16.99
Grades: 5 6 7 8   **Fic**
1. Novels in verse 2. England -- Fiction 3. Swimming -- Fiction 4. Race relations -- Fiction 5. Coventry (England) -- Fiction 6. Immigrants -- England -- Fiction 7. Mothers and daughters -- Fiction
ISBN 1599909677; 9781599909677
LC 2012038645
In this book, "12-year-old Kasienka moves with Mama from Gdansk, Poland, to Coventry, England, to find Tata, her father. The adjustment is difficult. At school, Kasienka is ostracized. At home, she questions why they are searching for a man who ran from them. When Kasienka complains, Mama questions her love. Kasienka feels powerful only when she swims at the pool—something Tata taught her to do. That is also where William, a schoolmate, first notices her." (Kirkus Reviews)

Crossley-Holland, Kevin
★ **Crossing** to Paradise. Arthur A. Levine Books 2008 339p $17.99
Grades: 7 8 9 10   **Fic**
1. Kings 2. Singing -- Fiction 3. Literacy -- Fiction 4. Middle Ages -- Fiction 5. Christian life -- Fiction 6. Pilgrims and pilgrimages -- Fiction 7. Great Britain -- History -- 1154-1399, Plantagenets -- Fiction
ISBN 978-0-545-05866-7; 0-545-05866-X; 978-0-545-05868-1 pa; 0-545-05868-6 pa
LC 2007-51853
First published 2006 in the United Kingdom with title: Gatty's tale
Gatty, the field-girl who appeared in the author's trilogy about King Arthur, is now an orphan. When she is selected for a pilgrimage, she travels from her home on an English estate to London, Venice, and eventually Jerusalem. "Grades six to ten." (Bull Cent Child Books)
"Gatty, the irrepressible peasant girl first introduced in Crossley-Holland's 'Arthur' trilogy . . . comes into her own in this sweeping, vibrant story." SLJ

Crowder, Melanie
Parched; by Melanie Crowder. New York""||"Harcourt Children's Books, Houghton Mifflin Harcourt 2013 160 p. (hardback) $15.99
Grades: 5 6 7 8   **Fic**
1. Voyages and travels -- Fiction 2. Dogs -- Fiction 3. Africa -- Fiction 4. Drought -- Fiction 5. Survival -- Fiction 6. Rhodesian ridgeback -- Fiction
ISBN 0547976518; 9780547976518
LC 2013003914

This book "tells of two young teens working together to survive a devastating drought in southern Africa. Musa, an African boy, has been sold into slavery because of his dowsing ability. His cruel owners keep him alive only to use his talents. Sarel, a Caucasian girl, faces an uncertain future after her parents are brutally shot by thugs looking for water. . . . Musa escapes his captors and flees toward the only water source he senses—across the desert, near Sarel's home." (School Library Journal)

Crowe, Chris
Mississippi trial, 1955. Penguin Putnam 2002 231p pa $5.99; $17.99
Grades: 7 8 9 10   **Fic**
1. Children 2. Racism 3. Grandfathers 4. Murder victims 5. Fathers and sons 6. Racism -- Fiction 7. Grandfathers -- Fiction 8. Mississippi -- Race relations
ISBN 0-14-250192-1 pa; 0-8037-2745-3
LC 2001-40221
In Mississippi in 1955, a sixteen-year-old finds himself at odds with his grandfather over issues surrounding the kidnapping and murder of a fourteen-year-old African American from Chicago. "Grades seven to ten." (Bull Cent Child Books)
"By combining real events with their impact upon a single fictional character, Crowe makes the issues in this novel hard-hitting and personal. The characters are complex." Voice Youth Advocates

Crowley, Cath
A **little** wanting song. Knopf 2010 265p $16.99; lib bdg $19.99
Grades: 8 9 10 11 12   **Fic**
1. Shyness -- Fiction 2. Australia -- Fiction 3. Musicians -- Fiction 4. Friendship -- Fiction 5. Loneliness -- Fiction
ISBN 978-0-375-86096-6; 0-375-86096-7; 978-0-375-96096-3 lib bdg; 0-375-96096-1 lib bdg
LC 2009-20305
First published 2005 in Australia with title: Chasing Charlie Duskin
One Australian summer, two very different sixteen-year-old girls—Charlie, a talented but shy musician, and Rose, a confident student longing to escape her tiny town—are drawn into an unexpected friendship, as told in their alternating voices
"Crowley's prose is lyrical and lovely, her characters are beautifully crafted, and her portrayal of teen life in Australia is a delight. . . . Female readers especially will enjoy this upbeat tale." Voice Youth Advocates

Crowley, James
Starfish; illustrations by Jim Madsen. Disney/Hyperion Books 2010 310p il $16.99
Grades: 4 5 6 7   **Fic**
1. Adventure fiction 2. Montana -- Fiction 3. Siblings -- Fiction 4. Siksika Indians -- Fiction 5. Runaway children -- Fiction
ISBN 978-1-4231-2588-4; 1-4231-2588-6
In the early part of the 1900s, Beatrice and Lionel, two Blackfeet Indian children, escape from the Chalk Bluff Indian Boarding School in Montana to find their grandfather,

and must elude their pursuers and make a life for themselves in the wilderness.

"This is a fast-paced and interesting novel that will maintain reader interest. Readers will be drawn into the plight of Native Americans trying to survive brutal conditions." Libr Media Connect

Crowley, Suzanne

The **stolen** one. Greenwillow Books 2009 406p $17.99; lib bdg $18.89

Grades: 8 9 10 11 12 **Fic**

1. Queens 2. Orphans -- Fiction 3. London (England) -- Fiction 4. Great Britain -- History -- 1485-1603, Tudors -- Fiction

ISBN 978-0-06-123200-8; 0-06-123200-9; 978-0-06-123201-5 lib bdg; 0-06-123201-7 lib bdg

LC 2008-15039

After the death of her foster mother, sixteen-year-old Kat goes to London to seek the answers to her parentage, and surprisingly finds herself invited into Queen Elizabeth's court.

"Intrigue, romance, and period details abound in this riveting story of Tudor England. . . . The sophisticated writing flows well, and the author does a terrific job of integrating historical details." SLJ

Crutcher, Chris

★ **Deadline**. Greenwillow Books 2007 316p $16.99; lib bdg $17.89; pa $8.99

Grades: 8 9 10 11 12 **Fic**

1. School stories 2. Death -- Fiction 3. Terminally ill -- Fiction

ISBN 978-0-06-085089-0; 0-06-085089-2; 978-0-06-085090-6 lib bdg; 0-06-085090-6 lib bdg; 978-0-06-085091-3 pa; 0-06-085091-4 pa

LC 2006-31526

Given the medical diagnosis of one year to live, high school senior Ben Wolf decides to fulfill his greatest fantasies, ponders his life's purpose and legacy, and converses through dreams with a spiritual guide known as "Hey-Soos."

"Ben's sensitive voice uses self-deprecating humor, philosophical pondering, and effective dramatic irony." Voice Youth Advocates

Ironman; a novel. Greenwillow Bks. 1995 181p $16.99; pa $6.99

Grades: 8 9 10 11 12 **Fic**

1. School stories 2. Triathlon -- Fiction 3. Father-son relationship -- Fiction

ISBN 0-688-13503-X; 0-06-059840-9 pa

LC 94-1657

While training for a triathlon, seventeen-year-old Bo attends Mr. Nak's anger management group at school which leads him to examine his relationship with his father.

"Through Crutcher's masterful character development, readers will believe in Bo, empathize with the other members of the anger-management group, absorb the wisdom of Mr. Nak and despise, yet at times pity, the boy's father. This is not a light read, as many serious issues surface, though the author's trademark dark humor (and colorful use of street language) is abundant." SLJ

Running loose. Greenwillow Bks. 1983 190p hardcover o.p. pa $8.99; pa $6.99

Grades: 7 8 9 10 **Fic**

1. School stories

ISBN 9780060094911 pa; 0-688-02002-X; 0-06-009491-5 pa

LC 82-20935

ALA YALSA Margaret A. Edwards Award (2000)

"Louie Banks tells what happened to him in his senior year in a small town Idaho high school. Besides falling in love with Becky and losing her in a senseless accident, Louie takes a stand against the coach when he sets the team up to injure a black player on an opposing team, and learns that you can't be honorable with dishonorable men. . . . Grade seven and up." (Voice Youth Advocates)

"Louie Banks tells what happened to him in his senior year in a small town Idaho high school. Besides falling in love with Becky and losing her in a senseless accident, Louie takes a stand against the coach when he sets the team up to injure a black player on an opposing team, and learns that you can't be honorable with dishonorable men." Voice Youth Advocates

Staying fat for Sarah Byrnes. Greenwillow Bks. 1993 216p hardcover o.p. pa $6.99

Grades: 7 8 9 10 **Fic**

1. Obesity -- Fiction 2. Swimming -- Fiction 3. Friendship -- Fiction 4. Child abuse -- Fiction

ISBN 0-688-11552-7; 0-06-009489-3 pa

LC 91-40097

ALA YALSA Margaret A. Edwards Award (2000)

"An obese boy and a disfigured girl suffer the emotional scars of years of mockery at the hands of their peers. They share a hard-boiled view of the world until events in their senior year hurl them in very different directions. A story about a friendship with staying power, written with pathos and pointed humor." SLJ

Stotan! HarperTempest 2003 261p pa $6.99

Grades: 7 8 9 10 **Fic**

1. Swimming -- Fiction

ISBN 0-06-009492-3

LC 85-12712

First published 1986

ALA YALSA Margaret A. Edwards Award (2000)

A high school coach invites members of his swimming team to a memorable week of rigorous training that tests their moral fiber as well as their physical stamina.

"A subplot involving the boys' fight against local Neo-Nazi activists provides some immediate action, while the various characters' conflicts tighten the middle and ending. The pace lags through the story's introduction; nevertheless, this is a searching sports novel, with a tone varying from macho-tough to sensitive." Bull Cent Child Books

Whale talk. Greenwillow Bks. 2001 220p $15.99; pa $8.99

Grades: 7 8 9 10 **Fic**

1. School stories 2. Swimming -- Fiction 3. Racially mixed people -- Fiction

ISBN 0-688-18019-1; 0-06-177131-7 pa

LC 00-59292

Intellectually and athletically gifted, TJ, a multiracial, adopted teenager, shuns organized sports and the gung-ho athletes at his high school until he agrees to form a swimming team and recruits some of the school's less popular students

"This remarkable novel is vintage Crutcher: heart-pounding athletic competitions, raw emotion, an insufferable high school atmosphere that allows bullying and reveres athletes, and a larger-than-life teen hero who champions the underdog while skewering both racists and abusers with his rapier-sharp wit." Book Rep

Cullen, Lynn

★ **I** am Rembrandt's daughter. Bloomsbury Children's Books 2007 307p $16.95

Grades: 7 8 9 10 **Fic**

1. Artists 2. Etchers 3. Painters 4. Drafters 5. Plague -- Fiction 6. Artists -- Fiction 7. Poverty -- Fiction 8. Netherlands -- Fiction 9. Father-daughter relationship -- Fiction

ISBN 978-1-59990-046-9; 1-59990-046-7

LC 2006-28197

In Amsterdam in the mid-1600s, Cornelia's life as the illegitimate child of renowned painter Rembrandt is marked by plague, poverty, and despair at ever earning her father's love, until she sees hope for a better future in the eyes of a weathy suitor.

"Historical fiction, mystery, and romance are masterfully woven. . . . Cullen's novel is a reader's delight." Voice Youth Advocates

Cummings, Priscilla

★ **Blindsided**. Dutton Children's Books 2010 226p $16.99

Grades: 7 8 9 10 **Fic**

1. School stories 2. Blind -- Fiction 3. Maryland -- Fiction

ISBN 978-0-525-42161-0; 0-525-42161-0

LC 2009-25092

"Natalie, 14, knows that her future is becoming dimmer as the loss of her eyesight is a nightmare she can't avoid. . . . Part of going from denial to acceptance is attending a boarding school for the blind. . . . Natalie is a credible character and her fear is palpable and painful. . . . Readers will enjoy the high drama and heroics." SLJ

The **journey** back; Priscilla Cummings. Dutton Children's Books 2012 243 p. (hardcover) $16.99

Grades: 7 8 9 10 **Fic**

1. Fugitives from justice -- Fiction 2. Camping -- Fiction 3. Maryland -- Fiction 4. Coming of age -- Fiction 5. Conduct of life -- Fiction 6. Voyages and travels -- Fiction 7. Fugitives from justice -- Fiction 8. Juvenile detention homes -- Fiction

ISBN 0525423621; 9780525423621

LC 2012003818

In this novel by Priscilla Cummings Digger is "escaped and on the run. . . . His bold escape from a juvenile detention facility nearly kills him, but soon an angry fourteen-year-old Digger is . . . hijacking a tractor trailer, 'borrowing' a bicycle, and stealing a canoe. When injuries stop him, Digger hides at a riverside campground . . . New friends, a job caring for rescued horses, and risking his life to save another

make Digger realize that the journey back is not just about getting home." (Publisher's note)

Red kayak; Priscilla Cummings. 1st ed; Dutton Children's Books 2004 209p $15.99; pa $6.99

Grades: 7 8 9 10 **Fic**

1. Death -- Fiction 2. Maryland -- Fiction 3. Friendship -- Fiction

ISBN 0-525-47317-3; 0-14-240573-4 pa

LC 2003-63532

Living near the water on Maryland's Eastern Shore, thirteen-year-old Brady and his best friends J.T. and Digger become entangled in a tragedy which tests their friendship and their ideas about right and wrong.

"This well-crafted story will have broad appeal." SLJ

Currier, Katrina Saltonstall

Kai's journey to Gold Mountain; an Angel Island story. illustrated by Gabhor Utomo. Angel Island Association 2005 39p il $16.95

Grades: 4 5 6 7 **Fic**

1. Immigrants -- Fiction 2. Chinese Americans -- Fiction 3. Los Angeles (Calif.) -- Fiction

ISBN 0-9667352-4-2

LC 2004-14821

In 1934, twelve-year-old Kai leaves China to join his father in America, but first he must take a long sea voyage, then endure weeks of crowded conditions and harsh examinations on Angel Island, fearing that he or his new friend will be sent home.

"The character Kai is based on a real person, whose photos, then and now, are part of the historical notes at the back of the book. Opposite each page of the intensely moving, detailed text are beautiful full-page watercolor-and-pencil illustrations that capture the crowded holding place, and, in unforgettable closeups, the characters' heartbreak and strength." Booklist

Curry, Jane Louise

The **Black** Canary. Margaret K. McElderry Books 2005 279p $16.95

Grades: 5 6 7 8 **Fic**

1. Generals 2. Courtiers 3. Conspirators 4. Royal favorites 5. Singers -- Fiction 6. London (England) -- Fiction 7. Racially mixed people -- Fiction 8. Great Britain -- History -- 1485-1603, Tudors -- Fiction

ISBN 0-689-86478-7

LC 2003-26150

As the child of two musicians, twelve-year-old James has no interest in music until he discovers a portal to seventeenth-century London in his uncle's basement, and finds himself in a situation where his beautiful voice and the fact that he is biracial might serve him well.

"A genuinely good story that conveys a sense of darkness and mystery in the textured backdrop of a storied time and place." Booklist

Curtis, Christopher Paul

★ **Bud,** not Buddy. Delacorte Press 1999 245p $16.95; pa $6.50

Grades: 4 5 6 7 **Fic**

1. Orphans -- Fiction 2. African Americans -- Fiction

3. Great Depression, 1929-1939 -- Fiction
ISBN 0-385-32306-9; 0-440-41328-1 pa

LC 99-10614

Awarded the Newbery Medal, 2000
Coretta Scott King Award for text

Ten-year-old Bud, a motherless boy living in Flint, Michigan, during the Great Depression, escapes a bad foster home and sets out in search of the man he believes to be his father—the renowned bandleader, H. E. Calloway of Grand Rapids

"Curtis says in a afterword that some of the characters are based on real people, including his own grandfathers, so it's not surprising that the rich blend of tall tale, slapstick, sorrow, and sweetness has the wry, teasing warmth of family folklore." Booklist

★ **Elijah** of Buxton. Scholastic 2007 341p $16.99; pa $7.99

Grades: 5 6 7 8   Fic

1. Canada -- Fiction 2. Slavery -- Fiction
ISBN 0-439-02344-0; 978-0-439-02344-3; 0-439-02345-9 pa; 978-0-439-02345-0 pa

LC 2007-05181

A Newbery Medal honor book, 2008

In 1859, eleven-year-old Elijah Freeman, the first freeborn child in Buxton, Canada, which is a haven for slaves fleeing the American south, uses his wits and skills to try to bring to justice the lying preacher who has stolen money that was to be used to buy a family's freedom.

"Many readers drawn to the book by humor will find themselves at times on the edges of their seats in suspense and, at other moments, moved to tears." Booklist

★ The **Watsons** go to Birmingham--1963; a novel. Delacorte Press 1995 210p $16.95; pa $6.50

Grades: 4 5 6 7   Fic

1. Prejudices -- Fiction 2. Family life -- Fiction 3. African Americans -- Fiction
ISBN 0-385-32175-9; 0-440-41412-1 pa

LC 95-7091

A Newbery Medal honor book, 1996

The ordinary interactions and everyday routines of the Watsons, an African American family living in Flint, Michigan, are drastically changed after they go to visit Grandma in Alabama in the summer of 1963

"Curtis's ability to switch from fun and funky to pinpoint-accurate psychological imagery works unusually well. . . . Ribald humor, sly sibling digs, and a totally believable child's view of the world will make this book an instant hit." SLJ

Curtis, Christopher Paul, 1953-

★ The **madman** of Piney Woods; Christopher Paul Curtis. Scholastic Press 2014 384 p. $16.99 Fic

1. Adventure fiction 2. n 3. Freedmen -- Fiction 4. Veterans -- Fiction 5. Immigrants -- Fiction 6. Irish -- Canada -- Fiction 7. Blacks -- Canada -- Fiction 8. Canada -- History -- 1867-1914 -- Fiction 9. Post-traumatic stress disorder -- Fiction 10. Chatham (Ont.) -- History -- 20th century -- Fiction 11. North Buxton

(Ont.) -- History -- 20th century -- Fiction
ISBN 0545156645; 9780545156646; 9780545156653; 9780545633765

LC 2014003493

"Benji and Red couldn't be more different. They aren't friends. They don't even live in the same town. But their fates are entwined. A chance meeting leads the boys to discover that they have more in common than meets the eye. Both of them have encountered a strange presence in the forest, watching them, tracking them. Could the Madman of Piney Woods be real?" (Publisher's note)

Cushman, Karen

★ **Alchemy** and Meggy Swann. Clarion Books 2010 167p $16

Grades: 5 6 7 8   Fic

1. Alchemy -- Fiction 2. Poverty -- Fiction 3. Physically disabled -- Fiction 4. London (England) -- Fiction 5. Father-daughter relationship -- Fiction 6. Great Britain -- History -- 1485-1603, Tudors -- Fiction
ISBN 978-0-547-23184-6; 0-547-23184-9

LC 2009-16387

In 1573, the crippled, scorned, and destitute Meggy Swann goes to London, where she meets her father, an impoverished alchemist, and eventually discovers that although her legs are bent and weak, she has many other strengths.

"Writing with admirable economy and a lively ability to recreate the past believably, Cushman creates a memorable portrayal of a troubled, rather mulish girl who begins to use her strong will in positive ways." Booklist

The **ballad** of Lucy Whipple. Clarion Bks. 1996 195p $15; $16.00

Grades: 5 6 7 8   Fic

1. Family life -- Fiction 2. Frontier and pioneer life -- Fiction 3. California -- Gold discoveries -- Fiction
ISBN 0-395-72806-1; 9780395728062

LC 95-45257

"Twelve-year-old Lucy is taken by her mother from their comfortable 19th-century home in Massachusetts to the rough-and-tumble California goldfields. Lucy's younger siblings don't object to this new life, but Lucy dislikes the dirt, hard work, and lack of civilization—especially reading material. When not helping Mama run Mr. Scatter's boarding house for miners, Lucy spends her time complaining or scheming a return to her beloved Massachusetts. Despite the losses she suffers in the makeshift town of Lucky Diggins, Lucy makes some surprising discoveries about herself and what she's gained in the West." (Christ Sci Monit) "Grades five to eight." (Booklist)

"Cushman's heroine is a delightful character, and the historical setting is authentically portrayed." SLJ

★ **Catherine,** called Birdy. Clarion Bks. 1994 169p $16

Grades: 6 7 8 9   Fic

1. Middle Ages -- Fiction 2. Great Britain -- Fiction
ISBN 0-395-68186-3

LC 93-23333

A Newbery Medal honor book, 1995

The fourteen-year-old daughter of an English country knight keeps a journal in which she records the events of her life, particularly her longing for adventures beyond the usual role of women and her efforts to avoid being married off

"In the process of telling the routines of her young life, Birdy lays before readers a feast of details about medieval England. . . . Superb historical fiction." SLJ

The **loud** silence of Francine Green. Clarion Books 2006 225p $16

Grades: 6 7 8 9   **Fic**

  1. School stories 2. Family life -- Fiction 3. Los Angeles (Calif.) -- Fiction 4. United States -- Politics and government -- 1945-1953 -- Fiction

  ISBN 978-0-618-50455-8; 0-618-50455-9

                LC 2005-29774

In 1949, thirteen-year-old Francine goes to Catholic school in Los Angeles where she becomes best friends with a girl who questions authority and is frequently punished by the nuns, causing Francine to question her own values.

Readers will "savor the story of friends and family tensions, the sly humor, and the questions about patriotism, activism, and freedom." Booklist

★ The **midwife's** apprentice. Clarion Bks. 1995 122p $12; pa $5.99

Grades: 6 7 8 9   **Fic**

  1. Midwives -- Fiction 2. Middle Ages -- Fiction 3. Great Britain -- Fiction

  ISBN 0-395-69229-6; 0-06-440630-X pa

                LC 94-13792

Awarded the Newbery Medal, 1996

In medieval England, a nameless, homeless girl is taken in by a sharp-tempered midwife, and in spite of obstacles and hardship, eventually gains the three things she most wants: a full belly, a contented heart, and a place in this world

"Earthy humor, the foibles of humans both high and low, and a fascinating mix of superstition and genuinely helpful herbal remedies attached to childbirth make this a truly delightful introduction to a world seldom seen in children's literature." SLJ

★ **Rodzina.** Clarion Bks. 2003 215p $16; pa $6.50

Grades: 5 6 7 8   **Fic**

  1. Orphans -- Fiction 2. Polish Americans -- Fiction

  ISBN 0-618-13351-8; 0-440-41993-X pa

                LC 2002-15976

A twelve-year-old Polish American girl is boarded onto an orphan train in Chicago with fears about traveling to the West and a life of unpaid slavery

"The story features engaging characters, a vivid setting, and a prickly but endearing heroine. . . . Rodzina's musings and observations provide poignancy, humor, and a keen sense of the human and topographical landscape." SLJ

Includes bibliographical references

★ **Will** Sparrow's road; Karen Cushman. Clarion Books 2012 216 p. (hardback) $16.99

Grades: 5 6 7 8   **Fic**

  1. Historical fiction 2. Runaway children -- Fiction 3. Swindlers and swindling -- Fiction 4. Runaways -- Fiction 5. Freak shows -- Fiction 6. Conduct of life -- Fiction 7. Great Britain -- History -- Elizabeth, 1558-

1603 -- Fiction

  ISBN 0547739621; 9780547739625

                LC 2011045898

In this book by Karen Cushman, set in Elizabethan England, "Will Sparrow, liar and thief, becomes a runaway. On the road, he encounters a series of con artists . . . and learns that others are more adept than he at lying and thieving. Then he reluctantly joins a traveling troupe of 'oddities,' including a dwarf and a cat-faced girl. . . . At last Will is forced to understand that appearances are misleading and that he has been his own worst deceiver." (Publisher's note)

Includes bibliographical references.

Cypess, Leah

Death sworn; by Leah Cypess. Greenwillow Books, an imprint of HarperCollinsPublishers 2014 352 p. (hardback) $17.99

Grades: 7 8 9 10 11 12   **Fic**

  1. Love stories 2. Fantasy fiction 3. Magic -- Fiction 4. Assassins -- Fiction 5. Fantasy 6. Love -- Fiction 7. Secrets -- Fiction

  ISBN 0062221213; 9780062221216

                LC 2013037379

In this book, by Leah Cypress, "when a young sorceress is exiled to teach magic to a clan of assassins, she will find that secrets can be even deadlier than swords. . . . Ileni is losing her magic. And that means she's losing everything: her position as the rising star of her people, her purpose in life, and even the young man she loves. . . . Sent to the assassins' cave, . . . she'll find an ally in Sorin, the deadly young man who could be the assassins' next leader. . . . Sparks--magical and romantic--will fly." (Publisher's note)

"As seventeen-year-old Ileni's magic begins to fade, she's sent to the Black Mountain to tutor assassins in sorcery. With the help of Sorin, her student and assigned protector, she must discover who killed her predecessors before someone kills her. Ileni proves a compelling protagonist, and the blend of romance, assassins, magic, and murder-mystery consistently raises the stakes." Horn Book

Mistwood. Greenwillow Books 2010 304p $16.99

Grades: 7 8 9 10   **Fic**

  1. Fantasy fiction 2. Magic -- Fiction 3. Kings and rulers -- Fiction

  ISBN 978-0-06-195699-7; 0-06-195699-6

                LC 2009-23051

Brought back from the Mistwood to protect the royal family, a girl who has no memory of being a shape-shifter encounters political and magical intrigue as she struggles with her growing feelings for the prince.

"A traditional premise is transformed into a graceful meditation on the ramifications of loyalty, duty and purpose. . . . Astonishing and inspiring." Kirkus

Nightspell. Greenwillow Books 2011 326p $16.99

Grades: 7 8 9 10   **Fic**

  1. Ghost stories 2. Dead -- Fiction 3. Sisters -- Fiction 4. Kings and rulers -- Fiction

  ISBN 978-0-06-195702-4; 0-06-195702-X

                LC 2010012637

Sent by her father, the king of Raellia, who is trying to forge an empire out of warring tribes, Darri arrives in Ghostland and discovers that her sister, whom she planned to rescue, may not want to leave this land where the dead mingle freely with the living.

"Swordfights, blood, and double-dealing pack the pages as this action-filled story races to a surprising conclusion." Booklist

D'Adamo, Francesco

Iqbal; a novel. written by Francesco D'Adamo; translated by Ann Leonori. Atheneum Bks. for Young Readers 2003 120p $15.95; pa $4.99

Grades: 5 6 7 8　　　　　　　　　　　　　　　**Fic**

1. Murder victims 2. Factory workers 3. Pakistan -- Fiction 4. Child labor -- Fiction 5. Children's rights advocates

ISBN 0-689-85445-5; 1-4169-0329-1 pa

LC 2002-153498

Original Italian edition, 2001

A fictionalized account of the Pakistani child who escaped from bondage in a carpet factory and went on to help liberate other children like him before being gunned down at the age of thirteen

"The situation and setting are made clear in this novel. Readers cannot help but be moved by the plight of these youngsters. . . . This readable book will certainly add breadth to most collections." SLJ

D'Lacey, Chris

The **fire** ascending; by Chris D'Lacey. 1st Scholastic ed. Orchard Books 2012 560 p. (hardcover) $18.99

Grades: 6 7 8 9　　　　　　　　　　　　　　　**Fic**

1. Fantasy fiction 2. Fantasy 3. Magic -- Fiction 4. Dragons -- Fiction 5. Voyages and travels -- Fiction 6. Quests (Expeditions) -- Fiction

ISBN 0545402166; 9780545402163

LC 2012003120

This book is the seventh installment of Chris D'Lacey's Last Dragon Chronicles series. The story follows "a young boy named Agawin. He's raised by a seer and lives near the peak of Kasgarden where the dragon Galen has gone to shed its dying tear. . . . Evil comes in the forms of Sybyl's like Hilde and Gwilanna, then there's the darkling army led by Voss in search of the fraas (sparks emitted from a dying dragon's tear)." (Children's Literature)

The **fire** within. Orchard Books 2005 340p $15.99

Grades: 6 7 8 9　　　　　　　　　　　　　　　**Fic**

1. Dragons -- Fiction 2. Authorship -- Fiction 3. Supernatural -- Fiction

ISBN 0-439-67244-9

LC 2004-58327

When college student David Rain rents a room in an unusual boardinghouse full of clay dragons, he has no idea that they, along with some lively squirrels, will help jumpstart his writing career.

This "has a satisfying domestic reality, spiced with some very unusual dragons." SLJ

Other titles in this series are:

Icefire (2006)

Fire star (2007)
The fire eternal (2008)
Dark fire (2010)
Fire world (2011)

Dagg, Carole Estby

★ The **year** we were famous. Clarion Books 2011 250p $16.99

Grades: 6 7 8 9 10　　　　　　　　　　　　　**Fic**

1. Adventure fiction 2. Voyages and travels -- Fiction 3. Mother-daughter relationship -- Fiction

ISBN 978-0-618-99983-5; 0-618-99983-3

"Dagg writes a captivating story about the determination of a mother and daughter, who in 1896 walked from Washington State to New York City. . . . Clara's free-spirited but unreliable mother suggests that they walk nearly 4,000 miles to save their farm from foreclosure (a publisher offers them a 10,000 advance if they make it in seven months) and bring attention to the suffragist movement. . . . The pages go by quickly. . . . The journey in itself is amazing, but Dagg's tender portrayal of a mother and daughter who learn to appreciate and forgive each other makes it unforgettable." Publ Wkly

Dakin, Glenn

The **Society** of Dread. Egmont USA 2010 318p (Candle Man) $15.99

Grades: 5 6 7 8　　　　　　　　　　　　　　　**Fic**

1. Adventure fiction 2. Superheroes -- Fiction

ISBN 978-1-60684-019-1; 1-60684-019-3

LC 2010023104

Sequel to: The Society of Unrelenting Vigilance (2009)

Now head of the Society of Good Works, teenaged Theo must reluctantly use his mysterious ability to melt evil when he ventures underground to face villains of old.

"This appealing contemporary fantasy has a fast-paced plot and enough inventive monsters and villains to captivate even the most reluctant readers." SLJ

The **Society** of Unrelenting Vigilance; [illustrations by Greg Swearingen] Egmont 2009 300p il (Candle Man) $15.99; lib bdg $18.99

Grades: 4 5 6 7　　　　　　　　　　　　　　　**Fic**

1. Adventure fiction 2. Superheroes -- Fiction

ISBN 978-1-60684-015-3; 1-60684-015-0; 978-1-60684-047-4 lib bdg; 1-60684-047-9 lib bdg

LC 2009-14035

Thirteen-year-old Theo, who has lived in seclusion his entire life, discovers he is the descendant of the Candle Man, a Victorian vigilante with the ability to melt criminals with a single touch.

This is a "lighthearted, action-driven adventure. . . . With the help of a cast of appealing characters, the nonstop action rolls to a satisfying conclusion." SLJ

Followed by: The Society of Dread (2010)

Daley, James Ryan

Jesus Jackson; James Ryan Daley. First edition Poisoned Pencil Press 2014 viii, 267 p (trade pbk : alk. paper) $10.95

Grades: 8 9 10 11 12　　　　　　　　　　　　**Fic**

1. Mystery fiction 2. Religion -- Fiction 3. High school

students -- Fiction 4. Death 5. Faith 6. Teenage boys 7. Brothers -- Death 8. Brothers and sisters
ISBN 1929345062; 9781929345069

LC 2014938496

"Jonathan Stiles is a 14-year-old atheist who is coping with his first day of ninth grade at the fervently religious St. Soren's Academy when his idolized older brother Ryan is found dead at the bottom of a ravine behind the school. As his world crumbles, Jonathan meets an eccentric stranger who bears an uncanny resemblance to Jesus Christ (except for his white linen leisure suit and sparkling gold chains)." (Publisher's note)

"The book excels, sidestepping holier-than-thou rhetoric and addressing the pain of loss head-on as well as painting a wonderful depiction of a young man coming to terms with how he was raised and how he wants to lead his own life. The mystery element and minor romance are icing on the cake: well-executed and finely tuned, complementing the book's major themes in all the right ways.Smart and sweet, comforting and moving. " Kirkus

Dallas, Sandra

The **quilt** walk; by Sandra Dallas. Sleeping Bear Press 2012 213 p. (hardcover) $15.95
Grades: 3 4 5 6 7   Fic
1. Oregon Trail 2. Quilts -- Fiction 3. Frontier and pioneer life 4. Historical fiction 5. Quilting -- Fiction 6. Friendship -- Fiction 7. Wagon trains -- Fiction 8. Frontier and pioneer life -- Fiction
ISBN 1585368008; 9781585367993; 9781585368006

LC 2012005863

This children's historical story, by Sandra Dallas, begins in "1863 and Emily Blue Hatchett has been told by her father that, come spring, their family will leave their farm . . . in Quincy, Illinois and travel the Overland Trail to a new home in Golden, Colorado. . . . When Emmy s grandmother comes to say goodbye, she gives Emmy a special gift, something to occupy her time along the trail. The journey by wagon train is long and full of hardships." (Publisher's note)

Daly, Cathleen

★ **Flirt** Club. Roaring Brook Press 2011 281p $15.99
Grades: 5 6 7 8   Fic
1. School stories 2. Clubs -- Fiction 3. Friendship -- Fiction
ISBN 978-1-59643-572-8; 1-59643-572-0

LC 2010-27473

Through notes and journal entries, best friends and self-proclaimed "drama geeks" Cisco (Izzy) and the Bean (Annie) write of the trials of middle school, as well as their efforts to attract boys by forming a Flirt Club.

"Told through very funny notes to each other, journal entries, and minutes from Flirt Club meetings, Daly's debut sparkles with wit, and her protagonists brim with enthusiasm and heart. . . . It's refreshing to see these girls counter middle-school drama with silliness rather than angst and hand-wringing." Publ Wkly

Damico, Gina

Croak; by Gina Damico. Houghton Mifflin Harcourt 2012 311 p. $8.99

Grades: 7 8 9 10   Fic
1. Mystery fiction 2. Soul -- Fiction 3. Death -- Fiction 4. Justice -- Fiction 5. Future life -- Fiction
ISBN 9780547608327

LC 2011017125

This book tells the story of "sixteen-year-old bad girl Lex Bartleby [who] is shipped off to her uncle Mort's farm, supposedly to figure out her anger issues with the help of manual labor. Instead, she learns that "farmer" Mort is a reaper of another kind entirely and that, as mayor of Croak, a small collection of Grim Reapers, he will be teaching Lex the family business. Although she initially takes to ferrying souls into the Afterlife with aplomb, Lex begins to question the roles of Reapers as silent witnesses to the world's injustices, especially when their knowledge of people's deaths would allow them to wreak karmic justice upon the murderers and rapists that otherwise get away with their crimes." (Bulletin of the Center for Children's Books)

Rogue; by Gina Damico. Graphia 2013 336 p. (paperback) $8.99
Grades: 8 9 10   Fic
1. Future life -- Fiction 2. Grim Reaper (Symbolic character) -- Fiction 3. Death -- Fiction 4. Humorous stories 5. Ghosts -- Fiction
ISBN 0544108841; 9780544108844

LC 2013004154

This book by Gina Damico follows a "band of surly teenage grim reapers risking everything on their mission to save the Afterlife. Uncle Mort's plan to save the Afterlife by enlisting Junior Grims to help destroy the portals that access it is full of risks, loopholes and secrets—and fiery-tempered, impulsive Lex is the plan's unstable lynchpin." (Kirkus Reviews)

Scorch; Gina Damico. Houghton Mifflin Harcourt 2012 332 p. (paperback) $8.99
Grades: 7 8 9 10   Fic
1. Fantasy fiction 2. Death -- Fiction 3. Humorous stories 4. Future life -- Fiction
ISBN 0547624573; 9780547624570

LC 2012014799

In this novel by Gina Damico "Lex is a full-time teenage grim reaper -- but now has the bizarre ability to Damn souls. . . . [S]he and her friends embark on a wild road trip to DeMyse. Though this sparkling desert oasis is full of luxuries and amusements, it feels like a prison to Lex. Her best chance at escape would be to stop all the senseless violence that she caused—but how can she do that from DeMyse, where the Grims seem mysteriously oblivious to the bloodshed?" (Publisher's note)

Daneshvari, Gitty

Class is not dismissed! [illustrations by Carrie Gifford] Little, Brown and Company 2010 307p il $16.99
Grades: 4 5 6   Fic
1. School stories 2. Phobias -- Fiction
ISBN 978-0-316-03328-2; 0-316-03328-6

LC 2010006889

Sequel to: School of Fear (2009)

Thirteen-year-olds Madeleine, Theo, and Lulu, fourteen-year-old Garrison, and ten-year-old new "contestant" Hyacinth, must face their phobias and join forces to learn who is stealing wigs and pageant trophies from the School of Fear.

"Filled with an eclectic, and often eccentric, cast of characters, this sequel uses the wry humor and outrageous situations that characterized the first book and makes for an entertaining read." SLJ

School of Fear; illustrated by Carrie Gifford. Little, Brown Books for Young Readers 2009 339p il $15.99

Grades: 4 5 6   **Fic**
1. School stories 2. Phobias -- Fiction
ISBN 978-0-316-03326-8; 0-316-03326-X
LC 2008051309

Twelve-year-olds Madeleine, Theo, and Lulu, and thirteen-year-old Garrison, are sent to a remote Massachusetts school to overcome their phobias, but tragedy strikes and the quartet must work together—with no adult assistance—to face their fears.

This is "tautly paced, spine-tingling and quite funny." Publ Wkly

Followed by: Class is not dismissed! (2010)

Danziger, Paula

The **cat** ate my gymsuit; [by] Paula Danziger. 30th anniversary edition; G.P. Putnam's Sons 2004 151p $15.99; pa $5.99

Grades: 4 5 6 7   **Fic**
1. School stories 2. Teachers -- Fiction
ISBN 0-399-24307-0; 0-14-240654-6 pa
LC 2004001892

A reissue of the title first published 1974 by Delacorte Press

When the unconventional English teacher who helped her conquer many of her feelings of insecurity is fired, thirteen-year-old Marcy Lewis uses her new found courage to campaign for the teacher's reinstatement.

"Paula Danziger's compassionate and accurate portrayal of a young girl struggling to find her own voice rings as true today as it did 30 years ago. A full cast brings this modern American classic of teenage angst to life with humor and pathos." SLJ

The **Divorce** Express. Delacorte Press 1982 148p il hardcover o.p. pa $5.99

Grades: 6 7 8 9   **Fic**
1. Divorce -- Fiction 2. Parent-child relationship -- Fiction
ISBN 0-14-240712-7 pa
LC 82-70318

This is "a warm, tender book for adolescents who must deal with the complexities of growing up." Child Book Rev Serv

The protagonist, fourteen year old Phoebe, shuttles "back and forth between her father's home in Woodstock and her mother's apartment in Manhattan via the bus she calls 'The Divorce Express' because there are so many children like her who ride it. She has not become adjusted to the man her mother is planning to marry, and feels more and more at home in Woodstock, especially when she makes a

new friend, Rosie, whose parents . . . are also divorced." Bull Cent Child Books

Dashner, James

The **kill** order; James Dashner. Delacorte Press 2012 329 p. $17.99

Grades: 7 8 9 10 11 12   **Fic**
1. Viruses -- Fiction 2. Survival skills -- Fiction 3. Natural disasters -- Fiction 4. Science fiction 5. Survival -- Fiction 6. Virus diseases -- Fiction
ISBN 9780307979117; 9780375990823; 9780385742887; 0385742886
LC 2012016790

In this book by James Dashner "sun flares hit the earth and mankind fell to disease. Mark and Trina were there when it happened, and they survived. But surviving the sun flares was easy compared to what came next. Now a disease of rage and lunacy races across the eastern United States, and there's something suspicious about its origin. Worse yet, it's mutating, and all evidence suggests that it will bring humanity to its knees." (Publisher's note)

★ The **maze** runner. Delacorte Press 2009 375p $16.99; lib bdg $19.99

Grades: 7 8 9 10 11 12   **Fic**
1. Science fiction 2. Amnesia -- Fiction
ISBN 0-385-73794-7; 0-385-90702-8 lib bdg; 978-0-385-73794-4; 978-0-385-90702-6 lib bdg
LC 2009-1345

Sixteen-year-old Thomas wakes up with no memory in the middle of a maze and realizes he must work with the community in which he finds himself if he is to escape.

"With a fast-paced narrative steadily answering the myriad questions that arise and an ever-increasing air of tension, Dashner's suspenseful adventure will keep readers guessing until the very end." Publ Wkly

Other titles in this series are:
The scorch trials (2010)
The death cure (2011)

Daswani, Kavita

Indie girl. Simon Pulse 2007 232p pa $8.99

Grades: 7 8 9 10   **Fic**
1. Fashion -- Fiction 2. Journalists -- Fiction 3. East Indian Americans -- Fiction
ISBN 1-4169-4892-9

"What sets this novel apart is Daswani's nuanced take on her character's Indian-American subculture, the pressure she feels to be like her more conventional cousins, her desire for independence, American-style, and her pride in her heritage. Indie is a heroine worth meeting." Publ Wkly

David, Keren

★ **When** I was Joe. Frances Lincoln 2010 364p $16.95; pa $8.95

Grades: 7 8 9 10   **Fic**
1. Crime -- Fiction 2. Witnesses -- Fiction
ISBN 978-1-84780-131-9; 1-84780-131-5; 978-1-84780-100-5 pa; 1-84780-100-5 pa

After he witnesses a murder by some ruthless gangsters, Ty and his mother go into hiding under police protection.

Even with a new identity, the killers will stop at nothing to silence him.

"This book has an intriguing premise and a cast of likable and realistic characters." SLJ

Followed by Almost true (2011)

Davies, Jacqueline

Lost. Marshall Cavendish 2009 242p $16.99

Grades: 7 8 9 10   **Fic**

1. Sisters -- Fiction 2. Factories -- Fiction 3. Bereavement -- Fiction 4. New York (N.Y.) -- Fiction 5. Triangle Shirtwaist Company, Inc. -- Fiction

ISBN 978-0-7614-5535-6; 0-7614-5535-3

LC 2008-40560

In 1911 New York, sixteen-year-old Essie Rosenfeld must stop taking care of her irrepressible six-year-old sister when she goes to work at the Triangle Waist Company, where she befriends a missing heiress who is in hiding from her family and who seems to understand the feelings of heartache and grief that Essie is trying desperately to escape.

The "unusual pacing adds depth and intrigue as the plot unfolds. There are many layers to this story, which will appeal to a variety of interests and age levels." SLJ

Where the ground meets the sky. Marshall Cavendish 2002 224p hardcover o.p. pa $5.95

Grades: 5 6 7 8   **Fic**

1. New Mexico -- Fiction 2. Manhattan Project -- Fiction 3. World War, 1939-1945 -- Fiction

ISBN 0-7614-5105-6; 0-7614-5187-0 pa

LC 2001-32519

During World War II, a twelve-year-old girl is uprooted from her quiet, East coast life and moved to a secluded army post in the New Mexico desert where her father and other scientists are working on a top secret project

"The story is told in Hazel's lively, if self-conscious voice. . . . Davies skillfully describes the secrecy and intensity of the work and how it affected every aspect of the researchers' and their families' lives." Booklist

Davies, Katie

The **great** dog disaster; Katie Davies ; illustrated by Hannah Shaw. Beach Lane Books 2013 208 p. (hardback) $12.99

Grades: 3 4 5 6 7   **Fic**

1. Dogs -- Fiction 2. Humorous stories 3. England -- Fiction 4. Newfoundland dog -- Fiction 5. Brothers and sisters -- Fiction 6. Family life -- England -- Fiction

ISBN 1442445173; 9781442445178; 9781442445185; 9781442445192

LC 2012041868

This book is the final book in the Great Critter Capers series by Katie Davies. Here, Suzanne is "thrilled to inherit Aunt Deidra's Beatrice, an ancient, smelly, incontinent Newfoundland who remains stubbornly inert until" Suzanne and her friend Anna realize: "Beatrice is depressed! To boost her spirits, the girls bathe her in Suzanne's baby brother's bath." But "a huge vet bill with the promise of more to come has Suzanne's parents murmuring that Beatrice would be better off elsewhere." (Kirkus Reviews)

Davies, Nicola, 1958-

The **Promise**; Nicola Davies, illustrated by Laura Carlin. Candlewick Press 2014 40 p. $16.99

Grades: K 1 2 3 4   **Fic**

1. Girls -- Fiction 2. Life change events -- Fiction 3. Acorns -- Fiction 4. Promises -- Fiction

ISBN 0763666335; 9780763666330

LC 2013934311

In this children's book by Nicola Davies, illustrated by Laura Carlin, "on a mean street in a mean, broken city, a young girl tries to snatch an old woman's bag. But the frail old woman, holding on with the strength of heroes, says the thief can't have it without giving something in return: the promise. It is the beginning of a journey that will change the thieving girl's life--and a chance to change the world, for good." (Publisher's note)

"A girl, with no name and of no particular age, describes a place as gritty as its people are hard: When I was young, I lived in a city that was mean and hard and ugly. She lives by stealing, and one day, she wrestles with an old woman for her bag, which the lady finally lets go of, with a condition: If you promise to plant them...Bright hues and plenty of greenery enliven the pages and lift the spirits. Lots to look at, think about, and discuss here." Booklist

Davies, Stephen

Hacking Timbuktu. Clarion Books 2010 264p map $16.00

Grades: 7 8 9 10   **Fic**

1. Adventure fiction 2. Computers -- Fiction 3. Buried treasure -- Fiction 4. Tombouctou (Mali) -- Fiction

ISBN 0-547-39016-5; 978-0-547-39016-1

LC 2009-45352

London sixteen-year-old Danny Temple and friend Omar use their computer and parkour skills to elude pursuers as they follow clues in an Arabic manuscript to the mysterious cliffs of Bandiagara in sub-Saharan Africa seeking an ancient treasure.

"Davies delivers a satisfying mix of history, exotic locales, computer hacking, and parkour in this well-constructed adventure story." Booklist

★ **Outlaw**. Clarion Books 2011 192p $16.99

Grades: 7 8 9 10   **Fic**

1. Africa -- Fiction 2. Siblings -- Fiction 3. Terrorism -- Fiction 4. Kidnapping -- Fiction 5. Sahara Desert -- Fiction 6. Social problems -- Fiction

ISBN 978-0-547-39017-8; 0-547-39017-3

LC 2011009643

The children of Britain's ambassador to Burkina Faso, fifteen-year-old Jake, who loves technology and adventure, and thirteen-year-old Kas, a budding social activist, are abducted and spend time in the Sahara desert with Yakuuba Sor, who some call a terrorist but others consider a modern-day Robin Hood.

"Stephen Davies has crafted a novel full of intrigue, fast-paced action, and sly humor. The fast moving story will draw in many readers, including those who usually shy away from books." Voice Youth Advocates

Davis, Heather

Never cry werewolf. HarperTeen 2009 216p
$16.99

Grades: 7 8 9 10   **Fic**

1. Camps -- Fiction 2. Werewolves -- Fiction
ISBN 978-0-06-134923-2; 0-06-134923-2

LC 2008-51967

Forced to attend a camp for teens with behavior problems, sixteen-year-old Shelby Locke's attempts to follow the
rules go astray when she meets a handsome British werewolf.

"Davis weaves together a fast-paced action adventure
story with issues of peer pressure, divorce, betrayal, friendship, acceptance, and, of course, romance." SLJ

Davis, Katie

The **curse** of Addy McMahon. Greenwillow
Books 2008 271p $16.99; lib bdg $17.89

Grades: 4 5 6   **Fic**

1. Authorship -- Fiction 2. Friendship -- Fiction 3.
Bereavement -- Fiction 4. Family life -- Fiction 5.
Cartoons and caricatures -- Fiction
ISBN 978-0-06-128711-4; 0-06-128711-3; 978-0-06-
128712-1 lib bdg; 0-06-128712-1 lib bdg

LC 2007041154

After her father's death, aspiring sixth-grade writer Addy
McMahon feels like she is cursed with bad luck, and when
she temporarily loses her best friend, and is forced to admit
that her mother is dating again, she vows she will never write
another word

"Peppered with authentic preteen conversations, the
novel combines traditional narrative with graphic-novel
stories, emails, and IMs. . . . . The book is a fast-paced and
interesting read." SLJ

Davis, Rebecca Fjelland

Chasing AllieCat. Flux 2011 277p pa $9.95

Grades: 7 8 9 10   **Fic**

1. Violence -- Fiction 2. Minnesota -- Fiction 3.
Bereavement -- Fiction 4. Mountain biking -- Fiction
ISBN 978-0-7387-2130-9; 0-7387-2130-1

LC 2010038217

When she is left with relatives in rural Minnesota for
the summer, Sadie meets Allie, a spiky-haired off-road biker,
and Joe, who team up to train for a race, but when they find
a priest badly beaten and near death in the woods, Allie mysteriously disappears leaving Sadie and Joe to discover the
dangerous secrets she is hiding.

Davis "constructs a succinct, compelling story that combines romance, suspense, and the theme of overcoming challenges. The strong sense of place, character development,
and love triangle dynamics should engage cycling enthusiasts as well as a broader audience." Publ Wkly

Davis, Tanita S.

A **la** carte. Alfred A. Knopf Books for Young
Readers 2008 288p $15.99; lib bdg $18.99

Grades: 7 8 9 10   **Fic**

1. Cooking -- Fiction 2. African Americans -- Fiction
ISBN 978-0-375-84815-5; 0-375-84815-0; 978-0-375-
94815-2 lib bdg; 0-375-94815-5 lib bdg

LC 2007-49656

Lainey, a high school senior and aspiring celebrity chef,
is forced to question her priorities after her best friend (and
secret crush) runs away from home.

"The relationships and characters in this book are authentic. The actions and dialogue seem true to those represented. Even though it is a quick read, the story is a meaningful one." Voice Youth Advocate

Mare's war. Alfred A. Knopf 2009 341p $16.99;
lib bdg $19.99

Grades: 7 8 9 10   **Fic**

1. Alabama -- Fiction 2. Sisters -- Fiction 3.
Grandmothers -- Fiction 4. African Americans -- Fiction
5. Automobile travel -- Fiction 6. World War, 1939-
1945 -- Fiction 7. United States -- Army -- Women's
Army Corps -- Fiction
ISBN 978-0-375-85714-0; 0-375-85714-1; 978-0-375-
95714-7 lib bdg; 0-375-95714-6 lib bdg

LC 2008-33744

ALA EMIERT Coretta Scott King Author Award Honor
Book (2010)

Teens Octavia and Tali learn about strength, independence, and courage when they are forced to take a car trip
with their grandmother, who tells about growing up Black in
1940s Alabama and serving in Europe during World War II
as a member of the Women's Army Corps.

"The parallel travel narratives are masterfully managed,
with postcards from Octavia and Tali to the folks back home
in San Francisco signaling the shift between 'then' and
'now.' Absolutely essential reading." Kirkus

Day, Karen

A **million** miles from Boston. Wendy Lamb
Books 2011 215p $15.99; lib bdg $18.99

Grades: 4 5 6 7   **Fic**

1. Dogs -- Fiction 2. Maine -- Fiction 3. Summer --
Fiction 4. Vacations -- Fiction 5. Friendship -- Fiction
6. Family life -- Fiction 7. Single parent family -- Fiction
ISBN 978-0-385-73899-6; 0-385-73899-4; 978-0-385-
90763-7 lib bdg; 0-385-90763-X lib bdg

LC 2010-16475

Rising seventh-grader Lucy plans on a perfect summer
at the Maine lake where her family has owned a cottage for
decades, but family of a classmate she dislikes has bought a
home there and her widowed father is bringing a girlfriend
to visit.

"Day delivers a well-paced, realistic 'summer of change'
story. . . . Day persuasively renders Lucy's uneasiness with
her complex shifting emotions and memories." Publ Wkly

No cream puffs; 1st ed.; Wendy Lamb Books
2008 209p $15.99; lib bdg $18.99

Grades: 6 7 8 9   **Fic**

1. Baseball -- Fiction 2. Michigan -- Fiction 3. Sex
role -- Fiction 4. Friendship -- Fiction
ISBN 978-0-375-83775-3; 0-375-83775-2; 978-0-375-
93775-0 lib bdg; 0-375-93775-7 lib bdg

LC 2007030018

In 1980, when twelve-year-old Madison, who loves to
play baseball, decides to play in her town's baseball league,
she never envisions the uproar it causes when she becomes
the first girl to join.

This is a "perceptive, enjoyable title, packed with exciting baseball." Booklist

De Goldi, Kate

★ The **10** p.m. question. Candlewick Press 2010 245p $15.99

Grades: 7 8 9 10 11 12   **Fic**

1. School stories 2. Worry -- Fiction 3. Agoraphobia -- Fiction 4. Family life -- Fiction 5. New Zealand -- Fiction 6. Eccentrics and eccentricities -- Fiction

ISBN 978-0-7636-4939-5; 0-7636-4939-2

LC 2009-49726

First published 2008 in New Zealand

Twelve-year-old Frankie Parsons has a quirky family, a wonderful best friend, and a head full of worrying questions that he shares with his mother each night, but when free-spirited Sydney arrives at school with questions of her own, Frankie is forced to face the ultimate ten p.m. question.

"De Goldi's novel is an achingly poignant, wryly comic story of early adolescence. . . . Nearly every character . . . is a loving, talented, unforgettable eccentric whose dialogue, much like De Goldi's richly phrased narration, combines heart-stopping tenderness with perfectly timed, deliciously zany humor." Booklist

The **ACB** with Honora Lee; by Kate De Goldi ; drawings by Gregory O'Brien. Longacre 2012 124 p. ill. (chiefly col.) (hardcover) $17.99

Grades: 4 5 6 7   **Fic**

1. Patience 2. Alphabet -- Fiction 3. Grandparent-grandchild relationship 4. Rest homes -- Fiction 5. Grandparent and child -- Fiction

ISBN 1770497226; 9781869799892; 9781770497221

LC 2012515235

In this juvenile book, by Kate De Goldi, illustrated by Gregory O'Brien, "Perry's mother and father are busy people . . . they're impatient, they're tired, they get cross easily. And they think that only children, like Perry, should be kept busy. . . . Perry . . . discovers her Gran has an unconventional interest in the alphabet, so Perry decides to make an alphabet book. . . . Soon everyone is interested in Perry's book project." (Publisher's note)

"Nine-year-old Perry, an only child, spends Thursday afternoons with her grandmother, Honora Lee, who lives at the Santa Lucia nursing home and suffers from dementia. With Honora Lee's help, Perry writes and illustrates an alphabet book about the residents. Fans of middle grade novels with quirky female protagonists will enjoy this story and its stylish color illustrations, which suit the mood of the text." Horn Book

De la Peña, Matt

The **living**; Matt de la Peña. Delacorte Press 2013 320 p.

Grades: 8 9 10 11 12   **Fic**

1. Cruise ships -- Fiction 2. Natural disasters -- Fiction 3. Survival after airplane accidents, shipwrecks, etc. -- Fiction 4. Diseases -- Fiction 5. Survival -- Fiction 6. Mexican Americans -- Fiction

ISBN 9780375989919; 9780385741200

LC 2012050778

Pura Belpre Author Award (2014)

In this book, by Matt de la Peña, "Shy took [a] summer job to make some money. In a few months on a luxury cruise liner, he'll rake in the tips and be able to help his mom and sister out with the bills. . . . But everything changes when the Big One hits. Shy's only weeks out at sea when an earthquake more massive than ever before recorded hits California, and his life is forever changed. The earthquake is only the first disaster. Suddenly it's a fight to survive for those left living." (Publisher's note)

"Shy Espinoza's summer job on Paradise Cruise Lines is, literally, a disaster. A series of catastrophes befall the cruise and eventually threaten civilization as he knows it; Shy finds himself on a life raft in the Pacific Ocean with a racist "spoiled-ass blond chick." Readers wanting a fast-paced survival story with plenty of action won't mind the over-the-top plot." (Horn Book)

Mexican whiteboy. Delacorte Press 2008 249p $15.99; lib bdg $18.99

Grades: 8 9 10 11 12   **Fic**

1. Cousins -- Fiction 2. California -- Fiction 3. Mexican Americans -- Fiction 5. Racially mixed people -- Fiction

ISBN 978-0-385-73310-6; 0-385-73310-0; 978-0-385-90329-5 lib bdg; 0-385-90329-4 lib bdg

LC 2007-32302

Sixteen-year-old Danny searches for his identity amidst the confusion of being half-Mexican and half-white while spending a summer with his cousin and new friends on the baseball fields and back alleys of San Diego County, California.

"The author juggles his many plotlines well, and the portrayal of Danny's friends and neighborhood is rich and lively." Booklist

We were here. Delacorte Press 2009 357p $17.99; lib bdg $20.99

Grades: 7 8 9 10 11 12   **Fic**

1. Brothers -- Fiction 2. California -- Fiction 3. Friendship -- Fiction 4. Runaway teenagers -- Fiction 5. Juvenile delinquency -- Fiction

ISBN 978-0-385-73667-1; 0-385-73667-3; 978-0-385-90622-7 lib bdg; 0-385-90622-6 lib bdg

LC 2008-44568

Haunted by the event that sentences him to time in a group home, Miguel breaks out with two unlikely companions and together they begin their journey down the California coast hoping to get to Mexico and a new life.

"The contemporary survival adventure will keep readers hooked, as will the tension that builds from the story's secrets." Booklist

De Lint, Charles

The **blue** girl; Charles de Lint. Viking 2004 368p hardcover o.p. pa $7.99

Grades: 7 8 9 10   **Fic**

1. Ghost stories 2. School stories 3. Fairies -- Fiction

ISBN 0-670-05924-2; 0-14-240545-0 pa

LC 2004-19051

New at her high school, Imogene enlists the help of her introverted friend Maxine and the ghost of a boy who haunts the school after receiving warnings through her dreams that soul-eaters are threatening her life

"The book combines the turmoil of high school intertwined with rich, detailed imagery drawn from traditional folklore and complex characters with realistic relationships. . . . This book is not just another ghost story, but a novel infused with the true sense of wonder and magic that is De Lint at his best. It is strongly recommended." Voice Youth Advocates

De Quidt, Jeremy

★ The **toymaker**; with illustrations by Gary Blythe. David Fickling Books 2010 356p il $16.99; lib bdg $19.99

Grades: 5 6 7 8   **Fic**

1. Adventure fiction 2. Toys -- Fiction
ISBN 978-0-385-75180-3; 0-385-75180-X; 978-0-385-75181-0 lib bdg; 0-385-75181-8 lib bdg

"Mathias . . . upon the death of his conjurer grandfather, is spirited away from the decrepit carnival they called home. His unknown new guardian appears to be after the secret contained on an inherited piece of paper, which is now in Mathias' possession. . . . Moving briskly across an atmospheric Germanic setting, the characters are chased by howling wolves, a dangerous dwarf, and unforgiving cold in a bloody, mysterious, and darkly thrilling quest." Booklist

Dee, Barbara

Just another day in my insanely real life; a novel. Margaret K. McElderry Books 2006 252p $15.95; pa $5.99

Grades: 5 6 7 8   **Fic**

1. Authorship -- Fiction 2. Single parent family -- Fiction
ISBN 978-1-4169-0861-6; 1-4169-0861-7; 978-1-4169-4739-4 pa; 1-4169-4739-6 pa

With her father "out of the picture" and her mother working long hours, twelve-year-old Cassie unconsciously describes her anger and confusion in a fantasy novel she is writing for school.

"It's the drama and seething anger in Cassie's first-person narrative that's so compelling." Booklist

Deebs, Tracy

Tempest rising. Walker & Co. 2011 344p $16.99

Grades: 8 9 10 11 12   **Fic**

1. War stories 2. Mermaids and mermen -- Fiction
ISBN 978-0-8027-2231-7; 0-8027-2231-8

LC 2010-34339

On her seventeenth birthday, Tempest must decide whether to remain a human and live on land or submit to her mermaid half, like her mother before her, and enter into a long-running war under the sea.

"Tempest is a gutsy, independent heroine with more than enough agency to save herself from danger. . . . For readers wanting a solid, familiar, but slightly different paranormal romance." Booklist

Deedy, Carmen Agra

★ The **Cheshire** Cheese cat; a Dickens of a tale. Peachtree Publishers 2011 228p il $16.95

Grades: 5 6 7 8   **Fic**

1. Cats -- Fiction 2. Mice -- Fiction 3. London (England) -- Fiction 4. Great Britain -- History -- 19th century -- Fiction
ISBN 978-1-56145-595-9; 1-56145-595-4

LC 2010052275

"The vagaries of tavern life in 19th-century London come alive in this delightful tale. . . . The fast-moving plot is a masterwork of intricate detail that will keep readers enthralled, and the characters are well-rounded and believable. Language is a highlight of the novel; words both elegant and colorful fill the pages. . . . Combined with Moser's precise pencil sketches of personality-filled characters, the book is a success in every way." SLJ

DeFelice, Cynthia C.

Fort; Cynthia DeFelice. Farrar, Straus & Giroux 2015 208 p. (hardback) $16.99

Grades: 4 5 6 7   **Fic**

1. Summer -- Fiction 2. Bullies -- Fiction 3. Friendship -- Fiction 4. Bullying -- Fiction 5. Great-aunts -- Fiction 6. Best friends -- Fiction 7. Great-uncles -- Fiction
ISBN 0374324271; 9780374324278

LC 2014040167

This book by Cynthia DeFelice "is told as a flashback in the 'What I Did on My Summer Vacation' essay that" narrator Wyatt "has no intention of showing to a teacher." (Booklist) "When older boys tear apart the fort where they have been enjoying a wonderful summer, Wyatt and Augie team up with another bullied kid to exact revenge, with unexpected consequences." (Publisher's Note)

"Wyatt and Augie's friendship is strong despite the fact that they only see each other in the summer. This particular summer, Wyatt's eleventh, is told as a flashback in the "What I Did on My Summer Vacation" essay that he has no intention of showing to a teacher... Stuffed full of clever pranks and summertime nostalgia, this is a story of kindness and adventure, and a rare breed in the middle-grade canon that doesn't rely on cheap humor to hold attention. A boisterous and poignant coming-of-age tale." Booklist

The **ghost** and Mrs. Hobbs; [by] Cynthia DeFelice. Farrar, Straus & Giroux 2001 180p $16; pa $5.99

Grades: 4 5 6   **Fic**

1. Ghost stories
ISBN 0-374-38046-5; 0-06-001172-6 pa

LC 00-52827

Hindered by a fight with her friend Dub and a series of mysterious fires, eleven-year-old Allie investigates the fire seventeen years earlier which claimed the lives of the husband and infant son of a school cafeteria worker, as well as the handsome young man whose ghost asks Allie for help

"This is a diverting and suspenseful ghost story offering a likable protagonist and a thrilling romantic spark." Horn Book

The **ghost** of Cutler Creek; [by] Cynthia DeFelice. 1st ed; Farrar, Straus and Giroux 2004 181p $16; pa $5.95

Grades: 4 5 6   **Fic**

1. Ghost stories 2. Mystery fiction 3. Dogs -- Fiction
ISBN 0-374-38058-9; 0-374-40004-0 pa

LC 2003-49051

When Allie is contacted by the ghost of a dog, she and Dub investigate the surly new boy at school and his father, who may be running a puppy mill, to see if they are involved.

"DeFelice has created a suspenseful tale that will leave readers rapidly turning pages." SLJ

★ The **ghost** of Fossil Glen; by Cynthia De-Felice. Farrar, Straus & Giroux 1998 167p (Ghost Mysteries) $16; pa $7.99

Grades: 4 5 6 **Fic**

1. Ghost stories

ISBN 0-374-31787-9; 9780312602130 pa

LC 97-33230

"Strange events begin when a calm, unknown voice prevents Allie from panicking and falling from a dangerous cliff while fossil hunting. Then, an old journal mysteriously appears in her mailbox. Allie often feels a presence nearby and dreams of a girl falling from the cliff. She then discovers the grave marker of an 11-year-old girl who was missing and presumed dead in 1994. Because of her reputation for telling stories, Allie cannot convince anyone to believe her except her longtime friend and fellow fossil hunter, Dub. Driven to pursue the mystery, Allie finds an old diary that provides her with facts about the girl's death. Foolishly, she reveals what she knows and endangers her own life. . . . Grades four to six." (SLJ)

"Sixth-grader Allie Nichols encounters the ghost of Lucy Stiles and becomes involved with Lucy's unsolved death, eventually finding proof that Lucy was murdered." Horn Book Guide

The **ghost** of Poplar Point; [by] Cynthia DeFelice. 1st ed.; Farrar, Straus and Giroux 2007 183p $16

Grades: 4 5 6 7 **Fic**

1. Ghost stories 2. Seneca Indians -- Fiction 3. New York (State) -- Fiction

ISBN 0-374-32540-5; 978-0-374-32540-4

LC 2006047329

Prompted by the ghost of a young Seneca Indian girl, twelve-year-old Allie and her friend Dub are determined, despite the opposition of an unscrupulous property developer, that the historical pageant celebrating the founding of their town tells the truth about the fate of the Seneca people who lived there during the Revolutionary War.

"This engaging book moves along quickly to a satisfying conclusion." Booklist

★ **Signal**. Farrar, Straus and Giroux 2009 151p $16.99

Grades: 5 6 7 8 **Fic**

1. Moving -- Fiction 2. Friendship -- Fiction 3. Loneliness -- Fiction 4. Child abuse -- Fiction 5. Country life -- Fiction

ISBN 978-0-374-39915-3; 0-374-39915-8

LC 2008-09278

After moving with his emotionally distant father to the Finger Lakes region of upstate New York, twelve-year-old Owen faces a lonely summer until he meets an abused girl who may be a space alien.

"Well-drawn secondary characters create a threatening backdrop to the developing mystery, while Owen's poignant relationship with his work-driven father elicits sympathy.

The tension builds on several fronts to a gripping climax and satisfying conclusion. Owen's likable voice, the plot's quick pace and the science fiction overtones make this a winner." Publ Wkly

Defoe, Daniel

Robinson Crusoe; edited with an introduction by Thomas Keymer and notes by Thomas Keymer and James Kelly. New ed.; Oxford University Press 2009 lii, 321p il (Oxford world's classics) pa $7.95

Grades: 8 9 10 11 12 Adult **Fic**

1. Adventure fiction 2. Islands -- Fiction 3. Survival after airplane accidents, shipwrecks, etc. -- Fiction

ISBN 978-0-19-955397-6

LC 2006-26022

First published 1719

"A minutely circumstantial account of the hero's shipwreck and escape to an uninhabited island, and the methodical industry whereby he makes himself a comfortable home. The story is founded on the actual experiences of Alexander Selkirk, who spent four years on the island of Juan Fernandez in the early 18th century." Lenrow. Reader's Guide to Prose Fic

DeKeyser, Stacy

The **Brixen** Witch; Stacy DeKeyser. Margaret K. McElderry Books 2012 208 p. (hardcover) $15.99

Grades: 4 5 6 7 8 **Fic**

1. Horror fiction 2. Occult fiction 3. Witches -- Fiction 4. Rats -- Fiction 5. Magic -- Fiction 6. Witchcraft -- Fiction 7. Community life -- Fiction

ISBN 9781442433281; 9781442433304

LC 2011033680

In this book, "12-year-old Rudi Bauer thinks he's found a treasure, [but] no good can come from taking something that belongs to the Brixen Witch. His sleep is plagued by nightmares, but when they stop there's no relief--the village is infested with rats. . . . As his Oma points out, young Rudi, the one child left behind after the children disappear and the one who precipitated the crisis, is the one to make things right." (Kirkus Reviews)

Delaney, Joseph

The **ghost** prison; Joseph Delaney. Sourcebooks Fire 2013 112 p. (hc : alk. paper) $12.99

Grades: 4 5 6 7 8 **Fic**

1. Horror fiction 2. Prisons -- Fiction 3. Horror stories 4. Ghosts -- Fiction 5. Orphans -- Fiction 6. Supernatural -- Fiction

ISBN 1402293186; 9781402293184

LC 2013017898

This novella is set in the same universe as Joseph Delaney's Last Apprentice series. The story "is narrated by orphan Billy Calder, who is apprehensive about the new job he has landed: helping guard an infamously haunted prison on the night shift. The ghosts and dangers turn out to be all too real, as Billy learns about the prison's bloody history and has a life-altering encounter one night while on the job." (Publishers Weekly)

A **new** darkness; 1 Joseph Delaney. Greenwillow Books, an imprint of HarperCollinsPublishers

2014 352 p. 22 cm (Starblade Chronicles) (hardback)
$17.99

Grades: 7 8 9 10   **Fic**

1. Horror fiction 2. Witches -- Fiction 3. Monsters
-- Fiction 4. Apprentices -- Fiction 5. Supernatural
-- Fiction 6. Horror stories

ISBN 0062334530; 9780062334534

LC 2014011963

"Tom Ward is the Spook, the one person who can defend
the county from bloodthirsty creatures of the dark. But he's
only seventeen, and his apprenticeship was cut short when
his master died in battle. . . . [F]ifteen-year-old . . . Jenny . .
. is a seventh daughter of a seventh daughter, and she wants
to be Tom's first apprentice. . . . Together, Tom and Jenny
will uncover the grave danger heading straight toward the
county." (Publisher's note)

"A plethora of action involving ghastly creatures, sword
fights, and magic coupled with just enough backstory and
description make this novel engaging enough to keep even
the most reluctant reader turning pages until the end. Tom's
story has a doozy of a cliff-hanger that is sure to bring teens
back for more." - SLJ Reviews

★ **Revenge** of the witch; illustrations by Patrick
Arrasmith. Greenwillow Bks. 2005 344p il (The
last apprentice) $14.99; lib bdg $15.89; pa $7.99

Grades: 5 6 7 8   **Fic**

1. Witches -- Fiction 2. Supernatural -- Fiction

ISBN 0-06-076618-2; 0-06-076619-0 lib bdg; 0-06-
076620-4 pa

LC 2004-54003

Young Tom, the seventh son of a seventh son, starts work
as an apprentice for the village spook, whose job is to protect ordinary folk from "ghouls, boggarts, and all manner of
wicked beasties"

"Delaney grabs readers by the throat and gives them a
good shake in a smartly crafted story. . . . This is a gristly
thriller. . . . Yet the twisted horror is amply buffered by an
exquisitely normal young hero, matter-of-fact prose, and a
workaday normalcy." Booklist

Other titles in this series are:
Curse of the bane (2006)
Night of the soul-stealer (2007)
Attack of the fiend (2008)
Wrath of the Bloodeye (2008)
Clash of the demons (2009)
Rise of the huntress (2010)
Rage of the fallen (2011)

Rise of the huntress; illustrations by Patrick Arrasmith. Greenwillow Books 2010 436p (The last
apprentice) $17.99; pa $7.99

Grades: 5 6 7 8   **Fic**

1. Horror fiction 2. Witches -- Fiction 3. Apprentices
-- Fiction 4. Supernatural -- Fiction

ISBN 978-0-06-171510-5; 0-06-171510-7; 978-0-06-
171512-9 pa; 0-06-171512-3 pa

LC 2009044188

Sequel to: Clash of the demons (2009)

Returning from Greece, Tom and the Spook find that
their home, including the Spook's precious library of knowl-

edge, has been burned to the ground, and that their battle
against the denizens of the dark must continue.

"Delaney once again combines chills with character
development. . . . Arrasmith's black-and-white illustrations
reinforce the idea that the supernatural creatures, even Tom's
temporary cohorts, are worth a shudder." Horn Book Guide

The **Spook's** Bestiary; illustrated by Julek Heller. Greenwillow Books 2011 222p il (The last
apprentice) $16.99

Grades: 5 6 7 8   **Fic**

1. Horror fiction 2. Apprentices -- Fiction 3.
Supernatural -- Fiction

ISBN 978-0-06-208114-8; 0-06-208114-4

LC 2010049856

Ready to be presented to the last apprentice, Tom Ward,
the spook's notebook contains instructions for vanquishing
boggarts, witches, the unquiet dead, and other dark creatures
and spirits.

"Heller's creepy drawings fill the pages and, like the
whole book, they should delight fans of the series." SLJ

Wrath of the Bloodeye; [by] Joseph Delaney; illustrations by Patrick Arrasmith. 1st ed.; Greenwillow
Books 2008 511p il (The last apprentice) $17.99; lib
bdg $18.89; pa $7.99

Grades: 5 6 7 8   **Fic**

1. Witches -- Fiction 2. Apprentices -- Fiction 3.
Supernatural -- Fiction

ISBN 978-0-06-134459-6; 0-06-134459-1; 978-0-06-
134460-2 lib bdg; 0-06-134460-5 lib bdg; 978-0-06-
134461-9 pa; 0-06-134461-3 pa

LC 2008017920

The continuing adventures of Tom, the seventh son of
a seventh son and apprentice to the local Spook, who faces danger and death daily in his job protecting the region
from evil.

Delsol, Wendy

Flock; Wendy Delsol. Candlewick Press 2012
384 p. (hardback) $16.99

Grades: 7 8 9 10   **Fic**

1. Occult fiction 2. Infants -- Fiction 3. Sisters --
Fiction 4. Schools -- Fiction 5. High schools -- Fiction
6. Supernatural -- Fiction 7. Students, Foreign --
Fiction 8. Interpersonal relations -- Fiction

ISBN 0763660108; 9780763660109

LC 2011048371

Sequel to: Frost

This book is the final in the "Stork" trilogy. Protagonist
Katla has returned to her high school life after saving her
boyfriend Jack in Iceland. But "her hopes of dodging unfinished business are dashed by the arrival of two Icelandic
exchange students: Marik . . . and Jinky . . . . It seems Katla
not only enraged the Snow Queen by rescuing . . . Jack,
she also was tricked into promising her frail baby sister to
the water queen — and Marik has come to collect. What's
worse, Katla doesn't dare confide in anyone lest she endanger them, so even her soul mate, Jack, is growing suspicious.
And now Katla's stork dreams, her guide for matching babies with mothers, have become strange and menacing as
well. (Amazon.com)

Frost. Candlewick Press 2011 376p $15.99

Grades: 7 8 9 10 **Fic**

1. School stories 2. Snow -- Fiction 3. Supernatural -- Fiction 4. Arctic regions -- Fiction

ISBN 978-0-7636-5386-6; 0-7636-5386-1

LC 2010047656

Sequel to Stork (2010)

After her boyfriend Jack conjures up a record-breaking snow storm, sixteen-year-old Kat LeBlanc finds herself facing an unusual rival in the form of an environmental researcher from Greenland who is drawn to their small town of Norse Falls, Minnesota, by the storm.

"Well-paced narration will keep readers interested—a superior paranormal adventure." Kirkus

Stork. Candlewick Press 2010 357p $15.99; pa $8.99

Grades: 7 8 9 10 **Fic**

1. School stories 2. Minnesota -- Fiction 3. Supernatural -- Fiction

ISBN 978-0-7636-4844-2; 0-7636-4844-2; 978-0-7636-5687-4 pa; 0-7636-5687-9 pa

LC 2009-51357

After her parents' divorce, Katla and her mother move from Los Angeles to Norse Falls, Minnesota, where Kat immediately alienates two boys at her high school and, improbably, discovers a kinship with a mysterious group of elderly women—the Icelandic Stork Society—who "deliver souls."

"This snappy, lighthearted supernatural romance blends Norse mythology and contemporary issues with an easy touch." Booklist

Followed by: Frost (2011)

DeMatteis, J. M.

Imaginalis. Katherine Tegen Books 2010 248p $16.99

Grades: 5 6 7 8 **Fic**

1. Fantasy fiction 2. Magic -- Fiction 3. Imagination -- Fiction 4. Books and reading -- Fiction

ISBN 978-0-06-173286-7; 0-06-173286-9

Devastated that her favorite fantasy book series will not be completed, twelve-year-old Mehera discovers that only her belief, imagination, and courage will save the land of Imaginalis and its inhabitants from being lost forever.

This is "a sure-footed fantasy. . . . The well-drawn characters, abundant action and humor, and hopeful message about the power of reading and belief keep it afloat." Publ Wkly

Dennard, Susan

Something strange and deadly; Susan Dennard. 1st ed. Harpercollins Childrens Books 2012 388 p. (hardback) $17.99; (paperback) $9.99

Grades: 7 8 9 10 11 12 **Fic**

1. Fairs 2. Ghost stories 3. Zombies -- Fiction 4. Horror stories 5. Dead -- Fiction 6. Magic -- fiction 7. Brothers and sisters -- Fiction 8. Philadelphia (Pa.) -- History -- 19th century -- Fiction

ISBN 0062083260; 9780062083265; 9780062083272

LC 2011042114

Author Susan Dennard's protagonist Eleanor Fitt "and her dear Mama have just about run out of funds, and she

misses [her brother] Elijah terribly [while he is on a] . . . three-year odyssey abroad. So when . . . he's been detained, she is mightily distressed. The next day, the determined teen is off for some help from the Spirit-Hunters. . . . Her can-do attitude finds her at one point systematically disabling a throng of zombies by smashing their kneecaps with her parasol." (Kirkus Reviews)

Followed by A Darkness Strange and Lovely (2013)

Derby, Sally

Kyle's island. Charlesbridge 2010 191p $16.95

Grades: 5 6 7 8 **Fic**

1. Lakes -- Fiction 2. Islands -- Fiction 3. Michigan -- Fiction 4. Siblings -- Fiction 5. Family life -- Fiction

ISBN 978-1-58089-316-9; 1-58089-316-3

LC 2009-17581

Kile, almost thirteen, spends much of the summer yearning to explore a nearby island, striving to be a good brother, fishing with an elderly neighbor, and fuming at his parents over their separation that is forcing his mother to sell the family's cabin on a Michigan lake.

"Derby writes a subtle coming-of-age novel that is engaging from start to finish. Kyle's character is so well developed that many readers will be able to understand the realistic emotions and situations taking place." Libr Media Connect

Deriso, Christine Hurley

Then I met my sister. Flux 2011 269p pa $9.95

Grades: 8 9 10 11 12 **Fic**

1. Death -- Fiction 2. Diaries -- Fiction 3. Sisters -- Fiction

ISBN 978-0-7387-2581-9; 0-7387-2581-1

LC 2010-45239

Summer Stetson has always lived in the shadow of her dead sister, knowing she can never measure up in any way, but on her seventeenth birthday her aunt gives her Shannon's diary, which reveals painful but liberating truths about Summer's family and herself.

"The journey Summer goes on to 'meet' her sister is compelling, but equally interesting are her discoveries about herself and her relationships. . . . This is a book intriguing enough to read in one sitting." SLJ

Derting, Kimberly

★ The **body** finder. Harper 2009 329p $16.99

Grades: 7 8 9 10 11 12 **Fic**

1. Mystery fiction 2. Dead -- Fiction 3. Supernatural -- Fiction 4. Extrasensory perception -- Fiction

ISBN 978-0-06-177981-7; 0-06-177981-4

LC 2009-39675

"Violet Ambrose can find dead bodies. Their aura of sound, color, or even taste imprints itself on their murderers, and Violet's extrasensory perception picks up on those elements. . . . Derting has written a suspenseful mystery and sensual love story that will captivate readers who enjoy authentic high-school settings, snappy dialogue, sweet romance, and heart-stopping drama." Booklist

Followed by: Desires of the dead (2011)

Desires of the dead. HarperCollins 2011 358p $16.99

Grades: 7 8 9 10   **Fic**
1. School stories 2. Homicide -- Fiction 3. Friendship
-- Fiction 4. Supernatural -- Fiction 5. Washington
(State) -- Fiction 6. Extrasensory perception -- Fiction
7. United States -- Federal Bureau of Investigation --
Fiction
ISBN 978-0-06-177984-8; 0-06-177984-9
LC 2010017838
Sequel to: The body finder (2010)
Sixteen-year-old Violet Ambrose's ability to find murder
victims and their killers draws the attention of the FBI just as
her relationship with Jay, her best-friend-turned-boyfriend,
heats up.

"The author paces the story beautifully, weaving together several story lines as she inches up to the final, desperate scene. . . . Imaginative, convincing and successful
suspense." Kirkus

The **last** echo; Kimberly Derting. Harper 2012
360 p. (hbk.) $17.99
Grades: 7 8 9 10 11 12   **Fic**
1. Love stories 2. Parapsychology -- Fiction 3.
Serial killers -- Fiction 4. Dead -- Fiction 5. Schools
-- Fiction 6. Friendship -- Fiction 7. Best friends --
Fiction 8. High schools -- Fiction 9. Serial murders
-- Fiction 10. Psychic ability -- Fiction 11. Washington
(State) -- Fiction
ISBN 0062082191; 9780062082190
LC 2011044633
Sequel to: Desires of the dead (2011)
This book, "the third installment of the Body Finder se-
ries," begins with protagonist Violet "working for a secret
agency that specializes in using paranormal powers to fight
crime. . . . She still loves her normal boyfriend Jay, so she
worries about the strong physical response she feels when-
ever she touches Rafe, a member of the team. Meanwhile,
Violet doesn't know she's become the target of a terrifying
serial killer." (Kirkus Reviews)

"As always, this author writes a gripping tale... Personalities come across quite strongly, as several of the characters
tend toward the eccentric." Kirkus

The **pledge**. Margaret K. McElderry Books 2011
323p $16.99
Grades: 7 8 9 10   **Fic**
1. Fantasy fiction 2. Ability -- Fiction 3. Social classes
-- Fiction 4. Language and languages -- Fiction
ISBN 978-1-4424-2201-8; 1-4424-2201-7; 978-1-
4424-2202-5 e-book
LC 2010053773
In a dystopian kingdom where the classes are separated
by the languages they speak, Charlaina 'Charlie' Hart has
a secret gift that is revealed when she meets a mysterious
young man named Max.

Derting "keeps her story consistently engaging through
vivid description and brisk pacing. . . . Great suspense from a
prolific new writer with a vibrant imagination." Kirkus

Despain, Bree
The **dark** Divine. Egmont USA 2010 372p
$17.99; lib bdg $20.99

Grades: 7 8 9 10 11   **Fic**
1. School stories 2. Minnesota -- Fiction 3. Family
life -- Fiction 4. Supernatural -- Fiction 5. Christian
life -- Fiction
ISBN 978-1-60684-057-3; 1-60684-057-6; 978-1-
60684-065-8 lib bdg; 1-60684-065-7 lib bdg
LC 2009-18680
Grace Divine, almost seventeen, learns a dark secret
when her childhood friend—practically a brother—returns,
upsetting her pastor-father and the rest of her family, around
the time strange things are happening in and near their small
Minnesota town.

"Despain raises complex issues of responsibility and
forgiveness and offers no easy answers. Atmospheric and
compelling." Booklist
Followed by: The lost saint (2010)

Despeyroux, Denise
The **big** book of vampires; by Denise Despeyroux. Tundra Books of Northern New York 2013
108 p. (hardcover) $17.95
Grades: 5 6 7   **Fic**
1. Vampires -- Fiction
ISBN 1770493719; 9781770493711
LC 2011932738
"The most noted and significant terror/vampire stories and legends are adapted and included in this large and
elaborately illustrated book. There are nine adaptations of
this literary genre of the nineteenth century and four legends
in the folk tradition. The legends, all about the adventures
of vampires, originated in China, Spain, Poland, and Denmark. . . . Each of the two sections has a page listing the
books along with several sentences of information." (Children's Literature)

Dessen, Sarah
★ **Along** for the ride; a novel. Viking 2009
383p $19.99
Grades: 7 8 9 10   **Fic**
1. Divorce -- Fiction 2. Infants -- Fiction 3. Stepfamilies
-- Fiction 4. Dating (Social customs) -- Fiction
ISBN 978-0-670-01194-0; 0-670-01194-0
LC 2009-5661
When Auden impulsively goes to stay with her father,
stepmother, and new baby sister the summer before she
starts college, all the trauma of her parents' divorce is revived, even as she is making new friends and having new
experiences such as learning to ride a bike and dating.

"Dessen explores the dynamics of an extended family
headed by two opposing, flawed personalities, revealing
their parental failures with wicked precision yet still managing to create real, even sympathetic characters. . . . [This
book] provides the interpersonal intricacies fans expect from
a Dessen plot." Horn Book

Lock and key; a novel. Viking Children's Books
2008 422p $18.99
Grades: 7 8 9 10   **Fic**
1. Child abuse -- Fiction 2. Family life -- Fiction 3.
Abandoned children -- Fiction
ISBN 978-0-670-01088-2; 0-670-01088-X
LC 2007-25370

When she is abandoned by her alcoholic mother, high school senior Ruby winds up living with Cora, the sister she has not seen for ten years, and learns about Cora's new life, what makes a family, how to allow people to help her when she needs it, and that she too has something to offer others.

"The dialogue, especially between Ruby and Cora, is crisp, layered, and natural. The slow unfolding adds to an anticipatory mood. . . . Recommend this one to patient, sophisticated readers." SLJ

The **moon** and more; by Sarah Dessen. Viking 2013 384 p. (hardcover) $19.99

Grades: 7 8 9 10   Fic

1. Bildungsromans 2. Dating (Social customs) -- Fiction 3. Father-daughter relationship -- Fiction 4. Beaches -- Fiction 5. Resorts -- Fiction 6. Coming of age -- Fiction 7. Fathers and daughters -- Fiction 8. Family-owned business enterprises -- Fiction 9. Documentary films -- Production and direction -- Fiction
ISBN 0670785601; 9780670785605

LC 2012035720

In this novel, by Sarah Dessen, "Luke is the perfect boyfriend. . . . But now, in the summer before college, Emaline wonders if perfect is good enough. Enter Theo, a super-ambitious outsider. . . . Emaline's . . . father, too, thinks Emaline should have a bigger life. . . . Emaline is attracted to the bright future that Theo and her father promise. But she also clings to the deep roots of her loving mother, stepfather, and sisters." (Publisher's note)

"Dessen's characters behave as deliciously unpredictably as people do in real life, and just as in real life, they sometimes have to make difficult choices with not-so-predictable outcomes... Completely engaging." Kirkus

That summer. Orchard Books 1996 198p hardcover o.p. pa $8.99

Grades: 7 8 9 10   Fic

1. Sisters -- Fiction 2. Weddings -- Fiction
ISBN 0-531-09538-X; 0-531-08888-X lib bdg; 978-0-14-240172-9 pa; 0-14-240172-2 pa

LC 96-7643

During the summer of her divorced father's remarriage and her sister's wedding, fifteen-year-old Haven comes into her own by letting go of the myths of the past

"Dessen adds a fresh twist to a traditional sister-of-the-bride story with her keenly observant narrative full of witty ironies. Her combination of unforgettable characters and unexpected events generates hilarity as well as warmth." Publ Wkly

The **truth** about forever. Viking 2004 382p $16.99; pa $6.50

Grades: 7 8 9 10   Fic

1. Death -- Fiction 2. Catering -- Fiction
ISBN 0-670-03639-0; 0-440-21928-0 pa

LC 2003-28298

The summer following her father's death, Macy plans to work at the library and wait for her brainy boyfriend to return from camp, but instead she goes to work at a catering business where she makes new friends and finally faces her grief.

"All of Dessen's characters . . . are fully and beautifully drawn. Their dialogue is natural and believable, and their care for one another is palpable. . . . Dessen charts Macy's navigation of grief in such an honest way it will touch every reader who meets her." SLJ

What happened to goodbye. Viking 2011 402p $19.99

Grades: 8 9 10 11 12   Fic

1. School stories 2. Divorce -- Fiction
ISBN 978-0-670-01294-7; 0-670-01294-7

LC 2010-41041

"The novel nimbly weaves together familiar story lines of divorce, high-school happiness and angst, and teen-identity struggles with likable, authentic adult and teen characters and intriguing yet credible situations." Booklist

DeStefano, Lauren

Perfect ruin; by Lauren DeStefano and illustrated by Teagan White. Simon and Schuster Books for Young Readers 2013 368 p. (The Internment chronicles) (hardcover : alk. paper) $17.99

Grades: 7 8 9 10   Fic

1. Utopias 2. Imaginary places 3. Criminal investigation -- Fiction 4. Science fiction 5. Utopias -- Fiction
ISBN 1442480610; 9781442480612

LC 2013014392

In this book by Lauren DeStefano "Morgan Stockhour knows getting too close to the edge of Internment, the floating city in the clouds where she lives, can lead to madness. Then a murder, the first in a generation, rocks the city. With whispers swirling and fear on the wind, Morgan can no longer stop herself from investigating, especially once she meets Judas. Betrothed to the victim, he is the boy being blamed for the murder, but Morgan is convinced of his innocence." (Publisher's note)

Detorie, Rick

★ The **accidental** genius of Weasel High. Egmont USA 2011 197p il pa $9.99

Grades: 5 6 7 8   Fic

1. Motion pictures -- Fiction
ISBN 1-60684-149-1 pa; 978-1-60684-149-5 pa

LC 2011-02776

Larkin Pace, a film-obsessed high school freshman, chronicles his experiences as he tries to raise money for a new camcorder and get a date with the girl who has been his best friend since third grade. "Grades five to eight." (Bull Cent Child Books)

"Larkin serves as a relatable 'everykid,' and many readers will enjoy spending some time with him." SLJ

Deuker, Carl

★ **Gym** candy. Houghton Mifflin Company 2007 313p $16

Grades: 7 8 9 10 11 12   Fic

1. School stories 2. Football -- Fiction 3. Steroids -- Fiction 4. Washington (State) -- Fiction 5. Father-son relationship -- Fiction
ISBN 978-0-618-77713-6; 0-618-77713-X

LC 2007-12749

Groomed by his father to be a star player, football is the only thing that has ever really mattered to Mick Johnson, who works hard for a spot on the varsity team his freshman year, then tries to hold onto his edge by using steroids, despite the consequences to his health and social life.

"Deuker skillfully complements a sobering message with plenty of exciting on-field action and locker-room drama, while depicting Mick's emotional struggles with loneliness and insecurity as sensitively and realistically as his physical ones." Booklist

High heat. Houghton Mifflin 2003 277p $16; pa $6.99

Grades: 7 8 9 10   **Fic**
1. School stories 2. Fathers -- Fiction
ISBN 0-618-31117-3; 0-06-057248-5 pa
                                               LC 2002-15324
When high school sophomore Shane Hunter's father is arrested for money laundering at his Lexus dealership, the star pitcher's life of affluence and private school begins to fall apart

This is "a story that delivers baseball action along with a rich psychological portrait, told through a compelling first-person narration." SLJ

Night hoops. Houghton Mifflin 2000 212p $15; pa $8.99

Grades: 7 8 9 10   **Fic**
1. Basketball -- Fiction 2. Friendship -- Fiction
ISBN 0-395-97936-6; 0-547-24891-1 pa
                                                LC 99-47882
While trying to prove that he is good enough to be on his high school's varsity basketball team, Nick must also deal with his parents' divorce and erratic behavior of a troubled classmate who lives across the street

"The descriptions of the games are well written and accurate. Best of all, the complexities of basketball are contrasted with the complexities of life." SLJ

Painting the black. Avon Books 1999 248p pa $5.99

Grades: 8 9 10 11 12   **Fic**
1. School stories 2. Baseball -- Fiction
ISBN 0-380-73104-5
First published 1997 by Houghton Mifflin
"After a disastrous fall from a tree, senior Ryan Ward wrote off baseball. But he is swept back into the game when cocky, charismatic Josh Daniels—a star quarterback with the perfect spiral pass as well as a pitcher with a mean slider—moves into the neighborhood. . . . The well-written sports scenes—baseball and football—will draw reluctant readers, but it is Ryan's moral courage that will linger when the reading is done." Booklist

★ **Payback** time. Houghton Mifflin Harcourt 2010 298p $16

Grades: 7 8 9 10   **Fic**
1. School stories 2. Courage -- Fiction 3. Obesity -- Fiction 4. Football -- Fiction 5. Journalists -- Fiction
ISBN 978-0-547-27981-7; 0-547-27981-7
                                               LC 2010-6779

Deuker "really cranks up the suspense in his newest page-turner. . . . The game action alone is riveting . . . but Deuker enriches the tale with several well-tuned subplots and memorable narrator/protagonist." Booklist

Swagger; Carl Deuker. Houghton Mifflin Harcourt 2013 304 p. $17.99

Grades: 7 8 9 10 11 12   **Fic**
1. Basketball -- Fiction 2. Child sexual abuse -- Fiction 3. Sexual abuse -- Fiction
ISBN 0547974590; 9780547974590
                                               LC 2012045062
In this book, by Carl Deuker, "high school senior Jonas moves to Seattle [and] is glad to meet Levi, a nice, soft-spoken guy and fellow basketball player." Then, readers are introduced to "Ryan Hartwell, a charismatic basketball coach and sexual predator. When Levi reluctantly tells Jonas that Hartwell abused him, Jonas has to decide whether he should risk his future career to report the coach." (Publisher's note)

"When his family moves to Seattle, high school basketball star Jonas befriends new neighbor Levi, who plays power forward. Assistant coach Ryan Hartwell appreciates Jonas's fast-breaking style, but something about Hartwell feels wrong. Eventually his misdeeds lead to tragedy, and Jonas must find the courage to do what's right. Basketball fans will love the realistic hardwood action and the story's quick pacing." (Horn Book)

DeVillers, Julia

Lynn Visible. Dutton Children's Books 2010 278p il $16.99

Grades: 6 7 8 9   **Fic**
1. School stories 2. Fashion -- Fiction 3. Pennsylvania -- Fiction
ISBN 978-0-525-47691-7; 0-525-47691-1
                                               LC 2009-23058
"Lynn Vincent knows all the latest trends and isn't afraid to flaunt her funky style. The problem is, in small-town Pennsylvania, being fashion forward makes Lynn socially backward. . . . But when one of Lynn's unique creations makes it into the hands of a famous designer and onto the runway, it seems that Lynn might finally get her moment in the spotlight." Publisher's note

Devlin, Ivy

Low red moon. Bloomsbury Children's Books 2010 244p $16.99

Grades: 7 8 9 10   **Fic**
1. Wolves -- Fiction 2. Homicide -- Fiction 3. Grandmothers -- Fiction 4. Supernatural -- Fiction 5. Forests and forestry -- Fiction
ISBN 978-1-59990-510-5; 1-59990-510-8
                                               LC 2010-03480
Seventeen-year-old Avery can remember nothing to explain her parents' violent death in the woods where they live, but after meeting Ben, a mysterious new neighbor, she begins to believe some of the stories she has heard about creatures of the forest.

This is "an eerie and engrossing paranormal murder mystery. . . . The emotion pouring off the pages should sweep readers into this haunting story." Publ Wkly

Diamand, Emily

Flood and fire. Chicken House/Scholastic 2011
351p il (Raiders' ransom) $17.99
Grades: 4 5 6 7 **Fic**
1. Science fiction 2. Adventure fiction 3. Cats --
Fiction 4. Robots -- Fiction 5. Computers -- Fiction 6.
Terrorism -- Fiction 7. Great Britain -- Fiction
ISBN 978-0-545-24268-4; 0-545-24268-1
LC 2010023544
Sequel to: Raiders' ransom (2009)
In 22nd-century Cambridge, England, thirteen-year-old
Lilly Melkun must try to stop the strange, uncontrollable
robots that were activated when a sinister-looking chip in
her hand-held computer triggered a false anti-terrorist alert.
"The rare combination of action at breakneck speed and
significant, believable character development makes this just
about impossible to put down." Kirkus

★ **Raiders'** ransom. Chicken House/Scholastic
2009 334p map $17.99
Grades: 4 5 6 7 **Fic**
1. Science fiction 2. Adventure fiction 3. Pirates --
Fiction 4. Kidnapping -- Fiction 5. Great Britain --
Fiction 6. Environmental degradation -- Fiction
ISBN 978-0-545-14297-7; 0-545-14297-0
LC 2008-43692
It's the 22nd century and, because of climate change,
much of England is underwater. Poor Lilly is out fishing with
her trusty sea-cat when greedy raiders pillage the town—and
kidnap the prime minister's daughter. Her village blamed,
Lilly decides to find the girl.
This is a "captivating story. . . . A well-drawn world, plot
twists galore and spunky characters make this one a true
page-turner." Kirkus
Folllowed by: Flood and fire (2011)

DiCamillo, Kate

★ **Because** of Winn-Dixie. Candlewick Press
2000 182p $15.99; pa $6.99
Grades: 4 5 6 7 **Fic**
1. Dogs -- Fiction 2. Florida -- Fiction
ISBN 978-0-7636-0776-0; 0-7636-0776-2; 978-0-
7636-4432-1 pa; 0-7636-4432-3 pa
LC 99-34260
A Newbery honor book, 2001
Ten-year-old India Opal Buloni describes her first summer in the town of Naomi, Florida, and all the good things
that happen to her because of her big ugly dog Winn-Dixie
"This well-crafted, realistic, and heartwarming story will
be read and reread as a new favorite deserving a long-term
place on library shelves." SLJ

★ **Flora** and Ulysses; The Illuminated Adventures. by Kate DiCamillo; illustrated by K. G. Campbell. Candlewick Press 2013 240 p. ill. (reinforced)
$17.99
Grades: 5 6 7 8 **Fic**
1. Fantasy fiction 2. Adventure fiction 3. Girls --
fiction 4. Squirrels -- fiction 5. Superheroes -- fiction
ISBN 076366040X; 9780763660406
LC 2012947748
Parents' Choice Awards: Gold Medal Fiction (2013)

Newberry Medal (2014)
In this book by Kate DiCamillo, "bitter about her parents' divorce, Flora Buckman has withdrawn into her favorite comic book The Amazing Incandesto! and memorized
the advisories in its ongoing bonus feature, Terrible Things
Can Happen to You! She puts those life-saving tips into action when a squirrel is swallowed whole by a neighbor's new
vacuum cleaner. . . . Flora resuscitates the squirrel," who
now has superpowers. (Publishers Weekly)

★ The **magician's** elephant; illustrated by Yoko
Tanaka. Candlewick Press 2009 201p il $16.99
Grades: 4 5 6 7 **Fic**
1. Adventure fiction 2. Orphans -- Fiction 3. Siblings
-- Fiction 4. Elephants -- Fiction 5. Missing children
-- Fiction
ISBN 978-0-7636-4410-9; 0-7636-4410-2
LC 2009-07359
When ten-year-old orphan Peter Augustus Duchene
encounters a fortune teller in the marketplace one day and
she tells him that his sister, who is presumed dead, is in fact
alive, he embarks on a remarkable series of adventures as he
desperately tries to find her.
"The profound and deeply affecting emotions at work in
the story are bouyed up by the tale's succinct, lyrical text;
gentle touches of humor; and uplifting message." Booklist

Dickens, Charles

A **Christmas** carol; [by] Charles Dickens; illus-
trated by P.J. Lynch. Candlewick Press 2006 156p
il $19.99
Grades: 5 6 7 8 **Fic**
1. Ghost stories 2. Christmas -- Fiction 3. Great
Britain -- History -- 19th century -- Fiction
ISBN 978-0-7636-3120-8; 0-7636-3120-5
LC 2005058122
A miser learns the true meaning of Christmas when three
ghostly visitors review his past and foretell his future
Lynch's "watercolor-and-gouache illustrations lavishly
enhance this handsome edition." SLJ

Dickerson, Melanie

The **merchant's** daughter. Zondervan 2011
284p pa $9.99
Grades: 7 8 9 10 11 12 **Fic**
1. Love -- Fiction 2. Middle Ages -- Fiction 3. Christian
life -- Fiction 4. Contract labor -- Fiction 5. Great
Britain -- History -- 1154-1399, Plantagenets -- Fiction
ISBN 978-0-31072761-3
LC 2011034338
In 1352 England, seventeen-year-old Annabel, granddaughter of a knight and a would-be nun, eludes a lecherous
bailiff but falls in love with Lord Le Wyse, the ferocious
and disfigured man to whom her family owes three years of
indentured servitude, in this tale loosely based on Beauty
and the Beast.
Dickerson "manages a heartfelt romance that will stick
with readers, not only for its morality but also for the exploration of a woman's place within fourteenth-century English
Christianity." Booklist

Dickinson, Peter

★ **Angel** Isle; illustrations by Ian Andrew. Wendy Lamb Books 2007 500p il $17.99; lib bdg $20.99

Grades: 7 8 9 10   **Fic**
    1. Fantasy fiction 2. Magic -- Fiction
    ISBN 978-0-385-74690-8; 978-0-385-90928-0 lib bdg
                                                                LC 2007-7053
Sequel to The Ropemaker (2001)

While seeking the Ropemaker to restore the ancient magic that will protect their valley, Saranja, Maja, and Ribek must outwit twenty-four of the empire's most powerful and evil magicians.

"The characters are as well developed as those in the first book, and the complex, multilayered story includes more heady explorations of time and magic, joined here by thoughts on the meaning of true love." Booklist

★ **Eva**. Delacorte Press 1989 219p hardcover o.p. pa $6.50; pa $7.99

Grades: 7 8 9 10   **Fic**
    1. Science fiction 2. Chimpanzees -- Fiction
    ISBN 0-385-29702-5; 0-440-20766-5 pa;
    9780440207665 pa
                                                                LC 88-29435
"Eva wakes up from a deep coma that was the result of a terrible car accident and finds herself drastically altered. The accident leaves her so badly injured that her parents consent to a radical experiment to transplant her brain and memory into the body of a research chimpanzee. With the aid of a computer for communication, Eva slowly adjusts to her new existence while scientists monitor her progress, feelings, and insight into the animal world." Voice Youth Advocates

★ The **ropemaker**. Delacorte Press 2001 375p $15.95; pa $7.95

Grades: 7 8 9 10   **Fic**
    1. Fantasy fiction 2. Magic -- Fiction
    ISBN 0-385-72921-9; 0-385-73063-2 pa
                                                                LC 2001-17422
Michael L. Printz Award honor book, 2002

When the magic that protects their Valley starts to fail, Tilja and her companions journey into the evil Empire to find the ancient magician Faheel, who originally cast those spells

"The suspense does not let up until the very last pages. While on one level this tale is a fantasy, it is also a wonderful coming-of-age story." SLJ

Followed by: Angel Isle

Dionne, Erin

Models don't eat chocolate cookies. Dial Books for Young Readers 2009 243p pa $7.99

Grades: 6 7 8 9   **Fic**
    1. Obesity -- Fiction 2. Fashion models -- Fiction
    ISBN 978-0-8037-3296-4; 0-8037-3296-1
                                                                LC 2008-20612
Overweight thirteen-year-old Celeste begins a campaign to lose weight in order to make sure she does not win the Miss HuskeyPeach modeling challenge, in which her mother and aunt have entered her--against her wishes.

"Wry first-person narrative also provides convincing views of middle-school friendships, family dynamics, and

incremental personal growth. . . . A light, well-paced first novel." Booklist

Moxie and the art of rule breaking; a 14 day mystery. by Erin Dionne. Dial Books for Young Readers, an imprint of Penguin Group (USA) Inc. 2013 256 p. (hardcover) $16.99

Grades: 5 6 7 8   **Fic**
    1. Art thefts -- Fiction 2. Boston (Mass.) -- Fiction 3. Criminal investigation -- Fiction 4. Gangsters -- Fiction 5. Grandfathers -- Fiction 6. Mystery and detective stories
    ISBN 0803738714; 9780803738713
                                                                LC 2012022306
In this novel by Erin Dionne "Moxie Fleece opens her front door to a mysterious stranger. Suddenly Moxie is involved in Boston's . . . Isabella Stewart Gardner Museum art heist. Moxie has two weeks to find the art, otherwise she and the people she loves will be in . . . danger. Her tools? Ollie, a geocaching addict [and] her Alzheimer's suffering grandfather, Grumps, who knows lots more than he lets on; and a geometry proof that she sets up to sort out the clues." (Publisher's note)

Includes bibliographical resources

Ollie and the science of treasure hunting; a 14 day mystery. by Erin Dionne. Dial Books for Young Readers, an imprint of Penguin Group (USA) Inc. 2014 288 p. (hardcover) $16.99

Grades: 5 6 7 8   **Fic**
    1. Mystery fiction 2. Camps -- Fiction 3. Adventure fiction 4. Buried treasure -- Fiction 5. Mystery and detective stories 6. Vietnamese Americans -- Fiction 7. Racially mixed people -- Fiction 8. Boston Harbor Islands (Mass.) -- Fiction
    ISBN 9780803738720; 0803738722
                                                                LC 2013031211
"While at Wilderness camp on the Boston Harbor Islands, Ollie must navigate new friends, new enemies, and a high-stakes game of tag, so the last thing he needs is a mystery. But then Ollie meets Grey, an elusive girl with knowledge of the island's secrets, including the legend of a lost pirate treasure, which may not be a legend after all." (Publisher's note)

"A cast of likable campers, each with his or her own quirks --midnight swimmer, sensitive to sun, cartography genius--drive this fast-paced adventure led by a camp ranger with a gambling problem. Nothing should surprise readers in this thoroughly satisfying tale of friendship, intrigue, and Boston Harbor Island topography." Booklist

Includes bibliographical references

Companion to:

Moxie and the Art of Rule Breaking (2013)

The **total** tragedy of a girl named Hamlet. Dial Books for Young Readers 2010 290p $16.99

Grades: 6 7 8 9   **Fic**
    1. School stories 2. Sisters -- Fiction 3. Theater -- Fiction
    ISBN 978-0-8037-3298-8; 0-8037-3298-8
"Some sisterly bonding, the sweet flutterings of a first romance, and a creatively contrived comeuppance for the

mean girls make this a cheerful read for younger middle-schoolers." Booklist

DiTerlizzi, Tony

The **battle** for WondLa; Tony DiTerlizzi; with illustrations by the author. 1st edition Simon & Schuster Books for Young Readers 2014 480 p. col. ill., col. map (The search for WondLa) (hardcover) $17.99

Grades: 2 3 4 5   **Fic**
   1. Fantasy fiction 2. Extraterrestrial beings -- Fiction 3. War -- Fiction 4. Science fiction 5. Human-alien encounters -- Fiction
   ISBN 1416983147; 9781416983149
                                                    LC 2013035219
"All hope for a peaceful coexistence between humankind and aliens seems lost in the third installment of the WondLa trilogy. Eva Nine has gone into hiding for fear of luring the wicked Loroc to her companions. However, news of the city Solas being captured by the human leader, Cadmus Pryde, forces Eva into action once again." (Publisher's note)

"Of particular interest is Eva's development into a young woman of unwavering compassion and courage, even in the face of betrayal, loss, and injury. DiTerlizzi's beautiful illustrations are worth the price of admission, as usual, and they do much to help the reader distinguish among the plethora of strange creatures." Booklist

A **hero** for WondLa; by Tony DiTerlizzi; with illustrations by the author. Simon & Schuster Books for Young Readers 2012 445 p. (hardcover) $17.99
Grades: 5 6 7 8   **Fic**
   1. Science fiction 2. Rescue work -- Fiction 3. Life on other planets -- Fiction 4. Identity -- Fiction 5. Human-alien encounters -- Fiction
   ISBN 1416983120; 9781416983125; 9781442450844
                                                    LC 2011037031
Author Tony DiTerlizzi tells a science fiction story. "Eva Nine had never seen another human, but after a human boy named Hailey rescues her along with her companions, she couldn't be happier. Eva thinks she has everything she's ever dreamed of, especially when Hailey brings her and her friends to the colony of New Attica, where humans of all shapes and sizes live in apparent peace and harmony. But all is not idyllic in New Attica, and Eva Nine soon realizes that something sinister is going on . . . [that] could mean the end of everything and everyone on planet Orbona." (Publisher's note)

★ The **search** for WondLa; with illustrations by the author. Simon & Schuster Books for Young Readers 2010 477p il $17.99
Grades: 5 6 7 8   **Fic**
   1. Science fiction 2. Extraterrestrial beings -- Fiction
   ISBN 978-1-4169-8310-1; 1-4169-8310-4
                                                    LC 2010-01326
Living in isolation with a robot on what appears to be an alien world populated with bizarre life forms, a twelve-year-old human girl called Eva Nine sets out on a journey to find others like her.

"The abundant illustrations, drawn in a flat, two-tone style, are lush and enhance readers' understanding of this

unique universe. . . . DiTerlizzi is pushing the envelope in his latest work, nearly creating a new format that combines a traditional novel with a graphic novel and with the interactivity of the computer. Yet, beneath this impressive package lies a theme readers will easily relate to: the need to belong, to connect, to figure out one's place in the world. The novel's ending is a stunning shocker that will leave kids frantically awaiting the next installment." SLJ

Divakaruni, Chitra Banerjee

The **conch** bearer. Roaring Brook Press 2003 265p (Brotherhood of the conch) $16.95; lib bdg $23.90
Grades: 5 6 7 8   **Fic**
   1. India -- Fiction 2. Magic -- Fiction
   ISBN 978-0-7613-1935-1; 0-7613-1935-2; 978-0-7613-2793-6 lib bdg; 0-7613-2793-2 lib bdg
                                                    LC 2003-8578
In India, a healer invites twelve-year-old Anand to join him on a quest to return a magical conch to its safe and rightful home, high in the Himalayan mountains

"Divakaruni keeps her tale fresh and riveting." Publ Wkly
   Other titles in this series are:
   The mirror of fire and dreaming (2005)
   Shadowland (2009)

Dixon, Heather

★ **Entwined**. Greenwillow Books 2011 472p
Grades: 7 8 9 10   **Fic**
   1. Fantasy fiction 2. Dance -- Fiction 3. Death -- Fiction 4. Magic -- Fiction 5. Princesses -- Fiction 6. Kings and rulers -- Fiction 7. Father-daughter relationship -- Fiction
   ISBN 0-06-200103-5; 978-0-06-200103-0
                                                    LC 2010-11686
Confined to their dreary castle while mourning their mother's death, Princess Azalea and her eleven sisters join The Keeper, who is trapped in a magic passageway, in a nightly dance that soon becomes nightmarish.

"The story gracefully explores significant themes of grief and loss, mercy and love. Full of mystery, lush settings, and fully orbed characters, Dixon's debut is both suspenseful and rewarding." Booklist

Dobkin, Bonnie

Neptune's children; [by] Bonnie Dobkin. Walker & Co. 2008 262p map $16.99
Grades: 7 8 9 10   **Fic**
   1. Terrorism -- Fiction 2. Amusement parks -- Fiction 3. Resistance to government -- Fiction
   ISBN 978-0-8027-9734-6; 0-8027-9734-2
                                                    LC 2008-2680
When a biological terrorist attack kills all adults on Earth, children stranded at an amusement park work together to survive, led by Milo whose father was an engineer there, but when new threats arise and suspicions grow, rebellion erupts.

"This thriller has gripping writing that makes it hard to put down. The characterizations of the older children are well done. . . . Even with the large number of survival stories on the market, this is one worth adding to your collection." SLJ

Docherty, James

The **ice** cream con; [by] Jimmy Docherty. Scholastic 2008 250p $16.99

Grades: 5 6 7 8 9   **Fic**

1. Bullies -- Fiction 2. Thieves -- Fiction 3. Scotland -- Fiction

ISBN 978-0-545-02885-1; 0-545-02885-X

LC 2007-35321

In Glasgow, Scotland, after getting mugged twice in ten minutes, thirteen-year-old Jake comes up with a plan to con the criminals on his estate with the help of his closest friends, until events start to snowball out of control.

"Docherty keeps the action coming fast and furious from beginning to end. . . . It is bound to be a huge hit with tween boys and especially reluctant readers." Voice Youth Advocates

Doctorow, Cory

★ **Little** brother. Tor Teen 2008 380p

Grades: 8 9 10 11 12   **Fic**

1. Computers -- Fiction 2. Terrorism -- Fiction 3. Civil rights -- Fiction 4. San Francisco (Calif.) -- Fiction 5. United States -- Dept. of Homeland Security -- Fiction

ISBN 0765319853; 9780765319852

LC 2008-1827

After being interrogated for days by the Department of Homeland Security in the aftermath of a terrorist attack on San Francisco, California, 17-year-old Marcus, released into what is now a police state, decides to use his expertise in computer hacking to set things right. "High school." (Horn Book)

"The author manages to explain naturally the necessary technical tools and scientific concepts in this fast-paced and well-written story. . . . The reader is privy to Marcus's gut-wrenching angst, frustration, and terror, thankfully offset by his self-awareness and humorous observations." Voice Youth Advocates

Pirate cinema; Cory Doctorow. 1st ed. Tor Teen 2012 384 p. (hardback) $19.99; (paperback) $9.99; (audiobook) $24.00

Grades: 7 8 9 10   **Fic**

1. Copyright 2. Runaway teenagers -- Fiction 3. Science fiction 4. England -- Fiction 5. Internet -- Fiction 6. Protest movements -- Fiction 7. Motion pictures -- Production and direction -- Fiction

ISBN 0765329085; 9780765329080; 9781429943185; 9780765329097; 9780307879585

LC 2012019871

In this book, author Cory Doctorow tells the story of Trent McCauley, a boy who "has an irrepressible drive to create . . . [films] through illegal downloading, and when he's caught, . . . [he] runs away to London, where he's taken under the wing of streetwise Jem Dodger. . . . He meets 26 and creates the persona Cecil B. DeVil. Pulled by 26 into the politics of copyright and the lobbyist money that purchases laws, Cecil becomes a creative figurehead for reform against escalating laws that aggressively jail kids." (Kirkus Reviews)

Dogar, Sharon

★ **Annexed**. Houghton Mifflin Harcourt 2010 333p $17

Grades: 8 9 10 11 12   **Fic**

1. Children 2. Diarists 3. Holocaust victims 4. Netherlands -- Fiction 5. Holocaust, 1933-1945 -- Fiction

ISBN 978-0-547-50195-6; 0-547-50195-1

LC 2010-282410

"On July 13, 1942, 15-year-old Peter van Pels and his parents entered the attic that became their home for two years. Peter is angry that he is hiding and not fighting Nazis. He is also not happy to be sharing cramped living quarters with the Franks, especially know-it-all Anne. In this novel, Dogar 'reimagines' what happened between the families who lived in the secret annex immortalized in Anne Frank's diary. In doing so, she creates a captivating historical novel and fully fleshes out the character of Peter, a boy whom teens will easily relate to." SLJ

Doherty, Berlie

The **girl** who saw lions. Roaring Brook Press 2008 249p $16.95

Grades: 6 7 8 9   **Fic**

1. Adoption -- Fiction 2. Tanzania -- Fiction 3. Great Britain -- Fiction 4. AIDS (Disease) -- Fiction

ISBN 978-1-59643-377-9; 1-59643-377-9

LC 2007-44054

In alternating voices, thirteen-year-old Rosa and her mother are trying to adopt a Tanzanian child in England, while in Tanzania, nine-year-old Abela watches her family die and her uncle illegally sends her to England, in the hopes of selling her.

"Packs in a great deal of information about the AIDS crisis in Africa, female genital mutilation, international adoptions, the foster care system, and the many challenges facing parentless children and the social workers who try to place them. Girls will love this emotionally powerful novel." Voice Youth Advocates

Doktorski, Jennifer Salvato

Famous last words; Jennifer Salvato Doktorski. Henry Holt and Company 2013 288 p. (hardcover) $17.99

Grades: 7 8 9 10   **Fic**

1. Women journalists -- Fiction 2. Internship programs -- Fiction 3. Journalism -- Fiction 4. Newspapers -- Fiction 5. Self-perception -- Fiction 6. Dating (Social customs) -- Fiction

ISBN 0805093672; 9780805093674

LC 2012046312

In this book, "aspiring reporter Sam D'Angelo, 16, is interning at her local New Jersey paper for the summer, stuck writing obituaries with her occasionally annoying, college-age fellow intern AJ. When she's not taking phone calls about dead people, Sam writes humorous imaginary obits (including one for herself); spends time with her grandmother; lusts after the 'incredibly hot' features intern, Tony Roma; and covertly investigates the shady mayor with AJ." (Publishers Weekly)

"Something of a love note to print journalism, the story is nevertheless snappy and contemporary, furthered by

Sam's wry, self-deprecating narration and convincingly colloquial dialogue. Cleverly titled, realistically written, and on the whole engaging and sympathetic, this story rings true." Kirkus

Dolamore, Jaclyn

★ **Magic** under glass. Bloomsbury Children's Books 2010 225p $16.99

Grades: 7 8 9 10 11 12   **Fic**

1. Fantasy fiction 2. Magic -- Fiction 3. Robots -- Fiction 4. Fairies -- Fiction 5. Singers -- Fiction

ISBN 978-1-59990-430-6; 1-59990-430-6

LC 2009-20944

A wealthy sorcerer's invitation to sing with his automaton leads seventeen-year-old Nimira, whose family's disgrace brought her from a palace to poverty, into political intrigue, enchantments, and a friendship with a fairy prince who needs her help.

"Delamore successfully juggles several elements that might have stymied even a more experienced writer: intriguing plot elements, sophisticated characterizations, and a subtle boost of girl power." Booklist

Dominy, Amy Fellner

OyMG. Walker & Co. 2011 247p $16.99

Grades: 6 7 8 9   **Fic**

1. Camps -- Fiction 2. Arizona -- Fiction 3. Prejudices -- Fiction 4. Jews -- United States -- Fiction

ISBN 978-0-8027-2177-8; 0-8027-2177-X

LC 2010-34581

Fourteen-year-old Ellie will do almost anything to win a scholarship to the best speech school in the country, but must decide if she is willing to hide her Jewish heritage while at a Phoenix, Arizona, summer camp that could help her reach her goal.

"Readers will be pulled into the thoughtful exploration of one girl's emotional connection to her religion and family heritage, her struggle to balance ambition with honesty and self respect, and her delicate negotiation of being different when that difference isn't outwardly apparent." Bull Cent Child Books

Donaldson, Julia

Running on the cracks. Henry Holt 2009 218p $16.99

Grades: 6 7 8 9   **Fic**

1. Orphans -- Fiction 2. Scotland -- Fiction 3. Runaway teenagers -- Fiction 4. Child sexual abuse -- Fiction 5. Racially mixed people -- Fiction

ISBN 978-0-8050-9054-3; 0-8050-9054-1

LC 2008-50278

After her parents are killed in an accident, English teenager Leonora Watts-Chan runs away to Glasgow, Scotland, to find her Chinese grandparents

"The characters in Donaldson's . . . YA debut are well drawn and their imperfections are authentic, particularly Mary's battle with mental illness. Despite heavy themes, the story is neither bleak nor gritty. The fast pace and short chapters should appeal to readers, who will celebrate the hopeful ending." Publ Wkly

Donovan, John

I'll get there, it better be worth the trip; 40th anniversary edition; Flux 2010 228p pa $9.95

Grades: 7 8 9 10 11   **Fic**

1. Alcoholism -- Fiction 2. Friendship -- Fiction 3. Homosexuality -- Fiction 4. New York (N.Y.) -- Fiction

ISBN 978-0-7387-2134-7 pa; 0-7387-2134-4 pa

LC 2010014266

First published 1969 by Harper & Row

While trying to cope with his alcoholic mother and absent father, a lonely New York City teenager develops a confusing crush on another boy.

"Donovan's novel is startlingly outspoken and honest in its presentation of a young teen questioning his sexuality. . . . Such is the author's skill that the reader knows this young man's journey of self-discovery will get him to his 'there,' wherever it may be. This welcome fortieth-anniversary edition of a YA classic is an essential purchase for all libraries." Voice Youth Advocates

Dooley, Sarah

Body of water. Feiwel and Friends 2011 324p $16.99

Grades: 7 8 9   **Fic**

1. Arson -- Fiction 2. Camping -- Fiction 3. Family life -- Fiction 4. West Virginia -- Fiction 5. Homeless persons -- Fiction

ISBN 978-0-312-61254-2; 0-312-61254-0

LC 2011023523

After their trailer home and all their belongings are burned, twelve-year-old Ember and her Wiccan family move to a lakeside campground where Ember's anguish over losing her dog, as well as her friendship with the boy she fears started the fire, stops her from making new friends and moving on.

"Dooley puts readers directly into the center of Ember's plight with a heartfelt first-person narration. An enthralling tale that demystifies Wicca, humanizes homeless families and inspires reflection on friendship, forgiveness and moving forward." Kirkus

Dorris, Michael

Morning Girl. Hyperion Bks. for Children 1992 74p hardcover o.p. pa $4.99

Grades: 4 5 6 7   **Fic**

1. Taino Indians -- Fiction 2. America -- Exploration -- Fiction

ISBN 0-7868-1358-X pa

LC 92-52989

Twelve year old Morning Girl, a Taino Indian who loves the day, and her younger brother Star Boy, who loves the night, take turns describing their life on a Bahamian island in 1492; in Morning Girl's last narrative, she witnesses the arrival of the first Europeans to her world

"The author uses a lyrical, yet easy-to-follow, style to place these compelling characters in historical context. . . . Dorris does a superb job of showing that family dynamics are complicated, regardless of time and place. . . . A touching glimpse into the humanity that connects us all." Horn Book

Sees Behind Trees. Hyperion Bks. for Children 1996 104p hardcover o.p. pa $4.99

Grades: 4 5 6 7   **Fic**
1. Native Americans -- Fiction 2. Vision disorders --
Fiction
ISBN 0-7868-1357-1 pa
LC 96-15859

"For the partially sighted Walnut, it is impossible to
prove his right to a grown-up name by hitting a target with
his bow and arrow. With his highly developed senses, however, he demonstrates that he can do something even better:
he can see 'what cannot be seen' which earns him the name
Sees Behind Trees.... Set in sixteenth-century America, this
richly imagined and gorgeously written rite-of-passage story
has the gravity of legend. Moreover, it has buoyant humor
and the immediacy of a compelling story that is peopled with
multidimensional characters." Booklist

Dowd, Siobhan

★ **Bog** child. David Fickling Books 2008 321p
Grades: 8 9 10 11 12   **Fic**
1. Mummies -- Fiction 2. Prisoners -- Fiction
3. Terrorism -- Fiction 4. Family life -- Fiction 5.
Northern Ireland -- Fiction
ISBN 0-385-75170-2 lib bdg; 978-0-385-75169-8;
0-385-75169-9; 978-0-385-75170-4 lib bdg
LC 2008-2998

This novel is set in Northern Ireland in 1981. 18-year-old
Fergus is distracted from his upcoming A-level exams by
the discovery of a girl's body in a peat bog, his imprisoned
brother's hunger strike, and the stress of being a courier for
Sinn Fein. "Grades eight to twelve." (Bull Cent Child Books)

"Dowd raises questions about moral choices within a
compelling plot that is full of surprises, powerfully bringing
home the impact of political conflict on innocent bystanders." Publ Wkly

★ The **London** Eye mystery. David Fickling
Books 2008 322p $15.99; lib bdg $18.99; pa $7.50
Grades: 5 6 7 8   **Fic**
1. Mystery fiction 2. Cousins -- Fiction 3. Siblings
-- Fiction 4. London (England) -- Fiction 5. Missing
children -- Fiction 6. Asperger's syndrome -- Fiction
ISBN 978-0-375-84976-3; 0-375-84976-9; 978-0-375-
94976-0 lib bdg; 0-375-84976-3 lib bdg; 978-0-385-
75184-1 pa; 0-385-75184-2 pa
LC 2007-15119

First published 2007 in the United Kingdom

When Ted and Kat's cousin Salim disappears from the
London Eye ferris wheel, the two siblings must work together—Ted with his brain that is "wired differently" and
impatient Kat—to try to solve the mystery of what happened
to Salim.

"Everything rings true here, the family relationships, the
quirky connections of Ted's mental circuitry, and . . . the
mystery. . . . A page turner with heft." Booklist

Dowell, Frances O'Roark

Chicken boy. Atheneum Books for Young Readers 2005 201p $15.95; pa $5.99
Grades: 4 5 6 7   **Fic**
1. Chickens -- Fiction 2. Friendship -- Fiction 3.

Family life -- Fiction
ISBN 0-689-85816-7; 1-4169-3482-0 pa
LC 2004-10928

Since the death of his mother, Tobin's family life and
school life have been in disarray, but after he starts raising
chickens with his seventh-grade classmate, Henry, everything starts to fall into place. "Intermediate, middle school."
(Horn Book)

"There is no glib resolution, here. But the strong narration and the child's struggle with forgiveness make for poignant, aching drama." Booklist

★ **Dovey** Coe. Atheneum Bks. for Young Read-
ers 2000 181p $16; pa $5.99
Grades: 5 6 7 8   **Fic**
1. Mountain life -- Fiction 2. North Carolina -- Fiction
ISBN 0-689-83174-9; 0-689-84667-3 pa
LC 99-46870

When accused of murder in her North Carolina mountain
town in 1928, Dovey Coe, a stronged-willed twelve-year-old
girl, comes to a new understanding of others, including her
deaf brother

"Dowell has created a memorable character in Dovey,
quick-witted and honest to a fault. . . . This is a delightful
book, thoughtful and full of substance." Booklist

★ **Falling** in. Atheneum Books for Young Read-
ers 2010 245p il $16.99
Grades: 4 5 6 7   **Fic**
1. Fantasy fiction
ISBN 978-1-4169-5032-5; 1-4169-5032-X
LC 2009-10412

Middle-schooler Isabelle Bean follows a mouse's squeak
into a closet and falls into a parallel universe where the children believe she is the witch they have feared for years, finally come to devour them.

"This perfectly paced story has enough realistic elements to appeal even to nonfantasy readers." Booklist

The **kind** of friends we used to be. Atheneum
Books for Young Readers 2009 234p $16.99
Grades: 5 6 7 8   **Fic**
1. School stories 2. Friendship -- Fiction
ISBN 978-1-4169-5031-8; 1-4169-5031-1
LC 2008-22245

Sequel to: The secret language of girls (2004)

Twelve-year-olds Kate and Marylin, friends since preschool, draw further apart as Marylin becomes involved in
student government and cheerleading, while Kate wants
to play guitar and write songs, and both develop unlikely
friendships with other girls and boys.

"Dowell gets middle-school dynamics exactly right, and
while her empathetic portraits of Kate and Marylin are genuine and heartfelt, even secondary characters are memorable.
A realistic and humorous look at the trials and tribulations of
growing up and growing independent." SLJ

★ The **second** life of Abigail Walker; Frances
O'Roark Dowell. Atheneum Books for Young Readers 2012 228 p. (hardcover) $16.99
Grades: 4 5 6 7   **Fic**
1. Self-confidence -- Fiction 2. Middle schools --

Fiction 4. Friendship -- Fiction 5. Overweight persons -- Fiction 6. Human-animal relationships -- Fiction
ISBN 1442405937; 9781442405936

LC 2012010646

This novel, by Frances O'Roark Dowell, follows a youth struggling with popularity. "Seventeen pounds. That's the difference between . . . chubby and slim, between teased and taunting. Abby is fine with her body, . . . so she speaks out against Kristen and her groupies--and becomes officially unpopular. Embracing her new status, Abby heads to an abandoned lot across the street and crosses an unfamiliar stream that leads her to a boy who's as different as they come." (Publisher's note)

★ **Shooting** the moon. Atheneum Books for Young Readers 2008 163p $16.99; pa $5.99
Grades: 4 5 6 7 **Fic**
1. Soldiers -- Fiction 2. Family life -- Fiction 3. Vietnam War, 1961-1975 -- Fiction
ISBN 978-1-4169-2690-0; 1-4169-2690-9; 978-1-4169-7986-9 pa; 1-4169-7986-7 pa

LC 2006-100347

Boston Globe-Horn Book Award honor book: Fiction and Poetry (2008)

When her brother is sent to fight in Vietnam, twelve-year-old Jamie begins to reconsider the army world that she has grown up in.

"The clear, well-paced first-person prose is perfectly matched to this novel's spare setting and restrained plot. . . . This [is a] thoughtful and satisfying story. . . . Readers will find beauty in its resolution, and will leave this eloquent heroine reluctantly." SLJ

The **sound** of your voice, only really far away; by Frances O'Roark Dowell. Atheneum Books for Young Readers 2013 192 p. (hardcover) $16.99
Grades: 5 6 7 8 **Fic**
1. Friendship -- Fiction 2. High school students -- Fiction 3. Interpersonal relations -- Fiction 4. Schools -- Fiction 5. Popularity -- Fiction 6. Best friends -- Fiction 7. Middle schools -- Fiction
ISBN 1442432896; 9781442432895; 9781442432918

LC 2012030308

Sequel to: The kind of friends we used to be

In this novel by Frances O'Roark Dowell "Marylin and Kate find that boys can be just as complicated as friendship. As a middle school cheerleader . . . Marylin [learns] there are also rules about whom she's allowed to like—and Benjamin, the student body president, is . . . unacceptable. She'll pretend that she's using him to get new cheerleading uniforms. When Matthew tells Kate that the school's Audio Lab needs funding . . ., she decides to . . . help him get it. There isn't enough money to go around, and it soon becomes clear that only one of the two girls can get her way." (Publisher's note)

Ten miles past normal. Atheneum Books for Young Readers 2011 211p $16.99
Grades: 6 7 8 9 10 **Fic**
1. School stories 2. Farm life -- Fiction 3. Bands (Music) -- Fiction 4. North Carolina -- Fiction
ISBN 1-4169-9585-4; 978-1-4169-9585-2

LC 2010-22041

Because living with "modern-hippy" parents on a goat farm means fourteen-year-old Janie Gorman cannot have a normal high school life, she tries joining Jam Band, making friends with Monster, and spending time with elderly former civil rights workers.

"Janie narrates her first year in high school with her sure, smart, sarcastic voice. . . . Dowell gets all the details of ninth grade right." Horn Book

Downer, Ann

The **dragon** of Never-Was. Atheneum Books for Young Readers 2006 305p il hardcover o.p. pa $5.99
Grades: 4 5 6 7 **Fic**
1. Magic -- Fiction 2. Dragons -- Fiction 3. Scotland -- Fiction
ISBN 978-0-689-85571-9; 0-689-85571-0; 978-1-4169-5453-8 pa; 1-4169-5453-8 pa

LC 2005017727

Sequel to Hatching magic (2003)

With the help of a bottle of blue fire and a magical brooch, Theodora searches for a dragon on an island off the coast of Scotland before it causes any harm.

"Smart, observant, and self-aware, Theodora makes a sympathetic character, convincing even in the most supernatural circumstances." Booklist

★ **Hatching** magic. Atheneum Bks. for Young Readers 2003 242p $16.95; pa $5.99
Grades: 4 5 6 7 **Fic**
1. Magic -- Fiction 2. Dragons -- Fiction
ISBN 0-689-83400-4; 0-689-87057-4 pa

LC 00-56570

When a thirteenth-century wizard confronts twenty-first century Boston while seeking his pet dragon, he is followed by a rival wizard and a very unhappy demon, but eleven-year-old Theodora Oglethorpe may hold the secret to setting everything right

"With likable characters, and laced with plenty of humor and adventure, Downer's fantasy will have solid appeal for young genre fans." Booklist

Another title about Theodora is:
The dragon of never-was (2006)

Downey, Jen Swann

The **ninja** librarians; the accidental keyhand. Jen Swann Downey. Sourcebooks Jabberwocky 2014 384 p. (hc : alk. paper) $16.99
Grades: 4 5 6 7 **Fic**
1. Adventure fiction 2. Libraries -- Fiction 3. Librarians -- Fiction 4. Censorship -- Fiction 5. Space and time -- Fiction 6. Secret societies -- Fiction
ISBN 1402287704; 9781402287701

LC 2013049956

Kirkus (March 15, 2014)

In this adventure story by Jen Swann Downey, "when Dorrie and her brother Marcus chase Moe--an unusually foul-tempered mongoose--into the janitor's closet of their local library, they make an astonishing discovery: the headquarters of a secret society of ninja librarians. Their mission: protect those whose words get them into trouble, anywhere in the world and at any time in history." (Publisher's note)

"Delightfully funny from the first page, where Dorrie laments having never been bitten by anything more bloodthirsty than her little sister, this middle-grade time-travel adventure is surprisingly full of fun and action (and a madcap mongoose). Downey's hilarious debut is perfect for any library-loving reader as well as those who never considered librarians to be cool." - Booklist

Accidental keyhand

Downham, Jenny

★ **Before** I die. David Fickling Books 2007 326p hardcover o.p. pa $9.99

Grades: 8 9 10 11 12   **Fic**

1. Death -- Fiction 2. Terminally ill -- Fiction
ISBN 978-0-385-75155-1; 978-0-385-75183-4 pa
LC 2007-20284

A terminally ill teenaged girl makes and carries out a list of things to do before she dies.

"Downham holds nothing back in her wrenchingly and exceptionally vibrant story." Publ Wkly

Dowswell, Paul

The **Auslander**. Bloomsbury Children's Books 2011 295p $16.99

Grades: 7 8 9 10   **Fic**

1. Orphans -- Fiction 2. Adoption -- Fiction 3. Insurgency -- Fiction 4. Berlin (Germany) -- Fiction 5. National socialism -- Fiction 6. World War, 1939-1945 -- Fiction 7. Germany -- History -- 1933-1945 -- Fiction
ISBN 1599906333; 9781599906331
LC 2010035626

First published 2009 in the United Kingdom

German soldiers take Peter from a Warsaw orphanage, and soon he is adopted by Professor Kaltenbach, a prominent Nazi, but Peter forms his own ideas about what he sees and hears and decides to take a risk that is most dangerous in 1942 Berlin.

"The characters are rich and nuanced; . . . the action is swift and suspenseful; and the juxtaposition of wartime nobility and wartime cruelty is timeless." Horn Book

Powder monkey; adventures of Sam Witchall. [by] Paul Dowswell. 1st U.S. ed.; Bloomsbury Pub. 2005 275p $16.95

Grades: 6 7 8 9   **Fic**

1. Sea stories 2. Adventure fiction 3. France -- History -- 1799-1815 -- Fiction 4. Great Britain -- History -- 1714-1837 -- Fiction
ISBN 978-1-58234-675-5; 1-58234-675-5
LC 2005013049

Thirteen-year-old Sam endures harsh conditions, battles, and a shipwreck after being pressed into service aboard the HMS Miranda during the Napoleonic Wars.

"Readers will be absorbed in the day-to-day life of young Sam, and his vivid tale will keep them on edge." SLJ

Other titles in this series are:
Prison ship (2006)
Battle fleet (2008)

Doyle, Arthur Conan, Sir, 1859-1930

The **adventures** and the memoirs of Sherlock Holmes; by Arthur Conan Doyle; illustrated by Scott McKowen. Sterling Pub. Co. 2004 vi, 569 p.p ill. (hardcover) $9.95

Grades: 7 8 9 10 11 12 Adult   **Fic**

1. Mystery fiction 2. Detective and mystery stories, English 3. Private investigators -- England -- Fiction 4. Holmes, Sherlock (Fictitious character) -- Fiction
ISBN 140271453X; 9781402714535
LC 2004016067

This book is a collection of Sir Arthur Conan Doyle's mystery stories featuring detective "Sherlock Holmes, with his unequalled powers of deduction." This edition has illustrations created by Scott McKowen "in scratchboard, an engraving medium which evokes the look of popular art from the period of these stories." (Publisher's note)

Doyle, Brian

Boy O'Boy. Douglas & McIntyre 2003 161p hardcover o.p. pa $12.95

Grades: 6 7 8 9   **Fic**

1. Canada -- Fiction 2. Child sexual abuse -- Fiction
ISBN 0-88899-588-1; 0-88899-590-3 pa

Living in Ottawa in 1945, Martin O'Boy must deal with a drunken father, an overburdened mother, a disabled twin brother, and a sexual predator at his church.

"Martin O'Boy is an expert observer and narrator. . . . Martin's world is believably real. Even the description of the sexual encounter seems like what a confused 11 or 12-year-old might say." SLJ

Followed by: Pure Spring

Pure Spring. Groundwood Books 2007 158p $16.95; pa $8.95

Grades: 6 7 8 9   **Fic**

1. Canada -- Fiction
ISBN 978-0-88899-774-6; 978-0-88899-775-3 pa

Sequel to: Boy O'Boy

It's spring in post-World War II Ottawa and Martin has found a true home. He's also working even though he had to lie about his age to get the job. Martin is also in love, but his boss is robbing the family of the one he loves.

"Doyle lovingly shapes his characters. . . . Doyle rounds out the grimness with comedic scenes." Horn Book

Doyle, Eugenie F.

According to Kit; [by] Eugenie Doyle. Front Street 2009 215p $17.95

Grades: 7 8 9 10   **Fic**

1. Ballet -- Fiction 2. Vermont -- Fiction 3. Farm life -- Fiction 4. Family life -- Fiction 5. Home schooling -- Fiction 6. Mother-daughter relationship -- Fiction
ISBN 978-1-59078-474-7; 1-59078-474-X
LC 2009-7032

As fifteen-year-old Kit does chores on her family's Vermont farm, she puzzles over her mother's apparent unhappiness, complains about being homeschooled after a minor incident at school, and strives to communicate just how important dance is to her.

Doyle's "characters are complicated and authentic. . . . Kit's obsession with ballet . . . will ring true for all teens equally focused on their own talents." Booklist

Doyle, Marissa

Betraying season. Henry Holt and Co. 2009 330p $16.99

Grades: 7 8 9 10 **Fic**

1. Magic -- Fiction 2. Ireland -- Fiction 3. Witches -- Fiction 4. Great Britain -- History -- 19th century -- Fiction

ISBN 978-0-8050-8252-4; 0-8050-8252-2

LC 2008-40593

Sequel to: Bewitching season (2008)

In 1838, Penelope Leland goes to Ireland to study magic and prove to herself that she is as good a witch as her twin sister Persy, but when Niall Keating begins to pay her court, she cannot help being distracted.

"This is a full-bodied story that wonderfully combines elements of romance, fantasy, and history. . . . Whether Doyle is describing the Irish countryside, a magical incantation, or a lover's kiss, her writing is compelling, and it will be hard for readers not to be swept away by this invigorating story." Booklist

★ **Bewitching** season. Henry Holt 2008 346p $16.95; pa $8.99

Grades: 7 8 9 10 **Fic**

1. Magic -- Fiction 2. Twins -- Fiction 3. Sisters -- Fiction 4. Missing persons -- Fiction 5. London (England) -- Fiction 6. Great Britain -- History -- 19th century -- Fiction

ISBN 978-0-8050-8251-7; 0-8050-8251-4; 978-0-312-59695-8 pa; 0-312-59695-2 pa

In 1837, as seventeen-year-old twins, Persephone and Penelope, are starting their first London Season they find that their beloved governess, who has taught them everything they know about magic, has disappeared.

"Doyle takes as much care with characters . . . as with story details. This [is a] delightful mélange of genres." Booklist

Followed by: Betraying season (2009)

Courtship and curses; Marissa Doyle. Henry Holt 2012 343 p. (hc) $17.99

Grades: 7 8 9 10 **Fic**

1. Regency novels 2. Mystery fiction 3. Magic -- Fiction 4. Witches -- Fiction 5. Self-acceptance -- Fiction 6. People with disabilities -- Fiction 7. Aristocracy (Social class) -- Fiction 8. Brussels (Belgium) -- History -- Fiction 9. Belgium -- History -- 1814-1830 -- Fiction 10. Great Britain -- History -- 1800-1837 -- Fiction

ISBN 0805091874; 9780805091878

LC 2011031999

This book tells the story of "Lady Sophronia Rosier (Sophie)," who is preparing "for her entrance into London society," despite a disability incurred from illness. She has help from "her new best friend, Parthenope" and "begins her procession into society." It soon becomes clear that someone is using magic to target her and her father. "Sophie and Parthenope begin to investigate while playing their roles in society, dreadfully aware that lives are at stake." (Voice of Youth Advocates)

Doyle, Roddy, 1958-

★ A **greyhound** of a girl; Roddy Doyle. Amulet Books 2012 208 p. (hbk.) $16.95

Grades: 7 8 9 10 11 12 **Fic**

1. Dog racing -- Fiction 2. Family life -- Fiction 3. Dublin (Ireland) -- Fiction 4. Women -- Ireland -- Fiction 5. Death -- Fiction 6. Ghosts -- Fiction 7. Ireland -- Fiction 8. Voyages and travels -- Fiction 9. Mothers and daughters -- Fiction

ISBN 9781407129334 Marion Lloyd; 1407129333 Marion Lloyd; 9781419701689 Amulet; 1419701681 Amulet

LC 2011042200

This book tells the story of "Twelve-year-old Mary O'Hara," an Irish girl who "is surrounded by good-humored women . . . her mum at home, her mum's mum, who is dying in Dublin's Sacred Heart Hospital, and her mum's mum's mum, who has just materialized as a ghost on her street. . . . [Roddy] Doyle divides up the novel by character, giving readers first-hand glimpses into the nature of each woman through time." (Kirkus)

Wilderness. Arthur A. Levine Books 2007 211p $16.99

Grades: 6 7 8 9 **Fic**

1. Finland -- Fiction 2. Mothers -- Fiction 3. Sledding -- Fiction 4. Wilderness survival -- Fiction

ISBN 978-0-439-02356-6; 0-439-02356-4

LC 2007-11688

As Irish teenager Gráinne anxiously prepares for a reunion with her mother, who abandoned the family years before, Gráinne's half-brothers and their mother take a dog-sledding vacation in Finland.

"The drama and adventure are leavened by generous helpings of Doyle's characteristic charm, laugh-out-loud humor, and wonderful way with words." SLJ

Drago, Ty

The **Undertakers**; rise of the Corpses. Sourcebooks Jabberwocky 2011 465p pa $10.99

Grades: 4 5 6 7 **Fic**

1. Horror fiction 2. Zombies -- Fiction

ISBN 978-1-4022-4785-9; 1-4022-4785-0

"Whatever you do, do not call them zombies! These are Corpses 'reanimated bodies that have been possessed,' and they are everywhere, although they are only visible to a select few, including 12-year-old Will Ritter. After realizing suddenly that he is able to see, Will is taken in by the Undertakers, a rogue group that rescues other, similarly targeted teens and fights to defeat the Corpses' evil plans to conquer Phildelphia and, ultimately, the world. . . . Calling into action a cast of distinctive characters with authentic voices and behaviors, . . . Will's breathless adventures . . . are thoughtful and exciting, and the descriptions of decaying flesh will likely both disgust and delight readers." Booklist

Draper, Sharon M.

The **Battle** of Jericho. Atheneum Books for Young Readers 2003 297p $16.95; pa $6.99

Grades: 7 8 9 10 **Fic**

1. School stories 2. Clubs -- Fiction 3. Death -- Fiction 4. Cousins -- Fiction

ISBN 0-689-84232-5; 0-689-84233-3 pa

LC 2002-8612

"This title is a compelling read that drives home important lessons about making choices." SLJ

Other titles in this series are:

Just another hero (2009)

November blues (2007)

Double Dutch. Atheneum Bks. for Young Readers 2002 183p $16; pa $4.99

Grades: 6 7 8 9　　　　　　　　　　　　　　**Fic**

1. Friendship -- Fiction 2. Rope skipping -- Fiction 3. African Americans -- Fiction

ISBN 0-689-84230-9; 0-689-84231-7 pa

LC 00-50247

Three eighth-grade friends, preparing for the International Double Dutch Championship jump rope competition in their home town of Cincinnati, Ohio, cope with Randy's missing father, Delia's inability to read, and Yo Yo's encounter with the class bullies

"Teens will like the high-spirited, authentic dialogue . . . the honest look at tough issues, and the team workout scenes that show how sports can transform young lives." Booklist

★ **Fire** from the rock. Dutton Children's Books 2007 229p $16.99

Grades: 6 7 8 9　　　　　　　　　　　　　　**Fic**

1. School stories 2. Arkansas -- Fiction 3. Race relations -- Fiction 4. African Americans -- Fiction 5. Central High School (Little Rock, Ark.) -- Fiction

ISBN 978-0-525-47720-4; 0-525-47720-9

LC 2006-102952

In 1957, Sylvia Patterson's life is disrupted by the impending integration of Little Rock's Central High when she is selected to be one of the first black students to attend the previously all white school.

"This historical fiction novel is a must have. It keeps the reader engaged with vivid depictions of a time that most young people can only imagine." Voice Youth Advocates

★ **Out** of my mind. Atheneum 2010 295p $16.99

Grades: 5 6 7 8　　　　　　　　　　　　　　**Fic**

1. Cerebral palsy -- Fiction

ISBN 978-1-4169-7170-2; 1-4169-7170-X

LC 2009-18404

Josette Frank Award for Fiction, 2011

"Fifth-grader Melody has cerebral palsy, a condition that affects her body but not her mind. Although she is unable to walk, talk, or feed or care for herself, she can read, think, and feel. A brilliant person is trapped inside her body, determined to make her mark in the world despite her physical limitations. . . . Told in Melody's voice, this highly readable, compelling novel quickly establishes her determination and intelligence and the almost insurmountable challenges she faces. . . . Uplifting and upsetting." Booklist

Stella by starlight; Sharon Draper. Atheneum Books for Young Readers 2015 336 p. (hardcover) $16.99

Grades: 4 5 6 7 8　　　　　　　　　　　　**Fic**

1. Ku Klux Klan 2. Segregation -- Fiction 3. Southern States -- Fiction 4. Prejudices -- Fiction 5. Civil rights -- Fiction 6. African Americans -- Fiction 7. Ku Klux

Klan (1915-) -- Fiction 8. North Carolina -- History -- 20th century -- Fiction

ISBN 1442494972; 9781442494978; 9781442494985

LC 2014038728

In this novel by Sharon M. Draper "when the Ku Klux Klan's unwelcome reappearance rattles Stella's segregated southern town, bravery battles prejudice in this Depression-era tour de force. As Stella's community--her world--is upended, she decides to fight fire with fire. And she learns that ashes don't necessarily signify an end." (Publisher's note)

"Coretta Scott King Award winner Draper draws inspiration from her grandmother's journal to tell the absorbing story of a young girl growing up in Depression-era, segregated North Carolina...This is an engrossing historical fiction novel with an amiable and humble heroine who does not recognize her own bravery or the power of her words. She provides inspiration not only to her fellow characters but also to readers who will relate to her and her situation. Storytelling at its finest." SLJ

Duble, Kathleen Benner

Hearts of iron. Margaret K. McElderry Books 2006 248p $15.95

Grades: 6 7 8 9　　　　　　　　　　　　　　**Fic**

1. Connecticut -- Fiction 2. Iron industry -- Fiction

ISBN 1-4169-0850-1

LC 2005-29258

In early 1800s Connecticut, fifteen-year-old Lucy tries to decide whether to marry her childhood friend who unhappily toils at the Mt. Riga iron furnace or the young man from Boston who has come to work in her father's store.

"Well-written historical fiction with a unique setting and a touch of mystery, Lucy's story will both inform and entertain readers." SLJ

Phantoms in the snow. Scholastic Press 2011 226p $17.99

Grades: 6 7 8 9　　　　　　　　　　　　　　**Fic**

1. Italy -- Fiction 2. Uncles -- Fiction 3. Orphans -- Fiction 4. Colorado -- Fiction 5. Pacifism -- Fiction 6. Soldiers -- Fiction 7. Military bases -- Fiction 8. World War, 1939-1945 -- Italy -- Fiction 9. United States -- Army -- Mountain Division, 10th -- Fiction

ISBN 978-0-545-19770-0; 0-545-19770-8

LC 2010016898

In 1944, fifteen-year-old Noah Garrett, recently orphaned, is sent to live at Camp Hale, Colorado, with an uncle he has never met, and there he finds his pacifist views put to the test.

"Duble has created a likable character in Noah, whose struggles to find out who he is and where he belongs in a world at war are convincingly portrayed and realistically resolved." Kirkus

Quest; 1st ed.; Margaret K. McElderry Books 2008 240p $16.99

Grades: 7 8 9 10　　　　　　　　　　　　　**Fic**

1. Explorers 2. Spies -- Fiction 3. Explorers -- Fiction 4. Netherlands -- Fiction 5. Seafaring life -- Fiction 6. America -- Exploration -- Fiction

ISBN 978-1-4169-3386-1; 1-4169-3386-7

LC 2006102712

Relates events of explorer Henry Hudson's final voyage in 1602 from four points of view, those of his seventeen-year-old son aboard ship, a younger son left in London, a crewmember, and a young English woman acting as a spy in Holland in hopes of restoring honor to her family's name.

"The author's skillful juxtaposition of these four narratives creates an absorbing work of historical fiction that manages to incorporate the viewpoints of explorers, investors, sailors, governments, family members, and neighbors of those who played a part in this fascinating era." SLJ

The **sacrifice**. Margaret K. McElderry Books 2005 211p $15.95

Grades: 6 7 8 9 **Fic**

1. Puritans -- Fiction 2. Witchcraft -- Fiction 3. Massachusetts -- History -- 1600-1775, Colonial period -- Fiction

ISBN 0-689-87650-5

LC 2004-18355

Two sisters, aged ten and twelve, are accused of witchcraft in Andover, Massachusetts, in 1692 and await trial in a miserable prison while their mother desperately searches for some way to obtain their freedom.

"Well written with accessible language, this book will appeal to a wide range of readers." SLJ

Includes bibliographical references

Dubosarsky, Ursula

★ The **golden** day; by Ursula Dubosarsky. Candlewick 2013 160 p. $15.99

Grades: 7 8 9 10 **Fic**

1. Mystery fiction 2. Friendship -- Fiction 3. Missing persons -- Fiction

ISBN 0763663999; 9780763663995; 9781742374710

LC 2012452201

In this novel by Ursula Dubosarsky "eleven schoolgirls embrace their own chilling history when their teacher abruptly goes missing on a field trip. Who was the mysterious poet they had met in the Garden? What actually happened in the seaside cave that day? And most important — who can they tell about it?" (Publisher's note)

"Spare and well written, this slim novel covers the days following a teacher's disappearance during a class outing. Eleven girls must make their way back to school where they are determined to keep their teacher's rendezvous with the local park's gardener a secret. The book's chilling atmosphere and mature tone are best suited for older readers." (Horn Book)

Dudley, David L.

Caleb's wars. Clarion Books 2011 263p $16.99

Grades: 7 8 9 10 **Fic**

1. Georgia -- Fiction 2. Germans -- Fiction 3. Family life -- Fiction 4. Segregation -- Fiction 5. Race relations -- Fiction 6. Prisoners of war -- Fiction 7. African Americans -- Fiction 8. World War, 1939-1945 -- Fiction

ISBN 978-0-547-23997-2; 0-547-23997-1

LC 2011009644

Fifteen-year-old Caleb's courageous commitment to justice grows as he faces a power struggle with his father, fights to keep both his temper and self-respect in dealing with whites, and puzzles over the German prisoners of war brought to his rural Georgia community during World War II.

"Caleb is compelling and believable, and Dudley's rich writing is impressive, clearly showing the various wars black Americans were fighting in the 1940s, both abroad and closer to home." SLJ

Duey, Kathleen

Sacred scars. Atheneum Books for Young Readers 2009 554p il (A resurrection of magic) $17.99

Grades: 7 8 9 10 **Fic**

1. School stories 2. Fantasy fiction 3. Magic -- Fiction

ISBN 978-0-689-84095-1; 0-689-84095-0

LC 2008-56044

In alternate chapters, Sadima works to free captive boys forced to copy documents in the caverns of Limori, and Hahp makes a pact with the remaining students of a wizards' academy in hopes that all will survive their training, as both learn valuable lessons about loyalty.

"The text so successfully portrays Hahp's experience in this grueling, cold-blooded wizard 'academy'—isolation, starvation, abuse and constant, unsolvable puzzles—that readers may absorb his strain, confusion and desolation themselves. . . . Absorbing and unwaveringly suspenseful." Kirkus

Skin hunger. Atheneum Books for Young Readers 2007 357p (Resurrection of magic) hardcover o.p. pa $9.99

Grades: 7 8 9 10 **Fic**

1. Fantasy fiction 2. Magic -- Fiction

ISBN 978-0-689-84093-7; 0-689-84093-4; 978-0-689-84094-4 pa; 0-689-84094-2 pa

LC 2006-34819

In alternate chapters, Sadima travels from her farm home to the city and becomes assistant to a heartless man who is trying to restore knowledge of magic to the world, and a group of boys fights to survive in the academy that has resulted from his efforts.

This is a "compelling new fantasy. . . . Duey sweeps readers up in the page-turning excitement." Horn Book

Followed by: Scared scars (2009)

Dumas, Alexandre

The **three** musketeers; translated by Jacques Le Clercq. Modern Library 1999 xxi, 598 p.p (hardcover) $26.00

Grades: 7 8 9 10 11 12 Adult **Fic**

1. Adventure 2. France -- Gascony 3. France -- 17th century 4. Courts and courtiers -- France 5. France -- History -- 1589-1789, Bourbons -- Fiction

ISBN 0679603328; 9780679603320

Original French edition, 1844

"D'Artagnan arrives in Paris one day in 1625 and manages to be involved in three duels with three musketeers . . . Athos, Porthos and Aramis. They become d'Artagnan's best friends. The account of their adventures from 1625 on develops against the rich historical background of the reign of Louis XIII and the early part of that of Louis XIV, the main plot being furnished by the antagonism between Cardinal de

Richelieu and Queen Anne d'Autriche." Haydn. Thesaurus of Book Dig

Dunagan, Ted M.

The **salvation** of Miss Lucretia; Ted M. Dunagan. NewSouth Books 2014 208 p. (hardcover) $21.95

Grades: 6 7 8 9   Fic

1. Historical fiction 2. Friendship -- Fiction 3. Southern States -- Fiction 4. Vodou 5. Friendship 6. Race relations 7. Alabama -- History -- 1819-1950

ISBN 1588382931; 9781588382931; 9781603062558

LC 2014933021

In this book, by Ted M. Dunagan, "young friends Ted and Poudlum continue their friendship despite the racial divide in the rural segregated South of the 1940s. On a trip to the forest . . . they stumble upon Miss Lucretia, the last of the voodoo queens. . . . Through a series of adventures, Ted and Poudlum resolve to follow their own unique moral compasses and do what's right despite the pressures of the time in which they live." (Publisher's note)

"Dunagan gives enough information about the pair (Ted is white, Poudlum is African American) and the setting (rural Alabama, 1949) to make jumping into this in-progress series easy." Booklist

Duncan, Lois

I know what you did last summer. Little, Brown 1973 199p hardcover o.p. pa $6.50

Grades: 7 8 9 10 11 12   Fic

1. Mystery fiction

ISBN 0-440-22844-1 pa

ALA YALSA Margaret A. Edwards Award (1992)

This book "has vivid characterization, good balance, and the boding sense of impending danger that adds excitement to the best mystery stories." Bull Cent Child Books

★ **Killing** Mr. Griffin. Dell 1990 223p hardcover o.p. pa $6.50

Grades: 7 8 9 10   Fic

1. School stories 2. Kidnapping -- Fiction

ISBN 0-440-94515-1 pa

First published 1978 by Little, Brown

ALA YALSA Margaret A. Edwards Award (1992)

The author's "skillful plotting builds layers of tension that draws readers into the eye of the conflict. The ending is nicely handled in a manner which provides relief without removing any of the chilling implications." SLJ

Locked in time. Little, Brown 1985 210p hardcover o.p. pa $6.50

Grades: 7 8 9 10   Fic

1. Mystery fiction 2. Louisiana -- Fiction

ISBN 0-316-19555-3; 0-440-94942-4 pa

LC 85-23

This "is the story of a domineering mother, Lisette, and her two teenage children, Gabe and Josie, who have all drunk from the cup of eternal youth. Seventeen-year-old Nore Robbins goes to visit her father, Charles, and her new stepfamily, Lisette, Gabe and Josie, at Lisette's beautiful old estate deep in the Louisiana bayou country. Nore discovers her stepfamily's secret and, in an attempt to expose this

knowledge, becomes Lisette's target for death. . . . Grades seven to ten." (SLJ)

"The writing style is smooth, the characters strongly developed, and the plot, which has excellent pace and momentum, is an adroit blending of fantasy and realism." Bull Cent Child Books

Stranger with my face. Little, Brown 1981 250p hardcover o.p. pa $8.95

Grades: 7 8 9 10   Fic

1. Twins -- Fiction 2. Supernatural -- Fiction

ISBN 0-440-98356-8

LC 81-8299

"The ghostly Lia is deliciously evil; the idea of astral projection—Lia's method of travel—is novel; the island setting is vivid; and the relationships among the young people are realistic in the smoothly written supernatural tale." Horn Book

Dunkle, Clare B.

The **house** of dead maids; illustrations by Patrick Arrasmith. Henry Holt and Co. 2010 146p il $15.99

Grades: 8 9 10 11 12   Fic

1. Ghost stories 2. Orphans -- Fiction 3. Great Britain -- Fiction 4. Household employees -- Fiction

ISBN 978-0-8050-9116-8; 0-8050-9116-5

LC 2009-50769

Eleven-year-old Tabby Aykroyd, who would later serve as housekeeper for thirty years to the Brontë sisters, is taken from an orphanage to a ghost-filled house, where she and a wild young boy are needed for a pagan ritual.

"The author manages to stay true to the essence of Wuthering Heights while creating a deliciously chilling ghost story that stands on its own. Readers do not have to be at all familiar with Brontë's gothic story of destructive love to be scared out of their wits by this one: cognoscenti, though, will recognize a few sly nods to the original." Bull Cent Child Books

★ The **sky** inside. Atheneum Books for Young Readers 2008 229p $16.99

Grades: 6 7 8 9   Fic

1. Science fiction

ISBN 978-1-41692-422-7; 1-41692-422-1

After the disappearance of his sister, Cassie, and other children who ask questions about their carefully choreographed life in a domed suburb cut off from the outside world, Martin and his intelligent dog investigate.

"Dunkle surrounds her protagonists with an enthralling range of settings, a memorable cast of characters. . . . Fans of the author will . . . recognize her evocative storytelling and intricate plotting." Bull Cent Child Books

Followed by: The walls have eyes (2009)

The **walls** have eyes. Atheneum Books for Young Readers 2009 225p $16.99

Grades: 6 7 8 9   Fic

1. Science fiction 2. Dogs -- Fiction 3. Robots -- Fiction 4. Family life -- Fiction 5. Genetic engineering

-- Fiction

ISBN 978-1-41695-379-1; 1-41695-379-5

LC 2008038298

Sequel to: The sky inside (2008)

Having spirited his parents out of their domed suburb, Martin goes to the school for help and finds that his sister, Cassie, and the other Wonder Babies are gone again, but his AllDog, Chip, may hold the means to save them all.

"Throughout, Dunkle creates a vivid sense of imminent danger. . . . The book is recommended for readers who enjoyed the first volume." Booklist

Dunlap, Susanne

In the shadow of the lamp; [by] Susanne Dunlap. Bloomsbury Children's Books 2011 293p $16.99
Grades: 7 8 9 10   **Fic**

1. Nurses 2. Nurses -- Fiction 3. Nonfiction writers 4. Crimean War, 1853-1856 -- Fiction 5. Great Britain -- History -- 19th century -- Fiction

ISBN 978-1-59990-565-5; 1-59990-565-5

LC 2010-21158

Sixteen-year-old Molly Fraser works as a nurse with Florence Nightingale during the Crimean War to earn a salary to help her family survive in nineteenth-century England.

"Dunlap has written a story with roots deep in research about Florence Nightingale and the women who served as nurses during the Crimean War. . . . [She] . . . delivers another extraordinary novel that feels relevant even today." Libr Media Connect

The musician's daughter; [by] Susanne Dunlap. Bloomsbury 2009 322p $16.99
Grades: 8 9 10 11 12   **Fic**

1. Composers 2. Mystery fiction 3. Gypsies -- Fiction 4. Homicide -- Fiction 5. Musicians -- Fiction 6. Vienna (Austria) -- Fiction

ISBN 978-1-59990-332-3; 1-59990-332-6

LC 2008-30307

In eighteenth-century Vienna, Austria, fifteen-year-old Theresa seeks a way to help her mother and brother financially while investigating the murder of her father, a renowned violinist in Haydn's orchestra at the court of Prince Esterhazy, after his body is found near a gypsy camp.

"Dunlap skillfully builds suspense until the final page. . . . Readers will root for courageous Theresa through the exciting intrigue even as they absorb deeper messages about music and art's power to lift souls and inspire change." Booklist

Dunmore, Helen

The deep. HarperCollinsPublishers 2009 326p $16.99
Grades: 6 7 8 9   **Fic**

1. Fantasy fiction 2. Mermaids and mermen -- Fiction

ISBN 978-0-06-081858-6; 0-06-081858-1

Sequel to: The tide knot (2008)

When the ferocious shape-shifting Kraken awakes after thousands of years and threatens the Mer, Sapphire agrees to help them by going with her brother Conor and their friend Faro into the Deep to lull the monster back to sleep.

The author "evokes setting well, and her descriptions of the sea world are lovely. She writes knowledgably about the sperm whale." Voice Youth Advocates

Ingo. HarperCollins Pubs. 2005 328p $16.99; lib bdg $17.89
Grades: 6 7 8 9   **Fic**

1. Great Britain -- Fiction 2. Mermaids and mermen -- Fiction

ISBN 978-0-06-081852-4; 0-06-081852-2; 978-0-06-081853-1 lib bdg; 0-06-081853-0 lib bdg

LC 2005-19079

As they search for their missing father near their Cornwall home, Sapphy and her brother Conor learn about their family's connection to the domains of air and of water.

"Strong character development combines with an engaging plot and magical elements to make this a fine choice for fantasy readers, who will look forward to the next installments in this planned trilogy." SLJ

Other titles about Sapphire are:

The tide knot (2008)

The deep (2009)

Tide knot. HarperCollins Publishers 2008 330p $16.99; $17.89
Grades: 6 7 8 9   **Fic**

1. Great Britain -- Fiction 2. Mermaids and mermen -- Fiction

ISBN 978-0-06-081855-5; 0-06-081855-7; 978-0-06-081856-2 lib bdg; 0-06-081856-5 lib bdg

LC 2007-06991

Sequel to: Ingo (2006)

First published 2006 in the United Kingdom

Two years after the disappearance of their father, Sapphire and Conor, having moved with their mother to the town of St. Pirans, try to make a new life for themselves, but Sapphire, unlike her mother and brother, finds it increasingly difficult to adjust to her new circumstances and is drawn more and more to the undersea world of Ingo.

"Supporting the brightly adventurous plot are believably flawed and conflicted characters." Horn Book

Followed by: The deep (2009)

DuPrau, Jeanne

★ The **city** of Ember. Random House 2003 270p (Books of Ember) $15.95; lib bdg $17.99; pa $6.99
Grades: 5 6 7 8   **Fic**

1. Science fiction

ISBN 0-375-82273-9; 0-375-92274-1 lib bdg; 0-385-73628-2 pa

LC 2002-10239

"The writing and storytelling are agreeably spare and remarkably suspenseful." Horn Book

Other titles in this series are:

The people of Sparks (2004)

The prophet of Yonwood (2006)

The diamond of Darkhold (2008)

Durango, Julia

The **walls** of Cartagena; by Julia Durango; illustrated by Tom Pohrt. Simon & Schuster Books for Young Readers 2008 152p il $15.99

Grades: 5 6 7 8   **Fic**

1. Leprosy -- Fiction 2. Slavery -- Fiction 3. Colombia -- Fiction 4. Catholic Church -- Fiction

ISBN 978-1-4169-4102-6; 1-4169-4102-9

LC 2007041861

Thirteen-year-old Calepino, an African slave in the seventeenth-century Caribbean city of Cartagena, works as a translator for a Jesuit priest who tends to newly-arrived slaves and, after working for a Jewish doctor in a leper colony and helping an Angolan boy and his mother escape, he realizes his true calling

"Illustrated with occasional small ink sketches, the ultimate rescue adventure is gripping, but more compelling is the authentic history of people desperate and brave." Booklist

Durbin, William

The **broken** blade. Delacorte Press 1997 163p hardcover o.p. pa $5.50

Grades: 5 6 7 8   **Fic**

1. Canada -- Fiction 2. Fur trade -- Fiction

ISBN 0-385-32224-0; 0-440-41184-X

LC 96-22114

When an injury prevents his father from going into northern Canada with fur traders, thirteen-year-old Pierre decides to take his father's place as a voyageur

"This look at the early nineteenth-century Canadian fur trade should appeal to reluctant readers as well as adventure buffs, and it may be a welcome suggestion for middle-school historical fiction reports." Bull Cent Child Books

The **darkest** evening. Orchard Books 2004 232p $15.95

Grades: 6 7 8 9   **Fic**

1. Russia -- Fiction 2. Communism -- Fiction 3. Finnish Americans -- Fiction

ISBN 0-439-37307-7

LC 2003-20255

In the 1930s, a young Finnish-American boy reluctantly moves with his family to Karelia, a communist-Finnish state founded in Russia, where his idealistic father soon realizes that his conception of a communist utopia is flawed.

"Many readers who enjoy tales of courage under fire . . . will find this exciting stuff." Booklist

The **Winter** War; [by] William Durbin. 1st ed.; Wendy Lamb Books 2008 231p $15.99; lib bdg $18.99

Grades: 6 7 8 9   **Fic**

1. Finland -- Fiction 2. Soldiers -- Fiction 3. Poliomyelitis -- Fiction 4. Russo-Finnish War, 1939-1940 -- Fiction

ISBN 978-0-385-74652-6; 0-385-74652-0; 978-0-385-90889-4 lib bdg; 0-385-90889-X lib bdg

LC 2007007048

When Russian troops invade Finland during the winter of 1939–40, Marko, a young polio victim determined to keep his homeland free, joins the Finnish Army as a messenger boy.

"Durbin's graphic depictions of the realities of war are not for the faint of heart. . . . More than a war story, though, this is a tale of resilience and self-discovery. . . . An engaging novel for adventure lovers and fans of historical fiction alike." SLJ

Includes bibliographical references

Durham, Paul

Fork-tongue charmers; Paul Durham; illustrations by Petur Antonsson. Harper, an imprint of HarperCollinsPublishers 2015 416 p. illustrations, maps (The Luck Uglies) (hardcover) $16.99

Grades: 4 5 6 7 8   **Fic**

1. Magic -- Fiction 2. Criminals -- Fiction 3. Fantasy 4. Monsters -- Fiction 5. Secret societies -- Fiction 6. Adventure and adventurers -- Fiction

ISBN 0062271539; 9780062271532

LC 2014038648

Sequel to: The Luck Uglies (2014)

In this novel by Paul Durham, illustrated by Petur Antonsson, "Rye O'Chanter was shocked to discover that her father was the leader . . . of outlaws known as the Luck Uglies. Now she too has been declared a criminal . . . and she must flee to the strange and remote Isle of Pest while her father faces off against . . . the Fork-Tongue Charmers, on the mainland. When the battle moves to the shores of Pest . . . Rye must . . . lead the charge in defending the island." (Publisher's note)

"The second volume in Durham's spirited series starts with a mysterious summons for Rye O'Chanter from her father, Harmless, now known to her as the High Chieftain of the Luck Uglies. . . . There is not a single dull moment in this story, which packs in as many clever twists and fully fleshed characters as the first book. And the writing remains a total delight: witty, richly layered, and capable of creating a world as real as this one. A bittersweet ending assures the reader that Rye's adventures are not over yet." Booklist

The **luck** uglies; Paul Durham; illustrations by Petur Antonsson. Harper, an imprint of HarperCollinsPublishers 2014 400 p. (hardback) $16.99

Grades: 4 5 6 7 8   **Fic**

1. Fantasy fiction 2. Secret societies -- Fiction 3. Monsters -- Fiction 4. Adventure and adventurers -- Fiction

ISBN 0062271504; 9780062271501

LC 2013047720

In this book, by Paul Durham, "a terrifying encounter has eleven-year-old Rye O'Chanter convinced that the monstrous, supposedly extinct Bog Noblins have returned. Now Rye's only hope is an exiled secret society so notorious its name can't be spoken aloud: the Luck Uglies. As Rye dives into Village Drowning's maze of secrets, rules, and lies, she'll discover the truth behind the village's legends of outlaws and beasts . . . and that it may take a villain to save them from the monsters." (Publisher's note)

"Rye O'Chanter and her friends Quinn and Folly live in Drowning, which is ruled by the tyrannical Earl Longchance, who bans women from reading. When the earl does nothing to protect the villagers from marauding monsters, Drowning's only hope is the Luck Uglies, a notorious outlaw gang--that may or may not exist. Durham's fast-paced narrative and clever characters enhance this humorous and engaging tale." Horn Book

Durrant, Lynda

Imperfections. Clarion Books 2008 172p $16

Grades: 6 7 8 9   **Fic**

1. Shakers -- Fiction 2. Kentucky -- Fiction 3. Siblings -- Fiction 4. Abandoned children -- Fiction 5. United States -- History -- 1861-1865, Civil War -- Fiction

ISBN 978-0-5470-0357-3; 0-5470-0357-9

LC 2008-23533

In 1862 Pleasant Hill, Kentucky, fourteen-year-old Rosemary Elizabeth strives to fit in with the Shaker sisters of this "Heaven on Earth," but yearns to be reunited with her mother and siblings from whom she was separated when they sought refuge from her abusive father. Includes facts about Shakers and Morgan's Raiders.

"This fine coming-of-age novel rewards readers with an unusual glimpse into a rarely portrayed religion as well as a different perspective on the Civil War." Booklist

Includes bibliographical references

My last skirt; the story of Jennie Hodgers, Union soldier. by Lynda Durrant. Clarion Books 2006 199p $16

Grades: 6 7 8 9   **Fic**

1. Soldiers 2. Male impersonators 3. Sex role -- Fiction 4. Irish Americans -- Fiction 5. United States -- History -- 1861-1865, Civil War -- Fiction

ISBN 978-0-618-57490-2; 0-618-57490-5

LC 2005027746

Enjoying the freedom afforded her while dressing as a boy in order to earn higher pay after emigrating from Ireland, Jennie Hodgers serves in the 95th Illinois Infantry as Private Albert Cashier, a Union soldier in the American Civil War.

"Based on a true story, Jennie's tale is gripping. . . . Her loneliness, longing, and missed opportunities will resonate deeply with readers." SLJ

Includes bibliographical references

Durst, Sarah Beth

Ice. Margaret K. McElderry Books 2009 308p $16.99

Grades: 7 8 9 10   **Fic**

1. Fairy tales 2. Polar bear -- Fiction 3. Scientists -- Fiction 4. Supernatural -- Fiction 5. Arctic regions -- Fiction

ISBN 978-1-4169-8643-0; 1-4169-8643-X

LC 2009-8618

A modern-day retelling of "East o' the Sun, West o' the Moon" in which eighteen-year-old Cassie learns that her grandmother's fairy tale is true when a Polar Bear King comes to claim her for his bride and she must decide whether to go with him and save her long-lost mother, or continue helping her father with his research

"Told in a descriptive style that perfectly captures the changing settings, Durst's novel is a page-turner that readers who enjoy adventure mixed with fairy-tale romance will find hard to put down." Booklist

Into the Wild. Razorbill 2007 260p $15.99

Grades: 6 7 8 9   **Fic**

1. Fairy tales 2. Magic -- Fiction

ISBN 978-1-59514-156-9; 1-59514-156-1

LC 2007-01942

Having escaped from the Wild and the preordained fairy tale plots it imposes, Rapunzel, along with her daughter Julie Marchen, tries to live a fairly normal life, but when the Wild breaks free and takes over their town, it is Julie who has to prevent everyone from being trapped in the events of a story.

"The novel is a creative romp through the fairy tale genre, highlighting the strength of the female characters whose stories we all know so well." Kliatt

Another title about Julie is:

Out of the wild (2008)

Vessel; Sarah Beth Durst. Margaret K. McElderry Books 2012 424 p. (hardcover) $16.99

Grades: 7 8 9 10   **Fic**

1. Deserts -- Fiction 2. Fantasy fiction 3. Adventure fiction 4. Gods and goddesses 5. Fantasy 6. Survival -- Fiction 7. Goddesses -- Fiction 8. Fate and fatalism -- Fiction

ISBN 1442423765; 9781442423763; 9781442423787

LC 2011044691

In this book by Sarah Beth Durst, "Liyana has trained all her life to be the vessel for her desert tribe's goddess Bayla. . . . "Bayla never shows up, but the trickster god Korbyn appears in human form and gives Liyana some startling news: the gods have all been imprisoned in false vessels, and he and Liyana must retrieve the various tribes' unsuccessful vessels, figure out where the deities are being held, and rescue them." (Bulletin of the Center for Children's Books)

Eames, Brian

The **dagger** Quick. Simon & Schuster Books for Young Readers 2011 320p $15.99

Grades: 4 5 6 7   **Fic**

1. Sea stories 2. Adventure fiction 3. Pirates -- Fiction 4. People with Disabilities -- Fiction

ISBN 978-1-4424-2311-4; 1-4424-2311-0

LC 2011-04405

Twelve-year-old Christopher "Kitto" Wheale, a club-footed boy seemingly doomed to follow in the boring footsteps of his father as a cooper in seventeenth-century England, finds himself on a dangerous seafaring adventure with his newly discovered uncle, the infamous pirate William Quick.

"Thoroughly researched, fast-paced, and tense, this coming-of-age adventure doesn't sugarcoat the dangers of the era, even as it embraces the mythical glamour of a pirate's life." Publ Wkly

Edgar, Elsbeth

The **Visconti** house. Candlewick Press 2011 287p $16.99

Grades: 4 5 6 7   **Fic**

1. Houses -- Fiction 2. Australia -- Fiction 3. Family life -- Fiction

ISBN 0-7636-5019-6; 978-0-7636-5019-3

LC 2010-39172

Laura Horton has always been an outsider, more interested in writing, drawing, or spending time with her free-spirited family than in her fellow teens, but she is drawn to Leon, a new student, as together they explore the mysteries of her eccentric old house.

"Convincing dialogue and well-drawn characters, both major and minor, bring energy to the story. . . . A fine, sensitive first novel." Booklist

Edge, Christopher

Twelve minutes to midnight; Christopher Edge; illustrations by Eric Orchard. Albert Whitman & Company 2014 256 p. $16.99

Grades: 4 5 6 7 **Fic**

1. Orphans -- Fiction 2. Supernatural -- Fiction 3. Psychiatric hospitals -- Fiction 4. Great Britain -- History -- Victoria, 1837-1901 -- Fiction 5. Authorship -- Fiction 6. Mystery and detective stories 7. Publishers and publishing -- Fiction 8. London (England) -- History -- 19th century -- Fiction

ISBN 080758133X; 9780807581339

LC 2013029481

In this book, by Christopher Edge, "Penelope Tredwell is the . . . orphan heiress of Victorian Britain's bestselling magazine, the Penny Dreadful. Her . . . tales--concealed under the pen name Montgomery Finch--are gripping the public. One day she receives a letter from the governor of the Bedlam madhouse requesting Finch's help to investigate the asylum's strange goings-on. Every night at precisely twelve minutes to midnight, the inmates all begin feverishly writing-incoherent ramblings." (Publisher's note)

"In Twelve Minutes to Midnight, readers meet Penelope Tredwell, the 13-year-old newspaper heiress and ghostwriter who pens tales of horror and mystery as Montgomery Flinch. She must keep her true identity secret, going so far as to hire an actor to play Montgomery at public appearances. In Shadows of the Silver Screen, a filmmaker wants to transform Penelope's stories into a motion picture. The protagonist soon finds that her terrifying tales are bleeding into reality. An atmospheric and spine-tingling series for middle graders who love old-fashioned mysteries." SLJ

Edwards, Janet

★ **Earth** girl; by Janet Edwards. Pyr 2013 350 p. (Earth girl trilogy) hbk $17.95

Grades: 7 8 9 10 **Fic**

1. Science fiction 2. People with disabilities -- Fiction

ISBN 9781616147655; 1616147652

LC 2012044570

In this young adult novel set in the future, Jarra and other Handicapped are discriminated against by the Norms. "Jarra decides to show them that she is just as good as they are and applies to an off-world college conducting an archaeology dig on the abandoned buildings of New York. Reinventing herself as Jarra Military Kid, JMK watches vids and takes combat lessons. . . . Since she grew up on Earth and has been to the New York digs many times, her skills quickly allow her to shine." (School Library Journal)

"The future that Edwards constructs is creative and the dig descriptions are well thought out. . . . The 'person against nature' conflict with unstable dig conditions and solar flares makes a refreshing change." SLJ

★ **Earth** star; Janet Edwards. Pyr, an imprint of Prometheus Books 2014 360 p. (hardback) $17.99

Grades: 7 8 9 10 11 12 **Fic**

1. Children with disabilities -- Abuse of -- Fiction

ISBN 1616148977; 9781616148973

LC 2013040057

In this sequel to Janet Edwards's "Earth Girl," "it's 2789. People portal between planets in seconds, often many times per day--except the Handicapped, like Jarra, whose immune systems can survive only on Earth. . . . She plans to continue studying prehistory by excavating sites of long-dead cities. But before the next dig begins, Jarra and boyfriend Fian are whisked off to a military base and inexplicably sworn in as officers. An unidentified alien sphere is hovering above Africa." (Kirkus Reviews)

"This far-future science-fiction sequel skips tired genre tropes to offer a fresh and thrilling adventure about hazardous archaeological excavation, a mystery in the sky and a potential threat to all of humanity...Nitty-gritty archaeology details are vivid, and easy slang creates color ("Twoing" is dating; "amaz" means amazing). Edwards shows that speculative fiction needn't be dystopic, conspiracy-filled or love-triangled to be riveting and satisfying. Amaz—simply amaz." (Kirkus)

Edwardson, Debby Dahl

★ **Blessing's** bead. Farrar, Straus & Giroux 2009 178p $16.99

Grades: 6 7 8 9 10 **Fic**

1. Alaska -- Fiction 2. Inupiat -- Fiction 3. Villages -- Fiction 4. Influenza -- Fiction 5. Alcoholism -- Fiction

ISBN 978-0-374-30805-6; 0-374-30805-5

LC 2008-26726

In 1917, Aaluk leaves for Siberia while her sister Nutaaq remains in their Alaskan village and becomes one of the few survivors of an influenza epidemic, then in 1986, Nunaaq's great-granddaughter leaves her mother due to a different kind of sickness and returns to the village where they were born

"It's the Nutaag's rhythmic, indelible voices—both as steady and elemental as the beat of a drum or a heart—that will move readers most. A unique, powerful debut." Booklist

★ **My** name is not easy. Marshall Cavendish 2011 248p $17.99; e-book $17.99

Grades: 7 8 9 10 **Fic**

1. School stories 2. Alaska -- Fiction 3. Native Americans -- Fiction

ISBN 978-0-7614-5980-4; 0-7614-5980-4; 978-0-7614-6091-6 e-book

LC 2011002108

"Edwardson's skillful use of dialogue and her descriptions of rural Alaska as well as boarding-school life invoke a strong sense of empathy and compassion in readers. . . Edwardson is to be applauded for her depth of research and her ability to portray all sides of the equation in a fair and balanced manner while still creating a very enjoyable read." SLJ

Efaw, Amy

Battle dress. HarperCollins Pubs. 2000 291p hardcover o.p. lib bdg $16.89

Grades: 7 8 9 10   **Fic**

1. Military education -- Fiction 2. Women in the armed forces -- Fiction 3. United States Military Academy -- Fiction

ISBN 0-06-028411-0 lib bdg; 0-06-053520-2

LC 99-34516

As a newly arrived freshman at West Point, seventeen-year-old Andi finds herself gaining both confidence and self esteem as she struggles to get through the grueling six weeks of new cadet training known as the Beast

"This book by a West Point graduate is a gripping, hard-to-put-down look at a young woman's struggle to succeed in a traditionally all-male environment." Voice Youth Advocates

Ehrenberg, Pamela

★ **Ethan,** suspended; written by Pamela Ehrenberg. Eerdmans Books for Young Readers 2007 266p $16

Grades: 7 8 9 10   **Fic**

1. Jews -- Fiction 2. Grandparents -- Fiction 3. Race relations -- Fiction 4. Washington (D.C.) -- Fiction

ISBN 978-0-8028-5324-0

LC 2006032697

After a school suspension and his parents' separation, Ethan is sent to live with his grandparents in Washington, D.C., which is worlds apart from his home in a Philadelphia suburb.

"Ehrenberg focuses on themes of race and class without sounding preachy. . . . Best of all are the portraits of [Ethan's] scrappy Jewish grandparents." Booklist

Ehrenhaft, Daniel

Friend is not a verb; a novel. HarperTeen 2010 241p $16.99

Grades: 7 8 9 10   **Fic**

1. Siblings -- Fiction 2. Rock music -- Fiction 3. Family life -- Fiction 4. Bands (Music) -- Fiction 5. New York (N.Y.) -- Fiction

ISBN 978-0-06-113106-6; 0-06-113106-7

LC 2009-44006

While sixteen-year-old Hen's family and friends try to make his supposed dreams of becoming a rock star come true, he deals with the reality of being in a band with an ex-girlfriend, a friendship that may become love, and his older sister's mysterious disappearance and reappearance.

"Offbeat characters, an intriguing mystery, and a sweet romance make Ehrenhaft's . . . . coming-of-age story stand out. . . . The mystery—and romance—wrap up rather neatly, but readers should be impressed by the clever surprise ending." Publ Wkly

Ehrlich, Esther

Nest; by Esther Ehrlich. Wendy Lamb Books, an imprint of Random House Children's Books 2014 336 p. (lib. bdg.) $19.99; (hbk) $16.99

Grades: 4 5 6 7   **Fic**

1. Bird watching -- Fiction 2. Cape Cod (Mass.) -- Fiction 3. Multiple sclerosis -- Fiction 4. Sick --

Fiction 5. Schools -- Fiction 6. Family life -- Fiction

ISBN 0385386087; 9780385386081; 9780385386104; 9780385386074

LC 2013036245

"In 1972 home is a cozy nest on Cape Cod for eleven-year-old Naomi 'Chirp' Orenstein, her older sister, Rachel; her psychiatrist father; and her dancer mother. But then Chirp's mom develops symptoms of a serious disease, and everything changes. Chirp finds comfort in watching her beloved wild birds. She also finds a true friend in Joey, the mysterious boy who lives across the street." (Publisher's note)

"The focus on nature and the outdoors helps set the pace as the seasonal changes quietly indicate the passage of time. Sensitive readers should be aware of the tough issues that it addresses--suicide, depression, and personal loss. However, the story also offers a hopeful message." SLJ

Elfman, Eric

Tesla's attic; by Neal Shusterman and Eric Elfman. Disney-Hyperion Books 2014 256 p. (Accelerati trilogy) $16.99

Grades: 5 6 7 8   **Fic**

1. Houses -- Fiction 2. Tesla, Nikola, 1856-1943 3. Science fiction 4. Inventions -- Fiction 5. Colorado Springs (Colo.) -- Fiction

ISBN 1423148037; 9781423148036

LC 2012039773

This children's novel, by Eric Elfman and Neal Shusterman, is the first book of "The Accelerati Trilogy." "After getting rid of . . . odd antiques in a garage sale, Nick befriends some local kids . . . and they discover that all of the objects have extraordinary properties. What's more, Nick figures out that the attic is a strange magnetic vortex, which attracts all sorts of trouble. It's as if the attic itself has an intelligence . . . . and a purpose." (Publisher's note)

"Lively, intelligent prose elevates this story of teenagers versus mad scientists, the third-person point of view offering a stage to various players in their play of galactic consequence." Kirkus

Elkeles, Simone

How to ruin my teenage life. Flux 2007 281p pa $8.95

Grades: 7 8 9 10 11 12   **Fic**

1. Jews -- Fiction 2. Israelis -- Fiction 3. Chicago (Ill.) -- Fiction 4. Father-daughter relationship -- Fiction

ISBN 978-0-7387-0961-1; 0-7387-1019-9

LC 2007005535

Living with her Israeli father in Chicago, seventeen-year-old Amy Nelson-Barak feels like a walking disaster, worried about her "non-boyfriend" in the Israeli army, her mother, new stepfather, and the baby they are expecting, a new boy named Nathan who has moved into her apartment building and goes to her school, and whether or not she really is the selfish snob that Nathan says she is.

"This book has laugh-out-loud moments. . . . . Amy's thoughtfulness and depth raise this book above most of the chick-lit genre." Voice Youth Advocates

Other titles in this series are:

How to ruin a summer vacation (2006)

How to ruin your boyfriend's reputation (2009)

Elliott, Laura

Across a war-tossed sea; L.M. Elliott. Disney-Hyperion Books 2014 256 p. (hardback) $16.99

Grades: 7 8 9 10 **Fic**

1. Brothers -- Fiction 2. Virginia -- Fiction 3. World War, 1939-1945 -- United States -- Fiction 4. World War, 1939-1945 -- Evacuation of civilians -- Fiction 5. British -- United States -- Fiction 6. Richmond (Va.) -- History -- 20th century -- Fiction

ISBN 1423157559; 9781423157557

LC 2013035303

In this book, by L.M. Elliott, "it's 1943, and World War II is raging. To escape the terror of the Blitz, ten-year-old Wesley and fourteen-year-old Charles were evacuated from England to America. After a few near misses with German U-boats and a treacherous ocean crossing, the brothers arrived in Virginia. The culture shock is intense as the London boys adjust to rural farm life and have to learn new sports, customs, and spellings, plus contend with racial segregation and bullying." (Publisher's note)

"Brothers Charles, fourteen, and Wesley, ten, are evacuated from London's 1943 Blitz and sent to live with a Virginian family. Adjusting to an American lifestyle and reconciling their misperceptions about it is stressful enough, but then they learn of Germans in a nearby POW camp. Evocative setting details and deft character portrayals make this a well-defined historical story. Includes an informative afterword." Horn Book

Give me liberty; [by] L. M. Elliott. Katherine Tegen Books 2006 376p $16.99; lib bdg $17.89; pa $7.99

Grades: 5 6 7 8 **Fic**

1. Virginia -- Fiction 2. United States -- History -- 1775-1783, Revolution -- Fiction

ISBN 0-06-074421-9; 0-06-074422-7 lib bdg; 0-06-074423-5 pa

Follows the life of thirteen-year-old Nathaniel Dunn, from May 1774 to December 1775, as he serves his indentureship with a music teacher in Williamsburg, Virginia, and witnesses the growing rift between patriots and loyalists, culminating in the American Revolution.

"Elliott packs a great deal of historical detail into a novel already filled with action, well-drawn characters, and a sympathetic understanding of many points of view." Booklist

A troubled peace; by L. M. Elliott. Katherine Tegen Books 2009 289p $16.99; lib bdg $17.89

Grades: 7 8 9 10 **Fic**

1. France -- Fiction 2. Veterans -- Fiction 3. World War, 1939-1945 -- Fiction

ISBN 978-0-06-074427-4; 0-06-074427-8; 978-0-06-074428-1 lib bdg; 0-06-074428-6 lib bdg

Sequel to: Under a war-torn sky (2001)

"It's near the end of World War II. Nineteen-year-old bomber pilot hero Henry Forester is back home in Virginia, suffering from nightmares and starting at every loud noise. . . . [He needs] to go back to France and search for the young boy who jeopardized his own life helping Henry escape. Returning and new readers alike will find action, well-devel-

oped characters, and deep details about the privations war brings." Booklist

Under a war-torn sky; [by] L.M. Elliott. Hyperion Bks. for Children 2001 284p hardcover o.p. pa $5.99

Grades: 7 8 9 10 **Fic**

1. France -- Fiction 2. World War, 1939-1945 -- Fiction

ISBN 0-7868-0755-5; 0-7868-1753-4 pa

LC 2001-16633

After his plane is shot down by Hitler's Luftwaffe, nineteen-year-old Henry Forester of Richmond, Virginia, strives to walk across occupied France, with the help of the French Resistance, in hopes of rejoining his unit

"It's packed with action, intrigue, and suspense, but this novel celebrates acts of kindness and heroism without glorifying war." Booklist

Followed by: A troubled peace (2009)

Elliott, Patricia

★ The **Pale** Assassin. Holiday House 2009 336p $17.95

Grades: 7 8 9 10 **Fic**

1. Adventure fiction 2. Siblings -- Fiction 3. France -- History -- 1789-1799, Revolution -- Fiction

ISBN 978-0-8234-2250-0; 0-8234-2250-X

LC 2009-7554

In early 1790s Paris, as the Revolution gains momentum, young and sheltered Eugenie de Boncoeur finds it difficult to tell friend from foe as she and the royalist brother she relies on become the focus of "le Fantome," the sinister spymaster with a long-held grudge against their family.

"The best aspect of this excellent work of historical fiction is Eugenie herself. Her gradual coming of age and growing political awareness provides resonant depth to what becomes a highly suspenseful survival tale." Booklist

Followed by: The traitor's smile (2011)

The **traitor's** smile. Holiday House 2011 304p $17.95

Grades: 7 8 9 10 **Fic**

1. Adventure fiction 2. Cousins -- Fiction 3. France -- History -- 1789-1799, Revolution -- Fiction

ISBN 978-0-8234-2361-3; 0-8234-2361-1

Sequel to: The Pale Assassin (2009)

First published 2010 in the United Kingdom

As the French Revolutin rages around her, wealthy and beautiful Eugenie de Boncoeur is no longer safe in her own country. She flees the bloody streeets of Paris for her cousin Hetta's house in England, narrowly excaping the clutches of the evil Pale Assassin, who is determined to force her to marry him.

Ellis, Ann Dee

Everything is fine. Little, Brown and Co. Books for Young Readers 2009 154p il $16.99

Grades: 6 7 8 9 10 **Fic**

1. Mothers -- Fiction 2. Bereavement -- Fiction 3. Family life -- Fiction 4. Depression (Psychology) -- Fiction

ISBN 978-0-316-01364-2; 0-316-01364-1

LC 2008-5847

When her father leaves for a job out of town, Mazzy is left at home to try to cope with her mother, who has been severely depressed since the death of Mazzy's baby sister.

"What makes [this book] so extraordinary is the narrative device that Ellis employs to searing effect. . . . [This] is a story so painful you want to read it with your eyes closed. It is a stunning novel." Voice Youth Advocates

★ **This** is what I did. Little, Brown 2007 157p $16.99

Grades: 6 7 8 9   **Fic**

1. School stories 2. Bullies -- Fiction
ISBN 978-0-316-01363-5; 0-316-01363-3
                    LC 2006-01388

Bullied because of an incident in his past, eighth-grader Logan is unhappy at his new school and has difficulty relating to others until he meets a quirky girl and a counselor who believe in him.

"Part staccato prose, part transcript, this haunting first novel will grip readers right from the start. . . . A particularly attractive book design incorporates small drawings between each segment of text." Publ Wkly

Ellis, Deborah

Bifocal; [by] Deborah Ellis and Eric Walters. Fitzhenry & Whiteside 2007 280p $18.95; pa $12.95

Grades: 7 8 9 10   **Fic**

1. School stories 2. Muslims -- Fiction 3. Prejudices -- Fiction
ISBN 978-1-55455-036-4; 1-55455-036-X; 978-1-55455-062-3 pa; 1-55455-062-9 pa

When a Muslim boy is arrested at a high school on suspicion of terrorist affiliations, growing racial tensions divide the student population.

"The story is told in the alternating voices of two students. . . . Their individual struggles to understand the flaring prejudice and their journeys toward self-discovery are subtle and authentic. . . . This is a story that will leave readers looking at their schools and themselves with new eyes." Booklist

My name is Parvana. Groundwood Books/House of Anansi Press 2012 201 p. (hardcover) $16.95

Grades: 5 6 7 8   **Fic**

1. Afghanistan -- Fiction 2. Interrogation -- Fiction 3. Women -- Afghanistan -- Fiction
ISBN 1554982979; 9781554982974

In this novel by Deborah Ellis "15-year-old Parvana is imprisoned and interrogated as a suspected terrorist in Afghanistan. . . . Parvana's captors" read "aloud the words in her notebook to decide if the angry written sentiments of a teenage girl can be evidence of guilt. . . . The interrogation, the words of the notebook and the effective third-person narration combine for a . . . portrait of a girl and her country." (Kirkus Reviews)

★ **No** ordinary day. Groundwood Books 2011 160p $16.95

Grades: 5 6 7   **Fic**

1. India -- Fiction 2. Leprosy -- Fiction 3. Orphans -- Fiction 4. Poverty -- Fiction 5. Homeless persons

-- Fiction
ISBN 978-1-55498-134-2; 1-55498-134-4

"Valli, about 10, lives in the poverty-stricken town of Jharia, India, where she is a coal picker. When she makes a shocking discovery about her family, she runs away and, after a series of harrowing events, reaches the bustling city of Kolkata. . . . While begging for change one day, she is befriended by a kind doctor who recognizes Valli's symptoms of leprosy. . . . With the help of the doctor and other leprosy patients, Valli gets treatment and education, learns tolerance for people different from herself, and simultaneously realizes her own self-worth. Although many important lessons are presented in this even-paced, clearly written story, it is never heavyhanded or didactic. Valli is a well-developed, realistic, and engaging narrator. . . . An important, inspiring tale." SLJ

Ellis, Sarah

Odd man out. Groundwood Books/House of Anansi Press 2006 162p $18.95; pa $9.95

Grades: 5 6 7 8   **Fic**

1. Cousins -- Fiction 2. Fathers -- Fiction 3. Grandmothers -- Fiction
ISBN 0-88899-702-7; 978-0-88899-703-6 pa; 0-88899-703-5 pa

"This is a thoughtful and often funny book of a boy on the verge of adolescence challenged to think—of his father, mother, cousins, life—in a different way." SLJ

Outside in; by Sarah Ellis. Pgw 2014 206 p. $16.95

Grades: 5 6 7 8   **Fic**

1. Canada -- Fiction 2. Teenage girls -- Fiction 3. Mother-daughter relationship -- Fiction 4. Eccentrics and eccentricities -- Fiction 5. Friendship -- Fiction 6. Homeless girls -- Fiction
ISBN 1554983673; 9781554983674

In this book, by Sarah Ellis, "Lynn is a typical 13-year-old Canadian, navigating through life. . . . Things start to fall apart when her mom wrecks her relationship with the only man who has ever stuck around and Lynn's passport doesn't come in time for her to take the choir trip with the rest of her friends, who leave for Portland. . . . Then a mysterious girl named Blossom is thrust into her life and introduces her to a wonderful world within their city called the Underland." (Publisher's note)

"—With the exception of her quirky, unmarried mother, Lynn is a typical 13-year-old Canadian, navigating through life filled with choir practice, projects, best friends, and school...Lynn's difficult relationship with her mother and her strong bonds with friends make this story very relatable. A thoughtful, exciting read that makes everything ordinary suddenly have the possibility to be extraordinary.—" (SLJ

Ellsworth, Loretta

★ **Unforgettable**. Walker Books for Young Readers 2011 256p $16.99

Grades: 6 7 8 9   **Fic**

1. School stories 2. Memory -- Fiction 3. Synesthesia -- Fiction 4. Dating (Social customs) -- Fiction
ISBN 978-0-8027-2305-5; 0-8027-2305-5
                    LC 2010049590

When Baxter Green was three years old he developed a condition that causes him to remember absolutely everything, and now that he is fifteen, he and his mother have moved to Minnesota to escape her criminal boyfriend and, Baxter hopes, to reconnect with a girl he has been thinking about since kindergarten.

"A lot is going here—an exploration of of synesthesia and memory, a crime story, an environmental drama, family relationships and a sweet, earnest love story. . . . But everything works." Kirkus

Elston, Ashley

The **rules** for disappearing; Ashley Elston. 1st ed. Hyperion 2013 320 p. (reinforced) $16.99

Grades: 7 8 9 10 11 12   **Fic**

1. Witnesses -- Fiction 2. Friendship -- Fiction 3. Dysfunctional families -- Fiction 4. Schools -- Fiction 5. High schools -- Fiction 6. Moving, Household -- Fiction 7. Natchitoches (La.) -- Fiction 8. Family life -- Louisiana -- Fiction 9. Natchitoches (La.) -- Fiction 10. Witness protection programs -- Fiction
ISBN 1423168976; 9781423168973

LC 2012035122

In this book by Ashley Elston, "seventeen-year-old Meg Jones . . . and her family are in the witness protection program, and they've changed towns six times in less than a year. . . . Meg's mother is an alcoholic, her father is depressed and secretive, and her 11-year-old sister is having trouble coping with all of the change. Fed up, Meg wants out of the program and will do anything to save her family, including digging up what her father did to get them into this mess." (Publishers Weekly)

"The fresh first-person narration serves the story well, providing grounding in reality as events spin out of control. Though the plot may seem a bit far-fetched at times, the realistic setting, believable romance and spunky protagonist will make this one worth the trip for mystery and romance fans." Kirkus

Emond, Stephen

★ **Happyface**. Little, Brown and Co. 2010 307p il $16.99

Grades: 7 8 9 10   **Fic**

1. School stories 2. Diaries -- Fiction 3. Divorce -- Fiction 4. Dating (Social customs) -- Fiction
ISBN 978-0-316-04100-3; 0-316-04100-9

LC 2008-47386

After going through traumatic times, a troubled, socially awkward teenager moves to a new school where he tries to reinvent himself.

"The illustrations range from comics to more fleshed-out drawings. Just like Happyface's writing, they can be whimsical, thoughtful, boyishly sarcastic, off-the-cuff, or achingly beautiful." Publ Wkly

★ **Winter** town; Story and art by Stephen Emond. Little, Brown 2011 336p il $17.99

Grades: 7 8 9   **Fic**

1. Love stories 2. Teenagers -- Fiction 3. High school students -- Fiction 4. Cartoons and caricatures -- Fiction
ISBN 0316133329; 9780316133326

LC 2011012966

Evan and Lucy, childhood best friends who grew apart after years of seeing one another only during Christmas break, begin a romance at age seventeen but his choice to mindlessly follow his father's plans for an Ivy League education rather than becoming the cartoonist he longs to be, and her more destructive choices in the wake of family problems, pull them apart.

This is a "remarkable illustrated work of contemporary fiction. . . . Interspersed throughout are both realistic illustrations and drawings of a comic strip being created by Evan and Lucy; these black-and-white, almost chibi-style panels form an effective parallel with the plot and appeal mightily on their own. Compelling, honest and true—this musing about art and self-discovery, replete with pitch-perfect dialogue, will have wide appeal." Kirkus

Enderle, Dotti

Crosswire. Calkins Creek 2010 143p $17.95

Grades: 5 6 7 8   **Fic**

1. Texas -- Fiction 2. Brothers -- Fiction 3. Droughts -- Fiction 4. Ranch life -- Fiction 5. Father-son relationship -- Fiction
ISBN 978-1-59078-751-9; 1-59078-751-X

LC 2010-07522

When an 1883 drought drives free-range cattlemen to shred Texas ranchers' barbed wire fences and steal water, thirteen-year-old Jesse works hard to help while dealing with his father and brother's falling-out and his own fear of guns.

"Enderle writes with restraint, her research neatly woven into the story, her characters carefully drawn. A small gem of a story." Kirkus

Includes bibliographical references

Engdahl, Sylvia Louise

★ **Enchantress** from the stars; foreword by Lois Lowry. Firebird 2003 288p pa $6.99

Grades: 7 8 9 10 11 12   **Fic**

1. Science fiction
ISBN 0-14-250037-2

A reissue of the title first published 1970 by Atheneum Pubs.

A Newbery Medal honor book, 1971

When young Elana unexpectedly joins the team leaving the spaceship to study the planet Andrecia, she becomes an integral part of an adventure involving three very different civilizations, each one centered on the third planet from the star in its own solar system

"Emphasis is on the intricate pattern of events rather than on characterization, and readers will find fascinating symbolism—and philosophical parallels to what they may have observed or thought. The book is completely absorbing and should have a wider appeal than much science fiction." Horn Book

Engle, Margarita

★ **Firefly** letters; a suffragette's journey to Cuba. Henry Holt & Co. 2010 151p $16.99

Grades: 7 8 9 10 11 12   **Fic**

1. Authors 2. Novelists 3. Novels in verse 4. Cuba

-- Fiction 5. Slavery -- Fiction 6. Sex role -- Fiction
ISBN 978-0-8050-9082-6; 0-8050-9082-7

LC 2009-23445

"This engaging title documents 50-year-old Swedish suffragette and novelist Fredrika Bremer's three-month travels around Cuba in 1851. Based in the home of a wealthy sugar planter, Bremer journeys around the country with her host's teenaged slave Cecilia, who longs for her mother and home in the Congo. Elena, the planter's privileged 12-year-old daughter, begins to accompany them on their trips into the countryside. . . . Using elegant free verse and alternating among each character's point of view, Engle offers powerful glimpses into Cuban life at that time. Along the way, she comments on slavery, the rights of women, and the stark contrast between Cuba's rich and poor." SLJ

Hurricane dancers; the first Caribbean pirate shipwreck. Henry Holt and Co. 2011 145p $16.99
Grades: 6 7 8 9 10   **Fic**
1. Novels in verse 2. Pirates -- Fiction 3. Shipwrecks -- Fiction 4. Caribbean region -- Fiction 5. Native Americans -- West Indies -- Fiction
ISBN 978-0-8050-9240-0; 0-8050-9240-4

LC 2010-11690

This is an "accomplished historical novel in verse set in the Caribbean. . . . The son of a Taíno Indian mother and a Spanish father, [Quebrado] is taken in 1510 from his village on the island that is present-day Cuba and enslaved on a pirate's ship, where a brutal conquistador . . . is held captive for ransom. When a hurricane destroys the boat, Quebrado is pulled from the water by a fisherman, Naridó, whose village welcomes him, but escape from the past proves nearly impossible. . . . Engle fictionalizes historical fact in a powerful, original story. . . . Engle distills the emotion in each episode with potent rhythms, sounds, and original, unforgettable imagery." Booklist

★ The **Lightning** Dreamer; Cuba's Greatest Abolitionist. Margarita Engle. Houghton Mifflin Harcourt 2013 192 p. $16.99
Grades: 6 7 8 9 10   **Fic**
1. Historical fiction 2. Novels in verse 3. Authors -- Fiction 4. Feminists -- Fiction 5. Abolitionists -- Fiction
ISBN 0547807430; 9780547807430

LC 2013003913

Pura Belpre Author Honor Book (2014)

This book is a "work of historical fiction about Cuban poet, author, antislavery activist and feminist Gertrudis Gómez de Avellaneda. Written in free verse, the story tells of how Tula, which was her childhood nickname, grows up in libraries, which she calls 'a safe place to heal/ and dream . . .,' influenced by the poetry of Jose Maria Heredia." (School Library Journal)

Includes bibliographical references.

Silver people; voices from the Panama Canal. Margarita Engle. Houghton Mifflin Harcourt 2014 272 p. (hardback) $17.99
Grades: 5 6 7 8   **Fic**
1. Panama Canal 2. Novels in verse 3. Rain forests -- Fiction 4. Migrant labor -- Fiction 5. Racism -- Fiction

6. Segregation -- Fiction 7. Panama Canal (Panama) -- History -- Fiction
ISBN 0544109414; 9780544109414

LC 2013037485

This children's book, by Margarita Engle, is an "exploration of the construction of the Panama Canal. . . . Mateo, a 14-year-old Cuban lured by promises of wealth, journeys to Panama only to discover the recruiters' lies and a life of harsh labor. However, through his relationships with Anita, an 'herb girl,' Henry, a black Jamaican worker, and Augusto, a Puerto Rican geologist, Mateo is able to find a place in his new land." (Kirkus Reviews)

"In melodic verses, Engle offers the voices of the dark-skinned workers (known as the 'silver people'), whose back-breaking labor helped build the Panama Canal, along with the perspective of a local girl. Interspersed are occasional echoes from flora and fauna as well as cameo appearances by historical figures. Together, they provide an illuminating picture of the project's ecological sacrifices and human costs." Horn Book

Includes bibliographical references

★ **Tropical** secrets; Holocaust refugees in Cuba. Henry Holt 2009 199p $16.95
Grades: 7 8 9 10 11   **Fic**
1. Novels in verse 2. Cuba -- Fiction 3. Jews -- Fiction 4. Refugees -- Fiction 5. Holocaust, 1933-1945 -- Fiction
ISBN 978-0-8050-8936-3; 0-8050-8936-5

LC 2008-36782

Escaping from Nazi Germany to Cuba in 1939, a young Jewish refugee dreams of finding his parents again, befriends a local girl with painful secrets of her own, and discovers that the Nazi darkness is never far away.

"Readers who think they might not like a novel in verse will be pleasantly surprised at how quickly and smoothly the story flows. . . . The book will provide great fodder for discussion of the Holocaust, self-reliance, ethnic and religious bias, and more." Voice Youth Advocates

The **wild** book; Margarita Engle. Harcourt Children's Books 2012 133p $16.99
Grades: 5 6 7 8   **Fic**
1. Novels in verse 2. Children's stories 3. Dyslexia -- Fiction 4. Cuba -- History -- 1909-1933 -- Fiction
ISBN 9780547581316

LC 2011027320

This book tells the story of "Josefa 'Fefa' de la Caridad Uría Peña. . . . Diagnosed with 'word blindness' (a misnomer for dyslexia), Fefa struggles at school. . . . Discounting a doctor's opinion . . . her mother gives her a blank diary: 'Let the words sprout / like seedlings, / then relax and watch / as your wild diary / grows.' . . . Her reading difficulties are heightened when bandits begin roving the countryside, kidnapping local children for ransom." (Kirkus Reviews)

English, Karen
★ **Francie**. Farrar, Straus & Giroux 1999 199p hardcover o.p. $17
Grades: 5 6 7 8   **Fic**
1. Alabama -- Fiction 2. Race relations -- Fiction 3.

African Americans -- Fiction
ISBN 0-374-32456-5; 0-374-42459-4 pa

LC 98-53047

Coretta Scott King honor book for text, 2000

"The best student in her small, all-black school in pre-integration Alabama, 12-year-old Francie hopes for a better life. . . . When Jessie, an older school friend who is without family, is forced on the run by a racist employer, Francie leaves her mother's labeled canned food for him in the woods. Only when the sheriff begins searching their woods . . . does she realize the depth of the danger she may have brought to her family. Francie's smooth-flowing, well-paced narration is gently assisted by just the right touch of the vernacular. Characterization is evenhanded and believable, while place and time envelop readers." SLJ

Ephron, Delia

Frannie in pieces; drawings by Chad W. Beckerman. HarperTeen 2007 374p il $16.99; pa $8.99
Grades: 7 8 9 10   **Fic**

1. Puzzles -- Fiction 2. Bereavement -- Fiction 3. Father-daughter relationship -- Fiction
ISBN 978-0-06-074716-9; 0-06-074716-1; 978-0-06-074718-3 pa; 0-06-074718-8 pa

LC 2007-10909

When fifteen-year-old Frannie's father dies, only a mysterious jigsaw puzzle that he leaves behind can help her come to terms with his death.

"This is a tender, moving story dealing with grief and growing up and the power of art to heal." SLJ

The **girl** with the mermaid hair. HarperTeen 2010 312p $16.99
Grades: 7 8 9 10   **Fic**

1. Family life -- Fiction 2. Personal appearance -- Fiction 3. Perfectionism (Personality trait) -- Fiction
ISBN 978-0-06-154260-2; 0-06-154260-1

LC 2009-03061

A vain teenaged girl is obsessed with beauty and perfection until she uncovers a devastating family secret.

"A solid and perceptive realistic drama, this will particularly satisfy readers beginning to reconsider their own familial assumptions." Bull Cent Child Books

Epstein, Adam Jay

Circle of heroes; Adam Jay Epstein & Andrew Jacobson. Harper 2012 327 p. (The familiars) (trade bdg.) $16.99
Grades: 4 5 6   **Fic**

1. Fantasy 2. Magic -- Fiction 3. Animals -- Fiction 4. Wizards -- Fiction 5. Zombies -- Fiction
ISBN 0061961140; 9780061961144

LC 2012005740

"Aldwyn, a street-smart alley cat, pretended he had telekinetic powers so young wizard Jack would chose him as a familiar. Aldwyn then learned that he and two other familiars—Skylar the blue jay and Gilbert the tree frog—were destined to undertake a perilous quest to defeat Paksahara, an evil hare who'd been familiar to the queen. In Circle of Heroes, the third book of The Familiars series for middle-grade readers, Paksahara and her undead animal army control the Shifting Fortress. Aldwyn and his friends have to

recapture it to return magic to the queendom of Vastia." (Publisher's Note)

"In this third installment, cat Aldwyn, frog Gilbert, and blue jay Skylar, the prophesied familiars, embark on a quest to unite seven magical animal descendants before the evil hare Paksahara and her Dead Army of zombie animals forever rid the world of human magic. Rollicking adventure and playful humor add whimsy to this series' theme of fulfilling destiny." Horn Book

Epstein, Robin

God is in the pancakes. Dial Books 2010 265p $16.99
Grades: 7 8 9 10   **Fic**

1. Old age -- Fiction 2. Sisters -- Fiction 3. Religion -- Fiction 4. Euthanasia -- Fiction 5. Dating (Social customs) -- Fiction
ISBN 978-0-8037-3382-4; 0-8037-3382-8

Fifteen-year-old Grace, having turned her back on religion when her father left, now finds herself praying for help with her home and love life, and especially with whether she should help a beloved elderly friend die with dignity.

"Everything comes together in an authentic, breezy read that asks difficult questions and doesn't shy away from direct answers, or the reality that answers may not exist. With well-developed adults and a teen seeking help from God and anyone she perceives as wise, this memorable novel offers food for thought and sustenance for the soul." Booklist

Erdrich, Louise

★ The **birchbark** house. Hyperion Bks. for Children 1999 244p il hardcover o.p. pa $6.99
Grades: 5 6 7 8   **Fic**

1. Ojibwa Indians -- Fiction
ISBN 0-7868-0300-2; 0-7868-1454-3 pa

LC 98-46366

Omakayas, a seven-year-old Native American girl of the Ojibwa tribe, lives through the joys of summer and the perils of winter on an island in Lake Superior in 1847.

"Erdrich crafts images of tender beauty while weaving Ojibwa words seamlessly into the text. Her gentle spot art throughout complements this first of several projected stories that will 'attempt to retrace [her] own family's history.'" Horn Book Guide

Followed by: The game of silence (2004)

★ **Chickadee**; Louise Erdrich. Harper 2012 256p. (trade bdg.) $16.99
Grades: 5 6 7 8   **Fic**

1. Brothers -- Fiction 2. Ojibwe Indians -- Fiction 3. Voyages and travels -- Fiction 4. Kidnapping -- Fiction 5. Family life -- Fiction 6. Métis -- Fiction 7. Ojibwa Indians -- Fiction 8. Great Plains -- History -- 19th century -- Fiction 9. Superior, Lake, Region -- History -- 19th century -- Fiction
ISBN 9780060577902; 9780060577919

LC 2012006565

Sequel to: The porcupine year.

Scott O'Dell Award for Historical Fiction (2013)

This book is the "fourth book of The Birchbark House Series. Omakayas is now a young mother with lively 8-year-old twins named Chickadee and Makoons." Makoons plays a trick on the tribe's bully, resulting in the bully's sons kidnapping Chickadee. He escapes, then "runs into his Uncle Quill driving an ox cart of furs to sell in St. Paul. Quill and Chickadee travel with fellow traders on the Red River ox cart trail, arriving in Pembina to find Makoons seriously ill." (Kirkus)

★ The **game** of silence; [by] Louise Erdrich. HarperCollins 2004 256p $15.99; lib bdg $16.89; pa $5.99

Grades: 5 6 7 8   **Fic**
    1. Ojibwa Indians -- Fiction
    ISBN 0-06-029789-1; 0-06-029790-5 lib bdg; 0-06-441029-3 pa
                                        LC 2004-6018
    Sequel to: The birchbark house (1999)
    Nine-year-old Omakayas, of the Ojibwa tribe, moves west with her family in 1849
    "Erdrich's captivating tale of four seasons portrays a deep appreciation of our environment, our history, and our Native American sisters and brothers." SLJ
    Followed by: The porcupine year (2008)

★ The **porcupine** year. HarperCollinsPublishers 2008 193p $15.99; lib bdg $16.89

Grades: 5 6 7 8   **Fic**
    1. Family life -- Fiction 2. Ojibwa Indians -- Fiction 3. Voyages and travels -- Fiction
    ISBN 978-0-06-029787-9; 0-06-029787-5; 978-0-06-029788-6 lib bdg; 0-06-029788-3 lib bdg
                                        LC 2008000757
    Sequel to: The game of silence (2004)
    In 1852, forced by the United States government to leave their beloved Island of the Golden Breasted Woodpecker, fourteen-year-old Omokayas and her Ojibwe family travel in search of a new home.
    "Based on Erdrich's own family history, this celebration of life will move readers with its mischief, its anger, and its sadness. What is left unspoken is as powerful as the story told." Booklist

Ernst, Kathleen

    Hearts of stone; [by] Kathleen Ernst. 1st ed.; Dutton Children's Books 2006 248p $16.99

Grades: 6 7 8 9   **Fic**
    1. Orphans -- Fiction 2. Tennessee -- Fiction 3. United States -- History -- 1861-1865, Civil War -- Fiction
    ISBN 0-525-47686-5
                                        LC 2005032756
    Orphaned when her father dies fighting for the Union and her mother expires from exhaustion, and also estranged from their Confederate neighbors, fifteen-year-old Hannah struggles to find a way for her family to survive during the Civil War in Tennessee.
    "Ernst movingly shows that the calamity and upheaval of war extends far beyond the battlefields." Booklist

Erskine, Kathryn

    The **absolute** value of Mike. Philomel Books 2011 247p $16.99

Grades: 5 6 7 8   **Fic**
    1. Pennsylvania -- Fiction 2. Business enterprises

-- Fiction 3. Father-son relationship -- Fiction 4. Eccentrics and eccentricities -- Fiction
    ISBN 978-0-399-25505-2; 0-399-25505-2
                                        LC 2010-13333
    Fourteen-year-old Mike, whose father is a brilliant mathematician but who has no math aptitude himself, spends the summer in rural Pennsylvania with his elderly and eccentric relatives Moo and Poppy, helping the townspeople raise money to adopt a Romanian orphan.
    "Erskine weaves together a large but entertaining cast of characters. . . . Despite many laugh-out-loud moments, the heart of the book is essentially serious." Horn Book

    The **badger** knight; Kathryn Erskine. Scholastic Press 2014 352 p. illustrations $17.99

Grades: 5 6 7 8   **Fic**
    1. Paganism 2. War stories 3. Medieval civilization 4. Adventure stories 5. Archers -- Fiction 6. Runaways -- Fiction 7. Friendship -- Fiction 8. Albinos and albinism -- Fiction 9. Great Britain -- History -- Edward III, 1327-1377 -- Fiction
    ISBN 0545464420; 9780545464420; 9780545464437; 9780545662932
                                        LC 2013042527
    In this book by Kathryn Erskine, "13-year-old Adrian--small, asthmatic, and an albino--dreams of becoming a soldier and fighting the 'pagan Scots' that threaten 1346 England. Perceived as weak and touched by the devil, the self-dubbed 'Badger' is a skilled archer and has the rare ability to read and write. When his amiable friend Hugh joins the English army, Adrian runs away to follow him." (Publishers Weekly)
    "--Erskine hits the bull's-eye in her retelling of the hero's journey through the eyes of a young, medieval archer determined to prove his worth through battle... Erskine excels at combining action, historical tidbits (Badger hides in an ancient Roman latrine and muses on the soldiers who came before him), and thoroughly likable characters with modern sensibilities. Much like Karen Cushman's notable books, Erskine's latest deserves a place in most middle school libraries." SLJ

    Quaking. Philomel Books 2007 236p $16.99

Grades: 7 8 9 10   **Fic**
    1. School stories 2. Patriotism -- Fiction 3. Toleration -- Fiction 4. Family life -- Fiction 5. Pennsylvania -- Fiction 6. Society of Friends -- Fiction
    ISBN 978-0-399-24774-3; 0-399-24774-2
                                        LC 2006-34563
    In a Pennsylvania town where antiwar sentiments are treated with contempt and violence, Matt, a fourteen-year-old girl living with a Quaker family, deals with the demons of her past as she battles bullies of the present, eventually learning to trust in others as well as herself.
    "This is a compelling story, which enfolds the political issues into a deeper focus on the characters' personal stories." Booklist

    Seeing red; by Kathryn Erskine. Scholastic Press 2013 352 p. $16.99

Grades: 5 6 7 8   **Fic**
    1. Family -- Fiction 2. Friendship -- Fiction 3. Race

relations -- Fiction 4. Grief -- Fiction 5. Bereavement
-- Fiction 6. Family life -- Virginia -- Fiction 7. Virginia
-- History -- Fiction 9. Families -- Virginia -- Fiction
10. Virginia -- History -- 20th century -- Fiction 11.
Virginia -- Race relations -- Fiction
ISBN 0545464404; 9780545464406; 9780545464413;
9780545576451

LC 2013004261

Author Kathryn Erskin presents a "story of family,
friendship, and race relations in the South. Red's daddy,
his idol, has just died, leaving Red and Mama with some
hard decisions and a whole lot of doubt. Should they sell the
Porter family business? When Red discovers the injustices
that have been happening in Rocky Gap since before he was
born, he's faced with unsettling questions about his family's
legacy." (Publisher's note)

Esckilsen, Erik E.
The **last** mall rat. Houghton Mifflin 2003 182p
$15; pa $5.95
Grades: 7 8 9 10   **Fic**
1. Shopping centers and malls -- Fiction
ISBN 0-618-23417-9; 0-618-60896-6 pa

LC 2002-14436

Too young to get a job at the Onion River Mall, fifteen-
year-old Mitch earns money from salesclerks to harrass
rude shoppers

"Realistic dialogue and a keen sense of what matters to
teens will draw them to this quick read." Booklist

Eulberg, Elizabeth
Revenge of the Girl With the Great Personality;
Elizabeth Eulberg. Scholastic 2013 272 p. (hard-
cover) $17.99
Grades: 7 8 9 10   **Fic**
1. Sisters -- Fiction 2. Beauty contests -- Fiction
ISBN 9780545476997; 0545476992

"Everybody loves Lexi. She's popular, smart, funny . . .
but she's never been one of . . . the pretty ones who get all the
attention from guys. And on top of that, her seven-year-old
sister, Mackenzie, is a terror in a tiara. . . . Lexi's sick of it. .
. . The time has come for Lexi to step out from the sidelines.
Girls without great personalities aren't going to know what
hit them. Because Lexi's going to play the beauty game."
(Publisher's note)

Evangelista, Beth
Gifted. Walker & Co. 2005 180p $16.95; pa
$6.95
Grades: 5 6 7 8   **Fic**
1. Bullies -- Fiction 2. Camping -- Fiction 3. Gifted
children -- Fiction
ISBN 0-8027-8994-3; 0-8027-9644-3 pa

Arrogant, mentally gifted George Clark has dreaded the
eighth-grade class camping trip and its inevitable bullying,
but a hurricane and a friend's loyalty make him realize what
is important in life.

"It's hard to write a successful book with an unlikable
protagonist . . . but that's what first-time author Evangelista
has done. . . . Fresh and funny." Booklist

Evans, Lissa
Horten's miraculous mechanisms; magic, mys-
tery & a very strange adventure. by Lissa Evans.
Sterling 2012 270 p. $14.95
Grades: 3 4 5 6 7   **Fic**
1. Mystery fiction 2. Adventure fiction 3. Children's
stories 4. Inventors -- Fiction 5. Magicians -- Fiction
ISBN 9781402798061

In this book, author Lissa "Evans borrows several classic
tropes and themes--magic, riddles, a quest, and even a night
at a museum--for the . . . story of 10-year-old Stuart Horten
. . . who stumbles into a family mystery when he and his
parents move to the small British town of Beeton. There,
Stuart discovers that his Great-Uncle Tony Horten, who disappeared years ago without a trace, was both an inventor of
mechanical devices and a magician. A chance phone call in
a broken phone booth is the first step in a journey that leads
Stuart around town, as he unearths his great-uncle's legacy
and secrets. Stuart also draws the attention of April, May,
and June (the journalistically inclined triplets next door),
as well as Beeton residents with more sinister intentions."
(Publishers Weekly)

Evans, Richard Paul
Battle of the Ampere; 3 Richard Paul Evans.
Mercury Ink/Simon Pulse 2013 307 p. $17.99
Grades: 6 7 8 9   **Fic**
1. Science fiction 2. Electricity -- Fiction 3. Friendship
-- Fiction 4. Tourette syndrome -- Fiction
ISBN 1442475110; 9781442475113; 9781442475137

LC 2013026653

This young adult science fiction novel, by Richard Paul
Evans, part three in the "Michael Vey" series, "Michael,
Taylor, Ostin and the rest of the Electroclan have destroyed
the largest of the Elgen Starxource plants, but now they're
on the run. The Elgen have teamed up with the Peruvian
army to capture them, and only Michael remains free. With
his friends due to stand trial for terrorism . . . Michael will
need all his wits and his abilities if he's to save them." (Publisher's note)

"Though the Electroclan's destruction of the Starxource
plant was a major victory over the Elgen, the Peruvian government has branded it a terroristic act. Hunted by both the
army and the Elgen fleet, Michael and friends must evade
capture as they plan their next move against Dr. Hatch. Evans develops character relationships better in this third installment, which continues to be exciting." Horn Book

Other titles in the series include:
The Prisoner of Cell 25 (2011)
Rise of the Elgen (2012)
Hunt for Jade Drago (2014)

Michael Vey; rise of the Elgen. by Richard
Paul Evans. Mercury Ink/Simon Pulse 2012 335 p.
(hardcover) $17.99
Grades: 6 7 8 9   **Fic**
1. Fantasy fiction 2. Voyages and travels -- Fiction
3. Peru -- Fiction 4. Science fiction 5. Friendship --
Fiction 6. Electricity -- Fiction 7. Tourette syndrome

-- Fiction

ISBN 1442454148; 9781442454149; 9781442454620; 9781442475106

LC 2012022717

Sequel to: Michael Vey, the prisoner of cell 25

This is the second book in Richard Paul Evans's Michael Vey series. Here, "after using their wits and powers to narrowly escape an Elgen trap, a mysterious voice leads the Electroclan to the jungles of Peru in search of Michael's mother. Once there, they discover that Dr. Hatch and the Elgen are far more powerful than anyone realizes. . . . Only the Electroclan and an anonymous voice now stand in the way of the Elgen's plan for global domination." (Publisher's note)

Fagan, Deva

Circus Galacticus. Harcourt 2011 291p $16.99

Grades: 6 7 8 9   **Fic**

1. Science fiction 2. Circus -- Fiction 3. Orphans -- Fiction

ISBN 978-0-547-58136-1; 0-547-58136-X

LC 2011009594

Trix's life in boarding school as an orphan charity case has been hard but when an alluring young Ringmaster invites her, a gymnast, to join Circus Galacticus she gains an entire universe of deadly enemies and potential friends, along with a chance to unravel secrets of her own past.

"Fagan's story makes SF fun. It's loaded with wild coincidences and easily spotted inspirations (X-Men, Doctor Who), yet the underlying idea of valuing diversity, friendship, and self-esteem shines, carried by Fagan's solid writing, appealing characters, and sprinkles of whimsy." Publ Wkly

Fortune's folly. Henry Holt 2009 260p $17.95

Grades: 5 6 7 8   **Fic**

1. Fairy tales 2. Adventure fiction 3. Prophecies -- Fiction

ISBN 978-0-8050-8742-0; 0-8050-8742-7

LC 2008-36780

Ever since her mother died and her father lost his shoe-making skills, Fortunata has survived by pretending to tell fortunes, but when she is tricked into telling the fortune of a prince, she is faced with the impossible task of fulfilling her wild prophecy to save her father's life.

"Fagan's language evokes images of fairy tales and legends, and the protagonist's first-person narrative sparkles with humor. In this book, words are powerful, impressive, mystical, and, sometimes, downright silly." SLJ

Fahy, Thomas Richard

The **unspoken**; [by] Tom Fahy. Simon & Schuster Books for Young Readers 2008 166p $15.99

Grades: 8 9 10 11 12   **Fic**

1. Horror fiction 2. Cults -- Fiction

ISBN 978-1-4169-4007-4; 1-4169-4007-3

LC 2007-00850

Six teens are drawn back to the small, North Carolina town where they once lived and, one by one, begin to die of their worst fears, as prophesied by the cult leader they killed five years earlier, and who they believe poisoned their parents.

"Teeth-clenching suspenseful at times and deliciously creepy at others, Fahy . . . delivers a classic horror story." Publ Wkly

Fairlie, Emily

The **lost** treasure of Tuckernuck; Emily Fairlie. Katherine Tegen Books 2012 283 p. (hardback) $16.99

Grades: 4 5 6 7 8   **Fic**

1. Mystery fiction 2. Buried treasure -- Fiction 3. Historic buildings -- Fiction 4. Schools -- Fiction 5. Mystery and detective stories 6. Treasure hunt (Game) -- Fiction

ISBN 0062118900; 9780062118905

LC 2012025279

This book by Emily Fairlie "tells the story of Bud and Laurie's quest to find the infamous Tutweiler Treasure. They're hot (or at least lukewarm) on the trail of clues, but time is running out -- the school board wants to tear down Tuckernuck Hall. Can Bud and Laurie find the treasure before it's lost forever?" (Publisher's note)

Falkner, Brian

The **project**. Random House 2011 275p $17.99

Grades: 6 7 8 9 10   **Fic**

1. Adventure fiction 2. Time travel -- Fiction 3. National socialism -- Fiction 4. World War, 1939-1945 -- Fiction

ISBN 978-0-375-96945-4; 0-375-96945-4

LC 2010033449

After discovering a terrible secret hidden in the most boring book in the world, Iowa fifteen-year-olds Luke and Tommy find out that members of a secret Nazi organization intend to use this information to rewrite history.

"The wacky unbelievability of this story in no way detracts from its enjoyment. It reads like an action movie, with plenty of chases, explosions, and by-a-hair escapes." SLJ

Falls, Kat

Dark life. Scholastic Press 2010 297p $16.99; pa $6.99

Grades: 4 5 6 7   **Fic**

1. Science fiction 2. Ocean -- Fiction

ISBN 978-0-545-17814-3; 0-545-17814-2; 978-0-545-17815-0 pa; 0-545-17815-0 pa

LC 2009-24907

"Ty has lived subsea his entire life. His family members moved below the water to make a better life for themselves. In this future, the climate changes on Earth have been so drastic that hardly any solid ground exits anymore. . . . This book will appeal to middle grade readers, who will enjoy the novel's mystery and suspense. It is a definite must-read for SF fans." Voice Youth Advocates

Followed by: Rip tide (2011)

Inhuman; Kat Falls. Scholastic Press 2013 384 p. $17.99

Grades: 7 8 9 10   **Fic**

1. Dystopian fiction 2. Apocalyptic fiction 3. Survival 4. Dystopias 5. Science fiction 6. Survival -- Fiction 7. Quarantine -- Fiction 8. Virus diseases -- Fiction 9.

Fathers and daughters -- Fiction
ISBN 054537099X; 9780545370998

LC 2013026360

In this dystopian novel by Kat Falls, "the United States east of the Mississippi has been abandoned. Now called the Feral Zone, a reference to the virus that turned millions of people into bloodthirsty savages, the entire area is off-limits. . . . [Protagonist] Lane gets the shock of her life when she learns that someone close to her has crossed into the Feral Zone." (Publisher's note)

"Years ago, the U.S. was bisected by a pandemic (spread by biting) that causes humans to mutate into feral human-animal hybrids. When pampered teenager Lane is blackmailed into the Feral Zone, she joins the search for a cure and discovers the gray area between human and feral. While Lane and her love triangle are bland, the zombie-apocalypse-meets-wereanimals-gone-wild setup captures the imagination." (Horn Book)

Rip tide. Scholastic Press 2011 320p $16.99
Grades: 4 5 6 7   Fic
1. Science fiction 2. Ocean -- Fiction
ISBN 0-545-17843-6; 978-0-545-17843-3
Sequel to: Dark life (2010)

"While preparing to sell the season's seaweed crop, Ty stumbles across an abandoned township, its doors chained shut and its residents murdered. Soon after, the colonists' deal with another township goes bad, and Ty's parents are kidnapped. As Ty and Gemma try to track down those responsible and save their loved ones, they're forced to join up with the notorious Seablite Gang, infiltrate the rough-and-tumble town of Rip Tide, fight for their lives against sea monsters and human predators, and discover who's killing entire townships—and why. . . . There's no shortage of action, intrigue, or daring exploits in this aquatic thriller. Atmospheric and tense, built around an expertly used post-apocalyptic meets Wild West setting, this story's a whole lot of fun." Publ Wkly

Fama, Elizabeth

Overboard; Elizabeth Fama. Cricket Books 2002 158p. maps (Cloth : alk. paper) $15.95
Grades: 7 8 9 10   Fic
1. Muslims -- Fiction 2. Indonesia -- Fiction 3. Shipwrecks -- Fiction 4. Survival after airplane accidents, shipwrecks, etc. -- Fiction 5. Survival -- Fiction 6. Sumatra (Indonesia) -- Fiction
ISBN 0812626524; 9780553494365

LC 20020592

In this "novel based on a 1996 ferry accident off the coast of Sumatra, Emily, a 14-year-old American living in Indonesia with her doctor parents, boards an overcrowded, tilting ferry (without her parents' knowledge) after her uncle invites her to visit him on a nearby island. As the ship lists to 'an unnatural angle,' the captain distributes life vests. Emily hands hers to a younger boy who is trying to hang on to the railing. . . . The girl then becomes trapped in the life-vest locker, which immediately fills with water. . . . [The plot continues with a] chronicle of Emily's nightlong struggle to survive. . . . During the course of the evening, she [encounters] . . . a Muslim child who explains some of the tenets of his faith as they bob along in the water." (Publishers Weekly)

Fantaskey, Beth

Buzz kill; by Beth Fantaskey. Houghton Mifflin Harcourt 2014 368 p. $17.99
Grades: 8 9 10 11 12   Fic
1. Murder -- Fiction 2. High schools -- Fiction 3. Football -- Coaching -- Fiction 4. Mystery and detective stories 5. Coaches (Athletics) -- Fiction 6. Dating (Social customs) -- Fiction
ISBN 0547393105; 9780547393100

LC 2013011423

In this book, by Beth Fantaskey, "when the widely disliked Honeywell Stingers football coach is found murdered, 17-year-old Millie is determined to investigate. She is chasing a lead for the school newspaper--and looking to clear her father, the assistant coach, and prime suspect. . . . Millie joins forces with her mysterious classmate Chase who seems to want to help her even while covering up secrets of his own." (Publisher's note)

"When the head football coach is killed, seventeen-year-old Millie, a school reporter obsessed with Nancy Drew, sets out to learn the truth and clear her assistant-coach father of any suspicion. She gets some unexpected help from dreamy quarterback Chase, who's hiding some secrets. This entertaining sleuth story is a good choice for teens now graduated from books featuring Millie's literary hero." Horn Book

Jessica's guide to dating on the dark side. Harcourt 2009 354p $17
Grades: 8 9 10 11 12   Fic
1. Vampires -- Fiction
ISBN 978-0-15-206384-9; 0-15-206384-6

LC 2007-49002

Seventeen-year-old Jessica, adopted and raised in Pennsylvania, learns that she is descended from a royal line of Romanian vampires and that she is betrothed to a vampire prince, who poses as a foreign exchange student while courting her.

"Fantaskey makes this premise work by playing up its absurdities without laughing at them. . . . The romance sizzles, the plot develops ingeniously and suspensefully, and the satire sings." Publ Wkly

Farber, E. S.

Seagulls don't eat pickles; by Erica Farber; illustrated by Jason Beene. Chronicle Books 2013 184 p. (Fish Finelli) (alk. paper) $15.99
Grades: 4 5 6 7   Fic
1. Pirates -- Fiction 2. Adventure fiction 3. Librarians -- Fiction 4. Historic sites -- Fiction 5. Buried treasure -- Fiction 6. Mystery and detective stories 7. Treasure troves -- Fiction 8. Historic sites -- Conservation and restoration -- Fiction
ISBN 145210820X; 9781452108209

LC 2012027739

This is the first book in E.S. Farber's Fish Finelli series. "Fish Finelli wants nothing more . . . than to fix up his boat with a supercharged Seagull motor and win Whooping Hollow's annual Captain Kidd Classic boat race," but has only saved half the necessary funds. "When local bully Bryce Billings baits Fish into a bet that he and his friends Roger and T.J. can't find Captain Kidd's fabled lost treasure, . . .

Fish finds himself knee-deep in a mysterious pirate adventure." (School Library Journal)

Fardell, John

The **7** professors of the Far North. G. P. Putnam's Sons 2005 217p il hardcover o.p. pa $6.99

Grades: 4 5 6 7 **Fic**

1. Science fiction 2. Adventure fiction 3. Arctic regions -- Fiction

ISBN 0-399-24381-X; 0-14-240735-6 pa

Eleven-year-old Sam finds himself involved in a dangerous adventure when he and his new friends, brother and sister Ben and Zara, set off for the Arctic to try and rescue the siblings' great-uncle and five other professors from the mad scientist holding them prisoner.

"Action is nonstop and very exciting. This inventive, funny, suspenseful, and exciting book will appeal to most readers." SLJ

Followed by: The flight of the Silver Turtle (2006)

Farinango, Maria Virginia

★ The **Queen** of Water. Delacorte Press 2011 352p $16.99; lib bdg $19.99

Grades: 8 9 10 11 12 **Fic**

1. Ecuador -- Fiction 2. Social classes -- Fiction

ISBN 978-0-385-73897-2; 0-385-73897-8; 978-0-385-90761-3 lib bdg; 0-385-90761-3 lib bdg

LC 2010-10512

"The complexities of class and ethnicity within Ecuadorian society are explained seamlessly within the context of the first-person narrative, and a glossary and pronunciation guide further help to plunge readers into the novel's world. By turns heartbreaking, infuriating and ultimately inspiring." Kirkus

Farizan, Sara

★ **If** you could be mine; a novel. Sara Farizan. Algonquin 2013 256 p. (hardcover) $16.95

Grades: 8 9 10 11 12 **Fic**

1. Sex reassignment surgery -- Fiction 2. Iran -- Social conditions -- Fiction 3. Iran -- Fiction 4. Love -- Fiction 5. Lesbians -- Fiction 6. Friendship -- Fiction 7. Best friends -- Fiction

ISBN 1616202513; 9781616202514

LC 2013008931

Rainbow List (2014)

Lambda Literary Awards Wiiner - LGBT Children's/YA (2014)

This novel, set in Iran, 17-year-old Sahar, who has wanted to marry her best friend Nasrin since they were six years old, dreams of living openly with her lover. Nasrin prefers to accept an arranged marriage, while intending to continue their illicit affair. Exposed to a world of sexual diversity by her gay cousin and made desperate by Nasrin's impending marriage, Sahar explores the one legal option for the two of them to be together: her own sex reassignment surgery." (Publishers Weekly)

"Rich with details of life in contemporary Iran, this is a GLBTQ story that we haven't seen before in YA fiction." SLJ

Farmer, Nancy

★ The **Ear,** the Eye, and the Arm; a novel. Puffin Books 1995 311p pa $6.99

Grades: 6 7 8 9 10 **Fic**

1. Science fiction 2. Zimbabwe -- Fiction

ISBN 978-0-14-131109-8; 0-14-131109-6

LC 95019982

First published 1994 by Orchard Books

A Newbery Medal honor book, 1995

In 2194 in Zimbabwe, General Matsika's three children are kidnapped and put to work in a plastic mine while three mutant detectives use their special powers to search for them

"Throughout the story, it's the thrilling adventure that will grab readers, who will also like the comic, tender characterizations." Booklist

A **girl** named Disaster. Orchard Bks. 1996 309p $19.95; pa $7.99

Grades: 6 7 8 9 **Fic**

1. Adventure fiction 2. Zimbabwe -- Fiction 3. Mozambique -- Fiction 4. Supernatural -- Fiction

ISBN 0-531-09539-8; 0-14-038635-1 pa

LC 96-15141

A Newbery Medal honor book, 1997

While journeying from Mozambique to Zimbabwe to escape an arranged marriage, eleven-year-old Nhamo struggles to escape drowning and starvation and in so doing comes close to the luminous world of the African spirits

"This story is humorous and heartwrenching, complex and multilayered." SLJ

★ The **house** of the scorpion. Atheneum Bks. for Young Readers 2002 380p $17.95; pa $7.99

Grades: 7 8 9 10 **Fic**

1. Science fiction 2. Cloning -- Fiction

ISBN 0-689-85222-3; 0-689-85223-1 pa

LC 2001-56594

A Newbery Medal honor book, 2003

In a future where humans despise clones, Matt enjoys special status as the young clone of El Patrón, the 140-year-old leader of a corrupt drug empire nestled between Mexico and the United States.

"This is a powerful, ultimately hopeful, story that builds on today's sociopolitical, ethical, and scientific issues and prognosticates a compelling picture of what the future could bring." Booklist

★ The **lord** of Opium; Nancy Farmer. Atheneum Books for Young Readers 2013 432 p. (hardcover) $17.99

Grades: 7 8 9 10 **Fic**

1. Fantasy fiction 2. Drug traffic -- Fiction 3. Science fiction 4. Cloning -- Fiction 5. Environmental degradation -- Fiction

ISBN 1442482540; 9781442482548

LC 2012030418

Sequel to: House of the scorpion (2002)

This book is the sequel to Nancy Farmer's "The House of the Scorpion." Here, "Matt was a clone of El Patrón, drug lord of Opium, but with El Patrón dead, Matt is now considered by international law to be fully human and El Patrón's rightful heir. But it's a corrupt land . . . ruled over by drug lords and worked by armies of Illegals turned into 'eejits,' or zombies. Matt wants to bring reform." (Kirkus Reviews)

★ The **Sea** of Trolls. Atheneum Books for Young Readers 2004 459p $17.95; pa $9.99

Grades: 5 6 7 8 9   **Fic**

1. Fantasy fiction 2. Vikings -- Fiction 3. Norse mythology -- Fiction 4. Druids and Druidism -- Fiction

ISBN 0-689-86744-1; 0-689-86746-8 pa

LC 2003-19091

After Jack becomes apprenticed to a Druid bard, he and his little sister Lucy are captured by Viking Berserkers and taken to the home of King Ivar the Boneless and his half-troll queen, leading Jack to undertake a vital quest to Jotunheim, home of the trolls.

"This exciting and original fantasy will capture the hearts and imaginations of readers." SLJ

Includes bibliographical references

Other titles in this series are:

The Land of the Silver Apples (2007)

The Islands of the Blessed (2009)

Farr, Richard

Emperors of the ice; a true story of disaster and survival in the Antarctic, 1910-13. Farrar, Straus & Giroux 2008 215p il map $19.95

Grades: 6 7 8 9   **Fic**

1. Painters 2. Explorers 3. Physicians 4. Penguins -- Fiction 5. Explorers -- Fiction 6. Antarctica -- Fiction 7. British Antarctic ("Terra Nova") Expedition (1910-1913) (1910-1913): -- Fiction

ISBN 978-0-374-31975-5; 0-374-31975-8

LC 2007-52347

Apsley 'Cherry' Cherry-Garrard shares his adventures as the youngest member of Robert Scott's expedition to Antarctica in the early twentieth century, during which he and Edward Wilson try to learn the evolutionary history of emperor penguins. Includes historical notes.

"Heavily illustrated with paintings, photos, and documents from the actual expedition, the book brings vividly to life the explorers and scientists of nearly a century ago." Voice Youth Advocates

Includes bibliographical references

Farrant, Natasha

After Iris; by Natasha Farrant. Dial Books for Young Readers 2013 272 p. (hardcover) $16.99

Grades: 5 6 7 8   **Fic**

1. Grief -- Fiction 2. Babysitters -- Fiction 3. Twins -- Fiction 4. Diaries -- Fiction 5. Au pairs -- Fiction 6. Brothers and sisters -- Fiction 7. Family life -- England -- London -- Fiction 8. Video recordings -- Production and direction -- Fiction

ISBN 0803739826; 9780803739826

LC 2012039136

In this book, 12-year-old "Bluebell Gadsby's family has been collapsing ever since Blue's twin sister, Iris, died three years ago. Blue's father is working on the other side of the country, and their mother is traveling overseas, which leaves new au pair Zoran in charge. Between Blue's older sister Flora's rebelliousness, her two younger siblings' antics, and

the family's pet rats, which live in the garden of their London home, Zoran has his hands full." (Publishers Weekly)

Farrar, Josh

Rules to rock by. Walker Books for Young Readers 2010 244p $16.99

Grades: 4 5 6 7   **Fic**

1. Moving -- Fiction 2. Bullies -- Fiction 3. Rock music -- Fiction 4. Rhode Island -- Fiction 5. Rock musicians -- Fiction

ISBN 978-0-8027-2079-5; 0-8027-2079-X

Annabella Cabrera tries to start a rock band at her new middle school in Providence, Rhode Island, but has trouble when the members of a rival band bully her and she develops a case of writer's block.

"Rock prevails in this spirited, never-say-die story about a girl and her dream. Farrar's first novel hits home about tween life, especially among the creative set, and for anyone who has ever been bullied." SLJ

Farrey, Brian

The **Grimjinx** rebellion; Brian Farrey. HarperCollins 2014 432 p. illustrations (hardcover) $16.99

Grades: 4 5 6 7   **Fic**

1. Fantasy fiction 2. Magic -- Fiction 3. Brothers and sisters -- Fiction 4. Swindlers and swindling -- Fiction 5. Fantasy

ISBN 0062049348; 9780062049346

LC 2013043194

In this book, by Brian Farrey, "Jaxter Grimjinx and his family haven't had much time for thieving. Through no fault of their own, they've been too busy saving the day. But the danger in the Five Provinces is only just beginning. The Palatinate Mages are almost ready to unveil their master plan, and legendary monsters will soon roam the land once more. Then Jaxter's sister, Aubrin, is kidnapped by the Mages." (Publisher's note)

"When mage sentinels carry off Jaxter Grimjinx's little sister Aubrin to be their new augur, the family's quest to get her back leads to the opening elements of a prophecy in which Jaxter will save the Five Provinces from a deadly scourge but die doing so. The twisted but coherent puzzle plot unfolds swiftly, speeded along by irreverent Grimjinx humor." Horn Book

Other titles in the series include:

The Vengekeep Prophecies (2012)

The Shadowhand Covenant (2013)

The **Shadowhand** Covenant; by Brian Farrey and illustrated by Brett Helquist. HarperCollins 2013 384 p. (hardback) $16.99

Grades: 4 5 6 7 8   **Fic**

1. Thieves -- Fiction 2. Conspiracies -- Fiction 3. Secret societies -- Fiction 4. Fantasy

ISBN 0062049313; 9780062049315

LC 2013021825

Sequel to: The Vengekeep prophecies

In this book by Brian Farrey, "trouble is brewing in the Five Provinces. Mysterious magical artifacts have gone missing from the royal vaults. Master thieves from a secret society known as the Shadowhands are disappearing. And without explanation, the High Laird has begun imprisoning the peaceful Sarosan people. Jaxter Grimjinx and his parents receive a summons from the Shadowhands—a summons that they would be foolish to ignore—and Jaxter is thrust into the heart of the conspiracy." (Publisher's note)

The **Vengekeep** prophecies; Brian Farrey; illustrated by Brett Helquist. Harper 2012 390 p. (hardback) $16.99

Grades: 4 5 6 7   **Fic**

1. Magic -- Fiction 2. Prophecies -- Fiction 3. Swindlers and swindling -- Fiction 4. Fantasy 5. Monsters -- Fiction

ISBN 0062049283; 9780062049285

LC 2012025282

In this book by Brian Farrey, "12-year-old Jaxter Grimjinx is anxious to prove himself at the family business: thievery. Jaxter's first attempt at burglary ends with . . . his family being jailed, but his parents have . . . replaced the prophetic tapestry that predicts the year ahead . . . with one that shows the Grimjinx family as heroes. The family quickly discovers, however, that the fake tapestry is actually enchanted, and every disaster it depicts is coming true." (Publishers Weekly)

Fawcett, Katie Pickard

To come and go like magic. Alfred A. Knopf 2010 263p $16.99; lib bdg $19.99

Grades: 5 6 7 8   **Fic**

1. Kentucky -- Fiction 2. Family life -- Fiction 3. Country life -- Fiction

ISBN 978-0-375-85846-8; 0-375-85846-6; 978-0-375-95846-5 lib bdg; 0-375-95846-0 lib bdg

LC 2008-52188

In the 1970s, twelve-year-old Chili Sue Mahoney longs to escape her tiny Kentucky home town and see the world, but she also learns to recognize beauty in the people and places around her.

"Chili's first-person narrative stretches from poetic thoughts . . . , to more down-to-earth observations. Her insights are absorbing and her setbacks heartbreaking, as she weighs the only home she's ever known against the possibilities that loom farther afield." Publ Wkly

Federle, Tim

★ **Better** Nate than ever; Tim Federle. Simon & Schuster Books for Young Readers 2013 288 p. (hardcover) $16.99

Grades: 5 6 7 8   **Fic**

1. Theater -- Fiction 2. Musicals -- Fiction 3. Auditions -- Fiction 4. New York (N.Y.) -- Fiction 5. Broadway (New York, N.Y.) -- Fiction

ISBN 1442446897; 9781442446892; 9781442446908

LC 2011050388

Odyssey Honor Recording (2014)

Rainbow List (2014)

Stonewall Honor Book: Children and Young Adult (2014)

Lambda Literary Awards Finalist (2014)

In author Tim Federle's book, "Nate Foster has big dreams. His whole life, he's wanted to star in a Broadway show. (Heck, he'd settle for seeing a Broadway show.) But how is Nate supposed to make his dreams come true when

he's stuck in Jankburg, Pennsylvania . . . ? With Libby's help, Nate plans a daring overnight escape to New York. There's an open casting call for 'E.T.: The Musical,' and Nate knows this could be the difference between small-town blues and big-time stardom." (Publisher's note)

Five, six, seven, Nate! by Tim Federle. Simon & Schuster Books for Young Readers 2014 304 p. (hardcover) $16.99

Grades: 5 6 7 8   **Fic**

1. Theater 2. Actors -- Fiction 3. Theater -- Fiction 4. Musicals -- Fiction 5. Friendship -- Fiction 6. Best friends -- Fiction 7. New York (N.Y.) -- Fiction 8. Broadway (New York, N.Y.) -- Fiction

ISBN 1442446935; 9781442446939

LC 2012051239

Sequel to: Better Nate than ever

In this book, by Tim Federle, "Nate is off to start rehearsals for 'E.T.: The Broadway Musical.' It's everything he ever practiced his autograph for! But as thrilling as Broadway is, rehearsals are nothing like Nate expects: full of intimidating child stars, cut-throat understudies, and a director who can't even remember Nate's name." (Publisher's note)

"Nate successfully auditioned for Broadway's E.T.: The Musical in Better Nate Than Ever. Of course, he's actually only an understudy's understudy, his chorus part keeps diminishing, and rehearsals are going poorly, but good-humored Nate takes it all in stride. Federle addresses his likable character's burgeoning interest in boys in a laudably straightforward way, making this entertaining backstage pass especially rewarding." (Horn Book)

Fehlbaum, Beth

Big fat disaster; Beth Fehlbaum. Merit Press, an imprint of F+W Media, Inc. 2014 288 p. (pb) $17.99

Grades: 7 8 9 10   **Fic**

1. Moving -- Fiction 2. Family life -- Fiction 3. Eating disorders -- Fiction 4. Overweight teenagers -- Fiction 5. Texas -- Fiction 6. Schools -- Fiction 7. High schools -- Fiction 8. Moving, Household -- Fiction

ISBN 1440570485; 9781440570483

LC 2013044512

In this book, by Beth Fehlbaum, "insecure, shy, and way overweight, Colby hates the limelight as much as her pageant-pretty mom and sisters love it. It's her life: Dad's a superstar, running for office on a family values platform. Then suddenly, he ditches his marriage for a younger woman and gets caught stealing money from the campaign. Everyone hates Colby for finding out and blowing the whistle on him. From a mansion, they end up in a poor relative's trailer." (Publisher's note)

"Colby's life as the heavy daughter of a disapproving former Miss Texas beauty queen is difficult enough, but it gets worse very quickly once she discovers a photo of her politician father kissing another woman...Colby's experiences, while extreme, ring true, and the fast pace, lively and profane dialogue, and timely topic make it a quick and enjoyable read." (Kirkus)

Fehler, Gene

Beanball; by Gene Fehler. Clarion Books 2008 119p $16

Grades: 7 8 9 10   **Fic**

1. School stories 2. Novels in verse 3. Baseball -- Fiction

ISBN 0-618-84348-5; 978-0-618-84348-0

LC 2007013058

Relates, from diverse points of view, events surrounding the critical injury of popular and talented high school athlete, Luke "Wizard" Wallace, when he is hit in the face by a fastball.

This is a "moving baseball novel in free verse. . . . This swift read will appeal to both reluctant readers and baseball players." KLIATT

Feinstein, John

Last shot; a Final Four mystery. Knopf 2005 251p $16.95; lib bdg $18.99

Grades: 6 7 8 9   **Fic**

1. Mystery fiction 2. Basketball -- Fiction 3. Journalists -- Fiction

ISBN 0-375-83168-1; 0-375-93168-6 lib bdg

LC 2004-26535

After winning a basketball reporting contest, eighth graders Stevie and Susan Carol are sent to cover the Final Four tournament, where they discover that a talented player is being blackmailed into throwing the final game.

"The action on the court is vividly described. . . . Mystery fans will find enough suspense in this fast-paced narrative to keep them hooked." SLJ

Other titles in this series are:

Vanishing act (2006)

Cover-up (2007)

Change-up (2009)

Rivalry (2010)

Feldman, Ruth Tenzer

Blue thread; Ruth Tenzer Feldman. Ooligan Press 2012 302 p. $12.95

Grades: 7 8 9 10   **Fic**

1. Historical fiction 2. Jewish women -- Fiction 3. Women's rights -- Fiction

ISBN 1932010416; 9781932010411

LC 2011024382

This young adult novel focuses on Miriam, a young Jewish girl in 1912 Portland, Oregon. "While her mother plans their trip to New York City to find her a husband, Miriam gets caught up in the fight for women's suffrage. At first she's nervous about going against her parents' wishes, but curiosity gets the better of her . . . . However, after a mysterious girl named Serakh whisks Miriam back to biblical times, her desire to be a larger part of the movement becomes stronger." (School Library Journal)

Fergus, Maureen

Ortega. Kids Can Press 2010 224p $16.95

Grades: 5 6 7 8   **Fic**

1. Science fiction 2. Gorillas -- Fiction

ISBN 978-1-55453-474-6; 1-55453-474-7

Eleven years ago, an infant lowland gorilla was acquired by a privately funded laboratory. An elite surgical team undertook a series of radical procedures designed to make it physically possible for the infant gorilla to acquire speech.

"The story's excitement and suspense as well as the emotional drama will ensnare readers. This interesting, affecting novel will definitely find an audience." SLJ

Recipe for disaster. Kids Can Press 2009 252p $18.95; pa $8.95

Grades: 7 8 9   **Fic**

1. Baking -- Fiction 2. Friendship -- Fiction

ISBN 978-1-55453-319-0; 1-55453-319-8; 978-1-55453-320-6 pa; 1-55453-320-1 pa

Francie was born to bake and dreams of one day starring in her own baking show. Her life is almost perfect until the new girl at school shows up.

"Francie is a delight. Her own special brand of humor touches every aspect of the tale. . . . This breezy, appealing read covers personal growth, the sacrifices of friendship, and the mistakes made along the way." SLJ

Ferraiolo, Jack D.

The big splash; by Jack D. Ferraiolo. Amulet Books 2008 277p $15.95

Grades: 4 5 6 7   **Fic**

1. School stories 2. Mystery fiction

ISBN 978-0-8109-7067-0; 0-8109-7067-8

LC 2007-49978

Matt Stevens, an average middle schooler with a glib tongue and a knack for solving crimes, uncovers a mystery while working with "the organization," a mafia-like syndicate run by seventh-grader Vincent "Mr. Biggs" Biggio, specializing in forged hall passes, test-copying rings, black market candy selling, and taking out hits with water guns.

This "novel delivers plenty of laughs, especially in the opening chapters, and fans of private-eye spoofs will enjoy this entertaining read." Booklist

★ Sidekicks. Amulet 2011 309p $16.95

Grades: 6 7 8 9   **Fic**

1. Superheroes -- Fiction

ISBN 978-0-8109-9803-2; 0-8109-9803-3

"By all outward appearances, Bright Boy is an average middle-school student, but at night, he becomes the sidekick to superhero Rogue Warrior. . . . Ferraiolo is delightfully unafraid to inject irreverence into the superhero formula, adding plenty of humor to the high-adventure high jinks." Booklist

Ferris, Jean

Much ado about Grubstake. Harcourt 2006 265p $17

Grades: 5 6 7 8   **Fic**

1. Orphans -- Fiction 2. Colorado -- Fiction 3. City and town life -- Fiction 4. Gold mines and mining -- Fiction

ISBN 0-15-205706-4

When two city folks arrive in the depressed mining town of Grubstake, Colorado in 1888, sixteen-year-old orphaned Arley tries to discover why they want to buy the supposedly worthless mines in the area

"Ferris combines adventure, love, and off-the-wall characters in a page-turning story full of good laughs and common sense messages." Voice Youth Advocates

Once upon a Marigold; by Jean Ferris. Harcourt 2002 266 p. $17

Grades: 5 6 7 8   **Fic**

1. Love -- Fiction 2. Princesses -- Fiction 3. Triangles (Interpersonal relations) -- Fiction 4. Fairy tales 5. Princesses/Fiction

ISBN 0152050841; 0152167919; 9780152167912

LC 2002000311

Marigold series

This novel by Jean Ferris focuses on Christian, who did not know "love could be so amazing. He was clueless when he started spying on the royal family. He lives in a cave with a troll for a dad. If his dad had only warned him about all that mind-boggling love stuff, maybe things wouldn't be such a mess. But then, maybe, Princess Marigold would be dead. And now that he's fallen for the princess, it's up to him to untwist an odd love triangle . . . and foil a scheming queen." (Publisher's note)

"This complex, fast-paced plot, a mixture of fantasy, romance, comedy, and coming-of-age novel, succeeds because these characters are compelling, well developed, and sympathetic." SLJ

Followed by: Twice upon a Marigold (2008)

Twice upon a Marigold. Harcourt 2008 297p $17

Grades: 5 6 7 8   **Fic**

1. Fairy tales 2. Princesses -- Fiction 3. Kings and rulers -- Fiction

ISBN 978-0-15-206382-5; 0-15-206382-X

LC 200735761

Sequel to: Once upon a Marigold (2002)

After a quiet, happy year in a small town, Queen Olympia regains her memory and initiates new plots and manipulations, as the residents of Zandelphia and Beaurivage, now ruled by Christian, Marigold, and Swithbert, feel the effects of her bad energy.

"Appealing new characters and fresh plot twists give this sequel a life of its own, though fans of the earlier book will enjoy the continuation of its story line, wry humor, and offbeat sense of fun." Booklist

Fforde, Jasper

The **Eye** of Zoltar; 2 by Jasper Fforde. Houghton Mifflin Harcourt 2014 416 p. (The Chronicles of Kazam) (hardback) $16.99

Grades: 7 8 9 10   **Fic**

1. Fantasy fiction 2. Magic -- Fiction 3. Orphans -- Fiction 4. Voyages and travels -- Fiction 5. Fantasy

ISBN 0547738498; 9780547738499

LC 2014001381

In this book, by Jasper Fforde, "although she's an orphan in indentured servitude, sixteen-year-old Jennifer Strange is pretty good at her job of managing the unpredictable crew at Kazam Mystical Arts Management. She already solved the Dragon Problem, avoided mass destruction by Quarkbeast, and helped save magic in the Ununited Kingdoms. Yet even Jennifer may be defeated when the long-absent Mighty

Shandar makes an astonishing appearance and commands her to find the Eye of Zoltar." (Publisher's note)

"This installment is darker than the first two outings and contains a Grand Canyon–sized cliff-hanger of an ending. Fans of strong, brave, intelligent females will root for Jennifer and her gang, and wait impatiently for the next book." SLJ

★ The **last** Dragonslayer; Jasper Fforde. Hodder & Stoughton 2010 281 p. (The Chronicles of Kazam) $16.99; (hbk.) $16.99

Grades: 7 8 9 10   **Fic**

1. Magic -- Fiction 2. Dragons -- Fiction 3. Employment agencies -- Fiction

ISBN 978-0547738475; 1444707175; 1444707191; 9781444707175; 9781444707199

LC 2010551874

In this book by Jasper Fforde, part of the Chronicles of Kazam series, "magic is fading. . . . Fifteen-year-old foundling Jennifer Strange runs Kazam, an employment agency for magicians -- but it's hard to stay in business when magic is drying up. And then the visions start, predicting the death of the world's last dragon at the hands of an unnamed Dragonslayer. If the visions are true, everything will change for Kazam -- and for Jennifer." (Publisher's note)

The **song** of the Quarkbeast; Jasper Fforde. Houghton Mifflin Harcourt 2013 304 p. (The chronicles of Kazam) $16.99

Grades: 7 8 9 10   **Fic**

1. Fantasy 2. Magic -- Fiction

ISBN 054773848X; 9780547738482

LC 2012047318

This is the second book in Jasper Fforde's Chronicles of Kazam series. Here, now "that magical power is on the rise again, the despotic King Snodd IV hopes to cash in, specifically by putting the wizards who work at Kazam Mystical Arts Management under his control by proposing they merge with iMagic, the rival house led by the Amazing Blix, a questionable character with a new royal appointment: Court Mystician." (Publishers Weekly)

Fichera, Liz

Played; Liz Fichera. Harlequin Books 2014 352 p. $9.99

Grades: 9 10 11 12   **Fic**

1. Love stories

ISBN 0373210949; 9780373210947

LC 2014001537

"Sam Tracy likes to stay under the radar and hang out with his friends from the Rez. But when he saves rich suburban princess Riley Berenger from falling off a mountain, she decides to try to save him. Riley promises to help Sam win the heart of the girl he can't get over, and suddenly Sam is mad popular and on everyone's hot list. Except now Riley's trying out some brand-new bad-girl moves." (Publisher's note)

"...the plot is a perfect mix of real-life scenarios and swoon-worthy romance, while the issues of race and class that Fichera interweaves into Sam and Riley's story add substance. In an alternating first-person narration style similar to Rainbow Rowell's Eleanor and Park (St. Martin's, 2013), readers are given insight into the characters' thoughts and feelings. The tale sticks to the formula, but the captivating ways in which the sequence of events plays out keep this take fresh and exciting." -SLJ

Fienberg, Anna

Number 8. Walker 2007 288p $16.95

Grades: 7 8 9 10   **Fic**

1. Singers -- Fiction 2. Australia -- Fiction 3. Family life -- Fiction 4. Mathematics -- Fiction 5. Organized crime -- Fiction

ISBN 978-0-8027-9660-8; 0-8027-9660-5

LC 2007-14706

While hiding out from the mob in the suburbs with his mother, a singer, Jackson uses his fascination with math and numbers to make friends, but strange phone calls and even greater threats endanger not only Jackson and his mother, but his new girlfriend, as well.

"The fact that each character has an idiosyncratic passion that somehow helps them understand the others adds dimension to an already effective suspense plot." Bull Cent Child Books

Fink, Mark

The **summer** I got a life. WestSide 2009 196p $15.95

Grades: 7 8 9   **Fic**

1. Love stories 2. Wisconsin -- Fiction 3. People with disabilitis -- Fiction

ISBN 978-1-934813-12-6; 1-934813-12-5

"Andy is pumped that his freshman year is over and his vacation is about to begin. Then his dad's promotion changes everything. Instead of Hawaii, Andy is spending two weeks on a farm in Wisconsin with his somewhat odd, but well-meaning, aunt and uncle. Once there, though, he finds that things aren't so bad particularly when he spots 'the most incredible-looking girl he has ever seen.' . . . Andy discovers that an accident at age four has left Laura confined to a wheelchair. . . . This is an engaging novel filled with life lessons, a little romance, humor, sports, and fraternal love." SLJ

Finn, Mary

★ **Belladonna**. Candlewick Press 2011 371p $16.99

Grades: 7 8 9 10   **Fic**

1. Artists 2. Painters 3. Horses -- Fiction 4. Great Britain -- History -- 1714-1837 -- Fiction

ISBN 978-0-7636-5106-0; 0-7636-5106-0

LC 2010038707

This book is set "[i]n rural England in 1757, [where] Thomas Rose is on the verge of becoming a man. Clever, but unable to learn reading and writing . . . Tom meets the enigmatic Hélène, a circus performer who goes by the name of Ling . . . Enchanted with Ling's stories of her life in the circus as much as with the girl herself, Tom commits to helping her find her beloved horse, Belladonna . . . Their search leads them to George Stubbs, known in the village as a horse butcher . . . the teens discover that Stubbs is a painter who is completing an anatomical study of horses that involves dissection of the animals. Stubbs takes Tom on as an apprentice and secures Ling a position in the household of the

wealthy family that purchased Belladonna, not knowing that the girl's ultimate goal is to escape with her horse." (School Libr J)

"A touch of intrigue and interesting details about horses, early necropsy, and everyday life add a rich frame to this historical coming-of-age story, unique in both its setting and subject." Booklist

Finneyfrock, Karen

The **sweet** revenge of Celia Door; by Karen Finneyfrock. Viking 2013 272 p. (hardcover) $16.99

Grades: 7 8 9 10   **Fic**

1. School stories 2. Revenge -- Fiction 3. Teenagers -- Fiction 4. Gays -- Fiction 5. Poetry -- Fiction 6. Schools -- Fiction 7. High schools -- Fiction 8. Hershey (Pa.) -- Fiction 9. Family life -- Pennsylvania -- Hershey -- Fiction

ISBN 0670012750; 9780670012756

LC 2011047221

In this teen novel, by Karen Finneyfrock, "Celia Door enters her freshman year . . . with giant boots, dark eyeliner, and a thirst for revenge against Sandy Firestone. . . . But then Celia meets Drake, the cool new kid from New York City who entrusts her with his deepest, darkest secret. When Celia's quest for justice threatens her relationship with Drake, she's forced to decide which is sweeter: revenge or friendship." (Publisher's note)

Fisher, Catherine

The **dark** city. Dial Books for Young Readers 2011 376p (Relic master) $16.99

Grades: 6 7 8 9   **Fic**

1. Fantasy fiction 2. Apprentices -- Fiction

ISBN 978-0-8037-3673-3; 0-8037-3673-8

LC 2010028801

"Relic Master Galen injured both his body and his mind when he dismantled an ancient technological artifact. While his physical injuries have healed, the loss of his psychic gifts has left him reluctantly dependent on his talented young apprentice, Raffi. Together they travel the dangerous road to the ruined Antaran city of Tasceron, where Galen hopes to reclaim his abilities from a shadowy figure known only as the Crow." Booklist

"Well-crafted storytelling provides more than the sum of its parts." Kirkus

Darkwater; by Catherine Fisher. Penguin Group USA 2012 229p (hardcover) $16.99

Grades: 6 7 8 9 10 11 12   **Fic**

1. Sin 2. Teenagers -- Fiction 3. Private schools -- Fiction 4. Soul -- Fiction 5. Twins -- Fiction 6. England -- Fiction 7. Schools -- Fiction 8. Brothers -- Fiction 9. Supernatural -- Fiction 10. Great Britain -- History -- Edward VII, 1901-1910 -- Fiction

ISBN 9780803738188

LC 2011048063

In author Catherine Fisher's book, "Sarah Trevelyan would give anything to regain the power and wealth her family has lost, so she makes a bargain with Azrael, Lord of Darkwater Hall. He gives her one hundred years and the means to accomplish her objective--in exchange for her soul. Fast-forward a hundred years to Tom, a fifteen-year-old boy who dreams of attending Darkwater Hall School but doesn't believe he has the talent. Until he meets a professor named Azrael, who offers him a bargain. Will Sarah be able to stop Tom from making the same mistake she did a century ago?" (Publisher's note)

Day of the scarab; book three of The Oracle Prophecies. Greenwillow Books 2006 400p (Oracle prophecies) $16.99; lib bdg $17.89
Grades: 7 8 9 10   Fic
 1. Fantasy fiction
 ISBN 0-06-057163-2; 0-06-057164-0;
 9780060571634 lib bdg
         LC 2005052626
As she works to return peace to Two Lands, Mirany travels through the Gates of the Underworld.
"Vivid, complicated, and thoroughly engossing, this fast-paced adventure keeps readers avidly turning pages until the majestic conclusion." Horn Book

The **hidden** Coronet. Dial Books for Young Readers 2011 421p (Relic master) $16.99
Grades: 6 7 8 9   Fic
 1. Fantasy fiction 2. Apprentices -- Fiction
 ISBN 978-0-8037-3675-7; 0-8037-3675-4
         LC 2010039315
Sequel to: The lost heiress (2011)
Sixteen-year-old Raffi and Master Galen continue to evade the Watch as they seek the Coronet, a potent ancient relic that could be their only hope for defeating the power that is destroying Anara.
"The climactic integration of visionary mysticism and gee-whiz gadgetry, rendered bittersweet by all-too human failures, leads directly to a cliffhanger ending." Kirkus

★ **Incarceron**. Dial Books 2010 442p $17.99
Grades: 7 8 9 10   Fic
 1. Fantasy fiction 2. Prisoners -- Fiction
 ISBN 978-0-8037-3396-1; 0-8037-3396-8
         LC 2008-46254
First published 2007 in the United Kingdom
To free herself from an upcoming arranged marriage, Claudia, the daughter of the Warden of Incarceron, a futuristic prison with a mind of its own, decides to help a young prisoner escape.
"Complex and inventive, with numerous and rewarding mysteries, this tale is certain to please." Publ Wkly
Followed by Sapphique (2011)

The **lost** heiress. Dial Books for Young Readers 2011 375p (Relic master) $16.99
Grades: 6 7 8 9   Fic
 1. Fantasy fiction 2. Apprentices -- Fiction
 ISBN 978-0-8037-3674-0; 0-8037-3674-6
         LC 2010038156
Sequel to: Dark city (2011)
Even though the city of Tasceron and its emperor have fallen, when Master Galen and his sixteen-year-old apprentice Raffi hear a rumor that the heiress to the throne still lives, they must try to find her and keep her safe.

"Separate plot threads intertwine in a satisfying climax, posing puzzles to keep readers ensnared while providing pleasing narrative momentum to the overall series." Kirkus
Followed by: The hidden coronet (2011)

The **Margrave**. Dial Books for Young Readers 2011 464p (Relic master) $16.99
Grades: 6 7 8 9   Fic
 1. Fantasy fiction 2. Apprentices -- Fiction
 ISBN 978-0-8037-3676-4; 0-8037-3676-2
         LC 2010043237
Their quest to find a secret relic with great power leads Master Galen and his sixteen-year-old apprentice Raffi into the Pit of Maar and the deep evil world at the heart of the Watch.
"The conclusion to Fisher's science-fantasy quartet satisfies." Kirkus

The **obsidian** mirror; by Catherine Fisher. Dial Books 2013 384 p. (Obsidian Mirror) (hardcover) $17.99
Grades: 7 8 9 10 11 12   Fic
 1. Fantasy fiction 2. Science fiction 3. Fathers -- Fiction 4. Time travel -- Fiction 5. Missing persons -- Fiction
 ISBN 0803739699; 9780803739697
         LC 2012019459
This book is the first in a trilogy from Catherine Fisher. The "mirror of the title, a dangerous gateway to other time periods, is being pursued by not one but three equally unpleasant and obsessive mad scientists. One of them, Oberon Venn, is the master of spooky Wintercombe Abbey. . . . Jake Wilde, Venn's teenage godson and his equal in arrogance, has been expelled from boarding school and shipped off to Wintercombe, where the boy plans to accuse Venn of having murdered Jake's father." (Publishers Weekly)

Obsidian mirror; the slanted worlds. by Catherine Fisher. Dial Books, an imprint of Penguin Group (USA) Inc. 2014 368 p. (hardcover : alk. paper) $17.99
Grades: 7 8 9 10 11 12   Fic
 1. Fantasy fiction 2. Apocalyptic fiction 3. Time travel -- Fiction 4. Missing persons -- Fiction 5. Coins -- Fiction 6. Fathers -- Fiction
 ISBN 0803739702; 9780803739703
         LC 2013018259
This book, by Catherine Fisher, is a "genre-blend of time travel, dark fantasy and post-apocalyptic thriller. . . . It starts with a literal explosion, as most of the cast of teenagers, adventurers, schoolmasters, changelings, ghosts and duplicated cats hunker down at the crumbling Wintercombe Abbey, desperately trying to master the Chronoptika excepting Sarah, sent from a ravaged future to destroy the enigmatic device, and Jake, trapped in the London Blitz." (Kirkus Reviews)
"This second in a projected trilogy provides a sumptuous genre-blend of time travel, dark fantasy and post-apocalyptic thriller, along with more complications than answers. . . . The fiendishly labyrinthine plot twists back and forth through perspectives and centuries, from England to medieval Florence to the dreamlike illusions of the Summerland,

but elegant prose, deft characterization and an acute eye for telling details keep readers anchored. . . . Gorgeous, atmospheric, and addictive but ultimately frustrating; absolutely necessary wherever the first has fans." Kirkus

Slanted worlds

The **oracle** betrayed; book one of The Oracle Prophecies. by Catherine Fisher. 1st American ed; Greenwillow Books 2004 341p (Oracle prophecies) $16.99; lib bdg $17.89; pa $6.99

Grades: 7 8 9 10   **Fic**
1. Fantasy fiction
ISBN 0-06-057157-8; 0-06-057158-6 lib bdg; 0-06-057159-4 pa

LC 2003-48498

After she is chosen to be "Bearer-of-the-god," Mirany questions the established order and sets out, along with a musician and a scribe, to find the legitimate heir of the religious leader known as the Archon.

"This [is] a well-developed world with its own culture, some sharply realized settings, and several strong, distinctive characters." Booklist

Other titles in this series :

Day of the scarab: book three of The Oracle Prophecies (2006)

The Sphere of Secrets: book two of The Oracle Prophecies (2005)

Sapphique. Dial Books 2011 460p $17.99

Grades: 7 8 9 10   **Fic**
1. Fantasy fiction 2. Computers -- Fiction 3. Prisoners -- Fiction 4. Identity (Psychology) -- Fiction
ISBN 978-0-8037-3397-8; 0-8037-3397-6

LC 2009-31479

Sequel to: Incarceron (2010)

After his escape from the sentient prison, Incarceron, Finn finds that the Realm is not at all what he expected, and he does not know whether he is to be its king, how to free his imprisoned friends, or how to stop Incarceron's quest to be free of its own nature.

"Fisher's superb world-building marks this title, effectively drawing the reader in to a place so rife with secrets even its inhabitants don't entirely understand the depth of its illusions." Bull Cent Child Books

The **sphere** of secrets; book two of The Oracle Prophecies. Greenwillow Books 2005 370p (Oracle prophecies) $16.99; lib bdg $17.89

Grades: 7 8 9 10   **Fic**
1. Fantasy fiction
ISBN 0-06-057161-6; 0-06-057162-4 lib bdg

LC 2004-42436

First published 2004 in the United Kingdom

Together with Alexos, Seth, Oblek, and a fallen silver star, Mirany is forced to continue the battle against the evil general Argelin.

"This second book in the series has the same power, adventure, and amazement as TheOracleBetrayed. . . . This compelling novel makes a satisfying sequel but can also stand on its own and may encourage readers to become immersed in the series." SLJ

Fitzgerald, Dawn

Soccer chick rules. Roaring Brook Press 2006 150p $16.95

Grades: 5 6 7 8   **Fic**
1. School stories 2. Soccer -- Fiction 3. Politics -- Fiction
ISBN 1-59643-137-7

While trying to focus on a winning soccer season, thirteen-year-old Tess becomes involved in local politics when she learns that all sports programs at her school will be stopped unless a tax levy is passed. "Grades five to eight." (Bull Cent Child Books)

This is "a fast-moving, true-to-life, amusing take on school life. The dialogue is especially spot-on." Booklist

Fitzmaurice, Kathryn

Destiny, rewritten; Kathryn Fitzmaurice; [edited by] Molly O'Neill. Katherine Tegen Books 2013 352 p. (hardcover) $16.99

Grades: 4 5 6 7   **Fic**
1. Father-daughter relationship -- Fiction
ISBN 0061625019; 9780061625015

LC 2012945971

In this novel, sixth-grader Emily, named for the poet Emily Dickinson, is pushed to become a poet by her mother "(she even commemorates the important moments of Emily's life in a first edition of Dickinson's poetry). Emily, however, thrives on predictability and order, and has no feel for poetry." She wants to find "her unknown father. . . . Just as Emily learns his name is hidden in the Dickinson book, it is accidentally taken and Emily sets out to find it." (Publishers Weekly)

A **diamond** in the desert; Kathryn Fitzmaurice. Viking 2012 258 p. (hardcover) $16.99

Grades: 5 6 7 8   **Fic**
1. Baseball -- Fiction 2. Father-son relationship -- Fiction 3. World War, 1939-1945 -- United States -- Fiction 4. Japanese Americans -- Evacuation and relocation, 1942-1945 -- Fiction 5. Guilt -- Fiction 6. Gila River Relocation Center -- Fiction
ISBN 0670012920; 9780670012923

LC 2011012041

In this book, "Tetsu is twelve when he and his mother and sister are relocated by World War II's infamous Executive Order 9066, which justified the internment of Japanese-Americans, to the camp at Gila River. His father, a leader in the Japanese-American community, is detained separately in another location, and Tetsu generally takes his responsibility as the oldest male in the immediate family very seriously. He's particularly solicitous of his younger sister, Kimi, who is . . . traumatized by the lack of privacy in the camp. . . . Kimi . . . wanders out into the desert, where she nearly dies. Guilt-stricken, Tetsu withdraws from baseball and from his friends, until his father arrives at Gila River and rekindles his son's interest in life." (Bulletin of the Center for Children's Books)

Includes bibliographical references (p. 255)

Fixmer, Elizabeth

★ **Saint** training. Zonderkidz 2010 239p $14.99

Grades: 5 6 7 8 **Fic**
1. School stories 2. Catholics -- Fiction 3. Family life
-- Fiction 4. Christian life -- Fiction
ISBN 978-0-310-72018-8; 0-310-72018-4
LC 2010010831

During the turbulent 1960s, sixth-grader Mary Clare
makes a deal with God: she will try to become a saint if He
provides for her large, cash-strapped family.

"The politically fervent period of the late 1960s, with its
dramatic upheavals in family, gender, social, and religious
conventions, comes to life with pathos and humor in this
powerful debut." Publ Wkly

Flack, Sophie
★ **Bunheads**. Poppy 2011 294p $17.99
Grades: 8 9 10 11 12 **Fic**
1. Ballet -- Fiction 2. New York (N.Y.) -- Fiction 3.
Dating (Social customs) -- Fiction
ISBN 978-0-316-12653-3; 0-316-12653-5
LC 2011009715

Hannah Ward, nineteen, revels in the competition, intense rehearsals, and dazzling performances that come with
being a member of Manhattan Ballet Company's corps de
ballet, but after meeting handsome musician Jacob she begins to realize there could be more to her life.

"Readers, both dancers and 'pedestrians' (the corps'
term for nondancers), will find Hannah's struggle a gripping
read." Publ Wkly

Flake, Sharon G.
Bang! Jump at the Sun/Hyperion Books for Chil-
dren 2005 298p hardcover o.p. pa $7.99
Grades: 8 9 10 11 12 **Fic**
1. Violence -- Fiction 2. Family life -- Fiction 3.
African Americans -- Fiction
ISBN 0-7868-1844-1; 0-7868-4955-X pa
LC 2005-47434

A teenage boy must face the harsh realities of inner city
life, a disintegrating family, and destructive temptations as
he struggles to find his identity as a young man.

"This disturbing, thought-provoking novel will leave
readers with plenty of food for thought and should fuel lively
discussions." SLJ

★ The **broken** bike boy and the Queen of 33rd
Street. Jump at the Sun/Hyperion Books for Children
2007 132p il $15.99; pa $5.99
Grades: 4 5 6 7 **Fic**
1. School stories 2. Friendship -- Fiction 3. African
Americans -- Fiction
ISBN 978-1-4231-0032-4; 1-4231-0032-8; 978-1-
4231-0035-5 pa; 1-4231-0035-2 pa
LC 2006-35590

Ten-year-old Queen, a spoiled and conceited African
American girl who is disliked by most of her classmates,
learns a lesson about friendship from an unlikely "knight in
shining armor."

"Complex intergenerational characters and a rich urban
setting defy stereotyping. . . . Infrequent detailed pencil illustrations . . . add a welcome dimension." Horn Book

The **skin** I'm in. Jump at the Sun 1998 171p
$14.95; pa $5.99
Grades: 6 7 8 9 **Fic**
1. School stories 2. Teachers -- Fiction 3. African
Americans -- Fiction
ISBN 0-7868-0444-0; 0-7868-1307-5 pa
LC 98-19615

Thirteen-year-old Maleeka, uncomfortable because her
skin is extremely dark, meets a new teacher with a birthmark
on her face and makes some discoveries about how to love
who she is and what she looks like

This "novel is fast-paced and realistic." Horn Book Guide

Flanagan, John
The **hunters**; John Flanagan. Philomel 2012
403 p. (hardback) $18.99
Grades: 5 6 7 8 **Fic**
1. Adventure fiction 2. Fantasy 3. Courage -- Fiction 4.
Pirates -- Fiction 5. Friendship -- Fiction 6. Seafaring
life -- Fiction 7. Adventure and adventurers -- Fiction
ISBN 0399256210; 9780399256219
LC 2012020986

This book by John Flanagan is part of the Brotherband
Chronicles series. "Hal and his brotherband crew are hot on
the trail of the pirate Zavac and they have one thing only on
their minds: Stopping the bloodthirsty thief before he can do
more damage. Of course, they also know Zavac has the Andomal, the priceless Skandian artifact stolen when the brotherband let down their guard. The chase leads down mighty
rivers, terrifying rapids, to the lawless fortress of Ragusa."
(Publisher's note)

The **invaders**; John Flanagan. Philomel Books
2012 429 p. (The Brotherband chronicles) (hardback) $18.99
Grades: 5 6 7 8 **Fic**
1. Fantasy 2. Courage -- Fiction 3. Pirates -- Fiction
4. Friendship -- Fiction 5. Seafaring life -- Fiction
ISBN 0399256202; 9780399256202
LC 2012000424

This book by John Flanagan is part of the Brotherband
Chronicles series. "Hal and the Herons have done the impossible. This group of outsiders has beaten out the strongest, most skilled young warriors in all of Skandia to win
the Brotherband competition. But their celebration comes
to an abrupt end when the Skandians' most sacred artifact,
the Andomal, is stolen--and the Herons are to blame." (Publisher's note)

★ The **outcasts**. Philomel Books 2011 434p
(Brotherband chronicles) $18.99
Grades: 5 6 7 8 **Fic**
1. Fantasy fiction 2. Adventure fiction 3. Friendship
-- Fiction
ISBN 978-0-399-25619-6; 0-399-25619-9

Hal, who does not fit into Skandian society, ends up in
a brotherband, a group of boys learning the skills that they
need to become warriors, with other outcasts, and they compete with other brotherbands in a series of challenges.

"This enjoyable, old-fashioned tale should have easy appeal for Flanagan's many fans, who are already invested in the world he's created." Publ Wkly

★ The **royal** ranger; John Flanagan. Philomel Books, an imprint of Penguin Group (USA) Inc. 2013 464 p.
Grades: 5 6 7 8   **Fic**
1. Fantasy fiction 2. Adventure and adventurers -- Fiction 3. Fantasy 4. Apprentices -- Fiction
ISBN 9780399163609

LC 2013015910

In this book, by John Flanagan, "Will Treaty has come a long way from the small boy with dreams of knighthood. Life had other plans for him, and as an apprentice Ranger under Halt, he grew into a legend. . . . The time has come to take on an apprentice of his own, and it's the last person he ever would have expected. Fighting his personal demons, Will has to win the trust and respect of his difficult new companion—a task that at times seems almost impossible." (Publisher's note)

"Taking place at least 16 years after the original 10 volumes of the Ranger's Apprentice series, this sequel sees Will training 15-year-old Maddie, the first girl to become a ranger's apprentice... Series fans will hang on every word of this adventure; Maddie emerges as a strong character and could easily develop a following among readers who enjoy Tamora Pierce's books about Alanna, another resourceful, independent-minded heroine." (Booklist)

★ The **ruins** of Gorlan. Philomel Books 2005 249p (Ranger's apprentice) $15.99; pa $7.99
Grades: 5 6 7 8   **Fic**
1. Fantasy fiction
ISBN 0-399-24454-9; 0-14-240663-5 pa
When fifteen-year-old Will is rejected by battleschool, he becomes the reluctant apprentice to the mysterious Ranger Halt, and winds up protecting the kingdom from danger.

"Flanagan concentrates on character, offering readers a young protagonist they will care about and relationships that develop believably over time." Booklist
Other titles in this series are:
The burning bridge (2006)
The icebound land (2007)
The battle for Skandia (2008)
The socerer of the north (2008)
The siege of Macindaw (2009)
Erak's ransom (2010)
The kings of Clonmel (2010)
Halt's peril (2010)
The Emperor of Nihon-Ja (2011)

Fleischman, Paul
★ **Bull** Run; woodcuts by David Frampton. HarperCollins Pubs. 1993 104p il pa $4.99
Grades: 6 7 8 9   **Fic**
1. Bull Run, 1st Battle of, 1861 -- Fiction 2. United States -- History -- 1861-1865, Civil War -- Fiction
ISBN 0-06-440588-5 pa

LC 92-14745

"Abandoning the conventions of narrative fiction, Fleischman tells a vivid, many-sided story in this original and

moving book. An excellent choice for readers' theater in the classroom or on stage." Booklist

Seek. Simon Pulse 2003 167p pa $7.99
Grades: 7 8 9 10   **Fic**
1. Radio -- Fiction 2. Fathers -- Fiction
ISBN 0-689-85402-1
First published 2001 by Front St./Cricket Bks.
"Fleischman has orchestrated a symphony that is both joyful and poignant with this book designed for reader's theatre." Voice Youth Advocates

Fleischman, Sid
The **entertainer** and the dybbuk. Greenwillow Books 2007 180p lib bdg $17.89; pa $6.99; $16.99
Grades: 6 7 8 9   **Fic**
1. Ghost stories 2. Jews -- Fiction 3. Supernatural -- Fiction 4. Ventriloquism -- Fiction 5. Holocaust, 1933-1945 -- Fiction
ISBN 0-06-13444-1; 978-0-06-134446-6 lib bdg; 0-06-134446-X lib bdg; 978-0-06-177140-8 pa; 0-06-177140-6 pa; 978-0-06-134445-9

LC 2007-17267

A struggling American ventriloquist in post-World War II Europe is possessed by the mischievous spirit of a young Jewish boy killed in the Holocaust.

"This exciting and thought-provoking book belongs in every collection." SLJ

The **whipping** boy; illustrations by Peter Sis. Greenwillow Bks. 1986 90p il $16.99; pa $5.99
Grades: 5 6 7 8   **Fic**
1. Adventure fiction 2. Thieves -- Fiction
ISBN 0-688-06216-4; 0-06-052122-8 pa

LC 85-17555

Awarded the Newbery Medal, 1987
"A round tale of adventure and humor, this follows the fortunes of Prince Roland (better known as Prince Brat) and his whipping boy, Jemmy, who has received all the hard knocks for the prince's mischief. . . . There's not a moment's lag in pace, and the stock characters, from Hold-Your-Nose Billy to Betsy's dancing bear Petunia, have enough inventive twists to project a lively air to it all." Bull Cent Child Books

Fleming, David
★ The **Saturday** boy; by David Fleming. Viking Children's 2013 240 p. (hardcover) $16.99
Grades: 5 6 7 8   **Fic**
1. School stories 2. Families of soldiers -- Fiction 3. Bullies -- Fiction 4. Schools -- Fiction 5. Behavior -- Fiction 6. Family life -- Fiction 7. Families of military personnel -- Fiction
ISBN 0670785512; 9780670785513

LC 2012029680

In this book, Derek is the son of "a soldier who flies Apache helicopters and is stationed in Afghanistan for another tour. . . . Derek is a good-hearted kid who just naturally attracts trouble--he doesn't mean to, but he's always in the wrong place at the wrong time and often the victim. He's also impulsive and has a hard time staying focused, which adds to his problems." Then one day, "he sees his dad on the news and his world falls apart." (School Library Journal)

Fletcher, Charlie

Stoneheart. Hyperion Books for Children 2007 450p (Stoneheart trilogy) $16.99; pa $7.99

Grades: 5 6 7 8   Fic

1. Fantasy fiction

ISBN 978-1-4231-0175-8; 1-4231-0175-8; 978-1-4231-0176-5 pa; 1-4231-0176-6 pa

LC 2007-01138

When twelve-year-old George accidentally decapitates a stone statue in London, England, he falls into a parallel dimension where he must battle ancient "live" statues and solve a dangerous riddle.

This "is an action-packed fantasy filled with battles, chases, and an intriguing variety of characters." SLJ

Other titles in this series are:

Ironhand (2008)

Silvertongue (2009)

Fletcher, Ralph

The **one** o'clock chop; [by] Ralph Fletcher. 1st ed.; Henry Holt 2007 183p $16.95

Grades: 7 8 9 10   Fic

1. Cousins -- Fiction 2. New York (State) -- Fiction 3. Boats and boating -- Fiction

ISBN 978-0-8050-8143-5; 0-8050-8143-7

LC 2006035470

In New York, fourteen-year-old Matt spends the summer of 1973 digging clams to earn money for his own boat and falling for Jazzy, a beautiful and talented girl from Hawaii who happens to be his first cousin.

"Plenty of universal teen fascinations and concerns exist for those readers willing to enter Matt's world and give themselves over to this smoothly paced and competently written novel." SLJ

Fletcher, Susan

Alphabet of dreams. Atheneum Books for Young Readers 2006 294p map $16.95

Grades: 6 7 8 9 10   Fic

1. Iran -- Fiction 2. Dreams -- Fiction 3. Zoroastrianism -- Fiction

ISBN 0-689-85042-5

In this book by Susan Fletcher, "Mitra comes from Persian royalty, but now that her family is dead, she disguises herself as a boy, stealing food and sheltering in burial caves with her younger brother, Babak. A journey is set in motion when Babak dreams of a portentous star, and the siblings follow Melchior and his two magi companions as they seek the king it represents." (Booklist)

"The characters are vivid and whole, the plot compelling, and the setting vast." Voice Youth Advocates

Ancient, strange, and lovely. Atheneum Books for Young Readers 2010 315p il (The dragon chronicles) $16.99

Grades: 6 7 8 9   Fic

1. Fantasy fiction 2. Dragons -- Fiction 3. Poaching -- Fiction

ISBN 978-1-4169-5786-7; 1-4169-5786-3

LC 2009053797

Fourteen-year-old Bryn must try to find a way to save a baby dragon from a dangerous modern world that seems to have no place for something so ancient.

"This book offers a wondrous mix of dystopic science fiction and magical fantasy. . . . Fletcher has done an outstanding job of creating a believable place and space for this story to unfold. The plot flows smoothly and quickly with a lot of action." SLJ

Dragon's milk. Atheneum Pubs. 1989 242p hardcover o.p. pa $5.99

Grades: 7 8 9 10   Fic

1. Fantasy fiction 2. Dragons -- Fiction

ISBN 0-689-31579-1; 0-689-71623-0 pa

LC 88-35059

Kaeldra, an outsider adopted by an Elythian family as a baby, possesses the power to understand dragons and uses this power to try to save her younger sister who needs dragon's milk to recover from an illness

"High-fantasy fans will delight in the clash of swords, the flash of magic, the many escape-and-rescue scenes." Booklist

Other titles in this series are:

Flight of the Dragon Kyn (1993)

Sign of the dove (1996)

Walk across the sea. Atheneum Bks. for Young Readers 2001 214p hardcover o.p. pa $4.99

Grades: 5 6 7 8   Fic

1. Prejudices -- Fiction 2. Chinese Americans -- Fiction

ISBN 0-689-84133-7; 0-689-85707-1 pa

LC 00-50246

In late nineteenth-century California, when Chinese immigrants are being driven out or even killed for fear they will take jobs from whites, fifteen-year-old Eliza Jane McCully defies the townspeople and her lighthouse-keeper father to help a Chinese boy who has been kind to her

"This is a gripping and complex story, and Fletcher's lyrical depiction of 19th-century life, her exceptionally well-drawn protagonist, and her deft analysis of racial discrimination make the book even more powerful." SLJ

Flinn, Alex

Beastly. HarperTeen 2007 304p $16.99; lib bdg $17.89; pa $8.99

Grades: 6 7 8 9 10   Fic

1. Fantasy fiction 2. New York (N.Y.) -- Fiction

ISBN 978-0-06-087416-2; 0-06-087416-3; 978-0-06-087417-9 lib bdg; 0-06-087417-1 lib bdg; 978-0-06-196328-5 pa; 0-06-196328-3 pa

LC 2006-36241

A modern retelling of "Beauty and the Beast" from the point of view of the Beast, a vain Manhattan private school student who is turned into a monster and must find true love before he can return to his human form.

This "is creative enough to make it an engaging read. . . . [This is an] engrossing tale that will have appeal for fans of fantasy and realistic fiction." Voice Youth Advocates

Cloaked. HarperTeen 2011 341p $16.99

Grades: 6 7 8 9   Fic

1. Fairy tales 2. Magic -- Fiction 3. Shoes -- Fiction 4.

Animals -- Fiction 5. Florida -- Fiction 6. Princesses -- Fiction 7. Missing persons -- Fiction
ISBN 978-0-06-087422-3; 0-06-087422-8

LC 2009-53387

Seventeen-year-old Johnny is approached at his family's struggling shoe repair shop in a Miami, Florida, hotel by Alorian Princess Victoriana, who asks him to find her brother who was turned into a frog.

"A diverting, whimsical romp through fairy-tale tropes." Bull Cent Child Books

A **kiss** in time. HarperTeen 2009 384p $16.99; pa $8.99

Grades: 7 8 9 10 11 12   **Fic**

1. Florida -- Fiction 2. Witches -- Fiction 3. Princesses -- Fiction
ISBN 978-0-06-087419-3; 0-06-087419-8; 978-0-06-087421-6 pa; 0-06-087421-X pa

LC 2008-22582

Sixteen-year-old Princess Talia persuades seventeen-year-old Jack, the modern-day American who kissed her awake after a 300-year sleep, to take her to her Miami home, where she hopes to win his love before the witch who cursed her can spirit her away.

This is a "clever and humorous retelling of 'Sleeping Beauty.' . . . Alternating between the teenagers' distinctive points of view, Flinn skillfully delineates how their upbringings set them apart while drawing parallels between their family conflicts. Fans of happily-ever-after endings will delight in the upbeat resolution." Publ Wkly

Flood, Nancy Bo

★ **Warriors** in the crossfire. Front Street 2010 142p $17.95

Grades: 6 7 8 9   **Fic**

1. World War, 1939-1945 -- Fiction 2. Islands of the Pacific -- Fiction
ISBN 978-1-59078-661-1; 1-59078-661-0

Twelve-year-old Joseph helps his family to survive when the natives of Saipan are caught in the crossfire between Japanese and American soldiers towards the end of World War II.

"Intense and powerful reading that avoids bleakness by celebrating family, culture, and a longing for peace." Booklist

Flores-Gabis, Enrique

★ **90** miles to Havana. Roaring Brook Press 2010 292p $17.99

Grades: 5 6 7 8   **Fic**

1. Cuba -- Fiction 2. Florida -- Fiction 3. Cuban refugees -- Fiction
ISBN 978-1-59643-168-3; 1-59643-168-7

"Drawing on his own experience as a child refugee from Cuba, Flores-Galbis offers a gripping historical novel about children who were evacuated from Cuba to the U.S. during Operation Pedro Pan in 1961. Julian, a young Cuban boy, experiences the violent revolution and watches mobs throw out his family's furniture and move into their home. For his safety, his parents send him to a refugee camp in Miami. . . . This is a seldom-told refugee story that will move readers with the first-person, present-tense rescue narrative, filled with betrayal, kindness, and waiting for what may never come." Booklist

Flores-Scott, Patrick

Jumped in; Patrick Flores-Scott. Christy Ottaviano Books, Henry Holt and Company 2013 304 p. (hardback) $16.99

Grades: 8 9 10   **Fic**

1. Gangs -- Fiction 2. Friendship -- Fiction 3. Slam poetry -- Fiction 4. Poetry -- Fiction 5. Schools -- Fiction 6. High schools -- Fiction 7. Mexican Americans -- Fiction 8. Des Moines (Wash.) -- Fiction 9. Interpersonal relations -- Fiction
ISBN 0805095144; 9780805095142

LC 2013018844

In this book, "grunge-rock devotee Sam has been trying to avoid the attention of teachers and other students ever since his mom left town two years earlier. Then the equally quiet Luis Cárdenas arrives in Sam's English class. . . . Sam doesn't see Luis' true colors until Ms. Cassidy announces that the class will have a poetry slam. Luis not only throws himself into creating a poem, he inspires Sam to do the same." (Kirkus Reviews)

Fogelin, Adrian

The **big** nothing; 1st ed; Peachtree 2004 235p $14.95

Grades: 7 8 9 10   **Fic**

1. Pianists -- Fiction 2. Family life -- Fiction
ISBN 1-56145-326-9

LC 2004-6327

Thirteen-year-old Justin Riggs struggles to cope with major family problems, including a brother who might be heading for the Persian Gulf, but finds an escape in piano lessons and the dream of a romance with a popular girl.

"Serious and humorous by turns, this seemingly simple story is actually quite complex but not weighty and will be enthusiastically embraced." SLJ

The **real** question. Peachtree 2006 234p $15.95

Grades: 7 8 9 10   **Fic**

1. Florida -- Fiction 2. Father-son relationship -- Fiction
ISBN 1-56145-383-8

LC 2006013996

Fisher Brown, a sixteen-year-old over-achiever, is on the verge of academic burnout when he impulsively decides to stop cramming for the SATs for one weekend and accompany his ne'erdowell neighbor to an out-of-town job repairing a roof.

"Fisher's first-person narration is dead-on. . . . This amazing title . . . should be required reading for every teen . . . who feels the weight of a parent's expectations but cannot quite figure out what to do about it." Voice Youth Advocates

Foley, Lizzie K.

Remarkable; a novel. by Lizzie K. Foley. Dial Books for Young Readers 2012 325 p. (hardcover) $16.99

Grades: 3 4 5 6 7   **Fic**

1. Fantasy fiction 2. Humorous fiction 3. Ability -- Fiction 4. Community life -- Fiction 5. Humorous stories 6. Pirates -- Fiction 7. Secrets -- Fiction 8.

Eccentrics and eccentricities -- Fiction
ISBN 9780803737068

LC 2011021641

This book presents the story of an average girl named Jane Doe who lives in "the town of Remarkable, so named for its abundance of talented citizens, everyone lives up to its reputation. . . . Jane should be just as remarkable. Instead, this average 10-year-old girl is usually overlooked. . . . Mix in a rival town's dispute over jelly, hints of a Loch Ness Monster-like creature and a psychic pizzeria owner who sees the future in her reflective pizza pans. . . . With the help of her quiet Grandpa John, who's also forgotten most of the time, Jane learns to be true to herself and celebrate the ordinary in life." (Kirkus)

Fombelle, Timothée de, 1973-

Toby alone; translated by Sarah Ardizzone; illustrated by Francois Place. Candlewick Press 2009 384p il $17.99; pa $8.99

Grades: 5 6 7 8   Fic

1. Fantasy fiction 2. Trees -- Fiction
ISBN 0-7636-4181-2; 0-7636-4815-9 pa; 978-0-7636-4181-8; 978-0-7636-4815-2 pa
Original French edition 2006

Toby is just one and a half millimeters tall, and he's the most wanted person in his world of the great oak Tree. When Toby's father discovers that the Tree is alive, he realizes that exploiting it could do damage to their world. Refusing to reveal the secret to an enraged community, Toby's parents have been imprisoned. Only Toby has managed to escape, but for how long?

"The impressive debut novel from French playwright de Fombelle deftly weaves mature political commentary, broad humor and some subtle satire into a thoroughly enjoyable adventure." Publ Wkly

Toby and the secrets of the tree; illustrated by Francois Place; translated by Sarah Ardizzone. Candlewick Press 2010 414p il $16.99

Grades: 5 6 7 8   Fic

1. Fantasy fiction 2. Trees -- Fiction
ISBN 978-0-7636-4655-4; 0-7636-4655-5

LC 2009014833

Sequel to: Toby alone (2009)

Thirteen-year-old Toby's tiny world is under greater threat than ever as Leo Blue holds Elisha prisoner while hunting the Grass People and anyone who stands in the way of his devastating plans for the oak Tree in which they all live, but this time Toby is not alone.

"Place's pen-and-ink illustrations are scattered generously throughout and enhance the overall quirkiness. . . . This interesting piece of eco-fantasy provides a satisfying conclusion for those who enjoyed the first book." SLJ

Vango; between sky and earth. Timothee de Fombelle. Candlewick Press 2014 432 p. illustrations hc $17.99

Grades: 9 10 11 12   Fic

1. Adventure fiction 2. Clergy -- Fiction 3. Historical fiction 4. Friendship -- Fiction 5. False accusation

-- Fiction
ISBN 9780763671969; 0763671967

LC 2013955696

In this book, by Timothée de Fombelle, translated by Sarah Ardizzone, "minutes from joining the priesthood in 1934, Vango, who was found washed ashore on a tiny Italian island as a toddler, must suddenly avoid both arrest and a simultaneous assassination attempt. Establishing his innocence while on the run across Europe requires untangling his mysterious past." (Kirkus Reviews)

"de Fombelle has written a brilliant, wonderfully exciting story of flight and pursuit, filled with colorful characters and head-scratching mystery. As the novel proceeds, the suspense is ratcheted up to breathtaking levels as the boy remains only one step ahead of his relentless pursuers." Booklist

Fontes, Justine

Benito runs. Darby Creek 2011 104p (Surviving Southside) lib bdg $27.93; pa $7.99

Grades: 7 8 9 10   Fic

1. Fathers -- Fiction 2. Hispanic Americans -- Fiction 3. Post-traumatic stress disorder -- Fiction
ISBN 978-0-7613-6151-0 lib bdg; 0-7613-6151-0; 978-0-7613-6165-7 pa; 0-7613-6165-0 pa

LC 2010023820

This "well-written [story reinforces] the importance of family, friends, values, and thoughtful decision-making. . . . [An] excellent [purchase, this book] will attract and engage reluctant readers." SLJ

"Benito's dad comes home from the war in Iraq. The family has been looking forward to his return, but he now has PTSD and is prone to loud, embarrassing outbursts. Ultimately, Benito leaves the house on an ill-fated bus journey." Voice Youth Advocates

Forbes, Esther

Johnny Tremain; a novel for old & young. with illustrations by Lynd Ward. Houghton Mifflin Books for Children 1943 256p il $17; pa $6.99

Grades: 5 6 7 8   Fic

1. United States -- History -- 1775-1783, Revolution -- Fiction
ISBN 978-0-395-06766-6; 0-395-06766-9; 978-0-440-44250-9 pa; 0-440-44250-8 pa
Awarded the Newbery Medal, 1944

"Johnny, an orphan, works as a favored apprentice to an aging silversmith until he burns his hand severely while working on an important project. During the Revolutionary War he serves as a dispatch rider for the Committee on Public Safety, meeting such men as Paul Revere and John Hancock. An outcast for a time, he finally learns on the battlefield of Lexington that his crippled hand can be put to use." Shapiro. Fic for Youth. 3d edition

Ford, John C.

The **morgue** and me. Viking 2009 313p $17.99

Grades: 8 9 10 11 12   Fic

1. Mystery fiction 2. Homicide -- Fiction 3. Michigan -- Fiction 4. Journalists -- Fiction 5. Criminal

investigation -- Fiction

ISBN 978-0-670-01096-7; 0-670-01096-0

LC 2009-1956

Eighteen-year-old Christopher, who plans to be a spy, learns of a murder cover-up through his summer job as a morgue assistant and teams up with Tina, a gorgeous newspaper reporter, to investigate, despite great danger.

"Ford spins a tale that's complex but not confusing, never whitewashing some of the harsher crimes people commit. The result is a story that holds its own as a mainstream mystery as well as a teen novel." Publ Wkly

Ford, Michael

The **Fire** of Ares. Walker & Co. 2008 244p (Spartan quest) $16.95; pa $7.99

Grades: 6 7 8 9   **Fic**

1. Admirals 2. Generals 3. Slavery -- Fiction 4. Social classes -- Fiction 5. Greece -- History -- Fiction 6. Sparta (Extinct city) -- Fiction

ISBN 978-0-8027-9744-5; 0-8027-9744-X; 978-0-8027-9827-5 pa; 0-8027-9827-6 pa

LC 2007024237

When slaves rebel in ancient Sparta, twelve-year-old Lysander, guarded by an heirloom amulet, the Fire of Ares, is caught between the Spartan ruling class, with whom he has been training as a warrior since his noble heritage was revealed, and those among whom he was recently laboring as a slave.

"Middle-grade boys who love action and vividly depicted battles will seize upon Ford's children's book debut . . . and they'll encounter a large number of interesting facts about ancient Greece along the way." Booklist

Other titles in this series are:

Birth of a warrior (2008)

Legacy of blood (2009)

★ The **poisoned** house. Albert Whitman 2011 319p $16.99

Grades: 6 7 8 9 10   **Fic**

1. Ghost stories 2. Supernatural -- Fiction 3. London (England) -- Fiction 4. Household employees -- Fiction 5. Great Britain -- History -- 19th century -- Fiction

ISBN 978-0-8075-6589-6; 0-8075-6589-X

LC 2010048250

As the widowed master of an elegant house in Victorian-era London slips slowly into madness and his tyrannical housekeeper takes on more power, a ghostly presence distracts a teenaged maidservant with clues to a deadly secret.

"This ghost story is light fare, chilling, and suspenseful." SLJ

Ford, Michael Thomas

Z. HarperTeen 2010 276p $16.99; lib bdg $17.89

Grades: 7 8 9 10   **Fic**

1. Science fiction 2. Games -- Fiction 3. Zombies -- Fiction

ISBN 978-0-06-073758-0; 0-06-073758-1; 978-0-06-073759-7 lib bdg; 0-06-073759-X lib bdg

LC 2009-44005

In the year 2032, after a virus that turned people into zombies has been eradicated, Josh is invited to join an un-

derground gaming society, where the gamers hunt zombies and the action is more dangerous than it seems.

"This book is a thriller, and the clever plot and characters will have readers hoping for more." SLJ

Forester, Victoria

★ The **girl** who could fly. Feiwel and Friends 2008 329p $16.95

Grades: 4 5 6 7   **Fic**

1. School stories 2. Science fiction 3. Flight -- Fiction

ISBN 978-0-312-37462-4; 0-312-37462-3

LC 2008-06882

When homeschooled farm girl Piper McCloud reveals her ability to fly, she is quickly taken to a secret government facility to be trained with other exceptional children, but she soon realizes that something is very wrong and begins working with brilliant and wealthy Conrad to escape.

"The story soars, just like Piper, with enough loop-de-loops to keep kids uncertain about what will come next. . . . Best of all are the book's strong, lightly wrapped messages about friendship and authenticity and the difference between doing well and doing good." Booklist

Forman, Gayle

★ **If** I stay; a novel. Dutton Children's Books 2009 201p $16.99

Grades: 7 8 9 10   **Fic**

1. Coma -- Fiction 2. Death -- Fiction 3. Oregon -- Fiction 4. Medical care -- Fiction

ISBN 0-525-42103-3; 978-0-525-42103-0

LC 2008-23938

While in a coma following an automobile accident that killed her parents and younger brother, seventeen-year-old Mia, a gifted cellist, weights whether to live with her grief or join her family in death.

"Intensely moving, the novel will force readers to take stock of their lives and the people and things that make them worth living." Publ Wkly

Followed by: Where she went (2011)

Where she went. Dutton Books 2011 264p $16.99

Grades: 7 8 9 10   **Fic**

1. Musicians -- Fiction 2. Rock music -- Fiction 3. Violoncellos -- Fiction 4. New York (N.Y.) -- Fiction

ISBN 978-0-525-42294-5; 0-525-42294-3

LC 2010-13474

"Both characters spring to life, and their pain-filled back story and current realities provide depth and will hold readers fast." Kirkus

Forward, Toby

Fireborn; by Toby Forward. Bloomsbury 2013 432 p. (hardback) $16.99

Grades: 6 7 8   **Fic**

1. Fire 2. Magic -- Fiction 3. Fantasy 4. Fire -- Fiction 5. Wizards -- Fiction 6. Apprentices -- Fiction

ISBN 1599908891; 9781599908892

LC 2013012055

In this book, the prequel to Toby Forward's book "Dragonborn," "when greedy wizard Slowin steals both name and power from his apprentice, Bee, the conflagration affects magic everywhere. Meanwhile, twelve-year-old Cabbage's own master, Flaxfield, suddenly loses all his magic, and Cabbage finds that he and a newm friend, Perry the (Hobbit-like) roffle, are the only ones with the ability to amend the situation." (Horn Book Magazine)

Foxlee, Karen

★ The **anatomy** of wings. Alfred A. Knopf 2009 361p $16.99; lib bdg $19.99

Grades: 8 9 10 11 12   **Fic**

1. Sisters -- Fiction 2. Suicide -- Fiction 3. Australia -- Fiction 4. Bereavement -- Fiction 5. Family life -- Fiction

ISBN 978-0-375-85643-3; 0-375-85643-9; 978-0-375-95643-0 lib bdg; 0-375-95643-3 lib bdg

LC 2008-19373

First published 2007 in Australia

After the suicide of her troubled teenage sister, eleven-year-old Jenny struggles to understand what actually happened.

Jenny's "observations are . . . poetic and washed with magic realism. . . . With heart-stopping accuracy and sly symbolism, Foxlee captures the small ways that humans reveal themselves, the mysterious intensity of female ado-lescence, and the surreal quiet of a grieving house, which slowly and with astonishing resilience fills again with sound and music." Booklist

★ **Ophelia** and the marvelous boy; by Karen Foxlee. Alfred A. Knopf 2014 240 p. $16.99

Grades: 4 5 6 7 8   **Fic**

1. Snow -- Fiction 2. Museums -- Fiction 3. Prisoners -- Fiction 4. Magic -- Fiction 5. Heroes -- Fiction 6. Wizards -- Fiction 7. Kings, queens, rulers, etc. -- Fiction

ISBN 0385753543; 9780385753548; 9780385753555

LC 2013012236

In this book, by Karen Foxlee, "Ophelia Jane Worthing-ton-Whittard . . . and her sister Alice are still grieving for their dead mother when their father takes a job in a strange museum in a city where it always snows. On her very first day in the museum Ophelia discovers a boy locked away in a long forgotten room. He is a prisoner of Her Majesty the Snow Queen. As Ophelia embarks on an incredible journey to rescue the boy everything that she believes will be tested." (Publisher's note)

"Ophelia discovers a boy who's imprisoned...by the Snow Queen; to rescue him, Ophelia must find the boy s missing sword. This is a fable of psychic healing, in which Ophelia, mourning her mother, must battle the Queen armed only with her powers as "defender of goodness and happi-ness and hope." Foxlee's deftness with characterization and setting makes this a satisfying fantasy." (Horn Book)

Frank, E. R.

Life is funny; a novel. Puffin Books 2002 263p pa $7.99

Grades: 7 8 9 10   **Fic**

1. Family life -- Fiction 2. Brooklyn (New York, N.Y.) -- Fiction

ISBN 0-14-230083-7

LC 2001-48436

First published 2000 by DK Ink

The lives of a number of young people of different races, economic backgrounds, and family situations living in Brooklyn, New York, become intertwined over a seven year period.

"The voices ring true, and the talk is painful, vulgar, rough, sexy, funny, fearful, furious, gentle." Booklist

Wrecked. Atheneum Books for Young Readers 2005 247p $15.95

Grades: 8 9 10 11 12   **Fic**

1. Bereavement -- Fiction 2. Traffic accidents -- Fiction

ISBN 0-689-87383-2

LC 2004-18448

After a car accident seriously injures her best friend and kills her brother's girlfriend, sixteen-year-old Anna tries to cope with her guilt and grief, while learning some truths about her family and herself.

"This story is compulsively readable both because Anna is likable and imperfect and because Frank's writing is so fluid." SLJ

Franklin, Emily

The **other** half of me. Delacorte Press 2007 247p $15.99; pa $6.50

Grades: 8 9 10 11 12   **Fic**

1. Artists -- Fiction 2. Sisters -- Fiction 3. Identity (Psychology) -- Fiction

ISBN 978-0-385-73445-5; 0-385-73445-X; 978-0-385-73446-2 pa; 0385-73446-8 pa

LC 2006-36825

Feeling out of place in her athletic family, artistic six-teen-year-old Jenny Fitzgerald, whose biological father was a sperm donor, finds her half sister through the Sibling Do-nor Registry and contacts her, hoping that this will finally make her feel complete.

"Franklin offers readers an engaging protagonist whose humor and unusual situation highlight the lonely and dis-placed feelings common to many teens." SLJ

Frazier, Angie

The **Eternal** Sea. Scholastic Press 2011 362p $17.99

Grades: 8 9 10 11 12   **Fic**

1. Adventure fiction 2. Egypt -- Fiction 3. Supernatural -- Fiction

ISBN 978-0-545-11475-2; 0-545-11475-6

Sequel to: Everlasting (2010)

Realizing that the magic of Umandu, the stone that grants immortality, is not done, seventeen-year-old Camille accompanies Oscar, Ira, and Randall to Egypt, where all their lives are in grave danger.

"Readers who enjoy sea romances won't go wrong." SLJ

Everlasting. Scholastic Press 2010 329p $17.99

Grades: 8 9 10 11 12   **Fic**

1. Adventure fiction 2. Australia -- Fiction 3. Shipwrecks -- Fiction 4. Supernatural -- Fiction 5. Seafaring life -- Fiction 6. Father-daughter relationship -- Fiction

ISBN 978-0-545-11473-8; 0-545-11473-X

LC 2009-20519

In 1855, seventeen-year-old Camille sets out from San Francisco, California, on her last sea voyage before entering a loveless marriage, but when her father's ship is destroyed, she and a friend embark on a cross-Australian quest to find her long-lost mother who holds a map to a magical stone.

"Although this novel takes place in the nineteenth century, many of the themes are relevant for today's teens. The author does a nice job of developing strong and funny characters while keeping the plot moving at a readable pace." Voice Youth Advocates

Followed by: The eternal sea (2011)

The **mastermind** plot; by Angie Frazier. Scholastic Press 2012 231 p. (Suzanna Snow mysteries) (hardcover : alk. paper) $16.99

Grades: 4 5 6 7 **Fic**

1. Mystery fiction 2. Adventure fiction 3. Children's stories 4. Arson -- Fiction 5. Uncles -- Fiction 6. Schools -- Fiction 7. Grandmothers -- Fiction 8. Mystery and detective stories 9. Family life -- Massachusetts -- Boston -- Fiction 10. Boston (Mass.) -- History -- 20th century -- Fiction

ISBN 0545208645; 9780545208642

LC 2011003770

Sequel to: The midnight tunnel

This children's mystery by Angie Frazier continues the adventures of Suzanna Snow. "She's just arrived in Boston, the city she's wanted to visit for as long as she can remember. . . . Her grandmother and cousin, Will, welcome her warmly, but her famous detective uncle, Bruce Snow, seems anything but pleased. He doesn't want [her] meddling in his current case involving a string of mysterious warehouse fires along the harbor front. But Zanna can't help herself. Is someone setting the fires? Just when she thinks she's on to something, a strange man starts following her. Is he a threat? Zanna needs to solve the case before she has the chance to find out." (Publisher's note)

The **midnight** tunnel; a Suzanna Snow mystery. Scholastic Press 2011 283p $16.99

Grades: 4 5 6 7 **Fic**

1. Mystery fiction 2. Canada -- Fiction 3. Uncles -- Fiction 4. Missing children -- Fiction 5. Hotels and motels -- Fiction

ISBN 978-0-545-20862-8; 0-545-20862-9

LC 2010-26770

In 1905, Suzanna is in training to be a well-mannered hostess at a Loch Harbor, New Brunswick, hotel, but her dream of being a detective gets a boost when a seven-year-old guest goes missing and Suzanna's uncle, a famous detective, comes to solve the case.

"What Zanna lacks in grace and composure, she makes up for in pluck, persistence and cleverness, emerging a likely and likable Edwardian Nancy Drew." Kirkus

Frazier, Sundee Tucker

★ The **other** half of my heart; [by] Sundee T. Frazier. Delacorte Press 2010 296p $16.99

Grades: 5 6 7 8 **Fic**

1. Twins -- Fiction 2. Sisters -- Fiction 3. Prejudices -- Fiction 4. Grandmothers -- Fiction 5. Beauty contests -- Fiction 6. African Americans -- Fiction 7. Racially

mixed people -- Fiction

ISBN 978-0-385-73440-0; 0-385-73440-9

LC 2009013209

Twin daughters of interracial parents, eleven-year-olds Keira and Minna have very different skin tones and personalities, but it is not until their African American grandmother enters them in the Miss Black Pearl Pre-Teen competition in North Carolina that red-haired and pale-skinned Minna realizes what life in their small town in the Pacific Northwest has been like for her more outgoing, darker-skinned sister.

"Frazier addresses issues faced by mixed-race children with a grace and humor that keep her from being pedantic. The story is enjoyable in its own right, and will also encourage readers to rethink racial boundries and what it means to be black or white in America." SLJ

Frederick, Heather Vogel

The **voyage** of Patience Goodspeed. Simon & Schuster Bks. for Young Readers 2002 219p hardcover o.p. pa $4.99

Grades: 5 6 7 8 **Fic**

1. Whaling -- Fiction 2. Navigation -- Fiction 3. Seafaring life -- Fiction

ISBN 0-689-84851-X; 0-689-84869-2 pa

LC 2001-49039

Following their mother's death in Nantucket, Captain Goodspeed brings twelve-year-old Patience and six-year-old Tad aboard his whaling ship, where a new crew member incites a mutiny and Patience puts her mathematical ability to good use

"This is an exciting voyage of peril and self-discovery." N Y Times Book Rev

Another title about Patience is:

The education of Patience Goodspeed (2004)

Fredericks, Mariah

Head games. Atheneum Books for Young Readers 2004 260p $15.95

Grades: 7 8 9 10 **Fic**

1. School stories 2. Dating (Social customs) -- Fiction

ISBN 0-689-85532-X

LC 2003-17012

Two teenagers connect online in a roleplaying game which leads them into their own face-to-face, half-acknowledged courtship.

"This novel realistically portrays young adults trying to find themselves, fit in, and resist the labels put on them." SLJ

Love; illustrated by Liselotte Watkins. Atheneum Books for Young Readers 2007 270p il (In the cards) $15.99

Grades: 5 6 7 8 **Fic**

1. School stories 2. Tarot -- Fiction 3. Friendship -- Fiction 4. Fortune telling -- Fiction

ISBN 978-0-689-87654-7; 0-689-87654-8

LC 2005-31956

Thirteen-year-old Anna hopes that her newly inherited tarot cards will predict an exciting future, including becoming the girlfriend of eighth-grade hottie, Declan Kelso.

"Fredericks displays a keen ear for dialogue and a knack for expressing some complex, real middle school emotions." SLJ

Other titles in this series are:
Fame (2008)
Life (2008)

Freedman, Paula J.

★ **My** basmati bat mitzvah; by Paula J. Freedman. Harry N. Abrams 2013 256 p. (alk. paper) $16.95

Grades: 4 5 6 **Fic**

1. Bat mitzvah -- Fiction 2. Jewish children -- Fiction 3. Judaism -- Fiction 4. East Indian Americans -- Fiction 5. Jews -- United States -- Fiction
ISBN 1419708066; 9781419708060

LC 2013005791

In this book, by Paula J. Freedman, "during the fall leading up to her bat mitzvah, Tara Feinstein has a lot more than her Torah portion on her mind. Between Hebrew school and study sessions with the rabbi, there doesn't seem to be enough time to hang out with her best friend Ben-O--who might also be her boyfriend--and her other best friend, Rebecca. Amid all this drama, Tara considers how to balance her Indian and Jewish identities and what it means to have a bat mitzvah while questioning her faith." (Publisher's note)

"How could Tara let know-it-all Sheila Rosenberg get away with saying, "You're not even Jewish," when Tara's Indian-born mother converted "way before I was even born"? With her bat mitzvah on the horizon, Tara secretly wonders: "Was I about to become more Jewish, or less Indian?" A light, warm, humorous story about cultural identity, inner harmony, and ordinary middle-school trials and tribulations. Glos." (Horn Book)

Freitas, Donna

★ The **possibilities** of sainthood. Farrar, Straus & Giroux 2008 272p $16.95

Grades: 7 8 9 10 11 12 **Fic**

1. School stories 2. Saints -- Fiction 3. Catholics -- Fiction 4. Family life -- Fiction 5. Rhode Island -- Fiction 6. Italian Americans -- Fiction
ISBN 978-0-374-36087-0; 0-374-36087-1

LC 2007-33298

While regularly petitioning the Vatican to make her the first living saint, fifteen-year-old Antonia Labella prays to assorted patron saints for everything from help with preparing the family's fig trees for a Rhode Island winter to getting her first kiss from the right boy.

"With a satisfying ending, this novel about the realistic struggles of a chaste teen is a great addition to all collections." SLJ

The **Survival** Kit. Farrar Straus Giroux 2011 351p $16.99

Grades: 7 8 9 10 **Fic**

1. Death -- Fiction 2. Bereavement -- Fiction
ISBN 978-0-374-39917-7; 0-374-39917-4

LC 2010041294

"The premise of the survival kit, a real-life tradition from Freitas's own mother, begs to be discussed and glued-and-scissored with friends, students, teachers, and librarians. A copy of The Survival Kit would be a worthy addition for a teen coping with her own loss or struggling to help friends or family cope with theirs." Voice Youth Advocates

French, Vivian

The **bag** of bones; [illustrated by] Ross Collins. Candlewick Press 2009 247p il (Tales from the five kingdoms) $14.99

Grades: 4 5 6 **Fic**

1. Fairy tales 2. Bats -- Fiction 3. Magic -- Fiction 4. Trolls -- Fiction 5. Orphans -- Fiction 6. Witches -- Fiction
ISBN 978-0-7636-4255-6; 0-7636-4255-X

Sequel to: The robe of skulls (2008)

"The Five Kingdoms almost come in for a spot of trouble . . . when a witch from beyond the More Enchanted Forest arrives with evil intentions and a bagful of forbidden Deep Magic. . . . [Readers] will be much amused by all the dashing about, the quick brushes with danger and the undercurrents of budding, clumsy romance." Kirkus

The **flight** of dragons; the fourth tales from the five kingdoms. illustrations by Ross Collins. Candlewick Press 2011 (Tales from the five kingdoms) $15.99

Grades: 4 5 6 **Fic**

1. Fairy tales 2. Bats -- Fiction 3. Dragons -- Fiction
ISBN 978-0-7636-5083-4; 0-7636-5083-8; 9780763650834; 0763650838

LC 2010040130

On Gracie Gillypot's birthday, greedy, chocolate-hungry twins awaken the banished Old Malignant One, and unless Gracie can find a powerful, long-forgotten dragon's egg, the Five Kingdoms may succumb to evil magic and Total Oblivion.

"In this romping, fractured fairy tale, illustrations by Collins appear often enough to remind readers of characters they might have forgotten." Booklist

The **heart** of glass; illustrated by Ross Collins. Candlewick Press 2010 244p il (Tales from the five kingdoms) $14.99; pa $5.99

Grades: 4 5 6 **Fic**

1. Fairy tales 2. Bats -- Fiction 3. Trolls -- Fiction 4. Orphans -- Fiction 5. Witches -- Fiction
ISBN 978-0-7636-4814-5; 0-7636-4814-0; 978-0-7636-5132-9 pa; 0-7636-5132-X pa

Sequel to: The bag of bones (2009)

Gracie Gillypott and Prince Marcus embark on a dwarf-watching outing, not knowing that the dwarves are working frantically making crowns for a royal wedding and that they have enlisted some unreliable trolls to help them, thus putting the humans' expedition in peril.

"French tells the tale in breezy tones—ably reflected in Collins's occasional, comically gothic ink drawings—and folds numerous complications into the plot, along with generous assortment of dwarves, trolls, mystic crones, spolied princesses and talking bats." Kirkus

The **robe** of skulls; [illustrated by] Ross Collins. Candlewick Press 2008 208p il (Tales from the five kingdoms) $14.99; pa $5.99

Grades: 4 5 6 **Fic**

1. Fairy tales 2. Bats -- Fiction 3. Magic -- Fiction 4.

Trolls -- Fiction
ISBN 0-7636-3531-6; 0-7636-4364-5 pa; 978-0-
7636-3531-2; 978-0-7636-4364-5 pa

LC 2007-38290

The sorceress Lady Lamorna has her heart set on a very expensive new robe, and she will stop at nothing—including kidnapping and black magic—to get the money to pay for it.

"Collins' black-and-white line drawings, dropped haphazardly into the text, perfectly complement the story, offering visual metaphors for the heady narrative mix of melodrama and humor." Bull Cent Child Books

Freymann-Weyr, Garret

My heartbeat. Houghton Mifflin 2002 154p $15
Grades: 7 8 9 10   **Fic**
1. Siblings -- Fiction 2. Homosexuality -- Fiction
ISBN 0-618-14181-2

LC 2001-47059

Michael L. Printz Award honor book, 2003

As she tries to understand the closeness between her older brother and his best friend, fourteen-year-old Ellen finds her relationship with each of them changing

"This beautiful novel tells a frank, upbeat story of teen bisexual love in all its uncertainty, pain, and joy. . . . The fast, clipped dialogue will sweep teens into the story, as will Ellen's immediate first-person, present-tense narrative." Booklist

Fridrik Erlingsson

Benjamin Dove. North-South 2007 206p
$15.95; pa $7.95
Grades: 6 7 8 9   **Fic**
1. Friendship -- Fiction
ISBN 978-0-7358-2150-7; 0-7358-2150-X; 978-0-
7358-2149-1 pa; 0-7358-2149-6 pa

"Benjamin tells the story of the summer her was 12, when free-spirited Roland moved into the neighborhood and changed the lives of Benjamin and his friends Jeff and Manny forever. . . . This is a well-written, attention-grabbing tale of desire for acceptance, conflict between good and evil, and coming-of-age." SLJ

Friedman, Aimee

The **year** my sister got lucky. Scholastic 2008
370p $16.99
Grades: 7 8 9 10   **Fic**
1. Moving -- Fiction 2. Sisters -- Fiction 3. Country life -- Fiction 4. New York (State) -- Fiction 5. City and town life -- Fiction
ISBN 978-0-439-92227-2; 0-439-92227-5

LC 2007-16416

When fourteen-year-old Katie and her older sister, Michaela, move from New York City to upstate New York, Katie is horrified by the country lifestyle but is even more shocked when her sister adapts effortlessly, enjoying their new life, unlike Katie.

"Friedman gets the push and pull of the sister bond just right in this delightful, funny, insightful journey." Booklist

Friedman, D. Dina

Escaping into the night. Simon & Schuster for Young Readers 2006 199p $17.99; pa $7.99

Grades: 6 7 8 9   **Fic**
1. Poland -- Fiction 2. Jewish refugees -- Fiction 3. Holocaust, 1933-1945 -- Fiction 4. World War, 1939-1945 -- Fiction
ISBN 978-1-4169-0258-4; 1-4169-0258-9; 978-1-4169-8648-5 pa; 1-4169-86480 pa

"Halina, a Jewish teen, is expelled from her Polish ghetto just before residents are being exterminated or sent to concentration camps. She joins a group of refugees who have banded together in an underground encampment in the Belorussian forests during World War II. . . . This compelling story offers an unusual insight into a different war experience." Voice Youth Advocates

Friedman, Laurie B.

Can you say catastrophe? by Laurie Friedman. Darby Creek 2013 151 p. (The mostly miserable life of April Sinclair) (trade hard cover : alk. paper) $17.95

Grades: 5 6 7 8   **Fic**
1. Summer -- Fiction 2. Family life -- Fiction 3. Dating (Social customs) -- Fiction
ISBN 1467709255; 9781467709255

LC 2012048867

In this book, by Laurie Friedman, "April Sinclair just wants what any normal thirteen-year-old would want: to disown her parents and obnoxious little sisters; to escape to summer camp ASAP with her two best friends, Billy and Brynn; and to make a good impression on Matt Parker. . . . Unfortunately, Matt witnesses April's utter humiliation at her birthday party. Then Billy kisses her. Just as April is trying to figure things out, her parents cancel her camp plans in lieu of a family RV trip." (Publisher's note)

"Irked by her parents, annoyed by her younger siblings and bewildered by the recent behavior of Billy, one of her best friends, April's teen years are off to an inauspicious start. In journal-style entries, April contemplates the ups and downs of her life, beginning with her momentous--and monumentally embarrassing--13th birthday...By tale's end, it is evident that this humorous, spirited teen is poised to triumph over the challenges of adolescence." Kirkus

Other titles include:
Love or Something Like It (2015)

Too good to be true; by Laurie Friedman. Darby Creek 2014 158 p. (The mostly miserable life of April Sinclair) (trade hard cover : alk. paper) $17.95
Grades: 5 6 7 8   **Fic**
1. Diaries -- Fiction 2. Friendship -- Fiction 3. Dating (Social customs) -- Fiction 4. Interpersonal relations -- Fiction
ISBN 1467709263; 9781467709262

LC 2013026434

In this book, by Laurie Friedman, "eighth grade is off to a surprisingly promising start for April Sinclair. . . Making the dance team is the icing on the cake. But with one unexpected move from her hot neighbor, Matt Parker, April's life starts to spin out of control. In the blink of an eye, her best friend is furious, her boyfriend dumps her, and the girls on the dance team don't want anything to do with her. How could things go so wrong so fast?" (Publisher's note)

"April (Can You Say Catastrophe?) begins eighth grade with great news: she's selected for a highly coveted spot on the high school dance team. The team's grueling schedule, however, leads to hard feelings between April and her boyfriend, and her best friend. Readers will relate to April's struggle to maintain old friendships while forging new ones, and cheer for her as she navigates the aftermath of a bad romantic decision." Horn Book

Friend, Catherine

Barn boot blues. Marshall Cavendish 2011 142p $16.99
Grades: 5 6 7 8   Fic
1. Moving -- Fiction 2. Farm life -- Fiction 3. Minnesota -- Fiction
ISBN 978-0-7614-5827-2; 0-7614-5827-1
                                          LC 2011001909
When her parents swap urban life in Minneapolis for rural life on a farm 100 miles away, twelve-year-old Taylor feels as if she is living on another planet.

"In this refreshingly compact novel, readers learn interesting, authentic details about everything from spinning wool to collecting eggs to in a kind-of-gross, kind-of-wonderful climax birthing lambs. In Taylor, Friend has created a plucky, lightly sarcastic protagonist whose frustration at her situation is palpable but who never comes off as unlikable or bratty." Horn Book

Friend, Natasha

★ **Bounce**; [by] Natasha Friend. Scholastic Press 2007 188p $16.99
Grades: 6 7 8 9   Fic
1. Moving -- Fiction 2. Remarriage -- Fiction 3. Stepfamilies -- Fiction 4. Massachusetts -- Fiction
ISBN 978-0-439-85350-7; 0-439-85350-8
                                          LC 2006038126
Thirteen-year-old Evyn's world is turned upside-down when her father, widowed since she was a toddler, suddenly decides to remarry a woman with six children, move with Ev and her brother from Maine to Boston, and enroll her in private school.

The author "presents, through hip conversations and humor, believable characters and a feel-good story with a satisfying amount of pathos." SLJ

Lush. Scholastic Press 2006 178p $16.99
Grades: 7 8 9 10   Fic
1. Fathers -- Fiction 2. Alcoholism -- Fiction
ISBN 0-439-85346-X
                                          LC 2005-031333
Unable to cope with her father's alcoholism, thirteen-year-old Sam corresponds with an older student, sharing her family problems and asking for advice.

"Friend adeptly takes a teen problem and turns it into a believable, sensitive, character-driven story, with realistic dialogue." Booklist

My life in black and white; by Natasha Friend. Penguin Group USA 2012 294 p. (hardcover) $17.99; (paperback) $8.99
Grades: 8 9 10 11   Fic
1. Sisters 2. Self-perception 3. Self-consciousness

4. Boxing -- Fiction 5. Friendship -- Fiction 6. Peer pressure -- Fiction 7. Self-acceptance -- Fiction 8. Beauty, Personal -- Fiction 9. Dating (Social customs) -- Fiction
ISBN 067001303X; 9780670013036; 9780670784943
                                          LC 2011021436
Author Natasha Friend tells the story of Lexi and her best friend Taylor. "After finding her boyfriend . . . and Taylor making out at a party, . . . an argument quickly escalates, leading to an accident that changes Lexi's life forever. . . . It isn't until her sister, Ruthie, and [friend] Theo . . . are honest with her that Lexi starts peeling away the plastic life she once had and discovers the real one underneath." (Kirkus Reviews)

Perfect. Milkweed Editions 2004 172p $16.95; pa $6.95
Grades: 6 7 8 9   Fic
1. Bulimia -- Fiction 2. Bereavement -- Fiction
ISBN 1-57131-652-3; 1-57131-651-5 pa
                                          LC 2004-6371
Following the death of her father, thirteen-year-old Isabelle uses bulimia as a way to avoid her mother's and ten-year-old sister's grief, as well as her own.

"Isabelle's grief and anger are movingly and honestly portrayed, and her eventual empathy for her mother is believable and touching." Booklist

Friesen, Gayle

The **Isabel** factor. KCP Fiction 2005 252p $16.95; pa $6.95
Grades: 7 8 9 10   Fic
1. Camps -- Fiction 2. Friendship -- Fiction
ISBN 1-55337-737-0; 1-55337-738-9 pa
"Anna and Zoe are inseparable—at least until Zoe breaks her arm and Anna finds herself on her way to summer camp without her best friend. . . . By the time Zoe arrives at camp (with her arm still in a sling), Anna is already embroiled in keeping peace between the individualistic Isabel and everyone else in Cabin 7. . . . Girls addicted to friendship stories will welcome this particularly well-crafted novel." Booklist

Friesen, Jonathan

★ The **last** Martin. Zonderkidz 2011 266p $14.99
Grades: 4 5 6 7   Fic
1. Family life -- Fiction
ISBN 978-0-310-72080-5; 0-310-72080-X
                                          LC 2010-48275
Thirteen-year-old Martin Boyle struggles to break a family curse after discovering that he has twelve weeks to live.

"Spiced with plenty of slapstick, the yarn speeds its protagonist through a succession of highs, lows and improbable triumphs on the way to a hilariously melodramatic finish." Kirkus

Friesner, Esther M.

Nobody's princess; [by] Esther Friesner. Random House 2007 305p hardcover o.p. pa $7.99
Grades: 6 7 8 9 10   Fic
1. Adventure fiction 2. Sex role -- Fiction 3. Classical mythology -- Fiction 4. Helen of Troy (Legendary

character) -- Fiction

ISBN 978-0-375-87528-1; 0-375-87528-X; 978-0-375-87529-8 pa; 0-375-87529-8 pa

LC 2006-06515

Determined to fend for herself in a world where only men have real freedom, headstrong Helen, who will be called queen of Sparta and Helen of Troy one day, learns to fight, hunt, and ride horses while disguised as a boy, and goes on an adventure throughout the Mediterranean world.

This "is a fascinating portrait. . . . Along the way, Friesner skillfully exposes larger issues of women's rights, human bondage, and individual destiny. It's a rollicking good story." Booklist

Followed by: Nobody's prize (2008)

Nobody's prize. Random House 2008 320p $16.99; lib bdg $19.99

Grades: 6 7 8 9　　　　　　　　　　　　**Fic**

1. Adventure fiction 2. Sex role -- Fiction 3. Jason (Greek mythology) -- Fiction 4. Helen of Troy (Legendary character) -- Fiction

ISBN 978-0-375-87531-1; 0-375-87531-X; 978-0-375-97531-8 lib bdg; 0-375-97531-4 lib bdg

LC 2007-08395

Sequel to Nobody's princess (2007)

Still longing for adventure, Princess Helen of Sparta maintains her disguise as a boy to join her unsuspecting brothers as part of the crew of the Argo, the ship commanded by Prince Jason in his quest for the Golden Fleece.

"Friesner is an accomplished writer who is able to interweave a contemporary feel for these ancient characters with pieces of history and mythology. She can also be funny. . . . It is possible for readers to begin with this book. . . . But it is surely best enjoyed as part of a series, and libraries with the first book will want to make sure fans get their second helping." Voice Youth Advocates

Sphinx's princess. Random House 2009 370p il map $17.99; lib bdg $20.99

Grades: 8 9 10 11 12　　　　　　　　　　**Fic**

1. Queens 2. Queens -- Fiction 3. Egypt -- History -- Fiction

ISBN 978-0-375-85654-9; 0-375-85654-4; 978-0-375-95654-6 lib bdg; 0-375-95654-9 lib bdg

LC 2009-13719

Although she is a dutiful daughter, Nefertiti's dancing abilities, remarkable beauty, and intelligence garner attention near and far, so much so that her family is summoned to the Egyptian royal court, where Nefertiti becomes a pawn in the power play of her scheming aunt, Queen Tiye.

"Dramatic plot twists, a powerful female subject, and engrossing details of life in ancient Egypt make for lively historical fiction." Booklist

Followed by: Sphinx's queen (2010)

Sphinx's queen. Random House 2010 352p $17.99; lib bdg $29.99

Grades: 8 9 10 11 12　　　　　　　　　　**Fic**

1. Queens 2. Queens -- Fiction 3. Egypt -- History

-- Fiction

ISBN 978-0-375-85657-0; 0-375-85657-9; 978-0-375-95657-7 lib bdg; 0-375-95657-3 lib bdg

LC 2010-13769

Sequel to: Sphinx's princess (2009)

Chased after by the prince and his soldiers for a crime she did not commit, Nefertiti finds temporary refuge in the wild hills along the Nile's west bank before returning to the royal court to plead her case to the Pharaoh.

This is written "in fine prose that expresses the questioning of religion that most young people experience as they approach maturity. . . . This deeply moral book tells a good story; or, rather, this good story reveals deeply moral truths." SLJ

Spirit's princess; Esther Friesner. 1st ed. Random House Childrens Books 2012 449 p. (trade) $17.99; (paperback) $10.99; (ebook) $53.97; (lib bdg.) $20.99

Grades: 7 8 9 10　　　　　　　　　　　　**Fic**

1. Family -- Fiction 2. Father-daughter relationship -- Fiction 3. Children with physical disabilities -- Fiction 4. Magic -- Fiction 5. Shamans -- Fiction 6. Spirits -- Fiction 7. Sex role -- Fiction 8. Japan -- History -- To 645 -- Fiction

ISBN 0375869077; 9780375869075; 9780375873140; 9780375873157; 9780375899904; 9780375969072

LC 2011010468

In the book by Esther Friesner, "Himiko's chieftain father adores her, as do her older brother and her father's wives. Despite their love and affection, none of them takes Himiko seriously when she insists she is a shaman. Himiko herself isn't sure she can achieve her goal; with one leg lame since she was a child, she can't do a shaman's dances. Though the current shaman insists Himiko will be her heir, it can't happen until Himiko is ready to stand up to her father." (Kirkus Reviews)

Threads and flames. Viking 2010 390p $17.99

Grades: 6 7 8 9 10　　　　　　　　　　　**Fic**

1. Jews -- Fiction 2. Fires -- Fiction 3. Immigrants -- Fiction 4. New York (N.Y.) -- Fiction 5. Polish Americans -- Fiction 6. Triangle Shirtwaist Company, Inc. -- Fiction

ISBN 978-0-670-01245-9; 0-670-01245-9

"Friesner's sparkling prose makes the immigrant experience in New York's Lower East Side come alive. . . . Readers will turn the pages with rapt attention to follow the characters' intrepid, risk-all adventures in building new lives." Booklist

Frost, Helen

The **braid**. Farrar, Straus and Giroux 2006 95p $16

Grades: 7 8 9 10　　　　　　　　　　　　**Fic**

1. Novels in verse 2. Canada -- Fiction 3. Sisters -- Fiction 4. Scotland -- Fiction 5. Immigrants -- Fiction

ISBN 0-374-30962-0

LC 2005-40148

Two Scottish sisters, living on the western island of Barra in the 1850s, relate, in alternate voices and linked narrative poems, their experiences after their family is forcible evicted and separated with one sister accompanying their parents and younger siblings to Cape Breton, Canada, and the other staying behind with other family on the small island of Mingulay.

"The book will inspire both students and teachers to go back and study how the taut poetic lines manage to contain the powerful feelings." Booklist

★ **Crossing** stones. Farrar, Straus and Giroux 2009 184p $16.99

Grades: 6 7 8 9 10   **Fic**

1. War stories 2. Novels in verse 3. Soldiers -- Fiction 4. Family life -- Fiction 5. Women -- Suffrage -- Fiction 6. World War, 1914-1918 -- Fiction

ISBN 0-374-31653-8; 978-0-374-31653-2

LC 2008-20755

In their own voices, four young people, Muriel, Frank, Emma, and Ollie, tell their experiences during the first World War, as the boys enlist and are sent overseas, Emma finishes school, and Muriel fights for peace and women's suffrage.

"Beautifully written in formally structured verse. . . . This [is a] beautifully written, gently told story." Voice Youth Advocates

Diamond Willow. Farrar, Straus and Giroux 2008 111p $16

Grades: 5 6 7 8   **Fic**

1. Novels in verse 2. Dogs -- Fiction 3. Alaska -- Fiction 4. Athapascan Indians -- Fiction

ISBN 978-0-374-31776-8; 0-374-31776-3

LC 2006-37438

In a remote area of Alaska, twelve-year-old Willow helps her father with their sleigh dogs when she is not at school, all the while unaware that the animals surrounding her carry the spirits of dead ancestors and friends who care for her. "Grades six to nine." (Bull Cent Child Books)

"Willow relates her story in one-page poems, each of which contains a hidden message printed in darker type. . . . Her poems offer pensive imagery and glimpses of character, and strong emotion. This complex and elegant novel will resonate with readers who savor powerful drama and multifaceted characters." SLJ

★ **Hidden**. Farrar Straus Giroux 2011 147p $16.99

Grades: 6 7 8 9 10   **Fic**

1. Novels in verse 2. Camps -- Fiction 3. Friendship -- Fiction

ISBN 0-374-38221-2; 978-0-374-38221-6

LC 2010-24854

When Wren Abbott and Darra Monson are eight years old, Darra's father steals a minivan. He doesn't know that Wren is hiding in the back. Years later, in a chance encounter at camp, the girls face each other for the first time.

"This novel in verse stands out through its deliberate use of form to illuminate emotions and cleverly hide secrets in the text." Booklist

Keesha's house. Frances Foster Bks./Farrar, Straus & Giroux 2003 116p hardcover o.p. pa $8

Grades: 7 8 9 10   **Fic**

1. Home -- Fiction

ISBN 0-374-34064-1; 0-374-40012-1 pa

LC 2002-22698

Michael L. Printz Award honor book, 2004

Seven teens facing such problems as pregnancy, closeted homosexuality, and abuse each describe in poetic forms what caused them to leave home and where they found home again

"Spare, eloquent, and elegantly concise. . . . Public, private, or correctional educators and librarians should put this must-read on their shelves." Voice Youth Advocates

★ **Salt**; by Helen Frost. Farrar, Straus, and Giroux 2013 160 p. (hardcover) $17.99

Grades: 5 6 7 8   **Fic**

1. War stories 2. Native Americans 3. Historical fiction 4. War of 1812 -- Fiction 5. Novels in verse 6. Friendship -- Fiction 7. Miami Indians -- Fiction 8. Trading posts -- Fiction 9. Frontier and pioneer life -- Indiana -- Fiction 10. United States -- History -- War of 1812 -- Fiction 11. Fort Wayne (Ind.) -- History -- 19th century -- Fiction

ISBN 0374363870; 9780374363871

LC 2012029521

This book, by Helen Frost, "set during the War of 1812 . . . is the story of the friendship between Anikwa, a Miami Indian boy, and James, the son of a trader. As both British and American armies advance on the area, other Native American peoples arrive hoping to fight with the British against the Americans. The plan fails, and Anikwa's peaceful people must flee. Will they have to abandon their traditional home, and will the friendship between the boys be sundered?" (Publisher's note)

Frost, Mark

Alliance; Mark Frost. Random House Inc 2014 352 p. (The Paladin Prophecy) (hardback) $17.99

Grades: 7 8 9 10   **Fic**

1. Supernatural -- Fiction 2. Secret societies -- Fiction 3. Superheroes -- Fiction 4. Good and evil -- Fiction

ISBN 0375870466; 9780375870460

LC 2013041891

This book is part of Mark Frost's "Paladin Prophecy" series. "Several months have passed since Will and his roommates defeated the Knights of Charlemagne, but many questions remain about the Knights, their ties to the monsters of the Never-Was and the disappearance of Will's parents. A wealthy school donor emerges as a major player in the conspiracy, so Will and his friends develop a risky plan to use their extraordinary abilities . . . to infiltrate and search his island home." (Kirkus Reviews)

"This second entry in the Paladin Prophecy trilogy brings readers up to date and includes a list in the first chapter to show the strengths possessed by the main characters. Basically, this is another book involving the adventures of a group of young people against the forces of evil, set against a school backdrop...There are discoveries, including caves and a hidden lab, very real threats, and of course, more villains in book two, which ends on a cliff-hanger—with the final confrontation for the fate of the world still to come in the third book." (VOYA)

Fry, Michael

The **Odd** Squad; Bully Bait. by Michael Fry. Disney Hyperion 2013 224 p. (hardcover) $12.99

Grades: 4 5 6 7   **Fic**

1. Friendship -- Fiction 2. School stories 3. Bullies -- Fiction 4. Schools -- Fiction 5. Middle schools -- Fiction 6. Interpersonal relations -- Fiction

ISBN 1423169247; 9781423169246

LC 2012014286

This children's story, by Michael Fry, is part of the "Odd Squad" series. "Nick is the shortest seventh-grader in the history of the world . . . , doesn't fit in . . . , and spends more time inside than outside his locker. . . . When a well-intentioned guidance counselor forces Nick to join the school's lamest club . . . , what starts off as a reluctant band of hopeless oddballs morphs into an effective and empowered team ready to face whatever middle school throws at them." (Publisher's note)

"Cartoonist Fry humorously mines the world of middle school as seen through the eyes of bullied Nick to answer the question: Can three oddballs team together to take down the school bully? ...Abundant cartoon-style illustrations enhance the book's silly yet sensitive portrayal of bullying and unlikely friendships." Kirkus

Fukuda, Andrew

The **Prey**; Andrew Fukuda. St Martins Press 2013 336 p. $18.99

Grades: 7 8 9 10 11 12   **Fic**

1. Horror fiction 2. Occult fiction 3. Survival skills -- Fiction

ISBN 1250005116; 9781250005113

LC 2013002667

This teen horror thriller, by Andrew Fukuda, is book 2 of the "Hunt" series. "With death only a heartbeat away, Gene and the remaining humans must find a way . . . to escape the hungry predators chasing them through the night. . . . Their escape takes them to a refuge of humans living high in the mountains. Gene and his friends think they're finally safe, but not everything here is as it seems." (Publisher's note)

Funke, Cornelia Caroline

Fearless; Cornelia Funke. Little, Brown Books for Young Readers 2013 432 p. (hardcover) $19.99

Grades: 6 7 8 9   **Fic**

1. Fantasy fiction 2. Brothers -- Fiction 3. Blessing and cursing -- Fiction 4. Fantasy 5. Magic -- Fiction 6. Adventure and adventurers -- Fiction

ISBN 0316056103; 9780316056106

LC 2012028742

This fantasy novel, by Cornelia Funke, translated by Oliver Latsch, is part of the "Mirrorworld" series. "Jacob Reckless has . . . tried everything to shake the Fairy curse that traded his life for his brother's. . . . But . . . they hear of one last possibility . . . : a crossbow that can kill thousands, or heal one, when shot through the heart. But a Goyl treasure hunter is also searching for the prized crossbow." (Publisher's note)

"Adroitly building on layers of European fairy tale, Funke's original, rapid-fire narrative fearlessly transports Jacob and a bevy of ominous, multifaceted fantastical characters

through a dark, decaying landscape in which death waits and honor is rare. Provocative, harrowing, engrossing." Kirkus

Inkdeath; [by] Cornelia Funke; translated from the German by Anthea Bell. Scholastic 2008 683p il map $24.99

Grades: 5 6 7 8   **Fic**

1. Fantasy fiction 2. Kidnapping -- Fiction 3. Books and reading -- Fiction

ISBN 978-0-439-86628-6; 0-439-86628-6

LC 2008-19922

Sequel to: Inkspell (2005)

As Bluejay—Mo's fictitious double—tries to keep the Book of Immortality from unraveling, Adderhead kidnaps all the children in the kingdom, asking for Bluejay's surrender or the children will be doomed to slavery in the silver mines.

"The assortment of villains is vivid and frightening. . . . The finale includes a thoroughly engrossing climax." SLJ

★ **Inkheart**; [by] Cornelia Funke; translated from the German by Anthea Bell. Scholastic 2003 534p $19.95; pa $9.99

Grades: 5 6 7 8   **Fic**

1. Fantasy fiction 2. Books and reading -- Fiction

ISBN 0-439-53164-0; 0-439-70910-5 pa

LC 2003-45844

Twelve-year-old Meggie learns that her father, who repairs and binds books for a living, can "read" fictional characters to life when one of those characters abducts them and tries to force him into service.

The author "proves the power of her imagination; readers will be captivated by the chilling and thrilling world she has created here." Publ Wkly

Other titles in this series are:

Inkspell (2005)

Inkdeath (2008)

★ **Reckless**; written and illustrated by Cornelia Funke; translated by Oliver Latsch. Little, Brown 2010 394p il $19.99

Grades: 6 7 8 9   **Fic**

1. Fantasy fiction 2. Adventure fiction 3. Magic -- Fiction 4. Brothers -- Fiction

ISBN 978-0-316-05609-0; 0-316-05609-X; 031605609X; 9780316056090

LC 2010006877

Jacob and Will Reckless have looked out for each other ever since their father disappeared, but when Jacob discovers a magical mirror that transports him to a warring world populated by witches, giants, and ogres, he keeps it to himself until Will follows him one day, with dire consequences.

"The fluid, fast-paced narrative exposes Jacob's complex character, his complicated sibling relationship and a densely textured world brimming with vile villains and fairy-tale detritus." Kirkus

Fuqua, Jonathon Scott

The **Willoughby** Spit wonder. Candlewick 2004 145p $15.99

Grades: 5 6 7 8   **Fic**

1. Sick -- Fiction 2. Virginia -- Fiction 3. Father-son

relationship -- Fiction
ISBN 0-7636-1776-8

LC 2002-41141

In 1950s Norfolk, Virginia, as Carter and his sister watch their dying father struggle to remain cheerful, Carter decides to emulate Prince Namor, comic superhero, in order to inspire his father to stay alive.

"Carter . . . is a compelling character, and his growing understanding and acceptance of the world is shown quietly through an array of accurately observed details. A subtle, engaging novel." Booklist

Fusco, Kimberly Newton

Beholding Bee; Kimberly Newton Fusco. Alfred A. Knopf 2013 336 p. $16.99

Grades: 5 6 7 8 **Fic**

1. Ghost stories 2. Orphans -- Fiction 3. Carnivals -- Fiction 4. Identity -- Fiction 5. Runaways -- Fiction 6. Self-esteem -- Fiction 7. Disfigured persons -- Fiction
ISBN 0375868364; 9780375868368; 9780375898860; 9780375968365

LC 2012005091

In this book by Kimberly Newton Fusco, "11-year-old orphan Bee travels with a carnival, assisting her guardian at the hot-dog stand and shielding the diamond-shaped birthmark on her face from stares and taunts. . . . When Pauline and her new boyfriend are sent away by the sinister carnival owner . . . Bee runs away. . . . She comes upon an inviting old house and is welcomed by two elderly women only she can see: Mrs. Potter . . . and Mrs. Swift, a prickly suffragette." (School Library Journal)

★ The **wonder** of Charlie Anne. Alfred A. Knopf 2010 272p $16.99; lib bdg $19.99

Grades: 5 6 7 8 **Fic**

1. Farm life -- Fiction 2. Friendship -- Fiction 3. Massachusetts -- Fiction 4. Race relations -- Fiction 5. African Americans -- Fiction 6. Great Depression, 1929-1939 -- Fiction
ISBN 978-0-375-86104-8; 0-375-86104-1; 978-0-375-96104-5 lib bdg; 0-375-96104-6 lib bdg

LC 2009-38831

In a 1930s Massachusetts farm town torn by the Depression, racial tension, and other hardships, Charlie Anne and her black next-door neighbor Phoebe form a friendship that begins to transform their community.

"Good humor, kindness and courage triumph in this warm, richly nuanced novel that cheers the heart like a song sweetly sung." Kirkus

Fusilli, Jim

Marley Z and the bloodstained violin. Dutton Children's Books 2008 164p $16.99

Grades: 5 6 7 8 **Fic**

1. School stories 2. Mystery fiction 3. Theft -- Fiction 4. Violins -- Fiction
ISBN 978-0-525-47907-9; 0-525-47907-4

Fourteen-year-old Marley Zimmerman is convinced that her friend did not steal a valuable violin from the Julliard School, despite surveillance video evidence, and enlists the other members of her would-be band, the Kingston Cowboys, to help her find the truth.

"Marley is a fully drawn character, and the supporting cast members are developed well enough to make them compelling and interesting. This mystery keeps pages turning to its surprise ending." SLJ

Gagnon, Michelle

Don't let go; Michelle Gagnon. Harper, an imprint of HarperCollinsPublishers 2014 352 p. (hardback) $17.99

Grades: 7 8 9 10 11 12 **Fic**

1. Dystopian fiction 2. Experiments -- Fiction 3. Computer hackers -- Fiction 4. Foster home care -- Fiction 5. Abandoned children -- Fiction 6. Adventure and adventurers -- Fiction
ISBN 0062102966; 9780062102966

LC 2014001880

Sequel to: Don't look now

This novel by Michelle Gagnon is the "finale to the Don't Turn Around trilogy," in which "Noa Torson is out of options. On the run with Peter and the two remaining teens of Persephone's Army, and with quickly failing health, she is up against immeasurable odds. The group is outnumbered, outsmarted, and outrun. But they will not give up. They know they must return to where this all began." (Publisher's note)

"Noa and three friends are on the run. They are toting heavy backpacks loaded with hard drives that contain the encrypted information they need to bring to the authorities to prove what experiments Pike has been doing on live people...A look into a future marred by what powerful people will do to fulfill their needs and wants is a little scary. It is heartening to see that young people who discover the truth can band together and battle what seems like overwhelming odds to triumph in the end." VOYA

Do not let go

Don't Look Now; Michelle Gagnon. Harpercollins Childrens Books 2013 336 p. $17.99

Grades: 7 8 9 10 11 12 **Fic**

1. Computer hackers -- Fiction 2. Abandoned children -- Fiction 3. Experiments -- Fiction 4. Foster home care -- Fiction
ISBN 0062102931; 9780062102935

LC 2013021823

In this book, by Michelle Gagnon, "Noa Torsen is on the run. Having outsmarted the sinister Project Persephone, Noa and her friend Zeke now move stealthily across the country . . . Back in Boston, Peter anxiously follows Noa's movements from his computer, using his hacker skills to feed her the information she needs to stay alive. . . . It will take everything Noa and Peter have to bring down the Project before it gets them first." (Publisher's note)

"Still suffering strange side effects from her stint as a human lab rat at Pike & Dolan, Noa (Don't Turn Around) leads a group of homeless teens bent on sabotaging the corporation. In Boston, her "hacktivist" friend Peter and his ex-girlfriend, Amanda, uncover new evidence that places them all in danger. This tense, suspenseful tech-thriller will engage readers from beginning to end." (Horn Book)

Don't turn around; by Michelle Gagnon. Harper 2012 320 p. (trade bdg.) $17.99

Grades: 7 8 9 10 11 12　　　　**Fic**
1. Dystopian fiction 2. Teenagers -- Fiction 3. Conspiracies -- Fiction 4. Computer hackers -- Fiction 5. Experiments -- Fiction 6. Foster home care -- Fiction 7. Abandoned children -- Fiction
ISBN 0062102907; 9780062102904
　　　　　　　　　　　　　LC 2012009691

This book tells the story of "[t]eenage hackers Noa and Peter." Orphan Noa escapes a hospital after waking up from an operation she has no memory of. After having his computer seized when he investigated his father's files, "Peter enlists his hacktivist group /ALLIANCE/ (of which Noa is a member) to" investigate and counterattack. "The attack only serves to dig the teens in deeper when they uncover a frightening conspiracy of human experimentation and corporate malfeasance." (Kirkus Reviews)

Strangelets; by Michelle Gagnon. Soho Teen 2013 1 p. (alk. paper) $17.99
Grades: 8 9 10 11 12　　　　**Fic**
1. Horror fiction 2. Mystery fiction 3. Science fiction 4. Escapes -- Fiction 5. Survival -- Fiction 6. Near-death experiences -- Fiction
ISBN 1616951370; 9781616951375
　　　　　　　　　　　　　LC 2012038333

This book by Michelle Gagnon shows the "horror endured by six teens trapped in a hospital-like bunker. They come from every point on the globe: cancer-stricken Sophie from California, petty thief Declan from Ireland, military trainee Anat from Israel, hiker Nico from Switzerland, shy Yosh from Japan, and studious Zain from India." They must figure out why they are there. (Publishers Weekly)

Gaiman, Neil, 1960-
★ **Coraline**; [by] Neil Gaiman; with illustrations by Dave McKean. HarperCollins Pubs. 2002 162p il pa $6.99; $16.99
Grades: 5 6 7 8　　　　**Fic**
1. Horror fiction 2. Supernatural -- Fiction
ISBN 0-380-80734-3 pa; 0-380-97778-8
　　　　　　　　　　　　　LC 2002-18937

Looking for excitement, Coraline ventures through a mysterious door into a world that is similar, yet disturbingly different from her own, where she must challenge a gruesome entity in order to save herself, her parents, and the souls of three others

"Gaiman twines his taut tale with a menacing tone and crisp prose fraught with memorable imagery . . . yet keeps the narrative just this side of terrifying." Publ Wkly

★ **Fortunately,** the milk; by Neil Gaiman; illustrated by Skottie Young. Harper, an imprint of HarperCollinsPublishers 2013 128 p. (hardcover bdgs) $14.99
Grades: 4 5 6 7　　　　**Fic**
1. Humorous stories 2. Fathers -- Fiction 3. Space and time -- Fiction 4. Adventure and adventurers -- Fiction
ISBN 0062224077; 9780062224071
　　　　　　　　　　　　　LC 2012050670

This children's picture book by Neil Gaiman is "about a father who has taken an excessively long time to return from the corner store with milk for his children's breakfast." He

"is abducted by aliens, made to walk the plank by pirates, and rescued by a stegosaurus in a balloon, among other outrageous escapades." (Publishers Weekly)

★ The **graveyard** book; with illustrations by Dave McKean. HarperCollins 2008 312p il $17.99; lib bdg $18.89
Grades: 5 6 7 8 9 10　　　　**Fic**
1. Death -- Fiction 2. Cemeteries -- Fiction 3. Supernatural -- Fiction
ISBN 0-06-053092-8; 0-06-053093-6 lib bdg; 978-0-06-053092-1; 978-0-06-053093-8 lib bdg
　　　　　　　　　　　　　LC 2008-13860

Awarded the Newbery Medal (2009)

Nobody Owens, nicknamed Bod, is a normal boy, except that he has been raised by in a graveyard by ghosts. "Grades five to nine." (Bull Cent Child Books)

"Gaiman writes with charm and humor, and again he has a real winner." Voice Youth Advocates

Interworld; [by] Neil Gaiman [and] Michael Reaves. Eos 2007 239p $16.99; lib bdg $17.89
Grades: 6 7 8 9 10　　　　**Fic**
1. Science fiction 2. Space and time -- Fiction
ISBN 978-0-06-123896-3; 978-0-06-123897-0 lib bdg
　　　　　　　　　　　　　LC 2007-08617

At nearly fifteen years of age, Joey Harker learns that he is able to travel between dimensions. Soon, he joins a team of different versions of himself, each from another dimension, to fight the evil forces striving to conquer all the worlds.

This offers "vivid, well-imagined settings and characters. . . . [A] rousing sf/fantasy hybrid." Booklist

Stardust. Avon Bks. 1999 238p hardcover o.p. pa $13.95; $30.00
Grades: 8 9 10 11 12 Adult　　　　**Fic**
1. Fantasy fiction 2. Fantasies
ISBN 0-380-97728-1; 0-06-114202-6 pa; 9780062200396
　　　　　　　　　　　　　LC 98-8773

"Young Tristran Thorn has grown up in the isolated village of Wall, on the edge of the realm of Faerie. When Tristran and the lovely Victoria see a falling star during the special market fair, Victoria impulsively offers him his heart's desire if he will retrieve the star for her. Tristran crosses the border into Faerie and encounters witches, unicorns, and other strange creatures." Libr J

Galante, Cecilia
The **patron** saint of butterflies. Bloomsbury 2008 292p $16.95
Grades: 6 7 8 9 10　　　　**Fic**
1. Cults -- Fiction 2. Christian life -- Fiction
ISBN 978-1-59990-249-4; 1-59990-249-4
　　　　　　　　　　　　　LC 2007-51368

When her grandmother takes fourteen-year-old Agnes, her younger brother, and best friend Honey and escapes Mount Blessing, a Connecticut religious commune, Agnes clings to the faith she loves while Honey looks toward a future free of control, cruelty, and preferential treatment.

"If both girls occasionally seem wise beyond their years, readers will nevertheless cheer them on as they ponder the limits of faith and duty." SLJ

The **summer** of May. Aladdin 2011 252p $16.99

Grades: 5 6 7 8   Fic
1. Anger -- Fiction 2. Summer -- Fiction 3. Teachers -- Fiction 4. Loss (Psychology) -- Fiction 5. Mother-daughter relationship -- Fiction
ISBN 1-4169-8023-7; 978-1-4169-8023-0

LC 2010-15879

An angry thirteen-year-old girl and her hated English teacher spend a summer school class together, learning surprising things about each other. "Grades four to seven." (Bull Cent Child Books)

"May's voice is sometimes humorous, at times heart-breaking, and always authentic. . . . A taut and believable novel." SLJ

Willowood. Simon & Schuster 2010 265p $16.99

Grades: 4 5 6 7   Fic
1. Geckos -- Fiction 2. Moving -- Fiction 3. Friendship -- Fiction 4. Single parent family -- Fiction
ISBN 978-1-4169-8022-3; 1-4169-8022-9

Eleven-year-old Lily has trouble leaving her best friend behind and moving to the city when her mother changes jobs, but she makes some very unlikely friends that soon become like family members.

"The characters . . . are fully realized individuals. . . . [This book has a] finely tuned plot and poetic language. . . . Children will enjoy the story of Lily's first few months in the big city." SLJ

Gale, Eric Kahn

The **Bully** Book; Eric Kahn Gale. Harpercollins Childrens Books 2012 240 p. $16.99

Grades: 4 5 6 7 8   Fic
1. School stories 2. Bullies -- Fiction 3. Friendship -- Fiction 4. Middle schools -- Fiction 5. Diaries -- Fiction
ISBN 0062125117; 9780062125118

LC 2012050677

Originally published in a different format as an ebook by the author

"When the author was eleven, he was bullied. This book is loosely based on incidents that happened to him in sixth grade. Eric Haskins, the new sixth-grade bully target, is searching for answers. And unlike many of us who experienced something awful growing up, he finds them. Though they may not be what he expected." (Publisher's note)

"The juxtaposition of Eric's journal against the Bully Book allows readers to see both the bullies' methodology and Eric's unwitting complicity. . . . A compelling and unusual look at a complex and intractable problem that succeeds admirably as story as well." Kirkus

The **Zoo** at the Edge of the World; by Eric Kahn Gale; illustrations by Matthew Howley. Balzer + Bray, an imprint of HarperCollinsPublishers 2014 240 p. illustrations (hardback) $16.99

Grades: 4 5 6 7   Fic
1. Zoos -- Fiction 2. Stuttering -- Fiction 3. Jungle animals -- Fiction 4. Human-animal communication -- Fiction
ISBN 0062125168; 9780062125163

LC 2014002144

In this book, by Eric Kahn Gale, "Marlin is not slow, or mute; what he is is a stutterer, and that makes it impossible for him to convince people otherwise. What he is also is a Rackham: the youngest son of the world-famous explorer Roland Rackham, who is the owner and proprietor of the Zoo at the Edge of the World, a resort where the well-to-do from all over the world can come to experience the last bit of the wild left in the world at the end of the nineteenth century." (Publisher's note)

"The stuttering son of a famous explorer discovers a new ability that will change his life and his world forever. Marlin Rackham doesn't have an ordinary childhood. He works alongside his brother, Tim, and father, Ronan, in the family's exotic South American zoo, a zoo so renowned that rich and famous people from all over the world travel to visit the resort. But Marlin has a problem: He stutters. His stutter is so bad he can barely communicate with people. Many think he's mute. However, there is one group Marlin can talk to with no problem: the animals. And when his father brings a jaguar back from an expedition, the beast's mystical ways make it possible for the animals to talk back. . . . A secondary plot concerning Marlin's relationships with his father and brother is equally nuanced and powerful, making the book a formidable read on two fronts. The romantic setting and striking prose are icing on the cake, creating an intoxicatingly charming book. Beautiful and fully absorbing." Kirkus

Gansworth, Eric

If I ever get out of here; Eric Gansworth. Arthur A. Levine Books 2013 368 p. (hardcover : alk. paper) $17.99

Grades: 5 6 7 8   Fic
1. Native Americans -- Fiction 2. Native Americans -- Reservations -- Fiction 3. Friendship -- Fiction 4. Race relations -- Fiction 5. Tuscarora Indians -- Fiction 6. Tuscarora Nation Reservation (N.Y.) -- Fiction 7. New York (State) -- History -- 20th century -- Fiction 8. Indians of North America -- New York (State) -- Fiction 9. New York (State) -- Ethnic relations -- Fiction
ISBN 0545417309; 9780545417303; 9780545417310

LC 2012030553

American Indian Youth Literature Awards Honor Book: Young Adult (2014)

In this book "Lewis lives in abject poverty on the reservation. . . . He's the only Indian in the class for smart kids. And he's in middle school. Times are tough. When George, a military kid, arrives, the two bond over their mutual appreciation of music. Lewis shares select pieces of his life with George. . . . Forces of nature eventually compel Lewis to face everything: the bully, what he is hiding and his own shame." (Kirkus Reviews)

Gantos, Jack

★ **Dead** end in Norvelt; Jack Gantos. Farrar Straus Giroux 2011 341p. $15.99

Grades: 4 5 6 7   **Fic**
1. Old age -- Fiction 2. Pennsylvania -- Fiction
ISBN 978-0-374-37993-3; 0-374-37993-9
LC 2010054009
Newbery Medal (2012)
Scott O'Dell Historical Fiction Award (2012)
In the historic town of Norvelt, Pennsylvania, twelve-year-old Jack Gantos spends the summer of 1962 grounded for various offenses until he is assigned to help an elderly neighbor with a most unusual chore involving the newly dead, molten wax, twisted promises, Girl Scout cookies, underage driving, lessons from history, typewriting, and countless bloody noses.
This is a "wildly entertaining meld of truth and fiction. . . . Memorable in every way." Publ Wkly

★ **From** Norvelt to nowhere; Jack Gantos. Farrar, Straus and Giroux 2013 288 p. (hardback) $16.99
Grades: 4 5 6 7   **Fic**
1. Old age -- Fiction 2. Friendship -- Fiction 3. Humorous stories 4. Mystery and detective stories 5. Norvelt (Pa.) -- History -- 20th century -- Fiction
ISBN 0374379947; 9780374379940
LC 2013022251
Sequel to: Dead end in Norvelt
Author Jack Gantos' book "opens deep in the shadow of the Cuban missile crisis. But . . . other kinds of trouble are raining down on young Jack Gantos. . . . After an explosion, a new crime by an old murderer, and the sad passing of the town's founder, twelve-year-old Jack will soon find himself launched on a mission that takes him hundreds of miles away, escorting his slightly mental elderly mentor, Miss Volker, on her relentless pursuit of the oddest of outlaws." (Publisher's note)

Heads or tails; stories from the sixth grade. Farrar, Straus Giroux 1994 151p il $16; pa $4.95
Grades: 5 6 7 8   **Fic**
1. School stories 2. Diaries -- Fiction 3. Family life -- Fiction
ISBN 0-374-32909-5; 0-374-42923-5 pa
LC 93-43117
"Jack is trying to survive his sixth-grade year, and he narrates, through a series of short-stories-cum-chapters, his difficulties in dodging the obstacles life throws in his path. . . . The writing is zingy and specific, with snappily authentic dialogue and a vivid sense of juvenile experience. . . . Jack and his family have a recognizably thorny relationship. This is a distinctive and lively sequence of everyday-life stories." Bull Cent Child Books
Other titles about Jack are:
Jack adrift (2003)
Jack on the tracks (1999)
Jack's black book (1997)
Jack's new power (1995)

★ **Jack** on the tracks; four seasons of fifth grade. Farrar, Straus & Giroux 1999 182p il $16; pa $5.95
Grades: 5 6 7 8   **Fic**
1. School stories 2. Family life -- Fiction 3. Miami (Fla.) -- Fiction
ISBN 0-374-33665-2; 0-374-43717-3 pa
LC 99-27897
Moving with his unbearable sister to Miami, Florida, Jack tries to break some of his bad habits but finds himself irresistibly drawn to things disgusting, gross, and weird
"Jack is a likable and appealing fifth grader. His first-person preadolescent musings and worries are poignant, funny, and real." SLJ
Other titles in this series are:
Heads or tails (1994)
Jack's black book (1997)
Jack's new power (1995)

Joey Pigza loses control. Farrar, Straus & Giroux 2000 195p $16
Grades: 5 6 7 8   **Fic**
1. Father-son relationship -- Fiction 2. Attention deficit disorder -- Fiction
ISBN 0-374-39989-1
LC 00-20098
A Newbery Medal honor book, 2001
Joey, who is still taking medication to keep him from getting too wired, goes to spend the summer with the hard-drinking father he has never known and tries to help the baseball team he coaches win the championship
"This high-voltage, honest novel mixes humor, pain, fear and courage with deceptive ease." Publ Wkly

★ **Joey** Pigza swallowed the key. Farrar, Straus & Giroux 1998 153p $16.99
Grades: 5 6 7 8   **Fic**
1. School stories 2. Schools -- Fiction 3. Single-parent families -- Fiction 4. Attention deficit disorder -- Fiction 5. Attention-deficit hyperactivity disorder -- Fiction
ISBN 0-374-33664-4
LC 98-24264
To the constant disappointment of his mother and his teachers, Joey has trouble paying attention or controlling his mood swings when his prescription meds wear off and he starts getting worked up and acting wired
This "frenetic narrative pulls at heartstrings and tickles funny bones." SLJ
Other titles about Joey Pigza are:
Joey Pigza loses control (2000)
What would Joey do? (2002)
I am not Joey Pigza (2007)
The key that swallowed Joey Pigza (2014)

★ **The key** that swallowed Joey Pigza; Jack Gantos. Fararr, Straus & Giroux 2014 160 p. (hardback) $16.99
Grades: 4 5 6 7   **Fic**
1. Boys -- Fiction 2. Family life -- Fiction 3. Babies -- Fiction 4. Brothers -- Fiction 5. Single-parent families -- Fiction 6. Attention-deficit hyperactivity disorder -- Fiction
ISBN 0374300836; 9780374300838
LC 2014023370
First edition
This book by Jack Gantos is "the fifth and final book in the groundbreaking Joey Pigza series. . . . With his dad MIA

in the wake of appearance-altering plastic surgery, Joey must give up school to look after his new baby brother and fill in for his mom, who hospitalizes herself to deal with a bad case of postpartum blues." (Publisher's note)

"Joey's indomitable spirit, grounded in his fierce, tender devotion to baby Carter and expressed through Gantos' inimitable comic tone, shows the fragile adults around him just what it looks like to be the man of the house." Booklist

Garcia, Cristina

★ **I** wanna be your shoebox. Simon & Schuster Books for Children 2008 198p $16.99; pa $6.99

Grades: 4 5 6 7 **Fic**

1. Jews -- Fiction 2. California -- Fiction 3. Family life -- Fiction 4. Grandfathers -- Fiction 5. Cuban Americans -- Fiction 6. Racially mixed people -- Fiction

ISBN 978-1-4169-3928-3; 1-4169-3928-8; 978-1-4169-7904-3 pa; 1-4169-7904-2 pa

LC 2008-51306

Thirteen-year-old, clarinet-playing, Southern California surfer, Yumi Ruiz-Hirsch, comes from a complex family—her father is Jewish-Japanese, her mother is Cuban, and her parents are divorced—and when her grandfather Saul is diagnosed with terminal cancer, Yumi asks him to tell her his life story, which helps her to understand her own history and identity.

"García's . . . exceptional ability to channel a range of voices lights up her first children's novel. . . . The large personalities propel the story and bring tenderness and credibility to a classic message about change." Publ Wkly

Garcia, Kami

Beautiful creatures; by Kami Garcia & Margie Stohl. Little, Brown and Co. 2010 563p $17.99

Grades: 7 8 9 10 **Fic**

1. Love stories 2. School stories 3. Supernatural -- Fiction 4. South Carolina -- Fiction 5. Extrasensory perception -- Fiction 6. United States -- History -- 1861-1865, Civil War -- Fiction

ISBN 0-316-04267-6; 978-0-316-04267-3

LC 2008-51306

ALA YALSA Morris Award Finalist, 2010

This novel is set in a small South Carolina town. Ethan is powerfully drawn to Lena, a new classmate with whom he shares a psychic connection and whose family hides a secret that my be revealed on her sixteenth birthday. "Grades eight to ten." (Bull Cent Child Books)

"The intensity of Ethan and Lena's need to be together is palpable, the detailed descriptions create a vivid, authentic world, and the allure of this story is the power of love. The satisfying conclusion is sure to lead directly into a sequel." SLJ

Followed by Beautiful darkness (2010)

Beautiful darkness; by Kami Garcia & Margaret Stohl. Little, Brown 2010 503p $17.99; pa $9.99

Grades: 8 9 10 11 12 **Fic**

1. Love stories 2. Supernatural -- Fiction 3. South Carolina -- Fiction 4. Extrasensory perception -- Fiction

ISBN 978-0-316-07705-7; 0-316-07705-7; 978-0-316-07704-0 pa; 0-316-07704-6 pa

LC 2010-7015

Sequel to: Beautiful creatures (2010)

In a small southern town with a secret world hidden in plain sight, sixteen-year-old Lena, who possesses supernatural powers and faces a life-altering decision, draws away from her true love, Ethan, a mortal with frightening visions.

"The southern gothic atmosphere, several new characters, and the surprising fate of one old favorite will keep readers going until the next book, which promises new surprises as '18 moons' approaches." Booklist

Unbreakable; by Kami Garcia. Little Brown & Co 2013 320 p. (international) $18

Grades: 7 8 9 10 **Fic**

1. Occult fiction 2. Secret societies -- Fiction 3. Love -- Fiction 4. Demonology -- Fiction 5. Supernatural -- Fiction

ISBN 9780316210171; 031621017X

LC 2012048435

In this young adult paranormal novel, by Kami Garcia, "when Kennedy Waters finds her mother dead, she doesn't realize that paranormal forces are responsible--not until mysterious identical twins Jared and Lukas Lockhart break into her room and destroy a deadly spirit sent to kill her. Kennedy learns that her mother's death was no accident, and now she has to take her place in the Legion of the Black Dove--a secret society whose five members were all murdered on the same night." (Publisher's note)

"Readers are quickly drawn into the action, from the murder at the beginning to the cliff-hanger at the end. It's the horror aspect more than the fast-paced intrigue, however, that is the book's strong point. The Legion members must travel from one terrifying location to another, and Garcia describes these chilling locations with flawless detail." - SLJ reviews

Garden, Nancy

Endgame. Harcourt 2006 287p $17

Grades: 8 9 10 11 12 **Fic**

1. School stories 2. Bullies -- Fiction 3. Violence -- Fiction 4. Family life -- Fiction

ISBN 0-15-205416-2; 978-0-15-205416-8

LC 2005-19486

Fifteen-year-old Gray Wilton, bullied at school and ridiculed by an unfeeling father for preferring drums to hunting, goes on a shooting rampage at his high school.

"This is a hard-hitting and eloquent look at the impact of bullying, and the resulting destruction of lives touched by the violence." SLJ

Gardner, Lyn

★ **Into** the woods; pictures by Mini Grey. David Fickling Books 2007 427p il $16.99; lib bdg $19.99; pa $7.50

Grades: 4 5 6 7 8 **Fic**

1. Fantasy fiction 2. Sisters -- Fiction

ISBN 978-0-385-75115-5; 0-385-75115-X; 978-0-385-75116-2 lib bdg; 0-385-75116-8 lib bdg; 978-0-440-42223-5 pa; 0-440-42223-X pa

LC 2006-24350

Pursued by the sinister Dr. DeWilde and his ravenous wolves, three sisters—Storm, the inheritor of a special musical pipe, the elder Aurora, and the baby Any—flee into the woods and begin a journey filled with danger as they try to find a way to defeat their pursuer and keep him from taking the pipe and control of the entire land. "Grades five to eight." (Bull Cent Child Books)

"Gardner's fast-paced fantasy-adventure cleverly borrows from well-known fairy tales, and astute readers will enjoy identifying the many folkloric references. . . . Grey's appealing black-and-white illustrations add humor and detail to the story." Booklist

Followed by: Out of the woods (2010)

Out of the woods; pictures by Mini Grey. David Fickling Books 2010 348p il $17.99; lib bdg $20.99

Grades: 4 5 6 7 8   **Fic**

1. Fantasy fiction 2. Sisters -- Fiction

ISBN 978-0-385-75154-4; 0-385-75154-0; 978-0-385-75156-8 lib bdg; 0-385-75156-7 lib bdg

Sequel to: Into the woods (2007)

This is a sequel to Into the Woods (2007). The Eden sisters "are being lured into a wicked witch's lair. . . . Belladonna wants Aurora's heart and Storm's all-powerful musical pipe, and she will stop at nothing to get them." (Publisher's note) "Grades five to eight." (Bull Cent Child Books)

"Aurora, Storm, and Any Eden thought their troubles were over when Storm tossed the Pied Piper's powerful, seductive pipe . . . into the sea and defeated the pipe's erstwhile owner, the villainous Dr. DeWilde. . . . But it seems their troubles have only begun. . . . A missing prince, a cowardly lion, a marauding dragon, seven dwarfs, and even the Grimm brothers all make appearances, and while the fractured fairy-tale stew is considerably more haphazard than that of the sisters' first outing, it's a well-conceived and entertaining mash-up nonetheless." Horn Book

Gardner, Sally

I, Coriander; [illustrations by Lydia Corry] Dial Bks. 2005 280p il $16.99

Grades: 6 7 8 9   **Fic**

1. Magic -- Fiction 2. Fairies -- Fiction

ISBN 0-8037-3099-3

LC 2005--06050

In 17th century London, Coriander, a girl who has inherited magic from her mother, must find a way to use this magic in order to save both herself and an inhabitant of the fairy world where her mother was born

"Seamlessly meshing fact and fantasy, the author composes a suspenseful masterpiece that will have audience members gladly suspending their disbelief." Publ Wkly

★ **Maggot** moon; Sally Gardner. Candlewick Press 2013 288 p. (reinforced) $16.99

Grades: 7 8 9 10 11 12   **Fic**

1. Dystopian Fiction 2. Alternative histories

ISBN 0763665533; 9780763665531

LC 2012947247

Costa Children's Book Award Winner 2012

Printz Honor Book (2014)

In this dystopian novel, "Standish Treadwell, 15, has lost parents, neighbors, best friend: All disappeared from Zone Seven, a post-war occupied territory, into the hellish clutches of the Motherland. Now a new horror approaches. . . . Standish and [his friend] Hector spin fantasies about the far-

off tantalizing consumer culture they glimpsed on television (now banned), but they lack a vision of the future beyond vague dreams of rescue." (Kirkus Reviews)

★ The **red** necklace; a story of the French Revolution. Dial Books 2008 378p $16.99

Grades: 8 9 10 11 12   **Fic**

1. Adventure fiction 2. Gypsies -- Fiction 3. Orphans -- Fiction 4. Social classes -- Fiction 5. France -- History -- 1789-1799, Revolution -- Fiction

ISBN 978-0-8037-3100-4; 0-8037-3100-0

LC 2007-39813

In the late eighteenth-century, Sido, the twelve-year-old daughter of a self-indulgent marquis, and Yann, a fourteen-year-old Gypsy orphan raised to perform in a magic show, face a common enemy at the start of the French Revolution.

"Scores are waiting to be settled on every page; this is a heart-stopper." Booklist

Followed by: The silver blade (2009)

The **Silver** Blade. Dial Books 2009 362p $16.99

Grades: 8 9 10 11 12   **Fic**

1. Adventure fiction 2. Magic -- Fiction 3. France -- History -- 1789-1799, Revolution -- Fiction

ISBN 978-0-8037-3377-0; 0-8037-3377-1

LC 2009-9282

Sequel to: The red necklace (2008)

As the Revolution descends into the ferocious Reign of Terror, Yann, now an extraordinary practioner of magic, uses his skills to confound his enemies and help spirit refugees out of France, but the question of his true identity and the kidnapping of his true love, Sido, expose him to dangers that threaten to destroy him.

"A luscious melodrama, rich in sensuous detail from horrific to sublime, with an iridescent overlay of magic." Kirkus

Garner, Em

Contaminated; by Em Garner. Egmont USA 2013 336 p. (hardcover) $17.99; (ebook) $17.99

Grades: 7 8 9 10   **Fic**

1. Horror fiction 2. Dystopian fiction 3. Horror stories 4. Science fiction 5. Mothers -- Fiction

ISBN 1606843540; 9781606843543; 9781606843550

LC 2012024472

This book is set two years after "a diet drink with genetically modified ingredients transformed countless Americans into mindlessly violent animals" Now, "the Contaminated are controlled by electronic collars, and the unclaimed are housed in kennels like that in which Velvet Ellis, 17, finds her mother." Velvet and her sister's "shaky hold on normal life is finally upended when Velvet brings their mother home, facing anger and fear from neighbors and eviction from their landlord." (Kirkus Reviews)

Garretson, Dee

Wildfire run. Harper 2010 261p $16.99; pa $6.99

Grades: 5 6 7 8   **Fic**

1. Adventure fiction 2. Fires -- Fiction 3. Presidents -- Fiction 4. Earthquakes -- Fiction 5. Wilderness

survival -- Fiction
ISBN 978-0-06-195347-7; 0-06-195347-4; 978-0-06-195350-7 pa; 0-06-195350-4 pa
LC 2009049482

A relaxing retreat to Camp David turns deadly after a faraway earthquake sets off a chain of disastrous events that traps the president's twelve-year-old son, Luke, and his two friends within the compound.

"Along with a breathlessly paced plot, Garretson crafts a preteen protagonist who grows out of being a whiny, moody sort and, with his companions, displays generous measures of courage and ingenuity in rising to the occasion." Booklist

Gavin, Jamila

See no evil. Farrar, Straus and Giroux 2009 198p $16.95

Grades: 5 6 7 8 9   **Fic**
1. Spies -- Fiction 2. Wealth -- Fiction 3. Illegal aliens -- Fiction 4. Organized crime -- Fiction 5. London (England) -- Fiction 6. Household employees -- Fiction
ISBN 978-0-374-36333-8; 0-374-36333-1
LC 2008-5123

First published 2008 in the United Kingdom with title: Robber baron's daughter

Twelve-year-old Nettie's sheltered and privileged life changes after her beloved tutor mysteriously disappears and Nettie, aided by the son of a household employee, begins to learn the truth about her father, whose wealth began with trafficking in illegal aliens.

"This well-written novel has descriptive language, atmosphere, and lots of intrigue as it moves to a stunning conclusion." SLJ

Gavin, Rohan

Knightley and son; Rohan Gavin. Bloomsbury 2014 320 p. (hardback) $16.99 **Fic**
1. Mystery fiction 2. Organized crime -- Fiction 3. Father-son relationship -- Fiction 4. Conspiracies -- Fiction 5. Fathers and sons -- Fiction 6. Mystery and detective stories
ISBN 1619631539; 9781619631533
LC 2013034316

In this novel by Rohan Gavin, "since 13-year-old Darkus Knightley's parents split, he sees his father, Alan--a detective of obsessive professional dedication--once a week. Darkus' sponge of a brain has absorbed the details of every former case of his father's, which fuel conversation during their visits. The conversations tend to be one-sided, though, as Alan has been comatose for four years. One evening, Alan miraculously wakes from his coma, ready to investigate a series of bizarre crimes." (Kirkus Reviews)

Gear, Kathleen O'Neal

Children of the Dawnland; [by] Kathleen O'Neal Gear and W. Michael Gear. Starscape 2009 336p $17.95

Grades: 6 7 8 9   **Fic**
1. Great Lakes region -- Fiction 2. Prehistoric peoples -- Fiction
ISBN 978-0-7653-2019-3; 0-7653-2019-3
LC 2008035761

13,000 years ago in the Great Lakes Region, twelve-year-old Twig, a Spirit Dreamer who can see into the future, teams up with best friend Greyhawk and the unpopular shaman Screech Owl to warn villagers of an impending natural disaster that could have devastating environmental effects.

"Those looking for an exciting fantasy novel will be pleased by the unusual setting, the well-paced action and the individual lens on culture change at a massive scale." Kirkus

Gebhart, Ryan

★ **There** will be bears; Ryan Gebhart. First edition Candlewick Press 2014 224 p. $16.99

Grades: 6 7 8   **Fic**
1. Bears -- Fiction 2. Grandfathers -- Fiction 3. Wilderness survival -- Fiction
ISBN 0763665215; 9780763665210
LC 2013946620

In this book, by Ryan Gebhart, "thirteen-year-old Tyson loves hanging out with his . . . Grandpa Gene. . . . So when Grandpa Gene has to move to a nursing home that can manage his kidney disease, Tyson feels like he's losing his only friend. Not only that, but Tyson was counting on Grandpa Gene to take him on his first big hunt. So in defiance of Mom and Dad's strict orders, and despite reports of a . . . man-eating grizzly named Sandy, the two sneak off to the Grand Tetons." (Publisher's note)

"Fully developed characters, complex and realistic relationships (especially between Tyson and Gramps), and Tyson's spot-on narrative voice--which balances faux bravado, risqué humor, and real emotional pain--make this story stand out." Pub Wkly

★ **Salt.** Orca Book Publishers 2009 252p map (The Salt trilogy) $18; pa $12.95

Grades: 6 7 8 9 10   **Fic**
1. Fantasy fiction 2. Extrasensory perception -- Fiction
ISBN 978-1-55469-209-5; 1-55469-209-1; 978-1-55469-369-6 pa; 1-55469-369-1 pa

"Hari lives in Blood Burrow, a hellacious, rat-infested slum. . . . Pearl is a pampered daughter of Company, her only purpose in life to be married off to cement one of her father's political alliances. When both young people, who share rare psychic gifts, revolt against their fates, they find themselves on a desperate journey across a hostile landscape, with the forces of Company at their heels. . . . A compelling tale of anger and moral development that also powerfully explores the evils of colonialism and racism." Publ Wkly

Other titles in this series are:
Gool (2010)
The Limping Man (2011)

Gensler, Sonia

The **revenant.** Alfred A. Knopf 2011 336p $16.99; lib bdg $19.99

Grades: 7 8 9 10   **Fic**
1. Ghost stories 2. School stories 3. Oklahoma -- Fiction 4. Teachers -- Fiction 5. Cherokee Indians -- Fiction 6. Cherokee National Female Seminary -- Fiction
ISBN 978-0-375-86701-9; 0-375-86701-5; 978-0-375-96701-6 lib bdg; 0-375-96701-X lib bdg
LC 2010-28701

When seventeen-year-old Willemina Hammond fakes credentials to get a teaching position at a school for Cherokee girls in nineteenth-century Oklahoma, she is haunted by the ghost of a drowned student.

"Gensler makes a solid debut with an eerie and suspenseful work of historical fiction in which everyone is a murder suspect. . . . The layers of detail address the complex social structure of the period, and Gensler's characters and dialogue are believably crafted." Publ Wkly

George, Jean Craighead

Charlie's raven; written and illustrated by Jean Craighead George. Dutton Children's Books 2004 190p il hardcover o.p. pa $6.99

Grades: 5 6 7 8 **Fic**

1. Ravens -- Fiction 2. Naturalists -- Fiction 3. Grandfathers -- Fiction

ISBN 0-525-47219-3; 0-14-240547-7 pa

Charlie's friend, Singing Bird, a Teton Sioux, tells him that ravens have curing powers, so Charlie steals a baby bird from its nest, hoping to heal his ailing Granddad, a retired naturalist.

"The story is technically accurate and offers a vivid sense of place and a window into Native American beliefs through storytelling." SLJ

George, Jessica Day

Dragon flight; [by] Jessica Day George. 1st U.S. ed.; Bloomsbury Children's Books 2008 262p $16.95

Grades: 5 6 7 8 **Fic**

1. Fantasy fiction 2. Dragons -- Fiction

ISBN 978-1-59990-110-7; 1-59990-110-2

LC 2007050762

Sequel to: Dragon slippers (2007)

Young seamstress Creel finds herself strategizing with the dragon king Shardas once again when a renegade dragon in a distant country launches a war against their country, bringing an entire army of dragons into the mix.

"Fans of the first book will find the same strengths here: the imaginatively detailed scenes; the thrilling, spell-fueled action; the possibility of romance with a prince; and the appealing, brave heroine." Booklist

Dragon slippers. Bloomsbury Children's Books 2007 324p $16.95; pa $7.99

Grades: 5 6 7 8 **Fic**

1. Fantasy fiction 2. Dragons -- Fiction 3. Orphans -- Fiction

ISBN 978-1-59990-057-5; 1-59990-057-2; 978-1-59990-275-3 pa; 1-59990-275-3 pa

LC 2006-21142

Orphaned after a fever epidemic, Creel befriends a dragon and unknowingly inherits an object that can either save or destroy her kingdom.

"The plot is fast paced with all the right touches of romance and adventure. . . . The characters are wonderfully drawn." Voice Youth Advocates

Followed by: Dragon flight (2008)

★ **Princess** of glass. Bloomsbury Children's Books 2010 266p $16.99

Grades: 6 7 8 9 10

1. Fairy tales 2. Princesses -- Fiction

ISBN 978-1-59990-478-8; 1-59990-478-0

Sequel to: Princess of the Midnight Ball (2009)

In the midst of maneuverings to create political alliances through marriage, sixteen-year-old Poppy, one of the infamous twelve dancing princesses, becomes the target of a vengeful witch while Prince Christian tries to save her.

"In a clever reworking of the Cinderella story, George once again proves adept at spinning her own magical tale." Booklist

★ **Princess** of the midnight ball. Bloomsbury Children's Books 2009 280p $16.99

Grades: 6 7 8 9 10 **Fic**

1. Fairy tales

ISBN 978-1-59990-322-4; 1-59990-322-9

LC 2008-30310

A retelling of the tale of twelve princesses who wear out their shoes dancing every night, and of Galen, a former soldier now working in the king's gardens, who follows them in hopes of breaking the curse.

"Fans of fairy-tale retellings . . . will enjoy this story for its magic, humor, and touch of romance." SLJ

Followed by: Princess of glass (2010)

Sun and moon, ice and snow. Bloomsbury 2008 336p $16.95

Grades: 7 8 9 10 11 12 **Fic**

1. Fairy tales 2. Fantasy fiction 3. Folklore -- Norway

ISBN 1-59990-109-9; 978-1-59990-109-1

LC 2007030848

A girl travels east of the sun and west of the moon to free her beloved prince from a magic spell. "Grades seven to twelve." (Bull Cent Child Books)

"George has adapted Norse myths and fairy tales to create this eerily beautiful, often terrifying world. . . . Mystery, adventure, and the supernatural, and a touch of love are woven together to create a vivid, well-crafted, poetic fantasy." Booklist

George, Madeleine

The **difference** between you and me; by Madeleine George. Viking 2012 256 p. (hardcover) $16.99

Grades: 7 8 9 10 11 12 **Fic**

1. Secrecy -- Fiction 2. Lesbians -- Fiction 3. High school students -- Fiction 4. Schools -- Fiction 5. High schools -- Fiction 6. Protest movements -- Fiction

ISBN 9780670011285

LC 2011012192

This young adult novel uses a trio of alternating narrators to tell the story of "self-proclaimed misfit and outspoken manifesto-author Jesse [who] deals daily with the hazards of being out and proud in high school. She's also carrying on a secret affair with image-conscious Emily, the girlfriend of a popular boy at school. Meeting weekly in the bathroom of the local public library, the two experience an inexplicable chemistry, even though Emily will barely acknowledge Jesse at any other time. Switching perspective among Emily, Jesse and a third girl, Esther, this . . . tale . . . explor[es] . . . attraction and shame. Jesse hides her relationship from her warmly quirky and accepting parents not because it is with a girl, but because she knows they will disapprove of its secrecy." (Kirkus)

★ **Looks**. Viking 2008 240p $16.99; pa $7.99
Grades: 8 9 10 11 12   **Fic**
1. School stories 2. Obesity -- Fiction 3. Friendship -- Fiction 4. Anorexia nervosa -- Fiction
ISBN 978-0-670-06167-9; 0-670-06167-0; 978-0-14-241419-4 pa; 0-14-241419-0 pa
LC 2007-38218

"Meghan and Aimee are on opposite ends of the outcast spectrum. Meghan is extremely overweight. . . . Aimee, on the other hand, is classic anorexic. Both girls have been hurt by one of the popular girls at school. They join forces to bring Cara down in a stunning bit of public humiliation. . . . The story will make readers think about the various issues touched upon, and it is difficult to put down." SLJ

Gephart, Donna

★ **How** to survive middle school. Delacorte Press 2010 247p $15.99; lib bdg $18.99
Grades: 5 6 7 8   **Fic**
1. School stories 2. Family life -- Fiction
ISBN 978-0-385-73793-7; 0-385-73793-9; 978-0-385-90701-9 lib bdg; 0-385-90701-X lib bdg
LC 2009-21809

When thirteen-year-old David Greenberg's best friend makes the start of middle school even worse than he feared it could be, David becomes friends with Penny, who shares his love of television shows and posts one of their skits on YouTube, making them wildly popular—online, at least.

"Gephart crafts for her likable protagonist an engaging, feel-good transition into adolescence that's well stocked with tears and laughter." Booklist

Olivia Bean, trivia queen; Donna Gephart. Delacorte Press 2012 278 p. $16.99
Grades: 3 4 5 6 7   **Fic**
1. Game shows -- Fiction 2. Children of divorced parents -- Fiction 3. Father-daughter relationship -- Fiction 4. Divorce -- Fiction 5. Fathers -- Fiction 6. Curiosities and wonders -- Fiction 7. Jeopardy (Television program) -- Fiction
ISBN 0385740522; 9780385740524
LC 2011006023

In this book, "Olivia Bean has watched 'Jeopardy!' every evening since she was a little girl, but the nightly tradition just hasn't been the same since her father . . . took off for California two years ago. When the show announces auditions for Kids Week, Olivia is intent on making the cut, not only to compete but, more importantly, to get a plane ticket out to the show's taping in L.A. with the hopes of meeting up with her estranged dad." (Bulletin of the Center for Children's Books).

Geras, Adele

★ **Ithaka**. Harcourt 2006 360p $17; pa $6.95
Grades: 7 8 9 10   **Fic**
1. Trojan War -- Fiction 2. Classical mythology --

Fiction 3. Odysseus (Greek mythology) -- Fiction
ISBN 0-15-205603-3; 0-15-206104-5 pa
LC 2005-7569

Companion volume to: Troy

The island of Ithaka is overrun with uncouth suitors demanding that Penelope choose a new husband, as she patiently awaits the return of Odysseus from the Trojan War.

This book "can introduce young people to the power of story in Homer's epics as well as being a beautifully written story in its own right." Voice Youth Advocates

★ **Troy**. Harcourt 2001 340p hardcover o.p. pa $6.95
Grades: 7 8 9 10   **Fic**
1. Trojan War -- Fiction
ISBN 0-15-216492-8; 0-15-204570-8 pa
LC 00-57262

"Mythology buffs will savor the author's ability to embellish stories of old without diminishing their original flavor, while the uninitiated will find this a captivating introduction to a pivotal event in classic Greek literature." Publ Wkly

Geus, Mireille

Piggy; translated by Nancy Forest-Flier. Front Street 2008 110p $14.95
Grades: 6 7 8 9   **Fic**
1. Autism -- Fiction 2. Bullies -- Fiction 3. Friendship -- Fiction 4. Criminal investigation -- Fiction
ISBN 978-1-59078-636-9; 1-59078-636-X
LC 2007-48847

Original Dutch edition 2005

Lizzie struggles to overcome the closed, internal world of autism when a new girl moves into her neighborhood, befriends her, then insists that Lizzie join her in seeking revenge on the boys who tease them.

"The title's compactness adds accessibility for readers who prefer sprint reads to distance, and this would be a natural discussion-starter for readers ranging from reluctant to adventurous." Bull Cent Child Books

Gewirtz, Adina Rishe

Zebra forest; Adina Rishe Gewirtz. Candlewick Press 2013 208 p. (reinforced) $15.99
Grades: 5 6 7 8   **Fic**
1. Hostages -- Fiction 2. Siblings -- Fiction
ISBN 0763660418; 9780763660413
LC 2012947251

In this novel, by Adina Rishe Gewirtz, "an escaped fugitive upends everything two siblings think they know about their family, their past, and themselves. . . . A rattling at the back door, an escapee from the prison holding them hostage in their own home, four lives that will never be the same. . . . [The book] portrays an unfolding standoff of truth against family secrets." (Publisher's note)

"Debut author Gewirtz successfully conveys the terror and tedium of being trapped. . . While the situation may frighten some readers, the matter-of-fact way [the protagonists] make the best of difficult circumstances . . . may be comforting to those whose families don't match the ideal. An emotionally honest family story with an ending that's hopeful without being implausibly upbeat." Pub Wkly

Gibbs, Stuart

Belly up. Simon & Schuster Books for Young Readers 2010 294p $15.99; pa $6.99

Grades: 4 5 6 7 **Fic**

1. Mystery fiction 2. Zoos -- Fiction 3. Hippopotamus -- Fiction

ISBN 1-4169-8731-2; 1-4169-8732-0 pa; 978-1-4169-8731-4; 978-1-4169-8732-1 pa

LC 2009-34860

Twelve-year-old Teddy investigates when a popular Texas zoo's star attraction, Henry the hippopotamus, is murdered.

"The characters are well-developed and believable, making this book appealing to reluctant readers and those who enjoy animal stories and mysteries." Libr Media Connect

The last musketeer. Harper 2011 244p $16.99

Grades: 5 6 7 8 **Fic**

1. Cardinals 2. Statesmen 3. Adventure fiction 4. Time travel -- Fiction 5. France -- History -- 1589-1789, Bourbons -- Fiction

ISBN 978-0-06-204838-7; 0-06-204838-4

LC 2011019376

In Paris with his parents to sell family heirlooms, fourteen-year-old Greg Rich suddenly finds himself four hundred years in the past, and is aided by boys who will one day be known as 'The Three Musketeers.'

"From the gripping first sentence . . . the excitement never flags in this newly imagined Musketeer adventure. . . . Using Alexandre Dumas' stories as a jumping-off point, Gibbs mixes fact, fantasy and thrills to create a galloping swashbuckler." Kirkus

Poached; Stuart Gibbs. Simon & Schuster Books for Young Readers 2014 329 pages (hardcover) $15.99

Grades: 4 5 6 7 **Fic**

1. Mystery fiction 2. Zoos -- Fiction 3. Koalas -- Fiction 4. Bullies -- Fiction 5. Texas -- Fiction 6. Zoo animals -- Fiction 7. Mystery and detective stories 8. Family life -- Texas -- Fiction

ISBN 1442467770; 9781442467774

LC 2013000539

In this sequel to "Belly Up," by Stuart Gibbs, "12-year-old trouble-magnet Teddy is still living at FunJungle, a massive zoo and amusement park, with his primatologist mother and wildlife photographer father. . . . When the school bully, Vance, forces Teddy to throw a fake arm into the shark tank . . . [it] has a large-scale snowball effect that positions Teddy as the key suspect in the theft of Kazoo, a koala on loan from Australia." (Kirkus Reviews)

"In Belly Up's sequel, twelve-year-old Teddy contends with bullies at school. At FunJungle, the zoo where he lives with his primatologist mother and wildlife-photographer father, things are even worse: Teddy's the prime suspect in a koala kidnapping. Gibbs weaves interesting trivia (newborn koalas are jellybean-size) and plenty of humor (a poop-throwing chimp helps ID an industrial spy/saboteur) into his action-packed mystery." Horn Book

Spy camp; Stuart Gibbs. 1st ed. Simon & Schuster Books for Young Readers 2013 336 p. (hardcover) $17.99

Grades: 4 5 6 7 **Fic**

1. Spies -- Fiction 2. Camping -- Fiction 3. Camps -- Fiction 4. Survival -- Fiction

ISBN 1442457538; 9781442457539

LC 2012019416

Sequel to: Spy school

In this story by Stuart Gibbs, "Ben Ripley is a middle-schooler . . . [who] spent the last year training to be a top-level spy and dodging all sorts of associated danger. So now that summer's finally here, Ben's ready to have some fun and relax. Except . . . a spy-in-training's work is never done, and the threats from SPYDER, an enemy spy organization, are as unavoidable as the summer heat. Will Ben be able to keep his cover--and his cool?" (Publisher's note)

"After escaping assassination by the top-secret organization SPYDER, Ben Ripley (Spy School) is looking forward to chilling out this summer. But SPYDER is turning up the heat, insisting that Ben come to work for them. Gorgeous fellow-spy-in-training Erica is ready to help, and her legendary grandfather also appears on the scene. Clever descriptions and plot twists make this a top-notch summer read." Horn Book

Gibson, Julia Mary

Copper magic; Julia Mary Gibson. Starscape 2014 336 p. map (hardback) $16.99

Grades: 4 5 6 7 8 **Fic**

1. Magic -- Fiction 2. Historical fiction 3. Great Lakes region -- Fiction 4. Talismans -- Fiction 5. Teenage girls -- Fiction 6. United States -- History -- 20th century -- Fiction

ISBN 0765332116; 9780765332110

LC 2014014660

"The year is 1906, and on the shores of Lake Michigan twelve-year-old Violet Blake unearths an ancient talisman--a copper hand. Violet's touch warms the copper hand and it begins to reveal glimpses of another time." (Publisher's note)

"The summer of 1906 promises to be an exciting one for twelve-year-old Violet Blake: she gets her first job as an assistant for a visiting photographer; she meets a new friend; and best of all, she discovers an ancient copper talisman in the shape of a hand buried near the creek where her mother used to harvest medicinal herbs. . . . The presence of magic is subtle in the story, but in the end, it matters little whether the copper hand has magical power or not. Instead it is Violet's growth from a self-centered child to one who carefully considers the feelings and needs of those around her that give this story weight." VOYA

Gidwitz, Adam

The Grimm conclusion; by Adam Gidwitz and illustrated by Hugh D'Andrade. Dutton Children's Books 2013 368 p. (hardcover) $16.99

Grades: 4 5 6 **Fic**

1. Fairy tales 2. Horror fiction 3. Humorous stories 4. Brothers and sisters -- Fiction 5. Characters in literature -- Fiction 6. Adventure and adventurers -- Fiction

ISBN 0525426159; 9780525426158

LC 2013021686

In this book by Adam Gidwitz and illustrated by Hugh D'Andrade, "two children venture through forests, flee kingdoms, face ogres and demons and monsters, and, ultimately, find their way home. Oh yes, and they may die. Just once or twice." (Publisher's note) "An omniscient narrator comments throughout, offering warnings, consolation, and explanations." (Horn Book Magazine)

★ A **tale** dark & Grimm. Dutton 2010 256p il $16.99

Grades: 5 6 7 8 **Fic**
1. Fairy tales 2. Siblings -- Fiction
ISBN 978-0-525-42334-8; 0-525-42334-6;
9780525425816

LC 2009-53289

This book follows Hansel and Gretel as they walk out of their own story and into eight more tales. "Age ten and up." (N Y Times Book Rev)

"An audacious debut that's wicked smart and wicked funny." Publ Wkly

Gier, Kerstin

Emerald green; Kerstin Gier; translated by Anthea Bell. Henry Holt and Co 2013 464 p. (hardback) $17.99

Grades: 7 8 9 10 **Fic**
1. Love stories 2. Time travel -- Fiction 3. Secret societies -- Fiction 4. Love -- Fiction 5. England -- Fiction 6. London (England) -- Fiction 7. Great Britain -- History -- Fiction 8. Family life -- England -- London -- Fiction
ISBN 0805092676; 9780805092677

LC 2013017885

Sequel to: Sapphire blue
In the conclusion to author Kerstin Gier's Ruby Red trilogy, Gwen has "recently learned that she is the Ruby, the final member of the time-traveling Circle of Twelve, and since then nothing has been going right. She suspects the founder of the Circle, Count Saint-German, is up to something nefarious, but nobody will believe her. And she's just learned that her charming time-traveling partner, Gideon, has probably been using her all along." (Publisher's note)

"The conclusion to the Ruby Red series has as many twists as the two previous books in the trilogy. Gwen has endured danger and flirted with romance throughout the two weeks (!) since she learned she's the final member of the time-traveling Circle of Twelve. Now, the questions aren't resolved until the final few pages as she tries to counteract the plans of the dastardly Count Saint-Germain. The bestselling series has been blessed with a clever heroine, a hysterical gargoyle, and a guy as good looking as he is enigmatic. With loooong lives ahead of them, perhaps this not the end after all. " (Booklist)

★ **Ruby** red; translated from the German by Anthea Bell. Henry Holt 2011 330p $16.99

Grades: 7 8 9 10 **Fic**
1. Family life -- Fiction 2. Time travel -- Fiction 3. London (England) -- Fiction 4. Secret societies -- Fiction
ISBN 978-0-8050-9252-3; 0-8050-9252-8

LC 2010-49223

Original German edition, 2009

"Sixteen-year-old Gwyneth has known all her life that a time-traveling gene runs in her family: her cousin, Charlotte, has been trained as the carrier since birth. Gwyneth starts to experience time traveling symptoms. When she suddenly finds herself sent to different eras three times within forty-eight hours, she begins to wonder whether her family made a mistake about who was to inherit the gene." (VOYA)

"Adventure, humor, and mystery all have satisfying roles here." Booklist

Sapphire blue; Kerstin Gier; translated from the German by Anthea Bell. Henry Holt 2012 362 p. (hc) $16.99

Grades: 7 8 9 10 **Fic**
1. Fantasy fiction 2. Time travel -- Fiction 3. Secret societies -- Fiction 4. England -- Fiction 5. London (England) -- Fiction 6. Great Britain -- History -- Fiction 7. Family life -- England -- London -- Fiction
ISBN 0805092668; 9780805092660

LC 2011034011

Sequel to: Ruby red
In this young adult fantasy novel, by Kerstin Gier, "16-year-old Gwen continues her time-traveling adventures as the newest member of the Circle of Twelve. . . . Her life's now controlled by . . . a secret society monitoring time travel. . . . All 12 time travelers must be introduced into the chronograph so the Circle can be closed, and the Guardians have assigned Gwen and irresistible Gideon de Villiers the task of locating four missing time travelers." (Kirkus Reviews)

Giff, Patricia Reilly

Eleven. Wendy Lamb Books 2008 164p $15.99; lib bdg $18.99; pa $6.50

Grades: 4 5 6 7 **Fic**
1. Woodwork -- Fiction 2. Friendship -- Fiction 3. Kidnapping -- Fiction 4. Learning disabilities -- Fiction
ISBN 978-0-385-73069-3; 978-0-385-90098-0 lib bdg; 978-0-440-23802-7 pa

LC 2007-12638

When Sam, who can barely read, discovers an old newspaper clipping just before his eleventh birthday, it brings forth memories from his past, and, with the help of a new friend at school and the castle they are building for a school project, his questions are eventually answered.

This is an "exquisitely rendered story of self-discovery." Publ Wkly

Lily's crossing. Delacorte Press 1997 180p $15.95; pa $6.50; $15.95

Grades: 4 5 6 7 **Fic**
1. Friendship -- Fiction 2. World War, 1939-1945 -- Fiction
ISBN 0-385-32142-2; 0-440-41453-9 pa; 9780385321426

LC 96-23021

A Newbery Medal honor book, 1998
"Set during World War II, this . . . story tells of the war's impact on two children, one an American and one a Hungarian refugee. Lily Mollahan, a spirited, sensitive youngster being raised by her grandmother and Poppy, her widower father, has a comfortable routine that includes the family's

annual summer migration to Gram's beach house in Rocka-way, NY. Lily looks forward to summer's freedom and fishing outings with Poppy. She meets Albert, a Hungarian boy who is staying at a neighbor's house. . . . Eventually the two become good friends. The war interferes directly with Lily's life when Poppy, an engineer, is sent to Europe to help with clean-up operations." (SLJ) "Grades five to eight." (Booklist)

"Gentle elements of danger and suspense . . . keep the plot moving forward, while the delicate balance of charac-ters and setting gently coalesces into an emotional whole that is fully satisfying." Bull Cent Child Books

Maggie's door. Wendy Lamb Bks. 2003 158p pa $6.50

Grades: 5 6 7 8 **Fic**

1. Ireland -- Fiction 2. Immigrants -- Fiction
ISBN 0-385-32658-0; 0-385-90095-3 lib bdg; 0-440-41581-0 pa

LC 2003-2415

Sequel to: Nory Ryan's song (2000)

In the mid-1800s, Nory and her neighbor and friend, Sean, set out separately on a dangerous journey from fam-ine-plagued Ireland, hoping to reach a better life in America

"Giff uses vivid language and precisely detailed obser-vation to convey both experience and emotion." Horn Book

★ **Nory** Ryan's song. Delacorte Press 2000 148p hardcover o.p. pa $5.99

Grades: 5 6 7 8 **Fic**

1. Famines -- Fiction 2. Ireland -- Fiction
ISBN 0-385-32141-4; 0-440-41829-1 pa

LC 00-27690

When a terrible blight attacks Ireland's potato crop in 1845, twelve-year-old Nory Ryan's courage and ingenuity help her family and neighbors survive

"Giff brings the landscape and the cultural particulars of the era vividly to life and creates in Nory a heroine to cheer for. A beautiful, heart-wrenching novel that makes a devas-tating event understandable." Booklist

Another title about Nory is:
Maggie's door (2003)

Pictures of Hollis Woods. Wendy Lamb Bks. 2002 166p $15.95; pa $6.50

Grades: 5 6 7 8 **Fic**

1. Artists -- Fiction 2. Old age -- Fiction 3. Foster home care -- Fiction
ISBN 0-385-32655-6; 0-440-41578-0 pa

LC 2002-426

A Newbery Medal honor book, 2003

"She was named for the place where she was found as an abandoned baby. Twelve-year-old Hollis Woods has been through many foster homes—and she runs away, every time. In her latest placement, with an artist named Josie, the tightly wound Hollis begins to relax ever so slightly. . . . But Josie is slowly slipping into dementia, and Hollis knows that she'll be taken away from her if Josie is found out. . . . Giff has a sure hand with language, and the narrative is taut and absorbing." Booklist

R my name is Rachel. Wendy Lamb Books 2011 166p $15.99; lib bdg $18.99; e-book $10.99

Grades: 4 5 6 7 **Fic**

1. Moving -- Fiction 2. Siblings -- Fiction 3. Farm life -- Fiction 4. Great Depression, 1929-1939 -- Fiction
ISBN 978-0-375-83889-7; 0-375-83889-9; 978-0-375-93889-4 lib bdg; 0-375-93889-3; 978-0-375-98389-4 e-book

LC 2011004303

Three city siblings, now living on a farm during the Great Depression, must survive on their own when their fa-ther takes a construction job miles away.

"Rachel's searing, present-tense narrative exposes her fears, determination, and hopefulness in the face of wrench-ing challenges. Recurring motifs—color, flowers, and draw-ings by a neighbor that Rachel discovers in unlikely places—add lyricism to this story of family solidarity." Publ Wkly

Storyteller. Wendy Lamb Books 2010 166p $15.99; lib bdg $18.99

Grades: 5 6 7 8 **Fic**

1. Aunts -- Fiction 2. Family life -- Fiction 3. New York (State) -- Fiction 4. Father-daughter relationship -- Fiction 5. United States -- History -- 1775-1783, Revolution -- Fiction
ISBN 978-0-375-83888-0; 0-375-83888-0; 978-0-375-93888-7 lib bdg; 0-375-93888-5 lib bdg

LC 2009-48130

Forced to spend months at an aunt's house, Elizabeth feel a connection to her ancestor Zee, whose picture hangs on the wall, and who reveals her story of hardships during the Revolutionary War as Elizabeth comes to terms with her own troubles

"As she brings these characters and history alive, Giff again demostrates her own gift for storytelling." Publ Wkly

Water Street. Wendy Lamb Books 2006 164p $15.95; lib bdg $17.99; pa $6.50

Grades: 5 6 7 8 **Fic**

1. Family life -- Fiction 2. Irish Americans -- Fiction 3. Brooklyn (New York, N.Y.) -- Fiction
ISBN 978-0-385-90097-3; 0-385-73068-3; 978-0-385-90097-3 lib bdg; 0-385-90097-X lib bdg; 978-0-440-41921-1 pa; 0-440-41921-2 pa

LC 2006-02024

In the shadow of the construction of the Brooklyn Bridge, eighth-graders and new neighbors Bird Mallon and Thomas Neary make some decisions about what they want to do with their lives.

"Continuing the Irish American immigration story be-gun in Nory Ryan's Song (2000) and Maggie's Door (2003), [this] novel, set in 1875, is about the next generation. . . . A poignant immigration story of friendship, work, and the meaning of home." Booklist

Winter sky; by Patricia Reilly Giff. Wendy Lamb Books, an imprint of Random House Children's Books 2014 160 p. illustrations (hardback) $15.99

Grades: 4 5 6 7 **Fic**

1. Courage -- Fiction 2. Friendship -- Fiction 3. Family

life -- Fiction 4. Fire fighters -- Fiction
ISBN 0375838929; 9780375838927; 9780385371926
LC 2013022399

In this book, by Patricia Reilly Giff, "Siria's dad is a firefighter who doesn't know that someone special watches out for him; each time his daughter hears a siren, she sneaks out of her apartment building to chase his fire truck and make sure he is safe. During one such nightly pursuit, Siria discovers evidence of what she believes to be arson. Who could be purposely setting fires? When clues point to someone close to home, Siria must find the strength to unravel the mystery." (School Library Journal)

"Worried about her firefighter father's safety, every time a siren wails eleven-year-old Siria sneaks out and chases the truck, watching to make sure he escapes harm. Over Christmas break, Siria notices small fires being set all over town and decides to investigate on her own. Unadorned but engaging prose and Giff's well-drawn characters add depth to a simple story about courage and friendship." Horn Book

Giles, Gail
Right behind you. Little, Brown 2007 292p hardcover o.p. pa $7.99
Grades: 8 9 10 11 12 **Fic**
1. Homicide -- Fiction 2. Family life -- Fiction 3. Psychotherapy -- Fiction
ISBN 978-0-316-16636-2; 0-316-16636-7; 978-0-316-16637-9 pa; 0-316-16637-5 pa
LC 2007-12336

After spending over four years in a mental institution for murdering a friend in Alaska, fourteen-year-old Kip begins a completely new life in Indiana with his father and stepmother under a different name, but not only has trouble fitting in, he finds there are still problems to deal with from his childhood.

"The story-behind-the-headlines flavor gives this a voyeuristic appeal, while the capable writing and sympathetic yet troubled protagonist will suck readers right into the action." Bull Cent Child Books

Gill, David Macinnis
★ **Black** hole sun. Greenwillow Books 2010 340p $16.99
Grades: 8 9 10 11 12 **Fic**
1. Science fiction 2. Miners -- Fiction 3. Mars (Planet) -- Fiction
ISBN 0-06-167304-8; 978-0-06-167304-7
LC 2009-23050

"Now that life on Mars has evolved beyond mere survival, humans have increasingly brought their corruption and vices from Earth to the newly inhabited planet. As the story opens, Durango and his crew of teenage bounty hunters are working to liberate the daughter of a wealthy aristocrat from the clutches of a kidnapper. Their next assignment takes them to Mars's South Pole to defend poor miners against the attacks of savage cannibals. . . . High school." (Horn Book)

"Durango is the 16-year-old chief of a team of mercenaries who eke out a living on Mars by earning meager commissions for their dangerous work. Their current job, and the main thrust of this high-energy, action-filled, sciencefiction romp, is to protect South Pole miners from the Dræu, a cannibalistic group who are after the miners' treasure. . . . Throughout the novel, the dialogue crackles with expertly

delivered sarcastic wit and venom. . . . Readers will have a hard time turning the pages fast enough as the body count rises to the climactic, satisfying ending." Booklist

Invisible sun; by David Macinnis Gill. 1st ed. Greenwillow Books 2012 370 p. (Black Hole Sun Trilogy) (paperback) $9.99; (trade bdg.) $16.99
Grades: 8 9 10 11 **Fic**
1. Science fiction 2. Mars (Planet) -- Fiction 3. Adventure fiction 4. Adventure and adventurers -- Fiction
ISBN 9780062073334; 006207332X; 9780062073327
LC 2011002841
Sequel to Black Hole Sun.

This science fiction adventure story, by David Macinnis Gill, is the sequel to "Black Hole Sun," continuing to describe how "Martian freedom fighters Durango and Vienne infiltrate an evil government compound in search of missing data they hope will render the planet safe from future harm. This . . . novel is packed with . . . death-defying escapes, ambushes and . . . shootouts." (Kirkus)

Shadow on the sun; David Macinnis Gill. 1st ed. Greenwillow Books, an imprint of HarperCollins Publishers 2013 432 p. (Black Hole Sun Trilogy) (hardcover) $17.99
Grades: 8 9 10 11 **Fic**
1. Science fiction 2. Mars (Planet) -- Fiction
ISBN 0062073354; 9780062073358
LC 2013008361

This young adult science fiction novel, by David Macinnis Gill, is the sequel to "Invisible Sun." "Ex-Regulators Durango and Vienne are at it again in a race against time on a dangerous Martian landscape. Shocked to have learned that his father heads up the enemy forces who captured him at the end of the previous book, wisecracking teen soldier Durango fights to escape the clutches of his evil dad and to reunite with his ex-assassin sidekick and love interest, Vienne." (Kirkus Reviews)

"This sequel doesn't stand alone, and Gill inserts just enough left turns and red herrings to keep seasoned series readers guessing. . . . A refreshingly nondystopic sci-fi adventure." Kirkus

Gilman, Charles
Professor Gargoyle; Charlie Ward. Quirk Books 2012 175 p. (hardcover) $13.99
Grades: 7 8 9 10 **Fic**
1. Horror fiction 2. School stories 3. Monsters -- Fiction 4. Teachers -- Fiction 5. Middle schools -- Fiction
ISBN 1594745919; 9781594745911
LC 2011946052

In this novel by Charles Gilman "Strange things are happening at Lovecraft Middle School. Rats are leaping from lockers. Students are disappearing. The school library is a labyrinth of secret corridors. And the science teacher is acting very peculiar -- in fact, he just might be a monster-in-disguise. Twelve-year-old Robert Arthur knew that seventh grade was going to be weird, but this is ridiculous!" (Publisher's note)

Gilman, David

The **devil's** breath. Delacorte Press 2008 391p
(Danger zone) $15.99; lib bdg $18.99

Grades: 7 8 9 10 11 12   **Fic**

1. Adventure fiction 2. Namibia -- Fiction 3.
Environmental protection -- Fiction
ISBN 978-0-385-73560-5; 978-0-385-90546-6 lib bdg
LC 2007-46744

When fifteen-year-old Max Gordon's environmentalist-
adventurer father goes missing while working in Namibia
and Max becomes the target of a would-be assassin at his
school in England, he decides he must follow his father to
Africa and find him before they both are killed.

"The action is relentless. . . . Gilman has a flair for making the preposterous seem possible." Booklist

Other titles in this series are:
Ice claw (2010)
Blood sun (2011)

Gilman, Laura Anne

Grail quest: the Camelot spell; book one. HarperCollins 2006 291p $10.99; lib bdg $14.89

Grades: 5 6 7 8   **Fic**

1. Kings 2. Magic -- Fiction 3. Middle Ages -- Fiction
4. Knights and knighthood -- Fiction
ISBN 0-06-077279-4; 0-06-077280-8 lib bdg

Three teenagers living in Camelot are forced to undertake a dangerous mission when King Arthur's court falls
under a mysterious enchantment on the eve of the quest for
the Holy Grail.

"The believable dialogue, succint plot, and uncomplicated references to court life will appeal to middle graders
who are beginning to explore Aurthurian legend." Voice
Youth Advocates

Other titles in this series are:
Grail quest: Morgain's revenge (2006)
Grail quest: The shadow companion (2006)

Gilmore, Kate

The **exchange** student. Houghton Mifflin 1999
216p $15; pa $6.95

Grades: 7 8 9 10   **Fic**

1. Science fiction 2. Extraterrestrial beings -- Fiction
ISBN 0-395-57511-7; 0-618-68948-6 pa
LC 97-47162

When her mother arranges to host one of the young people coming to Earth from Chela, Daria is both pleased and
intrigued by the keen interest shown by the Chelan in her
work breeding endangered species

"Gilmore makes a farfetched premise seem more reasonable with everyday details of life in the twenty-first century,
sympathetic characters, and logical consequences. . . . A
story that will appeal to readers on many levels." Booklist

Gipson, Frederick Benjamin

Old Yeller; [by] Fred Gipson; drawings by Carl
Burger. Harper & Row 1956 158p il $23; pa $5.99

Grades: 6 7 8 9   **Fic**

1. Dogs -- Fiction 2. Texas -- Fiction 3. Frontier and
pioneer life -- Fiction
ISBN 0-06-011545-9; 0-06-440382-3 pa
LC 56-8780

A Newbery Medal honor book, 1957

"Travis at fourteen was the man of the family during the
hard summer of 1860 when his father drove his herd of cattle
from Texas to the Kansas market. It was the summer when
an old yellow dog attached himself to the family and won
Travis' reluctant friendship. Before the summer was over,
Old Yeller proved more than a match for thieving raccoons,
fighting bulls, grizzly bears, and mad wolves. This is a skillful tale of a boy's love for a dog as well as a description of
a pioneer boyhood and it can't miss with any dog lover."
Horn Book

Glatstein, Jacob

Emil and Karl; by Yankev Glatshteyn; translated by Jeffrey Shandler. Roaring Brook Press 2006
194p $17.95; pa $6.99

Grades: 5 6 7 8   **Fic**

1. Jews -- Fiction 2. Friendship -- Fiction 3. Vienna
(Austria) -- Fiction 4. Holocaust, 1933-1945 -- Fiction
ISBN 1-59643-119-9; 0-312-37387-2 pa
LC 2005-26800

Original Yiddish edition 1940

A story about the dilemma faced by two young boys—
one Jewish, the other not—when they suddenly find themselves without homes or families in Vienna on the eve of
World War II.

"The fast-moving prose is stark and immediate.
Glatshteyn was, of course, writing about what was happening to children in his time. . . . The translation, 65 years
after the novel's original publication, is nothing short of
haunting." Booklist

Gleason, Colleen

The **clockwork** scarab; Colleen Gleason.
Chronicle Books 2013 356 p. (Stoker & Holmes)
(alk. paper) $17.99

Grades: 7 8 9 10   **Fic**

1. Mystery fiction 2. Historical fiction 3. Scarabs
-- Fiction 4. Time travel -- Fiction 5. Secret societies
-- Fiction 6. Detective and mystery stories 7. Mystery
and detective stories 8. Great Britain -- History -- 1837-
1901 -- Fiction 9. London (England) -- History -- 19th
century -- Fiction
ISBN 1452110700; 9781452110707
LC 2012036578

This is the first book in Colleen Gleason's Stoker and
Holmes series. The "narrative switches between two young
women living in 1889 London: observant and cerebral Al-
vermina Holmes (she goes by Mina . . .), the niece of Sherlock Holmes; and Evaline Stoker, the headstrong (and physically strong) younger sister to Bram, and member of a proud
line of vampire hunters." They "investigate the connection
between the disappearance of a young woman and several
recent murders." (Publishers Weekly)

Gleitzman, Morris

Now; Morris Gleitzman. Henry Holt 2012 184
p. (hc) $16.99

Grades: 7 8 9 10   **Fic**

1. Psychological fiction 2. Family life -- Fiction 3.
Grandfathers -- Fiction 4. Holocaust survivors --
Fiction 5. Australia -- Fiction 6. Wildfires -- Fiction 7.

Jews -- Australia -- Fiction 8. Separation (Psychology) -- Fiction
ISBN 0805093788; 9780805093780

LC 2011033496

Sequel to: Then

This novel by Morris Gleitzman is "[s]et in the current day, this is the final book in the series that began with Once, continued with Then and is . . . Now. . . . While her physician-parents are working in Africa, eleven-year-old Zelda is living with her grandfather, eighty-year-old Holocaust-survivor Felix Salinger, in Australia . . . He has achieved much in his life and is widely admired in the community. He has mostly buried the painful memories of his childhood . . . when a disaster leads them both to deal with unresolved feelings about the first Zelda, Felix's childhood friend." (Publisher's note)

★ **Once.** Henry Holt and Company 2010 163p $16.99

Grades: 7 8 9 10   **Fic**
1. Jews -- Poland -- Fiction 2. Holocaust, 1933-1945 -- Fiction
ISBN 978-0-8050-9026-0; 0-8050-9026-6

LC 2009-24153

"The horror of the Holocaust is told here through the eyes of a Polish Jewish child, Felix, who loses his innocence as he witnesses Nazi-led roundups, shootings, and deportations. . . . Most moving is the lack of any idealization. . . . Felix escapes, but one and a half million Jewish children did not, and this gripping novel will make readers want to find out more about them." Booklist

Followed by: Then (2011)

Then. Henry Holt 2010 198p $16.99

Grades: 7 8 9 10   **Fic**
1. Poland -- Fiction 2. Orphans -- Fiction 3. Jews -- Poland -- Fiction 4. Holocaust, 1933-1945 -- Fiction 5. World War, 1939-1945 -- Fiction
ISBN 978-0-8050-9027-7; 0-8050-9027-4

LC 2009050774

Sequel to: Once (2010)

In early 1940s Poland, ten-year-old Felix and his friend Zelda escape from a cattle car headed to the Nazi death camps and struggle to survive, first on their own and then with Genia, a farmer with her own reasons for hating Germans.

"There is no triumphant climax, and right up until the shocking end, the story of hidden children will grab readers with its details of the daily tension of rescue and betrayal." Booklist

Glewwe, Eleanor

Sparkers; Eleanor Glewwe. Viking, published by the Penguin Group 2014 336 p. (hardcover) $16.99

Grades: 5 6 7 8   **Fic**
1. Fantasy fiction 2. Magic -- Fiction 3. Diseases -- Fiction 4. Social classes -- Fiction 5. Fantasy
ISBN 0451468767; 9780451468765

LC 2013038475

In this book, by Eleanor Glewwe, "Marah Levi is halani--one of the lower class, unable to do magic like members of the elite class, the kasiri. . . . When she impulsively saves

a young kasir girl, Sarah, from being hurt in a crowd, the girl invites her home, where she finds a kindred spirit in Sarah's brother Azariah. . . . Together they find the cure for a disease. . . . Their work uncovers a sinister plot, however, putting them in grave danger." (Bulletin of the Center for Children's books)

"In the city of Ashara those with magical power (the "kasir") lord it over those without (the "halani," or "sparkers"). That changes when Marah Levi, a fourteen-year-old halan with a gift for music and languages, translates a forbidden spell to save her loved ones from a deadly illness. An unusual protagonist and a South Asian inspired setting make this a promising fantasy debut." Horn Book

Goeglein, T. M.

Cold fury; T.M. Goeglein. G.P. Putnam's Sons 2012 312 p. (hardcover) $17.99

Grades: 8 9 10 11 12   **Fic**
1. Mafia -- Fiction 2. Chicago (Ill.) -- Fiction 3. Missing persons -- Fiction 4. Violence -- Fiction 5. Secret societies -- Fiction 6. Mystery and detective stories
ISBN 0399257209; 9780399257209

LC 2011025824

This book by T. M. Goeglein follows "Sara Jane Rispoli . . . a normal sixteen-year-old coping with school and a budding romance--until her parents and brother are kidnapped and she discovers her family is deeply embedded in the Chicago Outfit (aka the mob). Now on the run from a masked assassin, rogue cops and her turncoat uncle, Sara Jane is chased and attacked at every turn, fighting back with cold fury as she searches for her family." (Publisher's note)

Goelman, Ari

The path of names; by Ari Goelman. Arthur A. Levine Books 2013 352 p. (hard cover : alk. paper) $16.99

Grades: 7 8 9 10   **Fic**
1. Ghost stories 2. Mystery fiction 3. Camps -- Fiction 4. Magic -- Fiction 5. Cabala 6. Labyrinths -- Fiction 7. Brothers and sisters -- Fiction 8. Jews -- United States -- Fiction
ISBN 0545474302; 9780545474306; 9780545474313; 9780545540148

LC 2012030554

This book features Dahlia whom "her parents have sent . . . to Camp Arava. . . . When Dahlia first sees two young girls disappear through the cabin wall, she's convinced it's a great magic trick, but soon she realizes that they're actually ghosts. . . . These strange phenomena begin to converge around a mysterious garden maze on the campgrounds, a maze that is rumored to be connected to the disappearance of children and that is ferociously guarded by the skulking camp caretaker." (Bulletin of the Center for Children's Books)

"Thirteen-year-old magic nerd Dahlia loathes her Jewish summer camp until she starts dreaming about a Jewish teen in 1940s New York City who seems to be connected to a pair of ghosts haunting the camp. Readers with an interest in Jewish mysticism will enjoy the book's paranormal elements and tweens will appreciate the realistic relationships among the campers." (Horn Book)

Going, K. L.

★ **Fat** kid rules the world. Putnam 2003 187p
$17.99; pa $6.99

Grades: 7 8 9 10   **Fic**
1. Obesity -- Fiction 2. Musicians -- Fiction 3.
Friendship -- Fiction
ISBN 0-399-23990-1; 0-14-240208-7 pa
LC 2002-67956

Michael L. Printz Award honor book, 2004

Seventeen-year-old Troy, depressed, suicidal, and
weighing nearly 300 pounds, gets a new perspective on life
when a homeless teenager who is a genius on guitar wants
Troy to be the drummer in his rock band

"Going has put together an amazing assortment of characters. . . . This is an impressive debut that offers hope for
all kids." Booklist

The **garden** of Eve. Harcourt 2007 234p $17;
pa $6.99

Grades: 4 5 6 7   **Fic**
1. Death -- Fiction 2. Magic -- Fiction 3. Bereavement
-- Fiction 4. New York (State) -- Fiction
ISBN 978-0-15-205986-6; 0-15-205986-5; 978-0-15-
206614-7 pa; 0-15-206614-4 pa
LC 2007-05074

Eve gave up her belief in stories and magic after her
mother's death, but a mysterious seed given to her as an
eleventh-birthday gift by someone she has never met takes
her and a boy who claims to be a ghost on a strange journey,
to where their supposedly cursed town of Beaumont, New
York, flourishes.

"Believably and with delicacy, Going paints a suspenseful story suffused with the poignant questions of what it
means to be alive, and what might await on the other side."
Horn Book

Goldblatt, Mark

Finding the worm; Mark Goldblatt. Random
House Inc 2015 352 p. (lib. bdg.) $19.99

Grades: 5 6 7 8   **Fic**
1. School discipline 2. Teenagers -- Fiction 3.
Vandalism -- Fiction 4. Friendship -- Fiction 5. Bar
mitzvah -- Fiction 6. Conduct of life -- Fiction 7. Jews
-- United States -- Fiction 8. Queens (New York, N.Y.)
-- History -- 20th century -- Fiction
ISBN 0385391099; 9780385391085; 9780385391092
LC 2014004052

Sequel to: Twerp

In this novel by Mark Goldblatt "trouble always seems
to find thirteen-year-old Julian Twerski. He's been accused
of vandalizing a painting. The principal doesn't want to
suspend him again, so instead, he asks Julian to write a
200-word essay on good citizenship. Being falsely accused
is bad enough, but outside of school, Julian's dealing with
even bigger issues. His friend Quentin has been really sick.
How can life be fair when the nicest guy in your group has
cancer?" (Publishers' note)

"Julian Twerski and the gang from Twerp (Random,
2013) are now in seventh grade, and it seems like they're
dealing with an even bigger set of challenges than last year.
When Julian is accused of vandalizing a painting at school,
he gets locked into a battle with his new principal that he

surely can't win.An excellent companion to Twerp, this
novel also stands alone." SLJ

Goldblatt, Stacey

Stray; a novel. Delacorte Press 2007 276p
$15.99; lib bdg $18.99

Grades: 7 8 9 10 11 12   **Fic**
1. Dogs -- Fiction 2. Dating (Social customs) -- Fiction
3. Mother-daughter relationship -- Fiction
ISBN 978-0-385-73443-1; 0-385-73443-3; 978-0-385-
90448-3 lib bdg; 0-385-90448-7 lib bdg
LC 2006-31828

Natalie's mother, a veterinarian with a dogs-only practice, has the sixteen-year-old on such a short leash that, when
the teenaged son of her old school friend comes to stay with
them for the summer, Natalie is tempted to break her mother's rules and follow her own instincts for a change.

"This fresh treatment of a familiar teen feeling will
attract readers who love dogs as well as a good first-love
story." Booklist

Golden, Christopher

The **sea** wolves; by Christopher Golden & Tim
Lebbon; with illustrations by Greg Ruth. Harper
2012 384 p. $16.99

Grades: 7 8 9 10   **Fic**
1. Sea stories 2. Adventure fiction 3. Monsters --
Fiction 4. Pirates -- Fiction 5. Supernatural -- Fiction
6. Adventure and adventurers -- Fiction
ISBN 0061863203; 9780061863202; 9780061863219
LC 2011010031

This young adult fantasy adventure novel by Christopher Golden and Tim Lebbon follows "Jack London . . . a
writer who lived his own real-life adventures. But . . . even
he couldn't set down [all his adventures] in writing. Terrifying, mysterious, bizarre, and magical. . . . Clinging to life
after he is captured in an attack by savage pirates, Jack is
unprepared for what he faces at the hands of the crew and
their charismatic, murderous captain, Ghost. For these mari-
ners are not mortal men but hungry beasts chasing gold and
death across the North Pacific. Jack's only hope lies with
Sabine—a sad, sultry captive of Ghost's insatiable hunger.
But on these waters, nothing is as it seems, and Sabine may
be hiding dangerous secrets of her own.— (Publisher's note)

The **wild**; by Christopher Golden & Tim Lebbon;
with illustrations by Greg Ruth. Harper 2011 348p
il (The secret journeys of Jack London) $15.99; lib
bdg $16.89

Grades: 7 8 9 10   **Fic**
1. Authors 2. Novelists 3. Adventure fiction 4. Wolves
-- Fiction 5. Short story writers 6. Supernatural --
Fiction 7. Wilderness survival -- Fiction 8. Gold mines
and mining -- Fiction 9. Yukon River valley (Yukon and
Alaska) -- Fiction
ISBN 978-0-06-186317-2; 0-06-186317-3; 978-0-06-
186318-9 lib bdg; 0-06-186318-1 lib bdg
LC 2010-07475

Seventeen-year-old Jack London makes the arduous
journey to the Yukon's gold fields in 1893, becoming increasingly uneasy about supernatural forces in the wilderness that seem to have taken a special interest in him.

"Golden and Lebbon write with a gritty assurance that brings the fantasy elements . . . down to earth. . . . Occasional sketches add a bit of cinematic drama." Booklist

Golden, Laura

Every day after; Laura Golden. 1st ed. Delacorte Press 2013 216 p. (ebook) $47.97; (library) $18.99; (hardcover) $15.99

Grades: 5 6 7 **Fic**

1. Historical fiction 2. Great Depression, 1929-1939 -- Fiction 3. Self-reliance -- Fiction 4. Family problems -- Fiction 5. Abandoned children -- Fiction 6. Depressions -- 1929 -- Fiction 7. Alabama -- History -- 1819-1950 -- Fiction

ISBN 0385743262; 9780307983121; 9780375991035; 9780385743266

LC 2012015770

This book, set in 1932 in small-town Alabama, "details the struggles and injustices facing 11-year-old Lizzie Hawkins after her father loses his job and leaves town. Stuck with an overdue mortgage and a mother paralyzed by depression, Lizzie believes she just has to hold it together until her father returns, as she is sure he will." (Publishers Weekly)

Golding, Julia

★ The **diamond** of Drury Lane. Roaring Brook Press 2008 424p (Cat Royal Quartet) $16.99; pa $7.99

Grades: 6 7 8 9 **Fic**

1. Orphans -- Fiction 2. Theater -- Fiction 3. London (England) -- Fiction 4. Drury Lane Theatre (London, England) -- Fiction 5. Great Britain -- History -- 1714-1837 -- Fiction

ISBN 978-1-59643-351-9; 1-59643-351-5; 978-0-312-56123-9 pa; 0-312-56123-7 pa

LC 2007-23604

Orphan Catherine "Cat" Royal, living at the Drury Lane Theater in 1790s London, tries to find the "diamond" supposedly hidden in the theater, which unmasks a treasonous political cartoonist, and involves her in the street gangs of Covent Garden and the world of nobility.

This is "a story with as many cliff-hangers as there are chapters. But the real thrills also come from the varied, sharply drawn cast. . . . [Golding] offers a view of London readers can grasp with all their senses." Booklist

Other titles in this series are:

Cat among the pigeons (2008)

Den of thieves (2009)

Cat o' nine tails (2009)

Secret of the sirens; [by] Julia Golding. 1st Marshall Cavendish ed.; Marshall Cavendish 2007 357p (The companions quartet) $16.99

Grades: 7 8 9 10 **Fic**

1. Supernatural -- Fiction 2. Mythical animals -- Fiction 3. Environmental protection -- Fiction

ISBN 978-0-7614-5371-0; 0-7614-5371-7

LC 2006052799

First published 2006 in the United Kingdom

Upon moving to her aunt's seaside home in the British Isles, Connie becomes part of a secret society that shelters mythical creatures, and must use her ability to communicate

with these beings to protect them from evil and the incursions of humans.

This "packs a serious environmental message, yet never feels heavyhanded. . . . The contemporary setting and its modern villains . . . make for an entertaining read." Publ Wkly

Other titles in this series are:

The gorgon's gaze (2007)

Mines of the minotaur (2008)

The chimera's curse (2008)

The **silver** sea. Marshall Cavendish 2010 334p $17.99

Grades: 6 7 8 9 **Fic**

1. Kings 2. Norway -- Fiction 3. Pirates -- Fiction 4. Slavery -- Fiction 5. Vikings -- Fiction 6. Middle Ages -- Fiction 7. Father-daughter relationship -- Fiction

ISBN 978-0-7614-5725-1; 0-7614-5725-9

LC 2009-51263

When pirates raid a village in ninth-century Norway, eighteen-year-old Toki is captured as a prize, while Freydis, his younger sister, is taken to a friendly village where she and her African slave, Enno, learn that their fates are linked by prophecy.

"The straightforward emotions and lack of complicated politics enable younger readers to traverse the landscapes of the Dark Ages with ease, . . . while following a well-wrought story of romance, revenge, and familial loyalty." Bull Cent Child Books

Golding, William

Lord of the flies; introduction by E. M. Forster; with a biographical and critical note by E. L. Epstein; illustrated by Ben Gibson. 50th anniversary ed; Berkley 2003 315p $23.95; pa $13

Grades: 8 9 10 11 12 **Fic**

1. Allegories 2. Boys -- Fiction 3. Survival after airplane accidents, shipwrecks, etc. -- Fiction

ISBN 0-399-52920-9; 0-399-50148-7 pa

LC 2003-54825

First published 1954 in the United Kingdom; first United States edition, 1955, by Coward-McCann

"Stranded on an island, a group of English schoolboys leave innocence behind in a struggle for survival. A political structure modeled after English government is set up and a hierarchy develops, but forces of anarchy and aggression surface. The boys' existence begins to degenerate into a savage one. They are rescued from their microcosmic society to return to an adult, stylized milieu filled with the same psychological tensions and moral voids. Adventure and allegory are brilliantly combined in this novel." Shapiro. Fic for Youth. 3d edition

Golds, Cassandra

The **museum** of Mary Child. Kane Miller 2009 329p $16.99

Grades: 6 7 8 9 10 **Fic**

1. Dolls -- Fiction 2. Museums -- Fiction

ISBN 978-1-935279-13-6; 1-935279-13-0

LC 2009-922719

"Lonely Heloise wants only to be loved, but lives as if jailed in the house of her stern and sometimes cruel godmother. One day Heloise uncovers a beautiful doll, Maria, hidden under the floorboards of her room, and it is love at first sight. Heloise hides Maria from her godmother, whose personal Ten Commandments include forbidding play, 'pretty clothes' and the possession of a doll. . . . Once Maria is discovered, Heloise finds out the horrible truth about the museum that adjoins her godmother's cottage and is thrust down a strange and magical path that reveals how sheltered she has been. . . . Golds's novel is pure fun, filled with mystery and nearly impossible to put down." Publ Wkly

Gonzalez, Christina Diaz

★ The **red** umbrella. Alfred A. Knopf 2010 284p $16.99; lib bdg $19.99

Grades: 6 7 8 9   **Fic**

1. Cuba -- Fiction 2. Family life -- Fiction
ISBN 0375861904; 0375961909 lib bdg; 9780375861901; 9780375961908 lib bdg

LC 2009022309

In 1961 after Fidel Castro comes to power in Cuba, fourteen-year-old Lucia and her seven-year-old brother are sent to the United States because her parents fear that the children will be taken away from them as others have been. "Grades five to eight." (Bull Cent Child Books)

"The pain of the revolution for those who disagreed is made clear and pressing, and the text manages to balance between being informative and entertaining. This could prove a helpful tie-in for classroom history lessons or a solid recommendation for fans of quietly engaging historical fiction." Bull Cent Child Books

Gonzalez, Julie

Imaginary enemy. Delacorte Press 2008 241p $15.99; lib bdg $18.99

Grades: 6 7 8 9 10   **Fic**

1. Imaginary playmates -- Fiction
ISBN 978-0-385-73552-0; 0-385-73552-9; 978-0-385-90530-5 lib bdg; 0-385-90530-0 lib bdg

LC 2007-45752

Although her impetuous behavior, smart-mouthed comments, and slacker ways have landed her in trouble over the years, sixteen-year-old Jane has always put the blame on her "imaginary enemy," until a new development forces her to decide whether or not to assume responsibility for her actions.

"Gonzalez has written a witty, realistic novel . . . peppered with funny, authentic dialogue." Booklist

Goobie, Beth

Before wings; a novel. Orca Bk. Pubs. 2001 203p hardcover o.p. pa $8.95

Grades: 7 8 9 10   **Fic**

1. Camps -- Fiction 2. Death -- Fiction
ISBN 1-55143-161-0; 1-55143-163-7 pa

LC 00-105582

"Full of magic realism and beautifully written, this is a story of good triumphing over evil, life triumphing over death, the power of love, friendship, and the hope for an afterlife." Booklist

Goodman, Alison

★ **Eon**: Dragoneye reborn. Viking 2009 531p $19.99

Grades: 7 8 9 10   **Fic**

1. Fantasy fiction 2. Magic -- Fiction 3. Dragons -- Fiction 4. Sex role -- Fiction 5. Apprentices -- Fiction
ISBN 978-0-670-06227-0; 0-670-06227-8

LC 2008-33223

Sixteen-year-old Eon hopes to become an apprentice to one of the twelve energy dragons of good fortune and learn to be its main interpreter, but to do so will require much, including keeping secret that she is a girl.

"Entangled politics and fierce battle scenes provide a pulse-quickening pace, while the intriguing characters add interest and depth." Booklist

Followed by: Eona: The last Dragoneye (2011)

Eona: the last Dragoneye. Viking 2011 637p il $19.99

Grades: 7 8 9 10   **Fic**

1. Fantasy fiction 2. Magic -- Fiction 3. Dragons -- Fiction 4. Apprentices -- Fiction
ISBN 978-0-670-06311-6; 0-670-06311-8

LC 2011-02997

Sequel to: Eon: Dragoneye reborn (2009)

Eon has been revealed as Eona, the first female Dragoneye in hundreds of years. Along with fellow rebels Ryko and Lady Dela, she is on the run from High Lord Sethon's army. The renegades are on a quest for the black folio, stolen by the drug-riddled Dillon; they must also find Kygo, the young Pearl Emperor, who needs Eona's power and the black folio if he is to wrest back his throne from the self-styled "Emperor" Sethon.

"One of those rare and welcome fantasies that complicate black-and-white morality." Kirkus

Singing the Dogstar blues. Viking 2003 261p $16.99

Grades: 7 8 9 10   **Fic**

1. Science fiction 2. Australia -- Fiction
ISBN 0-670-03610-2

LC 2002-12161

First published 1998 in Australia

In a future Australia, the saucy eighteen-year-old daughter of a famous newscaster and a sperm donor teams up with a hermaphrodite from the planet Choria in a time travel adventure that may significantly change both of their lives

"This wildly entertaining novel successfully mixes adventure, humor, mystery, and sf into a fast-paced, thrilling story that will appeal to a wide audience." Booklist

Gordon, Roderick

Tunnels; [by] Roderick Gordon, Brian Williams. Chicken House/Scholastic 2008 480p il $17.99

Grades: 6 7 8 9   **Fic**

1. Adventure fiction 2. London (England) -- Fiction
ISBN 978-0-439-87177-8; 0-439-87177-8

LC 2007-09169

When Will Burrows and his friend Chester embark on a quest to find Will's archaeologist father, who has inexplicably disappeared, they are led to a labyrinthine world underneath London, full of sinister inhabitants with evil intentions toward "Topsoilers" like Will and his father.

This is "compelling. . . . The authors add distinctive, vivid touches to the . . . premise . . . and the murderous, refreshingly competant Styx makes an uncommonly challenging adversary." Booklist

Other titles in this series are:
Deeper (2009)
Freefall (2010)
Closer (2011)

Gorman, Carol

Games. HarperCollinsPublishers 2007 279p $16.99; lib bdg $17.89

Grades: 6 7 8 9   **Fic**

1. School stories 2. Games -- Fiction
ISBN 978-0-06-057027-9; 0-06-057027-X; 978-0-06-057028-6 lib bdg; 0-06-057028-8 lib bdg
       LC 2006-31759

When fourteen-year-old rivals Boot Quinn and Mick Sullivan fight once too often, the new principal devises the punishment of having to play games together at his office, where they learn which battles are worth fighting.

"This novel is a great book for middle school students, well scripted, realistic, and entertaining. The characters are true and understandable." Voice Youth Advocates

Gosselink, John

The **defense** of Thaddeus A. Ledbetter; a novel. drawings by Jason Rosenstock. Amulet Books 2010 231p il $14.95

Grades: 4 5 6 7   **Fic**

1. School stories
ISBN 978-0-8109-8977-1; 0-8109-8977-8
       LC 2009052209

Twelve-year-old Thaddeus A. Ledbetter, who considers it a duty to share his knowledge and talent with others, refutes each of the charges which have sent him to "In-School Suspension" for the remainder of seventh grade.

"This original and entertaining book, with its smarty-pants narrator and case-file format, will draw comparisons to the Wimpy Kid series." Booklist

Goto, Hiromi

★ **Half** World; illustrations by Jillian Tamaki. Viking 2010 221p il $16.99

Grades: 7 8 9 10   **Fic**

1. Fantasy fiction 2. Mother-daughter relationship -- Fiction
ISBN 978-0-670-01220-6; 0-670-01220-3

"Raised in impoverished circumstances by her single mother, overweight 14-year-old Melanie is the target of ridicule at school and leads a lonely, introverted life. Then an evil being named Mr. Glueskin kidnaps her mother, forcing Melanie to travel to Half World, a colorless land that has been sundered from the realms of flesh and spirit, its deceased inhabitants cursed to relive the most traumatic moments of their lives. . . . Goto writes the hellish Half World as miserably surreal yet horrifyingly believable. . . . It's a fast-moving and provocative journey with cosmically high stakes, and one that should readily appeal to fans of dark, nightmarish fantasy." Publ Wkly

Gourlay, Candy

★ **Tall** story. David Fickling Books 2011 295p $16.99; $19.99

Grades: 6 7 8 9   **Fic**

1. Size -- Fiction 2. Giants -- Fiction 3. Siblings -- Fiction 4. Basketball -- Fiction 5. Philippines -- Fiction 6. Culture conflict -- Fiction 7. London (England) -- Fiction
ISBN 0385752172; 0385752180 lib bdg; 978-0-385-75217-6; 9780385752183 lib bdg
       LC 2010011891

In this book, "Bernardo, who suffers from gigantism, lives in a world where real life and magic collide. . . . To his younger sister, Andi, born and raised in London, Bernardo is both the brother she has always loved and the freakishly tall boy who is going to draw way too much attention at school. . . . When an earthquake devastates San Andres just after Bernardo leaves, he's sure it's his fault. He believes that he brings destruction and danger wherever he goes, but everyone else thinks that Bernardo brings miracles." (School Library Journal)

"This will capture the hearts and minds of sports lovers—and just about everyone else as well." Booklist

Grabenstein, Chris

The **crossroads**. Random House 2008 325p (Haunted places mystery) $16.99; lib bdg $19.99; pa $6.99

Grades: 5 6 7 8   **Fic**

1. Ghost stories 2. Connecticut -- Fiction 3. Stepmothers -- Fiction
ISBN 978-0-375-84697-7; 0-375-84697-2; 978-0-375-94697-4 lib bdg; 0-375-94697-7 lib bdg; 978-0-375-84698-4 pa; 0-375-84698-0 pa
       LC 2007024803

When eleven-year-old Zack Jennings moves to Connecticut with his father and new stepmother, they must deal with the ghosts left behind by a terrible accident, as well as another kind of ghost from Zack's past

"An absorbing psychological thriller . . . as well as a rip-roaring ghost story, this switches points of view among humans, trees, and ghosts with astonishing élan." Booklist

Other titles in this series are:
The Hanging Hill (2009)
The smoky corridor (2010)
The Black Heart Crypt (2011)

Escape from Mr. Lemoncello's library; Chris Grabenstein. 1st ed. Random House Inc. 2013 304 p. (hardcover) $16.99; (library) $19.99

Grades: 5 6 7   **Fic**

1. Contests -- Fiction 2. Games -- Fiction 3. Libraries -- Fiction 4. Books and reading -- Fiction
ISBN 037587089X; 9780375870897; 9780375970894
       LC 2012048122

In this book, twelve "seventh-graders win a chance to spend an overnight lock-in previewing their town's new public library," which was "conceived by Luigi Lemoncello, the . . . founder of Mr. Lemoncello's Imagination Factory, which is a source for every kind of game imaginable. During the lock-in the winners . . . are offered a further challenge: 'Find your way out of the library using only what's in the library.' The winner will become spokesperson for the Imagination Factory." (Publishers Weekly)

My brother the robot; James Patterson and Chris Grabenstein; illustrated by Juliana Neufeld. Little, Brown & Co. 2014 352 p. illustrations

Grades: 4 5 6 7 8   **Fic**

1. School stories 2. Robots -- Fiction 3. Humorous stories 4. Schools -- Fiction 5. Inventors -- Fiction 6. Family life -- Fiction 7. Middle schools -- Fiction
ISBN 9780316405911

LC 2013041672

In this graphic novel by James Patterson and Chris Grabenstein, "an extraordinary robot signs up for an ordinary fifth grade class. It was never easy for Sammy Hayes-Rodriguez to fit in, so he's dreading the day when his genius mom insists he bring her newest invention to school: a walking, talking robot he calls E--for 'Error.' Sammy's no stranger to robots--his house is full of a colorful cast of them. But this one not only thinks it's Sammy's brother... it's actually even nerdier than Sammy." (Publisher's note)

"Sammy Hayes-Rodriguez has never had an easy time fitting in at school. His mother is an inventor, his father is a graphic novel artist, and his beloved little sister has an immune condition that keeps her confined to the house. His best friend Trip has a talent for saying the wrong thing at the wrong time. And then, there are the robots: a houseful of his mother's creations, programmed to do everything from housework to tutoring, plus some that don't do anything useful at all...A fast-moving plot, lots of jokes, and a host of weird robots will draw readers in, especially those looking for books similar to series such as "Diary of a Wimpy Kid" (Abrams/Amulet) and "Timmy Failure" (Candlewick)." SLJ

Grace, Amanda

In too deep; Amanda Grace. Flux 2012 228 p. $9.95

Grades: 7 8 9 10 11 12   **Fic**

1. Rape -- Fiction 2. Honesty -- Fiction 3. False accusation -- Fiction 4. High school students -- Fiction 5. Teenagers -- Conduct of life -- Fiction 6. Rumor -- Fiction 7. Schools -- Fiction 8. High schools -- Fiction 9. Conduct of life -- Fiction
ISBN 0738726001; 9780738726007

LC 2011028806

In this young adult novel, a "girl gets caught in a lie she didn't tell but doesn't have the courage to correct. . . . Samantha wants to spark some romantic interest from her best friend and secret heartthrob Nick, so she makes a play for popularity-magnet Carter. He rebuffs her, but someone sees her leaving his bedroom in tears and jumps to the false conclusion that Carter assaulted her. Sam doesn't hear about the resulting rumors until she returns to school. Soon she feels too overwhelmed by social pressure to deny them. Sam finds many opportunities to confess the truth, but she can't bring herself to exonerate Carter. . . . Complicating matters, Sam knows that because of the deception, she's likely to lose Nick, who finally has declared his love for her.— (Kirkus)

Graff, Lisa

★ **Absolutely** almost; Lisa Graff. Philomel Books, an imprint of Penguin Group (USA) 2014 304 p. $16.99

Grades: 4 5 6 7   **Fic**

1. Self-esteem -- Fiction 2. Babysitters -- Fiction 3. Ability -- Fiction 4. Schools -- Fiction 5. Babysitters -- Fiction 6. Racially mixed people -- Fiction 7. Family life -- New York (State) -- New York -- Fiction
ISBN 0399164057; 9780399164057

LC 2013023620

In this book, by Lisa Graff, "Albie has never been the smartest kid in his class. He has never been the tallest. Or the best at gym. Or the greatest artist. Or the most musical. In fact, Albie has a long list of the things he's not very good at. But then Albie gets a new babysitter, Calista, who helps him figure out all of the things he is good at and how he can take pride in himself." (Publisher's note)

"Ten-year-old New Yorker Albie is a middle-of-the-road (at best) student. He's buoyed by small successes in math club and on spelling tests, and by his new babysitter's low-key approach to confidence-boosting. Albie is a sweet, vulnerable kid who just needs a little extra help and to whom readers may well relate. Short chapters add to the story's accessibility and keep the pace moving." (Horn Book)

★ **Lost** in the sun; Lisa Graff. Philomel Books, an imprint of Penguin Group (USA) 2015 304 p. $16.99

Grades: 4 5 6 7 8 9   **Fic**

1. Guilt -- Fiction 2. Brothers -- Fiction 3. Friendship -- Fiction 4. Remarriage -- Fiction 5. Tricks -- Fiction
ISBN 0399164065; 9780399164064

LC 2014027868

In this book by Lisa Graff, "Trent knows nothing could be worse than the year he had in fifth grade, when a freak accident on Cedar Lake left one kid dead, and Trent with a brain full of terrible thoughts he can't get rid of. Trent's pretty positive the entire disaster was his fault. . . . It isn't until Trent gets caught up in the whirlwind that is Fallon Little--the girl with the mysterious scar across her face--that things begin to change." (Publisher's note)

"Trent Zimmerman is consumed by rage. The universe has been manifestly unfair to him and he doesn't know how to handle it. Seven months ago, he struck a hockey puck at a bad angle, sending it like a missile into the chest of a boy with a previously undiagnosed heart ailment. That boy died and Trent feels responsible...Weighty matters deftly handled with humor and grace will give this book wide appeal." SLJ

A **tangle** of knots; Lisa Graff. Philomel Books 2013 240 p. $16.99

Grades: 3 4 5 6   **Fic**

1. Baking -- Fiction 2. Orphans -- Fiction 3. Ability -- Fiction 4. Identity -- Fiction 5. Poughkeepsie (N.Y.) -- Fiction 6. Family life -- New York -- Fiction
ISBN 0399255176; 9780399255175

LC 2012009573

Parents' Choice: Gold Medal Fiction (2013)

This juvenile novel, by Lisa Graff, is set "in a slightly magical world where everyone has a Talent. . . . Eleven-year-old Cady is an orphan with a phenomenal Talent for cake baking. . . . And her destiny leads her to a mysterious address that houses a lost luggage emporium, an old recipe, a family of children searching for their own Talents, and a Talent Thief who will alter her life forever. However, these encounters hold the key to Cady's past and how she became an orphan." (Publisher's note)

Grant, K. M.

Blaze of silver; [by] K. M. Grant. Walker & Co. 2007 261p $16.95

Grades: 6 7 8 9   **Fic**

1. Horses -- Fiction 2. Muslims -- Fiction 3. Knights and knighthood -- Fiction 4. Great Britain -- History -- 1154-1399, Plantagenets -- Fiction

ISBN 978-0-8027-9625-7; 0-8027-9625-7

LC 2006012098

Sequel to Green jasper (2006)

Using principles of their shared Muslim faith to persuade him, an agent of the Old Man of the Mountain convinces Kamil to lead Will and Ellie into a trap, but Kamil repents and seeks a way to save his friends and redeem himself.

"This last volume of The de Granville Trilogy presents an exciting, appropriate end to the story." Voice Youth Advocates

Blood red horse. Walker & Co. 2005 277p $16.95; pa $8.99

Grades: 6 7 8 9   **Fic**

1. Horses -- Fiction 2. Crusades -- Fiction 3. Middle Ages -- Fiction

ISBN 0-8027-8960-9; 0-8027-7734-8 pa

LC 2005-42280

First published 2004 in the United Kingdom

A special horse named Hosanna changes the lives of two English brothers and those around them as they fight with King Richard I against Saladin's armies during the Third Crusades.

This "story . . . transcends boundaries of gender and genre, with something to offer fans of equestrian fare, historical fiction, and battlefield drama alike." Booklist

Other titles in this series are:

Green jasper (2006)

Blaze of silver (2007)

★ **Blue** flame; book one of the Perfect Fire trilogy. Walker & Co. 2008 246p (Perfect fire trilogy) $16.99

Grades: 7 8 9 10   **Fic**

1. Middle Ages -- Fiction 2. Knights and knighthood -- Fiction 3. France -- History -- 0-1328 -- Fiction

ISBN 978-0-8027-9694-3; 0-8027-9694-X

LC 2007-51384

In 1242 in the restive Languedoc region of France, Parsifal, having been charged as a child to guard an important religious relic, has lived in hiding for much of his life until he befriends a young couple on opposite sides of the escalating conflict between the Catholics and the Cathars.

"Characters are as complex as the moral issues they face, and Grant's nuanced, thought-provoking look at the religious conflicts they face will resonate today." Booklist

Other books in this series are Paradise red (2010)

White heat (2009)

★ **How** the hangman lost his heart. Walker & Co. 2007 244p $16.95

Grades: 7 8 9 10   **Fic**

1. Adventure fiction 2. Great Britain -- History -- 1714-1837 -- Fiction

ISBN 978-0-8027-9672-1; 0-8027-9672-9

LC 2006-53182

When her Uncle Frank is executed for treason against England's King George in 1746, and his severed head is mounted on a pike for public viewing, daring Alice tries to reclaim the head for a proper burial, finding an unlikely ally in the softhearted executioner, while incurring the wrath of the royal guard.

"The story is filled with action and interesting characters. . . . This is a rousing read." SLJ

Paradise red; by K.M. Grant. Walker & Co. 2010 279 p. (hardcover) $17.99

Grades: 7 8 9 10   **Fic**

1. Love stories 2. Fantasy fiction 3. Albigenses -- Fiction 4. Middle Ages -- Fiction 5. Knights and knighthood -- Fiction 6. France -- History -- Louis IX, 1226-1270 -- Fiction 7. Languedoc (France) -- History -- 13th century -- Fiction 8. Montségur (France) -- History -- 13th century -- Fiction

ISBN 0802796966; 9780802796967

LC 2009054214

This is the final book in K.M. Grant's Perfect Fire trilogy. The novel "concludes the story of Raimon's quest to save the mystical blue flame which is at the heart of his love for the land he grew up in. This runs alongside the complicated story of his relationship with Yolanda who has made a political marriage to one of the enemy." (School Librarian)

White heat. Walker & Co. 2009 260p (Perfect fire trilogy) $16.99

Grades: 7 8 9 10   **Fic**

1. Inquisition -- Fiction 2. Middle Ages -- Fiction 3. Knights and knighthood -- Fiction 4. France -- History -- 0-1328 -- Fiction

ISBN 978-0-8027-9695-0; 0-8027-9695-8

LC 2008-46984

Sequel to: Blue heat (2008)

As the conflict in Languedoc, also called Occitan, intensifies, Raimon, having escaped the pyre, suppresses his longing to find his beloved Yolanda and, together with Parsifal, carries the Blue Flame to the mountains where it serves to rally loyal Occitanians to organize against the formidable French forces set to invade their beloved country.

"With thorough scholarship and an immersion into medieval sights, sounds, and points of view, Grant invites readers on a thrilling trip back in time." Horn Book

Grant, Katy

Hide and seek. Peachtree 2010 230p $15.95

Grades: 5 6 7 8   **Fic**

1. Arizona -- Fiction 2. Divorce -- Fiction 3. Kidnapping -- Fiction 4. Family life -- Fiction 5.

Wilderness survival -- Fiction
ISBN 978-1-56145-542-3; 1-56145-542-3

LC 2009040519

In the remote mountains of Arizona where he lives with his mother, stepfather, and two sisters, fourteen-year-old Chase discovers two kidnapped boys and gets caught up in a dangerous adventure when he comes up with a plan to get them to safety.

"Mystery and adventure propel this readable survival story that will hit the spot with Gary Paulsen's fans and may also entice reluctant readers." SLJ

Grant, Michael, 1954-

★ The call; Michael Grant. 1st ed. Katherine Tegen Books 2010 243 p. ill. (The Magnificent 12) (hardcover) $16.99

Grades: 4 5 6   Fic

1. Fantasy fiction 2. Adventure fiction 3. Fantasy 4. Humorous stories 5. Good and evil -- Fiction 6. Adventure and adventurers -- Fiction
ISBN 0061833665; 9780061833663

LC 2009044815

A seemingly average twelve-year-old learns that he is destined to gather a team of similarly gifted children to try to save the world from a nameless evil, which is threatening to reappear after an absence of three thousand years. "Age ten and up." (Publisher's note)

"The author keeps the story moving at a brisk pace with suspenseful action and laugh-out-loud humor." Kirkus

Followed by: The trap (2011)

Fear. Katherine Tegen Books 2011 576p (Gone) $17.99; lib bdg $18.89

Grades: 7 8 9 10   Fic

1. Fear -- Fiction 2. Supernatural -- Fiction 3. Good and evil -- Fiction
ISBN 978-0-06-144915-4; 0-06-144915-6; 978-0-06-144916-1 lib bdg; 0-06-144916-4 lib bdg

LC 2011019374

As the young residents of Perdido Beach begin to better comprehend the truths of who they are and their relationships to one another, the Darkness finds a new way to be born, bringing their understanding of fear to a new level.

"Fans can count on more excellent storytelling, multi-dimensional characters who continue to develop in unexpected ways, and some mighty fine eye-popping moments." Voice Youth Advocates

★ Gone. HarperTeen 2008 576p $17.99; lib bdg $18.89; pa $9.99

Grades: 7 8 9 10   Fic

1. Supernatural -- Fiction 2. Good and evil -- Fiction
ISBN 978-0-06-144876-8; 978-0-06-144877-5 lib bdg; 978-0-06-144878-2 pa

LC 2007-36734

In a small town on the coast of California, everyone over the age of fourteen suddenly disappears, setting up a battle between the remaining town residents and the students from a local private school, as well as those who have "The Power" and are able to perform supernatural feats and those who do not.

"A tour de force that will leave readers dazed, disturbed, and utterly breathless." Booklist

Other titles in this series are:
Hunger (2009)
Lies (2010)
Plague (2011)
Fear (2012)

Hunger; a Gone novel. HarperTeen 2009 590p $17.99; lib bdg $18.89

Grades: 7 8 9 10   Fic

1. Horror fiction 2. Supernatural -- Fiction 3. Good and evil -- Fiction
ISBN 978-0-06-144906-2; 0-06-144906-7; 978-0-06-144907-9 lib bdg; 0-06-144907-5 lib bdg

LC 2008-36465

Sequel to: Gone (2008)

Conditions worsen for the remaining young residents of a small California coastal town isolated by supernatural events when their food supplies dwindle and the Darkness underground awakens.

"Readers will be unable to avoid involuntarily gasping, shuddering, or flinching while reading this suspense-filled story. The tension starts in the first chapter and does not let up until the end." Voice Youth Advocates

Followed by: Lies (2010)

Lies; a Gone novel. Katherine Tegen Books 2010 447p (Gone) $17.99; lib bdg $18.89; pa $9.99

Grades: 7 8 9 10   Fic

1. Supernatural -- Fiction 2. Good and evil -- Fiction
ISBN 978-0-06-144909-3; 0-06-144909-1; 978-0-06-144910-9 lib bdg; 0-06-144910-5 lib bdg; 978-0-06-144911-6 pa; 0-06-144911-3 pa
Sequel to: Hunger (2009)

A girl who died now walks among the living; Zil and the Human Crew set fire to Perdido Beach; and amid the flames and smoke, Sam sees the figure of the boy he fears the most: Drake. But Drake is dead. Sam and Caine defeated him along with the Darkness—or so they thought.

"This book retains all the action, unexpected twists, and engaging characters of the previous stories; readers will learn answers to old questions but new questions will proliferate. . . . Fascinating, frightening and absolutely worth an obsessive wait for the next installment, mature teen readers will embrace this thrill ride tempered with a touch of smart social commentary." Voice Youth Advocates

Followed by: Plague (2011)

Plague; a Gone novel. Katherine Tegen Books 2011 492p (Gone) $17.99; lib bdg $18.89

Grades: 7 8 9 10   Fic

1. Plague -- Fiction 2. Supernatural -- Fiction 3. Good and evil -- Fiction
ISBN 978-0-06-144912-3; 0-06-144912-1; 978-0-06-144913-0 lib bdg; 0-06-144913-X lib bdg

LC 2010021834

Sequel to: Lies (2010)

A deadly, flu-like epidemic and a plague of flesh-eating creatures threaten the lives of the children at Perdido Beach while Sam, Astrid, Caine, and Diana each struggle with doubts and uncertainties.

"Grant's sf-fantasy thrillers continue to be the very definition of page-turner." Booklist

The **trap**. Katherine Tegen Books 2011 294p (The Magnificent 12) $16.99

Grades: 4 5 6   **Fic**

1. Fantasy fiction 2. Adventure fiction 3. Good and evil -- Fiction

ISBN 0-06-183368-1; 978-0-06-183368-7

LC 2010040580

Sequel to: The call (2010)

Mack MacAvoy, an average-seeming twelve-year-old boy who happens to have special powers, travels to China in an effort to assemble an elite team of his peers to help him thwart the evil Pale Queen.

Grant, Vicki

Quid pro quo. Orca 2005 160p $16.95; pa $7.95

Grades: 7 8 9 10   **Fic**

1. Mystery fiction 2. Lawyers -- Fiction 3. Missing persons -- Fiction 4. Mother-son relationship -- Fiction

ISBN 1-55143-394-X; 1-55143-370-2 pa

"Cyril Floyd MacIntyre, 13, is perplexed over the disappearance of his mother, a 28-year-old law-school graduate. . . . Cyril becomes involved in a web of intrigue and deceit searching for her. His discovery of resurfacing shady characters who played a role in Andy's disappearance makes for a suspense-filled, well-plotted legal thriller." SLJ

Followed by: Res judicata (2008)

Res judicata. Orca Book Publishers 2008 172p pa $9.95

Grades: 7 8 9 10   **Fic**

1. Mystery fiction 2. Lawyers -- Fiction 3. Criminals -- Fiction 4. Mother-son relationship -- Fiction

ISBN 978-1-55143940-2; 1-55143940-9

Sequel to: Quid pro quo (2005)

Cyril MacIntyre is on the case again, working for his eccentric mother and giving new meaning to the term "legal aid" in this sequel to Quid Pro Quo.

"The novel features laugh-out-loud bits between mother and son and plenty of hilarious insights from Cyril about life and the law. Students who enjoy quick-witted writing and good mysteries will enjoy how well Vicki Grant cracks the case." Libr Media Connect

Gratz, Alan

★ The **Brooklyn** nine; a novel in nine innings. Dial Books 2009 299p $16.99

Grades: 5 6 7 8 9   **Fic**

1. Baseball -- Fiction 2. Family life -- Fiction 3. German Americans -- Fiction 4. United States -- History -- Fiction 5. Brooklyn (New York, N.Y.) -- Fiction

ISBN 978-0-8037-3224-7; 0-8037-3224-4

LC 2008-21263

This novel follows the fortunes of a German immigrant family through nine generations, beginning in 1845, as they experience American life and play baseball. "Grades five to nine." (Bull Cent Child Books)

Gratz "builds this novel upon a clever . . . conceit . . . and executes it with polish and precision." Booklist

The **League** of Seven; Alan Gratz; illustrated by Brett Helquist. Starscape 2014 352 p. map (hardback) $16.99

Grades: 5 6 7 8   **Fic**

1. Steampunk fiction 2. United States -- History -- Fiction 3. Science fiction 4. Monsters -- Fiction 5. Secret societies -- Fiction 6. Adventure and adventurers -- Fiction

ISBN 076533822X; 9780765338228

LC 2014015435

"'The League of Seven' is the first book in [a] steampunk series by the acclaimed author of 'Samurai Shortstop,' Alan Gratz. In an alternate 1875 America electricity is forbidden, Native Americans and Yankees are united, and eldritch evil lurks in the shadows. Young Archie Dent knows there really are monsters in the world. His parents are members of the Septemberist Society, whose job it is to protect humanity from hideous giants called the Mangleborn." (Publisher's note)

"This hybrid of steampunk and alternate American history features a hell-raising girl's school, Atlantis, and three highly likable leads in a yarn rip-roaring from start to finish. . . . Moments of humor and pathos enliven the history and fantasy." Booklist

Samurai shortstop. Dial Books 2006 280p hardcover o.p. pa $7.99

Grades: 7 8 9 10   **Fic**

1. School stories 2. Baseball -- Fiction 3. Tokyo (Japan) -- Fiction 4. Father-son relationship -- Fiction

ISBN 0-8037-3075-6; 978-0-8037-3075-5; 0-14-241099-3 pa; 978-0-14-24099-8 pa

LC 2005-22081

While obtaining a Western education at a prestigious Japanese boarding school in 1890, sixteen-year-old Toyo also receives traditional samurai training which has profound effects on both his baseball game and his relationship with his father. This book features some scenes of graphic violence.

"This is an intense read about a fascinating time and place in world history." Publ Wkly

Graves, Keith

The **orphan** of Awkward Falls. Chronicle Books 2011 337p $16.99

Grades: 4 5 6 7   **Fic**

1. Mystery fiction 2. Orphans -- Fiction 3. Homicide -- Fiction 4. Inventors -- Fiction 5. Mentally ill -- Fiction 6. Science -- Experiments -- Fiction

ISBN 978-0-8118-7814-2; 0-8118-7814-7

LC 2011008008

Josephine Cravitz, the new girl in Awkward Falls, and her neighbor Thaddeus Hibble, a reclusive and orphaned boy inventor, become the targets of a mad cannibal from the local asylum for the criminally insane.

"Graves crafts a quick-moving plot composed of macabre twists. . . . Wordless opening and closing sequences, plus a handful of interior illustrations, both fill in background detail and intensify the overall macabre atmosphere." Kirkus

Gray, Claudia

Spellcaster; Claudia Gray. HarperTeen 2013 400 p. (hardback) $17.99

Grades: 8 9 10 11 12   **Fic**

1. Occult fiction 2. Witches -- Fiction 3. Love stories 4. Horror stories 5. Magic -- Fiction 6. Schools -- Fiction 7. High schools -- Fiction 8. Rhode Island -- Fiction 9. Blessing and cursing -- Fiction

ISBN 0061961205; 9780061961205

LC 2012025331

This young adult paranormal romance story, by Claudia Gray, follows a teenage girl with magical powers. "Descended from witches, Nadia can sense that a spell has been cast over the tiny Rhode Island town--a sickness infecting everyone and everything in it. The magic at work is darker and more powerful than anything she's come across and has sunk its claws most deeply into Mateo . . . her rescuer, her friend, and the guy she yearns to get closer to even as he pushes her away." (Publisher's note)

Steadfast; a Spellcaster novel. Claudia Gray. HarperTeen 2014 352 p. (hardcover bdg.) $17.99

Grades: 8 9 10 11 12   **Fic**

1. Imaginary places 2. Magic -- Fiction 3. Horror stories 4. Schools -- Fiction 5. Witches -- Fiction 6. High schools -- Fiction 7. Rhode Island -- Fiction 8. Blessing and cursing -- Fiction 9. Family life -- Rhode Island -- Fiction

ISBN 0061961221; 9780061961229

LC 2013015445

Sequel to: Spellcaster

In this book, by Claudia Gray, "Nadia, Mateo, and Verlaine saved Captive's Sound from the dark sorceress Elizabeth . . . or so they thought. But despite their best efforts, a crack opened and a new, greater evil seeped through. With Mateo as her Steadfast, Nadia's magic is magnified but her training is still incomplete. And a darker magic has begun to call Nadia. With her Steadfast, Mateo, and her best friend, Verlaine, Nadia must fight the black magic that tempts her and stop the One Beneath." (Publisher's note)

"The first barrier between our world and the evil entity known as The One Beneath has been breached and redemption is impossible—unless untrained teen witch Nadia, along with her steadfast Mateo and friend Verlaine, can resist a seemingly invincible sorceress' power and a demon's meddling, all while remaining true to their friendship and ideals...Gray uses unique and lyrical free-verse spells, spoken by both Nadia and the dark sorceress Elizabeth, as inroads to sets of memories—a clever tactic that helps readers understand motivation while providing backstories that make it easy to bond with Nadia and her friends. The ending will provide terrific fodder for book discussions, so make sure you have enough copies to go around." (Booklist)

A thousand pieces of you; Claudia Gray. HarperTeen, an imprint of HarperCollinsPublishers 2014 368 p. (hardcover) $17.99

Grades: 8 9 10 11   **Fic**

1. Science fiction 2. Adventure fiction 3. Murder -- Fiction 4. Family life -- Fiction 5. Space and time

-- Fiction 6. Adventure and adventurers -- Fiction

ISBN 0062278967; 9780062278968

LC 2014001894

This book, by Claudia Gray, is "about a girl who must chase her father's killer through multiple dimensions. Marguerite Caine's physicist parents are known for their groundbreaking achievements. Their most astonishing invention, called the Firebird, allows users to jump into multiple universes. . . . But then Marguerite's father is murdered, and the killer--her parent's handsome, enigmatic assistant Paul--escapes into another dimension before the law can touch him." (Publisher's note)

"Readers will appreciate Marguerite's determination to help her parents, even though she is a misfit, the lone artist in a family of scientific geniuses. The secondary players are equally well rounded, and their various incarnations in each dimension make for intriguing character explorations. In resourceful Marguerite's first-person narration, the story moves quickly, and the science is explained enough to make the plot clear, but not so much as to bog things down." Booklist

Gray, Dianne E.

Tomorrow, the river; [illustrations by Stephanie Cooper] Houghton Mifflin Company 2006 233p il $16

Grades: 6 7 8 9   **Fic**

1. Sisters -- Fiction 2. Steamboats -- Fiction 3. Photography -- Fiction 4. Mississippi River -- Fiction

ISBN 978-0-618-56329-6; 0-618-56329-6

LC 2005038068

In 1896, fourteen-year-old Megan joins her sister and family on their steamboat for the summer riding up the Mississippi River towards St. Paul, Minnesota, and through all of their adventures, Megan realizes what is her "true calling."

"History and river life are skillfully woven into the fast-moving plot, and the characters are fully realized." SLJ

Gray, Keith

★ **Ostrich** boys. Random House 2010 297p $17.99; lib bdg $20.99

Grades: 8 9 10 11 12   **Fic**

1. Death -- Fiction 2. Scotland -- Fiction 3. Friendship -- Fiction 4. Great Britain -- Fiction

ISBN 978-0-375-85843-7; 0-375-85843-1; 978-0-375-95843-4 lib bdg; 0-375-95843-6 lib bdg

LC 2008-21729

After their best friend Ross dies, English teenagers Blake, Kenny, and Sim plan a proper memorial by taking his ashes to Ross, Scotland, an adventure-filled journey that tests their loyalty to each other and forces them to question what friendship means.

"Gray's writing is cheeky, crisp, and realistic. He has created funny, bright characters whom readers cannot help but root for." SLJ

Green, Tim

Baseball great. HarperCollinsPublishers 2009 250p $16.99; lib bdg $17.89

Grades: 5 6 7 8   **Fic**

1. School stories 2. Baseball -- Fiction 3. Father-son

relationship -- Fiction
ISBN 978-0-06-162686-9; 0-06-162686-4; 978-0-06-162687-6 lib bdg; 0-06-162687-2 lib bdg

LC 2008051778

All twelve-year-old Josh wants to do is play baseball but when his father, a minor league pitcher, signs him up for a youth championship team, Josh finds himself embroiled in a situation with potentially illegal consequences.

"Issues of peer and family pressure are well handled, and the short, punchy chapters and crisp dialogue are likely to hold the attention of young baseball fans." SLJ

Other titles in this series are:
Rivals (2010)
Best of the best (2011)

Football genius. HarperCollinsPublishers 2007 244p $16.99; lib bdg $17.89; pa $6.99
Grades: 5 6 7 8   **Fic**
1. Football -- Fiction 2. Atlanta (Ga.) -- Fiction
ISBN 978-0-06-112270-5; 0-06-112270-X; 978-0-06-112272-9 lib bdg; 0-06-112272-6 lib bdg; 978-0-06-112273-6 pa; 0-06-112273-4 pa

LC 2006-29470

Troy, a sixth-grader with an unusual gift for predicting football plays before they occur, attempts to use his ability to help his favorite team, the Atlanta Falcons, but he must first prove himself to the coach and players.

The author "imparts many insider details that football fans will love. Green makes Troy a winning hero, and he ties everything together with a fast-moving plot." Booklist

Other titles in this series are:
Football champ (2009)
The big time (2010)
Deep zone (2011)

Football hero. HarperCollinsPublishers 2008 297p $16.99; lib bdg $17.89; pa $6.99
Grades: 5 6 7 8   **Fic**
1. Mafia -- Fiction 2. Football -- Fiction 3. New Jersey -- Fiction
ISBN 978-0-06-112274-3; 0-06-112274-2; 978-0-06-112275-0 lib bdg; 0-06-112275-0 lib bdg; 978-0-06-112276-7 pa; 0-06-112276-9 pa

LC 2007-24184

When twelve-year-old Ty's brother Thane is recruited out of college to play for the New York Jets, their Uncle Gus uses Ty to get insider information for his gambling ring, landing Ty and Thane in trouble with the Mafia.

"The novel is briskly paced and undemanding, and might be a good bet for sports-minded reluctant readers." SLJ

Force out; Tim Green. 1st ed. Harper 2013 288 p. (hardcover) $16.99
Grades: 4 5 6   **Fic**
1. Baseball -- Fiction 2. Friendship -- Fiction 3. Best friends -- Fiction 4. Conduct of life -- Fiction 5. Competition (Psychology) -- Fiction
ISBN 0062089595; 9780062089595

LC 2012026752

In this juvenile novel, by Tim Green, "Joey and Zach have always been best friends. They're also two of the best baseball players in their league, and shoo-ins for the all-star

team at the end of the season. Their dream is to play together on the Center State select team, and they will do anything to help each other get there. . . . Then the unthinkable happens: The boys learn there's only one open spot on the select team." (Publisher's note)

"Though Green is no stylist, he does a better job of avoiding the sports fantasy and sticking to real life than usual. There's plenty of play-by-play for those who want the sports to be the focus, but the interactions off the field are never shortchanged. . . . A slice of life for middle school readers who know that their sport is a microcosm of the larger world." Kirkus

New kid; Tim Green. HarperCollins 2014 320 p. (hardback) $16.99
Grades: 4 5 6 7 8   **Fic**
1. School stories 2. Moving -- Fiction 3. Baseball players -- Fiction 4. Schools -- Fiction 5. Baseball -- Fiction 6. Fathers and sons -- Fiction 7. Moving, Household -- Fiction 8. Interpersonal relations -- Fiction
ISBN 0062208721; 9780062208729

LC 2013032816

In this "baseball novel," by Tim Green, "Tommy's the new kid in town--who now goes by the name Brock--and he's having a hard time fitting in. Thanks to a prank gone wrong, he may be able to settle in on the baseball team. But can he prove himself before he becomes a new kid . . . again?" (Publisher's note)

"A teenage baseball star struggles not only with game-day stress, but also with the ever-present fear that his world is about to end. . . . His dad's job is mysterious and dangerous, and it requires them to stay on the run. Moving abruptly has only gotten harder as Brock gets older, and when he finds a great baseball coach and a good friend—and a potential girlfriend—the thought of leaving it all behind terrifies him even more. Best-selling author and former NFL defensive end Green delivers a riveting book about the complexities of being a teenager caught in unusual circumstances beyond his control. His writing is both compelling and intelligent, and even the implausible scenes—like a visit from a baseball great—still maintain a feel of authenticity. Even readers who aren't sports fans will find plenty of familiar drama and entertainment in this book. Exciting, romantic and thought-provoking, this book scores a home run." Kirkus

Greenwald, Lisa

Dog Beach; The Seagate Summers Book One. Lisa Greenwald. Amulet Books 2014 272 p. (alk. paper) $15.95
Grades: 5 6 7 8   **Fic**
1. Dogs -- Fiction 2. Summer -- Fiction 3. Beaches -- Fiction 4. Friendship -- Fiction 5. Vacations -- Fiction 6. Dog walking -- Fiction
ISBN 1419710184; 9781419710186

LC 2013023282

In this book, by Lisa Greenwald, "Eleven-year-old Remy loves Seagate, the island where her grandmother had a house and where her family spends every summer vacation. But this year's different. Remy misses her dog, Danish, who recently passed away. The usual Seagate traditions don't feel the same—and neither does her relationship with her two best friends, Micayla and Bennett. . . . Remy takes comfort in the company of Dog Beach." (Publisher's note)

"For 11-year-old Remy, Seagate Island, where her family vacations every year, is perfect because "summer after summer, it always stays the same." But this summer is different. Her beloved dog, Danish, has died, and Remy misses him terribly...Greenwald's gentle read is tailor-made for those on the cusp of friendship misunderstandings, burgeoning popularity awareness, awkward crushes, and the wobbly feeling that can come from deviating from comfortable routine. All of Remy's worries are soothed eventually, and happiness is well earned. This sweet series opener promises an agreeable journey." Booklist

★ **My** life in pink and green. Amulet Books 2010 288 p. (hbk.) $16.95

Grades: 4 5 6 7 **Fic**

1. Cosmetics -- Fiction 2. Environmental protection -- Fiction 3. Mother-daughter relationship -- Fiction
ISBN 0810983524; 0810989840 pa; 9780810983526; 9780810989849

LC 2008025577

When the family's drugstore is failing, seventh-grader Lucy uses her problem solving talents to come up with solution that might resuscitate the business, along with helping the environment.

"Greenwald deftly blends eco-facts and makeup tips, friendship dynamics, and spot-on middle-school politics into a warm, uplifting story." Booklist

Sweet treats, secret crushes. Amulet Books 2010 291p $16.95

Grades: 5 6 7 8 **Fic**

1. Friendship -- Fiction 2. Valentine's Day -- Fiction 3. Apartment houses -- Fiction 4. Brooklyn (New York, N.Y.) -- Fiction
ISBN 978-0-8109-8990-0; 0-8109-8990-5

LC 2009052208

When a snowstorm keeps thirteen-year-old best friends Olivia, Kate, and Georgia inside their Brooklyn, New York, apartment building on Valentine's Day, they connect with their neighbors by distributing homemade fortune cookies and uncover one another's secrets along the way.

"An affectionate, insightful ode to friendship. An enjoyable, sure-to-be popular read." Booklist

Greenwald, Tommy

★ **Charlie** Joe Jackson's guide to not reading. Roaring Brook Press 2011 220p il $14.99

Grades: 4 5 6 7 **Fic**

1. School stories 2. Books and reading -- Fiction
ISBN 978-1-59643-691-6; 1-59643-691-3

LC 2010-24079

Middle schooler Charlie Joe is proud of his success at avoiding reading, but eventually his schemes go too far.

"With its subversive humor and contemporary details drawn straight from kids' worlds, this clever title should attract a wide following." Booklist

Charlie Joe Jackson's guide to summer vacation; by Tommy Greenwald; illustrated by J. P. Coovert. 1st ed. Roaring Brook Press 2013 231 p. ill. (hardcover) $14.99

Grades: 4 5 6 7 **Fic**

1. Reading -- Fiction 2. Vacations -- Fiction 3. Camps -- Fiction 4. Humorous stories 5. Interpersonal relations -- Fiction
ISBN 159643757X; 9781596437579; 9781596438804

LC 2012034249

In this graphic novel by Tommy Greenwald "Charlie Joe Jackson finds himself in a terrible dream he can't wake up from: Camp Rituhbukkee . . . a place filled with grammar workshops, Read-a-Ramas, and kids who actually like reading. But Charlie Joe is determined to convince the entire camp to hate reading and writing—one genius at a time. Tommy Greenwald's 'Charlie Joe Jackson's Guide to Summer Vacation' is another . . . installment in the life of a reluctant reader." (Publisher's note)

Gregg, Stacy

The **princess** and the foal; Stacy Gregg. Philomel Books, an imprint of Penguin Group (USA) 2014 272 p. illustrations (hardback) $16.99

Grades: PreK 5 6 7 8 **Fic**

1. Horses -- Fiction 2. Princesses -- Fiction 3. Jordan -- Fiction 4. Show jumping -- Fiction 5. Animals -- Infancy -- Fiction
ISBN 0399168877; 9780399168871

LC 2014005307

In this juvenile novel, by Stacy Gregg, "when Queen Alia is killed in a tragic accident, Princess Haya is devastated. Knowing how unhappy she is and how much she loves horses, Haya's father, King Hussein, gives her a special present: a foal of her very own, And this foal changes Princess Haya's world completely." (Publisher's note)

"It's also a refreshingly active story—Haya is riding and leaping and playing outdoors (when she's not grounded) on nearly every page. Empowering and vigorous, this is a story sure to please princess fans, horse fans and, yes, even tomboys." Kirkus

Griffin, Adele

The **Julian** game. G.P. Putnam's Sons 2010 200p $16.99

Grades: 8 9 10 11 12 **Fic**

1. School stories 2. Bullies -- Fiction
ISBN 978-0-399-25460-4; 0-399-25460-9

LC 2010-2281

In an effort to improve her social status, a new scholarship student at an exclusive girls' school uses a fake online profile to help a popular girl get back at her ex-boyfriend, but the consequences are difficult to handle.

This is a "perceptive novel. . . . Canny use of details makes Griffin's characters fully realized and believable. . . . Strong pacing and a sympathetic protagonist ought to keep readers hooked." Publ Wkly

Where I want to be. G.P. Putnam's Sons 2005 150p pa $6.99

Grades: 7 8 9 10 **Fic**

1. Death -- Fiction 2. Sisters -- Fiction 3. Rhode Island -- Fiction 4. Mental illness -- Fiction
ISBN 0-399-23783-6; 0-14-240948-0 pa

LC 2004-1887

Two teenaged sisters, separated by death but still connected, work through their feelings of loss over the closeness they shared as children that was later destroyed by one's mental illness, and finally make peace with each other

"Thoughtful, unique, and ultimately life-affirming, this is a fascinating take on the literary device of a main character speaking after death." SLJ

Griffin, Claire J.

Nowhere to run; Claire J. Griffin. 1st ed. Namelos llc 2013 118 p. (hardcover) $18.95

Grades: 7 8 9 10   **Fic**

1. School stories 2. Juvenile delinquency -- Fiction
ISBN 1608981444; 9781608981441; 9781608981458

LC 2012951212

In this novel, by Claire J. Griffin, "Calvin has Deej--and a coach who thinks Calvin can win the championship in the 100-meter dash, a little brother who looks up to him, a boss who trusts him with the keys to the car shop, and Momma, who made him promise to stay in school. And then there's Junior, the girlfriend of Calvin's dreams. . . . But when Calvin and Deej get suspended from school on a trumped-up charge, things start to fall apart." (Publisher's note)

Griffin, Paul

Ten Mile River. Dial Books 2008 188p $16.99

Grades: 8 9 10 11 12   **Fic**

1. New York (N.Y.) -- Fiction 2. Homeless persons -- Fiction 3. Runaway teenagers -- Fiction 4. Juvenile delinquency -- Fiction
ISBN 978-0-8037-3284-1; 0-8037-3284-8

LC 2007-047870

Having escaped from juvenile detention centers and foster care, two teenaged boys live on their own in an abandoned shack in a New York City park, making their way by stealing, occasionally working, and trying to keep from being arrested.

"The language is tough but convincing, the setting authentic, the characters memorable and their struggles played out with a complexity that respects the audience's intelligence." Publ Wkly

Griffin, Peni R.

The ghost sitter. Dutton Children's Bks. 2001 131p $14.99; pa $5.99

Grades: 4 5 6 7   **Fic**

1. Ghost stories
ISBN 0-525-46676-2; 0-14-230216-3 pa

LC 00-65859

When she realizes that her new house is haunted by the ghost of a ten-year-old girl who used to live there, Charlotte tries to help her find peace

"Griffin's book has several strong appeals: new best friends solving a mystery together, a just-scary-enough ghost girl, and a deathless bond between sisters that provides the book with its resoundingly satisfying conclusion and bang-up last sentence." Horn Book

Grimes, Nikki

★ **Bronx** masquerade. Dial Bks. 2002 167p $16.99; pa $5.99

Grades: 7 8 9 10   **Fic**

1. School stories 2. African Americans -- Fiction 3. Bronx (New York, N.Y.) -- Fiction
ISBN 0-8037-2569-8; 0-14-250189-1 pa

LC 00-31701

While studying the Harlem Renaissance, students at a Bronx high school read aloud poems they've written, revealing their innermost thoughts and fears to their formerly clueless classmates

"Funny and painful, awkward and abstract, the poems talk about race, abuse, parental love, neglect, death, and body image. . . . Readers will enjoy the lively, smart voices that talk bravely about real issues and secret fears. A fantastic choice for readers' theater." Booklist

Dark sons. Jump at the Sun 2005 216p $15.99

Grades: 6 7 8 9 10   **Fic**

1. Novels in verse 2. Stepfamilies -- Fiction 3. Father-son relationship -- Fiction
ISBN 0-7868-1888-3

LC 2004-54208

Alternating poems compare and contrast the conflicted feelings of Ishmael, son of the Biblical patriarch Abraham, and Sam, a teenager in New York City, as they try to come to terms with being abandoned by their fathers and with the love they feel for their younger stepbrothers.

"The simple words eloquently reveal what it's like to miss someone. . . . but even more moving is the struggle to forgive and the affection each boy feels for the baby that displaces him. The elemental connections and the hope . . . will speak to a wide audience." Booklist

A **girl** named Mister. Zondervan 2010 223p $15.99

Grades: 8 9 10 11   **Fic**

1. Saints 2. Novels in verse 3. Pregnancy -- Fiction 4. Christian life -- Fiction 5. African Americans -- Fiction
ISBN 978-0-310-72078-2; 0-310-72078-8

LC 2010-10830

A pregnant teenager finds support and forgiveness from God through a book of poetry presented from the Virgin Mary's perspective.

"Writing in lovely prose with lyrical, forthright language that avoids over-moralizing while driving home the big issues of teen pregnancy, award-winning Nikki Grimes just may help a few young women make different choices. At the same time, she effectively makes the case for parents and schools to continue to educate, educate, educate." Voice Youth Advocates

★ **Jazmin's** notebook. Dial Bks. 1998 102p $15.99

Grades: 6 7 8 9   **Fic**

1. Authorship -- Fiction 2. African Americans -- Fiction 3. Harlem (New York, N.Y.) -- Fiction
ISBN 0-8037-2224-9

LC 97-5850

A Coretta Scott King honor book for text, 1999

Jazmin, an Afro-American fourteen-year-old who lives with her older sister in a small Harlem apartment in the 1960s, finds strength in writing poetry and keeping a record of the events in her sometimes difficult life

"An articulate, admirable heroine, Jazmin leaps over life's hurdles with agility and integrity." Publ Wkly

★ **Planet** Middle School. Bloomsbury Childrens 2011 154p $15.99

Grades: 4 5 6 7   Fic
1. School stories 2. Novels in verse 3. Basketball -- Fiction 4. Friendship -- Fiction 5. Family life -- Fiction
ISBN 978-1-59990-284-5; 1-59990-284-2
LC 2010050744

A series of poems describes all the baffling changes at home and at school in twelve-year-old Joylin's transition from tomboy basketball player to not-quite-girly girl.

"In freeflowing free-verse poems, multi–awardwinning author and poet Grimes . . . explores the riot of hormones and expected gender roles that can make negotiating the preteen years such a challenge. . . . A work that should help adolescent readers find the courage and humor to grow into the individuals they already are." Kirkus

The **road** to Paris. G. P. Putnam's Sons 2006 153p $15.99; pa $6.99

Grades: 4 5 6 7   Fic
1. Siblings -- Fiction 2. Foster home care -- Fiction 3. Racially mixed people -- Fiction
ISBN 0-399-24537-5; 978-0-399-24537-4; 978-0-14-241082-0 pa; 0-14-241082-9 pa
LC 2005-28920

Inconsolable at being separated from her older brother, eight-year-old Paris is apprehensive about her new foster family but just as she learns to trust them, she faces a life-changing decision.

"In clear, short chapters, Grimes tells a beautiful story of family, friendship, and faith from the viewpoint of a child in search of home in a harsh world." Booklist

Grisham, John, 1955-

The **accused**; by John Grisham. 1st ed. Dutton Children's Books 2012 271 p. (hardcover) $16.99

Grades: 4 5 6 7   Fic
1. Legal stories 2. Stalking -- Fiction 3. Courts -- Fiction 4. Lawyers -- Fiction 5. Stealing -- Fiction
ISBN 0525425764; 9780525425762
LC 2012013972

In this book by John Grisham, "Theodore Boone is being stalked. His lawyer parents are involved in a high-profile case. On the last day of the trial, Theo discovers that his locker has been broken into. Later that day, one of his bike tires is slashed. . . . The 13-year-old becomes the main suspect after a local store is robbed and computers are found in his locker. With the help of his uncle, Theo uses his investigative skills to determine who is behind these crimes." (School Library Journal)

Theodore Boone: the abduction. Dutton Children's Books 2011 217p $16.99

Grades: 4 5 6 7   Fic
1. Lawyers -- Fiction 2. Kidnapping -- Fiction
ISBN 978-0-525-42557-1; 0-525-42557-8
LC 2011006060

When his best friend disappears from her bedroom in the middle of the night, thirteen-year-old Theo uses his legal knowledge and investigative skills to chase down the truth and save April.

"The book is smoothly written, and there's a mild tutorial on the criminal justice system." Publ Wkly

Theodore Boone: kid lawyer. Dutton Children's Books 2010 263p $16.99

Grades: 4 5 6 7   Fic
1. Mystery fiction 2. Lawyers -- Fiction
ISBN 0-525-42384-2; 978-0-525-42384-3

With two attorneys for parents, thirteen-year-old Theodore Boone knows more about the law than most lawyers do. But when a high profile murder trial comes to his small town and Theo gets pulled into it, it's up to this amateur attorney to save the day.

"Grisham serves up a dandy legal adventure that moves along quickly. Without intruding on the story's trajectory, he gives plenty of background about the legal process and explores various ethical questions." Horn Book Guide

Grossman, Nancy

A **world** away; Nancy Grossman. Hyperion 2012 394 p. $16.99

Grades: 7 8 9 10   Fic
1. Bildungsromans 2. Amish -- Fiction 3. Adolescence -- Fiction 4. Aunts -- Fiction 5. Self-realization -- Fiction
ISBN 1423151534; 9781423151531
LC 2011032890

This book is the story of 16-year-old Eliza, who "feels trapped by the conservative traditions of her Amish community. During her 'rumspringa,' a time when Amish teenagers are allowed to 'step out of the plain world,' she" works as "a nanny . . . . Eliza is thrilled with her new contemporary wardrobe and the modern conveniences available to her, but she didn't anticipate falling in love with a neighbor . . . or discovering secrets that will significantly change her view of her family." (Publishers Weekly)

Grove, S. E.

★ The **glass** sentence; S.E. Grove. Viking, an imprint of Penguin Group (USA) 2014 512 p. (Mapmakers) (hardcover) $17.99

Grades: 6 7 8 9 10   Fic
1. Historical fiction 2. Kidnapping -- Fiction 3. Fantasy 4. Maps -- Fiction
ISBN 0670785024; 9780670785025
LC 2013025832

In this young adult novel by S. E. Grove, part of The Mapmakers Trilogy, "Shadrack is kidnapped. And Sophia, who has rarely been outside of Boston, is the only one who can search for him. Together with Theo, a refugee from the West, she travels over rough terrain and uncharted ocean, encounters pirates and traders, and relies on a combination of Shadrack's maps, common sense, and her own slantwise powers of observation." (Publisher's note)

"In a world fractured into disparate eras during the Great Disruption, Sophia Tims is entrusted with the Tracing Glass (containing a memory thought to be the cause of the Disruption) when her uncle, the cartographer Shadrack Elli, is kidnapped. An intricate fantasy with a Gilded-Age feel, this solidly constructed quest features maps of all kinds and unusual steampunk-flavored elements." Horn Book

Guibord, Maurissa

★ **Warped**. Delacorte Press 2011 339p $16.99; lib bdg $19.99

Grades: 7 8 9 10   **Fic**

1. Magic -- Fiction 2. Tapestry -- Fiction 3. Time travel 4. Great Britain -- History -- 1485-1603, Tudors -- Fiction

ISBN 0-385-73891-9; 0-385-90758-3 lib bdg; 978-0-385-73891-0; 978-0-385-90758-3 lib bdg

LC 2009-53654

When seventeen-year-old Tessa Brody comes into possession of an ancient unicorn tapestry, she is thrust into sixteenth-century England, where her life is intertwined with that of a handsome nobleman. "Grades seven to ten." (Bull Cent Child Books)

"This has it all—fantasy, romance, witchcraft, life-threatening situations, detective work, chase scenes, and a smattering of violence. Imaginative and compelling, it's impossible to put down." SLJ

Gurevich, Margaret

Chloe by design; making the cut. by Margaret Gurevich; illustrated by Brooke Hagel. Capstone Young Readers, a Capstone imprint" 2014 384 p. (Chloe by design) (paper over board) $14.95

Grades: 5 6 7 8 9   **813.6**

1. Teenage girls -- Fiction 2. Fashion designers -- Fiction 3. Fashion design -- Fiction 4. Television game shows -- Fiction 5. Competition (Psychology) -- Fiction 6. Reality television programs -- Fiction

ISBN 1623701120; 9781623701123

LC 2013050317

In this novel by Margaret Gurevich "Chloe has always loved everything to do with fashion. And when she finds out a new reality series for aspiring teenage designers is holding auditions in her town, she's desperate to win a spot on the show. Chloe knows this is her chance. But before Chloe can realize her dreams, she has to survive the competition." (Publisher's note)

"Project Runway meets Mean Girls in this fashion-inspired first volume of the Chloe by Design series. Chloe Montgomery has always dreamed of becoming a fashion designer, so when her favorite reality show, Design Diva, offers up a teen version of the show, Chloe knows she has to audition—the show's wild challenges will push her creatively. She gets in, but can she overcome her shy instincts and handle criticism from both the judges and her fashion nemesis?...While the outcome is predictable, Chloe's journey (and the fashions that accompany it) make for an enjoyable, fluffy read. Perfect for readers obsessed with fashion, clothing design, and reality TV." Booklist

Another book about Chloe is:
Balancing act (2015)

Gurtler, Janet

I'm not her. Sourcebooks Fire 2011 288p pa $9.99

Grades: 7 8 9 10   **Fic**

1. Cancer -- Fiction 2. Sisters -- Fiction 3. Identity

(Psychology) -- Fiction

ISBN 978-1-4022-5636-3; 1-4022-5636-1

Brainy Tess Smith is the younger sibling of the beautiful, popular, volleyball-scholarship-bound Kristina. When Kristina is diagnosed with bone cancer, it drastically changes both sisters' lives.

"This quick and heartbreaking read realistically shows how one person's illness affects an entire community." SLJ

Gutman, Dan

Abner & me; a baseball card adventure. HarperCollins 2005 166p (Baseball card adventure) $16.99; lib bdg $17.89; pa $5.99

Grades: 4 5 6 7   **Fic**

1. Baseball -- Fiction 2. Gettysburg (Pa.), Battle of, 1863 -- Fiction 3. United States -- History -- 1861-1865, Civil War -- Fiction

ISBN 0-06-053443-5; 0-06-053444-3 lib bdg; 0-06-053445-1 pa

LC 2004-6315

With his ability to travel through time using baseball cards and photographs, thirteen-year-old Joe and his mother go back to 1863 to ask Abner Doubleday whether he invented baseball, but instead find themselves in the middle of the Battle of Gettysburg.

Babe & me; a baseball card adventure. Avon Bks. 2000 161p il (Baseball card adventure) $15.99

Grades: 4 5 6 7   **Fic**

1. Baseball players 2. Baseball -- Fiction

ISBN 0-380-97739-7

LC 99-36778

With their ability to travel through time using vintage baseball cards, Joe and his father have the opportunity to find out whether Babe Ruth really did call his shot when he hit that homerun in the third game of the 1932 World Series against the Chicago Cubs

"Readers will enjoy the action, the rich baseball lore, and the sense of adventure." Booklist

Honus & me; a baseball card adventure. Avon Bks. 1997 140p il (Baseball card adventure) $16.99; pa $5.99

Grades: 4 5 6 7   **Fic**

1. Baseball players 2. Baseball coaches 3. Baseball managers 4. Baseball -- Fiction

ISBN 0-380-97350-2; 0-380-78878-0 pa

LC 96-31439

Joey, who loves baseball but is not very good at it, finds a valuable 1909 Honus Wagner card and travels back in time to meet Honus

"This clever adventure will capture the hearts of anyone who has ever held a baseball bat in his or her hands. Gutman's voice rings true from start to finish." SLJ

Jackie & me; a baseball card adventure. Avon Bks. 1999 145p il (Baseball card adventure) $15.99; pa $5.99

Grades: 4 5 6 7   **Fic**

1. Baseball players 2. Army officers 3. Baseball --

Fiction
ISBN 0-380-97685-4; 0-380-80084-5 pa
LC 98-53347

With his ability to travel through time by using baseball cards, Joe goes back to 1947 to meet Jackie Robinson, turning into a black boy in the process

"Full of action, this title will spark history discussions and be a good choice for book reports and leisure reading." SLJ

Jim & me; a baseball card adventure. Harper-Collins Publishers 2008 195p (Baseball card adventure) $15.99; lib bdg $16.89

Grades: 4 5 6 7   Fic
1. Decathletes 2. Pentathletes 3. Olympic athletes 4. Baseball -- Fiction
ISBN 978-0-06-059494-7; 978-0-06-059495-4 lib bdg
LC 2007030703

Joe and his longtime enemy, Bobby Fuller, use a vintage baseball card to travel in time, hoping to stop Jim Thorpe from participating in the 1912 Olympics and losing his medals, but instead they watch Thorpe struggle during his first season with the New York Giants.

Mickey & me; a baseball card adventure. HarperCollins Pubs. 2003 152p il (Baseball card adventure) $15.99; pa $5.99

Grades: 4 5 6 7   Fic
1. Baseball players 2. Baseball -- Fiction
ISBN 0-06-029247-4; 0-06-029248-2 lib bdg; 0-06-447258-2 pa
LC 2002-5641

When Joe travels back in time to 1944, he meets the Milwaukee Chicks, one of the only all-female professional baseball teams in the history of the game

"Like the other books in the series, this one delivers a fast-moving plot, lots of action, and colorful depictions of famous sports heroes of the past." Booklist

The **million** dollar shot. Hyperion Bks. for Children 1997 114p hardcover o.p. pa $5.99

Grades: 4 5 6 7   Fic
1. Contests -- Fiction 2. Basketball -- Fiction
ISBN 0-7868-2275-9; 1-4231-0084-0 pa
LC 97-6461

Eleven-year-old Eddie gets a chance to win a million dollars by sinking a foul shot at the National Basketball Association finals

This "will appeal to both sports readers and general audiences. Gutman's subtle humor, exciting sports action, and excruciating suspense make this title an outstanding choice for reluctant readers." SLJ

Mission unstoppable. Harper 2011 293p (The genius files) $16.99; lib bdg $17.89

Grades: 5 6 7 8   Fic
1. Adventure fiction 2. Twins -- Fiction 3. Genius -- Fiction 4. Siblings -- Fiction 5. Family life -- Fiction
ISBN 0-06-182764-9; 0-06-182765-7 lib bdg; 978-0-06-182764-8; 978-0-06-182765-5 lib bdg
LC 2010-09390

On a cross-country vacation with their parents, twins Coke and Pepsi, soon to be thirteen, fend off strange assassins as they try to come to terms with their being part of a top-secret government organization known as The Genius Files.

"Gutman's novel offers a quirky look at Americana that will engage curious minds. . . . Those looking for a fun and suspenseful read . . . will not be disappointed." Booklist

Another title in this series is:
Never say genius (2012)

Never say genius. Harper 2012 (Genius files) $16.99; lib bdg $17.89

Grades: 5 6 7 8   Fic
1. Adventure fiction 2. Twins -- Fiction 3. Genius -- Fiction 4. Siblings -- Fiction 5. Family life -- Fiction
ISBN 978-0-06-182767-9; 0-0-6182767-3; 978-0-06-182768-6 lib bdg; 0-06-182768-1 lib bdg
LC 2011019363

As their cross-country journey with their parents continues through the midwest, twins Coke and Pepsi, now thirteen, again face strange assassins at such places as the first McDonald's restaurant and Cedar Point amusement park.

"The author brings his confused but resourceful youngsters to an explosive climax and a shocking revelation that guarantees further adventures on the road back to the left coast." Kirkus

Ray & me; a baseball card adventure. HarperCollinsPublishers 2009 173p (Baseball card adventure) $15.99

Grades: 4 5 6 7   Fic
1. Baseball players 2. Baseball -- Fiction
ISBN 978-0-06-123481-1; 0-06-123481-8; 978-0-06-123482-8 lib bdg
LC 2008019645

After recovering from being hit in the head during a baseball game, Stosh travels back in time to try to save Ray Chapman, a batter who was killed by a pitch in New York in 1920.

Roberto & me; a baseball card adventure. Harper 2010 180p (Baseball card adventure) $15.99; lib bdg $16.89

Grades: 4 5 6 7   Fic
1. Baseball players 2. Baseball -- Fiction
ISBN 978-0-06-123484-2; 0-06-123484-2; 978-0-06-123485-9 lib bdg; 0-06-123485-0 lib bdg
LC 2009014267

Stosh travels back to 1969 to try to prevent the untimely death of Roberto Clemente, a legendary baseball player and humanitarian, but upon his return to the present, he meets his own great-grandson who takes him into the future, and what he finds there is more shocking than anything he has encountered in his travels to the past.

"This series entry is both amusing and informative." Booklist

Satch & me; a baseball card adventure. HarperCollins 2006 175p (Baseball card adventures) $15.99; lib bdg $16.89

Grades: 4 5 6 7 **Fic**
1. Baseball players 2. Baseball -- Fiction
ISBN 978-0-06-059491-6; 0-06-059491-8; 978-0-06-059492-3 lib bdg; 0-06-059492-6 lib bdg
LC 2005005717

With his ability to travel through time using vintage baseball cards, Joe takes Flip with him to find out whether Satchel Paige really was the fastest pitcher ever.

"Enhancing the action-driven story are plenty of well-written baseball scenes, black-and-white photos, and the appearance of Negro League players Josh Gibson, Cool Papa Bell, and Buck ONeil." SLJ

Shoeless Joe & me; a baseball card adventure. HarperCollins Pubs. 2002 163p (Baseball card adventures) hardcover o.p. lib bdg $17.89; pa $5.99
Grades: 4 5 6 7 **Fic**
1. Baseball players 2. Baseball -- Fiction
ISBN 0-06-029253-9; 0-06-029254-7 lib bdg; 0-06-447259-0 pa
LC 2001-24638

Joe Stoshack travels back to 1919, where he meets Shoeless Joe Jackson and tries to prevent the fixing of the World Series in which Jackson was wrongly implicated

"Shoeless Joe is compelling, and Joe's adventures are exciting." Voice Youth Advocates

Other titles in the Baseball card adventures series are:
Abner & me (2005)
Babe & me (2000)
Honus & me (1997)
Jackie & me (1999)
Jim & me (2008)
Mickey & me (2003)
Ray & me (2009)
Roberto & me (2010)
Satch & me (2006)

Gwaltney, Doris

Homefront. Simon & Schuster Books for Young Readers 2006 310p $16.99; pa $6.99
Grades: 5 6 7 8 **Fic**
1. Virginia -- Fiction 2. Family life -- Fiction 3. World War, 1939-1945 -- Fiction
ISBN 0-689-86842-1; 1-4169-9572-2 pa
LC 2006-283492

"As Margaret Ann Motley looks forward to seventh grade, the only changes she sees on the horizon are her sister's leaving for college and, immediately afterwards, moving . . . into her sister's old room. With the U.S. on the brink of World War II, though, greater changes are in store. . . . Gwaltney provides vivid character portrayals. . . . Well grounded in the Tidewater area of Virginia, the novel's social context is made real." Booklist

Haber, Melissa Glenn

Dear Anjali. Aladdin 2010 282p $16.99
Grades: 5 6 7 8 **Fic**
1. Letters -- Fiction 2. Friendship -- Fiction 3. Bereavement -- Fiction
ISBN 978-1-4169-9599-9; 1-4169-9599-4

When her best friend dies at the age of thirteen, Meredith writes letters to her as she tries to endure her grief and other confusing emotions.

"Haber skillfully handles the child's heartache, her loneliness, and the conflicting desires. . . . By placing the story between the keys of Meredith's dad's old typewriter, the author gives the narrative a believable realism. . . . The realistic, not-too-tidy ending brings truth to this novel, underscoring that life is complicated." SLJ

Haddix, Margaret Peterson

The **always** war. Simon & Schuster Books for Young Readers 2011 197p $16.99
Grades: 7 8 9 10 **Fic**
1. War stories 2. Science fiction 3. Computers -- Fiction 4. Heroes and heroines -- Fiction 5. Post-traumatic stress disorder -- Fiction
ISBN 978-1-4169-9526-5; 1-4169-9526-9
LC 2010033344

In a war-torn future United States, fifteen-year-old Tessa, her childhood friend Gideon, now a traumatized military hero, and Dek, a streetwise orphan, enter enemy territory and discover the shocking truth about a war that began more than seventy-five years earlier.

"The short chapters with cliff-hanger endings and the action-packed plot make this book and excellent choice for reluctant readers." SLJ

★ **Among** the hidden. Simon & Schuster Bks. for Young Readers 1998 153p $16.95; pa $5.99
Grades: 5 6 7 8 **Fic**
1. Science fiction
ISBN 0-689-81700-2; 0-689-82475-0 pa
LC 97-33052

In a future where the Population Police enforce the law limiting a family to only two children, Luke has lived all his twelve years in isolation and fear on his family's farm, until another 'third' convinces him that the government is wrong

"The fully realized setting, honest characters, and fast paced plot combine for a suspenseful tale." ALAN

Other titles in this series are:
Among the Barons (2003)
Among the betrayed (2002)
Among the brave (2004)
Among the enemy (2005)
Among the free (2006)
Among the impostors (2001)

Caught; Book 5 Margaret Peterson Haddix. Simon & Schuster Books for Young Readers 2012 343 p. (The Missing) (hardcover : alk. paper) $16.99
Grades: 5 6 7 8 **Fic**
1. Science fiction 2. Time travel -- Fiction 3. Einstein, Albert, 1879-1955 -- Fiction 4. Space and time -- Fiction 5. Serbia -- History -- 1804-1918 -- Fiction 6. Switzerland -- History -- 20th century -- Fiction
ISBN 141698982X; 9781416989820; 9781442422889
LC 2011018654

In this fifth installment of Margaret Peterson Haddix's "Missing" series, "Jonah and Katherine are accustomed to traveling through time, but when learn they next have to return Albert Einstein's daughter to history, they think it's a joke -- they've only heard of his sons. But it turns out that Albert Einstein really did have a daughter, Lieserl, whose 1902 birth and subsequent disappearance was shrouded in mystery." (Publisher's note)

★ **Double** identity. Simon & Schuster Books for Young Readers 2005 218p $15.95

Grades: 5 6 7 8 **Fic**

1. Science fiction 2. Cloning -- Fiction

ISBN 0-689-87374-3

LC 2004-13448

Thirteen-year-old Bethany's parents have always been overprotective, but when they suddenly drop out of sight with no explanation, leaving her with an aunt she never knew existed, Bethany uncovers shocking secrets that make her question everything she thought she knew about herself and her family.

This is a "suspenseful sf novel guaranteed to keep readers riveted." Booklist

★ **Found**. Simon & Schuster Books for Young Readers 2008 314p (The missing) $15.99; pa $6.99

Grades: 5 6 7 8 9 **Fic**

1. Science fiction 2. Adoption -- Fiction

ISBN 978-1-4169-5417-0; 1-4169-5417-1; 978-1-4169-5421-7 pa; 1-4169-5421-X pa

LC 2007-23614

When thirteen-year-olds Jonah and Chip, who are both adopted, learn they were discovered on a plane that appeared out of nowhere, full of babies with no adults on board, they realize that they have uncovered a mystery involving time travel and two opposing forces, each trying to repair the fabric of time.

This is "a tantalizing opener to a new series. . . . Readers will be hard-pressed to wait for the next installment." Publ Wkly

Other titles in this series are:

Sent (2009)

Sabotaged (2010)

Torn (2011)

Full ride; Margaret Peterson Haddix. Simon & Schuster Books for Young Readers 2013 352 p. (hardcover) $16.99

Grades: 6 7 8 9 10 11 12 **Fic**

1. Scholarships -- Fiction 2. Family secrets -- Fiction 3. Ohio -- Fiction 4. Schools -- Fiction 5. Secrets -- Fiction 6. Criminals -- Fiction 7. High schools -- Fiction 8. Mothers and daughters -- Fiction

ISBN 1442442786; 9781442442788; 9781442442795; 9781442442801

LC 2012038146

In this book, by Margaret Peterson Haddix, "Becca's claim to fame is one she's been hiding from for the past three years: Her father is a notorious embezzler. . . . Three years after the trial and imprisonment that destroyed Becca's life, she and her mother have started over again and are living in a town where no one knows their secret. But as college--and its cost--looms large, Becca begins to wonder how they'll afford it. And how she can apply for financial aid without divulging her secret?" (Publisher's note)

"Her father in prison for embezzlement, fourteen-year-old Becca and her mother flee to an Ohio suburb to hide from the media and start new lives. Years later, a chain of events reveals layers of secrets behind Becca's father's crimes, his victims, and her mother's motivations. Haddix deftly emphasizes relatable issues: moving, losing faith in a parent, and falling out of economic comfort." (Horn Book)

Just Ella. Simon & Schuster Bks. for Young Readers 1999 185p hardcover o.p. pa $5.99

Grades: 7 8 9 10 **Fic**

1. Sex role -- Fiction 2. Princesses -- Fiction

ISBN 0-689-82186-7; 0-689-83128-5 pa

LC 98-8384

In this continuation of the Cinderella story, fifteen-year-old Ella finds that accepting Prince Charming's proposal ensnares her in a suffocating tangle of palace rules and royal etiquette, so she plots to escape.

"In lively prose, with well-developed characters, creative plot twists, wit, and drama, Haddix transforms the Cinderella tale into an insightful coming-of-age story." Booklist

Risked; Margaret Peterson Haddix. Simon & Schuster Books for Young Readers 2013 320 p. (The missing) (hardcover : alk. paper) $16.99

Grades: 5 6 7 8 9 **Fic**

1. Soviet Union -- History -- 1917-1921, Revolution -- Fiction 2. Science fiction 3. Time travel -- Fiction 4. Soviet Union -- History -- Revolution, 1917-1921 -- Fiction

ISBN 1416989846; 9781416989844; 9781442426474

LC 2012006770

In this book, by Margaret Peterson Haddix, "When Jonah and Katherine find themselves on a mission to return Alexei and Anastasia Romanov to history and then save them from the Russian Revolution, they are at a loss. Because in their own time, the bones of Alexei and Anastasia have been positively identified through DNA testing. What hope do they have of saving Alexis and Anastasia's lives when the twenty-first century has proof of their deaths?" (Publisher's note)

Sabotaged. Simon & Schuster Books for Young Readers 2010 377p (The missing) $16.99

Grades: 5 6 7 8 9 **Fic**

1. Science fiction 2. Colonists 3. Roanoke Island (N.C.) -- History -- Fiction

ISBN 978-1-4169-5424-8; 1-4169-5424-4

Sequel to: Sent (2009)

Time-travelers Jonah and Katherine are summoned to help another missing child from history, this time Virginia Dare from the Roanoke Colony, but their journey is sabotaged and goes dangerously awry, leaving them in the wrong time period. Includes author's note about the history of Roanoke Colony and Virginia Dare.

Sent. Simon & Schuster Books for Young Readers 2009 313p (The missing) $15.99; pa $6.99

Grades: 5 6 7 8 9 **Fic**

1. Science fiction 2. Kings 3. Time travel -- Fiction 4.

Great Britain -- Fiction

ISBN 978-1-4169-5422-4; 1-4169-5422-8; 978-1-4169-5423-1 pa; 1-4169-5423-6 pa

LC 2008-11552

Sequel to: Found (2008)

Jonah, Katherine, Chip, and Alex suddenly find themselves in 1483 at the Tower of London, where they discover that Chip and Alex are Prince Edward V and Richard of Shrewsbury, imprisoned by their uncle, King Richard III, but trying to repair history without knowing what is supposed to happen proves challenging. Author's note includes historical facts about the princes and king

"Haddix conveys quite a bit of real history painlessly to her target audience and even mixes in some physics. . . . Valuable fun for tweens." Kirkus

Followed by: Sabotaged (2010)

Torn. Simon & Schuster Books for Young Readers 2011 345p (The missing) $15.99

Grades: 5 6 7 8 **Fic**

1. Explorers 2. Science fiction 3. Time travel -- Fiction 4. Voyages and travels -- Fiction

ISBN 978-1-4169-8980-6; 1-4169-8980-3

LC 2010019645

Time travelers Jonah and Katherine arrive in 1611 to rescue missing child John Hudson, son of the explorer Henry Hudson, but just as the mutiny on the Discovery is supposed to start, Jonah and Katherine's knowledge of history is tested once again, and they fear that more is at stake than just one boy's life. Author's note includes facts about Henry Hudson's explorations.

"Hudson's ill-fated explorations provide an excellent opportunity for readers to learn about sailing ships, survival, and mutiny. Plenty of action and an extended author's note sustain this fourth entry in the Missing series." Booklist

★ **Uprising.** Simon & Schuster Books for Young Readers 2007 346p $16.99; pa $7.99

Grades: 6 7 8 9 10 **Fic**

1. Fires -- Fiction 2. Strikes -- Fiction 3. Triangle Shirtwaist Company, Inc. -- Fiction

ISBN 978-1-4169-1171-5; 1-4169-1171-5; 978-1-4169-1172-2 pa; 1-4169-1172-3 pa

LC 2006-34870

In 1927, at the urging of twenty-one-year-old Harriet, Mrs. Livingston reluctantly recalls her experiences at the Triangle Shirtwaist factory, including miserable working conditions that led to a strike, then the fire that took the lives of her two best friends, when Harriet, the boss's daughter, was only five years old. Includes historical notes.

"This deftly crafted historical novel unfolds dramatically with an absorbing story and well-drawn characters who readily evoke empathy and compassion." SLJ

Hagen, George

★ **Gabriel** Finley and the raven's riddle; George Hagen. Schwartz & Wade Books 2014 384 p. illustrations, maps (lib bdg) $19.99

Grades: 5 6 7 8 **Fic**

1. Fantasy fiction 2. Ravens -- Fiction 3. Magic -- Fiction 4. Missing persons -- Fiction 5. Voyages and travels -- Fiction 6. Adventure and adventurers --

Fiction

ISBN 9780385371049; 0385371047; 9780385371032

LC 2013032533

This fantasy by George Hagen follows the "twelve-year-old Gabriel [trying to] find his missing father, who seems to have vanished without a trace. . . . With the help of Paladin--a young raven with whom he has a magical bond that enables them to become one creature--he flies to the foreboding land of Aviopolis, where he must face a series of difficult challenges and unanswerable riddles that could lead to his . . . or to his death." (Publisher's note)

"The world-building and narrative tension are solid, fairly fresh, and rich, forgiving the obvious plot and slightly cardboard characters." Horn Book

Gabriel Finley and the raven's riddle

Hagerup, Klaus

Markus and the girls; translated by Tara Chace. Front Street 2009 208p $17.95

Grades: 6 7 8 9 **Fic**

1. School stories 2. Love -- Fiction 3. Norway -- Fiction

ISBN 978-1-59078-520-1; 1-59078-520-7

LC 2007048850

Sequel to: Markus and Diana (2006)

Only two months into his first year of junior high school, Markus has already fallen in love with all of the girls in his class.

"Hagerup's romp of Shakespearean comedic complexity is balanced by a healthy dose of slapstick." Horn Book Guide

Hahn, Mary Downing

★ The **ghost** of Crutchfield Hall. Clarion Books 2010 153p $17

Grades: 5 6 7 8 **Fic**

1. Ghost stories 2. Cousins -- Fiction 3. Orphans -- Fiction 4. Great Britain -- History -- 19th century -- Fiction

ISBN 978-0-547-38560-0; 0-547-38560-9

In the nineteenth century, ten-year-old Florence Crutchfield leaves a London orphanage to live with her great-uncle, great-aunt, and sickly cousin James, but she soon realizes the home has another resident, who means to do her and James harm.

"A deliciously spine-tingling tale that even the most reluctant readers will enjoy." SLJ

★ **Hear** the wind blow. Clarion Bks. 2003 212p $15

Grades: 5 6 7 8 **Fic**

1. Siblings -- Fiction 2. United States -- History -- 1861-1865, Civil War -- Fiction

ISBN 0-618-18190-3

LC 2002-15977

With their mother dead and their home burned, a thirteen-year-old boy and his little sister set out across Virginia in search of relatives during the final days of the Civil War

The author "gives readers an entertaining and thought-provoking combination: a strong adventure inextricably bound to a specific time and place, but one that resonates with universal themes." Horn Book

Mister Death's blue-eyed girls; Mary Downing Hahn. Clarion Books 2012 330 p. $16.99

Grades: 8 9 10 11 12 **Fic**

1. Mystery fiction 2. Historical fiction 3. Homicide -- Fiction 4. Grief -- Fiction 5. Murder -- Fiction 6. Coming of age -- Fiction 7. Baltimore (Md.) -- History -- 20th century -- Fiction

ISBN 0547760620; 9780547760629

LC 2011025950

In this work of historical fiction, "[t]he high-school year is almost over, there's a party in the park and Mister Death will soon be there, rifle in hand. . . . Two girls, Cheryl and Bobbi Jo, never make it to school the next day, their bloody bodies found in the park where they were shot. [Mary Downing] Hahn's . . . story traces the effects of a crime on everyone involved, including Buddy Novak, accused of a crime he didn't commit." (Kirkus Reviews)

Promises to the dead. Clarion Bks. 2000 202p hardcover o.p. pa $5.99

Grades: 5 6 7 8 **Fic**

1. Slavery -- Fiction 2. Maryland -- Fiction 3. United States -- History -- 1861-1865, Civil War -- Fiction

ISBN 0-395-96394-X; 0-547-25838-0 pa

LC 99-48525

Twelve-year-old Jesse leaves his home on Maryland's Eastern Shore to help a young runaway slave find a safe haven in the early days of the Civil War

"Hahn skillfully blends the language and customs of the Civil War era with an exciting plot." Voice Youth Advocates

★ **Stepping** on the cracks. Clarion Bks. 1991 216p $16; pa $6.99

Grades: 5 6 7 8 **Fic**

1. World War, 1939-1945 -- Fiction

ISBN 0-395-58507-4; 0-547-07660-6 pa

LC 91-7706

In 1944, while her brother is overseas fighting in World War II, eleven-year-old Margaret gets a new view of the school bully Gordy when she finds him hiding his own brother, an army deserter, and decides to help him

"Well-drawn characters and a satisfying plot. . . . There is plenty of action and page-turning suspense to please those who want a quick read, but there is much to ponder and reflect on as well." SLJ

★ **Wait** till Helen comes; a ghost story. Clarion Bks. 1986 184p $15; pa $5.95; pa $6.99

Grades: 4 5 6 **Fic**

1. Ghost stories 2. Stepchildren -- Fiction

ISBN 0-89919-453-2; 0-547-02864-4 pa; 9780380704422 pa

LC 86-2648

"Molly, the 12-year-old narrator, and her brother Michael dislike their bratty 5-year-old stepsister Heather and resent the family move to an isolated converted church in the country. The adjourning graveyard frightens Molly, but Heather seems drawn to it. Molly discovers that the ghost of a child (Helen) who died in a fire a century ago wants to lure Heather to her doom. Molly determines to save her stepsister. In so doing, she learns that Heather's strange behavior stems from her feelings of guilt at having accidentally caused her mother's death by playing near a stove and starting a fire. Eventually, Molly wrests Heather from Helen's arms as the ghost attempts to drown them. The girls discover the skeletons of Helen's parents, and their burial finally puts to rest Helen's spirit. . . . Grades four to seven." (SLJ)

"Intertwined with the ghost story is the question of Molly's moral imperative to save a child she truly dislikes. Though the emotional turnaround may be a bit quick for some, this still scores as a first-rate thriller." Booklist

Hahn, Rebecca

A **creature** of moonlight; Rebecca Hahn. Houghton Mifflin Harcourt 2014 224 p. $17.99

Grades: 7 8 9 10 11 12 **Fic**

1. Fantasy fiction 2. Dragons -- Fiction 3. Fantasy 4. Magic -- Fiction 5. Flowers -- Fiction 6. Identity -- Fiction 7. Princesses -- Fiction 8. Forests and forestry -- Fiction

ISBN 054410935X; 9780544109353

LC 2013020188

In this novel, by Rebecca Hahn, "as the only heir to the throne, Marni should have been surrounded by wealth and privilege, not living in exile--but now the time has come when she must choose between claiming her birthright as princess of a realm whose king wants her dead, and life with the father she has never known: a wild dragon who is sending his magical woods to capture her." (Publisher's note)

"Marni lives in a shack at the edge of the woods with her Gramps, where she tends flowers, as she's done for most of her life. Yet change is afoot... This book's greatest strength lies in the vivid woodland scenes and the rich detail that describes the mystical pieces of Marni's tale." (School Library Journal)

Haines, Kathryn Miller

★ The **girl** is murder. Roaring Brook Press 2011 352p $16.99

Grades: 7 8 9 10 **Fic**

1. Mystery fiction 2. Social classes -- Fiction 3. Missing persons -- Fiction 4. New York (N.Y.) -- Fiction 5. Father-daughter relationship -- Fiction

ISBN 978-1-59643-609-1; 1-59643-609-3

LC 2010-32935

In 1942 New York City, fifteen-year-old Iris grieves for her mother who committed suicide, and secretly helps her father with his detective business since he, having lost a leg at Pearl Harbor, struggles to make ends meet. "Grades six to ten." (Bull Cent Child Books)

This is "a smart offering that gives both mysteries and historical fiction a good name. . . . The mystery is solid, but what makes this such a standout is the cast. . . . The characters, young and old, leap off the pages." Booklist

The **girl** is trouble; Kathryn Miller Haines. Roaring Brook Press 2012 336p. $17.99

Grades: 6 7 8 **Fic**

1. Mystery fiction 2. Historical fiction 3. Women detectives -- Fiction

ISBN 9781596436107

LC 2011031806

This book is set in "the Fall of 1942 and Iris's world is rapidly changing. Her Pop is back from the war with a missing leg, limiting his ability to do the physically grueling part of his detective work. Iris is dying to help, especially when she discovers that one of Pop's cases involves a boy at her school. Now, instead of sitting at home watching Deanna Durbin movies, Iris is sneaking out of the house, double crossing her friends, and dancing at the Savoy till all hours of the night. There's certainly never a dull moment in the private eye business." (Publisher's note)

Halam, Ann

Snakehead. Wendy Lamb Books 2008 289p il map $16.99; lib bdg $19.99

Grades: 6 7 8 9 10   **Fic**

1. Gods and goddesses -- Fiction 2. Classical mythology -- Fiction 3. Medusa (Greek mythology) -- Fiction 4. Perseus (Greek mythology) -- Fiction

ISBN 978-0-375-84108-8; 978-0-375-94108-5 lib bdg

LC 2007-28318

Compelled by his father Zeus to accept the evil king Polydectes's challenge to bring the head of the monstrous Medusa to the Aegean island of Serifos, Perseus, although questioning the gods' interference in human lives, sets out, accompanied by his beloved Andromeda, a princess with her own harsh destiny to fulfill.

"Mythology buffs will appreciate the plethora of classical figures, while periodic references to contemporary culture (e.g., a band of rich, rowdy teens are dubbed the Yacht Club kids) and occasional slang drive the story home for the target audience without sacrificing its heroic dimensions." Publ Wkly

Hale, Marian

The **goodbye** season. Henry Holt and Co. 2009 271p $16.99

Grades: 7 8 9 10   **Fic**

1. Texas -- Fiction 2. Bereavement -- Fiction 3. Family life -- Fiction 4. Household employees -- Fiction 5. Mother-daughter relationship -- Fiction

ISBN 978-0-8050-8855-7; 0-8050-8855-5

LC 2008-50275

In Canton, Texas, seventeen-year-old Mercy's dreams of a different life than her mother's are postponed by harsh circumstances, including the influenza epidemic of 1918-19, which forces her into doing domestic work for a loving, if troubled, family.

This is a "compelling, tautly written novel." SLJ

The **truth** about sparrows. Henry Holt & Co. 2004 260p $16.95; pa $6.99

Grades: 5 6 7 8   **Fic**

1. Moving -- Fiction 2. Friendship -- Fiction 3. Great Depression, 1929-1939 -- Fiction

ISBN 0-8050-7584-4; 0-312-37133-0 pa

LC 2003-56981

Twelve-year-old Sadie promises that she will always be Wilma's best friend when their families leave drought-stricken Missouri in 1933, but once in Texas, Sadie learns that she must try to make a new home—and new friends, too

"Rich with social history, this first novel is informative, enjoyable, and evocative." SLJ

Hale, Shannon

★ **Book** of a thousand days; illustrations by James Noel Smith. Bloomsbury Children's Books 2007 305p il $17.95

Grades: 7 8 9 10   **Fic**

1. Love stories 2. Fantasy fiction

ISBN 978-1-59990-051-3; 1-59990-051-3

LC 2006-36999

Fifteen-year-old Dashti, sworn to obey her sixteen-year-old mistress, the Lady Saren, shares Saren's years of punishment locked in a tower, then brings her safely to the lands of her true love, where both must hide who they are as they work as kitchen maids.

This is a "captivating fantasy filled with romance, magic, and strong female characters." Booklist

The **Goose** girl. Bloomsbury Children's Books 2003 383p $17.95; pa $8.99

Grades: 6 7 8 9   **Fic**

1. Fairy tales 2. Princesses -- Fiction

ISBN 1-58234-843-X; 1-58234-990-8 pa

LC 2002-28336

On her way to marry a prince she's never met, Princess Anidori is betrayed by her guards and her lady-in-waiting and must become a goose girl to survive until she can reveal her true identity and reclaim the crown that is rightfully hers

"A fine adventure tale full of danger, suspense, surprising twists, and a satisfying conclusion." Booklist

Other titles in this series are:

Enna burning (2004)

River secrets (2006)

Forest born (2009)

Princess Academy; Palace of Stone. Shannon Hale. Bloomsbury 2012 321 p. (hardcover) $17.99

Grades: 5 6 7 8   **Fic**

1. Fantasy fiction 2. Princesses -- Fiction 3. Revolutions -- Fiction 4. Telepathy -- Fiction 5. Self-confidence -- Fiction 6. Kings, queens, rulers, etc. -- Fiction

ISBN 1599908735; 9781599908731

LC 2012003875

Author Shannon Hale's "sequel to 'Princess Academy' (2005) returns Miri and several of the girls from Mount Eskel to Asland to prepare for the wedding of Miri's best friend Britta to Prince Steffan. Times are dire: The people are destitute or starving, and the king . . . seems indifferent and distant. [Miri] uses not only rhetoric and ethics but the emotions of her people, which are held in the linder stone that comprises the palace, to hold the violence of the revolution in check." (Kirkus Reviews)

"A literary and engaging coming-of-age story, the elements of class tension, home, family, friendship, and self discovery ring true." VOYA

The **storybook** of legends; by Shannon Hale. Little Brown & Co 2013 320 p. (Ever After High) (hardback) $14.99

Grades: 4 5 6 7   **Fic**

1. Fairy tales 2. School stories 3. Schools -- Fiction 4. Friendship -- Fiction 5. Fairy tales -- Fiction 6. Boarding schools -- Fiction 7. Fate and fatalism --

Fiction 8. Characters in literature -- Fiction
ISBN 0316401226; 9780316401227

LC 2013024496

In this middle grades story by Shannon Hale, "At Ever After High, an enchanting boarding school, the children of fairytale legends prepare themselves to fulfill their destinies as the next generation of Snow Whites, Prince Charmings and Evil Queens . . . whether they want to or not. Each year on Legacy Day, students sign the Storybook of Legends to seal their scripted fates." (Publisher's note)

"Raven Queen and Apple White, the daughters of famous fairy-tale characters, begin their much-anticipated Legacy Year at Ever After High. They investigate the mystery of a lost story, and Raven realizes that being evil might not be her only path. Fans of the Inkheart and Sisters Grimm series will enjoy the "hexellent" fairy-tale-infused lingo and lively characters." Horn Book

Hall, C. Aubrey

Crystal bones. Marshall Cavendish Children's Books 2011 313p (The Faelin chronicles) $17.99
Grades: 7 8 9 10   Fic
1. Fantasy fiction 2. Fairies -- Fiction 3. Orphans -- Fiction
ISBN 0-7614-5828-X; 978-0-7614-5828-9

LC 2010015435

Suddenly and violently orphaned, Diello and his sister Cynthe learn secrets about their heritage when their parents' goblin enemies come searching for a powerful sword that has been kept hidden for many years.

"Though these are somewhat serious, heavy issues, the book has an underlying innocence that makes it amenable for a wide range of readers." Booklist

Hall, Teri

Away. Dial Books 2011 234 p. $16.99
Grades: 5 6 7 8   Fic
1. Science fiction 2. Resistance to government -- Fiction
ISBN 9780803735026; 0803735022

LC 2011001163

Sequel to: The Line (2010)

After helping heal Malgam, Rachel learns that her father is still living in the devastated territory of Away, captured by members of another clan who are planning to use him to make a deal with the government on the other side of the Line, and she joins the rescue party that must risk much to save him.

"This worthy sequel . . . continues to build a dystopian world rich with suspense and moral choices." Kirkus

The Line. Dial Books 2010 219p $16.99
Grades: 5 6 7 8   Fic
1. Science fiction
ISBN 978-0-8037-3466-1; 0-8037-3466-2

LC 2009-12301

Rachel thinks that she and her mother are safe working for Ms. Moore at her estate close to The Line, an invisible border of the Unified States, but when Rachel has an opportunity to Cross into the forbidden zone, she is both frightened and intrigued

This "sets readers up for a series about another world that might have come from situations too close to our own." Libr Media Connect

Followed by: Away (2011)

Halpern, Julie

Get well soon. Feiwel & Friends 2007 193p $16.95; pa $8.99
Grades: 7 8 9 10   Fic
1. Mental illness -- Fiction 2. Psychiatric hospitals -- Fiction
ISBN 0-312-36795-3; 978-0-312-36795-4; 0-312-58148-3 pa; 978-0-312-58148-0 pa

LC 2006-32358

When her parents confine her to a mental hospital, Anna, an overweight teenage girl who suffers from panic attacks, describes her experiences in a series of letters to a friend.

"Halpern creates a narrative that reflects the changes in Anna with each passing day that includes self-reflection and a good dose of humor." Voice Youth Advocates

Have a nice day; Julie Halpern. Feiwel and Friends 2012 325 p. $16.99
Grades: 7 8 9 10 11 12   Fic
1. Mental illness -- Fiction 2. Self-perception 3. Parent-child relationship -- Fiction
ISBN 0312606605; 9780312606602

In author Julie Halpern's book, "Anna Bloom has just come home from a three-week stay in a mental hospital. She feels...okay. It's time to get back to some sort of normal life, whatever that means. She has to go back to school, where teachers and friends are dying to know what happened to her, but are too afraid to ask. And Anna is dying to know what's going on back at the hospital with her crush, Justin, but is too afraid to ask. Meanwhile, Anna's parents are"t getting along, and she wonders if she's the cause of her family's troubles." (Publisher's note)

Halpin, Brendan

★ Shutout. Farrar, Straus and Giroux 2010 183p $16.99
Grades: 6 7 8 9   Fic
1. Soccer -- Fiction 2. Friendship -- Fiction
ISBN 978-0-374-36899-9; 0-374-36899-6

LC 2009-32972

Fourteen-year-old Amanda and her best friend Lena start high school looking forward to playing on the varsity soccer team, but when Lena makes varsity and Amanda only makes junior varsity, their long friendship rapidly changes.

"The dialogue is spot-on, and the characters are fully fleshed out. . . . While there is plenty of soccer action for fans of the sport, the book will also appeal to teens looking for a solid friendship story." SLJ

Hamilton, K. R.

★ Tyger tyger; by Kersten Hamilton. Clarion Books 2010 308p (Goblin wars) $17
Grades: 7 8 9 10   Fic
1. Fantasy fiction 2. Magic -- Fiction 3. Goblins -- Fiction 4. Irish Americans -- Fiction 5. Mentally

disabled children -- Fiction
ISBN 978-0-547-33008-2; 0-547-33008-1
LC 2010-01337

Soon after the mysterious and alluring Finn arrives at her family's home, sixteen-year-old Teagan Wylltson and her disabled brother are drawn into the battle Finn's family has fought since the thirteenth century, when Finn MacCumhaill angered the goblin king. "Grades eight to ten." (Bull Cent Child Books)

"Laced with humor, packed with surprises and driven by suspense, the plot grabs readers from the start using the stylistic tactics of the best fantasy writing. Major characters are beautifully drawn, and many of the secondary characters are equally distinct." Kirkus

Followed by: In the forests of the night (2011) and When the Stars Threw Down Their Spears (2013)

Hamilton, Kersten

In the forests of the night; Kersten Hamilton. Clarion Books 2011 295 p. $16.99
Grades: 7 8 9 10   **Fic**
1. Fantasy fiction 2. Goblins -- Fiction 3. Zoos -- Fiction 4. Magic -- Fiction 5. Finn MacCool -- Fiction 6. Irish Americans -- Fiction 7. Imaginary creatures -- Fiction 8. People with mental disabilities -- Fiction
ISBN 0547435606; 9780547435602
LC 2011009846

This book is the second in Kersten Hamilton's Goblin Wars series. Here, "Teagan and her friends must cope with the aftermath of escaping from the Dark Man's forces as well as new dangers. As she picks up the pieces of her life, Teagan begins a tentative relationship with goblin hunter Finn and struggles with her newly revealed goblin heritage." (School Library Journal)

"In her second book, high schooler Teagan (who found out in Tyger, Tyger that she's half-goblin) is back safely from Mag Mell. While she, her little brother Aiden, and love interest Finn Mac Cumhaill (Finn MacCool from Irish folklore) regroup at home in Chicago, wicked forces track them. Well-incorporated folklore elements blend nicely with everyday concerns (e.g., Teagan's post-high-school plans; best friend/boyfriend rivalry)." (Horn Book)

When the stars threw down their spears; by Kersten Hamilton. Clarion Books 2013 400 p. (hardback) $16.99
Grades: 7 8 9 10   **Fic**
1. Love stories 2. Magic -- Fiction 3. Goblins -- Fiction 4. Zoos -- Fiction 5. Horror & Ghost Stories 6. Finn MacCool -- Fiction 7. Chicago (Ill.) -- Fiction 8. Irish Americans -- Fiction 9. Imaginary creatures -- Fiction 10. People with mental disabilities -- Fiction
ISBN 0547739648; 9780547739649
LC 2012029195

In this novel by Kersten Hamilton "magical creatures are tumbling through mysterious portals from Mag Mell, the world-between-worlds, into the streets of Chicago. Meanwhile, the romance between seventeen-year-old Teagan, who is part goblin, and the alluring bad boy Finn Mac Cumhaill is heating up . . . . which is awkward, to say the least, considering he is bound by a family curse to fight goblins his entire life." (Publisher's note)

"In this third book, Teagan and her friends deal with the evil creatures seeping out of Mag Mell and into the streets of Chicago. Teagan and Finn work together to fight the darkness while their love continues to grow, even though it's now forbidden. Fans of fast-paced adventures and Irish folklore will find the two components nicely intertwined." (Horn Book)

Hamilton, Kiki

The **faerie** ring. Tor Teen 2011 343p $17.99
Grades: 7 8 9 10   **Fic**
1. Fantasy fiction 2. Fairies -- Fiction 3. Orphans -- Fiction 4. Thieves -- Fiction 5. London (England) -- Fiction 6. Great Britain -- History -- 19th century -- Fiction
ISBN 978-0-7653-2722-2; 0-7653-2722-8
LC 2011021577

"In 1871 London, a ragged girl pickpocket steals a ring that enforces a truce between the British Crown and the Faery world, setting off a struggle between the realms. . . . The story keeps suspense high with one crisis after another, until it escalates into a final exciting showdown." Kirkus

Hamilton, Virginia

★ The **house** of Dies Drear; illustrated by Eros Keith. Macmillan 1968 246p il hardcover o.p. pa $5.99
Grades: 5 6 7 8   **Fic**
1. Mystery fiction 2. Ohio -- Fiction 3. African Americans -- Fiction
ISBN 0-02-742500-2; 1-4169-1405-6 pa

"The answer to the mystery comes in a startling dramatic dénouement that is pure theater. This is gifted writing; the characterization is unforgettable, the plot imbued with mounting tension." Saturday Rev

Followed by The mystery of Drear House (1987)

★ The **planet** of Junior Brown. Macmillan 1971 210p hardcover o.p. pa $5.99
Grades: 6 7 8 9   **Fic**
1. Friendship -- Fiction 2. African Americans -- Fiction
ISBN 0-689-71721-0; 1-4169-1410-2 pa
A Newbery Medal honor book, 1972

"This is the story of a crucial week in the lives of two black, eighth-grade dropouts who have been spending their time with the school janitor. Each boy is presented as a distinct individual. Jr. is a three-hundred pound musical prodigy as neurotic as his overprotective mother. Buddy has learned to live by his wits in a world of homeless children. Buddy becomes Jr. Brown's protector and says to the other boys, 'We are together because we have to learn to live for each other.'" Read Ladders for Hum Relat. 6th edition

Hamley, Dennis

Without warning; Ellen's story 1914-1918. [by] Dennis Hamley. 1st U.S. ed.; Candlewick Press 2007 326p $17.99
Grades: 6 7 8 9   **Fic**
1. Great Britain -- Fiction 2. World War, 1914-1918 -- Fiction
ISBN 978-0-7636-3338-7; 0-7636-3338-0
LC 2007025248

First published 2006 in the United Kingdom with title: Ellen's people

During World War I, an English teenager leaves the safety of home and begins a journey of self-discovery that takes her close to the front lines to pursue her calling as a nurse.

"This intense narrative dramatically offers insight into the effects of World War I on the English home front. . . . This is a highly readable selection with many well-drawn characters." SLJ

Han, Jenny

Shug; [by] Jenny Han. 1st ed.; Simon & Schuster Books for Young Readers 2006 248p $14.95

Grades: 5 6 7 8   **Fic**

1. School stories 2. Family life -- Fiction
ISBN 978-1-4169-0942-2; 1-4169-0942-7

LC 2005009367

"Tall, freckled, gawky seventh-grader Annemarie Wilcox (whose family calls her Shug) has a beautiful, popular older sister; a gorgeous, alcoholic mother who doesn't fit in their small Georgia town; and a father who's always away on business. She also has a huge crush on Mark, the neighborhood boy who has always been her best friend. . . . Shug's direct, honest narration reveals a wholly believable, endearing, hot-tempered young woman who faces painful truths and survives." Booklist

★ The **summer** I turned pretty. Simon & Schuster Books for Young Readers 2009 276p $16.99

Grades: 7 8 9 10   **Fic**

1. Summer -- Fiction 2. Beaches -- Fiction 3. Vacations -- Fiction 4. Friendship -- Fiction
ISBN 978-1-4169-6823-8; 1-4169-6823-7

LC 2008-27070

Belly spends the summer she turns sixteen at the beach just like every other summer of her life, but this time things are very different.

"Romantic and heartbreakingly real. . . . The novel perfectly blends romance, family drama, and a coming-of-age tale, one that is substantially deeper than most." SLJ

Other titles in this series are:

It's not summer without you (2010)
We'll always have summer (2011)

Handler, Daniel, 1970-

★ **Why** we broke up; art by Maira Kalman. Little, Brown 2012 354p il $19.99

Grades: 8 9 10 11 12   **Fic**

1. Man-woman relationship -- Fiction 2. Breaking up (Interpersonal relations) 3. Letters -- Fiction 4. Dating (Social customs) -- Fiction
ISBN 978-0-316-12725-7

LC 2011009714

Printz Honor Book (2012)

Sixteen-year-old Min Green writes a letter to Ed Slaterton in which she breaks up with him, documenting their relationship and how items in the accompanying box, from bottle caps to a cookbook, foretell the end.

Hannan, Peter

My big mouth; 10 songs I wrote that almost got me killed. Scholastic Press 2011 235p il $16.99

Grades: 6 7 8 9   **Fic**

1. School stories 2. Bullies -- Fiction 3. Rock music -- Fiction 4. Bands (Music) -- Fiction
ISBN 978-0-545-16210-4; 0-545-16210-6

LC 2010034426

"Hannan's abundant cartoons set the tone for the misadventures of Davis Delaware, the new kid in ninth grade. Davis's attempts to blend in quickly land him on the wrong side of school bully Gerald 'the Butcher' when he forms a band with Gerald's cute girlfriend, Molly, and her dweeby friend, Edwin. . . . Hannan's edgy, exaggerated style suits the humor-driven narrative well. Give this to readers who enjoy light, entertaining realistic fiction." SLJ

Hannigan, Katherine

True (. . . sort of) Greenwillow Books 2011 360p $16.99; lib bdg $17.89

Grades: 4 5 6   **Fic**

1. School stories 2. Siblings -- Fiction 3. Friendship -- Fiction 4. Family life -- Fiction
ISBN 978-0-06-196873-0; 0-06-196873-0; 978-0-06-196874-7 lib bdg; 0-06-196874-9 lib bdg

For most of her eleven years, Delly has been in trouble without knowing why, until her little brother, R. B., and a strange, silent new friend, Ferris, help her find a way to be good—and happy—again.

"Told in carefully crafted language that begs to be read aloud, the story runs the gamut from laugh-out-loud funny to emotionally wrenching." SLJ

Hansen, Joyce

The **gift** -giver. Clarion Bks. 1980 118p pa $6.95

Grades: 4 5 6 7   **Fic**

1. School stories 2. Friendship -- Fiction 3. Foster home care -- Fiction 4. African Americans -- Fiction 5. Bronx (New York, N.Y.) -- Fiction
ISBN 0-618-61123-1

LC 80-12969

Doris tells the story of her friendship with Amir, a foster child in her Bronx neighborhood, and how it brings her into closer understanding with her family even though it divides her from her old friends.

This "has well-developed plot threads that are nicely knit, a memorable depiction of a person whose understanding and compassion are gifts to his friends, and a poignantly realistic ending." Bull Cent Child Books

Followed by: Yellow Bird and me

Home is with our family; [illustrated by] E. B. Lewis. Hyperion 2010 272p il (Black pioneers) $16.99

Grades: 4 5 6 7   **Fic**

1. Abolitionists -- Fiction 2. African Americans -- Fiction
ISBN 978-0-7868-5217-8; 0-7868-5217-8

Maria Peterson is looking forward to turning 13. She envisions new adult prestige and responsibility, like attending abolitionist meetings and listening to inspiring speakers like Sojourner Truth. However, she doesn't bank on all the unexpected changes that her 13th year brings.

"The plot flows quickly and has enough action to hold a reader's attention. Teachers can use this book to provide their students with a deeper understanding of the Fugitive Slave Act." Libr Media Connect

One true friend. Clarion Bks. 2001 154p hardcover o.p. pa $6.95

Grades: 4 5 6 7 **Fic**

1. Friendship -- Fiction 2. Foster home care -- Fiction 3. New York (State) -- Fiction 4. African Americans -- Fiction 5. Bronx (New York, N.Y.) -- Fiction

ISBN 0-395-84983-7; 0-618-60991-1 pa

LC 2001-28483

Fourteen-year-old orphan Amir, living in Syracuse, exchanges letters with his friend Doris, still living in their old Bronx neighborhood, in which they share their lives and give each other advice on friendship, family, foster care, and making decisions

"Both sad and hopeful, this story dramatizes the struggle for survival, the primal pull of family, and the gift of 'one true friend.'" Booklist

Other titles about Amir and Doris are:

The gift-giver (1980)

Yellow Bird and me (1985)

Yellow Bird and me. Clarion Bks. 1985 155p hardcover o.p. pa $6.95

Grades: 4 5 6 7 **Fic**

1. Dyslexia -- Fiction 2. Friendship -- Fiction 3. New York (State) -- Fiction 4. African Americans -- Fiction 5. Bronx (New York, N.Y.) -- Fiction

ISBN 0-89919-335-8; 0-618-61116-9 pa

LC 85-484

"Hansen's familiarity with reading problems and young people is evident in her credible characters and lively dialogue that rings true." SLJ

Hardinge, Frances

★ **Fly** by night. HarperCollinsPublishers 2006 487p hardcover o.p. lib bdg $17.89; pa $7.99

Grades: 5 6 7 8 **Fic**

1. Fantasy fiction

ISBN 978-0-06-087627-2; 0-06-087627-1; 978-0-06-087629-6 lib bdg; 0-06-087629-8 lib bdg; 978-0-06-087630-2 pa; 0-06-087630-1 pa

LC 2005-20598

Mosca Mye and her homicidal goose, Saracen, travel to the city of Mandelion on the heels of smooth-talking conman, Eponymous Clent.

"Through rich, colorful language and a sure sense of plot and pacing, Hardinge has created a distinctly imaginative world full of engaging characters, robust humor, and true suspense." SLJ

Followed by: Fly trap (2011)

Fly trap. Harper 2011 584p $16.99

Grades: 5 6 7 8 **Fic**

1. Fantasy fiction

ISBN 978-0-06-088044-6; 0-06-088044-9

LC 2010027755

Sequel to: Fly by night (2006)

Adventurous orphan Mosca Mye, her savage goose, Saracen, and their sometimes-loyal companion, Eponymous Clent, become embroiled in the intrigues of Toll, a town that changes entirely as day turns to night.

Crammed with eccentric, Dickensian characters, unexpected plot turns, and numerous very niche gods and goddesses . . . , Hardinge's world is rich enough to fuel two or three fantasy novels. It's a beautifully written tale, by turns humorous and heartbreaking and a sheer pleasure to read. Publ Wkly

★ The **lost** conspiracy. Harper 2009 568p $16.99; lib bdg $17.89

Grades: 6 7 8 9 10 **Fic**

1. Fantasy fiction 2. Sisters -- Fiction

ISBN 978-0-06-088041-5; 0-06-088041-4; 978-0-06-088042-2 lib bdg; 0-06-088042-2 lib bdg

LC 2008-45380

Published in the United Kingdom with title: Gullstruck Island

When a lie is exposed and their tribe turns against them, Hathin must find a way to save her sister Arilou—once considered the tribe's oracle—and herself.

"A deeply imaginative story, with nuanced characters, intricate plotting, and an amazingly original setting. . . . A perfectly pitched, hopeful ending caps off this standout adventure." Booklist

Hardy, Janice

The **shifter**. Balzer + Bray 2009 370p (The Healing Wars) $16.99; pa $7.99

Grades: 5 6 7 8 **Fic**

1. War stories 2. Fantasy fiction 3. Orphans -- Fiction 4. Sisters -- Fiction

ISBN 978-0-06-174704-5; 0-06-174704-1; 978-0-06-174708-3 pa; 0-06-174708-4 pa

LC 2008-47673

Nya is an orphan struggling for survival in a city crippled by war. She is also a Taker—with her touch, she can heal injuries, pulling pain from another person into her own body. But unlike her sister, Tali, and the other Takers who become Healers' League apprentices, Nya's skill is flawed: She can't push that pain into pynvium, the enchanted metal used to store it. All she can do is shift it into another person

"The ethical dilemmas raised . . . provide thoughtful discussion material and also make the story accessible to more than just fantasy readers." Booklist

Other titles in this series are:

Blue fire (2010)

Darkfall (2011)

Harland, Richard

Liberator; Richard Harland. 1st ed. Simon & Schuster Book for Young Readers 2012 487 p. maps (paperback) $9.99; (hardcover) $17.99

Grades: 6 7 8 9 10 **Fic**

1. Steampunk fiction 2. Revolutions -- Fiction 3. Social conflict -- Fiction 4. Fantasy 5. Social classes -- Fiction

ISBN 9781442423343; 1442423331; 9781442423336; 9781442423350

LC 2010050911

This is the "second of [Richard] Harland's steampunk series." Here, "[a]fter the Filthies revolted, Col Porpentine and his family were among the few swanks to stay aboard the juggernaut now called the 'Liberator.' But the new regime has troubles galore: A saboteur stalks the halls, an anti-Swank zealot joins the Revolutionary Council and people are disappearing. It's hard for Col to maintain a blossoming romance with revolutionary Filthy Riff in this atmosphere." (Kirkus Reviews)

Worldshaker. Simon & Schuster Books for Young Readers 2010 388p $16.99

Grades: 6 7 8 9 10 **Fic**

1. Fantasy fiction 2. Social classes -- Fiction
ISBN 978-1-4169-9552-4; 1-4169-9552-8

LC 2009-16924

Sixteen-year-old Col Porpentine is being groomed as the next Commander of Worldshaker, a juggernaut where elite families live on the upper decks while the Filthies toil below, but when he meets Riff, a Filthy girl on the run, he discovers how ignorant he is of his home and its residents.

"Harland's steampunk alternate history is filled with oppression, class struggle, and war, showing their devastation on a personal level through Col's privileged eyes. . . . The writing is sharp and the story fast-paced, demonstrating that, despite his elite status, Col may be just as trapped as any Filthy." Publ Wkly

Harlow, Joan Hiatt

The **watcher**; Joan Hiatt Harlow. Margaret K. McElderry Books 2014 290 p. (hardback) $16.99

Grades: K 5 6 7 **Fic**

1. Germany -- Fiction 2. Identity -- Fiction 3. Parental kidnapping -- Fiction 4. World War, 1939-1945 -- Fiction 5. Mother-daughter relationship -- Fiction 6. National socialism -- History -- Fiction 7. Nazis -- Fiction 8. Mothers and daughters -- Fiction 9. Germany -- History -- 1933-1945 -- Fiction 10. World War, 1939-1945 -- Germany -- Berlin -- Fiction 11. World War, 1939-1945 -- Underground movements -- Germany -- Fiction
ISBN 1442429119; 9781442429116; 9781442429123

LC 2014030259

"Wendy is kidnapped . . . by her own mother, who is actually a Nazi spy. As a new Berliner—and now a German—Wendy is expected to speak in a language she's never known and support a cause she doesn't believe in. There are allies, though, among the Germans. Allies who have been watching over Wendy since she arrived. And Wendy, along with her new German shepherd puppy, must confront them. If only she can find them." (Publisher's note)

"Harlow knows how to develop a story that will draw students in and keep their attention to the very end. The story combines adventure and suspense, with a heartwarming story of friendship and loyalty. The historical aspect also makes it well-suited to Social Studies classes covering World War II." Lib Med Con

Includes bibliographical references

Harmel, Kristin

When you wish; [by] Kristin Harmel. 1st ed.; Delacorte Press 2008 273p $15.99; lib bdg $18.99

Grades: 7 8 9 10 **Fic**

1. Fame -- Fiction 2. Florida -- Fiction 3. Singers -- Fiction 4. Father-daughter relationship -- Fiction 5. Mother-daughter relationship -- Fiction
ISBN 978-0-385-73475-2; 0-385-73475-1; 978-0-385-90474-2 lib bdg; 0-385-90474-6 lib bdg

LC 2007020472

When sixteen-year-old pop singing sensation Star Beck learns that her father, who left when she was three, has been writing to her for six years, she disguises herself, leaves her controlling mother and adoring fans behind, and goes to find him—and, perhaps, a normal life—in St. Petersburg, Florida.

"Harmel has created a character and a story that will have wide appeal. There is enough complexity to hold the interest of a more demanding reader, even while remaining basically an entertaining reading experience." KLIATT

Harness, Cheryl

Just for you to know. HarperCollins 2006 308p $16.99; lib bdg $17.89

Grades: 5 6 7 8 **Fic**

1. Death -- Fiction 2. Missouri -- Fiction 3. Family life -- Fiction
ISBN 0-06-078313-3; 0-06-078314-1 lib bdg

LC 2006-281855

In Independence, Missouri, in 1963, twelve-year-old Carmen already has her hands full dealing with a dreamy mother, a sometimes reckless father, and five noisy little brothers, but must find a way to hold onto her own dreams when tragedy strikes.

"Carmen's pain and loneliness are brought to life through her narrative. The writing flows nicely." SLJ

Harper, Charise Mericle

Alien encounter; Charise Mericle Harper. First edition Christy Ottaviano Books, Henry Holt & Company 2014 208 p. illustrations (Sasquatch and aliens) (hardback) $12.99

Grades: 3 4 5 6 **Fic**

1. Yeti -- Fiction 2. Friendship -- Fiction 3. Family life -- Fiction 4. Extraterrestrial beings -- Fiction 5. Humorous stories 6. Family life -- Northwest, Pacific -- Fiction
ISBN 0805096213; 9780805096217

LC 2013039906

This book, the first in Charise Mericle Harper's "Sasquatch and Aliens" series, "introduces a pair of nine-year-old boys who are propelled into an adventure that may or may not involve otherworldly creatures. Anxiety-prone Morgan first meets new kid Lewis as Lewis is hanging from a tree by his underwear. After Morgan reluctantly rescues Lewis (whose family just bought a creepy motel), a tentative friendship is born." (Publishers Weekly)

"With an authentic, zany splash of fourth-grade humor, perspective, and imagination, this inaugural series title targets boys and will captivate elementary readers...Like Grace in Harper's popular "Just Grace" series (Houghton Harcourt), Morgan is a spunky, verbal, resourceful protagonist whose nonstop adventures resonate with self-discovery, family relationships, friendships, and creative problem-solving.—" SLJ

Harper, Suzanne

The **Juliet** club. Greenwillow Books 2008 402p $17.99; lib bdg $18.89

Grades: 8 9 10 11 12 **Fic**

1. Poets 2. Authors 3. Dramatists 4. Italy -- Fiction 5. Letters -- Fiction

ISBN 978-0-06-136691-8; 0-06-136691-9; 978-0-06-136692-5 lib bdg; 0-06-136692-7 lib bdg

LC 2007-41315

When high school junior Kate wins an essay contest that sends her to Verona, Italy, to study Shakespeare's 'Romeo and Juliet' over the summer, she meets both American and Italian students and learns not just about Shakespeare, but also about star-crossed lovers—and herself.

"An amalgam of familiar Shakespearean plot elements, character names, and devices make up this delightful, light, and romantic read. . . . The chapter titles are each given act and scene designations to keep the structure of a play. Following the formula of a Shakespearean comedy, the novel ends with a grand ball where misunderstandings are resolved and couples are revealed in a magical evening." Voice Youth Advocates

The **secret** life of Sparrow Delaney. Greenwillow Books 2007 364p $16.99; lib bdg $17.89

Grades: 7 8 9 10 **Fic**

1. Family life -- Fiction 2. Spiritualism -- Fiction 3. New York (State) -- Fiction

ISBN 978-0-06-113158-5; 0-06-113158-X; 978-0-06-113159-2 lib bdg; 0-06-113159-8 lib bdg

LC 2006-41339

In Lily Dale, New York, a community dedicated to the religion of Spiritualism, tenth-grader Sparrow Delaney, the youngest daughter in an eccentric family of psychics, agonizes over whether or not to reveal her special abilities in order to help a friend.

"For all of the imagination the author displays in inventing a spirit world, she shows equal skill in probing the nuances of tender emotions, too." Publ Wkly

Harrington, Karen

Courage for beginners; by Karen Harrington. Little, Brown and Co. 2014 304 p. (hardcover) $17

Grades: 4 5 6 7 8 **Fic**

1. Texas -- Fiction 2. Friendship -- Fiction 3. Schools -- Fiction 4. Agoraphobia -- Fiction 5. Middle schools -- Fiction 6. Family problems -- Fiction

ISBN 031621048X; 9780316210485

LC 2013021596

Sequel to: Sure Signs of Crazy (2013)

"Twelve-year-old Mysti Murphy wishes she were a character in a book. If her life were fictional, she'd magically know how to deal with the fact that her best friend, Anibal Gomez, has abandoned her in favor of being a 'hipster.' She'd be able to take care of everyone when her dad has to spend time in the hospital. And she'd certainly be able to change her family's secret." (Publisher's note)

"Mysti's curatorial narration--as if she were describing paintings or book characters--works on multiple levels, showing off her snark and emphasizing her mother's sheltered influence. Her mother is flawed but sympathetic; she knows her fears are disproportionate, but their debilitating

effect is real. With gallows humor and believable small victories, this unusual novel is a window into making friends and facing fears." Kirkus

Sure signs of crazy; by Karen Harrington. 1st ed. Little Brown & Co 2013 288 p. (hardcover) $17

Grades: 4 5 6 7 8 **Fic**

1. Adolescence -- Fiction 2. Parent-child relationship -- Fiction 3. Texas -- Fiction 4. Coming of age -- Fiction 5. Mental illness -- Fiction 6. Family problems -- Fiction

ISBN 0316210587; 9780316210584

LC 2012030683

Parents' Choice: Silver Medal Fiction (2013)

In this book, "worried that she will grow up to be crazy like her mother or alcoholic like her father, rising seventh-grader Sarah Nelson takes courage from Harper Lee's 'To Kill a Mockingbird,' writing letters to Atticus Finch and discovering her own strengths. . . . She describes the events of the summer she turns 12, gets her period, develops a crush on a neighbor and fellow word lover, and comes to terms with her parents' failings." (Kirkus Reviews)

Harris, Joanne

Runemarks. Alfred A. Knopf 2008 526p map $18.99; lib bdg $21.99

Grades: 7 8 9 10 11 12 **Fic**

1. Fantasy fiction 2. Magic -- Fiction 3. Norse mythology -- Fiction

ISBN 978-0-375-84444-7; 978-0-375-94444-4 lib bdg; 0-375-84444-9; 0-375-94444-3 lib bdg

LC 2007-28928

Maddy Smith, who bears the mysterious mark of a rune on her hand, learns that she is destined to join the gods of Norse mythology and play a role in the fate of the world.

"Harris demonstrates a knack for moving seamlessly between the serious and comic. . . . She creates a glorious and complex world replete with rune-based magic spells, bickering gods, exciting adventures, and difficult moral issues." Publ Wkly

Harris, Lewis

A **taste** for red. Clarion Books 2009 169p $16

Grades: 4 5 6 **Fic**

1. Vampires -- Fiction 2. Friendship -- Fiction 3. Missing children -- Fiction

ISBN 978-0-547-14462-7; 0-547-14462-8

LC 2008-25318

When some of her classmates disappear, sixth-grader Svetlana, along with her new friends go in search of the missing students using her newfound ability as an Olfactive, one who has heightened smell, hearing, and the ability to detect vampires.

"Svetlana comes across as a strong character. . . . Her first-person narrative is fast-paced and witty, and her mild scorn for everything she encounters at school will appeal to angst-ridden tweens. Sure to be a crowd-pleaser." SLJ

Harris, Teresa E.

The **perfect** place; Teresa E. Harris. Clarion Books 2014 272 p. (hardcover) $16.99

Grades: 5 6 7 8 **Fic**

1. Aunts -- Fiction 2. Family life -- Fiction 3. African Americans -- Fiction 4. Home -- Fiction 5. Virginia -- Fiction 6. Great-aunts -- Fiction 7. Segregation -- Fiction 8. Moving, Household -- Fiction 9. Family life -- Virginia -- Fiction

ISBN 0547255195; 9780547255194

LC 2013036214

In this book, "12-year-old Treasure is tired of moving from place to place every time her unreliable father leaves the family. At the opening of the novel, Treasure's father is gone and her mother leaves her and her younger sister, Tiffany, with their Great-Aunt Grace in the small town of Black Lake, Virginia. Treasure does not want to be there, and her introduction to her no-nonsense relative only strengthens her resolve to stay detached during her mother's absence." (School Library Journal)

"Two months after 12-year-old Treasure's dad left without further word, her mom decides to search for him, and she takes Treasure and her younger sister to stay with their cantankerous Great-Aunt Grace in Black Lake, Virginia... Readers will find sly humor here as well as the pleasure of seeing justice done on several levels. A satisfying first novel with a realistic but heartening ending." Booklist

Harrison, Cora

I was Jane Austen's best friend; illustrated by Susan Hellard. Delacorte Press 2010 342p il $17.99; lib bdg $20.99

Grades: 7 8 9 10 **Fic**

1. Authors 2. Novelists 3. Cousins -- Fiction 4. Diaries -- Fiction 5. Friendship -- Fiction 6. Great Britain -- History -- 1714-1837 -- Fiction

ISBN 0-385-73940-0; 0-385-90787-7 lib bdg; 978-0-385-73940-5; 978-0-385-90787-3 lib bdg

LC 2010-15309

In a series of journal entries, Jenny Cooper describes her stay with cousin Jane Austen in the 1790s. (Bull Cent Child Books)

"This is a lovely, simple coming-of-age story with a strong historical setting. . . . The situations and locations are unmistakable and will be pleasingly familiar to readers of Austen's works." Voice of Youth Advocates

Harrison, Michelle

13 curses. Little, Brown 2011 486p (13 Treasures Trilogy) $15.99; pa $6.99

Grades: 5 6 7 8 **Fic**

1. Magic -- Fiction 2. Fairies -- Fiction 3. Orphans -- Fiction 4. Kidnapping -- Fiction

ISBN 978-0-316-04150-8; 0-316-04150-5; 978-0316041492 pa

Sequel to: 13 treasures (2010)

When fairies steal her brother, thirteen-year-old Rowan Fox promises that in exchange for his return she will find the thirteen charms that the fairies have enchanted and hidden in the human world.

"The sure-handed storytelling creates a completely credible setting—by turns violent and tender, sinister and poignant. . . . Contrasts between human emotion and commitment and the cold, often cruel magic and mischief of the fairy realm create terrific tension and afford opportunities for heroism for the young protagonists." Kirkus

★ **13** treasures. Little, Brown Books for Young Readers 2010 355p il $15.99

Grades: 5 6 7 8 **Fic**

1. Mystery fiction 2. Fairies -- Fiction 3. Grandmothers -- Fiction 4. Great Britain -- Fiction

ISBN 978-0-316-04148-5; 0-316-04148-3

LC 2008-45511

Bedeviled by evil fairies that only she can see, thirteen-year-old Tanya is sent to stay with her cold and distant grandmother at Elvesden Manor, where she and the caretaker's son solve a disturbing mystery that leads them to the discovery that Tanya's life is in danger.

"Harrison writes with great assuredness, creating a seductive setting and memorable, fully developed characters. . . . . It's an excellent choice for fans of the Spiderwick Chronicles and other modern-day fairy tales." Publ Wkly

Followed by: 13 curses (2011)

Harrison, Troon

The **horse** road; by Troon Harrison. Bloomsbury 2012 320 p. (alk. paper) $16.99

Grades: 4 5 6 7 **Fic**

1. Horses -- Fiction 2. Historical fiction 3. Horsemanship -- Fiction 4. Central Asia -- History -- Fiction 5. Fergana Valley -- History -- Fiction

ISBN 1599908468; 9781599908465

LC 2012014010

This book is "the first of a projected trio of horse-centered historical novels. . . . Kalli, shy and stammering everywhere but on a horse, begins to prove herself when she and her friend Batu catch a glimpse over a mountainside of thousands of Middle Kingdom warriors preparing to attack their town. . . . When her own mare, Swan, is stolen, she dons armor and weapons and rides to the rescue. In the end, she wins Swan not in battle, but through shrewd bargaining." (Kirkus Reviews)

"Densely descriptive prose, rife with historical and equine detail for horse-fiction fans, vividly portrays aspects of daily life and culture." Booklist

Harrold, A. F.

The **imaginary**; by A.F. Harrold; illustrations by Emily Gravett. Bloomsbury 2015 224 p. illustrations (some color) (hardcover) $16.99

Grades: 4 5 6 7 8 **Fic**

1. Friendship -- Fiction 2. Supernatural -- Fiction 3. Adventure and adventurers 4. Imaginary playmates -- Fiction 5. Mother-daughter relationship -- Fiction 6. Best friends -- Fiction 7. Mothers and daughters -- Fiction 8. Adventure and adventurers -- Fiction

ISBN 0802738117; 9780802738110; 9781619636965

LC 2014016677

"Rudger is Amanda Shuffleup's imaginary friend. Nobody else can see Rudger-until the evil Mr. Bunting arrives at Amanda's door. Mr. Bunting hunts imaginaries. Rumor has it that he even eats them. And now he's found Rudger. Soon Rudger is alone, and running for his imaginary life. He needs to find Amanda before Mr. Bunting catches him-and before Amanda forgets him and he fades away to nothing." (Publisher's note)

"This inventive mix of humor and suspense starts with the amusing appearance of Amanda's imaginary friend, Rudger. Their summer of make-believe adventures quickly darkens, though, when Mr. Bunting shows up. He's a grown-up who can not only see "Imaginaries" like Rudger, but also eats them to prolong his own life. . . . A great choice for readers who like fantastic tales with a dose of true scariness." SLJ

Hart, Alison

Gabriel's horses; by Alison Hart. 1st ed.; Peachtree 2007 161p (Racing to freedom) $14.95
Grades: 6 7 8 9 **Fic**
1. Slavery -- Fiction 2. Kentucky -- Fiction 3. Horse racing -- Fiction 4. African Americans -- Fiction 5. United States -- History -- 1861-1865, Civil War -- Fiction
ISBN 978-1-56145-398-6; 1-56145-398-6
LC 2006027697

In Kentucky, during the Civil War, the twelve-year-old slave Gabriel, contends with a cruel new horse trainer and skirmishes with Confederate soldiers as he pursues his dream of becoming a jockey.

"The author grounds this fast-paced tale in historical fact by providing a nonfiction epilogue. Readers will find this wonderful blend of history and horses appealing." SLJ

Another title in this series is:
Gabriel's triumph (2007)

Gabriel's triumph; by Alison Hart. 1st ed.; Peachtree 2007 164p (Racing to freedom) $14.95
Grades: 6 7 8 9 **Fic**
1. Kentucky -- Fiction 2. Horse racing -- Fiction 3. African Americans -- Fiction 4. United States -- History -- 1861-1865, Civil War -- Fiction
ISBN 978-1-56145-410-5
LC 2007001430

Sequel to: Gabriel's horses (2007)

A thirteen-year-old newly-freed slave faces the challenges of freedom and horse racing as he pursues his dream of becoming a famous jockey in Civil War Kentucky and New York.

"Thrilling horse racing once again frames a stirring Civil War story." Booklist

Hartinger, Brent

Project Sweet Life. HarperTeen 2009 282p $16.99
Grades: 6 7 8 9 **Fic**
1. Friendship -- Fiction 2. Summer employment -- Fiction 3. Washington (State) -- Fiction
ISBN 978-0-06-082411-2; 0-06-082411-5
LC 2008-19644

When their fathers insist that they get summer jobs, three fifteen-year-old friends in Tacoma, Washington, dedicate their summer vacation to fooling their parents into thinking that they are working, which proves to be even harder than having real jobs would have been.

This "will keep readers laughing and engaged." SLJ

Hartman, Rachel

★ **Seraphina**; a novel. by Rachel Hartman. Random House 2012 465 p. (hardcover) $17.99
Grades: 7 8 9 10•11 12 **Fic**
1. Fantasy fiction 2. Dragons -- Fiction 3. Kings and rulers -- Fiction 4. Fantasy 5. Music -- Fiction 6. Secrets -- Fiction 7. Identity -- Fiction 8. Courts and courtiers -- Fiction 9. Self-actualization (Psychology) -- Fiction
ISBN 9780375866562; 9780375896583; 9780375966569; 0375866566
LC 2011003015

William C. Morris Award (2013)
Boston Globe-Horn Book Honor: Fiction (2013).

In this book, "[a]fter 40 years of peace between human and dragon kingdoms, their much-maligned treaty is on the verge of collapse. Tensions are already high with an influx of dragons, reluctantly shifted to human forms, arriving for their ruler Ardmagar Comonot's anniversary. But when Prince Rufus is found murdered in the fashion of dragons--that is, his head has been bitten off--things reach a fever pitch." (Booklist)

Followed by: Shadow Scale (2015)

Hartnett, Sonya, 1968-

★ **Butterfly**. Candlewick Press 2010 232p $16.99
Grades: 7 8 9 10 11 12 **Fic**
1. Australia -- Fiction 2. Family life -- Fiction
ISBN 0-7636-4760-8; 978-0-7636-4760-5
LC 2009046549

In 1980s Australia, nearly fourteen-year-old Ariella "Plum" Coyle fears the disapproval of her friends, feels inferior to her older brothers, and hates her awkward, adolescent body but when her glamorous neighbor befriends her, Plum starts to become what she wants to be—until she discovers her neighbor's ulterior motive.

"The deliberate pacing, insight into teen angst, and masterful word choice make this a captivating read to savor." SLJ

★ The **children** of the King; Sonya Hartnett. 1st U.S. edition Penguin Books (Australia) 2012 265 p. ill. $16.99
Grades: 5 6 7 8 **Fic**
1. Historical fiction 2. Friendship -- Fiction 3. World War, 1939-1945 -- Great Britain -- Fiction 4. World War, 1939-1945 -- Evacuation of civilians -- Fiction 5. England -- Fiction 6. World War, 1939-1945 -- Children -- Great Britain -- Fiction 7. World War, 1939-1945 -- Evacuation of civilians -- England -- Fiction
ISBN 0763667358; 9780670076130; 9780763667351
LC 2013414845

This book, by Sonya Hartnett, "takes place in England during World War II. . . . Siblings Cecily and Jeremy, along with their mother Heloise, are sent to the northern countryside to live with Heloise's brother, Peregrine Lockwood, in mysterious Heron Hall. . . . The family winds up taking in May Bright, a 10-year-old refugee from London. The two girls become fast friends and . . . come across two boys in the ruins of a nearby castle." (School Library Journal)

"Twelve-year-old Cecily, her older brother Jeremy, and their mother flee WWII London for the safety of Uncle Peregrine's country manor. Once there, Cecily discovers two boys hiding in some nearby ruins. Hartnett's gift for language deftly conveys both the sublime and the mundane in life. She grounds the book's fantasy elements with a heartfelt examination of the hardships endured by civilians in wartime." Horn Book

What the birds see. Candlewick Press 2003 196p $15.99

Grades: 7 8 9 10   **Fic**
1. Missing children -- Fiction
ISBN 0-7636-2092-0

                        LC 2002-73717

While the residents of his town concern themselves with the disappearance of three children, a lonely, rejected nine-year-old boy worries that he may inherit his mother's insanity.

"Tightly composed and ripe with symbolism, this complex book will offer opportunities for rich discussion." SLJ

Hartry, Nancy

Watching Jimmy. Tundra Books 2009 152p $16.95

Grades: 5 6 7 8   **Fic**
1. Child abuse -- Fiction 2. Brain -- Wounds and injuries -- Fiction
ISBN 0-88776-871-7; 978-0-88776-871-2

This story takes place in Canadia in 1958. Eleven-year-old Carolyn walks an emotional tightrope knowing what really happened to her best friend, Jimmy, the day his Uncle Ted chose to teach him a lesson that left Jimmy brain-damaged. But when Uncle Ted threatens his beleaguered family with even more abuse and the loss of their home, Carolyn must find the courage to match wits with him and to speak out, using the truth as her only weapon. "Age nine and up." (Quill Quire)

"Like a steady beat that pulses louder and louder, the story unfolds against a backdrop of postwar social and political concerns and Remembrance Day. Carolyn is a passionate and feisty character, delineated with love and precision, and readers will be drawn to her. A compelling and satisfying novel." SLJ

Harvey, Alyxandra

Haunting Violet. Walker Books for Young Readers 2011 352p $17.99

Grades: 7 8 9 10   **Fic**
1. Ghost stories 2. Mystery fiction 3. Spiritualism -- Fiction 4. Social classes -- Fiction 5. Great Britain -- History -- 19th century -- Fiction
ISBN 978-0-8027-9839-8; 0-8027-9839-X

                        LC 2010-31077

Sixteen-year-old Violet Willoughby has been part of her mother's Spiritualist scam since she was nine, but during an 1872 house party in Hampshire, England, she is horrified to learn that she can actually see ghosts, one of whom wants Violet to solve her murder.

"A well-paced, clever and scary supernatural-suspense story." Kirkus

Hearts at stake. Walker & Co. 2010 248p (The Drake chronicles) $16.99; pa $9.99

Grades: 8 9 10 11 12   **Fic**
1. Siblings -- Fiction 2. Vampires -- Fiction 3. Friendship -- Fiction
ISBN 978-0-8027-9840-4; 0-8027-9840-3; 978-0-8027-2074-0 pa; 0-8027-2074-9 pa

                        LC 2009-23156

As her momentous sixteenth birthday approaches, Solange Drake, the only born female vampire in 900 years, is protected by her large family of brothers and her human best friend Lucy from increasingly persistent attempts on her life by the powerful vampire queen and her followers.

"Witty, sly, and never disappointing." Booklist
Other titles in this series are:
Blood feud (2010)
Out for blood (2011)

Harvey, Sarah N.

Death benefits. Orca Book Publishers 2010 212p pa $12.95

Grades: 7 8 9 10   **Fic**
1. Old age -- Fiction 2. Grandfathers -- Fiction
ISBN 978-1-55469-226-2 pa; 1-55469-226-1 pa

Royce is pressed into service as a caregiver for his ninety-five-year-old grandfather and gradually comes to appreciate the cantankerous old man.

"Harvey's writing is energetic, and Royce's snarky narration is sure to keep readers' attention." Publ Wkly

Haskell, Merrie

Handbook for dragon slayers; Merrie Haskell. 1st ed. HarperCollins 2013 336 p. (hardcover) $16.99

Grades: 6 7 8   **Fic**
1. Fantasy fiction 2. Fairy tales 3. Dragons -- Fiction 4. Authorship -- Fiction 5. Princesses -- Fiction 6. Books and reading -- Fiction 7. People with disabilities -- Fiction 8. Adventure and adventurers -- Fiction
ISBN 0062008161; 9780062008169

                        LC 2012022159

Schneider Family Book Awards: Middle School (2014)

In this juvenile fantasy story, by Merrie Haskell, "political upheaval sends Princess Tilda fleeing from her kingdom in the company of two hopeful dragon slayers. The princess never had any interest in chasing dragons. . . . But the princess finds herself making friends with magical horses, facing the Wild Hunt, and pointing a sword at the fire-breathing creatures. While doing things she never imagined, Tilda finds qualities in herself she never knew she possessed." (Publisher's note)

The princess curse. Harper 2011 325p $16.99

Grades: 4 5 6 7   **Fic**
1. Fairy tales 2. Magic -- Fiction 3. Princesses -- Fiction
ISBN 978-0-06-200813-8; 0-06-200813-7

                        LC 2010040424

"Author Haskell has her way with the story of 'The Twelve Dancing Princesses,' incorporating references to other myths and legends and adding many twists of her own, not least of which is making the royals' attempted rescuer a strong-willed, 13-year-old apprentice herbalist, Reveka. . . . When Vasile offers the hand of any of his daughters in marriage to anyone who banishes the curse (or a 'fabulous dowry' if the curse-breaker is female), Reveka is determined to win the reward. . . . With a good sense of humor, an able and empowered protagonist, and a highly original take on this tale, Haskell's story gives readers much to enjoy." Publ Wkly

Hatfield, Ruth

The **Book** of Storms; Ruth Hatfield. Henry Holt & Co 2014 368 p. $16.99

Grades: 5 6 7 8   **Fic**

1. Missing persons 2. Adventure fiction 3. Storms -- Fiction 4. Supernatural -- Fiction 5. Missing persons -- Fiction 6. Adventure and adventurers -- Fiction 7. Human-animal communication -- Fiction
ISBN 0805099980; 9780805099980

           LC 2014029352

In this juvenile novel, by Ruth Hatfield, illustrated by Greg Call, when "Danny O'Neill . . . wakes the morning after a storm to find his house empty, his parents gone, and himself able to hear the thoughts of a dying tree, he has no choice but to set out to find answers. He soon learns that the enigmatic Book of Storms holds the key to what he seeks . . . but unraveling its mysteries won't be easy." (Publisher's note)

"This debut novel is an entertaining fantasy adventure set across a modern European landscape. The book follows 11-year-old Danny O'Neill as he struggles to piece together the seemingly incomprehensible details left behind by a devastating storm. The quest takes him deep within himself where he must find courage that he never knew he possessed...Not only does Hatfield take readers inside the thoughts and minds of all sorts of flora and fauna, but she uses their observable traits to guide their humanistic presence in very believable ways." SLJ

Hathaway, Barbara

Letters to Missy Violet. Houghton Mifflin 2012 157p $15.99

Grades: 4 5 6   **Fic**

1. Letters -- Fiction 2. Southern States -- Fiction 3. African Americans -- Fiction
ISBN 9780547363004

           LC 2011012162

While her friend Missy Violet, the town midwife, is away in Florida, eleven-year-old Viney concerns herself with ailing neighbors, schoolmates, and her irrepressible cousin Charles, who feels superior because he has been to Harlem in New York City.

"This Depression-era gem . . . offers a child's-eye view on America's racial inequities. . . . Like a warm cup of alphabet soup, this offering packs several essential ingredients-hope, love, despair, courage, family, honor-into a hearty, child-size blend." Kirkus

Missy Violet & me. Houghton 2004 100p $15

Grades: 4 5 6   **Fic**

1. Midwives -- Fiction 2. Childbirth -- Fiction 3. African Americans -- Fiction
ISBN 978-0-618-37163-1; 0-618-37163-X

Coretta Scott King/John Steptoe New Talent Award, 2005

During the early 1900s, eleven-year-old Viney spends her summer working for the local midwife and learns first-hand about birth, death, and "catchin' babies."

"Unspooled as leisurely as a summer afternoon spent on the front porch, this appealingly nostalgic tale conveys the tenor of the time as well as the affable narrator's growth during one momentous summer." Publ Wkly

Followed by: Letters to Missy Violet (2012)

Hausman, Gerald

A **mind** with wings; the story of Henry David Thoreau. [by] Gerald & Loretta Hausman. 1st ed; Trumpeter Books for Young Readers 2006 148p $15.95

Grades: 6 7 8 9   **Fic**

1. Authors 2. Naturalists 3. Essayists 4. Pacifists 5. Writers on nature 6. Nonfiction writers 7. Naturalists -- Fiction 8. Massachusetts -- Fiction
ISBN 1-59030-228-1

           LC 2005018094

"This well-researched novel expertly captures Thoreau's character and life in mid-19th-century Massachusetts. . . . Careful readers will have much to mull over, and they will savor the adventures of this great American thinker." SLJ

Includes bibliographical references

Hautman, Pete

★ **All-in.** Simon & Schuster Books for Young Readers 2007 181p hardcover o.p. pa $5.99

Grades: 7 8 9 10   **Fic**

1. Poker -- Fiction 2. Gambling -- Fiction 3. Las Vegas (Nev.) -- Fiction
ISBN 978-1-4169-1325-2; 1-4169-1325-4; 978-1-4169-1326-9 pa; 1-4169-1326-9 pa

           LC 2006-23871

Sequel to No limit (2005)

Having won thousands of dollars playing high-stakes poker in Las Vegas, seventeen-year-old Denn Doyle hits a losing streak after falling in love with a young casino card dealer named Cattie Hart.

"Skillfully using the multiple-voice approach, Hautman brings to life the intricacies of poker, crafting a thrilling story of loss, good versus evil, and redemption." Voice Youth Advocates

★ The **big** crunch. Scholastic Press 2011 280p $17.99

Grades: 8 9 10 11 12   **Fic**

1. School stories 2. Dating (Social customs) -- Fiction
ISBN 978-0-545-24075-8; 0-545-24075-1

           LC 2010-40011

"Wes Andrews has just ended a suffocating relationship with Izzy. June is new to the school—her sixth in the last four years. Like Wes, she's not looking to get entangled. . . . But in the high-school world of 'users, posers, geeks, skanks, preps, gangstas, macho-morons, punks, burnouts, and so forth,' the two relatively normal, nice kids do find each other . . . eventually. Hautman uses a third-person point of view to weave a humorous and bittersweet tale of romance and the convoluted, uncertain paths that bring two people together. A poignant and quiet tale in which the only special effect is love—refreshing." Kirkus

Blank confession. Simon & Schuster Books for Young Readers 2010 170p $16.99
Grades: 7 8 9 10   **Fic**
> 1. School stories 2. Bullies -- Fiction 3. Drug traffic -- Fiction
> ISBN 978-1-4169-1327-6; 1-4169-1327-0
> > LC 2009-50169

A new and enigmatic student named Shayne appears at high school one day, befriends the smallest boy in the school, and takes on a notorious drug dealer before turning himself in to the police for killing someone.

"Masterfully written with simple prose, solid dialogue and memorable characters, the tale will grip readers from the start and keep the reading in one big gulp, in the hope of seeing behind Shayne's mask. A sure hit with teen readers." Kirkus

★ The **Cydonian** pyramid; Pete Hautman. Candlewick Press 2013 368 p. (The Klaatu Diskos) (reinforced) $16.99
Grades: 7 8 9 10 11 12   **Fic**
> 1. Science fiction 2. Time travel -- Fiction
> ISBN 0763654043; 9780763654047
> > LC 2012942673

This novel, by Pete Hautman, is part of the "Klaatu Diskos" series. "More than half a millennium in the future, in the shadow of the looming Cydonian Pyramid, a pampered girl named Lah Lia has been raised for one purpose: to be sacrificed. . . . But just as she is about to be killed, a strange boy appears from the diskos, providing a cover of chaos that allows her to escape and launching her on a time-spinning journey in which her fate is irreversibly linked to his." (Publisher's note)

★ **Godless.** Simon & Schuster Books for Young Readers 2004 208p $15.95; pa $8.99
Grades: 7 8 9 10   **Fic**
> 1. Religion -- Fiction
> ISBN 0-689-86278-4; 1-4169-0816-1 pa
> > LC 2003-10468

When sixteen-year-old Jason Bock and his friends create their own religion to worship the town's water tower, what started out as a joke begins to take on a power of its own

"The witty text and provocative subject will make this a supremely enjoyable discussion-starter as well as pleasurable read." Bull Cent Child Books

Hole in the sky. Simon & Schuster Bks. for Young Readers 2001 179p $16; pa $11.95
Grades: 7 8 9 10   **Fic**
> 1. Science fiction 2. Grand Canyon (Ariz.) -- Fiction
> ISBN 0-689-83118-8; 1-4169-6822-9 pa
> > LC 00-58324

In a future world ravaged by a mutant virus, sixteen-year-old Ceej and three other teenagers seek to save the Grand Canyon from being flooded, while trying to avoid capture by a band of renegade Survivors

"Readers will appreciate the novel's intense action and fascinating premise." Horn Book Guide

How to steal a car. Scholastic Press 2009 170p $16.99
Grades: 7 8 9 10   **Fic**
> 1. Theft -- Fiction 2. Family life -- Fiction
> ISBN 978-0-545-11318-2; 0-545-11318-0
> > LC 2008-54146

Fifteen-year-old, suburban high school student Kelleigh, who has her learner's permit, recounts how she began stealing cars one summer, for reasons that seem unclear even to her.

"A sharply observed, subversive coming-of-age tale." Kirkus

The **Klaatu** terminus; Pete Hautman. Candlewick Press 2014 368 p. (The Klaatu diskos) $16.99
Grades: 7 8 9 10 11 12   **Fic**
> 1. Science fiction 2. Dystopian fiction 3. Apocalyptic fiction
> ISBN 0763654051; 9780763654054
> > LC 2013944132

In this series finale, Pete Hautman "weaves several diverging time streams into one . . . masterwork. . . . In a far distant future, Tucker Feye and . . . Lia find themselves atop a crumbling pyramid in an abandoned city. In present-day Hopewell, Tucker's uncle Kosh faces armed resistance . . . as he attempts to help a terrorized woman named Emma. . . . And on a train platform in 1997, a seventeen-year-old Kosh is given an instruction that will change his life." (Publisher's note)

"Tucker and Lia (The Obsidian Blade; The Cydonian Pyramid) join together in the end stage of their journey through the millennia and the final confrontation with the murderous Lah Sept; Tucker uncovers his own role in Lah Sept history. Pulling together elaborate strands of the first two books, this conclusion rewards readers with a surprising yet cogent and satisfying chronicle across time." Horn Book

The **obsidian** blade. Candlewick Press 2012 308p $16.99
Grades: 7 8 9 10   **Fic**
> 1. Uncles -- Fiction 2. Religion -- Fiction 3. Supernatural -- Fiction 4. Space and time -- Fiction 5. Missing persons -- Fiction
> ISBN 978-0-7636-5403-0
> > LC 2011018617

After thirteen-year-old Tucker Feye's parents disappear, he suspects that the strange disks of shimmering air that he keeps seeing are somehow involved, and when he steps inside of one he is whisked on a time-twisting journey trailed by a shadowy sect of priests and haunted by ghostlike figures.

Snatched; [by] Pete Hautman and Mary Logue. Putnam 2006 200p (Bloodwater mysteries) $15.99
Grades: 7 8 9 10   **Fic**
> 1. Mystery fiction 2. Kidnapping -- Fiction
> ISBN 0-399-24377-1
> > LC 2005-28558

Too curious for her own good, Roni, crime reporter for her high school newspaper, teams up with Brian, freshman science geek, to investigate the beating and kidnapping of a classmate.

"Give this solid marks for plotting and characterization, as well as for suspense." Booklist

Other titles in this series are:

Skullduggery (2007)

Doppelganger (2008)

Sweetblood. Simon & Schuster Bks. for Young Readers 2003 180p $16.95; pa $6.99

Grades: 7 8 9 10   **Fic**

1. Diabetes -- Fiction

ISBN 0-689-85048-4; 0-689-87324-7 pa

LC 2002-11179

"Hautman does an outstanding job of making Lucy's theory and her struggle to accept herself credible. . . . Lucy's clever, self-deprecating voice is endlessly original." Booklist

Hawkins, Aaron R.

The **year** money grew on trees; written and illustrated by Aaron R. Hawkins. Houghton Mifflin 2010 293p il $16

Grades: 5 6 7 8   **Fic**

1. Apples -- Fiction 2. Cousins -- Fiction 3. Siblings -- Fiction 4. Farm life -- Fiction 5. New Mexico -- Fiction 6. Money-making projects for children -- Fiction

ISBN 978-0-547-27977-0; 0-547-27977-9

In early 1980s New Mexico, thirteen-year-old Jackson Jones recruits his cousins and sisters to help tend an elderly neighbor's neglected apple orchard for the chance to make big money and, perhaps, to own the orchard.

"Hawkins's children's book debut is rich with details that feel drawn from memory, . . . and Jackson's narration sparkles. His hard work, setbacks, and motivations make this a highly relatable adventure in entrepreneurship." Publ Wkly

Hawkins, Rachel

Demonglass; a Hex Hall novel. Hyperion 2011 359p $16.99

Grades: 7 8 9 10   **Fic**

1. Ghost stories 2. Magic -- Fiction 3. Witches -- Fiction 4. Supernatural -- Fiction 5. Great Britain -- Fiction 6. Father-daughter relationship -- Fiction

ISBN 978-1-4231-2131-2; 1-4231-2131-7

LC 2010-10511

Sequel to: Hex Hall (2010)

After learning that she is capable of dangerous magic, Sophie Mercer goes to England with her father, friend Jenna, and Cal hoping to have her powers removed, but soon she learns that she is being hunted by the Eye—and haunted by Elodie.

"Narrator Sophie's delivery is . . . delightfully bold, and the many action scenes lend a cinematic feel." Booklist

Hex Hall. Disney/Hyperion Books 2010 323p $16.99

Grades: 7 8 9 10   **Fic**

1. School stories 2. Witches -- Fiction 3. Supernatural -- Fiction

ISBN 1423121309; 9781423121305

When Sophie attracts too much human attention for a prom-night spell gone horribly wrong, she is exiled to Hex Hall, an isolated reform school for witches, faeries, and shapeshifters. "Grades seven to ten." (Bull Cent Child Books)

"Sixteen-year-old Sophie Mercer, whose absentee father is a warlock, discovered both her heritage and her powers at age 13. While at her school prom, Sophie happens upon a miserable girl sobbing in the bathroom and tries to perform a love spell to help her out. It misfires, and Sophie finds herself at Hecate (aka Hex) Hall, a boarding school for delinquent Prodigium (witches, warlocks, faeries, shape-shifters, and the occasional vampire). What makes this fast-paced romp work is Hawkins' wry humor and sharp eye for teen dynamics." Booklist

Followed by: Demonglass (2011)

Hayes, Rosemary

Payback. Frances Lincoln 2009 207p pa $8.95

Grades: 7 8 9 10   **Fic**

1. Muslims -- Fiction 2. Pakistan -- Fiction 3. London (England) -- Fiction

ISBN 978-1-84507-935-2 pa; 1-84507-935-3 pa

Halima, a teenaged Muslim girl living in London, discovers her father owes a favor to a distant relative in Pakistan and must repay the debt by forcing Halima into marriage

"In this tale of clashing cultures set against a backdrop of strong family ties and traditional Muslim faith, Hayes writes clearly and concisely, switching the narrative voice among the characters and letting the dynamics of the story simmer and build realistically." SLJ

Hayles, Marsha

Breathing room; Marsha Hayles. Henry Holt and Co. 2012 244 p. (hc) $17.99

Grades: 5 6 7 8   **Fic**

1. Bildungsromans 2. Historical fiction 3. Teenagers -- Fiction 4. Tuberculosis -- Fiction 5. Sick -- Fiction 6. Hospitals -- Fiction 7. Coming of age -- Fiction 8. Minnesota -- History -- 20th century -- Fiction

ISBN 0805089616; 9780805089615

LC 2011034055

Author Marsha Hayles' book is "set in 1940 at a sanitarium in Loon Lake, Minn. . . . Thirteen-year-old Evvy Hoffmeister has tuberculosis and feels abandoned by her family when she's sent to the sanitarium to be cured. The cold nurses, strict rules, mind-numbing routines, and endless bed rest are dispiriting for Evvy and her roommates: kind Beverly, glamorous Pearl, and defensive Dena. . . . Nonetheless, the girls find strength in each other and discover creative ways to bring cheer." (Publishers Weekly)

Headley, Justina Chen

★ **North** of beautiful. Little, Brown 2009 373p $16.99

Grades: 7 8 9 10 11 12   **Fic**

1. Aesthetics -- Fiction

ISBN 978-0-316-02505-8; 0-316-02505-4

LC 2008-09260

Headley's "finely crafted novel traces a teen's uncharted quest to find beauty. Two things block Terra's happiness: a port-wine stain on her face and her verbally abusive father. . . . . A car accident brings her together with Jacob, an Asian-born adoptee with unconventional ideas. . . . . . The author confidently addresses very large, slippery questions about the meaning of art, travel, love and of course, beauty." Publ Wkly

Healey, Karen

The **shattering**. Little, Brown 2011 311p $17.99
Grades: 7 8 9 10   **Fic**
1. Mystery fiction 2. Suicide -- Fiction 3. Homicide -- Fiction 4. New Zealand -- Fiction 5. Supernatural -- Fiction
ISBN 978-0-316-12572-7; 0-316-12572-5
                             LC 2010047996

When a rash of suicides disturbs Summerton, an oddly perfect tourist town on the west coast of New Zealand, the younger siblings of the dead boys become suspicious and begin an investigation that reveals dark secrets and puts them in grave danger.

"Juggling multiple viewpoints, Healey skillfully keeps her characters on an emotional roller-coaster even as they deal with physical threats. The climax delivers a gut punch that only underscores the sensitivity of the subject matter (without lessening the thrill at all)." Publ Wkly

When we wake; Karen Healey. Little, Brown Books for Young Readers 2013 304 p. (hardcover) $17.99
Grades: 7 8 9 10 11 12   **Fic**
1. Science fiction 2. Dystopian fiction 3. Science Fiction 4. Australia -- Fiction
ISBN 031620076X; 9780316200769
                             LC 2012028739

"Sixteen-year-old Tegan is just like every other girl living in 2027--But on what should have been the best day of Tegan's life, she dies--and wakes up a hundred years in the future, locked in a government facility with no idea what happened. . . . But the future isn't all she hoped it would be, and when . . . secrets come to light, Tegan must make a choice: Does she keep her head down and survive, or fight for a better future?" (Publisher's note)

While we run; by Karen Healey. Little Brown & Co 2014 336 p. (hardcover) $18
Grades: 7 8 9 10 11 12   **Fic**
1. Cryonics 2. Science fiction 3. Cryonics -- Fiction 4. Australia -- Fiction
ISBN 031623382X; 9780316233828
                             LC 2013022281

Sequel to: When we wake

In this science fiction novel by Karen Healey, "Abdi Taalib thought he was moving to Australia for a music scholarship. But after meeting the beautiful and brazen Tegan Oglietti, his world was turned upside down. Tegan's no ordinary girl--she died in 2027, only to be frozen and brought back to life in Abdi's time, 100 years later." (Publisher's note)

"In When We Wake, Tegan and Abdi revealed the government's plan to populate a new planet with cryogenically frozen slaves. Abdi begins narrating six months after their capture by the government. Like its predecessor, Run succeeds simply as a sci-fi thriller, but it's elevated by its social

commentary, emphasizing the importance of fighting for justice in a world that has little of it." Horn Book

Healy, Christopher

The **Hero's** Guide to Being an Outlaw; Christopher Healy, illustrated by Todd Harris. Harpercollins Childrens Books 2014 528 p. illustrations (The Hero's guide; book 3) $16.99
Grades: 4 5 6 7   **Fic**
1. Fantasy fiction 2. Princes -- Fiction
ISBN 006211848X; 9780062118486
                             LC 2014018251

"The League of Princes returns in the hilariously epic conclusion to the hit series that began with Christopher Healy's 'The Hero's Guide to Saving Your Kingdom.' . . . Posters plastered across the thirteen kingdoms are saying that Briar Rose has been murdered--and the four Princes Charming are the prime suspects. Now they're on the run in a desperate attempt to clear their names." (Publisher's note)

"Throughout the heroes' and heroines' travels, the antiprince conspiracy is revealed in each kingdom—it's directly related to loose ends from The Hero's Guide to Storming the Castle (2013). Side characters make comedic final appearances, and a surprise villain team-up provides closure to the trilogy. Part screwball comedy, part sly wit and all fun." Kirkus

The **hero's** guide to saving your kingdom; written by Christopher Healy; with drawings by Todd Harris. Walden Pond Press 2012 438 p. ill., map $16.99
Grades: 4 5 6 7   **Fic**
1. Princes -- Fiction 2. Fairy tales -- Fiction 3. Heroes and heroines -- Fiction 4. Fairy tales 5. Humorous stories 6. Witches -- Fiction
ISBN 0062117432; 9780062117434
                             LC 2011053347

In this book, "four Princes . . . must team up on a . . . quest to save their kingdoms. . . . Cinderella wants adventure more than sheltered Prince Frederic does. Prince Gustav's pride is still badly damaged from having needed Rapunzel's teary-eyed rescue. Through Sleeping Beauty, Prince Liam learns kissing someone out of enchanted sleep doesn't guarantee compatibility. . . . Although she loves wacky Prince Duncan, Snow White needs some solitude." (Kirkus Reviews)

The **hero's** guide to storming the castle; by Christopher Healy; with drawings by Todd Harris. Walden Pond Press, an imprint of HarperCollinsPublishers 2013 496 p. (Hero's Guide) (hardcover) $16.99
Grades: 4 5 6 7   **Fic**
1. Fractured fairy tales 2. Humorous fiction 3. Fairy tales 4. Humorous stories 5. Heroes -- Fiction 6. Princes -- Fiction 7. Characters in literature -- Fiction
ISBN 0062118455; 9780062118455
                             LC 2012050668

Sequel to: The hero's guide to saving your kingdom

In this humorous, middle-grade fantasy story, by Christopher Healy, illustrated by Todd Harris, "the charming princes from the fairy tales of Cinderella, Rapunzel, Snow White, and Briar Rose, saved the countryside from an evil witch in 'The Hero's Guide to Saving Your Kingdom.' And now, they have to save the day again, by keeping a magical object from falling into the hands of power-mad warlords who would use it for evil." (Publisher's note)

Hearn, Julie

Hazel; a novel. Atheneum Books for Young Readers 2009 389p $17.99

Grades: 8 9 10 11   **Fic**

1. Slavery -- Fiction 2. Social classes -- Fiction 3. Caribbean region -- Fiction 4. London (England) -- Fiction 5. Racially mixed people -- Fiction

ISBN 978-1-4169-2504-0; 1-4169-2504-X

LC 2008-53961

Thirteen-year-old Hazel leaves her comfortable, if somewhat unconventional, London home in 1913 after her father has a breakdown, and goes to live in the Caribbean on her grandparents' sugar plantation where she discovers some shocking family secrets.

"Hearn's characters vividly reveal class distinctions and racial prejudices prevalent in 1913." Voice Youth Advocates

★ **Ivy**; a novel. Atheneum Books for Young Readers 2008 355p $17.99; pa $9.99

Grades: 8 9 10 11 12   **Fic**

1. Artists -- Fiction 2. Criminals -- Fiction 3. Drug abuse -- Fiction 4. London (England) -- Fiction 5. Great Britain -- History -- 19th century -- Fiction

ISBN 978-1-4169-2506-4; 1-4169-2506-6; 978-1-4169-2507-1 pa; 1-4169-2507-4 pa

LC 2007-045463

In mid-nineteenth-century London, young, mistreated, and destitute Ivy, whose main asset is her beautiful red hair, comes to the attention of an aspiring painter of the pre-Raphaelite school of artists who, with the connivance of Ivy's unsavory family, is determined to make her his model and muse.

"Quirky characters, darkly humorous situations, and quick action make this enjoyable historical fiction." SLJ

The **minister's** daughter. Atheneum Books for Young Readers 2005 263p hardcover o.p. pa $7.99

Grades: 7 8 9 10   **Fic**

1. Witchcraft -- Fiction 2. Supernatural -- Fiction 3. Salem (Mass.) -- Fiction 4. Great Britain -- History -- 1642-1660, Civil War and Commonwealth -- Fiction

ISBN 0-689-87690-4; 0-689-87691-2 pa

LC 2004-18324

In 1645 in England, the daughters of the town minister successfully accuse a local healer and her granddaughter of witchcraft to conceal an out-of-wedlock pregnancy, but years later during the 1692 Salem trials their lie has unexpected repercussions.

"With its thought-provoking perceptions about human nature, magic and persecution, this tale will surely cast a spell over readers." Publ Wkly

Heath, Jack

The **Lab**. Scholastic Press 2008 311p $17.99

Grades: 7 8 9 10   **Fic**

1. Science fiction 2. Adventure fiction 3. Spies -- Fiction 4. Genetic engineering -- Fiction

ISBN 978-0-545-06860-4; 0-545-06860-6

"A gritty dystopic world exists under the iron rule of the mega-corporation Chao-Sonic, with only a few vigilante groups around to act as resistance. Six of Hearts is easily the best agent on one such group, the Deck, and he is fiercely dedicated to justice, using his extensive genetic modifications to his advantage. . . . The compelling and memorable protagonist stands out even against the intricately described and disturbing city whose vividness makes the place's questionable fate a suspenseful issue in its own right." Bull Cent Child Books

Followed by: Remote control (2010)

Money run; by Jack Heath. 1st American ed. Scholastic Press 2013 245 p. (hardcover) $17.99

Grades: 8 9 10   **Fic**

1. Crime -- Fiction 2. Adventure fiction 3. Stealing -- Fiction 4. Assassins -- Fiction 5. Theft 6. Thieves -- Fiction 7. Robbers and outlaws -- Fiction

ISBN 0545512662; 9780545512664

LC 2013004005

In this book, "Ashley and Benjamin are two teen partners in crime--real crime, as in major heists--who rely on their youth to avoid suspicion. . . . Their prey today happens to be a billionaire businessman who has sponsored an essay contest with a prize of $10,000 (Ash has won with an essay ghostwritten by Benjamin), but that's peanuts compared to the $2 million they hope to loot." (Kirkus Reviews)

Remote control. Scholastic Press 2010 326p $17.99

Grades: 7 8 9 10   **Fic**

1. Science fiction 2. Adventure fiction 3. Spies -- Fiction 4. Genetic engineering -- Fiction

ISBN 978-0-545-07591-6; 0-545-07591-2

Sequel to: The Lab (2008)

First published 2007 in Australia

Agent Six of Hearts, 16-year-old superhuman, is on a mission. His brother Kyntak has been kidnapped. A strange and sinister new figure is rising in power. Six is suspected of being a double agent. The Deck has been put into lockdown by the Queen of Spades. A mysterious girl has appeared who acts as Six's guardian angel. Who can he trust?

"The technothriller begun in The Lab (2008) takes several intriguing twists . . . on its way to a satisfying, if temporary, resolution." Booklist

Hegamin, Tonya

M +O 4evr; [by] Tonya Cherie Hegamin. Houghton Mifflin Co. 2008 165p $16

Grades: 8 9 10 11   **Fic**

1. Death -- Fiction 2. Slavery -- Fiction 3. Lesbians -- Fiction 4. Friendship -- Fiction 5. Family life -- Fiction 6. Pennsylvania -- Fiction

ISBN 978-0-618-49570-2; 0-618-49570-3

LC 2007-34293

In parallel stories, Hannah, a slave, finds love while fleeing a Maryland plantation in 1842, and in the present, Opal watches her life-long best friend, Marianne, pull away and eventually lose her life in the same Pennsylvania ravine where Hannah died.

"Hegamin's first novel is richly imaginative as it deals with difficult subjects. . . . [The] parallel stories of love and loss blend seamlessly in this small book that packs a big wallop." SLJ

Pemba's song; a ghost story. [by] Tonya Hegamin & Marilyn Nelson. Scholastic Press 2008 109p $16.99

Grades: 7 8 9 10 **Fic**

1. Moving -- Fiction 2. Slavery -- Fiction 3. Connecticut -- Fiction 4. Parapsychology -- Fiction 5. African Americans -- Fiction

ISBN 978-0-545-02076-3; 0-545-02076-X

LC 2007051044

As fifteen-year-old Pemba adjusts to leaving her Brooklyn, New York, home for small-town Connecticut, a Black history researcher helps her understand the paranormal experiences drawing her into the life of a mulatto girl who was once a slave in her house.

"Written in shifting voices and styles, this vivid, collaborative novella tells a supernatural story of a young girl's connection with history." Booklist

Hegedus, Bethany

Between us Baxters. WestSide Books 2009 306p $17.95

Grades: 7 8 9 10 **Fic**

1. Friendship -- Fiction 2. Race relations -- Fiction

ISBN 978-1-934813-02-7; 1-934813-02-8

"In 1959, in Holcolm County, GA, there is a palpable tension. Times are slowly changing, causing resentment among some folks and optimism among others. The volatile mix sets the tone for this story of family, friendship, and racial discrimination. . . .When suspicious fires, vandalism, and threats to successful black business owners cause fear and distrust among the townspeople, the strength of Polly and Timbre Ann's bond is tested. . . . The connection between the two girls and their families is beautifully described and believable, and the richness of the characters is apparent. The pacing of the story is deliberate and suspenseful with twists and turns that add to the bittersweet conclusion." SLJ

Helgerson, Joseph

Crows & cards; a novel. written with diligence by Mr. Joseph Helgerson; to which are added fine illustrations by Mr. Peter Desève; also included is Dictionarium Americannicum; being the words herein most arcane and alien and their definitions. Houghton Mifflin Harcourt 2009 344p il $16; pa $5.99

Grades: 4 5 6 7 **Fic**

1. Slavery -- Fiction 2. Gambling -- Fiction 3. Apprentices -- Fiction 4. Native Americans -- Fiction 5. Saint Louis (Mo.) -- Fiction

ISBN 978-0-618-88395-0; 0-618-88395-9; 978-0-547-33909-2 pa; 0-547-33909-7 pa

LC 2008013308

In 1849, Zeb's parents ship him off to St. Louis to become an apprentice tanner, but the naive twelve-year-old rebels, casting his lot with a cheating riverboat gambler, while a slave and an Indian medicine man try to get Zeb back on the right path. Includes historical notes, glossary, and bibliographical references

"Helgerson surrounds Zeb with a lively cast. . . . A solid choice for fans of high-spun yarns and not-too-tall tales." Booklist

★ **Horns** & wrinkles. Houghton Mifflin 2006 357p il $16; pa $4.95

Grades: 4 5 6 7 **Fic**

1. Magic -- Fiction 2. Trolls -- Fiction 3. Bullies -- Fiction 4. Mississippi River -- Fiction

ISBN 0-618-61679-9; 0-618-98178-0 pa

LC 2005025448

Along a magic-saturated stretch of the Mississippi River near Blue Wing, Minnesota, twelve-year-old Claire and her bullying cousin Duke are drawn into an adventure involving Bodacious Deepthink the Great Rock Troll, a helpful fairy, and a group of trolls searching for their fathers.

"Tongue-in-cheek humor brings a delightful zing to the playfully inventive storytelling and fast-paced plot. Enchanting sketches foreshadow each chapter, adding to the wonder." SLJ

Hemingway, Edith Morris

Road to Tater Hill; [by] Edith M. Hemingway. Delacorte Press 2009 213p map $16.99; lib bdg $19.99

Grades: 5 6 7 8 **Fic**

1. Friendship -- Fiction 2. Bereavement -- Fiction 3. Grandparents -- Fiction 4. Mountain life -- Fiction 5. North Carolina -- Fiction 6. Depression (Psychology) -- Fiction

ISBN 978-0-385-73677-0; 0-385-73677-0; 978-0-385-90627-2 lib bdg; 0-385-90627-7 lib bdg

LC 2008-24906

At her grandparents' North Carolina mountain home during the summer of 1963, eleven-year-old Annie Winters, grief-stricken by the death of her newborn sister and isolated by her mother's deepening depression, finds comfort in holding an oblong stone 'rock baby' and in the friendship of a neighbor boy and a reclusive mountain woman with a devastating secret

"Drawing on the author's childhood roots, the heart of this first novel is the sense of place, described in simple lyrical words. . . . True to Annie's viewpoint, the particulars tell a universal drama of childhood grief, complete in all its sadness, anger, loneliness, and healing." Booklist

Hemphill, Helen

★ The **adventurous** deeds of Deadwood Jones. Front Street 2008 228p $16.95

Grades: 5 6 7 8 **Fic**

1. Cousins -- Fiction 2. Cowhands -- Fiction 3. West (U.S.) -- Fiction 4. Race relations -- Fiction 5. African Americans -- Fiction

ISBN 978-1-59078-637-6; 1-59078-637-8

LC 2008005422

Thirteen-year-old Prometheus Jones and his eleven-year-old cousin Omer flee Tennessee and join a cattle drive that will eventually take them to Texas, where Prometheus hopes his father lives, and they find adventure and face challenges as African Americans in a land still recovering from the Civil War.

"Prometheus is an always sympathetic and engaging character, and the dangers and misadventures he encounters . . . make for compelling reading." Booklist

Long gone daddy. Front Street 2006 176p $16.95

Grades: 8 9 10 11 12   **Fic**
1. Grandfathers -- Fiction 2. Christian life -- Fiction 3. Las Vegas (Nev.) -- Fiction 4. Father-son relationship -- Fiction
ISBN 1-932425-38-1

LC 2005-25105

Young Harlan Q. Stank gets a taste of life in the fast lane when he accompanies his preacher father on a road trip to Las Vegas to bury his grandfather and to fulfill the terms of the old man's will.

"Many teens will see their own questions about faith, worship, and independence in Harlan's heart-twisting feelings." Booklist

Hemphill, Michael
    Stonewall Hinkleman and the Battle of Bull Run; [by] Michael Hemphill and Sam Riddleburger. Dial Books for Young Readers 2009 168p $16.99

Grades: 4 5 6   **Fic**
1. Time travel -- Fiction 2. Bull Run, 1st Battle of, 1861 -- Fiction 3. United States -- History -- 1861-1865, Civil War -- Fiction
ISBN 978-0-8037-3179-0; 0-8037-3179-5

LC 2008-15795

While participating in a reenactment of the Battle of Bull Run, twelve-year-old Stonewall Hinkleman is transported back to the actual Civil War battle by means of a magic bugle.

This is a "well-paced time-travel novel. . . . Stonewall is a likable character whose attitude changes for the better in the story. . . . A good choice for historical fiction fans." SLJ

Hemphill, Stephanie
    Hideous love; the story of the girl who wrote Frankenstein. Stephanie Hemphill. Balzer + Bray, an imprint of HarperCollinsPublishers 2013 320 p. (hardcover bdg.) $17.99

Grades: 9 10 11 12   **Fic**
1. Novels in verse 2. Historical fiction 3. Love -- Fiction 4. Authorship -- Fiction
ISBN 0061853313; 9780061853319

LC 2013000237

This book is a "fictionalized verse biography of" author Mary Shelley. Stephanie Hemphill "explores the particular challenges facing a gifted female artist who allies herself with a renowned male poet. Central to the plot is the parentage of Mary Wollstonecraft Godwin Shelley, daughter of Mary Wollstonecraft, the pioneering feminist philosopher who died days after Mary was born, and William Godwin, a radical political philosopher who espoused free love for all but his daughters." (Kirkus Reviews)

Sisters of glass; Stephanie Hemphill. Alfred A. Knopf 2012 150 p. $16.99

Grades: 7 8 9 10   **Fic**
1. Love stories 2. Novels in verse 3. Historical fiction 4. Families -- Fiction 5. Family life -- Fiction 6. Venice (Italy) -- Fiction 7. Families -- Fiction 8. Glassworkers -- Fiction 9. Venice (Italy) -- Fiction 10. Glass blowing and working -- Fiction
ISBN 0375861092; 0375961097; 9780375861093; 9780375961090

LC 2011277551

This book presents "[a] . . . tale of destiny, fidelity, and true love" set in "fourteenth-century Murano, Italy (of glass-making renown) and . . . told through verse. . . . Maria is disdainful of her training to be a society woman and yearns instead to spend her time with her art or in the family's furnaces with Luca, an employee whose skill with glass is the marvel that leads Maria, who once aspired to be a glassblower, to fall in love with him." (Booklist)

★ **Wicked** girls; a novel of the Salem witch trials. Balzer + Bray 2010 408p il $17.99; lib bdg $17.89

Grades: 7 8 9 10 11 12   **Fic**
1. Novels in verse 2. Trials -- Fiction 3. Witchcraft -- Fiction 4. Salem (Mass.) -- Fiction
ISBN 0-06-185328-3; 0-06-185329-1 lib bdg; 978-0-06-185328-9; 978-0-06-185329-6 lib bdg

LC 2010-9593

This is "a fictionalized account of the Salem witch trials told from the perspectives of three of the real young women living in Salem in 1692. Ann Putnam Jr. plays the queen bee. When her father suggests that a spate of illnesses within the village is the result of witchcraft, Ann . . . puts in motion a chain of events that will change the lives of the people around her forever. Mercy Lewis, the beautiful servant in Ann's house, inspires adulation in some and envy in others. With a troubled past, she seizes her only chance at safety. Margaret Walcott, Ann's cousin, is desperately in love and consumed with fiery jealousy. She is torn between staying loyal to her friends and pursuing the life she dreams of with her betrothed." (Publisher's note) "Middle school, high school." (Horn Book)

"Hemphill's raw, intimate poetry probes behind the abstract facts and creates characters that pulse with complex emotion." Booklist

Includes bibliographical references

Henderson, Jan-Andrew
    Bunker 10. Harcourt 2007 253p $17

Grades: 7 8 9 10   **Fic**
1. Virtual reality -- Fiction 2. Genetic engineering -- Fiction
ISBN 978-0-15-206240-8; 0-15-206240-8

LC 2006-38694

Something is going terribly wrong at the top secret Pinewood Military Installation as the teenage geniuses who study and work there are about to discover a horrible truth.

"Henderson ably balances intriguing plot twists and hauntingly well-developed characters with gripping pace and dramatic showdowns." Bull Cent Child Books

Henderson, Jason

The **Triumph** of Death; Jason Henderson. HarperTeen 2012 310 p.

Grades: 8 9 10 11 12   **Fic**

1. Occult fiction 2. Adventure fiction 3. Horror stories 4. Witches -- Fiction 5. Vampires -- Fiction 6. Supernatural -- Fiction

ISBN 9780061951039

LC 2012004297

This young adult paranormal adventure, by Jason Henderson, is book three of the "Alex Van Helsing" series. "There is a famous painting in Madrid that holds the key to an apocalypse only Alex Van Helsing can stop . . . [and] a newly risen vampire queen threatens the fate of the world. . . . Teaming up with a motorcycle-riding witch, Alex jets between Switzerland, the UK, and Spain in a frantic race to prevent the queen from . . . [plunging] the world into darkness." (Publisher's note)

★ **Vampire** rising. HarperTeen 2010 249p (Alex Van Helsing) $16.99

Grades: 6 7 8 9 10   **Fic**

1. Horror fiction 2. School stories 3. Vampires -- Fiction 4. Switzerland -- Fiction 5. Supernatural -- Fiction

ISBN 978-0-06-195099-5; 0-06-195099-8

LC 2009-39663

At a boarding school in Switzerland, fourteen-year-old Alex Van Helsing learns that vampires are real, that he has a natural ability to sense them, and that an agency called the Polidorium has been helping his family fight them since 1821.

"Henderson references Mary Shelley's Frankenstein to weave a great story line full of action, suspense, and adventure. The satisfying story captivates readers with a modern-day spin of James Bond meets Dracula." SLJ

Another title about Alex Van Helsing is:

Voice of the undead (2011)

Voice of the undead. HarperTeen 2011 297p (Alex Van Helsing) $16.99

Grades: 6 7 8 9 10   **Fic**

1. Horror fiction 2. School stories 3. Vampires -- Fiction 4. Switzerland -- Fiction 5. Supernatural -- Fiction

ISBN 978-0-06-195101-5; 0-06-195101-3

LC 2010045554

Sequel to: Vampire rising (2010)

After a fire damages his boarding school in Switzerland, fourteen-year-old Alex and his friends move to the girls' school across the lake, where supernatural happenings are disturbing the peace, and in the meantime, more Van Helsing family secrets are revealed.

"Henderson continues to spin a James Bond-type of action adventure story with a supernatural twist. It's an entertaining read that is full of suspense and intrigue." SLJ

Heneghan, James

Payback. Groundwood/House of Anansi Press 2007 184p $16.95; pa $8.95

Grades: 6 7 8 9   **Fic**

1. Guilt -- Fiction 2. Bullies -- Fiction 3. Suicide

-- Fiction 4. Immigrants -- Fiction 5. Irish -- Canada -- Fiction

ISBN 0-88899-701-9; 978-0-88899-701-2; 978-0-88899-704-3 pa; 0-88899-704-3 pa

"After his eighth-grade classmate Benny commits suicide, Charley blames himself. . . . Why did he do nothing when he saw the bullies torment Benny and call him 'fag'? Was it because, as a new Irish immigrant in Vancouver, Charley himself was threatened and bullied? . . . The drama of guilt, sorrow, and redemption is honest and heartfelt, told in Charley's spare, fast, first-person narrative." Booklist

Safe house. Orca Book Publishers 2006 151p pa $7.95

Grades: 6 7 8 9   **Fic**

1. Belfast (Northern Ireland) -- Fiction

ISBN 1-55143-640-X pa; 978-1-55143-640-1 pa

"Readers will be drawn by the fast action and the breathless escape adventure, but they'll also respond to the politics of war in Belfast." Booklist

Henkes, Kevin

★ **Bird** Lake moon. Greenwillow Books 2008 179p $15.99; lib bdg $16.89; pa $5.99

Grades: 4 5 6 7   **Fic**

1. Lakes -- Fiction 2. Divorce -- Fiction 3. Wisconsin -- Fiction 4. Friendship -- Fiction 5. Bereavement -- Fiction 6. Family life -- Fiction

ISBN 978-0-06-147076-9; 0-06-147076-7; 978-0-06-147078-3 lib bdg; 0-06-147078-3 lib bdg; 978-0-06-147079-0 pa; 0-06-147079-1 pa

LC 2007-36564

Twelve-year-old Mitch and his mother are spending the summer with his grandparents at Bird Lake after his parents separate, and ten-year-old Spencer and his family have returned to the lake where Spencer's little brother drowned long ago, and as the boys become friends and spend time together, each of them begins to heal

"Characters are gently and believably developed as the story weaves in and around the beautiful Wisconsin setting. The superbly crafted plot moves smoothly and unhurriedly, mirroring a slow summer pace." SLJ

★ **Olive's** ocean. Greenwillow Bks. 2003 217p $15.99; pa $6.99

Grades: 5 6 7 8   **Fic**

1. Family life -- Fiction 2. Grandmothers -- Fiction

ISBN 0-06-053543-1; 0-06-053545-8 pa

LC 2002-29782

A Newbery Medal honor book, 2004

On a summer visit to her grandmother's cottage by the ocean, twelve-year-old Martha gains perspective on the death of a classmate, on her relationship with her grandmother, on her feelings for an older boy, and on her plans to be a writer.

"Rich characterizations move this compelling novel to its satisfying and emotionally authentic conclusion." SLJ

Protecting Marie. Greenwillow Bks. 1995 195p $18.99; pa $5.99

Grades: 5 6 7 8   **Fic**

1. Dogs -- Fiction 2. Father-daughter relationship --

Fiction
ISBN 0-688-13958-2; 0-06-053545-8 pa
LC 94-16387

Relates twelve-year-old Fanny's love-hate relationship with her father, a temperamental artist, who has given Fanny a new dog

"The characters ring heartbreakingly true in this quiet, wise story; they are complex and difficult—like all of us—and worthy of our attention." Horn Book

Henry, April

Torched. G.P. Putnam's Sons 2009 224p $16.99

Grades: 8 9 10 11   **Fic**

1. Terrorism -- Fiction 2. Environmental movement -- Fiction

ISBN 978-0-399-24645-6; 0-399-24645-2
LC 2008-01145

In order to save her parents from going to jail for possession of marijuana, sixteen-year-old Ellie must help the FBI uncover the intentions of a radical environmental group by going undercover.

"The mix of politics and thrilling action will grab teens. . . This suspenseful story will spark discussion about what it means to fight for right 'by any means necessary.'" Booklist

Henry, O.

The **gift** of the Magi; illustrations by P.J. Lynch. Candlewick Press 2008 un il $15.99

Grades: 5 6 7 8   **Fic**

1. Gifts -- Fiction 2. Christmas -- Fiction

ISBN 978-0-7636-3530-5; 0-7636-3530-8
LC 2007052028

A husband and wife sacrifice treasured possessions in order to buy each other Christmas presents.

The story "enjoys a gentle new interpretation through watercolor illustrations in worn grays and warm brown tones. . . . Lynch's illustrations of wintry landscapes and the protagonists' animated faces add an accessible level of storytelling to the sophisticated prose." Horn Book Guide

Hensley, Joy N.

Rites of passage; Joy N. Hensley. First edition HarperTeen 2014 416 p. (hardback) $17.99

Grades: 7 8 9 10   **Fic**

1. School stories 2. Bullies -- Fiction 3. Secret societies -- Fiction 4. Schools -- Fiction 5. Bullying -- Fiction 6. Sex role -- Fiction 7. Military training -- Fiction 8. Blue Ridge Mountains -- Fiction

ISBN 0062295195; 9780062295194
LC 2014010022

In this novel by Joy N. Hensley, "sixteen-year-old Sam McKenna discovers that becoming one of the first girls to attend a revered military academy means living with a target on her back. As Sam struggles to prove herself, she learns that a decades-old secret society is alive and active . . . and determined to force her out." (Publisher's note)

"The narrative flows along terrifically as Sam courageously battles to make it even while the forces against her increase. The characters stand out as individual and real; readers will cheer Sam on throughout. Absolutely compelling." Kirkus

Henson, Heather

Dream of Night. Atheneum 2010 218p $15.99

Grades: 6 7 8 9   **Fic**

1. Horses -- Fiction 2. Child abuse -- Fiction 3. Foster home care -- Fiction

ISBN 978-1-4169-4899-5; 1-4169-4899-6

"Once Dream of Night was a champion racehorse, but by the time Jess DiLima gets him he's nearly dead from starvation and pneumonia, and his thin hide is covered in scars. Twelve-year-old Shiloh is scarred, too, both from physical abuse and from the emotional withering of years in foster care. . . . [Henson's] novel, like her characters, shimmers with anger and hope. She doesn't pull her punches—the scenes and flashbacks of abuse are realistically graphic—but she also never lets the details overwhelm the narrative, always offering the possibility of redemption." Kirkus

Hepler, Heather

The **cupcake** queen. Dutton 2009 242p $16.99; pa $7.99

Grades: 6 7 8 9   **Fic**

1. Baking -- Fiction 2. Moving -- Fiction 3. Family life -- Fiction

ISBN 978-0-525-42157-3; 0-525-42157-2; 978-0-14-241668-6 pa; 0-14-241668-1 pa
LC 2008-48971

While longing to return to life in New York City, thirteen-year-old Penny helps her mother and grandmother run a cupcake bakery in Hog's Hollow, tries to avoid the beastly popular girls, to be a good friend to quirky Tally, and to catch the eye of enigmatic Marcus.

"An endearing and poignant story about standing up to adversity and finding peace in what it is, rather than holding out for what it could be." Publ Wkly

Herbach, Geoff

I'm with stupid; Geoff Herbach. Sourcebooks Fire 2013 320 p. (tp : alk. paper) $9.99

Grades: 7 8 9 10   **Fic**

1. Suicide -- Fiction 2. Football players -- Fiction 3. Father-son relationship -- Fiction 4. Anxiety -- Fiction 5. Schools -- Fiction 6. Athletes -- Fiction 7. Identity -- Fiction 8. Wisconsin -- Fiction 9. High schools -- Fiction

ISBN 1402277911; 9781402277917
LC 2012042814

Sequel to: Stupid fast

This book explores a "Wisconsin football phenom's high-school years. The pressure is truly on as Felton, a senior, has to cope with the stresses of college recruitment. When his girlfriend, Aleah, breaks off their long-distance romance, and the brother of the bullied freshman he mentors kills himself, Felton violently unravels. Identifying with Shakespeare's Hamlet, Felton struggles with his own royal role as sports hero and his father's legacy as angry suicide." (Booklist)

Nothing special; Geoff Herbach. Sourcebooks Inc. 2012 290 p. (paperback) $9.99; (ebook) $9.99

Grades: 6 7 8 9 10   **Fic**

1. Friendship -- Fiction 2. Dysfunctional families --

Fiction 3. Teenagers -- Conduct of life -- Fiction
ISBN 1402265077; 9781402265075; 9781402265099

In this book, author Geoff Herbach tells the story of Felton, a football and track star who deals with his girlfriend Aleah abroad in Germany and "the possibility that his younger brother Andrew could be falling apart. Andrew has convinced their mother to let him go to band camp, but Felton discovers that Andrew, usually the sane member of the family, has in fact run away to Florida. An impromptu road trip with erstwhile best friend Gus turns up surprising reasons for Andrew's escape." (Kirkus Reviews)

Stupid fast. Sourcebooks 2011 311p pa $9.99
Grades: 6 7 8 9 10   **Fic**
1. Boys -- Fiction 2. Football -- Fiction
ISBN 978-1-4022-5630-1; 1-4022-5630-2

"Herbach is at his peak limning the confusion and frustration of a young man who no longer recognizes his own body, and Felton's self-deprecating take on his newly awarded A-list status is funny and compelling." Bull Cent Child Books

Herlong, Madaline

The **great** wide sea; [by] M. H. Herlong. Viking Children's Books 2008 283p $16.99; pa $6.99
Grades: 7 8 9 10   **Fic**
1. Sailing -- Fiction 2. Brothers -- Fiction 3. Bereavement -- Fiction 4. Father-son relationship -- Fiction 5. Survival after airplane accidents, shipwrecks, etc. -- Fiction
ISBN 978-0-670-06330-7; 0-670-06330-4; 978-0-14-241670-9 pa; 0-14-241670-3 pa
LC 2008-08384

Still mourning the death of their mother, three brothers go with their father on an extended sailing trip off the Florida Keys and have an adventure at sea

"Herlong makes the most of the three boys' characters, each exceptionally well developed here, to make this as much a novel of brotherhood as a sea story." Bull Cent Child Books

Herrera, Robin

Hope is a ferris wheel; Robin Herrera. Amulet Books 2014 272 p. (alk. paper) $16.95
Grades: 4 5 6 7   **Fic**
1. Clubs -- Fiction 2. Moving -- Fiction 3. Poetry -- Fiction 4. Trailer parks -- Fiction 5. Trailer camps -- Fiction
ISBN 1419710397; 9781419710391
LC 2013026392

In this book, by Robin Herrera, "ten-year-old Star Mackie lives in a trailer park with her flaky mom and her melancholy older sister. . . . Moving to a new town has made it difficult for Star to make friends, when her classmates tease her because of where she lives and because of her layered blue hair. But when Star starts a poetry club, she develops a love of Emily Dickinson and . . . learns some important lessons about herself and comes to terms with her hopes for the future." (Publisher's note)

"Star Mackie is a fifth-grader overflowing with hope—especially for friends. But that seems impossible at her new school since she is teased for living in a pink trailer and hav-

ing strangely layered blue hair. In her debut, Herrera has created a delightful narrator with a memorable voice and surrounded her with a unique supporting cast. Got fans of Joan Bauer in your neck of the woods? Send them this way.: Booklist

Herrick, Amy

The **Time** Fetch; a novel. Amy Herrick. Algonquin Young Readers 2013 320 p. $16.95
Grades: 5 6 7 8   **Fic**
1. Time travel -- Fiction 2. Science fiction 3. Space and time -- Fiction 4. Adventure and adventurers -- Fiction
ISBN 1616202203; 9781616202200
LC 2013008612

In this book, "when eighth-grader Edward picks up what he thinks is a rock for science class, he accidentally disturbs a Time Fetch, little knowing it's full of time-eating foragers. Soon, he and three classmates—athletic Danton, painfully shy Brigit, and abrasive Feenix—are pulled into a quest to prevent the out-of-control foragers from destroying everything." (Publishers Weekly)

Herrick, Steven

By the river. Front Street 2006 238p $16.95
Grades: 8 9 10 11 12   **Fic**
1. Death -- Fiction 2. Brothers -- Fiction 3. Australia -- Fiction 4. Single parent family -- Fiction
ISBN 1-932425-72-1
LC 2005-23967

First published 2004 in the United Kingdom

A fourteen-year-old describes, through prose poems, his life in a small Australian town in 1962, where, since their mother's death, he and his brother have been mainly on their own to learn about life, death, and love.

"The poems are simple but potent in their simplicity, blending together in a compelling, evocative story of a gentle, intelligent boy growing up and learning to deal with a sometimes-ugly little world that he . . . will eventually escape." Voice Youth Advocates

Hesse, Karen

★ **Brooklyn** Bridge; a novel. Feiwel and Friends 2008 229p il map $17.95
Grades: 5 6 7 8 9 10   **Fic**
1. Immigrants -- Fiction 2. Family life -- Fiction 3. Social classes -- Fiction 4. Homeless persons -- Fiction 5. Russian Americans -- Fiction 6. Brooklyn (New York, N.Y.) -- Fiction
ISBN 978-0-312-37886-8; 0-312-37886-6
LC 2008-05624

In 1903 Brooklyn, fourteen-year-old Joseph Michtom's life changes for the worse when his parents, Russian immigrants, invent the teddy bear and turn their apartment into a factory, while nearby the glitter of Coney Island contrasts with the dismal lives of children dwelling under the Brooklyn Bridge.

Hesse "applies her gift for narrative voice to this memorable story. . . . The novel explodes with dark drama before its eerie but moving resolution." Publ Wkly

★ **Letters** from Rifka. Holt & Co. 1992 148p
$16.95; pa $6.99

Grades: 5 6 7 8   **Fic**
1. Jews -- Fiction 2. Letters -- Fiction 3. Immigrants
-- Fiction
ISBN 0-8050-1964-2; 0-312-53561-9 pa
LC 91-48007

In letters to her cousin, Rifka, a young Jewish girl, chronicles her family's flight from Russia in 1919 and her own experiences when she must be left in Belgium for a while when the others emigrate to America

"Based on the true story of the author's great-aunt, the moving account of a brave young girl's story brings to life the day-to-day trials and horrors experienced by many immigrants as well as the resourcefulness and strength they found within themselves." Horn Book

★ **Out** of the dust. Scholastic 1997 227p $16.95; pa $6.99
Grades: 5 6 7 8   **Fic**
1. Novels in verse 2. Oklahoma -- Fiction 3. Farm life
-- Fiction 4. Dust storms -- Fiction 5. Great Depression, 1929-1939 -- Fiction
ISBN 0-590-36080-9; 0-590-37125-8 pa
LC 96-40344

Awarded the Newbery Medal, 1998

"Hesse's writing transcends the gloom and transforms it into a powerfully compelling tale of a girl with enormous strength, courage, and love. The entire novel is written in very readable blank verse." Booklist

Safekeeping; Karen Hesse. Feiwel and Friends 2012 294 p. ill., map $17.99
Grades: 7 8 9 10 11 12   **Fic**
1. Alternative histories 2. Revolutions -- Fiction 3. Voyages and travels -- Fiction
ISBN 1250011345; 9781250011343
LC 2012288414

In this book, a "group of rebels called the American People's Party has taken control" in the U.S. "Radley, an American teenager returning home from doing volunteer work in Haiti, finds her parents gone and her Vermont home abandoned. Not knowing whom to trust or where she'll be safe, she sets out on foot to Canada, befriending a reticent girl along the way. The two form a tentative friendship and manage to cross into Canada." (Publishers Weekly)

Witness. Scholastic Press 2001 161p $16.95; pa $5.99
Grades: 6 7 8 9   **Fic**
1. Novels in verse 2. Vermont -- Fiction 3. Prejudices
-- Fiction 4. Ku Klux Klan -- Fiction
ISBN 0-439-27199-1; 0-439-27200-9 pa
LC 00-54139

A series of poems express the views of eleven people in a small Vermont town, including a young black girl and a young Jewish girl, during the early 1920s when the Ku Klux Klan is trying to infiltrate the town

"The story is divided into five acts, and would lend itself beautifully to performance. The plot unfolds smoothly, and the author creates multidimensional characters." SLJ

Hesser, Terry Spencer
Kissing doorknobs. Delacorte Press 1998 149p hardcover o.p. pa $6.50
Grades: 7 8 9 10   **Fic**
1. Obsessive-compulsive disorder -- Fiction
ISBN 0-385-32329-8; 0-440-41314-1 pa
LC 97-26937

Fourteen-year-old Tara describes how her increasingly strange compulsions begin to take over her life and affect her relationships with her family and friends

"An honest, fresh, and multilayered story to which readers will instantly relate. . . . The prose is forthright, economical, and peppered with wry humor." SLJ

Hiaasen, Carl
★ **Flush**. Knopf 2005 263p $16.95; lib bdg $18.99; pa $8.99
Grades: 5 6 7 8   **Fic**
1. Florida -- Fiction 2. Boats and boating -- Fiction 3. Environmental protection -- Fiction
ISBN 0-375-82182-1; 0-375-92182-6 lib bdg; 0-375-84185-7 pa
LC 2005-05259

With their father jailed for sinking a river boat, Noah Underwood and his younger sister, Abbey, must gather evidence that the owner of this floating casino is emptying his bilge tanks into the protected waters around their Florida Keys home

"This quick-reading, fun, family adventure harkens back to the Hardy Boys in its simplicity and quirky characters." SLJ

★ **Hoot**. Knopf 2002 292p $15.95; pa $8.95
Grades: 5 6 7 8   **Fic**
1. Owls -- Fiction 2. Florida -- Fiction 3. Environmental protection -- Fiction
ISBN 0-375-82181-3; 0-375-82916-4 pa
LC 2002-25478

A Newbery Medal honor book, 2003

Roy, who is new to his small Florida community, becomes involved in another boy's attempt to save a colony of burrowing owls from a proposed construction site

"The story is full of offbeat humor, buffoonish yet charming supporting characters, and genuinely touching scenes of children enjoying the wildness of nature." Booklist

★ **Scat**. Knopf 2009 371p $16.99; lib bdg $19.99; pa $8.99
Grades: 5 6 7 8   **Fic**
1. Florida -- Fiction 2. Teachers -- Fiction 3. Missing persons -- Fiction 4. Wildlife conservation -- Fiction
ISBN 978-0-375-83486-8; 0-375-83486-9; 978-0-375-93486-5 lib bdg; 0-375-93486-3 lib bdg; 978-0-375-83487-5 pa; 0-375-83487-7 pa
LC 2008-28266

Nick and his friend Marta decide to investigate when a mysterious fire starts near a Florida wildlife preserve and an unpopular teacher goes missing.

"Once again, Hiaasen has written an edge-of-the-seat eco-thriller. . . . From the first sentence, readers will be hooked. . . . This well-written and smoothly plotted story, with fully realized characters, will certainly appeal to mystery lovers." SLJ

Hickam, Homer H., 1943-

　Crater; a Helium-3 novel. Homer Hickam. Thomas Nelson 2012 311 p.

Grades: 6 7 8　　　　　　　　　　　　　　**Fic**

　　1. Moon -- Fiction 2. Science fiction 3. Orphans -- Fiction 4. Trucking -- Fiction 5. Space flight -- Fiction

　　ISBN 1595546642; 9781595546647

　　　　　　　　　　　　　　　LC 2011051931

This young adult science fiction novel tells the story of "[l]ong-haul trucking on the Moon . . . with raiders, romance and a secret mission. Teenage orphan Crater Trueblood was plucked from the Helium-3 mines by lunar kingpin Colonel Medaris. . . . Trueblood suddenly finds himself scouting for a convoy headed for Armstrong City and charged with picking up a mysterious package. In the course of an eventful trip, Crater survives numerous natural hazards out in the "big suck," learns how to deal with rambunctious truckers (much like herding cats) and plays various high-speed low-gravity sports. He also hooks up with the Colonel's mercurial granddaughter Maria and battles genetically altered superwarriors with help from a vacuum-suited horse and a Tribble-like supercomputer." (Kirkus)

　Crescent; second in the Helium-3 series. by Homer Hickam. Thomas Nelson 2013 336 p. (A Helium-3 novel) (pbk.) $9.99

Grades: 7 8 9 10 11 12　　　　　　　　　**Fic**

　　1. Moon -- Fiction 2. Fugitives from justice -- Fiction 3. War -- Fiction 4. Science fiction 5. Prejudices -- Fiction 6. Prisoners of war -- Fiction

　　ISBN 1595546634; 9781595546630

　　　　　　　　　　　　　　　LC 2012051410

This book is the sequel to author Homer Hickam's "Crater". "Weary of the war with the Unified Countries of the World . . . Crater Trueblood captures Crescent--a short, mouthy and thoroughly deadly genetically altered superwarrior from Earth. He is then faced with the tall task of keeping her from killing, or being killed by, the vengeful citizens of Moontown. Meanwhile, his estranged sweetheart, Maria, . . . barely blasts her way out of a UCW kidnap attempt." (Kirkus Reviews)

　"Expertly blending space opera and hard sci-fi, romance, and even mystery (there's a detour for a nifty whodunit), this is fast paced, packed with intriguing ideas." Booklist

Hicks, Deron R.

　The **secrets** of Shakespeare's grave; by Deron R. Hicks; [illustrated by Mark Edward Geyer] Houghton Mifflin Harcourt 2012 273 p. (hardcover) $16.99

Grades: 4 5 6　　　　　　　　　　　　　**Fic**

　　1. Mystery fiction 2. Shakespeare, William, 1564-1616 -- Fiction 3. Cousins -- Fiction 4. Mystery and detective stories 5. Brothers and sisters -- Fiction 6. Adventure and adventurers -- Fiction

　　ISBN 0547840349; 9780547840345

　　　　　　　　　　　　　　　LC 2012014801

In this book by Deron R. Hicks "Twelve-year-old Colophon Letterford has a serious mystery on her hands. Will she discover the link between her family's literary legacy and Shakespeare's tomb before it's too late? Antique paintings, secret passages, locked mausoleums, a four-hundred-year-old treasure, and a cast of quirky (and some ignoble) characters all add up to a . . . journey through literary time and space in real-world locales from Mont St. Michel to Stratford-Upon-Avon to Central Park!" (Publisher's note)

Higgins, F. E.

　★ The **Black** Book of Secrets. Feiwel and Friends 2007 273p $14.95

Grades: 4 5 6 7　　　　　　　　　　　　**Fic**

　　1. Apprentices -- Fiction 2. Pawnbrokers -- Fiction

　　ISBN 978-0-312-36844-9; 0-312-36844-5

　　　　　　　　　　　　　　　LC 2007-32559

When Ludlow Fitch runs away from his thieving parents in the City, he meets up with the mysterious Joe Zabbidou, who calls himself a secret pawnbroker, and who takes Ludlow as an apprentice to record the confessions of the townspeople of Pagus Parvus, where resentments are many and trust is scarce.

　This is "an intriguing blend of adventure and historical fiction spiced with a light touch of the fantastic." Voice of Youth Advocates

　The **Eyeball** Collector. Feiwel & Friends 2009 251p $14.99

Grades: 7 8 9 10　　　　　　　　　　　　**Fic**

　　1. Horror fiction 2. Mystery fiction

　　ISBN 978-0-312-56681-4; 0-312-56681-6

　"In what the author dubs a 'polyquel' that partially bridges her Black Book of Secrets (2007) and its prequel Bone Magician (2008), Higgins sends a suddenly penniless young orphan from the filthy streets of Urbs Umida's South Side to an extravagantly rococo estate house in search of vengeance for his family's ruin. . . . Readers with a taste for lurid prose, macabre twists, riddles, exotic poisons, high-society caricatures, murderous schemes and scenes of stomach-churning degeneracy will find some or all of these in every chapter, and though the author trots in multiple characters and references from previous episodes, this one stands sturdily on its own." Kirkus

　The **lunatic's** curse. Feiwel and Friends 2011 336p $15.99

Grades: 6 7 8 9　　　　　　　　　　　　**Fic**

　　1. Horror fiction

　　ISBN 978-0-312-56682-1; 0-312-56682-4

　"The prosperous town of Oppum Oppidulum, the deep and cold adjacent Lake Beluarum and the Asylum for the Peculiar and Bizarre that sits on an island in said lake all hold horrifying secrets. Young Rex discovers this when his father is confined to the Asylum after suddenly going mad and eating his own hand—to the open glee of Rex's sinister new stepmother Acantha Grammaticus. . . . Strewing her narrative with dark hints, obscure clues, assorted lunatics and, in particular, both macabre cuisine and a panoply of noxious or tantalizingly evocative odors, the author contrives a highly atmospheric experience. Readers with strong stomachs and a taste for melodramatic narratives . . . will devour this yarn with relish." Kirkus

Higgins, Jack

★ **Sure** fire; [by] Jack Higgins with Justin Richards. G.P. Putnam's Sons 2007 237p $16.99

Grades: 6 7 8 9 **Fic**

1. Adventure fiction 2. Spies -- Fiction 3. Twins -- Fiction 4. Fathers -- Fiction

ISBN 978-0-399-24784-2; 0-399-24784-X

LC 2007008144

First published 2006 in the United Kingdom

Resentful of having to go and live with their estranged father after the death of their mother, fifteen-year-old twins, Rich and Jade, soon find they have more complicated problems when their father is kidnapped and their attempts to rescue him involve them in a dangerous international plot to control the world's oil.

This is a "standout YA spy novel. . . . Each chapter ends with a cliff-hanger, maintaining the high level of suspense." Publ Wkly

Other titles in this series are:

Death run (2008)

Sharp shot (2009)

First strike (2010)

Higgins, Joanna

Waiting for the queen; Joanna Higgins. Milkweed Editions 2013 256 p. (alk. paper) $16.95

Grades: 6 7 8 9 10 **Fic**

1. Historical fiction 2. Immigrants -- United States 3. Shakers -- Fiction 4. Slavery -- Fiction 5. Friendship -- Fiction 6. Social classes -- Fiction 7. Pennsylvania -- History -- 1775-1865 -- Fiction 8. Frontier and pioneer life -- Pennsylvania -- Fiction 9. France -- History -- Revolution, 1789-1799 -- Fiction

ISBN 1571317007; 9781571317001

LC 2012042167

In this book, "Eugenie, 15 and haunted by the horrors [of the French Revolution] they've escaped, arrives unprepared for the harshly primitive conditions they find [in America], and she's annoyed by her unrealistic mother's matchmaking with an unpleasant young noble. In alternating chapters, her story is contrasted with that of Quaker Hannah, who . . . has been hired to help the French out for a year but whose faith keeps her from the subservience the noblemen demand." (Kirkus Reviews)

Higgins, M. G.

Bi -Normal; M. G. Higgins. Saddleback Pub 2013 191 p. (paperback) $9.95

Grades: 7 8 9 10 11 12 **Fic**

1. School stories 2. Gay teenagers -- Fiction

ISBN 1622500040; 9781622500048

In this book, "a teen football player with a girlfriend discovers he has feelings for another boy. When Brett first notices his attraction to Zach, a boy who sits next to him in art class, he wants to push it away Brett and his friends are the kind of guys who ogle girls' bodies and pick on boys they perceive as gay. As his feelings intensify, however, Brett is torn between acting on his attraction and acting out of his denial." (Kirkus Reviews)

Higgins, Simon

Moonshadow; rise of the ninja. Little Brown & Co. 2010 325p il $15.99

Grades: 4 5 6 7 **Fic**

1. Japan -- Fiction 2. Ninja -- Fiction 3. Spies -- Fiction 4. Secret societies -- Fiction

ISBN 978-0-316-05531-4; 0-316-05531-X

First published 2008 in Australia with title: Moonshadow: eye of the beast

It's the dawn of an age of peace in medieval Japan. But a power-hungry warlord is plotting to plunge the national into a deadly civil war. Enter Moonshadow, the newest agent for the Grey Light Order, a secret brotherhood of ninja spy warriors. Can Moonshadow defeat the evil warlord or will his first mission be his last?

"The swordplay is fast and furious, and Japanese terms and places are integrated in a manner that reluctant readers will find accessible. This adventure is part spy novel, part magic, and all fun." SLJ

Followed by: The nightmare ninja (2011)

The **nightmare** ninja. Little, Brown 2011 368p (Moonshadow) $15.99

Grades: 4 5 6 7 **Fic**

1. Japan -- Fiction 2. Ninja -- Fiction 3. Orphans -- Fiction 4. Supernatural -- Fiction

ISBN 978-0-316-05533-8; 0-316-05533-6

LC 2010043177

Sequel to: Moonshadow: rise of the ninja (2010)

Battling a power-hungry warlord in medieval Japan, teenaged Moonshadow, an orphaned ninja in the shogun's secret service with the ability to see through the eyes of animals, encounters a weaponless assassin who enters the mind of his victims during their sleep.

"Higgins effectively uses this work to set the stage for a compelling third installment." Kirkus

Hill, C. J.

Erasing time; C. J. Hill. Katherine Tegen Books 2012 361 p. $17.99

Grades: 8 9 10 11 **Fic**

1. Secrecy -- Fiction 2. Resistance to government 3. Future life 4. Science fiction 5. Twins -- Fiction 6. Sisters -- Fiction 7. Time travel -- Fiction 8. Government, Resistance to -- Fiction

ISBN 0062123920; 9780062123923

LC 2011044624

"When twins Sheridan and Taylor wake up 400 years in the future, they find a changed world: domed cities, no animals, and a language that's so different, it barely sounds like English. And the worst news: They can't go back home.

The twenty-fifth-century government transported the girls to their city hoping to find a famous scientist to help perfect a devastating new weapon. The same government has implanted tracking devices in the citizens, limiting and examining everything they do. Taylor and Sheridan have to find a way out of the city before the government discovers their secrets." (Publisher's note)

Slayers; friends and traitors. by C. J. Hill. Feiwel & Friends 2013 390 p. $16.99

Grades: 7 8 9 10 11 12   **Fic**

1. Dragons -- Fiction 2. Teenagers -- Fiction
ISBN 1250024617; 9781250024619

In this book, by C. J. Hill, "Tori's got a problem. She thought she'd have one more summer to train as a dragon Slayer, but time has run out. When Tori hears the horrifying sound of dragon eggs hatching, she knows the Slayers are in trouble. In less than a year, the dragons will be fully grown and completely lethal. The Slayers are well-prepared, but their group is still not complete, and Tori is determined to track down Ryker--the mysterious missing Slayer." (Publisher's note)

"When Tori breaks the rules that keep the dragon slayers safe, all the slayers are endangered unless they can figure out which one of them is a traitor. A steamy love triangle takes center stage over the dragon-fighting in this installment; though many characters from the first book only show up fleetingly, fans of Slayers will find plenty to entertain them." (Horn Book)

Hill, Kirkpatrick

Do not pass go. Margaret K. McElderry Books 2007 229p $15.99

Grades: 6 7 8 9   **Fic**

1. Alaska -- Fiction 2. Fathers -- Fiction 3. Prisoners -- Fiction
ISBN 978-1-4169-1400-6; 1-4169-1400-5

LC 2006-03254

When Deet's father is jailed for using drugs, Deet learns that prison is not what he expected, nor are other people necessarily the way he thought they were.

"Hill does not sugar-coat the hardships that plague Deet's family. . . . Deet emerges as a sensitive, courageous protagonist who is smart enough and open-minded enough to look past people's mistakes." Publ Wkly

Hilmo, Tess

Skies like these; Tess Hilmo. Margaret Ferguson Books, Farrar Straus Giroux 2014 240 p. (hardback) $16.99

Grades: 4 5 6 7   **Fic**

1. Western stories 2. Friendship -- Fiction 3. Aunts -- Fiction 4. Wyoming -- Fiction 5. Eccentrics and eccentricities -- Fiction
ISBN 0374369984; 9780374369989

LC 2013033675

"Twelve-year-old Jade's perfect summers have always been spent reading and watching TV reruns, so she's not happy when her parents send her off to Wyoming to her aunt's house. She meets a boy who calls himself Roy Parker--just like the real name of the legendary rebel cowboy Butch Cassidy. . . . Jade wants to be a good friend, but she's not so sure about Roy's schemes." (Publisher's note)

"In Hilmo's second middle-grade novel, a 12-year-old city girl spends a month in Wyoming and finds big skies, a boy who idolizes Butch Cassidy, and her own sense of adventure. . . . But rest assured, if there's a sequel, their future big plans will likely center around climbing Grand Teton rather than robbing banks." Booklist

★ **With** a name like Love. Margaret Ferguson Books/Farrar Straus Giroux 2011 249p $16.99

Grades: 5 6 7 8   **Fic**

1. Mystery fiction 2. Arkansas -- Fiction 3. Country life -- Fiction 4. Christian life -- Fiction 5. Conduct of life -- Fiction
ISBN 978-0-374-38465-4; 0-374-38465-7

LC 2010036314

Thirteen-year-old Olivene Love gets tangled up in a murder mystery when her itinerant preaching family arrives in the small town of Binder, Arkansas in 1957.

"Hilmo creates a family, town and a mystery that readers won't soon forget." Kirkus

Hinton, S. E.

★ The **outsiders**. Viking 1967 188p $17.99; pa $9.99

Grades: 7 8 9 10   **Fic**

1. Social classes -- Fiction 2. Juvenile delinquency -- Fiction
ISBN 0-670-53257-6; 0-14-038572-X pa
ALA YALSA Margaret A. Edwards Award (1988)

"This remarkable novel by a seventeen-year-old girl gives a moving, credible view of the outsiders from the inside—their loyalty to each other, their sensitivity under tough crusts, their understanding of self and society." Horn Book

Hinwood, Christine

The **returning**. Dial Books 2011 302p map $17.99

Grades: 6 7 8 9 10   **Fic**

1. War stories 2. Villages -- Fiction
ISBN 978-0-8037-3528-6; 0-8037-3528-6

LC 2010-08398

First published 2009 in Australia with title: Bloodflower

When the twelve-year war between the Uplanders and Downlanders is over and Cam returns home to his village, questions dog him, from how he lost an arm to why he was the only one of his fellow soldiers to survive, such that he must leave until his own suspicions are resolved.

"Themes of rebuilding and redemption are powerful, but it is in the small, acutely observed details of debut author Hinwood's world that her story truly shines." Publ Wkly

Hirahara, Naomi

1001 cranes. Delacorte Press 2008 230p $15.99; lib bdg $18.99; pa $6.50

Grades: 5 6 7 8   **Fic**

1. Family life -- Fiction 2. Grandparents -- Fiction 3. Japanese Americans -- Fiction
ISBN 978-0-385-73556-8; 0-385-73556-1; 978-0-385-90541-1 lib bdg; 0-385-90541-6 lib bdg; 978-0-440-42234-1 pa; 0-440-42234-5 pa

LC 2007-27655

With her parents on the verge of separating, Angela, a twelve-year-old Japanese American girl, spends the summer in Los Angeles with her grandparents, where she folds paper cranes into wedding displays, becomes involved with a young skateboarder, and learns how complicated relationships can be.

Angela's "colorful, bold voice captures the excitement of her first love as well as the anxiety of not understanding the many secrets of the adults around her. By experiencing her family's support, by learning about her Japanese heritage, and by acknowledging the various ways that love is expressed, Angela emerges into a strong, caring person." SLJ

Hiranandani, Veera

★ The **whole** story of half a girl. Delacorte Press 2012 $16.99; lib bdg $19.99

Grades: 4 5 6 7   **Fic**

1. School stories 2. East Indian Americans -- Fiction 3. Racially mixed people -- Fiction 4. Depression (Psychology) -- Fiction

ISBN 978-0-385-74128-6; 0-385-74128-6; 978-0-375-98995-7 lib bdg; 0-375-98995-1 lib bdg; 978-0-375-98441-9 ebook

                LC 2011026178

In this book, "[w]hen Sonia's father loses his job at the end of her fifth-grade year, it means she can't return to her beloved private school and instead must navigate the rocky waters of public school for the first time. Up until this point, eleven-year-old Sonia has never thought that much about her identity as the daughter of an Indian father and a Jewish-American mother, but she is suddenly faced with questions that she can't always answer about her race, her ethnicity, and her core values. She . . . . begins two friendships: with Kate, a very perky, popular girl who encourages Sonia to try out for cheerleading but seems very keen on transforming her into something she isn't, and with Alisha, who, like Sonia, aspires to be a writer." (Bulletin of the Center for Children's Books).

"Sonia's struggles are painfully realistic. . . True to life, her problems do not wrap up neatly, but Sonia's growth is deeply rewarding in this thoughtful and beautifully wrought novel." Publ Wkly

Hirsch, Jeff

The **39** clues: Breakaway; unstoppable: breakaway. Jeff Hirsch. Scholastic 2014 192 p. (The 39 clues: unstoppable) (paper over board) $12.99

Grades: 4 5 6 7   **Fic**

1. Betrayal 2. Adventure stories 3. Brothers and sisters -- Fiction

ISBN 0545521424; 9780545521420

                LC 2013942298

In this 39 Clues series book by Jeff Hirsch, "Dan and Amy are facing their greatest threat yet, an enemy who has found a way to use the source of the Cahill family power against them. To stop him, Dan and Amy must set out on a desperate mission that will take them from one of the world's hottest regions all the way to the frozen blast of the Arctic Circle. But with the enemy closing in, Dan finds himself facing the one terror he never imagined--being betrayed by his own sister." (Publisher's note)

The **eleventh** plague. Scholastic Press 2011 278p $17.99

Grades: 7 8 9 10   **Fic**

1. Science fiction

ISBN 978-0-545-29014-2; 0-545-29014-7

                LC 2010048966

Twenty years after the start of the war that caused the Collapse, fifteen-year-old Stephen, his father, and grandfather travel post-Collapse America scavenging, but when his

grandfather dies and his father decides to risk everything to save the lives of two strangers, Stephen's life is turned upside down.

This "novel is an impressive story with strong characters. . . . Hirsch delivers a tight, well-crafted story." Publ Wkly

Hirsch, Odo

Darius Bell and the glitter pool. Kane/Miller 2010 214p $15.99

Grades: 4 5 6 7   **Fic**

1. Gifts -- Fiction 2. Poverty -- Fiction

ISBN 978-1-935279-65-5; 1-935279-65-3

First published 2009 in Australia

The Bell family's ancestors were showered with honours, gifts and grants of land. In exchange, they have bestowed a Gift, once every 25 years, on the town. Now it's Darius's father's turn and there is no money for an impressive gift. When an earthquake reveals a glorious cave, with the most beautiful minerals lining the walls, he thinks he's found the answer.

"With an inventive cast of characters and a surprise twist at the end, this gentle, appealing story would make a terrific read-aloud for a young audience." Booklist

Hitchcock, Shannon

The **ballad** of Jessie Pearl; Shannon Hitchcock. 1st ed. Namelos llc 2012 131 p. ill. (hardcover) $18.95

Grades: 5 6 7 8   **Fic**

1. Love stories 2. Historical fiction 3. Tuberculosis -- Fiction

ISBN 160898141X; 9781608981410; 9781608981427

                LC 2012936706

In this novel, by Shannon Hitchcock, "it's 1922, and Jessie has big plans for her future, but that's before tuberculosis strikes. Though she has no talent for cooking, cleaning, or nursing, Jessie puts her dreams on hold to help her family. She falls in love for the first time ever, and suddenly what she wants is not so simple anymore." (Publisher's note)

Hobbs, Valerie

★ The **last** best days of summer. Frances Foster Books 2010 197p $16.99

Grades: 5 6 7 8   **Fic**

1. Artists -- Fiction 2. Old age -- Fiction 3. Popularity -- Fiction 4. Grandmothers -- Fiction 5. Down syndrome -- Fiction

ISBN 978-0-374-34670-6; 0-374-34670-4

                LC 2008-47145

During a summer visit, twelve-year-old Lucy must come to terms with both her grandmother's failing memory and how her mentally-challenged neighbor will impact her popularity when both enter the same middle school in the fall.

"The story's finely tuned realism is refreshing, particularly in Lucy's yearning for social acceptance and in the fully drawn and wholly memorable characters." Booklist

Hobbs, Will

Beardance. Atheneum Pubs. 1993 197p il pa $5.99

Grades: 7 8 9 10 **Fic**
1. Bears -- Fiction 2. Ute Indians -- Fiction
ISBN 0-689-31867-7; 0-689-87072-8 pa

LC 92-44874

Sequel to Bearstone

While accompanying an elderly rancher on a trip into the San Juan Mountains, Cloyd, a Ute Indian boy, tries to help two orphaned grizzly cubs survive the winter and, at the same time, completes his spirit mission.

"The story offers plenty of action and memorable characters, and the descriptions of Ute rituals and legends, the setting, and Cloyd's first experiences with spirit dreams are particularly well done." Horn Book Guide

★ **Bearstone**. Atheneum Pubs. 1989 154p hardcover o.p. pa $4.99
Grades: 7 8 9 10 **Fic**
1. Ute Indians -- Fiction
ISBN 0-689-87071-X pa

LC 89-6641

"The growth and maturity that Cloyd acquires as the summer progresses is juxtaposed poetically against the majestic Colorado landscape. Hobbs has creatively blended myth and reality as Cloyd forges a new identity for himself." Voice Youth Advocates

Followed by Beardance (1993)

Crossing the wire. HarperCollins 2006 216p $15.99; lib bdg $16.89; pa $5.99
Grades: 5 6 7 8 **Fic**
1. Mexicans -- Fiction 2. Illegal aliens -- Fiction
ISBN 978-0-06-074138-9; 0-06-074138-4; 978-0-06-074139-6 lib bdg; 0-06-074139-2 lib bdg; 978-0-06-074140-2 pa; 0-06-074140-6 pa

LC 2005-19697

Fifteen-year-old Victor Flores journeys north in a desperate attempt to cross the Arizona border and find work in the United States to support his family in central Mexico.

This is "an exciting story in a vital contemporary setting." Voice Youth Advocates

Downriver. Atheneum Pubs. 1991 204p hardcover o.p. pa $6.99
Grades: 7 8 9 10 **Fic**
1. White-water canoeing -- Fiction
ISBN 0-689-31690-9; 0-440-22673-2 pa

LC 90-1044

Fifteen-year-old Jessie and the other rebellious teenage members of a wilderness survival school team abandon their adult leader, hijack his boats, and try to run the dangerous white water at the bottom of the Grand Canyon

"The book is exquisitely plotted, with nail-biting suspense and excitement." SLJ

Ghost canoe. Morrow Junior Bks. 1997 195p $16.99
Grades: 5 6 7 8 **Fic**
1. Adventure fiction 2. Buried treasure -- Fiction 3. Pacific Northwest -- Fiction
ISBN 0-688-14193-5

LC 96-34417

Fourteen-year-old Nathan, fishing with the Makah in the Pacific Northwest, finds himself holding a vital clue when a mysterious stranger comes to town looking for Spanish treasure

"Hobbs blends together a number of elements to create an exciting adventure set in 1874..., A winning tale that artfully combines history, nature, and suspense." SLJ

★ **Go** big or go home. HarperCollinsPublishers 2008 185p $15.99; lib bdg $16.89; pa $5.99
Grades: 6 7 8 9 **Fic**
1. Science fiction 2. Cousins -- Fiction 3. Meteorites -- Fiction 4. South Dakota -- Fiction
ISBN 0-06-074141-4; 0-06-074142-2 lib bdg; 0-06-074143-0 pa; 978-0-06-074141-9; 978-0-06-074142-6 lib bdg; 978-0-06-074143-3 pa

LC 2006100440

Fourteen-year-old Brady and his cousin Quinn love extreme sports, but nothing could prepare them for the aftermath of Brady's close encounter with a meteorite after it crashes into his Black Hills, South Dakota, bedroom.

"The sense of place is powerful, with bits of lore about the region making the reader feel immersed in the story and its setting, and the characterizations are especially strong." Voice Youth Advocates

★ **Jason's** gold. Morrow Junior Bks. 1999 221p $16.99; pa $5.99
Grades: 5 6 7 8 **Fic**
1. Orphans -- Fiction 2. Voyages and travels -- Fiction 3. Klondike River Valley (Yukon) -- Gold discoveries -- Fiction
ISBN 0-688-15093-4; 0-380-72914-8 pa

LC 99-17973

When news of the discovery of gold in Canada's Yukon Territory in 1897 reaches fifteen-year-old Jason, he embarks on a 10,000-mile journey to strike it rich

"The successful presentation of a fascinating era, coupled with plenty of action, makes this a good historical fiction choice." SLJ

Followed by Down the Yukon (2001)

Leaving Protection. HarperCollins 2004 178p il map $15.99; pa $5.99
Grades: 7 8 9 10 **Fic**
1. Alaska -- Fiction 2. Fishing -- Fiction 3. Buried treasure -- Fiction
ISBN 0-688-17475-2; 0-380-73312-9 pa

LC 2003-15545

Sixteen-year-old Robbie Daniels, happy to get a job aboard a troller fishing for king salmon off southeastern Alaska, finds himself in danger when he discovers that his mysterious captain is searching for long-buried Russian plaques that lay claim to Alaska and the Northwest

This "nautical thriller brims with detail about the fishing life and weaves in historical facts as well. . . . Robbie's doubts build to a climactic finale involving a dramatic and fateful storm at sea, grippingly rendered. Fans of maritime tales will relish the atmosphere and the bursts of action." Publ Wkly

Never say die; by Will Hobbs. HarperCollins Children's Books 2012 224 p. (trade bdg.) $16.99

Grades: 4 5 6 7   **Fic**

1. Canada -- Fiction 2. Wilderness survival -- Fiction 3. Adventure fiction 4. Bears -- Fiction 5. Caribou -- Fiction 6. Eskimos -- Fiction 7. Brothers -- Fiction 8. Inuit -- Canada -- Fiction 9. Photojournalism -- Fiction 10. Aklavik (N.W.T.) -- Fiction 11. Climatic changes -- Fiction 12. Adventure and adventurers -- Fiction

ISBN 006170878X; 9780061708787; 9780061708794

LC 2011053289

This juvenile adventure novel, by Will Hobbs, is set "in Canada's Arctic, [where] Nick Thrasher is an accomplished Inuit hunter at fifteen. . . . Ryan Powers . . , invites Nick to come along and help him find the caribou. Barely down the river, disaster strikes. . . . With nothing but the clothes on his back and the knife on his hip, Nick is up against it in a world of wolves, caribou, and grizzlies. All the while, the monstrous grolar bear stalks the land." (Publisher's note)

Take me to the river. HarperCollins 2011 184p $15.99; lib bdg $16.89

Grades: 5 6 7 8   **Fic**

1. Texas -- Fiction 2. Cousins -- Fiction 3. Canoes and canoeing -- Fiction

ISBN 978-0-06-074144-0; 0-06-074144-9; 978-0-06-074145-7 lib bdg; 0-06-074145-7 lib bdg

LC 2010003147

When North Carolina fourteen-year-old Dylan Sands joins his fifteen-year-old cousin Rio in running the Rio Grande River, they face a tropical storm and a fugitive kidnapper.

"The story unfolds in a disarming manner. The pace is quick, and the challenges are relentless, but the writing is so grounded in physical details and emotional realism that every turn of events seems convincing within the context of the story." Booklist

Wild Man Island. HarperCollins Pubs. 2002 184p $15.99; lib bdg $16.89; pa $5.99

Grades: 6 7 8 9   **Fic**

1. Alaska -- Fiction 2. Wilderness survival -- Fiction

ISBN 0-688-17473-6; 0-06-029810-3 lib bdg; 0-380-73310-2 pa

LC 2001-39818

After fourteen-year-old Andy slips away from his kayaking group to visit the wilderness site of his archaeologist father's death, a storm strands him on Admiralty Island, Alaska, where he manages to survive, encounters unexpected animal and human inhabitants, and looks for traces of the earliest prehistoric immigrants to America

"A well-paced adventure, this novel combines survival saga, mystery, and archaeological expedition." Voice Youth Advocates

Hocking, Amanda

Wake; Amanda Hocking. St. Martin's Griffin 2012 309 p. (hardback) $17.99

Grades: 7 8 9 10   **Fic**

1. Occult fiction 2. Fantasy fiction 3. Sirens (Mythology) -- Fiction 4. Love -- Fiction 5. Sisters -- Fiction 6. Supernatural -- Fiction 7. Seaside resorts

-- Fiction

ISBN 1250008123; 9781250008121; 9781429956581

LC 2012014630

This is the first in Amanda Hocking's Watersong series. Here, "Gemma Fisher is happy—she's a star on the swim team, her family is loving and supportive, and the crush-worthy boy next door returns her interest. The only downside: three gorgeous but creepy new girls who have her in their sights." These girls ultimately turn out to be Sirens who trick Gemma into drinking potion that turns her into a Siren as well. (Publishers Weekly)

Followed by Lullaby (2012) and Tidal (2013)

Hodge, Rosamund

Cruel Beauty; Rosamund Hodge. Balzer + Bray, an imprint of HarperCollinsPublishers 2014 352 p. (hardcover) $17.99

Grades: 8 9 10 11 12   **Fic**

1. Love stories 2. Imaginary places 3. Magic -- Fiction 4. Fantasy

ISBN 0062224735; 9780062224736

LC 2013015418

In this book, by Rosamund Hodge, "betrothed to the evil ruler of her kingdom, Nyx has always known her fate was to marry him, kill him, and free her people from his tyranny. On her seventeenth birthday, when she moves into his castle high on the kingdom's mountaintop, nothing is as she expected. Nyx knows she must save her homeland at all costs, yet she can't resist the pull of her sworn enemy--who's gotten in her way by stealing her heart." (Publisher's note)

"Hodge's story infuses elements of Greek mythology and classic fairy tales. The plot moves quickly, and the characters are well formed; their transgressions make them interesting and authentic. The complex relationship between Nyx and Ignifex is especially engaging. An entertaining read for teens who enjoy romantic fantasy.—" (School Library Journal)

Hodkin, Michelle

The **evolution** of Mara Dyer; Michelle Hodkin. Simon & Schuster Books for Young Readers 2012 527 p. (hardcover) $17.99

Grades: 7 8 9 10 11 12   **Fic**

1. Stalkers -- Fiction 2. Supernatural -- Fiction 3. Post-traumatic stress disorder -- Fiction 4. Love -- Fiction 5. Florida -- Fiction

ISBN 1442421797; 9781442421790; 9781442421813

LC 2012019195

Sequel to: The unbecoming of Mara Dyer

In this novel by Michelle Hodkin, part of the Mara Dyer Trilogy, "Mara continues her relationship with wealthy Noah. . . . Meanwhile, Mara insists that her supposedly dead former boyfriend, Jude, continues to stalk her. She is being treated as an outpatient for PTSD after causing (as she originally believed) the deaths of Jude and her friends. . . . Noah uses his wits and wealth to try to protect her and to investigate the possibility that Jude indeed survived." (Kirkus)

The **unbecoming** of Mara Dyer. Simon & Schuster 2011 456p $16.99

Grades: 7 8 9 10 11 12   **Fic**

1. School stories 2. Florida -- Fiction 3. Family life

-- Fiction 4. Supernatural -- Fiction 5. Post-traumatic
stress disorder -- Fiction

ISBN 978-1-4424-2176-9; 1-4424-2176-2

LC 2010050862

Seventeen-year-old Mara cannot remember the accident
that took the lives of three of her friends but, after moving
from Rhode Island to Florida, finding love with Noah, and
more deaths, she realizes uncovering something buried in
her memory might save her family and her future.

"The characters are real and wonderful, and the supernatural story is riveting." SLJ

Hof, Marjolijn

Mother number zero. Groundwood Books 2011
179p $16.95

Grades: 4 5 6 7   **Fic**
1. Adoption -- Fiction 2. Siblings -- Fiction 3. Family
life -- Fiction 4. Netherlands -- Fiction

ISBN 978-1-55498-078-9; 1-55498-078-X

Fay "and his older sister An Bing Wa were both adopted;
she was an abandoned baby in China, and he was born to a
mother traumatized in the Bosnian conflict. A new girl in the
neighborhood, Maud, takes a keen interest in Fay's story and
urges him to find his birth mother. . . . Hof . . . writes Fay's
narration with a calm, matter-of-fact voice that possesses a
literalness and simplicity in keeping with his youth. . . . The
story nonetheless treats the characters with quiet percipi-
ence. . . . Younger fans of domestic novels who like a tale
with more gravitas if not reading difficulty will appreciate
this thoughtful family story." Bull Cent Child Books

Hoffman, Alice

Green angel. Scholastic Press 2003 116p pa
$5.99

Grades: 7 8 9 10   **Fic**
1. Gardening -- Fiction

ISBN 0-439-44384-9; 0-545-20411-9 pa

LC 2002-6980

Haunted by grief and by her past after losing her family
in a fire, fifteen-year-old Green retreats into her ruined garden as she struggles to survive emotionally and physically
on her own

"A powerfully written and thought-provoking
selection." SLJ

★ **Green** witch. Scholastic Press 2010 135p
$17.99

Grades: 7 8 9 10 11 12   **Fic**
1. Orphans -- Fiction 2. Gardening -- Fiction 3.
Bereavement -- Fiction 4. Storytelling -- Fiction 5.
Supernatural -- Fiction 6. Missing persons -- Fiction

ISBN 978-0-545-14195-6; 0-545-14195-8

LC 2009-17606

A year after her world was nearly destroyed, sixteen-
year-old Green has become the one villagers turn to for aid,
especially to record their stories, but Green will need the
help of other women who, like herself, are believed to be
witches if she is to find her best friend and her one true love.

"Haunting, philosophical, and filled with poetic imagery
. . . this book will leave an indelible mark." Publ Wkly

Hoffman, Mary

★ The **falconer's** knot; a story of friars, flirtation and foul play. Bloomsbury Children's Books
2007 297p $16.95

Grades: 7 8 9 10   **Fic**
1. Renaissance -- Fiction 2. Religious life -- Fiction 3.
Italy -- History -- 0-1559 -- Fiction

ISBN 978-1-59990-056-8; 1-59990-056-4

LC 2006-16365

Silvano and Chiara, teens sent to live in a friary and a
nunnery in Renaissance Italy, are drawn to one another and
dream of a future together, but when murders are committed
in the friary, they must discover who is behind the crimes
before they can realize their love.

"Hoffman creates utterly engaging characters and vivid
settings, and she skillfully turns up the suspense, wrapping
her varied plot threads into a satisfying whole." Booklist

Hoffman, Nina Kiriki

A **stir** of bones. Viking 2003 211p $15.99

Grades: 7 8 9 10   **Fic**
1. Ghost stories 2. Wife abuse -- Fiction

ISBN 0-670-03551-3

LC 2003-5029

Prequel to the author's adult novels, A red heart of memories (1999) and Past the size of dreaming (2000)

Fourteen-year-old Susan Blackstrom "begins the painful
process of breaking away from her abusive father, with help
from allies both human and supernatural. A chance encounter with three classmates leads Susan to an abandoned house
that . . . harbors an uncommonly substantial ghost named
Nathan. . . . Richly endowed with complex relationships, a
strange and subtle brand of magic, evocative language, and
suspenseful storytelling, this will draw readers into a world
less safe and simple than it seems at first glance." Booklist

Hokenson, Terry

The **winter** road; 1st ed.; Front Street 2006
175p $16.95

Grades: 7 8 9 10   **Fic**
1. Canada -- Fiction 2. Survival after airplane accidents,
shipwrecks, etc. -- Fiction

ISBN 1-932425-45-4

LC 2005027030

Seventeen-year-old Willa, still grieving over the death
of her older brother and the neglect of her father, decides
to fly a small plane to fetch her mother from Northern
Ontario, but when the plane crashes she is all alone in the
snowy wilderness.

"The mortal challenges Willa faces make for a gripping
narrative, one sharpened by visceral details." Booklist

Holczer, Tracy

The **secret** hum of a daisy; Tracy Holczer. G.P.
Putnam's Sons, an imprint of Penguin Group (USA)
2014 320 p. (hardback) $16.99

Grades: 5 6 7 8   **Fic**
1. Home -- Fiction 2. Death -- Fiction 3. Moving
-- Fiction 4. Grandmothers -- Fiction 5. Treasure hunt
(Game) -- Fiction 6. Moving, Household -- Fiction

ISBN 039916393X; 9780399163937

LC 2013039962

In this book, by Tracy Holczer, "twelve-year-old Grace and her mother . . . [travel] from place to place like gypsies. But Grace wants to finally have a home all their own. Just when she thinks she's found it her mother says it's time to move again. Grace summons the courage to tell her mother how she really feels and will always regret that her last words to her were angry ones. After her mother's sudden death, Grace is forced to live with a grandmother she's never met." (Publisher's note)

"Twelve-year-old Grace, mourning her mother's death, goes to live with her grandmother in Mama's hometown. Grace refuses to forgive Grandma for sending Mama away as a pregnant teen. In talking to townspeople, who help fill in gaps about her family's past, Grace finds the hope, peace, and home she's been looking for. Holczer weaves healing symbols (birds, daisies) and poetry into her lyrical text." Horn Book

Holder, Nancy

Crusade; by Nancy Holder and Debbie Viguie. Simon Pulse 2010 470p $16.99

Grades: 7 8 9 10 11   **Fic**

1. Horror fiction 2. Sisters -- Fiction 3. Vampires -- Fiction 4. Supernatural -- Fiction

ISBN 978-1-4169-9802-0; 1-4169-9802-0

LC 2010-9094

An international team of six teenaged vampire hunters, trained in Salamanca, Spain, goes to New Orleans seeking to rescue team-member Jenn's younger sister as the vampires escalate their efforts to take over the Earth.

"The cinematic writing and apocalyptic scenario should find a ready audience." Publ Wkly

Followed by: Damned (2011)

Damned; by Nancy Holder and Debbie Viguie. Simon Pulse 2011 $16.99; pa $9.99

Grades: 7 8 9 10   **Fic**

1. Horror fiction 2. Vampires -- Fiction 3. Supernatural -- Fiction

ISBN 978-1-4169-9804-4; 1-4169-9804-7; 978-1-4169-9805-1 pa; 1-4169-9805-5 pa

LC 2011005474

Sequel to: Crusade (2010)

As the newly appointed Hunter, teenager Jenn leads the fighting teams who defend against the Cursed Ones--the vampires who are taking over Earth--but an even more sinister force now threatens the teams of hunters, with the fate of humanity at stake.

Holm, Jennifer L.

★ **Boston** Jane: an adventure. HarperCollins Pubs. 2001 273p hardcover o.p. pa $6.99

Grades: 6 7 8 9   **Fic**

1. Chinook Indians -- Fiction 2. Washington (State) -- Fiction 3. Frontier and pioneer life -- Fiction

ISBN 0-06-028738-1; 0-06-028739-X; 0-06-440849-3 pa

LC 2001-16753

Schooled in the lessons of etiquette for young ladies of 1854, Miss Jane Peck of Philadelphia finds little use for manners during her long sea voyage to the Pacific Northwest

and while living among the American traders and Chinook Indians of Washington Territory

"Strong characterizations, meticulous attention to historical details . . . and a perceptive understanding of human nature make this a first-rate story not to be missed." Booklist

Other titles about Boston Jane are:

Boston Jane: the claim (2004)

Boston Jane: wilderness days (2002)

Boston Jane: the claim. HarperCollins Pub. 2004 230p hardcover o.p. pa $7.99 **Fic**

1. Chinook Indians -- Fiction 2. Washington (State) -- Fiction 3. Frontier and pioneer life -- Fiction

ISBN 0-06-029045-5; 0-06-029046-3 lib bdg; 0-375-86206-4 pa

LC 2003-9556

Sequel to Boston Jane: wilderness days

The arrival from Philadelphia of her spiteful nemesis Sally Biddle and the return of her corrupt ex-fiance Richard Baldt spell trouble for seventeen-year-old Miss Jane Peck, who has survived on her own in Shoalwater Bay, a community of white settlers and Chinook Indians in 1850s Washington Territory

"The story is fast paced and lively, and Holm successfully campaigns for diversity and feminism without making her plot seem like a thinly disguised message." Voice Youth Advocates

Boston Jane: wilderness days. HarperCollins Pubs. 2002 242p hardcover o.p. pa $7.99

Grades: 6 7 8 9   **Fic**

1. Washington (State) -- Fiction 2. Frontier and pioneer life -- Fiction

ISBN 0-06-029043-9; 0-06-029044-7 lib bdg; 0-375-86205-6 pa

LC 2002-1473

Sequel to: Boston Jane: an adventure

Far from her native Philadelphia, Miss Jane Peck continues to prove that she's more than an etiquette-schooled graduate of Miss Hepplewhite's Young Ladies Academy as she braves the untamed wilderness of Washington Territory in the mid 1850s

"Holm once again delivers an action-packed story with a strong female protagonist." SLJ

Followed by: Boston Jane: the claim

The fourteenth goldfish; Jennifer L. Holm. Random House Inc 2014 208 p. (hardcover) $16.99; (library binding) $19.99

Grades: 4 5 6 7   **Fic**

1. Scientists -- Fiction 2. Grandfathers -- Fiction 3. Aging -- Fiction 4. Family life -- Fiction

ISBN 0375870644; 9780375870644; 9780375970641

LC 2013035052

"Eleven-year-old Ellie has never liked change. She misses fifth grade. She misses her old best friend. She even misses her dearly departed goldfish. Then one day a strange boy shows up. He's bossy. He's cranky. And weirdly enough . . . he looks a lot like Ellie's grandfather, a scientist who's always been slightly obsessed with immortality." (Publisher's note)

"With humor and heart, Holm has crafted a story about life, family, and finding one's passion that will appeal to readers willing to imagine the possible." SLJ

Includes bibliographical references

★ **Middle** school is worse than meatloaf; a year told through stuff. by Jennifer L. Holm; pictures by Elicia Castaldi. Atheneum Books for Young Readers 2007 un il $12.99

Grades: 5 6 7 8   **Fic**

1. School stories 2. Family life -- Fiction

ISBN 0-689-85281-9

"Ginny Davis begins seventh grade with a list of items to accomplish. This list, along with lots of other 'stuff'—including diary entries, refrigerator notes, cards from Grandpa, and IM screen messages—convey a year full of ups and downs. Digitally rendered collage illustrations realistically depict the various means of communication, and the story flows easily from one colorful page to the next. . . . The story combines honesty and humor to create a believable and appealing voice." SLJ

★ **Our** only May Amelia. HarperCollins Pubs. 1999 253p il hardcover o.p. pa $5.99

Grades: 5 6 7 8   **Fic**

1. Family life -- Fiction 2. Finnish Americans -- Fiction 3. Washington (State) -- Fiction 4. Frontier and pioneer life -- Fiction

ISBN 0-06-027822-6; 0-06-440856-6 pa

LC 98-47504

A Newbery Medal honor book, 2000

As the only girl in a Finnish American family of seven brothers, May Amelia Jackson resents being expected to act like a lady while growing up in Washington State in 1899

"The voice of the colloquial first-person narrative rings true and provides a vivid picture of frontier and pioneer life. . . . An afterword discusses Holm's research into her own family's history and that of other Finnish immigrants." Horn Book Guide

Followed by: The trouble with May Amelia (2011)

★ **Penny** from heaven. Random House 2006 274p il $15.95; lib bdg $17.99; pa $6.99

Grades: 5 6 7 8   **Fic**

1. New Jersey -- Fiction 2. Family life -- Fiction 3. Italian Americans -- Fiction

ISBN 0-375-83687-X; 0-375-93687-4 lib bdg; 0-375-83689-6 pa

LC 2005-13896

A Newbery Medal honor book, 2007

As she turns twelve during the summer of 1953, Penny gains new insights into herself and her family while also learning a secret about her father's death.

"Holm impressively wraps pathos with comedy in this coming-of-age story, populated by a cast of vivid characters." Booklist

The **trouble** with May Amelia; illustrated by Adam Gustavson. Atheneum Books for Young Readers 2011 204p il $15.99

Grades: 5 6 7 8   **Fic**

1. Sex role -- Fiction 2. Siblings -- Fiction 3. Finnish

Americans -- Fiction 4. Washington (State) -- Fiction 5. Frontier and pioneer life -- Fiction

ISBN 1-4169-1373-4; 978-1-4169-1373-3

LC 2010042092

Sequel to: Our only May Amelia (1999)

Living with seven brothers and her father, who thinks girls are useless, a thirteen-year-old Finnish American farm girl is determined to prove her worth when a enterprising gentleman tries to purchase their cash-strapped family settlement in Washington State in 1900.

"Holm gets her heroine just right. Narrating events in dryly witty, plainspoken first-person, this indomitable teen draws readers in with her account, through which her world comes alive." Kirkus

Holmes, Sara Lewis

★ **Operation** Yes. Arthur A. Levine Books 2009 234p $16.99

Grades: 5 6 7 8   **Fic**

1. School stories 2. Acting -- Fiction 3. Cousins -- Fiction 4. Teachers -- Fiction 5. Military bases -- Fiction

ISBN 978-0-545-10795-2; 0-545-10795-4; 978-0-545-10796-9 pa; 0-545-10796-2 pa

LC 2008053732

In her first ever teaching job, Miss Loupe uses improvisational acting exercises with her sixth-grade students at an Air Force base school, and when she experiences a family tragedy, her previously skeptical class members use what they have learned to help her, her brother, and other wounded soldiers

"Quick, funny, sad, full of heart, and irresistibly absorbing." Booklist

Holt, Kimberly Willis

★ The **water** seeker. Henry Holt 2010 309p $16.99

Grades: 4 5 6 7   **Fic**

1. Father-son relationship -- Fiction 2. Frontier and pioneer life -- Fiction 3. Overland journeys to the Pacific -- Fiction

ISBN 978-0-8050-8020-9; 0-8050-8020-1

LC 2009-24149

Traces the hard life, filled with losses, adversity, and adventure, of Amos, son of a trapper and dowser, from 1833 when his mother dies giving birth to him until 1859, when he himself has grown up and has a son of his own.

"Drawing on such diverse themes as Manifest Destiny, personal identity and cross-cultural relationships, the author has crafted a satisfying all-ages story that hosts a dazzling array of richly realized secondary characters . . . and flows as effortlessly as the Platte River." Kirkus

★ **When** Zachary Beaver came to town. Holt & Co. 1999 227p $17.99

Grades: 5 6 7 8   **Fic**

1. Texas -- Fiction 2. Obesity -- Fiction 3. Friendship -- Fiction

ISBN 0-8050-6116-9

LC 99-27998

During the summer of 1971 in a small Texas town, thirteen-year-old Toby and his best friend Cal meet the star of a sideshow act, 600-pound Zachary, the fattest boy in the world

"Holt writes with a subtle sense of humor and sensitivity, and reading her work is a delightful experience." Voice Youth Advocates

Holub, Josef

An **innocent** soldier; translated by Michael Hofmann. Arthur A. Levine Books 2005 231p $16.99

Grades: 8 9 10 11 12   **Fic**

1. War stories 2. Russia -- Fiction 3. France -- History -- 1799-1815 -- Fiction

ISBN 0-439-62771-0

A sixteen-year-old farmhand is tricked into fighting in the Napoleonic Wars by the farmer for whom he works, who secretly substitutes him for the farmer's own son.

"This is a well-wrought psychological tale. . . . [It] has a lot to offer to those seeking to build a deep historical fiction collection." SLJ

Holyoke, Polly

The **Neptune** Project; Polly Holyoke. 1st ed. Disney-Hyperion Books 2013 352 p. (reinforced) $16.99

Grades: 4 5 6 7   **Fic**

1. Science fiction 2. Ocean -- Fiction 3. Genetic engineering -- Fiction 4. Survival -- Fiction 5. Undersea colonies -- Fiction 6. Environmental degradation -- Fiction

ISBN 1423157567; 9781423157564

LC 2013000353

In this novel, by Polly Holyoke, "Nere . . . is one of a group of kids who . . . have been genetically altered to survive in the ocean. . . . In order to reach the safe haven of the Neptune colony, Nere and her fellow mutates must swim through hundreds of miles of dangerous waters, relying only on their wits, dolphins, and each other to evade terrifying undersea creatures and a government that will stop at nothing to capture the Neptune kids." (Publisher's note)

Hoobler, Dorothy

The **demon** in the teahouse; [by] Dorothy and Thomas Hoobler. Philomel Bks. 2001 181p $17.99

Grades: 6 7 8 9   **Fic**

1. Mystery fiction 2. Japan -- Fiction

ISBN 0-399-23499-3

LC 00-50184

In eighteenth-century Japan, fourteen-year-old Seikei, a merchant's son in training to be a samurai, helps his patron investigate a series of murders and arson in the capital city of Edo, each of which is associated in some way with a popular geisha

"Details of Shogun-era Japan are seamlessly woven into a gripping story." Horn Book Guide

★ The **ghost** in the Tokaido Inn; [by] Dorothy and Thomas Hoobler. Philomel Bks. 1999 214p $17.99; pa $6.99

Grades: 6 7 8 9   **Fic**

1. Mystery fiction 2. Japan -- Fiction

ISBN 0-399-23330-X; 0-698-11879-0 pa

LC 98-14089

While attempting to solve the mystery of a stolen jewel, Seikei, a merchant's son who longs to be a samurai, joins a group of kabuki actors in eighteenth-century Japan

"Precise characterization, suspenseful plot twists, and a pace defined by swift and sometimes violent action make this a lively period thriller." Bull Cent Child Books

Other titles about Seikei are:

The demon in the teahouse (2001)

In darkess, death (2004)

The sword that cut the burning grass (2005)

A samurai never fears death (2007)

Seven paths to death (2008)

Seven paths to death; a samurai mystery. [by] Dorothy and Thomas Hoobler. Philomel Books 2008 192p $14.99

Grades: 6 7 8 9   **Fic**

1. Mystery fiction 2. Maps -- Fiction 3. Japan -- Fiction 4. Samurai -- Fiction 5. Tattooing -- Fiction

ISBN 978-0-399-24610-4; 0-399-24610-X

LC 2007042092

Samurai Seikei and Judge Ooka, his foster-father, seek seven men who have seven maps on their backs in order to locate a cache of dangerous weapons before they fall into the wrong hands.

"This is a successful historical mystery, chockablock with adventure . . . and cultural details." Booklist

The **sword** that cut the burning grass; a samurai mystery. [by] Dorothy & Thomas Hoobler. Sleuth/Philomel 2005 211p $10.99

Grades: 6 7 8 9   **Fic**

1. Mystery fiction 2. Japan -- Fiction

ISBN 0-399-24272-4

In his latest adventure in eighteenth-century Japan, fourteen-year-old samurai apprentice Seikei, with the help of a servant girl and an imperious old man, sets out to rescue the young Emperor Yasuhito from his kidnappers.

"There's plenty of rousing action to propel the story forward, and, as always, Seikei makes a thoughtful hero." Booklist

Hooper, Mary

Fallen Grace. Bloomsbury 2011 309p $16.99

Grades: 7 8 9 10   **Fic**

1. Orphans -- Fiction 2. Poverty -- Fiction 3. Sisters -- Fiction 4. London (England) -- Fiction 5. Mentally disabled -- Fiction 6. Swindlers and swindling -- Fiction 7. Funeral rites and ceremonies -- Fiction 8. Great Britain -- History -- 19th century -- Fiction

ISBN 978-1-59990-564-8; 1-59990-564-7

LC 2010-25498

In Victorian London, impoverished fifteen-year-old orphan Grace takes care of her older but mentally unfit sister Lily, and after enduring many harsh and painful experiences, the two become the victims of a fraud perpetrated by the wealthy owners of several funeral businesses.

Hooper "packs her brisk Dickensian fable with colorful characters and suspenseful, satisfying plot twists. The sobering realities of child poverty and exploitation are vividly conveyed, along with fascinating details of the Victorian funeral trade." Kirkus

Includes bibliographical references

Hopkins, Ellen

Rumble; Ellen Hopkins. Margaret K. McElderry Books 2014 560 p. (hardcover) $19.99

Grades: 8 9 10 11 12   **Fic**

1. Novels in verse 2. Grief -- Fiction 3. Suicide -- Fiction 4. Schools -- Fiction 5. High schools -- Fiction 6. Family problems -- Fiction

ISBN 1442482842; 9781442482845

LC 2013037681

In this young adult verse novel by Ellen Hopkins, "Matthew Turner doesn't have faith in anything. Not in family--his is a shambles after his younger brother was bullied into suicide. Not in so-called friends who turn their backs when things get tough. Not in some all-powerful creator who lets too much bad stuff happen. . . . No matter what his girlfriend Hayden says about faith and forgiveness, there's no way Matt's letting go of blame." (Publisher's note)

"Matt is a wonderfully faceted character that readers will alternately sympathize with and dislike. His actions are directly related to his emotional turmoil, and teens will understand his pain and admire his intellect, even while shaking their heads over his actions.." SLJ

Hopkinson, Deborah

The **Great** Trouble; a mystery of London, the blue death, and a boy called Eel. by Deborah Hopkinson. Alfred A. Knopf 2013 256 p. (hard cover) $16.99

Grades: 4 5 6 7 8   **Fic**

1. Cholera 2. Orphans -- Fiction 3. London (England) -- Fiction 4. Cholera -- Fiction 5. Epidemics -- Fiction 6. London (England) -- History -- 19th century -- Fiction 7. Great Britain -- History -- Victoria, 1837-1901 -- Fiction

ISBN 0375848185; 9780375848186; 9780375948183

LC 2012032799

Author Deborah Hopkinson's book, "equal parts medical mystery, historical novel, and survival story about the 1854 London cholera outbreak, . . . introduces Eel, a boy trying to make ends meet on Broad Street. When he visits one of his regular employers, he learns the man has fallen ill. Eel enlists the help of Dr. Snow, and together they work to solve the mystery of what exactly is causing the spread of cholera and how they can prevent it." (Booklist)

Includes bibliographical references (p. 245-247)

Into the firestorm; a novel of San Francisco, 1906. Alfred A. Knopf 2006 200p hardcover o.p. pa $5.99

Grades: 5 6 7 8   **Fic**

1. Orphans -- Fiction 2. Earthquakes -- Fiction 3. San Francisco (Calif.) -- Fiction

ISBN 0-375-83652-7; 0-440-42129-2 pa

LC 2005-37189

Days after arriving in San Francisco from Texas, eleven-year-old orphan Nicholas Dray tries to help his new neighbors survive the 1906 San Francisco earthquake and the subsequent fires.

"The terror of the 1906 disaster is brought powerfully alive in this fast-paced tale. . . . Nick is a thoroughly developed protagonist, as are the supporting characters." SLJ

Includes bibliographical references

Hopkinson, Nalo

The **Chaos**; Nalo Hopkinson. Margaret K. McElderry Books 2012 241p. (hardcover) $16.99

Grades: 7 8 9 10 11 12   **Fic**

1. Science fiction 2. Toronto (Ont.) -- Fiction 3. Siblings -- Fiction 4. Racially mixed people -- Fiction 5. Canada -- Fiction 6. Identity -- Fiction 7. Supernatural -- Fiction 8. Brothers and sisters -- Fiction 9. Family life -- Canada -- Fiction 10. Interpersonal relations -- Fiction

ISBN 1416954880; 9781416954880; 9781442409552

LC 2011018154

In this young adult science fiction novel, "Scotch's womanly build and mixed heritage (white Jamaican dad, black American mom) made her the target of small-town school bullies. Since moving to Toronto, she's found friends and status. . . . When a giant bubble appears at an open-mic event, Scotch dares her brother, Rich, to touch it. He disappears, a volcano rises from Lake Ontario and chaos ripples across city and world, transforming reality in ways bizarre." (Kirkus Reviews)

Horowitz, Anthony

Ark angel. Philomel Books 2006 326p (An Alex Rider adventure) $17.99; pa $8.99

Grades: 5 6 7 8   **Fic**

1. Adventure fiction 2. Spies -- Fiction 3. Orphans -- Fiction 4. Terrorism -- Fiction

ISBN 0-399-24152-3; 0-14-240738-0 pa

LC 2005-48884

After recovering from a near fatal gunshot wound, teenage spy Alex Rider embarks on a new mission to stop a group of eco-terrorists from sabotaging the launch of the first outer space hotel.

"What's impossible to resist are the imaginative gadgets and the breakneck action, which Horowitz handles with his usual assurance and skill." Booklist

Crocodile tears. Philomel Books 2009 388p (Alex Rider)

Grades: 5 6 7 8   **Fic**

1. Adventure fiction 2. Spies -- Fiction 3. Orphans -- Fiction

ISBN 0-399-25056-5; 978-0-399-25056-9

Alex Rider does battle with a con artist who has invested millions of dollars in a form of genetically modified corn that can release an airborne strain of virus capable of eliminating an entire country in a single day. "Age ten and up." (N Y Times Book Rev)

"The book is chock-full of excitement and suspense from the first page to the last." SLJ

Eagle Strike. Philomel Books 2004 256p (An Alex Rider adventure) $17.99; pa $8.99

Grades: 5 6 7 8 **Fic**
1. Adventure fiction 2. Spies -- Fiction
ISBN 0-399-23979-0; 0-14-240613-9 pa
LC 2003-12523
First published 2003 in the United Kingdom
After a chance encounter with assassin Yassen Grego-rovich in the South of France, teenage spy Alex Rider in-vestigates international pop star and philanthropist Damian Cray whose new video game venture hides sinister motives involving Air Force One, nuclear missiles, and the interna-tional drug trade.

"In this heart-racing novel, Horowitz combines fast-paced action with ingenious gadgets that Alex either has on his side or is forced to battle against. The straightforward writing will appeal to a wide audience." SLJ

Evil star; book two of the Gatekeepers. Scholas-tic Press 2006 318p (Gatekeepers) $17.99
Grades: 6 7 8 9 **Fic**
1. Peru -- Fiction 2. Incas -- Fiction
ISBN 0-439-67996-6
Sequel to Raven's gate
Having locked the Raven's gate, fourteen-year-old Matt travels to Peru where he meets the second of the five gate-keepers and works with him to try to stop the opening of a second gate somehow related to the Nazca Lines.

"Though this is the second installment in this series, new readers will catch on quickly. . . . The plot turns and emo-tional relationships will more than satisfy thrill seekers." SLJ
Followed by Nightrise

The **Falcon's** Malteser; a Diamond brothers mystery. [by] Anthony Horowitz. 1st American ed; Philomel Books 2004 191p $16.99
Grades: 5 6 7 8 **Fic**
1. Mystery fiction
ISBN 0-399-24153-1
LC 2004-48322
After his older brother, a fledgling private detective, agrees to safeguard a package for a dwarf who does not live long, thirteen-year-old Nick scampers to solve the mystery while also trying to stay one step ahead of an assortment of thugs.

"The Diamond Brothers stories are invariably funny and full of excitement. Mystery readers with a sense of humor will enjoy [this tale]." Voice Youth Advocates

The **Greek** who stole Christmas; a Diamond Brothers mystery. [by] Anthony Horowitz. Puffin Books 2008 105p pa $6.99
Grades: 5 6 7 8 **Fic**
1. Mystery fiction
ISBN 978-0-14-240375-4 pa; 0-14-240375-X pa
LC 2008025944
Fourteen-year-old Nick and his brother, an ineffectual private detective, try to prevent the threatened murder of an international pop star in London at Christmas time.

"The witty banter between the characters keeps this short novel moving at breakneck speed." SLJ

Necropolis. Levithan/Scholastic Press 2009 389p (Gatekeepers) $17.99

Grades: 6 7 8 9 **Fic**
1. Supernatural -- Fiction 2. Hong Kong (China) -- Fiction
ISBN 978-0-439-68003-5; 0-439-68003-4
LC 2008-44892
Sequel to: Nightrise (2007)
To stop the evil corporation Nightrise from unleashing its devastating power around the globe, fifteen-year-old Matt and three other Gatekeepers travel to Hong Kong to find Scarlet, the final Gatekeeper, whose fate is inextricably joined to their own.

"There are many action-filled sequences and Scarlett is an interesting new addition to the cast of characters. . . . Fans of the series will naturally want to read it and prepare themselves for the final great battle." Voice Youth Advocates

Nightrise; book three of the Gatekeepers. [by] Anthony Horowitz. Scholastic Press 2007 365p (Gatekeepers) $17.99
Grades: 6 7 8 9 **Fic**
1. Twins -- Fiction 2. Nevada -- Fiction 3. Brothers -- Fiction 4. Telepathy -- Fiction 5. Supernatural -- Fiction
ISBN 978-0-439-68001-1; 0-439-68001-8
LC 2006035882
Sequel to Evil star
As fourteen-year-old telepathic twins struggle to escape the clutches of the Nightrise Corporation, one of them trav-els through dreams to a time when the evil Old Ones ruled and learns the role that he, his brother, and three other Gate-keepers must play to keep the world safe from the Old Ones' return.

"There's no lack of plot or action in this breathless fan-tasy thriller." Kliatt

Point blank. Philomel Bks. 2002 215p (An Alex Rider adventure) $17.99; pa $7.99
Grades: 5 6 7 8 **Fic**
1. Adventure fiction 2. Spies -- Fiction 3. Cloning -- Fiction
ISBN 0-399-23621-X; 0-14-240612-0 pa
LC 2001-33926
Sequel to Stormbreaker
First published 2001 in the United Kingdom with title: Point blanc
"After two influential businessmen die in separate freak accidents, MI6, England's spy network, once again calls upon 14-year-old Alex Rider to infiltrate Point Blanc, a pri-vate school in the French Alps. . . . He stumbles upon an evil mad scientist's plot to take over the world using clones as replacements for prominent sons. Spy gadgets, chase scenes, mysteries, and a cliff-hanger ending will keep even reluctant readers interested in the second novel in this series." SLJ

★ **Public** enemy number two; a Diamond broth-ers mystery. Philomel Books 2004 190p $16.99; pa $5.99
Grades: 5 6 7 8 **Fic**
1. Mystery fiction
ISBN 0-399-24154-X; 0-14-240218-4 pa
LC 2004-10418

When thirteen-year-old Nick is framed for a jewel robbery, he and his brother, the bumbling detective Tim Diamond, attempt to clear his name by capturing the master criminal known as the Fence.

"Horowitz has a knack for puns and humor, and he successfully combines it with a nonstop action mystery that has everything from hydraulically controlled buses to secret caverns. A readable and exciting adventure." SLJ

Other titles in the Diamond Brothers Mystery series are:

The falcon's Maltester (2004)

South by southeast (2005)

Three of Diamonds (2005)

The Greek who stole Christmas (2008)

Raven's gate; book one of the Gatekeepers. [by] Anthony Horowitz. 1st ed; Scholastic Press 2005 254p (Gatekeepers) $17.95; pa $7.99

Grades: 6 7 8 9   **Fic**

1. Witchcraft -- Fiction 2. Supernatural -- Fiction 3. Great Britain -- Fiction

ISBN 0-439-67995-8; 0-439-68009-7 pa

LC 2004-21512

Sent to live in a foster home in a remote Yorkshire village, Matt, a troubled fourteen-year-old English boy, uncovers an evil plot involving witchcraft and the site of an ancient stone circle.

"The creepy activities and the overall atmosphere of fear are well defined, and once the action starts, it doesn't let up. . . . This powerful struggle between good and evil is a real page-turner." SLJ

Other titles in the Gatekeepers series are:

Evil star (2006)

Nightrise (2007)

Necropolis (2009)

Scorpia. Philomel Books 2005 312p (An Alex Rider adventure) $17.99; pa $8.99

Grades: 5 6 7 8   **Fic**

1. Adventure fiction 2. Italy -- Fiction 3. Spies -- Fiction 4. Orphans -- Fiction 5. Terrorism -- Fiction 6. London (England) -- Fiction

ISBN 978-0-399-24151-2; 0-399-24151-5; 978-0-14-240578-9 pa; 0-14-240578-7 pa

LC 2004009089

First published 2004 in the United Kingdom

After being told that his father was an assassin for a criminal organization, fourteen-year-old Alex goes to Italy to find out more and becomes involved in a plan to kill thousands of English schoolchildren.

"High-tech and low-tech machinations will rivet readers." Booklist

Scorpia rising. Philomel Books 2011 402p (Alex Rider) $17.99

Grades: 5 6 7 8   **Fic**

1. Spies -- Fiction 2. Orphans -- Fiction 3. Terrorism -- Fiction 4. Middle East -- Fiction 5. London (England) -- Fiction

ISBN 978-0-399-25057-6; 0-399-25057-3

LC 2010043344

When the world's deadliest terrorist organization, Scorpia, stirs up trouble in the Middle East, it is up to fourteen-year-old MI6 agent Alex Rider to thwart their plans.

Skeleton Key. Philomel Bks. 2003 264p (An Alex Rider adventure) $17.99; pa $8.99 **Fic**

1. Adventure fiction 2. Spies -- Fiction 3. Tennis -- Fiction

ISBN 0-399-23777-1; 0-14-240613-9 pa

LC 2002-13507

First published 2002 in the United Kingdom

Reluctant teenage-spy Alex Rider, on a routine mission at the Wimbledon tennis championships, gets caught up in Chinese gangs, illegal nuclear weapons, and the suspect plans of his Russian host, General Sarov

"This page-turning thriller leaves readers breathless with anticipation." SLJ

Snakehead; [by] Anthony Horowitz. 1st American ed.; Philomel Books 2007 un $17.99

Grades: 5 6 7 8   **Fic**

1. Adventure fiction 2. Spies -- Fiction 3. Orphans -- Fiction

ISBN 978-0-399-24161-1

LC 2007020505

Sequel to Ark Angel

While working with the Australian Secret Service on a dangerous mission, teenaged spy Alex Rider uncovers information about his parents.

"The convoluted plot, nearly constant action, and clever gadgets will intrigue readers." Booklist

South by southeast; a Diamond brothers mystery. [by] Anthony Horowitz. Philomel Bks. 2005 148p $16.99; pa $5.99

Grades: 5 6 7 8   **Fic**

1. Mystery fiction

ISBN 0-399-24155-8; 0-14-240374-1 pa

LC 2005043169

First published 1997 in the United Kingdom

Fourteen-year-old Nick and his bumbling detective brother Tim Diamond investigate a mystery involving international spies and assassins.

"Horowitz has created another well-written, well-paced spy melodrama." SLJ

★ **Stormbreaker**. Philomel Books 2001 192p (An Alex Rider adventure) $17.99; pa $7.99

Grades: 5 6 7 8   **Fic**

1. Adventure fiction 2. Spies -- Fiction 3. Orphans -- Fiction 4. Terrorism -- Fiction 5. Great Britain -- Fiction

ISBN 0-399-23620-1; 0-14-240611-2 pa

LC 00-63683

First published 2000 in the United Kingdom

After the death of the uncle who had been his guardian, fourteen-year-old Alex Rider is coerced to continue his uncle's dangerous work for Britain's intelligence agency, MI6

"Horowitz thoughtfully balances Alex's super-spy finesse with typical teen insecurities to create a likable hero living a fantasy come true. An entertaining, nicely layered novel." Booklist

Other titles about Alex Rider are:

Point blank (2002)
Skeleton key (2003)
Eagle strike (2004)
Scorpia (2005)
Alex Rider, the gadgets (2006)
Ark angel (2006)
Snakehead (2007)
Crocodile tears (2009)
Scorpia rising (2011)

Three of diamonds; three Diamonds Brothers mysteries. [by] Anthony Horowitz. Philomel Books 2005 214p $16.99

Grades: 5 6 7 8   **Fic**

1. Mystery fiction
ISBN 0-399-24157-4

LC 2005276176

A collection of three Diamond Brothers mysteries in which Tim and Nick bungle their way through a search for a missing philanthropist, find themselves in a Parisian prison, and are stranded on a Scottish island with a murderer.

"Nick is a realistic character with a voice that is sarcastic and fresh, while Tim's lack of intelligence makes even the most dangerous situations laughable. Plenty of plays on words add to the humor." SLJ

Horvath, Polly

The **canning** season. Farrar, Straus & Giroux 2003 195p $16; pa $6.95

Grades: 6 7 8 9   **Fic**

1. Aunts -- Fiction
ISBN 0-374-39956-5; 0-374-41042-9 pa

LC 2002-66296

Thirteen-year-old Ratchet spends a summer in Maine with her eccentric great-aunts Tilly and Penpen, hearing strange stories from the past and encountering a variety of unusual and colorful characters

"Offbeat, slapstick humor is mitigated by poignancy in Horvath's distinctive rollicking style. There is occasional use of strong language, and the family stories are woven with death, often gruesomely described. . . . Readers are in for a wise and wacky ride when they open this novel." SLJ

The **Corps** of the Bare-Boned Plane. Farrar, Straus and Giroux 2007 261p $17

Grades: 7 8 9 10 11 12   **Fic**

1. Death -- Fiction 2. Uncles -- Fiction 3. Cousins -- Fiction 4. Islands -- Fiction 5. Airplanes -- Fiction 6. Bereavement -- Fiction 7. British Columbia -- Fiction
ISBN 978-0-374-31553-5; 0-374-31553-1

LC 2006-41281

When their parents are killed in a train accident, cousins Meline and Jocelyn, who have little in common, are sent to live with their wealthy, eccentric, and isolated Uncle Marten on his island off the coast of British Columbia, where they are soon joined by other oddly disconnected and troubled people.

"The savagely dark humor allows Horvath to place her characters in increasingly bizarre psychic positions, building

to an almost painful crescendo in a remarkable examination of the extremes of emotional distress." Horn Book

Everything on a waffle. Farrar, Straus & Giroux 2001 149p hardcover o.p. $16

Grades: 4 5 6 7   **Fic**

1. Uncles -- Fiction 2. British Columbia -- Fiction
ISBN 0-374-32236-8; 0-374-42208-7 pa

LC 00-35399

A Newbery Medal honor book, 2002

Eleven-year-old Primrose living in a small fishing village in British Columbia recounts her experiences and all that she learns about human nature and the unpredictability of life in the months after her parents are lost at sea

"The story is full of subtle humor and wisdom, presented through the eyes of a uniquely appealing young protagonist." SLJ

★ **My** one hundred adventures. Schwartz & Wade Books 2008 260p $16.99; lib bdg $19.99; pa $7.99

Grades: 4 5 6 7   **Fic**

1. Summer -- Fiction 2. Beaches -- Fiction 3. Siblings -- Fiction 4. Babysitters -- Fiction 5. Single parent family -- Fiction
ISBN 978-0-375-84582-6; 0-375-84582-8; 978-0-375-95582-2 lib bdg; 0-375-95582-8 lib bdg; 978-0-375-85526-9 pa; 0-375-85526-2 pa

LC 2008-02243

Twelve-year-old Jane, who lives at the beach in a run-down old house with her mother, two brothers, and sister, has an eventful summer accompanying her pastor on bible deliveries, meeting former boyfriends of her mother's, and being coerced into babysitting for a family of ill-mannered children.

With writing as foamy as waves, as gritty as sand, or as deep as the sea, this book may startle readers with the freedom given the heroine. . . . Unconventionality is Horvath's stock and trade, but here the high quirkiness quotient rests easily against Jane's inner story with its honest, childlike core. Booklist

Followed by: Northward to the Moon (2010)

Northward to the moon. Schwartz & Wade Books 2010 244p $17.99; lib bdg $20.99

Grades: 4 5 6 7   **Fic**

1. Canada -- Fiction 2. Nevada -- Fiction 3. Ranch life -- Fiction 4. Family life -- Fiction 5. Grandmothers -- Fiction 6. Massachusetts -- Fiction 7. Automobile travel -- Fiction
ISBN 978-0-375-86110-9; 0-375-86110-6; 978-0-375-96110-6 lib bdg; 0-375-96110-0 lib bdg

LC 2009-10133

Sequel to: My one hundred adventures (2008)

When her stepfather loses his job in Saskatchewan, Jane and the rest of the family set off on a car trip, ending up in Nevada after improbably being given a bag full of possibly stolen money.

"Many characters here are distinct, wonderfully idiosyncratic individuals, and Horvath's fine-tuned observations are conveyed with subtlety and precision." Booklist

★ **One** year in Coal Harbor; Polly Horvath. Schwartz & Wade Books 2012 216 p. (hardcover) $16.99

Grades: 5 6 7 **Fic**

1. Cookbooks -- Fiction 2. Friendship -- Fiction 3. British Columbia -- Fiction 4. Self-reliance -- Fiction 5. Family problems -- Fiction 6. Foster home care -- Fiction 7. Interpersonal relations -- Fiction 8. Eccentrics and eccentricities -- Fiction

ISBN 0375869700; 9780375869709; 9780375969706

LC 2011023591

In this book by Polly Horvath, "Primrose Squab . . . . chronicl[es] the latest goings-on in her British Columbian fishing village. Now 12 and happily reunited with her parents, Primrose has set her sights on compiling a cookbook. . . . When Ked, a foster child, arrives in town, Primrose gains an accomplice in her culinary efforts and an ally in opposing a local logging operation. More importantly, she hopes she has found a true best friend." (Publishers Weekly)

The **vacation**; [by] Polly Horvath. 1st ed; Farrar, Straus & Giroux 2005 197p $16

Grades: 5 6 7 8 **Fic**

1. Aunts -- Fiction 2. Vacations -- Fiction 3. Family life -- Fiction 4. Automobile travel -- Fiction

ISBN 0-374-38070-8

LC 2004-57667

When his parents go to Africa to work as missionaries, twelve-year-old Henry's eccentric aunts, Pigg and Mag, take him on a cross-country car trip, allowing him to gain insight into his family and himself.

"Horvath spins another delightfully offbeat yarn, complete with her signature cast of eccentric characters, wacky situations, poignant moments, and snappy dialogue." SLJ

Hosler, Jay

The **last** of the sandwalkers; written and illustrated by Jay Hosler. First Second 2015 312 p. illustrations (paperback) $16.99

Grades: 5 6 7 8 9 10 **Fic**

1. Graphic novels 2. Science fiction 3. Adventure fiction 4. Beetles -- Fiction 5. Scientific expeditions -- Fiction

ISBN 162672024X; 9781626720244

LC 2014045542

This book, by Jay Hosler, is about a "civilization of beetles. In this bug's paradise, beetles write books, run restaurants, and even do scientific research. But not too much scientific research is allowed by the powerful elders, who guard a terrible secret about the world outside. . . . Lucy is not one to quietly cooperate, however. This tiny field scientist defies the law of her safe but authoritarian home and leads a team of researchers out into the desert." (Publisher's note)

"Hosler's cartooning is no less meticulous than his writing and similarly retains a sense of animated energy and humor, engaging readers with characters that are far from human, but filled with humanity." Booklist

Includes bibliographical references

House, Silas

★ **Eli** the Good. Candlewick Press 2009 295p $16.99

Grades: 5 6 7 8 **Fic**

1. Aunts -- Fiction 2. Veterans -- Fiction 3. Friendship -- Fiction 4. Family life -- Fiction 5. Post-traumatic stress disorder -- Fiction

ISBN 978-0-7636-4341-6; 0-7636-4341-6

LC 2009004589

In the summer of 1976, ten-year-old Eli Book's excitement over Bicentennial celebrations is tempered by his father's flashbacks to the Vietnam War and other family problems, as well as concern about his tough but troubled best friend, Edie.

"House writes beautifully, with a gentle tone. He lays out Eli's world in exquisite detail. . . . The story flows along as steadily as a stream. . . . Eli is good company and children will enjoy accompanying him on his journey." SLJ

Houston, Julian

New boy. Houghton Mifflin Co. 2005 282p $16

Grades: 8 9 10 11 12 **Fic**

1. School stories 2. Prejudices -- Fiction 3. African Americans -- Fiction

ISBN 0-618-43253-1

LC 2004-27207

"As the first black student in an elite Connecticut boarding school in the late 1950s, Rob Garrett, 16, knows he is making history. . . . When his friends in the South plan a sit-in against segregation, he knows he must be part of it. . . . The honest first-person narrative makes stirring drama. . . . This brings up much for discussion about then and now." Booklist

Houtman, Jacqueline

The **reinvention** of Edison Thomas. Front Street 2010 189p $17.95

Grades: 6 7 8 9 **Fic**

1. School stories 2. Friendship -- Fiction 3. Inventions -- Fiction

ISBN 978-1-59078-708-3; 1-59078-708-0

Middle school student Eddy Thomas loves science and inventing, but has trouble with people. Finally he meets some friends who appreciate his abilities and respect his unique view of the world.

"A perceptive look at a complicated mind, the novel is steeped in the world of science (binomial nomenclature appears throughout), and the quirky humor and authentic characters should have wide appeal." Publ Wkly

Houts, Michelle

The **Beef** Princess of Practical County. Delacorte Press 2009 226p $16.99; lib bdg $19.99

Grades: 6 7 8 9 **Fic**

1. Cattle -- Fiction 2. Indiana -- Fiction 3. Farm life -- Fiction

ISBN 978-0-385-73584-1; 978-0-385-90568-8 lib bdg

LC 2008-34712

Twelve-year-old Libby, the daughter of an Indiana cattle farmer, raises two calves in hopes of winning the annual steer competition at the county fair, but fails to follow her father's warning about developing a bond with animals that are destined to be sold at auction.

"Houts paints an idyllic yet authentic picture of farm life as she takes Libby and her family through the ups and downs of cattle raising and fair showing with sly humor and a flair for description and characterization." Booklist

Howard, Ellen

The **crimson** cap. Holiday House 2009 177p $16.95

Grades: 5 6 7 8   **Fic**

1. Explorers 2. Texas -- Fiction 3. Explorers -- Fiction 4. Native Americans -- Fiction 5. America -- Exploration -- Fiction

ISBN 978-0-8234-2152-7; 0-8234-2152-X

LC 2009-25551

In 1684, wearing his father's faded cap, eleven-year-old Pierre Talon joins explorer Rene-Robert Cavelier on an ill-fated expedition to seek the Mississippi River, but after the expedition falls apart Pierre, deathly ill, is taken in by Hasi-nai Indians. Includes historical facts.

"A riveting adventure that will prove to be hard to put down. Howard's fast-paced writing brings the story to life. This solid coming-of-age story is based on real events and historical figures." SLJ

Howard, J. J.

That time I joined the circus; J.J. Howard. Point 2013 272 p. (hardcover) $17.99

Grades: 7 8 9 10   **Fic**

1. Circus -- Fiction 2. Absent mothers -- Fiction 3. Florida -- Fiction 4. Friendship -- Fiction 5. Best friends -- Fiction 6. New York (N.Y.) -- Fiction 7. Mothers and daughters -- Fiction 8. Single-parent families -- Fiction

ISBN 0545433819; 9780545433815

LC 2012016715

In this novel, 17-year-old Lexi lives with her father Gavin, a musician in New York City. Her "long-absent mother . . . has apparently joined the circus. When Gavin dies unexpectedly, leaving his daughter penniless, her only option is to track down her mother in Florida. Failing to find her, Lexi gratefully accepts work with the Circus Europa." (Publishers Weekly)

Howe, James, 1946-

Addie on the inside; James Howe. Atheneum Books for Young Readers 2011 206 p. $16.99

Grades: 5 6 7 8   **Fic**

1. School stories 2. Novels in verse 3. Self-acceptance -- Fiction 4. Interpersonal relations -- Fiction 5. Grandmothers -- Fiction 6. Identity (Psychology) -- Fiction

ISBN 141691384X; 9781416913849

LC 2010024497

This book, by James Howe, "follows 13-year-old Ad-die's struggles to define herself according to her own terms. Through her poems, Addie reflects on her life and life in general: her first boyfriend, what it means to be accepted and her endeavors to promote equality. Addie is at her most fragile when she examines her relationship with her boyfriend and the cruel behavior of her former best friend. Her forthright observations address serious topics with a maturity beyond her age." (Kirkus Reviews)

"Howe's artfully crafted lines show Addie's intelligence and wit, and his imagery evokes the aura of sadness sur-rounding 'this purgatory of/ the middle school years/ when

so many things/ that never mattered before/ and will never matter again/ matter.' Readers will empathize with Addie's anguish and admire her courage to keep fighting." Publ Wkly

Also known as Elvis; James Howe. Atheneum Books for Young Readers 2014 288 p. (Misfits) (hardcover) $16.99

Grades: 5 6 7 8 9   **Fic**

1. Friendship -- Fiction 2. Family life -- Fiction 3. Summer employment -- Fiction 4. Single-parent families -- fiction 5. Fathers and sons -- Fiction 6. Mothers and sons -- Fiction 7. Single-parent families -- Fiction

ISBN 1442445106; 9781442445109; 9781442445116

LC 2013015974

In this book, by James Howe, "Skeezie Tookis, also known as Elvis, isn't looking forward to this summer in Paintbrush Falls. While his best friends Bobby, Joe, and Ad-die are off on exciting adventures, he's stuck at home, taking care of his sisters and working five days a week to help out his mom. True, he gets to hang out at the Candy Kitchen with the awesome HellomynameisSteffi, but he also has to contend with Kevin Hennessey's never-ending bullying." (Publisher's note)

"As an adult, Skeezie reflects on the summer when his absent father returned home seeking reconciliation. As Skee-zie tries to hold his fragile family life together, he explores his own emotions toward his parents and sisters, and is sur-prised by the bonds he feels. A satisfying conclusion to the Misfit books, with glimpses into adulthood for each member of the Gang of Five." Horn Book

The **misfits**; James Howe. Atheneum Books for Young Readers 2001 274 p. $17.99

Grades: 5 6 7 8   **Fic**

1. School stories 2. Bullies -- Fiction 3. Elections -- Fiction 4. Friendship -- Fiction 5. Teasing

ISBN 0689839553; 9780689839559

LC 0066390

This book, by James Howe, is "about junior high school politics and nasty name calling. . . . Bobby Goodspeed [is] an overweight seventh grader who belongs to the Gang of Five, which (ironically) is made up of four not five kids who consider themselves misfits. The student council elections are coming up, and [the Gang of Five] decide to run on the 'No-Name Party,' which promises to bring an end to all name calling in the school." (School Library Journal)

This is a "timely, sensitive, laugh-out-loud must-read for all middle school students and teachers." Voice Youth Advocates

★ **Totally** Joe; James Howe. Atheneum Books for Young Readers 2005 189 p. $17.99

Grades: 5 6 7 8 9   **Fic**

1. School stories 2. Friendship -- Fiction 3. Adolescence -- Fiction 4. Homosexuality -- Fiction

ISBN 068983957X; 9780689839573

LC 2004022242

In this book, by James Howe, "Joe's teacher asks his sev-enth-grade class to write an alphabiography throughout the year, presenting themselves and their lives in entries from A to Z. Joe's essays begin and end with friends, from Addie, a long-time pal and confidant, to Zachary, a new student who, like Joe, has a unique approach to life. . . . Joe demonstrates that he truly is a one-of-a-kind kid, mostly comfortable with himself but still struggling with common adolescent issues." (School Library Journal)

"Joe, one of the characters in The Misfits (2001), has his say, in a voice uniquely his own. Twelve-year-old Joe knows he is gay. He played with Barbies as a young child, prefers cooking to sports, and has a crush on a male classmate...Joe himself often comes off as a cross between Niles Crane and Harvey Fierstein. But he also reacts like a kid, and readers in his situation will wish for the love and support he receives from friends and family, as well as the happy life he so clearly envisions." Booklist

Howe, Katherine

Conversion; Katherine Howe. G. P. Putnam's Sons 2014 432 p. (hardback) $18.99

Grades: 7 8 9 10 11 12 **Fic**

1. School stories 2. Salem witch trials 3. Schools -- Fiction 4. Epidemics -- Fiction 5. Friendship -- Fiction 6. Massachusetts -- Fiction 7. Preparatory schools -- Fiction

ISBN 0399167773; 9780399167775

LC 2014000397

In this young adult novel by Katherine Howe, "It's senior year at St. Joan's Academy, and school is a pressure cooker. College applications, the battle for valedictorian, deciphering boys' texts: Through it all, Colleen Rowley and her friends are expected to keep it together. Until they can't. . . . Only Colleen--who's been reading 'The Crucible' for extra credit--comes to realize what nobody else has: Danvers was once Salem Village." (Publisher's note)

"St. Joan's Academy in Danvers, Massachusetts, a well-to-do private girl's school for the best and brightest, is usually only home to hysteria of the college-admissions kind. But when Clara starts convulsing in class, a media frenzy fixates on the St. Joan's mystery disease...A simmering blend of relatable high-school drama with a persistent pinprick of unearthliness in the background." Booklist

Howe, Peter

Waggit again; drawings by Omar Rayyan. HarperCollinsPublishers 2009 292p il $16.99; lib bdg $17.89

Grades: 5 6 7 **Fic**

1. Dogs -- Fiction

ISBN 978-0-06-124264-9; 0-06-124264-0; 978-0-06-124265-6 lib bdg; 0-06-124265-9 lib bdg

LC 2008020213

Sequel to: Waggit's tale (2008)

After being left in the country by his owner, Waggit sets out on the long journey to New York City and meets some unexpected friends along the way.

Felicia's "relationship with the dogs is made wonderfully plausible. Waggit's growth in self-understanding is also fully developed and well handled, and the ending will satisfy readers deeply." Kirkus

Waggit's tale; drawings by Omar Rayyan. HarperCollinsPublishers 2008 288p il $16.99; lib bdg $17.89; pa $6.99

Grades: 5 6 7 **Fic**

1. Dogs -- Fiction

ISBN 978-0-06-124261-8; 0-06-124261-6; 978-0-06-124262-5 lib bdg; 0-06-124262-4 lib bdg; 978-0-06-124263-2 pa; 0-06-124263-2 pa

LC 2007020878

Followed by: Waggit again (2009)

When Waggit is abandoned by his owner as a puppy, he meets a pack of wild dogs who become his friends and teach him to survive in the city park, but when he has a chance to go home with a kind woman who wants to adopt him, he takes it

"The novel celebrates the wild freedom of the feral dog pack, while also emphasizing the many hazards of urban life for homeless companion animals." Voice Youth Advocates

Howell, Troy

The **dragon** of Cripple Creek; a novel. Amulet Books 2011 385p $19.95

Grades: 5 6 7 8 **Fic**

1. Fantasy fiction 2. Adventure fiction 3. Gold -- Fiction 4. Dragons -- Fiction 5. Colorado -- Fiction

ISBN 978-0-8109-9713-4; 0-8109-9713-4

LC 2010-34362

When Kat, her father, and brother visit an old gold mine that has been turned into an amusement park, she falls down a shaft and meets an ancient dragon, the last of his kind, and inadvertently triggers a twenty-first century gold rush.

"Writing in Kat's first person narrative, which is wry and funny, clipped and eloquent, Howell, best known as an illustrator, mixes fantasy adventure with a moving conservation story in a debut that blends sadness, secrecy, and pure fantasy." Booklist

Howland, Leila

Forget-me-not summer; Leila Howland. First edition Harpercollins 2015 352 p. illustrations (hardcover) $16.99

Grades: 4 5 6 7 **Fic**

1. Summer -- Fiction 2. Vacations -- Fiction 3. Sisters -- Fiction 4. Great aunts -- Fiction 5. Cape Cod (Mass.) -- Fiction 6. Actors and actresses -- Fiction 7. Interpersonal relations -- Fiction

ISBN 0062318691; 9780062318695

LC 2014027413

In this children's book by Leiland Howard, "though Marigold, Zinnia, and Lily Silver couldn't be more different, they're all excited about their various plans for summer vacation. But any expectation of summer fun comes crashing down when the sisters' parents send them to Cape Cod to visit their aunt Sunny. Small-town life is not what these L.A. girls had in mind. They must adjust, however, to things like sharing a room and living without a TV." (Publisher's note)

"An old-fashioned story well-told, with engaging characters—a beach read for preteens that is as comfortable as the old tennis shoes worn on the Massachusetts shore." Kirkus

Nantucket blue; Leila Howland. 1st ed. Hyperion 2013 304 p. (reinforced) $16.99

Grades: 8 9 10 11 12 **Fic**

1. Summer -- Fiction 2. Female friendship -- Fiction 3. Interpersonal relations -- Fiction 4. Grief -- Fiction

5. Divorce -- Fiction 6. Friendship -- Fiction 7. Best friends -- Fiction 8. Grief -- Fiction 9. Best friends 10. Dating (Social customs) -- Fiction 11. Nantucket Island (Mass.) -- Fiction 12. Children of divorced parents -- Fiction 13. Interpersonal relations in adolescence -- Fiction

ISBN 1423160517; 9781423160519

LC 2012035121

This novel, by Leila Howland, follows a girl named "Cricket Thompson. . . . When Jules and her family suffer a devastating tragedy that forces the girls apart, Jules becomes a stranger whom Cricket wonders whether she ever really knew. . . . But it's the things Cricket hadn't counted on—most of all, falling hard for someone who should be completely off-limits—that turn her dreams into an exhilarating, bitter-sweet reality." (Publisher's note)

"Lacrosse-champ Cricket Thompson has always been welcomed by her best friend Jules's affluent family. But when Nina, Jules's mother, dies suddenly, big changes en-sue. Expecting her usual warm reception, Cricket shows up at Jules's family home on Nantucket to find herself shunned. There's some emotional heaviness to the story, but it's also a breezy, beach-ready tale of self-awakening and first love." (Horn Book)

Hrdlitschka, Shelley

Allegra; by Shelley Hrdlitschka. Orca Book Publishers 2013 280 p. (paperback) $12.95; (ebook) $12.99; (ebook) $12.99

Grades: 7 8 9 10   **Fic**

1. School stories 2. Teacher-student relationship -- Fiction 3. Performing arts high schools 4. Teacher-student relationships

ISBN 1459801970; 9781459801974; 9781459801998; 9781459801981

LC 2012952952

In this book, Allegra, daughter of two musicians, is thrilled to be at Deer Lake School for the Fine and Perform-ing Arts. She "has her sights set on becoming a professional dancer. However, her excitement is dimmed by the school's requirement that she take a music-theory class. Despite her initial reluctance, Allegra soon begins to enjoy the class due to the charisma of its young and attractive teacher," Mr. Rocchelli. Is their relationship too close? (School Library Journal)

★ **Sister** wife. Orca 2008 269p pa $12.95

Grades: 8 9 10 11 12   **Fic**

1. Polygamy -- Fiction

ISBN 978-1-55143-927-3; 1-55143-927-1

In a remote polygamist community, Celeste struggles to accept her destiny while longing to be free to live her life her way.

"This compelling story combines with authentic charac-ters to pique the interest of a wide array of teens and get them talking about faith and free will." Voice Youth Advocates

Hubbard, Amanda

Ripple; [by] Mandy Hubbard. Razorbill 2011 260p $16.99

Grades: 8 9 10 11 12   **Fic**

1. Love stories 2. Fantasy fiction 3. Sirens (Mythology)

ISBN 978-1-59514-423-2; 1-59514-423-4

"Lexi, 18, is responsible for the death of Steven, her friend Siena's brother and the only boy she ever loved. That was two years ago, right before discovering that she is a siren, cursed to swim each night and sing out haunting melodies that will lure men to their deaths in the water. She has been protecting herself and those around her by keep-ing everyone at a distance and swimming in an isolated lake where no one will hear her song. But as the new school year begins, Lexi finds herself pursued by two boys whom she can't ignore. . . . In this new twist on a supernatural romance, Hubbard expands the genre by including both a siren and a nix in among the high school drama. . . . Fans of girl dramas, mysteries, and fantasy romance will devour the story." SLJ

Hudson, Tara

Hereafter. HarperTeen 2011 407p $17.99

Grades: 8 9 10 11 12   **Fic**

1. Ghost stories 2. Oklahoma -- Fiction 3. Family life -- Fiction 4. Future life -- Fiction 5. Good and evil -- Fiction 6. Near-death experiences -- Fiction

ISBN 978-0-06-202677-4; 0-06-202677-1

LC 2010045622

Amelia, long a ghost, forms a strong bond with eighteen-year-old Joshua, who nearly drowned where she did and who awakens in her long-forgotten senses and memories even as Eli, a spirit, tries to draw her away.

"A must for collections given the genre's popularity." Booklist

Hughes, Dean

Missing in action. Atheneum Books for Young Readers 2010 228p $16.99; pa $6.99

Grades: 6 7 8 9   **Fic**

1. Utah -- Fiction 2. Baseball -- Fiction 3. Prejudices -- Fiction 4. Family life -- Fiction 5. Grandparents -- Fiction 6. World War, 1939-1945 -- Fiction 7. Racially mixed people -- Fiction 8. Japanese Americans -- Evacuation and relocation, 1942-1945 -- Fiction

ISBN 978-1-4169-1502-7; 1-4169-1502-8; 978-1-4424-1248-4 pa; 1-4424-1248-8 pa

LC 2009-11276

While his father is missing in action in the Pacific dur-ing World War II, twelve-year-old Jay moves with his mother to small-town Utah, where he sees prejudice from both sides, as a part-Navajo himself and through an unlikely friendship with Japanese American Ken from the nearby internment camp.

"Jay's pain and eventual resolution will touch readers in this sure-to-be-popular work of historical fiction." Booklist

Search and destroy. Atheneum Books for Young Readers 2006 216p $16.95

Grades: 7 8 9 10   **Fic**

1. Vietnam War, 1961-1975 -- Fiction

ISBN 0-689-87023-X

LC 2005-11255

Recent high school graduate Rick Ward, undecided about his future and eager to escape his unhappy home life, joins the army and experiences the horrors of the war in Vietnam.

"This is a compelling, insightful story about the emotional, physical, and psychological scars that wars leave upon soldiers." Booklist

Soldier boys. Atheneum Bks. for Young Readers 2001 162p $16.95; pa $5.99

Grades: 7 8 9 10   **Fic**

1. Soldiers -- Fiction 2. World War, 1939-1945 -- Fiction 3. Ardennes, Battle of the, 1944-1945 -- Fiction
ISBN 0-689-81748-7; 0-689-86021-8 pa

LC 00-46920

"This World War II novel tells the parallel stories of two young soldiers fighting on opposite sides of the conflict—a paratrooper from Utah and a Hitler Youth who joins the German army. Spence and Dieter's paths cross briefly on a snow-covered Belgian hill in a scene both compassionate and tragic. Hughes tells their tales in assured prose that's harrowing without being exploitive." Horn Book Guide

Hughes, Gregory

Unhooking the moon; by Gregory Hughes. Quercus 2010 374 p. (hardcover) $16.95

Grades: 6 7 8   **Fic**

1. Orphans -- Fiction 2. Voyages and travels -- Fiction 3. United States -- Fiction
ISBN 1623650208; 9781623650209

LC 2010478376

In this book, orphans Bob and Marie Claire (aka Rat) travel from Winnipeg to New York City in search of their drug dealer uncle. "For lack of a better plan, they wander Manhattan and the Bronx asking passersby if they know him. This strategy leads to encounters with a host of colorful city types, notably a pair of softhearted con men and a lonely rising rap star." (Kirkus Reviews)

Hughes, Mark Peter

A **crack** in the sky. Delacorte Press 2010 405p il $16.99; lib bdg $19.99

Grades: 5 6 7 8   **Fic**

1. Science fiction
ISBN 978-0-385-73708-1; 0-385-73708-4; 978-0-385-90645-6 lib bdg; 0-385-90645-5 lib bdg

LC 2009-43532

In a post-apocalyptic world, thirteen-year-old Eli, part of the most powerful family in the world, keeps noticing problems with the operations of his domed city but his family denies them, while in the surrounding desert, the Outsiders struggle to survive while awaiting a prophesied savior.

"Hughes keeps his protagonist an individual, and in fact an amiable, scrappy one with whom readers will identify." Bull Cent Child Books

Hughes, Pat Raccio

★ **Five** 4ths of July; by Pat Raccio Hughes. Viking 2011 278p $16.99

Grades: 7 8 9 10   **Fic**

1. Adventure fiction 2. Connecticut -- Fiction 3. United States -- History -- 1775-1783, Revolution -- Fiction
ISBN 978-0-670-01207-7; 0-670-01207-6

LC 2010-49521

On July 4th, 1777, fourteen-year-old Jake Mallory and his friends are celebrating their new nation's independence,

but over the next four years Jake finds himself in increasingly adventurous circumstances as he battles British forces, barely survives captivity on a prison ship, and finally returns home to Connecticut, war-torn and weary, but hopeful for America's future.

This is a "straightforward and well-conceived novel. . . . A fine addition to collections on the war and an eye-opening look at the horrors of British prison ships." Kirkus

Hughes, Shirley, 1927-

★ **Hero** on a bicycle; Shirley Hughes. Candlewick Press 2013 224 p. $15.99

Grades: 5 6 7   **Fic**

1. Historical fiction 2. World War, 1939-1945 -- Fiction
ISBN 076366037X; 9780763660376

LC 2012943650

This book is set in Italy during World War II. "The narrative focuses on a city under German occupation, events being perceived principally through the eyes of three members of the Crivelli family: teenager Paolo, his older sister Constanza and Rosemary, their English-born mother. . . . When an opportunity arises for Paolo, Constanza and Rosemary to lend their practical support to the Partisan cause Paolo, in particular, seizes it enthusiastically." (School Librarian)

Hull, Nancy L.

On rough seas; [by] Nancy L. Hull. Clarion Books 2008 261p $16

Grades: 6 7 8 9   **Fic**

1. Great Britain -- Fiction 2. World War, 1939-1945 -- Fiction 3. Dunkerque (France), Battle of, 1940 -- Fiction
ISBN 978-0-618-89743-8; 0-618-89743-8

LC 2007-37933

In Dover, England in 1940, fourteen-year-old Alec Curtis wants nothing more than to go to sea, to absolve himself of the guilt he feels over the earlier drowning of his cousin and to help the war effort, but when he sneaks aboard a small boat going across the English Channel to Dunkirk, his experience changes him forever.

"Hull offers a sensitive portrayal of Alec's seesawing emotions and gradual recognition of what matters to him, culminating in subtle changes that show his newfound maturity in sometimes unexpected yet wholly convincing ways. A well-researched historical novel." Booklist

Hulme, John

★ The **glitch** in sleep; [by] John Hulme and Michael Wexler; illustrations by Gideon Kendall. Bloomsbury Children's Books 2007 277p il (The Seems) $16.95; pa $7.99

Grades: 4 5 6 7   **Fic**

1. Science fiction 2. Sleep -- Fiction
ISBN 978-1-59990-129-9; 1-59990-129-3; 978-1-59990-298-2 pa; 1-59990-298-2 pa

LC 2007-2598

When twelve-year-old Becker Drane is recruited by The Seems, a parallel universe that runs everything in The World, he must fix a disastrous glitch in the Department of Sleep that threatens everyone's ability to ever fall asleep again

"The story is upbeat and full of humor. . . . Dynamic full-page illustrations appear throughout." SLJ

Another title in this series is:
The split second (2008)

The **lost** train of thought; by John Hulme and Michael Wexler; illustrated by Gideon Kendall. 1st U.S. ed. Bloomsbury 2009 289 p. ill. (alk. paper) $16.99

Grades: 5 6 7 8 **Fic**
  1. Fantasy fiction 2. Voyages and travels -- Fiction 3. Technology -- Fiction 4. Space and time -- Fiction 5. Thought and thinking -- Fiction
  ISBN 1599901315; 9781599901312

LC 2009002145

This is the third book in John Hulme's Seems series. Here, "Becker Drane's coolest job in The World—as a Fixer in The Seems—is in jeopardy. So when a trainload of Thought goes missing, Becker reluctantly agrees to join a veteran team of Fixers on a mission in The Middle of Nowhere. Turns out getting the train back on track is just a temporary Fix, and Becker's real mission just might end his Fixing days forever." (Publisher's note)

The **split** second; by John Hulme and Michael Wexler; illustrations by Gideon Kendall. 1st U.S. ed.; Bloomsbury Children's Books 2008 301p il (The Seems) $16.99

Grades: 5 6 7 8 **Fic**
  1. Science fiction 2. Terrorism -- Fiction
  ISBN 978-1-599-90130-5; 1-599-90130-7

LC 2008012241

Sequel to: The glitch in sleep (2007)

Now thirteen-years-old and still a Fixer in the parallel universe called the Seems, Becker Drane is called upon to repair the damage caused by an enormous bomb planted in the Department of Time, an act of terrorism perpetrated by the evil members of the Tide, a group that is trying to destroy the World.

"This sequel continues to develop a truly ingenious setting while proving every bit as much of a nail-biter as the first." Booklist

Humphreys, Chris

The **hunt** of the unicorn. Alfred A. Knopf 2011 345p $16.99; lib bdg $19.99; e-book $16.99

Grades: 6 7 8 9 **Fic**
  1. Fantasy fiction 2. Unicorns -- Fiction
  ISBN 978-0-375-85872-7; 0-375-85872-7; 978-0-375-95872-4 lib bdg; 0-375-95872-4; 978-0-375-89624-8 e-book

LC 2010-30852

Despite strange dreams and her ailing father's firm belief in the family lore of a long-ago ancestor's connection to the mythical unicorn, fifteen-year-old New Yorker Elayne remains skeptical until, during a school visit to the unicorn tapestries in the Cloisters, she finds herself entering a tumultuous world where she must fulfill the legacy of her ancestors by taming the unicorn and bringing a tyrant to justice.

"This is wish fulfillment at its finest, with Elayne playing the everyday gal turned spunky heroine. . . . With references to our world's overpopulation and pollution, there is a heady dose of environmentalism here, but it is nicely

tempered with a fair amount of humor and adventure." Bull Cent Child Books

Hunt, Lynda Mullaly

One for the Murphys; Lynda Mullaly Hunt. Nancy Paulsen Books 2012 224 p. (hardback) $16.99

Grades: 5 6 7 8 **Fic**
  1. Girls -- Fiction 2. Family -- Fiction 3. Foster children -- Fiction 4. Connecticut -- Fiction 5. Stepfathers -- Fiction 6. Family problems -- Fiction 7. Foster home care -- Fiction 8. Mothers and daughters -- Fiction 9. Family life -- Connecticut -- Fiction
  ISBN 0399256156; 9780399256158

LC 2011046708

This book by Lynda Mullaly Hunt follows "eighth-grader Carley Connors [as she] learns about a different kind of family life, first resisting and then resisting having to leave the loving, loyal Murphys. . . . She's torn between her love for her mother and her memory of the fight that sent her to the hospital, when her mother caught and held her for her stepfather. Slowly won over at home . . . Carley also finds a friend at school in the prickly, Wicked-obsessed Toni." (Kirkus Reviews)

Hunter, Erin

Code of the clans; illustrated by Wayne McLoughlin. HarperCollinsPublishers 2009 156p il (Warriors) $16.99; lib bdg $17.89

Grades: 6 7 8 9 **Fic**
  1. Fantasy fiction 2. Cats -- Fiction
  ISBN 978-0-06-166009-2; 0-06-166009-4; 978-0-06-166010-8 lib bdg; 0-06-166010-8 lib bdg

LC 2008045061

Explores the fifteen rules that govern the daily life of a warrior cat.

Dawn; [by] Erin Hunter. 1st ed.; HarperCollins 2005 335p (Warriors: the new prophecy) $15.99; lib bdg $17.89; pa $6.99

Grades: 6 7 8 9 **Fic**
  1. Fantasy fiction 2. Cats -- Fiction
  ISBN 978-0-06-074455-7; 0-06-074455-3; 978-0-06-074456-4 lib bdg; 0-06-074456-1 lib bdg; 978-0-06-074457-1 pa; 0-06-074457-X pa

LC 2005009175

Sequel to Moonrise (2005)

The questing cats return to a forest devastated by the Twolegs, where they must find a way to convince their Clans to leave in search of a new home, even though they have no idea where they are going.

"Fans will relish this eminently satisfying episode." Booklist

Followed by Starlight (2006)

Fire and ice; [by] Erin Hunter. 1st ed; HarperCollins 2003 317p (Warriors) $15.99; lib bdg $16.89

Grades: 6 7 8 9 **Fic**
  ISBN 0-06-000003-1; 0-06-052556-8 lib bdg

LC 2002-14415

Sequel to In the wild (2003)

Fireheart, a full-fledged warrior cat, must confront questions of loyalty and identity as he faces the possibility of betrayal from within his own forest clan.

"Characters remain true to their feline natures, adding to the plausibility of events in this tension-filled story." Booklist

Followed by Forest of secrets (2003)

★ **Into** the wild. HarperCollins Pubs. 2003 272p il map (Warriors) $15.99; lib bdg $16.89; pa $5.99

Grades: 6 7 8 9   **Fic**

1. Fantasy fiction 2. Cats -- Fiction

ISBN 0-06-000002-3; 0-06-052548-7 lib bdg; 0-06-052550-9 pa

For generations, four clans of wild cats have shared the forest. When their warrior code is threatened by mysterious deaths, a house cat named Rusty may turn out to be the bravest warrior of all.

"The author has created an intriguing world with an intricate structure and mythology, and an engaging young hero." SLJ

Other titles in the Warriors series are:

Code of the clans (2009)

A dangerous path (2004)

The darkest hour (2004)

Fire and ice (2003)

Forest of secrets (2003)

Rising storm (2004)

The **sight**; [by] Erin Hunter. HarperCollins Pub. 2007 363p (Warriors: power of three) $16.99; lib bdg $17.89

Grades: 6 7 8 9   **Fic**

1. Fantasy fiction 2. Cats -- Fiction

ISBN 978-0-06-089201-2; 0-06-089201-3; 978-0-06-089203-6 lib bdg; 0-06-089203-X lib bdg

LC 2007-11860

In a troubled time for the Clans, three young cats, grandchildren of the legendary Firestar, begin their training as warriors and, in the course of many adventures, discover their true destiny.

"Plenty of action and solid characterizations make this an enticing choice for fans of the long-running enterprise." Booklist

Other titles in this series are:

Dark river (2008)

Outcast (2008)

Eclipse (2008)

Long shadows (2009)

Sunrise (2009)

Huntley, Amy

The **everafter**. Balzer + Bray 2009 144p $16.99; lib bdg $17.89; pa $8.99

Grades: 7 8 9 10   **Fic**

1. Dead -- Fiction 2. Death -- Fiction 3. Friendship -- Fiction 4. Lost and found possessions -- Fiction

ISBN 978-0-06-177679-3; 0-06-177679-3; 978-0-06-177680-9 lib bdg; 0-06-177680-7 lib bdg; 978-0-06-177681-6 pa; 0-06-177681-5 pa

LC 2008-46149

ALA YALSA Morris Award Finalist, 2010

Madison Stanton doesn't know where she is or how she got there. But she does know this—she is dead. And alone in a vast, dark space. The only company Maddy has in this place are luminescent objects that turn out to be all the things she lost while she was alive. And soon she discovers that, with these artifacts, she can re-experience—and even—change moments from her life.

"This fresh take on a teen's journey of self-exploration is a compelling and highly enjoyable tale. Huntley expertly combines a coming-of-age story with a supernatural mystery that keeps readers engrossed until the climactic ending. This touching story will appeal to those looking for a ghost story, romance, or family drama." SLJ

Hurley, Tonya

★ **Ghostgirl**. Little, Brown 2008 328p $17.99

Grades: 7 8 9 10   **Fic**

1. Ghost stories 2. School stories 3. Death -- Fiction 4. Popularity -- Fiction

ISBN 978-0-316-11357-1; 0-316-11357-3

LC 2007-31541

After dying, high school senior Charlotte Usher is as invisible to nearly everyone as she always felt, but despite what she learns in a sort of alternative high school for dead teens, she clings to life while seeking a way to go to the Fall Ball with the boy of her dreams.

"Hurley combines afterlife antics, gothic gore, and high school hell to produce an original, hilarious satire. . . . . Tim Burton and Edgar Allan Poe devotees will die for this fantastic, phantasmal read." SLJ

Other titles in this series are:

Ghostgirl: Homecoming (2009)

Ghostgirl: Lovesick (2010)

Hurst, Carol Otis

Through the lock. Houghton Mifflin 2001 160p $15

Grades: 5 6 7 8   **Fic**

1. Canals -- Fiction 2. Orphans -- Fiction 3. Connecticut -- Fiction

ISBN 0-618-03036-0

LC 99-28510

Etta, a twelve-year-old orphan in nineteenth-century Connecticut, meets Walter, a boy living in an abandoned cabin on the New Haven and Northampton Canal and has adventures with him while trying to be reunited with her siblings

"Etta and Walter's terse conversations, anguished and funny, are the best part of the book, and the history is fascinating." Booklist

Hurwitz, Michele Weber

The **summer** I saved the world-- in 65 days; by Michele Weber Hurwitz. Wendy Lamb Books, an imprint of Random House Children's Books 2014 272 p. (trade) $16.99

Grades: 5 6 7 8   **Fic**

1. Summer -- Fiction 2. Neighbors -- Fiction 3. Family life -- Fiction 4. Helping behavior -- Fiction 5. Illinois -- Fiction 6. Friendship -- Fiction 7. Helpfulness -- Fiction 8. Conduct of life -- Fiction 9. Family life

-- Illinois -- Fiction
ISBN 0385371063; 9780385371063; 9780385371070; 9780385371094

LC 2013016843

In this book, by Michele Weber Hurwitz, "thirteen-year-old Nina Ross is feeling kind of lost. . . . This summer, Nina decides to change things. She hatches a plan. There are sixty-five days of summer. Every day, she'll anonymously do one small but remarkable good thing for someone in her neighborhood, and find out: does doing good actually make a difference? Along the way, she discovers that her neighborhood, and her family, are full of surprises and secrets." (Publisher's note)

"The summer before ninth grade, Nina is adrift: she's growing apart from her best friend, and her family hardly speaks to one another. Then she decides to do one small, anonymous kind act each day, hoping to bring some good to her neighborhood. Nina is a thoughtful, inspiring hero who proves that one person really can make a difference." Horn Book

Hyde, Catherine Ryan

The **year** of my miraculous reappearance. Alfred A. Knopf 2007 228p $15.99; lib bdg $18.99

Grades: 7 8 9 10   **Fic**
1. Siblings -- Fiction 2. Alcoholism -- Fiction 3. Down syndrome -- Fiction
ISBN 978-0-375-83257-4; 978-0-375-93257-1 lib bdg; 0-375-83257-2; 0-375-93257-7 lib bdg

LC 2006-29194

Thirteen-year-old Cynnie has had to deal with her mother's alcoholism and stream of boyfriends all her life, but when her grandparents take custody of her brother, Bill, who has Down Syndrome, Cynnie becomes self-destructive and winds up in court-mandated Alcoholics Anonymous meetings.

"Cynnie's love for and devotion to Bill are wholly believable, as are her attempts to snare a stable adult presence in her life. Secondary characters are multidimensional and well drawn." Booklist

Ibbitson, John

★ The **Landing**; a novel. KCP Fiction 2008 160p $17.95; pa $7.95

Grades: 7 8 9 10   **Fic**
1. Canada -- Fiction 2. Uncles -- Fiction 3. Violinists -- Fiction
ISBN 978-1-55453-234-6; 1-55453-234-5; 978-1-55453-238-4 pa; 1-55453-238-8 pa

Ben thinks he will always be stuck at Cook's Landing, barely making ends meet like his uncle. But when he meets a wealthy widow from New York City, he sees himself there too. When she hires him to play his violin, he realizes his gift could unlock the possibilities of the world. Then, during a stormy night on Lake Muskoka, everything changes.

"With lovely prose, Ibbitson brings to life the rugged beauty and the devastating poverty of the Lake Muskoka region. His characters are as strong and remote as their surroundings." Voice Youth Advocates

Ibbotson, Eva

The **beasts** of Clawstone Castle; illustrated by Kevin Hawkes. Dutton Children's Books 2006 243p il hardcover o.p. $16.99

Grades: 4 5 6   **Fic**
1. Ghost stories 2. Cattle -- Fiction 3. Castles -- Fiction 4. Great Britain -- Fiction
ISBN 0-14-240931-6 pa; 0-525-47719-5

LC 2005-29188

While spending the summer with elderly relatives at Clawstone Castle in northern England, Madlyn and her brother Rollo, with the help of several ghosts, attempt to save the rare cattle that live on the castle grounds. "Grades four to seven." (Bull Cent Child Books)

"Ibbotson's charismatic ghosts are great. . .—as human as they are horrific—and there's plenty of quirky humor in this energetic, diverting read, loaded with charm." Booklist

★ The **dragonfly** pool; illustrated by Kevin Hawkes. Dutton Children's Books 2008 377p il $17.99; pa $7.99

Grades: 5 6 7 8   **Fic**
1. School stories 2. World War, 1939-1945 -- Fiction
ISBN 978-0-525-42064-4; 0-525-42064-9; 978-0-14-241486-6 pa; 0-14-241486-7 pa

"Ibbotson's trademark eccentric characters and strongly contrasted principles of right and wrong brighten and broaden this uplifting tale." Booklist

★ The **Ogre** of Oglefort; [illustrations by Lisa K. Weber] Dutton Children's Books 2011 246p il $16.99

Grades: 4 5 6   **Fic**
1. Fairy tales 2. Magic -- Fiction 3. Orphans -- Fiction 4. Princesses -- Fiction
ISBN 978-0-525-42382-9; 0-525-42382-6

LC 2010038137

When the Hag of Dribble, an orphan boy, and a troll called Ulf are sent to rescue a princess from an ogre, it turns out to be far from the routine magical mission they expect.

"Magical creatures abound in this effervescent fairy tale that effectively merges classic tropes with modern sensibilities." Bull Cent Child Books

One dog and his boy; by Eva Ibbotson. Scholastic Press 2012 271 p. $16.99

Grades: 3 4 5 6   **Fic**
1. Children's stories 2. Pets -- Fiction 3. Dogs -- Fiction 4. Wealth -- Fiction 5. England -- Fiction 6. London (England) -- Fiction 7. Voyages and travels -- Fiction 8. Human-animal relationships -- Fiction 9. Family life -- England -- London -- Fiction
ISBN 0545351960; 9780545351966

LC 2011003773

In this book, by Eva Ibbotson, "[all] Hal has ever wanted is a dog. His busy parents, hoping that he'll tire of the idea, rent a dog from Easy Pets, run by the heartless Mr. and Mrs. Carker. Hal and Fleck, the dog he chooses, bond immediately, and they are both heartbroken when Hal's mother, realizing that Hal's interest isn't waning, sneaks the dog back to

Easy Pets. Hal decides to get Fleck back and run away to his grandparents." (Bulletin of the Center for Children's Books)

★ The **star** of Kazan; illustrated by Kevin Hawkes. Dutton 2004 405p il $16.99; pa $7.99

Grades: 5 6 7 8   **Fic**

1. Mystery fiction 2. Germany -- Fiction 3. Vienna (Austria) -- Fiction

ISBN 0-525-47347-5; 0-14-240582-5 pa

LC 2004-45455

After twelve-year-old Annika, a foundling living in late nineteenth-century Vienna, inherits a trunk of costume jewelry, a woman claiming to be her aristocratic mother arrives and takes her to live in a strangely decrepit mansion in Germany

"This is a rich saga . . . full of stalwart friends, sly villains, a brave heroine, and good triumphing over evil. . . . An intensely satisfying read." SLJ

Ingold, Jeanette

The **Big** Burn. Harcourt 2002 295p $17; pa $6.95

Grades: 7 8 9 10   **Fic**

1. Forest fires -- Fiction

ISBN 0-15-216470-7; 0-15-204924-X pa

LC 2001-5667

Three teenagers battle the flames of the Big Burn of 1910, one of the century's biggest wildfires

"A solid adventure story with a well-realized setting." Booklist

Includes bibliographical references (p. {293}-295)

Hitch. Harcourt, Inc 2005 272p $17; pa $6.95

Grades: 7 8 9 10   **Fic**

1. Montana -- Fiction 2. Great Depression, 1929-1939 -- Fiction 3. Civilian Conservation Corps (U.S.) -- Fiction

ISBN 0-15-204747-6; 0-15-20561-9 pa

LC 2004-19447

To help his family during the Depression and avoid becoming a drunk like his father, Moss Trawnley joins the Civilian Conservation Corps, helps build a new camp near Monroe, Montana, and leads the other men in making the camp a success.

This is "a credible, involving story. . . . Both [the author's] writing style and her 1930s setting feels totally true to the time." Booklist

Mountain solo. Harcourt 2003 309p $17; pa $6.95

Grades: 7 8 9 10   **Fic**

1. Violinists -- Fiction 2. Family life -- Fiction

ISBN 0-15-202670-3; 0-15-205358-1 pa

LC 2003-42326

Back at her childhood home in Missoula, Montana, after a disastrous concert in Germany, a teenage violin prodigy contemplates giving up life with her mother in New York City and her music as she, her father, stepmother, and stepsister hike to a pioneer homesite where another violinist once faced difficult decisions of his own

"Mountain Solo is a good read for anyone fascinated by the power of music and its effects on individuals' lives." SLJ

Includes bibliographical references (p. {307}-309)

Irving, Washington

The **Legend** of Sleepy Hollow; illustrated by Gris Grimly. Atheneum Books for Young Readers 2007 un il $16.99

Grades: 4 5 6   **Fic**

1. Ghost stories 2. New York (State) -- Fiction

ISBN 1-4169-0625-8; 978-1-4169-0625-4

LC 2005-27502

A superstitious schoolmaster, in love with a wealthy farmer's daughter, has a terrifying encounter with a headless horseman.

"The tale, . . . slightly condensed but with language and ambiguities intact, is reimagined here with humor, vigor, [and] clarity. . . . Irving's language is challenging . . . but Grimly's numerous Halloween-hued panel and spot illustrations . . . parse it into comprehensible tidbits. The comically amplified emotions and warm yellow and orange tones balance the horror aspects of the text." Horn Book

Isbell, Tom

The **Prey**; Tom Isbell. Harperteen 2015 416 p. $17.99

Grades: 7 8 9 10   **Fic**

1. Science fiction 2. Dystopian fiction 3. Twins -- Fiction 4. Orphans -- Fiction 5. Survival -- Fiction

ISBN 0062216015; 9780062216014

In this young adult science fiction novel, by Tom Isbell, "orphaned teens, soon to be hunted for sport, must flee their resettlement camps in their fight for survival and a better life. For in the Republic of the True America, it's always hunting season. . . . As unlikely Book and fearless Hope lead their quest for freedom, these teens must find the best in themselves to fight the worst in their enemies." (Publisher's note)

"An electromagnetic pulse followed by radiation—they called it Omega, the end—destroyed civilization as it once existed. The survivors established the Republic of the True America. But the future still looks like a dead end for Book and Hope, two teens who find themselves in the camps that purport to be orphanages...Careful readers will appreciate the irony and subtle, deeper meanings in character and location names as Isbell shapes his own vision of a dark world..." Booklist

Jackson, Alison

Rainmaker. Boyds Mills Press 2005 192p $16.95

Grades: 5 6 7 8   **Fic**

1. Florida -- Fiction 2. Droughts -- Fiction 3. Great Depression, 1929-1939 -- Fiction

ISBN 1-59078-309-3

"For 13-year-old Pidge Martin, the summer of 1939 brings changes and challenges. Her town, Frostfree, Florida, faces its longest drought in 40 years, and if it doesn't rain soon, area families . . . may lose their farms. A miracle is in order, and Pidge's father hopes a rainmaker can provide one. . . . Pidge is a well-characterized, sympathetic protagonist that readers will connect with." Booklist

Jacobson, Jennifer Richard, 1958-

The **complete** history of why I hate her; [by] Jennifer Richard Jacobson. Atheneum Books for Young Readers 2010 181p $16.99

Grades: 7 8 9 10   **Fic**

1. Maine -- Fiction 2. Cancer -- Fiction 3. Resorts -- Fiction 4. Sisters -- Fiction 5. Personality disorders -- Fiction

ISBN 978-0-689-87800-8; 0-689-87800-1

LC 2008-42959

Wanting a break from being known only for her sister's cancer, seventeen-year-old Nola leaves Boston for a waitressing job at a summer resort in Maine, but soon feels as if her new best friend is taking over her life.

"A compelling story of self-discovery with plenty of insights into the motivations that drive relationships." Booklist

Paper things; Jennifer Richard Jacobson. Candlewick Press 2015 384 p. $16.99

Grades: 5 6 7 8   **Fic**

1. Maine -- Fiction 2. Orphans -- Fiction 3. Siblings -- Fiction 4. Middle schools -- Fiction 5. Homeless persons -- Fiction 6. Promises -- Fiction 7. Gifted girls -- Fiction

ISBN 0763663239; 9780763663230

LC 2014944677

In this book, by Jennifer Richard Jacobson, "when Ari's mother died four years ago, she had two final wishes: that Ari and her older brother, Gage, would stay together always, and that Ari would go to Carter, the middle school for gifted students. So when nineteen-year-old Gage decides he can no longer live with their bossy guardian, Janna, Ari knows she has to go with him. But it's been two months, and Gage still hasn't found them an apartment." (Publisher's note)

"Before her death four years earlier, Ari and Gage's mother had urged them to "stay together always." Now it has been two months since nineteen-year-old Gage and eleven-year-old Ari left their overbearing guardian's home to strike out on their own, and the challenges of finding a permanent job and stable living situation have frayed Gage's confidence... In this poignant view of one child's experience with homelessness, Jacobson deftly shows how easily it can happen, an insidious downward spiral with heart-wrenching consequences." Horn Book

★ **Small** as an elephant; [by] Jennifer Richard Jacobson. Candlewick Press 2011 275p $15.99

Grades: 5 6 7 8   **Fic**

1. Adventure fiction 2. New England -- Fiction 3. Abandoned children -- Fiction 4. Mother-son relationship -- Fiction

ISBN 0-7636-4155-3; 978-0-7636-4155-9

LC 2010039175

When his mother disappears from an Acadia National Park campground, Jack tries to make his way back home to Boston, with only a small toy elephant for company. "Intermediate, middle school." (Horn Book)

"Jacobson masterfully puts readers into Jack's mind—he loves and understands his mother, but sometimes his judgments are not always good, and readers understand. . . . Jack's journey to a new kind of family is inspiring and never sappy." Kirkus

Jacques, Brian

Castaways of the Flying Dutchman; illustrated by Ian Schoenherr. Philomel Bks. 2001 327p il $22.95; pa $7.99

Grades: 6 7 8 9   **Fic**

1. Adventure fiction 2. Dogs -- Fiction 3. Angels -- Fiction 4. Orphans -- Fiction

ISBN 0-399-23601-5; 0-14-250118-2 pa

LC 00-59822

In 1620, a boy and his dog are rescued from the doomed ship, Flying Dutchman, by an angel who guides them in travelling the world, eternally helping those in great need

"The swashbuckling language brims with color and melodrama; the villains are dastardly and stupid; and buried treasure, mysterious clues, and luscious culinary descriptions . . . keep the pages turning." Booklist

Other titles in this series are:
The angel's command (2003)
Voyage of slaves (2006)

Mariel of Redwall; illustrated by Gary Chalk. Philomel Bks. 1992 387p il $24.99; pa $7.99

Grades: 5 6 7 8 9   **Fic**

1. Fantasy fiction 2. Mice -- Fiction 3. Animals -- Fiction

ISBN 978-0-399-22144-6; 0-399-22144-1; 978-0-441-00694-6 pa; 0-441-00694-9 pa

LC 91-17157

"Jacques' characters are fully developed and true to their natures; his dialectal dialog resounds with wit; the plot is filled with action, drama, and larger-than-life violence; and good conquers all. A satisfying tale with wide appeal that extends beyond its intended audience." Booklist

★ **Redwall**; illustrated by Gary Chalk. 20th anniversary ed.; Philomel 2007 351p il $23.99; pa $7.99

Grades: 5 6 7 8 9   **Fic**

1. Fantasy fiction 2. Mice -- Fiction 3. Animals -- Fiction

ISBN 978-0-399-24794-1; 0-399-24794-7; 978-0-441-00548-2 pa; 0-441-00548-9 pa

First published 1986

"Thoroughly engrossing, this novel captivates despite its length. . . . The theme will linger long after the story is finished." Booklist

Other titles in this series are:
The Bellmaker (1995)
Doomwyte (2008)
Eulalia! (2007)
High Rhulain (2005)
The legend of Luke (2000)
Loamhedge (2003)
The long patrol (1998)
Lord Brocktree (2000)
Mariel of Redwall (1992)
Marlfox (1998)
Martin the Warrior (1994)
Mattimeo (1990)
Mossflower (1998)
The outcast of Redwall (1996)
Pearls of Lutra (1997)

Rakkety Tam (2004)
The Rogue Crew (2011)
Sable Quean (2009)
Salamandastron (1993)
Taggerung (2001)
Triss (2002)

Jaden, Denise

Losing Faith. Simon Pulse 2010 381p pa $9.99

Grades: 7 8 9 10 11 12   **Fic**

1. School stories 2. Cults -- Fiction 3. Death -- Fiction
4. Sisters -- Fiction 5. Bereavement -- Fiction 6.
Christian life -- Fiction

ISBN 978-1-4169-9609-5; 1-4169-9609-5

LC 2010-7296

Brie tries to cope with her grief over her older sister
Faith's sudden death by trying to learn more about the religious "home group" Faith secretly joined and never talked
about with Brie or her parents.

"With pitch-perfect portrayals of high school social life
and a nuanced view into a variety of Christian experiences of
faith, this first novel gives readers much to think about." SLJ

James, Helen Foster

Paper son; Lee's journey to America. written
by Helen Foster James and Virginia Shin-Mui Loh;
illustrated by Wilson Ong. Sleeping Bear Press 2013
32 p. ill. (reinforced) $16.99

Grades: 5 6 7 8   **Fic**

1. Historical fiction 2. Immigrants -- United States --
Fiction 3. Orphans -- Fiction 4. Immigrants -- Fiction
5. Chinese Americans -- Fiction 6. Emigration and
immigration -- Fiction 7. Angel Island Immigration
Station (Calif.) -- Fiction 8. Angel Island (Calif.) --
History -- 20th century -- Fiction

ISBN 1585368334; 9781585368334

LC 2012033691

This historical novel, by Helen Foster James, Virginia
Shin-Mui Loh, and illustrated by Wilson Ong, is part of the
"Tales of Young Americans" series. "In 1926, 12-year-old
Fu Lee['s] . . . parents . . . spent all of their money buying
a 'paper son slot' for Lee to go to America. Being a 'paper
son' means pretending to be the son of a family already in
America. . . . But first he must pass the test at Angel Island
Immigration Station in San Francisco." (Publisher's note)

Jansen, Hanna

Over a thousand hills I walk with you; translated
from the German by Elizabeth D. Crawford. Carolrhoda Books 2006 342p $16.95

Grades: 7 8 9 10   **Fic**

1. Rwanda -- Fiction

ISBN 1-57505-927-4; 978-1-57505-927-3

LC 2005-21123

Original German edition, 2002

"Eight-year-old Jeanne was the only one of her family
to survive the 1994 Rwanda genocide. Then a German family adopted her, and her adoptive mother now tells Jeanne's
story in a compelling fictionalized biography that stays true
to the traumatized child's bewildered viewpoint." Booklist

Jaramillo, Ann

La linea. Roaring Brook Press 2006 131p
$16.95; pa $7.99

Grades: 5 6 7 8   **Fic**

1. Mexicans -- Fiction 2. Siblings -- Fiction 3.
Immigrants -- Fiction

ISBN 1-59643-154-7; 0-312-37354-6 pa

LC 2005-20133

When fifteen-year-old Miguel's time finally comes to
leave his poor Mexican village, cross the border illegally,
and join his parents in California, his younger sister's determination to join him soon imperils them both.

"A gripping contemporary survival adventure, this spare
first novel is also a heart-wrenching family story of courage,
betrayal, and love." Booklist

Jarzab, Anna

All unquiet things. Delacorte Press 2010 339p
$17.99

Grades: 8 9 10 11 12   **Fic**

1. School stories 2. Mystery fiction 3. Homicide --
Fiction 4. California -- Fiction 5. Social classes --
Fiction

ISBN 978-0-385-73835-4; 0-385-73835-8; 978-0-385-
90723-1 lib bdg; 0-385-90723-0 lib bdg

LC 2009-11557

After the death of his ex-girlfriend Carly, northern California high school student Neily joins forces with Carly's
cousin Audrey to try to solve her murder.

"A year after Carly's murder, friends Neily and Audrey
team up to find her killer. Their investigation exposes unsettling secrets about her final months. Jarzab's deft construction of alternating narratives by Neily and Audrey reveals
not only Carly's mysterious last days but also the girls'
relationship with one another. The murder mystery, while
suspenseful, is not as well developed as the fully realized
characters." Horn Book

The opposite of hallelujah; Anna Jarzab. Delacorte Press 2012 452 p. (hc) $16.99

Grades: 7 8 9 10   **Fic**

1. Ex-nuns -- Fiction 2. Secrets -- Fiction 3. Sisters
-- Fiction 4. Nuns -- Fiction 5. Guilt -- Fiction 6.
Children's secrets -- Fiction

ISBN 0385738366; 9780375894084; 9780385738361;
9780385907248

LC 2012010882

In this book by Anna Jarzab "Caro's parents drop the
bombshell news that [her sister] Hannah is returning to live
with them. . . . Unable to understand Hannah, Caro resorts
to telling lies about her mysterious reappearance. . . . And as
she unearths a clue from Hannah's past--one that could save
Hannah from the dark secret that possesses her--Caro begins
to see her sister in a whole new light." (Publisher's note)

Jeffrey, Mark

Max Quick: the pocket and the pendant. Harper
2011 294p $15.99

Grades: 4 5 6 7   **Fic**

1. Science fiction 2. Time -- Fiction 3. Voyages and

travels -- Fiction 4. Identity (Psychology) -- Fiction
ISBN 978-0-06-198892-9; 0-06-198892-8

LC 2010-42663

First released 2005 as a podcast audiobook

Young Max, a troubled boy with a mysterious past, joins two other youths unaffected when the rest of the world was frozen in time on a journey across America—and time it-self—seeking the source of the "Time-stop."

"This fast-paced adventure . . . will keep readers turning pages." SLJ

Jenkins, A. M.

Night road. HarperTeen 2008 362p $16.99; lib bdg $17.89; pa $8.99

Grades: 8 9 10 11 12 **Fic**

1. Horror fiction 2. Vampires -- Fiction 3. Automobile travel -- Fiction
ISBN 978-0-06-054604-5; 0-06-054604-2; 978-0-06-054605-2 lib bdg; 0-06-054605-0 lib bdg; 978-0-06-054606-9 pa; 0-06-054606-9 pa

LC 2007-31703

Battling his own memories and fears, Cole, an extraordi-narily conscientious vampire, and Sandor, a more impulsive acquaintance, spend a few months on the road, trying to train a young man who recently joined their ranks.

"The real strength of the novel lies in the noirish at-mosphere, accessible prose, and crisp, sharp dialogue." Horn Book

Repossessed. HarperTeen 2007 218p $15.99

Grades: 7 8 9 10 **Fic**

1. School stories 2. Devil -- Fiction 3. Demoniac possession -- Fiction
ISBN 978-0-06-083568-2; 0-06-083568-0

LC 2007-09142

Michael L. Printz Award honor book, 2008

A fallen angel, tired of being unappreciated while do-ing his pointless, demeaning job, leaves Hell, enters the body of a seventeen-year-old boy, and tries to experience the full range of human feelings before being caught and punished, while the boy's family and friends puzzle over his changed behavior.

"Funny and clever. . . . It's a quick, quirky and entertain-ing read, with some meaty ideas in it, too." Kliatt

Jennings, Patrick

Odd, weird, and little; Patrick Jennings. Egmont USA 2014 160 p. (hardcover) $15.99

Grades: 4 5 6 7 **Fic**

1. Owls -- Fiction 2. Bullies -- Fiction 3. Schools -- Fiction 4. Friendship -- Fiction 5. Middle schools -- Fiction 6. Eccentrics and eccentricities -- Fiction
ISBN 1606843745; 9781606843741

LC 2013018248

In this book, by Patrick Jennings, "Woodrow and his classmates are surprised at the old-fashioned clothing and the tiny, delicate appearance of Toulouse, a newly arrived student from Canada. . . . Woodrow risks regaining his place as top [bullying] victim as he decides to befriend and protect Toulouse. . . . Readers also learn about the psychology behind bullying and about self-empowerment." (Kirkus Reviews)

Jennings, Richard W.

Ghost town. Houghton Mifflin 2009 167p $16

Grades: 7 8 9 10 **Fic**

1. Kansas -- Fiction 2. Ghost towns -- Fiction 3. Imaginary playmates -- Fiction 4. Business enterprises -- Fiction
ISBN 978-0-547-19471-4; 0-547-19471-4

LC 2008036781

Thirteen-year-old Spencer Honesty and his imaginary friend, an Indian called Chief Leopard Frog, improbably achieve fame and riches in the abandoned town of Paisley, Kansas, when Spencer begins taking photographs with his deceased father's ancient camera and Chief Leopard Frog has his poems published by a shady businessman in the Cayman Islands.

"Jennings has a dry wit, and the protagonist's matter-of-fact observations make the most outlandish scenes seem possible. This is a coming-of-age story/tall tale that's full of charm." SLJ

★ **Orwell's** luck; [by] Richard Jennings. Hough-ton Mifflin 2000 146p $15; pa $6.95

Grades: 5 6 7 8 **Fic**

1. Magic -- Fiction 2. Rabbits -- Fiction
ISBN 0-618-03628-8; 0-618-69335-1 pa

LC 99-33501

While caring for an injured rabbit which becomes her confidant, horoscope writer, and source of good luck, a thoughtful seventh grade girl learns to see things in more than one way

"This absolutely captivating tale is about everyday magic . . . filled with quiet humor and seamless inven-tion. The characters . . . are the sort that readers fall in love with." Booklist

Stink City. Houghton Mifflin Company 2006 186p $16

Grades: 5 6 7 8 **Fic**

1. Fishing -- Fiction 2. Animal rights movement -- Fiction
ISBN 978-0-618-55248-1; 0-618-55248-0

LC 2006-05863

As fifteen-year-old Cade gets involved in animal rights activism in his struggle to atone for the suffering of fish used in his family's smelly catfish bait business, his neighbor Leigh Ann tries to keep him out of trouble

"Many kids will enjoy the fishing lore, eccentric di-versions, and exaggerated humor in this whopper of a yarn." Booklist

Jeschonek, Robert T.

My favorite band does not exist. Clarion Books 2011 327p $16.99

Grades: 8 9 10 11 12 **Fic**

1. Fantasy fiction
ISBN 978-0-547-37027-9; 0-547-37027-X

Sixteen-year-old Idea Deity, who believes that he is a character in a novel who will die in the sixty-fourth chap-ter, has created a fictional underground rock band on the internet which, it turns out, may actually exist, and whose members are wondering who is broadcasting all their personal information.

"Jeschonek has created a quirky, time and space-bending adventure that might just gather a cult following of its own. . . . Libraries looking for a strong addition to their science-fiction collections will want to invest in this sophisticated novel." SLJ

Jeter, Derek, 1974-

The **contract**; Derek Jeter; with Paul Mantell. Jeter Publishing, Simon & Schuster Books for Young Readers 2014 176 p. (hardcover) $16.99

Grades: 5 6 7   **Fic**

1. Sports -- Fiction 2. Baseball -- Fiction 3. Goal (Psychology) -- Fiction 4. Teamwork (Sports) -- Fiction
ISBN 1481423126; 9781481423120

LC 2014004045

This book, by baseball player Derek Jeter, "is a middle grade baseball novel. . . . As a young boy, Derek Jeter dreams of being the shortstop for the New York Yankees. He even imagines himself in the World Series. So when Derek is chosen for the Little League Tigers, he hopes to play shortstop. But on the day of the assignments, Derek Starts at second base. Still, he tries his best while he wishes and dreams of that shortstop spot." (Publisher's note)

"A boy named Derek Jeter chases his dreams of playing in the Major Leagues. The author's note states the story is "based on some of my experiences growing up and playing baseball," and the book's "theme" is: "Set Your Goals High." Third-grade Derek (the character) is remarkably--and unrealistically--self-possessed and self-aware, but fans will get a kick out of this kid-version of their hero." Horn Book

Jimenez, Francisco

★ **Breaking** through. Houghton Mifflin 2001 195p il $15; pa $6.95

Grades: 7 8 9 10 11 12   **Fic**

1. California -- Fiction 2. Migrant labor -- Fiction 3. Mexican Americans -- Fiction
ISBN 0-618-01173-0; 0-618-34248-6 pa

LC 2001-16941

Sequel to: The circuit (1997)

Having come from Mexico to California ten years ago, fourteen-year-old Francisco is still working in the fields but fighting to improve his life and complete his education

"For all its recounting of deprivation, this is a hopeful book, told with rectitude and dignity." Horn Book

★ The **circuit**: stories from the life of a migrant child. Houghton Mifflin 1999 $16

Grades: 7 8 9 10 11 12   **Fic**

1. California -- Fiction 2. Family life -- Fiction 3. Migrant labor -- Fiction 4. Mexican Americans -- Fiction
ISBN 0-395-7902-1; 978-0-395-97902-0

First published 1997 by University of New Mexico Press

The story "begins in Mexico when the author is very young and his parents inform him that they are going on a very long trip to 'El Norte.' What follows is a series of stories of the family's unending migration from one farm to another as they search for the next harvesting job. Each story is told from the point of view of the author as a young child. The simple and direct narrative stays true to this perspective. . . . Lifting the story up from the mundane, Jiménez

deftly portrays the strong bonds of love that hold this family together." Publ Wkly

Followed by: Breaking through (2001)

★ **Reaching** out. Houghton Mifflin 2008 196p $16; pa $6.99

Grades: 7 8 9 10 11 12   **Fic**

1. California -- Fiction 2. Mexican Americans -- Fiction 3. Father-son relationship -- Fiction
ISBN 978-0-618-03851-0; 0-618-03851-5; 978-0-547-25030-4 pa; 0-547-25030-4 pa

Sequel to: Breaking through (2001)

A Pura Belpre Author Award honor book, 2009

"Papa's raging depression intensifies young Jiménez's personal guilt and conflict in the 1960s. . . . He is the first in his Mexican American migrant family to attend college in California. . . . Like his other fictionalized autobiographies, The Circuit (1997) and Breaking Through (2001), this sequel tells Jiménez's personal story in self-contained chapters that join together in a stirring narrative. . . . The spare episodes will draw readers with the quiet daily detail of work, anger, sorrow, and hope." Booklist

Jinks, Catherine

The **abused** werewolf rescue group. Harcourt 2011 409p $16.99

Grades: 8 9 10 11 12   **Fic**

1. Mystery fiction 2. Werewolves -- Fiction
ISBN 978-0-15-206615-4; 0-15-206615-2

Sequel to: The reformed vampire support group (2009)

When Tobias wakes up in a hospital with no memory of the night before, a mysterious man tells him he has a dangerous condition, and he finds himself involved with a group of werewolves convinced he needs their help.

Jinks "weaves an action-packed story that has a tempo all its own. The constant plot twists and turns thrust the characters into bizarre situations that are at times as humorous as they are scary." SLJ

Babylonne; [by] Catherine Jinks. Candlewick Press 2008 384p map $18.99

Grades: 7 8 9 10 11 12   **Fic**

1. War stories 2. Orphans -- Fiction 3. Middle Ages -- Fiction 4. France -- History -- 0-1328 -- Fiction
ISBN 978-0-7636-3650-0; 0-7636-3650-9

LC 2007-21958

In the violent and predatory world of thirteenth-century Languedoc, Pagan's sixteen-year-old daughter disguises herself as a boy and runs away with a priest who claims to be a friend of her dead father and mother, not knowing whether or not she can trust him, or anyone.

"Complete with snappy dialogue, humorous asides, and colorful descriptions . . . this novel stands on its own as a very fine historical fiction book about a period in history that is not commonly written about for teens." Voice Youth Advocates

★ **Evil** genius. Harcourt 2007 486p $17

Grades: 7 8 9 10   **Fic**

1. School stories 2. Crime -- Fiction 3. Genius -- Fiction 4. Australia -- Fiction 5. Good and evil --

Fiction
ISBN 978-0-15-205988-0; 0-15-205988-1
LC 2006-14476

First published 2005 in Australia

Child prodigy Cadel Piggot, an antisocial computer hacker, discovers his true identity when he enrolls as a first-year student at an advanced crime academy.

"Cadel's turnabout is convincingly hampered by his difficulty recognizing appropriate outlets for rage, and Jinks' whiplash-inducing suspense writing will gratify fans of Anthony Horowitz's high-tech spy scenarios." Booklist

Other titles about Cadel Piggot are:
Genius squad (2008)
Genius wars (2010)

Genius squad. Harcourt 2008 436p $17
Grades: 7 8 9 10   **Fic**
1. Crime -- Fiction 2. Genius -- Fiction 3. Australia -- Fiction 4. Good and evil -- Fiction
ISBN 978-0-15-205985-9; 0-15-205985-7

After the Axis Institute is blown up, fifteen-year-old Cadell Piggot is unhappily stuck in foster care with constant police surveillance to protect him from the evil Prosper English until he gets an offer to join a mysterious group called Genius Squad.

"Readers who loved Evil Genius will find this sequel as gripping, devilish and wonderfully dark as its predecessor." Publ Wkly

The **genius** wars. Harcourt 2010 378p $17
Grades: 7 8 9 10   **Fic**
1. Science fiction 2. Crime -- Fiction 3. Genius -- Fiction 4. Australia -- Fiction 5. Good and evil -- Fiction
ISBN 978-0-15-206619-2; 0-15-206619-5
LC 2009-49979

Fifteen-year-old genius Cadel Piggot Greenaus sets aside his new, crime-free life when his best friend Sonja is attacked, and he crosses oceans and continents trying to track down his nemesis Prosper English, breaking whatever rules he must.

"The climax is taut, absorbing and tantalizingly ambiguous." Kirkus

★ **How** to catch a bogle; by Catherine Jinks; illustrated by Sarah Watts. Harcourt Children's Books 2013 320 p. ill. (hardcover) $16.99
Grades: 5 6 7 8   **Fic**
1. Fantasy fiction 2. Alternative histories 3. Orphans -- Fiction 4. Monsters -- Fiction 5. Apprentices -- Fiction 6. Supernatural -- Fiction 7. London (England) -- History -- 19th century -- Fiction 8. Great Britain -- History -- Victoria, 1837-1901 -- Fiction
ISBN 0544087089; 9780544087088
LC 2012045936

This is the first in a historical fantasy trilogy from Catherine Jinks. Here, "child-eating bogles infest Victorian London, providing work aplenty for 'Go-Devil Man' Alfred Bunce and his intrepid young apprentice, Birdie." Birdie is kidnapped by "would-be warlock Roswell Morton, out to capture one of the monsters for his own evil uses." She also must deal with the unwanted "attentions of Miss Edith

Eames," who wants "to see Birdie cleaned up and educated in the social graces." (Kirkus Reviews)

Living hell. Harcourt 2010 256p $17
Grades: 7 8 9 10   **Fic**
1. Science fiction
ISBN 978-0-15-206193-7; 0-15-206193-2
LC 2009-18938

Chronicles the transformation of a spaceship into a living organism, as seventeen-year-old Cheney leads the hundreds of inhabitants in a fight for survival while machines turn on them, treating all humans as parasites.

"Jinks' well-thought-out environs and rational characters help ground this otherwise out-of-control interstellar thriller." Booklist

The **reformed** vampire support group. Houghton Mifflin Harcourt 2009 362p $17; pa $8.99
Grades: 8 9 10 11 12   **Fic**
1. Mystery fiction 2. Vampires -- Fiction
ISBN 978-0-15-206609-3; 0-15-206609-8; 978-0-547-41166-8 pa; 0-547-41166-9 pa
LC 2008-25115

Fifteen-year-old vampire Nina has been stuck for fifty-one years in a boring support group for vampires, and nothing exciting has ever happened to them—until one of them is murdered and the others must try to solve the crime.

"Those tired of torrid bloodsucker stories or looking for a comic riff on the trend will feel refreshed by the vomitous, guinea-pig-drinking accidental heroics of Nina and her pals." Kirkus

Followed by: The abused werewolf rescue group (2011)

Saving Thanehaven; by Catherine Jinks. Egmont USA 2013 384 p. (hardcover) $17.99
Grades: 4 5 6 7   **Fic**
1. Fantasy fiction 2. Science fiction 3. Computer games -- Fiction 4. Virtual reality -- Fiction 5. Knights and knighthood -- Fiction
ISBN 1606842749; 9781606842744
LC 2012046190

In this book, "Noble is just an earnest knight in the computer game 'Thanehaven Slayer' when he encounters young Rufus, who strongly suggests that he may be doomed if he doesn't drop all the heroics and start thinking for himself. With Rufus' mantra 'you don't have to do this' ringing in his ears, Noble sets out to change his computer world." (Kirkus Reviews)

Jobling, Curtis
The **rise** of the wolf. Viking Childrens Books 2011 412p (Wereworld) $16.99
Grades: 4 5 6 7   **Fic**
1. Fantasy fiction 2. Adventure fiction 3. Werewolves -- Fiction
ISBN 978-0-670-01330-2; 0-670-01330-7
LC 2010049517

When a vicious beast invades his father's farm and sixteen-year-old Drew suddenly transforms into a werewolf, he runs away from his family, seeking refuge in the most out of the way parts of Lyssia, only to be captured by Lord

Bergan's men and forced to battle numerous werecreatures while trying to prove that he is not the enemy.

"Jobling's characterizations are solid, his world-building is complex and fascinating, and the combat scenes are suitably exciting. The book's themes are familiar—lost prince in exile, voyage of self-discovery, young heroes rebelling against injustice and evil—but Jobling uses them to tell a thoroughly enjoyable adventure that makes particularly inventive use of its shapeshifter elements and mythology." Publ Wkly

Jocelyn, Marthe

Folly. Wendy Lamb Books 2010 249p $15.99; lib bdg $18.99

Grades: 8 9 10 11 12 **Fic**

1. London (England) -- Fiction 2. Abandoned children -- Fiction 3. Household employees -- Fiction 4. Foundling Hospital (London, England) -- Fiction 5. Great Britain -- History -- 19th century -- Fiction
ISBN 978-0-385-73846-0; 0-385-73846-3; 978-0-385-90731-6 lib bdg; 0-385-90731-1 lib bdg

LC 2009-23116

In a parallel narrative set in late nineteenth-century England, teenaged country girl Mary Finn relates the unhappy conclusion to her experiences as a young servant in an aristocratic London household while, years later, young James Nelligan describes how he comes to leave his beloved foster family to live and be educated at London's famous Foundling Hospital.

"Mary's spry narration (James's chapters unfold in third-person) combined with the tale's texture and fervent emotion will seduce readers." Horn Book Guide

★ **How** it happened in Peach Hill. Wendy Lamb Books 2007 232p $15.99; lib bdg $18.99

Grades: 6 7 8 9 **Fic**

1. Clairvoyance -- Fiction 2. New York (State) -- Fiction 3. Swindlers and swindling -- Fiction 4. Mother-daughter relationship -- Fiction
ISBN 978-0-375-83701-2; 0-375-93701-9; 978-0-375-93701-9 lib bdg; 0-375-93701-3 lib bdg

LC 2006-26688

When fifteen-year-old Annie Grey and her "clairvoyant" mother arrive in Peach Hill, New York, in 1924, each finds a reason for wanting to finally settle down, but to reach their goals they will have to do some serious lying and Annie will have to stand up for herself.

"The blend of coming-of-age, adventure, and intrigue, framed by details of small-town life and a classic con, will appeal to fans of spunky female characters and readers of historical fiction alike." Booklist

Mable Riley; a reliable record of humdrum, peril, and romance. Candlewick Press 2004 279p $15.99; pa $6.99

Grades: 5 6 7 8 **Fic**

1. Canada -- Fiction 2. Teachers -- Fiction 3. Women's rights -- Fiction
ISBN 0-7636-2120-X; 0-7636-3287-2 pa

LC 2003-55322

In 1901, fourteen-year-old Mable Riley dreams of being a writer and having adventures while stuck in Perth County,

Ontario, assisting her sister in teaching school and secretly becoming friends with a neighbor who holds scandalous opinions on women's rights.

"This book is a funny and inspiring tale of a young girl finding her voice and the courage to make it heard." Voice Youth Advocates

Viminy Crowe's comic book; Marthe Jocelyn, Richard Scrimger. Tundra Books of Northern New York 2014 317 p. illustrations (hardcover) $17.99

Grades: 4 5 6 7 **Fic**

1. Adventure fiction 2. Comic books, strips, etc. 3. Adventure stories 4. Steampunk fiction 5. Caricatures and cartoons -- Fiction. 6. Congresses and conventions -- Fiction
ISBN 1770494790; 9781770494794; 9781770494800

LC 2013943886

"Is there a personality conflict? Oh, yes. Addy wants to go home; Wylder wants to stay and explore the world of Viminy Crowe's comic book. Do things go wrong? You bet they do, from the very start, when Addy loses her pet rat, Catnip, and almost gets shot by a Red Rider. All the while the actual comic book story is going on around them." (Publisher's note)

"A bathroom portal at ComicFest launches two kids, Wylder Wallace and Addy Crowe, into the pages of a comic book. Suspense builds as the kids' presence affects the story, their adventures shown (in interspersed comic panels) in Davila's clear, humorous illustrations. It's a clever concept that's well executed by Jocelyn and Scrimger." Horn Book

★ **Would** you. Wendy Lamb Books 2008 165p $15.99; lib bdg $18.99; pa $6.50

Grades: 8 9 10 11 12 **Fic**

1. Coma -- Fiction 2. Sisters -- Fiction 3. Family life -- Fiction 4. Medical care -- Fiction 5. Traffic accidents -- Fiction
ISBN 978-0-375-83703-6; 0-375-83703-5; 978-0-375-93703-3 lib bdg; 0-375-93703-X lib bdg; 978-0-375-83704-3 pa; 0-375-83704-3 pa

LC 2007-18913

When her beloved sister, Claire, steps in front of a car and winds up in a coma, Nat's anticipated summer of working, hanging around with friends, and seeing Claire off to college is transformed into a nightmare of doctors, hospitals, and well-meaning neighbors.

"Jocelyn captures a teen's thoughts and reactions in a time of incredible anguish without making her overly dramatic. Readers will fly through the pages of this book, crying, laughing, and crying some more." SLJ

John, Antony

Five flavors of dumb. Dial Books 2010 337p $16.99

Grades: 7 8 9 10 **Fic**

1. Deaf -- Fiction 2. Rock musicians -- Fiction 3. Seattle (Wash.) -- Fiction
ISBN 978-0-8037-3433-3; 0-8037-3433-6

LC 2009-44449

Eighteen-year-old Piper is profoundly hearing impaired and resents her parent's decision raid her college fund to get cochlear implants for her baby sister. She becomes the manager for her classmates' popular rock band, called Dumb, giving her the chance to prove her capabilities to her parents and others, if only she can get the band members to get along.

"Readers interested in any of the narrative strands . . . will find a solid, satisfyingly complex story here." Bull Cent Child Books

Johnson, Angela, 1961-

★ A **certain** October; Angela Johnson. Simon & Schuster Books For Young Readers 2012 176 p. (hardback) $16.99

Grades: 7 8 9 10 11 12   **Fic**

1. Bildungsromans 2. Death -- Fiction 3. Guilt -- Fiction 4. Teenagers -- Fiction 5. Autism -- Fiction 6. Friendship -- Fiction 7. High schools -- Fiction

ISBN 9781442417267; 9780689865053; 9780689870651

         LC 2012001595

In this book, "when a terrible accident occurs, Scotty feels responsible for the loss of someone she hardly knew, and the world goes wrong. She cannot tell what is a dream and what is real. Her friends are having a hard time getting through to her and her family is preoccupied with their own trauma. But the prospect of a boy, a dance, and the possibility that everything can fall back into place soon help Scotty realize that she is capable of adding her own flavor to life." (Publisher's note)

★ A **cool** moonlight. Dial Bks. 2003 133p hardcover o.p. pa $6.99

Grades: 4 5 6   **Fic**

1. Skin -- Diseases -- Fiction

ISBN 0-8037-2846-8; 0-14-240284-2 pa

         LC 2002-31521

Nine-year-old Lila, born with xeroderma pigmentosum, a skin disease that make her sensitive to sunlight, makes secret plans to feel the sun's rays on her tenth birthday

"The book's real magic resides in the spell cast by Johnson's spare, lucid, lyrical prose. Using simple words and vivid sensory images, she creates Lila's inner world as a place of quiet intensity." Booklist

★ The **first** part last. Simon & Schuster Bks. for Young Readers 2003 131p $15.95

Grades: 7 8 9 10   **Fic**

1. Infants -- Fiction 2. Teenage fathers -- Fiction 3. African Americans -- Fiction

ISBN 0-689-84922-2

         LC 2002-36512

Prequel to Heaven (1998)

Michael L. Printz Award, 2004

Bobby's carefree teenage life changes forever when he becomes a father and must care for his adored baby daughter.

"Brief, poetic, and absolutely riveting." SLJ

Followed by: Sweet hereafter (2010)

★ **Heaven.** Simon & Schuster Bks. for Young Readers 1998 138p $16.95; pa $7.99

Grades: 6 7 8 9   **Fic**

1. Adoption -- Fiction 2. African Americans -- Fiction

ISBN 0-689-82229-4; 1-4424-0342-X pa

         LC 98-3291

Coretta Scott King Award for text, 1999

Fourteen-year-old Marley's seemingly perfect life in the small town of Heaven is disrupted when she discovers that her father and mother are not her real parents

"In spare, often poetic prose . . . Johnson relates Marley's insightful quest into what makes a family." SLJ

Sweet, hereafter. Simon & Schuster Books for Young Readers 2010 118p $16.99

Grades: 7 8 9 10   **Fic**

1. Iraq War, 2003- -- Fiction 2. African Americans -- Fiction

ISBN 978-0-689-87385-0; 0-689-87385-9

Sweet leaves her family and goes to live in a cabin in the woods with the quiet but understanding Curtis, to whom she feels intensely connected, just as he is called back to serve again in Iraq.

"With heartfelt empathy, we share in Shoogy's personal loss and her need for a new direction. Characters from the two other titles reappear, and we get a glimpse of how their lives are moving forward. This book belongs in all junior and senior high school collections, especially those who already own the first two titles. . . . Johnson now has one more well-woven character development novel to her name." Libr Media Connect

★ **Toning** the sweep. Orchard Bks. 1993 103p hardcover o.p. pa $5.99

Grades: 6 7 8 9   **Fic**

1. Death -- Fiction 2. Family life -- Fiction 3. Grandmothers -- Fiction 4. African Americans -- Fiction

ISBN 0-531-05476-4; 0-531-08626-7 lib bdg; 978-0-590-48142-7 pa; 0-590-48142-8 pa

         LC 92-34062

Coretta Scott King Award for text

On a visit to her grandmother Ola, who is dying of cancer in her house in the desert, fourteen-year-old Emmie hears many stories about the past and her family history and comes to a better understanding of relatives both dead and living

"Full of subtle nuance, the novel is overlaid with meaning about the connections of family and the power of friendship." SLJ

Johnson, J. J.

★ The **theory** of everything; by Jen Wichman. Peachtree Publishers 2012 334 p. ill. (hardcover) $16.95

Grades: 7 8 9 10   **Fic**

1. Bereavement -- Fiction 2. Interpersonal relations -- Fiction 3. Grief -- Fiction 4. Friendship -- Fiction 5. Best friends -- Fiction 6. New York (State) -- Fiction 7. Loss (Psychology) -- Fiction 8. Family life -- New York (State) -- Fiction

ISBN 1561456233; 9781561456239

         LC 2011020973

In this novel, by J. J. Johnson, "ever since Sarah Jones's best friend Jamie died in a freak accident, life has felt sort of . . . random. Sarah has always followed the rules. . . . Now what? . . . In a last ditch effort to pull it together, Sarah ends up working for Roy, a local eccentric who owns a Christmas tree farm, and who might also be trying to understand the rules, patterns, and connections in life." (Publisher's note)

Johnson, Jaleigh

★ The **mark** of the dragonfly; Jaleigh Johnson. First edition Delacorte Press 2014 400 p. map (glb) $19.99; (hc) $16.99

Grades: 5 6 7 8   **Fic**
    1. Magic -- Fiction 2. Fantasy fiction 3. Adventure and adventurers -- Fiction 4. Fantasy
    ISBN 0385376456; 9780385376457; 9780385376150
                      LC 2013019716

This book, by Jaleigh Johnson, is an "adventure story about a mysterious girl and a fearless boy, set in a magical world. . . . Piper has never seen the Mark of the Dragonfly until she finds the girl amid the wreckage of a caravan in the Meteor Fields. The girl doesn't remember a thing about her life, but the intricate tattoo on her arm is proof that she's from the Dragonfly Territories and that she's protected by the king. Which means a reward for Piper if she can get the girl home." (Publisher's note)

    "Heart, brains and courage find a home in a steampunk fantasy worthy of a nod from Baum. . . . A well-imagined world of veritable adventure." Kirkus

Johnson, Lindsay Lee

Worlds apart. Front Street 2005 166p il $16.95

Grades: 7 8 9 10   **Fic**
    1. Moving -- Fiction 2. Psychiatric hospitals -- Fiction
    ISBN 1-932425-28-4
                      LC 2005-12052

A thirteen-year-old daughter of a surgeon finds herself wrenched away from a comfortable lifestyle to a home on the grounds of a mental hospital, where her father has accepted a five year contract.

    "This story brings bias and prejudice to the forefront in a discussable and readable narrative." SLJ

Johnson, Maureen

13 little blue envelopes. HarperCollins Publishers 2005 317p $15.99; pa $8.99

Grades: 8 9 10 11 12   **Fic**
    1. Aunts -- Fiction 2. Europe -- Fiction 3. Voyages and travels -- Fiction
    ISBN 0-06-054141-5; 0-06-054143-1 pa
                      LC 2005-02658

When seventeen-year-old Ginny receives a packet of mysterious envelopes from her favorite aunt, she leaves New Jersey to criss-cross Europe on a sort of scavenger hunt that transforms her life.

    "Equal parts poignant, funny and inspiring, this tale is sure to spark wanderlust." Publ Wkly

    Followed by: The last little blue envelope (2011)

The **last** little blue envelope. HarperTeen 2011 282p $16.99

Grades: 8 9 10 11 12   **Fic**
    1. Aunts -- Fiction 2. Europe -- Fiction 3. Artists -- Fiction 4. Letters -- Fiction 5. Voyages and travels

-- Fiction 6. Swindlers and swindling -- Fiction
    ISBN 978-0-06-197679-7; 0-06-197679-2
                      LC 2010033580

"Ginny's narrative, told in an intelligent, third-person voice, establishes her firmly as a sympathetic, often hilarious everygirl, whose efforts to understand herself and who she'd like to be are fraught with moments both romantic and heartbreaking. Johnson's skill in creating secondary characters that are unusual, realistically flawed and utterly believable is again on display here. . . . This is an appealingly smart and honest read that fans of the first will find deeply satisfying." Kirkus

★ The **madness** underneath; Maureen Johnson. G. P. Putnam's Sons 2013 304 p. (Shades of London) (hardback) $17.99

Grades: 6 7 8 9 10   **Fic**
    1. Ghost stories 2. Occult fiction 3. Mystery fiction 4. Ghosts -- Fiction 5. Murder -- Fiction 6. England -- Fiction 7. Schools -- Fiction 8. Boarding schools -- Fiction 9. London (England) -- Fiction
    ISBN 039925661X; 9780399256615
                      LC 2012026755

This paranormal mystery novel, by Maureen Johnson, is book two of "The Shades of London Trilogy." "After her near-fatal run-in with the Jack the Ripper copycat, Rory Devereaux . . . [has] become a human terminus, with the power to eliminate ghosts on contact. . . . The Ripper may be gone, but now there is a string of new inexplicable deaths threatening London. Rory has evidence that the deaths are no coincidence. Something much more sinister is going on." (Publisher's note)

The **name** of the star. G. P. Putnam's Sons 2011 384p $16.99

Grades: 6 7 8 9 10   **Fic**
    1. Ghost stories 2. School stories 3. Homicide -- Fiction 4. Witnesses -- Fiction 5. London (England) -- Fiction
    ISBN 978-0-399-25660-8; 0-399-25660-1; 9780399256608; 0399256601
                      LC 2011009003

"Johnson's trademark sense of humor serves to counterbalance some grisly murders in this page-turner, which opens her Shades of London series. . . . As one mutilated body after another turns up, Johnson . . . amplifies the story's mysteries with smart use of and subtle commentary on modern media shenanigans and London's infamously extensive surveillance network. . . . Readers looking for nonstop fun, action, and a little gore have come to the right place." Publ Wkly

Scarlett fever. Point/Scholastic 2010 336p $16.99

Grades: 7 8 9 10   **Fic**
    1. School stories 2. Actors -- Fiction 3. Family life -- Fiction 4. New York (N.Y.) -- Fiction 5. Hotels and motels -- Fiction 6. Dating (Social customs) -- Fiction
    ISBN 978-0-439-89928-4; 0-439-89928-1
    Sequel to: Suite Scarlett (2008)

Fifteen-year-old Scarlett, who is beginning to get over her breakup with Eric, stays busy as assistant to her theatrical-agent friend who is not only promoting Scarlett's brother Spencer, but also a new client whose bad-boy brother has transferred to Scarlett's school.

"While the novel may be enjoyed for the light if slightly madcap romance that it is, it is notable for its attention to social class and to the Martins' struggles with money." SLJ

★ **Suite** Scarlett. Scholastic Point 2008 353p $16.99

Grades: 6 7 8 9 10   **Fic**

  1. Authorship -- Fiction 2. Family life -- Fiction 3. New York (N.Y.) -- Fiction 4. Hotels and motels -- Fiction

ISBN 978-0-439-89927-7; 0-439-89927-3

                   LC 2007-041903

Fifteen-year-old Scarlett Marvin is stuck in New York City for the summer working at her quirky family's historic hotel, but her brother's attractive new friend and a seasonal guest who offers her an intriguing and challenging writing project improve her outlook.

"Utterly winning, madcap Manhattan farce, crafted with a winking, urbane narrative and tight, wry dialogue." Booklist

Another title about Scarlett is:

Scarlett fever (2010)

Johnson, Peter

★ **What** happened. Front Street 2007 133p $16.95

Grades: 8 9 10 11 12   **Fic**

  1. Traffic accidents -- Fiction 2. Father-son relationship -- Fiction

ISBN 978-1-932425-67-3; 1-932425-67-5

                   LC 2006-12028

When Duane is involved in a hit-and-run accident during a snowstorm, passengers Kyle and his younger brother must face Duane's powerful father, a man whose hatred of their own absent father may lead him to harm the boys.

"The voice that Johnson has given this boy . . . is breathtakingly good, each word conspiring with every other word to create an irresistibly seductive tone that is a haunting combination of sadness and fragile hope." Booklist

Johnson, Terry Lynn

  Ice dogs; by Terry Lynn Johnson. Houghton Mifflin, Houghton Mifflin Harcourt 2013 288 p. $16.99

Grades: 5 6 7 8 9   **Fic**

  1. Wilderness survival -- Fiction 2. Sled dog racing -- Fiction 3. Dogs -- Fiction 4. Alaska -- Fiction 5. Survival -- Fiction 6. Sled dogs -- Fiction 7. Dogsledding -- Fiction 8. Wilderness areas -- Fiction

ISBN 0547899262; 9780547899268

                   LC 2012045061

In this book, by Terry Lynn Johnson, "Victoria Secord, a fourteen-year-old Alaskan dogsled racer, loses her way on a routine outing with her dogs. With food gone and temperatures dropping, her survival and that of her dogs and the mysterious boy she meets in the woods is entirely up to her." (Publisher's note)

Johnson, Varian

  The **great** Greene heist; by Varian Johnson. Arthur A. Levine Books 2014 240 p. (hardcover) $16.99

Grades: 5 6 7 8   **Fic**

  1. School stories 2. Schools -- Fiction 3. Elections -- Fiction 4. Friendship -- Fiction 5. Best friends -- Fiction 6. Middle schools -- Fiction 7. Practical jokes -- Fiction

ISBN 0545525527; 9780545525534; 0545525535; 9780545525527

                   LC 2013029145

"Jackson Greene has reformed. No, really he has. He was once the best con artist at Maplewood Middle School, and everyone still talks about his Blitz at the Fitz.... But after Principal Kelsey caught him in his office, Jackson swore off scheming for good. Then Keith Sinclair--loser of the Blitz--announces he's running for school president, against Jackson's former almost-girlfriend Gaby de la Cruz." (Publisher's note)

"This fast-paced caper reads like Ocean's 11 for the middle-school set, and that's no coincidence: Johnson (Saving Maddie, 2010) openly credits the film as inspiration, and he has pretty much pulled it off, right down to the dizzying plot twists, incredulous access to the latest tech, and unflappable swagger. " Booklist

Johnson-Shelton, Nils

  The **Invisible** Tower. HarperCollins 2011 335p (Otherworld chronicles) $16.99

Grades: 4 5 6 7   **Fic**

  1. Adventure fiction 2. Kings

ISBN 978-0-06-207086-9; 0-06-207086-X

                   LC 2011022928

A twelve-year-old boy learns that he is actually King Arthur brought back to life in the twenty-first century—and that the fate of the universe rests in his hands.

"This new take on the Arthurian legends, told in third-person, pits wisecracking contemporary teens with their contemporary banter. . . . against all manner of obstacles. . . . It's always high-spirited and fun. Gives new life to Arthurian legends and may just send readers back to more traditional tellings." Kirkus

  The **seven** swords; Nils Johnson-Shelton. HarperCollins 2013 368 p. (Otherworld chronicles) (hardback) $16.99

Grades: 4 5 6 7   **Fic**

  1. Arthurian romances -- Adaptations 2. Fantasy fiction 3. Adventure fiction

ISBN 0062070940; 9780062070944

                   LC 2012019088

This juvenile adventure fantasy, by Nils Johnson-Shelton, second in the "Otherworld Chronicles," follows "Artie Kingfisher, the new King Arthur. On a quest to recover seven magical swords of the Dark Ages, Artie and Kay gather 'New Knights of the Round Table' and try to unite two worlds. Standing in their way is Lordess Morgaine. . . . Artie and his band travel from Ohio via crossover points between worlds in search of swords in Sweden, France and Japan." (Kirkus Reviews)

Johnston, E. K.

Prairie fire; E.K. Johnston. Carolrhoda Books 2015 304 p. (trade hard cover : alk. paper) $18.99

Grades: 7 8 9 10 11 12   **Fic**

1. Dragons -- Fiction 2. Friendship -- Fiction 3. Fame -- Fiction 4. High schools -- Fiction 5. Bards and bardism -- Fiction 6. Family life -- Canada -- Fiction 7. Adventure and adventurers -- Fiction

ISBN 146773909X; 9781467739092; 9781467761819; 9781467776790; 9781467776806; 9781467776813

LC 2014008995

Sequel to: The story of Owen

In this young adult novel by E. K. Johnston, the sequel to "The Story of Owen," "Every dragon slayer owes the Oil Watch a period of service, and young Owen was no exception. What made him different was that he did not enlist alone. His two closest friends stood with him shoulder to shoulder. . . . But the arc of history is long and hardened by dragon fire. Try as they might, Owen and his friends could not twist it to their will." (Publisher's note)

"A fantasy YA novel that steers clear of love triangles, teen angst, and a tidy ending is hard to come by; Prairie Fire and its prequel are must-haves." SLJ

The **story** of Owen; dragon slayer of Trondheim. E. K. Johnston. Carolrhoda Lab 2014 305 p. (hardcover) $17.95

Grades: 7 8 9 10 11 12   **Fic**

1. Adventure fiction 2. Canada -- Fiction 3. Dragons -- Fiction 4. Family life -- Fiction 5. Fame -- Fiction 6. Schools -- Fiction 7. High schools -- Fiction 8. Bards and bardism -- Fiction 9. Family life -- Canada -- Fiction 10. Adventure and adventurers -- Fiction

ISBN 9781467710664; 1467710660

LC 2013020492

William C. Morris Finalist (2015)

In this book, author E. K. Johnston, "envisions an Earth nearly identical to our own, with one key difference: dragons. . . . After 16-year-old Siobhan McQuaid agrees to become the bard for dragon-slayer-in-training Owen Thorskard, who has moved with his famous dragon-slaying family to her small Ontario town, she winds up at the center of a grassroots effort to understand an odd spike in dragon numbers." (Publishers Weekly)

"Humor, pathos and wry social commentary unite in a cleverly drawn, marvelously diverse world. Refreshingly, the focus is on the pair as friends and partners, not on potential romance." Kirkus

Johnston, Julie

Little red lies; by Julie Johnston. Tundra Books 2013 352 p. (hardcover) $19.95

Grades: 7 8 9   **Fic**

1. Family life -- Fiction 2. College and school drama 3. Teenage girls -- Fiction

ISBN 1770493131; 9781770493131; 9781770493148

LC 2012947608

In this book by Julie Johnston "the war is over, but for thirteen-year-old Rachel, the battle has just begun. Putting childhood behind her, she knows what she wants--to prove she has acting talent worthy of the school drama club, and

what she doesn't want--to romantically fall for someone completely inappropriate. Ultimately, she finds a way to come to terms with life as it reaches an end and life as it begins." (Publisher's note)

A **very** fine line. Tundra Books 2006 198p $18.95; pa $10.95

Grades: 5 6 7 8   **Fic**

1. Canada -- Fiction 2. Clairvoyance -- Fiction

ISBN 978-0-88776-746-3; 0-88776-746-X; 978-0-88776-829-3 pa; 0-88776-829-6 pa

Then thirteen-year-old Rosalind's "aunt informs her that as the seventh daughter of a seventh daughter, she can . . . see glimpses of the future, she balks. . . . The story begins in Kepston, Ontario, in 1941. . . . Readers who come to the book intrigued by the idea of clairvoyance will fine much more: several vivid characters, a well-realized setting, and a sensitively nuanced resolution." Booklist

Johnston, Tony

Any small goodness; a novel of the barrio. illustrations by Raúl Colón. Blue Sky Press (NY) 2001 128p il $16.95; pa $4.99

Grades: 4 5 6 7   **Fic**

1. Mexican Americans -- Fiction 2. Los Angeles (Calif.) -- Fiction

ISBN 0-439-18936-5; 0-439-23384-4 pa

LC 99-59877

Arturo and his family and friends share all kinds of experiences living in the barrio of East Los Angeles—reclaiming their names, playing basketball, championing the school librarian, and even starting their own gang

"The characters are likable and warm. . . . The message is positive and the episodes, while occasionally serious, are more often humorous and gratifying." SLJ

Jolin, Paula

In the name of God. Roaring Brook Press 2007 208p $16.95

Grades: 8 9 10 11 12   **Fic**

1. Syria -- Fiction 2. Muslims -- Fiction 3. Family life -- Fiction 4. Islamic fundamentalism -- Fiction

ISBN 978-1-59643-211-6; 1-59643-211-X

LC 2006-23834

Determined to follow the laws set down in the Qur'an, seventeen-year-old Nadia becomes involved in a violent revolutionary movement aimed at supporting Muslim rule in Syria and opposing the Western politics and materialism that increasingly affect her family.

"The well-written prose and short chapters give stories in the news a face and a character. Readers of this book will not be able to read or watch the news in the same way." Voice Youth Advocates

Jones, Allan Frewin

Destiny's path; [by] Frewin Jones. HarperTeen 2009 329p $16.99

Grades: 8 9 10 11 12   **Fic**

1. War stories 2. Magic -- Fiction 3. Wales -- Fiction 4. Princesses -- Fiction 5. Fate and fatalism -- Fiction

ISBN 978-0-06-087146-8; 0-06-087146-6

LC 2009-14587

Sequel to: Warrior princess (2009)

When fifteen-year-old Princess Branwen tries to turn away from her destiny as the one who will save Wales from the Saxons, the Shining Ones send an owl in the form of a young girl called Blodwedd to guide her and Rhodri on the right path.

"Branwen's compelling story leaves readers waiting for the sequel." Booklist

Followed by: The emerald flame (2010)

Jones, Diana Wynne, 1934-2011

★ **Enchanted** glass. Greenwillow Books 2010 292p $16.99

Grades: 6 7 8 9   **Fic**

1. Magic -- Fiction 2. Orphans -- Fiction 3. Villages -- Fiction 4. Great Britain -- Fiction

ISBN 978-0-06-186684-5; 0-06-186684-9

LC 2009006195

After his grandfather dies, Andrew Hope inherits a house and surrounding land in an English village, but things become very complicated when young orphan Aidan shows up and suddenly a host of variously magical townsfolk and interlopers start intruding on their lives.

"Jones hits all the bases, combining fluid storytelling, sly humor, and exquisitely drawn characters." Booklist

House of many ways. Greenwillow Books 2008 404p $17.99; lib bdg $18.89; pa $8.99

Grades: 5 6 7 8   **Fic**

1. Fantasy fiction 2. Magic -- Fiction 3. Houses -- Fiction 4. Uncles -- Fiction

ISBN 978-0-06-147795-9; 0-06-147795-8; 978-0-06-147796-6 lib bdg; 0-06-147796-6 lib bdg; 978-0-06-147797-3 pa; 0-06-147797-4 pa

LC 2007036147

Sequel to: Howl's moving castle (1986)

When Charmain is asked to housesit for Great Uncle William, the Royal Wizard of Norland, she is ecstatic to get away from her parents, but finds that his house is much more than it seems.

This is "a buoyantly entertaining read. . . . [Jones'] comic pacing and wit are amply evident." Horn Book

★ **Howl's** moving castle. Greenwillow Books 1986 212p hardcover o.p. pa $6.99

Grades: 5 6 7 8   **Fic**

1. Fantasy fiction

ISBN 0-06-147878-4 pa; 0-688-06233-4; 978-0-06-147878-9 pa

LC 85-21981

Sophie "resigns herself to making a living as a hatter and helping her younger sisters prepare to make their fortunes. But adventure seeks her out in the shop where she sits alone dreaming over her hats. The wicked Witch of the Waste, angered by 'competition' in the area, turns her into an old woman, so she seeks refuge inside the strange moving castle of the wizard Howl. Howl, advertised by his apprentice as an eater of souls, lives a mad, frantic life trying to escape the curse the witch has placed on him, find the perfect girl of his dreams and end the contract he and his fire demon have entered. Sophie, against her best instincts and at first

unaware of her own powers, falls in love. . . . Grade six and up." (SLJ)

"Satisfyingly, Sophie meets a fate far exceeding her dreary expectations. This novel is an exciting, multi-faceted puzzle, peopled with vibrant, captivating characters. A generous sprinkling of humor adds potency to this skillful author's spell." Voice Youth Advocates

Followed by: House of many ways (2008)

Jones, Kimberly K.

Sand dollar summer. Margaret K. McElderry Books 2006 206p $15.95; pa $5.99

Grades: 5 6 7 8   **Fic**

1. Maine -- Fiction 2. Islands -- Fiction 3. Family life -- Fiction

ISBN 978-1-4169-0362-8; 1-4169-0362-3; 978-1-4169-5834-5 pa; 1-4169-5834-7 pa

LC 2005012740

When twelve-year-old Lise spends the summer on an island in Maine with her self-reliant mother and bright—but oddly mute—younger brother, her formerly safe world is complicated by an aged Indian neighbor, her mother's childhood friend, and a hurricane.

"The drama in [the] smart, tough, first-person narrative is understated; the spaces between the words are as eloquent as what is said. . . . The family story . . . is exquisitely told." Booklist

Jones, Patrick

★ **Bridge**; Patrick Jones. Darby Creek 2014 92 p. (The alternative) $7.95

Grades: 6 7 8 9 10 11 12   **Fic**

1. School stories 2. Family life -- Fiction 3. High schools -- Fiction 4. Illegal aliens -- Fiction 5. Hispanic Americans -- Fiction 6. Work -- Fiction 7. Schools -- Fiction 8. Spanish language -- Fiction

ISBN 1467744824; 9781467739030; 9781467744829

LC 2013041390

"José can't keep up. As the only English speaker in a family of undocumented immigrants, he handles everything from taking family members to the doctor to bargaining with the landlord. Plus he works two jobs. With all this responsibility, he's missing a lot of school. . . . José knows he has to turn things around if he wants to graduate from Rondo Alternative High School. Can he raise his grades enough to have a shot at college and a better life?" (Publisher's note)

"The author's effective use of flashbacks and crisp portraits of positive adult characters add further emotional depth to this emotional glimpse at the high-pressure difficulties facing children in immigrant families. References to O'Brien's book will likely spark the interest of readers in that title as well." PW Reviews

Jones, Rob Lloyd

Wild boy; Rob Lloyd Jones. Candlewick Press 2013 304 p. $16.99

Grades: 5 6 7 8   **Fic**

1. Mystery fiction 2. Steampunk fiction

ISBN 0763662526; 9780763662523

LC 2013931467

In this book, "Wild Boy's head-to-toe fur has garnered him scorn and abuse from commoners, but his extraordinary

intellectual gifts eventually win him a future with a powerful, elite group called the Gentlemen. . . . When Wild Boy is
about to be hanged by the unseemly circus crew for a murder
he did not commit, teen acrobat Clarissa helps him escape.
Together, they follow clues through sewers and back alleys,
learning about an extraordinary electrical device linked to
the murder." (Kirkus Reviews)

Wild boy and the black terror; Rob Lloyd Jones.
Candlewick Press 2015 336 p. illustrations, map
$16.99

Grades: 5 6 7 8   **Fic**
1. Serial killers -- Fiction 2. Circus performers --
Fiction 3. Great Britain -- History -- Victoria, 1837-
1901 -- Fiction 4. Children's stories 5. Murderers--
England--London 6. Detective and mystery stories
ISBN 0763662534; 9780763662530

LC 2014945722

This novel by Rob Lloyd Jones is set in "London, 1842.
Wild Boy, master detective and former freak-show performer, and Clarissa, circus acrobat and troublemaker, are the secret last hope of a city beset by horror. A poisoner stalks the
streets, leaving victims mad with terror--and then dead. Can
the Black Terror be traced to a demon called Malphas? Can
Wild Boy and Clarissa uncover a cure in time to save the
queen and the city?" (Publisher's note)

"Adventure, conspiracy and adrenaline intermingle with
dark deeds, devil worship and blood diamonds in this sequel to Wild Boy (2013). . . . The queen and the Gentlemen
need them to unearth the cause of a mysterious sickness that
blackens veins and sends victims into a stupor of madness
before tragic death. . . . Can the duo save all of London from
a hellbent killer? Diamonds are a Wild Boy's worst enemy in
this steampunk romp not intended for the faint—or black—
of heart." Kirkus

Jones, Traci L.
Finding my place. Farrar Straus Giroux 2010
181p $16.99

Grades: 6 7 8 9   **Fic**
1. School stories 2. Moving -- Fiction 3. Colorado --
Fiction 4. Friendship -- Fiction 5. Prejudices -- Fiction
6. Race relations -- Fiction 7. African Americans --
Fiction
ISBN 978-0-374-33573-1; 0-374-33573-7

LC 2008-54433

After moving to an affluent suburb of Denver in 1975,
ninth-grader Tiphanie feels lonely at her nearly all-white
high school until she befriends another "outsider" and discovers that prejudice exists in many forms.

"Tiphanie is refreshingly witty and open-minded. .
. . Jones handles the intricacies of race relations splendidly and excels in the frankness of her prose. . . . This
immediate, engaging novel will appeal to readers of all
backgrounds." Booklist

★ **Silhouetted** by the blue. Farrar, Straus & Giroux 2011 200p $16.99

Grades: 5 6 7 8   **Fic**
1. School stories 2. Theater -- Fiction 3. Bereavement
-- Fiction 4. African Americans -- Fiction 5. Depression

(Psychology) -- Fiction
ISBN 978-0-374-36914-9; 0-374-36914-3

LC 2010008419

After the death of her mother in an automobile accident,
seventh-grader Serena, who has gotten the lead in her middle
school play, is left to handle the day-to-day challenges of
caring for herself and her younger brother when their father
cannot pull himself out of his depression.

"Jones has written another winner with this beautiful,
haunting tale rich in story and characterization." Booklist

Standing against the wind; 1st ed.; Farrar, Straus
and Giroux 2006 184p $16

Grades: 6 7 8 9   **Fic**
1. School stories 2. African Americans -- Fiction 3.
City and town life -- Fiction
ISBN 978-0-374-37174-6; 0-374-37174-1

LC 2005-51226

As she tries to escape her poor Chicago neighborhood
by winning a scholarship to a prestigious boarding school,
shy and studious eighth-grader Patrice discovers that she has
more options in life than she previously realized.

"Handled without obscenity, the lively street talk will
draw readers to the gripping story of a contemporary kid
who works to make her dreams come true." Booklist

Jones, Ursula
The **islands** of Chaldea; by Diana Wynne Jones;
completed by Ursula Jones. Greenwillow Books,
an imprint of HarperCollinsPublishers 2013 368 p.
(trade ed.) $17.99

Grades: 4 5 6 7 8   **Fic**
1. Cats -- Fiction 2. Fantasy fiction 3. Aunts -- Fiction
4. Magic -- Fiction 5. Fantasy 6. Self-confidence --
Fiction 7. Voyages and travels -- Fiction
ISBN 0062295071; 9780062295071

LC 2013036422

In this book, by Diana Wynne Jones and Ursula Jones,
"Aileen comes from a long line of magic makers, and her
Aunt Beck is the most powerful magician on Skarr. But even
though she is old enough, Aileen's magic has yet to reveal
itself. When Aileen is sent over the sea on a mission for the
King, she worries that she'll be useless and in the way. A
powerful (but mostly invisible) cat changes all of that—and
with every obstacle Aileen faces, she becomes stronger and
more confident and her magic blooms." (Publisher's note)

"Diana Wynne Jones's humor, insight, and brisk, inventive style shine in this posthumously published novel. Aileen
is embarrassed when she fails her Wise Woman initiation.
She discovers her own "very vigorous" powers on a quest
with her Wise Aunt Beck, a prince, and his attendant through
the islands of Chaldea. Jones's imaginative vigor is unabated
in this last, picaresque novel." Horn Book

Jordan, Rosa
Lost Goat Lane. Peachtree Publisher 2004 197p
$14.95

Grades: 5 6 7 8   **Fic**
1. Goats -- Fiction 2. Florida -- Fiction 3. Race
relations -- Fiction 4. African Americans -- Fiction
ISBN 1-56145-325-0

LC 2004-5343

Two families—one white, one black—living near one another in rural Florida overcome their suspicions of each other and find ways to work together, with the help of their children and a few goats

"The fully realized characters and the warmth of the story make up for the small sermons. A tender, satisfying offering." SLJ

Other titles in this series are:

The goatnappers (2007)

The last wild place (2008)

Joseph, Lynn

The **color** of my words. HarperCollins Pubs. 2000 138p hardcover o.p. pa $5.99

Grades: 5 6 7 8   **Fic**

1. Siblings -- Fiction 2. Family life -- Fiction 3. Dominican Republic -- Fiction

ISBN 0-06-028232-0; 0-06-447204-3 pa

LC 00-22440

When life gets difficult for Ana Rosa, a twelve-year-old would-be writer living in a small village in the Dominican Republic, she can depend on her older brother to make her feel better—until the life-changing events on her thirteenth birthday

"A finely crafted novel, lovely and lyrical." SLJ

Flowers in the sky; by Lynn Joseph. HarperTeen 2013 240 p. (hardcover) $17.99

Grades: 8 9 10 11 12   **Fic**

1. Bildungsromans 2. New York (N.Y.) -- Fiction 3. Brothers and sisters -- Fiction 4. Love -- Fiction 5. Immigrants -- Fiction 6. Coming of age -- Fiction 7. Dominican Republic -- Fiction 8. Dominican Americans -- Fiction

ISBN 0060297948; 9780060297947

LC 2012038122

In this novel, by Lynn Joseph, "fifteen-year-old Nina Perez . . . must leave her . . . lush island home in Samana, Dominican Republic, when she's sent . . . to live with her brother, Darrio, in New York, to seek out a better life. . . . But then she meets . . . [a] tall, green-eyed boy . . . , who just might help her learn to see beauty in spite of tragedy." (Publisher's note)

Joyce, Graham, 1954-

The **exchange**. Viking 2008 241p $16.99

Grades: 7 8 9 10   **Fic**

1. Tattooing -- Fiction 2. Supernatural -- Fiction 3. Single parent family -- Fiction 4. Dating (Social customs) -- Fiction

ISBN 978-0-670-06207-2; 0-670-06207-3

LC 2007-32160

Cursed by the elderly recluse whose home she and a friend were creeping through late one night, fourteen-year-old Caz soon finds her life disintegrating and realizes she must find a way of lifting the curse—or at least understanding its power.

"Joyce has crafted a bizarre, magically realistic tale. . . . It's a wild ride with subtly moralistic undertones and a surprisingly happy ending that will stay with readers." Booklist

Juby, Susan

Another kind of cowboy. HarperTeen 2007 344p $16.99

Grades: 8 9 10 11 12   **Fic**

1. Horses -- Fiction 2. Friendship -- Fiction 3. Horsemanship -- Fiction 4. Homosexuality -- Fiction 5. British Columbia -- Fiction

ISBN 0-06-076517-8; 978-0-06-076517-0

LC 2006-36336

In Vancouver, British Columbia, two teenage dressage riders, one a spoiled rich girl and the other a closeted gay sixteen-year-old boy, come to terms with their identities and learn to accept themselves.

"Wry humor infuses this quiet story with a gentle warmth, and the secondary characters are well developed." Booklist

Getting the girl; a guide to private investigation, surveillance, and cookery. [by] S. Juby. HarperTeen 2008 341p $16.99; lib bdg $17.89; pa $8.99

Grades: 6 7 8 9 10   **Fic**

1. School stories 2. Mystery fiction 3. Popularity -- Fiction 4. British Columbia -- Fiction

ISBN 978-0-06-076525-5; 0-06-076525-9; 978-0-06-076527-9 lib bdg; 0-06-076527-5 lib bdg; 978-0-06-076528-6 pa; 0-06-076528-3 pa

LC 2008-00788

Ninth-grader Sherman Mack investigates the "Defilers," a secret group at his British Columbia high school that marks certain female students as pariahs, at first because he is trying to protect the girl he has a crush on, but later as a matter of principle.

Juby "applies her signature brand of humor to a detective novel. . . . [This offers a] strong and memorable female cast. . . . Here's hoping that Juby delivers on the promise of sequels." Horn Book

Jung, Mike

Geeks, girls, and secret identities; by Mike Jung; with illustrations by Mike Maihack. Arthur A. Levine Books 2012 307 p. (hardcover : alk. paper) $16.99

Grades: 3 4 5 6 7   **Fic**

1. Boys' clubs 2. Secrecy -- Fiction 3. Friendship -- Fiction 4. Science fiction 5. Clubs -- Fiction 6. Humorous stories 7. Robots -- Fiction 8. Schools -- Fiction 9. Superheroes -- Fiction 10. Middle schools -- Fiction

ISBN 0545335485; 9780545335485; 9780545335492; 9780545392518

LC 2011042548

In author Mike Jung's book, "Vincent Wu is Captain Stupendous's No. 1 Fan, but even he has to admit that Captain Stupendous has been a little off lately. During Professor Mayhem's latest attack, Captain Stupendous barely made it out alive, although he did manage to save Vincent from a giant monster robot. It's Vincent's dream come true . . . until he finds out Captain Stupendous's secret identity: It's Polly Winnicott-Lee, the girl Vincent happens to have a crush on." (Publisher's note)

Kade, J. V.

Bot Wars; by J.V. Kade. Dial Books for Young Readers 2013 368 p. (hardcover) $16.99

Grades: 5 6 7 8　　　　　　　　　　　**Fic**

1. Science fiction 2. Apocalyptic fiction 3. Father-son relationship -- Fiction 4. War -- Fiction 5. Robots -- Fiction 6. Fathers -- Fiction 7. Missing persons -- Fiction

ISBN 0803738609; 9780803738607

LC 2012017682

This book is set in the future, where the "Robot Wars [have] left the U.S. in shambles, divided between Bot Territory and the United Districts. Even though the wars ended months ago, 12-year-old Trout St. Kroix is still waiting for his soldier father to come home. When Trout makes one last desperate attempt to bring attention to his father's plight, he discovers the surprising truth about where his father is and what he's been up to." (Publishers Weekly)

Kade, Stacey

The **ghost** and the goth. Hyperion 2010 281p $16.99

Grades: 8 9 10 11 12　　　　　　　　　**Fic**

1. Ghost stories 2. School stories

ISBN 1-4231-2197-X; 978-1-4231-2197-8

LC 2010-8135

After being hit by a bus and killed, a high school homecoming queen gets stuck in the land of the living, with only a loser classmate—who happens to be able to see and hear ghosts—to help her.

"The tale is absorbing, and Kade successfully portrays a typical present-day high school. This novel will appeal to fans of romances and ghost stories alike." SLJ

Followed by: Queen of the dead (2011)

Queen of the dead. Hyperion 2011 266p $16.99

Grades: 8 9 10 11 12　　　　　　　　　**Fic**

1. Ghost stories 2. Family life -- Fiction 3. Secret societies -- Fiction

ISBN 978-1-4231-3467-1; 1-4231-3467-2

LC 2010029226

Sequel to: Ghost and the goth (2010)

Will gets involved with The Order, a group consisting of ghost-talkers like himself, as he continues to help spirits into the light, while Alona, his vain, self-centered, and cranky spirit guide begins to learn the value of helping others.

"This sequel to The Ghost and the Goth (2010) has exchanged some of the lighter humor for a more complex story line. Characters are more fully developed, and the momentum is stronger." Booklist

The **rules**; Stacey Kade. Hyperion 2013 416 p. $17.99

Grades: 7 8 9 10 11 12　　　　　　　　**Fic**

1. Science fiction 2. Schools -- Fiction 3. Identity -- Fiction 4. High schools -- Fiction 5. Genetic engineering -- Fiction 6. Fathers and daughters -- Fiction 7. Extraterrestrial beings -- Fiction 8. Interpersonal relations -- Fiction

ISBN 9781423153283

LC 2012033732

In this book, rescued "from a genetics lab by her adoptive father, Ariane Tucker has spent the last ten years hiding" that she's "a human-extraterrestrial hybrid, created by GenTex Labs as part of Project Paper Doll. She must follow 'the rules' set out by her father to avoid being detected by her classmates or GTX. Blend in, do not get noticed, trust no one, and never forget that they are searching for her." But Ariane breaks the rules when she catches the eye of Zane Bradshaw. (Voice of Youth Advocates)

Kadohata, Cynthia

Cracker! the best dog in Vietnam. Atheneum Books for Young Readers 2007 312p $16.99; pa $7.99

Grades: 5 6 7 8　　　　　　　　　　　**Fic**

1. Dogs -- Fiction 2. Vietnam War, 1961-1975 -- Fiction

ISBN 978-1-4169-0637-7; 1-4169-0637-1; 978-1-4169-0638-4 pa; 1-4169-0638-X pa

LC 2006-22022

The author "tells a stirring, realistic story of America's war in Vietnam, using the alternating viewpoints of an army dog named Cracker and her 17-year-old handler, Rick Hanski. . . . The heartfelt tale explores the close bond of the scout-dog team." Booklist

Half a world away; Cynthia Kadohata. Atheneum Books for Young Readers 2014 240 p. hbk $16.99

Grades: 5 6 7 8　　　　　　　　　　　**Fic**

1. Adoptees -- Fiction 2. Adoption -- Fiction 3. Love -- Fiction 4. Abandoned children -- Fiction 5. Emotional problems -- Fiction

ISBN 1442412755; 9781442412750

LC 2013031627

In this middle grade book by Cynthia Kadohata, "eleven-year-old Jaden is adopted, and he knows he's an 'epic fail.' That's why his family is traveling to Kazakhstan to adopt a new baby--to replace him, he's sure. . . . But when they get to Kazakhstan, it turns out the infant they've travelled for has already been adopted, and literally within minutes are faced with having to choose from six other babies." (Publisher's note)

"Twelve-year-old Jaden, adopted from Romania and suffering from attachment disorder, travels to Kazakhstan with his parents, who have decided to adopt a second child. As his parents struggle to bond with an emotionally unresponsive infant, Jaden bonds with disabled toddler Dimash--a breakthrough for Jaden. This story about a troubled adoptee and the equally troubling issues of international adoption is compelling and involving." Horn Book

★ **Kira** -Kira. Atheneum Bks. for Young Readers 2004 244p $15.95; pa $6.99

Grades: 5 6 7 8　　　　　　　　　　　**Fic**

1. Death -- Fiction 2. Georgia -- Fiction 3. Sisters -- Fiction 4. Japanese Americans -- Fiction

ISBN 0-689-85639-3; 0-689-85640-7 pa

Awarded the Newbery Medal, 2005

Chronicles the close friendship between two Japanese-American sisters growing up in rural Georgia during the late 1950s and early 1960s, and the despair when one sister becomes terminally ill.

"This beautifully written story tells of a girl struggling to find her own way in a family torn by illness and horrendous work conditions. . . . All of the characters are believable and well developed." SLJ

★ **A million** shades of gray. Atheneum Books for Young Readers 2010 216p $16.99
Grades: 5 6 7 8   **Fic**
1. Vietnam -- Fiction 2. Elephants -- Fiction 3. Wilderness survival -- Fiction
ISBN 1-4169-1883-3; 978-1-4169-1883-7
LC 2009-33307
In 1975 after American troops pull out of Vietnam, a thirteen-year-old boy and his beloved elephant escape into the jungle when the Viet Cong attack his village. "Grades five to eight." (Bull Cent Child Books)
"Kadohata delves deep into the soul of her protagonist while making a faraway place and stark consequences of war seem very near." Publ Wkly

★ **Outside** beauty. Atheneum Books for Young Readers 2008 265p $16.99; pa $8.99
Grades: 5 6 7 8   **Fic**
1. Sisters -- Fiction 2. Japanese Americans -- Fiction 3. Father-daughter relationship -- Fiction 4. Mother-daughter relationship -- Fiction
ISBN 978-0-689-86575-6; 0-689-86575-9; 978-1-4169-9818-1 pa; 1-4169-9818-7 pa
LC 2007-39711
Thirteen-year-old Shelby and her three sisters must go to live with their respective fathers while their mother, who has trained them to rely on their looks, recovers from a car accident that scarred her face
Kadohata's "gifts for creating and containing drama and for careful definition of character prove as powerful as ever in this wise, tender and compelling novel." Publ Wkly

★ The **thing** about luck; Cynthia Kadohata; illustrated by Julia Kuo. 1st ed. Atheneum Books for Young Readers 2013 288 p. (hardcover) $16.99
Grades: 5 6 7 8   **Fic**
1. Luck -- Fiction 2. Japanese Americans -- Fiction 3. Brothers and sisters -- Fiction 4. Kansas -- Fiction 5. Grandparents -- Fiction 6. Farm life -- Kansas -- Fiction
ISBN 1416918825; 9781416918820; 9781442474673
LC 2012021287
National Book Award Finalist (2013)
Parents' Choice: Silver Medal Fiction (2013)
Asian/Pacific American Awards for Literature: Children's Literature Winner (2014)
In this novel, by Newbery Medalist Cynthia Kadohata, "Summer knows that kouun means 'good luck' in Japanese, and this year her family has none of it. Just when she thinks nothing else can possibly go wrong, an emergency whisks her parents away to Japan--right before harvest season. Summer and her little brother, Jaz, are left in the care of their grandparents, who come out of retirement in order to harvest wheat and help pay the bills." (Publisher's note)
"Kadohata expertly captures the uncertainties of the tween years as Summer navigates the balance of childlike concerns with the onset of increasingly grown-up responsibilities." (SLJ)

Weedflower. Atheneum Books for Young Readers 2006 260p $16.95; pa $5.99
Grades: 5 6 7 8   **Fic**
1. Arizona -- Fiction 2. World War, 1939-1945 -- Fiction 3. Japanese Americans -- Evacuation and relocation, 1942-1945 -- Fiction
ISBN 0-689-86574-0; 1-4169-7566-7 pa
LC 2004-24912
After twelve-year-old Sumiko and her Japanese-American family are relocated from their flower farm in southern California to an internment camp on a Mojave Indian reservation in Arizona, she helps her family and neighbors, becomes friends with a local Indian boy, and tries to hold on to her dream of owning a flower shop.
Sumiko "is a sympathetic heroine, surrounded by well-crafted, fascinating people. The concise yet lyrical prose conveys her story in a compelling narrative." SLJ

Kagawa, Julie
The **Eternity** Cure; Julie Kagawa. Harlequin Books 2013 448 p. (hardcover) $16.99
Grades: 7 8 9 10 11 12   **Fic**
1. Science fiction 2. Vampires -- Fiction 3. Epidemics -- Fiction
ISBN 0373210698; 9780373210695
This vampire novel, by Julie Kagawa, is part of the "Blood of Eden" series. "Allie will follow the call of blood to save her creator, Kanin, from the psychotic vampire Sarren. But when the trail leads to Allie's birthplace in New Covington, what Allie finds there will change the world forever. . . . There's a new plague on the rise, a strain of the Red Lung virus that wiped out most of humanity generations ago--and this strain is deadly to humans and vampires alike." (Publisher's note)

★ The **immortal** rules; a legend begins. Julie Kagawa. Harlequin Teen 2012 504 p. (Blood of Eden) (hardcover) $18.99
Grades: 7 8 9 10 11 12   **Fic**
1. Love stories 2. Diseases -- Fiction 3. Vampires -- Fiction
ISBN 0373210515; 9780373210510
LC 2011279454
In this book, "[r]abids, vicious hybrid creatures born of the plague, prowl the land beyond the walled vampire cities. . . . When Allie is savagely attacked by a rabid, . . . a mysterious vampire offers her the choice of a human death or 'life' as a vampire. . . . Allie's determination to remain more human than monster is put to the test, particularly when she joins a band of humans on a desperate journey to safety on the island of Eden. Particularly when she falls in love." (Kirkus)
"Kagawa wraps excellent writing and skillful plotting around a well-developed concept and engaging characters, resulting in a fresh and imaginative thrill-ride that deserves a wide audience." Pub Wkly

Talon; by Julie Kagawa. Harlequin Books Teen 2014 464 p. $17.99
Grades: 8 9 10 11   **Fic**
1. Fantasy fiction 2. Dragons -- Fiction 3. Brothers and

sisters -- Fiction 4. Shapeshifting
ISBN 0373211392; 9780373211395

In this book, by Julie Kagawa, "dragons were hunted to near extinction by the Order of St. George, a legendary society of dragon slayers. Hiding in human form and growing their numbers in secret, the dragons of Talon have become strong and cunning. . . . Ember and Dante Hill are the only sister and brother known to dragonkind. Trained to infiltrate society, Ember wants to live the teen experience and enjoy a summer of freedom before taking her destined place in Talon." (Publisher's note)

"Young love, sibling rivalry, rogue dragons, and plots for world domination create an intriguing mix in this new series." Horn Book

Kang, Hildi

Chengli and the Silk Road caravan. Tanglewood 2011 178p $14.95

Grades: 5 6 7 8   **Fic**

1. China -- Fiction 2. Fathers -- Fiction 3. Princesses -- Fiction 4. Trade routes -- Fiction
ISBN 978-1-933718-54-5; 1-933718-54-4

LC 2010047359

Called to follow the wind and search for information about his father who disappeared many years ago, thirteen-year-old Chengli, carrying a piece of jade with strange writing that had belonged to his father, joins a caravan charged with giving safe passage to the Emperor's daughter as it navigates the constant dangers of the Silk Road in 630 A.D.

"This fast-paced adventure is filled with friendship, historical detail, changing scenery, and action. It will appeal to a wide range of readers." SLJ

Kantor, Melissa

The **breakup** bible; a novel. Hyperion Books for Children 2007 272p $15.99

Grades: 8 9 10 11 12   **Fic**

1. Dating (Social customs) -- Fiction
ISBN 978-0-7868-0962-2

Jennifer thinks she and Max are the perfect couple, until he decides he just wants to be friends.

"Written with wit and featuring a few fine plot twists, this will have teen girls nodding sympathetically." Booklist

Girlfriend material. Disney/Hyperion Books 2009 251p $15.99

Grades: 7 8 9 10   **Fic**

1. Summer -- Fiction 2. Cape Cod (Mass.) -- Fiction
ISBN 978-1-4231-0849-8; 1-4231-0849-3

Kate has never had a boyfriend. But while crashing at her mother's wealthy friends' home at Cape Cod for the summer, Kate meets Adam. But when her breezy summer romance with Adam becomes more complicated, Kate asks herself if she is girlfriend material.

"The changes in Kate are both gradual and realistic. . . . Her emotional journey and acute self-consciousness are likely to strike a chord." Publ Wkly

Karim, Sheba

Skunk girl. Farrar, Straus & Giroux 2009 231p $16.95

Grades: 8 9 10 11 12   **Fic**

1. School stories 2. Muslims -- Fiction 3. Family life -- Fiction 4. New York (State) -- Fiction 5. Pakistani Americans -- Fiction 6. Dating (Social customs) -- Fiction
ISBN 978-0-374-37011-4; 0-374-37011-7

LC 2008-7482

Nina Khan is not just the only Asian or Muslim student in her small-town high school in upstate New York, she is also faces the legacy of her "Supernerd" older sister, body hair, and the pain of having a crush when her parents forbid her to date.

This novel is "rife with smart, self-deprecating humor." Kirkus

Karr, Kathleen

Fortune's fool. Alfred A. Knopf 2008 201p $15.99; lib bdg $18.99; pa $6.50

Grades: 5 6 7 8   **Fic**

1. Middle Ages -- Fiction 2. Fools and jesters -- Fiction 3. Germany -- History -- 0-1517 -- Fiction
ISBN 978-0-375-84816-2; 0-375-84816-9; 978-0-375-94816-9 lib bdg; 0-375-84816-3 lib bdg; 978-0-375-84307-5 pa; 0-375-84307-8 pa

LC 2007-49034

In medieval Germany, fifteen-year-old Conrad, a court jester, and his beloved Christa, a servant girl, escape from a cruel master and journey through the countryside on a quest to find a kind lord who will give them sanctuary.

"Karr does an splendid job of recreating the medieval milieu, especially the life of a professional entertainer with all of its challenges and hardships." Booklist

Katcher, Brian

Playing with matches. Delacorte Press 2008 294p $15.99; lib bdg $18.99

Grades: 8 9 10 11 12   **Fic**

1. School stories 2. Missouri -- Fiction 3. Burns and scalds -- Fiction 4. Dating (Social customs) -- Fiction
ISBN 978-0-385-73544-5; 0-385-73544-8; 978-0-385-90525-1 lib bdg; 0-385-90525-4 lib bdg

LC 2007-27654

While trying to find a girl who will date him, Missouri high school junior Leon Sanders befriends a lonely, disfigured female classmate.

"This is a strong debut novel with a cast of quirky, multidimensional characters struggling with issues of acceptance, sexuality, identity, and self-worth." SLJ

Keating, Jess

How to outrun a crocodile when your shoes are untied; by Jess Keating. Sourcebooks Jabberwocky 2014 288 p. (My Life Is A Zoo) (trade pbk) $7.99

Grades: 5 6 7 8   **Fic**

1. Zoos -- Fiction 2. Middle schools -- Fiction 3. Twins -- Fiction 4. Popularity -- Fiction 5. Family life -- Fiction
ISBN 1572339470; 9781402297557

LC 2014006806

In this middle grades book by Jess Keating, "Ana Wright's social life is now officially on the endangered list: she lives in a zoo (umm, elephant droppings!?), her best friend lives on the other side of the world, and the Sneerers are making junior high miserable. All Ana wants is to fade into the background." (Publisher's note)

"Humor, poignancy and fascinating zoological facts infuse the narrative with a warm conversational tone that welcomes readers into the drama that is middle school." Kirkus

Kehoe, Stasia Ward

The **sound** of letting go; by Stasia Ward Kehoe. Viking, published by Penguin Group 2014 400 p. (hardcover) $17.99

Grades: 7 8 9 10 11 12   **Fic**

1. Autism -- Fiction 2. Family life -- Fiction 3. High school students -- Fiction 4. Alienation (Social psychology) -- Fiction 5. Jazz -- Fiction 6. Novels in verse 7. Schools -- Fiction 8. Trumpet -- Fiction 9. High schools -- Fiction 10. Family problems -- Fiction
ISBN 0670015539; 9780670015535

LC 2013013098

In this book, by Stasia Ward Kehoe, "for sixteen years, Daisy has been good. A good daughter, helping out with her autistic younger brother uncomplainingly. A good friend, even when her best friend makes her feel like a third wheel. When her parents announce they're sending her brother to an institution--without consulting her--Daisy's furious, and decides the best way to be a good sister is to start being bad. She quits jazz band and orchestra, slacks in school, and falls for bad-boy Dave." (Publisher's note)

"Kehoe's second novel-in-verse, after 2011's Audition, movingly evokes the conflicting emotions of 17-year-old Daisy Meehan as her family teeters on the edge of falling apart due to her younger brother Steven's violent episodes. . . . This painfully honest portrait of a family in crisis raises questions about love, responsibility, and self-sacrifice as it moves gracefully to a difficult but realistic resolution." Pub Wkly

Kehret, Peg

Abduction! Dutton Children's Books 2004 215p $16.99; pa $6.99

Grades: 5 6 7 8   **Fic**

1. Kidnapping -- Fiction
ISBN 0-525-47294-0; 0-14-240617-1 pa

LC 2003-63531

Thirteen-year-old Bonnie has a feeling of foreboding on the very day that her six-year-old brother Matt and their dog Pookie are abducted, and she becomes involved in a major search effort as well as a frightening adventure

"This novel has enough suspense to keep children interested, and it will also appeal to reluctant readers." SLJ

The **ghost's** grave. Dutton Children's Books 2005 210p $16.99; pa $5.99

Grades: 5 6 7 8   **Fic**

1. Ghost stories 2. Coal miners -- Fiction 3. Washington (State) -- Fiction
ISBN 0-525-46162-0; 0-14-240819-0 pa

LC 2004022064

Apprehensive about spending the summer in Washington State with his Aunt Ethel when his parents get an overseas job, twelve-year-old Josh soon finds adventure when he meets the ghost of a coal miner.

"This fast-paced and engaging book should be a hit with fans of ghost stories. Josh is a rich character to whom readers can relate." SLJ

Keith, Harold

★ **Rifles** for Watie. Crowell 1957 332p $16.89; pa $5.99

Grades: 6 7 8 9   **Fic**

1. Generals 2. Indian leaders 3. United States -- History -- 1861-1865, Civil War -- Fiction
ISBN 0-690-04907-2; 0-06-447030-X pa
Awarded the Newbery Medal, 1958

"An exceptionally well-written story of the Civil War as it was fought in the western states." Bull Cent Child Books

Keller, Julia

★ **Back** home. Egmont USA 2009 194p $15.99; lib bdg $18.99

Grades: 6 7 8 9   **Fic**

1. Fathers -- Fiction 2. Soldiers -- Fiction 3. Family life -- Fiction 4. Iraq War, 2003- -- Fiction 5. Brain -- Wounds and injuries -- Fiction
ISBN 978-1-60684-005-4; 1-60684-005-3; 978-1-60684-048-1 lib bdg; 1-60684-048-7 lib bdg

LC 2009-15877

Thirteen-year-old Rachel Browning understands that her father will be different after being injured in the Iraq War, but no one is prepared for the impact that his traumatic brain injury and other wounds have on the entire family

"No one who reads this heartbreaking book will ever forget it. With integrity, authenticity, and immediacy, Keller has captured the extraordinary complexity and challenge of unexpected change and, to her everlasting credit, unsparingly shares the whole truth of it with her readers." Booklist

Kelley, Jane

The **girl** behind the glass; [by] Jane Kelley. Random House 2011 183p $16.99; lib bdg $19.99; e-book $16.99

Grades: 4 5 6 7   **Fic**

1. Ghost stories 2. Twins -- Fiction 3. Moving -- Fiction 4. Sisters -- Fiction 5. Family life -- Fiction
ISBN 978-0-375-86220-5; 0-375-86220-X; 978-0-375-96220-2 lib bdg; 0-375-96220-4 lib bdg; 978-0-375-88996-7 e-book

LC 2010-43568

Moving from Brooklyn to a rental house in the country strains the relationship between eleven-year-old identical twins Hannah and Anna Zimmer, a situation made worse by the ghost of a girl who is trapped in the house because of problems with her own sister eighty years before.

"Both chilling and lyrical. . . . The tensions within the Zimmer family are especially well-observed, and Kelley . . . conveys an impressive amount of emotion with few words. The ethereal tone and steady parceling out of warning, clues, and bits of information . . . . maintain the novel's intrigue and will keep readers invested in the unfolding mystery." Publ Wkly

Kelly, Erin Entrada

Blackbird fly; by Erin Entrada Kelly. Greenwillow Books, an imprint of HarperCollinsPublishers 2015 304 p. (hardback) $16.99

Grades: 4 5 6 7 8 **Fic**
1. School stories 2. Music -- Fiction 3. Bullies -- Fiction 4. Guitar -- Fiction 5. Middle schools -- Fiction 6. Filipino Americans -- Fiction
ISBN 0062238612; 9780062238610
LC 2014029444

In this novel by Erin Entrada Kelly, "Apple has always felt a little different from her classmates. . . . It becomes unbearable in middle school, when the boys . . . in Apple's class put her name on the Dog Log, the list of the most unpopular girls in school. When Apple's friends turn on her and everything about her life starts to seem weird and embarrassing, Apple turns to music." (Publisher's note)

"Debut author Kelly skillfully weaves together the story of misfit Apple, her love of music, and a budding romance with a new boy at school, while never losing focus on the central issue of what it is like to be the 'other. . .'" Booklist

Kelly, Jacqueline

★ The **evolution** of Calpurnia Tate. Henry Holt and Co. 2009 340p $16.99

Grades: 4 5 6 7 **Fic**
1. Texas -- Fiction 2. Nature -- Fiction 3. Family life -- Fiction 4. Naturalists -- Fiction 5. Grandfathers -- Fiction
ISBN 0-8050-8841-5; 978-0-8050-8841-0
LC 2008-40595

A Newbery Medal honor book (2010)

In central Texas in 1899, eleven-year-old Callie Vee Tate is instructed to be a lady by her mother, learns about love from the older three of her six brothers, and studies the natural world with her grandfather. "Grades five to eight." (Bull Cent Child Books)

"Callie is a charming, inquisitive protagonist; a joyous, bright, and thoughtful creation. . . . Several scenes . . . mix gentle humor and pathos to great effect." SLJ

Kelly, Lynne

Chained; Lynne Kelly. Farrar Straus Giroux 2012 248 p. (hardcover) $16.99

Grades: 4 5 6 **Fic**
1. Debt 2. Circus performers -- Fiction 3. Human-animal relationship -- Fiction 4. India -- Fiction 5. Circus -- Fiction 6. Elephants -- Fiction 7. Child labor -- Fiction 8. Conduct of life -- Fiction 9. Animals -- Treatment -- Fiction
ISBN 0374312370; 9780374312374; 9780374312503
LC 2011031767

In author Lynne Kelly's book, "after ten-year-old Hastin's family borrows money to pay for his sister's hospital bill, he leaves his village in northern India to take a job as an elephant keeper and work off the debt. . . . The crowds that come to the circus see a lively animal . . . but Hastin sees Nandita, a sweet elephant and his best friend, who is chained when she's not performing and hurt with a hook until she learns tricks perfectly. Hastin protects Nandita as best as he can, knowing that the only way they will both survive is if he can find a way for them to escape." (Publisher's note)

Kelsey, Marybeth

A **recipe** 4 robbery. Greenwillow Books 2009 282p $16.99; lib bdg $17.89

Grades: 4 5 6 **Fic**
1. Mystery fiction
ISBN 978-0-06-128843-2; 0-06-128843-8; 978-0-06-128845-6 lib bdg; 0-06-128845-4 lib bdg
LC 2008-29145

An unsupervised goose, missing family heirlooms, and some suspicious characters turn the annual cucumber festival into a robbery investigation for three sixth-grade friends.

"The novel is full of likable characters and fun twists and turns. The plot moves quickly, and Kelsey writes with wit and verve." SLJ

Kenneally, Miranda

Racing Savannah; Miranda Kenneally. Sourcebooks Fire 2013 304 p. (tp : alk. paper) $9.99

Grades: 8 9 10 11 12 **Fic**
1. Horsemanship -- Fiction 2. Love -- Fiction 3. Horses -- Fiction 4. Tennessee -- Fiction
ISBN 1402284764; 9781402284762
LC 2013023322

In this book, by Miranda Kenneally, "Savannah has always been much more comfortable around horses than boys. Especially boys like Jack Goodwin. . . . She knows the rules: no mixing between the staff and the Goodwin family. But Jack has no such boundaries. With her dream of becoming a jockey, Savannah isn't exactly one to follow the rules either." (Publisher's note)

"Kenneally (Stealing Parker, 2012) again looks at sports through a female lens, this time tackling male-dominated horse racing, in this fourth Hundred Oaks novel. Savannah, her widowed horse-trainer father, and her father's pregnant girlfriend move to Tennessee's Cedar Hill, a farm that trains horses for races including the Kentucky Derby...The author's knack for weaving forbidden romance, breezy dialogue, and details of this lesser-known sports venue places it in the winner's circle for reluctant readers and chick-lit fans." (Booklist)

Kennedy, James

The **Order** of Odd-Fish; [by] James Kennedy. Delacorte Press 2008 403p $15.99; lib bdg $18.99

Grades: 6 7 8 9 **Fic**
1. Adventure fiction 2. Aunts -- Fiction
ISBN 978-0-385-73543-8; 0-385-73543-X; 978-0-385-90524-4 lib bdg; 0-385-90524-6 lib bdg
LC 2008-00711

Thirteen-year-old Jo suddenly finds her humdrum life turned upside down when Colonel Anatoly Kordakov shows up at her aunt's party and announces he has come to protect her.

"This clever, creative story will keep readers engaged and laughing." Libr Media Connect

Kent, Rose

Kimchi & calamari. HarperCollinsPublishers 2007 220p $15.99; lib bdg $16.89

Grades: 4 5 6 7 **Fic**
1. Adoption -- Fiction 2. Korean Americans -- Fiction

3. Italian Americans -- Fiction
ISBN 978-0-06-083769-3; 0-06-083769-1; 978-0-06-083770-9 lib bdg; 0-06-083770-5 lib bdg

LC 2006-20041

"Fourteen-year-old Korean adoptee Joseph Calderaro is stumped when his social studies teacher assigns an ancestry essay. . . . Kent's debut novel humorously captures the feelings of a young teen who thoroughly enjoys his Italian-American family but still wonders about his birth parents." Booklist

Kent, Trilby

★ **Medina** Hill. Tundra Books 2009 172p $19.95

Grades: 6 7 8 9   Fic

1. Great Britain -- Fiction
ISBN 978-0-88776-888-0; 0-88776-888-1

This is a "highly original debut." Booklist

Stones for my father. Tundra Books 2011 170p $19.95

Grades: 6 7 8 9   Fic

1. Afrikaners -- Fiction 2. South Africa -- Fiction 3. South African War, 1899-1902 -- Fiction
ISBN 978-1-77049-252-3; 1-77049-252-6

"This meticulously researched novel about a white Afrikaner girl caught up in the Boer War at the turn of the 19th century brings to light a hitherto overlooked aspect of South African history. Corlie Roux is living with her harsh mother and younger brothers on an isolated farm in what was the South African Republic (now Mpumalanga). As the war reaches their farm, they flee, but are captured and interned in a concentration camp. . . . Kent tackles the challenge of depicting the complex relationships between Afrikaner colonists and English imperialists, and also the relationships of both these groups to the indigenous Africans." SLJ

Kephart, Beth

Dangerous neighbors; a novel. Egmont USA 2010 176p $16.99; lib bdg $19.99

Grades: 7 8 9 10   Fic

1. Death -- Fiction 2. Guilt -- Fiction 3. Twins -- Fiction 4. Sisters -- Fiction 5. Bereavement -- Fiction 6. Philadelphia (Pa.) -- Fiction 7. Centennial Exhibition (1876: Philadelphia, Pa.) -- Fiction
ISBN 978-1-60684-080-1; 1-60684-080-0; 978-1-60684-106-8 lib bdg; 1-60684-106-8 lib bdg

LC 2010-11249

Set against the backdrop of the 1876 Centennial Exhibition in Philadelphia, Katherine cannot forgive herself when her beloved twin sister dies, and she feels that her only course of action is to follow suit.

"Exceptionally graceful prose . . . and flashbacks are so realistically drawn and deftly integrated that readers will be as startled as Katherine to find themselves yanked out of morose memories and surrounded by noisy fairgoers." Bull Cent Child Books

Dr. Radway's Sarsaparilla Resolvent; by Beth Kephart; illustrated by William Sulit. Temple Univ Pr 2013 198 p. ill. (paperback) $15.95

Grades: 6 7 8 9   Fic

1. Grief -- Fiction 2. Police brutality -- Fiction
ISBN 0984042962; 9780984042968

This book by Beth Kephart follows 14-year-old protagonist William Quinn. "With his father in the Cherry Hill prison and his genially wayward older brother, Francis, recently beaten to death by a brutal policeman, his mother has ground herself into unbearable, paralyzing grief, and the boy has to find a way to save them both. . . . Gradually, William finds a way to make right some terrible wrongs." (Kirkus Reviews)

★ **Going** over; Beth Kephart. Chronicle Books 2014 262 p. map (alk. paper) $17.99

Grades: 8 9 10 11 12   Fic

1. Love -- Fiction 2. Family life -- Fiction 3. Berlin (Germany) -- Fiction 4. Berlin Wall (1961-1989) -- Fiction 5. Family life -- Germany -- Fiction 6. Germany -- History -- 1945-1990 -- Fiction 7. Berlin Wall, Berlin, Germany, 1961-1989 -- Fiction 8. Berlin (Germany) -- History -- 1945-1989 -- Fiction
ISBN 1452124574; 9781452124575

LC 2012046894

In this book, by Beth Kephart, "Ada lives among the rebels, punkers, and immigrants of Kreuzberg in West Berlin. Stefan lives in East Berlin, in a faceless apartment bunker of Friedrichshain. Bound by love and separated by circumstance, their only chance for a life together lies in a high-risk escape. But will Stefan find the courage to leap? Or will forces beyond his control stand in his way?" (Publisher's note)

"In a present-tense narration alternating between Ada's first-person and Stefan's second-person, the young lovers on opposite sides of the Berlin Wall in 1983 plan for Stefan's escape to the West. Kephart works romantic chemistry into a danger-packed plot with moving results in this captivating glimpse into an underrepresented era that will appeal to older readers with a taste for literary historical fiction." Horn Book

★ The **heart** is not a size. HarperTeen 2010 244p $16.99

Grades: 7 8 9 10   Fic

1. Mexico -- Fiction 2. Poverty -- Fiction 3. Friendship -- Fiction 4. Volunteer work -- Fiction
ISBN 978-0-06-147048-6; 0-06-147048-1

LC 2008-55721

Fifteen-year-old Georgia learns a great deal about herself and her troubled best friend Riley when they become part of a group of suburban Pennsylvania teenagers that go to Anapra, a squatters village in the border town of Juarez, Mexico, to undertake a community construction project.

"Kephart's prose is typically poetic. She pens a faster-paced novel that explores teens' inner selves. . . . The writing is vivid, enabling readers to visualize Anapra's desolation and hope." Voice Youth Advocates

★ **House** of Dance. HarperTeen 2008 263p $16.99; lib bdg $17.89; pa $10.99

Grades: 7 8 9 10   Fic

1. Death -- Fiction 2. Cancer -- Fiction 3. Dancers -- Fiction 4. Grandfathers -- Fiction 5. Mother-daughter

relationship -- Fiction
ISBN 978-0-06-142928-6; 0-06-142928-7; 978-0-06-142929-3 lib bdg; 0-06-142929-5 lib bdg; 978-0-06-142930-9 pa; 0-06-142930-9 pa

LC 2007-26011

During one of her daily visits across town to visit her dying grandfather, fifteen-year-old Rosie discovers a dance studio that helps her find a way to bring her family members together.

This is "distinguished more by its sharp, eloquent prose than by its plot. . . . Poetically expressed memories and moving dialogue both anchor and amplify the characters' emotions." Publ Wkly

Nothing but ghosts. HarperTeen 2009 278p $17.95

Grades: 8 9 10 11 12 **Fic**
1. Art -- Fiction 2. Mothers -- Fiction 3. Gardening -- Fiction 4. Bereavement -- Fiction 5. Loss (Psychology) -- Fiction
ISBN 978-0-06-166796-1; 0-06-166796-X

LC 2008-26024

After her mother's death, sixteen-year-old Katie copes with her grief by working in the garden of an old estate, where she becomes intrigued by the story of a reclusive millionaire, while her father, an art restorer, manages in his own way to come to terms with the death of his wife.

"Kephart's evocative writing and gentle resolution offer healing and hope as her characters come to terms with their losses." Publ Wkly

★ **Undercover**. HarperTeen 2007 278p $16.99; lib bdg $17.89; pa $8.99

Grades: 8 9 10 11 12 **Fic**
1. School stories 2. Poetry -- Fiction 3. Family life -- Fiction
ISBN 978-0-06-123893-2; 0-06-123893-7; 978-0-06-123894-9 lib bdg; 0-06-123894-5 lib bdg; 978-0-06-123895-6 pa; 0-06-123895-3 pa

LC 2007-2981

High school sophomore Elisa is used to observing while going unnoticed except when classmates ask her to write love notes for them, but a teacher's recognition of her talent, a "client's" desire for her friendship, a love of ice skating, and her parent's marital problems draw her out of herself.

"Kephart tells a moving story. . . . Readers will fall easily into the compelling premise and Elisa's memorable, graceful voice." Booklist

You are my only; a novel. Egmont USA 2011 240p $16.99

Grades: 7 8 9 10 **Fic**
1. Kidnapping -- Fiction 2. Home schooling -- Fiction 3. Mother-daughter relationship -- Fiction
ISBN 978-1-60684-272-0; 1-60684-272-2

LC 2010052662

Tells, in their separate voices and at a space of fourteen years, of Emmy, whose baby has been stolen, and Sophie, a teenager who defies her nomadic, controlling mother by making friends with a neighbor boy and his elderly aunts.

This is a "a psychologically taut novel. . . . Succinct, emotionally packed chapters capture similarities between

mother and daughter, the depth of their despair, their common desire to be free, and their poetic vision of the world." Publ Wkly

Kerley, Barbara

Greetings from planet Earth. Scholastic Press 2007 246p $16.99

Grades: 5 6 7 8 **Fic**
1. Family life -- Fiction 2. Vietnam War, 1961-1975 -- Fiction 3. Father-son relationship -- Fiction
ISBN 0-439-80203-2; 978-0-439-80203-1

LC 2006-11300

In 1977, as twelve-year-old Theo struggles with a science class project on space exploration, questions emerge about why his father never returned from Vietnam and why Theo's mother has been keeping secrets for many years.

"The novel convincingly portrays a family overshadowed by secrets." Booklist

Kerr, M. E.

Gentlehands. Harper & Row 1978 183p hardcover o.p. pa $5.99

Grades: 7 8 9 10 **Fic**
1. Criminals -- Fiction 2. Grandfathers -- Fiction 3. Social classes -- Fiction
ISBN 978-0-06-447067-4 pa; 0-06-447067-9 pa

LC 77-11860

ALA YALSA Margaret A. Edwards Award (1993)

"Buddy Boyle falls for Skye and her affluent, breezy way of life. Finding his own parents not 'cultured' enough for this new relationship, Buddy turns to his grandfather, whose love of opera and other refinements make him more suitable to make Skye's acquaintance. A shocking surprise awaits Buddy when Mr. DeLucca, pursuer of an infamous Nazi, finally identifies his quarry." Shapiro. Fic for youth. 3rd edition

If I love you, am I trapped forever? Marshall Cavendish 2008 178p $16.99

Grades: 8 9 10 11 12 **Fic**
1. School stories 2. Newspapers -- Fiction 3. New York (N.Y.) -- Fiction 4. Dating (Social customs) -- Fiction 5. Father-son relationship -- Fiction
ISBN 978-0-7614-5545-5

LC 2007051768

A reissue of the title first published 1973 by Harper & Row

Alan, a popular senior high school student, faces painful changes after a new student, Duncan "Doomed" Stein, comes to town and starts an influential underground newspaper.

"Extremely humorous at times, the story is also occasionally touched with sadness and poignancy." Horn Book Guide

Kerz, Anna

Better than weird. Orca Book Publishers 2011 218p pa $9.95

Grades: 4 5 6 7 **Fic**
1. School stories 2. Autism -- Fiction 3. Bullies -- Fiction 4. Father-son relationship -- Fiction
ISBN 978-1-55469-362-7 pa; 1-55469-362-4 pa

When Aaron's long-absent father returns, Aaron must cope with bullying at school, his grandmother's illness and his father's pregnant new wife.

"Yet another in a long line of recent books about kids with autism, Kerz's effort nevertheless shines. . . . A heart-warming read for fans of realistic fiction." Booklist

The **gnome's** eye. Orca Book Publishers 2010 210p pa $12.95

Grades: 4 5 6 7   **Fic**

1. Fear -- Fiction 2. Canada -- Fiction 3. Immigrants -- Fiction

ISBN 978-1-55469-195-1 pa; 1-55469-195-8 pa

When Theresa and her family immigrate to Canada after World War II, she confronts her many fears with the help of a talisman given to her by a friend in Austria.

"Both laughter and genuine concern will be evident through Theresa's imaginative storytelling and descriptive narrative." SLJ

Kessler, Jackie Morse

Breath; Jackie Morse Kessler. Graphia 2013 336 p. (paperback) $8.99

Grades: 8 9 10 11 12   **Fic**

1. Death -- Fiction 2. Depression (Psychology) -- Fiction 3. Four Horsemen of the Apocalypse -- Fiction

ISBN 0547970439; 9780547970431

LC 2012023509

In this book by Jackie Morse Kessler, "the fourth and final title in the 'Riders of the Apocalypse' series, Death is suicidal. Because his soul mate did not follow him into the world of sadness and dying, the Grim Reaper has decided to end it all, a decision that will mean the end of humanity. Fortunately, he doesn't consider the fact that high-school senior Xander Atwood, although similarly depressed, might worm his way into Death's heart and provide insight that could change his mind." (Booklist)

"Kessler once again highlights a common teen affliction, this time depression, in her allegory of hopelessness turned to hope. . . . The series is a strong and unique attempt to encourage troubled teens to consider their options and accept the help they need, while exposing all readers to the pain their friends may be experiencing." Booklist

Loss; Jackie Morse Kessler. Graphia 2012 258 p. pa $8.99

Grades: 8 9 10 11 12   **Fic**

1. Fantasy fiction 2. Plague -- Fiction 3. Bullies -- Fiction 4. Apocalyptic fiction 5. Schools -- Fiction 6. Diseases -- Fiction 7. Self-esteem -- Fiction 8. Time travel -- Fiction 9. High schools -- Fiction 10. Four Horsemen of the Apocalypse -- Fiction

ISBN 0547712154; 9780547712154

LC 2011031490

This young adult novel is part of Jackie Morse Kessler's Riders of the Apocalypse

series in which "[f]ifteen-year-old Billy Ballard is the kid that everyone picks on. But things change drastically when Death tells Billy he must stand in as Pestilence, the White Rider of the Apocalypse. Now armed with a Bow that allows him to strike with disease from a distance, Billy lashes out at his tormentors . . . and accidentally causes an

outbreak of meningitis. Horrified by his actions, Billy begs Death to take back the Bow. For that to happen, says Death, Billy must track down the real White Rider, and stop him from unleashing something awful on humanity . . . that could make the Black Plague look like a summer cold. Does one bullied teenager have the strength to stand his ground—and the courage to save the world?" (Publisher's note)

Key, Watt

Alabama moon. Farrar, Straus & Giroux 2006 294p $16; pa $6.99

Grades: 5 6 7 8   **Fic**

1. Alabama -- Fiction 2. Orphans -- Fiction 3. Wilderness survival -- Fiction

ISBN 0-374-30184-0; 0-312-38428-9 pa

LC 2005-40165

After the death of his father, ten-year-old Moon leaves their forest shelter home and is sent to an Alabama institution, becoming entangled in the outside world he has never known and making good friends, a relentless enemy, and finally a new life

"The book is well written with a flowing style, plenty of dialogue, and lots of action. The characters are well drawn and three-dimensional." SLJ

Followed by: Dirt road home (2010)

Dirt road home. Farrar Straus Giroux 2010 211p $16.99

Grades: 5 6 7 8   **Fic**

1. Gangs -- Fiction 2. Alabama -- Fiction 3. Violence -- Fiction 4. Reformatories -- Fiction 5. Father-son relationship -- Fiction

ISBN 978-0-374-30863-6; 0-374-30863-2

LC 2010-11319

Sequel to: Alabama moon (2006)

At Hellenweiler, a reformatory for second-offenders, fourteen-year-old Hal Mitchell will soon be free if he can avoid the gang violence of his fellow inmates, but the real enemy may lie elsewhere.

"With authentic characters and a candid first-person narrative, Key's story offers a disturbing appraisal of life in a juvenile facility, and a riveting battle for justice." Publ Wkly

★ **Fourmile**; Watt Key. Farrar Straus Giroux 2012 227 p, (hardcover) $16.99

Grades: 5 6   **Fic**

1. Child abuse -- Fiction 2. Father-son relationship -- Fiction 3. Mother-son relationship -- Fiction 4. Alabama -- Fiction 5. Violence -- Fiction 6. Loss (Psychology) -- Fiction 7. Farm life -- Alabama -- Fiction

ISBN 0374350957; 9780374324414; 9780374350956

LC 2012003220

In the book by Watt Key, "[m]iddle schooler Foster and his mother have been barely getting by since his father's death a year ago. . . . Mother has begun a relationship with dangerous, unpleasant Dax, a man she seems powerless to keep from abusing both Foster and his dog, Joe. Then Gary shows up, hiking along the rural road. . . . Foster, desperate to find some steady ground in his life, connects to Gary immediately." (Kirkus Reviews)

Khan, Rukhsana

Wanting Mor. Groundwood/House of Anansi Books 2009 190p $17.95

Grades: 6 7 8 9   **Fic**

1. Sex role -- Fiction 2. Afghanistan -- Fiction 3. Bereavement -- Fiction 4. Birth defects -- Fiction
ISBN 0-88899-858-9; 978-0-88899-858-3; 978-0-88899-862-0 pa

Jameela and her family live in a poor, war-torn village in Afghanistan. Even with her cleft lip and lack of educational opportunities, Jameela feels relatively secure, sustained by her Muslim faith and the love of her mother, Mor. But when Mor dies, Jameela's father impulsively decides to start a new life in Kabul.

"This compelling story is based on real incidents. Jameela's matter-of-fact, first person narrative will awaken young readers to life and conditions in Afghanistan." Booklist

Khoury, Jessica

Origin; Jessica Khoury. Razorbill 2012 393 p. (hardcover) $17.99

Grades: 6 7 8   **Fic**

1. Science fiction 2. Immortality -- Fiction 3. Science -- Experiments -- Fiction 4. Rain forests -- Fiction 5. Indigenous peoples -- Fiction 6. Amazon River Region -- Fiction
ISBN 1595145958; 9781595145956

LC 2012014447

In this young adult novel by Jessica Khoury "Pia has grown up in a secret laboratory hidden deep in the Amazon rainforest. She was raised by a team of scientists who have created her to be the start of a new immortal race. But on the night of her seventeenth birthday . . . and sneaks outside the compound for the first time in her life . . . Pia meets Eio, a boy from a nearby village. Together, they embark on a race against time to discover the truth about Pia's origin." (Author's note)

Kidd, Ronald

The **year** of the bomb. Simon & Schuster Books for Young Readers 2009 202p $15.99

Grades: 6 7 8 9   **Fic**

1. Fear -- Fiction 2. Cold war -- Fiction 3. California -- Fiction 4. Blacklisting of entertainers -- Fiction 5. Motion pictures -- Production and direction -- Fiction
ISBN 978-1-4169-5892-5; 1-4169-5892-4

LC 2008023646

In 1955 California, as "Invasion of the Body Snatchers" is filmed in their hometown, thirteen-year-old Arnie discovers a real enemy when he and three friends go against a young government agent determined to find communists at a neaby university or on the movie set.

"The book is vividly imbued with historical detail; parallels between the Red Scare witch hunters and the movie's body-invading aliens are particularly effective." Horn Book Guide

Kilworth, Garry

Attica. Little, Brown 2009 334p pa $11.95

Grades: 5 6 7 8   **Fic**

1. Fantasy fiction 2. Stepfamilies -- Fiction
ISBN 978-1-904233-56-5 pa; 1-904233-56-2 pa

"The children have distinct personalities and react to Attica in realistic ways, finding their own strengths in this exhilarating, unpredictable environment. This book is a rare find." Booklist

Kimmel, Elizabeth Cody

★ The **reinvention** of Moxie Roosevelt. Dial Books for Young Readers 2010 256p $16.99

Grades: 4 5 6 7   **Fic**

1. School stories
ISBN 978-0-8037-3303-9; 0-8037-3303-8

LC 2009-37939

On her first day of boarding school, a thirteen-year-old girl who feels boring and invisible decides to change her personality to match her unusual name.

"Kimmel's sharply observed novel reflects a keen understanding of the agony of self-definition that is adolescence. Readers will cheer for Moxie as she charts her path toward self-acceptance." Kirkus

Kinard, Kami

The **Boy** Project; notes and observations of Kara McAllister. Scholastic Press 2012 $12.99

Grades: 6 7 8 9   **Fic**

1. School stories 2. Science projects -- Fiction 3. Dating (Social customs) -- Fiction
ISBN 978-0-545-34515-6; 0-545-34515-4

LC 2011008332

Eighth-grader Kara McAllister chronicles her efforts when she tries to use the scientific method to transform her social blunders into romantic victories.

"This middle-school drama is hip to the moment, with breakup texting, kissing and popularity tug of wars. . . . Kara's irrepressible spirit, clever wit and introspection save this story from vapidity." Kirkus

Kindl, Patrice

Keeping the castle; a tale of romance, riches, and real estate. by Patrice Kindl. Viking Childrens Books 2012 261 p. $16.99; (hardcover) $16.99

Grades: 7 8 9 10 11   **Fic**

1. Love stories 2. Regency novels 3. Marriage -- Fiction 4. Castles -- Fiction 5. Courtship -- Fiction 6. Social classes -- Fiction 7. Great Britain -- History -- 1789-1820 -- Fiction 8. England -- Social life and customs -- 19th century -- Fiction
ISBN 0670014389; 9780670014385

LC 2011033185

In this book, "[s]eventeen-year-old Althea Crawley is . . . on a quest to marry rich so that she may secure the family's only inheritance, a dilapidated castle on the edge of the North Sea. . . . Marriage prospects in tiny Lesser Hoo are slim, to say the least, until dashing and wealthy Lord Boring arrives on the scene. Matters are further complicated by a revolving cast of potential suitors, including Lord Boring's cousin, Mr. Fredericks." (Booklist)

King, Caro

Seven sorcerers; Caro King. Aladdin 2011 324 p. (hbk.) $15.99

Grades: 5 6 7 8   **Fic**

1. Fantasy 2. Missing children -- Fiction 3. Brothers

and sisters -- Fiction 4. Adventure and adventurers -- Fiction
ISBN 1442420421; 9781442420427

LC 2011001432

Sequel: Shadow spell

First published 2009 in the United Kingdom

"Nineveh 'Nin' Redstone is 11 years old and resolutely ordinary. Her four-year-old brother is nothing but a nuisance until the awful Wednesday when she wakes up and he's gone. Worse, no one but Nin remembers he exists. It's left to her to reclaim him from Skerridge (a bogeyman) and the Terrible House of Strood." (Publishers Weekly)

A "complex, intelligent fantasy that is at turns funny and terrifying." Booklist

Kinney, Jeff

Diary of a wimpy kid; the ugly truth. by Jeff Kinney. Amulet Books 2010 217 p. ill. (hardcover) $13.95

Grades: 5 6 7 8   **Fic**

1. Adolescence 2. School stories 3. Humorous stories 4. Diaries -- Fiction 5. Friendship -- Fiction 6. Family life -- Fiction 7. Maturation (Psychology) -- Fiction
ISBN 0810984911; 9780810984912

LC 2010033360

This is the fifth book in Laura Oliver's Diary of Wimpy Kid series. Here, "Greg Heffly is seeking a replacement for his best friend, Rowley, as he faces the new school year. . . . But that's not all. Greg also faces issues relating to bathroom etiquette, acne, his mother returning to school, the family gathering at Grandma's for Uncle Gary's wedding, Advance Health class (sex education), girls, brotherly quandaries, and dealing with friends on Facebook." (School Library Journal)

Diary of a wimpy kid: dog days. Amulet Books 2009 224p

Grades: 5 6 7 8   **Fic**

1. Summer -- Fiction 2. Vacations -- Fiction
ISBN 0810983915; 9780810983915

LC 2009024953

In the of middle-schooler Greg Heffley, he records his attempts to spend his summer vacation sensibly indoors playing video games and watching television, despite his mother's other ideas.

"Kinney's gift for telling, pitch-perfect details in both his writing and art remains." Publ Wkly

★ **Diary** of a wimpy kid: Greg Heffley's journal. Amulet Books 2007 217p pa $14.95

Grades: 5 6 7 8   **Fic**

1. School stories 2. Friendship -- Fiction
ISBN 978-0-8109-9313-6 pa; 0-8109-9313-9 pa

LC 2006-31847

Greg records his sixth grade experiences in a middle school where he and his best friend, Rowley, undersized weaklings amid boys who need to shave twice daily, hope just to survive, but when Rowley grows more popular, Greg must take drastic measures to save their friendship

"Kinney's background as a cartoonist is apparent in this hybrid book that falls somewhere between traditional prose and graphic novel. . . . The pace moves quickly. The first of three installments, it is an excellent choice for reluctant

readers, but more experienced readers will also find much to enjoy and relate to." SLJ

Other titles about Greg are:

Diary of a wimpy kid: Rodrick rules (2008)

Diary of a wimpy kid: the last straw (2009)

Diary of a wimpy kid: dog days (2009)

Diary of a wimpy kid: Rodrick rules. Amulet Books 2008 216p il $12.95

Grades: 5 6 7 8   **Fic**

1. School stories 2. Family life -- Fiction
ISBN 978-0-8109-9473-7; 0-8109-9473-9

LC 2007-32296

Companion volume to: Diary of a wimpy kid: Greg Heffley's journal (2007)

Greg Heffley tells about his summer vacation and his attempts to steer clear of trouble when he returns to middle school and tries to keep his older brother Rodrick from telling everyone about Greg's most humiliating experience of the summer.

"Once again diarist Greg chronicles a hilarious litany of problems. . . . As before, he peppers his journal entries with his own cartoons. . . . He comes across as a real kid, and his story is one that will appeal to all those real kids who feel just like him." Booklist

Diary of a wimpy kid: the last straw. Amulet Books 2009 217p il $12.95

Grades: 5 6 7 8   **Fic**

1. School stories 2. Family life -- Fiction
ISBN 978-0-8109-7068-7; 0-8109-7068-6

LC 2008060022

Middle-schooler Greg Heffley nimbly sidesteps his father's attempts to change Greg's wimpy ways until his father threatens to send him to military school.

"Kinney's spot-on humor and winning formula of deadpan text set against cartoons are back in full force." Publ Wkly

The **third** wheel; Jeff Kinney. Amulet Books 2012 217 p. (Diary of a wimpy kid) $13.95; $13.95

Grades: 5 6 7 8   **Fic**

1. Dance -- Fiction 2. School stories 3. Humorous fiction
ISBN 1419705849; 9781419705847

This children's story, by Jeff Kinney, is book 7 in the "Diary of a Wimpy Kid" series. "A dance at Greg's middle school has everyone scrambling to find a partner, and Greg is determined not to be left by the wayside. So he concocts a desperate plan to find someone . . . to go with on the big night. But Greg's schemes go hilariously awry, and his only option is to attend the dance with his best friend, Rowley Jefferson, and a female classmate as a 'group of friends.'" (Publisher's note)

Kinsey-Warnock, Natalie

True colors; by Natalie Kinsey-Warnock. Alfred A. Knopf Books for Young Readers 2012 242 p. (hard cover) $15.99

Grades: 4 5 6 7   **Fic**

1. Absent mothers -- Fiction 2. Orphans -- Fiction 3. Abandoned children -- Fiction 4. Identity (Psychology)

-- Fiction 5. Identity -- Fiction 6. Foundlings -- Fiction
7. Farm life -- Vermont -- Fiction 8. People with mental
disabilities -- Fiction 9. Vermont -- History -- 20th
century -- Fiction
ISBN 0375860991; 9780375854538; 9780375860997;
9780375897061; 9780375960994

LC 2011037863

This book by Natalie Kinsey-Warnock "tells the story
of one girl's journey to find the mother she never had, set
against the period backdrop of a small farming town in
1950s Vermont. For her entire life, 10-year-old Blue has
never known her mother. . . . Over the course of one summer,
she resolves to finally find out who she is. . . . Her search
leads her down a road of self-discovery that will change her
life forever." (Publisher's note)

Kipling, Rudyard, 1865-1936

★ The **jungle** book; by Rudyard Kipling; il-
lustrated by Robert R. Ingpen. Sterling Children's
Books 2012 192 p. ill. (hardcover) $19.95
Grades: 4 5 6 7   Fic
1. Picture books for children 2. Fantasy fiction
ISBN 1402782845; 9781402782848

This book is an illustrated version of Rudyard Kipling's
1894 children's story collection "The Jungle Book." Illustrations by Robert Ingpen accompany the stories "of the
boy Mowgli, rescued and raised by tigers in the heart of the
jungle. The tales feature such . . . creatures such as Bagheera,
the graceful black panther; Baloo, the kindly brown bear;
and Kaa, the snake with the hypnotic stare." The stories
'Rikki-Tikki-Tavi,' 'The White Seal,' and 'Toomai of the
Elephants'" are included, too. (Publisher's note)

Kirby, Jessi

Golden; Jessi Kirby. 1st ed. Simon & Schuster
Books for Young Readers 2013 288 p. (hardcover)
$16.99
Grades: 7 8 9 10 11 12   Fic
1. Love stories 2. Mystery fiction 3. Diaries -- Fiction
4. Love -- Fiction 5. Choice -- Fiction 6. Family
problems -- Fiction 7. Mothers and daughters -- Fiction
ISBN 1442452161; 9781442452169; 9781442452183;
9781442452251

LC 2012042216

In this novel, by Jessi Kirby, "seventeen-year-old Parker
Frost has never taken the road less traveled. . . . Julianna Far-
netti and Shane Cruz are remembered as the golden couple
of Summit Lakes High . . . but Julianna's journal tells . . .
. the secrets that were swept away with her the night that
Shane's jeep plunged into an icy river. . . . Reading Julianna's journal gives Parker . . . reasons to question what really happened the night of the accident." (Publisher's note)

"Kirby's . . . third novel is inspirational and contemplative in its mood and tone. Multifaceted characters and dashes
of mystery and romance come together in a successful mediation on the value of taking an active role in one's life."
Pub Wkly

Moonglass. Simon & Schuster Books for Young
Readers 2011 232p $16.99; ebook $9.99
Grades: 8 9 10 11 12   Fic
1. Guilt -- Fiction 2. Moving -- Fiction 3. Beaches

-- Fiction 4. Suicide -- Fiction 5. California -- Fiction
6. Father-daughter relationship -- Fiction
ISBN 978-1-4424-1694-9; 1-4424-1694-7; 978-1-
4424-1696-3 ebook; 1-4424-1696-3 ebook

LC 2010-37389

At age seven, Anna watched her mother walk into the
surf and drown, but nine years later, when she moves with
her father to the beach where her parents fell in love, she
joins the cross-country team, makes new friends, and faces
her guilt.

"Kirby creates a cast of sympathetic and credible characters, each imperfect but well intentioned. There's action as
well as introspection here." Booklist

Kirby, Matthew J.

★ The **clockwork** three. Scholastic Press 2010
391p $17.99
Grades: 5 6 7 8   Fic
1. Fantasy fiction 2. Friendship -- Fiction 3. Clocks
and watches -- Fiction
ISBN 978-0-545-20337-1; 0-545-20337-6

LC 2009-37879

As mysterious circumstances bring Giuseppe, Frederick,
and Hannah together, their lives soon interlock like the turning gears in a clock and they realize that each one holds a
key to solving the others' mysteries

This is a "riveting historical fantasy. . . . Kirby has assembled all the ingredients for a rousing adventure, which he
delivers with rich, transporting prose." Publ Wkly

Icefall. Scholastic Press 2011 325p $17.99
Grades: 5 6 7 8   Fic
1. Fantasy fiction 2. Ice -- Fiction 3. Winter -- Fiction
4. Storytelling -- Fiction
ISBN 978-0-545-27424-1; 0-545-27424-9

LC 2011000890

"Kirby turns in a claustrophobic, thought-provoking
coming-of-age adventure that shows a young woman growing into her own, while demonstrating the power of myth
and legend. Kirby's attention to detail and stark descriptions
make this an effective mood piece." Publ Wkly

Kittle, Katrina

Reasons to be happy. Sourcebooks Jabberwocky
2011 281p pa $7.99
Grades: 7 8 9 10   Fic
1. School stories 2. Ghana -- Fiction 3. Bulimia --
Fiction 4. Popularity -- Fiction 5. Bereavement --
Fiction 6. Personal appearance -- Fiction
ISBN 978-1-4022-6020-9; 1-4022-6020-2

LC 2011020276

Eighth-grader Hannah Carlisle feels unattractive compared to her movie star parents and cliquish Beverly Hills
classmates, and when her mother's cancer worsens and her
father starts drinking heavily, Hannah's grief and anger turn
into bulimia, which only her aunt, a documentary filmmaker,
understands.

"Hannah's believability as a character as well as
the realistic, painful depiction of bulimia make this a
standout." Booklist

Kittredge, Caitlin

The **Iron** Thorn. Delacorte Press 2011 493p (Iron Codex) $17.99; lib bdg $20.99

Grades: 7 8 9 10   **Fic**

1. Fantasy fiction

ISBN 0-385-73829-3; 0-385-90720-6 lib bdg; 978-0-385-73829-3; 978-0-385-90720-0 lib bdg

          LC 2010-00972

In an alternate 1950s, mechanically gifted fifteen-year-old Aoife Grayson, whose family has a history of going mad at sixteen, must leave the totalitarian city of Lovecraft and venture into the world of magic to solve the mystery of her brother's disappearance and the mysteries surrounding her father and the Land of Thorn.

"Steampunk fans will delight in this first title in the sure-to-be-popular Iron Codex series. . . . There's plenty of tame but satisfying romance, too, and plot twists galore. Aoife is a caustic-tongued, feisty, and independent young woman, with plenty of nerve and courage." Booklist

The **nightmare** garden; Caitlin Kittredge. Delacorte Press 2012 417 p. (The iron codex) (hardback) $17.99

Grades: 7 8 9 10   **Fic**

1. Fantasy fiction 2. Adventure fiction 3. Steampunk fiction 4. Metaphysics -- Fiction 5. Voyages and travels -- Fiction 6. Fantasy 7. Magic -- Fiction

ISBN 9780375985690; 9780385738316; 9780385907217

          LC 2011038306

Sequel to: The Iron Thorn.

This book is the second novel in Caitlin Kittredge's 'Iron Codex' series. "Spoiled, inconsistent, often-thoughtless heroine Aoife Grayson nearly destroyed the world when she broke the Lovecraft Engine and sundered the gates between the worlds of human and Fae. But she's not going to let a little thing like that stop her, so she sets off on an exhausting, somewhat episodic adventure through the steampunk-horror '50s nightmare that is her world . . . . The ending promises even bigger adventures to come." (Kirkus)

Kizer, Amber

A **matter** of days; Amber Kizer. 1st ed. Delacorte Press 2013 288 p. (ebook) $50.97; (hardcover) $16.99; (library) $19.99

Grades: 7 8 9 10   **Fic**

1. Apocalyptic fiction 2. Voyages and travels 3. Science fiction 4. Survival -- Fiction 5. Epidemics -- Fiction 6. Virus diseases -- Fiction 7. Brothers and sisters -- Fiction

ISBN 0385908040; 9780375898259; 9780385739733; 9780385908047

          LC 2012012200

In this book, "Nadia and Rabbit's military doctor uncle, Bean, visited them and insisted on injecting them with a vaccine for a 'new bug.' Not long afterward, the disease XRD TB . . . starts ravaging the world, and 16-year-old Nadia and 11-year-old Rabbit are the only survivors in their entire town. With the assorted survival gear their uncle ordered for them, they attempt to make their way from their Seattle suburb to their grandfather in West Virginia." (Publishers Weekly)

"This post-apocalyptic tale is particularly frightening as it doesn't take place in some distant, imagined future. A solid, realistically imagined survival tale with a strong female protagonist." Kirkus

Meridian. Delacorte Press 2009 305p $16.99; lib bdg $19.99

Grades: 7 8 9 10   **Fic**

1. Death -- Fiction 2. Angels -- Fiction 3. Colorado -- Fiction 4. Supernatural -- Fiction 5. Good and evil -- Fiction

ISBN 978-0-385-73668-8; 0-385-73668-1; 978-0-385-90621-0 lib bdg; 0-385-90621-8 lib bdg

          LC 2008-35666

On her sixteenth birthday, Meridian is whisked off to her great-aunt's home in Revelation, Colorado, where she learns that she is a Fenestra, the half-human, half-angel link between the living and the dead, and must learn to help human souls to the afterlife before the dark forces reach them.

"The author brings a fresh voice to the realm of teen paranormal romantic fiction. . . . The characters are compelling and the themes of good and evil, life and death will keep readers engaged." SLJ

Followed by: Wildcat fireflies (2011)

Wildcat fireflies. Delacorte Press 2011 508p $16.99

Grades: 7 8 9 10   **Fic**

1. Death -- Fiction 2. Angels -- Fiction 3. Supernatural -- Fiction 4. Good and evil -- Fiction

ISBN 978-0-385-73971-9; 0-385-73971-0

          LC 2010-30405

Sequel to: Meridian (2010)

Teenaged Meridian Sozu, a half-human, half-angel link between the living and the dead known as a Fenestra, hits the road with Tens, her love and sworn protector, in hopes of finding another person with Meridian's ability to help souls transition safely into the afterlife.

"Some of the day-to-day events may be hard to believe, but this is a book about angels and demons after all; fans will forgive." Kirkus

Kladstrup, Kristin

Garden princess; Kristin Kladstrup. Candlewick Press 2013 272 p. $15.99

Grades: 6 7 8   **Fic**

1. Occult fiction 2. Fantasy fiction

ISBN 0763656852; 9780763656850

          LC 2012943642

This book features a garden where "every flower in it is always in bloom, but Princess Adela, a gardening expert and enthusiast, is sure that can't be true. When the princess's friend Garth receives a mysterious invitation to Hortensia's garden party, Adela arranges to accompany him. . . . Wandering among flowers she knows shouldn't be in bloom, Adela learns the frightening secret of Hortensia's magic garden and finds herself in terrible danger." (School Library Journal)

Klages, Ellen

★ The **green** glass sea. Viking 2006 321p $16.99; pa $7.99

Grades: 5 6 7 8   **Fic**
1. New Mexico -- Fiction 2. Scientists -- Fiction 3.
Atomic bomb -- Fiction 4. World War, 1939-1945 --
Fiction
ISBN 0-670-06134-4; 0-14-241149-3 pa

It is 1943, and 11-year-old Dewey Kerrigan is traveling
west on a train to live with her scientist father—but no one
will tell her exactly where he is. When she reaches Los Alamos, New Mexico, she learns why: he's working on a top
secret government program.

"Many readers will know as little about the true nature
of the project as the girls do, so the gradual revelation of
facts is especially effective, while those who already know
about Los Alamos's historical significance will experience
the story in a different, but equally powerful, way." SLJ

Followed by: White sands, red menace (2008)

White sands, red menace. Viking 2008 337p
$16.99
Grades: 5 6 7 8   **Fic**
1. Cold war -- Fiction 2. New Mexico -- Fiction 3.
Scientists -- Fiction 4. Atomic bomb -- Fiction
ISBN 978-0-670-06235-5; 0-670-06235-9

Sequel to: The green glass sea (2006)

"The groundbreaking science is part of daily life for the
smart techno-teens, and the adult characters are as compelling as the kids. . . . Along with . . . global issues, Klages'
compelling story explores personal relationships and what it
means to be a family." Booklist

Klass, David
Firestorm. Frances Foster Books 2006 289p
(The Caretaker trilogy) $17
Grades: 8 9 10 11 12   **Fic**
1. Science fiction
ISBN 0-374-32307-0
                                  LC 2005-52112
After learning that he has been sent from the future for
a special purpose, eighteen-year-old Jack receives help from
an unusual dog and a shape-shifting female fighter.

"The sobering events and tone are leavened with engaging humor, and the characters are multidimensional. The
relentless pace, coupled with issues of ecology, time travel,
self-identity, and sexual awakening, makes for a thrilling
and memorable read." SLJ

Other books in the Caretaker Trilogy are:
Whirlwind (2008)
Timelock (2009)

Second impact; David Klass and Perri Klass.
Frances Foster Books 2013 288 p. (hardback)
$16.99
Grades: 8 9 10 11 12   **Fic**
1. School stories 2. Brain -- Wounds and injuries
-- Fiction 3. Blogs -- Fiction 4. Schools -- Fiction
5. Football -- Fiction 6. High schools -- Fiction 7.
Conduct of life -- Fiction 8. Sports injuries -- Fiction
ISBN 0374379963; 9780374379964
                                  LC 2012040873
In this book, "Carla Jenson, sports reporter for her school
paper, convinces Jerry Downing, star quarterback and excel-
lent writer, to blog about the team's season—a novel idea

with unexpected repercussions." This is especially true once
Carla latches onto the topic of "sports-related concussions
even though she is opposed by Jerry and practically everyone else in the school and town as the controversy escalates." (Kirkus Reviews)

★ **Stuck** on Earth. Farrar Straus & Giroux 2010
227p $16.99
Grades: 4 5 6 7   **Fic**
1. Science fiction 2. Bullies -- Fiction 3. Extraterrestrial
beings -- Fiction
ISBN 978-0-374-39951-1; 0-374-39951-4
                                  LC 2008--48133
On a secret mission to evaluate whether the human race
should be annihilated, a space alien inhabits the body of a
bullied fourteen-year-old boy.

"Klass's . . . thoughtful, often wrenching book offers
plenty to think about, from what's really going on in Tom's
head to questions about human responsibility to the planet
and each other. It takes 'alienation' to a whole new level."
Publ Wkly

Timelock. Farrar, Straus and Giroux 2009 246p
(The Caretaker trilogy) $17.99
Grades: 8 9 10 11 12   **Fic**
1. Science fiction 2. Ecology -- Fiction 3. Time travel
-- Fiction
ISBN 978-0-374-32309-7; 0-374-32309-7
                                  LC 2008-23280
Sequel to: Whirlwind (2008)

Jack discovers that the only way to protect the Earth
from ecological disaster at the hands of the Dark Army is to
lock time, and he must choose between staying in the present
or returning to the future world from which he came.

"Every bit as fast paced, thrilling, and similar to a gripping computer game as its predecessors, this final volume in
the trilogy will keep readers absorbed while presenting them
with a valuable warning about the need for environmental
awareness." SLJ

Whirlwind; [by] David Klass. 1st ed.; Farrar
Straus Giroux 2008 295p (The Caretaker trilogy)
$17.95; pa $8.99
Grades: 8 9 10 11 12   **Fic**
1. Science fiction
ISBN 978-0-374-32308-0; 0-374-32308-9; 978-0-312-
38429-6 pa; 0-312-38429-7 pa
                                  LC 2007014160
Sequel to: Firestorm (2006)

Jack finds himself embroiled in another dangerous adventure when, after a six-month absence, he returns to the
Hudson River town where he grew up to find his girlfriend
PJ only to discover that she is missing and everyone believes
him to be responsible for her disappearance and the death of
his family.

"The fast-paced, gripping plot is an excellent vehicle for
presenting a significant environmental message to an audience that might not hear it otherwise." SLJ

Followed by: Timelock (2009)

Klass, Sheila Solomon

★ **Soldier's** secret; the story of Deborah Sampson. Henry Holt 2009 215p $17.95

Grades: 6 7 8 9 10   **Fic**

1. Soldiers 2. Memoirists 3. Soldiers -- Fiction 4. United States -- History -- 1775-1783, Revolution -- Fiction

ISBN 978-0-8050-8200-5; 0-8050-8200-X

             LC 2008-36783

During the Revolutionary War, a young woman named Deborah Sampson disguises herself as a man in order to serve in the Continental Army.

In this novel, Sampson "is strong, brave, and witty. . . . Klass doesn't shy away from the horrors of battle; she also is blunt regarding details young readers will wonder about, like how Sampson dealt with bathing, urination, and menstruation. . . . Sampson's romantic yearnings for a fellow soldier . . . is given just the right notes or restraint and realism." Booklist

Klause, Annette Curtis

The **silver** kiss. Delacorte Press 1990 198p hardcover o.p. pa $5.99

Grades: 8 9 10 11 12   **Fic**

1. Death -- Fiction 2. Vampires -- Fiction

ISBN 0-385-30160-X; 0-440-21346-0 pa

             LC 89-48880

"There's inherent romantic appeal in the vampire legend, and Klause weaves all the gory details into a poignant love story that becomes both sensuous and suspenseful." Booklist

Klavan, Andrew

MindWar; a novel. Andrew Klavan. Thomas Nelson, Inc. 2014 352 p. (The MindWar Trilogy) (hardback) $15.99

Grades: 7 8 9 10   **Fic**

1. Teenagers -- Fiction 2. Video games -- Fiction 3. Virtual reality -- Fiction 4. Undercover operations -- Fiction 5. Cyberterrorism -- Prevention -- Fiction

ISBN 1401688926; 9781401688929

             LC 2013050887

In this novel by Andrew Klaven "high school football star Rick Dial . . . immerses himself in video games after a car accident leaves his legs painfully useless. The teen is recruited to fight real life baddies. . . a virtual reality world created by Kurodar, a terrorist out to destroy the free world. He must fight for his life, because what happens to you in this virtual world affects your body in real life." (School Library Journal)

"Edgar Award–winning Klavan's well-orchestrated fantasy thriller features brisk but compelling character development, a touch of wry humor, Christian sensitivity that doesn't proselytize, and an imaginative mix of gaming action with real-life stakes. With just the right cliff-hanger ending, this trilogy opener shows promise." Booklist

Mind War

Klein, Lisa M.

Cate of the Lost Colony; by Lisa Klein. Bloomsbury 2010 329p $16.99

Grades: 8 9 10 11 12   **Fic**

1. Poets 2. Queens 3. Authors 4. Explorers 5. Historians 6. Courtiers 7. Travel writers 8. Orphans -- Fiction 9. Lumbee Indians -- Fiction 10. Roanoke Island (N.C.) -- History -- Fiction 11. Great Britain -- History -- 1485-1603, Tudors -- Fiction

ISBN 978-1-59990-507-5; 1-59990-507-8

             LC 2010-8299

When her dalliance with Sir Walter Ralegh is discovered by Queen Elizabeth in 1587, lady-in-waiting Catherine Archer is banished to the struggling colony of Roanoke, where she and the other English settlers must rely on a Croatoan Indian for their survival. Includes author's note on the mystery surrounding the Lost Colony.

"This robust, convincing portrait of the Elizabethan world with complex, rounded characters wraps an intriguingly plausible solution to the 'lost colony' mystery inside a compelling love story of subtle thematic depth." Kirkus

Includes bibliographical references

Lady Macbeth's daughter. Bloomsbury 2009 291p $16.99

Grades: 7 8 9 10   **Fic**

1. Poets 2. Authors 3. Dramatists 4. Kings 5. Homicide -- Fiction 6. Scotland -- Fiction 7. Witchcraft -- Fiction 8. Kings and rulers -- Fiction 9. Physically disabled -- Fiction

ISBN 978-1-59990-347-7; 1-59990-347-4

             LC 2009-6717

In alternating chapters, ambitious Lady Macbeth tries to bear a son and win the throne of Scotland for her husband, and Albia, their daughter who was banished at birth and raised by three weird sisters, falls in love, learns of her parentage, and seeks to free Scotland from tyranny in this tale based on Shakespeare's Macbeth.

"The writing is crisp and clear and makes good use of Shakespeare's language and its times. The characters are well-developed and the story being told from the perspective of the mother and daughter makes for age-old conflict. This tale will keep readers asking the ultimate question of whether or not power is ultimately worth the price." Libr Media Connect

Klise, Kate

★ **Grounded.** Feiwel and Friends 2010 196p $16.99

Grades: 4 5 6 7   **Fic**

1. Death -- Fiction 2. Missouri -- Fiction 3. Bereavement -- Fiction 4. Swindlers and swindling -- Fiction

ISBN 978-0-312-57039-2; 0-312-57039-2

             LC 2010013008

After her father, brother, and sister are killed in a plane crash, twelve-year-old Daralynn's life in tiny Digginsville, Missouri, proceeds as her mother turns angry and embittered, her grandmother becomes senile, and her flamboyant aunt continues to run the Summer Sunset Retirement Home for Distinguished Gentlemen, while being courted by the owner of the town's new crematorium.

"Dark humor melds with genuine pathos in Klise's moving novel. . . . This quiet story illuminates and celebrates the human need for connection beyond the grave." Booklist

Homesick; Kate Klise. 1st ed. Feiwel and Friends 2012 192 p. (hardcover) $16.99
Grades: 4 5 6 7 8   **Fic**
1. Divorce -- Fiction 2. Family life -- Fiction
ISBN 1250008425; 9781250008428
In this book by Kate Klise, "Benny's parents are splitting up. . . . Benny's dad has always liked clutter, but now, he begins hoarding everything. . . . As his house grows more cluttered and his father grows more distant, Benny tries to sort out whether he can change anything at all. Meanwhile, a local teacher enters their quiet Missouri town in America's Most Charming Small Town contest, and the pressure is on to clean up the area, especially Benny's ramshackle of a house." (Publisher's note)

Letters from camp; illustrated by M. Sarah Klise. Avon Bks. 1999 178p il hardcover o.p. pa $5.99
Grades: 4 5 6 7   **Fic**
1. Camps -- Fiction 2. Letters -- Fiction 3. Siblings -- Fiction
ISBN 0-380-97539-4; 0-380-79348-2 pa
LC 98-52315
Sent to Camp Happy Harmony to learn how to get along with each other, pairs of brothers and sisters chronicle in letters home how they come to suspect the intentions of the singing family running the camp
This is a "delightfully wacky story. . . . The humor is very gentle and tongue-in-cheek. . . . An entirely satisfying camp adventure." Booklist

Regarding the sink; where, oh where, did Waters go? illustrated by M. Sarah Klise. Harcourt 2004 127p il $15
Grades: 4 5 6 7   **Fic**
1. School stories
ISBN 0-15-205019-1
LC 2003-26560
A series of letters reveals the selection of the famous fountain designer, Florence Waters, to design a new sink for the Geyser Creek Middle School cafeteria, her subsequent disappearance, and the efforts of a class of sixth-graders to find her
"Piecing the story and clues together is satisfying. Introduce this book to savvy readers who are ready for the jump to a clever, unconventional reading experience." SLJ
Other titles in this series are:
Regarding the bathrooms (2006)
Regarding the bees (2007)
Regarding the fountain (1998)
Regarding the trees (2005)

Kluger, Jeffrey
★ **Freedom** stone. Philomel Books 2011 316p $16.99
Grades: 4 5 6   **Fic**
1. Magic -- Fiction 2. Slavery -- Fiction 3. African Americans -- Fiction 4. United States -- History -- 1861-1865, Civil War -- Fiction
ISBN 978-0-399-25214-3; 0-399-25214-2
LC 2010-06028

With the help of a magical stone from Africa, a thirteen-year-old slave travels to the battle of Vicksburg to clear her father's name and free her family from bondage.
Kluger "adeptly mixes drama, fantasy, romance, and history, while creating characters so determined to survive that readers can't help being drawn into their plights. In a climax that breaks with reality but that will keep readers hungry to learn the outcome, Kluger proves his storytelling prowess." Publ Wkly

Kluger, Steve
★ **My** most excellent year; a novel of love, Mary Poppins, & Fenway Park. Dial Books 2008 403p $16.99; pa $8.99
Grades: 8 9 10 11 12   **Fic**
1. Friendship -- Fiction 2. Boston (Mass.) -- Fiction
ISBN 978-0-8037-3227-8; 0-8037-3227-9; 978-0-14-241343-2 pa; 0-14-2413437 pa
LC 2007-26651
"Three bright and funny Brookline, MA, eleventh graders look back on their most excellent year—ninth grade—for a school report. Told in alternating chapters by each of them, this enchanting, life-affirming coming-of-age story unfolds through instant messages, emails, memos, diary entries, and letters. . . . This is a rich and humorous novel for older readers." SLJ

Knowles, Jo
See you at Harry's; Jo Knowles. 1st ed. Candlewick Press 2012 310 p. $16.99
Grades: 6 7 8 9 10 11   **Fic**
1. Siblings -- Fiction 2. Bereavement -- Fiction 3. Restaurants -- Fiction 4. Gay teenagers -- Fiction 5. Family 6. Grief -- Fiction 7. Family life -- Fiction 8. Homosexuality -- Fiction 9. Family problems -- Fiction 10. Brothers and sisters -- Fiction
ISBN 9780763654078
LC 2011018619
In this children's novel, "seventh grader Fern . . . relates the . . . tragedies of her family. Her high-school-freshman older brother Holden has come to the place in his life where he's acknowledged that he's gay. . . . Fern offers him support and love. . . . And then there's 3-year-old Charlie, always messy, often annoying, but deeply loved. Fern's busy, distracted parents leave all of the kids wanting for more attention--until a tragic accident tears the family apart." (Kirkus Reviews)

Knox, Elizabeth
Dreamhunter; book one of the Dreamhunter duet. Farrar, Straus & Giroux 2006 365p (Dreamhunter duet) $19; pa $8.99
Grades: 7 8 9 10   **Fic**
1. Fantasy fiction 2. Dreams -- Fiction
ISBN 0-374-31853-0; 0-312-53571-6 pa
LC 2005-46366
First published 2005 in the United Kingdom
In a world where select people can enter "The Place" and find dreams of every kind to share with others for a fee, a fifteen-year-old girl is training to be a dreamhunter when her father disappears, leaving her to carry on his mysterious mission. "Grades nine to twelve." (Bull Cent Child Books)

This first of a two-book series is "a highly original exploration of the idea of a collective unconscious, mixed with imagery from the raising of Lazarus and with the brave, dark qualities of the psyche of an adolescent female." Horn Book Guide

Followed by Dreamquake (2007)

Dreamquake; book two of the Dreamhunter duet. Farrar, Straus & Giroux 2007 449p map (Dreamhunter duet) $19

Grades: 7 8 9 10   **Fic**
1. Fantasy fiction 2. Dreams -- Fiction
ISBN 978-0-374-31854-3; 0-374-31854-9
LC 2006-48109

Sequel to Dreamhunter

Michael L. Printz Award honor book, 2008

Aided by her family and her creation, Nown, Laura investigates the powerful Regulatory Body's involvement in mysterious disappearances and activities and learns, in the process, the true nature of the Place in which dreams are found.

The author's "haunting, invigorating storytelling will leave readers eager to return to its puzzles—and to reap its rewards." Booklist

Mortal fire; by Elizabeth Knox. 1st ed. Frances Foster Books 2013 448 p. (hardcover) $17.99

Grades: 7 8 9 10 11   **Fic**
1. Occult fiction 2. Fantasy fiction 3. Magic -- Fiction 4. Identity -- Fiction 5. Stepbrothers -- Fiction 6. Islands of the Pacific -- Fiction
ISBN 0374388296; 9780374388294
LC 2012040872

This novel, set in a fictional area of New Zealand, stars Canny, a "16-year-old Ma'eu, taciturn, antisocial, and exceptionally gifted in math." She has what she calls "Extra," an "ethereal script that Canny alone can see, attached to plants, buildings, or nothing at all." When she and friends "come upon a valley dense with the Extra, Canny realizes that there is more to her visions than her own oddness—there are people, the Zarenes, whose existence is interwoven with this magical language." (Publishers Weekly)

Knudsen, Michelle

★ The **dragon** of Trelian. Candlewick Press 2009 407p $16.99

Grades: 4 5 6 7   **Fic**
1. Fantasy fiction 2. Magic -- Fiction 3. Dragons -- Fiction 4. Princesses -- Fiction
ISBN 978-0-7636-3455-1; 0-7636-3455-7
LC 2008025378

A mage's apprentice, a princess, and a dragon combine their strength and magic to bring down a traitor and restore peace to the kingdom of Trelian.

"Knudsen does a fantastic job of creating sympathetic and realistic characters that really drive the story. The tale is adventurous and exciting with many twists and turns along the way." SLJ

Followed by: The princess of Trelian (2012)

The **princess** of Trelian; Michelle Knudsen. Candlewick Press 2012 437 p. (reinforced) $16.99

Grades: 4 5 6 7   **Fic**
1. Fantasy fiction 2. Fantasy 3. Magic -- Fiction 4. Dragons -- Fiction 5. Princesses -- Fiction
ISBN 0763650625; 9780763650629
LC 2011047174

Sequel to: The dragon of Trelian (2009)

In this juvenile fantasy novel, by Michelle Knudsen, a "sequel to 'The Dragon of Trelian,' . . . Princess Meg is now heir to the throne, but her subjects are uneasy about her . . . dragon, and it only becomes worse when a neighboring king accuses the dragon of ravaging the countryside. . . . Meanwhile, Meg's best friend Calen has earned his mage's mark, but a mysterious, magical attack occurs. . . . [T]he deposed villain from the previous book is behind all the mischief." (Horn Book Magazine)

Knutsson, Catherine

Shadows cast by stars; Catherine Knutsson. 1st ed. Atheneum Books for Young Readers 2012 456 p. (hardcover) $17.99; (paperback) $9.99

Grades: 7 8 9 10   **Fic**
1. Blood 2. Science fiction 3. Plague -- Fiction 4. Twins -- Fiction 5. Spirits -- Fiction 6. Family life -- Fiction 7. Brothers and sisters -- Fiction 8. Indians of North America -- Fiction
ISBN 1442401915; 9781442401914; 9781442401938; 9781442401921
LC 2011038419

Author Catherine Knutsson tells the story of Native American Cassandra Mercredi. The "sixteen-year-old . . . [may] be immune to Plague, but that doesn't mean she's safe--government forces are searching for those of aboriginal heritage to harvest their blood. When a search threatens Cassandra and her family, they flee to the Island: a mysterious and idyllic territory protected by the Band, a group of guerilla warriors--and by an enigmatic energy barrier that keeps outsiders out and the spirit world in." (Publisher's note)

Koertge, Ronald

Now playing; Stoner & Spaz II. [by] Ron Koertge. Candlewick Press 2011 208p $16.99

Grades: 8 9 10 11 12   **Fic**
1. School stories 2. Drug abuse -- Fiction 3. Cerebral palsy -- Fiction 4. Self-acceptance -- Fiction 5. Dating (Social customs) -- Fiction
ISBN 978-0-7636-5081-0; 0-7636-5081-1
LC 2010040151

Sequel to: Stoner & Spaz (2002)

High schooler Ben Bancroft, a budding filmmaker with cerebral palsy, struggles to understand his relationship with drug-addict Colleen while he explores a new friendship with A.J., who shares his obsession with movies and makes a good impression on Ben's grandmother.

"Koertge writes sharp dialogue and vivid scenes." Publ Wkly

★ **Shakespeare** makes the playoffs; [by] Ron Koertge. Candlewick Press 2010 170p lib bdg $15.99; pa $5.99

Grades: 6 7 8 9   **Fic**
1. Novels in verse 2. Poetry -- Fiction 3. Baseball

-- Fiction

ISBN 978-0-7636-4435-2 lib bdg; 0-7636-4435-8 lib bdg; 978-0-7636-5852-6 pa

LC 2009-14519

Sequel to: Shakespeare bats cleanup (2003)

Fourteen-year-old Kevin Boland, poet and first baseman, is torn between his cute girlfriend Mira and Amy, who is funny, plays Chopin on the piano, and is also a poet.

"The well-crafted poetry is firmly rooted in the experiences of regular teens and addresses subjects that range from breakups to baseball.... Appealing and accessible." Booklist

★ **Stoner** & Spaz; [by] Ron Koertge. Candlewick Press 2002 169p hardcover o.p. pa $6.99

Grades: 8 9 10 11 12   **Fic**

1. School stories 2. Cerebral palsy -- Fiction

ISBN 0-7636-1608-7; 0-7636-2150-1 pa

LC 2001-43050

A troubled youth with cerebral palsy struggles toward self-acceptance with the help of a drug-addicted young woman

"Funny, touching, and surprising, it is a hopeful yet realistic view of things as they are and as they could be." Booklist

Followed by: Now Playing: Stoner & Spaz II (2011)

★ **Strays**; [by] Ron Koertge. Candlewick Press 2007 167p $16.99

Grades: 7 8 9 10 11 12   **Fic**

1. Orphans -- Fiction 2. Foster home care -- Fiction

ISBN 978-0-7636-2705-8; 0-7636-2705-4

LC 2007-24096

After his parents are killed in a car accident, high school senior Sam wonders whether he will ever feel again or if he will remain numbed by grief.

"Though Koertge never soft pedals the horrors faced by some foster children, this thoughtful novel about the lost and abandoned is a hopeful one." Booklist

Koja, Kathe

★ **Buddha** boy. Speak 2004 117p pa $5.99

Grades: 7 8 9 10   **Fic**

1. School stories 2. Artists -- Fiction 3. Buddhism -- Fiction 4. Conduct of life -- Fiction

ISBN 0-14-240209-5

LC 2004041669

First published 2003 by Farrar, Straus & Giroux

Justin spends time with Jinsen, the unusual and artistic new student whom the school bullies torment and call Buddha Boy, and ends up making choices that impact Jinsen, himself, and the entire school.

"A compelling introduction to Buddhism and a credible portrait of how true friendship brings out the best in people." Publ Wkly

★ **Headlong**. Farrar, Straus and Giroux 2008 195p $16.95

Grades: 8 9 10 11 12   **Fic**

1. School stories 2. Orphans -- Fiction 3. Social classes -- Fiction

ISBN 978-0-374-32912-9; 0-374-32912-5

LC 2007-23612

High school sophomore Lily opens herself to new possibilities when, despite warnings, she becomes friends with 'ghetto girl' Hazel, a new student at the private Vaughn School which Lily, following in her elitist mother's footsteps, has attended since preschool.

"Class, identity and friendship are the intersecting subjects of this intelligent novel. . . . [The author] relays this story with her usual insight and, through her lightning-fast characterizations, an ability to project multiple perspectives simultaneously." Publ Wkly

★ **Kissing** the bee. Farrar, Straus and Giroux 2007 121p $16

Grades: 8 9 10 11 12   **Fic**

1. Love stories 2. School stories 3. Bees -- Fiction 4. Friendship -- Fiction

ISBN 978-0-374-39938-2; 0-374-39938-7

LC 2006-37378

While working on a bee project for her advanced biology class, quiet high school senior Dana reflects on her relationship with gorgeous best friend Avra and Avra's boyfriend Emil, whom Dana secretly loves.

The "understated, tightly focused language evokes vivid scenes and heady emotions." Publ Wkly

Konigsberg, Bill

★ **Openly** straight; Bill Konigsberg. Arthur A. Levine Books 2013 336 p. (hard cover : alk. paper) $17.99

Grades: 8 9 10 11   **Fic**

1. School stories 2. Gay teenagers -- Fiction 3. Schools -- Fiction 4. Identity -- Fiction 5. Homosexuality -- Fiction 6. Massachusetts -- Fiction 7. Preparatory schools -- Fiction 8. Preparatory schools -- Massachusetts -- Fiction

ISBN 0545509890; 9780545509893; 9780545509909

LC 2012030552

Lambda Literary Awards Finalist (2014)

In this book, "Coloradan Rafe Goldberg has always been the token gay kid. He's been out since eighth grade. His parents and community are totally supportive. . . . On the outside, Rafe seems fine, but on the inside, he's looking for change, which comes with the opportunity to reinvent himself at the prestigious Natick Academy in Massachusetts. There for his junior year, Rafe cloaks his gayness in order to be just like one of the other guys." All is well until he falls for a straight friend. (Kirkus Reviews)

"Rafe is sick of being the poster child for all things gay at his uber-liberal Colorado high school, so when he gets into a Massachusetts boarding school for his junior year, he decides to reboot himself as "openly straight." Konigsberg slyly demonstrates how thoroughly assumptions of straightness are embedded in everyday interactions. For a thought-provoking take on the coming-out story, look no further." (Horn Book)

Konigsburg, E. L.

The **mysterious** edge of the heroic world. Atheneum Books for Young Readers 2007 244p $16.99; pa $5.99

Grades: 5 6 7 8   **Fic**

1. Florida -- Fiction 2. Friendship -- Fiction 3. Art

museums -- Fiction

ISBN 978-1-4169-4972-5; 1-4169-4972-0; 978-1-4169-5353-1 pa; 1-4169-5353-1 pa

"This humorous, poignant, tragic, and mysterious story has intertwining plots that peel away like the layers of an onion." SLJ

The **outcasts** of 19 Schuyler Place. Atheneum Bks. for Young Readers 2004 296p $16.95

Grades: 5 6 7 8   **Fic**

1. Social action -- Fiction

ISBN 0-689-86636-4

LC 2003-8067

A prequel to Silent to the bone

Upon leaving an oppressive summer camp, twelve-year-old Margaret Rose Kane spearheads a campaign to preserve three unique towers her grand uncles have been building in their back yard for over forty years

"The plot is well paced and has excellent foreshadowing. Konigsburg's characters are particularly well motivated. . . . Funny and thought-provoking by turns, this is Konigsburg at her masterful best." SLJ

Silent to the bone. Atheneum Bks. for Young Readers 2000 261p hardcover o.p. pa $5.99

Grades: 7 8 9 10   **Fic**

1. Mystery fiction 2. Siblings -- Fiction 3. Babysitters -- Fiction

ISBN 0-689-83601-5; 0-689-83602-3 pa

LC 00-20043

When he is wrongly accused of gravely injuring his baby half-sister, thirteen-year-old Branwell loses his power of speech and only his friend Connor is able to reach him and uncover the truth about what really happened

"A compelling mystery that is also a moving story of family, friendship, and seduction." Booklist

★ The **view** from Saturday. Atheneum Bks. for Young Readers 1996 163p $16.95; pa $5.99

Grades: 4 5 6 7   **Fic**

1. School stories 2. Friendship -- Fiction 3. Physically disabled -- Fiction

ISBN 0-689-80993-X; 0-689-81721-5 pa

LC 95-52624

Awarded the Newbery Medal, 1997

Four students, with their own individual stories, develop a special bond and attract the attention of their teacher, a paraplegic, who choses them to represent their sixth-grade class in the Academic Bowl competition

"Glowing with humor and dusted with magic. . . . Wrought with deep compassion and a keen sense of balance." Publ Wkly

Korman, Gordon

★ The **Juvie** three. Hyperion 2008 249p lib bdg $15.99

Grades: 7 8 9 10   **Fic**

1. Friendship -- Fiction 2. Juvenile delinquency -- Fiction

ISBN 978-1-4231-0158-1; 1-4231-0158-8

LC 2008-19087

Gecko, Arjay, and Terence, all in trouble with the law, must find a way to keep their halfway house open in order to stay out of juvenile detention.

"Korman keeps lots of balls in the air as he handles each boy's distinct voice and character—as well as the increasingly absurd situation—with humor and flashes of sadness." Booklist

No more dead dogs. Hyperion Bks. for Children 2000 180p $15.99; pa $5.99

Grades: 5 6 7 8   **Fic**

1. School stories 2. Theater -- Fiction

ISBN 0-7868-0531-5; 0-7868-1601-5 pa

LC 00-24313

Eighth-grade football hero Wallace Wallace is sentenced to detention attending rehearsals of the school play where, in spite of himself, he becomes wrapped up in the production and begins to suggest changes that improve not only the play but his life as well

"Humor abounds here, but underlying is the true angst of the middle school student." Voice Youth Advocates

★ **Schooled**. Hyperion Books for Children 2007 208p $15.99

Grades: 6 7 8 9   **Fic**

1. School stories 2. Hippies -- Fiction

ISBN 0-7868-5692-0

Homeschooled by his hippie grandmother, Capricorn (Cap) Anderson has never watched television, tasted a pizza, or even heard of a wedgie. But when his grandmother lands in the hospital, Cap is forced to move in with a guidance counselor and attend the local middle school.

"This rewarding novel features an engaging main character and some memorable moments of comedy, tenderness, and reflection." Booklist

★ **Son** of the mob. Hyperion Bks. for Children 2002 262p hardcover o.p. pa $7.99

Grades: 7 8 9 10   **Fic**

1. Mafia -- Fiction

ISBN 0-7868-0769-5; 0-7868-1593-0 pa

LC 2002-68672

Seventeen-year-old Vince's life is constantly complicated by the fact that he is the son of a powerful Mafia boss, a relationship that threatens to destroy his romance with the daughter of an FBI agent

"The fast-paced, tightly focused story addresses the problems of being an honest kid in a family of outlaws—and loving them anyway. Korman doesn't ignore the seamier side of mob life, but even when the subject matter gets violent . . . he keeps things light by relating his tale in the first-person voice of a humorously sarcastic yet law-abiding wise guy." Horn Book

Another title about Vince is:

Son of the mob: Hollywood hustle (2004)

Swindle. Scholastic Press 2008 252p (Swindle)

Grades: 4 5 6   **Fic**

1. Baseball cards -- Fiction 2. Swindlers and swindling

-- Fiction

ISBN 0-439-90344-0; 0-439-90345-9 pa; 978-0-439-90344-8; 978-0-439-90345-5 pa

LC 2007-17225

After unscrupulous collector S. Wendell Palomino cons him out of a valuable baseball card, sixth-grader Griffin Bing puts together a band of misfits to break into Palomino's store and steal the card back, planning to use the money to finance his father's failing invention, the SmartPick fruit picker. "Grades four to six." (Bull Cent Child Books)

"The plot is the main attraction, and its clever intricacies—silly, deceptively predictable, and seasoned with the occasional unexpected twist—do not disappoint." Booklist

Ungifted; Gordon Korman. Balzer + Bray 2012 280 p. $16.99

Grades: 4 5 6　　　　　　　　　　　　　　**Fic**

1. School stories 2. Humorous fiction 3. Humorous stories 4. Robots -- Fiction 5. Schools -- Fiction 6. Behavior -- Fiction 7. Robotics -- Fiction 8. Middle schools -- Fiction 9. Gifted children -- Fiction

ISBN 006174266X; 9780061742668

LC 2012008408

In this children's book, "hyperactive, heedless Donovan Curtis whacks a school statue of Atlas with a stick, which sends the huge metal globe on Atlas's shoulders rolling into the gym during a basketball game, which lands Donovan in the superintendent's office, where his name is mistakenly entered by the irate administrator onto a list of candidates for the district's middle-school gifted program." The plot includes "Donovan's shallow yet indispensable contribution to his team's robotics competition." (Bulletin of the Center for Children's Books)

Zoobreak. Scholastic Press 2009 230p $16.99; pa $6.99

Grades: 3 4 5 6　　　　　　　　　　　　　**Fic**

1. Adventure fiction 2. Zoos -- Fiction 3. Theft -- Fiction 4. Long Island (N.Y.) -- Fiction 5. Lost and found possessions -- Fiction

ISBN 978-0-545-12499-7; 0-545-12499-9; 978-0-545-12500-0 pa; 0-545-12500-6 pa

LC 2009015456

Sequel to: Swindle (2008)

After a class trip to a floating zoo where animals are mistreated and Savannah's missing pet monkey is found in a cage, Long Island sixth-grader Griffin Bing and his band of misfits plan a rescue.

"Both children and adults will find the story fast moving and enjoyable. The often-unpredictable plot is interesting, full of humor, and good fun." Voice Youth Advocates

Kositsky, Lynne

The **thought** of high windows. Kids Can Press 2004 175p hardcover o.p. pa $6.95

Grades: 7 8 9 10　　　　　　　　　　　　**Fic**

1. Jews -- Fiction 2. Holocaust, 1933-1945 -- Fiction

ISBN 1-55337-621-8; 1-55337-622-6 pa

"Esther describes her life as one of a group of Jewish children taken from Germany to France by the Red Cross during World War II. The novel begins when she is 15 and living in a French castle; her childhood in Berlin is described

through flashbacks. . . . Based on true events, this is an immediate, painfully honest story." SLJ

Koss, Amy Goldman

The **girls**. Dial Bks. for Young Readers 2000 121p $16.99; pa $5.99

Grades: 5 6 7 8　　　　　　　　　　　　**Fic**

1. Friendship -- Fiction

ISBN 0-8037-2494-2; 0-14-230033-0 pa

LC 99-19318

"This provocative page-turner will be passed from one girl to the next." SLJ

Poison Ivy. Roaring Brook Press 2006 166p $16.96

Grades: 7 8 9 10　　　　　　　　　　　**Fic**

1. School stories 2. Bullies -- Fiction

ISBN 1-59643-118-0

LC 2005-17256

In a government class three popular girls undergo a mock trial for their ruthless bullying of a classmate.

"Realistic dialogue and fast-paced action will hold interest, and the final verdict is unsettling, but not unexpected." SLJ

Side effects; 1st ed.; Roaring Brook Press 2006 143p $16.95

Grades: 6 7 8 9　　　　　　　　　　　　**Fic**

1. Cancer -- Fiction

ISBN 978-1-59643-167-6; 1-59643-167-9

LC 2005-31473

Everything changes for Isabelle, not quite fifteen, when she is diagnosed with lymphoma—but eventually she survives and even thrives.

"Koss refuses to glamorize Issy's illness or treatment. Instead, she settles for an honesty and frankness that will both challenge and enlighten readers." Booklist

Kostick, Conor

★ **Epic**. Viking 2007 364p $17.99

Grades: 7 8 9 10　　　　　　　　　　　**Fic**

1. Fantasy fiction 2. Video games -- Fiction

ISBN 0-670-06179-4; 978-0-670-06179-2

LC 2006-19958

On New Earth, a world based on a video role-playing game, fourteen-year-old Erik persuades his friends to aid him in some unusual gambits in order to save his father from exile and safeguard the futures of each of their families.

"There is intrigue and mystery throughout this captivating page-turner. Veins of moral and ethical social situations and decisions provide some great opportunities for discussion. Well written and engaging." SLJ

Other titles in this series are:

Edda (2011)

Saga (2008)

Krieg, Jim

★ **Griff** Carver, hallway patrol. Razorbill 2010 224p $15.99

Grades: 4 5 6 7　　　　　　　　　　　　**Fic**

1. School stories 2. Counterfeits and counterfeiting --

Fiction
ISBN 978-1-59514-276-4; 1-59514-276-2

LC 2009-32553

Legendary Griff Carver joins the Rampart Middle
School Hallway Patrol and, with the help of his friend Tommy, Griff solves the case of counterfeit hall passes.

"With comically over-the-top cop lingo . . . Griff and
Tommy tell their stories through incident reports and interviews, adding drama and humor to the most mundane aspects
of school. . . . Krieg will keep readers chuckling through the
hilarious but action-packed showdown." Publ Wkly

Krisher, Trudy
  Fallout. Holiday House 2006 315p $17.95
Grades: 7 8 9 10   Fic
  1. Friendship -- Fiction 2. Prejudices -- Fiction 3.
North Carolina -- Fiction
  ISBN 978-0-8234-2035-3; 0-8234-2035-3

LC 2006-41193

The move of an unconventional Hollywood family to a
coastal North Carolina town in the early 1950s results not
only in an unlikely friendship between high school age Genevieve and newcomer Brenda but also in a challenge to traditional ways of thinking.

"This is an excellent novel for teens searching for a
good story with a well-paced and action-filled plot that challenges them to think about the importance of voicing their
opinions." SLJ

Krishnaswami, Uma
  ★ The **grand** plan to fix everything; [illustra-
tions by Abigail Halpin] Atheneum Books for Young
Readers 2011 224p il $16.99
Grades: 4 5 6 7   Fic
  1. India -- Fiction 2. Actors -- Fiction 3. Moving
-- Fiction 4. Friendship -- Fiction 5. East Indian
Americans -- Fiction
  ISBN 978-1-4169-9589-0; 1-4169-9589-7

LC 2010035145

Eleven-year-old Dini loves movies, and so when she
learns that her family is moving to India for two years,
her devastation over leaving her best friend in Maryland is
tempered by the possibility of meeting her favorite actress,
Dolly Singh.

"An out-of-the-ordinary setting, a distinctive middle-
grade character with an unusual passion, and the pace of
a lively Bollywood 'fillum' make this novel a delight."
Publ Wkly

Krokos, Dan
  False memory; Dan Krokos. Disney Press 2012
327 p. $17.99
Grades: 6 7 8 9   Fic
  1. Secrecy -- Fiction 2. Teenagers -- Fiction 3. Genetic
transformation 4. Science fiction 5. Memory -- Fiction
6. Genetic engineering -- Fiction
  ISBN 1423149769; 9781423149767

LC 2011053532

In author Dan Krokos' book, "Miranda North wakes up
alone on a park bench with no memory. In her panic, she
releases a mysterious energy that incites pure terror in everyone around her . . . Miranda discovers she was trained

to be a weapon and is part of an elite force of genetically-
altered teens who possess flawless combat skills and powers
strong enough to destroy a city . . . Then Miranda uncovers a dark truth that sets her team on the run. Suddenly her
past doesn't seem to matter when there may not be a future."
(Publisher's note)

Kuehn, Stephanie
  Complicit; Stephanie Kuehn. St. Martin's Griffin
2014 256 p. illustrations (hardback) $19.99
Grades: 8 9 10 11 12   Fic
  1. Orphans -- Fiction 2. Mental illness -- Fiction 3.
Private schools -- Fiction 4. Brothers and sisters --
Fiction 5. Amnesia -- Fiction 6. Schools -- Fiction
  ISBN 1250044596; 9781250044594

LC 2014008117

"Cate is out of juvie. For her little brother, 17-year-old
Jamie, that's bad. It's been two years since Cate horribly injured a rival by setting a barn on fire. This was the last in
a long series of tempestuous, violent acts Cate committed
since she and Jamie were adopted following the murder of
their mother. With Cate locked up, Jamie is almost a whole
being. . . . But Cate's return brings everything flooding
back." (Booklist)

"...every page shows a firm, surprising choice, whether
you like it or not. Cate, naturally, is the main event, the alter-
natingly irrational, gentle, explosive, and enigmatic center
of this fast, black whirlpool of a novel." (Booklist)

Kuhlman, Evan
  ★ The **last** invisible boy; written by Evan Kuhlman; illustrated by J. P. Coovert. Atheneum Books
for Young Readers 2008 233p il $16.99; pa $5.99
Grades: 4 5 6 7   Fic
  1. School stories 2. Ohio -- Fiction 3. Bereavement
-- Fiction 4. Family life -- Fiction 5. Father-son
relationship -- Fiction
  ISBN 978-1-4169-5797-3; 1-4169-5797-9; 978-1-
4169-6089-8 pa; 1-4169-6089-9 pa

LC 2007-40258

In the wake of his father's sudden death, twelve-year-
old Finn feels he is becoming invisible as his hair and skin
become whiter by the day, and so he writes and illustrates a
book to try to understand what is happening and to hold on
to himself and his father

"Vivid details . . . add depth to the characterizations and
grow in meaning as the story progresses. . . . Finn's distinct
narrative voice, and the sweet precision with which the story
unfolds, give this title a touching resonance." Booklist

Kurti, Richard
  Monkey wars; Richard Kurti. Delacorte Press
2015 416 p. (hardcover) $17.99
Grades: 7 8 9 10 11 12   Fic
  1. War 2. Monkeys -- Fiction 3. Human-animal
relationship -- Fiction 4. War -- Fiction 5. Langurs
-- Fiction 6. Rhesus monkey -- Fiction
  ISBN 0385744412; 9780375991653; 9780385744416

LC 2014038203

In this novel by Richard Kurti, "when rhesus monkeys
are brutally massacred on the dusty streets of Kolkata by
a troop of power-hungry langur monkeys, Mico, a privi-

leged langur, becomes entangled in the secrets at the heart of his troop's leadership. He feels compelled to help the few surviving rhesus, especially Papina, a young female he befriends, even though doing so goes against everything he's been taught." (Publisher's note)

"Teens will enjoy this page-turner parable of war through the eyes of rival monkey troops in India. The gentle rhesus monkeys are invaded by their enemies, the langur, in a territorial land grab. . . . This book will be useful in discussions about apathy versus taking a stand, the domination of one culture over another through time, ethnic cleansing, relocation, boundaries, and genocide. Highly recommended, this book is great fodder for debate and discussion." VOYA

Kurtz, Chris

The **adventures** of a South Pole pig; a novel of snow and courage. Chris Kurtz; illustrations by Jennifer Black Reinhardt. Harcourt Children's Books, Houghton Mifflin Harcourt 2013 288 p. $16.99

Grades: 4 5 6 7   **Fic**

1. Sled dog racing -- Fiction 2. Adventure fiction 3. Dogs -- Fiction 4. Pigs -- Fiction 5. Sled dogs -- Fiction 6. Antarctica -- Fiction 7. Dogsledding -- Fiction 8. Adventure and adventurers -- Fiction

ISBN 0547634552; 9780547634555

LC 2012027226

In this children's story, by Chris Kurtz, illustrated by Jennifer Black Reinhardt, "the day Flora spots a team of sled dogs is the day she sets her heart on becoming a sled pig. Before she knows it, she's on board a ship to Antarctica for the most exhilarating--and dangerous--adventure of her life." (Publisher's note)

Kwasney, Michelle D.

Itch; [by] Michelle D. Kwasney. Henry Holt 2008 240p $16.95

Grades: 5 6 7 8   **Fic**

1. School stories 2. Ohio -- Fiction 3. Mothers -- Fiction 4. Friendship -- Fiction 5. Child abuse -- Fiction 6. Grandparents -- Fiction

ISBN 978-0-8050-8083-4; 0-8050-8083-X

LC 2007027573

In 1968, after the death of her beloved Gramps, Delores "Itch" Colchester and her grandmother move from Florida to an Ohio trailer park, where she meets new people and, when she learns that a friend is being abused by her mother, tries her best to emulate her plain-spoken grandfather

"The 1960s references provide the realistic backdrop for this moving, believable story. Sympathetic well-drawn characters draw the reader into Delores' personal struggles." Booklist

L'Engle, Madeleine

★ A **wrinkle** in time. Farrar, Straus & Giroux 1962 211p $17; pa $7.99

Grades: 5 6 7 8 9 10   **Fic**

1. Fantasy fiction

ISBN 0-374-38613-7; 0-312-36754-6 pa

Awarded The Newbery Medal, 1963

ALA YALSA Margaret A. Edwards Award (1998)

This book "makes unusual demands on the imagination and consequently gives great rewards." Horn Book

Other titles in this series are:
A swiftly tilting planet (1978)
A wind in the door (1973)

La Fevers, R. L.

Theodosia and the eyes of Horus; [illustrated by Yoko Tanaka] Houghton Mifflin Harcourt 2010 375p il $16

Grades: 4 5 6 7   **Fic**

1. Adventure fiction 2. Magic -- Fiction 3. Museums -- Fiction 4. Family life -- Fiction 5. London (England) -- Fiction

ISBN 978-0-547-22592-0; 0-547-22592-X

Eleven-year-old Theodosia's ability to detect black magic raises her suspicions about a magician known as the Great Awi Bubu, while Henry, home for the spring holidays, discovers an artifact at the Museum of Legends and Antiquities that is coveted by every black-cloaked occultist in London.

"Once again, supernaturally talented Theodosia navigates around her etiquette-obsessed grandmother and absentminded parents in a suspenseful, satisfying fantasy that's filled with the specifics of magical ritual sure to delight readers." Booklist

Theodosia and the last pharaoh; illustrated by Yoko Tanaka. Houghton Mifflin Harcourt 2011 394p il $16.99

Grades: 4 5 6 7   **Fic**

1. Adventure fiction 2. Egypt -- Fiction 3. Magic -- Fiction 4. Museums -- Fiction 5. Family life -- Fiction

ISBN 978-0-547-39018-5; 0-547-39018-1

LC 2010032224

When eleven-year-old Theodosia and her cat, Isis, travel to Egypt to return the Orb of Ra and the Emerald Tablet, she hopes to learn more about her origins but finds, instead, the Serpents of Chaos and a precious treasure that suddenly appears and disappears.

"Tanaka's drawings nicely extend the action." Booklist

Theodosia and the Serpents of Chaos; illustrated by Yoko Tanaka. Houghton Mifflin 2007 343p il $16; pa $6.99

Grades: 4 5 6 7   **Fic**

1. Adventure fiction 2. Egypt -- Fiction 3. Magic -- Fiction 4. Museums -- Fiction 5. London (England) -- Fiction

ISBN 978-0-618-75638-4; 0-618-75638-8; 978-0-618-99976-7 pa; 0-618-99976-0 pa

LC 2006-34284

Set in 1906 London and Cairo, this mystery adventure introduces an intrepid heroine—Theodosia Throckmorton, who is thrust into the heart of a mystery when she learns an ancient Egyptian amulet carries a curse that threatens to crumble the British Empire

"It's the delicious, precise, and atmospheric details (nicely extended in Tanaka's few, stylized illustrations) that will capture and hold readers." Booklist

Other titles about Theodosia are:
Theodosia and the Staff of Osiris (2008)
Theodosia and the Eyes of Horus (2010)
Theodosia and the last Pharoah (2011)

Theodosia and the Staff of Osiris; [by] R.L. LaFevers; illustrated by Yoko Tanaka. Houghton Mifflin Co. 2008 387p il $16

Grades: 4 5 6 7 **Fic**

1. Adventure fiction 2. Magic -- Fiction 3. Mummies -- Fiction 4. Museums -- Fiction 5. Family life -- Fiction 6. London (England) -- Fiction

ISBN 978-0-618-92764-7; 0-618-92764-6

LC 2008007277

When mummies go missing all over London, eleven-year-old Theodosia puts aside her fight against the Serpents of Chaos to save her father, who is suspected in the thefts, all the while avoiding a string of new governesses.

"Clever and exciting just like the previous book, this also features a layered relationship between Theodosia and her grandmother." Booklist

La Valley, Josanne

The **Vine** basket; by Josanne La Valley. Clarion Books 2013 252 p. (hardcover) $16.99

Grades: 4 5 6 7 8 **Fic**

1. China -- Fiction 2. Farm life -- Fiction 3. Basket making -- Fiction 4. Ethnic relations -- Fiction 5. Farm life -- China -- Fiction 6. Fathers and daughters -- Fiction 7. Uighur (Turkic people) -- Fiction

ISBN 0547848013; 9780547848013

LC 2012021007

Asian/Pacific American Awards for Literature: Children's Literature Honor (2014)

In this novel, by Josanne La Valley, "things aren't looking good for fourteen-year-old Mehrigul. She yearns to be in school, but she's needed on the family farm. . . . Her only hope is an American woman who buys one of her decorative vine baskets for a staggering sum and says she will return in three weeks for more. Mehrigul must brave terrible storms, torn-up hands from working the fields, and her father's scorn to get the baskets done." (Publisher's note)

"The vivid and authentic sense of place, custom, and politics serves as an effective vehicle for the skillfully characterized, emotionally charged story. . . . The realistic and satisfying resolution will resonate with readers . . . . An absorbing read and an excellent choice for expanding global understanding." SLJ

Laban, Elizabeth

The **Tragedy** Paper; Elizabeth LaBan. Alfred A. Knopf 2013 320 p. $17.99

Grades: 7 8 9 10 11 12 **Fic**

1. Love stories 2. School stories 3. Albinos and albinism -- Fiction 4. Schools -- Fiction 5. High schools -- Fiction 6. Boarding schools -- Fiction 7. Dating (Social customs) -- Fiction 8. Interpersonal relations -- Fiction

ISBN 0375870407; 9780375870408; 9780375970405; 9780375989124

LC 2012011294

This novel by Elizabeth Laban "follows the story of Tim Macbeth, a seventeen-year-old albino and a recent transfer to the prestigious Irving School. . . . He finds himself falling for the quintessential 'It' girl, Vanessa Sheller. . . . Vanessa is into him, too, but she can kiss her social status goodbye if anyone ever finds out. Tim and Vanessa begin a clandestine romance, but looming over them is the Tragedy Paper, Irving's version of a senior year thesis." (Publisher's note)

Lacey, Josh

Island of Thieves; Josh Lacey. Houghton Mifflin 2012 228 p.

Grades: 4 5 6 7 8 **Fic**

1. Peru -- Fiction 2. Adventure fiction 3. Uncles -- Fiction 4. Pirates -- Fiction 5. Buried treasure -- Fiction 6. Islands -- Fiction 7. Mystery and detective stories 8. Adventure and adventurers -- Fiction

ISBN 0547763271; 9780547763279

LC 2011033893

In this children's novel, a boy takes part in "swashbuckling adventures in faraway places, freed from the strictures of parents, school, siblings and caregivers. . . . Tom nearly ruins his parents' vacation by accidentally burning down the shed in his backyard. . . . Harvey welcomes Tom . . . but as soon as Tom's parents leave, he starts packing for Peru. . . . When he tells Tom it's because he has an opportunity to hunt for pirate treasure, Tom blackmails his uncle into taking him along." (Kirkus)

LaFaye, A.

Stella stands alone; [by] A. LaFaye. Simon & Schuster Books for Young Readers 2008 245p map $16.99

Grades: 7 8 9 10 **Fic**

1. Orphans -- Fiction 2. African Americans -- Fiction 3. Swindlers and swindling -- Fiction 4. Reconstruction (1865-1876) -- Fiction

ISBN 978-1-4169-1164-7; 1-4169-1164-2

LC 2007-38725

Fourteen-year-old Stella, orphaned just after the Civil War, fights to keep her family's plantation and fulfill her father's desire to turn land over to the people who have worked on it for generations, but first she must find her father's hidden deed and will.

"Readers will be drawn along by Stella's refusal to act helpless and sweet and her discovery of strength and kindness in unexpected places. The sadness and anger, and the wrenching legacy of slavery are present throughout." Booklist

Water steps. Milkweed Editions 2009 175p $16.95; pa $6.95

Grades: 4 5 6 7 **Fic**

1. Water -- Fiction 2. Phobias -- Fiction 3. Irish Americans -- Fiction

ISBN 978-1-57131-687-5; 1-57131-687-6; 978-1-57131-686-8 pa; 1-57131-686-8 pa

LC 2008011684

Eleven-year-old Kyna, terrified of water since her family drowned in a storm that nearly took her life as well, works to overcome her phobia when her adoptive parents, Irish immigrants with a mysterious past, rent a cabin on Lake Champlain for the summer.

"The language is almost poetic with its use of sensory detail, alliteration, and precise word choices. A satisfying story of overcoming one's fears and discovering secrets." SLJ

LaFleur, Suzanne M.

★ **Love,** Aubrey. Wendy Lamb Books 2009 262p $15.99; lib bdg $18.99

Grades: 5 6 7 8 **Fic**

1. School stories 2. Letters -- Fiction 3. Vermont -- Fiction 4. Friendship -- Fiction 5. Bereavement -- Fiction 6. Grandmothers -- Fiction 7. Abandoned children -- Fiction 8. Depression (Psychology) -- Fiction

ISBN 978-0-385-73774-6; 0-385-73774-2; 978-0-385-90686-9 lib bdg; 0-385-90686-2 lib bdg

LC 2008-31742

While living with her Gram in Vermont, eleven-year-old Aubrey writes letters as a way of dealing with losing her father and sister in a car accident, and then being abandoned by her grief-stricken mother.

Aubrey's "detailed progression from denial to acceptance makes her both brave and credible in this honest and realistic portrayal of grief." Kirkus

Lai, Thanhha

★ **Inside** out and back again. Harper 2011 262p $15.99

Grades: 4 5 6 7 **Fic**

1. Novels in verse 2. Alabama -- Fiction 3. Vietnam -- Fiction 4. Immigrants -- Fiction 5. Vietnamese Americans -- Fiction

ISBN 978-0-06-196278-3; 0-06-196278-3

LC 2010007855

"For all the ten years of her life, Hà has only known Saigon: the thrills of its markets, the joy of its traditions, and the warmth of her friends close by. But now the Vietnam War has reached her home. Hà and her family are forced to flee as Saigon falls, and they board a ship headed toward hope. In America, Hà discovers the foreign world of Alabama: the coldness of its strangers, the dullness of its food . . . and the strength of her very own family." (Publisher's note)

"Based on Lai's personal experience, this first novel captures a child-refugee's struggle with rare honesty. Written in accessible, short free-verse poems." Booklist

★ **Listen**, Slowly; Thanhha Lai. Harpercollins Childrens Books 2015 272 p. illustration $16.99

Grades: 4 5 6 7 8 **Fic**

1. Culture 2. Family -- Fiction 3. Vietnam -- Fiction 4. Families -- Fiction 5. Grandmothers -- Fiction 6. Vietnam War, 1961-1975 -- Missing in action -- Fiction

ISBN 0062229184; 9780062229182

"A California girl born and raised, Mai . . . has to travel to Vietnam with her grandmother, who is going back to find out what really happened to her husband during the Vietnam War. Mai's parents think this trip will be a great opportunity for their out-of-touch daughter to learn more about her culture. But to Mai, those are their roots, not her own. To survive her trip, Mai must find a balance between her two completely different worlds." (Publisher's note)

"Gracefully written and enriched by apposite figures of speech, Listen, Slowly is a superb, sometimes humorous, always thought-provoking coming-of-age story." Booklist

Lairamore, Dawn

Ivy and the meanstalk. Holiday House 2011 227p $16.95

Grades: 4 5 6 7 **Fic**

1. Fairy tales 2. Giants -- Fiction 3. Dragons -- Fiction 4. Princesses -- Fiction

ISBN 978-0-8234-2392-7; 0-8234-2392-1

LC 2010048627

Sequel to: Ivy's ever after (2010)

Fourteen-year-old Princess Ivy wants nothing more than to have a little fun in the company of her dragon friend, Elridge, but unless she can recover the magical harp snatched by a thieving youth named Jack long ago, her entire kingdom will suffer an unspeakable fate.

This is "delightful and humorous. . . . Lairamore's well-developed characters are excellent riffs on fairy-tale traditions. . . . Various settings are depicted in rich detail while never detracting from the narrative. The plot is filled with action-packed scenes." SLJ

★ **Ivy's** ever after. Holiday House 2010 311p $16.95

Grades: 4 5 6 7 **Fic**

1. Fairy tales 2. Dragons -- Fiction 3. Princesses -- Fiction

ISBN 978-0-8234-2261-6; 0-8234-2261-5

LC 2009-43288

Fourteen-year-old Ivy, a most unroyal princess, befriends Elridge, the dragon sent to keep her in a tower, and together they set out on a perilous quest to find Ivy's fairy godmother, who may be able to save both from their dire fates.

"Ivy is an engaging alternative to the standard damsel-in-distress figure, and with a lushly vivid setting, witty dialogue, and lots of adventure, this well-plotted first novel will appeal to fans of Vivian Vande Velde's A Hidden Magic (1985) and A Well-Timed Enchantment (1990)." Booklist

Followed by: Ivy and the meanstalk (2011)

Laird, Elizabeth

The **betrayal** of Maggie Blair. Houghton Mifflin 2011 423p il $16.99

Grades: 7 8 9 10 **Fic**

1. Uncles -- Fiction 2. Witchcraft -- Fiction 3. Scotland -- History -- 17th century -- Fiction

ISBN 978-0-547-34126-2; 0-547-34126-1

LC 2010-25120

In seventeenth-century Scotland, sixteen-year-old Maggie Blair is sentenced to be hanged as a witch but escapes to the home of her uncle, placing him and his family in great danger as she risks her life to save them all from the King's men.

"Laird seamlessly weaves a fairly comprehensive history lesson into an engaging, lively story." Bull Cent Child Books

A **little** piece of ground; [by] Elizabeth Laird; with Sonia Nimr. Haymarket Books 2006 216p pa $9.95

Grades: 6 7 8 9 10 **Fic**

1. Palestine -- Fiction 2. Israel-Arab conflicts -- Fiction

ISBN 978-1-931859-38-7; 1-931859-38-8

LC 2006008707

During the Israeli occupation of Ramallah in the West Bank of Palestine, twelve-year-old Karim and his friends create a secret place for themselves where they can momentarily forget the horrors of war.

"Throughout this powerful narrative, the authors remain true to Karim's character and reactions. He is a typical self-centered adolescent. . . . [This book] deserves serious attention and discussion." SLJ

Lake, Nick

Blood ninja II: the revenge of Lord Oda. Simon and Schuster Books for Young Readers 2010 377p $16.99

Grades: 7 8 9 10 11   **Fic**

1. Japan -- Fiction 2. Ninja -- Fiction 3. Vampires -- Fiction

ISBN 978-1-4169-8629-4; 1-4169-8629-4

LC 2010-10110

Sequel to: Blood ninja (2009)

In sixteenth-century Japan, Taro, a vampire like all ninja warriors, tries to protect his mother and defeat the power-hungry Lord Oda, who he believed was dead.

"Ghosts and Zen Buddhist philosophy add a surprising and sometimes effective depth to the story." Booklist

Lancaster, Mike A.

The future we left behind; Mike A. Lancaster. Egmont USA 2012 367 p. (hardback) $16.99

Grades: 7 8 9 10   **Fic**

1. Science fiction 2. Cults -- Fiction 3. England -- Fiction 4. Computer programs -- Fiction 5. Family life -- England -- Fiction 6. Technological innovations -- Fiction

ISBN 1606844105; 9781606844106; 9781606844113

LC 2012003794

Sequel to: Human.4

This sequel to "Human.4" is set in the future. Here, "Peter is the son of the man who saved the world by inventing robot bees. Destined by his wealthy genius father for a future in science, Peter rebels against both by enrolling in a literature class and befriending Alpha, a girl in a wacky religious cult. Alpha is a Strakerite, following the ancient tapes of Kyle Straker. Kyle and his girlfriend Lilly believed humans are regularly upgraded by aliens. Skeptical at first, Peter is soon convinced." (Kirkus)

★ Human.4. Egmont USA 2011 231p $16.99

Grades: 7 8 9 10   **Fic**

1. Science fiction 2. Computers -- Fiction 3. Family life -- Fiction 4. Great Britain -- Fiction

ISBN 978-1-6068-4099-3; 1-6068-4099-1

LC 2010030313

Twenty-first century fourteen-year-old Kyle was hypnotized when humanity was upgraded to 1.0 and he, incompatible with the new technology, exposes its terrifying impact in a tape-recording found by the superhumans of the future.

"Lancaster fashions a fast-paced, upsetting little thriller punctuated by ominous editorial notes that translate Kyle's details for the futuristic audience." Booklist

Landon, Kristen

The limit. Aladdin 2010 291p $15.99

Grades: 6 7 8 9   **Fic**

1. Science fiction

ISBN 978-1-4424-0271-3; 1-4424-0271-7

LC 2010-12707

When his family exceeds its legal debt limit, thirteen-year-old Matt is sent to the Federal Debt Rehabilitation Agency workhouse, where he discovers illicit activities are being carried out using the children who have been placed there.

"From the first sentence . . . Landon captures readers' attention and keeps it. This first-person, part realistic fiction, part fantasy should appeal to readers looking for high-action adventure." Booklist

Landy, Derek

★ Skulduggery Pleasant. HarperCollinsPublishers 2007 392p $17.99; lib bdg $18.89; pa $7.99

Grades: 4 5 6 7   **Fic**

1. Fantasy fiction 2. Magic -- Fiction

ISBN 978-0-06-123115-5; 0-06-123115-0; 978-0-06-123116-2 lib bdg; 0-06-123116-9 lib bdg; 978-0-06-123117-9 pa; 0-06-123117-7 pa

LC 2006-29403

When twelve-year-old Stephanie inherits her weird uncle's estate, she must join forces with Skulduggery Pleasant, a skeleton mage, to save the world from the Faceless Ones

This "is a rich fantasy that is as engaging in its creative protagonists and villains as it is in the lightning-paced plot and sharp humor." Bulletin Cent Child Books

Other titles in this series are:

Playing with fire (2008)

The faceless ones (2009)

Lane, Andrew

Black ice; Andrew Lane. Farrar Straus Giroux 2013 288 p. (Sherlock Holmes. The legend begins) (hardcover) $17.99

Grades: 5 6 7 8   **Fic**

1. Mystery fiction 2. Holmes, Sherlock (Fictional character) -- Fiction 3. Murder -- Fiction 4. Mystery and detective stories 5. Moscow (Russia) -- History -- 19th century -- Fiction 6. Russia -- History -- Alexander II, 1855-1881 -- Fiction 7. Great Britain -- History -- Victoria, 1837-1901 -- Fiction

ISBN 0374387699; 9780374387693

LC 2012004996

This novel, by Andrew Lane, is the third book of the "Sherlock Holmes: The Legend Begins" series. "When Sherlock and Amyus Crowe, his American tutor, visit Sherlock's brother, Mycroft, in London, all they are expecting is lunch and some polite conversation. What they find shocks both of them to the core: a locked room, a dead body, and Mycroft holding a knife. . . . Threatened with the gallows, Mycroft needs Sherlock to save him." (Publisher's note)

Rebel fire; Andrew Lane. Farrar Straus Giroux 2012 343 p. (Sherlock Holmes. The legend begins) $16.99

Grades: 5 6 7 8   **Fic**

1. Mystery fiction 2. Holmes, Sherlock (Fictional character) -- Fiction 3. Mystery and detective stories 4. Great Britain -- History -- Victoria, 1837-1901 -- Fiction

ISBN 0374387680; 9780374387686

LC 2011000124

This novel, by Andrew Lane, is part of the "Sherlock Holmes: The Legend Begins" series. "Fourteen-year-old Sherlock Holmes knows that Amyus Crowe, his mysterious American tutor, has some dark secrets. But he didn't expect to find John Wilkes Booth, the notorious assassin, apparently alive and well in England--and Crowe somehow mixed up in it. . . . And so begins an adventure that will take Sherlock across the Atlantic, to the center of a deadly web." (Publisher's note)

Includes bibliographical references

Lane, Dakota

Gothic Lolita; a mystical thriller. words and photographs by Dakota Lane. Atheneum Books for Young Readers 2008 194p il $17.99

Grades: 8 9 10 11 12 **Fic**

1. Japan -- Fiction 2. Weblogs -- Fiction 3. Bereavement -- Fiction 4. Hollywood (Calif.) -- Fiction 5. Racially mixed people -- Fiction

ISBN 978-1-4169-1396-2; 1-4169-1396-3

LC 2008-15390

Lane "focuses on two half-Japanese, half-American girls who forge an unusual bond over their blogs, loneliness and fascination with the gothic Lolita subculture. Chelsea is in L.A. and Miya is in Japan. . . . Readers will find themselves quickly engrossed." Publ Wkly

Lange, Erin Jade

Butter; Erin Jade Lange. Bloomsbury 2012 296 p. (hardback) $16.99

Grades: 8 9 10 11 12 **Fic**

1. Eating habits 2. Suicide -- Fiction 3. Teenagers -- Fiction 4. Obesity -- Fiction 5. Eating disorders -- Fiction

ISBN 1599907801; 9781599907802

LC 2011045509

In author Erin Jade Lange's book, a "lonely obese boy everyone calls 'Butter' is about to make history. He is going to eat himself to death-live on the Internet-and everyone is invited to watch. When he first makes the announcement online to his classmates, Butter expects pity, insults, and possibly sheer indifference. What he gets are morbid cheerleaders rallying around his deadly plan. Yet as their dark encouragement grows, it begins to feel a lot like popularity . . . But what happens when Butter reaches his suicide deadline?" (Publisher's note)

Langrish, Katherine

★ **The shadow** hunt. Harper 2010 322p $16.99

Grades: 6 7 8 9 **Fic**

1. Fantasy fiction

ISBN 978-0-06-111676-6; 0-06-111676-9

LC 2009-930446

First published 2009 in the United Kingdom

"Thirteen-year-old Wolf is running away from the abbey where he was raised when he unexpectedly meets renowned knight Sir Hugo. Together, they capture a mysterious elf-child and return to Hugo's castle, where Wolf will be allowed to stay—if he gets the elf-child to speak. . . . In this medieval fantasy, Langrish . . . provides a vividly rendered, engrossing tale. Epic themes—good and evil, faith and doubt, sin and redemption—are made personal and poignant

through the losses and longings of the notably well-drawn, dimensional main characters." Booklist

Larbalestier, Justine

How to ditch your fairy. Bloomsbury 2008 307p $16.99

Grades: 6 7 8 9 10 **Fic**

1. Magic -- Fiction 2. Fairies -- Fiction

ISBN 978-1-59990-301-9; 1-59990-301-6

LC 2008-02408

In a world in which everyone has a personal fairy who tends to one aspect of daily life, fourteen-year-old Charlie decides she does not want hers—a parking fairy—and embarks on a series of misadventures designed to rid herself of the invisible sprite and replace it with a better one, like her friend Rochelle's shopping fairy.

"Charlie is totally likable, smart, and sarcastic, a perfectly self-involved, insecure teen. At its core, this is a typical coming-of-age story, but the addition of the fairies, the slightly alternative setting, and the made-up slang make it much more." SLJ

Magic lessons. Razorbill 2006 275p $16.99; pa $7.99

Grades: 8 9 10 11 12 **Fic**

1. Magic -- Fiction 2. Australia -- Fiction 3. Space and time -- Fiction 4. New York (N.Y.) -- Fiction

ISBN 1-59514-054-9; 1-59514-124-3 pa

LC 2005-23870

Sequel to Magic or madness (2005)

When fifteen-year-old Reason is pulled through the magical door connecting New York City with the Sydney, Australia, home of her grandmother, she encounters an impossibly ancient man who seems to have some purpose in mind for her.

"Larbalestier creates complex relationships among her characters, and their realistic flaws, combined with the sense of danger throughout, make this a good choice for even reluctant readers." SLJ

Followed by Magic's child (2007)

Magic or madness. Razorbill 2005 288p $16.99; pa $7.99

Grades: 8 9 10 11 12 **Fic**

1. Magic -- Fiction 2. Australia -- Fiction 3. Grandmothers -- Fiction 4. Space and time -- Fiction 5. New York (N.Y.) -- Fiction

ISBN 1-59514-022-0; 1-59514-124-3 pa

LC 2004-18263

From the Sydney, Australia home of a grandmother she believes is a witch, fifteen-year-old Reason Cansino is magically transported to New York City, where she discovers that friends and foes can be hard to distinguish

"Readers looking for layered, understated fantasy will follow the looping paths of Larbalestier's fine writing . . . with gratitude and awe." Booklist

Other titles about Reason Cansino are:

Magic lessons (2006)

Magic's child (2007)

Larson, Kirby

Dash; Kirby Larson. Scholastic Press 2014 256 p. (hardcover) $16.99

Grades: 4 5 6 7   **Fic**

1. Dogs -- Fiction 2. Japanese Americans -- Evacuation and relocation, 1942-1945 3. World War, 1939-1945 -- Fiction 4. Japanese American children -- Fiction 5. Puyallup Assembly Center (Puyallup, Wash.) -- Fiction 6. Japanese Americans -- Evacuation and relocation, 1942-1945 -- Fiction

ISBN 0545416353; 9780545416351

LC 2013042525

"Although Mitsi Kashino and her family are swept up in the wave of anti-Japanese sentiment following the attack on Pearl Harbor, Mitsi never expects to lose her home--or her beloved dog, Dash. But, as World War II rages and people of Japanese descent are forced into incarceration camps, Mitsi is separated from Dash, her classmates, and life as she knows it." (Publisher's note)

"Spot-on dialogue, careful cultural details and the inclusion of specific historical characters such as artist Eddie Sato make this an educational read as well as a heartwarming one. An author's note adds further authenticity. This emotionally satisfying and thought-provoking book will have readers pulling for Mitsi and Dash." Kirkus

Hattie Big Sky. Delacorte Press 2006 289p hardcover o.p. pa $6.99

Grades: 6 7 8 9 10   **Fic**

1. Montana -- Fiction 2. Orphans -- Fiction 3. World War, 1914-1918 -- Fiction 4. Frontier and pioneer life -- Fiction

ISBN 0-385-73313-5; 0-385-73595-2 pa

LC 2005-35039

A Newbery Medal honor book, 2007

After inheriting her uncle's homesteading claim in Montana, sixteen-year-old-orphan Hattie Brooks travels from Iowa in 1917 to make a home for herself, befriends a German-American family and encounters some unexpected problems related to the war in Europe. "Grades six to nine." (Bull Cent Child Books)

This is "a richly textured novel full of memorable characters." Booklist

Hattie ever after; Kirby Larson. Delacorte Press 2013 240 p. (hc) $16.99

Grades: 6 7 8 9 10   **Fic**

1. Historical fiction 2. Orphans -- Fiction 3. Reporters and reporting -- Fiction 4. Self-reliance -- Fiction 5. San Francisco (Calif.) -- History -- 20th century -- Fiction

ISBN 0385737467; 9780307979681; 9780385737463; 9780385906685

LC 2012007068

Sequel to: Hattie Big Sky

In this novel, by Newbury Honor award-winning author Kirby Larson, "after leaving Uncle Chester's homestead claim, orphan Hattie Brooks throws a lasso around a new dream, even bigger than the Montana sky. She wants to be a reporter . . . , go to Grand Places, and do Grand Things, like Hattie's hero Nellie Bly. Another girl might be stymied by

this, but . . . nothing can squash her desire to write for a big city newspaper." (Publisher's note)

Includes bibliographical references

Larson, M. A.

Pennyroyal Academy; M. A. Larson. G. P. Putnam's Sons, an imprint of Penguin Group (USA) 2014 304 p. maps (hardback) $16.99

Grades: 5 6 7 8   **Fic**

1. Schools 2. Princesses -- Fiction 3. Knights and knighthood -- Fiction 4. Fantasy 5. Dragons -- Fiction 6. Schools -- Fiction 7. Witches -- Fiction 8. Military education -- Fiction 9. Adventure and adventurers -- Fiction

ISBN 0399163247; 9780399163241

LC 2014014516

In this novel by M.A. Larson, "a girl from the forest arrives in a bustling kingdom with no name and no idea why she is there, only to find herself at the center of a world at war. She enlists at Pennyroyal Academy, where princesses and knights are trained to battle the two great menaces of the day: witches and dragons. As Evie learns what it truly means to be a princess, she realizes surprising things about herself and her family." (Publisher's note)

"Forget the notion of traditional princesses. At Pennyroyal Academy, princesses are trained to fight witches and save kingdoms, and, yes, knights learn to slay dragons...the focus and detailed character development is on the young women, their hopes and dreams (sometimes dreadfully scary), their real fears, and their disappointments in themselves, their friends, and the adults around them. Since the book ends with some of the princesses and knights selected to return for another school year, Larson has left the door open for a welcome second year at Pennyroyal with Evie and her friends." Booklist

Larwood, Kieran

Freaks; Kieran Larwood. Chicken House/Scholastic 2013 256 p. $16.99

Grades: 5 6 7 8   **Fic**

1. Mystery fiction 2. Circus performers -- Fiction 3. Freak shows -- Fiction 4. Mystery and detective stories 5. Abnormalities, Human -- Fiction 6. London (England) -- History -- 19th century -- Fiction 7. Great Britain -- History -- Victoria, 1837-1901 -- Fiction

ISBN 0545474248; 9780545474245; 9780545474252

LC 2012002639

In this book, 10-year-old "Sheba, better known as the Wolfgirl for her layer of fur and ability to sprout fangs and claws, is an orphan who ends up as part of Plumpscuttle's Peculiars, a freak show that also stars a teenage ninja, a trash-talking monkey boy, a romance-writing strongman, and a woman who talks to rats. This gang of unlikely heroes gets caught up in a mystery involving missing street urchins, steampunk monstrosities, and a fiendish set of villains." (Publishers Weekly)

Laskas, Gretchen Moran

The **miner's** daughter. Simon & Schuster Books for Young Readers 2007 250p $15.99

Grades: 8 9 10 11 12   **Fic**

1. Family life -- Fiction 2. West Virginia -- Fiction 3.

Coal mines and mining -- Fiction 4. Great Depression, 1929-1939 -- Fiction
ISBN 978-1-4169-1262-0; 1-4169-1262-2

LC 2006-00684

Sixteen-year-old Willa, living in a Depression-era West Virginia mining town, works hard to help her family, experiences love and friendship, and finds an outlet for her writing when her family becomes part of the Arthurdale, West Virginia, community supported by Eleanor Roosevelt.

"Richly drawn characters and plot make this an excellent novel that explores the struggles endured by many in America in the 1930s." SLJ

Lasky, Kathryn

★ **Ashes**. Viking 2010 318p $16.99

Grades: 6 7 8 9 10 11 12 **Fic**

1. Germany -- Fiction 2. National socialism -- Fiction
ISBN 978-0-670-01157-5; 0-670-01157-6

LC 2009-33127

In 1932 Berlin, thirteen-year-old Gaby Schramm witnesses the beginning of Hitler's rise to power, as soldiers become ubiquitous, her beloved literature teacher starts wearing a jewelled swastika pin, and the family's dear friend, Albert Einstein, leaves the country while Gaby's parents secretly bury his books and papers in their small yard.

"Gaby's questioning but assertive nature helps form a compelling, readable portrait of pre-WWII Germany." Publ Wkly

Chasing Orion. Candlewick Press 2010 362p $17.99

Grades: 6 7 8 9 **Fic**

1. Indiana -- Fiction 2. Friendship -- Fiction 3. Poliomyelitis -- Fiction
ISBN 978-0-7636-3982-2; 0-7636-3982-6

LC 2009007327

In 1952, when Georgie is eleven years old, her family moves to a new Indiana neighborhood where her teenaged neighbor has polio and is in an iron lung.

"A truly extraordinary page-turner that embraces life's big and small aspects with humor and a healthy respect for its profound contradictions." Kirkus

The **escape**; Kathryn Lasky. Scholastic Press 2014 240 p. illustrations (Horses of the dawn) (hardcover) $16.99

Grades: 4 5 6 7 8 **Fic**

1. Horses -- Fiction 2. Mother-daughter relationship -- Fiction 3. Responsibility -- Fiction 4. North America -- History -- Fiction
ISBN 9780545397162; 0545397162

LC 2013037215

This book "reimagines the history of the reintroduction of horses to North America by Spanish conquistadors through the eyes of the horses they brought with them. Estrella, a plucky foal unexpectedly born on board a Spanish ship bound for the New World, is strong, brave, and wise beyond her years. She, along with three others, survives being tossed overboard into shark-infested waters by swimming to the Yucatan Peninsula. Thus begins her quest to find the land of the sweet grass only she can smell." (Booklist)

"Lasky successfully fuses fantasy and fact as she gives her equine characters credible emotional depth and underscores the tensions and disparity between Old and New World sensibilities." Pub Wkly

Hawksmaid; the untold story of Robin Hood and Maid Marian. Harper 2010 292p $16.99

Grades: 5 6 7 8 **Fic**

1. Falconry -- Fiction 2. Robin Hood (Legendary character) -- Fiction 3. Maid Marian (Legendary character) -- Fiction 4. Great Britain -- History -- 1154-1399, Plantagenets -- Fiction
ISBN 978-0-06-000071-4; 0-06-000071-6

In twelfth-century England, Matty grows up to be a master falconer, able to communicate with the devoted birds who later help her and Fynn, also known as Robin Hood, to foil Prince John's plot to steal the crown.

"Lasky nicely weaves details of 12th-century life into this suspenseful adventure whose fantasy ending may surprise but will certainly please readers." SLJ

Lone wolf. Scholastic Press 2010 219p il map (Wolves of the Beyond) $16.99

Grades: 5 6 7 8 **Fic**

1. Fantasy fiction 2. Wolves -- Fiction
ISBN 978-0-545-09310-1; 0-545-09310-4

LC 2009-17007

Abandoned by his pack, a baby wolf with a mysterious mark on his deformed paw survives and embarks on a journey that will change the world of the wolves of the Beyond.

"Lasky merges anthropomorphic fantasy with realistic details about wolves and bears to produce an almost plausible emotional narrative, complete with dialogue and personalities. . . . . The author builds a captivating world of forest, snow and volcanoes populated by intelligent animals and weaves a compelling story sure to bring readers back for the second installment." Kirkus

Other titles in this series are:

Shadow wolf (2010)
Watch wolf (2011)
Frost worlf (2011)

Latham, Irene

Leaving Gee's Bend. G.P. Putnam's Sons 2010 230p $16.99

Grades: 5 6 7 8 **Fic**

1. Quilts -- Fiction 2. Alabama -- Fiction 3. African Americans -- Fiction
ISBN 978-0-399-25179-5; 0-399-25179-0

LC 2009-08732

Ludelphia Bennett, a determined, ten-year-old African American girl in 1932 Gee's Bend, Alabama, leaves home in an effort to find medical help for her sick mother, and she recounts her ensuing adventures in a quilt she is making.

"Ludelphia's voice is authentic and memorable, and Latham captures the tension of her dangerous journey and the racism she encounters." Booklist

Lavender, William

Aftershocks. Harcourt 2006 344p $17

Grades: 8 9 10 11 12 **Fic**

1. Sex role -- Fiction 2. Earthquakes -- Fiction 3.

Chinese Americans -- Fiction 4. San Francisco (Calif.) -- Fiction 5. Father-daughter relationship -- Fiction
ISBN 0-15-205882-6

LC 2005-19695

In San Francisco from 1903 to 1908, teenager Jessie Wainwright determines to reach her goal of becoming a doctor while also trying to care for the illegitimate child of a liaison between her father and their Chinese maid.

This "is readable historical fiction about an engrossing event in U.S. history." Voice Youth Advocates

Law, Ingrid

★ **Savvy**. Dial Books for Young Readers 2008 342p $16.99

Grades: 4 5 6 7 **Fic**

1. Magic -- Fiction 2. Family life -- Fiction 3. Voyages and travels -- Fiction
ISBN 978-0-8037-3306-0; 0-8037-3306-2

LC 2007-39814

Boston Globe-Horn Book Award honor book: Fiction and Poetry (2008)

A Newbery Medal honor book, 2009

Recounts the adventures of Mississippi (Mibs) Beaumont, whose thirteenth birthday has revealed her "savvy"—a magical power unique to each member of her family—just as her father is injured in a terrible accident.

"Short chapters and cliffhangers keep the pace quick, while the mix of traditional language and vernacular helps the story feel both fresh and timeless. . . . [This is] a vibrant and cinematic novel that readers are going to love." Publ Wkly

Other titles in this series are:
Scrumble (2010)
Switch (2015)

★ **Scumble**. Dial Books for Young Readers 2010 400p il $16.99

Grades: 4 5 6 7 **Fic**

1. Magic -- Fiction 2. Wyoming -- Fiction 3. Ranch life -- Fiction
ISBN 978-0-8037-3307-7; 0-8037-3307-0

LC 2010-02444

Mibs's cousin Ledge is disappointed to discover that his "savvy" —the magical power unique to each member of their family—is to make things fall apart, which endangers his uncle Autry's ranch and reveals the family secret to future reporter Sarah.

This provides a "satisfying plot, delightful characters, alliterative language, and rich imagery." Booklist

Lawlor, Laurie

Dead reckoning; a pirate voyage with Captain Drake. Simon & Schuster Books for Young Readers 2005 254p $15.95

Grades: 7 8 9 10 **Fic**

1. Admirals 2. Explorers 3. Orphans -- Fiction 4. Pirates -- Fiction 5. Seafaring life -- Fiction
ISBN 0-689-86577-5

LC 2004-21682

Emmet, a fifteen-year-old orphan, learns hard lessons about survival when he sails from England in 1577 as a servant aboard the Golden Hind—the ship of his cousin, the explorer and pirate Francis Drake—on its three-year circumnavigation of the world.

"The tone is dark and grim, and there are scenes that might horrify younger readers. . . . But the story is authentic and harrowing, and the historical details are well done. This book would be perfect for older teens who love historical fiction, or want more on pirates." SLJ

He will go fearless; [by] Laurie Lawlor. Simon & Schuster Books for Young Readers 2006 210p $15.95

Grades: 5 6 7 8 **Fic**

1. Father-son relationship -- Fiction 2. Overland journeys to the Pacific -- Fiction 3. United States -- History -- 1865-1898 -- Fiction
ISBN 0-689-86579-1

LC 2005-06129

With the Civil War ended and Reconstruction begun, fifteen-year-old Billy resolves to make the dangerous and challenging journey West in search of real fortune – his true father.

"Danger, adventure, and survival combine to make this a richly detailed story." SLJ

Lawrence, Caroline

★ The **case** of the deadly desperados; Caroline Lawrence. G.P. Putnam's Sons 2011 279 p. (Western mysteries) $16.99

Grades: 4 5 6 7 8 **Fic**

1. Mystery fiction 2. Western stories 3. Children's stories 4. Orphans -- Fiction 5. Racially mixed people -- Fiction 6. Disguise -- Fiction 7. Mystery and detective stories 8. Nevada -- History -- 19th century -- Fiction
ISBN 9780399256332

LC 2011013305

In this book, Caroline "Lawrence shifts her sleuthing . . . [to] Virginia City, Montana in the 1860s. . . . Whittlin' Walt . . . has just scalped and slain the foster parents of twelve-year-old P. K. (Pinky) Pinkerton, . . . who holds a coveted deed to an entire region of silver mines. Pinky hightails it to Virginia City . . . to register his claim, . . . [then] to Chicago, where he wants to join the detective whom he believes to be his father." (Bulletin of the Center for Children's Books)

★ **P.K.** Pinkerton and the petrified man; Caroline Lawrence. G.P. Putnam's Sons 2013 320 p. (hardcover) $16.99

Grades: 4 5 6 7 8 **Fic**

1. Mystery fiction 2. Western stories 3. Orphans -- Fiction 4. Disguise -- Fiction 5. Mystery and detective stories 6. Racially mixed people -- Fiction 7. Nevada -- History -- 19th century -- Fiction
ISBN 0399256342; 9780399256349

LC 2012026737

This western mystery adventure novel, by Caroline Lawrence, is "starring Master-of-Disguise, P.K. Pinkerton. After vanquishing three notorious Desperados, twelve-year-old P.K. Pinkerton opens a private-eye business in Virginia City. P.K.'s skills are quickly put to the test: When a maid named

Martha witnesses a murder, she hires the young detective to track the killer before he finds her too." (Publisher's note)

★ **P.K.** Pinkerton and the pistol-packing widows; Caroline Lawrence. G.P. Putnam's Sons, an imprint of Penguin Group (USA) Inc. 2014 304 p. maps (hardcover) $16.99

Grades: 4 5 6 7 8   Fic
1. Mystery fiction 2. Nevada -- Fiction 3. Disguise -- Fiction 4. Detectives -- Fiction 5. Orphans -- Fiction 6. Mystery and detective stories 7. Racially mixed people -- Fiction 8. Nevada -- History -- 19th century -- Fiction
ISBN 0399256350; 9780399256356
LC 2013000211

In this book, by Caroline Lawrence, "P.K. Pinkerton's detective agency is thriving in Virginia City--until the evening P.K. is abruptly stuffed into a turnip sack and tossed into the back of a wagon! Surfacing in Chinatown, P.K. is forced into taking a job trailing the abductor's fiancé in Carson City. Danger lurks at every turn. P.K. must battle quicksand, escape the despicable former Deputy Marshall, Jack Williams, and save Poker Face Jace from certain death." (Publisher's note)

"In this third rousing series entry, P.K. is going to Carson City to investigate Poker Face Jace, who Opal Blossom believes is her two-timing fiancí. P.K. must navigate twists and turns in a case involving Nevada Territory's bid for statehood. A big reveal should have readers thinking about P.K.'s art of disguise and looking at our hero in a new light." Horn Book

Lawrence, Iain
★ The **giant** -slayer. Delacorte Press 2009 292p $16.99

Grades: 5 6 7 8   Fic
1. Imagination -- Fiction 2. Medical care -- Fiction 3. Storytelling -- Fiction 4. Poliomyelitis -- Fiction 5. Father-daughter relationship -- Fiction
ISBN 978-0-385-73376-2; 0-385-73376-3
LC 2008-35409

When her eight-year-old neighbor is stricken with polio in 1955, eleven-year-old Laurie discovers that there is power in her imagination as she weaves a story during her visits with him and other patients confined to iron lung machines.

This is "compelling. . . . This effectively shows how children face life-changing challenges with incredible determination." Booklist

The **seance**. Delacorte Press 2008 262p il $15.99; lib bdg $18.99; pa $6.99

Grades: 4 5 6 7   Fic
1. Magicians 2. Mystery fiction 3. Nonfiction writers 4. Magicians -- Fiction 5. Spiritualism -- Fiction
ISBN 978-0-385-73375-5; 0-385-73375-5; 978-0-385-90392-9 lib bdg; 0-385-90392-8 lib bdg; 978-0-440-23970-3 pa; 0-440-23970-2 pa
LC 2007-27994

In 1926, magician Harry Houdini arrives in the city to perform magic and to expose fradulent mediums but thirteen-year-old Scooter King, who works for his mother making her seances seem real, needs Houdini's help to solve a murder.

"Mystery lovers will get a kick out of this rollicking whodunit featuring swashbuckling soothsayers, outlandish séances, magic tricks and more." Publ Wkly

★ The **wreckers**. Delacorte Press 1998 196p hardcover o.p.   pa $5.99

Grades: 5 6 7 8   Fic
1. Adventure fiction 2. Shipwrecks -- Fiction 3. Great Britain -- History -- 1714-1837 -- Fiction
ISBN 0-385-32535-5; 0-440-41545-4 pa
LC 97-31625

"In 1799 fourteen-year-old John Spencer survives a shipwreck on the coast of Cornwall. To his horror, he soon learns that the villagers are not rescuers, but pirates who lure ships ashore in order to plunder their cargoes. . . . Lawrence creates an edge-of-the-chair survival/mystery story. Fast-moving, mesmerizing." Horn Book Guide

Other titles in this series are:
The smugglers (1999)
The buccaneers (2001)

Le Guin, Ursula K.
Gifts. Harcourt 2004 274p $17; $17; pa $7.95

Grades: 7 8 9 10   Fic
1. Fantasy fiction
ISBN 9780152051235; 0-15-205123-6; 0-15-205124-4 pa
LC 2003-21449

"Brantors, or chiefs, of the various clans of the Uplands have powers passed down through generations, powers to call animals to the hunt, start fires, cast a wasting disease, or undo the very essence of a life or thing. The clans live isolated from the inhabitants of the Lowland cities in an uneasy truce, where each people's ambitions are kept at bay by fear of the other's vengeance. Two Upland teenagers, Gry and Orrec, have grown from childhood friendship into romance and also into a repudiation of their hereditary powers. . . . Rejecting traditions that bind them to roles unwanted and undesired, Gry and Orrec decide to leave their homes and seek a freer if less privileged life in the Lowlands. . . . Grades seven to twelve." (Bull Cent Child Books)

"Although intriguing as a coming-of-age allegory, Orrec's story is also rich in . . . earthy magic and intelligent plot twists." Booklist

Powers. Harcourt 2007 502p map $17; pa $7.99

Grades: 7 8 9 10   Fic
1. Fantasy fiction
ISBN 978-0-15-205770-1; 0-15-205770-6; 978-0-15-206674-1 pa; 0-15-206674-8 pa
LC 2006-13549

Sequel to Voices (2006)

When young Gavir's sister is brutally killed, he escapes from slavery and sets out to explore the world and his own psychic abilities.

"Le Guin uses her own prodigious power as a writer to craft lyrical, precise sentences, evoking a palpable sense of place and believable characters." SLJ

Voices. Harcourt 2006 341p $17

Grades: 7 8 9 10 **Fic**
1. Fantasy fiction
ISBN 978-015-205678-0; 0-15-205678-5
LC 2005020753
Sequel to Gifts (2004)
Young Memer takes on a pivotal role in freeing her war-torn homeland from its oppressive captors.
"While her prose is simple and unadorned, Le Guin's superior narrative voice and storytelling power make even small moments ring with truth, and often with beauty." SLJ
Followed by Powers (2007)

★ A **wizard** of Earthsea; [by] Ursula K. Le Guin; illustrated by Ruth Robbins. Bantam trade pbk. ed.; Bantam Books 2004 182p il pa $15
Grades: 6 7 8 9 **Fic**
1. Fantasy fiction 2. Science fiction 3. Magic -- Fiction
ISBN 0-553-38304-3; 978-0-553-38304-1
LC 2004558962
A reissue of the title first published 1968 by Parnassus Press
ALA YALSA Margaret A. Edwards Award (2004)
A "powerful fantasy-allegory. Though set as prose, the rhythms of the langauge are truly and consistently poetical." Read Ladders for Hum Relat. 5th edition
Other titles in this series are:
The Tombs of Atuan (1971)
The farthest shore (1972)
Tehanu (1990)

Leal, Ann Haywood
Also known as Harper. Henry Holt 2009 246p $16.95
Grades: 4 5 6 7 **Fic**
1. Poets -- Fiction 2. Siblings -- Fiction 3. People with disabilities -- Fiction 4. Single parent family -- Fiction
ISBN 978-0-8050-8881-6; 0-8050-8881-4
LC 2008-36940
Writing poetry helps fifth-grader Harper Lee Morgan cope with her father's absence, being evicted, and having to skip school to care for her brother while their mother works, and things look even brighter after she befriends a mute girl and a kindly disabled woman.
"The characters are memorable as are the descriptive passages. . . . Most touching are Harper's pithy poems that expose the raw emotions of a bright but disadvantaged girl. This book is rich with discussion opportunity for middle school students." Voice Youth Advocates

A **finders** -keepers place. Henry Holt 2010 259p $16.99
Grades: 5 6 7 **Fic**
1. School stories 2. Sisters -- Fiction 3. Mental illness -- Fiction 4. Missing persons -- Fiction 5. Single parent family -- Fiction 6. Manic-depressive illness -- Fiction
ISBN 978-0-8050-8882-3; 0-8050-8882-2
LC 2009-50771
As their mother's manic-depression grows worse, eleven-year-old Esther and her sister Ruth visit various churches hoping to find their father, a preacher named Ezekiel who left them seven years before in 1966.

"Leal excels in pithy characterization, mainly through spot-on dialogue, yielding sympathetic characters, a gripping plot, and no shortage of heartbreaking moments." Publ Wkly

Lean, Sarah
★ A **dog** called Homeless; Sarah Lean. Katherine Tegen Books 2012 202 p. (trade bdg) $16.99
Grades: 3 4 5 6 7 **Fic**
1. Dogs -- Fiction 2. Blind -- Fiction 3. Grief -- Fiction 4. Hearing impaired -- Fiction 5. Selective mutism -- Fiction 6. Single-parent families -- Fiction 7. People with disabilities -- Fiction
ISBN 0062122207; 9780062122209
LC 2011044628
Schneider Family Book Award (2013)
In this book by Sarah Lean, "a girl grieving for her dead mother gives up talking when she becomes convinced that what she says doesn't matter. . . . Cally begins to see her mother . . . dressed in a red raincoat and sometimes accompanied by a very large dog. . . . Cally also meets Mrs. Cooper, a neighbor in their new apartment building who lovingly cares for her blind, nearly deaf 11-year-old son, Sam." (Kirkus Reviews)

Leavitt, Lindsey
Going vintage; by Lindsey Leavitt. 1st U.S. ed. Bloomsbury 2013 320 p. (hardcover) $16.99
Grades: 7 8 9 10 **Fic**
1. School stories 2. Sisters -- Fiction 3. Dating (Social customs) -- Fiction 4. Lists -- Fiction 5. Schools -- Fiction 6. California -- Fiction 7. High schools -- Fiction 8. JUVENILE FICTION -- Love & Romance 9. Family life -- California -- Fiction 10. JUVENILE FICTION -- Family -- Siblings
ISBN 1599907879; 9781599907871
LC 2012023269
In this book, "after discovering her boyfriend has a serious online relationship with another girl, Mallory very publicly dumps him on his social media site. She complicates the situation by deciding to try to fulfill a to-do list her grandmother crafted at the beginning of her junior year of high school in 1962, a time Mallory thinks must have been much simpler than today. . . . She's aided by her loyal younger sister, Ginnie, and the growing affection of her ex's cousin, charming Oliver." (Kirkus)

Sean Griswold's head. Bloomsbury 2011 276p $16.99
Grades: 7 8 9 10 **Fic**
1. School stories 2. Family life -- Fiction 3. Pennsylvania -- Fiction 4. Multiple sclerosis -- Fiction
ISBN 978-1-59990-498-6; 1-59990-498-5
LC 2010-06949
"Leavitt capably handles the issues of chronic illness with sensitivity, making this an insightful, humorous, and ultimately uplifting family drama." Bull Cent Child Books

Leavitt, Martine
My book of life by Angel; Martine Leavitt. Farrar, Straus and Giroux Books for Young Readers 2012 252 p. $17.99; (hardback) $17.99; (ebook) $12.95

Grades: 8 9 10 11   **Fic**

1. Novels in verse 2. Runaway teenagers -- Fiction 3. Juvenile prostitution -- Fiction 4. Runaways -- Fiction 5. Drug abuse -- Fiction 6. Prostitution -- Fiction 7. Vancouver (B.C.) -- Fiction

ISBN 0374351236; 9780374351236; 9781554983179

LC 2011044563

This "novel in verse tells the story of 16-year-old Angel, who has been working as a prostitute in Vancouver. . . . After Angel's friend Serena disappears, Angel decides to give up" the drugs her pimp Call feeds her "and try to return home. Angel's withdrawal is severe . . . but it's nothing compared to the pain she feels when Call brings home an 11-year-old girl, Melli, to follow in Angel's footsteps. Angel is determined to keep Melli safe, even while other women continue to disappear." (Publishers Weekly)

Lecesne, James

★ **Absolute** brightness. HarperTeen 2008 472p $17.99; lib bdg $18.89

Grades: 7 8 9 10   **Fic**

1. Cousins -- Fiction 2. New Jersey -- Fiction 3. Good and evil -- Fiction 4. Homosexuality -- Fiction

ISBN 978-0-06-125627-1; 0-06-125627-7; 978-0-06-125628-8 lib bdg; 0-06-125628-5 lib bdg

LC 2007-02988

ALA YALSA Morris Award Finalist, 2009

In the beach town of Neptune, New Jersey, Phoebe's life is changed irrevocably when her gay cousin moves into her house and soon goes missing.

"This thoughtful novel is beautifully written; its themes are haunting, and in spite of the central tragedy, it's often laugh-out-loud funny." Kliatt

Leck, James

★ The **adventures** of Jack Lime; written by James Leck. Kids Can Press 2010 126p $16.95; pa $8.95

Grades: 5 6 7 8   **Fic**

1. Mystery fiction 2. Narcolepsy -- Fiction

ISBN 978-1-55453-364-0; 1-55453-364-3; 978-1-55453-365-7 pa; 1-55453-365-1 pa

"Jack Lime is the guy you come to if you've got a problem. . . . He'll find out what needs finding out. . . . This slim volume contains three cases. In the first, Jack susses out the whereabouts of a missing bike. In the second, he shakes down a hamster-napping and blackmail scheme. And in the final, he recounts his first case on the job. . . . All the touchstones that make for great noir are translated for kids. . . . The lingo that makes hard-boiled reading so much fun is here, but never schticky, and Leck knows that a great hero needs a debilitating flaw: for Jack, it's his narcolepsy." Booklist

Lee, Harper

★ To kill a mockingbird; Harper Lee. 50th anniversary ed; Harper 2010 323p $25.00

Grades: 8 9 10 11 12 Adult   **Fic**

1. Alabama -- Fiction 2. Race relations -- Fiction

ISBN 9780061743528

"Scout, as Jean Louise is called, is a precocious child. She relates her impressions of the time when her lawyer father, Atticus Finch, is defending a black man accused of raping a white woman in a small Alabama town during the 1930's. Atticus's courageous act brings the violence and injustice that exists in their world sharply into focus as it intrudes into the lighthearted life that Scout and her brother Jem have enjoyed until that time." Shapiro. Fic for Youth. 3d edition

Lee, Tanith

Piratica; being a daring tale of a singular girl's adventure upon the high seas. presented most handsomely by the notorious Tanith Lee. Dutton Children's Books 2004 288p $17.99

Grades: 6 7 8 9   **Fic**

1. Adventure fiction 2. Pirates -- Fiction 3. Sex role -- Fiction

ISBN 0-525-47324-6

First published 2003 in the United Kingdom

A bump on the head restores Art's memories of her mother and the exciting life they led, so the sixteen-year-old leaves Angels Academy for Young Maidens, seeks out the pirates who were her family before her mother's death, and leads them back to adventure on the high seas.

"Piratica is a refreshing, tongue-in-cheek, tangled tale that will entice readers who crave adventure and fantasy." SLJ

Followed by Piratica II: return to Parrot Island (2006)

Piratica II: return to Parrot Island; being the return of a most intrepid heroine to sea and secrets. Dutton Children's Books 2006 320p $17.99

Grades: 6 7 8 9   **Fic**

1. Adventure fiction 2. Pirates -- Fiction 3. Sex role -- Fiction

ISBN 0-525-47769-1

Sequel to Piratica (2004)

Art Blastside is bored with life ashore, so she jumps at the chance to return to sea.

"Lee's writing is complex, and she uses her skill to craft subtle pundit humor and lush description." Voice Youth Advocates

Lee, Ying S.

A **spy** in the house. Candlewick Press 2010 335p (The Agency) $16.99

Grades: 8 9 10 11 12   **Fic**

1. Mystery fiction 2. Orphans -- Fiction 3. Household employees -- Fiction 4. Swindlers and swindling -- Fiction 5. Great Britain -- History -- 19th century -- Fiction

ISBN 978-0-7636-4067-5; 0-7636-4067-0

LC 2009-32736

Rescued from the gallows in 1850s London, young orphan and thief Mary Quinn is offered a place at Miss Scrimshaw's Academy for Girls where she is trained to be part of an all-female investigative unit called The Agency and, at age seventeen, she infiltrates a rich merchant's home in hopes of tracing his missing cargo ships.

"Lee fills the story with classic elements of Victorian mystery and melodrama. Class differences, love gone awry, racial discrimination, London's growing pains in the 1850s, and the status of women in society are all addressed. Historical details are woven seamlessly into the plot, and descriptive writing allows readers to be part of each scene." SLJ

Other titles in this series are:

The body at the tower (2010)

The traitor in the tunnel (2012)

Leeds, Constance

The **unfortunate** son; by Constance Leeds. Viking Childrens Books 2012 302 p. (hardcover) $16.99

Grades: 4 5 6 7   **Fic**

1. Bildungsromans 2. Historical fiction 3. Pirates -- Fiction 4. Kidnapping -- Fiction 5. Luck -- Fiction 6. Fishing -- Fiction 7. Slavery -- Fiction 8. Identity -- Fiction 9. Abnormalities, Human -- Fiction 10. Africa -- History -- To 1498 -- Fiction 11. France -- History -- 15th century -- Fiction

ISBN 0670013986; 9780670013982

LC 2011027530

This book is the story of Luc, whose "father hates him, seemingly without reason, so" the boy runs away "to apprentice with a local fisherman. . . . Living with the fisherman's family he grows close to their ward, the beautiful Beatrice, and things seem to be looking up . . . until he's kidnapped by pirates and sold to a Tunisian in North Africa. While Luc receives an education from his learned master, Beatrice" attempts to unravel Luc's past. (Kirkus Reviews)

Lennon, Tom

When love comes to town; Tom Lennon. Albert Whitman 2013 304 p. (reinforced) $15.99

Grades: 8 9 10 11 12   **Fic**

1. Historical fiction 2. Gay teenagers -- Fiction 3. Gays -- Fiction 4. Ireland -- Fiction 5. Coming out (Sexual orientation) -- Fiction

ISBN 0807589160; 9780807589168

LC 2012020160

In this novel, by Tom Lennon, "the year is 1990, and in his hometown of Dublin, Ireland, Neil Byrne plays rugby, keeps up with the in-crowd at his school, and is just a regular guy. A guy who's gay. It's a secret he keeps from the wider world as he explores the city at night and struggles to figure out how to reveal his real self--and to whom." (Publisher's note)

Leonard, Julia Platt

Cold case. Aladdin 2011 281p $15.99

Grades: 6 7 8 9   **Fic**

1. Mystery fiction 2. Spies -- Fiction 3. Brothers -- Fiction 4. Homicide -- Fiction 5. Family life -- Fiction 6. Restaurants -- Fiction 7. Santa Fe (N.M.) -- Fiction

ISBN 978-1-4424-2009-0; 1-4424-2009-X

LC 2010041854

When thirteen-year-old Oz Keillor finds a dead body in his family's Santa Fe, New Mexico, restaurant, he is determined to solve the mystery in which his older brother is implicated, but which also involves their long-dead father, who was accused of being a spy.

"The well-plotted double mystery is propped up by a few choice details about restaurant life, some sly red herrings, and a cast of nicely rounded characters." Booklist

Lerangis, Peter

The **colossus** rises; Peter Lerangis. Harper 2013 348 p. (Seven wonders) (hardcover bdg.) $17.99; (pbk.) $6.99

Grades: 4 5 6 7 8 9   **Fic**

1. Fantasy fiction 2. Adventure fiction 3. Science fiction 4. Ability -- Fiction 5. Friendship -- Fiction 6. Adventure and adventurers -- Fiction 7. Atlantis (Legendary place) -- Fiction

ISBN 0062070401; 006207041X; 9780062070401; 9780062070418

LC 2012025334

This children's fantasy story, by Peter Lerangis, illustrated by Torstein Norstrand and Mike Reagan, is the first of the "Seven Wonders" series. "13-year-old Jack McKinley will die unless he can locate the magic Loculi containing the ancient powers of Atlantis. . . . The problem is that . . . Atlantis was . . . divided into seven containers and hidden in the Seven Wonders of the Ancient World. Finding the powers will not only save Jack's life, but also give him superpowers." (Kirkus Reviews)

Teens Jack, Marco, Aly, and Cass begin a quest to find seven pieces of Atlantis' power that were hidden long ago and that will, if returned to Atlantis, save them from certain death due to the genetic abnormality that also gives them superior abilities.

Lost in babylon; by Peter Lerangis and translated by Torstein Norstrand. HarperCollins 2013 384 p. (Seven wonders) (hardcover bdg.) $17.99

Grades: 4 5 6 7 8 9   **Fic**

1. Occult fiction 2. Adventure fiction 3. Seven Wonders of the World -- Fiction

ISBN 0062070436; 9780062070432

LC 2013942765

This book, by Peter Lerangis, "chronicles Jack McKinley and his friends as they carry on their mission to save their lives—and the world—by locating seven magic orbs called Loculi, which are hidden in the Seven Wonders of the Ancient World. After defeating the Colossus of Rhodes and capturing the first of the Loculi, their friend Marco has disappeared. With no leads, no clues, and no one else to turn to, the kids have no choice but to trust Professor Bhegad and the Karai Institute again as they head off to Babylon." (Publisher's note)

Tomb of shadows; Peter Lerangis, Torstein Norstrand; [edited by] David Linker. HarperCollins 2014 352 p. (Seven wonders) (hardcover) $17.99

Grades: 4 5 6 7 8 9   **Fic**

1. Fantasy fiction 2. Seven Wonders of the World -- Fiction 3. Adventure stories 4. Betrayal -- Fiction

ISBN 0062070460; 9780062070463

LC 2014931071

This middle grades fantasy novel by Peter Lerangis, illustrated by Torstein Norstrand, part of the Seven Wonders series, "chronicles the adventures of Jack McKinley and his friends in a life-or-death race to the Mausoleum at Halicarnassus. In the rubble of this Wonder of the Ancient World, they have to face down their own demons and engage in an epic battle with foes long gone." (Publisher's note)

"—Jack, Ally, and Cass continue their quest to save the world—even as their friend Marco joins the enemy's side. Epic battles and fast-moving chapters will keep fans of this "Percy Jackson"-like series engaged." SLJ

Other titles in the series include:

The Colossus Rises (2013)

Lost in Bablyon (2013)

Les Becquets, Diane

Season of ice. Bloomsbury U.S.A. Children's Books 2008 281p $16.95

Grades: 8 9 10 11 12   **Fic**

1. Lakes -- Fiction 2. Maine -- Fiction 3. Stepfamilies -- Fiction 4. Missing persons -- Fiction 5. Father-daughter relationship -- Fiction

ISBN 978-1-59990-063-6; 1-59990-063-7

LC 2007-30845

When seventeen-year-old Genesis Sommer's father disappears on Moosehead Lake near their small-town Maine home in mid-November, she must cope with the pressure of keeping her family together, even while rumors about the event plague her.

This is "a heartbreaking story from the very beginning, but Les Becquets turns it into something well beyond a mere tearjerker. . . . It's a tender story of a tough, smart, loving girl who finds that she can rise to the challenge of what she's lost because of what she's gained. Readers will understand her and admire her, and find her difficult indeed to forget." Bull Cent Child Books

Lester, Alison

Quicksand pony. Houghton Mifflin 1998 136p $15

Grades: 5 6 7 8   **Fic**

1. Horses -- Fiction 2. Australia -- Fiction

ISBN 0-395-93749-3

LC 98-6930

First published 1997 in Australia

After her pony Bella, trapped in quicksand, is rescued by a mysterious unseen person, ten-year-old Biddy follows the trail into the Australian bush and discovers the solution to a disappearance that happened years ago

"A multilayered story of survival, love, mystery, and family relationships." SLJ

Lester, Joan Steinau

★ **Black**, white, other. Zondervan 2011 222p $15.99

Grades: 7 8 9 10   **Fic**

1. Divorce -- Fiction 2. Slavery -- Fiction 3. California -- Fiction 4. Family life -- Fiction 5. Grandmothers -- Fiction 6. Race relations -- Fiction 7. Racially mixed people -- Fiction

ISBN 978-0-310-72763-7; 0-310-72763-4

LC 2011015208

Twenty miles from Oakland, California, where fires have led to racial tension, multi-racial fifteen-year-old Nina faces the bigotry of long-time friends, her parents' divorce, and her brother's misbehavior, while learning of her great-great grandmother Sarah's escape from slavery.

"Lester . . . conjures a credible plot and complications; divorce is a fact of life and racially mixed heritage is con-

spicuously becoming one. The simple contrapuntal narrative of Sarah Armstrong's escaping slavery distinguishes the book emotionally and psychologically, raising it above other issue-oriented YA novels. Lester writes with social sensitivity and an ear for teen language and concerns. This is engaging treatment of a challenging subject that comes with little precedent." Publ Wkly

Includes bibliographical references

Lester, Julius

Day of tears; a novel in dialogue. Hyperion 2005 177p hardcover o.p. pa $7.99

Grades: 7 8 9 10   **Fic**

1. Slavery -- Fiction 2. African Americans -- Fiction

ISBN 0-7868-0490-4; 1-42310-409-9 pa

Coretta Scott King Award for text

Emma has taken care of the Butler children since Sarah and Frances's mother, Fanny, left. Emma wants to raise the girls to have good hearts, as a rift over slavery has ripped the Butler household apart. Now, to pay off debts, Pierce Butler wants to cash in his slave "assets", possibly including Emma.

"The horror of the auction and its aftermath is unforgettable. . . . The racism is virulent (there's widespread use of the n-word). The personal voices make this a stirring text for group discussion." Booklist

★ **Guardian**. Amistad/HarperTeen 2008 129p $16.99; lib bdg $17.89

Grades: 7 8 9 10   **Fic**

1. Lynching -- Fiction 2. Race relations -- Fiction 3. Southern States -- Fiction 4. African Americans -- Fiction

ISBN 978-0-06-155890-0; 0-06-155890-7; 978-0-06-155891-7 lib bdg; 0-06-155891-5 lib bdg

LC 2008-14251

In a rural southern town in 1946, a white man and his son witness the lynching of an innocent black man. Includes historical note on lynching.

"The author's understated, haunting prose is as compelling as it is dark; . . . [the story] leaves a deep impression." Publ Wkly

Includes bibliographical references

Time's memory. Farrar, Straus & Giroux 2006 230p $17

Grades: 8 9 10 11 12   **Fic**

1. Slavery -- Fiction 2. African Americans -- Fiction

ISBN 0-374-37178-4; 978-0-374-37178-4

LC 2005-47716

Ekundayo, a Dogon spirit brought to America from Africa, inhabits the body of a young African American slave on a Virginia plantation, where he experiences loss, sorrow, and reconciliation in the months preceding the Civil War.

"More than a picture of slavery through the eyes of those enslaved or their captors, Lester's narrative evokes spiritual images of Mali's Dogon people." SLJ

Levine, Gail Carson

Ella enchanted. HarperCollins Pubs. 1997 232p $16.99; lib bdg $17.89; pa $6.50

Grades: 5 6 7 8   **Fic**
1. Fantasy fiction
ISBN 0-06-027510-3; 0-06-027511-1 lib bdg; 0-06-440705-5 pa

LC 96-30734

A Newbery Medal honor book, 1998

"Ella is blessed by a fairy at birth with the gift of obedience. But the blessing is a horror for Ella, who must literally do what everyone tells her, from sweeping the floor to giving up a beloved heirloom necklace. After her mother dies, and her covetous, caustic father leaves on a trading trip, Ella's world is turned upside down. She battles both ogres and wicked stepsisters, makes friends and loses them, and must deny her love for her prince, Charmont, to save his life and his realm. In making this ultimate sacrifice, she breaks the curse." (Booklist) "Grades five to eight." (Bull Cent Child Books)

"As finely designed as a tapestry, Ella's story both neatly incorporates elements of the original tale and mightily expands them." Booklist

Ever. HarperCollinsPublishers 2008 256p $16.99; lib bdg $17.89; pa $6.99
Grades: 5 6 7 8   **Fic**
1. Winds -- Fiction 2. Immortality -- Fiction 3. Fate and fatalism -- Fiction 4. Gods and goddesses -- Fiction
ISBN 978-0-06-122962-6; 0-06-122962-8; 978-0-06-122963-3 lib bdg; 0-06-122963-6 lib bdg; 978-0-06-122964-0 pa; 0-06-122964-4 pa

LC 2007-32289

Fourteen-year-old Kezi and Olus, Akkan god of the winds, fall in love and together try to change her fate—to be sacrificed to a Hyte god because of a rash promise her father made—through a series of quests that might make her immortal.

"Levine conducts a riveting journey, offering passion and profound pondering along the way." Publ Wkly

Fairest. HarperCollins 2006 326p $16.99
Grades: 6 7 8 9   **Fic**
1. Fairy tales 2. Singing -- Fiction
ISBN 978-0-06-073408-4; 0-06-073408-6

LC 2006-00337

In a land where beauty and singing are valued above all else, Aza eventually comes to reconcile her unconventional appearance and her magical voice, and learns to accept herself for who she truly is.

"The plot is fast-paced, and Aza's growth and maturity are well crafted and believable." SLJ

★ A **tale** of Two Castles. Harper 2011 328p $16.99; lib bdg $17.89
Grades: 4 5 6   **Fic**
1. Fantasy fiction 2. Mystery fiction 3. Dragons -- Fiction 4. Apprentices -- Fiction 5. Kings and rulers -- Fiction
ISBN 978-0-06-122965-7; 0-06-122965-2; 978-0-06-122966-4 lib bdg; 0-06-122966-0 lib bdg

LC 2010027756

"Hoping to apprentice as an actor, Elodie travels from her rural home to the city of Two Castles. . . . When she's robbed and then rejected as an actor, she apprentices her-self to crafty dragon Meenore as a detective. Shape-shifting Count Jonty Um, a kindly ogre, is their first client. . . . But who is to be trusted and who isn't? . . . Intermediate, middle school." (Horn Book)

"Readers are certain to be pulled, like Elodie herself, right into the midst of the rich and swirling life of Two Castles." SLJ

Levine, Kristin

★ The **best** bad luck I ever had. Putnam 2009 266p $16.99
Grades: 5 6 7 8   **Fic**
1. Alabama -- Fiction 2. Friendship -- Fiction 3. Prejudices -- Fiction 4. Family life -- Fiction 5. Country life -- Fiction 6. Race relations -- Fiction
ISBN 978-0-399-25090-3; 0-399-25090-5

LC 2008-11570

In Moundville, Alabama, in 1917, twelve-year-old Dit hopes the new postmaster will have a son his age, but instead he meets Emma, who is black, and their friendship challenges accepted ways of thinking and leads them to save the life of a condemned man.

"Tension builds just below the surface of this energetic, seamlessly narrated . . . novel. . . . Levine handles the setting with grace and nuance." Publ Wkly

★ The **lions** of Little Rock; Kristin Levine. G. P. Putnam's Sons 2012 298p.
Grades: 5 6 7 8   **Fic**
1. School stories 2. African Americans -- Fiction 3. School integration -- Fiction 4. Schools -- Fiction 5. Friendship -- Fiction 6. Bashfulness -- Fiction 7. Middle schools -- Fiction 8. Race relations -- Fiction 9. Family life -- Arkansas -- Fiction 10. Little Rock (Ark.) -- History -- 20th century -- Fiction
ISBN 9780399256448

LC 2011031835

This book presents a "portrait of 1958 Little Rock, Ark., the tumultuous year when the governor refused integration by closing local high schools. The story is told through the . . . voice of painfully quiet 12-year-old Marlee Nisbett, who makes a rare friend in Liz, a new student at her middle school. Liz instills some much-needed confidence in Marlee, but when it's revealed that Liz is 'passing' as a white student, Liz must leave school abruptly, putting their friendship to the test. The girls meet in secret, and Marlee joins an antisegregationist organization, both actions inviting serious risk amid escalating racist threats." (Publishers Weekly)

The **paper** cowboy; Kristin Levine. Putnam Juvenile 2014 352 p. (hardback) $16.99
Grades: 5 6 7 8   **Fic**
1. Family -- Fiction 2. Neighbors -- Fiction 3. Conduct of life -- Fiction 4. Newspaper carriers -- Fiction 5. Communism -- Fiction 6. Neighborliness -- Fiction 7. Family problems -- Fiction 8. Illinois -- History -- 20th century -- Fiction
ISBN 039916328X; 9780399163289

LC 2014004421

In this book, by Kristin Levine, "Tommy is . . . a bully. He's always playing cruel jokes on classmates or stealing from the store. But Tommy has a reason: life at home is tough. His abusive mother isn't well; in fact, she may be mentally ill, and his sister, Mary Lou, is in the hospital badly burned from doing a chore it was really Tommy's turn to do. To make amends, Tommy takes over Mary Lou's paper route." (Publisher's note)

"Twelve-year-old Tommy wants to be a cowboy. That's not so easy, though, in 1950s Downers Grove, Illinois. After he plays a prank that ends up costing the local grocery store owner his business, a remorseful Tommy goes about becoming a different kind of cowboy--one "who stands up for others." Themes of bullying, community, and growing up in a dysfunctional family are explored sensitively." Horn Book

Levithan, David

Two boys kissing; by David Levithan. Alfred A. Knopf 2013 208 p. (hardcover library binding) $19.99

Grades: 8 9 10 11 12   **Fic**
1. School stories 2. Gay teenagers -- Fiction 3. Gays -- Fiction 4. Love -- Fiction 5. Homosexuality -- Fiction 6. Social change -- Fiction
ISBN 0307931900; 0375971122; 9780307931900; 9780307931917; 9780375971129
LC 2012047089
Lambda Literary Awards Winner - LGBT Children's/YA (2014)
Stonewall Honor Book: Children and Young Adult (2014)

In this book, students Craig and Henry are trying to set a world record for the longest kiss They "are no longer dating, throwing an element of uncertainty into an act that's romantic, political, and personal. Neil and Peter have been dating for a year and are beginning to wonder what's next. Avery, 'born a boy that the rest of the world saw as a girl,' and Ryan are caught up in the dizzying excitement of meeting someone new. And Cooper is rapidly losing himself into a digital oblivion." (Publishers Weekly)

"Craig and Harry attempt to break the world record for longest kiss, which, in turn, affects the lives of the people around them. Narrated by a ghostly chorus of past generations of gay men who died of AIDS, Levithan's latest novel weaves together an informed (sometimes melodramatic) perspective on the past with the present-day stories of seven boys constructing their own sexual identities." (Horn Book)

Levitin, Sonia

★ **Strange** relations. Alfred A. Knopf 2007 298p hardcover o.p. pa $6.50

Grades: 7 8 9 10   **Fic**
1. Jews -- Fiction 2. Hawaii -- Fiction 3. Cousins -- Fiction 4. Religion -- Fiction
ISBN 978-0-375-83751-7; 0-375-83751-5; 978-0-440-23963-5 pa; 0-440-23963-X pa
LC 2006-33275
Fifteen-year-old Marne is excited to be able to spend her summer vacation in Hawaii, not realizing the change in her lifestyle it would bring staying with her aunt, seven cousins, and uncle who is a Chasidic rabbi.

"It's rare to find such well-developed characters, empathetic and sensitive religious treatment, and carefully crafted plotlines in one novel." SLJ

Levy, Dana Alison

The **misadventures** of the family Fletcher; Dana Levy. Delacorte Press 2014 272 p. (glb) $18.99

Grades: 4 5 6 7   **Fic**
1. Interracial adoption 2. Children of gay parents -- Fiction 3. Humorous stories 4. Schools -- Fiction 5. Adoption -- Fiction 6. Brothers -- Fiction 7. Neighbors -- Fiction 8. Family life -- Fiction
ISBN 0385376545; 9780385376525; 9780385376549
LC 2013026320

In this middle grades book by Dana Alison Levy, "With four brothers, a dog, a cat, school projects, soccer matches, and a grumpy neighbor, the Fletchers are your typical American family . . . with two dads, and siblings who are adopted kids from various ethnic backgrounds. While 12-year-old Sam ponders . . . trying out for the school play . . . , 10-year-old Jax negotiates changing friendships and a veteran project that involves talking to the unfriendly Vietnam vet next door." (School Library Journal)

"Four adopted (and racially diverse) brothers and two dads star in this Penderwicks-esque chronicle of a year in their lives. Focusing each chapter on one boy while still keeping the whole family in the picture, Levy provides a compelling, compassionate, and frequently hilarious look at their daily concerns. Readers will want to be part of (or at least friends with) this delightful family." Horn Book

Lewis, C. S.

★ The **lion,** the witch, and the wardrobe; illustrated by Pauline Baynes. HarperCollins Pubs. 1994 189p il (The chronicles of Narnia) $17.99; lib bdg $18.89; pa $7.99

Grades: 4 5 6 7   **Fic**
1. Fantasy fiction
ISBN 0-06-023481-4; 0-06-023482-2 lib bdg; 0-06-440499-4 pa
LC 93-8889
A reissue of the title first published 1950 by Macmillan
Four English schoolchildren find their way through the back of a wardrobe into the magic land of Narnia and assist Aslan, the golden lion, to triumph over the White Witch, who has cursed the land with eternal winter

This begins "the 'Narnia' stories, outstanding modern fairy tales with an underlying theme of good overcoming evil." Child Books Too Good to Miss

Other titles in this series are:
Prince Caspian (1951)
The voyage of the Dawn Treader (1952)
The silver chair (1953)
The horse and his boy (1954)
The magician's nephew (1956)
The last battle (1956)

Lewis, Gill

One white dolphin; Gill Lewis; illustrated by Raquel Aparicio. Atheneum Books for Young Readers 2012 p. cm. (hardback) $15.99

Grades: 5 6 7   **Fic**
1. Ecology -- Fiction 2. England -- Fiction 3. Dolphins -- Fiction 4. Seashore -- Fiction 5. Marine ecology -- Fiction 6. Wildlife rescue -- Fiction 7. Environmental

protection -- Fiction
ISBN 9781442414471; 9781442414501
LC 2012009182

In this book, "a boy with cerebral palsy and an injured albino dolphin calf help Kara Wood come to terms with her mother's death and the sale of the family's boat, Moana. Kara's mother vanished a year ago on a dolphin-saving trip to the South Pacific. With debts mounting, her father plans to sell the sailboat they built. . . . The temporary protection of the reef near their British coastal home is about to expire." (Kirkus Reviews)

★ **Wild** wings; illustrated by Yuta Onoda. Atheneum Books for Young Readers 2011 287p il $15.99

Grades: 4 5 6 7   **Fic**

1. Gambia -- Fiction 2. Ospreys -- Fiction 3. Scotland -- Fiction 4. Farm life -- Fiction 5. Friendship -- Fiction
ISBN 1-4424-1445-6; 978-1-4424-1445-7
LC 2010-49228

Callum becomes friends with Iona, a practically feral classmate who has discovered an osprey, thought to be gone from Scotland, on Callum's family farm, and they eventually share the secret with others, including Jeneba who encounters the same bird at her home in Gambia.

This is a "rich, moving tale. . . . The suspenseful story line is surrounded with precise details. . . . Short chapters, some with cliffhanging endings, will read-aloud well. . . . A powerfully memorable story." Kirkus

Lewis, Stewart

The **secret** ingredient; Stewart Lewis. Delacorte Press 2013 256 p. (hc) $17.99

Grades: 7 8 9 10   **Fic**

1. Cooking -- Fiction 2. Mothers -- Fiction 3. Interpersonal relations -- Fiction 4. Self-realization -- Fiction 5. Los Angeles (Calif.) -- Fiction
ISBN 0385743319; 9780375991066; 9780385743310
LC 2012027203

This novel by Stewart Lewis is a "journey of family, food, romance, and self-discovery as Olivia, a teen chef living in L.A., finds a vintage cookbook and begins a search for her birthmother that will change her life forever. A new job leads Olivia to a gorgeous, mysterious boy named Theo. And as Olivia cooks the recipes from a vintage cookbook she stumbles upon, she begins to wonder if the mother she's never known might be the secret ingredient she's been lacking." (Publisher's note)

"Adopted by two dads, Olivia begins to sense a void in her life. Serendipitously, Olivia finds her supposedly "nameless" birth mother but quickly realizes that maybe the secret ingredient to a fulfilled life is appreciating what one already has. Lewis's mature protagonist adapts remarkably well to her nontraditional life in this story that limns themes of adolescence, adoption, illness, and financial instability." (Horn Book)

Lewis, Sylvia

Beautiful decay; Sylvia Lewis. Running Press Teens 2013 303 p. $9.95

Grades: 7 8 9 10 11 12   **Fic**

1. Supernatural -- Fiction 2. Alienation (Social

psychology) -- Fiction
ISBN 0762446110; 9780762446117
LC 2012951788

This "paranormal horror novel" follows "17-year-old Ellie. . . . A touch of her bare skin can cause anyone or anything to decay. No one wants to be near her, even though she wears gloves to avoid contact with anyone. . . . Things at school improve when Nate, the new guy, seems more curious than grossed out by her. . . . Ellie finds the strength she didn't know she had to break away from her lonely, 'bleached and gloved' existence to help him." (School Library Journal)

"Ellie Miller lives a lonely life. Her parents are rarely home when she is, her mother spends her time bleaching the house, and her only friend, Mackenzie, lives two states away and communicates via computer. Isolated by classmates due to an "immunity disorder," she wears gloves and dares not touch anything or anyone...Fans of paranormal will flock to Lewis' fast-paced debut that offers a unique take on being different. Many questions are left unanswered, laying the groundwork for a sequel." (Booklist)

LeZotte, Ann Clare

T4; a novel in verse. written by Ann Clare LeZotte. Houghton Mifflin Co. 2008 108p $14

Grades: 6 7 8 9 10   **Fic**

1. Novels in verse 2. Deaf -- Fiction 3. Euthanasia -- Fiction 4. Germany -- History -- 1933-1945 -- Fiction
ISBN 978-0-547-04684-6; 0-547-04684-7
LC 2007-47737

When the Nazi party takes control of Germany, thirteen-year-old Paula, who is deaf, finds her world-as-she-knows-it turned upside down, as she is taken into hiding to protect her from the new law nicknamed T4.

"This novel will have a lasting effect on readers, giving insight into an often-forgotten aspect of the horrors of the Third Reich." SLJ

Lieberman, Leanne

Lauren Yanofsky hates the Holocaust; Leanne Lieberman. Orca Book Publishers 2013 240 p. (paperback) $12.95; (ebook) $12.99

Grades: 7 8 9 10   **Fic**

1. Jews -- Fiction 2. Holocaust, 1939-1945 -- Fiction
ISBN 1459801091; 9781459801097; 9781459801103 pdf; 9781459801110
LC 2012952950

In this novel, by Leanne Lieberman, "Lauren Yanofsky doesn't want to be Jewish anymore. Her father, a noted Holocaust historian, keeps giving her Holocaust memoirs to read, and her mother doesn't understand why Lauren hates the idea of Jewish youth camps and family vacations to Holocaust memorials. But when Lauren sees some of her friends . . . playing Nazi war games, she is faced with a terrible choice: betray her friends or betray her heritage." (Publisher's note)

"Lieberman . . . smoothly weaves humor and knowledge about Judaism through Lauren's story. Lauren's narration is contemplative and from the heart, and readers should relate to her attempts to identify her beliefs and tackle life's big questions." Pub Wkly

Off pointe; Leanne Lieberman. Orca Book Publishers 2015 128 p. (Orca limelights) (pbk.) $9.95

Grades: 6 7 8 9 **Fic**

1. Ballet -- Fiction 2. Dancers -- Fiction 3. Friendship -- Fiction 4. Camps -- Fiction 5. Ballet dancers -- Fiction

ISBN 1459802802; 9781459802803; 9781459802810; 9781459802827

LC 2014935396

In this novel by Leanne Lieberman "Meg's summer ballet program is canceled and her ballet teacher suggests she attend Camp Dance to learn new dance styles. At camp, Meg struggles to learn contemporary dance. A girl named Logan, who is jealous of Meg's ballet technique and her friendship with Nio . . . . makes Meg's life even more difficult. When Meg, Nio and Logan have to work together to create a piece for the final show, arguments threaten to ruin their dance. " (Publisher's note)

"No dreadful swerves or lethal surprises here; the books lead the reader to expect a happy ending and, after the requisite hardships, that is where they arrive. The journey may be bittersweet, but the message is one of hope and encouragement: no success without failure, no learning without doing, no joy without daring." Voya

Lieurance, Suzanne

The **locket**; surviving the Triangle Shirtwaist fire. [by] Suzanne Lieurance. Enslow Publishers 2008 160p il (Historical fiction adventures) lib bdg $27.93

Grades: 4 5 6 7 **Fic**

1. Sisters -- Fiction 2. Factories -- Fiction 3. Immigrants -- Fiction 4. Jews -- United States -- Fiction 5. Triangle Shirtwaist Company, Inc. -- Fiction

ISBN 978-0-7660-2928-6 lib bdg; 0-7660-2928-X lib bdg

LC 2007-5281

After Galena, an eleven-year-old Russian immigrant, survives a terrible fire at the non-unionized Triangle Shirtwaist factory while her older sister and many others do not, she begins fighting for improved working conditions in New York City factories.

"Woven together in perfect compatibility, the historical background and fictional plot give readers a clear insight into Jewish immigrants and . . . . unfair labor practices, and there is excellent foreshadowing of the fire." SLJ

Includes bibliographical references

Lin, Grace

★ **Starry** River of the Sky; by Grace Lin. Little, Brown 2012 288 p. col. ill. $17.99

Grades: 3 4 5 6 **Fic**

1. Fairy tales 2. Moon -- Fiction 3. Villages -- Fiction 4. Storytelling -- Fiction

ISBN 0316125954; 9780316125956

LC 2012012651

In this novel by Grace Lin, "the moon is missing from the remote Village of Clear Sky, but only a young boy named Rendi seems to notice! Rendi has run away from home and is now working as a chore boy at the village inn. He can't help but notice the village's peculiar inhabitants and their problems . . . but one day, a mysterious lady arrives at the

Inn with the gift of storytelling, and slowly transforms the villagers and Rendi himself." (Publisher's note)

Includes bibliographical references.

★ **Where** the mountain meets the moon. Little, Brown and Co. 2009 278p il $16.99

Grades: 4 5 6 7 **Fic**

1. Fairy tales 2. Moon -- Fiction 3. Dragons -- Fiction

ISBN 978-0-316-11427-1; 0-316-11427-8

LC 2008-32818

A Newbery Medal honor book, 2010

Minli, an adventurous girl from a poor village, buys a magical goldfish, and then joins a dragon who cannot fly on a quest to find the Old Man of the Moon in hopes of bringing life to Fruitless Mountain and freshness to Jade River

"With beautiful language, Lin creates a strong, memorable heroine and a mystical land. . . . Children will embrace this accessible, timeless story about the evil of greed and the joy of gratitude." Booklist

Lindelauf, Benny

★ **Nine** Open Arms; Benny Lindelauf; translated from the Dutch by John Nieuwenhuizen; jacket and interior art by Dasha Tolstikova. Enchanted Lion 2014 264 p. illustrations, map $16.95

Grades: 5 6 7 8 9 **Fic**

1. Dutch literature 2. Historical fiction 3. Family life -- Fiction

ISBN 1592701469; 9781592701469

LC 2014014977

Mildred L. Batchelder Honor Book (2015)

"A ghost story, a fantasy, a historical novel, and literary fiction all wrapped into one, this highly awarded novel for young readers begins with the Boon family's move to an isolated, dilapidated house. Is it the site of a haunting tragedy, as one of the daughters believes, or an end to all their worries, as their father hopes?" (Publisher's note)

"Every element of the tale has a purpose, and in the end, the multiple layers of past and present separate and come together in surprising, often discomfiting twists and turns. A challenging and entirely unique Dutch import." Kirkus

Lippert-Martin, Kristen

Tabula rasa; Kristen Lippert-Martin. Egmont USA 2014 335 p. (hardcover) $17.99

Grades: 6 7 8 9 **Fic**

1. Science fiction 2. Adventure fiction 3. Memory -- Fiction 4. Hospitals -- Fiction 5. Adventure and adventurers -- Fiction

ISBN 1606845187; 9781606845189

LC 2013030315

In this book, by Kristen Lippert-Martin, "Sarah starts a crazy battle for her life within the walls of her hospital-turned-prison when a procedure to eliminate her memory goes awry and she starts to remember snatches of her past. Was she an urban terrorist or vigilante? Has the procedure been her salvation or her destruction? The answers lie trapped within her mind. To access them, she'll need the help of the teen computer hacker who's trying to bring the hospital down for his own reasons." (Publisher's note)

"Mysteries stack upon mysteries in this gripping, multifaceted thriller. A page-turning adventure that will leave readers hoping for a sequel." Horn Book

Lipsyte, Robert

★ The **contender**. Harper & Row 1967 182p hardcover o.p. pa $5.99

Grades: 7 8 9 10 **Fic**

1. Boxing -- Fiction 2. African Americans -- Fiction 3. Harlem (New York, N.Y.) -- Fiction

ISBN 0-06-447039-3

ALA YALSA Margaret A. Edwards Award (2001)

"After a street fight in which he is the chief target, Alfred wanders into a gym in his neighborhood. He decides not only to improve his physical condition but also to become a boxer. Because of this interest Alfred's life is completely changed. He assumes a more positive outlook on his immediate future, even within the confines of a black ghetto." Shapiro. Fic for Youth. 3d edition

Followed by The brave (1991) and The chief (1993)

★ **One** fat summer. Harper & Row 1977 152p hardcover o.p. pa $5.99

Grades: 7 8 9 10 **Fic**

1. Obesity -- Fiction 2. Weight loss -- Fiction

ISBN 0-06-023895-X; 0-06-447073-3 pa

LC 76-49746

ALA YALSA Margaret A. Edwards Award (2001)

"This is far superior to most of the summer-of-change stories; any change that takes place is logical and the protagonist learns by action and reaction to be both self-reliant and compassionate." Bull Cent Child Books

Followed by Summer rules (1981) and The summerboy (1982)

The **twinning** project; by Robert Lipsyte. Clarion Books 2012 269 p. (hardback) $16.99

Grades: 4 5 6 7 **Fic**

1. Science fiction 2. Twins -- Fiction 3. Parallel universes -- Fiction 4. Schools -- Fiction 5. Middle schools -- Fiction 6. Space and time -- Fiction

ISBN 0547645716; 9780547645711

LC 2011050252

This book by Robert Lipsyte follows protagonist Tom, who has been "expelled from school after school for fighting bullies. . . . The boy's only comfort comes from talking through his problems with his imaginary twin, Eddie, a jock who lives on a version of Earth 50 years behind Tom's. . . . When the boys' 'grandfather' on both Earths reveals that the twin planets were created by alien scientists, the boys switch places to fight for the survival of both Earths." (Publishers Weekly)

Lisle, Holly

★ The **Ruby** Key. Orchard Books 2008 361p (Moon & sun) $16.99; pa $7.99

Grades: 5 6 7 8 **Fic**

1. Fantasy fiction 2. Siblings -- Fiction

ISBN 978-0-545-00012-3; 0-545-00012-2; 978-0-545-00013-0 pa; 0-545-00013-0 pa

LC 2007-30217

In a world where an uneasy peace binds Humans and Nightlings, fourteen-year-old Genna and her twelve-year-old brother Dan learn of their uncle's plot to gain immortality in exchange for human lives, and the two strike their own bargain with the Nightling lord, which sets them on a dangerous journey along the Moonroads in search of a key.

"Lisle's fertile imagination provides the nightworlds with monsters . . . but it is her clever plotting in this . . . fantasy, leading up to a thrilling finish . . . That will bewitch her audience." Horn Book

Followed by: The silver door (2009)

The **silver** door. Orchard Books 2009 366p (Moon & sun) $17.99

Grades: 5 6 7 8 **Fic**

1. War stories 2. Fantasy fiction

ISBN 978-0-545-00014-7; 0-545-00014-9

LC 2008-40153

When Genna is chosen as the Sunrider of prophecy, her destiny is to unite the magic of the sun and the moon for the good of both Nightlings and humans.

"This second book of the Moon & Sun series has jarring stop-start feel, but the complexities of the interlaced human and nightling societies continue to unfold in fascinating way, creating a multi-hued, fully realized world for readers to explore." Horn Book

Littke, Lael

Lake of secrets. Holt & Co. 2002 202p $16.95

Grades: 7 8 9 10 **Fic**

1. Mystery fiction 2. Reincarnation -- Fiction

ISBN 0-8050-6730-2

LC 2001-39933

Having arrived in her mother's home town to try to find her long-missing brother, who disappeared three years before she was born, fifteen-year-old Carlene finds herself haunted by memories from a past life

"The realistic characters and plot make the idea compelling, and the story will intrigue teens." Booklist

Little, Kimberley Griffiths

★ **Circle** of secrets. Scholastic Press 2011 326p $17.99

Grades: 5 6 7 8 **Fic**

1. Ghost stories 2. Guilt -- Fiction 3. Louisiana -- Fiction 4. Mother-daughter relationship -- Fiction

ISBN 978-0-545-16561-7; 0-545-16561-X

LC 2011000889

A year after her mother has deserted the family, eleven-year-old Shelby goes to stay with her, deep in the Louisiana bayou, where they both confront old hurts and regrets.

"The gently spooky ghost angle is handled nicely with some religious overtones. A very dramatic climax leads to a sweet, satisfying ending with some surprising twists and with reconciliation occurring for several characters." Kirkus

The **healing** spell. Scholastic Press 2010 354p $17.99

Grades: 5 6 7 8 **Fic**

1. Coma -- Fiction 2. Guilt -- Fiction 3. Mother-

daughter relationship -- Fiction
ISBN 978-0-545-16559-4; 0-545-16559-8
LC 2009-28016

Twelve-year-old Livie is living with a secret and it's crushing her. She knows she is responsible for her mother's coma, but she can't tell anyone. It's up to her to find a way to wake her momma up.

"Little explores the extremes of childhood guilt and its consequences in this harsh yet well-crafted story about fully drawn people. The bayou, with its rich culture, is an atmospheric character that overlays the story with mystery and dread." Booklist

The **time** of the fireflies; Kimberley Griffiths Little. Scholastic Press 2014 368 p. (jacketed hardcover) $18.99

Grades: 5 6 7 8　　　　　　　　　　　　　　Fic
1. Mystery fiction 2. Family secrets -- Fiction 3. Secrets -- Fiction 4. Fireflies -- Fiction 5. Louisiana -- Fiction 6. Family life -- Fiction 7. Time travel -- Fiction 8. Family problems -- Fiction
ISBN 0545165636; 9780545165631
LC 2013027396

In this middle grades book by Kimberley Griffiths Little, "When Larissa Renaud starts receiving eerie phone calls on a disconnected old phone in her family's antique shop, she knows she's in for a strange summer. A series of clues leads her to the muddy river banks. . . . It soon becomes clear that it is up to Larissa to prevent history from repeating itself and a fatal tragedy from striking the people she loves." (Publisher's note)

"Twelve-year-old Larissa's parents own Bayou Bridge Antiques, which features a wall of old phones. When one of the phones begins ringing, Larissa hesitantly picks it up. The female voice on the other end begs Larissa to find the fireflies. . . . [F]ans of Mary Downing Hahn's books will appreciate the spooky porcelain dolls and family curse." Booklist

Littlefield, Sophie

Infected; Sophie Littlefield. First edition Delacorte Press 2015 256 p. (hc : alk. paper) $17.99

Grades: 7 8 9 10　　　　　　　　　　　　　　Fic
1. Conspiracies -- Fiction 2. Family secrets -- Fiction 3. National security -- United States 4. Spies -- Fiction 5. Survival -- Fiction 6. Dating (Social customs) -- Fiction
ISBN 0385741065; 9780375989834; 9780385741064
LC 2013046923

"Carina's senior year is spiraling downward. Fast. Both her mother and her uncle, the only two family members she's ever known, are dead. Their deaths were accidents, unfortunate results of the highly confidential research they performed for a national security organization. The people Carina loved kept dangerous secrets, Secrets that make her question the life she's been living up to now." (Publisher's note)

"Nail-biting action with a scientifically and technologically involved plotline gives this novel an edge, and, moreover, the character development is surprisingly rich given the fast pace of the narrative. The weight of the themes also keeps the story from reading like a movie script. Red herrings keep the reader guessing until the end. Hard to put down." Booklist

Littman, Sarah

Backlash; Sarah Darer Littman. First edition Scholastic Press 2015 325 p. $17.99

Grades: 7 8 9　　　　　　　　　　　　　　Fic
1. Bullies -- Fiction 2. Sisters -- Fiction 3. Suicide -- Fiction 4. Neighbors -- Fiction 5. Friendship -- Fiction 6. Family life -- Fiction 7. Cyberbullying -- Fiction 8. Bullying -- Fiction
ISBN 0545651263; 9780545651264; 9780545651271; 9780545755023
LC 2014020226

In this book, by Sarah Darer Littman, "Lara just got told off on Facebook. She thought that Christian liked her, that he was finally going to ask her to his school's homecoming dance. It's been a long time since Lara's felt this bad, this depressed. . . . Bree used to be BBFs with overweight, depressed Lara in middle school, but constantly listening to Lara's problems got to be too much. Bree's secretly glad that Christian's pointed out Lara's flaws to the world." (Publisher's note)

"The depression and bullying are handled realistically without sugarcoating, and fortunately, consequences are applied. An excellent choice for any antibullying campaign." Booklist

Life, after; [by] Sarah Darer Littman. Scholastic Press 2010 281p $17.99

Grades: 7 8 9 10 11 12　　　　　　　　　　Fic
1. Argentina -- Fiction 2. Terrorism -- Fiction 3. Immigrants -- Fiction
ISBN 978-0-545-15144-3; 0-545-15144-9

After a terrorist attack kills Dani's aunt and unborn cousin, life in Argentina—private school, a boyfriend, a loving family—crumbles quickly. In order to escape a country that is sinking under their feet, Dani and her family move to the United States.

The author "weaves sensitively articulated themes . . . and credible teen banter into an emotionally complex tale." Booklist

Llewellyn, Sam

Darksolstice. Orchard Books 2010 365p map (Lyonesse) $17.99

Grades: 5 6 7 8　　　　　　　　　　　　　　Fic
1. Fantasy fiction 2. Kings
ISBN 978-0-439-93471-8; 0-439-93471-0
LC 2009006283

Sequel to: The well between the worlds (2009)

While Idris Limpet, Rightful King of the Land of Lyonesse, is making the treacherous journey to the distant land of Aegypt to rescue his dear friend and sister, Morgan, he meets a company of friends who shall become his Knights of the Round Table and lead armies to battle the evil regent, Fisheagle.

The **well** between the worlds. Orchard Books 2009 339p (Lyonesse) $17.99

Grades: 5 6 7 8　　　　　　　　　　　　　　Fic
1. Fantasy fiction 2. Kings
ISBN 978-0-439-93469-5; 0-439-93469-9
LC 2008-20075

Eleven-year-old Idris Limpet, living with his family in the once noble but now evil and corrupt island country of Lyonesse, finds his life taking a dramatic turn when, after a near-drowning incident, he is accused of being allied to the feared sea monsters and is rescued from a death sentence by a mysterious and fearsome stranger.

"Seldom does one find a new fantasy that is so richly textured, so original in concept, and with such a wonderfully interesting story.... Fantasy lovers will be impatient to find out where their paths take them." Voice Youth Advocates

Followed by: Darksolstice (2010)

Lloyd, Alison

Year of the tiger. Holiday House 2010 194p $16.95

Grades: 5 6 7 8   **Fic**

1. Adventure fiction 2. China -- Fiction 3. Archery -- Fiction 4. Social classes -- Fiction

ISBN 978-0-8234-2277-7; 0-8234-2277-1

LC 2009033651

First published 2008 in Australia

In ancient China, Hu and Ren forge an unlikely alliance in an effort to become expert archers and, ultimately, to save their city from invading barbarians.

"Brimming with details of daily life in the Han Dynasty, this fast-paced story alternates in the third person between Hu and Ren." Kirkus

Lloyd, Natalie

★ A **snicker** of magic; by Natalie Lloyd. Scholastic Press 2014 320 p. hbk $16.99

Grades: 4 5 6 7   **Fic**

1. Magic -- Fiction 2. Curses -- Fiction 3. Tennessee -- Fiction 4. Friendship -- Fiction 5. Family life -- Fiction 6. Mothers and daughters -- Fiction

ISBN 9780545552707; 0545552702

LC 2013027779

"Midnight Gulch used to be a magical place, a town where people could sing up thunderstorms and dance up sunflowers. But that was long ago, before a curse drove the magic away. Twelve-year-old Felicity knows all about things like that; her nomadic mother is cursed with a wandering heart.... But when she arrives in Midnight Gulch, Felicity thinks her luck's about to change." (Publisher's note)

"The unusual language, showing a tinge of Tennessee mountain dialect, spins a web around the story that touches on helping others, budding friendships, and strength of family." Booklist

Lloyd, Saci

★ The **carbon** diaries 2015. Holiday House 2009 330p il map $17.95

Grades: 8 9 10 11 12   **Fic**

1. Science fiction 2. Family life -- Fiction 3. Great Britain -- Fiction 4. Conservation of natural resources -- Fiction

ISBN 978-0-8234-2190-9; 0-8234-2190-2

LC 2008-19712

First published 2008 in the United Kingdom

In 2015, when England becomes the first nation to introduce carbon dioxide rationing in a drastic bid to combat climate change, sixteen-year-old Laura documents the first year of rationing as her family spirals out of control.

"Deeply compulsive and urgently compulsory reading." Booklist

Includes bibliographical references

Followed by The carbon diaries 2017 (2010)

The **carbon** diaries 2017. Holiday House 2010 326p il map $17.95

Grades: 8 9 10 11 12   **Fic**

1. Science fiction 2. College students -- Fiction 3. London (England) -- Fiction 4. Conservation of natural resources -- Fiction

ISBN 978-0-8234-2260-9; 0-8234-2260-7

Sequel to: The carbon diaries 2015 (2009)

First published 2009 in the United Kingdom

Two years after England introduces carbon dioxide rationing to combat climatic change, eighteen-year-old Laura chronicles her first year at a London university as natural disasters and political upheaval disrupt her studies.

"The friction of living life in times of radical upheaval remains potent, sobering, and awfully exciting." Booklist

Lloyd-Jones, Emily

Illusive; Emily Lloyd-Jones. Little, Brown & Co. 2014 416 p. (hardcover) $18

Grades: 7 8 9 10 11 12   **Fic**

1. Science fiction 2. Dystopian fiction 3. Vaccines -- Fiction 4. Superheroes -- Fiction 5. Organized crime -- Fiction 6. Robbers and outlaws -- Fiction 7. Adventure and adventurers -- Fiction

ISBN 0316254568; 9780316254564

LC 2013025295

In this young adult science fiction novel by Emily Lloyd-Jones, "When the MK virus swept across the planet, a vaccine was created to stop the epidemic, but it came with some unexpected side effects. A small percentage of the population developed superhero-like powers. Seventeen-year-old Ciere Giba has the handy ability to change her appearance at will. She's what's known as an illusionist...She's also a thief." (Publisher's note)

"Ciere, a teenage career criminal with the ability to create illusions, lives in a dystopian future where a vaccine gone wrong created a feared minority of people with superpowers. Her latest job pulls her and her Dickensian gang of misfit allies into a power struggle involving the future of the vaccine. Innovative world-building and a scrappy protagonist strengthen this high-stakes caper." Horn Book

Lockhart, E.

★ The **disreputable** history of Frankie Landau-Banks. Hyperion 2008 352p $16.99; pa $8.99

Grades: 7 8 9 10 11 12   **Fic**

1. School stories

ISBN 0-7868-3818-3; 0-7868-3819-1 pa; 978-0-7868-3818-9; 978-0-7868-3819-6 pa

Michael L. Printz Award honor book, 2009

"Frankie Landau-Banks at age 14: Debate Club. Her father's 'bunny rabbit.' A mildly geeky girl attending a highly competitive boarding school. Frankie Landau-Banks at age 15: A knockout figure. A sharp tongue. A chip on her shoulder. And a gorgeous new senior boyfriend: ... Matthew

Livingston. Frankie Landau-Banks. No longer the kind of girl to take 'no' for an answer. Especially when 'no' means she's excluded from her boyfriend's all-male secret society. . . . Not when she knows she's smarter than any of them. When she knows Matthew's lying to her. . . . Frankie Banks at age 16: Possibly a criminal mastermind. This is the story of how she got that way." (Publisher's note) "Grades nine to twelve." (Bull Cent Child Books)

"On her return to Alabaster Prep . . . [Frankie] attracts the attention of gorgeous Matthew . . . [who] is a member of the Loyal Order of the Basset Hounds, an all-male Alabaster secret society. . . . Frankie engineers her own guerilla membership by assuming a false online identity. . . . Lockhart creates a unique, indelible character. . . . Teens will be galvanized." Booklist

★ **Dramarama.** Hyperion 2007 311p $15.99
Grades: 7 8 9 10 11 12   Fic
1. School stories 2. Actors -- Fiction 3. Friendship -- Fiction
ISBN 0-7868-3815-9; 978-0-7868-3815-8
LC 2006-49599

Spending their summer at Wildewood Academy, an elite boarding school for the performing arts, tests the bond between best friends Sadye and Demi.

"Teens will identify strongly with both the heartbreak and the humor in this authentic portrayal of friendships maturing and decaying." SLJ

★ **We** were liars; E. Lockhart. Delacorte Press 2014 240 p. (hardback) $17.99
Grades: 7 8 9 10 11 12   Fic
1. Summer -- Fiction 2. Wealth -- Fiction 3. Family life 4. Love -- Fiction 5. Amnesia -- Fiction 6. Families -- Fiction 7. Friendship -- Fiction
ISBN 038574126X; 9780375989940; 9780385741262
LC 2013042127

In this book, by E. Lockhart, "Cadence Sinclair Eastman is the oldest grandchild of a preeminent family. The Sinclairs have . . . a private island off the coast of Massachusetts called Beechwood. Harris, the family patriarch, has three daughters: Bess, Carrie, and Penny, who is Cadence's mother. And then there is the next generation, 'the Liars': Cadence, Johnny, . . . Mirren, . . . and outsider Gat, an Indian boy and the nephew of Carrie's boyfriend." (Booklist)

"Cadence Sinclair Easton comes from an old-money family, headed by a patriarch who owns a private island off of Cape Cod. Each summer, the extended family gathers at the various houses on the island, and Cadence, her cousins Johnny and Mirren, and friend Gat (the four "Liars"), have been inseparable since age eight....The story, while lightly touching on issues of class and race, more fully focuses on dysfunctional family drama, a heart-wrenching romance between Cadence and Gat, and, ultimately, the suspense of what happened during that fateful summer. The ending is a stunner that will haunt readers for a long time to come." (School Library Journal)

Lockwood, Vicki

The **magnificent** Lizzie Brown and the mysterious phantom; by Vicki Lockwood; illustrated by Stephanie Hans. Stone Arch Books, a Capstone im-

print 2014 200 p. (The magnificent Lizzie Brown) (paper over board) $10.95
Grades: 5 6 7 8   Fic
1. Circus 2. Mystery fiction 3. Circus -- Fiction 4. Criminals -- Fiction 5. Psychic ability -- Fiction 6. Mystery and detective stories
ISBN 1623700698; 9781434279408; 9781434279422; 9781623700690
LC 2013050830

Sequel to: The Magnificent Lizzie Brown and the Devil's Hound (2014)

In this juvenile novel, by Vicki Lockwood, illustrated by Stephanie Hans, "a mysterious Phantom is terrorizing London, and when Lizzie realizes she has a talent that will let her stop the crimes before they happen she and her new circus friends feel compelled to intervene. But when one of their own is blamed for the crimes instead, their investigation takes a turn for the worse." (Publisher's note)

"In Victorian London, a twelve-year-old escapes grinding poverty and an abusive father by joining a traveling circus and finding first work, then acceptance and love, and finally a vocation: she becomes the circus fortuneteller. Despite plot contrivances and conversational anachronisms, Lizzie is an appealing heroine and these first two series entries are satisfying." Horn Book

Loftin, Nikki

Nightingale's nest; Nikki Loftin. Razorbill 2014 256 p. 22 cm (hardcover) $16.99
Grades: 4 5 6 7   Fic
1. Boys -- Fiction 2. Friendship -- Fiction 3. Birds -- Fiction 4. Magic -- Fiction 5. Singing -- Fiction 6. Family problems -- Fiction 7. Foster home care -- Fiction 8. Dysfunctional families -- fiction
ISBN 159514546X; 9781595145468
LC 2013047556

"Twelve-year-old John Fischer Jr. . . . is spending his summer helping his father with his tree removal business, clearing brush for Mr. King, the wealthy owner of a chain of Texas dollar stores, when he hears a beautiful song that transfixes him. Inspired by a Hans Christian Andersen story, 'Nightingale's Nest' is a . . . novel about a boy with the weight of the world on his shoulders and a girl with the gift of healing in her voice." (Publisher's note)

"John narrates his story in fluid, lyrical prose, Loftin blending the raw realism of a boy who makes the wrong choice with the fairy-tale magic of a girl with a nightingale voice. Unusual, finely crafted story of loss, betrayal and healing." Kirkus

Wish girl; Nikki Loftin. Razorbill 2015 256 p. (hardcover) $16.99
Grades: 4 5 6 7   Fic
1. Friendship -- Fiction 2. Cancer patients -- Fiction 3. Runaway children -- Fiction 4. Texas -- Fiction 5. Cancer -- Fiction 6. Best friends -- Fiction 7. Individuality -- Fiction 8. Family problems -- Fiction 9. Family life -- Texas -- Fiction
ISBN 1595146865; 9781595146861
LC 2014031004

In this children's novel by Nikki Loftin "when his family moves to the Texas Hill Country, ... Peter finds a tranquil, natural valley where he can, at last, hear himself think. There, he meets a girl his age: Annie Blythe . . . a 'Make-A-Wish Girl.' And in two weeks she will begin a dangerous treatment to try and stop her cancer from spreading. Annie and Peter hatch a plan to escape into the valley. But the pair soon discovers that the valley--and life--may have other plans for them." (Publisher's note)

"In this companion to Nightingale's Nest (Razorbill, 2014), 12-year-old Peter Stone's new home in rural Texas is completely unlike his previous life in San Antonio. Even in the quiet of the country, his family is too loud. They never stop to understand sensitive, introverted Peter...This emotional story will be loved by fans of Nightingale's Nest, as the plot structure, atmosphere, and characters are similar." SLJ

Companion to:
Nightingale's Nest (2014)

Loizeaux, William

★ **Clarence** Cochran, a human boy; pictures by Anne Wilsdorf. Farrar, Straus and Giroux 2009 152p il $16

Grades: 4 5 6 **Fic**
1. Toleration -- Fiction 2. Cockroaches -- Fiction 3. Environmental protection -- Fiction
ISBN 978-0-374-31323-4; 0-374-31323-7

LC 2007-35358

With the threat of extermination looming, a cockroach who has been transformed into a tiny human learns to communicate with his human hosts, leading to an agreement both sides can live with, and a friendship between Clarence and ten-year-old Mimi, a human environmentalist.

"There's a serious message here about environmentalism and the power of words, and the action and suspense make this a good read-aloud or classroom-discussion choice." SLJ

London, Alex

Guardian; Alex London. Philomel Books, an imprint of Penguin Group (USA) Inc. 2014 352 p. $17.99

Grades: 7 8 9 **Fic**
1. Science fiction 2. Dystopian fiction 3. Epidemics -- Fiction 4. Social classes -- Fiction 5. Gays -- Fiction
ISBN 0399165762; 9780399165764

LC 2013025938

Sequel to: Proxy

"It's a grave new world when the revolution a reluctant hero inspired could mean the death of everyone he tried to save, including himself. In this sequel to Proxy (2013), radical groups form in the wake of the Jubilee. The Reconciliation staunchly endorses tech-free purity, while Machinists demand a renaissance of the networks. Reluctant 16-year-old hero Syd is paraded as a political puppet, labeled a savior by supporters and marked a target by the opposition. His importance as a mascot for the Reconciliation necessitates a bodyguard, 17-year-old Liam. Liam is strong (he has a killer metal hand), silent (too shy for vocal eloquence) and will do anything to remain near Syd for reasons other than professional integrity. Amid political upheaval, an illness begins to spread, rendering victims' blue blood black and diminishing their mental faculties. Syd has been a hesitant political

figure but knows he is the only hope for ending the illness." (Kirkus)

"Nonstop action and breakneck pace characterize this exceptional thriller. London provides his audience with an intricate plot, enriched by fine world-building and believable characters. The ample backstory will enable readers to enjoy Guardian without having read Proxy, although most will want to read these in sequence. This thought-provoking and breathtaking novel belongs in all collections serving young adults." VOYA

Proxy; Alex London. Philomel 2013 379 p. $17.99

Grades: 7 8 9 10 **Fic**
1. Science fiction 2. Dystopian fiction 3. Gays -- Fiction 4. Social classes -- Fiction
ISBN 0399257764; 9780399257766

LC 2012039704

In this book, "Knox is a 'patron,' a privileged and wealthy citizen of Mountain City. His only concerns are hacking, scoring with girls, and causing trouble while angering his bigwig dad. His proxy, a person who is contractually obligated to serve out Knox's punishments, is a gay teen. In exchange for working as a proxy, Syd is able to pay off his debts. When Knox accidentally kills a girl, 16 years at the Old Sterling Work Colony is too great a punishment for Syd to bear, so he escapes." (School Library Journal)

London, Jack

★ The **call** of the wild; pictures by Wendell Minor. Atheneum Books for Young Readers 1999 112p il $24; pa $4.95

Grades: 5 6 7 8 9 10 11 12 Adult **Fic**
1. Dogs -- Fiction 2. Alaska -- Fiction 3. Yukon River valley (Yukon and Alaska) -- Fiction
ISBN 0-689-81836-X; 1-4165-0019-7 pa

LC 97-45019

First published 1903 by Macmillan

"Buck, half-St. Bernard, half-Scottish sheepdog, is stolen from his comfortable home in California and pressed into service as a sledge dog in the Klondike. At first he is abused by both man and dog, but he learns to fight ruthlessly. He becomes lead dog on a sledge team, after bettering Spitz, the vicious old leader, in a brutal fight to the death. In John Thornton, he finally finds a master whom he can respect and love. When Thornton is killed by Indians, Buck breaks away to the wilds and becomes the leader of a wolf pack, returning each year to the site of Thornton's death." Reader's Ency. 4th edition

Long, Ruth Frances

The **treachery** of beautiful things; by Ruth Frances Long. Dial Books 2012 363 p. (hardcover) $17.99

Grades: 7 8 9 10 11 12 **Fic**
1. Fantasy fiction 2. Fairies -- Fiction 3. Forests and forestry -- Fiction 4. Fantasy 5. Love -- Fiction 6. Kings, queens, rulers, etc. -- Fiction
ISBN 0803735804; 9780803735804

LC 2011027165

In this book by Ruth Long, "the trees swallowed her brother whole, and Jenny was there to see it. Now seventeen, she revisits the woods where Tom was taken. . . . . She's lured into the trees, where she finds strange and dangerous creatures. . . . Among them is Jack, mercurial and magnetic, with secrets of his own. Determined to find her brother, with or without Jack's help, Jenny struggles to navigate a faerie world where stunning beauty masks some of the most treacherous evils." (Publisher's note)

Lopez, Diana

Ask my mood ring how I feel; by Diana Lopez. 1st ed. Little, Brown and Co. 2013 324 p. (hardcover) $17

Grades: 4 5 6 7   **Fic**
1. Breast cancer -- Fiction 2. Children of cancer patients -- Fiction 3. Cancer -- Fiction 4. Promises -- Fiction 5. Friendship -- Fiction 6. Fund-raising -- Fiction 7. Christian life -- Fiction 8. Hispanic Americans -- Fiction 9. San Antonio (Tex.) -- Fiction 10. Family life -- Texas -- Fiction
ISBN 0316209961; 9780316209960
LC 2012029856

In this book, Chia's "mother is diagnosed with breast cancer, which spurs . . . changes throughout their family. . . . After visiting the Basilica of Our Lady of San Juan del Valle in southern Texas, Chia dedicates herself to a promesa, vowing to secure 500 sponsors for a Walk for the Cure in exchange (she hopes) for her mother's recovery." (Publishers Weekly)

Confetti girl. Little, Brown and Company 2009 198p $15.99

Grades: 4 5 6 7   **Fic**
1. School stories 2. Texas -- Fiction 3. Friendship -- Fiction 4. Bereavement -- Fiction 5. Mexican Americans -- Fiction 6. Father-daughter relationship -- Fiction
ISBN 978-0-316-02955-1; 0-316-02955-6
LC 2008032819

After the death of her mother, Texas sixth-grader Lina's grades and mood drop as she watches her father lose himself more and more in books, while her best friend uses Lina as an excuse to secretly meet her boyfriend.

"Lopez effectively portrays the Texas setting and the characters' Latino heritage. . . . This . . . novel puts at its center a likable girl facing realistic problems on her own terms." Booklist

Lord, Cynthia

Half a chance; Cynthia Lord. Scholastic Press 2014 224 p. (hc) $16.99

Grades: 4 5 6 7   **Fic**
1. Photography -- Fiction 2. Father-daughter relationship -- Fiction 3. Friendship -- Fiction 4. New Hampshire -- Fiction
ISBN 0545035333; 9780545035330
LC 2013013431

"When Lucy's family moves to an old house on a lake, Lucy tries to see her new home through her camera's lens, as her father has taught her--he's a famous photographer, away on a shoot. . . . When she discovers that he's judging a photo contest, Lucy decides to enter anonymously. She wants to find out if her eye for photography is really special--or only good enough." (Publisher's note)

"The story is moving, and readers will find themselves caught up in sensitive Lucy's honest and thoughtful narration." Horn Book

★ **Touch** blue. Scholastic Press 2010 186p $16.99

Grades: 4 5 6 7   **Fic**
1. Maine -- Fiction 2. Islands -- Fiction 3. Foster home care -- Fiction
ISBN 978-0-545-03531-6; 0-545-03531-7
LC 2009042306

When the state of Maine threatens to shut down their island's one-room schoolhouse because of dwindling enrollment, eleven-year-old Tess, a strong believer in luck, and her family take in a trumpet-playing foster child named Aaron to increase the school's population.

"Aaron's relationship with his foster family . . . develops believably. The tight-knit community and lobster-catching details make for a warm, colorful environment. This is a feel-good story." Booklist

Lottridge, Celia Barker

The **listening** tree. Fitzhenry & Whiteside 2011 172p $11.95

Grades: 4 5 6 7   **Fic**
1. Canada -- Fiction 2. Courage -- Fiction 3. Great Depression, 1929-1939 -- Fiction
ISBN 978-1-55455-052-4; 1-55455-052-1

It's 1935, and Ellen and her mother must leave their dried-up Saskatchewan farm to board with Aunt Gladys in Toronto. Intimidated by her new surroundings, Ellen chooses to hide in the branches of the large leafy tree outside her window and watch the neighbourhood children playing, rather than joining in their games. But when Ellen overhears a plan to evict the family-next-door from their home, she must overcome her fears and help her neighbours.

"Lottridge provides a wealth of well-developed, believable characters, especially Ellen. The story is a deftly-written, heartbreaking, and heartwarming tale of friendship and the perseverance to withstand hardships. This is a great book to introduce young readers to the impact of the Great Depression." Voice Youth Advocates

Love, D. Anne

Defying the diva; [by] D. Anne Love. Margaret K. McElderry Books 2008 257p $16.99

Grades: 7 8 9 10   **Fic**
1. School stories 2. Bullies -- Fiction
ISBN 978-1-4169-3481-3; 1-4169-3481-2
LC 2007-10945

During Haley's freshman year of high school, a campaign of gossip and bullying causes her to be socially ostracized, but after spending the summer living with her aunt, working at a resort, making new friends, and dating a hunky lifeguard, she learns how to stand up for herself and begins to trust again.

"Concluding with a serious author's note on harassment, which includes information on getting help, this text skillfully captures the painful reality of teen bullying while also telling Haley's humorous and sincere story of growing up." Kirkus

Semiprecious. Margaret K. McElderry Books 2006 293p $16.95; pa $6.99

Grades: 5 6 7 8   Fic

1. Oklahoma -- Fiction 2. Family life -- Fiction
ISBN 978-0-689-85638-9; 0-689-85638-5; 978-0-689-87389-8 pa; 0-689-87389-1 pa

LC 2005-14906

Uprooted and living with an aunt in 1960s Oklahoma, thirteen-year-old Garnet and her older sister Opal brave their mother's desertion and their father's recovery from an accident, learning that "the best home of all is the one you make inside yourself"

"An involving novel of hurt, healing, and adjustment." Booklist

Lovejoy, Sharon

Running out of night; Sharon Lovejoy. Delacorte Press 2014 304 p. (hc) $16.99

Grades: 5 6 7   Fic

1. Friendship -- Fiction 2. Fugitive slaves -- Fiction 3. Runaways -- Fiction 4. Race relations -- Fiction 5. African Americans -- Fiction
ISBN 0385744099; 9780375991479; 9780385744096

LC 2013026375

In this novel by Sharon Lovejoy "when Zenobia, a fugitive slave, creeps onto the porch of an 1858 Virginia home, the white girl inside schemes to prevent her abusive father from spotting the escapee. Denied a name and mistreated by her motherless family, the girl quickly concludes that her circumstances look little better than plucky Zenobia's and the two resolve to flee together." (School Library Journal)

"In 1858, twelve-year-old Girl, white, lower-class, and abused, flees her Virginia home and travels toward Quaker Waterford with runaway slaves. As she befriends the slaves, first-person narrator Girl (renamed Lark) astutely differentiates between her own subjugation and that of black slaves. Unfortunately, several characters' near-miraculous recoveries from escape-related injuries undermine an otherwise head-on look at multiple forms of enslavement. Websites. Bib., glos." Horn Book

Low, Dene

The **entomological** tales of Augustus T. Percival; Petronella saves nearly everyone. Houghton Mifflin 2009 196p $16.00

Grades: 7 8 9 10   Fic

1. Uncles -- Fiction 2. Insects -- Fiction 3. Missing persons -- Fiction 4. London (England) -- Fiction
ISBN 0-547-15250-7; 978-0-547-15250-9

Petronella's fashionable friends are arriving at her country estate near London to celebrate her sixteenth birthday and her coming out party. During the festivities, important guests are disappearing, kidnapping notes are appearing, many of the clues are insects, and Uncle Augustus (who has developed a bug eating compulsion) is surreptitiously devouring evidence.

"Archetypical characters are skillfully drawn, time and place are clearly evoked, and excitement and intrigue abound amid the hilarity." SLJ

Lowry, Lois

Anastasia at your service; decorations by Diane DeGroat. Houghton Mifflin 1982 149p il pa $5.50

Grades: 4 5 6   Fic

1. Friendship -- Fiction 2. Household employees -- Fiction
ISBN 0-395-32865-9; 0-440-40290-5 pa

LC 82009231

Twelve-year-old Anastasia has a series of disastrous experiences when, expecting to get a job as a lady's companion, she is hired instead to be a maid.

★ **Anastasia** Krupnik. Houghton Mifflin 1979 113p $17; pa $5.99

Grades: 4 5 6   Fic

1. Family life -- Fiction
ISBN 0-395-28629-8; 0-440-40852-0 pa

Anastasia's 10th year has some good things like falling in love and really getting to know her grandmother and some bad things like finding out about an impending baby brother

"Anastasia's father and mother—an English professor and an artist—are among the most humorous, sensible, and understanding parents to be found in . . . children's fiction, and Anastasia herself is an amusing and engaging heroine." Horn Book

Other titles about Anastasia Krupnik are:
Anastasia again! (1981)
Anastasia at your service (1982)
Anastasia, ask your analyst (1984)
Anastasia on her own (1985)
Anastasia has the answers (1986)
Anastasia's chosen career (1987)
Anastasia at this address (1991)
Anastasia, absolutely (1995)

Gathering blue. Houghton Mifflin 2000 215p $16; pa $8.95

Grades: 5 6 7 8   Fic

1. Science fiction
ISBN 0-618-05581-9; 0-385-73256-2 pa

LC 00-24359

Lame and suddenly orphaned, Kira is mysteriously removed from her squalid village to live in the palatial Council Edifice, where she is expected to use her gifts as a weaver to do the bidding of the all-powerful Guardians

"Lowry has once again created a fully realized world full of drama, suspense, and even humor." SLJ

★ The **giver**. Houghton Mifflin 1993 180p pa $8.95; $17

Grades: 6 7 8 9 10   Fic

1. Science fiction
ISBN 0-385-73255-4 pa; 0-395-64566-2

LC 92-15034

Awarded the Newbery Medal, 1994

This novel is set in a future society "without conflict, poverty, unemployment, divorce, injustice, or inequality. . . . December is the time of the annual Ceremony at which each twelve-year-old receives a life assignment determined by the Elders. . . . Jonas has been chosen for something special. When his selection leads him to an unnamed man—the man called only the Giver—he begins to sense the dark secrets that underlie the fragile perfection of his world." (Publisher's note) "Grades five to eight." (Bull Cent Child Books)

"A riveting, chilling story that inspires a new appreciation for diversity, love, and even pain. Truly memorable." SLJ

★ **Number** the Stars; Lois Lowry. 25th Anniversary Edition Houghton Mifflin Harcourt 2014 137 p. $17.99

Grades: 4 5 6 7　　　　　　　　　　　　**Fic**
　1. Jews -- Fiction 2. Denmark -- Fiction 3. Friendship -- Fiction 4. World War, 1939-1945 -- Fiction
　ISBN 0544340000; 9780544340008

LC 8837134

First published 1989

Newbery Medal (1990)

"As the German troops begin their campaign to 'relocate' all the Jews of Denmark, Annemarie Johansen's family takes in Annemarie's best friend, Ellen Rosen, and conceals her as part of the family. Through the eyes of ten-year-old Annemarie, we watch as the Danish Resistance smuggles almost the entire Jewish population of Denmark, nearly seven thousand people, across the sea to Sweden." (Publisher's note)

"The appendix details the historical incidents upon which Lowry bases her plot. . . . The whole work is seamless, compelling, and memorable." Horn Book

Awarded the Newbery Medal, 1990

In 1943, during the German occupation of Denmark, ten-year-old Annemarie learns how to be brave and courageous when she helps shelter her Jewish friend from the Nazis

"The appended details the historical incidents upon which Lowry bases her plot. . . . The whole work is seamless, compelling, and memorable." Horn Book

The **silent** boy. Houghton Mifflin 2003 178p $15

Grades: 4 5 6 7　　　　　　　　　　　　**Fic**
　1. Mentally disabled -- Fiction
　ISBN 0-618-28231-9

LC 2002-9072

Katy, the precocious eight-year-old daughter of the town doctor, befriends a retarded boy

"The author balances humor and generosity with the obstacles and injustice of Katy's world to depict a complete picture of the turn of the 20th century." Publ Wkly

★ **Son**; by Lois Lowry. Houghton Mifflin 2012 393 p. $17.99

Grades: 6 7 8 9 10 11 12　　　　　　　　**Fic**
　1. Science fiction 2. Dystopian fiction 3. Amnesia -- Fiction 4. Mothers -- Fiction 5. Secrecy -- Fiction 6. Identity -- Fiction 7. Mother-child relationship -- Fiction 8. Mother and child -- Fiction 9. Separation (Psychology) -- Fiction
　ISBN 0547887205; 9780547887203

LC 2012014034

Author Lois Lowry tells the story of "14-year-old Claire, [who] has no contact with her baby Gabe until she surreptitiously bonds with him in the community Nurturing Center. . . . After living for years with Alys, a childless healer, Claire's memory returns. Intent on finding Gabe, she . . . encounters the sinister Trademaster and exchanges her youth for

his help in finding her child, now living in the same village as middle-aged Jonas and his wife Kira. Elderly and failing, Claire reveals her identity to Gabe, who must use his unique talent to save the village." (Kirkus Reviews)

Lu, Marie

★ **Champion**; a Legend novel. Marie Lu. G.P. Putnam's Sons, an imprint of Penguin Group (USA) 2013 384 p. (hardback) $18.99

Grades: 8 9 10 11 12　　　　　　　　　　**Fic**
　1. Love -- Fiction 2. Dystopian fiction 3. Plague -- Fiction 4. Science fiction
　ISBN 0399256776; 9780399256776

LC 2013028221

In this novel, by Marie Lu, "June and Day have sacrificed so much for the people of the Republic—and each other—and now their country is on the brink of a new existence. June is back in the good graces of the Republic, working within the government's elite circles as Princeps Elect while Day has been assigned a high level military position. But neither could have predicted the circumstances that will reunite them once again." (Publisher's note)

"Having been diagnosed with a terminal illness, Day (Legend; Prodigy) takes care of his brother, Eden, victim of the Republic's experiments in biological warfare. International diplomacy raises the stakes in this final volume of the trilogy, but readers will likely care more about whether Day and June (the Republic's prodigy) can repair their passionate romance. Lu's storytelling is compulsively readable." (Horn Book)

★ **Legend**. G. P. Putnam's Sons 2011 305p $17.99

Grades: 8 9 10 11 12　　　　　　　　　　**Fic**
　1. War stories 2. Science fiction 3. Plague -- Fiction 4. Siblings -- Fiction 5. Soldiers -- Fiction 6. Criminals -- Fiction 7. Resistance to government -- Fiction
　ISBN 978-0-399-25675-2; 0-399-25675-X

LC 2011002003

"The characters are likable, the plot moves at a good pace, and the adventure is solid." SLJ

★ **Prodigy**; a Legend novel. Marie Lu. G. P. Putnam's Sons 2012 384 p. (Legend) $17.99

Grades: 8 9 10 11 12　　　　　　　　　　**Fic**
　1. Science fiction 2. Dystopian fiction 3. Fugitives from justice -- Fiction 4. Resistance to government -- Fiction 5. War -- Fiction 6. Soldiers -- Fiction 7. Criminals -- Fiction 8. Assassination -- Fiction 9. Government, Resistance to -- Fiction
　ISBN 0399256768; 9780399256769

LC 2012003773

This young adult science fiction adventure novel, by Marie Lu, is the sequel to her novel "Legend." "Injured and on the run, it has been seven days since June and Day barely escaped Los Angeles and the Republic with their lives. Day is believed dead. . . . June is now the Republic's most wanted traitor. Desperate for help, they turn to the Patriots--a vigilante rebel group sworn to bring down the Republic. But can they trust them?" (Publisher's note)

"This is a well-molded mixture of intrigue, romance, and action, where things can change with almost any turn of the page, and frequently do." Booklist

The **Young** Elites; Marie Lu. Putnam Publishing Group 2014 368 p. map (hardback) $18.99
Grades: 8 9 10 11 12 **Fic**
1. Fantasy fiction 2. Supernatural -- Fiction 3. Secret societies -- Fiction 4. Ability -- Fiction 5. Adventure and adventurers -- Fiction
ISBN 0399167838; 9780399167836
LC 2014025732

In this fantasy novel, by Marie Lu, "Adelina Amouteru is a survivor of the blood fever. . . . But some of the fever's survivors are rumored to possess . . . mysterious and powerful gifts, and though their identities remain secret, they have come to be called the Young Elites. . . . Teren Santoro . . . , as Leader of the Inquisition Axis, it is his job to seek out the Young Elites. . . . Enzo Valenciano is a member of . . . [a] secret sect of Young Elites [that] seeks out others like them before the Inquisition Axis can." (Publisher's note)

"In a gorgeously constructed world that somewhat resembles Renaissance Italy but with its own pantheon, geography and fauna, the multiethnic and multisexual Young Elites offer a cinematically perfect ensemble of gorgeous-but-unusual illusionists, animal speakers, fire summoners and wind callers. A must for fans of Kristin Cashore's Fire (2009) and other totally immersive fantasies." Kirkus

Lubar, David
Hidden talents. TOR Bks. 1999 213p il hardcover o.p. pa $5.99
Grades: 6 7 8 9 **Fic**
1. School stories 2. Extrasensory perception -- Fiction
ISBN 0-312-86646-1; 0-7653-4265-0 pa
LC 99-24560

When thirteen-year-old Martin arrives at an alternative school for misfits and problem students, he falls in with a group of boys with psychic powers and discovers something surprising about himself

The author "serves up great fun, along with an insight or two for those whose powers are only too human." Publ Wkly

Followed by: True talents

★ **Sleeping** freshmen never lie. Dutton Books 2005 279p $16.99; pa $6.99
Grades: 7 8 9 10 **Fic**
1. School stories 2. Authorship -- Fiction
ISBN 0-525-47311-4; 0-14-240780-1 pa
LC 2004-23067

While navigating his first year of high school and awaiting the birth of his new baby brother, Scott loses old friends and gains some unlikely new ones as he hones his skills as a writer

"The plot is framed by Scott's journal of advice for the unborn baby. The novel's absurd, comical mood is evident in its entries. . . . The author brings the protagonist to three-dimensional life by combining these introspective musings with active, hilarious narration." SLJ

True talents. Tom Doherty Associates 2007 315p $17.95; pa $5.99

Grades: 6 7 8 9 **Fic**
1. Friendship -- Fiction 2. Kidnapping -- Fiction 3. Extrasensory perception -- Fiction
ISBN 978-0-7653-0977-8; 0-7653-0977-7; 978-0-7653-4856-2 pa; 0-7653-4856-X pa
LC 2006-39763

Sequel to: Hidden talents

Over a year after fourteen-year-old Eddie "Trash" Thalmeyer and his friends from Edgeview Alternative School find out about their psychic abilities, Trash is kidnapped and Torchie, Cheater, Lucky, Flinch, and Martin must join forces to rescue their friend, discovering their true talents in the process.

This is "a gripping page-turner, with a flawlessly structured plot and compelling, struggling characters who never let each other down." Voice Youth Advocates

Lucier, Makiia
A **death** -struck year; Makiia Lucier. Houghton Mifflin Harcourt 2014 288 p. (hardback) $17.99
Grades: 9 10 11 12 **Fic**
1. Nurses -- Fiction 2. Epidemics -- Fiction 3. Influenza -- Fiction 4. Portland (Or.) -- Fiction 5. Influenza Epidemic, 1918-1919 -- Fiction 6. Portland (Or.) -- History -- 20th century -- Fiction 7. Influenza Epidemic, 1918-1919 -- Oregon -- Portland -- Fiction
ISBN 0544164504; 9780544164505
LC 2013037482

In this novel, by Makiia Lucier, "the Spanish influenza is devastating . . . Pacific Northwest. Schools, churches, and theaters are shut down. The entire city [of Portland, Oregon] is thrust into survival mode--and into a panic. Seventeen-year-old Cleo is told to stay put in her quarantined boarding school, but when the Red Cross pleads for volunteers, she cannot ignore the call for help." (Publisher's note)

"A teen girl struggles to survive the Spanish influenza pandemic of 1918...Readers will be swept up in the story as Cleo builds friendships and manages to find hope amid disease and death. A notable debut." (Kirkus)

Includes bibliographical references

Luddy, Karon
★ **Spelldown**. Simon & Schuster Books for Young Readers 2007 211p $15.99; pa $5.99
Grades: 5 6 7 8 **Fic**
1. School stories 2. Spelling bees -- Fiction 3. South Carolina -- Fiction
ISBN 1-4169-1610-5; 978-1-4169-1610-9; 1-4169-5452-X pa; 978-1-4169-5452-1 pa
LC 2006-21956

In 1969, the town of Red Clover, South Carolina, led by an enthusiastic new Latin teacher, supports thirteen-year-old Karlene as she wins her school spelling bee and strives to qualify for the National Bee, despite family problems and a growing desire for romance.

"This heartrending and funny debut novel deftly evokes place, time and character." Publ Wkly

Luper, Eric
Bug boy. Farrar, Straus and Giroux 2009 248p $16.99

Grades: 7 8 9 10   **Fic**

1. Gambling -- Fiction 2. Horse racing -- Fiction 3. New York (State) -- Fiction 4. Father-son relationship -- Fiction 5. Swindlers and swindling -- Fiction

ISBN 978-0-374-31000-4; 0-374-31000-9

LC 2008-26730

In 1934 Saratoga, New York, just as fifteen-year-old Jack Walsh finally realizes his dream of becoming a jockey, complications arise in the form of a female bookie, an unexpected visit from his father, and a man who wants him to "fix" a race.

"This well-written, engaging story effectively captures the desperate times of the Depression and the hard-edged world of horse racing." SLJ

Lupica, Mike

The **batboy**. Philomel Books 2010 247p $17.99

Grades: 5 6 7 8   **Fic**

1. Baseball -- Fiction 2. Detroit (Mich.) -- Fiction 3. Mother-son relationship -- Fiction 4. Detroit Tigers (Baseball team) -- Fiction

ISBN 978-0-399-25000-2; 0-399-25000-X

LC 2009015067

Even though his mother feels baseball ruined her marriage to his father, she allows fourteen-year-old Brian to become a bat boy for the Detroit Tigers, who have just drafted his favorite player back onto the team.

Lupica gives "his readers a behind-the-scenes look at major league sports. In this novel, he adds genuine insights into family dynamics and the emotional state of his hero." Booklist

The **big** field. Philomel Books 2008 243p $17.99

Grades: 5 6 7 8   **Fic**

1. Baseball -- Fiction 2. Father-son relationship -- Fiction

ISBN 978-0-399-24625-8; 0-399-24625-8

LC 2007-23647

When fourteen-year-old baseball player Hutch feels threatened by the arrival of a new teammate named Darryl, he tries to work through his insecurities about both Darryl and his remote and silent father, who was once a great ballplayer too.

"Writing in typically fluid prose and laying in a strong supporting lineup, Lupica strikes the right balance between personal issues and game action." Booklist

Fantasy league; Mike Lupica. Philomel, an imprint of Penguin Group (USA) 2014 304 p. (hardback) $17.99

Grades: 5 6 7 8   **Fic**

1. Football -- Fiction 2. Football teams -- fiction 3. Fantasy football -- fiction

ISBN 0399256075; 9780399256073

LC 2014007442

In this book, by Mike Lupica, "12-year-old Charlie is a fantasy football guru. He may be just a bench warmer for his school's football team, but when it comes to knowing and loving the game, he's first-string. He even becomes a celebrity when his podcast gets noticed by a sports radio host, who plays Charlie's fantasy picks for all of Los Angeles to

hear. Soon Charlie befriends the elderly owner of the L.A. Bulldogs . . . and convinces him to take a chance on an aging quarterback." (Publisher's note)

"Usually a football book is about whether or not the kid makes the team and the problems that follow. So it's refreshing that those issues are only a part of 12-year-old Charlie Gains' story. See, Charlie is known as the Brain, because he is a football stats genius. He understands which players should be playing where and why. . . . There's a lot of football here: pro and fantasy teams and Charlie's own Pop Warner career. Veteran sportswriter Lupica handles it all very well. However, it's the heart and depth he adds to the story depicting Charlie's relationships with a sterling cast of characters that make this unique. This Moneyball story with kids is on the money." Booklist

Heat. Philomel Books 2006 220p $16.99

Grades: 5 6 7 8   **Fic**

1. Cubans -- Fiction 2. Orphans -- Fiction 3. Baseball -- Fiction 4. Illegal aliens -- Fiction

ISBN 0-14-240757-7 pa; 0-399-24301-1

LC 2005013521

Pitching prodigy Michael Arroyo is on the run from social services after being banned from playing Little League baseball because rival coaches doubt he is only twelve years old and he has no parents to offer them proof. "Grades five to eight." (Bull Cent Child Books)

"The dialogue crackles, and the rich cast of supporting characters' . . . nearly steals the show. Topnotch entertainment." Booklist

Heavy hitters; Mike Lupica. Scholastic 2014 219 p. hbk $16.99

Grades: 3 4 5 6 7   **Fic**

1. Baseball -- Fiction 2. Children of divorced parents -- Fiction 3. Fear -- Fiction 4. Friendship -- Fiction 5. Baseball players -- Fiction 6. Dysfunctional families -- Fiction

ISBN 0545381843; 9780545381840

LC 2014430128

In this middle grade book by Mike Lupica, part of the Game Changers series, "Ben and his friends, the Core Four Plus One, are so excited to play in their town's All-Star Baseball league. But in the first game of the season Ben gets hit by a pitch. It's never happened to him before and it shakes him up. . . . Ben discovers that Justin's parents are getting a divorce and Justin is thinking about quitting the team." (Publisher's note)

"Charismatic Ben McBain joins his favorite sidekicks . . . for another sports season, this time All-Star baseball. Conflict comes quickly when Ben slumps after being hit by a pitch and Justin struggles with his parent's divorce. By trying to help one another, the friends also help themselves. Lupica's captivating play-by-play details pull the reader into the games, right alongside these sports-loving characters." Horn Book

Other titles in this series are:
Game changers (2012)
Play makers (2013)

Hero. Philomel Books 2010 289p $17.99

Grades: 6 7 8 9   **Fic**

1. Adventure fiction 2. Death -- Fiction 3. Politics

-- Fiction 4. Family life -- Fiction 5. Superheroes --
Fiction 6. New York (N.Y.) -- Fiction 7. Father-son
relationship -- Fiction

ISBN 978-0-399-25283-9; 0-399-25283-5

LC 2010-01772

Fourteen-year-old Zach learns he has the same special
abilities as his father, who was the President's globe-trotting
troubleshooter until "the Bads" killed him, and now Zach
must decide whether to use his powers in the same way at
the risk of his own life.

"Lupica effectively unfolds this high-adventure
story." Booklist

Miracle on 49th Street. Philomel Books 2006
246p $17.99; pa $7.99

Grades: 5 6 7 8 **Fic**

1. Basketball -- Fiction 2. Boston (Mass.) -- Fiction 3.
Father-daughter relationship -- Fiction

ISBN 0-399-24488-3; 0-14-240942-1 pa

LC 2005-32648

After her mother's death, twelve-year-old Molly learns
that her father is a basketball star for the Boston Celtics.

"Lupica creates intriguing, complex characters . . . and
he paces his story well, with enough twists and cliff-hangers
to keep the pages turning." SLJ

The **only** game; Mike Lupica. Simon & Schuster
Books for Young Readers 2015 320 p. (hardcover)
$16.99

Grades: 4 5 6 7 **Fic**

1. Baseball -- Fiction 2. Brothers -- Fiction 3.
Friendship -- Fiction 4. Grief -- Fiction 5. Bullies
-- Fiction

ISBN 1481409956; 9781481409957; 9781481409964

LC 2014015989

"Jack Callahan is the star of his baseball team and sixth
grade is supposed to be his year. That is, until he up and
quits. Jack's brother has passed away, and though [everyone]
thinks baseball is just the thing he needs to move on, Jack
feels it's anything but. Time spent with . . . new friends
unlocks something within Jack, and with their help . . . Jack
discovers sometimes it's more than just the love of the game
that keeps us moving." (Publisher's note)

"Although the story is sports related, this is more than a
baseball book and will appeal to a wide variety of readers.
A must-buy." SLJ

Summer ball; [by] Mike Lupica. Philomel
Books 2007 244p $17.99

Grades: 6 7 8 9 **Fic**

1. Camps -- Fiction 2. Basketball -- Fiction

ISBN 978-0-399-24487-2

LC 2006021781

Sequel to Travel team (2004)

Thirteen-year-old Danny must prove himself all over
again for a disapproving coach and against new rivals at a
summer basketball camp.

"Lupica breathes life into both characters and story.
Danny is . . . sympathetic and engaging. He is surrounded by
a cast of supporting characters who add humor and whose
interactions ring true." SLJ

Lurie, April

The **latent** powers of Dylan Fontaine. Delacorte
Press 2008 208p $15.99; lib bdg $18.99

Grades: 8 9 10 11 12 **Fic**

1. Family life -- Fiction 2. New York (N.Y.) -- Fiction

ISBN 978-0-385-73125-6; 978-0-385-90153-6 lib bdg

LC 2007-32313

Fifteen-year-old Dylan's friend Angie is making a film
about him while he is busy trying to keep his older brother
from getting caught with drugs, to deal with his mother having left the family, and to figure out how to get Angie to
think of him as more than just a friend.

"This is a story about guys, primarily . . . brothers; fathers and sons; lonely young men who are feeling somewhat
lost. Any reader will care for each one of them. Lurie does a
wonderful job of making them real." KLIATT

Ly, Many

Roots and wings; [by] Many Ly. Delacorte Press
2008 262p $15.99; lib bdg $18.99

Grades: 6 7 8 9 10 **Fic**

1. Buddhism -- Fiction 2. Cambodian Americans --
Fiction

ISBN 978-0-385-73500-1; 978-0-385-90494-0 lib
bdg; 0-385-73500-6; 0-385-90494-0 lib bdg

LC 2008-00474

While in St. Petersburg, Florida, to give her grandmother a Cambodian funeral, fourteen-year-old Grace, who was
raised in Pennsylvania, finally gets some answers about the
father she never met, her mother's and grandmother's youth,
and her Asian-American heritage.

"The book is beautifully written . . . [and] the author allows family secrets to unfold carefully and explores them
with sincerity." SLJ

Lyga, Barry

Archvillain. Scholastic Press 2010 180p $16.99

Grades: 4 5 6 7 **Fic**

1. Science fiction 2. Superheroes -- Fiction 3. Good
and evil -- Fiction 4. Extraterrestrial beings -- Fiction

ISBN 978-0-545-19649-9; 0-545-19649-3

LC 2010-05291

Twelve-year-old Kyle Camden develops greater mental agility and superpowers during a plasma storm that also
brings Mighty Mike, an alien, to the town of Bouring, but
while each does what he thinks is best, Kyle is labeled a villain and Mike a hero.

"Comic book fans in particular will appreciate this
clever origin story, first in a new series. . . . Lyga . . . laces
his story with ample humor. . . . Readers will find plenty to
ponder." Publ Wkly

★ The **astonishing** adventures of Fanboy &
Goth Girl. Houghton Mifflin 2006 311p $16.95

Grades: 8 9 10 11 12 **Fic**

1. School stories 2. Friendship -- Fiction 3. Cartoons
and caricatures -- Fiction

ISBN 0-618-72392-7

LC 2005-33259

A fifteen-year-old "geek" who keeps a list of the high
school jocks and others who torment him, and pours his energy into creating a great graphic novel, encounters Kyra,

Goth Girl, who helps change his outlook on almost everything, including himself.

"This engaging first novel has good characterization with genuine voices. . . . The book is compulsively readable." Voice Youth Advocates

Followed by: Goth Girl rising (2009)

Goth girl rising. Houghton Mifflin Harcourt 2009 390p $17

Grades: 8 9 10 11 12   **Fic**

1. School stories 2. Psychotherapy -- Fiction

ISBN 978-0-547-07664-5; 0-547-07664-9

Sequel to: The astonishing adventures of Fanboy and Goth Girl (2006)

"After six months in a mental hospital, Kyra, the newly shaven-headed heroine of The Astonishing Adventures of Fan Boy and Goth Girl (2006), has only one plan: to exact embarrassing revenge on sweet, loyal Fan Boy for not contacting her while she was away. . . . Goth teens and fans of the first novel will be drawn into the darkness that is her life." Kirkus

Hero -type. Houghton Mifflin Co. 2008 295p $16

Grades: 7 8 9 10   **Fic**

1. School stories 2. Maryland -- Fiction 3. Patriotism -- Fiction 4. Heroes and heroines -- Fiction

ISBN 978-0-547-07663-8; 0-547-07663-0

LC 2008-7276

Feeling awkward and ugly is only one reason sixteen-year-old Kevin is uncomfortable with the publicity surrounding his act of accidental heroism, but when a reporter photographs him apparently being unpatriotic, he steps into the limelight to encourage people to think about what the symbols of freedom really mean.

"Leavened by much humor . . . this neatly plotted look at what real patriotism and heroism mean will get readers thinking." KLIATT

The **mad** mask; by Barry Lyga. Scholastic Press 2012 226 p. (Archvillain) $6.99

Grades: 5 6 7 8   **Fic**

1. Science fiction 2. Robots -- Fiction 3. Superheroes -- Fiction 4. Good and evil -- Fiction 5. Extraterrestrial beings -- Fiction

ISBN 0545196531; 9780545196512; 9780545196536

LC 2011001085

This is the second book in Barry Lyga's Archvillain series. "Endowed with extraordinary strength and brainpower by a mysterious 'space plasma,' sixth-grader Kyle (aka the Azure Avenger) . . . is working on a new device to expose [his rival Mighty Mike] when he is contacted by yet another would-be archvillain. Calling himself the Mad Mask, the newcomer . . . needs Kyle's help to finish his Ultitron robot and promises assistance against Mighty Mike in return." (School Library Journal)

Lynch, Chris

Angry young man. Simon & Schuster BFYR 2011 167p $16.99

Grades: 7 8 9 10   **Fic**

1. Brothers -- Fiction 2. Conduct of life -- Fiction

3. Single parent family -- Fiction 4. Mother-son relationship -- Fiction

ISBN 0-689-84790-4; 978-0-689-84790-5

LC 2009-52832

Eighteen-year-old Robert tries to help his half-brother Xan, a seventeen-year-old misfit, to make better choices as he becomes increasingly attracted to a variety of protesters, anarchists, and the like.

"For those who wonder about the roots of homegrown terror and extremism, . . . Lynch pushes the spotlight from the individual to society in a story that can be brutal and ugly, yet isn't devoid of hope." Publ Wkly

The **Big** Game of Everything. HarperTeen 2008 275p $16.99; lib bdg $17.89

Grades: 7 8 9 10   **Fic**

1. Golf -- Fiction 2. Family life -- Fiction 3. Grandfathers -- Fiction 4. Summer employment -- Fiction

ISBN 978-0-06-074034-4; 0-06-074034-5; 978-0-06-074035-1 lib bdg; 0-06-074035-3 lib bdg

LC 2007-49578

Jock and his eccentric family spend the summer working at Grampus's golf complex, where they end up learning the rules of "The Big Game of Everything."

"This Printz Honor-winning author offers up another touching and offbeat novel full of delightfully skewed humor." Voice Youth Advocates

Casualties of war; Chris Lynch. Scholastic Press 2013 192 p. (hc) $16.99

Grades: 8 9 10 11 12   **Fic**

1. War stories 2. Soldiers -- Fiction 3. Vietnam War, 1961-1975 -- Fiction 4. Airmen -- Fiction 5. Agent Orange -- Fiction 6. United States. Air Force -- Fiction 7. Vietnam -- History -- 1945-1975 -- Fiction

ISBN 0545270235; 9780545270236; 9780545270243

LC 2012014434

This book concludes "[Chris] Lynch's Vietnam War series . . . with the final narrative of four friends caught in the chaos of war. Morris, Ivan and Rudi have told their stories; it's Beck's turn. Beck, now in the Air Force, was always the smart one, the one bound for college. . . . And in Vietnam, Beck does feel as if he has 'just been handed the keys to the universe itself.' He is, literally, above it all, as he watches the war from on high in his C-123 aircraft." (Kirkus)

★ **Hothouse**. HarperTeen 2010 198p $16.99

Grades: 8 9 10 11 12   **Fic**

1. Death -- Fiction 2. Friendship -- Fiction 3. Bereavement -- Fiction 4. Fire fighters -- Fiction 5. Father-son relationship -- Fiction

ISBN 978-0-06-167379-5; 0-06-167379-X

LC 2010-3145

Teens D.J. and Russell, life-long friends and neighbors, had drifted apart but when their firefighter fathers are both killed, they try to help one another come to terms with the tragedy and its aftermath.

"Lynch fully commits to the first-person voice, giving into Russ' second-by-second conflicts and contradictions. The author also has a strong grasp of the garrulous slaps and punches that make up many male relationships. Russ' friend-

ships are so real they hurt. The story hurts, too, but that's
how it should be." Booklist

★ **Inexcusable**. Atheneum Books for Young
Readers 2005 165p $16.95; pa $6.99
Grades: 8 9 10 11 12   **Fic**
1. School stories 2. Rape -- Fiction 3. Football --
Fiction
ISBN 0-689-84789-0; 1-416-93972-5 pa
LC 2004-30874

High school senior and football player Keir sets out to
enjoy himself on graduation night, but when he attempts to
comfort a friend whose date has left her stranded, things go
terribly wrong

"This finely crafted and thought-provoking page-turner
carefully conveys that it is simply inexcusable to whitewash
wrongs, and that those responsible should (and hopefully
will) pay the price." SLJ

Pieces; Chris Lynch. Simon & Schuster Books
for Young Readers 2013 176 p. (hardcover) $16.99
Grades: 7 8 9 10 11 12   **Fic**
1. Brothers -- Fiction 2. Bereavement -- Fiction 3.
Donation of organs, tissues, etc. -- Fiction 4. Death --
Fiction 5. Grief -- Fiction 6. Interpersonal relations
-- Fiction
ISBN 1416927034; 9781416927037; 9781442453111
LC 2011042049

In this book, "a year after his 20-year-old brother Duane
died in a diving accident, 18-year-old Eric still can't seem to
move forward. In an attempt to keep the 'nothingness that is
filling the Duane space' from taking hold, he reaches out to
three of the donors who received his brother's 'pieces.' After
meeting shy, redheaded Phil, brassy Barry and sweet single
mom Melinda, Eric finds himself constantly asking the questions, 'Who are these people? Who are they, to me? Who am
I, to them?'" (Kirkus Reviews)

Lyon, Annabel
All -season Edie. Orca Book Publishers 2008
179p pa $8.95
Grades: 5 6 7 8   **Fic**
1. Canada -- Fiction 2. Family life -- Fiction 3.
Grandfathers -- Fiction
ISBN 978-1-55143-713-2 pa; 1-55143-713-9 pa

"Wry, fast, and funny. . . . Set in a Vancouver suburb . . .
[this book] gets the preteen voice perfectly." Booklist

Lyon, Steve
The **gift** moves. Houghton Mifflin 2004 230p
$15
Grades: 5 6 7 8   **Fic**
1. Science fiction
ISBN 0-618-39128-2
LC 2003-12293

In a futuristic United States devoid of wealth and material things, a teenage baker befriends a talented weaver's
apprentice who holds a dark secret.

"Lyon mixes elements of magical realism with a coming-of-age story, incorporating issues that teens will relate
to. . . . This is an unusual story that is sure to inspire much
thought and contemplation." SLJ

Lyons, Mary E.
Letters from a slave boy; the story of Joseph
Jacobs. Atheneum Books for Young Readers 2007
197p il map $15.99; pa $5.99
Grades: 6 7 8 9   **Fic**
1. Slaves 2. Letters -- Fiction 3. Slavery -- Fiction 4.
African Americans -- Fiction
ISBN 978-0-689-87867-1; 0-689-87867-2; 978-0-689-
87868-8 pa; 0-689-87868-0 pa
LC 2006-01277

Companion volume to Letters from a Slave Girl (1992)
A fictionalized look at the life of Joseph Jacobs, son of
a slave, told in the form of letters that he might have written
during his life in pre-Civil War North Carolina, on a whaling expedition, in New York, New England, and finally in
California during the Gold Rush.

"The 'letters' are short and the pace is quick. The dialect
and spelling give authenticity without making the text difficult to read and understand. . . . This title stands on its own,
but children who appreciated the forthright perspective of
the first book will want to read this one as well." SLJ

★ **Letters** from a slave girl; the story of Harriet
Jacobs. Scribner 1992 146p il hardcover o.p. pa
$5.99; pa $5.99
Grades: 6 7 8 9   **Fic**
1. Slaves 2. Authors 3. Domestics 4. Memoirists
5. Letters -- Fiction 6. Slavery -- Fiction 7. African
Americans -- Fiction
ISBN 0-684-19446-5; 1-4169-3637-8 pa;
9781416936374 pa
LC 91-45778

This is a fictionalized version of the life of Harriet Jacobs, told in the form of letters that she might have written
during her slavery in North Carolina and as she prepared for
escape to the North in 1842. Glossary. Bibliography. "Age
twelve and up." (Horn Book)

This "is historical fiction at its best. . . . Mary Lyons has
remained faithful to Jacobs's actual autobiography throughout her readable, compelling novel. . . . Her observations
of the horrors of slavery are concise and lucid. The letters
are written in dialect, based on Jacobs's own writing and on
other slave narrations of the period." Horn Book

Maberry, Jonathan
The **orphan** army; Jonathan Maberry. Simon &
Schuster Books for Young Readers 2015 400 p. (The
Nightsiders) (hardcover) $16.99
Grades: 5 6 7 8   **Fic**
1. Science fiction 2. Monsters -- Fiction 3. Heroes
and heroines -- Fiction 4. Magic -- Fiction 5. Heroes
-- Fiction 6. Supernatural -- Fiction 7. Extraterrestrial
beings -- Fiction
ISBN 1481415751; 9781481415750
LC 2014014576

In this juvenile novel, by Jonathan Maberry, part of "The
Nightsiders" series, set "in a slightly futuristic world, where
ruthless insectlike monsters are exterminating humans and
the Earth itself, Milo discovers secrets that change the tides
of war in a serious way. The Nightsiders are a group of mystical beasts leading the fight to defend Earth and its inhabitants from the maleficent Bugs." (School Library Journal)

"Milo Silk is not a hero. This mantra of Milo's, repeated throughout much of this series opener, couldn't be further from the truth. In a slightly futuristic world, where ruthless insectlike monsters are exterminating humans and the Earth itself, Milo discovers secrets that change the tides of war in a serious way... must-have for fans of Maberry's previous books and middle grade sci-fi." SLJ

Rot & ruin. Simon & Schuster Books for Young Readers 2010 458p $17.99

Grades: 9 10 11 12   **Fic**
1. Horror fiction 2. Zombies -- Fiction 3. Brothers -- Fiction
ISBN 1-4424-0232-6; 978-1-4424-0232-4
LC 2009-46041

In a post-apocalyptic world where fences and border patrols guard the few people left from the zombies that have overtaken civilization, fifteen-year-old Benny Imura is finally convinced that he must follow in his older brother's footsteps and become a bounty hunter.

"In turns mythic and down-to-earth, this intense novel combines adventure and philosophy to tell a truly memorable zombie story." Publ Wkly

Followed by: Dust & decay (2011)

MacColl, Michaela

Nobody's secret; by Michaela MacColl. Chronicle Books 2013 288 p. (reinforced) $16.99

Grades: 7 8 9 10   **Fic**
1. Mystery fiction 2. Historical fiction 3. Poets -- Fiction 4. Mystery and detective stories 5. Women poets, American -- 19th century -- Fiction 6. Amherst (Mass.) -- History -- 19th century -- Fiction
ISBN 1452108609; 9781452108605
LC 2012030364

In this book, when "15-year-old Emily Dickinson meets and flirts with a handsome stranger, she feels the first flicker of romance. Then the young man is found dead in her family's pond, and the budding poet is sure that he was a victim of foul play. Determined to see that justice is done, she and her younger sister, Vinnie, investigate and discover that he is James Wentworth, heir to a fortune from which his aunt and uncle have defrauded him. Suspecting murder, Emily sets out to solve the case." (School Library Journal)

★ **Prisoners** in the palace; how Victoria became queen with the help of her maid, a reporter, and a scoundrel; a novel of intrigue and romance. Chronicle Books 2010 367p $16.99

Grades: 7 8 9 10   **Fic**
1. Queens 2. Orphans -- Fiction 3. London (England) -- Fiction 4. Household employees -- Fiction 5. Great Britain -- History -- 19th century -- Fiction
ISBN 978-0-8118-7300-0; 0-8118-7300-5
LC 2010-8257

Recently orphaned and destitute, seventeen-year-old Liza Hastings earns a position as a lady's maid to sixteen-year-old Princess Victoria at Kensington Palace in 1836, the year before Victoria becomes Queen of England.

"This novel is full of historical detail, vivid settings, and richly drawn characters, and themes of friendship and romance give the story teen appeal." Booklist

Promise the night. Chronicle Books 2011 $16.99

Grades: 6 7 8 9   **Fic**
1. Air pilots 2. Memoirists 3. Horse trainers 4. Kenya -- Fiction 5. Women air pilots -- Fiction
ISBN 978-0-8118-7625-4; 0-8118-7625-X
LC 2011010938

This novel explores the early life of Beryl Markham, who grew up on a farm in Kenya, and became the first person to fly solo across the Atlantic from east to west.

"MacColl vividly portrays her headstrong protagonist . . . with fierce, exuberant spirit." Booklist

Rory's promise; Michaela MacColl, Rosemary Nichols. Calkins Creek 2014 288 p. (Hidden Histories) $16.95

Grades: 5 6 7 8   **Fic**
1. Orphans -- Fiction 2. Interracial adoption 3. Sisters -- Fiction 4. Orphanages -- Fiction 5. Orphan trains -- Fiction 6. New York (N.Y.) -- Fiction 7. New York Foundling Hospital -- Fiction
ISBN 1620916231; 9781620916230
LC 2014935295

In this novel by Michaela MacColl and Rosemary Nichols "Rory and her little sister, Violet are . . . together in the Catholic Foundling Hospital in New York City. But in 1904 the hospital begins to send orphans to the Arizona Territory to be adopted by devout Catholic families. Too old to be adopted, Rory is desperate to find a way to accompany Violet. Rory soon discovers that the families the Sisters have chosen for the white orphans are actually Mexican immigrant families." (Publisher's note)

"Outspoken twelve-year-old Rory, who lives in NYC's Catholic Foundling Hospital in 1904, vows to protect her sister, Violet. When Violet is placed with a family in racially divided Arizona Territory, Rory sneaks aboard the train headed west. Despite some lackluster dialogue and underdeveloped characters, Rory is a feisty and compelling protagonist in an action-packed story based on historical events." Horn Book

MacCullough, Carolyn

Always a witch. Clarion Books 2011 276p $16.99

Grades: 8 9 10 11 12   **Fic**
1. Witches -- Fiction 2. Time travel -- Fiction 3. Good and evil -- Fiction 4. New York (N.Y.) -- Fiction
ISBN 978-0-547-22485-5; 0-547-22485-0
LC 2011008148

Sequel to: Once a witch (2009)

Haunted by her grandmother's prophecy that she will soon be forced to make a terrible decision, witch Tamsin Greene risks everything to travel back in time to 1887 New York to confront the enemy that wants to destroy her family.

This is "an enjoyable magical adventure." Kirkus

Drawing the ocean. Roaring Brook Press 2006 170p $16.95

Grades: 7 8 9 10   **Fic**
1. Ghost stories 2. Death -- Fiction 3. Twins -- Fiction
4. Siblings -- Fiction
ISBN 978-1-59643-092-1; 1-59643-092-3
           LC 2005-31471

A gifted artist, Sadie is determined to fit in at her new
school, but her deceased twin brother Ollie keeps appearing
to her.

"Characters of every age come to life with vivid descriptions and dialogue that make this spare mood piece
work." SLJ

★ **Once** a witch. Clarion Books 2009 292p $16
Grades: 8 9 10 11 12   **Fic**
1. Sisters -- Fiction 2. Witches -- Fiction 3. Time travel
-- Fiction 4. Good and evil -- Fiction 5. New York
(N.Y.) -- Fiction
ISBN 978-0-547-22399-5; 0-547-22399-4
           LC 2008-49234

Born into a family of witches, seventeen-year-old Tamsin is raised believing that she alone lacks a magical "Talent," but when her beautiful and powerful sister is taken by
an age-old rival of the family in an attempt to change the
balance of power, Tamsin discovers her true destiny.

"The book will appeal to teen readers who enjoy stories
with romance, magic, or time travel, along with hardcore
fantasy aficionados, and it is appropriate for all young adult
collections." Voice Youth Advocates

Followed by: Always a witch (2011)

MacDonald, Anne Louise
Seeing red. KCP Fiction 2009 220p $17.95;
pa $8.95
Grades: 6 7 8 9   **Fic**
1. Dreams -- Fiction 2. Extrasensory perception --
Fiction
ISBN 978-1-55453-291-9; 1-55453-291-4; 978-1-
55453-292-6 pa; 1-55453-292-2 pa

"From the time he was a young child, Frankie's dreams
invoked meaningful colors and seemed like premonitions
that he was powerless to change. . . . . He develops an unexpected friendship with an unpopular classmate whom he is
convinced is a mind reader and who also sees colors. The
dilemmas faced by Frankie and some of the other characters
are intriguing as they struggle with their fears, disappointments, and aspirations. The story has several touching moments and unexpected turns in a plot." SLJ

MacDonald, Bailey
The **secret** of the sealed room; a mystery of
young Benjamin Franklin. Aladdin 2010 208p
$16.99
Grades: 4 5 6 7   **Fic**
1. Authors 2. Diplomats 3. Inventors 4. Statesmen
5. Scientists 6. Mystery fiction 7. Writers on science
8. Members of Congress 9. Boston (Mass.) -- Fiction
ISBN 978-1-4169-9760-3; 1-4169-9760-1

When she runs away after her master dies, indentured
servant Patience Martin is accused of stealing and needs the
help of a young Benjamin Franklin to prove her innocence.

"MacDonald creates a series of events that could very
well be factual and leaves the reader curious to know more.

Replete with historical facts without being blatant, the well-
developed plot will keep mystery lovers guessing until the
very last chapter." Booklist

Wicked Will. Aladdin 2009 201p $16.99
Grades: 5 6 7   **Fic**
1. Poets 2. Authors 3. Dramatists 4. Mystery fiction
5. Orphans -- Fiction 6. Theater -- Fiction 7. Great
Britain -- History -- 1485-1603, Tudors -- Fiction
ISBN 1-4169-8660-X; 978-1-4169-8660-7
           LC 2008-50818

Performing in the English town of Stratford-on-Avon in
1576, Viola, a young actress (disguised as a boy) and a local lad named Will Shakespeare uncover a murder mystery.

"The chapters themselves logically reveal the twists and
turns of the plot in concise, readable prose. The realistic details put flesh on the bones of not only the primary characters, but also of the secondary personages as well." SLJ

Macdonald, Maryann
Odette's secrets; by Maryann Macdonald.
Bloomsbury 2013 240 p. (hardback) $16.99
Grades: 6 7 8 9   **Fic**
1. Novels in verse 2. Hidden children (Holocaust)
-- Fiction 3. France -- History -- 1940-1945, German
occupation -- Fiction 4. Identity -- Fiction 5. Jews
-- France -- Fiction 6. Holocaust, Jewish (1939-1945)
-- Fiction 7. France -- History -- German occupation,
1940-1945 -- Fiction
ISBN 159990750X; 9781599907505
           LC 2012015549

This biographical story-in-verse, by Maryann Macdonald, takes place in Nazi-occupied France. "Odette is a young
Jewish girl living in Paris during a dangerous time. . . . After
Odette's father enlists in the French army and her mother
joins the Resistance, Odette is sent to the countryside until it
is safe to return. On the surface, she leads the life of a regular
girl . . . but inside, she is burning with secrets about the life
she left behind and her true identity." (Publisher's note)

MacHale, D. J.
★ The **pilgrims** of Rayne. Simon & Schuster
Books for Young Readers 2007 547p (Pendragon)
$16.99; pa $8.99
Grades: 7 8 9 10   **Fic**
1. Fantasy fiction 2. Adventure fiction
ISBN 978-1-4169-1416-7; 1-4169-1416-1; 978-1-
4169-1417-4 pa; 1-4169-1417-X pa
           LC 2006038131

With Saint Dane seemingly on the verge of toppling all
of the territories, Pendragon and Courtney set out to rescue
Mark and find themselves traveling—and battling—their
way through different worlds as they try to save all of Halla.

This is "packed . . . with nonstop action, mind-
boggling plot twists, and well-imagined locales." Voice
Youth Advocates

Other titles in this series are:
The merchant of death (2002)
The lost city of Faar (2003)
The never war (2003)
The reality bug (2003)
Black water (2004)

The rivers of Zadaa (2005)
Quillan games (2006)
Raven rise (2008)
The soldiers of Halla (2009)

SYLO; by D.J. MacHale. Penguin Group USA
2013 416 p. (hardcover) $17.99
Grades: 5 6 7 8 9   Fic
1. Dystopian Fiction 2. Adventure fiction
ISBN 1595146652; 9781595146656

This is the first book in a proposed trilogy from D.J.
MacHale. Here, Tucker Pierce has a small but satisfying life
on a small island. But when the island is quarantined by the
U.S. Navy, things start to fall apart. . . . People start dying.
The girl he wants to get to know a whole lot better, Tori, is
captured along with Tucker and imprisoned behind barbed
wire." They must escape to the mainland and try to figure
out what this SYLO organization that is imprisoning them
is. (Kirkus Reviews)

Mack, Tracy

The **fall** of the Amazing Zalindas; casebook no.
1. by Tracy Mack and Michael Citrin; illustrations by
Greg Ruth. Orchard Books 2006 259p il (Sherlock
Holmes and the Baker Street irregulars) $16.99; pa
$6.99
Grades: 4 5 6 7   Fic
1. Mystery fiction 2. Circus -- Fiction 3. Great Britain
-- Fiction
ISBN 0-439-82836-8; 0-545-06939-4 pa
LC 2005-34000

The ragamuffin boys known as the Baker Street Irregulars help Sherlock Holmes solve the mysterious deaths of a
family of circus tightrope walkers.

"Colorful, well-defined characters . . . and plenty of
historical detail, Cockney slang . . . and Sherlockian references bring Victorian England to life. Vintage-style design
elements and evocative black-and-white illustrations further
the effect." Booklist

The **mystery** of the conjured man; [by] Tracy
Mack & Michael Citrin; [illustrations by Greg Ruth]
Orchard Books 2009 il (Sherlock Holmes and the
Baker Street Irregulars) hardcover o.p.
Grades: 4 5 6   Fic
1. Mystery fiction 2. Spiritualism -- Fiction 3. Great
Britain -- Fiction 4. Swindlers and swindling -- Fiction
ISBN 978-0-439-83667-8 pa
LC 2006035701

The ragtag group of orphan boys known as the Baker
Street Irregulars faces shady characters and seemingly real
ghosts when they assist the famous detective, Sherlock
Holmes, in investigating the mysterious death of Greta Ber-
linger during a seance.

"A great addition to an entertaining series." SLJ

Mack, W. C.

Athlete vs. mathlete; by W.C. Mack. Bloomsbury. Distributed to the trade by Macmillan 2013
208 p. (hardback) $16.99

Grades: 5 6 7   Fic
1. Sibling rivalry -- Fiction 2. Twins -- Fiction 3.
Schools -- Fiction 4. Brothers -- Fiction 5. Basketball
-- Fiction 6. Competition (Psychology) -- Fiction
ISBN 1599909154; 9781599908588; 9781599909158
LC 2012014146

This book "introduces athletic seventh-grader Owen and
his klutzy, academic-minded fraternal twin, Russell. The
boys are content with their respective roles until the new
school basketball coach, impressed by Russell's height, invites him to try out for the team. No one is more shocked
than Russell when he makes the cut, along with Owen, but
his victory precipitates a flurry of conflicts for both boys."
The story is "told from the boys' alternating points of view."
(Publishers Weekly)

Mackall, Dandi Daley

The **silence** of murder. Alfred A. Knopf 2011
327p $16.99; lib bdg $19.99
Grades: 7 8 9 10   Fic
1. Mystery fiction 2. Homicide -- Fiction 3. Siblings
-- Fiction 4. Mentally disabled -- Fiction
ISBN 978-0-375-86896-2; 978-0-375-96896-9 lib bdg
LC 2010035991

Sixteen-year-old Hope must defend her developmentally disabled brother (who has not spoken a word since he
was seven) when he is accused of murdering a beloved high
school baseball coach.

"The well-plotted mystery is intriguing, and Hope's determined efforts to solve it have an authentic feel." Booklist

Mackel, Kathy

★ **Boost**. Dial Books 2008 248p $16.99; pa
$7.99
Grades: 6 7 8 9   Fic
1. Steroids -- Fiction 2. Basketball -- Fiction
ISBN 978-0-8037-3240-7; 0-8037-3240-6; 978-0-14-
241539-9 pa; 0-14-241539-1 pa
LC 2007-49441

Thirteen-year-old Savvy's dreams of starting for her
elite basketball team are in danger when she is accused of
taking steroids

"Mackel has turned a tough subject in the world of teen
competitive sports into a highly readable blend of intense
action, interfamily relationships, and intrigue." SLJ

Mackey, Heather

Dreamwood; Heather Mackey. G.P. Putnam's
Sons 2014 336 p. (hardback) $16.99
Grades: 4 5 6 7 8   Fic
1. Supernatural -- Fiction 2. Missing persons -- Fiction
3. Runaway children -- Fiction 4. Forests and forestry
-- Fiction 5. Runaways -- Fiction 6. Adventure and
adventurers -- Fiction 7. Northwest, Pacific -- History
-- 19th century -- Fiction
ISBN 0399250670; 9780399250675
LC 2013039402

In this book, by Heather Mackey, "Lucy Darrington has
no choice but to run away from boarding school. Her father, an expert on the supernatural, has been away for too
long while doing research in Saarthe, a remote territory in
the Pacific Northwest populated by towering redwoods,

timber barons, and the Lupine people. But upon arriving, she learns her father is missing: Rumor has it he's gone in search of dreamwood, a rare tree with magical properties." (Publisher's note)

"Lucy Darrington's adventures begin on a train as she flees a starched ladies finishing school to join her ghost-chasing father on the west coast of the vaguely Victorian, slightly steampunk American States...Dialogue and perilous situations nudge the story along at a steady clip, with the second half a breathless page turner. Dreamwood will please character-focused readers. Hand this to children who want an environmental adventure like Eva Ibbotson's Journey to the River Sea (Dutton, 2002) or a character-grounded speculation like Kenneth Oppel's Airborn (HarperCollins, 2004)." SLJ

Mackey, Weezie Kerr

Throwing like a girl; [by] Weezie Kerr Mackey. Marshall Cavendish 2007 271p $16.99

Grades: 6 7 8 9   **Fic**

1. School stories 2. Texas -- Fiction 3. Softball -- Fiction 4. Family life -- Fiction
ISBN 978-0-7614-5342-0

LC 2006030233

After moving from Chicago to Dallas in the spring of her sophomore year, fifteen-year-old Ella finds that joining the softball team at her private school not only helps her make friends, it also provides unexpected opportunities to learn and grow.

"Readers will be delighted with how well the athletics and the girly stuff work in tandem." Booklist

Mackler, Carolyn

The **earth,** my butt, and other big, round things. Candlewick Press 2003 246p $15.99; pa $8.99

Grades: 7 8 9 10   **Fic**

1. School stories 2. Obesity -- Fiction 3. Family life -- Fiction 4. New York (N.Y.) -- Fiction
ISBN 0-7636-1958-2; 0-7636-2091-2 pa

LC 2002-73921

Michael L. Printz Award honor book, 2004

Feeling like she does not fit in with the other members of her family, who are all thin, brilliant, and good-looking, fifteen-year-old Virginia tries to deal with her self-image, her first physical relationship, and her disillusionment with some of the people closest to her

"The e-mails [Virginia] exchanges . . . and the lists she makes (e.g., 'The Fat Girl Code of Conduct') add both realism and insight to her character. The heroine's transformation into someone who finds her own style and speaks her own mind is believable—and worthy of applause." Publ Wkly

Tangled. HarperTeen 2010 308p $16.99

Grades: 8 9 10 11 12   **Fic**

1. Vacations -- Fiction 2. Friendship -- Fiction 3. Caribbean region -- Fiction 4. New York (State) -- Fiction
ISBN 978-0-06-173104-4; 0-06-173104-8

LC 2009-7286

The lives of four very different teenagers become entangled in ways that none of them could have imagined after a short stay at a Caribbean resort

"The various viewpoints weave together to create a compelling and cohesive whole. Themes of understanding, respecting others, and the power of good communication are carefully and effectively woven throughout a story that begs for discussion." SLJ

MacLachlan, Patricia, 1938-

Kindred souls; Patricia MacLachlan. Harper-Collins 2012 119 p. (trade bdg.) $16.99

Grades: 4 5 6   **Fic**

1. Bereavement -- Fiction 2. Family life -- Fiction 3. Family farms -- Fiction 4. Grandfathers -- Fiction 5. Houses -- Remodeling -- Fiction 6. Dogs -- Fiction 7. Old age -- Fiction 8. Prairies -- Fiction 9. Farm life -- Fiction 10. Sod houses -- Fiction
ISBN 9780060522971; 9780060522988

LC 2011016617

This book follows narrator Jake and his 88-year-old grandfather Billy, the eponymous kindred souls of the story's title. The pair "live on a farm that their family has owned for generations; in fact, Billy was born in a sod house he remembers fondly, the ruins of which still exist on the property." To comfort their dying grandfather, "Jake and his siblings undertake a remarkably ambitious project: They rebuild the sod house; Billy moves into it, and he eventually passes away there." The "first-person account of a boy coping with his grandfather's death . . . portrays . . . the opportunity to grieve for a loved one even while he is still alive." (Kirkus)

MacLean, Jill

★ The **nine** lives of Travis Keating. Fitzhenry & Whiteside 2008 217p pa $11.95

Grades: 5 6 7 8   **Fic**

1. Cats -- Fiction 2. Bullies -- Fiction 3. Newfoundland -- Fiction
ISBN 978-1-55455-104-0; 1-55455-104-8

After his mother's death, Travis Keating and his father move to Ratchet, Newfoundland, to start a new life. Things are tough for Travis (Hud, the school bully, being the toughest) until, putting aside his own problems, he starts to care for a colony of feral cats.

"This is a solid piece of contemporary fiction with an interesting story. It should have broad appeal." SLJ

Nix Minus One; by Jill Maclean. Pajama Press 2013 296 p. (hardcover) $21.95

Grades: 7 8 9 10   **Fic**

1. School stories 2. Novels in verse
ISBN 192748524X; 9781927485248

This novel in verse focuses on 15-year-old Nix. "Formerly known as 'Fatty Humbolt,' he is struggling with his crush on Loren Cody, the girlfriend of the best player on the hockey team, and his love-hate relationship with his older sister, Roxy." Nix is shy while Roxy is the opposite. "Then Roxy falls for Bryan Sykes, a popular but notorious cad and politician's son, and Nix is forced to come out of his shell and find his voice." (School Library Journal)

Madden, Kerry

Gentle's Holler. Viking 2005 237p $16.99; pa $6.99

Grades: 5 6 7 8   **Fic**

1. Poverty -- Fiction 2. Family life -- Fiction 3. North Carolina -- Fiction

ISBN 0-670-05998-6; 0-14-240751-8 pa

LC 2004-18424

In the early 1960s, twelve-year-old songwriter Livy Two Weems dreams of seeing the world beyond the Maggie Valley, North Carolina, holler where she lives in poverty with her parents and eight brothers and sisters, but understands that she must put family first.

"Livy's narration rings true and is wonderfully voiced, and Madden's message about the importance of forgiveness will be well received." SLJ

Other titles in this series are:

Louisiana's song (2007)

Jessie's mountain (2008)

Maddox, Jake

Free throw; by Jake Maddox; illustrated by Sean Tiffany; text by Anastasia Suen. Stone Arch Books 2007 65p il lib bdg $22.60; pa $5.95

Grades: 4 5 6 7   **Fic**

1. Basketball -- Fiction

ISBN 978-1-59889-060-0 lib bdg; 1-59889-060-3 lib bdg; 978-1-59889-238-3 pa; 1-59889-238-X pa

LC 2006006076

Since Derek is now the tallest player on his basketball team, the coach decides to have him play center but Jason, the former center, has little confidence in Derek and will not pass him the ball.

"The clear descriptions, realistic dialogue, abundant action, and touches of humor will appeal to younger children, as well as to middle school or older readers who are working to bolster their skills. They will appreciate the large font and the comic-book-style drawings that illuminate the [text]." SLJ

Madigan, L. K.

★ The **mermaid's** mirror. Houghton Mifflin Harcourt 2010 316p $16

Grades: 8 9 10 11 12   **Fic**

1. Magic -- Fiction 2. Surfing -- Fiction 3. California -- Fiction 4. Family life -- Fiction 5. Mermaids and mermen -- Fiction 6. Father-daughter relationship -- Fiction

ISBN 978-0-547-19491-2; 0-547-19491-9

LC 2010-6771

Lena, almost sixteen, has always felt drawn to the waters of San Francisco Bay despite the fears of her father, a former surfer, but after she glimpses a beautiful woman with a tail, nothing can keep Lena from seeking the mermaid in the dangerous waves at Magic Crescent Cove.

"The characters . . . are well rounded and integrated into the plot. . . . With highly imagistic descriptions and savvy dialogue, Madigan offers a rewarding and credible story that uses fantasy elements to bare truths about family ties." Booklist

Madison, Bennett

Lulu Dark and the summer of the Fox; a mystery. by Bennett Madison. Razorbill 2006 $10.99

Grades: 7 8 9 10   **Fic**

1. Mystery fiction

ISBN 1-59514-086-7

LC 2006004960

Companion volume to Lulu Dark can see through walls (2005)

When a mysterious person called the Fox begins to threaten young starlets, Lulu Dark investigates, even though she suspects that her own mother—an aging actress—might be behind it all.

"Teens will enjoy this smart, funny chick-lit heroine who has real problems and a satirical outlook." SLJ

Magnin, Joyce

Carrying Mason; [by] Joyce Magnin. Zonderkidz 2011 153p $14.99

Grades: 5 6 7 8   **Fic**

1. Family life -- Fiction 2. Country life -- Fiction 3. Pennsylvania -- Fiction 4. Mentally disabled -- Fiction

ISBN 978-0-310-72681-4; 0-310-72681-6

LC 2011014462

In rural Pennsylvania in 1958, when thirteen-year-old Luna's best friend Mason dies, she decides to move in with his mentally disabled mother and care for her as Mason did.

"Gently, deliberately paced, Luna's first-person tale provides a fresh look at mental disabilities and the additional burden of negative attitudes. While Ruby's disability is apparent, this effort also celebrates her capabilities. Although the primary focus is Luna, her quirky father, supportive mother and boy-crazy older sister are also sufficiently developed to provide additional depth. A quiet coming-of-age tale with heart offers a fresh look at mentally disabled adults." Kirkus

Magoon, Kekla

Camo girl. Aladdin 2010 218p $16.99

Grades: 5 6 7 8   **Fic**

1. Friendship -- Fiction 2. Prejudices -- Fiction 3. Racially mixed people -- Fiction

ISBN 978-1-4169-7804-6; 1-4169-7804-6

A novel about a biracial girl living in the suburbs of Las Vegas examines the friendships that grow out of, and despite, her race.

"Magoon . . . offers a sensitive and articulate portrayal of a pair of middle-school outsiders. . . . This poetic and nuanced story addresses the courage it takes to truly know and support someone, as well as the difficult choices that come with growing up." Publ Wkly

Fire in the streets; by Kekla Magoon. 1st Aladdin hardcover ed. Aladdin 2012 336 p. $15.99

Grades: 7 8 9 10   **Fic**

1. Historical fiction 2. Black nationalism -- Fiction 3. African Americans -- Civil rights -- Fiction 4. Racism -- Fiction 5. African Americans -- Fiction 6. Black Panther Party -- Fiction 7. Brothers and sisters -- Fiction 8. Civil rights movements -- Fiction 9. Civil rights movements -- Fiction 10. United States -- History -- 20th century -- Fiction 11. Chicago (Ill.) -- History

-- 20th century -- Fiction
ISBN 1442422300; 9781442422308

LC 2011039129

Sequel to: The rock and the river

This historical novel by Kekla Magoon, is set "in the sweltering Chicago summer of 1968. [Maxie] is a Black Panther--or at least she wants to be one. . . . At fourteen, she's allowed to help out in the office, but she certainly can't help patrol the streets. Then Maxie realizes that there is a traitor in their midst, and if she can figure out who it is, it may be her ticket to becoming a real Panther. But when she learns the truth, the knowledge threatens to destroy her world." (Publisher's note)

★ The **rock** and the river. Aladdin 2009 290p $15.99

Grades: 7 8 9 10   **Fic**

1. Brothers -- Fiction 2. Chicago (Ill.) -- Fiction 3. African Americans -- Fiction 4. Black Panther Party -- Fiction
ISBN 978-1-4169-7582-3; 1-4169-7582-9

LC 2008-29170

ALA EMIERT Coretta Scott King John Steptoe New Talent Award (2010)

In 1968 Chicago, fourteen-year-old Sam Childs is caught in a conflict between his father's nonviolent approach to seeking civil rights for African Americans and his older brother, who has joined the Black Panther Party.

This "novel will make readers feel what it was like to be young, black, and militant 40 years ago, including the seething fury and desperation over the daily discrimination that drove the oppressed to fight back." Booklist

Maguire, Gregory, 1954-

★ **Egg** & spoon; a novel by Gregory Maguire. Candlewick Press 2014 475 p. hbk $17.99

Grades: 7 8 9 10 11 12   **Fic**

1. Poor -- Fiction 2. Girls -- Fiction 3. Russia -- Fiction 4. Monks 5. Princes 6. Mistaken identity 7. Baba Yaga (Legendary Character)
ISBN 0763672203; 9780763672201

LC 2014931834

Boston Globe-Horn Book Honor: Fiction (2015)

In this young adult novel by Gregory Maguire, "Elena Rudina lives in the impoverished Russian countryside. Her father has been dead for years. . . . Her mother is dying, slowly, in their tiny cabin. And there is no food. But then a train arrives in the village, a train carrying untold wealth, a cornucopia of food, and a noble family destined to visit the Tsar in Saint Petersburg." (Publisher's note)

"With one brother conscripted into the Tsar's army and another bound to serve a local landowner, Elena is left alone to care for her widowed and ailing mother in early 20th-century Russia. When an elegant train bearing a noble her age rolls through their barren village, Elena and her counterpart, Cat, accidentally swap places. . . . The author weaves a lyrical tale full of magic and promise, yet checkered with the desperation of poverty and the treacherous prospect of a world gone completely awry. Egg and Spoon is a beautiful reminder that fairy tales are at their best when they illuminate the precarious balance between lighthearted childhood and the darkness and danger of adulthood." SLJ

What -the-Dickens; the story of a rogue tooth fairy. Candlewick Press 2007 295p $15.99; pa $6.99

Grades: 4 5 6 7   **Fic**

1. Storms -- Fiction 2. Cousins -- Fiction 3. Fairies -- Fiction 4. Orphans -- Fiction 5. Storytelling -- Fiction
ISBN 978-0-7636-2961-8; 0-7636-2961-8; 978-0-7636-4307-2 pa; 0-7636-4307-6 pa

LC 2007-24186

As a terrible storm rages, ten-year-old Dinah and her brother and sister listen to their cousin Gage's tale of a newly-hatched, orphaned, skibberee, or tooth fairy, called What-the-Dickens, who hopes to find a home among the skibbereen tribe, if only he can stay out of trouble.

"The immediacy of the story and combination of fantasy and reality will grip even reluctant readers." SLJ

Mah, Adeline Yen

Chinese Cinderella and the Secret Dragon Society; [by] Adeline Yen Mah. 1st ed; HarperCollins 2005 242p $15.99; lib bdg $16.89

Grades: 5 6 7 8   **Fic**

1. China -- Fiction 2. Martial arts -- Fiction 3. World War, 1939-1945 -- Fiction
ISBN 0-06-056734-1; 0-06-056735-X lib bdg

LC 2004-8852

During the Japanese occupation of parts of China, twelve-year-old Ye Xian is thrown out of her father's and stepmother's home, joins a martial arts group, and tries to help her aunt and the Americans in their struggle against the Japanese invaders.

"Full of adventure and contrivance, this somewhat old-fashioned, plot-driven novel is clear about the values that are important to the author. . . . These young people are courageous, creative, and open-minded." SLJ

Mahoney, Karen

The **iron** witch. Flux 2011 299p pa $9.95

Grades: 6 7 8 9 10   **Fic**

1. Magic -- Fiction 2. Alchemy -- Fiction 3. Orphans -- Fiction 4. Kidnapping -- Fiction
ISBN 0-7387-2582-X; 978-0-7387-2582-6

LC 2010037692

Seventeen-year-old Donna Underwood is considered a freak, cursed by the magical heritage that destroyed her alchemist parents, but when vicious wood elves abduct her best friend Navin, Donna must betray all her parents fought for and join the battle between the humans and the fey.

"Adventurous, dark and dangerous. The Iron Witch will have teen readers clamoring for more." Libr Media Connect

Mahy, Margaret

Maddigan's Fantasia. Margaret K. McElderry Books 2007 499p $15.99

Grades: 4 5 6 7   **Fic**

1. Fantasy fiction 2. Magic -- Fiction 3. Circus -- Fiction
ISBN 1-4169-1812-4; 978-1-4169-1817-7

LC 2006-15512

In a world made uncertain by "the Chaos," two time-traveling boys, fifteen-year-old Timon and eleven-year-old Eden, seek to protect a magic talisman, aided by twelve-year-old Garland, a member of a traveling circus known as Maddigan's Fantasia.

"A well-drawn character, Garland resembles other Mahy protagonists—cranky, assertive and filled with self-doubt—and her adventures are invariably exciting." Publ Wkly

The **Magician** of Hoad. Margaret K. McElderry Books 2009 411p $18.99

Grades: 7 8 9 10   **Fic**

1. Fantasy fiction 2. Magicians -- Fiction

ISBN 978-1-4169-7807-7; 1-4169-7807-0

LC 2008-23000

A young farm boy who possesses mysterious powers is chosen by the king to be the court's royal magician.

"Mahy majestically deploys the poetic language of fantasy to portray the changes and challenges of adolescence; here, and epic quest for identity is wrapped up in terror, romance, surprise, and suspense—always sustained by luminous imagery and intelligent, musical prose." Horn Book

Maizel, Rebecca

Infinite days; a vampire queen novel. St. Martin's Griffin 2010 325p (Vampire queen) pa $9.99

Grades: 7 8 9 10   **Fic**

1. School stories 2. Vampires -- Fiction 3. Supernatural -- Fiction

ISBN 978-0-312-64991-3; 0-312-64991-6

At a New England boarding school, Lenah Beaudonte tries to act like a normal sixteen-year-old although she was, before a hundred-year hibernation, a centuries-old vampire queen whose bloodthirsty, abandoned coven is seeking her.

"The story is filled with action, romance, longing, deception, and sacrifice. It will leave vampire fans thirsting for more." SLJ

Stolen nights; a Vampire queen novel. Rebecca Maizel. St. Martin's Griffin 2013 303 p. (paperback) $9.99

Grades: 7 8 9 10   **Fic**

1. Love -- Fiction 2. Vampires -- Fiction 3. Supernatural -- Fiction 4. Schools -- Fiction 5. Boarding schools -- Fiction

ISBN 0312649924; 9780312649920

LC 2012038339

This book, the second in author Rebecca Maizel's Vampire Queen series, follows Lenah Beaudonte . . . a vampire who has just become human again. . . . Lenah and her lover, Rhode, are now both human teens. . . . [T]hey are confronted . . . by the Aeris, a sort of supernatural communion of the elements, who . . .give them a choice: they can either go back to their original times . . . or stay in the present day with the caveat of not being able to be romantically linked to each other." (VOYA)

"At first, this novel seems to lack luster in its genre, but timeless themes of love and the search for identity, in addition to the cliff-hanger ending, leave readers pondering Lenah's choices and keenly anticipating the next installment." SLJ

Malaghan, Michael

Greek ransom. Andersen Press 2010 264p pa $9.99

Grades: 5 6 7 8   **Fic**

1. Adventure fiction 2. Greece -- Fiction 3. Siblings -- Fiction 4. Kidnapping -- Fiction

ISBN 978-184270-786-9; 1-84270-786-8

"Nick and Callie Latham are on the Greek island of Theta with their archaeologist parents for a working vacation. Then the children discover that Mum and Dad have lost the family's money in a reckless bid to locate the lost treasure of King Akanon. A shifty businessman kidnaps the couple in order to acquire it for himself. After Nick and Callie barely escape capture themselves, it's up to them to find a way to free their parents. . . . Readers will be on the edge of their seats throughout to see what happens next. . . . The relationship between Nick and Callie is spot-on, and kids will enjoy this high-spirited tale." SLJ

Malchow, Alex

The **Sword** of Darrow; [by] Alex and Hal Malchow. BenBella 2011 531p map $17.99

Grades: 5 6 7 8   **Fic**

1. Fantasy fiction 2. Magic -- Fiction 3. Fairies -- Fiction 4. Princesses -- Fiction

ISBN 978-1-9356-1846-1; 1-9356-1846-6

LC 2011012233

"For 10 years the people of Sonnencrest endured the cruel and tyrannical rule of the Goblins. Then Princess Babette, the only surviving member of the royal family, and Darrow, a crippled boy, become the unlikely forces in the fight against the oppressors. The authors paint convincing portraits of the characters. . . . Readers will be drawn to this fledgling rebellion and follow it to its spectacular success. Magic, monsters, and wizards add to the excitement." SLJ

Maldonado, Torrey

Secret Saturdays. G.P. Putnam's Sons 2010 195p $16.99

Grades: 6 7 8 9   **Fic**

1. School stories 2. African Americans -- Fiction 3. Single parent family -- Fiction 4. Racially mixed people -- Fiction 5. Brooklyn (New York, N.Y.) -- Fiction

ISBN 978-0-399-25158-0; 0-399-25158-8

LC 2009-10361

Twelve-year-old boys living in a rough part of New York confront questions about what it means to be a friend, a father, and a man.

"Maldonado convincingly portrays roughneck playgrounds where boys are expected to be 'hard' and . . . Justin's narration resonates with the authenticity of a preteen doing his best in an urban landscape that has taught him all he knows. . . . The book remains a moving portrayal of the hope to be found through honest relationships." Publ Wkly

Malley, Gemma

The **Declaration**. Bloomsbury 2007 300p $16.95

Grades: 7 8 9 10   **Fic**

1. Science fiction 2. Immortality -- Fiction 3. Great Britain -- Fiction

ISBN 978-1-59990-119-0; 1-59990-119-6

LC 2006-102138

In 2140 England, where drugs enable people to live forever and children are illegal, teenaged Anna, an obedient

"Surplus" training to become a house servant, discovers that her birth parents are trying to find her.

This is "gripping. . . . The indoctrinated teen's awakening to massive injustice makes compulsive reading." Booklist

Other titles in this series are:
The legacy (2011)
The resistance (2008)

Mangum, Lisa

After hello; Lisa Mangum. Shadow Mountain 2012 272 p. (hardbound : alk. paper) $17.99

Grades: 7 8 9 10   **Fic**
1. Friendship -- Fiction 2. Photographers -- Fiction 3. Man-woman relationship -- Fiction 4. Trust -- Fiction 5. New York (N.Y.) -- Fiction 6. Dating (Social customs) -- Fiction 7. Interpersonal relations -- Fiction
ISBN 1609070100; 9781609070106

LC 2012017735

Author Lisa Mangum focuses on Sara, a girl whose "first trip to New York City . . . turns into 24 hours she will never forget. An amateur photographer, Sara walks around the city taking pictures; when a boy named Sam wanders into her lens, she is intrigued by him and follows him on his missions to find and trade things for people . . . As Sam and Sara travel from St. John the Divine Cathedral to Central Park and Times Square, they meet a string of artists and musicians and reluctantly discuss their turbulent pasts." (Barnes & Noble)

Manivong, Laura

Escaping the tiger. Harper 2010 216p il $15.99

Grades: 6 7 8 9   **Fic**
1. Laos -- Fiction 2. Refugees -- Fiction 3. Thailand -- Fiction 4. Family life -- Fiction
ISBN 978-0-06-166177-8; 0-06-166177-5

LC 2009-24095

In 1982, twelve-year-old Vonlai, his parents, and sister, Dalah, escape from Laos to a Thai refugee camp, where they spend four long years struggling to survive in hopes on one day reaching America.

"This compelling novel offers significant historical background. This is certainly a book to prompt purposeful discussion to increase historical and multicultural awareness." SLJ

Mankell, Henning

★ A **bridge** to the stars. Delacorte Press 2007 164p $15.99; lib bdg $18.99; pa $8.99

Grades: 6 7 8 9   **Fic**
1. Sweden -- Fiction 2. Father-son relationship -- Fiction
ISBN 978-0-385-73495-0; 0-385-73495-6; 978-0-385-90489-6 lib bdg; 0-385-90489-4 lib bdg; 978-0-440-24042-6 pa; 0-440-24042-5 pa

LC 2006-26901

In Sweden in 1956, eleven-year-old Joel and his father, a logger who was once a sailor, live alone with their secrets, including Joel's secret society that meets at night and his father's new romantic interest.

This is a "quiet but deeply satisfying coming-of-age story. . . . Those who welcome character-driven fiction will treasure this beautifully realized novel." Booklist

Other titles in this series are:
Shadows in the twilight (2008)

When the snow fell (2009)

Mantchev, Lisa

Eyes like stars. Feiwel and Friends 2009 356p $16.99

Grades: 8 9 10 11 12   **Fic**
1. Magic -- Fiction 2. Actors -- Fiction 3. Orphans -- Fiction 4. Theater -- Fiction 5. Books and reading -- Fiction
ISBN 978-0-312-38096-0; 0-312-38096-8

LC 2008-15317

Thirteen-year-old Bertie strives to save Theater Illuminata, the only home she has ever known, but is hindered by the Players who magically live on there, especially Ariel, who is willing to destroy the Book at the center of the magic in order to escape into the outside world.

"The story contains enough mystery and mayhem to keep readers engaged, even as they analyze." Voice Youth Advocates

Other titles in this series include:
Perchance to dream (2010)
So silver bright (2011)

Perchance to dream. Feiwel and Friends 2010 337p $16.99; pa $9.99

Grades: 8 9 10 11 12   **Fic**
1. Magic -- Fiction 2. Fairies -- Fiction 3. Orphans -- Fiction 4. Theater -- Fiction
ISBN 978-0-312-38097-7; 0-312-38097-6; 978-0-312-67510-3 pa; 0-312-67510-0 pa
Sequel to Eyes like stars (2009)

Bertie, who is blessed with word magic, and her fairy sidekicks seek to save Nate, who has been kidnapped by the Sea Witch, but Bertie is torn between Nate and Ariel, an air spirit who loves Bertie enough to die for her.

"The pace is fast and furious . . . but it's Mantchev's fresh, intelligent style that delights most. . . . This fantastical romp—an absolute must for theater buffs—might stand alone, but it'd be a pity not to start with the first." Kirkus

Followed by So silver bright (2011)

So silver bright. Feiwel and Friends 2011 356p $16.99; ebook $9.99

Grades: 8 9 10 11 12   **Fic**
1. Magic -- Fiction 2. Actors -- Fiction 3. Fairies -- Fiction 4. Theater -- Fiction 5. Books and reading -- Fiction
ISBN 978-0-312-38098-4; 978-1-4299-9540-5 ebook

LC 2011023907

Bertie thinks that to complete her quest to have a true family she need only reunite her father, the Scrimshander, with her mother, Ophelia, but complications arise and she is torn between her responsibilities and the dream of flying free, just as she is torn between Nate and Ariel.

Manzano, Sonia

★ The **revolution** of Evelyn Serrano; Sonia Manzano. Scholastic 2012 205 p. $17.99

Grades: 6 7 8 9 10   **Fic**
1. Historical fiction 2. Puerto Ricans -- Fiction 3. Puerto Ricans -- New York (N.Y.) 4. Identity -- Fiction 5. Grandmothers -- Fiction 6. Protest movements --

Fiction 7. Grandparent and child -- Fiction 8. Identity (Psychology) -- Fiction 9. Puerto Rican families -- Fiction 10. New York (N.Y.) -- History -- Fiction 11. East Harlem (New York, N.Y.) -- Fiction 12. Family life -- New York (State) -- Harlem -- Fiction 13. New York (N.Y.) -- History -- 20th century -- Fiction 14. Puerto Ricans -- New York (State) -- New York -- Fiction 15. East Harlem (New York, N.Y.) -- History -- 20th century -- Fiction

ISBN 0545325056; 9780545325059; 9780545325066

LC 2012009240

Pura Belpré Author Honor Book (2013)

This novel, by Sonia Manzano, is set "in New York's El Barrio in 1969. . . . The Young Lords, a Puerto Rican activist group, dump garbage in the street and set it on fire, igniting a powerful protest. When Abuela steps in to take charge, Evelyn is thrust into the action. . . . Evelyn learns important truths about her Latino heritage and the history makers who shaped a nation." (Publisher's note)

Includes bibliographical references

Marchetta, Melina

★ **Finnikin** of the rock. Candlewick Press 2010 399p map $18.99

Grades: 8 9 10 11 12   **Fic**

1. Fantasy fiction

ISBN 0-7636-4361-0; 978-0-7636-4361-4

LC 2009-28046

In this fantasy novel, "Finnikin was only a child during the five days of the unspeakable, when the royal family of Lumatere were brutally murdered, and an imposter seized the throne. . . . Finnikin, now on the cusp of manhood, is compelled to join forces with an arrogant and enigmatic young novice named Evanjalin, who claims that her dark dreams will lead the exiles to a surviving royal child and a way to pierce the cursed barrier and regain the land of Lumatere." (Publisher's note)

"The skillful world building includes just enough detail to create a vivid sense of place, and Marchetta maintains suspense with unexpected story arcs. It is the achingly real characters, though, and the relationships that emerge through the captivating dialogue that drive the story. Filled with questions about the impact of exile and the human need to belong, this standout fantasy quickly reveals that its real magic lies in its accomplished writing." Booklist

★ **Froi** of the exiles. Candlewick 2012 608 p.

Grades: 8 9 10 11 12   **Fic**

1. Exiles 2. War stories 3. Fantasy fiction

ISBN 9780763647599

In this fantasy book, "Froi, a former street thief who has started a new life in Lumatere, is sent to Charyn in disguise to assassinate its king, but his worldview is shaken by revelations about his own unknown past. Tensions between the two kingdoms ratchet up, and Froi's loyalties are tested as he becomes entrenched in the chaotic political situation in Charyn and is drawn to its unpredictable princess, Quintana, who has been horribly abused in an attempt to break Charyn's curse." (Publishers Weekly)

★ **Quintana** of Charyn; Melina Marchetta. Candlewick Press 2013 528 p. (Lumatere chronicles) $18.99

Grades: 8 9 10 11 12   **Fic**

1. War stories 2. Fantasy fiction

ISBN 0763658359; 9780763658359

LC 2012955120

This is the conclusion of Melina Marchetta's trilogy which began with "Finnikin of the Rock." Here, "the kingdoms of Lumatere and Charyn attempt to bridge past atrocities through a new generation of leaders. Although tragedies arise, unity and healing are core themes, compared to the horrors of the previous books. As the title suggests, Quintana--the rightful ruler of Charyn, hidden following the uprising in the kingdom in Froi of the Exiles--is at the center of this final book." (Publishers Weekly)

Marciano, John Bemelmans

The **9** lives of Alexander Baddenfield; by John Bemelmans Marciano. Viking Published by Penguin Group 2013 144 p. (hardcover) $16.99

Grades: 4 5 6 7 8   **Fic**

1. Fantasy fiction 2. Cats -- Fiction 3. Death -- Fiction 4. Humorous stories 5. Wealth -- Fiction 6. Orphans -- Fiction 7. Reincarnation -- Fiction 8. Conduct of life -- Fiction

ISBN 0670014060; 9780670014064

LC 2012048448

In this book, "Alexander Baddenfield is a horrible boy . . . who is the last in a long line of lying, thieving scoundrels. One day, Alexander has an astonishing idea. Why not transplant the nine lives from his cat into himself? Suddenly, Alexander has lives to spare, and goes about using them up, attempting the most outrageous feats he can imagine. Only when his lives start running out, and he is left with only one just like everyone else, does he realize how reckless he has been." (Publisher's note)

Marcus, Kimberly

Exposed. Random House 2011 260p $16.99; lib bdg $19.99

Grades: 8 9 10   **Fic**

1. School stories 2. Novels in verse 3. Rape -- Fiction 4. Guilt -- Fiction 5. Friendship -- Fiction 6. Photography -- Fiction

ISBN 0-375-86693-0; 0-375-96693-5 lib bdg; 978-0-375-86693-7; 978-0-375-89724-5 e-book; 978-0-375-96693-4 lib bdg

LC 2009-51545

High school senior Liz, a gifted photographer, can no longer see things clearly after her best friend accuses Liz's older brother of a terrible crime.

"The narrative largely zooms in on Liz's pain and her struggle to ground herself in her photography and gain admission to art school as events swirl around her. As a result of tethering the narrative to Liz's perspective, the ongoing discussion of Kate's rape and ensuing trial are not heavy-handed or gratuitous. In Liz, Marcus has created a sympathetic lead. A worthy addition to any collection." SLJ

Margolis, Leslie

Everybody bugs out. Bloomsbury Children's Books 2011 195p $15.99

Grades: 4 5 6 **Fic**

1. School stories 2. California -- Fiction 3. Friendship -- Fiction 4. Family life -- Fiction

ISBN 1-59990-526-4; 978-1-59990-526-6

LC 2010035628

Sixth-grader Annabelle realizes that she has a crush on Oliver, with whom she is doing a science fair project, just before the Valentine's Day dance—and just before her friend Claire announces her crush on him.

"Margolis' breezy tone nicely conveys the peaks and valleys of middle-school life." Kirkus

Girl's best friend. Bloomsbury USA Childrens Books 2010 261p $14.99

Grades: 4 5 6 7 **Fic**

1. School stories 2. Mystery fiction 3. Dogs -- Fiction 4. Twins -- Fiction 5. Siblings -- Fiction 6. Family life -- Fiction 7. Brooklyn (New York, N.Y.) -- Fiction

ISBN 978-1-59990-525-9; 1-59990-525-6

LC 2010000562

In Brooklyn, New York, twelve-year-old dog-walker Maggie, aided by her twin brother Finn and best friend Lucy, investigates someone she believes is stealing pets.

"Characters are well-developed, typical preteens. Readers will easily identify with these seventh graders, and they will love the eccentric landlady who adds a bit of humor. Mystery fans will enjoy this lighthearted whodunit." SLJ

Girls acting catty. Bloomsbury 2009 179p $15.99

Grades: 4 5 6 **Fic**

1. School stories 2. California -- Fiction 3. Remarriage -- Fiction 4. Family life -- Fiction

ISBN 978-1-59990-237-1; 1-59990-237-0

LC 2009002144

Sequel to: Boys are dogs (2008)

Sixth-grader Annabelle spends autumn coping with competing groups of friends at school, her mother's pre-wedding stress, learning to get along with a cute stepbrother-to-be, and such momentous events as wearing her first bra and learning to shave her legs.

"Margolis handles Annabelle's minor crises with sensitivity and humor." SLJ

Marillier, Juliet

★ **Cybele's** secret. Alfred A. Knopf 2008 432p $17.99; lib bdg $20.99

Grades: 7 8 9 10 **Fic**

1. Magic -- Fiction 2. Turkey -- Fiction 3. Sisters -- Fiction 4. Supernatural -- Fiction

ISBN 978-0-375-83365-6; 0-375-83365-X; 978-0-375-93365-3 lib bdg; 0-375-93365-4 lib bdg

LC 2008-4758

Scholarly eighteen-year-old Paula and her merchant father journey from Transylvania to Istanbul to buy an ancient pagan artifact rumored to be charmed, but others, including a handsome Portuguese pirate and an envoy from the magical Wildwood, want to acquire the item, as well.

This is a "honeyed draught of a [novel]. . . . Marillier embroiders Ottoman Empire cultural details into every fold and drape of her story." Booklist

Raven flight; a Shadowfell novel. Juliet Marillier. Alfred A. Knopf 2013 416 p.

Grades: 7 8 9 10 **Fic**

1. Occult fiction 2. Fantasy fiction 3. Fantasy 4. Magic -- Fiction 5. Orphans -- Fiction 6. Insurgency -- Fiction 7. Voyages and travels -- Fiction

ISBN 9780375869556; 9780375969553

LC 2012039483

This is the second volume of Juliet Marillier's Shadowfell series. Here, "Neryn's time among the rebels has left her stronger and healthier but no closer to grasping her power and becoming a true Caller. When a potential ally sets a time limit for rebelling against tyrannical King Keldec, Neryn can no longer hide and sets off to find the Hag of the Isles and the Lord of the North." (Kirkus Reviews)

Shadowfell; Juliet Marillier. Alfred A. Knopf 2012 410 p. map (trade) $16.99

Grades: 7 8 9 10 11 12 **Fic**

1. Fantasy fiction 2. Magic -- Fiction 3. Adventure fiction 4. Fantasy 5. Orphans -- Fiction 6. Insurgency -- Fiction 7. Voyages and travels -- Fiction

ISBN 0375869549; 9780375869549; 9780375969546; 9780375983665

LC 2011041050

Originally published: Sydney, N.S.W. : Pan Macmillan, 2012.

In this novel by Juliet Marillier "Fifteen-year-old Neryn is alone in the land of Alban, where the oppressive king has ordered anyone with magical strengths captured and brought before him. Eager to hide her own canny skill--a uniquely powerful ability to communicate with the fairy-like Good Folk--Neryn sets out for the legendary Shadowfell, a home and training ground for a secret rebel group determined to overthrow the evil King Keldec." (Publisher's note)

Wildwood dancing. Knopf 2007 416p $16.99; lib bdg $18.99

Grades: 7 8 9 10 **Fic**

1. Magic -- Fiction 2. Sisters -- Fiction 3. Supernatural -- Fiction

ISBN 0-375-83364-1; 0-375-93364-6 lib bdg

LC 2006-16075

Five sisters who live with their merchant father in Transylvania use a hidden portal in their home to cross over into a magical world, the Wildwood.

This is told "with a striking sense of place, magical elements, beautifully portrayed characters, strong heroines, and an emotional core that touches the heart." Voice Youth Advocates

Followed by: Cybele's secret (2008)

Mariz, Rae

The **Unidentified**. Balzer + Bray 2010 296p $16.99

Grades: 7 8 9 10   **Fic**
1. School stories 2. Science fiction
ISBN 978-0-06-180208-9; 0-06-180208-5
LC 2009-54254

In a futuristic alternative school set in a shopping mall where video game-playing students are observed and used by corporate sponsors for market research, Katey "Kid" Dade struggles to figure out where she fits in and whether she even wants to.

"An all-too-logical extrapolation of today's trends, this story of conformity, rebellion, and seeking one's identity is evocative of Scott Westerfeld and Cory Doctorow, injecting a dystopian setting with an optimistic, antiestablishment undercurrent." Publ Wkly

Marr, Melissa, 1972-

Loki's wolves; by K.L. Armstrong and M.A. Marr. 1st ed. Little, Brown and Co. 2013 368 p. ill. (The Blackwell pages) (hardcover) $16.99
Grades: 4 5 6 7 8   **Fic**
1. Norse mythology -- Fiction 2. Adventure fiction 3. Gods -- Fiction 4. Monsters -- Fiction 5. Supernatural -- Fiction 6. Shapeshifting -- Fiction 7. Mythology, Norse -- Fiction 8. Adventure and adventurers -- Fiction
ISBN 031620496X; 9780316204965
LC 2012029851

This juvenile fantasy novel, by K. L. Armstrong and M. A. Marr, is the first book in the "Blackwell Pages" series. "Matt hears the words, but he can't believe them. He's Thor's representative? Destined to fight trolls, monstrous wolves and giant serpents . . . or the world ends? He's only thirteen. . . . But now Ragnarok is coming, and it's up to the champions to fight in the place of the long-dead gods." (Publisher's note)

"It is so methodically constructed that readers will welcome the action Ragnarök will offer. . . . Norse mythology brought to life with engaging contemporary characters and future volumes that promise explosive action; ideal for Percy Jackson fans who want to branch out." Kirkus

Odin's ravens; K.L. Armstrong; M.A. Marr. First edition Little, Brown and Co. 2014 352 p. illustrations (The Blackwell pages) (hardcover) $17
Grades: 4 5 6 7 8   **Fic**
1. Adventure fiction 2. Supernatural -- Fiction 3. Norse mythology -- Fiction 4. Gods and goddesses -- Fiction 5. Gods -- Fiction 6. Monsters -- Fiction 7. Valhalla -- Fiction 8. Shapeshifting -- Fiction 9. Mythology, Norse -- Fiction 10. Adventure and adventurers -- Fiction
ISBN 0316204986; 9780316204989
LC 2013018519

In this sequel to "Loki's Wolves," by K.L. Armstrong and M.A. Marr, "when thirteen-year-old Matt Thorsen, a modern day descendant of the Norse god Thor, was chosen to represent Thor in an epic battle to prevent the apocalypse he thought he knew how things would play out. Gather the descendants standing in for gods like Loki and Odin, defeat a giant serpent, and save the world. No problem, right?" (Publisher's note)

"This sequel stands by itself, as essential details of the first are neatly woven throughout. Intense action, well-crafted scenes and humor-laced dialogue add up to a sure winner.

Just enough black-and-white illustrations add a visual dimension to the vivid text. What Riordan has done for Greek and Egyptian mythology, Armstrong and Marr are doing for Norse myths, and readers will come away knowing much about Valkyries, Berserkers, wulfenkind and draugr. A Hel of a good read." -Kirkus

Wicked lovely. HarperTeen 2007 328p il $16.99; lib bdg $17.89
Grades: 8 9 10 11 12   **Fic**
1. Fantasy fiction 2. Fairies -- Fiction 3. Kings and rulers -- Fiction
ISBN 978-0-06-121465-3; 0-06-121465-5; 978-0-06-121466-0 lib bdg; 0-06-121466-3 lib bdg
LC 2007-09143

Seventeen-year-old Aislinn, who has the rare ability to see faeries, is drawn against her will into a centuries-old battle between the Summer King and the Winter Queen, and the survival of her life, her love, and summer all hang in the balance.

"This story explores the themes of love, commitment, and what it really means to give of oneself for the greater good to save everyone else. It is the unusual combination of past legends and modern-day life that gives a unique twist to this 'fairy' tale." SLJ

Other titles in this series are:
Darkest mercy (2011)
Fragile eternity (2009)
Ink exchange (2008)
Radiant shadows (2010)

Marriott, Zoe

The **swan** kingdom. Candlewick Press 2008 272p $16.99; pa $8.99
Grades: 6 7 8 9 10 11 12   **Fic**
1. Fantasy fiction 2. Magic -- Fiction
ISBN 978-0-7636-3481-0; 0-7636-3481-6; 978-0-7636-4293-8 pa; 0-7636-4293-2 pa
LC 2007-38291

When Alexa's mother is killed, her father marries a cunning and powerful woman and her brothers disappear, sending Alexa on a long, dangerous journey as she attempts to harness the mystical power she inherited from her mother and restore the kingdom to its proper balance.

"The mix of magic, royalty and romance will compel many teens." Publ Wkly

Marsden, Carolyn, 1950-

My Own Revolution; Carolyn Marsden. Candlewick Press 2012 174 p. $16.99
Grades: 7 8 9 10 11 12   **Fic**
1. Czechoslovakia -- Fiction 2. Communist countries -- Fiction 3. Resistance to government -- Fiction
ISBN 0763653950; 9780763653958
LC 2012942296

This young adult novel, by Carolyn Marsden, takes place "in 1960s Czechoslovakia, [where] . . . . fourteen-year-old Patrik rebels against the communist regime in small ways whenever he gets the chance. . . . But anti-Party sentiment is risky, and when party interference cuts a little too close to home, Patrik and his family find themselves faced with a decision . . . that will change everything." (Publisher's note)

Sahwira; an African friendship. [by] Carolyn Marsden and Philip Matzigkeit. Candlewick Press 2009 189p $15.99

Grades: 5 6 7 8   **Fic**

1. Clergy -- Fiction 2. Zimbabwe -- Fiction 3. Friendship -- Fiction 4. Race relations -- Fiction

ISBN 978-0-7636-3575-6; 0-7636-3575-8

The strong friendship between two boys, one black and one white, who live on a mission in Rhodesia, begins to unravel as protests against white colonial rule intensify in 1964.

"The book looks beyond race to examine questions about the meaning of being Christian, fear of Communism, family loyalty, and ethical choices. Marsden and Matzigkeit . . . deftly navigate the dynamic forces at play in the two boys' lives. . . . The story crosses genres to bring in elements of historical fiction, intrigue, and mystery." Bull Cent Child Books

★ **Take** me with you. Candlewick Press 2010 160p $14.99

Grades: 4 5 6 7   **Fic**

1. Italy -- Fiction 2. Orphans -- Fiction 3. Friendship -- Fiction 4. Racially mixed people -- Fiction

ISBN 978-0-7636-3739-2; 0-7636-3739-4

LC 2009-38053

This story is set in "Italy after World War II. Pina and Susanna have lived at their Naples orphanage since they were babies. . . . Pina, pretty and blonde, . . . is sure the nuns tell prospective parents she is bad. Susanna is the daughter of an Italian woman and a black American solider. . .; no one looks like her. Then two very different parents come into the girls' lives. . . . Both satisfy the girls' dreams in unexpected ways. Marsden often puts crafts like sewing or crocheting into her stories, and in many ways she is like a master craftsman, using words instead of stitches for her deceptively simple design." Booklist

Marsden, John

Circle of flight; [by] John Marsden. Scholastic 2009 307p (The Ellie chronicles) pa $7.99

Grades: 7 8 9 10   **Fic**

1. War stories 2. Orphans -- Fiction 3. Australia -- Fiction

ISBN 978-0-439-78321-7; 0-439-78321-6 pa

The Ellie Chronicles, the follow-up to the Tomorrow Series, tells of post-invasion Australia as witnessed by teenage Ellie. In this final installment, Ellie's responsibility for her surrogate brother Gavin is threatened by both enemy forces and the government and she finds herself fighting both but on different fields of battle.

Incurable. Scholastic 2008 245p (The Ellie chronicles) pa $7.99

Grades: 7 8 9 10   **Fic**

1. War stories 2. Australia -- Fiction

ISBN 978-0-439-78322-4 pa; 0-439-78322-4 pa

First published 2005 in Australia

Ellie has struggled to put the war behind her and lead a normal life. Although what's normal about your parents having been murdered; trying to run a farm and go to school; and bringing up a young boy who's hiding terrible secrets about his past?

While I live. Scholastic 2007 299p (The Ellie chronicles) $16.99

Grades: 7 8 9 10   **Fic**

1. War stories 2. Australia -- Fiction

ISBN 978-0-439-78318-7; 0-439-78318-6

Officially the war is over, but Ellie can not seem to escape it and resume a normal life especially after her parents are murdered and she becomes the ward of an unscrupulous lawyer who wants to acquire her family's property.

"Fans of 16-year-old Ellie Linton . . . will be overjoyed that she's back in an exciting series of her own. The realistic and shocking war-related violence that characterized the earlier titles is just as prevalent here." SLJ

Other titles about Ellie Linton are:

Circle of flight (2009)

Incurable (2008)

★ **Tomorrow,** when the war began. Houghton Mifflin 1995 286p pa $9.99

Grades: 7 8 9 10   **Fic**

1. War stories 2. Australia -- Fiction

ISBN 9780439829106; 0395706734

LC 94-29299

First published 1993 in Australia

"Australian teenager Ellie and six of her friends return from a winter break camping trip to find their homes burned or deserted, their families imprisoned, and their country occupied by a foreign military force in league with a band of disaffected Australians. As their shock wears off, the seven decide they must stick together if they are to survive. After a life-threatening skirmish with the occupiers, the teens retreat to their isolated campsite in the bush country and make plans to fight a guerilla war against the invaders." (School Library Journal)

"The novel is a riveting adventure through which Marsden explores the capacity for evil and the necessity of working together to oppose it." Horn Book

Marsh, Katherine

★ **Jepp,** who defied the stars; Katherine Marsh. Hyperion 2012 385 p. (hardback) $16.99

Grades: 6 7 8 9 10   **Fic**

1. Bildungsromans 2. Dwarfs -- Fiction 3. Historical fiction 4. Renaissance -- Fiction 5. Voyages and travels -- Fiction 6. Courts and courtiers -- Fiction 7. Europe -- History -- 16th century -- Fiction

ISBN 1423135008; 9781423135005

LC 2011053065

This book tells the story of "a 15-year-old dwarf named Jepp. . . . The first of the book's three sections finds a battered and beaten Jepp being transported ignobly in a cage to an unknown destination; along the way, he recalls the events that led him there, from his humble upbringing in an inn to becoming a court dwarf in Brussels. . . . Jepp's fortunes continue to wax and wane in the later sections, as

he arrives at the island castle of astronomer Tycho Brahe."
(Publishers Weekly)

★ The **night** tourist; [by] Katherine Marsh. 1st
ed.; Hyperion Books for Children 2007 232p $17.99
Grades: 6 7 8 9   **Fic**
   1. Death -- Fiction 2. New York (N.Y.) -- Fiction 3.
Classical mythology -- Fiction
   ISBN 978-1-4231-0689-0; 1-4231-0689-X
                     LC 2007013311

After fourteen-year-old classics prodigy Jack Perdu has
a near fatal accident he meets Euri, a young ghost who introduces him to New York's Underworld, where those who died
in New York reside until they are ready to move on, and Jack
vows to find his dead mother there.

   "Mixing numerous references to mythology and classical literature with deft touches of humor and extensive
historical details . . . . this intelligent and self-assured debut
will compel readers from its outset and leave them satisfied."
Publ Wkly

   Followed by: The twilight prisoner (2009)

The **twilight** prisoner; [by] Katherine Marsh.
1st ed.; Hyperion Books for Children 2009 246p
$17.99
Grades: 6 7 8 9   **Fic**
   1. Death -- Fiction 2. New York (N.Y.) -- Fiction 3.
Classical mythology -- Fiction
   ISBN 978-1-4231-0693-7; 1-4231-0693-8
                     LC 2008013938
   Sequel to: The night tourist (2007)
   In an effort to impress a female classmate, high school
sophomore Jack Perdu endangers both of their lives by taking her to New York City's Underworld, where those who
died in New York reside until they are ready to move on.

   "Readers should be drawn in by the complex relationships between Marsh's protagonists and Jack's continuing
existential struggles, caught between the worlds of the living
and the dead." Publ Wkly

Martin, Ann M.

   Better to wish; Ann M. Martin. 1st ed. Scholas-
tic 2013 240 p. (Family tree) (hardcover) $16.99
Grades: 3 4 5 6 7   **Fic**
   1. Discrimination -- Fiction 2. Historical fiction 3.
Depressions -- 1929 -- Fiction 4. Family life -- Maine --
Fiction 5. Families -- Maine -- Fiction 6. Depressions
-- 1929 -- Fiction 7. Maine -- History -- 20th century
-- Fiction
   ISBN 0545359422; 9780545359429
                     LC 2012047940

This is the first book in Ann M. Martin's Family Tree
series. "Growing up in Maine, eight-year-old Abby Nichols
is the oldest daughter of an ambitious carpenter eager to realize the American Dream. But his prejudices are strong, too:
he won't let Abby associate with her Irish Catholic neighbor,
Orrin. . . . As Abby's father gains success, she enjoys more
privileges, . . . but the family's newfound prosperity doesn't
ease her outrage over her father's mistreatment of the less
fortunate." (Publishers Weekly)

A **corner** of the universe. Scholastic Press 2002
189p $15.95; pa $5.99
Grades: 5 6 7 8   **Fic**
   1. Uncles -- Fiction 2. Friendship -- Fiction 3. Mentally
disabled -- Fiction
   ISBN 0-439-38880-5; 0-439-38881-3 pa
                     LC 2001-57611
   A Newbery Medal honor book, 2003
   The summer that Hattie turns twelve, she meets the
childlike uncle she never knew and becomes friends with
a girl who works at the carnival that comes to Hattie's
small town
   "Martin delivers wonderfully real characters and an engrossing plot through the viewpoint of a girl who tries so
earnestly to connect with those around her." SLJ

Everything for a dog. Feiwel and Friends 2009
211p $16.99
Grades: 5 6 7 8   **Fic**
   1. Dogs -- Fiction 2. Loneliness -- Fiction 3.
Bereavement -- Fiction
   ISBN 978-0-312-38651-1; 0-312-38651-6
                     LC 2008-34747
   In parallel stories, Bone, an orphaned dog, finds and
loses a series of homes, Molly, a family pet, helps Charlie
through the grief and other after-effects of his brother's
death, and lonely Henry pleads for a dog of his own
   "This is a sensitive, gentle read that surrounds its
occasional heartbreak with plenty of hope and warm
feelings." Booklist

Here today. Scholastic 2004 308p $16.95; pa
$5.99
Grades: 5 6 7 8   **Fic**
   1. Mothers -- Fiction 2. Family life -- Fiction
   ISBN 0-439-57944-9; 0-439-57945-7 pa
                     LC 2004-41620
   In 1963, Ellie's mother was crowned a grocery store
beauty queen, her classmates treated her cruelly, and President Kennedy was killed. It was also when Ellie realized that
in trying to keep her life together she had to let pieces of it go
   "Martin paints a well-articulated picture of the times,
but it is her memorable child and adult characters that shine
here." SLJ

★ **Rain** Reign; Ann M. Martin. Feiwel &
Friends 2014 240 p. $16.99
Grades: 4 5 6 7   **Fic**
   1. Dogs -- Fiction 2. English language -- Homonyms 3.
Lost items -- Fiction 4. Asperger's syndrome -- Fiction
   ISBN 0312643004; 9780312643003
   Schneider Family Book Award (Ages 11 - 13) (2015)
   In this middle grades novel by Ann M. Martin, "Rose
Howard is obsessed with homonyms. She's thrilled that her
own name is a homonym, and she purposely gave her dog
Rain a name with two homonyms (Reign, Rein), which, ac-
cording to Rose's rules of homonyms, is very special. . . .
When a storm hits their rural town, rivers overflow, the roads
are flooded, and Rain goes missing. . . . Now Rose has to find
her dog, even if it means leaving her routines and safe places
to search." (Publisher's note)

"Rose, a fifth-grader who has been diagnosed with Asperger syndrome, is often teased at school about her obsession with homonyms and her steadfast conviction that everyone should follow the rules at all times. Rose lives with her harsh, troubled father, but it's Uncle Weldon who cares for her in the ways that matter most. Still, her father did give her Rain, a stray dog that comforts and protects Rose. After Rain is lost in a storm and recovered, Rose learns that her dog has an identification microchip...Rose is driven by the unwavering belief that she must follow the rules, find Rain's former owners, and give the dog back to them... Readers will be moved by the raw portrayal of Rose's difficult home life, her separation from other kids at school, and her loss of the dog that has loved her and provided a buffer from painful experiences. A strong story told in a nuanced, highly accessible way." (Booklist)

Martin, Rafe

Birdwing; [by] Rafe Martin. 1st ed; Arthur A. Levine Books 2005 359p $16.99

Grades: 6 7 8 9   **Fic**

1. Fairy tales

ISBN 0-439-21167-0

LC 2004-11695

Prince Ardwin, known as Birdwing, the youngest of six brothers turned into swans by their stepmother, is unable to complete the transformation back into human form, so he undertakes a journey to discover whether his feathered arm will be a curse or a blessing to him.

"The many original characters and unusual adventure scenes ensure that readers will remember this well-paced fantasy." Booklist

Martinez, Claudia Guadalupe

Pig Park; by Claudia Guadalupe Martinez. First edition Cinco Puntos Press 2014 248 p. illustrations (hardback) $15.95

Grades: 8 9 10 11   **Fic**

1. Ghost towns 2. Community life 3. Building -- Fiction 4. Neighborhoods -- Fiction 5. Hispanic Americans -- Fiction 6. Bakers and bakeries -- Fiction 7. Family life -- Illinois -- Chicago -- Fiction

ISBN 1935955764; 9781935955764; 9781935955771

LC 2013040645

In this novel by Claudia Guadalupe Martinez "Masi Burciaga hauls bricks to help build a giant pyramid in her neighborhood park. Her neighborhood is becoming more of a ghost town each day since the lard company moved away. As a last resort, the neighborhood grown-ups enlist all the remaining able-bodied boys and girls into this scheme in hopes of luring visitors. But something's not right about the entrepreneur behind it all." (Publisher's note)

"Martinez uses nicely specific physical details to relate Masi's experiences, and the moments in the bakery seem particularly authentic and are suffused with love.The warm, diverse community setting and the realistic family interactions help overcome the somewhat jumbled plotlines." Kirkus

The **smell** of old lady perfume. Cinco Puntos Press 2008 249p il $15.95

Grades: 5 6 7 8   **Fic**

1. School stories 2. Death -- Fiction 3. Grandmothers

-- Fiction 4. Hispanic Americans -- Fiction

ISBN 978-1-9336-9318-7; 1-9336-9318-5

LC 2007-38296

When sixth-grader Chela Gonzalez's father has a stroke and her grandmother moves in to help take care of the family, her world is turned upside down.

"Short, well-crafted chapters offer perceptive glimpses into life on the border, the dynamics of middle-grade girls, and a family in turmoil." Horn Book Guide

Martinez, Jessica

★ **Virtuosity**. Simon Pulse 2011 294p $16.99

Grades: 8 9 10 11 12   **Fic**

1. Musicians -- Fiction 2. Drug abuse -- Fiction 3. Violinists -- Fiction 4. Chicago (Ill.) -- Fiction 5. Mother-daughter relationship -- Fiction

ISBN 978-1-4424-2052-6; 1-4424-2052-9

LC 2010042513

This is a "riveting novel. . . . The portrayal of Carmen's world . . . is unique and convincing. . . . Even readers without much interest in music will enjoy this exceptional novel." SLJ

Mary-Todd, Jonathan

Shot down; Jonathan Mary-Todd. Darby Creek 2012 92 p. (lib. bdg. : alk. paper) $27.93

Grades: 7 8 9 10 11 12   **Fic**

1. Adventure fiction 2. Apocalyptic fiction 3. Survival skills -- Fiction 4. Survival after airplane accidents, shipwrecks, etc. -- Fiction 5. Science fiction 6. Hunting -- Fiction 7. Kentucky -- Fiction 8. Survival -- Fiction

ISBN 0761383298; 9780761383291

LC 2012006864

This young adult novel, by Jonathan Mary-Todd, is a post-apocalyptic adventure story. "When a bullet knocks Malik and the Captain's hot-air balloon out of the sky, Malik goes into wilderness survival mode. . . . Whatever the crisis, he's always counted on the Gene Matterhorn Wilderness Survival Guidebook when things got crazy. Now he and the Captain are in the middle of miles of Kentucky wilderness, being chased by manhunters." (Publisher's note)

Mason, Prue

Camel rider; [by] Prue Mason. 1st U.S. ed.; Charlesbridge 2007 204p $15.95

Grades: 6 7 8 9   **Fic**

1. War stories 2. Deserts -- Fiction 3. Persian Gulf region -- Fiction 4. Wilderness survival -- Fiction

ISBN 978-1-58089-314-5; 1-58089-314-7

LC 2006034125

Two expatriates living in a Middle Eastern country, twelve-year-old Adam from Australia and Walid from Bangladesh, must rely on one another when war breaks out and they find themselves in the desert, both trying to reach the same city with no water, little food, and no common language.

"The suspense is sustained and the wildly improbable happy ending is very satisfying." SLJ

Mason, Timothy

The **last** synapsid. Delacorte Press 2009 311p il $16.99; lib bdg $19.99

Grades: 5 6 7 8   **Fic**

1. Colorado -- Fiction 2. Time travel -- Fiction 3. Space and time -- Fiction 4. Prehistoric animals -- Fiction
ISBN 978-0-385-73581-0; 0-385-73581-2; 978-0-385-90567-1 lib bdg; 0-385-90567-X lib bdg

LC 2008-35678

On a mountain near their tiny town of Faith, Colorado, best friends Rob and Phoebe discover a squat, drooly creature from thirty million years before the dinosaurs, that needs their help in tracking down a violent carnivore that must be returned to its proper place in time, or humans will never evolve.

"Mason has written a highly engaging fantasy that includes something for all readers. . . . Readers will find it difficult to put this book down until they have reached the last page." Libr Media Connect

Mass, Wendy

★ **Every** soul a star; a novel. Little, Brown and Co. 2008 322p $15.99; pa $6.99

Grades: 5 6 7 8   **Fic**

1. Friendship -- Fiction 2. Solar eclipses -- Fiction
ISBN 978-0-316-00256-1; 0-316-00256-9; 978-0-316-00257-8 pa; 0-316-00257-7 pa

LC 2008009259

Ally, Bree, and Jack meet at the one place the Great Eclipse can be seen in totality, each carrying the burden of different personal problems, which become dim when compared to the task they embark upon and the friendship they find.

Mass "combines astronomy and storytelling for a well-balanced look at friendships and the role they play in shaping identity. . . . Information about solar eclipses and astronomy is carefully woven into the plot to build drama and will almost certainly intrigue readers." Publ Wkly

Includes bibliographical references

Heaven looks a lot like the mall; a novel. Little, Brown 2007 251p $16.99

Grades: 8 9 10 11 12   **Fic**

1. School stories 2. Coma -- Fiction 3. Shopping centers and malls -- Fiction
ISBN 978-0-316-05851-3; 0-316-05851-3

LC 2007-12333

When high school junior Tessa Reynolds falls into a coma after getting hit in the head during gym class, she experiences heaven as the mall where her parents work, and she revisits key events from her life, causing her to reevaluate herself and how she wants to live.

"Tessa's journey and authentic voice is one that readers will appreciate. . . . Funny, thought-provoking, and at times heartbreaking, this story will entertain and inspire readers." SLJ

Jeremy Fink and the meaning of life. Little, Brown 2006 289p $15.99; pa $6.99

Grades: 5 6 7 8   **Fic**

1. Conduct of life -- Fiction 2. Father-son relationship -- Fiction
ISBN 978-0-316-05829-2; 0-316-05829-7; 978-0-316-05849-0 pa; 0-316-05849-1 pa

LC 2005037291

Just before his thirteenth birthday, Jeremy Fink receives a keyless locked box—set aside by his father before his death five years earlier—that purportedly contains the meaning of life.

"Mass fashions an adventure in which both journey and destination are worth the trip." Horn Book

A **mango** -shaped space; a novel. Little, Brown 2003 220p $16.95

Grades: 5 6 7 8   **Fic**

1. School stories 2. Synesthesia -- Fiction
ISBN 0-316-52388-7

LC 2002-72989

Afraid that she is crazy, thirteen-year-old Mia, who sees a special color with every letter, number, and sound, keeps this a secret until she becomes overwhelmed by school, changing relationships, and the loss of something important to her

"Mass skillfully conveys Mia's emotions, and readers will be intrigued with this fictional depiction of an actual, and fascinating, condition." Horn Book Guide

Pi in the sky; Wendy Mass. 1st ed. Little, Brown and Co. 2013 256 p. (hardcover) $17

Grades: 3 4 5 6 7   **Fic**

1. Creation -- Fiction 2. Science fiction 3. Earth -- Fiction 4. Universe -- Fiction
ISBN 0316089168; 9780316089166

LC 2012030638

In this humorous children's novel, by Wendy Mass, "Joss is the seventh son of the Supreme Overlord of the Universe, and all he gets to do is deliver pies. . . . But when Earth suddenly disappears, Joss is tasked with the not-so-simple job of bringing it back. With the help of an outspoken girl from Earth named Annika, Joss embarks on the adventure of a lifetime and learns that the universe is an even stranger place than he'd imagined." (Publisher's note)

Masson, Sophie

The **madman** of Venice. Delacorte Press 2010 276p $17.99; lib bdg $20.99

Grades: 6 7 8 9   **Fic**

1. Venice (Italy) -- Fiction 2. Missing persons -- Fiction
ISBN 978-0-385-73843-9; 0-385-73843-9; 978-0-385-90729-3 lib bdg; 0-385-90729-X lib bdg

LC 2009022369

First published 2009 in the United Kingdom

"An exotic setting and delicious intrigue combine to make intense historical fiction in this tale of missing persons, murder, and, of course, romance. English merchant Master Ashby heads to Venice in 1602 to investigate the murder of his agent Salerio and the strange disappearance of a young Jewish girl accused of witchcraft by the cruel, conniving wife of the Count of Montemaro. . . . Ashby and his alchemist friend Dr. Leone soon find themselves entangled in a morass that involves Venetian pirates, mistaken identities, and the poisoning of the Count." SLJ

Snow, fire, sword; 1st American ed.; Eos 2006 359p $15.99; lib bdg $16.89

Grades: 6 7 8 9 **Fic**

1. Fantasy fiction 2. Magic -- Fiction
ISBN 978-0-06-079091-2; 0-06-079091-1; 978-0-06-079092-9 lib bdg; 0-06-079092-X lib bdg

LC 2005-18149

In the mythical, Indonesia-like country of Jayangan, a village girl and an apprentice swordmaker embark on a magical journey to defeat a hidden evil that threatens their land.

"The sense of a permeable membrane between spirit worlds and contemporary reality will fascinate many readers, as will the shifting images of water buffaloes and motorbikes, villages and cities, and sacred and secular ways." Booklist

Master, Irfan

★ A **beautiful** lie; by Irfan Master. Albert Whitman 2012 301 p. (hardcover) $16.99

Grades: 7 8 9 10 **Fic**

1. Deception -- Fiction 2. India -- History -- Fiction 3. Father-son relationship -- Fiction 4. Honesty -- Fiction 5. Terminally ill -- Fiction 6. Fathers and sons -- Fiction 7. India -- History -- Partition, 1947 -- Fiction 8. Pakistan -- History -- 20th century -- Fiction 9. India -- History -- Partition, 1947
ISBN 0807505978; 9780807505977

LC 2011051132

In this book by Irfan Master, set "in India in 1947, the country is coming apart -- and so is thirteen-year-old Bilal's life. He is determined to protect his dying father from the news of Partition, news that he knows will break his father's heart. With spirit and determination, and with the help of his good friends, Bilal builds an elaborate deception, even printing false pages of the local newspaper to hide the signs of national unrest." (Publisher's note)

Matas, Carol

After the war. Simon & Schuster Bks. for Young Readers 1996 116p map hardcover o.p. pa $4.99

Grades: 7 8 9 10 **Fic**

1. Jews -- Fiction 2. Holocaust, 1933-1945 -- Fiction
ISBN 0-689-80350-8; 0-689-80722-8

LC 95-43613

After being released from Buchenwald at the end of World War II, fifteen-year-old Ruth risks her life to lead a group of children across Europe to Palestine

"Rich in texture and simple in its honesty, this story resonates with feeling." Voice Youth Advocates

Followed by The garden

Sparks fly upward. Clarion Bks. 2002 180p $15

Grades: 4 5 6 7 **Fic**

1. Jews -- Fiction 2. Canada -- Fiction 3. Prejudices -- Fiction
ISBN 0-618-15964-9

LC 2001-47188

In 1910, when a family of Russian Jews moves from Saskatchewan to Winnipeg, Canada, twelve-year-old Rebecca must live with Christians temporarily and struggles with anti-Semitism, confusion about God, and changing relationships with family and friends

"There's no sentimentality in the characterization . . . and the history is well researched. Most compelling, though, is Rebecca's personal struggle with faith, friendship, and loyalty." Booklist

The **whirlwind**. Orca 2007 128p pa $8.95

Grades: 6 7 8 9 **Fic**

1. Jews -- Fiction 2. Immigrants -- Fiction 3. World War, 1939-1945 -- Fiction
ISBN 978-1-55143-703-3 pa; 1-55143-703-1 pa

"Benjamin Friedman, a 15-year-old Jewish boy, fears for his life in Nazi Germany. Fortunately, his family is able to escape Hitler, arriving in Seattle in the summer of 1941. Ben is relieved to be there but is upset and confused by his experiences. . . . This unique and thought-provoking story shows what prejudice and indifference to suffering and wrongdoing can lead to. It imparts an understanding of the Holocaust and World War II." SLJ

Matson, Morgan

Since you've been gone; Morgan Matson. Simon & Schuster Books for Young Readers 2014 464 p. (hardback) $17.99

Grades: 7 8 9 10 **Fic**

1. Friendship -- Fiction 2. Family life -- Fiction 3. Self-reliance -- Fiction 4. Dating (Social customs) -- Fiction 5. Connecticut -- Fiction 6. Best friends -- Fiction 7. Family life -- Connecticut -- Fiction
ISBN 1442435003; 9781442435001; 9781442435018

LC 2013041617

In this book, by Morgan Matson, "Emily is about to take some risks and have the most unexpected summer ever. . . . Before Sloane, Emily didn't go to parties, she barely talked to guys, and she didn't do anything crazy. Enter Sloane, social tornado and the best kind of best friend—someone who yanks you out of your shell. But right before what should have been an epic summer, Sloane just disappears. . . . There's just a random to-do list with thirteen bizarre tasks that Emily would never try." (Publisher's note)

"Emily feels lost when her best friend, Sloane, disappears without explanation. But Sloane left Emily a daunting to-do list (with items like 'kiss a stranger'), and Emily bravely takes on each task, finding new friends, confidence, and a crush along the way. A perfectly awkward protagonist; well-rounded, quirky supporting characters; and spot-on dialogue make this novel of self-discovery stand out." Horn Book

Matthews, Andrew

The **way** of the warrior. Dutton Children's Books 2008 152p $15.99

Grades: 7 8 9 10 **Fic**

1. Japan -- Fiction 2. Samurai -- Fiction
ISBN 978-0-525-42063-7; 0-525-42063-0

"In 1565, when Jimmu is 10 years old, he witnesses his father commit seppuku, a ritual suicide, to avoid bringing dishonor to his family. . . . Jimmu spends the next seven years learning the art of the samurai . . . with the sole intention of avenging his father . . . . The . . . story is an honest and engaging portrayal of a young man's struggle to do the right thing. . . . The vivid depictions of a soldier's life in 16th-century Japan will captivate samurai enthusiasts, and the amount of action that Matthews packs into this relatively short novel will appeal to reluctant readers." SLJ

Matthews, L. S.

Lexi. Delacorte Press 2008 200p $14.99; lib bdg $17.99

Grades: 4 5 6 7   **Fic**

1. Twins -- Fiction 2. Amnesia -- Fiction 3. Orphans -- Fiction 4. Sisters -- Fiction 5. Homeless persons -- Fiction

ISBN 978-0-385-73574-2; 0-385-73574-X; 978-0-385-90563-3 lib bdg; 0-385-90563-7 lib bdg

LC 2007-46745

When twelve-year-old Lexi wakes up in the middle of a forest with no memory of her name or anything else, she slowly reconstructs her forgotten life with the help of some shelter workers, an ex-boxer, and her long-lost grandmother.

"This is a story of improbable, sometimes frightening events told by a child narrator, in which extraordinary things seem perfectly plausible. . . . Fans of Matthews's previous work will appreciate its sense of childlike wonder and fantasy." SLJ

The **outcasts.** Delacorte Press 2007 259p $15.99; lib bdg $18.99

Grades: 7 8 9 10   **Fic**

1. School stories 2. Supernatural -- Fiction 3. Great Britain -- Fiction

ISBN 978-0-385-73367-0; 978-0-385-90382-0 lib bdg

LC 2006-50872

First published 2005 in the United Kingdom

A much-anticipated school trip to England's West Country turns into a life-changing adventure for five high school misfits when they fall into another dimension while exploring the house in which they are staying.

"A fun, wild, and thoughtfully layered adventure." Booklist

Matthews, Tom L.

Danger in the dark; a Houdini & Nate mystery. [by] Tom Lalicki; pictures by Carlyn Cerniglia. Farrar, Straus and Giroux 2006 186p il $14.95

Grades: 4 5 6 7   **Fic**

1. Magicians 2. Mystery fiction 3. Nonfiction writers 4. Magicians -- Fiction 5. Spiritualism -- Fiction

ISBN 0-374-31680-5

LC 2005052111

Thirteen-year-old Nathaniel, aided by the famous magician Harry Houdini, plots to unmask a phony spirit advisor attempting to relieve the boy's great-aunt of her fortune.

"The action is nonstop, and even a flurry of enormous coincidences won't spoil enthusiasm for this entertaining story." Booklist

Other titles in this series are:

Shots at sea (2007)

Frame-up on the Bowery (2009)

Matti, Truus

★ **Departure** time; translated from the Dutch by Nancy Forest-Flier. Namelos 2010 214p $18.95; pa $9.95

Grades: 5 6 7 8   **Fic**

1. Memory -- Fiction 2. Father-daughter relationship -- Fiction

ISBN 978-1-60898-087-1; 1-60898-087-1; 978-1-60898-009-3 pa; 1-60898-009-X pa

Original Dutch edition 2009

"A 10-year-old girl is lost in a surrealistic landscape—a red-earth desert threatened by an approaching storm. Nothing looks familiar. She can't remember how she got to this place. Alternating with this classic bad-dream setting, which is narrated in the third person, is a first-person, furious tirade by a girl who feels abandoned by her father and neglected by her mother. Readers will be intrigued by the way Matti interweaves these stories and tantalizes with the possible connections between them. . . . Remarkable and arresting and wholly original, this novel lingers in the mind long after the last page has been read." SLJ

★ **Mister** Orange; Truus Matti; translated from the Dutch by Laura Watkinson. Enchanted Lion Books 2013 156 p. (hardcover) $16.95

Grades: 5 6 7 8   **Fic**

1. Historical fiction 2. Friendship -- Fiction 3. Child-adult relationship -- Fiction 4. Artists -- Fiction 5. World War, 1939-1945 -- Fiction 6. New York (N.Y.) -- History -- 1898-1951 -- Fiction 7. Family life -- New York (State) -- New York -- Fiction

ISBN 159270123X; 9781592701230

LC 2012051313

Mildred L. Batchelder Award (2014)

This children's story, by Truus Matti, translated by Laura Watkinson, is set in Manhattan in "1943. . . . Linus Muller works at the family grocery store in the east 70s. . . . One of his customers . . . arranges to have a crate of oranges delivered every other week. Over the course of these deliveries, an intimacy develops between Linus and . . . Mister Orange. In the peacefulness of Mister Orange's spare kitchen, they discuss the war, the future, freedom and imagination." (Publisher's note)

May, Kyla

Kiki; my stylish life. by Kyla May. Scholastic Inc. 2013 96 p.

Grades: 7 8 9 10 11 12   **Fic**

1. Diaries -- Fiction 2. Friendship -- Fiction 3. Clubs -- Fiction 4. Fashion -- Fiction 5. Schools -- Fiction 6. Popularity -- Fiction 7. Best friends -- Fiction 8. Elementary schools -- Fiction 9. Friendship 10. Fashion design -- Fiction

ISBN 9780545445122; 9780545496131; 9780545496803; 0545496136

LC 2012034246

In this book by Kyla May, "Kiki, Coco, and Lulu are the BEST of friends. They even have their very own club! But Mika, the new girl, is shaking things up on Lotus Lane. This first book is written as Kiki's diary--with illustrations and doodles throughout. Kiki LOVES creating cool outfits, hanging out with friends, and collecting fun facts." (Publisher's note)

Mayall, Beth

Mermaid Park. Razorbill 2005 248p $16.99

Grades: 7 8 9 10 **Fic**
1. Swimming -- Fiction 2. New Jersey -- Fiction 3. Family life -- Fiction 4. Summer employment -- Fiction
ISBN 1-59514-029-8

Sixteen-year-old Amy escapes family difficulties by immersing herself in her job at a mermaid-themed water show.
"This is a good read that deals with real growing-up issues." SLJ

Mazer, Harry

A **boy** at war; a novel of Pearl Harbor. Simon & Schuster Bks. for Young Readers 2001 104p il hardcover o.p. pa $4.99
Grades: 7 8 9 10 **Fic**
1. Pearl Harbor (Oahu, Hawaii), Attack on, 1941 -- Fiction
ISBN 0-689-84161-2; 0-689-84160-4 pa

LC 00-49687

While fishing with his friends off Honolulu on December 7, 1941, teenaged Adam is caught in the midst of the Japanese attack and through the chaos of the subsequent days tries to find his father, a naval officer who was serving on the U.S.S. Arizona when the bombs fell

"Mazer's graphic, sensory descriptions give the narrative immediacy, putting readers alongside Adam, watching with him as 'pieces of the ship and pieces of men rained down around him.' . . . This is a thought-provoking, sobering account of the human costs of war." Horn Book Guide

Other titles in this series are:
A boy no more (2004)
Heroes don't run (2005)

★ The **last** mission. Dell 1981 188p pa $5.99
Grades: 7 8 9 10 **Fic**
1. Jews -- Fiction 2. Prisoners of war -- Fiction 3. World War, 1939-1945 -- Fiction
ISBN 0-440-94797-9
First published 1979 by Delacorte Press

In 1944 a 15-year-old Jewish boy tells his family he will travel in the West but instead, enlists in the United States Air Corps and is subsequently taken prisoner by the Germans.

"Told in a rapid journalistic style, occasionally peppered with barrack-room vulgarities, the story is a vivid and moving account of a boy's experience during World War II as well as a skillful, convincing portrayal of his misgivings as a Jew on enemy soil and of his ability to size up—in mature human fashion—the misery around him." Horn Book

My brother Abe; Sally Lincoln's story. Simon & Schuster Books for Young Readers 2009 202p $15.99
Grades: 4 5 6 7 **Fic**
1. Lawyers 2. Presidents 3. State legislators 4. Members of Congress 5. Parents of prominent persons 6. Frontier and pioneer life -- Fiction
ISBN 978-1-4169-3884-2; 1-4169-3884-2

LC 2008-01106

Forced off their land in Kentucky in 1816, nine-year-old Sarah Lincoln, known as Sally, and her family, including younger brother Abe, move to the Indiana frontier.

"Drawing on a limber imagination and knack for storytelling, Mazer . . . turns a few facts from Abraham Lincoln's childhood into a vivid historical novel. . . . Abe's older sister, Sally, about whom little is known, serves as the personable narrator and protagonist." Publ Wkly

★ **Snow** bound. Delacorte Press 1973 146p hardcover o.p. pa $5.99
Grades: 7 8 9 10 **Fic**
1. Runaway children -- Fiction 2. Wilderness survival -- Fiction
ISBN 0-440-96134-3

LC 72-7958

"Tony Laporte is angry when his parents will not allow him to keep a stray dog, so he takes off in his mother's old car. Driving without a license in the middle of a snowstorm that soon becomes a blizzard, Tony picks up a hitchhiker, Cindy Reichert. Trying to impress the slightly older girl with his driving skill, Tony wrecks the car, leaving the two stranded in a desolate area far from a main highway, with little likelihood of rescue for days." Shapiro. Fic for Youth. 3d edition

Somebody, please tell me who I am; Harry Mazer and Peter Lerangis. 1st ed; Simon & Schuster Books for Young Readers 2012 148p. $15.99
Grades: 6 7 8 9 10 11 12 **Fic**
1. Family -- Fiction 2. Amnesia -- Fiction 3. Veterans -- Fiction
ISBN 9781416938958 (hardcover)

LC 2011006010

Schneider Family Book Award (2013)

In this book, "[i]n May, Ben tells his family and friends he's joining the army after graduation; in June, he goes off to basic training; in July, he's deployed to Iraq; in September, . . . [he] return[s] stateside with a traumatic brain injury. His girlfriend, his best friend, and his family, all sick with grief and worry, come together to support Ben as he struggles to recover and communicate." (Bulletin of the Center for Children's Books)

Mazer, Norma Fox

After the rain. Morrow 1987 291p hardcover o.p. pa $5.99
Grades: 6 7 8 9 **Fic**
1. Death -- Fiction 2. Grandfathers -- Fiction
ISBN 0-688-06867-7; 0-380-75025-2 pa

LC 86-33270

A Newbery Medal honor book, 1988

"A powerful book, dealing with death and dying and the strength of family affection." Horn Book

"Adolescent Rachel has always been a little afraid of Grandpa Izzy, her mother's father; sharp-tongued and irritable, the old man seems to have no kindness or softness in his nature. After the family learns that he has terminal cancer (which Izzy isn't told), Rachel begins to visit him and walk with him daily, and by the time he is near the end and hospitalized, she has come to love him." Bull Cent Child Books

Girlhearts. HarperCollins Pubs. 2001 210p hardcover o.p. lib bdg $16.89; pa $6.99

Grades: 6 7 8 9 **Fic**
1. Death -- Fiction 2. Orphans -- Fiction
ISBN 0-688-13350-9; 0-688-06866-9 lib bdg; 0-380-72290-9 pa

LC 00-63202

Thirteen-year-old Sarabeth Silver's life is turned upside-down when her mother dies suddenly, leaving her orphaned, confused, and at the mercy of everyone who seems to know what is best for her

"Mazer's intimate portrait of grief is convincing and well drawn." Horn Book Guide

The **missing** girl. HarperTeen 2008 288p $16.99; lib bdg $17.89

Grades: 7 8 9 10 **Fic**
1. Sisters -- Fiction 2. Kidnapping -- Fiction 3. New York (State) -- Fiction 4. Child sexual abuse -- Fiction
ISBN 978-0-06-623776-3; 978-0-06-623777-0 lib bdg

LC 2007-09136

In Mallory, New York, as five sisters, aged eleven to seventeen, deal with assorted problems, conflicts, fears, and yearnings, a mysterious middle-aged man watches them, fascinated, deciding which one he likes the best.

"Fans of . . . classic tales of high-tension peril will appreciate the way this successfully plays on their deepest fears." Bull Cent Child Books

McBride, Regina

The **fire** opal. Delacorte Press 2010 293p $16.99; lib bdg $19.99

Grades: 7 8 9 10 **Fic**
1. Ireland -- Fiction 2. Family life -- Fiction 3. Supernatural -- Fiction 4. Celtic mythology -- Fiction
ISBN 978-0-385-73781-4; 0-385-73781-5; 978-0-385-90692-0 lib bdg; 0-385-90692-7 lib bdg

LC 2009-07573

While invading English soldiers do battle in sixteenth-century Ireland, Maeve grows up with a mystical connection to a queen who, centuries before, faced enemies of her own.

"Filled with fantastic creatures and hair-raising adventure, this mystical, imaginative tale should appeal to fantasy fans of all ages. A compelling, addictive read." Voice Youth Advocates

McCaffrey, Anne

Dragon's fire; [by] Anne McCaffrey, Todd McCaffrey. 1st ed.; Del Rey/Ballantine Books 2006 366p $24.95

Grades: 7 8 9 10 11 12 **Fic**
1. Fantasy fiction 2. Dragons -- Fiction
ISBN 0-345-48028-7

LC 2006040236

"The deadly Thread has not fallen on Pern for nearly 200 turns, but it is due to in another 18, and the firestone needed by the dragons to breathe fire and fight Thread is in short supply. . . . A number of well-limned major characters move the plot forward with the long series' expected momentum, and as usual, the interactions between humans, dragons, fire lizards, and whers put the richly detailed story on a par with the rest of the Pern canon." Booklist

Dragonflight; volume 1 of The Dragonriders of Pern. Ballantine Bks. 1978 337p il (Dragonriders of Pern) hardcover o.p. pa $12.95

Grades: 8 9 10 11 12 Adult **Fic**
1. Fantasy fiction 2. Science fiction 3. Dragons -- Fiction
ISBN 0-345-27749-X; 0-345-48426-6 pa

LC 78-16707

First published 1968 in paperback. Based on two award winning stories entitled: Weyr search and Dragonrider. Many titles co-written by Todd McCaffrey

ALA YALSA Margaret A. Edwards Award (1999)

The planet Pern, originally colonized from Earth but long out of contact with it, has been periodically threatened by the deadly silver Threads which fall from the wandering Red Star. To combat them a life form on the planet was developed into winged, fire-breathing dragons. Humans with a high degree of empathy and telepathic power are needed to train and preserve these creatures. As the story begins, Pern has fallen into decay, the threat of the Red Star has been forgotten, the Dragonriders and dragons are reduced in number and in disrepute, and the evil Lord Fax has begun conquering neighboring holds.

Fantasy titles set on Pern include:
All the Weyrs of Pern (1991)
The chronicles of Pern: first fall (1993)
Dragon Harper (2007)
Dragon's fire (2006)
Dragon's kin (2003)
Dragon's time (2011)
Dragondrums (1979)
Dragonquest (1971)
Dragonsdawn (1988)
Dragonseye (1997)
Dragonsinger (1977)
Dragonsong (1976)
The masterharper of Pern (1998)
Morets: Dragonlady of Pern (1983)
Nerilka's story (1986)
The Renegades of Pern (1989)
The skies of Pern (2001)
White dragon (1978)

McCahan, Erin

Love and other foreign words; by Erin McCahan. Dial Books, an imprint of Penguin Group (USA) Inc. 2014 336 p. (hardcover) $17.99

Grades: 8 9 10 11 12 **Fic**
1. Love stories 2. Love -- Fiction 3. Sisters -- Fiction 4. Friendship -- Fiction 5. Interpersonal relations -- Fiction 6. Best friends -- Fiction 7. Interpersonal communication -- Fiction
ISBN 0803740514; 9780803740518

LC 2013027095

In this book, by Erin McCahan, "[s]ixteen-year-old Josie lives her life in translation. She speaks High School, College, Friends, Boyfriends, Break-ups, and even the language of Beautiful Girls. But none of these is her native tongue--the only people who speak that are her best friend Stu and her sister Kate. So when Kate gets engaged to an epically insufferable guy, how can Josie see it as anything but the mistake of a lifetime?" (Publisher's note)

"Josie doesn't like change. So when her sister Kate announces she's going to marry Geoff, Josie immediately tries everything to alienate him. But she also becomes curious about the nature of love and, with the help of her friends and family, tries to understand it. The highlight of this effectively drawn, often funny novel is its smart, precocious, and irrepressibly inquisitive protagonist." Horn Book

Mccall, Guadalupe Garcia

★ **Under** the mesquite. Lee & Low Books 2011 224p $17.95

Grades: 7 8 9 10 11 12   **Fic**

1. Texas -- Fiction 2. Cancer -- Fiction 3. Family life -- Fiction 4. Mexican Americans -- Fiction
ISBN 978-1-60060-429-4; 1-60060-429-3; 978-1-60060-875-9 ebook

LC 2010052567

"With poignant imagery and well-placed Spanish, the author effectively captures the complex lives of teenagers in many Latino and/or immigrant families." Kirkus

McCarthy, Maureen

When you wish upon a rat; by Maureen McCarthy. Amulet Books 2012 281 p. $16.95

Grades: 4 5 6   **Fic**

1. Rats -- Fiction 2. Dysfunctional families -- Fiction 3. Wishes -- Fiction 4. Family life -- Fiction
ISBN 1419701614; 9781419701610

LC 2012015626

In this Middle school novel, by Maureen McCarthy, "With an absentminded inventor for a father and a flighty artist for a mother, it's always reliable Ruth [Craze] who ends up doing the dishes, paying the bills, and finding lost socks. . . . So when Rodney the Rat--a slightly sinister stuffed animal that was a gift from her favorite aunt--suggests a way out, Ruth is ready to risk everything. Three wishes. Three chances to create her perfect life. A million ways to get it wrong." (Publisher's note)

McCaughrean, Geraldine

★ The **death** -defying Pepper Roux. Harper 2010 328p $16.99; lib bdg $17.89

Grades: 5 6 7 8   **Fic**

1. Adventure fiction 2. France -- Fiction 3. Fate and fatalism -- Fiction
ISBN 978-0-06-183665-7; 0-06-183665-6; 978-0-06-183666-4 lib bdg; 0-06-183666-4 lib bdg

LC 2009-39665

Having been raised believing he will die before he reaches the age of fourteen, Pepper Roux runs away on his fourteenth birthday in an attempt to elude his fate, assumes another identity, and continues to try to outrun death, no matter the consequences.

"McCaughrean's exuberant prose and whirling humor animate an unforgettable cast of characters." Booklist

★ The **glorious** adventures of the Sunshine Queen. Harper 2011 325p $16.99

Grades: 5 6 7 8   **Fic**

1. Adventure fiction 2. Theater -- Fiction 3. Missouri

River -- Fiction
ISBN 978-0-06-200806-0; 0-06-200806-4

LC 2010021958

Sequel to: Stop the train! (2003)

When a diphtheria outbreak forces twelve-year-old Cissy to leave her Oklahoma hometown in the 1890s, she and her two classmates embark on a wild adventure down the Missouri River with a team of traveling actors who are living on a dilapidated paddle steamer.

"McCaughrean invests her characters with humanity and shows a farcical sense for dialogue, while her arch narrative voice, includes the theatrical and clever turns of phrase." Booklist

★ The **kite** rider; a novel. HarperCollins Pubs. 2002 272p maps hardcover o.p. pa $6.99

Grades: 5 6 7 8   **Fic**

1. Kings 2. China -- Fiction 3. Kites -- Fiction
ISBN 0-06-623874-9; 0-06-441091-9 pa

LC 2001-39522

In thirteenth-century China, after trying to save his widowed mother from a horrendous second marriage, twelve-year-old Haoyou has life-changing adventures when he takes to the sky as a circus kite rider and ends up meeting the great Mongol ruler Kublai Khan

"The story is a genuine page-turner. . . . McCaughrean fully immerses her memorable characters in the culture and lore of the ancient Chinese and Mongols, which make this not only a solid adventure story but also a window to a fascinating time and place." Booklist

Not the end of the world; a novel. HarperTempest 2005 244p $16.99; lib bdg $17.89

Grades: 7 8 9 10   **Fic**

1. Noah's ark -- Fiction
ISBN 0-06-076030-3; 0-06-076031-1 lib bdg

LC 2004-14786

Noah's daughter, daughters-in-law, sons, wife, and the animals describe what it was like to be aboard the ark while they watched everyone around them drown.

"This frightening retelling of the biblical Noah's Ark story is written beautifully and with brutal clarity." Voice Youth Advocates

McClain, Lee

Sizzle. Marshall Cavendish 2011 190p $17.99

Grades: 6 7 8 9   **Fic**

1. Moving -- Fiction 2. Cooking -- Fiction 3. Orphans -- Fiction 4. Pennsylvania -- Fiction 5. Foster home care -- Fiction 6. Mexican Americans -- Fiction
ISBN 978-0-7614-5981-1; 0-7614-5981-2

LC 2011001234

When the aunt she lives with becomes ill, orphaned Linda Delgado must leave Arizona for Philadelphia, where she struggles to adapt to a huge foster family, eating canned food, and finding an outlet for her love of cooking.

"Linda's friendly narration is compelling and easy to read. Chapters are broken up with screen shots of her food blog. With a light but honest touch, this book addresses many serious matters." SLJ

McClintock, Norah

About that night; Norah McClintock. Orca Book Publishers 2014 248 p. (pbk.) $12.95

Grades: 7 8 9 10   **Fic**

1. Murder -- Fiction 2. Missing persons -- Fiction 3. High school students -- Fiction 4. Triangles (Interpersonal relations) -- Fiction 5. Missing persons 6. Detective and mystery stories

ISBN 1459805941; 9781459805941; 9781459805958; 9781459805965

LC 2014935377

"Derek is staying with his new girlfriend and her parents while his family is out of town. He can't believe his luck--Jordie is the hottest girl in school, and he's going out with her. When Ronan, school bad boy and Jordie's ex-boyfriend, shows up, Jordie decides that maybe Derek isn't the one after all. But before she can end it with him, Derek disappears. Did he run away? Or did something happen to him?" (Publisher's note)

"Mystery fans will appreciate the thoughtful plotting, the complex characters, and an ambiguous ending that guarantees readers will be mulling over the story long after they finish. Of special note are the descriptions of landscape and weather: cold, forbidding, and characters in themselves, with their own secrets and dangers." Booklist

Masked; written by Norah McClintock. Orca Book Publishers 2010 108p (Orca soundings) pa $9.95

Grades: 7 8 9 10   **Fic**

1. Mystery fiction

ISBN 978-1-55469-364-1; 1-55469-364-0

Rosie walks in on an armed robbery in her father's convenience store. Who is that masked man? And why is the loser from school there?

"Tight plotting, swift pacing, and tension that intensifies with each page mark this entry in the always-reliable Orca Soundings series for reluctant readers." Booklist

She said/she saw. Orca Book Publishers 2011 211p pa $12.95

Grades: 7 8 9 10   **Fic**

1. Homicide -- Fiction 2. Witnesses -- Fiction 3. Criminal investigation -- Fiction

ISBN 1-55469-335-7 pa; 978-1-55469-335-1 pa

When Tegan's two best friends are gunned down in front of her, nobody believes her that she didn't see who did it and doesn't know why.

"The brisk pace, solid character development and inventive structuring make for fast, page-turning reading, and at all wraps up with an unpredictable plot twist and ending. Mysterious and haunting, packed with hard truths about adolescence." Kirkus

Taken. Orca Book Publishers 2009 166p pa $12.95

Grades: 7 8 9 10   **Fic**

1. Kidnapping -- Fiction 2. Wilderness survival -- Fiction

ISBN 978-1-55469-152-4; 1-55469-152-4

"After two girls from a nearby town go missing everyone goes on high alert, suspecting a serial killer, and while walking home, Stephanie is grabbed from behind and injected with a drug that knocks her out. She awakens hours later to find herself tied up in an abandoned cabin deep in a densely wooded area. . . . Her harrowing journey back to safety propels this plot-driven, fast-paced tale forward. . . . Told in the first person, this suspenseful survival story is sure to have strong appeal." Kirkus

McClymer, Kelly

Must love black. Simon Pulse 2008 167p pa $8.99

Grades: 6 7 8 9   **Fic**

1. Twins -- Fiction 2. Sisters -- Fiction 3. Babysitters -- Fiction

ISBN 978-1-4169-6994-5; 1-4169-4903-8

"Philippa does not consider herself a Goth but she loves the color black. When she answers a classified ad for a summer nanny position, it is the advertisement's one specification 'must love black' that attracts her to the job. . . . McClymer's novel combines understated gothic elements with traditional teen romance tropes and succeeds as a light and funny read." SLJ

McCormick, Patricia

Cut. Front St. 2000 168p $16.95

Grades: 7 8 9 10   **Fic**

1. Family problems 2. Self-mutilation 3. Emotional problems 4. Psychiatric hospitals 5. Self-mutilation -- Fiction 6. Psychiatric hospitals -- Fiction

ISBN 1-88691-061-8

LC 00-34840

While confined to a mental hospital, thirteen-year-old Callie slowly comes to understand some of the reasons behind her self-mutilation, and gradually starts to get better. "Age twelve and up." (N Y Times Book Rev)

"Realistic, sensitive, and heartfelt." Voice Youth Advocates

My brother's keeper. Hyperion Books for Children 2004 187p $15.99

Grades: 7 8 9 10   **Fic**

1. Baseball -- Fiction 2. Brothers -- Fiction 3. Drug abuse -- Fiction

ISBN 0-7868-5173-2

LC 2004-55233

Thirteen-year-old Toby, a prematurely gray-haired Pittsburgh Pirates fan and baseball card collector, tries to cope with his brother's drug use, his father's absence, and his mother dating Stanley the Food King.

"This is a clever and believable first-person narrative by a responsible, caring, and appealing kid who is doing his utmost to hold together people he loves." Booklist

Purple Heart. Balzer + Bray 2009 198p $16.99; lib bdg $17.89; pa $8.99

Grades: 7 8 9 10   **Fic**

1. Memory -- Fiction 2. Soldiers -- Fiction 3. Hospitals -- Fiction 4. Iraq War, 2003- -- Fiction 5. Brain --

Wounds and injuries -- Fiction
ISBN 978-0-06-173090-0; 0-06-173090-4; 978-0-06-173091-7 lib bdg; 0-06-173091-2 lib bdg; 978-0-06-173092-4 pa; 0-06-173092-0 pa

LC 2009-1757

While recuperating in a Baghdad hospital from a traumatic brain injury sustained during the Iraq War, eighteen-year-old soldier Matt Duffy struggles to recall what happened to him and how it relates to his ten-year-old friend, Ali.

"Strong characters heighten the drama. . . . McCormick raises moral questions without judgment and will have readers examining not only this conflict but the nature of heroism and war." Publ Wkly

McCoy, Chris

Scurvy Goonda. Alfred A. Knopf 2009 324p $16.99; lib bdg $19.99
Grades: 4 5 6 7 8   Fic
1. Adventure fiction 2. Pirates -- Fiction 3. Family life -- Fiction 4. Massachusetts -- Fiction 5. Imaginary playmates -- Fiction
ISBN 978-0-375-85598-6; 0-375-85598-X; 978-0-375-95598-3 lib bdg; 0-375-95598-4 lib bdg

LC 2008-39290

At age fourteen, Ted Merritt is eager to replace his imaginary friend, a bacon-loving pirate, with real friends but soon he is led from Cape Cod, Massachusetts, into a world of discarded 'abstract companions' who are intent on wreaking vengeance on the human race.

"Refreshingly hilarious, slighty disgusting, and utterly original, this nutty underdog caper finishes with a rousing climax and a satisfying resolution." Bull Cent Child Books

McCrite, K. D.

In front of God and everybody. Thomas Nelson 2011 298p (Confessions of April Grace) pa $9.99
Grades: 4 5 6 7   Fic
1. Arkansas -- Fiction 2. Farm life -- Fiction 3. Christian life -- Fiction 4. Swindlers and swindling -- Fiction
ISBN 978-1-4003-1722-6; 1-4003-1722-3

LC 2011005583

In the summer of 1986, eleven-year-old April Grace, who lives on a rural Arkansas farm with her family, across a field from her grandmother, has her sense of Christian charity tested when a snooty couple from San Francisco moves into a dilapidated house down the road and her grandmother takes up with a loud, obnoxious, and suspicious-acting Texan.

"With keen eyes and good humor, April Grace notes the quirks, presumptions, and motivations of family and neighbors; she has plenty of fodder—the characters' personalities are dialed up to 11." Publ Wkly

McDaniel, Lurlene

Breathless. Delacorte Press 2009 165p $13.99
Grades: 8 9 10 11 12   Fic
1. Cancer -- Fiction 2. Suicide -- Fiction 3. Siblings -- Fiction 4. Friendship -- Fiction
ISBN 978-0-385-90458-2; 0-385-90458-4

LC 2008-18427

A high school diving champion develops bone cancer in this story told from the points of view of the diver, his best friend, his sister, and his girlfriend.

"This is a heartstrings-tugging read that retains the central character's dignity and peace in the face of insurmountable odds. A sensitive book on a delicate topic." SLJ

Hit and run; [by] Lurlene McDaniel. 1st ed.; Delacorte Press 2007 180p $10.99
Grades: 8 9 10 11 12   Fic
1. School stories 2. Traffic accidents -- Fiction
ISBN 978-0-385-73161-4

LC 2006012738

Events surrounding the hit and run accident of a popular high school student are told from the viewpoints of those involved, including the victim.

This "demonstrates the power of love and making choices. McDaniel, known for her inspiring novels, has a simplistic style, but a weighty message—it's the way you respond to a given situation that defines who you are and who you will be." SLJ

McDonald, Abby

The anti -prom. Candlewick Press 2011 280p $16.99
Grades: 8 9 10 11   Fic
1. School stories
ISBN 978-0-7636-4956-2; 0-7636-4956-2

LC 2010-39170

On prom night, Bliss, Jolene, and Meg, students from the same high school who barely know one another, band together to get revenge against Bliss's boyfriend and her best friend, whom she caught together in the limousine they rented.

"McDonald instills more intelligence than you'd expect from such a plot while not skimping on the simple pleasures, either." Booklist

McDonald, Ian

Be my enemy; by Ian McDonald. Pyr 2012 280 p. (hardcover) $16.95
Grades: 7 8 9 10   Fic
1. Science fiction 2. Kidnapping -- Fiction 3. Technology -- Fiction 4. Father-son relationship -- Fiction
ISBN 1616146788; 9781616146788

LC 2012018572

Sequel to: Planesrunner (2011)

This book by Ian McDonald is the second in the Everness Series. "Everett Singh has escaped with the Infundibulum from the clutches of Charlotte Villiers and the Order, but at a terrible price. His father is missing, banished to one of the billions of parallel universes of the Panoply of All Worlds, and Everett and the crew of the airship Everness have taken a wild Heisenberg jump to a random parallel plane." (Publisher's note)

Empress of the sun; by Ian McDonald. Pyr 2014 290 p. (Everness) (hardback) $17.99
Grades: 7 8 9 10   Fic
1. War stories 2. Airships -- Fiction 3. Human-alien encounters -- Fiction 4. Science fiction 5. Adventure

and adventurers -- Fiction

ISBN 1616148659; 9781616148652

LC 2013036315

In this book by Ian McDonald, "the The airship Everness [enters an] . . . alternate Earth unlike any her crew has ever seen. Everett, Sen, and the crew find themselves above a plain that goes on forever in every direction without any horizon. There they find an Alderson Disc, an astronomical megastructure of incredibly strong material. Then they meet the Jiju, the dominant species on a plane where the dinosaurs didn't die out. War between their kingdoms is inevitable, total and terrible." (Publisher's note)

"The marvelous Everness series takes readers to a world with highly evolved dinosaurs in this third voyage through parallel universes...Fans might wish for more focus on the original Everett, but eventually, the three storylines weave themselves together nicely, setting up another sequel with hints of forthcoming romance. Endlessly fascinating and fun." (Kirkus)

★ **Planesrunner**. Pyr 2011 269p (Everness) $16.95

Grades: 6 7 8 9   **Fic**

1. Science fiction

ISBN 978-1-61614-541-5; 1-61614-541-2

LC 2011032751

When fourteen-year-old Everett Singh's scientist father is kidnapped from the streets of London, he leaves a mysterious app on Everett's computer giving him access to the Infundibulum—a map of parallel earths—which is being sought by technologically advanced dark powers that Everett must somehow elude while he tries to rescue his father.

"McDonald writes with scientific and literary sophistication, as well as a wicked sense of humor. Add nonstop action, eccentric characters, and expert universe building, and this first volume of the Everness series is a winner." Publ Wkly

McDonald, Janet

Harlem Hustle. Frances Foster Books 2006 182p $16

Grades: 8 9 10 11   **Fic**

1. Rap music -- Fiction 2. African Americans -- Fiction 3. Harlem (New York, N.Y.) -- Fiction

ISBN 978-0-374-37184-5; 0-374-37184-9

LC 2005-52108

Eric "Hustle" Samson, a smart and streetwise seventeen-year-old dropout from Harlem, aspires to rap stardom, a dream he naively believes is about to come true.

"The author nails the hip-hop lingo and the street slang, and her characters strike just the right attitude. . . . Young adults will love this book." SLJ

★ **Off** -color. Farrar, Straus and Giroux 2007 163p $16

Grades: 7 8 9 10 11 12   **Fic**

1. Single parent family -- Fiction 2. Racially mixed people -- Fiction 3. Brooklyn (New York, N.Y.) -- Fiction 4. Mother-daughter relationship -- Fiction

ISBN 0-374-37196-2

LC 2006-47334

Fifteen-year-old Cameron living with her single mother in Brooklyn finds her search for identity further chal-

lenged when she discovers that she is the product of a biracial relationship.

"McDonald dramatizes the big issues from the inside, showing the hard times and the joy in fast-talking dialogue that is honest, insulting, angry, tender, and very funny." Booklist

McDonnell, Margot

Torn to pieces. Delacorte Press 2008 258p $15.99; lib bdg $18.99

Grades: 8 9 10 11 12   **Fic**

1. Friendship -- Fiction 2. Grandparents -- Fiction 3. Missing persons -- Fiction 4. Mother-daughter relationship -- Fiction

ISBN 978-0-385-73559-9; 0-385-73559-6; 978-0-385-90542-8 lib bdg; 0-385-90542-4 lib bdg

LC 2007-41536

When her mother disappears during a business trip, seventeen-year-old Anne discovers that her family harbors many dark secrets.

"This teen thriller . . . builds to a gripping conclusion with a final twist that will shock and satisfy teen readers." Booklist

McDowell, Marilyn Taylor

★ **Carolina** Harmony. Delacorte 2009 288p $16.99; lib bdg $19.99

Grades: 4 5 6 7   **Fic**

1. Orphans -- Fiction 2. Farm life -- Fiction 3. Blue Ridge Mountains region -- Fiction

ISBN 978-0-385-73590-2; 0-385-73590-1; 978-0-385-90575-6 lib bdg; 0-385-90575-0 lib bdg

"After Carolina's beloved Auntie Shen suffers a stroke, Carolina escapes from an unpleasant foster placement. The orphaned 10-year-old finds love at Harmony Farm, but the web of lies she spins almost leads to losing that home too. . . . This third-person narrative unwinds leisurely, with plenty of backtracking to fill in details of Carolina's life and the glories of her world in the Blue Ridge Mountains. . . . McDowell reveals her love for this part of the world, savoring the language, the environment, and the traditions of mountain culture." Booklist

McElligott, Matthew

Benjamin Franklinstein lives! [by] Matthew McElligott & Larry Tuxbury; illustrated by Matthew McElligott. G. P. Putnam's Sons 2010 121p il $12.99

Grades: 4 5 6 7   **Fic**

1. Authors 2. Diplomats 3. Inventors 4. Statesmen 5. Scientists 6. Science fiction 7. Writers on science 8. Zombies -- Fiction 9. Members of Congress

ISBN 978-0-399-25229-7; 0-399-25229-0

While working on a science fair project, a Philadelphia school boy discovers both a secret laboratory in his basement and Benjamin Franklin, who comes to life after receiving a jolt of electricity.

"It's a light fun read, and McElligott's many diagrams, graphs, and drawings are a nice addition." Booklist

Followed by: Benjamin Franklinstein meets the fright brothers (2011)

Benjamin Franklinstein meets the Fright brothers; by Matthew McElligott and Larry Tuxbury; [illustrated by Matthew McElligott] G. P. Putnam's Sons 2011 147p il $16.99

Grades: 4 5 6 7 **Fic**

1. Authors 2. Diplomats 3. Inventors 4. Statesmen 5. Scientists 6. Writers on science 7. Members of Congress 8. Scientists -- Fiction 9. Secret societies -- Fiction

ISBN 978-0-399-25480-2; 0-399-25480-3

LC 2010040431

Sequel to: Benjamin Franklinstein lives! (2010)

Victor and his friends, aided by Benjamin Franklin, uncover an evil scheme involving giant bats and two mysterious brothers, and learn more about the secretive Modern Order of Prometheus.

"Enhanced by frequent charts, diagrams, lists and other visual aids, a spirit of rational (if often reckless) scientific inquiry pervades the tale, as Ben and his allies translate coded messages, analyze evidence, get a lesson in meteorology and conduct experiments using both real and science-fictional gear on the way to a literally electrifying climax. . . . The authors have way too much fun taking the opener's premise and evil conspiracy to the next level. Readers will too." Kirkus

McEntire, Myra

Hourglass. Egmont USA 2011 390p $17.99

Grades: 7 8 9 10 **Fic**

1. Science fiction 2. Orphans -- Fiction 3. Homicide -- Fiction 4. Siblings -- Fiction 5. Parapsychology -- Fiction 6. Space and time -- Fiction

ISBN 1-60684-144-0; 978-1-60684-144-0

LC 2010-43618

Seventeen-year-old Emerson uses her power to manipulate time to help Michael, a consultant hired by her father, to prevent a murder that happened six months ago. "Grades seven to ten." (Bull Cent Child Books)

"Em is an entertainingly cheeky narrator and appealingly resilient heroine. . . . McEntire deftly juggles plot, characters and dialogue; her portrait of grief is particularly poignant." Kirkus

McGhee, Alison

All rivers flow to the sea. Candlewick Press 2005 168p $15.99

Grades: 8 9 10 11 12 **Fic**

1. Sisters -- Fiction 2. Bereavement -- Fiction 3. Traffic accidents -- Fiction 4. Adirondack Mountains (N.Y.) -- Fiction

ISBN 0-7636-2591-4

LC 2004-54609

After a car accident in the Adirondacks leaves her older sister Ivy brain-dead, seventeen-year-old Rose struggles with her grief and guilt as she slowly learns to let her sister go.

"This somber, philosophical look at loss and the reestablishment of identity is sensitive and perceptive, and includes passages of beautiful writing. Supporting characters are complex and lovingly rendered." Booklist

McGowan, Keith

The **witch's** guide to cooking with children; illustrated by Yoko Tanaka. Henry Holt and Co. 2009 180p il $15.99

Grades: 5 6 7 8 **Fic**

1. Germany -- Fiction 2. Witches -- Fiction 3. Siblings -- Fiction

ISBN 978-0-8050-8668-3; 0-8050-8668-4

LC 2008-50269

Eleven-year-old inventor Sol must recover his self-confidence if he and his eight-year-old sister, Connie, are to escape the clutches of Hansel and Gretel's witch, to whom they have been led by their new stepmother and the man they believe to be their father.

"McGowan's modern retelling of the Hansel and Gretel plot is nuanced, fascinating, and gratifyingly dark without being graphic or horrific. . . . Tanaka's frequent softly shaded monochromatic illustrations are atmospheric and haunting, and the human figures' oversized eyes and exaggerated noses echo the disturbing strangeness of the story. Hand this to kids who like their folktales on the scary side." Bull Cent Child Books

McGraw, Eloise Jarvis

The **moorchild**; [by] Eloise McGraw. Margaret K. McElderry Bks. 1996 241p $17; pa $5.99

Grades: 4 5 6 7 **Fic**

1. Fantasy fiction 2. Fairies -- Fiction

ISBN 0-689-80654-X; 1-4169-2768-9 pa

LC 95-34107

A Newbery Medal honor book, 1997

"Incorporating some classic fantasy motifs and icons, McGraw . . . conjures up an appreciably familiar world that, as evidence of her storytelling power, still strikes an original chord." Publ Wkly

McGuigan, Mary Ann

Morning in a different place. Front Street 2009 195p $17.95

Grades: 7 8 9 10 **Fic**

1. Friendship -- Fiction 2. Race relations -- Fiction 3. African Americans -- Fiction 4. Bronx (New York, N.Y.) -- Fiction

ISBN 978-1-59078-551-5; 1-59078-551-7

LC 2007-17547

In 1963 in the Bronx, New York, eighth-graders Fiona and Yolanda help one another face hard decisions at home despite family and social opposition to their interracial friendship, but Fiona is on her own when popular classmates start paying attention to her and give her a glimpse of both a different way of life and a new kind of hatefulness.

This book is "never didactic. McGuigan's writing is spare and low-key, and her metaphors are acute." Booklist

McKay, Hilary, 1959-

★ **Binny** for short; by Hilary McKay and illustrated by Micah Player. Margaret K. McElderry Books 2013 291 p. (hardcover) $16.99

Grades: 3 4 5 6 **Fic**

1. Aunts -- Fiction 2. Family -- Fiction 3. Ghosts 4. Family life -- Fiction 5. Loss (Psychology) -- Fiction 6.

Moving, Household -- Fiction
ISBN 1442482753; 9781442482753

LC 2013000053

In this book, by Hilary McKay and illustrated by Micah Player, "Aunty Violet has died, and left Binny and her family an old house in a seaside town. Binny is faced with a new crush, a new frenemy, and a ghost. It seems Aunty Violet may not have completely departed. [For Binny] it's odd being haunted by her aunt, but there is also the warmth of a busy and loving mother, a musical older sister, and a hilarious little brother, who is busy with his experiments." (Publisher's note)

★ **Saffy's** angel. Margaret K. McElderry Bks. 2002 152p $16; pa $4.99

Grades: 5 6 7 8   **Fic**
1. Adoption -- Fiction 2. Family life -- Fiction 3. Great Britain -- Fiction
ISBN 0-689-84933-8; 0-689-84934-6 pa

LC 2001-44110

First published 2001 in the United Kingdom

After learning that she was adopted, thirteen-year-old Saffron's relationship with her eccentric, artistic family changes, until they help her go back to Italy where she was born to find a special momento of her past

"Like the Casson household itself, the plot is a chaotic whirl that careens off in several directions simultaneously. But McKay always skillfully draws each clearly defined character back into the story with witty, well-edited details; rapid dialogue; and fine pacing." Booklist

Other titles in this series are:
Indigo's star (2004)
Permanent Rose (2005)
Caddy ever after (2006)
Forever Rose (2008)

McKay, Sharon E.
Enemy territory; Sharon McKay. Annick Press 2012 184 p. $21.95

Grades: 6 7 8 9 10 11 12   **Fic**
1. Toleration -- Fiction 2. Friendship -- Fiction 3. Israel-Arab conflicts -- Fiction
ISBN 1554514312; 9781554514311

In author Sharon E. McKay's book, "Sam, an Israeli teen whose leg may have to be amputated, and Yusuf, a Palestinian teen who has lost his left eye, find themselves uneasy roommates in a Jerusalem hospital. One night, the boys decide to slip away while the nurses aren't looking and go on an adventure to the Old City. . . . They band together to find their way home and to defend themselves against unfriendly locals, arrest by the military police, and an encounter with a deadly desert snake." (Publisher's note)

Thunder over Kandahar; photographs by Rafal Gerszak. Annick Press 2010 260p il $21.95; pa $12.95

Grades: 7 8 9 10 11 12   **Fic**
1. Afghanistan -- Fiction 2. Afghan War, 2001- -- Fiction
ISBN 978-1-55451-267-6; 1-55451-267-0; 978-1-55451-266-9 pa; 1-55451-266-2 pa

"When her British and American-educated parents' return to Afghanistan is cut short by a terrible attack, 14-year-old Yasmine is sent to Kandahar for safety. Instead, the driver abandons her and her friend Tamanna along the way, and they must travel on their own through Taliban-controlled mountains. . . . In spite of unrelenting violence, along with grinding poverty, restrictive customs, and the horrors of war, what shines through this sad narrative is the love Afghans have for their country. . . . [The author] traveled to Afghanistan and provides numerous credits for this gripping tale." SLJ

McKenzie, Nancy
Guinevere's gamble. Alfred A. Knopf 2009 361p (The Chrysalis Queen quartet) $16.99; lib bdg $19.99

Grades: 7 8 9 10   **Fic**
1. Kings 2. Merlin (Legendary character) -- Fiction 3. Guinevere (Legendary character) -- Fiction 4. Great Britain -- History -- 0-1066 -- Fiction 5. Morgan le Fay (Legendary character) -- Fiction
ISBN 978-0-375-84346-4; 0-375-84346-9; 978-0-375-94346-1 lib bdg; 0-375-94346-3 lib bdg

LC 2008-50617

Sequel to: Guinevere's gift (2008)

Thirteen-year-old Guinevere learns more about her destiny when she accompanies her aunt and uncle to an important council of Welsh kings and finds that she has a powerful enemy in the High King's sister Morgan.

"Readers who are familiar with Arthurian legends as well as those who are not will find this continuing story enjoyable." SLJ

Guinevere's gift. Alfred A. Knopf 2008 327p (The Chrysalis Queen quartet) $15.99; lib bdg $18.99

Grades: 7 8 9 10   **Fic**
1. Cousins -- Fiction 2. Guinevere (Legendary character) -- Fiction 3. Great Britain -- History -- 0-1066 -- Fiction
ISBN 978-0-375-84345-7; 0-375-84345-0; 978-0-375-94345-4 lib bdg; 0-375-94345-5 lib bdg

LC 2007-28782

When the orphaned Guinevere is twelve years old, living with Queen Alyse and King Pellinore of Gwynedd, she fearlessly helps rescue her cousin from kidnappers who are plotting to seize the palace and overthrow the king, even as the queen despairs of Guinevere's rebellious nature.

"Adventure seekers can be content with this tale of a heroine and her castle while dedicated legend fans will appreciate where it fits in the overall tapestry." Bull Cent Child Books

Another title in this series is:
Guinevere's gamble (2009)

McKernan, Victoria
★ The **devil's** paintbox. Alfred A. Knopf 2009 359p $16.99; lib bdg $19.99

Grades: 6 7 8 9 10   **Fic**
1. Orphans -- Fiction 2. Siblings -- Fiction 3. Frontier and pioneer life -- Fiction 4. Overland journeys to the

Pacific -- Fiction
ISBN 978-0-375-83750-0; 0-375-83750-7; 978-0-375-93750-7 lib bdg; 0-375-93750-1 lib bdg
LC 2008-4749

In 1866, fifteen-year-old Aidan and his thirteen-year-old sister Maddy, penniless orphans, leave drought-stricken Kansas on a wagon train hoping for a better life in Seattle, but find there are still many hardships to be faced.

This is a "gripping novel. . . . Attention to detail and steady pacing keep readers fully engaged." Publ Wkly

Shackleton's stowaway. Knopf 2005 336p $15.95; lib bdg $17.99

Grades: 7 8 9 10   **Fic**
1. Explorers 2. Adventure fiction 3. Endurance (Ship) -- Fiction 4. Survival after airplane accidents, shipwrecks, etc. -- Fiction
ISBN 0-375-82691-2; 0-375-92691-7 lib bdg
LC 2004-10313

A fictionalized account of the adventures of eighteen-year-old Perce Blackborow, who stowed away for the 1914 Shackleton Antarctic expedition and, after their ship Endurance was crushed by ice, endured many hardships, including the loss of his left foot to frostbite, during the nearly two-year return journey across sea and ice

"This book provides historical information for history and geography classes who are interested in exploration, the Antarctic, and early history of great sea voyages." Libr Media Connect

McKinlay, Meg

Below; Meg McKinlay. Candlewick Press 2013 224 p. (reinforced) $15.99

Grades: 4 5 6 7   **Fic**
1. Reservoirs -- Fiction 2. Extinct cities -- Fiction
ISBN 0763661260; 9780763661267
LC 2012943652

In this book by Meg McKinlay, "Cassie was . . . the first baby born in the Australian town of New Lower Grange, which was established after the intentional flooding of the previous town to accommodate a dam. . . . [S]he feels the pull of the forbidden lake above Old Lower Grange. There, she is joined by Liam, a classmate whose life was altered in a tragic accident, and together they search for the truth about the town's past as its centenary celebration approaches." (Publishers Weekly)

"Although the author does a masterful job of making sure all the pieces fit at the end, the central mystery is hard to buy. This is mitigated by a reasonably suspenseful climax, an earned family solidarity message and the lesson: that to find the truth, one must delve below the surface. A quietly intriguing meditation on history and truth." Kirkus

McKinlay, Robin

★ **Beauty**; a retelling of the story of Beauty & the beast. Harper & Row 1978 247p $15.99; pa $5.99

Grades: 7 8 9 10   **Fic**
1. Fairy tales
ISBN 0-06-024149-7; 0-06-440477-3 pa
LC 77-25636

"McKinley's version of this folktale is embellished with rich descriptions and settings and detailed characterizations. The author has not modernized the story but varied the traditional version to attract modern readers. The values of love, honor, and beauty are placed in a magical setting that will please the reader of fantasy." Shapiro. Fic for Youth. 3d edition

★ The **blue** sword. Greenwillow Bks. 1982 272p $17.99; pa $6.99

Grades: 7 8 9 10   **Fic**
1. Fantasy fiction
ISBN 0-688-00938-7; 0-441-06880-4 pa
LC 82-2895

A Newbery Medal honor book, 1983

Harry, bored with her sheltered life in the remote orange-growing colony of Daria, discovers magic in herself when she is kidnapped by a native king with mysterious powers.

"This is a zesty, romantic, heroic fantasy with an appealing stalwart heroine, a finely realixed mythical kingdom, and a grounding in reality." Booklist

Chalice. G.P. Putnam's Sons 2008 263p $18.99

Grades: 7 8 9 10 11 12   **Fic**
1. Fantasy fiction 2. Bees -- Fiction
ISBN 978-0-399-24676-0; 0-399-24676-2
LC 2008-704

A beekeeper by trade, Mirasol's life changes completely when she is named the new Chalice, the most important advisor to the new Master, a former priest of fire.

"The fantasy realm is evoked in thorough and telling detail. . . . A lavish and lasting treat." Publ Wkly

Dragonhaven. G.P. Putnam's Sons 2007 342p $17.99

Grades: 7 8 9 10 11 12   **Fic**
1. Fantasy fiction 2. Dragons -- Fiction
ISBN 0-399-24675-4; 978-0-399-24675-3
LC 2007-8197

When Jake Mendoza, who lives in the Smokehill National Park where his father runs the Makepeace Institute of Integrated Dragon Studies, goes on his first solo overnight in the park, he finds an infant dragon whose mother has been killed by a poacher. "Grades eight to ten." (Bull Cent Child Books)

Readers "will be engaged by McKinley's well-drawn characters and want to root for the Smokehill community's fight to save the ultimate endangered species." SLJ

★ The **hero** and the crown. Greenwillow Bks. 1985 246p lib bdg $16.99

Grades: 6 7 8 9   **Fic**
1. Fantasy fiction
ISBN 0-688-02593-5
LC 84-4074

Awarded the Newbery Medal, 1985

The author "has in this suspenseful prequel . . . created an utterly engrossing fantasy, replete with a fairly mature romantic subplot as well as adventure." N Y Times Book Rev

Pegasus. G.P. Putnam's Sons 2010 404p $18.99

Grades: 8 9 10 11 12   **Fic**
1. Fantasy fiction 2. Magic -- Fiction 3. Princesses --
Fiction 4. Pegasus (Greek mythology) -- Fiction
ISBN 0-399-24677-0; 978-0-399-24677-7
LC 2010-2279

Because of a thousand-year-old alliance between humans and pegasi, Princess Sylvi is ceremonially bound to Ebon, her own pegasus, on her twelfth birthday, but the closeness of their bond becomes a threat to the status quo and possibly to the safety of their two nations.

"McKinley's storytelling is to be savored. She lavishes page after page upon rituals and ceremonies, basks in the awe of her intricately constructed world, and displays a masterful sense of pegasi physicality and mannerisms." Booklist

Rose daughter. Greenwillow Bks. 1997 306p
pa $7.99
Grades: 7 8 9 10   **Fic**
1. Fairy tales
ISBN 0-688-15439-5; 0-441-00583-7 pa
LC 96-48783

Compared to Beauty, this "is fuller bodied, with richer characterizations and a more mystical, darker edge. . . . There is more background on the Beast in this version . . . and Beauty's choice at the end, a departure from that in Beauty, is just so right. Readers will be enchanted, in the best sense of the word." Booklist

McKinney-Whitaker, Courtney

The **last** sister; Courtney McKinney-Whitaker. University of South Carolina Press 2014 232 p. (Young Palmetto books) (hardback) $39.95
Grades: 7 8 9 10   **Fic**
1. Historical fiction 2. Native Americans -- Wars -- Fiction 3. Frontier and pioneer life -- Fiction 4. Cherokee Indians -- Wars, 1759-1761 -- Fiction 5. South Carolina -- History -- 1775-1865 -- Fiction 6. Frontier and pioneer life -- South Carolina -- Fiction
ISBN 1611174295; 9781611174298; 9781611174304
LC 2014011484

This young adult historical novel, by Courtney McKinney-Whitaker, "set during the Anglo-Cherokee War (1758-61), . . . traces a young woman's journey through grief, vengeance, guilt, and love in the unpredictable world of the early American frontier. After a band of fellow settlers fakes a Cherokee raid to conceal their murder of her family, seventeen-year-old Catriona 'Catie' Blair embarks on a quest to report the crime and bring the murderers to justice." (Publisher's note)

"This historical novel is set in the Carolinas during the Cherokee Wars, concurrent with Thomas Jefferson and John Adams writing the Declaration of Independence and George Washington navigating the Delaware River. Seventeen-year-old Catie Blair is forced to conjure up maturity and responsibility when tragedy strikes her family . . . A unique historical fiction title with a compelling plot and unique backdrop, taking place during a little-known skirmish in a pivotal time of American history." SLJ

McKinnon, Hannah Roberts

★ **Franny** Parker. Farrar Straus Giroux 2009
149p $16

Grades: 5 6 7 8   **Fic**
1. Droughts -- Fiction 2. Oklahoma -- Fiction 3. Violence -- Fiction 4. Family life -- Fiction
ISBN 978-0-374-32469-8; 0-374-32469-7
LC 2008-01702

Through a hot, dry Oklahoma summer, twelve-year-old Franny tends wild animals brought by her neighbors, hears gossip during a weekly quilting bee, befriends a new neighbor who has some big secrets, and learns to hope.

"Franny is a relatable and consistent narrator, the homey rural setting is throughtfully rendered and the easy prose should appeal to reluctant readers." Publ Wkly

The **properties** of water. Farrar, Straus, and Giroux 2010 166p $16.99
Grades: 5 6 7 8   **Fic**
1. Sisters -- Fiction 2. Accidents -- Fiction
ISBN 978-0-374-36145-7; 0-374-36145-2

When her older sister, Marni, is paralyzed jumping off the cliffs into the lake near their house, twelve-year-old Lace feels responsible for the accident and struggles to find a way to help heal her family.

"McKinnon "has created a cast of believably imperfect characters, and Lace's emotions ring true." Publ Wkly

McKissack, Fredrick

★ **Shooting** star. Atheneum Books for Young Readers 2009 273p $16.99
Grades: 8 9 10 11 12   **Fic**
1. School stories 2. Football -- Fiction 3. Steroids -- Fiction 4. African Americans -- Fiction
ISBN 978-1-4169-4745-5; 1-4169-4745-0
LC 2008-55525

Jomo Rogers, a naturally talented athlete, starts taking performance enhancing drugs in order to be an even better high school football player, but finds his life spinning out of control as his game improves.

"Profane and scatological language abounds, but it is not outside the realm of what one could hear any day in a school locker room. Top-notch sports fiction." SLJ

McKissack, Patricia C.

The **clone** codes; [by] Patricia C. McKissack, Fredrick L. McKissack [and] John McKissack. Scholastic 2010 173p $16.99
Grades: 4 5 6 7   **Fic**
1. Science fiction 2. Cloning -- Fiction 3. Segregation -- Fiction 4. Identity (Psychology) -- Fiction
ISBN 978-0-439-92983-7; 0-439-92983-0
LC 2009-24076

On the run from a bounty hunter who arrested her mother for being part of a secret society devoted to freeing clones, thirteen-year-old Leanna learns amazing truths about herself and her family as she is forced to consider the value of freedom and what it really means to be human in 2170 America.

"The story is tight and fast-paced, yet makes room for historical parallels that are vivid without being preachy. An intriguing start to a planned trilogy." Publ Wkly

Followed by: Cyborg (2011)

Cyborg; a Clone codes novel. [by] Patricia C. McKissack, Fredrick L. McKissack, John P. McKissack. Scholastic Press 2011 107p $16.99

Grades: 4 5 6 7   **Fic**

1. Science fiction 2. Civil rights -- Fiction 3. Artificial intelligence -- Fiction

ISBN 978-0-439-92985-1; 0-439-92985-7

LC 2010016075

Sequel to: Clone codes (2010)

Seventeen-year-old Houston, a cyborg since the age of seven, and a fugitive living on the Moon, joins with other cyborgs all over the world in non-violent protest marches to challenge the Cyborg Act 2130 and hopefully secure increased civil liberties.

"The McKissacks continue to successfully draw parallels between a futuristic world that tries to control those considered different and historic racial struggles. . . . The worldbuilding is intriguing, there is plenty of action and ethnic diversity in a science-fiction tale is welcome." Kirkus

A **friendship** for today. Scholastic Press 2007 172p $16.99

Grades: 4 5 6 7   **Fic**

1. Divorce -- Fiction 2. Missouri -- Fiction 3. Friendship -- Fiction 4. Race relations -- Fiction 5. African Americans -- Fiction 6. School integration -- Fiction

ISBN 978-0-439-66098-3

LC 2006-29293

In 1954, when desegregation comes to Kirkland, Missouri, ten-year-old Rosemary faces many changes and challenges at school and at home as her parents separate.

"A real, at times raw tale about a winning and insightful young heroine during a bittersweet era." Publ Wkly

★ **Let** my people go; Bible stories told by a freeman of color to his daughter, Charlotte, in Charleston, South Carolina, 1806-16. by Patricia and Fredrick McKissack; illustrated by James Ransome. Atheneum Bks. for Young Readers 1998 134p il $20

Grades: 4 5 6 7   **Fic**

1. Bible stories 2. Slavery -- Fiction 3. African Americans -- Fiction

ISBN 0-689-80856-9

LC 97-19983

Charlotte, the daughter of a free black man who worked as a blacksmith in Charleston, South Carolina, in the early 1800s recalls the stories from the Bible that her father shared with her, relating them to the experiences of African Americans

"The poignant juxtaposition of the Biblical characters and Charlotte's personal narrative is authentic and moving. . . . The occasional illustrations are powerful oil paintings in rich colors, emotional and evocative." SLJ

Includes bibliographical references

★ **Nzingha,** warrior queen of Matamba; by Patricia McKissack. Scholastic 2000 136p (Royal diaries) $10.95

Grades: 5 6 7 8   **Fic**

1. Queens 2. Angola -- Fiction 3. Princesses -- Fiction

4. Slave trade -- Fiction

ISBN 0-439-11210-9

LC 00-24216

Presents the diary of thirteen-year-old Nzingha, a sixteenth-century West African princess who loves to hunt and hopes to lead her kingdom one day against the invasion of the Portuguese slave traders

"The diary format will appeal to readers and the author's use of time lines, seasons, and actual place names makes the story believable and interesting." SLJ

McLaren, Clemence

Inside the walls of Troy; a novel of the women who lived the Trojan War. Atheneum Bks. for Young Readers 1996 199p hardcover o.p. pa $5.99

Grades: 7 8 9 10   **Fic**

1. Helen of Troy (Legendary character) -- Fiction

ISBN 0-689-31820-0; 0-689-87397-2 pa

LC 93-8127

The events surrounding the famous battle between the Greeks and the Trojans are told from the points of view of two women, the beautiful Helen and the prophetic Cassandra

"These ancient stories are made as fresh and vivid as any modern tale by the electrifying characters and sensual details." Booklist

McLoughlin, Jane

At Yellow Lake. Frances Lincoln Children's Books 2012 358 p. (paperback) $8.99

Grades: 7 8 9 10   **Fic**

1. Mystery fiction 2. Teenagers -- Fiction 3. Native Americans -- Fiction

ISBN 1847802877; 9781847802873

In this book by Jane McLoughlin, "Etta, Peter and Jonah all find themselves at a cabin by the shore of Yellow Lake. . . . Jonah has come to Yellow Lake to try to get in touch with his Ojibwe roots. Peter is there to bury a lock of his mother's hair -- her final request. Etta is on the run from her mother's creepy boyfriend. . . . But as the three take shelter in the cabin . . . they soon realise that they have inadvertently stumbled onto the scene of a horrifying crime." (Publisher's note)

McMann, Lisa

Cryer's Cross. Simon Pulse 2011 232p $16.99

Grades: 7 8 9 10   **Fic**

1. Mystery fiction 2. Montana -- Fiction 3. Supernatural -- Fiction 4. Missing persons -- Fiction 5. Obsessive-compulsive disorder -- Fiction

ISBN 978-1-4169-9481-7; 1-4169-9481-5; 978-1-4169-9483-1 ebook

LC 2010-15410

"Kendall is a unique character, and the details of her OCD compulsions are well drawn. Haunting passages from another world, which provide just enough detail to intrigue and disturb readers, are intertwined with Kendall's story. Part mystery, part ghost story, and part romance, this book has enough to satisfy a variety of readers." Booklist

Wake. Simon Pulse 2008 210p $15.99; pa $8.99

Grades: 7 8 9 10   **Fic**

1. School stories 2. Dreams -- Fiction

ISBN 978-1-4169-5357-9; 1-4169-5357-4; 978-1-4169-7447-5 pa; 1-4169-7447-4 pa

LC 2007036267

Ever since she was eight years old, high school student Janie Hannagan has been uncontrollably drawn into other people's dreams, but it is not until she befriends an elderly nursing home patient and becomes involved with an enigmatic fellow-student that she discovers her true power.

"A fast pace, a great mix of teen angst and supernatural experiences, and an eerie, attention-grabbing cover will make this a hit." Booklist

Other titles in this series are:

Fade (2009)

Gone (2010)

McMullan, Margaret

Cashay. Houghton Mifflin Harcourt 2009 166p $15

Grades: 7 8 9 10   **Fic**

1. Anger -- Fiction 2. Mentoring -- Fiction 3. Bereavement -- Fiction 4. Racially mixed people -- Fiction

ISBN 978-0-547-07656-0; 0-547-07656-8

LC 2008-36111

When her world is turned upside down by her sister's death, a mentor is assigned to fourteen-year-old Cashay to help her through her anger and grief.

"Cashay's spirited voice and non-frothy prose will draw both confirmed and newer fans of inner-city drama." Kirkus

★ **How** I found the Strong; a Civil War story. Houghton Mifflin 2004 136p $15

Grades: 5 6 7 8   **Fic**

1. Slavery -- Fiction 2. Mississippi -- Fiction 3. United States -- History -- 1861-1865, Civil War -- Fiction

ISBN 0-618-35008-X

LC 2003-12294

Frank Russell, known as Shanks, wishes he could have gone with his father and brother to fight for Mississippi and the Confederacy, but his experiences with the war and his changing relationship with the family slave, Buck, change his thinking.

"The crisply written narrative is full of regional speech and detail, creating a vivid portrait." Voice Youth Advocates

★ **Sources** of light. Houghton Mifflin 2010 233p $15

Grades: 6 7 8 9   **Fic**

1. Mississippi -- Fiction 2. Photography -- Fiction 3. Race relations -- Fiction 4. African Americans -- Civil rights -- Fiction

ISBN 978-0-547-07659-1; 0-547-07659-2

LC 2009-49708

"When 14-year-old Samantha Thomas moves to Jackson, Miss., in 1962, following her father's death in Vietnam, she learns about love and hate all in the same year. Her mother meets Perry Walker, a photographer who teaches Sam about taking photographs and seeing the world in new ways, but what she begins seeing and pondering is the racial situation in Jackson—lunch-counter sit-ins, voter-registra-

tion protests and the violent reprisals of many in the white community, including the father of the boy she begins to like. . . . This offers a superb portrait of a place and time and a memorable character trying to make sense of a world both ugly and beautiful." Kirkus

★ **When** I crossed No-Bob. Houghton Mifflin Company 2007 209p $16

Grades: 5 6 7 8   **Fic**

1. Farm life -- Fiction 2. Mississippi -- Fiction 3. Race relations -- Fiction 4. Abandoned children -- Fiction 5. Reconstruction (1865-1876) -- Fiction

ISBN 978-0-618-71715-6; 0-618-71715-3

LC 2007-12753

Ten years after the Civil War's end, twelve-year-old Addy, abandoned by her parents, is taken from the horrid town of No-Bob by schoolteacher Frank Russell and his bride, but when her father returns to claim her she must find another way to leave her O'Donnell past behind.

"The simple prose can be pure poetry. . . . Readers will be drawn by the history close-up and by the elemental moral choice." Booklist

McNab, Andy

Traitor; [by] Andy McNab and Robert Rigby. G.P. Putnam's Sons 2005 265p $15.99

Grades: 7 8 9 10   **Fic**

1. Spies -- Fiction 2. Orphans -- Fiction 3. Grandfathers -- Fiction 4. Great Britain -- Fiction

ISBN 0-399-24464-6

LC 2005-6701

"Orphaned Londoner Danny Watts wants nothing to do with his estranged grandfather, a traitor who went MIA years ago, until the British military offers Danny a proposition: find his grandfather and he'll receive a scholarship. . . . With help from his best friend, Elena, he sets off to find his relative and the truth. . . . The well-crafted language includes a few coarse phrases. . . . With its brisk plot and unpredictable characters, this story of intrigue rises above many standard adventure stories." Booklist

Other titles in this series are:

Payback (2006)

Avenger (2007)

Meltdown (2008)

McNamee, Eoin

The **Navigator**. Wendy Lamb Books 2007 342p il (Navigator trilogy) $15.99; pa $6.99

Grades: 6 7 8 9   **Fic**

1. Fantasy fiction 2. Time -- Fiction

ISBN 978-0-375-83910-8; 0-375-83910-0; 978-0-385-73554-4 pa; 0-385-73554-5 pa

LC 2006-26691

Owen has always been different, and not only because his father committed suicide, but he is not prepared for the knowledge that he has a mission to help the Wakeful—the custodians of time—to stop the Harsh from reversing the flow of time.

McNamee "shows a deft hand in writing for children. Excellent world-building, a thrilling and propulsive plot, internal consistency and a multitude of child heroes guarantee a following for this exciting fantasy." Kirkus

Other titles in this series are:
City of Time (2008)
The Frost Child (2009)

McNamee, Graham

Acceleration. Wendy Lamb Bks. 2003 210p
hardcover o.p. pa $6.99
Grades: 8 9 10 11 12   **Fic**
1. Mystery fiction 2. Canada -- Fiction 3. Homicide
-- Fiction
ISBN 0-385-73119-1; 0-440-23836-6 pa
LC 2003-3708

Stuck working in the Lost and Found of the Toronto
Transit Authority for the summer, seventeen-year-old Duncan finds the diary of a serial killer and sets out to stop him

"Never overexploits the sensational potential of the subject and builds suspense layer upon layer, while injecting
some surprising comedy relief." Booklist

Bonechiller; [by] Graham McNamee. 1st ed.;
Wendy Lamb Books 2008 294p $15.99; lib bdg
$18.99
Grades: 7 8 9 10 11 12   **Fic**
1. Canada -- Fiction 2. Monsters -- Fiction 3.
Bereavement -- Fiction 4. Supernatural -- Fiction
ISBN 978-0-385-74658-8; 0-385-74658-X; 978-0-
385-90895-5 lib bdg; 0-385-90895-4 lib bdg
LC 2007039383

Four high school students face off against a soul-stealing
beast that has been making young people disappear their
small Ontario, Canada, town for centuries.

"This will be an easy booktalk and a spendidly enjoyable read sure to please those who respond with both hope
and dread when things go bump in the night." Bull Cent
Child Books

McNaughton, Janet

An **earthly** knight. HarperCollins Publishers
2004 261p $15.99; lib bdg $16.89
Grades: 7 8 9 10   **Fic**
1. Fantasy fiction 2. Scotland -- Fiction
ISBN 0-06-008992-X; 0-06-008993-8 lib bdg
LC 2003-9561
First published 2003 in Canada

In 1162 in Scotland, sixteen-year-old Jenny Avenel falls
in love with the mysterious Tam Lin while being courted by
the king's brother and must navigate the tides of tradition
and the power of ancient magic to define her own destiny.

"The author does an excellent job of interweaving legend and history to create an exciting and engaging tale." SLJ

McNeal, Laura

★ **Dark** water. Alfred A. Knopf 2010 287p
$16.99; lib bdg $19.99
Grades: 7 8 9 10   **Fic**
1. Fires -- Fiction 2. Divorce -- Fiction 3. California
-- Fiction 4. Family life -- Fiction 5. Illegal aliens --
Fiction 6. Homeless persons -- Fiction
ISBN 978-0-375-84973-2; 0-375-84973-4; 978-0-375-
94973-9 lib bdg; 0-375-94973-9 lib bdg
LC 2009-43249

Living in a cottage on her uncle's southern California
avocado ranch since her parent's messy divorce, fifteen-
year-old Pearl Dewitt meets and falls in love with an illegal
migrant worker, and is trapped with him when wildfires approach his makeshift forest home.

"Notable for well-drawn characters, an engaging plot
and, especially, hauntingly beautiful language, this is an outstanding book." Kirkus

The **decoding** of Lana Morris; [by] Laura & Tom
McNeal. Alfred A. Knopf 2007 289p $15.99
Grades: 7 8 9 10 11 12   **Fic**
1. Drawing -- Fiction 2. Nebraska -- Fiction 3.
Disabled -- Fiction 4. Supernatural -- Fiction 5. Foster
home care -- Fiction
ISBN 0-375-83106-1; 978-0-375-83106-5
LC 2006-23950

For sixteen-year-old Lana life is often difficult, with a
flirtatious foster father, an ice queen foster mother, a houseful of special needs children to care for, and bullies harrass-
ing her, until the day she ventures into an antique shop and
buys a drawing set that may change her life.

This is "a colorful character drama with genuine spice
and impact." Bull Cent Child Books

McNeal, Tom

★ **Far** far away; by Tom McNeal. 1st ed. Alfred A. Knopf Books for Young Readers 2013 371
p. (hardcover) $17.99; (ebook) $53.97; (library)
$20.99
Grades: 7 8 9 10   **Fic**
1. Occult fiction 2. Fantasy fiction 3. Ghosts -- Fiction
4. Friendship -- Fiction 5. Supernatural -- Fiction 6.
Missing persons -- Fiction
ISBN 0375849726; 9780375849725; 9780375896989;
9780375949722
LC 2012020603

Parents' Choice: Gold Medal Fiction (2013)

This book "is narrated by the ghost of Jacob Grimm . . . ,
unhappily caught in the Zwischenraum (a plane of existence
between life and death). For now, he is the nearly constant
companion of Jeremy Johnson," who hears voices. This ability "has made him an object of derision for many in his little
town, though—thrillingly—not to the electrifyingly vibrant
Ginger Boultinghouse, who is more than happy to lure Jeremy into more trouble than he's ever encountered." (School
Library Journal)

McNicoll, Sylvia

Last chance for Paris. Fitzhenry & Whiteside
2008 204p pa $11.95
Grades: 6 7 8 9   **Fic**
1. Twins -- Fiction 2. Canada -- Fiction 3. Wolves
-- Fiction 4. Siblings -- Fiction
ISBN 978-1-5545-5061-6 pa; 1-5545-5061-0 pa

Fourteen-year-old Zanna goes to the Alberta ice fields
with her father and twin brother, Martin, where they find a
wolf pup which they name Paris. When Martin is lost, Paris
helps find him.

"Written with elements of wry humor and romance,
this Canadian novel features a narrator whose disarmingly
candid opinions make her an appealing guide for read-

ers who usually veer away from backwoods or survival stories." Booklist

McNish, Cliff

★ **Angel**. Carolrhoda Books 2008 312p $16.95

Grades: 7 8 9 10   **Fic**

1. School stories 2. Angels -- Fiction 3. Bullies -- Fiction 4. Popularity -- Fiction 5. Mental illness -- Fiction

ISBN 978-0-8225-8900-6; 0-8225-8900-1

LC 2007-9664

An unlikely friendship develops between fourteen-year-olds Stephanie, an angel-obsessed social outcast, and Freya, a popular student whose visions of angels sent her to a mental institution and who is now seeing a dark angel at every turn.

"The author beautifully melds a tale of the fantastic and the mundane." Voice Youth Advocates

The **silver** child; by Cliff McNish. 1st American ed; Carolrhoda Books 2005 192p lib bdg $15.95

Grades: 6 7 8 9   **Fic**

1. Fantasy fiction

ISBN 1-57505-825-1

LC 2004-12407

Drawn to a wasteland of garbage dumps called Coldharbour, six children undergo mysterious transformations and band together to face an unknown enemy.

The author "writes a darkly compelling fantasy, using alternating narratives to add to the suspense. His vivid, often lyrical prose will engage readers." Booklist

Other titles in this series are:

Silver City (2006)

Silver world (2007)

McPhee, Peter

New blood. James Lorimer 2008 167p pa $8.95

Grades: 6 7 8 9 10   **Fic**

1. School stories 2. Canada -- Fiction 3. Bullies -- Fiction

ISBN 978-1-55028-996-1; 1-55028-996-9

When his family moves from the tough streets of Glasgow to Winnipeg, Canada, Callum finds that his high school days of dealing with bullies are far from over.

"The Scottish culture, which becomes a colorful character, adds to the fullness of the story. The writing, rich in dialogue, does not waste words and keeps the reader involved and cheering for this gutsy hero who fights his fear to stand against abuse aimed at himself and others." Voice Youth Advocates

McQuein, Josin L.

Arclight; Josin L. McQuein. 1st ed. Greenwillow Books, an imprint of HarperCollins Publishers 2013 416 p. (hardcover) $17.99

Grades: 8 9 10 11 12   **Fic**

1. Orphans -- Fiction 2. Fantasy fiction 3. Science fiction 4. Amnesia -- Fiction 5. Identity -- Fiction

ISBN 0062130145; 9780062130143

LC 2013002929

In this book, "Marina was pulled from the Dark at the cost of nine lives, and she is paying the price. Ostracized

and abused by those whose parents died for her sake, Marina is all but alone in the Arclight, a safe zone where it is never dark. The Fade live in the Dark—chameleons, they steal humans from the light to an unknown fate. Marina dreams of their voices and frets that she has no memory of her life before her rescue." She seeks answers about her past. (Publishers Weekly)

McQuerry, Maureen Doyle

★ **Beyond** the door; Maureen Doyle McQuerry. Amulet Books 2014 384 p. (Time out of time) $16.95

Grades: 4 5 6 7 8   **Fic**

1. Adventure fiction 2. Magic -- Fiction 3. Celtic mythology -- Fiction 4. Brothers and sisters -- Fiction 5. Space and time -- Fiction 6. Animals, Mythical -- Fiction 7. Mythology, Celtic -- Fiction 8. Adventure and adventurers -- Fiction

ISBN 1419710168; 9781419710162

LC 2013025513

This book, by Maureen Doyle McQuerry, "weaves a . . . coming-of-age story with fantasy and mythology. With his love of learning and the game of Scrabble, Timothy James feels like the only person who understands him is his older sister, Sarah. . . . One night, while his parents and sister are away, the door opens, and mythical creatures appear in his own living room! Soon, a mystery of unparalleled proportions begins to unfold, revealing an age-old battle of Light against Dark." (Publisher's note)

"Scrabble-loving loner Timothy and his older sister Sarah access an ancient mythological prophecy when Timothy saves his school tormentor Jessica from being hunted on Beltane, the Gaelic May Day festival. Heavy reliance on Celtic mythology and symbolism doesn't help an awkwardly disjointed plot, though the strong good/evil dichotomy will attract fans to the new series. A code in Ogham script runs along each page." Horn Book

The **Peculiars**; a novel. Maureen Doyle McQuerry. Amulet Books 2012 359 p. (hardback) $16.95

Grades: 7 8 9 10 11 12   **Fic**

1. Fantasy fiction 2. Voyages and travels -- Fiction 3. Father-daughter relationship -- Fiction 4. Goblins -- Fiction 5. Identity -- Fiction 6. Abnormalities, Human -- Fiction 7. Adventure and adventurers -- Fiction

ISBN 1419701789; 9781419701788

LC 2012000844

This is the story of Lena Mattacascar, who at age 18 "travel[s] to Scree, an uncharted wilderness of 'indigenous folks' and deported convicts," sitting on the train with young librarian "Jimson Quiggley," with "marshal Thomas Saltre" watching them. "Lena cannot stop thinking about her mysterious father" or the possibility that she's part Peculiar (goblin). "Scree is the place where Lena's questions might be answered, but arriving there just multiplies them." (Publishers Weekly)

McStay, Moriah

Everything that makes you; Moriah McStay. First edition Katherine Tegen Books, an imprint of

HarperCollins Children's Books 2015 346 p. 22 cm
(hardcover) $17.99

Grades: 8 9 10 11 **Fic**
1. Accidents -- Fiction 2. Family life -- Fiction 3.
Self-confidence -- Fiction 4. Interpersonal relations --
Fiction 5. Disfigured persons -- Fiction
ISBN 0062295489; 9780062295484
LC 2014005864

In this book, by Moriah McStay, "Fiona Doyle's face
was horribly scarred as a child. She writes about her frustrations and dreams in notebooks, penning song lyrics. But
she'd never be brave enough to sing those songs in public. Fi
Doyle . . . [is] the best lacrosse player in the state and can't
be distracted by her friend who wants to be more than that.
But then her luck on the field goes south. Alternating chapters between Fiona and Fi tell two stories about the same
girl." (Publisher's note)

"Entertaining and intellectually stimulating, the novel
invites discussion about how much of a person's life is determined by events and whether some tendencies are inborn."
Publishers Weekly

McWilliams, Kelly

Doormat; a novel. Delacorte Press 2004 131p
$15.95; lib bdg $17.99

Grades: 6 7 8 9 **Fic**
1. Theater -- Fiction 2. Pregnancy -- Fiction 3.
Friendship -- Fiction
ISBN 0-385-73168-X; 0-385-90204-2 lib bdg
LC 2003-19675

Fourteen-year-old Jaime has always been a doormat, but
her diary reveals how getting the lead in a school play, finding her first boyfriend, discovering her dream, and helping
her best friend cope with being pregnant transform her life.

"McWilliams' first-person, present-tense vignettes are
taut, funny, and touching, the dialogue is authentic, and both
the teen and adult characters ring true." Booklist

Mead, Alice

Dawn and dusk. Farrar, Straus and Giroux 2007
151p $16

Grades: 6 7 8 9 **Fic**
1. Iran -- Fiction 2. Refugees -- Fiction 3. Iran-Iraq
War, 1980-1988 -- Fiction
ISBN 0-374-31708-9; 978-0-374-31708-9
LC 2006-40850

As thirteen-year-old Azad tries desperately to cling to
the life he has known, the political situation in Iran during
the war with Iraq finally forces his family to flee their home
and seek safety elsewhere.

"Azad is an appealing protagonist, and it is his simple
and direct story that will draw readers through the complexities of a multinational ethnic longing for self-determination
that remains at the heart of an international tinderbox." SLJ

★ **Swimming** to America; Alice Mead. 1st ed;
Farrar, Straus and Giroux 2005 153p $16

Grades: 6 7 8 9 **Fic**
1. Immigrants -- Fiction 2. Brooklyn (New York, N.Y.)
-- Fiction
ISBN 0-374-38047-3
LC 2004-53249

Eighth grader Linda Berati struggles to understand who
she is within the context of her mother's secrecy about the
family background, her discomfort with her old girlfriends,
her involvement with the family problems of her Cuban-
American friend Ramon, and an opportunity to attend a
school for "free spirits" like herself.

Written with "sensitivity and optimism. . . . [This is] an
informative, empathetic, contemporary portrait of the immigrant experience." SLJ

Mebus, Scott

Gods of Manhattan. Dutton Children's Books
2008 372p (Gods of Manhattan) $17.99

Grades: 6 7 8 9 **Fic**
1. Fantasy fiction 2. Adventure fiction 3. Space and
time -- Fiction 4. New York (N.Y.) -- Fiction 5. Gods
and goddesses -- Fiction
ISBN 978-0-525-47955-0; 0-525-47955-4
LC 2007-18113

"Rory, 13, and his sister Bridget, 9, live in present-day
New York City unaware of the spirits from Manhattan's or
'Mannahatta's' past that coexist alongside them. Rory has a
gift for seeing this other world but has repressed this ability
until the day he notices a cockroach riding a rat, an ancient
Indian warrior, a papier-mâché boy, and other oddities. . . .
The use of real historical figures and events lends authentici-
ty to this compulsively readable and fast-paced fantasy." SLJ

Other titles in this series are:
Spirits in the park (2009)
The sorcerer's secret (2010)

Medina, Meg

★ **Milagros**; girl from Away. Henry Holt and
Co. 2008 279p $17.89

Grades: 6 7 8 9 **Fic**
1. Magic -- Fiction 2. Maine -- Fiction 3. Islands
-- Fiction 4. West Indies -- Fiction 5. Rays (Fishes) --
Fiction 6. Mother-daughter relationship -- Fiction
ISBN 978-0-8050-8230-2; 0-8050-8230-1
LC 2007-46939

Twelve-year-old Milagros barely survives an invasion
of her tiny, Caribbean island home, escapes with the help
of mysterious sea creatures, reunites briefly with her pirate-
father, and learns about a mother's love when cast ashore on
another island.

"Medina's use of magical realism keeps readers tantalizingly off-balance as she navigates among settings. . . . [This]
haunting tale . . . will remain with readers." Horn Book

Meehan, Kierin

★ **Hannah's** winter. Kane/Miller Book Publishers 2009 212p $15.95

Grades: 5 6 7 8 **Fic**
1. Adventure fiction 2. Japan -- Fiction
ISBN 978-1-933605-98-2; 1-933605-98-7
First published 2001 in Australia

Hannah would much rather be back in Australia, starting
high school with her friends. But Japan turns out to be nothing like she'd imagined. When Hannah and her new friend

Miki find an ancient message in the stationery shop, they are drawn into involving a mysterious riddle.

"Meehan utilizes beautifully crafted similes and metaphors as she creates a loving and detailed portrayal of Japan and its people. . . . The tale remains so grounded in reality that it never defies belief. A fine fantasy." Kirkus

Meehl, Brian

★ **Suck** it up. Delacorte Press 2008 323p $15.99; pa $8.99

Grades: 8 9 10 11   **Fic**

1. Vampires -- Fiction

ISBN 978-0-385-73300-7; 0-385-73300-3; 978-0-440-42091-0 pa; 0-440-42091-1 pa

LC 2007-27995

After graduating from the International Vampire League, a scrawny, teenaged vampire named Morning is given the chance to fulfill his childhood dream of becoming a superhero when he embarks on a League mission to become the first vampire to reveal his identity to humans and to demonstrate how peacefully-evolved, blood-substitute-drinking vampires can use their powers to help humanity.

This "an original and light variation on the current trend in brooding teen vampire protagonists. . . . Puns abound in this lengthy, complicated romp. . . . Teens will find it delightful." Booklist

Melling, O. R.

The **book** of dreams. Amulet Books 2009 698p map (Chronicles of Faerie) $19.95

Grades: 7 8 9 10   **Fic**

1. Magic -- Fiction 2. Canada -- Fiction 3. Fairies -- Fiction 4. Native Americans -- Fiction 5. Voyages and travels -- Fiction

ISBN 978-0-8109-8346-5; 0-8109-8346-X

LC 2008-24689

Sequel to The Light-Bearer's daughter (2007)

Now thirteen and depressed, Dana has been living with her father and his new wife in Canada for two years, and when she finds that her gateway to the land of Faerie has been mysteriously shattered, she must travel the length and breadth of Canada to find the secret that will re-open the Faerie world.

"The author's exploration of folk traditions across cultures makes the book unique." Voice Youth Advocates

The **Hunter's** Moon. Amulet Books 2005 284p (Chronicles of Faerie) $16.95; pa $7.95

Grades: 7 8 9 10   **Fic**

1. Magic -- Fiction 2. Ireland -- Fiction

ISBN 0-8109-5857-0; 0-8109-9214-0 pa

LC 2004-22216

First published 1992 in Ireland

Two teenage cousins, one Irish, the other from the United States, set out to find a magic doorway to the Faraway Country, where humans must bow to the little people.

"This novel is a compelling blend of Irish mythology and geography. Characters that breathe and connect with readers, and a picturesque landscape that shifts between the present and the past, bring readers into the experience." SLJ

Other available titles in this series are:
The book of dreams (2009)

The Light-Bearer's daughter (2007)
The Summer King (2006)

The **Light** -Bearer's daughter. Amulet Books 2007 348p map (Chronicles of Faerie) hardcover o.p. pa $7.95

Grades: 7 8 9 10 11   **Fic**

1. Magic -- Fiction 2. Ireland -- Fiction

ISBN 978-0-8109-0781-2; 0-8109-0781-X; 978-0-8109-7123-3 pa; 0-8109-7123-2 pa

LC 2006-33517

Sequel to The Summer King (2006)

In exchange for the granting of her heart's desire, twelve-year-old Dana agrees to make an arduous journey to Lugnaquillia through the land of Faerie in order to warn King Lugh, second in command to the High King, that an evil destroyer has entered the Mountain Kingdom.

"The richly integrated, vivid fantasy scenes balance the strident calls for environmental protection and world peace, and the characters' private passages through 'layers of storied memory' will bring the issues home for readers." Booklist

Followed by The book of dreams (2009)

The **Summer** King. Amulet Books 2006 359p map (Chronicles of Faerie) $16.95

Grades: 7 8 9 10   **Fic**

1. Magic -- Fiction 2. Ireland -- Fiction

ISBN 0-8109-5969-0

LC 2005-15083

Seventeen-year-old Laurel returns to her grandparents' home in Ireland, where she encounters the roly-poly man, a cluricaun who sets Laurel on a quest to free her twin sister, thought to be dead, to live with her lover in the legendary world of Faerie.

"Fans of Melling's first title in the Chronicles of Faerie, The Hunter's Moon (2005), will recognize similarly thrilling action, fascinating Irish mythology, and magnificently detailed magic." Booklist

Meloy, Colin

Under Wildwood; Colin Meloy; illustrated by Carson Ellis. Balzer + Bray 2012 559 p. (hardback) $17.99

Grades: 5 6 7 8   **Fic**

1. Fantasy fiction 2. Adventure fiction 3. Fantasy 4. Animals -- Fiction 5. Portland (Or.) -- Fiction

ISBN 006202471X; 9780062024718

LC 2012019040

Sequel to: Wildwood

This children's picture book is a sequel to "Wildwood." Here, bookish "Prue and bandit-in-training Curtis team up once again to fight a nefarious governess and evil science teacher in this fast-paced fantasy set in Oregon. . . . In this strange land, it can be difficult to tell friend from foe, making for deliciously suspenseful adventures with a rat named Septimus and a circus bear with hooks instead of paws." (Children's Literature)

★ **Wildwood**; illustrations by Carson Ellis. Balzer + Bray 2011 541p il $16.99

Grades: 5 6 7 8   **Fic**

1. Fantasy fiction 2. Animals -- Fiction 3. Siblings --

Fiction 4. Portland (Or.) -- Fiction 5. Missing persons
-- Fiction
ISBN 978-0-06-202468-8; 0-06-202468-X

LC 2011010072

When her baby brother is kidnapped by crows, seventh-grader Prue McKeel ventures into the forbidden Impassable Wilderness—a dangerous and magical forest in the middle of Portland, Oregon—and soon finds herself involved in a war among the various inhabitants.

"Illustrations by Ellis . . . bring forest and inhabitants to gently whimsical life. A satisfying blend of fantasy, adventure story, eco-fable and political satire with broad appeal." Kirkus

Wildwood imperium; Colin Meloy; illustrations by Carson Ellis. Balzer + Bray 2014 592 p. ill (some col.), maps (Wildwood chronicles) (hardcover) $17.99

Grades: 5 6 7 8 **Fic**
1. Fairy tales 2. Fantasy fiction 3. Orphans -- Fiction 4. Friendship -- Fiction
ISBN 0062024744; 9780062024749

LC 2013953784

Kirkus (December 15, 2013)

This fairy tale, by Colin Meloy, is the third book in the fantasy "Wildwood" series. "A young girl's midnight séance awakens a long-slumbering malevolent spirit. . . . A band of runaway orphans allies with an underground collective of saboteurs and plans a daring rescue of their friends, imprisoned in . . . an industrial wasteland. . . . Two old friends draw closer to their goal of bringing together a pair of exiled toy makers in order to reanimate a mechanical boy prince." (Publisher's note)

"Dramatic shifts in tone and mood--by turns politically astute and subversively witty, elegiac, droll and philosophical--are par for the course, while narrative style ranges from intimate to intergalactically distant." Kirkus

Meloy, Maile

★ The **apothecary**. G. P. Putnam's Sons 2011 353p $16.99

Grades: 6 7 8 9 **Fic**
1. Adventure fiction 2. Alchemy -- Fiction 3. Cold war -- Fiction 4. Great Britain -- Fiction 5. London (England) -- Fiction
ISBN 978-0-399-25627-1; 0-399-25627-X

LC 2010045003

"With evocative, confident prose and equally atmospheric spot art from Schoenherr, adult author Meloy's first book for young readers is an auspicious one." Publ Wkly

The **apprentices**; by Maile Meloy; illustrated by Ian Schoenherr. G.P. Putnam's Sons, an imprint of Penguin Group (USA) Inc. 2013 432 p. (hardcover) $16.99

Grades: 6 7 8 9 **Fic**
1. Magic -- Fiction 2. Alchemy -- Fiction 3. Voyages and travels -- Fiction 4. Adventure and adventurers -- Fiction 5. Southeast Asia -- History -- 1945- -- Fiction
ISBN 9780399162459

LC 2012048715

In this book by Maile Meloy is the sequel to "The Apothecary". "Janie, now 16, is alone at an elite American boarding school, unaware of the whereabouts of her first boyfriend, Benjamin, and his apothecary father. After she is wrongly expelled, she realizes she is the victim of a nefarious scheme, which again poses a threat to world peace. The . . . plot spans the globe as the heroes find their way back to each other." (Publishers Weekly)

Meltzer, Milton

Tough times; by Milton Meltzer. Clarion Books 2007 168p $16

Grades: 5 6 7 8 **Fic**
1. Jews -- Fiction 2. Family life -- Fiction 3. Massachusetts -- Fiction 4. Great Depression, 1929-1939 -- Fiction
ISBN 978-0-618-87445-3; 0-618-87445-3

LC 2006102765

In 1931 Worcester, Massachusetts, Joey Singer, the teenaged son of Jewish immigrants, suffers with his family through the early part of the Great Depression, trying to finish high school, working a milk delivery route, marching on Washington, and eventually even becoming a hobo, all the while trying to figure out how to go to college and realize his dream of becoming a writer.

"Joey's strong voice makes this a valuable addition to the historical-fiction shelves." Booklist

Meminger, Neesha

Shine, coconut moon. Margaret K. McElderry Books 2009 256p $16.99; pa $8.99

Grades: 7 8 9 10 **Fic**
1. School stories 2. Prejudices -- Fiction 3. East Indian Americans -- Fiction 4. September 11 terrorist attacks, 2001 -- Fiction
ISBN 978-1-4169-5495-8; 1-4169-5495-3; 978-1-4424-0305-5 pa; 1-4424-0305-5 pa

LC 2008-9836

In the days and weeks following the terrorist attacks on September 11, 2001, Samar, who is of Punjabi heritage but has been raised with no knowledge of her past by her single mother, wants to learn about her family's history and to get in touch with the grandparents her mother shuns.

"Meminger's debut book is a beautiful and sensitive portrait of a young woman's journey from self-absorbed navet to selfless, unified awareness." SLJ

Merrill, Jean

★ The **pushcart** war; by Jean Merrill; with illustrations by Ronni Solbert. Bantam Doubleday Dell Books for Young Readers 1987 222p il pa $6.50

Grades: 5 6 7 8 **Fic**
1. Trucks -- Fiction 2. New York (N.Y.) -- Fiction
ISBN 0-440-47147-8

A reissue of the title first published 1964 by W. R. Scott

The outbreak of a war between truck drivers and pushcart peddlers brings the mounting problems of traffic to the attention of both the city of New York and the world.

"A book that is both humorous and downright funny. . . . Such a lively book will need little introducing." Horn Book

Messer, Stephen

The **death** of Yorik Mortwell; illustrated by
Gris Grimly. Random House Children's Books 2011
173p il $15.99; lib bdg $18.99; e-book $15.95

Grades: 5 6 7 8   **Fic**

1. Ghost stories 2. Fantasy fiction 3. Magic -- Fiction
4. Siblings -- Fiction 5. Demonology -- Fiction 6.
Good and evil -- Fiction 7. Social classes -- Fiction
ISBN 978-0-375-86858-0; 978-0-375-96858-7 lib
bdg; 978-0-375-89928-7 e-book

LC 2010014255

Following his death at the hands of fellow twelve-year-
old, Lord Thomas, Yorik returns as a ghost to protect his
sister from a similar fate but soon learns of ancient magical beings, both good and evil, who are vying for power at
the Estate.

"Full-page, macabre illustrations appear throughout.
Lemony Snicket, Harry Potter, and Neil Gaiman enthusiasts
will appreciate this engaging, eccentric adventure." SLJ

★ **Windblowne**. Random House 2010 304p
$16.99

Grades: 4 5 6 7   **Fic**

1. Fantasy fiction 2. Kites -- Fiction 3. Uncles --
Fiction 4. Space and time -- Fiction
ISBN 978-0-375-86195-6; 0-375-86195-5

LC 2008-43777

Hapless Oliver, who lives in the trees in the town of
Windblowne, seeks his eccentric great-uncle Gilbert's help
in creating a kite for the all-important kite festival, but when
Gilbert suddenly disappears, Oliver is guided by one of Gilbert's kites in a quest through different worlds to find him.

"Messer constructs a tale that moves along at a powerful,
steady pace to a climactic faceoff, and Oliver's realization
that the gateway to worlds is open for those who can truly
listen to the wind's voices sparks a memorable sea change in
his self-image." Kirkus

Messner, Kate

The **brilliant** fall of Gianna Z. Walker 2009
198p $16.99

Grades: 5 6 7 8   **Fic**

1. Trees -- Fiction 2. Old age -- Fiction 3. Running
-- Fiction 4. Vermont -- Fiction 5. Grandmothers --
Fiction
ISBN 978-0-8027-9842-8; 0-8027-9842-X

Gianna has less than one week to complete her leaf project if she wants to compete in the upcoming cross-country
sectionals, but issues like procrastination, disorganization—
and her grandmother's declining health—seem destined to
keep her from finishing.

"Youngsters will find much to relate to in this likable
protagonist's struggle to balance family and academic com-
mitments. . . . Plot twists keep readers engaged, and Messner's warm and humorous tone will capture even reluctant
readers." SLJ

Sugar and ice. Walker & Co. 2010 275p $16.99

Grades: 4 5 6 7   **Fic**

1. Ice skating -- Fiction 2. New York (State) -- Fiction
ISBN 978-0-8027-2081-8; 0-8027-2081-1

LC 2009-54217

When Russian skating coach Andrei Grosheva offers
farm girl Claire a scholarship to train with the elite in Lake
Placid, she encounters a world of mean girls on ice, where
competition is everything

"The dialogue between classmates and siblings is realistic, and the intergenerational or extended family relationships are interesting. The author shows the intensity of the
world of competitive skating without dwelling on its rough
edges, making it accessible not only to tween readers, but
also to those who might have Olympic aspirations." SLJ

Meyer, Carolyn

Beware, Princess Elizabeth. Harcourt 2001
214p (Young royals) hardcover o.p. pa $5.95

Grades: 7 8 9 10   **Fic**

1. Queens 2. Great Britain -- History -- 1485-1603,
Tudors -- Fiction
ISBN 0-15-202659-2; 0-15-204556-2 pa

LC 00-11700

After the death of her father, King Henry VIII, in 1547,
thirteen-year-old Elizabeth must endure the political intrigues and dangers of the reigns of her half-brother Edward
and her half-sister Mary before finally becoming Queen of
England eleven years later

"The story moves along swiftly with hints of romance, life-and-death plots, and snippets of everyday life."
Book Rep

Cleopatra confesses. Simon & Schuster Books
for Young Readers 2011 289p $16.99

Grades: 6 7 8 9   **Fic**

1. Queens 2. Queens -- Fiction 3. Princesses -- Fiction
4. Egypt -- History -- Fiction
ISBN 978-1-4169-8727-7; 1-4169-8727-4

LC 2010025989

Princess Cleopatra, the third (and favorite) daughter of
King Ptolemy XII, comes of age in ancient Egypt, accumulating power and discovering love.

Meyer's "lush, detail-rich prose ably evokes Cleopatra's
life as a young princess, beginning at age 10 and continuing
on until she turns 22. . . . Narrating with the poise and confidence of a born leader, this Cleopatra should win readers
over." Publ Wkly

Includes bibliographical references

Duchessina; a novel of Catherine de' Medici.
Harcourt 2007 261p (Young royals) $17

Grades: 7 8 9 10   **Fic**

1. Queens 2. Regents 3. Italy -- Fiction 4. Queens
-- Fiction 5. Orphans -- Fiction
ISBN 978-0-15-205588-2; 0-15-205588-6

LC 2006028876

While her tyrannical family is out of favor in Italy,
young Catherine de Medici is raised in convents, then in
1533, when she is fourteen, her uncle, Pope Clement VII,
arranges for her marriage to prince Henri of France, who is
destined to become king.

"With meticulous historical detail, sensitive characterizations, and Catherine's strong narration, Meyer's memorable story of a fascinating young woman who relies on her

intelligence, rather than her beauty, will hit home with many teens." Booklist

The **true** adventures of Charley Darwin. Harcourt 2009 321p il $17

Grades: 7 8 9 10   **Fic**

1. Naturalists 2. Travel writers 3. Writers on science 4. Natural history -- Fiction 5. Voyages around the world -- Fiction 6. Beagle Expedition (1831-1836) -- Fiction

ISBN 978-0-15-206194-4; 0-15-206194-0

LC 2008-17451

In nineteenth-century England, young Charles Darwin rejects the more traditional careers of physician and clergyman, choosing instead to embark on a dangerous five-year journey by ship to explore the natural world.

"Meyer's writing has a light touch that capitalizes on the humorous, romantic, and exciting events in the man's life while introducing his scientific pursuits and the beliefs of his time. . . . This novel paints a readable and detailed portrait of the young Charles Darwin." SLJ

Includes bibliographical references

Meyer, Kai

The **water** mirror; translated by Elizabeth D. Crawford. Margaret K. McElderry Books 2005 250p (Dark reflections) $15.95

Grades: 5 6 7 8   **Fic**

1. Fantasy fiction 2. Orphans -- Fiction 3. Mermaids and mermen -- Fiction

ISBN 0-689-87787-0

LC 2005-11943

Original German edition 2001

In Venice two teenaged orphans, apprenticed to a maker of magic mirrors, begin to realize that their fates are tied to the magical protector of the city known as the Flowing Queen and to the ruler of Hell, respectively.

An "inventive and original fantasy . . . A powerful mix of political intrigue, adventure, and magic." SLJ

Other titles in this series are:

The stone light (2007)

The glass word (2008)

Meyer, L. A.

★ **Bloody** Jack; being an account of the curious adventures of Mary Jacky Faber, ship's boy. Harcourt 2002 278p hardcover o.p. pa $6.95

Grades: 7 8 9 10   **Fic**

1. Adventure fiction 2. Orphans -- Fiction 3. Pirates -- Fiction 4. Sex role -- Fiction 5. Seafaring life -- Fiction

ISBN 0-15-216731-5; 0-15-205085-X pa

LC 2002-759

Reduced to begging and thievery in the streets of 18th-century London, a thirteen-year-old orphan disguises herself as a boy and connives her way onto a British warship set for high sea adventure in search of pirates

"From shooting a pirate in battle to foiling a shipmate's sexual attack to surviving when stranded alone on a Caribbean island, the action in Jacky's tale will entertain readers with a taste for adventure." Booklist

Other titles in this series are:

Curse of the blue tattoo (2004)

In the belly of The Bloodhound (2006)

The mark of the golden dragon (2011)

Mississippi Jack (2007)

My bonny light horseman (2008)

Rapture of the deep (2009)

Under the Jolly Roger (2005)

The wake of the Lorelei Lee (2010)

Viva Jacquelina! being an account of the further adventures of Jacky Faber, over the hills and far away. written by L.A. Meyer. Harcourt 2012 p. cm. $16.99

Grades: 7 8 9 10   **Fic**

1. Spain -- History -- Fiction 2. Adventure fiction 3. Historical fiction 4. Spies -- Fiction 5. Sex role -- Fiction 6. Seafaring life -- Fiction 7. Adventure and adventurers -- Fiction 8. Europe -- History -- 1789-1815 -- Fiction 9. Great Britain -- History -- George III, 1760-1820 -- Fiction

ISBN 9780547763507

LC 2011041931

This young adult adventure novel, by L. A. Meyer, continues the "Bloody Jack Adventures" series. "Once again under the thumb of British Intelligence, Jacky is sent to Spain to spy for the Crown during the early days of the nineteenth-century Peninsular War. She finds herself in the company of guerilla freedom fighters, poses for the famous artist Goya, runs with the bulls, is kidnapped by the Spanish Inquisition, and travels with a caravan of gypsies." (Publisher's note)

Meyer, Marissa, 1984-

★ **Cinder**; Marissa Meyer. Feiwel & Friends 2012 320 p. $17.99

Grades: 7 8 9 10 11 12   **Fic**

1. Fairy tales 2. Science fiction 3. Robots -- Fiction

ISBN 9780312641894

LC 2011036123

In this book, "as plague ravages the overcrowded Earth, observed by a ruthless lunar people, Cinder, a gifted mechanic and cyborg, becomes involved with handsome Prince Kai and must uncover secrets about her past in order to protect the world in this futuristic take on the Cinderella story." (Publisher's note)

Followed by: Scarlet (2013)

★ **Cress**; Marissa Meyer. Feiwel & Friends 2014 560 p. $18.99

Grades: 7 8 9 10 11 12   **Fic**

1. Fugitives from justice -- Fiction 2. Human-alien encounters -- Fiction

ISBN 0312642970; 9780312642976

In this book by Marissa Meyer, third in her Lunar Chronicles series, "Cinder and Captain Thorne are fugitives on the run, now with Scarlet and Wolf in tow. Together, they're plotting to overthrow Queen Levana and prevent her army from invading Earth. Their best hope lies with Cress, a girl trapped on a satellite since childhood. When a daring rescue of Cress goes awry, the group is splintered. Meanwhile, Queen Levana will let nothing prevent her marriage to Emperor Kai." (Publisher's note)

"—Cress is locked away in a floating satellite. She dreams of visiting Earth, the planet she has been forced to spy on, and meeting Carswell Thorne, the handsome ship captain who teamed up with Cinder in Scarlet (Feiwel & Friends, 2013)....Cress fills in more historical details about Earth and Luna's relationship—most of which will be of no surprise to the reader—and Cinder's rebirth as a cyborg. Fans of Scarlet and Wolf may be disappointed that their relationship takes a backseat to the newly introduced pairing. As always, Meyer excels at interweaving new characters that extend beyond the archetypes of their fairy tale into the main story. Readers will eagerly await the final installment of this highly appealing and well-constructed series." (School Library Journal)

★ **Scarlet**; Marissa Meyer. Feiwel and Friends 2013 464 p. $17.99

Grades: 7 8 9 10 11 12   **Fic**

1. Science fiction 2. Fractured fairy tales 3. Cyborgs -- Fiction 4. Missing persons -- Fiction 5. Extraterrestrial beings -- Fiction

ISBN 0312642962; 9780312642969

                 LC 2012034060

This novel, by Marissa Meyer, is the second book of the "Lunar Chronicles" series. "Cinder, the cyborg mechanic, . . . [is] trying to break out of prison. . . . [Meanwhile,] Scarlet Benoit's grandmother is missing. . . . When Scarlet encounters Wolf, a street fighter who may have information . . . , she is loath to trust this stranger. . . . As Scarlet and Wolf unravel one mystery, they encounter another when they meet Cinder." (Publisher's note)

Meyer, Stephenie

New moon. Little, Brown and Co. 2006 563p $17.99

Grades: 8 9 10 11 12   **Fic**

1. School stories 2. Vampires -- Fiction 3. Washington (State) -- Fiction

ISBN 978-0-316-16019-3; 0-316-16019-9

                 LC 2006012309

Sequel to Twilight (2005)

When the Cullens, including her beloved Edward, leave Forks rather than risk revealing that they are vampires, it is almost too much for eighteen-year-old Bella to bear, but she finds solace in her friend Jacob until he is drawn into a "cult" and changes in terrible ways.

"Vampire aficionados will voraciously consume this mighty tome in one sitting, then flip back and read it once more. It maintains a brisk pace and near-genius balance of breathtaking romance and action." Voice Youth Advocates

Followed by Eclipse (2007)

★ **Twilight**. Little, Brown and Co. 2005 498p $17.99; pa $8.99

Grades: 8 9 10 11 12   **Fic**

1. School stories 2. Vampires -- Fiction 3. Washington (State) -- Fiction

ISBN 0-316-16017-2; 0-316-01584-9 pa

                 LC 2004-24730

When seventeen-year-old Bella leaves Phoenix to live with her father in Forks, Washington, she meets an exquisitely handsome boy at school for whom she feels an overwhelming attraction and who she comes to realize is not wholly human.

"Realistic, subtle, succinct, and easy to follow, . . . [this book] will have readers dying to sink their teeth into it." SLJ

Other titles in this series are:

Breaking dawn (2008)

Eclipse (2007)

New moon (2006)

Meyer, Susan

Black radishes; [by] Susan Lynn Meyer. Delacorte Press 2010 228p map $16.99; lib bdg $19.99

Grades: 5 6 7 8   **Fic**

1. France -- Fiction 2. Jews -- France -- Fiction 3. Paris (France) -- Fiction 4. Holocaust, 1933-1945 -- Fiction

ISBN 978-0-385-73881-1; 0-385-73881-1; 978-0-385-90748-4 lib bdg; 0-385-90748-6 lib bdg

                 LC 2009-47613

"Set in France during World War II, this historical novel follows eleven-year-old Gustave as his family escapes Paris for safer quarters in the small, provincial town of Saint-Georges. . . . Not long after Gustave's family arrives in Saint-Georges, the Nazis invade and occupy Paris and establish a demarcation line between occupied northern France and unoccupied Vichy France in the south. . . . The episodic narrative offers abundant detail, and the wartime dangers, especially Gustave's father's illicit travel between occupied and unoccupied zones, adds considerable suspense. Gustave's growth over the course of the novel is both realistic and relatable, making this an appealing topical entry for the upper elementary/middle school set." Bull Cent Child Books

Meyerhoff, Jenny

Queen of secrets. Farrar, Straus and Giroux 2010 230p $16.99

Grades: 8 9 10 11 12   **Fic**

1. School stories 2. Cousins -- Fiction 3. Orphans -- Fiction 4. Grandparents -- Fiction 5. Jews -- United States -- Fiction

ISBN 978-0-374-32628-9; 0-374-32628-2

                 LC 2008-55561

Fifteen-year-old Essie Green, an orphan who has been raised by her secular Jewish grandparents in Michigan, experiences conflicting loyalties and confusing emotions when her aunt, uncle, and cousin move back from New York, and her very religious cousin tries to fit in with the other football players at Essie's high school, one of whom is Essie's popular new boyfriend.

"Compelling characters, dramatic tension, and thoughtful exploration of how teenagers create their own identity amid familial and cultural influences should give this story wide appeal." Publ Wkly

Michael, Jan

★ **City** boy. Clarion Books 2009 186p $16

Grades: 5 6 7 8   **Fic**

1. Malawi -- Fiction 2. Orphans -- Fiction 3. Country life -- Fiction

ISBN 978-0-547-22310-0; 0-547-22310-2

                 LC 2008-37418

First published in the United Kingdom with title: Leaving home

In the southern African country of Malawi, after the AIDS-related deaths of both of his parents, a boy leaves his affluent life in the city to live in a rural village, sharing a one-roomed hut with his aunt, his cousins, and other orphans.

"This is a powerful portrait of poverty and hardship, evenly balanced with shades of hope. Michael's simple prose subtly layers detail, building full-bodied descriptions of landscapes and characters, leaving no room for shortcuts. . . . A stoic tale of surviving life's uncertainties." Kirkus

Michael, Livi

City of dogs. G. P. Putnam's Sons 2007 250p $16.99

Grades: 5 6 7 8   **Fic**

1. Fantasy fiction 2. Dogs -- Fiction 3. Norse mythology -- Fiction
ISBN 978-0-399-24356-1; 0-399-24356-9

LC 2006-26539

Jenny, a mysterious dog, shows up on Sam's birthday and pulls many of the other dogs in the neighborhood into her quest to prevent the destruction of the world.

"Fantasy readers seeking a thoughtful novel into which to sink their teeth will especially appreciate the unhurried pace, the frequently shifting perspectives . . . and the offbeat but quite effective dogcentric narration." Bull Cent Child Books

Michaelis, Antonia

★ Tiger moon; translated from the German by Anthea Bell. Amulet Books 2008 453p pa $9.95; $19.95

Grades: 8 9 10 11 12   **Fic**

1. India -- Fiction 2. Tigers -- Fiction 3. Thieves -- Fiction 4. Princesses -- Fiction 5. Storytelling -- Fiction
ISBN 0-8109-4499-5 pa; 0-8109-9481-X; 978-0-8109-4499-2 pa; 978-0-8109-9481-2

LC 2007-22823

Sold to be the eighth wife of a rich and cruel merchant, Safia, also called Raka, tries to escape her fate by telling stories of Farhad the thief, his companion Nitish the white tiger, and their travels across India to retrieve a famous jewel that will save a kidnapped princess from becoming the bride of a demon king. "Grades eight to ten." (Bull Cent Child Books)

"The plot is fast paced and exciting, and the story gives an excellent overview of the conflicts of India at the time of British occupation, and of Hindu religious beliefs." SLJ

Michaels, Rune

★ Genesis Alpha; [by] Rune Michaels. 1st ed.; Atheneum Books for Young Readers 2007 193p $15.99

Grades: 7 8 9 10   **Fic**

1. Brothers -- Fiction 2. Homicide -- Fiction 3. Video games -- Fiction 4. Genetic engineering -- Fiction
ISBN 978-1-4169-1886-8; 1-4169-1886-8

LC 2007001446

When thirteen-year-old Josh's beloved older brother, Max, is arrested for murder, the victim's sister leads Josh to evidence of Max's guilt—and her own—hidden in their favorite online role-playing game. Josh, who was conceived to save Max's life years earlier, must consider whether he shares that guilt.

"Skillfully interweaving science fiction and cyberspace into a murder mystery, Michaels gives readers a story that is not only difficult to put down but also poses questions that will linger long after the last page is turned." Voice Youth Advocates

Nobel genes. Simon & Schuster 2010 181p $16.99

Grades: 6 7 8 9 10   **Fic**

1. Mentally ill -- Fiction 2. Mother-son relationship -- Fiction 3. Manic-depressive illness -- Fiction
ISBN 978-1-4169-1259-0; 1-4169-1259-2

LC 2009-36665

A boy whose manic-depressive mother has always told him that his father won a Nobel Prize, spends his time taking care of her and searching for clues to the identity of the Nobel Prizewinning sperm donor, eventually finding a truth he must learn to accept.

This is a "skillful, deeply disconcerting tale. . . . Michaels . . . makes effective use of first-person narration to give readers a highly believable protagonist and a riveting, from-the-trenches look at what it is like to live with a parent who suffers from a serious mental illness." Publ Wkly

The reminder. Atheneum Books for Young Readers 2008 182p $16.99; pa $8.99

Grades: 6 7 8 9 10   **Fic**

1. Robots -- Fiction 2. Mothers -- Fiction 3. Bereavement -- Fiction
ISBN 978-1-4169-4131-6; 1-4169-4131-2; 978-1-4424-0253-9 pa; 1-4424-0253-9 pa

LC 2008-15391

A teenaged girl who hears her dead mother's voice makes a startling discovery after breaking into her father's industrial robotics lab and finding his latest secret project: a lifelike replica of her mother's head that looks, talks, moves, and even smiles just like her mother.

"An intriguing story about loss and survival, with elements of science fiction." Booklist

Mieville, China

★ Un Lun Dun. Ballantine Books 2007 432p il hardcover o.p. pa $9

Grades: 5 6 7 8 9   **Fic**

1. Fantasy fiction
ISBN 978-0-345-49516-7; 0-345-49516-0; 978-0-345-45844-5 pa; 0-345-45844-3 pa

LC 2007-296921

When 12-year-old Zanna and her friend Deeba find a secret entrance leading out of London and into the strange city of Un Lun Dun, it appears that an ancient prophesy is coming true at last

"Miéville's fantastical city is vivid and splendidly crafted. . . . The story is exceptional and the action moves along at a quick pace." SLJ

Mikaelsen, Ben

Ghost of Spirit Bear; [by] Ben Mikaelsen. 1st ed.; HarperCollins Publishers 2008 154p $16.99; lib bdg $17.89

Grades: 6 7 8 9   **Fic**
1. School stories 2. Bullies -- Fiction
ISBN 978-0-06-009007-4; 0-06-009007-3; 978-0-06-
009008-1 lib bdg; 0-06-009008-1 lib bdg
LC 2007036732
Sequel to: Touching Spirit Bear (2001)
After a year in exile on an Alaskan island as punishment
for severely beating a fellow student, Cole Matthews returns
to school in Minneapolis having made peace with himself
and his victim--but he finds that surviving the violence
and hatred of high school is even harder than surviving in
the wilderness.
This is "gripping and fast moving. . . [this novel] will
appeal to boys especially and to reluctant readers." KLIATT

Touching Spirit Bear. HarperCollins Pubs. 2001
241p $15.99; lib bdg $16.89; pa $5.99
Grades: 6 7 8 9   **Fic**
1. Bears -- Fiction 2. Alaska -- Fiction 3. Wilderness
survival -- Fiction
ISBN 0-380-97744-3; 0-06-029149-4 lib bdg; 0-380-
80560-X pa
LC 00-40702
After his anger erupts into violence, Cole, in order to
avoid going to prison, agrees to participate in a sentencing
alternative based on the native American Circle Justice, and
he is sent to a remote Alaskan Island where an encounter
with a huge Spirit Bear changes his life
"Mikaelsen's portrayal of this angry, manipulative, damaged teen is dead on. . . . Gross details about Cole eating
raw worms, a mouse, and worse will appeal to fans of the
outdoor adventure/survival genre." SLJ
Followed by: Ghost of Spirit Bear (2008)

Miklowitz, Gloria D.
The **enemy** has a face. Eerdmans Bks. for Young
Readers 2003 139p $16; pa $8
Grades: 7 8 9 10   **Fic**
1. Missing persons -- Fiction
ISBN 0-8028-5243-2; 0-8028-5261-0 pa
LC 2002-9233
Netta and her family have relocated temporarily from Israel to Los Angeles, and when her seventeen-year-old brother mysteriously disappears, she becomes convinced that he
has been abducted by Palestinian terrorists
"Almost unbearably suspenseful, the plot will keep
readers turning pages as fast as they can. Nicely interspersed
with the events is a thoughtful examination of some of the
reasons behind the age-old strife between Palestinians and
Israelis. Readers come away with a greater understanding of
the conflict, and Netta is given the opportunity to modify her
attitude about her former enemies." SLJ

Milford, Kate
★ The **Boneshaker**; [illustrations by Andrea Of-
fermann] Clarion Books 2010 372p il $17
Grades: 5 6 7 8 9   **Fic**
1. Bicycles -- Fiction 2. Missouri -- Fiction 3.
Demonology -- Fiction 4. Supernatural -- Fiction
ISBN 978-0-547-24187-6; 0-547-24187-9
LC 2009-45350

When Jake Limberleg brings his traveling medicine
show to a small Missouri town in 1913, thirteen-year-old
Natalie senses that something is wrong and, after investigating, learns that her love of automata and other machines
make her the only one who can set things right.
"Natalie is a well-drawn protagonist with sturdy supporting characters around her. The tension built into the solidly
constructed plot is complemented by themes that explore the
literal and metaphorical role of crossroads and that thin line
between good and evil." Kirkus

The **Broken** Lands; by Kate Milford; with illustrations by Andrea Offermann. Clarion Books 2012
455 p. ill. (hardback) $16.99
Grades: 5 6 7 8 9 10   **Fic**
1. Bridges -- Fiction 2. Supernatural -- Fiction 3.
New York (N.Y.) -- Fiction 4. Orphans -- Fiction 5.
Demonology -- Fiction 6. Good and evil -- Fiction
7. New York (N.Y.) -- History -- 1865-1898 -- Fiction
8. Coney Island (New York, N.Y.) -- History -- 19th
century -- Fiction
ISBN 0547739664; 9780547739663
LC 2011049466
This book, a prequel to "Kate Milford's 'The Boneshaker,' [is] set in . . . nineteenth-century Coney Island and
New York City. Few crossroads compare to the one being
formed by the Brooklyn Bridge and the East River, and as
the bridge's construction progresses, forces of unimaginable
evil seek to bend that power to their advantage. . . . Can the
teenagers Sam, a card sharp, and Jin, a fireworks expert, stop
them before it's too late?" (Publisher's note)

Greenglass House; by Kate Milford; with illus-
trations by Jaime Zollars. Clarion Books, Houghton
Mifflin Harcourt 2014 384 p. (hardback) $17.99
Grades: 5 6 7 8   **Fic**
1. Mystery fiction 2. Hotels and motels -- Fiction 3.
Magic -- Fiction 4. Adoption -- Fiction 5. Mystery and
detective stories 6. Hotels, motels, etc. -- Fiction
ISBN 0544052706; 9780544052703
LC 2013036212
Edgar Award: Best Juvenile (2015)
In this middle grades book by Kate Milford, illustrated
by Jaime Zollars, "it's wintertime at Greenglass House. The
creaky smuggler's inn is always quiet during this season,
and twelve-year-old Milo, the innkeepers' adopted son,
plans to spend his holidays relaxing. . . . As objects go missing and tempers flare, Milo and Meddy, the cook's daughter, must decipher clues and untangle the web of deepening
mysteries to discover the truth about Greenglass House--and
themselves." (Publisher's note)

Millard, Glenda
★ A **small** free kiss in the dark. Holiday House
2010 180p $16.95
Grades: 6 7 8 9   **Fic**
1. War stories 2. Infants -- Fiction 3. Refugees --
Fiction 4. Australia -- Fiction 5. Homeless persons
-- Fiction
ISBN 978-0-8234-2264-7; 0-8234-2264-X
LC 2009-27212
First published 2009 in Australia

Skip "narrates with an artist's attention to detail and rich use of visual metaphor. . . . Skip's optimism against the apocalyptic background lends the story a haunting quality that is not to be easily forgotten." SLJ

"When a war comes without warning, Skip, an abused 12-year-old runaway, finds an unlikely family in a homeless elderly man, an abandoned child, and a young dancer who, though only 15, is already the mother of a baby girl. They find a home in an abandoned amusement park until the soldiers come and their very existence is threatened." Booklist

Miller, Kirsten

All you desire; can you trust your heart? Razorbill 2011 423p $17.99

Grades: 6 7 8 9 10 **Fic**

1. Love stories 2. Reincarnation -- Fiction 3. New York (N.Y.) -- Fiction 4. Fate and fatalism -- Fiction
ISBN 978-1-59514-323-5; 1-59514-323-8

Haven Moore and Iain Morrow have been living a blissful life in Rome, an ocean way from the Ouroboros Society and its diabolical leader. But paradise is not to last. The mysterious disappearance of Haven's best friend, Beau, sends the pair running back to New York, where they encounter the Horae, an underground group of women who have spent centuries scheming to destroy Adam Rosier.

"A multi-layered mystery with (mostly) rounded characters." Kirkus

★ The **eternal** ones. Razorbill 2010 411p $17.99

Grades: 6 7 8 9 10 **Fic**

1. Love stories 2. Faith -- Fiction 3. Tennessee -- Fiction 4. Reincarnation -- Fiction 5. New York (N.Y.) -- Fiction 6. Fate and fatalism -- Fiction
ISBN 978-1-59514-308-2; 1-59514-308-4

LC 2010-22775

Seventeen-year-old Haven Moore leaves East Tennessee to attend the Fashion Institute of Technology in New York City, where she meets playboy Iain Morrow, whose fate may be tied to hers through a series of past lives.

"Miller's writing elevates the supernatural romance well beyond typical fare, and Haven's mix of naïveté and determination makes her a solid, credible heroine." Publ Wkly

Followed by: All you desire (2011)

Kiki Strike; the darkness dwellers. by Kirsten Miller. Bloomsbury 2013 416 p. (hardback) $17.99

Grades: 5 6 7 8 **Fic**

1. Girls -- Fiction 2. Adventure fiction 3. Teenagers -- Fiction 4. Crime -- Fiction 5. France -- Fiction 6. Identity -- Fiction 7. Paris (France) -- Fiction 8. New York (N.Y.) -- Fiction
ISBN 1599907364; 9781599907369

LC 2012023303

This teen adventure novel, by Kirsten Miller, is part of the "Kiki Strike" series. "First they ventured deep under New York to save the city itself. Then things got personal as the Irregulars ventured into a haunted mansion in Chinatown to uncover an evil twin. Now, . . . this . . . group of delinquent geniuses jump feet first into a[n] . . . international pursuit,

going underground in Paris to pursue a pair of treacherous royals who have killed Kiki's parents." (Publisher's note)

★ **Kiki** Strike: inside the shadow city; [by] Kirsten Miller. Bloomsbury Children's Books 2006 387p $16.95

Grades: 5 6 7 8 **Fic**

1. Mystery fiction 2. New York (N.Y.) -- Fiction
ISBN 978-1-58234-960-2; 1-58234-960-6

LC 2005030945

Life becomes more interesting for Ananka Fishbein when, at the age of twelve, she discovers an underground room in the park across from her New York City apartment and meets a mysterious girl called Kiki Strike who claims that she, too, wants to explore the subterranean world

"If a 12-year-old can be a hardboiled detective, Ananka Fishbein is one. Her narration is fresh and funny, and the author's unadorned, economical, yet descriptive style carries her character through with verve." SLJ

Another title about Kiki Strike is:
Kiki Strike: The empress's tomb (2007)

Kiki Strike: the Empress's tomb. Bloomsbury Children's Books 2007 369p $16.95

Grades: 5 6 7 8 **Fic**

1. Mystery fiction 2. New York (N.Y.) -- Fiction
ISBN 978-1-59990-047-6; 1-59990-047-5

LC 2007012000

Companion volume to Kiki Strike: inside the shadow city (2006)

Fourteen-year-olds Ananka Fishbein, Kiki Strike, and the other Irregulars encounter a Chinese mummy, a ghost, trained squirrels, and old enemies as they try to stop an art forgery ring and safeguard the secret streets hidden beneath New York City.

"A must-have for libraries where the first book is popular and a recommended purchase for collections that could use a good ghost/spy/action/mystery/story." SLJ

Miller, Sarah

The **lost** crown. Atheneum Books for Young Readers 2011 412p $17.99

Grades: 8 9 10 11 12 **Fic**

1. Emperors 2. Sisters -- Fiction 3. Kings and rulers -- Fiction 4. World War, 1914-1918 -- Fiction 5. Russia -- History -- 1905, Revolution -- Fiction
ISBN 978-1-4169-8340-8; 1-4169-8340-6

LC 2010037001

In alternating chapters, Grand Duchesses Olga, Tatiana, Maria, and Anastasia tell how their privileged lives as the daughters of the tsar in early twentieth-century Russia are transformed by world war and revolution.

"Each Grand Duchess comes across as a unique personality. . . . Like the best historical novels, this allows modern-day teens to see themselves in very different people." Booklist

★ **Miss** Spitfire; reaching Helen Keller. Atheneum Books for Young Readers 2007 208p $16.99

Grades: 7 8 9 10 11 **Fic**

1. Deaf 2. Blind 3. Authors 4. Memoirists 5. Humanitarians 6. Deaf -- Fiction 7. Blind -- Fiction

8. Teachers -- Fiction 9. Teachers of the deaf 10. Inspirational writers 11. Teachers of the blind 12. Social welfare leaders

ISBN 978-1-4169-2542-2; 1-4169-2542-2

LC 2006014738

At age twenty-one, partially-blind, lonely but spirited Annie Sullivan travels from Massachusetts to Alabama to try and teach six-year-old Helen Keller, deaf and blind since age two, self-discipline and communication skills. Includes historical notes and timeline.

"This excellent novel is compelling reading even for those familiar with the Keller/Sullivan experience." SLJ

Includes bibliographical references

Millet, Lydia

The **fires** beneath the sea. Big Mouth House 2011 256p (The dissenters) $16.95

Grades: 4 5 6 7   **Fic**

1. Otters -- Fiction 2. Mothers -- Fiction 3. Supernatural -- Fiction 4. Cape Cod (Mass.) -- Fiction

ISBN 978-1-931520-71-3; 1-931520-71-2

"Mom vanished two months ago, and summer's ending. While swimming in the ocean, Cara spots a sea otter—but sea otters don't belong on Atlantic beaches. Cara reaches out her fingertips, and the otter streams words into Cara's mind. . . . Millet's prose is lyrically evocative. . . . A lush and intelligent opener for a topical eco-fantasy series." Kirkus

Mills, Claudia

One square inch. Farrar, Straus and Giroux 2010 168p $16.99

Grades: 4 5 6 7   **Fic**

1. Mothers -- Fiction 2. Siblings -- Fiction 3. Imagination -- Fiction 4. Manic-depressive illness -- Fiction

ISBN 978-0-374-35652-1; 0-374-35652-1

When their mother's behavior changes and she starts to neglect her children, seventh-grader Cooper and his little sister take refuge in Inchland, an imaginary country inspired by deeds to one square inch of land that their grandfather gave them.

Mills "delivers a compassionate story about life with a bipolar parent. . . . The twist of [Cooper's] emotions and depth of his concern for his mother and sister are believable and deeply moving." Publ Wkly

Mills, Rob

Charlie's key. Orca Book Publishers 2011 254p pa $9.99

Grades: 5 6 7 8 9   **Fic**

1. Mystery fiction 2. Orphans -- Fiction

ISBN 978-1-55469-872-1; 1-55469-872-3

A young orphan struggles to unlock the significance of an old key left by his dying father.

"A fast-paced, often riveting mystery with a plausible, thrilling climax." Kirkus

Mills, Sam

The **viper** within; [by] Sam Mills. 1st American ed.; Alfred A. Knopf 2008 296p $16.99; lib bdg $19.99

Grades: 7 8 9 10   **Fic**

1. Cults -- Fiction 2. Divorce -- Fiction 3. Religion -- Fiction 4. Kidnapping -- Fiction

ISBN 978-0-375-84465-2; 0-375-84465-1; 978-0-375-94465-9 lib bdg; 0-375-94465-6 lib bdg

LC 2007031952

Bitter and angry after his parents' divorce, Jon joins a cult, The Religion of Hebetheus, at his high school and soon becomes embroiled in a plot to kidnap a fellow student and suspected terrorist, but their plans go terribly wrong.

"Thought provoking, tension packed, and suspenseful, Mill's novel forces readers to grapple with multiple perspectives on terrorism, cults, religion, victimization, fidelity, embedded misogyny and conscience." Voice Youth Advocates

Milway, Alex

The **mousehunter**; written and illustrated by Alex Milway. Little, Brown 2009 422p il map $15.99

Grades: 4 5 6 7   **Fic**

1. Adventure fiction 2. Mice -- Fiction 3. Pirates -- Fiction

ISBN 978-0-316-02454-9; 0-316-02454-6

Captain Mousebeard is a feared mousehunting pirate. He seeks out the rarest and most precious breeds of mice to collect and trade. Emeline, a mousekeeper, wants the bounty her master puts on Mousebeard's head. So she heads off to adventure to capture the pirate.

"Milway has created an atmospheric and engaging world filled with hundreds of varieties of mice with different coloring, temperaments, and abilities. New creatures are introduced both within the text and in pages with information and illustrations from The Mousehunter's Almanac interspersed between chapters. Readers will enjoy the action, chases, and plot twists." SLJ

Miranda, Megan

Soulprint; by Megan Miranda. Bloomsbury/Walker 2015 368 p. (hardcover) $17.99

Grades: 7 8 9 10   **Fic**

1. Science fiction 2. Reincarnation -- Fiction 3. Fugitives from justice -- Fiction 4. Soul -- Fiction 5. Guilt -- Fiction 6. Prisoners -- Fiction 7. Conduct of life -- Fiction

ISBN 0802737749; 9780802737748

LC 2014009921

This novel by Megan Miranda is set "in a future where reincarnation can be scientifically tracked. . . .17-year-old half-Hispanic Alina Chase has spent her life isolated, allegedly for her own protection. She carries within her the soul of a charismatic and destructive whistleblower turned blackmailer, June Calahan. Broken out of confinement by a daring trio barely older than she is, Alina finds she still cannot escape June's shadow." (Publishers Weekly)

"A unique spin on recent dystopian reads featuring genetic heritability . . . [Soulprint] will fascinate teens already enthralled with questions about what they might do with their lives. A surprising new sf thriller with just enough of a touch of romance." Booklist

Mitchard, Jacquelyn

★ **All** we know of heaven; a novel. HarperTeen 2008 312p $16.99; lib bdg $17.89

Grades: 7 8 9 10 11 12   **Fic**

1. Death -- Fiction 2. Bereavement -- Fiction 3. Traffic accidents -- Fiction

ISBN 978-0-06-134578-4; 0-06-134578-4; 978-0-06-134579-1 lib bdg; 0-06-134579-2 lib bdg

When Maureen and Bridget, two sixteen-year-old best friends who look like sisters, are in a terrible car accident and one of them dies, they are at first incorrectly identified at the hospital, and then, as Maureen achieves a remarkable recovery, she must deal with the repercussions of the accident, the mixup, and some choices she made while she was getting better.

"Riveting, compassionate and psychologically nuanced. . . . Utterly gripping." Publ Wkly

Look both ways. Razorbill 2009 271p $16.99

Grades: 6 7 8 9   **Fic**

1. Twins -- Fiction 2. Sisters -- Fiction 3. Cheerleading -- Fiction 4. Clairvoyance -- Fiction 5. Native Americans -- Fiction

ISBN 978-159514-161-3; 1-59514-161-8

LC 2008028997

When psychic twin Mallory Brynn starts seeing images of a white wildcat in her dreams, she tries to figure out the connection of her images to an injured cheerleader and her Native American friend Eden.

"The mix of prophetic visions and dreams, friends in dire straits, and cheerleading tryouts will keep some readers turning pages." Booklist

The **midnight** twins. Razorbill 2008 235p $16.99; pa $8.99

Grades: 6 7 8 9   **Fic**

1. Twins -- Fiction 2. Telepathy -- Fiction 3. Clairvoyance -- Fiction

ISBN 978-1-59514-160-6; 1-59514-160-X; 978-1-59514-226-9 pa; 1-59514-226-6 pa

LC 2007-31139

Identical twins Meredith and Mallory Brynn have always shared one another's thoughts, even as they dream, but their connection diminishes as they approach their thirteenth birthday, and one begins to see the future, the other the past, leading them to discover that a high school student they know is doing horrible things that place the twins, and others, in grave danger.

"The plot moves quickly, propelled by the mysteries of the sisters' relationship. . . . The girls' supernatural knowledge is a delicious bonus." Publ Wkly

Other titles about Meredith and Mallory are:

Look both ways (2009)
Watch for me by moonlight (2010)

Watch for me by moonlight; a Midnight Twins novel. Razorbill 2010 283p $16.99

Grades: 6 7 8 9   **Fic**

1. Twins -- Fiction 2. Sisters -- Fiction 3. Kidnapping -- Fiction 4. Clairvoyance -- Fiction

ISBN 978-1-59514-277-1; 1-59514-277-0

Mally and Merry's supernatural dream visions are put to the test when their baby brother is kidnapped—and by someone who has grown very close to the Brynn family.

Mitchell, Saundra

The **vespertine**. Harcourt 2011 296p $16.99

Grades: 8 9 10 11 12   **Fic**

1. Clairvoyance -- Fiction 2. Baltimore (Md.) -- Fiction

ISBN 978-0-547-48247-7; 0-547-48247-7

It's the summer of 1889, and Amelia van den Broek is new to Baltimore and eager to take in all the pleasures the city has to offer. But her gaiety is interrupted by disturbing, dreamlike visions she has only at sunset—visions that offer glimpses of the future. Soon, friends and strangers alike call on Amelia to hear her prophecies. However, a forbidden romance with Nathaniel, an artist, threatens the new life Amelia is building in Baltimore.

"Nathaniel's forbidden charms will most certainly have readers swooning. . . . There's . . . considerable fun to be had here, and Amelia's supernatural power is believably portrayed." Bull Cent Child Books

Miéville, China, 1972-

★ **Railsea**; China Mieville. Del Rey/Ballantine Books 2012 424 p. ill. (hbk. : alk. paper) $18.00

Grades: 7 8 9 10   **Fic**

1. Adventure fiction 2. Steampunk fiction 3. Railroads -- Fiction 4. Imaginary places -- Fiction

ISBN 0345524527; 9780345524522; 9780345524546

LC 2012009516

This book presents "a steampunk spin on 'Moby-Dick' . . . . Instead of chasing whales on the sea, the crew of the diesel train Medes hunt moldywarpes—enormous, maneating, molelike creatures who are only one of the countless menacing species who burrow in the perilous earth beneath a tangled ocean of train tracks. And it is one moldywarpe in particular, the great Mocker-Jack, that Captain Naphi is after—it's trendy for any captain worth her iron to have such a defining obsession, and she is fully aware that they hunt metaphor in beast form. Aboard for the grand adventure is your hero, young Sham (don't call him Ishmael)." (Booklist)

Mlawski, Shana

Hammer of witches; by Shana Mlawski. Tu Books 2013 400 p. (reinforced) $18.95

Grades: 6 7 8 9   **Fic**

1. Fantasy fiction 2. Storytelling -- Fiction 3. Magic -- Fiction 4. Wizards -- Fiction 5. Explorers -- Fiction 6. America -- Discovery and exploration -- Spanish -- Fiction

ISBN 1600609872; 9781600609879

LC 2012048627

In this novel, by Shana Mlawski, "Baltasar Infante . . . encounters a monster straight out of stories one night . . . Captured by . . . a mysterious witch-hunting arm of the Spanish Inquisition, . . . the Inquisitor demands he reveal the whereabouts of Amir al-Katib, a legendary Moorish sorcerer who can bring myths and the creatures within them to life. Now Baltasar must escape, find al-Katib, and defeat a dreadful power that may destroy the world." (Publisher's note)

"Newcomer Mlawski delivers a fast-paced coming-of-age adventure, respectfully evoking the complexities and cultural landscape of the period. She draws from a variety of sources, including Jewish and Biblical myth, offering an accessible, attention-grabbing story that seamlessly inserts its magical elements into historical fact." Pub Wkly

Mlynowski, Sarah

Don't even think about it; Sarah Mlynowski. Delacorte Press 2014 336 p. (hc : alk. paper) $17.99
Grades: 7 8 9 10   **Fic**
1. Telepathy -- Fiction 2. Extrasensory perception -- Fiction 3. Schools -- Fiction 4. High schools -- Fiction 5. New York (N.Y.) -- Fiction 6. TriBeCa (New York, N.Y.) -- Fiction
ISBN 0385737386; 9780385737388; 9780385906623
LC 2012050777
This book, by Sarah Mlynowski, follows three girls who "used to be average New York City high school sophomores" but develop "telepathic powers." The girls use their powers to find about "romance, secrets, [and] scandals" involving their friends, boyfriends and students at their high school. (Publisher's note)

"When a group of Manhattan 10th graders inadvertently receives telepathic abilities from tainted flu shots, things rapidly get chaotic (and noisy). Finding out too much information dramatically upends family relationships, friendships, and romances. . . . Filled with heartbreak, hilarity, and some brutal truths, Mlynowski's novel will leave readers thinking about the gaps between our private and public selves and the lies we tell others and ourselves." Pub Wkly

Do not even think about it

Gimme a call. Delacorte Press 2010 301p $17.99; lib bdg $20.99
Grades: 7 8 9 10   **Fic**
1. School stories 2. Time travel -- Fiction
ISBN 978-0-385-73588-9; 0-385-73588-X; 978-0-385-90574-9 lib bdg; 0-385-90574-2 lib bdg
LC 2009-20020
"When Devi's high-school sweetheart breaks up with her right before their senior prom, she is devastated. Not only is she dateless but she is also friendless and relegated to a mediocre college because she has concentrated on her boyfriend instead of academics. . . . In a fresh twist on time travel, she contacts her freshman self via cell phone and proceeds to change their future. Of course, one small change leads to others, and both girls begin to wonder about the wisdom of this collaboration. Mlynowski has given herself a complicated, challenging story, and she is particularly effective in conveying the differences in maturity and perspective between a freshman and a senior." Booklist

Ten things we did (and probably shouldn't have) HarperTeen 2011 357p $16.99; ebook $9.99
Grades: 7 8 9 10   **Fic**
1. Friendship -- Fiction 2. Connecticut -- Fiction
ISBN 978-0-06-170124-5; 0-06-170124-6; 978-0-06-208461-3 ebook; 0-06-208461-5 ebook
LC 2010-45556
Sixteen-year-old April, a high school junior, and her friend Vi, a senior, get a crash course in reality as the list of things they should not do becomes a list of things they

did while living parent-free in Westport, Connecticut, for the semester.

"With wit, energy, and an uncanny understanding of teenage logic, Mlynowski . . . weighs the pros and cons of independence in this modern cautionary tale. . . . Mlynowski avoids sermonizing, offering 10 madcap and remarkably tense escapades that will have readers laughing, cringing, and guessing how April will get out of the next pickle." Publ Wkly

Mobley, Jeannie

★ **Katerina's** wish; Jeannie Mobley. Margaret K. McElderry Books 2012 256 p. (hardcover) $15.99
Grades: 4 5 6 7   **Fic**
1. Wishes -- Fiction 2. Historical fiction 3. Immigrants -- Fiction 4. Czech Americans -- Fiction 5. Coal mines and mining -- Fiction 6. Family life -- Colorado -- Fiction 7. Colorado -- History -- 1876-1950 -- Fiction
ISBN 1442433434; 9781442433434; 9781442433458
LC 2011044392

In this young adult novel, Katerina and her family have immigrated from Bohemia and "settled in a coal mining camp, [where] they are still buried in work and trapped by debt. Then Trina sees a fish that reminds her of a fairy tale about a magic carp; soon after, her two younger sisters' frivolous wishes are granted. Initially skeptical, Trina eventually makes her wish: for a farm that will make her family happy." (Publishers Weekly)

Searching for Silverheels; Jeannie Mobley. Margaret K. McElderry Books 2014 304 p. (hardcover) $16.99
Grades: 5 6 7   **Fic**
1. Legends 2. United States -- History -- 19th century 3. Sex role -- Fiction 4. Colorado -- History -- 1876-1950 -- Fiction 5. World War, 1914-1918 -- United States -- Fiction
ISBN 1481400290; 9781481400299; 9781481400305
LC 2013033485
In this novel by Jeannine Mobley "Pearl spends the summers helping her mother run the family café and entertaining tourists with the legend of Silverheels, a beautiful dancer who nursed miners through a smallpox epidemic in 1861 and then mysteriously disappeared. Josie says that Silverheels was a crook, not a savior, and she challenges Pearl to a bet: prove that Silverheels was the kindhearted angel of legend, or help Josie pass out the suffragist pamphlets that . . . drive away the tourists." (Publisher's note)

"Pearl Barnell and her small town of Como, Colorado are in for a change. The shift begins when Josie, a local suffragette, challenges the legend of Silverheels that Pearl shares with some tourists who enter her family's café. Readers follow Pearl in her quest to learn the truth about the dancer nicknamed Silverheels, and they see her shed her complacence for a determination to do right, no matter the cost...etween the search for the real Silverheels, Pearl's transformation and romantic decisions, and the tension between Josie and the townspeople, there is enough to keep readers interested in the story." SLJ

Mochizuki, Ken

Beacon Hill boys. Scholastic Press 2002 201p $16.95; pa $5.99

Grades: 7 8 9 10   **Fic**

1. Japanese Americans -- Fiction 2. Washington (State) -- Fiction

ISBN 0-439-26749-8; 0-439-24906-6 pa

LC 2002-2343

In 1972 in Seattle, a teenager in a Japanese American family struggles for his own identity, along with a group of three friends who share his anger and confusion

"The author nicely balances universal experiences of male adolescence . . . with scenes that bring readers right into the complicated era, and his important, thought-provoking story asks tough questions about racial and cultural identity, prejudice, and family." Booklist

Molloy, Michael

Peter Raven under fire. Scholastic 2005 502p il maps $17.95

Grades: 6 7 8 9   **Fic**

1. Sea stories 2. Adventure fiction 3. France -- History -- 1799-1815 -- Fiction

ISBN 0-439-72454-6

"In 1800, continuous war has depleted France's treasury, but Napoleon still wants to expand his empire. To this end, he needs money to defeat the superior British Navy and to exploit Louisiana for the greatest gain. In England, midshipman Peter Raven, 13, is assigned to HMS Torren. When powerful, sadistic pirates murder everyone on the ship except Peter and jack-of-all-trades Matthew Book, the protagonist finds himself apprenticed to a British spy. . . . Fast paced with multiple plot twists. . . . Molloy's writing is intelligent and engaging." SLJ

Moloney, James

The **Book** of Lies. HarperCollinsPublishers 2007 360p $16.99; lib bdg $17.89

Grades: 5 6 7 8   **Fic**

1. Fantasy fiction 2. Magic -- Fiction 3. Orphans -- Fiction

ISBN 978-0-06-057842-8; 0-06-057842-4; 978-0-06-057843-5 lib bdg; 0-06-057843-2 lib bdg

LC 2006-29874

On the night he was brought to an orphanage, Marcel's memories were taken by a sorceror and replaced with new ones by his Book of Lies, but Bea, a girl with the ability to make herself invisible, was watching and is determined to help him discover his true identity.

"Readers who enjoy the mixture of mystery, riddles, action, and camaraderie will be pleased that the open-ended conclusion leads to a planned sequel." Booklist

Monaghan, Annabel

A **girl** named Digit; by Annabel Monaghan. Houghton Mifflin Harcourt 2012 187 p. $16.99; $16.99

Grades: 7 8 9   **Fic**

1. School stories 2. Terrorism -- Fiction 3. Cryptography -- Fiction 4. Kidnapping -- Fiction 5. Interpersonal relations -- Fiction 6. Adventure and adventurers -- Fiction

ISBN 054766852X; 9780547668529; 9780544022485

LC 2011012239

In this book, "saddled with the nickname Digit, Farrah resolved to fit in once she reached high school by hiding her math skills. Then Farrah stumbles upon an eco-terrorist organization after their suicide bomb attack on JFK Airport, and the terrorists want her dead. . . . Farrah's FBI protector, the cute, young rookie agent John Bennett, . . . works with Farrah to uncover a blackmail scheme involving the attack's bomber." (Kirkus Reviews)

Mone, Gregory

Fish. Scholastic Press 2010 241p $16.99

Grades: 4 5 6 7   **Fic**

1. Adventure fiction 2. Ciphers -- Fiction 3. Pirates -- Fiction 4. Buried treasure -- Fiction

ISBN 978-0-545-11632-9; 0-545-11632-5

Eleven-year-old Fish, seeking a way to help his family financially, becomes a reluctant cabin boy on a pirate ship, where he soon makes friends—and enemies—and is asked to help decipher clues that might lead to a legendary treasure.

"Mone seamlessly integrates factual information into his tale of friendship, loyalty, and exploration. . . . Fish makes a splashing good addition to adventure fiction." SLJ

Monninger, Joseph

★ **Finding** somewhere. Delacorte Press 2011 $17.99; lib bdg $20.99; e-book $17.99

Grades: 7 8 9 10   **Fic**

1. Horses -- Fiction 2. Friendship -- Fiction 3. Automobile travel -- Fiction

ISBN 978-0-385-73942-9; 978-0-385-90789-7 lib bdg; 978-0-375-86214-4 e-book

LC 2010053551

Sixteen-year-old Hattie and eighteen-year-old Delores set off on a road trip that takes unexpected turns as they discover the healing power of friendship and confront what each of them is fleeing from.

"Monninger's writing is delicious, evocative and, especially during horse-focused scenes, moving. Horse story, road trip, coming-of-age tale: It's any and all of these, but mostly a tender and authentic voyage into the mind of a wise, funny and wholly likable protagonist." Kirkus

★ **Hippie** chick. Front Street 2008 156p $16.95

Grades: 8 9 10 11 12   **Fic**

1. Manatees -- Fiction 2. Shipwrecks -- Fiction 3. Everglades (Fla.) -- Fiction 4. Survival after airplane accidents, shipwrecks, etc. -- Fiction

ISBN 978-1-59078-598-0; 1-59078-598-3

LC 2007-51976

After her sailboat capsizes, fifteen-year-old Lolly Emmerson is rescued by manatees and taken to a mangrove key in the Everglades, where she forms a bond with her aquatic companions while struggling to survive.

"It's an affecting account, beautifully told." SLJ

Wish. Delacorte Press 2010 193p $17.99; lib bdg $20.99

Grades: 6 7 8 9 10   **Fic**

1. Sharks -- Fiction 2. Wishes -- Fiction 3. Siblings

-- Fiction 4. Cystic fibrosis -- Fiction
ISBN 978-0-385-73941-2; 0-385-73941-9; 978-0-385-
90788-0 lib bdg; 0-385-90788-5 lib bdg

LC 2010-09958

Bee's brother, Tommy, knows everything there is to
know about sharks. He also knows that his life will be cut
short by cystic fibrosis. And so does Bee. That's why she
wants to make his wish-foundation-sponsored trip to swim
with a great white shark an unforgettable memory. Only
when Bee takes Tommy to meet a famous shark attack survivor and hard-core surfer does Tommy have the chance to
live one day to the fullest.

"Fans of Monninger's other works will recognize the
fluid, thoughtful writing and vivid characters, and this could
be an eye-opener for shark aficionados looking to take
their interest beyond the glitz of shark week." Bull Cent
Child Books

Moodie, Craig

Into the trap. Roaring Brook Press 2011 199p
$15.99

Grades: 5 6 7 8   **Fic**

1. Adventure fiction 2. Islands -- Fiction 3. Thieves
-- Fiction 4. Lobsters -- Fiction
ISBN 978-1-59643-585-8; 1-59643-585-2

LC 2010029238

Twelve-year-old Eddie Atwell accidentally learns who
has been stealing lobsters from Fog Island lobstermen and
enlists thirteen-year-old Briggs Fairfield, a summer visitor,
to help foil their plans.

"Set over a single, tense day, the novel's chapter titles
track the hours and give the book an immediate, real-time
pace. An exciting drama." Booklist

Moon bear; Gill Lewis; illustrated by Alessandro
Gottardo. Atheneum Books for Young Readers
2015 384 p. illustrations (hardcover) $16.99

Grades: 4 5 6 7 8   **Fic**

1. Laos -- Fiction 2. Bears -- Fiction 3. Asiatic black
bear -- Fiction 4. Animals -- Treatment -- Fiction
ISBN 1481400940; 9781481400947; 9781481400954

LC 2013049285

In this book, by Gill Lewis, "[t]welve-year-old Tam, on
a dare, ventures into a moon bear den in the mountains of
Northern Laos. His goal is to steal the cub and sell it, making
a fortune for his family. But the mother bear's unexpected
return upends Tam's plan, and he barely escapes with his
life. And then his life implodes anyway. . . . Tam is forced to
work hundreds of miles away in the city, at a moon bear farm
where bile from bear gall bladders is used for medicine."
(Publisher's note)

"Through Tam's selfless quest to get the bear back to the
wild, and his protection of the cub at the expense of his own
well-being, readers witness the depths of his bravery, compassion, and strong moral compass." Pub Wkly

Moore, Carley

The **stalker** chronicles; Carley Moore. Farrar
Straus Giroux 2012 230 p. (hardcover) $16.99

Grades: 8 9 10 11 12   **Fic**

1. School stories 2. Divorce -- Fiction 3. Interpersonal
relations -- Fiction 4. Schools -- Fiction 5. Friendship

-- Fiction 6. Best friends -- Fiction 7. High schools
-- Fiction 8. New York (State) -- Fiction 9. Family life
-- New York (State) -- Fiction
ISBN 9780374371807; 9781429961752

LC 2011013093

This book features "Cammie, a high-school sophomore,
whose history has involved such intense interest in guys .
. . that she's now known around school as a stalker. When
cute new guy Toby turns up in her small town, Cammie's
determined that she'll change her ways, . . . and finally get
the relationship she's been longing for. . . . The dissolution
of Cammie's parents' marriage . . . brings her dysfunctional
patterns into sharp relief." (Bulletin of the Center for Children's Books)

Moore, Derrick

Always upbeat / All that; Stephanie Perry Moore;
All that / Stephanie Perry Moore & Derrick Moore.
Saddleback 2012 314 p. $14.95

Grades: 7 8 9 10 11 12   **Fic**

1. Football players 2. Cheerleading -- Fiction 3. High
school students -- Fiction
ISBN 1616518847; 9781616518844

This book by Stephanie Perry Moore and Derrick Moore
"deliver[s] a pair of intersecting but distinct stories from the
points of view of a cheerleader and a quarterback at a predominantly African-American Atlanta high school. Spoiled,
confident Charli Black and driven athlete Blake Strong have
been together for two years. Now, at the start of their junior
year, they are growing apart. Blake wants to 'take [their]
relationship to the next level,' but Charli wants to wait."
(Kirkus Reviews)

Moore, Perry

Hero. Hyperion 2007 428p $16.99

Grades: 7 8 9 10 11 12   **Fic**

1. Science fiction 2. Superheroes -- Fiction 3.
Homosexuality -- Fiction 4. Father-son relationship --
Fiction
ISBN 978-1-4231-0195-6; 1-4231-0195-2

Thom Creed, the gay son of a disowned superhero, finds
that he, too, has special powers and is asked to join the very
League that rejected his father, and it is there that Thom finds
other misfits whom he can finally trust.

"The combination of mystery, fantasy, thriller, and romance create a delightful and compelling read." Voice
Youth Advocates

Moore, Peter

Red moon rising. Hyperion 2011 328p $16.99

Grades: 7 8 9 10   **Fic**

1. Vampires -- Fiction 2. Werewolves -- Fiction
ISBN 978-1-4231-1665-3; 1-4231-1665-8

LC 2009-40375

In a world where vampires dominate and werewolves
are despised, a teenaged half-vampire discovers his reces-
sive werewolf genes are developing with the approaching
full moon.

"The details are imaginative and believable, as are the
social interactions at school and in Danny's home." Booklist

V is for villain; Peter Moore. Hyperion 2014
336 p. $17.99

Grades: 7 8 9 10 **Fic**
1. Adventure fiction 2. Ability -- Fiction 3. Brothers
-- Fiction 4. Superheroes -- Fiction 5. Good and evil
-- Fiction
ISBN 1423157494; 9781423157496
LC 2013026304
Publishers Weekly (March 17, 2014)

"When Brad makes friends who are more into political
action than weight lifting, he's happy to join a new crew-
especially since it means spending more time with Layla, a
girl who may or may not have a totally illegal, totally secret
super-power. And with her help, Brad begins to hone a dangerous new power of his own." (Publisher's note)

"Some of the characterizations in this quasi-dystopian
novel can be a little heavy-handed, but with plenty of plot
twists, dastardly conspiracies, and a snarky narrator, the latest from Moore." - Booklist

Moran, Katy
Bloodline. Candlewick Press 2009 297p il map
$16.99

Grades: 7 8 9 10 **Fic**
1. War stories 2. Adventure fiction 3. Middle Ages
-- Fiction 4. Great Britain -- History -- 0-1066 -- Fiction
ISBN 978-07636-4083-5; 0-7636-4083-2
LC 2008-21413

While traveling through early seventh-century Britain
trying to stop an impending war, Essa, who bears the blood
of native British tribes and of the invading Anglish, makes
discoveries that divide his loyalties.

"Essa is a complex, sympathetic protagonist: prickly
and quick of temper, but also clever, determined and of
unflinching integrity. If his struggle is authentically gory
and ultimately tragic, it is not without glimpses of love and
hope." Kirkus

Followed by: Bloodline rising (2011)

Bloodline rising. Candlewick Press 2011 328p
map $16.99

Grades: 7 8 9 10 **Fic**
1. Slaves -- Fiction 2. Criminals -- Fiction 3. Middle
Ages -- Fiction 4. Great Britain -- History -- 0-1066
-- Fiction
ISBN 978-0-7636-4508-3; 0-7636-4508-7
LC 2010-46692
Sequel to: Bloodline (2009)

Cai, a thief in seventh-century Constantinople, finds
himself held captive on a trading ship bound for Britain—
the home his father, a ruthless barbarian assassin, fled long
ago—where he discovers that his Anglish captors know
more about the secrets of his family than he does.

"At its heart, this is the story of a boy's turbulent relationship with his father, torn between resentment and admiration, rivalry and respect, which renders the tale both as
intimate as heartbreak and universal as hope. Grim, lyrical
and unforgettable." Kirkus

Mordecai, Martin
Blue Mountain trouble. Arthur A. Levine Books
2009 341p $16.99

Grades: 5 6 7 8 **Fic**
1. Twins -- Fiction 2. Jamaica -- Fiction 3. Siblings
-- Fiction 4. Family life -- Fiction 5. Mountain life
-- Fiction
ISBN 978-0-545-04156-0; 0-545-04156-2
LC 2008042648

After being saved from a disastrous landslide by an extraordinary goat that blocks their usual way to school, twins
Pollyread and Jackson, living with their parents high in the
mountains of Jamaica, find the strange goat reappearing at
crucial intervals as their day-to-day life is changed by series
of mysterious events involving the return of a local troublemaker and secrets from their family's past.

"Mordecai has written a nostalgic valentine to his native
island that is . . . always rich in characterization with a beautifully realized setting. The elements of magic and mystery
intriguing, too." Booklist

Morden, Simon
The **lost** art. David Fickling Books 2008 521p
$16.99; lib bdg $19.99

Grades: 8 9 10 11 12 **Fic**
1. Science fiction 2. Religion and science -- Fiction
ISBN 978-0-385-75147-6; 0-385-75147-8; 978-0-385-
75148-3 lib bdg; 0-385-75148-6 lib bdg
LC 2007-35591

A millennium after a devastating war changed the direction of Earth's rotation, when the Church keeps science and
technology suppressed, magician-like Benzamir and Va, a
killer-for-hire turned monk, seek Solomon, who is surreptitiously spreading technology for nefarious purposes.

"This original and engaging science fiction adventure
features adult protagonists, though they deal with classic
coming-of-age questions about their place in the world."
Horn Book Guide

Morgan, Nicola
The **highwayman's** footsteps. Candlewick Press
2007 354p $16.99

Grades: 6 7 8 9 **Fic**
1. Adventure fiction 2. Great Britain -- History -- 1714-
1837 -- Fiction
ISBN 978-0-7636-3472-8; 0-7636-3472-7
LC 2007-25997

In eighteenth-century England, William runs away from
his father, only to be captured by an armed highwayman
who turns out to be a girl. Together, they seek vengeance
against William's cruel father and the soldiers who killed
the girl's parents.

"Alfred Noyes' romantic epic . . . provides the jumping
off point for this beautifully written historical novel. . . . Excellent for both recreational reading and curriculum support
in the humanities." Booklist

Morgan, Page
The **beautiful** and the cursed; by Page Morgan. 1st ed. Delacorte Press 2013 352 p. (library)
$21.99; (hardcover) $18.99

Grades: 7 8 9 10 11 12 **Fic**
1. Love stories 2. Gargoyles -- Fiction 3. Brothers and
sisters -- Fiction 4. Sisters -- Fiction 5. Supernatural
-- Fiction 6. Paris (France) -- History -- 1870-1940 --

Fiction 7. France -- History -- Third Republic, 1870-1940 -- Fiction

ISBN 0385743114; 9780375990953; 9780385743112

LC 2012022378

In this book by Page Morgan, "Ingrid, her sister Gabby, and their mom arrive at the abandoned abbey that they plan to turn into an art gallery. Grayson, Ingrid's twin brother, had procured the place and was supposed to meet them there. Grayson, however, does not show up and the girls are surprised to learn that he has actually been missing for several days. . . . . [Ingrid] and Gabby . . .discover a world of living gargoyles that can transform into humans." (Children's Literature)

Morgenstern, Susie Hoch

Secret letters from 0 to 10; translated by Gill Rosner. Viking 1998 137p $16.99; pa $4.99

Grades: 4 5 6   **Fic**

1. School stories 2. Friendship -- Fiction 3. Paris (France) -- Fiction

ISBN 0-670-88007-8; 0-14-130819-2 pa

LC 98-5559

Ten-year-old Ernest lives a boring existence in Paris with his grandmother until a lively girl named Victory enters his class at school

"Morgenstern has created extremely well-drawn, distinct, and sometimes quirky characters with eloquent dialogue." SLJ

Moriarty, Chris

The **inquisitor's** apprentice; illustrations by Mark Edward Geyer. Harcourt Children's Books 2011 345p il $16.99

Grades: 4 5 6 7   **Fic**

1. Inventors 2. Gangs -- Fiction 3. Magic -- Fiction 4. Witches -- Fiction 5. Apprentices -- Fiction 6. New York (N.Y.) -- Fiction 7. Jews -- United States -- Fiction

ISBN 978-0-547-58135-4; 0-547-58135-1

In early twentieth-century New York, Sacha Kessler's ability to see witches earns him an apprenticeship to the police department's star Inquisitor, Maximillian Wolf, to help stop magical crime and, with fellow apprentice Lily Astral, Sacha investigates who is trying to kill Thomas Edison, whose mechanical witch detector that could unleash the worst witch-hunt in American history.

"Sacha, Lily and Inspector Wolf are all fully developed and multilayered characters, as are the many other distinctive personalities that appear in the tale. The author employs rich language and syntax that please the ear and touch the senses, making it all come alive." Kirkus

The **watcher** in the shadows; Chris Moriarty; [illustrated by] Mark Edward Geyer. Harcourt Children's Books 2013 336 p. (hardcover) $16.99

Grades: 4 5 6 7   **Fic**

1. Fantasy fiction 2. Jews -- Fiction 3. Mystery fiction 4. New York (N.Y.) -- History -- 20th century -- Fiction

ISBN 0547466323; 9780547466323

LC 2013003919

This juvenile novel, by Chris Moriarty, is part of the "Inquisitor's Apprentice" series. "New York's Bowery District becomes the scene of a terrible murder when the Klezmer

King gets fried to a crisp by his Electric Tuxedo--on stage! The Inquisitor's apprentice, thirteen-year-old Sacha Kessler, tries to help find the killer, but the closer he gets to solving the crime, the more it sounds as if the creature that haunted him in his first adventure is back." (Publisher's note)

"Rich language, colorful syntax, vivid description and a brilliant cast of characters beckon readers right into both the adventure and the heartfelt emotional landscape. Exciting, action-packed and absolutely marvelous." Kirkus

Moriarty, Jaclyn

★ A **corner** of white; Jaclyn Moriarty. Arthur A. Levine Books 2013 384 p. (Colors of Madeleine trilogy) (hardcover) $17.99

Grades: 7 8 9 10 11 12   **Fic**

1. Fantasy fiction 2. Epistolary fiction 3. Color -- Fiction 4. Magic -- Fiction 5. England -- Fiction 6. Princesses -- Fiction 7. Missing persons -- Fiction 8. Cambridge (England) -- Fiction 9. Interpersonal relations -- Fiction

ISBN 0545397367; 9780545397360

LC 2012016582

Boston Globe-Horn Book Honor: Fiction (2013).

This opening volume of a fantasy series from Jaclyn Moriarty focuses on 14-year-old Madeleine, who "lives in Cambridge, England, with her zany mother in uncertain circumstances, having run away from their fabulously privileged international existence. Meanwhile, Elliot lives in Bonfire, The Farms, Cello, a parallel reality. . . . Through a crack between their worlds, they begin exchanging letters." (Kirkus Reviews)

"Australian writer Moriarty's marvelously original fantasy is quirky and clever... [she] captures the proud iconoclasm of many homeschoolers and does not shy away from tenderness and poignancy." BookList

★ The **cracks** in the kingdom; Jaclyn Moriarty. Arthur A. Levine Books, an imprint of Scholastic Inc. 2014 480 p. (The colors of Madeleine) (hardcover : alk. paper) $18.99

Grades: 7 8 9 10 11 12   **Fic**

1. Fantasy fiction 2. Princesses -- Fiction 3. Missing persons -- Fiction 4. Color -- Fiction 5. Magic -- Fiction 6. England -- Fiction 7. Cambridge (England) -- Fiction 8. Interpersonal relations -- Fiction

ISBN 0545397383; 9780545397384; 9780545397391

LC 2013022827

In this book, by Jaclyn Moriarty, "Princess Ko's been bluffing about the mysterious absence of her father. . . . . If she can't get him back in a matter of weeks, the consequence may be a devastating war. So under the guise of a publicity stunt she gathers a group of teens - each with a special ability - from across the kingdom to crack the unsolvable case of the missing royals of Cello." (Publisher's note)

"In this lively follow-up to A Corner of White (Scholastic, 2013), Moriarty chronicles the ever-intertwining lives of Cambridge resident Madeline Tully and her secret correspondent Elliot Baranski, a quick-witted farm boy from the Kingdom of Cello...The RYA's work around Cello expands an already complex and intricately drawn world. Readers will be clamoring for the next title after the thrilling yet satisfying conclusion.—" (School Library Journal)

The **ghosts** of Ashbury High. Arthur A. Levine Books 2010 480p $18.99
Grades: 8 9 10 11 12   **Fic**
  1. School stories 2. Australia -- Fiction
  ISBN 978-0-545-06972-4; 0-545-06972-6
                      LC 2009-32651
Student essays, scholarship committee members' notes, and other writings reveal interactions between a group of modern-day students at an exclusive New South Wales high school and their strange connection to a young Irishman transported to Australia in the early 1800s.
"The off-the-rails zaniness . . . is . . . satisfying, and in between all the irreverence, Moriarty slips in plenty of sharp-eyed, poignant observations." SLJ

The **murder** of Bindy Mackenzie. Arthur A. Levine Books 2006 494p $16.99
Grades: 8 9 10 11 12   **Fic**
  1. School stories 2. Australia -- Fiction
  ISBN 0-439-74051-7; 0-439-74052-5 pa
                      LC 2006-07562
Class brain Bindy Mackenzie has alienated her entire high school but when she realizes someone is trying to kill her, she has to make friends in order to get help.
"The truths about family, school, and social pressures and Bindy's unforgettable, earnest, hilariously high-strung voice . . . will capture and hold readers." Booklist

The **year** of secret assignments. Arthur A. Levine Books 2004 340p $16.95; pa $7.99
Grades: 8 9 10 11 12   **Fic**
  1. School stories 2. Australia -- Fiction 3. Friendship -- Fiction
  ISBN 0-439-49881-3; 0-439-49882-1 pa
                      LC 2003-14278
Three female students from Ashbury High write to three male students from rival Brookfield High as part of a pen pal program, leading to romance, humiliation, revenge plots, and war between the schools
"There are a few coarse moments—a reference to a blow job and some caustic outbursts. . . . This is an unusual novel with an exhilarating pace, irrepressible characters, and a screwball humor that will easily attract teens." Booklist
  Other titles set at Ashbury High are:
  The ghosts of Ashbury High (2010)
  The murder of Bindy Mackenzie (2006)

Morpurgo, Michael

The **amazing** story of Adolphus Tips; [by] Michael Morpurgo. Scholastic Press 2006 140p $15.99
Grades: 4 5 6 7   **Fic**
  1. Cats -- Fiction 2. Grandmothers -- Fiction 3. World War, 1939-1945 -- Fiction
  ISBN 0-439-79661-X
                      LC 2005049038
When Boowie reads the diary that his grandmother sends him, he learns of her childhood in World War II England when American and British soldiers practiced for D-Day's

invasion in the area of her home, and about her beloved cat, Adolphus Tips, and the cat's namesake
"The personal story of anger and love is as gripping as the war drama, and Morpurgo includes a fascinating note about the invasion rehearsal and why its history is seldom told." Booklist

An **elephant** in the garden. Feiwel and Friends 2011 199p $16.99
Grades: 6 7 8 9   **Fic**
  1. Zoos -- Fiction 2. Germany -- Fiction 3. Elephants -- Fiction 4. World War, 1939-1945 -- Fiction
  ISBN 978-0-312-59369-8; 0-312-59369-4
Lizzie and Karl's mother is a zoo keeper; the family has become attached to an orphaned elephant named Marlene, who will be destroyed as a precautionary measure so she and the other animals don't run wild should the zoo be hit by bombs. The family persuades the zoo director to let Marlene stay in their garden instead. When the city is bombed, the family flees with thousands of others, but how can they walk the same route when they have an elephant in tow, and keep themselves safe?
"This well-paced, heartwarming narrative by a master storyteller will appeal to readers on several levels—as a tale of adventure and suspense, as a commentary on human trauma and animal welfare during war, as a perspective on the hardships facing the German people in the final months of World War II, and as a tribute to the rich memories and experiences of an older generation." SLJ

Half a man; Michael Morpurgo, illustrated by Gemma O'Callaghan. Candlewick Press 2015 64 p. $16.99
Grades: 7 8 9 10   **Fic**
  1. Grandfathers -- Fiction 2. World War, 1939-1945 -- Fiction 3. Veterans -- Fiction 4. Grandparent and child -- Fiction
  ISBN 0763677477; 9780763677473
                      LC 2014939339
In this book, "author Michael Morpurgo evokes the postwar Britain of his childhood. . . . From a young age, Michael was both fascinated by and afraid of his grandfather. Grandpa's ship was torpedoed during the Second World War, leaving him with terrible burns. . . . As he grows older, Michael stays with his grandfather during the summer holidays and learns the story behind Grandpa's injuries, finally getting to know the real man behind the solemn figure from his childhood." (Publisher's note)
"Morpurgo has penned an extraordinary little book of pain and triumph. It is a fictionalized tale but is based on the heroic work of Dr. McIndoe, a pioneering plastic surgeon who treated severely burned soldiers during World War II... This title will resonate with a variety of readers, including children who are interested in World War II, fans of R.J. Palacio's Wonder (Random, 2012), and is an outstanding choice for reluctant readers. With our returning wounded warriors of today, this is a timely and superb addition to all collections and not to be missed." SLJ

★ **Kensuke's** kingdom. Scholastic Press 2003 164p hardcover o.p. pa $5.99

Grades: 4 5 6 7　　　　　　　　　　　**Fic**
1. Survival after airplane accidents, shipwrecks, etc. --
Fiction
ISBN 0-439-38202-5; 0-439-59181-3 pa
　　　　　　　　　　　　　　LC 2002-9078
First published 1999 in the United Kingdom
When Michael is swept off his family's yacht, he washes
up on a desert island, where he struggles to survive—until
he finds he is not alone
This is "highly readable. . . . The end is bittersweet but
believable, and the epilogue is a sad commentary on the
long-lasting effects of war." Booklist

The **Mozart** question; [by] Michael Morpurgo;
illustrated by Michael Foreman. Candlewick Press
2008 66p il $15.99
Grades: 4 5 6 7　　　　　　　　　　　**Fic**
1. Violinists -- Fiction 2. Venice (Italy) -- Fiction 3.
Holocaust, 1933-1945 -- Fiction
ISBN 978-0-7636-3552-7; 0-7636-3552-9
A young journalist goes to Venice, Italy, to interview a
famous violinist, who tells the story of his parents' incarceration by the Nazis, and explains why they can no longer
listen to the music of Mozart.
"Morpurgo breathes life into this touching tale, which is
conveyed with compassion and honesty. Foreman's watercolors enrich the narrative." SLJ

Private Peaceful. Scholastic Press 2004 202p
$16.95; pa $5.99
Grades: 7 8 9 10　　　　　　　　　　**Fic**
1. Great Britain -- Fiction 2. World War, 1914-1918
-- Fiction
ISBN 0-439-63648-5; 0-439-63653-1 pa
　　　　　　　　　　　　　　LC 2003-65347
First published 2003 in the United Kingdom
When Thomas Peaceful's older brother is forced to join
the British Army, Thomas decides to sign up as well, although he is only fourteen years old, to prove himself to his
country, his family, his childhood love, Molly, and himself
"In this World War I story, the terse and beautiful narrative of a young English soldier is as compelling about the
world left behind as about the horrific daily details of trench
warfare. . . . Suspense builds right to the end, which is shocking, honest, and unforgettable." Booklist

War horse; by Michael Morpurgo. Scholastic
2007 165p $16.99
Grades: 5 6 7 8　　　　　　　　　　　**Fic**
1. Horses -- Fiction 2. World War, 1914-1918 -- Fiction
ISBN 978-0-439-79663-7; 0-439-79663-6
　　　　　　　　　　　　　　LC 2006044368
First published 1982 in the United Kingdom
Joey the horse recalls his experiences growing up on an
English farm, his struggle for survival as a cavalry horse
during World War I, and his reunion with his beloved master
"At times deeply affecting, the story balances the horror
with moments of respite and care." Horn Book Guide

Morris, Gerald
★ The **squire's** tale. Houghton Mifflin 1998
212p (The squire's tales) $15; pa $5.50

Grades: 6 7 8 9　　　　　　　　　　　**Fic**
1. Knights and knighthood -- Fiction 2. Gawain
(Legendary character) -- Fiction 3. Great Britain --
History -- 0-1066 -- Fiction
ISBN 0-395-86959-5; 0-440-22823-9 pa
　　　　　　　　　　　　　　LC 97-12447
In medieval England, fourteen-year-old Terence finds
his tranquil existence suddenly changed when he becomes
the squire of the young Gawain of Orkney and accompanies
him on a long quest, proving Gawain's worth as a knight
and revealing an important secret about his own true identity
"Well-drawn characters, excellent, snappy dialogue, de-
tailed descriptions of medieval life, and a dry wit put a new
spin on this engaging tale of the characters and events of
King Arthur's time." Booklist
Other titles in this series are:
The squire, his knight, & his lady (1999)
The savage damsel and the dwarf (2000)
Parsifal's page (2001)
The ballad of Sir Dinadan (2003)
The princess, the crone, and the dung-cart knight (2004)
The lionness & her knight (2005)
The quest of the Fair Unknown (2006)
The squire's quest (2009)
The legend of the king (2010)

Morris, Paula
Ruined; a novel. Point 2009 309p $16.99
Grades: 6 7 8 9 10　　　　　　　　　　**Fic**
1. Ghost stories 2. New Orleans (La.) -- Fiction
ISBN 978-0-545-04215-4; 0-545-04215-1
Set in New Orleans, this is "the story of 15-year-old Rebecca Brown, a proud New Yorker sent to live with a family friend while her father travels overseas. Ostracized as
an outsider, Rebecca struggles to fit in and cope with her
new surroundings. When she befriends Lisette, a ghost who
has haunted the cemetery ever since her mysterious death
155 years earlier, Rebecca is drawn into an eerie story of
betrayal, loss, old curses and family secrets. . . . This moody
tale thoroughly embraces the rich history, occult lore and
complex issues of race, ethnicity, class and culture that have
defined New Orleans for centuries." Publ Wkly

Morrison, Meg
Grounded; the tale of Rapunzel. Megan Morrison. Arthur A. Levine Books, an imprint of Scholastic Inc. 2015 384 p. (Tyme) (alk. paper) $17.99
Grades: 5 6 7 8　　　　　　　　　　　**Fic**
1. Fractured fairy tales 2. Thieves -- Fiction 3. Fairy
tales 4. Magic -- Fiction 5. Fairies -- Fiction 6.
Witches -- Fiction 7. Robbers and outlaws -- Fiction
8. Characters in literature -- Fiction 9. Adventure and
adventurers -- Fiction
ISBN 0545638267; 9780545638265; 9780545642699;
9780545642705; 9780545754682
　　　　　　　　　　　　　　LC 2014027138
This juvenile story, by Megan Morrison, is a retelling of
the Rapunzel legend. "In all of Tyme, . . . no one is as lucky
as Rapunzel. . . . And she knows this because Witch tells her
so--her beloved Witch. . . . [Then] Rapunzel descends to the
ground for the first time, and finds a world filled with more

peril than Witch promised . . . and more beauty, wonder, and adventure than she could have dreamed." (Publisher's note)

Morton-Shaw, Christine

The **hunt** for the seventh. HarperCollins 2008 273p il map $16.99; lib bdg $17.89; pa $6.99

Grades: 6 7 8 9   **Fic**

1. Ghost stories 2. Mystery fiction 3. Father-son relationship -- Fiction

ISBN 978-0-06-072822-9; 0-06-072822-1; 978-0-06-072823-6 lib bdg; 0-06-072823-X lib bdg; 978-0-06-072824-3 pa; 0-06-072824-8 pa

LC 2007-38885

When his father starts a new job at Minerva Hall as gardener, twelve-year-old Jim discovers an ancient curse that needs to be unraveled before disaster happens.

"Morton-Shaw skillfully weaves ancient lore into a gripping mystery. The fine plotting keeps readers turning the pages as suspense builds to the surprising end." SLJ

The **riddles** of Epsilon. Katherine Tegen Books 2005 375p $16.99; lib bdg $17.89

Grades: 7 8 9 10   **Fic**

1. Supernatural -- Fiction 2. Great Britain -- Fiction

ISBN 0-06-072819-1; 0-06-072820-5 lib bdg

LC 2004-14641

After moving with her parents to a remote English island, fourteen-year-old Jess attempts to dispel an ancient curse by solving a series of riddles, aided by Epsilon, a supernatural being.

Moses, Shelia P.

Joseph. Margaret K. McElderry Books 2008 174p $16.99; pa $8.99

Grades: 7 8 9 10   **Fic**

1. Drug abuse -- Fiction 2. African Americans -- Fiction 3. Mother-son relationship -- Fiction

ISBN 978-1-4169-1752-6; 1-4169-1752-7; 978-4169-9442-8 pa; 1-4169-9442-4 pa

Fourteen-year-old Joseph tries to avoid trouble and keep in touch with his father, who is serving in Iraq, as he and his alcoholic, drug-addicted mother move from one homeless shelter to another.

"Moses creates a compelling character in Joseph. His struggle to survive his current situation intact is fascinating to read. . . . Negative influences such as drug dealers and users are described in a clear, cold light. Education and hard work are praised for their positive influences. Middle school and junior high teens will enjoy this story." Voice Youth Advocates

Followed by: Joseph's grace (2010)

The **legend** of Buddy Bush. Margaret K. McElderry Books 2004 216p $15.95

Grades: 6 7 8 9   **Fic**

1. North Carolina -- Fiction 2. Race relations -- Fiction 3. African Americans -- Fiction

ISBN 0-689-85839-6

LC 2003-8024

In 1947, twelve-year-old Pattie Mae is sustained by her dreams of escaping Rich Square, North Carolina, and moving to Harlem when her Uncle Buddy is arrested for attempt-

ed rape of a white woman and her grandfather is diagnosed with a terminal brain tumor.

"Patti Mae's first-person voice, steeped in the inflections of the South, rings true, and her observations richly evoke a time, place, and a resilient African American community." Booklist

Another title about Buddy Bush is:
The return of Buddy Bush (2005)

The **return** of Buddy Bush. Simon & Schuster 2006 143p il $15.95

Grades: 6 7 8 9   **Fic**

1. Family life -- Fiction 2. North Carolina -- Fiction 3. Race relations -- Fiction 4. African Americans -- Fiction

ISBN 0-689-87431-6

Sequel to: The legend of Buddy Bush

Pattie Mae goes to Harlem to visit her sister after the death of her beloved grandfather. She hopes to soak up the Northern lifestyle and is on a secret mission to find her Uncle Buddy, who is hiding out after being falsely accused of rape in their North Carolina hometown.

"Pattie Mae's voice is fresh and colloquial, and her spunky narration will speak to readers." SLJ

Mosley, Walter

47. Little, Brown 2005 232p $16.99

Grades: 7 8 9 10   **Fic**

1. Magic -- Fiction 2. Slavery -- Fiction 3. African Americans -- Fiction

ISBN 0-316-11035-3

LC 2004-12500

Number 47, a fourteen-year-old slave boy growing up under the watchful eye of a brutal master in 1832, meets the mysterious Tall John, who introduces him to a magical science and also teaches him the meaning of freedom.

"Time travel, shape-shifting, and intergalactic conflict add unusual, provocative elements to this story. And yet, well-drawn characters; lively dialogue filled with gritty, regional dialect; vivid descriptions; and poignant reflections ground it in harsh reality." SLJ

Moss, Jenny

Shadow. Scholastic Press 2010 377p $17.99

Grades: 7 8 9 10   **Fic**

1. Fairy tales 2. Kings and rulers -- Fiction

ISBN 978-0-545-03641-2; 0-545-03641-0

LC 2009-14209

When Shadow, whose job all her life has been to stay close to the young queen and prevent her prophecied death at the age of sixteen, fails in her task and the castle is thrown into chaos, she escapes along with a young knight, embarking upon a journey that eventually reveals her true identity.

"With its dashing knights, pretentious queen, and put-upon protagonist, the story starts out like any other garden-variety fairytale, but it soon takes a turn for the darkly subversive world of pagan religions and political scheming. . . . A nuanced coming of age story with a fairy-tale setting, this is sure to please." Bull Cent Child Books

Winnie's war. Walker & Co. 2009 178p $16.99

Grades: 5 6 7 8   **Fic**

1. Texas -- Fiction 2. Epidemics -- Fiction 3. Influenza

-- Fiction 4. Family life -- Fiction
ISBN 978-0-8027-9819-0; 0-8027-9819-5

LC 2008-23233

Living in the shadow of a Texas cemetery, twelve-year-old Winnie Grace struggles to keep the Spanish influenza of 1918 from touching her family—her coffin-building father, her troubled mother, and her two baby sisters.

"The small town of Coward Creek comes to life in Moss's writing. . . . Winnie and the others populate a solid plot, but it is the setting and the characters that will make this book last as a popular favorite with a space on shelves well into the future." Voice Youth Advocates

Moulton, Courtney Allison

Angelfire; 1st ed. Katherine Tegen Books 2011 453 p. (trade bdg.) $17.99

Grades: 7 8 9 10   Fic

1. Horror fiction 2. Horror stories 3. Souls -- Fiction 4. Youths' writings 5. Angels -- Fiction 6. Monsters -- Fiction 7. Reincarnation -- Fiction
ISBN 9780062002327; 9780062002341

LC 2010012821

A seventeen-year-old girl discovers that she has the reincarnated soul of an ancient warrior destined to battle the reapers --creatures who devour humans and send their souls to Hell. --Grades nine to twelve. -- (Bull Cent Child Books)

"The author has introduced a dark and compelling world of action and intrigue, albeit with enough 'normal' drama and humor sprinkled throughout to lighten it. . . . Older junior and senior high school readers will find themselves engrossed in the story until its powerful conclusion—then anxiously awaiting the second installment." Voice Youth Advocates

Mourlevat, Jean-Claude

★ The **pull** of the ocean; [by] Jean-Claude Mourlevat; translated from the French by Y. Maudet. Delacorte Press 2006 190p hardcover o.p. lib bdg $17.99; pa $6.50

Grades: 5 6 7   Fic

1. Size -- Fiction 2. Twins -- Fiction 3. France -- Fiction 4. Brothers -- Fiction
ISBN 978-0-385-73348-9; 0-385-73348-8; 978-0-385-90364-6 lib bdg; 0-385-90364-2 lib bdg; 978-0-385-73666-4 pa; 0-385-73666-5 pa

LC 2006001802

Loosely based on Charles Perrault's "Tom Thumb," seven brothers in modern-day France flee their poor parents' farm, led by the youngest who, although mute and unusually small, is exceptionally wise.

This "is a memorable novel that readers will find engaging and intellectually satisfying." SLJ

★ **Winter's** end; translated by Anthea Bell. Candlewick Press 2009 415p lib bdg $21.99

Grades: 8 9 10 11 12   Fic

1. Fantasy fiction 2. Adventure fiction 3. Orphans -- Fiction 4. Despotism -- Fiction 5. Resistance to government -- Fiction
ISBN 978-0-7636-4450-5; 0-7636-4450-1

LC 2009-8456

Fleeing across icy mountains from a pack of terrifying dog-men sent to hunt them down, four teenagers escape from their prison-like boarding schools to take up the fight against the tyrannical government that murdered their parents fifteen years earlier.

"Teeming with heroic acts, heartbreaking instances of sacrifice and intriguing characters . . . the book will keep readers absorbed and set imaginations spinning." Publ Wkly

Mulder, Michelle, 1976-

Out of the box. Orca Book Publishers 2011 150p pa $9.95

Grades: 6 7 8 9   Fic

1. Aunts -- Fiction 2. Canada -- Fiction 3. Family life -- Fiction 4. Mother-daughter relationship -- Fiction
ISBN 978-1-55469-328-3 pa; 1-55469-328-4 pa

Ellie's passion for tango music leads to an interest in Argentine history and a desire to separate herself from her parents' problems.

"Ellie's narration authentically conveys her gradual growth, the insecurities that surround her developing friendships, her role in a dysfunctional family, and the pleasure she takes in music. Adults and their relationships are portrayed credibly. . . . A bit of Argentine history rounds out the believable plot." SLJ

Mull, Brandon

Rogue Knight; by Brandon Mull. Aladdin 2014 480 p. (Five kingdoms) (hardback) $17.99

Grades: 4 5 6 7   Fic

1. Fantasy fiction 2. Knights and knighthood -- Fiction 3. Adventure and adventurers -- Fiction
ISBN 1442497033; 9781442497030; 9781442497047

LC 2014025800

Sequel to: Sky Raiders (2014)

In this novel, by Brandon Mull, book two of the "Five Kingdoms" series, "young Cole enters the second of five kingdoms in the otherworldly Outskirts, is exposed to a second culture and a second flavor of magic, and battles a second monster made of stolen magic as he continues the search for his fellow earthly kidnappees." (Kirkus Reviews)

"After adventuring in the Outskirts in Sky Raiders (2014), Cole Randolph is still stuck in the amazing, confusing world of the Five Kingdoms. Luckily, he is not alone--his friends Mira, Jace, Twitch, and Joe are along for the ride as they set out to rescue Mira's sister from danger in the kingdom of Elloweer. . . . Cole is a relatable and brave Everykid hero, and his friends bring different perspectives to this ongoing tale. Mull's latest series continues to be excellent, and it should easily find a home among fans of middle-grade fantasy stories." Booklist

Sky Raiders; by Brandon Mull. Aladdin 2014 432 p. (Five kingdoms) (hardback) $16.99

Grades: 4 5 6 7   Fic

1. Fantasy fiction 2. Adventure fiction
ISBN 1442497009; 9781442497009

LC 2013032734

"Cole Randolph was just trying to have a fun time with his friends on Halloween (and maybe get to know Jenna Hunt a little better). But when a spooky haunted house turns out to be a portal to something much creepier, Cole finds himself on an adventure on a whole different level." (Publisher's note)

"Although Mull packs quite a bit into this initial installment, he skillfully mixes the capricious logic of dreams with high stakes and constant danger. The intriguing premise, strong world-building, and numerous twists make this a real page-turner." Pub Wkly

Spirit animals; 1 wild born. Brandon Mull. Scholastic Press 2013 224 p. (Spirit animals) $12.99

Grades: 4 5 6 7   **Fic**
1. Spirits -- Fiction 2. Children and animals 3. Magic
ISBN 0545522439; 9780545522434

LC 2013932302

This book, by Brandon Mull, is set in "the world of Erdas, where every child who comes of age must discover if they have a spirit animal, a rare bond between human and beast that bestows great powers to both. A dark force has risen from distant and long-forgotten lands, and has begun an onslaught that will ravage the world. Now the fate of Erdas has fallen on the shoulders of four young strangers." (Publisher's note)

★ A **world** without heroes. Aladdin 2011 454p (Beyonders) $19.99

Grades: 4 5 6 7   **Fic**
1. Fantasy fiction 2. Magic -- Fiction 3. Space and time -- Fiction 4. Heroes and heroines -- Fiction
ISBN 978-1-4169-9792-4; 1-4169-9792-X

LC 2010-23437

Fourteen-year-old Jason Walker is transported to a strange world called Lyrian, where he joins Rachel, who was also drawn there from our world, and a few rebels, to piece together the Word that can destroy the malicious wizard emperor, Surroth.

"Mull moves his story at a brisk pace, preventing the tragedies from overwhelming the adventure, while offering ample action and feisty dialogue to keep fantasy lovers entertained." Publ Wkly

Muller, Rachel Dunstan

Squeeze; written by Rachel Dunstan Muller. Orca Book Publishers 2010 166p (Orca sports) pa $9.95

Grades: 6 7 8 9   **Fic**
1. Caves -- Fiction 2. Brothers -- Fiction 3. Accidents -- Fiction
ISBN 978-1-55469-324-5; 1-55469-324-1

On a caving trip with his older brother, Byron discovers a new cave but has to make some life-or-death decisions when his brother is seriously injured.

"A fast-paced, compulsively readable book. . . . Information about caving is woven seamlessly into the narrative, and descriptions of the beauty of underground rock formations are often quite lyrical." SLJ

Mulligan, Andy

★ **Trash**. David Fickling Books 2010 232p $16.99; lib bdg $19.99

Grades: 6 7 8 9   **Fic**
1. Mystery fiction 2. Poverty -- Fiction 3. Political corruption -- Fiction 4. Refuse and refuse disposal --

Fiction
ISBN 978-0-385-75214-5; 0-385-75214-8; 978-0-385-75215-2 lib bdg; 0-385-75215-6 lib bdg

LC 2010-15940

Fourteen-year-olds Raphael and Gardo team up with a younger boy, Rat, to figure out the mysteries surrounding a bag Raphael finds during their daily life of sorting through trash in a third-world country's dump.

"While on the surface the book reads like a fast-paced adventure title, it also makes a larger statement about the horrors of poverty and injustice in the world. . . . Trash is a compelling read." SLJ

Murdock, Catherine Gilbert

★ **Dairy** Queen; a novel. Houghton Mifflin 2006 275p $16

Grades: 7 8 9 10   **Fic**
1. Football -- Fiction 2. Farm life -- Fiction
ISBN 0-618-68307-0

LC 2005-19077

After spending her summer running the family farm and training the quarterback for her school's rival football team, sixteen-year-old D.J. decides to go out for the sport herself, not anticipating the reactions of those around her.

"D. J.'s voice is funny, frank, and intelligent, and her story is not easily pigeonholed." Voice Youth Advocates

Other titles about D.J. Schwenk are:
Front and center (2009)
The off season (2007)

Front and center. Houghton Mifflin 2009 256p (The dairy queen trilogy) $16

Grades: 7 8 9 10   **Fic**
1. Farm life -- Fiction 2. Basketball -- Fiction
ISBN 978-0-618-95982-2; 0-618-95982-3

LC 2009-24167

Sequel to: The off season (2007)

"In the third and final book . . . about farm girl, linebacker, and basketball star D.J. Schwenk, the self-aggrandizing heroine must decide her future: is she up to playing basketball for the Big Ten schools that are starting to recruit her, or should she choose a smaller college, where the game is less brutal but also less challenging? . . . D.J.'s voice is intimate and compelling, her story both universal and unique, familiar and eye-opening." Horn Book

The off season. Houghton Mifflin 2007 277p $16

Grades: 7 8 9 10   **Fic**
1. Football -- Fiction 2. Farm life -- Fiction
ISBN 978-0-618-68695-7; 0-618-68695-9

LC 2006029278

Sequel to: Dairy Queen (2006)

High school junior D.J. staggers under the weight of caring for her badly injured brother, her responsibilities on the dairy farm, a changing relationship with her friend Brian, and her own athletic aspirations.

This "depicts a believably maturing D.J., a young woman whose character shines through even as she struggles to find her voice. Readers will root for her at every tragicomic turn." SLJ

Followed by: Front and center (2009)

★ **Princess** Ben; being a wholly truthful account of her various discoveries and misadventures, recounted to the best of her recollection, in four parts. written by Catherine Gilbert Murdock. Houghton Mifflin 2008 344p $16; pa $8.99

Grades: 7 8 9 10   **Fic**

1. Fairy tales 2. Magic -- Fiction 3. Princesses -- Fiction 4. Courts and courtiers -- Fiction

ISBN 978-0-618-95971-6; 0-618-95971-8; 978-0-547-22325-4 pa; 0-547-22325-0 pa

LC 2007-34300

A girl is transformed, through instruction in life at court, determination, and magic, from sullen, pudgy, graceless Ben into Crown Princess Benevolence, a fit ruler of the kindgom of Montagne as it faces war with neighboring Drachensbett.

"Murdock's prose sweeps the reader up and never falters, blending a formal syntax and vocabulary with an intimate tone that bonds the reader with Ben." Horn Book

★ **Wisdom's** kiss; a thrilling and romantic adventure, incorporating magic, villany and a cat. written by Catherine Gilbert Murdock. Houghton Mifflin 2011 284p $16.99

Grades: 7 8 9 10   **Fic**

1. Fairy tales 2. Cats -- Fiction 3. Orphans -- Fiction 4. Soldiers -- Fiction 5. Princesses -- Fiction 6. Supernatural -- Fiction 7. Household employees -- Fiction

ISBN 978-0-547-56687-0; 0-547-56687-5

LC 2011003708

Princess Wisdom, who yearns for a life of adventure beyond the kingdom of Montagne, Tips, a soldier keeping his true life secret from his family, Fortitude, an orphaned maid who longs for Tips, and Magic the cat form an uneasy alliance as they try to save the kingdom from certain destruction. Told through diaries, memoirs, encyclopedia entries, letters, biographies, and a stage play.

"Packed with double entendres, humorous dialogue and situations, and a black cat that will capture the reader's imagination, this is a joyful, timeless fantasy that teens will savor." Booklist

Murphy, Claire Rudolf

Free radical. Clarion Bks. 2002 198p $15

Grades: 7 8 9 10   **Fic**

1. Baseball -- Fiction

ISBN 0-618-11134-4

LC 2001-42268

In Fairbanks, Alaska, in the middle of the summer Little League baseball season, fifteen-year-old Luke is stunned when his mother confesses that she is wanted by the FBI for her role in the death of a student during an anti-Vietnam War protest thirty years ago

"The fast action of the baseball scenes will lure teens to the sports story, and the thought-provoking issues of guilt and responsibility will hold their interest." Booklist

Murphy, Jim

Desperate journey. Scholastic Press 2006 278p il map $16.99

Grades: 5 6 7 8   **Fic**

1. Family life -- Fiction 2. Erie Canal (N.Y.) -- Fiction

ISBN 0-439-07806-7

LC 2006-02526

In the mid-1800s, with both her father and her uncle in jail on an assault charge, Maggie, her brother, and her ailing mother rush their barge along the Erie Canal to deliver their heavy cargo or lose everything.

This is a "gripping novel." Booklist

Murphy, Rita

Bird. Delacorte Press 2008 151p $15.99; lib bdg $18.99

Grades: 5 6 7 8   **Fic**

1. Kites -- Fiction 2. Flight -- Fiction 3. Houses -- Fiction 4. Vermont -- Fiction 5. Supernatural -- Fiction

ISBN 978-0-385-73018-1; 0-385-73018-7; 978-0-385-90557-2 lib bdg; 0-385-90557-2 lib bdg

LC 2008-04690

Miranda, a small, delicate girl easily carried off by the wind, lands at Bourne Manor on the coast of Lake Champlain and is raised by the dour Wysteria Barrows, but she begins to believe rumors that the Manor is cursed and, aided by a new friend and kites secreted in an attic, seeks to escape.

"This enchanting novel is well written with lyrical text and beautiful descriptions. . . . Good for middle school students, this book will make a nice addition to school and public libraries alike." Libr Media Connect

Looking for Lucy Buick. Delacorte Press 2005 165p $15.95; lib bdg $17.99

Grades: 7 8 9 10   **Fic**

1. Family life -- Fiction 2. Abandoned children -- Fiction

ISBN 0-385-72939-1; 0-385-90176-3 lib bdg

LC 2004-20128

Following the death of her favorite adoptive aunt, Lucy goes searching for her biological family who abandoned her in an old Buick eighteen years before.

"What wins the day are the people in Lucy's life, living and dead . . . who pop off the pages, and Murphy's voice . . . which tells the story with a steadfastness and sweetness." Booklist

Murray, Kirsty

The **secret** life of Maeve Lee Kwong; by Kirsty Murray. Allen & Unwin 2008 252p (Children of the wind) pa $8.95

Grades: 5 6 7 8   **Fic**

1. Chinese -- Fiction 2. Ireland -- Fiction 3. Australia -- Fiction 4. Racially mixed people -- Fiction

ISBN 978-1-86508-737-5 pa; 1-86508-737-8 pa

"Being half-Chinese and half-Irish never bothered Maeve Lee Kwong much. A lot of Australians have mixed heritages, and she considers herself fully Aussie. Then her mother dies in a car accident, and Maeve no longer knows who she is, or where she belongs. . . . This book has a lot going for it, including short and highly varied scenes that propel the story forward at a brisk pace. With settings in

Australia, Hong Kong, and Ireland, the descriptions are lush and appealing." SLJ

Murray, Martine

How to make a bird. Arthur A. Levine Books 2010 233p $17.99

Grades: 7 8 9 10 **Fic**

1. Australia -- Fiction 2. Bereavement -- Fiction 3. Family life -- Fiction 4. Runaway teenagers -- Fiction

ISBN 978-0-439-66951-1; 0-439-66951-0

LC 2009-27453

When seventeen-year-old, small-town Australian girl Manon Clarkeson leaves home in the middle of the night, wearing her mother's long, inappropriate red silk dress and riding her bike, she is heading for Melbourne, not exactly sure what she is looking for but not wanting to stay at home alone with her father anymore.

"Although Mannie's defining attributes—acute self-consciousness and claustrophobic intensity—are hallmarks of many YA heroines, Murray's powerful lyrical voice and close observation breathe new life into them. . . . The novel offers an especially vivid sense of place—the harsh but open rural landscape and densely populated yet lonely, urban Melbourne." Kirkus

Mussi, Sarah

★ The **door** of no return. Margaret K. McElderry Books 2008 394p $17.99; pa $8.99

Grades: 8 9 10 11 12 **Fic**

1. Adventure fiction 2. Ghana -- Fiction 3. Blacks -- Fiction 4. Homicide -- Fiction 5. Great Britain -- Fiction 6. Buried treasure -- Fiction

ISBN 978-1-4169-1550-8; 1-4169-1550-8; 978-1-4169-6825-2 pa; 1-4169-6825-3 pa

LC 2007-18670

Sixteen-year-old Zac never believed his grandfather's tales about their enslaved ancestors being descended from an African king, but when his grandfather is murdered and the villains come after Zac, he sets out for Ghana to find King Baktu's long-lost treasure before the murderers do.

"This exciting narrative takes place in England and Africa; in jungles, dark caves, and on the sea. . . . Overall, this is a complex, masterful story for confident readers." SLJ

Myer, Andy

Henry Hubble's book of troubles; Andy Myer. First edition Delacorte Press 2015 151 p. illustrations (hardback) $15.99

Grades: 4 5 6 **Fic**

1. School stories 2. Humorous fiction 3. Humorous stories 4. Diaries -- Fiction 5. Schools -- Fiction 6. Middle schools -- Fiction

ISBN 0385744390; 9780375991646; 9780385744393

LC 2014044043

In this middle grades book, by Andy Myer, "Henry Hubble . . . [is] in a world of trouble. From class-trip bathroom breaks to Halloween-costume catastrophes to lunchroom-table love drama, Henry is always in the middle of a debacle. That is . . . until [his] journal . . . makes Henry a media mogul and one of the most popular sixth graders in the world." (Publisher's note)

"Mixing realistic and farcical elements, Henry's peppy narrative features amusing digressions and commentary—and occasional potty humor—further enlivened by "Henry's" interspersed drawings and droll verse, in an entertaining, fast-paced read." Booklist

Myers, Anna

Assassin; [by] Anna Myers. Walker & Company 2005 212p $16.95

Grades: 7 8 9 10 **Fic**

1. Actors 2. Lawyers 3. Presidents 4. Murderers 5. State legislators 6. Members of Congress 7. United States -- History -- 1861-1865, Civil War -- Fiction

ISBN 0-8027-8989-7

LC 2005042275

In alternating passages, a young White House seamstress named Bella and the actor John Wilkes Booth describe the events that lead to the latter's assassination of Abraham Lincoln.

"The novel offers a good opportunity for discussion about the assassin, his motivations, and, in this case, how he drew an unsuspecting girl into his scheme." SLJ

The **grave** robber's secret. Walker & Co. 2011 196p $16.99

Grades: 7 8 9 10 **Fic**

1. Homicide -- Fiction 2. Grave robbing -- Fiction 3. Philadelphia (Pa.) -- Fiction

ISBN 978-0-8027-2183-9; 0-8027-2183-4

LC 2010018097

In Philadelphia in the 1800s, twelve-year-old Robbie is forced to help his father rob graves, then when he suspects his dad of murder, Robbie makes a life-changing decision.

"The story is well written and the characterization is excellent. Readers will connect to Robby on several levels and will feel for Martha Burke." Libr Media Connect

Spy! [by] Anna Myers. Walker & Co. 2008 211p $16.99

Grades: 5 6 7 8 9 **Fic**

1. Revolutionaries 2. Spies -- Fiction 3. Orphans -- Fiction 4. Teachers -- Fiction 5. United States -- History -- 1775-1783, Revolution -- Fiction

ISBN 978-0-8027-9742-1; 0-8027-9742-3

LC 2008-254

In 1774, twelve-year-old Jonah becomes a pupil of Nathan Hale, who inspires him to question his beliefs about the impending revolution, and two years later, Jonah makes a decision that leads to Nathan's execution.

"Set against clearly delineated historical events, the story employs personal thoughts and feelings to show the conflicts facing the colonists. This well-written novel is a good supplement to American history studies." SLJ

Time of the witches. Walker & Co. 2009 197p $16.99

Grades: 6 7 8 9 **Fic**

1. Trials -- Fiction 2. Orphans -- Fiction 3. Witchcraft -- Fiction 4. Salem (Mass.) -- Fiction

ISBN 978-0-8027-9820-6; 0-8027-9820-9

LC 2008-54278

Orphaned Drucilla finds a home with the beautiful but troubled Mistress Putnam as accusations of witchcraft start to swirl in Salem Village.

"Myers brings a time of mass hysteria to life. . . . Myers draws heavily from the actual participants in the events. . . . A solid piece of historical fiction." SLJ

Tulsa burning. Walker & Co. 2002 152p $16.95; pa $6.95

Grades: 7 8 9 10 **Fic**

1. Riots -- Fiction 2. Oklahoma -- Fiction 3. Race relations -- Fiction

ISBN 0-8027-8829-7; 0-8027-7696-5 pa

LC 2002-23457

In 1921, fifteen-year-old Noble Chase hates the sheriff of Wekiwa, Oklahoma, and is more than willing to cross him to help his best friend, a black man, who is injured during race riots in nearby Tulsa

"In this emotional page-turner, Myers expertly captures an era of poisonous racism while conveying the strong, true voice of a courageous young man." Booklist

Wart; [by] Anna Myers. Walker & Co. 2007 215p $16.95

Grades: 5 6 7 8 **Fic**

1. Remarriage -- Fiction 2. Witchcraft -- Fiction

ISBN 978-0-8027-8977-8; 0-8027-8977-3

LC 2007006218

Regretting his part in his father's decision not to marry the town librarian, Stewart has many misgivings about the latest woman in their lives, although her spells and charms might make Stewart popular and improve his basketball game.

"The plot moves quickly and the characters are appealing and unique." SLJ

Myers, Edward

★ **Storyteller**; by Edward Myers. Clarion Books 2008 283p $16

Grades: 6 7 8 9 **Fic**

1. Fairy tales 2. Storytelling -- Fiction 3. Kings and rulers -- Fiction

ISBN 978-0-618-69541-6; 0-618-69541-9

LC 2007031031

Jack, a seventeen-year-old storyteller, goes to the royal city seeking his fortune and soon attracts the attention of the grief-stricken king, his beautiful eldest daughter, and his cruel young son, and he attempts to help them—and the entire kingdom—through his stories.

"This old-fashioned story has the timeless appeal of adventure, humor, and light romance, all woven together by an able teller of tales." Booklist

Myers, Walter Dean, 1937-2014

Amiri & Odette; a love story. a poem by Walter Dean Myers; paintings by Javaka Steptoe. Scholastic Press 2009 un il $17.99

Grades: 7 8 9 10 **Fic**

1. Fairy tales 2. Love stories 3. Novels in verse 4. African Americans -- Fiction

ISBN 978-0-590-68041-7; 0-590-68041-2

LC 2008-11563

Presents a modern, urban retelling in verse of the ballet in which brave Amiri falls in love with beautiful Odette and fights evil Big Red for her on the streets of the Swan Lake Projects.

"Myers's verse is almost overwrought—as it should be to suit the story, and the intensity of teenage love. The melodrama combines with an energy and beat that—heightened by dynamic text design—makes this ideal for performance. Steptoe's collage-on-cinderblock illustrations have a roughness, darkness, and density that suit the tone." SLJ

Carmen; an urban adaptation of the opera. Egmont USA 2011 various pagings $16.99

Grades: 8 9 10 11 12 **Fic**

1. Love -- Fiction 2. New York (N.Y.) -- Fiction 3. Hispanic Americans -- Fiction

ISBN 978-1-60684-115-0; 1-60684-115-7; 978-1-60684-199-0 e-book

LC 2011002491

A policeman's obsessive love for a tempestuous wig factory worker ends in tragedy in this updated version of Bizet's Carmen, set in Spanish Harlem, and told in screenplay format.

"Myers seamlessly pulls off the drama's transportation to a contemporary urban setting and, true to form, renders it accessible to today's teens. . . . An excellent choice for reluctant readers, urban or otherwise." SLJ

★ The **Cruisers**; Walter Dean Myers. Scholastic Press 2010 126 p. $15.99

Grades: 6 7 8 9 **Fic**

1. Schools -- Fiction 2. Newspapers -- Fiction 3. Middle schools -- Fiction 4. Race relations -- Fiction 5. African Americans -- Fiction 6. Freedom of speech -- Fiction 7. Harlem (New York, N.Y.) -- Fiction

ISBN 978-0-439-91626-4; 0-439-91626-7; 9780439916264

LC 2009052426

Friends Zander, Kambui, LaShonda, and Bobbi, caught in the middle of a mock Civil War at DaVinci Academy, learn the true cost of freedom of speech when they use their alternative newspaper, The Cruiser, to try to make peace.

"A finely crafted look at smart, urban underachievers. . . . [The book offers] fleet pacing, a spot-on voice, good characters, great dialogue, smart ideas, and an unusual story that can maneuver whip-quick from light to heavy and right back again." Booklist

Another title in this series is:

The Cruisers: checkmate (2011)

The **Cruisers**: checkmate. Scholastic Press 2011 133p $16.99

Grades: 6 7 8 9 **Fic**

1. School stories 2. Chess -- Fiction 3. Newspapers -- Fiction 4. Gifted children -- Fiction 5. African Americans -- Fiction 6. Harlem (New York, N.Y.) -- Fiction

ISBN 978-0-439-91627-1; 0-439-91627-5

LC 2010045106

Sequel to: Cruisers (2010)

Four middle-schoolers who publish an alternative newspaper at their Harlem academy for gifted students investigate why a classmate—one of the best chess players in New York City—was caught trying to buy drugs.

"Though less provocative than the first volume, this has the same breezy tone and effortless attitude and has plenty to say (always in the most natural of ways) about addicts and prison." Booklist

★ **Darius** & Twig; Walter Dean Myers. 1st ed. Harper, an imprint of HarperCollinsPublishers 2013 208 p. (hardcover) $17.99

Grades: 8 9 10 11 12   **Fic**
1. Friendship -- Fiction 2. Harlem (New York, N.Y.) -- Fiction 3. Running -- Fiction 4. Authorship -- Fiction 5. Best friends -- Fiction 6. New York (N.Y.) -- Fiction 7. African Americans -- Fiction 8. Dominican Americans -- Fiction
ISBN 0061728233; 9780061728235; 9780061728242
LC 2012050678
Coretta Scott King Honor Book: Author (2014)

In this book by Walter Dean Myers, "Harlem teenager Darius, a writer, wants to get out of his neighborhood and make it to college, but his grades aren't good enough. He's hoping that if he can get a story published, he might nab a college scholarship. His best friend Twig is a track star, and sees athletics as his escape. Both are skeptical of the hype they are fed about how hard work pays off, and they face obstacles ranging from school bullies . . . to indifferent educators." (Publishers Weekly)

"This encouraging text may inspire teens who feel trapped by their surroundings...Told in Darius's voice, the prose is poetic but concise. This would be a worthwhile addition to any middle or high school media center or public library shelf and would make a valuable book for discussion in a middle school classroom.—" VOYA

Dope sick. HarperTeen/Amistad 2009 186p $16.99; lib bdg $17.89

Grades: 8 9 10 11 12   **Fic**
1. Drug abuse -- Fiction 2. Supernatural -- Fiction 3. African Americans -- Fiction 4. Harlem (New York, N.Y.) -- Fiction
ISBN 978-0-06-121477-6; 0-06-121477-9; 978-0-06-121478-3 lib bdg; 0-06-121478-7 lib bdg
LC 2008-10568

Seeing no way out of his difficult life in Harlem, seventeen-year-old Jeremy "Lil J" Dance flees into a house after a drug deal goes awry and meets a weird man who shows different turning points in Lil J's life when he could have made better choices.

"Myers uses street-style lingo to cover Lil J's sorry history of drug use, jail time, irresponsible fatherhood and his own childhood grief. A didn't-see-that-coming ending wraps up the story on a note of well-earned hope and will leave readers with plenty to think about." Publ Wkly

★ **Fallen** angels; Walter Dean Myers. Scholastic Paperbacks 2008 336 p. hardcover o.p. (pbk.) $7.99

Grades: 8 9 10 11 12 Adult   **Fic**
1. Vietnam War, 1961-1975 -- Fiction 2. African American soldiers -- Fiction
ISBN 9780545055765; 0545055768

First published 1988
ALA YALSA Margaret A. Edwards Award (1994)

"Black, seventeen, perceptive and sensitive, Richie (the narrator) has enlisted and been sent to Vietnam; in telling the story of his year of active service, Richie is candid about the horror of killing and the fear of being killed, the fear and bravery and confusion and tragedy of the war." Bull Cent Child Books

"Except for occasional outbursts, the narration is remarkably direct and understated; and the dialogue, with morbid humor sometimes adding comic relief, is steeped in natural vulgarity, without which verisimilitude would be unthinkable. In fact, the foul talk, which serves as the story's linguistic setting, is not nearly as obscene as the events." Horn Book

Game. HarperTeen 2008 218p $16.99; lib bdg $17.89

Grades: 8 9 10 11 12   **Fic**
1. School stories 2. Basketball -- Fiction 3. Czech Americans -- Fiction 4. African Americans -- Fiction 5. Harlem (New York, N.Y.) -- Fiction
ISBN 978-0-06-058294-4; 978-0-06-058295-1 lib bdg
LC 2007-18370

If Harlem high school senior Drew Lawson is going to realize his dream of playing college, then professional, basketball, he will have to improve at being coached and being a team player, especially after a new—white—student threatens to take the scouts' attention away from him.

"Basketball fans will love the long passages of detailed court action. . . . The authentic thoughts of a strong, likable, African American teen whose anxieties, sharp insights, and belief in his own abilities will captivate readers of all backgrounds." Booklist

Harlem summer. Scholastic Press 2007 176p il $16.99

Grades: 6 7 8 9   **Fic**
1. African Americans -- Fiction 2. Harlem Renaissance -- Fiction 3. Harlem (New York, N.Y.) -- Fiction
ISBN 978-0-439-36843-8; 0-439-36843-X
LC 2006-46812

In 1920s Harlem, sixteen-year-old Mark Purvis, an aspiring jazz saxophonist, gets a summer job as an errand boy for the publishers of the groundbreaking African American magazine, "The Crisis," but soon finds himself on the enemy list of mobster Dutch Shultz.

"Readers will be delighted to accompany the teen on his action-packed adventures." Booklist

★ **Hoops**; a novel. Delacorte Press 1981 183p hardcover o.p. pa $5.99

Grades: 7 8 9 10   **Fic**
1. Basketball -- Fiction 2. African Americans -- Fiction 3. Harlem (New York, N.Y.) -- Fiction
ISBN 0-440-93884-8 pa
LC 81-65497
ALA YALSA Margaret A. Edwards Award (1994)

"This story offers the reader some fast, descriptive basketball action, a love story between Lonnie and girlfriend Mary-Ann, peer friendship problems, and gangster intrigues. Most importantly, however, it portrays the growth of a trusting and deeply caring father-son relationship between [the coach] Cal and [fatherless] Lonnie." Voice Youth Advocates

Followed by The outside shot (1988)

Invasion! Walter Dean Myers. Scholastic Press 2013 224 p. $17.99

Grades: 7 8 9 10 **Fic**

1. Friendship -- Fiction 2. Normandy (France), Attack on, 1944 -- Fiction 3. War -- Fiction 4. African American soldiers -- Fiction 5. France -- History -- 20th century -- Fiction 6. Normandy (France) -- History -- 20th century -- Fiction 7. Segregation -- United States -- History -- 20th century -- Fiction 8. World War, 1939-1945 -- Campaigns -- France -- Normandy -- Fiction 9. Segregation -- United States -- History -- 20th century -- Fiction 10. World War, 1939-1945 -- Participation, African American

ISBN 0545384281; 9780545384285; 9780545384292; 9780545576598

LC 2013005595

In this book by Walter Dean Myers, "old friends Josiah 'Woody' Wedgewood and Marcus Perry see each other in England prior to the invasion of Normandy. Woody is with the 29th Infantry, and Marcus, who's black, is with the Transportation Corps, the segregation of their Virginia hometown following them right into wartime. Their friendship frames the story, as the two occasionally encounter each other in the horrific days ahead." (Kirkus Reviews)

"Myers eloquently conveys how exhausting war is physically and emotionally. . . . [T]his novel can be hard to read, but it is also hard to put down." SLJ

Kick; [by] Walter Dean Myers and Ross Workman. HarperTeen 2011 197p $16.99; lib bdg $17.89

Grades: 7 8 9 10 **Fic**

1. Police -- Fiction 2. Soccer -- Fiction 3. Mentoring -- Fiction 4. New Jersey -- Fiction 5. Family life -- Fiction 6. Criminal investigation -- Fiction

ISBN 978-0-06-200489-5; 0-06-200489-1; 978-0-06-200490-1 lib bdg; 0-06-200490-5 lib bdg

LC 2010-18441

Told in their separate voices, thirteen-year-old soccer star Kevin and police sergeant Brown, who knew his father, try to keep Kevin out of juvenile hall after he is arrested on very serious charges.

"Workman is a genuine talent, writing short, declarative sentences that move that narrative forward with assurance and a page-turning tempo. Myers, of course, is a master. . . . The respective voices and characters play off each other as successfully as a high-stakes soccer match." Booklist

Lockdown. Amistad 2010 247p $16.99; lib bdg $17.89

Grades: 8 9 10 11 12 **Fic**

1. Old age -- Fiction 2. Friendship -- Fiction 3. African Americans -- Fiction 4. Juvenile delinquency -- Fiction

ISBN 978-0-06-121480-6; 0-06-121480-9; 978-0-06-121481-3 lib bdg; 0-06-121481-7 lib bdg

LC 2009-7287

Coretta Scott King Author Award honor book, 2011

Teenage Reese, serving time at a juvenile detention facility, gets a lesson in making it through hard times from an unlikely friend with a harrowing past.

"Reese's first-person narration rings with authenticity. . . . Myers' storytelling skills ensure that the messages he offers are never heavy-handed." Booklist

★ **Monster**; illustrations by Christopher Myers. HarperCollins Pubs. 1999 281p il $14.95; lib bdg $14.89; pa $8.99

Grades: 7 8 9 10 **Fic**

1. Trials -- Fiction 2. African Americans -- Fiction

ISBN 0-06-028077-8; 0-06-028078-6 lib bdg; 0-06-440731-4 pa

LC 98-40958

Michael L. Printz Award, 2000

While on trial as an accomplice to a murder, sixteen-year-old Steve Harmon records his experiences in prison and in the courtroom in the form of a film script as he tries to come to terms with the course his life has taken.

"Balancing courtroom drama and a sordid jailhouse setting with flashbacks to the crime, Myers adeptly allows each character to speak for him or herself, leaving readers to judge for themselves the truthfulness of the defendants, witnesses, lawyers, and, most compellingly, Steve himself." Horn Book Guide

Oh, Snap! by Walter Dean Myers. Scholastic 2013 128 p. (hardcover) $17.99

Grades: 6 7 8 9 **Fic**

1. Theft -- Fiction 2. Journalists -- Fiction

ISBN 0439916291; 9780439916295

This is the fourth book in Walter Dean Myers's Cruisers series. Here, the "four budding urban journalists are psyched that their underground publication, 'The Cruiser,' was named the third-best school newspaper in the city, an honor that doesn't sit well with the official school newspaper, which ups its game. This pushes narrator Zander to hastily get involved with the case of Phat Tony, a wannabe rapper classmate who may be involved in a robbery." (Booklist)

On a clear day; Walter Dean Myers. First edition Crown Books for Young Readers, an imprint of Random House Children's Books 2014 256 p. (hardcover) $17.99

Grades: 6 7 8 9 10 **Fic**

1. Science fiction 2. Dystopian fiction 3. Teenagers -- Fiction 4. Social action -- Fiction 5. Interpersonal relations -- Fiction 6. England -- Fiction

ISBN 0385387539; 9780385387538; 9780385387545

LC 2013046708

Kirkus (August 2014)

In this book, by Walter Dean Myers, "[y]oung heroes decide that they are not too young or too powerless to change their world. . . . It is 2035. Teens, armed only with their ideals, must wage war on the power elite. Dahlia is a Low Gater. . . . The Gaters live in closed safe communities, protected from the Sturmers, mercenary thugs. And the C-8, a consortium of giant companies, control global access to finance, media, food, water, and energy resources." (Publisher's note)

"Readers are left to question what actions are possible, what actions are needed and what actions are right in a world where inaction is an impossibility. A clarion call from a beloved, much-missed master." Kirkus

★ **Riot.** Egmont 2009 164p $16.99; lib bdg $19.99; pa $8.99

Grades: 7 8 9 10 11 12   **Fic**

1. Riots -- Fiction 2. Race relations -- Fiction 3. Irish Americans -- Fiction 4. New York (N.Y.) -- Fiction 5. African Americans -- Fiction 6. Racially mixed people -- Fiction

ISBN 978-1-60684-000-9; 1-60684-000-2; 978-1-60684-042-9 lib bdg; 1-60684-042-8 lib bdg; 978-1-60684-209-6 pa; 1-60684-209-9 pa

LC 2009-14638

In 1863, fifteen-year-old Claire, the daughter of an Irish mother and a black father, faces ugly truths and great danger when Irish immigrants, enraged by the Civil War and a federal draft, lash out against blacks and wealthy "swells" of New York City.

"In this fast, dramatic novel told in screenplay format, Myers takes on a controversial historical conflict that is seldom written about. . . . There are no easy resolutions, idealized characters, or stereotypes, and the conflicts are unforgettable." Booklist

Scorpions. Harper & Row 1988 216p $16.99; lib bdg $16.89; pa $5.99

Grades: 6 7 8 9   **Fic**

1. African Americans -- Fiction 2. Juvenile delinquency -- Fiction 3. Harlem (New York, N.Y.) -- Fiction

ISBN 0-06-024364-3; 0-06-024365-1 lib bdg; 0-06-447066-0 pa

LC 85-45815

A Newbery Medal honor book, 1989

Set in Harlem, this "story presents a brutally honest picture of the tragic influence of gang membership and pressures on a young black adolescent. Jamal Hicks, age twelve, reluctantly follows the orders of his older brother, now serving time in prison for robbery, and takes his place as leader of the Scorpions. When Jamal's leadership is challenged, disaster follows and Jamal learns some tragic lessons about friendship and owning a gun." Child Book Rev Serv

★ **Slam!** Scholastic Press 1996 266p hardcover o.p. pa $5.99

Grades: 7 8 9 10   **Fic**

1. School stories 2. Basketball -- Fiction 3. African Americans -- Fiction

ISBN 0-590-48667-5; 0-590-48668-3 pa

LC 95-46647

Coretta Scott King Award for text

Seventeen-year-old "Slam" Harris is counting on his noteworthy basketball talents to get him out of the inner city and give him a chance to succeed in life, but his coach sees things differently

Myers "descriptions of Slam on the court . . . use crisp details, not flowery language, to achieve their muscular poetry, and Myers is equally vivid in relating the torment Slam feels as he stares at a page of indecipherable algebra formulas. . . . [This is an] admirably realistic coming-of-age novel." Booklist

A **star** is born; Walter Dean Myers. Scholastic 2012 176 p. (Cruisers) (ebook) $17.99; (hardcover) $17.99

Grades: 6 7 8 9   **Fic**

1. School stories 2. Autism -- Fiction 3. Siblings -- Fiction 4. Gifted children -- Fiction 5. Schools -- Fiction 6. Theater -- Fiction 7. Middle schools -- Fiction 8. African Americans -- Fiction 9. Brothers and sisters -- Fiction 10. Harlem (New York, N.Y.) -- Fiction

ISBN 9780545512688; 9780439916288

LC 2011030333

This book is the third in the Cruisers series. "For 14-year-old LaShonda Powell, real life is a lot tougher than solving for x and y in algebra class. She's been offered a full scholarship to the Virginia Woolf Society Program for Young Ladies, thanks to her costume designs for the recent class play, and if she completes the program, she'll qualify for future college scholarships. The problem is that LaShonda lives in a group home with her autistic brother, Chris, and the two are inseparable." (Kirkus)

Street love. Amistad/Harper Tempest 2006 134p $15.99; lib bdg $16.89

Grades: 8 9 10 11 12   **Fic**

1. Novels in verse 2. African Americans -- Fiction 3. Harlem (New York, N.Y.) -- Fiction

ISBN 978-0-06-028079-6; 0-06-028079-4; 978-0-06-028080-2 lib bdg; 0-06-028080-8 lib bdg

LC 2006-02457

This story told in free verse is set against a background of street gangs and poverty in Harlem in which seventeen-year-old African American Damien takes a bold step to ensure that he and his new love will not be separated.

"The realistic drama on the street and at home tells a gripping story." Booklist

★ **Sunrise** over Fallujah. Scholastic Press 2008 290p $17.99

Grades: 8 9 10 11 12   **Fic**

1. Iraq War, 2003- -- Fiction 2. African Americans -- Fiction

ISBN 978-0-439-91624-0; 0-439-91624-0

LC 2007-25444

"Instead of heading to college as his father wishes, Robin leaves Harlem and joins the army to stand up for his country after 9/11. While stationed in Iraq with a war looming that he hopes will be averted, he begins writing letters home to his parents and to his Uncle Richie. . . . Myers brilliantly freeze-frames the opening months of the current Iraq War by realistically capturing its pivotal moments in 2003 and creating a vivid setting. Memorable characters share instances of wry levity that balance the story without deflecting its serious tone." SLJ

Myklusch, Matt

Jack Blank and the Imagine Nation. Aladdin 2010 480p $16.99

Grades: 4 5 6 7   **Fic**

1. Fantasy fiction 2. Science fiction 3. Orphans -- Fiction 4. Superheroes -- Fiction

ISBN 978-1-4169-9561-6; 1-4169-9561-7

Twelve-year-old Jack, freed from a dismal orphanage, makes his way to the elusive and impossible Imagine Nation, where a mentor saves him from dissection and trains him to use his superpower, despite the virus he carries that makes him a threat.

This creates "a richly imagined world with strong appeal to fans of comics. The island is populated by a fun cast of heroes and villains. . . . Brisk narration captures the superhero world with a mixture of fast-paced action, wry humor, and occasional heartfelt speeches about courage and friendship." SLJ

Followed by: Jack Blank and the secret war (2011)

The **secret** war. Aladdin 2011 529p $16.99

Grades: 4 5 6 7   **Fic**

1. Fantasy fiction 2. Orphans -- Fiction 3. Viruses -- Fiction 4. Superheroes -- Fiction

ISBN 978-1-4169-9564-7; 1-4169-9564-1

      LC 2010041779

Sequel to: Jack Blank and the Imagine Nation (2010)

Twelve-year-old Jack may be the Imagine Nation's only hope of fending off a new Rustov attack, with the help of his fellow superheroes-in-training, but the virus he carries, and Jonas's suspicions, provide new complications.

Myracle, Lauren

Eleven. Dutton Children's Books 2004 201p (The Winnie years) $16.99; pa $6.99

Grades: 4 5 6 7   **Fic**

1. Friendship -- Fiction 2. Family life -- Fiction

ISBN 0-525-47165-0; 0-14-240346-6 pa

      LC 2003-49076

The year between turning eleven and turning twelve bring many changes for Winnie and her friends

"The inclusion of details about the everyday lives of these girls . . . will make this novel enjoyable, even for reluctant readers. However, it's the book's occasional revelation of harder truths that lifts it out of the ordinary." SLJ

Other titles in this series are:

Twelve (2007)

Thirteen (2008)

Thirteen plus one (2010)

Ten (2011)

★ **Luv** ya bunches. Amulet Books 2009 335p $15.95

Grades: 4 5 6   **Fic**

1. School stories 2. Friendship -- Fiction

ISBN 978-0-8109-4211-0; 0-8109-4211-9

      LC 2009012585

Four friends—each named after a flower—navigate the ups and downs of fifth grade. Told through text messages, blog posts, screenplay, and straight narrative

Myracle "displays a shining awareness of and sensitivity to the highly textured society of tween girls. . . . This is a fun, challenging, and gently edifying story." Booklist

Another title about these characters is:

Violet in bloom (2010)

Peace, love, and baby ducks. Dutton Children's Books 2009 292p $16.99; pa $8.99

Grades: 8 9 10 11 12   **Fic**

1. Sisters -- Fiction 2. Atlanta (Ga.) -- Fiction

ISBN 978-0-525-47743-3; 0-525-47743-8; 978-0-14-241527-6 pa; 0-14-241527-8 pa

      LC 2008-34221

Fifteen-year-old Carly's summer volunteer experience makes her feel more real than her life of privilege in Atlanta ever did, but her younger sister starts high school pretending to be what she is not, and both find their relationships suffering.

"Myracle empathetically explores issues of socioeconomic class, sibling rivalry, and parental influence in a story that is deeper and more nuanced than the title and cutesy cover." Booklist

Violet in bloom; a flower power book. Amulet Books 2010 366p $15.95

Grades: 4 5 6   **Fic**

1. School stories 2. Food -- Fiction 3. California -- Fiction 4. Friendship -- Fiction

ISBN 978-0-8109-8983-2; 0-8109-8983-2

      LC 2010-24319

Fifth-graders Katie-Rose, Violet, Milla, and Yasaman seem to have little in common except their flower-related names, but they nurture their new friendship through a social-networking site and a campaign to have healthier snacks served at school.

This is "a realistic, easy-to-relate-to riot of pre-adolescent exuberance. A triumph." Kirkus

Na, An

★ A **step** from heaven. Front St. 2000 156p $15.95

Grades: 7 8 9 10   **Fic**

1. Family life -- Fiction 2. Korean Americans -- Fiction

ISBN 1-88691-058-8

      LC 00-41083

Michael L. Printz Award, 2002

A young Korean girl and her family find it difficult to learn English and adjust to life in America

"This isn't a quick read, especially at the beginning when the child is trying to decipher American words and customs, but the coming-of-age drama will grab teens and make them think of their own conflicts between home and outside. As in the best writing, the particulars make the story universal." Booklist

Wait for me. Putnam 2006 169p hardcover o.p. pa $7.99

Grades: 8 9 10 11 12   **Fic**

1. Deaf -- Fiction 2. Sisters -- Fiction 3. Korean Americans -- Fiction 4. Mother-daughter relationship -- Fiction

ISBN 0-399-24275-9; 0-14-240918-9 pa

      LC 2005-30931

As her senior year in high school approaches, Mina yearns to find her own path in life but working at the family business, taking care of her little sister, and dealing with her mother's impossible expectations are as stifling as the southern California heat, until she falls in love with a man who offers a way out.

"This is a well-crafted tale, sensitively told. . . . The mother-daughter conflict will resonate with teens of any culture who have wrestled parents for the right to choose their own paths." Bull Cent Child Books

Naftali, Joel

The **rendering**; [by] Joel Naftali. Egmont USA 2011 275p $15.99

Grades: 5 6 7 8 **Fic**

1. Science fiction 2. Adventure fiction 3. Weblogs -- Fiction

ISBN 978-1-60684-118-1; 1-60684-118-1

LC 2010-36640

Thirteen-year-old Doug relates in a series of blog posts the story of how he saved the world but was falsely branded a terrorist and murderer, forced to fight the evil Dr. Roach and his armored biodroid army with an electronics-destroying superpower of his own.

"Naftali balances tragedy and absurd humor with aplomb, not an easy task when dealing with horrific explosions and giant wisecracking skunks. Readers seeking a fast-paced, action-packed adventure will find this eminently suitable." Bull Cent Child Books

Naidoo, Beverley

★ **Burn** my heart. HarperCollins 2009 209p $15.99; lib bdg $16.89

Grades: 7 8 9 10 11 12 **Fic**

1. Kenya -- Fiction 2. Friendship -- Fiction 3. Race relations -- Fiction

ISBN 978-0-06-143297-2; 0-06-143297-0; 978-0-06-143298-9 lib bdg; 0-06-143298-9 lib bdg

LC 2008-928322

First published 2007 in the United Kingdom

This "is an interesting story of which few people will be aware but might wish to know more. This solid novel would be a good multicultural addition to a teen collection." Voice Youth Advocates

★ **Journey** to Jo'burg; a South African story. illustrations by Eric Velasquez. Lippincott 1986 80p il hardcover o.p. pa $4.99

Grades: 5 6 7 8 **Fic**

1. South Africa -- Race relations -- Fiction

ISBN 0-06-440237-1 pa

LC 85-45508

"This touching novel graphically depicts the plight of Africans living in the horror of South Africa. Thirteen-year-old Maledi and her 9-year-old brother leave their small village, take the perilous journey to the city, and encounter, firsthand, the painful struggle for justice, freedom, and dignity in the 'City of Gold.' A provocative story with a message readers will long remember." Soc Educ

Followed by Chain of fire (1990)

★ The **other** side of truth. HarperCollins Pubs. 2001 252p hardcover o.p. pa $5.99

Grades: 5 6 7 8 **Fic**

1. Nigeria -- Fiction 2. Africans -- Fiction 3. Refugees -- Fiction 4. London (England) -- Fiction

ISBN 0-06-029628-3; 0-06-441002-1 pa

LC 00-54112

First published 2000 in the United Kingdom

Smuggled out of Nigeria after their mother's murder, Sade and her younger brother are abandoned in London when their uncle fails to meet them at the airport and they are fearful of their new surroundings and of what may have happened to their journalist father back in Nigeria

"Part survival adventure, part docudrama, the narrative stays true to Sade's viewpoint. . . . This powerful novel brings the news images very close." Booklist

Followed by Web of lies (2006)

Web of lies. HarperCollins Pub. 2006 256p lib bdg $16.89; $15.99

Grades: 6 7 8 9 **Fic**

1. Gangs -- Fiction 2. Africans -- Fiction 3. Refugees -- Fiction 4. London (England) -- Fiction

ISBN 0-06-076077-X lib bdg; 0-06-076075-3

"In The Other Side of Truth (2001), Naidoo brings politics close through the eyes of Sade, who, following the assassination of her mother in Nigeria, flees to London with her brother, Femi. Now, two years later, the children have been reunited with their father, as the refugee family waits for asylum. The focus this time is on Femi, 12, who succumbs to pressure to join a violent gang. . . . Readers will want to talk about the issues Naidoo raises here." Booklist

Nails, Jennifer

Next to Mexico; by Jennifer Nails. Houghton Mifflin Harcourt 2008 235p $16

Grades: 4 5 6 **Fic**

1. School stories 2. Arizona -- Fiction 3. Friendship -- Fiction 4. Mexican Americans -- Fiction

ISBN 978-0-618-96635-6; 0-618-96635-8

LC 2008007268

Outspoken, impulsive Lylice has skipped fifth grade, but she finds that getting along at Susan B. Anthony Middle School is more difficult than she expected, until she is assigned to be the English Buddy to Mexico Mendoza, a recent immigrant.

"Lylice humorously narrates this lively, thought-provoking story, becoming increasingly likeable and endearing." Voice Youth Advocates

Namioka, Lensey

Mismatch; a novel. Delacorte Press 2006 217p $15.95; lib bdg $17.99

Grades: 7 8 9 10 **Fic**

1. Prejudices -- Fiction 2. Chinese Americans -- Fiction 3. Japanese Americans -- Fiction 4. Dating (Social customs) -- Fiction

ISBN 0-385-73183-3; 0-385-90220-4 lib bdg

Their families clash when Andy, a Japanese-American teenaged boy, starts dating Sue, a Chinese-American teenaged girl.

"A story that is current, relevant, and upbeat." SLJ

★ An **ocean** apart, a world away. Delacorte Press 2002 197p hardcover o.p. pa $5.50

Grades: 5 6 7 8 **Fic**

1. Chinese -- United States -- Fiction

ISBN 0-385-73002-0; 0-440-22973-1 pa

LC 2002-73550

Despite the odds facing her decision to become a doctor in 1920's Nanking, China, teenaged Yanyan leaves her family to study at Cornell University where, along with hard work, she finds prejudice and loneliness as well as friendship and a new sense of accomplishment

"Without heavy messages, Namioka explores what it means to be independent." Booklist

Ties that bind, ties that break; a novel. Delacorte Press 1999 154p hardcover o.p. pa $5.50

Grades: 5 6 7 8   **Fic**
1. China -- Fiction 2. Sex role -- Fiction 3. Footbinding -- Fiction 4. Individuality -- Fiction 5. China -- History -- 1912-1928
ISBN 0-385-32666-1; 0-440-41599-3 pa
LC 98-27877

Ailin's life takes a different turn when she defies the traditions of upper class Chinese society by refusing to have her feet bound. "Grades seven to ten." (SLJ)

"In lyrical, descriptive prose, Namioka compassionately portrays a young girl's coming-of-age in a repressive, challenging time." Booklist

Nance, Andrew
Daemon Hall; [by] Andrew Nance; with illustrations by Coleman Polhemus. Henry Holt 2007 259p $16.95

Grades: 7 8 9 10   **Fic**
1. Horror fiction 2. Authorship -- Fiction
ISBN 978-0-8050-8171-8; 0-8050-8171-2
LC 2006-31044

Famous horror story writer R. U. Tremblin comes to the town of Maplewood to hold a short story writing contest, offering the five finalists the chance to spend what turns out to be a terrifying—and deadly—night with him in a haunted house.

"Readers looking for creepy chills and thrills will find plenty of satisfaction in this fast-paced book." Booklist

Followed by: Return to Daemon hall (2011)

Return to Daemon Hall: evil roots; with illustrations by Coleman Polhemus. Henry Holt 2011 240p il $16.99

Grades: 7 8 9 10   **Fic**
1. Horror fiction 2. Authors -- Fiction 3. Contests -- Fiction 4. Authorship -- Fiction 5. Storytelling -- Fiction
ISBN 978-0-8050-8748-2; 0-8050-8748-6
LC 2010048609

Sequel to: Daemon Hall (2007)

Wade and Demarius go to author Ian Tremblin's home as judges of the second writing contest but soon are mysteriously transported to Daemon Hall, where they and the three finalists must tell—and act out—the stories each has written.

"Polhemus' stark artwork builds the mood, with heavy lines and crosshatching complementing the campfire nature of the tales." Kirkus

Nanji, Shenaaz
Child of dandelions. Front Street 2008 214p $17.95

Grades: 7 8 9 10 11 12   **Fic**
1. Generals 2. Presidents 3. Uganda -- Fiction 4. Family life -- Fiction 5. East Indians -- Fiction
ISBN 978-1-93242-593-2; 1-93242-593-4
LC 2007-31576

In Uganda in 1972, fifteen-year-old Sabine and her family, wealthy citizens of Indian descent, try to preserve their normal life during the ninety days allowed by President Idi Amin for all foreign Indians to leave the country, while soldiers and others terrorize them and people disappear.

"This is an absorbing story rich with historical detail and human dynamics." Bull Cent Child Books

Napoli, Donna Jo
Alligator bayou. Wendy Lamb Books 2009 280p $16.99; lib bdg $19.99

Grades: 6 7 8 9 10   **Fic**
1. Uncles -- Fiction 2. Louisiana -- Fiction 3. Prejudices -- Fiction 4. Country life -- Fiction 5. Italian Americans -- Fiction 6. United States -- History -- Fiction
ISBN 978-0-385-74654-0; 0-385-74654-7; 978-0-385-90891-7 lib bdg; 0-385-90891-1 lib bdg
LC 2008-14504

Fourteen-year-old Calogero Scalise and his Sicilian uncles and cousin live in small-town Louisiana in 1898, when Jim Crow laws rule and anti-immigration sentiment is strong, so despite his attempts to be polite and to follow American customs, disaster dogs his family at every turn.

"Napoli's skillful pacing and fascinating detail combine in a gripping story that sheds cold, new light on Southern history and on the nature of racial prejudice." Booklist

★ **Beast**. Atheneum Bks. for Young Readers 2000 260p hardcover o.p. pa $8

Grades: 7 8 9 10   **Fic**
1. Fairy tales 2. Iran -- Fiction
ISBN 0-689-83589-2; 0-689-87005-1 pa
LC 99-89923

"The reader is immersed in the imagery and spirituality of ancient Persia. . . . Although Napoli uses Farsi (Persian) and Arabic words in the text (there is a glossary), this only adds to the texture and richness of her remarkable piece of writing." Book Rep

Bound. Atheneum Books for Young Readers 2004 186p hardcover o.p. pa $5.99

Grades: 8 9 10 11 12   **Fic**
1. China -- Fiction 2. Sex role -- Fiction
ISBN 0-689-86175-3; 0-689-86178-8 pa
LC 2004-365

In a novel based on Chinese Cinderella tales, fourteen-year-old stepchild Xing-Xing endures a life of neglect and servitude, as her stepmother cruelly mutilates her own child's feet so that she alone might marry well

The author "fleshes out and enriches the story with well-rounded characters and with accurate information about a specific time and place in Chinese history; the result is a dramatic and masterful retelling." SLJ

Fire in the hills. Dutton Children's Books 2006 215p hardcover o.p. pa $7.99

Grades: 5 6 7 8   **Fic**
1. Italy -- Fiction 2. World War, 1939-1945 -- Fiction
ISBN 0-525-47751-9; 0-14-241200-7 pa
Sequel to Stones in water (1997)
Upon returning to Italy, fourteen-year-old Roberto struggles to survive, first on his own, then as a member of the resistance, fighting against the Nazi occupiers while yearning to reach home safely and for an end to the war.
"This well-written book grips the reader from the beginning and on through Roberto's adventures." Voice Youth Advocates

The **great** god Pan. Wendy Lamb Bks. 2003 149p $15.95; lib bdg $17.99
Grades: 7 8 9 10   **Fic**
1. Pan (Greek deity) -- Fiction 2. Classical mythology -- Fiction
ISBN 0-385-32777-3; 0-385-90120-8 lib bdg
    LC 2002-13139
A retelling of the Greek myths about Pan, both goat and god, whose reed flute frolicking leads him to a meeting with Iphigenia, a human raised as the daughter of King Agamemnon and Queen Clytemnestra
"Filling in gaps that appear in other myths about Pan and Iphigenia, Napoli creates a novel filled with breathtaking language about nature, music, and desire. Teen readers will swoon." Booklist

★ **Hush**; an Irish princess' tale. Atheneum Books for Young Readers 2007 308p $16.99
Grades: 8 9 10 11 12   **Fic**
1. Ireland -- Fiction 2. Slavery -- Fiction 3. Princesses -- Fiction 4. Middle Ages -- Fiction
ISBN 978-0-689-86176-5; 0-689-86176-1
    LC 2007-2676
Fifteen-year-old Melkorka, an Irish princess, is kidnapped by Russian slave traders and not only learns how to survive but to challenge some of the brutality of her captors, who are fascinated by her apparent muteness and the possibility that she is enchanted.
This is a "powerful survival story. . . . Napoli does not shy from detailing practices that will make readers wince . . . and the Russian crew repeatedly gang-rapes an older captive. . . . The tension over Mel's hopes for escape paces this story like a thriller." Publ Wkly

Lights on the Nile. HarperCollins 2011 278p $16.99; lib bdg $17.89
Grades: 4 5 6 7   **Fic**
1. Baboons -- Fiction 2. Fairies -- Fiction 3. Kidnapping -- Fiction 4. Egypt -- History -- Fiction
ISBN 978-0-06-166793-0; 0-06-166793-5; 978-0-06-166794-7 lib bdg; 0-06-166794-3 lib bdg
    LC 2011010179
Ten-year-old Kepi, a young girl in ancient Egypt, embarks on a journey to save her family when she is unexpectedly taken captive, along with the baby baboon she has rescued from a crocodile.
Napoli "crafts a mystical coming-of-age tale and a love letter of sorts to Egypt, saturated with proverbs, intriguing details of everyday life at the time, and rich descriptions of

the places Kepi visits. . . . Kepi's survival skills and perspective are challenged in this absorbing adventure." Publ Wkly

The **smile**. Dutton Children's Books 2008 260p $17.99
Grades: 7 8 9 10   **Fic**
1. Artists 2. Painters 3. Scientists 4. Artists -- Fiction 5. Writers on science 6. Renaissance -- Fiction 7. Italy -- History -- 0-1559 -- Fiction
ISBN 978-0-525-47999-4; 0-525-47999-6
    LC 2007-48522
In Renaissance Italy, Elisabetta longs for romance, and when Leonardo da Vinci introduces her to Guiliano de Medici, whose family rules Florence but is about to be deposed, she has no inkling of the romance—and sorrow—that will ensue.
"Napoli skillfully draws readers into the vibrant settings . . . with tangible, sensory details that enliven the novel's intriguing references to history and art. Elisabetta's strength and individuality . . . will captivate readers." Booklist

★ **Stones** in water. Dutton Children's Bks. 1997 209p hardcover o.p. pa $5.99
Grades: 5 6 7 8   **Fic**
1. World War, 1939-1945 -- Fiction
ISBN 0-525-45842-5; 0-14-130600-9 pa
    LC 97-14253
After being taken by German soldiers from a local movie theater along with other Italian boys including his Jewish friend, Roberto is forced to work in Germany, escapes into the Ukrainian winter, before desperately trying to make his way back home to Venice
This is a "gripping, meticulously researched story (loosely based on the life of an actual survivor)." Publ Wkly

Storm; Donna Jo Napoli. Simon & Schuster 2014 350 p. (hardback) $17.99
Grades: 8 9 10 11 12   **Fic**
1. Noah's ark -- Fiction 2. Survival after airplane accidents, shipwrecks, etc. -- Fiction 3. Deluge -- Fiction 4. Animals -- Fiction 5. Survival -- Fiction
ISBN 1481403028; 9781481403023
    LC 2013026808
National Jewish Book Award: Children's and Young Adult (2014)
This young adult novel, by Donna Jo Napoli, is a reimagining of the Noah flood myth. "After days of downpour, her family lost, Sebah . . . is tempted just to die in the flames rather than succumb to a slow, watery death. Instead, she and Aban build a raft. What they find on the stormy seas is beyond imagining: a gigantic ark. But Sebah does not know what she'll find on board, and Aban is too weak to leave their raft." (Publisher's note)
"Sixteen-year-old Sebah, a Canaanite girl, survives a massive flood that kills her family. As the rains continue, she encounters a giant boat--Noah's ark. Exhausted and grief-stricken, Sebah finds herself in a cage with a pair of bonobos, with whom she soon bonds. The characters that Napoli creates to flesh out her retelling of the classic story add depth." Horn Book

The **wager**. Henry Holt 2010 262p il $16.99

Grades: 8 9 10 11 12 **Fic**
1. Fairy tales 2. Devil -- Fiction 3. Sicily (Italy) -- Fiction
ISBN 978-0-8050-8781-9; 0-8050-8781-8
LC 2009-23436

Having lost everything in a tidal wave in 1169 Sicily, nineteen-year-old Don Giovanni makes a simple-sounding wager with a stranger he recognizes as the devil but, while desperate enough to surrender his pride and good looks for three years, he is not willing to give up his soul.

"Evocative of Hermann Hesse's Siddhartha, this marvelous story is well told, and the rich, sophisticated language will grip skilled readers." SLJ

Naylor, Phyllis Reynolds
Alice in April. Atheneum Pubs. 1993 164p hardcover o.p. pa $5.99
Grades: 5 6 7 8 **Fic**
1. School stories 2. Family life -- Fiction
ISBN 0-689-31805-7; 978-1-442-42757-0 pa; 1-442-42757-4 pa
LC 92-17016

While trying to survive seventh grade, Alice discovers that turning thirteen will make her the Woman of the House at home, so she starts a campaign to get more appreciated for taking care of her father and older brother

"Deftly written dialogue and an empathetic tone neatly balance substantial themes with plain good fun." Publ Wkly

Alice in lace. Atheneum Bks. for Young Readers 1996 139p hardcover o.p. pa $5.99
Grades: 5 6 7 8 **Fic**
1. School stories 2. Family life -- Fiction
ISBN 0-689-80358-3; 0-689-80597-7 pa
LC 95-30903

"In this newest stage of Alice's journey to adulthood, the appealing heroine begins eighth grade with a million questions and few answers. . . . Naylor obviously has fun exploring friendship, family, relationships, and even love. With all of these issues permeating the story, Alice and her friends are a little more serious than in previous titles, but readers will still find plenty to laugh at and cheer about." SLJ

Alice in rapture, sort of. Atheneum Pubs. 1989 166p hardcover o.p. pa $5.99
Grades: 5 6 7 8 **Fic**
1. Family life -- Fiction
ISBN 0-689-31466-3; 1-442-42362-5 pa
LC 88-8174

The summer before she enters the seventh grade becomes the summer of Alice's first boyfriend, and she discovers that love is about the most mixed-up thing that can possibly happen to you, especially since she has no mother to go to for advice

"A book that is wise, perceptive, and hilarious." SLJ

Alice in-between. Atheneum Pubs. 1994 144p pa $5.99
Grades: 4 5 6 7 **Fic**
1. Family life -- Fiction
ISBN 0-689-31890-1; 1-416-96770-2 pa
LC 93-8167

When motherless Alice turns thirteen she feels in-between, no longer a child but not yet a woman, and discovers that growing up can be both frustrating and wonderful

"This is bound to reassure the many adolescent fans who can identify with the 'in-between blues.'" SLJ

Alice on her way. Atheneum Books for Young Readers 2005 322p hardcover o.p. pa $6.99
Grades: 7 8 9 10 **Fic**
1. School stories 2. Family life -- Fiction 3. Stepmothers -- Fiction
ISBN 0-689-87090-6; 0-689-87091-4 pa
LC 2004-21203

Alice is adjusting to her new stepmother, her brother's new apartment, her ex-boyfriend, and getting a driver's license.

"Naylor depicts her character confronting contemporary coming-of-age issues, big and small, with openness, humor, intimacy, and surprise." Booklist

Alice the brave. Atheneum Bks. for Young Readers 1995 130p pa $7.99
Grades: 5 6 7 8 **Fic**
1. Fear -- Fiction 2. Family life -- Fiction
ISBN 0-689-80095-9; 1-416-97542-X pa
LC 94-32340

The summer before eighth grade, Alice tries to confront her fears, not the least of which is a fear of deep water.

"Alice's wry, funny, vulnerable voice expresses every girl's fears about what is 'normal' in an imperfect world." Booklist

All but Alice. Atheneum Pubs. 1992 151p hardcover o.p. pa $5.99
Grades: 5 6 7 8 **Fic**
1. School stories 2. Clubs -- Fiction
ISBN 0-689-31773-5; 1-442-42756-6 pa
LC 91-28722

Seventh grader Alice decides that the only way to stave off personal and social disasters is to be part of the crowd, especially the "in" crowd, no matter how boring and, potentially, difficult

"Naylor's light, but deft touch with important thematic concerns is most appealing." SLJ

Almost Alice. Atheneum Books for Young Readers 2008 272p $16.99
Grades: 9 10 11 12 **Fic**
1. School stories 2. Friendship -- Fiction
ISBN 978-0-689-87096-5; 0-689-87096-5
LC 2007-037457

In the second semester of her junior year of high school, Alice gets back together with her old boyfriend Patrick, gets a promotion on the student newspaper, and remains a reliable, trusted friend.

"Naylor confronts head-on the serious realities of an unplanned pregnancy and the decisions that need to be made." Horn Book

Cricket man. Atheneum Books for Young Readers 2008 208p $16.99

Grades: 6 7 8 9 **Fic**

1. School stories 2. Maryland -- Fiction 3. Pregnancy -- Fiction 4. Family life -- Fiction 5. Skateboarding -- Fiction 6. Heroes and heroines -- Fiction
ISBN 978-1-416-94981-7; 1-416-94981-X

LC 2008-05889

Thirteen-year-old Kenny secretly calls himself "Cricket Man" after a summer of rescuing creatures from his family's Bethesda, Maryland, pool, which gives him more self-confidence and an urge to be a hero, especially for his depressed sixteen-year-old neighbor, Jodie.

"Naylor sketches a sensitive portrayal of life in middle school. . . . An involving novel by a fine storyteller." Booklist

Dangerously Alice. Atheneum Books for Young Readers 2007 294p $15.99

Grades: 7 8 9 10 **Fic**

1. School stories 2. Maryland -- Fiction 3. Family life -- Fiction
ISBN 978-0-689-87094-1; 0-689-87094-9

LC 2006-24181

During fall semester of her junior year of high school, Alice decides to change her good girl image, while major remodeling begins at home and some important relationships begin to change.

"The dialogue is right-on, and . . . teens will love the funny, honest, nonmessagey drama on the edge." Booklist

Faith, hope, and Ivy June. Delacorte Press 2009 280p $16.99; lib bdg $19.99

Grades: 5 6 7 8 **Fic**

1. School stories 2. Kentucky -- Fiction 3. Appalachian region -- Fiction
ISBN 978-0-385-73615-2; 0-385-73615-0; 978-0-385-90588-6 lib bdg; 0-385-90588-2 lib bdg

LC 2008-19625

During a student exchange program, seventh-graders Ivy June and Catherine share their lives, homes, and communities, and find that although their lifestyles are total opposites they have a lot in common.

"This finely crafted novel . . . depicts a deep friendship growing slowly through understanding. As both girls wait out tragedies at the book's end, they cling to hope—and each other—in a thoroughly real and unaffected way. Naylor depicts Appalachia with sympathetic realism." Kirkus

Incredibly Alice. Atheneum Books for Young Readers 2011 278p $16.99

Grades: 7 8 9 10 **Fic**

1. School stories 2. Theater -- Fiction 3. Maryland -- Fiction 4. Family life -- Fiction 5. Dating (Social customs) -- Fiction
ISBN 978-1-4169-7553-3; 1-4169-7553-5

LC 2010036982

Maryland teenager Alice McKinley spends her last semester of high school performing in the school play, working on the student paper, worrying about being away from her boyfriend, who will be studying in Spain, and anticipating her future in college.

"Realistic and satisfying, Alice and friends' bittersweet senior year's ending and their preparations for adulthood's exciting and intimidating world will resonate with any high school female." Voice Youth Advocates

Intensely Alice. Atheneum Books for Young Readers 2009 269p $16.99; pa $6.99

Grades: 7 8 9 10 **Fic**

1. Summer -- Fiction 2. Maryland -- Fiction
ISBN 978-1-4169-7551-9; 1-4169-7551-9; 978-1-4169-7554-0 pa; 1-4169-7554-3 pa

LC 2008-49047

During the summer between her junior and senior years of high school, Maryland teenager Alice McKinley volunteers at a local soup kitchen, tries to do "something wild" without getting arrested, and wonders if her trip to Chicago to visit boyfriend Patrick will result in a sleepover.

"As candid, funny, and touching as the rest of the series." Booklist

Outrageously Alice. Atheneum Bks. for Young Readers 1997 133p $16.99; pa $5.99

Grades: 5 6 7 8 **Fic**

1. School stories 2. Family life -- Fiction
ISBN 0-689-80354-0; 0-689-80596-9 pa

LC 96-7744

"Alice is, as always, likable, humorous, and true to life." SLJ

★ **Reluctantly** Alice. Atheneum Pubs. 1991 182p $16; pa $4.99

Grades: 7 8 9 10 **Fic**

1. School stories 2. Family life -- Fiction
ISBN 0-689-31681-X; 0-689-81688-X pa

LC 90-37956

Alice experiences the joys and embarrassments of seventh grade while advising her father and older brother on their love lives

"Naylor combines laugh-out-loud scenes with moments of sudden gentleness. . . . The characters are complex, the dialogue is droll, the junior high world authentic." Booklist

Other titles about Alice are:
Achingly Alice (1998)
Alice alone (2001)
Alice in-between (1994)
Alice in lace (1996)
Alice in the know (2006)
Alice on her way (2005)
Alice on the outside (1999)
Alice the brave (1995)
All but Alice (1992)
Almost Alice (2008)
Intensely Alice (2009)
Dangerously Alice (2007)
The grooming of Alice (2000)
Including Alice (2004)
Outrageously Alice (1997)
Patiently Alice (2003)
Simply Alice (2002)

Saving Shiloh. Atheneum Bks. for Young Readers 1997 137p $17.99; pa $5.99

Grades: 4 5 6 **Fic**

1. Dogs -- Fiction 2. West Virginia -- Fiction

ISBN 0-689-81460-7; 0-689-83582-5 pa

LC 96-37373

Sequel to: Shiloh season (1996)

Marty and his family try to help their rough neighbor, Judd Travers, change his mean ways, even though their West Virginia community continues to expect the worst of him

"The West Virginia setting is wonderfully rendered, the dialect is authentic, the characters are memorable, and the narration is nicely paced." SLJ

★ **Shiloh**. Atheneum Pubs. 1991 144p $16.95; pa $6.99

Grades: 4 5 6 **Fic**

1. Dogs -- Fiction 2. West Virginia -- Fiction

ISBN 0-689-31614-3; 0-689-83582-5 pa

LC 90-603

Awarded the Newbery Medal, 1992

When he finds a lost beagle in the hills behind his West Virginia home, Marty tries to hide it from his family and the dog's real owner, a mean-spirited man known to shoot deer out of season and to mistreat his dogs

"A credible plot and characters, a well-drawn setting, and nicely paced narration combine in a story that leaves the reader feeling good." Horn Book

Other titles about Shiloh are:

Shiloh season (1996)

Saving Shiloh (1997)

Shiloh season. Atheneum Bks. for Young Readers 1996 120p pa $5.99

Grades: 4 5 6 **Fic**

1. Dogs -- Fiction 2. West Virginia -- Fiction

ISBN 0-689-80647-7; 0-689-80646-9 pa

LC 95-32558

Sequel to: Shiloh (1991)

"Although Marty has earned Shiloh by working for the dog's loathsome former owner, Judd Travers now wants Shiloh back. What's more, the resentful Judd is now drunk most of the time and hunting illegally on the Preston's property. . . Taut with suspense, touched by a fine sense of humanity, and narrated in an authentic West Virginia dialect, this compelling page-turner will be in justifiable demand." Booklist

Followed by: Saving Shiloh (1997)

Simply Alice. Atheneum Bks. for Young Readers 2002 222p $16; pa $5.99

Grades: 7 8 9 10 **Fic**

1. School stories

ISBN 0-689-82635-4; 0-689-85965-1 pa

LC 2001-35539

In her high school freshman year, fourteen-year-old Alice experiences changes and challenges with friends, family, and school activities, which leave her feeling better about herself than ever before

"The messages are neither superficial nor overearnest. Fans will grab this for the funny, honest daily drama of a teenager growing up now." Booklist

Neely, Cynthia

Unearthly; [by] Cynthia Hand. HarperTeen 2011 435p $17.99

Grades: 7 8 9 10 **Fic**

1. School stories 2. Angels -- Fiction 3. Moving -- Fiction 4. Wyoming -- Fiction 5. Supernatural -- Fiction

ISBN 978-0-06-199616-0; 0-06-199616-5

LC 2010-17849

Sixteen-year-old Clara Gardner's purpose as an angel-blood begins to manifest itself, forcing her family to pull up stakes and move to Jackson, Wyoming, where she learns that danger and heartbreak come with her powers.

"Hand avoids overt discussion of religion while telling an engaging and romantic tale with a solid backstory. Her characters deal realistically with the uncertainty of being on the cusp of maturity without wrapping themselves in angst." Publ Wkly

Neff, Henry H.

The **hound** of Rowan. Random House 2007 414p il (The tapestry) $17.99; lib bdg $20.99; pa $6.99

Grades: 6 7 8 9 **Fic**

1. School stories 2. Magic -- Fiction

ISBN 978-0-375-83894-1; 0-375-83894-5; 978-0-375-93894-8 lib bdg; 0-375-93894-4 lib bdg; 978-0-375-83895-8 pa; 0-375-83895-3 pa

LC 2006-20970

After glimpsing a hint of his destiny in a mysterious tapestry, twelve-year-old Max McDaniels becomes a student at Rowan Academy, where he trains in "mystics and combat" in preparation for war with an ancient enemy that has been kidnapping children like him.

"Max's intelligence and goodhearted nature give the story a solid emotional core even as the surprising twists and turns keep the pages turning." Voice Youth Advocates

Other titles in this series are:

The second siege (2008)

The fiend and the forge (2011)

Nelson, Blake

Destroy all cars. Scholastic Press 2009 218p $17.99

Grades: 7 8 9 10 **Fic**

1. School stories 2. Ecology -- Fiction 3. Social action -- Fiction

ISBN 978-0-545-10474-6; 0-545-10474-2

LC 2008-34850

Through assignments for English class, seventeen-year-old James Hoff rants against consumerism and his classmates' apathy, puzzles over his feelings for his ex-girlfriend, and expresses disdain for his emotionally-distant parents.

Nelson "offers an elegant and bittersweet story of a teenager who is finding his voice and trying to make meaning in a world he often finds hopeless." Publ Wkly

They came from below. Tor 2007 299p $17.95

Grades: 7 8 9 10 **Fic**

1. Beaches -- Fiction 2. Supernatural -- Fiction 3. Cape

Cod (Mass.) -- Fiction 4. Marine pollution -- Fiction
ISBN 978-0-7653-1423-9; 0-7653-1423-1

LC 2007-09542

While vacationing on Cape Cod, best friends Emily, age sixteen, and Reese, seventeen, meet Steve and Dave, who seem too good to be true, and whose presence turns out to be related to a dire threat of global pollution.

"Offering wittiness, suspense and ideologies borrowed from Eastern religions, Nelson reaches a new level of depth and creativity with this intriguing depiction of one very weird summer." Publ Wkly

Nelson, James

On the volcano. G.P. Putnam's Sons 2011 275p $16.99

Grades: 7 8 9 10   **Fic**
1. Violence -- Fiction 2. Volcanoes -- Fiction 3. Wilderness areas -- Fiction 4. Frontier and pioneer life -- Fiction
ISBN 978-0-399-25282-2; 0-399-25282-7

LC 2008-53557

In the 1870s, sixteen-year-old Katie has grown up in a remote cabin on the edge of a volcano with her father and their friend Lorraine, the only people she has ever seen, but, after eagerly anticipating it for so long, her first trip into a town ultimately brings tragedy into their lives.

"Nelson has created a moving tale of frontier life. Katie shows tremendous fighting spirit as she deal with the trials in her life. . . . [This] is perfect for historical fiction fans." Voice Youth Advocates

Nelson, Nina

Bringing the boy home; by N.A. Nelson. HarperCollinsPublishers 2008 211p $15.99; lib bdg $16.89

Grades: 5 6 7 8   **Fic**
1. Rain forests -- Fiction 2. Amazon River valley -- Fiction 3. Senses and sensation -- Fiction 4. Extrasensory perception -- Fiction
ISBN 978-0-06-088698-1; 0-06-088698-6; 978-0-06-088699-8 lib bdg; 0-06-088699-4 lib bdg

LC 2007-31702

As two Takunami youths approach their thirteenth birthdays, Luka reaches the culmination of his mother's training for the tribe's manhood test while Tirio, raised in Miami, Florida, by his adoptive mother, feels called to begin preparations to prove himself during his upcoming visit to the Amazon rain forest where he was born.

"The vivid setting, imagined cultural particulars . . . and magical realism will captivate readers." Booklist

Nelson, R. A.

Days of Little Texas. Alfred A. Knopf 2009 388p $16.99; lib bdg $19.99

Grades: 8 9 10 11 12   **Fic**
1. Ghost stories 2. Slavery -- Fiction 3. Supernatural -- Fiction 4. Good and evil -- Fiction 5. Christian life -- Fiction 6. Evangelistic work -- Fiction
ISBN 978-0-375-85593-1; 0-375-85593-9; 978-0-375-95593-8 lib bdg; 0-375-95593-3 lib bdg

LC 2008-33855

Sixteen-year-old Ronald Earl King, who has been a charismatic evangelist since he was ten years old, is about to preach at a huge revival meeting on the grounds of an old plantation, where, with confusing help from the ghost of a girl he could not heal, he becomes engaged in an epic battle between good and evil.

"Chapters are brief, the pace is rapid, and the tension is high as Ronald wrestles with demons both temporal and spiritual to find his place in the world. An affecting and sharply written story." SLJ

Nelson, Theresa

Ruby electric; a novel. Atheneum Bks. for Young Readers 2003 264p hardcover o.p. pa $5.99

Grades: 5 6 7 8   **Fic**
1. Fathers -- Fiction 2. Siblings -- Fiction 3. Authorship -- Fiction 4. California -- Fiction
ISBN 0-689-83852-2; 0-689-87146-5 pa

LC 2002-8034

Twelve-year-old Ruby Miller, movie buff and aspiring screen writer, tries to resolve the mysteries surrounding her little brother's stuffed woolly mammoth and their father's five year absence

"Ruby's voice is electric, and she is an unforgettable character with courage, a cause, and imagination." Booklist

Nelson, Vaunda Micheaux

No crystal stair; a documentary novel of the life and work of Lewis Michaux, Harlem bookseller. by Vaunda Micheaux Nelson; art work by R. Gregory Christie. Carolrhoda Lab 2012 188p. ill.

Grades: 6 7 8 9 10 11 12   **Fic**
1. Harlem (New York, N.Y.) 2. African American authors 3. Booksellers and bookselling 4. Harlem (New York, N.Y.) -- Fiction 5. African Americans -- Books and reading -- Fiction 6. Bookstores -- New York (State) -- New York -- Fiction
ISBN 9780761361695

LC 2011021251

Coretta Scott King Author Honor Book (2013)

This "biographical novel presents the life and work of a man whose Harlem bookstore became an intellectual, literary haven for African Americans from 1939 until 1975. [The book proceeds t]hrough alternating voices of actual family members, acquaintances, journalists, and the subject himself, [Lewis] Michaux. . . . Influenced by the nationalism of Marcus Garvey and the intellect of Frederick Douglass, he believed that black people needed to educate themselves . . . [and h]e opened the National Memorial African Bookstore. . . . He accumulated works by black writers and talked to customers and passersby about cultural awareness and self-improvement. His bookstore attracted Harlem residents; civil-rights activists, including Malcolm X and Muhammad Ali; and political attention." (School Libr J)

Nemeth, Sally

The heights, the depths, and everything in between. Alfred A. Knopf 2006 263p hardcover o.p. lib bdg $17.99; pa $6.99

Grades: 5 6 7 8   **Fic**
1. Size -- Fiction 2. Dwarfism -- Fiction 3. Friendship

-- Fiction
ISBN 0-375-83458-3; 0-375-93458-8 lib bdg; 0-553-49499-6 pa

LC 2005-33273

In 1977, best friends Lucy Small, a seventh grader from Wilmington, Delaware, who is five feet ten inches tall, and Jake Little, a dwarf, try unsuccessfully to go unnoticed during their first year of junior high school

"Playwright Nemeth has a real gift for capturing teen dialogue and emotions. . . . Readers will relate to this satisfying tale." Booklist

Neri, G.

Chess rumble; by G. Neri; art by Jesse Joshua Watson. Lee & Low Books 2007 64p il $18.95

Grades: 5 6 7 8   **Fic**

1. Chess -- Fiction 2. African Americans -- Fiction
ISBN 978-1-58430-279-7

LC 2007010772

Branded a troublemaker due to his anger over everything from being bullied to his sister's death a year before, Marcus begins to control himself and cope with his problems at home and at his inner-city school when an unlikely mentor teaches him to play chess

"Neri expertly captures Marcus's voice and delicately teases out his alternating vulnerability and rage. The cadence and emotion of the verse are masterfully echoed through Watson's expressive acrylic illustrations." SLJ

Ghetto cowboy; [by] G. Neri; illustrated by Jesse Joshua Watson. Candlewick Press 2011 218p il $15.99

Grades: 4 5 6 7   **Fic**

1. Horses -- Fiction 2. Moving -- Fiction 3. African Americans -- Fiction 4. City and town life -- Fiction 5. Philadelphia (Pa.) -- Fiction 6. Father-son relationship -- Fiction
ISBN 978-0-7636-4922-7; 0-7636-4922-8

LC 2010007565

Twelve-year-old Cole's behavior causes his mother to drive him from Detroit to Philadelphia to live with a father he has never known, but who soon has Cole involved with a group of African-American "cowboys" who rescue horses and use them to steer youths away from drugs and gangs.

"This well-written book is based on a true story of urban cowboys in Philadelphia and New York. Cole's spot-on emotional insight is conveyed through believable dialogue. . . . Watson's illustrations punctuate the intriguing aspects of the story and make the novel more appealing." SLJ

Ness, Patrick

The **Ask** and the Answer; a novel. Candlewick Press 2009 519p (Chaos walking) $18.99

Grades: 8 9 10 11 12   **Fic**

1. Science fiction 2. Telepathy -- Fiction 3. Space colonies -- Fiction 4. Social problems -- Fiction
ISBN 978-0-7636-4490-1; 0-7636-4490-0

LC 2009-7329

Sequel to: The knife of never letting go (2008)

Alternate chapters follow teenagers Todd and Viola, who become separated as the Mayor's oppressive new regime

takes power in New Prentisstown, a space colony where residents can hear each other's thoughts.

"Provocative questions about gender bias, racism, the meaning of war and the price of peace are thoughtfully threaded throughout a breathless, often violent plot peopled with heartbreakingly real characters." Kirkus

Followed by: Monsters of men (2010)

★ The **knife** of never letting go. Candlewick Press 2008 479p (Chaos walking) $18.99

Grades: 8 9 10 11 12   **Fic**

1. Boys -- Fiction 2. Science fiction 3. Dystopian fiction 4. Psychics -- Fiction 5. Telepathy -- Fiction 6. Space colonies -- Fiction
ISBN 978-0-7636-3931-0; 0-7636-3931-1

LC 2007-52334

Pursued by power-hungry Prentiss and mad minister Aaron, young Todd and Viola set out across New World searching for answers about his colony's true past and seeking a way to warn the ship bringing hopeful settlers from Old World.

"This troubling, unforgettable opener to the Chaos Walking trilogy is a penetrating look at the ways in which we reveal ourselves to one another, and what it takes to be a man in a society gone horribly wrong." Booklist

★ A **monster** calls; a novel. inspired by an idea from Siobhan Dowd; illustrations by Jim Kay. Candlewick Press 2011 204p il $15.99

Grades: 6 7 8 9 10   **Fic**

1. School stories 2. Cancer -- Fiction 3. Monsters -- Fiction 4. Great Britain -- Fiction 5. Loss (Psychology) -- Fiction 6. Mother-son relationship -- Fiction
ISBN 978-0-7636-5559-4; 0-7636-5559-7

LC 2010040741

"Conor O'Malley is struggling with his mother's illness and terrorized by nightmares which seem to come to life. The monster who visits him tells Conor three allegorical stories, each time instructing Conor that he will have to tell his own truth in the fourth and final story. Conor's daily life and "truth" are even more haunting than the monster." (Library Media Connection)

This is a "profoundly moving, expertly crafted tale of unaccountable loss. . . . A singular masterpiece, exceptionally well-served by Kay's atmospheric and ominous illustrations." Publ Wkly

Monsters of men. Candlewick Press 2010 603p (Chaos walking) $18.99; pa $9.99

Grades: 8 9 10 11 12   **Fic**

1. War stories 2. Science fiction 3. Telepathy -- Fiction 4. Space colonies -- Fiction 5. Social problems -- Fiction
ISBN 978-0-7636-4751-3; 0-7636-4751-9; 978-0-7636-5665-2 pa; 0-7636-5665-8 pa

Sequel to: The Ask and the Answer (2009)

As a world-ending war surges to life around them, Todd and Viola face monstrous decisions, questioning all they have ever known as they try to step back from the darkness and find the best way to achieve peace.

"The Chaos Walking trilogy comes to a powerful conclusion in this grueling but triumphant tale." Publ Wkly

Neumeier, Rachel

★ The **City** in the Lake. Alfred A. Knopf 2008
304p $15.99; lib bdg $18.99

Grades: 8 9 10 11 12   **Fic**

1. Fantasy fiction 2. Magic -- Fiction
ISBN 978-0-375-84704-2; 0-375-84704-9; 978-0-375-
94704-9 lib bdg; 0-375-94704-3 lib bdg

LC 2008-08941

Seventeen-year-old Timou, who is learning to be a mage,
must save her mysterious, magical homeland, The Kingdom,
from a powerful force that is trying to control it.

"Neumeier structures her story around archetypal fantasy elements. . . . It's the poetic, shimmering language and
fascinating unfolding of worlds that elevates this engrossing
story beyond its formula." Booklist

The **Floating** Islands. Alfred A. Knopf 2011
388p map $16.99; lib bdg $19.99

Grades: 5 6 7   **Fic**

1. Fantasy fiction 2. Magic -- Fiction 3. Flight --
Fiction 4. Cousins -- Fiction
ISBN 0-375-84705-7; 0-375-94705-1 lib bdg; 978-0-
375-84705-9; 978-0-375-94705-6 lib bdg

LC 2010-12772

The adventures of two teenaged cousins who live in a
place called The Floating Islands, one of whom is studying to become a mage and the other one of the legendary
island flyers.

"The author delineates complex characters, geographies
and societies alike with a dab hand, deftly weaves them all—
along with dragons of several sorts, mouthwatering kitchen
talk, flashes of humor and a late-blooming romance—into
a suspenseful plot and delivers and outstanding tale that is
self-contained but full of promise for sequels." Kirkus

Newbery, Linda

At the firefly gate. David Fickling Books 2007
152p hardcover o.p. pa $6.50

Grades: 5 6 7 8   **Fic**

1. Supernatural -- Fiction 2. Great Britain -- Fiction 3.
World War, 1939-1945 -- Fiction
ISBN 978-0-385-75113-1; 978-0-440-42188-7 pa

LC 2006-01796

After moving with his parents from London to Suffolk
near a former World War II airfield, Henry sees the shadowy
image of a man by the orchard gate and feels an unusual affinity with an eldery woman who lives next door

"This is a well-written book, with an old-fashioned
tone, that emphasizes character and feelings over plot. It's
for thoughtful readers who appreciate a book that lingers in
their minds." SLJ

Catcall; illustrated by Ian P. Benfold Haywood.
David Fickling Books 2008 179p il $15.99; lib
bdg $18.99

Grades: 5 6 7 8   **Fic**

1. Cats -- Fiction 2. Family life -- Fiction 3.
Stepfamilies -- Fiction 4. Great Britain -- Fiction
ISBN 978-0-385-75164-3; 0-385-75164-8; 978-0-385-
75165-0 lib bdg; 0-385-75165-6 lib bdg

LC 2008-1910

When eight-year-old Jamie becomes almost possessed
by a lion he encountered in a wild animal park, his blended
family, especially his cat-loving older brother Josh, struggles
to connect with the boy they love

"In addition to the likable characters, the story provides an example of people working through problems
without yelling or abuse. It is refreshing to read about this
loving family, reminiscent of those created by Madeleine
L'Engle." SLJ

Flightsend. David Fickling Books 2010 241p
$15.99; lib bdg $18.99

Grades: 7 8 9 10   **Fic**

1. Moving -- Fiction 2. Bereavement -- Fiction 3.
Great Britain -- Fiction 4. Mother-daughter relationship
-- Fiction
ISBN 978-0-385-75203-9; 0-385-75203-2; 978-0-385-
75205-3 lib bdg; 0-385-75205-9 lib bdg

First published 1999 in the United Kingdom

Just when her life seems to be falling apart, an English
teen named Charlie gains a fresh perspective when she and
her mother relocate to a rural village.

"The characters are wonderfully developed. The leisurely plot unfolds quietly, meandering through Charlie's life
and endearing her to readers." SLJ

Lost boy. David Fickling Books 2008 194p
$15.99; lib bdg $18.99

Grades: 4 5 6 7   **Fic**

1. Ghost stories 2. Mystery fiction 3. Wales -- Fiction
4. Traffic accidents -- Fiction
ISBN 978-0-375-84574-1; 978-0-375-93617-3 lib bdg

LC 2007-15041

First published 2005 in the United Kingdom

After Matt moves to Hay-on-Wye in Wales, a boy his age
who bears the same initials and was killed in a car accident
many years earlier, appears to Matt.

"With its imaginative melding of present-day concerns, good storytelling, lush descriptions of the landscape
and even a faithful dog, this novel will ensnare readers."
Publ Wkly

Newbound, Andrew

Ghoul strike! Chicken House 2010 309p $16.99

Grades: 4 5 6 7   **Fic**

1. Angels -- Fiction 2. Monsters -- Fiction 3.
Supernatural -- Fiction
ISBN 978-0-545-22938-8; 0-545-22938-3

LC 2010013580

When twelve-year-old, psychic ghost hunter Alannah
Malarra faces demons from another dimension, rather than
the treasure-hoarding ghosts she is used to, she needs the
help of protectors from the Attack-ready Network of Global
Evanescent Law-enforcers (A.N.G.E.L.) police force to help
her quell the dangerous uprising

"Alannah is a great female hero. . . . The other main
characters are also multidimensional, and descriptions of the
various creatures are detailed and entertaining. Readers will
enjoy the fast-paced plot and the friendship between Alannah and Wortley." SLJ

Newton, Robert

Runner. Alfred A. Knopf 2007 209p $15.99; lib bdg $18.99

Grades: 6 7 8 9 **Fic**

1. Poverty -- Fiction 2. Running -- Fiction 3. Australia -- Fiction 4. Criminals -- Fiction

ISBN 978-0-375-83744-9; 978-0-375-93744-6 lib bdg; 0-375-83744-2; 0-375-93744-7 lib bdg

LC 2006-29275

In Richmond, Australia, in 1919, fifteen-year-old Charlie Feehan becomes an errand boy for a notorious mobster, hoping that his ability to run will help him, his widowed mother, and his baby brother to escape poverty.

"Rich dialogue in Australian dialect creates a colorful picture of the historical urban setting, suspenseful plot, and warm characterizations." SLJ

Nicholls, Sally

★ **Season** of secrets. Arthur A. Levine Books 2011 225p $16.99

Grades: 4 5 6 **Fic**

1. Sisters -- Fiction 2. Bereavement -- Fiction 3. Family life -- Fiction 4. Great Britain -- Fiction

ISBN 978-0-545-21825-2; 0-545-21825-X

LC 2010017070

Sent by their father to live in the country with their grandparents after the sudden death of their mother, Molly's older sister Hannah expresses her grief in a raging rebellion while imaginative Molly finds herself increasingly distracted by visions, that seemingly only she can see, of a strange hunt in the nearby forest.

"Written in gently flowing prose, the plot appropriately transitions from autumn into summer as Molly emerges from grief to acceptance and hope. A poignant story of healing tinged with mystery." Kirkus

★ **Ways** to live forever; [by] Sally Nicholls. Arthur A. Levine Books 2008 212p il $16.99

Grades: 4 5 6 7 **Fic**

1. Death -- Fiction 2. Leukemia -- Fiction 3. Authorship -- Fiction 4. Family life -- Fiction

ISBN 978-0-545-06948-9; 0-545-06948-3

LC 2007047341

Eleven-year-old Sam McQueen, who has leukemia, writes a book during the last three months of his life, in which he tells about what he would like to accomplish, how he feels, and things that have happened to him.

This "skirts easy sentiment to confront the hard questions head-on, intelligently and realistically and with an enormous range of feeling." Publ Wkly

Nichols, Janet

★ **Messed** up; [by] Janet Nichols Lynch. Holiday House 2009 250p $17.95

Grades: 7 8 9 10 **Fic**

1. School stories 2. California -- Fiction 3. Family life -- Fiction 4. Abandoned children -- Fiction 5. Hispanic Americans -- Fiction

ISBN 978-0-8234-2185-5; 0-8234-2185-6

LC 2008-22577

Fifteen-year-old RD is repeating the eighth grade, planning to have an easy year, but after his grandmother walks out her boyfriend is no longer able to care for him, which leaves RD to fend for himself while avoiding being caught.

"A memorable story of grit and survival, and helping hands along the way." Kirkus

Nicholson, William

Seeker. Harcourt 2006 413p (Noble warriors) $17; pa $7.95

Grades: 7 8 9 10 **Fic**

1. Fantasy fiction

ISBN 978-0-15-205768-8; 0-15-205768-4; 978-0-15-205866-1 pa; 0-15-205866-4 pa

LC 2005-17171

"The classic coming-of-age tale is combined with a rich setting of cold villains, strange powers, and disturbing warriors." Voice Youth Advocates

Other titles in this series are:
Jango (2007)
Noman (2008)

Nielsen, Jennifer A.

Elliot and the Yeti threat; illustrated by Gideon Kendall. Sourcebooks Jabberwocky 2012 il $12.99

Grades: 4 5 6 7 **Fic**

1. Fantasy fiction 2. Yeti -- Fiction

ISBN 978-1-4022-4021-8; 1-4022-4021-X

Being King of the Brownies is no easy job! Elliot outsmarted the Goblins and foiled the Pixie Plot, but now he's being threatened by a giant Yeti. Oh, and there's a mermaid hiding in his bathtub. Elliot might be able to survive some unusual self-defense lessons and a kingnapping plot, but can he withstand the friendship of the neighbor girl—his arch—nemesis–Cami Wortson?

The **false** prince; by Jennifer A. Nielsen. Scholastic Press 2012 342 p. (The ascendance trilogy) hbk $17.99

Grades: 4 5 6 7 8 **Fic**

1. Fantasy fiction 2. Adventure fiction 3. Impersonation -- Fiction 4. Secrets -- Fiction 5. Courts and courtiers -- Fiction

ISBN 9780545284134

LC 2011006692

This fantasy book depicts the adventures of Sage, a "brazen 15-year-old orphan living in the imaginary kingdom of Carthya [who] becomes embroiled in a treasonous powerplay to install a false prince on the vacant throne." He is selected with three other boys from the orphanage by Bevin Connor to compete to impersonate the missing Prince Jaron and act as Connor's pawn on the throne. "Sage's disdain, defiance and reckless arrogance mark him for failure, but his boldness, instinct and innate decency indicate there's more than meets the eye. Could Sage become Prince Jaron?" Jennifer A. Nielsen's story features "ruthless ambition, fierce action and plotting . . . . and lots of sword play and hidden passages." (Kirkus)

Mark of the thief; by Jennifer A. Nielsen. Scholastic Press 2015 352 p. (Praetor war) (jacketed hardcover) $17.99

Grades: 5 6 7 8 9 **Fic**

1. Rome -- Fiction 2. Magic -- Fiction 3. Slaves --

Fiction 4. Amulets -- Fiction 5. Slavery -- Fiction 6. Insurgency -- Fiction 7. Rome -- Antiquities -- Fiction 8. Rome -- History -- Empire, 30 B.C.-476 A.D. -- Fiction

ISBN 054556154X; 9780545561549

LC 2014017068

In this novel by Jennifer A. Nielsen, "when Nic, a slave in the mines outside of Rome, is forced to enter a sealed cavern containing the lost treasures of Julius Caesar, he finds much more than gold and gemstones: He discovers an ancient bulla, an amulet that belonged to the great Caesar and is filled with a magic once reserved for the Gods. He finds himself at the center of a ruthless conspiracy to overthrow the emperor and spark the Praetor War." (Publisher's note)

"A fantastical alternate history set in ancient Rome. Nicolas Calva and his sister are slaves in the mines outside of Rome. When Nic is forced to retrieve treasure from Julius Caesar's cave, he assumes he is going to his death...This genre mash-up of history, fantasy, and action/adventure is fast-paced and explores themes such as class struggles, familial ties, and the immorality of slavery. Readers will have lots to digest as they quickly flip through the pages to see how Nic will escape his enemies to become a free man." SLJ

The **runaway** king; Jennifer A. Nielsen. Scholastic Press 2013 352 p. (The ascendance trilogy) (hardcover) $17.99

Grades: 4 5 6 7 8   Fic

1. Fantasy fiction 2. Kings and rulers -- Fiction 3. Princesses -- Fiction 4. Conspiracies -- Fiction 5. Courts and courtiers -- Fiction 6. Kings, queens, rulers, etc. -- Fiction

ISBN 0545284155; 9780545284158

LC 2012035290

"Just weeks after Jaron has taken the throne, an assassination attempt forces him into a deadly situation. Rumors of a coming war are winding their way between the castle walls, and Jaron feels the pressure quietly mounting within Carthya. Soon, it becomes clear that deserting the kingdom may be his only hope of saving it." (Publisher's note)

The **shadow** throne; Jennifer A. Nielsen. First edition Scholastic Press 2014 336 p. (Ascendance trilogy) (hardcover) $17.99

Grades: 4 5 6 7 8   Fic

1. Kings and rulers 2. Adventure fiction 3. Battles -- Fiction 4. Adventure stories 5. Rescues -- Fiction 6. Adventure and adventurers -- Fiction

ISBN 9780545284172; 0545284171

LC 2013021841

This book, by Jennifer A. Nielsen, is the "finale of the Ascendance Trilogy. . . . Jaron learns than King Vargan of Avenia and allies from Gelyn and Mendenwal have invaded Carthya and captured Jaron's friend Imogen. Determined to save Imogen, Jaron attempts a rescue and fails, leaving him a prisoner and Imogen presumed dead. As he tries to cope with Imogen's death, captive Jaron discovers how much he loved her." (Kirkus Reviews)

"There's enough adventure, mystery, and romance in this concluding volume to please a variety of genre readers." Horn Book

Nielsen, Susin

Dear George Clooney; please marry my mom. Tundra Books 2010 229p $15.95

Grades: 5 6 7 8   Fic

1. Divorce -- Fiction 2. Letters -- Fiction

ISBN 978-0-88776-977-1; 0-88776-977-2

"Smarting from her parent's divorce—her director father left her mother to marry an actress—Violet is fed up with all the 'losers' her mother has since dated. . . . She pens a letter to George Clooney . . . explaining that she's trying to find a suitable suitor for her parent. . . . Nielsen skillfully balances her story's keen humor . . . with poignancy." Publ Wkly

The **reluctant** journal of Henry K. Larsen; Susin Nielsen. Tundra Books of Northern New York 2012 243 p. (hardcover) $17.95

Grades: 7 8 9 10 11 12   Fic

1. Bullies 2. Grief -- Fiction 3. Diaries -- Fiction

ISBN 1770493727; 9781770493728

LC 2011938782

In this novel, by Susin Nielsen, "thirteen-year-old Henry's happy life abruptly ends when his older brother kills the boy who bullied him in school and then takes his own life. Henry refers to this tragedy as 'IT.' He moves to a new city . . . for a fresh start. To help him cope with IT, Henry's therapist recommends he keep a journal. Henry hates the suggestion but soon finds himself recording his thoughts and feelings constantly, even updating it multiple times per day." (Kirkus Reviews)

★ **Word** nerd. Tundra Books 2008 248p $18.95; pa $12.95

Grades: 5 6 7 8   Fic

1. Friendship -- Fiction 2. Scrabble (Game) -- Fiction 3. Mother-son relationship -- Fiction

ISBN 978-0-88776-875-0; 0-88776-875-X; 978-0-88776-990-0 pa; 0-88776-990-X pa

"Twelve-year-old Ambrose Bukowski and his widowed, overprotective mother . . . move frequently. When he almost dies after he bites into a peanut that bullies put in his sandwich, just to see if he is really allergic, Irene . . . decides to homeschool him. . . . Ambrose gets to know 25-year-old Cosmo, recently released from jail and the son of the Bukowskis' . . . landlords. . . . Ambrose . . . talks Cosmo into taking him to a Scrabble Club. . . . This is a tender, often funny story with some really interesting characters. It will appeal to word nerds, but even more to anyone who has ever longed for acceptance or had to fight unreasonable parental restrictions." SLJ

Nielson, Sheila A.

Forbidden sea. Scholastic 2010 296p $17.99

Grades: 5 6 7 8   Fic

1. Fantasy fiction 2. Islands -- Fiction 3. Superstition -- Fiction 4. Mermaids and mermen -- Fiction

ISBN 978-0-545-09734-5; 0-545-09734-7

LC 2009-22993

When a mermaid attempts to lure her into the sea, fourteen-year-old Adrianne, who lives in a superstitious island community, must choose between the promise of an underwater paradise and those she loves.

"The plot pacing is steady and suspenseful as more details about the protagonist's current life and past are revealed through her absorbing first-person narration. Nielsen's new spin on a traditional fantasy setup is sure to appeal." SLJ

Nigg, Joe

How to raise and keep a dragon; by John Topsell; executive editor, Joseph Nigg; illustrations, Dan Malone. Barron's 2006 128p il $18.99

Grades: 5 6 7 8   **Fic**

1. Dragons -- Fiction

ISBN 0-7641-5920-8

"Posing as dragon-breeder John Topsell . . . Nigg instructs readers in selecting and caring for a breed of dragon suited for them. . . . While not intended as a serious book on mythology, Nigg does share many bits of real dragon lore while spinning out details of what it might be like to live in a world where people breed, register, and show these creatures. Malone's full-color illustrations on every page offer fans many cool pictures to copy or sketch. With its tongue firmly in cheek, this book is a lot of lighthearted fun." SLJ

Nimmo, Jenny

Midnight for Charlie Bone. Orchard Bks. 2003 401p (Children of the Red King) $12.99

Grades: 5 6 7 8   **Fic**

1. School stories 2. Magic -- Fiction 3. Great Britain -- Fiction

ISBN 978-0-439-47429-0; 0-439-47429-9

LC 2002-30738

First published 2002 in the United Kingdom

Charlie Bone's life with his widowed mother and two grandmothers undergoes a dramatic change when he discovers that he can hear people in photographs talking.

"This marvelous fantasy is able to stand on its own despite inevitable comparisons to the students of Hogwarts." Voice Youth Advocates

Other titles in this series are:

Charlie Bone and the time twister (2003)

Charlie Bone and the invisible boy (2004)

Charlie Bone and the castle of mirrors (2005)

Charlie Bone and the hidden king (2006)

Charlie Bone and the beast (2007)

Charlie Bone and the shadow (2008)

Charlie Bone and the Red Knight (2010)

★ The **snow** spider; [by] Jenny Nimmo. Orchard Books 2006 146p (Magician trilogy) $9.99

Grades: 4 5 6 7   **Fic**

1. Magic -- Fiction 2. Wales -- Fiction 3. Father-son relationship -- Fiction

ISBN 978-0-439-84675-2; 0-439-84675-7

LC 2006009445

A reissue of the title first published 1987 by Dutton

Gifts from Gwyn's grandmother on his ninth birthday open up a whole new world to him, as he discovers he has magical powers that help him heal the breach with his father that has existed ever since his sister's mysterious disappearance four years before

"The narration is paced well and builds in excitement along with the tale." SLJ

Other titles in this series are:

Emlyn's moon (2007)

Chestnut solider (2007)

The **stones** of Ravenglass; Jenny Nimmo. Scholastic Press 2012 250 p. (Chronicles of the red king) (jacketed hardcover) $16.99

Grades: 4 5 6   **Fic**

1. Magicians -- Fiction 2. Prisoners -- Fiction 3. Kings and rulers -- Fiction 4. Magic -- Fiction 5. Camels -- Fiction 6. Voyages and travels -- Fiction 7. Brothers and sisters -- Fiction 8. Voyages and travels -- Fiction 9. Brothers and sisters -- Fiction

ISBN 0439846749; 9780439846745

LC 2012003034

This book, part of author Jenny Nimmo's Chronicles of the Red King series, chronicles "the origin and the adventures of Charlie Bone's magical ancestor, the Red King! Timoken, a magician king, has found a new home in a castle in Britain. But when an evil steward takes control of the castle, he imprisons Timoken. With the help of Gabar, the talking camel, Timoken escapes and embarks on a quest to find and rescue his friends, and build himself a kingdom to call home for good." (Publisher's note)

Nix, Garth, 1963-

★ **Clariel**; the lost Abhorsen. Garth Nix. HarperCollins 2014 400 p. maps (hardcover) $18.99

Grades: 7 8 9 10   **Fic**

1. Fantasy fiction 2. Magic -- Fiction

ISBN 006156155X; 9780061561559

LC 2013047958

In this fantasy novel by Garth Nix, part of the Old Kingdom series, "Clariel is the daughter of one of the most notable families in the Old Kingdom, with blood relations to the Abhorsen and, most important, to the King. She dreams of living a simple life but discovers this is hard to achieve when a dangerous Free Magic creature is loose in the city, her parents want to marry her off to a killer, and there is a plot brewing against the old and withdrawn King Orrikan." (Publisher's note)

"Nix's intricate world building reveals more Old Kingdom history and its ever-shifting alliance between the political and magical. Themes of freedom and destiny underpin Clariel's harrowing, bittersweet story, and readers will delight in the telling." Booklist

Mister Monday; Keys to the kingdom, book one. Scholastic 2003 361p (Keys to the kingdom) $15.99; pa $5.99

Grades: 6 7 8 9   **Fic**

1. Fantasy fiction

ISBN 0-439-70370-0; 0-439-55123-4 pa

LC 2004-540574

Arthur Penhaligon is supposed to die at a young age, but is saved by a key that is shaped like the minute hand of a clock. The key causes bizarre creatures to come from another realm, bringing with them a plague. A man named Mister Monday will stop at nothing to get the key back. Arthur goes to a mysterious house that only he can see, so that he can learn the truth about himself and the key

"The first in a seven part series for middle graders is every bit as exciting and suspenseful as the author's previous young adult novels." SLJ

Other titles in the Keys to the Kingdom series are:
Grim Tuesday (2004)
Drowned Wednesday (2005)
Sir Thursday (2006)
Lady Friday (2007)
Superior Saturday (2008)
Lord Sunday (2010)

★ **Sabriel**. HarperCollins Pubs. 1996 292p hardcover o.p. pa $7.99
Grades: 7 8 9 10   Fic
1. Fantasy fiction
ISBN 0-06-027322-4; 0-06-447183-7 pa
LC 96-1295

First published 1995 in Australia

Sabriel, daughter of the necromancer Abhorsen, must journey into the mysterious and magical Old Kingdom to rescue her father from the Land of the Dead.

"The final battle is gripping, and the bloody cost of combat is forcefully presented. The story is remarkable for the level of originality of the fantastic elements . . . and for the subtle presentation, which leaves readers to explore for themselves the complex structure and significance of the magic elements." Horn Book

Other titles in this series are:
Abhorsen (2003)
Across the wall (2005)
Clariel (2014)
Lirael, daughter of the Clayr (2001)

Shade's children. HarperCollins Pubs. 1997 310p $18.99; pa $6.99
Grades: 7 8 9 10   Fic
1. Science fiction
ISBN 0-06-027324-0; 0-06-447196-9 pa
LC 97-3841

In a savage postnuclear world, four young fugitives attempt to overthrow the bloodthirsty rule of the Overlords with the help of Shade, their mysterious mentor

"Grim, unusual, and fascinating." Horn Book

Troubletwisters; [by] Garth Nix and Sean Williams. Scholastic Press 2011 293p $16.99
Grades: 5 6 7 8   Fic
1. Fantasy fiction 2. Magic -- Fiction 3. Twins -- Fiction 4. Siblings -- Fiction 5. Grandmothers -- Fiction
ISBN 978-0-545-25897-5; 0-545-25897-9
LC 2011015765

When their house mysteriously explodes and they are sent to live with an unknown relative named Grandma X, twelve-year-old twins Jaide and Jack Shield learn that they are troubletwisters, young Wardens just coming into their powers, who must protect humanity from The Evil trying to break into Earth's dimension.

"Full of adventure and the unexpected, . . . [this] is delightfully twisted. The pacing is perfect, the setting is eerily dark, the faceless Evil rings true, and the resolution is satisfying." Booklist

Nixon, Joan Lowery
The **haunting**. Delacorte Press 1998 184p hardcover o.p. pa $5.50
Grades: 7 8 9 10   Fic
1. Ghost stories 2. Louisiana -- Fiction
ISBN 0-385-32247-X; 0-440-22008-4 pa
LC 97-32658

When her mother inherits an old plantation house in the Louisiana countryside, fifteen-year-old Lia seeks to rid it of the evil spirit that haunts it

"This title has it all - a hint of romance, some really scary scenes, and a plucky heroine who successfully routs both outer and inner demons." Horn Book Guide

Laugh till you cry. Delacorte Press 2004 99p hardcover o.p. lib bdg $17.99
Grades: 5 6 7 8   Fic
1. School stories 2. Moving -- Fiction 3. Family life -- Fiction
ISBN 0-385-73027-6; 0-385-90186-0 lib bdg
LC 2004-9557

Thirteen years old and a budding comedian, Cody has little to laugh about after he and his mother move from California to Texas to help his sick grandmother and he finds himself framed by his jealous cousin for calling in bomb threats to their school.

"The pacing of the story, Cody's humorous side, and the book's length make this mystery ideal for reluctant readers." SLJ

Nightmare. Delacorte Press 2003 166p hardcover o.p. lib bdg $17.99; pa $5.99
Grades: 6 7 8 9   Fic
1. Mystery fiction 2. Camps -- Fiction 3. Homicide -- Fiction
ISBN 0-385-73026-8; 0-385-90151-8 lib bdg; 0-4402-3773-4 pa
LC 2003-43434

Emily is sent to a camp for underachievers where she discovers a murderer on the staff who might provide an explanation for her recurring nightmares

"Elements of suspense and mystery are cleverly integrated with the teen's problems resulting from what she witnessed as a child. Readers will once again fall under Nixon's spell as they enjoy this page-turner." SLJ

Noel, Alyson
Radiance. Square Fish 2010 183p pa $7.99
Grades: 5 6 7 8   Fic
1. Ghost stories 2. Dead -- Fiction 3. Future life -- Fiction
ISBN 978-0-312-62917-5; 0-312-62917-6
LC 2010015840

After crossing the bridge into the afterlife, a place called Here where the time is always Now, Riley's existence continues in much the same way as when she was alive until she is given the job of Soul Catcher and, together with her teacher Bodhi, returns to earth for her first assignment, a ghost called the Radiant Boy who has been haunting an English castle for centuries and resisted all previous attempts to get him across the bridge.

"Narrating in a contemporary voice with an honest and comfortable cadence, Riley is imperfect, but always likable. . . . In the midst of this wildly fanciful setting, Noël is able to capture with nail-on-the-head accuracy common worries and concerns of today's tweens." SLJ

Other titles in this series are:

Dreamland (2011)

Simmer (2011)

Nolan, Han

★ **Crazy**. Harcourt 2010 348p $17

Grades: 7 8 9 10   **Fic**

1. School stories 2. Friendship -- Fiction 3. Bereavement -- Fiction 4. Mental illness -- Fiction 5. Father-son relationship -- Fiction

ISBN 978-0-15-205109-9; 0-15-205109-0

LC 2009-49969

Fifteen-year-old loner Jason struggles to hide father's declining mental condition after his mother's death, but when his father disappears he must confide in the other members of a therapy group he has been forced to join at school.

"Nolan leavens this haunting but hopeful story with spot-on humor and a well-developed cast of characters." Booklist

A **face** in every window. Harcourt Brace & Co. 1999 264p hardcover o.p. pa $6.95

Grades: 7 8 9 10   **Fic**

1. Mentally disabled -- Fiction

ISBN 0-15-201915-4; 0-15-206418-4 pa

LC 99-14230

After the death of his grandmother, who held the family together, teenage JP is left with a mentally challenged father and a mother who seems ineffectual and constantly sick, and he feels everything sliding out of control

"Only a writer as talented as Nolan could make this improbable story line and bizarre cast of characters not only believable but also ultimately uplifting, intriguing, and memorable." Booklist

A **summer** of Kings. Harcourt 2006 334p $17

Grades: 6 7 8 9   **Fic**

1. Black Muslims -- Fiction 2. Race relations -- Fiction 3. African Americans -- Fiction

ISBN 0-15-205108-2

LC 2005-19487

Over the course of the summer of 1963, fourteen-year-old Esther Young discovers the passion within her when eighteen-year-old King-Roy Johnson, accused of murdering a white man in Alabama, comes to live with her family.

"Infused with rhetoric that is as meaningful today as it was two generations ago, this young teen's account of a life-changing summer not only opens a window to history, but also displays Nolan's brilliant gift for crafting profoundly appealing protagonists." SLJ

Nolen, Jerdine

Eliza's freedom road; an Underground Railroad diary. Simon & Schuster Books for Young Readers 2011 139p il map $14.99

Grades: 4 5 6 7   **Fic**

1. Diaries -- Fiction 2. Slavery -- Fiction 3. African

Americans -- Fiction 4. Underground railroad -- Fiction

ISBN 1-4169-5814-2; 978-1-4169-5814-7

LC 2010-20931

A twelve-year-old slave girl begins writing in a journal where she documents her journey via the Underground Railroad from Alexandria, Virginia, to freedom in St. Catharines, Canada.

"Nolen reveals some of the traumas and tragedies of slavery but keeps her focus on those things that allow Eliza the power to escape: literacy, her mother's legacy, a bit of luck and a great deal of courage." Kirkus

Includes bibliographical references

Nooks & crannies; Jessica Lawson. First edition Simon & Schuster Books for Young Readers 2015 336 p. illustrations (hardcover) $16.99

Grades: 3 4 5 6 7   **Fic**

1. Aristocracy -- Fiction 2. Mystery fiction 3. Inheritance and succession -- Fiction 4. Identity -- Fiction 5. Mystery and detective stories 6. Aristocracy (Social class) -- Fiction 7. Inheritance and succession -- Fiction 8. Great Britain -- History -- Edward VII, 1901-1910 -- Fiction

ISBN 1481419218; 9781481419215; 9781481419222

LC 2014023223

In this children's mystery story, by Jessica Lawson and illustrated by Natalie Andrewson, "Tabitha Crum . . . receives one of six invitations to the country estate of wealthy Countess Camilla DeMoss. . . . Then the children beginning disappearing, one by one. So Tabitha takes a cue from her favorite detective novels and, with [her pet mouse] Pemberley by her side, attempts to solve the case and rescue the other children." (Publisher's note)

"Lawson offers a compelling puzzle, vividly drawn characters, and a clever and capable young detective, who bravely sniffs out clues before the final secrets are revealed—with everyone together in the parlor, naturally." Booklist

Nooks and crannies

Norcliffe, James

The **boy** who could fly. Egmont USA 2010 312p $15.99

Grades: 5 6 7 8   **Fic**

1. Fantasy fiction 2. Flight -- Fiction 3. Siblings -- Fiction 4. Abandoned children -- Fiction

ISBN 978-1-60684-084-9; 1-60684-084-3

LC 2009-41167

First published 2009 in New Zealand with title: The loblolly boy

Having grown up in a miserable home for abandoned children, a young boy jumps at the chance to exchange places with the mysterious, flying "loblolly boy," but once he takes on this new identity, he discovers what a harsh price he must pay.

"Norcliffe has written an imaginative and richly atmospheric fantasy with sympathetic characters. . . . This is . . . a haunting tale that will capture most readers' imaginations." Booklist

Nordin, Sofia

In the wild; translated by Maria Lundin. House of Anansi Press 2005 115p hardcover o.p. pa $6.95

Grades: 4 5 6 7 **Fic**
1. Bullies -- Fiction 2. Wilderness survival -- Fiction
ISBN 0-88899-648-9; 0-88899-663-2 pa
Originally published in Swedish

"Amanda, the target of harassment by her classmates, is on an adventure trip with her sixth-grade class. When she and one of the bullies, Philip, are separated from the group and become lost in the wilderness, they are forced to work together to survive. . . . Nordin realistically depicts the psychological effects of relentless hounding. . . . The translation is smooth and the text flows naturally. . . . Well written, and a lightning-fast read." SLJ

North, Pearl

The **boy** from Ilysies. Tor 2010 316p $17.99
Grades: 7 8 9 10 **Fic**
1. Fantasy fiction 2. Books and reading -- Fiction
ISBN 978-0-7653-2097-1; 0-7653-2097-5
LC 2010-36676
Sequel to Libyrinth (2009)

Cast out of the Libyrinth after being tricked into committing a crime, young Po may return only if he completes a dangerous mission to retrieve a legendary artifact that could either be the answer to all of the Libyrinth's problems, or could destroy the world.

"North has created that rare thing: a second book in a series that is stronger than the first." SLJ

Libyrinth. Tor Teen 2009 332p $17.95
Grades: 7 8 9 10 **Fic**
1. Fantasy fiction 2. Books and reading -- Fiction
ISBN 978-0-7653-2096-4; 0-7653-2096-7
LC 2009-1514

In a distant future where Libyrarians preserve and protect the ancient books that are housed in the fortress-like Libyrinth, Haly is imprisoned by Eradicants, who believe that the written word is evil, and she must try to mend the rift between the two groups before their war for knowledge destroys them all.

"Among this novel's pleasures are the many anonymous quotations scattered throughout, snatches of prose that Haly hears as she goes about her chores . . . all of which are carefully identified at the end. The complex moral issues posed by this thoughtful and exciting tale are just as fascinating." Publ Wkly

Followed by: The boy from Ilysies (2010)

North, Phoebe

Starglass; by Phoebe North. 1st ed. Simon & Schuster Books for Young Readers 2013 448 p. (hardcover) $17.99
Grades: 7 8 9 10 **Fic**
1. Jews -- Fiction 2. Underground movements -- Fiction 3. Interplanetary voyages -- Fiction 4. Science fiction 5. Insurgency -- Fiction 6. Fathers and daughters -- Fiction
ISBN 1442459530; 9781442459533; 9781442459557
LC 2012021171

In this book by Phoebe North, "[o]n a generation ship that left Earth 500 years ago, a teenager grapples with disillusionment and emotional isolation as her society nears the planet it intends to land on. Terra lives with her harsh, alco-

holic father and awaits her adult job assignment . . . from the strict ruling Council." She "discovers a secret rebellion aboard the Asherah." (Kirkus Reviews)

Northrop, Michael

Plunked; Michael Northrop. Scholastic Press 2012 247 p. (jacketed hardcover) $16.99
Grades: 4 5 6 7 8 **Fic**
1. Ethics -- Fiction 2. Fear -- Fiction 3. Schools -- Fiction 4. Baseball -- Fiction 5. Perseverance (Ethics) -- Fiction
ISBN 0545297141; 9780545297141
LC 2011032737

This children's story by Michael Northrop centers on the "Sixth grader Jack Mogens [who] has it all figured out: He's got his batting routine down, and his outfielding earns him a starting spot alongside his best friend Andy on their Little League team, the Tall Pines Braves. He even manages to have a not-totally-embarrassing conversation with Katie, the team's killer shortstop. But in the first game of the season, a powerful stray pitch brings everything Jack's worked so hard for crashing down around his ears. . . ." Jack then has to face his fears and anxieties and return to the game. (Publisher's note)

Trapped. Scholastic Press 2011 225p $17.99
Grades: 7 8 9 10 **Fic**
1. School stories 2. Blizzards -- Fiction
ISBN 978-0-545-21012-6; 0-545-21012-7
LC 2010-36595

Seven high school students are stranded at their New England high school during a week-long blizzard that shuts down the power and heat, freezes the pipes, and leaves them wondering if they will survive.

"Northrop is cooly brilliant in his setup, amassing the tension along with the snow, shrewdly observing the shifting social dynamics within the group." Bull Cent Child Books

Norville, Rod

Moonshine express; with a history of moonshine today and yesterday. Four Seasons Pub. 2003 xxix, 195p pa $13.95
Grades: 6 7 8 9 **Fic**
1. Florida -- Fiction 2. Moonshining -- Fiction
ISBN 1-89129-99-2
"This is an edge-of-the-seat thriller." SLJ

Nuzum, K. A.

A **small** white scar; [by] K.A. Nuzum. 1st ed.; Joanna Cotler Books 2006 180p $15.99; lib bdg $16.89
Grades: 6 7 8 9 **Fic**
1. Twins -- Fiction 2. Brothers -- Fiction 3. Colorado -- Fiction 4. Cowhands -- Fiction 5. Mentally disabled
ISBN 978-0-06-075639-0; 0-06-075639-X; 978-0-06-075640-6 lib bdg; 0-06-075640-3 lib bdg
LC 2005017721

Fifteen-year-old Will Bennon leaves his family and begins life as a cowboy, but his mentally retarded twin brother follows him and joins the journey.

"The images of the stark 1940s Colorado countryside suffering from drought, and the wild animals that populate it, are clearly drawn with poetic turns of phrase. Characters, plot, and theme all combine to make a compelling story." SLJ

Nye, Naomi Shihab

Going going. Greenwillow Books 2005 232p il $15.99; lib bdg $16.89

Grades: 7 8 9 10   Fic

1. Small business -- Fiction 2. San Antonio (Tex.) -- Fiction 3. Political activists -- Fiction

ISBN 0-688-16185-5; 0-06-029366-7 lib bdg

LC 2004-10146

In San Antonio, Texas, sixteen-year-old Florrie leads her friends and a new boyfriend in a campaign which supports small businesses and protests the effects of chain stores.

The "novel's strong message belongs honestly to Florrie, whose vivid individualism will engage readers. Nye evokes history through small details, inviting readers to view their own cities and towns with a new perspective." Horn Book Guide

★ **Habibi**. Simon & Schuster Bks. for Young Readers 1997 259p $16; pa $5.99

Grades: 7 8 9 10   Fic

1. Jerusalem -- Fiction 2. Jewish-Arab relations -- Fiction

ISBN 0-689-80149-1; 0-689-82523-4 pa

LC 97-10943

When fourteen-year-old Liyanne Abboud, her younger brother, and her parents move from St. Louis to a new home between Jerusalem and the Palestinian village where her father was born, they face many changes and must deal with the tensions between Jews and Palestinians

"Poetically imaged and leavened with humor, the story renders layered and complex history understandable through character and incident." SLJ

Nylund, Eric S.

The **Resisters**; [by] Eric Nylund. Random House 2011 210p $16.99; lib bdg $19.99

Grades: 5 6 7 8   Fic

1. Science fiction 2. Brainwashing -- Fiction 3. Extraterrestrial beings -- Fiction

ISBN 978-0-375-86856-6; 0-375-86856-9; 978-0-375-96856-3 lib bdg; 0-375-96856-3 lib bdg

LC 2010-19230

When twelve-year-olds Madison and Felix kidnap him, Ethan learns that the Earth has been taken over by aliens and that all the adults in the world are under mind control.

"Ethan, Felix, and Madison are multidimensional characters with authentic emotions and realistic attitudes and motives. This book mixes considerable background exposition with fast-moving action. While the immediate plot issues are resolved, there are plenty of threads left dangling. Middle school boys will enjoy the high-tech battle action and will look forward to the next installment." SLJ

Nyoka, Gail

Mella and the N'anga; an African tale. Sumach Press 2006 158p pa $9.95

Grades: 5 6 7 8   Fic

1. Fantasy fiction 2. Zimbabwe -- Fiction

ISBN 1-894549-49-X

In ancient mythical Zimbabwe, Mella and two other girls train with the N'anga, a mysterious, spiritual advisor, to become Daughters of the Hunt and rescue their people.

"The language reinforces the sense of the ancient court setting, and many passages glimmer with mysticism linked to the beauty of the natural world. Mella's thrilling, magical, girl-powered quest will attract many readers." Booklist

O Guilin, Peadar

The **inferior**. David Fickling Books 2008 439p $16.99

Grades: 8 9 10 11 12   Fic

1. Science fiction 2. Hunting -- Fiction 3. Cannibalism -- Fiction

ISBN 978-0-385-75145-2; 0-385-75145-1

LC 2007-34496

In a brutal world where hunting and cannibalism are necessary for survival, something is going terribly wrong as even the globes on the roof of the world are fighting, but one young man, influenced by a beautiful and mysterious stranger, begins to envision new possibilities.

This is an "epic story of survival, betrayal, and community. . . . This well-paced fantasy/science fiction blend perfectly introduces community conflict at a base level. . . . Easy to follow and intriguing at every turn, TheInferior will hold readers from page to page, chapter to chapter, to the very end." SLJ

O'Brien, Annemarie

Lara's gift; by Annemarie O'Brien. Alfred A. Knopf 2013 176 p. (hardcover) $16.99; (ebook) $50.97; (library binding) 19.99

Grades: 5 6 7 8 9   Fic

1. Historical fiction 2. Dogs -- Breeding 3. Dogs -- Fiction 4. Borzoi -- Fiction 5. Visions -- Fiction 6. Sex role -- Fiction 7. Family life -- Russia -- Fiction 8. Fathers and daughters -- Fiction 9. Russia -- History -- 1904-1914 -- Fiction

ISBN 0307931749; 9780307931740; 9780307975485; 9780375971051

LC 2012034070

In this book, on "a remote estate in 1910s Russia, Lara must prove herself capable of following in her father's footsteps as the head of a prestigious borzoi breeding kennel. There are so many things between her and the realization of her dream. That she is female is the biggest obstacle, but she must also hide the fact that she has visions of future occurrences that involve the dogs and the dangerous wolves that populate the estate." (Kirkus Reviews)

O'Brien, Caragh M.

★ **Birthmarked**. Roaring Brook Press 2010 362p map $16.99

Grades: 6 7 8 9 10   Fic

1. Science fiction 2. Midwives -- Fiction 3. Genetic engineering -- Fiction

ISBN 978-1-59643-569-8; 1-59643-569-0

LC 2010-281716

In a future world baked dry by the sun and divided into those who live inside the wall and those who live outside it, sixteen-year-old midwife Gaia Stone is forced into a difficult choice when her parents are arrested and taken into the city.

"Readers who enjoy adventures with a strong heroine standing up to authority against the odds will enjoy this compelling tale." SLJ

The **vault** of dreamers; Caragh M. O'Brien. First edition Roaring Brook Press 2014 432 p. illustrations (hardback) $17.99

Grades: 8 9 10 11 **Fic**
    1. Science fiction 2. Dreams -- Fiction 3. High schools -- Fiction 4. Schools -- Fiction 5. Reality television programs -- Fiction
    ISBN 1596439386; 9781596439382; 9781596439399
    LC 2014013322
    In this novel, by Caragh M. O'Brien, "the Forge School is the most prestigious arts school in the country. The secret to its success: every moment of the students' lives is televised as part of the insanely popular Forge Show, and the students' schedule includes twelve hours of induced sleep meant to enhance creativity. But when first year student Rosie Sinclair skips her sleeping pill, she discovers there is something off about Forge." (Publisher's note)
    "Like O'Brien's Birthmarked trilogy, this dystopian, sci-fi, psychological-thriller hybrid raises ethical and moral questions about science. This might have been a difficult story to pull off, given the environment, but with a likable narrator who is thoroughly unimpressed with herself, it works. The end is abrupt, hinting at a sequel, and there is a good measure of predictability." Booklist

O'Brien, Johnny
    Day of deliverance; a Jack Christie adventure. Templar Books 2010 183p $15.99

Grades: 5 6 7 8 **Fic**
    1. Queens 2. Science fiction 3. Adventure fiction 4. Time travel -- Fiction 5. Great Britain -- History -- 1485-1603, Tudors -- Fiction
    ISBN 978-0-7636-5075-9; 0-7636-5075-7
    LC 2010010710
    To thwart their arch-enemy, Pendlesharp, and his misguided notion of changing history, schoolboy Jack Christie and his friend Angus travel back in time to foil a plot to assassinate Elizabeth I, meeting playwright Christopher Marlowe and a young actor named William Shakespeare along the way.
    "Readers will enjoy the nonstop action, as well as the glimpses of historical figures." Kirkus

    Day of the assassins; a Jack Christie novel. [illustrated by Nick Hardcastle] Templar Books 2009 211p il $15.99

Grades: 5 6 7 8 **Fic**
    1. Princes 2. Science fiction 3. Adventure fiction 4. Time travel -- Fiction 5. World War, 1914-1918 -- Fiction 6. Europe -- History -- 1871-1918 -- Fiction
    ISBN 978-0-7636-4595-3; 0-7636-4595-8
    LC 2009023630
    Fifteen-year-old Jack is sent to 1914 Europe as a pawn in the battle between his long-lost father, who has built a time

machine, and a secret network of scientists who want to prevent him from trying to use it to change history for the better.

    "From an explosive escape out of captivity to a much-anticipated scene that decides the fate of World War I, the end of the book has plenty of action. Historical information and photographs about the events and people central to the period enhance this title even more." SLJ
    Another title about Jack is:
    Day of deliverance (2010)

O'Brien, Robert C.
    ★ **Mrs.** Frisby and the rats of NIMH; [by] Robert C. O'Brien; illustrated by Zena Bernstein. Atheneum Books for Young Readers 2006 233p il $18; pa $6.99

Grades: 4 5 6 7 **Fic**
    1. Mice -- Fiction 2. Rats -- Fiction
    ISBN 978-0-689-20651-1; 0-689-20651-8; 978-0-689-71068-1 pa; 0-689-71068-2 pa
    A reissue of the title first published 1971
    Awarded the Newbery Medal, 1972
    Having no one to help her with her problems, a widowed mouse visits the rats whose former imprisonment in a laboratory made them wise and long lived.
    "The story is fresh and ingenious, the style witty, and the plot both hilarious and convincing." Saturday Rev

    ★ **Z** for Zachariah. Atheneum Pubs. 1975 246p hardcover o.p. pa $7.99

Grades: 7 8 9 10 **Fic**
    1. Science fiction
    ISBN 0-689-30442-0; 1-416-93921-0 pa
    Seemingly the only person left alive after a nuclear war, a sixteen-year-old girl is relieved to see a man arrive into her valley until she realizes that he is a tyrant and she must somehow escape.
    "The journal form is used by O'Brien very effectively, with no lack of drama and contrast, and the pace and suspense of the story are adroitly maintained until the dramatic and surprising ending." Bull Cent Child Books

O'Connell, Tyne
    True love, the sphinx, and other unsolvable riddles; a comedy in four voices. [by] Tyne O'Connell. 1st U.S. ed.; Bloomsbury 2007 225p $16.95

Grades: 7 8 9 10 **Fic**
    1. Love stories 2. School stories 3. Egypt -- Fiction 4. Friendship -- Fiction
    ISBN 978-1-59990-050-6; 1-59990-050-5
    LC 2007002596
    While on a class trip in Egypt, two teenaged best friends from an American private boys' school and two teenaged best friends from a British private girls' school meet each other, and must endure many misunderstandings on their path to true love.
    "This flirty, fun romcom, told from four distinctive points of view, reads like an old-time comedy of errors. O'Connell describes Egypt with such vitality and richness that it shines as a separate character." SLJ

O'Connor, Barbara

Fame and glory in Freedom, Georgia. Farrar, Straus & Giroux 2003 104p $16; pa $6.95

Grades: 4 5 6 7   **Fic**

1. School stories 2. Contests -- Fiction

ISBN 0-374-32258-9; 0-374-40018-0 pa

LC 2002-190212

Unpopular sixth-grader Burdette Bird Weaver persuades the new boy at school, whom everyone thinks is mean and dumb, to be her partner for a spelling bee that might win her everything she's ever wanted

"An idiosyncratic group of characters play out this touching and well-paced story about friendship, family, and connection." Horn Books

Greetings from nowhere. Farrar, Straus and Giroux 2008 198p $16

Grades: 4 5 6 7   **Fic**

1. North Carolina -- Fiction 2. Hotels and motels -- Fiction

ISBN 978-0-374-39937-5; 0-374-39937-9

LC 2006-37439

In North Carolina's Great Smoky Mountains, a troubled boy and his mother, a happy family seeking adventure, a man and his lonely daughter, and the widow who must sell the rundown motel that has been her home for decades, meet and are transformed by their shared experiences.

"The plainspoken text is clean, direct, and honest in its portrayal of pain and hope." Booklist

★ **How** to steal a dog; a novel. Farrar, Straus & Giroux 2007 170p pa $6.99; $16

Grades: 4 5 6   **Fic**

1. Dogs -- Fiction 2. Siblings -- Fiction 3. Homeless persons -- Fiction

ISBN 0-312-56112-1 pa; 0-374-33497-8; 978-0-312-56112-3 pa; 978-0-374-33497-0

LC 2005-40166

Living in the family car in their small North Carolina town, Georgina persuades her younger brother to help her in an elaborate scheme to get money by stealing a dog and then claiming the reward that the owners are bound to offer

This is told "in stripped-down, unsentimental prose. . . . The myriad effects of homelessness and the realistic picture of a moral quandary will surely generate discussion." Booklist

O'Connor, Sheila

★ **Sparrow** Road. G. P. Putnam's Sons 2011 247p $16.99

Grades: 5 6 7 8   **Fic**

1. Artists -- Fiction

ISBN 978-0-399-25458-1; 0-399-25458-7

LC 2010-28290

Twelve-year-old Raine spends the summer at a mysterious artists colony and discovers a secret about her past.

This is a "beautifully written novel. . . . Readers finding themselves in this quiet world will find plenty of space to imagine and dream for themselves." Kirkus

O'Dell, Kathleen

Agnes Parker . . . girl in progress. Dial Bks. 2003 156p hardcover o.p. pa $6.99

Grades: 4 5 6 7   **Fic**

1. School stories 2. Friendship -- Fiction

ISBN 0-8037-2648-1; 0-14-240228-1 pa

LC 2001-58256

As she starts in the sixth grade, Agnes faces challenges with her old best friend, a longtime bully, a wonderful new classmate and neighbor, and herself

"This is a thoughtful, gently humorous, and resonant cusp-of-coming-of-age novel." Horn Book Guide

Other titles about Agnes Parker are:

Agnes Parker . . . Happy camper? (2005)

Agnes Parker . . . Keeping cool in middle school (2007)

Agnes Parker . . . keeping cool in middle school; [by] Kathleen O'Dell. Dial Books for Young Readers 2007 156p $16.99

Grades: 4 5 6   **Fic**

1. School stories 2. Friendship -- Fiction

ISBN 978-0-8037-3078-6

LC 2006021320

Agnes Parker tries to maintain her old persona and keep a low profile in middle school, but her best friend Prejean's problems, persistent harassment from the eighth-grade boys, and a friendship with an interesting boy in her art class make it difficult.

"Agnes is just as likable in this latest installment which is poignant, light, and never saccharine." Booklist

Agnes Parker. . . happy camper? [illustrations by Charise Mericle Harper] Dial Books for Young Readers 2005 160p il $16.95; pa $5.99

Grades: 4 5 6 7   **Fic**

1. Camps -- Fiction 2. Friendship -- Fiction

ISBN 0-8037-2962-6; 0-14-240618-X pa

LC 2004-8101

Science camp brings pranks, fun, rivalries, and a new and somewhat unsettling view of a longtime best friend.

"O'Dell writes knowingly of preteen anxieties and concerns, and her characters ring true." Booklist

O'Dell, Scott

★ **Island** of the Blue Dolphins; illustrated by Ted Lewin. 50th anniversary ed.; Houghton Mifflin Books for Children 2010 177p il $22

Grades: 5 6 7 8   **Fic**

1. Native Americans -- Fiction 2. Wilderness survival -- Fiction 3. San Nicolas Island (Calif.) -- Fiction

ISBN 978-0-547-42483-5; 0-547-42483-3

A reissue of the newly illustrated edition published 1990; first published 1960

Awarded the Newbery Medal, 1961

Left alone on a beautiful but isolated island off the coast of California, a young Indian girl spends eighteen years, not only merely surviving through her enormous courage and self-reliance, but also finding a measure of happiness in her solitary life.

The edition illustrated by Ted Lewin "features twelve full-page, full-color watercolors in purple and blue hues that are appropriate to the island setting. This handsome gift-edition version includes a new introduction by Lois Lowry to commemorate the book's fiftieth anniversary." Horn Book Guide

Sing down the moon. Houghton Mifflin 1970 137p hardcover o.p. pa $6.99

Grades: 5 6 7 8   **Fic**

1. Navajo Indians -- Fiction

ISBN 0-395-10919-1; 978-0-547-40632-9 pa; 0-547-40632-0 pa

A Newbery Medal honor book, 1971

"There is a poetic sonority of style, a sense of identification, and a note of indomitable courage and stoicism that is touching and impressive." Saturday Rev

Streams to the river, river to the sea; a novel of Sacagawea. Houghton Mifflin 1986 191p hardcover o.p. pa $6.99

Grades: 5 6 7 8   **Fic**

1. Interpreters 2. Guides (Persons) 3. Native Americans -- Fiction 4. Lewis and Clark Expedition (1804-1806) -- Fiction

ISBN 0-395-40430-4; 0-618-96642-0 pa

LC 86-936

"An informative and involving choice for American history students and pioneer-adventure readers." Bull Cent Child Books

Thunder rolling in the mountains; [by] Scott O'Dell and Elizabeth Hall. Houghton Mifflin 1992 128p map $17

Grades: 5 6 7 8   **Fic**

1. Nez Percé Indians -- Fiction

ISBN 0-395-59966-0

LC 91-15961

"This is a sad, dark-hued story told in Mr. O'Dell's lean, affecting prose." Child Book Rev Serv

★ **Zia**. Houghton Mifflin 1976 179p hardcover o.p. pa $6.95

Grades: 5 6 7 8   **Fic**

1. Native Americans -- Fiction 2. Christian missions -- Fiction

ISBN 0-395-24393-9; 978-0-547-40633-6 pa; 0-547-40633-9 pa

LC 75-44156

"Zia is an excellent story in its own right, written in a clear, quiet, and reflective style which is in harmony with the plot and characterization." SLJ

O'Hearn, Kate

Elspeth. Kane Miller 2010 303p (Shadow of the dragon) $16.99

Grades: 6 7 8 9   **Fic**

1. Fantasy fiction 2. Dragons -- Fiction 3. Sisters -- Fiction 4. Time travel -- Fiction

ISBN 978-1-935279-18-1; 1-935279-18-1

Sequel to: Kira (2009)

"The author does a great job of creating an action-packed adventure filled with suspense and even a little romance. The

characters are well developed, and the plot is fast-paced and entertaining." SLJ

Kira. Kane Miller 2009 309p (Shadow of the dragon) $16.99

Grades: 6 7 8 9   **Fic**

1. Fantasy fiction 2. Dragons -- Fiction 3. Prisoners -- Fiction

ISBN 978-1-935279-05-1; 1-935279-05-X

"With plenty of exciting action sequences, this debut fantasy will appeal to girls clamoring for a hearty heroine, and the cliff-hanger ending will have readers checking the release date for the next book." Booklist

Another title in this series is:

Elspeth (2010)

O'Neal, Eilis

★ The **false** princess. Egmont USA 2010 319p $16.99

Grades: 6 7 8 9   **Fic**

1. Magic -- Fiction 2. Princesses -- Fiction 3. Witchcraft -- Fiction 4. Conspiracies -- Fiction 5. Identity (Psychology) -- Fiction

ISBN 978-1-60684-079-5; 1-60684-079-7

LC 2009040903

This is a "compelling fantasy, which is filled with magic, political drama, and romance." Publ Wkly

O'Rourke, Erica

Tangled; Erica O'Rourke. KTeen/Kensington 2012 ix, 326 p.p (trade pbk.) $9.95

Grades: 7 8 9 10   **Fic**

1. Occult fiction 2. Magic -- Fiction 3. Interpersonal relations -- Fiction 4. Secrets -- Fiction 5. Friendship -- Fiction 6. Secrecy -- Fiction

ISBN 0758267053; 9780758267054

LC 2011277358

Sequel to: Torn.

This is the second in the "Torn" trilogy. To help her dead friend's sister, Mo must "summon Luc for help. But help for Constance comes with a price—the Quartoren, leaders of the Arcs, want Mo to repair the ley lines from which they draw their power." Several others require her attention as well, pulling Mo in several directions and exacerbating her struggle of living in both the human and magical worlds. (Kirkus)

Torn. Kensington 2011 310p pa $9.95

Grades: 7 8 9 10   **Fic**

1. Magic -- Fiction 2. Homicide -- Fiction 3. Friendship -- Fiction

ISBN 978-0-7582-6703-0; 0-7582-6703-7

Mo Fitzgerald knows about secrets. But when she witnesses her best friend's murder, she discovers Verity was hiding things she never could have guessed. To find the answers she needs and the vengeance she craves, Mo will have to enter a world of raw magic and shifting alliances. And she'll have to choose between two very different, equally dangerous guys.

"O'Rourke's heroine is refreshing: determined, spunky, and unpredictable. . . . Torn should . . . satisfy readers with an insatiable thirst for well-written, fast-paced fantasy and leave them eager for the next installment in the series." SLJ

Oakes, Cory Putnam

Dinosaur boy; Cory Putman Oakes. Sourcebooks Jabberwocky 2015 224 p. illustrations (alk. paper) $12.99

Grades: 4 5 6 7   **Fic**

1. Bullies -- fiction 2. School superintendants and principals -- Fiction 3. Rescues -- Fiction 4. Schools -- Fiction 5. Bullying -- Fiction 6. Dinosaurs -- Fiction 7. Stegosaurus -- Fiction 8. Extraterrestrial beings -- Fiction

ISBN 1492605379; 9781492605379

LC 2014030138

In this children's book by Cory Putnam Oakes about a boy with dinosaur genes, "despite the Principal's Zero Tolerance Policy, Sawyer becomes a bully magnet, befriended only by Elliot aka 'Gigantor' and the weird new girl. When the bullies start disappearing, Sawyer is relieved-until he discovers a secret about the principal that's more shocking than Dino DNA. The bullies are in for a galactically horrible fate...and it's up to Sawyer and his friends to rescue them." (Publisher's note)

"A fun mix of school drama, science fiction, and humor, the story explores the daily hassles of living as part dinosaur, along with the real pain of bullying. First in a planned series, it should find a wide audience." Booklist

Oaks, J. Adams

★ **Why** I fight; a novel. Atheneum Books for Young Readers 2009 228p $16.99; pa $8.99

Grades: 8 9 10 11 12   **Fic**

1. Uncles -- Fiction 2. Violence -- Fiction 3. Criminals -- Fiction

ISBN 978-1-4169-1177-7; 1-4169-1177-4; 978-1-4424-0254-6 pa; 1-4424-0254-7 pa

LC 2007-46433

After his house burns down, twelve-year-old Wyatt Reaves takes off with his uncle, and the two of them drive from town to town for six years, earning money mostly by fighting, until Wyatt finally confronts his parents one last time.

"Oaks' first novel is a breathtaking debut with an unforgettable protagonist. . . . The voice Oaks has created for Wyatt to tell his painful and poignant story is a wonderful combination of the unlettered and the eloquent." Booklist

Oates, Joyce Carol

★ **Big** Mouth & Ugly Girl. HarperCollins Pubs. 2002 265p hardcover o.p. pa $7.99

Grades: 7 8 9 10   **Fic**

1. School stories 2. Friendship -- Fiction

ISBN 0-06-623756-4; 0-06-447347-3 pa

LC 2001-24601

When sixteen-year-old Matt is falsely accused of threatening to blow up his high school and his friends turn against him, an unlikely classmate comes to his aid.

"Readers will be propelled through these pages by an intense curiosity to learn how events will play out. Oates has written a fast-moving, timely, compelling story." SLJ

Freaky green eyes. Harper Tempest 2003 341p hardcover o.p. pa $6.99

Grades: 7 8 9 10   **Fic**

1. Domestic violence -- Fiction

ISBN 0-06-623757-2 lib bdg; 0-06-447348-1 pa

LC 2002-32868

Fifteen-year-old Frankie relates the events of the year leading up to her mother's mysterious disappearance and her own struggle to discover and accept the truth about her parents' relationship.

"Oates pulls readers into a fast-paced, first-person thriller. . . . An absorbing page-turner." Booklist

Okimoto, Jean Davies

Maya and the cotton candy boy. Endicott and Hugh 2011 $16.99; pa $9.99

Grades: 4 5 6 7   **Fic**

1. School stories 2. Siblings -- Fiction 3. Immigrants -- Fiction

ISBN 978-0-9823167-4-0; 0-9823167-4-7; 978-0-9823167-5-7 pa; 0-9823167-5-5 pa

Newly arrived from Kazakhstan, twelve-year-old Maya Alazova resents the way her mother babies her brother, but when she leaves her English Language Learner program for mainstream classes and has to deal with a boy, a bully, and conflict at home, she finds her brother can help with their new culture in ways their parents can't.

"Maya tells her story well, and observant readers will come away with a better understanding of the sacrifices made by similar families." SLJ

Okorafor, Nnedi

Akata witch. Viking 2011 349p $16.99

Grades: 6 7 8 9   **Fic**

1. Fantasy fiction 2. Nigeria -- Fiction 3. Witchcraft -- Fiction 4. Albinos and albinism -- Fiction

ISBN 978-0-670-01196-4; 0-670-01196-7

"Although 12-year-old Sunny is Nigerian, she was born in America, and her Nigerian classmates see her as an outsider. Worse, she's an albino, an obvious target for bullies and suspected of being a ghost or a witch. Things change, however, when she has a vision of impending nuclear war. Then her classmate Orlu and his friend Chichi turn out to be Leopard People—witches—and insist that she is, too. . . . This tale is filled with marvels and is sure to appeal to teens whose interest in fantasy goes beyond dwarves and fairies." Publ Wkly

The **shadow** speaker; [by] Nnedi Okorafor-Mbachu. Jump at the Sun/Hyperion Books for Children 2007 336p hardcover o.p. pa $8.99

Grades: 7 8 9 10   **Fic**

1. Fantasy fiction 2. Science fiction 3. West Africa -- Fiction 4. Sahara Desert -- Fiction

ISBN 978-1-4231-0033-1; 1-4231-0033-6; 978-1-4231-0036-2 pa; 1-4231-0036-0 pa

LC 2007-13313

In West Africa in 2070, after fifteen-year-old "shadow speaker" Ejii witnesses her father's beheading, she embarks on a dangerous journey across the Sahara to find Jaa, her father's killer, and upon finding her, she also discovers a greater purpose to her life and to the mystical powers she possesses.

"Okorafor-Mbachu does an excellent job of combining both science fiction and fantasy elements into this novel. . . . The action moves along at a quick pace and will keep most readers on their toes and wanting more at the end of the novel." Voice Youth Advocates

Zahrah the Windseeker; by Nnedi Okorafor-Mbachu. Houghton Mifflin 2005 308p il $16

Grades: 5 6 7 8   **Fic**

1. Fantasy fiction

ISBN 0-618-34090-4

LC 2004-15783

Zahrah, a timid thirteen-year-old girl, undertakes a dangerous quest into the Forbidden Greeny Jungle to seek the antidote for her best friend after he is bitten by a snake, and finds knowledge, courage, and hidden powers along the way.

"Okorafor-Mbachu's evocative setting will draw experienced fantasy readers with its heady mix of the familiar and the strange." Booklist

Oliver, Jana G.

The **demon** trapper's daughter; a demon trapper novel. [by] Jana Oliver. St. Martin's Griffin 2011 355p pa $9.99

Grades: 7 8 9 10   **Fic**

1. Demonology -- Fiction 2. Apprentices -- Fiction 3. Supernatural -- Fiction 4. Atlanta (Ga.) -- Fiction 5. Father-daughter relationship -- Fiction

ISBN 978-0-312-61478-2; 0-312-61478-0

LC 2010-38860

In 2018 Atlanta, Georgia, after a demon threatens seventeen-year-old Riley Blackthorne's life and murders her father, a legendary demon trapper to whom she was apprenticed, her father's partner, Beck, steps in to care for her, knowing she hates him.

"With a strong female heroine, a fascinating setting, and a complex, thrill-soaked story, this series is off to a strong start." Publ Wkly

Followed by Soul thief (2011)

Soul thief; [by] Jana Oliver. St. Martin's Griffin 2011 339p (A demon trappers novel) pa $9.99

Grades: 7 8 9 10   **Fic**

1. Orphans -- Fiction 2. Demonology -- Fiction 3. Apprentices -- Fiction 4. Supernatural -- Fiction 5. Atlanta (Ga.) -- Fiction

ISBN 978-0-312-61479-9

LC 2011019930

Sequel to The demon trapper's daughter (2011)

In 2018 Atlanta, Georgia, seventeen-year-old apprentice Demon Trapper Riley Blackthorne must deal with unwanted fame, an unofficial bodyguard, an overprotective friend, the Vatican's own Demon Trappers, and an extremely powerful Grade Five demon who is stalking her.

Oliver, Lauren

★ **Liesl** & Po; illustrated by Kei Acedera. Harper 2011 307p il $16.99

Grades: 4 5 6 7   **Fic**

1. Ghost stories 2. Fantasy fiction 3. Magic -- Fiction 4. Bereavement -- Fiction

ISBN 978-0-06-201451-1; 0-06-201451-X

Liesl lives in a tiny attic bedroom, locked away by her cruel stepmother. Her only friends are the shadows and the mice—until one night a ghost appears from the darkness. It is Po, who comes from the Other Side. That same night, an alchemist's apprentice, Will, accidentally bungles an important delivery. He switches a box containing the most powerful magic in the world with one containing something decidedly less remarkable.

This is a "charming, insightful fantasy. . . . This original fairy tale, told by a wise and humorous omniscient narrator and peopled with broadly drawn but instantly recognizable characters, avoids sentimentality to show the magic of accepting loss without letting go and finding joy in the lives left behind." Booklist

Pandemonium; Lauren Oliver. 1st ed.; HarperCollinsPublishers 2012 375p $17.99

Grades: 8 9 10 11   **Fic**

1. Science fiction 2. Love -- Fiction 3. Resistance to government -- Fiction

ISBN 978-0-06-197806-7

LC 2011024241

Sequel to Delirium (2011)

After falling in love, Lena and Alex flee their oppressive society where love is outlawed and everyone must receive "the cure"—an operation that makes them immune to the delirium of love—but Lena alone manages to find her way to a community of resistance fighters, and although she is bereft without the boy she loves, her struggles seem to be leading her toward a new love.

Requiem; Lauren Oliver. Harper 2013 432 p. (hardcover) $18.99

Grades: 8 9 10 11 12   **Fic**

1. Science fiction 2. Resistance to government -- Fiction 3. Love -- Fiction 4. Maine -- Fiction 5. Marriage -- Fiction 6. Friendship -- Fiction 7. Best friends -- Fiction 8. Government, Resistance to -- Fiction

ISBN 0062014536; 9780062014535

LC 2012030236

Sequel to: Pandemonium

This young adult novel, by Lauren Oliver, is the conclusion to the "Delirium" trilogy. "The nascent rebellion . . . has ignited into an all-out revolution . . . , and Lena is at the center of the fight. After rescuing Julian from a death sentence, Lena and her friends fled to the Wilds. But the Wilds are no longer a safe haven. . . . As Lena navigates the increasingly dangerous terrain of the Wilds, her best friend, Hana, lives a safe, loveless life in Portland." (Publisher's note)

★ The **spindlers**; Lauren Oliver; illustrated by Iacopo Bruno. 1st ed. Harper 2012 246 p. ill. (hardcover) $16.99

Grades: 4 5 6   **Fic**

1. Monsters -- Fiction 2. Fantasy fiction 3. Fantasy 4. Soul -- Fiction 5. Brothers and sisters -- Fiction

ISBN 0061978086; 9780061978081

LC 2012009698

This children's fantasy novel, by Lauren Oliver, is about a young girl who travels to a fantasy realm to rescue her younger brother from monsters. "When Liza's brother, Patrick, changes overnight, Liza knows exactly what has happened: The spindlers have gotten to him and stolen his soul. . . . To rescue Patrick, Liza must go Below, armed with little more than her wits and a broom. There, she uncovers a vast world populated with . . . terrible dangers." (Publisher's note)

Olsen, Sylvia

The **girl** with a baby. Sono Nis Press 2004 203p pa $8.95

Grades: 7 8 9 10 **Fic**

1. Canada -- Fiction 2. Teenage mothers -- Fiction 3. Native Americans -- Fiction

ISBN 1-55039-142-9

This "novel tells of teenage mother Jane, 14, who wants to stay in school and raise her baby, Destiny, to be respectful of tradition and smart in the new ways. Jane's family left the reservation because of resentment against Dad, who is white; now in a white area, they face prejudice for being Indian. . . . Jane's home . . . is drawn without romanticism, and . . . Jane's first-person narrative never denies how hard life is, and how thrilling." Booklist

White girl. Sono Nis Press 2004 235p pa $8.95

Grades: 7 8 9 10 **Fic**

1. Prejudices -- Fiction 2. Native Americans -- Fiction

ISBN 1-5503-9147-X

"The talk is contemporary and relaxed, and the characters will hold readers as much as the novel's extraordinary sense of place." Booklist

Olson, Gretchen

Call me Hope; a novel. by Gretchen Olson. Little, Brown & Company 2007 272p hardcover o.p. pa $5.99

Grades: 4 5 6 **Fic**

1. Oregon -- Fiction 2. Child abuse -- Fiction 3. Mother-daughter relationship -- Fiction

ISBN 978-0-316-01236-2; 0-316-01236-X; 978-0-316-01239-3 pa; 0-316-01239-4 pa

LC 2006027896

In Oregon, eleven-year-old Hope begins coping with her mother's verbal abuse by devising survival strategies for herself based on a history unit about the Holocaust, and meanwhile she works toward buying a pair of purple hiking boots by helping at a second-hand shop

"Hope is a winsome character whose bravery and determination will resonate with middle-grade readers." Booklist

Omololu, Cynthia Jaynes

Dirty little secrets; [by] C.J. Omololu. Walker & Co. 2010 212p $16.99

Grades: 8 9 10 11 12 **Fic**

1. School stories 2. Death -- Fiction 3. Compulsive behavior -- Fiction 4. Mother-daughter relationship -- Fiction

ISBN 978-0-8027-8660-9; 0-8027-8660-X

LC 2009-22461

When her unstable mother dies unexpectedly, sixteen-year-old Lucy must take control and find a way to keep the long-held secret of her mother's compulsive hoarding from being revealed to friends, neighbors, and especially the media.

"As a valuable new addition to heartbreaking but honest books about teens immersed in emotionally distressed families, . . . this potent and creatively woven page-turner brings a traumatic situation front and center." SLJ

Oppel, Kenneth

Airborn. Eos 2004 355p $16.99; lib bdg $17.89

Grades: 7 8 9 10 **Fic**

1. Fantasy 2. Pirates 3. Airships 4. Fantasy fiction 5. Airships -- Fiction 6. Imaginary creatures

ISBN 0-06-053180-0; 0-06-053181-9 lib bdg

LC 2003-15642

Michael L. Printz Award honor book, 2005

Matt, a young cabin boy aboard an airship, and Kate, a wealthy young girl traveling with her chaperone, team up to search for the existence of mysterious winged creatures reportedly living hundreds of feet above the Earth's surface.

"This rousing adventure has something for everyone: appealing and enterprising characters, nasty villains, and a little romance." SLJ

Other titles in this series are:

Skybreaker (2005)

Starclimber (2009)

★ The **Boundless**; Kenneth Oppel. First edition Simon & Schuster Books for Young Readers 2014 332 p. illustrations (hardcover : alk. paper) $16.99

Grades: 4 5 6 7 8 **Fic**

1. Adventure fiction 2. Circus -- Fiction 3. Railroads -- Fiction 4. Canada -- History -- Fiction 5. Railroad trains -- Fiction 6. Adventure and adventurers -- Fiction 7. Canada -- History -- 1867-1914 -- Fiction

ISBN 144247288X; 9781442472884; 9781442472891

LC 2013009879

In this book, by Kenneth Oppel, "The Boundless . . . is on its maiden voyage across the country, and first-class passenger Will Everett is about to embark on the adventure of his life! When Will ends up in possession of the key to a train car containing priceless treasures, he becomes the target of sinister figures from his past. In order to survive, Will must join a traveling circus, enlisting the aid of Mr. Dorian, the ringmaster and leader of the troupe." (Publisher's note)

"Will's father is driving the Boundless, the longest train ever, on her maiden voyage. After a series of adventures (involving a sasquatch and a murder), Will finds himself stranded in the caboose, where, with the help of a cute tightrope walker, he dodges a nefarious villain. The third-person present-tense narrative creates suspense as the well-drawn characters travel through an alternate-universe Canadian wilderness." (Horn Book)

★ **Half** brother. Scholastic Press 2010 375p $17.99

Grades: 7 8 9 10 **Fic**

1. Canada -- Fiction 2. Research -- Fiction 3. Chimpanzees -- Fiction 4. Family life -- Fiction

ISBN 978-0-545-22925-8; 0-545-22925-1

LC 2010-2696

In 1973, when a renowned Canadian behavioral psychologist pursues his latest research project—an experiment to determine whether chimpanzees can acquire advanced language skills—he brings home a baby chimp named Zan and asks his thirteen-year-old son to treat Zan like a little brother.

"Oppel has taken a fascinating subject and molded it into a topnotch read. Deftly integrating family dynamics, animal-rights issues, and the painful lessons of growing up, Half Brother draws readers in from the beginning and doesn't let go." SLJ

Silverwing. Simon & Schuster Bks. for Young Readers 1997 217p hardcover o.p. pa $6.99

Grades: 5 6 7 8   **Fic**
1. Bats -- Fiction
ISBN 0-689-81529-8; 1-4169-4998-4 pa

LC 97-10977

When a newborn bat named Shade but sometimes called "Runt" becomes separated from his colony during migration, he grows in ways that prepare him for even greater journeys

"Oppel's bats are fully developed characters who, if not quite cuddly, will certainly earn readers' sympathy and re-spect. In Silverwing the author has created an intriguing mi-crocosm of rival species, factions, and religions." Horn Book

Other titles in this series are:
Sunwing (2000)
Firewing (2003)
Darkwing (2007)

Such wicked intent; Kenneth Oppel. Simon & Schuster Books For Young Readers 2012 320 p. (hardback) $16.99; (paperback) $9.99

Grades: 7 8 9 10   **Fic**
1. Love stories 2. Death -- Fiction 3. Friendship -- Fiction 4. Horror stories 5. Dead -- Fiction 6. Twins -- Fiction 7. Alchemy -- Fiction 8. Brothers -- Fiction 9. Supernatural -- Fiction 10. Geneva (Republic) -- History -- 18th century -- Fiction
ISBN 1442403187; 9781442403185; 9781442403208; 9781442403192

LC 2011042843

This book by Kenneth Oppel is part of the "Apprentice-ship of Victor Frankenstein" series. "[T]hree weeks after [his twin] Konrad's death, Victor plucks a mysterious box from the still-warm ashes of the books of the Dark Library. Demonstrating tremendous hubris, Victor aims to return Konrad to the living world and still win Elizabeth, Kon-rad's grief-stricken love and the boys' childhood friend." (Kirkus Reviews)

★ **This** dark endeavor; the apprenticeship of Victor Frankenstein. Simon & Schuster Books for Young Readers 2011 298p $17.99

Grades: 7 8 9 10   **Fic**
1. Horror fiction 2. Twins -- Fiction 3. Alchemy -- Fiction 4. Brothers -- Fiction
ISBN 1-4424-0315-2; 1-4424-0317-9 ebook; 978-1-4424-0315-4; 978-1-4424-0317-8 ebook

LC 2011016974

When his twin brother falls ill in the family's chateau in the independent republic of Geneva in the eighteenth century, sixteen-year-old Victor Frankenstein embarks on a dangerous and uncertain quest to create the forbidden Elixir of Life described in an ancient text in the family's secret Biblioteka Obscura.

"Written in a readable approximation of early 19th-cen-tury style, Oppel's . . . tale is melodramatic, exciting, disqui-eting, and intentionally over the top." Publ Wkly

Orenstein, Denise Gosliner
★ The **secret** twin. Katherine Tegen Books 2007 385p $16.99; lib bdg $17.89

Grades: 7 8 9 10   **Fic**
1. Twins -- Fiction 2. Orphans -- Fiction 3. Siamese twins -- Fiction
ISBN 978-0-06-078564-2; 0-06-078564-0; 978-0-06-078565-9 lib bdg; 0-06-078565-9 lib bdg

LC 2006-03876

Born a conjoined twin, thirteen-year-old Noah bears the secret guilt of being the only survivor, and now finds himself in the care of a stranger with a secret of her own.

"This spellbinding story will entangle readers at the first sentence. . . . Orenstein's writing is magic—every word and phrase precisely chosen." Booklist

Unseen companion. Katherine Tegen Bks. 2003 357p lib bdg $16.89; pa $7.99

Grades: 7 8 9 10   **Fic**
1. Inuit -- Fiction 2. Alaska -- Fiction
ISBN 0-06-052057-4 lib bdg; 0-06-052058-2 pa

LC 2002-152944

"In distinctive voices, the four narrators tell their own involving stories. . . . A sensitive observer and a compelling storyteller, Orenstein offers a novel that is both touching and harsh." Booklist

Orlev, Uri
Run, boy, run; a novel. translated from the He-brew by Hillel Halkin. Houghton Mifflin 2003 186p $15

Grades: 7 8 9 10   **Fic**
1. Jews -- Poland -- Fiction 2. Holocaust, 1933-1945 -- Fiction
ISBN 0-618-16465-0

LC 2003-1550

Original Hebrew edition, 2001

Based on the true story of a nine-year-old boy who es-capes the Warsaw Ghetto and must survive throughout the war in the Nazi-occupied Polish countryside

"The story is totally engrossing as it vividly describes the hardships faced by so many youngsters during the war. Orlev has . . . successfully used historical fiction to illustrate the Holocaust experience." SLJ

★ The **song** of the whales; translated by Hillel Halkin. Houghton Mifflin Books for Children 2010 108p $16

Grades: 5 6 7 8   **Fic**
1. Jews -- Fiction 2. Dreams -- Fiction 3. Israel -- Fiction 4. Old age -- Fiction 5. Jerusalem -- Fiction 6. Family life -- Fiction 7. Grandfathers -- Fiction
ISBN 978-0-547-25752-5; 0-547-25752-X

LC 2009-49720

At age eight, Mikha'el knows he is different from other boys, but over the course of three years as he helps his par-ents care for his elderly grandfather in Jerusalem, Grandpa teaches Mikha'el to use the gift they share of making other people's dreams sweeter.

This is "the sort of story that operates on many different levels. . . . With a clean sense that less is more, Orlev has crafted a sweetly mysterious and quietly moving read." Booklist

Ortiz Cofer, Judith

Call me Maria; a novel. Orchard Books 2004 127p $16.95

Grades: 7 8 9 10   **Fic**

1. Puerto Ricans -- Fiction 2. New York (N.Y.) -- Fiction

ISBN 0-439-38577-6

LC 2004-2674

Fifteen-year-old Maria leaves her mother and their Puerto Rican home to live in the barrio of New York with her father, feeling torn between the two cultures in which she has been raised.

"Through a mixture of poems, letters, and prose, María gradually reveals herself as a true student of language and life. . . . Understated but with a brilliant combination of all the right words to convey events, Cofer aptly relates the complexities of María's two homes, her parents' lives, and the difficulty of her choice between them." SLJ

If I could fly. Farrar Straus & Giroux 2011 195p $16.99

Grades: 8 9 10 11 12   **Fic**

1. Pigeons -- Fiction 2. Singers -- Fiction 3. New Jersey -- Fiction 4. Family life -- Fiction 5. Puerto Ricans -- Fiction

ISBN 978-0-374-33517-5; 0-374-33517-6

LC 2010022309

When fifteen-year-old Doris's mother, a professional singer, returns to Puerto Rico and her father finds a girlfriend, Doris cares for a neighbor's pigeons and relies on friends as she begins to find her own voice and wings.

"A familiar story of mother/daughter relationships delivered lyrically, simply and inspirationally." Kirkus

Orwell, George, 1903-1950

Animal farm; a fairy story. with a foreword to the Centennial edition by Ann Patchett; with a preface by Russell Baker; introduction by C.M. Woodhouse. Centennial ed.; Harcourt Brace 2003 xxix, 97p $14

Grades: 7 8 9 10 11 12 Adult   **Fic**

1. Animals -- Fiction 2. Totalitarianism -- Fiction

ISBN 978-0-45228-424-1; 0-45228-424-4

First published 1945 in the United Kingdom; first United States edition 1946

Orwell's 1945 fable about the power struggles among animals on a farm parallels the situation in Russia at the time as Orwell saw it; the characters include the ruthless pig Stalin, his idealistic Trotsky-like adversary, and the simple, kindly horse who represents the common man.

Osa, Nancy

Cuba 15. Delacorte Press 2003 277p hardcover o.p. pa $7.95

Grades: 7 8 9 10   **Fic**

1. Cuban Americans -- Fiction

ISBN 0-385-73021-7; 0-385-73233-3 pa

LC 2002-13389

Violet Paz, who is half Cuban American, half Polish American, reluctantly prepares for her upcoming "quince," a Spanish nickname for the celebration of an Hispanic girl's fifteenth birthday

"Violet's hilarious, cool first-person narrative veers between slapstick and tenderness, denial and truth." Booklist

Osterlund, Anne

Aurelia. Speak 2008 246p pa $8.99

Grades: 8 9 10 11   **Fic**

1. Mystery fiction 2. Princesses -- Fiction

ISBN 978-0-14-240579-6; 0-14-240579-5

LC 2007-36074

The king sends for Robert, whose father was a trusted spy, when someone tries to assassinate Aurelia, the stubborn and feisty crown princess of Tyralt.

"Osterlund's characters are both believable, relatable, and enviable, which makes this book enjoyable to read. Even though the book might seem to fit the mold of a quintessential princess fairy tale, Aurelia's spitfire attitude and her resulting actions lend the story a unique twist." Voice Youth Advocates

Followed by: Exile (2011)

Exile. Speak 2011 295p pa $8.99

Grades: 8 9 10 11   **Fic**

1. Princesses -- Fiction 2. Voyages and travels -- Fiction

ISBN 978-0-14-241739-3; 0-14-241739-4

LC 2010009645

Sequel to Aurelia (2008)

In exile, Princess Aurelia is free of responsibilities, able to travel the country and meet the people of Tyralt, but when her journey erupts in a fiery conflagration that puts the fate of the kingdom in peril, she and her companion Robert must determine whether they have the strength and the will to complete their mission.

Ostlere, Cathy

★ **Karma;** a novel in verse. Razorbill 2011 517p map $18.99

Grades: 7 8 9 10 11 12   **Fic**

1. Novels in verse 2. India -- Fiction 3. Violence -- Fiction 4. Culture conflict -- Fiction

ISBN 978-1-59514-338-9; 1-59514-338-6

"The novel's pace and tension will compel readers to read at a gallop, but then stop again and again to turn a finely crafted phrase, whether to appreciate the richness of the language and imagery or to reconsider the layers beneath a thought. This is a book in which readers will consider the roots and realities of destiny and chance. Karma is a spectacular, sophisticated tale that will stick with readers long after they're done considering its last lines." SLJ

Ostow, Micol

Emily Goldberg learns to salsa. Razorbill 2006 200p $16.99

Grades: 7 8 9 10   **Fic**

1. Jews -- Fiction 2. Family life -- Fiction 3. Puerto

Ricans -- Fiction 4. Racially mixed people -- Fiction
ISBN 1-59514-081-6

LC 2006-14651

Forced to stay with her mother in Puerto Rico for weeks after her grandmother's funeral, half-Jewish Emily, who has just graduated from a Westchester, New York high school, does not find it easy to connect with her Puerto Rican heritage and relatives she had never met.

This is "a moving story that has a solid plotline and plenty of family secrets." Booklist

★ **So** punk rock (and other ways to disappoint your mother) a novel. with art by David Ostow. Flux 2009 246p il pa $9.95

Grades: 8 9 10 11 12   **Fic**

1. School stories 2. New Jersey -- Fiction 3. Rock music -- Fiction 4. Bands (Music) -- Fiction 5. Jews -- United States -- Fiction

ISBN 978-0-7387-1471-4; 0-7387-1471-2

LC 2009-8216

Four suburban New Jersey students from the Leo R. Gittleman Jewish Day School form a rock band that becomes inexplicably popular, creating exhiliration, friction, confrontation, and soul-searching among its members.

The "comic-strip-style illustrations are true show-stoppers. . . . A rollicking, witty, and ultra-contemporary book that drums on the funny bone and reverberates through the heart." Booklist

Oswald, Nancy

Nothing here but stones; a Jewish pioneer story. [by] Nancy Oswald. Henry Holt 2004 215p $16.95

Grades: 5 6 7 8   **Fic**

1. Jews -- Fiction 2. Colorado -- Fiction 3. Immigrants -- Fiction 4. Frontier and pioneer life -- Fiction

ISBN 0-8050-7465-1

LC 2003-56969

In 1882, ten-year-old Emma and her family, along with other Russian Jewish immigrants, arrive in Cotopaxi, Colorado, where they face inhospitable conditions as they attempt to start an agricultural colony, and lonely Emma is comforted by the horse whose life she saved

"This well-paced, vivid account should capture readers' attention." SLJ

Owen, James A.

Here, there be dragons; written and illustrated by James A. Owen. Simon & Schuster Books for Young Readers 2006 326p il (The Chronicles of the Imaginarium Geographica) $17.95

Grades: 8 9 10 11 12   **Fic**

1. Fantasy fiction

ISBN 978-1-4169-1227-9; 1-4169-1227-4

LC 2005-30486

Three young men are entrusted with the Imaginarium Geographica, an atlas of fantastical places to which they travel in hopes of defeating the Winter King whose bid for power is related to the First World War raging in the Real World.

"From the arresting prologue, the reader is gripped by a finely crafted fantasy tale and compelled to continue. . . . This superb saga has interesting characters and plenty of action." Voice Youth Advocates

Other titles in this series are:
The search for the Red Dragon (2007)
The indigo king (2008)
The shadow dragons (2009)
The dragon's apprentice (2010)

Oz, Amos, 1939-

★ **Suddenly** in the depths of the forest; translated from the Hebrew by Sondra Silverston. Harcourt 2011 134p $15.99

Grades: 4 5 6 7   **Fic**

1. Fables 2. Animals -- Fiction

ISBN 978-0-547-55153-1; 0-547-55153-3

LC 2011-08664

In a gray and gloomy village, all of the animals—from dogs and cats to fish and snails—disappeared years before. No one talks about it and no one knows why, though everyone agrees that the village has been cursed. But when two children see a fish—a tiny one and just for a second—they become determined to unravel the mystery of where the animals have gone.

"In this swiftly moving fable . . . . Oz creates palpable tension with a repetitive, almost hypnotic rhythm and lyrical language that twists a discussion-provoking morality tale into something much more enchanting." Booklist

Padian, Maria

Brett McCarthy: work in progress. Knopf 2008 276p $15.99; lib bdg $18.99

Grades: 5 6 7 8   **Fic**

1. School stories 2. Maine -- Fiction 3. Cancer -- Fiction 4. Friendship -- Fiction 5. Family life -- Fiction 6. Grandmothers -- Fiction

ISBN 978-0-375-84675-5; 0-375-84675-1; 978-0-375-94675-2 lib bdg; 0-375-94675-6 lib bdg

LC 2007-04415

Eighth-grader Brett McCarthy—once good student and best-friend-to-Diane, now suspended and friendless—faces school and family troubles as she grapples with her redefined life.

"It is Padian's fully developed characters and ear for teenage voices that make this a story that will resonate with anyone who has ever felt isolated in the middle of a crowd." SLJ

Jersey tomatoes are the best. Alfred A. Knopf 2011 344p $16.99; lib bdg $19.99

Grades: 7 8 9 10   **Fic**

1. Camps -- Fiction 2. Ballet -- Fiction 3. Tennis -- Fiction 4. Friendship -- Fiction 5. Anorexia nervosa -- Fiction

ISBN 978-0-375-86579-4; 0-375-86579-9; 978-0-375-96579-1 lib bdg; 0-375-96579-3 lib bdg

LC 2010-11827

When fifteen-year-old best friends Henry and Eve leave New Jersey, one for tennis camp in Florida and one for ballet camp in New York, each faces challenges that put her long-cherished dreams of the future to the test.

"Padian's writing and plotting are clean and clear, and her handling of the duo's dilemmas never stoops to melodrama. An excellent read for sports lovers who desire some meaty beefsteak in their stories." Booklist

Palacio, R. J.

★ **Wonder**; by R.J. Palacio. Alfred A. Knopf 2012 315 p. (hardcover) $15.99

Grades: 3 4 5 6   **Fic**

1. Middle schools 2. Interpersonal relations 3. Birth defects -- Fiction 4. Schools -- Fiction 5. Middle schools -- Fiction 6. Self-acceptance -- Fiction 7. Abnormalities, Human -- Fiction

ISBN 9780375869020; 9780375899881; 9780375969027

LC 2011027133

In this book, "[a]fter being homeschooled for years, Auggie Pullman is about to start fifth grade, but he's worried: How will he fit into middle-school life when he looks so different from everyone else? Auggie has had 27 surgeries to correct facial anomalies he was born with, but he still has a face that has earned him such cruel nicknames as Freak, Freddy Krueger, Gross-out and Lizard face. . . . Palacio divides the novel into eight parts, interspersing Auggie's first-person narrative with the voices of family members and classmates, . . . expanding the story beyond Auggie's viewpoint and demonstrating that Auggie's arrival at school doesn't test only him, it affects everyone in the community." (Kirkus)

Paley, Sasha

Huge. Simon & Schuster Books for Young Readers 2007 259p $15.99

Grades: 7 8 9   **Fic**

1. Camps -- Fiction 2. Obesity -- Fiction 3. Friendship -- Fiction

ISBN 978-1-4169-3517-9; 1-4169-3517-7

LC 2007-03510

When Wilhelmina and April find themselves roommates at a fat camp, both with very different goals, they find they have very little in common until they are both humiliated by the same person.

"The characters are sharply drawn, and the often-amusing story does a good job of showing how everyday concerns are often overshadowed by the issue of weight." Booklist

Palma, Felix J.

The **map** of the sky; a novel. by Felix J. Palma. 1st Atria Books hardcover ed. Atria Books 2012 594 p. (hardcover : alk. paper) $26.00; (paperback) $16.00; (ebook) $24.99

Grades: 6 7 8 9 10 11 12 Adult   **Fic**

1. Time travel -- Fiction 2. Extraterrestrial beings -- Fiction 3. Wells, H. G. (Herbert George), 1866-1946 -- Fiction 4. Fiances -- Fiction 5. Writers -- Fiction 6. Socialites -- New York (State) -- New York -- Fiction

ISBN 1451660316; 9781451660319; 9781451660326; 9781921942907

LC 2012028794

Sequel to: The map of time

In this book by Felix J. Palma, "H. G. Wells . . . meet[s] . . . Garrett Serviss, the man who dared write a sequel to his 'War of the Worlds.'. . . An alcohol-infused sense of camaraderie and adventure inspire the two men to set off to view a hidden secret -- a Martian kept in a locked room in the Natural History Museum. As alien forces converge on London,

a group of citizens struggle to preserve the once-proud city against destruction." (Library Journal)

The **map** of time; Félix J. Palma; translated by Nick Caistor. Atria Books 2011 611p. (hbk.) $26.00

Grades: 6 7 8 9 10 11 12 Adult   **Fic**

1. Science fiction 2. Historical fiction 3. Time travel -- Fiction

ISBN 9781439167397; 1439167397; 143916746X; 9781439167465

LC 2010047304

Originally published in Spain in 2008.

Col. ill. on lining papers.

This book, the first in a trilogy is a "thriller that explores the ramifications of time travel in three intersecting narratives. In the opening chapter, set in 1896 England, aristocratic Andrew Harrington plans to take his own life, despondent over the death years earlier of his lover, the last victim of Jack the Ripper. Meanwhile, 21-year-old Claire Haggerty plots to escape her restrictive role as a woman in Victorian society by journeying to the year 2000. A new commercial concern, Murray's Time Travel, offers such a trip for a hefty fee. Finally, Scotland Yarder Colin Garrett believes that the fatal wound on a murder victim could only have been caused by a weapon from the future. Linking all three stories is H.G. Wells, the author of The Time Machine." (Publisher's Wkly)

Palmer, Robin

The **Corner** of Bitter and Sweet; by Robin Palmer. Penguin Group USA 2013 400 p. $9.99

Grades: 7 8 9 10 11 12   **Fic**

1. Children of alcoholics -- Fiction 2. Television personalities -- Fiction 3. Mother-daughter relationship -- Fiction

ISBN 0142412503; 9780142412503

In this book by Robin Palmer, "a teenage girl and her showbiz mom are forced to re-evaluate their relationship after rehab. . . . To learn how to cope, Annabelle joins Alateen. But when Janie scores a role in a new movie with hot young superstar Billy Barrett, Annabelle frets that if anything goes wrong, it could put her mom right back on the bottle. Fortunately she's distracted by her own crush on small-town boy Matt and the lure of a college photography fellowship." (Kirkus Reviews)

Yours truly, Lucy B. Parker: girl vs. superstar. G. P. Putnam's Sons 2010 215p $15.99; pa $6.99

Grades: 5 6 7 8   **Fic**

1. Celebrities -- Fiction 2. Stepfamilies -- Fiction

ISBN 978-0-399-25489-5; 0-399-25489-7; 978-0-14-241500-9 pa; 0-14-241500-6 pa

"Lucy B. Parker, 12, is having a difficult time. Her best friend dumps her, she still hasn't gotten her period, and her mom insists that she wear a bra. Just when things can't get any worse, her mom announces that she's going to marry the father of Laurel Moses, a TV-music-movie star . . . who happens to hate Lucy's guts. . . . Readers will relate to the lessons learned, but they aren't preachy or in-your-face. The writing is easy to follow, and this book will definitely be enjoyed by preteens who long for Laurel's glamorous life, while also appreciating with Lucy's stable home." SLJ

Another title about Lucy is:

Sealed with a kiss (2010)

Paolini, Christopher

★ **Eragon**. Knopf 2003 509p (Inheritance) $18.95; lib bdg $20.99; pa $6.99

Grades: 7 8 9 10 **Fic**

1. Fantasy fiction 2. Dragons -- Fiction

ISBN 0-375-82668-8; 0-375-92668-2 lib bdg; 0-440-23848-X pa

LC 2003-47481

First published 2002 in different form by Paolini International

In Aagaesia, a fifteen-year-old boy of unknown lineage called Eragon finds a mysterious stone that weaves his life into an intricate tapestry of destiny, magic, and power, peopled with dragons, elves, and monsters

"This unusual, powerful tale . . . is the first book in the planned Inheritance trilogy. . . . The telling remains constantly fresh and fluid, and [the author] has done a fine job of creating an appealing and convincing relationship between the youth and the dragon." Booklist

Other titles in this series are:

Brisningr (2008)

Eldest (2005)

Papademetriou, Lisa

Drop. Alfred A. Knopf 2008 169p $15.99; lib bdg $18.99

Grades: 8 9 10 11 12 **Fic**

1. Gambling -- Fiction 2. Las Vegas (Nev.) -- Fiction

ISBN 978-0-375-84244-3; 0-375-84244-6; 978-0-375-94244-0 lib bdg; 0-375-94244-0 lib bdg

LC 2008-02568

Sixteen-year-old math prodigy Jerrica discovers she has the ability to predict outcomes in blackjack and roulette, and joins forces with Sanjay and Kat to develop her theories while helping them get the money they desperately need.

"The characters are well drawn and the excitement of the gambling scenes is well executed. Additionally, some surprising details about the teens turn the story upside down, unraveling everything that readers thought they knew about them. A page-turner." SLJ

Homeroom diaries; by James Patterson and Lisa Papademetriou; illustrated by Keino. First Edition Little, Brown and Co. 2014 272 p. illustrations (hardcover) $18

Grades: 7 8 9 10 **Fic**

1. School stories 2. Teenage girls -- Fiction 3. Diaries -- Fiction 4. Friendship -- Fiction 5. High schools -- Fiction 6. Foster home care -- Fiction 7. Interpersonal relations -- Fiction

ISBN 0316207624; 9780316207621

LC 2013016061

In this young adult novel by James Patterson and Lisa Papademetriou, illustrated by Keino, "Margaret 'Cuckoo' Clarke recently had a brief stay in a mental institution following an emotional breakdown, but she's turning over a new leaf with her 'Operation Happiness.' She's determined to beat down the bad vibes of the Haters, the Terror Teachers, and all of the trials and tribulations of high school by writing and drawing in her diary." (Publisher's note)

"Despite the fact that serious issues (a negligent mother, an attempted sexual assault, and an incident of cyberbullying) are at play, the lighthearted tone adds levity to the work. The novel is fully illustrated with humorous artwork that contributes to the story in a meaningful way. Fans of the popular "diary fiction" genre (as well as those simply looking for an approachable and quick read) will find much to enjoy here." SLJ

M or F? a novel. [by] Lisa Papademetriou and Chris Tebbetts. Razorbill 2005 296p $16.99

Grades: 8 9 10 11 12 **Fic**

1. Friendship -- Fiction 2. Homosexuality -- Fiction

ISBN 1-59514-034-4

LC 2005008149

Gay teen Marcus helps his friend Frannie chat up her crush online, but then becomes convinced that the crush is falling for him instead.

"This is a creative, funny romance, written with style and sophistication." Booklist

Paquette, Ammi-Joan

Nowhere girl. Walker & Co. 2011 246p $16.99

Grades: 6 7 8 9 **Fic**

1. Fathers -- Fiction 2. Thailand -- Fiction 3. Voyages and travels -- Fiction

ISBN 978-0-8027-2297-3; 0-8027-2297-0

LC 2010049591

Fair-skinned and blond-haired, thirteen-year-old Luchi was born in a Thai prison where her American mother was being held and she has never had any other home, but when her mother dies Luchi sets out into the world to search for the family and home she has always dreamed of.

"The classic quest story gets expanded here with contemporary details in spare lyrical prose that intensify the perilous, archetypal journey. . . . The realistic specifics . . . make the story of betrayal and kindness immediate and universal." Booklist

Paratore, Coleen

Forget me not; from the life of Willa Havisham. by Coleen Murtagh Paratore. Scholastic Press 2009 178p $16.99

Grades: 5 6 7 8 **Fic**

1. Dogs -- Fiction 2. Weddings -- Fiction 3. Friendship -- Fiction 4. Cape Cod (Mass.) -- Fiction 5. Dating (Social customs) -- Fiction 6. Mother-daughter relationship -- Fiction

ISBN 978-0-545-09401-6; 0-545-09401-1; 978-0-545-09404-7 pa; 0-545-09404-6 pa

LC 2008-40712

During a Cape Cod summer, Willa is enjoying her relationship with 'JFK' Kennelly and the challenges of planning a wedding all by herself, but when jealousy enters her love life, best friend Tina pulls away, and the bride proves impossible to please, a sweet dog begins to turn things around.

The **wedding** planner's daughter; [by] Coleen Murtagh Paratore. Simon & Schuster Books for Young Readers 2005 200p $15.95; pa $5.99

Grades: 5 6 7 8 **Fic**

1. Weddings -- Fiction 2. Mother-daughter relationship

-- Fiction

ISBN 0-689-87340-9; 1-4169-1854-X pa

LC 2004-14502

Willa, a romantic girl who wants a father, tries to find a husband for her mother, Cape Cod's most popular wedding planner.

"This book is as sweet a confection as the cherry cordials its 12-year-old protagonist is so fond of eating. . . . The girl's letter to her mother . . . provides emotional heft to what has up to that point been just a pleasant story." SLJ

Other titles about Willa are:

The cupid chronicles (2007)

Willa by heart (2008)

Forget me not (2009)

Willa by heart; [by] Coleen Murtagh Paratore. Simon & Schuster Books for Young Readers 2008 228p $15.99

Grades: 5 6 7 8   Fic

1. Theater -- Fiction 2. Weddings -- Fiction 3. Pregnancy -- Fiction 4. Cape Cod (Mass.) -- Fiction 5. Hotels and motels -- Fiction

ISBN 978-1-4169-4076-0; 1-4169-4076-6

LC 2007016203

As her freshman year nears an end, fourteen-year-old Willa finds herself helping plan two weddings, auditioning for 'Our Town,' organizing a book drive, fighting jealousy over her boyfriend's beautiful new friend, and preparing to become a big sister.

"Willa's spirited first-person narrative is abundantly sprinkled with literary allusions and quotes from titles collected in an appended booklist." Booklist

Park, Barbara

The **graduation** of Jake Moon. Atheneum Bks. for Young Readers 2000 115p $15; pa $4.99

Grades: 4 5 6 7   Fic

1. Grandfathers -- Fiction 2. Alzheimer's disease -- Fiction

ISBN 0-689-83912-X; 0-689-83985-5 pa

LC 99-87475

Fourteen-year-old Jake recalls how he has spent the last four years of his life watching his grandfather descend slowly but surely into the horrors of Alzheimer's disease

"Jake is a well-rounded and believable character surrounded by colorful and equally realistic supporting characters. . . . This novel . . . is written in an accessible style that will appeal to a wide audience." SLJ

Park, Linda Sue

Archer's quest. Clarion Books 2006 167p $16; pa $6.50

Grades: 4 5 6 7   Fic

1. Science fiction 2. Korea -- Fiction 3. Korean Americans -- Fiction

ISBN 978-0-618-59631-7; 0-618-59631-3; 978-0-440-42204-4 pa; 0-440-42204-3 pa

LC 2005-29789

Twelve-year-old Kevin Kim helps Chu-mong, a legendary king of ancient Korea, return to his own time

This "is a breezy, fun read." Voice Youth Advocates

Click; [by] Linda Sue Park [et al.] Arthur A. Levine Books 2007 217p $16.99

Grades: 7 8 9 10   Fic

1. Adventure fiction 2. Photojournalism -- Fiction

ISBN 0-439-41138-6; 978-0-439-41138-7

LC 2006-100069

"Ten distinguished authors each write a chapter of this intriguing novel of mystery and family, which examines the lives touched by a photojournalist George Keane, aka Gee. . . . The authors' distinctive styles remain evident; although readers expecting a more straightforward or linear story may find the leaps through time and place challenging, the thematic currents help the chapters gel into a cohesive whole." Publ Wkly

Project Mulberry; a novel. Clarion 2005 225p $16; pa $6.99

Grades: 5 6 7 8   Fic

1. Korean Americans -- Fiction

ISBN 0-618-47786-1; 0-440-42163-2 pa

LC 2004-18159

While working on a project for an afterschool club, Julia, a Korean American girl, and her friend Patrick learn not just about silkworms, but also about tolerance, prejudice, friendship, patience, and more. Between the chapters are short dialogues between the author and main character about the writing of the book

"The unforgettable family and friendship story, the quiet, almost unspoken racism, and the excitement of the science make this a great cross-curriculum title." Booklist

★ A **single** shard. Clarion Bks. 2001 152p $15; pa $6.99

Grades: 5 6 7 8   Fic

1. Korea -- Fiction 2. Pottery -- Fiction

ISBN 0-395-97827-0; 0-440-41851-8 pa

LC 00-43102

Awarded the Newbery Medal, 2002

Tree-ear, a thirteen-year-old orphan in medieval Korea, lives under a bridge in a potters' village, and longs to learn how to throw the delicate celadon ceramics himself

"This quiet, but involving, story draws readers into a very different time and place. . . . A well-crafted novel with an unusual setting." Booklist

Storm warning. Scholastic 2010 190p (The 39 clues) $12.99

Grades: 4 5 6 7   Fic

1. Ciphers -- Fiction

ISBN 978-0-545-06049-3; 0-545-06049-4

Sequel to: The emperor's code by Gordon Korman (2010)

Amy and Dan hit the high seas as they follow the trail of some infamous ancestors to track down a long lost treasure. However, the real prize isn't hidden in a chest. It's the discovery of the Madrigals' most dangerous secret and, even more shockingly, the true identity of the mysterious man in black.

Followed by: Into the gauntlet by Margaret Peterson Haddix (2010)

When my name was Keoko. Clarion Bks. 2002 199p $16; pa $6.99

Grades: 5 6 7 8   **Fic**

1. Korea -- Fiction 2. World War, 1939-1945 -- Fiction
ISBN 0-618-13335-6; 0-440-41944-1 pa

LC 2001-32487

With national pride and occasional fear, a brother and sister face the increasingly oppressive occupation of Korea by Japan during World War II, which threatens to suppress Korean culture entirely

"Park is a masterful prose stylist, and her characters are developed beautifully. She excels at making traditional Korean culture accessible to Western readers." Voice Youth Advocates

Includes bibliographical references

Park, Linda Sue, 1960-

Keeping score. Clarion Books 2008 202p map $16; pa $6.99

Grades: 4 5 6 7   **Fic**

1. Baseball -- Fiction 2. Family life -- Fiction 3. Brooklyn (New York, N.Y.) -- Fiction
ISBN 978-0-618-92799-9; 0-618-92799-9; 978-0-547-24897-4 pa; 0-547-24897-0 pa

LC 2007-46522

"Maggie's perspective is authentically childlike and engaging, and her relations with her family and friends ring true. . . . This finely crafted novel should resonate with a wide audience of readers." SLJ

★ A **long** walk to water; based on a true story. Clarion Books 2010 121p map $16

Grades: 6 7 8 9 10   **Fic**

1. Refugees 2. Relief workers 3. Water -- Fiction 4. Africans -- Fiction 5. Refugees -- Fiction 6. Sudan -- History -- Civil War, 1983-2005 -- Fiction
ISBN 0-547-25127-0; 978-0-547-25127-1

LC 2009-48857

When the Sudanese civil war reaches his village in 1985, eleven-year-old Salva becomes separated from his family and must walk with other Dinka tribe members through southern Sudan, Ethiopia, and Kenya in search of safe haven. Based on the life of Salva Dut, who, after emigrating to America in 1996, began a project to dig water wells in Sudan.

This is a "spare, immediate account. . . . Young readers will be stunned by the triumphant climax of the former refugee who makes a difference." Booklist

Trust no one; Linda Sue Park. 1st ed. Scholastic Press 2013 190 p. (reinforced) $12.99

Grades: 4 5 6 7   **Fic**

1. Spy stories 2. Mystery fiction
ISBN 0545298431; 9780545298438

LC 2012939109

This is the fifth installment of Linda Sue Park's Cahills vs. Vespers series. Here, "Amy and Dan discover that one of their friends is a spy for the Vespers, a group of evil agents who kidnapped seven of their family members. But which friend is it? The shocking secrets continue when the Cahill siblings finally figure out the Vespers' real plan, and it's much worse than they originally thought." (Owl Magazine)

Parker, Marjorie Hodgson

David and the Mighty Eighth; a British boy and a Texas airman in World War II. by Marjorie Hodgson Parker; illustrated by Mark Postlethwaite. Bright Sky Press 2007 176p il $17.95

Grades: 4 5 6 7   **Fic**

1. Great Britain -- Fiction 2. World War, 1939-1945 -- Fiction
ISBN 978-1-931721-93-6; 1-931721-93-9

LC 2007025999

When, during the London Blitz, he and his older sister are evacuated to go live on their grandparents' East Anglia farm, a young English boy finds it difficult to adjust to his new life until the arrival of the pilots and crews of the U.S. Eight Air Force at nearby airfields brings excitement, friendship, and hope for the future.

This is an "exciting novel, based on a true story. . . . The story is framed by extensive historical notes. . . . Spacious type, thick paper, and an occasional black-and-white drawings make this an appealing package all around." Booklist

Parker, Robert B.

Chasing the bear; a young Spenser novel. Philomel Books 2009 169p $14.99

Grades: 7 8 9 10   **Fic**

1. Bullies -- Fiction 2. Friendship -- Fiction 3. Kidnapping -- Fiction 4. Child abuse -- Fiction
ISBN 978-0-399-24776-7; 0-399-24776-9

LC 2008-52725

Spenser reflects back to when he was fourteen-years-old and how he helped his best friend Jeannie when she was abducted by her abusive father.

"A clean, sharp jab of a read." Booklist

The **Edenville** Owls. Philomel Books 2007 194p $17.99

Grades: 6 7 8 9   **Fic**

1. Mystery fiction 2. Teachers -- Fiction 3. Basketball -- Fiction 4. Friendship -- Fiction 5. Massachusetts -- Fiction
ISBN 978-0-399-24656-2; 0-399-24656-8

LC 2006-34533

Fourteen-year-old Bobby, living in a small Massachusetts town just after World War II, finds himself facing many new challenges as he tries to pull together his coachless basketball team, cope with new feelings for his old friend Joanie, and discover the identity of the mysterious stranger who seems to be threatening his teacher.

"The poignant, well-articulated coming-of-age moments deepen the heart-pounding suspense." Booklist

Parkinson, Curtis

Domenic's war; a story of the Battle of Monte Cassino. Tundra Books 2006 191p pa $9.95

Grades: 6 7 8 9   **Fic**

1. Italy -- Fiction 2. World War, 1939-1945 -- Fiction
ISBN 0-88776-751-6

"Based on actual experiences, this World War II novel tells the stories of Italians living near Monte Cassino, caught between the German army and the Allied forces. Young Domenic Luppino and his family live north of the fighting, but fear the advancing troops. Fifteen-year-old Antonio lost his entire family when fighting moved into the town, and now he's on his own. Both boys face hardships and risk their lives for friends and family. Their stories of strength, resourcefulness, and survival are deftly placed within the context of the Monte Cassino campaign and will give readers a poignant look at the ways in which the war affected average citizens." SLJ

Parkinson, Siobhan

Blue like Friday. Roaring Brook Press 2008 160p $16.95

Grades: 4 5 6 7 **Fic**

1. Ireland -- Fiction 2. Family life -- Fiction 3. Synesthesia -- Fiction 4. Missing persons -- Fiction
ISBN 978-1-59643-340-3; 1-59643-340-X

When Olivia helps her quirky friend Hal, whose synesthesia causes him to experience everything in colors, with a prank intended to get rid of Hal's potential stepfather, there are unexpected consequences, including the disappearance of Hal's mother.

"Parkinson creates a warm, moving story of real families facing real problems. . . . The economy of her prose is admirable; all the characters are well drawn." Booklist

Parkinson, Siobhán

Long story short. Roaring Brook Press 2011 160p $16.99

Grades: 6 7 8 9 10 **Fic**

1. Ireland -- Fiction 2. Siblings -- Fiction 3. Runaway children -- Fiction
ISBN 978-1-59643-647-3; 1-59643-647-6
LC 2010-29023

Fourteen-year-old Jono and his eight-year-old sister Julie run away when, soon after their grandmother's death, their alcoholic mother hits Julie, but when the police find them in Galway, Jono learns he is in big trouble.

"A deeply affecting story about what can go wrong when adults fail children and the choices available to them are all bad." Publ Wkly

Parnell, Robyn

The **mighty** Quinn; by Robyn Parnell; illustrated by Aaron and Katie DeYoe. 1st ed. Scarletta Press 2013 263 p. ill. (paperback) $10.95

Grades: 4 5 6 7 **Fic**

1. School stories 2. Oregon -- Fiction 3. Bullies -- Fiction 4. Schools -- Fiction 5. Friendship -- Fiction
ISBN 1938063104; 9781938063107
LC 2012031518

In this story, by Robyn Parnell, "Quinn Andrews-Lee . . . faces a dismal school year. His little sister outshines him . . . , he yearns for a service award his peers disdain, and charismatic bigot Matt Barker's goal in life is to torment Quinn. . . . When Quinn reports an act of vandalism, he is accused of injuring Matt. . . . A free-spirited new kid in Quinn's class, helps Quinn deduce who hurt Matt, but Matt would probably die . . . before admitting the truth." (Publisher's note)

Parry, Rosanne

Heart of a shepherd; [by] Rosanne Parry. Random House Children's Books 2009 161p lib bdg $18.99; $15.99

Grades: 4 5 6 7 **Fic**

1. Oregon -- Fiction 2. Ranch life -- Fiction 3. Family life -- Fiction 4. Christian life -- Fiction 5. Iraq War, 2003- -- Fiction
ISBN 0-375-84802-9; 978-0-375-94802-2 lib bdg; 0-375-94802-3 lib bdg; 978-0-375-84802-5
LC 2007-48094

Ignatius 'Brother' Alderman, nearly twelve, promises to help his grandparents keep the family's Oregon ranch the same while his brothers are away and his father is deployed to Iraq, but as he comes to accept the inevitability of change, he also sees the man he is meant to be

There is "more action than introspection afoot, with sibling tensions, a wildfire, and the grandfather's death along the journey. It's refreshing . . . to find a protagonist with his eyes and heart open to positive adult examples . . . and who matches his mettle to theirs." Bull Cent Child Books

Second fiddle. Random House 2011 233p map $16.99; lib bdg $19.99

Grades: 5 6 7 8 **Fic**

1. Music -- Fiction 2. France -- Fiction 3. Germany -- Fiction 4. Soldiers -- Fiction 5. Paris (France) -- Fiction 6. Berlin (Germany) -- Fiction
ISBN 978-0-375-86196-3; 0-375-86196-3; 978-0-375-96196-0 lib bdg; 0-375-96196-8 lib bdg; 978-0-375-89350-6 e-book
LC 2009-33324

Six months after the fall of the Berlin Wall, three eighth-grade girls living on an American military base with their families in Berlin try to save a Russian soldier, who has been beaten and left for dead, by smuggling him to Paris, where they are going to perform in a music competition.

"This reads like first-class historical fiction; Parry . . . vividly conjures the political tensions of the period, the challenges of life as an army brat, and the redemptive power of music." Publ Wkly

Written in stone; Rosanne Parry. Random House Inc 2013 208 p. (jacketed hardcover) $16.99

Grades: 5 6 7 **Fic**

1. Historical fiction 3. Orphans -- Fiction 4. Makah Indians -- Fiction 5. Northwest, Pacific -- History -- 20th century -- Fiction 6. Indians of North America -- Northwest, Pacific -- Fiction
ISBN 0375869719; 9780375869716; 9780375871351; 9780375969713; 9780375985348
LC 2012012491

In this book, five "years after her mother and baby sister die in the 1918 flu pandemic, Pearl's father is lost in the last Makah whale hunt. Pearl, 13, is determined to create a future for herself that honors her distinguished heritage; still, her extended family's unaccustomed financial hardship and loss of status stings. The New York collector interested in their masks and carvings might offer a way out, but does he have a secret agenda?" (Kirkus Reviews)

Includes bibliographical references ( )

Partridge, Elizabeth

★ **Dogtag** summer. Bloomsbury Books for Young Readers 2011 226p $16.99

Grades: 4 5 6 7   **Fic**

1. Hippies -- Fiction 2. Adoption -- Fiction 3. California -- Fiction 4. Family life -- Fiction 5. Vietnamese Americans -- Fiction 6. Racially mixed people -- Fiction 7. Vietnam War, 1961-1975 -- Fiction

ISBN 978-1-59990-183-1; 1-59990-183-8

LC 2010-25515

In the summer of 1980 before she starts junior high school in Santa Rosa, California, Tracy, who was adopted from Vietnam when she was six years old, finds an old ammo box with a dog tag and picture that bring up painful memories for both her Vietnam-veteran father and her.

"This gripping yet tender coming-of-age story reveals multiple nuanced perspectives of the Vietnam War and its aftermath. . . . Powerful historical fiction." Publ Wkly

Pastis, Stephan

Timmy failure; we meet again. Stephan Pastis. Candlewick Press 2014 272 p. illustrations $14.99

Grades: 4 5 6 7   **Fic**

1. Boys -- Fiction 2. Polar bear -- Fiction 3. Private investigators -- Fiction

ISBN 0763673757; 9780763673758

LC 2014933979

This illustrated children's book, by Stephan Pastis, the third in the "Timmy Failure" series, continues to follow "Timmy Failure. And his detective agency is on the verge of global domination. Global riches. Global fame. And yet the gods keep throwing him curveballs: for starters, academic probation. The coveted Miracle Report is the key to everything, including a good grade." (Publisher's note)

"In this third story about the world's greatest detective (who really isn't), Timmy Failure is allowed back to school on academic probation, and he and his mother (and polar bear Total) have moved again now that she has a new job...While he is not yet ready for prime time, there are signs that, with the support of people who find him lovable in spite of himself, Timmy Failure will not live up to his name." Booklist

Timmy failure : now look what you've done; Now Look What You've Done. Stephan Pastis. Candlewick Press 2014 288 p. illustrations $14.99

Grades: 4 5 6 7   **Fic**

1. Detectives -- Fiction 2. Polar bear -- Fiction 3. Problem solving -- Fiction 4. Self-confidence -- Fiction 5. Globes 6. Schools 7. Contests 8. Humorous stories 9. Detective and mystery stories

ISBN 0763660515; 9780763660512

LC 2013944145

In this book, by Stephan Pastis, "the too-smart-for-his-own-good kid detective is back for a second zany installment, along with his 1500-pound polar/bear business partner, Total. Timmy has big dreams for his crime-solving empire, fueled by his complete self-confidence, delusions of grandeur, and his assured win in a competition to find a stolen globe worth $500. But first, shenanigans are afoot and must be thwarted." (School Library Journal)

"Timmy is back, clueless as ever, his sleuthing even clumsier than in the first installment. Timmy and his polar bear sidekick, Total, haplessly plow through the shenanigans thwarting Timmy's domination of the school detective competition. Great-aunt Coriander and her own wacky aspirations add a new layer to the winning combination of sardonically humorous text and pen-and-ink cartoons that has won Timmy many fans." Horn Book

Paterson, Katherine

Bread and roses, too. Clarion Books 2006 275p $16; pa $6.99

Grades: 5 6 7 8   **Fic**

1. Strikes -- Fiction 2. Immigrants -- Fiction 3. Lawrence (Mass.) -- Fiction 4. United States -- History -- 1898-1919 -- Fiction

ISBN 978-0-618-65479-6; 0-618-65479-8; 978-0-547-07651-5 pa; 0-547-07651-7 pa

LC 2005-31702

Jake and Rosa, two children, form an unlikely friendship as they try to survive and understand the 1912 Bread and Roses strike of mill workers in Lawrence, Massachusetts.

"Paterson has skillfully woven true events and real historical figures into the fictional story and created vivid settings, clearly drawn characters, and a strong sense of the hardship and injustice faced by the mostly immigrant mill workers." SLJ

★ **Bridge** to Terabithia; illustrated by Donna Diamond. Crowell 1977 128p il $15.99; lib bdg $16.89; pa $5.99

Grades: 4 5 6 7   **Fic**

1. Death -- Fiction 2. Virginia -- Fiction 3. Friendship -- Fiction

ISBN 0-690-01359-0; 0-690-04635-9 lib bdg; 0-06-440184-7 pa

LC 77-2221

Awarded the Newbery Medal, 1978

The life of Jess, a ten-year-old boy in rural Virginia expands when he becomes friends with a newcomer who subsequently meets an untimely death trying to reach their hideaway, Terabithia, during a storm

"Jess and his family are magnificently characterized; the book abounds in descriptive vignettes, humorous sidelights on the clash of cultures, and realistic depictions of rural school life." Horn Book

The **day** of the pelican. Clarion Books 2009 145p $16

Grades: 6 7 8 9   **Fic**

1. Muslims -- Fiction 2. Refugees -- Fiction 3. Albanians -- Fiction 4. Kosovo (Serbia) -- Fiction

ISBN 978-0-547-18188-2; 0-547-18188-4

LC 2009-14998

In 1998 when the Kosovo hostilities escalate, thirteen-year-old Meli's life as an ethnic Albanian, changes forever after her brother escapes his Serbian captors and the entire family flees from one refugee camp to another until they are able to immigrate to America.

"Paterson offers a realistic and provocative account of these refugees' plight, balanced by the hope of new beginnings and the resilience of the human spirit." Publ Wkly

★ The **great** Gilly Hopkins. Crowell 1978 148p $15.99; lib bdg $16.89; pa $5.99

Grades: 5 6 7 8   **Fic**

1. Foster home care -- Fiction

ISBN 0-690-03837-2; 0-690-03838-0 lib bdg; 0-06-440201-0 pa

           LC 77-27075

A Newbery Medal honor book, 1979

"A well-structured story, [this] has vitality of writing style, natural dialogue, deep insight in characterization, and a keen sense of the fluid dynamics in human relationships." Bull Cent Child Books

★ **Jacob** have I loved. Crowell 1980 216p $15.99; lib bdg $17.89; pa $6.99

Grades: 5 6 7 8   **Fic**

1. Twins -- Fiction 2. Sisters -- Fiction 3. Chesapeake Bay (Md. and Va.) -- Fiction

ISBN 0-690-04078-4; 0-690-04079-2 lib bdg; 0-06-440368-8 pa

           LC 80-668

Awarded the Newbery Medal, 1981

Filled with resentment over the attention showered upon her twin sister, and awaiting the day she can leave her town behind, young Louise meets a wise old sea captain and begins learning how to let go of her anger.

"Each incident and feeling in the life of her young protagonist rings true because the younger voice is so alive and direct. This is a book full of humor and compassion and sharpness." Bull Cent Child Books

Jip; his story. Lodestar Bks. 1996 181p hardcover o.p. pa $6.99

Grades: 5 6 7 8   **Fic**

1. Slavery -- Fiction 2. Vermont -- Fiction 3. African Americans -- Fiction 4. Racially mixed people -- Fiction

ISBN 0-525-67543-4; 0-14-240411-X pa

           LC 96-2680

While living on a Vermont poor farm during 1855 and 1856, Jip learns that his mother was a runaway slave, and that his father, the plantation owner, plans to reclaim him as property

"This historically accurate story is full of revelations and surprises, one of which is the return appearance of the heroine of Lyddie. . . . The taut, extremely readable narrative and its tender depictions of friendship and loyalty provide first-rate entertainment." Publ Wkly

★ **Lyddie**. Lodestar Bks. 1991 182p $17.99; pa $6.99

Grades: 5 6 7 8 9   **Fic**

1. Factories -- Fiction 2. Massachusetts -- Fiction 3. United States -- History -- 1815-1861 -- Fiction

ISBN 0-525-67338-5; 0-14-240254-0 pa

           LC 90-42944

Impoverished Vermont farm girl Lyddie Worthen is determined to gain her independence by becoming a factory worker in Lowell, Massachusetts, in the 1840s

"Not only does the book contain a riveting plot, engaging characters, and a splendid setting, but the language—graceful, evocative, and rhythmic—incorporates the rural speech patterns of Lyddie's folk, the simple Quaker expressions of the farm neighbors, and the lilt of fellow mill girl Bridget's Irish brogue. . . . A superb story of grit, determination, and personal growth." Horn Book

Park's quest. Lodestar Bks. 1988 148p hardcover o.p. pa $5.99

Grades: 5 6 7 8   **Fic**

1. Farm life -- Fiction 2. Vietnamese Americans -- Fiction

ISBN 0-14-034262-1 pa

           LC 87-32422

Eleven-year-old Park makes some startling discoveries when he travels to his grandfather's farm in Virginia to learn about his father who died in the Vietnam War and meets a Vietnamese-American girl named Thanh

The author "confronts the complexity, the ambiguity, of the war and the emotions of those it involved with an honesty that young readers are sure to recognize and appreciate." N Y Times Book Rev

Preacher's boy. Clarion Bks. 1999 168p $15; pa $4.95

Grades: 5 6 7 8   **Fic**

1. Vermont -- Fiction 2. Family life -- Fiction 3. Christian life -- Fiction

ISBN 0-395-83897-5; 0-06-447233-7 pa

           LC 98-50083

In 1899, ten-year-old Robbie, son of a preacher in a small Vermont town, gets himself into all kinds of trouble when he decides to give up being Christian in order to make the most of his life before the end of the world

"With warmth, humor, and her powerful yet plain style, Paterson draws empathetic and memorable characters." SLJ

The **same** stuff as stars. Clarion Bks. 2002 242p $15

Grades: 5 6 7 8   **Fic**

1. Brothers and sisters -- Fiction

ISBN 0-618-24744-0

           LC 2002-3967

When Angel's self-absorbed mother leaves her and her younger brother Bernie with their poor great-grandmother, the eleven-year-old girl worries not only about her mother and brother, her imprisoned father, the frail old woman, but also about a mysterious man who begins sharing with her the wonder of the stars. "Intermediate." (Horn Book)

"Paterson's deft hand at characterization, her insight into the human soul, and her glorious prose make this book one to rejoice over." Voice Youth Advocates

Patneaude, David

A **piece** of the sky; [by] David Patneaude; [cover illustration by Layne Johnson] Albert Whitman 2007 178p il $15.95

Grades: 5 6 7 8   **Fic**

1. Oregon -- Fiction 2. Meteorites -- Fiction 3.

Mountaineering -- Fiction
ISBN 978-0-8075-6536-0

LC 2006023529

Fourteen-year-old Russell, his friend Phoebe, and her brother Isaac must find a legendary meteor in the Oregon mountains before it is exploited

"This old-fashioned adventure story has contemporary appeal." Booklist

Thin wood walls. Houghton Mifflin 2004 231p $16

Grades: 7 8 9 10   **Fic**
1. World War, 1939-1945 -- Fiction 2. Japanese Americans -- Evacuation and relocation, 1942-1945 -- Fiction
ISBN 0-618-34290-7

LC 2004-1014

When the Japanese bomb Pearl Harbor, Joe Hamada and his family face growing prejudice, eventually being torn away from their home and sent to a relocation camp in California, even as his older brother joins the United States Army to fight in the war.

"Basing his story on extensive research and interviews, the author does a fine job of bringing the daily experience up close through the story of an American kid torn from home." Booklist

Paton Walsh, Jill

A **parcel** of patterns. Farrar, Straus & Giroux 1983 136p hardcover o.p. pa $5.95

Grades: 7 8 9 10   **Fic**
1. Plague -- Fiction 2. Great Britain -- Fiction
ISBN 0-374-35750-1; 0-374-45743-3 pa

LC 83-48143

Mall Percival tells how the plague came to her Derbyshire village of Eyam in the year 1665, how the villagers determined to isolate themselves to prevent further spread of the disease, and how three-fourths of them died before the end of the following year.

"Historical in broad outline, the narrative blends superb characterizations, skillful plotting, and convincing speech for a hauntingly memorable story that offers a richly textured picture of the period." Child Book Rev Serv

Patrick, Cat

Forgotten; a novel. Little, Brown 2011 288p $17.99

Grades: 7 8 9 10 11   **Fic**
1. School stories 2. Memory -- Fiction 3. Family life -- Fiction 4. Dating (Social customs) -- Fiction
ISBN 978-0-316-09461-0; 0-316-09461-7

LC 2010-43032

Sixteen-year-old London Lane forgets everything each night and must use notes to struggle through the day, even to recall her wonderful boyfriend, but she "remembers" future events and as her "flashforwards" become more disturbing she realizes she must learn more about the past lest it destroy her future.

"Patrick raises philosophical issues of real interest. . . . Thoughtful readers will enjoy the mind games, romance readers will enjoy the relationship dynamics, and all read-

ers will find themselves inexorably pulled into a logical yet surprising and compelling finish." Booklist

The **Originals**; Cat Patrick. 1st ed. Little, Brown and Co. 2013 304 p. (hardcover) $18

Grades: 8 9 10 11 12   **Fic**
1. Sisters -- Fiction 2. Human cloning -- Fiction 3. Dating (Social customs) -- Fiction 4. Cloning -- Fiction 5. Individuality -- Fiction 6. Single-parent families -- Fiction
ISBN 0316219436; 9780316219433

LC 2012029853

In this novel, by Cat Patrick, "17-year-olds Lizzie, Ella, and Betsey Best grew up as identical triplets . . . until they discovered a shocking family secret. They're actually closer than sisters, they're clones . . . , hiding from a government agency that would expose them. . . . Then Lizzie meets Sean Kelly. . . . As their relationship develops, Lizzie realizes that she's not a carbon copy of her sisters; she's an individual with unique dreams and desires." (Publisher's note)

Revived; by Cat Patrick. 1st ed. Little, Brown & Co. 2012 336 p. (hardcover) $17.99; (paperback) $8.99

Grades: 7 8 9 10 11 12   **Fic**
1. Drugs -- Testing 2. Secrecy -- Fiction 3. Science -- Experiments -- Fiction 4. Death -- Fiction 5. Drugs -- Fiction 6. Schools -- Fiction 7. High schools -- Fiction 8. Moving, Household -- Fiction
ISBN 0316094625; 9780316094627; 9780316094634

LC 2011026950

This book, by Cat Patrick, follows Daisy, who since the age of five has been "part of a top-secret clinical trial for a drug called Revive that can bring the deceased back to life. . . . Daisy uncovers some secrets within the program: a mysterious extra case file, a new test batch of Revive, some unexplained car crashes, and the erratic behavior of the mysterious man at the top, nicknamed God." (Bulletin of the Center for Children's Books)

Patrick, Denise Lewis

A **matter** of souls; Denise Lewis Patrick. Carolrhoda Lab 2014 186 p. (trade hard cover : alk. paper) $16.95

Grades: 7 8 9 10 11 12   **Fic**
1. American short stories 2. Race relations -- Fiction 3. Southern States -- Fiction 4. African Americans -- History 5. Southern States -- History -- Fiction 6. African Americans -- Southern States -- Fiction
ISBN 0761392807; 9780761392804

LC 2013017597

This collection of short stories, by Denise Lewis Patrick, "considers the souls of black men and women across centuries and continents. In each, she takes the measure of their dignity, describes their dreams, and catalogs their fears. Brutality, beauty, laughter, rage, and love all take their turns in each story, but the final impression is of indomitable, luminous, and connected souls." (Publisher's note)

"Eight short stories with long memory cut to the quick— all the more as they could be true. Patrick's tales from the distant and not-so-distant past shed fresh light on interracial and intraracial conflicts that shape and often distort the realities of African-Americans. . . . The plots and characters change from one story to the next, but each one artfully tells a poignant truth without flinching. Shocking, informative and powerful, this volume offers spectacular literary snapshots of black history and culture." Kirkus

Patron, Susan

Behind the masks; the diary of Angeline Reddy. Susan Patron. Scholastic 2012 293 p. ill., map (paper-over-board) $12.99

Grades: 5 6 7 8 9 **Fic**

1. Mystery fiction 2. Diaries -- Fiction 3. Thieves -- Fiction 4. Gold mines and mining -- Fiction 5. Frontier and pioneer life -- California -- Fiction 6. Lawyers -- Fiction 7. Mystery and detective stories 8. Robbers and outlaws -- Fiction 9. California -- History -- 19th century -- Fiction

ISBN 9780545304375

LC 2011023826

"[T]his Dear America series title [is] set in Bodie, California, in 1880. Fourteen-year-old diarist and would-be dramatist Angeline Reddy does not believe her father, criminal lawyer Patrick Reddy, has been murdered. Convinced his disappearance is purposeful, Angie investigates his 'demise' and tries to bring him back to their rough-and-tumble mining community. Assisted by friends, a dashing young Wells Fargo clerk, and the members of a local theater troupe, . . . Angie offers a revealing look at frontier life "especially preoccupations with thespian entertainments, racial and social prejudices, and vigilante justice."(Booklist)

Patt, Beverly

★ **Best** friends forever; a World War II scrapbook. with illustrations by Shula Klinger. Marshall Cavendish 2010 92p il $17.99

Grades: 5 6 7 8 **Fic**

1. Friendship -- Fiction 2. Washington (State) -- Fiction 3. World War, 1939-1945 -- Fiction 4. Puyallup Assembly Center (Wash.) -- Fiction 5. Japanese Americans -- Evacuation and relocation, 1942-1945 -- Fiction

ISBN 978-0-7614-5577-6; 0-7614-5577-9

LC 2008-20875

Fourteen-year-old Louise keeps a scrapbook detailing the events in her life after her best friend, Dottie, a Japanese-American girl, and her family are sent to a relocation camp during World War II.

"If the drama of the girls separation isn't enough, a romantic subplot and the antics of Dottie's goofy dog (living with Louise in her absence) will surely keep young readers interested. This heartwarming tale of steadfast friendship makes a wonderful access point for learning more about World War II and Japanese internment." SLJ

Includes bibliographical references

Patten, E. J.

Return to Exile; illustrated by John Rocco. Simon & Schuster 2011 512p (The Hunter chronicles) $16.99

Grades: 5 6 7 8 **Fic**

1. Fantasy fiction 2. Uncles -- Fiction 3. Monsters

-- Fiction

ISBN 978-1-4424-2032-8; 1-4424-2032-4; 978-1-4169-8259-3 e-book

LC 2010053480

"Sky's twelfth birthday is a mix. His mother's delicious homemade goulash cannot overshadow the disappearance of his beloved uncle, Phineas, or the family's return to the small town of Exile. Sky has grown up reading about the Hunters of Legend, but he never dreamed that they were real until monsters appear in Exile and make Sky their target. . . . Patten's first novel excels at world building and pacing; the monsters . . . are fully formed and vividly drawn. . . . Interspersed with humor to keep an otherwise dark story from becoming overbearing, the balance is just right." Booklist

Patterson, James

Maximum Ride: the angel experiment. Little, Brown 2005 422p (Maximum Ride) $16.99

Grades: 7 8 9 10 **Fic**

1. Science fiction 2. Genetic engineering -- Fiction

ISBN 0-316-15556-X

LC 2004-18623

After the mutant Erasers abduct the youngest member of their group, the "bird kids," who are the result of genetic experimentation, take off in pursuit and find themselves struggling to understand their own origins and purpose.

"Smart-mouthed sympathetic characters and copious butt-kicking make this fast read pure escapist pleasure." Horn Book Guide

Other titles in this series are:
School's out forever (2006)
Saving the world and other extreme sports (2007)
Final warning (2008)
Max (2009)
Fang (2010)
Angel (2011)

★ **Middle** school, the worst years of my life; [by] James Patterson and Chris Tebbetts; illustrated by Laura Park. Little, Brown 2011 281p il $15.99

Grades: 4 5 6 7 **Fic**

1. School stories 2. Bereavement -- Fiction 3. Family life -- Fiction

ISBN 0-316-10187-7; 978-0-316-10187-5

LC 2010022852

When Rafe Kane enters middle school, he teams up with his best friend, "Leo the Silent," to create a game to make school more fun by trying to break every rule in the school's code of conduct.

"The book's ultrashort chapters, dynamic artwork, and message that 'normal is boring' should go a long way toward assuring kids who don't fit the mold that there's a place for them, too." Publ Wkly

Patterson, Valerie O.

The **other** side of blue. Clarion Books 2009 223p $16

Grades: 7 8 9 10 **Fic**

1. Artists -- Fiction 2. Curacao -- Fiction 3. Bereavement -- Fiction 4. Mother-daughter relationship

-- Fiction

ISBN 978-0-547-24436-5; 0-547-24436-3

LC 2008-49233

The summer after her father drowned off the island of Curacao, Cyan and her mother, a painter, return to the house they stay at every summer, along with the daughter of her mother's fiance, but Cyan blames her mother and spends her time trying to find out what really happened to her father

"In her memorable first-person voice, filled with the minute observations of a young artist, Cyan sketches out with believable detail the beautiful setting, the unspoken family tension, and her fragile recovery of hope after loss." Booklist

Pattou, Edith

East. Harcourt 2003 498p hardcover o.p. pa $8.95

Grades: 7 8 9 10   **Fic**

1. Fairy tales 2. Bears -- Fiction

ISBN 0-15-204563-5; 0-15-205221-6 pa

LC 2003-2338

A young woman journeys to a distant castle on the back of a great white bear who is the victim of a cruel enchantment

"Readers with a taste for fantasy and folklore will embrace Pattou's . . . lushly rendered retelling of 'East of the Sun and West of the Moon'." Publ Wkly

Pauley, Kimberly

Cat Girl's day off; Kimberly Pauley. Tu Books 2012 334 p. (hardcover : alk. paper) $17.95

Grades: 6 7 8 9 10   **Fic**

1. Cats -- Fiction 2. Mystery fiction 3. Adventure fiction 4. High school students -- Fiction 5. Parapsychology 6. Schools -- Fiction 7. High schools -- Fiction 8. Chicago (Ill.) -- Fiction 9. Mystery and detective stories 10. Human-animal communication -- Fiction 11. Family life -- Illinois -- Chicago -- Fiction 12. Motion pictures -- Production and direction -- Fiction

ISBN 1600608833; 9781600608834; 9781600608841

LC 2011042997

In this young adult novel, "High school sophomore Natalie 'Nat' Ng has a 'Talent' she's not proud of: the ability to talk to cats. Her younger sister is a 'supergenius' with chameleonlike abilities; her older sister is proficient in truth divination and levitation, and has X-ray vision; and her parents work for the Bureau of Extrasensory Regulation and Management. When a film crew comes to Nat's Chicago high school to shoot a takeoff of 'Ferris Bueller's Day Off' things get fishy: the female star isn't acting like herself, and Nat learns from a cat that celebrity blogger Easton West may not be who she claims to be. Along with her friends Oscar and Melly, Nat gets dragged into a whirlwind adventure to find out what happened to the real Easton." (Publishers Weekly)

Paulsen, Gary

Crush; the theory, practice, and destructive properties of love. Gary Paulsen. Wendy Lamb Books 2012 136 p.

Grades: 5 6 7 8   **Fic**

1. Love -- Fiction 2. Humorous fiction 3. Crushes -- Fiction 4. High school students -- Fiction 5. Dating (Social customs) -- Fiction 6. Humorous stories 7.

Interpersonal relations -- Fiction

ISBN 0385742304; 9780307974532; 9780375990540; 9780385742306; 9780385742313

LC 2011028915

In this book, "Tina, aka the most beautiful girl he's ever seen, has stolen Kevin's heart, although she's blissfully oblivious to the effect she has on him. . . . Rather than reveal his ardor outright, Kevin decides it's safer to first make a scientific study of just how love works by setting up romantic opportunities for his victims (otherwise known as study subjects). He starts by trying to create a candlelit dinner for his parents, although he accidentally causes a fire." (Kirkus Reviews)

★ **Dogsong**. Atheneum Books for Young Readers 2000 177p $17.99; pa $6.99

Grades: 6 7 8 9   **Fic**

1. Inuit -- Fiction 2. Arctic regions -- Fiction 3. Sled dog racing -- Fiction

ISBN 0-689-83960-X; 1-416-93962-8 pa

A reissue of the title first published 1985 by Bradbury Press

A Newbery Medal honor book, 1986

A fourteen-year-old Eskimo boy who feels assailed by the modernity of his life takes a 1400-mile journey by dog sled across ice, tunda, and mountains seeking his own "song" of himself

The author's "mystical tone and blunt prose style are well suited to the spare landscape of his story, and his depictions of Russell's icebound existence add both authenticity and color to a slick rendition of the vision-quest plot, which incorporates human tragedy as well as promise." Booklist

Flat broke. Wendy Lamb Books 2011 118p $12.99; lib bdg $15.99

Grades: 4 5 6   **Fic**

1. Friendship -- Fiction 2. Family life -- Fiction 3. Business enterprises -- Fiction 4. Money-making projects for children -- Fiction

ISBN 978-0-385-74002-9; 0-385-74002-6; 978-0-385-90818-4 lib bdg; 0-385-90818-0 lib bdg

LC 2010049415

Sequel to: Liar, liar (2011)

Fourteen-year-old Kevin is a hard worker, so when his income is cut off he begins a series of businesses, from poker games to selling snacks, earning money to take a girl to a dance, but his partners soon tire of his methods.

"A jocular, fast-paced voyage into the sometimes simple but never quiet mind of an ambitious eighth grader." Kirkus

★ **Harris** and me; a summer remembered. Harcourt Brace & Co. 1993 157p $16

Grades: 5 6 7 8   **Fic**

1. Cousins -- Fiction 2. Farm life -- Fiction

ISBN 0-15-292877-4

LC 93-19788

Sent to live with relatives on their farm because of his unhappy home life, an eleven-year-old city boy meets his distant cousin Harris and is given an introduction to a whole new world

"Readers will experience hearts as large as farmers' appetites, humor as broad as the country landscape and adventures as wild as boyhood imaginations. All this adds up to a hearty helping of old-fashioned, rip-roaring entertainment." Publ Wkly

★ **Hatchet**; [by] Gary Paulsen; illustrated by Drew Willis. 20th anniversary ed.; Simon & Schuster Books for Young Readers 2007 188p il $19.99; pa $6.99

Grades: 6 7 8 9 **Fic**

1. Divorce -- Fiction 2. Survival after airplane accidents, shipwrecks, etc. -- Fiction

ISBN 978-1-416-92508-8; 1-416-92508-2; 978-1-416-93647-3 pa; 1-416-93647-5 pa

A reissue of the title first published 1987 by Bradbury Press

A Newbery Medal honor book, 1988

After a plane crash, thirteen-year-old Brian spends fifty-four days in the wilderness, learning to survive initially with only the aid of a hatchet given him by his mother, and learning also to survive his parents' divorce

"Paulsen's knowledge of our national wilderness is obvious and beautifully shared." Voice Youth Advocates

Other titles in this series are:

The river (1991)

Brian's winter (1996)

Brian's return (1999)

Brian's hunt (2003)

The **island**. Orchard Bks. 1988 202p hardcover o.p. pa $5.99

Grades: 8 9 10 11 12 **Fic**

1. Islands -- Fiction

ISBN 0-531-05749-6; 0-439-78662-2 pa

LC 87-24761

"With humor and psychological genius, Paulsen develops strong adolescent characters who lend new power to youth's plea to be allowed to apply individual skills in their risk-taking." Voice Youth Advocates

Liar, liar; the theory, practice, and destructive properties of deception. Wendy Lamb Books 2011 120p $12.99; lib bdg $15.99

Grades: 4 5 6 **Fic**

1. School stories 2. Family life -- Fiction 3. Truthfulness and falsehood -- Fiction

ISBN 0-385-74001-8; 0-385-90817-2 lib bdg; 978-0-385-74001-2; 978-0-385-90817-7 lib bdg

LC 2010-28356

Fourteen-year-old Kevin is very good at lying and doing so makes life easier, until he finds himself in big trouble with his friends, family, and teachers. "Ages eight to twelve." (Publisher's note)

"Kevin's grappling with family troubles adds . . . emotional dimension to Paulsen's novel." Publ Wkly

Followed by: Flat broke (2011)

Nightjohn. Delacorte Press 1993 92p $15.95; pa $5.99

Grades: 7 8 9 10 **Fic**

1. Reading -- Fiction 2. Slavery -- Fiction 3. African

Americans -- Fiction

ISBN 0-385-30838-8; 0-440-21936-1 pa

LC 92-1222

Twelve-year-old Sarny's brutal life as a slave becomes even more dangerous when a newly arrived slave offers to teach her how to read

"Paulsen is at his best here: the writing is stark and bare-boned, without stylistic pretensions of any kind. The narrator's voice is strong and true, the violence real but stylized with an almost mythic tone. . . . The simplicity of the text will make the book ideal for older reluctant readers who can handle violence but can't or won't handle fancy writing in long books. Best of all, the metaphor of reading as an act of freedom speaks for itself through striking action unembroidered by didactic messages." Bull Cent Child Books

Notes from the dog. Wendy Lamb Books 2009 133p $15.99; lib bdg $18.99

Grades: 5 6 7 8 **Fic**

1. Cancer -- Fiction 2. Gardening -- Fiction

ISBN 0-385-73845-5; 0-385-90730-3 lib bdg; 978-0-385-73845-3; 978-0-385-90730-9 lib bdg

LC 2009-13300

When Johanna shows up at the beginning of summer to house-sit next door to Finn, he has no idea of the profound effect she will have on his life by the time summer vacation is over.

"The plot is straightforward, but Paulsen's thoughtful characters are compelling and their interactions realistic. This emotional, coming-of-age journey about taking responsibilty for one's own happiness and making personal connections will not disappoint." Publ Wkly

Road trip; by Jim and Gary Paulsen. Wendy Lamb Books 2013 128 p. (trade) $12.99

Grades: 5 6 7 8 **Fic**

1. Dogs -- Fiction 2. Automobile travel -- Fiction 3. Father-child relationship -- Fiction 4. Border collie -- Fiction 5. Animal shelters -- Fiction 6. Fathers and sons -- Fiction

ISBN 038574191X; 9780307930866; 9780375988578; 9780375990311; 9780385741910

LC 2012014284

In this book, by Gary Paulsen and Jim Paulsen, "Dad and Ben haven't been getting along recently and Dad hopes a road trip to rescue a border collie will help them reconnect. But Ben is on to Dad's plan and invites Ben's thuggish buddy, Theo. The family dog, Atticus, comes along too and the story is told by Ben and Atticus. . . . Only sharp-eyed Atticus realizes that Theo is on the run—and someone is following them." (Publisher's note)

The **Schernoff** discoveries. Delacorte Press 1997 103p pa $4.99

Grades: 5 6 7 8 **Fic**

1. School stories 2. Friendship -- Fiction

ISBN 0440414636

LC 96045390

This "novel, narrated by a 14-year-old, self-confessed geek, focuses on the narrator's friend, Harold. Equally geeky and brainy as well, Harold takes the lead in {a} . . . series of adventures ranging from the unusual but pragmatic (enrolling in home economics to meet girls) to the sneaky and possibly suicidal (taking revenge on the football players who broke his slide rule by giving them a cake flavored with 43 boxes of chocolate laxatives)." (Booklist) "Grades four to eight." (SLJ)

"The tone is breezy, funny, and sometimes touching (but not too mushy) and bound to keep the most reluctant reader chuckling." Bull Cent Child Books

Soldier's heart; a novel of the Civil War. Delacorte Press 1998 106p $15.95; pa $5.99
Grades: 7 8 9 10　　　　　　　　　　　　　**Fic**
　1. Post-traumatic stress disorder -- Fiction　2. United States -- History -- 1861-1865, Civil War -- Fiction
　ISBN 0-385-32498-7; 0-440-22838-7 pa
　　　　　　　　　　　　　　　　　LC 98-10038
"This compelling and realistic depiction of war is based on a true story. . . . Paulsen's writing is crisp and fast-paced, and this soldier's story will haunt readers long after they finish reading the novel." Book Rep

The **Transall** saga. Delacorte Press 1998 248p pa $6.50
Grades: 5 6 7 8　　　　　　　　　　　　　**Fic**
　1. Science fiction
　ISBN 0-440-21976-0 pa
　　　　　　　　　　　　　　　　　LC 97-40773
While backpacking in the desert, thirteen-year-old Mark falls into a tube of blue light and is transported into a more primitive world, where he must use his knowledge and skills to survive

"A riveting tale of adventure and action." Voice Youth Advocates

Vote; the theory, practice, and destructive properties of politics. Gary Paulsen. 1st ed. Wendy Lamb Books 2013 144 p. (hardcover) $12.99; (ebook) $38.97; (hardcover) $12.99
Grades: 5 6 7 8　　　　　　　　　　　　　**Fic**
　1. School stories　2. Humorous fiction　3. Elections -- Fiction　4. Humorous stories　5. Schools -- Fiction　6. Middle schools -- Fiction　7. Politics, Practical -- Fiction　8. Interpersonal relations -- Fiction
　ISBN 0385742282; 9780307974525; 9780375990533; 9780385742283 trade; 9780385742290
　　　　　　　　　　　　　　　　　LC 2012023059
In this humorous children's novel, by Gary Paulsen, the author's lead character from previous stories is reprised when he runs for school office. "Kevin Spencer . . . has a knack for tackling big ideas and goofing up, so what's next? Politics, of course! He's running for office, and his campaign is truly unique." (Publisher's note)

"Those who started this four-book series at the beginning may sense that our protagonist is maturing a wee bit, but not so much as to dampen the humor for fans or newcomers. . . . Fast-paced action and Kevin's penchant for getting into ridiculous situations make this the perfect book bait for not-so-eager readers." BookList

The **winter** room. Orchard Bks. 1989 103p $16.95; pa $5.99

Grades: 5 6 7 8　　　　　　　　　　　　　**Fic**
　1. Farm life -- Fiction　2. Minnesota -- Fiction
　ISBN 0-531-05839-5; 0-545-08534-9 pa
　　　　　　　　　　　　　　　　　LC 89-42541
A Newbery Medal honor book, 1990
A young boy growing up on a northern Minnesota farm describes the scenes around him and recounts his old Norwegian uncle's tales of an almost mythological logging past

"While this seems at first to be a collection of anecdotes organized around the progression of the farm calendar, Paulsen subtly builds a conflict that becomes apparent in the last brief chapters, forceful and well-prepared. . . . Lyrical and only occasionally sentimental, the prose is clean, clear, and deceptively simple." Bull Cent Child Books

★ **Woods** runner. Wendy Lamb Books 2010 164p $15.99; lib bdg $18.99
Grades: 6 7 8 9　　　　　　　　　　　　　**Fic**
　1. Spies -- Fiction　2. Soldiers -- Fiction　3. Kidnapping -- Fiction　4. Pennsylvania -- Fiction　5. Native Americans -- Fiction　6. Frontier and pioneer life -- Fiction　7. United States -- History -- 1775-1783, Revolution -- Fiction
　ISBN 978-0-385-73884-2; 0-385-73884-6; 978-0-385-90751-4 lib bdg; 0-385-90751-6 lib bdg
　　　　　　　　　　　　　　　　　LC 2009-27397
From his 1776 Pennsylvania homestead, thirteen-year-old Samuel, who is a highly-skilled woodsman, sets out toward New York City to rescue his parents from the band of British soldiers and Indians who kidnapped them after slaughtering most of their community. Includes historical notes.

"Paulsen fortifies this illuminating and gripping story with interspersed historical sections that offer details about frontier life and the war (such as technology, alliances, and other period information), helping place Sam's struggles in context." Publ Wkly

Pausewang, Gudrun
Dark hours; translated by John Brownjohn. Annick Press 2006 208p $21.95
Grades: 6 7 8 9　　　　　　　　　　　　　**Fic**
　1. Germany -- Fiction　2. Refugees -- Fiction　3. World War, 1939-1945 -- Fiction
　ISBN 1-55451-042-2
"Well written with suspense and powerful sentiments, this story will spark discussion." SLJ

Traitor; translated from the German by Rachel Ward. Carolrhoda Books 2006 220p hardcover o.p. pa $9.95
Grades: 7 8 9 10　　　　　　　　　　　　　**Fic**
　1. Germany -- Fiction　2. Prisoners of war -- Fiction　3. World War, 1939-1945 -- Fiction
　ISBN 0-8225-6195-6; 0-7613-6571-0 pa
　　　　　　　　　　　　　　　　　LC 2005-33379
During the closing months of World War II, a fifteen-year-old German girl must decide whether or not to help an escaped Russian prisoner of war, despite the serious consequences if she does so.

"Pausewang presents an exciting and thought-provoking novel." SLJ

Paver, Michelle

Wolf brother. HarperCollins 2005 295p (Chronicles of ancient darkness) $16.99; lib bdg $17.89; pa $6.99

Grades: 5 6 7 8   **Fic**

1. Bears -- Fiction 2. Wolves -- Fiction 3. Demoniac possession -- Fiction 4. Prehistoric peoples -- Fiction
ISBN 0-06-072825-6; 0-06-072826-4 lib bdg; 0-06-072827-2 pa

LC 2004-8857

First published 2004 in the United Kingdom

6,000 years in the past, twelve-year-old Tarak and his guide, a wolf cub, set out on a dangerous journey to fulfill an oath the boy made to his dying father—to travel to the Mountain of the World Spirit seeking a way to destroy a demon-possessed bear that threatens all the clans

"Paver's depth of research into the spiritual world of primitive peoples makes this impressive British import, slated to be the first in a six-book series, intriguing and believable." SLJ

Other titles in this series are:
Spirit walker (2006)
Soul eater (2007)
Outcast (2008)
Oath breaker (2009)
Ghost hunter (2010)

Peacock, Carol Antoinette

Red thread sisters; by Carol Antoinette Peacock. Viking 2012 236 p. (hardcover) $15.99

Grades: 4 5 6 7 8   **Fic**

1. Adoptees -- Fiction 2. Friendship -- Fiction 3. Chinese Americans -- Fiction 4. Adoption -- Fiction 5. Family life -- Fiction 6. Interracial adoption -- Fiction 7. Intercountry adoption -- Fiction
ISBN 0670013862; 9780670013869

LC 2012019511

This novel, by Carol Antoinette Peacock, offers a "story of friendship, family, and love. Wen has spent the first eleven years of her life at an orphanage in rural China . . . [with] her best friend, Shu Ling. When Wen is adopted by an American couple, she struggles . . . knowing that Shu Ling remains back at the orphanage, alone. Wen knows that her best friend deserves a family and a future, too. But finding a home for Shu Ling isn't easy, and time is running out." (Publisher's note)

Peacock, Shane

★ **Eye** of the crow. Tundra Books 2007 264p (The boy Sherlock Holmes) $24.99; pa $9.95

Grades: 6 7 8 9 10   **Fic**

1. Mystery fiction 2. Great Britain -- History -- 19th century -- Fiction
ISBN 978-0-88776-850-7; 0-88776-850-4; 978-0-88776-919-1 pa; 0-88776-919-5 pa

"A young woman is brutally murdered in a dark back street of Whitechapel; a young Arab is discovered with the bloody murder weapon; and a thirteen-year-old Sherlock Holmes, who was seen speaking with the alleged killer as he was hauled into jail, is suspected to be his accomplice. . . . Although imaginative reconstruction of Holmes childhood has been the subject of literary and cinematic endeavors,

Peacock's take ranks among the most successful." Bull Cent Child Books

Other titles in this series are:
Death in the air (2008)
The dragon turn (2011)
The secret fiend (2010)
Vanishing girl (2009)

Pearce, Jackson

As you wish. HarperTeen 2009 298p $16.99

Grades: 6 7 8 9   **Fic**

1. School stories 2. Wishes -- Fiction 3. Artists -- Fiction 4. Popularity -- Fiction 5. Homosexuality -- Fiction
ISBN 006166152X; 0061661538; 0061661546; 9780061661525; 9780061661532; 9780061661549

LC 2008-44033

When a genie arrives to grant sixteen-year-old Viola's wish to feel she belongs, as she did before her best friend/boyfriend announced that he is gay, her delay in making wishes gives her and the mysterious Jinn time to fall in love. "Grades seven to ten." (Bull Cent Child Books)

"Written in alternating chapters between Jinn and Viola, the story unfolds to rapidly change from the regular 'genie in the bottle' saga to a poignant tale of love and sacrifices made in the name of love. . . . The result is a fabulous fantasy from a first time author." Voice Youth Advocates

Pearce, Jacqueline

Manga touch; [by] Jacqueline Pearce. Orca Books 2007 105p pa $8.95

Grades: 6 7 8   **Fic**

1. Japan -- Fiction 2. Travel -- Fiction
ISBN 978-1-55143-746-0 pa; 1-55143-746-5 pa

Dana takes a school trip to Japan to learn about Japanese culture and artwork. She surprisingly discovers she has a lot to learn about people as well as manga art.

"Readers will enjoy the skillful way Pearce weaves in facts regarding Japanese culture while still keeping things interesting." Voice Youth Advocates

Pearsall, Shelley

All of the above; a novel. illustrations by Javaka Steptoe. Little, Brown 2006 234p il hardcover o.p. pa $5.99

Grades: 5 6 7 8   **Fic**

1. School stories 2. City and town life -- Fiction
ISBN 0-316-11524-X; 978-0-316-11524-7; 978-0-316-11526-1 pa; 0-316-11526-6 pa

LC 2005-33109

Five urban middle school students, their teacher, and other community members relate how a school project to build the world's largest tetrahedron affects the lives of everyone involved.

"Pearsall's novel, based on a real event in 2002—is a delightful story about the power of a vision and the importance of a goal. The authentic voices of the students and the well-intentioned, supportive adults surrounding them illustrate all that is good about schools, family, friendship, and community." Booklist

All shook up; [by] Shelley Pearsall. Alfred A. Knopf 2008 261p il $15.99; lib bdg $18.99

Grades: 6 7 8 9   **Fic**

1. Chicago (Ill.) -- Fiction 2. Father-son relationship -- Fiction

ISBN 978-0-375-83698-5; 0-375-83698-5; 978-0-375-93698-2 lib bdg; 0-375-93698-X lib bdg

LC 2007-22931

When thirteen-year-old Josh goes to stay with his father in Chicago for a few months, he discovers—to his horror—that his dad has become an Elvis impersonator.

"This affecting story of a typical, clever middle-school boy dealing with divorce and the new families that sometimes replace the old is also a very funny tale told by a terrifically engaging young narrator." Voice Youth Advocates

Jump into the sky; Shelley Pearsall. Alfred A. Knopf 2012 344 p. (hbk.) $16.99

Grades: 4 5 6 7   **Fic**

1. Historical fiction 2. Father-son relationship -- Fiction 3. World War, 1939-1945 -- Children -- Fiction 4. World War, 1939-1945 -- African Americans -- Fiction 5. Prejudices -- Fiction 6. Segregation -- Fiction 7. Fathers and sons -- Fiction 8. African Americans -- Fiction 9. Prejudices -- Fiction 10. United States -- History -- World War, 1939-1945 -- Fiction 11. United States. Army. Parachute Infantry Battalion, 555th -- Fiction 12. United States -- History -- World War, 1939-1945 -- Fiction 13. United States. Army. Parachute Infantry Battalion, 555th -- Fiction

ISBN 0375836993; 0375895485; 0375936998; 0440421403; 9780375836992; 9780375895487; 9780375936999; 9780440421405

LC 2011024935

This novel by Shelley Pearsall presents a "tale of the 555th Parachute Infantry Battalion, little known all-black paratroopers serving during WWII. . . . Her tale of 13-year-old Levi Battle's struggle to find his place in the world during World War II . . . [is the] story of a displaced boy hungry to connect with the war-hero father who is more legend than parent. . . . Levi is [sent to] his father at a base in North Carolina. . . . [and] is plunged into the racist South." (Kirkus Reviews)

Pearson, Joanna

The **rites** & wrongs of Janice Wills. Arthur A. Levine Books 2011 218p $16.99

Grades: 8 9 10 11 12   **Fic**

1. School stories 2. Anthropology -- Fiction 3. North Carolina -- Fiction

ISBN 978-0-545-19773-1; 0-545-19773-2

LC 2010029348

Aspiring anthropologist Janice Wills reports on the sociocultural ordeals of being an almost-seventeen-year-old in Melva, North Carolina, including "Beautiful Rich Girls," parties, and the Miss Livermush pageant.

"This anthropological observation-style novel is unique and provides a great social commentary on the life of teenagers. It is a cute story that includes mentions of bisexuality, some strong language, and the hint that the Hot Theater Guy might push Janice too far, but it remains a fun look at life in small town Southern society." Voice Youth Advocates

Pearson, Mary E.

★ The **adoration** of Jenna Fox; [by] Mary E. Pearson. Henry Holt and Co. 2008 272p $16.95; pa $8.99

Grades: 7 8 9 10 11 12   **Fic**

1. Science fiction 2. Bioethics -- Fiction

ISBN 978-0-8050-7668-4; 0-8050-7668-9; 978-0-312-59441-1 pa; 0-312-59441-0 pa

LC 2007-27314

In the not-too-distant future, when biotechnological advances have made synthetic bodies and brains possible but illegal, a seventeen-year-old girl, recovering from a serious accident and suffering from memory lapses, learns a startling secret about her existence.

"The science . . . and the science fiction are fascinating, but what will hold readers most are the moral issues of betrayal, loyalty, sacrifice, and survival." Booklist

Followed by The Fox inheritance (2011)

Fox forever; Mary E. Pearson. Henry Holt and Company 2013 304 p. (hardcover) $17.99

Grades: 7 8 9 10 11 12   **Fic**

1. Science fiction 2. Dystopian fiction 3. Bioethics -- Fiction 4. Biotechnology -- Fiction 5. Medical ethics -- Fiction 6. Government, resistance to -- Fiction

ISBN 0805094342; 9780805094343

LC 2012027677

This young adult novel, by Mary E. Pearson, is the conclusion to the "Jenna Fox Chronicles." "After . . . 260 years as a disembodied mind in a little black box, [Lock Jenkins] has a . . . body. But . . . he'll have to return the Favor he accepted from the . . . Network. Locke must infiltrate the home of a government official by gaining the trust of his daughter, seventeen-year-old Raine, and he soon finds himself pulled deep into the world of the resistance--and into Raine's life." (Publisher's note)

The **Fox** Inheritance; [by] Mary E. Pearson. Henry Holt 2011 384p $16.99

Grades: 7 8 9 10 11 12   **Fic**

1. Science fiction 2. Bioethics -- Fiction

ISBN 0805088296; 9780805088298

LC 2011004800

Sequel to: The adoration of Jenna Fox (2008)

Two-hundred-sixty years after a terrible accident destroyed their bodies, sixteen-year-old Locke and seventeen-year-old Kara have been brought back to life in newly bioengineered bodies, with many questions about the world they find themselves in and more than two centuries of horrible memories of being trapped in a digital netherworld wondering what would become of them.

"Pearson delivers another spellbinding thriller. . . . A dazzling blend of science fiction, mystery, and teen friendship drama." Publ Wkly

Peck, Richard

Are you in the house alone? Viking 1976 156p pa $5.99

Grades: 8 9 10 11 12   **Fic**

1. Rape -- Fiction

ISBN 0-14-130693-9 pa

LC 76-28810

ALA YALSA Margaret A. Edwards Award (1990)

"Gail is frightened by the obscene telephone calls she receives and the notes that are left on her school locker. It is after she has been raped by a classmate while she is babysitting that she begins to understand the real meaning of fear. Although she is a victim, she is doubted by her family, friends, and the police. Most unendurable is the fact that she is forced frequently to cross the path of her attacker, the son of a prominent member of the community." Shapiro. Fic for Youth. 2d edition

Fair weather; a novel. Dial Bks. 2001 130p il $16.99; pa $5.99

Grades: 5 6 7 8   **Fic**

1. Actors 2. Singers 3. Scouts 4. Hunters 5. Circus executives 6. Circus performers 7. Family life -- Fiction 8. Chicago (Ill.) -- Fiction

ISBN 0-8037-2516-7; 0-14-250034-8 pa

LC 00-55561

In 1893, thirteen-year-old Rosie and members of her family travel from their Illinois farm to Chicago to visit Aunt Euterpe and attend the World's Columbian Exposition which, along with an encounter with Buffalo Bill and Lillian Russell, turns out to be a life-changing experience for everyone

"Peck's unforgettable characters, cunning dialogue and fast-paced action will keep readers in stitches." Publ Wkly

Here lies the librarian. Dial Books 2006 145p $16.99; pa $6.99

Grades: 4 5 6   **Fic**

1. Indiana -- Fiction 2. Librarians -- Fiction 3. Automobiles -- Fiction 4. Country life -- Fiction

ISBN 0-8037-3080-2; 0-14-240908-1 pa

LC 2005-20279

Fourteen-year-old Eleanor "Peewee" McGrath, a tomboy and automobile enthusiast, discovers new possibilities for her future after the 1914 arrival in her small Indiana town of four young librarians.

"Another gem from Peck, with his signature combination of quirky characters, poignancy, and outrageous farce." SLJ

★ A **long** way from Chicago; a novel in stories. Dial Bks. for Young Readers 1998 148p pa $5.99; $15.99

Grades: 5 6 7 8   **Fic**

1. Illinois -- Fiction 2. Grandmothers -- Fiction 3. Depressions -- 1929 -- Fiction 4. Country life -- Illinois -- Fiction 5. Great Depression, 1929-1939 -- Fiction

ISBN 0-14-240110-2 pa; 0-8037-2290-7

LC 98-10953

A Newbery Medal honor book, 1999

Joe recounts his annual summer trips to rural Illinois with his sister during the Great Depression to visit their larger-than-life grandmother

"The novel reveals a strong sense of place, a depth of characterization, and a rich sense of humor." Horn Book

Followed by: A year down yonder (2000)

★ **On** the wings of heroes. Dial Books 2007 148p $16.99; pa $6.99

Grades: 4 5 6 7   **Fic**

1. Illinois -- Fiction 2. World War, 1939-1945 -- Fiction

ISBN 0-8037-3081-0; 0-14-241204-X pa

LC 2006011906

A boy in Illinois remembers the homefront years of World War II, especially his two heroes, his brother in the Air Force and his father, who fought in the previous war.

"Peck's masterful, detail-rich prose describes wartime in the United States. . . . Peck's characters are memorable. . . . This book is an absolute delight." SLJ

The **river** between us. Dial Bks. 2003 164p $16.99; pa $6.99

Grades: 7 8 9 10   **Fic**

1. Race relations -- Fiction 2. Racially mixed people -- Fiction 3. United States -- History -- 1861-1865, Civil War -- Fiction

ISBN 0-8037-2735-6; 0-14-240310-5 pa

LC 2002-34815

During the early days of the Civil War, the Pruitt family takes in two mysterious young ladies who have fled New Orleans to come north to Illinois

"The harsh realities of war are brutally related in a complex, always surprising plot that resonates on mutiple levels." Horn Book Guide

★ A **season** of gifts. Dial Books for Young Readers 2009 156p $16.99

Grades: 5 6 7 8   **Fic**

1. Moving -- Fiction 2. Illinois -- Fiction

ISBN 978-0-8037-3082-3; 0-8037-3082-9

LC 2008-48050

Relates the surprising gifts bestowed on twelve-year-old Bob Barnhart and his family, who have recently moved to a small Illinois town in 1958, by their larger-than-life neighbor, Mrs. Dowdel.

"The type of down-home humor and vibrant characterizations Peck fans have come to adore re-emerge in full as Peck resurrects Mrs. Dowdel, the irrepressible, self-sufficient grandmother featured in A Year Down Yonder and A Long Way from Chicago." Publ Wkly

★ The **teacher's** funeral; a comedy in three parts. Dial Books 2004 190p $16.99; pa $6.99

Grades: 5 6 7 8   **Fic**

1. Indiana -- Fiction 2. Teachers -- Fiction 3. Country life -- Fiction

ISBN 0-8037-2736-4; 0-14-240507-8 pa

LC 2004-4361

In rural Indiana in 1904, fifteen-year-old Russell's dream of quitting school and joining a wheat threshing crew is disrupted when his older sister takes over the teaching at his one-room schoolhouse after mean, old Myrt Arbuckle "hauls off and dies."

"The dry wit and unpretentious tone make the story's events comical, its characters memorable, and its conclusion unexpectedly moving." Booklist

Three -quarters dead. Dial Books 2010 193p $16.99

Grades: 7 8 9 10 11 12   **Fic**

1. Ghost stories 2. Horror fiction 3. Dead -- Fiction 4.

Friendship -- Fiction

ISBN 978-0-8037-3454-8; 0-8037-3454-9

LC 2009-49362

Sophomore loner Kerry is overjoyed when three popular senior girls pick her to be in their clique, until a shocking accident sets off a string of supernatural occurrences that become more and more threatening.

"This staccato-sentenced chiller is not so much a ghost story as it is a smart, sly treatise on friendship, bullying and the timeless power of high-school hierarchies. . . . [The author's] real-life depictions of adolescent egotism and backstabbing cruelty are spot-on." Kirkus

★ A **year** down yonder. Dial Bks. for Young Readers 2000 130p $16.99; pa $5.99

Grades: 5 6 7 8 **Fic**

1. Grandmothers -- Fiction 2. Great Depression, 1929-1939 -- Fiction

ISBN 0-8037-2518-3; 0-14-230070-5 pa

LC 99-43159

Awarded the Newbery Medal, 2001

"Peck has created a delightful, insightful tale that resounds with a storyteller's wit, humor, and vivid description." SLJ

Peck, Robert Newton

★ A **day** no pigs would die. Knopf 1973 150p $25; pa $5.50

Grades: 6 7 8 9 **Fic**

1. Pigs -- Fiction 2. Shakers -- Fiction 3. Vermont -- Fiction 4. Farm life -- Fiction 5. Family life -- Fiction 6. Father-son relationship -- Fiction

ISBN 0-394-48235-2; 0-679-85306-5 pa

"Rob lives a rigorous life on a Shaker farm in Vermont in the 1920s. Since farm life is earthy, this book is filled with Yankee humor and explicit descriptions of animals mating. A painful incident that involves the slaughter of Rob's beloved pet pig is instrumental in urging him toward adulthood. The death of his father completes the process of his accepting responsibility." Shapiro. Fic for Youth. 3d edition

Peet, Mal

Mysterious traveler; Mal Peet, Elspeth Graham, illustrated by P. J. Lynch. Candlewick Press 2013 48 p. $15.99

Grades: 3 4 5 **Fic**

1. Sahara Desert -- Fiction 2. Picture books for children

ISBN 0763662321; 9780763662325

LC 2012947823

This children's picture book was "inspired by the guides who navigate the Sahara in Mali." An old man named Issa rescues a baby wearing a valuable necklace and "raises the infant as his granddaughter, relying more and more on young Mariama once his eyesight begins to fail. . . . After a trio of arrogant visitors rejects Issa's guidance, he and Mariama rescue them just as a potentially deadly sandstorm swirls up." One of the boys turns out to be Mariama's brother. (School Library Journal)

★ **Tamar**. Candlewick Press 2007 424p $17.99

Grades: 8 9 10 11 12 **Fic**

1. Netherlands -- Fiction 2. Grandfathers -- Fiction 3.

World War, 1939-1945 -- Fiction

ISBN 978-0-7636-3488-9; 0-7636-3488-3

LC 2006-51837

In 1995, 15-year-old Tamar inherits a box containing a series of coded messages from his late grandfather. The messages show Tamar the life that his grandfather lived during World War II the life of an Allied undercover operative in Nazi-occupied Holland.

"Peet's plot is tightly constructed, and striking, descriptive language, full of metaphor, grounds the story." Booklist

Pellegrino, Marge

Journey of dreams. Frances Lincoln Children's Books 2009 250p map $15.95

Grades: 6 7 8 9 **Fic**

1. Refugees -- Fiction 2. Guatemala -- Fiction

ISBN 978-1-84780-061-9; 1-84780-061-0

"This novel will captivate both Latin American survivors of civil war and their peers. Outstanding." Kirkus

Includes glossary

The **Penderwicks** in spring; Jeanne Birdsall. Knopf Books for Young Readers 2015 352 p. (The Penderwicks) (hardback) $16.99; (lib. bdg.) $19.99

Grades: 4 5 6 7 **Fic**

1. Birthdays -- Fiction 2. Family life -- Fiction 3. Massachusetts -- Fiction 4. Money-making projects for children -- Fiction 5. Singing -- Fiction 6. Surprise -- Fiction 7. Moneymaking projects -- Fiction 8. Single-parent families -- Fiction 9. Family life -- Massachusetts -- Fiction

ISBN 0375870776; 9780375870774; 9780375970771

LC 2014023537

Sequel to: The Penderwicks at Point Mouette (2011)

In this book, by Jeanne Birdsall, "springtime is finally arriving on Gardam Street, and there are surprises in store for each member of the family. Some surprises are just wonderful, like neighbor Nick Geiger coming home from war. And some are ridiculous, like Batty's new dog-walking business. Batty is saving up her dog-walking money for an extra-special surprise for her family, which she plans to present on her upcoming birthday." (Publisher's note)

"[T]he compelling story line examines the guilt that Batty feels over both the death of her mother and her inability to keep the family dog, Hound, alive--and it does so in touching ways. Batty is the narrator most of the time, but younger Ben takes over on occasion, and 2-year-old Lydia is an eccentric presence." Booklist

Pennington, Kate

Brief candle; [by] Kate Pennington. Hodder Children's 2004 262p pa $12.95

Grades: 6 7 8 9 **Fic**

1. Poets 2. Authors 3. Novelists 4. Great Britain -- Fiction

ISBN 0-12-92965-2

"Along with losing herself in romantic poetry, 14-year-old Emily Bronte loves to wander the wild landscape around her father's parsonage. . . . Her two passions thrillingly collide when she encounters a distraught young man, whose courtship of a girl outside his station has left him jobless and desperate.... Pennington's homage offers the most to teens familiar with Bronte's Wuthering Heights. . . . But even readers without much previous knowledge about the book's underpinnings . . . will enjoy the universally accessible view of an ill-fated love and the dreamy restless teen who acts on its behalf." SLJ

Pennypacker, Sara, 1951-

★ The **summer** of the gypsy moths; Sara Pennypacker. Balzer + Bray 2012 275 p. (tr. bdg.) $15.99

Grades: 4 5 6   **Fic**

1. Siblings -- Fiction 2. Family life -- Fiction 3. Foster children -- Fiction 4. Death -- Fiction 5. Secrets -- Fiction 6. Great aunts -- Fiction 7. Cape Cod (Mass.) -- Fiction 8. Loss (Psychology) -- Fiction

ISBN 0061964204; 9780061964206

LC 2011026095

This middle reader story by Sara Pennypacker follows "Stella[, who] loves living with Great-aunt Louise in her big old house near the water on Cape Cod . . . since her mom is . . . unreliable. So while Mom 'finds herself,' Stella fantasizes that someday she'll come back to the Cape and settle down. The only obstacle to her plan? Angel, the foster kid Louise has taken in. . . . [T]he girls hardly speak to each other. But when tragedy unexpectedly strikes, Stella and Angel are forced to rely on each other to survive." (Publisher's note)

Perera, Anna

★ **Guantanamo** boy. Albert Whitman 2011 339p $17.99

Grades: 7 8 9 10 11 12   **Fic**

1. Cousins -- Fiction 2. Muslims -- Fiction 3. Torture -- Fiction 4. Prisoners -- Fiction 5. Prejudices -- Fiction 6. Guantanamo Bay Naval Base (Cuba) -- Detention Camp -- Fiction

ISBN 978-0-8075-3077-1; 0-8075-3077-8

LC 2010048016

"Readers will feel every ounce of Khalid's terror, frustration, and helplessness in this disturbing look at a sad, ongoing chapter in contemporary history." Publ Wkly

Perez, Ashley Hope

What can(t) wait. Carolrhoda 2011 234p $17.95

Grades: 7 8 9 10   **Fic**

1. Family life -- Fiction 2. Mexican Americans -- Fiction

ISBN 978-0-7613-6155-8; 0-7613-6155-3

LC 2010-28175

"Pérez fills a hole in YA lit by giving Marisa an authentic voice that smoothly blends Spanish phrases into dialogue and captures the pressures of both Latina life and being caught between two cultures." Kirkus

Perez, L. King

Remember as you pass me by. Milkweed 2007 184p $16.95; pa $6.95

Grades: 5 6 7 8   **Fic**

1. Texas -- Fiction 2. Friendship -- Fiction 3. Race relations -- Fiction 4. African Americans -- Fiction

ISBN 978-1-57131-677-6; 978-1-57131-678-3 pa

In small-town Texas in the mid-1950s, twelve-year-old Silvy tries to make sense of her parent's financial problems,

a Supreme Court ruling that will integrate her school, the prejudice of her family and friends, and her own behavior, which always seems to be wrong

"The story flows chronologically with enough drama to keep readers turning the pages." SLJ

Perez, Marlene

Dead is a battlefield; Marlene Perez. Graphia 2012 227 p.

Grades: 7 8 9 10   **Fic**

1. Zombies -- Fiction 2. Perfumes -- Fiction 3. Supernatural -- Fiction 4. Female friendship -- Fiction 5. High school students -- Fiction 6. Schools -- Fiction 7. High schools -- Fiction 8. Interpersonal relations -- Fiction

ISBN 0547607342; 9780547607344

LC 2011031489

In this young adult novel, a "high-school freshman learns that she's one of a group of women who fight evil beasties in her supernatural town of Nightshade, Calif. In this sixth installment of the "Dead Is . . ." series, Jessica discovers to her dismay that she's a "virago," a woman warrior destined to fight paranormal baddies. Jessica worries, too, about her very best friend in the whole world, Eva, who's been acting strangely since she discovered a new perfume. . . . Jessica also finds herself attracted to Dominic . . . while she's juggling dates with Connor. . . . Meanwhile, Eva joins the groupies hanging around creepy Edgar and becomes ever more hostile toward Jessica, even trying to bite her. It seems that Edgar's perfume turns girls into zombies. Now Jessica has to find a cure and drive Edgar out of town." (Kirkus)

Dead is a killer tune; Marlene Perez. Graphia 2012 204 p. (paperback) $7.99

Grades: 8 9 10 11 12   **Fic**

1. Accidents -- Fiction 2. Bands (Music) -- Fiction 3. Mystery fiction 4. Music -- Fiction 5. Schools -- Fiction 6. High schools -- Fiction 7. Supernatural -- Fiction 8. Interpersonal relations -- Fiction

ISBN 0547608349; 9780547608341

LC 2012014798

Author Marlene Perez tells the story of a Battle of the Bands competition. "Jessica's romance with Dominic hasn't exactly progressed smoothly . . . Dominic's band, Side Effects May Vary, finds competition in an out-of-town act followed by a large entourage of obsessed fans--Hamlin, fronted by Brett Piper. When the most competitive bands start losing members to recklessness and bizarre accidents, Jessica must not only get to the bottom of the mystery, but also step into the spotlight as a musician herself." (Kirkus)

Dead is just a dream; by Marlene Perez. Houghton Mifflin Harcourt 2013 164 p. (Dead is) (hardback) $16.99

Grades: 8 9 10   **Fic**

1. Fantasy fiction 2. Clowns -- Fiction 3. Homicide -- Fiction 4. Murder -- Fiction 5. Schools -- Fiction 6. Nightmares -- Fiction 7. High schools -- Fiction 8. Supernatural -- Fiction 9. Psychic ability -- Fiction 10. Interpersonal relations -- Fiction

ISBN 0544102622; 9780544102620

LC 2013003883

In this book, by Marlene Perez "Jessica and her virago friends are . . . .in the midst of four murders, all seemingly connected to creepy paintings being installed in the homes of Nightshade's most influential citizens. Just when the girls think they've solved the mystery, a bloody clown begins to stalk Jessica, confounding their original suspicions. Jessica and Dominic's status as a happy couple is also threatened when Dominic announces he will be touring with his band during part of their senior year." (Booklist)

"Jessica and her virago friends are back in this latest Dead Is series entry. This time they're in the midst of four murders, all seemingly connected to creepy paintings being installed in the homes of Nightshade's most influential citizens. Just when the girls think they've solved the mystery, a bloody clown begins to stalk Jessica, confounding their original suspicions...Girl drama, sweet romance, and murder - —what more could young teens want in a breezy read?" Booklist

Dead is the new black. Harcourt 2008 190p pa $7.95

Grades: 7 8 9 10   **Fic**
  1. School stories 2. Cheerleading -- Fiction 3. Supernatural -- Fiction 4. Extrasensory perception -- Fiction
  ISBN 978-0-15-206408-2; 0-15-206408-7
                             LC 2007027677

While dealing with her first boyfriend and suddenly being pressed into service as a substitute cheerleader, seventeen-year-old Daisy Giordano, daughter and sister of psychics but herself a 'normal', attempts to help her mother discover who is behind a series of bizarre attacks on teenage girls in their little town of Nightshade, California.

"This is the witty and humorous first installment in a series; it provides romance, mystery, friendship, adventure, and the supernatural all rolled up in a fast-paced, plot-twisting story." SLJ

  Other titles in this series are:
  Dead is a state of mind (2009)
  Dead is so last year (2009)
  Dead is just a rumor (2010)
  Dead is not an option (2011)

Perkins, Lynne Rae

  All alone in the universe. Greenwillow Bks. 1999 140p il hardcover o.p. pa $5.99

Grades: 5 6 7 8   **Fic**
  1. Friendship -- Fiction
  ISBN 0-688-16881-7; 0-380-73302-1 pa
                              LC 98-50093

Debbie is dismayed when her best friend Maureen starts spending time with ordinary, boring Glenna

"A poignant story written with sensitivity and tenderness." SLJ

  ★ **As** easy as falling off the face of the earth. Greenwillow Books 2010 352p il $16.99

Grades: 8 9 10 11 12   **Fic**
  1. Adventure fiction 2. Chance -- Fiction 3. Accidents -- Fiction
  ISBN 978-0-06-187090-3; 0-06-187090-0
                            LC 2009-42524

A teenaged boy encounters one comedic calamity after another when his train strands him in the middle of nowhere, and everything comes down to luck.

"The real pleasure is Perkins' relentlessly entertaining writing. . . . Wallowing in the wry humor, small but potent truths, and cheerful implausibility is an absolute delight." Booklist

  ★ **Criss** cross. Greenwillow Books 2005 337p $16.99; lib bdg $17.89; pa $6.99

Grades: 6 7 8 9   **Fic**
  1. Nineteen sixties -- Fiction 2. Identity (Psychology) -- Fiction
  ISBN 0-06-009272-6; 0-06-009273-4 lib bdg; 0-06-009274-2 pa
                            LC 2004-54023

Awarded the Newbery Medal, 2006

Teenagers in a small town in the 1960s experience new thoughts and feelings, question their identities, connect, and disconnect as they search for the meaning of life and love. "Grades five to eight." (Bull Cent Child Books)

"Debbie . . . and Hector . . . narrate most of the novel. Both are 14 years old. Hector is a fabulous character with a wry humor and an appealing sense of self-awareness. . . . The descriptive, measured writing includes poems, prose, haiku, and question-and-answer formats. There is a great deal of humor in this gentle story." SLJ

Perkins, Mitali

  ★ **Bamboo** people. Charlesbridge 2010 272p $16.95

Grades: 5 6 7 8   **Fic**
  1. Myanmar -- Fiction 2. Wilderness survival -- Fiction
  ISBN 978-1-58089-328-2; 1-58089-328-7
                            LC 2009005495

Two Burmese boys, one a Karenni refugee and the other the son of an imprisoned Burmese doctor, meet in the jungle and in order to survive they must learn to trust each other.

"Perkins seamlessly blends cultural, political, religious, and philosophical context into her story, which is distinguished by humor, astute insights into human nature, and memorable characters." Publ Wkly

  Secret keeper. Delacorte Press 2009 225p $16.99; lib bdg $19.99

Grades: 7 8 9 10   **Fic**
  1. India -- Fiction 2. Sisters -- Fiction 3. Family life -- Fiction
  ISBN 978-0-385-73340-3; 0-385-73340-2; 978-0-385-90356-1 lib bdg; 0-385-90356-1 lib bdg
                            LC 2008-21475

In 1974 when her father leaves New Delhi, India, to seek a job in New York, Ashi, a tomboy at the advanced age of sixteen, feels thwarted in the home of her extended family in Calcutta where she, her mother, and sister must stay, and when her father dies before he can send for them, they must remain with their relatives and observe the old-fashioned traditions that Ashi hates.

"The plot is full of surprising secrets rooted in the characters' conflicts and deep connections with each other. The two sisters and their mutual sacrifices are both heartbreaking and hopeful." Booklist

Tiger boy; Mitali Perkins; illustrated by Jamie Hogan. Charlesbridge 2015 144 p. (reinforced for library use) $14.95

Grades: 3 4 5 6   **813.6**

1. Tigers -- Fiction 2. Bangladesh -- Fiction 3. Family life -- Fiction 4. Animal rescue -- Fiction 5. Tiger -- Fiction 6. Wildlife rescue -- Fiction 7. Family life -- Bangladesh -- Fiction 8. Families -- Bangladesh -- Fiction 9. Sundarbans (Bangladesh and India) -- Fiction

ISBN 158089660X; 9781580896603; 9781607345435; 9781607346647

LC 2013049028

In this book, by Mitali Perkins, "[w]hen a tiger cub goes missing from the reserve, Neel is determined to find her before the greedy Gupta gets his hands on her to kill her and sell her body parts on the black market. Neel's parents, however, are counting on him to study hard and win a prestigious scholarship to study in Kolkata. Neel doesn't want to leave his family or his island home and he struggles with his familial duty." (Publisher's note)

Perkins, Stephanie

Anna and the French kiss. Dutton 2010 372p $16.99

Grades: 7 8 9 10   **Fic**

1. School stories 2. France -- Fiction 3. Foreign study -- Fiction 4. Paris (France) -- Fiction

ISBN 978-0-525-42327-0; 0-525-42327-3

LC 2009-53290

"Perkin's debut surpasses the usual chick-lit fare with smart dialogue, fresh characters and plenty of tingly interactions, all set amid pastries, parks and walks along the Seine in arguably the most romantic city in the world." Kirkus

Perl, Lila

Isabel's War; Lila Perl. Lizzie Skurnick Books 2014 224 p. $12.95

Grades: 5 6 7 8   **Fic**

1. Historical fiction 2. World War, 1939-1945 -- Refugees -- Fiction 3. Refugees -- Fiction 4. Holocaust, Jewish (1939-1945) -- Fiction 5. Kindertransports (Rescue operations) -- Fiction

ISBN 1939601274; 1939601363; 9781939601278; 9781939601360

Sydney Taylor Book Awards Honor Book (2013)

In this novel, by Lila Perl, "introduces us to Isabel Brandt, . . . twelve-year-old New Yorker who's more interested in boys and bobbing her nose than the distant war across the Pacific. . . . Things change when Helga . . . comes to live with Isabel and her family. Helga is everything Isabel's not--cool, blonde, and vaguely aloof. She's also a German war refugee, with a past that gives a growing Isabel something more important to think about than boys and her own looks." (Publisher's note)

"Isabel Brandt is a typical 12-year-girl who dreams of Frank Sinatra, boys, and being popular in school. But it is 1942, and the war in Europe and the Pacific becomes very significant for this Jewish girl from the Bronx. As her family begins their summer vacation in the Catskills, Isabel meets Helga, her new roommate...As Isabel learns about the war

and the treatment of Jews by Nazis, her relationship with Helga and her outlook on life radically changes. Readers will identify with the protagonist as she discovers what things are truly important." SLJ

Perro, Bryan

The **key** of Braha; Bryan Perro; translated from the French by Y. Maudet. Delacorte Press 2012 184 p. (hc) $16.99

Grades: 4 5 6 7   **Fic**

1. Fantasy fiction 2. Adventure fiction 3. Dead -- Fiction 4. Mythology -- Fiction 5. Fantasy 6. Good and evil -- Fiction 7. Adventure and adventurers -- Fiction

ISBN 0385907672; 9780375896941; 9780385739047; 9780385907675

LC 2011026173

This book is the second in Bryan Perro's 'Amos Daragon' young adult fantasy series, translated from French, in which a 12-year-old sorcerer named Amos, "unwittingly takes on a hazardous mission: He's killed so he can pass into and fix a netherworld crowded with dead souls who aren't being permitted to pass on to their appointed fates. . . . Once there Amos receives aid against numerous enemies from a varied cast of . . . characters, many of whom are figures from mythology (explained in a lexicon)." (Kirkus)

The **mask** wearer; translated from the French by Y. Maudet. Delacorte Press 2011 167p (Amos Paragon) $16.99; lib bdg $19.99

Grades: 4 5 6 7   **Fic**

1. Fantasy fiction 2. Adventure fiction 3. Good and evil -- Fiction

ISBN 0-385-73903-6; 0-385-90766-4 lib bdg; 978-0-385-73903-0; 978-0-385-90766-8 lib bdg

LC 2010023725

To defeat the forces of evil which threaten his world, young Amos Daragon, aided by mythical animal friends, sets out on a journey to find four masks that harness the forces of nature and sixteen powerful stones that give the masks their magic.

"Amos's journey of self-discovery and his quick thinking are sure to keep readers turning the pages to discover the truth behind the never-ending chaos." SLJ

Peterfreund, Diana

Omega City; by Diana Peterfreund. Harpercollins Childrens Books 2015 336 p. $16.99

Grades: 4 5 6 7   **Fic**

1. Adventure fiction 2. Cold war -- Fiction 3. Scientists -- Fiction 4. Conspiracies -- Fiction

ISBN 0062310852; 9780062310859

In this middle grades book, by Diana Peterfreund, "Gillian Seagret doesn't listen to people who say her father's a crackpot. His conspiracy theories about the lost technology of Cold War-era rocket scientist Dr. Aloysius Underberg may have cost him his job and forced them to move to the middle of nowhere, but Gillian knows he's right and plans to prove it. . . . Gillian sets off on a journey into the ruins of Omega City, a vast doomsday bunker deep inside the earth." (Publisher's note)

Peters, Julie Anne

Between Mom and Jo. Little, Brown 2006 232p $16.99

Grades: 7 8 9 10 **Fic**

1. Lesbians -- Fiction 2. Prejudices -- Fiction 3. Family life -- Fiction 4. Mother-son relationship -- Fiction

ISBN 0-316-73906-5

LC 2005-22012

Fourteen-year-old Nick has a three-legged dog named Lucky 2, some pet fish, and two mothers, whose relationship complicates his entire life as they face prejudice, work problems, alcoholism, cancer, and finally separation.

"A powerful, moving examination of the relationships we forge within the family we are given." Horn Book Guide

★ **By** the time you read this, I'll be dead. Disney/Hyperion Books 2010 200p $16.99

Grades: 8 9 10 11 12 **Fic**

1. Bullies -- Fiction 2. Obesity -- Fiction 3. Suicide -- Fiction 4. Depression (Psychology) -- Fiction

ISBN 1-4231-1618-6; 978-1-4231-1618-9

LC 2009-8315

High school student Daelyn Rice, who has been bullied throughout her school career and has more than once attempted suicide, again makes plans to kill herself, in spite of the persistent attempts of an unusual boy to draw her out.

"Powerfully portrayed in the first person, the protagonist's account offers compelling insight into just how spiritually and emotionally devastating bullying can be." Voice Youth Advocates

Define normal; a novel. Little, Brown 2000 196p $14.95; pa $5.95

Grades: 7 8 9 10 **Fic**

1. School stories 2. Friendship -- Fiction

ISBN 0-316-70631-0; 0-316-73489-6 pa

LC 99-42774

When she agrees to meet with Jasmine as a peer counselor at their middle school, Antonia never dreams that this girl with the black lipstick and pierced eyebrow will end up helping her deal with the serious problems she faces at home and become a good friend

"Readers who are looking for believable characters and a good story about friendship, being different, and growing wiser will appreciate Define 'Normal'" Voice Youth Advocates

Luna; a novel. Little, Brown 2003 248p hardcover o.p. pa $7.99

Grades: 9 10 11 12 **Fic**

1. Siblings -- Fiction 2. Transsexualism -- Fiction

ISBN 0-316-73369-5; 0-316-01127-4 pa

LC 2003-58913

"Regan's brother Liam can't stand the person he is during the day... His true self, Luna, only reveals herself at night. In the secrecy of his basement bedroom Liam transforms himself into the beautiful girl he longs to be, with help from his sister's clothes and makeup...But are Liam's family and friends ready to welcome Luna into their lives? Compelling and provocative, this is an unforgettable novel about a transgender teen's struggle for self-identity and acceptance." (Publisher's Note)

"The author gradually reveals the issues facing a transgender teen, educating readers without feeling too instructional (Luna and Regan discuss lingo, hormones and even sex change operations). Flashbacks throughout help round out the story, explaining Liam/Luna's longtime struggle with a dual existence, and funny, sarcastic-but-strong Regan narrates with an authentic voice that will draw readers into this new territory." Publ Wkly

Petersen, P. J.

Wild river. Delacorte Press 2009 120p $14.99; lib bdg $17.99

Grades: 4 5 6 7 **Fic**

1. Brothers -- Fiction 2. Kayaks and kayaking -- Fiction 3. Wilderness survival -- Fiction

ISBN 978-0-385-73724-1; 0-385-73724-6; 978-0-385-90656-2 lib bdg; 0-385-90656-0 lib bdg

LC 2008-24921

Considered lazy and unathletic, twelve-year-old Ryan discovers a heroic side of himself when a kayak trip with his older brother goes horribly awry.

"The compelling first-person narration sets this apart from other adventure stories. . . . With sharp pacing, short sentences, and an unintimidating length, this is a strong, accessible choice for younger readers." Booklist

Peterson, Lois J.

Beyond repair; [by] Lois Peterson. Orca Book Publishers 2011 121p (Orca currents) pa $9.95

Grades: 6 7 8 9 **Fic**

1. Bereavement -- Fiction

ISBN 978-1-55469-816-5; 1-55469-816-2

Cam, still grieving over the death of his father, is worried that he is being stalked.

"Compact, dialogue driven writing keeps the atmosphere tense as Cam races toward a confrontation with his father's killer. . . . A resonant, quick read from a reliable reluctant reader series." Booklist

Silver rain; [by] Lois Peterson. Orca Book Publishers 2010 181p pa $9.95

Grades: 6 7 8 9 **Fic**

1. Canada -- Fiction 2. Missing persons -- Fiction 3. Great Depression, 1929-1939 -- Fiction

ISBN 978-1-55469-280-4; 1-55469-280-6

Elsie's father has disappeared and, as the Depression wears on, the family becomes desperate for money.

"Terse, grim, and funny, the plainspoken narrative from Elsie's viewpoint beautifully conveys a child's sense of the times." Booklist

Peterson, Will

Triskellion; [by] Will Peterson. Candlewick Press 2008 365p $16.99

Grades: 6 7 8 9 **Fic**

1. Twins -- Fiction 2. Siblings -- Fiction 3. Supernatural -- Fiction 4. Great Britain -- Fiction

ISBN 978-0-7636-3971-6; 0-7636-3971-0

After their parents' divorce, Rachel and Adam are sent to live with their grandmother in the English village of Triskellion, where they find danger and paranormal activity as they discover hidden secrets that some will kill to keep buried.

"The plot moves along at a brisk pace, and there's plenty of adventure, dark and creepy atmosphere, and a touch of the paranormal." SLJ

Followed by: Triskellion 2: The burning (2009)

Triskellion 2: The burning. Candlewick Press 2009 461p $16.99

Grades: 6 7 8 9   **Fic**

1. Twins -- Fiction 2. Siblings -- Fiction 3. Archeology -- Fiction 4. Supernatural -- Fiction 5. Great Britain -- Fiction

ISBN 978-0-7636-4223-5; 0-7636-4223-1

LC 2009006657

Sequel to: Triskellion (2008)

Fourteen-year-old twins Adam and Rachel, pursued by both their former 'Hope Project' benefactors and followers of a zombie-like figure, flee London for Paris, Seville, and finally Morocco, where they unearth an ancient secret more startling than the first.

This is an "action-packed sequel. . . . [It is] imaginative and centered on two likable teens." SLJ

Petrucha, Stefan

The **Rule** of Won. Walker & Co. 2008 227p $16.99

Grades: 8 9 10 11 12   **Fic**

1. School stories 2. Clubs -- Fiction 3. Supernatural -- Fiction 4. Books and reading -- Fiction

ISBN 978-0-8027-9651-6; 0-8027-9651-6

LC 2008-00255

Caleb Dunne, the quintessential slacker, is pressured by his girlfriend to join a high school club based on The Rule of Won, which promises to fulfill members' every "crave," but when nonbelievers start being ostracized and even hurt, Caleb must act.

"The book is fast paced and gripping enough to draw in reluctant readers. . . . Raising questions about issues such as personal responsibility, freedom of speech and the press, and standing up for unpopular beliefs, this novel would be a terrific choice for book-group and class discussions." SLJ

Split. Walker Books for Young Readers 2010 257p $16.99

Grades: 7 8 9 10   **Fic**

1. Computers -- Fiction 2. Space and time -- Fiction

ISBN 978-0-8027-9372-0; 0-8027-9372-X

LC 2009-8889

After his mother dies, Wade Jackson cannot decide whether to become a musician or a scholar, so he does both—splitting his consciousness into two distinct worlds.

"The shifting action keeps the fast-paced dual plots moving, and teens will be entertained by the two Wades' embodiment of the tension between being success oriented and following your whims." Booklist

★ **Teen,** Inc. [by] Stefan Petrucha. Walker 2007 244p $16.95

Grades: 8 9 10 11 12   **Fic**

1. Orphans -- Fiction 2. Pollution -- Fiction 3. Business ethics -- Fiction

ISBN 978-0-8027-9650-9; 0-8027-9650-8

LC 2007-2368

Fourteen-year-old Jaiden has been raised by NECorp. since his parents were killed when he was a baby, so when he discovers that the corporation has been lying about producing illegal levels of mercury emissions, he and his two friends decide to try to do something about it.

"Witty and provocative without being preachy, this novel has both daring characters and a heady plot." Booklist

Petruck, Rebecca

Steering toward normal; Rebecca Petruck. Amulet Books 2014 336 p. illustrations (hardback) $16.95

Grades: 5 6 7 8   **Fic**

1. Brothers -- Fiction 2. Ranch life -- Fiction 3. Sibling rivalry -- Fiction

ISBN 1419707329; 9781419707322

LC 2013045512

In this book, by Rebecca Petruck, "eighth grade is set to be a good year for Diggy Lawson. He's chosen a great calf to compete at the Minnesota State Fair, he'll see a lot of July, the girl he secretly likes at 4-H, and he and his dad Pop have big plans for April Fool's Day. But everything changes when classmate Wayne Graf's mother dies, which brings to light the secret that Pop is Wayne's father, too. Suddenly, Diggy has a half brother, who moves in and messes up his life." (Publisher's note)

"Diggy Lawson has high hopes for eighth grade, including plans to win Grand Champion at the State Fair with his calf, Joker. Then it's revealed that Diggy's classmate Wayne is actually his half-brother, upending Diggy's family and their community. Petruck handles her characters with a balanced mix of humor and heart, allowing them to emerge as real boys with complicated emotions." Horn Book

Pfeffer, Susan Beth

Life as we knew it. Harcourt 2006 337p $17

Grades: 7 8 9 10   **Fic**

1. Science fiction 2. Family life -- Fiction 3. Natural disasters -- Fiction

ISBN 0-15-205826-5; 978-0-15-205826-5

LC 2005-36321

Through journal entries sixteen-year-old Miranda describes her family's struggle to survive after a meteor hits the moon, causing worldwide tsunamis, earthquakes, and volcanic eruptions.

"Each page is filled with events both wearying and terrifying and infused with honest emotions. Pfeffer brings cataclysmic tragedy very close." Booklist

Other titles in this series are:

The dead & gone (2008)

This world we live in (2010)

Philbin, Joanna

The **daughters.** Little, Brown 2010 275p il $16.99

Grades: 6 7 8 9   **Fic**

1. School stories 2. Fame -- Fiction 3. Wealth -- Fiction 4. Friendship -- Fiction 5. New York (N.Y.) -- Fiction

ISBN 978-0-316-04900-9; 0-316-04900-X

In New York City, three fourteen-year-old best friends who are all daughters of celebrities watch out for each other as they try to strike a balance between ordinary high school events, such as finding a date for the homecoming dance, and family functions like walking the red carpet with their famous parents.

This is a "fun, quick read. . . . Readers will be intrigued by the well-drawn characters and their growth over the course of several months." SLJ

Other titles in this series are:

The daughters break the rules (2010)

The daughters take the stage (2011)

Philbrick, Rodman

Zane and the hurricane; a story of Katrina. Rodman Philbrick. The Blue Sky Press, an imprint of Scholastic Inc. 2014 181 p. maps (hardback) $16.99

Grades: 5 6 7 8   **Fic**

1. Rescue work -- Fiction 2. Hurricane Katrina, 2005 -- Fiction 3. Survival -- Fiction 4. African Americans -- Fiction 5. New Orleans (La.) -- Fiction 6. Racially mixed people -- Fiction

ISBN 0545342384; 9780545342384

LC 2013025489

In this children's novel, by Rodman Philbrick, "Zane Dupree is a charismatic 12-year-old boy of mixed race visiting a relative in New Orleans when Hurricane Katrina hits. Unexpectedly separated from all family, Zane and his dog experience the terror of Katrina's wind, rain, and horrific flooding. Facing death, they are rescued from an attic air vent by a kind, elderly musician and a scrappy young girl." (Publisher's note)

"Careful attention to detail in representations of the storm, the city and local dialect give this tale a realistic feel. Zane's perspective as an outsider allows Philbrick to weave in social commentary on race, class, greed and morality, offering rich fodder for reflection and discussion." Kirkus

Philbrick, W. R.

★ The **mostly** true adventures of Homer P. Figg; [by] Rodman Philbrick. Blue Sky Press 2009 224p $16.99

Grades: 5 6 7 8   **Fic**

1. Adventure fiction 2. Orphans -- Fiction 3. Brothers -- Fiction 4. United States -- History -- 1861-1865, Civil War -- Fiction

ISBN 978-0-439-66818-7; 0-439-66818-2

LC 2008-16925

A Newbery Medal honor book, 2010

Twelve-year-old Homer, a poor but clever orphan, has extraordinary adventures after running away from his evil uncle to rescue his brother, who has been sold into service in the Civil War

"The book wouldn't be nearly as much fun without Homer's tall tales, but there are serious moments, too, and the horror of war and injustice of slavery ring clearly above the din of playful exaggerations." Publ Wkly

Pierce, Tamora

Bloodhound. Random House 2009 551p il (Beka Cooper) $18.99; lib bdg $21.99; pa $10.99

Grades: 7 8 9 10   **Fic**

1. Fantasy fiction 2. Police -- Fiction 3. Counterfeits

and counterfeiting -- Fiction

ISBN 978-0-375-81469-3; 0-375-81469-8; 978-0-375-91469-0 lib bdg; 0-375-91469-2 lib bdg; 978-0-375-83817-0 pa; 0-375-83817-1 pa

LC 2008025838

Sequel to Terrier (2006)

Having been promoted from "Puppy" to "Dog," Beka, now a full-fledged member of the Provost's Guard, and her former partner head to a neighboring port city to investigate a case of counterfeit coins.

"Quirky, endearing characters save the story." Booklist

Followed by Mastiff (2011)

★ **First** test. Random House 1999 216p (Protector of the small) hardcover o.p. pa $5.99

Grades: 6 7 8 9   **Fic**

1. Fantasy fiction

ISBN 0-679-88914-0; 0-679-98914-5 lib bdg; 0-679-88917-5 pa

LC 98-30903

First title in the Protector of the small series. Ten-year-old Keladry of Mindalen, daughter of nobles, serves as a page but must prove herself to the males around her if she is ever to fulfill her dream of becoming a knight

"Pierce spins a whopping good yarn, her plot balanced on a solid base of action and characterization." Bull Cent Child Books

Other titles in this series are:

Page (2001)

Squire (2002)

Lady knight (2002)

★ **Melting** stones. Scholastic Press 2008 312p $17.99

Grades: 8 9 10 11 12   **Fic**

1. Fantasy fiction 2. Magic -- Fiction

ISBN 978-0-545-05264-1; 0-545-05264-5

LC 2007045036

Residents of the island of Starns send for help from Winding Circle temple, and when prickly green mage Rosethorn and young stone mage trainee Evvy respond, Evvy finds that the problem is with a long-dormant volcano and tries to use her talents to avert the looming destruction.

This "is a riveting story that has many inventive and exciting plot twists and turns. . . . The story features excellent character development." SLJ

★ **Sandry's** book. Scholastic Press 1997 252p (Circle of magic) hardcover o.p. pa $6.99

Grades: 6 7 8 9   **Fic**

1. Fantasy fiction 2. Magic -- Fiction

ISBN 0-590-55356-9; 0-590-55408-5 pa

LC 95-39540

Four young misfits find themselves living in a strictly disciplined temple community where they become friends while also learning to do crafts and to use their powers, especially magic

"Pierce has created an excellent new world where magic is a science and utterly believable and populated it with a cast of well-developed characters." Booklist

Other available titles in this series are:

Tris's book (1998)

Daja's book (1998)
Briar's book (1999)

★ **Terrier**. Random House 2006 581p il map
(Beka Cooper) hardcover o.p. pa $9.99

Grades: 7 8 9 10 **Fic**
1. Fantasy fiction 2. Magic -- Fiction 3. Police --
Fiction
ISBN 978-0-375-81468-6; 0-375-81468-X; 978-0-
375-83816-3 pa; 0-375-83816-3 pa
LC 2006-14834

When sixteen-year-old Beka becomes "Puppy" to a
pair of "Dogs," as the Provost's Guards are called, she uses
her police training, natural abilities and a touch of magic
to help them solve the case of a murdered baby in Tortall's
Lower City.

"Pierce deftly handles the novel's journal structure,
and her clear homage to the police-procedural genre applies a welcome twist to the girl-legend-in-the-making story
line." Booklist

Other titles featuring Beka Cooper are:
Bloodhound (2009)
Mastiff (2011)

★ **Trickster's** choice. Random House 2003
422p $17.95; pa $8.95

Grades: 7 8 9 10 **Fic**
1. Fantasy fiction
ISBN 0-375-81466-3; 0-375-82879-6 pa
LC 2003-5202

Alianne must call forth her mother Alanna's courage and her father's wit in order to survive on the Copper Isles in a royal court rife with political intrigue and
murderous conspiracy

"This series opener is packed with Pierce's alluring mix
of fantasy, adventure, romance, and humor, making the book
an essential purchase for school and public libraries." Voice
Youth Advocates

Another title in this series is:
Trickster's queen (2004)

★ The **will** of the empress. Scholastic Press
2005 550p $17.99; pa $8.99

Grades: 8 9 10 11 12 **Fic**
1. Fantasy fiction
ISBN 0-439-44171-4; 0-439-44172-2 pa
LC 2005-02874

On visit to Namorn to visit her vast landholdings and her
devious cousin, Empress Berenene, eighteen-year-old Sandry must rely on her childhood friends and fellow mages,
Daja, Tris, and Briar, despite the distance that has grown
between them

"This novel begins two years after the Circle of Magic
and The Circle Opens series. . . . Readers will enjoy being
reacquainted with these older but still very well-developed
characters." SLJ

Pierce, Tamora, 1954-
Alanna: the first adventure; Tamora Pierce. Atheneum Pubs. 1983 241p $12.95

Grades: 7 8 9 10 **Fic**
1. Fantasy fiction 2. Gender role -- Fiction 3. Knights

and knighthood -- Fiction
ISBN 0-689-30994-5
LC 83-2595

"Neither Alanna nor her twin brother Thom were happy
with their father's decision to send Alanna to a convent and
Thom to court. The two decide to switch places and Alanna
posing as 'Alan' becomes a page at court while Tom goes
to the convent to learn sorcery. Alanna finds life as a page
hard, particularly as she is lighter and smaller than the other
pages, but she struggles hard to overcome these disadvantages. She makes many friends at court, including . . . Prince
Jonathan whose life she saves using her magical gift of healing." (Voice Youth Advocates)

Other titles in this series are:
In the hand of the goddess
The woman who rides like a man
Lioness rampant

Pierpoint, Eric
The **last** ride of Caleb O'Toole; Eric Pierpoint.
Sourcebooks Jabberwocky 2013 304 p. (tp : alk.
paper) $7.99

Grades: 4 5 6 7 **Fic**
1. Oregon Trail -- Fiction 2. Historical fiction 3.
Orphans -- Fiction 4. Wagon trains -- Fiction 5.
Bozeman Trail -- Fiction 6. Coming of age -- Fiction
7. Brothers and sisters -- Fiction 8. Adventure and
adventurers -- Fiction 9. Oregon National Historic Trail
-- Fiction 10. West (U.S.) -- History -- 1860-1890 --
Fiction
ISBN 1402281714; 9781402281716
LC 2013011800

In this book, it's "1877 in Great Bend, Kan., and cholera has panicked citizens and killed scores, including Caleb
O'Toole's father. The story opens as 12-year-old Caleb races
through town to find one of his sisters while his mother lies
dying of the disease and a mob threatens to burn down their
house. Caleb then witnesses a murder, and the O'Toole children escape amid an explosive gunfight, after agreeing to
. . . take the Oregon Trail to their aunt's ranch in Montana
Territory." (Publishers Weekly)

Pierson, D. C.
The **boy** who couldn't sleep and never had to; a
novel. DC Pierson. Vintage Books 2010 226 p. ill.
$14.95

Grades: 11 12 Adult **Fic**
1. Science fiction 2. Teenagers -- Fiction 3. Friendship
-- Fiction 4. Sleep disorders -- Fiction 5. Sleep --
Fiction 6. Schools -- Fiction 7. High schools -- Fiction
8. Cartoons and comics -- Fiction
ISBN 9780307474612
LC 2009021984

Alex Award (2011)

In this book, the recipient of a 2010 ALA Alex Award,
"[w]hen [high-school student] Darren Bennett meets [class-
mate] Eric Lederer, there's an instant connection. They share
a love of drawing, the bottom rung on the cruel high school
social ladder and a pathological fear of girls. Then Eric reveals a secret: He doesn't sleep. Ever. When word leaks out
about Eric's condition, he and Darren find themselves on the
run. Is it the government trying to tap into Eric's mind, or

something far darker? It could be that not sleeping is only part of what Eric's capable of, and the truth is both better and worse than they could ever imagine." (Publisher's note)

Crap kingdom; by DC Pierson. Viking 2013 368 p. (hardcover) $17.99

Grades: 7 8 9 10 11 12   **Fic**

1. Fantasy fiction 2. Humorous fiction 3. Fantasy 4. Heroes -- Fiction

ISBN 067001432X; 9780670014323

LC 2012015578

In this comic novel, by D. C. Pierson, "with [a] . . . mysterious yet oddly ordinary-looking prophecy, Tom's fate is sealed: he's . . . whisked away to a magical kingdom to be its Chosen One. There's just one problem: The kingdom is mostly made of garbage from Earth. . . . When Tom turns down the job of Chosen One, he thinks he's making a smart decision. But when Tom discovers he's been replaced by his best friend Kyle, . . . Tom wants Crap Kingdom back--at any cost." (Publisher's note)

Pignat, Caroline

★ **Greener** grass; the famine years. Red Deer Press 2009 276p pa $12.95

Grades: 7 8 9 10   **Fic**

1. Famines -- Fiction 2. Ireland -- Fiction

ISBN 978-0-88995-402-1; 0-88995-402-X

"In 1847, 15-year-old Kit is jailed for digging up potatoes on confiscated land to feed her starving family, and during the three weeks that she is incarcerated, she reflects on the past year in Ireland: the blight, the famine, evictions, and deaths. . . . True to Kat's voice, the plain, rhythmic language . . . is lyrical but never ornate. The tension in the story and in the well-developed characters is always rooted in daily detail." Booklist

Followed by: Wild geese (2010)

Wild geese. Red Deer Press 2010 335p pa $12.95

Grades: 7 8 9 10   **Fic**

1. Irish -- Fiction 2. Canada -- Fiction 3. Immigrants -- Fiction 4. Seafaring life -- Fiction

ISBN 978-0-88995-432-8 pa; 0-88995-432-1 pa

Sequel to: Greener grass (2009)

"Kit, pursued as a criminal, has safely made it on board an immigrant 'coffin' ship bound for Canada, disguised as a boy and accompanied by Mick, her best friend. Along the way, with historically gritty authenticity, she encounters a lethal fever, near-starvation conditions and terrifying storms. . . . When she finally reaches Canada, there is more disease and separation." Kirkus

Pike, Aprilynne

Earthbound. Penguin Group USA 2013 352 p. $17.99

Grades: 7 8 9 10   **Fic**

1. Occult fiction 2. Science fiction

ISBN 1595146504; 9781595146502

This is the first book in a series from Aprilynne Pike. Here, plane crash survivor Tavia "is in rehab and finishing her senior year online. She has time to look at the world with attentive eyes, and what she sees is often unnerving:

glowing triangles on the historic houses of Portsmouth, N.H., or pedestrians who flicker. She tries to attribute these visions to the brain injury she sustained in the crash, but she can't dismiss the stalker with a blond ponytail so easily." (Publishers Weekly)

"The characters are well developed and the narrative is easy to follow... Pike does take a while to get to the heart of the matter, but overall the story is compelling. Readers of supernatural romances will be clamoring." SLJ

Wings. HarperTeen 2009 294p $16.99; lib bdg $17.89; pa $8.99

Grades: 7 8 9 10   **Fic**

1. Fantasy fiction 2. Plants -- Fiction 3. Trolls -- Fiction 4. Fairies -- Fiction

ISBN 978-0-06-166803-6; 0-06-166803-6; 978-0-06-166804-3 lib bdg; 0-06-166804-4 lib bdg; 978-0-06-166805-0 pa; 0-06-166805-2 pa

LC 2008-24653

When a plant blooms out of fifteen-year-old Laurel's back, it leads her to discover the fact that she is a faerie and that she has a crucial role to play in keeping the world safe from the encroaching enemy trolls.

"Replete with budding romance, teen heroics, a good smattering of evil individuals, and an ending that serves up a ready sequel, this novel nonetheless provides an unusual approach to middle level fantasy through its startlingly creative premise that faeries are of the plant world and not the animal world. . . . Both male and female fantasy readers will enjoy this fast-paced action fantasy." Voice Youth Advocates

Other titles in this series are:

Illusions (2011)

Spells (2010)

Pileggi, Leah

Prisoner 88; Leah Pileggi. Charlesbridge 2013 142 p. (reinforced for library use) $16.95

Grades: 4 5 6 7 8   **Fic**

1. Prisons -- Fiction 2. Prisoners -- Fiction 3. Prisons -- Idaho Territory -- Fiction 4. Prisoners -- Idaho Territory -- Fiction 5. Idaho Territory -- History -- 19th century -- Fiction

ISBN 1580895603; 9781580895606; 9781607345343; 9781607346111

LC 2012024443

In this book, by Leah Pileggi, "ten-year-old Jake Evans has just received a five-year sentence for manslaughter. . . . The warden and guards are at a bit of a loss on how to treat so young a convict, and . . . Jake's life improves considerably in the aftermath of his conviction." But "there are hardened criminals who would like to take Jake down just for the grim pleasure of it, and Jake is drawn into the turmoil of an jailbreak attempt." (Bulletin of the Center for Children's Literature)

Prisoner Eighty-eight

Pincus, Greg

The **14** fibs of Gregory K; Greg Pincus. Arthur A. Levine Books 2013 240 p. (hardcover : alk. paper) $17.99

Grades: 4 5 6 7   **Fic**

1. Truthfulness and falsehood 2. Honesty -- Fiction

3. Schools -- Fiction 4. Mathematics -- Fiction 5. Middle schools -- Fiction 6. Creative writing -- Fiction 7. Fathers and sons -- Fiction 8. Brothers and sisters -- Fiction 9. Middle-born children -- Fiction
ISBN 0439912997; 9780439912990; 9780439913003
LC 2012044117

In this book, by Greg Pincus, "Gregory K is the middle child in a family of mathematical geniuses. But if he claimed to love math? Well, he'd be fibbing. What he really wants most is to go to Author Camp. But to get his parents' permission he's going to have to pass his math class, which has a probability of 0. THAT much he can understand!" (Publisher's note)

"Eleven-year-old Gregory doesn't love math, but everyone in his family does. He yearns to go to Author Camp with his best friend, Kelly. To please his family, he tells a series of lies and then has to fix the resulting problems. Unconvincing secondary characters weaken the plot, but the story might appeal to those who feel they just don't fit in." (Horn Book)

Fourteen fibs of Gregory K

Pinkney, Andrea Davis

★ **Bird** in a box; illustrations by Sean Qualls. Little, Brown Books for Young Readers 2011 278p il $16.99

Grades: 4 5 6 7 **Fic**
1. Boxing -- Fiction 2. African Americans -- Fiction 3. Radio broadcasting -- Fiction 4. Harlem (New York, N.Y.) -- Fiction 5. Great Depression, 1929-1939 -- Fiction
ISBN 978-0-316-07403-2; 0-316-07403-9
LC 2010-22851

In 1936, three children meet at the Mercy Home for Negro Orphans in New York State, and while not all three are orphans, they are all dealing with grief and loss which together, along with the help of a sympathetic staff member and the boxing matches of Joe Louis, they manage to overcome.

"Pinkney weaves quite a bit of 1930s history into her story and succeeds admirably in showing how Louis came to represent so much more than his sport. Her detailed notes make this an accessible and inspiring piece of historical fiction that belongs in most collections." SLJ

★ The **red** pencil; a novel told in poems, pictures, and possibilities. by Andrea Davis Pinkney; illustrated by Shane Evans. First edition Little, Brown & Co. 2014 336 p. illustrations, map (hardcover) $17

Grades: 4 5 6 7 **Fic**
1. Sudan -- Fiction 2. Refugees -- Fiction 3. Novels in verse 4. Blacks -- Sudan -- Fiction
ISBN 9780316247801; 0316247804
LC 2013044753

Amelia Bloomer Project (2014)

"Amira is twelve. . . . Maybe old enough to go to school in Nyala--Amira's one true dream. But life in her peaceful Sudanese village is shattered when the Janjaweed arrive. . . . After she loses nearly everything, Amira needs . . . to make the long journey . . . to safety at a refugee camp. Her days are tough at the camp, until the gift of a simple red pencil opens her mind." (Publisher's note)

"Amira's thoughts and drawings are vividly brought to life through Pinkney's lyrical verse and Evans's lucid line illustrations, which infuse the narrative with emotional intensity." SLJ

With the might of angels; the diary of Dawnie Rae Johnson. Scholastic 2011 324p il map (Dear America) $12.99

Grades: 5 6 7 8 **Fic**
1. School stories 2. Diaries -- Fiction 3. Virginia -- Fiction 4. Family life -- Fiction 5. Race relations -- Fiction 6. African Americans -- Fiction 7. School integration -- Fiction
ISBN 0-545-29705-2; 978-0-545-29705-9
LC 2011001363

In 1955 Hadley, Virginia, twelve-year-old Dawnie Rae Johnson, a tomboy who excels at baseball and at her studies, becomes the first African American student to attend the all-white Prettyman Coburn school, turning her world upside down. Includes historical notes about the period.

"Dawnie's journal is realistic, encompassing thoughts and emotions one would expect of someone so stressed. . . . The author seamlessly incorporates historical events into the child's journal. The end matter contains age-appropriate photographs, a time line, and brief biographical sketches of the people mentioned. A first purchase." SLJ

Pinkwater, Daniel Manus

Adventures of a cat-whiskered girl; illustrations by Calef Brown. Houghton Mifflin Books for Children 2010 268p il $16

Grades: 4 5 6 **Fic**
1. Science fiction 2. Cats -- Fiction 3. Extraterrestrial beings -- Fiction
ISBN 978-0-547-22324-7; 0-547-22324-2

Big Audrey, who has catlike whiskers, and her telepathic friend Molly set out on a journey to find out why flying saucers are landing behind the old stone barn in Poughkeepsie, New York, and, more importantly, to determine whether another cat-whiskered girl really exists.

"Mixing the absurd with the profound, Pinkwater's odd narration will have even the most serious readers laughing at the chaos." Booklist

Bushman lives! written by Daniel Pinkwater; illustrated by Calef Brown. Houghton Mifflin Harcourt 2012 247 p. $16.99

Grades: 5 6 7 8 **Fic**
1. Gorillas -- Fiction 2. Teenagers -- Fiction 3. Friendship -- Fiction 4. Humorous stories 5. Artists -- Fiction 6. Coming of age -- Fiction 7. Adventure and adventurers -- Fiction 8. Chicago (Ill.) -- History -- 20th century -- Fiction
ISBN 0547385390; 9780547385396
LC 2011048211

In author Daniel Pinkwater's book, "Harold Knishke has no idea he wants to be an artist until the guy in the army cap in Bughouse Square just asks him. Almost immediately Harold is taking drawing classes from a taxidermist and acquires a studio of his own in a building so mysterious he can't tell a soul about it . . . . He also has a best friend who is convinced that Bushman, the 427-pound gorilla who once lived in the

Lincoln Park Zoo and is now stuffed and on display in the Field Museum of Natural History, is still alive." (Kirkus)

The **Neddiad**; how Neddie took the train, went to Hollywood, and saved civilization. by Daniel Pinkwater; illustrations by Calef Brown. Houghton Mifflin 2007 307p il $16

Grades: 5 6 7 8   **Fic**

1. Turtles -- Fiction 2. Los Angeles (Calif.) -- Fiction
ISBN 978-0-618-59444-3; 0-618-59444-2

LC 2006033944

Followed by: The Yggyssey (2009)

When shoelace heir Neddie Wentworthstein and his family take the train from Chicago to Los Angeles in the 1940s, he winds up in possession of a valuable Indian turtle artifact whose owner is supposed to be able to prevent the impending destruction of the world, but he is not sure exactly how.

"A bright and breezy adventure with a smart and funny narrator. . . . [This is a] goofy and lovingly nostalgic historical fantasy." SLJ

The **Yggyssey**; how Iggy wondered what happened to all the ghosts, found out where they went, and went there. illustrations by Calef Brown. Houghton Mifflin Co. 2009 245p il $16

Grades: 4 5 6   **Fic**

1. Ghost stories 2. Hotels and motels -- Fiction 3. Hollywood (Calif.) -- Fiction
ISBN 978-0-618-59445-0; 0-618-59445-0

LC 2008-01874

Sequel to: The Neddiad

In the mid-1950s, Yggdrasil Birnbaum and her friends, Seamus and Neddie, journey to Old New Hackensack, which is on another plane, to try to learn why ghosts are disappearing from the Birnbaum's hotel and other Hollywood, California, locations.

"Once again, Pinkwater combines a goofy plot, myth and fairy tale references, and an obvious affection for yesteryear Los Angeles in a supernaturally funny read." Booklist

Pinter, Jason

Zeke Bartholomew, superspy. Sourcebooks Jabberwocky 2011 256p pa $7.99

Grades: 4 5 6 7   **Fic**

1. Adventure fiction 2. Spies -- Fiction
ISBN 978-1-4022-5755-1; 1-4022-5755-4

Zeke Bartholomew has always dreamed of being a spy. But when a case of mistaken identity goes horribly wrong, he's thrust into a world of real-life espionage beyond his wildest dreams. Soon this 7th grade nobody finds himself hunted by the lava-powered behemoth Ragnarok, aided by a mysterious butt-kicking girl who goes only by the codename 'Sparrow.'

"Zeke's first-person narration and ample one-liners provide plenty of laughs in a novel that combines espionage, wild sci-fi, and a satiric take on the ever-growing kids-save-the-world subgenre." Booklist

Pitcher, Annabel

My sister lives on the mantelpiece; a novel. Annabel Pitcher. 1st US ed. Little, Brown & Co. 2012 214 p. (hardcover) $17.99

Grades: 6 7 8 9 10   **Fic**

1. Bullies 2. Religions 3. Prejudices 4. Grief -- Fiction 5. England -- Fiction 6. Family problems -- Fiction
ISBN 0316176907; 9780316176903

LC 2011027350

In this book, Annabel Pitcher tells a story about "grief, prejudice, religion, bullying, and familial instability. . . . Jamie and his family are still dealing with his sister Rose's death in a terrorist bombing five years earlier. . . . The family falls apart--their mother runs off with another man, and their alcoholic father moves from London to the Lake District with the children, where he lavishes attention on Rose's urn. . . . Jamie's pivotal friendship with a Muslim girl, Sunya, is a standout." (Publishers Weekly)

Pixley, Marcella

★ **Freak**. Farrar, Straus and Giroux 2007 131p $16

Grades: 6 7 8 9 10   **Fic**

1. School stories 2. Bullies -- Fiction
ISBN 0-374-32453-0; 978-0-374-32453-7

LC 2006-50683

Twelve-year-old Miriam, poetic, smart, and quirky, is considered a freak by the popular girls at her middle school, and she eventually explodes in response to their bullying, revealing an inner strength she did not know she had.

"The story's conflicts are exceptionally riveting and believable." Booklist

★ **Without** Tess. Farrar Straus Giroux 2011 280p $16.99

Grades: 7 8 9 10   **Fic**

1. Death -- Fiction 2. Guilt -- Fiction 3. Sisters -- Fiction 4. Mental illness -- Fiction 5. Jews -- United States -- Fiction
ISBN 978-0-374-36174-7; 0-374-36174-6

LC 2011001469

Fifteen-year-old Lizzie Cohen recalls what it was like growing up with her imaginative but disturbed older sister Tess, and how she is striving to reclaim her own life since Tess died.

The author "plumbs the emotional depths of a tough subject with sensitivity and insight into the complexities of human nature and sibling bonds." Kirkus

Platt, Chris

Astra. Peachtree 2010 144p $15.95

Grades: 5 6 7 8   **Fic**

1. Horses -- Fiction 2. Father-daughter relationship -- Fiction
ISBN 978-1-56145-541-6; 1-56145-541-5

LC 2010001654

Forbidden to ride after her mother's death in a riding accident, thirteen-year-old Lily nurses her mother's beloved horse, Astra, back to health, hoping that someday Astra will win the Tevis Cup endurance race

"Filled with information about endurance racing as well as a cast of interesting supporting characters, including the dishy new boy in town, this novel is a quick and enjoyable read." SLJ

Platt, Randall Beth

Hellie Jondoe; [by] Randall Platt. Texas Tech University Press 2009 216p pa $16.95

Grades: 5 6 7 8   Fic

1. Oregon -- Fiction 2. Orphans -- Fiction

ISBN 978-0-89672-663-5 pa; 0-89672-663-0 pa

LC 2009-21514

In 1918, as the Great War ends and the Spanish influenza pandemic begins, thirteen-year-old Hellie Jondoe survives on the streets of New York as a beggar and pickpocket until she boards the orphan train to Oregon, where she learns about loyalty, honesty, and the meaning of family

"This is solid historical fiction with a scrappy heroine who is genuinely tough and a true survivor. Irrepressible and irreverent." Kirkus

Plum, Amy

Die for me. HarperTeen 2011 344p $17.99

Grades: 8 9 10 11   Fic

1. Love stories 2. Dead -- Fiction 3. Sisters -- Fiction 4. Bereavement -- Fiction 5. Supernatural -- Fiction 6. Paris (France) -- Fiction

ISBN 978-0-06-200401-7; 0-06-200401-8

LC 2010-30785

After their parents are killed in a car accident, sixteen-year-old Kate Mercier and her older sister Georgia, each grieving in her own way, move to Paris to live with their grandparents and Kate finds herself powerfully drawn to the handsome but elusive Vincent who seems to harbor a mysterious and dangerous secret.

"Plum deftly navigates the real world and the fantastical. Her characters are authentic, and their romances are believable. Plum introduces a world and a story that are sure to intrigue teen readers and will easily attract fans of the Twilight series." Booklist

Poblocki, Dan

The haunting of Gabriel Ashe; Dan Poblocki. Scholastic Press 2013 288 p. (hardcover) $16.99

Grades: 6 7 8   Fic

1. Horror fiction 2. School stories 3. Horror tales 4. Horror stories 5. Monsters -- Fiction 6. Friendship -- Fiction 7. Imagination -- Fiction 8. Imagination -- Fiction

ISBN 0545402700; 9780545402705

LC 2013004009

In this book, after "a fire destroys his home, Gabe and his family move into his grandmother's mansion in a small Massachusetts town. Gabe quickly befriends his neighbor, Seth Hopper, and the two play a dark fantasy game in the woods between their houses." Worried about his status at school, Gabe is concerned when he realizes Seth might be the class dork. Increasingly dark pranks begin to occur. (Kirkus Reviews)

The nightmarys. Random House 2010 325p $16.99; lib bdg $19.99

Grades: 6 7 8 9   Fic

1. Mystery fiction 2. Supernatural -- Fiction

ISBN 978-0-375-84256-6; 0-375-84256-X; 978-0-375-94256-3 lib bdg; 0-375-94256-4 lib bdg

LC 2009-50690

Seventh-grader Timothy July and his new friend Abigail try to break a curse that is causing them and others to be tormented by their greatest fears brought to life.

Poblocki "offers plenty of grisly, cinematically creepy imagery for readers who like a good scare, and the tightly wound narrative and ongoing tension between Timothy and Abigail will keep readers holding their breath until even after what they think is the climax." Publ Wkly

The stone child. Random House 2009 274p $15.99; lib bdg $18.99

Grades: 5 6 7 8   Fic

1. Authors -- Fiction 2. Monsters -- Fiction 3. Supernatural -- Fiction 4. Books and reading -- Fiction

ISBN 978-0-375-84254-2; 0-375-84254-3; 978-0-375-94254-9 lib bdg; 0-375-94254-8 lib bdg

LC 2008-21722

When friends Eddie, Harris, and Maggie discover that the scary adventures in their favorite author's fictional books come true, they must find a way to close the portal that allows evil creatures and witches to enter their hometown of Gatesweed.

"The creep factor is high but not graphic, and the kids act and react like real kids. . . . This briskly paced novel is sure to be popular with fans of scary stuff." SLJ

Polak, Monique

The middle of everywhere. Orca Book Publishers 2009 200p pa $12.95

Grades: 7 8 9 10   Fic

1. Inuit -- Fiction 2. Arctic regions -- Fiction 3. Québec (Province) -- Fiction 4. Wilderness survival -- Fiction

ISBN 978-1-55469-090-9; 1-55469-090-0

Noah spends a school term in George River, in Quebec's Far North, trying to understand the Inuit culture, which he finds both threatening and puzzling.

"Although the survival-adventure details will engage reluctant readers, the story has elements of romance when Noah strives to impress an Inuit classmate." SLJ

★ What world is left. Orca Book Pub. 2008 215p pa $12.95

Grades: 7 8 9 10 11 12   Fic

1. Jews -- Netherlands -- Fiction 2. Holocaust, 1933-1945 -- Fiction 3. World War, 1939-1945 -- Netherlands -- Fiction 4. Netherlands -- History -- 1940-1945, German occupation -- Fiction

ISBN 978-1-5514-3847-4; 1-5514-3847-X

"Growing up in a secular Jewish home in Holland, Anneke cares little about Judaism, so she has no faith to lose when, in 1943, her family is deported to Theresienstadt, the Nazi concentration camp. . . . Based on the experiences of the author's mother . . . this novel is narrated in Anneke's first-person, present-tense voice. The details are unforgettable. . . . An important addition to the Holocaust curriculum." Booklist

Polisner, Gae

The **pull** of gravity. Frances Foster Books 2011 202p $16.99

Grades: 6 7 8 9   **Fic**

1. Death -- Fiction 2. Bereavement -- Fiction 3. Family life -- Fiction 4. Father-son relationship -- Fiction

ISBN 978-0-374-37193-7; 0-374-37193-8

LC 2010-21749

When their friend Scooter dies of a rare disease, teenagers Nick Gardner and Jaycee Amato set out on a secret journey to find the father who abandoned "The Scoot" when he was an infant, and give him a signed first edition of "Of Mice and Men."

"Polisner's first novel begins with a bang and ends with another . . . . There is a great deal to enjoy throughout, and literary kids will surely enjoy a subplot involving John Steinbeck." Booklist

Pollock, Tom

★ The **city's** son; Tom Pollock. Flux 2012 460p $16.99

Grades: 6 7 8   **Fic**

1. London (England) -- Fiction 2. Fantasy fiction 3. Magic -- Fiction 4. England -- Fiction 5. Supernatural -- Fiction 6. London (Eng.) -- Fiction 7. Family problems -- Fiction

ISBN 9780738734309

LC 2012010589

This novel, by Tom Pollock, follows "teenage graffiti artist Beth Bradley . . . [and] Filius, the ragged crown prince of London's underworld. . . . Reach, the malign god of demolition, is on a rampage . . . to lay claim to the skyscraper throne. Caught up in helping Filius raise an alleyway army to battle Reach, Beth soon forgets her old life. But when the enemy claims her best friend, Beth must choose between the acceptance she finds in the streets and the life she left behind." (Publisher's note)

Polonsky, Ami

Gracefully Grayson; Ami Polonsky. Hyperion 2014 256 p. $16.99

Grades: 6 7 8 9   **Fic**

1. School stories 2. Transgender teenagers 3. Teacher-student relationship -- Fiction 4. Orphans -- Fiction 5. Theater -- Fiction 6. Family life -- Fiction 7. Middle schools -- Fiction 8. Self-acceptance -- Fiction 9. Transgender people -- Fiction

ISBN 1423185277; 9781423185277

LC 2014010155

In this novel by Ami Polonsky "Grayson Sender has been holding onto a secret for what seems like forever: 'he' is a girl on the inside, stuck in the wrong gender's body. The weight of this secret is crushing, but sharing it would mean facing ridicule, scorn, rejection, or worse. Despite the risks, Grayson's true self itches to break free. Will new strength from an unexpected friendship and a caring teacher's wisdom be enough to help Grayson?" (Publisher's note)

"Sixth grader Grayson daydreams about being a girl, despite being seen by everyone as male. Grayson keeps people at a distance until Amelia moves to town. After landing the (female) lead in a play, Grayson fights for the right to present her truest self to others--both on and off stage. Polonsky

captures her protagonist's loneliness, then courage, in an immediate and intimate narrative." Horn Book

Porter, Sarah

Lost voices. Houghton Mifflin Harcourt 2011 291p $16.99

Grades: 7 8 9 10   **Fic**

1. Singing -- Fiction 2. Supernatural -- Fiction 3. Mermaids and mermen -- Fiction

ISBN 978-0-547-48250-7; 0-547-48250-7

LC 2011008438

Assaulted and left on the cliffs outside of her grim Alaskan fishing village by her abusive, alcoholic uncle, fourteen-year-old Luce expects to die when she tumbles into the icy waters below, but when she instead transforms into a mermaid she is faced with struggles and choices she could never have imagined.

"Porter's writing is expressive and graceful. . . . A captivatingly different story." Booklist

Porter, Tracey

★ **Billy** Creekmore. Joanna Cotler Books 2007 305p $16.99; lib bdg $17.89; pa $6.99

Grades: 5 6 7 8   **Fic**

1. Circus -- Fiction 2. Orphanages -- Fiction 3. West Virginia -- Fiction 4. Coal mines and mining -- Fiction

ISBN 978-0-06-077570-4; 0-06-0-77570-X; 978-0-06-077571-1 lib bdg; 0-06-077571-8 lib bdg; 978-0-06-077572-8 pa; 0-06-077572-6 pa

LC 2007-00001

In 1905, ten-year-old Billy is taken from an orphanage to live with an aunt and uncle he never knew he had, and he enjoys his first taste of family life until his work in a coal mine and involvement with a union brings trouble, then he joins a circus in hopes of finding his father.

"Porter's writing is strong, and the story, told in Billy's steadfast yet child-true voice, makes the shocking history about the lives of children at the turn of the last century come alive for today's readers." Booklist

Potter, Ellen

The **humming** room; Ellen Potter. 1st ed. Feiwel & Friends 2012 184 p. $16.99

Grades: 4 5 6 7   **Fic**

1. Children's stories 2. Family -- Fiction 3. Haunted houses -- Fiction 4. Foster children -- Fiction 5. Gardens -- Fiction 6. Islands -- Fiction 7. Orphans -- Fiction

ISBN 0312644388; 9780312644383

LC 2011033583

In this book by Ellen Potter, "[h]idden under the family trailer, Roo hears . . . the murder of her drug-dealing father. . . . [S]he is sent to live with her . . . reclusive uncle on Cough Rock, a spooky old house named for its former use as a sanitarium. . . . [The cast of characters includes a] personal assistant, a cheerful local servant, a mysterious wild boy, and a secluded boy cousin with a fearful temper who is not expected to live." (Bulletin of the Center for Children's Books)

★ **Slob**. Philomel Books 2009 199p $16.99

Grades: 5 6 7 8   **Fic**

1. Obesity -- Fiction 2. Orphans -- Fiction 3. Siblings

-- Fiction 4. Inventions -- Fiction 5. Bereavement -- Fiction 6. New York (N.Y.) -- Fiction
ISBN 978-0-399-24705-7; 0-399-24705-X

LC 2008-40476

Picked on, overweight genius Owen tries to invent a television that can see the past to find out what happened the day his parents were killed.

"An intriguingly offbeat mystery, . . . at turns humorous, suspenseful and poignant." Kirkus

Powell, Laura

Burn mark; by Laura Powell. Bloomsbury Children's Books 2012 403p. (hardback) $17.99
Grades: 7 8 9 10 11 12   **Fic**
1. Occult fiction 2. Witches -- Fiction 3. Supernatural -- Fiction 4. England -- Fiction 5. London (England) -- Fiction
ISBN 1599908433; 9781599908434

LC 2011034464

This young adult fantasy, by Laura Powell, is set "in a modern world where witches are hunted down and burned at the stake. . . . Glory is from a family of witches, and is desperate to develop her 'Fae' powers. . . . Lucas is the son of the Chief Prosecutor for the Inquisition with a privileged life very different from the witches he is being trained to prosecute. And then one day, both Glory and Lucas develop the Fae . . . [and] their lives are inextricably bound together." (Publisher's note)

The **game** of triumphs. Alfred A. Knopf 2011 269p $16.99; lib bdg $19.99; ebook $10.99
Grades: 7 8 9 10   **Fic**
1. Games -- Fiction 2. Tarot -- Fiction 3. Supernatural -- Fiction 4. Space and time -- Fiction 5. London (England) -- Fiction
ISBN 978-0-375-86587-9; 0-375-86587-X; 978-0-375-96587-6 lib bdg; 0-375-96587-4 lib bdg; 978-0-375-89774-0 ebook

LC 2010021813

Fifteen-year-old Cat and three other London teens are drawn into a dangerous game in which Tarot cards open doorways into a different dimension and while there is everything to win, losing can be fatal.

"Original and engrossing." Kirkus

The **Master** of Misrule; Laura Powell. Alfred A. Knopf 2012 363 p. (trade hardcover) $16.99
Grades: 7 8 9 10 11 12   **Fic**
1. Games -- Fiction 2. Tarot -- Fiction 3. Supernatural -- Fiction 4. England -- Fiction 5. Role playing -- Fiction 6. Space and time -- Fiction 7. London (England) -- Fiction
ISBN 0375865888; 9780375865664; 9780375865886; 9780375897849; 9780375965883

LC 2011021135

Sequel to: The Game of Triumphs

In this book, "despite holding the Triumphs that promise answers to their various back stories (including the murder of Cat's parents, Blaine's abusive stepfather and Flora's comatose sister, all related to the Game of Triumphs), resolution eludes Cat and her friends. They must fight the Fool, now the Master of Misrule, whom they released in the first

volume, not only for their own success, but to save the world." (Kirkus Reviews)

"This fast-paced novel mixes fantasy and reality in an intricately described setting... Packed with mystery, action, and even a hint of romance, The Master of Misrule will appeal to fans of role-playing games or anyone seeking an adventurous read.—" VOYA

Powell, Randy

Swiss mist. Farrar, Straus & Giroux 2008 210p $16.95
Grades: 6 7 8 9 10   **Fic**
1. Divorce -- Fiction 2. Washington (State) -- Fiction
ISBN 978-0-374-37356-6; 0-374-37356-6

LC 2007-27680

Follows Milo from fifth grade, when his mother and philosopher father get divorced, through tenth grade, when his mother has married a wealthy businessman and Milo is still a bit of a loner, looking for the meaning of life.

"This book is rewardingly remarkable for the characters and bits of truth that Milo never stops pursuing, even as he learns that truth is not what matters most." SLJ

Three clams and an oyster. Farrar, Straus & Giroux 2002 216p hardcover o.p. pa $6.95
Grades: 7 8 9 10   **Fic**
1. Football -- Fiction 2. Friendship -- Fiction
ISBN 0-374-37526-7; 0-374-40007-5 pa

LC 2001-54833

During their humorous search to find a fourth player for their flag football team, three high school juniors are forced to examine their long friendship, their individual flaws, and their inability to try new experiences

"Sometimes philosophical, sometimes comical, but always touching, Randy Powell writes an unusually moving story of adolescent male friends." Book Rep

Powell, William Campbell

Expiration day; William Campbell Powell. Tor Teen 2014 336 p. (hardback) $17.99
Grades: 8 9 10 11 12   **Fic**
1. Bildungsromans 2. Science fiction 3. Robots -- Fiction 4. Diaries -- Fiction 5. England -- Fiction 6. Coming of age -- Fiction
ISBN 0765338289; 9780765338280

LC 2013025453

In this book, by William Campbell Powell, "it is the year 2049, and humanity is on the brink of extinction. . . . Tania Deeley has always been told that she's a rarity: a human child in a world where most children are sophisticated androids manufactured by Oxted Corporation. . . . Though she has always been aware of the existence of teknoids, it is not until her first day at The Lady Maud High School for Girls that Tania realizes that her best friend, Siân, may be one." (Publisher's note)

"In this coming-of-age diary, a girl navigates life in a dystopic near-future. By the year 2049, the world has become a rather unfriendly place for humans and robots alike. England is divided into color-coded zones, parts of the African continent are shadowed in mystery, and very few humans are still able to procreate....The author pays homage to the genre's giants while combining realistic characters (both human and android) and detailed worldbuilding with an unpredictably optimistic conclusion. In the end, the thoughtful balance of narrative and description and the well-paced plot are marred only by a mildly distracting subplot that unreels in interstitial "Intervals." An auspicious debut. " (Kirkus)

Powers, J. L.

This thing called the future; a novel. Cinco Puntos 2011 213p $16.95

Grades: 8 9 10 11 12   **Fic**

1. Sick -- Fiction 2. South Africa -- Fiction 3. Mother-daughter relationship -- Fiction

ISBN 978-1-933693-95-8; 1-933693-95-9

Powers "composes a compelling, often harrowing portrait of a struggling country, where old beliefs and rituals still have power, but can't erase the problems of the present. Readers will be fully invested in Khosi's efforts to secure a better future." Publ Wkly

Pratchett, Terry

★ The **amazing** Maurice and his educated rodents. HarperCollins Pubs. 2001 241p hardcover o.p. pa $6.99

Grades: 7 8 9 10   **Fic**

1. Fantasy fiction 2. Cats -- Fiction 3. Rats -- Fiction

ISBN 0-06-001233-1; 0-06-001235-8 pa

LC 2001-42411

A talking cat, intelligent rats, and a strange boy cooperate in a Pied Piper scam until they try to con the wrong town and are confronted by a deadly evil rat king

"In this laugh-out-loud fantasy, his first 'Discworld' novel for younger readers, Pratchett rethinks a classic story and comes up with a winner." SLJ

★ **Dodger**; by Terry Pratchett. HarperCollins 2012 360 p. (hardback) $17.99

Grades: 7 8 9 10   **Fic**

1. Lifesaving 2. Love stories 3. Historical fiction 4. Love -- Fiction 5. Humorous stories 6. Conduct of life -- Fiction 7. Adventure and adventurers -- Fiction 8. Todd, Sweeney (Legendary character) -- Fiction 9. London (England) -- History -- 19th century -- Fiction 10. Great Britain -- History -- Victoria, 1837-1901 -- Fiction

ISBN 0062009494; 9780062009494; 9780062009500

LC 2012022155

Michael L. Printz Honor Book (2013)

Author Terry Pratchett presents a story of historical fiction. "Dodger is a guttersnipe and a tosher . . . [and] a petty criminal but also (generally) one of the good guys. One night he rescues a beautiful young woman and finds himself hobnobbing quite literally with the likes of Charlie Dickens . . . and Ben Disraeli . . . And when he attempts to smarten himself up to impress the damsel in distress, he unexpectedly comes face to face with . . . Sweeney Todd." (Kirkus)

A **hat** full of sky. HarperCollins 2004 288p $16.99; lib bdg $17.89

Grades: 7 8 9 10   **Fic**

1. Fantasy fiction 2. Fairies -- Fiction 3. Witches

-- Fiction

ISBN 0-06-058660-5; 0-06-058661-3 lib bdg

LC 2003-21443

Sequel to: The Wee Free Men (2003)

Tiffany Aching, a young witch-in-training, learns about magic and responsibility as she battles a disembodied monster with the assistance of the six-inch-high Wee Free Men and Mistress Weatherwax, the greatest witch in the world.

"This book is full of irreverent humor, laugh-out-loud dialogue, and many memorable characters." SLJ

Followed by: Wintersmith (2006)

★ **I** shall wear midnight. Harper 2010 355p $16.99

Grades: 7 8 9 10   **Fic**

1. Ghost stories 2. Fantasy fiction 3. Fairies -- Fiction 4. Witches -- Fiction

ISBN 978-0-06-143304-7; 0-06-143304-7

LC 2010-24442

Sequel to: Wintersmith (2006)

Fifteen-year-old Tiffany Aching, the witch of the Chalk, seeks her place amid a troublesome populace and tries to control the ill-behaved, six-inch-high Wee Free Men who follow her as she faces an ancient evil that agitates against witches.

"The final adventure in Pratchett's Tiffany Aching series brings this subset of Discworld novels to a moving and highly satisfactory conclusion." Publ Wkly

Johnny and the bomb. HarperCollins 2007 245p hardcover o.p. lib bdg $17.89; pa $6.99

Grades: 5 6 7 8   **Fic**

1. Science fiction 2. Great Britain -- Fiction 3. World War, 1939-1945 -- Fiction

ISBN 978-0-06-054191-0; 0-06-054191-1; 978-0-06-054192-7 lib bdg; 0-06-054192-X lib bdg; 978-0-06-054193-4 pa; 0-06-054193-8 pa

LC 2006-00555

Third in the trilogy which began with Only you can save mankind (2005) and Johnny and the dead (2006)

Thirteen-year-old Johnny Maxwell acquires the neighborhood homeless woman's shopping cart when she is injured and discovers that its contents have the ability to send him back in time from 1996 to 1941 England

"This trilogy ends with a bang. . . . Johnny's quirky sidekicks are back, each sidesplittingly portrayed and effectively advancing the plot." SLJ

Johnny and the dead. HarperCollins 2006 213p hardcover o.p. pa $7.99

Grades: 5 6 7 8   **Fic**

1. Ghost stories 2. Great Britain -- Fiction

ISBN 978-0-06-054188-0; 0-06-054188-1; 978-0-06-054190-3 pa; 0-06-054190-3 pa

LC 2005-05073

Sequel to Only you can save mankind

First published 1993 in the United Kingdom

After twelve-year-old Johnny Maxwell suddenly starts seeing and talking to ghosts, he and his friends become involved in a battle to save the local cemetery

"Readers will take immense pleasure in the jokes, some broad and some subtle and dry, that come sailing at them from all sides." SLJ

Followed by Johnny and the bomb (2006)

★ **Nation.** HarperCollins 2008 367p $16.99; lib bdg $17.89; pa $8.99

Grades: 7 8 9 10 11 12 Fic

1. Islands -- Fiction 2. Tsunamis -- Fiction 3. Survival after airplane accidents, shipwrecks, etc. -- Fiction
ISBN 978-0-06-143301-6; 0-06-143301-2; 978-0-06-143302-3 lib bdg; 0-06-143302-0 lib bdg; 978-0-06-143303-0 pa; 0-06-143303-9 pa

LC 2008-20211

Boston Globe-Horn Book Award: Fiction (2009)

After a devastating tsunami destroys all that they have ever known, Mau, an island boy, and Daphne, an aristocratic English girl, together with a small band of refugees, set about rebuilding their community and all the things that are important in their lives.

"Quirky wit and broad vision make this a fascinating survival story on many levels." Booklist

★ **Only** you can save mankind. HarperCollins 2005 207p hardcover o.p. lib bdg $16.89; pa $6.99

Grades: 5 6 7 8 Fic

1. War stories 2. Computer games -- Fiction
ISBN 0-06-054185-7; 0-06-054186-5 lib bdg; 0-06-054187-3 pa

First published 1992 in the United Kingdom

Twelve-year-old Johnny endures tensions between his parents, watches television coverage of the Gulf War, and plays a computer game called Only You Can Save Mankind, in which he is increasingly drawn into the reality of the alien ScreeWee

This is "a wild ride, full of Pratchett's trademark humor; digs at primitive, low-resolution games . . .; and some not-so-subtle philosophy about war and peace." Booklist

Other titles in this trilogy are:
Johnny and the dead (2006)
Johnny and the bomb (2006)

The **Wee** Free Men. HarperCollins Pubs. 2003 263p hardcover o.p. pa $9.99

Grades: 7 8 9 10 Fic

1. Fantasy fiction 2. Witches -- Fiction
ISBN 0-06-001236-6; 0-06-201217-7 pa

LC 2002-15396

A young witch-to-be named Tiffany teams up with the Wee Free Men, a clan of six-inch-high blue men, to rescue her baby brother and ward off a sinister invasion from Fairyland

"Pratchett invites readers into his well-established realm of Discworld where action, magic, and characters are firmly rooted in literary reality. Humor ripples throughout, making tense, dangerous moments stand out in stark contrast." Bull Cent Child Books

Other titles about Tiffany are:
A hat full of sky (2004)
I shall wear midnight (2010)
Wintersmith (2006)

Wintersmith. HarperTempest 2006 323p $16.99; lib bdg $17.99

Grades: 7 8 9 10 Fic

1. Fantasy fiction 2. Winter -- Fiction 3. Witches -- Fiction
ISBN 978-0-06-089031-5; 0-06-089031-2; 978-0-06-089032-2 lib bdg; 0-06-089032-0 lib bdg

LC 2006-03705

Sequel to: A hat full of sky (2004)

When witch-in-training Tiffany Aching accidentally interrupts the Dance of the Seasons and awakens the interest of the elemental spirit of Winter, she requires the help of the six-inch-high, sword-wielding, sheepstealing Wee Free Men to put the seasons aright.

"Yet another rollicking, clever, and quite charming adventure is brought to readers, who will find themselves delighted again—or for the first time—by Pratchett's exuberant storytelling." Booklist

Followed by: I shall wear midnight (2010)

Preller, James

★ **Bystander.** Feiwel and Friends 2009 226p $16.99

Grades: 5 6 7 8 Fic

1. School stories 2. Moving -- Fiction 3. Bullies -- Fiction 4. Divorce -- Fiction 5. Family life -- Fiction 6. Long Island (N.Y.) -- Fiction
ISBN 0312379064; 9780312379063

LC 2008-28554

Thirteen-year-old Eric discovers there are consequences to not standing by and watching as the bully at his new school hurts people, but although school officials are aware of the problem, Eric may be the one with a solution.

"Although there are no pat answers, the message (that a bystander is hardly better than an instigator) is clear, and Preller's well-shaped characters, strong writing, and realistic treatment of middle-school life deliver it cleanly." Booklist

★ **Six** innings; a game in the life. Feiwel and Friends 2008 147p $16.95

Grades: 4 5 6 7 Fic

1. Cancer -- Fiction 2. Baseball -- Fiction
ISBN 978-0-312-36763-3; 0-312-36763-5

LC 2007-32846

Earl Grubb's Pool Supplies plays Northeast Gas & Electric in the Little League championship game, while Sam, who has cancer and is in a wheelchair, has to call the play-by-play instead of participating in the game.

"The outcome is predictable but the journey is nailbitingly tense. Kids will be nodding in agreement at the truths laid bare." Publ Wkly

Preus, Margi

★ **Heart** of a samurai; based on the true story of Nakahama Manjiro. Abrams/Amulet 2010 301p il $15.95

Grades: 7 8 9 10 11 12 Fic

1. Interpreters 2. Japanese -- United States -- Fiction 3. Survival after airplane accidents, shipwrecks, etc. -- Fiction
ISBN 978-0-8109-8981-8; 0-8109-8981-6

LC 2009-51634

A Newbery Medal honor book, 2011

In 1841, rescued by an American whaler after a terrible shipwreck leaves him and his four companions castaways on a remote island, fourteen-year-old Manjiro, who dreams of becoming a samurai, learns new laws and customs as he becomes the first Japanese person to set foot in the United States.

The author "mixes fact with fiction in a tale that is at once adventurous, heartwarming, sprawling, and nerve-racking in its depictions of early anti-Asian sentiment. She succeeds in making readers feel every bit as 'other' as Manjiro, while showing America at its best and worst through his eyes." Publ Wkly

Includes bibliographical references

Shadow on the mountain; a novel inspired by the true adventures of a wartime spy. by Margi Preus. Amulet Books 2012 286 p. (alk. paper) $16.95
Grades: 6 7 8 9 **Fic**
1. Adventure fiction 2. Historical fiction 3. World War, 1939-1945 -- Fiction 4. Spies -- Fiction 5. Norway -- History -- German occupation, 1940-1945 -- Fiction 6. World War, 1939-1945 -- Underground movements -- Norway -- Fiction
ISBN 1419704249; 9781419704246
LC 2012015623

This juvenile historical fiction novel, by Margi Preus, "recounts the adventures of a 14-year-old Norwegian boy named Espen during World War II. After Nazi Germany invades and occupies Norway, Espen and his friends are swept up in the Norwegian resistance movement. Espen gets his start by delivering illegal newspapers, then graduates to the role of courier and finally becomes a spy, dodging the Gestapo along the way." (Publisher's note)

Includes bibliographical references.

West of the moon; Margi Preus. Amulet Books 2014 224 p. (alk. paper) $16.95
Grades: 5 6 7 8 **Fic**
1. Norway -- Fiction 2. Folklore -- Norway 3. Human trafficking -- Fiction 4. United States -- Immigration and emigration -- Fiction 5. Norway -- History -- 19th century -- Fiction
ISBN 1419708961; 9781419708961
LC 2013023250

Author Margi Preus "weaves original fiction with myth and folktale to tell the story of Astri, a young Norwegian girl desperate to join her father in America. After being separated from her sister and sold to a cruel goat farmer, Astri makes a daring escape. She quickly retrieves her little sister, and, armed with a troll treasure, a book of spells and curses, and a possibly magic hairbrush, they set off for America." (Publisher's note)

"In the Scandinavian fairy tale "East of the Sun and West of the Moon," a young girl is taken from her home to a magnificent castle by a great bear, whom she discovers is really a prince... Like dun silk shot through with gold, Preus (Heart of a Samurai, 2010) interweaves the mesmerizing tale of Astri's treacherous and harrowing mid-nineteenth-century immigration to America with bewitching tales of magic. A fascinating author's note only adds to the wonder." Bklst

Includes bibliographical references

Prevost, Guillaume

The **book** of time; [by] Guillaume Prévost; translated by William Rodarmor. Arthur A. Levine Books 2007 213p $16.99; pa $6.99
Grades: 5 6 7 8 **Fic**
1. Science fiction 2. Missing persons -- Fiction
ISBN 978-0-439-88375-7; 0-439-88375-X; 978-0-439-88379-5 pa; 0-439-88379-2 pa
LC 2006-38446

Original French edition 2006

Sam Faulkner travels back in time to medieval Ireland, ancient Egypt and Renaissance Bruges in search of his missing father

"The appeal of the novel . . . comes from both well-drawn characters and a swiftly moving story." Booklist

Other titles in this series are:
The gate of days (2008)
The circle of gold (2009)

Price, Charlie
★ **Desert** Angel. Farrar Straus Giroux 2011 176p $15.99
Grades: 8 9 10 11 12 **Fic**
1. Violence -- Fiction 2. California -- Fiction 3. Illegal aliens -- Fiction 4. Mexican Americans -- Fiction
ISBN 978-0-374-31775-1; 0-374-31775-5
LC 2010044122

"Price's pacing is tight, aided by direct, clipped prose that underscores Scotty's brutality and Angel's fragile emotional state. Both the best and worst of humanity shine through in this gripping novel." Publ Wkly

Price, Lissa
Enders; by Lissa Price. Delacorte Press 2014 288 p. (hc : alk. paper) $17.99
Grades: 7 8 9 10 **Fic**
1. Brainwashing 2. Teenagers -- Fiction 3. Science -- Experiments -- Fiction 4. Science fiction
ISBN 0385742495; 9780375990618; 9780385742498
LC 2013011679

Sequel to: Starters

In this book by Lissa Price, the conclusion to her Starters series, "someone is after Starters like Callie and Michael-teens with chips in their brains. They want to experiment on anyone left over from Prime Destinations--Starters who can be controlled and manipulated. With the body bank destroyed, Callie no longer has to rent herself out to creepy Enders. But Enders can still get inside her mind and make her do things she doesn't want to do." (Publisher's note)

"Some glossed-over twists stretch believability, though the threat (and villain's secret plan), smaller-scale than in Starters, is personal in a creepy way. Metals can be controlled remotely, and Callie's modified chip keeps her awake and aware, leading to a delightfully disturbing climax. It's not as intense as Starters, but it offers some answers and a solid conclusion that will repay readers." (Kirkus)

Starters; Lissa Price. Delacorte Press 2012 336 p. (paperback) $9.99; (ebook) $53.97; (glb) $20.99; (hardcover) $17.99

Grades: 7 8 9 10   **Fic**

1. Science fiction 2. Orphans -- Fiction 3. Intergenerational relations -- Fiction 4. Brothers and sisters -- Fiction

ISBN 9780385742481; 0385742371; 9780307975232; 9780375990601; 9780385742375

LC 2011040820

In this book, "[w]hen a deadly virus wipes out the entire population of the U.S. save the elderly and the young, . . . the result is a dysfunctional society polarized between young 'Starters' and the increasingly long-lived 'Enders.' Children who are unclaimed by surviving relatives are institutionalized, and many -- like Callie and her little brother, Tyler -- learn to fend for themselves in virtual hiding from the law to escape that fate." (Bulletin of the Center for Children's Books)

Price, Nora

Zoe letting go; Nora Price. Razorbill 2012 279 p. $17.99

Grades: 8 9 10 11 12   **Fic**

1. Rehabilitation -- Fiction 2. Eating disorders -- Fiction 3. Diaries -- Fiction 4. Letters -- Fiction 5. Friendship -- Fiction 6. Anorexia nervosa -- Fiction 7. Emotional problems -- Fiction

ISBN 1595144668; 9781595144669

LC 2012012257

This book tells the story of 16-year-old Zoe, who "finds herself in a small rehabilitation center for girls with eating disorders," which she feels "must be some kind of mistake" because "she feels in control of her cautious dietary habits. Through letters to her mysteriously silent best friend, Elise, as well as a personal journal," it becomes clear that Zoe is in denial and "that she is, in fact, a girl with a disorder that is spiraling out of control." (School Library Journal)

Priestly, Chris

Mister Creecher. Bloomsbury 2011 390p $16.99

Grades: 6 7 8 9   **Fic**

1. Horror fiction 2. Frankenstein (Fictional character)

ISBN 978-1-59990-703-1; 1-59990-703-8

Billy is a street urchin, a pickpocket, and a petty thief. Mister Creecher is a giant of a man whose appearance terrifies everyone he meets. A bond develops between these two misfits as they embark on a bloody journey that will take them from London northward on the trail of their target . . . Doctor Victor Frankenstein.

"Priestly's love of Shelley is evident. Here, he restores Shelley's original creature—not a lurching, moaning monster but an eloquent, profoundly flawed being—imbuing him with the deep desire to be loved and accepted." Booklist

Prineas, Sarah

★ The **magic** thief; illustrations by Antonio Javier Caparo. HarperCollins Pubs. 2008 419p il map

Grades: 4 5 6 7   **Fic**

1. Fantasy fiction 2. Magic -- Fiction 3. Thieves --

Fiction 4. Apprentices -- Fiction

ISBN 0-06-137587-X; 0-06-137588-8 lib bdg; 0-06-137590-X pa; 978-0-06-137587-3; 978-0-06-137588-0 lib bdg; 978-0-06-137590-3 pa

LC 2007031704

Conn is a young thief who is drawn into a life of adventure after picking the pocket of the wizard Nevery Flinglas. Finglas has returned from exile to try to reverse the decline of magic in Wellmet City. "Grades five to nine." (Bull Cent Child Books)

"Conn is a thief but, through desire and inevitability, becomes a wizard . . . This evolution begins when Conn picks the pocket of the wizard Nevery. . . . What works wonderfully well here is the boy's irresistable voice." Booklist

Other titles in this series are:

Lost (2009)

Found (2010)

Prinz, Yvonne

The **Vinyl** Princess. HarperTeen 2010 313p $16.99

Grades: 8 9 10 11 12   **Fic**

1. Music -- Fiction 2. Zines -- Fiction 3. Weblogs -- Fiction 4. California -- Fiction 5. Sound recordings -- Fiction

ISBN 978-0-06-171583-9; 0-06-171583-2

LC 2009-14270

Allie, a sixteen-year-old who is obsessed with LPs, works at the used record store on Telegraph Ave. and deals with crushes—her own and her mother's—her increasingly popular blog and zine, and generally grows up over the course of one summer in her hometown of Berkeley, California.

Prinz "writes with a genuine passion for music that readers who live to listen will recognize, and in this heartfelt, often-hilarious story, she shows the profound ways that music can shape lives." Booklist

Proimos, James, 1958-

12 things to do before you crash and burn. Roaring Brook Press 2011 121p $14.99

Grades: 7 8 9 10   **Fic**

1. Uncles -- Fiction 2. Bereavement -- Fiction 3. Baltimore (Md.) -- Fiction 4. Father-son relationship -- Fiction

ISBN 978-1-59643-595-7; 1-59643-595-X

LC 2010043935

Sixteen-year-old James 'Hercules' Martino completes twelve tasks while spending two weeks in Baltimore with his Uncle Anthony, and gains insights into himself, his uncle, and his recently deceased father, a self-help author and daytime talk show host who was beloved by the public but a terrible father.

"Proimos fully inhabits the mind and voice of his hero, whose almost mythic journey offers moments hilarious, heartbreaking, and triumphant." Publ Wkly

Prose, Francine

After. HarperCollins Pubs. 2003 330p $15.99; lib bdg $16.89

Grades: 7 8 9 10   **Fic**

1. School stories 2. Conspiracies -- Fiction 3. School

violence -- Fiction
ISBN 0-06-008081-7; 0-06-008082-5 lib bdg
LC 2002-14386

In the aftermath of a nearby school shooting, a grief and crisis counselor takes over Central High School and enacts increasingly harsh measures to control students, while those who do not comply disappear

"This drama raises all-too-relevant questions about the fine line between safety as a means of protection versus encroachment on individual rights and free will. Sure to spur heated discussions." Publ Wkly

Touch. HarperTeen 2009 262p $16.99; lib bdg $17.89

Grades: 7 8 9 10 **Fic**
1. School stories 2. Friendship -- Fiction 3. Family life -- Fiction 4. Stepmothers -- Fiction
ISBN 978-0-06-137517-0; 0-06-137517-9; 978-0-06-137518-7 lib bdg; 0-06-137518-7 lib bdg
LC 2008-20208

Ninth-grader Maisie's concepts of friendship, loyalty, self-acceptance, and truth are tested to their limit after a schoolbus incident with the three boys who have been her best friends since early childhood.

"Readers will be fascinated by this convincing tale and the questions that it raises, from its gripping first chapter to its poignant and surprising conclusion." Voice Youth Advocates

The **turning**; by Francine Prose. HarperTeen 2012 256 p. (hardcover) $17.99

Grades: 7 8 9 10 **Fic**
1. Ghost stories 2. Horror fiction 3. Babysitters -- Fiction 4. Ghosts -- Fiction
ISBN 0061999660; 9780061999666
LC 2012019090

This book by Francine Prose is an "epistolary retelling of Henry James's 'The Turn of the Screw' [which] traces a contemporary babysitter's supernatural encounters. The protagonist, Jack, is hoping to earn some money for college when he agrees to care for orphan siblings on Crackstone's Landing, a remote island without phones, Internet, or TV. . . . Jack is spooked by two ethereal figures, perhaps the ghosts of the children's former governess and her beau." (Publishers Weekly)

Pryor, Bonnie

The **iron** dragon; the courageous story of Lee Chin. Enslow Publishers 2010 160p (Historical fiction adventures) lib bdg $27.93; pa $14.95

Grades: 4 5 6 **Fic**
1. Railroads -- Fiction 2. California -- Fiction 3. Immigrants -- Fiction 4. Chinese Americans -- Fiction
ISBN 978-0-7660-3389-4 lib bdg; 0-7660-3389-9 lib bdg; 978-1-59845-215-0 pa; 1-59845-215-0 pa
LC 2009017930

In the mid-nineteenth century, teenager Lee Chin and his father leave China for California to work on the transcontinental railroad, where Lee defies his father's wishes and saves money to free his younger sister from slavery in China, then brings her to join him in beginning a new life in America. Includes historical note about the Chinese who helped build the transcontinental railroad

"Lee Chin's tale is compellingly told. . . . Historical information is accurate and honest about the period depicted." SLJ

Simon's escape; a story of the Holocaust. Enslow Publishers 2010 160p (Historical fiction adventures) lib bdg $27.93; pa $14.95

Grades: 4 5 6 **Fic**
1. Poland -- Fiction 2. Jews -- Poland -- Fiction 3. Holocaust, 1933-1945 -- Fiction 4. World War, 1939-1945 -- Fiction
ISBN 978-0-7660-3388-7 lib bdg; 0-7660-3388-0 lib bdg; 978-1-59845-216-7 pa; 1-59845-216-9 pa
LC 2009029322

Simon, a young Polish Jew, and his family are forced by Nazis to leave their home for the filth and hunger of the Warsaw ghetto then, when his family is all taken away, he escapes to fight for survival in the countryside. Includes facts about the Holocaust

This "is a compelling, informative introduction to Holocaust history." Booklist

Pullman, Philip, 1946-

The **amber** spyglass; His Dark Materials book III. [appendix illustrations by Ian Beck] Deluxe ed.; Alfred A. Knopf 2007 518p il $22.99; lib bdg $25.99

Grades: 7 8 9 10 11 12 **Fic**
1. Fantasy fiction
ISBN 978-0-375-84673-1; 978-0-375-94673-8 lib bdg
LC 2006-48865

Sequel to: The subtle knife
First published 2000

Third volume in His Dark Materials trilogy "starts where The Subtle Knife . . . left off. Lyra has been hidden away by her mother, and Will is determined to find her. Meanwhile, Lord Asriel is preparing to fight the forces of the Church's Consistorial Court, as well as the God-like Authority's Lieutenant, Metatron, who hungers for ultimate power over all worlds. At the heart of this discord is Dust, the mysterious substance that is linked irrevocably to consciousness; it is streaming away at an increasing rate, causing havoc in its wake. It is Lyra and Will's destiny to determine the outcome of this situation." SLJ

★ The **golden** compass; his dark materials book I. [appendix illustrations by Ian Beck] Deluxe 10th anniversary ed.; Alfred A. Knopf 2006 399p il $22.95

Grades: 7 8 9 10 11 12 **Fic**
1. Fantasy fiction
ISBN 978-0-375-83830-9; 0-375-83830-9
LC 2005-32556

First published 1995 in the United Kingdom with title: Northern lights

This first title in a fantasy trilogy "introduces the characters and sets up the basic conflict, namely, a race to unlock the mystery of a newly discovered type of charged particles simply called 'dust' that may be a bridge to an alternate universe. The action follows 11-year-old protagonist Lyra Belacqua from her home at Oxford University to the frozen wastes of the North on a quest to save dozens of kidnapped children from the evil 'Gobblers,' who are using them as part of a sinister experiment involving dust." Libr J [review of 1996 edition]

Other titles in the His dark materials series are:

The amber spyglass (2000)

The subtle knife (1997)

★ **Once** upon a time in the North; illustrated by John Lawrence. Knopf 2008 95p il $12.99

Grades: 7 8 9 10 11 12   **Fic**

1. Fantasy fiction

ISBN 978-0-375-84510-9; 0-375-84510-0

LC 2007-43993

Prequel to: The golden compass

In a time before Lyra Silvertongue was born, the tough American balloonist Lee Scoresby and the great armoured bear Iorek Byrnison meet when Lee and his hare daemon Hester crash-land their trading balloon onto a port in the far Arctic North and find themselves right in the middle of a political powder keg.

"The precise narrative prose is spiced up with Lee's flights of 'oratorical flamboyancy,' and the sardonic banter between Lee and his daemon Hester is as amusing as ever. [Illustrated with] engraved spot illustrations and 'reproduced' documents." Horn Book

The **subtle** knife; His Dark Materials book II. [appendix illustrations by Ian Beck] Deluxe 10th anniversary ed.; Alfred A. Knopf 2007 326p il $22.99; lib bdg $25.99

Grades: 7 8 9 10 11 12   **Fic**

1. Fantasy fiction

ISBN 978-0-375-84672-4; 978-0-375-94672-1 lib bdg

LC 2006-48866

Sequel to: The golden compass

First published 1997

In the second volume of His dark materials trilogy the boundaries between worlds begin to dissolve. Lyra and her daemon help Will Parry in his search for his father and for a powerful, magical knife.

"More than fulfilling the promise of The Golden Compass, this second volume in the His Dark Materials trilogy starts off at a heart-thumping pace and never slows down." Publ Wkly

Followed by: The amber spyglass

Two crafty criminals! and how they were captured by the daring detectives of the New Cut Gang; including Thunderbolt's Waxwork & the gas-fitters' ball. Philip Pullman. Alfred A. Knopf 2012 281 p. (hardback) $16.99

Grades: 5 6 7 8   **Fic**

1. Mystery fiction 2. Crime -- Fiction 3. Gangs -- Fiction 4. Humorous fiction 5. Children's stories 6. Humorous stories 7. Mystery and detective stories 8. Adventure and adventurers -- Fiction 9. London (England) -- History -- 19th century -- Fiction 10. Great Britain -- History -- Victoria, 1837-1901 -- Fiction

ISBN 9780375870293; 9780375970290; 9780375988684

LC 2011042391

This children's book by Philip Pullman was published in 1994 as two novellas: "Thunderbolt's Waxwork" and "The Gas-Fitters' Ball," which are set in "1894 London . . . [and] star . . . the intrepid boy and girl detectives of the New Cut Gang. . . . Thunderbolt Dobney sees his own father hauled off to jail for what he thinks must be 'coining.' . . . [H]e and the New Cut Gang expose the real criminal. . . . In 'The Gas-Fitters' Ball,' . . . the Gas-Fitters' Hall is burgled." (Kirkus Reviews)

Pyron, Bobbie

★ A **dog's** way home. Katherine Tegen Books 2011 321p lib bdg $17.89; $16.99

Grades: 4 5 6 7   **Fic**

1. Dogs -- Fiction 2. North Carolina -- Fiction 3. Traffic accidents -- Fiction

ISBN 0-06-198673-9 lib bdg; 0-06-198674-7; 978-0-06-198673-4 lib bdg; 978-0-06-198674-1

LC 2010006960

After a car accident strands them at opposite ends of the Blue Ridge Parkway, eleven-year-old Abby and her beloved sheltie Tam overcome months filled with physical and emotional challenges to find their way back to each other.

"A heartwarming, suspenseful tale . . . With vibrant, sympathetic characterizations, Pyron creates an inspiring portrayal of devotion and survival against all odds." Publ Wkly

The **dogs** of winter; by Bobbie Pyron. Arthur A. Levine Books 2012 312 p. (hardcover : alk. paper) $16.99

Grades: 5 6 7 8   **Fic**

1. Wild dogs -- Fiction 2. Abandoned children -- Fiction 3. Wilderness survival -- Fiction 4. Dogs -- Fiction 5. Gangs -- Fiction 6. Moscow (Russia) -- Fiction 7. Street children -- Fiction 8. Homeless persons -- Fiction 9. Russia (Federation) -- Fiction 10. Human-animal relationships -- Fiction

ISBN 0545399300; 9780545399302; 9780545399319; 9780545469852

LC 2011051519

In this book by Bobbie Pyron "Ivan's mother disappears, [and] he's abandoned on the streets of Moscow, with little chance to make it through the harsh winter. But help comes in an unexpected form: Ivan is adopted by a pack of dogs, and the dogs quickly become more than just his street companions: They become his family. Soon Ivan, who used to love reading fairytales, is practically living in one." But "when help is finally offered to him, will he be able to accept it?" (Publisher's note)

Lucky strike; Bobbie Pyron. Arthur A. Levine Books, an imprint of Scholastic Inc. 2015 262 p. hbk $16.99

Grades: 4 5 6 7   **Fic**

1. Luck -- Fiction 2. Florida -- Fiction 3. Lightning -- Fiction 4. Grandparent-grandchild relationship -- Fiction 5. Grandparent and child -- Fiction 6. Franklin County (Fla.) -- Fiction

ISBN 9780545592178; 0545592178; 0545592186; 9780545592185

LC 2014013764

In this book, by Bobbie Pyron, "Nate Harlow has never had a lucky day in his life. . . . His best friend, Genesis Beam (aka Gen), believes in science and logic, and she doesn't think for one second that there's such a thing as luck, good or bad. But only an extremely unlucky person could be struck by lightning on his birthday... and that person is Nate Harlow. By some miracle, though, Nate survives, and the strike seems to have changed his luck." (Publisher's note)

"The quirkiness of the characters and the town never goes too far, and there is an overall cozy feeling to the book. Genesis's dad is the preacher at The Church of the One True Redeemer and Everlasting Light, but she is a scientist through and through, which adds complexity to the text, including musings on destiny, fate, probability, and weather." SLJ

Qamar, Amjed

Beneath my mother's feet. Atheneum Books for Young Readers 2008 198p $16.99

Grades: 7 8 9 10   **Fic**

1. Poverty -- Fiction 2. Pakistan -- Fiction 3. Sex role -- Fiction 4. Household employees -- Fiction

ISBN 978-1-4169-4728-8; 1-4169-4728-0

LC 2007-19001

When her father is injured, fourteen-year-old Nazia is pulled away from school, her friends, and her preparations for an arranged marriage, to help her mother clean houses in a wealthy part of Karachi, Pakistan, where she finally rebels against the destiny that is planned for her.

This novel "provides a fascinating glimpse into a world remarkably distant from that of most American teens, and would be an excellent suggestion for readers who want to know about how other young people live." SLJ

Quick, Barbara

A **golden** web. HarperTeen 2010 266p $16.99

Grades: 7 8 9 10   **Fic**

1. Biologists 2. Italy -- Fiction 3. Anatomy -- Fiction 4. Sex role -- Fiction 5. Middle Ages -- Fiction

ISBN 978-0-06-144887-4; 0-06-144887-7

LC 2009-14265

In fourteenth-century Bologna, Alessandra Giliani, a brilliant young girl, defies convention and risks death in order to attend medical school at the university so that she can study anatomy.

"Alessandra's intellectual curiosity is wonderfully depicted, her philosophical musings are entertaining, and her commitment to the pursuit of biological knowledge enlivens the plot. Quick's prose is fluid and authentic, bright and engaging." Publ Wkly

Quick, Matthew

★ **Sorta** like a rockstar; a novel. Little, Brown 2010 355p $16.99; pa $8.99

Grades: 7 8 9 10 11   **Fic**

1. School stories 2. Homeless persons -- Fiction 3. Depression (Psychology) -- Fiction

ISBN 978-0-316-04352-6; 0-316-04352-4; 978-0-316-04353-3 pa; 0-316-04353-2 pa

LC 2008-46746

Although seventeen-year-old Amber Appleton is homeless, living in a school bus with her unfit mother, she is a relentless optimist who visits the elderly at a nursing home, teaches English to Korean Catholic women with the use of rhythm and blues music, and befriends a solitary Vietnam veteran and his dog, but eventually she experiences one burden more than she can bear and slips into a deep depression.

"This book is the answer to all those angst-ridden and painfully grim novels in the shortcut lingo of short attention-span theater. Hugely enjoyable." SLJ

Quintero, Sofia

★ **Efrain's** secret. Alfred A. Knopf 2010 265p $16.99; lib bdg $19.99

Grades: 8 9 10 11 12   **Fic**

1. School stories 2. Violence -- Fiction 3. Drug traffic -- Fiction 4. Hispanic Americans -- Fiction 5. Bronx (New York, N.Y.) -- Fiction

ISBN 978-0-375-84706-6; 0-375-84706-5; 978-0-375-94706-3 lib bdg; 0-375-94706-X lib bdg

LC 2009-8493

Ambitious high school senior and honor student Efrain Rodriguez makes some questionable choices in pursuit of his dream to escape the South Bronx and attend an Ivy League college.

"Quintero imbues her characters with unexpected grace and charm. . . . Mostly, though, it is Quintero's effortless grasp of teen slang that gives her first-person story its heart." Booklist

Rabin, Staton

Black powder. Margaret K. McElderry Books 2005 245p $16.95

Grades: 6 7 8 9   **Fic**

1. Science fiction 2. African Americans -- Fiction

ISBN 0-689-86876-4

This is "a touching story of two great scientific minds discovering the humanity behind the ideas. Langston is particularly well-developed as an intelligent, mostly responsible African-American finding his way." SLJ

Raedeke, Christy

The **daykeeper's** grimoire. Flux 2010 352p (Prophecy of days) pa $9.95

Grades: 7 8 9 10   **Fic**

1. Mayas -- Fiction 2. Scotland -- Fiction 3. Prophecies -- Fiction 4. Conspiracies -- Fiction 5. Secret societies -- Fiction

ISBN 978-0-7387-1576-6; 0-7387-1576-X

LC 2009-30668

Caity Mac Fireland of San Francisco accompanies her parents to an isle off the coast of Scotland where she finds a Mayan relic and, guided by a motley crew of advisors, uncovers an incredible secret that an elite group of powerbrokers will stop at nothing to control.

"A delightful heroine, she's funny, frank, and mostly true to the way a real teen would act if she found herself in such an odd circumstance. Readers will want to follow Caity's adventure." Booklist

Followed by: The serpent's coil (2011)

The **serpent's** coil. Flux 2011 298p (Prophecy of days) $9.95

Grades: 7 8 9 10   **Fic**
1. Travel -- Fiction 2. Prophecies -- Fiction 3.
Conspiracies -- Fiction 4. Native Americans -- Fiction
ISBN 978-0-7387-1577-3; 0-7387-1577-8
                                    LC 2011004573
Sequel to: The daykeeper's grimoire (2010)

While attending a boarding school that allows her to
travel around the globe, Caity continues her mission to fulfill
a Mayan prophecy and mobilize the world's young people to
stop the devastating global reign of the Fraternitas.

"Conspiracies abound in the second book of the Prophecy of Days series, which, if possible, moves at an even
greater pace than the first. Raedeke weaves together an impressive array of mysticism, ancient knowledge, and conspiracy theories while keeping the main plot, if not all the
details, easy to follow." Voice Youth Advocates

Raf, Mindy

The **symptoms** of my insanity; Mindy Raf. Dial
2013 384 p. (hardcover) $17.99
Grades: 8 9 10 11 12   **Fic**
1. School stories 2. Puberty -- Fiction 3. Teenage
girls -- Fiction 4. Mothers -- Fiction 5. High schools
-- Fiction 6. Hypochondria -- Fiction
ISBN 0803732414; 9780803732414
                                    LC 2012024708
In this novel, by Mindy Raf, "a teenage hypochondriac
with large breasts learns to deal with life's pressure and find
self-acceptance." Izzy's "ever-expanding chest is the brunt
of ogling and inappropriate jokes." She is then pranked by a
basketball player, exposing a picture of her on the Internet.
"Her internal questioning of the incident exemplifies what
many teenage girls feel about sexual expectations and misguided culpability in sexual assaults." (Kirkus Reviews)

"While the plot is predictable . . . Izzy's self-deprecating
humor and wry observations bring fresh air to tired tropes.
Raf's background in comedy serves her well and gives
her protagonist an authenticity that will make readers feel
invested in her story. A fairly standard contribution to the
genre, but a solid one." SLJ

Railsback, Lisa

Noonie's masterpiece; art by Sarajo Frieden.
Chronicle Books 2010 208p il $18.99
Grades: 4 5 6 7   **Fic**
1. School stories 2. Artists -- Fiction 3. Family life
-- Fiction 4. Father-daughter relationship -- Fiction 5.
Eccentrics and eccentricities -- Fiction
ISBN 978-0-8118-6654-5; 0-8118-6654-8
                                    LC 2008-26831
Upon learning that her deceased mother, an artist, went
through a "Purple Period," ten-year-old Noonie decides to
do the same, hoping that this will bring her archaeologist
father home to see her win a school art contest and that the
aunt, uncle, and cousin she lives with will come to understand her just a little.

"Noonie may be an unreliable and even unlikable narrator at times, but her pain and vulnerability are as evident as
her belief in herself as an artist, and by the end of the story,
she'll have readers in her corner. The ink-and-watercolor illustrations, appearing throughout the book, have a 1960s-
retro look." Booklist

Rallison, Janette

Just one wish. G. P. Putnam's Sons 2009 264p
$16.99; pa $7.99
Grades: 7 8 9 10   **Fic**
1. Actors -- Fiction 2. Cancer -- Fiction 3. Siblings
-- Fiction
ISBN 978-0-399-24618-0; 0-399-24618-5; 978-0-14-
241599-3 pa; 0-14-241599-5 pa
                                    LC 2008-9297
Seventeen-year-old Annika tries to cheer up her little
brother Jeremy before his surgery to remove a cancerous
tumor by bringing home his favorite television actor, Steve
Raleigh, the star of "Teen Robin Hood"

"Annika's wacky encounters . . . and anxiety for her
brother make the story both comical and poignant." Horn
Book Guide

Randall, Thomas

Dreams of the dead. Bloomsbury Children's
Books 2009 276p (The waking) pa $8.99
Grades: 8 9 10 11 12   **Fic**
1. School stories 2. Death -- Fiction 3. Japan -- Fiction
4. Supernatural -- Fiction
ISBN 978-1-59990-250-0; 1-59990-250-8
                                    LC 2008-30844
After her mother dies, sixteen-year-old Kara and her father move to Japan, where he teaches and she attends school,
but she is haunted by a series of frightening nightmares and
deaths that might be revenge—or something worse

"The story has suspense, mystery, and horror. It will
be a great hit with fans of manga, anime, or Japanese
culture." SLJ

Followed by: Spirits of the Noh (2011)

Spirits of the Noh. Bloomsbury U.S.A. Children's Books 2010 264p (The waking) $8.99
Grades: 8 9 10 11 12   **Fic**
1. Horror fiction 2. School stories 3. Japan -- Fiction
4. Monsters -- Fiction 5. Supernatural -- Fiction
ISBN 978-1-59990-251-7; 1-59990-251-6
                                    LC 2009018251
Sequel to: Dreams of the dead (2009)

Just as Kara and her friends at the Monju-no-Chie
school in Japan are beginning to get over the horrifying
deaths of two students, another monster emerges to terrorize
the school.

"Using all the usual horror elements, Randall constructs
a fine teen chiller complete with mean-girl drama, a dash of
romance and the angst of teens who believe that adults do
not understand them." Kirkus

Ransom, Candice

Rebel McKenzie; Candice Ransom. Disney Hyperion 2012 270 p. $16.99
Grades: 4 5 6 7   **Fic**
1. Country life -- Fiction 2. Beauty contests -- Fiction
3. Money-making projects for children -- Fiction 4.
Nephews -- Fiction 5. Virginia -- Fiction 6. Trailer
camps -- Fiction 7. Loss (Psychology) -- Fiction 8.
Country life -- Virginia -- Fiction
ISBN 1423145399; 9781423145394
                                    LC 2011032729

In this novel by Candice Ransom "Rebel McKenzie wants to spend her summer attending . . . a camp where kids discover prehistoric bones, right alongside real paleontologists. But digs cost money, and Rebel is broker than four o'clock. When she finds out her annoying neighbor Bambi Lovering won five hundred dollars by playing a ukulele behind her head in a beauty contest, Rebel decides to win the Frog Level Volunteer Fire Department's beauty pageant." (Publisher's note)

Rapp, Adam

The **children** and the wolves; Adam Rapp. Candlewick Press 2011 152 p. $16.99

Grades: 8 9 10   **Fic**

1. Kidnapping -- Fiction 2. Psychological fiction 3. Juvenile delinquency -- Fiction 4. Illinois -- Fiction 5. Drug abuse -- Fiction 6. Single parent family -- Fiction
ISBN 0763653373; 9780763653378

LC 2011013676

This book by Printz Honor-winning author Adam Rapp presents a story "about three disaffected teens and a kidnapped child. Three teenagers—a sharp, well-to-do girl named Bounce and two struggling boys named Wiggins and Orange—are holding a four-year old girl hostage in Orange's basement. The little girl answers to 'the Frog' and seems content to play a video game about wolves all day long, a game that parallels the reality around her. As the stakes grow higher and the guilt and tension mount, Wiggins cracks and finally brings Frog to a trusted adult." (Publisher's note)

Raskin, Joyce

My misadventures as a teenage rock star; written by Joyce Raskin; illustrations by Carol Chu. Graphia 2011 107p il pa $8.99

Grades: 7 8 9 10   **Fic**

1. New Jersey -- Fiction 2. Popularity -- Fiction 3. Rock music -- Fiction 4. Family life -- Fiction 5. Bands (Music) -- Fiction
ISBN 978-0-547-39311-7 pa; 0-547-39311-3 pa

LC 2010-27456

Fourteen-year-old Alex, a short, pasty, shy, greasy-haired girl with acne, gains self-confidence when her brother convinces her to play bass in a rock band, but she finds that being 'cool' has its drawbacks.

"The unintimidating length and layout, direct prose, and swift-moving plot make thsi a particularly fine choice for reluctant readers." Bull Cent Child Books

Ravel, Edeet

The **saver**. Groundwood Books/House of Anansi Press 2008 214p $17.95; pa $8.95

Grades: 7 8 9 10 11   **Fic**

1. Death -- Fiction 2. Uncles -- Fiction 3. Orphans -- Fiction
ISBN 978-0-88899-882-8; 0-88899-882-1; 978-0-88899-883-5 pa; 0-88899-883-X pa

When 17-year-old Fern's mother dies of a heart attack, she has to make her own way in the world. She takes over her mother's housecleaning jobs, takes a job as a janitor, and adds two other part-time jobs. Then her Uncle Jack, whom she's never met, shows up to help her.

"Written as a series of letters to an imaginary friend on another planet, this is a compelling story of determination and the will to survive." SLJ

Rawlings, Marjorie Kinnan

The **yearling**; with pictures by N. C. Wyeth. Scribner 1985 400p il hardcover o.p. pa $5.95

Grades: 5 6 7 8   **Fic**

1. Deer -- Fiction 2. Florida -- Fiction
ISBN 0-684-18461-3; 0-02-044931-3 pa

LC 85-40301

Reissue of the title first published 1938; awarded Pulitzer Prize, 1939

"With its excellent descriptions of Florida scrub landscapes, its skillful use of native vernacular, its tender relation between Jody and his pet fawn, The Yearling is a simply written, picturesque story of boyhood." Time

Rawls, Wilson

Where the red fern grows; the story of two dogs and a boy. Bantam Bks. 1996 212p $16.95; pa $5.99

Grades: 4 5 6 7   **Fic**

1. Dogs -- Fiction 2. Ozark Mountains -- Fiction
ISBN 0-385-32330-1; 0-440-41267-6 pa

First published 1961 by Doubleday

"Looking back more than 50 years to his boyhood in the Ozarks, the narrator recalls how he achieved his heart's desire in the ownership of two redbone hounds, how he taught them all the tricks of hunting, and how they won the championship coon hunt before Old Dan was killed by a mountain lion and Little Ann died of grief. Although some readers may find this novel hackneyed and entirely too sentimental, others will enjoy the fine coonhunting episodes and appreciate the author's feelings for nature." Booklist

Ray, Delia

Ghost girl; a Blue Ridge Mountain story. Clarion Bks. 2003 216p il $15

Grades: 5 6 7 8   **Fic**

1. Presidents 2. School stories 3. Philanthropists 4. Teachers -- Fiction 5. Virginia -- Fiction 6. Spouses of presidents 7. Secretaries of commerce
ISBN 0-618-33377-0

LC 2003-4115

Eleven-year-old April is delighted when President and Mrs. Hoover build a school near her Madison County, Virginia, home but her family's poverty, grief over the accidental death of her brother, and other problems may mean that April can never learn to read from the wonderful teacher, Miss Vest

"This excellent portrayal of four important years in a girl's life rises to the top. Based on a real school and teacher, this novel seamlessly incorporates historical facts into the narrative." SLJ

Here lies Linc. Alfred A. Knopf 2011 308p $16.99; lib bdg $19.99

Grades: 5 6 7 8   **Fic**

1. School stories 2. Iowa -- Fiction 3. Death -- Fiction

4. Cemeteries -- Fiction 5. Family life -- Fiction
ISBN 978-0-375-86757-6; 0-375-86757-0; 978-0-375-
96756-6 lib bdg; 0-375-96756-7 lib bdg

LC 2010030004

While researching a rumored-to-be-haunted grave for a
local history project, twelve-year-old Lincoln Crenshaw unearths some startling truths about his own family.

"Ray's tale, which centers around a real legend, strikes
the perfect balance of humor, realistic chills and near-teen
angst." Kirkus

Singing hands. Clarion Books 2006 248p il
$16

Grades: 4 5 6 7   **Fic**
1. Deaf -- Fiction 2. Clergy -- Fiction 3. Alabama --
Fiction 4. Family life -- Fiction
ISBN 0-618-65762-2

LC 2005-22972

In the late 1940s, twelve-year-old Gussie, a minister's
daughter, learns the definition of integrity while helping
with a celebration at the Alabama School for the Deaf—
her punishment for misdeeds against her deaf parents and
their boarders.

"While the portrayal of a signing household is natural and convincing, the focus is on Gussie's rebellion and
growth, the real heart of the story." Horn Book Guide

Reedy, Trent
Words in the dust. Arthur A. Levine Books 2011
266p $17.99

Grades: 5 6 7 8   **Fic**
1. Literacy -- Fiction 2. Sex role -- Fiction 3.
Afghanistan -- Fiction 4. Birth defects -- Fiction
ISBN 0-545-26125-2; 978-0-545-26125-8

LC 2010-26160

Zulaikha, a thirteen-year-old girl in Afghanistan, faces a
series of frightening but exhilarating changes in her life as
she defies her father and secretly meets with an old woman
who teaches her to read, her older sister gets married, and
American troops offer her surgery to fix her disfiguring
cleft lip.

"The evolution of key relationships presents a nuanced
look at family dynamics and Afghan culture. Though unsentimental and fraught with tragedy, Reedy's narrative offers
hope and will go a long way toward helping readers understand the people behind the headlines." Publ Wkly

Rees, Celia
The **fool's** girl. Bloomsbury 2010 297p $16.99

Grades: 8 9 10 11 12   **Fic**
1. Poets 2. Authors 3. Dramatists 4. Adventure
fiction 5. London (England) -- Fiction 6. Great Britain
-- History -- 1485-1603, Tudors -- Fiction
ISBN 978-1-59990-486-3; 1-59990-486-1

LC 2009-51894

Violetta and Feste have come to London to rescue a holy
relic taken from a church in Illyria by the evil Malvolio, and
once there, they tell the story of their adventures to playwright William Shakespeare, who turns it into a play.

"Expertly livening the proceedings with intrigues, japes,
kisses, mildly bawdy comments, . . . colorful characters, plot
twists, quick violence, and an occasional breath of the su-

pernatural, Rees dishes up a quick-paced tale that builds to a
suspenseful climax." Booklist

Rees, Douglas C.
Vampire High. Delacorte Press 2003 226p
$15.95; lib bdg $17.99

Grades: 7 8 9 10   **Fic**
1. School stories 2. Vampires -- Fiction 3.
Massachusetts -- Fiction
ISBN 0-385-73117-5; 0-385-90143-7 lib bdg

LC 2003-41992

When his family moves from California to New Sodom,
Massachusetts and Cody enters Vlad Dracul Magnet School,
many things seem strange, from the dark-haired, pale-
skinned, supernaturally strong students to Charon, the wolf
who guides him around campus on the first day

"There's barely a false note in this rollicking tale of horror, humor, and light romance that will appeal to both girls
and boys." Booklist

Another title in this series is:
Vampire High: sophomore year (2010)

Vampire High: sophomore year. Delacorte 2010
247p $16.99; lib bdg $17.89

Grades: 7 8 9 10   **Fic**
1. School stories 2. Vampires -- Fiction 3.
Massachusetts -- Fiction
ISBN 978-0-385-73725-8; 0-385-73725-4; 978-0-385-
90657-9 lib bdg; 0-385-90657-9 lib bdg
Sequel to: Vampire High (2003)

When Cody's Goth cousin Turk moves into his house,
enrolls at Vlad Dracul, and decides to turn an abandoned
nineteenth-century mill into an art center, the vampire (Jenti)
students are not pleased, and Cody's hopes for a great sophomore year are blighted.

"Rees's fast-paced and action-packed story line tackles
important teen issues like identity, belonging, friendship,
and acceptance in a way that is not overbearing or preachy.
With lots of humor and strong, engaging characters, this
novel has an appeal factor that is sure to make its mark (or
bite) on readers of this genre." SLJ

Reeve, Philip
★ **Fever** Crumb. Scholastic Press 2010 325p
$17.99

Grades: 6 7 8 9 10   **Fic**
1. Science fiction 2. Orphans -- Fiction 3. Sex role
-- Fiction 4. London (England) -- Fiction
ISBN 978-0-545-20719-5; 0-545-20719-3

LC 2009-15457

Prequel to: The Hungry City Chronicles series
Foundling Fever Crumb has been raised as an engineer
although females in the future London, England, are not believed capable of rational thought, but at age fourteen she
leaves her sheltered world and begins to learn startling truths
about her past while facing danger in the present.

"Reeve's captivating flights of imagination play as vital
a role in the story as his endearing heroine, hiss-worthy villains, and nifty array of supporting characters." Booklist
Followed by A web of air (2011)

★ **Here** lies Arthur. Scholastic Press 2008 339p $16.99

Grades: 7 8 9 10 **Fic**

1. Kings 2. Magic -- Fiction 3. Great Britain -- History -- 0-1066 -- Fiction

ISBN 978-0-545-09334-7; 0-545-09334-1

LC 2008-05787

When her village is attacked and burned, Gwyna seeks protection from the bard Myrddin, who uses Gwyna in his plan to transform young Arthur into the heroic King Arthur.

"Powerfully inventive. . . . Events rush headlong toward the inevitable ending, but Gwyna's observations illuminate them in a new way." Booklist

Mothstorm; or the horror from beyond Georgium Sidus!; or a tale of two shapers. as told by Art Mumby to Philip Reeve; decorated throughout by David Wyatt. Bloomsbury U.S.A. Children's Books 2008 390p il $16.99; pa $7.99

Grades: 5 6 7 8 **Fic**

1. Science fiction 2. Adventure fiction 3. Siblings -- Fiction

ISBN 978-1-59990-303-3; 1-59990-303-2; 978-1-59990-382-8 pa; 1-59990-382-2 pa

LC 2008008192

Sequel to: Starcross (2007)

Reports of a strange phenomenon at the fringe of the galaxy and its connection to one of Father's old friends send the entire Mumby family, accompanied by Jack and other friends, to a far-off planet where they must find a way to prevent a new invasion of the solar system by giant moths.

This "is a clever blending of genres including science fiction, historical fiction, fantasy, and adventure with a liberal dash of British humor and style." SLJ

No such thing as dragons. Scholastic Press 2010 186p $16.99

Grades: 4 5 6 7 **Fic**

1. Fantasy fiction 2. Dragons -- Fiction

ISBN 978-0-545-22224-2; 0-545-22224-9

A young, mute boy who is apprenticed to a dragon-slayer suspects that the winged beasts do not exist, until he—and his master—learn the truth.

"This is certainly different from anything that Reeve has done previously, but is still shot through with his trademark imagination and feel for action. It will be eagerly devoured by young readers." SLJ

Scrivener's moon; the third book in the Fever Crumb series. Philip Reeve. Scholastic Press 2012 341 p. (Fever Crumb series) (hardcover) $17.99

Grades: 6 7 8 9 10 **Fic**

1. Steampunk fiction 2. Technology -- Fiction 3. Science fiction 4. England -- Fiction 5. Identity -- Fiction 6. London (England) -- Fiction 7. Dystopias -- Fiction 8. Mutation (Biology) -- Fiction 9. Technology -- Fiction 10. London (England) -- Fiction 11. Identity (Psychology) -- Fiction

ISBN 0545222184; 9780545222181

LC 2012008124

This young adult steampunk adventure novel, by Philip Reeve, is the conclusion to the "Fever Crumb" trilogy. "The Scriven people are brilliant, mad--and dead. All except one, whose monstrous creation is nearly complete--a giant city on wheels. New London terrifies the rest of the world, and an army of mammoth-riders gathers to fight it. Meanwhile, young Fever Crumb begins a hunt for Ancient technology in the icy strongholds of the north." (Publisher's note)

Starcross; or The coming of the moobs!, or, Our adventures in the fourth dimension: a stirring adventure of spies, time travel and curious hats. as narrated by Art Mumby, (& Miss Myrtle Mumby) to their amanuensis, Philip Reeve & illustrated throughout by David Wyatt. Bloomsbury U.S.A. Children's Books 2007 368p il $16.95; pa $7.99

Grades: 5 6 7 8 **Fic**

1. Science fiction

ISBN 978-1-59990-121-3; 1-59990-121-8; 978-1-59990-296-8 pa; 1-59990-296-6 pa

LC 2007-12002

Sequel to: Larklight (2006)

Young Arthur Mumby, his sister Myrtle, and their mother accept an invitation to take a holiday at an up-and-coming resort in the asteroid belt, where they become involved in a dastardly plot involving spies, time travel, and mind-altering clothing

"It's all very tongue-in-cheek with plenty of jokes and puns in the best traditions of British humor." Booklist

Followed by: Mothstorm (2008)

A **Web** of Air. Scholastic Press 2011 293p $17.99

Grades: 6 7 8 9 10 **Fic**

1. Science fiction 2. Flight -- Fiction 3. Orphans -- Fiction

ISBN 0-545-22216-8; 978-0-545-22216-7

LC 2010043341

Sequel to: Fever Crumb (2010)

Two years ago, Fever Crumb escaped the wartorn city of London in a traveling theater. Now, she arrives in the extraordinary city of Mayda, where buildings ascend the cliffs on funicular rails, and a mysterious recluse is building a machine that can fly.

"It's clear that Reeve . . . is building toward an epic, and his remarkable storytelling gifts, coupled with a trenchant understanding of human nature, make these projected volumes worth the wait." Horn Book

Reger, Rob

Emily the Strange: dark times. Harper 2010 226p il $16.99

Grades: 7 8 9 10 **Fic**

1. Adventure fiction 2. Aunts -- Fiction 3. Family -- Fiction 4. Time travel -- Fiction 5. Supernatural -- Fiction

ISBN 978-0-06-145235-2; 0-06-145235-1

LC 2009032256

Traveling in her homemade TimeOut Machine, Emily journeys to the eighteenth century to uncover the truth behind a Strange family rumor.

"Entertaining and thought-provoking, Emily's adventures maintain the series' popularity and present an interesting choice for a mother/daughter reading group." Voice Youth Advocates

Emily the Strange: stranger and stranger. Harper 2010 263p $16.99

Grades: 7 8 9 10   **Fic**

1. Moving -- Fiction 2. Supernatural -- Fiction

ISBN 978-0-06-145232-1; 0-06-145232-7

LC 2009007289

After moving to a new town with her mother, Emily the Strange finds her troubles multiplying when she accidentally duplicates herself.

"Emily's second journal, a sequel to The Lost Days (HarperCollins, 2009), is a dark delight, filled with all kinds of Strangeness. . . . Fans of the first book and newcomers alike will thoroughly enjoy the zaniness and clamor for more." SLJ

Emily the Strange: the lost days; [by] Rob Reger and Jessica Gruner; illustrated by Rob Reger and Buzz Parker. Harper 2009 266p il $16.99; lib bdg $17.89

Grades: 7 8 9 10   **Fic**

1. Adventure fiction 2. Amnesia -- Fiction 3. Runaway teenagers -- Fiction

ISBN 978-0-06-145229-1; 0-06-145229-7; 978-0-06-145230-7 lib bdg; 0-06-145230-0 lib bdg

LC 2008027225

Emily the Strange has lost her memory and finds herself in the town of Blackrock with nothing more than her diary, her slingshot, and the clothes on her back

"The action moves along with no lulls, and none of the entries or illustrations are superfluous. This is a highly enjoyable read." SLJ

Other titles about Emily the Strange are:

Emily the Strange: stranger and stranger (2010)

Emily the Strange: dark times (2010)

Reh, Rusalka

Pizzicato; the abduction of the magic violin. translated by David Henry Wilson. AmazonCrossing 2011 124p pa $9.95

Grades: 4 5 6 7   **Fic**

1. Magic -- Fiction 2. Germany -- Fiction 3. Orphans -- Fiction 4. Violins -- Fiction

ISBN 978-1-6110-9004-8; 1-6110-9004-0

Darius is none too pleased to be paired with Archibald Archinola, a master violinmaker, for a school project, especially when he thinks about his rival—fellow orphan and constant nemesis Max—being surrounded by Porsches at Auto Frederick for the same assignment. But when Darius discovers an old violin in a glass case and strikes the chords, a cut on his hand magically disappears, and suddenly studying with the violinmaker proves to be anything but dull.

This story "has an Old World European charm, from the cast of eccentric, lovable characters to the scenes of café life. Readers will delight in watching the buffoonish villains get their comeuppance, but it's Darius' wish-fulfillment . . . that will satisfy readers most." Booklist

Reichs, Kathleen J.

Seizure; [by] Kathy Reichs. 2011 491p $17.99

Grades: 6 7 8 9 10   **Fic**

1. Adventure fiction 2. Supernatural -- Fiction

ISBN 9781595143945; 1595143947

Sequel to: Virals (2010)

"Tory Brennan, 14, and her friends are still trying to determine exactly what happened to them following the events of the series opener (Virals, 2010). The teens have been exposed to an experimental virus that altered their DNA, giving them characteristics comparable to wolves, enhancing their natural senses and creating a human pack. . . . Due to the economy, funding has been pulled on [Kit's father's] research project, necessitating a change of job and a move away from South Carolina and her pack mates. . . . Dodging bullets, slipping out after curfew, following obscure clues into underground tunnels, not to mention Cotillion duties and snarky classmates, are just part of the adventure. . . . Reichs taps into the angst of teens, fear of separation and the uncertainty of today's economy and wraps it all in an entertaining yarn of history, pirates and modern technology." Kirkus

★ **Virals**; [by] Kathy Reichs. Penguin/Razorbill 2010 454p map $17.99

Grades: 6 7 8 9 10   **Fic**

1. Mystery fiction 2. Viruses -- Fiction 3. Missing persons -- Fiction

ISBN 978-1-59514-342-6; 1-59514-342-4

LC 2010-42384

Tory Brennan is the leader of a band of teenage "sci-philes" who live on an island off the coast of South Carolina and when the group rescues a dog caged for medical testing, they are exposed to an experimental strain of canine parvovirus that changes their lives forever.

"From the opening sentence to the last word, readers will be absorbed in Tory Brennan's world. . . . Reichs has found a pitch-perfect voice for Tory that will ring true with today's teens, capturing and entirely new audience." Kirkus

Followed by: Seizure (2011)

Reinhardt, Dana

★ **How** to build a house; a novel. Wendy Lamb Books 2008 227p $15.99; lib bdg $18.99

Grades: 8 9 10 11 12   **Fic**

1. Divorce -- Fiction 2. Building -- Fiction 3. Tennessee -- Fiction 4. Stepfamilies -- Fiction 5. Volunteer work -- Fiction

ISBN 978-0-375-84453-9; 0-375-84453-8; 978-0-375-94454-3 lib bdg; 0-375-94454-0 lib bdg

LC 2007-33403

Seventeen-year-old Harper Evans hopes to escape the effects of her father's divorce on her family and friendships by volunteering her summer to build a house in a small Tennessee town devastated by a tornado.

"This meticulously crafted book illustrates how both homes and relationships can be resurrected through hard work, hope and teamwork." Publ Wkly

Odessa again; Dana Reinhardt. 1st ed. Wendy Lamb Books 2013 208 p. (ebook) $47.97; (hardcover) $15.99; (library) $18.99

Grades: 4 5 6 7   **Fic**
1. Remarriage -- Fiction 2. Time travel -- Fiction
ISBN 0385739567; 9780375897887; 9780385739566; 9780385907934

                                      LC 2012008231
In this children's novel, by Dana Reinhardt, "fourth grader Odessa Green-Light lives with her mom and her toad of a little brother, Oliver. Her dad is getting remarried. . . . Meanwhile, Odessa moves into the attic room of their new house. One day [it] . . . turns out that Odessa has gone back in time a whole day! With this new power she can fix all sorts of things--embarrassing moments, big mistakes, and even help Oliver be less of a toad. Her biggest goal: reunite Mom and Dad." (Publisher's note)
"Realistically drawn, Odessa is a believable, likable kid on the brink of growing up, struggling with family changes. . . . With humor as well as depth, this is an endearing story of a spunky girl who realizes that life gets more, not less, confusing as she grows up." Kirkus

The **summer** I learned to fly. Wendy Lamb Books 2011 216p $15.99; lib bdg $18.99; e-book $15.99
Grades: 5 6 7 8   **Fic**
1. Rats -- Fiction 2. California -- Fiction 3. Family life -- Fiction 4. Retail trade -- Fiction 5. Single parent family -- Fiction
ISBN 978-0-385-73954-2; 0-385-73954-0; 978-0-385-90792-7 lib bdg; 0-385-90792-3 lib bdg; 978-0-375-89787-0 e-book; 0-375-89787-9 e-book

                                      LC 2010029412
Thirteen-year-old Drew starts the summer of 1986 helping in her mother's cheese shop and dreaming about co-worker Nick, but when her widowed mother begins dating, Drew's father's book of lists, her pet rat, and Emmett, a boy on a quest, help her cope.
"This quiet novel invites readers to share in its heroine's deepest yearnings, changing moods, and difficult realizations." Publ Wkly

★ The **things** a brother knows. Wendy Lamb Books 2010 245p $16.99; lib bdg $19.99
Grades: 7 8 9 10 11 12   **Fic**
1. Brothers -- Fiction 2. Soldiers -- Fiction 3. Family life -- Fiction 4. Boston (Mass.) -- Fiction 5. Jews -- United States -- Fiction
ISBN 978-0-375-84455-3; 0-375-84455-4; 978-0-375-94455-9 lib bdg; 0-375-94455-9 lib bdg

Although they have never gotten along well, seventeen-year-old Levi follows his older brother Boaz, an ex-Marine, on a walking trip from Boston to Washington, D.C. in hopes of learning why Boaz is completely withdrawn.
"Reinhardt's poignant story of a soldier coping with survivor's guilt and trauma, and his Israeli American family's struggle to understand and help, is timely and honest." Booklist

Reisman, Michael
★ **Simon** Bloom, the gravity keeper. Dutton Children's Books 2007 298p $15.99; pa $8.99
Grades: 5 6 7 8   **Fic**
1. Science fiction 2. Physics -- Fiction 3. Extraterrestrial

beings -- Fiction
ISBN 978-0-525-47922-2; 978-0-14-241368-5 pa

                                    LC 2006039046
Nerdy sixth-grader Simon Bloom finds a book that enables him to control the laws of physics, but when two thugs come after him, he needs the formulas in the book to save himself
This is a "fast-paced, cinematic . . . novel. . . . It makes scientific concepts interesting and accessible." Publ Wkly
Another title about Simon Bloom is:
Simon Bloom, the octopus effect (2009)

Simon Bloom, the octopus effect. Dutton Children's Books/Walden Media 2009 360p $16.99
Grades: 5 6 7 8   **Fic**
1. Science fiction 2. Physics -- Fiction 3. Space and time -- Fiction
ISBN 978-0-525-42082-8; 0-525-42082-7

                                    LC 2008-13896
When twelve-year-old Simon becomes the official Keeper of the Order of Physics, he and his friends Owen and Alysha face extreme danger as they try to protect the Universe from destruction by evil forces

Renn, Diana
Latitude zero; by Diana Renn. Viking, published by Penguin Group 2014 448 p. (hardback) $17.99
Grades: 7 8 9 10   **Fic**
1. Mystery fiction 2. Murder -- Fiction 3. Bicycles -- Fiction 4. Journalists -- Fiction 5. Organized crime -- Fiction 6. Ecuador -- Fiction 7. Bicycle racing -- Fiction 8. Mystery and detective stories 9. Bicycles and bicycling -- Fiction 10. Reporters and reporting -- Fiction 11. Investigative journalists -- Fiction
ISBN 067001558X; 9780670015580

                                    LC 2013043837
In this book, by Diana Renn, "[w]hen star cyclist Juan Carlos Macias-Leon is murdered during the course of a charity bicycle race, Tess, one of the last to see him alive, finds herself involved and, as she begins to investigate, in jeopardy. Determined, nevertheless, to find the truth, she travels to Juan Carlos' native country, Ecuador (the latitude zero of the title). There, she discovers that danger has pursued her, and the more she investigates, the more questions she has." (Booklist)
"Renn has constructed a salient "Whodunit" totally upon the sport of professional bike racing, injecting the plot with adrenaline at every twist, and throwing the reader in tandem with the characters. Furthermore, this diverse array of talented teen characters makes Latitude Zero an inspiring read for the adolescent reader." VOYA

Tokyo heist; by Diana Renn. Viking 2012 373 p. (hardcover) $17.99
Grades: 7 8 9 10 11 12   **Fic**
1. Mystery fiction 2. Art thefts -- Fiction 3. Tokyo (Japan) -- Fiction 4. Seattle (Wash.) -- Fiction 5. Mystery and detective stories 6. Fathers and daughters -- Fiction
ISBN 0670013323; 9780670013326

                                    LC 2011043364

In this book "when sixteen-year-old Violet agrees to spend the summer with her father, an up-and-coming artist in Seattle, she has no idea what she's walking into. Her father's newest clients, the Yamada family, are the victims of a high-profile art robbery: van Gogh sketches have been stolen from their home, and, until they can produce the corresponding painting, everyone's lives are in danger." (Publisher's note)

"The plot has lots of twists and turns, leaving readers on edge, and a hint of romance... Teens will learn about Japanese culture, and fans of manga and art students will rejoice that they can relate to the protagonist and story." LJ

Rennison, Louise

The **taming** of the tights; Louise Rennison. HarperTeen 2013 306 p. (trade bdg.) $17.99

Grades: 7 8 9 10 11 12   Fic

1. Love stories 2. School stories 3. Actresses -- Fiction 4. Teenagers -- Fiction 5. Humorous stories 6. England -- Fiction 7. Schools -- Fiction 8. High schools -- Fiction 9. Performing arts -- Fiction 10. Yorkshire (England) -- Fiction 11. Dating (Social customs) -- Fiction

ISBN 0062226207; 9780062226204

LC 2013021359

Sequel to: A midsummer tights dream

In this book, by Louise Rennison, "Tallulah and her mates are back to finish their winter term at the Dother Hall performing arts program. And Tallulah is determined to finally show the world she's a true star of the stage! She's distracted by bad-boy Cain and trying her best to keep her accidental snog-session with him a secret. And although she is slowly beginning to think that maybe he's not so bad after all, she also continues to wonder about unavailable Charlie and dreamy Alex." (Publisher's note)

"Tallulah (A Midsummer Tights Dream) and the Tree Sisters are back for another term at performing arts college where they comically reinterpret another Shakespeare play. But drama follows Tallulah offstage as she debates who is better boyfriend material: Cain or Charlie. Though the book is light on plot, readers will welcome the return of Tallulah's humorous musings and this distinctly British, quirky cast of characters." (Horn Book)

Withering tights. HarperTeen 2011 274p (Misadventures of Tallulah Casey) $16.99

Grades: 7 8 9 10   Fic

1. Camps -- Fiction 2. Acting -- Fiction 3. York (England) -- Fiction

ISBN 0-06-179931-9; 978-0-06-179931-0

LC 2010045552

Self-conscious about her knobby knees but confident in her acting ability, fourteen-year-old Tallulah spends the summer at a Yorkshire performing arts camp that, she is surprised to learn, is for girls only. "Grades six to nine." (Bull Cent Child Books)

"Tallulah is a vivacious and hilarious character who will speak to every girl." SLJ

Repka, Janice

The **clueless** girl's guide to being a genius. Dutton Children's Books 2011 218p $16.99

Grades: 4 5 6   Fic

1. School stories 2. Genius -- Fiction 3. Teachers -- Fiction 4. Friendship -- Fiction 5. Mathematics -- Fiction 6. Baton twirling -- Fiction

ISBN 978-0-525-42333-1; 0-525-42333-8

LC 2010038139

When Aphrodite Wigglesmith, a thirteen-year-old, Harvard-educated mathematics genius, returns home to teach remedial math to middle school students, both she and her students end up getting unexpected lessons.

"A lighthearted, funny and often bizarre saga of middle-school mayhem. . . . Equal parts silly and endearing." Kirkus

Resau, Laura

The **indigo** notebook. Delacorte Press 2009 324p $16.99; lib bdg $19.99; pa $9.99

Grades: 7 8 9 10 11 12   Fic

1. Ecuador -- Fiction 2. Fathers -- Fiction 3. Single parent family -- Fiction 4. Mother-daughter relationship -- Fiction

ISBN 978-0-385-73652-7; 0-385-73652-5; 978-0-385-90614-2 lib bdg; 0-385-90614-5 lib bdg; 978-0-375-84524-6 pa; 0-375-84524-0 pa

LC 2008-40519

Fifteen-year-old Zeeta comes to terms with her flighty mother and their itinerant life when, soon after moving to Ecuador, she helps an American teenager find his birth father in a nearby village

"Observant, aware, and occasionally wry, Zeeta's first-person narration will attract readers and hold them." Booklist

Followed by: The ruby notebook (2010)

★ **Red** glass. Delacorte Press 2007 275p $15.99; lib bdg $18.99

Grades: 7 8 9 10   Fic

1. Mexico -- Fiction 2. Orphans -- Fiction 3. Guatemala -- Fiction 4. Family life -- Fiction 5. Automobile travel -- Fiction

ISBN 978-0-385-73466-0; 0-385-73466-2; 978-0-385-90464-3 lib bdg; 0-385-90464-9 lib bdg

LC 2007-02408

Sixteen-year-old Sophie has been frail and delicate since her premature birth, but discovers her true strength during a journey through Mexico, where the six-year-old orphan her family hopes to adopt was born, and to Guatemala, where her would-be boyfriend hopes to find his mother and plans to remain.

"The vivid characters, the fine imagery, and the satisfying story arc make this a rewarding novel." Booklist

The **ruby** notebook. Delacorte Press 2010 373p $16.99; lib bdg $19.99

Grades: 7 8 9 10   Fic

1. France -- Fiction 2. Single parent family -- Fiction 3. Mother-daughter relationship -- Fiction

ISBN 978-0-385-73653-4; 0-385-73653-3; 978-0-385-90615-9 lib bdg; 0-385-90615-3 lib bdg

LC 2009-51965

Sequel to: The indigo notebook (2009)

When sixteen-year-old Zeeta and her itinerant mother move to Aix-en-Provence, France, Zeeta is haunted by a mysterious admirer who keeps leaving mementoes for her, and when her Ecuadorian boyfriend comes to visit, their relationship seems to have changed.

"Weaving bits of magic, city lore and bittersweet romance into each of the many plot lines, Resau has again crafted a complex and satisfying novel. . . . Characters are rich and vibrant." Kirkus

★ **What** the moon saw; a novel. Delacorte Press 2006 258p $15.95; pa $5.99

Grades: 5 6 7 8 **Fic**

1. Mexico -- Fiction 2. Country life -- Fiction 3. Grandparents -- Fiction

ISBN 0-385-73343-7; 0-440-23957-5 pa

LC 2006-04571

Fourteen-year-old Clara Luna spends the summer with her grandparents in the tiny, remote village of Yucuyoo, Mexico, learning about her grandmother's life as a healer, her father's decision to leave home for the United States, and her own place in the world.

This is an "exquisitely crafted narrative. . . . The characters are well developed. . . . Resau does an exceptional job of portraying the agricultural society sympathetically and realistically." SLJ

Restrepo, Bettina

★ **Illegal**. Katherine Tegen Books 2011 251p $16.99

Grades: 7 8 9 10 **Fic**

1. Texas -- Fiction 2. Mexicans -- Fiction 3. Illegal aliens -- Fiction

ISBN 978-0-06-195342-2; 0-06-195342-3

LC 2010-19451

Nora, a fifteen-year-old Mexican girl, faces the challenges of being an illegal immigrant in Texas when she and her mother cross the border in search of Nora's father.

"Restrepo's novel offers an unsparing immigrant story that is both gritty and redemptive. . . . This is urban realism meets quest tale, told with great emotional immediacy, and it will appeal to many teen readers." Bull Cent Child Books

Revis, Beth

Across the universe. Razorbill 2011 398p $17.99

Grades: 7 8 9 10 **Fic**

1. Science fiction 2. Dictators -- Fiction 3. Space vehicles -- Fiction

ISBN 978-1-59514-397-6; 1-59514-397-1

LC 2010-51834

Amy, a cryogenically frozen passenger aboard the vast spaceship Godspeed, is nearly killed when her cyro chamber is unplugged fifty years before Godspeed's scheduled landing. All she knows is that she must race to unlock Godspeed's hidden secrets before whoever woke her tries to kill again—and she doesn't know who she can trust on a ship ruled by a tyrant.

"Revis's tale hits all of the standard dystopian notes, while presenting a believable romance and a series of tantalizing mysteries that will hold readers' attention." Publ Wkly

Rex, Adam

Champions of breakfast; Adam Rex. Balzer + Bray 2014 368 p. (The cold cereal saga) (hardcover bdg. : alk. paper) $16.99

Grades: 4 5 6 7 **Fic**

1. Imaginary places 2. Magic -- Fiction 3. Fairies -- Fiction 4. Cereals, Prepared -- Fiction 5. Adventure and adventurers -- Fiction

ISBN 0062060082; 9780062060082

LC 2013021387

In this book by Adam Rex, part of the Cold Cereal Saga series, "time is quickly running out before Nimue, who has been working with the corrupt Goodco Cereal Company, finds another portal and uses it to bring the mythical dragon Saxbriton into our world--and launch the terrible fairy invasion. In the end, it's up to Scott and his companions to save the fate of two worlds." (Publisher's note)

"Scott, Polly, Emily, and Erno, together with a large supporting cast, rescue the miniaturized Queen of England and quell a fairy invasion by killing the dragon Saxbriton and healing the rift between the worlds. The superabundance of characters is hard to keep track of, but for readers following the Arthurian-reimagining trilogy, action, magic, and humor combine for a whiz-bang conclusion." (Horn Book)

★ **Cold** cereal. Balzer + Bray 2012 421p il $16.99

Grades: 4 5 6 7 **Fic**

1. Adventure fiction 2. Food -- Fiction 3. Magic -- Fiction 4. Twins -- Fiction 5. Siblings -- Fiction

ISBN 978-0-06-206002-0; 0-06-206002-3

LC 2011019538

A boy who may be part changeling, twins involved in a bizarre secret experiment, and a clurichaun in a red tracksuit try to save the world from an evil cereal company whose ultimate goal is world domination.

"The author tucks in portrait illustrations and hilariously odd TV-commercial storyboards, along with a hooded Secret Society, figures from Arthurian legend, magical spells and potions, a certain amount of violence, many wonderful throwaway lines. . . . All in all, it's a mad scramble that culminates in the revelation of a dastardly plot that will require sequels to foil." Kirkus

Smek for president! Adam Rex. Disney-Hyperion Books 2014 272 p. illustrations (hardback) $16.99

Grades: 5 6 7 8 **Fic**

1. Science fiction 2. Humorous fiction 3. Adventure and adventurers 4. Human-alien encounters -- Fiction 5. Extraterrestrial beings -- Fiction 6. Humorous stories 7. Interplanetary voyages -- Fiction 8. Adventure and adventurers -- Fiction

ISBN 1484709519; 9781484709511

LC 2014010764

Sequel to: The True Meaning of Smekday (2007)

In this book, by Adam Rex, "Tip and J.Lo are back for another hilarious intergalactic adventure. . . . After Tip and J.Lo banished the Gorg from Earth in a scheme involving the cloning of many, many cats, the pair is notorious--but not for their heroics. Instead, human Dan Landry has taken credit for conquering the Gorg, and the Boov blame J.Lo for ruining their colonization of the planet." (Publisher's note)

"After successfully banishing the Gorg and ruining the Boovs's plans to colonize planet Earth, J.Lo and Gratuity (Tip to her friends) are back in this sequel to The True Meaning of Smekday (Hyperion, 2007)... Hilarious cartoons will please graphic novel aficionados. Don't skip Appendix A: Rules for Stickyfish." SLJ

★ The **true** meaning of Smekday. Hyperion Books for Children 2007 423p il $16.99; pa $6.99
Grades: 5 6 7 8 **Fic**
1. Science fiction 2. End of the world -- Fiction 3. Extraterrestrial beings -- Fiction
ISBN 0-7868-4900-2; 978-0-7868-4900-0; 0-7868-4901-0 pa; 978-0-7868-4901-7 pa
When her mother is abducted by aliens on Christmas Eve (or "Smekday" Eve since the Boov invasion), 11 year-old Tip hops in the family car and heads south to find her and meets an alien Boov mechanic who agrees to help her and save the planet from disaster.

"Incorporating dozens of his weird and wonderful illustrations and fruitfully manipulating the narrative structure, Rex skewers any number of subjects." Publ Wkly

Unlucky charms; Adam Rex. Balzer + Bray 2013 400 p. (The cold cereal saga) (hardback) $16.99
Grades: 4 5 6 7 **Fic**
1. Fantasy fiction 2. Humorous fiction 3. Prepared cereals -- Fiction 4. Magic -- Fiction 5. Twins -- Fiction 6. Cereals, Prepared -- Fiction 7. Brothers and sisters -- Fiction
ISBN 0062060058; 9780062060051
LC 2012026714
This humorous juvenile fantasy book, by Adam Rex, is part of the "Cold Cereal Saga." "In this hectic middle volume, [Adam] Rex's notably diverse crew of human, part-human and nonhuman allies splits up in hopes of scotching the schemes of the sorceress Nimue, who is out to create a worldwide army of mind-controlled 'sugar zombies' through magically enhanced breakfast cereal." (Kirkus Reviews)

Reynolds, Marilyn
Shut up! Morning Glory Press 2009 245p $15.95; pa $9.95
Grades: 8 9 10 11 12 **Fic**
1. Brothers -- Fiction 2. Child sexual abuse -- Fiction
ISBN 978-1-932538-93-9; 1-932538-93-3; 978-1-932538-88-5 pa; 1-932538-88-7 pa
LC 2008-933535
This book "presents a marginalized issue—sexual abuse of boys—in a frank, thoughtful, and sensitive manner." Voice Youth Advocates

Rhodes, Jewell Parker
★ **Ninth** Ward. Little, Brown 2010 217p $15.99
Grades: 5 6 7 8 **Fic**
1. New Orleans (La.) -- Fiction 2. Extrasensory perception -- Fiction 3. Hurricane Katrina, 2005 --

Fiction
ISBN 978-0-316-04307-6; 0-316-04307-9
LC 2009-34423
Coretta Scott King Author Award honor book, 2011
In New Orleans' Ninth Ward, twelve-year-old Lanesha, who can see spirits, and her adopted grandmother have no choice but to stay and weather the storm as Hurricane Katrina bears down upon them.

"The dynamics of the diverse community enrich the survival story, and the contemporary struggle of one brave child humanizes the historic tragedy." Booklist

Sugar; Jewell Parker Rhodes. 1st ed. Little, Brown and Co. 2013 288 p. (hardcover) $16.99
Grades: 3 4 5 6 7 8 **Fic**
1. Plantation life -- Fiction 2. Historical fiction 3. Race relations -- Fiction 4. African Americans -- Fiction 5. Chinese Americans -- Fiction 6. Plantation life -- Louisiana -- Fiction 7. Louisiana -- History -- 1865-1950 -- Fiction 8. Reconstruction (U.S. history, 1865-1877) -- Fiction
ISBN 0316043052; 9780316043052
LC 2012026218
In this historical novel, by Jewell Parker Rhodes, "ten-year-old Sugar lives on the River Road sugar plantation along the banks of the Mississippi. Slavery is over, but laboring in the fields all day doesn't make her feel very free. . . . Here's another tale of a strong, spirited young girl who rises beyond her circumstances and inspires others to work toward a brighter future." (Publisher's note)

"Sugar's clipped narration is personable and engaging, strongly evoking the novel's historical setting and myriad racial tensions, making them accessible and meaningful to beginning readers." Pub Wkly

Rhuday-Perkovich, Olugbemisola
8th grade superzero. Arthur A. Levine Books 2010 324p $16.99
Grades: 6 7 8 9 **Fic**
1. School stories 2. Politics -- Fiction 3. Volunteer work -- Fiction 4. Homeless persons -- Fiction 5. African Americans -- Fiction
ISBN 978-0-545-09676-8; 0-545-09676-6
LC 2009-19850
After halfheartedly joining his church youth group's project at a homeless shelter near his Brooklyn middle school, eighth-grade "loser" Reggie McKnight is inspired to run for school office on a platform of making a real difference in the community.

The author "manages to bring both passion and compassion to a story that has its moments of humor and genuine emotion, and will be highly useful for classroom discussion." Booklist

Rich, Naomi
★ **Alis**. Viking Children's Books 2009 274p $17.99
Grades: 7 8 9 10 **Fic**
1. Marriage -- Fiction 2. Religion -- Fiction 3. Runaway teenagers -- Fiction
ISBN 978-0-670-01125-4; 0-670-01125-8
LC 2008-23234

Raised within the strict religious confines of the Community of the Book, Alis flees from an arranged marriage to the much older Minister of her town and her life takes a series of unexpected twists before she returns to accept her fate.

"Rich's sympathetic portrayal of Alis and her desperate struggle to exercise free will in a theocracy will have audiences firmly gripped." Publ Wkly

Richards, Jame

★ **Three** rivers rising; a novel of the Johnstown flood. Alfred A. Knopf 2010 293p $16.99; lib bdg $19.99

Grades: 6 7 8 9 10 **Fic**

1. Novels in verse 2. Floods -- Fiction 3. Pennsylvania -- Fiction 4. Social classes -- Fiction

ISBN 978-0-375-85885-7; 0-375-85885-7; 978-0-375-95885-4 lib bdg; 0-375-95885-1 lib bdg

LC 2009-4251

Sixteen-year-old Celestia is a wealthy member of the South Fork Fishing and Hunting Club, where she meets and falls in love with Peter, a hired hand who lives in the valley below, and by the time of the torrential rains that lead to the disastrous Johnstown flood of 1889, she has been disowned by her family and is staying with him in Johnstown. Includes an author's note and historical timeline.

This is a "striking novel in verse. . . . Richards builds strong characters with few words and artfully interweaves the lives of these independent thinkers." Publ Wkly

Includes bibliographical references

Richards, Jasmine

The **book** of wonders. HarperCollins 2012 400p $14.99

Grades: 4 5 6 7 **Fic**

1. Fantasy fiction 2. Adventure fiction 3. Friendship -- Fiction

ISBN 978-0-06-201007-0; 0-06-201007-7

LC 2011009153

In a tale loosely based on the Arabian nights, thirteen-year-old Zardi and her best friend, Ridhan, join forces with Captain Sinbad to defeat an evil sultan and restore magic to the world of Arribitha.

"This buoyant debut offers a fresh plot, brisk pacing and engaging characters. . . . Richards deftly borrows from lesser-known tales of the 1001 Arabian Nights to enrich her complex storyline while keeping style and syntax simple and direct." Kirkus

Richter, Conrad

The **light** in the forest. Everyman's Library 2005 176p $14.95; pa $6.50

Grades: 7 8 9 10 **Fic**

1. Delaware Indians -- Fiction 2. Frontier and pioneer life -- Fiction

ISBN 1-4000-4426-X; 1-4000-7788-5 pa

First published 1953 by Knopf

"A boy stolen in early childhood and brought up by the Delawares is at fifteen suddenly returned to the family he has forgotten. He resents his loss of independence, hates the brutality of the white man's civilization, and longs only for a return to the Indians whom he remembers as peace-loving

and kind. His return to the Delawares does not, however, bring him peace; rather, he must make a bitter choice between helping his indian brothers kill a group of unsuspecting white men or helping the white men escape. This is both vivid re-creation of outdoor life and a provocative study in conflicting loyalties." Horn Book

Richter, Jutta

Beyond the station lies the sea; translated from the German by Anna Brailovsky. Milkweed Editions 2009 81p $14

Grades: 4 5 6 7 **Fic**

1. Angels -- Fiction 2. Homeless persons -- Fiction

ISBN 978-1-57131-690-5; 1-57131-690-6

LC 2009018135

Trying to get to the beach where it is warm, two homeless boys enlist the aid of a rich woman who gives them money in exchange for a guardian angel.

"Richter presents a darkly poetic, masterfully crafted view of life on the streets." Publ Wkly

Riel, Jorn

The **shipwreck**; translated from Danish by John Mason; illustrated by Helen Cann. Barefoot Books 2011 il (The Inuk quartet) pa $12.99

Grades: 4 5 6 **Fic**

1. Adventure fiction 2. Inuit -- Fiction 3. Vikings -- Fiction

ISBN 978-1-84686-335-6; 1-84686-335-X

"This beautifully illustrated epic adventure, set circa 1000 CE, begins with the shocking, retaliatory beheading of young Viking Leiv's father by Thorstein Gunnarsson. The playful boy becomes withdrawn and vows to take revenge. When Thorstein casts off from Iceland for Greenland to serve out his sentence of exile, Leiv stows away onboard but is swept into the sea during a storm. An Inuit brother and sister, Apuluk, 12, and Narua, 11, find him and care for him in secret. . . . The narrative is straightforward and well paced, with several engaging dramatic episodes. Riel skillfully interweaves information about the Inuit culture, language, and environment without being didactic. . . . Vocabulary may pose a challenge for less-advanced readers, and mention of beheadings and amputations may be unsuitable for others. But Cann's ethereal watercolor, graphite, and collage illustrations in cool blue tones and browns have a calmer mood that will enchant readers with the beauty of the Arctic landscape." SLJ

Riggs, Ransom

Hollow city; by Ransom Riggs. Quirk Books 2014 399 p. (Novel of Miss Peregrine's Peculiar Children) $17.99

Grades: 6 7 8 9 **Fic**

1. Supernatural -- Fiction 2. London (England) -- Fiction 3. Escapes -- Fiction 4. Escapes 5. Orphanages -- Fiction 6. London

ISBN 1594746125; 9781594746123

This book, by Ransom Riggs, "begins in 1940, immediately after the first book [of the 'Miss Peregrine's Home for Peculiar Childrenthe' ended. Having escaped Miss Peregrine's island by the skin of their teeth, Jacob and his new friends must journey to London, the peculiar capital of the world. Along the way, they encounter new allies, a menagerie of peculiar animals, and other unexpected surprises." (Publisher's note)

"Hard on the heels of Riggs' first hugely successful effort, Miss Peregrine's Home for Peculiar Children (2011), comes this equally creepy sequel, which picks up where the first book left off... Like the first volume, this one is generously illustrated with peculiar period photographs that capture and enhance the eerie mood and mode. Fans will be pleased with this second volume and downright delighted to know that a third in the series is in the offing." (Booklist)

Miss Peregrine's home for peculiar children. Quirk Books 2011 352p il $17.99

Grades: 6 7 8 9   **Fic**

1. Ghost stories 2. Wales -- Fiction

ISBN 978-1-59474-476-1; 1-59474-476-9

"When Jacob's grandfather, Abe, a WWII veteran, is savagely murdered, Jacob has a nervous breakdown, in part because he believes that his grandfather was killed by a monster that only they could see. On his psychiatrist's advice, Jacob and his father travel from their home in Florida to Cairnholm Island off the coast of Wales, which, during the war, housed Miss Peregrine's Home for Peculiar Children. . . . Nearly 50 unsettling vintage photographs appear throughout, forming the framework of this dark but empowering tale, as Riggs creates supernatural backstories and identities for those pictured in them. . . . It's an enjoyable, eccentric read, distinguished by well-developed characters, a believable Welsh setting, and some very creepy monsters." Publ Wkly

Riley, James

Half upon a time. Aladdin 2010 385p $15.99

Grades: 5 6 7 8   **Fic**

1. Fairy tales 2. Adventure fiction

ISBN 978-1-4169-9593-7; 1-4169-9593-5

                        LC 2010012714

In the village of Giant's Hand Jack's grandfather has been pushing him to find a princess and get married, so when a young lady falls out of the sky wearing a shirt that says "Punk Princess," and she tells Jack that her grandmother, who looks suspiciously like the long-missing Snow White, has been kidnapped, Jack decides to help her.

"Riley does a wonderful job of combining the 21st century with the world in which fairies are alive, as well as creating characters that middle school students will relate to." Libr Media Connect

Story thieves; James Riley. Aladdin 2015 400 p. (Story Thieves) (hardcover : alk. paper) $16.99

Grades: 5 6 7 8   **Fic**

1. Adventure fiction 2. Magic -- Fiction 3. Books and reading -- Fiction 4. Characters in literature -- Fiction 5. Adventure and adventurers -- Fiction

ISBN 1481409190; 9781481409193; 9781481409209

                        LC 2014028133

In this juvenile novel, by James Riley, "[l]ife is boring when you live in the real world, instead of starring in your own book series. Owen knows that better than anyone, what with the real world's homework and chores. But everything changes the day Owen sees the impossible happen: his class-

mate Bethany climb out of a book in the library. It turns out Bethany's half-fictional and has been searching every book she can find for her missing father, a fictional character." (Publisher's note)

"When Owen sees Bethany climb out of a book, he learns that she is half fictional and is searching for her missing father. While Owen sympathizes, he also immediately sees the possibilities for fame, fortune, and glory...Owen learns a lot about how to be a true friend and what courage really is in this fast-paced, action-packed tale. A fun book for fans who enjoyed Riley's "Half Upon a Time" (Aladdin) series." SLJ

Rinaldi, Ann

Come Juneteenth. Harcourt 2007 246p (Great episodes) $17; pa $6.99

Grades: 6 7 8 9   **Fic**

1. Texas -- Fiction 2. Slavery -- Fiction 3. Juneteenth -- Fiction 4. Family life -- Fiction 5. African Americans -- Fiction

ISBN 978-0-15-05947-7; 0-15-205947-4; 978-0-15-206392-4 pa; 0-15-206392-7 pa

                        LC 2006-21458

Fourteen-year-old Luli and her family face tragedy after failing to tell their slaves that President Lincoln's Emancipation Proclamation made them free.

"Luli's authentic voice demonstrates Rinaldi's ability to evoke the human side of history." SLJ

★ The **fifth** of March; a story of the Boston Massacre. Harcourt Brace & Co. 1993 335p (Great episodes) pa $6.95

Grades: 7 8 9 10   **Fic**

1. Political leaders 2. Boston Massacre, 1770 -- Fiction 3. United States -- History -- 1600-1775, Colonial period -- Fiction

ISBN 0-15-205078-7 pa

                        LC 93-17821

Fourteen-year-old Rachel Marsh, an indentured servant in the Boston household of John and Abigail Adams, is caught up in the colonists' unrest that eventually escalates into the massacre of March 5, 1770.

"The story moves along briskly, and details of life in 18th-century Boston are woven into the narrative." SLJ

Girl in blue. Scholastic Press 2001 310p hardcover o.p. pa $5.99

Grades: 6 7 8 9   **Fic**

1. Spies 2. Spies -- Fiction 3. Sex role -- Fiction 4. United States -- History -- 1861-1865, Civil War -- Fiction

ISBN 0-439-07336-7; 0-439-67646-0 pa

                        LC 00-41945

To escape an abusive father and an arranged marriage, fourteen-year-old Sarah, dressed as a boy, leaves her Michigan home to enlist in the Union Army, and becomes a soldier on the battlefields of Virginia as well as a Union spy working in the house of Confederate sympathizer Rose O'Neal Greenhow in Washington, D.C.

"This first-person novel will engage readers through its sympathetic main character and exciting action." Booklist

The **redheaded** princess. HarperCollinsPublishers 2008 214p $15.99; lib bdg $16.89

Grades: 6 7 8 9 **Fic**

1. Queens 2. Great Britain -- History -- 1485-1603, Tudors -- Fiction

ISBN 978-0-06-073374-2; 0-06-073374-8; 978-0-06-073375-9 lib bdg; 0-06-073375-6 lib bdg

LC 2007-18577

In 1542, nine-year-old Lady Elizabeth lives on an estate near London, striving to get back into the good graces of her father, King Henry VIII, and as the years pass she faces his death and those of other close relatives until she finds herself next in line to ascend the throne of England in 1558.

"The rich scene-setting and believable, appealing heroine will satisfy Rinaldi's many fans." Booklist

An **unlikely** friendship; a novel of Mary Todd Lincoln and Elizabeth Keckley. Harcourt 2007 241p $17

Grades: 6 7 8 9 **Fic**

1. Memoirists 2. Dressmakers 3. Slavery -- Fiction 4. Friendship -- Fiction 5. Spouses of presidents

ISBN 0-15-205597-5

LC 2005-30210

Relates the lives of Mary Todd Lincoln, raised in a wealthy Virginia family, and Lizzy Keckley, a dressmaker born a slave, as they grow up separately then become best friends when Mary's childhood dream of living in the White House comes true.

This "story is fascinating and filled with remarkable gems of historical memorabilia to create a very satisfying read." Voice Youth Advocates

Riordan, Rick

The **battle** of the Labyrinth. Hyperion Books for Children 2008 361p (Percy Jackson & the Olympians) lib bdg $17.99; pa $7.99

Grades: 5 6 7 8 9 **Fic**

1. Classical mythology -- Fiction

ISBN 978-1-4231-0146-8 lib bdg; 1-4231-0146-4 lib bdg; 978-1-4231-0149-9 pa; 1-4231-0149-9 pa

LC 2007-42957

Sequel to: The Titan's curse (2007)

When demonic cheerleaders invade his high school, Percy Jackson hurries to Camp Half Blood, from whence he and his demigod friends set out on a quest through the Labyrinth, while the war between the Olympians and the evil Titan lord Kronos draws near.

"The wit, rousing swordplay and breakneck pace will once again keep kids hooked." Publ Wkly

Followed by: The last Olympian (2009)

The **blood** of Olympus; Rick Riordan. 1st edition Disney-Hyperion Books 2014 528 p. (The heroes of Olympus) (hardback) $19.99

Grades: 5 6 7 8 **Fic**

1. Adventure fiction 2. Classical mythology -- Fiction 3. Mythology, Greek -- Fiction 4. Mythology, Roman -- Fiction 5. Gaia (Greek deity) -- Fiction

ISBN 1423146735; 9781423146735

LC 2014017392

In this novel by Rick Riordan, book 5 of the "The Heroes of Olympus" series, "though the Greek and Roman crewmembers of the Argo II have made progress in their many quests, they still seem no closer to defeating the earth mother, Gaea. Her giants have risen . . . and they're stronger than ever. They must be stopped before the Feast of Spes, when Gaea plans to have two demigods sacrificed in Athens." (Publisher's note)

"Readers looking forward to the battle scenes will find plenty here, but the young heroes also rely on their wits as they dupe, charm, and negotiate their way through a series of encounters with gods, goddesses, and mythological creatures." Booklist

The **house** of Hades; Rick Riordan. Disney-Hyperion 2013 597 p. (Heroes of Olympus) (hardback) $19.99

Grades: 5 6 7 8 **Fic**

1. Hell -- Fiction 2. Gods and goddesses -- Fiction 3. Classical mythology -- Fiction 4. Camps -- Fiction 5. Giants -- Fiction 6. Mythology, Greek -- Fiction 7. Mythology, Roman -- Fiction 8. Gaia (Greek deity) -- Fiction 9. Hera (Greek deity) -- Fiction

ISBN 1423146727; 9781423146728

LC 2013015946

In this book, by Rick Riordan, "Annabeth and Percy tumble into a pit leading straight to the Underworld. The other five demigods have to put aside their grief and follow Percy's instructions to find the mortal side of the Doors of Death. If they can fight their way through the Gaea's forces, and Percy and Annabeth can survive the House of Hades, then the Seven will be able to seal the Doors from both sides and prevent the giants from raising Gaea." (Publisher's note)

"In this fourth in Riordan's series pitting Roman and Greek demigods against an awakening goddess Gaea, Percy and Annabeth trek through Tartarus to escape through the Doors of Death, while their friends fight their way to the Doors' mortal side to rescue them. The wisecracking teens reveal emotional depths while overcoming monsters and personal obstacles in this high velocity continuation of the gripping franchise." Horn Book

The **last** Olympian. Hyperion Books for Children 2009 381p map (Percy Jackson & the Olympians) $17.99

Grades: 5 6 7 8 9 **Fic**

1. Classical mythology -- Fiction

ISBN 978-1-4231-0147-5; 1-4231-0147-5

Sequel to: The battle of the Labyrinth (2008)

All year the half-bloods have been preparing for battle against the Titans. Now it's up to Percy Jackson and an army of young demi-gods to stop the Lord of Time.

"Riordan masterfully orchestrates the huge cast of characters and manages a coherent, powerful tale at once exciting, philosophical and tear-jerking." Kirkus

★ The **lightning** thief. Miramax Books/Hyperion Books for Children 2005 377p (Percy Jackson & the Olympians) pa $7.99

Grades: 5 6 7 8 9 **Fic**
1. Classical mythology -- Fiction
ISBN 0-7868-5629-7; 1-4231-3494-X pa; 978-0-
6417-2344-5; 978-1-4231-3494-7 pa

LC 2005-299400

Twelve-year-old Percy Jackson learns he is a demigod,
the son of a mortal woman and Poseidon, god of the sea. His
mother sends him to a summer camp for demigods where
he and his new friends set out on a quest to prevent a war
between the gods.

"Riordan's fast-paced adventure is fresh, dangerous, and
funny." Booklist

The **lost** hero. Disney/Hyperion Books 2010
553p $18.99
Grades: 5 6 7 8 **Fic**
1. Camps -- Fiction 2. Monsters -- Fiction 3. Classical
mythology -- Fiction
ISBN 978-1-4231-1339-3; 1-4231-1339-X

LC 2010015469

"Completely in control of pacing and tone, . . . [Riordan]
. . . balances a faultless comic banter against deeper notes
that reveal the characters' vulnerabilities." Horn Book

★ The **maze** of bones. Scholastic 2008 220p il
(The 39 clues) $12.99
Grades: 4 5 6 7 **Fic**
1. Family -- Fiction 2. Ciphers -- Fiction
ISBN 978-0-545-06039-4; 0-545-06039-7

At the reading of their grandmother's will, Dan and Amy
Cahill are given the choice of receiving a million dollars or
uncovering the 39 clues hidden around the world that will
lead to the source of the family's power, but by taking on
the clues, they end up in a dangerous race against their own
family members.

"Adeptly incorporating a genuine kids' perspective, the
narrative unfolds like a boulder rolling downhill and keeps
readers glued to the pages. . . . The book dazzles with suspense, plot twists, and snappy humor." SLJ

Other titles in this series are:
One false note by Gordon Korman (2008)
The sword thief by Peter Lerangis (2009)
The black circle by Patrick Carman (2009)
Beyond the grave by Jude Watson (2009)
In too deep by Jude Watson (2010)
The viper's nest by Peter Lerangis (2010)
The emperor's code by Gordon Korman (2010)
Storm warning by Linda Sue Park (2010)
Into the gauntlet by Margaret Peterson Haddix (2010)

Percy Jackson's Greek Gods; Rick Riordan; illustrated by John Rocco. Disney-Hyperion 2014
336 p. color illustrations (hardback) $24.99
Grades: 5 6 7 8 **Fic**
1. Greek mythology 2. Gods and goddesses -- Fiction
3. Gods, Greek -- Fiction
ISBN 1423183649; 9781423183648

LC 2013034612

"Riordan takes the classic guide to Greek myths and
makes it his own, with an introduction and narration by beloved character Percy Jackson. With 19 chapters, this oversize hardcover includes a variety of stories, from the early

tales of Gaea and the Titans to individual tales of gods readers encounter in the 'Percy Jackson' series. . ., such as Ares,
Apollo, and Dionysus." (School Library Journal)

"Combining the sarcasm and wit of Percy Jackson with
the original Greek myths is a great way to hook tweens and
teens on the stories without boring them. The beautiful illustrations by John Rocco enhance each story without taking
away from the action and drama." VOYA

Includes bibliographical references and index

The **Sea** of Monsters. Miramax Books/Hyperion
Books for Children 2006 279p (Percy Jackson & the
Olympians) $17.95; pa $7.99
Grades: 5 6 7 8 9 **Fic**
1. Classical mythology -- Fiction
ISBN 978-0-7868-5686-2; 0-7868-5686-6; 978-1-
4231-0334-9 pa; 1-4231-0334-3 pa

LC 2006280771

Sequel to: The lightning thief (2005)

Demigod Percy Jackson and his friends must journey
into the Sea of Monsters to save their camp. But first Percy
will discover a secret that makes him wonder whether being
claimed as Poseidon's son is an honor or a cruel joke

"Adventure follows chaotic adventure at a rapid pace,
and readers with even a passing acquaintance with the Odyssey will enjoy this fresh use of familiar stories." SLJ

Followed by: The Titan's curse (2007)

The **Serpent's** Shadow; Rick Riordan. Disney/
Hyperion Books 2012 viii, 406 p.p (hardcover)
$19.99
Grades: 4 5 6 7 **Fic**
1. Adventure fiction 2. Supernatural -- Fiction 3.
Mythology -- Fiction 4. Magic -- Fiction 5. Mythology,
Egyptian -- Fiction 6. Voyages and travels -- Fiction
7. Brothers and sisters -- Fiction 8. Adventure and
adventurers -- Fiction
ISBN 1423140575; 9781423140573

LC 2012454979

This book by Rick Riordan is the third installment of
the Kane Chronicles series. "Despite their best efforts, Carter and Sadie Kane can't seem to keep Apophis, the chaos
snake, down. Now Apophis is threatening to plunge the
world into eternal darkness, and the Kanes are faced with
the impossible task of having to destroy him once and for
all." (Publisher's note)

The **son** of Neptune. Disney/Hyperion Books
2011 521p (The heroes of Olympus) $19.99
Grades: 5 6 7 8 **Fic**
1. Camps -- Fiction 2. Monsters -- Fiction 3. Prophecies
-- Fiction 4. Classical mythology -- Fiction
ISBN 978-1-4231-4059-7; 1-4231-4059-1

LC 2011017658

Demigod Percy Jackson, still with no memory, and his
new friends from Camp Jupiter, Hazel and Frank, go on
a quest to free Death, but their bigger task is to unite the
Greek and Roman camps so that the Prophecy of Seven can
be fulfilled.

The **throne** of fire; Rick Riordan. Disney/Hy-
perion Books 2011 (Kane chronicles) $18.99

Grades: 4 5 6 7   **Fic**
  ISBN 978-1-4231-4056-6; 1-4231-4056-7;
  1423140567; 9781423140566
  Sequel to: The red pyramid (2010)
  Carter and Sadie, offspring of the brilliant Egyptologist
Dr. Julius Kane, embark on a worldwide search for the Book
of Ra, but the House of Life and the gods of chaos are deter-
mined to stop them.
  "Lit by flashes of humor, this fantasy adventure is an
engaging addition to the Kane Chronicles series." Booklist

  The **Titan's** curse. Miramax Books/Hyperion
Books for Children 2007 312p (Percy Jackson &
the Olympians) $17.95
Grades: 5 6 7 8 9   **Fic**
  1. Classical mythology -- Fiction
  ISBN 1423101456; 1423101480 pa; 9781423101451
                      LC 2006-35731
  Sequel to The Sea of Monsters (2006)
  When the goddess Artemis disappears while hunting a
rare, ancient monster, a group of her followers joins Percy
and his friends in an attempt to find and rescue her before
the winter solstice, when her influence is needed to sway the
Olympian Council regarding the war with the Titans.
  "Intricate prophecies and relationships are neatly braid-
ed into the adventurous plot." SLJ
  Followed by The battle of the Layrinth (2008)

  Vespers rising; [by] Rick Riordan, Peter Lerangis, Gordon Korman, Jude Watson. Scholastic 2011
238p (The 39 clues) $12.99
Grades: 4 5 6 7   **Fic**
  1. Ciphers -- Fiction
  ISBN 978-0-545-29059-3; 0-545-32606-0
  Fourteen-year-old Amy Cahill and her younger brother
Dan thought they could return to their regular lives when
they found the 39 clues. But the Vespers, powerful enemies,
will stop at nothing to get the clues. And with the Vespers
rising, the world is in jeopardy.

Ritter, John H.
  The **boy** who saved baseball. Philomel Books
2003 216p $17.99; pa $6.99
Grades: 5 6 7 8   **Fic**
  1. Baseball -- Fiction
  ISBN 0-399-23622-8; 0-14-240286-9 pa
                      LC 2002-15792
  A prequel to this title is: The desperado who stole baseball (2009)
  The fate of a small California town rests on the outcome
of one baseball game, and Tom Gallagher hopes to lead his
team to victory with the secrets of the now disgraced player,
Dante Del Gato
  "This tale is peppered with both optimism and dilemmas; it has plenty of play-by-play action, lots of humor, and
a triumphant ending." SLJ

  Choosing up sides. Philomel Bks. 1998 166p
$17.99; pa $5.99
Grades: 6 7 8 9   **Fic**
  1. Baseball -- Fiction 2. Father-son relationship --

Fiction 3. Left- and right-handedness -- Fiction
  ISBN 0-399-23185-4; 0-689-11840-5 pa
                      LC 97-39779
  "This is an entertaining and thought-provoking coming-
of-age story." Book Rep
  "In 1921 Ohio, a minister's son is condemned by his fa-
ther because of his natural inclination for using his left hand.
Luke discovers he has a talent for playing baseball, although
Pa disdains sports—especially a game that utilizes Luke's
'evil' hand." Horn Book Guide

  The **desperado** who stole baseball. Philomel
Books 2009 260p il $17.99
Grades: 5 6 7 8   **Fic**
  1. Outlaws 2. Orphans -- Fiction 3. Baseball -- Fiction
  4. California -- Fiction 5. Frontier and pioneer life --
Fiction
  ISBN 978-0-399-24664-7; 0-399-24664-9
                      LC 2008-16901
  Prequel to: The boy who saved baseball
  In 1881, the scrappy, rough-and-tumble baseball team in
a California mining town enlists the help of a quick-witted
twelve-year-old orphan and the notorious outlaw Billy the
Kid to win a big game against the National League Champion Chicago White Stockings
  "This tall-tale page-turner stands alone though it will be
most appreciated by fans of Ritter's earlier works." SLJ

Rivers, Karen
  Finding Ruby Starling; by Karen Rivers. Arthur
A. Levine Books, an imprint of Scholastic Inc. 2014
288 p. (hardcover) $17.99
Grades: 5 6 7 8   **Fic**
  1. Twins -- Fiction 2. Adoption -- Fiction 3. Blogs
-- Fiction 4. Email -- Fiction 5. Sisters -- Fiction 6.
Mothers and daughters -- Fiction
  ISBN 0545534798; 9780545534796
                      LC 2014002269
  In this middle grade book by Karen Rivers, "when Ruby
Starling gets a message from a Ruth Quayle proclaiming
them to be long-lost twin sisters, she doesn't know what to
do with it. . . . Ruth is an extroverted American girl. Ruby
is a shy English one. As they investigate the truth of their
birth and the circumstances of their separation, they also
share lives full of friends, family, and possible romances."
(Publisher's note)
  "In this epistolary, dual-narrator story, Ruth, an American twelve-year-old, e-finds her identical twin, Ruby, in
England. As with any novel in letters (in this case emails,
handwritten notes, and the occasional Tumblr posting),
voice is everything, and Ruth and Ruby have distinctive, convincing, and entertaining writing styles. Subplots
abound, including the backstory of two complicated families. Hectic, highly textured, and good-natured without being soppy." Horn Book

Robert, Na'ima B.
  Boy vs. girl. Frances Lincoln Children's 2011
260p $15.95
Grades: 6 7 8 9 10   **Fic**
  1. Twins -- Fiction 2. Muslims -- Fiction 3. Ramadan
-- Fiction 4. Siblings -- Fiction 5. Great Britain --

Fiction 6. Pakistanis -- Great Britain -- Fiction
ISBN 978-1-84780-150-0; 1-84780-150-1

"Twins Farhana and Faraz determine to fast during Ramadan now that they are 16. . . . As first-generation Brits, they must respond to the demands of their Pakistani family, their secular schools, and their friends. . . . The characters are realistic. . . . A well-balanced chord is struck here between storytelling and exploring the complex and sometimes conflicting pulls of tradition, family, friends, and lifestyle." Booklist

Robert, Na'ima bint

From Somalia with love; [by] Na'ima B. Robert. Frances Lincoln Children's Books 2008 159p $15.95; pa $7.95

Grades: 7 8 9 10 **Fic**

1. Muslims -- Fiction 2. Somalia -- Fiction 3. London (England) -- Fiction 4. Father-daughter relationship -- Fiction

ISBN 978-1-84507-831-7; 1-84507-831-4; 978-1-84507-832-4 pa; 1-84507-832-2 pa

"Safia has grown up believing her father died in the fighting in Somalia. When she finds out that he is alive and on his way to London to join the family, she is apprehensive about the difference his presence will make in her life. . . . This is a unique title that will be popular in regions that have large Somali populations or where Randa Abdel-Fattah's books are popular." SLJ

Includes glossary

Roberts, Jeyn

Dark inside. Simon & Schuster Books for Young Readers 2011 327p $17.99

Grades: 7 8 9 10 **Fic**

1. Science fiction 2. Monsters -- Fiction 3. Good and evil -- Fiction

ISBN 978-1-4424-2351-0; 1-4424-2351-X

LC 2011008642

After tremendous earthquakes destroy the Earth's major cities, an ancient evil emerges, turning ordinary people into hunters, killers, and insane monsters but a small group of teens comes together in a fight for survival and safety.

"Well-balanced, realistic suspense." Kirkus

Rage within; Jeyn Roberts. Simon & Schuster Books for Young Readers 2012 357 p. (hardcover) $17.99

Grades: 7 8 9 10 **Fic**

1. Science fiction 2. Apocalyptic fiction 3. Monsters -- Fiction 4. Survival -- Fiction 5. Good and evil -- Fiction

ISBN 1442423544; 9781442423541; 9781442423565
LC 2011047396

Sequel to: Dark inside

In author Jeyn Roberts' "apocalyptic sequel to 'Dark Inside' . . . Aries, Clementine, Michael, and Mason have survived the first wave of the apocalypse that wiped out most of the world's population and turned many of the rest into murderous Baggers. Now they're hiding out in an abandoned house . . . trying to figure out their next move. As the Baggers begin to create a new world order, these four teens

will have to trust and rely on each other in order to survive." (Publisher's note)

Roberts, Laura Peyton

Green. Delacorte Press 2010 261p $16.99; lib bdg $19.99

Grades: 5 6 7 8 **Fic**

1. Fantasy fiction 2. Leprechauns -- Fiction 3. Grandmothers -- Fiction

ISBN 978-0-385-73558-2; 0-385-73558-8; 978-0-385-90543-5 lib bdg; 0-385-90543-2 lib bdg

LC 2008-54241

Abducted by leprechauns on her thirteenth birthday, Lilybet Green learns that there is more to her family tree—and to her bond with her late grandmother—than she ever imagined.

"A fun, fresh take on leprechaun lore that pushes well past typical depictions to embrace banking transactions, lepro-human relations, and some creative problem-solving. Lily is a credible hero, by turns scared and confident, and definitely one young readers will enjoy following." Booklist

Roberts, Marion

Sunny side up. Wendy Lamb Books 2009 244p il $15.99; lib bdg $18.99

Grades: 4 5 6 7 **Fic**

1. Australia -- Fiction 2. Friendship -- Fiction 3. Family life -- Fiction

ISBN 978-0-385-73672-5; 0-385-73672-X; 978-0-385-90624-1 lib bdg; 0-385-90624-2 lib bdg

LC 2008-08633

First published 2008 in Australia

As the hot Australian summer draws to an end, eleven-year-old Sunny, content to be an only child with amicably divorced parents, finds her life getting much too complicated when her mother's boyfriend moves in with his two children, her best friend begins to develop an interest in boys, and she is contacted by her long-estranged grandmother.

"Character development is strong, as the girl is quick to observe and comment on the people in her life, and the setting forms an interesting backdrop. Small black-and-white photos are liberally scattered throughout." SLJ

Roberts, Willo Davis

The kidnappers. Atheneum Bks. for Young Readers 1998 137p hardcover o.p. pa $4.99

Grades: 4 5 6 7 **Fic**

1. Wealth -- Fiction 2. Kidnapping -- Fiction 3. New York (N.Y.) -- Fiction

ISBN 0-689-81394-5; 0-689-81393-7 pa

LC 96-53677

No one believes eleven-year-old Joey, who has a reputation for telling tall tales, when he claims to have witnessed the kidnapping of the class bully outside their expensive New York City private school

"The combination of a witty narrative and a suspenseful plot makes this a good page-turner that will leave even the most reluctant readers glued to their seats." Booklist

Robinet, Harriette Gillem

Walking to the bus-rider blues. Atheneum Bks. for Young Readers 2000 146p hardcover o.p. pa $4.99

Grades: 5 6 7 8   **Fic**

1. Race relations -- Fiction 2. African Americans -- Fiction
ISBN 0-689-83191-9; 0-689-83886-7 pa

LC 99-29054

Twelve-year-old Alfa Merryfield, his older sister, and their grandmother struggle for rent money, food, and their dignity as they participate in the Montgomery, Alabama bus boycott in the summer of 1956

"Ingredients of mystery, suspense, and humor enhance and personalize this well-constructed story that offers insight into a troubled era." SLJ

Robinson, A. M.

Vampire crush. HarperTeen 2011 404p pa $8.99

Grades: 7 8 9 10   **Fic**

1. Vampires -- Fiction
ISBN 978-0-06-198971-1 pa; 0-06-198971-1 pa

LC 2010-09397

Sixteen-year-old journalist Sophie McGee's junior year is filled with unexpected drama—and romance—when she discovers that her new classmates are hiding a dark secret, while the "boy next door" from her childhood re-enters her life.

"Sophie is smart, funny, and determined, and her narration adds humor and wit to the story. The quirky supporting cast is pretty much what you'd expect in a teen vampire tale. An original and entertaining entry to the genre that won't disappoint." Booklist

Robinson, Barbara

★ The **best** Christmas pageant ever; pictures by Judith Gwyn Brown. Harper & Row 1972 80p il $15.99; lib bdg $16.89; pa $5.99

Grades: 4 5 6   **Fic**

1. Pageants -- Fiction 2. Christmas -- Fiction
ISBN 0-06-025043-7; 0-06-025044-5 lib bdg; 0-06-440275-4 pa

In this story the six Herdmans, "absolutely the worst kids in the history of the world," discover the meaning of Christmas when they bully their way into the leading roles of the local church nativity play

The story "romps through the festive preparations with comic relish, and if the Herdmans are so gauche as to seem exaggerated, they are still enjoyable, as are the not-so-subtle pokes at pageant-planning in general." Bull Cent Child Books

Other titles about the Herdmans are:
The best Halloween ever (2004)
The best school year ever (1994)

Robinson, Gary

Little Brother of War; Gary Robinson. 7th Generation 2013 120 p. (pbk.) $9.95

Grades: 6 7 8   **Fic**

1. Ball games -- Fiction 2. Brothers -- Fiction 3.

Ball games -- Fiction 4. Mississippi -- Fiction 5. Individuality -- Fiction 6. Choctaw Indians -- Fiction 7. Family life -- Mississippi -- Fiction 8. Indians of North America -- Mississippi -- Fiction
ISBN 1939053021; 9781939053022

LC 2013013182

This book by Gary Robinson is part of the "PathFinders series about Native American teens, written by Native authors. Randy is pressured to pursue high school sports, like his father and recently deceased war-hero brother before him. But the 16-year-old discovers that he loves--and has a talent for--Choctaw stickball or toli, an ancient game similar to lacrosse that isn't a school sport and that his father thinks is a relic." (Publishers Weekly)

Rocco, John

Swim that rock; John Rocco, Jay Primiano. Candlewick Press 2014 304 p. ill., map $16.99

Grades: 7 8 9 10   **Fic**

1. Bildungsromans 2. Fishing -- Fiction 3. Family life -- Fiction 4. Rhode Island -- Fiction
ISBN 0763669059; 9780763669058

LC 2013952797

In this book, by John Rocco and Jay Primiano, "a young working-class teen fights to save his family's diner after his father is lost in a fishing-boat accident. . . . In Narragansett Bay, scrabbling out a living as a quahogger isn't easy, but with the help of some local clammers, Jake is determined to work hard and earn enough money to ensure his family's security and save the diner in time." (Publisher's note)

"When his fisherman father went missing, Jake and his mother lost their house, and now the family diner is in danger of being repossessed. A mysterious character named Captain and seasoned fisherman Gene Hassard help Jake earn money by learning the ways of the bay. With a lushly detailed sense of place and character, the story examines a boy coming to terms with his situation." Horn Book

Rodda, Emily

★ The **key** to Rondo. Scholastic Press 2008 342p $16.99; pa $6.99

Grades: 5 6 7 8   **Fic**

1. Fantasy fiction 2. Magic -- Fiction 3. Cousins -- Fiction
ISBN 0-545-03535-X; 978-0-545-03535-4; 0-545-03536-8 pa; 978-0-545-03536-1 pa

LC 2007-16873

Through an heirloom music box, Leo, a serious, responsible boy, and his badly-behaved cousin Mimi enter the magical world of Rondo to rescue Mimi's dog from a sorceress, who wishes to exchange him for the key that allows free travel between worlds.

"Rodda fills the cousins' quest with image-rich prose and compelling action." Bull Cent Child Books

Another title about Rondo is:
The Wizard of Rondo (2009)

The **Wizard** of Rondo. Scholastic Press 2009 385p $16.99

Grades: 5 6 7 8   **Fic**

1. Fantasy fiction 2. Magic -- Fiction 3. Cousins --

Fiction

ISBN 978-0-545-11516-2; 0-545-11516-7

LC 2009004375

Sequel to: The key to Rondo (2008)

Cousins Leo and Mimi return to the world of Rondo through their family's enchanted music box to rescue a missing wizard and foil the plans of the evil Blue Queen.

"Folklore buffs and Rodda's fans are sure to enjoy." Booklist

Rodgers, Mary

Freaky Friday. Harper & Row 1972 145p hardcover o.p. pa $5.99

Grades: 4 5 6 7   **Fic**

1. Mother-daughter relationship -- Fiction

ISBN 0-06-025048-8; 0-06-025049-6 lib bdg; 0-06-057010-5 pa

"A fresh, imaginative, and entertaining story." Bull Cent Child Books

"'When I woke up this morning, I found I'd turned into my mother.' So begins the most bizarre day in the life of 13-year-old Annabel Andrews, who discovers one Friday morning she has taken on her mother's physical characteristics while retaining her own personality. Readers will giggle in anticipation as Annabel plunges madly from one disaster to another trying to cope with various adult situations." Publ Wkly

Rodkey, Geoff

The **Tapper** twins go to war (with each other) Geoff Rodkey. Little, Brown & Co. 2015 240 p. illustrations (Tapper twins) (hardcover) $13.99

Grades: 4 5 6 7   **Fic**

1. School stories 2. Twins -- Fiction 3. New York (N.Y.) -- Fiction 4. Practical jokes -- Fiction 5. Brothers and sisters -- Fiction 6. Schools -- Fiction 7. Oral history -- Fiction 8. Internet games -- Fiction 9. Family life -- New York (State) -- New York -- Fiction

ISBN 0316297798; 9780316297790

LC 2014015918

This book, by Geoff Rodkey, is a "comedy featuring twelve-year-old fraternal twins, Claudia and Reese, who couldn't be more different...except in their determination to come out on top in a vicious prank war! But when the competition escalates into an all-out battle that's fought from the cafeteria of their New York City private school all the way to the fictional universe of an online video game, the twins have to decide if their efforts to destroy each other are worth the price." (Publisher's note)

"t started with words. Or maybe with the missing toaster pastry. But when Reese Tapper called his twin sister, Claudia, "Princess Farts-a-Lot" in front of the whole sixth grade, the war was on. Through oral-history interviews, text messages, e-mails, chat-room comments, photographs, and margin notes, Claudia documents the history of the Tapper twins' war...Thanks to the inclusion of various points of view, Claudia's reasonably balanced narrative offers plenty of humorous insight, and occasional doodles and photos keep it peppy." Booklist

Another title in this series is:

The Tapper twins tear up New York (2015)

Rodman, Mary Ann

★ **Jimmy's** stars. Farrar, Straus & Giroux 2008 257p $16.95

Grades: 5 6 7 8   **Fic**

1. Siblings -- Fiction 2. Soldiers -- Fiction 3. Family life -- Fiction 4. Pittsburgh (Pa.) -- Fiction 5. World War, 1939-1945 -- Fiction

ISBN 978-0-374-33703-2; 0-374-33703-9

LC 2007-05091

In 1943, eleven-year-old Ellie is her brother Jimmy's "best girl," and when he leaves Pittsburgh just before Thanksgiving to fight in World War II, he promises he will return, asks her to leave the Christmas tree up until he does, and reminds her to "let the joy out."

Rodman "finds beauty in every emotional nuance... . The lively spirit of working-class Pittsburgh . . . extends Ellie's person story with a broader sense of home-front life." Booklist

Rodman, Sean

Infiltration. Orca Book Publishers 2011 130p (Orca soundings) lib bdg $16.95; pa $9.95

Grades: 7 8 9 10   **Fic**

1. City and town life -- Fiction

ISBN 978-1-55469-986-5 lib bdg; 1-55469-986-X lib bdg; 978-1-55469-985-8 pa; 1-55469-985-1 pa

Bex breaks into locked and abandoned buildings just because he can, but when a new friend's behavior becomes more and more risky, he has to do the right thing.

This "is a fast-paced action-adventure story. . . . The page-turning suspense it generates and the fascinating hook of urban-exploration should grab any reader." Booklist

Rodriguez, Cindy L.

When reason breaks; by Cindy L. Rodriguez. Bloomsbury Publishing 2015 294 p. (hardcover) $17.99

Grades: 8 9 10 11   **Fic**

1. Suicide -- Fiction 2. Family life -- Fiction 3. High schools -- Fiction 4. Schools -- Fiction 5. Family problems -- Fiction 6. Emotional problems -- Fiction 7. Hispanic Americans -- Fiction 8. Goth culture (Subculture) -- Fiction

ISBN 1619634120; 9781619634121

LC 2014009109

In this book, by Cindy L. Rodriguez, "Elizabeth Davis must learn to control her anger before it destroys her. Emily Delgado appears to be a smart, sweet girl, with a normal life, but as depression clutches at her, she struggles to feel normal. Both girls are in Ms. Diaz's English class, where they connect to the words of Emily Dickinson. . . . And with Dickinson's poetry as their guide, both girls must conquer their personal demons to ever be happy." (Publisher's note)

"A sharply drawn, emotionally resonant tale of two girls—one gripped by uncontrollable rage, the other by unrelenting numbness—that will speak to many teens." Kirkus

Roecker, Laura

★ The **Liar** Society; by Lisa and Laura Roecker. Sourcebooks Fire 2011 361p pa $9.99

Grades: 7 8 9 10   **Fic**

1. School stories 2. Mystery fiction 3. Secret societies

-- Fiction

ISBN 978-1-4022-5633-2; 1-4022-5633-7

When Kate receives a mysterious e-mail from her dead friend Grace, she must prove that Grace's death was not an accident, but finds that her elite private school holds secrets so big people are willing to kill to protect them.

This is a "smartly paced and plotted first novel, full of twists, clues, and sleuthing. Add this to your go-to list of mysteries." Booklist

The **lies** that bind; Lisa and Laura Roecker. Sourcebooks Fire 2012 314 p. (The Liar Society) (tp : alk. paper) $9.99

Grades: 7 8 9 10 **Fic**

1. School stories 2. Missing persons -- Fiction 3. Secret societies -- Fiction 4. Schools -- Fiction 5. High schools -- Fiction

ISBN 1402270240; 9781402270246

LC 2012035855

This young adult school mystery, by Lisa and Laura Roecker, is part of "The Liar Society" series. "Kate has heard of messages from beyond the grave, but she never expected to find one in a fortune cookie. Especially from her best friend, Grace--who's supposed to be dead. At the elite Pemberly Brown Academy, . . . a popular girl has gone missing, and Kate owes it to Grace's memory to find out what happened. But in a school ruled by secret societies, who can she trust?" (Publisher's note)

The **third** lie's the charm; Third lie is the charm. Lisa & Laura Roecker. Sourcebooks Fire 2013 288 p. (The Liar Society) (tp : alk. paper) $9.99

Grades: 7 8 9 10 **Fic**

1. School stories 2. Mystery fiction 3. Schools -- Fiction 4. High schools -- Fiction 5. Secret societies -- Fiction

ISBN 1402285930; 9781402285936

LC 2013023321

In this young adult mystery by Lisa Roecker and Laura Roecker, part of The Liar Society series, "Katie Lowry knows she could've stopped Alistair from doing something stupid if only she'd picked up the phone. Now she has to live with the guilt. She's sick of the lies, sick of the secret societies that rule life at Pemberly Brown Academy." (Publisher's note)

Third lie is the charm

Rollins, James

Jake Ransom and the howling sphinx. Harper 2011 369p il map $16.99

Grades: 5 6 7 8 **Fic**

1. Science fiction 2. Adventure fiction 3. Egypt -- Fiction 4. Siblings -- Fiction 5. Archeology -- Fiction 6. Prehistoric animals -- Fiction

ISBN 978-0-06-147382-1; 0-06-147382-0

LC 2010045619

Sequel to: Jake Ransom and the Skull King's shadow (2009)

When Connecticut middle-schooler Jake and his older sister Kady are transported back to Pangaea, the strange world of lost civilizations, they must find the truth behind the mythic Fire Opal Eye in order to survive.

"Likely to win Jake more fans, this will have adventure seekers of both genders clamoring for volume three." Kirkus

Jake Ransom and the Skull King's shadow. HarperCollins 2009 399p il map $16.99; lib bdg $17.89; pa $7.99

Grades: 5 6 7 8 **Fic**

1. Adventure fiction 2. Mayas -- Fiction 3. Siblings -- Fiction 4. Archeology -- Fiction

ISBN 978-0-06-147379-1; 0-06-147379-0; 978-0-06-147380-7 lib bdg; 0-06-147380-4 lib bdg; 978-0-06-147381-4 pa; 0-06-147381-2 pa

LC 2009-14570

Connecticut middle-schooler Jake and his older sister Kady are transported by a Mayan artifact to a strange world inhabited by a mix of people from long-lost civilizations who are threatened by prehistoric creatures and an evil alchemist, the Skull King.

This is an "exciting time-travel adventure. . . . Rollins . . . presents a wide range of interesting historical information while telling a rollicking good story that should please a wide range of readers." Publ Wkly

Another title about Jake Ransom is:

Jake Ransom and the howling sphinx (2011)

Rorby, Ginny

Lost in the river of grass. Carolrhoda Lab 2011 255p $17.95

Grades: 7 8 9 10 **Fic**

1. Everglades (Fla.) -- Fiction 2. Wilderness survival -- Fiction

ISBN 978-0-7613-5685-1; 0-7613-5685-1

LC 2009-53999

"In this authentic survival adventure, Sarah, a 13-year-old scholarship student, leaves her preppy classmates on a weekend trip to the Everglades and takes off with Andy, 15 . . . who offers her a brief guided tour in his airboat. After the boat sinks, they walk for three days through the swamp . . . until, finally, helicopters rescue them. What comes through best here is not only the teens' courage and mutual support but also the realism of their fights and weaknesses." Booklist

The **outside** of a horse; a novel. Dial Books for Young Readers 2010 343p $16.99

Grades: 7 8 9 10 **Fic**

1. Horses -- Fiction 2. Amputees -- Fiction 3. Veterans -- Fiction 4. Father-daughter relationship -- Fiction

ISBN 978-0-8037-3478-4; 0-8037-3478-6

LC 2009-25101

When her father returns from the Iraq War as an amputee with post-traumatic stress disorder, Hannah escapes by volunteering to work with rescued horses, never thinking that the abused horses could also help her father recover.

Hannah "comes across as a believable teen. As a backdrop to the story, Rorby has interwoven a good deal of disturbing information about animal cruelty. Horse lovers and most others will saddle up right away with this poignant tale." Booklist

Rose, Caroline Starr

★ **May** B. a novel-in-verse. Schwartz & Wade Books 2012 $15.99; lib bdg $18.99

Grades: 4 5 6 7   **Fic**
1. Novels in verse 2. Kansas -- Fiction 3. Frontier and
pioneer life -- Fiction
ISBN 978-1-58246-393-3; 1-58246-393-X; 978-1-
58246-412-1 lib bdg; 1-58246-412-X lib bdg
                                        LC 2010033222
When a failed wheat crop nearly bankrupts the Betterly
family, Pa pulls twelve-year-old May from school and hires
her out to a couple new to the Kansas frontier.

"If May is a brave, stubborn fighter, the short, free-verse
lines are one-two punches in this Laura Ingalls Wilder-in-
spired ode to the human spirit." Kirkus

Rosen, Michael J.

Sailing the unknown; around the world with
Captain Cook. written by Michael J. Rosen; illustrated by Maria Cristina Pritelli. Creative Editions 2012
37 p. $17.99

Grades: 3 4 5 6 7   **Fic**
1. Sea stories 2. Explorers -- Fiction 3. Voyages
around the world -- Fiction 4. Diaries -- Fiction
ISBN 1568462166; 9781568462165
                                        LC 2011040840
This children's book, by Michael J. Rosen, illustrated
by Maria Cristina Pritelli, tells the story of "an 11-year-old
sailor named Nicholas, . . . [who in 1768] took to the seas
with British explorer James Cook on a 3-year expedition
of discovery, venturing into an uncharted world filled with
strange lands, mysterious peoples, and peculiar creatures."
(Publisher's note)

Rosen, Renee

★ **Every** crooked pot. St. Martin's Griffin 2007
227p pa $8.95

Grades: 7 8 9 10   **Fic**
1. Birth defects -- Fiction 2. Father-daughter
relationship -- Fiction
ISBN 978-0-312-36543-1; 0-312-36543-8
                                        LC 2007-10457
"Rosen looks back at the life of Nina Goldman, whose
growing up is tied to two pillars: a port-wine stain around
her eye and her inimitable father, Artie. The birthmark, she
hates; her father, she loves. Both shape her in ways that merit
Rosen's minute investigation. . . . There's real power in the
writing." Booklist

Rosoff, Meg

★ **Picture** me gone; by Meg Rosoff. G.P. Putnam's Sons 2013 256 p. $17.99

Grades: 7 8 9   **Fic**
1. Missing persons -- Fiction 2. Parent-child relationship
-- Fiction 3. Coming of age -- Fiction 4. Mystery and
detective stories 5. Fathers and daughters -- Fiction
ISBN 0399257659; 9780399257650
                                        LC 2012048974
This book by Meg Rosoff is a story "about the relationship between parents and children, love and loss. Mila has an
exceptional talent for reading a room—sensing hidden facts
and unspoken emotions from clues that others overlook. So
when her father's best friend, Matthew, goes missing from
his upstate New York home, Mila and her beloved father
travel from London to find him. Just when she's closest to

solving the mystery, a shocking betrayal calls into question
her trust." (Publisher's note)

"Sensitive Londoner Mila, twelve, travels with her father, Gil, to upstate New York to search for Gil's boyhood
friend, who has inexplicably disappeared. The subject of this
road-trip novel--how much guilt and tragedy can a person
bear before he gives up on life?--is adult, but the writing is
up to Rosoff's usual standards of originality, depth, wit, and
insight." (Horn Book)

★ **There** is no dog; Meg Rosoff. G. P. Putnam's
Sons 2011 243p. $17.99

Grades: 7 8 9   **Fic**
1. Love stories 2. God -- Fiction 3. Man-woman
relationship -- Fiction
ISBN 9780399257643
                                        LC 2011020651
This book "looks at the world's natural disasters, injustices, and chaos and presents a[n] . . . explanation: God is a
horny teenage boy. According to this . . . account, God, aka
'Bob,' was given Earth by his mother, who won the planet in
a poker game. Bob showed flashes of brilliance during Creation, but he feels little responsibility for the planet. When he
falls head-over-heels in lust with a beautiful zoo employee,
Lucy, Bob's passion and growing anger toward those who
would keep them apart is manifested through wildly fluctu-
ating weather and rampant flooding." (Publishers Weekly)

Ross, Elizabeth

Belle epoque; Elizabeth Ross. Delacorte Press
2013 336 p. (ebook) $53.97; (library) $20.99;
(hardcover) $17.99

Grades: 7 8 9 10 11 12   **Fic**
1. Love stories 2. Historical fiction 3. Female friendship
-- Fiction 4. Runaways -- Fiction 5. Social classes --
Fiction 6. Conduct of life -- Fiction 7. Beauty, Personal
-- Fiction 8. Interpersonal relations -- Fiction 9. Paris
(France) -- History -- 1870-1940 -- Fiction 10. France
-- History -- Third Republic, 1870-1940 -- Fiction
ISBN 0375990054; 9780375985270; 9780375990052;
9780385741460
                                        LC 2012034694
William C. Morris Honor Book (2014)
In this book, "sixteen-year-old runaway Maude Pichon
is ugly—so much so that she lands a job as a 'repoussoir,' an
unattractive girl paid to be seen with a lovelier girl to make
her appear even more beautiful by comparison . . . . Maude
is humiliated by the idea, but her poverty leaves her few options." Then "chance sends a dashing composer Maude's
way, and a countess hires her to befriend her independent-
minded daughter, Isabelle." (Publishers Weekly)

"Ross models her plot on an 1866 story by Zola, "Les
Repoussoirs," expanding its focus to highlight Maude's
plight and using that to illuminate the chasm that existed between the wealthy and the poor... A refreshingly relevant and
inspiring historical venture." Kirkus

Ross, Jeff

The **drop**. Orca Book Publishers 2011 157p
(Orca sports) pa $9.95

Grades: 6 7 8 9 **Fic**

1. Snowboarding -- Fiction

ISBN 978-1-55469-392-4; 1-55469-392-6

When Alex and three other snowboarders find themselves in trouble in the remote mountains of British Columbia, Alex must confront his fears and lead them to safety.

"Readers need not be regular snowboarders to appreciate the extended descriptions of the sport: they will feel the exhilaration of every turn and jump. The writing is crisp, and the plot moves along quickly." SLJ

Ross, Joel

The **Fog** diver; Joel Ross. HarperCollins 2015 336 p. (hardback) $16.99

Grades: 4 5 6 7 **Fic**

1. Aeronautics -- Fiction 2. Science fiction 3. Science fiction 4. Orphans -- Fiction 5. Survival -- Fiction 6. Recycling (Waste) -- Fiction 7. Adventure and adventurers -- Fiction 8. Environmental degradation -- Fiction

ISBN 0062352938; 9780062352934

LC 2014034154

In this juvenile novel, by Joel Ross, "living in the sky is the new reality and a few determined slum kids just might become heroes. . . . Thirteen-year-old Chess and his friends Hazel, Bea, and Swedish sail their rickety air raft over the deadly Fog, scavenging the ruins for anything they can sell to survive. But now survival isn't enough. They must risk everything to get to the miraculous city of Port Oro, the only place where their beloved Mrs. E can be cured of fogsickness." (Publisher's note)

"[A] fresh approach, convincingly delivered, with overtones reminiscent of Dickens the only thing missing is a sequel, which readers will hope won't be far behind." Kirkus

Rossetti, Rinsai

The **girl** with borrowed wings; by Rinsai Rossetti. Dial Books 2012 300 p. (hardcover) $17.99

Grades: 7 8 9 10 11 12 **Fic**

1. Cats -- Fiction 2. Voyages and travels -- Fiction 3. Father-daughter relationship -- Fiction 4. Love -- Fiction 5. Flying -- Fiction 6. Deserts -- Fiction 7. Shapeshifting -- Fiction

ISBN 0803735669; 9780803735668

LC 2011027164

This is Rinsai Rossetti's debut, a coming-of-age novel. Of "Thai descent, 17-year-old Frenenqer Paje has grown up" with "her coldly overbearing father . . . . [S]he disobeys her father by rescuing a mistreated cat" who "is actually a shapeshifting 'Free person' named Sangris . . . . By night, he flies Frenenqer around the world to places both real and magical, slowly chipping away at the defenses she has built up to withstand her father's callous cruelty." (Publishers Weekly)

Rossi, Veronica

Under the never sky; Veronica Rossi. HarperCollins 2012 376 p. (hardback) $17.99

Grades: 6 7 8 9 10 11 12 **Fic**

1. Science fiction 2. Apocalyptic fiction 3. Cannibalism -- Fiction 4. Man-woman relationship -- Fiction

ISBN 9780062072030

LC 2011044631

This book tells the story of "Aria [who] knows her chances of surviving in the outer wasteland--known as The Death Shop--are slim. . . . Then Aria meets an Outsider named Perry. He's wild--a savage--and her only hope of staying alive. A hunter for his tribe in a merciless landscape, Perry views Aria as sheltered and fragile--everything he would expect from a Dweller. . . . Opposites in nearly every way, Aria and Perry must accept each other to survive." (Publisher's note)

Rottman, S. L.

Out of the blue; written by S.L. Rottman. Peachtree Publishers 2009 297p $16.95

Grades: 6 7 8 9 **Fic**

1. Moving -- Fiction 2. Child abuse -- Fiction 3. Military bases -- Fiction

ISBN 978-1-56145-499-0; 1-56145-499-0

LC 2008052839

After moving to Minot, North Dakota, with his mother, the new female base commander, Air Force dependent Stu Ballentyne gradually becomes aware that something terrible is going on in his neighbor's house.

"The story offers both a realistic interpretation of teenage life on an Air Force base and the teen's feeling of powerlessness upon witnessing child abuse—both physical and verbal—in action." SLJ

Rowen, Michelle

Reign check. Walker 2010 292p (Demon princess) $16.99; pa $9.99

Grades: 7 8 9 10 **Fic**

1. School stories 2. Canada -- Fiction 3. Fairies -- Fiction 4. Demonology -- Fiction 5. Friendship -- Fiction

ISBN 978-0-8027-2093-1; 0-8027-2093-5; 978-0-8027-9549-6 pa; 0-8027-9549-8 pa

LC 2009028796

Sequel to: Reign or shine (2009)

Sixteen-year-old Nikki is again summoned to the Underworld to appear before the Demon Council, the king of the faerie realm enrolls at her small-town Canada high school to experience human life, and her mother begins dating one of her teachers.

"Another chilling, sometimes violent, romantic fantasy that moves from the mundane world to the Shadowlands to the dungeons of the Underground before Nikki can finish her Christmas shopping." Booklist

Reign or shine. Walker & Co. 2009 284p (Demon princess) $16.99; pa $9.99

Grades: 7 8 9 10 **Fic**

1. School stories 2. Canada -- Fiction 3. Moving -- Fiction 4. Demonology -- Fiction 5. Remarriage -- Fiction

ISBN 978-0-8027-8492-6; 0-8027-8492-5; 978-0-8027-9534-2 pa; 0-8027-9534-X pa

LC 2009000205

In small-town Canada after her mother's fourth marriage, sixteen-year-old Nikki learns that her long-lost father is king of the demons, a fact that threatens to destroy her newfound popularity and sense of belonging.

Rowen "skillfully balances a lighthearted teen voice with emotional maturity. . . . Nikki's engaging voice and

several intriguing secondary characters make this a winner."
Publ Wkly

Followed by: Reign check (2010)

Rowling, J. K.

★ **Harry** Potter and the Sorcerer's Stone; illustrations by Mary Grandpré. Arthur A. Levine Bks.
1998 309p il $22.99; pa $8.99

Grades: 4 5 6 7 8 9 10   **Fic**

1. Fantasy fiction 2. Witches -- Fiction
ISBN 0-590-35340-3; 0-590-35342-X pa
LC 97-39059

First published 1997 in the United Kingdom with title:
Harry Potter and the Philosopher's Stone

Rescued from the outrageous neglect of his aunt and uncle, a young boy with a great destiny proves his worth while
attending Hogwarts School for Witchcraft and Wizardry.

This "is a brilliantly imagined and beautifully written
fantasy." Booklist

Other titles in this series are:
Harry Potter and the Chamber of Secrets (1999)
Harry Potter and the Deathly Hallows (2007)
Harry Potter and Goblet of Fire (2000)
Harry Potter and the Half-Blood Prince (2005)
Harry Potter and the Order of the Phoenix (2003)
Harry Potter and the prisoner of Azkaban (1999)

Roy, Carter

The **blood** guard; Carter Roy. Two Lions 2014
288 p. (trade pbk. : alk. paper) $17.99

Grades: 5 6 7 8   **Fic**

1. Fantasy fiction 2. Adventure and adventurers 3.
Survival skills -- Fiction 4. Secret societies -- Fiction 5.
Adventure stories 6. Kidnapping -- Fiction
ISBN 1477847251; 9781477847251
LC 2013958330

In this book, by Carter Roy, "when thirteen-year-old
Ronan Truelove's . . . . mom snatches him from school, then
sets off on a high speed car chase, Ronan is shocked. His
. . . dad has been kidnapped? And the kidnappers are after
him, too? His mom, he quickly learns, is . . . a member of an
ancient order of knights, the Blood Guard, a sword-wielding
secret society sworn to protect the Pure—thirty-six noble
souls whose safety is crucial if the world as we know it is to
survive." (Publisher's note)

:Ronan thought he was just a regular kid leading a mostly
normal life until his parents disappeared. He teams up with
a former classmate and a two-hundred-year-old pickpocket
for a life or death struggle against evil. As Ronan embarks
on a hero's journey, familiar tropes of righting wrongs and
self-discovery persist but nevertheless remain entertaining
as mystery, mysticism, and action abound." Horn Book

Roy, James

Max Quigley; technically not a bully. written
and illustrated by James Roy. Houghton Mifflin Harcourt 2009 202p il $12.95

Grades: 4 5 6   **Fic**

1. Bullies -- Fiction 2. Friendship -- Fiction
ISBN 978-0-547-15263-9; 0-547-15263-9
LC 2008-36110

First published 2007 in Australia

After playing a prank on one of his "geeky" classmates,
sixth-grader Max Quigley's punishment is to be tutored
by him.

"Straightforward chronology, believable dialogue, self-contained chapters, and plenty of humor make this accessible to reluctant readers and particularly appealing to boys
who may see a bit of themselves in this realistic school
story." Booklist

Roy, Jennifer Rozines

★ **Mindblind**; [by] Jennifer Roy. Marshall Cavendish 2010 248p il $15.99

Grades: 7 8 9 10 11   **Fic**

1. Genius -- Fiction 2. Bands (Music) -- Fiction 3.
Asperger's syndrome -- Fiction
ISBN 978-0-7614-5716-9; 0-7614-5716-X
LC 2010-6966

Fourteen-year-old Nathaniel Clark, who has Asperger's
Syndrome, tries to prove that he is a genius by writing songs
for his rock band, so that he can become a member of the
prestigious Aldus Institute, the premier organization for the
profoundly gifted.

"Mature readers will empathize with Nathaniel as his
friends, Jessa and Cooper, do. This book is for teens who
appreciate a story about self-discovery, dreams, and friendship." Voice Youth Advocates

★ **Yellow** star; by Jennifer Roy. Marshall Cavendish 2006 227p $16.95

Grades: 5 6 7 8   **Fic**

1. Jews -- Fiction 2. Poland -- Fiction 3. Holocaust,
1933-1945 -- Fiction
ISBN 0-7614-5277-X; 978-0-7614-5277-5
LC 2005-50788

From 1939, when Syvia is four and a half years old, to
1945 when she has just turned ten, a Jewish girl and her family struggle to survive in Poland's Lodz ghetto during the
Nazi occupation.

"In a thoughtful, vividly descriptive, almost poetic
prose, Roy retells the true story of her Aunt Syvia's experiences. . . . This book is a standout in the genre of Holocaust
literature." SLJ

Rubens, Michael

Sons of the 613; Mike Rubens. Clarion Books
2012 305 p. (hardcover) $16.99

Grades: 7 8 9 10   **Fic**

1. Brothers -- Fiction 2. Bar mitzvah -- Fiction 3.
Masculinity -- Fiction 4. Schools -- Fiction 5.
Minnesota -- Fiction 6. Coming of age -- Fiction 7.
Junior high schools -- Fiction 8. Jews -- United States
-- Fiction 9. Family life -- Minnesota -- Fiction
ISBN 0547612168; 9780547612164
LC 2011044352

In this book by Michael Rubens, "Isaac's parents have
abandoned him for a trip to Italy in the final days before his
bar mitzvah. And even worse, his hotheaded older brother,
Josh, has been left in charge. . . . When Josh declares that
there is more to becoming a man than memorization, the
mad 'quest' begins for Isaac. . . . But when Isaac begins to
fall for Josh's girlfriend, Leslie, the challenges escalate from
bad to worse." (Publisher's note)

Ruby, Laura

Bad apple. HarperTeen 2009 247p $16.99; pa $8.99

Grades: 8 9 10 11 12   **Fic**

1. School stories 2. Bullies -- Fiction 3. Divorce -- Fiction 4. Teacher-student relationship -- Fiction

ISBN 978-0-06-124330-1; 0-06-124330-2; 978-0-06-124333-2 pa; 0-06-124333-7 pa

             LC 2009-1409

Tola Riley, a high school junior, struggles to tell the truth when she and her art teacher are accused of having an affair.

"Tola and her family are fascinating, quirky-yet-believable, and wholly likable. Ruby works in traditional fairy-tale elements . . . with wry humor." Booklist

Ruby, Lois

The **secret** of Laurel Oaks. Tom Doherty Associates 2008 282p $16.95

Grades: 6 7 8 9   **Fic**

1. Ghost stories 2. Slavery -- Fiction 3. Louisiana -- Fiction

ISBN 978-0-7653-1366-9; 0-7653-1366-9

             LC 2008-28395

While staying with her family in Louisiana's Laurel Oaks Plantation, purported to be one of the most haunted places in America, thirteen-year-old Lila is contacted by the ghost of a slave girl unjustly convicted of murder. Story inspired by the author's visit to the Myrtles Plantation in Louisiana.

"Ruby succeeds in writing a captivating story about a time long gone, portraying the horror of slavery effectively." Libr Media Connect

Shanghai shadows. Holiday House 2006 284p $16.95

Grades: 7 8 9 10   **Fic**

1. Jews -- Fiction 2. China -- Fiction 3. World War, 1939-1945 -- Fiction

ISBN 0-8234-1960-6; 978-0-8234-1960-9

             LC 2005-50342

From 1939 to 1945, a Jewish family struggles to survive in occupied China; young Ilse by remaining optimistic, her older brother by joining a resistance movement, her mother by maintaining connections to the past, and her father by playing the violin that had been his livelihood.

The author's "careful research, courageous characters, low-key descriptions of fear and misery, and understated examples of love, friendship, and courage will further readers' understanding and personalize the often-horrifying epoch." Booklist

Includes bibliographical references

Rue, Ginger

Brand new Emily; a novel. Tricycle Press 2009 240p $14.99

Grades: 7 8 9 10   **Fic**

1. School stories 2. Ohio -- Fiction 3. Poets -- Fiction 4. Publicity -- Fiction 5. Popularity -- Fiction

ISBN 978-1-58246-269-1; 1-58246-269-0

             LC 2008011357

Tired of being picked on by a trio of popular girls, fourteen-year-old poet Emily hires a major public relations firm to change her image and soon finds herself "re-branded" as Em, one of the most important teens not only in her middle school, but in celebrity magazines, as well.

"It's a smart premise, and besides having something pertinent to say about kindness, hubris and the perils of popularity, Rue also imparts insight into how celebrities are designed and marketed. . . . The material is so enjoyable that readers might not even notice that they've learned something." Kirkus

Ruiz Zafon, Carlos, 1964-

Marina; Carlos Ruiz Zafon; translated by Lucia Graves. Little, Brown & Co. 2014 336 p. (hardcover) $19

Grades: 8 9 10 11 12   **Fic**

1. Suspense fiction 2. Barcelona (Spain) -- Fiction 3. Love -- Fiction 4. Supernatural -- Fiction 5. Mystery and detective stories 6. Spain -- History -- 20th century -- Fiction

ISBN 0316044717; 9780316044714

             LC 2013016666

In this novel by Carlos Ruiz Zafón, "15-year-old Oscar Drai suddenly vanishes from his boarding school in the old quarter of Barcelona. For seven days and nights no one knows his whereabouts. . . . His story begins in the heart of old Barcelona when he meets Marina and her father German Blau, a portrait painter." (Publisher's note)

"Set in Barcelona, Spain from late 1979 to May 1980, this gothic novel centers around 15-year-old boarding school student Oscar Drai. Instead of studying during his free time, the teen explores the city, and one day ends up in an area that seems deserted. Drawn in by music coming from an old dilapidated house, Oscar is given a scare by the owner, an eccentric and haunted German artist...With elements of romance, mystery, and horror, none of them overwhelming the other, this complex volume that hints at Mary Shelley's Frankenstein manages to weave together three separate stories for a cohesive and eerie result." SLJ

The **Midnight** Palace; translated by Lucia Graves. Little, Brown 2011 298p $17.99

Grades: 7 8 9 10   **Fic**

1. India -- Fiction 2. Twins -- Fiction 3. Orphans -- Fiction 4. Siblings -- Fiction 5. Demonology -- Fiction 6. Calcutta (India) -- Fiction 7. Secret societies -- Fiction

ISBN 978-0-316-04473-8; 0-316-04473-3

             LC 2010-43131

Original Spanish edition 1994

When a mysterious threat reenters the lives of twins Ben and Sheere, separated as babies and reunited as teenagers in 1930s Calcutta, the siblings must confront an unspeakable terror, with the help of their secret society of fellow orphans.

"The sense of dread and mystery that pervades the story, and the themes of lost innocence and sacrifice keep readers turning the pages." SLJ

★ The **Prince** of Mist; translated by Lucia Graves. Little, Brown 2010 320p $17.99

Grades: 6 7 8 9 10   **Fic**

1. Dead -- Fiction 2. Magic -- Fiction 3. Siblings -- Fiction 4. Shipwrecks -- Fiction 5. Supernatural

-- Fiction 6. Europe -- History -- 1918-1945 -- Fiction
ISBN 978-0-316-04477-6; 0-316-04477-6
LC 2009-51256

In 1943, in a seaside town where their family has gone
to be safe from war, thirteen-year-old Max Carver and sister, fifteen-year-old Alicia, with new friend Roland, face off
against an evil magician who is striving to complete a bargain made before he died.

"Zafon is a master storyteller. From the first page, the
reader is drawn into the mystery and suspense that the young
people encounter when they move into the Fleischmann
house. . . . This book can be read and enjoyed by every level
of reader." Voice Youth Advocates

Rumley, Crickett

Never sit down in a hoopskirt and other things I
learned in Southern belle hell. Egmont USA 2011
296p pa $8.99

Grades: 8 9 10 11 12   Fic
1. Alabama -- Fiction 2. Etiquette -- Fiction 3.
Grandmothers -- Fiction 4. Beauty contests -- Fiction
5. Father-daughter relationship -- Fiction
ISBN 978-1-60684-131-0; 1-60684-131-9
LC 2010043617

After being ousted from yet another elite boarding
school, seventeen-year-old Jane returns to her Alabama
hometown, where her grandmother persuades her to enter
the Magnolia Maid pageant.

"Rumley works in nice points about shaking up the status quo while still keeping things light and bright." Booklist

Rundell, Katherine

★ **Cartwheeling** in thunderstorms; Katherine
Rundell. Simon & Schuster Books for Young Readers 2014 256 p. (hardcover) $16.99

Grades: 4 5 6 7 8   Fic
1. School stories 2. Bullies -- Fiction 3. Orphans --
Fiction 4. Boarding schools -- Fiction 5. Interpersonal
relations -- Fiction 6. Zimbabweans -- England --
London -- Fiction
ISBN 1442490616; 9781442490611; 9781442490635
LC 2013021053

Boston Globe-Horn Book Award: Fiction (2015)

In this middle grade novel by Katherine Rundell, illustrated by Melissa Castrillón, "Wilhelmina Silver's world is
golden. Living half-wild on an African farm with her horse,
her monkey, and her best friend, every day is beautiful. But
when her home is sold and Will is sent away to boarding
school in England, the world becomes impossibly difficult.
Lions and hyenas are nothing compared to packs of vicious
schoolgirls." (Publisher's note)

"Wilhelmina, daughter of William Silver, white foreman
of the Two Tree Hill Farm in Zimbabwe, leads a 'wildcat'
life. Her idyll ends abruptly and tragically with her father's
death from malaria, after which she's shipped off to boarding school in England. Rundell's finely drawn etchings of
the people in Will's sphere and rich descriptions of African
colonial farm life sprawl across the pages." Horn Book

Rooftoppers; by Katherine Rundell and illustrated by Terry Fan. Simon & Schuster Books for Young
Readers 2013 288 p. (hardcover) $16.99

Grades: 4 5 6 7   Fic
1. Orphans -- Fiction 2. Mother-daughter relationship
-- Fiction 3. Roofs -- Fiction 4. France -- Fiction 5.
Paris (France) -- Fiction 6. Missing persons -- Fiction
7. Homeless persons -- Fiction 8. Guardian and ward
-- Fiction
ISBN 1442490586; 9781442490581
LC 2012049469

In this book, by Katherine Rundell, "everyone thinks
that Sophie is an orphan. . . . Her guardian tells her it is
almost impossible that her mother is still alive. . . . When
the Welfare Agency writes to her guardian, threatening to
send Sophie to an orphanage, she takes matters into her own
hands and flees to Paris to look for her mother. . . . She meets
Matteo and his network of rooftoppers--urchins who live in
the hidden spaces above the city. Together they scour the city
in a search for Sophie's mother." (Publisher's note)

Runholt, Susan

Adventure at Simba Hill. Viking 2011 273p
$16.99

Grades: 5 6 7 8   Fic
1. Mystery fiction 2. Kenya -- Fiction 3. Africans
-- Fiction 4. Smuggling -- Fiction 5. Archeology --
Fiction 6. Friendship -- Fiction
ISBN 978-0-670-01201-5; 0-670-01201-7
LC 2010024533

When fourteen-year-old best friends Kari and Lucas
travel to an archaeological dig in Kenya with Kari's uncle
Geoff, they help expose a smuggling ring.

"Lighthearted and yet mostly based on logic, this outing
allows readers to get a taste of Africa's pleasures. . . . The
cast of suspects and rapidly made friends keeps the mood
frothy and the sinister actions nicely removed." Kirkus

The **mystery** of the third Lucretia. Viking Childrens Books 2008 288p $16.99; pa $6.99

Grades: 5 6 7 8   Fic
1. Mystery fiction 2. Art -- Fiction 3. Europe -- Fiction
4. Friendship -- Fiction
ISBN 978-0-670-06252-2; 0-670-06252-9; 978-0-14-
241338-8 pa; 0-14-241338-0 pa
LC 2007-24009

While traveling in London, Paris, and Amsterdam, fourteen-year-old best friends Kari and Lucas solve an international art forgery mystery.

"There are enough artistic details for fans of art mysteries and enough spying and fleeing for fans of detective
adventure." Bull Cent Child Books

Other titles about Kari and Lucas are:
Rescuing Seneca Crane (2009)
The adventure at Simba Hill (2011)

Rescuing Seneca Crane. Viking Childrens Books
2009 276p $16.99

Grades: 5 6 7 8   Fic
1. Mystery fiction 2. Scotland -- Fiction 3. Friendship
-- Fiction 4. Kidnapping -- Fiction
ISBN 978-0-670-06291-1; 0-670-06291-X
LC 2008037648

While accompanying her mother on a business trip to Scotland, fourteen-year-old Kari and her best friend Lucas attempt to solve a kidnapping mystery.

"Reluctant readers will enjoy the pacing, which neither rushes the mystery nor drags out the clues. The author skillfully weaves facts about Scottish culture and geography into the narrative." SLJ

Runyon, Brent

Surface tension; a novel in four summers. Alfred A. Knopf 2009 197p $16.99; lib bdg $19.99

Grades: 8 9 10 11   **Fic**

1. Vacations -- Fiction 2. Family life -- Fiction 3. New York (State) -- Fiction

ISBN 978-0-375-84446-1; 0-375-84446-5; 978-0-375-94446-8 lib bdg; 0-375-94446-X lib bdg

LC 2008-9193

During the summer vacations of his thirteenth through his sixteenth year at the family's lake cottage, Luke realizes that although some things stay the same over the years that many more change.

"With sensitivity and candor, Runyon reveals how life changes us all and how these unavoidable changes can be full of both turmoil and wonder." Kirkus

Rupp, Rebecca

After Eli; Rebecca Rupp. 1st ed. Candlewick 2012 245 p. (hardcover) $15.99; (ebook) $15.99

Grades: 4 5 6 7 8   **Fic**

1. Bildungsromans 2. Family -- Fiction 3. Brothers -- Fiction 4. Bereavement -- Fiction 5. Death -- Fiction 6. Books and reading -- Fiction 7. Interpersonal relations -- Fiction

ISBN 0763658103; 9780763658106; 9780763661946

LC 2011048344

In this book, "Daniel, a wry and thoughtful narrator, looks back on the summer when he was 14, three years after his older brother, Eli, died in Iraq at age 22." Daniel's "memories of larger-than-life Eli and his lingering anger about his death" are interwoven with "Daniel's day-to-day challenges, including his dysfunctional family . . .; his frustrations with his . . . friends; his attraction to Isabelle, a . . . newcomer to town; and his nascent friendship with school outcast Walter." (Publishers Weekly)

★ **Octavia** Boone's big questions about life, the universe, and everything. Candlewick Press 2010 185p $15.99

Grades: 5 6 7 8   **Fic**

1. School stories 2. Vermont -- Fiction 3. Religion -- Fiction 4. Family life -- Fiction 5. Christian life -- Fiction

ISBN 978-0-7636-4491-8; 0-7636-4491-9

LC 2009-47408

Seventh-grader Octavia puzzles over life's biggest questions when her mother seems to find the answers in a conservative Christian church, while her artist father believes the writings of Henry David Thoreau hold the key.

"This hopeful novel highlights the resilience of children and the courage of those who seek truth in a complicated world." Publ Wkly

Rush, Jennifer

Altered; by Jennifer Rush. 1st ed. Little, Brown and Co. 2013 336 p. (hardcover) $17.99

Grades: 7 8 9 10 11 12   **Fic**

1. Science fiction 2. Runaway teenagers -- Fiction 3. Memory -- Fiction 4. Identity -- Fiction 5. Runaways -- Fiction 6. Genetic engineering -- Fiction 7. Fathers and daughters -- Fiction

ISBN 0316197084; 9780316197083

LC 2012007545

This is the debut novel in a series from Jennifer Rush. Here, "homeschooled 18-year-old Anna Mason has a life ruled by secrecy. Her widower father works for a clandestine organization called the Branch, and four gorgeous genetically altered teenage boys live in the basement laboratory of their New York State farmhouse. . . . When the Branch tries to collect 'the units,' chaos erupts, and Sam, Anna, and the others take off on the run." (Publishers Weekly)

"[T]his debut's strengths--pacing and plot twists, especially--outweigh the deficits. Riveting." Kirkus

Russell, Christopher

Dogboy. Greenwillow Books 2006 259p $15.99; $15.99; lib bdg $16.89

Grades: 5 6 7 8   **Fic**

1. Dogs -- Fiction 2. Orphans -- Fiction 3. Middle Ages -- Fiction 4. Knights and knighthood -- Fiction 5. Hundred Years' War, 1339-1453 -- Fiction

ISBN 978-0-06-084116-4; 0-06-084116-8; 978-0-06-084117-1 lib bdg; 0-06-084117-6 lib bdg

LC 2005-08525

First published 2005 in the United Kingdom

In 1346, twelve-year-old Brind, an orphaned kennel boy raised with hunting dogs at an English manor, accompanies his master, along with half of the manor's prized mastiffs, to France, where he must fend for himself when both his master and the dogs are lost at the decisive battle of Crécy

"The action is fast-paced with narrow escapes at every turn and elements of dry humor at the most unlikely times." SLJ

Followed by: Hunted (2007)

Russell, Krista

Chasing the Nightbird. Peachtree 2011 200p $15.95

Grades: 5 6 7 8   **Fic**

1. Sailors -- Fiction 2. Slavery -- Fiction 3. Abolitionists -- Fiction 4. Massachusetts -- Fiction

ISBN 1561455970; 9781561455973

LC 2011002665

In 1851 New Bedford, Massachusetts, fourteen-year-old Cape Verdean sailor Lucky Valera is kidnapped by his estranged half-brother and forced to work in a mill, but while Lucky is plotting his escape he meets a former slave and a young Quaker girl who influence his plans.

"Without slowing the story's pace, Russell gives readers plenty to think about regarding the turbulent racial dynamics of the period—Lucky, who is dark-skinned yet free, initially sees little connection between his life and the plight of slaves. Strong-willed and goodhearted, Lucky is an especially vibrant hero in this multifaceted and suspenseful historical adventure." Publ Wkly

Russell, Randy

Dead rules. HarperTeen 2011 376p $16.99

Grades: 7 8 9 10   **Fic**

1. School stories 2. Dead -- Fiction 3. Future life -- Fiction 4. Supernatural -- Fiction

ISBN 978-0-06-19867-03; 0-06-19867-04

LC 2010032452

When high school junior Jana Webster dies suddenly, she finds herself in Dead School, where she faces choices that will determine when she, a Riser, will move on, but she strives to become a Slider instead, for the chance to be with the love of her life—even if it means killing him.

"Sarcastic quips and double entendres drive the story's humor, but it's the sensitivity of the supporting characters . . . that allows Jana (and readers) to see laughter within tragedy." Kirkus

Rutkoski, Marie

★ The **Cabinet** of Wonders; [by] Marie Rutkoski. Farrar Straus Giroux 2008 258p (The Kronos Chronicles) $16.95; pa $6.99

Grades: 5 6 7 8   **Fic**

1. Fantasy fiction 2. Magic -- Fiction 3. Gypsies -- Fiction 4. Princes -- Fiction

ISBN 978-0-374-31026-4; 0-374-31026-2; 978-0-312-60239-0 pa; 0-312-60239-1 pa

LC 2007037702

Twelve-year-old Petra, accompanied by her magical tin spider, goes to Prague hoping to retrieve the enchanted eyes the Prince of Bohemia took from her father, and is aided in her quest by a Roma boy and his sister.

"Add this heady mix of history and enchantment to the season's list of astonishingly accomplished first novels. . . . Infusions of folklore (and Rutkowski's embellishments of them) don't slow the fast plot but more deeply entrance readers." Publ Wkly

Other titles in this series are:

The Celestial Globe (2009)

The Jewel of the Kalderash (2011)

★ The **shadow** society; Marie Rutkoski. Farrar, Straus and Giroux 2012 408 p. $17.99

Grades: 7 8 9 10 11 12   **Fic**

1. Science fiction 2. Alternative histories 3. Supernatural -- Fiction 4. Schools -- Fiction 5. Identity -- Fiction 6. Illinois -- Fiction 7. High schools -- Fiction 8. Foster home care -- Fiction

ISBN 0374349053; 9780374349059

LC 2011033158

In this novel by Marie Rutkoski "Darcy Jones doesn't remember anything before the day she was abandoned as a child outside a Chicago firehouse. . . . But she couldn't have guessed that she comes from an alternate world where the Great Chicago Fire didn't happen and deadly creatures called Shades terrorize the human population. Memories begin to haunt Darcy when a new boy arrives at her high school, and he makes her feel both desire and desired in a way she hadn't thought possible." (Publisher's note)

★ The **winner's** curse; Marie Rutkoski. Farrar Straus & Giroux 2014 368 p. (The winner's trilogy) (hardcover) $17.99

Grades: 7 8 9 10 11 12   **Fic**

1. Love -- Fiction 2. Slavery -- Fiction 3. Imperialism -- Fiction

ISBN 0374384673; 9780374384678

LC 2013000312

In this book, by Marie Rutkoski, "winning what you want may cost you everything you love. As a general's daughter in a vast empire that revels in war and enslaves those it conquers, seventeen-year-old Kestrel has two choices: she can join the military or get married. But Kestrel has other intentions. One day, she is startled to find a kindred spirit in a young slave up for auction. Arin's eyes seem to defy everything and everyone. Following her instinct, Kestrel buys him." (Publisher's note)

"As 17-year-old Kestrel comes to know Arin, the Herrani slave she purchased on a whim, she puts both herself and him at risk. Arin, 19, also finds himself falling for this daughter of the Valorian general who conquered his homeland...Full-bodied characters explore issues of loyalty, class, and values (for example, arts versus military strengths), without sacrificing any of the relationship-related tension that is a hallmark of this kind of story. A tasty twist of an ending virtually locks readers in for subsequent entries in the series. Fans may want to revisit this one while they wait for future books; maybe get more than one copy? " (Booklist)

Ryan, Amy Kathleen

Flame; a Sky Chasers novel. Amy Kathleen Ryan. St. Martin's Griffin 2014 336 p. (Sky Chasers) (hardback) $18.99

Grades: 8 9 10 11 12   **Fic**

1. War stories 2. Airships -- Fiction 3. Science fiction

ISBN 0312621361; 9780312621360

LC 2013039416

In this novel, the conclusion to author Amy Kathleen Ryan's Sky Chasers series, "Waverly and the other members of the Empyrean have been scattered, and their home ship destroyed. Their mission to rescue their parents didn't go as planned, and now they're at an even greater disadvantage: trapped with their enemies on the New Horizon. Seth's situation is even worse. After setting out from the Empyrean on his own, with only a vague strategy to guide him, he is a fugitive aboard the New Horizon." (Publisher's note)

"When this meaty, harrowing conclusion to the Sky Chasers series opens, the inhabitants of the vessel Empyrean are fleeing their destroyed spacecraft to join their former enemies on board the New Horizon. Action begins immediately, and the story shifts mainly among the points of view of Waverly, Kieran and Seth...The pace is at times methodical, and much of the suspense comes from characters' and readers' uncertainty as to whom to trust. Stakes are high, however, and readers witness graphic (though generally not gory) violence and bodily harm as the three teens work to both overthrow and defend Pastor Anne Mather, the New Horizon's leader. It all comes to a head in a climax that is tense and viscerally frightening. Detailed and gripping, with a thorough and satisfying resolution." (Kirkus)

★ **Glow**. St. Martin's Griffin 2011 307p (Sky chasers) $17.99

Grades: 8 9 10 11 12   **Fic**
1. Science fiction
ISBN 978-0-312-59056-7; 0-312-59056-3
LC 2011020385

Part of the first generation to be conceived in deep space, fifteen-year-old Waverly is expected to marry young and have children to populate a new planet, but a violent betrayal by the dogmatic leader of their sister ship could have devastating consequences.

"The themes of survival, morality, religion, and power are well developed, and the characters are equally complex. The author has also created a unique and vivid outer-space setting that is exciting and easy to imagine." SLJ

Spark; a Sky chasers novel. Amy Kathleen Ryan. 1st ed. St. Martin's Press 2012 309 p. (hardcover) $17.99; (paperback) $9.99
Grades: 8 9 10 11 12   **Fic**
1. Mystery fiction 2. Friendship -- Fiction 3. Parent-child relationship -- Fiction 4. Science fiction
ISBN 0312621353; 9780312621353; 9781250014160; 9781250031952
LC 2012004631

Author Amy Kathleen Ryan's character "Waverly Marshall has endured and committed terrible acts aboard the 'New Horizon.' . . . [Kieran] delivers sermons designed to promote both unity and loyalty. . . . Meanwhile, Seth . . . escapes the brig under mysterious circumstances and discovers a major threat to the ship. As Waverly, Kieran, [and] Seth . . . work . . . to keep the peace, secure the ship and rescue their parents from the 'New Horizon,' . . . political and moral questions arise." (Kirkus Reviews)

Ryan, Carrie

The **map** to everywhere; by Carrie Ryan & John Parke Davis. Little, Brown & Co. 2014 448 p. illustrations (The map to everywhere) (hardcover) $17
Grades: 4 5 6 7   **Fic**
1. Fantasy fiction 2. Pirates -- Fiction 3. Fantasy 4. Maps -- Fiction 5. Magic -- Fiction 6. Wizards -- Fiction 7. Stealing -- Fiction 8. Adventure and adventurers -- Fiction
ISBN 031624077X; 9780316240772
LC 2013044752

In this juvenile novel, by Carrie Ryan and John Parke Davis, "to Master Thief Fin, an orphan from the murky pirate world of the Khaznot Quay, the Map is the key to finding his mother. To suburban schoolgirl Marrill, it's her only way home after getting stranded on the Pirate Stream, the magical waterway that connects every world in creation. With the help of a bumbling wizard and his crew, they must scour the many worlds of the Pirate Stream to gather the pieces of the Map to Everywhere." (Publisher's note)

"Two displaced young adventurers sail streams of raw magic from world to world in this vividly cast series opener. Convergent plotlines bring together Marrill, who impulsively climbs aboard the four-master that floats into view atop a shimmering mirage in an Arizona parking lot, and Fin, another world's scruffy orphan/thief who literally passes "out of sight, out of mind" with everyone he meets. Nearly everyone, that is: To his shock, Marrill actually remembers him when he's not in view. . . . Multifaceted characters, high

stakes, imaginative magic, and hints of hidden twists and complexities to come add up to a memorable start to a projected four-volume voyage." Kirkus

Ryan, Pam Muñoz

★ The **dreamer**; drawings by Peter Sís. Scholastic Press 2010 372p il $17.99
Grades: 4 5 6 7   **Fic**
1. Authors 2. Diplomats 3. Novelists 4. Novelist 5. Nobel laureates for peace 6. Nobel laureates for literature 7. Father-son relationship -- Fiction 8. Biography, Individual
ISBN 978-0-439-26970-4; 0-439-26970-9
Boston Globe-Horn Book Award honor book: Fiction (2010)

Neftali finds beauty and wonder everywhere. He loves to collect treasures, daydream, and write—pastimes his authoritarian father thinks are for fools. Against all odds, Neftali prevails against his father's cruelty and his own crippling shyness to become one of the most widely read poets in the world, Pablo Neruda.

"Ryan loads the narrative with vivid sensory details. And although it isn't poetry, it eloquently evokes the sensation of experiencing the world as someone who savors the rhythms of words and gets lost in the intricate surprises of nature. The neat squares of Sis' meticulously stippled illustrations, richly symbolic in their own right, complement and deepen the lyrical quality of the book." Booklist

★ **Echo**; by Pam Muñoz Ryan. Scholastic Press 2015 585 p. $19.99
Grades: 4 5 6 7 8   **Fic**
1. Music -- Fiction 2. Fate and fatalism -- Fiction 3. Harmonica -- Fiction 4. Family life -- Fiction 5. Germany -- History -- Fiction 6. California -- History -- Fiction 7. Pennsylvania -- History -- Fiction
ISBN 0439874025; 9780439874021
LC 2014021482

In this novel by Pam Muñoz Ryan, "lost and alone in a forbidden forest, Otto meets three mysterious sisters and suddenly finds himself entwined in a puzzling quest involving a prophecy, a promise, and a harmonica. Decades later, Friedrich in Germany, Mike in Pennsylvania, and Ivy in California each, in turn, become interwoven when the very same harmonica lands in their lives." (Publisher's note)

"The harmonica and the love of music serve as the unifying threads for these tales of young people who save the lives and spirits of their families and neighbors, each in a time marked by bigotry and violence. It's an ambitious device, but Ryan's storytelling prowess and vivid voice lead readers expertly through a hefty tome illuminated by layers of history, adventure, and the seemingly magical but ultimately very human spirit of music." Horn Book

Esperanza rising. Scholastic Press 2000 262p $15.95; pa $4.99
Grades: 5 6 7 8   **Fic**
1. California -- Fiction 2. Mexican Americans -- Fiction 3. Agricultural laborers -- Fiction
ISBN 0-439-12041-1; 0-439-12042-X pa
LC 00-24186

Esperanza and her mother are forced to leave their life of wealth and privilege in Mexico to go work in the labor camps of Southern California, where they must adapt to the harsh circumstances facing Mexican farm workers on the eve of the Great Depression

"Ryan writes movingly in clear, poetic language that children will sink into, and the [book] offers excellent opportunities for discussion and curriculum support." Booklist

Rylander, Chris

The **fourth** stall. Walden Pond Press 2011 314p $15.99

Grades: 4 5 6 7   **Fic**

1. School stories 2. Bullies -- Fiction 3. Friendship -- Fiction 4. Business enterprises -- Fiction

ISBN 978-0-06-199496-8; 0-06-199496-0

LC 2010016280

Sixth-graders Mac and Vince operate a business charging schoolmates for protection from bullies and for help to negotiate conflicts peacefully, with amazing challenges and results.

"Rylander mines a substantial amount of humor and heart from this combination hardboiled crime novel and middle-grade character piece. . . . A light and enjoyable caper." Publ Wkly

Rylant, Cynthia

★ A **fine** white dust. Simon & Schuster 2000 106p $25; pa $4.99

Grades: 5 6 7 8   **Fic**

1. Religion -- Fiction 2. Friendship -- Fiction 3. Family life -- Fiction

ISBN 978-0-689-84087-6; 0-689-84087-X; 978-1-4169-2769-3 pa; 1-4169-2769-7 pa

A reissue of the title first published 1986 by Bradbury Press

A Newbery Medal honor book, 1987

The visit of the traveling Preacher Man to his small North Carolina town gives new impetus to thirteen-year-old Peter's struggle to reconcile his own deeply felt religious belief with the beliefs and non-beliefs of his family and friends

"Blending humor and intense emotion with a poetic use of language, Cynthia Rylant has created a taut, finely drawn portrait of a boy's growth from seeking for belief, through seduction and betrayal, to a spiritual acceptance and a readiness 'for something whole.'" Horn Book

★ **God** got a dog; Cynthia Rylant; illustrated by Marla Frazee. 1st Beach Lane Books ed. Beach Lane Books 2013 48 p. ill. (hardcover) $17.99

Grades: 5 6 7 8   **Fic**

1. God -- Poetry 2. Picture books for children 3. Femininity of God -- Poetry 4. God -- Fiction 5. Novels in verse

ISBN 1442465182; 9781442465183

LC 2013005577

This book is an illustrated collection of poetry from Cynthia Rylant. A major theme is the multiplicity of God, which Maria Frazee's illustrations expand on, "depicting Him or Her as a black, tattooed nail artist; a middle-aged white woman eating by herself; a little dark-skinned boy on roller skates . . .; a bearded, dark-skinned dude playing poker with

Gabriel; a homeless black woman. An illustration appears opposite each poem." (Kirkus Reviews)

★ **Missing** May. Orchard Bks. 1992 89p hardcover o.p. pa $5.99

Grades: 5 6 7 8   **Fic**

1. Death -- Fiction 2. West Virginia -- Fiction

ISBN 0-531-05996-0; 0-439-61383-3 pa

LC 91-23303

Awarded the Newbery Medal, 1993

After the death of the beloved aunt who has raised her, twelve-year-old Summer and her uncle Ob leave their West Virginia trailer in search of the strength to go on living

"There is much to ponder here, from the meaning of life and death to the power of love. That it all succeeds is a tribute to a fine writer who brings to the task a natural grace of language, an earthly sense of humor, and a well-grounded sense of the spiritual." SLJ

Sachar, Louis

★ The **cardturner**; a novel about a king, a queen, and a joker. Delacorte Press 2010 336p $17.99; lib bdg $20.99

Grades: 8 9 10 11 12   **Fic**

1. Uncles -- Fiction 2. Family life -- Fiction 3. Bridge (Game) -- Fiction

ISBN 978-0-385-73662-6; 0-385-73662-2; 978-0-385-90619-7 lib bdg; 0-385-90619-6 lib bdg

LC 2009-27585

"Alton gets roped into serving as a card turner for his great-uncle, Lester Trapp, a bridge whizz who recently lost his eyesight. . . . To Alton's surprise, he becomes enamored of the game and begins to bond with his crusty uncle. . . . With dry, understated humor, Alton makes the intricacies of bridge accessible, while his relationships with and observations about family members and friends . . . form a portrait of a reflective teenager whose life is infinitely enriched by connections he never expected to make." Publ Wkly

★ **Holes**; [by] Louis Sachar. 10th anniversary ed.; Farrar, Straus and Giroux 2008 265p $18

Grades: 5 6 7 8   **Fic**

1. Friendship -- Fiction 2. Buried treasure -- Fiction 3. Homeless persons -- Fiction 4. Juvenile delinquency -- Fiction

ISBN 978-0-374-33266-2; 0-374-33266-5

LC 2007045430

A reissue of the title first published 1998. Includes additional information about the author and his Newbery acceptance speech

Awarded the Newbery Medal, 1999

As further evidence of his family's bad fortune which they attribute to a curse on a distant relative, Stanley Yelnats is sent to a hellish correctional camp in the Texas desert where he finds his first real friend, a treasure, and a new sense of himself

"This delightfully clever story is well-crafted and thought-provoking, with a bit of a folklore thrown in for good measure." Voice Youth Advocates

Small steps; [by] Louis Sachar. Delacorte Press 2006 257p $16.95; lib bdg $19.99

Grades: 5 6 7 8   **Fic**
1. Cerebral palsy -- Fiction 2. African Americans --
Fiction 3. Juvenile delinquency -- Fiction
ISBN 0-385-73314-3; 0-385-90333-2 lib bdg
LC 2005-09102
Sequel to Holes

Three years after being released from Camp Green Lake,
Armpit is trying hard to keep his life on track, but when his
old pal X-Ray shows up with a tempting plan to make some
easy money scalping concert tickets, Armpit reluctantly
goes along.

This "is a story of redemption, of the triumph of the
human spirit, of self-sacrifice, and of doing the right thing.
Sachar is a master storyteller who creates memorable
characters." SLJ

Saenz, Benjamin Alire
★ **He** forgot to say good-bye. Simon & Schuster
2008 321p $16.99
Grades: 8 9 10 11   **Fic**
1. Drug abuse -- Fiction 2. Mexican Americans --
Fiction
ISBN 978-1-4169-4963-3; 1-4169-4963-1
LC 2007-21959

Two teenaged boys with very different lives find that
they share a common bond—fathers they have never met
who left when they were small boys—and in spite of their
differences, they become close when they each need someone who understands.

"The affirming and hopeful ending is well-earned for the
characters and a great payoff for the reader. . . . Characters
are well-developed and complex. . . . Overall it is a strong
novel with broad teenage appeal." Voice Youth Advocates

Sage, Angie
Darke; illustrations by Mark Zug. Katherine Te-
gen Books 2011 641p il (Septimus Heap) $17.99;
lib bdg $18.89
Grades: 5 6 7 8   **Fic**
1. Fantasy fiction 2. Magic -- Fiction 3. Witchcraft
-- Fiction 4. Apprentices -- Fiction
ISBN 978-0-06-124242-7; 0-06-124242-X; 978-0-06-
124243-4 lib bdg; 0-06-124243-8 lib bdg
LC 2011010180

Apprentice Septimus Heap must enter the Darke to save
the Castle and the Wizard Tower from destruction, but he
needs the help of many to battle the spreading Darkenesse.

"Sage expertly weaves multiple new and continuing
plotlines together. An appendix ties up what loose ends it
can while leaving the door open for the conclusion. . . . A
memorable, edge-of-the-seat escapade that will enthrall confirmed fans and newbies alike." Kirkus

★ **Magyk**; Septimus Heap, book one. illustrations by Mark Zug. Katherine Tegen Books 2005
576p il $16.99; lib bdg $17.89; pa $7.99
Grades: 5 6 7 8   **Fic**
1. Fantasy fiction 2. Magic -- Fiction
ISBN 0-06-057731-2; 0-06-057732-0 lib bdg; 0-06-
057733-9 pa
LC 2003-28185

After learning that she is the Princess, Jenna is whisked
from her home and carried toward safety by the Extraordinary Wizard, those she always believed were her father and
brother, and a young guard known only as Boy 412, pursued
by agents of those who killed her mother ten years earlier.

"Youngsters will lose themselves happily in Sage's flu-
ent, charismatic storytelling, which enfolds supportive allies
and horrific enemies, abundant quirky details, and poignant
moments of self-discovery." Booklist
Other titles in this series are:
Flyte (2006)
Physik (2007)
Queste (2008)
Syren (2009)
Darke (2011)

The **Magykal** papers; illustrations by Mark Zug.
Katherine Tegen Books 2009 167p il (Septimus
Heap)
Grades: 5 6 7 8   **Fic**
1. Fantasy fiction 2. Magic -- Fiction 3. Princesses
-- Fiction
ISBN 0-06-170416-4; 978-0-06-170416-1
LC 2008027110

Purports to be a compilation of pamphlets, journals,
restaurant reviews, maps, historical information, and other
never-before-published papers from the world of the apprentice alchemist, Septimus Heap.

"Fans of Sage's saga will rejoice in the little pieces
if 'magyk' collected here. Beautifully rendered in full
color." SLJ

Pathfinder; Angie Sage; illustrations by Mark
Zug. Katherine Tegen Books, an imprint of Harper-
CollinsPublishers 2014 480 p. (Septimus Heap :
TodHunter moon) (hardback) $17.99
Grades: 5 6 7   **Fic**
1. Imaginary places 2. Magic -- Fiction 3. Fantasy 4.
Wizards -- Fiction 5. Kidnapping -- Fiction
ISBN 0062272454; 9780062272454
LC 2013051281

This novel by Angie Sage "tells the story of Alice Tod-
Hunter Moon, a young PathFinder who leaves her seaside
village in search of her friend Ferdie. Rumor has it that Ferdie has been taken by mysterious creatures called Garmin
under orders from the malevolent Lady." (Publisher's note)

"After Tod's father and village are kidnapped, she must
learn PathFinder Magyk and team up with Septimus to save
them. Fans of the Septimus Heap books will enjoy seeing
the old characters in this spinoff series, but the sheer number
of cameos bogs down the plot; new secondary characters are
flat, but Tod has a clear, relatable voice." Horn Book

Saint-Exupery, Antoine de
The **little** prince; written and illustrated by An-
toine de Saint-Exupery; translated from the French by
Richard Howard. Harcourt 2000 83p il $18; pa
$12
Grades: 4 5 6 7 8 9 10 11 12 Adult   **Fic**
1. Fantasy fiction 2. Princes -- Fiction 3. Air pilots

-- Fiction 4. Extraterrestrial beings -- Fiction
ISBN 0-15-202398-4; 0-15-601219-7 pa

LC 99-50439

A new translation of the title first published 1943 by
Reynal & Hitchcock.

"This many-dimensional fable of an airplane pilot who
has crashed in the desert is for readers of all ages. The pilot
comes upon the little prince soon after the crash. The prince
tells of his adventures on different planets and on Earth as he
attempts to learn about the universe in order to live peacefully on his own small planet. A spiritual quality enhances
the seemingly simple observations of the little prince." Shapiro. Fic for Youth. 3d edition

Saldaña, René

Dancing with the devil and other tales from beyond; Bailando con el diablo y otros cuentos del más
allá. by por René Saldaña, Jr.; Spanish translation by
traducción al español de Gabriela Baeza Ventura. Piñata Books 2012 81 p. (alk. paper) $9.95

Grades: 5 6 7 8 9   Fic
1. Short stories 2. Mexican Americans -- Fiction 3.
Spanish language materials -- Bilingual 4. Children's
stories, American -- Translations into Spanish
ISBN 1558857443; 9781558857445

LC 2012008729

Author Rene Saldaña Jr. presents a book of short stories.
"Lauro and Miguel run for their lives--with La Llorona's
cold breath on their necks-- after being caught smoking
cigarettes down by the river. There's Felipe, who's so determined to win back the Peñitas Grand Master Marble Champion title that he's willing to make a deal for a shooter with
a supernatural edge. And when Louie's leg swells up after he
cuts his toe playing with a knife, he can't help but wonder if
his mom's warning could be true." (Publisher's note)

Saldin, Erin

★ The **girls** of No Return. Arthur A. Levine
Books 2012 345p $17.99

Grades: 7 8 9 10   Fic
1. School stories 2. Idaho -- Fiction 3. Wilderness
areas -- Fiction
ISBN 978-0-545-31026-0; 0-545-31026-1; 978-0-545-
39253-2 e-book

LC 2011024214

A troubled sixteen-year-old girl attending a wilderness
school in the Idaho mountains must finally face the consequences of her complicated friendships with two of the other
girls at the school.

"Teen and adult characters that matter are complex
and intriguing. Saldin keeps readers intrigued by both
withholding information and sharing Lida's retrospective
thoughts without ever seeming manipulative. This debut
is richly rewarding and will linger for its subtle examination of human behavior and emotions-love, trust, guilt and
forgiveness." Kirkus

Salerni, Dianne K.

We hear the dead. Sourcebooks Fire 2010 422p
pa $9.99

Grades: 7 8 9 10   Fic
1. Mediums 2. Sisters -- Fiction 3. Spiritualism --

Fiction 4. New York (State) -- Fiction
ISBN 978-1-4022-3092-9; 1-4022-3092-3

The author "paints vivid scenes of life in upstate New
York during a time when exposed ankles were shocking and
the Underground Railroad offered a dangerous route to freedom for both conductors and slaves. Historical fiction at its
best." SLJ

Sales, Leila

Past perfect. Simon Pulse 2011 306p $16.99

Grades: 7 8 9 10   Fic
1. New England -- Fiction 2. Summer employment --
Fiction 3. Dating (Social customs) -- Fiction
ISBN 978-1-4424-0682-7; 1-4424-0682-8

LC 2011025811

"Chelsea is an appealing narrator with a sharp sense of
humor, and readers will tear through this novel to find out
whether she reunites with Ezra or gets together with Dan
from the rival museum. . . . This is a satisfying and fun
read." SLJ

This song will save your life; Leila Sales. Farrar
Straus & Giroux 2013 288 p. (hard) $17.99

Grades: 8 9 10 11 12   Fic
1. Bullies -- Fiction 2. Disc jockeys -- Fiction 3.
Schools -- Fiction 4. Suicide -- Fiction 5. Popularity
-- Fiction 6. High schools -- Fiction 7. Interpersonal
relations -- Fiction
ISBN 0374351384; 9780374351380

LC 2012050408

In this book, "Elise has endured a lifetime of social
isolation and bullying at school. Walking alone one night
soon after a halfhearted suicide attempt, the 16-year-old inadvertently ends up at an underground nightclub. There, an
aspiring musician befriends her, and she catches the eye of
Char, a cute DJ who agrees to teach her to mix music. But
as talented, driven Elise spends more nights sneaking out to
learn how to DJ (and kiss Char), her double life spins out of
control." (Publishers Weekly)

Salisbury, Graham

★ **Eyes** of the emperor. Wendy Lamb Books
2005 228p hardcover o.p. pa $6.99

Grades: 7 8 9 10   Fic
1. Japanese Americans -- Fiction 2. World War, 1939-
1945 -- Fiction
ISBN 0-385-72971-5; 0-440-22956-1 pa

LC 2004-15142

Following orders from the United States Army, several young Japanese American men train K-9 units to hunt
Asians during World War II.

"Based on the experiences of 26 Hawaiian-Americans
of Japanese ancestry, this novel tells an uncomfortable story.
Yet it tells of belief in honor, respect, and love of country."
Libr Media Connect

★ **House** of the red fish. Wendy Lamb Books
2006 291p $16.95; lib bdg $17.99

Grades: 6 7 8 9   Fic
1. Hawaii -- Fiction 2. Japanese Americans -- Fiction

3. World War, 1939-1945 -- Fiction
ISBN 0-385-73121-3; 0-385-90145-3 lib bdg
LC 2006-07544
Sequel to Under the blood-red sun (1994)

Over a year after Japan's attack on Pearl Harbor and the arrest of Tomi's father and grandfather, Tomi and his friends, battling anti-Japanese-American sentiment in Hawaii, try to find a way to salvage his father's sunken fishing boat.

"Many readers, even those who don't enjoy historical fiction, will like the portrayal of the work and the male camaraderie." Booklist

Lord of the deep. Delacorte Press 2001 182p hardcover o.p. pa $7.99
Grades: 5 6 7 8   **Fic**
1. Hawaii -- Fiction 2. Fishing -- Fiction 3. Stepfathers
-- Fiction
ISBN 0-385-72918-9; 0-440-22911-1 pa
LC 00-60280

Working for Bill, his stepfather, on a charter fishing boat in Hawaii teaches thirteen-year-old Mikey about fishing, and about taking risks, making sacrifices, and facing some of life's difficult choices

"With its vivid Hawaiian setting, this fine novel is a natural for book-discussion groups that enjoy pondering moral ambiguity. Its action-packed scenes will also lure in reluctant readers." SLJ

★ **Night** of the howling dogs; a novel. Wendy Lamb Books 2007 191p $16.99; lib bdg $19.99; pa $6.50
Grades: 5 6 7 8   **Fic**
1. Hawaii -- Fiction 2. Camping -- Fiction 3. Tsunamis
-- Fiction 4. Earthquakes -- Fiction 5. Boy Scouts of America -- Fiction 6. Survival after airplane accidents, shipwrecks, etc. -- Fiction
ISBN 978-0-385-73122-5; 978-0-385-90146-8 lib bdg; 978-0-440-23839-3 pa
LC 2007-07054

In 1975, eleven Boy Scouts, their leaders, and some new friends camping at Halape, Hawaii, find their survival skills put to the test when a massive earthquake strikes, followed by a tsunami.

This is a "vivid adventure. . . . Salisbury weaves Hawaiian legend into the modern-day narrative to create a haunting, unusual novel." Booklist

Under the blood-red sun. Delacorte Press 1994 246p hardcover o.p. pa $5.99
Grades: 5 6 7 8 9 10   **Fic**
1. Hawaii -- Fiction 2. Japanese Americans -- Fiction
3. World War, 1939-1945 -- Fiction 4. Pearl Harbor (Oahu, Hawaii), Attack on, 1941 -- Fiction
ISBN 0-385-32099-X; 0-440-41139-4 pa
LC 94-444

Tomikazu Nakaji's biggest concerns are baseball, homework, and a local bully, until life with his Japanese family in Hawaii changes drastically after the bombing of Pearl Harbor in December 1941

"Character development of major figures is good, the setting is warmly realized, and the pace of the story moves gently though inexorably forward." SLJ

Followed by: House of the red fish (2006)

Salisbury, Sandy, 1944-
Hunt for the bamboo rat; by Graham Salisbury. Wendy Lamb Books, an imprint of Random House Children's Books 2014 336 p. illustration (hardback) $16.99
Grades: 6 7 8 9 10   **Fic**
1. Spy stories 2. Japanese Americans -- Fiction 3. World War, 1939-1945 -- Fiction 4. Spies -- Fiction 5. Survival -- Fiction 6. Prisoners of war -- Fiction 7. World War, 1939-1945 -- Philippines -- Fiction 8. Philippines -- History -- Japanese occupation, 1942-1945 -- Fiction
ISBN 0375842667; 9780375842665; 9780375940705
LC 2014005743

This book by Graham Salisbury is set "in August 1941. . . . Seventeen-year-old Zenji Watanabe . . . is Nisei, speaks perfect English and Japanese, and is recruited by the U.S. Army as a special undercover intelligence agent working in Manila, code name: Bamboo Rat. It's a dangerous assignment to be in the Philippines on the eve of Japanese invasion and imminent American involvement. He's American, but looks Japanese, and soon finds himself caught in the middle." (Horn Book Magazine)

"Written in short, rapid-fire paragraphs that move the plot along at a brisk pace, the story will leave readers spellbound. A gripping saga of wartime survival. (maps, author's note, glossary, resources)" Kirkus

Saller, Carol Fisher
Eddie's war; [by] Carol Fisher Saller. Namelos 2011 ix, 194p $18.95
Grades: 5 6 7 8   **Fic**
1. Novels in verse 2. Brothers -- Fiction 3. Farm life -- Fiction 4. World War, 1939-1945 -- Fiction
ISBN 1-60898-108-8; 1-60898-109-6 pa; 978-1-60898-108-3; 978-1-60898-109-0 pa

"When we meet him in 1934, Eddie is five, Tom ten. In the next ten years the brothers develop friendships, discover family secrets, . . . and ponder the causes of European conflict . . . as well as the virulent prejudice rife in their own farming community. Tom's enlisting in 1943 unveils the real nature of war that has inspired the boys' games. Narrated by Eddie, these seventy-six vignettes are beautifully phrased and vividly revealing of character." Horn Book

Sanchez, Alex
★ **Bait**. Simon & Schuster Books for Young Readers 2009 239p $16.99
Grades: 7 8 9 10   **Fic**
1. Stepfathers -- Fiction 2. Mexican Americans -- Fiction 3. Child sexual abuse -- Fiction
ISBN 978-1-4169-3772-2; 1-4169-3772-2
LC 2008-38815

Diego keeps getting into trouble because of his explosive temper until he finally finds a probation officer who helps him get to the root of his anger so that he can stop running from his past.

"This groundbreaking novel brings to life an appealing young man who is neither totally a victim nor a victimizer, one who struggles to handle conflicts that derail many young lives. . . . High interest and accessible, this coming-of-age story belongs in every collection." SLJ

So hard to say; Alex Sanchez. 1st ed; Simon & Schuster Books for Young Readers 2004 230p $14.95

Grades: 6 7 8 9   **Fic**
   1. California -- Fiction 2. Homosexuality -- Fiction 3. Mexican Americans -- Fiction
   ISBN 0-689-86564-3
                  LC 2003-21128
Thirteen-year-old Xio, a Mexican American girl, and Frederick, who has just moved to California from Wisconsin, quickly become close friends, but when Xio starts thinking of Frederick as her boyfriend, he must confront his feelings of confusion and face the fear that he might be gay.

"Adventurous, multifaceted, funny, and unpredictably insightful, Sanchez's novel . . . gels well-rounded characterizations with the universal excitement of first love." SLJ

Sandell, Lisa Ann
   A **map** of the known world. Scholastic Press 2009 273p $16.99

Grades: 7 8 9 10   **Fic**
   1. School stories 2. Art -- Fiction 3. Bereavement -- Fiction 4. Family life -- Fiction
   ISBN 978-0-545-06970-0; 0-545-06970-X
                  LC 2008-50745
Devastated, along with her parents, by the death of her older brother and apprehensive about being a freshman in the same high school he attended, fourteen-year-old Cora finds unexpected solace in art.

Sandell's "fluid phrasing and choice of metaphors give her prose a quiet poetic ambience." Publ Wkly

Sanders, Scott Loring
   Gray baby; a novel. Houghton Mifflin Harcourt 2009 321p $17

Grades: 7 8 9 10   **Fic**
   1. Homicide -- Fiction 2. Virginia -- Fiction 3. Alcoholism -- Fiction 4. Country life -- Fiction 5. Single parent family -- Fiction 6. Racially mixed people -- Fiction
   ISBN 978-0-547-07661-4; 0-547-07661-4
                  LC 2008-36810
Clifton has grown up in rural Virginia with the memory of his African American father being beaten to death by policemen, causing his white mother to slip into alcoholism and depression, but after befriending an old man who listens to his problems, Clifton finally feels less alone in the world.

"Unflinching and raw, the story, set in the late 1980s, explores the destructiveness of racism." Horn Book Guide

Sanders, Shelly
   Rachel's secret. Second Story Press 2012 248 p. $12.95

Grades: 6 7 8 9 10   **Fic**
   1. Historical fiction 2. Antisemitism -- Fiction 3. Judaism -- Relations -- Christianity -- Fiction
   ISBN 1926920376; 9781926920375
This book follows "14-year-old Rachel . . . living under Russian rule in Kishinev in 1903, [she] was one of the last

people to see her Christian friend Mikhail alive when she witnessed his murder at the hands of disgruntled relatives who stood to lose out on an inheritance. His death is blamed on Jews, however, and a vicious pogrom is unleashed on the city. Rachel's anguish about knowing what happened stems from a justified fear of not being believed if she comes forward, thus evoking more turmoil. She also harbors guilt that her somewhat risky friendship with a non-Jewish boy somehow triggered the calamity. . . . [W]hile Rachel does act courageously and courtroom justice is meted out, virulent anti-Semitism still rules the day." (Booklist)

Sanderson, Brandon
   ★ **Alcatraz** versus the evil Librarians. Scholastic Press 2007 308p $16.99; pa $6.99

Grades: 4 5 6 7   **Fic**
   1. Fantasy fiction 2. Librarians -- Fiction 3. Grandfathers -- Fiction
   ISBN 0-439-92550-9; 978-0-439-92550-1; 0-439-92552-5 pa; 978-0-439-92552-5 pa
                  LC 2006-38378
On his thirteenth birthday, foster child Alcatraz Smedry receives a bag of sand which is immediately stolen by the evil Librarians who are trying to take over the world. Soon, Alcatraz is introduced to his grandfather and his own special talent, and told that he must use it to save civilization.

"Readers whose sense of humor runs toward the subversive will be instantly captivated. . . . This nutty novel isn't for everyone, but it's also sure to win passionate fans." Publ Wkly

Other titles about Alcatraz are:
Alcatraz versus the scrivener's bones (2008)
Alcatraz versus the Knights of Crystallia (2009)
Alcatraz versus the shattered lens (2010)

   Alcatraz versus the Knights of Crystallia. Scholastic Press 2009 299p $16.99

Grades: 4 5 6 7   **Fic**
   1. Fantasy fiction 2. Mothers -- Fiction 3. Librarians -- Fiction
   ISBN 0-439-92555-X; 978-0-439-92555-6
When Alcatraz and Grandpa Smedry make a pilgrimage to the Free Kingdom city of Crystallia, they are shocked to find the city under seige by the Evil Librarians—led by Alcatraz's own mother.

"Offbeat humor, a budding romance, plenty of magic, creative world building, smart references to science fiction luminaries, clever word play, and good action scenes make this one a strong choice." Voice Youth Advocates

   Alcatraz versus the Scrivener's Bones. Scholastic Press 2008 322p

Grades: 4 5 6 7   **Fic**
   1. Fantasy fiction 2. Librarians -- Fiction 3. Grandfathers -- Fiction
   ISBN 0-439-92553-3; 978-0-439-92553-2
                  LC 2007039985
This is a sequel to Alcatraz Versus the Evil Librarians (2007). Thirteen-year-old Alcatraz Smedry and his companions track Al's father and grandfather in the Great Library of Alexandria, where they are confronted by un-

dead, soul-stealing wraiths. "Intermediate, middle school.". (Horn Book)

"Sanderson's second middle grade fantasy is every bit as clever, fast-paced, and original as Alcatraz Versus the Evil Librarians." Voice Youth Advocates

Alcatraz versus the shattered lens. Scholastic Press 2010 292p $17.99

Grades: 4 5 6 7   **Fic**

1. Fantasy fiction 2. Librarians -- Fiction

ISBN 0-439-92557-6; 978-0-439-92557-0

When a hero is needed to save the doomed kingdom of Mokia from the evil Librarians, thirteen-year-old Alcatraz Smedry, whose family talents include getting lost and breaking things, answers the call.

The **Rithmatist**; Brandon Sanderson. Tor Teen 2013 384 p. ill. (hardcover) $17.99

Grades: 7 8 9 10   **Fic**

1. Fantasy fiction 2. Magic -- Fiction 3. Fantasy

ISBN 0765320320; 9780765320322

LC 2012043417

In this young adult fantasy novel, by Brandon Sanderson, "Joel wants to be a Rithmatist. Chosen by the Master in a mysterious inception ceremony, Rithmatists have the power to infuse life into two-dimensional figures known as Chalklings. Rithmatists are humanity's only defense against the Wild Chalklings--merciless creatures that leave mangled corpses in their wake. Having nearly overrun the territory of Nebrask, the Wild Chalklings now threaten all of the American Isles." (Publisher's note)

Sandler, Karen

Rebellion; Karen Sandler. First edition Tu Books 2014 396 p. map (Tankborn) (hardcover) $19.95

Grades: 7 8 9 10   **Fic**

1. Science fiction 2. Terrorism -- Fiction 3. Genetic engineering -- Fiction 4. Kidnapping -- Fiction

ISBN 9781600609848; 1600609848

LC 2014002775

Sequel to: Awakening

In this young adult science fiction novel by Karen Sandler, part of the Tankborn Trilogy series, "Kayla is a GEN--a genetically engineered nonhuman--in a world torn apart by castes separating GENs from 'real' humans. In the wake of a devastating bomb blast, Kayla finds herself at the headquarters of the organization that planted the bomb--and many others like it in GEN food warehouses and homes." (Publisher's note)

"Sandler tackles caste systems, slavery and terrorism (including its muddled logic) head-on. . . . With rebellions, ideological questions and a nonwhite, not-entirely-heterosexual cast, this series is a strong addition to the genre." Kirkus

Tankborn. Tu Books 2011 373p map $17.95

Grades: 7 8 9 10   **Fic**

1. Science fiction 2. Genetic engineering -- Fiction

ISBN 978-1-60060-662-5; 1-60060-662-8

LC 2011014589

Kayla and Mishalla, two genetically engineered nonhuman slaves (GENs), fall in love with higher-status boys,

discover deep secrets about the creation of GENs, and in the process find out what it means to be human.

"Sandler has created a fascinating dystopian world. . . . The author's speculative vision of the darker side of future possibilities in genetic engineering and mind control is both chilling and thought-provoking." SLJ

Saunders, Kate

★ **Beswitched**. Delacorte Press 2011 244p $16.99

Grades: 4 5 6 7   **Fic**

1. School stories 2. Magic -- Fiction 3. Time travel -- Fiction 4. Great Britain -- Fiction

ISBN 978-0-385-74075-3

LC 2011000747

First published 2010 in the United Kingdom

On her way, reluctantly, to a boarding school in present-day England, Flora suddenly finds herself in 1935, the new girl at St. Winifred's, having been summoned via a magic spell by her new dormitory mates.

"This absorbing novel . . . features a dimensional, delightful protagonist, whose personality and growth ring true. . . . Along with the entertaining magical elements, the universal themes of self-discovery and looking beyond appearances combine into a wholly engaging and enjoyable read." Booklist

The **Whizz** Pop Chocolate Shop; Kate Saunders. 1st ed. Delacorte Press 2013 293 p. (hardcover) $16.99

Grades: 5 6 7 8   **Fic**

1. Chocolate -- Fiction 2. Fantasy fiction 3. Cats -- Fiction 4. Magic -- Fiction 5. Twins -- Fiction 6. England -- Fiction 7. Immortality -- Fiction 8. London (England) -- Fiction 9. Brothers and sisters -- Fiction 10. Adventure and adventurers -- Fiction

ISBN 0385743017; 9780385743013

LC 2011053081

In this children's story, by Kate Saunders, "the family of eleven-year-old twins Oz and Lily have inherited [a house], together with the mysterious shop downstairs. Long ago, the shop's famous chocolate-makers . . . were clever sorcerers. Now evil villains are hunting for the secret of their greatest recipe. . . . This magic chocolate [has] the ability to destroy the world. . . . It's up to them to stop the villains and keep the magical chocolate recipe out of harm's way." (Publisher's note)

Scaletta, Kurtis

Mamba Point. Alfred A. Knopf 2010 268p il $16.99; lib bdg $19.99

Grades: 5 6 7 8   **Fic**

1. Fear -- Fiction 2. Snakes -- Fiction 3. Liberia -- Fiction

ISBN 978-0-375-86180-2; 0-375-86180-7; 978-0-375-96180-9 lib bdg; 0-375-96180-1 lib bdg

LC 2009-22084

After moving with his family to Liberia, twelve-year-old Linus discovers that he has a mystical connection with the black mamba, one of the deadliest snakes in Africa, which he is told will give him some of the snake's characteristics.

Includes facts about the author's experiences as a thirteen-year-old American living in Liberia in 1982

Scaletta "has created an appealing, well-written protagonist whose everyday and extraordinary experiences . . . change his life in unexpected, positive ways. . . . The engaging first-person narrative and array of diversely drawn characters further enliven the novel." Booklist

Mudville. Alfred A. Knopf 2009 265p $16.99; lib bdg $19.99; pa $7.99

Grades: 5 6 7 8   **Fic**

1. Rain -- Fiction 2. Baseball -- Fiction 3. Minnesota -- Fiction 4. Family life -- Fiction 5. Dakota Indians -- Fiction 6. Foster home care -- Fiction
ISBN 978-0-375-85579-5; 0-375-85579-3; 978-0-375-95579-2 lib bdg; 0-375-95579-8 lib bdg; 978-0-375-84472-0 pa; 0-375-84472-4 pa

LC 2008000166

For twenty-two years, since a fateful baseball game against their rival town, it has rained in Moundville, so when the rain finally stops, twelve-year-old Roy, his friends, and foster brother Sturgis dare to face the curse and form a team

The author "balances perceptive explorations of personal and domestic issues perfectly with fine baseball talk and . . . absorbing play-by-play." SLJ

Scalzi, John

Fuzzy nation. Tor 2011 301p $24.99

Grades: 8 9 10   **Fic**

1. Science fiction 2. Space colonies -- Fiction 3. Life on other planets -- Fiction
ISBN 978-0-7653-2854-0; 0-7653-2854-2

LC 2010038178

Jack Holloway, prospecting on Zara XXIII for ZaraCorp, finds an immensely valuable stream of sunstone. But when he forwards footage of the planet's catlike, native "fuzzies" to a biologist friend who believes the "fuzzies" are sentient-hired company thugs, murder, and arson soon follow to protect ZaraCorp's mining interests

"Readers drawn to books with themes related to ethics, ecology, and science will appreciate this smart novel." Voice Youth Advocates

Scanlon, Liz Garton

The **great** good summer; Liz Garton Scanlon. Beach Lane Books 2015 224 p. (hardcover) $16.99

Grades: 4 5 6 7   **Fic**

1. Summer -- Fiction 2. Friendship -- Fiction 3. Runaway children -- Fiction 4. Runaways -- Fiction 5. Bus travel -- Fiction 6. Friendship -- Fiction 7. Christian life -- Fiction 8. Mothers and daughters -- Fiction
ISBN 1481411470; 9781481411479; 9781481411486

LC 2014014988

In this children's story, by Liz Garton Scanlon, "Ivy and Paul are both having a crummy summer. . . . Ivy's mama hasn't been herself since the spring, when wildfires destroyed everything. . . . Meanwhile, Paul is sad because NASA's space shuttle program is being shut down and now he will never be able to become an astronaut. . . . The two become an unlikely pair when they hatch a plan to find Mama and say goodbye to the space shuttle." (School Library Journal)

Scarrow, Alex

Day of the predator. Walker Books for Young Readers 2011 404p (TimeRiders) $16.99

Grades: 7 8 9 10   **Fic**

1. Science fiction 2. Time travel -- Fiction
ISBN 978-0-8027-2296-6; 0-8027-2296-2

LC 2010040987

Sequel to: TimeRiders (2010)

With teens Maddy, Liam, and Sal on their first solo assignment for a secret agency, Liam is sent back in time to prevent the murder of the father of time travel by a terrorist group, but due to a nuclear accident, he ends up in the late cretaceous period where the biggest threat is not from the legendary tyrannosaur.

"Readers will be intrigued, puzzled—and ready for the next one." Kirkus

TimeRiders. Walker & Co. 2010 405p $16.99

Grades: 7 8 9 10   **Fic**

1. Science fiction 2. Time travel -- Fiction 3. Environmental protection -- Fiction 4. September 11 terrorist attacks, 2001 -- Fiction
ISBN 978-0-8027-2172-3; 0-8027-2172-9

LC 2009-53166

Rescued from imminent death, teens Maddy, Liam, and Sal join forces in 2001 Manhattan to correct changes in history made by other time travelers, using a "time bubble" surrounding the attack on the Twin Towers to hide their journeys.

"The characters are expertly developed, each displaying vulnerabilities and quirks that make them memorable as individuals. . . . This is a brilliantly paced, fascinating look at the ways in which one seemingly small change can ripple out to—literally—the end of the world." Bull Cent Child Books

Another title in this series is:
Day of the predator (2011)

Scheibe, Lindsey

Riptide; one summer, endless possibilities. Lindsey Scheibe. 1st ed. Flux 2013 277 p. (paperback) $9.99

Grades: 7 8 9 10 11 12   **Fic**

1. Surfing -- Fiction 2. Teenage girls -- Fiction 3. Friendship -- Fiction 4. Child abuse -- Fiction 5. Best friends -- Fiction 6. San Diego (Calif.) -- Fiction 7. Dating (Social customs) -- Fiction
ISBN 0738735949; 9780738735948

LC 2012048951

In this novel, by Lindsey Scheibe, "signing up for her first surf competition, Grace has just one summer to train and impress the university scouts who will be judging the comp. But summer is about more than just big waves. As romances ignite and her feelings for Ford threaten to reach the point of no return, Grace must face the biggest challenges of her life." (Publisher's note)

Schindler, Holly

Playing hurt. Flux 2011 303p pa $9.95

Grades: 7 8 9 10   **Fic**

1. Love stories 2. Resorts -- Fiction 3. Minnesota --

Fiction 4. Loss (Psychology) -- Fiction
ISBN 978-0-7387-2287-0; 0-7387-2287-1

LC 2010-44173

Chelsea Keyes, a high school basketball star whose promising career has been cut short by a terrible accident on the court, and Clint Morgan, a nineteen-year-old ex-hockey player who gave up his sport following a game-related tragedy, meet at a Minnesota lake resort and find themselves drawn together by the losses they have suffered.

"Both heartbreaking and thrilling, the emotional journey that Clint and Chelsea embark on together is more than a heady romance; the characters are realistically drawn, and the book does not shy away from the reality of the characters' experiences: anger and grief mixed with desire and yearning. The book speaks to personal struggles and triumphs and the ability of the human spirit to heal." Voice Youth Advocates

Schlitz, Laura Amy

★ A **drowned** maiden's hair; a melodrama.
Candlewick Press 2006 389p $15.99

Grades: 5 6 7 8 **Fic**

1. Orphans -- Fiction 2. Spiritualism -- Fiction
ISBN 978-0-7636-2930-4; 0-7636-2930-8

LC 2006-49056

At the Barbary Asylum for Female Orphans, eleven-year-old Maud is adopted by three spinster sisters moonlighting as mediums who take her home and reveal to her the role she will play in their seances.

"Filled with heavy atmosphere and suspense, this story recreates life in early-20th-century New England. . . . Maud is a charismatic, three-dimensional character." SLJ

★ **Splendors** and glooms; Laura Amy Schlitz.
Candlewick 2012 384 p. (reinforced trade ed.)
$17.99

Grades: 4 5 6 7 **Fic**

1. Mystery fiction 2. Orphans -- Fiction 3. Kidnapping -- Fiction 4. Puppets and puppet plays -- Fiction 5. Puppets -- Fiction 6. Witches -- Fiction 7. Blessing and cursing -- Fiction 8. London (England) -- History -- 19th century -- Fiction 9. Great Britain -- History -- Victoria, 1837-1901 -- Fiction
ISBN 0763653802; 9780763653804

LC 2011048366

John Newbery Honor Book (2013)

In this book by Laura Amy Schlitz "Clara Wintermute . . . invites . . . the master puppeteer, Gaspare Grisini, . . . to entertain at her birthday party. . . . When Clara vanishes that night, suspicion of kidnapping falls upon the puppeteer and, by association, Lizzie Rose and Parsefall. As they seek to puzzle out Clara's whereabouts, Lizzie and Parse uncover Grisini's criminal past." (Publisher's note)

Schmatz, Pat

★ **Bluefish**. Candlewick Press 2011 226p
$15.99

Grades: 5 6 7 8 **Fic**

1. School stories 2. Literacy -- Fiction 3. Teachers -- Fiction
ISBN 978-0-7636-5334-7; 0-7636-5334-9

LC 2010044815

"A cast of richly developed characters peoples this work of contemporary fiction, told in the third person from Travis' point of view, with first-person vignettes from Velveeta's perspective peppered throughout. . . . A story rife with unusual honesty and hope." Kirkus

"Travis is missing his old home in the country, and he's missing his old hound, Rosco. Now there's just the cramped place he shares with his well-meaning but alcoholic grandpa, a new school, and the dreaded routine of passing when he's called on to read out loud. But that's before Travis meets Mr. McQueen, who doesn't take "pass" for an answer--a rare teacher whose savvy persistence has Travis slowly unlocking a book on the natural world. And it's before Travis is noticed by Velveeta, a girl whose wry banter and colorful scarves belie some hard secrets of her own." (Publisher's Note)

Schmid, Susan Maupin

Lost time. Philomel Books 2008 169p $16.99

Grades: 6 7 8 9 **Fic**

1. Science fiction 2. Missing persons -- Fiction
ISBN 978-0-399-24460-5; 0-399-24460-3

LC 2007-42095

Violynne, the twelve-year-old daughter of missing archaeologists on the planet Lindos, must solve the puzzle of her parents' disappearance before the dictatorial Arbiter captures her and forces her to do his bidding.

"Lively, descriptive prose incorporates mystery, action-adventure, and sci-fi elements, including exotic beings, landscapes, and devices. . . . [An] enjoyable, suspenseful read." Booklist

Schmidt, Gary D.

★ **Lizzie** Bright and the Buckminster boy. Clarion Books 2004 219p $15; pa $6.99

Grades: 7 8 9 10 **Fic**

1. Maine -- Fiction 2. Race relations -- Fiction
ISBN 0-618-43929-3; 0-553-49495-3 pa

LC 2003-20967

A Newbery Medal honor book, 2005

In 1911, Turner Buckminster hates his new home of Phippsburg, Maine, but things improve when he meets Lizzie Bright Griffin, a girl from a poor, nearby island community founded by former slaves that the town fathers—and Turner's—want to change into a tourist spot

"Although the story is hauntingly sad, there is much humor, too. Schmidt's writing is infused with feeling and rich in imagery. With fully developed, memorable characters and a fascinating, little-known piece of history, this novel will leave a powerful impression on readers." SLJ

★ **Okay** for now. Clarion Books 2011 360p
il $16.99

Grades: 4 5 6 7 **Fic**

1. Moving -- Fiction 2. New York (State) -- Fiction 3. City and town life -- Fiction
ISBN 978-0-547-15260-8; 0-547-15260-4

LC 2010942981

"It's 1968. The Vietnam War and Apollo 11 are in the background, and . . . Doug Swieteck starts a new life in tiny Marysville, N.Y. . . . He may have moved away, but his cruel father and abusive brothers are still with him. . . . This is

Schmidt's best novel yet—darker than The Wednesday Wars and written with more restraint, but with the same expert attention to voice, character and big ideas." Kirkus

★ **Trouble**. Clarion Books 2008 297p $16

Grades: 6 7 8 9 10 **Fic**

1. Death -- Fiction 2. Prejudices -- Fiction 3. Family life -- Fiction 4. Traffic accidents -- Fiction 5. Cambodian Americans -- Fiction

ISBN 978-0-618-92766-1; 0-618-92766-2

LC 2007-40104

Fourteen-year-old Henry, wishing to honor his brother Franklin's dying wish, sets out to hike Maine's Mount Katahdin with his best friend and dog, but fate adds another companion—the Cambodian refugee accused of fatally injuring Franklin—and reveals troubles that predate the accident.

"Schmidt creates a rich and credible world peopled with fully developed characters who have a lot of complex reckoning to do. . . . [The author's prose] is flawless, and Henry's odyssey of growth and understanding is pitch-perfect and deeply satisfying." Bull Cent Child Books

★ The **Wednesday** wars. Clarion Books 2007 264p pa $6.99; $16

Grades: 5 6 7 8 **Fic**

1. Poets 2. Authors 3. Dramatists 4. School stories

ISBN 054723760X; 0618724834; 9780547237602; 9780618724833

LC 2006-23660

A Newbery Medal honor book, 2008

During the 1967 school year, on Wednesday afternoons when all his classmates go to either Catechism or Hebrew school, seventh-grader Holling Hoodhound stays in Mrs. Baker's classroom where they read the plays of William Shakespeare and Holling learns something of value about the world he lives in. "Grades five to seven." (Bull Cent Child Books)

"The serious issues are leavened with ample humor, and the supporting cast . . . is fully dimensional. Best of all is the hero." Publ Wkly

Schneider, Robyn

Knightley Academy; by Violet Haberdasher. Aladdin 2010 469p $15.99

Grades: 5 6 7 8 **Fic**

1. School stories 2. Orphans -- Fiction 3. Knights and knighthood -- Fiction

ISBN 978-1-4169-9143-4; 1-4169-9143-3

LC 2009-23443

In an alternate Victorian England, fourteen-year-old orphan Henry Grim, a maltreated servant at an exclusive school for the "sons of Gentry and Quality," begins a new life when he unexpectedly becomes the first commoner to be accepted at Knightley Academy, a prestigious boarding school for knights.

"Robyn Schneider . . . writing as the pseudonymous Haberdasher, delivers a cute novel that balances its simple plot with a solid lead character, witty dialogue, and a jaunty narrative voice. . . . The nebulous historical setting and focus on military training and chivalry are a welcome change of pace from fictional academies that revolve around magic." Publ Wkly

Followed by: The secret prince (2011)

The **secret** prince; [by] Violet Haberdasher. Aladdin 2011 503p $16.99

Grades: 5 6 7 8 **Fic**

1. School stories 2. Orphans -- Fiction 3. Secret societies -- Fiction 4. Knights and knighthood -- Fiction

ISBN 978-1-4169-9145-8; 1-4169-9145-X

LC 2010038855

Sequel to: Knightley Academy (2010)

Fourteen-year-old orphan Henry Grim's schooling at the prestigious Knightley Academy continues, as he and some friends discover an old classroom filled with forgotten weapons which lead them into a dangerous adventure.

"Though some of the past events can be gleaned from this book, it's more enjoyable for those who have read Knightley Academy. . . . The fast-moving plotline in this installment is wrapped up nicely, but enough is left hanging and the characters are interesting enough to make readers eagerly anticipate the next in the series." SLJ

Schraff, Anne E.

A **boy** called Twister; [by] Anne Schraff. Saddleback Educational 2010 180p (Urban underground) pa $8.95

Grades: 6 7 8 9 10 **Fic**

1. Texas -- Fiction 2. Moving -- Fiction 3. Fathers -- Fiction 4. Prisoners -- Fiction 5. California -- Fiction 6. Track athletics -- Fiction

ISBN 978-1-61651-002-2 pa; 1-61651-002-1 pa

"After his beloved mother dies, Kevin, 16, moves from Texas to his grandparents' home in California. He quickly settles in and makes new friends, begins a romance, stars on the track team, and confronts the school bully, Marco. Throughout it all, though, he keeps the secret that his dad was sent to prison for second-degree murder and died in a prison riot when Kevin was 6. . . . This small, fast-paced paperback will grab even reluctant readers with the suspenseful story, cool dialogue, and sports action, which never distracts from Kevin's personal struggle." Booklist

Schreck, Karen

While he was away; Karen Schreck. Sourcebooks Fire 2012 249 p. $8.99

Grades: 7 8 9 10 **Fic**

1. Love stories 2. Loneliness -- Fiction 3. Iraq War, 2003-2011 -- Fiction

ISBN 140226402X; 9781402264023

This book follows a couple, Penna and David, as David "leaves for a stint in Iraq. . . . Penna is anxious and devastated, but eventually she finds ways to cope. . . . In Iraq, David struggles with the mind-numbing work of patrols and the terror that interrupts it, and he focuses on an orphanage for Iraqi refugee children as a way to be useful. . . . Paralleling Penna's story is her discovery of a grandmother who lost her first husband in World War II." (Kirkus Reviews)

"With realistic characters and interesting dialogue, While He Was Away is both insightful and tragic." VOYA

Schrefer, Eliot

The **deadly** sister. Scholastic Press 2010 310p $17.99

Grades: 8 9 10 11 12   **Fic**
1. Mystery fiction 2. Sisters -- Fiction 3. Homicide
-- Fiction
ISBN 978-0-545-16574-7; 0-545-16574-1
LC 2010-281733

Abby Goodwin has always covered for her sister, Maya,
but now Maya has been accused of murder, and Abby's not
sure she'll be able to cover for her sister anymore. Abby
helps Maya escape. But when Abby begins investigating
the death, she find that you can't trust anyone, not even the
people you think you know.

"Well-drawn characters, realistic dialogue, and suspenseful twists and turns add to the appeal. Teens crave
mystery, and this book will suit them just fine." SLJ

★ **Endangered**; Eliot Schrefer. Scholastic Press
2012 264 p. (reinforced) $17.99
Grades: 7 8 9 10 11 12   **Fic**
1. Animal sanctuaries -- Fiction 2. Wildlife conservation
-- Fiction 3. Congo (Democratic Republic) -- Fiction
4. Apes -- Fiction 5. Bonobo -- Fiction 6. Divorce
-- Fiction 7. Wildlife rescue -- Fiction 8. Racially
mixed people -- Fiction 9. Blacks -- Congo (Democratic
Republic) -- Fiction 10. Children of divorced parents
-- Fiction
ISBN 0545165768; 9780545165761
LC 2012030877

This book by Eliot Schrefer was a 2012 National Book
Award Finalist for Young People's Literature. "When one
girl has to follow her mother to her sanctuary for bonobos,
she's not thrilled to be there. It's her mother's passion, and
she'd rather have nothing to do with it. But when revolution
breaks out and their sanctuary is attacked, she must rescue
the bonobos and hide in the jungle. Together, they will fight
to keep safe, to eat, and to survive." (Publisher's note)

★ **Threatened**; Eliot Schrefer. Scholastic Press
2014 288 p. map (jacketed hardcover) $17.99
Grades: 7 8 9 10 11 12   **Fic**
1. Orphans -- Fiction 2. Chimpanzees -- Fiction
3. Animal rescue -- Fiction 4. Gabon -- Fiction 5.
Adventure stories 6. Wildlife rescue -- Fiction 7.
Orphans -- Gabon -- Fiction
ISBN 0545551439; 9780545551434
LC 2013018599

National Book Award Shortlist: Young People's Literature (2014)

In this juvenile story, by Eliot Schrefer, "Luc and Prof
head into the rough, dangerous jungle in order to study the
elusive chimpanzees. There, Luc finally finds a new family-
-and must act when that family comes under attack. . . . [It] is
the story of a boy fleeing his present, a man fleeing his past,
and a trio of chimpanzees who are struggling not to flee at
all." (Publisher's note)

"After the death of his mother and sister, Luc is left in the
hands of a moneylender, Monsieur Tatagani. One of many
orphans forced to do Tatagani's bidding, Luc has found a
way to be useful and earn a few coins wiping glasses in a
bar in Gabon...There are times when Luc's voice as an uneducated orphan adolescent seems vivid and real, at other
times less so. Still, the valor and soul of Luc is captivating. Fascinating and sure to lead to discussion." (School
Library Journal)

Schreiber, Ellen
Vampire kisses. Katherine Tegen Books 2003
197p $15.99; lib bdg $16.89
Grades: 7 8 9 10   **Fic**
1. Vampires -- Fiction
ISBN 0-06-009334-X; 0-06-009335-8 lib bdg
LC 2002-155506

Sixteen-year-old Raven, an outcast who always wears
black and hopes to become a vampire some day, falls in love
with the mysterious new boy in town, eager to find out if he
can make her dreams come true

"Schreiber uses a careful balance of humor, irony, pathos, and romance." Booklist

Other titles in this series are:
Vampire kisses 2: Kissing coffins (2005)
Vampire kisses 3: Vampireville (2006)
Vampire kisses 4: Dance with a vampire (2007)
Vampire kisses 5: The Coffin Club (2008)
Vampire kisses 6: Royal Blood (2009)
Vampire kisses 7: Love bites (2010)
Vampire kisses 8: Cryptic cravings (2011)

Schreiber, Joe
Game over, Pete Watson; by Joe Schreiber.
Houghton Mifflin Harcourt 2014 224 p. (hardback)
$16.99
Grades: 4 5 6 7   **Fic**
1. Humorous fiction 2. Spies -- Fiction 3. Video
games -- Fiction 4. Father-son relationship -- Fiction
5. Humorous stories
ISBN 0544157567; 9780544157569
LC 2013024335

In this book, by Joe Schreiber, "after he sells a vintage
console of his dad's to the neighborhood exterminator,
[Pete's] dad gets kidnapped before his eyes. Pete discovers
that his father is a CIA agent and is now trapped in the gaming system, which also doubles as a database for government
secrets. Aided by his geeky ex-best friend Wesley and Wesley's attractive older sister, Pete must stop the supervillain .
. . by going into the game himself." (Bulletin of the Center
for Children's Books)

"When talented gamer Pete Watson sells a dated video-
game console to get cash for the newest Brawl-A-Thon release, he unknowingly gets his father kidnapped and puts
United States security at risk. With rapid-fire plot twists,
slapstick comedy, and interactive illustrations complete
with an "eight-bit" Pete animated through the page turns,
this light read champions video-game history and skills."
Horn Book

Schroder, Monika
The **dog** in the wood. Front Street 2009 163p
$17.95
Grades: 6 7 8 9   **Fic**
1. Russians -- Fiction 2. Family life -- Fiction 3.
Political prisoners -- Fiction 4. World War, 1939-1945
-- Fiction 5. Germany -- History -- 1933-1945 -- Fiction
ISBN 978-1-59078-701-4; 1-59078-701-3
LC 2009-04970

As World War II draws to an end, Russian soldiers occupy Schwartz, Germany, bringing both friendship and hardship to the family of ten-year-old Fritz, whose grandfather

was a Nazi sympathizer, eventually forcing them to leave their farm, then arresting Fritz's mother and her hired hand.

"The action in this important addition of WWII literature will grab readers, and Schröder's story is an excellent, authentic portrait of children in war." Booklist

My brother's shadow. Farrar Straus Giroux 2011 217p $16.99

Grades: 6 7 8 9 10   **Fic**

1. Germany -- Fiction 2. Journalism -- Fiction 3. Family life -- Fiction 4. Political activists -- Fiction 5. World War, 1914-1918 -- Fiction

ISBN 978-0-374-35122-9; 0-374-35122-8

LC 2010033107

In 1918 Berlin, Germany, sixteen-year-old Moritz struggles to do what is right on his newspaper job, in his relationship with his mother and sister who are outspoken socialists, and with his brother, who returns from the war physically and emotionally scarred.

"In this nuanced and realistic work of historical fiction, Schröder . . . immerses readers in her setting with meticulous details and dynamic characters that contribute to a palpable sense of tension." Publ Wkly

Saraswati's way. Farrar Straus Giroux 2010 233p $15.99

Grades: 5 6 7 8   **Fic**

1. India -- Fiction 2. Education -- Fiction 3. Mathematics -- Fiction

ISBN 978-0-374-36411-3; 0-374-36411-7

LC 2009-37286

Leaving his village in rural India to find a better education, mathematically gifted, twelve-year-old Akash ends up at the New Delhi train station, where he relies on Saraswati, the Hindu goddess of knowledge, to guide him as he negotiates life on the street, resists the temptations of easy money, and learns whom he can trust.

"With skillfully integrated cultural details . . . and a fully realized child's story, Schröder presents a view, sobering and inspiring, of remarkably resilient young people surviving poverty without losing themselves." Booklist

Schroeder, Lisa

Chasing Brooklyn. Simon Pulse 2010 412p $15.99

Grades: 7 8 9 10   **Fic**

1. Novels in verse 2. Dreams -- Fiction 3. Bereavement -- Fiction

ISBN 978-1-4169-9168-7; 1-4169-9168-9

LC 2009-19442

As teenagers Brooklyn and Nico work to help each other recover from the deaths of Brooklyn's boyfriend—Nico's brother Lucca—and their friend Gabe, the two begin to rediscover their passion for life, and a newly blossoming passion for one another.

"Chasing Brooklyn is told in a verse format that enables the author to cut right to the emotional quick. The short sentences and minimal dialogue keep the focus on the pain and fear of the two main characters. . . . While the wrenching impact will leave readers raw, the ultimately hopeful ending is comforting. A quick read, but one with substance." SLJ

My secret guide to Paris; by Lisa Schroeder. First edition Scholastic Press 2015 216 p. (alk. paper) $16.99

Grades: 4 5 6   **Fic**

1. Bereavement -- Fiction 2. Family life -- Fiction 3. Grandmothers -- Fiction 4. Paris (France) -- Fiction 5. Grandparent-grandchild relationship -- Fiction 6. Grief -- Fiction 7. France -- Fiction 8. Families 9. Bereavement 10. Mothers and daughters -- Fiction 11. Family life -- France -- Paris -- Fiction 12. Grandparent and child -- Fiction

ISBN 0545708087; 9780545708081

LC 2014017073

In this book, by Lisa Schroeder, "Nora loves everything about Paris. . . . Of course, she's never actually been there -- she's only visited through her Grandma Sylvia's stories. And just when they've finally planned a trip together, Grandma Sylvia is suddenly gone. . . . She misses her grandmother terribly, but she still wants to see the city they both loved. So when Nora finds letters and a Paris treasure map among her Grandma Sylvia's things, she dares to dream again." (Publisher's note)

"The bittersweet circumstances of the Paris trip are offset by strong elements of wish fulfillment, including gowns and a fancy fashion show. This is a sweet, reassuring contemporary read about handling grief and reconnecting with family." Booklist

Schumacher, Julie

★ **Black** box; a novel. Delacorte Press 2008 168p $15.99; lib bdg $18.99

Grades: 8 9 10 11 12   **Fic**

1. School stories 2. Sisters -- Fiction 3. Family life -- Fiction 4. Depression (Psychology) -- Fiction

ISBN 978-0-385-73542-1; 0-385-73542-1; 978-0-385-90523-7 lib bdg; 0-385-90523-8 lib bdg

LC 2007-45774

When her sixteen-year-old sister is hospitalized for depression and her parents want to keep it a secret, fourteen-year-old Elena tries to cope with her own anxiety and feelings of guilt that she is determined to conceal from outsiders.

"The writing is spare, direct, and honest. Written in the first person, this is a readable, ultimately uplifting book about a difficult subject." SLJ

Schwab, Victoria

The **Near** Witch. Hyperion Books 2011 282p $16.99

Grades: 7 8 9 10   **Fic**

1. Witches -- Fiction 2. Villages -- Fiction 3. Supernatural -- Fiction

ISBN 978-1-4231-3787-0; 1-4231-3787-6

LC 2010036289

Sixteen-year-old Lexi, who lives on an enchanted moor at the edge of the village of Near, must solve the mystery when, the day after a mysterious boy appears in town, children start disappearing.

"Part fairy tale, part legend with a little romance, this well-written mystery will capture the attention of teens." SLJ

Schwabach, Karen

The **storm** before Atlanta. Random House 2010 307p $16.99; lib bdg $19.99

Grades: 5 6 7 8   **Fic**

1. Freedom -- Fiction 2. Slavery -- Fiction 3. Soldiers -- Fiction 4. Runaway children -- Fiction 5. United States -- History -- 1861-1865, Civil War -- Fiction

ISBN 978-0-375-85866-6; 0-375-85866-0; 978-0-375-95866-3 lib bdg; 0-375-95866-5 lib bdg

LC 2010014514

In 1863 northwestern Georgia, an unlikely alliance forms between ten-year-old New York drummer boy Jeremy, fourteen-year-old Confederate Charlie, and runaway slave Dulcie as they learn truths about the Civil War, slavery, and freedom.

"Richly detailed and well paced, the story provides both well-developed characters and plenty of suspense and gore. For those who like to know the facts behind historical fiction, the author provides historical notes and selected sources. An appealing Civil War title for readers with strong stomachs." Kirkus

Schwartz, Ellen

Cellular; written by Ellen Schwartz. Orca Book Publishers 2010 115p (Orca soundings) pa $9.95

Grades: 7 8 9 10   **Fic**

1. Leukemia -- Fiction 2. Friendship -- Fiction

ISBN 978-1-55469-296-5; 1-55469-296-2

When Brendan is diagnosed with leukemia, his life is turned upside down. With smothering family, and distant friends, all seems hopeless until he meets Lark, terminally ill, and yet full of life.

"In this emotional entry in the Orca Soundings series, Lark's sweetness and wisdom spin out on a trajectory that readers just know will not end happily for her, even though Brendan realizes she has touched his life mightily." Booklist

Stealing home. Tundra Books 2006 217p pa $8.95

Grades: 5 6 7 8   **Fic**

1. Jews -- Fiction 2. Orphans -- Fiction 3. Family life -- Fiction 4. Racially mixed people -- Fiction

ISBN 978-0-88776-765-4 pa; 0-88776-765-6 pa

"Joey, an orphaned, mixed-race 10-year-old isn't the only one who has to make adjustments after he's taken in by Jewish relatives he never knew he had. Wondering why his mother never told him about her side of the family, Joey moves to Brooklyn—to find a warm welcome from Aunt Frieda, an instant ally in baseball-loving cousin Bobbie, and a decidedly cold shoulder from his grandfather. . . . Keenly felt internal conflicts, lightened by some sparky banter, put this more than a cut above the average." Booklist

Schwartz, Virginia Frances

Send one angel down. Holiday House 2000 163p $15.95 **Fic**

1. Cousins -- Fiction 2. Slavery -- Fiction 3. African Americans -- Fiction 4. Racially mixed people -- Fiction

ISBN 0-8234-1484-1

LC 99-52818

Abram, a young slave tries to hide the horrors of slavery from his younger cousin Eliza, a light-skinned slave who is the daughter of the plantation owner

"Schwartz's well-developed characters are full of humanity and personality, and the story vividly acknowledges the sustaining power of music . . . in the lives of the slaves. This is a profoundly moving tale that is ultimately hopeful but never glosses over the horrific treatment of slaves." Booklist

Scott, Elaine

Secrets of the Cirque Medrano. Charlesbridge 2008 216p lib bdg $15.95

Grades: 4 5 6 7   **Fic**

1. Artists 2. Painters 3. Circus -- Fiction 4. Orphans -- Fiction 5. Restaurants -- Fiction 6. Paris (France) -- Fiction

ISBN 978-1-57091-712-7 lib bdg; 1-57091-712-4 lib bdg

LC 2007-2329

In the Paris village of Montmartre in 1904, fourteen-year-old Brigitte works long hours in her aunt's cafe, where she serves such regular customers as the young artist Pablo Picasso, encounters Russian revolutionaries, and longs to attend the exciting circus nearby. Includes author's note on the Picasso painting "Family of Saltimbanques"

This "places an interesting historical moment within the grasp of middle-schoolers." Kirkus

Scott, Elizabeth

Perfect you. Simon Pulse 2008 304p pa $9.99

Grades: 7 8 9 10   **Fic**

1. School stories 2. Friendship -- Fiction 3. Family life -- Fiction

ISBN 978-1-4169-5355-5 pa; 1-4169-5355-8 pa

LC 2007-929324

"Kate's father quit his job and is now living his dream by selling infomercial vitamins at a mall kiosk. The teen's college-graduate brother is living on the couch, her mother is working two jobs, and her friend Anna isn't talking to her now that Anna has lost weight and become popular. Making Kate's life completely miserable, her overbearing grandmother has moved in, and Will, the boy Kate tries to pretend she doesn't like because of their contentious history, is constantly making approaches. . . . Scott does a good job portraying a teen who is simultaneously self-centered and sympathetic. . . . Supporting characters are well fleshed out, and the ending, while encouraging, isn't all sunshine and roses, making it believable as well as hopeful." SLJ

Stealing Heaven. HarperTeen 2008 307p $16.99; lib bdg $17.89; pa $8.99

Grades: 7 8 9 10   **Fic**

1. Thieves -- Fiction 2. Mother-daughter relationship -- Fiction

ISBN 978-0-06-112280-4; 0-06-112280-7; 978-0-06-112281-1 lib bdg; 0-06-112281-5 lib bdg; 978-0-06-112282-8 pa; 0-06-112282-3 pa

Eighteen-year-old Dani grows weary of her life as a thief when she and her mother move to a town where Dani feels like she can put down roots.

"Witty dialogue gives a new perspective full of hope to YAs who feel trapped between family and friends." KLIATT

Scott, Kieran, 1974-

Geek magnet; a novel in five acts. G.P. Putnam's Sons 2008 308p $16.99

Grades: 7 8 9 10   **Fic**

1. School stories 2. Theater -- Fiction 3. Dating (Social customs) -- Fiction

ISBN 978-0-399-24760-6; 0-399-24760-2

LC 2007-28707

Seventeen-year-old KJ Miller is determined to lose the label of "geek magnet" and get the guy of her dreams, all while stage managing the high school musical, with the help of the most popular girl in school.

"An enjoyable, touching read about self-discovery with a hopeful ending that avoids too-neat resolutions." Booklist

The **princess** & the pauper; [by] Kate Brian. Simon & Schuster Bks. for Young Readers 2003 266p hardcover o.p. pa $8.99

Grades: 7 8 9 10   **Fic**

1. Princesses -- Fiction 2. Los Angeles (Calif.) -- Fiction

ISBN 0-689-86173-7; 1-4169-5369-8 pa

LC 2003-7380

When sixteen-year-old Julia, of Los Angeles, and sixteen-year-old Princess Carina, of Vineland, switch places, Julia dances at the ball with the incredible Markus and Carina escapes rigid protocol to spend time with a rock star

"Although the plot is pure fairy tale, the humor is incisive, the characters of the two girls are well drawn, and the touch of sweet, G-rated romance will thrill the intended audience." Booklist

This is so not happening; Kieran Scott. Simon & Schuster BFYR. 2012 315 p. (hardcover) $16.99

Grades: 7 8 9 10   **Fic**

1. Love stories 2. Teenage parents -- Fiction 3. Dating (Social customs) -- Fiction 4. Babies -- Fiction 5. Schools -- Fiction 6. New Jersey -- Fiction 7. High schools -- Fiction 8. Social classes -- Fiction 9. Teenage fathers -- Fiction 10. Teenage mothers -- Fiction 11. Family life -- New Jersey -- Fiction

ISBN 1416999558; 9781416999553

LC 2011041612

In this book, the third in a series, "constantly thwarted lovers Ally and Jake finally establish a firm boyfriend-girlfriend relationship during their senior year in high school. . . Ally learns that her former best friend Chloe is pregnant and saying that Jake is the father. Because the brief encounter between the two occurred outside of their formal relationship, Ally decides to forgive Jake and stick with him, even as he becomes ever more obsessed with the baby." (Kirkus Reviews)

Scott, Michael

★ The **alchemyst**. Delacorte Press 2007 375p (The secrets of the immortal Nicholas Flammel) $16.99; lib bdg $19.99

Grades: 7 8 9 10   **Fic**

1. Magicians 2. Mathematicians 3. Alchemists 4. Astrologers 5. Biographers 6. Magic -- Fiction 7. Twins -- Fiction 8. Alchemy -- Fiction 9. Writers on science 10. Siblings -- Fiction 11. San Francisco (Calif.) -- Fiction

ISBN 978-0-385-73357-1; 0-385-73357-7; 978-0-385-90372-1 lib bdg; 0-385-90372-3 lib bdg

LC 2006-24417

While working at pleasant but mundane summer jobs in San Francisco, fifteen-year-old twins, Sophie and Josh, suddenly find themselves caught up in the deadly, centuries-old struggle between rival alchemists, Nicholas Flamel and John Dee, over the possession of an ancient and powerful book holding the secret formulas for alchemy and everlasting life.

"Scott uses a gigantic canvas for this riveting fantasy. . . . A fabulous read." SLJ

Other titles in this series are:

The magician (2008)

The sorceress (2009)

The necromancer (2010)

The warlock (2011)

The **enchantress**; Michael Scott. Delacorte Press 2012 517 p. $18.99

Grades: 7 8 9 10   **Fic**

1. Atlantis -- Fiction 2. Monsters -- Fiction 3. Time travel -- Fiction 4. Flamel, Nicolas, d. 1418 -- Fiction 5. Magic -- Fiction 6. Twins -- Fiction 7. Alchemists -- Fiction 8. Supernatural -- Fiction 9. Brothers and sisters -- Fiction

ISBN 0385735359; 9780385735353

LC 2012006497

In this book, the final installment of the "Secrets of the Immortal Nicholas Flamel" series, "Nicholas Flamel and his beloved wife, Perenelle, are making a final stand to save San Francisco from an attack of monsters large and small, launched from Alcatraz Island by Quetzalcoatl. Twins Josh (Gold) and Sophie (Silver) are being staged to take power from Aten and become rulers of an overthrown Danu Talis 10,000 years earlier." (Booklist)

"[Scott] fully fleshes out his main characters in their final roles, realistically and sometimes surprisingly melding their lives, their deaths, and their futures. This is a powerful and tidy conclusion to [the] series." Booklist

Scott, Mindi

Freefall. Simon Pulse 2010 315p pa $7.99

Grades: 8 9 10 11 12   **Fic**

1. Alcoholism -- Fiction 2. Bereavement -- Fiction 3. Rock musicians -- Fiction

ISBN 978-1-4424-0278-2; 1-4424-0278-4

LC 2010-12663

Seth, a bass guitar player in a teen rock band, deals with alcoholism, his best friend's death, and first love.

"Seth's character arc is fully realized, without the burden of too much introspection or weighty insight to bog down the pace of the narrative. . . . This is a solid exploration of what you can and can't do to help your friends, built on top of an engaging story of boy meets girl." Bull Cent Child Books

Scotto, Michael

Postcards from Pismo; Michael Scotto; [edited by] Ashley Mortimer. Midlandia Press 2012 180 p. (paperback) $10.99

Grades: 4 5 6   **Fic**

1. Afghan War, 2001- -- Fiction 2. Filipino Americans -- Fiction 3. Military personnel -- United States -- Correspondence -- Fiction

ISBN 0983724369; 9780983724360

LC 2011943050

In this book, a "class assignment blossoms into friendship as a fourth-grade (later fifth-) Californian showers a young soldier stationed in Afghanistan with letters, e-mail messages and postcards. [Michael] Scotto supplies only chatty Felix's side of the continuing correspondence. . . . Felix queries his pen pal about what soldiers do while detailing his own interests, teachers, town, hard-working Filipino American parents (and their reactions when his restless big brother enlists)." (Kirkus)

Scrimger, Richard

Me & death; an afterlife adventure. Tundra Books 2010 187p pa $12.95

Grades: 7 8 9 10   **Fic**

1. Death -- Fiction 2. Future life -- Fiction

ISBN 978-0-88776-796-8 pa; 0-88776-796-6 pa

"Jim isn't an easy guy to like. . . . While he is chasing another kid, he falls in front of an oncoming car. So begins his epic journey into the afterlife, in which he is shown scenes from his past by three different ghosts, all of whom have a key to his future in the real world. . . . Scrimger creates unpredictable, sad, and authentic scenes that enliven the story. . . . Scrimger's novel is a difficult, compelling read that taps into teens' fascination with death, as well as the line between good and bad behavior." Booklist

Sedgwick, Marcus

★ My swordhand is singing. Wendy Lamb Books 2007 205p hardcover o.p. pa $6.99

Grades: 7 8 9 10   **Fic**

1. Horror fiction 2. Gypsies -- Fiction 3. Vampires -- Fiction 4. Supernatural -- Fiction

ISBN 978-0-375-84689-2; 978-0-375-84690-8 pa

LC 2007-07051

In the dangerous dark of winter in an Eastern European village during the early seventeenth century, Peter learns from a gypsy girl that the Shadow Queen is behind the recent murders and reanimations, and his father's secret past may hold the key to stopping her.

"Sedgwick writes a compellingly fresh vampire story, combining elements from ancient myths and legends to create a believable and frightening tale." Voice Youth Advocates

★ Revolver. Roaring Brook Press 2010 204p $16.99

Grades: 7 8 9 10   **Fic**

1. Death -- Fiction 2. Siblings -- Fiction 3. Arctic regions -- Fiction 4. Alaska -- Gold discoveries -- Fiction

ISBN 978-1-59643-592-6; 1-59643-592-5

First published 2009 in the United Kingdom

A Michael L. Printz honor book, 2011

In an isolated cabin, fourteen-year-old Sig is alone with a corpse: his father, who has fallen through the ice and frozen to death only hours earlier. Then comes a stranger claiming that Sig's father owes him a share of a horde of stolen gold. Sig's only protection is a loaded Colt revolver hidden in the cabin's storeroom.

"Tight plotting and a wealth of moral concerns—good versus evil; faith, love, and hope; the presence of God; survival in a bleak landscape; trusting the lessons parents teach—make this a memorable tale." Horn Book

★ She is not invisible; Marcus Sedgwick. Roaring Brook Press 2014 224 p. (hardback) $16.99

Grades: 7 8 9 10 11 12   **Fic**

1. Mystery fiction 2. Blind -- Fiction 3. Missing persons -- Fiction 4. Brothers and sisters -- Fiction 5. Fathers -- Fiction 6. Mystery and detective stories 7. People with disabilities -- Fiction

ISBN 1596438010; 9781596438019

LC 2013029561

In this book, by Marcus Sedgwick, "Laureth Peak's father has taught her to look for recurring events, patterns, and numbers - a skill at which she's remarkably talented. Her secret: She is blind. But when her father goes missing, Laureth and her 7-year-old brother Benjamin are thrust into a mystery that takes them to New York City where surviving will take all her skill at spotting the amazing, shocking, and sometimes dangerous connections in a world full of darkness." (Publisher's note)

"Laureth is sixteen, smart, self-doubting, and blind. She is also desperate to find her missing famous writer father -- desperate enough to boost her mother's credit card to buy two plane tickets from London to New York City, forge travel documents, and "abduct" her beloved seven-year-old brother in order to disguise her blindness... Laureth herself is worth the journey. The tricks she uses to negotiate in a sighted world.. her determination to fight the tendency of sighted people to treat blind people as stupid or deaf or, most insidiously, invisible -- all are presented matter-of-factly and sympathetically. Readers will applaud Laureth's believable evolution into a more confident -- and definitely more visible -- young woman." (Horn Book)

★ White crow. Roaring Brook Press 2011 234p $15.99

Grades: 8 9 10 11 12   **Fic**

1. Horror fiction 2. Villages -- Fiction 3. Friendship -- Fiction 4. Good and evil -- Fiction 5. Great Britain -- Fiction

ISBN 978-1-59643-594-0; 1-59643-594-1

LC 2010034053

"Showing his customary skill with a gothic setting and morally troubled characters, Sedgwick keeps readers guessing to the very end." Publ Wkly

"Sixteen-year-old Rebecca moves with her father from London to a small, seaside village, where she befriends another motherless girl and they spend the summer together exploring the village's sinister history." (Publisher's Note)

Selfors, Suzanne

Coffeehouse angel. Walker & Co. 2009 276p $16.99

Grades: 7 8 9 10   **Fic**
1. School stories 2. Angels -- Fiction 3. Wishes --
Fiction 4. Grandmothers -- Fiction
ISBN 978-0-8027-9812-1; 0-8027-9812-8
                                          LC 2008-33333
Sixteen-year-old Katrina's kindness to a man she finds
sleeping behind her grandmother's coffeehouse leads to
a strange reward as Malcolm, who is actually a teenage
guardian angel, insists on rewarding her by granting her
deepest wish.

"This light read is right for teens struggling with self-
confidence issues. . . . Although the protagonist deals with
loneliness, illness, aging, and competition in this coming-
of-age novel, it is a humorous read." Voice Youth Advocates

Fortune's magic farm; illustrated by Catia Chien.
Little, Brown 2009 264p il $14.99; pa $5.99
Grades: 4 5 6   **Fic**
1. Farms -- Fiction 2. Magic -- Fiction 3. Orphans
-- Fiction
ISBN 978-0-316-01818-0; 0-316-01818-X; 978-0-
316-01819-7 pa; 0-316-01819-8 pa
                                          LC 2008-12493
Rescued from a rainy, boggy town where she works in a
dismal factory, ten-year-old orphan Isabelle learns that she is
the last surviving member of a family that tends the world's
only remaining magic-producing farm.

"Readers will cozy up to the tale's quirky characters and enjoy the many twists and turns of this magical
adventure." Kirkus

★ **Saving** Juliet. Walker & Co. 2008 242p
$16.95
Grades: 7 8 9 10 11 12   **Fic**
1. Poets 2. Authors 3. Dramatists 4. Italy -- Fiction
5. Actors -- Fiction 6. Theater -- Fiction 7. Space and
time -- Fiction
ISBN 978-0-8027-9740-7; 0-8027-9740-7
                                          LC 2007-18528
Seventeen-year-old Mimi Wallingford's stage fright and
fight with her mother on the closing night of Romeo and Juliet are nothing compared to the troubles she faces when she
and her leading man are transported to Shakespeare's Verona, where she decides to give the real Juliet a happy ending.

This is "hilarious and often very clever. . . . Readers will
have fun with the characters. . . . Mimi . . . is an honest savvy
narrator." Publ Wkly

Smells like dog. Little, Brown 2010 360p
$15.99
Grades: 4 5 6 7   **Fic**
1. Dogs -- Fiction 2. Uncles -- Fiction 3. Buried
treasure -- Fiction
ISBN 978-0-316-04398-4; 0-316-04398-2
When farm boy Homer Pudding's explorer-uncle dies
and leaves him a droopy dog with a mysterious coin hid-
den on its collar, it leads him to The City, where they meet
Madame La Directeur, the conniving head of the Natural
History Museum, who is trying to steal the coin and take
Homer's place in a secret society of adventurers.

"Full of fantasy, fun, and humorous dialogue, this will
attract dog lovers, mystery enthusiasts, adventure addicts,

and reluctant readers. A thoroughly enjoyable read." Voice
Youth Advocates
Another title about Homer Pudding is:
Smells like treasure (2011)

Smells like treasure. Little, Brown and Company
2011 407p $15.99
Grades: 4 5 6 7   **Fic**
1. Mystery fiction 2. Adventure fiction 3. Dogs --
Fiction 4. Buried treasure -- Fiction 5. Secret societies
-- Fiction
ISBN 978-0-316-04399-1; 0-316-04399-0
                                          LC 2010041541
Sequel to: Smells like dog (2010)
Farm boy Homer faces another challenger for his
uncle's spot in the society of Legends, Objects, Secrets,
and Treasures but Dog's hidden ability to smell treasure
guides the duo as clues lead them to fantastic mansions and
hidden islands.

"The author weaves in enough details of the earlier
book to refesh readers' memories in this droll, satisfying
sequel. The suspense of the challenge . . . will keep readers
turning the pages. . . . There was plenty of rip-roaring fun
here." Kirkus

The **sweetest** spell; Suzanne Selfors. Walker &
Co. 2012 404 p. (hardback) $16.99
Grades: 7 8 9 10 11 12   **Fic**
1. Love stories 2. Fantasy fiction 3. People with
physical disabilities -- Fiction 4. Fantasy 5. Magic --
Fiction 6. Chocolate -- Fiction 7. Prejudices -- Fiction
8. People with disabilities -- Fiction
ISBN 0802723764; 9780802723765
                                          LC 2011034591
This book follows "Emmeline . . . an outcast among
her people, the Kell. When the king enslaves the men and
her village is destroyed in a flood, Emmeline is taken in by
Owen Oak and his family. She discovers that she can churn
butter into chocolate -- a food that's been lost for years in the
land of Anglund. Romance blossoms, but the two are separated when the girl is kidnapped for her magical abilities."
(School Library Journal)

"Selfors's story line initially comes across as chaotic,
but the pacing is strong, and the elements of her tale fall
into place in a logical and entirely satisfying manner. An
exhilarating, romantic, and frequently funny story of self-
discovery." Pub Wkly

Selzer, Adam
How to get suspended and influence people; a
novel. Delacorte Press 2007 183p $15.99; lib bdg
$18.99
Grades: 6 7 8 9   **Fic**
1. School stories 2. Censorship -- Fiction 3. Motion
pictures -- Fiction
ISBN 978-0-385-73369-4; 978-0-385-90384-4 lib bdg
                                          LC 2006-20438
Gifted eighth-grader Leon Harris becomes an instant celebrity when the film he makes for a class project sends him
to in-school suspension.

"This funny, fast-paced novel is filled with characters who epitomize the middle school experience, and it presents a lesson or two about free speech as well." SLJ

Another title about Leon is:

Pirates of the retail wasteland (2008)

I kissed a zombie, and I liked it. Delacorte Press 2010 177p lib bdg $12.99; pa $7.99

Grades: 7 8 9 10 **Fic**

1. Zombies -- Fiction 2. Vampires -- Fiction 3. Dating (Social customs) -- Fiction

ISBN 978-0-385-90497-1 lib bdg; 0-385-90497-5 lib bdg; 978-0-385-73503-2 pa; 0-385-73503-0 pa

LC 2009-24052

Living in the post-human era when the undead are part of everyday life, high schooler Alley breaks her no-dating rule when Doug catches her eye, but classmate Will demands to turn her into a vampire and her zombie boyfriend may be unable to stop him.

"With snappy dialogue and a light, funny touch, Selzer creates a readable examination of love, self-sacrifice, and where to draw the line before you lose yourself." Publ Wkly

I put a spell on you; from the files of Chrissie Woodward, spelling bee detective. Delacorte Press 2008 247p $15.99; lib bdg $18.99

Grades: 4 5 6 7 **Fic**

1. School stories 2. Mystery fiction 3. Spelling bees -- Fiction

ISBN 978-0-385-73504-9; 0-385-73504-9; 978-0-385-90498-8 lib bdg; 0-385-90498-3 lib bdg

LC 2008035673

When Gordon Liddy Community School's resident tattletale-detective, Chrissie Woodward, realizes that the adults are out to fix the big spelling bee, she transfers her loyalty to her fellow students and starts collecting evidence. Told through in-class letters, administrative memos, file notes from Chrissie's investigation, and testimony from spelling bee contestants

"The wit in this school story is directed almost entirely against the grownups in a scathingly funny indictment of a shady principal and insanely competitive parents." Horn Book

Pirates of the retail wasteland. Delacorte Press 2008 197p $15.99; lib bdg $18.99

Grades: 6 7 8 9 **Fic**

1. Schools -- Fiction. 2. Middle schools -- Fiction. 3. Gifted children -- Fiction. 4. Motion pictures -- Production and direction -- Fiction.

ISBN 978-0-385-73482-0; 0-385-73482-4; 978-0-385-90480-3 lib bdg; 0-385-90480-0 lib bdg

LC 2007-27602

When eighth-grader Leon decides what to do for his project in the gifted program, it involves coffee houses, pirates, and filmmaking.

"The clever repartee and humor will amuse junior high students." KLIATT

Selznick, Brian

★ The **invention** of Hugo Cabret; a novel in words and pictures. Scholastic Press 2007 533p il $22.95

Grades: 4 5 6 7 **Fic**

1. Robots -- Fiction 2. Orphans -- Fiction 3. Motion picture directors 4. Paris (France) -- Fiction 5. Motion pictures -- Fiction

ISBN 0-439-81378-6

LC 2006-07119

Awarded the Caldecott Medal, 2008

When twelve-year-old Hugo, an orphan living and repairing clocks within the walls of a Paris train station in 1931, meets a mysterious toyseller and his goddaughter, his undercover life and his biggest secret are jeopardized.

"With characteristic intelligence, exquisite images, and a breathtaking design, Selznick shatters conventions related to the art of bookmaking." SLJ

★ **Wonderstruck**; a novel in words and pictures. Scholastic Press 2011 637p il $29.99

Grades: 4 5 6 7 **Fic**

1. Deaf -- Fiction 2. Museums -- Fiction 3. New York (N.Y.) -- Fiction 4. Runaway children -- Fiction 5. American Museum of Natural History -- Fiction

ISBN 978-0-545-02789-2; 0-545-02789-6

LC 2011009113

"Readers know that the two stories will converge, but Selznick keeps them guessing, cutting back and forth with expert precision. . . . Both stories are equally immersive and impeccably paced. . . . Visually stunning, completely compelling." Kirkus

Sensel, Joni

The **Farwalker's** quest. Bloomsbury U.S.A Children's Books 2009 372p $16.99

Grades: 5 6 7 8 **Fic**

1. Fantasy fiction

ISBN 978-1-59990-272-2; 1-59990-272-9

LC 2008-30523

When twelve-year-old Ariel and her friend Zeke find a mysterious artifact the like of which has not been seen in a long time, it proves to be the beginning of a long and arduous journey that will untimately reveal to them their true identities.

"This is a solid and well-paced fantasy in which the journey is more important than the conclusion." SLJ

Followed by: The timekeeper's moon (2010)

The **timekeeper's** moon; [drawings by Yelena Safronova] Bloomsbury 2010 339p il $16.99

Grades: 5 6 7 8 **Fic**

1. Fantasy fiction

ISBN 978-1-59990-457-3; 1-59990-457-8

LC 2009-16690

Sequel to: The Farwalker's quest (2009)

Summoned by the moon to embark on a dangerous journey, thirteen-year-old Ariel Farwalker, knowing she must obey or risk destruction, sets out with her guardian, Scarl, to follow a mysterious map to an unknown entity called "Timekeeper"

"Vivid world building and tight pacing mark this sequel . . . further distinguished by rich characters with believable relationships." Booklist

Sepetys, Ruta

★ **Between** shades of gray; Ruta Sepetys. Philomel Books 2011 344p map $17.99

Grades: 8 9 10 11 12   **Fic**

1. Lithuania -- Fiction 2. Soviet Union -- Fiction
ISBN 978-0-399-25412-3; 0-399-25412-9

LC 2009-50092

In this novel by Ruta Sepetys, "Fifteen-year-old Lina is a Lithuanian girl living an ordinary life--until Soviet officers invade her home and tear her family apart. Separated from her father and forced onto a crowded train, Lina, her mother, and her young brother make their way to a Siberian work camp, where they are forced to fight for their lives." (Publisher's note)

"A harrowing page-turner, made all the more so for its basis in historical fact, the novel illuminates the persecution suffered by Stalin's victims (20 million were killed), while presenting memorable characters who retain their will to survive even after more than a decade in exile." Publ Wkly

Service, Pamela F.

Tomorrow's magic; [by] Pamela F. Service. 1st ed.; Random House 2007 437p $15.99; lib bdg $18.99; pa $7.99

Grades: 7 8 9 10   **Fic**

1. Fantasy fiction 2. Science fiction 3. Kings 4. Magic -- Fiction 5. Merlin (Legendary character) -- Fiction 6. Morgan le Fay (Legendary character) -- Fiction
ISBN 978-0-375-84087-6; 0-375-84087-7; 978-0-375-94087-3 lib bdg; 0-375-94087-1 lib bdg; 978-0-375-84087-6 pa; 0-375-84088-5 pa

LC 2006016131

First published in two volumes by Atheneum: Winter of magic's return (1985), Tomorrow's magic (1987)

Two novels in which a young, resurrected Merlin and two friends attempt to bring King Arthur back to Britain, then struggle against the evil plots of Morgan Le Fey to build a new and better civilization in the wake of a nuclear holocaust.

"Service has done a terrific job melding futuristic science fiction with ancient Arthurian legend." Horn Book Guide

Followed by: Yesterday's magic (2008)

Yesterday's magic; [by] Pamela F. Service. Random House 2008 216p $16.99

Grades: 7 8 9 10   **Fic**

1. Fantasy fiction 2. Science fiction 3. Kings 4. Magic -- Fiction 5. Merlin (Legendary character) -- Fiction 6. Morgan le Fay (Legendary character) -- Fiction
ISBN 978-0-375-85577-1; 0-375-85577-7

Sequel to: Tomorrow's magic (2007)

"When Heather McKenna is kidnapped by the sorceress Morgan LeFay, it is up to Heather's friend Welly and the wizard Merlin . . . to rescue her. Set 500 years in the future, following a nuclear devastation, the technological world has ground to a halt, but magic is beginning to take hold again." Publisher's note

Shahan, Sherry

Death mountain; [by] Sherry Shahan. 1st ed.; Peachtree 2005 202p $15.95

Grades: 5 6 7 8   **Fic**

1. Wilderness survival -- Fiction 2. Sierra Nevada Mountains -- Fiction
ISBN 1-56145-353-6

LC 2005010820

"A day trip to a mountain lake turns to disaster when lightning strikes a pack mule, a mud slide kills a horse, and hikers scatter, seeking shelter. Erin, 14, leaves her new friend Levi with the injured hikers to search for his sister, Mae, who has run off-trail in the confusion. . . . A great addition to the adventure-survival genre." SLJ

Ice island. Delacorte Press 2012 $10.99; lib bdg $18.99; ebook $10.99

Grades: 4 5 6 7   **Fic**

1. Dogs -- Fiction 2. Alaska -- Fiction 3. Sled dog racing -- Fiction 4. Wilderness survival -- Fiction 5. Iditarod Trail Sled Dog Race, Alaska -- Fiction
ISBN 978-0-385-74154-5; 0-385-74154-5; 978-0-375-99009-0 lib bdg; 0-375-99009-7 lib bdg; 978-0-375-98575-1 ebook

LC 2011003838

Thirteen-year-old Tatum's dream of competing in the grueling 1,049-mile Iditerod Trail Sled Dog Race may be at an end when she becomes lost in a freak snowstorm during a training run on Alaska's remote Santa Ysabel Island.

"Riveting and atmospheric. . . . This survival adventure creates an almost otherworldly experience within a treacherous and bracingly beautiful landscape." Kirkus

Shan, Darren

Lord Loss; [by] Darren Shan. 1st U.S. ed.; Little, Brown 2005 233p (Demonata) hardcover o.p. pa $8.99

Grades: 7 8 9 10   **Fic**

1. Horror fiction
ISBN 0-316-11499-5; 0-316-01233-5 pa

LC 2005-0145

Presumably the only witness to the horrific and bloody murder of his entire family, a teenage boy must outwit not only the mental health professionals determined to cure his delusion, but also the demonic forces only he can see.

"The plot rolls along at high speed, but Shan is still quite adept when it comes to capturing Grubbs' roller-coaster emotions." Booklist

Other titles in this series are:
Demon thief (2006)
Slawter (2006)
Bec (2007)
Blood beast (2007)
Demon apocalypse (2008)
Death's shadow (2008)
Wolf island (2009)
Dark calling (2009)

Shanahan, Lisa

★ The **sweet,** terrible, glorious year I truly, completely lost it. Delacorte Press 2007 297p $15.99; lib bdg $18.99

Grades: 7 8 9 10   **Fic**

1. School stories 2. Theater -- Fiction 3. Australia -- Fiction 4. Family life -- Fiction

ISBN 978-0-385-73516-2; 0-385-73516-2; 978-0-385-90505-3 lib bdg; 0-385-90505-X lib bdg

LC 2006-101158

Fourteen-year-old Gemma Stone struggles to understand her shifting emotions as her older sister plans her wedding, she overcomes her nerves and tries out for the school play, and she gets to know one of the most notorious boys in her class.

"Shanahan's quirky characters are a riot, but the depth of Gemma's growth and heartbreak is profound." SLJ

Shang, Wendy Wan-Long

★ The **way** home looks now; Wendy Wan-Long Shang. Scholastic Press 2015 272 p. $16.99

Grades: 4 5 6 7 8   **Fic**

1. Grief -- Fiction 2. Baseball -- Fiction 3. Pittsburgh (Pa.) -- Fiction 4. Chinese Americans -- Fiction 5. Traffic accidents -- Fiction 6. Bereavement 7. Baseball stories 8. Traffic accidents 9. Little League baseball -- Fiction 10. Chinese American families -- Pennsylvania -- Pittsburgh

ISBN 0545609569; 9780545609562

LC 2014028707

This middle grades book, by Wendy Wan-Long Shang, is a "story of family and loss, healing and friendship, and the great American pastime, baseball. Twelve-year-old Peter Lee and his family are baseball lovers, who bond over back lot games and talk of the Pittsburgh Pirates. But when tragedy strikes, the family flies apart and baseball no longer seems to matter. Is that true? Peter wonders if just maybe the game they love can pull them together and bring them back." (Publisher's note)

"Twelve-year-old Peter just wants his home to be the way it was before—before his mother stopped talking, before she started sitting on the couch staring at the TV, and before his older brother died in a car accident. Peter's father is a strict Chinese immigrant who stresses homework, emphasizes respect for authority, and forbids baseball...Peter is a fully realized character, but the rest of his family and most of the players on his team fall flat. VERDICT Though the plot occasionally gets bogged down with too many side stories, this heartwarming story is still a worthy purchase." SLJ

Sharenow, Rob

★ The **Berlin** Boxing Club. HarperTeen 2011 404p il $17.99

Grades: 7 8 9 10   **Fic**

1. Boxers (Persons) 2. Boxing -- Fiction 3. Family life -- Fiction 4. Jews -- Germany -- Fiction 5. Berlin (Germany) -- Fiction 6. National socialism -- Fiction 7. Holocaust, 1933-1945 -- Fiction 8. Germany -- History -- 1933-1945 -- Fiction

ISBN 978-0-06-157968-4; 0-06-157968-8

LC 2010024446

"Readers will be drawn by the sports detail and by the close-up narrative of the daily oppression." Booklist

"Karl Stern has never thought of himself as a Jew. But the bullies at his school in Nazi-era Berlin, don't care that Karl has never been in a synagogue or that his family doesn't

practice religion. . . . So when Max Schmeling, champion boxer and German national hero, makes a deal with Karl's father to give Karl boxing lessons. . . . it seems like the perfect chance to reinvent himself." (Publisher's Note)

My mother the cheerleader; a novel. Laura Geringer Books 2007 288p hardcover o.p. pa $8.99

Grades: 7 8 9 10   **Fic**

1. Race relations -- Fiction 2. New Orleans (La.) -- Fiction 3. School integration -- Fiction 4. Mother-daughter relationship -- Fiction

ISBN 978-0-06-114896-5; 0-06-114896-2; 978-0-06-114898-9 pa; 0-06-114898-9 pa

LC 2006-21716

Thirteen-year-old Louise uncovers secrets about her family and her neighborhood during the violent protests over school desegregation in 1960 New Orleans.

"Through inquisitive Louise's perspective, readers get a wrenching look at the era's turmoil and pervasive racism." Publ Wkly

Shaw, Liane

Fostergirls. Second Story Press 2011 256p pa $11.95

Grades: 6 7 8 9   **Fic**

1. Foster home care -- Fiction

ISBN 978-1-897187-90-6; 1-897187-90-4

"Her name is Sadie, but she might as well be called Fostergirl. Grouphomegirl. That's how everyone thinks of her. Sadie doesn't care. . . . Her goal is to go unnoticed, to disappear. Nothing good comes from being noticed, especially if you're a fostergirl. Another new high school, another new group home. This one is lucky number 13, but who's counting? Except, this time there's a girl at her school named Rhiannon who won't let Sadie be invisible. In fact, she insists on being her friend. This friendship, and the dawning feeling that she finally belongs, might be able to restore Sadie's belief in others, and—ultimately—herself." (Publisher's note) "Age thirteen and up." (Quill Quire)

"Shaw's biggest challenge is making caustic, self-deprecating, and distrustful Sadie likable. Fortunately, she succeeds. Sadie, though tough as nails, narrates her story with an amusing edginess that works. Shaw keeps things PG-rated . . . while highlighting the reality of life as a foster child. . . . Readers seeking an honest account of how a girl without parents survives, this story delivers." Publ Wkly

Shaw, Susan

One of the survivors. Margaret K. McElderry Books 2009 199p $15.99

Grades: 6 7 8 9   **Fic**

1. School stories 2. Anger -- Fiction 3. Death -- Fiction 4. Fires -- Fiction 5. Guilt -- Fiction 6. Bereavement -- Fiction

ISBN 978-1-4169-6129-1; 1-4169-6129-1

LC 2008035965

When his classmates die in a school fire, fourteen-year-old Joey is haunted by their deaths and struggles to survive amidst suspicion and anger from the town.

"Shaw tackles a gut-wrenching situation in honest, solution-oriented terms that should appeal to reluctant readers. The novel is short, the plot and suspense build slowly, and the decisions required by the teens make for thought-provoking discussions." SLJ

★ **Safe**. Dutton Books 2007 168p $16.99
Grades: 7 8 9 10   **Fic**
    1. Rape -- Fiction 2. Mothers -- Fiction
    ISBN 978-0-525-47829-4; 0-525-47829-9
                                        LC 2006-36428
    When thirteen-year-old Tracy, whose mother died when she was three years old, is raped and beaten on the last day of school, all her feelings of security disappear and she does not know how to cope with the fear and dread that engulf her.
    This is an "extraordinarily tender novel. . . . Intimate, first-person narrative honestly expresses Tracy's full range of emotions." Publ Wkly

    Tunnel vision. Margaret K. McElderry Books 2011 272p $16.99
Grades: 5 6 7 8   **Fic**
    1. Crime -- Fiction 2. Homicide -- Fiction 3. Witnesses -- Fiction 4. Organized crime -- Fiction
    ISBN 978-1-4424-0839-5; 1-4424-0839-1
                                        LC 2010036306
    After witnessing her mother's murder, sixteen-year-old high school student Liza Wellington and her father go into the witness protection program.
    "The author creates a completely believable character in Liza, who often reverts to childlike emotions only to learn the hard way that cold reality takes precedence over even dearly held wishes. Kudos for the unexpected double ending, both illusory and realistic, giving readers a choice." Kirkus

Shecter, Vicky Alvear
    Cleopatra's moon. Arthur A. Levine Books 2011 353p $18.99
Grades: 8 9 10 11 12   **Fic**
    1. Queens 2. Generals 3. Statesmen 4. Orators 5. Egypt -- Fiction 6. Princesses -- Fiction 7. Rome -- History -- Fiction
    ISBN 978-0-545-22130-6; 0-545-22130-7
                                        LC 2010028818
    Cleopatra Selene, the only surviving daughter of Cleopatra and Marc Antony, recalls her life of pomp and splendor in Egypt and, after her parents' deaths, capitivity and treachery in Rome.
    "This novel has romance, drama, heartbreak, and adventure, all rooted in an accurate and descriptive historical setting. Shecter writes about the world of ancient Egypt and Rome with wonderful detail. . . . Her characters are skillfully fictionalized." SLJ

Sheinmel, Alyssa B.
    The **lucky** kind. Alfred A. Knopf 2011 201p $16.99; lib bdg $19.99
Grades: 8 9 10 11 12   **Fic**
    1. Adoption -- Fiction 2. Friendship -- Fiction 3. Family life -- Fiction 4. New York (N.Y.) -- Fiction
    ISBN 978-0-375-86785-9; 0-375-86785-6; 978-0-375-96785-6 lib bdg; 0-375-96785-0 lib bdg; 978-0-375-89866-2 e-book
                                        LC 2010-27967

    Having always felt secure within his small family, Manhattan high school junior Nick is unsettled to discover the existence of an older brother that his father put up for adoption many years ago.
    "Nick's narration, ruminative yet straightforward, gives him a credible voice as he lurches unwillingly toward adulthood, and the book deftly conveys that he's really a good guy even if the situation is causing him to sink below his usual standards. The well-crafted family story offers an excellent stage for depicting the challenge facing every young adult—how to accept human responsibilty and fraility as we go through life." Bull Cent Child Books

Sheinmel, Courtney
    All the things you are. Simon & Schuster Books for Young Readers 2011 244p $15.99
Grades: 5 6 7 8   **Fic**
    1. Theft -- Fiction 2. Friendship -- Fiction 3. Family life -- Fiction 4. Stepfamilies -- Fiction 5. New York (N.Y.) -- Fiction
    ISBN 978-1-4169-9717-7; 1-4169-9717-2
                                        LC 2010010090
    When Carly Wheeler's mother is arrested for embezzling, Carly's perfect life begins to fall apart as friends at her prestigious private school stop talking to her, her beloved stepfather starts worrying about finances, and her image of herself and her family changes.
    "Sheinmel persuasively and sensitively conveys Carly's conflicting emotions and her attempts to make sense of what's been thrust upon her." Publ Wkly

    Positively. Simon & Schuster Books for Young Readers 2009 216p $15.99
Grades: 6 7 8 9 10   **Fic**
    1. Camps -- Fiction 2. Death -- Fiction 3. Friendship -- Fiction 4. Bereavement -- Fiction 5. Stepfamilies -- Fiction 6. AIDS (Disease) -- Fiction
    ISBN 978-1-4169-7169-6; 1-4169-7169-6
                                        LC 2008-35447
    Thirteen-year-old Emmy, grieving over her mother who died of AIDS, resentful of having to live with her father and pregnant stepmother, and despairing about her future, finds hope at a summer camp for HIV-positive girls like herself. Includes facts about Elizabeth Glaser, one of the founders of the Pediatric AIDS Foundation.
    "This valuable story discusses uncertainty, very human fears, and most important, hope. . . . It is a terrific introduction to a complex and important topic." Voice Youth Advocates

Sheldon, Dyan
    Confessions of a Hollywood star. Candlewick Press 2006 202p $15.99
Grades: 7 8 9 10   **Fic**
    1. Actors -- Fiction 2. Motion pictures -- Fiction
    ISBN 0-7636-3075-6
    Upon learning at the end of her senior year of high school that a Hollywood film is being made in her hometown, Lola stops at nothing to get a part and upstage her nemesis, Carla Santini.
    "Lola's voice is once again an uproariously funny delight." Booklist

The **crazy** things girls do for love. Candlewick Press 2011 $15.99

Grades: 7 8 9 10   **Fic**
1. School stories 2. Environmental protection -- Fiction
ISBN 978-0-7636-5018-6; 0-7636-5018-8

LC 2010048434

When fashionista Sicilee, arty Maya, and antisocial Waneeda risk their reputations by joining Clifton Springs High School's Environmental Club to be near gorgeous new student Cody Lightfoot, each finds a new way of looking at the world.

"The details are laugh-out-loud funny. . . . With plenty of wry romance, the story builds to a save-the-trees climax that also brings a change in Cody." Booklist

My perfect life. Candlewick Press 2002 201p $16.99; pa $5.99

Grades: 7 8 9 10   **Fic**
1. School stories 2. Elections -- Fiction
ISBN 0-7636-1839-X; 0-7636-2436-5 pa

LC 2001-58118

Ella has no interest in running for class president at her suburban high school, but her off-beat friend Lola tricks her into challenging the rich and overbearing Carla Santini in a less-than-friendly race

"The story is entertaining and well written. The characters reflect the personalities and cliques of kids in any high school." SLJ

Shen, Prudence

Nothing Can Possibly Go Wrong; by Prudence Shen, illustrated by Faith Erin Hicks. First Second 2013 288 p. (paperback) $16.99

Grades: 7 8 9 10   **Fic**
1. Robots -- Fiction 2. Cheerleading -- Fiction 3. School stories -- Graphic novels
ISBN 159643659X; 9781596436596

In this juvenile graphic novel, by Prudence Shen, illustrated by Faith Erin Hicks, "you wouldn't expect Nate and Charlie to be friends. Charlie's the laid-back captain of the basketball team, and Nate is the neurotic, scheming president of the robotics club. But they are friends, however unlikely--until Nate declares war on the cheerleaders. At stake is funding that will either cover a robotics competition or new cheerleading uniforms--but not both." (Publisher's note)

"Shen's plot ably balances drama, humor, angst, and robotic geekery, giving the book an immediate YA appeal, but one that's broad enough to be enjoyable to older readers, as well. Visually, Hicks's wide-eyed, inky b&w panels infuse the characters with real emotion and personality, capturing the book's heartfelt youthfulness." Pub Wkly

Sherlock, Patti

Letters from Wolfie. Viking 2004 232p $16.99; pa $6.99

Grades: 5 6 7 8   **Fic**
1. Dogs -- Fiction 2. Vietnam War, 1961-1975 -- Fiction
ISBN 0-670-03694-3; 0-14-240358-X pa

LC 2003-24316

Certain that he is doing the right thing by donating his dog, Wolfie, to the Army's scout program in Vietnam, thir-teen-year-old Mark begins to have second thoughts when the Army refuses to say when and if Wolfie will ever return.

"In this topnotch novel, Sherlock weaves together numerous threads of emotion, information, and plot so seamlessly that readers will be surprised by how much they've learned by the time they finish this deceptively simple story." SLJ

Sherman, Deborah

The **BEDMAS** conspiracy. Fitzhenry & White-side 2011 170p pa $9.95

Grades: 4 5 6 7   **Fic**
1. School stories 2. Bands (Music) -- Fiction
ISBN 978-1-55455-181-1; 1-55455-181-1

Adam's band, Sick on a Snow Day, is challenged by more than just an unusual name: Adam is mistakenly accused of cheating on a test and must maintain a clean record and B-average if he wants to stay in the band. Then his lead singer, Daniela, gets stage fright.

"Adam's academic difficulties and Daniela's stage fright are only two of the challenges thrown their way, but both are handled imaginatively and with humor. . . . A genial read." SLJ

Sherman, Delia

Changeling. Viking 2006 292p $16.99; pa $8.99

Grades: 5 6 7 8   **Fic**
1. Fantasy fiction 2. New York (N.Y.) -- Fiction
ISBN 0-670-05967-6; 0-14-241188-4 pa

"Neef is a changeling, a human baby stolen by fairies. She lives in 'New York Between,' an invisible parallel city, and she was raised under the protection of her godmother (a white rat) and the Green Lady of Central Park. . . . After breaking Fairy Law, Neef is expelled, and she must complete a heroic quest . . . in order to regain entry to her community. . . . Silly, profound, and lightning paced all at once, this novel will please adventure fans and fantasy readers alike." Bull Cent Child Books

Another title about Neef is:

The Magic Mirror of the Mermaid Queen (2009)

★ The **freedom** maze. Big Mouth House 2011 267p $16.95

Grades: 7 8 9 10   **Fic**
1. Slavery -- Fiction 2. Louisiana -- Fiction 3. Time travel -- Fiction 4. Race relations -- Fiction 5. Plantation life -- Fiction
ISBN 978-1-931520-30-0; 1-931520-30-5

"It's 1960, but on the decayed Fairchild sugar plantation in rural Louisiana, vestiges of a grimmer past remain-the old cottage, overgrown garden maze, relations between white and black races. Stuck for the summer in the family ancestral home under the thumb of her cranky, imperious grandmother, Sophie, 13, makes a reckless wish that lands her in 1860, enslaved-by her own ancestors. . . . Plantation life for whites and blacks unfolds in compelling, often excruciating detail. . . . Multilayered, compassionate and thought-provoking." Kirkus

The **Magic** Mirror of the Mermaid Queen. Viking 2009 290p $17.99

Grades: 5 6 7 8   **Fic**
1. School stories 2. Fantasy fiction 3. New York (N.Y.)
-- Fiction
ISBN 978-0-670-01089-9; 0-670-01089-8
                                    LC 2009000850
Sequel to: Changeling (2006)

In New York Between, a parallel Manhattan that is home
to various creatures of folklore, Neef meets her counterparts at Miss Van Loon's school for human changelings,
where Neef learns the basics of diplomacy and soon gets
into trouble.

"Spiced with just enough background information, it
works just fine on its own, but it will create immediate desire
to read Changeling as well." SLJ

Sherrard, Valerie
The **glory** wind. Fitzhenry & Whiteside 2011
222p pa $12.95

Grades: 5 6 7 8   **Fic**
1. Ontario -- Fiction 2. Prejudices -- Fiction 3. Country
life -- Fiction
ISBN 978-1-55455-170-5; 1-55455-170-6

Eleven-year-old Luke must come to terms with the moral prejudices of his small town in rural 1950s Ontario when
he befriends Gracie, the daughter of a young widow who
moves in next door.

"Luke's first person narration is fresh and emotionally
true. . . . The haunting depiction of small-mindedness will
leave readers wondering, as Luke comes to, about Gracie's
true nature: heavenly child—or angel?" Kirkus

Sherry, Maureen
Walls within walls; illustrated by Adam Stower.
Katherine Tegen Books 2010 349p il $16.99

Grades: 4 5 6 7   **Fic**
1. Mystery fiction 2. Siblings -- Fiction 3. New York
(N.Y.) -- Fiction
ISBN 978-0-06-176700-5; 0-06-176700-X
                                    LC 2010-09494
When the Smithfork family moves into a lavish Manhattan apartment building, they discover clues to a decades-old
mystery hidden behind the walls of their new home.

This "packs all sorts of interesting information about
topics like history and architecture into a mystery that kids
can (almost) solve. . . . Readers will get a real feel for the
uniqueness that is New York City." Booklist

Sheth, Kashmira
Blue jasmine; [by] Kashmira Sheth. Hyperion
Books for Children 2004 186p $15.99; pa $5.99

Grades: 5 6 7 8   **Fic**
1. India -- Fiction 2. Immigrants -- Fiction 3. East
Indians -- Fiction
ISBN 0-7868-1855-7; 0-7868-5565-7 pa
                                    LC 2003-50818
When twelve-year-old Seema moves to Iowa City with
her parents and younger sister, she leaves friends and family behind in her native India but gradually begins to feel at
home in her new country

"Seema's story, which articulates the ache for distant
home and family, will resonate with fellow immigrants and
enlighten their classmates." Booklist

Boys without names. Balzer & Bray 2010 316p
$15.99

Grades: 4 5 6 7   **Fic**
1. India -- Fiction 2. Slavery -- Fiction 3. Child labor
-- Fiction 4. Missing persons -- Fiction
ISBN 978-0-06-185760-7; 0-06-185760-2
                                    LC 2009-11747
Eleven-year-old Gopal and his family leave their rural
Indian village for life with his uncle in Mumbai, but when
they arrive his father goes missing and Gopal ends up locked
in a sweatshop from which there is no escape.

"Readers quickly come to care for this clever, perceptive boy who tries hard to do the right thing. . . . The author
includes more about child labor at the end of this well-told
survival story with a social conscience." SLJ

★ **Keeping** corner. Hyperion 2007 281p hardcover o.p. pa $5.99

Grades: 7 8 9 10 11 12   **Fic**
1. Authors 2. Journalists 3. Essayists 4. Pacifists 5.
Memoirists 6. India -- Fiction 7. Political leaders 8.
Widows -- Fiction 9. Writers on politics 10. Women's
rights -- Fiction
ISBN 978-0-7868-3859-2; 0-7868-3859-0; 978-0-
7868-3860-8 pa; 0-7868-3860-4 pa
                                    LC 2007-15314
In India in the 1940s, twelve-year-old Leela's happy,
spoiled childhood ends when her husband since age nine,
whom she barely knows, dies, leaving her a widow whose
only hope of happiness could come from Mahatma Ghandi's
social and political reforms.

Sheth "sets up a thrilling premise in which politics become achingly personal." Booklist

Shimko, Bonnie
★ The **private** thoughts of Amelia E. Rye. Farrar, Straus Giroux 2010 234p $16.99

Grades: 5 6 7 8   **Fic**
1. Friendship -- Fiction 2. New York (State) -- Fiction
3. Mother-daughter relationship -- Fiction
ISBN 978-0-374-36131-0; 0-374-36131-2
                                    LC 2008048092
Growing up in a small town in upstate New York during the 1960s, 13-year-old Amelia E. Ryel, unwanted by her
mother, searches for love and acceptance.

"The book is peopled with believable, multilayered
characters. . . . Shimko's . . . story is original, and Amelia's
distinctive voice and likable nature will have readers rooting
for her in times of trouble and cheering her ultimate good
fortune." Publ Wkly

Shinn, Sharon
★ **Gateway**. Viking 2009 280p $17.99

Grades: 6 7 8 9 10   **Fic**
1. Space and time -- Fiction 2. Chinese Americans --
Fiction
ISBN 978-0-670-01178-0; 0-670-01178-9
                                    LC 2009-14002

While passing through the Arch in St. Louis, Missouri, a Chinese American teenager is transported to a parallel world where she is given a dangerous assignment.

The author's "fantasy finds the right balance between adventure and romance, while illuminating how seductive evil can be and that sometimes the best weapon one can possess is a skeptical mind." Publ Wkly

Shoemaker, Tim

Back before dark; Timothy Shoemaker. Zondervan 2013 384 p. (hardcover) $14.99

Grades: 7 8 9 10   **Fic**

1. Friendship -- Fiction 2. Kidnapping -- Fiction 3. Best friends -- Fiction 4. Christian life -- Fiction 5. Conduct of life -- Fiction 6. Mystery and detective stories

ISBN 0310734991; 9780310734994

LC 2012049855

"Every kid's worst nightmare, a ride through the park gets Gordy abducted. The kids find themselves in the wrong place at the wrong time. It's every kid's worst nightmare, when a ride through the park gets Gordy abducted. Their powers of observation are put to the test like never before, as they fight the clock to find their friend. In the dark, things are never what they seem." (Publisher's Note)

"In this sequel to Code of Silence, Gordy is kidnapped and his friends Hiro, Cooper, and Lunk decide to take his rescue into their own hands. While the suspense is vitiated by an excess of description and a slow pace, Shoemaker raises interesting questions about law and morality as the friends find themselves resorting to dubious means to catch the criminal." Horn Book

Code of silence; Tim Shoemaker. Zondervan 2012 331 p. (hardcover) $14.99

Grades: 7 8 9 10   **Fic**

1. Youth -- Fiction 2. Secrecy -- Fiction 3. Deception -- Fiction 4. Witnesses -- Fiction 5. Christian life -- Fiction 6. Conduct of life -- Fiction 7. Robbers and outlaws -- Fiction

ISBN 9780310726531

LC 2011048880

In this crime novel for young adults by Tim Shoemaker, "thirteen-year-olds Cooper, Gordy, and Hiro are snacking at their favorite burger joint, Frank 'n Stein's, when they witness a brutal robbery. Two men, masked as a clown and Elvis, savagely beat the owner and steal his considerable stash of cash. The kids manage to escape, and with the security camera hard drive to boot, but Clown gets a good look at Cooper and swears he'll find him. Afraid to go to the police (the robbers were wearing cop pants), Cooper convinces his friends to enact a code of silence. As the maybe-crooked police and other possible suspects get closer to identifying the witnesses, the kids' lies to their parents, their teachers, and one another set off increasingly desperate maneuvers and dangerous infighting" (Booklist)

Showalter, Gena

Intertwined. Harlequin Teen 2009 440p $15.99

Grades: 7 8 9 10   **Fic**

1. Vampires -- Fiction 2. Werewolves -- Fiction 3.

Supernatural -- Fiction

ISBN 978-0-373-21002-2; 0-373-21002-7

"This fast-paced, action-driven plot has many unexpected twists and turns. Well written, with a unique story line and strong characters." SLJ

Other titles in this series are:

Unraveled (2010)

Twisted (2011)

Shreve, Susan

The **lovely** shoes; [by] Susan Shreve. Arthur A. Levine Books 2011 252p $16.99

Grades: 6 7 8 9   **Fic**

1. Shoemakers 2. School stories 3. Shoe designers 4. Shoes -- Fiction 5. Birth defects -- Fiction 6. Florence (Italy) -- Fiction 7. Mother-daughter relationship -- Fiction

ISBN 978-0-439-68049-3; 0-439-68049-2

LC 2010027937

In 1950s Ohio, ninth-grader Franny feels isolated and self-conscious at high school because of her deformed leg and feet, but her irrepressibly high-spirited mother is determined to find shoes for Franny to wear at the school dances.

"Celebrating the rewards of determination and a positive attitude, this atmospheric novel credibly depicts Franny's internal growth and changing attitude. The contrast between smalltown Ohio and splendorous Florence provides an intriguing framework for the book's classic themes." Publ Wkly

Shulman, Mark

★ **Scrawl**. Roaring Brook Press 2010 234p $16.99

Grades: 6 7 8 9 10   **Fic**

1. School stories 2. Bullies -- Fiction 3. Diaries -- Fiction 4. Poverty -- Fiction 5. Self-perception -- Fiction

ISBN 978-1-59643-417-2; 1-59643-417-1

LC 2010-10521

When eighth-grade school bully Tod and his friends get caught committing a crime on school property, his penalty—staying after school and writing in a journal under the eye of the school guidance counsellor—reveals aspects of himself that he prefers to keep hidden.

"Blackmail, cliques, and a sense of hopelessness from both students and teachers sets up an unexpected ending that will leave readers with a new appreciation for how difficult high school can be. With the potential to occupy the rarified air of titles like S.E. Hinton's The Outsiders and Chris Crutcher's Staying Fat for Sarah Byrnes . . ., Scrawl paints the stereotypical school bully in a different, poignant light." Voice Youth Advocates

Treasure hunters; by James Patterson, Chris Grabenstein, and Mark Shulman and illustrated by Juliana Neufeld. Little, Brown and Company 2013 480 p. (Treasure hunters) $14.99

Grades: 3 4 5 6   **Fic**

1. Pirates -- Fiction 2. Siblings -- Fiction 3. Buried treasure -- Fiction 4. Twins -- Fiction 5. Seafaring life -- Fiction 6. Missing persons -- Fiction 7. New York (N.Y.) -- Fiction 8. Brothers and sisters -- Fiction 9.

Adventure and adventurers -- Fiction
ISBN 031620756X; 9780316207560

LC 2012040968

In this book, by James Patterson, Chris Grabenstein and Mark Shulman, "the Kidd siblings have grown up diving down to shipwrecks and traveling the world, helping their famous parents recover everything from swords to gold doubloons from the bottom of the ocean. But after their parents disappear n the job, the kids are suddenly thrust into the biggest treasure hunt of their lives." (Publisher's note)

Shulman, Polly

Enthusiasm. G. P. Putnam's Sons 2006 198p hardcover o.p. pa $7.99

Grades: 7 8 9 10   **Fic**

1. School stories
ISBN 0-399-24389-5; 0-14-240935-9 pa

LC 2005-13490

Julie and Ashleigh, high school sophomores and Jane Austen fans, seem to fall for the same Mr. Darcy-like boy and struggle to hide their true feelings from one another while rehearsing for a school musical.

"While familiarity with Austen's world through her books or, more likely, the movie renditions will deepen readers' appreciation for Shulman's impressive . . . novel, it is by no means a prerequisite to enjoying this involving and often amusing narrative of friendship, courtship, and (of course) true love." Booklist

★ The **Grimm** Legacy. G. P. Putnam's Sons 2010 325p $16.99

Grades: 5 6 7 8   **Fic**

1. Fantasy fiction 2. Magic -- Fiction 3. Libraries -- Fiction 4. New York (N.Y.) -- Fiction
ISBN 0-399-25096-4; 978-0-399-25096-5

LC 2009028919

New York high school student Elizabeth gets an after-school job as a page at the "New-York Circulating Material Repository," and when she gains coveted access to its Grimm Collection of magical objects, she and the other pages are drawn into a series of frightening adventures involving mythical creatures and stolen goods.

"This modern fantasy has intrigue, adventure, and romance, and the magical aspects of the tale are both clever and intricately woven. . . . Shulman's prose is fast paced, filled with humor, and peopled with characters who are either true to life or delightfully bizarre." SLJ

The **Wells** Bequest; by Polly Shulman. Nancy Paulsen Books, an imprint of Penguin Group (USA) Inc. 2013 272 p. (hardcover) $16.99

Grades: 5 6 7 8   **Fic**

1. Fantasy fiction 2. Science fiction 3. Time travel -- Fiction
ISBN 0399256466; 9780399256462

LC 2012036571

This book is a companion to Polly Shulman's "The Grimm Legacy." Here, New York Circulating Material Repository page "Leo notices an object materializing on the floor. The glittering, football-sized machine has 'gears and rods and knobs and a little saddle' —and two miniscule humans, one of whom is himself." He discovers that he and his

fellow page Jaya must travel in time to prevent another page from misusing Nikola Tesla's death ray. (Kirkus Reviews)

Shurtliff, Liesl

Rump; the true story of Rumpelstiltskin. Liesl Shurtliff. 1st ed. Alfred A. Knopf 2013 272 p. (hardcover) $16.99

Grades: 3 4 5 6 7   **Fic**

1. Fractured fairy tales 2. Magic -- Fiction 3. Fairy tales 4. Gold -- Fiction 5. Humorous stories 6. Magic -- Fiction 7. Names, Personal -- Fiction
ISBN 0307977935; 9780307977939 trade; 9780307977946; 9780307977953; 9780307977960

LC 2012005093

In this fractured fairy tale, by Liesl Shurtliff, "12-year-old [Rumpelstiltskin] . . . finds an old spinning wheel, . . . [and] discovers he has a gift for spinning straw into gold. His best friend, Red Riding Hood, warns him that magic is dangerous, and she's right. With each thread he spins, he weaves himself deeper into a curse. To break the spell, Rump must go on a perilous quest, fighting off pixies, trolls, poison apples, and a wickedly foolish queen." (Publisher's note)

"Debut author Shurtliff upends the traditional characterization of this fairy tale's antihero, recasting Rumpelstiltskin as a sympathetic and tragically doomed protagonist. . . . [T] he picaresque-style narrative gives the maligned character a refreshingly plainspoken voice, while honoring the original story's hauntingly strange events." Pub Wkly

Shusterman, Neal

★ **Antsy** does time. Dutton Children's Books 2008 247p $16.99

Grades: 5 6 7 8   **Fic**

1. School stories 2. Death -- Fiction 3. Brooklyn (New York, N.Y.) -- Fiction
ISBN 978-0-525-47825-6; 0-525-47825-6

LC 2008-00459

Sequel to: The Schwa was here (2004)

Fourteen-year-old Anthony "Antsy" Bonano learns about life, death, and a lot more when he tries to help a friend with a terminal illness feel hopeful about the future.

"Featuring a terrific supporting cast led by Antsy's wise, acerbic mother, an expert blend of comedy and near tragedy, and the wry observations of a narrator . . . this will keep tween readers hooked from start to finish." Booklist

Bruiser. HarperTeen 2010 328p $16.99; lib bdg $17.89

Grades: 8 9 10 11 12   **Fic**

1. Twins -- Fiction 2. Siblings -- Fiction 3. Child abuse -- Fiction 4. Supernatural -- Fiction
ISBN 978-0-06-113408-1; 0-06-113408-2; 978-0-06-113409-8 lib bdg; 0-06-113409-0 lib bdg

LC 2009-30930

Inexplicable events start to occur when sixteen-year-old twins Tennyson and Bronte befriend a troubled and misunderstood outcast, aptly nicknamed Bruiser, and his little brother, Cody.

"Narrated in turns by Tennyson, Bronte, Bruiser, and Bruiser's little brother, Cody, the story is a fascinating study in the art of self-deception and the way our best intentions for others are often based in the selfish desires of our deepest selves. . . . This eloquent and thoughtful story will most certainly leave its mark." Bull Cent Child Books

★ **Downsiders**. Simon & Schuster Bks. for Young Readers 1999 246p hardcover o.p. pa $8.99
Grades: 9 10 11 12   **Fic**
  1. Subways -- Fiction 2. New York (N.Y.) -- Fiction
  ISBN 0-689-80375-3; 1-4169-9747-4 pa
              LC 98-38555

When fourteen-year-old Lindsay meets Talon and discovers the Downsiders world which had evolved from the subway built in New York in 1867 by Alfred Ely Beach, she and her new friend experience the clash of their two cultures.

"Shusterman has invented an alternate world in the Downside that is both original and humorous." Voice Youth Advocates

★ **Everlost**. Simon & Schuster Books for Young Readers 2006 313p (The Skinjacker trilogy) $16.95; pa $8.99
Grades: 8 9 10 11 12   **Fic**
  1. Death -- Fiction 2. Future life -- Fiction 3. Traffic accidents -- Fiction
  ISBN 978-0-689-87237-2; 0-689-87237-2; 978-1-4169-9749-8 pa; 1-4169-9749-0 pa
              LC 2005-32244

When Nick and Allie are killed in a car crash, they end up in Everlost, or limbo for lost souls, where although Nick is satisfied, Allie will stop at nothing—even skinjacking—to break free.

"Shusterman has reimagined what happens after death and questions power and the meaning of charity. While all this is going on, he has also managed to write a rip-roaring adventure complete with monsters, blimps, and high-diving horses." SLJ

Other titles in this series are:
Everfound (2011)
Everwild (2009)

Full tilt; a novel. Simon & Schuster Bks. for Young Readers 2003 201p $16.95; pa $8.99
Grades: 7 8 9 10   **Fic**
  1. Horror fiction 2. Brothers -- Fiction 3. Amusement parks -- Fiction
  ISBN 0-689-80374-5; 1-4169-9748-2 pa
              LC 2002-13867

"Shusterman has created a surreal, scary fantasy, packed with suspenseful psychological drama." Booklist

"An older, alluring, and slightly mysterious girl invites Blake to an amusement park that's only open from midnight to dawn. The rules: he must finish seven rides, all before sunrise, or the park absorbs him. Blake comes to realize that each ride takes him to his deepest fears." Horn Book Guide

The **Schwa** was here; [by] Neal Shusterman. 1st ed; Dutton Children's Books 2004 228p $15.99
Grades: 5 6 7 8   **Fic**
  1. Friendship -- Fiction 2. Brooklyn (New York, N.Y.) -- Fiction
  ISBN 0-525-47182-0
              LC 2004-45072

A Brooklyn eighth-grader nicknamed Antsy befriends the Schwa, an "invisible-ish" boy who is tired of blending into his surroundings and going unnoticed by nearly everyone.

"Antsy is one funny narrator. . . . Shusterman has created yet another very readable and refreshingly different story." Voice Youth Advocates

Followed by: Antsy does time (2008)

Ship out of luck; a companion to The Schwa was here. Neal Shusterman. Dutton Books, an imprint of Penguin Group (USA) Inc. 2013 256 p. (hardcover : alk. paper) $16.99
Grades: 6 7 8   **Fic**
  1. Smuggling -- Fiction 2. Cruise ships -- Fiction 3. Caribbean Area -- Fiction 4. Adventure and adventurers -- Fiction
  ISBN 0525422269; 9780525422266
              LC 2013000031

In this book, "Old Man Crawley, a filthy-rich irascible codger with a soft spot for his blind, 16-year-old granddaughter, Lexie, is about to turn 80. To celebrate, he invites--commands, really--Antsy and his family to join him and Lexie for a week aboard the incredibly fabulous cruise ship Plethora of the Deep." During the trip, Antsy meets and tries to help "Tilde, who claims she's a stowaway and smuggler of illegal immigrants." (Kirkus Reviews)

UnSouled; Neal Shusterman. Simon & Schuster Books for Young Readers 2013 416 p. (Unwind trilogy) (hardback) $17.99
Grades: 6 7 8 9 10 11 12   **Fic**
  1. Science fiction 2. Traffic accidents 3. Travel -- Fiction 4. Identity -- Fiction 5. Survival -- Fiction 6. Revolutionaries -- Fiction 7. Fugitives from justice -- Fiction
  ISBN 1442423692; 9781442423695
              LC 2013022703

In this book, the third in author Neal Shusterman's Un-Wholly series, "Lev and Connor are on the road again. Their destination is back to Ohio where Sonia, an antiques dealer with an important past, will help them end Unwinding once and for all. After a bizarre car accident . . . they wind up on a Native American reservation. Here, readers learn a lot more about Lev's past, and Connor meets up with Cam, the one and only Rewind." (School Library Journal)

"In the third of his projected four-volume Unwind "dystology" Shusterman brings most of his central cast of teenage fugitives together and introduces an important new character, who is exempt from being unwound (legally disassembled for body parts) because she has a mild spectrum disorder. Frequent references to events in previous episodes slow the pace somewhat but the present-tense tale remains suspenseful, the overall premise is as hauntingly plausible as ever, and an electrifying revelation at the end points the way to a possible resolution." (Booklist)

UnWholly; Neal Shusterman. Simon & Schuster Books For Young Readers 2012 402 p. (hardback) $17.99
Grades: 6 7 8 9 10 11 12   **Fic**
  1. Science fiction 2. Identity -- Fiction 3. Survival skills -- Fiction 4. Survival -- Fiction 5. Revolutionaries

-- Fiction 6. Fugitives from justice -- Fiction
ISBN 1442423668; 9781442423664; 9781442423688

LC 2012002729

Sequel to: Unwind

This sequel to Neal Shusterman's book "Unwind" follows "Cam . . . a product of unwinding; made entirely out of the parts of other unwinds, he is a teen who does not technically exist. A futuristic Frankenstein, Cam struggles with a search for identity and meaning. . . . And when the actions of a sadistic bounty hunter cause Cam's fate to become inextricably bound with the fates of Connor, Risa, and Lev, he'll have to question humanity itself." (Publisher's note)

★ **Unwind.** Simon & Schuster Books for Young Readers 2007 335p $17.99

Grades: 6 7 8 9 10 11 12　　　　　　　　　**Fic**

1. Science fiction
ISBN 1-4169-1204-5; 1-4169-1205-3 pa; 978-1-4169-1204-0; 978-1-4169-1205-7 pa

LC 2006032689

In a future world where those between the ages of thirteen and eighteen can have their lives "unwound" and their body parts harvested for use by others, three teens go to extreme lengths to uphold their beliefs—and, perhaps, save their own lives. "Grades eight to ten." (Bull Cent Child Books)

"Poignant, compelling, and ultimately terrifying." Voice Youth Advocates

Siegelson, Kim L.

Honey Bea; [by] Kim L. Siegelson. 1st ed; Jump at the Sun/Hyperion Books for Children 2006 276p $15.99

Grades: 7 8 9 10　　　　　　　　　　　　**Fic**

1. Magic -- Fiction 2. Slavery -- Fiction 3. Louisiana -- Fiction 4. Plantation life -- Fiction
ISBN 0-7868-0853-5

LC 2003-61888

On a Louisiana sugar plantation, a young slave girl struggles with the magical powers that have been passed down from her grandmother and mother to her, unsure of the responsibilities and consequences that accompany this power.

"Siegelson crafts a mesmerizing tale heavy with the scent of honey and flowers and rooted in Louisiana soil." Booklist

Silberberg, Alan

★ **Milo**; sticky notes and brain freeze. written and illustrated by Alan Silberberg. Aladdin 2010 275p il $15.99

Grades: 5 6 7 8　　　　　　　　　　　　　**Fic**

1. Death -- Fiction 2. Mothers -- Fiction 3. Friendship -- Fiction 4. Bereavement -- Fiction
ISBN 978-1-4169-9430-5; 1-4169-9430-0

LC 2010012708

"This is more than just another funny story about a middle school misfit who is the new kid in the neighborhood. While Milo does struggle with all the normal tween anxieties and self-consciousness about his family, there is more. Silberberg details the daily events with Wimpy Kid-like drawings and quick-witted humor that will keep the pages turning. Milo's new friendships with classmates Marshall and Hillary and elderly neighbor Sylvia Poole allow readers to glimpse at the deeper truth--Milo's mother's

death--as it emerges between laugh lines. Silberberg takes on a tough topic and always stays true to the age of the character through dialogue and artwork while maintaining that wisecracking, 12-year-old humor." SLJ

Silvey, Craig

★ **Jasper** Jones; a novel. Alfred A. Knopf 2011 312p $16.99

Grades: 6 7 8 9 10　　　　　　　　　　　**Fic**

1. Mystery fiction 2. Homicide -- Fiction 3. Australia -- Fiction 4. Family life -- Fiction
ISBN 0-375-86666-3; 0-375-96666-8 lib bdg; 978-0-375-86666-1; 978-0-375-96666-8 lib bdg

LC 2010-9364

In small-town Australia, teens Jasper and Charlie form an unlikely friendship when one asks the other to help him cover up a murder until they can prove who is responsible.

"Silvey infuses his prose with a musician's sensibility—Charlie's pounding heart is echoed in the terse staccato sentences of the opening scenes, alternating with legato phrases laden with meaning. The author's keen ear for dialogue is evident in the humorous verbal sparring between Charlie and Jeffrey, typical of smart 13-year-old boys. . . . A richly rewarding exploration of truth and lies by a masterful storyteller." Kirkus

Simmons, Michael

Alien feast; [by] Michael Simmons; illustrated by George O'Connor. Roaring Brook Press 2008 240p il (Chronicles of the first invasion) $9.95

Grades: 5 6 7 8　　　　　　　　　　　　　**Fic**

1. Science fiction 2. Orphans -- Fiction 3. Kidnapping -- Fiction 4. Extraterrestrial beings -- Fiction
ISBN 978-1-59643-281-9; 1-59643-281-0

LC 2007-44050

In 2017, human-eating aliens have kidnapped two scientists who might cure the disease that is destroying them, and twelve-year-old William Aitkin, his elderly, ailing Uncle Maynard, and the scientists' daughter, Sophie, set out to rescue them.

"The youngsters are nicely developed, and, refreshingly, they act as you'd expect kids to behave in such a stressful situation, not like miniature adults. O'Connor's artwork adds to the humor." SLJ

Simner, Janni Lee

Bones of Faerie. Random House 2009 247p $16.99; lib bdg $19.99

Grades: 7 8 9 10　　　　　　　　　　　　**Fic**

1. Fantasy fiction 2. Magic -- Fiction 3. Fairies -- Fiction
ISBN 978-0-375-84563-5; 978-0-375-94563-2 lib bdg

LC 2008-2022

Fifteen-year-old Liza travels through war-ravaged territory, accompanied by two companions, in a struggle to bridge the faerie and human worlds and to bring back her mother while learning of her own powers and that magic can be controlled.

This is a "compelling developed, highly vulnerable trio whose resolute defiance against the status quo will resonate with readers long after specific details of the story may be forgotten." Bull Cent Child Books

Followed by: Faerie winter (2011)

Faerie after; Janni Lee Simner. Random House Inc. 2013 272 p. (ebook) $50.97; (hardcover) $16.99; (library) $19.99

Grades: 7 8 9 10 **Fic**
1. Occult fiction 2. Fantasy fiction 3. Fairies -- Fiction 4. Magic -- Fiction 5. Coming of age -- Fiction
ISBN 0375870695; 9780307974556; 9780375870699; 9780375970696

LC 2012006430

Sequel to: Faerie winter

This is the third book in Janni Lee's Bones of Faerie trilogy. "Relative peace has descended upon Liza's town, where she practices her summoner magic and waits for her half-faerie baby sister to be born. But the forest is showing new dangers, though subtle ones," particularly a strange dust. "Liza's quest to find out what's wrong reveals fresh disasters." (Kirkus)

Faerie winter. Random House Children's Books 2011 270p $16.99; lib bdg $19.99

Grades: 7 8 9 10 **Fic**
1. Magic -- Fiction 2. Fairies -- Fiction 3. Mother-daughter relationship -- Fiction
ISBN 978-0-375-86671-5; 0-375-86671-X; 978-0-375-96671-2 lib bdg; 0-375-96671-4 lib bdg

LC 2010014250

Sequel to: Bones of Faerie (2009)

Unable to get answers from her mother, sixteen-year-old Liza learns from Karin that while her own actions may have doomed the fairy and human worlds, she may be able to save them with more training, if the Faerie Queen can first be stopped.

"Simner tells a more streamlined story this time around and keeps up the dark atmospherics of her high-appeal blend of unsettling speculative-fiction scenarios." Booklist

Thief eyes. Random House 2010 272p $16.99

Grades: 7 8 9 10 **Fic**
1. Fantasy fiction 2. Magic -- Fiction 3. Iceland -- Fiction 4. Missing persons -- Fiction
ISBN 978-0-375-86670-8; 0-375-86670-1

LC 2009-18166

Haley's mother disappeared while on a trip to Iceland, and a year later, when her father takes her there to find out what happened, Haley finds herself deeply involved in an ancient saga that began with her Nordic ancestors.

"Simner skillfully weaves Haley and Ari's modern emotional struggles into the ancient saga and enlivens the story with an intriguing cast of characters from the original tale." Booklist

Simon, Charnan

Plan B. Darby Creek 2011 104p (Surviving Southside) lib bdg $27.93; pa $7.95

Grades: 7 8 9 10 **Fic**
1. School stories 2. Pregnancy -- Fiction
ISBN 978-0-7613-6149-7 lib bdg; 0-7613-6149-9 lib bdg; 978-0-7613-6163-3 pa; 0-7613-6163-4 pa

LC 2010023819

Lucy has her life planned out: she'll graduate and then join her boyfriend, Luke, at college in Austin. She'll become a Spanish teacher and of course they'll get married. But then Lucy gets pregnant. Together, she and Luke will have to make the most difficult decision of their lives.

This "well-written [story reinforces] the importance of family, friends, values, and thoughtful decision-making. . . . [An] excellent [purchase, this book] will attract and engage reluctant readers." SLJ

Singer, Nicky

Gem X. Holiday House 2008 311p $16.95

Grades: 7 8 9 10 **Fic**
1. Science fiction 2. Cloning -- Fiction 3. Genetic engineering -- Fiction 4. Political corruption -- Fiction
ISBN 978-0-8234-2108-4; 0-8234-2108-2

LC 2007-14975

Sixteen-year-old Maxo Strang, the most perfect human ever made, suddenly discovers a 'crack' in his face, which leads him to expose his community's dark underworld of secret scientific research and the city's corrupt supreme leader.

"This intelligent, fast-paced novel will appeal to those teens who . . . want speculative fiction with bite and satire." SLJ

Singleton, Linda Joy

Dead girl dancing; Linda Joy Singleton. Flux 2009 259 p. pa $9.95

Grades: 8 9 10 11 12 **Fic**
1. Fantasy fiction 2. Stalkers -- Fiction 3. Supernatural -- Fiction 4. Identity -- Fiction 5. Friendship -- Fiction 6. Future life -- Fiction 7. Self-esteem -- Fiction 8. Best friends -- Fiction 9. Emotional problems -- Fiction
ISBN 9780738714066

LC 2008044037

This paranormal young adult book, the second book in Linda Joy Singleton's "Dead Girl" series after "Dead Girl Watching," continues the story of Amber, who is a "Temp Lifer," or someone who has the ability to "step[. . .] into someone's life--and their body." In this installment, Amber is stuck in the body of "[her] boyfriend's older sister, who is getting ready to go wild on spring break--while being pursued by a psycho stalker and a Dark Lifer." (Publisher's note)

Dead girl in love; Linda Joy Singleton. Flux 2009 283 p. $9.95

Grades: 8 9 10 11 12 **Fic**
1. Fantasy fiction 2. Supernatural -- Fiction 3. Female friendship -- Fiction 4. Identity -- Fiction 5. Friendship -- Fiction 6. Future life -- Fiction 7. Best friends -- Fiction 8. Grandmothers -- Fiction 9. Mothers and daughters -- Fiction
ISBN 0738714070; 9780738714073

LC 2009009049

This paranormal young adult book, the third book in Linda Joy Singleton's "Dead Girl" series after "Dead Girl Dancing," continues the story of Amber, whose "dead grandmother keeps finding people who have big problems and then [Amber has] the freaky experience of stepping into their life—and their body!—to provide help. This time, [she's] in the body of [her] BFF, Alyce. Since Alyce and

[Amber] know everything about each other," Amber thinks she "won't have to do a lot of detective work" with this case. However, she's alarmed to discover that a question she does have to answer is why Alyce's body is in a coffin. (Publisher's note)

Dead girl walking; [by] Linda Joy Singleton. Flux 2008 308p (Dead girl) $9.95

Grades: 8 9 10 11 12   **Fic**
1. School stories 2. Death -- Fiction 3. Future life -- Fiction
ISBN 978-0-7387-1405-9; 0-7387-1405-4
LC 2008012991

When Amber, a smart, middle-class, high school student, is hit by a truck, she meets her deceased grandmother in a dreamlike place, then takes a wrong turn and awakens in the body of a wealthy, beautiful, popular classmate with serious problems.

"This page-turner has wit, love, courage, adventure, and remarkable insight." SLJ

Sitomer, Alan Lawrence

★ The **downside** of being up. G.P. Putnam's Sons 2011 215p $16.99

Grades: 6 7 8 9   **Fic**
1. School stories 2. Puberty -- Fiction 3. Family life -- Fiction
ISBN 978-0-399-25498-7; 0-399-25498-6
LC 2010044203

All Bobby Connor wants is to survive middle school, but puberty is making that difficult for him as his body conspires against him.

"It is impossible to dislike this pun-filled tale. . . . This fiction provides some long-needed realism, served up by a narrator who knows what he is talking about." Booklist

The **secret** story of Sonia Rodriguez. Jump at the Sun/Hyperion Books For Children 2008 312p lib bdg $17.99

Grades: 7 8 9 10   **Fic**
1. Family life -- Fiction 2. Mexican Americans -- Fiction
ISBN 978-1-4231-1072-9; 1-4231-1072-2
LC 2007-45265

Tenth-grader Sonia reveals secrets about her life and her Hispanic family as she studies hard to become the first Rodriguez to finish high school.

"Sonia's immediate voice will hold teens with its mix of anger, sorrow, tenderness, and humor." Booklist

Skelton, Matthew

★ **Endymion** Spring. Delacorte Press 2006 392p il $17.95; lib bdg $19.99; pa $9.99

Grades: 5 6 7 8   **Fic**
1. Inventors 2. Printers 3. Magic -- Fiction 4. Great Britain -- Fiction 5. Books and reading -- Fiction
ISBN 0-385-73380-1; 0-385-90397-9 lib bdg; 0-385-73456-5 pa
LC 2006-46259

Having reluctantly accompanied his academic mother and pesky younger sister to Oxford, twelve-year-old Blake Winters is at loose ends until he stumbles across an ancient

and magical book, secretly brought to England in 1453 by Gutenberg's mute apprentice to save it from evil forces, and which now draws Blake into a dangerous and life-threatening quest

"This book is certain to reach an audience looking for a page-turner, and it just might motivate readers to explore the . . . facts behind the fiction." SLJ

★ The **story** of Cirrus Flux. Delacorte Press 2010 288p il $17.99; lib bdg $20.99

Grades: 4 5 6 7   **Fic**
1. Adventure fiction 2. Orphans -- Fiction 3. Supernatural -- Fiction 4. London (England) -- Fiction 5. Great Britain -- History -- 1714-1837 -- Fiction
ISBN 978-0-385-73381-6; 0-385-73381-X; 978-0-385-90398-1 lib bdg; 0-385-90398-7 lib bdg
LC 2009-18987

In 1783 London, the destiny of an orphaned boy and girl becomes intertwined as the boy, Cirrus Flux, is pursued by a sinister woman mesmerist, a tiny man with an all-seeing eye, and a skull-collecting scoundrel, all of whom believe that he possesses an orb containing a divine power.

Skelton "neatly weaves touches of fantasy into a late-eighteenth century London setting. . . . His literary sensibility and grubby atmospherics are strong enough to carry the tale." Booklist

Skurzynski, Gloria

The **Virtual** War. Simon & Schuster Bks. for Young Readers 1997 152p hardcover o.p. pa $10.95

Grades: 6 7 8 9   **Fic**
1. Science fiction 2. Virtual reality -- Fiction
ISBN 0-689-81374-0; 1-4169-7577-2 pa
LC 96-35346

In a future world where global contamination has necessitated limited human contact, three young people with unique genetically engineered abilities are teamed up to wage a war in virtual reality

"Skurzynski's anti-war message is clear yet never didactic; her characters are complex and fully realized, the pacing brisk, and the story compelling." Bull Cent Child Books

Other titles in this series are:
The choice (2006)
The clones (2002)
The revolt (2005)

Slade, Arthur

★ The **hunchback** assignments; [by] Arthur Slade. Wendy Lamb Books 2009 278p $15.99; lib bdg $18.99

Grades: 7 8 9 10   **Fic**
1. Science fiction 2. Spies -- Fiction 3. Supernatural -- Fiction 4. London (England) -- Fiction 5. Physically disabled -- Fiction 6. Great Britain -- History -- 19th century -- Fiction
ISBN 978-0-385-73784-5; 0-385-73784-X; 978-0-385-90694-4 lib bdg; 0-385-90694-3 lib bdg
LC 2008-54378

In Victorian London, fourteen-year-old Modo, a shape-changing hunchback, becomes a secret agent for the Permanent Association, which strives to protect the world from the evil machinations of the Clockwork Guild.

"A solid story line and well-crafted writing make for a pleasing and evocative adventure." Booklist

Other titles in the series are:

The dark deeps (2010)

Empire of ruins (2011)

Followed by: The dark deeps (2010)

Jolted; Newton Starker's rules for survival. [by] Arthur Slade. Wendy Lamb Books 2009 227p $15.99; lib bdg $18.99

Grades: 5 6 7 8   Fic

1. School stories 2. Lightning -- Fiction

ISBN 978-0-385-74700-4; 0-385-74700-4; 978-0-385-90944-0 lib bdg; 0-385-90944-6 lib bdg

LC 2008-8632

First published 2008 in Canada

Many of Newton Starker's ancestors, including his mother, have been killed by lightning strikes, so when he enrolls at the eccentric Jerry Potts Academy of Higher Learning and Survival in Moose Jaw, Saskatchewan, he tries to be a model student so that he can avoid the same fate.

"The premise will snag readers immediately [and] . . . Slade's portrayal of Newton's sweep of emotions as he deals with his perceived fate–fear, fury, dogged determination–is especially convincing." Publ Wkly

Slater, Adam

The **Shadowing**: Hunted. Egmont 2011 208p $16.99

Grades: 7 8 9 10   Fic

1. Ghost stories 2. Horror fiction 3. Supernatural -- Fiction

ISBN 978-1-6068-426-1; 1-60684-261-7

"Callum Scott sees ghosts. . . . It's because he is a 'chime child,' born on a full moon between midnight Friday and dawn Saturday. . . . When a huge, particularly evil-looking black dog and a pale boy dripping blood start following him, he is unnerved. . . . The barrier between the human world and the demon realm is disintegrating like it does every hundred years, and only the chime children can keep humanity safe. Slater shows a knack for building tension and terror and readers . . . will gulp this series opener and ask for more." Booklist

Slayton, Fran Cannon

★ **When** the whistle blows. Philomel Books 2009 162p $16.99

Grades: 7 8 9 10   Fic

1. Railroads -- Fiction 2. Family life -- Fiction 3. Country life -- Fiction 4. West Virginia -- Fiction

ISBN 978-0-399-25189-4; 0-399-25189-8

LC 2008-38435

Jimmy Cannon tells about his life in the 1940s as the son of a West Virginia railroad man, loving the trains and expecting one day to work on the railroad like his father and brothers.

"Telling details and gentle humor help set the scene and reveal a great deal about these characters and their lives. . . . A polished paean to a bygone time and place." SLJ

Sleator, William

★ The **duplicate**. Dutton 1988 154p hardcover o.p. pa $5.99

Grades: 7 8 9 10   Fic

1. Science fiction

ISBN 0-14-130431-6

LC 87-30562

Sixteen-year-old David, finding a strange machine that creates replicas of living organisms, duplicates himself and suffers the horrible consequences when the duplicate turns against him

"There are some points in the story when the roles of the clones (referred to as Duplicates A and B) become congested to the detriment of the book's pace, but fantasy fans will doubtless find the concept fresh enough and eerie enough to compensate for this, and Sleator is, as always, economical in casting and structuring his story." Bull Cent Child Books

★ **Interstellar** pig. Dutton 1984 197p hardcover o.p. pa $6.99

Grades: 5 6 7 8   Fic

1. Science fiction

ISBN 0-14-037595-3 pa

LC 84-4132

Barney's boring seaside vacation suddenly becomes more interesting when the cottage next door is occupied by three exotic neighbors who are addicted to a game they call "Interstellar Pig."

The author "draws the reader in with intimations of danger and horror, but the climactic battle is more slapstick than horrific, and the victor's prize could scarcely be more ironic. Problematic as straight science fiction but great fun as a spoof on human-alien contact." Booklist

Another title about Barney is:

Parasite Pig (2002)

Singularity. Dutton 1985 170p hardcover o.p. pa $5.99

Grades: 7 8 9 10   Fic

1. Science fiction 2. Twins -- Fiction

ISBN 0-525-44161-1; 0-14-037598-8 pa

LC 84-26075

Sixteen-year-old twins Harry and Barry stumble across a gateway to another universe, where a distortion in time and space causes a dramatic change in their competitive relationship

"The book has a title with a fine double entendre and is an unusual, suspenseful yarn told by a master storyteller." Horn Book

Sloan, Holly Goldberg

★ **Counting** by 7s; by Holly Goldberg Sloan. Dial Books for Young Readers 2012 384 p. (hardcover) $16.99

Grades: 4 5 6 7   Fic

1. Genius -- Fiction 2. Orphans -- Fiction 3. Alienation (Social psychology) -- Fiction 4. Schools -- Fiction 5. Gardening -- Fiction 6. High schools -- Fiction 7. Eccentrics and eccentricities -- Fiction

ISBN 0803738552; 9780803738553

LC 2012004994

This book follows "Willow Chance . . . an extremely precocious and analytical 12-year-old 'genius'. . . . Despite Willow's social difficulties, she makes an impression on everyone around her--whether it's Dell Duke, a lonely and ineffectual school district counselor, or Jairo Hernandez, the taxi driver Willow hires to drive her to her meetings with Dell. After Willow's parents die in a car crash, her new friend Mai Nguyen persuades her mother to take Willow in." (Publishers Weekly)

★ **I'll** be there. Little, Brown 2011 392p $17.99
Grades: 7 8 9 10 **Fic**
1. Brothers -- Fiction 2. Family life -- Fiction 3. Mental illness -- Fiction 4. Father-son relationship -- Fiction
ISBN 978-0-316-12279-5; 0-316-12279-3
LC 2010-42994
"This riveting story will keep readers interested and guessing until the end." SLJ

"Protecting his mute younger brother from their unstable father and the factors that force them to continuously move and prevent their school attendance, Sam finds everything changing when he meets Emily, who tempts them to consider a normal life. A first novel." (Publisher's Note)

Smelcer, John E.
The **Great** Death; [by] John Smelcer. Henry Holt and Co. 2009 166p $15.99
Grades: 6 7 8 9 **Fic**
1. Death -- Fiction 2. Alaska -- Fiction 3. Orphans -- Fiction 4. Sisters -- Fiction 5. Epidemics -- Fiction 6. Native Americans -- Fiction 7. Voyages and travels -- Fiction
ISBN 978-0-8050-8100-8; 0-8050-8100-3
LC 2008-51113
As their Alaskan village's only survivors of sickness brought by white men one winter early in the twentieth century, sisters Millie, aged thirteen, and Maura, ten, make their way south in hopes of finding someone alive.
"An engaging tale of survival." Kirkus

The **trap**; [by] John Smelcer. Henry Holt and Co. 2006 170p $15.95
Grades: 6 7 8 9 **Fic**
1. Alaska -- Fiction 2. Grandfathers -- Fiction 3. Native Americans -- Fiction 4. Survival after airplane accidents, shipwrecks, etc. -- Fiction
ISBN 978-0-8050-7939-5; 0-8050-7939-4
LC 2005035740
In alternating chapters, seventeen-year-old Johnny Least-Weasel worries about his missing grandfather, and the grandfather, Albert Least-Weasel, struggles to survive, caught in his own steel trap in the Alaskan winter.
"In this story, Smelcer . . . seems to straddle the line flawlessly between an ancient legend and contemporary fiction. . . . His characters act with quiet dignity. . . . The suspense is played on an everyday level, which is why it works." Voice Youth Advocates

Smibert, Angie
Memento Nora. Marshall Cavendish 2011 184p $16.99

Grades: 8 9 10 11 12 **Fic**
1. Science fiction 2. Memory -- Fiction 3. Terrorism -- Fiction 4. Cartoons and caricatures -- Fiction 5. Resistance to government -- Fiction
ISBN 0-7614-5829-8; 978-0-7614-5829-6
LC 2010011816
In a near future in which terrorism is commonplace but memories of horrors witnessed can be obliterated by a pill, teens Nora, Winter, and Micah, create an underground comic to share with their classmates the experiences they want to remember.
This offers "a multi-threaded plot that manages to be both complex and comfortably easy to follow. . . . The fast pace encourages readers to fall headfirst into a gripping suspense-adventure ride." Bull Cent Child Books

Smiley, Jane, 1949-
Gee Whiz; Jane Smiley; with illustrations by Elaine Clayton. Alfred A. Knopf 2013 272 p. (The horses of Oak Valley Ranch) (library binding) $19.99
Grades: 4 5 6 7 **Fic**
1. Ranch life -- Fiction 2. Horses -- Fiction 3. Christian life -- Fiction 4. Horses -- Training -- Fiction 5. Ranch life -- California -- Fiction 6. Family life -- California -- Fiction 7. California -- History -- 1950- -- Fiction
ISBN 0375969691; 9780375869693; 9780375969690; 9780375985331
LC 2012024370
In this book, by Jane Smiley, "Gee Whiz is a striking horse, and only part of that is because of his size. . . . When Abby is confronted with an onslaught of reminders of just how little of the world she has seen, she finds herself connecting with Gee Whiz's calm and curious nature, and his desire to know more." (Publisher's note)

★ The **Georges** and the Jewels; with illustrations by Elaine Clayton. Alfred A. Knopf 2009 232p il $16.99; lib bdg $19.99
Grades: 4 5 6 7 **Fic**
1. Horses -- Fiction 2. California -- Fiction 3. Ranch life -- Fiction 4. Christian life -- Fiction
ISBN 978-0-375-86227-4; 0-375-86227-7; 978-0-375-96227-1 lib bdg; 0-375-96227-1 lib bdg
LC 2009-06241
Seventh-grader Abby Lovitt grows up on her family's California horse ranch in the 1960s, learning to train the horses her father sells and trying to reconcile her strict religious upbringing with her own ideas about life.
"As might be expected from the skilled hands of Smiley . . . there are synchronous storylines . . . [and] many will find it difficult to say goodbye to Abby, Jack and especially to Ornery George." Publ Wkly
Other titles in this series are:
A good horse (2010)
True blue (2011)

Pie in the Sky; Book Four of the Horses of Oak Valley Ranch. Jane Smiley; with illustrations by Elaine Clayton. Alfred A. Knopf Books for Young Readers 2012 257 p. (hardback) $16.99
Grades: 4 5 6 7 **Fic**
1. Horsemanship -- Fiction 2. Horses -- Fiction

3. Schools -- Fiction 4. High schools -- Fiction 5. Christian life -- Fiction 6. Horses -- Training -- Fiction 7. Ranch life -- California -- Fiction 8. Family life -- California -- Fiction 9. California -- History -- 1950- -- Fiction

ISBN 0375869689; 9780375869686; 9780375969683; 9780375985324

LC 2011044104

In this book, by Jane Smiley, "Abby Lovitt doesn't realize how unprepared she is when she takes her beloved horse, True Blue, to a clinic led by the most famous equestrian anyone knows. The biggest surprise, though, is that Sophia . . . stops riding. Who will ride her horse? Abby's dad seems to think it will be Abby. Pie in the Sky is the most expensive horse Abby has ever ridden. But he is proud and irritable, and he takes Abby's attention away from the continuing mystery that is True Blue." (Publisher's note)

Smith, Alexander Gordon

Lockdown. Farrar, Straus and Giroux 2009 273p (Escape from Furnace) $14.99

Grades: 7 8 9 10   **Fic**

1. Science fiction 2. Escapes -- Fiction 3. Prisoners -- Fiction

ISBN 978-0-374-32491-9; 0-374-32491-3

LC 2008-43439

When fourteen-year-old Alex is framed for murder, he becomes an inmate in the Furnace Penitentiary, where brutal inmates and sadistic guards reign, boys who disappear in the middle of the night sometimes return weirdly altered, and escape might just be possible.

"Once a plot is hatched, readers will be turning pages without pause, and the cliffhanger ending will have them anticipating the next installment. Most appealing is Smith's flowing writing style, filled with kid-speak, colorful adjectives, and amusing analogies." SLJ

Other titles in this series are:
Death sentence (2011)
Solitary (2010)

Smith, Cynthia Leitich

Feral nights; Cynthia Leitich Smith. Candlewick Press 2013 304 p. $17.99

Grades: 9 10 11 12   **Fic**

1. Occult fiction 2. Monsters -- Fiction

ISBN 0763659096; 9780763659097

LC 2012942377

This young adult paranormal fantasy story, by Cynthia Leitich Smith, is the first entry in the series "Feral." "When sexy, free-spirited werecat Yoshi tracks his sister, Ruby, to Austin, he discovers that she is not only MIA, but also the key suspect in a murder investigation. Meanwhile, werepossum Clyde and human Aimee have set out to do a little detective work of their own, sworn to avenge the brutal killing of werearmadillo pal Travis." (Publisher's note)

Rain is not my Indian name. HarperCollins Pubs. 2001 135p $15.99; lib bdg $16.89

Grades: 6 7 8 9   **Fic**

1. Death -- Fiction 2. Photography -- Fiction 3. Native

Americans -- Fiction

ISBN 0-688-17397-7; 0-06-029504-X lib bdg

LC 00-59705

Tired of staying in seclusion since the death of her best friend, a fourteen-year-old Native American girl takes on a photographic assignment with her local newspaper to cover events at the Native American summer youth camp

"The engaging first-person narrative convincingly portrays Rain's grieving process and addresses the varying degrees of prejudice she encounters." Horn Book Guide

Smith, D. James

The **boys** of San Joaquin; a novel. Atheneum Books for Young Readers 2005 231p $15.95; pa $5.99

Grades: 5 6 7 8   **Fic**

1. Deaf -- Fiction 2. California -- Fiction 3. Family life -- Fiction 4. Italian Americans -- Fiction

ISBN 0-689-87606-8; 1-4169-1619-9 pa

LC 2004-3075

In a small California town in 1951, twelve-year-old Paolo and his deaf cousin Billy get caught up in a search for money missing from the church collection, leading them to complicated discoveries about themselves, other family members, and townspeople they thought they knew

"Narrator Paolo has an appealingly distinctive voice and a keen eye for observing people, and the supporting characters are equally memorable." Booklist

Other titles about Paolo and Billy are:
Probably the world's best story about a dog and the girl who loved me (2006)
It was September when we ran away the first time (2008)

It was September when we ran away the first time; [by] D. James Smith. Atheneum Books for Young Readers 2008 240p $16.99

Grades: 5 6 7 8   **Fic**

1. Deaf -- Fiction 2. California -- Fiction 3. Race relations -- Fiction 4. Chinese Americans -- Fiction

ISBN 978-1-4169-3809-5; 1-4169-3809-5

LC 2008-4819

In Orange Grove, California, in 1951, plans for an upcoming carnival and running away part-time fall by the wayside when twelve-year-old Paolo, his six-year-old brother Georgie, and their ten-year-old deaf cousin Billy become victims of prejudice after Billy befriends a Chinese American girl

"The plot twists and turns with real surprises . . . and the story is rooted in a . . . diverse community consumed with cold war paranoia. Paolo's scrappy bond with Billy is the heart of the story as they sign together about their anger, confusion and sense of lasting friendship." Booklist

Probably the world's best story about a dog and the girl who loved me. Atheneum Books for Young Readers 2006 234p $15.95

Grades: 5 6 7 8   **Fic**

1. Deaf -- Fiction 2. California -- Fiction 3. Family life -- Fiction 4. Italian Americans -- Fiction

ISBN 1-4169-0542-1

LC 2005-12334

Sequel to: The boys of San Joaquin

The further adventures and misadventures of twelve-year-old Paolo, his six-year-old brother Georgie, and their nine-year-old deaf cousin Billy as they try to find their missing dog, cope with a new paper route, and discover romance in their small California town in 1951

"Paolo's struggle to understand Theresa's bewildering effect on him feels just right, and the nostalgic story . . . winds around like a pleasant small-town street until it reaches a satisfying end." Booklist

Followed by: It was Sepetmber when we ran away the first time (2008)

Smith, Emily Wing

Back when you were easier to love. Dutton Books 2011 296p $16.99

Grades: 8 9 10 11 12   Fic

1. Love stories 2. Mormons -- Fiction 3. Automobile travel -- Fiction

ISBN 978-0-525-42199-3; 0-525-42199-8

LC 2010-13469

When her boyfriend Zan leaves high school in Utah a year early to attend Pitzer College, a broken-hearted Joy and Zan's best friend Noah take off on a road trip to California seeking "closure."

Smith "effectively reconstructs Zan and Joy's relationship. . . . Joy's voice is sturdy, and her articulations about loss and belief are thoughtful and often moving. Self-acceptance and both the comforts and restrictions of the Mormon religion and identity are central themes in this sweet story." Publ Wkly

★ The **way** he lived; [by] Emily Wing Smith. 1st ed.; Flux 2008 232p pa $9.95

Grades: 8 9 10 11 12   Fic

1. Utah -- Fiction 2. Death -- Fiction 3. Mormons -- Fiction

ISBN 978-0-7387-1404-2 pa

LC 2008024416

"The author preserves each narrator's complexity. . . It's a testament to Smith's skills that although her central character speaks only through other people's recollections, his identity emerges distinctly by the end of the novel." Publ Wkly

Smith, Hope Anita

★ **Keeping** the night watch; with illustrations by E.B. Lewis. Henry Holt 2008 73p il $18.95

Grades: 4 5 6 7   Fic

1. Novels in verse 2. Fathers -- Fiction 3. Family life -- Fiction 4. African Americans -- Fiction

ISBN 978-0-8050-7202-0; 0-8050-7202-0

LC 2007-12372

Sequel to: The way a door closes (2003)

Coretta Scott King honor book for text, 2009

A thirteen-year-old African American boy chronicles what happens to his family when his father, who temporarily left, returns home and they all must deal with their feelings of anger, hope, abandonment, and fear.

"The words are simple . . . and the beautiful watercolor pictures of the African American family have the same quiet

intensity as pictures in the first book. . . . Although mainly in free verse, there's also a sonnet." Booklist

The **way** a door closes; [by] Hope Anita Smith; with illustrations by Shane W. Evans. Holt & Co. 2003 52p il $18.95

Grades: 4 5 6 7   Fic

1. Novels in verse 2. Fathers -- Fiction 3. Family life -- Fiction 4. African Americans -- Fiction

ISBN 0-8050-6477-X

LC 2002-67884

In this novel in verse "readers are drawn into the thoughts and feelings of a 13-year-old African American as he tries to understand and cope with a parent's departure from the family. . . . In carefully chosen, straightforward language, Smith conveys the boy's roller-coaster emotions with pinpoint accuracy. The results are poems that are heartbreaking, angry, and tender. Done in warm shades of mostly brown, blue, and gold, Evans's color spot and full-page paintings have a realistic, slightly sculptural appearance and are a perfect complement to the poems." SLJ

Followed by: Keeping the night watch (2008)

Smith, Icy

Half spoon of rice; a survival story of the Cambodian genocide. written by Icy Smith; illustrated by Sopaul Nhem. East West Discovery Press 2010 42p il

Grades: 5 6 7 8   Fic

1. Cambodia -- Fiction 2. Genocide -- Fiction

ISBN 0-9821675-8-X; 978-0-9821675-8-8

LC 2009002973

Nine-year-old Nat and his family are forced from their home on April 17, 1975, marched for many days, separated from each other, and forced to work in the rice fields, where Nat concentrates on survival. Includes historical notes and photographs documenting the Cambodian genocide

"Bold, impressionistic oil paintings, mainly full page but some full spreads, speak volumes, and archival photographs are appended. This powerful child's eye view of war is harsh and realistic—like its subject—though accessible and thought-provoking." SLJ

Smith, Jennifer E.

The **comeback** season. Simon & Schuster Books for Young Readers 2008 246p $15.99

Grades: 6 7 8 9 10   Fic

1. Baseball -- Fiction 2. Bereavement -- Fiction 3. Family life -- Fiction 4. Chicago (Ill.) -- Fiction 5. Father-daughter relationship -- Fiction

ISBN 978-1-4169-3847-7; 1-4169-3847-8

LC 2007-17067

High school freshman Ryan Walsh, a Chicago Cubs fan, meets Nick when they both skip school on opening day, and their blossoming relationship becomes difficult for Ryan when she discovers that Nick is seriously ill and she again feels the pain of losing her father five years earlier.

"Smith deftly twines strands of grief, romance, baseball, family, and friendships lost and regained into this tale. . . . The present-tense narrative has an immediacy that will engage readers and the supporting cast is unusually vivid." Booklist

The **geography** of you and me; Jennifer E. Smith. Little, Brown & Co. 2014 352 p. (hardcover) $18

Grades: 7 8 9 10 11 12   **Fic**

1. Love -- Fiction 2. Social classes -- Fiction 3. Voyages and travels -- Fiction 4. Electric power failures -- Fiction 5. New York (N.Y.) -- Fiction

ISBN 0316254770; 9780316254779

LC 2013022845

In this book, by Jennifer E. Smith, "Lucy lives on the 24th floor. Owen lives in the basement. It's fitting, then, that they meet in the middle–stuck between two floors of a New York City apartment building, on an elevator rendered useless by a citywide blackout. After they're rescued, Lucy and Owen spend the night wandering the darkened streets. . . . But once the power is back, so is reality. Lucy soon moves abroad with her parents, while Owen heads out west with his father." (Publisher's note)

"Owen and Lucy meet during a citywide blackout in New York and spend a memorable (chaste) night together. Soon afterward, Lucy's parents take her to Europe, and Owen and his dad move to San Francisco, but even on opposite sides of the world, they think about each other. Smith's fans will recognize the alternating narration; reflective, deliberate writing style; and serendipitous coincidences." Horn Book

Smith, Lindsay

Sekret; Lindsay Smith. Roaring Brook Press 2014 345 p. (hardback) $17.99

Grades: 8 9 10 11 12   **Fic**

1. Spies -- Fiction 2. Psychics -- Fiction 3. Soviet Union -- Fiction 4. Russia -- History -- 1917-1991, Soviet Union -- Fiction 5. KGB -- Fiction 6. Psychic ability -- Fiction 7. Soviet Union -- History -- 1953-1985 -- Fiction

ISBN 1596438924; 9781596438927

LC 2013027913

In this book, by Lindsay Smith, "Yulia's father always taught her to hide her thoughts and control her emotions to survive the harsh realities of Soviet Russia. But when she's captured by the KGB and forced to work as a psychic spy with a mission to undermine the U.S. space program, she's thrust into a world of suspicion, deceit, and horrifying power." (Publisher's note)

"We the Living meets Genius Squad, this novel follows the misfortunes of Yulia, one of a group of psychic teens pressed into the service of the 1960s KGB. The concept is ambitious and the heroine fiery, but there is a surfeit of plot elements (including a hokey love triangle) and the writing is frequently turgid." Horn Book

Smith, Patricia Clark

Weetamoo, heart of the Pocassets. Scholastic 2003 203p il (Royal diaries) $10.95

Grades: 6 7 8 9   **Fic**

1. Massachusetts -- Fiction 2. Native Americans -- Fiction

ISBN 0-439-12910-9

LC 00-49243

The 1653-1654 diary of a fourteen-year-old Pocasset Indian girl, destined to become a leader of her tribe, describes how her life changes with the seasons, after a ritual fast she undertakes, and with her tribe's interaction with the English "Coat-men" of the nearby Plymouth Colony

This is "a lively yet ultimately tragic tale that vividly evokes the time period." Booklist

Smith, Roland

Chupacabra; Roland Smith. Scholastic Press 2013 336 p. illustrations $16.99

Grades: 5 6 7 8   **Fic**

1. Cryptozoology 2. Kidnapping -- Fiction 3. Mythical animals -- Fiction 4. Father-daughter relationship -- Fiction 5. Chupacabras -- Fiction 6. Missing persons -- Fiction 7. Adventure and adventurers -- Fiction

ISBN 0545178177; 9780545178174

LC 2013404665

This book, part of the Cryptid Hunters series, by Roland Smith, "reunites Marty and his unusual uncle, cryptozoologist Travis Wolfe, as they search the world for Wolfe's daughter, Grace. Grace has been kidnapped by her grandfather, the ruthless and dangerous Noah Blackwood. . . . Now, with word that the mysterious creature known as Chupacabra has been sighted again, Wolfe is torn between his obsession with finding cryptids and his desperate need to rescue his daughter." (Publisher's note)

"Plunging readers in where Tentacles (Scholastic, 2009) left off, this fast-paced novel opens right after Grace discovers that her twin brother, Marty, is in fact her cousin, and that her father's unscrupulous enemy, Noah Blackwood, is actually her grandfather...Though this sequel suffers in comparison to the previous books in the series, Smith adeptly adds enough new characters, dangers, and cool science to reel in reluctant readers and keep them turning pages long after their lights should have been turned off.—" SLJ

Other titles in the series include:
Cryptid Hunters (2005)
Mutation (2014)
Tentacles (2009)

Cryptid hunters. Hyperion Books for Children 2005 348p $15.99; pa $5.99

Grades: 5 6 7 8   **Fic**

1. Adventure fiction 2. Twins -- Fiction 3. Congo (Republic) -- Fiction

ISBN 0-7868-5161-9; 0-7868-5162-7 pa

Twins, Grace and Marty, along with a mysterious uncle, are dropped into the middle of the Congolese jungle in search of their missing photojournalist parents.

"The action is nonstop in this well-paced jungle adventure, and Smith adds a deeper layer in scenes of Marty and Grace discovering truths about their complicated family relationships." Booklist

Followed by: Tentacles (2009)

Elephant run. Hyperion Books for Children 2007 318p $15.99

Grades: 6 7 8 9 10 11 12   **Fic**

1. Myanmar -- Fiction 2. Elephants -- Fiction 3. Prisoners of war -- Fiction 4. World War, 1939-1945

-- Fiction

ISBN 978-1-4231-0402-5; 1-4231-0402-1

LC 2007-13310

Nick endures servitude, beatings, and more after his British father's plantation in Burma is invaded by the Japanese in 1941.

"The Burmese setting and the role of elephants in the lumbering industry are exceptionally well integrated into this wartime adventure tale." Bull Cent Child Books

Eruption; Roland Smith. Scholastic Press 2012 156 p. (Storm runners.)

Grades: 5 6 7 8 **Fic**

1. Circus -- Fiction 2. Rescue work -- Fiction 3. Volcanoes -- Mexico -- Fiction 4. Earthquakes -- Mexico -- Fiction 5. Father-son relationship -- Fiction 6. Mexico -- Fiction 7. Survival -- Fiction 8. Volcanoes -- Fiction 9. Earthquakes -- Fiction 10. Storm chasers -- Fiction 11. Circus animals -- Fiction 12. Fathers and sons -- Fiction

ISBN 0545081742; 9780545081740

LC 2011042743

In the third "installment in the 'Storm Runners' series, Chase and his father are off to Mexico to find the missing Rossi Family Circus. . . . [T]hey end up near a rumbling volcano. [Roland] Smith . . . gives the survival story an extra dose of octane with some escaped wild animals—in this case, a tiger that nearly devours Chase." (Booklist) ". . . [A]ll contact has been lost with the Rossi Brothers' Circus, on tour near Mexico City, in the wake of a major earthquake. This sends a crew headed by catastrophe experts Chase and his father John to the rescue. . . . [They find themselves on] Popocatepetl's shaking, landslide ridden slopes amid clouds of ash to discover human corpses, dead elephants and big cats, desperados, trapped refugees, dozens of badly injured villagers and . . . an escaped tiger." (Kirkus)

I, Q.: book one, Independence Hall. Sleeping Bear Press 2008 302p pa $8.95

Grades: 5 6 7 8 **Fic**

1. Adventure fiction 2. Spies -- Fiction 3. Terrorism -- Fiction

ISBN 978-1-58536-325-4 pa; 1-58536-325-1 pa

In Philadelphia, Angela realizes she's being followed, and Q soon learns the secret about Angela's real mother, a former Secret Service agent

"Adventure, suspense, humor, fascinating characters, and plot twists galore will draw middle-graders to this series starter." Booklist

Followed by: I, Q.: book two, The White House (2009)

I. Q.: book two, The White House. Sleeping Bear Press 2010 pa $8.95

Grades: 5 6 7 8 **Fic**

1. Spies -- Fiction 2. Siblings -- Fiction 3. Terrorism -- Fiction 4. Remarriage -- Fiction 5. Washington (D.C.) -- Fiction 6. Philadelphia (Pa.) -- Fiction 7. White House (Washington, D.C.) -- Fiction

ISBN 978-1-58536-456-5; 1-58536-456-8

LC 2011378292

Q (Quest) and Angela make it to the White House in Washington, D.C. to find that it is even harder to determine who are the 'good' and 'bad' guys than ever before.

"This spellbinding James Bond genre espionage novel for the middle school set will leave readers breathlessly waiting for the next installment." Voice Youth Advocates

★ **Peak**. Harcourt 2007 246p $17

Grades: 7 8 9 10 **Fic**

1. Mountaineering -- Fiction 2. Father-son relationship -- Fiction 3. Mount Everest (China and Nepal) -- Fiction

ISBN 978-0-15-202417-8

LC 2006024325

After fourteen-year-old Peak Marcello is arrested for scaling a New York City skyscraper, he is sent to live with his long-lost father, who wants him to be the youngest person to reach the Everest summit.

"This is a thrilling, multifaceted adventure story. Smith includes plenty of mountaineering facts told in vivid detail. . . . But he also explores other issues, such as the selfishness that nearly always accompanies the intensely single-minded." Booklist

Storm runners. Scholastic Press 2011 143p $16.99

Grades: 5 6 7 8 **Fic**

1. Florida -- Fiction 2. Hurricanes -- Fiction 3. Father-son relationship -- Fiction

ISBN 978-0-545-08175-7; 0-545-08175-0

LC 2010-32720

Twelve-year-old Chase Masters travels the country with his father, a "storm runner," but he is tested in ways he never could have imagined when he and a new friend are caught in a hurricane near St. Petersburg, Florida.

"This is an exciting, quick read. . . . Readers will feel engaged with Chase and his friends in their struggles to survive." SLJ

Followed by: The surge (2011)

The **surge**. Scholastic Press 2011 133p il (Storm runners) $16.99

Grades: 5 6 7 8 **Fic**

1. Circus -- Fiction 2. Storms -- Fiction 3. Florida -- Fiction 4. Hurricanes -- Fiction

ISBN 978-0-545-08179-5; 0-545-08179-3

LC 2011017358

After barely surviving a terrifying hurricane, Chase and his friends Nicole and Rashawn have made it to the safety of Nicole's family farm, which is also the winter home of the Rossi Brothers Circus, where flood waters are rising and dangerous circus animals are on the loose.

"A high-velocity page-turner." Kirkus

Tentacles. Scholastic Press 2009 318p $16.99

Grades: 5 6 7 8 **Fic**

1. Mystery fiction 2. Adventure fiction 3. Squids -- Fiction 4. New Zealand -- Fiction

ISBN 978-0-545-16688-1; 0-545-16688-8

LC 2009011125

Sequel to: Cryptid hunters (2005)

After the mysterious disappearance of their parents, Marty and Grace go to live with their scientist uncle and accompany him on, what soon becomes, an increasingly dangerous expedition to New Zealand to track a giant squid.

Smith, Roland C., 1951-

Mutation; Roland Smith. Scholastic Press 2014 352 p. (Cryptid hunters) (hardback) $16.99

Grades: 5 6 7 8   **Fic**

1. Brazil -- Fiction 2. Missing persons -- Fiction 3. Jungles -- Fiction 4. Animals, Mythical -- Fiction 5. Adventure and adventurers -- Fiction

ISBN 0545081807; 9780545081801; 9780545081818
LC 2014017169

In this book by Roland Smith "Marty and his best friend, Luther, have managed to rescue Marty's cousin Grace from the clutches of the nefarious pseudo-naturalist Noah Blackwood, but . . . Marty's parents have been missing in Brazil for months. With time running out, Marty and the Cryptos Island crew race off for Brazil -- where they discover that Noah Blackwood has twisted the natural order of things beyond their wildest, most terrifying dreams." (Publisher's note)

"Marty, Grace, and friends make their way to Brazil to continue their twofold quest: find Marty's missing parents and stop the evil Noah Blackwood from continuing his unethical genetic experiments. Action, adventure, and high-tech gadgetry all combine into an exciting but over-the-top story. Stunning revelations and other dramatic turns provide additional impetus to keep readers turning the pages." Horn Book

Smith, Sarah

The **other** side of dark. Atheneum Books for Young Readers 2010 312p $16.99

Grades: 6 7 8 9 10   **Fic**

1. Ghost stories 2. Orphans -- Fiction 3. Supernatural -- Fiction 4. Boston (Mass.) -- Fiction 5. Race relations -- Fiction 6. African Americans -- Fiction

ISBN 978-1-4424-0280-5; 1-4424-0280-6
LC 2010-14690

Since losing both of her parents, fifteen-year-old Katie can see and talk to ghosts, which makes her a loner until fellow student Law sees her drawing of a historic house and together they seek a treasure rumored to be hidden there by illegal slave-traders.

The author "weaves complicated racial issues into a romantic, mysterious novel." Booklist

Smith, Sherri L.

★ **Flygirl**. G.P. Putnam's Sons 2009 275p $16.99

Grades: 7 8 9 10   **Fic**

1. Air pilots -- Fiction 2. Women air pilots -- Fiction 3. African Americans -- Fiction 4. World War, 1939-1945 -- Fiction

ISBN 978-0-399-24709-5; 0-399-24709-2
LC 2008-25407

During World War II, a light-skinned African American girl "passes" for white in order to join the Women Airforce Service Pilots.

"The details about navigation are exciting, but tougher than any flight maneuver are Ida Mae's loneliness, shame,

and fear that she will be thrown out of the the military, feelings that culminate in an unforgettable climax." Booklist

Snicket, Lemony, 1970-

File under: 13 suspicious incidents; by Lemony Snicket; art by Seth. Little Brown & Co 2014 259 p. (All the wrong questions) (hardback) $12

Grades: 4 5 6 7   **Fic**

1. Mystery fiction 2. Humorous fiction 3. Apprentices -- Fiction 4. City and town life -- Fiction 5. Humorous stories 6. Mystery and detective stories

ISBN 0316284033; 9780316284035
LC 2013037873

This book, by Lemony Snicket, presents "thirteen mini-mysteries. Paintings have been falling off of walls, a loud and loyal dog has gone missing, a specter has been seen walking the pier at midnight--strange things are happening all over the town of Stain'd-By-The-Sea. . . . Join the investigation and tackle the mysteries alongside Snicket, then turn to the back of the book to see the solution revealed." (Publisher's note)

"Kid-detective Lemony Snicket treats us to thirteen short mysteries (missing newt, ghostly appearance, series of break-ins) in which he leaves readers poised just before the reveal, with a chance to solve the mystery themselves before they flip to the back of the book. (It's Encyclopedia Brown for Snicket-Hipsters.) The actual puzzles are dandy, and the format is ideal for the author's comic avalanche." Horn Book

Other titles in the series include:
Who Could That be at This Hour
When Did You See Her Last
Shouldn't You Be in School

Shouldn't you be in school? Lemony Snicket. Little, Brown & Co. 2014 325 p. illustrations (some color) (All the wrong questions) (hardcover) $16

Grades: 4 5 6 7   **Fic**

1. School stories 2. Mystery fiction 3. Arson -- Fiction 4. Humorous stories 5. Apprentices -- Fiction 6. Detective and mystery stories 7. Arson investigation -- Fiction

ISBN 0316123064; 9780316123068; 9780316225045; 9780316279703; 9780316409681
LC 2014933203

In this children's book by Lemony Snicket "Lemony Snicket must work together with his incompetent chaperone to figure out who is burning down all of the buildings in the quaint town of Stain'd-by-the-Sea. Snicket is part of a special program, the V.F.D., and spends his days sleuthing with his chaperone, Theodora, in an attempt to catch the elusive and mysterious Hangfire, who is supposedly to blame for all of the mysterious happenings." (School Library Journal)

"In his third adventure, twelve-year-old Lemony Snicket, apprentice investigator, tackles a series of arsons in the economically depressed and highly mysterious town of Stain'd-by-the-Sea. Readers already hooked by this series will be pleased to check in with heroic librarian Qwerty, investigative journalist Moxie Mallahan, and the bickering Officers Mitchum and their bullying son, Stewart...As to the actual story, clues of the gray-matter sort (such as anagrams) combine with escapes, attacks, cliffhangers, and looming bad guys, keeping the whole crazy plot buoyant. Just." Horn Book

Other titles in the series include:

Who Could That Be at this Hour (2012)

When Did You See Her Last (2013)

When did you see her last? Lemony Snicket; illustrated by Seth. Little Brown & Co 2013 288 p. (All the wrong questions) (hardcover) $16

Grades: 4 5 6 7   **Fic**

1. Missing persons -- Fiction 2. Mystery fiction

ISBN 0316123056; 9780316123051; 9780316251952

LC 2012955921

Parents' Choice: Silver Medal Fiction (2013)

In this book, author Lemony Snicket "has a new case to solve when he and his chaperone are hired to find a missing girl. Is the girl a runaway? Or was she kidnapped? Was she seen last at the grocery store? Or could she have stopped at the diner? Is it really any of your business? These are All The Wrong Questions." (Publisher's note)

"A further adventure for the young private eye Lemony Snicket involves the disappearance of a brilliant young chemist, the only hope for rejuvenation of the town of Stain'd-by-the-Sea. In the course of Snicket's investigation he reconnects with characters from "Who Could That Be at This Hour?". This tongue-in-cheek adventure is peppered with references to classic children's books." (Horn Book)

★ **Who** could that be at this hour? by Lemony Snicket; art by Seth. Little, Brown 2012 272 p. $15.99

Grades: 4 5 6 7   **Fic**

1. Bildungsromans 2. Mystery fiction 3. Humorous fiction 4. Statues -- Fiction 5. Stealing -- Fiction 6. Apprentices -- Fiction

ISBN 0316123080; 9780316123082

LC 2012012657

This children's adventure mystery, by Lemony Snicket, begins in "Stain'd-by-the-Sea, the mostly deserted town where 12-year-old Lemony Snicket takes his first case as apprentice to chaperone S. Theodora Markson. They have been hired by Mrs. Murphy Sallis to retrieve a vastly valuable statue of the local legend, the Bombinating Beast. . . . With the help and/or hindrance of girls Moxie and Ellington, can Snicket keep his promises and come close to solving a mystery?" (Kirkus Reviews)

Sniegoski, Tom

Quest for the Spark; Book 2 written by Tom Sniegoski; illustrated by Jeff Smith; color by Steve Hamaker. Graphix 2012 234 p. (hardcover : alk. paper) $22.99

Grades: 4 5 6 7   **Fic**

1. Fantasy fiction 2. Magic -- Fiction 3. Adventure fiction 4. Dreams -- Fiction 5. Dragons -- Fiction 6. Fantasy 7. Humorous stories 8. Heroes -- Fiction 9. Adventure and adventurers -- Fiction

ISBN 9780545141031; 9780545141048

LC 2011020281

This book is set in the world of illustrator Jeff Smith's "Bone" graphic novels. Here, author Tom Sniegoski tells the story of "Tom, a Valley turnip farmer" who "receives a vi-

sion that the peaceful otherworld of the Dreaming is under attack. The evil Nacht, a renegade Dragon, seeks to control the dreamland, and through it, the Waking World as well. A mysterious forest woman tells Tom that he has been chosen to lead a quest to find the scattered pieces of the Spark--the light of creation that can drive back the dark power. When his family falls under the Nacht's corrupted sleep spell, Tom realizes that he has no choice and sets out with his best friend, a talking raccoon." (School Libr J)

Quest for the spark; book one. written by Tom Sniegoski; illustrated by Jeff Smith; color by Steve Hamaker. Graphix 2011 218p il (Bone) $22.99; pa $10.99

Grades: 4 5 6 7   **Fic**

1. Fantasy fiction 2. Adventure fiction 3. Magic -- Fiction 4. Dreams -- Fiction 5. Heroes and heroines -- Fiction

ISBN 978-0-545-14101-7; 0-545-14101-X; 978-0-545-14102-4 pa; 0-545-14102-8 pa

LC 2010017002

Twelve-year-old Tom Elm, his raccoon friend Roderick, Percival, Abbey, and Barclay Bone, warrior-priest Randolf, and forest-woman Lorimar join in a quest to find the pieces of the Spark that can save Dreaming—and the Waking World—from a Darkness created by the Nacht.

"At long last . . . we return to the Valley that was the setting for Smith's comics-landscape-changing Bone, though this adventure takes place in prose rather than panels. . . . As long as fans are not expecting a repeat of the old magic and not too disappointed that there isn't nearly enough of Smith's always excellent full-color, full-page artwork helping out, it looks as if they're in for a cheery jaunt back through a beloved world." Booklist

Sleeper code; by Tom Sniegoski. Razorbill 2006 278p (Sleeper conspiracy) pa $6.99

Grades: 8 9 10 11 12   **Fic**

1. Conspiracies -- Fiction 2. Sleep disorders -- Fiction 3. Multiple personality -- Fiction

ISBN 1-59514-052-2

LC 2006009102

Just when he has met a beautiful girl and his outlook is improving, sixteen-year-old narcoleptic Tom Lovett begins to suspect that his dreams and hallucinations of killing people may be something more real and terrifying.

"Readers looking for fast-paced action and espionage will enjoy this first book in the two-part Sleeper Conspiracy." SLJ

Snow, Alan

Here be monsters! an adventure involving magic, trolls, and other creatures. written and illustrated by Alan Snow. Atheneum Books for Young Readers 2006 529p il (The Ratbridge chronicles) $17.95; pa $8.99

Grades: 4 5 6 7   **Fic**

1. Fantasy fiction 2. Monsters -- Fiction

ISBN 978-0-689-87047-7; 0-689-87047-7; 978-0-689-87048-4 pa; 0-689-87048-5 pa

LC 2005-24438

While gathering food to bring to his grandfather, young Arthur becomes trapped in the city of Ratbridge, where he and some new friends try to stop a plot to shrink the monsters of Arthur's home, the Underworld, for a nefarious purpose

"Helpful in creating the settings and bringing the more fantastic characters to life, the illustrations, which are often amusing, also make the book accessible to younger children who like lengthy books. Snow's inventive fantasy . . . combines stout hearts, terrible troubles, and inspired lunacy." Booklist

Snow, Carol

Snap. HarperTeen 2009 221p $16.99

Grades: 7 8 9 10   **Fic**
1. Beaches -- Fiction 2. Cameras -- Fiction 3. Friendship -- Fiction 4. Family life -- Fiction 5. Photography -- Fiction 6. Supernatural -- Fiction
ISBN 978-0-06-145211-6; 0-06-145211-4
                                            LC 2009-14581
When fifteen-year-old Madison's parents, who are having problems, bring her to a seedy beachside town, she relies on some quirky new friends for help figuring out how her camera is taking pictures of people who are not there, and who later suffer tragedies.

"Snow's novel is a page-turning blend of romance, mystery, and the supernatural. . . . Characters are well developed." SLJ

Switch. HarperTeen 2008 215p $16.99; pa $8.99

Grades: 8 9 10 11 12   **Fic**
1. Supernatural -- Fiction
ISBN 978-0-06-145208-6; 0-06-145208-4; 978-0-06-145210-9 pa; 0-06-145210-6 pa
                                            LC 2008020220
Living in a small beach community with her mother, fifteen-year-old Claire, an accomplished swimmer, discovers that, like her long-dead but, still very much present, grandmother, she has the ability to inhabit other people's bodies while asleep.

"Claire's quick-paced narration comes laced with bolts of sarcasm; the realistic problems blend successfully into a suspenseful, mystical story." Kirkus

Snow, Maya

Sisters of the sword. HarperCollins 2008 275p (Sisters of the sword) $16.99; lib bdg $17.89; pa $6.99

Grades: 5 6 7 8   **Fic**
1. Japan -- Fiction 2. Samurai -- Fiction 3. Sisters -- Fiction 4. Sex role -- Fiction
ISBN 978-0-06-124387-5; 0-06-124387-6; 978-0-06-124388-2 lib bdg; 0-06-124388-4 lib bdg; 978-0-06-124389-9 pa; 0-06-124389-2 pa
                                            LC 2007-029610
Two aristocratic sisters in ancient Japan disguise themselves as samurai warriors to take revenge on the uncle who betrayed their family.

"This rousing new series . . . starts off with a bang, or more accurately, the silent thrust of a sword." Booklist
Other titles in this series are:
Chasing the secret (2009)

Journey through fire (2009)

Snyder, Laurel

Any which wall; drawings by LeUyen Pham. Random House 2009 242p il $16.99; lib bdg $19.99

Grades: 4 5 6 7   **Fic**
1. Iowa -- Fiction 2. Magic -- Fiction 3. Wishes -- Fiction 4. Siblings -- Fiction 5. Space and time -- Fiction
ISBN 978-0-375-85560-3; 0-375-85560-2; 978-0-375-95560-0 lib bdg; 0-375-95560-7 lib bdg
                                            LC 2008-22605
In the middle of an Iowa cornfield, four children find a magic wall that enables them to travel through time and space.

"Snyder's fresh, down-to-earth voice is complemented by Pham's energetic illustrations, which seem at once retro and modern. Fantasy fans will enjoy this novel, but so will readers who like stories about ordinary kids." SLJ

Snyder, Zilpha Keatley

The magic nation thing; [by] Zilpha Keatley Snyder. Delacorte Press 2005 164p hardcover o.p. pa $6.50

Grades: 4 5 6 7   **Fic**
1. San Francisco (Calif.) -- Fiction 2. Extrasensory perception -- Fiction
ISBN 0-385-73085-3; 0-440-41931-X pa
                                            LC 2004-10105
Although twelve-year-old Abby has always tried to deny that she has some kind of weird psychic power, she takes advantage of it to help her mother, a struggling private investigator, and, more importantly, to find her best friend's little brother when he goes missing at a ski resort

"Readers will delight in Snyder's vivid descriptions of Abby's special powers, but what will draw them most is the warm, believable story." Booklist

William S. and the great escape. Atheneum Books for Young Readers 2009 214p $16.99

Grades: 5 6 7 8   **Fic**
1. Acting -- Fiction 2. Siblings -- Fiction
ISBN 978-1-4169-6763-7; 1-4169-6763-X
                                            LC 2008-10377
In 1938, twelve-year-old William has already decided to leave home when his younger sister informs him that she and their brother and sister are going too, and right away, but complications arise when an acquaintance decides to "help" them.

"Wit and pluck are rewarded in this quick-paced, high-drama adventure, which may also whet young appetites for Shakespeare." Publ Wkly
Followed by: William's midsummer dreams (2011)

William's midsummer dreams. Atheneum Books for Young Readers 2011 209p $16.99

Grades: 5 6 7 8   **Fic**
1. Aunts -- Fiction 2. Acting -- Fiction 3. Theater -- Fiction 4. Adoption -- Fiction 5. Siblings -- Fiction
ISBN 978-1-4424-1997-1; 9781442419995 e-book
                                            LC 2010036958

Sequel to: William S. and the great escape (2009)

Now permanently settled with Aunt Fiona, who has adopted him and his siblings, thirteen-year-old William gets the chance to play Puck in a professional production of A Midsummer Night's Dream.

"An adventure story with a lot to say about identity, ambition and character." Kirkus

Somper, Justin

Demons of the ocean. Little, Brown 2006 330p (Vampirates) $15.99

Grades: 6 7 8 9   **Fic**

1. Adventure fiction 2. Twins -- Fiction 3. Pirates -- Fiction 4. Vampires -- Fiction
ISBN 0-316-01373-0

When twins Connor and Grace's ship is wrecked in a storm and Connor is rescued by pirates, he believes that Grace has been taken aboard the mythical Vampirate's ship, and he is determined to find her.

"This winning fantasy features both pirates and vampires with adventure, bloodcurling action, and sinister characters." Voice Youth Advocates

Other titles in this series are:
Tide of terror (2007)
Blood Captain (2008)
Black heart (2009)
Empire of night (2010)

Son, John

Finding my hat. Orchard Bks. 2003 185p (First person fiction) $16.95; pa $6.99

Grades: 5 6 7 8   **Fic**

1. Family life -- Fiction 2. Korean Americans -- Fiction
ISBN 0-439-43538-2; 0-439-43539-0 pa

LC 2002-44998

Jin-Han describes his life growing up with his mother and father, immigrants from Korea, and his little sister as they move to different cities with his parents' business

This is "a beautifully written and deeply personal account of growing up." SLJ

Sones, Sonya

Stop pretending; what happened when my big sister went crazy. HarperCollins Pubs. 1999 149p lib bdg $14.89; pa $6.99

Grades: 6 7 8 9   **Fic**

1. Sisters -- Fiction 2. Mental illness -- Fiction
ISBN 0-06-028386-6 lib bdg; 0-06-446218-8 pa

LC 99-11473

"Based on the journals Sones wrote at the age of 13 when her 19-year-old sister was hospitalized due to manic depression, the simply crafted but deeply felt poems reflect her thoughts, fears, hopes, and dreams during that troubling time." SLJ

★ **What** my girlfriend doesn't know. Simon & Schuster Books for Young Readers 2007 291p $16.99

Grades: 7 8 9 10   **Fic**

1. School stories 2. Artists -- Fiction 3. Boston (Mass.)

-- Fiction 4. Dating (Social customs) -- Fiction
ISBN 978-0-689-87602-8; 0-689-87602-5

LC 2006-14682

Sequel to What my mother doesn't know (2001)

Fourteen-year-old Robin Murphy is so unpopular at high school that his name is slang for "loser," and so when he begins dating the beautiful and popular Sophie her reputation plummets, but he finds acceptance as a student in a drawing class at Harvard.

"Robin's believable voice is distinctive, and Sones uses her spare words (and a few drawings) to expert effect." Booklist

★ **What** my mother doesn't know. Simon & Schuster Bks. for Young Readers 2001 259p hardcover o.p. pa $7.99

Grades: 7 8 9 10   **Fic**

1. Novels in verse 2. Dating (Social customs) -- Fiction
ISBN 0-689-84114-0; 0-689-85553-2 pa

LC 00-52634

This is "a fast, funny, touching book. . . . The very short, sometimes rhythmic lines make each page fly. Sophie's voice is colloquial and intimate." Booklist

Followed by What my girlfriend doesn't know (2007)

Sonnenblick, Jordan

★ **After** ever after. Scholastic Press 2010 260p $16.99

Grades: 5 6 7 8   **Fic**

1. School stories 2. Cancer -- Fiction 3. Friendship -- Fiction 4. Family life -- Fiction
ISBN 978-0-439-83706-4; 0-439-83706-5

Jeffery's cancer is in remission but the chemotherapy and radiation treatments have left him with concentration problems, and he worries about school work, his friends, his family, and a girl who likes him

"Sonnenblick imbues Jeffrey with a smooth, likable, and unaffected voice. . . . As hilarious as it is tragic, and as honest as it is hopeful . . . [this book is] irresistable reading." Booklist

Drums, girls, & dangerous pie. Scholastic Press 2005 273p $16.99

Grades: 5 6 7 8   **Fic**

1. Brothers -- Fiction 2. Leukemia -- Fiction
ISBN 0-439-75519-0

LC 2004-62563

First published 2004 by Turning Tide Press

When his younger brother is diagnosed with leukemia, thirteen-year-old Steven tries to deal with his complicated emotions, his school life, and his desire to support his family.

"A story that could have morphed into melodrama is saved by reality, rawness, and the wit Sonnenblick infuses into Steven's first-person voice." Booklist

Followed by: After ever after (2010)

★ **Notes** from the midnight driver. Scholastic Press 2006 265p $16.99

Grades: 8 9 10 11 12   **Fic**

1. Old age -- Fiction 2. Musicians -- Fiction 3.

Friendship -- Fiction
ISBN 0-439-75779-7

LC 2005-27972

After being assigned to perform community service at a nursing home, sixteen-year-old Alex befriends a cantankerous old man who has some lessons to impart about jazz guitar playing, love, and forgiveness.

The author "deftly infiltrates the teenage mind to produce a first-person narrative riddled with enough hapless confusion, mulish equivocation, and beleaguered deadpan humor to have readers nodding with recognition, sighing with sympathy, and gasping with laughter—often on the same page." Horn Book

★ **Zen** and the art of faking it. Scholastic Press 2007 264p $16.99; pa $7.99

Grades: 5 6 7 8   Fic

1. School stories 2. Pennsylvania -- Fiction 3. Zen Buddhism -- Fiction 4. Asian Americans -- Fiction
ISBN 978-0-439-83707-1; 0-439-83707-3; 978-0-439-83709-5 pa; 0-439-83709-X pa

LC 2006-28841

When thirteen-year-old San Lee moves to a new town and school for the umpteenth time, he is looking for a way to stand out when his knowledge of Zen Buddhism, gained in his previous school, provides the answer—and the need to quickly become a convincing Zen master.

The author gives readers "plenty to laugh at. . . . Mixed with more serious scenes, . . . lighter moments take a basic message about the importance of honesty and forgiveness and treat it with panache." Publ Wkly

Sonnichsen, A.L.

Red butterfly; A. L. Sonnichsen, illustrated by Amy June Bates. Simon & Schuster Books for Young Readers 2015 392 p. hardcover $16.99

Grades: 4 5 6 7   Fic

1. China 2. Adopted children 3. Novels in verse 4. China -- Fiction 5. Adoption -- Fiction 6. Families -- Fiction 7. Foundlings -- Fiction 8. Abnormalities, Human -- Fiction 9. Intercountry adoption -- Fiction
ISBN 1481411098; 9781481411097

LC 2013050300

In this book by A. L. Sonnichsen, "Kara never met her birth mother. Abandoned as an infant, she was taken in by an American woman living in China. Now eleven, Kara spends most of her time in their apartment, wondering why she and Mama cannot leave the city of Tianjin and go live with Daddy in Montana. Mama tells Kara to be content with what she has but what if Kara secretly wants more?" (Publisher's Note)

"An innocent victim of China's adoption system, Kara was left in a basket and rescued by an American woman. An unwanted female baby with a deformed hand set Kara apart from birth, but Mama, her savior, was a 60-year-old Montana woman living on an expired visa...Sympathetic readers will appreciate that Kara learns to build trust with those who demonstrate their compassion in constructive attempts to right some of the wrongs of her difficult beginnings." Booklist

Sorrells, Walter

Erratum; 1st ed.; Dutton 2008 298p $17.99

Grades: 4 5 6 7   Fic

1. Science fiction 2. Space and time -- Fiction 3. Books and reading -- Fiction
ISBN 978-0-525-47832-4; 0-525-47832-9

LC 2007052647

When Jessica finds--and then loses--an unfinished book about her life, she learns that if she cannot keep it from falling into the wrong hands, the balance of the universe is in peril.

"Highly imaginative, fast-paced and a bit disorienting. . . . Sorrell presents a stew of hearty concepts, including string theory, alternate dimensions and mind control. Readers with a taste for science or science fiction will be especially intrigued." Publ Wkly

★ **First** shot. Dutton Children's Books 2007 279p hardcover o.p. pa $7.99

Grades: 7 8 9 10 11 12   Fic

1. Mystery fiction 2. Homicide -- Fiction 3. Father-son relationship -- Fiction
ISBN 978-0-525-47801-0; 0-525-47801-9; 978-0-14-241421-7 pa; 0-14-241421-2 pa

As David enters his senior year of high school, a family secret emerges that could solve the mystery of why his mother was murdered two years ago.

"David's first person narration pulls readers into the young man's torment. . . . This is a fast-paced, intriguing read." Booklist

Whiteout. Dutton Children's Books 2009 312p (Hunted) $15.99

Grades: 7 8 9 10   Fic

1. Mystery fiction 2. Homicide -- Fiction 3. Blizzards -- Fiction 4. Minnesota -- Fiction 5. Mother-daughter relationship -- Fiction
ISBN 978-0-525-42141-2; 0-525-42141-6

Sixteen-year-old Chass makes her way through a Minnesota blizzard, seeking not only the murderer of a beloved music teacher, but also something belonging to the killer who has been chasing her mother and herself around the country.

"There is . . . plenty of suspense to propel even a reluctant reader, and a number of false turns to keep the reader guessing." Voice Youth Advocates

Soto, Gary, 1952-

Accidental love; [by] Gary Soto. Harcourt 2006 179p $16

Grades: 6 7 8 9   Fic

1. Love stories 2. School stories 3. Hispanic Americans -- Fiction
ISBN 0-15-205497-9

LC 2004-29900

In this book by Gary Soto, "Marisa is in her first year of high school, a little overweight and always ready to pick a fight. After punching her best friend's cheating boyfriend in an elevator, she gets home to find she has someone else's cell phone-and realizes she must have switched phones with the nerdy kid who was in the elevator with them. When she meets Rene, she immediately notices his white socks and flood pants, and yet, she can't help wanting to hang around him." (Kirkus Reviews)

This is a "warmhearted, humorous novel." SLJ

★ **Buried** onions. Harcourt Brace & Co. 1997 149p hardcover o.p. pa $6.95

Grades: 8 9 10 11 12   **Fic**

1. Violence -- Fiction 2. Mexican Americans -- Fiction
ISBN 0-15-201333-4; 0-15-206265-3 pa

LC 96-53112

When nineteen-year-old Eddie drops out of college, he struggles to find a place for himself as a Mexican American living in a violence-infested neighborhood of Fresno, California.

"Soto has created a beautiful, touching, and truthful story. . . . The lyrical language and Spanish phrases add to the immediacy of setting and to the sensitivity the author brings to his character's life." Voice Youth Advocates

★ **Taking** sides. Harcourt Brace Jovanovich 1991 138p hardcover o.p. pa $5.95

Grades: 5 6 7 8   **Fic**

1. Basketball -- Fiction 2. Hispanic Americans -- Fiction
ISBN 0-15-284076-1; 0-15-204694-1 pa

LC 91-11082

Fourteen-year-old Lincoln Mendoza, an aspiring basketball player, must come to terms with his divided loyalties when he moves from the Hispanic inner city to a white suburban neighborhood

This is a "light but appealing story. . . . Because of its subject matter and its clear, straightforward prose, it will be especially good for reluctant readers." SLJ

Includes glossary

Sovern, Megan Jean

★ The **meaning** of Maggie; by Megan Jean Sovern. Chronicle Books 2014 224 p. (alk. paper) $16.99

Grades: 4 5 6 7   **813.6**

1. Family life -- Fiction 2. Middle schools -- Fiction
3. Multiple sclerosis -- Fiction 4. Father-daughter relationship -- Fiction 5. Fathers and daughters -- Fiction
ISBN 1452110212; 9781452110219

LC 2013029644

In this book, by Megan Jean Sovern, "Maggie Mayfield has decided to write a memoir of the past year of her life. And what a banner year it's been! During this period she's Student of the Month on a regular basis, an official shareholder of Coca-Cola stock, and defending Science Fair champion. Most importantly, though, this is the year Maggie has to pull up her bootstraps (the family motto) and finally learn why her cool-dude dad is in a wheelchair, no matter how scary that is." (Publisher's note)

"In her debut novel, Sovern introduces readers to determined eleven-year-old Maggie Mayfield. Thinking there's nothing she can't conquer, Maggie is stymied by her dad's mysterious illness--slowly revealed as multiple sclerosis. Maggie's self-realizations come quickly, but her distinct voice, with a snarky superiority that often masks her true

vulnerability, creates a character who's not easy to love but tough to forget." Horn Book

Sparrow, Rebecca

The **year** Nick McGowan came to stay; [by] Rebecca Sparrow. 1st American ed.; Alfred A. Knopf 2008 198p $15.99; lib bdg $18.99

Grades: 8 9 10 11   **Fic**

1. School stories 2. Australia -- Fiction
ISBN 978-0-375-84570-3; 0-375-84570-4; 978-0-375-94570-0 lib bdg; 0-375-84570-9 lib bdg

LC 2007020758

First published 2006 in Australia

In her final year of high school in 1989, Australian teenager Rachel has her world turned upside down when the most popular (and disturbed) boy in school comes to live with her family for a semester.

"This book is full of laugh-out-loud moments. . . . Sparrow is adept at accurately portraying her teenage characters and placing them in realistic scenarios that most readers will find pertinent." SLJ

Speare, Elizabeth George, 1908-1994

Calico Captive; illustrated by W. T. Mars. Sandpiper 2001 274p ill. (pbk.) $6.95

Grades: 6 7 8   **Fic**

1. Historical fiction 2. Prisoners -- Fiction 3. Native Americans -- Fiction 4. United States -- History -- 1755-1763, French and Indian War -- Fiction
ISBN 9780618150762

LC 57009017

In this book, set "[i]n the year 1754, the stillness of Charlestown, New Hampshire, is shattered by the terrifying cries of an Indian raid. Young Miriam Willard . . . finds herself . . . a captive on a forest trail, caught up in the ebb and flow of the French and Indian War. It is a harrowing march north. . . . At the end of the trail waits a life of hard work and, perhaps, even a life of slavery. . . . Miriam and her companions finally reach Montreal, a city of shifting loyalties filled with the intrigue of war, and here, by a sudden twist of fortune, Miriam meets the prominent Du Quesne family, who introduce her to a life she has never imagined. Based on an actual narrative diary published in 1807, . . . [the book] reenacts a . . . facet of history." (Publisher's note)

★ The **sign** of the beaver. Houghton Mifflin 1983 135p $16

Grades: 5 6 7 8   **Fic**

1. Friendship -- Fiction 2. Native Americans -- Fiction 3. Frontier and pioneer life -- Fiction
ISBN 0-395-33890-5

LC 83-118

A Newbery Medal honor book, 1984

Left alone to guard the family's wilderness home in eighteenth-century Maine, Matt is hard-pressed to survive until local Indians teach him their skills

Matt "begins to understand the Indians' ingenuity and respect for nature and the devastating impact of the encroachment of the white man. In a quiet but not unsuspenseful story . . . the author articulates historical facts along with the adventures and the thoughts, emotions, and developing insights of a young adolescent." Horn Book

★ The **witch** of Blackbird Pond. Houghton Mifflin 1958 249p $17

Grades: 6 7 8 9   Fic

1. Puritans -- Fiction 2. Witchcraft -- Fiction 3. Connecticut -- History -- 1600-1775, Colonial period -- Fiction

ISBN 0-395-07114-3

LC 58-11063

Awarded the Newbery Medal, 1959

"Headstrong and undisciplined, Barbados-bred Kit Tyler is an embarrassment to her Puritan relatives, and her sincere attempts to aid a reputed witch soon bring her to trial as a suspect." Child Books Too Good to Miss

Spillebeen, Geert

Age 14; translated by Terese Edelstein. Houghton Mifflin 2009 216p $16

Grades: 8 9 10 11 12   Fic

1. Soldiers -- Fiction 2. World War, 1914-1918 -- Fiction

ISBN 978-0-547-05342-4; 0-547-05342-8

LC 2010-277732

"Based on a true story, this spare, powerful novel . . . focuses on Patrick, a poor Irish kid who is just 13 when war breaks out. He dreams of escaping his dreary future and abusive dad and finding adventure and glory in the army. . . . The recruiters knowingly accept him into the service when he claims that he is a 17-year-old named John. . . . Spillebeen brings to the story to a realistic, grim conclusion." Booklist

Kipling's choice; written by Geert Spillebeen; translated by Terese Edelstein. Houghton Mifflin Co 2005 147p $16; pa $7.99

Grades: 7 8 9 10   Fic

1. Army officers 2. France -- Fiction 3. Children of prominent persons 4. World War, 1914-1918 -- Fiction

ISBN 0-618-43124-1; 0-618-80035-2 pa

LC 2004-20856

In 1915, mortally wounded in Loos, France, eighteen-year-old John Kipling, son of writer Rudyard Kipling, remembers his boyhood and the events leading to what is to be his first and last World War I battle.

"This well-written novel combines facts with speculation about John Kipling's short life and gruesome death. A riveting account of World War I." SLJ

Spinelli, Jerry

★ **Crash**. Knopf 1996 162p hardcover o.p. pa $6.99; lib bdg $17.99

Grades: 5 6 7 8   Fic

1. Football -- Fiction 2. Friendship -- Fiction 3. Grandfathers -- Fiction

ISBN 0440238579; 0679879579; 0679979573

LC 95030942

"Crash is a star football player. He torments Penn, a classmate who is everything Crash is not—friendly, small, and a pacifist. When his beloved grandfather comes to live with his family and suffers a debilitating stroke, Crash be-

gins to see value in many of the things he has scorned." Horn Book Guide

Hokey Pokey; by Jerry Spinelli. Alfred A. Knopf Books for Young Readers 2013 304 p. (hard cover) $15.99

Grades: 5 6 7 8   Fic

1. Bildungsromans 2. Fantasy fiction 3. Imaginary places 4. Play -- Fiction 5. Growth -- Fiction

ISBN 0375831983; 9780307975706; 9780375831980; 9780375832017; 9780375931987

LC 2012004177

In this book, Jerry Spinelli "creates a surreal landscape." There are no adults in "Hokey Pokey, where boys and girls dine on flavored ice and spend their days watching cartoons, playing cowboy games, and using their bicycles as trusty steeds. Jack's bike, Scramjet, is . . . stolen by his archenemy, Jubilee. This marks the first of a series of unsettling events that give Jack, a boy on the brink of adolescence, the eerie impression that 'things have shifted.'" (Publishers Weekly)

Jake and Lily; Jerry Spinelli. 1st ed. Balzer + Bray 2012 335 p. (hardback) $15.99

Grades: 3 4 5 6 7   Fic

1. Twins -- Fiction 2. Bullies -- Fiction 3. Children's stories 4. Friendship -- Fiction 5. Individuality -- Fiction 6. Brothers and sisters -- Fiction

ISBN 9780060281359; 9780060281366

LC 2011053362

This book offers a "story about a pair of twins growing apart. For almost as long as they can remember, Jake and Lily have shared a 'special sense,' which they call 'goombla.' . . . Lily tries to find out who she is without her brother, but it's hard work, and most of her attempts are unsuccessful. . . . Though the twins eventually rediscover their 'goombla,' . . . [author Jerry] Spinelli doesn't suggest that the two will go back to being the people they once were." (Publishers Weekly)

Love, Stargirl; [by] Jerry Spinelli. Alfred A. Knopf 2007 274p $16.99; lib bdg $19.99

Grades: 7 8 9 10   Fic

1. Letters -- Fiction 2. Pennsylvania -- Fiction

ISBN 978-0-375-81375-7; 978-0-375-91375-4 lib bdg

LC 2007002308

Still moping months after being dumped by her Arizona boyfriend Leo, fifteen-year-old Stargirl, a home-schooled free spirit, writes "the world's longest letter" to Leo, describing her new life in Pennsylvania.

"Fans of Stargirl will be charmed by this satisfying sequel." Kliatt

★ **Maniac** Magee; a novel. Little, Brown 1990 184p $16.99; pa $6.99

Grades: 5 6 7 8   Fic

1. Orphans -- Fiction 2. Race relations -- Fiction 3. Homeless persons -- Fiction

ISBN 0-316-80722-2; 0-316-80906-3 pa

LC 89-27144

Awarded the Newbery Medal, 1991

"Orphaned at three, Jeffery Lionel Magee, after eight unhappy years with relatives, one day takes off running. A year later, he ends up 200 miles away in Two Mills, a highly segregated community. Part tall tale and part contemporary realistic fiction, this unusual novel magically weaves timely issues of homelessness, racial prejudice, and illiteracy into an energetic story that bursts with creativity, enthusiasm, and hope for the future. In short, it's a celebration of life." Booklist

Smiles to go. Joanna Cotler Books 2008 248p $16.99; lib bdg $17.89; pa $6.99

Grades: 6 7 8 9 10   **Fic**

1. School stories 2. Siblings -- Fiction 3. Friendship -- Fiction 4. Family life -- Fiction

ISBN 978-0-06-028133-5; 0-06-028133-2; 978-0-06-028134-2 lib bdg; 0-06-028134-0 lib bdg; 978-0-06-447197-8 pa; 0-06-447197-7 pa

LC 2007-29563

Will Tuppence's life has always been ruled by science and common sense but in ninth grade, shaken up by the discovery that protons decay, he begins to see the entire world differently and gains new perspective on his relationships with his little sister and two closest friends.

"What makes a Spinelli novel isn't plotting so much as character, dialogue, voice and humor. The Spinelli touch remains true in this funny and thoroughly enjoyable read." Publ Wkly

★ **Stargirl**. Knopf 2000 186p pa $8.95; $15.95; lib bdg $17.99

Grades: 7 8 9 10   **Fic**

1. School stories 2. Arizona 3. Schools 4. Popularity 5. High schools 6. Individuality 7. Arizona -- Fiction 8. Eccentrics and eccentricities

ISBN 0-375-82233-X pa; 0-679-88637-0; 0-679-98637-5 lib bdg

LC 99-87944

In this story about the perils of popularity, the courage of nonconformity, and the thrill of first love, an eccentric student named Stargirl changes Mica High School forever

"As always respectful of his audience, Spinelli poses searching questions about loyalty to one's friends and oneself and leaves readers to form their own answers." Publ Wkly

Another title about Stargirl is:

Love, Stargirl (2007)

There's a girl in my hammerlock. Simon & Schuster Bks. for Young Readers 1991 199p hardcover o.p. pa $5.99

Grades: 5 6 7 8   **Fic**

1. School stories 2. Sex role -- Fiction 3. Wrestling -- Fiction

ISBN 1-4169-3937-7 pa

LC 91-8765

Thirteen-year-old Maisie joins her school's formerly all-male wrestling team and tries to last through the season, despite opposition from other students, her best friend, and her own teammates

The author "tackles a meaty subject—traditional gender roles—with his usual humor and finesse. The result, written

in a breezy, first-person style, is a rattling good sports story that is clever, witty and tightly written." Publ Wkly

★ **Wringer**. HarperCollins Pubs. 1997 228p $16.99; lib bdg $16.89; pa $6.50

Grades: 4 5 6 7   **Fic**

1. Courage -- Fiction 2. Pigeons -- Fiction 3. Violence -- Fiction

ISBN 0-06-024913-7; 0-06-024914-5 lib bdg; 0-06-440578-8 pa

LC 96-37897

A Newbery Medal honor book, 1998

"Palmer LaRue is running out of birthdays. For as long as he can remember, he's dreaded the day he turns ten -- the day he'll take his place beside all the other ten-year-old boys in town, the day he'll be a wringer. But Palmer doesn't want to be a wringer...Palmer can't stop himself from being a wringer just like he can't stop himself from growing one year older, just like he can't stand up to a whole town -- right?" (Publisher's note)

"During the annual pigeon shoot, it is a town tradition for 10-year-old boys to break the necks of wounded birds. In this riveting story told with verve and suspense, Palmer rebels." SLJ

Spinner, Stephanie

Damosel; in which the Lady of the Lake renders a frank and often startling account of her wondrous life and times. Alfred A. Knopf 2008 198p $16.99; lib bdg $19.99

Grades: 7 8 9 10   **Fic**

1. Kings 2. Magic -- Fiction 3. Dwarfs -- Fiction 4. Fools and jesters -- Fiction 5. Great Britain -- History -- 0-1066 -- Fiction

ISBN 978-0-375-83634-3; 0-375-83634-9; 978-0-375-93634-0 lib bdg; 0-375-93634-3 lib bdg

LC 2007-43519

Damosel, a rule-bound Lady of the Lake, and Twixt, a seventeen-year-old dwarf, relate their experiences as they strive to help King Arthur face Morgause, Morgan, and Mordred, one through her magic and the other through his humble loyalty.

"The magic is exciting and palpable. . . . Spinner's elegant language, strong characterizations, energetic dialogue, and lively plot combine in a memorable, accessible novel." Booklist

Quicksilver. Knopf 2005 229p hardcover o.p. pa $5.99

Grades: 7 8 9 10   **Fic**

1. Classical mythology -- Fiction

ISBN 0-375-82638-6; 0-440-23845-5 pa

LC 2004-10311

Hermes, Prince of Thieves and son of Zeus, relates why the seasons change, the history of the Trojan War, his friendship with Pegasus, and many more adventures.

"Spinner seamlessly weaves necessary background information about the cast of celestial characters into a narrative filled with thrilling action and violence that is drawn straight from the original stories. Teens will connect with Hermes' immediate, often very funny voice." Booklist

Quiver. Knopf 2002 177p $15.95; lib bdg $17.99; pa $5.99

Grades: 7 8 9 10   **Fic**

1. Atalanta (Greek mythology) -- Fiction

ISBN 0-375-81489-2; 0-375-91489-7 lib bdg; 0-440-23819-6 pa

LC 2002-5451

When her father commands that she produce an heir, the huntress Atalanta gives her suitors a seemingly impossible task in order to uphold her pledge of chastity, as the gods of ancient Greece look on

"Spinner gives this Greek myth a fresh face and makes Atalanta a strong heroine." SLJ

Spooner, Michael

Last Child. Henry Holt 2005 230p $16.95

Grades: 7 8 9 10   **Fic**

1. Smallpox -- Fiction 2. North Dakota -- Fiction 3. Mandan Indians -- Fiction 4. Racially mixed people -- Fiction

ISBN 0-8050-7739-1

LC 2005-9957

"Action-packed prose; sharp, witty dialogue; and strong characterization make this novel an entertaining read." Voice Youth Advocates

"The horror of the smallpox epidemic that killed more than 20,000 Indians from the Upper Missouri nations in the late 1830s is told from the perspective of a young girl at a fur-company outpost, who is caught between her loving Scottish dad, who calls her Rosalie, and her Mandan family that calls her Last Child." Booklist

Spradlin, Michael P.

Keeper of the Grail. G.P. Putnam's Sons 2008 248p (The youngest Templar) $17.99

Grades: 6 7 8 9   **Fic**

1. Grail -- Fiction 2. Crusades -- Fiction 3. Middle Ages -- Fiction 4. Knights and knighthood -- Fiction

ISBN 978-0-399-24763-7; 0-399-24763-7

LC 2007-36143

In 1191, fifteen-year-old Tristan, a youth of unknown origin raised in an English abbey, becomes a Templar Knight's squire during the Third Crusade and soon finds himself on a mission to bring the Holy Grail to safety.

"The deadly action, uncompromising in many of its descriptions, may take center stage, but Spradlin smartly doesn't neglect story. . . . The stirring story ends with a true cliff-hanger, priming fans for the next installment." Booklist

Other titles in this series are:

Trail of fate (2009)

Orphan of destiny (2010)

Springer, Kristina

My fake boyfriend is better than yours. Farrar, Straus and Giroux 2010 180p $15.99

Grades: 5 6 7   **Fic**

1. Honesty -- Fiction 2. Friendship -- Fiction 3. Imagination -- Fiction

ISBN 978-0-374-39910-8; 0-374-39910-7

LC 2009-32981

When her best friend Sea returns from her summer vacation claiming to have a boyfriend, twelve-year-old Tori is

sure she is lying and makes up her own boyfriend, who just so happens to do everything better than Sea's boyfriend.

"Springer writes in authentic tween language. . . . Tori is a well-rounded character, both likable and relatable. The themes will resonate with any girl who's ever gone through the hardships of middle school. . . . A fun read." SLJ

Springer, Nancy

The **case** of the bizarre bouquets; an Enola Holmes mystery. [by] Nancy Springer. Philomel Books 2008 170p $14.99

Grades: 5 6 7 8   **Fic**

1. Mystery fiction 2. Missing persons -- Fiction 3. London (England) -- Fiction

ISBN 978-0-399-24518-3; 0-399-24518-9

LC 2007020435

Fourteen-year-old Enola Holmes, disguised as a beautiful woman, finds clues in floral bouquets as she searches for the missing Doctor Watson, a companion of her famous older brother, Sherlock.

"Springer's descriptions of late-19th-century England are vivid, the mystery is intriguing, and Enola's cleverness and capability will appeal to readers who like their heroines both sprightly and savvy." SLJ

The **case** of the cryptic crinoline; an Enola Holmes mystery. Philomel Books 2009 160p $14.99

Grades: 5 6 7 8   **Fic**

1. Nurses 2. Mystery fiction 3. Nonfiction writers 4. Great Britain -- Fiction 5. Missing persons -- Fiction 6. London (England) -- Fiction

ISBN 978-0-399-24781-1; 0-399-24781-5

LC 2008040475

In late nineteenth-century London, fourteen-year-old Enola Holmes, much younger sister of detective Sherlock Holmes, turns to Florence Nightingale for help when her investigation into the disappearance of a Crimean War widow grows cold.

"From the riveting prologue to the satisfying conclusion, readers are hurled headlong into Enola Holmes's latest case." SLJ

The **case** of the gypsy good-bye; an Enola Holmes mystery. Philomel Books 2010 166p

Grades: 5 6 7 8   **Fic**

1. Mystery fiction 2. Missing persons -- Fiction

ISBN 0399252363; 9780399252365

This is the concluding volume in the Enola Holmes mystery series. "As Enola searches for the missing Lady Blanchefleur del Campo, she discovers that her brother Sherlock is just as diligently searching for Enola herself. . . . He is in possession of a . . . message from their long-lost mother that only Enola can decipher. Sherlock, along with their brother Mycroft, must follow Enola into the reeking tunnels of London's dark underbelly as they solve a triple mystery: What has happened to their mother? And to Lady Blanchefleur? And what does either have to do with Mycroft, who holds Enola's future in his hands?" (Publisher's note) "Intermediate, middle school." (Horn Book)

"The series that features Enola Holmes, the (much) younger sister of Sherlock, continues to be flat-out among the best mysteries being written for young people today. Not only are the mysteries sharp attention holders but the conclusions are well thought out, with i's dotted and t's crossed in true Holmesian fashion." Booklist

The **case** of the left-handed lady; an Enola Holmes mystery. [by] Nancy Springer. Philomel Books 2007 234p $12.95
Grades: 5 6 7 8   **Fic**
1. Mystery fiction 2. Kidnapping -- Fiction 3. London (England) -- Fiction
ISBN 978-0-399-24517-6
LC 2006008261
Pursued by her much older brother, famed detective Sherlock Holmes, fourteen-year-old Enola, disguised and using false names, attempts to solve the kidnapping of a baronet's sixteen-year-old daughter in nineteenth-century London.
"Enola is beautifully drawn, as are the sights and sounds of late-nineteenth-century London." Booklist

★ The **case** of the missing marquess; an Enola Holmes mystery. Philomel Books 2006 216p pa $6.99; $10.99
Grades: 5 6 7 8   **Fic**
1. Mystery fiction 2. Missing persons -- Fiction 3. London (England) -- Fiction
ISBN 0-14-240933-2 pa; 0-399-24304-6
Enola Holmes, much younger sister of detective Sherlock Holmes, must travel to London in disguise to unravel the disappearance of her missing mother. "Grades four to eight." (Bull Cent Child Books)
"Enola's loneliness, intelligence, sense of humor, and sheer pluck make her an extremely appealing heroine." SLJ
Other titles about Enola Holmes are:
The case of the left-handed lady (2007)
The case of the bizarre bouquets (2008)
The case of the peculiar pink fan (2008)
The case of the cryptic crinoline (2009)
The case of the gypsy good-bye (2010)

The **case** of the peculiar pink fan; an Enola Holmes mystery. [by] Nancy Springer. Philomel Books 2008 183p $14.99
Grades: 5 6 7 8   **Fic**
1. Mystery fiction 2. London (England) -- Fiction 3. Lost and found possessions -- Fiction
ISBN 978-0-399-24780-4; 0-399-24780-7
LC 2008006933
While fourteen-year-old Enola Holmes endeavors to save her friend Lady Cecily Alistair from an unwelcome arranged marriage, she meets with some assistance from her older brother, Sherlock, and interference by the eldest, Mycroft.
"This features a strong mystery, intriguing family relationships, and the continuing thread of a daughter and mother lost to each other. . . . A rousing read with plenty of terrific Victorian detail." Booklist

I am Mordred; a tale from Camelot. Philomel Bks. 1998 184p hardcover o.p. pa $6.99
Grades: 7 8 9 10   **Fic**
1. Kings 2. Mordred (Legendary character) -- Fiction

3. Great Britain -- History -- 0-1066 -- Fiction
ISBN 0-399-23143-9; 0-698-11841-3 pa
LC 97-39740
"Springer humanizes Arthurian archvillain Mordred in a thoroughly captivating and poignant tale." Booklist

I am Morgan le Fay; a tale from Camelot. Philomel Bks. 2001 227p hardcover o.p. pa $5.99
Grades: 7 8 9 10   **Fic**
1. Kings 2. Great Britain -- History -- 0-1066 -- Fiction 3. Morgan le Fay (Legendary character) -- Fiction
ISBN 0-399-23451-9; 0-698-11974-6 pa
LC 99-52847
In a war-torn England where her half-brother Arthur will eventually become king, the young Morgan le Fay comes to realize that she has magic powers and links to the faerie world
"Introspective, yet threaded with intrigue and adventure, this compelling study of the legendary villainess explores the ways that love, hate, jealousy, and the desire for power shape one young woman's fate and affect the destiny of others." Horn Book

Lionclaw; a tale of Rowan Hood. Philomel Bks. 2002 122p $16.99
Grades: 4 5 6 7   **Fic**
1. Adventure fiction 2. Middle Ages -- Fiction 3. Robin Hood (Legendary character) -- Fiction
ISBN 0-399-23716-X
LC 2001-45929
Sequel to: Rowan Hood, outlaw girl of Sherwood Forest (2001)
Young Lionel, minstrel in the outlaw band of Rowan Hood, daughter of Robin, tries to find his courage when she is abducted from Sherwood Forest
"Springer excels at keeping the action and adventure in high gear, and she creates strong characters with clear motivations." Booklist
Followed by: Outlaw princess of Sherwood (2003)

Rowan Hood returns; the final chapter. Philomel Bks. 2005 169p il $16.99
Grades: 4 5 6 7   **Fic**
1. Adventure fiction 2. Middle Ages -- Fiction 3. Robin Hood (Legendary character) -- Fiction
ISBN 0-399-24206-6
When she finds out who murdered her mother, Celandine, Rowan Hood returns to her former home to seek revenge.

★ **Rowan** Hood, outlaw girl of Sherwood Forest. Philomel Bks. 2001 170p hardcover o.p. pa $5.99
Grades: 4 5 6 7   **Fic**
1. Adventure fiction 2. Middle Ages -- Fiction 3. Robin Hood (Legendary character) -- Fiction
ISBN 0-399-23368-7; 0-698-11972-X pa
LC 00-63694
In her quest to connect with Robin Hood, the father she has never met, thirteen-year-old Rosemary disguises herself as a boy, befriends a half-wolf, half-dog, a runaway princess, and an overgrown boy whose singing is hypnotic, and makes peace with her elfin heritage

"This tale is a charmer, filled with exciting action, plenty of humor, engaging characters, and a nice fantasy twist." Booklist

Other titles about Rowan Hood are:
Lionclaw (2002)
Outlaw princess of Sherwood (2003)
Wild boy (2004)
Rowan Hood returns (2005)

Wild boy, a tale of Rowan Hood. Philomel Books 2004 115p hardcover o.p. pa $5.99

Grades: 4 5 6 7 **Fic**
1. Adventure fiction 2. Middle Ages -- Fiction 3. Robin Hood (Legendary character) -- Fiction
ISBN 0-399-24015-2; 978-0-14-240395-2 pa; 0-14-240395-4 pa

LC 2003-19146

Sequel to: Outlaw princess of Sherwood (2003)

Determined to avenge the death of his swineherd father at the hands of the Sheriff of Nottingham, Rook finally gets his chance when the Sheriff's son is captured by Robin Hood.

This includes "plenty of merrie-olde-England atmosphere and action." Booklist

Followed by: Rowan Hood returns (2005)

St. Antoine, Sara

Three bird summer; Sara St. Antoine. Candlewick Press 2014 256 p. $16.99

Grades: 5 6 7 **Fic**
1. Mystery fiction 2. Lakes -- Fiction 3. Summer -- Fiction 4. Neighbors -- Fiction 5. Grandmothers -- Fiction 6. Vacations -- Fiction 7. Summer resorts -- Fiction
ISBN 0763665649; 9780763665647

LC 2013946623

In this book, by Sara St. Antoine, "[f]or as long as he can remember, Adam and his parents have spent their summers at his grandmother's rustic cabin on Three Bird Lake. But this year will be different. There will be no rowdy cousins running around tormenting Adam. There will be no Uncle John or Aunt Jean. And there'll be no Dad to fight with Mom. This year, the lake will belong just to Adam. But then Adam meets Alice, the girl next door, who seems to want to become friends." (Publisher's note)

"Summertime for twelve-year-old Adam has always meant traveling to Grandma's rustic cabin in Minnesota. This summer is different: his parents have divorced, and Grandma is showing signs of dementia. St. Antoine's setting is remarkably palpable and lyrically described: pine trees are "spindly giants in pointy hats." And her characters are well realized, with Grandma both strong-willed and fragile and loner Adam experiencing true friendship." Horn Book

St. Crow, Lili

Strange angels. Razorbill 2009 293p pa $9.99

Grades: 8 9 10 11 12 **Fic**
1. Orphans -- Fiction 2. Vampires -- Fiction 3. Werewolves -- Fiction 4. Supernatural -- Fiction 5. Extrasensory perception -- Fiction
ISBN 978-1-59514-251-1; 1-59514-251-7

LC 2008-39720

Sixteen-year-old Dru's psychic abilities helped her father battle zombies and other creatures of the "Real World," but now she must rely on herself, a "werwulf"-bitten friend, and a half-human vampire hunter to learn who murdered her parents, and why.

"The book grabs readers by the throat, sets hearts beating loudly and never lets go." Kirkus

Other titles in this series are:
Betrayals (2009)
Defiance (2011)
Jealousy (2010)

St. John, Lauren

The **white** giraffe; illustrated by David Dean. Dial Books for Young Readers 2007 180p il $16.99; pa $6.99

Grades: 4 5 6 7 **Fic**
1. Orphans -- Fiction 2. Giraffes -- Fiction 3. South Africa -- Fiction 4. Mythical animals -- Fiction
ISBN 978-0-8037-3211-7; 0-8037-3211-2; 978-0-14-241152-0 pa; 0-14-241152-3 pa

LC 2006-21323

After a fire kills her parents, eleven-year-old Martine must leave England to live with her grandmother on a wildlife game reserve in South Africa, where she befriends a mythical white giraffe

"The story is captivating and well spun." SLJ

Other titles in this series are:
Dolphin song (2008)
Last leopard (2009)
The elephant's tale (2010)

Stahler, David

Doppelganger; [by] David Stahler, Jr. HarperCollins Publishers 2006 258p hardcover o.p. pa $8.99

Grades: 8 9 10 11 12 **Fic**
1. Horror fiction 2. Child abuse -- Fiction 3. Family life -- Fiction 4. Supernatural -- Fiction
ISBN 978-0-06-087232-8; 0-06-087232-2; 978-0-06-087234-2 pa; 0-06-087234-9 pa

LC 2005-28484

When a sixteen-year-old member of a race of shapeshifting killers called doppelgangers assumes the life of a troubled teen, he becomes unexpectedly embroiled in human life—and it is nothing like what he has seen on television.

"This brooding story of literally stepping into someone else's shoes combines romance, horror, and angst to create a distinctive story of redemption. The abusive relationships in Chris's family are portrayed with realism and sensitivity." Voice Youth Advocates

Spinning out; by David Stahler Jr. Chronicle Books 2012 285p $16.99

Grades: 7 8 9 10 **Fic**
1. Authors 2. Dramatists 3. School stories 4. Screenwriters 5. Theater -- Fiction 6. Vermont -- Fiction 7. Friendship -- Fiction 8. Schizophrenia -- Fiction 9. Television scriptwriters 10. Mental illness -- Fiction
ISBN 978-0-8118-7780-0; 0-8118-7780-9

LC 2010039392

Frenchy and Stewart, two Northern Vermont high school seniors, try out for the school musical, 'Man of La Mancha,' but when Stewart is cast as Don Quixote he soon becomes obsessed with his role and Frenchy must try to overcome his own demons to help his friend stay grounded in reality.

"Stahler creates a solid narrator in Frenchy, ably balancing his grief, confusion over Stewart's deteriorating mental state, and elation at his dawning relationship with stage manager Kaela. The resulting denouement is chaotic and heart-wrenching." Publ Wkly

Standiford, Natalie

The **secret** tree; Natalie Standiford. Scholastic Press 2012 245 p. $16.99

Grades: 4 5 6 7   **Fic**

1. Bildungsromans 2. Mystery fiction 3. Children's stories 4. Friendship

ISBN 0545334799; 9780545334792

This coming of age story combines "[m]iddle-school dynamics, pesky sibling relations, a rumored haunted house, . . . and a mystery. . . . When 10-year-old Minty discovers a hollow tree in the woods . . . [and] find[s] a secret written on a scrap of paper stashed inside, it sets the stage for a . . . mystery. . . . [W]hile Minty tries to figure out what's going on, she . . . befriend[s] an apparently parentless kid, Raymond, who seems to live in an abandoned spec house." (Kirkus)

Switched at birthday; Natalie Standiford. Scholastic Press 2014 240 p. (jacketed hardcover) $16.99

Grades: 4 5 6 7   **Fic**

1. Change -- Fiction 2. Change (Psychology) 3. Birthdays -- Fiction 4. Friendship -- Fiction 5. Identity (Psychology) -- Fiction 6. Magic -- Fiction 7. Schools -- Fiction 8. Identity -- Fiction 9. Middle schools -- Fiction 10. Change (Psychology) -- Fiction

ISBN 0545346509; 9780545346504

LC 2013018598

In this book, by Natalie Standiford, "Lavender and Scarlet are nothing alike. . . . There's only one thing Lavender and Scarlet know for sure they have in common: the same birthday. . . . They've never swapped presents. But this year, because of two wishes that turned all too true, they are about to swap something much bigger than presents. Because the morning after their birthdays, Lavender is going to wake up in Scarlet's body . . . and Scarlet is going to make up in Lavender's." (Publisher's note)

"Shortly before she turns 13, Lavender sums up her situation mathematically: 'Short hairy cavegirl + glasses = loser.' Her few friends are outnumbered by the group of cool girls who, routinely, publicly put her down. When popular Scarlet magically and inadvertently switches bodies with Lavender on their thirteenth birthdays, each girl is thrown into a new family and a new set of friends, as well as sudden, unforeseen challenges. . . . This well-paced novel will appeal to readers who loved Wendy Mass' popular 11 Birthdays (2009), which it resembles both in tone and in its use of a magical element." Booklist

Staniszewski, Anna

My sort of fairy tale ending; Anna Staniszewski. Sourcebooks Jabberwocky 2013 224 p. (tp : alk. paper) $6.99

Grades: 4 5 6 7   **Fic**

1. Magic -- Fiction 2. Fairies -- Fiction 3. Rescues -- Fiction 4. Families -- Fiction 5. Adventure and adventurers -- Fiction

ISBN 1402279337; 9781402279331

LC 2013017896

Sequel to: My epic fairy tale fail

In this book, by Anna Staniszewski, "Jenny only wants to rescue her parents . . . She's certain that the Queen Fairy has captured them, but when the queen captures Jenny too, the plot becomes complex. It turns out that the Queen Fairy is more than a bit insane. . . . When Jenny actually finds her parents, she must concoct a plan to rescue them, but with no power and her friends disappearing, she faces difficulties. . . . Of course Jenny will prevail, but how?" (Kirkus Reviews)

My very unfairy tale life. Sourcebooks Jabberwocky 2011 198p pa $6.99

Grades: 4 5 6 7   **Fic**

1. Fairy tales 2. Magic -- Fiction

ISBN 978-1-4022-5946-3; 1-4022-5946-8

Jenny, a professional adventurer, would prefer spending time with her friends over helping magical kingdoms around the universe, but soon she is given the choice to return to her normal life or go into a battle she doesn't think she can win.

"An eye for imaginative detail mixes with these likable characters and a theme of empathy for others to keep the story appropriate to a younger audience, who easily will identify with Jenny. Charming." Kirkus

Stanley, Diane

★ **Bella** at midnight; illustrated by Bagram Ibatoulline. HarperCollins Pubs. 2006 278p il $15.99; lib bdg $16.89; pa $6.99

Grades: 5 6 7 8   **Fic**

1. Fairy tales 2. Knights and knighthood -- Fiction

ISBN 978-0-06-077573-5; 0-06-077573-4; 978-0-06-077574-2 lib bdg; 0-06-077574-2 lib bdg; 978-0-06-077575-9 pa; 0-06-077575-0 pa

LC 2005-05906

Raised by peasants, Bella discovers that she is actually the daughter of a knight and finds herself caught up in a terrible plot that will change her life and the kingdom forever

"What raises this above other recreated fairy tales is the quality of the writing, dotted with jeweled description and anchored by the strong values—loyalty, truth, honor." Booklist

The **cup** and the crown; Diane Stanley. Harper 2012 344 p. (hardback) $16.99

Grades: 5 6 7 8   **Fic**

1. Fantasy fiction 2. Magic -- Fiction 3. Fantasy 4. Identity -- Fiction 5. Clairvoyance -- Fiction 6. Drinking cups -- Fiction

ISBN 0061963216; 9780061963216

LC 2012025280

In this fantasy novel by Diane Stanley "Molly has visions of a beautiful goblet: one of her grandfather's loving cups, which he filled with magic that bound people together. So it hardly surprises Molly when handsome King Alaric asks her to find a loving cup to help him win the heart of the beautiful Princess of Cortova. As Molly and her friends

Winifred and Tobias journey far beyond the safe borders of Westria, a mysterious raven appears to guide their quest." (Publisher's note)

The mysterious case of the Allbright Academy. HarperCollinsPublishers 2008 258p $16.99; lib bdg $17.89

Grades: 4 5 6 7   **Fic**
1. School stories 2. Mystery fiction
ISBN 978-0-06-085817-9; 0-06-085817-6; 978-0-06-085818-6 lib bdg; 0-06-085818-4 lib bdg
LC 2007-10910
Eighth-grader Franny and her friends investigate why most of the students at their exclusive boarding school are brilliant, beautiful, and perfectly behaved.
"Stanley delivers another humorous and thoroughly enjoyable mystery." Publ Wkly

The mysterious matter of I.M. Fine. HarperCollins Pubs. 2001 201p hardcover o.p. pa $5.99

Grades: 4 5 6 7   **Fic**
1. Mystery fiction 2. Magic -- Fiction 3. Books and reading -- Fiction
ISBN 0-688-17546-5; 0-380-73327-7 pa
LC 00-54040
Noticing that a popular series of horror novels is having a bizarre effect on the behavior of its readers, Franny and Beamer set out to find the mysterious author
"The solidly constructed mystery, well-rounded characters, and playful jab at wildly successful horror writers go down a treat." Horn Book Guide
Another title about Franny and her friends is:
The mysterious case of the Allbright Academy (2008)

★ **The princess** of Cortova; Diane Stanley. Harper, an imprint of HarperCollinsPublishers 2013 320 p. (hardback) $16.99

Grades: 5 6 7 8   **Fic**
1. Betrothal -- Fiction 2. Occult fiction 3. Alternative histories 4. Fantasy 5. Magic -- Fiction 6. Princesses -- Fiction 7. Clairvoyance -- Fiction 8. Courts and courtiers -- Fiction 9. Kings, queens, rulers, etc. -- Fiction
ISBN 0062047302; 9780062047304; 9780062047311
LC 2013021824
Sequel to: The cup and the crown
This book is the final one in Diane Stanley's trilogy about prescient Molly and her friends. Here, Molly and "young Kind Alaric and . . . Tobias journey from Westria to the Kingdom of Cortova in search of an alliance that will include Alaric's betrothal to Princess Elizabetta. To complicate matters, however, Alaric's cousin, the foxy Reynard, King of Austlind, has arrived with a similar goal. Who will win the hand of the fair Elizabetta?" (Booklist)

★ **Saving** Sky. Harper 2010 199p $15.99

Grades: 5 6 7 8   **Fic**
1. Terrorism -- Fiction 2. Immigrants -- Fiction 3. New Mexico -- Fiction 4. Prejudices -- Fiction 5. Ranch life -- Fiction 6. Family life -- Fiction
ISBN 978-0-06-123905-2; 0-06-123905-4
LC 2010-09393

In an America that has suffered continual terrorist attacks since 9/11, seventh-grader Sky stands up for what is right and helps a classmate of Middle Eastern descent, although doing so places her and her family at great risk.
"Readers will have much to discuss after finishing this beautifully written, disturbing book." Booklist

★ **The silver** bowl. Harper 2011 307p $16.99

Grades: 5 6 7 8   **Fic**
1. Fantasy fiction 2. Clairvoyance -- Fiction
ISBN 978-0-06-157543-3; 0-06-157543-7
"Molly is a young scullery maid in the castle of King Edmund, and like her mother before her, she sees visions and hears voices that offer glimpses of the future. But is this a blessing or a curse?. . . . The girl's choice of silence . . . is challenged when she learns that a rumored curse on the royal family is true and only by sharing her visions might they be saved. Combining carefully chosen details of setting with a richly realized fantasy premise, Stanley succeeds in creating a believable world large enough to accommodate not only menace and evil but also loyalty, enduring friendship, and love." Booklist

Stanley, George Edward

Night fires; a novel. Aladdin 2009 183p $15.99

Grades: 7 8 9 10   **Fic**
1. Moving -- Fiction 2. Oklahoma -- Fiction 3. Bereavement -- Fiction 4. Race relations -- Fiction 5. Ku Klux Klan (1915-) -- Fiction
ISBN 978-1-4169-7559-5; 1-4169-7559-4
LC 2008051607
In 1922, thirteen-year-old Woodrow Harper and his recently-widowed mother move to his father's childhood home in Lawton, Oklahoma, where he is torn between the "right people" of the Ku Klux Klan and those who encourage him to follow the path of his "nigra-loving" father.
"A thought-provoking novel. . . . Stanley's highly charged, emotional story tells of a very dark period in this country's history." SLJ

Staples, Suzanne Fisher

Dangerous skies. Farrar, Straus & Giroux 1996 231p hardcover o.p. pa $7.95

Grades: 7 8 9 10   **Fic**
1. Friendship -- Fiction 2. Prejudices -- Fiction 3. African Americans -- Fiction
ISBN 0-374-31694-5; 0-374-41670-2 pa
LC 95-45529
"At twelve, white boy Buck and black girl Tunes Smith are best friends. . . . The adolescents' idyllic world of fishing and observing nature is shattered when their much older friend Jorge Rodrigues is murdered, and Tunes is accused of the crime. . . . Staples's beautifully written and chilling tale of contemporary racism should keep young adult readers turning pages until they reach the heart-breaking end." Voice Youth Advocates

Shabanu; daughter of the wind. Knopf 1989 240p hardcover o.p. pa $6.50

Grades: 8 9 10 11 12　　　　　　　　　**Fic**
1. Pakistan -- Fiction 2. Sex role -- Fiction
ISBN 0-394-84815-2; 0-440-23856-0 pa
　　　　　　　　　　　　　　LC 89-2714
A Newbery Medal honor book, 1990

When eleven-year-old Shabanu, the daughter of a no-mad in the Cholistan Desert of present-day Pakistan, is pledged in marriage to an older man whose money will bring prestige to the family, she must either accept the decision, as is the custom, or risk the consequences of defying her father's wishes

"Interspersing native words throughout adds realism, but may trip up readers, who must be patient enough to find meaning through context. This use of language is, however, an important element in helping Staples paint an evocative picture of life in the desert that includes references to the hard facts of reality." Booklist

Other titles in this series are:
Haveli (1993)
The house of djinn (2008)

★ **Under** the Persimmon tree. Farrar, Straus & Giroux 2005 275p $17
Grades: 7 8 9 10　　　　　　　　　**Fic**
1. Pakistan -- Fiction 2. Afghanistan -- Fiction
ISBN 0-374-38025-2

During the 2001 Afghan War, the lives of Najmal, a young refugee from Kunduz, Afghanistan, and Nusrat, an American teacher who has converted to Islam, intersect at a school in Peshawar, Pakistan. "Grades four to six." (MultiCult Rev)

"Staples weaves a lot of history and politics into her story. . . . But . . . it's the personal story . . . that compels as it takes readers beyond the modern stereotypes of Mus-lims as fundamentalist fanatics. There are no sweet reunions, but there's hope in heartbreaking scenes of kindness and courage." Booklist

Starke, Ruth

Noodle pie. Kane Miller 2010 187p il $15.99
Grades: 4 5 6 7　　　　　　　　　**Fic**
1. Vietnam -- Fiction 2. Vietnamese -- Fiction
ISBN 978-1-935279-25-9; 1-935279-25-4

"Eleven-year-old Andy's first trip to Vietnam with his father, a 'Viet Kieu' (someone born in Vietnam who now lives overseas), exposes him to internalized prejudices about his heritage. . . . Andy distinguishes himself from his pushy relatives by emphasizing his Australian citizenship and criti-cizing customs that seem unfair. . . . This humorous, touch-ing novel is a delicious cross-cultural treat, and includes an appendix of Vietnamese recipes." Publ Wkly

Starmer, Aaron

The **only** ones. Delacorte Press 2011 321p $17.99; lib bdg $20.99; e-book $17.99
Grades: 4 5 6 7　　　　　　　　　**Fic**
1. Supernatural -- Fiction
ISBN 978-0-385-74043-2; 0-385-74043-3; 978-0-385-90839-9 lib bdg; 0-385-90839-3 lib bdg; 978-0-375-89919-5 e-book
　　　　　　　　　　　　　　LC 2010040383

After setting off from the island where he has been lead-ing a solitary existence, thirteen-year-old Martin discovers a village with other children who have been living simi-larly without any adults, since the grown-ups have all been spirited away.

"Both literary and engaging, this is the kind of book readers will want to return to for new discoveries." Kirkus

The **Riverman**; Aaron Starmer. Farrar Straus Giroux 2014 320 p. (hardback) $15.99
Grades: 5 6 7 8 9　　　　　　　　　**Fic**
1. Fantasy fiction 2. Imaginary places 3. Friendship -- Fiction 4. Missing children -- Fiction 5. Fantasy 6. Space and time 7. Missing children
ISBN 0374363099; 9780374363093
　　　　　　　　　　　　　　LC 2013027900

In this book, by Aaron Starmer, "Fiona Loomis shows up at Alistair's door asking him to pen her biography and begins to tell him of a strange land she's visited called Aquavania. . . . Fiona warns Alistair that the Riverman is stealing the souls of children and that she is next. Alistair, drawn into Fiona's story, wants to protect her—if only he can discover the full truth." (Booklist)

"When Fiona Loomis shows up at Alistair's door asking him to pen her biography and begins to tell him of a strange land she's visited called Aquavania, Alistair isn't sure he be-lieves any of it. . . . Fiona warns Alistair that the Riverman is stealing the souls of children and that she is next. . . . While the ending is left a bit up in the air, this magical tale is sure to please readers of urban fantasy, and with its theme of missing children and changing friendships, it will be perfect for fans of Neil Gaiman and Charles de Lint, too." Booklist

Stauffacher, Sue

Harry Sue. Knopf 2005 288p hardcover o.p. lib bdg $17.99; pa $6.50
Grades: 5 6 7 8　　　　　　　　　**Fic**
1. Prisoners -- Fiction 2. People with disabilities -- Fiction 3. Mother-daughter relationship -- Fiction
ISBN 0-375-83274-2; 0-375-93274-7 lib bdg; 0-440-42064-4 pa
　　　　　　　　　　　　　　LC 2004-16945

Although tough-talking Harry Sue would like to start a life of crime in order to be "sent up" and find her incarcer-ated mother, she must first protect the children at her ne-glectful grandmother's home day care center and befriend a paralyzed boy.

"This is a riveting story, dramatically and well told, with characters whom readers won't soon forget." SLJ

Stead, Rebecca

First light. Wendy Lamb Books 2007 328p $15.99; lib bdg $18.99; pa $6.99
Grades: 5 6 7 8　　　　　　　　　**Fic**
1. Greenland -- Fiction 2. Supernatural -- Fiction 3. Greenhouse effect -- Fiction
ISBN 978-0-375-84017-3; 0-375-84017-6; 987-0-375-094017-0 lib bdg; 0-375-94017-0 lib bdg; 978-0-440-42222-8 pa; 0-440-42222-1 pa
　　　　　　　　　　　　　　LC 2006-39733

This "novel is an exciting, engaging mix of science fiction, mystery, and adventure. . . . Peter and Thea are fully developed main characters." SLJ

Liar & spy; by Rebecca Stead. Wendy Lamb Books 2012 180 p. (hardback) $15.99

Grades: 4 5 6 7 8 **Fic**

1. Spy stories 2. Boys -- Fiction 3. Neighbors -- Fiction 4. Friendship -- Fiction 5. Spies -- Fiction 6. Schools -- Fiction 7. Middle schools -- Fiction 8. Apartment houses -- Fiction 9. Brooklyn (New York, N.Y.) -- Fiction 10. Family life -- New York (State) -- New York -- Fiction

ISBN 0385737432; 9780375899539; 9780385737432; 9780385906654

LC 2011042674

In this book, protagonist "Georges has a lot going on. Dad was laid off so Mom has started working extra shifts at the hospital, and they had to sell their house in Brooklyn and move into an apartment. One good thing about the new building is Safer, an unusual boy who lives on the top floor. He's determined to teach Georges how to be a spy. Their main case: spy on the mysterious Mr. X in the apartment above Georges. As Georges and Safer go deeper into their Mr. X plan, the line between games, lies, and reality begin to blur." (Barnes and Noble)

★ **When** you reach me. Wendy Lamb Books 2009 199p $15.99; lib bdg $18.99

Grades: 5 6 7 8 **Fic**

1. Space and time -- Fiction 2. New York (N.Y.) -- Fiction

ISBN 0-385-73742-4; 0-385-90664-1 lib bdg; 978-0-385-73742-5; 978-0-385-90664-7 lib bdg

LC 2008-24998

Awarded the Newbery Medal, 2010

As her mother prepares to be a contestant on the 1980s television game show, The 20,000 Pyramid, a twelve-year-old New York City girl tries to make sense of a series of mysterious notes received from an anonymous source. "Ages nine to fourteen." (Publisher's note)

"The '70s New York setting is an honest reverberation of the era; the mental gymnastics required of readers are invigorating; and the characters . . . . are honest bits of humanity." Booklist

Steele, Allen

Apollo's outcasts; by Allen Steele. Pyr 2012 311 p. (hardcover) $16.99

Grades: 7 8 9 10 **Fic**

1. Science fiction 2. People with disabilities -- Fiction 3. United States -- Fiction 4. Space colonies -- Fiction 5. Coups d'état -- Fiction 6. Regression (Civilization) -- Fiction 7. Children with disabilities -- Fiction

ISBN 1616146869; 9781616146863

LC 2012023582

This book from Hugo Award-winning author Allen Steele sends "a handful of kids to the Moon in the wake of a political coup in America. Jamey Barlowe, 16, was born on the Moon but raised on Earth; as a result of a low-gravity infancy, Jamey uses a multifunctional 'mobil' chair to get around. . . . Anxious to do something productive upon ar-

riving in Apollo (and able to walk for the first time), Jamey joins the elite Lunar Search and Rescue, just in time to end up on the front lines." (Publishers Weekly)

Steer, Dugald

The **dragon** diary; [by] Dugald A. Steer; illustrated by Douglas Carrel. Candlewick Press 2009 248p il (Dragonology chronicles) $16.99

Grades: 5 6 7 8 **Fic**

1. Fantasy fiction 2. Dragons -- Fiction 3. Siblings -- Fiction

ISBN 978-0-7636-3425-4; 0-7636-3425-5

LC 2009005795

Apprentice dragonologists Daniel and Beatrice Cook's mentor is called away at a crucial time, leaving the brother and sister alone to search for an ancient diary that could cure some gravely ill dragons

"This fast-paced fantasy features sibling rivalry, multitudes of dragons, and mid-air heroics." Horn Book Guide

Stein, Tammar

High dive. Alfred A. Knopf 2008 201p $15.99; lib bdg $18.99

Grades: 7 8 9 10 **Fic**

1. Europe -- Fiction 2. Vacations -- Fiction 3. Friendship -- Fiction 4. Loss (Psychology) -- Fiction 5. Single parent family -- Fiction

ISBN 978-0-375-83024-2; 0-375-83024-3; 978-0-375-93024-9 lib bdg; 0-375-93024-8 lib bdg

LC 2007049657

With her mother stationed in Iraq as an Army nurse, Vanderbilt University student Arden Vogel, whose father was killed in a traffic accident a few years earlier, impulsively ends up on a tour of Europe with a group of college girls she meets on her way to attend to some family business in Sardinia.

"Ideal for the thoughtful armchair traveler, this story is engaging enough for readers on the long flight to the enduring wonders of Europe and emerging adulthood." SLJ

Kindred. Alfred A. Knopf 2011 266p $16.99; lib bdg $19.99

Grades: 7 8 9 10 **Fic**

1. Twins -- Fiction 2. Angels -- Fiction 3. Siblings -- Fiction 4. Supernatural -- Fiction 5. Good and evil -- Fiction

ISBN 978-0-375-85871-0; 0-375-85871-7; 978-0-375-95871-7 lib bdg; 0-375-95871-1 lib bdg

LC 2010-07071

Spiritual warfare breaks out when the Archangel Raphael and the Devil deliver assignments to eighteen-year-old fraternal twins Miriam and Moses.

"Skillfully intertwining family, medical, and supernatural dramas with a sweet romantic subplot, Stein . . . unleashes cosmic battles to play out among the inhabitants of smalltown Hamilton, Tenn., a setting replete with Civil War history. . . . Miriam's initial interpretation of her illness as divine punishment gives way to more complex theological reflections in this riveting tale, an angel book that stands out from the chorus." Publ Wkly

Light years; a novel. Knopf 2005 263p hardcover o.p. pa $6.99

Grades: 7 8 9 10   **Fic**

1. Bereavement -- Fiction 2. Israel-Arab conflicts -- Fiction

ISBN 0-375-83023-5; 0-440-23902-8 pa

LC 2004-7776

Maya Laor leaves her home in Israel to study astronomy at the University of Virginia after the tragic death of her boyfriend in a suicide bombing.

"This well-paced first novel, a moving study of grief and recovery, is also a love story that should appeal particularly to students interested in other ways of seeing the world." SLJ

Includes bibliographical references

Steinbeck, John

The **pearl**; John Steinbeck centennial ed; Penguin Books 2002 87p pa $11

Grades: 7 8 9 10   **Fic**

1. Mexico -- Fiction 2. Poverty -- Fiction

ISBN 0-14-200069-8

LC 2001-56113

First published 1947

"Kino, a poor pearl-fisher, lives a happy albeit spartan life with his wife and their child. When he finds a magnificent pearl, the Pearl of the World, he is besieged by dishonest pearl merchants and envious neighbors. Even a greedy doctor ties his professional treatment of their baby when it is bitten by a scorpion to the possible acquisition of the pearl. After a series of disasters, Kino throws the pearl away since it has brought him only unhappiness." Shapiro. Fic for Youth. 3d edition

The **red** pony. Viking 1993 100p pa $9

Grades: 4 5 6 7 8   **Fic**

1. Horses -- Fiction 2. California -- Fiction 3. Ranch life -- Fiction

ISBN 0-670-59184-X; 0-14-017736-1 pa

LC 86-1610

First published 1937

"Jody Tiflin, ten years old, begins to grow up in these four vignettes describing his life on a farm in California. He takes responsibility for his red pony and suffers when it dies. An old man arouses Jody's curiosity about what is beyond the mountains, and he anxiously awaits the birth of a colt. His grandfather's tales are a source of interest and wonder for Jody." Shapiro. Fic for Youth. 3d edition

Steinmetz, Karen

The **mourning** wars. Roaring Brook Press 2010 232p $17.99

Grades: 7 8 9 10   **Fic**

1. Mohawk Indians -- Fiction 2. United States -- History -- 1702-1713, Queen Anne's War -- Fiction

ISBN 978-1-59643-290-1; 1-59643-290-X

LC 2010-11735

In 1704, Mohawk Indians attack the frontier village of Deerfield, Massachusetts, kidnapping over 100 residents, including seven-year-old Eunice Williams. Based on a true story.

"Eunice's largely imagined life makes a fascinating story with a setting that is vividly and dramatically evoked. The book will be especially useful in the classroom." Booklist

Includes bibliographical references

Stellings, Caroline

The **contest**. Seventh Generation 2009 123p pa $9.95

Grades: 4 5 6 7   **Fic**

1. Canada -- Fiction 2. Poverty -- Fiction 3. Contests -- Fiction 4. Friendship -- Fiction 5. Books and reading -- Fiction 6. Racially mixed people -- Fiction

ISBN 978-0-9779183-5-5 pa; 0-9779183-5-1 pa

LC 2009-20294

Rosy, a poor, eleven-year-old, half-Mohawk girl from Hamilton, Ontario, Canada enters an Anne of Green Gables look-alike contest in hopes of winning a set of Anne books, and gains a new friend and deeper understanding of Anne's character

"Readers will enjoy Rosy and her spunky attitude. . . . Some readers will finish this book and go seeking the Anne series to read, and those already familiar with the Anne books will enjoy the connection." Libr Media Connect

Stephens, John

The **black** reckoning; John Stephens. Alfred A. Knopf 2015 432 p. (Books of beginning) (hardback) $17.99

Grades: 4 5 6 7   **Fic**

1. Magic -- Fiction 2. Identity -- Fiction 3. Monsters -- Fiction 4. Prophecies -- Fiction 5. Space and time -- Fiction 6. Brothers and sisters -- Fiction 7. Books and reading -- Fiction

ISBN 0375868720; 9780375868726; 9780375968723

LC 2014023538

In this novel, by John Stephens, part of the Books of Beginning series, "the adventures of siblings Kate, Michael, and Emma come to a stunning conclusion when they must find the last Book of Beginning--the Book of Death--before the Dire Magnus does, for when all three books are united, their combined power will be unstoppable." (Publisher's note)

"Heartbreaking sacrifices, joyous reunions, and poignant partings round out this rousing old-school fantasy adventure." Horn Book

Other titles in the trilogy are:
The Emerald Atlas (2011)
The Fire Chronicle (2012)

★ The **emerald** atlas. Alfred A. Knopf 2011 417p (The books of beginning) $17.99; lib bdg $20.99

Grades: 4 5 6   **Fic**

1. Magic -- Fiction 2. Monsters -- Fiction 3. Siblings -- Fiction 4. Prophecies -- Fiction 5. Space and time -- Fiction 6. Books and reading -- Fiction

ISBN 978-0-375-86870-2; 0-375-86870-4; 978-0-375-96870-9 lib bdg; 0-375-96870-9 lib bdg

LC 2010029100

Kate, Michael, and Emma have passed from one orphanage to another in the ten years since their parents disappeared to protect them, but now they learn that they have special powers, a prophesied quest to find a magical book, and a fearsome enemy.

"This fast-paced, fully imagined fantasy is by turns frightening and funny, and the siblings are well-crafted and empathetic heroes. Highly enjoyable, it should find many readers." Publ Wkly

★ The **fire** chronicle; John Stephens. Alfred A. Knopf 2012 437 p. (hardback) $17.99

Grades: 4 5 6   **Fic**

1. Fantasy fiction 2. Adventure fiction 3. Time travel -- Fiction 4. Magic -- Fiction 5. Identity -- Fiction 6. Monsters -- Fiction 7. Prophecies -- Fiction 8. Space and time -- Fiction 9. Books and reading -- Fiction 10. Brothers and sisters -- Fiction 11. New York (N.Y.) -- History -- 1898-1951 -- Fiction

ISBN 0375868712; 9780375868719; 9780375899560; 9780375968716

LC 2012016139

In this novel by John Stephens, part of the Books of Beginning series, "Kate, Michael, and Emma long to continue the hunt for their missing parents. . . .A frantic chase sends Kate a hundred years into the past, to a perilous, enchanted New York City. . . . Meanwhile, Michael and Emma have set off to find the second of the Books of Beginning. A series of clues leads them into a hidden world where they must brave harsh polar storms, track down an ancient order of warriors, and confront terrible monsters." (Publisher's note)

Sternberg, Libby

The **case** against my brother. Bancroft Press 2007 201p $19.95

Grades: 6 7 8 9   **Fic**

1. Brothers -- Fiction 2. Prejudices -- Fiction 3. Portland (Or.) -- Fiction 4. Polish Americans -- Fiction

ISBN 978-1-890862-51-0; 1-890862-51-7

"In 1922, when their widowed mother dies, Carl Matiuski and his older brother, Adam, move to Portland, OR, to live with an uncle. . . . When [Adam] is accused of a crime he didn't commit, Carl steps in . . . to try to clear his brother's name. . . . Readers are easily swept up in the adventure as the eye-opening mystery unfolds." SLJ

Stevens, Robin

Murder is bad manners; Robin Stevens. Simon & Schuster Books for Young Readers 2015 320 p. (hardcover) $16.99

Grades: 4 5 6 7   **Fic**

1. School stories 2. Mystery fiction 3. Murder -- Fiction 4. Friendship -- Fiction 5. Boarding schools -- Fiction 6. Chinese -- England -- Fiction 7. Mystery and detective stories

ISBN 148142212X; 9781481422123; 9781481422130

LC 2014003939

In this middle grades book, by Robin Stevens, "Daisy Wells and Hazel Wong are best friends at Deepdean School for Girls, and they both have a penchant for solving mysteries. . . . [T]hey form their own (secret!) detective agency. The only problem? They have nothing to investigate. But that changes once Hazel discovers the body of their science teacher, Miss Bell - and the body subsequently disappears." (Publisher's note)

"Here's a mystery import, set in the 1930s, that does justice to its British roots. Hazel Wong has come from Hong Kong to attend Deepdean boarding school. An outcast until she is accepted by upper-crust Daisy Wells, Hazel is happy to be half of a two-girl detective agency...Hazel makes a good narrator, and while the mystery plods a bit and has too many teachers—though a cast list helps—not every reader will guess the ending. Nancy Drew, meet Wells and Wong." Booklist

Stevenson, Robert Louis

Kidnapped; [by] Robert Louis Stevenson; with an introduction by Sid Hite. F. Watts 2007 213p (Scholastic classics) $25.50

Grades: 7 8 9 10 11 12 Adult   **Fic**

1. Adventure fiction 2. Scotland -- Fiction 3. Kidnapping -- Fiction

ISBN 978-0-531-16990-2; 0-531-16990-1

LC 2006006816

First published 1886

A sixteen-year-old orphan is kidnapped by his villainous uncle, but later escapes and becomes involved in the struggle of the Scottish highlanders against English rule.

Treasure Island; Robert Louis Stevenson; illustrated by John Lawrence. 1st U.S. ed. Candlewick Press 2009 269 p. col. ill. (reinforced) $24.99

Grades: 5 6 7 8 9 10 11 12 Adult   **Fic**

1. Adventure fiction 2. Pirates -- Fiction 3. Buried treasure -- Fiction

ISBN 0763644455; 9780763644451

LC 2009007338

First published in 1883.

While going through the possessions of a deceased guest who owed them money, the mistress of the inn and her son find a treasure map that leads them to a notorious pirate's fortune

"Lawrence evokes the essence of classic adventure stories with his vinyl-cut illustrations, as thick black shapes are tempered by muted tones of blue, gold and green. . . . Readers will feel they've discovered a true relic with this edition." Publ Wkly

Stevenson, Robin H.

Dead in the water; [by] Robin Stevenson. Orca Book Publishers 2008 169p (Orca sports) pa $9.95

Grades: 6 7 8 9   **Fic**

1. Adventure fiction 2. Sailing -- Fiction 3. British Columbia -- Fiction 4. Endangered species -- Fiction

ISBN 978-1-5514-3962-4 pa; 1-5514-3962-X pa

"Simon ('Spacey') joins three other teenagers for a weeklong sailing course in British Columbia, Canada. . . . His weird shipmate, Olivia, insists that the men on a nearby cabin cruiser are smuggling abalone, a threatened shellfish species, and she persuades Simon to help her investigate. . . . Stevenson . . . delivers plenty of realistic, gripping detail about handling a boat in screaming winds and crashing waves, as well as a solid story about a crucial environmental issue." Booklist

Escape velocity. Orca Book Publishers 2011 232p pa $12.95

Grades: 6 7 8 9 **Fic**
1. Mother-daughter relationship -- Fiction
ISBN 978-1-55469-866-0; 1-55469-866-9

Forced to live with the mother who abandoned her at birth, Lou goes looking for truth in her mother's fiction.

"Lou is a fully rounded, attractive character. Zoe's emotional insensitivity toward her, while painful, becomes understandable as her believable back story emerges. Other characters are also nicely, authentically fleshed out, adding depth and a strong sense of reality. A quiet, moving exploration of what it means to be a mother—or a daughter—even when the relationship is unconventional." Kirkus

Liars and fools; written by Robin Stevenson. Orca Book Publishers 2010 246p pa $9.95
Grades: 5 6 7 8 **Fic**
1. Canada -- Fiction 2. Bereavement -- Fiction
ISBN 978-1-55469-248-4 pa; 1-55469-248-2 pa

Still grieving the loss of her mother, Fiona resists the idea of moving on with her life, especially when her father starts dating a psychic.

"Fiona is a believable character trying to deal with her grief. . . . Her relationship with her best (and only) friend, Abby, is realistic, and the banter between the two girls adds humor." Booklist

Out of order; written by Robin Stevenson. Orca Book Publishers 2007 221p pa $8.95
Grades: 8 9 10 11 12 **Fic**
1. School stories 2. Canada -- Fiction 3. Friendship -- Fiction
ISBN 978-1-55143-693-7; 1-55143-693-0

When Sophie moves to Victoria, she hopes to leave the bullying she experienced in Ontario behind, but when she makes two new friends who are polar opposites, she finds that friendships can both help and harm her sense of self.

"The visceral, emotional reactions of the characters ring true. . . . Despite weighty themes, this story is about friendship and self-worth." Voice Youth Advocates

Stevermer, Caroline
Magic below stairs. Dial Books for Young Readers 2010 199p $16.99
Grades: 4 5 6 7 **Fic**
1. Magic -- Fiction 2. Orphans -- Fiction 3. Household employees -- Fiction 4. Great Britain -- History -- 19th century -- Fiction
ISBN 978-0-8037-3467-8; 0-8037-3467-0
LC 2009-25100

Ten-year-old Frederick, who is surreptitiously watched over by a household elf, is plucked from a London orphanage to be a servant to a wealthy wizard, and eventually his uncanny abilities lead him to become the wizard's apprentice.

"A well-developed fictional world and the many concrete details of belowstairs life make the magical events in this engaging chapter book more believable." Booklist

Stewart, Alex
Dragonwood; Alex Stewart. Evans 2010 56 p. pa $7.99
Grades: 7 8 9 10 **Fic**
1. Fantasy fiction 2. Mystery fiction 3. Elves -- Fiction

4. Criminals -- Fiction
ISBN 0237541351; 145174465X; 9780237541354; 9781451744651
LC 2011287528

This book is part of "the Shades series . . . from Britain" and "presents a fantasy story that dispenses with the massive casting and large chunks of world building" found in other fantasy stories. The story "follows a Halfling bounty hunter, Pip, who has been paid by an elven prince to track down and return the head of an orcish outlaw, who is rumored to have slain the prince's sister. He soon enough finds reason to doubt his employer's word, but Pip is sworn to carry out his mission one way or another." Author Alex Stewart offers "a conflicted-private-eye story in a fantasy setting." (Booklist)

Stewart, Paul
The **curse** of the night wolf; [by] Paul Stewart and Chris Riddell; illustrated by Chris Riddell. David Fickling Books 2008 204p il (Barnaby Grimes) $15.99; lib bdg $18.99
Grades: 4 5 6 7 **Fic**
1. Mystery fiction 2. Physicians -- Fiction 3. Werewolves -- Fiction 4. London (England) -- Fiction 5. Great Britain -- History -- 19th century -- Fiction
ISBN 978-0-385-75125-4; 0-385-75125-7; 978-0-385-75126-1 lib bdg; 0-385-75126-5 lib bdg
LC 2008-01697

Soon after Victorian messenger Barnaby Grimes is attacked by a huge beast while crossing London's rooftops, he becomes entangled in a mystery involving patent medicine, impoverished patients, and very expensive furs.

"Moody, highly detailed pen-and-ink drawings provide ornamentation throughout, lending a classic Victorian feel to help punctuate the drama. . . . Possessing an easy confidence and quick wit . . . Barnaby is an appealing character." Booklist

Other titles in this series are:
Return of the emerald skull (2009)
Legion of the Dead (2010)

Phantom of Blood Alley; [by] Paul Stewart & Chris Riddell; illustrated by Chris Riddell. David Fickling Books 2010 201p il (Barnaby Grimes) $16.99
Grades: 4 5 6 7 **Fic**
1. Mystery fiction 2. Photography -- Fiction 3. Supernatural -- Fiction 4. Great Britain -- History -- 19th century -- Fiction
ISBN 978-0-385-75134-6; 0-385-75134-6
First published 2009 in the United Kingdom

Barnaby finds himself in the fiercely competitive world of early photography, where the rewards are immense but so are the risks. After an experiment goes disastrously wrong, Barnaby is on the trail of a mad chemist with a talent for disappearing into thin air.

Stewart, Trenton Lee
The **extraordinary** education of Nicholas Benedict; by Trenton Lee Stewart; illustrated by Diana Sudyka. Little, Brown 2012 470 p. $17.99
Grades: 4 5 6 7 8 **Fic**
1. Bullies -- Fiction 2. Orphans -- Fiction 3. Friendship

-- Fiction 4. Narcolepsy -- Fiction 5. Orphanages -- Fiction 6. Genius -- Fiction 7. Mystery and detective stories 8. Adventure and adventurers -- Fiction
ISBN 9780316176194

LC 2011031690

This book tells the story of Nicholas Benedict who "is just 9 years. . . . Small in physical stature but intellectually gifted, he has an 'unfortunate' nose . . . and a medical condition that prompts 'unpredictable sleeping episodes' that drop 'him from consciousness like a trapdoor into a black dungeon' at the least opportune of times. . . . What has long made him a nuisance to less intelligent adults and target practice for bullies also makes him a curiosity for a slightly older boy who befriends him at his new home -- the ominously named Rothschild's End. The orphanage is housed in a two-story mansion. . . . [The book] revolves around . . . the . . . themes . . . [of] orphans, friendship and the sorts of surrogate families that form as a result." (LA Times)

★ The **mysterious** Benedict Society; illustrated by Carson Ellis. Little, Brown 2007 485p il $16.99; pa $6.99

Grades: 5 6 7 8 **Fic**
1. Science fiction 2. Adventure fiction
ISBN 978-0-316-05777-6; 0-316-05777-0; 978-0-316-00395-7 pa; 0-316-00395-6 pa

LC 2006-09925

After passing a series of mind-bending tests, four children are selected for a secret mission that requires them to go undercover at the Learning Institute for the Very Enlightened, where the only rule is that there are no rules

"Stewart's unusual characters, threatening villains, and dramatic plot twists will grab and hold readers' attention." SLJ

Other titles about the Benedict Society are:
The mysterious Benedict Society and the perilous journey (2008)
The mysterious Benedict Society and the prisoner's dilemma (2009)

The **mysterious** Benedict Society and the perilous journey; by Trenton Lee Stewart; illustrated by Carson Ellis. Little, Brown and Co. 2008 440p il $16.99

Grades: 5 6 7 8 **Fic**
1. Science fiction 2. Adventure fiction
ISBN 978-0-316-05780-6; 0-316-05780-0

LC 2007031540

Sequel to: The mysterious Benedict Society (2007)

Reynie, Kate, Sticky, and Constance, all graduates of the Learning Institute for the Very Enlightened and members of the Benedict Society, embark on a scavenger hunt that turns into a desperate search for the missing Mr. Benedict.

"This is pure adventure—lots of racing, scheming, fighting." Booklist

Stiefvater, Maggie
★ The **dream** thieves; Maggie Stiefvater. Scholastic 2013 416 p. (Raven cycle) (jacketed hardcover) $18.99

Grades: 8 9 10 11 12 **Fic**
1. Occult fiction 2. Fantasy fiction 3. Magic -- Fiction

4. Dreams -- Fiction 5. Paranormal fiction 6. Secrets -- Fiction 7. Occultism -- Fiction 8. Family secrets -- Fiction
ISBN 0545424941; 9780545424943

LC 2013018731

This is the second book in Maggie Stiefvater's Raven Cycle series. Here, after "the transformative events at Cabeswater . . . , the context in which Gansey, Blue, Adam, Ronan, and Noah operate is further altered by the arrival of the Gray Man, a self-described hit man. . . . The Gray Man brings with him the machinations of larger, previously unknown forces as he takes orders from a voice on the phone to hunt the Greywaren, the identity of which is revealed early on." (Publishers Weekly)

"In this darker second book (The Raven Boys), Gansey, Blue, and the search for Glendower take a backseat to the exploration of Ronan's and Adam's tortured personalities. Stiefvater's descriptive prose reveals a complicated plot, multiple viewpoints, and detailed backstories. Many mysteries remain, but the cliffhanger ending makes it clear that Glendower will resurface as the main focus of book three." (Horn Book)

Hunted; Maggie Stiefvater. Scholastic Inc. 2014 192 p. map (Spirit animals) (paper-over-board) $12.99

Grades: 4 5 6 7 **Fic**
1. Fantasy fiction 2. Wolves -- Fiction 3. Human-animal relationship -- Fiction
ISBN 0545522447; 9780545522441; 9780545522564; 9780545599726

LC 2013947126

This fantasy novel by Maggie Stiefvater, part of the Spirit Animals series, describes how its "four young heroes have barely had time to come together as a team, and their own spirit animal bonds are still greatly untested. But now they face a brutal confrontation against an enemy who will break any rule to defeat them." (Publisher's note)

"Stiefvater blends Mull's brilliant world building with her talent of writing memorable villains." Booklist

★ The **raven** boys; Maggie Stiefvater. Scholastic Press 2012 409 p. (hardcover) $18.99

Grades: 8 9 10 11 12 **Fic**
1. Magic -- Fiction 2. Supernatural -- Fiction 3. Private schools -- Fiction 4. Paranormal fiction 5. Occultism -- Fiction 6. Clairvoyance -- Fiction
ISBN 0545424925; 9780545424929

LC 2012030880

This book is the first in Maggie Stiefvater's series the "Raven Cycle". It follows "16-year-old Blue Sargent, daughter of a small-town psychic, [who] has lived her whole life under a prophecy: If she kisses her true love, he will die. . . . She sees a vision of a dying Raven boy named Gansey. The Raven Boys--students at Aglionby, a nearby prep school, so-called because of the ravens on their school crest--soon encounter Blue in person." (Kirkus Reviews)

★ The **Scorpio** Races. Scholastic Press 2011 409p $17.99

Grades: 8 9 10 11 12 **Fic**
1. Love stories 2. Fantasy fiction 3. Horses -- Fiction

4. Racing -- Fiction 5. Orphans -- Fiction
ISBN 978-0-545-22490-1; 0-545-22490-X

LC 2011015775

"Stiefvater's narration is as much about atmospherics as it is about event, and the water horses are the environment in which Sean and Puck move, allies and rivals to the end. It's not a feel-good story—dread, loss, and hard choices are the islanders' lot. As a study of courage and loyalty tested, however, it is an utterly compelling read." Publ Wkly

Stier, Catherine

The **terrible** secrets of the Tell-All Club. Albert Whitman & Co. 2009 125p $14.99

Grades: 4 5 6   **Fic**

1. School stories 2. Clubs -- Fiction 3. Friendship -- Fiction

ISBN 978-0-8075-7798-1; 0-8075-7798-7

LC 2008055704

When four fifth-grade friends complete a "tell-all" survey, tensions arise and come to a head during an overnight class trip

"Told in the four voices of the club members, the story shows the characters' insecurities and the family issues they face. Reluctant readers will find it fast paced, easy to follow, and populated with likable personalities." SLJ

Stoffels, Karlijn

★ **Heartsinger**; translated by Laura Watkinson. Arthur A. Levine Books 2009 134p $16.99

Grades: 8 9 10 11   **Fic**

1. Fantasy fiction 2. Love -- Fiction 3. Voyages and travels -- Fiction

ISBN 978-0-545-06929-8; 0-545-06929-7; 978-0-545-06968-7 pa; 0-545-06968-8 pa

LC 2008-17785

In this meditation on various kinds of love, Mee travels across the country to the court of the Princess Esperanza, singing the life stories of some of the people he meets.

"Written with clarity and grace. . . . This unusual novel offers readers limpid writing, strong storytelling, and the unblinking recognition of love in many forms." Booklist

Stolz, Joelle

The **shadows** of Ghadames; translated from the French by Catherine Temerson. Delacorte Press 2004 119p $15.95; lib bdg $17.99

Grades: 5 6 7 8   **Fic**

1. Libya -- Fiction 2. Muslims -- Fiction 3. Sex role -- Fiction

ISBN 0-385-73104-3; 0-385-90131-3 lib bdg

LC 2003-21656

At the end of the nineteenth century in Libya, eleven-year-old Malika simultaneously enjoys and feels constricted by the narrow world of women, but an injured stranger enters her home and disrupts the traditional order of things.

"Stolz invigorates her tale with elegant prose and a deft portrayal of a girl verging on adolescence. The vivid backdrop is intoxicating." Booklist

Stone, Phoebe

The **boy** on Cinnamon Street; by Phoebe Stone. Arthur A. Levine Books 2012 234 p. (alk. paper) $16.99

Grades: 3 4 5 6 7 8   **Fic**

1. Girls -- Psychology 2. Friendship -- Fiction 3. Memory -- Fiction 4. Grandparent-grandchild relationship 5. Memory -- Fiction 6. Schools -- Fiction 7. Best friends -- Fiction 8. Grandparents -- Fiction 9. Massachusetts -- Fiction

ISBN 0545215129; 9780545215121

LC 2011017862

This book tells the story of "seventh-grader [Louise who] lives with her grandparents in their condo and she's quit [gymnastics], . . . instead spending her time with friends Reni and her brother Henderson Elliot, whose warm and embracing family she adores. When a cute ninth-grader turns up on her doorstep delivering pizza, and she then finds a note under the mat confessing interest in Louise, she's transported into her first serious crush." (Bulletin of the Center for Children's Books)

Deep down popular; a novel. by Phoebe Stone. Arthur A. Levine Books 2008 280p $16.99; pa $4.99

Grades: 4 5 6 7   **Fic**

1. School stories 2. Virginia -- Fiction 3. Friendship -- Fiction 4. Family life -- Fiction 5. Country life -- Fiction

ISBN 978-0-439-80245-1; 0-439-80245-8; 978-0-439-80244-4 pa; 0-439-80244-X pa

LC 2007017198

In a small Virginia town, sixth-grader Jessie Lou Ferguson has a crush on the hugely popular Conrad Parker Smith, and when he suddenly develops a medical problem and the teacher asks Jessie Lou to help him, they become friends, to her surprise

"Jessie Lou tells her tale with the strong, rough-edged purity of a young poet, which she is; equally strong are the story's underpinnings, longing and laughter, and a willingness to believe in something despite the facts." Booklist

★ The **Romeo** and Juliet code. Arthur A. Levine Books 2011 300p $16.99

Grades: 4 5 6 7   **Fic**

1. Maine -- Fiction 2. Ciphers -- Fiction 3. Family life -- Fiction 4. World War, 1939-1945 -- United States -- Fiction 5. World War, 1939-1945 -- Evacuation of civilians -- Fiction

ISBN 978-0-545-21511-4; 0-545-21511-0

LC 2010-30005

During World War II, eleven-year-old Felicity is sent from London to Bottlebay, Maine, to live with her grandmother, aunt, uncle, and a reclusive boy who helps her decode mysterious letters that contain the truth about her missing parents.

Felicity "is endearingly portrayed, and the back story, so gradually revealed, provides a peek into the depths of the souls of some of the adults. The pacing is deliberately slow, yet Felicity's growing awareness of how she can help heal the troubled adults makes this an eminently satisfying read." Kirkus

Romeo blue; by Phoebe Stone. 1st ed. Arthur A. Levine Books 2013 352 p. (hardcover) $16.99

Grades: 4 5 6 7   **Fic**

1. Espionage -- Fiction 2. World War, 1939-1945 -- Children -- Fiction 3. World War, 1939-1945 -- Evacuation of civilians -- Fiction 4. Identity -- Fiction 5. Foster children -- Fiction 6. Families -- Fiction 7. Family life -- Maine -- Fiction 8. World War, 1939-1945 -- Maine -- Fiction 9. Maine -- History -- 20th century -- Fiction 10. Foster children -- Maine -- Fiction 11. World War, 1939-1945 -- Maine -- Fiction 12. Maine -- History -- 20th century -- Fiction 13. World War, 1939-1945 -- Evacuation of civilians -- Great Britain -- Fiction

ISBN 0545443601; 9780545443609

LC 2012038060

Parents' Choice: Silver Medal Fiction (2013)

"In this sequel to the WWII historical mystery 'The Romeo and Juliet Code,' . . . twelve-year old . . . Flissy now knows her Uncle Gideon is actually her biological father. . . . And she knows her whole family are some kind of spies, but she does not know . . . if they are still alive. And she has no idea why the creepy neighbor, Mr. Fitzwilliam, has invited her and adopted cousin Derek for tea, how he seems to know about her parents' secret activities." (Children's Literature)

Stone, Tamara Ireland

Time between us; Tamara Ireland Stone. Hyperion 2012 384 p. (hardcover) $17.99

Grades: 7 8 9 10   **Fic**

1. Love stories 2. Time travel -- Fiction 3. Love -- Fiction 4. Schools -- Fiction 5. Illinois -- Fiction 6. High schools -- Fiction 7. Space and time -- Fiction 8. Family life -- Illinois -- Fiction

ISBN 142315956X; 9781423159568

LC 2011053368

This book by Tamara Ireland Stone follows "Anna and Bennett," a couple who "were never supposed to meet: she lives in 1995 Chicago and he lives in 2012 San Francisco. But Bennett's unique ability to travel through time and space brings him into Anna's life, and with him, a new world of adventure and possibility. As their relationship deepens, they face the reality that time might knock Bennett back where he belongs." (Publisher's note)

Stork, Francisco X.

★ The **last** summer of the death warriors. Arthur A. Levine Books 2010 344p $17.99

Grades: 8 9 10 11 12   **Fic**

1. Death -- Fiction 2. Orphans -- Fiction 3. New Mexico -- Fiction 4. Mexican Americans -- Fiction

ISBN 978-0-545-15133-7; 0-545-15133-3

LC 2009-19853

"This novel, in the way of the best literary fiction, is an invitation to careful reading that rewards serious analysis and discussion. Thoughtful readers will be delighted by both the challenge and Stork's respect for their abilities." Booklist

★ **Marcelo** in the real world. Arthur A. Levine Books 2009 312p $17.99

Grades: 8 9 10 11 12   **Fic**

1. Autism -- Fiction 2. Asperger's syndrome -- Fiction

ISBN 0-545-05474-5; 978-0-545-05474-4

LC 2008-14729

ALA Schneider Family Book Award Honor Book (2010)

This book features "Marcelo Sandoval [who] is a 17-year-old looking forward to his senior year in high school. Living with something akin to Asperger's syndrome, Marcelo has spent his life learning step by step how to do things that many people learn intuitively. . . . Marcelo's father makes a deal with him: if he will spend the summer working at his father's law firm and successfully follow the rules of the real world, he can choose where he will spend his senior year." (Christian Century)

"Stork introduces ethical dilemmas, the possibility of love, and other 'real world' conflicts, all the while preserving the integrity of his characterizations and intensifying the novel's psychological and emotional stakes." Publ Wkly

Strasser, Todd

Boot camp. Simon & Schuster Books for Young Readers 2007 238p hardcover o.p. pa $6.99

Grades: 8 9 10 11 12   **Fic**

1. Torture -- Fiction 2. Juvenile delinquency -- Fiction

ISBN 978-1-4169-0848-7; 1-4169-0848-X; 978-1-4169-5942-7 pa; 1-4169-5942-4 pa

LC 2006-13634

After ignoring several warnings to stop dating his former teacher, Garrett is sent to Lake Harmony, a boot camp that uses brutal methods to train students to obey their parents.

"The ending is both realistic and disturbing. . . . Writing in the teen's mature and perceptive voice, Strasser creates characters who will provoke strong reactions from readers. . . . [This is a] fast-paced and revealing story." SLJ

Can't get there from here. Simon & Schuster Books for Young Readers 2004 198p $15.95

Grades: 7 8 9 10   **Fic**

1. New York (N.Y.) -- Fiction 2. Homeless persons -- Fiction 3. Runaway teenagers -- Fiction

ISBN 0-689-84169-8

LC 2003-170

Tired of being hungry, cold, and dirty from living on the streets of New York City with a tribe of other homeless teenagers who are dying, one by one, a girl named Maybe ponders her future and longs for someone to care about her

"While the events described in this cautionary tale are shocking, the language is not, making these all-too-real problems accessible to a wide readership." SLJ

Fallout; Todd Strasser. Candlewick Press 2013 272 p. $16.99

Grades: 5 6 7 8   **Fic**

ISBN 0763655341; 9780763655341

LC 2012955123

This book is an alternate history novel by Todd Strasser. "In the summer of 1962, the possibility of nuclear war is all anyone talks about. But Scott's dad is the only one in the neighborhood who actually prepares for the worst. . . . . . When the unthinkable happens," their neighbors "force their way into the shelter. . . . With not enough room, not enough food, and not enough air, life inside the shelter is filthy, physically draining, and emotionally fraught." (Publisher's note)

Famous. Simon & Schuster Books for Young Readers 2011 257p $15.99

Grades: 7 8 9 10   **Fic**

1. Fame -- Fiction 2. Actors -- Fiction 3. Celebrities -- Fiction 4. Hollywood (Calif.) -- Fiction

ISBN 978-1-4169-7511-3; 1-4169-7511-X

LC 2009-48163

Sixteen-year-old Jamie Gordon had a taste of praise and recognition at age fourteen when her unflattering photograph of an actress was published, but as she pursues her dream of being a celebrity photographer, she becomes immersed in the dark side of fame.

"The book makes some astute observations about America's reality-television culture and its obsession with fame. . . . This well-crafted novel clearly belongs in all public, junior high, and high school libraries." Voice Youth Advocates

If I grow up. Simon & Schuster Books for Young Readers 2009 222p $16.99

Grades: 7 8 9 10   **Fic**

1. Gangs -- Fiction 2. Poverty -- Fiction 3. Violence -- Fiction 4. African Americans -- Fiction

ISBN 978-1-4169-2523-1; 1-4169-2523-6

LC 2008-00655

Growing up in the inner-city projects, DeShawn is reluctantly forced into the gang world by circumstances beyond his control.

"Strasser's writing puts the reader in the midst of the projects and offers totally real characters." Voice Youth Advocates

Includes bibliographical references

No place; Todd Strasser. Simon & Schuster Books for Young Readers 2014 272 p. (hardcover) $17.99

Grades: 7 8 9 10   **Fic**

1. Homelessness 2. Homeless persons -- Fiction 3. Poverty -- Fiction

ISBN 144245721X; 9781442457218

LC 2012043701

In this novel, by Todd Strasser, "It seems like Dan has it all. . . . Then his family loses their home. Forced to move into the town's Tent City, Dan feels his world shifting. . . . As Dan struggles to adjust to his new life, he gets involved with the people who are fighting for better conditions and services for the residents of Tent City. But someone wants Tent City gone, and will stop at nothing until it's destroyed." (Publisher's note)

"High school senior Dan Halprin is the star pitcher on the baseball team, has been offered a scholarship to Rice University, and is dating wealthy Talia. When his parents lose their jobs as a stockbroker and youth athletics coach, and then their home, the family is forced to move into Dignityville, a tent community in the center of town. Humiliated and angry, Dan struggles to maintain his self-confidence, relationships, and aspirations...Coping with their personal financial catastrophe, wanting to stay in their familiar town, finding work, accepting charity, and maintaining self-respect are issues that weigh heavily on Dan and his parents. Read-

ers will be drawn into this contemporary story." (School Library Journal)

Stratton, Allan

  ★ **Borderline**. HarperTeen 2010 298p $16.99; lib bdg $17.89

Grades: 6 7 8 9 10   **Fic**

1. Muslims -- Fiction 2. Terrorism -- Fiction 3. Friendship -- Fiction 4. Prejudices -- Fiction 5. Father-son relationship -- Fiction

ISBN 978-0-06-145111-9; 0-06-145111-8; 978-0-06-145112-6 lib bdg; 0-06-145112-6 lib bdg

LC 2009-5241

Despite the strained relationship between them, teenaged Sami Sabiri risks his life to uncover the truth when his father is implicated in a terrorist plot.

This is "a powerful story and excellent resource for teaching tolerance, with a message that extends well beyond the timely subject matter." Publ Wkly

Chanda's secrets. Annick Press 2004 193p $19.95; pa $8.95

Grades: 7 8 9 10   **Fic**

1. Africa -- Fiction 2. AIDS (Disease) -- Fiction

ISBN 1-55037-835-X; 1-55037-834-1 pa

Michael L. Printz Award honor book, 2005

"The details of sub-Saharan African life are convincing and smoothly woven into this moving story of poverty and courage, but the real insight for readers will be the appalling treatment of the AIDS victims. Strong language and frank description are appropriate to the subject matter." SLJ

Another title about Chanda is:

Chanda's war (2007)

Chanda's wars; with an afterword by Roméo Dallaire. HarperCollinsPublishers 2008 384p $17.99; lib bdg $18.89; pa $8.99

Grades: 8 9 10 11 12   **Fic**

1. War stories 2. Africa -- Fiction 3. Orphans -- Fiction 4. Kidnapping -- Fiction

ISBN 978-0-06-087262-5; 0-06-087262-4; 978-0-06-087264-9 lib bdg; 0-06-087264-0 lib bdg; 978-0-06-087265-6 pa; 0-06-087265-9 pa

LC 2007-10829

Sequel to: Chanda's secrets (2004)

Chanda Kabelo, a teenaged African girl, must save her younger siblings after they are kidnapped and forced to serve as child soldiers in General Mandiki's rebel army.

"The characters are drawn without sentimentality, and the story is a moving portrayal of betrayal and love. The army's brutality and the traumas of the child soldiers are graphic and disturbing." Booklist

Strauss, Victoria

  Passion blue; by Victoria Strauss. Marshall Cavendish Children 2012 346 p. (hardcover) $17.99

Grades: 7 8 9 10 11 12   **Fic**

1. Historical fiction 2. Convents -- Fiction 3. Women artists -- Fiction 4. Self-realization -- Fiction 5. Nuns -- Fiction 6. Magic -- Fiction 7. Artists -- Fiction 8. Talismans -- Fiction 9. Italy -- History -- 15th century

-- Fiction
ISBN 0761462309; 9780761462309; 9780761462316
LC 2011040133

In this book by Victoria Strauss, when "Giulia is forced into a convent . . . she is surprised to learn of the beauty within, and that nuns and novices have vocations. . . . Her world expands as she learns the tools, materials, and techniques of great Renaissance painters. By chance, she meets a young male artisan repairing a convent masterpiece. They begin a clandestine romance. Her two desires -- painting and a husband -- war within as she contemplates her future." (School Library Journal)

Strickland, Brad

The **house** where nobody lived; a John Bellairs mystery featuring Lewis Barnavelt. [by] Brad Strickland. Sleuth 2006 173p $16.99
Grades: 4 5 6 7   **Fic**
  1. Witchcraft -- Fiction
  ISBN 0-8037-3148-5
                 LC 2006001673

Twelve-year-old Lewis and his best friend Rose Rita investigate a strange old house in their home town and discover that they may be dealing with powerful ancient Hawaiian spirits.

"Filled with likable, kooky characters, this mystery is fast paced and funny." SLJ

John Bellairs's Lewis Barnavelt in The whistle, the grave, and the ghost. Dial Bks. for Young Readers 2003 152p $16.99
Grades: 4 5 6 7   **Fic**
  1. Witchcraft -- Fiction
  ISBN 0-8037-2622-8
                 LC 2002-10817

In the woods near his home in Michigan, thirteen-year-old Lewis Barnavelt stumbles upon an ancient grave and silver whistle that draw him, his best friend Rose Rita Pottinger, his uncle Jonathan, and their friend Mrs. Zimmermann into a battle with an ancient evil

"Strickland excels at heart-in-your-throat suspense that he maintains until the final paragraphs." Booklist

The **sign** of the sinister sorcerer; [by] Brad Strickland. Dial Books for Young Readers 2008 168p $16.99
Grades: 4 5 6 7   **Fic**
  1. Mystery fiction 2. Magic -- Fiction 3. Uncles -- Fiction 4. Orphans -- Fiction 5. Witches -- Fiction 6. Michigan -- Fiction 7. Supernatural -- Fiction
  ISBN 978-0-8037-3151-6; 0-8037-3151-5
                 LC 2008007698

In Michigan in the mid-1950s, Lewis Barnavelt is convinced that the series of accidents he and his uncle are experiencing are the result of a curse by a mysterious, hooded figure that may be part of his uncle's past.

"For readers who enjoy trying to solve the mystery as they read, there are abundant clues including an anagram. A quick, exciting read." SLJ

Other titles about Lewis Barnavelt by Brad Strickland are:

The beast under the wizard's bridge (2000)

The house where nobody lived (2006)
The spector from the magician's museum (1998)
The tower at the end of the world (2001)
The whistle, the grave, and the ghost (2003)

Stringer, Helen

The **midnight** gate. Feiwel and Friends 2011 376p $17.99
Grades: 5 6 7 8   **Fic**
  1. Ghost stories 2. School stories 3. Orphans -- Fiction 4. Supernatural -- Fiction 5. Great Britain -- Fiction
  ISBN 0-312-38764-4; 978-0-312-38764-8
                 LC 2010036476

Sequel to: Spellbinder (2009)

Twelve-year-old Belladonna Johnson, who lives with the ghosts of her parents, once again teams up with her classmate Steve, whose mother has suddenly disappeared, when they are given a dangerous assignment by a ghostly monk involving a return to the Dark Times.

"Stringer's vivid descriptions and irreverent nods to all sorts of mythology, along with well-paced cliff-hangers throughout, are just right for fantasy and adventure buffs." Booklist

★ **Spellbinder**. Feiwel and Friends 2009 372p $17.99
Grades: 5 6 7 8   **Fic**
  1. Ghost stories 2. Dead -- Fiction 3. Great Britain -- Fiction
  ISBN 978-0-312-38763-1; 0-312-38763-6
                 LC 2008-28552

Twelve-year-old Belladonna Johnson, who lives with the ghosts of her parents in the north of England, teams up with an always-in-trouble classmate to investigate why all of the ghosts in the world have suddenly disappeared.

"Magical creatures, amulets, and verses are all a part of this delightful tale. . . . Stringer maintains the humor and logic of preteens who are awkwardly coming into their magical destinies." SLJ

Followed by: The midnight gate (2011)

Strohmeyer, Sarah

How Zoe made her dreams (mostly) come true; Sarah Strohmeyer. Balzer + Bray 2013 320 p. (pbk. bdg.) $9.99
Grades: 7 8 9 10   **Fic**
  1. Amusement parks -- Fiction 2. Summer employment -- Fiction 3. Internship programs -- Fiction 4. Cousins -- Fiction 5. New Jersey -- Fiction
  ISBN 0062187457; 9780062187451
                 LC 2012038163

In this book, "Zoe Kiefer, 17, and her cousin, Jess, are interns at Fairyland Kingdom, an over-the-top theme park in New Jersey. These internships are coveted. . . . Jess gets cast as a Little Red Riding Hood and Zoe is tasked with being the demanding Queen's personal assistant (aka slave). Zoe worries that these subpar positions won't put them in the running for the Dream and Do grant, a $25,000 prize that both girls desperately need." (School Library Journal)

Smart girls get what they want; by Sarah Stroh-meyer. 1st ed. Harpercollins Childrens Books 2012 348 p. (tr. bdg.) $17.99; (paperback) $9.99

Grades: 7 8 9 10 11 12   Fic

1. Female friendship -- Fiction 2. Grading and marking (Education) 3. High school students -- Fiction 4. Schools -- Fiction 5. Friendship -- Fiction 6. Best friends -- Fiction 7. High schools -- Fiction 8. Interpersonal relations -- Fiction

ISBN 0061953407; 9780061953408; 9780061953415

LC 2011026094

Author Sarah Strohmeyer tells the story of Gigi, Neerja, and Bea, three friends who "stumble upon . . . [Neerja's sister] Parad's signature-less yearbook, making them think that maybe studying isn't everything. . . . When Gigi is accused of cheating on the AP Chemistry midterm along with Mike, a Man Clan wannabe who calls her 'Einstein,' the girls launch into action. Gigi finds herself running for student rep against Will, the new guy from California. . . . Neerja tries out for the lead in Romeo and Juliet and Bea convinces Gigi to join the ski team with her." (Kirkus Reviews)

Stroud, Jonathan

★ The **Amulet** of Samarkand. Hyperion Bks. for Children 2003 462p (Bartimaeus trilogy) $17.95; pa $7.99

Grades: 7 8 9 10   Fic

1. Fantasy fiction

ISBN 0-7868-1859-X; 0-7868-5255-0 pa

LC 2003-49904

Nathaniel, a magician's apprentice, summons up the djinni Bartimaeus and instructs him to steal the Amulet of Samarkand from the powerful magician Simon Lovelace.

"There is plenty of action, mystery, and humor to keep readers turning the pages. This title, the first in a trilogy, is a must for fantasy fans." SLJ

Other titles in this series are:

The golem's eye (2004)

Ptolemy's gate (2006)

★ **Heroes** of the valley. Hyperion Books for Children 2009 483p $17.99

Grades: 7 8 9 10   Fic

1. Adventure fiction 2. Middle Ages -- Fiction

ISBN 978-1-4231-0966-2; 1-4231-0966-X

"Twelve Houses control sections of a valley. Halli Sveinsson—at 15, the youngest child of the rulers of the House of Svein—goes against tradition when he sets out to avenge the death of his murdered uncle, and his actions result in warfare among Houses for the first time in generations. . . . Smart, funny dialogue and prose, revealing passages about the exploits of the hero Svein, bouts of action and a touch of romance briskly move the story along." Publ Wkly

★ The **ring** of Solomon; a Bartimaeus novel. Disney/Hyperion Books 2010 398p $17.99

Grades: 7 8 9 10   Fic

1. Fantasy fiction 2. Kings 3. Magic -- Fiction 4. Jerusalem -- Fiction 5. Witchcraft -- Fiction

ISBN 978-1-4231-2372-9; 1-4231-2372-7

LC 2010015468

Wise-cracking djinni Bartimaeus finds himself at the court of King Solomon with an unpleasant master, a sinister servant, and King Solomon's magic ring.

"In this exciting prequel set in ancient Israel, Stroud presents an early adventure of his sharp-tongued djinn, Bartimaeus. . . . This is a superior fantasy that should have fans racing back to those books." Publ Wkly

Stroud, Jonathan, 1970-

★ The **screaming** staircase; by Jonathan Stroud. Disney-Hyperion 2013 400 p. (Lockwood & Co.) hbk $16.99

Grades: 4 5 6 7   Fic

1. Adventure fiction 2. Ghosts -- Fiction 3. Supernatural -- Fiction 4. Haunted houses -- Fiction 5. Psychic ability -- Fiction

ISBN 1423164911; 9781423164913

LC 2013000352

This is the first book in Jonathan Stroud's Lockwood & Co. series. Lucy Carlyle has joined the Lockwood & Co. firm to help with England's ghost problem. "As its third member, she teams up with glib, ambitious Anthony Lockwood and slovenly-but-capable scholar George Cubbins to entrap malign spirits for hire. The work is fraught with peril, not only because a ghost's merest touch is generally fatal, but also, as it turns out, as none of the three is particularly good at careful planning." (Kirkus Reviews)

The **whispering** skull; by Jonathan Stroud. Disney-Hyperion 2014 448 p. illustrations (Lockwood & Co.) (hardback) $17.99

Grades: 4 5 6 7   Fic

1. Occult fiction 2. Mystery fiction 3. Ghosts -- Fiction 4. England -- Fiction 5. Supernatural -- Fiction 6. Psychic ability -- Fiction 7. London (England) -- Fiction 8. Mystery and detective stories

ISBN 142316492X; 9781423164920

LC 2014014683

This novel, by Jonathan Stroud, is book 2 in the "Lockwood & Co." supernatural mystery series. "In the six months since Anthony, Lucy, and George survived a night in the most haunted house in England, Lockwood & Co. hasn't made much progress. . . . A new client, Mr. Saunders, hires Lockwood & Co. to be present at the excavation of Edmund Bickerstaff. . . . Saunders needs the coffin sealed with silver to prevent any supernatural trouble. All goes well-until George's curiosity attracts a horrible phantom." (Publisher's note)

"In this sequel to The Screaming Staircase (2013), Stroud delivers another riveting narrative in which the three young psychic investigators deal with malevolent supernatural forces in an alternate London. Narrator Lucy Carlyle, the newest member of Lockwood & Company, develops the rare ability to converse with a mysterious skull kept in a sealed jar. Though this captive spirit has the firsthand knowledge the group needs to solve its latest case, Lucy suspects that beyond his entreaties and wisecracks, the tortured skull is manipulating them with misleading information. Physically and psychologically taxing, the case strains the bond that Anthony Lockwood, Lucy, and their colleague, George, share. Stroud writes with a fine ear for dialogue, a wry sense of humor, and a knack for describing haunted places. Creating tension that ebbs and flows, he slowly builds the dramatic narrative to a resounding crescendo, and he makes the quieter scenes that follow just as compelling. The second entry in the Lockwood & Company series, this imaginative adventure features one of the most hair-raising chase scenes in children's fiction. At the book's end, when the enigmatic Lockwood reveals a chilling secret, readers can only hope that more sequels are in the offing. High-Demand Backstory: Stroud, of Bartimaeus fame, is no stranger to the New York Times best-seller list, and this second installment of his new series looks primed to keep him there." Booklist

Strykowski, Marcia

Call Me Amy; Marcia Strykowski. Midpoint Trade Books Inc 2013 180 p. (hardcover) $24.95
Grades: 6 7 8   **Fic**
1. Adolescence -- Fiction 2. Animal rescue -- Fiction 3. Historical fiction
ISBN 1935462768; 9781935462767
In this novel, set in Maine in 1973, eighth-grader Amy Henderson is dealing with acne, her faraway best friend, and overall nervousness. "But the sudden appearance of an injured harbor seal brings her closer to two unlikely allies as they care for the seal, dubbed 'Pup,' in secret: loudmouthed Craig, whose carefree personality is a cover for underlying insecurities and family problems, and elderly Miss Cogshell, who proves to be worldly and kind." (Publishers Weekly)
"Well-drawn, sympathetic characters and the developing spark between Amy and Craig combine to create a pleasant, satisfying read." Kirkus

Stuber, Barbara

★ **Crossing** the tracks. Margarert K. McElderry Books 2010 258p $16.99
Grades: 6 7 8 9   **Fic**
1. Missouri -- Fiction 2. Household employees -- Fiction 3. Father-daughter relationship -- Fiction
ISBN 978-1-4169-9703-0; 1-4169-9703-2
          LC 2009-42672
In Missouri in 1926, fifteen-year-old Iris Baldwin discovers what family truly means when her father hires her out for the summer as a companion to a country doctor's invalid mother.
"Thought-provoking and tenderhearted, Iris's story is one of a mature young woman who faces life with courage and common sense. . . . This thoughtful novel offers strong character development and an engaging protagonist." SLJ

Sturtevant, Katherine

The **brothers** story. Farrar, Straus and Giroux 2009 271p $16.99
Grades: 7 8 9 10 11   **Fic**
1. Twins -- Fiction 2. Brothers -- Fiction 3. Apprentices -- Fiction 4. Great Britain -- Fiction 5. Mentally disabled children -- Fiction
ISBN 978-0-374-30992-3; 0-374-30992-2
          LC 2008-35513
In the late seventeenth century, fifteen-year-old Kit, driven to desperation by the starvation of one brother and mistreatment of his own simpleminded twin, realizes his dream of becoming an apprentice in London but feels drawn by duty to return home to Essex.

"Readers will quickly empathize with Kit; his conflicted feelings toward his brother, a mixture of great tenderness and shame, are sensitively drawn. He experiences the beginnings of his sexual awakening in scenes that are occasionally ribald but never gratuitous. Sturtevant invokes the cacophony of noises, smells, and sights of London, along with the sorrows and kindnesses found in daily life." SLJ

A **true** and faithful narrative. Farrar, Straus & Giroux 2006 247p $17
Grades: 6 7 8 9   **Fic**
1. London (England) -- Fiction 2. Great Britain -- History -- 1603-1714, Stuarts -- Fiction
ISBN 0-374-37809-6
          LC 2005046922
Sequel to At the sign of the star (2000)
A sequel to At the Sign of the Star (2000), this title is set in Restoration England. "Meg Moore, the literarily inclined heroine, . . . is now sixteen and in a position to be courted—although she'd much rather be writing books. . . . Middle school, high school." (Horn Book)
The author "offers readers a story depicted with great clarity and many vivid details of everyday life. Written in the first-person, the narrative reveals Meg as a strong-willed yet vulnerable young woman who emerges as a well-rounded, convincing individual." Booklist

Sullivan, Laura L.

Guardian of the Green Hill; [illustrations by David Wyatt] Henry Holt and Company 2011 293p il $16.99
Grades: 5 6 7 8   **Fic**
1. Fantasy fiction 2. Fairies -- Fiction 3. Siblings -- Fiction 4. Supernatural -- Fiction 5. Great Britain -- Fiction
ISBN 978-0-8050-8985-1; 0-8050-8985-3
          LC 2010029231
Sequel to: Under the Green Hill (2010)
After the Midsummer War ends, Meg Morgan faces a madman in the battle for control of the last bastion of fairies in England, aided by her siblings Rowan, Silly, and James, and American neighbors Dickie Rhys, and Finn Fachan.
"Sullivan's writing has a timelessness that contrasts nicely with Meg's distinctly modern ideas and weaves a compelling story that will pull readers along." SLJ

Under the green hill. Henry Holt and Company 2010 308p $16.99
Grades: 5 6 7 8   **Fic**
1. Fantasy fiction 2. Fairies -- Fiction 3. Siblings -- Fiction 4. Supernatural -- Fiction
ISBN 978-0-8050-8984-4; 0-8050-8984-5
          LC 2009-50772
While staying with distant relatives in England, Americans Rowan, Meg, Silly, and James Morgan, with their neighbors Dickie Rhys and Finn Fachan, learn that one of them must fight to the death in the Midsummer War required by the local fairies
"Sullivan draws heavily on her knowledge of Middle English folklore and creates a story rich with memorable characters and evocative language." SLJ
Followed by: Guardian of the green hill (2011)

Sullivan, Mary

Dear Blue Sky; Mary Sullivan. Nancy Paulsen Books 2012 248 p. (hardcover) $16.99

Grades: 4 5 6 7   **Fic**

1. Children and war 2. Siblings -- Fiction 3. Brothers -- Fiction 4. War -- Fiction 5. Pen pals -- Fiction 6. Family life -- Fiction 7. Down syndrome -- Fiction 8. Iraq War, 2003-2011 -- Fiction 9. Brothers and sisters -- Fiction

ISBN 0399256849; 9780399256844

LC 2011046952

In the book by Mary Sullivan, "Cassie's whole world changes when her beloved older brother, Sef, goes to war in Iraq . . . While her parents are preoccupied, her best friend, Sonia, inexplicably stops talking to her; her older sister, Van, tests out risky behaviors; and her developmentally delayed younger brother, Jack, becomes altogether silent. When a seventh-grade social-studies project leads her to a blog called Blue Sky, written by an Iraqi girl of similar age, Cassie starts to see the war from a different perspective." (Kirkus)

Sullivan, Tara

Golden boy; Tara Sullivan. G.P. Putnam's Sons, an imprint of Penguin Group (USA) Inc. 2013 368 p. (hardcover) $16.99

Grades: 7 8 9 10 11 12   **Fic**

1. Voyages and travels -- Fiction 2. Albinos and albinism -- Fiction 3. Survival -- Fiction 4. Tanzania -- Fiction 5. Human rights -- Fiction 6. Human skin color -- Fiction

ISBN 0399161120; 9780399161124

LC 2012043310

In this book, an albino boy named Habo does not fit in with his Tanzanian family, who shun him. "Only Habo's sister, Asu, protects and nurtures him. Poverty forces the family from their rural home near Arusha to Mwanza, hundreds of miles away, to stay with relatives. After their bus fare runs out, they hitch a ride across the Serengeti with an ivory poacher who sees opportunity in Habo. Forced to flee for his life, the boy eventually becomes an apprentice to Kweli, a wise, blind carver." (Kirkus)

Suma, Nova Ren

Dani noir. Aladdin 2009 266p $15.99

Grades: 6 7 8 9   **Fic**

1. Mystery fiction 2. Divorce -- Fiction 3. Remarriage -- Fiction 4. Motion pictures -- Fiction 5. Mother-daughter relationship -- Fiction

ISBN 978-1-4169-7564-9; 1-4169-7564-0

LC 2009-22270

Imaginative thirteen-year-old Dani feels trapped in her small mountain town with only film noir at the local art theater and her depressed mother for company, but while trying to solve a real mystery she learns much about herself and life.

"Suma's watertight debut displays an expert balance of the realities of teenage life, humor and intrigue." Publ Wkly

Summers, Courtney

This is not a test; Courtney Summers. St. Martin's Griffin 2012 336 p. $9.99; (pbk.) $9.99

Grades: 7 8 9 10 11 12   **Fic**

1. Adventure fiction 2. Zombies -- Fiction 3. Child abuse -- Fiction 4. Horror stories 5. Schools -- Fiction 6. Survival -- Fiction 7. High schools -- Fiction 8. Family problems -- Fiction

ISBN 0312656742; 9780312656744; 9781250011817

LC 2012004633

In this book, "six teens who barely know or like each other seek refuge in their high school while the undead hordes lurk outside. . . . The end of the world unfolds through the eyes of high school junior Sloane Price, who has been contemplating suicide since her older sister ran away six months earlier, leaving Sloane with their physically abusive father. But these worries are pushed aside as Sloane tries to keep her fellow students alive." (Publishers Weekly)

Sun, Amanda

Ink; Amanda Sun. Harlequin Books 2013 304 p. (paperback) $9.99

Grades: 7 8 9 10 11 12   **Fic**

1. Love stories 2. Fantasy fiction 3. Japan -- Fiction

ISBN 037321071X; 9780373210718

In this teen romance novel, by Amanda Sun, part of "The Paper Gods" series, "Katie Greene must move halfway across the world. Stuck with her aunt in Shizuoka, Japan, Katie feels lost. Alone. . . . When Katie meets aloof but gorgeous Tomohiro, the star of the school's kendo team, she is intrigued by him. . . . Somehow Tomo is connected to the kami, powerful ancient beings who once ruled Japan--and as feelings develop between Katie and Tomo, things begin to spiral out of control." (Publisher's note)

"Katie's tendency to jump to conclusions, cry, and act before she thinks is frustrating, but it leaves plenty of room for growth. The descriptions of life in Japan—particularly teen life— create a strong sense of place, and set a vivid backdrop for this intriguing series opener by a debut author." BookList

Supplee, Suzanne

Somebody everybody listens to. Dutton 2010 245p $16.99

Grades: 7 8 9 10 11 12   **Fic**

1. Singers -- Fiction 2. Country music -- Fiction 3. Nashville (Tenn.) -- Fiction

ISBN 978-0-525-42242-6; 0-525-42242-0

LC 2009-25089

Retta Lee Jones is blessed with a beautiful voice and has big dreams of leaving her tiny Tennessee hometown. With a beaten down car, a pocketful of hard-earned waitressing money, and stars in her eyes, Retta sets out to make it big in Nashville.

"While a must read for country music lovers, . . . [this book] will appeal to a wide audience, especially those who long to pursue a dream against the odds." Publ Wkly

Sutcliff, Rosemary

Sword song. Farrar, Straus & Giroux 1998 271p hardcover o.p. pa $6.95

Grades: 7 8 9 10   **Fic**

1. Vikings -- Fiction 2. Great Britain -- History -- 0-1066 -- Fiction

ISBN 0-374-37363-9; 0-374-46984-9 pa

LC 98-16827

At sixteen, Bjarni is cast out of the Norse settlement in the Angles' Land for an act of oath-breaking and spends five years sailing the west coast of Scotland and witnessing the feuds of the clan chiefs living there

"This is a well-crafted story that will appeal to sophisticated readers." SLJ

Sutton, Kelsey

Some quiet place; by Kelsey Sutton. 1st ed. Flux 2013 336 p. (paperback) $9.99

Grades: 7 8 9 10   **Fic**
1. Occult fiction 2. School stories 3. Fear -- Fiction 4. Schools -- Fiction 5. Emotions -- Fiction 6. Wisconsin -- Fiction 7. High schools -- Fiction 8. Supernatural -- Fiction 9. Family problems -- Fiction 10. Farm life -- Wisconsin -- Fiction

ISBN 0738736430; 9780738736433

LC 2013005021

In this book, "Elizabeth Caldwell's best friend is dying of cancer, one of the cutest boys in school loves her, and her alcoholic father beats her—but Elizabeth doesn't care about any of it. Her only meaningful interactions are with the Emotions, immortal personifications of the feelings she can't experience. With them, she does not have to pretend, as she must when she tries to muster believable social responses." The book explores the reasons behind Elizabeth's coldness. (Publishers Weekly)

"Haunting, chilling and achingly romantic, Sutton's debut novel for teens will keep readers up until the wee hours, unable to tear themselves away from this strange and beautifully crafted story. Elizabeth Caldwell can't feel emotions, yet she sees them everywhere, human in appearance, standing alongside their "summons.".Chills and goose bumps of the very best kind accompany this haunting, memorable achievement." (Kirkus)

Sweeney, Joyce

The **guardian**. Henry Holt and Co. 2009 177p $16.95

Grades: 7 8 9 10   **Fic**
1. School stories 2. Bullies -- Fiction 3. Siblings -- Fiction 4. Foster home care -- Fiction 5. Father-son relationship -- Fiction

ISBN 978-0-8050-8019-3; 0-8050-8019-8

LC 2008-40602

When thirteen-year-old Hunter, struggling to deal with a harsh, money-grubbing foster mother, three challenging foster sisters, and a school bully, returns to his childhood faith and prays to St. Gabriel, he instantly becomes aware that he does, indeed, have a guardian.

"Sweeney's prose is insightful and realistic, with cleverly delivered descriptions. The peripheral characters are believable, and the religious undercurrent supports the plot. Well-paced, and with a satisfying conclusion." SLJ

Swift, Jonathan

Gulliver's travels; illustrated by Scott McKowen. Sterling Pub. Co. 2007 293p il (Sterling unabridged classics) $9.95

Grades: 7 8 9 10 11 12 Adult   **Fic**
1. Fantasy fiction 2. Voyages and travels -- Fiction

ISBN 978-1-4027-4339-9; 1-4027-4339-4

LC 2007003974

First published 1726

"In the account of his four wonder-countries Swift satirizes contemporary manners and morals, art and politics-in fact the whole social scheme-from four different points of view. The huge Brobdingnagians reduce man to his natural insignificance, the little people of Lilliput parody Europe and its petty broils, in Laputa philosophers are ridiculed, and finally all Swift's hatred and contempt find their satisfaction in degrading humanity to a bestial condition." Baker. Guide to the Best Fic

Swinburne, Stephen R.

Wiff and Dirty George: the Z.E.B.R.A. Incident. Boyds Mills Press 2010 167p il $17.95

Grades: 4 5 6 7   **Fic**
1. Nineteen sixties -- Fiction 2. Great Britain -- Fiction

ISBN 978-1-59078-755-7; 1-59078-755-2

Witt and Dirty George give chase to the notorious Basil King, a criminal genius who is best on taking over Great Britain. "Grades four to seven." (Bull Cent Child Books)

"London in 1969 was a trippy place, no doubt, but it's made even more psychodelic with the adventures of Wiff and Dirty George, two twelve-year-olds who follow their noses into a world of trouble. While on a morning train, the boys are slightly horrified when everyone's pants fall down, but instead of worrying overmuch about their own embarrassment, they take off after the large white rabbit who seems to be the instigator of the mass humiliation. . . . The humor is more situational than verbal; the characters are all comedic straight men in a twisted, absurd world. . . . Delightfully daft 'clues' precede each chapter, and a glossary of Britishisms will help young Yanks navigate the dialect." Bull Cent Child Books

Tak, Bibi Dumon

Soldier bear; written by Bibi Dumon Tak; illustrated by Philip Hopman; translated by Laura Watkinson. Eerdmans Books for Young Readers 2011 145p il $13

Grades: 4 5 6 7   **Fic**
1. Iran -- Fiction 2. Bears -- Fiction 3. Italy -- Fiction 4. Poland -- Fiction 5. Soldiers -- Fiction 6. World War, 1939-1945 -- Fiction

ISBN 978-0-8028-5375-2; 0-8028-5375-7

LC 2011013963

Original Dutch edition 2008

An orphaned Syrian brown bear cub is adopted by Polish soldiers during World War II and serves for five years as their mischievous mascot in Iran and Italy. Based on a true story.

"This is smoothly translated and engagingly illustrated with sketches and helpful maps. Funny, fresh and heartwarming." Kirkus

Takako, Shimura

Wandering son; Volume One. Shimura Takako; translated by Matt Thorn. Fantagraphics 2011 192 p. ill. (hardcover) $19.99

Grades: 7 8 9 10   **Fic**

1. Manga 2. Puberty -- Graphic novels 3. Bildungsromans -- Graphic novels 4. Transgender people -- Graphic novels 5. Graphic novels 6. Sex role -- Graphic novels

ISBN 1606994166; 9781606994160

This manga "tells the story of a friendship between Shuichi, a young boy who wishes he were a girl, and Yoshino, a young girl who wishes she were a boy. . . . Shuichi's impulses toward a female identity feel confusing and shameful to him, and it's the girls in his life—first Yoshino, and then Saori—who point out his difference and encourage it. . . . Both children are teased mercilessly by their classmates, whose sexual development, while perhaps more socially normative, is just as confusing to them." (Publishers Weekly)

This graphic novel "tells the story of a friendship between Shuichi, a young boy who wishes he were a girl, and Yoshino, a young girl who wishes she were a boy." Publ Wkly

Tal, Eve

Cursing Columbus. Cinco Puntos Press 2009 248p $17.95

Grades: 7 8 9 10   **Fic**

1. Jews -- Fiction 2. Immigrants -- Fiction 3. Family life -- Fiction 4. New York (N.Y.) -- Fiction 5. Russian Americans -- Fiction

ISBN 978-1-933693-59-0; 1-933693-59-2

LC 2009-15834

Sequel to: Double crossing (2005)

In 1907, fourteen-year-old Raizel, who has lived in New York City for three years, and her brother Lemmel, newly-arrived, respond very differently to the challenges of living as Ukrainian Jews in the Lower East Side as Raizel works toward fitting in and getting ahead, while Lemmel joins a gang and lives on the streets

"The story offers a realistic and poignant picture of a bygone time." SLJ

Double crossing. Cinco Puntos Press 2005 261p $16.95

Grades: 7 8 9 10   **Fic**

1. Jews -- Fiction 2. Immigrants -- Fiction

ISBN 0-938317-94-6

LC 2005-8188

In 1905, as life becomes increasingly difficult for Jews in Ukraine, eleven-year-old Raizel and her father flee to America in hopes of earning money to bring the rest of the family there, but her father's health and Orthodox faith become barriers.

"Tal's fictionalized account of her grandfather's journey to America is fast paced, full of suspense, and highly readable." SLJ

Followed by: Cursing Columbus (2009)

Tanner, Lian

City of lies. Delacorte Press 2011 278 p. (The Keeper's trilogy) lib bdg $20.99; $17.99

Grades: 5 6 7 8   **Fic**

1. Fantasy fiction 2. Adventure fiction 3. Thieves --

Fiction 4. Kidnapping -- Fiction

ISBN 0385739060; 0385907699 lib bdg; 9780385907699 lib bdg; 9780385739061

LC 2010048579

Sequel to: Museum of thieves (2010)

Twelve-year-old Goldie, impulsive and bold, relies on her skills as a liar and a thief to try to rescue her captured friends from the child-stealers running rampant in the City of Spoke.

Museum of thieves. Delacorte Press 2010 312p (The Keepers Trilogy) $16.99; lib bdg $19.99

Grades: 5 6 7 8   **Fic**

1. Fantasy fiction 2. Adventure fiction 3. Museums -- Fiction 4. Thieves -- Fiction

ISBN 978-0-385-73905-4; 0-385-73905-2; 978-0-385-90768-2 lib bdg; 0-385-90768-0 lib bdg

LC 2009053655

Goldie, an impulsive and bold twelve-year-old, escapes the oppressive city of Jewel, where children are required to wear guardchains for their protection, and finds refuge in the extraordinary Museum of Dunt, an ever-shifting world where she discovers a useful talent for thievery and mysterious secrets that threaten her city and everyone she loves.

"Readers will be quickly caught up in the highly dramatic chases, the intriguing museum that shifts layout at will, and the nifty otherworld elements. There's depth beneath that, though. . . . [The book] may set young readers thinking about their own world's choices." Bull Cent Child Books

Followed by: City of lies (2011)

Tarshis, Lauren

Emma-Jean Lazarus fell in love. Dial Books for Young Readers 2009 169p $16.99; pa $6.99

Grades: 5 6 7   **Fic**

1. School stories 2. Friendship -- Fiction

ISBN 978-0-8037-3321-3; 0-8037-3321-6; 978-0-14-241568-9 pa; 0-14-241568-5 pa

Sequel to: Emma-Jean Lazarus fell out of a tree (2007)

Seventh-grader Emma-Jean Lazarus uses her logical, scientific mind to navigate the mysteries of the upcoming Spring Fling, her friend Colleen's secret admirer, and other love-related dilemmas

"Tarshis deftly weaves in important details from the previous book . . . providing those new to Emma-Jean some necessary back story. . . . Fans will appreciate the continuity and relish the reappearance of familiar characters, especially Ms Wright, the lovable school janitor, and the rest of Emma Jean's true blue friends. The story ends on a happy note with the possibility of more adventures to come." Kirkus

★ **Emma**-Jean Lazarus fell out of a tree. Dial Books for Young Readers 2007 199p $16.99

Grades: 5 6 7   **Fic**

1. School stories 2. Friendship -- Fiction

ISBN 978-0-8037-3164-6; 0-8037-3164-7

LC 2006-18428

A quirky and utterly logical seventh-grade girl named Emma-Jean Lazarus discovers some interesting results when she gets involved in the messy everyday problems of her peers.

"Readers will be fascinated by Emma-Jean's emotionless observations and her adult-level vocabulary. Tarshis pulls off a balancing act, showing the child's detachment yet making her a sympathetic character. Exceptionally fleshed-out secondary characters add warmth to the story." SLJ

Followed by: Emma-Jean Lazarus fell in love (2009)

I survived the Battle of Gettysburg, 1863; Lauren Tarshis. Scholastic 2013 89 p. (paperback) $4.99
Grades: 3 4 5 6 **Fic**
1. Fugitive slaves -- Fiction 2. Gettysburg (Pa.), Battle of, 1863 -- Fiction
ISBN 0545459362; 9780545459365

This children's book, by Lauren Tarshis, is book 7 in the "I Survived" series. "It's 1863, and Thomas and his little sister, Birdie, have fled the farm where they were born and raised as slaves. . . . They soon cross paths with a Union soldier . . ., marching with the army. But then orders come through: The men are called to battle in Pennsylvania. Thomas has made it so far . . . but does he have what it takes to survive Gettysburg?" (Publisher's note)

Tashjian, Janet
The **gospel** according to Larry. Holt & Co. 2001 227p il $16.95; pa $5.99
Grades: 7 8 9 10 **Fic**
1. Web sites -- Fiction
ISBN 0-8050-6378-1; 0-440-23792-0 pa
LC 2001-24568

Seventeen-year-old Josh, a loner-philosopher who wants to make a difference in the world, tries to maintain his secret identity as the author of a web site that is receiving national attention

"Tashjian fabricates a cleverly constructed scenario and expertly carries it out to the bittersweet end." Horn Book Guide

Other titles about Larry are:
Vote for Larry (2004)
Larry and the meaning of life (2008)

Larry and the meaning of life. Henry Holt and Co. 2008 211p $16.95
Grades: 7 8 9 10 **Fic**
1. Authors 2. Naturalists 3. Essayists 4. Pacifists 5. Writers on nature 6. Nonfiction writers 7. Massachusetts -- Fiction 8. Political activists -- Fiction 9. Identity (Psychology) -- Fiction
ISBN 978-0-8050-7735-3; 0-8050-7735-9
LC 2007-46936

Larry (otherwise known as Josh) is in the doldrums, but after meeting a spiritual guru at Walden Pond who convinces him to join his study group, he starts to question his grasp of reality.

★ **My** life as a book; with cartoons by Jake Tashjian. Henry Holt 2010 211p il $16.99; pa $6.99
Grades: 4 5 6 7 **Fic**
1. Summer -- Fiction 2. Animals -- Fiction 3. Family life -- Fiction 4. Books and reading -- Fiction
ISBN 978-0-8050-8903-5; 0-8050-8903-9; 978-0-312-67289-8 pa; 0-312-67289-6 pa
LC 2009-18909

Dubbed a "reluctant reader" by his teacher, twelve-year-old Derek spends summer vacation learning important lessons even though he does not complete his summer reading list.

"The protagonist is by turns likable and irritating, but always interesting. He is sure to engage fans of Jeff Kinney's 'Diary of a Wimpy Kid' books . . . as well as those looking for a spunky, contemporary boy with a mystery to solve. Reluctant readers will appreciate the book's large print and quick-paced story." SLJ

"Another title about Derek is:
My life as a stuntboy (2011)

My life as a cartoonist; Janet Tashjian; with cartoons by Jake Tashjian. Henry Holt and Company 2013 272 p. illustrations (hardcover) $13.99
Grades: 4 5 6 7 **Fic**
1. Cartoonists 2. School stories 3. People with disabilities -- Fiction 4. Schools -- Fiction 5. Cartoonists -- Fiction 6. Wheelchairs -- Fiction
ISBN 0805096094; 9780805096095
LC 2012046201

In this book, by Janet Tashjian, "[t]here's a new kid in Derek Fallon's class. His name is Umberto and he uses a wheelchair. Derek's family is still fostering Frank the monkey, and Derek thinks it would be great to train Frank to assist Umberto. But Derek quickly realizes that Umberto is definitely not looking for any help. Derek soon becomes the butt of Umberto's jokes. On top of that, Umberto starts stealing Derek's cartoon ideas and claiming them as his own." (Publisher's note)

"Cartoonist Derek grapples with a perplexing association between disability and bullying in this stand-alone sequel to My Life as a Book (2010) and My Life as a Stuntboy (2011). . . . This entertaining read leaves some provoking questions unanswered--usefully." Kirkus

Companion titles include:
My Life as a Book (2010)
My Life as a Stuntboy (2011)
My Life as a Joke (2014)
My Life as a Gamer (2015)

My life as a joke; Janet Tashjian; with cartoons by Jake Tashjian. Henry Holt and Company 2014 252 p. illustrations (hardback) $13.99
Grades: 4 5 6 7 **Fic**
1. School stories 2. Middle schools -- Fiction 3. Friendship -- Fiction 4. Maturation (Psychology) -- Fiction 5. Family life -- California -- Los Angeles -- Fiction
ISBN 080509850X; 9780805098501
LC 2013046395

In this middle grade book by Janet Tashjian, illustrated by Jake Tashjian, "Derek Fallon discovers all the angst that comes with being twelve--he just wants to feel grown up, but life gets in the way with a series of mishaps that make him look like a baby. . . . Why isn't being in middle school as great as Derek imagined?" (Publisher's note)

"In his fourth appearance, twelve-year-old Derek resolves to appear more mature, but he's constantly a laughingstock. . . . Fans will enjoy the fast plot, Derek's supportive friends, and cartoon marginalia representing Derek's ever-expanding collection of vocabulary words." Horn Book

My life as a stuntboy; with cartoons by Jake Tashjian. Henry Holt and Company 2011 256p il $13.99

Grades: 4 5 6 7   **Fic**

1. School stories 2. Monkeys -- Fiction 3. Stunt flying -- Fiction 4. Motion pictures -- Fiction

ISBN 978-0-8050-8904-2; 0-8050-8904-7

LC 2010029884

Twelve-year-old Derek Fallon has the opportunity of a lifetime--to perform stunts in a movie featuring a popular twelve-year-old star—but complications arise involving his best friend, a capuchin monkey, and Derek's chronic inability to concentrate on schoolwork.

"The generous margins are filled with Derek's often quite clever stick-figure cartoons illustrating vocabulary words such as 'flabbergasted' and 'camouflage'—all rendered by the author's teenage son. Another fun, emotionally resonant read for the Wimpy Kid set and beyond." Kirkus

Vote for Larry. Henry Holt and Co 2004 224p $16.95

Grades: 7 8 9 10   **Fic**

1. Politics -- Fiction 2. Elections -- Fiction

ISBN 0-8050-7201-2

LC 2003-56578

Sequel to: The gospel according to Larry (2005)

Not yet eighteen years old, Josh, a.k.a. Larry, comes out of hiding and returns to public life, this time to run for President as an advocate for issues of concern to youth and to encourage voter turnout.

"A solid and timely work that will make readers laugh, but more important, will make them think." Voice Youth Advocates

Followed by: Larry and the meanin of life (2008)

Tate, Eleanora E.

Celeste's Harlem Renaissance. Little, Brown 2007 279p $15.99; pa $5.99

Grades: 4 5 6 7   **Fic**

1. Aunts -- Fiction 2. African Americans -- Fiction 3. Harlem Renaissance -- Fiction 4. Harlem (New York, N.Y.) -- Fiction

ISBN 978-0-316-52394-3; 978-0-316-11362-5 pa

In 1921, thirteen-year-old Celeste leaves North Carolina to stay with her glamorous Aunt Valentina in Harlem, New York, where she discovers the vibrant Harlem Renaissance in full swing, even though her aunt's life is not exactly what she was led to believe.

"Both sobering and inspiring, Tate's novel is a moving portrait of growing up black and female in 1920s America." Booklist

Taub, Melinda

Still star-crossed; by Melinda Taub. 1st ed. Random House Childrens Books 2013 352 p. (library) $19.99; (hardcover) $16.99

Grades: 7 8 9 10 11 12   **Fic**

1. Love stories 2. Historical fiction 3. Love -- Fiction 4. Families -- Fiction 5. Vendetta -- Fiction 6. Characters in literature -- Fiction 7. Italy -- History -- 1559-1789 -- Fiction 8. Verona (Italy) -- History -- 16th century -- Fiction

ISBN 0385743505; 9780375991189; 9780385743501

LC 2012032626

This young adult novel is a sequel to the events of the play "Romeo and Juliet." The "peace purchased with Romeo's and Juliet's deaths lasts two weeks before the Capulets and Montagues renew their fight in the streets of Verona. . . . Prince Escalus attempts to force the feuding families into concord by arranging a marriage between Rosaline and Benvolio." (Kirkus Reviews)

Tayleur, Karen

Chasing boys. Walker & Co. 2009 244p $16.99

Grades: 7 8 9 10 11   **Fic**

1. School stories 2. Fathers -- Fiction

ISBN 978-0-8027-9830-5; 0-8027-9830-6

LC 2008-23241

First published 2007 by Black Dog Books

With her father gone and her family dealing with financial problems, El transfers to a new school, where she falls for one of the popular boys and then must decide whether to remain true to herself or become like the girls she scorns.

"All the ingredients of El's life are blended seamlessly, never downplaying the audience's intelligence, as Tayleur captures the all-consuming nature of a teenage crush without making El ridiculous. Moody, poetic, and intimate, this book is billed as the 'romance for girls who don't like pink,' but is much more than that." Booklist

Taylor, Chloe

Ready to wear; Chloe Taylor. 1st ed. Simon Spotlight 2013 176 p. (Sew Zoey) (paperback) $5.99; (hardcover) $15.99

Grades: 3 4 5 6 7   **Fic**

1. Fashion 2. Middle schools -- Fiction 3. School stories

ISBN 1442479345; 9781442479333; 9781442479340

LC 2013935204

In this children's novel, by Chloe Taylor, illustrated by Nancy Zhang, "fashion-loving Zoey Webber gets the best news ever: Her middle school is getting rid of uniforms! . . . Zoey has sketchbooks full of fashion designs, but nothing to wear! So with a little help from her best friends Kate and Priti, she learns to make her own clothes. She even begins to post her fashion design sketches online in a blog. That's how the Sew Zoey blog begins, and soon it becomes much more." (Publisher's note)

Taylor, Greg

The girl who became a Beatle. Feiwel and Friends 2011 281p $16.99; pa $9.99

Grades: 6 7 8 9   **Fic**

1. Fame -- Fiction 2. Beatles -- Fiction 3. Rock music -- Fiction 4. Space and time -- Fiction 5. Conduct of

life -- Fiction

ISBN 978-0-312-65259-3; 0-312-65259-3; 978-0-312-60683-1 pa; 0-312-60683-4 pa

LC 2010-41450

Regina Bloomsbury, a sixteen-year-old, Beatles-obsessed rocker, takes a trip to an alternate reality where the Beatles never existed and her band, the Caverns, are the rock-and-roll superstars.

"Teens will likely skim over the fantasy's shaky logistical questions and enjoy the vicarious view of stardom's perks and pitfalls, which Taylor deepens with Regina's lingering, real-world sorrow over her parents' divorce." Booklist

Killer Pizza. Feiwel and Friends 2009 346p $16.99

Grades: 6 7 8 9   **Fic**

1. Horror fiction 2. Monsters -- Fiction

ISBN 978-0-312-37379-5; 0-312-37379-1

LC 2008028543

While working as summer employees in a local pizza parlor, three teenagers are recruited by an underground organization of monster hunters.

"Toby is an easygoing and relatable young adult, and young teens will enjoy the fun, slightly scary read." Voice Youth Advocates

Followed by: Killer pizza: the slice (2011)

Killer Pizza: the slice. Feiwel and Friends 2011 341p $16.99

Grades: 6 7 8 9   **Fic**

1. Horror fiction 2. Adventure fiction 3. Monsters -- Fiction

ISBN 978-0-312-58088-9; 0-312-58088-6

LC 2010048928

Sequel to: Killer pizza (2009)

Having passed the tests to become Monster Combat Officers, teens Toby, Annabel, and Strobe are sent on a secret mission to deliver to the Monster Protection Program a beautiful fourteen-year-old monster who wants to defect, regardless of the considerable dangers this poses.

Taylor, Laini

Blackbringer. G. P. Putnam's Sons 2007 437p (Faeries of Dreamdark) $17.99

Grades: 6 7 8 9   **Fic**

1. Fantasy fiction 2. Magic -- Fiction 3. Fairies -- Fiction

ISBN 978-0-399-24630-2; 0-399-24630-4

LC 2006026540

Magpie Windwitch, faerie, devil hunter, and granddaughter of the West Wind, must defeat an ancient evil creature, the Blackbringer, who has escaped from his bottle and threatens to unmake all of creation.

"Taylor drives the story forward by slowly teasing the reader with twists and turns in the plot. . . . Teen readers will identify with this faerie's humanness." Voice Youth Advocates

★ **Daughter** of smoke and bone. Little, Brown 2011 418p $18.99

Grades: 8 9 10 11 12   **Fic**

1. Love stories 2. Occult fiction 3. Fantasy fiction 4.

School stories 5. Angels -- Fiction 6. Artists -- Fiction 7. Supernatural -- Fiction 8. Classical mythology -- Fiction

ISBN 978-0-316-13402-6; 0-316-13402-3; 9780316196192

LC 2010045802

Seventeen-year-old Karou, a lovely, enigmatic art student in a Prague boarding school, carries a sketchbook of hideous, frightening monsters—the chimaerae who form the only family she has ever known.

Taylor "again weaves a masterful mix of reality and fantasy with cross-genre appeal. Exquisitely written and beautifully paced." Publ Wkly

★ **Days** of blood & starlight; Laini Taylor. 1st ed. Little, Brown Books for Young Readers 2012 528 p. maps (Daughter of smoke and bone trilogy) (hardcover) $18.99

Grades: 9 10 11 12   **Fic**

1. Occult fiction 2. Fantasy fiction 3. Angels -- Fiction 4. Demonology -- Fiction 5. Supernatural -- Fiction 6. Czech Republic -- Fiction 7. Mythology, Greek -- Fiction 8. Prague (Czech Republic) -- Fiction 9. Chimera (Greek mythology) -- Fiction

ISBN 0316133973; 9780316133975

LC 2012028752

Sequel to: Daughter of smoke and bone

In this fantasy sequel to "Daughter of Smoke and Bone," "Karou . . . has taken up the resurrection work . . . under the direction of the dangerous chimaera leader, Thiago. . . . The angel army is menacing the countryside in an attempt to kill the remaining chimaera, so she is designing and resurrecting stronger, more effective winged warriors to protect her people." (Bulletin of the Center for Children's Books)

Dreams of gods & monsters; by Laini Taylor. Little, Brown and Co. 2014 624 p. (hardback) $19

Grades: 8 9 10 11 12   **Fic**

1. Angels -- Fiction 2. Supernatural -- Fiction 3. Good and evil -- Fiction 4. Greek mythology -- Fiction 5. Fantasy 6. Demonology -- Fiction 7. Mythology, Greek -- Fiction 8. Chimera (Greek mythology) -- Fiction

ISBN 0316134074; 9780316134071

LC 2014003645

"In Taylor's third and final installment in her Daughter of Smoke and Bone trilogy, Karou and Akiva's dream of peace and a life together comes tantalizingly close, only to be repeatedly thwarted by their peoples' separate and conflicting histories, both mystical and real. Joined by angels and chimaera, Karou and Akiva lead their armies and fight side by side to prevent the apocalypse by banishing Jael, captain of the Dominion of Seraphim, from the earth he is determined to destroy." (Booklist)

"Eliza Jones, a research fellow at Smithsonian's National Museum of Natural History, wakes from a recurring nightmare to the discovery that angels have appeared in the sky above Uzbekistan. Unbeknownst to Eliza, she is the linchpin upon which the salvation of worlds depends. The battle is well and truly on in this finale to the "Daughter of Smoke and Bone" trilogy (Little, Brown)... The conclusion promises resurrection, renewal, and long-postponed love happily resolved, and that should satisfy even the most meticulous fans." (School Library Journal(

Dreams of gods and monsters

Silksinger; illustrations by Jim Di Bartolo. G.P. Putnam's Sons 2009 449p il (Dreamdark) $18.99

Grades: 6 7 8 9 　　　　　　　　　**Fic**

1. Fantasy fiction 2. Fairies -- Fiction 3. Mercenary soldiers -- Fiction 4. Good and evil -- Fiction

ISBN 978-0-399-24631-9; 0-399-24631-2

　　　　　　　　　　　　　　　LC 2008047981

While journeying by dragonfly caravan over the Sayash Mountains, warrior-faerie Whisper Silksinger, hunted by devils, meets a young mercenary with an ancient scimitar and secrets of his own.

"With excellent world-building and deft pacing, this story is difficult to put down. The characters are well developed, and their close relationships and rapid-fire dialogue enhance the story." SLJ

Taylor, Mildred D.

The **friendship**; pictures by Max Ginsburg. Dial Bks. for Young Readers 1987 53p il $15.99; pa $4.99

Grades: 4 5 6 7 　　　　　　　　　**Fic**

1. Mississippi -- Fiction 2. Race relations -- Fiction 3. African Americans -- Fiction

ISBN 0-8037-0417-8; 0-14-038964-4 pa

　　　　　　　　　　　　　　　LC 86-29309

Coretta Scott King Award for text

This "story about race relations in rural Mississippi during the Depression focuses on an incident between an old Black man, Mr. Tom Bee, and a white storekeeper, Mr. John Wallace. Indebted to Tom for saving his life as a young man, John had promised they would always be friends. But now, years later, John insists that Tom call him 'Mister' and shoots the old man for defiantly—and publicly—calling him by his first name. Narrator Cassie Logan and her brothers . . . are verbally abused by Wallace's villainous sons before witnessing the encounter." Bull Cent Child Books

★ The **gold** Cadillac; pictures by Michael Hays. Dial Bks. for Young Readers 1987 43p il $16.99; pa $4.99

Grades: 4 5 6 7 　　　　　　　　　**Fic**

1. Prejudices -- Fiction 2. Race relations -- Fiction 3. African Americans -- Fiction

ISBN 0-8037-0342-2; 0-14-038963-6 pa

　　　　　　　　　　　　　　　LC 86-11526

"Full-page sepia paintings effectively portray the characters, setting, and mood of the story events as Hays ably demonstrates his understanding of the social and emotional environments which existed for blacks during this period." SLJ

"The shiny gold Cadillac that Daddy brings home one summer evening marks a stepping stone in the lives of Wilma and [Lois,] two black sisters growing up in Ohio during the fifties. At first neighbors and relatives shower them with attention. But when the family begins the long journey to the South to show off the car to their Mississippi relatives, the girls, for the first time, encounter the undisguised ugliness of racial prejudice." Horn Book

★ The **land**. Phyllis Fogelman Bks. 2001 375p $17.99; pa $6.99

Grades: 7 8 9 10 　　　　　　　　　**Fic**

1. Race relations -- Fiction 2. African Americans -- Fiction 3. Racially mixed people -- Fiction

ISBN 0-8037-1950-7; 0-14-250146-8 pa

　　　　　　　　　　　　　　　LC 00-39329

Prequel to Roll of Thunder, Hear My Cry

Coretta Scott King Award for text

After the Civil War Paul-Edward Logan, the son of a white father and a black mother, finds himself caught between the two worlds of colored folks and white folks as he pursues his dream of owning land of his own.

"Taylor masterfully uses harsh historical realities to frame a powerful coming-of-age story that stands on its own merits." Horn Book Guide

★ **Let** the circle be unbroken. Dial Bks. for Young Readers 1981 394p $17.99; pa $7.99

Grades: 4 5 6 7 　　　　　　　　　**Fic**

1. Mississippi -- Fiction 2. African Americans -- Fiction 3. Great Depression, 1929-1939 -- Fiction

ISBN 0-8037-4748-9; 0-14-034892-1 pa

　　　　　　　　　　　　　　　LC 81-65854

Sequel to: Roll of thunder, hear my cry

The author "provides her readers with a literal sense of witnessing important American history. . . . Moreover, [she] never neglects the details of her volatile 9-year-old heroine's interior life. The daydreams, the jealousy, the incredible ardor of that age come alive." N Y Times Book Rev

★ The **road** to Memphis; by Mildred Taylor. Dial Bks. 1989 290p pa $6.99; $18.99

Grades: 4 5 6 7 　　　　　　　　　**Fic**

1. Mississippi -- Fiction 2. Race relations -- Fiction 3. African Americans -- Fiction

ISBN 0-14-036077-8 pa; 0-8037-0340-6

　　　　　　　　　　　　　　　LC 88-33654

Coretta Scott King Award for text

This is a sequel to Let the Circle Be Unbroken (BRD 1982). "The time is 1941, with the U.S. on the verge of war; Cassie {Logan} . . . is sure that nothing will stop her from college and career. When her friend Moe is humiliated and ridiculed by local bigots, he loses control and attacks three men with a crowbar. Cassie and her brothers and friends (including one white friend, Jeremy Simms) help Moe escape. . . . Grades seven to twelve." (Booklist)

"Taylor's continued smooth, easy language provides readability for all ages, with a focus on universal human pride, worthy values, and individual responsibility. This action-packed drama is highly recommended." Voice Youth Advocates

★ **Roll** of thunder, hear my cry; 25th anniversary ed; Phyllis Fogelman Books 2001 276p $17.99; pa $7.99

Grades: 4 5 6 7 8 9 　　　　　　　　　**Fic**

1. Mississippi -- Fiction 2. African Americans -- Fiction

ISBN 0-8037-2647-3; 0-14-240112-9 pa

　　　　　　　　　　　　　　　LC 00-39378

First published 1976 by Dial Press

Awarded the Newbery Medal, 1977

"The time is 1933. The place is Spokane, Mississippi where the Logans, the only black family who own their own land, wage a courageous struggle to remain independent, displeasing a white plantation owner bent on taking their land. But this suspenseful tale is also about the story's young narrator, Cassie, and her three brothers who decide to wage their own personal battles to maintain the self-dignity and pride with which they were raised. . . . Ms. Taylor's richly textured novel shows a strong, proud black family . . . resisting rather than succumbing to oppression." Child Book Rev Serv

The **well**; David's story. Dial Bks. for Young Readers 1995 92p hardcover o.p. pa $5.99

Grades: 4 5 6 7 **Fic**

1. Mississippi -- Fiction 2. Race relations -- Fiction 3. African Americans -- Fiction

ISBN 0-8037-1802-0; 0-14-038642-4 pa

LC 94-25360

This story "delivers an emotional wallop in a concentrated span of time and action. . . . This story reverberates in the heart long after the final paragraph is read." Horn Book

"David Logan (Cassie's father) tells this story from his childhood. . . . There's a drought, and the Logans possess the only well in the area that has not gone dry. Black and white alike come for water freely given by the family, but the Simms boys can't seem to stand the necessary charity, and their resentment explodes when David's big brother Hammer beats Charlie Simms after Charlie hits David." Bull Cent Child Books

Taylor, S. S.

The **Expeditioners** and the Treasure of Drowned Man's Canyon; and the Treasure of Drowned Man's Canyon. by S. S. Taylor; illustrated by Katherine Roy. Pgw 2012 320 p. $22

Grades: 5 6 7 8 **Fic**

1. Adventure fiction 2. Maps -- Fiction 3. Exploration -- Fiction

ISBN 1938073061; 9781938073069

In this book by S. S. Taylor, illustrated by Katherine Roy, "computers have failed, electricity is extinct, and the race to discover new lands is underway! Brilliant explorer Alexander West has just died under mysterious circumstances, but not before smuggling half of a strange map to his intrepid children--Kit the brain, M.K. the tinkerer, and Zander the brave. Why are so many government agents trying to steal the half-map? (And where is the other half?)" (Publisher's note)

Taylor, Theodore

★ The **cay**. Delacorte Press 1987 137p $16.95; pa $5.50

Grades: 5 6 7 8 **Fic**

1. Blind -- Fiction 2. Race relations -- Fiction 3. Caribbean region -- Fiction 4. Survival after airplane accidents, shipwrecks, etc. -- Fiction

ISBN 0-385-07906-0; 0-440-22912-X pa

A reissue of the title first published 1969

When the freighter on which they are traveling is torpedoed by a German submarine during World War II, Phillip, an adolescent white boy blinded by a blow on the head, and Timothy, an old black man, are stranded on a tiny Caribbean island where the boy acquires a new kind of vision, courage, and love from his old companion

"Starkly dramatic, believable and compelling." Saturday Rev

Followed by: Timothy of the cay

★ **Timothy** of the cay. Harcourt Brace & Co. 1993 161p hardcover o.p. pa $5.95

Grades: 5 6 7 8 **Fic**

1. Blind -- Fiction 2. Race relations -- Fiction 3. Caribbean region -- Fiction 4. Survival after airplane accidents, shipwrecks, etc. -- Fiction

ISBN 0-15-288358-4; 0-15-206320-X pa

LC 93-7898

Sequel to: The cay

Having survived being blinded and shipwrecked on a tiny Caribbean island with the old black man Timothy, twelve-year-old white Phillip is rescued and hopes to regain his sight with an operation. Alternate chapters follow the life of Timothy from his days as a young cabin boy

"Somewhat more thoughtful than its well-loved antecedent, this boldly drawn novel is no less commanding." Publ Wkly

Teague, David

★ **Saving** Lucas Biggs; by Marisa de los Santos and David Teague. Harper, an imprint of HarperCollinsPublishers 2014 288 p. (hardback) $16.99

Grades: 5 6 7 8 **Fic**

1. Girls -- Fiction 2. Time travel -- Fiction 3. Detective and mystery stories

ISBN 0062274627; 9780062274625

LC 2013043189

This "time-travel story from husband-and-wife team Marisa de los Santos and David Teague follows one girl's race to change the past in order to save her father's future. Thirteen-year-old Margaret knows her father is innocent, but that doesn't stop the cruel Judge Biggs from sentencing him to death. Margaret is determined to save her dad, even if it means using her family's secret--and forbidden--ability to time travel." (Publisher's note)

"...The authors weave a tale of justice and family bonds with threads of historical fiction accented with the fantastical physics of time travel. The heroine begins to realize that the very stuff that makes people who they are—that combination of all their life experiences—can sometimes shift the very fabric of history. At least that's what Margaret is hoping, because the only way to save her father is to first save corrupt Lucas Biggs from himself.—" SLJ

Teague, Mark

★ The **doom** machine; a novel. Blue Sky Press 2009 376p $17.99

Grades: 4 5 6 7 **Fic**

1. Science fiction 2. Space and time -- Fiction 3. Extraterrestrial beings -- Fiction

ISBN 978-0-545-15142-9; 0-545-15142-2

LC 2009-14262

When a spaceship lands in the small town of Vern Hollow in 1956, juvenile delinquent Jack Creedle and prim, studious Isadora Shumway form an unexpected alliance as they try to keep a group of extraterrestrials from stealing eccentric Uncle Bud's space travel machine.

"This book is filled with humor and dramatic figurative language that makes the setting completely approachable. It is a great fit for science fiction, humor, and adventure genre fans." Voice Youth Advocates

Teller, Janne

★ **Nothing**; translated from the Danish by Martin Aitken. Atheneum Books for Young Readers 2010 227p $16.99

Grades: 7 8 9 10 11 12 **Fic**

1. School stories 2. Meaning (Philosophy) -- Fiction
ISBN 978-1-4169-8579-2; 1-4169-8579-4

LC 2009-19784

Michael J. Printz honor book, 2011

When thirteen-year-old Pierre Anthon leaves school to sit in a plum tree and train for becoming part of nothing, his seventh grade classmates set out on a desperate quest for the meaning of life.

"Indelible, elusive, and timeless, this uncompromising novel has all the marks of a classic." Booklist

TenNapel, Doug

Cardboard; Doug TenNapel. Graphix / Scholastic 2012 288 p. $24.99

Grades: 5 6 7 8 **Fic**

1. Boxes -- Fiction 2. Gifts -- Graphic novels 3. Magic -- Graphic novels 4. Bullies -- Graphic novels 5. Father-son relationship -- Graphic novels
ISBN 0545418720; 9780545418720; 9780545418737

LC 2011934533

In this graphic novel, "Cam Howerton's out-of-work father is so broke, the best he can do for Cam's birthday is an empty cardboard box purchased from a toy seller with two mysterious rules: return every unused scrap of cardboard and don't ask for any more. . . . [T]he box becomes a project. What should father and son make out of the box? 'A boxer,' Cam suggests. . . . 'Boxer Bill,' created from inanimate material, comes alive. Unfortunately, Marcus, the neighborhood bully . . . steals the scrap materials, and begins turning out a whole evil empire of cardboard monsters. . . . [A]fter losing control of them he must unite with Cam and his father to defeat the massive cardboard army. . . . [Q]uestions are raised about what it means to be a man, what makes a good man, and what forms people's character." (Horn Book)

Terry, Chris L.

Zero fade; Chris L Terry. Curbside Splendor Publishing 2013 294 p. $12

Grades: 7 8 9 10 **Fic**

1. School stories 2. Bullies -- Fiction 3. Historical fiction
ISBN 0988480433; 9780988480438

LC 2013944486

This book focuses on Kevin Phifer, "a black seventh-grader in 1990s Richmond, Va." He "wants a fade, thinking the stylish haircut will bolster his shaky standing in the cut-throat world of middle school, where he's just one friend away from eating lunch alone. But his mother, a church secretary and solo parent studying for a nursing degree at night, won't even try. Expressing his frustration leads to a week's

grounding. Tyrell and his entourage of bullies make Kevin's life miserable at school." (Kirkus Reviews)

"Original, hilarious, thought-provoking and wicked smart: not to be missed." (Kirkus)

Terry, Teri

Fractured; Teri Terry. Nancy Paulsen Books 2013 336 p. (Slated trilogy) $17.99

Grades: 7 8 9 10 **Fic**

1. Dystopian fiction 2. Memory -- Fiction 3. Science fiction 4. England -- Fiction 5. Schools -- Fiction 6. Identity -- Fiction 7. Terrorism -- Fiction 8. High schools -- Fiction 9. England -- Fiction 10. Dystopias -- Fiction
ISBN 0399161732; 9780399161735

LC 2012044317

Author Teri Terry presents the "second installment of the Slated trilogy . . . set in a future where violent teens have their memory erased as an alternative to jail. Kyla has been Slated--her personality wiped blank, her memories lost to her forever. Or so she thought. When a mysterious man from her past comes back into her life and wants her help, she thinks she's on her way to finding the truth." (Publisher's note)

"Kyla's memories, wiped by the government in Slated, are slowly returning; she's been found by an anti-government group that claims she's a member and wants her to complete one last mission. Kyla's struggles to uncover her identity and think through the consequences of her actions are realistic and add an emotional backbone to this fast-paced middle volume of the trilogy." (Horn Book)

Slated; Teri Terry. Nancy Paulsen Books 2013 346 p. (hardcover) $17.99

Grades: 7 8 9 10 **Fic**

1. Science fiction 2. Memory -- Fiction 3. Identity -- Fiction 4. Schools -- Fiction 5. High schools -- Fiction 6. Family life -- England -- Fiction
ISBN 0399161724; 9780399161728

LC 2012020873

In this novel, by Teri Terry, "Kyla has been Slated--her memory and personality erased as punishment for committing a crime she can't remember. The government has taught her how to walk and talk again, given her a new identity and a new family, and told her to be grateful for this second chance that she doesn't deserve. It's also her last chance--because they'll be watching to make sure she plays by their rules." (Publisher's note)

Testa, Dom

★ The **comet's** curse. Tor Teen 2009 236p (Galahad) $16.95

Grades: 7 8 9 10 11 12 **Fic**

1. Science fiction 2. Interplanetary voyages -- Fiction
ISBN 978-0-7653-2107-7; 0-7653-2107-6

LC 2008-35620

First published 2005 by Profound Impact Group

Desperate to save the human race after a comet's deadly particles devastate the adult population, scientists create a ship that will carry a crew of 251 teenagers to a home in a distant solar system.

This book is "both a mystery and an adventure, combining a solid cast of characters with humor, pathos, growing pains and just a hint of romance." Kirkus

Other titles in this series are:
The Cassini code (2010)
Cosmic storm (2011)
The dark zone (2011)
The web of Titan (2009)

Tharp, Tim

Knights of the hill country. Alfred A. Knopf 2006 233p hardcover o.p. pa $6.99

Grades: 8 9 10 11 12   Fic

1. School stories 2. Football -- Fiction 3. Oklahoma -- Fiction

ISBN 978-0-375-83653-4; 0-375-83653-5; 978-0-553-49513-3 pa; 0-553-49513-5 pa

LC 2005-33279

In his senior year, high school star linebacker Hampton Greene finally begins to think for himself and discovers that he might be interested in more than just football.

"Taut scenes on the football field and the dilemmas about choosing what feels right over what's expected are all made memorable by Hamp's unforgettable, colloquial voice." Booklist

Thomas, Erin

Boarder patrol; written by Erin Thomas. Orca Book Publishers 2010 170p (Orca sports) pa $9.95

Grades: 6 7 8 9   Fic

1. Mystery fiction 2. Skiing -- Fiction 3. Cousins -- Fiction 4. Snowboarding -- Fiction

ISBN 978-1-55469-294-1 pa; 1-55469-294-6 pa

"Ryan, 16, works as a Junior Ski Patrol volunteer in order to earn a free lift pass. His dream is to pursue snowboarding professionally. His cousin, Kevin, who works at the lifts, starts acting strangely, especially when Ryan begins investigating the disappearance of some ski equipment, including his own, on the mountain. . . . The story includes vivid descriptions of snowboarding and mountain rescue, and the mystery is involving." SLJ

Thomason, Mark

Moonrunner. Kane/Miller 2009 217p $15.95

Grades: 4 5 6 7   Fic

1. Horses -- Fiction 2. Australia -- Fiction

ISBN 978-1-935279-03-7; 1-935279-03-3

First published 2008 in Australia

"In the 1890s, Casey and his parents immigrate to Australia, to a homestead that they inherited from his grandfather. The 12-year-old finds the change difficult. He is bullied at school, and he misses his baseball team in Montana and his horse. Then he happens upon a magnificent wild stallion, and he is determined to befriend the brumby, whom he names Moonrunner. . . . This well-paced story effectively portrays the family's struggles. Casey is a strong, engaging protagonist whose interactions with the other characters are believable and interesting." SLJ

Thompson, Holly

The **language** inside; Holly Thompson. 1st ed. Delacorte Press 2013 528 p. (hardcover) $17.99

Grades: 7 8 9 10 11 12   Fic

1. Novels in verse 2. Moving -- Fiction 3. Interpersonal relations -- Fiction 4. Japan -- Fiction 5. Cancer -- Fiction 6. Tsunamis -- Fiction 7. Massachusetts -- Fiction 8. Moving, Household -- Fiction 9. Family life -- Massachusetts -- Fiction

ISBN 0385739796; 9780375898358; 9780385739795; 9780385908078

LC 2012030596

Includes bibliographical references (p. 520).

In this novel in verse, by Holly Thompson, "Emma's family moves to a town outside Lowell, Massachusetts, to stay with Emma's grandmother while her mom undergoes treatment. Emma feels out of place in the United States. She begins to have migraines, and longs to be back in Japan. At her grandmother's urging, she volunteers in a long-term care center to help Zena, a patient with locked-in syndrome, write down her poems." (Publisher's note)

★ **Orchards**; Holly Thompson; illustrations by Grady McFerrin. Delacorte Press 2011 327p il $17.99; lib bdg $20.99

Grades: 7 8 9 10   Fic

1. Novels in verse 2. Japan -- Fiction 3. Suicide -- Fiction 4. Bereavement -- Fiction 5. Family life -- Fiction 6. Racially mixed people -- Fiction

ISBN 978-0-385-73977-1; 0-385-73977-X; 978-0-385-90806-1 lib bdg; 0-385-90806-7 lib bdg

LC 2010-23724

"After a classmate commits suicide, Kana, a half-Japanese, half-Jewish American eighth grader, is sent to her maternal grandmother's farm in rural Japan for personal reflection. Kana tells her story in poignantly straightforward verse directed at the deceased classmate as she struggles with blame and regret, wondering if she and her friends are responsible because they took part in ostracizing the girl. She struggles, too, with her biracial, bicultural identity, feeling isolated in her new surroundings." (School Library Journal)

"Kanako's urgent teen voice, written in rapid free verse and illustrated with occasional black-and-white sketches, will hold readers with its nonreverential family story." Booklist

Thompson, J. E.

The **girl** from Felony Bay; John Thompson. Walden Pond Press, an imprint of HarperCollinsPublishers 2013 384 p. (hardcover bdg.) $16.99

Grades: 4 5 6 7   Fic

1. Theft -- Fiction 2. Mystery fiction 3. Coma -- Fiction 4. Fathers -- Fiction 5. Families -- Fiction 6. Charleston (S.C.) -- Fiction 7. Mystery and detective stories

ISBN 0062104462; 9780062104465

LC 2012025338

In this book, 12-year-old Abbey Force's "father has suffered an accident and now lies in the hospital in a coma. Meanwhile, he has been accused of stealing from a client named Miss Lydia Jenkins, and his law firm . . . has sold the Force family home, Reward Plantation, in order to repay her." Abbey makes friends with the new owners' daughter Bee and the girls "stumble upon a mystery--someone is digging holes at Felony Bay, perhaps in search of buried treasure." (Kirkus Reviews)

Thompson, Kate

★ The **new** policeman. Greenwillow Books 2007 442p hardcover o.p. pa $8.99

Grades: 7 8 9 10　　　　　　　**Fic**

1. Fantasy fiction 2. Music -- Fiction 3. Fairies -- Fiction 4. Ireland -- Fiction 5. Space and time -- Fiction
ISBN 978-0-06-117427-8; 0-06-117427-0; 978-0-06-117429-2 pa; 0-06-117429-7 pa

LC 2006-8246

First published 2005 in the United Kingdom

Irish teenager JJ Liddy discovers that time is leaking from his world into Tir na nOg, the land of the fairies, and when he attempts to stop the leak he finds out a lot about his family history, the music that he loves, and a crime his great-grandfather may or may not have committed.

"Mesmerizing and captivating, this book is guaranteed to charm fantasy fans." Voice Youth Advocates

Other titles in this series are:

The last of the High Kings (2008)

The white horse trick (2010)

Origins. Bloomsbury 2007 313p (Missing link trilogy) $17.95

Grades: 6 7 8 9　　　　　　　**Fic**

1. Science fiction 2. Animals -- Fiction 3. Future life -- Fiction 4. Genetic engineering -- Fiction
ISBN 978-1-58234-652-6; 1-58234-652-6

LC 2007-06924

Sequel to Only human (2006)

Christy 's souvenir stone from the yeti's cave proves to be fatal for many of the inhabitants of Fourth World leaving among the survivors a pair of genetically-altered twins whose eventual descendants face an uncertain future in a stone age world of nuclear devastation and disease.

This is "a post-apolcalyptic stunner. [It blends] weighty science fiction themes like genetic engineering and the future of human evolution with equally thought-provoking allegorical fable." Publ Wkly

Thompson, Paul B.

The **devil's** door; a Salem witchcraft story. Enslow Publishers 2010 160p (Historical fiction adventures) lib bdg $27.93; pa $14.95

Grades: 4 5 6　　　　　　　**Fic**

1. Trials -- Fiction 2. Witchcraft -- Fiction 3. Salem (Mass.) -- Fiction
ISBN 978-0-7660-3387-0 lib bdg; 0-7660-3387-2 lib bdg; 978-1-59845-214-3 pa; 1-59845-214-2 pa

Sarah Wright and her father Ephraim move to Salem Village, Massachusetts, in 1692, where they witness the Salem witchcraft hysteria, during which Ephraim is arrested and Sarah must try to help him escape from jail.

"Factual material is incorporated into the narrative, creating a fast-paced, fascinating read." SLJ

Thompson, Ricki

City of cannibals. Front Street 2010 269p $18.95

Grades: 8 9 10 11 12　　　　　　　**Fic**

1. Monks -- Fiction 2. Persecution -- Fiction 3. Runaway teenagers -- Fiction 4. Great Britain -- History -- 1485-1603, Tudors -- Fiction
ISBN 978-1-59078-623-9; 1-59078-623-8

LC 2010-2105

In 1536 England, sixteen-year-old Dell runs away from her brutal father and life in a cave carrying only a handmade puppet to travel to London, where she learns truths about her mother's death and the conflict between King Henry VIII and the Catholic Church.

"Thompson's England is authentically vulgar, and her grasp of period slang—as well as Dell's burgeoning sexual desires—is expert. Packed with rich metaphor, this is a challenging but rewarding read." Booklist

Thomson, Jamie

Dark Lord, the early years; by Jamie Thomson. Walker & Co. 2012 290 p. (hardcover) $16.99

Grades: 6 7 8 9　　　　　　　**Fic**

1. School stories 2. Fantasy fiction 3. Fantasy 4. Humorous stories 5. Magic -- Fiction 6. Identity -- Fiction
ISBN 0802728499; 9780802728494

LC 2012007152

In this book by Jamie Thomson, "the Dark Lord—renamed Dirk Lloyd by confused, puny Earthlings—is taken to the Hospital Lockup and then to a House of Detention" after waking up in a parking lot "trapped in the body of a 12-year-old human." People think he's crazy, "but thankfully, Christopher, the child of his captors, agrees to be a minion, as does goth girl Sooz. Dirk must find a way back to his Darklands" before he loses his evil abilities. (Kirkus)

Thomson, Sarah L.

The **secret** of the Rose; 1st ed.; Greenwillow Books 2006 296p $16.99; lib bdg $17.89

Grades: 6 7 8 9　　　　　　　**Fic**

1. Authors 2. Dramatists 3. Theater -- Fiction 4. Sex role -- Fiction 5. Catholics -- Fiction 6. Great Britain -- History -- 1485-1603, Tudors -- Fiction
ISBN 978-0-06-087250-2; 0-06-087250-0; 978-0-06-087251-9 lib bdg; 0-06-087251-9 lib bdg

LC 2005-22177

When her father is imprisoned in 1592 England for being Catholic, fourteen-year-old Rosalind disguises herself as a boy and finds an ultimately dangerous job as servant to playwright Christopher Marlowe.

"Part historical mystery, part suspense, this fast-paced story is propelled by Rosalind's desire not just to survive but also to learn who she is." Voice Youth Advocates

Thor, Annika

Deep sea; Annika Thor ; translated from the Swedish by Linda Schenck. First American edition Delacorte Press 2015 240 p. (hc) $17.99

Grades: 7 8 9 10 11 12　　　　　　　**Fic**

1. Jews -- Fiction 2. Sweden -- Fiction 3. Sisters -- Fiction 4. Refugees -- Fiction 5. Friendship -- Fiction 6. World War, 1939-1945 -- Refugees -- Fiction 7. Schools -- Fiction 8. Jews -- Sweden -- Fiction 9.

Sweden -- History -- Gustav V, 1907-1950 -- Fiction
ISBN 0385743858; 9780375991325; 9780385743853
LC 2014005586

In this book, by Annika Thor, "Stephie and her younger sister, Nellie, escaped the Nazis in Vienna and fled to an island in Sweden, where they were taken in by different families. . . . Nellie wants to be adopted by her foster family. Stephie, on the other hand, can't stop thinking about her parents, who are in a Nazi camp in Austria." (Publisher's note)

"This novel about coming of age during a complicated, tragic time in history is both delicate and poignant, as when Stephie and Nellie sit on the dock, remembering a lullaby their mother sang. Thor's novel capably demonstrates the loneliness, powerlessness, and prejudice Stephie faces, as well as her growing inner strength." PW Annex

★ A **faraway** island; translated from the Swedish by Linda Schenck. Delacorte Press 2009 247p map $16.99; lib bdg $19.99

Grades: 4 5 6 7   **Fic**
1. Jews -- Fiction 2. Sweden -- Fiction 3. Islands -- Fiction 4. Sisters -- Fiction 5. Refugees -- Fiction 6. World War, 1939-1945 -- Fiction
ISBN 978-0-385-73617-6; 0-385-73617-7; 978-0-385-90590-9 lib bdg; 0-385-90590-4 lib bdg
LC 2009-15420

ALA ALSC Batchelder Award (2010)
In 1939 Sweden, two Jewish sisters wait for their parents to flee the Nazis in Austria, but while eight-year-old Nellie settles in quickly, twelve-year-old Stephie feels stranded at the end of the world, with a foster mother who is as cold and unforgiving as the island on which they live.

"Children will readily empathize with Stephie's courage. Both sisters are well-drawn, likable characters. This is the first of four books Thor has written about the two girls." SLJ
Followed by: The lily pond (2011)

The **lily** pond. Delacorte Press 2011 217p $16.99; lib bdg $19.99

Grades: 4 5 6 7   **Fic**
1. School stories 2. Sweden -- Fiction 3. Refugees -- Fiction 4. Friendship -- Fiction 5. Jews -- Sweden -- Fiction 6. World War, 1939-1945 -- Fiction
ISBN 978-0-385-74039-5; 0-385-74039-5; 978-0-385-90838-2 lib bdg; 0-385-90838-5 lib bdg; 978-0-375-89914-0 e-book
LC 2010053548

"A year after Stephie Steiner and her younger sister, Nellie, left Nazi-occupied Vienna, Stephie has finally adapted to life on the rugged Swedish island where she now lives. But more change awaits Stephie: her foster parents have allowed her to enroll in school on the mainland, in Goteberg. Stephie is eager to go. Not only will she be pursuing her studies, she'll be living in a cultured city again—under the same roof as Sven, the son of the lodgers who rented her foster parents' cottage for the summer." (Publisher's note)

Thurlo, Aimee
The **spirit** line; [by] Aimeé & David Thurlo. Viking 2004 216p $15.99

Grades: 6 7 8 9   **Fic**
1. New Mexico -- Fiction 2. Navajo Indians -- Fiction
ISBN 0-670-03645-5

When the special rug Crystal Manyfeathers is weaving for her kinaaldá, the traditional Navajo womanhood ceremony, is stolen from her loom, there are any number of suspects.

"Carefully combining humor and seriousness, this well-paced story contains accurate portrayals of Navajo customs, mostly believable teen dialogue, and a realistic depiction of the conflicts modern Native young people face." SLJ

Tiernan, Cate
Balefire. Razorbill 2011 974p pa $8.99

Grades: 8 9 10 11 12   **Fic**
1. Twins -- Fiction 2. Sisters -- Fiction 3. Witchcraft -- Fiction 4. New Orleans (La.) -- Fiction
ISBN 978-1-59514-411-9

An omnibus edition of four titles previously published separately, the first three of which were first published 2005. The last, A necklace of water, was first published 2006

Separated since birth, seventeen-year-old twins Thais and Clio unexpectedly meet in New Orleans where they seem to be pursued by a coven of witches who want to harness the twins' magical powers for its own ends.

Tingle, Tim
Danny Blackgoat, Navajo prisoner; Tim Tingle. 7th Generation 2013 160 p. (pbk.) $9.95

Grades: 6 7 8   **Fic**
1. Navajo Indians -- Fiction 2. Navajo Long Walk, 1863-1867 3. Bullies -- Fiction 4. Prisoners -- Fiction 5. Conduct of life -- Fiction 6. Navajo Long Walk, 1863-1867 -- Fiction 7. Indians of North America -- Texas -- Fiction 8. Fort Davis National Historic Site (Tex.) -- Fiction
ISBN 193905303X; 9781939053039
LC 2013013183

American Indian Youth Literature Awards Honor Book: Middle School (2014)
In this book, "Danny Blackgoat is a teenager in Navajo country when soldiers burn down his home, kill his sheep and capture his family. During the Long Walk of 1864, Danny is labeled a troublemaker. . . . Refusing to accept captivity, he is sent to Fort Davis, Texas, a Civil War prisoner outpost. There . . . he meets Jim Davis. Jim teaches Danny how to hold his anger and . . . aids Danny in a daring and dangerous escape." (Publisher's note)

How I became a ghost; a Choctaw trail of tears story. by Tim Tingle. RoadRunner Press 2013 160 p. (The how I became a ghost series) (hardcover : alk. paper) $18.95

Grades: 4 5 6 7   **Fic**
1. Ghost stories 2. Choctaw Indians -- Fiction
ISBN 1937054535; 9781937054533; 9781937054540; 9781937054557
LC 2013935579

American Indian Youth Literature Award Winner (2014)
In this book, "a 10-year-old Choctaw boy recounts the beginnings of the forced resettlement of his people from their Mississippi-area homelands in 1830. . . . Even as the

Choctaw prepare to leave their homes, Isaac begins to have unsettling visions. . . [The] visions begin to come true, as some are burned to death by the Nahullos and others perish due to smallpox-infested blankets. . . . But the Choctaw barrier between life and death is a fluid one, and ghosts follow Isaac, providing reassurance." (Kirkus Reviews)

Tocher, Timothy

Bill Pennant, Babe Ruth, and me. Cricket Books 2009 178p $16.95

Grades: 5 6 7 8   Fic

1. Baseball players 2. Baseball managers 3. Baseball -- Fiction 4. New York Giants (Baseball team) -- Fiction 5. New York Yankees (Baseball team) -- Fiction.
ISBN 978-0-8126-2755-8; 0-8126-2755-5

LC 2008026829

In 1920, sixteen-year-old Hank finds his loyalties divided when he is assigned to care for the Giants' mascot, a wildcat named Bill Pennant, as well as keep an eye on Babe Ruth in Ruth's first season with the New York Yankees.

The author "seamlessly blends fact and fiction. He recreates the era with scrupulous attention to its syntax and slang, as well as details of daily life. Ruth, McGraw and the other historical figures come alive for readers, and the fictional Hank is a sympathetic, fully developed character." Kirkus

Chief Sunrise, John McGraw, and me; Timothy Tocher. 1st ed; Cricket Books 2004 154p $15.95

Grades: 5 6 7 8 9   Fic

1. Baseball -- Fiction 2. Race relations -- Fiction 3. Runaway teenagers -- Fiction
ISBN 0-8126-2711-3

LC 2003-23407

In 1919, fifteen-year-old Hank escapes an abusive father and goes looking for a chance to become a baseball player, accompanied by a man who calls himself Chief Sunrise and claims to be a full-blooded Seminole.

"The story is both entertaining and thought-provoking." Booklist

Todd, Pamela

The **blind** faith hotel; [by] Pamela Todd. Margaret K. McElderry Books 2008 312p $16.99; pa $8.99

Grades: 8 9 10   Fic

1. Nature -- Fiction 2. Prairies -- Fiction 3. Family life -- Fiction
ISBN 978-1-4169-5494-1; 1-4169-5494-5; 978-1-4169-9509-8 pa; 1-4169-9509-9 pa

LC 2007-43912

When her parents separate and she and her siblings move with their mother from the northwest coast to a midwest prairie farmhouse, fourteen-year-old Zoe, miserably unhappy to be away from the ocean and her father, begins to develop a deep attachment to her new surroundings, when, after a shoplifting episode, she is assigned to work at a nature preserve.

"This touching novel tackles many difficult issues; beautiful imagery and language keep the story vibrant." Horn Book Guide

Toft, Di

The **twilight** circus. Chicken House/Scholastic Inc. 2011 372p $17.99

Grades: 5 6 7 8   Fic

1. Circus -- Fiction 2. Vampires -- Fiction 3. Werewolves -- Fiction 4. Grandfathers -- Fiction 5. Supernatural -- Fiction 6. Great Britain -- Fiction
ISBN 0-545-29492-4; 978-0-545-29492-8

LC 2010054231

Sequel to: Wolven (2011)

After a summer spent dodging mutant werewolves and mad scientists, Nat Carver and shapeshifter Woody join the Twilight Circus of Illusion and are caught up in a struggle against a black widow vampire and her terrifying hive.

"Definitely a continuation rather than a freestanding episode, but the author keeps her ongoing plot galloping along and adds an assortment of marvelous new creatures to the cast." Kirkus

Wolven. Scholastic 2010 322p $16.99; pa $7.99

Grades: 5 6 7 8   Fic

1. Werewolves -- Fiction 2. Supernatural -- Fiction 3. Great Britain -- Fiction
ISBN 978-0-545-17109-0; 0-545-17109-1; 978-0-545-17110-6 pa; 0-545-17110-5 pa

Twelve-year-old Nat, with help from his friends, and his "pet" Woody, a wolf that turns into a boy, must face werewolves that have been altered as part of a dastardly plan.

"Toft spins an incredible tale full of action, mystery, and suspense. This hair-raising adventure with its fresh perspective on werewolf lore is perfect for audiences not ready for some of the edgier material out there. A satisfying read with a fly-off-the-shelves cover." SLJ

Another title in this series is:
The twilight circus (2011)

Toksvig, Sandi

★ **Hitler's** canary. Roaring Brook Press 2007 191p $16.95

Grades: 5 6 7 8   Fic

1. Jews -- Fiction 2. Denmark -- Fiction 3. World War, 1939-1945 -- Fiction
ISBN 978-1-59643-247-5; 1-59643-247-0

LC 2006-16607

Ten-year-old Bamse and his Jewish friend Anton participate in the Danish Resistance during World War II.

"Though . . . suspenseful episodes will thrill readers, it is Bamse's growing courage and deepening understanding that drive the story." Booklist

Tolan, Stephanie S.

★ **Surviving** the Applewhites. HarperCollins Pubs. 2002 216p $15.99; lib bdg $17.89; pa $5.99

Grades: 5 6 7 8   Fic

1. Theater -- Fiction 2. Family life -- Fiction 3. Eccentrics and eccentricities -- Fiction
ISBN 0-06-623602-9; 0-06-623603-7 lib bdg; 0-06-441044-7 pa

LC 2002-1474

A Newbery Medal honor book, 2003

Jake, a budding juvenile delinquent, is sent for home schooling to the arty and eccentric Applewhite family's Creative Academy, where he discovers talents and interests he never knew he had

This is a "thoroughly enjoyable book with humor, well-drawn characters, and a super cover." Voice Youth Advocates

Toliver, Wendy

Lifted. Simon Pulse 2010 309p pa $9.99
Grades: 7 8 9 10   **Fic**
1. School stories 2. Texas -- Fiction 3. Theft -- Fiction 4. Moving -- Fiction
ISBN 978-1-4169-9048-2; 1-4169-9048-8

"Poppy isn't happy with her single mother for moving her to Texas and enrolling the decidedly secular 16-year-old in a private Baptist high school. Soon, however, she becomes fascinated with the two most elite girls in class. . . . Her new friends, despite their pious attitudes, are shoplifters. Toliver does a good job of making clear the thefts are less about the desire for things like designer jeans than about the adrenaline rush of getting away with something. . . . Will appeal to all teens interested in wayward behavior." Booklist

Tolkien, J. R. R. (John Ronald Reuel), 1892-1973

★ The **hobbit,** or, There and back again. Houghton Mifflin 2001 330p il $18; pa $10
Grades: 5 6 7 8 9 10 11 12 Adult   **Fic**
1. Fantasy fiction
ISBN 0-618-16221-6; 0-618-26030-7 pa
                                                 LC 2001276594
A reissue of the title first published 1938

"This fantasy features the adventures of hobbit Bilbo Baggins, who joins a band of dwarves led by Gandalf the Wizard. Together they seek to recover the stolen treasure that is hidden in Lonely Mountain and guarded by Smaug the Dragon. This book precedes the Lord of the Rings trilogy." Shapiro. Fic for Youth. 3d edition

Followed by: The lord of the rings trilogy: The fellowship of the ring; The two towers; The return of the king

The **hobbit**; or, There and back again. illustrated by Michael Hague. Houghton Mifflin 1984 290p il $29.95
Grades: 5 6 7 8 9 10 11 12 Adult   **Fic**
1. Magic 2. Satire 3. Allegories 4. Fantasy fiction 5. Fantasies 6. Imaginary kingdoms
ISBN 0-395-36290-3
                                                    LC 84-9023
First published 1937 in the United Kingdom; first United States edition 1938

Bilbo Baggins, a respectable, well-to-do hobbit, lives comfortably in his hobbit-hole until the day the wandering wizard Gandalf chooses him to share in an adventure from which he may never return. "Grades four to eight." (Bull Cent Child Books)

"It must be understood that this is a children's book only in the sense that the first of many readings can be undertaken in the nursery. . . . [The hobbit] will be funniest to its youngest readers, and only years later, at a tenth or twentieth reading, will they begin to realize what deft scholarship and pro-

found reflection have gone to make everything in it so ripe, so friendly, and in its own way so true." Times Lit Suppl

★ The **lord** of the rings; 50th Anniversary ed; Houghton Mifflin 2004 xxv, 1157p il map slip case $100
Grades: 7 8 9 10 11 12 Adult   **Fic**
1. Fantasy fiction
ISBN 0-618-51765-0
                                                 LC 2004-275215
First published 1954 in the United Kingdom

"This is a tale of imaginary gnomelike creatures who battle against evil. Led by Frodo, the hobbits embark on a journey to prevent a magic ring from falling into the grasp of the powers of darkness. The forces of good succeed in their fight against the Dark Lord of evil, and Frodo and Sam bring the Ring to Mount Doom, where it is destroyed." Shapiro. Fic for Youth. 3d edition

Tomlinson, Heather

★ **Aurelie**; a faerie tale. Henry Holt 2008 184p $16.95
Grades: 7 8 9 10   **Fic**
1. Fantasy fiction 2. Music -- Fiction 3. Fairies -- Fiction 4. Princesses -- Fiction
ISBN 978-0-8050-8276-0; 0-8050-8276-X
                                                  LC 2007-41958
Heartsick at losing her two dearest companions, Princess Aurelie finds comfort in the glorious music of the faeries, but the duties of the court call her, as do the needs of her friends.

"Graceful prose leads the reader through a complex chronological narrative and a Shakespearean tangle of love stories." Booklist

★ The **swan** maiden. Henry Holt 2007 292p $16.95
Grades: 6 7 8 9   **Fic**
1. Fairy tales 2. Magic -- Fiction
ISBN 978-0-8050-8275-3; 0-8050-8275-1
                                                  LC 2006-33774
Raised as a chastelaine-in-training unlike her sisters who are learning the arts of sorcery, Doucette discovers when she is sixteen years old that she too has magic in her blood, and she must brave her mother's wrath-and the loss of the man she loves-in order to follow her birthright.

"Layered, elegantly written, and filled with unexpected twists and turns, TheSwan Maiden soars with grace and power." Booklist

★ **Toads** and diamonds. Henry Holt 2010 278p $16.99
Grades: 8 9 10 11 12   **Fic**
1. Fairy tales 2. India -- Fiction
ISBN 978-0-8050-8968-4; 0-8050-8968-3
                                                  LC 2009-23448
A retelling of the Perrault fairy tale set in pre-colonial India, in which two stepsisters receive gifts from a goddess and each walks her own path to find her gift's purpose, discovering romance along the way.

The author "creates a vivid setting. Lavish details starkly contrast the two girls' lives and personalities. . . . The complexities of the cultural backstory pose a challenge to readers, but this beautifully embroidered adventure is well worth the effort." Booklist

Tooke, Wes

King of the mound; my summer with Satchel Paige. Simon & Schuster Books for Young Readers 2012 155p $15.99

Grades: 4 5 6　　　　　　　　　　　　　　　**Fic**

1. Baseball players 2. Baseball -- Fiction 3. People with disabilities -- Fiction 4. Poliomyelitis -- Fiction 5. African Americans -- Fiction 6. Father-son relationship -- Fiction

ISBN 978-1-4424-3346-5; 1-4424-3346-9

LC 2011012740

Twelve-year-old Nick loves baseball so after a year in the hospital fighting polio and with a brace on one leg, Nick takes a job with the minor league team for which his father is catcher and gets to see the great pitcher, Satchel Paige, play during the 1935 season. Includes historical notes.

"Tooke sticks closely to historical records, with the addition of a few extra Paige exploits and aphorisms, and . . . the fictional overlay offers a comfortably predictable 'hard work brings just rewards' arc. Nourishing fare for Matt Christopher graduates." Kirkus

Towell, Ann

Grease town. Tundra Books 2010 232p $19.99

Grades: 5 6 7 8　　　　　　　　　　　　　　**Fic**

1. Canada -- Fiction 2. Race relations -- Fiction

ISBN 0-88776-983-7; 978-0-88776-983-2

"When twelve-year-old Titus Sullivan decides to run away to join his Uncle Amos and older brother, Lem, he finds an alien and exciting world in Oil Springs, the first Canadian oil boomtown of the 19th century. The Enniskillen swamp is slick with oil, and it takes enterprising folk to plumb its depths. The adventurers who work there are a tough lot of individuals. In this hard world, Titus becomes friends with a young black boy, the child of slaves who came to Canada on the Underground Railroad. When tragedy strikes in the form of a race riot, Titus's loyalties are tested." (Publisher's note) "Ages ten to fourteen." (Quill Quire)

"In 1863, oil has recently been discovered in Oil Springs, Ontario, and a variety of people, black and white, and from many different walks of life, are settling there. Orphans Lem and Titus Sullivan live in their aunt's stuffy and regimented house. When 19-year-old Lem sets out for Oil Springs, 13-year-old Titus stows away in his brother's wagon. . . . Towell skillfully creates the setting of this mucky little town and its colorful inhabitants. Titus, who narrates, has a voice that is believable and uncontrived. . . . Supporting characters are equally strong and well developed. . . . Towell has created a strong narrator and a compelling plot." SLJ

Towell, Katy

Skary childrin and the carousel of sorrow. Alfred A. Knopf 2011 265p $16.99; lib bdg $19.99; ebook $16.99

Grades: 4 5 6 7　　　　　　　　　　　　　　**Fic**

1. Ghost stories 2. School stories 3. Supernatural

-- Fiction

ISBN 978-0-375-86859-7; 0-375-86859-3; 978-0-375-96860-0 lib bdg; 0-375-96860-1 lib bdg; 978-0-375-89931-7 e-book; 0-375-89931-6 e-book

LC 2010-38830

In Widowsbury, an isolated village where people believe "known is good, new is bad," three outcasts from the girls' school join forces with a home-schooled boy to uncover and combat the evil that is making people disappear.

"Towell tucks violent tempests, maggoty slime, hideous transformations, nightmares, sudden terrors and like atmosphere-building elements into a rousingly melodramatic literary debut." Kirkus

Townley, Rod

The blue shoe; a tale of thievery, villainy, sorcery, and shoes. by Roderick Townley; illustrated by Mary GrandPré. Alfred A. Knopf 2009 254p il $16.99; lib bdg $19.99

Grades: 4 5 6 7　　　　　　　　　　　　　　**Fic**

1. Fables 2. Fairy tales

ISBN 978-0-375-85600-6; 0-375-85600-5; 978-0-375-95600-3 lib bdg; 0-375-95600-X lib bdg

LC 2008-43851

A mysterious stranger commissions a single, valuable shoe from a humble cobbler, changing the cobbler's life and the life of his young apprentice forever.

"This is a "fun, whimsical fairy tale. . . . The good-versus-evil plotline, dynamic cast of characters, . . . light romance between Hap and Sophia, and copious amounts of magic and intrigue will be a hit with a wide range of readers." Booklist

Sky; a novel in three sets and an encore. by Roderick Townley. 1st ed; Atheneum Books for Young Readers 2004 265p $16.95

Grades: 7 8 9 10　　　　　　　　　　　　　**Fic**

1. Jazz musicians -- Fiction 2. New York (N.Y.) -- Fiction

ISBN 0-689-85712-8

LC 2003-11354

In New York City in 1959, fifteen-year-old Alec Schuyler, at odds with his widowed father over his love of music, finds a mentor and friend in a blind, black jazz musician.

"Townley presents a compassionate portrait of a young man who is battling for his own place in life and sets the story in the exciting time of the beat poets and the explosive development of jazz music." SLJ

Townley, Roderick

The door in the forest; [by] Roderick Townley. Alfred A. Knopf 2011 245p $16.99; lib bdg $19.99

Grades: 4 5 6　　　　　　　　　　　　　　　**Fic**

1. Magic -- Fiction 2. Honesty -- Fiction 3. Soldiers -- Fiction 4. Space and time -- Fiction

ISBN 0-375-85601-3; 0-375-95601-8 lib bdg; 978-0-375-85601-3; 978-0-375-95601-0 lib bdg

LC 2010034710

While trying to outwit the soldiers who are occupying their small town, fourteen-year-old Daniel, who cannot lie, and Emily, who discovers she has magical powers, are inexplicably drawn to a mysterious island in the heart of the forest where townsfolk have been warned never to go. "Intermediate." (Horn Book)

"Townley's fanciful story swings like a pendulum from Wild West tall tale to a vague mysticism that is enlivened by colorful imagery. . . . At its considerable best, it is quirky and engaging; sentences hurry purposefully along, deepening atmosphere, theme, and plot." Horn Book

Townsend, Wendy

★ **Lizard** love; [by] Wendy Townsend. Front Street 2008 196p $17.95

Grades: 6 7 8 9   **Fic**
   1. Reptiles -- Fiction 2. Country life -- Fiction 3. New York (N.Y.) -- Fiction 4. City and town life -- Fiction
   ISBN 978-1-932425-34-5; 1-932425-34-9
                      LC 2007017975

Grace, a teenager, and her mother have moved to Manhattan where she feels alienated and out of place, far from the ponds and farm where she grew up playing with bullfrogs and lizards, until she finds Fang & Claw, a reptile store, and meets the owner's son, Walter.

"Townsend displays a remarkable narrative gift. . . . Her sensitive herpetological descriptions are unflinching, evocative, and positively elegant. Even minor characterizations are full and complex." Booklist

★ The **sundown** rule. Namelos 2011 128p $18.95

Grades: 5 6 7 8   **Fic**
   1. Aunts -- Fiction 2. Uncles -- Fiction 3. Wildlife conservation -- Fiction 4. Father-daughter relationship -- Fiction
   ISBN 1-60898-099-5; 978-1-60898-099-4

Louise and her dad live an idyllic life surrounded by nature. When he gets an assignment to go to Brazil to write an article for a magazine, Louise has to go live in a suburb with her aunt and uncle, leaving her cat, Cash, behind, since Aunt Kay is allergic to animals. Her dad says that it will be for only six weeks, and that everything will be okay. But it isn't, especially when Cash gets hit by a car and dies. And when a new friend's dad shoots a crow for no reason. And when her own dad gets sick, really sick, and might not be coming home.

"Townsend builds a rich, moving story that is refreshing for its subject matter and lyrical realism." Publ Wkly

Tracy, Kristen

Bessica Lefter bites back; by Kristen Tracy. Delacorte Press 2012 263 p. $16.99

Grades: 4 5 6 7   **Fic**
   1. Gifts -- Fiction 2. Mascots -- Fiction 3. Middle schools -- Fiction 4. School children -- Fiction 5. Friendship -- Fiction 6. Schools -- Fiction
   ISBN 9780385740692; 0385740697
                      LC 2011045677

In this children's book, "[s]ixth-grader Bessica's new middle-school persona meets a host of problems, including mending a friendship damaged by mean text messages, facing a bully in her first outing as team mascot and coming to terms with her grandmother's boyfriend. . . . Rumor has it the opposing mascot in the first game will facebomb her. Neither Bessica nor readers learn what facebombing

actually is in this context until after the disastrous event." (Kirkus Reviews)

The **reinvention** of Bessica Lefter. Delacorte Press 2011 305p $15.99

Grades: 4 5 6 7   **Fic**
   1. School stories 2. Idaho -- Fiction 3. Friendship -- Fiction
   ISBN 978-0-385-90634-0; 0-385-90634-X
                      LC 2010-04844

Eleven-year-old Bessica's plans to begin North Teton Middle School as a new person begin to fall apart even before school begins.

Tracy "offers a positive and comforting message about learning to make adjustments, ending the book on a happy note, with Bessica finding her niche as school mascot." Publ Wkly

Sharks & boys. Hyperion 2011 272p $16.99

Grades: 6 7 8 9   **Fic**
   1. Ships -- Fiction 2. Twins -- Fiction 3. Siblings -- Fiction 4. Survival after airplane accidents, shipwrecks, etc. -- Fiction
   ISBN 978-1-4231-4354-3; 1-4231-4354-X
                      LC 2011-04803

Feeling betrayed, fifteen-year-old Enid follows her boyfriend, Wick, from Vermont to Maryland where he and six others they know from twin studies rent a yacht, but after she sneaks aboard a storm sets them adrift without food or water, fighting for survival.

"A page-turning thriller, . . . this emotionally complex novel makes everyone's worst beach nightmare palpable and provides a fascinating character study that explores what happens when instincts are pitted against relationships." Booklist

Too cool for this school; Kristen Tracy. Delacorte Press 2013 288 p. (hardback) $16.99

Grades: 5 6 7   **Fic**
   1. School stories 2. Female friendship -- Fiction 3. Cousins -- Fiction 4. Schools -- Fiction 5. Friendship -- Fiction 6. Family life -- Fiction 7. Middle schools -- Fiction 8. Conduct of life -- Fiction
   ISBN 0385740700; 9780375989629; 9780385740708
                      LC 2013011084

In this book, "Lane Cisco works hard to be popular and, as a result, her life is pretty perfect. She has three amazing best friends and a 'secret boyfriend' . . . . Best of all, Lane has just been chosen to be sixth-grade class captain, a pinnacle of popularity. These successes are thrown into flux when her Alaskan cousin Angelina (nicknamed Mint) comes to stay for a month." Mint ignores all social cues, befriends Lane's secret boyfriend, and goes after Lane's friend Ava's crush. (Publishers Weekly)

Trafton, Jennifer

★ The **rise** and fall of Mount Majestic; illustrations by Brett Helquist. Dial Books for Young Readers 2010 338p il $16.99

Grades: 4 5 6 7   **Fic**
1. Fairy tales 2. Adventure fiction 3. Giants -- Fiction
ISBN 978-0-8037-3375-6; 0-8037-3375-5

LC 2009-51659

Ten-year-old Persimmony Smudge, who longs for heroic adventures, overhears a secret that thrusts her into the middle of a dangerous mission that could destroy the island on which she lives.

"Trafton imbues her tale with a delightful sense of fun and fascinating, well-rounded characters-playful wordsmithing and flowing dialogue make this an excellent choice for bedtime read-aloud." Publ Wkly

Tregay, Sarah

Love and leftovers; a novel in verse. Katherine Tegen Books 2011 432p $17.99

Grades: 7 8 9 10   **Fic**
1. Novels in verse 2. Iowa -- Fiction 3. Moving -- Fiction 4. Bisexuality -- Fiction 5. Family life -- Fiction 6. New Hampshire -- Fiction
ISBN 978-0-06-202358-2; 0-06-202358-6

LC 2011019367

When her father starts dating a man, fifteen-year-old Marcie's depressed mother takes her to New Hampshire but just as Marcie starts falling for a great guy her father brings her back to Iowa, where all of her relationships have become strained.

"Tregay's choice to write in verse works well, her spare but effective language artfully evoking what otherwise might be a conventional highschool romance. . . . The father's completely accepted gay relationship, although mostly in the background, adds an element of interest. It all feels realistic and makes for an interesting, attractive novel. A verse novel with real depth." Kirkus

Treggiari, Jo

Ashes, ashes. Scholastic Press 2011 360p $17.99

Grades: 7 8 9 10   **Fic**
1. Science fiction 2. Dogs -- Fiction 3. Epidemics -- Fiction 4. New York (N.Y.) -- Fiction
ISBN 978-0-545-25563-9; 0-545-25563-5

LC 2010032398

In a future Manhattan devastated by environmental catastrophes and epidemics, sixteen-year-old Lucy survives alone until vicious hounds target her and force her to join Aidan and his band, but soon they learn that she is the target of Sweepers, who kidnap and infect people with plague.

"The tense plot, cinematic moments, and highly capable protagonists make this a fast, gripping read." Publ Wkly

Trigiani, Adriana

Viola in reel life. HarperTeen 2009 282p $16.99

Grades: 7 8 9 10   **Fic**
1. Ghost stories 2. School stories 3. Indiana -- Fiction 4. Video recording -- Fiction 5. Dating (Social customs) -- Fiction
ISBN 978-0-06-145102-7; 0-06-145102-9

LC 2009-14269

When fourteen-year-old Viola is sent from her beloved Brooklyn to boarding school in Indiana for ninth grade, she overcomes her initial reservations as she makes friends

with her roommates, goes on a real date, and uses the unsettling ghost she keeps seeing as the subject of a short film—her first.

This "is a sweet, character-driven story. Viola is very real, as are her feelings, hopes, desires, and dreams." SLJ

Followed by: Viola in the spotlight (2011)

Viola in the spotlight. HarperTeen 2011 283p $16.99

Grades: 7 8 9 10   **Fic**
1. Theater -- Fiction 2. Family life -- Fiction 3. Dating (Social customs) -- Fiction 4. Brooklyn (New York, N.Y.) -- Fiction
ISBN 978-0-06-145105-8; 0-06-145105-3

LC 2010045553

Sequel to: Viola in reel life (2009)

Back home in Brooklyn, fifteen-year-old Viola has big summer plans but with one best friend going to camp and the other not only working but experiencing her first crush, Viola is glad to be overworked as an unpaid lighting intern when her grandmother's play goes to Broadway.

"An equally enjoyable follow-up to Viola in Reel Life." Booklist

Tripp, Ben

The **accidental** highwayman; being the tale of Kit Bristol, his horse Midnight, a mysterious princess, and sundry magical persons besides. Ben Tripp. Tor Teen 2014 304 p. illustrations (hardback) $17.99

Grades: 7 8 9 10   **Fic**
1. Magic -- Fiction 2. Adventure fiction 3. Fairies -- Fiction 4. Princesses -- Fiction 5. Great Britain -- Fiction 6. Fate and fatalism -- Fiction 7. Robbers and outlaws -- Fiction 8. Adventure and adventurers -- Fiction 9. Great Britain -- History -- George III, 1760-1820 -- Fiction
ISBN 0765335492; 9780765335494

LC 2014033724

In this book, by Ben Tripp, "Christopher 'Kit' Bristol is the unwitting servant of notorious highwayman Whistling Jack. One dark night, Kit finds his master bleeding from a mortal wound, dons the man's riding cloak to seek help, and changes the course of his life forever. Mistaken for Whistling Jack and on the run from redcoats . . . Kit takes up his master's quest to rescue a rebellious fairy princess from an arranged marriage to King George III of England." (Publisher's note)

"Readers will root for star-crossed lovers, Kit and Morgana, and delight in their 'opposites attract' romance, drawn onward by a rollicking plot . . . Fantasy readers, especially fans of Cathrynne Valente's work, will enjoy the author's elegant turns of phrase. A first purchase for all fantasy collections." SLJ

Trueman, Terry

★ **7** days at the hot corner. HarperTempest 2007 160p $15.99

Grades: 7 8 9 10   **Fic**
1. Baseball -- Fiction 2. Friendship -- Fiction 3. Homosexuality -- Fiction
ISBN 978-0-06-057494-9; 0-06-057494-1

LC 2006-03706

Varsity baseball player Scott Latimer struggles with his own prejudices and those of others when his best friend reveals that he is gay.

This "suspenseful story is enhanced by some late-inning surprises, the gay subplot is treated with honesty and integrity, and Scott and Travis are believable, sympathetic characters." Booklist

★ **Cruise** control; 1st ed; HarperTempest 2004 149p $15.99; lib bdg $16.89; pa $8.99

Grades: 7 8 9 10   **Fic**
   1. Brothers -- Fiction 2. Basketball -- Fiction 3. Cerebral palsy -- Fiction 4. Father-son relationship -- Fiction
   ISBN 0-06-623960-5; 0-06-623961-3 lib bdg; 0-06-447377-5 pa
                                                          LC 2003-19822

A talented basketball player struggles to deal with the helplessness and anger that come with having a brother rendered completely dysfunctional by severe cerebral palsy and a father who deserted the family.

"This powerful tale is extremely well written and will give readers an understanding of what it's like to have a challenged sibling." SLJ

Hurricane; a novel. HarperCollins 2008 137p $15.99; lib bdg $16.89

Grades: 5 6 7   **Fic**
   1. Honduras -- Fiction 2. Hurricanes -- Fiction 3. Survival after airplane accidents, shipwrecks, etc. -- Fiction
   ISBN 978-0-06-000018-9; 0-06-000018-X; 978-0-06-000019-6 lib bdg; 0-06-000019-8 lib bdg
                                                          LC 2007-02990

A revised edition of Swallowing the sun, published 2004 in the United Kingdom

"Thirteen-year-old Jose lives with his family in Honduras. A hurricane hits, causing the recently clear-cut hillside adjacent to his village to become a mudslide that smothers and kills most of its fifty inhabitants. . . . Jose quickly takes charge and becomes a resourceful member of his ailing community. This survival tale is concise but engaging. Trueman's descriptions of the village buried in mud and of the difficulties it creates for the survivors are vivid." Voice Youth Advocates

★ **Inside** out. HarperTempest 2003 117p hardcover o.p. pa $8.99

Grades: 7 8 9 10   **Fic**
   1. Suicide -- Fiction 2. Hostages -- Fiction 3. Mentally ill -- Fiction 4. Schizophrenia -- Fiction 5. Juvenile delinquency -- Fiction
   ISBN 0-06-623962-1; 0-06-447376-7 pa
                                                          LC 2002-151604

A sixteen-year-old with schizophrenia is caught up in the events surrounding an attempted robbery by two other teens who eventually hold him hostage.

"Trueman sometimes captures moments of heartbreaking truth, and his swift, suspenseful plot will have particular appeal to reluctant readers." Booklist

Life happens next; a novel. Terry Trueman. HarperTeen 2012 132 p. (trade bdg.) $17.99

Grades: 7 8 9 10   **Fic**
   1. Love stories 2. Down syndrome -- Fiction 3. Cerebral palsy -- Fiction 4. Dogs -- Fiction 5. Communication -- Fiction 6. Seattle (Wash.) -- Fiction 7. Special education -- Fiction 8. People with disabilities -- Fiction 9. Family life -- Washington (State) -- Seattle -- Fiction
   ISBN 0062028030; 9780062028037; 9780062028051
                                                          LC 2011044627

Sequel to: Stuck in neutral

This book is the sequel to author Terry Trueman's "Stuck in Neutral." Here, Shawn McDaniel, who has cerebral palsy, "fantasizes about his sister's best friend, Ally, and what it would be like if he ever got up the courage to tell her how he felt about her." He is also dealing with "Debi, [who] moves in with them. . . . Debi has Down's syndrome and is often disruptive, but . . . she becomes the first person to connect with Shawn on more than a surface level." (Voice of Youth Advocates)

★ **Stuck** in neutral. HarperCollins Pubs. 2000 114p $14.95; lib bdg $16.89; pa $6.99

Grades: 7 8 9 10   **Fic**
   1. Euthanasia -- Fiction 2. Cerebral palsy -- Fiction 3. Father-son relationship -- Fiction
   ISBN 0-06-028519-2; 0-06-028518-4 lib bdg; 0-06-447213-2 pa
                                                          LC 99-37098

Michael L. Printz Award honor book, 2001

Fourteen-year-old Shawn McDaniel, who suffers from severe cerebral palsy and cannot function, relates his perceptions of his life, his family, and his condition, especially as he believes his father is planning to kill him.

"Trueman has created a compelling novel that poses questions about ability and existence while fostering sympathy for people with severe physical limitations." Bull Cent Child Books

Tubb, Kristin O'Donnell

The **13th** sign; Kristin O'Donnell Tubb. Feiwel and Friends 2013 272 p. $16.99

Grades: 6 7 8 9   **Fic**
   1. Astrology -- Fiction 2. Occult fiction 3. Zodiac -- Fiction 4. Supernatural -- Fiction 5. Books and reading -- Fiction 6. New Orleans (La.) -- Fiction 7. Adventure and adventurers -- Fiction
   ISBN 0312583524; 9780312583521
                                                          LC 2012034058

In this juvenile astrology-themed fantasy novel, by Kristin O'Donnell Tubb, "when a teen accidentally unlocks the lost 13th zodiac sign, everyone's personality shifts, and she must confront 12 Keepers of the zodiac to restore global order. . . . Unless she can find and restore Ophiuchus to the heavens within 23 hours, all personality changes will be permanent. To do this, Jalen must destroy 12 Keepers who protect Ophiuchus." (Kirkus Reviews)

★ **Selling** hope. Feiwel and Friends 2010 215p $16.99

Grades: 6 7 8   **Fic**
   1. Comets -- Fiction 2. Mothers -- Fiction 3. Magic

tricks -- Fiction 4. Single parent family -- Fiction

ISBN 978-0-312-61122-4; 0-312-61122-6

LC 2010-12571

In 1910, just before the earth passes through the tail of Halley's Comet, thirteen-year-old Hope McDaniels, whose father is a magician in a traveling vaudeville show, tries to earn enough money to quit the circuit by selling "anti-comet pills," with the help of fellow-performer Buster Keaton.

"Tubb deftly ingrains a thoughtful ethical question into the story . . . but never overdoes it in this bouncy tale populated by a terrific cast of characters." Booklist

Tullson, Diane

Riley Park. Orca Book Publishers 2009 102p (Orca soundings) $16.95; pa $9.95

Grades: 7 8 9 10   **Fic**

1. Homicide -- Fiction 2. Friendship -- Fiction 3. Bereavement -- Fiction 4. Brain -- Wounds and injuries -- Fiction

ISBN 978-1-55469-124-1; 1-55469-124-9; 978-1-55469-123-4 pa; 1-55469-123-0 pa

After Corbin and his best friend Darius are attacked in Riley Park, Corbin must cope with the loss of his friend, his physical impairments, and finding the culprit.

This is "a suspenseful, tightly plotted story that manages . . . to create both a memorable protagonist and a thought-provoking, emotionally involving story." Booklist

Tunnell, Michael O.

Moon without magic. Dutton Children's Books 2007 218p hardcover o.p. pa $8.99

Grades: 6 7 8 9   **Fic**

1. Magic -- Fiction 2. Orphans -- Fiction 3. Middle East -- Fiction

ISBN 978-0-525-47729-7; 978-1-461-11288-4 pa; 1-461-11288-5 pa

LC 2006102951

Sequel to: Wishing moon (2004)

Aminah's magic lamp is stolen, and the primary suspect is Idris the storyteller.

This is a "fast-paced adventure." SLJ

Wishing moon. Dutton Children's Books 2004 272p hardcover o.p. pa $9.99

Grades: 6 7 8 9   **Fic**

1. Magic -- Fiction 2. Orphans -- Fiction 3. Middle East -- Fiction

ISBN 0-525-47193-6; 978-1-460-93919-2 pa; 1-460-93919-0 pa

LC 2003-62486

After a fourteen-year-old orphan named Aminah comes to possess a magic lamp, the wishes granted her by the genie inside it allow her to alter her life by choosing prosperity, purpose, and romance.

"Aminah strives to do good with her magic, and yet the tale skips preachiness and goes for rich characterizations and a strong, suspenseful plot worthy of the Arabian Nights." Booklist

Another title about Aminah is:

Moon without magic (2007)

Turnage, Sheila

★ The **ghosts** of Tupelo Landing; by Sheila Turnage. Kathy Dawson Books 2014 368 p. (hardcover) $16.99

Grades: 5 6 7 8   **Fic**

1. Ghost stories 2. Hotels and motels 3. City and town life -- Fiction 4. Ghosts -- Fiction 5. Hotels -- Fiction 6. Identity -- Fiction 7. Foundlings -- Fiction 8. Haunted places -- Fiction 9. North Carolina -- Fiction 10. Mystery and detective stories 11. Community life -- North Carolina -- Fiction

ISBN 0803736711; 9780803736719

LC 2013019376

In this book, by Sheila Turnage, "when Miss Lana makes an Accidental Bid at the Tupelo auction and winds up the mortified owner of an old inn, she doesn't realize there's a ghost in the fine print. Naturally, Desperado Detective Agency (aka Mo and Dale) opens a paranormal division to solve the mystery of the ghost's identity. But Mo and Dale start to realize . . . [p]eople can also be haunted by their own past." (Publisher's note)

★ **Three** times lucky; by Sheila Turnage. Dial Books for Young Readers 2012 256 p. (hardcover) $16.99

Grades: 5 6 7 8   **Fic**

1. Absent mothers -- Fiction 2. Adopted children -- Fiction 3. Abandoned children -- Fiction 4. Murder -- Fiction 5. Identity -- Fiction 6. Foundlings -- Fiction 7. Restaurants -- Fiction 8. North Carolina -- Fiction 9. Mystery and detective stories 10. Community life -- North Carolina -- Fiction

ISBN 0803736703; 9780803736702

LC 2011035027

John Newbery Honor Book (2013)

This is the story of Mo LoBeau, who washed downstream as an infant 11 years ago and who has since been in the care of the Colonel, "a stranger who can't remember anything about his own past," and "Miss Lana, owner of the Tupelo Cafe. Mo . . . loves the Colonel and Lana, but" wonders about her origins. She "send[s] messages in bottles to her 'Upstream Mother.'" Also featured are "an out-of-town detective, a dead body . . . , a long-forgotten bank robbery, and a kidnapping." (Publishers Weekly)

Turner, Ann Warren

Father of lies; [by] Ann Turner. HarperTeen 2011 247p $16.99

Grades: 7 8 9 10   **Fic**

1. Witchcraft -- Fiction 2. Salem (Mass.) -- Fiction 3. Manic-depressive illness -- Fiction

ISBN 978-0-06-137085-4; 0-06-137085-1

LC 2010-15224

In 1692 when a plague of accusations descends on Salem Village in Massachusetts and "witch fever" erupts, fourteen-year-old Lidda, who has begun to experience visions and hear voices, tries to expose the lies of the witch trials without being hanged as a witch herself. Includes author's notes about the Salem Witch Trials and bipolar disease.

"Turner perfectly captures the nightmare nature of Salem's witchcraft period and of some of the outside forces that may have fueled it. . . . Yet the town's issues play a secondary role in Lidda's own believable struggles with enc-roaching insanity—or an otherworldly paranormal force: an appraisal left for engaged readers to make." Kirkus

Includes bibliographical references

Hard hit; [by] Ann Turner. Scholastic Press 2006 167p $16.99

Grades: 7 8 9 10 **Fic**

1. Novels in verse 2. Death -- Fiction 3. Cancer -- Fiction 4. Baseball -- Fiction 5. Father-son relationship -- Fiction

ISBN 0-439-29680-3

LC 2005-49906

A rising high school baseball star faces his most difficult challenge when his father is diagnosed with pancreatic cancer.

This is a "novel in verse that speaks volumes long after the book is closed." Voice Youth Advocates

Turner, Max

End of days. St. Martin's Griffin 2010 296p (Night runner) pa $9.99

Grades: 7 8 9 10 **Fic**

1. Vampires -- Fiction 2. Supernatural -- Fiction

ISBN 978-0-312-59252-3; 0-312-59252-3

LC 2010-30191

Sequel to: Night runner (2009)

While Charlie struggles with his vampirism, he, Zack, and their friends are pulled into a conflict with the mysterious Mr. Hyde, a creature who hunts vampires.

"The well-developed characters add dimension to the story line, and Zack's witty and sarcastic humor makes this a truly enjoyable read." SLJ

Night runner. St. Martin's Griffin 2009 261p pa $9.99

Grades: 7 8 9 10 **Fic**

1. Vampires -- Fiction

ISBN 978-0-312-59228-8; 0-312-59228-0

LC 2009-16672

Fifteen-year-old Zach is quite content living in a mental ward because of his unusual allergies until dark secrets about his past, his parents, and his strange sickness slowly surface, placing him in great danger

"This fast-paced vampire story featuring a likable character with a strong voice will appeal to a broad teen audience." Booklist

Followed by: End of days (2010)

Turner, Megan Whalen

A **conspiracy** of kings. Greenwillow Books 2010 316p $16.99; lib bdg $17.89

Grades: 7 8 9 10 **Fic**

1. Adventure fiction 2. Princes -- Fiction 3. Kidnapping -- Fiction 4. Kings and rulers -- Fiction

ISBN 978-0-06-187093-4; 0-06-187093-5; 978-0-06-187094-1 lib bdg; 0-06-187094-3 lib bdg

LC 2009-23052

Boston Globe-Horn Book Honor: Fiction (2010)

Kidnapped and sold into slavery, Sophos, an unwilling prince, tries to save his country from being destroyed by rebellion and exploited by the conniving Mede empire.

"Given the complexity of Turner's plot, readers should reread the first three books before beginning this one, which derives its power from the intricate construction of Turner's imagined world, a realm in which her founding mythology is as impressive as her descriptions of the land itself. . . . Strong evidence emerges that the story doesn't end here, and fans will savor this while they wait for more." Publ Wkly

★ The **thief**. Greenwillow Bks. 1996 219p $17.99; pa $6.99

Grades: 7 8 9 10 **Fic**

1. Adventure fiction 2. Thieves -- Fiction

ISBN 0-688-14627-9; 0-06-082497-2 pa

LC 95-41040

A Newbery Medal honor book, 1997

"A tantalizing, suspenseful, exceptionally clever novel. . . . The author's characterization of Gen is simply superb." Horn Book

"Gen languishes in prison for boasting of his skill as a thief. The magus—the king's powerful advisor—needing a clever thief to find an ancient ring that gives the owner the right to rule a neighboring country, bails Gen out. Their journey toward the treasure is marked by danger and political intrigue, and features a motley cast, tales of old gods, and the revelation of Gen's true identity." Publisher's note

Other titles in this series are:

A conspiracy of kings (2010)

The King of Attolia (2006)

The Queen of Attolia (2000)

Twain, Mark, 1835-1910

★ The **adventures** of Tom Sawyer; illustrated by Barry Moser; afterword by Peter Glassman. Books of Wonder 1989 261p il $24.99

Grades: 5 6 7 8 **Fic**

1. Missouri -- Fiction 2. Mississippi River -- Fiction

ISBN 0-688-07510-X

First published 1876

The adventures and pranks of a mischievous boy growing up in a Mississippi River town on the early nineteenth century.

The **prince** and the pauper; introduction by Christopher Paul Curtis. Modern Library 2003 211p (The Modern Library classics) pa $8.95

Grades: 5 6 7 8 9 10 11 12 Adult **Fic**

1. Kings 2. Great Britain -- History -- 1485-1603, Tudors -- Fiction

ISBN 0-375-76112-8

LC 2002-26302

First published 1881

"Edward VI of England and a little pauper change places a few days before Henry VIII's death. The prince wanders in rags, while Tom Canty suffers the horrors of princedom. At the last moment, the mistake is rectified." Reader's Ency. 4th edition

Twomey, Cathleen

Beachmont letters. Boyds Mills Press 2003 223p $16.95

Grades: 7 8 9 10   **Fic**
1. Fires -- Fiction 2. Burns and scalds -- Fiction
ISBN 1-59078-050-7
LC 2002-111301

Scarred by a fire that killed her father, a seventeen-year-old girl begins a correspondence with a young soldier in 1944

This "has plenty of atmosphere and an appealing, courageous heroine who gradually realizes her own strength. This unusual survivor/love story is certain to be a three-hanky read." Booklist

Uchida, Yoshiko

★ A **jar** of dreams. Atheneum Pubs. 1981 131p hardcover o.p. pa $4.99
Grades: 5 6 7 8   **Fic**
1. California -- Fiction 2. Prejudices -- Fiction 3. Family life -- Fiction 4. Japanese Americans -- Fiction
ISBN 0-689-50210-9; 0-689-71672-9 pa
LC 81-3480

"Rinko in her guilelessness is genuine and refreshing, and her worries and concerns seem wholly natural, honest, and convincing." Horn Book

"A story of the Depression Era is told by eleven-year-old Rinko, the only girl in a Japanese-American family living in Oakland and suffering under the double burden of financial pressure and the prejudice that had increased with the tension of economic competition. Into the household comes a visitor who is a catalyst for change." Bull Cent Child Books

Other titles about Rinko Tsujimura and her family are:
The best bad thing (1983)
The happiest ending (1985)

★ **Journey** to Topaz; a story of the Japanese-American evacuation. illustrated by Donald Carrick. Heyday Books 2005 149p il pa $9.95
Grades: 5 6 7 8   **Fic**
1. World War, 1939-1945 -- Fiction 2. Japanese Americans -- Evacuation and relocation, 1942-1945 -- Fiction
ISBN 978-1-890771-91-1 pa; 1-890771-91-0 pa
LC 2004-16537
First published 1971 by Scribner

After the Pearl Harbor attack an eleven-year-old Japanese-American girl and her family are forced to go to an aliens camp in Utah
Followed by: Journey home (1978)

Uehashi, Nahoko

★ **Moribito**; Guardian of the Spirit. [by] Nahoko Uehashi; translated by Cathy Hirano; illustrated by Yuko Shimizu. Arthur A. Levine Books 2008 248p il $17.99
Grades: 6 7 8 9   **Fic**
1. Fantasy fiction 2. Japan -- Fiction 3. Martial arts -- Fiction
ISBN 978-0-5450-0542-5; 0-5450-0542-6

The wandering warrior Balsa is hired to protect Prince Chagum from both a mysterious monster and the prince's father, the Mikado.

"This book is first in a series of ten that have garnered literary and popular success in Japan. . . . Balsa and Cha-

gum's story is brought to America with a strong translation. . . . Readers who are fans of action manga, especially with strong female characters, will enjoy the ninja-like fighting scenes. . . . The exciting premise, combined with an attractive cover, should insure that this title will circulate well." Voice Youth Advocates

Followed by: Moribito II: Guardian of the Darkness (2009)

Moribito II; Guardian of the Darkness. by Nahoko Uehashi; translated by Cathy Hirano; illustrated by Yuko Shimizu. Arthur A. Levine Books 2009 245p il $17.99
Grades: 6 7 8 9   **Fic**
1. Fantasy fiction
ISBN 978-0-545-10295-7; 0-545-10295-2
LC 2008-37444
Sequel to: Moribito: Guardian of the Spirit (2008)
ALA ALSC Batchelder Award Honor Book (2010)

The wandering female bodyguard Balsa returns to her native country of Kanbal, where she uncovers a conspiracy to frame her mentor and herself.

"Once again, Uehashi immerses readers in the culture, traditions, mythology--even diet--of the populace, creating a full, captivating world. . . . This growing series has something for everyone." Publ Wkly

Umansky, Kaye

Solomon Snow and the stolen jewel. Candlewick Press 2007 245p $12.99
Grades: 5 6 7 8   **Fic**
1. Orphans -- Fiction
ISBN 978-0-7636-2793-5; 0-7636-2793-3
LC 2006-47331
Sequel to: The silver spoon of Solomon Snow (2005)

While trying to rescue Prudence's father from prison, Solomon, Prudence, the Infant Prodigy, and Mr. Skippy the rabbit find themselves caught up in the mad plans of the villainous Dr. Calimari to steal a fabulous and cursed ruby.

"Fans of Lemony Snicket will enjoy this fast-paced read. . . . Reluctant readers might find the short chapters, silly comedy, and simple characters attractive." SLJ

Unsworth, Tania

The **one** safe place; a novel. by Tania Unsworth. Algonquin Young Readers 2014 304 p. $15.95
Grades: 6 7 8 9 10   **Fic**
1. Dystopian fiction 2. Orphans -- Fiction 3. Survival skills -- Fiction 4. Abandoned children -- Fiction 5. Science fiction 6. Survival -- Fiction
ISBN 1616203293; 9781616203290
LC 2013043145

This book, by Tania Unsworth, is a "near-future dystopia. . . . Devin doesn't remember life before the world got hot; he has grown up farming the scorched earth with his grandfather in their remote valley. When his grandfather dies, Devin heads for the city. Once there, among the stark glass buildings, he finds scores of children, just like him, living alone on the streets. They tell him rumors of a place for abandoned children, . . . but only the luckiest get there." (Publisher's note)

"Orphaned twelve-year-old Devin is invited to live at the paradisaical Home for Childhood, but something terrifying is happening to the children there. Devin's synesthesia, which makes him interesting to the Home's sinister Administrator, may provide the key to their escape. Set in a world of post climate change desperation, Unsworth's story thoughtfully explores the theme of adults' nostalgia for childhood." Horn Book

Updale, Eleanor

★ **Montmorency**; thief, liar, gentleman? Orchard Books 2004 232p $16.95

Grades: 6 7 8 9 10   **Fic**

1. Thieves -- Fiction 2. London (England) -- Fiction 3. Great Britain -- History -- 19th century -- Fiction

ISBN 0-439-58035-8

LC 2003-56345

First published 2003 in the United Kingdom

In Victorian London, after his life is saved by a young physician, a thief utilizes the knowledge he gains in prison and from the scientific lectures he attends as the physician's case study exhibit to create a new, highly successful, double life for himself.

"Updale adroitly works the tradition of devilish schemes and narrow escapes, and the plot moves as nimbly as the master thief himself." Bull Cent Child Books

Other titles about Montmorency are:

Montmorency and the assassins (2006)

Montmorency on the rocks: doctor, aristocrat, murderer? (2005)

Montmorency's revenge (2007)

Montmorency and the assassins. Orchard Books 2006 404p lib bdg $16.99

Grades: 6 7 8 9   **Fic**

1. Thieves -- Fiction 2. Great Britain -- Fiction 3. London (England) -- Fiction

ISBN 0-439-68343-2 lib bdg

LC 2005-11980

After twenty years as a gentleman, Montmorency is glad to be free of Scarper, his wretched alter-ego, but when a young friend is caught in the middle of a murderous political plot, Montmorency may have no choice but to call upon Scarper for help.

Montmorency on the rocks; doctor, aristocrat, murderer? Orchard Books 2005 362p $16.95; pa $6.99

Grades: 6 7 8 9 10   **Fic**

1. Thieves -- Fiction 2. London (England) -- Fiction 3. Great Britain -- History -- 19th century -- Fiction

ISBN 0-439-60676-4; 978-0-439-60676-9; 0-439-60677-2 pa; 978-0-439-60677-6 pa

LC 2004-15368

Sequel to Montmorency and the assassins (2006)

First published 2004 in the United Kingdom

In Victorian London, when Montmorency and his alter ego, Scarper, reunite with Dr. Farcett, the two cooperate to capture a bomber and become involved in solving the mystery of the poisoning of a village of Scottish children.

Montmorency's revenge. Orchard Books 2007 289p $16.99

Grades: 6 7 8 9   **Fic**

1. Criminals -- Fiction 2. London (England) -- Fiction 3. Great Britain -- History -- 19th century -- Fiction

ISBN 0-439-81373-5; 978-0-439-81373-0

LC 2006-09745

As Queen Victoria lies dying and with her family in danger, a group of friends races to track down the anarchists responsible for George's death, even as Montmorency seeks to teach a new generation to forgive.

"With all the fast-forward energy and finely detailed settings . . . of his earlier adventures, this one is as easy to fall into, and it ends with a breath-catching cliffhanger." Voice Youth Advocates

Upjohn, Rebecca

The **secret** of the village fool; by Rebecca Upjohn; illustrated by Renne Benoit. Second Story Press 2012 32 p. $18.95

Grades: 5 6 7 8   **Fic**

1. World War, 1939-1945 -- Jews -- Fiction 2. World War, 1939-1945 -- Poland -- Fiction 3. World War, 1939-1945 -- Children -- Fiction

ISBN 1926920759; 9781926920757

In this children's book by Rebecca Upjohn, illustrated by Renne Benoit, "Milek and his brother Munio live in a sleepy village in Poland. . . . They reluctantly do as their mother asks when she asks them to visit their neighbor Anton, knowing that the rest of the village laughs at him because of his strange habits of speaking to animals and only eating vegetables. Things change quickly when war comes to their town in the form of Nazi soldiers searching for Jewish families like that of Milek and Munio." (Publisher's note)

Urban, Linda

★ The **center** of everything; by Linda Urban. Houghton Mifflin Harcourt 2013 208 p. $15.99

Grades: 4 5 6 7   **Fic**

1. Wishes -- Fiction 2. Bereavement -- Fiction

ISBN 0547763484; 9780547763484

LC 2012954515

In this book, "months after her grandmother's death, 12-year-old Ruby Pepperdine composes a winning essay honoring her New Hampshire town's namesake" and will get to read it to the community. But she's more concerned that "she didn't listen to her grandmother's final words before she died. Ruby thinks that maybe if she wishes hard enough, 'everything will be back to how it is supposed to be,' but making a wish the right way is a tricky business." (Publishers Weekly)

Ursu, Anne

★ **Breadcrumbs**; drawings by Erin McGuire. Walden Pond Press 2011 313p il $16.99

Grades: 4 5 6 7   **Fic**

1. Fairy tales 2. Magic -- Fiction 3. Friendship -- Fiction

ISBN 978-0-06-201505-1; 0-06-201505-2

LC 2010045666

"Fifth-grader Hazel embarks on a memorable journey into the Minnesota woods to find her best friend Jack, who vanishes after a shard of glass pierces his eye. . . . Hazel enters the woods to find 'an entirely different place,' populated by creatures from the pages of Hans Christian Andersen. . . . [This is a] multi-layered, artfully crafted, transforming testament to the power of friendship." Kirkus

Usher, Mark David

The **golden** ass of Lucius Apuleius; adapted from the Latin original by M.D. Usher; illustrations by T. Motley. David R. Godine 2011 85p il $17.95

Grades: 4 5 6 7   **Fic**

1. Magic -- Fiction 2. Social classes -- Fiction 3. Classical mythology -- Fiction

ISBN 978-1-56792-418-3; 1-56792-418-2

LC 2010032978

Lucius Apuleius, a young nobleman fascinated by magic, accidentally turns himself into an ass and then sets out on a journey that reveals to him the conditions of peasants and slaves in and around Thessaly and leads him to find redemption as a follower of Isis and Osiris.

"A faithful (if relatively clean) version of the world's oldest surviving complete novel. . . . Though all of the sex and most of the dissolute behavior has been excised, the lad's first transformation is milked throughout for double entendres . . . and there are plenty of silly incidents and names . . . to lighten the overall tone. Motley's elaborate illustrated initials and pen-and-ink drawings add satiric bite. . . . An entertaining romp." Kirkus

Vail, Rachel

Kiss me again; Rachel Vail. HarperTeen 2013 256 p. (hardcover) $17.99

Grades: 7 8 9 10   **Fic**

1. Love stories 2. Kissing -- Fiction 3. Teenagers -- Sexual behavior -- Fiction 4. Schools -- Fiction 5. Remarriage -- Fiction 6. High schools -- Fiction 7. Stepfamilies -- Fiction 8. Dating (Social customs) -- Fiction 9. Interpersonal relations -- Fiction

ISBN 0061947172; 9780061947179

LC 2012011521

In this book, "ninth-grader Charlie Collins has lived with her mother, a divorced Harvard professor, for many years. Now Mom's new husband, Joe, has moved into the spacious house, along with his sweet 9-year-old daughter, Samantha, and his notoriously flirtatious ninth-grade son, Kevin. . . . Charlie copes with a mutual crush on Kevin; an increasingly tenuous relationship with her best friend, Tess; her first paying job; and other trials and triumphs of growing up." (Kirkus)

Lucky. HarperTeen 2008 233p $16.99; lib bdg $17.89

Grades: 7 8 9 10   **Fic**

1. School stories 2. Wealth -- Fiction 3. Friendship -- Fiction

ISBN 978-0-06-089043-8; 978-0-06-089044-5 lib bdg

As Phoebe and her clique of privileged girlfriends get ready to graduate from eighth grade, a financial scandal threatens her family's security—as well as Phoebe's social status—but ultimately it teaches her the real meaning of friendship.

"Vail's insightful characterizations of teen girls and their shifting loyalties is right on target." Booklist

Other titles in this series are:

Gorgeous (2009)

Brilliant (2010)

Unfriended; Rachel Vail. Viking, published by Penguin Group 2014 288 p. (hardback) $16.99

Grades: 6 7 8 9   **Fic**

1. Social media 2. Middle schools -- Fiction 3. Schools -- Fiction 4. Friendship -- Fiction 5. Popularity -- Fiction 6. Social media -- Fiction

ISBN 0670013072; 9780670013074

LC 2014006247

In this young adult novel by Rachel Vail, "when Truly is invited to sit at the Popular Table with the group she has dreamed of joining, she can hardly believe her luck. Everyone seems so nice, so kind to one another. But all is not as it seems with her new friends, and soon she's caught in a maelstrom of lies, misunderstandings, accusations and counter-accusations, all happening very publicly in the relentless, hyperconnected social media world from which there is no escape." (Publisher's note)

"The points of view allow the reader to be drawn into the teens' motivations and illustrate the importance of clear communication, the dangers of online bullying, and the universal struggles teens face. Mean girls, misunderstood girls, awkward boys, friendship, popularity, social misfits, all play into this book that epitomizes the roller coaster that is middle school." Lib Med Con

Valente, Catherynne M.

The boy who lost Fairyland; Catherynne M. Valente; illustrated by Ana Juan. Feiwel & Friends 2015 240 p. (Fairyland) (hardback) $16.99

Grades: 5 6 7 8   **Fic**

1. Fantasy fiction 2. Trolls -- Fiction 3. Fantasy 4. Changelings -- Fiction

ISBN 1250023491; 9781250023490; 9781250073327

LC 2014042417

In this novel, by Catherynne M. Valente, illustrated by Ana Juan, "when a young troll named Hawthorn is stolen from Fairyland by the Golden Wind, he becomes a changeling--a human boy--in the strange city of Chicago. . . . Left with a human family, Hawthorn struggles with his troll nature and his changeling fate. But when he turns twelve, he stumbles upon a way back home, to a Fairyland much changed from the one he remembers." (Publisher's note)

"In this fourth book in the fantastical series, a young troll named Hawthorn is stolen away by the Golden Wind and brought to live in Chicago as a changeling. When he turns 12, he finds a way back to Fairyland, a place now much changed from the magical realm he left...While readers unfamiliar with the series can certainly jump in with this novel, most will want to start at the beginning. A phenomenal fantasy series worthy of a spot in every library collection." SLJ

Other titles in this series are:

The Girl who Soared Over Fairyland and Cut the Moon in Two (2013)

The Girl who Circumnavigated Fairyland in a Ship of her Own Making (2011)

The Girl who Fell Beneath Fairyland and Led the Revels There (2012)

★ The **girl** who circumnavigated Fairyland in a ship of her own making; [by] Catherynne M. Valente; with illustrations by Ana Juan. Feiwel and Friends 2011 247p il $16.99

Grades: 4 5 6 7 8   **Fic**

1. Fantasy fiction
ISBN 978-0-312-64961-6; 0-312-64961-4

LC 2010050895

"The book's appeal is crystal clear from the outset: this is a kind of The Wonderful Wizard of Oz by way of Alice's Adventures in Wonderland, made vivid by Juan's Tenniel-inflected illustrations. . . . Those who thrill to lovingly wrought tales of fantasy and adventure . . . will be enchanted." Publ Wkly

The **girl** who fell beneath Fairyland and led the revels there; by Catherynne M. Valente; with illustrations by Ana Juan. Feiwel and Friends 2012 258 p. $16.99

Grades: 4 5 6 7 8   **Fic**

1. Fantasy fiction 2. Magic -- Fiction 3. Fairies -- Fiction
ISBN 0312649622; 9780312649623

In this book by Catherynne M. Valente, illustrated by Ana Juan, "September has longed to return to Fairyland after her first adventure there. And when she finally does, she learns that its inhabitants have been losing their shadows--and their magic--to the world of Fairyland Below. This underworld has a new ruler: Halloween, the Hollow Queen, who is September's shadow. And Halloween does not want to give Fairyland's shadows back." (Publisher's note)

The **Girl** Who Soared over Fairyland and Cut the Moon in Two; by Catherynne M. Valente; illustrated by Ana Juan. Feiwel & Friends 2013 256 p. $16.99

Grades: 4 5 6 7 8   **Fic**

1. Moon -- Fiction 2. Fairies -- Fiction 3. Female friendship -- Fiction
ISBN 1250023505; 9781250023506

In this book, by Catherynne M. Valente, September is "tasked with delivering a package to the moon, which has begun to shudder and shake with moonquakes because a . . . yeti is trying to break it to pieces. September and her friends traverse the moon, meet their fates, encounter older and younger versions of themselves, and wonder what, exactly, makes them who they are--all while trying to find the speedy yeti and stop him from his destructive plans." (Booklist)

"In this third volume, following The Girl Who Fell Beneath Fairyland and Led the Revels There, September returns to Fairyland and finds herself on a mission to stop a vengeful yeti from destroying his Fairy abusers--and everyone else on the moon. September is now wiser and sadder, and longs for autonomy; likewise, Fairyland and its inhabitants have become darker and more adult." (Horn Book)

Valente, Allyson

How (not) to find a boyfriend; by Allyson Valentine. Philomel Books 2013 304 p. (hardcover) $16.99

Grades: 7 8 9 10   **Fic**

1. School stories 2. Popularity -- Fiction 3. Genius -- Fiction 4. Schools -- Fiction 5. Cheerleading -- Fiction 6. High schools -- Fiction 7. Dating (Social customs) -- Fiction
ISBN 0399257713; 9780399257711

LC 2012019316

In this book, former nerd Nora Fulbright has worked hard to shed her geeky image since starting high school. "As sophomore year begins, she's made the cheerleading squad, and it looks like the handsome fullback is taking notice of her. . . . Worried that the cheer captain will mock her for taking AP classes, she switches her schedule, then has to switch it back so she'll have classes with Adam, the brainy and adorable new boy in school." (Publishers Weekly)

Valentine, Jenny

Broken soup. HarperTeen 2009 216p $16.99

Grades: 7 8 9 10   **Fic**

1. Bereavement -- Fiction 2. Family life -- Fiction 3. London (England) -- Fiction
ISBN 978-0-06-085071-5; 0-06-085071-X

LC 2008-11719

A photographic negative and two surprising new friends become the catalyst for healing as fifteen-year-old Rowan struggles to keep her family and her life together after her brother's death.

"The mystery Valentine sets in motion is quickly paced and packed with revelations. . . . The main appeal of the book, however, is her beautifully modulated tone. . . . Insightful details abound." Booklist

Double; Jenny Valentine. Disney-Hyperion 2012 246 p. (alk. paper) $16.99

Grades: 7 8 9 10 11 12   **Fic**

1. Mystery fiction 2. Identity -- Fiction 3. Homeless persons -- Fiction 4. London (England) -- Fiction 5. Missing children -- Fiction 6. England -- Fiction 7. Impersonation -- Fiction
ISBN 1423147146; 9781423147145

LC 2011010027

In this book, "[w]hat starts as a case of mistaken identity turns into a . . . mystery. . . . Homeless, 16-year-old Chap is . . . presented with . . . [the]opportunity of a lifetime: if he pretends to be Cassiel Roadnight, a teen who has been missing for two years and who looks just like Chap, Chap can have the life and family he's always dreamed of. As he tries to pass in his new identity . . . Chap begins to suspect that there's more to Cassiel's disappearance than meets the eye." (Publishers Weekly)

★ **Me,** the missing, and the dead. HarperTeen 2008 201p $16.99; lib bdg $17.89

Grades: 8 9 10 11   **Fic**

1. Death -- Fiction 2. Fathers -- Fiction 3. Missing persons -- Fiction 4. London (England) -- Fiction 5. Single parent family -- Fiction
ISBN 978-0-06-085068-5; 0-06-085068-X; 978-0-06-085069-2 lib bdg; 0-06-085069-8 lib bdg

LC 2007-14476

First published 2007 in the United Kingdom with title: Finding Violet Park

ALA YALSA Morris Award finalist, 2009

When a series of chance events leaves him in possession of an urn with ashes, sixteen-year-old Londoner Lucas Swain becomes convinced that its occupant, Violet Park, is communicating with him, initiating a voyage of self-discovery that forces him to finally confront the events surrounding his father's sudden disappearance.

"Part mystery, part magical realism, part story of personal growth, and in large part simply about a funny teenager making light of his and his family's pain, this short novel is engaging from start to finish." SLJ

Van Beirs, Pat

A **sword** in her hand; by Jean-Claude Van Rijckeghem and Pat Van Beirs; translated by John Nieuwenhuizen. Annick 2011 276p $21.95

Grades: 5 6 7 8   **Fic**

1. Plague -- Fiction 2. Princesses -- Fiction 3. Middle Ages -- Fiction 4. Father-daughter relationship -- Fiction

ISBN 978-1-55451-291-1; 1-55451-291-3

The Count of Flanders flies in a rage when his newborn child is not the expected male heir but a girl. Marguerite growing up under the disapproving eye of her heartless father learns to survive in the violent male world of the Middle Ages. Will she be able to resist the combined presure of politics, power and a foreign prince?

"The deft characterization of Marguerite and the sumptuous details woven throughout this captivating novel will engage readers." SLJ

Van de Ruit, John

Spud. Razorbill 2007 331p hardcover o.p. pa $9.99

Grades: 6 7 8 9 10   **Fic**

1. School stories 2. South Africa -- Fiction

ISBN 978-1-59514-170-5; 0-14-302484-1; 978-1-59514-187-3 pa; 1-59514-187-1 pa

LC 2007-6065

In 1990, thirteen-year-old John "Spud" Milton, a prepubescent choirboy, keeps a diary of his first year at an elite, boys-only boarding school in South Africa.

"This raucous autobiographical novel about a scholarship boy in an elite boys' boarding school in 1990 is mainly farce but also part coming-of-age tale." Booklist

Followed by Spud¿the madness continues... (2008)

Van Draanen, Wendelin, 1965-

Flipped. Knopf 2001 212p $14.95

Grades: 6 7 8 9   **Fic**

1. Family life 2. Conduct of life 3. Self-perception 4. Interpersonal relations

ISBN 9780375811746; 0-375-81174-5; 0-375-82544-4 pa

LC 2001-29238

In alternating chapters, two teenagers describe how their feelings about themselves, each other, and their families have changed over the years. "Grades six to nine." (Bull Cent Child Books)

"There's lots of laugh-out-loud egg puns and humor in this novel. There's also, however, a substantial amount of serious social commentary woven in, as well as an exploration of the importance of perspective in relationships." SLJ

Runaway. Knopf 2006 250p $15.95; lib bdg $17.99

Grades: 6 7 8 9   **Fic**

1. Orphans -- Fiction 2. Homeless persons -- Fiction 3. Runaway children -- Fiction

ISBN 0-375-83522-9; 0-375-93522-3 lib bdg

LC 2005-33276

After running away from her fifth foster home, Holly, a twelve-year-old orphan, travels across the country, keeping a journal of her experiences and struggle to survive.

"The ending of this taut, powerful story seems possible and deeply hopeful." Booklist

The **running** dream. Alfred A. Knopf 2011 336p $16.99; lib bdg $19.99

Grades: 7 8 9 10 11 12   **Fic**

1. School stories 2. Running -- Fiction 3. Amputees -- Fiction 4. People with disabilities -- Fiction

ISBN 978-0-375-86667-8; 0-375-86667-1; 978-0-375-96667-5 lib bdg; 0-375-96667-6 lib bdg

LC 2010-07072

"It's a classic problem novel in a lot of ways. . . . Overall, though, this is a tremendously upbeat book. . . . Van Draanen's extensive research into both running and amputees pays dividends." Booklist

★ **Sammy** Keyes and the hotel thief. Knopf 1998 163p il hardcover o.p. pa $6.50

Grades: 4 5 6 7   **Fic**

1. Mystery fiction

ISBN 978-0-679-88839-0; 0-679-89264-8 pa

LC 97-40776

Thirteen-year-old Sammy's penchant for speaking her mind gets her in trouble when she involves herself in the investigation of a robbery at the "seedy" hotel across the street from the seniors' building where she is living with her grandmother

"This is a breezy novel with vivid characters." Bull Cent Child Books

Other titles about Sammy Keyes are:

Sammy Keyes and the skeleton man (1998)
Sammy Keyes and the Sisters of Mercy (1999)
Sammy Keyes and the runaway elf (1999)
Sammy Keyes and the curse of Moustache Mary (2000)
Sammy Keyes and the Hollywood mummy (2001)
Sammy Keyes and the search for Snake Eyes (2002)
Sammy Keyes and the art of deception (2003)
Sammy Keyes and the psycho Kitty Queen (2004)
Sammy Keyes and the dead giveaway (2005)
Sammy Keyes and the wild things (2007)
Sammy Keyes and the cold hard cash (2008)
Sammy Keyes and the wedding crasher (2010)
Sammy Keyes and the night of skulls (2011)
Sammy Keyes and the power of Justice Jack (2012)
Sammy Keyes and the showdown in Sin City (2013)
Sammy Keyes and the killer cruise (2013)
Sammy Keyes and the kiss goodbye (2014)

Van Eekhout, Greg

The **boy** at the end of the world. Bloomsbury Children's Books 2011 212p $16.99

Grades: 4 5 6 7   **Fic**

1. Science fiction 2. Robots -- Fiction

ISBN 978-1-59990-524-2; 1-59990-524-8

LC 2010035741

Born half-grown in a world that is being destroyed, Fisher has instinctive knowledge of many things, including that he must avoid the robot that knows his name.

"A pleaser for readers who prefer their sf livened up with unpredictable elements and emotional complexity." Booklist

Van Etten, David

Likely story. Alfred A. Knopf 2008 230p il $15.99; lib bdg $18.99

Grades: 7 8 9 10   **Fic**

1. Television -- Fiction 2. Hollywood (Calif.) -- Fiction 3. Mother-daughter relationship -- Fiction

ISBN 978-0-375-84676-2; 0-375-84676-X; 978-0-375-94676-9 lib bdg; 0-375-94676-4 lib bdg

LC 2007-22724

Sixteen-year-old Mallory, daughter of the star of a long-running but faltering soap opera, writes her own soap opera script and becomes deeply involved in the day-to-day life of a Hollywood player, while trying to hold on to some shaky personal relationships.

"Strong-willed, quick-witted Mallory is a sympathetic heroine, and Van Etten engagingly weds melodrama to the more mundane, universal dramas of teenage life." Horn Book Guide

Other titles in this series are:

All that glitters (2008)

Red carpet riot (2009)

Van Leeuwen, Jean

★ **Cabin** on Trouble Creek. Dial Books for Young Readers 2004 119p $16.99; pa $6.99

Grades: 4 5 6 7   **Fic**

1. Ohio -- Fiction 2. Brothers -- Fiction 3. Frontier and pioneer life -- Fiction

ISBN 0-8037-2548-5; 0-14-241164-7 pa

LC 2003-14151

In 1803 in Ohio, two young brothers are left to finish the log cabin and guard the land while their father goes back to Pennsylvania to fetch their mother and younger siblings.

"Excellent pacing is what makes this novel work so well. . . . The suspense builds consistently. The boys' struggle is portrayed realistically, without sugarcoating nature's harshness." SLJ

Lucy was there-- Phyllis Fogelman Bks. 2002 165p $16.99

Grades: 4 5 6 7   **Fic**

1. Dogs -- Fiction 2. Death -- Fiction 3. Friendship -- Fiction

ISBN 0-8037-2738-0

LC 2001-33974

With the help of new friends and a very special dog, Morgan begins to come to terms with the loss of her mother and five-year-old brother, who boarded a plane and never came back. "Grades five to seven." (Bull Cent Child Books)

"Morgan's anguish is palpable but never overwrought, and the short chapters, appealing heroine, and well-told story leavened with humor give this solid . . . appeal." Booklist

Van Tol, Alex

Knifepoint; written by Alex Van Tol. Orca Book Publishers 2010 113p (Orca soundings) $16.95; pa $9.95

Grades: 7 8 9 10   **Fic**

1. Kidnapping -- Fiction

ISBN 978-1-55469-306-1; 1-55469-06-3; 978-1-55469-305-4 pa; 1-55469-305-5 pa

Jill is enduring a brutal job on a mountain ranch, guiding wannabe-cowboys on trail rides. On a solo ride with a handsome stranger she ends up in a fight for her life with no one to help her.

"The suspense is palpable. Both reluctant and avid readers who enjoy nail-biting tension will race through." Booklist

Van Vleet, Carmella

Eliza Bing is (not) a big, fat quitter; by Carmella Van Vleet; illustrated by Karen Donnelly. Holiday House 2014 165 p. (hardcover) $16.95

Grades: 3 4 5 6 7   **Fic**

1. Family life -- Fiction 2. Tae kwon do -- Fiction 3. Attention deficit disorder -- Fiction 4. Martial arts -- Fiction 5. Determination (Personality trait) -- Fiction 6. Attention-deficit hyperactivity disorder -- Fiction

ISBN 082342944X; 9780823429448

LC 2013015279

This novel, written by Carmella Van Vleet and illustrated by Karen Donnelly, is "about determination and the rewards of hard work[.] A preteen girl struggling with ADHD must stick with a summer taekwondo class to prove that she s dedicated enough to pursue her true passion: cake decorating." (Publisher's note)

"Eliza Bing, 11, is not a big, fat quitter, or is she? Her track record isn't great. She has a history of not following through with activities - —Junior Scouts, gymnastics, tap, piano . So, when she wants to sign up for a cake-decorating class with her bakery loving friend, her parents flat-out say no. Eliza strikes a nearly impossible deal with her parents: if she can finish a tae kwon do class over the summer, she can take cake decorating in the fall...Fast moving and humorous with chapter titles such as "Sticky Note to Self: Wear White Underwear on Wednesdays and Saturdays," feisty Eliza will have readers, especially those with ADHD, rooting for her." SLJ

Vance, Alexander

The **Heartbreak** Messenger. Feiwel & Friends 2013 288 p. $16.99

Grades: 6 7 8   **Fic**

1. School stories 2. Dating (Social customs) -- Fiction

ISBN 1250029694; 9781250029690

In this book by Alexander Vance, after "seventh-grader Quentin accepts $20 to deliver a breakup message for a friend's older brother, a new business is born: he becomes the 'Heartbreak Messenger,' hired to perform breakups for the weak-willed. Quentin believes his single mother, an auto mechanic, is struggling to pay their bills, so there's an altruistic side to his entrepreneurship, but he also enjoys the power the job gives him. Problems arise." (Publishers Weekly)

Vande Velde, Vivian

The **book** of Mordred; [illustrations by Justin Gerard] Houghton Mifflin 2005 342p hardcover o.p. pa $8.99

Grades: 8 9 10 11 12   **Fic**

1. Kings 2. Knights and knighthood -- Fiction 3. Mordred (Legendary character) -- Fiction 4. Great Britain -- History -- 0-1066 -- Fiction

ISBN 0-618-50754-X; 0-618-80916-3 pa

LC 2004-28223

As the peaceful King Arthur reigns, the five-year-old daughter of Lady Alayna, newly widowed of the village-wizard Toland, is abducted by knights who leave their barn burning and their only servant dead.

"All of the characters are well developed and have a strong presence throughout. . . . [This] provides an intriguing counterpoint to anyone who is interested in Arthurian legend." SLJ

Frogged; Vivian Vande Velde. Houghton Mifflin Harcourt 2013 208 p. $16.99

Grades: 5 6 7 8   **Fic**

1. Fantasy fiction 2. Fractured fairy tales 3. Fairy tales 4. Frogs -- Fiction 5. Humorous stories 6. Princesses -- Fiction 7. Self-perception -- Fiction

ISBN 054794215X; 9780547942155

LC 2013003905

In this alternate version of "The Frog Prince," "Princess Imogene, who is 12 and 'gawky,' is tired of falling short in her family's eyes. The real trouble begins when a . . . frog, who tells Imogene he's a prince beset by a witch's spell, tricks her into kissing him. He returns to his human form, but she is transformed into a frog as a result; worse, he was just the lowly son of a wagon maker. Too kind to use that sort of deceit on someone else, Imogene searches for another solution." (Publishers Weekly)

Heir apparent. Harcourt 2002 315p $17; pa $6.95

Grades: 6 7 8 9   **Fic**

1. Science fiction 2. Virtual reality -- Fiction

ISBN 0-15-204560-0; 0-15-205125-2 pa

LC 2002-2441

While playing a total immersion virtual reality game of kings and intrigue, fourteen-year-old Giannine learns that demonstrators have damaged the equipment to which she is connected, and she must win the game quickly or be damaged herself

"This adventure includes a cast of intriguing characters and personalities. The feisty heroine has a funny, sarcastic sense of humor and succeeds because of her ingenuity and determination." SLJ

Magic can be murder. Harcourt 2000 197p hardcover o.p. pa $6.99

Grades: 6 7 8 9 10   **Fic**

1. Mystery fiction 2. Witchcraft -- Fiction

ISBN 0-15-202665-7; 0-547-25872-0 pa

LC 00-8595

"Nola is a witch trained by her mother, Mary. . . . A scrying spell mistakenly left floating in a bucket threatens to expose the two women, and Nola's efforts to discover the urgency of their danger makes her magical witness to murder. . . . Grades seven to ten." (Bull Cent Child Books)

"The well-developed characters provide entertaining reading." SLJ

Remembering Raquel. Harcourt 2007 160p $16

Grades: 8 9 10 11   **Fic**

1. School stories 2. Death -- Fiction 3. Obesity -- Fiction

ISBN 978-0-15-205976-7

LC 2006-35769

Various people recall aspects of the life of Raquel Falcone, an unpopular, overweight freshman at Quail Run High School, including classmates, her parents, and the driver who struck and killed her as she was walking home from an animated film festival.

"Easily booktalked and deeper than it initially seems, this will be popular with reluctant readers." Booklist

★ **Stolen**. Marshall Cavendish 2008 158p $16.99

Grades: 6 7 8 9 10   **Fic**

1. Magic -- Fiction 2. Amnesia -- Fiction 3. Witches -- Fiction 4. Missing children -- Fiction

ISBN 978-0-7614-5515-8; 0-7614-5515-9

LC 2008-03184

A girl finds herself running through the forest at the edge of a village with no memory of anything, even her own name, and later learns that she might be twelve-year-old Isabelle, believed to be stolen by a witch six years before.

"Vande Velde, noted for her well-crafted riffs on fairy tales, has written her darkest yet, a story of greed, jealousy, and insidious evil that will haunt the reader for some time to come." Booklist

Vanderpool, Clare

★ **Moon** over Manifest. Delacorte Press 2010 351p $16.99; lib bdg $19.99

Grades: 5 6 7 8   **Fic**

1. Kansas -- Fiction 2. Fathers -- Fiction 3. Great Depression, 1929-1939 -- Fiction

ISBN 978-0-385-73883-5; 0-385-73883-8; 978-0-385-90750-7 lib bdg; 0-385-90750-8 lib bdg

LC 2009-40042

Awarded the Newbery Medal, 2011

Twelve-year-old Abilene Tucker is the daughter of a drifter who, in the summer of 1936, sends her to stay with an old friend in Manifest, Kansas, where he grew up, and where she hopes to find out some things about his past.

"The absolute necessity of story as a way to redemption and healing past wounds is at the heart of this beautiful debut, and readers will cherish every word up to the heartbreaking yet hopeful and deeply gratifying ending." Kirkus

Vanhee, Jason

Engines of the broken world; Jason Vanhee. Henry Holt and Company 2013 272 p. (hardcover) $16.99

Grades: 8 9 10 11 12 **Fic**
1. Supernatural -- Fiction 2. Brothers and sisters --
Fiction 3. Science fiction
ISBN 0805096299; 9780805096293

LC 2013026768

In this book, by Jason Vanhee, "Merciful Truth and her
brother, Gospel, have just pulled their dead mother into the
kitchen and stowed her under the table. It was a long illness, and they wanted to bury her--they did--but it's far too
cold outside, and they know they won't be able to dig into
the frozen ground. The Minister who lives with them, who
preaches through his animal form, doesn't make them feel
any better about what they've done." (Publisher's note)

"Unlike most action-packed dystopias, the story's slow-
er pace . . . allows readers to feel the fog encroaching on
Merciful and Gospel's rustic home, and hear every scratch
of their dead mother's awkward movements upon the cellar
stairs." Booklist

Vaughn, Carrie
Steel. HarperTeen 2011 294p $16.99; lib bdg
$17.89
Grades: 7 8 9 10 **Fic**
1. Fencing -- Fiction 2. Pirates -- Fiction 3. Time
travel -- Fiction 4. Caribbean region -- Fiction
ISBN 978-0-06-154791-1; 0-06-154791-3; 978-0-06-
195648-5 lib bdg; 0-06-195648-1 lib bdg

LC 2010012631

When Jill, a competitive high school fencer, goes with
her family on vacation to the Bahamas, she is magically
transported to an early-eighteenth-century pirate ship in the
middle of the ocean.

This is "thoroughly enjoyable. . . . Through her assertive,
appealing protagonist and a satisfying plot that sheds light on
lesser-known aspects of pirate life, Vaughn introduces readers to an intriguing sport with an ancient pedigree." Kirkus

Voices of dragons. HarperTeen 2010 309p
$16.99
Grades: 7 8 9 10 **Fic**
1. Fantasy fiction 2. Dragons -- Fiction
ISBN 978-0-06-179894-8; 0-06-179894-0

LC 2009-11604

In a parallel world where humans and dragons live in a
state of cold war, seventeen-year-old Kay and her dragon
friend, Artegal, struggle to find a way to show that dragons
and humans can coexist.

"Vaughn's story is charming and fast paced with a
strong, likable heroine." Publ Wkly

Vaught, Susan
Freaks like us; by Susan Vaught. Bloomsbury
2012 240 p. (hardcover) $16.99
Grades: 7 8 9 10 11 12 **Fic**
1. Friendship -- Fiction 2. Schizophrenia -- Fiction 3.
Mental illness -- Fiction 4. Missing persons -- Fiction
5. Love -- Fiction 6. Missing children -- Fiction 7.
Mystery and detective stories
ISBN 1599908727; 9781599908724

LC 2012004227

This is the story of Jason, whose selectively mute friend
Sunshine has "vanished, and Jason, whose schizophrenia

has shaped his life, is a suspect in her disappearance. Seniors
Jason, Drip and Sunshine have ridden the short bus and gone
through school labeled SED--that's 'Severely Emotionally
Disturbed.' Bullying at the hands of kids with behavioral
disabilities goes unreported and unpunished, but the trio's alliance made life bearable in their catchall special ed program
. . . . As the FBI investigates, Jason's always-shaky world
threatens to come apart. Not taking "fuzzy pills" keeps his
brain sharp, but the voices plaguing him grow louder. Jason
carries Sunshine's secrets--should he break his promise not
to tell?" (Kirkus)

Vaupel, Robin
My contract with Henry. Holiday House 2003
244p $16.95
Grades: 5 6 7 8 **Fic**
1. Authors 2. Naturalists 3. School stories 4. Essayists
5. Pacifists 6. Writers on nature 7. Nonfiction writers
8. Friendship -- Fiction
ISBN 0-8234-1701-8

LC 2002-27471

A mission that begins as an eighth-grade project on
Henry David Thoreau's experimental living at Walden Pond
becomes a life-changing experience for a group of outsider
students who become budding philosophers, environmental
activists, and loyal friends. "Grades six to nine." (Bull Cent
Child Books)

"Vaupel creates a painfully accurate portrayal of middle-
school social dynamics." Booklist

The **rules** of the universe by Austin W. Hale.
Holiday House 2007 265p $16.95
Grades: 4 5 6 7 **Fic**
1. Science fiction 2. Death -- Fiction 3. Grandfathers
-- Fiction
ISBN 978-0-8234-1811-4; 0-8234-1811-1

LC 2003-56751

Thirteen-year-old Austin Hale, an aspiring scientist and
disciple of his grandfather, a Nobel Prize-winning molecular
physicist, finds himself in control of a powerful energy force
that can turn back time and its orbit upside down

"The captivating blend of scientific research and magic
is effectively balanced against the stark realism of a boy facing his first significant losses; the overall tone is one of cautious optimism." Bull Cent Child Books

Vawter, Vince
★ **Paperboy**; Vince Vawter. 1st ed. Delacorte
Press 2013 240 p. (library) $19.99; (hardcover)
$16.99
Grades: 5 6 7 8 **Fic**
1. Stuttering -- Fiction 2. Race relations -- Fiction 3.
Newspaper carriers -- Fiction 4. Self-esteem -- Fiction
5. Interpersonal relations -- Fiction 6. Family life --
Tennessee -- Fiction 7. Memphis (Tenn.) -- History --
20th century -- Fiction
ISBN 0385742444; 9780307975058; 9780375990588;
9780385742443

LC 2012030546

Newbery Honor Book (2014)

In this book by Vince Vawter, "[a]fter an overthrown
baseball busts his best friend's lip, 11-year-old Victor

Vollmer takes over the boy's paper route. This is a particularly daunting task for the able-armed Victor, as he has a prominent stutter that embarrasses him. . . .Through the paper route he meets a number of people, gains a much-needed sense of self and community, and has a life-threatening showdown with a local cart man." (School Library Journal)

"Carefully crafted language, authenticity of setting and quirky characters that ring fully true all combine to make this a worthwhile read. Although Little Man's stutter holds up dialogue, that annoyance also powerfully reflects its stultifying impact on his life. An engaging and heartfelt presentation that never whitewashes the difficult time and situation as Little Man comes of age." Kirkus

Veciana-Suarez, Ana

The **flight** to freedom. Orchard Bks. 2002 215p (First person fiction) $16.95; pa $6.99

Grades: 6 7 8 9   **Fic**

1. Immigrants -- Fiction 2. Cuban Americans -- Fiction

ISBN 0-439-38199-1; 0-439-38200-9 pa

LC 2001-58783

Writing in the diary her father gave her, thirteen-year-old Yara describes life with her family in Havana, Cuba, in 1967 as well as her experiences in Miami, Florida, after immigrating there to be reunited with some relatives while leaving others behind. "Middle school, high school." (Horn Book)

"The story and characters ring true in their portrayal of loss, longing, and the hope of starting a new life." SLJ

Venkatraman, Padma

★ **Climbing** the stairs. G.P. Putnam's Sons 2008 247p $16.99

Grades: 6 7 8 9 10   **Fic**

1. Prejudices -- Fiction 2. Family life -- Fiction 3. Brain -- Wounds and injuries -- Fiction 4. India -- History -- 1765-1947, British occupation -- Fiction

ISBN 978-0-399-24746-0; 0-399-24746-7

LC 2007-21757

In India, in 1941, when her father becomes brain-damaged in a non-violent protest march, fifteen-year-old Vidya and her family are forced to move in with her father's extended family and become accustomed to a totally different way of life.

"Venkatraman paints an intricate and convincing backdrop of a conservative Brahmin home in a time of change. . . . The striking cover art . . . will draw readers to this vividly told story." Booklist

★ **Island's** end. G.P. Putnam's Sons 2011 240p $16.99

Grades: 5 6 7 8 9   **Fic**

1. India -- Fiction 2. Islands -- Fiction 3. Apprentices -- Fiction

ISBN 978-0-399-25099-6; 0-399-25099-9

LC 2010036298

"Uido's clear, intelligent, present-tense voice consistently engrosses as she pushes through doubt and loss to find the right path. The beach, jungle and cliff settings are palpable. . . . There is very little information known about Andaman Islanders, making it hard to gauge the authenticity of this portrayal; the author's note indicates a respectful and dili-

gent approach to her subject. . . . Refreshingly hopeful and beautifully written." Kirkus

★ A **time** to dance; Padma Venkatraman. Nancy Paulsen Books, an imprint of Penguin Group (USA) Inc. 2014 320 p. $17.99

Grades: 8 9 10 11 12   **Fic**

1. Novels in verse 2. Dance -- Fiction 3. India -- Fiction 4. Amputees -- Fiction 5. People with disabilities -- Fiction

ISBN 0399257101; 9780399257100

LC 2013024244

Author Padma Venkatraman's "story of a young girl's struggle to regain her passion and find a new peace is told lyrically through verse that captures the beauty and mystery of India and the ancient bharatanatyam dance form. . . . Veda, a classical dance prodigy in India, lives and breathes dance - so when an accident leaves her a below-knee amputee, her dreams are shattered. . . . But Veda refuses to let her disability rob her of her dreams, and she starts all over again." (Publisher's note)

"This free-verse novel set in contemporary India stars Veda, a teenage Bharatanatyam dancer. After a tragic accident, one of Veda's legs must be amputated below the knee. Veda tries a series of customized prosthetic legs, determined to return to dancing as soon as possible. Brief lines, powerful images, and motifs of sound communicate Veda's struggle to accept her changed body." Horn Book

Verday, Jessica

The **Hollow**. Simon Pulse 2009 515p $17.99

Grades: 7 8 9 10 11 12   **Fic**

1. Authors 2. Historians 3. Ghost stories 4. School stories 5. Essayists 6. Biographers 7. Children's authors 8. Bereavement -- Fiction 9. Supernatural -- Fiction 10. New York (State) -- Fiction

ISBN 1-4169-7893-3; 978-1-4169-7893-0

LC 2008042817

High-school junior Abbey struggles with the loss of her best friend Kristen, who vanished on a legendary bridge, but her grief is eased by Caspian, an attractive and mysterious stranger she meets in the Sleepy Hollow cemetery.

"Abbey's narration is heartfelt and authentically written." SLJ

Followed by: The haunted (2010)

Verne, Jules

★ **20,000** leagues under the sea; illustrated by the Dillons; translated by Anthony Bonner. Books of Wonder 2000 394p il $21.95

Grades: 5 6 7 8 9 10 11 12 Adult   **Fic**

1. Science fiction 2. Submarines -- Fiction

ISBN 0-688-10535-1

LC 00-24336

Original French edition, 1870

Retells the adventures of a French professor and his two companions as they sail above and below the world's oceans as prisoners on the fabulous electric submarine of the deranged Captain Nemo

Vernick, Audrey

★ **Water** balloon. Clarion Books 2011 312p $16.99

Grades: 4 5 6 7   **Fic**

1. Dogs -- Fiction 2. Divorce -- Fiction 3. Friendship -- Fiction 4. Babysitters -- Fiction 5. Father-daughter relationship -- Fiction

ISBN 978-0-547-59554-2; 0-547-59554-9

LC 2011009847

With her best friends pulling away from her, her newly-separated parents deciding she should spend the summer at her father's new home, and a babysitting job she does not want, Marley's life is already as precarious as an overfull water balloon when a cute boy enters the picture.

"The book moves along at a pace that will keep tweens interested, and the dialogue among the characters feels real. Marley's relationships with her friends and family are complex, and even the most reluctant readers will relate to her and the choices that she makes." SLJ

Vernick, Shirley Reva

The **blood** lie; a novel. Cinco Puntos Press 2011 141p $15.95

Grades: 5 6 7 8   **Fic**

1. Love -- Fiction 2. Prejudices -- Fiction 3. Antisemitism -- Fiction 4. New York (State) -- Fiction 5. Jews -- United States -- Fiction

ISBN 978-1-933693-84-2; 1-933693-84-3

LC 2011011429

"Based on an actual incident in Massena in 1928, the slim novel effectively mines layers of ignorance, fear, intolerance and manipulation, and it connects the incident to Henry Ford's anti-Semitic writing and to the lynching of Jewish businessman Leo Frank in 1915." Kirkus

Vigilante, Danette

Saving Baby Doe; Danette Vigilante. G.P. Putnam's Sons, an imprint of Penguin Group (USA) Inc. 2014 240 p. (hardback) $16.99

Grades: 5 6 7 8   **Fic**

1. Orphans -- Fiction 2. Friendship -- Fiction 3. Family life -- Fiction 4. Single-parent families -- fiction 5. Neighbors -- Fiction 6. Foundlings -- Fiction 7. Best friends -- Fiction 8. Conduct of life -- Fiction 9. Hispanic Americans -- Fiction 10. Single-parent families -- Fiction

ISBN 039925160X; 9780399251603

LC 2013022728

In this book, by Danette Vigilante, "a cry in a building-site portable toilet leads thirteen-year-old Lionel and his friend Anisa to the discovery of an abandoned newborn baby. . . . Lionel, himself abandoned by his father, fears that Baby Doe will be hurt by a similar loss, so he schemes to bring her home with him. Realizing baby supplies cost money, a rare commodity around his house, he reluctantly agrees to take on some work for a local drug dealer." (Bulletin of the Center for Children's Books)

"Thirteen-year-old Lionel Perez and his friend Anisa Torres stumble across a newborn baby. Despite his mother's efforts to tie up his time with piano lessons, Lionel gets mixed up with a drug dealer in the hopes of earning enough money to take care of the baby himself. Vigilante's finely tuned depiction of Lionel's Red Hook, Brooklyn, neighborhood is believable and engaging." Horn Book

Trouble with half a moon. G. P. Putnam's Sons 2011 181p $16.99

Grades: 5 6 7 8   **Fic**

1. Faith -- Fiction 2. Friendship -- Fiction 3. Bereavement -- Fiction 4. Child abuse -- Fiction 5. Puerto Ricans -- Fiction 6. City and town life -- Fiction 7. Jamaican Americans -- Fiction

ISBN 978-0-399-25159-7; 0-399-25159-6

LC 2010-07377

Overwhelmed by grief and guilt over her brother's death and its impact on her mother, and at odds with her best friend, thirteen-year-old Dellie reaches out to a neglected boy in her building in the projects and learns from a new neighbor to have faith in herself and others.

"The story is told with considerable appeal and accessibility, and kids won't have to lead the same life as Dellie to recognize her travails." Bull Cent Child Books

Villareal, Ray

Body slammed! by Ray Villareal. Piñata Books 2012 194 p. (alk. paper) $11.95

Grades: 7 8 9 10   **Fic**

1. Wrestling -- Fiction 2. Father-son relationship -- Fiction 3. Choice -- Fiction 4. Schools -- Fiction 5. High schools -- Fiction 6. Fathers and sons -- Fiction 7. Mexican Americans -- Fiction 8. San Antonio (Tex.) -- Fiction

ISBN 1558857494; 9781558857490

LC 2012003181

Sequel to: My father, the Angel of Death

This novel, by Ray Villareal, follows "[s]ixteen-year-old Jesse Baron . . . [who] is fed up with being cut down and dismissed, whether by the coach or his friends. . . . But it's through his dad that Jesse meets TJ Masters, a brash, new wrestling talent who's over 21, . . . TJ makes Jesse feel tough and confident. . . . But will Jesse listen to his family and friends when they warn him about hanging out with someone who's often reckless and irresponsible?" (Publisher's note)

Vincent, Zu

The **lucky** place. Front Street 2008 230p $17.95

Grades: 7 8 9 10   **Fic**

1. Death -- Fiction 2. Cancer -- Fiction 3. Alcoholism -- Fiction 4. Stepfathers -- Fiction 5. Father-daughter relationship -- Fiction

ISBN 978-1-932425-70-3; 1-932425-70-5

LC 2007-18357

"Readers meet Cassie when she is three years old and her inebriated father leaves her behind at the racetrack. . . . She is returned home by the police and their mother eventually realizes that this man is not a competent father. . . . Mom brings home Ellis, New Daddy, and Cassie can't help but feel his strength. . . . Cassie's voice changes as she grows into a 12-year-old who comes to know that inside herself is the real lucky place that she can truly count on. . . . Taking place in California in the late 1950s and early '60s . . . Vincent's novel ably creates a world that makes promises it can't keep. . . . A stunning fiction debut." SLJ

Vivian, Siobhan

The **list**; Siobhan Vivian. Scholastic 2012 333 p. (hardcover : alk. paper) $17.99

Grades: 7 8 9 10 11 12　　　　　**Fic**

1. Female friendship 2. Self-perception -- Fiction 3. Personal appearance -- Fiction 4. High school students -- Fiction 5. Identity (Psychology) -- Fiction 6. Friendship -- Fiction 7. Self-esteem -- Fiction 8. High schools -- Fiction

ISBN 0545169178; 9780545169172

LC 2012004248

This young adult novel presents an "exploration of physical appearance and the status it confers. . . . Every year during homecoming week, a list is posted anonymously at Mount Washington High naming the prettiest and ugliest girls in each class. . . . The list confers instant status, transforming formerly homeschooled sophomore Lauren from geeky to hot while consigning her counterpart . . . Candace, to pariah. But what the label mainly confers is anxiety. Prettiest junior Bridget despairs that she'll ever be thin enough to merit her title. . . . Jennifer, four-time 'ugliest' winner, tries to relish the notoriety. . . . Whether clued in or clueless to the intricate social complexities, boyfriends reinforce the status quo, while moms carry scars of their own past physical insecurities." (Kirkus)

A **little** friendly advice. Scholastic/Push 2008 248p $16.99

Grades: 7 8 9 10 11 12　　　　　**Fic**

1. Ohio -- Fiction 2. Divorce -- Fiction 3. Friendship -- Fiction 4. Father-daughter relationship -- Fiction

ISBN 978-0-545-00404-6; 0-545-00404-7

LC 2007-9905

When Ruby's divorced father shows up unexpectedly on her sixteenth birthday, the week that follows is full of confusing surprises, including discovering that her best friend has been keeping secrets from her, her mother has not been truthful about the past, and life is often complicated.

"Readers will find themselves and their relationships reflected in Ruby's story—for better and worse." Publ Wkly

Voelkel, J.

The **end** of the world club; [by] J&P Voelkel. Egmont USA 2011 384p (The Jaguar stones) $16.99

Grades: 4 5 6 7　　　　　**Fic**

1. Adventure fiction 2. Mayas -- Fiction 3. Supernatural -- Fiction 4. Central America -- Fiction

ISBN 978-1-60684-072-6; 1-60684-072-X

LC 2010036641

Sequel to: Middleworld (2007)

With the end of the Mayan calendar fast approaching, fourteen-year-old Max Murphy and his friend Lola, the Maya girl who saved his life in the perilous jungle, race against time to outwit the twelve villainous Lords of Death, following the trail of the conquistadors into a forgotten land steeped in legend and superstition.

"The authors use Maya mythology and terms and add interesting facts about Spain and Spanish culture. This is a fast-paced book, and the action starts right away." SLJ

Middleworld; [by] J & P Voelkel [i.e., Jon Voelkel, Pamela Craik Voelkel] Smith and Kraus Publishers 2007 397p il (The Jaguar stones) $17.95; pa $8.99

Grades: 4 5 6 7　　　　　**Fic**

1. Adventure fiction 2. Mayas -- Fiction 3. Central America -- Fiction

ISBN 978-1-57525-561-3; 1-57525-561-8; 978-1-60684-071-9 pa; 1-60684-071-1 pa

"Suspense and intrigue, human sacrifice, smuggling, and secret doors and escape routes through pyramids ensure that the novel, the first in a projected trilogy, is likely to win legions of fans." SLJ

"Newly arrived in 'the snake-infested dump' of San Xavier, a fictional Central American country, 14-year-old Max Murphy discovers that his archaeologist parents have disappeared. Aided in his search by resourceful Lola, a descendent of the Maya, Max learns that the gods of her people have chosen him for a mission involving powerful artifacts." Booklist

Followed by: The end of the world club (2010)

Voigt, Cynthia

Bad girls in love. Atheneum Bks. for Young Readers 2002 233p hardcover o.p. pa $11.99

Grades: 6 7 8 9　　　　　**Fic**

1. School stories 2. Friendship -- Fiction

ISBN 0-689-82471-8; 0-689-86620-8 pa

LC 2001-45898

Now in the eighth grade, best friends Mikey and Margalo try to figure out boys, crushes, and falling in love

It's the girls' "talk—insulting, furious, funny, needy, and smart—on the telephone, and in the school's cafeteria, bathrooms, and hallways that gets the junior-high jungle exactly right." Booklist

Other titles in this series are:

Bad, badder, baddest (1997)

Bad girls (1996)

Bad girls, bad girls, whatcha gonna do? (2006)

It's not easy being bad (2000)

★ **Dicey's** song. Atheneum Pubs. 1982 196p $17.95; pa $6.99

Grades: 5 6 7 8　　　　　**Fic**

1. Siblings -- Fiction 2. Grandmothers -- Fiction

ISBN 0-689-30944-9; 0-689-86362-4 pa

LC 82-3882

Sequel to Homecoming

Awarded the Newbery Medal, 1983

"The vividness of Dicey is striking; Voigt has plumbed and probed her character inside out to fashion a memorable protagonist." Booklist

Dicey "had brought her siblings to the grandmother they'd never seen when their mother (now in a mental institution) had been unable to cope. This is the story of the children's adjustment to Gram (and hers to them) and to a new school and a new life—but with some of the old problems." Bull Cent Child Books

★ **Homecoming**. Atheneum Pubs. 1981 312p $18.95; pa $6.99

Grades: 6 7 8 9 **Fic**
1. Siblings -- Fiction 2. Abandoned children -- Fiction
ISBN 0-689-30833-7; 0-689-86361-6 pa

LC 80-36723

ALA YALSA Margaret A. Edwards Award (1995)
"The characterizations of the children are original and intriguing, and there are a number of interesting minor characters encountered in their travels." SLJ

Followed by: Dicey's song

★ **Izzy**, willy-nilly; Rev. format ed.; Atheneum Books for Young Readers 2005 327p $17.95; pa $6.99

Grades: 7 8 9 10 **Fic**
1. Amputees -- Fiction 2. Friendship -- Fiction 3. Drunk driving -- Fiction
ISBN 978-1-4169-0340-6; 1-4169-0340-2; 978-1-4169-0339-0 pa; 1-4169-0339-9 pa

LC 2005299062

A reissue of the title first published 1986
ALA YALSA Margaret A. Edwards Award (1995)
A car accident causes fifteen-year-old Izzy to lose one leg and face the need to start building a new life as an amputee.
"Voigt shows unusual insight into the workings of a 15-year-old girl's mind. . . . Just as Voigt's perceptive empathy brings Izzy to life, other characterizations are memorable, whether of Izzy's shallow former friends or of her egocentric 10-year-old sister." Pub Wkly [review of 1986 edition]

Mister Max; the book of lost things. by Cynthia Voigt; illustrated by Iacopo Bruno. Alfred A. Knopf 2013 384 p. (hardcover) $16.99; (library) $19.99

Grades: 5 6 7 8 **Fic**
1. Abandoned children -- Fiction 2. Historical fiction 3. Self-reliance -- Fiction 4. Problem solving -- Fiction
ISBN 0307976815; 9780307976819; 9780307976826; 9780375971235

LC 2012033823

In this book, Max "is left at the dock when he misses a boat to India, where his [actor] parents supposedly have been invited by a maharajah to start a theater. . . . Although his wise yet bossy librarian grandmother lives next door, 12-year-old Max wants to earn his keep and be independent. Cleverly donning the costumes and different roles performed by his missing parents, Max discovers an aptitude for finding lost things. . . . He is a 'solutioneer,' solving people's problems." (Kirkus Reviews)

★ A **solitary** blue. Atheneum Pubs. 1983 189p hardcover o.p. pa $6.99

Grades: 7 8 9 10 **Fic**
1. Divorce -- Fiction 2. Parent-child relationship -- Fiction
ISBN 0689310080; 0689863608

LC 83-6007

A Newbery honor book, 1984
"Jefferson Greene, a minor character from Dicey's Song {BRD 1983}, is the subject of the new novel. Beginning when Jeff was seven years old and ending when he was in high school, the book overlaps and goes beyond the earlier one. . . . {This novel} explores the relationships among Jeff, his mother Melody, and his father 'the Professor.' After

Melody walked out on the family to pursue a long line of unrealistic causes, the Professor and his young son went on as if nothing had changed. Their . . . coexistence continued until Jeff at the age of eleven received an unexpected invitation to spend the summer with his mother and her family in South Carolina. . . . Age twelve and up." (Horn Book)
"This is the most mature and sophisticated of Voigt's novels. . . . Beautifully knit . . . compelling and intelligent." Bull Cent Child Books

Volponi, Paul

Black and white. Viking 2005 185p $15.99; pa $6.99

Grades: 7 8 9 10 **Fic**
1. Basketball -- Fiction 2. Race relations -- Fiction 3. African Americans -- Fiction
ISBN 0-670-06006-2; 0-14-240692-9 pa

LC 2004-24543

Two star high school basketball players, one black and one white, experience the justice system differently after committing a crime together and getting caught.
"These complex characters share a mutual respect and struggle with issues of loyalty, honesty, and courage. Social conflicts, basketball fervor, and tough personal choices make this title a gripping story." SLJ

The **hand** you're dealt. Atheneum Books for Young Readers 2008 176p $16.99

Grades: 8 9 10 11 **Fic**
1. School stories 2. Poker -- Fiction 3. Teachers -- Fiction
ISBN 978-1-4169-3989-4; 1-4169-3989-X

LC 2007-22988

When seventeen-year-old Huck's vindictive math teacher wins the town poker tournament and takes the winner's watch away from Huck's father while he is in a coma, Huck vows to get even with him no matter what it takes.
"The varied characters are unique and add to the book's interest quotient." Voice Youth Advocates

★ **Homestretch**. Atheneum Books for Young Readers 2009 151p $16.99

Grades: 6 7 8 9 10 **Fic**
1. Death -- Fiction 2. Prejudices -- Fiction 3. Horse racing -- Fiction 4. Mexican Americans -- Fiction 5. Father-son relationship -- Fiction
ISBN 978-1-4169-3987-0; 1-4169-3987-3

LC 2008-30024

Five months after losing his mother, seventeen-year-old Gas runs away from an abusive father and gets a job working at an Arkansas race track, surrounded by the illegal Mexican immigrants that he and his father blame for her death.
"Volponi continues his streak of well-written novels in this simply written, coming-of-age story." Voice Youth Advocates

★ **Hurricane** song; a novel of New Orleans. Viking Childrens Books 2008 144p $15.99

Grades: 7 8 9 10 11 12 **Fic**
1. Jazz music -- Fiction 2. New Orleans (La.) -- Fiction 3. Father-son relationship -- Fiction 4. Hurricane

Katrina, 2005 -- Fiction
ISBN 978-0-670-06160-0; 0-670-06160-3
                                    LC 2007-38215
Twelve-year-old Miles Shaw goes to live with his father, a jazz musician, in New Orleans, and together they
survive the horrors of Hurricane Katrina in the Superdome,
learning about each other and growing closer through their
painful experiences.

"A brilliant blend of reality and fiction, this novel hits
every chord just right." Voice Youth Advocates

Rikers High. Viking 2010 216p $16.99
Grades: 8 9 10 11 12   **Fic**
1. Prisoners -- Fiction 2. African Americans -- Fiction
3. Juvenile delinquency -- Fiction 4. Rikers Island
Prison (New York, N.Y.) -- Fiction
ISBN 978-0-670-01107-0; 0-670-01107-X
                                    LC 2009-22471
Based on the adult novel, Rikers, published in 2002 by
Black Heron Press

Arrested on a minor offense, a New York City teenager
attends high school in the jail facility on Rikers Island, as he
waits for his case to go to court.

"The author draws authentic situations and characters
from his six years of teaching at Rikers. . . . An absorbing
portrait of life in the stir. . . . Rare is the reader who won't
find his narrative sobering." Booklist

★ **Rucker** Park setup. Viking 2007 149p
$15.99
Grades: 7 8 9 10 11 12   **Fic**
1. Mystery fiction 2. Homicide -- Fiction 3. Basketball
-- Fiction 4. African Americans -- Fiction 5. Harlem
(New York, N.Y.) -- Fiction
ISBN 978-0-670-06130-3; 0-670-06130-1
                                    LC 2006-28463
While playing in a crucial basketball game on the very
court where his best friend was murdered, Mackey tries to
come to terms with his own part in that murder and decide
whether to maintain his silence or tell J.R.'s father and the
police what really happened.

The author's "description of playing pickup ball on one
of the toughest courts in the world feels wholly authentic.
The characters also feel real." Voice Youth Advocates

Voorhees, Coert
Lucky fools; Coert Voorhees. Hyperion Books
2012 293 p. $16.99
Grades: 8 9 10 11 12   **Fic**
1. College choice 2. Theater -- Fiction 3. Dating
(Social customs) -- Fiction 4. Schools -- Fiction 5.
College choice -- Fiction 6. Palo Alto (Calif.) -- Fiction
7. Preparatory schools -- Fiction
ISBN 1423123980; 9781423123989
                                    LC 2011026252
Author Coert Voorhees presents a story about an aspiring
high school actor. "For the seniors at prestigious Oak Fields
Prep, the pressure is on to get into an Ivy League school. .
. . But David Ellison, star of the school play . . . wants to
go to Juilliard instead. As David's Juilliard audition and the
play's opening night approach, he is plagued with doubts

about his acting ability and his relationships with two girls."
(Publishers Weekly)

Vrettos, Adrienne Maria
★ **Sight**; [by] Adrienne Maria Vrettos. Margaret
K. McElderry Books 2007 254p $16.99
Grades: 7 8 9 10   **Fic**
1. School stories 2. Parapsychology -- Fiction 3.
Missing persons -- Fiction 4. Criminal investigation
-- Fiction
ISBN 978-1-4169-0657-5; 1-4169-0657-6
                                    LC 2006-35999
Sixteen-year-old Dylan uses her psychic abilities to help
police solve crimes against children, but keeps her extracur-
ricular activities secret from her friends at school.

"Vrettos has created a creepy scenario with a taut plot
and a gripping climax. . . . She has crafted a believable setting and characters." Bull Cent Books

Skin. Margaret K. McElderry Books 2006 227p
$16.95
Grades: 7 8 9 10   **Fic**
1. Siblings -- Fiction 2. Anorexia nervosa -- Fiction
ISBN 1-4169-0655-X
                                    LC 2005001119
When his parents decide to separate, eighth-grader
Donnie watches with horror as the physical condition of
his sixteen-year old sister, Karen, deteriorates due to an
eating disorder.

"The overwhelming alienation Donnie endures will
speak to many teens, while his honest perspective will be
welcomed by boys." Booklist

Wagner, Hilary
Lords of Trillium; by Hilary Wagner; illustrated by Omar Rayyan. Holiday House 2014 224 p.
(Nightshade chronicles) (hardcover) $17.95
Grades: 5 6 7 8   **Fic**
1. Fantasy fiction 2. Rats -- Fiction 3. Animal
experimentation -- Fantasy
ISBN 0823424138; 9780823424139
                                    LC 2013031299
In this book, by Hilary Wagner, "when the albino rat Billycan left Trillium at the end of The White Assassin, he fled
to the island of Tosca. There, here learns that a former ally,
working undercover in Nightshade City, is plotting to free
Killdeer's imprisoned evil generals and seize power. . . . But
something even more sinister is afoot in Trillium City. . .
. They discover that Prince Pharmaceuticals, the insidious
corporation that tortured so many rats, is back in business."
(Publisher's note)

"Wagner reveals lingering secrets, along with intrigue,
rivalries, revenge, and redemption in the satisfying third
book in this complex animal fantasy series." Booklist

Nightshade City; [illustrations by Omar Rayyan]
Holiday House 2010 262p il $17.95
Grades: 5 6 7 8   **Fic**
1. Fantasy fiction 2. Rats -- Fiction
ISBN 978-0-8234-2285-2; 0-8234-2285-2
                                    LC 2010-02474

Eleven years after the cruel Killdeer took over the Catacombs far beneath the human's Trillium City, Juniper Belancourt, assisted by Vincent and Victor Nightshade, leads a maverick band of rats to escape and establish their own city.

"The themes of love, loss and loyalty resonate through the novel, and the moments of darkness and violence are ultimately overpowered by hope and redemption. A good story well-told." Kirkus

Followed by: The white assassin (2011)

The **white** assassin. Holiday House 2011 242p il (The Nightshade chronicles) $17.95
Grades: 5 6 7 8   **Fic**
  1. Fantasy fiction 2. Rats -- Fiction
  ISBN 978-0-8234-2333-0
                                           LC 2011009579
  Sequel to: Nightshade City (2010)
Snakes, bats, and rats join forces to save Nightshade from Billycan and his horde of brutal swamp rats, aided by an antidote to the drug that made Billycan the way he is, but the revelation of secrets proves an even more powerful weapon in the fight for peace.

Waite, Michael P.
The **witches** of Dredmoore Hollow; by Riford McKenzie; with illustrations by Peter Ferguson. Marshall Cavendish Children 2008 264p il $16.99
Grades: 4 5 6 7   **Fic**
  1. Aunts -- Fiction 2. Witches -- Fiction 3. New England -- Fiction
  ISBN 978-0-7614-5458-8; 0-7614-5458-6
                                            LC 2007-29781
Strange things begin happening at Elijah's New England home just before his twelfth birthday in 1927, especially after two aunts he had never met whisk him away to Moaning Marsh, where he realizes that they are witches who need something from him in order to remove a curse.

"The book has continuous action and piles of demonic atmosphere." SLJ

Walden, Mark
Dreadnought. Simon & Schuster 2011 297p (H.I.V.E.) $16.99
Grades: 5 6 7 8   **Fic**
  1. School stories 2. Science fiction 3. Genius -- Fiction 4. Good and evil -- Fiction 5. Artificial intelligence -- Fiction
  ISBN 978-1-4424-2186-8; 1-4424-2186-X
A renegade faction of the world's most powerful villains is intent on destroying G.L.O.V.E. (Global League of Villainous Enterprises) and showing the world the true face of evil. The Disciples begin by hijacking Diabolus Darkdoom's Airborne command post, then they kidnap his son and his son's best friend. Heading out to America, Otto, Wing et al embark on a rescue operation. Cut off from the support of H.I.V.E. (The Higher Institute of Villainous Education) and on the run from American security forces the hunt for their friends leads to one of the US military's most secret facilities.

This "series continues to entertain with its high-energy, tongue-in-cheek take on a league of supervillains and their secret school." Booklist

Escape velocity. Simon & Schuster 2011 344p (H.I.V.E.) $16.99
Grades: 5 6 7 8   **Fic**
  1. School stories 2. Science fiction 3. Genius -- Fiction 4. Good and evil -- Fiction 5. Artificial intelligence -- Fiction
  ISBN 978-1-4424-2185-1; 1-4424-2185-1
Pupils and staff at H.I.V.E., The Higher Institute of Villainous Education, are horrified to discover that Dr Nero has been captured by the forces of HOPE, the Hostile Operative Prosecution Executive, the world's newest and most ruthlessly efficient security force. Three months pass without any news of his fate, and Number One has decided to appoint a sinister new headmistress for the school.

"Fans of the series will enjoy that the action starts immediately." Booklist

H.I.V.E; The Higher Institute of Villainous Education. Simon & Schuster Books for Young Readers 2007 309p $15.99; pa $6.99
Grades: 5 6 7 8   **Fic**
  1. Criminals -- Fiction
  ISBN 1-4169-3571-1; 978-1-4169-3571-1; 978-1-4169-3572-8 pa; 1-4169-3572-X pa
                                           LC 2007-16205
"H.I.V.E. is operated on a volcanic island in a distant ocean by G.L.O.V.E., a shadowy organization of worldwide wickedness. And, as 13-year-old master of mischief Otto Malpense soon discovers, here the slickest of young tricksters, thieves, and hackers have been brought against their will to be trained as the next generation of supervillains. . . . [This] novel is a real page-turner; those who love superhero stories will eat it up." SLJ

Another title about H.I.V.E. is:
H.I.V.E.: The Overlord protocol (2008)
H.I.V.E.: Escape velocity (2011)
H.I.V.E.: Dreadnought (2011)

H.I.V.E.: the Overlord protocol. Simon & Schuster Books for Young Readers 2008 376p $15.99
Grades: 5 6 7 8   **Fic**
  1. Criminals -- Fiction
  ISBN 978-1-4169-3573-5; 1-4169-3573-8
  Sequel to: H.I.V.E. (2007)
Still trapped at the Higher Institute of Villainous Education, or H.I.V.E., evil-genius-in-training Otto Malpense is nearly assassinated and must now not only try to escape, but also find out who murdered his best friend—and save himself.

This is "a real page turner. . . . A wickedly compelling adventure." Booklist

Followed by: H.I.V.E.: Escape velocity (2011)

Waldorf, Heather
Tripping. Red Deer Press 2008 342p pa $12.95
Grades: 8 9 10 11 12   **Fic**
  1. Canada -- Fiction 2. Amputees -- Fiction 3. Voyages and travels -- Fiction 4. Wilderness survival -- Fiction
  ISBN 978-0-88995-426-7; 0-88995-426-7
"Rainey and five other teens begin an eight-week school-sponsored educational/survival trek across Canada. . . . Rainey's challenge is heightened because she has an artifi-

cial leg and she learns that her mother, who abandoned her as a baby, lives near one of their stops and wants to meet her. As the trip progresses, the individuals bond and become part of a team. . . . Waldorf has written a unique story in which six very different young people are united in a common cause. Told with wit and humor, this fast-paced novel has character development that is extraordinary." SLJ

Wallace, Bill

Skinny -dipping at Monster Lake. Simon & Schuster Bks. for Young Readers 2003 212p hardcover o.p. pa $5.99

Grades: 4 5 6 7   **Fic**

ISBN 0-689-85150-2; 0-689-85151-0 pa

LC 2002-152820

When twelve-year-old Kent helps his father in a daring underwater rescue, he wins the respect he has always craved.

"This old-fashioned adventure has wide appeal, and the youngsters' games and camaraderie will hook even reluctant readers." SLJ

Wallace, Jason

Out of shadows. Holiday House 2011 282p $17.95

Grades: 7 8 9 10 11 12   **Fic**

1. School stories 2. Bullies -- Fiction 3. Zimbabwe -- Fiction 4. Race relations -- Fiction

ISBN 978-0-8234-2342-2; 0-8234-2342-5

LC 2010-24372

In 1983, at an elite boys' boarding school in Zimbabwe, thirteen-year-old English lad Robert Jacklin finds himself torn between his black roommate and the white bullies still bitter over losing power through the recent civil war.

"This thought-provoking narrative offers teens a window into a distinctive time and place in history that is likely to be unfamiliar to most of them. A first purchase for high schools, especially those with a strong world cultures curriculum." SLJ

Wallace, Rich

One good punch. Alfred A. Knopf 2007 114p $15.99

Grades: 7 8 9 10 11 12   **Fic**

1. School stories 2. Journalism -- Fiction 3. Pennsylvania -- Fiction 4. Track athletics -- Fiction

ISBN 978-0-375-81352-8; 0-375-81352-7

LC 2006-33270

Eighteen-year-old Michael Kerrigan, writer of obituaries for the Scranton Observer and captain of the track team, is ready for the most important season of his life—until the police find four joints in his school locker, and he is faced with a choice that could change everything.

"This novel's success is in creating a multidimensional male character in a format that will appeal to all readers. The moral dilemma . . . makes this novel ripe for ethical discussions." Voice Youth Advocates

Perpetual check. Alfred A. Knopf 2009 112p $15.99; lib bdg $18.99

Grades: 8 9 10 11   **Fic**

1. Chess -- Fiction 2. Brothers -- Fiction 3. Father-son

relationship -- Fiction

ISBN 978-0-375-84058-6; 0-375-84058-3; 978-0-375-94058-3 lib bdg; 0-375-94058-8 lib bdg

LC 2008-04159

Brothers Zeke and Randy participate in an important chess tournament, playing against each other while also trying to deal with their father's intensely competitive tendencies.

"Wallace cleverly positions Randy and Zeke for a win-win conclusion in this satisfying, engaging, and deceptively simple story." SLJ

War and watermelon. Viking 2011 184p $15.99

Grades: 6 7 8 9   **Fic**

1. School stories 2. Brothers -- Fiction 3. Football -- Fiction 4. New Jersey -- Fiction 5. Family life -- Fiction 6. Vietnam War, 1961-1975 -- Fiction 7. Father-son relationship -- Fiction 8. United States -- History -- Fiction

ISBN 978-0-670-01152-0; 0-670-01152-5

LC 2010-41043

As the summer of 1969 turns to fall in their New Jersey town, twelve-year-old Brody plays football in his first year at junior high while his older brother's protest of the war in Vietnam causes tension with their father.

"Sixties culture and events . . . are well integrated into the story, and humorous vignettes . . . help lighten the mood." Booklist

Wicked cruel; Rich Wallace. Knopf Books for Young Readers 2013 208 p. (hardback) $16.99

Grades: 5 6 7 8   **Fic**

1. Ghost stories 2. Horror fiction 3. Schools -- Fiction 4. Halloween -- Fiction 5. Supernatural -- Fiction 6. New Hampshire -- Fiction 7. Folklore -- New Hampshire -- Fiction

ISBN 0375867481; 9780375865145; 9780375867484; 9780375967481

LC 2012042504

This book of three "ghostly stories explore urban legends--actually rural New England legends--and how they changed lives. A bullied boy moves away and dies from a brain injury, yet he is seen in a music video after his death. A team of horses drowns in a flooded brickyard, but on certain rainy nights, they run free. Five farm children die young, but one mysteriously communicates with a young boy who may be as afraid of girls as of ghosts." (Kirkus Reviews)

★ **Wrestling** Sturbridge. Knopf 1996 135p hardcover o.p. pa $4.99

Grades: 7 8 9 10   **Fic**

1. Wrestling -- Fiction 2. Friendship -- Fiction

ISBN 0-679-87803-3; 0-679-88555-2 pa

LC 95-20468

"The wresting scenes are thrilling. . . . Like Ben, whose voice is so strong and clear here, Wallace weighs his words carefully, making every one count in this excellent, understated first novel." Booklist

"Narrator Ben, a high school senior, doesn't want to be like his father and so many others in Sturbridge, Pa., who after graduating get a job at the cinder block plant. Seemingly his only alternative is to become a state wrestling champion and thus win an athletic scholarship. But his way is firmly blocked by his buddy Al, who reigns supreme in their weight class." Publ Wkly

Wallenfels, Stephen

POD. Namelos 2009 212p $18.95; pa $9.95

Grades: 7 8 9 10   **Fic**

1. Science fiction 2. Extraterrestrial beings -- Fiction
ISBN 978-1-60898-011-6; 1-60898-011-1; 978-1-60898-010-9 pa; 1-60898-010-3 pa

LC 2008-29721

As alien spacecrafts fill the sky and zap up any human being who dares to go outside, fifteen-year-old Josh and twelve-year-old Megs, living in different cities, describe what could be their last days on Earth.

"The dire circumstances don't negate the humor, the hormones, or the humanity found in the young narrators. This is solid, straightforward sci-fi." Booklist

Waller, Sharon Biggs

A **mad,** wicked folly; Sharon Biggs Waller. Viking, published by the Penguin Group 2014 448 p. map (hardback) $17.99

Grades: 8 9 10 11 12   **Fic**

1. Love -- Fiction 2. Gender role -- Fiction 3. London (England) -- Fiction 4. Great Britain -- History -- Edward VII, 1901-1910 -- Fiction 5. Artists -- Fiction 6. Sex role -- Fiction 7. London (England) -- History -- 20th century -- Fiction
ISBN 0670014680; 9780670014682

LC 2013029858

This book, by Sharon Biggs Waller, is "about a young English woman who is talented, beautiful, passionate, and wealthy. Despite these advantages, Victoria Darling struggles with the harsh limitations imposed upon women prior to and during the Edwardian era of 1901-1910, which curtail her attempts to attend art school. While Victoria does not initially associate with the Suffragette Movement, she ultimately discovers that her fate is intertwined with the cause." (School Library Journal)

"Victoria's dream of becoming an artist leads her naively into scandals, tempts her into a convenient marriage, and drives her to join the Women's Social and Political Union. Persistence eventually triumphs, and friendships, love, and art lessons are her rewards. Sound historical research provides the backbone for this warm novel about the development of women's opportunities in Edwardian London." Horn Book

Includes bibliographical references

Walliams, David

★ The **boy** in the dress; illustrated by Quentin Blake. Razorbill 2009 231p il $15.99

Grades: 4 5 6 7   **Fic**

1. School stories 2. Soccer -- Fiction 3. Great Britain -- Fiction 4. Transvestites -- Fiction
ISBN 978-1-59514-299-3; 1-59514-299-1

"Dennis is a bit surprised—but not terribly nonplussed—to discover that he enjoys wearing dresses. The 12-year-old does, however, realize this is not the kind of revelation he wants to share with his truck-driving dad, his older brother, or his mates on the school football team, where he is the star player. . . . Walliams . . . has written a witty, high-spirited,

and, well, sensible story about cross-dressing and other real-life issues." Booklist

Walrath, Dana

★ **Like** water on stone; Dana Walrath. Delacorte Press 2014 368 p. (hc) $16.99

Grades: 8 9 10 11 12   **Fic**

1. Orphans -- Fiction 2. Armenian massacres, 1915-1923 -- Fiction 3. Turkey -- History -- Ottoman Empire, 1288-1918 -- Fiction 4. Novels in verse 5. Genocide -- Fiction 6. Armenians -- Turkey -- Fiction 7. Brothers and sisters -- Fiction
ISBN 0385743971; 9780375991424; 9780385743976

LC 2013026323

"Shahen Donabedian dreams of going to New York. Sosi, his twin sister, never wants to leave her home, especially now that she is in love. But when the Ottoman pashas set in motion their plans to eliminate all Armenians, neither twin has a choice. They flee into the mountains . . . [b]ut the children are not alone. An eagle watches over them as they run at night and hide each day, making their way across mountain ridges and rivers red with blood." (Publisher's note)

"This beautiful, yet at times brutally vivid, historical verse novel will bring this horrifying, tragic period to life for astute, mature readers.... A cast of characters, and author note with historical background are thoughtfully included." SLJ

Walsh, Alice

A **Long** Way from Home. Orca Book Pub 2012 232 p. (paperback) $11.95

Grades: 7 8 9 10   **Fic**

1. Immigrants -- Fiction 2. Prejudices -- Fiction 3. September 11 terrorist attacks, 2001 -- Fiction
ISBN 1926920791; 9781926920795

In this book by Alice Walsh, "thirteen-year-old Rabia, along with her mother and younger brother, flees Afghanistan. . . . They take part in a program that is relocating refugee widows and orphans to America. . . . After the terrorist attack on the World Trade Center in New York City, their plane is diverted to Gander, Newfoundland. Also on the plane is a boy named Colin, who struggles with his prejudices against Rabia and her family." (Publisher's note)

Walsh, Pat

★ The **Crowfield** curse. Chicken House 2010 326p il $16.99

Grades: 5 6 7 8   **Fic**

1. Magic -- Fiction 2. Orphans -- Fiction 3. Monasteries -- Fiction 4. Great Britain -- History -- 1154-1399, Plantagenets -- Fiction
ISBN 0-545-22922-7; 978-0-545-22922-7

LC 2009-51483

In 1347, when fourteen-year-old orphan William Paynel, an impoverished servant at Crowfield Abbey, goes into the forest to gather wood and finds a magical creature caught in a trap, he discovers he has the ability to see fays and becomes embroiled in a strange mystery involving Old Magic, a bitter feud, and ancient secrets.

"This suspenseful and spooky story will thrill readers. . . . With fascinating attention to detail and an edgy battle between evil and good, Walsh sweeps readers almost effortlessly into another time and place." SLJ

The **Crowfield** demon; Pat Walsh. Scholastic 2012 360 p. $16.99

Grades: 5 6 7 8   **Fic**
1. Fantasy fiction 2. Adventure fiction 3. Children's stories 4. Demonology -- Fiction 5. Magic -- Fiction 6. Orphans -- Fiction 7. Identity -- Fiction 8. Monasteries -- Fiction 9. Blessing and cursing -- Fiction 10. Great Britain -- History -- 14th century -- Fiction
ISBN 054531769X; 9780545317696; 9780545373500
LC 2011029246
Sequel to: The Crowfield curse
This juvenile historical fantasy novel by Pat Walsh is the sequel to his earlier story 'The Crowfield Curse.' "In 'The Crowfield Curse,' young monks' apprentice Will learned he was gifted with the Sight: able to see beyond this mortal coil into the spirit realms of Old Magic. Protected by the warrior fay Shadlok -- and befriended by the wry, wary hobgoblin called Brother Walter -- the boy is just coming into his strange powers. But now, from its very foundations, Crowfield Abbey has begun to crumble. As Will slaves to salvage the chapel, he discovers something truly terrifying. A heathen creature from a pagan past is creeping up through the rubble -- avowed to unleash havoc on holy ground!" (Publisher's note)

Walters, Eric

Catboy. Orca Book Publishers 2011 229p pa $9.95

Grades: 4 5 6 7   **Fic**
1. Boys -- Fiction 2. Cats -- Fiction 3. Canada -- Fiction
ISBN 978-1-55469-953-7 pa; 1-55469-953-3 pa
The wild cat colony Taylor has been caring for is at risk of being destroyed, and in order to save it, Taylor will need the help of all his friends.
"Walters' story . . . moves fast and is plenty appealing. . . . Solid writing, strong kid characters, caring adults, and cute animals could make this a popular choice." Booklist

The **money** pit mystery. Fitzhenry & Whiteside 2011 289p pa $9.95

Grades: 4 5 6 7   **Fic**
1. Mystery fiction 2. Islands -- Fiction 3. Family life -- Fiction 4. Buried treasure -- Fiction
ISBN 978-1-55455-123-1; 1-55455-123-4
"Sam's grandfather and mother had a fight years ago, and now Sam, his sister, and their mother are visiting him for the first time in years. When they arrive on tiny Oak Island, they are shocked to discover how rundown the man's once-immaculate house has become. To make matters worse, he isn't even there. When Sam, Beth, and their friend, Buzz, do some exploring, they are surprised by some security guards at the town's 'money pit.' Some folks believe that Captain Kidd buried treasure here. . . . This is a well-thought-out mystery with lots of suspense and a fully realized picture of a struggling family." SLJ

Sketches; by Eric Walters. Viking 2008 232p $15.99

Grades: 7 8 9 10   **Fic**
1. Artists -- Fiction 2. Homeless persons -- Fiction 3. Runaway teenagers -- Fiction
ISBN 978-0-670-06294-2; 0-670-06294-4
LC 2007-23123
After running away from home, fifteen-year-old Dana finds friends on the Toronto streets, and, eventually, a way to come to terms with what has happened to her.
"The characters' well-portrayed camaraderie, resourcefulness, and resiliency carry the tale, which ends on a note of promise." SLJ

Special Edward. Orca Book Publishers 2009 108p (Orca currents) $16.95; pa $9.95

Grades: 7 8 9 10   **Fic**
1. School stories 2. Learning disabilities -- Fiction
ISBN 978-1-55469-096-1; 1-55469-096-X; 978-1-55469-092-3 pa; 1-55469-092-7 pa
In an attempt to gain lower expectations and extra time for tests, Edward tries to fake a special education designation.
"Walters has a good ear for teen talk, and Edward is as charming to read about as he is in the classroom. The author deftly weaves subtle clues into Edward's character that will leave readers nodding in agreement with his true condition. . . . A refreshing read." SLJ

Splat! written by Eric Walters. Orca Book Publishers 2008 112p $16.95; pa $9.95

Grades: 7 8 9 10   **Fic**
1. Canada -- Fiction 2. Tomatoes -- Fiction 3. Friendship -- Fiction
ISBN 978-1-55143-988-4; 1-55143-988-3; 978-1-55143-986-0 pa; 1-55143-986-7 pa
"The relationship between Keegan and narrator Alex, with their relentless and often quite funny smartassed exchanges, is the core of this speedy and readable novel." Bull Cent Child Books
"Keegan and Alex are the only kids in Leamington who haven't volunteered to help out with the town's annual tomato festival. In an attempt to teach them a sense of responsibility, their fathers put them in charge of the tomato toss. The boys decide it's their responsibility to add a little excitement to the event." Publisher's note

Ward, David

★ **Escape** the mask. Amulet Books 2008 195p (The grassland trilogy) $15.95

Grades: 7 8 9 10   **Fic**
1. Science fiction 2. Slavery -- Fiction
ISBN 978-0-8109-9477-5; 0-8109-9477-1
LC 2007028212
Six young friends, tortured by the Spears and forced to work as slaves in the harsh fields of Grassland, vow to escape to find the freedom that was stolen from them long ago, and their opportunity arises when Outsiders come and wage war against the Spears.
"Ward's novel bursts with action and is laden with tense scenes. His excellent descriptive writing allows the reader to visualize the action. In addition, Ward's fantasy world is so believable that the text almost reads as historical fiction." Voice Youth Advocates
Other titles in this series are:

Beneath the mask (2008)

Beyond the mask (2010)

Ward, Rachel

The **Chaos**. Chicken House 2011 339p $17.99

Grades: 8 9 10 11 12 **Fic**

1. Science fiction 2. Death -- Fiction 3. Orphans -- Fiction 4. London (England) -- Fiction 5. Blacks -- Great Britain -- Fiction 6. Extrasensory perception -- Fiction

ISBN 978-0-545-24269-1; 0-545-24269-X

Sequel to: Numbers (2010)

When rising flood waters force him and his grandmother to evacuate their coastal home and return to London, sixteen-year-old Adam, who has inherited his mother's curse of being able to see the day that someone will die when he looks into their eyes, becomes disturbed when he begins to see January 1, 2027, a date six months into the future, in nearly everyone around him.

"In this sequel to Numbers a fascinating premise is again worked out through gripping episodes and a lightly handled metaphysical dilemma." Horn Book

Infinity; Rachel Ward. Chicken House/Scholastic 2012 249 p. (Numbers) $17.99

Grades: 8 9 10 11 12 **Fic**

1. Death -- Fiction 2. England -- Fiction 3. Psychic ability -- Fiction 4. London (England) -- Fiction 5. Interpersonal relations -- Fiction 6. Blacks -- England -- London -- Fiction

ISBN 0545350921; 9780545350921; 9780545381918

LC 2011032709

This novel, by Rachel Ward, is the conclusion to the "Numbers" trilogy. "Sarah loves Adam, but can't bear the thought that every time he looks in her eyes, he can see her dying; can see her last day. It's 2029. Two years since the Chaos. . . . Little Mia was supposed to die that New Year's Day. The numbers don't lie. But somehow she changed her date. Mia's just a baby, oblivious to her special power. But ruthless people are hunting her down, determined to steal her secret." (Publisher's note)

★ **Numbers**. Chicken House/Scholastic 2010 325p $17.99

Grades: 8 9 10 11 12 **Fic**

1. Science fiction 2. Death -- Fiction 3. Runaway teenagers -- Fiction 4. Blacks -- Great Britain -- Fiction 5. Extrasensory perception -- Fiction

ISBN 978-0-545-14299-1; 0-545-14299-7

LC 2008-55440

"Ward's debut novel is gritty, bold, and utterly unique. Jem's isolation and pain, hidden beneath a veneer of toughness, are palpable, and the ending is a real shocker." SLJ

"Since the day her mother died, Jem has known about the numbers. Numbers that pop into her head when she looks into someone's eyes. They're dates, the numbers. Dates predicting with brute accuracy each person's death. Burdened by such grim knowledge, Jem avoids relationships. Until she meets Spider, another outsider, and takes a chance." Publisher's note

Followed by: The Chaos (2011)

Wardlaw, Lee

101 ways to bug your friends and enemies. Dial Books for Young Readers 2011 $16.99; pa $6.99

Grades: 4 5 6 7 **Fic**

1. School stories 2. Bullies -- Fiction 3. California -- Fiction 4. Inventions -- Fiction 5. Family life -- Fiction

ISBN 978-0-8037-3262-9; 978-0-14-241949-6 pa

LC 2011001161

Steve "Sneeze" Wyatt takes half of his classes at the high school, where he attracts the attention of a bully on the varsity golf team, while at middle school all of his friends seem to be falling in love—including Sneeze, himself.

"With a unique cast of characters (including supportive parents) and plenty of conflict and humor, this is a good choice for reluctant readers." SLJ

101 ways to bug your teacher; Lee Wardlaw. Dial Books 2004 246p hardcover o.p. pa $6.99

Grades: 4 5 6 7 **Fic**

1. School stories

ISBN 0-8037-2658-9; 0-14-240331-1 pa

LC 2003-20068

Steve "Sneeze" Wyatt attempts to thwart his parents' plan to have him skip eighth grade, but he has bigger problems when his friends disapprove of his new list and Mrs. "Fierce" Pierce threatens to keep him from the Invention Convention.

"In spite of the title, the characters show respect for their teachers and parents, and for one another. A delightful read." SLJ

Warner, Sally

It's only temporary; written and illustrated by Sally Warner. Viking Childrens Books 2008 182p il $15.99

Grades: 4 5 6 7 **Fic**

1. Bullies -- Fiction 2. Siblings -- Fiction 3. Grandmothers -- Fiction 4. Brain -- Wounds and injuries -- Fiction

ISBN 978-0-670-06111-2; 0-670-06111-5

LC 2007-038220

When Skye's older brother comes home after a devastating accident, she moves from Albuquerque, New Mexico, to California to live with her grandmother and attend middle school, where she somewhat reluctantly makes new friends, learns to stand up for herself and those she cares about, and begins to craft a new relationship with her changed brother.

"Warner deftly handles Skye's anger toward her brain-injured brother, also infusing her with a convincingly developed sense of compassion. Witty line art decorates some pages." Horn Book Guide

Wasserman, Robin

★ **Awakening**. Scholastic 2007 207p (Chasing yesterday) pa $5.99

Grades: 6 7 8 9 **Fic**

1. Amnesia -- Fiction

ISBN 978-0-439-93338-4

"A teenager wakes up just yards away from a mysterious industrial accident. . . . Although she is seriously injured and has amnesia, she should be dead. . . . As Jane Doe, or J.D., she receives national news attention. Then a woman shows up, claiming to be her mother, and J.D. goes 'home' to a house she cannot remember and begins psychiatric treatment with an old family friend, who unnervingly looks exactly like the monstrous doctor of her nightmares.... [Wasserman's] characters are well developed and believable, her plot is suspenseful, and her backgrounds ... are nicely detailed." Voice Youth Advocates

Another title in this series is:
Betrayal (2007)

Betrayal. Scholastic 2007 209p (Chasing yesterday) pa $5.99

Grades: 6 7 8 9   **Fic**

1. Memory -- Fiction 2. Psychokinesis -- Fiction
ISBN 978-0-439-93341-4; 0-439-93341-2
Sequel to: Awakening

"J.D. is on the run, searching for answers about her past, and about the dangerous powers she can't seem to control. She knows she can't trust the memories implanted in her mind by the mysterious Dr. Styron, but they still feel real and they won't stop haunting her. J.D. and Daniel must race to uncover the truth and unlock the dark secrets in her brain before it's too late." Publisher's note

The **book** of blood and shadow; by Robin Wasserman. Alfred A. Knopf 2012 352p. (trade hardcover) $17.99

Grades: 7 8 9   **Fic**

1. Mystery fiction 2. Suspense fiction 3. Homicide -- Fiction 4. Prague (Czech Republic) -- Fiction 5. Murder -- Fiction 6. Conspiracies -- Fiction 7. Supernatural -- Fiction 8. Czech Republic -- Fiction 9. Secret societies -- Fiction 10. Mystery and detective stories
ISBN 9780375868764; 9780375872778; 9780375899614; 9780375968761

           LC 2011003920

In this book, "Nora . . . help[s] an eccentric professor translate a sixteenth-century book by a notable alchemist (and the letters left by his daughter, Elizabeth), . . . spending more time with her best friend, Chris, and his roommate, Max, who are also working on the project. Just as quickly as Nora becomes invested in Elizabeth's life, Max transforms from a slightly creepy tagalong to a sweet, solicitous boyfriend. Then Chris is brutally murdered, his girlfriend Adriane is left without memory of the night, and Max (the main suspect in the crime) disappears. . . . Nora . . . continu[es] her translation of the secrets encrypted in Elizabeth's . . . communications and uncovering conspiracies . . . in which she herself is . . . a key figure." (Bulletin of the Center for Children's Books)

Waters, Dan

★ **Generation** dead. Hyperion 2008 382p $16.99

Grades: 7 8 9 10   **Fic**

1. School stories 2. Death -- Fiction 3. Zombies -- Fiction 4. Prejudices -- Fiction
ISBN 978-1-4231-0921-1; 1-4231-0921-X

           LC 2007-36361

When dead teenagers who have come back to life start showing up at her high school, Phoebe, a goth girl, becomes interested in the phenomenon, and when she starts dating

a "living impaired" boy, they encounter prejudice, fear, and hatred.

This "is a classic desegregation story that also skewers adult attempts to make teenagers play nice. . . . Motivational speakers, politically correct speech and encounter groups come in for special ridicule." N Y Times Book Rev

Followed by: Kiss of life (2009)

Waters, Zack C.

Blood moon rider; [by] Zack C. Waters. Pineapple Press 2006 126p $13.95

Grades: 5 6 7 8   **Fic**

1. Florida -- Fiction 2. Ranch life -- Fiction 3. Grandfathers -- Fiction 4. World War, 1939-1945 -- Fiction
ISBN 978-1-56164-350-9; 1-56164-350-5

           LC 2005030749

After his father's death in World War II, fourteen-year-old Harley Wallace tries to join the Marines but is, instead, sent to live with his grandfather in Peru Landing, Florida, where he soon joins a covert effort to stop Nazis from destroying a secret airbase on Tampa Bay

This is "an adventure filled with unexpected kindnesses and the irrepressibility of family ties, as well as a brush with espionage and a couple of suspenseful shoot'em-up scenes. A colorful cast of characters and a nod to teenage romance help make this a good choice for middle school boys." SLJ

Watkins, Steve

★ **Down** Sand Mountain. Candlewick Press 2008 327p $16.99

Grades: 7 8 9 10   **Fic**

1. School stories 2. Bullies -- Fiction 3. Florida -- Fiction 4. Family life -- Fiction 5. Race relations -- Fiction
ISBN 978-0-7636-3839-9; 0-7636-3839-0

           LC 2007-52159

In a small Florida mining town in 1966, twelve-year-old Dewey faces one worst-day-ever after another, but comes to know that the issues he faces about bullies, girls, race, and identity are part of the adult world, as well.

"The simple, beautiful prose remains totally true to the child's bewildered viewpoint. . . . Readers will be haunted by the disturbing drama of harsh secrets close to home." Booklist

Watkins, Yoko Kawashima

★ **My** brother, my sister, and I. Bradbury Press 1994 275p hardcover o.p. pa $5.99

Grades: 6 7 8 9   **Fic**

1. Japan -- Fiction 2. Korea -- Fiction 3. World War, 1939-1945 -- Fiction
ISBN 0-02-792526-9; 0-689-80656-6 pa

           LC 93-23535

"Watkins's first-person narrative is beautifully direct and emotionally honest." Publ Wkly

"The author continues her autobiographical account begun in So Far from the Bamboo Grove with the story of how the two sisters, Ko and Yoko, now reunited with their brother Hideyo, try to survive in postwar Japan." Horn Book

★ **So** far from the bamboo grove. Lothrop, Lee & Shepard Bks. 1986 183p map hardcover o.p. pa $5.99

Grades: 6 7 8 9   **Fic**

1. Japan -- Fiction 2. Korea -- Fiction 3. World War, 1939-1945 -- Fiction

ISBN 0-688-13115-8 pa

LC 85-15939

A fictionalized autobiography in which eight-year-old Yoko escapes from Korea to Japan with her mother and sister at the end of World War II

"An admirably told and absorbing novel." Horn Book

Followed by: My brother, my sister and I

Watson, Cristy

Benched. Orca Book Publishers 2011 123p (Orca currents) pa $9.95

Grades: 6 7 8 9   **Fic**

1. Gangs -- Fiction 2. Brothers -- Fiction

ISBN 1-55469-408-6; 978-1-55469-408-2

Cody and his friends get caught up in gang activity when they steal a park bench.

"Reluctant readers, especially, will be hooked as the tension builds, and the realistic story, which avoids a slick resolution, will spark discussion." Booklist

Watson, Geoff

Edison's gold. Egmont USA 2010 312p $15.99; lib bdg $18.99

Grades: 4 5 6 7   **Fic**

1. Inventors 2. Mystery fiction 3. Adventure fiction 4. Electrical engineers 5. Inventors -- Fiction 6. Secret societies -- Fiction

ISBN 978-1-60684-094-8; 1-60684-094-0; 978-1-60684-095-5 lib bdg; 1-60684-095-9 lib bdg

LC 2010-11312

Tom Edison and his friends become embroiled in a mystery involving his 'double-great' grandfather's inventions, a secret society, and a vendetta being carried out by a descendant of inventor Nikola Tesla.

This "is a fast-paced adventure filled mystery that middle schoolers will like." SLJ

Watson, Jude

The **39** clues; unstoppable: nowhere to run. Jude Watson. Scholastic 2013 272 p. (The 39 clues: unstoppable) (paper over board) $12.99

Grades: 4 5 6 7   **Fic**

1. Supernatural -- Fiction 2. Brothers and sisters -- Fiction 3. Adventure and adventurers -- Fiction

ISBN 9780545521376; 0545521378

LC 2013934701

In this book, by Jude Watson, "the Cahill family has a secret. For five hundred years, they have guarded the 39 Clues – thirty-nine ingredients in a serum that transforms whomever takes it into the most powerful person on earth. . . . Certain Cahills have always made it their mission to keep the serum safe. . . . Thirteen-year-old Dan Cahill and his older sister, Amy, are the latest guardians of the Clues. They think they've done everything right, but a tiny mistake leads to catastrophe." (Publisher's note)

"Six months after sixteen-year-old Amy and thirteen-year-old Dan defeated the Vespers, the Cahill siblings set out on another quest to stop the serum their family has protected for centuries from wreaking havoc on the world. This first entry in a new spinoff series is formulaic, but the suspense and high stakes that 39 Clues fans love are front and center." (Horn Book)

Beyond the grave. Scholastic 2009 190p (The 39 clues) $12.99

Grades: 4 5 6 7   **Fic**

1. Ciphers -- Fiction 2. Orphans -- Fiction 3. Siblings -- Fiction

ISBN 978-0-545-06044-8; 0-545-06044-3

Sequel to: The sword thief by Peter Lerangis (2009)

A clue sends Amy and Dan jetting off to find out just what's behind the fierce rivalry between the Tomas and Ekaterina branches of the Cahill family. Was a Clue stolen from the Tomas branch? Where is it now? And most important, can Amy and Dan get their hands on it before their rivals do?

"Like the previous books, historical information is woven into the fast-paced adventure." SLJ

Followed by: The black circle by Patrick Carman (2009)

In too deep. Scholastic 2009 206p (The 39 clues) $12.99

Grades: 4 5 6 7   **Fic**

1. Adventure fiction 2. Ciphers -- Fiction 3. Orphans -- Fiction 4. Siblings -- Fiction

ISBN 978-0-545-09064-3; 0-545-09064-4

Sequel to: Beyond the grave by Jude Watson (2009)

"Amy and Dan fly to Australia. Attemping to trace their late parents' journey eight years earlier, they link Amelia Earhart's last flight to their own family quest. . . . The spy-versus-spy mentality will keep readers guessing. . . . The series' fans will devour the breathless action scenes in this fast-paced adventure." Booklist

Followed by: The viper's nest by Peter Lerangis (2010)

Loot; how to steal a fortune. Jude Watson. Scholastic Press 2014 272 p. (alk. paper) $16.99

Grades: 4 5 6 7   **Fic**

1. Twins -- Fiction 2. Adventure fiction 3. Jewelry -- Fiction 4. Orphans -- Fiction 5. Robbers and outlaws -- Fiction 6. Brothers and sisters -- Fiction 7. Adventure and adventurers -- Fiction

ISBN 0545468027; 9780545468022

LC 2014001218

"When master jewel thief Alfie McQuinn dies, his stashed set of clues and cryptic last words to March, his 12-year-old son and apprentice, mark the beginning of a race against time. The first clue leads March to discover his twin sister, Jules, a traveling circus acrobat. Tossed into a group home, they meet Darius, a juvenile delinquent with a soft spot for Izzy, a code-cracking hacker." (Booklist)

"Pitch-perfect characters, from scheming criminals to a twisted former cop to the twins' father, move in and out of the narrative, but it's the four young teens that drive the tale forward with enviable schemes and ingenious plans.Taut, engrossing and unstoppable." Kirkus

Watson, Renee

What Momma left me. Bloomsbury 2010 224p
$15.99

Grades: 5 6 7 8   **Fic**
1. Orphans -- Fiction 2. Bereavement -- Fiction 3.
Family life -- Fiction 4. Grandparents -- Fiction 5.
Christian life -- Fiction 6. African Americans -- Fiction
ISBN 978-1-59990-446-7; 1-59990-446-2

LC 2009-18263

After the death of their mother, thirteen-year-old Serenity Evans and her younger brother go to live with their
grandparents, who try to keep them safe from bad influences
and help them come to terms with what has happened to
their family.

"Serenity's struggles and insights, as she wrestles with
her parents' legacy and an uncertain future, are inspiring,
authentic, and told in a straighforward yet poetic style. The
first-person narration is consistent, and the mystery of the
painful circumstances of her mother's death—as well as additional tragedies—propels the story." Publ Wkly

Watts, Irene N.

★ **No** moon. Tundra Books 2010 234p pa
$12.95

Grades: 6 7 8 9   **Fic**
1. Shipwrecks -- Fiction 2. Household employees --
Fiction 3. Titanic (Steamship) -- Fiction
ISBN 978-0-88776-971-9; 0-88776-971-3

Louisa Gardener is the fourteen-year-old nursemaid to
the young daughters of a wealthy, titled family living in
London, England, in 1912. The family decides to sail to
New York aboard the Titanic. An accident to the children's
nanny, only days prior to the sailing, means that Louisa must
go in her stead.

"Watts provides a fascinating account of what the
great unsinkable ship was like. The catastrophe is rendered in a heartbreakingly graceful style. . . . [This is a]
uniquely engaging and satisfying coming-of-age historical
adventure." Booklist

Weatherford, Carole Boston

★ **Becoming** Billie Holiday; art by Floyd Cooper. Wordsong 2008 116p il $19.95

Grades: 7 8 9 10   **Fic**
1. Singers 2. Blues musicians 3. Novels in verse 4.
Singers -- Fiction 5. Jazz music -- Fiction 6. African
Americans -- Fiction
ISBN 978-1-59078-507-2; 1-59078-507-X

LC 2007-51214

Coretta Scott King honor book for text, 2009

Jazz vocalist Billie Holiday looks back on her early
years in this fictional memoir written in verse.

"This captivating title places readers solidly into Holiday's world, and is suitable for independent reading as well
as a variety of classroom uses." SLJ

Includes bibliographical references

Weatherly, Lee

Angel burn; [by] L.A. Weatherly. Candlewick
Press 2011 449p $17.99

Grades: 8 9 10 11 12   **Fic**
1. Love -- Fiction 2. Angels -- Fiction 3. Supernatural

-- Fiction
ISBN 978-0-7636-5652-2; 0-7636-5652-6

LC 2010-44819

In a world where angels are fierce stalkers whose irresistible force allows them to feed off humans and drain
them of their vitality, a ruthless teenaged assassin of angels falls in love with a half-angel half-human girl, with
devastating consequences.

"Weatherly's plot and writing are first-rate, adrenaline-
fueled while still taking the time to thoughtfully develop the
characters and build the romance. This elevated twist on the
angel genre deserves to be spread far and wide." Publ Wkly

Kat got your tongue. David Fickling Books
2007 195p $15.99; lib bdg $18.99

Grades: 7 8 9 10   **Fic**
1. Amnesia -- Fiction 2. Great Britain -- Fiction
ISBN 978-0-385-75117-9; 0-385-75117-6; 978-0-385-
75122-3 lib bdg; 0-385-75122-2 lib bdg

LC 2006-24408

After being hit by a car, thirteen-year-old Kat wakes up
in the hospital with no memory of her previous life.

"Weatherby writes with fluid grace and makes this story
line compelling, sprinkling bits of humor into Kat's journey
toward recovery." Booklist

Weaver, Will

Defect. Farrar, Straus and Giroux 2007 199p
$16

Grades: 7 8 9 10 11 12   **Fic**
1. School stories 2. Minnesota -- Fiction 3. Birth
defects -- Fiction 4. Foster home care -- Fiction
ISBN 0-374-31725-9; 978-0-374-31725-6

LC 2006-49152

After spending most of his life in Minnesota foster
homes hiding a bizarre physical abnormality, fifteen-year-
old David is offered a chance at normalcy, but must decide
if giving up what makes him special is the right thing to do.

The author "skillfully interweaves the improbable
with twenty-first-century realities in this provocative novel of the ultimate cost of being so, so different." Voice
Youth Advocates

Full service. Farrar, Straus & Giroux 2005 231p
hardcover o.p. pa $8.99

Grades: 7 8 9 10   **Fic**
1. Farm life -- Fiction 2. Minnesota -- Fiction 3.
Service stations -- Fiction
ISBN 0-374-32485-9; 0-374-40022-9 pa

LC 2004-57671

In the summer of 1965, teenager Paul Sutton, a northern
Minnesota farm boy, takes a job at a gas station in town,
where his strict religious upbringing is challenged by new
people and experiences.

"Weaver is a wonderful stylist and his beautifully chosen
words put such a shine on his deeply felt story that most
teens will be able to find their own faces reflected in its
pages." Booklist

Saturday night dirt. Farrar, Straus and Giroux
2008 163p $14.95; pa $7.99

Grades: 8 9 10 11 **Fic**
1. Minnesota -- Fiction 2. Automobile racing -- Fiction
ISBN 978-0-374-35060-4; 0-374-35060-4; 978-0-312-56131-4 pa; 0-312-56131-8 pa

LC 2007-6988

In a small town in northern Minnesota, the much-anticipated Saturday night dirt-track race at the old-fashioned, barely viable, Headwaters Speedway becomes, in many ways, an important life-changing event for all the participants on and off the track.

"Weaver presents compelling character studies. . . . Young racing fans . . . will find much that rings true here." Booklist

Other titles in this series are Checkered flag cheater (2010)

Super stock rookie (2009)

Webb, Philip

Six days. Chicken House 2011 336p $17.99
Grades: 5 6 7 8 **Fic**
1. Science fiction 2. Siblings -- Fiction 3. Space and time -- Fiction 4. London (England) -- Fiction
ISBN 978-0-545-31767-2; 0-545-31767-3

LC 2010054233

Cass and her brother Wilbur scavenge in the ruins of a future London seeking an artifact for their Russian masters, but the search takes on a new urgency after the arrival of Erin and Peyto, strangers from afar who claim to hold the key to locating the mysterious object.

Webb "has created a complex and intriguing dystopia filled with devastation, clever devices . . . and lots of local color. . . . The novel's rapid pacing will hook readers and keep them turning pages." Booklist

Weber, David

★ A beautiful friendship. Baen Books 2011 361p $18.99
Grades: 6 7 8 9 **Fic**
1. Science fiction 2. Animals -- Fiction 3. Space colonies -- Fiction
ISBN 978-1-4516-3747-2; 1-4516-3747-0

LC 2011015815

Twelve-year-old Stephanie Harrington, a genetically-enhanced girl on the pioneer planet of Sphinx, bonds with a treecat, a telepathic and fully sentient animal, putting her in danger from highly placed enemies who want to ensure that the planet remains entirely in human hands.

"The environmenatal messages, human-animal friendship, humor, action, and inventive techology will make this series starter an easy hit with teen sf readers." Booklist

Weber, Lori

If you live like me. Lobster Press 2009 331p pa $14.95
Grades: 7 8 9 10 **Fic**
1. Family life -- Fiction 2. Newfoundland -- Fiction
ISBN 1-897550-12-X; 978-1-897550-12-0

Cheryl's unhappiness builds with each move as her family travels across Canada while her father does research for a book, and by the time they reach Newfoundland, she is planning her escape, but events cause her to re-examine her feelings

"Weber's depiction of Cheryl is true to life, an accurate account of an independent and intelligent teenager struggling with loneliness, acceptance of change, and her own approaching adulthood." SLJ

Wedekind, Annie

A horse of her own; by Annie Wedekind. Feiwel and Friends 2008 275p $16.95; pa $7.99
Grades: 5 6 7 8 **Fic**
1. Camps -- Fiction 2. Horses -- Fiction 3. Kentucky -- Fiction 4. Horsemanship -- Fiction
ISBN 978-0-312-36927-9; 0-312-36927-1; 978-0-312-58146-6 pa; 0-312-58146-7 pa

LC 2007032769

At summer camp Jane feels like an outsider among the cliquish rich girls who board their horses at Sunny Acres farm, and when the horse she has been riding is sold to another camper, she feels even worse until her teacher asks her to help train a beautiful but skittish new horse, and the experience brings out the best in her.

"Tenacious and thoughtful, Jane is an appealing protagonist who gradually recognizes that being accepted no longer matters to her. The plot . . . has enough twists, including a hint of romance, to sustain readers' interest." SLJ

Weeks, Sarah

As simple as it seems. Laura Geringer Books 2010 181p $15.99; lib bdg $16.89
Grades: 4 5 6 **Fic**
1. Ghost stories 2. Adoption -- Fiction 3. Friendship -- Fiction 4. Catskill Mountains (N.Y.) -- Fiction
ISBN 978-0-06-084663-3; 0-06-084663-1; 978-0-06-084664-0 lib bdg; 0-06-084664-X lib bdg

Eleven-year-old Verbena Polter gets through a difficult summer of turbulent emotions and the revelation of a disturbing family secret with an odd new friend who believes she is the ghost of a girl who drowned many years before.

"Weeks's characters are well rounded and her story line is engaging." Horn Book Guide

★ Jumping the scratch; a novel. Laura Geringer Books 2006 167p il $15.99; pa $5.99
Grades: 5 6 7 8 **Fic**
1. Aunts -- Fiction 2. Memory -- Fiction 3. Child sexual abuse -- Fiction
ISBN 978-0-06-054109-5; 0-06-054109-1; 978-0-06-054110-1 pa; 0-06-054111-3 pa

LC 2005-17776

After moving with his mother to a trailer park to care for an injured aunt, eleven-year-old Jamie Reardon struggles to cope with a deeply buried secret

"Weeks alludes to sexual abuse, but with a broad brush and no graphic details. . . . Weeks perfectly captures not only the guilt, shame, and pain of the abused boy but also the tenor of a fifth-grade classroom from the point of view of a new student who is friendless, targeted, and belittled by an insensitive teacher. Touches of humor ameliorate the pain and poignancy." SLJ

Pie. Scholastic Press 2011 183p $16.99

Grades: 4 5 6 7   **Fic**
   1. Cats -- Fiction 2. Pies -- Fiction 3. Aunts -- Fiction
ISBN 978-0-545-27011-3; 0-545-27011-1

In the 1950s in the small town of Ipswitch, PA, Polly
Portman dies and leaves the recipe for her prize-winning
piecrust to her cat Lardo, in the care of her niece Alice, but
then the cat is kidnapped and the bakery is trashed.

"Weeks deftly leavens moments of hilarity with the process of grieving in this sweet coming-of-age story in which
Alice learns from Aunt Polly to follow her heart and to open
it as well. Readers will close the book with a satisfied sigh
and may seek out an adult to help them bake a pie. Recipes
included." SLJ

Weichman, Kathy Cannon

Like a river; a civil war novel. Kathy Cannon
Wiechman. Calkins Creek 2015 336 p. $17.95
Grades: 5 6 7 8   **Fic**
   1. Historical fiction 2. United States -- History -- 1861-
1865, Civil War -- Fiction
ISBN 1629792098; 9781629792095
                                LC 2014945289

In this novel, by Kathy Cannon Wiechman, "Leander
and Polly are two teenage Union soldiers who carry deep,
dangerous secrets. Leander is underage when he enlists and
Polly follows her father into war disguised as his son. . . .
Polly mourns the death of her father, endures Andersonville
Prison, and narrowly escapes the Sultana steamboat disaster.
As the lives of these . . . soldiers intersect, each . . . learns
about the importance of loyalty, family, and love." (Publisher's note)

"Three years have passed since the beginning of the
Civil War, when two underage teens, West Virginian Paul
Settles and Ohioan Leander Jordan, both with secrets to
guard, enlist in the Union Army. Their paths cross in a military hospital, where their mysteries begin to unravel, but the
plot takes them in separate directions...A truly excellent first
purchase for all fans of historical fiction who enjoy a hint of
romance." SLJ

Weil, Cynthia

I'm glad I did; Cynthia Weil. Soho Teen 2015
272 p. (hardback) $18.99
Grades: 8 9 10 11 12   **Fic**
   1. Nineteen sixties 2. Rock music -- Fiction 3.
Songwriters and songwriting 4. Love -- Fiction 5.
Secrets -- Fiction 6. Composers -- Fiction 7. Popular
music -- Fiction
ISBN 161695356X; 9781616953560
                                LC 2014025047

In this novel by Cynthia Weil "it's the summer of 1963
and JJ Green is a born songwriter . . . [and] she takes an
internship at the Brill Building, the epicenter of a new sound
called rock and roll. She even finds herself a writing partner
in Luke Silver, a boy . . . who seems to connect instantly
with her music. Best of all, they'll be cutting their first demo
with legendary singer Dulcie Brown. But Dulcie's past is a
tangle of secrets." (Publisher's note)

"Grammy-winning songwriter Weil makes an impressive YA debut with this period novel set against the rapidly
changing music industry of the early 1960s. . . [s]howing
both the bright and the dark sides of the music business,

Weil crafts an enticing tale of a sheltered teenager's induction into a world where ambitions and morals are repeatedly
tested." PW

Wein, Elizabeth E.

  ★ **Black** dove, white raven; Elizabeth Wein.
Disney-Hyperion 2015 368 p. (hardback) $17.99
Grades: 8 9 10 11 12   **Fic**
   1. Adoption -- Fiction 2. Air pilots -- Fiction 3. Race
relations -- Fiction 4. Brothers and sisters -- Fiction 5.
Italo-Ethiopian War, 1935-1936 -- Fiction 6. Americans
-- Ethiopia -- Fiction 7. Adventure and adventurers --
Fiction 8. Ethiopia -- History -- 1889-1974 -- Fiction
ISBN 142318310X; 9781423183105
                                LC 2014044446

In this book, by Elizabeth Wein, "Emilia and Teo's
lives changed in a fiery, terrifying instant when a bird strike
brought down the plane their stunt pilot mothers were flying.
Teo's mother died immediately, but Em's survived, determined to raise Teo according to his late mother's wishes.
. . . But in 1930s America, a white woman raising a black
adoptive son alongside a white daughter is too often seen as
a threat." (Publisher's note)

"Em (white) and Teo (black) have grown up together,
their mothers American stunt-pilots who met after World
War I. After Teo's mother Delia dies in a crash, Em's mother moves the family to Ethiopia -- in part, to fulfill Delia's
dream for her son to live in the land of his father, where
his skin color won't bring discrimination...The intellectual,
psychological, and emotional substance of this story is formidable, and Wein makes it all approachable and engaging."
Horn Book

The **empty** kingdom. Viking 2008 217p (Mark
of Solomon) $16.99
Grades: 7 8 9 10   **Fic**
   1. Africa -- Fiction 2. Princes -- Fiction
ISBN 978-0-670-06273-7; 0-670-06273-1
                                LC 2007-29082

Sequel to: The lion hunter (2007)

Telemakos, imprisoned on the upper levels of Abreha's,
ruler of Himyar, twelve-story palace and lacking any way
to communicate his predicament to his family in faraway
Aksum, tries to find a subtle and effective way to regain
his freedom.

"Wein deftly balances the political with the personal. . . .
A unique, epic journey into adulthood." Horn Book

  ★ The **lion** hunter. Viking 2007 223p (Mark
of Solomon) $16.99
Grades: 7 8 9 10   **Fic**
   1. Kings 2. Africa -- Fiction 3. Princes -- Fiction
ISBN 978-0-670-06163-1; 0-670-03638-2

Still recovering from his ordeal as a government spy,
twelve-year-old Telemakos, the half-Ethiopian grandson
of King Artos of Britain, is sent with his sister to live with
Abreha, the ruler of Himyar. His Aunt Goewin warns him
that Abreha is a dangerous man, but just how dangerous remains to be seen.

"The vividly evoked setting provides a lush backdrop
for the story's seemingly casual permutations, and readers'
sympathies toward the embattled, wounded hero will draw

them on willingly while Wein weaves her web of loyalty and intrigue." Horn Book

Followed by: The empty kingdom (2008)

Weingarten, Lynn

Wherever Nina lies. Point 2009 316p $16.99

Grades: 8 9 10 11 12 **Fic**

1. Sisters -- Fiction 2. Missing persons -- Fiction
ISBN 978-0-545-06631-0; 0-545-06631-X

LC 2008-21527

"Sixteen-year-old Ellie Wrigley is desperate to find her unconventional, beloved older sister, Nina, who disappeared two years ago, seemingly without a trace. When Ellie uncovers a clue in a local secondhand shop . . . she is determined to investigate. . . . Ellie sets off on a cross-country chase with her new crush, Sean, who has also lost a sibling. . . . Weingarten's fast-paced, chatty style will keep readers tuned in." Publ Wkly

Weissman, Elissa Brent

The **short** seller; Elissa Brent Weissman. 1st ed. Atheneum Books for Young Readers 2013 256 p. (hardcover) $15.99

Grades: 3 4 5 6 **Fic**

1. Girls -- Fiction 2. Stocks -- Fiction 3. Friendship -- Fiction 4. Best friends -- Fiction 5. Mononucleosis -- Fiction 6. Electronic trading of securities -- Fiction
ISBN 1442452552; 9781442452558

LC 2012018632

In this middle-grade novel, by Elissa Brent Weissman, "a twelve-year-old takes on the stock market. . . . It all starts when seventh grader Lindy Sachs is granted $100 and access to her father's online trading account. . . . With trading talent and access to her parents' savings, the opportunity to make some real dough is too tempting to pass up. In fact, given how well Lindy's stocks are doing, it would be a disservice to not invest it all. . . . Right?" (Publisher's note)

The **trouble** with Mark Hopper. Dutton Children's Books 2009 227p $16.99

Grades: 5 6 7 8 **Fic**

1. School stories 2. Contests -- Fiction 3. Maryland -- Fiction 4. Identity (Psychology) -- Fiction
ISBN 978-0-525-42067-5; 0-525-42067-3

LC 2008-34211

When two eleven-year-olds with the same name, similar looks, and very different personalities go to the same Maryland middle school, confusion and bad feelings ensue, but things improve after a teacher insists that they become study partners.

"Realistic school interactions give Weissman's novel a lot of kid appeal with substance." Horn Book Guide

Welch, Sheila Kelly

Waiting to forget. Namelos 2011 170p $18.95

Grades: 5 6 7 8 **Fic**

1. Siblings -- Fiction 2. Foster home care -- Fiction
ISBN 978-1-60898-114-4; 1-60898-114-2

T.J. and his sister, Angela, learn how to move forward and be happy while in foster care.

"T.J.'s authentic voice and the multilayered presentation of his memories, shifting between the waiting room

and his past, make for a poignant, realistic tale of child-survivors." Kirkus

Wells, Ken

Rascal; a dog and his boy. illustrations by Christian Slade. Alfred A. Knopf 2010 201p il $16.99; lib bdg $19.99

Grades: 4 5 6 7 **Fic**

1. Dogs -- Fiction 2. Louisiana -- Fiction
ISBN 978-0-375-86652-4; 0-375-86652-3; 978-0-375-96652-1 lib bdg; 0-375-96652-8 lib bdg

LC 2009-37606

Rascal may be the happiest beagle ever to live. He used to live on Voclain's Farm, but now he lives with his very own boy, Meely. Together they explore the Louisiana bayou. But when Meely gets stuck on a rotting bridge deep in the bayou, it's up to Rascal to save his boy from danger.

"This is a cracking good animal story of classic pedigree. . . . Characterizations of both humans and animals are sharp and distinct. . . . [The] narration sings with the same lively Cajun-flavored spice as the dialogue, and it's an easy dialect to get the hang of." Bull Cent Child Books

Wells, Robison

Feedback; Robison Wells. HarperTeen 2012 312 p. (hardback) $17.99

Grades: 7 8 9 10 **Fic**

1. Private schools -- Fiction 2. School stories 3. Mystery fiction 4. Science fiction 5. Robots -- Fiction 6. Survival -- Fiction
ISBN 0062026100; 9780062026101; 9780062228307

LC 2012004296

Sequel to: Variant

In author Robison Wells' story, "Benson Fisher escaped from Maxfield Academy's deadly rules and brutal gangs. The worst was over. Or so he thought. But now he's trapped on the other side of the wall, in a different kind of prison. . . . [His friends] are all pawns in the school's twisted experiment, held captive and controlled by an unseen force. And while Benson struggles to figure out who, if anyone, can be trusted, he discovers that Maxfield Academy's plans are darker than anything he imagined--and they may be impossible to stop." (Publisher's note)

Variant. HarperTeen 2011 376p $17.99

Grades: 7 8 9 10 **Fic**

1. School stories 2. Science fiction
ISBN 978-0-06-202608-8; 0-06-202608-9

LC 2010042661

After years in foster homes, seventeen-year-old Benson Fisher applies to New Mexico's Maxfield Academy in hopes of securing a brighter future, but instead he finds that the school is a prison and no one is what he or she seems.

"Hard to put down from the very first page, this fast-paced novel with Stepford overtones answers only some of the questions it poses, holding some of the most tantalizing open for the next installment in a series that is anything but ordinary." Kirkus

Wells, Rosemary

My Havana; [by] Rosemary Wells with Secundino Fernandez; illustrated by Peter Ferguson. Candlewick Press 2010 65p il $17.99

Grades: 4 5 6 7   **Fic**

1. Architects 2. Cuba -- Fiction 3. Dictators -- Fiction 4. Family life -- Fiction

ISBN 978-0-7636-4305-8; 0-7636-4305-X

LC 2009-12053

Relates events in the childhood of architect Secundino Fernandez, who left his beloved Havana, Cuba, with his parents, first to spend a year in Spain, and later to move to New York City.

"Wells has chosen anecdotes wisely, and Ferguson's illustrations are atmospheric, capturing Dino's childlike enthusiasm and longing." Kirkus

★ On the Blue Comet; illustrated by Bagram Ibatoulline. Candlewick Press 2010 329p il $16.99

Grades: 5 6 7 8   **Fic**

1. Adventure fiction 2. Railroads -- Fiction 3. California -- Fiction 4. Space and time -- Fiction

ISBN 978-0-7636-3722-4; 0-7636-3722-X

LC 2009051358

During the Great Depression, Oscar's dad must sell their home and head west in search of work. Oscar meets a mysterious drifter and witnesses a crime so stunning it catapults Oscar on a train journey from coast to coast, from one decade to another.

"Ibatoulline's full-color, atmospheric Norman Rockwell-like vignettes enhance the nostalgic feel of this warm, cleverly crafted adventure." Kirkus

★ Red moon at Sharpsburg. Viking 2007 236p $16.99; pa $7.99

Grades: 6 7 8 9 10   **Fic**

1. United States -- History -- 1861-1865, Civil War -- Fiction

ISBN 0-670-03638-2; 978-0-670-03638-7; 0-14-241205-8 pa; 978-0-14-241205-3 pa

As the Civil War breaks out, India, a young Southern girl, summons her sharp intelligence and the courage she didn't know she had to survive the war that threatens to destroy her family, her Virginia home and the only life she has ever known.

"This powerful novel is unflinching in its depiction of war and the devastation it causes, yet shows the resilience and hope that can follow such a tragedy. India is a memorable, thoroughly believable character." SLJ

Welsh, M. L.

Heart of stone; a Verity Gallant tale. M.L. Welsh. David Fickling Books 2012 409 p. (hard cover) $16.99

Grades: 5 6 7 8   **Fic**

1. Love stories 2. Occult fiction 3. Witches -- Fiction 4. Fantasy 5. Sailing -- Fiction 6. Betrayal -- Fiction 7. Friendship -- Fiction 8. Family life -- Fiction 9. Books and reading -- Fiction

ISBN 0385752431; 9780375899164; 9780385752428; 9780385752435

LC 2011023878

Sequel to: Mistress of the Storm

This book is a "companion novel to 'Mistress Of The Storm' . . . tell[ing] the story of heroine Verity Gallant's fight against an evil force determined to put an end to all happily-ever-after stories. . . . The evil force appears to be trying to destroy Verity's cliffside hometown of Wellow, which is rapidly being eroded by white sand gathering as if it had a single motive—to erase all the 'Original Stories' with happy endings." (Voice of Youth Advocates)

★ Mistress of the Storm; a Verity Gallant tale. David Fickling Books 2011 318p $16.99; lib bdg $19.99

Grades: 5 6 7 8   **Fic**

1. Fantasy fiction 2. Sailing -- Fiction 3. Witches -- Fiction 4. Friendship -- Fiction 5. Family life -- Fiction 6. Books and reading -- Fiction

ISBN 978-0-385-75244-2; 0-385-75244-X; 978-0-385-75245-9 lib bdg; 0-385-75245-8 lib bdg

LC 2010018721

First published in the United Kingdom

After a stranger gives an ancient book to unpopular, twelve-year-old Verity Gallant, she and her new-found friends, Henry and Martha, uncover secrets stirring in the harbor town of Wellow and use them to face a powerful, vengeful witch.

"Welsh's prose is lovely, her characters are well-drawn, and the atmosphere of the town is palpable. In creating a place in the world where a story read aloud can become true, Welsh offers a benediction of sorts to readers, that 'every child who is alone or out of place will find the friends they need, and the love they deserve.'" Publ Wkly

Wendig, Chuck

Under the Empyrean Sky. Amazon Childrens Pub 2013 368 p. $17.99

Grades: 7 8 9 10   **Fic**

1. Science fiction 2. Apocalyptic fiction

ISBN 1477817204; 9781477817209

In this first book in Chuck Wendig's Heartland Trilogy, "the haves hover above ruined Earth in luxurious flotillas and the have-nots toil below in the Heartland, [are] told whom to marry and what to grow. . . . When Cael and his friends discover a trail of precious, prohibited vegetables growing deep in the corn, they stumble on a secret that may save them—or get them killed." (Kirkus Reviews)

Werlin, Nancy

Double helix. Dial Books 2004 252p hardcover o.p. pa $6.99

Grades: 7 8 9 10   **Fic**

1. Science fiction 2. Bioethics -- Fiction 3. Genetic engineering -- Fiction

ISBN 0-8037-2606-6; 0-14-240327-X pa

LC 2003-12269

Eighteen-year-old Eli discovers a shocking secret about his life and his family while working for a Nobel Prizewinning scientist whose specialty is genetic engineering.

"Werlin clearly and dramatically raises fundamental bioethical issues for teens to ponder. She also creates a riveting story with sharply etched characters and complex relationships that will stick with readers long after the book is closed." SLJ

★ **Extraordinary**. Dial Books for Young Readers 2010 393p il $17.99

Grades: 8 9 10 11 12   **Fic**

1. Fantasy fiction 2. Jews -- Fiction 3. Fairies -- Fiction 4. Friendship -- Fiction

ISBN 978-0-8037-3372-5; 0-8037-3372-0

           LC 2010-2086

Phoebe, a member of the wealthy Rothschilds family, befriends Mallory, an awkward new girl in school, and the two become as close as sisters, but Phoebe does not know that Mallory is a faerie, sent to the human world to trap the ordinary human girl into fulfilling a promise made by her ancestor Mayer to the queen of the faeries.

"The carefully nuanced, often sensual prose delivers a highly effective narrative. Characterizations are arresting and complex." SLJ

★ **Impossible**; a novel. Dial Books 2008 376p $17.99

Grades: 7 8 9 10   **Fic**

1. Magic -- Fiction 2. Pregnancy -- Fiction 3. Teenage mothers -- Fiction

ISBN 978-0-8037-3002-1; 0-8037-3002-0

           LC 2008-06633

When seventeen-year-old Lucy discovers her family is under an ancient curse by an evil Elfin Knight, she realizes to break the curse she must perform three impossible tasks before her daughter is born in order to save them both.

"Werlin earns high marks for the tale's graceful interplay between wild magic and contemporary reality." Booklist

★ The **killer's** cousin; [by] Nancy Werlin. Dial Books 2009 227p $16.99; pa $7.99

Grades: 7 8 9 10   **Fic**

1. Cousins -- Fiction 2. Homicide -- Fiction

ISBN 978-0-8037-3370-1; 0-8037-3370-4; 978-0-14-241373-9 pa; 0-14-241373-9 pa

           LC 2008-24294

A reissue of the title first published 1998 by Delacorte

After being acquitted of murder, seventeen-year-old David goes to stay with relatives in Cambridge, Massachusetts, where he finds himself forced to face his past as he learns more about his strange young cousin Lily.

"Teens will find this tautly plotted thriller, rich in complex, finely drawn characters, an absolute page-turner." Booklist

The **rules** of survival. Dial Books 2006 259p $16.99

Grades: 8 9 10 11 12   **Fic**

1. Siblings -- Fiction 2. Child abuse -- Fiction

ISBN 0-8037-3001-2

           LC 2006-1675

Seventeen-year-old Matthew recounts his attempts, starting at a young age, to free himself and his sisters from the grip of their emotionally and physically abusive mother.

The author "tackles the topic of child abuse with grace and insight. . . . Teens will empathize with these siblings and the secrets they keep in this psychological horror story." SLJ

West, Kasie

Pivot point; Kasie West. HarperTeen 2013 352 p. (hardback) $17.99

Grades: 7 8 9 10   **Fic**

1. Love stories 2. Occult fiction 3. Divorce -- Fiction 4. Love -- Fiction 5. Schools -- Fiction 6. High schools -- Fiction 7. Choice (Psychology) -- Fiction

ISBN 0062117378; 9780062117373

           LC 2012019089

This book tells the story of Addie Coleman, who has the ability to see into the future and choose between the better of two options. "She is a Searcher living in the Compound, the southern Texas home of the most gifted individuals in the county. When her parents decide to divorce, with her mother staying in the Compound, and her father opting to live in the normal world, she decides to use her ability to help her chose with whom to live." (Booklist)

Split second; Kasie West. HarperTeen, an imprint of HarperCollinsPublishers 2014 368 p. (hardcover bdg.) $17.99

Grades: 7 8 9 10   **Fic**

1. Love stories 2. Memory -- Fiction 3. Psychics -- Fiction 4. Love -- Fiction 5. Schools -- Fiction 6. Family life -- Fiction 7. High schools -- Fiction 8. Psychic ability -- Fiction 9. Choice (Psychology) -- Fiction

ISBN 0062117386; 9780062117380

           LC 2013008053

In this young adult novel, by Kasie West, Addie has lost her memories, so "when Addie's dad invites her to spend her winter break with him in the Norm world, she jumps at the chance. There she meets the handsome and achingly familiar Trevor. . . . But after witnessing secrets that were supposed to stay hidden, Trevor quickly seems more suspicious of Addie than interested in her. She wants to change that." (Publisher's note)

"—In this follow-up to Pivot Point (HarperCollins, 2013), Addie leaves the Compound after a bad breakup. As a Searcher, Addie can see two possible futures, and she finds it hard to believe this is the one she chose, the one in which she is betrayed by her best friend and her boyfriend... In this fast-paced fantasy, the plot is slow to begin but takes off after the first few chapters. Recommended for readers who love dystopian stories with a bit of romance." (School Library Journal)

Westerfeld, Scott

Blue noon; [by] Scott Westerfeld. 1st ed.; Eos 2006 378p (Midnighters) $15.99; lib bdg $16.89

Grades: 7 8 9 10   **Fic**

1. Science fiction

ISBN 0-06-051957-6; 0-06-051958-4 lib bdg

           LC 2005017597

The five midnighters from Bixby discover that the secret hour is starting to invade the daylight world, and if they cannot stop it, the darklings will soon be free to hunt again.

"The plot maintains an exciting pace. . . . This is fun recreational reading." SLJ

Extras. Simon Pulse 2011 399p $17.99; pa $9.99

Grades: 7 8 9 10   **Fic**
1. Science fiction
ISBN 978-1-4424-3007-5; 978-1-4424-1978-0 pa
Sequel to Specials (2006)
First published 2007

Aya is "an 'extra' (face rank stuck in the mid-400,000s)
in a city run on a 'reputation economy.' If Aya can win fame
as a 'kicker,' reporting with her trusty hovercam on a story
that captures the city's imagination, her face rank will soar.
. . . Westerfeld shows he has a finger on the pulse of our
reputation economy, alchemizing the cult of celebrity, advertising's constant competition for consumer attention."
Horn Book

★ **Leviathan**; written by Scott Westerfeld; illustrated by Keith Thompson. Simon Pulse 2009 440p
il map $19.99; pa $9.99
Grades: 7 8 9 10   **Fic**
1. War stories 2. Science fiction 3. Princes -- Fiction
4. Mythical animals -- Fiction 5. Genetic engineering
-- Fiction
ISBN 978-1-4169-7173-3; 1-4169-7173-4; 978-1-
4169-7174-0 pa; 1-4169-7174-2 pa
                                               LC 2009-881

In an alternate 1914 Europe, fifteen-year-old Austrian
Prince Alek, on the run from the Clanker Powers who are attempting to take over the globe using mechanical machinery,
forms an uneasy alliance with Deryn who, disguised as a boy
to join the British Air Service, is learning to fly genetically-
engineered beasts.

"The protagonists' stories are equally gripping and keep
the story moving, and Thompson's detail-rich panels bring
Westerfeld's unusual creations to life." Publ Wkly

Other titles in this series are:
Behemoth (2010)
Goliath (2011)

Pretties. Simon Pulse 2011 348p $17.99; pa
$9.99
Grades: 7 8 9 10   **Fic**
1. Science fiction
ISBN 978-1-4169-3639-8; 978-1-4424-1980-3 pa
Sequel to Uglies
First published 2005

Tally's transformation to perfect and popular including
her totally hot boyfriend is everything she always wanted.
But beneath the fun and freedom something is wrong and
now Tally has to fight for her life because what she knows
has put her in danger with the authorities.

"Riveting and compulsively readable, this action-packed
sequel does not disappoint." Booklist

Followed by Specials

★ **So** yesterday; a novel. Razorbill 2004 225p
$16.99; pa $7.99
Grades: 7 8 9 10   **Fic**
1. Mystery fiction 2. Missing persons -- Fiction 3.
New York (N.Y.) -- Fiction
ISBN 1-59514-000-X; 1-59514-032-8 pa
                                               LC 2004-2302

Hunter Braque, a New York City teenager who is paid
by corporations to spot what is "cool," combines his ana-

lytical skills with girlfriend Jen's creative talents to find a
missing person and thwart a conspiracy directed at the heart
of consumer culture

"This hip, fascinating thriller aggressively questions
consumer culture. . . . Teens will inhale this wholly entertaining, thought-provoking look at a system fueled by their
purchasing power." Booklist

Specials. Simon Pulse 2011 350p $17.99; pa
$9.99
Grades: 7 8 9 10   **Fic**
1. Science fiction
ISBN 978-1-4424-3008-2; 978-1-4424-1979-7 pa
Sequel to Pretties
First published 2006

Tally has been transformed from a repellent ugly to su-
permodel pretty. Now she's a super-amped fighting machine.
Her mission is to keep the uglies down and the pretties stupid. But Tally's never been good at playing by the rules.

"Readers who enjoyed Uglies and Pretties . . . will not
want to miss Specials. . . . Westerfeld's themes include van-
ity, environmental conservation, Utopian idealism, fascism,
violence, and love." SLJ

Followed by Extras

Uglies. Simon Pulse 2005 425p rpt $17.99
Grades: 7 8 9 10   **Fic**
1. Science fiction
ISBN 9781416936381

"Tally is an ugly, waiting eagerly for her sixteenth birthday, when surgery will make her into a Pretty and she can
join her old friend Peris in the life of the beautiful in New
Pretty Town. In the meantime, she revels in hoverboard-
ing and pulling tricks with her rebellious friend, Shay, who
doesn't share Tally's anticipation for joining the Pretty
world. When Shay runs away to join dissidents outside
the city, Tally is blackmailed by the city's Special Circumstances unit into following Shay and uncovering the location
of the anti-establishment rebels, a task that becomes more
difficult when Tally's sympathies begin to skew toward the
rebels, especially their charismatic leader, David. . . . Grades
six to ten." (Bull Cent Child Books)

"Fifteen-year-old Tally's eerily harmonious, postapocalyptic society gives extreme makeovers to teens on their sixteenth birthdays. . . . When a top-secret agency threatens to
leave Tally ugly forever unless she spies on runaway teens,
she agrees to infiltrate the Smoke, a shadowy colony of refugees from the 'tyranny of physical perfection.'" Booklist

Weston, Robert Paul
Dust city; a novel. by Robert Weston. Razorbill
2010 299p $16.99
Grades: 7 8 9 10   **Fic**
1. Magic -- Fiction 2. Wolves -- Fiction 3. Fairies --
Fiction 4. Father-son relationship -- Fiction
ISBN 978-1-59514-296-2; 1-59514-296-7
                                               LC 2010-36067

Henry Whelp, son of the Big Bad Wolf, investigates
what happened to the fairies that used to protect humans and
animalia, and what role the corporation that manufactures
synthetic fairy dust played in his father's crime.

"The premise is fractured fairy tale, but the play is pure noir. . . . The clever setup and gutting of fairy-tale tropes will garner plenty of enthusiasm." Booklist

★ **Zorgamazoo**. Razorbill 2008 281p il $15.99
Grades: 4 5 6 7   **Fic**
1. Novels in verse 2. Adventure fiction 3. Imagination -- Fiction
ISBN 978-1-59514-199-6; 1-59514-199-5
                                                    LC 2007-51682
Imaginative and adventurous Katrina eludes her maniacal guardian to help Morty, a member of a vanishing breed of zorgles, with his quest to uncover the fate of the fabled zorgles of Zorgamazoo as well as of other creatures that seem to have disappeared from the earth.

"This book is a natural descendant to the works of Dr. Seuss and Roald Dahl." Booklist

Westrick, A. B.
Brotherhood; Anne Westrick. Viking Juvenile 2013 368 p. (hardback) $17.99
Grades: 5 6 7 8 9   **Fic**
1. Historical fiction 2. Ku Klux Klan -- Fiction 3. Prejudices -- Fiction 4. Race relations -- Fiction 5. Family life -- Virginia -- Fiction 6. Ku Klux Klan (19th cent.) -- Fiction 7. Reconstruction (U.S. history, 1865-1877) -- Fiction 8. Richmond (Va.) -- History -- 19th century -- Fiction 9. Reconstruction (U.S. history, 1865-1877) -- Fiction
ISBN 0670014397; 9780670014392
                                                    LC 2013008272
In this historical novel, 14-year-old Shad Weaver's "life is full of secrets. Desperate to learn to read, he begins attending a school for African-Americans. . . . He is very careful not to be seen, especially by any members of the other secret group to which he belongs, the Klan. Shad is deeply ambivalent about the brotherhood, appreciating it for the camaraderie it fosters but becoming increasingly uncomfortable with the violence it perpetuates." He must make a stand when his teacher is murdered. (Kirkus Reviews)

Weyn, Suzanne
Distant waves; a novel of the Titanic. Scholastic Press 2009 330p $17.99
Grades: 8 9 10 11   **Fic**
1. Inventors 2. Journalists 3. Financiers 4. Fur traders 5. Sisters -- Fiction 6. Electrical engineers 7. Inventors -- Fiction 8. Spiritualism -- Fiction 9. Titanic (Steamship) -- Fiction 10. Mother-daughter relationship -- Fiction
ISBN 978-0-545-08572-4; 0-545-08572-1
                                                    LC 2008-40708
In the early twentieth century, four sisters and their widowed mother, a famed spiritualist, travel from New York to London, and as the Titanic conveys them and their acquaintances, journalist W.T. Stead, scientist Nikola Tesla, and industrialist John Jacob Astor, home, Tesla's inventions will either doom or save them all.

"The interplay of science, spirituality, history and romance will satisfy." Publ Wkly

Empty. Scholastic Press 2010 183p $17.99

Grades: 7 8 9 10   **Fic**
1. Science fiction 2. Ecology -- Fiction 3. Hurricanes -- Fiction 4. Energy resources -- Fiction 5. Environmental degradation -- Fiction
ISBN 978-0-545-17278-3; 0-545-17278-0
                                                    LC 2010-16743
When, just ten years in the future, oil supplies run out and global warming leads to devastating storms, senior high school classmates Tom, Niki, Gwen, Hector, and Brock realize that the world as they know it is ending and lead the way to a more environmentally-friendly society.

"The realistic and thought-provoking scenario is packaged into a speedy read, and given the popularity of dystopian fiction, it should find an audience." Booklist

Recruited. Darby Creek 2011 104p (Surviving Southside) lib bdg $27.93
Grades: 7 8 9 10   **Fic**
1. School stories 2. Football -- Fiction 3. African Americans -- Fiction
ISBN 978-0-7613-6153-4; 0-7613-6153-7
                                                    LC 2010023662
"Kadeem is ecstatic when scouts shower him with gifts, dinners, and parties and he realizes that his dream of playing college football may be coming true. His happiness quickly turns to dread, though, as he learns that the incentives offered to him are violations of recruitment policy. . . . [This] well-written [story reinforces] the importance of family, friends, values, and thoughtful decision-making. . . . [An] excellent [purchase, this book] will attract and engage reluctant readers." SLJ

Reincarnation; [by] Suzanne Weyn. Scholastic Press 2008 293p $17.99
Grades: 7 8 9 10   **Fic**
1. Love stories 2. Reincarnation -- Fiction 3. Space and time -- Fiction
ISBN 978-0-545-01323-9; 0-545-01323-2
                                                    LC 2007-08743
When a young couple dies in prehistoric times, their love—and link to various green stones—endures through the ages as they are reborn into new bodies and somehow find a way to connect.

"Readers with a romantic bent will be drawn to this story, which pushes the notion of eternal love to its limits: two spirits find each other again and again, at different moments in history." Publ Wkly

Wharton, Thomas
The **shadow** of Malabron. Candlewick Press 2009 382p (The perilous realm) $16.99
Grades: 5 6 7 8   **Fic**
1. Fantasy fiction
ISBN 978-0-7636-3911-2; 0-7636-3911-7
                                                    LC 2009-7768
When Will, a rebellious teen, stumbles from the present into the realm where stories come from, he learns he has a mission concerning the evil Malabron and, aided by some of the story folk, he faces a host of perils while seeking the gateless gate that will take him home.

"Lush descriptive prose, cleverly sustained suspense, a sprinkling of humor and an exciting climax will keep readers riveted to the story, while those who know their folklore will be delighted by Wharton's twisting of the tropes and tales of myth and legend." Kirkus

Whelan, Gloria

After the train. HarperCollins 2009 152p
$15.99; lib bdg $16.89

Grades: 6 7 8 9   **Fic**

1. Antisemitism -- Fiction 2. Jews -- Germany -- Fiction
3. Germany -- History -- 1945-1990 -- Fiction

ISBN 978-0-06-029596-7; 0-06-029596-1; 978-0-06-029597-4 lib bdg; 0-06-029597-X lib bdg

LC 2008-10185

Ten years after the end of the Second World War, the town of Rolfen, West Germany, looks just as peaceful and beautiful as ever, until young Peter Liebig discovers a secret about his past that leads him to question everything, including the town's calm facade and his own sense of comfort and belonging.

"The story offers effective suspense in the mystery of Peter's situation and a dramatic climax. . . . Fans of Whelan's middle-school-aimed historical fiction . . . will definitely want to get their hands on this title." Bull Cent Child Books

All my noble dreams and then what happens; Gloria Whelan. 1st ed. Simon & Schuster Books for Young Readers 2013 272 p. (hardcover) $15.99

Grades: 6 7 8 9 10   **Fic**

1. India -- History -- Fiction 2. Historical fiction 3. Aunts -- Fiction 4. Insurgency -- Fiction 5. Family life -- India -- Fiction 6. Great Britain -- History -- George V, 1910-1936 -- Fiction 7. India -- History -- British occupation, 1765-1947 -- Fiction 8. India -- History -- British occupation, 1765-1947 -- Fiction

ISBN 1442449764; 9781442449763; 9781442449770

LC 2012018599

Sequel to: Small acts of amazing courage

This novel is a sequel to Gloria Whelan's "Small Acts of Amazing Courage." Set "in India in the year 1921," here British-born protagonist Rosy has returned to "India, the land she considers home, after an extended stay in England. The household . . . is bustling with preparations for a visit by the Prince of Wales. Rosy has promised to deliver a letter written by Mahatma Gandhi, an appeal to Great Britain to give India its freedom." (Publishers Weekly)

Burying the sun. HarperCollins Publishers 2004 205p $15.99; lib bdg $16.89

Grades: 5 6 7 8   **Fic**

1. World War, 1939-1945 -- Fiction 2. Saint Petersburg (Russia) -- Siege, 1941-1944 -- Fiction

ISBN 0-06-054112-1; 0-06-054113-X lib bdg

LC 2003-12487

In Leningrad in 1941, when Russia and Germany are at war, fourteen-year-old Georgi vows to help his family and his city during the terrible siege.

"Haunting images and elegant prose make this companion to The Impossible Journey . . . and Angel on the Square . . . memorable. . . . The lilting writing style and simple dignity

of the characters help construct an honest portrait of everyday life in extraordinary circumstances." SLJ

Includes bibliographical references

Chu Ju's house. HarperCollins 2004 227p
$15.99; lib bdg $16.89

Grades: 5 6 7 8   **Fic**

1. China -- Fiction 2. Sex role -- Fiction 3. Runaway teenagers -- Fiction

ISBN 0-06-050724-1; 0-06-050725-X lib bdg

LC 2003-6979

In order to save her baby sister, fourteen-year-old Chu Ju leaves her rural home in modern China and earns food and shelter by working on a sampan, tending silk worms, and planting rice seedlings, while wondering if she will ever see her family again.

"Whelan tells a compelling adventure story, filled with rich cultural detail, about a smart, likable teenage girl who overcomes society's gender restrictions." Booklist

★ The **Disappeared**. Dial Books 2008 136p
$16.99; pa $6.99

Grades: 8 9 10 11 12   **Fic**

1. Siblings -- Fiction 2. Argentina -- Fiction

ISBN 978-0-8037-3275-9; 0-8037-3275-9; 978-0-14-241540-5 pa; 0-14-241540-5 pa

LC 2007-43750

Teenaged Silvia tries to save her brother, Eduardo, after he is captured by the military government in 1970s Argentina

"The deftly handled voices of Silvia and Eduardo follow the well-intentioned, but often grievous, mistakes of youth. Their compelling tale is a chilling account of the manipulative power of corruption." SLJ

Includes bibliographical references

Goodbye, Vietnam. Knopf 1992 135p hardcover o.p. pa $5.50

Grades: 4 5 6 7   **Fic**

1. Refugees -- Fiction 2. Vietnamese -- Fiction

ISBN 0-679-82376-X; 0-679-92263-6 pa

LC 91-3660

Thirteen-year-old Mai and her family embark on a dangerous sea voyage from Vietnam to Hong Kong to escape the unpredictable and often brutal Vietnamese government

"While the book has the suspense and appeal of any good escape story, Whelan is neither melodramatic nor sentimental, and the sometimes horrific details of the scary voyage are plain but understated." Bull Cent Child Books

★ **Homeless** bird. HarperCollins Pubs. 2000 216p hardcover o.p. pa $5.99

Grades: 6 7 8 9 10   **Fic**

1. India -- Fiction 2. Women -- India -- Fiction

ISBN 0-06-028454-4; 0-06-440819-1 pa

LC 99-33241

When thirteen-year-old Koly enters into an ill-fated arranged marriage, she must either suffer a destiny dictated by India's tradition or find the courage to oppose it.

"This beautifully told, inspiring story takes readers on a fascinating journey through modern India and the universal intricacies of a young woman's heart." Booklist

★ **Listening** for lions. HarperCollins 2005 194p $15.99; lib bdg $16.89; pa $5.99

Grades: 5 6 7 8 **Fic**

1. Orphans -- Fiction 2. Physicians -- Fiction 3. East Africa -- Fiction 4. Great Britain -- Fiction

ISBN 0-06-058174-3; 0-06-058175-1 lib bdg; 0-06-058176-X pa

Left an orphan after the influenza epidemic in British East Africa in 1918, thirteen-year-old Rachel is tricked into assuming a deceased neighbor's identity to travel to England, where her only dream is to return to Africa and rebuild her parents' mission hospital.

"In a straightforward, sympathetic voice, Rachel tells an involving, episodic story." Booklist

★ The **locked** garden. HarperCollins Children's Books 2009 168p $15.99

Grades: 4 5 6 7 **Fic**

1. Michigan -- Fiction 2. Family life -- Fiction 3. Mental illness -- Fiction 4. Psychiatric hospitals -- Fiction

ISBN 978-0-06-079094-3; 0-06-079094-6

LC 2008-24637

After their mother dies of typhoid, Verna and her younger sister Carlie move with their father, a psychiatrist, and stern Aunt Maude to an asylum for the mentally ill in early-twentieth-century Michigan, where new ideas in the treatment of mental illness are being proposed, but old prejudices still hold sway.

"Whelan establishes a strong sense of time, unusual setting and characters. . . . This convincing melodrama portrays an atypical attitude toward treating mental illness." Kirkus

See what I see. HarperTeen 2011 199p $16.99

Grades: 7 8 9 10 11 12 **Fic**

1. Sick -- Fiction 2. Artists -- Fiction 3. Detroit (Mich.) -- Fiction 4. Father-daughter relationship -- Fiction

ISBN 978-0-06-125545-8; 0-06-125545-9

LC 2010-03094

When eighteen-year-old Kate arrives on the Detroit doorstep of her long-estranged father, a famous painter, she is shocked to learn that he is dying and does not want to support her efforts to attend the local art school.

"With elegant prose, Whelan portrays a gradually developing and complex relationship built on guilt, curiosity, love, and a passion for art." Booklist

Small acts of amazing courage. Simon & Schuster Books for Young Readers 2011 217p $15.99

Grades: 6 7 8 9 10 **Fic**

1. Aunts -- Fiction 2. Bereavement -- Fiction 3. Great Britain -- Fiction 4. London (England) -- Fiction 5. India -- History -- 1765-1947, British occupation -- Fiction

ISBN 978-1-4424-0931-6; 1-4424-0931-2

LC 2010-13164

In 1919, independent-minded fifteen-year-old Rosalind lives in India with her English parents, and when they fear she has fallen in with some rebellious types who believe in Indian self-government, she is sent "home" to London, where she has never been before and where her older brother died, to stay with her two aunts.

"Whelan balances the facts with distinctive, sometimes comical characterizations and vibrant, original sensory descriptions. . . . Whelan's vibrant, episodic story explores the tension between doing what's right, rather than what's expected, and the infinite complexities of colonialism." Booklist

Whipple, Natalie

House of ivy and sorrow; Natalie Whipple. HarperTeen, an imprint of HarperCollinsPublishers 2014 368 p. (pbk. bdg.) $9.99

Grades: 8 9 10 11 12 **Fic**

1. Love stories 2. Fantasy fiction 3. Friendship -- Fiction 4. Witchcraft -- Fiction 5. Grandmothers -- Fiction 6. Blessing and cursing -- Fiction 7. Fathers and daughters -- Fiction 8. Dating (Social customs) -- Fiction

ISBN 0062120182; 9780062120182

LC 2013008052

In this young adult fantasy romance novel by Natalie Whipple, "Jo Hemlock is not your typical witch. Outside the walls of her grandmother's ivy-covered house, she's kept her magical life completely separate from her life in high school. But when the Curse that killed her mother resurfaces, it threatens to destroy not only her life but her grandmother's too--and keeping her secret may no longer be an option." (Publisher's note)

"Josephine, 17, lives with her grandmother in a house under the interstate where it's rumored that an old witch can make someone love you if you're willing to give her your pinkie finger. Jo knows that the rumors are true, because her grandmother is that witch...This is a fast-paced fantasy, with just the right amount of romance and realism. Readers will relate to Jo's relationships with her family, crush, and two best friends. Despite the current glut of supernatural and urban fantasy, this tale will stand out." SLJ

Whitaker, Alecia

The **queen** of Kentucky. Little, Brown 2011 375p $17.99

Grades: 7 8 9 10 **Fic**

1. School stories 2. Kentucky -- Fiction 3. Farm life -- Fiction 4. Friendship -- Fiction 5. Popularity -- Fiction 6. Dating (Social customs) -- Fiction

ISBN 978-0-316-12506-2; 0-316-12506-7

LC 2010045840

In this book, "Ricki Jo is determined to give herself an extreme makeover as she enters high school, . . . expanding her horizons beyond her life as a hard-working farm girl. Another new girl, Mackenzie, becomes her ally, and . . . they join up with an established group of friends who are . . . in the cool crowd. Ricki Jo, now Ericka, becomes a cheerleader, develops a crush on a much sought after boy who teases her mercilessly, experiments with alcohol, and reinvents her sense of style through magazines. Her transformation doesn't always go smoothly, and her best friend, Luke, tries his best to keep her grounded, but Ericka is determined to transform from her old self to what she considers her new and improved self." (Bulletin of the Center for Children's Books)

"This is familiar territory, but Whitaker's setting is fresh, and readers from rural areas will recognize the class differences. . . . Ericka's first-person voice is sassy and quite believable as she tries to figure out who she is—and who everybody else is, too." Booklist

White, Amy Brecount

Forget -her-nots. Greenwillow Books 2010 374p $16.99; lib bdg $17.89

Grades: 7 8 9 10   **Fic**

1. School stories 2. Magic -- Fiction 3. Flowers -- Fiction 4. Mother-daughter relationship -- Fiction

ISBN 978-0-06-167298-9; 0-06-167298-X; 978-0-06-167299-6 lib bdg; 0-06-167299-8 lib bdg

LC 2009-7105

At a Charlottesville, Virginia, boarding school, four-teen-year-old Laurel realizes that she shares her deceased mother's connection with flowers, but as she begins to learn their ancient language and share it with other students, she discovers powers that are beyond her control.

"A delicate sense of magical possibility and reverence for the natural world help elevate White's story from a typical prep-school drama into something more memorable." Publ Wkly

White, Andrea

Surviving Antarctica; reality TV 2083. Harp-erCollins Publishers 2005 327p hardcover o.p. pa $6.99

Grades: 7 8 9 10   **Fic**

1. Science fiction 2. Antarctica -- Fiction

ISBN 0-06-055454-1; 0-06-055456-8 pa

LC 2004-6249

In the year 2083, five fourteen-year-olds who were deprived by chance of the opportunity to continue their educations reenact Scott's 1910-1913 expedition to the South Pole as contestants on a reality television show, secretly aided by a Department of Entertainment employee

"A real page-turner, this novel will give readers pause as they ponder the ethics of teens risking their lives in adult-contrived situations for the entertainment of the masses." Booklist

Window boy. Bright Sky Press 2008 255p $17.95

Grades: 6 7 8 9   **Fic**

1. Statesmen 2. Historians 3. School stories 4. Prime ministers 5. Memoirists 6. Cabinet members 7. Members of Parliament 8. Cerebral palsy -- Fiction 9. Imaginary playmates -- Fiction 10. Nobel laureates for literature

ISBN 978-1-933979-14-4; 1-933979-14-3

LC 2008-492

After his mother finally convinces the principal of Greenfield Junior High to admit him, twelve-year-old Sam arrives for his first day of school, along with his imaginary friend Winston Churchill, who encourages him to persevere with his cerebral palsy.

"Strong character development is combined with an accurate representation of the lack of educational opportunities for those who were physically and mentally disabled pre-IDEA." SLJ

Windows on the world. Namelos 2011 $18.95; pa $9.95

Grades: 6 7 8 9   **Fic**

1. School stories 2. Science fiction 3. Birds -- Fiction 4. Orphans -- Fiction 5. Time travel -- Fiction

ISBN 978-1-60898-105-2; 1-60898-105-3; 978-1-60898-106-9 pa; 1-60898-106-1 pa

LC 2011003678

In 2083, orphan Shama Katooee, who has just stolen an expensive pet bird, is mysteriously selected to attend the elite Chronos Academy to be trained in the practice of Time-Watch, although she has no idea how or why she has been given this honor.

"The third-person narrative focuses mainly on Shama, with intermittent chapters on Maye Jones in NYC in 2001 and Lt. Bazel. White . . . subtly poses other questions surrounding advancements in technology and capitalism in this well-imagined and disturbing future." Kirkus

White, Ellen Emerson

Long live the queen. Feiwel and Friends 2008 312p pa $9.99

Grades: 7 8 9 10   **Fic**

1. Terrorism -- Fiction 2. Kidnapping -- Fiction

ISBN 0-312-37490-9; 978-0-312-37490-7

LC 2008-7124

First published 1989

The President's daughter is a victim of kidnapping by terrorists.

"The author pulls no punches in this gripping tale, and combines a stirring plot with complex characters." Publ Wkly

Long may she reign. Feiwel and Friends 2007 708p $15.95

Grades: 6 7 8 9 10   **Fic**

1. School stories 2. Presidents -- Fiction 3. Post-traumatic stress disorder -- Fiction

ISBN 978-0-312-36767-1; 0-312-36767-8

LC 2007-32635

Meg Powers, daughter of the president of the United States, is recovering from a brutal kidnapping, and in an effort to deal with her horrific experience and her anger at her mother—the president—for not negotiating for her release, Meg decides to go away for her second semester of college, where she encounters even more challenges.

"The hip dialogue will hook teens. . . . Beneath its chick-lit veneer, this book is a thought-provoking read." Voice Youth Advocates

The **President's** daughter. Feiwel and Friends 2008 304p pa $9.99

Grades: 7 8 9 10   **Fic**

1. Moving -- Fiction 2. Politics -- Fiction 3. Washington (D.C.) -- Fiction 4. Mother-daughter relationship -- Fiction

ISBN 0-312-37488-7; 978-0-312-37488-4

LC 2008-6888

First published 1984

Sixteen-year-old Meghan Powers' happy life in Massachusetts changes drastically when her mother, one of the most prestigious senators in the country, becomes the front-runner in the race for United States President.

"Besides offering a solid look at the political system, this [book] has very strong characterizations." Booklist

Other titles about Meg are:
White House autumn (2008)
Long live the queen (2008)
Long may she reign (2007)

White House autumn. Feiwel and Friends 2008 236p pa $9.99

Grades: 7 8 9 10   **Fic**

1. School stories 2. Politics -- Fiction 3. Presidents -- Fiction 4. Family life -- Fiction 5. Washington (D.C.) -- Fiction

ISBN 0-312-37489-5; 978-0-312-37489-1

LC 2008-6883

First published 1985

Seventeen-year-old Meg's surging emotions after her mother, the United States President, is shot, threaten her relationship with boyfriend Josh and best friend Beth, but she strives to maintain control to help her father and younger brothers.

"Apart from its novelistic merits, the book prompts thought on the burdens of public office, the need for character in the elect and their families." Publ Wkly

White, J. A.

The **Thickety**; a path begins. J.A. White. Katherine Tegen Books, an imprint of HarperCollinsPublishers 2014 496 p. (hardcover bdg.) $16.99

Grades: 5 6 7 8   **Fic**

1. Fantasy fiction 2. Magic -- Fiction 3. Witches -- Fiction

ISBN 0062257242; 9780062257246

LC 2013021509

This book, by J.A. White, "is the thrilling start of a new middle-grade fantasy series about a girl, a mysterious forest, and a book of untold magical powers. Kara and her brother, Taff, are shunned by their village because their mother was a witch. The villagers believe nothing is more evil than magic, except for what lurks in the nearby Thickety. But when Kara enters the forbidden forest, she discovers a strange book, a grimoire that might have belonged to her mother." (Publisher's note)

"When Kara was just a child, she was accused of witchcraft and forced to watch her mother executed for the same crime. Ever after, she and her family have lived in their isolated theocratic community as pariahs...White's persistent dark imagery, along with Offermann's eerie silhouette spot illustrations, adds to the overall dark atmosphere." Booklist

The **whispering** trees; J.A. White; illustrations by Andrea Offermann. Katherine Tegen Books, an imprint of HarperCollinsPublishers 2015 528 p. illustrations (The thickety) $16.99

Grades: 5 6 7 8   **Fic**

1. Fantasy fiction 2. Magic -- Fiction 3. Brothers and sisters -- Fiction 4. Human-animal communication -- Fiction 5. Fantasy

ISBN 0062257293; 9780062257291

LC 2014022226

In this book, by J.A. White, "[a]fter Kara Westfall's village turns on her for practicing witchcraft, she and her brother, Taff, flee to the one place they know they won't be followed: the Thickety. Only this time the Forest Demon, Sordyr, is intent on keeping them there. Sordyr is not the Thickety's only danger: unknown magic lurks behind every twist and shadow of the path." (Publisher's note)

"The menacing Thickety is forbidden, but it's safer for Kara and her little brother, Taff, than staying in the village, now that it's being controlled by a vicious witch. . . . He's created a vivid, unsettling environment of rich magic and terrifying horrors: monsters composed of bones and teeth, tentacled creatures that feed on feelings, shadows that consume bodies, and more. Kara still seems much older than her 12 years, but that's a minor complaint that doesn't distract from the lush descriptions of a spine-tingling, captivating place." Booklist

White, Kiersten

Paranormalcy. HarperTeen 2010 335p $16.99

Grades: 7 8 9 10 11 12   **Fic**

1. Police -- Fiction 2. Fairies -- Fiction 3. Prophecies -- Fiction 4. Supernatural -- Fiction

ISBN 978-0-06-198584-3; 0-06-198584-3

LC 2010-07027

When a dark prophecy begins to come true, sixteen-year-old Evie of the International Paranormal Containment Agency must not only try to stop it, she must also uncover its connection to herself and the alluring shapeshifter, Lend.

"White shows the technique and polish of a pro in this absorbing romance, which comes closer than most to hitting the Buffy mark. . . . The action is fast; fun and fear are in abundance; and Lend's father is actually a cool grownup." Publ Wkly

Followed by: Supernaturally (2011)

Supernaturally. HarperTeen 2011 342p $17.99

Grades: 7 8 9 10   **Fic**

1. Fairies -- Fiction 2. Prophecies -- Fiction 3. Supernatural -- Fiction

ISBN 978-0-06-198586-7; 0-06-198586-4

LC 2010040426

Sequel to: Paranormalcy (2010)

Sixteen-year-old Evie thinks she has left the International Paranormal Containment Agency, and her own paranormal activities, behind her when she is recruited to help at the Agency, where she discovers more about the dark faerie prophecy that threatens her future.

"Evie's voice is the best part of the story, as she balances her supernatural abilities against typical teen concerns and obsessions." Kirkus

White, Ruth

★ **Belle** Prater's boy. Farrar, Straus & Giroux 1996 196p $17

Grades: 5 6 7 8   **Fic**

1. Cousins -- Fiction 2. Virginia -- Fiction 3. Appalachian region -- Fiction

ISBN 0-374-30668-0

LC 94-43625

A Newbery Medal honor book, 1997

"Gypsy and her cousin Woodrow become close friends after Woodrow's mother disappears. Both sixth-graders feel deserted by their parents—Gypsy discovers that her father committed suicide—and need to define themselves apart from these tragedies. White's prose evokes the coal mining region of Virginia and the emotional quality of her characters' transformations." Horn Book Guide

Another title about Belle Prater is:
The search for Belle Prater (2005)

★ **Little** Audrey. Farrar, Straus & Giroux 2008 145p $16
Grades: 5 6 7 8   **Fic**
1. Death -- Fiction 2. Virginia -- Fiction 3. Coal miners -- Fiction 4. Country life -- Fiction
ISBN 978-0-374-34580-8; 0-374-34580-5
LC 2007-29310
In 1948, eleven-year-old Audrey lives with her father, mother, and three younger sisters in Jewell Valley, a coal mining camp in Southwest Virginia, where her mother still mourns the death of a baby, her father goes on drinking binges on paydays, and Audrey tries to recover from the scarlet fever that has left her skinny and needing to wear glasses.

"The setting is perfectly portrayed and the characterizations ring true." Voice Youth Advocates

Memories of Summer. Farrar, Straus & Giroux 2000 135p $16
Grades: 7 8 9 10   **Fic**
1. Sisters -- Fiction 2. Michigan -- Fiction 3. Mentally ill -- Fiction
ISBN 0-374-34945-2
LC 99-54793
In 1955, thirteen-year-old Lyric finds her whole life changing when her family moves from the hills of Virginia to a town in Michigan and her older sister Summer begins descending into mental illness

"A marvelous recreation of time and place and a poignant story that has much to say about compassion." SLJ

★ A **month** of Sundays. Margaret Ferguson Books/Farrar Straus Giroux 2011 168p $16.99
Grades: 6 7 8 9   **Fic**
1. Sick -- Fiction 2. Virginia -- Fiction 3. Family life -- Fiction 4. Country life -- Fiction 5. Christian life -- Fiction
ISBN 978-0-374-39912-2; 0-374-39912-3
LC 2010036311
In the summer of 1956 while her mother is in Florida searching for a job, fourteen-year-old April Garnet Rose, who has never met her father, stays with her terminally ill aunt in Virginia and accompanies her as she visits different churches, looking for God.

"White captures life in small-town America. . . . This heartwarming story has more than a touch of wonder. Expanding one's emotional life . . . is beautifully captured here." Booklist

The **treasure** of Way Down Deep; Ruth White. Margaret Ferguson Books 2013 176 p. (hardcover) $16.99

Grades: 5 6 7 8   **Fic**
1. Halloween -- Fiction 2. Buried treasure -- Fiction 3. Dogs -- Fiction 4. Orphans -- Fiction 5. Foundlings -- Fiction 6. Boardinghouses -- Fiction 7. Community life -- West Virginia -- Fiction 8. West Virginia -- History -- 1951- -- Fiction
ISBN 0374380678; 9780374377472; 9780374380670
LC 2012021665

Sequel to: Way Down Deep
Parents' Choice: Silver Medal Fiction (2013)
In this book by Ruth White, "Ruby loves her life, but things start turning when her pet goat dies and Miss Arbutus feels an ill wind blowing into town. Then the local mines start closing, and everyone in Way Down Deep feels the pinch. Can Ruby help save the town? Will the special button Rita gave her as a gift be part of the solution? And can the town come together when a treasure appears?" (Booklist)

★ **Way** Down Deep. Farrar, Straus and Giroux 2007 197p $16
Grades: 5 6 7 8   **Fic**
1. Orphans -- Fiction 2. West Virginia -- Fiction
ISBN 0-374-38251-4; 978-0-374-38251-3
LC 2006-46324
In the West Virginia town of Way Down Deep in the 1950s, a foundling called Ruby June is happily living with Miss Arbutus at the local boarding house when suddenly, after the arrival of a family of outsiders, the mystery of Ruby's past begins to unravel.

This is "a story as tender as a breeze and as sharp as a tack. . . . At the heart of the story are profound questions that readers will enjoy puzzling out." Booklist

You'll like it here (everybody does) Delacorte Press 2011 272p $16.99; lib bdg $19.99
Grades: 4 5 6 7   **Fic**
1. Science fiction 2. Family life -- Fiction 3. Interplanetary voyages -- Fiction 4. Extraterrestrial beings -- Fiction
ISBN 978-0-385-73998-6; 0-385-73998-2; 978-0-385-90813-9 lib bdg; 0-385-90813-X lib bdg
LC 2010-32153
Although Meggie Blue seems to be an average sixth-grader she is abnormally frightened when residents of her small, North Carolina town become fixated on aliens, and soon she and her family are forced to flee, making it clear that all is not as it seems.

White's "considerable writing skills elevate a story with many familiar elements, including the importance of individuality, the pitfalls of conformity, and the tyranny of a dictatorship. Kids will like this, but it's also a fun jumping off point for serious discussion." Booklist

White, T. H.
★ The **once** and future king. Putnam 1958 677p $25.95
Grades: 8 9 10 11 12 Adult   **Fic**
1. Fantasy fiction 2. Kings 3. Knights and knighthood -- Fiction 4. Great Britain -- History -- 0-1066 -- Fiction
ISBN 0-399-10597-2
LC 58-10760

"White's contemporary retelling of Malory's Le Morte d'Arthur is both romantic and exciting." Shapiro. Fic for Youth. 3d edition

Whitley, David

The **children** of the lost. Roaring Brook Press 2011 357p $16.99

Grades: 7 8 9 10   **Fic**

1. Fantasy fiction

ISBN 978-1-59643-614-5; 1-59643-614-X

LC 2010-28112

Sequel to: Midnight charter (2009)

Banished from Agora, the ancient city-state where absolutely everything must be bartered, Mark and Lily are happy to find the apparently perfect land of Giseth except that the inhabitants seem fearful, something strange lurks in the surrounding forest, and a mysterious woman keeps appearing in their dreams urging them to find the children of the lost.

This "explores tantalizing new territory and solidifies the Agora Trilogy as one of the more literary ambitious and complex fantasies going." Booklist

Midnight charter. Roaring Brook Press 2009 319p $17.99

Grades: 7 8 9 10   **Fic**

1. Science fiction

ISBN 978-1-59643-381-6; 1-59643-381-7

"Deft world-building and crafty plotting combine for a zinger of an ending that will leave readers poised for book two. Surprisingly sophisticated upper-middle-grade fare, with enough meat to satisfy older readers as well." Kirkus

Followed by: The children of the lost (2011)

Whitman, Emily

Wildwing. Greenwillow Books 2010 359p $16.99

Grades: 7 8 9 10   **Fic**

1. Falcons -- Fiction 2. Time travel -- Fiction 3. Social classes -- Fiction 4. Great Britain -- History -- 1066-1154, Norman period -- Fiction

ISBN 978-0-06-172452-7; 0-06-172452-1

LC 2009-44189

In 1913 London, fifteen-year-old Addy is a lowly servant, but when she gets inside an elevator car in her employer's study, she is suddenly transported to a castle in 1240 and discovers that she is mistaken for the lord's intended bride.

"Whitman populates both of her worlds with vivid, believable characters. . . . This historical novel with a time-travel twist of sci-fi will find an avid readership." SLJ

Whitney, Daisy

When you were here; by Daisy Whitney. Little, Brown and Co. 2013 272 p. $18

Grades: 7 8 9 10   **Fic**

1. Cancer -- Fiction 2. Tokyo (Japan) -- Fiction 3. Mother-son relationship -- Fiction 4. Grief -- Fiction 5. Japan -- Fiction 6. Mothers and sons -- Fiction

ISBN 0316209740; 9780316209748

LC 2012031409

In this novel by Daisy Whitney "when he gets a letter from his [deceased] mom's property manager in Tokyo, where she had been going for [cancer] treatment, it shows

. . . a side of his mother he never knew.Danny travels to Tokyo to connect with his mother's memory and make sense of her final months. Among the cherry blossoms, temples, and crowds, and with the help of a . . . girl, he begins to see how it may not have been ancient magic or mystical treatment that kept his mother going." (Publisher's note)

"Danny's mother has recently died from cancer, his father died years ago, his estranged sister lives in China, and he and Holland, the love of his life, have broken up. A trip to Japan is enlightening and helps him handle a shocking secret he learns about Holland. The extent of Danny's problems stretches credulity, but readers will be caught up in the drama." (Horn Book)

Whitney, Kim Ablon

The **other** half of life; a novel based on the true story of the MS St. Louis. Alfred A. Knopf 2009 237p $16.99; lib bdg $19.99

Grades: 6 7 8 9 10   **Fic**

1. Jews -- Germany -- Fiction 2. Holocaust, 1933-1945 -- Fiction

ISBN 978-0-375-85219-0; 0-375-85219-0; 978-0-375-95219-7 lib bdg; 0-375-95219-5 lib bdg

LC 2008-38949

In 1939, fifteen-year-old Thomas sails on a German ship bound for Cuba with more than nine hundred German Jews expecting to be granted safe haven in Cuba.

"The characters are intriguing enough, but it's the real-life history that provides the novel's energy." Horn Book Guide

Includes bibliographical references

Whittemore, Jo

Odd girl in. Simon & Schuster 2011 234p pa $6.99

Grades: 4 5 6   **Fic**

1. School stories 2. Siblings -- Fiction

ISBN 978-1-4424-1284-2; 1-4424-1284-4

"Spunky 12-year-old Alex doesn't really want friends or a social life. . . . She hates girly giggling parties and doesn't see any other girls in her middle school that she'd want to have as a friend, so she just concentrates on following in the footsteps of her prankster older twin brothers. . . . Alex's absent mother provides an element of drama in this otherwise witty, laugh-out-loud romp. Whittemore handles not only the comedy but deftly portrays Alex's and her brothers' advancement into a more mature state of mind. It should keep middle-schoolers laughing from start to finish." Kirkus

Whittenberg, Allison

Hollywood & Maine. Delacorte Press 2009 166p $15.99; lib bdg $18.99

Grades: 5 6 7 8   **Fic**

1. School stories 2. Family life -- Fiction 3. Pennsylvania -- Fiction 4. African Americans -- Fiction

ISBN 978-0-385-73671-8; 0-385-73671-1; 978-0-385-90623-4 lib bdg; 0-385-90623-4 lib bdg

LC 2008-35679

Sequel to: Sweet Thang (2006)

In 1976 Pennsylvania, middle-schooler Charmaine Upshaw contemplates a career as a model or actress while coping with boyfriend problems and the return of her uncle, a fugitive who cost her family $1,000 in bail money a year earlier.

"The family's personal trials, triumphs, individual growth, and many personalities are the book's focus and its heart. Zinger dialogue and clever narration promise laughs and an enjoyable read." SLJ

Life is fine. Delacorte Press 2008 181p $15.99; lib bdg $18.99

Grades: 8 9 10 11 12   **Fic**

1. Child abuse -- Fiction 2. African Americans -- Fiction 3. Mother-daughter relationship -- Fiction

ISBN 978-0-385-73480-6; 978-0-385-90478-0 lib bdg

LC 2007-27604

With a neglectful mother who has an abusive, live-in boyfriend, life for fifteen-year-old Samara is not fine, but when a substitute teacher walks into class one day and introduces her to poetry, she starts to view life from a different perspective.

"Samara's voice is sharp and convincing." Publ Wkly

Sweet Thang. Delacorte Press 2006 149p $15.95

Grades: 5 6 7 8   **Fic**

1. School stories 2. Family life -- Fiction 3. African Americans -- Fiction

ISBN 0-385-73292-9

LC 2005-03809

In 1975, life is not fair for fourteen-year-old Charmaine Upshaw, who shares a room with her brother, tries to impress a handsome classmate, and acts as caretaker for a rambunctious six-year-old cousin who has taken over the family.

"Whittenberg has created a refreshing cast and a good read." SLJ

Another title about the Upshaw family is:

Hollywood & Maine (2009)

Whyman, Matt

Goldstrike; a thriller. Atheneum Books for Young Readers 2010 262p $16.99

Grades: 7 8 9 10   **Fic**

1. Computer crimes -- Fiction 2. London (England) -- Fiction 3. United States -- Central Intelligence Agency -- Fiction

ISBN 978-1-4169-9510-4; 1-4169-9510-2

LC 2009-17830

Sequel to: Icecore (2007)

After escaping Camp Twilight, eighteen-year-old Carl Hobbes and Beth, his girlfriend, begin a new life in London, England, where he attempts to program Sphynx Cargo's highly intelligent supercomputer to help protect them from the CIA and assassins.

"The action sequences are believable and often realistically brutal, and the climactic battle is intense and entertaining." Publ Wkly

Icecore; a Carl Hobbes thriller. Atheneum Books for Young Readers 2007 307p $16.99; pa $8.99

Grades: 7 8 9 10   **Fic**

1. Torture -- Fiction 2. Prisoners -- Fiction 3. Arctic regions -- Fiction 4. Military bases -- Fiction 5.

Computer crimes -- Fiction

ISBN 978-1-4169-4907-7; 1-4169-4907-0; 978-1-4169-8960-8 pa; 1-4169-8960-9 pa

LC 2007-02674

Seventeen-year-old Englishman Carl Hobbes meant no harm when he hacked into Fort Knox's security system, but at Camp Twilight in the Arctic Circle, known as the Guantanamo Bay of the north, he is tortured to reveal information about a conspiracy of which he was never a part.

"Powered by a fast-paced narrative, this exploration of numerous timely themes . . . gives the eminently readable adventure a degree of depth." Publ Wkly

Followed by: Goldstrike (2010)

Wiggins, Bethany

Cured; by Bethany Wiggins. Bloomsbury/Walker 2014 320 p. (hardback) $17.99

Grades: 7 8 9 10 11 12   **Fic**

1. Science fiction 2. Apocalyptic fiction 3. Twins -- Fiction 4. Survival -- Fiction 5. Voyages and travels -- Fiction 6. Brothers and sisters -- Fiction

ISBN 0802734200; 9780802734204

LC 2013024935

Sequel to: Stung

In this book, by Bethany Wiggins, is a "reimagining of our world after an environmental catastrophe. . . . Now that Fiona Tarsis and her twin brother, Jonah, are no longer beasts, they set out to find their mother. . . . Heading for a safe settlement rumored to be in Wyoming . . . they are attacked by raiders. Luckily, they find a new ally in Kevin, who saves them and leads them to safety in his underground shelter. But the more they get to know Kevin, the more they suspect he has ties to the raiders." (Publisher's note)

"Jacqui lives as Jack in a dangerous zombie-ish dystopia caused by a vaccine's unforeseen effects. Searching for her missing older brother, Jacqui joins forces with Fiona Tarsis (Stung), who has the cure for the rabid vaccine recipients, but they are sidetracked by raiders. Mysterious romance and eleventh-hour reveals do not rescue this sequel from its meandering plot and clunky gender politics." Horn Book

Stung; Bethany Wiggins. Walker & Company 2013 304 p. (hardcover) $17.99

Grades: 7 8 9 10 11 12   **Fic**

1. Science fiction 2. Epidemics -- Fiction 3. Survival -- Fiction

ISBN 0802734189; 9780802734181

LC 2012027183

In this novel, by Bethany Wiggins, "a worldwide pandemic occurred and the government tried to bio-engineer a cure. Only the solution was deadlier than the original problem-the vaccination turned people into ferocious, deadly beasts who were branded as a warning to un-vaccinated survivors. Key people needed to rebuild society are protected from disease and beasts inside a fortress-like wall. But Fiona has awakened branded, alone-and on the wrong side of the wall." (Publisher's note)

"Wiggins. . . muses on the dangers of science and medicine and deftly maps out the chain of events that has led to catastrophe, creating a violent world vastly different from ours but still recognizable. With a stirring conclusion and space for a sequel, it's an altogether captivating story." Kirkus

Wignall, K. J.

Blood; [by] K. J. Wignall. Egmont USA 2011
264p (Mercian triology) $16.99; ebook $16.99

Grades: 7 8 9 10 11 12   **Fic**

1. Vampires -- Fiction 2. Good and evil -- Fiction
ISBN 978-1-60684-220-1; 1-60684-220-X; 978-1-
60684-258-4 ebook; 1-60684-258-7 ebook

LC 2011005899

A centuries-old vampire wakes up in the modern day to
find he is being hunted by an unknown enemy, and begins to
uncover the secrets of his origin and the path of his destiny.

Wignall "develops what could have been yet another
vampire story into a promising series opener with a sophisticated plot and elegant prose." Booklist

Wild, K.

Fight game; [by] Kate Wild. Chicken House/
Scholastic 2007 279p $16.99

Grades: 7 8 9 10   **Fic**

1. Science fiction 2. Spies -- Fiction 3. Martial arts
-- Fiction 4. Genetic engineering -- Fiction
ISBN 978-0-439-87175-4; 0-439-87175-1

LC 2006-32889

Fifteen-year-old Freedom Smith is a fighter, just like all
of his relatives who have the "Hercules gene," which leads
him to a choice between being jailed for attempted murder
or working with a covert law enforcement agency to break
up a mysterious, illegal fight ring.

"Intriguing supporting characters pepper Wild's debut
novel and bolster an already strong portagonist. . . . Wild's
story pulsates with raw energy." Voice Youth Advocates

Wildavsky, Rachel

The **secret** of Rover. Amulet Books 2011 351p
$16.95

Grades: 5 6 7 8   **Fic**

1. Twins -- Fiction 2. Uncles -- Fiction 3. Siblings
-- Fiction 4. Inventions -- Fiction 5. Kidnapping --
Fiction 6. Washington (D.C.) -- Fiction 7. Voyages and
travels -- Fiction
ISBN 0-8109-9710-X; 978-0-8109-9710-3

LC 2010-23450

Twelve-year-old twins Katie and David Bowen evade
foreign militants and make their way from Washington, D.C.
to their uncle's Vermont home, hoping he can help rescue
their parents, who were kidnapped because of their secret
invention, Rover.

"Kids making the transition from series mysteries to
more sophisticated thrillers will do well by this suspenseful
and age-appropriate drama." Bull Cent Child Books

Wiles, Deborah

★ The **Aurora** County All-Stars. Harcourt
2007 242p il $16; pa $5.99

Grades: 4 5 6   **Fic**

1. Death -- Fiction 2. Baseball -- Fiction 3. Mississippi
-- Fiction 4. Race relations -- Fiction
ISBN 978-0-15-206068-8; 0-15-206068-5; 978-0-15-
206626-0 pa; 0-15-206626-8 pa

LC 2006-102551

In a small Mississippi town, after the death of the old
man to whom twelve-year-old star pitcher House Jackson

has been secretly reading for a year, House uncovers secrets
about the man and the history of baseball in Aurora County.

"Quotations from Walt Whitman's poetry, baseball players and Aurora County news dispatches pepper the story and
add color. . . . A home run for Wiles." Publ Wkly

★ **Countdown**. Scholastic 2010 377p il (The
sixties trilogy) $17.99

Grades: 5 6 7 8   **Fic**

1. Cold war -- Fiction 2. Family life -- Fiction 3.
Cuban Missile Crisis, 1962 -- Fiction
ISBN 978-0-545-10605-4; 0-545-10605-2

It's 1962, and it seems everyone is living in fear. Twelve-
year-old Franny Chapman lives with her family in Washington, DC, during the days surrounding the Cuban Missile Crisis. Amidst the pervasive threat of nuclear war, Franny must
face the tension between herself and her younger brother,
figure out where she fits in with her family, and look beyond
outward appearances.

"Wiles skillfully keeps many balls in the air, giving readers a story that appeals across the decades as well as offering
enticing paths into the history." Booklist

★ **Revolution**; Deborah Wiles. First edition
Scholastic 2014 495 p. illustrations, map (The sixties trilogy) $19.99

Grades: 5 6 7 8   **Fic**

1. Family life -- Fiction 2. Nineteen sixties -- Fiction 3.
United States -- History -- Fiction 4. African Americans
-- Civil rights -- Fiction
ISBN 0545106079; 9780545106078

LC 2014935954

National Book Award Shortlist: Young People's Literature (2014)

In this book, by Deborah Wiles, "it's 1964, and Sunny's
town is being invaded. Or at least that's what the adults of
Greenwood, Mississippi are saying. All Sunny knows is that
people from up north are coming to help people register
to vote. They're calling it Freedom Summer. Meanwhile,
Sunny can't help but feel like her house is being invaded,
too. She has a new stepmother, a new brother, and a new
sister crowding her life, giving her little room to breathe."
(Publisher's note)

"Wiles does an excellent job of entwining the two plot
strands and seamlessly integrating her exhaustive research,
which is detailed at the book's conclusion. . . . As in Countdown, the outstanding period artwork, photographs, snippets of sayings, and songs interspersed throughout bring a
troubled time close." Booklist

Wilhelm, Doug

The **revealers**. Farrar, Straus & Giroux 2003
207p $16

Grades: 4 5 6 7   **Fic**

1. School stories 2. Internet -- Fiction 3. Friendship
-- Fiction
ISBN 0-374-36255-6

LC 2002-35321

Tired of being bullied and picked on, three seventh-
grade outcasts join forces and, using scientific methods and
the power of the Internet, begin to create a new atmosphere

at Parkland Middle School. "Grades five to nine." (Bull Cent Child Books)

"Briskly plotted, the novel shows how bringing the stories to light transforms stereotypes into real people and provides a vehicle for others to become involved. . . . The novel is effective and will fascinate even reluctant readers." SLJ

Wilkins, Ebony Joy

Sellout. Scholastic Press 2010 267p $17.99

Grades: 7 8 9 10   **Fic**

1. Social classes -- Fiction 2. African Americans -- Fiction

ISBN 978-0-545-10928-4; 0-545-10928-0

NaTasha loves her life of affluence in Park Adams, but her grandmother fears she has lost touch with her roots and whisks her off to Harlem, where NaTasha meets rough, streetwise girls at a crisis center and finds the courage to hold her own against them.

"Some elements of the story tie up too easily—NaTasha's greatest tormentors warm up to her a bit too quickly to be believed—but the message of staying true to oneself shines through." SLJ

Wilkinson, Lili

Pink. HarperTeen 2011 310p $16.99

Grades: 7 8 9 10 11 12   **Fic**

1. School stories 2. Theater -- Fiction 3. Australia -- Fiction 4. Homosexuality -- Fiction 5. Identity (Psychology) -- Fiction

ISBN 978-0-06-192653-2; 0-06-192653-1

LC 2010-9389

Sixteen-year-old Ava does not know who she is or where she belongs, but when she tries out a new personality—and sexual orientation—at a different school, her edgy girlfriend, potential boyfriend, and others are hurt by her lack of honesty.

"The novel is in turn laugh-out-loud funny, endearing, and heartbreaking as Ava repeatedly steps into teenage social land mines—with unexpected results. Because Wilkinson doesn't rely on stereotypes, the characters are well-developed, and interactions between them feel genuine." Voice Youth Advocates

Wilks, Mike

Mirrorscape. Egmont USA 2009 340p $16.99; lib bdg $19.99

Grades: 6 7 8 9   **Fic**

1. Fantasy fiction 2. Adventure fiction 3. Art -- Fiction 4. Artists -- Fiction 5. Apprentices -- Fiction

ISBN 978-1-60684-008-5; 1-60684-008-8; 978-1-60684-040-5 lib bdg; 1-60684-040-1 lib bdg

LC 2009-16245

In a world where all pleasures are severely restricted, Melkin Womper is apprenticed to a master painter where he discovers the Mirrorscape, a world inside paintings, and becomes entangled in a war between the restrictive Fifth Mystery and the rebels fighting to stop them

"In this innovative debut, readers will find an imaginative fantasy devoid of typical wizardry." Booklist

Willey, Margaret

Beetle Boy; by Margaret Willey. Carolrhoda Lab 2014 208 p. hbk $17.95

Grades: 8 9 10 11   **Fic**

1. Child authors -- Fiction 2. Father-son relationship -- Fiction 3. Family problems -- Fiction 4. Emotional problems -- Fiction 5. Dating (Social customs) -- Fiction

ISBN 1467726397; 9781467726399

LC 2013036853

"When he was seven, Charlie Porter never intended to become the world's youngest published author. . . . But Charlie's story not only made his father stop crying. It made him start planning. The story became a book, and then it became school events and book festivals, and a beetle costume, and a catchphrase--'I was born to write!' . . . Beetle Boy is a novel of a broken family, the long shadow of neglect, and the light of small kindnesses." (Publisher's note)

"Willey takes readers along on Charlie's painful journey back to physical and emotional health via a meandering timeline of flashbacks, dreams and wrenching conversations, skillfully weaving together the bits and pieces of his life. Innovative use of type brings an immediacy to Charlie's struggles as he slowly looks the truth--and his brother--squarely in the face." Kirkus

Williams, Alex

The **deep** freeze of Bartholomew Tullock. Philomel Books 2008 298p $16.99

Grades: 6 7 8 9   **Fic**

1. Adventure fiction 2. Dogs -- Fiction 3. Weather -- Fiction 4. Inventions -- Fiction

ISBN 978-0-399-25185-6; 0-399-25185-5

LC 2008-02663

Published in the United Kingdom with title: The storm maker

In a land of never-ending snow, Rufus Breeze and his mother must protect the family home from being seized by tyrant Bartholomew Tullock, while sister Madeline and her father, an inventor of fans that are now useless, join forces with a ne'er-do-well adventurer and his blue-haired terrier, hoping to make some money.

This offers "originality of setting, a full complement of truly heinous villains, insurmountable dangers cleverly surmounted, ingenious contraptions, and plucky, appealing underdogs. . . . William handles his material with fizz and verve." Bull Cent Child Books

The **talent** thief; an extraordinary tale of an ordinary boy. Philomel Books 2010 300p $16.99

Grades: 5 6 7 8   **Fic**

1. Adventure fiction 2. Orphans -- Fiction

ISBN 978-0-399-25278-5; 0-399-25278-9

Orphaned Cressida, a magnificent singer, and her twelve-year-old brother Adam attend the by-invitation-only Festival of Youthful Genius, where they join forces with a former race car driver to try to stop a bizarre creature from stealing the talents of the young prodigies.

"This is a story that fantasy and adventure fans will enjoy, and the well-paced action will propel them to the end." SLJ

Williams, Carol Lynch

The **chosen** one. St. Martin's Griffin 2009 213p $16.95

Grades: 7 8 9 10   **Fic**

1. Cults -- Fiction 2. Polygamy -- Fiction 3. Family life -- Fiction

ISBN 978-0-312-55511-5; 0-312-55511-3

LC 2009-4800

In a polygamous cult in the desert, Kyra, not yet fourteen, sees being chosen to be the seventh wife of her uncle as just punishment for having read books and kissed a boy, in violation of Prophet Childs' teachings, and is torn between facing her fate and running away from all that she knows and loves.

"This book is a highly emotional, terrifying read. It is not measured or objective. Physical abuse, fear, and even murder are constants. It is a girl-in-peril story, and as such, it is impossible to put down and holds tremendous teen appeal." Voice Youth Advocates

Glimpse. Simon & Schuster Books for Young Readers 2010 484p $16.99

Grades: 7 8 9 10   **Fic**

1. Novels in verse 2. Sisters -- Fiction 3. Suicide -- Fiction 4. Child sexual abuse -- Fiction 5. Mother-daughter relationship -- Fiction

ISBN 978-1-4169-9730-6; 1-4169-9730-X

LC 2009-41147

Living with their mother who earns money as a prostitute, two sisters take care of each other and when the older one attempts suicide, the younger one tries to uncover the reason.

"Williams leans hard on her free-verse line breaks for drama . . . and it works. A page-turner for Ellen Hopkins fans." Kirkus

Miles from ordinary; a novel. St. Martin's Press 2011 197p $16.99

Grades: 7 8 9 10   **Fic**

1. Family life -- Fiction 2. Mental illness -- Fiction 3. Mother-daughter relationship -- Fiction

ISBN 978-0-312-55512-2; 0-312-55512-1

LC 2010-40324

"The author has crafted both a riveting, unusual suspense tale and an absolutely convincing character in Lacey. The book truly is miles from ordinary, in the very best way. Outstanding." Kirkus

"Thirteen-year-old Lacey hopes that this summer day will be a new start. She has gotten her mother a job at Winn-Dixie because they desperately need the money, and Lacey will be following in her aunt Linda's footsteps by working at the public library. Lacey craves an opportunity to be "normal," to flirt with her neighbor Aaron and not have to watch over Momma, who seems so much better these days. But the day quickly spins out of control when Momma disappears." (Booklist)

Williams, Kathryn

Pizza, love, and other stuff that made me famous; Kathryn Williams. Henry Holt 2012 231 p. (hc) $16.99

Grades: 7 8 9 10   **Fic**

1. Cooking -- Fiction 2. Reality television programs -- Fiction 3. Restaurants -- Fiction 4. Interpersonal relations -- Fiction 5. Competition (Psychology) -- Fiction 6. Television -- Production and direction -- Fiction

ISBN 0805092854; 9780805092851

LC 2011034053

In this young adult novel by Kathryn Williams "Sixteen-year-old Sophie Nicolaides . . . audition[s] for a new reality show, 'Teen Test Kitchen.'. . . [T]he prize includes a full scholarship to one of America's finest culinary schools and a summer in Napa, California, not to mention fame. Once on set, Sophie immediately finds herself in the thick of the drama -- including a secret burn book, cutthroat celebrity judges, and a very cute French chef." (Publisher's note)

Williams, Katie

The **space** between trees. Chronicle Books 2010 274p $17.99

Grades: 8 9 10 11 12   **Fic**

1. School stories 2. Homicide -- Fiction

ISBN 978-0-8118-7175-4; 0-8118-7175-4

LC 2009-48561

When the body of a classmate is discovered in the woods, sixteen-year-old Evie's lies wind up involving her with the girl's best friend, trying to track down the killer.

"Evie's raw honesty and the choices she makes make for difficult reading, but also a darkly beautiful, emotionally honest story of personal growth." Publ Wkly

Williams, L. A.

The **witches'** kitchen; [by] Allen Williams. Little Brown 2010 276p il $16.99

Grades: 5 6 7 8   **Fic**

1. Magic -- Fiction 2. Toads -- Fiction 3. Witchcraft -- Fiction

ISBN 978-0-7595-2912-0; 0-7595-2912-4

LC 2009-45625

When Toad wakes up dangling over a bubbling witches' cauldron with no memory of her former life, she just manages to escape and, with the help of an imp, a fairy, and some other friends, she sets out to discover her identity.

Toad is "an engaging protagonist. . . . Her ragtag pals are elegantly described. . . . Intricate pencil drawings . . . pepper the text, adding details that elaborate on the spare descriptions." Bull Cent Child Books

Williams, Laura E.

Slant; [by] Laura E. Williams. Milkweed Editions 2008 149p $16.95; pa $6.95

Grades: 5 6 7 8 9   **Fic**

1. Mothers -- Fiction 2. Adoption -- Fiction 3. Friendship -- Fiction 4. Prejudices -- Fiction 5. Plastic surgery -- Fiction 6. Korean Americans -- Fiction

ISBN 978-1-57131-681-3; 1-57131-681-7; 978-1-57131-682-0 pa; 1-57131-682-5 pa

LC 2008007093

Thirteen-year-old Lauren, a Korean-American adoptee, is tired of being called "slant" and "gook," and longs to have plastic surgery on her eyes, but when her father finds out about her wish—and a long-kept secret about her mother's death is revealed—Lauren starts to question some of her own assumptions

"The characters are exceptionally well drawn, and the friendship between Julie and Lauren is not only believable, featuring humor, conflict, and true wit, but also captures both girls' gains in maturity." SLJ

Williams, Maiya

The **Fizzy** Whiz kid. Amulet Books 2010 273p $16.95

Grades: 5 6 7 8 **Fic**

1. Moving -- Fiction 2. Advertising -- Fiction 3. Hollywood (Calif.) -- Fiction

ISBN 978-0-8109-8347-2; 0-8109-8347-8

Moving to Hollywood with his academic parents, eleven-year-old Mitch feels like an outsider in his school where everyone has connections to the powerful and famous in the entertainment industry, until he is cast in a soda commercial that launches a popular catchphrase.

"Williams' breezy tale is as addictive and bubbly as a Fizzy Whiz itself, and her experience in the entertainment industry packs real value into her descriptions of auditions, movie sets, and agent negotiations. . . . Mitchell's realization that he is a product being assembled is both goofy and poignant." Booklist

Williams, Michael

Diamond boy; Michael Williams. First edition Little, Brown & Co. 2014 400 p. maps (hardcover) $18

Grades: 7 8 9 10 **Fic**

1. Blacks -- Fiction 2. Zimbabwe -- Fiction 3. Survival skills -- Fiction 4. Mines and mineral resources -- Fiction 5. Survival -- Fiction 6. Blacks -- Zimbabwe -- Fiction 7. Shona (African people) -- Fiction 8. Diamond mines and mining -- Fiction

ISBN 0316320692; 9780316320672; 9780316320696

LC 2013042071

Publishers Weekly (October 2014)

"Patson Moyo's life is perfectly ordinary. . . . His father, a teacher, is often a little dreamy but a wonderful storyteller. . . . Patson never would have guessed that his smart, university-graduate father . . . can barely make ends meet, due to government corruption and the massive devaluation of the Zimbabwean dollar. Egged on by Patson's stepmother, Sylvia, the Moyos decide to improve their situation by traveling to Marage." (School Library Journal)

"Written in diary format, the story brings the reader into the mind and soul of a young refugee suffering in a hell created by the greed and violence of powerful adults. More than simply a good read, Diamond Boy is a multilayered, teachable novel with a variety of approaches and is highly recommended for middle and high school collections." VOYA

★ **Now** is the time for running. Little, Brown 2011 233p $17.99

Grades: 6 7 8 9 10 **Fic**

1. Soccer -- Fiction 2. Brothers -- Fiction 3. Refugees -- Fiction 4. Zimbabwe -- Fiction 5. Homeless persons -- Fiction 6. Mentally disabled -- Fiction

ISBN 978-0-316-07790-3; 0-316-07790-9

LC 2010043460

"There is plenty of material to captivate readers: fast-paced soccer matches every bit as tough as the players; the determination of Deo and his fellow refugees to survive unthinkably harsh conditions; and raw depictions of violence. . . . But it's the tender relationship between Deo and Innocent, along with some heartbreaking twists of fate, that will endure in readers' minds." Publ Wkly

Williams, Sarah DeFord

★ **Palace** beautiful. G.P. Putnam's Sons 2010 232p $16.99

Grades: 6 7 8 9 **Fic**

1. Utah -- Fiction 2. Moving -- Fiction 3. Diaries -- Fiction 4. Influenza -- Fiction 5. Family life -- Fiction

ISBN 978-0-399-25298-3; 0-399-25298-3

LC 2009-03213

After her move in 1985 to Salt Lake City, thirteen-year-old Sadie finds a journal in a hidey-hole in the attic, and along with her sister and new friend she reads about the influenza epidemic of 1918.

"Williams does a super job with the characters in this beautifully written book, and it is satisfying to see how they develop." SLJ

Williams, Susan

Wind rider. HarperCollins 2006 309p $16.99

Grades: 7 8 9 10 **Fic**

1. Horses -- Fiction 2. Sex role -- Fiction 3. Prehistoric peoples -- Fiction

ISBN 978-0-06-087236-6; 0-06-087236-5; 978-0-06-087237-3 lib bdg; 0-06-087237-3 lib bdg

LC 2005028595

Fern, a teenager living in 4000 B.C., defies the expectations of her people by displaying a unique and new ability to tame horses and by also questioning many of the traditional activities of women.

"Fern aggressively strains against her mother's expectations and her society's traditional gender roles, and it is these timeless struggles, narrated in Fern's poetic voice, that transform Williams' impressively researched details into a vividly imagined, wholly captivating world." Booklist

Williams, Suzanne

Bull rider; [by] Suzanne Morgan Williams. Margaret K. McElderry Books 2009 241p $16.99

Grades: 7 8 9 10 **Fic**

1. Brothers -- Fiction 2. Veterans -- Fiction 3. Bull riding -- Fiction 4. Wounds and injuries -- Fiction

ISBN 978-1-4169-6130-7; 1-4169-6130-5

LC 2007-52518

When his older brother, a bull-riding champion, returns from the Iraq War partially paralyzed, fourteen-year-old Cam takes a break from skateboarding to enter a bull-riding contest, in hopes of winning the $15,000 prize and motivating his depressed brother to continue with his rehabilitation.

"The mix of wild macho action with family anguish and tenderness will grab teens. . . . [This is a] powerful contemporary story of family, community, and work." Booklist

Williams, Tad

The **dragons** of Ordinary Farm; by Tad Williams and Deborah Beale; pictures by Greg Swearingen. Harper 2009 412p il $16.99

Grades: 4 5 6 7   Fic

1. Farms -- Fiction 2. Uncles -- Fiction 3. Siblings -- Fiction 4. Supernatural -- Fiction 5. Mythical animals -- Fiction

ISBN 978-0-06-154345-6; 0-06-154345-4

LC 2008035298

When their great-uncle Gideon invites Tyler and Lucinda to his farm for the summer, they discover his animals are extremely unusual.

"Williams and Beale have created a gripping fantasy with realistic but appealing characters as well as scientific magic that explains the appearance of legendary creatures." SLJ

Williams-Garcia, Rita

★ **Gone** Crazy in Alabama; by Rita Williams-Garcia. Harpercollins Childrens Books 2015 304 p. $16.99

Grades: 4 5 6 7 8   Fic

1. Sisters -- Fiction 2. Family secrets -- Fiction 3. African American children -- Fiction 4. Mothers -- Fiction

ISBN 0062215876; 9780062215871

This novel by Rita Williams-Garcia "tells the story of the Gaither sisters, who are about to learn what it's like to be fish out of water as they travel from the streets of Brooklyn to the rural South for the summer of a lifetime. . . . As Delphine hears about her family history, she uncovers the surprising truth that's been keeping the sisters apart. But when tragedy strikes, Delphine discovers that the bonds of family run deeper than she ever knew possible." (Publisher's note)

"This well-crafted depiction of a close-knit community in rural Alabama works beautifully, with language that captures its humor, sorrow and resilience. Rich in all areas, Delphine and her sisters' third outing will fully satisfy the many fans of their first two." Kirkus

Previous books in the trilogy are:
One Crazy Summer (2010)
P.S. Be Eleven (2013)

★ **Jumped**. HarperTeen 2009 169p $16.99; lib bdg $17.89

Grades: 8 9 10 11 12   Fic

1. School stories 2. Bullies -- Fiction

ISBN 978-0-06-076091-5; 0-06-076091-5; 978-0-06-076092-2 lib bdg; 0-06-076092-3 lib bdg

LC 2008-22381

The lives of Leticia, Dominique, and Trina are irrevocably intertwined through the course of one day in an urban high school after Leticia overhears Dominique's plans to beat up Trina and must decide whether or not to get involved.

"In alternating chapters narrated by Leticia, Trina, and Dominique, Williams-Garcia has given her characters strong, individual voices that ring true to teenage speech, and she lets them make their choices without judgment or moralizing." SLJ

★ **Like** sisters on the homefront. Lodestar Bks. 1995 165p hardcover o.p. pa $5.99

Grades: 7 8 9 10   Fic

1. Family life -- Fiction 2. Teenage mothers -- Fiction 3. African Americans -- Fiction

ISBN 0-525-67465-9; 0-14-038561-4 pa

LC 95-3690

"Beautifully written, the text captures the cadence and rhythm of New York street talk and the dilemma of being poor, black, and uneducated. This is a gritty, realistic, well-told story." SLJ

"It's bad enough that 14-year-old Gayle has one baby, but when she becomes pregnant again by another boy, Mama's had enough. She takes Gayle for an abortion and then ships her and her baby south to stay with religious relatives. . . . With the help of her dying great-grandmother, who leaves Gayle the family's African-American oral tradition, she begins to mature and understand her place in the family and her future." Child Book Rev Serv

No laughter here. HarperCollins 2004 133p $15.99; lib bdg $16.89

Grades: 7 8 9 10   Fic

1. Friendship -- Fiction 2. New York (N.Y.) -- Fiction 3. African Americans -- Fiction 4. Female circumcision -- Fiction

ISBN 0-688-16247-9; 0-688-16248-7 lib bdg

LC 2003-9331

In Queens, New York, ten-year-old Akilah is determined to find out why her closest friend, Victoria, is silent and withdrawn after returning from a trip to her homeland, Nigeria.

This is a "disturbing and poignant coming-of-age novel. . . . This contemporary tale about the ancient rite of female circumcision will no doubt leave an indelible mark on pre-teens." Publ Wkly

★ **One** crazy summer. Amistad 2010 218p $15.99; lib bdg $16.89

Grades: 4 5 6 7 8   Fic

1. Poets -- Fiction 2. Mothers -- Fiction 3. Sisters -- Fiction 4. Black Panther Party -- Fiction. 5. African Americans -- Civil rights -- Fiction

ISBN 978-0-06-076088-5; 0-06-076088-5; 978-0-06-076089-2 lib bdg; 0-06-076089-3 lib bdg

LC 2009-09293

A Newbery Medal honor book, 2011

In the summer of 1968, after travelling from Brooklyn to Oakland, California, to spend a month with the mother they barely know, eleven-year-old Delphine and her two younger sisters arrive to a cold welcome as they discover that their mother, a dedicated poet and printer, is resentful of the intrusion of their visit and wants them to attend a nearby Black Panther summer camp.

"Delphine's growing awareness of injustice on a personal and universal level is smoothly woven into the story in poetic language that will stimulate and move readers." Publ Wkly

★ **P.S.** Be Eleven; Rita Williams-Garcia. Harpercollins Childrens Books 2013 288 p. $16.99

Grades: 4 5 6 7 8   Fic

1. Historical fiction 2. African American children -- Fiction

ISBN 0061938629; 9780061938627

Sequel to: One crazy summer.

Coretta Scott King Book Award Author Winner (2014)

This book is a follow-up to Rita Williams-Garcia's Newbery Honor-winning "One Crazy Summer." Here, "Delphine and her sisters return to Brooklyn from visiting their estranged mother, Cecile, a poet . . . . Change and conflict have the Gaither household in upheaval: Pa has a new girlfriend, Uncle Darnell returns from Vietnam a damaged young man, and the sixth-grade teacher Delphine hoped to get has been replaced by a man from Zambia." (Publishers Weekly)

"...Soars as a finely drawn portrait of a family in flux and as a memorable slice of a specific time in our nation's history." Booklist

Williamson, Jill

By darkness hid. Marcher Lord Press 2009 490p map (Blood of kings) $14.99

Grades: 7 8 9 10   **Fic**

1. Fantasy fiction 2. Gifted children -- Fiction 3. Knights and knighthood -- Fiction

ISBN 978-0-9821049-5-8; 0-9821049-5-2

"With no family, Achan Cham is marked as a stray and lives the brutal life of a slave. When he is lucky enough to be chosen to begin training as a Kingsguard Knight, his life changes completely, but he is left to wonder if it is for the better. . . . Wonderfully written with a superb plot, this book is a sure-fire hit with almost any reader. . . . The novel is a solid choice for any collection." Voice Youth Advocates

Followed by: To darkness fled (2010)

To darkness fled. Marcher Lord Press 2010 680p map (Blood of kings) pa $17.99

Grades: 7 8 9 10   **Fic**

1. Fantasy fiction 2. Knights and knighthood -- Fiction

ISBN 978-0-9825987-0-2; 0-9825987-0-X

Sequel to: By darkness hid (2009)

"Once again the superb writing enhances the thought-provoking story, making this a package too good to miss. . . . Reading this will certainly leave the reader anxiously awaiting the next installment." Voice Youth Advocates

Willingham, Bill

Down the Mysterly River; illustrations by Mark Buckingham. Tor/Starscape 2011 333p il $15.99

Grades: 4 5 6 7   **Fic**

1. Fantasy fiction 2. Memory -- Fiction 3. Animals -- Fiction 4. Forests and forestry -- Fiction

ISBN 978-0-7653-2792-5; 0-7653-2792-9

LC 2011018958

Top notch Boy Scout Max "the Wolf" cannot remember how he came to be in a strange forest, but soon he and three talking animals are on the run from the Blue Cutters, hunters who will alter the foursome's very essence if they can catch them.

"Willingham roles out his themes slowly, only fully spelling them out in the final scene, but they don't interfere with the rollicking story, nasty (but fully realized) villains, and heroic camaraderie. . . . [This] is a stellar example of a novel working both as an adventure tale and as metafiction." Publ Wkly

Willis, Cynthia Chapman

Buck fever. Feiwel and Friends 2009 228p $16.99

Grades: 7 8 9 10   **Fic**

1. Artists -- Fiction 2. Hunting -- Fiction 3. Siblings -- Fiction 4. Family life -- Fiction 5. Father-son relationship -- Fiction

ISBN 978-0-312-38297-1; 0-312-38297-9

LC 2008034748

Twelve-year-old Joey and his fifteen-year-old sister Philly relate their experiences trying to cope in a family already strained by the mother's extended travel, and pushed further apart by the father's disappointment that Joey is more interested in drawing deer than hunting them.

"The quietness of nature and small-town life is wonderfully reflected in Willis' patient and artful prose, and every hunting detail feels authentic. . . . An unusually sensitive and reflective boy-centric book." Booklist

Willner-Pardo, Gina

The **hard** kind of promise. Clarion Books/Houghton Mifflin Harcourt 2010 200p $16

Grades: 4 5 6 7   **Fic**

1. School stories 2. California -- Fiction 3. Friendship -- Fiction 4. Popularity -- Fiction

ISBN 978-0-547-24395-5; 0-547-24395-2

California seventh-graders Sarah and Marjorie made a promise in kindergarten to always be friends, but Marjorie is weird and Sarah, wanting to be at least somewhat popular, makes friends with a fellow choir member.

"Willner-Pardo's avoidance of overblown crises and dramatic climaxes creates a steadily paced, authentic story" Publ Wkly

Willocks, Tim

Doglands. Random House 2011 308p $16.99; lib bdg $19.99; ebook $16.99

Grades: 5 6 7 8   **Fic**

1. Adventure fiction 2. Dogs -- Fiction 3. Supernatural -- Fiction 4. Animal welfare -- Fiction

ISBN 978-0-375-86571-8; 0-375-86571-3; 978-0-375-96571-5 lib bdg; 0-375-96571-8 lib bdg; 978-0-375-89604-0 ebook; 0-375-89604-X ebook

LC 2009033328

Furgal, a half-greyhound puppy, escapes a cruel dog-track owner and sets out in the hope of finding his father and the fabled Doglands, later returning to try to free his mother, sisters, and the other abused dogs.

"The dogs each have distinct personalities, and the mystic lore of the Doglands adds a secondary fantasy layer to the narrative. Humans are only sketched in, which is fitting, since the tale is told from the dog point of view. A riveting dog tale with a healthy serving of savagery, not all on the part of the four-legged characters." Kirkus

Wilson, Diane L.

Black storm comin' Margaret K. McElderry Books 2005 295p $17.99

Grades: 7 8 9 10   **Fic**

1. Pony express -- Fiction 2. Racially mixed people --

Fiction 3. Frontier and pioneer life -- Fiction
ISBN 0-689-87137-6; 0-689-87138-2

LC 2004-9438

Twelve-year-old Colton, son of a black mother and a white father, takes a job with the Pony Express in 1860 after his father abandons the family on their California-bound wagon train, and risks his life to deliver an important letter that may affect the growing conflict between the North and South.

"Wilson masterfully creates a multidimensional character in Colton. . . . Readers will absorb greater lessons as they become engrossed in the excitement, beauty, and terror of Colton's journey to California and manhood." Booklist

★ **Firehorse**. Margaret K. McElderry Books 2006 325p $16.95

Grades: 7 8 9 10   **Fic**

1. Arson -- Fiction 2. Horses -- Fiction 3. Sex role -- Fiction 4. Family life -- Fiction 5. Boston (Mass.) -- Fiction 6. Veterinary medicine -- Fiction
ISBN 1-4169-1551-6; 978-1-4169-1551-5

LC 2005-30785

Spirited fifteen-year-old horse lover Rachel Selby determines to become a veterinarian, despite the opposition of her rigid father, her proper mother, and the norms of Boston in 1872, while that city faces a serial arsonist and an epidemic spreading through its firehorse population.

"Wilson paces the story well, with tension building. . . . The novel's finest achievement, though, is the convincing depiction of family dynamics in an era when men ruled the household and women, who had few opportunities, folded their dreams and put them away with the linens they embroidered." Booklist

Wilson, Jacqueline

Best friends. Roaring Brook Press 2008 229p $15.95; pa $7.99

Grades: 4 5 6 7   **Fic**

1. School stories 2. Scotland -- Fiction 3. Friendship -- Fiction
ISBN 978-1-59643-278-9; 1-59643-278-0; 978-0-312-58144-2 pa; 0-312-58144-0 pa

LC 2006-39716

Rambunctious and irrepressible Gemma has been best friends with Alice ever since they were born on the same day, so when Alice moves miles away to Scotland, Gemma is distraught over the idea that Alice might find a new best friend.

"Believable, sympathetic characters; recognizable home and school situations; and plenty of humor . . . will ensure that this becomes . . . a popular read for middle-grade girls." Booklist

Kiss. Roaring Brook Press 2010 248p $16.99

Grades: 7 8 9 10   **Fic**

1. Friendship -- Fiction
ISBN 978-1-59643-242-0; 1-59643-242-X

"Sylvie, 14, has always assumed she would marry her best friend, Carl, but lately he has been distant and doesn't even seem interested in their secret fantasy, Glassworld. When a game of spin the bottle results in Carl kissing Sylvie's new friend, Miranda, and refusing to kiss her, Sylvie

begins to doubt her attractiveness. But when Carl suddenly insists on including his new friend, Paul, on all their outings, especially his birthday party, Sylvie is even more confused. . . . With sharply drawn characters, Wilson handles the confusion and angst of teen love and sexuality with careful sensitivity." SLJ

Wilson, John

The **alchemist's** dream; [by] John Wilson. Key Porter Books 2007 248p pa $12.95

Grades: 7 8 9 10   **Fic**

1. Explorers 2. Explorers -- Fiction 3. Navigation -- Fiction 4. London (England) -- Fiction 5. Great Britain -- History -- 1603-1714, Stuarts -- Fiction
ISBN 978-1-55263-934-4 pa; 1-55263-934-7 pa

"Middle grade readers and high school readers who like historical fiction and stories of adventure with some mystery thrown in will be drawn to this book." Voice Youth Advocates

"In the fall of 1669, the Nonsuch returned to London with a load of fur from Hudson Bay. It brought something else, too—the lost journal from Henry Hudson's tragic search for a passage to Cathay in 1611. The journal finds its way to the aged Robert Bylot and triggers disturbing memories of his life." Publisher's note

And in the morning. Kids Can Press 2003 198p $16.95

Grades: 7 8 9 10   **Fic**

1. World War, 1914-1918 -- Fiction
ISBN 1-55337-400-2

"Jim Hay, 16, is caught up in the patriotic fervor sweeping across Scotland as the British troops prepare to enter World War I. . . . His father is killed in action and 10 days later his mother dies from shock and grief. Within weeks, Jim has signed up and is soon in the trenches. . . . A compelling, fascinating, and ultimately disturbing book that is not to be missed." SLJ

Ghost moon. Orca 2011 172p (Desert legends trilogy) pa $12.95

Grades: 6 7 8 9   **Fic**

1. Outlaws 2. New Mexico -- Fiction 3. West (U.S.) -- Fiction 4. Frontier and pioneer life -- Fiction
ISBN 978-1-55469-879-0; 1-55469-879-0

Sequel to: Written in blood (2010)

"A young wanderer lands in the middle of New Mexico's Lincoln County War. . . . 16-year-old James Doolen falls in with Bill Bonney (not yet known as 'Billy the Kid') a charming but decidedly mercurial teenager who hares off on a vicious killing spree after their new boss, John Tunstall, is murdered by a rival merchant's gang of hired gunmen. . . . Action fans will thrill to the gunplay and other dangers. James' conflicting feelings about his archetypically dangerous friend . . . introduce thought provoking elements. A tale of the Old West with a sturdy historical base and nary a dull moment." Kirkus

Victorio's war; John Wilson. Orca Book Publishers 2012 157p (paperback) $12.95

Grades: 6 7 8 9   **Fic**

1. Western stories 2. Historical fiction 3. Biographical

fiction
ISBN 9781554698820 pa; 9781554698837 (pdf);
9781554698844 (epub)

LC 2011942580

In this historical novel, by John Wilson, after "taking up a new job scouting for a troop of Buffalo Soldiers, Jim Doolen finds himself caught between friends in the military and friends riding with the Apaches they are chasing. . . . He is saved by his mystic old mentor Too-ah-yay-say from being killed . . . and held captive until a final massacre by Mexican soldiers." (Kirkus)

Written in blood. Orca Book Publishers 2010 157p (Desert legends trilogy) pa $12.95

Grades: 6 7 8 9   **Fic**

1. Fathers -- Fiction 2. West (U.S.) -- Fiction 3. Voyages and travels -- Fiction 4. Frontier and pioneer life -- Fiction
ISBN 978-1-55469-270-5 pa; 1-55469-270-9 pa

A young man's search for the father who abandoned him takes him through the wilds of the Arizona territory and northern Mexico during the 1870's and brings him in contact with an assortment of intriguing characters.

"Told in a terse, present-tense narrative, James' adventures will thrill all fans of traditional pulp-style oaters." Booklist

Followed by: Ghost moon (2011)

Wilson, N. D.

★ The **dragon's** tooth; [by] N. D. Wilson. Random House 2011 485p (Ashtown burials) $16.99; lib bdg $19.99; e-book $16.99

Grades: 5 6 7 8   **Fic**

1. Fantasy fiction 2. Magic -- Fiction 3. Siblings -- Fiction 4. Secret societies -- Fiction
ISBN 978-0-375-86439-1; 0-375-86439-3; 978-0-375-96439-8 lib bdg; 0-375-96439-8 lib bdg; 978-0-375-89572-2 e-book

LC 2009038651

"This fast-paced fantasy quickly draws readers in to its alternate reality. . . . Allusions to mythology and complex character development . . . make Wilson's first in a proposed series a gem." Booklist

★ **Leepike** Ridge; [by] N. D. Wilson. Random House 2007 224p $15.99; lib bdg $18.99; pa $6.99

Grades: 4 5 6 7   **Fic**

1. Adventure fiction 2. Caves -- Fiction 3. Missing persons -- Fiction 4. Mother-son relationship -- Fiction
ISBN 978-0-375-83873-6; 0-375-83873-2; 978-0-375-93873-3 lib bdg; 0-375-93873-7 lib bdg; 978-0-375-83874-3 pa; 0-375-83874-0 pa

LC 2006-13352

While his widowed mother continues to search for him, eleven-year-old Tom, presumed dead after drifting away down a river, finds himself trapped in a series of underground caves with another survivor and a dog, and pursued by murderous treasure-hunters

"While Leepike Ridge is primarily an adventure story involving murder, treachery, and betrayal, Wilson's rich imagination and his quirky characters are a true delight." SLJ

Wilson, Nancy Hope

Mountain pose. Farrar, Straus & Giroux 2001 233p $17

Grades: 5 6 7 8   **Fic**

1. Diaries -- Fiction 2. Vermont -- Fiction 3. Grandmothers -- Fiction
ISBN 0-374-35078-7

LC 00-57269

When twelve-year-old Ellie inherits an old Vermont farm from her cruel and heartless grandmother Aurelia, she reads a set of diaries written by an ancestor and discovers secrets from the past

"Beautifully written and suspenseful, this novel explores the many emotions associated with the tragedy of spousal and child abuse." Voice Youth Advocates

Winerip, Michael

Adam Canfield of the Slash. Candlewick Press 2005 326p $15.99; pa $6.99

Grades: 5 6 7 8   **Fic**

1. School stories 2. Journalism -- Fiction
ISBN 0-7636-2340-7; 0-7636-2794-1 pa

While serving as co-editors of their school newspaper, middle-schoolers Adam and Jennifer uncover fraud and corruption in their school and in the city's government.

"This is a deceptively fun read that somehow manages to present kids with some of the most subtle social and ethical questions currently shaping their futures." SLJ

Other titles about Adam Canfield are:
Adam Canfield, watch you back! (2007)
Adam Canfield, the last reporter (2009)

Adam Canfield, the last reporter. Candlewick Press 2009 377p $16.99

Grades: 5 6 7 8   **Fic**

1. School stories 2. Journalism -- Fiction
ISBN 978-0-7636-2342-5; 0-7636-2342-3

LC 2009007347

When the school board shuts down the student newspaper, the Ameche Brothers, two budding entrepreneurs with a knack for refurbishing junk but a shaky command of journalistic ethics, step in to help.

"The novel is packed with memorable characters, breezy laughs, a bit of romance, and heart-tugging quandaries." SLJ

Adam Canfield, watch your back! Candlewick Press 2007 329p $15.99; pa $7.99

Grades: 5 6 7 8   **Fic**

1. School stories 2. Bullies -- Fiction 3. Journalism -- Fiction
ISBN 978-0-7636-2341-8; 0-7636-2341-5; 978-0-7636-4412-3 pa; 0-7636-4412-9 pa

LC 2007-25245

Sequel to Adam Canfield of the Slash (2005)

A much-welcomed snow day turns into an embarrasing nightmare for middle-grader Adam Canfield when, after being mugged by high school bullies, he becomes the focus of major media attention just as his co-editors at The Slash are launching a contest to out bullies at their school.

"Winerip writes with lots of laugh-out-loud humor. . . . Yet in the midst of this humor, he tackles some tough ethical issues." SLJ

Winget, Dianna Dorisi

A **million** ways home; Dianna Dorisi Winget. Scholastic Press 2014 272 p. $16.99

Grades: 4 5 6 7   **Fic**

1. Dogs -- Fiction 2. Witnesses -- Fiction 3. Friendship -- Fiction 4. Grandmothers -- Fiction 5. Washington (State) -- Fiction 6. German shepherd dog -- Fiction 7. Spokane County (Wash.) -- Fiction 8. Witnesses -- Protection -- Fiction

ISBN 0545667062; 9780545667067; 9780545667074

LC 2014005037

"Poppy's life has been turned upside down after her grandma (and guardian) had a stroke and ended up in the hospital. . . . [W]hen she witnesses an armed robbery, 'back to normal' slips even further out of her reach. To keep Poppy safe, the budget-strapped police devise an unusual 'witness protection program,' wherein Poppy will stay with Detective Brannigan's mother." (Publisher's note)

"Readers will cheer on this sassy, relatable, pre-teen as they get to know her. Most of her trials are beyond Poppy's years and certainly out of her control. Even reluctant readers will enjoy the journey Poppy takes to find a new, perhaps unexpected, version of family, friendship, and home." Lib Med Con

Winston, Sherri

★ The **Kayla** chronicles; a novel. Little, Brown 2007 188p hardcover o.p. pa $7.99

Grades: 6 7 8 9 10   **Fic**

1. School stories 2. Dancers -- Fiction 3. Journalism -- Fiction 4. African Americans -- Fiction

ISBN 978-0-316-11430-1; 0-316-11430-8; 978-0-316-11431-8 pa; 0-316-11431-6 pa

LC 2006-933219

Kayla transforms herself from mild-mannered journalist to hot-trotting dance diva in order to properly investigate her high school's dance team, and has a hard time remaining true to her real self while in the role.

"Few recent novels for younger YAs mesh levity and substance this successfully." Booklist

Winters, Ben H.

The **mystery** of the missing everything. Harper 2011 263p $16.99

Grades: 4 5 6 7   **Fic**

1. School stories 2. Mystery fiction

ISBN 978-0-06-196544-9; 0-06-196544-8

LC 2011010167

Sequel to: The secret life of Ms. Finkleman (2010)

When a treasured trophy disappears from the display case at Mary Todd Lincoln Middle School and the principal cancels the eagerly anticipated eighth grade class trip, Bethesda Fielding has no choice but to solve the mystery.

"Featuring the same cast of eccentric teachers and eclectic students, this zany sequel offers another fast-moving middle-school puzzler, lots of pre and early teen humor and one relentless sleuth who's willing to admit when she's wrong. Fans will cheer more mystery and mayhem at Mary Todd Lincoln Middle School." Kirkus

The **secret** life of Ms. Finkleman. Harper 2010 247p $16.99

Grades: 4 5 6 7   **Fic**

1. School stories 2. Teachers -- Fiction 3. Musicians -- Fiction 4. Rock music -- Fiction

ISBN 978-0-06-196541-8; 0-06-196541-3

LC 2010-04601

Spurred by a special project from her social studies teacher, seventh-grader Bethesda Fielding uncovers the secret identity of her music teacher, which leads to a most unusual concert performance and a tutoring assignment.

"Liberally laced with humor and featuring an upbeat heroine, unexpected friendship and rock-music trivia, this witty middle-school drama offers a lighthearted lesson in the importance of getting the facts straight." Kirkus

Another title about Bethesda Fielding is:
The mystery of missing everything (2011)

Winters, Cat

★ **In** the shadow of blackbirds; Cat Winters. Amulet Books 2013 400 p. $16.95

Grades: 8 9 10 11 12   **Fic**

1. Occult fiction 2. Historical fiction 3. Ghosts -- Fiction 4. Spiritualism -- Fiction 5. World War, 1914-1918 -- Fiction 6. Influenza Epidemic, 1918-1919 -- Fiction 7. San Diego (Calif.) -- History -- 20th century -- Fiction

ISBN 141970530X; 9781419705304

LC 2012039262

William C. Morris Honor Book (2014)

In this book, sixteen-year-old Mary Shelley Black lives in 1918. "With WWI raging on and Mary's father on trial for treason, she goes to live with her Aunt Eva in San Diego, Calif. . . . Grieving for her childhood beau Stephen, who died while fighting overseas with the Army, Mary goes outside during a thunderstorm and is struck dead by lightning—for a few minutes. When Mary comes to, she discovers she can communicate with the dead, including Stephen." (Publishers Weekly)

"Winters strikes just the right balance between history and ghost story . . . . Vintage photographs contribute to the authenticity of the atmospheric and nicely paced storytelling." Kirkus

Winterson, Jeanette

Tanglewreck. Bloomsbury Children's Books 2006 414p $16.95; pa $6.95

Grades: 5 6 7 8   **Fic**

1. Science fiction 2. Space and time -- Fiction 3. Clocks and watches -- Fiction

ISBN 978-1-58234-919-0; 1-58234-919-3; 978-1-59990-081-0 pa; 1-59990-081-5 pa

LC 2005-30630

Eleven-year-old Silver sets out to find the Timekeeper—a clock that controls time—and to protect it from falling into the hands of two people who want to use the device for their own nefarious ends

"Winterson seamlessly combines rousing adventure with time warps, quantum physics, and a few wonderfully hapless flunkies." Booklist

Winthrop, Elizabeth

Counting on Grace. Wendy Lamb Books 2006 232p $15.95; lib bdg $17.99; pa $6.99

Grades: 5 6 7 8   **Fic**

1. Photographers 2. Vermont -- Fiction 3. Factories -- Fiction 4. Child labor -- Fiction 5. Photographers -- Fiction

ISBN 0-385-74644-X; 0-385-90878-4 lib bdg; 0-553-48783-3 pa

It's 1910 in Pownal, Vermont. At 12 Grace and her best friend Arthur must go to work in the mill, helping their mothers work the looms. Together Grace and Arthur write a secret letter to the Child Labor Board about underage children working in the mill. A few weeks later, Lewis Hine, a famous reformer, arrives undercover to gather evidence. Grace meets him and appears in some of his photographs, changing her life forever.

"Much information on early photography and the workings of the textile mills is conveyed, and history and fiction are woven seamlessly together in this beautifully written novel." SLJ

Wiseman, Eva

★ **Puppet;** a novel. Tundra Books 2009 243p $17.95

Grades: 7 8 9 10 11 12   **Fic**

1. Prejudices -- Fiction 2. Jews -- Hungary -- Fiction

ISBN 0-88776-828-8; 978-0-88776-828-6

"The year is 1882. A young servant girl named Esther disappears from a small Hungarian village. Several Jewish men from the village of Tisza Eszvar face the 'blood libel'— the centuries-old calumny that Jews murder Christian children for their blood. A fourteen-year-old Jewish boy named Morris Scharf becomes the star witness of corrupt authorities who coerce him into testifying against his fellow Jews, including his own father, at the trial. This . . . fictionalized account of one of the last blood libel trials in Europe is told through the eyes of Julie, a friend of the murdered Esther, and a servant at the jail where Morris is imprisoned." (Publisher's note) "Age eleven and up." (Quill Quire)

"Times are hard in Julie Vamosi's Hungarian village in the late nineteenth-century, and the townspeople . . . blame the Jews. After Julie's best friend, Esther, . . . disappears, the rumor spreads that the Jews cut her throat and drained her blood to drink with their Passover matzos. . . . Based on the records of a trial in 1883, this searing novel dramatizes virulent anti-Semitism from the viewpoint of a Christian child. . . . The climax is electrifying." Booklist

Wiseman, Rosalind

Boys, girls, and other hazardous materials. Putnam 2010 282p $17.99

Grades: 8 9 10 11 12   **Fic**

1. School stories

ISBN 978-0-399-247965; 0-399-24796-3

LC 2009-18446

Transferring to a new high school, freshman Charlotte "Charlie" Healey faces tough choices as she tries to shed her "mean girl" image.

Wiseman "succeeds in delivering realistic, likable characters whose challenges and mistakes are all too relatable." Bull Cent Child Books

Wisler, G. Clifton

Caleb's choice. Lodestar Bks. 1996 154p hardcover o.p. pa $4.99

Grades: 5 6 7 8   **Fic**

1. Slavery -- Fiction 2. Underground railroad -- Fiction

ISBN 0-14-038256-9 pa

LC 96-2339

"When 13-year-old Caleb Dulaney's father loses the family fortune in 1858, Caleb leaves his private school and privileged life to live with his grandmother in northern Texas. He adjusts easily to working in his grandmother's inn, but he struggles with the controversy surrounding the Fugitive Slave Law. Should he help two fugitive slaves escape to Kansas? Although he is not comfortable breaking the law, he agrees to assist because a runaway slave saved him from drowning." (Booklist) "Grades four to eight." (SLJ)

"This fast-paced, easy-to-read novel proves that history can be intriguing and exciting, Wisler draws readers into this masterful, and often humorous tale." ALAN

Red Cap. Lodestar Bks. 1991 160p hardcover o.p. pa $5.99

Grades: 4 5 6 7   **Fic**

1. Andersonville Prison -- Fiction 2. United States -- History -- 1861-1865, Civil War -- Fiction

ISBN 0-14-036936-8 pa

LC 90-21944

A young Yankee drummer boy displays great courage when he's captured and sent to Andersonville Prison

The author "presents a well-researched view of the war. He effectively interweaves the known facts of Powell's life with first-person accounts of other soldiers and prisoners to create an exciting story." SLJ

Withers, Pam

First descent. Tundra Books 2011 265p $17.95

Grades: 7 8 9 10   **Fic**

1. Colombia -- Fiction 2. Kayaks and kayaking -- Fiction

ISBN 978-1-77049-257-8; 1-77049-257-7

"Seventeen-year-old champion slalom kayaker Rex Scruggs is determined to kayak Colombia's Furioso River, when he meets a young woman, an Andean indigena, who both aids Rex in his quest and puts him in the crosshairs of Colombia's battling guerrillas and paramilitaries. . . . Withers flings the reader from one perilous adventure to another." Booklist

Wittlinger, Ellen

Hard love. Simon & Schuster Bks. for Young Readers 1999 224p hardcover o.p. pa $8.99

Grades: 7 8 9 10   **Fic**

1. Lesbians -- Fiction 2. Authorship -- Fiction

ISBN 0-689-82134-4; 0-689-84154-X pa

LC 98-6668

Michael L. Printz Award honor book, 2000

"John, cynical yet vulnerable, thinks he's immune to emotion until he meets bright, brittle Marisol, the author of his favorite zine. He falls in love, but Marisol, a lesbian, just wants to be friends. A love story of a different sort—funny, poignant, and thoughtful." Booklist

Followed by: Love & lies: Marisol's story (2008)

Love & lies; Marisol's story. Simon & Schuster Books for Young Readers 2008 245p $16.99

Grades: 7 8 9 10 **Fic**
1. Lesbians -- Fiction 2. Authorship -- Fiction 3. Massachusetts -- Fiction
ISBN 978-1-4169-1623-9; 1-4169-1623-7
LC 2007-18330

When Marisol, a self-confident eighteen-year-old lesbian, moves to Cambridge, Massachusetts to work and try to write a novel, she falls under the spell of her beautiful but deceitful writing teacher, while also befriending a shy, vulnerable girl from Indiana.

"The emotional morass of Marisol's life . . . . is complex and realistic; it will draw in both fans of the earlier novel . . . and realistic-fiction readers seeking a love story with depth." Bull Cent Child Books

Parrotfish. Simon & Schuster Books for Young Readers 2007 294p $16.99

Grades: 7 8 9 10 **Fic**
1. School stories 2. Family life -- Fiction 3. Transgender people -- Fiction
ISBN 978-1-4169-1622-2; 1-4169-1622-9
LC 2006-9689

Grady, a transgendered high school student, yearns for acceptance by his classmates and family as he struggles to adjust to his new identity as a male.

"The author demonstrates well the complexity faced by transgendered people and makes the teen's frustration with having to fit into a category fully apparent." Publ Wkly

This means war! Simon & Schuster Books for Young Readers 2010 224p $16.99

Grades: 5 6 7 8 **Fic**
1. Fear -- Fiction 2. Contests -- Fiction 3. Friendship -- Fiction
ISBN 978-1-4169-97101-6; 1-4169-7101-7
LC 2008-32586

In 1962, when her best friend Lowell begins to hang around new friends who think girls are losers, Juliet, a fearful fifth-grader, teams up with bold, brave Patsy who challenges the boys to a series of increasingly dangerous contests

"Wittlinger latches on to a poignant metaphor for war in the lively and readable tale set against the backdrop of the 1962 Cuban missile crisis." Booklist

Zigzag. Simon & Schuster Bks. for Young Readers 2003 267p $16.95

Grades: 7 8 9 10 **Fic**
1. Cousins -- Fiction 2. Automobile travel -- Fiction
ISBN 0-689-84996-6
LC 2002-2145

A high-school junior makes a trip with her aunt and two cousins, discovering places she did not know existed and strengths she did not know she had

"Teens will easily hear themselves in Robin's hilarious, sharp observations and feel her excitement as she travels through new country and discovers her own strength." Booklist

Woelfle, Gretchen

All the world's a stage; a novel in five acts. illustrated by Thomas Cox. Holiday House 2011 163p il $16.95

Grades: 4 5 6 7 **Fic**
1. Actors -- Fiction 2. Orphans -- Fiction 3. Theater -- Fiction 4. Apprentices -- Fiction 5. Globe Theatre (London, England) -- Fiction 6. Chamberlain's Men (Theater company) -- Fiction 7. Great Britain -- History -- 1485-1603, Tudors -- Fiction
ISBN 978-0-8234-2281-4; 0-8234-2281-X
LC 2010023474

Twelve-year-old orphan Christopher "Kit" Buckles becomes a stage boy in a London theater in 1598, tries his hand at acting, and later helps build the Globe Theater for playwright William Shakespeare and the Chamberlain's Men acting troupe.

"The most compelling drama is Kit's universal search for his calling and his shifting friendships. . . . Frequent charming drawings enhance the sense of time and place." Booklist

Includes glossary and bibliographical references

Wolf, Allan

New found land; Lewis and Clark's voyage of discovery: a novel. Candlewick Press 2004 500p map $18.99

Grades: 7 8 9 10 **Fic**
1. Lewis and Clark Expedition (1804-1806) -- Fiction
ISBN 0-7636-2113-7
LC 2003-65254

The letters and thoughts of Thomas Jefferson, members of the Corps of Discovery, their guide Sacagawea, and Captain Lewis's Newfoundland dog, all tell of the historic exploratory expedition to seek a water route to the Pacific Ocean.

"This is an extraordinary, engrossing book that would appeal most to serious readers, but it should definitely be added to any collection." SLJ

Includes glossary and bibliographical references

★ The **watch** that ends the night; voices from the Titanic. Candlewick Press 2011 466p $21.99

Grades: 7 8 9 10 **Fic**
1. Novels in verse 2. Shipwrecks -- Fiction 3. Titanic (Steamship) -- Fiction
ISBN 978-0-7636-3703-3
LC 2010040150

"A lyrical, monumental work of fact and imagination that reads like an oral history revved up by the drama of the event." Kirkus

"Millionaire John Jacob Astor hopes to bring home his pregnant teen bride with a minimum of media scandal. A beautiful Lebanese refugee, on her way to family in Florida, discovers the first stirrings of love. And an ancient iceberg glides south, anticipating its fateful encounter. The voices in this remarkable re-creation of the Titanic disaster span classes and stations, from Margaret ('the unsinkable Molly') Brown to the captain who went down with his ship; from the lookout and wireless men to a young boy in search of dragons and a gambler in search of marks." (Publisher's note)

Wolf, Joan M.

★ **Someone** named Eva. Clarion Books 2007 200p $16; pa $6.99

Grades: 5 6 7 8 **Fic**

1. School stories 2. National socialism -- Fiction 3. World War, 1939-1945 -- Fiction 4. Europe -- History -- 1918-1945 -- Fiction

ISBN 0-618-53579-9; 0-547-23766-9 pa

LC 2006-26070

From her home in Lidice, Czechoslovakia, in 1942, eleven-year-old Milada is taken with other blond, blue-eyed children to a school in Poland to be trained as "proper Germans" for adoption by German families, but all the while she remembers her true name and history.

"This amazing, eye-opening story, masterfully written, is an essential part of World War II literature and belongs on the shelves of every library." SLJ

Wolff, Virginia Euwer

★ **Make** lemonade. Holt & Co. 1993 200p $17.95; pa $7.95

Grades: 8 9 10 11 12 **Fic**

1. Novels in verse 2. Poverty -- Fiction 3. Babysitters -- Fiction 4. Teenage mothers -- Fiction

ISBN 978-0-8050-2228-5; 0-8050-2228-7; 978-0-8050-8070-4 pa; 0-8050-8070-8 pa

LC 92-41182

"Fourteen-year-old LaVaughn accepts the job of babysitting Jolly's two small children but quickly realizes that the young woman, a seventeen-year-old single mother, needs as much help and nurturing as her two neglected children. The four become something akin to a temporary family, and through their relationship each makes progress toward a better life. Sixty-six brief chapters, with words arranged on the page like poetry, perfectly echo the patterns of teenage speech." Horn Book Guide

Other titles in this trilogy are:

This full house (2009)

True believer (2001)

The **Mozart** season. Holt & Co. 1991 249p hardcover o.p. pa $6.99

Grades: 6 7 8 9 **Fic**

1. Violinists -- Fiction

ISBN 0-8050-1571-X; 0-312-36745-7 pa

LC 90-23635

Allegra spends her twelfth summer practicing a Mozart concerto for a violin competition and finding many significant connections in her world

"With a clear, fresh voice that never falters, Wolff gives readers a delightful heroine, a fully realized setting, and a slowly building tension that reaches a stunning climax." SLJ

★ **Probably** still Nick Swansen. Holt & Co. 1988 144p hardcover o.p. pa $7.99

Grades: 7 8 9 10 **Fic**

1. Learning disabilities -- Fiction

ISBN 0-8050-0701-6; 0-689-85226-6 pa

LC 88-13175

Sixteen-year-old learning-disabled Nick struggles to endure a life in which the other kids make fun of him, he has to take special classes, his date for the prom makes an excuse

not to go with him, and he is haunted by the memory of his older sister who drowned while he was watching

"It is a poignant, gentle, utterly believable narrative." Booklist

This full house. Bowen Press 2009 476p $17.99; lib bdg $18.89

Grades: 8 9 10 11 12 **Fic**

1. School stories 2. Novels in verse 3. Friendship -- Fiction

ISBN 978-0-06-158304-9; 0-06-158304-9; 978-0-06-158305-6 lib bdg; 0-06-158305-7 lib bdg

LC 2008-20157

Sequel to: True believer (2001)

High-school-senior LaVaughn's perceptions and expectations of her life begin to change as she learns about the many unexpected connections between the people she loves best.

"LaVaughn's ferocious determination and intelligence will wholly captivate readers, as will her beautifully articulated, elemental questions about integrity, faith, and how best to build a life." Booklist

True believer. Atheneum Bks. for Young Readers 2001 264p $17; pa $7.99

Grades: 8 9 10 11 12 **Fic**

1. Novels in verse 2. Poverty -- Fiction 3. Single parent family -- Fiction

ISBN 0-689-82827-6; 0-689-85288-6 pa

LC 00-32792

Sequel to: Make lemonade (1993)

Michael L. Printz Award honor book, 2002

Living in the inner city amidst guns and poverty, fifteen-year-old LaVaughn learns from old and new friends, and inspiring mentors, that life is what you make it—an occasion to rise to

"LaVaughn tells her own story in heart-stopping stream-of-consciousness that reveals her convincing naïveté and her blazing determination, intelligence, and growth. . . . Transcendent, raw, and fiercely optimistic, the novel answers some of its own questions about overcoming adversity." Booklist

Followed by: This full house (2009)

Wolfson, Jill

Home, and other big, fat lies. Henry Holt 2006 281p $16.95

Grades: 5 6 7 8 **Fic**

1. Nature -- Fiction 2. Foster home care -- Fiction 3. Environmental protection -- Fiction

ISBN 978-0-8050-7670-7; 0-8050-7670-0

LC 200035843

Eleven-year-old Termite, a foster child with an eye for the beauty of nature and a talent for getting into trouble, takes on the loggers in her new home town when she tries to save the biggest tree in the forest.

"Written with humor and sensitivity." Voice Youth Advocates

What I call life. Holt & Co. 2005 270p $16.95; pa $6.99

Grades: 5 6 7 8   **Fic**
  1. Foster home care -- Fiction
  ISBN 0-8050-7669-7; 0-312-37752-5 pa

Placed in a group foster home, eleven-year-old Cal Lavender learns how to cope with life from the four other girls who live there and from their storytelling guardian, the Knitting Lady.

"Wolfson paints her characters with delightful authenticity. Her debut novel is a treasure of quiet good humor and skillful storytelling that conveys subtle messages about kindness, compassion, and the gift of family regardless of its configuration." Booklist

Wolitzer, Meg

The **fingertips** of Duncan Dorfman. Dutton Childrens Books 2011 294p $16.99
Grades: 4 5 6 7   **Fic**
  1. Contests -- Fiction 2. Individualism -- Fiction 3. Scrabble (Game) -- Fiction
  ISBN 978-0-525-42304-1; 0-525-42304-4
                LC 2011005228

"The novel is shot through with Scrabble words and rules in a way that is reminiscent of Louis Sachar's The Cardturner (2010). Readers will identify with and root for the characters as their tales intertwine to a satisfying if slightly too cheery close. Word wizards aren't the only ones who will enjoy this readable rumination on ethics, competition and identity." Kirkus

Wollman, Jessica

Switched. Delacorte Press 2007 249p $15.99
Grades: 6 7 8 9   **Fic**
  1. School stories 2. Social classes -- Fiction 3. Household employees -- Fiction 4. Mother-daughter relationship -- Fiction
  ISBN 978-0-385-73396-0

Laura and Willa, born the same night seventeen years ago on opposite sides of Darien, Connecticut, are both unhappy with their lives and when they discover they look remarkably alike, they decide to try out one another's lives for four months.

"Wollman turns a potentially clichéd premise . . . into an entertaining and thoughtful novel. . . . Wollman creates credible characters who should endear themselves to readers." Publ Wkly

Wood, Frances

When Molly was a Harvey Girl; by Frances M. Wood. Kane/Miller 2010 226p $15.99
Grades: 6 7 8 9   **Fic**
  1. Sisters -- Fiction 2. New Mexico -- Fiction 3. Restaurants -- Fiction 4. Frontier and pioneer life -- Fiction
  ISBN 978-1-935279-51-8; 1-935279-51-3

"Thirteen-year-old Molly Gerry and her older sister Colleen's world is rocked when their father dies, leaving them penniless. Their best hope seems to be leaving their small Illinois town to work at the Harvey Eating House in Raton, New Mexico. . . . Inspired by the author's great-grandmother's experiences, this historical bildungsroman shows life out west in the 1800s in all its flash and grittiness.

Molly is a strongly drawn character. . . . [This is a] delightful tale." Booklist

Wood, June Rae

The **man** who loved clowns. Putnam 1992 224p hardcover o.p. pa $5.99
Grades: 5 6 7 8   **Fic**
  1. Uncles -- Fiction 2. Down syndrome -- Fiction 3. Mentally disabled -- Fiction
  ISBN 0-14-240422-5 pa
                LC 91-33861

Thirteen-year-old Delrita, whose unhappy life has caused her to hide from the world, loves her uncle Punky but sometimes feels ashamed of his behavior because he has Down's syndrome

"Wood's prose is strong and flowing, with a good balance of dialogue and narrative, and with several well-developed and memorable characters." SLJ
  Another title about Delrita is:
  Turtle on a fence post (1997)

Wood, Maggie L.

Captured. Lobster Press 2011 284p (The Divided Realms) $12.95
Grades: 6 7 8 9   **Fic**
  1. Fantasy fiction
  ISBN 978-1-77080-071-7 pa; 1-77080-071-9 pa

"Willow was brought up believing she was just a normal girl with a grandmother that had a penchant for telling fantastic stories about another realm where she was a princess and magic and fairies were everyday occurrences. . . . Or, at least that is what Willow thought until the day her Nana died and she was transported to the home she never knew to save a family she never knew she had. . . . Wood's characters must think outside the game to save their world. Sometimes it takes an outsider to see things that those on the inside cannot. This is a wonderful book—well written and likely to fly off the shelves while fantasy is still the hot genre." Voice Youth Advocates
  Followed by: The darkening (2011)

The **darkening**. Lobster Press 2011 283p (The Divided Realms) pa $12.95
Grades: 6 7 8 9   **Fic**
  1. Fantasy fiction 2. Fairies -- Fiction
  ISBN 978-1-77080-072-4 pa; 1-77080-072-7 pa
  Sequel to: Captured (2011)

"Willow travels to the faery realm, but when Brand breaks the all-important rules by stowing away in the magical transport spell, the faeries turn the pair over to the dark lord Jarlath Thornheart, who throws them into the terrifying goblin's gauntlet. . . . This story remains entertaining." Kirkus

Wood, Maryrose

My life the musical; by Maryrose Wood. 1st ed.; Delacorte Press 2008 228p $15.99; lib bdg $18.99
Grades: 7 8 9 10   **Fic**
  1. School stories 2. Theater -- Fiction 3. Musicals -- Fiction 4. New York (N.Y.) -- Fiction
  ISBN 978-0-385-73278-9; 0-385-73278-3; 978-0-385-90297-7 lib bdg; 0-385-90297-2 lib bdg
                LC 2007015034

Sixteen-year-old Emily Pearl's obsession with Broadway shows, and one musical in particular, lands her in trouble in school and at home, but it might also allow her and her best friend, Phillip, to find a dramatic solution to the problems.

"Teens will enjoy the fast pace and humor in this uplifting novel." SLJ

Nightshade; based on a concept by the Duchess of Northumberland. Balzer + Bray 2011 (The poison diaries) $17.99

Grades: 8 9 10   **Fic**
1. Plants -- Fiction 2. Medical care -- Fiction 3. Supernatural -- Fiction 4. Poisons and poisoning -- Fiction 5. Father-daughter relationship -- Fiction 6. Great Britain -- History -- 1714-1837 -- Fiction
ISBN 978-0-06-180242-3; 0-06-180242-5
LC 2011024911

In late eighteenth-century Northumberland, England, sixteen-year-old Jessamine Luxton is so desperate to find Weed, who her father says deserted her when she was at death's door, that she asks for help from the evil Oleander.

"Promising Weed's continued pursuit (and, hopefully, reviving the intriguing issue of Mr. Luxton's poisoning), part three's sure to levy as much page-turning enthrallment as its predecessors." Kirkus

The **poison** diaries; based on a concept by the Duchess of Northumberland. Balzer + Bray 2010 278p $16.99

Grades: 8 9 10 11   **Fic**
1. Plants -- Fiction 2. Supernatural -- Fiction 3. Great Britain -- Fiction 4. Poisons and poisoning -- Fiction 5. Father-daughter relationship -- Fiction
ISBN 978-0-06-180236-2; 0-06-180236-0
LC 2009-54427

In late eighteenth-century Northumberland, England, sixteen-year-old Jessamine Luxton and the mysterious Weed uncover the horrible secrets of poisons growing in Thomas Luxton's apothecary garden.

"This intriguing fantasy has many tendrils to wrap around teen hearts. . . . The haunting ending will leave readers wanting to talk about the themes of cruelty, honesty, and loyalty." Booklist

Another title in this series is:
Nightshade (2011)

The **unseen** guest; by Maryrose Wood; illustrated by Jon Klassen. Balzer + Bray 2012 340 p. (hardback) $15.99

Grades: 4 5 6   **Fic**
1. Mystery fiction 2. Wolves -- Fiction 3. Nannies -- Fiction 4. Wild children -- Fiction 5. Great Britain -- History -- 19th century -- Fiction 6. England -- Fiction 7. Orphans -- Fiction 8. Secrets -- Fiction 9. Governesses -- Fiction 10. Feral children -- Fiction 11. London (England) -- Fiction
ISBN 9780061791185
LC 2011053315

This young adult novel offers a "Victorian mystery [story about] teenage governess Penelope Lumley [who] takes on threats to her wolfish young charges that include a hustler after the Ashton fortune. . . . Once he meets the three feral children Penelope is charged with training up to be human, Faucet's scheme to finance the introduction of ostrich racing to the British Isles by marrying the Dowager Lady Ashton is transformed to visions of wolf racing and sideshow exhibitions. . . . Along with . . . pitching her plucky protagonist into one crisis after another . . . . the author slips in a few more seemingly significant Clues to the Ashtons' curious history and Penelope's apparent involvement in it." (Kirkus)

Wooding, Chris
★ The **haunting** of Alaizabel Cray. Orchard Bks. 2004 292p $16.95; pa $7.99

Grades: 7 8 9 10   **Fic**
1. Horror fiction 2. Supernatural -- Fiction 3. London (England) -- Fiction
ISBN 0-439-54656-7; 0-439-59851-6 pa
LC 2003-69108

First published 2001 in the United Kingdom

In a world similar to Victorian London, Thaniel, a seventeen-year-old hunter of deadly, demonic creatures called the wych-kin, takes in a lost, possessed girl, and becomes embroiled in a plot to unleash evil on the world

"Eerie and exhilarating. . . . [The author] fuses together his best storytelling skills . . . . to create a fabulously horrific and ultimately timeless underworld." SLJ

Havoc; illustrated by Dan Chernett. Scholastic Press 2010 396p il $16.99

Grades: 6 7 8 9   **Fic**
1. Magic -- Fiction 2. Good and evil -- Fiction 3. Comic books, strips, etc. -- Fiction
ISBN 978-0-545-16045-2; 0-545-16045-6
Sequel to: Malice (2009)

"As Seth makes his way back into Malice with the talismanic Shard and joins the effort to mount an attack on the dread Deadhouse, a new ally, Alicia, nervously tracks the House's sinister master Tall Jake to the decrepit English psychiatric hospital where Grendel—the mad, disturbed, misshapen graphic artist (and maybe god?) who has created both the comic and the world it depicts—is imprisoned. . . . This features expertly meshed multiple plotlines, colorful supporting characters . . . . frequent eerie skitterings and sudden feelings of dread plus nonstop action that breaks, occasionally, from prose into graphic-novel–style panels festooned with noisy sound effects." Kirkus

★ **Malice**; illustrated by Dan Chernett. Scholastic Press 2009 377p il $14.99; pa $8.99

Grades: 6 7 8 9 10   **Fic**
1. Horror fiction 2. Comic books, strips, etc. -- Fiction
ISBN 978-0-545-16043-8; 0-545-16043-X; 978-0-545-16044-5 pa; 0-545-16044-8 pa

Everyone's heard the rumors. Call on Tall Jake and he'll take you to Malice, a world that exists inside a horrifying comic book. A place most kids never leave. Seth and Kady think it's all a silly myth. But then their friend disappears.

"This nail-biter will keep readers glued to the story until the very last page is turned. . . . Seth and Kady are strong and exciting characters." SLJ

Followed by: Havoc (2010)

Poison. Orchard Bks. 2005 273p $16.99; pa $7.99

Grades: 7 8 9 10   **Fic**

1. Fantasy fiction 2. Fairies -- Fiction 3. Storytelling -- Fiction

ISBN 0-439-75570-0; 0-439-75571-9 pa

LC 2005-02174

First published 2003 in the United Kingdom

When Poison leaves her home in the marshes of Gull to retrieve the infant sister who was snatched by the fairies, she and a group of unusual friends survive encounters with the inhabitants of various Realms, and Poison herself confronts a surprising destiny.

"Poison's story should please crowds of horror fans who like their books fast-paced, darkly atmospheric, and melodramatic." SLJ

Silver; Chris Wooding. Scholastic Press 2014 320 p. (hc) $17.99

Grades: 7 8 9 10 11 12   **Fic**

1. Horror fiction 2. School stories 3. Schools -- Fiction 4. Survival -- Fiction 5. Boarding schools -- Fiction 6. Communicable diseases -- Fiction 7. Boarding school students -- Fiction

ISBN 0545603927; 9780545603928

LC 2013014037

In this young adult science fiction horror novel, by Chris Wooding, "without warning, a horrifying infection will spread across the school grounds [of Mortingham Boarding Academy], and a group of students with little in common will find themselves barricaded in a classroom, fighting for their lives. Some will live. Some will die. And then it will get even worse." (Publisher's note)

"When strange insects assault a remote boarding school in England, the kids try to save the day in this tense page-turner...Skillfully managed subplots keep the pages flying. It looks like the end of the world is nigh.... It's just all kinds of white-knuckle fun." (Kirkus)

The **storm** thief. Orchard Books 2006 310p $16.99

Grades: 6 7 8 9 10   **Fic**

1. Science fiction

ISBN 0-439-86513-1

LC 2005-35993

With the help of a golem, two teenaged thieves try to survive on the city island of Orokos, where unpredictable probability storms continually change both the landscape and the inhabitants.

The author "delivers memorable characters, such as Vago, whose plight—Who am I and where do I belong in the world?—will be understood by many teens. Wooding also creates a unique world for his characters to explore, and the setting serves as an excellent backdrop for the author to develop his theme of order versus chaos and the need for balance between the two." Voice Youth Advocates

Woodruff, Elvira

Dear Austin; letters from the Underground Railroad. illustrated by Nancy Carpenter. Knopf 1998 137p il $16; lib bdg $17.99; pa $5.50

Grades: 4 5 6   **Fic**

1. Slavery -- Fiction 2. Pennsylvania -- Fiction 3. African Americans -- Fiction 4. Underground railroad -- Fiction

ISBN 0-679-88594-3; 0-679-98594-8 lib bdg; 0-375-80356-4 pa

LC 98-5314

Sequel to Dear Levi (1994)

In 1853, in letters to his older brother, eleven-year-old Levi describes his adventures in the Pennsylvania countryside with his black friend Jupiter and his experiences with the Underground Railroad

"The smoothly written text is fast paced." Horn Book Guide

Fearless. Scholastic Press 2008 224p il $16.99; pa $6.99

Grades: 5 6 7 8   **Fic**

1. Artists 2. Engravers 3. Inventors 4. Architects 5. Adventure fiction 6. Orphans -- Fiction 7. Lighthouses -- Fiction 8. Great Britain -- History -- 1603-1714, Stuarts -- Fiction

ISBN 978-0-439-67703-5; 0-439-67703-3; 978-0-439-67704-2 pa; 0-439-67704-1 pa

LC 2006-10137

In late seventeenth-century England, eleven-year-old Digory, forced to leave his hometown after his father is lost at sea, becomes an apprentice to the architect Henry Winstanley, who built a lighthouse on the treacherous Eddystone Reef—the very rocks that sank Digory's grandfather's ship years before.

"This fascinating, well-written story is closely based on the life of the real Henry Winstanley. . . . The characters are finely drawn and the action is nonstop." SLJ

George Washington's spy; a time travel adventure. Scholastic Press 2010 229p $16.99

Grades: 4 5 6   **Fic**

1. Authors 2. Diplomats 3. Inventors 4. Statesmen 5. Scientists 6. Writers on science 7. Members of Congress 8. Time travel -- Fiction 9. Boston (Mass.) -- Fiction 10. United States -- History -- 1775-1783, Revolution -- Fiction

ISBN 978-0-545-10487-6; 0-545-10487-4

LC 2009032700

Sequel to: George Washington's socks (1991)

Ten-year-old Matt and six other children travel to 1776 Boston, living out American history as they meet Benjamin Franklin, learn about colonial medicine, and become part of a rebel spy ring

"Woodruff does an excellent job of conveying the complexities of war. . . . This is a great introduction to the Revolutionary period. . . . The story is fast paced, exciting, and informative." SLJ

Woods, Brenda

Emako Blue. G. P. Putnam's Sons 2004 124p $15.99

Grades: 7 8 9 10   **Fic**

1. African Americans -- Fiction 2. Los Angeles (Calif.)

-- Fiction

ISBN 0-399-24006-3

LC 2003-16647

Monterey, Savannah, Jamal, and Eddie have never had much to do with each other until Emako Blue shows up at chorus practice, but just as the lives of the five Los Angeles high school students become intertwined, tragedy tears them apart.

"This short, succinct, and poignant story of friendship, family, and overwhelming sadness will leave some readers in tears." SLJ

My name is Sally Little Song. G.P. Putnam's Sons 2006 182p $15.99; pa $5.99

Grades: 4 5 6 7   **Fic**

1. Florida -- Fiction 2. Georgia -- Fiction 3. Slavery -- Fiction 4. Seminole Indians -- Fiction 5. African Americans -- Fiction

ISBN 0-399-24312-7; 0-14-240943-X pa

LC 2005-32651

When their owner plans to sell one of them in 1802, twelve-year-old Sally and her family run away from their Georgia plantation to look for both freedom from slavery and a home in Florida with the Seminole Indians.

"Based on historical accounts, this novel provides readers with an alternative view of the realities of slavery—an escape to the South rather than North. . . . This accessible tale will prove a rich resource for study and discussion." SLJ

A **star** on the Hollywood Walk of Fame. G. P. Putnam's Sons 2010 164p il $16.99

Grades: 6 7 8 9 10 11 12   **Fic**

1. School stories 2. Authorship -- Fiction 3. Los Angeles (Calif.) -- Fiction

ISBN 978-0-399-24683-8; 0-399-24683-5

LC 2009-08750

Nine Los Angeles high school students use a creative writing class assignment to shed light on their own lives.

"Woods is such a master of pace and voice that her storytelling will rivet even reluctant readers to the page. Her use of dialect is flawless, and her quick transitions from one character's perspective to the next keep things lively." Bull Cent Child Books

Woods, Ron

The **hero**. Knopf 2002 215p hardcover o.p. pa $4.99

Grades: 5 6 7 8   **Fic**

1. Death -- Fiction 2. Rafting (Sports) -- Fiction

ISBN 0-375-80612-1; 0-440-22978-2 pa

LC 00-54460

In the summer of 1957 in Idaho, when 14 year old Jamie and his older cousin Jerry reluctantly include outsider Dennis in their rafting adventure, Dennis drowns and Jamie lies that Dennis made a heroic sacrifice

"The author deftly handles a convincing adventure with emotional depth and tenderness toward his characters." SLJ

Woodson, Jacqueline

★ **After** Tupac and D Foster. G.P. Putnam's Sons 2008 153p $15.99

Grades: 7 8 9 10   **Fic**

1. Poets 2. Actors 3. Rap musicians 4. Friendship -- Fiction 5. African Americans -- Fiction 6. Queens (New York, N.Y.) -- Fiction

ISBN 978-0-399-24654-8

LC 2007-23725

A Newbery honor book, 2009

In the New York City borough of Queens in 1996, three girls bond over their shared love of Tupac Shakur's music, as together they try to make sense of the unpredictable world in which they live.

"The subtlety and depth with which the author conveys the girls' relationships lend this novel exceptional vividness and staying power." Publ Wkly

★ **Feathers**. G.P. Putnam's Sons 2007 118p $15.99; pa $6.99

Grades: 4 5 6 7   **Fic**

1. Religion -- Fiction 2. Race relations -- Fiction 3. African Americans -- Fiction

ISBN 978-0-399-23989-2; 0-399-23989-8; 978-0-14-241198-8 pa; 0-14-241198-1 pa

LC 2006-24713

A Newbery Medal honor book, 2008

When a new, white student nicknamed "The Jesus Boy" joins her sixth grade class in the winter of 1971, Frannie's growing friendship with him makes her start to see some things in a new light.

"Woodson creates in Frannie a strong protagonist who thinks for herself and recognizes the value and meaning of family. The story ends with hope and thoughtfulness while speaking to those adolescents who struggle with race, faith, and prejudice." SLJ

★ **From** the notebooks of Melanin Sun. G.P. Putnam's Sons 2010 126p $17.99; pa $7.99

Grades: 7 8 9 10   **Fic**

1. Lesbians -- Fiction 2. African Americans -- Fiction 3. Mother-son relationship -- Fiction 4. Brooklyn (New York, N.Y.) -- Fiction

ISBN 978-0-399-25280-8; 0-399-25280-0; 978-0-14-241641-9 pa; 0-14-241641-X pa

LC 2009011314

A reissue of the title first published 1995 by Blue Sky Press

A Coretta Scott King honor book, 1996

Almost-fourteen-year-old Melanin Sun's comfortable, quiet life is shattered when his mother reveals she has fallen in love with a woman

"Offering no easy answers, Woodson teaches the reader that love can lead to acceptance of all manner of differences." Publ Wkly

Hush. Putnam 2002 181p $15.99; pa $5.99

Grades: 6 7 8 9   **Fic**

1. Witnesses -- Fiction 2. African Americans -- Fiction

ISBN 0-399-23114-5; 0-14-250049-6 pa

LC 2001-19710

Thirteen-year-old Toswiah finds her life changed when her family enters the witness protection program

The author's "poetic, low-key, yet vivid writing style perfectly conveys the story's atmosphere of quiet intensity." Horn Book

★ **If** you come softly. Putnam 1998 181p $15.99; pa $5.99

Grades: 7 8 9 10   **Fic**
  1. Race relations -- Fiction 2. New York (N.Y.) -- Fiction 3. African Americans -- Fiction
  ISBN 0-399-23112-9; 0-698-11862-6 pa

LC 97-32212

ALA YALSA Margaret A. Edwards Award (2006)

After meeting at their private school in New York, fifteen-year-old Jeremiah, who is black and whose parents are separated, and Ellie, who is white and whose mother has twice abandoned her, fall in love and then try to cope with people's reactions

"The gentle and melancholy tone of this book makes it ideal for thoughtful readers and fans of romance." Voice Youth Advocates

Another title about Jeremiah is:
Behind you (2004)

Lena; by Jacqueline Woodson. 1st G.P. Putnam's Sons ed.; G. P. Putnam's Sons 2006 135p $17.99

Grades: 6 7 8 9   **Fic**
  1. Sisters -- Fiction 2. Runaway teenagers -- Fiction
  ISBN 0-399-24469-7

LC 2005032666

Sequel to: I hadn't meant to tell you this (1994)

A reissue of the title first published 1999 by Delacorte Press

ALA YALSA Margaret A. Edwards Award (2006)

Thirteen-year-old Lena and her younger sister Dion mourn the death of their mother as they hitchhike from Ohio to Kentucky while running away from their abusive father.

"Soulful, wise and sometimes wrenching, this taut story never loses its grip on the reader." Publ Wkly

★ **Locomotion**. Putnam 2003 100p $17.99; pa $5.99

Grades: 4 5 6 7   **Fic**
  1. Novels in verse 2. Foster home care -- Fiction 3. African Americans -- Fiction
  ISBN 978-0-399-23115-5; 0-399-23115-3; 978-0-14-241552-8 pa; 0-14-241552-9 pa

LC 2002-69779

In a series of poems, eleven-year-old Lonnie writes about his life, after the death of his parents, separated from his younger sister, living in a foster home, and finding his poetic voice at school

"In a masterful use of voice, Woodson allows Lonnie's poems to tell a complex story of loss and grief and to create a gritty, urban environment. Despite the spare text, Lonnie's foster mother and the other minor characters are three-dimensional, making the boy's world a convincingly real one." SLJ

★ **Peace,** Locomotion. G.P. Putnam's Sons 2009 134p $15.99; pa $7.99

Grades: 4 5 6 7   **Fic**
  1. Letters -- Fiction 2. Orphans -- Fiction 3. Siblings -- Fiction 4. Foster home care -- Fiction 5. African Americans -- Fiction
  ISBN 978-0-399-24655-5; 0-399-24655-X; 978-0-14-241512-2 pa; 0-14-241512-X pa

LC 2008-18583

Through letters to his little sister, who is living in a different foster home, sixth-grader Lonnie, also known as "Locomotion," keeps a record of their lives while they are apart, describing his own foster family, including his foster brother who returns home after losing a leg in the Iraq War

"Woodson creates a full-bodied character in kind, sensitive Lonnie. Readers will understand his quest for peace, and appreciate the hard work he does to find it." Publ Wkly

Woodworth, Chris

  Double -click for trouble. Farrar, Straus and Giroux 2008 162p $16

Grades: 6 7 8 9   **Fic**
  1. Uncles -- Fiction 2. Indiana -- Fiction 3. Country life -- Fiction
  ISBN 978-0-374-30987-9; 0-374-30987-6

LC 2006-38351

After he is caught viewing inappropriate websites on the Internet, a fatherless, thirteen-year-old Chicago boy is sent to rural Indiana to spend school break with his eccentric great-uncle.

"Woodworth perfectly captures an eighth-grade boy on the cusp of adolescence, struggling with his identity as he learns about himself, his family, and what is really important in relationships." SLJ

When Ratboy lived next door. Farrar, Straus and Giroux 2005 181p $16

Grades: 6 7 8 9   **Fic**
  1. Indiana -- Fiction 2. Raccoons -- Fiction 3. Friendship -- Fiction
  ISBN 0-374-34677-1

LC 2004-50634

When his strange family moves into her quiet southern Indiana town, sixth-grader Lydia Carson initially despises her new neighbor and classmate, who seems as wild as the raccoon that is his closest companion.

"There are serious issues present, including poverty, alcoholism, abuse, learning disabilities, and bullying. The conflicts of the plot are effectively tied up, though not too neatly to lose believability. . . . An outstanding offering." SLJ

Woon, Yvonne

  Dead beautiful. Disney/Hyperion 2010 456p $16.99; pa $9.99

Grades: 7 8 9 10 11 12   **Fic**
  1. School stories 2. Maine -- Fiction 3. Immortality -- Fiction 4. Supernatural -- Fiction
  ISBN 978-1-4231-1956-2; 1-4231-1956-8; 978-1-4231-1961-6 pa; 1-4231-1961-4 pa

LC 2009-42850

After her parents die under mysterious circumstances, sixteen-year-old Renee Winters is sent from California to an old-fashioned boarding school in Maine, where she meets a fellow student to whom she seems strangely connected.

"This hefty novel takes a new and unconventional look at the undead, focusing on story and interesting characters and leaving gore and mayhem hidden in the background. . . . Well written, intriguing and, above all, different." Kirkus

Wrede, Patricia C., 1953-

Across the Great Barrier; Patricia C. Wrede. Scholastic Press 2011 339p (Frontier magic) $16.99

Grades: 7 8 9 10 11 12   **Fic**

1. Fantasy 2. Magic -- Fiction 3. Twins -- Fiction 4. Brothers and sisters -- Fiction 5. Frontier and pioneer life -- Fiction

ISBN 978-0-545-03343-5; 0-545-03343-8; 9780545033435

LC 2011032260

Sequel to: Thirteenth child (2009)

Eff is an unlucky thirteenth child. Her twin brother, Lan, is a powerful seventh son of a seventh son. And yet, Eff is the one who saved the day for the settlements west of the Great Barrier. Her unique ways of doing magic and seeing the world, and her fascination with the magical creatures and land in the Great Plains push Eff to work toward joining an expedition heading west. But things are changing on the frontier.

"Splendid worldbuilding and deliciously complex characterization continue to be the hallmarks of this standout fantasy." Kirkus

Dealing with dragons. Harcourt Brace Jovanovich 1990 212p (The Enchanted Forest Chronicles) hardcover o.p. pa $6.99

Grades: 5 6 7 8   **Fic**

1. Fairy tales 2. Magic -- Fiction 3. Dragons -- Fiction

ISBN 0-15-222900-0; 0-15-204566-X pa

LC 89-24599

Bored with traditional palace life, a princess goes off to live with a group of dragons and soon becomes involved with fighting against some disreputable wizards who want to steal away the dragons' kingdom

"A decidedly diverting novel with plenty of action and many slightly skewed fairy-tale conventions that add to the laugh-out-loud reading pleasure and give the story a wide appeal." Booklist

Other titles in this series are:

Searching for dragons (1991)

Calling on dragons (1993)

Talking to dragons (1993)

The Far West; Patricia C. Wrede. Scholastic Press 2012 378 p. $17.99

Grades: 7 8 9 10 11 12   **Fic**

1. Steampunk fiction 2. Fantasy fiction 3. Fantasy 4. Magic -- Fiction 5. Twins -- Fiction 6. Friendship -- Fiction

ISBN 0545033446; 9780545033442

LC 2012288790

This young adult speampunk novel, by Patricia C. Wrede, concludes the "Frontier Magic" trilogy. "Eff is an unlucky thirteenth child . . . but also the seventh daughter in her family. Her twin brother, Lan, is a powerful double seventh son. Her life at the edge of the Great Barrier Spell is different from anyone else's that she knows. . . . With Lan, William, Professor Torgeson, Wash, and Professor Ochiba,

Eff finds that nothing on the wild frontier is as they expected." (Publisher's note)

Sorcery and Cecelia, or, The enchanted chocolate pot; being the correspondence of two young ladies of quality regarding various magical scandals in London and the country. [by] Patricia C. Wrede and Caroline Stevermer. Harcourt 2003 316p $17; pa $6.95

Grades: 7 8 9 10   **Fic**

1. Cousins -- Fiction 2. Supernatural -- Fiction 3. Great Britain -- Fiction

ISBN 0-15-204615-1; 0-15-205300-X pa

LC 2002-38706

In 1817 in England, two young cousins, Cecilia living in the country and Kate in London, write letters to keep each other informed of their exploits, which take a sinister turn when they find themselves confronted by evil wizards

"This is a fun story that quickly draws in the reader." Voice Youth Advocates

Other titles about Kate and Cecilia are:

The grand tour (2004)

The mislaid magician (2006)

The thirteenth child. Scholastic Press 2009 344p (Frontier magic) $16.99

Grades: 7 8 9 10 11 12   **Fic**

1. School stories 2. Fantasy fiction 3. Magic -- Fiction 4. Twins -- Fiction 5. Frontier and pioneer life -- Fiction

ISBN 978-0-545-03342-8; 0-545-03342-X

LC 2008-34048

Eighteen-year-old Eff must finally get over believing she is bad luck and accept that her special training in Aphrikan magic, and being the twin of the seventh son of a seventh son, give her extraordinary power to combat magical creatures that threaten settlements on the western frontier.

Wrede "creates a rich world where steam dragons seem as normal as bears, and a sympathetic character in Eff." Publ Wkly

Followed by Across the Great Barrier (2011)

Wright, Bil

Putting makeup on the fat boy. Simon & Schuster Books for Young Readers 2011 219p $16.99

Grades: 7 8 9 10 11 12   **Fic**

1. School stories 2. Cosmetics -- Fiction 3. Homosexuality -- Fiction 4. New York (N.Y.) -- Fiction 5. Hispanic Americans -- Fiction 6. Single parent family -- Fiction

ISBN 978-1-4169-3996-2; 1-4169-3996-2

LC 2010032450

"Obviously, there's a whole lot going on in Wright's novel, but it's handled deftly and, for the most part, believably. Best of all, Carlos is not completely defined by his homosexuality." Booklist

When the black girl sings; [by] Bil Wright. Simon & Schuster Books for Young Readers 2007 266p $16.99; pa $5.99

Grades: 6 7 8 9 10   **Fic**

1. Divorce -- Fiction 2. Adoption -- Fiction 3.

Connecticut -- Fiction 4. African Americans -- Fiction
ISBN 978-1-4169-3995-5; 1-4169-3995-4; 978-1-
4169-4003-6 pa; 1-4169-4003-0 pa
LC 2006030837

Adopted by white parents and sent to an exclusive Connecticut girls' school where she is the only black student, fourteen-year-old Lahni Schuler feels like an outcast, particularly when her parents separate, but after attending a local church where she hears gospel music for the first time, she finds her voice.

"Readers will enjoy the distinctive characters, lively dialogue, and palette of adolescent and racial insecurities in this contemporary, upbeat story." SLJ

Wright, Denis
Violence 101; a novel. G. P. Putnam's Sons 2010 213p $16.99
Grades: 8 9 10   Fic
1. Genius -- Fiction 2. Violence -- Fiction 3. New Zealand -- Fiction 4. Reformatories -- Fiction 5. Race relations -- Fiction
ISBN 978-0-399-25493-2; 0-399-25493-5
LC 2010-02851
First published 2007 in New Zealand

In a New Zealand reformatory, Hamish Graham, an extremely intelligent fourteen-year-old who believes in the compulsory study of violence, learns that it is not always the answer.

"Wright's novel is clever and biting, a tragedy of society's failure to deal with kids like Hamish and a satire of society's winking condemnations of violence. Hamish's actions can be revolting, despite his justifications, but he still draws empathy as a product of the environment at large. Hardly a comfortable book to read, but a gripping one." Publ Wkly

Wulffson, Don L.
Soldier X. Viking 2001 226p $15.99; pa $6.99
Grades: 7 8 9 10   Fic
1. Russia -- Fiction 2. World War, 1939-1945 -- Fiction
ISBN 0-670-88863-X; 0-14-250073-9 pa
LC 99-49418

In 1943 sixteen-year-old Erik experiences the horrors of war when he is drafted into the German army and sent to fight on the Russian front

"Erik's first-person narrative records battlefield sequences with an unflinching—and occasionally numbing—brutality, in a story notable for its unusual perspective." Horn Book Guide

Wunder, Wendy
★ The **museum** of intangible things; Wendy Wunder. Razorbill 2014 304 p. (hardback) $17.99
Grades: 8 9 10 11 12   Fic
1. Mental illness -- Fiction 2. Female friendship -- Fiction 3. Runaway teenagers -- Fiction 4. Manic-depressive illness -- Fiction 5. Runaways -- Fiction 6. Friendship -- Fiction 7. Best friends -- Fiction 8. Automobile travel -- Fiction
ISBN 1595145141; 9781595145147
LC 2013030169

In this book, by Wendy Wunder, "Hannah and Zoe haven't had much in their lives, but they've always had each other. So when Zoe tells Hannah she needs to get out of their down-and-out New Jersey town, they . . . head west. . . . As they chase storms and make new friends, Zoe tells Hannah she wants more for her. She wants her to live bigger, dream grander, aim higher. And so Zoe begins teaching Hannah all about life's intangible things." (Publisher's note)

"As Hannah and best friend Zoe (diagnosed bipolar) embark on a cross-country road trip, Zoe gives Hannah "intangible lessons" (e.g., Hannah learns insouciance when they overnight in an IKEA). When Zoe's irrationality gets scary, Hannah learns betrayal and, later, forgiveness. With each lesson, Hannah becomes more confident, building her own distinct identity. Meanwhile, Zoe is a complex character--intelligent, loyal, and funny." Horn Book

★ The **probability** of miracles. Razorbill 2011 360p $17.99
Grades: 8 9 10 11 12   Fic
1. Death -- Fiction 2. Maine -- Fiction 3. Cancer -- Fiction 4. Miracles -- Fiction
ISBN 978-1-59514-368-6; 1-59514-368-8

"Faced with death, one teen discovers life in this bittersweet debut. . . . Cynical and loner Campbell Cooper (an Italian-Samoan-American) gave up on magic after her parents divorced, her father died and she developed neuroblastoma. . . . Having exhausted Western medicine, her single mother suggests spending the summer after Cam's graduation in Promise, Maine, a hidden town . . . known to have mysterious healing powers. . . . Exploring both sides of Cam's heritage, the story unfolds through narration as beautiful as the sun's daily 'everlasting gobstopper descent behind the lighthouse.' Irreverent humor, quirky small-town charm and surprises along the way help readers brace themselves for the tearjerker ending." Kirkus

Wynne-Jones, Tim
The **boy** in the burning house. Farrar, Straus & Giroux 2001 213p hardcover o.p. pa $5.95
Grades: 6 7 8 9   Fic
1. Mystery fiction 2. Canada -- Fiction
ISBN 0-374-30930-2; 0-374-40887-4 pa
LC 99-89534
First published 2000 in Canada

Trying to solve the mystery of his father's disappearance from their rural Canadian community, fourteen-year-old Jim gets help from the disturbed Ruth Rose, who suspects her stepfather, a local pastor

"A gripping, fast-moving plot offers the pure adrenaline rush of a thriller." Horn Book Guide

Wyss, Thelma Hatch
Bear dancer; the story of a Ute girl. Margaret K. McElderry Books 2005 181p il $15.95
Grades: 5 6 7 8   Fic
1. Ute Indians -- Fiction
ISBN 1-4169-0285-6
LC 2005-40620

In late nineteenth-century Colorado, Elk Girl, sister of Ute chief Ouray, is captured by Cheyenne and Arapaho warriors, rescued by the white "enemy," and finally returned to her home. Includes historical notes.

"This fascinating story is based on a real person. . . . An excellent addition to historical-fiction collections." SLJ

Yancey, Richard

The **extraordinary** adventures of Alfred Kropp; by Rick Yancey. Bloomsbury Pub. 2005 339p $16.95; pa $7.95

Grades: 7 8 9 10   **Fic**

1. Adventure fiction 2. Kings 3. Orphans -- Fiction
ISBN 1-58234-693-3; 1-59990-044-0 pa

LC 2005-13044

Through a series of dangerous and violent misadventures, teenage loser Alfred Kropp rescues King Arthur's legendary sword Excalibur from the forces of evil.

"True to its action-adventure genre, the story is lighthearted, entertaining, occasionally half-witted, but by and large fun." SLJ

Other titles about Alfred Kropp are:
Alfred Kropp: the seal of Solomon (2007)
Alfred Kropp: the thirteenth skull (2008)

Yang, Dori Jones

Daughter of Xanadu. Delacorte Press 2011 336p map $17.99

Grades: 7 8 9 10 11 12   **Fic**

1. Travelers 2. Love stories 3. Kings 4. Travel writers 5. China -- Fiction 6. Sex role -- Fiction 7. Soldiers -- Fiction
ISBN 0385739230; 0385907788; 9780385739238; 9780385907781

LC 2009-53652

Emmajin, the sixteen-year-old granddaughter of Khublai Khan, becomes a warrior and falls in love with explorer Marco Polo in thirteenth-century China. "Grades seven to ten." (Bull Cent Child Books)

"Daughter of Xanadu offers rich descriptions and vivid depictions of fictional characters and historical figures, making them charming and believable. A colorful and compelling read." SLJ

Yee, Lisa

Absolutely Maybe. Arthur A. Levine Books 2009 274p $16.99

Grades: 8 9 10 11 12   **Fic**

1. Fathers -- Fiction 2. Runaway teenagers -- Fiction 3. Los Angeles (Calif.) -- Fiction 4. Mother-daughter relationship -- Fiction
ISBN 978-0-439-83844-3; 0-439-83844-4

LC 2008-17787

When living with her mother, an alcoholic ex-beauty queen, becomes unbearable, almost seventeen-year-old Maybelline "Maybe" Chestnut runs away to California, where she finds work on a taco truck and tries to track down her birth father.

"The characters are complex and their friendships layered—they sweep readers up in their path." Publ Wkly

Millicent Min, girl genius. Arthur A. Levine Books 2003 248p $16.95; pa $4.99

Grades: 5 6 7   **Fic**

1. School stories 2. Gifted children -- Fiction 3. Chinese Americans -- Fiction
ISBN 0-439-42519-0; 0-439-42520-4 pa

LC 2003-3747

"At the tender age of eleven, Millicent Min has completed her junior year of high school. Summer school is Millie's idea of fun, so she is excited that her parents are allowing her to take a college poetry course. . . . The tension between Millie's formal, overly intellectual way of expressing herself and her emotional immaturity makes her a very funny narrator. . . . Readers considerably older than Millicent's eleven years will enjoy this strong debut novel." Voice Youth Advocates

Other titles about Millicent Min and her friends are:
Stanford Wong flunks big-time (2005)
So totally Emily Ebers (2007)

Warp speed. Arthur A. Levine Books 2011 310p $16.99

Grades: 5 6 7 8   **Fic**

1. School stories 2. Bullies -- Fiction 3. California -- Fiction 4. Popularity -- Fiction 5. Family life -- Fiction
ISBN 978-0-545-12276-4; 0-545-12276-7

LC 2010-24228

"Yee's combination of humor and sympathy works a charm here, giving Marley a life of his own and a chance at success in this solid addition to her prismatic look at middle school." Kirkus

"Entering 7th grade is no big deal for Marley Sandelski: Same old boring classes, same old boring life. The only thing he has to look forward to is the upcoming Star Trek convention. But when he inadvertently draws the attention of Digger Ronster, the biggest bully in school, his life has officially moved from boring to far too dramatic . . . from invisible to center stage." (Publisher's note)

Yee, Paul

Learning to fly; [by] Paul Yee. Orca Book Pub. 2008 108p (Orca soundings) $16.95

Grades: 7 8 9 10   **Fic**

1. Canada -- Fiction 2. Chinese -- Fiction 3. Drug abuse -- Fiction 4. Friendship -- Fiction 5. Immigrants -- Fiction 6. Prejudices -- Fiction 7. Native Americans -- Fiction
ISBN 978-1-55143-955-6; 1-55143-955-7

"Jason Chen, 17, wants to leave his small town in Canada and return to China. . . . His white high-school teachers do not know how smart he is, and his classmates jeer at him. Driven to join the crowd of potheads, he bonds especially with his Native American classmate, Charles ('Chief'). Narrated in Jason's wry, first-person, present-tense narrative, Yee's slim novel packs in a lot. . . . The clipped dialogue perfectly echoes the contemporary scene, the harsh prejudice felt by the new immigrant and the Native American, and their gripping friendship story." Booklist

Yelchin, Eugene

★ **Breaking** Stalin's nose; written and illustrated by Eugene Yelchin. Henry Holt and Company 2011 140p il $15.99

Grades: 4 5 6 7 **Fic**
1. Communism -- Fiction 2. Soviet Union -- Fiction 3.
Father-son relationship -- Fiction
ISBN 0-8050-9216-1; 978-0-8050-9216-5
LC 2011005792
In the Stalinist era of the Soviet Union, ten-year-old
Sasha idolizes his father, a devoted Communist, but when
police take his father away and leave Sasha homeless, he is
forced to examine his own perceptions, values, and beliefs.

"Readers will quickly pick up on the dichotomy between
Sasha's ardent beliefs and the reality of life under Stalin-
ism, and be glad for his ultimate disillusion, even as they
worry for his future. An author's note concisely presents the
chilling historical background and personal connection that
underlie the story." Publ Wkly

Yeomans, Ellen
Rubber houses; a novel. Little, Brown and
Company 2007 152p $15.99
Grades: 7 8 9 10 **Fic**
1. Novels in verse 2. Death -- Fiction 3. Siblings --
Fiction 4. Bereavement -- Fiction
ISBN 978-0-316-10647-4; 0-316-10647-X
LC 2005-37297
A novel in verse that relates seventeen-year-old Kit's ex-
periences as her younger brother is diagnosed with and dies
of cancer and as she withdraws into and gradually emerges
from her grief.

"This slim work speaks volumes about the grieving process. Yeomans has very precisely selected her words to convey the fear and the grief that Kit feels." SLJ

Yep, Laurence, 1948-
City of fire. Tom Doherty Associates 2009 320p
$15.99
Grades: 5 6 7 8 **Fic**
1. Fantasy fiction 2. Magic -- Fiction 3. Hawaii --
Fiction 4. Dragons -- Fiction
ISBN 978-0-7653-1924-1; 0-7653-1924-1
LC 2009016737
Twelve-year-old Scirye and her companions travel to
Houlani, a new Hawaiian island created by magic, where
they enlist the help of volcano goddess Pele in an attempt
to stop an evil dragon and a mysterious man from altering
the universe.

"Readers will be on tenterhooks awaiting the next episode of this exhilarating chase." Booklist
Followed by: City of ice (2011)

City of ice. Tor 2011 383p $17.99
Grades: 5 6 7 8 **Fic**
1. Fantasy fiction 2. Magic -- Fiction 3. Dragons --
Fiction 4. Arctic regions -- Fiction
ISBN 978-0-7653-1925-8; 0-7653-1925-X
LC 2011007411
Sequel to: City of fire (2009)
From the islands of Hawaii, Scirye and her loyal com-
panions pursue the villainous Mr. Roland and evil dragon
Badik all the way to the city of Nova Hafnia in the icy Arctic
Circle, to prevent Roland from obtaining the power to alter
the universe.

"Readers who enjoy inner conflicts, barbed dialogue,
casts replete with supernatural creatures and fantasy epics that don't take themselves too seriously will find it a
treat." Kirkus

Dragons of silk. Harper 2011 339p $15.99
Grades: 6 7 8 9 **Fic**
1. China -- Fiction 2. Silkworms -- Fiction 3. Chinese
Americans -- Fiction
ISBN 978-0-06-027518-1; 0-06-027518-9
LC 2011016553
Four generations of Chinese and Chinese-American
girls, beginning in 1835, are tied together by the tradi-
tion of raising silkworms and the legacy of the legendary
Weaving Maid.

"Yep doesn't shy away from some harsh historical truths:
the pervasiveness of opium addiction, bloody battles erupting between silk-factory owners and independent weavers
and severe exclusion laws. The earlier chapters, while slowly paced, are more interesting, as Yep deftly conjures the culture and spirit of long-ago China. . . . Overall, however, the
author captures the world of women well, and lush silk is a
prominent backdrop." Kirkus

★ **Dragon** road; Golden Mountain chronicles:
1939. HarperCollins 2008 291p $16.99; lib bdg
$17.89
Grades: 6 7 8 9 **Fic**
1. Basketball -- Fiction 2. Chinese Americans -- Fiction
3. Great Depression, 1929-1939 -- Fiction
ISBN 978-0-06-027520-4; 0-06-027520-0; 978-0-06-
027521-1 lib bdg; 0-06-027521-9 lib bdg
LC 2008-00784
In 1939, unable to find regular jobs because of the
Great Depression, long-time friends Cal Chin and Barney
Young tour the country as members of a Chinese American
basketball team.

"As always, Yep's history is impeccable; now he's written
an episode with appeal to basketball fans as well." Booklist
Includes bibliographical references

★ **Dragon's** gate; Golden Mountain chronicles:
1867. HarperCollins Pubs. 1993 273p $16.99; pa
$6.99
Grades: 6 7 8 9 **Fic**
1. Railroads -- Fiction 2. Chinese -- United States --
Fiction
ISBN 0-06-022971-3; 0-06-440489-7 pa
LC 92-43649
Sequel to The serpent's children (1984) and Mountain
light (1985)
A Newbery Medal honor book, 1994
When he accidentally kills a Manchu, a fifteen-year-old
Chinese boy is sent to America to join his father, an uncle,
and other Chinese working to build a tunnel for the trans-
continental railroad through the Sierra Nevada mountains
in 1867

"Yep has succeeded in realizing the primary characters
and the irrepressibly dramatic story. . . . The carefully researched details will move students to thought and discussion." Bull Cent Child Books

A **dragon's** guide to the care and feeding of humans; Laurence Yep & Joanne Ryder; Illustrations by Mary GrandPré. Crown Books for Young Readers 2015 160 p. illustrations (hc) $15.99

Grades: 4 5 6 7   **Fic**

1. Pets -- Fiction 2. Dragons -- Fiction 3. Magic -- Fiction 4. Artists -- Fiction 5. Friendship -- Fiction 6. Imaginary creatures -- Fiction

ISBN 0385392281; 9780385392280; 9780385392297

LC 2014017803

In this novel by Laurence Yep and Joanne Ryder, "crusty dragon Miss Drake has a new pet human, precocious Winnie. Oddly enough, Winnie seems to think Miss Drake is her pet. . . . Unknown to most . . . , the City by the Bay is home to many . . . fantastic creatures. . . . And Winnie wants to draw every new creature she encounters. . . . But Winnie's sketchbook is not what it seems. Somehow, her sketchlings have been set loose on the city streets!" (Publisher's note)

"With a black-and-white spot illustration opening most chapters, an engaging narrator, and a consistently fluid writing style, this title makes a fine dragon choice for readers not yet ready for more weighty fantasy novels." SLJ

★ **Dragonwings**; Golden Mountain chronicles: 1903. Harper & Row 1975 248p lib bdg $16.89; pa $6.99

Grades: 6 7 8 9   **Fic**

1. Chinese Americans -- Fiction 2. San Francisco (Calif.) -- Fiction

ISBN 0-06-026738-0 lib bdg; 0-06-440085-9 pa

A Newbery Medal honor book, 1976

"In 1903 Moon Shadow, eight years old, leaves China for the 'Land of the Golden Mountains,' San Francisco, to be with his father, Windrider, a father he has never seen. There, beset by the trials experienced by most foreigners in America, Moonrider shares his father's dream—to fly. This dream enables Windrider to endure the mockery of the other Chinese, the poverty he suffers in this hostile place—the land of the white demons—and his loneliness for his wife and his own country." Shapiro. Fic for Youth. 3d edition

Hiroshima; a novella. Scholastic 1995 56p hardcover o.p. pa $4.99

Grades: 4 5 6 7   **Fic**

1. Hiroshima (Japan) -- Bombardment, 1945 -- Fiction

ISBN 0-590-20832-2; 0-590-20833-0 pa

LC 94-18195

Through a "present-tense narration that moves back and forth between the experiences of a 12-year-old girl and the men on the Enola Gay, Yep's novella tells the events of the day the first atomic bomb was dropped and its aftermath. Sachi survives but is badly burned; her sister dies and her soldier father is killed in action. For three years the girl spends most of her time indoors, as newcomers to the city fear the scarred survivors. Then she travels to America for plastic surgery, which enables her to take part in her society again. She returns to Japan, hoping to help other victims. Yep ends with two chapters on the destructive potential of nuclear warfare and on some of the efforts being made toward disarmament." (SLJ) Bibliography. "Grades four to seven." (Booklist)

"This moving and detailed narrative chronicles the dropping of the atomic bomb on Hiroshima and its effects on its citizens, especially on twelve-year-old Sachi. Based on true accounts, this book describes the horrors and sadness as well as the courage and hope that result from war." Soc Educ

★ The **star** maker. Harper 2010 100p $15.99; lib bdg $16.89

Grades: 5 6 7 8   **Fic**

1. Uncles -- Fiction 2. Family life -- Fiction 3. Chinese New Year -- Fiction 4. Chinese Americans -- Fiction 5. San Francisco (Calif.) -- Fiction

ISBN 978-0-06-025315-8; 0-06-025315-0; 978-0-06-025316-5 lib bdg; 0-06-025316-9 lib bdg

LC 2010-07856

With the help of his popular Uncle Chester, a young Chinese American boy tries hard to fulfill a promise to have firecrackers for everyone on the Chinese New Year in 1954. Includes an afterword with information about the Chinese customs portrayed in the story.

"Yep skillfully portrays the significance and emotional nature of common childhood dramas, from fears of going back on one's word to worries of losing a favorite uncle to a new girlfriend. . . . Yep has crafted other memorable characters, including Chinatown itself, which sparkle with energy and camaraderie." Publ Wkly

Includes bibliographical references

★ The **traitor**; Golden Mountain chronicles, 1885. HarperCollins Pubs. 2003 310p hardcover o.p. pa $6.99

Grades: 5 6 7 8   **Fic**

1. Friendship -- Fiction 2. Prejudices -- Fiction 3. Chinese Americans -- Fiction

ISBN 0-06-027522-7; 0-06-000831-8 pa

LC 2002-22534

Sequel to: Dragon's gate

In 1885, a lonely illegitimate American boy and a lonely Chinese American boy develop an unlikely friendship in the midst of prejudices and racial tension in their coal mining town of Rock Springs, Wyoming

"The short chapters read quickly, and readers will become involved through the first-person voices that capture each boy's feelings of being an outsider and a traitor." Booklist

Yhard, Jo Ann

The **fossil** hunter of Sydney Mines. Nimbus Pub. 2010 169p il pa $10.95

Grades: 4 5 6 7   **Fic**

1. Mystery fiction 2. Fossils -- Fiction

ISBN 978-1-55109-760-2; 1-55109-760-5

"When a mining company wants to strip mine, Grace's father disagrees due to the damage it would do to the area's irreplaceable fossils. Grace and her father lead the protests, but the protests stop once her father disappears and is presumed dead in an accident. . . . Yhard excels at providing enough information to allow the reader to follow the clues and solve the crime. Nothing is too far-fetched nor too obvious as the suspense builds to a satisfying resolution." Libr Media Connect

Yohalem, Eve

★ **Escape** under the forever sky; a novel. Chronicle Books 2009 220p $16.99

Grades: 4 5 6 7 **Fic**

1. Ethiopia -- Fiction 2. Kidnapping -- Fiction 3. Wilderness survival -- Fiction 4. Mother-daughter relationship -- Fiction

ISBN 978-0-8118-6653-8; 0-8118-6653-X

LC 2008-19565

As a future conservation zoologist whose mother is the United States Ambassador to Ethiopia, thirteen-year-old Lucy uses her knowledge for survival when she is kidnapped and subsequently escapes.

"Lucy's past and present are gracefully woven together, through well-integrated flashbacks, into a powerful picture of the life of a foreigner in Ethiopia. The story should appeal to all with a sense of adventure." Publ Wkly

Yolen, Jane

B.U.G. (Big Ugly Guy) by Jane Yolen and Adam Stemple. Dutton Children's Books 2013 344 p.

Grades: 4 5 6 7 8 **Fic**

1. Golem -- Fiction 2. Magic -- Fiction 3. Bullies -- Fiction 4. Friendship -- Fiction 5. Bands (Music) -- Fiction 6. Klezmer music -- Fiction 7. Jews -- United States -- Fiction

ISBN 9780525422389

LC 2012018217

A constant target for bullies, Sammy Greenburg is glad to make friends with a boy named Skink, who even agrees to "start up a Klezmer fusion garage band after Sammy introduces Skink to the unique combination of jazz and Jewish folk music. When the bullies beat up Skink, however, Sammy decides enough is enough, and, using a formula he finds in his rabbi's study, he creates a golem to take vengeance on his enemies—and fill the missing drummer spot in his new band." (Bulletin of the Center for Children's Books)

★ **Briar** Rose. Doherty Assocs. 1992 190p (Fairy tale series) hardcover o.p. pa $6.99

Grades: 8 9 10 11 12 Adult **Fic**

1. Fantasy fiction 2. Grandmothers -- Fiction 3. Jews -- Poland -- Fiction 4. Holocaust, 1933-1945 -- Fiction

ISBN 0-312-85135-9; 0-7653-4230-8 pa

LC 92-25456

"Yolen takes the story of Briar Rose (commonly known as Sleeping Beauty) and links it to the Holocaust. . . . Rebecca Berlin, a young woman who has grown up hearing her grandmother Gemma tell an unusual and frightening version of the Sleeping Beauty legend, realizes when Gemma dies that the fairy tale offers one of the very few clues she has to her grandmother's past. . . . By interpolating Gemma's vivid and imaginative story into the larger narrative, Yolen has created an engrossing novel." Publ Wkly

Curse of the Thirteenth Fey; the True Tale of Sleeping Beauty. Jane Yolen. Philomel Books 2012 290 p. $16.99

Grades: 6 7 8 9 10 **Fic**

1. Curses -- Fiction 2. Princesses -- Fiction 3. Family life -- Fiction 4. Fairy tales 5. Elves -- Fiction 6. Magic -- Fiction 7. Fairies -- Fiction 8. Prophecies -- Fiction 9. Family life -- Fiction

ISBN 0399256644; 9780399256646

LC 2011038847

In author Jane Yolen's book, "Gorse is the thirteenth . . . in a family of fairies tied to the evil king's land and made to do his bidding. . . . When accident-prone Gorse falls ill just as the family is bid to bless the new princess . . . [she] races to the castle with the last piece of magic the family has left. . . . But that is when accident, mayhem, and magic combine to drive Gorse's story into the unthinkable, threatening the baby, the kingdom, and all." (Publisher's note)

Dragon's blood. Harcourt 2004 303p (Pit dragon chronicles) pa $6.95

Grades: 6 7 8 9 **Fic**

1. Fantasy fiction 2. Dragons -- Fiction

ISBN 0-15-205126-0

LC 2003-56661

A reissue of the title first published 1982 by Delacorte Press

Jakkin, a bond boy who works as a Keeper in a dragon nursery on the planet Austar IV, secretly trains a fighting pit dragon of his own in hopes of winning his freedom

"An original and engrossing fantasy." Horn Book

Other titles in this series are:

Heart's blood (2004)

Sending of dragons (2004)

Dragon's heart (2009)

Girl in a cage; [by] Jane Yolen & Robert J. Harris. Philomel Bks. 2002 234p hardcover o.p. pa $6.99

Grades: 7 8 9 10 **Fic**

1. Kings 2. Scotland -- Fiction

ISBN 0-399-23627-9; 0-14-240132-3 pa

LC 2001-55978

As English armies invade Scotland in 1306, eleven-year-old Princess Marjorie, daughter of the newly crowned Scottish king, Robert the Bruce, is captured by England's King Edward Longshanks and held in a cage on public display

"Marjorie's first-person narration of her captivity and the events leading up to it are exciting and moving, and her strategies for coping with a hideous imprisonment are models of ingenuity and staying true to oneself." SLJ

Hobby. Harcourt Brace & Co. 1996 90p (Young Merlin trilogy) $16

Grades: 4 5 6 7 **Fic**

1. Fantasy fiction 2. Merlin (Legendary character) -- Fiction

ISBN 0-15-200815-2

LC 95-36735

Sequel to Passager

"This second book of the Young Merlin trilogy (the sequel to Passager) continues the adventures of Merlin as a boy. When his adopted family dies in a tragic fire, the boy sets out to find a new life. On his journey, he is taken up by a sinister and cruel thief, but escapes to become the apprentice to an apparently kindly traveling magician, Ambrosius, who names him Hobby. He finds Ambrosius's magic deceptions distasteful, however, and realizes that only truth will serve him and his dreams in the future." (Horn Book) "Grades three to six." (SLJ)

"The characters are well drawn and appealing." SLJ

Followed by Merlin

Merlin; the young Merlin trilogy, book three. Harcourt Brace & Co. 1997 91p (Young Merlin trilogy) $15

Grades: 4 5 6 7 8 **Fic**

1. Fantasy fiction 2. Merlin (Legendary character) -- Fiction

ISBN 0-15-200814-4

LC 96-11683

Sequel to Hobby

This is the concluding volume of the trilogy about the youth of the Arthurian wizard that began with Passager and Hobby (both 1996). "Hawk-Hobby, whose true name is Merlin, takes refuge in the woods where his saga began. After he is saved from a pack of wild dogs by a wild man, the 12-year-old boy finds himself living in a forested village of wild folk. Imprisoned by the local women after they discover his prophetic powers, Hawk-Hobby escapes with the help of a small child named Cub, who happens to be the once and future King Arthur." (Booklist) "Grades four to eight." (SLJ)

This book is "written in stark but poetic language that will challenge some readers." SLJ

Passager. Harcourt Brace & Co. 1996 76p (Young Merlin trilogy) $16

Grades: 4 5 6 7 **Fic**

1. Fantasy fiction 2. Merlin (Legendary character) -- Fiction

ISBN 0-15-200391-6

LC 94-27101

"A feral child wanders the woods, sleeping in trees, fending for himself against cold, hunger, and wild animals. He has forgotten where he came from and lost his ability to speak. After some time, a kindly falconer comes across the wild boy; he captures and tames him. As the boy slowly recovers his ability to speak, he learns to be friends with the falconer's dogs and birds and . . . remembers that his name is Merlin." (Horn Book) "Grades three to eight." (SLJ)

A "stark, poignant, and absorbing tale. . . . This 'skinny' book will entice reluctant readers, but its rich language and poetic phrasing make it compelling and challenging." SLJ

Pay the piper; [by] Jane Yolen and Adam Stemple. Tor/Starscape 2005 175p $16.95

Grades: 6 7 8 9 **Fic**

1. Fantasy fiction 2. Rock music -- Fiction

ISBN 0-7653-1158-5

When Callie interviews the band, Brass Rat, for her school newspaper, her feelings are ambivalent, but when all the children of Northampton begin to disappear on Halloween, she knows where the dangerous search must begin.

The authors "have produced a rollicking good riff on the Pied Piper. . . . The authors keep the action moving. . . . An entertaining as well as meaty read." Booklist

The **queen's** own fool; a novel of Mary Queen of Scots. [by] Jane Yolen and Robert J. Harris. Philomel Bks. 2000 390p pa $7.99

Grades: 7 8 9 10 **Fic**

1. Queens 2. Scotland -- Fiction

ISBN 0-399-23380-6; 0-698-11918-5 pa

LC 99-55070

When twelve-year-old Nicola leaves Troupe Brufort and serves as the fool for Mary, Queen of Scots, she experiences the political and religious upheavals in both France and Scotland

"The authors have woven fiction and historical fact into a seamless tapestry." Horn Book Guide

★ The **Rogues**; [by] Jane Yolen & Robert J. Harris. Philomel Books 2007 277p $18.99

Grades: 7 8 9 10 **Fic**

1. Adventure fiction 2. Scotland -- Fiction

ISBN 978-0-399-23898-7

LC 2006-26434

After his family is evicted from their Scottish farm, fifteen-year-old Roddy forms an unlikely friendship with a notorious rogue who helps him outwit a tyrant landlord in order to find a family treasure and make his way to America.

"The suspense mounts and the plot races along flawlessly in this excellent historical adventure." Booklist

Snow in Summer. Philomel Books 2011 243p $16.99

Grades: 4 5 6 7 **Fic**

1. Fairy tales 2. Magic -- Fiction 3. Stepmothers -- Fiction 4. West Virginia -- Fiction

ISBN 0-399-25663-6; 978-0-399-25663-9

LC 2010044242

Recasts the tale of Snow White, setting it in West Virginia in the 1940s with a stepmother who is a snake-handler.

"This story is beautifully written and deliciously scary, with just enough differences from familiar versions to keep readers guessing." Publ Wkly

Troll Bridge; a rock 'n' roll fairy tale. [by] Jane Yolen and Adam Stemple. 1st ed.; Starscape 2006 240p $16.95; pa $5.99

Grades: 7 8 9 10 **Fic**

1. Fairy tales 2. Musicians -- Fiction

ISBN 0-7653-1426-6; 0-7653-5284-2 pa

LC 2005034517

Sixteen-year-old harpist prodigy Moira is transported to a strange and mystical wilderness, where she finds herself in the middle of a deadly struggle between a magical fox and a monstrous troll.

"The story ends with a grand twist that is totally satisfying. The writing is filled with humor and straightforward prose, and the song lyrics are so well written that one can almost hear the music that accompanies them." SLJ

Yoo, David

The **detention** club. Balzer + Bray 2011 299p $16.99

Grades: 5 6 7 8 **Fic**

1. School stories 2. Siblings -- Fiction 3. Popularity

-- Fiction 4. Korean Americans -- Fiction
ISBN 978-0-06-178378-4; 0-06-178378-1

LC 2010-46211

Sixth-grader Peter Lee, in a desperate attempt to regain the popularity he had in elementary school, discovers that serving detention can win him important friends, much to the dismay of his over-achieving eighth-grade sister, Sunny.

"Even readers who guess the thief's identity early on will be entertained by the boys' hijinks and empathize with their desire to fit in." Publ Wkly

Yoo, Paula

Good enough. HarperTeen 2008 322p $16.99; lib bdg $17.89

Grades: 7 8 9 10   **Fic**

1. Violinists -- Fiction 2. Korean Americans -- Fiction
ISBN 978-0-06-079085-1; 978-0-06-079086-8 lib bdg

LC 2007-02985

A Korean American teenager tries to please her parents by getting into an Ivy League college, but a new guy in school and her love of the violin tempt her in new directions.

"The frequent lists, . . . SAT questions, and even spam recipes are, like Patti's convincing narration, filled with laugh-out-loud lines, but it's the deeper questions about growing up with immigrant parents, confronting racism, and how best to find success and happiness that will stay with readers." Booklist

Young, E. L.

STORM: The Infinity Code. Dial 2008 311p il $16.99

Grades: 6 7 8 9   **Fic**

1. Adventure fiction 2. Spies -- Fiction 3. Great Britain -- Fiction
ISBN 978-0-8037-3265-0

In London, the teenaged geniuses of STORM, a secret organization dedicated to eliminating the world's misery through science and technology, uncover plans for a deadly weapon and race to find and dismantle it, then confront the corrupt scientist behind the scheme.

"Young's debut novel is full of unusual scientific creations—all based on real inventions. The novel is plot-driven and packed with unlikely escapes and improbable plot twists—exactly what many middle school and junior high readers crave." Voice Youth Advocates

Other titles in this series are:
STORM: The ghost machine (2008)
STORM: The black sphere (2009)

Young, Karen Romano

Doodlebug; a novel in doodles. Feiwel and Friends 2010 un il $14.99

Grades: 4 5 6 7   **Fic**

1. School stories 2. Moving -- Fiction 3. California -- Fiction 4. Family life -- Fiction 5. Racially mixed people -- Fiction
ISBN 978-0-312-56156-7; 0-312-56156-3

Doreen Bussey, aka Dodo, takes the nickname Doodlebug when her family moves from Los Angeles to San Francisco and she records her experiences in a notebook with words, scribbles, and drawings.

This offers "an engaging, originial heroine, a satisfying story and lots of great pictures. . . . Some details, like the fact that the family is interracial, are shown but not stated, rewarding careful examination of the artwork. . . . Charming and thoughtful." Kirkus

Young, Moira

Blood red road. Margaret K. McElderry Books 2011 512p (Dustlands trilogy) $17.99

Grades: 6 7 8 9 10   **Fic**

1. Science fiction 2. Twins -- Fiction 3. Orphans -- Fiction 4. Siblings -- Fiction 5. Kidnapping -- Fiction
ISBN 978-1-4424-2998-7; 1-4424-2998-4

LC 2011-03423

"When 18-year-old Saba's father is killed and her twin brother, Lugh, is kidnapped, she sets out to rescue him, along with their younger sister, Emmi, and Saba's intelligent raven, Nero. Their travels across the desert wasteland bring them to a violent city in which Saba is forced to fight for her life in an arena. When she escapes with the help of a group of women warriors, she and her new allies (including a handsome and infuriating male warrior named Jack) try to prevent Lugh from being sacrificed." (Publishers Weekly)

"Readers will . . . be riveted by the book's fast-paced mix of action and romance. It's a natural for Hunger Games fans." Publ Wkly

Young, Suzanne

A **need** so beautiful. Balzer + Bray 2011 267p $16.99; ebook $9.99

Grades: 8 9 10 11 12   **Fic**

1. Supernatural -- Fiction 2. Good and evil -- Fiction 3. Portland (Or.) -- Fiction
ISBN 978-0-06-200824-4; 0-06-200824-2; 978-0-06-208454-5 ebook; 0-06-208454-2 ebook

LC 2010040810

A compelling Need that Charlotte has felt all her life is growing stronger, forcing her to connect with people in crisis, but at the same time other changes are taking place and she is terrified by what Monroe, a doctor and family friend, says must happen next.

"Charlotte is an exceptionally likable character who demonstrates an extraordinary amount of personal growth as she learns to accept her fate. . . . A unique take on the age-old struggle of good vs. evil." SLJ

Yovanoff, Brenna

The **replacement**. Razorbill 2010 343p $17.99

Grades: 9 10 11 12   **Fic**

1. Fantasy fiction 2. Death -- Fiction 3. Siblings -- Fiction 4. Supernatural -- Fiction 5. Missing children -- Fiction
ISBN 978-1-59514-337-2; 1-59514-337-8

LC 2010-36066

Sixteen-year-old Mackie Doyle knows that he replaced a human child when he was just an infant, and when a friend's sister disappears he goes against his family's and town's deliberate denial of the problem to confront the beings that dwell under the town, tampering with human lives.

"Yovanoff's spare but haunting prose creates an atmosphere shrouded in gloom and secrecy so that readers, like Mackie, must attempt to make sense of a situation ruled by chaos and fear. The ethical complications of the town's deal with the creatures of Mayhem are clearly presented but never overwrought, while Mackie's problematic relationship to the townspeople as both an outsider and a savior is poignantly explored." Bull Cent Child Books

Zadoff, Allen

Food, girls, and other things I can't have. Egmont USA 2009 311p $16.99; lib bdg $19.99

Grades: 7 8 9 10   **Fic**

1. School stories 2. Obesity -- Fiction 3. Football -- Fiction 4. Popularity -- Fiction

ISBN 978-1-60684-004-7; 1-60684-004-5; 978-1-60684-051-1 lib bdg; 1-60684-051-7 lib bdg

LC 2009-16242

Fifteen-year-old Andrew Zansky, the second fattest student at his high school, joins the varsity football team to get the attention of a new girl on whom he has a crush.

"The author does not lead Andy down the expected path. When forced to make a decision, his choice is unique and the conclusion satisfying. . . . The possibly offensive locker room language is typical and lends credibility. More importantly, Andy's character is thoughtful and refreshing." SLJ

My life, the theater, and other tragedies; a novel. Egmont USA 2011 282p $16.99

Grades: 7 8 9 10   **Fic**

1. School stories 2. Theater -- Fiction 3. New Jersey -- Fiction 4. Bereavement -- Fiction

ISBN 978-1-60684-036-8; 1-60684-036-3

LC 2010043619

While working backstage on a high school production of 'A Midsummer Night's Dream,' sixteen-year-old Adam develops feelings for a beautiful actress—which violates an unwritten code—and begins to overcome the grief that has controlled him since his father's death nearly two years earlier.

"Zadoff captures the confusion, torn loyalties, and overwrought drama of teenage life—not to mention student theater." Publ Wkly

Zahler, Diane

The **thirteenth** princess. Harper 2009 243p

Grades: 4 5 6 7   **Fic**

1. Fairy tales 2. Magic -- Fiction 3. Sisters -- Fiction 4. Princesses -- Fiction 5. Household employees -- Fiction 6. Father-daughter relationship -- Fiction 7. Folklore -- Germany

ISBN 0-06-182498-4; 0-06-182499-2 lib bdg; 978-0-06-182498-2; 978-0-06-182499-9 lib bdg

LC 2009-14575

Zita, cast aside by her father and raised as a kitchen maid, learns when she is nearly twelve that she is a princess and that her twelve sisters love her, and so when she discovers they are victims of an evil enchantment, she desperately tries to save them. Inspired by the Grimm fairy tale, "The twelve dancing princesses."

Zahler "deftly and thoughtfully embellishes the tale's classic elements. . . . Zahler takes a light story and gives it gratifying depth, rounding out the characters and their motivations without betraying the source material and wrapping

it all together in a graceful and cohesive romantic drama." Publ Wkly

A **true** princess. Harper 2011 182p $15.99

Grades: 4 5 6   **Fic**

1. Fairy tales 2. Friendship -- Fiction 3. Princesses -- Fiction 4. Voyages and travels -- Fiction

ISBN 978-0-06-182501-9; 0-06-182501-8

LC 2010017846

Twelve-year-old Lilia goes north to seek the family she has never known, accompanied by her friends Kai and Karina and their dog Ove, on an adventure fraught with peril, especially when they become lost in Bitra Forest, the Elf King's domain. Inspired by the Hans Christian Andersen tale, The princess and the pea.

"Readers who enjoyed . . . Zahler's The Thirteenth Princess . . . will also relish this tale." SLJ

Zail, Suzy

Playing for the commandant; Suzy Zail. Candlewick Press 2014 256 p. $16.99

Grades: 7 8 9 10 11 12   **Fic**

1. Pianists -- Fiction 2. Holocaust, 1939-1945 -- Fiction 3. War stories 4. Historical fiction 5. Concentration camp inmates - Fiction

ISBN 0763664030; 9780763664039

LC 2013955694

In this young adult novel by Suzy Zail, "Before, Hanna was going to be a famous concert pianist. She was going to wear her yellow dress to a dance. And she was going to dance with a boy. But then the Nazis came. Now it is up to Hanna to do all she can to keep her mother and sister alive, even if that means playing piano for the commandant and his guests." (Publisher's note)

"Zail's story is as gut-wrenching as any Holocaust tale . . . The haunting, matter-of-fact tone of Hanna's story will likely resonate with teens learning about the Holocaust." Booklist

Zalben, Jane Breskin

Four seasons. Alfred A. Knopf 2011 322p $15.99; lib bdg $18.99

Grades: 6 7 8 9   **Fic**

1. Music -- Fiction 2. Pianists -- Fiction 3. New York (N.Y.) -- Fiction

ISBN 978-0-375-86222-9; 0-375-86222-6; 978-0-375-96222-6 lib bdg; 0-375-96222-0 lib bdg

LC 2010-12731

Over the course of a year, thirteen-year-old Allegra Katz, a student at the demanding Julliard School and the daughter of two musicians, tries to decide whether she wants to continue to pursue a career as a concert pianist or to do something else with her life.

"The warm, complicated relationships and respectful treatment of Ally's depression animate an involving, perceptive, and reassuring novel that will hit readers where they live." Bull Cent Child Books

Zarr, Sara

★ **How** to save a life; Sara Zarr. Little, Brown 2011 341 p. $17.99

Grades: 6 7 8 9 10 11 12   **Fic**

1. Adoption -- Fiction 2. Bereavement -- Fiction 3.

Mother-daughter relationship -- Fiction 4. Colorado -- Fiction 5. Pregnancy -- Fiction 6. Family life -- Fiction
ISBN 9780316036061

LC 2010045832

Told from their own viewpoints, seventeen-year-old Jill, in grief over the loss of her father, and Mandy, nearly nineteen, are thrown together when Jill's mother agrees to adopt Mandy's unborn child but nothing turns out as they had anticipated.

★ The **Lucy** variations; by Sara Zarr. 1st ed. Little, Brown and Co. 2013 320 p. (hardcover) $17.99

Grades: 7 8 9 10 11 12 **Fic**
1. Pianists -- Fiction 2. Brothers and sisters -- Fiction 3. Ability -- Fiction 4. San Francisco (Calif.) -- Fiction 5. Family life -- California -- Fiction 6. Self-actualization (Psychology) -- Fiction
ISBN 031620501X; 9780316205016

LC 2012029852

In this novel, by Sara Zarr, "Lucy Beck-Moreau once had a promising future as a concert pianist. . . . Now, at sixteen, it's over. A death, and a betrayal, led her to walk away. That leaves her talented ten-year-old brother, Gus, to shoulder the full weight of the Beck-Moreau family expectations. Then Gus gets a new piano teacher who is young, kind, and interested in helping Lucy rekindle her love of piano--on her own terms." (Publisher's note)

"The third-person narration focuses entirely on Lucy but allows readers enough distance to help them understand her behavior in ways Lucy cannot. Occasional flashbacks fill out the back story. The combination of sympathetic main character and unusual social and cultural world makes this satisfying coming-of-age story stand out." Kirkus

★ **Once** was lost. Little, Brown 2009 217p $16.99

Grades: 7 8 9 10 **Fic**
1. Clergy -- Fiction 2. Alcoholism -- Fiction 3. Kidnapping -- Fiction 4. Christian life -- Fiction
ISBN 978-0-316-03604-7; 0-316-03604-8

LC 2009-25187

As the tragedy of a missing girl unfolds in her small town, fifteen-year-old Samara, who feels emotionally abandoned by her parents, begins to question her faith.

"This multilayered exploration of the intersection of the spiritual life and imperfect people features suspense and packs an emotional wallop." SLJ

Roomies; Sara Zarr and Tara Altebrando. Little, Brown and Company 2014 288 p. $18

Grades: 9 10 11 12 **Fic**
1. Roommates -- Fiction 2. Teenage girls -- Fiction 3. Email -- Fiction 4. Friendship -- Fiction 5. Dating (Social customs) -- Fiction 6. Family life -- California -- Fiction 7. Family life -- New Jersey -- Fiction
ISBN 0316217492; 9780316217491

LC 2012048431

In this book, by Sara Zarr and Tara Altebrando, "Elizabeth receives her freshman-year roommate assignment at the beginning of summer [and] she shoots off an email to coordinate the basics. She can't wait to escape her New Jer-

sey beach town, and her mom, and start life over in California. The first note to Lauren in San Francisco comes as a surprise; she had requested a single. . . . Soon the girls are emailing back and forth, sharing secrets even though they've never met." (Publisher's note)

"Jersey girl Elizabeth (EB) and San Franciscan Lauren, soon to be college roommates, correspond throughout the summer; chapters with alternating perspectives unwrap each girl's backstory, personality, and coming-to-terms with changes looming on the horizon. The premise will have mass appeal with teens who fantasize about their post-high-school futures, and the authors succeed in presenting two distinct and relatable narrative voices." (Horn Book)

★ **Sweethearts**. Little, Brown and Co. 2008 217p $16.99

Grades: 8 9 10 11 12 **Fic**
1. Love stories 2. School stories 3. Utah -- Fiction 4. Weight loss -- Fiction
ISBN 978-0-316-01455-7; 0-316-01455-9

LC 2007-41099

After losing her soul mate, Cameron, when they were nine, Jennifer, now seventeen, transformed herself from the unpopular fat girl into the beautiful and popular Jenna, but Cameron's unexpected return dredges up memories that cause both social and emotional turmoil.

"Zarr's writing is remarkable. . . . She conveys great delicacy of feeling and shades of meaning, and the realistic, moving ending will inspire excellent discussion." Booklist

Zemser, Amy Bronwen

★ **Dear** Julia. Greenwillow Books 2008 327p $16.99; lib bdg $17.89

Grades: 7 8 9 10 **Fic**
1. Cooking -- Fiction 2. Contests -- Fiction 3. Feminism -- Fiction 4. Mother-daughter relationship -- Fiction
ISBN 978-0-06-029458-8; 0-06-029458-2; 978-0-06-029459-5 lib bdg; 0-06-029459-0 lib bdg

LC 2008-3824

Shy sixteen-year-old Elaine has long dreamed of being the next Julia Child, to the dismay of her feminist mother, but when her first friend, the outrageous Lucida Sans, convinces Elaine to enter a cooking contest, anything could happen.

"Readers will laugh throughout, but Zemser never loses sight of Elaine's frailties and hopes." Publ Wkly

Zenatti, Valerie

A **bottle** in the Gaza Sea; translated by Adriana Hunter. Bloomsbury Children's Books 2008 149p il $16.95

Grades: 7 8 9 10 11 12 **Fic**
1. Israel -- Fiction 2. Letters -- Fiction 3. Israel-Arab conflicts -- Fiction
ISBN 978-1-59990-200-5; 1-59990-200-1

LC 2007-42361

Original French edition, 2005

Seventeen-year-old Tal Levine of Jerusalem, despondent over the ongoing Arab-Israeli conflict, puts her hopes for peace in a bottle and asks her brother, a military nurse in the Gaza Strip, to toss it into the sea, leading ultimately to friendship and understanding between her and an 'enemy.'

"Zenatti uses short, riveting chapters, . . . to pack a punch with readers reluctant to voracious. The overall effect is one of a haunting relationship that will help teens understand both sides of the Israeli-Palestinian conflict." Kirkus

Zephaniah, Benjamin

Face. Bloomsbury Pub. 2002 207p $15.95; pa $6.95

Grades: 7 8 9 10   **Fic**

1. Great Britain -- Fiction 2. Burns and scalds -- Fiction
ISBN 1-58234-774-3; 1-58234-921-5 pa
LC 2002-22758

First published 1999 in the United Kingdom

"This book will not only be enjoyed by teen readers for its entertaining story, but also for its statement about prejudice." Voice Youth Advocates

"Something terrible has happened to Martin's face. An automobile crash and fire have left the handsome, popular 15-year-old boy horribly disfigured. . . . His life is about to change drastically." Booklist

Zettel, Sarah

Bad luck girl; Sarah Zettel. Random House Inc 2014 368 p. (The American fairy trilogy) (hardcover) $17.99

Grades: 7 8 9 10   **Fic**

1. Magic -- Fiction 2. Fairies -- Fiction 3. Chicago (Ill.) -- Fiction 4. Racially mixed people -- Fiction 5. Chicago (Ill.) -- History -- 20th century -- Fiction
ISBN 0375869409; 9780375869402; 9780375969409
LC 2013013855

In this book, by Sarah Zettel, "after rescuing her parents from the Seelie king at Hearst Castle, Callie is caught up in the war between the fairies of the Midnight Throne and the Sunlit Kingdoms. By accident, she discovers that fairies aren't the only magical creatures in the world. There's also Halfers, misfits that are half fairy and half other - laced with strange magic and big-city attitude. As the war heats up, Callie's world falls apart." (Publisher's note)

"Half-fairy, half-human Callie (Golden Girl; Dust Girl) has reunited with her family, thus starting a war between the two fairy kingdoms. Fleeing Los Angeles for Chicago, Callie realizes that to end the war she must stand and fight. Zettel brings the street life, locales, and culture of jazz-age Chicago into the imagery of her fantasy, packing the story with incident and adventure." Horn Book

Dust girl; Sarah Zettel. Random House 2012 292 p. (trade : alk. paper) $17.99

Grades: 6 7 8 9   **Fic**

1. Fairies -- Fiction 2. Voyages and travels -- Fiction 3. Father-daughter relationship -- Fiction 4. Magic -- Fiction
ISBN 9780375869389; 9780375873812; 9780375969386; 9780375983184
LC 2011043310

In this book, "a mixed-race girl in Dust Bowl Kansas discovers her long-lost father isn't just a black man: He's a fairy. . . . [A] strange man . . . tells Callie secrets of her never-met father. Soon Callie's walking the dusty roads with Jack, a ragged white kid. . . . Callie and Jack dodge fairy politics and dangers, from grasshopper people to enchanted food to

magic movie theaters--but the conventional dangers are no less threatening." (Kirkus Reviews)

Golden girl; by Sarah Zettel. 1st ed. Random House Inc. 2013 308 p. (The American fairy trilogy) (hardcover) $17.99; (library) $20.99

Grades: 7 8 9 10   **Fic**

1. Fairies -- Fiction 2. Fantasy fiction 3. Voyages and travels -- Fiction 4. Magic -- Fiction 5. Fairies -- Fiction 6. Racially mixed people -- Fiction 7. Hollywood (Los Angeles, Calif.) -- History -- 20th century -- Fiction
ISBN 0375869395; 9780375869396; 9780375969393
LC 2013006238

In this book, it's 1935, and Callie LeRoux has journeyed to Hollywood from Slow Run, Kan., in search of her white human mother and black fairy father. A fairy kidnap attempt is foiled by none other than the famous Renaissance man Paul Robeson, a human who seems impervious to fairy magic. . . . Callie just wants to find her parents and get the heck out of Dodge, but with a prophecy hanging over her head, it won't be easy." (Kirkus Reviews)

Palace of Spies; being a true, accurate, and complete account of the scandalous and wholly remarkable adventures of Margaret Preston Fitzroy... by Sarah Zettel. Harcourt, Houghton Mifflin Harcourt 2013 368 p. (Palace of spies) $16.99

Grades: 8 9 10   **Fic**

1. Spies -- Fiction 2. London (England) -- Fiction 3. Great Britain -- History -- 1714-1837 -- Fiction 4. Love -- Fiction 5. Orphans -- Fiction 6. Courts and courtiers -- Fiction 7. London (England) -- History -- 18th century -- Fiction 8. Great Britain -- History -- George I, 1714-1727 -- Fiction
ISBN 0544074114; 9780544074118
LC 2012046366

In author Sarah Zettel's book, "sixteen-year-old Peggy is a well-bred orphan who is coerced into posing as a lady in waiting at the palace of King George I. Life is grand, until Peggy starts to suspect that the girl she's impersonating might have been murdered. Unless Peggy can discover the truth, she might be doomed to the same terrible fate. But in a court of shadows and intrigue, anyone could be a spy--perhaps even the handsome young artist with whom Peggy is falling in love." (Publisher's note)

"In eighteenth-century London, destitute orphan Peggy Fitzroy agrees to impersonate the recently deceased spy Lady Francesca as maid of honor to Princess Caroline. With a war of succession, jilted love, and religious turmoil in the mix, Peggy must navigate intrigue and shady liaisons to uncover the truth behind her predecessor's death. The feisty narrator and lush period details will garner fans for this new series." (Horn Book)

Zevin, Gabrielle

Because it is my blood; Gabrielle Zevin. Farrar Straus Giroux 2012 350 p. $17.99

Grades: 7 8 9 10   **Fic**

1. Crime -- Fiction 2. Criminals -- Fiction 3. High school students -- Fiction 4. Science fiction 5. Mexico -- Fiction 6. Violence -- Fiction 7. Chocolate -- Fiction 8. Celebrities -- Fiction 9. New York (N.Y.) -- Fiction

10. Organized crime -- Fiction 11. Oaxaca de Juárez (Mexico) -- Fiction 12. Family life -- New York (State) -- New York -- Fiction

ISBN 0374380740; 9780374380748

LC 2011036991

In Gabrielle Zeven's book, "Anya Balanchine is determined to follow the straight and narrow . . . since her release from Liberty Children's Facility . . . Unfortunately, her criminal record is making it hard for her to do that. No high school wants her with a gun possession charge . . . But when old friends return demanding that certain debts be paid, Anya is thrown right back into the criminal world that she had been determined to escape." (Macmillan)

Elsewhere. Farrar, Straus & Giroux 2005 275p $16; pa $6.95

Grades: 7 8 9 10 **Fic**

1. Death -- Fiction 2. Future life -- Fiction

ISBN 0-374-32091-8; 0-312-36746-5 pa

LC 2004-56279

After fifteen-year-old Liz Hall is hit by a taxi and killed, she finds herself in a place that is both like and unlike Earth, where she must adjust to her new status and figure out how to "live."

"Zevin's third-person narrative calmly, but surely guides readers through the bumpy landscape of strongly delineated characters dealing with the most difficult issue that faces all of us. A quiet book that provides much to think about and discuss." SLJ

★ **Memoirs** of a teenage amnesiac. Farrar, Straus and Giroux 2007 271p $17; pa $8.99

Grades: 7 8 9 10 **Fic**

1. School stories 2. Amnesia -- Fiction 3. Friendship -- Fiction

ISBN 978-0-374-34946-2; 0-374-34946-0; 978-0-312-56128-4 pa; 0-312-56128-8 pa

LC 2006-35287

After a nasty fall, Naomi realizes that she has no memory of the last four years and finds herself reassessing every aspect of her life.

This is a "sensitive, joyful novel. . . . Pulled by the the heart-bruising love story, readers will pause to contemplate irresistible questions." Booklist

Zhang, Kat, 1991-

Once we were; the second book in the Hybrid chronicles. Kat Zhang. HarperTeen 2014 340 p. $17.99

Grades: 8 9 10 11 12 **Fic**

1. Science fiction 2. Sisters -- Fiction 3. Identity (Psychology) -- Fiction 4. Resistance to government -- Fiction 5. Identity -- Fiction 6. Government, Resistance to -- Fiction

ISBN 0062114905; 9780062114907; 9780062114914

LC 2013032811

In this sequel to "What's Left of Me," by Kat Zhang, "Eva and Addie struggle to share their body as they clash over romance and join the fight for hybrid freedom. . . . Addie and Eva escaped imprisonment at a horrific psychiatric hospital. Now they should be safe, living among an underground hybrid movement. But safety is starting to feel con-

stricting. Faced with the possibility of being in hiding forever, the girls are eager to help bring about change—now." (Publisher's note)

"Because sisters Addie and Eva grew up hiding their hybrid nature, they're now learning-along with readers-some of the nuances of what it means for two souls to share one body...hang has a unique challenge: she must give each character two distinct personalities, which she skillfully manages. While this book lacks some of the freshness of What's Left of Me (HarperCollins, 2012), simply by virtue of being a sequel, the lovely, atmospheric storytelling is still very much present. Zhang has envisioned a complex, unique world and deftly brings it to life." (School Library Journal)

What's left of me. Harper 2012 343 p. $17.99

Grades: 8 9 10 11 12 **Fic**

1. Twins -- Fiction 2. Dystopian Fiction 3. Science fiction

ISBN 0062114875; 9780062114877

LC 2012289047

This novel, by Kat Zhang, is the first book of the young adult science fiction "Hybrid Chronicles." "Eva and Addie started out the same way as everyone else--two souls woven together in one body, taking turns controlling their movements. . . . Finally Addie was pronounced healthy and Eva was declared gone. Except, she wasn't. . . . For the past three years, Eva has clung to the remnants of her life, . . . for a chance to smile, to twirl, to speak, Eva will do anything." (Publisher's note)

Ziegler, Jennifer

How not to be popular. Delacorte Press 2008 339p $15.99; lib bdg $18.99

Grades: 7 8 9 10 11 12 **Fic**

1. School stories 2. Texas -- Fiction 3. Hippies -- Fiction 4. Popularity -- Fiction

ISBN 978-0-385-73465-3; 0-385-73465-4; 978-0-385-90463-6 lib bdg; 0-385-90463-0 lib bdg

LC 2007-27603

Seventeen-year-old Sugar Magnolia Dempsey is tired of leaving friends behind every time her hippie parents decide to move, but her plan to be unpopular at her new school backfires when other students join her on the path to "supreme dorkdom."

This "balances laugh-out-loud, sardonic commentary with earnest reflections that will directly connect with teens." Booklist

Zielin, Lara

Donut days. G.P. Putnam's Sons 2009 246p $16.99

Grades: 7 8 9 10 **Fic**

1. Clergy -- Fiction 2. Sex role -- Fiction 3. Minnesota -- Fiction 4. Journalism -- Fiction 5. Christian life -- Fiction

ISBN 978-0-399-25066-8; 0-399-25066-2

LC 2008-26138

During a camp-out promoting the opening of a donut shop in a small Minnesota town, sixteen-year-old Emma, an aspiring journalist, begins to connect an ongoing pollution investigation with the turmoil in the evangelical Christian church where her parents are pastors.

This is a "sweet, satisfying treat. . . . Teens will enjoy this lighter look at some serious issues of faith and family." SLJ

Zimmer, Tracie Vaughn

42 miles; illustrated by Elaine Clayton. Clarion Books 2008 73p il $16

Grades: 4 5 6   **Fic**

1. Novels in verse 2. Divorce -- Fiction 3. Farm life -- Fiction 4. Family life -- Fiction 5. City and town life -- Fiction

ISBN 978-0-618-61867-5; 0-618-61867-8

LC 2007-31032

As her thirteenth birthday approaches, JoEllen decides to bring together her two separate lives—one as Joey, who enjoys weekends with her father and other relatives on a farm, and another as Ellen, who lives with her mother in an apartment near her school and friends.

"Using free verse, Zimmer shows the richness in both places, while black-and-white composit illustrations bright the bits and pieces together." Booklist

Reaching for sun. Bloomsbury Children's Books 2007 192p $14.95

Grades: 7 8 9 10   **Fic**

1. Novels in verse 2. Friendship -- Fiction 3. Cerebral palsy -- Fiction

ISBN 1-59990-037-8

LC 2006-13197

Josie, who lives with her mother and grandmother and has cerebral palsy, befriends a boy who moves into one of the rich houses behind her old farmhouse.

"Written in verse, this quick-reading, appealing story will capture readers' hearts with its winsome heroine and affecting situations." Booklist

Zindel, Paul

★ The **Pigman**; a novel. Harper & Row 1968 182p hardcover o.p. pa $6.99

Grades: 7 8 9 10   **Fic**

ISBN 0-06-026828-X; 0-06-0757353-3 pa

ALA YALSA Margaret A. Edwards Award (2002)

"John Conlan and Lorraine Jensen, high school sophomores, are both troubled young people who have problems at home. They become friendly with an elderly widower, Mr. Pignati, who welcomes them into his home and shares with them his simple pleasures, including his collection of ceramic pigs, of which he is proud. When the Pigman, as the young people call him, goes to the hospital after a heart attack, they take advantage of his house for a party that becomes destructive. The consequences are tragic and propel the two young friends into more responsible behavior." Shapiro. Fic for Youth. 3d edition

Another title about the Pigman is:
The Pigman's legacy (1980)

Zink, Michelle

Guardian of the Gate. Little, Brown 2010 340p $17.99

Grades: 7 8 9 10   **Fic**

1. Magic -- Fiction 2. Twins -- Fiction 3. Sisters -- Fiction 4. Supernatural -- Fiction 5. Good and evil

-- Fiction

ISBN 978-0-316-03447-0; 0-316-03447-9

Sequel to: Prophecy of the sisters (2009)

In 1891 London, sixteen-year-old orphan Lia Milthorpe continues her quest to end an ancient prophecy requiring her to search for missing pages and human "keys" and develop her powers for an inevitable final confrontation with her twin sister Alice.

"An intense and captivating story that gives a whole new meaning to sibling rivalry." Voice Youth Advocates

★ **Prophecy** of the sisters. Little, Brown 2009 343p $17.99

Grades: 7 8 9 10   **Fic**

1. Twins -- Fiction 2. Sisters -- Fiction 3. Supernatural -- Fiction 4. Good and evil -- Fiction

ISBN 978-0-316-02742-7; 0-316-02742-1

LC 2008-45290

In late nineteenth-century New York state, wealthy sixteen-year-old twin sisters Lia and Alice Milthorpe find that they are on opposite sides of an ancient prophecy that has destroyed their parents and seeks to do even more harm.

"This arresting story takes readers to other planes of existence." Booklist

Followed by: Guardian of the gate (2010)

Zinn, Bridget

Poison; by Bridget Zinn. 1st ed. Disney/Hyperion Books 2013 276 p. (hardcover) $16.99

Grades: 7 8 9 10 11 12   **Fic**

1. Occult fiction 2. Fantasy fiction 3. Fantasy 4. Magic -- Fiction 5. Heroes -- Fiction 6. Princesses -- Fiction 7. Impersonation -- Fiction 8. Fugitives from justice -- Fiction

ISBN 1423139933; 9781423139935

LC 2012008693

In this novel, sixteen-year-old "Kyra is on the run. She may be one of the Kingdom of Mohr's most highly skilled potions masters, but she has also just tried—and failed—to poison Princess Ariana. And Kyra is determined to finish her mission even if it means killing her best friend. . . . In order to save her kingdom from a nefarious plot, Kyra will have to come to terms with all the gifts she possesses." (School Library Journal)

Zucker, Naomi Flink

★ **Callie's** rules; by Naomi Zucker. Egmont USA 2009 240p $15.99; lib bdg $18.99

Grades: 4 5 6 7   **Fic**

1. School stories 2. Halloween -- Fiction 3. New Jersey -- Fiction 4. Family life -- Fiction

ISBN 978-1-60684-027-6; 1-60684-027-4; 978-1-60684-052-8 lib bdg; 1-60684-052-5 lib bdg

LC 2009-15419

Eleven-year-old Callie Jones tries to keep track of all the rules for fitting in that other middle schoolers seem to know, but when the town decides to replace Halloween with an Autumn Festival, Callie leads her large family in an unusual protest.

"Callie herself is both funny and resourceful. Worthwhile and entertaining." Kirkus

Followed by: Write on, Callie Jones (2010)

Write on, Callie Jones; by Naomi Zucker. Egmont USA 2010 188p $15.99

Grades: 4 5 6 7 **Fic**

1. School stories 2. Authorship -- Fiction 3. Newspapers -- Fiction

ISBN 978-1-60684-028-3; 1-60684-028-2

LC 2010-23134

Sequel to: Callie's rules (2009)

As she continues to establish rules for navigating middle school, aspiring author Callie writes for the school newspaper until the principal cancels her article and Callie's quest to have her voice heard leads to a series of unexpected consequences.

"Playful, entertaining writing peppers this novel. . . . A quick, easy read for fans of the first book." SLJ

Zuckerman, Linda

A **taste** for rabbit. Arthur A. Levine Books 2007 310p $16.99

Grades: 7 8 9 10 **Fic**

1. Foxes -- Fiction 2. Animals -- Fiction 3. Rabbits -- Fiction 4. Resistance to government -- Fiction

ISBN 0-439-86977-3; 978-0-439-86977-5

LC 2007-7787

Quentin, a rabbit who lives in a walled compound run by a militaristic government, must join forces with Harry, a fox, to stop the sinister disappearances of outspoken and rebellious rabbit citizens.

"The blend of adventure, mystery and morality in this heroic tale of honor and friendship will appeal to middle-school fantasy fans." Publ Wkly

Zusak, Markus, 1975-

★ The **book** thief. Knopf 2006 552p il $16.95; lib bdg $18.99

Grades: 8 9 10 11 12 **Fic**

1. Death -- Fiction 2. Jews -- Germany -- Fiction 3. Books and reading -- Fiction 4. Holocaust, 1933-1945 -- Fiction 5. World War, 1939-1945 -- Fiction

ISBN 0-375-83100-2; 0-375-93100-7 lib bdg

LC 2005-08942

Michael L. Printz Award honor book, 2007

Trying to make sense of the horrors of World War II, Death relates the story of Liesel—a young German girl whose book-stealing and storytelling talents help sustain her family and the Jewish man they are hiding, as well as their neighbors.

"This hefty volume is an achievement—a challenging book in both length and subject, and best suited to sophisticated older readers." Publ Wkly

Zweig, Eric

Fever season. Dundurn Press 2009 254p $10

Grades: 7 8 9 10 **Fic**

1. Canada -- Fiction 2. Hockey -- Fiction 3. Orphans -- Fiction 4. Influenza -- Fiction 5. Montreal (Quebec) -- Fiction

ISBN 978-1-55488-432-2; 1-55488-432-2

When David is orphaned by the Spanish influenza outbreak in 1919 Montreal, he needs to find his long-lost uncle if he wants to avoid the orphanage, and he gets his chance when he gets a job with the Montreal Canadiens.

"Zweig tells a good story while he weaves a vibrant tapestry of life in the early 1900's. . . . Dramatic descriptions of war nightmares and flu sick-rooms hung with bleach-dipped sheets make history come alive. Interesting tidbits about hockey and its stars such as Bad Joe Hall, coupled with play-by-play action and French Canadian expressions, give the story true hockey flavor." Voice Youth Advocates

S C STORY COLLECTIONS

13; thirteen stories that capture the agony and ecstasy of being thirteen. edited by James Howe. Atheneum Books for Young Readers 2003 278p $16.95; pa $7.99

Grades: 4 5 6 7 **S C**

1. Short stories

ISBN 0-689-82863-2; 1-416-92684-4 pa

"The stories are a mixture of humor, pathos, and poignancy, and most are based on personal experiences. . . . Howe has chosen excellent authors for this volume and they have written oh-so-true stories about that wonderful, terrible first year of being a teenager. " SLJ

Alexander, Lloyd

★ The **foundling** and other tales of Prydain; rev & expanded ed; Holt & Co. 1999 98p hardcover o.p. pa $5.99

Grades: 5 6 7 8 **S C**

1. Short stories 2. Fantasy fiction

ISBN 0-8050-6130-4; 0-8050-8053-8 pa

LC 98-42807

First published 1973; this revised and expanded edition includes two additional stories Coll and his white pig and The truthful harp, first published separately 1965 and 1967 respectively

Eight short stories dealing with events that preceded the birth of Taran, the Assistant Pig-Keeper and key figure in the author's five works on the Kingdom of Prydain which began with The book of three

"The stories are written with vivid grace and humor." Chicago. Children's Book Center [review of 1973 edition]

★ **American** eyes; new Asian-American short stories for young adults. introduction by Cynthia Kadohata. Fawcett Juniper 1996 138p pa $6.99

Grades: 7 8 9 10 **S C**

1. Short stories 2. Asian Americans -- Fiction

ISBN 0-449-70448-3

First published 1994 by Holt & Co.

These ten stories reflect the conflict Asian Americans face in balancing an ancient heritage and an unknown future.

This collection is distinguished by the "excellent quality of its writing, the acuteness of characterization, and the sophistication of its themes." SLJ

Amnesty International

Free?: stories about human rights; [edited by] Amnesty International. Candlewick Press 2010 202p il $17.99; pa $8.99

Grades: 7 8 9 10 **S C**

1. Short stories 2. Freedom -- Fiction 3. Human rights -- Fiction

ISBN 978-0-7636-4703-2; 0-7636-4703-9; 978-0-7636-4926-5 pa; 0-7636-4926-0 pa

LC 2009-14720

An anthology of fourteen stories by young adult authors from around the world, on such themes as asylum, law, education, and faith, compiled in honor of the sixtieth anniversary of the Universal Declaration of Human Rights.

"Margaret Mahy writes about class with wit and intensity, as does Jamila Gavin, who sets the class war in India, where a young girl's family throws her out for resisting an arranged marriage. . . . David Almond explores school power plays in a story about a boy who says no to a popular bully. Hurricane Katrina is Rita Williams-Garcia's setting. Two contemporary Palestinian stories compare the current occupation with Native American experiences of oppression. . . . Sure to spark discussion and perhaps participation in Amnesty International." Booklist

Appelt, Kathi

Kissing Tennessee and other stories from the Stardust Dance. Harcourt 2000 118p hardcover o.p. pa $5.95

Grades: 6 7 8 9 **S C**

1. Short stories 2. School stories

ISBN 0-15-202249-X; 0-15-205127-9 pa

LC 99-50505

Graduating eighth graders relate their stories of love and heartbreak that have brought them to Dogwood Junior High's magical Stardust Dance.

"This collection will spark conversation in contemporary literature discussions, will quietly unsettle readers, and will elevate the quality of short-story collections." SLJ

Asimov, Isaac

I, robot; Bantam hardcover ed.; Bantam Books 2004 224p (Robot series) $24; pa $7.99

Grades: 7 8 9 10 11 12 Adult **S C**

1. Short stories 2. Science fiction 3. Robots -- Fiction

ISBN 0-553-80370-0; 0-553-29438-5 pa

LC 2003-69139

First published 1950 by Gnome Press

"These loosely connected stories cover the career of Dr. Susan Calvin and United States Robots, the industry that she heads, from the time of the public's early distrust of these robots to its later dependency on them. This collection is an important introduction to a theme often found in science fiction: the encroachment of technology on our lives." Shapiro. Fic for Youth. 3d edition

Aspin, Diana

Ordinary miracles. Red Deer Press 2003 168p (Northern Lights young novels) pa $7.95

Grades: 7 8 9 10 **S C**

1. Short stories 2. Canada -- Fiction

ISBN 0-88995-277-9

A collection of 13 short stories concerning life in a small Canadian community, covering such topics as an old man's memories of abandonment by his mother and his abusive life as an orphan, a teen's struggle with his sexuality, and issues such as alcoholism, death, adultery, and poverty.

This is "a riveting collection. . . . The author has created a work that leaves readers awash with feelings of empathy for each young protagonist." SLJ

Avi

Strange happenings; five tales of transformation. Harcourt 2006 147p $15; pa $5.95

Grades: 5 6 7 8 **S C**

1. Short stories 2. Supernatural -- Fiction

ISBN 0-15-205790-0; 0-15-206461-3 pa

LC 2004-29579

"In this short story collection, Avi offers five fantastical tales, set in both contemporary and fairy-tale lands, that explore the notion of transformation. . . . The pieces are vividly imagined and shot through with a captivating, edgy spookiness, which, along with their brevity and some droll, crackling dialogue, makes them great choices for sharing aloud in class or as inspiration in creative-writing units." Booklist

What do fish have to do with anything? and other stories; illustrated by Tracy Mitchell. Candlewick Press 1997 202p il hardcover o.p. pa $6.99

Grades: 4 5 6 7 **S C**

1. Short stories

ISBN 0-7636-0329-5; 0-7636-2319-9 pa

LC 97-1354

"While Avi's endings are not tidy, they are effective: each story brings its protagonist beyond childhood self-absorption to the realization that one is an integral part of a bigger picture." Horn Book

"Willie believes a homeless man possesses a cure for unhappiness. A minister dares his devilish son to be good. Pet-obsessed Eve receives visitations from two deceased cats. . . . These are among seven . . . stories dealing with communication in troubled relationships." Publisher's note

Bachmann, Stefan

The **Cabinet** of Curiosities; 36 Tales Brief & Sinister. by Stefan Bachmann, Katherine Catmull, Claire Legrand and Emma Trevayne; illustrated by Alexander Jansson. Harpercollins Childrens Books 2014 496 p. illustrations $16.99

Grades: 3 4 5 6 7 **S C**

1. Short stories 2. Horror fiction 3. Mystery fiction

ISBN 0062331051; 9780062331052

LC 2013362532

This book, by Stefan Bachmann, Katherine Catmull, Claire Legrand and Emma Trevayne, is "a collection of thirty-six forty eerie, mysterious, intriguing, and very short stories. . . . The book features an introduction and commentary by the authors and black-and-white illustrations throughout." (Publisher's note)

"Many of these are moral tales in which nasty children or adults die horribly; others, though, feature perfectly nice people who meet similarly gruesome ends. Readers who enjoy their Halloween chills all year round will find this anthology a delight." Pub Wkly

★ **Baseball** crazy: ten short stories that cover all the bases; edited by Nancy E. Mercado. Dial Books for Young Readers 2008 191p $16.99; pa $6.99

Grades: 4 5 6 7   **S C**

1. Short stories 2. Baseball -- Fiction

ISBN 978-0-8037-3162-2; 0-8037-3162-0; 978-0-14-241371-5 pa; 0-14-241371-2 pa

LC 2007-26649

"There's no shortage of great writing in this collection of 10 stories. Baseball unifies the entries, but there the similarities end. . . . Readers will be drawn in by the masterful storytelling." Publ Wkly

The **beastly** bride; tales of the animal people. edited by Ellen Datlow & Terri Windling; introduction by Terri Windling; selected decorations by Charles Vess. Viking 2010 500p $19.99

Grades: 8 9 10 11 12   **S C**

1. Short stories 2. Supernatural -- Fiction

ISBN 978-0-670-01145-2; 0-670-01145-2

LC 2009-14317

A collection of stories and poems relating to animal transfiguration legends from around the world, retold and reimagined by various authors. Includes brief biographies, authors' notes, and suggestions for further reading

"The majority of these beastly tales make for fun, thoughtful, occasionally gripping, reading." Voice Youth Advocates

Book Wish Foundation

★ **What** you wish for; foreword by Mia Farrow. G.P. Putnam's Sons 2011 252p $17.99

Grades: 6 7 8 9   **S C**

ISBN 978-0-399-25454-3; 0-399-25454-4

LC 2011003215

A collection of stories and poems with the theme of wishes.

This is a "moving anthology. . . . There isn't a weak story in the book, but, of course, a few are standouts. . . . Here's a wish: that this collection might find the widest readership possible." Booklist

Brown, Dustin

The **sports** pages; edited and with an introduction by Jon Scieszka; stories by Dustin Brown, ... [et al.]; with illustrations by Dan Santat. Walden Pond Press 2012 245 p ill (Guys read) (paberback bdg.) $6.99; (hardcover bdg.) $16.99

Grades: 4 5 6 7 8   **S C**

1. Short stories 2. Sports -- Fiction

ISBN 9780061963773; 9780061963780

LC 2012012716

This book, edited and with an introduction by Jon Scieszka, "offers a smorgasbord of sportswriting--fiction and non-fiction--to appeal to every sports enthusiast. From baseball to football, ice hockey to track and mixed martial arts, there is plenty here for sports-minded readers to like, with lively

action, humor and even a dose of mysticism in the form of magical grapefruit and a witch doctor." (Kirkus Reviews)

"In the third volume of his Guys Read series (the first focused on humor, and the second on thrillers), editor Scieszka turns his attention to sports, serving up 10 stories. . . . In his introduction, Scieszka wisely notes that good stories and good games are alike: Both reveal character and truths bigger than the game or the story." Booklist

Campoy, F. Isabel

Yes! we are Latinos; by Alma Flor Ada and F. Isabel Campoy; illustrated by David Diaz. Charlesbridge 2013 96 p. ill. (reinforced) $18.95

Grades: 7 8 9 10   **S C**

1. Hispanic Americans -- Poetry 2. American poetry -- Latino authors 3. Short stories 4. Immigrants -- Fiction 5. Immigrants -- United States 6. Latin Americans -- United States 7. Emigration and immigration -- Fiction 8. Latin Americans -- Cultural assimilation 9. Latin Americans -- United States -- Fiction

ISBN 158089383X; 9781580893831

LC 2012027214

In this book, the authors "shape fictional portraits of 13 young people living in the U.S., who have diverse experiences and backgrounds but share a Latino heritage. The first-person narrative poems range from reflective to free-spirited, methodical to free-association. . . . Informative nonfictional interludes . . . address relevant subjects, including immigration, the challenges migrant workers face, and Cuba-U.S. history." (Publishers Weekly)

Includes bibliographical references and index

★ The **chronicles** of Harris Burdick; 14 amazing authors tell the tales. Houghton Mifflin Harcourt 2011 un il $24.99

Grades: 5 6 7 8 9   **S C**

1. Short stories

ISBN 978-0-547-54810-4; 0-547-54810-9; 0547548109; 9780547548104

LC 2011006564

"Van Allsburg's The Mysteries of Harris Burdick, published in 1984, paired foreboding sentences with cryptic, highly detailed charcoal-pencil illustrations. With mostly stimulating, sometimes conventional results, seasoned authors (and Van Allsburg himself) play the game children have for decades, incorporating the sentences and visual cues into new stories . . . that expand on the original's enigmas. The liveliest entries pick up on Van Allsburg's haunting ambiguity: Jon Scieszka ends with a cliffhanger, Gregory Maguire weaves a complex tale of magic, and M.T. Anderson concocts a chilling Halloween offering. For a lakeside picture of two children, Sherman Alexie writes a sinister narrative about exasperating twins who pretend to have a third sibling, until their creepy prank backfires. . . . This star-studded exercise in creative writing tests the wits of favorite authors and shows readers how even the big shots hone their craft." Publ Wkly

Cleavage; breakaway fiction for real girls. edited by Deb Loughead & Jocelyn Shipley. Sumach Press 2008 186p il pa $12.95

    Grades: 8 9 10 11 12   **S C**

    1. Short stories 2. Mother-daughter relationship -- Fiction

    ISBN 978-1-894549-76-9; 1-894549-76-7

"Alternately edgy, charming, funny, and sweet, these 15 stories address issues confronting adolescents. Integral to each selection is the complicated relationship between the girls and their mothers. . . . The selections touch on the multiple meanings of the word 'cleavage,' and together form an aptly named collection of stories about body image and mothers and daughters coming together and growing apart. A fresh, honest, and entertaining anthology." SLJ

Compestine, Ying Chang

    ★ A **banquet** for hungry ghosts; a collection of deliciously frightening tales. illustrated by Coleman Polhemus. Henry Holt and Co. 2009 180p il $16.99

    Grades: 6 7 8 9 10   **S C**

    1. Ghost stories 2. Short stories 3. China -- Fiction

    ISBN 978-0-8050-8208-1; 0-8050-8208-5

           LC 2008-50273

Presents and eight-course banquet of ghost stories centering around Chinese cooking and culture. Each story is followed by a recipe and historical notes

"The stories are laced with beautiful (as well as lurid) images and chilling illustrations of the ghosts and their victims. Like the ghosts themselves, Compestine's memorable stories should prove difficult to shake." Publ Wkly

Cornered; 14 stories of bullying and defiance. [edited by] Rhoda Belleza. Running Press Teens 2012 383 p. $9.95

    Grades: 7 8 9 10 11 12   **S C**

    1. Short stories 2. School stories 3. Bullies -- Fiction

    ISBN 9780762444281

           LC 2011943133

This book is a "bully-themed anthology" of stories that focus "not only on teens who are targets of bullying, but also those who perpetrate it—and many . . . do both. Bullying [in the stories] takes many forms, including a teacher ridiculing students, a viral racist email and hazing on a soccer team. The contributors largely delve into bullies' behavior without resting on cliché . . . Most contributors also . . . observe that family dynamics can have as much impact as those at school." (Kirkus)

Corsets & clockwork; 13 steampunk romances. edited by Trisha Telep. Running Press Teens 2011 437p pa $9.95

    Grades: 7 8 9 10   **S C**

    1. Love stories 2. Short stories

    ISBN 978-0-7624-4092-4; 0-7624-4092-9

Collects thirteen original stories set during the Victorian era, including tales of steam-powered machines, family secrets, and love.

"While not every story is exceptional, all are engaging. Some of them contain challenging vocabulary and concepts; however, the action and romance in the other selections would make them good choices for reluctant readers. The common flaw is that the stories end too soon, just when readers have begun to fall in love with the steampunk worlds the writers have created." SLJ

Crutcher, Chris

    ★ **Athletic** shorts; six short stories. Greenwillow Bks. 1991 154p $17.99; pa $6.99

    Grades: 7 8 9 10   **S C**

    1. Short stories 2. Sports -- Fiction

    ISBN 0-688-10816-4; 0-06-050783-7 pa

           LC 91-4418

    ALA YALSA Margaret A. Edwards Award (2000)

    A collection of short stories about high school sports

"The author seamlessly blends humor with more serious elements. . . These Athletic Shorts will speak to YAs, touch them deeply, and introduce them to characters they'll want to know better." SLJ

Dahl, Roald

    Skin and other stories. Viking 2000 212p $15.99; pa $8.99

    Grades: 7 8 9 10   **S C**

    1. Short stories

    ISBN 0-670-89184-3; 0-14-131034-0 pa

           LC 99-58600

    A collection of 13 of the author's short stories written for adults. "Full of irony and unexpected twists, they smack of the master's touch—every word carefully chosen, characters fully fleshed out in only a few pages, the sense of place immediate." Booklist

Del Negro, Janice

    ★ **Passion** and poison; tales of shape-shifters, ghosts, and spirited women. Marshall Cavendish 2007 64p il $16.99

    Grades: 5 6 7 8   **S C**

    1. Ghost stories 2. Short stories 3. Supernatural -- Fiction

    ISBN 978-0-7614-5361-1; 0-7614-5361-X

           LC 2007-07237

"Including both original tales and retellings, this collection of seven stories . . . features diverse female protagonists facing challenges and perils—from human bullies to ghosts. More eerie than scary, the tales of bravery, revenge, grief, and redemption share a gothic sensibility. . . . The black-and-white illustrations . . . evoke bygone times." Booklist

Delacre, Lulu

    ★ **Salsa** stories; stories and linocuts by Lulu Delacre. Scholastic Press 2000 105p il hardcover o.p. $16.99

    Grades: 4 5 6   **S C**

    1. Short stories 2. Latin America 3. Family life -- Fiction 4. Latin America -- Fiction

    ISBN 0-590-63118-7; 0-590-63121-7 pa

           LC 99-25534

A collection of stories within the story of a family celebration where the guests relate their memories of growing up in various Latin American countries. Also contains recipes

"Kids will respond to both the warmth and the anxiety of the family life described in the vivid writing, and in Delacre's nicely composed linocuts." Booklist

Delaney, Joseph

The **Spook's** tale and other horrors; illustrations by Patrick Arrasmith. Greenwillow Books 2009 166p il (The last apprentice) $10.95; lib bdg $14.89
Grades: 5 6 7 8   S C
1. Short stories 2. Witches -- Fiction 3. Supernatural -- Fiction
ISBN 978-0-06-173028-3; 0-06-173028-9; 978-0-06-173030-6 lib bdg; 0-06-173030-0 lib bdg
LC 2008042235

As sixty-year-old John Gregory reflects on the past, he reveals how the world of ghosts, ghasts, witches, and boggarts was exposed to him and he later became the Spook, even though his first intention had been to join the priesthood.

"These short stories are narrated by secondary characters from the popular series, giving insight into some of Tom Ward's well-known companions. A 'Gallery of Villains' section identifies additional characters and gives a citation to the novels. . . . This book would be perfect for pulling reluctant readers into the series. The occasional black-and-white illustrations add a creepy, atmospheric touch." SLJ

Destination unexpected: short stories; collected by Donald R. Gallo. Candlewick Press 2003 240p hardcover o.p. pa $8.99
Grades: 7 8 9 10   S C
1. Short stories
ISBN 0-7636-1764-4; 0-7636-3119-1 pa
LC 2002-71599

This collection "features teen protagonists experiencing a transforming experience while on some kind of journey. . . . Whether humorous or serious, the stories are consistently well written and engaging." Booklist

Does this book make me look fat? edited by Marissa Walsh. Clarion Books 2008 215p $16
Grades: 7 8 9 10 11 12   S C
1. Short stories 2. Obesity -- Fiction 3. Eating disorders -- Fiction
ISBN 978-0-547-01496-8; 0-547-01496-1
LC 2008-25070

"This star-studded collection tackles a popular topic—body image—with humor, sensitivity, and creativity. . . . [It includes] Megan McCafferty's story narrated by a pair of skinny jeans. Other highlights are Matt de la Peña's wrenching story of a young man coming to terms with his sister's devastating eating disorder, and Sarra Manning's feisty protagonist, who helps a co-worker find her own style and later faces her own body issues." Booklist

Don't cramp my style; stories about that time of the month. edited by Lisa Rowe Fraustino. Simon & Schuster for Young Readers 2004 295p $15.95
Grades: 7 8 9 10   S C
1. Short stories 2. Menstruation -- Fiction
ISBN 0-689-85882-5
A collection of eleven stories concerning menstruation.

"This highly recommended collection . . . encompasses an impressive variety of times, cultures, attitudes, and moods. . . . The writing . . . is consistently excellent." Voice Youth Advocates

Ellis, Deborah

Lunch with Lenin and other stories. Fitzhenry & Whiteside 2008 169p pa $14.95
Grades: 7 8 9 10 11 12   S C
1. Short stories 2. Drug abuse -- Fiction
ISBN 978-1-55455-105-7; 1-55455-105-6
A collection of short stories that explore the lives of teenagers affected directly or indirectly by drugs.

"The relatively short stories read quickly, offering neither judgment nor solutions but rather the opportunity for compassion and understanding. . . . The collection's quality . . . is high enough to justify placing this book in every library." Voice Youth Advocates

Enthralled; paranormal diversions. edited by Melissa Marr and Kelley Armstrong. HarperCollins 2011 452p $17.99; pa $9.99
Grades: 7 8 9 10   S C
1. Short stories 2. Supernatural -- Fiction 3. Voyages and travels -- Fiction
ISBN 978-0-06-201579-2; 0-06-201579-6; 978-0-06-201578-5 pa; 0-06-201578-8 pa
LC 2011019393

A collection of sixteen original short stories by writers of paranormal tales, featuring journeys made by teens and magical beings.

"These short stories are loosely connected by a very openly interpreted journey motif. Psychics, genies, angels and gargoyles join fairies and vampires to terrorize and romance their fellow characters. The diversity in authors allows for the sometimes-neglected horror implied in paranormal stories to be spotlighted. . . . This collection is ideal as a sampler tray for paranormal readers looking to pick up new authors to follow or to further explore the fictional worlds they already know." Kirkus

Estevis, Anne

Down Garrapata road; by Anne Estevis. Arte Piñata Books 2003 119p pa $12.95
Grades: 7 8 9 10   S C
1. Short stories 2. Texas -- Fiction 3. Mexican Americans -- Fiction
ISBN 1-55885-397-9
LC 2003-49837

A collection of short stories set in a small Mexican-American community in southern Texas during the 1940s and 1950s, revealing the traditions, love, and social concerns of the families living there.

"Sly, gentle, and written in lively, simple language, these are stories that will draw readers into the particulars of a culture while capturing universal family dramas." Booklist

★ **Every** man for himself; ten short stories about being a guy. edited by Nancy E. Mercado. Dial Books 2005 154p il hardcover o.p. pa $6.99

Grades: 7 8 9 10   S C

1. Short stories 2. Boys -- Fiction

ISBN 0-8037-2896-4; 0-14-240813-1 pa

LC 2004-24069

"This collection provides a refreshing look at the values, decisions, and friendships that ultimately shape a boy into a man. The stories themselves are diverse, ranging from humorous to serious." SLJ

Fear: 13 stories of suspense and horror; [selected by and with an] introduction by R.L. Stine. Dutton 2010 306p $16.99; pa $7.99

Grades: 7 8 9 10   S C

1. Short stories 2. Horror fiction

ISBN 978-0-525-42168-9; 0-525-42168-8; 978-0-14-241774-4 pa; 0-14-241774-2 pa

LC 2009-53284

"Thirteen highly suspenseful short stories. . . . [Stine] enlists some of the best in the business, such as Meg Cabot and F. Paul Wilson, Walter Sorrells and James Rollins, who offer plenty of heart-throbbing supernatural horror, crime suspense, shockers and sometimes a mixture of all three. . . . Fast-paced, shuddery-scary fun." Kirkus

Firebirds; an anthology of original fantasy and science fiction. edited by Sharyn November. Firebird Press 2003 420p il $19.99

Grades: 7 8 9 10 11 12   S C

1. Short stories 2. Fantasy fiction 3. Science fiction

ISBN 0-14-250142-5

"Teens will find much to savor and celebrate in this dazzling collection of 16 short stories by some of the best fantasy writers around." SLJ

Firebirds rising; an anthology of original science fiction and fantasy. edited by Sharyn November. Firebird 2006 530p hardcover o.p. pa $9.99

Grades: 7 8 9 10 11 12   S C

1. Short stories 2. Fantasy fiction 3. Science fiction

ISBN 0-14-240549-3; 978-0-14-240549-9; 0-14-240936-7 pa; 978-0-14-240936-7 pa

This is a collection of sixteen science fiction and fantasy stories.

"This anthology is a wonderful choice for any young adult collection." Voice Youth Advocates

Firebirds soaring; an anthology of original speculative fiction. [edited by Sharyn November; illustrated by Mike Dringenberg] Firebird 2009 574p il $19.99

Grades: 7 8 9 10 11 12   S C

1. Short stories 2. Fantasy fiction 3. Science fiction

ISBN 978-0-14-240552-9; 0-14-240552-3

LC 2008-29516

This anthology "contains 19 short stories by some of the top writers in this genre. . . . The selections vary in length, with some short stories, some novellas. Each work is introduced by an evocative illustration that beautifully sets the scene for the written work. The variety of styles and themes and a gathering together of so many talented writers in one work offer readers a banquet for the imagination. For fans of the genre, this is a must read." SLJ

Flake, Sharon G.

★ **Who** am I without him? short stories about girls and the boys in their lives. Jump at the Sun/Hyperion Books for Children 2004 168p $15.99; pa $7.99

Grades: 7 8 9 10   S C

1. Short stories 2. African Americans -- Fiction

ISBN 0-7868-0693-1; 1-4231-0383-1 pa

Ten short stories about African American teenage girls and their relationships with boys.

"Addressing issues and situations that many girls face in today's often complex society, this book is provocative and thought-provoking." SLJ

Flanagan, John

The **lost** stories. Philomel 2011 422p (Ranger's apprentice) $17.99

Grades: 5 6 7 8   S C

1. Short stories 2. Fantasy fiction

ISBN 978-0-399-25618-9; 0-399-25618-0

This is "a collection of nine stories showing events not recorded in the books [of the Ranger's Apprentice series] and following the familiar characters during certain unrecorded times. In the framework story, set in 1896, an archaeologist discovers the fabled lost stories of the medieval Kingdom of Araluen. . . . Inspired by questions from readers, these short stories retain the adventure and the camaraderis of the novels." Booklist

Fleischman, Paul

Graven images; three stories. by Paul Fleischman; illustrations by Bagram Ibatoulline. Candlewick Press 2006 116p il $16.99; pa $5.99

Grades: 5 6 7 8   S C

1. Short stories 2. Supernatural -- Fiction

ISBN 0-7636-2775-5; 0-7636-2984-7 pa

LC 2005054283

A newly illustrated edition with a new afterword of the title first published 1982 by Harper & Row

A Newbery Medal honor book, 1983

A collection of three stories about a child who reads the lips of those who whisper secrets into a statue's ear; a daydreaming shoemaker's apprentice who must find ways to make the girl he loves notice him; and a stone carver who creates a statue of a ghost.

"Readers will be delighted with the return to print of [this title] with haunting new acrylic gouache illustrations . . . evoking the spinetingling aspects of this trio of tales. . . . Via a new afterword, the author explains the stories' inspiration and describes this book's significance early in his career." Publ Wkly

Full house; 10 stories about poker. edited by Pete Hautman. G. P. Putnam's Sons 2007 161p $17.99

Grades: 7 8 9 10   **S C**

1. Short stories 2. Poker -- Fiction
ISBN 978-0-399-24528-2

LC 2007-14116

This is a "compilation of stories about teenage encounters with poker. The characters find themselves in high-stakes situations: playing with the Devil, competing in a scholarship game, fighting to defeat a deadbeat stepdad, and staying one step ahead of an Internet poker company. . . . The stories vary from the eerily realistic to amusingly farfetched. In all cases, teen poker players will recognize themselves and their opponents in this diverse collection." SLJ

Gaiman, Neil

★ **M** is for magic; illustrations by Teddy Kristiansen. HarperCollins Pub. 2007 260p il $16.99; lib bdg $17.89; pa $6.99

Grades: 7 8 9 10   **S C**

1. Short stories 2. Magic -- Fiction
ISBN 978-0-06-118642-4; 0-06-118642-2; 978-0-06-118645-5 lib bdg; 0-06-118645-7 lib bdg; 978-0-06-118647-9 pa; 0-06-118647-3 pa

LC 2007-14472

Gaiman "has selected nine of his short stories and a poem and added a segment from an upcoming children's title for this volume. . . . This well-chosen collection is sure to create a new generation of Gaiman fans who will not need to understand all the allusions to enjoy the stories." Booklist

Unnatural creatures; stories. Neil Gaiman; [edited by] Rosemary Brosnan. 1st ed. HarperCollins 2013 480 p. ill. (hardcover) $17.99

Grades: 8 9 10 11 12   **S C**

1. Short stories 2. Fantasy fiction 3. Monsters -- Fiction
ISBN 0062236296; 9780062236296; 9780062236302

LC 2013933032

This fantasy-horror short story collection, compiled by Neil Gaiman and edited by Maria Dahvana Headley, "is a collection of short stories about the fantastical things that exist only in our minds. . . . The sixteen stories . . . range from the whimsical to the terrifying. The magical creatures range from werewolves to sunbirds to beings never before classified. E. Nesbit, Diana Wynne Jones, Gahan Wilson, and other literary luminaries contribute to the anthology." (Publisher's note)

Gallo, Donald R.

Join in; multiethnic short stories by outstanding writers for young adults. edited by Donald R. Gallo. Delacorte Press 1993 256p hardcover o.p. pa $5.99

Grades: 7 8 9 10   **S C**

1. Short stories
ISBN 0-440-21957-4 pa

LC 92-43169

The compiler of this collection invited "'a number of authors from different ethnic backgrounds to write a story featuring American teenagers from specific cultural groups.'"

(Bull Cent Child Books) "Grades seven to twelve." (Booklist)

"The 17 stories cross the boundaries of race and culture and probe the universal themes of belonging, acceptance, family, and friendship." Booklist

★ **Owning** it; stories about teens with disabilities. edited by Donald R. Gallo. Candlewick Press 2008 215p pbk. $6.99

Grades: 7 8 9 10   **S C**

1. Short stories 2. Diseases -- Fiction 3. People with disbailities -- Fiction
ISBN 9780763646615

LC 2007-24963

This anthology presents ten stories of teenagers facing the challenges of school, parents, boyfriends and girlfriends, in addition to the additional complications that come with having a physical or psychological disability. "Grades seven to ten." (Bull Cent Child Books)

"Each of the stories is strong and will resonate with teens dealing with everything from drinking problems, migraines, Tourette's Syndrome, and even cancer." Libr Media Connect

Geektastic; stories from the nerd herd. edited by Holly Black and Cecil Castellucci. Little Brown & Co. 2009 403p il $16.99

Grades: 7 8 9 10   **S C**

1. Short stories
ISBN 978-0-316-00809-9; 0-316-00809-5

LC 2009-455709

A collection of twenty-nine short stories about geeks.

"Although not all geekdoms are covered, topics include cosplay (dressing as characters), cons (conventions), SF television and movies, RPGs (roleplaying games), fantasy books, baton-twirling, astronomy, Rocky Horror, quiz bowl, and dinosaurs. Geek-themed comics by Hope Larson and Bryan Lee O'Malley separate the stories. . . . Although readers need not necessarily be geeks to appreciate this well-written collection, it will help. Buy for all the geeks in your library—including the librarian." Voice Youth Advocates

Give me shelter; stories about children who seek asylum. edited by Tony Bradman. Frances Lincoln 2007 220p $16.95

Grades: 5 6 7 8   **S C**

1. Short stories 2. Refugees -- Fiction
ISBN 978-1-84507-522-4; 1-84507-522-6

This is a "moving collection of 11 powerful narratives, quite different in their particulars but astonishingly similar in their sense of loss and loneliness. . . . While most of the stories focus on current asylum-seekers in Britain, one looks back to a Vietnamese child's trip to Australia, and another is set in an unnamed Eastern European country." SLJ

Gothic! ten original dark tales. edited by Deborah Noyes. Candlewick Press 2004 241p hardcover o.p. pa $7.99

Grades: 7 8 9 10   **S C**

1. Short stories 2. Horror fiction
ISBN 0-7636-2243-5; 0-7636-2737-2 pa

LC 2004-45188

This "collection features short stories by noted young adult authors such as M. T. Anderson, Caitlín R. Kiernan, Garth Nix, Celia Rees, Janni Lee Simner, and Barry Your-grau. . . . These varied tales take place in the distant past and in the high-tech present. Some are humorous while others have surprising twists or are reminiscent of classic fairy tales full of malevolent characters, but all share a love of the surreal or supernatural. . . . A sophisticated, thought-provoking, and gripping read." SLJ

★ The **Great** War; an anthology of stories inspired by objects from the first World War. illustrated by Jim Kay. Candlewick Press 2014 304 p. illustrations

Grades: 3 4 5 6 7 8   S C
1. World War, 1914-1918 2. War stories 3. Historical fiction
ISBN 9780763675547

         LC 2013955699

In this book, illustrated by Jim Kay, "eleven internationally acclaimed writers draw on personal objects to bring the First World War to life. . . . Each author was invited to choose an object that had a connection to the war . . . and use it as the inspiration for an original short story." (Publisher's note)

"Each of the 11 original short stories in this superlative collection about WWI has been inspired by an object evoking the conflict. Thus, the catalyst for contributor Almond is a soldier's writing case; for Timothée de Fombelle, it's a Victoria Cross; for Adèle Geras, a wartime butter dish; for John Boyne, a recruitment poster; and so forth...Haunting black-and-white illustrations by Kate Greenaway Medal–winning illustrator Kay reinforce the stories' somber mood and cumulative power. This book is both beautifully designed and beautifully written." Booklist

★ **Guys** read: funny business; edited and with an introduction by Jon Scieszka; stories by Mac Barnett [et al.]; with illustrations by Adam Rex. Walden Pond Press 2010 268p il $16.99; pa $5.99

Grades: 4 5 6 7   S C
1. Short stories 2. Humorous fiction 3. Boys -- Fiction
ISBN 978-0-06-196374-2; 0-06-196374-7; 978-0-06-196373-5 pa; 0-06-196373-9 pa

         LC 2010-08122

A collection of humorous stories featuring a teenaged mummy, a homicidal turkey, and the world's largest pool of chocolate milk.

"A must-have collection for the boys in your library—and while you're at it, get a copy for the girls too!" Booklist

★ **Guys** read: thriller. Walden Pond Press 2011 viii, 272p $16.99; pa $6.99

Grades: 5 6 7 8   S C
1. Short stories 2. Adventure fiction
ISBN 978-0-06-196376-6; 0-06-196376-3; 978-0-06-196375-9 pa; 0-06-196375-5 pa

"Scieszka has gathered 10 thrilling stories from stellar writers. There are ghost stories, a deeply touching tale of a wish-granting machine and one about monsters that live in storm drains. . . . This anthology is brimming with choice

stuff for guys who appreciate the uncanny, the uncouth and the unput-down-able." Kirkus

★ **Half**-minute horrors; edited by Susan Rich. HarperCollinsPublishers 2009 141p il $12.99

Grades: 5 6 7 8   S C
1. Short stories 2. Horror fiction
ISBN 978-0-06-183379-3; 0-06-183379-7

         LC 2009-18293

An anthology of very short, scary stories by an assortment of authors and illustrators including Chris Raschka, Joyce Carol Oates, Neil Gaiman, Jack Gantos, and Lane Smith.

"This collection of more than 70 chilling snippets is ideal for campfires and car trips. The stories—some a couple sentences, some a few pages—range from darkly humorous . . . to outright creepy. . . . These are inherently quick reads, but with enough plot and detail to encourage further imagining." Publ Wkly

Hearne, Betsy Gould

The **canine** connection: stories about dogs and people; [by] Betsy Hearne. Margaret K. McElderry Bks. 2003 113p hardcover o.p. pa $8.95

Grades: 5 6 7 8   S C
1. Short stories 2. Dogs -- Fiction
ISBN 0-689-85258-4; 1-4169-6817-2 pa

         LC 2001-58991

Twelve short stories that reflect the varied ways that dogs and humans relate

"The emotions and dialogue are pitch perfect. . . . A rewarding collection that will stay with readers." Booklist

Holt, Kimberly Willis

Part of me; stories of a Louisiana family. 1st ed.; H. Holt 2006 208p $16.95

Grades: 7 8 9 10   S C
1. Short stories 2. Louisiana -- Fiction 3. Family life -- Fiction
ISBN 0-8050-6360-9; 978-0-8050-6360-8

         LC 2005-29676

Ten stories trace the connections between four generations of one Louisiana family from 1939 when a young girl leaves school to help support her family to 2006 when an eighty-year-old woman embarks on a book tour. "Grades five to seven." (Bull Cent Child Books)

"Holt once again excels at creating character and an evocative sense of place." SLJ

Kiss me deadly; 13 tales of paranormal love. edited by Trisha Telep. RP Teens 2010 430p pa $9.95

Grades: 7 8 9 10   S C
1. Love stories 2. Short stories 3. Supernatural -- Fiction
ISBN 978-0-7624-3949-2; 0-7624-3949-1

         LC 2010-926067

A collection of short stories combining dark seduction and modern romance presents a variety of tales featuring the romantic lives of humans and werewolves, ghosts, fallen angels, zombies, and shape-shifters.

The stories "have varying lengths and tones, representing an impressive range of writing styles; it is likely that any fantasy reader will find at least one memorable story that speaks directly to his or her preferences." Bull Cent Child Books

Le Guin, Ursula K.

Tales from Earthsea. Ace Books 2002 314p (The Earthsea cycle) rpt $16.99; pa $13.95
Grades: 11 12 Adult   S C
    1. Short stories 2. Fantasy fiction
    ISBN 9780547851402 rpt; 0-441-00932-8
                                               LC 2001-56673
"Inhabited by people no better or worse than ourselves, Earthsea is dominated by the practice of magic as precise as any science and as unpredictable in its social consequences. Since it is based entirely on language, Earthsea's magic serves as a metaphor for the writer's own sorcery. Yet despite Le Guin's strong bias toward the didactic there is no hint of by-the-numbers allegory here." N Y Times Book Rev

Lester, Julius

Long journey home: stories from black history. Dial Press (NY) 1972 147p hardcover o.p. pa $5.99
Grades: 6 7 8 9   S C
    1. Short stories 2. African Americans -- Fiction
    ISBN 0-14-038981-4 pa
"In a foreword, Julius Lester explains that he has chosen minor figures because the mass of people were the 'movers of history' while the great figures are their symbols. . . . The selections are diversified in their settings and alike in their sharply-etched effectiveness." Bull Cent Child Books

★ Life on Mars: tales from the new frontier; an original science fiction anthology. edited by Jonathan Strahan. Viking 2011 333p $19.99
Grades: 7 8 9 10   S C
    1. Short stories 2. Science fiction 3. Mars (Planet) -- Fiction
    ISBN 978-0-670-01216-9; 0-670-01216-5
                                               LC 2011-02998
"In this strong anthology, Strahan . . . collects stories by some of the most talented writers in science fiction. Ranging from the first Mars landing to the far future, they often make use of the most recent scientific data about the Red Planet. . . . Invoking some of the great authors of Martian tales, from Burroughs and Bradbury to Heinlein and Kim Stanley Robinson . . . , this anthology is sure to appeal to any teens who yearn to explore Earth's nearest neighbor." Publ Wkly

Love is hell; [by] Melissa Marr . . . [et al.] HarperTeen 2008 263p $16.99; pa $9.99
Grades: 7 8 9 10   S C
    1. Love stories 2. Short stories 3. Supernatural -- Fiction
    ISBN 978-0-06-144305-3; 0-06-144305-0; 978-0-06-144304-6 pa; 0-06-144304-2 pa
                                               LC 2007-49574
"Supernatural romance is the well-chosen theme of five original stories by as many authors. . . . There's enough variety to round out the central theme, and consistently supple storytelling will lure readers through all five entries." Publ Wkly

Lucky dog; twelve tales of rescued dogs. [by Kirby Larson ... et al.] Scholastic Press 2013 192 p. $15.99
Grades: 4 5 6 7   S C
    1. Short stories 2. Dogs -- Fiction 3. Dog rescue -- Fiction 4. Dog adoption -- Fiction
    ISBN 0545554519; 9780545554510
                                               LC 2013011309
This book is a collection of dog stories for children by authors such as Kirby Larson, Tui T. Sutherland, and Ellen Miles. "You'll meet Foxtrot, a feisty Pomeranian who can't bear the thought of leaving her best friend. And Beatrice, whose bark is definitely worse than her bite. And then there's Pumpkin, one of the 101 Chihuahuas who turn life at the center upside down." (Publisher's note)

"Troy, 'the new kid in town,' is comforted when he adopts a new dog at the shelter; Tilly is afraid of dogs and Buddy is happy at the shelter, but somehow the two bond. Each short story by a different popular author is connected through the Pawley Rescue Center, which places dogs with their families. Some of the stories lack a strong emotional core." Horn Book

Marston, Elsa

Santa Claus in Baghdad and other stories about teens in the Arab world. Indiana University Press 2008 198p pa $15.95
Grades: 6 7 8 9 10   S C
    1. Short stories 2. Middle East -- Fiction 3. Arab countries -- Fiction
    ISBN 978-0-253-22004-2; 0-253-22004-1
                                               LC 2007-50768
A collection of eight stories, most previously published in other anthologies, about what it is like to grow up in the Middle East today.

"Marston, who has lived and visited the countries of which she writes, offers a realistic portrait of the Middle East that mixes possiblity and bleakness in equal measure." Voice Youth Advocates

McKinley, Robin

The door in the hedge. Greenwillow Bks. 1981 216p hardcover o.p. pa $6.99
Grades: 7 8 9 10   S C
    1. Fairy tales 2. Short stories
    ISBN 0-688-00312-5; 0-698-11960-6 pa
                                               LC 80-21903
"These tales are well-written and enjoyable to read. It is too bad they lack illustrations." Child Book Rev Serv

The author "presents four romantic tales that elaborate— to a greater or lesser degree—upon the supernatural lore of fairy tale, myth, and legend. Two of the stories are original in plot and in characters. . . . The other two stories are literary recastings of Grimm tales, 'The Princess and the Frog' . . . {and} 'The Twelve Dancing Princesses.'" Horn Book

★ Fire: tales of elemental spirits; [by] Robin McKinley and Peter Dickinson. G. P. Putnam's Sons 2009 297p $19.99
Grades: 7 8 9 10   S C
    1. Short stories 2. Fire -- Fiction 3. Mythical animals

-- Fiction
ISBN 978-0-399-25289-1; 0-399-25289-4

LC 2009-4730

"The settings of these five tales range from ancient to modern, but they are all united by encounters with magical creatures with an affinity for fire. . . . This collection of beautifully crafted tales will find a warm welcome from fans of either author, as well as from fantasy readers in general." SLJ

Water; tales of elemental spirits; [by] Robin McKinley, Peter Dickinson. Putnam 2002 266p $18.99; pa $6.99

Grades: 7 8 9 10   S C
1. Short stories 2. Fantasy fiction 3. Mermaids and mermen -- Fiction
ISBN 0-399-23796-8; 0-14-240244-3 pa

LC 2001-41642

"The masterfully written stories all feature distinct, richly detailed casts and settings . . . and focus as strongly on action as on character. There's plenty here to excite, enthrall, and move even the pickiest readers." SLJ

McKissack, Patricia C.

★ **The dark -thirty**; Southern tales of the supernatural. illustrated by Brian Pinkney. Knopf 1992 122p il $18.95; lib bdg $20.99; pa $6.50

Grades: 4 5 6 7   S C
1. Ghost stories 2. Short stories 3. African Americans -- Fiction
ISBN 0-679-81863-4; 0-679-91853-9 lib bdg; 0-679-89006-8 pa

LC 92-3021

Coretta Scott King Award for text, 1993; A Newbery honor book, 1993

A collection of ghost stories with African American themes, designed to be told during the Dark Thirty—the half hour before sunset—when ghosts seem all too believable

"Strong characterizations are superbly drawn in a few words. The atmosphere of each selection is skillfully developed and sustained to the very end. Pinkney's stark scratchboard illustrations evoke an eerie mood, which heightens the suspense of each tale." SLJ

★ **Porch lies**; tales of slicksters, tricksters, and other wily characters. [by] Patricia C. McKissack; illustrated by André Carrilho. Schwartz & Wade Books 2006 146p il $18.95; lib bdg $22.99

Grades: 4 5 6 7   S C
1. Short stories 2. African Americans -- Fiction
ISBN 0-375-83619-5; 0-375-93619-X lib bdg

LC 2005-22048

The "original tales in this uproarious collection draw on African American oral tradition and blend history and legend with sly humor, creepy horror, villainous characters, and wild farce. McKissack based the stories on those she heard as a child while sitting on her grandparents' porch. . . . Carrilho's full-page illustrations—part cartoon, part portrait in silhouette—combine realistic characters with scary monsters." Booklist

McRobbie, David

A whole lot of Wayne; [by] David McRobbie. Allen & Unwin 2007 396p pa $12.95

Grades: 7 8 9 10   S C
1. Short stories 2. Boys -- Fiction
ISBN 978-1-74175-244-1; 1-74175-244-2

"McRobbie thoroughly entertains readers with this charming and heartwarming collection of stories starring Wayne Wilson. Accompanied by his friend Squocka Berrington, the teen finds himself in a variety of hilarious and oftentimes precarious situations." SLJ

★ **Moccasin thunder**; American Indians stories for today. edited by Lori Marie Carlson. HarperCollins 2005 156p $15.99

Grades: 7 8 9 10   S C
1. Short stories 2. Native Americans -- Fiction
ISBN 0-06-623957-5

LC 2004-22186

Presents ten short stories about contemporary Native American teens by members of tribes of the United States and Canada, including Louise Erdrich and Joseph Bruchac.

"This distinguished anthology offers powerful, beautifully written stories that are thoughtful and important for teens to hear." SLJ

Morpurgo, Michael

Singing for Mrs. Pettigrew; stories and essays from a writing life. illustrated by Peter Bailey. Candlewick Press 2009 263p il $18.99

Grades: 6 7 8 9   S C
1. Essays 2. Short stories 3. Voyages and travels -- Fiction
ISBN 978-0-7636-3624-1; 0-7636-3624-X

"Morpurgo's writing is thoroughly enjoyable in this collection of previously published short stories and poems with accompanying essays. The pieces cover a wide range of emotions. . . . Evocative fine-lined black-and-white illustrations appear throughout." Horn Book Guide

My dad's a punk; 12 stories about boys and their fathers. edited by Tony Bradman. Kingfisher 2006 271p pa $7.95

Grades: 7 8 9 10   S C
1. Short stories 2. Father-son relationship -- Fiction
ISBN 0-7534-5870-5

"Authors such as Ron Koertge, Tim Wynne-Jones, and Francis McCrickard explore father-son relationships in moving stories set in the past, present, and future. From bird watching to bird slaughter, divorced dads to gay dads, and close conversations to clandestine meetings on street corners, the situations and characters in each of these stories convey the depth and breadth of what it means to be a male in a family. A strong collection." Booklist

Myers, Walter Dean, 1937-2014

145th Street; short stories. Delacorte Press 2000 151p hardcover o.p. pa $5.50

Grades: 7 8 9 10   S C
1. Short stories 2. African Americans -- Fiction 3.

Harlem (New York, N.Y.) -- Fiction
ISBN 0-385-32137-6; 0-440-22916-2 pa

LC 99-36097

"These ten powerful stories create a vivid mosaic of life in the Harlem neighborhood of 145th Street. Memorable characters range from outgoing Big Joe, who decides to stage his own funeral party in Big Joe's funeral, to book-loving Monkeyman, who outsmarts the Tigros gang. . . . Beautifully told, Myers's stories offer an enticing collection for teens." Voice Youth Advocates

★ **What** they found; love on 145th street. Wendy Lamb Books 2007 243p $15.99; lib bdg $18.99
Grades: 8 9 10 11 12   S C
1. Short stories 2. Family life -- Fiction 3. African Americans -- Fiction 4. Harlem (New York, N.Y.) -- Fiction
ISBN 978-0-385-32138-9; 0-385-32138-4; 978-0-375-93709-5 lib bdg; 0-375-93709-9 lib bdg

LC 2007-7057

Companion volume to 145th street (2000)
Fifteen interrelated stories explore different aspects of love, such as a dying father's determination to help start a family business—a beauty salon—and the relationship of two teens who plan to remain celibate until they marry.

"Rich in both character and setting, these urban tales combine heartbreak and hope into a vivid tableau of a community. A priority purchase for all libraries, especially those in urban settings." SLJ

Na, An
No such thing as the real world; a short story collection. [by] An Na [et al.]; introduction by Jill Santopolo; [compiled by Laura Geringer and Jill Santopolo] HarperTeen 2009 246p $16.99
Grades: 8 9 10   S C
1. Short stories
ISBN 978-0-06-147058-5; 0-06-147058-9

LC 2008-22583

Six young adult authors present short stories featuring teens who have to face the "real world" for the first time.

"This unique collection will challenge students' intellect and have them questioning their own decision-making skills. A fine balance is straddled between sophisticated prose and authentic teen voices, uninhibited and peppered with profanity." SLJ

Naidoo, Beverley
Out of bounds: seven stories of conflict and hope. HarperCollins Pubs. 2003 175p $16.99; pa $5.99
Grades: 5 6 7 8   S C
1. Short stories 2. South Africa -- Race relations -- Fiction
ISBN 0-06-050799-3; 0-06-050801-9 pa

LC 2002-68901

First published 2001 in the United Kingdom
Seven stories, spanning the time period from 1948 to 2000, chronicle the experiences of young people from different races and ethnic groups as they try to cope with the restrictions placed on their lives by South Africa's apartheid laws

"Naidoo's book reveals our humanity and inhumanity with starkness and precision. . . . She honors her country's past, present, and future with these brave tales." Horn Book

Nayeri, Daniel
★ **Straw** house, Wood house, Brick house, Blow. Candlewick Press 2011 404p $19.99
Grades: 8 9 10 11 12   S C
1. Love stories 2. Short stories 3. Mystery fiction 4. Science fiction 5. West (U.S.) -- Fiction
ISBN 9780763655266; 0763655260

LC 2011013675

A collection of four novellas in different genres, including a western about a farmer who grows living toys and a rancher who grows half-living people; a science fiction story of the near-future in which the world is as easy to manipulate as the Internet; a crime story in which every wish comes true and only the Imaginary Crimes Unit can stop them; and a comedic love story in which Death describes himself as a charismatic hero.

"Four stylistically brilliant novellas offer readers a range of exquisite reading experiences in this collection." Bull Cent Child Books

Nix, Garth
★ **Across** the wall; a tale of the Abhorsen and other stories. Eos 2005 305p hardcover o.p. pa $7.99
Grades: 7 8 9 10   S C
1. Short stories 2. Fantasy fiction
ISBN 0-06-074713-7; 0-06-074715-3 pa
In Nicholas Sayre and the creature of case, the opening novella, "Nick encounters a bloodsucking Free Magic monster during a visit to Ancelstierre's top-secret intelligence agency. The story teasingly refers to British mysteries and spy fiction, parodic elements that will appeal most to Nix's adult fans. Even less-experienced readers, though, will enjoy getting to know Nick on his own terms. . . . The remaining 11 stories . . . include selections clearly intended for middle-graders as well as more sophisticated offerings containing frank references to sex and violence spattered with 'blood and brains and urine.' Buy this with the understanding that the packaging will attract the full spectrum of Nix's fans but that the younger ones may get more than they bargained for." Booklist

Noyes, Deborah
★ The **ghosts** of Kerfol. Candlewick Press 2008 163p $16.99
Grades: 8 9 10 11 12   S C
1. Ghost stories 2. Short stories 3. Supernatural -- Fiction
ISBN 978-0-7636-3000-3; 0-7636-3000-4

LC 2007-51884

Over the centuries, the inhabitants of author Edith Wharton's fictional mansion, Kerfol, are haunted by the ghosts of dead dogs, fractured relationships, and the taste of bitter revenge.

This collection includes "five wonderfully chilling short stories." Publ Wkly

The **restless** dead; ten original stories of the supernatural. edited by Deborah Noyes. Candlewick Press 2007 253p pbk. $7.99; $16.99

Grades: 8 9 10 11 12   **S C**

1. Short stories 2. Horror fiction 3. Supernatural -- Fiction

ISBN 9780763636715; 0-7636-2906-5; 978-0-7636-2906-9

LC 2007-22114

This is a companion volume to Gothic!: Ten Original Dark Tales. This is a collection of ten stories by Kelly Link, Chris Wooding, Annette Curtis Klause, Marcus Sedgwick, Herbie Brennan, Deobrah Noyes, Libba Bray, M.A. Anderson, Holly Black, and Nancy Etchemendy. "Grades seven to nine." (Bull Cent Child Books)

This is a "collection of terrifying stories from some of the most well-known authors writing for teens, including M. T. Anderson, Holly Black, Libby Bray, and Annette Curtis Klause. From vampires to vindictive ghosts, this diverse anthology has it all, and then some." Booklist

Nye, Naomi Shihab, 1952-

★ **There** is no long distance now; very short stories. Greenwillow Books 2011 201p $17.99

Grades: 7 8 9 10 11 12   **S C**

1. Short stories

ISBN 0-06-201965-1; 978-0-06-201965-3

LC 2010025559

"Very short stories offer glimpses into the everyday lives of young people. . . . As she does in her poetry, Nye achieves a perfect marriage of theme and structure in stories that reflect the moments, glimpses and epiphones of growing up." Kirkus

On the fringe; edited by Donald R. Gallo. Dial Bks. for Young Readers 2001 224p hardcover o.p. pa $6.99

Grades: 7 8 9 10   **S C**

1. Short stories

ISBN 0-8037-2656-2; 0-14-250026-7 pa

LC 00-40521

"Kids who are geeks, unathletic, poor, emotionally fragile, loners, or unattractive by current standards form the heart of this collection of exceptional stories by well-known YA authors such as Joan Bauer, Chris Crutcher, and M. E. Kerr." SLJ

Once upon a cuento; edited by Lyn Miller-Lachman. Curbstone Press 2003 243p pa $15.95

Grades: 9 10 11 12   **S C**

1. Short stories 2. Hispanic Americans -- Fiction

ISBN 1-88068-499-3

LC 2003-14667

"Writing quality is consisently high throughout. . . . This book . . . succeeds admirably in proving, through literature, that there is no single 'Latino experience.'" Voice Youth Advocates

"Fourteen Latino authors have contributed to this collection of 17 short stories" SLJ

Other worlds; edited by Jon Scieszka, illustrated by Greg Ruth. Walden Pond Press 2013 352 p. (Guys read) (hardback) $16.99

Grades: 4 5 6 7 8   **S C**

1. Short stories 2. Science fiction 3. Fantasy fiction

ISBN 0061963801; 9780061963797; 9780061963803

LC 2013021863

This book, edited by Jon Scieszka, is the fourth Guys Read collection of science fiction short stories. It "is anchored by Ray Bradbury's 1946 'Frost and Fire,' about colonists stranded for generations on a planet so harsh that the average life span is less than two weeks." Other topics include "unsuccessful alien invasions of Earth to Tom Angleberger's tale of smart clothes in rebellion, an eerie ghost story from Kenneth Oppel and . . . a 'girl in armor' episode from Shannon Hale." (Kirkus Reviews)

"Though most of the tales here are entertaining and 'mind-expandingly fun,' Shusterman's and Bradbury's especially stand out as intriguing, suspenseful, and thought-provoking." Horn Book

★ **Outside** rules; short stories about nonconformist youth. edited, with an introduction by Claire Robson. Persea Books 2007 178p pa $9.95

Grades: 7 8 9 10   **S C**

1. Short stories

ISBN 0-89255-316-2; 978-0-89255-316-7

LC 2006-22548

An anthology of fourteen short stories about youth who do not quite fit in because they are too brainy, unathletic, poor, the "wrong" religion, emotionally fragile, from non-traditional families, not model-thin, or simply bent on following a unique path.

"The collection is broadly multicultural, and the stories are consistently insightful, original, and discussion provoking in addition to being well written." Bull Cent Child Books

Paulsen, Gary

Paintings from the cave; three novellas. Wendy Lamb Books 2011 161p $15.99; lib bdg $18.99

Grades: 4 5 6 7   **S C**

1. Short stories 2. Art -- Fiction 3. Dogs -- Fiction 4. Violence -- Fiction 5. Homeless persons -- Fiction

ISBN 978-0-385-74684-7; 978-0-385-90921-1 lib bdg; 978-0-375-89743-6 e-book

LC 2011016287

"These novellas portray an unflinching look at children who have endured neglectful and abusive homes and are surviving on their own. The atmospheric first tale, 'Man of the Iron Heads,' is narrated by Jake, a boy of about 11, who hides from the local gang until he finds the courage to outsmart its violent leader. 'Jo-Jo the Dog-Faced Girl' presents a lonely girl with three adopted dogs who finds acceptance in befriending a girl with leukemia. Finally, 'Erik's Rules' celebrates the power of art and is told by Jamie, the younger of two homeless brothers, whose unstable existence changes after a chance encounter with a friendly volunteer at the animal shelter. By incorporating the solace found in dogs, art, libraries, and new friends into these tales of heartache and redemption, Paulsen provides his readers with hope of a better life." SLJ

Peck, Richard

Past perfect, present tense: new and collected stories. Dial Bks. 2004 177p hardcover o.p. pa $6.99
Grades: 7 8 9 10 11 12   S C
1. Short stories
ISBN 0-8037-2998-7; 0-14-240537-X pa
LC 2003-10904
A collection of short stories, including two previously unpublished ones, that deal with the way things could be.
"The stories perfectly highlight Peck's range and expertise at characterization. Almost every one is a superb read-aloud. . . . This superior collection is a must for every library." SLJ

★ Pick-up game; a full day of full court. edited by Marc Aronson & Charles R. Smith Jr. Candlewick Press 2011 170p il $15.99; pbk. $6.99
Grades: 7 8 9 10   S C
1. Short stories 2. Basketball -- Fiction 3. New York (N.Y.) -- Fiction
ISBN 0-7636-4562-1; 978-0-7636-4562-5; 9780763660680
A series of short stories by such authors as Walter Dean Myers, Rita Williams-Garcia, and Joseph Bruchac, interspersed with poems and photographs, provides different perspectives on a game of streetball played one steamy July day at the West 4th Street court in New York City known as The Cage.
"This anthology squeaks out a win. . . . Sharp-elbow action alternates with an almost spiritual grace." Booklist

Pierce, Tamora

★ Young warriors; stories of strength. edited by Tamora Pierce and Josepha Sherman. Random House 2005 312p hardcover o.p. pa $9.99
Grades: 7 8 9 10   S C
1. Short stories 2. Fantasy fiction
ISBN 0-375-82962-8; 978-0-375-82962-8; 0-375-82963-6 pa; 978-0-375-82963-5 pa
LC 2004-16432
This is a "collection of fifteen fantasy and alternative history stories featuring war and warriors. . . . Grades seven to twelve." (Bull Cent Child Books)
"This timely and appealing anthology will surely help swell the ranks of teenage fantasy readers." SLJ

Poe, Edgar Allan

Edgar Allan Poe's tales of death and dementia; illustrated by Gris Grimly. Atheneum Books for Young Readers 2009 136p il $18.99
Grades: 7 8 9 10   S C
1. Short stories 2. Horror fiction
ISBN 978-1-4169-5025-7; 1-4169-5025-7
LC 2009003056
"Four of Poe's morbid short stories are adapted for teens in this heavily illustrated presentation: 'The Tell-Tale Heart,' 'The System of Dr. Tarr and Professor Fether,' 'The Oblong Box,' and 'The Facts in the Case of M. Valdemar.' Grimly intersperses his horror-infused ink-and-watercolor cartoon art throughout Poe's putrid prose. The effect is an offering

that bridges graphic and traditional print formats. Great for readers who adore the gothic and the gruesome." SLJ

Edgar Allan Poe's tales of mystery and madness; illustrated by Gris Grimley. Atheneum Books for Young Readers 2004 135p il $17.95
Grades: 8 9 10 11 12   S C
1. Short stories 2. Horror fiction
ISBN 0-689-84837-4
LC 2003-10565
"With high-production values and gothic sensibilities thoroughly reflected in both text and art, this is an essential purchase for libraries. Adults can use it to lead young people to some great literature; readers will pluck it off the shelves themselves for creepy, entertaining fun." Booklist

Priestley, Chris

Uncle Montague's tales of terror; [by] Chris Priestley; illustrations by David Roberts. Bloomsbury Children's Books 2007 238p il $12.95
Grades: 5 6 7 8 9   S C
1. Short stories 2. Horror fiction 3. Uncles -- Fiction 4. Storytelling -- Fiction
ISBN 978-1-59990-118-3; 1-59990-118-8
"Ghosts, demons, jinns, and deadly trees populate these 10 chilly short stories set in the late 19th century, with the language and black-and-white illustrations capturing the feel of Victorian times. Young Edgar hears these tales while visiting his eccentric Uncle Montague, and each one is connected to a strange object in his uncle's study. . . . An enjoyable collection with enough creepy atmosphere (and some gruesome action) to hold readers' attention." SLJ

Rice, David

Crazy loco; stories about growing up Chicano in southern Texas. Dial Books for Young Readers 2001 135p hardcover o.p. pa $6.99
Grades: 7 8 9 10 11 12   S C
1. Short stories 2. Texas -- Fiction 3. Mexican Americans -- Fiction
ISBN 0-8037-2598-1; 0-14-250056-9 pa
LC 00-59042
A collection of nine stories about Mexican American kids growing up in the Rio Grande Valley of southern Texas.
"Two great strengths of these stories are the pitch-perfect sense for the speech and thought patterns of teens and the vivid depiction of the daily lives of Mexican-Americans in Texas's Rio Grande Valley." SLJ

Rowling, J. K.

The tales of Beedle the Bard; translated from the ancient runes by Hermione Granger; commentary by Albus Dumbledore; introduction, notes, and illustrations by J.K. Rowling. Arthur A. Levine 2008 111p il $12.99
Grades: 5 6 7 8 9 10 11 12   S C
1. Fairy tales 2. Short stories 3. Magic -- Fiction
ISBN 978-0-545-12828-5; 0-545-12828-5
A collection of tales from the world of Harry Potter.
"The introduction is captivating . . . [and] the tales themselves are entertaining. . . . Rowling is at the top of

her game as a superb storyteller, providing her legions of fans with an enchanting collection of wizard folklore." Voice Youth Advocates

San Souci, Robert

★ **Dare** to be scared; thirteen stories to chill and thrill. illustrations by David Ouimet. Cricket Bks. 2003 159p il $15.95

Grades: 4 5 6 7   S C

1. Short stories 2. Horror fiction

ISBN 0-8126-2688-5

LC 2002-152827

"With crisp, straightforward delivery and some intriguing endings, these 13 tales are great fun for young readers who like to be spooked." Booklist

Dare to be scared 4; thirteen more tales of terror. [by] Robert D. San Souci; illustrations by David Ouimet. Cricket Books 2009 275p il $17.95

Grades: 4 5 6 7   S C

1. Short stories 2. Horror fiction

ISBN 978-0-8126-2754-1; 0-8126-2754-7

LC 2009018490

"These deliciously shivery tales are perfect for campfire spookiness or as Halloween read-alouds. As in the previous books in the series, San Souci relies heavily on folklore and urban legends, giving the stories an even more chilling impact. . . . Strong themes such as death and murder are prevalent throughout. Ouimet's dark illustrations are paired perfectly with this creepy collection." SLJ

Haunted houses; [by] Robert D. San Souci; illustrated by Kelly Murphy and Antoine Revoy. Henry Holt 2010 276p il (Are you scared yet?) $16.99

Grades: 4 5 6 7   S C

1. Ghost stories 2. Short stories 3. Horror fiction

ISBN 978-0-8050-8750-5; 0-8050-8750-8

LC 2009-50763

"These 10 spooky stories include a classic Halloween scare: visitors get their admission fee of $25 back if they make it to the top floor of a haunted house—but can they? In another, the primary occupant of a dollhouse is a ghost of a child who needs help moving from one consciousness to another. . . . The stories are well paced and satisfyingly startling. . . . This book won't stay on the shelves for long. Murphy and Revoy's black-and-white illustrations heighten the fright factor, making San Souci's collection even more riveting." SLJ

Scary stories; illustrations by Barry Moser; introduction by Peter Glassman. Chronicle Books 2006 184p il $16.95

Grades: 6 7 8 9   S C

1. Short stories 2. Horror fiction

ISBN 978-0-8118-5414-6; 0-8118-5414-0

LC 2005025226

"A collection of 20 previously published stories, some by well-known writers of horror such as Stephen King and H. P. Lovecraft, others by authors not generally associated with the genre, like Winston Churchill. Each selection in-

cludes a chilling black-and-white engraving, often placed near the end of the story for maximum effect." SLJ

Sedgwick, Marcus

★ **Midwinterblood**; Marcus Sedgwick. Roaring Brook Press 2013 272 p. (hardcover) $17.99

Grades: 7 8 9 10 11 12   S C

1. Reincarnation -- Fiction 2. Love stories 3. Love -- Fiction 4. Islands -- Fiction 5. Scandinavia -- Fiction

ISBN 1596438002; 9781596438002

LC 2012013302

Printz Award Winner (2014)

Author Marcus Sedgwick presents seven stories about "an archaeologist who unearths a mysterious artifact, an airman who finds himself far from home, a painter, a ghost, a vampire, and a Viking." The stories "take place on the remote Scandinavian island of Blessed where a curiously powerful plant that resembles a dragon grows. . . . What secrets lurk beneath the surface of this idyllic countryside? And what might be powerful enough to break the cycle of midwinterblood?" (Publisher's note)

Shards and Ashes; edited by Melissa Marr and Kelley Armstrong; with additional stories by Veronica Roth, Kami Garcia, Margaret Stohl and more. Harpercollins Childrens Books 2013 x, 369 p.p (ebook) $7.99; (hardcover) $17.99

Grades: 7 8 9 10   S C

1. Science fiction 2. Dystopian fiction 3. Apocalyptic fiction

ISBN 9780062098474; 0062098462; 9780062098467

This book, edited by Melissa Marr and Kelley Armstrong, offers nine science fiction short stories. "The world is gone, destroyed by human, ecological, or supernatural causes. Survivors dodge chemical warfare and cruel gods; they travel the reaches of space and inhabit underground caverns. Their enemies are disease, corrupt corporations, and one another; their resources are few and their courage is tested." (Publisher's note)

Shattered: stories of children and war; edited by Jennifer Armstrong. Knopf 2002 166p hardcover o.p. pa $6.50

Grades: 7 8 9 10   S C

1. War stories 2. Short stories

ISBN 0-375-81112-5; 0-440-23765-3 pa

LC 2001-18609

"These selections will make teens cry, will make them angry, but most of all they will make them think." SLJ

★ **Shelf** life: stories by the book; edited by Gary Paulsen. Simon & Schuster Bks. for Young Readers 2003 173p $16.95

Grades: 5 6 7 8   S C

1. Short stories 2. Books and reading -- Fiction

ISBN 0-689-84180-9

LC 2002-66901

Ten short stories in which the lives of young people in different circumstances are changed by their encounters with books

"Covering almost every genre of fiction, including mystery, SF, fantasy and realism, these well-crafted stories by familiar authors offer sharply drawn characterizations and intriguing premises." Publ Wkly

Shusterman, Neal

Darkness creeping; twenty twisted tales. Puffin Books 2007 291p pa $7.99

Grades: 5 6 7 8   S C

1. Short stories 2. Horror fiction

ISBN 0-14-240721-6

"The author takes a walk on the dark side in this collection of spooky stories, some old, some new, all delightfully creepy. He knows his audience, providing enough horrific touches to appeal to the most challenging readers—those hard-to-reach middle school boys. Each story is introduced with a brief statement describing where he got the idea." Voice Youth Advocates

★ **Sideshow**; ten original tales of freaks, illusionists, and other matters odd and magical. edited by Deborah Noyes. Candlewick Press 2009 199p il $16.99

Grades: 7 8 9 10   S C

1. Short stories

ISBN 978-0-7636-3752-1; 0-7636-3752-1

LC 2008-37420

"This is a masterpiece of 10 short stories by world-class authors. Contributors include David Almond, Annette Curtis Klause, and Vivian Vande Velde. . . . Not all of the stories are traditional prose; several are graphic renditions, including Matt Phelan's masterfully drawn 'Jargo!' . . . Suspending disbelief, readers of this fantastic anthology may start investing in psychics and sleeping with the light on." SLJ

Sleator, William

★ **Oddballs**; stories. Dutton Children's Bks. 1993 134p hardcover o.p. pa $5.99

Grades: 6 7 8 9 10   S C

1. Short stories 2. Friendship -- Fiction 3. Family life -- Fiction

ISBN 0-525-45057-2; 0-14-037438-8 pa

LC 92-27666

A collection of stories based on experiences from the author's youth and peopled with an unusual assortment of family and friends.

"Fresh, funny, and slightly gross, the quasi-autobiographical glimpses will grab the reader's attention." Horn Book Guide

Soto, Gary

★ **Baseball** in April, and other stories; 10th anniversary ed; Harcourt Brace Jovanovich 2000 111p $16; pa $6

Grades: 5 6 7 8   S C

1. Short stories 2. California -- Fiction 3. Mexican Americans -- Fiction

ISBN 0-15-202573-1; 0-15-202567-7 pa

A reissue of the title first published 1990

A collection of eleven short stories focusing on the everyday adventures of Hispanic young people growing up in Fresno, California

Each story "gets at the heart of some aspect of growing up. The insecurities, the embarrassments, the triumphs, the inequities of it all are chronicled with wit and charm. Soto's characters ring true and his knowledge of, and affection for, their shared Mexican-American heritage is obvious and infectious." Voice Youth Advocates

★ **Help** wanted; stories. by Gary Soto. Harcourt 2005 216p $17; pa $6.95

Grades: 6 7 8 9   S C

1. Short stories 2. California -- Fiction 3. Mexican Americans -- Fiction

ISBN 0-15-205201-1; 978-0-15-205663-6 pa

LC 2004-7510

"The stories are sometimes funny, often poignant, and occasionally provocative." Booklist

"Ten original short stories about Mexican-American teens in central California. The fundamental theme of 'needing help' is the common thread among the stories, which range from the satirical to the peculiar to the humorous to the sad." SLJ

Hey 13! Holiday House 2011 197p $16.95

Grades: 6 7 8 9   S C

1. Short stories

ISBN 978-0-8234-2395-8; 0-8234-2395-6

LC 2011007709

A collection of thirteen short stories about the ups and downs of being thirteen years old.

"The author's skill and the short story format are both well utilized. . . . This title offers both comfort and fun for tween readers." Booklist

★ **Local** news. Harcourt Brace Jovanovich 1993 148p hardcover o.p. pa $5.95

Grades: 5 6 7 8   S C

1. Short stories 2. California -- Fiction 3. Mexican Americans -- Fiction

ISBN 0-15-248117-6; 0-15-204695-X pa

LC 92-37905

A collection of thirteen short stories about the everyday lives of Mexican American young people in California's Central Valley

"These stories resonate with integrity, verve, and compassion." Horn Book

Spinelli, Jerry

The **library** card. Scholastic 1997 148p pa $4.99

Grades: 4 5 6 7   S C

1. Short stories 2. Books and reading -- Fiction

ISBN 0-590-38633-6

LC 96-18412

"A library card is the magical object common to each of these four stories in which a budding street thug, a television addict, a homeless orphan, and a lonely girl are all transformed by the power and the possibilities that await them within the walls of the public library. Spinelli's characters . . . are unusual and memorable; his writing both humorous and convincing." Horn Book Guide

Starry-eyed; 16 stories that steal the spotlight. edited by Ted Michael and Josh Pultz. Running Press Teens 2013 400 p. $9.95

Grades: 7 8 9 10 11 12   S C

1. Performing arts 2. Actors -- Fiction 3. Singers -- Fiction

ISBN 0762449497; 9780762449491

LC 2013940578

Editors Ted Michael and Josh Pultz present a "collection of fictional short stories [that] highlight the struggles, hopes, failures, and triumphs of young aspiring singers, dancers, actors, actresses, and performers. While these characters may feel out of place during their everyday lives, they are able to find a home onstage and in rehearsals. Woven throughout the anthology are personal anecdotes from several of today's most celebrated performers of stage, screen, and television." (Publisher's note)

★ **Steampunk**! an anthology of fantastically rich and strange stories. edited by Kelly Link and Gavin J. Grant. Candlewick Press 2011 432p pbk. $12.99

Grades: 8 9 10 11 12   S C

1. Short stories 2. Fantasy fiction

ISBN 0763657972; 9780763657970

LC 2010040742

In this collection of short stories edited by Kelly Link and Gavin J. Grant "fourteen [authors] of speculative fiction, including two graphic storytellers, embrace the [steampunk] genre's established themes and refashion them in surprising ways and settings as diverse as Appalachia, ancient Rome, future Australia, and alternate California." (Publisher's note)

"Veteran editors Link and Grant serve up a delicious mix of original stories from 14 skilled writers and artists. . . . Chockful of gear-driven automatons, looming dirigibles, and wildly implausible time machines, these often baroque, intensely anachronistic tales should please steampunks of all ages." Publ Wkly

★ **Talking** leaves; contemporary native American short stories. introduced and edited by Craig Lesley; associate editor, Katheryn Stavrakis. Dell 1991 xxvi, 385p pa $16.95

Grades: 8 9 10 11 12 Adult   S C

1. Short stories 2. Native Americans -- Fiction

ISBN 0-385-31272-5

LC 92-139334

This anthology includes contributions by such authors as Louise Erdrich, Diane Glancy, Michael Dorris, N. Scott Momaday, Paula Gunn Allen, and Mary Tallmountain

"All these stories have a strong sense of person and place and engagingly inform of the Native American condition." Libr J

Tan, Shaun

★ **Lost** & found; 3 by Shaun Tan. Arthur A. Levine Books 2011 un il $21.99

Grades: 5 6 7 8   S C

1. Short stories

ISBN 978-0-545-22924-1; 0-545-22924-3

LC 2010030936

This book comprises three previously published stories by the Australian author-illustrator "In 'The Red Tree,' a young girl moves listlessly through her day with a sense of dreadful ennui that escalates with each page turn . . . until finally finding some hope at the end. In 'The Lost Thing,' a young boy discovers a most peculiar object and dutifully tries to find a proper home for it. . . . Finally, 'The Rabbits' (with a text by John Marsden) is a colonization fable, as rabbits invade and populate a new land, overwhelming the native animal population and severely altering the landscape. . . . Intermediate, middle school." (Horn Book)

"'The Red Tree' follows a solitary girl through a single, not very good day, exploring her feelings as they shift from disappointment and confusion to alienation and despair. The spare, lyrical text provides an anchor for Tan's large, moody, beautiful paintings. 'The Lost Thing' is a more upbeat tale of a boy who discovers an unusual object and then must decide what to do with it. Freedom and imagination are the themes in this story, and here the art includes fascinating and sometimes humorous bits of technical drawings. The prose of John Marsden's 'The Rabbits,' an allegory about imperialism, is so simple and melodic that it verges on poetry. The artist emphasizes the invasive foreignness of the rabbits by dressing them in baroque uniforms, drawing mystifying, gigantic machines and buildings for them to build and deploy in their inexorable drive to dominate." SLJ

★ **Tales** from outer suburbia. Arthur A. Levine Books 2009 92p il $19.99

Grades: 7 8 9 10   S C

1. Short stories 2. Suburban life -- Fiction

ISBN 0-545-05587-3; 978-0-545-05587-1

LC 2008-13784

This is a collection of fifteen illustrated stories set in the Australian suburbs. "Grades five to ten." (Bull Cent Child Books)

"The term 'suburbia' may conjure visions of vast and generic sameness, but in his hypnotic collection of 15 short stories and meditations, Tan does for the sprawling landscape what he did for the metropolis in The Arrival . . . . Ideas and imagery both beautiful and disturbing will linger." Publ Wkly

Taylor, Laini

★ **Lips** touch; three times. illustrations by Jim Di Bartolo. Arthur A. Levine Books 2009 265p il $17.99

Grades: 8 9 10 11 12   S C

1. Short stories 2. Kissing -- Fiction 3. Supernatural -- Fiction

ISBN 978-0-545-05585-7; 0-545-05585-7

LC 2009-5458

These three stories about kissing feature elements of the supernatural. "Grades nine to twelve." (Bull Cent Child Books)

"Taylor offers a powerful trio of tales, each founded upon the consequences of a kiss. . . . Contemporary Kizzy, who so yearns to be a normal, popular teenager that she forgets the rules of her Old Country upbringing and is seduced by a goblin in disguise; Anamique, living in British colonial India, silenced forever due to a spell cast upon her at birth; and Esmé, who at 14 discovers she is host to another—non-human—being. . . . Each is, in vividly distinctive fashion, a mesmerizing love story that comes to a satisfying but never predictable conclusion. Di Bartolo's illustrations provide tantalizing visual preludes to each tale." Publ Wkly

This family is driving me crazy; ten stories about surviving your family. edited by M. Jerry Weiss and Helen S. Weiss. G. P. Putnam's Sons 2009 224p $17.99

Grades: 6 7 8 9 10   **S C**

1. Short stories 2. Family life -- Fiction
ISBN 978-0-399-25040-8; 0-399-25040-9

LC 2009-06821

"Ten authors contribute short stories about family life. . . . The diversity of authors really provides something for everyone. . . . Enough gems are included here to make it a worthwhile purchase." Booklist

Tomo; friendship through fiction: an anthology of Japan teen stories. edited by Holly Thompson; cover and part-title illustrations by John Shelley. Stone Bridge Press 2012 383 p. (pbk.) $14.95

Grades: 7 8 9 10   **S C**

1. Japan -- Fiction 2. Short stories -- Collections 3. Teenagers -- Fiction 4. Friendship -- Fiction 5. Short stories 6. Japan -- Fiction 7. Children's stories, Japanese
ISBN 1611720060; 9781611720068

LC 2011051530

This book of short stories, edited by Holly Thompson, is an "anthology of authors with direct or indirect Japanese 'heritage or experience.' The 36 tales (all but six of which are new) were gathered as contributions to the relief effort for victims of the 2011 earthquake and tsunami." The various entries focus on stories about Japanese and half-Japanese teenagers in a variety of genres, including historical fiction, contemporary teenage drama, and fantasy. Stories are indexed by plot themes, including friendship, ghosts, super-powers, and family relationships. (Kirkus)

★ **Troll's** eye view; a book of villainous tales. Viking 2009 200p $16.99; pa $7.99

Grades: 5 6 7 8   **S C**

1. Fairy tales 2. Short stories
ISBN 978-0-670-06141-9; 0-670-06141-7; 978-0-14-241673-0 pa; 0-14-241673-8 pa

Everyone thinks they know the real story behind the villains in fairy tales—evil, no two ways about it. But the villains themselves beg to differ. In this anthology for younger readers, you'll hear from the Giant's wife (from Jack and the Beanstalk), Rumpelstiltskin, the oldest of the Twelve Dancing Princesses, and more.

"A mixed bag of funny, quirky, and downright creepy entries. . . . The collection is largely accessible and very enjoyable." Booklist

Under my hat; tales from the cauldron. edited by Jonathan Strahan. Random House 2012 415 p. (trade) $16.99

Grades: 5 6 7 8   **S C**

1. Short stories 2. Witches -- Fiction 3. Children's

stories
ISBN 0375868305; 9780375868047; 9780375868306; 9780375898815; 9780375968303

LC 2011031253

This book presents "eighteen short tales about witches. . . . Garth Nix's 'A Handful of Ashes' features a library and librarian. Delia Sherman's 'The Witch in the Woods' . . . [features] deer and bear shape-shifters and no small darkness. . . . Jane Yolen makes Hans Christian Andersen's life a tale itself." (Kirkus Reviews)

Under the moons of Mars; new adventures on Barsoom. edited by John Joseph Adams. Simon & Schuster Books for Young Readers 2012 xv, 352 p.p ill. (hardcover) $16.99

Grades: 6 7 8 9 10 11 12   **S C**

1. Science fiction 2. Adventure fiction 3. Short stories -- Collections 4. Short stories, American 5. Mars (Planet) -- Fiction 6. Science fiction, American 7. Carter, John (Fictitious character)
ISBN 9781442420304; 1442420294; 9781442420298; 9781442420311

LC 2011034391

This anthology, edited by John Joseph Adams, features several science fiction stories set in Edgar Rice Burroughs' Barsoom series. "Fans of all ages have marveled at the adventures of John Carter, an Earthman who suddenly finds himself in a strange new world. A century later, readers can enjoy this compilation of brand-new stories starring John Carter of Mars." (Publisher's note)

Under the weather; stories about climate change. edited by Tony Bradman. Frances Lincoln Children's 2009 215p pbk. $8.99; $16.95

Grades: 5 6 7 8   **S C**

1. Short stories 2. Greenhouse effect -- Fiction
ISBN 9781845079444; 1-84507-930-2; 978-1-84507-930-7

"Eight stories by a variety of authors attempt to make the facts about climate change and its global ramifications relevant to today's children. The majority of the selections are about youngsters enacting change and working toward solutions in tangible ways. For example, 'How to Build the Perfect Sandcastle' is about a Philippino boy who works to rebuild the coral reefs, which are dying due to the rise in ocean temperature. . . . Overall . . . this is a worthwhile effort that will appeal to children wanting to make a difference in their world as well as to teachers trying to make the scientific reality of climate change real to their students." SLJ

Vande Velde, Vivian

All Hallows' Eve; 13 stories. Harcourt 2006 225p $17

Grades: 7 8 9 10   **S C**

1. Short stories 2. Halloween -- Fiction 3. Supernatural -- Fiction
ISBN 978-0-15-205576-9; 0-15-205576-2

LC 2006-05439

Presents thirteen tales of Halloween horrors, including ghosts, vampires, and pranks gone awry.

"This mistress of the macabre draws readers in with her familiar conversational tone and easily recognizable situations . . . before skillfully shifting the narratives in unsettling, sometimes terrifying, directions. . . . Vande Velde's narrative tricks are a treat." Horn Book

★ **Being** dead; stories. Harcourt 2001 203p hardcover o.p. pa $6.95

Grades: 7 8 9 10   **S C**

1. Short stories 2. Horror fiction 3. Supernatural -- Fiction

ISBN 0-15-216320-4; 0-15-204912-6 pa

LC 00-12996

"Often humorous and sometimes evoking sympathy, this anthology will be enjoyed by lovers of mild horror as well as by those who like clever short stories." Voice Youth Advocates

Cloaked in red. Marshall Cavendish Children 2010 127p $15.99

Grades: 7 8 9 10   **S C**

1. Fairy tales 2. Short stories

ISBN 0-7614-5793-3; 978-0-7614-5793-0

LC 2009-51753

This book presents eight variations on the traditional tale of Little Red Riding Hood. "Grades five to eight." (Bull Cent Child Books)

The stories "blend wry contemporary commentary with fractured-fairy-tale elements, horror, and a subtle bit of sensuality. . . . The wacky tales can easily be used to inspire teens to make up versions of their own." Booklist

Visions: nineteen short stories by outstanding writers for young adults; edited by Donald R. Gallo. Delacorte Press 1987 228p hardcover o.p. pa $6.99

Grades: 7 8 9 10   **S C**

1. Short stories

ISBN 0-440-20208-6

LC 87-6787

"Information about the authors follows each of nineteen original short stories, most of them impressive examples of the genre, all of them written by established men and women. Among the familiar names: Joan Aiken, M.E. Kerr, Walter Dean Myers, Richard Peck. The tales are grouped under such headings as 'Adjustments' or 'Kinships,' and include both realistic and fanciful writing, most of the work being of fine quality and the rest only slightly less so." Bull Cent Child Books

Voices in first person; reflections on Latino identity. [edited by Lori Marie Carlson] Atheneum Books for Young Readers 2008 96p il $16.99

Grades: 6 7 8 9 10 11 12   **S C**

1. Short stories 2. American literature -- Hispanic American authors -- Collections

ISBN 978-1-4169-0635-3; 1-4169-0635-5

LC 2006-34161

A collection of brief fictional pieces about the experiences of Latinos in the United States, by such writers as Sandra Cisneros, Gary Soto, Oscar Hijuelos, and others.

"Carlson has drawn from both established and new writers, focusing on finding Latino voices that speak to contemporary readers. . . . This collection sparkles more than its predecessors because of its dynamic design, featuring black-and-white photographs and line illustrations incorporated with the text in a collage-like magazine layout." SLJ

★ **Welcome** to Bordertown; new stories and poems of the Borderlands. edited by Holly Black and Ellen Kushner; introduction by Terri Windling. Random House 2011 517p $19.99; lib bdg $22.99; e-book $19.99

Grades: 7 8 9 10   **S C**

1. Short stories 2. Fantasy fiction 3. Poetry -- Collections 4. Supernatural -- Fiction

ISBN 978-0-375-86705-7; 0-375-86705-8; 978-0-375-96705-4 lib bdg; 0-375-96705-2 lib bdg; 978-0-375-89745-0 e-book

LC 2010-35558

This collection of short stories and poems focuses on Bordertown, "a city on the border between our human world and the elfin realm. Runaway teens come from both sides of the border to find adventure, to find themselves. Elves play in rock bands and race down the street on spell-powered motorbikes. Human kids recreate themselves in the squats and clubs and artists' studios of Soho." (Publisher's note)

"This is punk-rock, DIY fantasy, full of harsh reality and incandescent magic . . . Many of the stories echo with loss and discomfort; standouts include 'Crossings' by Janni Lee Simner, a chilling look at the difference between dreams and reality, and 'A Tangle of Green Men,' Charles De Lint's heartbreaking examination of love, loss and life. Poems and songs (from Patricia A. McKillip, Neil Gaiman and Jane Yolen, among others) balance the fiction. . . . A masterful anthology." Kirkus

What are you afraid of? stories about phobias. edited by Donald R. Gallo. Candlewick Press 2006 189p $16.99

Grades: 6 7 8 9   **S C**

1. Short stories 2. Phobias -- Fiction

ISBN 0-7636-2654-6

LC 2004-62874

Presents ten short stories by well-known authors featuring teenagers with phobias, inluding fear of gaining weight, fear of clowns, and fear of cats.

"This is an excellent collection on a topic that holds a strange and fascinating allure." SLJ

Who do you think you are? stories of friends and enemies. selected by Hazel Rochman and Darlene Z. McCampbell. Little, Brown 1993 170p hardcover o.p. pa $9.99

Grades: 7 8 9 10   **S C**

1. Short stories 2. Friendship -- Fiction

ISBN 0-316-75320-3

LC 93-314

"Meticulously chosen and arranged, these works crystalize moments of vulnerability, sorrow and understanding; together, they serve as an excellent introduction to modern American writing." Publ Wkly

"Louise Erdrich, John Updike, Ray Bradbury, Joyce Carol Oates, Sandra Cisneros, Tim O'Brien, Richard Peck, and Maya Angelou are among the 15 writers represented in this anthology of stories [two prose excerpts and a poem] about friendship and loss of friendship." Booklist

You don't have a clue; Latino mystery stories for teens. [edited by Sarah Cortez] Pinata Books 2011 310p pa $16.95
Grades: 6 7 8 9 10   **S C**
1. Short stories 2. Hispanic Americans -- Fiction
ISBN 1-55885-692-7; 978-1-55885-692-9
                                            LC 2011-00117
These short stories are "set in schools and communities from New York City to Venice Beach, California." (Publisher's note) "Grades seven to ten." (Bull Cent Child Books)

You never did learn to knock; 14 stories about girls and their mothers. selected by Bel Mooney. Kingfisher 2006 254p pa $7.95
Grades: 7 8 9 10   **S C**
1. Short stories 2. Mother-daughter relationship -- Fiction
ISBN 0-7534-5877-2
In this collection of short stories about mothers and daughters "situations include adoption, girls manipulating their mothers, divorce, and terminal illness. . . . A solid, enjoyable collection due to its breezy style and content." SLJ

AUTHOR, TITLE, AND SUBJECT INDEX

This index to the books in the Classified Collection includes author, title, and subject entries; added entries for publishers' series, illustrators, joint authors, and editors of works entered under title; and name and subject cross-references; all arranged in one alphabet.

The number or symbol in bold face type at the end of each entry refers to the Dewey Decimal Classification or to the Fiction (Fic) or Story Collection (S C), or Easy Books (E) section where the main entry for the book will be found. Works classed in 92 will be found under the headings for the biographies' subject.

A & L do summer. Blazanin, J. **Fic**

10 inventors who changed the world. Gifford, C. **920**

10 kings & queens who changed the world. Gifford, C. **920**

The **10** p.m. question. De Goldi, K. **Fic**

10 plants that shook the world. Richardson, G. **630.9**

10,000 days of thunder. Caputo, P. **959.704**

100 hispanics you should know. Castro, I. A. **920**

100+ literacy lifesavers. Bacon, P. S. **428**

The **100-year-old** secret. Barrett, T. **Fic**

1001 cranes. Hirahara, N. **Fic**

The **101** best tropical fishes. Wood, K. **639.34**

101 essential tips [series]
Mills, D. Aquarium fish **639.34**

101 facts about bullying. Kevorkian, M. **302.3**

101 great bombers. **623.74**

101 great fighters. **623.74**

101 great tanks. **623.7**

101 great warships. **623.82**

101 great, ready-to-use book lists for children. Keane, N. J. **028.5**

101 great, ready-to-use book lists for teens. Keane, N. J. **028.5**

The 101 greatest weapons of all times [series]
101 great bombers **623.74**
101 great fighters **623.74**
101 great tanks **623.7**
101 great warships **623.82**

101 outstanding graphic novels. **741.5**

101 questions [series]
Brynie, F. H. 101 questions about food and digestion that have been eating at you . . . until now **612.3**
Brynie, F. H. 101 questions about muscles to stretch your mind and flex your brain **612.7**
Brynie, F. H. 101 questions about reproduction **612.6**
Brynie, F. H. 101 questions about sleep and dreams that kept you awake nights . . . until now **612.8**

101 questions about food and digestion that have been eating at you . . . until now. Brynie, F. H. **612.3**

101 questions about muscles to stretch your mind and flex your brain. Brynie, F. H. **612.7**

101 questions about reproduction. Brynie, F. H. **612.6**

101 questions about sleep and dreams that kept you awake nights . . . until now. Brynie, F. H. **612.8**

101 stories of the great ballets. **792.8**

101 success secrets for gifted kids. Fonseca, C. **155.45**

101 things you wish you'd invented--and some you wish no one had. Horne, R. **609**

101 ways to bug your friends and enemies. Wardlaw, L. **Fic**

101 ways to bug your teacher. Wardlaw, L. **Fic**

109 forgotten American heroes. Ying, C. **920**

12 things to do before you crash and burn. Proimos, J. **Fic**

13. **S**

13 American artists children should know. Finger, B. **709**

13 artists children should know. Wenzel, A. **709**

13 buildings children should know. Roeder, A. **720**

13 curses. Harrison, M. **Fic**

13 little blue envelopes. Johnson, M. **Fic**

13 photos children should know. Finger, B. **770**

13 planets. Aguilar, D. A. **523.2**

13 sculptures children should know. Wenzel, A. **731**

13 treasures. Harrison, M. **Fic**

13 Treasures Trilogy [series]
Harrison, M. 13 curses **Fic**

13 women artists children should know. Schumann, B. **709**

The **13th** sign. Tubb, K. O. **Fic**

The **14** fibs of Gregory K. Pincus, G. **Fic**

145th Street. Myers, W. D. **S**

The **15** lanthanides and the 15 actinides. Lew, K. **546**

1776. Kostyal, K. M. **973.3**

1898 to World War II. Hernandez, R. E. **305.8**

19 varieties of gazelle. Nye, N. S. **811**

The **1900s** decade in photos. Corrigan, J. **973.91**

The **1910s** decade in photos. Corrigan, J. **973.91**

The **1920s** and 1930s. McEvoy, A. **391**

The **1920s** decade in photos. Corrigan, J. **973.91**

The **1930s** decade in photos. Corrigan, J. **973.917**

The **1940s** decade in photos. Corrigan, J. **973.917**

1950S *See* Nineteen fifties

The **1950s** and 1960s. Rooney, A.   **391**

The **1950s** decade in photos. Corrigan, J.   **973.921**

1960S *See* Nineteen sixties

The **1960s** decade in photos. Corrigan, J.   **973.923**

1968. Kaufman, M. T.   **909.82**

The **1970s** decade in photos. Corrigan, J.   **973.924**

The **1980s** and 1990s. Clancy Steer, D.   **391**

The **1980s** decade in photos. Corrigan, J.   **973.927**

The **1990s** decade in photos. Corrigan, J.   **973.92**

20,000 leagues under the sea. Verne, J.   **Fic**

The **2000s** decade in photos. Corrigan, J.   **973.93**

2001: a space odyssey. Clarke, A. C.   **Fic**

The 20th century's most influential Hispanics [series]

  Kallen, S. A. Rigoberta Menchu, Indian rights activist   **92**

21st century debates [series]

  Fooks, L. The drug trade   **364.1**

21st Century skills innovation library. Makers as innovators [series]

  Soldering   **671.5**

21st-century counselors. Flath, C.   **362.2**

24 girls in 7 days. Bradley, A.   **Fic**

24/7 goes to war [series]

  DiConsiglio, J. Vietnam   **959.704**

  Dougherty, S. Pearl Harbor   **940.54**

  Johnson, J. Gettysburg   **973.7**

  Miller, T. D-Day   **940.54**

24/7, science behind the scenes [series]

  Brownlee, C. Cute, furry, and deadly   **614.4**

  Denega, D. Skulls and skeletons   **363.2**

  Tilden, T. E. L. Help! What's eating my flesh?   **614.4**

  Webber, D. Do you read me?   **363.2**

The **2nd** international cookbook for kids. Locricchio, M.   **641.5**

3 willows. Brashares, A.   **Fic**

3-D dinosaur. Woodward, J.   **567.9**

3-D human body. Walker, R.   **612**

3-D PHOTOGRAPHY *See* Three-dimensional photography

30 days to getting over the dork you used to call your boyfriend. Hantman, C.   **158**

365 more simple science experiments with everyday materials. Churchill, E. R.   **507.8**

The **39** clues. Watson, J.   **Fic**

The 39 clues [series]

  Park, L. S. Storm warning   **Fic**

  Riordan, R. The maze of bones   **Fic**

  Riordan, R. Vespers rising   **Fic**

  Watson, J. Beyond the grave   **Fic**

  Watson, J. In too deep   **Fic**

The **39** clues: Breakaway. Hirsch, J.   **Fic**

The 39 clues: unstoppable [series]

  Hirsch, J. The 39 clues: Breakaway   **Fic**

  Watson, J. The 39 clues   **Fic**

4-H CLUBS

  See also Agriculture -- Societies; Agriculture -- Study and teaching; Boys' clubs; Girls' clubs

4-H guide to digital photography. Johnson, D.   **775**

4-H guide to dog training and dog tricks. Rogers, T.   **636.7**

4-H guide to raising chickens. Kindschi, T.   **636.5**

4-H guide to training horses. Bowers, N.   **636.1**

42 miles. Zimmer, T. V.   **Fic**

46 science fair projects for the evil genius. Bonnet, R. L.   **507.8**

47. Mosley, W.   **Fic**

47 things you can do for the environment. Petronis, L.   **333.72**

5,000 miles to freedom. Fradin, J. B.   **326**

50 Cent (Musician), 1975-

  Playground   **Fic**

50 climate questions. Christie, P.   **551.609**

50 Questions [series]

  Christie, P. 50 climate questions   **551.609**

50 underwear questions.   **391.4**

500 great books for teens. Silvey, A.   **028.5**

7 days at the hot corner. Trueman, T.   **Fic**

The **7** professors of the Far North. Fardell, J.   **Fic**

8th grade superzero. Rhuday-Perkovich, O.   **Fic**

The **9** lives of Alexander Baddenfield.   **Fic**

90 miles to Havana. Flores-Gabis, E.   **Fic**

911: the book of help.   **810**

A

A to Z of American Indian women. Sonneborn, L.   **920.003**

A to Z of women in science and math. Yount, L.   **920.003**

The **A-Z** of health. Stoyles, P.   **616**

A. Philip Randolph and the African American labor movement. Miller, C. C.   **92**

Aaseng, Nathan

  Business builders in sweets and treats   **920**

  Construction: building the impossible   **624**

  Weird meat-eating plants   **583**

Abadzis, Nick

  Laika   **741.5**

ABANDONED CHILDREN

  Jocelyn, M. A home for foundlings   **362.7**

  Warren, A. Orphan train rider   **362.7**

ABANDONED CHILDREN

  See also Child welfare; Children

ABANDONED CHILDREN -- FICTION

  Gagnon, M. Don't Look Now   **Fic**

  Kinsey-Warnock, N. True colors   **Fic**

  Mister Max   **Fic**

  Pyron, B. The dogs of winter   **Fic**

  Turnage, S. Three times lucky   **Fic**

  Unsworth, T. The one safe place   **Fic**

L. 616.85

ADHESIVES

Knapp, B. J. Materials science 620.1

ADHESIVES

See also Materials

ADIRONDACK MOUNTAINS (N.Y.) -- FIC-TION

Auch, M. J. Guitar boy Fic

Bruchac, J. Bearwalker Fic

McGhee, A. All rivers flow to the sea Fic

ADJUSTMENT (PSYCHOLOGY)

See also Psychology

Adler, David A.

B. Franklin, printer 973.3

Don't talk to me about the war Fic

Frederick Douglass 92

Harriet Tubman and the Underground Railroad 973.7

Adler, Emily

Sweet 15 Fic

Adlington, L. J.

Cherry Heaven Fic

The diary of Pelly D Fic

Administering the school library media center. Morris, B. J. 027.8

ADMINISTRATION OF CRIMINAL JUSTICE

Jacobs, T. A. They broke the law, you be the judge 345

Rosaler, M. The devil on trial 345

See also Administration of justice; Criminal law

ADMINISTRATION OF JUSTICE

Jacobs, T. A. They broke the law, you be the judge 345

ADMIRALS

Bell, T. Nick of time Fic

Brager, B. L. John Paul Jones 92

Cooper, M. L. Hero of the high seas 92

Finkelstein, N. H. Three across 629.13

Ford, M. Birth of a warrior Fic

Ford, M. The Fire of Ares Fic

Ford, M. Legacy of blood Fic

Kirkpatrick, K. A. Snow baby 92

Lace, W. W. Sir Francis Drake 92

Lawlor, L. Dead reckoning Fic

Thimmesh, C. Girls think of everything 920

ADMIRALS

See also Military personnel; Navies

Adoff, Arnold

(ed) Hamilton, V. Virginia Hamilton: speeches, essays, and conversations 813

(ed) I am the darker brother 811

(ed) My black me 811

Adoff, Jaime

The song shoots out of my mouth 811

ADOLESCENCE

Bailey, J. Sex, puberty, and all that stuff 612.6

Bazelon, E. Sticks and stones 302.34

Burek Pierce, J. Sex, brains, and video games 027.62

Dunham, K. The girl's body book 613

Jukes, M. The guy book 305.235

Madaras, L. The what's happening to my body? book for boys 612.6

Madaras, L. The what's happening to my body? book for girls 612.6

Mar, J. The body book for boys 612.6

McCoy, K. The teenage body book 613

Pfeifer, K. G. American Medical Assocation boy's guide to becoming a teen 613

Shandler, S. Ophelia speaks 305.235

ADOLESCENCE -- FICTION

Anderson, J. D. Sidekicked Fic

Grossman, N. A world away Fic

Harrington, K. Sure signs of crazy Fic

Howe, J. Totally Joe Fic

Kinney, J. Diary of a wimpy kid Fic

Lee, H. To kill a mockingbird Fic

Strykowski, M. Call Me Amy Fic

ADOLESCENCE -- PSYCHOLOGY *See* Adolescent psychology

ADOLESCENT FATHERS *See* Teenage fathers

ADOLESCENT MOTHERS *See* Teenage mothers

ADOLESCENT PREGNANCY *See* Teenage pregnancy

ADOLESCENT PSYCHOLOGY

Bellenir, K. Mental health information for teens 616.89

Honos-Webb, L. The ADHD workbook for teens 616.85

Hugel, B. I did it without thinking 155.5

Mangan, T. How to feel good 305.23

Tarshis, T. P. Living with peer pressure and bullying 303.3

ADOLESCENT PSYCHOLOGY

See also Psychology

ADOLESCENTS *See* Teenagers

Adolf Hitler and Nazi Germany. Rice, E. 92

ADOPTED CHILDREN

Jansen, H. Over a thousand hills I walk with you Fic

Red butterfly Fic

Rhodes-Courter, A. M. Three little words 92

ADOPTED CHILDREN

See also Adoptees; Children

ADOPTED CHILDREN -- FICTION

Babbitt, N. The moon over High Street Fic

Turnage, S. Three times lucky Fic

ADOPTEES -- FICTION

Kadohata, C. Half a world away Fic

Peacock, C. A. Red thread sisters Fic

Adoption. 362.7

ADOPTION

AFRICAN AMERICAN ACTORS AND AC-
TRESSES *See* African American actors

The **African** American almanac. **305.8**

AFRICAN AMERICAN ART

Bolden, T. Wake up our souls **704**

AFRICAN AMERICAN ART

See also Art; Black art

AFRICAN AMERICAN ARTISTS

Art from her heart: folk artist Clementine Hunter **92**

Duggleby, J. Story painter: the life of Jacob Lawrence **759.13**

AFRICAN AMERICAN ARTISTS

See also Artists; Black artists

AFRICAN AMERICAN ARTS

Hill, L. C. Harlem stomp! **810**

Hillstrom, K. The Harlem Renaissance **810**

Robson, D. The Black arts movement **700**

AFRICAN AMERICAN ATHLETES

Brill, M. T. Marshall Major Taylor **92**

Burlingame, J. Jesse Owens **92**

Gigliotti, J. Jesse Owens **92**

Green, M. Y. A strong right arm: the story of Mamie Peanut Johnson **92**

McCormack, S. Cool Papa Bell **92**

McDougall, C. Jesse Owens **92**

Micklos, J. Muhammad Ali **92**

Myers, W. D. The greatest: Muhammad Ali **92**

Payment, S. Buck Leonard **92**

Robinson, S. Promises to keep: how Jackie Robinson changed America **92**

Roselius, J. C. Magic Johnson **92**

Smith, C. R. Twelve rounds to glory: the story of Muhammad Ali **92**

Sullivan, G. Knockout!: a photobiography of boxer Joe Louis **92**

Twemlow, N. Josh Gibson **92**

Williams, V. Venus & Serena **92**

Wukovits, J. F. Jackie Robinson and the integration of baseball **92**

AFRICAN AMERICAN ATHLETES

See also Athletes; Black athletes

AFRICAN AMERICAN AUTHORS

Abrams, D. Ernest J. Gaines **92**

Fradin, D. B. Zora! **813**

Hart, J. Native son: the story of Richard Wright **92**

Hinton, K. Jacqueline Woodson **92**

Levy, D. Richard Wright **92**

Litwin, L. B. Zora Neale Hurston **92**

Lyons, M. E. Sorrow's kitchen **92**

Myers, W. D. Bad boy **813**

No crystal stair **Fic**

Poetry from the masters: the pioneers **811**

Sapet, K. Rhythm and folklore **92**

Sickels, A. Walter Dean Myers **92**

AFRICAN AMERICAN BASEBALL PLAYERS

See also Baseball players

AFRICAN AMERICAN BUSINESSPEOPLE

Bundles, A. P. Madam C.J. Walker **92**

Ransom, C. F. Maggie L. Walker **92**

AFRICAN AMERICAN BUSINESSPEOPLE

See also Black businesspeople; Businesspeople

AFRICAN AMERICAN CHILDREN

Bolden, T. Tell all the children our story **305.8**

Flake, S. G. You don't even know me **808.8**

Mayer, R. H. When the children marched **323.1**

Partridge, E. Marching for freedom **323.1**

AFRICAN AMERICAN CHILDREN

See also Black children; Children

AFRICAN AMERICAN CHILDREN -- FICTION

Gone Crazy in Alabama **Fic**

Williams-Garcia, R. P.S. Be Eleven **Fic**

AFRICAN AMERICAN CIVIL RIGHTS WORKERS

March Book Two **92**

AFRICAN AMERICAN DANCERS

See also African Americans; Dancers

AFRICAN AMERICAN EDUCATORS

Hinman, B. Eternal vigilance: the story of Ida B. Wells-Barnett **92**

Washington, B. T. Up from slavery **92**

AFRICAN AMERICAN EDUCATORS

See also African Americans; Educators

AFRICAN AMERICAN FIGHTER PILOTS -- BIOGRAPHY

Greenly, L. Eugene Bullard **92**

African American folklore. Currie, S. **398.2**

African American history [series]

Howse, J. The Civil War **973.7**

Szulhan, R. Contemporary achievements **305.8**

African American history and culture [series]

The Black experience in America **305.8**

African American inventors. Currie, S. **500**

AFRICAN AMERICAN INVENTORS

See also African Americans; Inventors

Young, J. C. Inspiring African-American inventors **920**

AFRICAN AMERICAN INVENTORS -- BIOGRAPHY

Currie, S. African American inventors **500**

Davidson, T. African American scientists and inventors **509.2**

AFRICAN AMERICAN JOURNALISTS -- BIOGRAPHY

Hunter-Gault, C. To the mountaintop! **070.92**

AFRICAN AMERICAN LEGISLATORS

March Book Two **92**

AFRICAN AMERICAN LIBRARIANS

See also Black librarians; Librarians

AFRICAN AMERICAN MEN -- BIOGRAPHY

Moore, W. Discovering Wes Moore **975.2**

Pinkney, A. D. Hand in hand **973**

African American millionaires. Sullivan, O. R. **920**

AFRICAN AMERICAN MUSIC

Cooper, M. L. Slave spirituals and the Jubilee Singers **782.421**

Ellis, R. M. With a banjo on my knee **787.8**

Mendelson, A. A. American R & B **781.644**

Turck, M. Freedom song **323.1**

AFRICAN AMERICAN MUSIC

See also Black music; Music

African American musicians. Tate, E. E. **920**

AFRICAN AMERICAN MUSICIANS

See also Black musicians; Musicians

AFRICAN AMERICAN MUSICIANS

Gelfand, D. E. Jimi Hendrix **92**

Golus, C. Tupac Shakur **92**

Harris, A. R. Tupac Shakur **92**

Partridge, K. Louis Armstrong **92**

Pratt, M. Michael Jackson **92**

Stein, S. Duke Ellington **92**

Tate, E. E. African American musicians **920**

Willett, E. Jimi Hendrix **92**

Rice, E. Charlie Parker **788.7**

AFRICAN AMERICAN MUSICIANS -- POETRY

Lewis, J. P. Black cat bone **811**

AFRICAN AMERICAN NOVELISTS -- BIOGRAPHY

Kramer, B. Toni Morrison **813**

AFRICAN AMERICAN PAINTERS -- BIOGRAPHY

Duggleby, J. Story painter: the life of Jacob Lawrence **759.13**

AFRICAN AMERICAN PILOTS

De Capua, S. The Tuskegee airmen **940.54**

African American Poetry. **811**

AFRICAN AMERICAN POETRY *See* American poetry -- African American authors

AFRICAN AMERICAN POTTERS

Cheng, A. Etched in clay **92**

African American religious leaders. Haskins, J. **920**

AFRICAN AMERICAN SAILORS

Sheinkin, S. The Port Chicago 50 **940.54**

AFRICAN AMERICAN SCIENTISTS

Davidson, T. African American scientists and inventors **509.2**

African American scientists and inventors. Davidson, T. **509.2**

AFRICAN AMERICAN SINGERS

Cartlidge, C. Jennifer Hudson **92**

Duggleby, J. Uh huh!: the story of Ray Charles **92**

Freedman, R. The voice that challenged a nation **92**

Jones, V. G. Marian Anderson **92**

Slavicek, L. C. Paul Robeson **92**

Stone, T. L. Ella Fitzgerald **92**

Woog, A. Ray Charles and the birth of soul **92**

AFRICAN AMERICAN SINGERS

See also African Americans; Singers

AFRICAN AMERICAN SOLDIERS

Blair, M. W. Liberty or death **973.3**

DeFord, D. H. African Americans during the Civil War **973.7**

Howse, J. The Civil War **973.7**

Reis, R. A. African Americans and the Civil War **973.7**

Stone, T. L. Courage has no color, the true story of the Triple Nickles **940.54**

Trudeau, N. A. Like men of war **973.7**

AFRICAN AMERICAN SOLDIERS -- FICTION

Myers, W. D. Fallen angels **Fic**

Myers, W. D. Invasion! **Fic**

AFRICAN AMERICAN SONGS *See* African American music

AFRICAN AMERICAN STUDENTS -- ALABAMA -- BIRMINGHAM -- HISTORY -- 20TH CENTURY

Levinson, C. Y. We've got a job **323.1**

AFRICAN AMERICAN WOMEN

Allen, T. B. Harriet Tubman, secret agent **92**

Angelou, M. Maya Angelou **811**

Bolden, T. Maritcha **92**

Bolden, T. Searching for Sarah Rector **92**

Butler, M. G. Sojourner Truth **92**

Freedman, R. The voice that challenged a nation **92**

Jemison, M. C. Find where the wind goes **92**

Let it shine **920**

Parks, R. Rosa Parks: my story **976.1**

AFRICAN AMERICAN WOMEN

See also Black women; Women

AFRICAN AMERICAN WOMEN -- BIOGRAPHY

Adler, D. A. Harriet Tubman and the Underground Railroad **973.7**

Fradin, D. B. Zora! **813**

Horn, G. M. Sojourner Truth **305.5**

Mullenbach, C. Double victory **940.53**

Woodson, J. Brown girl dreaming **92**

AFRICAN AMERICAN WOMEN -- CIVIL RIGHTS -- HISTORY -- 20TH CENTURY

Mullenbach, C. Double victory **940.53**

AFRICAN AMERICAN WOMEN -- HEALTH AND HYGIENE

Fornay, A. Born beautiful **646.7**

AFRICAN AMERICAN WOMEN -- OKLAHOMA -- CREEK COUNTY -- BIOGRAPHY

Bolden, T. Searching for Sarah Rector **92**

AFRICAN AMERICAN WOMEN AEROSPACE ENGINEERS -- UNITED STATES -- BIOGRAPHY

Aerospace engineer Aprille Ericsson **629.409**

AFRICAN AMERICAN WOMEN AUTHORS -- BIOGRAPHY -- POETRY

Woodson, J. Brown girl dreaming **92**

DeMallie, H. R. Behind enemy lines   **940.54**

Earl, S. Benjamin O. Davis, Jr.   **92**

Finkelstein, N. H. Three across   **629.13**

Giblin, J. Charles A. Lindbergh   **629.13**

Tunnell, M. Candy bomber   **92**

AIR GUITAR

See also Guitars

AIR PILOTS

Brown, J. K. Amelia Earhart   **92**

DeMallie, H. R. Behind enemy lines   **940.54**

Finkelstein, N. H. Three across   **629.13**

Fleming, C. Amelia lost: the life and disappearance
of Amelia Earhart   **92**

Gherman, B. Anne Morrow Lindbergh   **92**

Giblin, J. Charles A. Lindbergh   **629.13**

Hense, M. How fighter pilots use math   **629.13**

MacColl, M. Promise the night   **Fic**

Micklos, J. Unsolved: what really happened to
Amelia Earhart?   **92**

Saint-Exupery, A. d. The little prince   **Fic**

Tanaka, S. Amelia Earhart   **92**

Tunnell, M. Candy bomber   **92**

AIR PILOTS

See also Aeronautics

AIR PILOTS -- FICTION

Black dove, white raven   **Fic**

AIR PIRACY *See* Hijacking of airplanes

AIR POLLUTION

Gardner, R. Air   **533**

Rapp, V. Protecting Earth's air quality   **363.7**

AIR POLLUTION

See also Environmental health; Pollution

AIR POLLUTION -- MEASUREMENT

See also Measurement

AIR POWER

See also Military aeronautics

AIR ROUTES *See* Aeronautics

AIR TRAVEL

See also Transportation; Travel; Voyages and
travels

AIR WARFARE *See* Military aeronautics; Military
airplanes

AIR-CUSHION VEHICLES

See also Vehicles

AIR-SHIPS *See* Airships

Airborn. Oppel, K.   **Fic**

Airborne: a photobiography of Wilbur and Orville
Wright. Collins, M.   **92**

AIRCRAFT *See* Airplanes; Airships; Balloons;
Gliders (Aeronautics); Helicopters

AIRCRAFT ACCIDENTS

Lace, W. W. The Hindenburg disaster of 1937 **363.1**

Sherman, J. The Hindenburg disaster   **363.1**

Vogel, C. G. The man who flies with birds **598**

AIRCRAFT ACCIDENTS -- FICTION

Brody, J. Unremembered   **Fic**

AIRCRAFT CARRIERS

See also Military aeronautics; Warships

AIRCRAFT INDUSTRY EXECUTIVES

Carson, M. K. The Wright Brothers for kids **629.13**

Collins, M. Airborne: a photobiography of Wilbur
and Orville Wright   **92**

Crompton, S. The Wright brothers   **92**

Finkelstein, N. H. Three across   **629.13**

Freedman, R. The Wright brothers: how they invented the airplane   **92**

Airhead. Cabot, M.   **Fic**

AIRLINES -- HIJACKING *See* Hijacking of airplanes

Airman. Colfer, E.   **Fic**

AIRMEN -- FICTION

Lynch, C. Casualties of war   **Fic**

The **airplane.** Faber, H.   **629.133**

AIRPLANE CRASHES *See* Aircraft accidents

AIRPLANE ENGINES

See also Engines

AIRPLANE HIJACKING *See* Hijacking of airplanes

AIRPLANE PILOTS *See* Air pilots

AIRPLANE RACING

Blair, M. W. The roaring 20   **797.5**

Airplanes. Oxlade, C.   **629.133**

AIRPLANES

See also Aeronautics

Faber, H. The airplane   **629.133**

Oxlade, C. Airplanes   **629.133**

AIRPLANES -- ACCIDENTS *See* Aircraft accidents

AIRPLANES -- DESIGN AND CONSTRUCTION

Rooney, A. Aerospace engineering and the principles of flight   **629.1**

AIRPLANES -- FICTION

Colfer, E. Airman   **Fic**

Horvath, P. The Corps of the Bare-Boned Plane **Fic**

AIRPLANES -- HIJACKING *See* Hijacking of
airplanes

AIRPLANES -- MATERIALS

See also Materials

AIRPLANES -- MODELS

Mercer, B. The flying machine book   **745.592**

AIRPLANES -- MODELS

See also Models and modelmaking

AIRPLANES -- NOISE

See also Noise; Noise pollution

AIRPLANES -- RACING *See* Airplane racing

AIRPORTS

See also Aeronautics

AIRSHIPS

Oppel, K. Airborn   **Fic**

Sherman, J. The Hindenburg disaster   **363.1**

AIRSHIPS

See also Aeronautics

ANIMISM

See also Religion

Anna and the French kiss. Perkins, S.   **Fic**

Anna Dressed in Blood. Blake, K.   **Fic**

Anna Sui. Darraj, S. M.   **92**

Anne Frank.   **92**

Anne Frank and the children of the Holocaust. Lee, C. A.   **940.53**

The **Anne** Frank Case: Simon Wiesenthal's search for the truth. Rubin, S. G.   **92**

Anne Frank Stichting

Rol, R. v. d. Anne Frank, beyond the diary   **940.53**

Anne Frank, beyond the diary. Rol, R. v. d.   **940.53**

Anne Frank: her life in words and pictures. Metselaar, M.   **92**

Anne Hutchinson. Stille, D. R.   **92**

Anne Morrow Lindbergh. Gherman, B.   **92**

Annenberg Foundation Trust at Sunnylands' adolescent mental health initiative [series]

Ford, E. What you must think of me   **616.85**

Annexed. Dogar, S.   **Fic**

Annie Oakley. Koestler-Grack, R. A.   **92**

Annie Oakley: a photographic story of a life. Wills, C. A.   **92**

Annotated book lists for every teen reader. Bartel, J.   **028.5**

The **annotated** Phantom tollbooth. Juster, N.   **813**

ANNUALS See Almanacs; Calendars; Periodicals; School yearbooks; Yearbooks

ANNUALS (PLANTS)

See also Cultivated plants; Flower gardening; Flowers

ANNUITIES

See also Investments; Retirement income

Anorexia. Stewart, G.   **616.85**

Anorexia. Parks, P. J.   **616.85**

Anorexia and bulimia. Sonenklar, C.   **616.85**

ANOREXIA NERVOSA

Parks, P. J. Anorexia   **616.85**

Silverstein, A. The eating disorders update   **616.85**

Sonenklar, C. Anorexia and bulimia   **616.85**

Stewart, G. Anorexia   **616.85**

ANOREXIA NERVOSA

See also Eating disorders

ANOREXIA NERVOSA -- FICTION

Anderson, L. H. Wintergirls   **Fic**

Burton, R. Leaving Jetty Road   **Fic**

George, M. Looks   **Fic**

Padian, M. Jersey tomatoes are the best   **Fic**

Price, N. Zoe letting go   **Fic**

Vrettos, A. M. Skin   **Fic**

ANOREXIA NERVOSA -- PERSONAL NARRATIVES

Binstock, M. Nourishment   **92**

Another kind of cowboy. Juby, S.   **Fic**

Ansel Adams. West, K.   **92**

ANSWERS TO QUESTIONS See Questions and answers

ANTARCTIC EXPEDITIONS See Antarctica -- Exploration

Antarctica. Tulloch, C.   **998**

ANTARCTICA

See also Earth; Polar regions

Antarctica. Myers, W. D.   **998**

ANTARCTICA

Baker, S. In the Antarctic   **508**

Bledsoe, L. J. How to survive in Antarctica   **998**

Johnson, R. L. Ernest Shackleton   **92**

Myers, W. D. Antarctica   **998**

Tulloch, C. Antarctica   **998**

Wade, R. Polar worlds   **998**

Walker, S. M. Frozen secrets   **998**

ANTARCTICA -- DISCOVERY AND EXPLORATION -- BRITISH

Bertozzi, N. Shackleton   **919.89**

ANTARCTICA -- EXPLORATION

Bertozzi, N. Shackleton   **919.89**

ANTARCTICA -- EXPLORATION

See also Exploration; Scientific expeditions

ANTARCTICA -- FICTION

Farr, R. Emperors of the ice   **Fic**

Kurtz, C. The adventures of a South Pole pig   **Fic**

Patterson, J. The final warning   **Fic**

White, A. Surviving Antarctica   **Fic**

Anthem for Jackson Dawes. Bryce, C.   **Fic**

Anthony Burns: the defeat and triumph of a fugitive slave. Hamilton, V.   **92**

Anthony Horowitz. Abrams, D.   **92**

Anthony, Joelle

Restoring harmony   **Fic**

Anthony, Susan B., 1820-1906

About

Colman, P. Elizabeth Cady Stanton and Susan B. Anthony   **92**

Monroe, J. The Susan B. Anthony women's voting rights trial   **324.6**

Todd, A. M. Susan B. Anthony   **92**

ANTHROPOGEOGRAPHY See Human geography

ANTHROPOLOGISTS

Hopping, L. J. Bone detective   **92**

Mark, J. T. Margaret Mead   **306**

Walker, S. M. Written in bone   **614**

ANTHROPOLOGY

Chrisp, P. History year by year   **909**

ANTHROPOLOGY -- FICTION

Pearson, J. The rites & wrongs of Janice Wills   **Fic**

ANTHROPOMETRY

See also Anthropology; Ethnology; Human beings

ANTI-APARTHEID MOVEMENT

Sonneborn, L. The end of apartheid in South Af-

Anya's ghost. Brosgol, V.   **741.5**
Anya's war. Alban, A.   **Fic**
Anything but typical. Baskin, N. R.   **Fic**
Anzovin, Steven
    Kane, J. N. Famous first facts   **031.02**
The **Apache**. Bial, R.   **970.004**
APACHE INDIANS
    Bial, R. The Apache   **970.004**
    Ehrlich, A. Wounded Knee: an Indian history of the
      American West   **970.004**
    Jastrzembski, J. C. The Apache wars   **970.004**
    Sullivan, G. Geronimo   **92**
The **Apache** wars. Jastrzembski, J. C.   **970.004**
APARTHEID
    Beecroft, S. The release of Nelson Mandela **968.06**
    Coster, P. The struggle against apartheid   **968**
    Downing, D. Apartheid in South Africa   **968**
    Sonneborn, L. The end of apartheid in South Af-
      rica   **968.06**
Apartheid in South Africa. Downing, D.   **968**
APARTMENT HOUSES
      See also Buildings; Domestic architecture;
      Houses; Housing
APARTMENT HOUSES -- FICTION
    Greenwald, L. Sweet treats, secret crushes   **Fic**
    Stead, R. Liar & spy   **Fic**
Ape-men.   **001.9**
Apelqvist, Eva
    LGBTQ families   **306.87**
APES
    Barker, D. Top 50 reasons to care about great
      apes   **599.8**
APES
      See also Primates
Apfelbaum, Nina
    Rosen, P. Bearing witness   **016**
APHRODITE (GREEK DEITY)
      See also Gods and goddesses
APICULTURE *See* Beekeeping
APOCALYPTIC FICTION
    Aguirre, A. Enclave   **Fic**
    Bacigalupi, P. The drowned cities   **Fic**
    Block, F. L. Love in the time of global warming **Fic**
    Coutts, A. Tumble & fall   **Fic**
    Falls, K. Inhuman   **Fic**
    Fisher, C. Obsidian mirror   **Fic**
    Hautman, P. The Klaatu terminus   **Fic**
    Kade, J. V. Bot Wars   **Fic**
    Kessler, J. Loss   **Fic**
    Kizer, A. A matter of days   **Fic**
    Mary-Todd, J. Shot down   **Fic**
    Roberts, J. Rage within   **Fic**
    Rossi, V. Under the never sky   **Fic**
    Shards and Ashes   **S**
    Wendig, C. Under the Empyrean Sky   **Fic**
    Wiggins, B. Cured   **Fic**

APOCALYPTIC FILMS
      See also Motion pictures
APOLLO (GREEK DEITY)
      See also Gods and goddesses
APOLLO 11 (SPACECRAFT)
    Platt, R. Moon landing   **629.45**
    Thimmesh, C. Team moon   **629.45**
APOLLO 13 (SPACECRAFT)
    Holden, H. M. Danger in space   **629.45**
APOLLO 17 (SPACECRAFT)
    Nardo, D. The Blue marble   **525.022**
APOLLO PROJECT
    Bodden, V. To the moon   **629.45**
    Holden, H. M. Danger in space   **629.45**
    Nardo, D. The Blue marble   **525.022**
APOLLO PROJECT
      See also Life support systems (Space envi-
      ronment); Orbital rendezvous (Space flight);
      Space flight to the moon
APOLLO PROJECT -- GRAPHIC NOVELS
    Ottaviani, J. T-Minus: the race to the moon **629.45**
APOLLO THEATRE (NEW YORK, N.Y.)
    Marx, T. Steel drumming at the Apollo   **785**
Apollo's outcasts. Steele, A.   **Fic**
Apolo Anton Ohno. Uschan, M. V.   **796.91**
The **apothecary**. Meloy, M.   **Fic**
Appalachia. Rylant, C.   **974**
APPALACHIAN REGION
    Rylant, C. Appalachia   **974**
APPALACHIAN REGION -- FICTION
    Cleaver, V. Where the lillies bloom   **Fic**
    Naylor, P. R. Faith, hope, and Ivy June   **Fic**
    White, R. Belle Prater's boy   **Fic**
APPARITIONS
    Matthews, R. Ghosts and spirits   **133.1**
APPARITIONS
      See also Parapsychology; Spirits
APPEARANCE, PERSONAL *See* Personal ap-
    pearance
Appelbaum, Susannah
    The Shepherd of Weeds   **Fic**
Appelbaum, Susannah
    The Hollow Bettle   **Fic**
    The Shepherd of Weeds   **Fic**
    The Tasters Guild   **Fic**
Appelt, Kathi
    Keeper   **Fic**
    Kissing Tennessee and other stories from the Star-
    dust Dance   **S**
    The true blue scouts of Sugarman Swamp   **Fic**
    The underneath   **Fic**
APPERCEPTION
      See also Educational psychology; Psychology
APPETITE DEPRESSANTS -- MISCELLANEA
    Parks, P. J. Diet drugs   **615.7**
APPETIZERS

AUTOMATA *See* Robots

AUTOMATED CATALOGING
See also Cataloging

AUTOMATONS *See* Robots

The **automobile.** Collier, J. L.   **629.222**

AUTOMOBILE ACCIDENTS *See* Traffic accidents

AUTOMOBILE EXECUTIVES
Copley, B. The tall Mexican: the life of Hank Aguirre, all-star pitcher, businessman, humanitarian   **92**
Mitchell, D. Driven   **92**

AUTOMOBILE INDUSTRY
Mitchell, D. Driven   **92**

AUTOMOBILE PARTS
See also Automobiles

AUTOMOBILE RACING
Arroyo, S. L. How race car drivers use math **796.72**
Blackwood, G. L. The Great Race   **796.72**
Eagen, R. NASCAR   **796.72**
Kelley, K. C. Hottest NASCAR machines   **796.72**
Morganelli, A. Formula One   **796.72**
Pimm, N. R. The Daytona 500   **796.72**
Sirvaitis, K. Danica Patrick   **92**

AUTOMOBILE RACING -- FICTION
Weaver, W. Saturday night dirt   **Fic**
Weaver, W. Super stock rookie   **Fic**

AUTOMOBILE RACING DRIVERS
Sirvaitis, K. Danica Patrick   **92**

AUTOMOBILE TOURING *See* Automobile travel

AUTOMOBILE TRAVEL
Julia and the art of practical travel   **Fic**

AUTOMOBILE TRAVEL
See also Transportation; Travel; Voyages and travels

AUTOMOBILE TRAVEL -- FICTION
Kinney, J. Diary of a wimpy kid   **Fic**
Paulsen, G. Road trip   **Fic**

AUTOMOBILE TRAVEL -- GUIDEBOOKS
See also Maps

AUTOMOBILES
Collier, J. L. The automobile   **629.222**
Harmon, D. First car smarts   **629.222**
Williams, B. Who invented the automobile?   **629.222**
Woods, B. Hottest muscle cars   **629.222**
Woods, B. Hottest sports cars   **629.222**

AUTOMOBILES
See also Highway transportation; Motor vehicles; Vehicles

AUTOMOBILES -- ACCIDENTS *See* Traffic accidents

AUTOMOBILES -- COLLISION AVOIDANCE SYSTEMS
Mara, W. From locusts to...automobile anti-collision systems   **629.2**

AUTOMOBILES -- DESIGN AND CONSTRUCTION
See also Industrial design

AUTOMOBILES -- FICTION
Camper, C. Lowriders in space   **741.5**

AUTOMOBILES -- FUEL CONSUMPTION
Bjornlund, L. What is the future of alternative energy cars?   **388.3**

AUTOMOBILES -- LAW AND LEGISLATION
See also Law; Legislation

AUTOMOBILES -- MODELS
Balmer, A. J. Doc Fizzix mousetrap racers **629.22**
Gabrielson, C. Kinetic contraptions   **621.46**
Rigsby, M. Amazing rubber band cars   **745.592**
Sobey, E. Radio-controlled car experiments **796.1**

AUTOMOBILES -- MODELS
See also Models and modelmaking

AUTOMOBILES -- MOTORS
See also Engines

AUTOMOBILES -- RACING *See* Automobile racing

AUTOMOBILES -- TECHNOLOGICAL INNOVATIONS
Bjornlund, L. What is the future of alternative energy cars?   **388.3**

AUTOMOBILES -- TECHNOLOGICAL INNOVATIONS
See also Technological innovations

AUTOMOBILES -- TOURING *See* Automobile travel

AUTOMOBILES, ELECTRIC *See* Electric automobiles

AUTOMOTIVE INDUSTRY *See* Automobile industry

AUTONOMY (PSYCHOLOGY)
See also Psychology

AUTUMN
See also Seasons

Auxier, Jonathan
The Night Gardener   **Fic**
Peter Nimble and his fantastic eyes   **Fic**

AVAILABILITY OF HEALTH SERVICES *See* Access to health care

AVALANCHES
See also Snow

Avalon. Arnett, M.   **Fic**

AVANT-GARDE (AESTHETICS)
See also Aesthetics; Modernism (Aesthetics)

AVARICE
See also Sin

Avenger. McNab, A.   **Fic**

The **avengers:** heroes assembled. Parker, J. **741.5**

AVERAGE
See also Arithmetic; Probabilities; Statistics

Aveyard, Victoria
Red queen   **Fic**

BOOK DISCUSSION GROUPS *See* Book clubs (Discussion groups)

BOOK ILLUSTRATION *See* Illustration of books

BOOK LISTS *See* Best books

Book of a thousand days. Hale, S.   **Fic**

The **book** of blood. Newquist, H.   **612.1**

The **book** of blood and shadow. Wasserman, R. **Fic**

The **Book** of dragons. Hague, M.   **808.83**

The **book** of dreams. Melling, O. R.   **Fic**

The **book** of gardening projects for kids. Cohen, W.   **635**

The **Book** of Lies. Moloney, J.   **Fic**

The **book** of magic. Barron, T. A.   **Fic**

The **Book** of monologues for aspiring actors. **808.82**

The **book** of Mordred. Vande Velde, V.   **Fic**

The **Book** of Mormon. Book of Mormon   **289.3**

Book of Mormon

The Book of Mormon   **289.3**

The **book** of North American owls. Sattler, H. R.   **598.9**

The **book** of pirates. Rose, J.   **910.4**

The **book** of potentially catastrophic science. Connolly, S.   **507.8**

The **Book** of Storms.   **Fic**

The Book of Tamarind [series]

Aguiar, N. The lost island of Tamarind   **Fic**

Aguiar, N. Secrets of Tamarind   **Fic**

The **book** of the Lion. Cadnum, M.   **Fic**

The **book** of the maidservant. Barnhouse, R. **Fic**

The **book** of three. Alexander, L.   **Fic**

The **book** of time. Prevost, G.   **Fic**

The **book** of wonders. Richards, J.   **Fic**

BOOK REVIEWING

See also Books and reading; Criticism

BOOK SELECTION

Keane, N. J. 101 great, ready-to-use book lists for teens   **028.5**

BOOK SELECTION

See also Libraries -- Acquisitions; Libraries -- Collection development

BOOK TALKS

Baxter, K. A. Gotcha again for guys!   **028.5**

Cannon, T. C. Cooler than fiction   **027.62**

Cole, S. Booktalking around the world   **021.7**

Diamant-Cohen, B. Booktalking bonanza   **028.5**

Gillespie, J. T. Classic teenplots   **011.6**

Keane, N. J. The tech-savvy booktalker   **021.7**

Langemack, C. The booktalker's bible   **021.7**

Mahood, K. Booktalking with teens   **021.7**

Schall, L. Genre talks for teens   **028.5**

Schall, L. Value-packed booktalks   **028.1**

York, S. Booktalking authentic multicultural literature   **021**

BOOK TALKS

See also Book reviews; Libraries -- Public relations; Public speaking

The **book** thief. Zusak, M.   **Fic**

BOOK TRADE *See* Book industry; Booksellers and bookselling; Publishers and publishing

The **book** whisperer. Miller, D.   **372.6**

Book Wish Foundation

What you wish for   **S**

The **Book** Without Words. Avi   **Fic**

Bookings & gigs. Witmer, S.   **781.66**

Bookmapping. Cavanaugh, T. W.   **372.6**

Bookmarked.   **809**

BOOKS -- APPRAISAL *See* Book reviewing; Books and reading; Criticism; Literature -- History and criticism

BOOKS -- CENSORSHIP

Books under fire   **016.098**

BOOKS -- CENSORSHIP

See also Censorship

BOOKS -- LARGE PRINT *See* Large print books

BOOKS -- PRICES

See also Booksellers and bookselling; Prices

BOOKS -- REVIEWS

Baxter, K. A. From cover to cover   **028.1**

BOOKS -- SELECTION *See* Book selection

Books about the Middle East. Al-Hazza, T. C. **016**

BOOKS AND READING

Aronson, M. Beyond the pale   **810**

Barr, C. Best books for middle school and junior high readers   **028.5**

Baxter, K. A. Gotcha good!   **028.5**

Diamant-Cohen, B. Booktalking bonanza   **028.5**

Gilmore, B. Speaking volumes   **028.5**

Grimes, S. Reading is our business   **027.8**

Keane, N. J. 101 great, ready-to-use book lists for teens   **028.5**

Krashen, S. D. The power of reading   **028.5**

Matthew, K. I. Neal-Schuman guide to recommended children's books and media for use with every elementary subject   **011.6**

Miller, D. The book whisperer   **372.6**

Nilsen, A. P. Literature for today's young adults   **028.5**

Reid, R. Reid's read-alouds   **011.6**

Reid, R. Reid's read-alouds 2   **011.6**

Saccardi, M. Books that teach kids to write   **028.5**

Shelf life: stories by the book   **S**

Skaggs, G. Look, it's books!   **021.7**

Stanley, D. The mysterious matter of I.M. Fine **Fic**

Temple, C. A. Children's books in children's hands   **028.5**

BOOKS AND READING

See also Communication; Education; Reading

BOOKS AND READING -- BEST BOOKS *See* Best books

BOOKS AND READING -- FICTION

Abbott, T. The postcard   **Fic**

Boxers. **741.5**

BOXERS (PERSONS)

Micklos, J. Muhammad Ali **92**

Myers, W. D. The greatest: Muhammad Ali **92**

Sharenow, R. The Berlin Boxing Club **Fic**

Smith, C. R. Twelve rounds to glory: the story of Muhammad Ali **92**

Sullivan, G. Knockout!: a photobiography of boxer Joe Louis **92**

BOXES

Explorer **741.5**

BOXES -- COLLECTORS AND COLLECTING

See also Collectors and collecting

BOXES -- FICTION

TenNapel, D. Cardboard **Fic**

Boxing. Mason, P. **796.8**

BOXING

Mason, P. Boxing **796.8**

BOXING -- BIOGRAPHY

Micklos, J. Muhammad Ali **92**

Myers, W. D. The greatest: Muhammad Ali **92**

Smith, C. R. Twelve rounds to glory: the story of Muhammad Ali **92**

Sullivan, G. Knockout!: a photobiography of boxer Joe Louis **92**

BOXING -- FICTION

Friend, N. My life in black and white **Fic**

Lipsyte, R. The contender **Fic**

Pinkney, A. D. Bird in a box **Fic**

Sharenow, R. The Berlin Boxing Club **Fic**

The **boy** at the end of the world. Van Eekhout, G. **Fic**

A **boy** at war. Mazer, H. **Fic**

A **boy** called Twister. Schraff, A. E. **Fic**

The **boy** from Ilysies. North, P. **Fic**

The **boy** in the burning house. Wynne-Jones, T. **Fic**

The **boy** in the dress. Walliams, D. **Fic**

A **boy** no more. Mazer, H. **Fic**

Boy O'Boy. Doyle, B. **Fic**

The **boy** on Cinnamon Street. Stone, P. **Fic**

Boy on the lion throne. Kimmel, E. C. **92**

The **boy** on the wooden box. Leyson, L. **92**

The **Boy** Project. Kinard, K. **Fic**

Boy proof. Castellucci, C. **Fic**

BOY SCOUTS

See also Boys' clubs; Scouts and scouting

BOY SCOUTS OF AMERICA -- FICTION

Salisbury, G. Night of the howling dogs **Fic**

The **boy** Sherlock Holmes [series]

Peacock, S. Death in the air **Fic**

Peacock, S. The dragon turn **Fic**

Peacock, S. Eye of the crow **Fic**

Peacock, S. The secret fiend **Fic**

Peacock, S. Vanishing girl **Fic**

Boy talk. **612.6**

Boy vs. girl. Robert, N. B. **Fic**

The **boy** who could fly. Norcliffe, J. **Fic**

The **boy** who couldn't sleep and never had to. Pierson, D. C. **Fic**

The **boy** who dared. Bartoletti, S. C. **Fic**

The **boy** who harnessed the wind. Kamkwamba, W. **92**

The **boy** who lost Fairyland. **Fic**

The **boy** who saved baseball. Ritter, J. H. **Fic**

The **Boy** who swam with piranhas. Almond, D. **Fic**

Boy2girl. Blacker, T. **Fic**

Boy: tales of childhood. Dahl, R. **92**

BOYCOTTS

See also Commerce; Consumers; Passive resistance

Boyd, Herb

Wright, S. Simeon's story **305.8**

Boyd, Maria

Will **Fic**

Boyle, Jordan

Examining geothermal energy **621.44**

Boyle, Robert, 1627-1691

About

Baxter, R. Skeptical chemist **92**

Boyne, John

Noah Barleywater runs away **Fic**

Boyology. Burningham, S. O. **306.7**

BOYS

Aronson, M. For boys only **031.02**

Boy talk **612.6**

Bradbury, R. Something wicked this way comes **Fic**

Dude! **810**

Gipson, F. B. Old Yeller **Fic**

Golding, W. Lord of the flies **Fic**

Iggulden, C. The dangerous book for boys **031.02**

Jukes, M. The guy book **305.235**

Mar, J. The body book for boys **612.6**

BOYS

See also Children

BOYS -- BOOKS AND READING

Aronson, M. For boys only **031.02**

Baxter, K. A. Gotcha again for guys! **028.5**

Sullivan, M. Connecting boys with books 2 **028.5**

Sullivan, M. Serving boys through readers' advisory **028.5**

Welch, R. J. The guy-friendly YA library **027.62**

Zbaracki, M. D. Best books for boys **028.5**

BOYS -- FICTION

Clifton, L. Freaky Fast Frankie Joe **Fic**

Gantos, J. The key that swallowed Joey Pigza **Fic**

Heap House **Fic**

Loftin, N. Nightingale's nest **Fic**

Ness, P. The knife of never letting go **Fic**

Pastis, S. Timmy failure **Fic**

Stead, R. Liar & spy **Fic**

BOYS -- HEALTH AND HYGIENE

Will puberty last my whole life? **613**

Brosgol, Vera
  Anya's ghost   **741.5**
Brosnan, Rosemary
  (ed) Unnatural creatures   **S**
Brotherband chronicles [series]
  Flanagan, J. The invaders   **Fic**
  Flanagan, J. The outcasts   **Fic**
Brotherhood. Westrick, A. B.   **Fic**
Brotherhood of the conch [series]
  Divakaruni, C. B. The conch bearer   **Fic**
BROTHERS
  Horowitz, A. The Falcon's Malteser   **Fic**
  Trueman, T. Cruise control   **Fic**
  Van Leeuwen, J. Cabin on Trouble Creek   **Fic**
BROTHERS
  See also Men; Siblings
BROTHERS -- DEATH
  Daley, J. R. Jesus Jackson   **Fic**
BROTHERS -- FICTION
  Alexander, K. The crossover   **Fic**
  Black, H. Black heart   **Fic**
  Clifton, L. Freaky Fast Frankie Joe   **Fic**
  Elliott, L. Across a war-tossed sea   **Fic**
  Erdrich, L. Chickadee   **Fic**
  Funke, C. Fearless   **Fic**
  Lost in the sun   **Fic**
  Lynch, C. Pieces   **Fic**
  The only game   **Fic**
  Petruck, R. Steering toward normal   **Fic**
  Rubens, M. Sons of the 613   **Fic**
  Rupp, R. After Eli   **Fic**
  Stealing the game   **Fic**
  Sullivan, M. Dear Blue Sky   **Fic**
  Wish You Weren't   **Fic**
BROTHERS -- GRAPHIC NOVELS
  Wood, D. Into the volcano   **741.5**
BROTHERS AND SISTERS *See* Siblings
BROTHERS AND SISTERS -- FICTION
  Angus, S. A Horse Called Hero   **Fic**
  Battle of the beasts   **Fic**
  Black dove, white raven   **Fic**
  The black reckoning   **Fic**
  Blume, J. BFF*   **Fic**
  Button Hill   **Fic**
  Collar, O. The Red Pyramid   **Fic**
  Daley, J. R. Jesus Jackson   **Fic**
  Dowell, F. O. Dovey Coe   **Fic**
  Farmer, N. The Sea of Trolls   **Fic**
  Freymann-Weyr, G. My heartbeat   **Fic**
  Farrey, B. The Grimjinx rebellion   **Fic**
  Gantos, J. Jack on the tracks   **Fic**
  Giff, P. R. Nory Ryan's song   **Fic**
  Griffin, P. R. The ghost sitter   **Fic**
  Hirsch, J. The 39 clues: Breakaway   **Fic**
  Joseph, L. Flowers in the sky   **Fic**
  Kadohata, C. The thing about luck   **Fic**

Kagawa, J. Talon   **Fic**
Kehret, P. Abduction!   **Fic**
Konigsburg, E. L. Silent to the bone   **Fic**
Kuehn, S. Complicit   **Fic**
Lowry, L. The silent boy   **Fic**
McKay, H. Saffy's angel   **Fic**
McQuerry, M. D. Beyond the door   **Fic**
Morgan, P. The beautiful and the cursed   **Fic**
Naidoo, B. The other side of truth   **Fic**
Naylor, P. R. Simply Alice   **Fic**
Paterson, K. The same stuff as stars   **Fic**
Peters, J. A. Luna   **Fic**
The red pyramid   **741.5**
Saunders, K. The Whizz Pop Chocolate Shop   **Fic**
Sedgwick, M. She is not invisible   **Fic**
The spindlers   **Fic**
The Tapper twins go to war (with each other)   **Fic**
Vanhee, J. Engines of the broken world   **Fic**
Waiting for Gonzo   **Fic**
The war that saved my life   **Fic**
Watson, J. The 39 clues   **Fic**
The whispering trees   **Fic**
Zarr, S. The Lucy variations   **Fic**
The **brothers** story. Sturtevant, K.   **Fic**
The **brothers'** war. Lewis, J. P.   **811**
Brothers, Meagan
  Debbie Harry sings in French   **Fic**
Brougham, Jason
  Abramson, A. S. Inside dinosaurs   **567.9**
Brouwer, Sigmund
  Devil's pass   **Fic**
Brower, David, 1912-2000
           About
  Byrnes, P. Environmental pioneers   **363.7**
BROWN BEAR
  Gish, M. Brown bears   **599.78**
BROWN BEAR -- LITERATURE
  Gish, M. Brown bears   **599.78**
Brown bears. Gish, M.   **599.78**
Brown girl dreaming. Woodson, J.   **92**
Brown v. Board of Education. Gold, S. D.   **344**
Brown v. Board of Education. Anderson, W.   **344**
Brown, Alan
  The Bible and Christianity   **220**
Brown, Cynthia Light
  Discover National Monuments, National Parks   **363.6**
Brown, Dee Alexander
  Bury my heart at Wounded Knee   **970.004**
  Dee Brown's folktales of the Native American   **398.2**
  Ehrlich, A. Wounded Knee: an Indian history of the American West   **970.004**
  Zimmerman, D. J. Saga of the Sioux   **970.004**
Brown, Don
  The great American dust bowl   **978**

Burns, Loree Griffin
Beetle busters **595.76**
Citizen scientists **590.72**
The hive detectives **638**
Tracking trash **551.46**
Burns, Raymond
Ames, L. J. Draw 50 holiday decorations **743**
Burr, Aaron, 1756-1836
About
St. George, J. The duel: the parallel lives of Alexander Hamilton and Aaron Burr **92**
Burr, Brooks M.
Page, L. M. Peterson field guide to freshwater fishes of North America north of Mexico **597**
Burroughs, John, 1837-1921
About
Wadsworth, G. John Burroughs **508**
BURROWING ANIMALS
Miller, S. S. Secret lives of burrowing beasts **591.7**
Burtenshaw, Jenna
Shadowcry **Fic**
Burton, Bonnie
Girls against girls **305.23**
Burton, Rebecca
Leaving Jetty Road **Fic**
Burton, Richard Francis Sir, 1821-1890
About
Young, S. Richard Francis Burton **92**
Bury my heart at Wounded Knee. Brown, D. A. **970.004**
BURYING GROUNDS See Burial; Cemeteries
Burying the sun. Whelan, G. **Fic**
BUS TRAVEL -- FICTION
Angleberger, T. Emperor Pickletine rides the bus **Fic**
The great good summer **Fic**
Busby, Cylin, 1970-
(ed) First kiss (then tell) **808.8**
About
Busby, C. The year we disappeared **92**
Busby, John, 1942-
About
Busby, C. The year we disappeared **92**
Buscemi, Karen
Split in two **306.874**
BUSES
See also Automobiles; Highway transportation; Local transit; Motor vehicles
BUSH SURVIVAL See Wilderness survival
Bush, Gail
(ed) Indivisible **811**
Bush, George W. (George Walker), 1946-
About
Burgan, M. George W. Bush **973.931**
Bushman lives! **Fic**
Bushman, Claudia L.

Mormons in America **289.3**
Bushman, Richard L.
Bushman, C. L. Mormons in America **289.3**
BUSINESS
See also Commerce; Economics
BUSINESS -- INFORMATION RESOURCES
See also Information resources
BUSINESS -- INTERNET RESOURCES
See also Internet resources
BUSINESS AND POLITICS
See also Politics
Business builders [series]
Aaseng, N. Business builders in sweets and treats **920**
Business builders in sweets and treats. Aaseng, N. **920**
BUSINESS CYCLES
Hollander, B. Booms, bubbles, and busts **338.5**
BUSINESS CYCLES
See also Cycles; Economic conditions
BUSINESS DEPRESSION, 1929-1939 See Great Depression, 1929-1939
BUSINESS ENTERPRISES
Rankin, K. Start it up **338**
BUSINESS ENTERPRISES -- FICTION
Chambers, V. Fifteen candles **Fic**
Connor, L. Crunch **Fic**
Cottrell Boyce, F. Framed **Fic**
Erskine, K. The absolute value of Mike **Fic**
Jennings, R. W. Ghost town **Fic**
Paulsen, G. Flat broke **Fic**
Rylander, C. The fourth stall **Fic**
BUSINESS ETHICS
See also Ethics; Professional ethics
BUSINESS ETHICS -- FICTION
Petrucha, S. Teen, Inc. **Fic**
BUSINESS ETIQUETTE
See also Etiquette
BUSINESS FORECASTING
See also Economic forecasting; Forecasting
Business leaders [series]
Baughan, B. Russell Simmons **92**
Hasday, J. L. Facebook and Mark Zuckerberg **92**
Johnson, A. J. Warren Buffett **92**
Sapet, K. Google founders: Larry Page and Sergey Brin **92**
Scally, R. Jeff Bezos **92**
Smith, C. Twitter **92**
BUSINESS LETTERS
See also Letter writing
BUSINESS MATHEMATICS
See also Mathematics
BUSINESS MORTALITY See Bankruptcy; Business failures
BUSINESS ORGANIZATIONS See Business enterprises

By darkness hid. Williamson, J.   **Fic**
By the river. Herrick, S.   **Fic**
By the time you read this, I'll be dead. Peters, J. A.   **Fic**
BY-PRODUCTS See Waste products
Byam, Michele
  Arms & armor   355.8
Byars, Betsy Cromer
  Cracker Jackson   **Fic**
  The dark stairs   **Fic**
  The keeper of the doves   **Fic**
        About
  Cammarano, R. Betsy Byars   813
Bye for now. Churchyard, K.   **Fic**
Byers, Ann
  Communications satellites   384.5
  Courageous teen resisters   940.53
  First credit cards and credit smarts   332.7
  Jobs as green builders and planners   690
  Rescuing the Danish Jews   940.53
  Saving children from the Holocaust   940.53
  Trapped--youth in the Nazi ghettos   940.53
  Youth destroyed--the Nazi camps   940.53
Bylines: a photobiography of Nellie Bly. Macy, S.   92
Bylot, Robert, fl. 1610-1616
        About
  Wilson, J. The alchemist's dream   **Fic**
BYRD ANTARCTIC EXPEDITION
    See also Antarctica -- Exploration
Byrd, Richard Evelyn, 1888-1957
        About
  Finkelstein, N. H. Three across   629.13
Byrd, Robert
  Schlitz, L. A. Good masters! Sweet ladies!   940.1
  Schlitz, L. A. The hero Schliemann   92
Byrnes, Patricia
  Environmental pioneers   363.7
Bystander. Preller, J.   **Fic**
BYZANTINE ARCHITECTURE
    See also Ancient architecture; Architecture; Medieval architecture
BYZANTINE ART
    See also Ancient art; Art; Medieval art
The **Byzantine** Empire. Vanvoorst, J. F.   949.5
BYZANTINE EMPIRE
  Feldman, R. T. The fall of Constantinople   949.5
BYZANTINE EMPIRE -- CIVILIZATION
  Vanvoorst, J. F. The Byzantine Empire   949.5

C

C. F. MARTIN & CO.
  VanHecke, S. Raggin', jazzin', rockin'   784.19
C. G. CONN LTD.
  VanHecke, S. Raggin', jazzin', rockin'   784.19
C. S. Lewis. Hamilton, J.   92

CABALA
  Judaism; Mysticism; Occultism
    See also Hebrew literature; Jewish literature;
CABALA -- FICTION
  Goelman, A. The path of names   **Fic**
Cabin on Trouble Creek. Van Leeuwen, J.   **Fic**
CABINET MEMBERS
  Abrams, D. Nicolas Sarkozy   92
  Bell, T. Nick of time   **Fic**
  Blashfield, J. F. Golda Meir   92
  Severance, J. B. Winston Churchill   92
  White, A. Window boy   **Fic**
The **Cabinet** of Curiosities. Bachmann, S.   **S**
The **Cabinet** of Wonders. Rutkoski, M.   **Fic**
CABINET OFFICERS
  Keller, E. Frances Perkins   92
CABLE RAILROADS
    See also Railroads
Cabot, John, 1450-1498
        About
  Fritz, J. Around the world in a hundred years   910.92
Cabot, Meg
  Airhead   **Fic**
  All-American girl   **Fic**
  Being Nikki   **Fic**
  From the notebooks of a middle school princess   **Fic**
  The princess diaries   **Fic**
  Runaway   **Fic**
Cabral, Pedro Alvares, 1460?-1526?
        About
  Fritz, J. Around the world in a hundred years   910.92
Caddy ever after. McKay, H.   **Fic**
Cadnum, Michael
  The book of the Lion   **Fic**
  Peril on the sea   **Fic**
Caduto, Michael J.
  Catch the wind, harness the sun   333.79
Caes, Charles J.
  Discovering the speed of light   535
Caesar, Julius, 100-44 B.C.
        About
  Galford, E. Julius Caesar   92
  McKeown, A. Julius Caesar   822.3
CAFES See Coffeehouses; Restaurants
Caffeine.   362.2
CAFFEINE
  Caffeine   362.2
The **cage.** Sender, R. M.   940.53
CAGE BIRDS
    See also Birds
Cahill, Sean
  LGBT youth in America's schools   371.82
CAI See Computer-assisted instruction
Caine, Rachel
  Prince of Shadows   **Fic**
Cairns, Sarah

Gutman, D. Ray & me **Fic**

Chapman, Robert L.
(ed) Dictionary of American slang **427**
(ed) Roget's international thesaurus **423**

CHARACTER
See also Ethics; Personality

CHARACTERS *See* Characters and characteristics in literature

CHARACTERS AND CHARACTERISTICS IN LITERATURE
Bodden, V. Creating the character **808.3**
Nilsen, A. P. Names and naming in young adult literature **813**
Rubin, C. M. The real Alice in Wonderland **92**

CHARACTERS AND CHARACTERISTICS IN LITERATURE
See also Literature

CHARACTERS IN LITERATURE -- FICTION
The Grimm conclusion **Fic**
Grounded **Fic**
Hale, S. The storybook of legends **Fic**
The hero's guide to storming the castle **Fic**
Story thieves **Fic**
Taub, M. Still star-crossed **Fic**

CHARADES
See also Amateur theater; Amusements; Literary recreations; Riddles

Charbonneau, Joelle
Graduation day **Fic**
Independent study **Fic**
The Testing **Fic**

CHARCOAL DRAWING
See also Drawing

Chari, Sheela
Vanished **Fic**

CHARISMATA *See* Spiritual gifts

CHARITABLE INSTITUTIONS *See* Charities; Institutional care; Orphanages

CHARITIES
Reusser, K. Celebrities giving back **361.7**

CHARITIES
See also Human services; Social work

CHARITY
See also Ethics; Virtue

CHARLATANS *See* Impostors and imposture

Charles A. Lindbergh. Giblin, J. **629.13**
Charles and Emma. Heiligman, D. **92**
Charles Babbage and the engines of perfection. Collier, B. **92**
Charles Darwin. Krull, K. **92**
Charles Darwin and the Beagle adventure. Wood, A. J. **508**
Charles Darwin and the evolution revolution. Stefoff, R. **575**
Charles Darwin and the mystery of mysteries. Eldredge, N. **92**

Charles Dickens. Wells-Cole, C. **823**
Charles Dickens and the street children of London. Warren, A. **92**

Charles, John
Mosley, S. The suffragists in literature for youth **016**

Charles, Ray
About
Duggleby, J. Uh huh!: the story of Ray Charles **92**
Woog, A. Ray Charles and the birth of soul **92**

CHARLESTON (S.C.) -- FICTION
Thompson, J. E. The girl from Felony Bay **Fic**

Charleyboy, Lisa
(ed) Dreaming in Indian **704.03**

Charlie Bone and the beast. Nimmo, J. **Fic**
Charlie Bone and the castle of mirrors. Nimmo, J. **Fic**
Charlie Bone and the hidden king. Nimmo, J. **Fic**
Charlie Bone and the invisible boy. Nimmo, J. **Fic**
Charlie Bone and the Red Knight. Nimmo, J. **Fic**
Charlie Bone and the shadow. Nimmo, J. **Fic**
Charlie Bone and the time twister. Nimmo, J. **Fic**
Charlie Joe Jackson's guide to not reading. Greenwald, T. **Fic**
Charlie Joe Jackson's guide to summer vacation. **Fic**
Charlie Parker. Rice, E. **788.7**
Charlie's key. Mills, R. **Fic**
Charlie's raven. George, J. C. **Fic**
A charm of dolphins. Hall, H. **599.5**

CHARMS
See also Folklore; Superstition

CHARMS -- FICTION
Cooper, I. Angel in my pocket **Fic**
Cremer, A. Invisibility **Fic**

CHARTER SCHOOLS
See also Schools

CHARTERS
See also History -- Sources
Charting the world. Panchyk, R. **912**

CHARTOGRAPHY *See* Maps

Chase, Richard
The Jack tales **398.2**
Chasing AllieCat. Davis, R. F. **Fic**
Chasing boys. Tayleur, K. **Fic**
Chasing Brooklyn. Schroeder, L. **Fic**
Chasing cheetahs. **599.75**
Chasing Lincoln's killer. Swanson, J. L. **973.7**
Chasing Orion. Lasky, K. **Fic**
Chasing the bear. Parker, R. B. **Fic**
Chasing the Nightbird. Russell, K. **Fic**
Chasing the secret. Snow, M. **Fic**
Chasing the storm. Miller, R. **551.55**
Chasing Vermeer. Balliett, B. **Fic**

Chasing yesterday [series]
Wasserman, R. Awakening **Fic**
Wasserman, R. Betrayal **Fic**

Chasse, Jill D.

CHOIRS (MUSIC) -- FICTION
Bauer, A. C. E. No castles here   **Fic**

Choldenko, Gennifer
Al Capone does my homework   **Fic**
Al Capone does my shirts   **Fic**
Al Capone shines my shoes   **Fic**
No passengers beyond this point   **Fic**
Notes from a liar and her dog   **Fic**

CHOLERA -- FICTION
Hopkinson, D. The Great Trouble   **Fic**

Choo, Jimmy, 1961-
About
Sapet, K. Jimmy Choo   **92**

Choosing up sides. Ritter, J. H.   **Fic**
Choosing Web 2.0 tools for learning and teaching in a digital world. Berger, P.   **025.04**
Chopin's world. Malaspina, A.   **92**

Chopin, Frédéric, 1810-1849
About
Malaspina, A. Chopin's world   **92**

Choppy socky blues. Briant, E.   **Fic**
Choreographer. Marsico, K.   **792.8**

CHOREOGRAPHERS
Bernier-Grand, C. T. Alicia Alonso   **92**
Freedman, R. Martha Graham, a dancer's life **792.8**
Marsico, K. Choreographer   **792.8**

The **chosen** one. Williams, C. L.   **Fic**
The **chosen** prince.   **Fic**

Chotjewitz, David
Daniel half human   **Fic**

Choyce, Lesley
Deconstructing Dylan   **Fic**

Chris Crutcher. Sommers, M. A.   **92**

Chrisp, Peter
Atlas of ancient worlds   **911**
History year by year   **909**
Warfare   **355**
World War II: fighting for freedom   **940.54**

CHRISTIAN ANTIQUITIES
See also Antiquities

CHRISTIAN ART
Connolly, S. New Testament miracles   **226**

CHRISTIAN ART
See also Art; Religious art

CHRISTIAN ART AND SYMBOLISM See Christian art; Christian symbolism

CHRISTIAN BIOGRAPHY
See also Biography; Religious biography

CHRISTIAN CIVILIZATION
See also Christianity; Civilization

CHRISTIAN ETHICS
See also Ethics

CHRISTIAN FUNDAMENTALISM
See also Christianity -- Doctrines; Religious fundamentalism

CHRISTIAN FUNDAMENTALISM -- FICTION

Americus   **741.5**

CHRISTIAN HOLIDAYS
See also Church year; Religious holidays

CHRISTIAN LEGENDS
See also Legends

CHRISTIAN LIFE
Fletcher, S. Walk across the sea   **Fic**

CHRISTIAN LIFE -- FICTION
Bickle, L. The hallowed ones   **Fic**
Bickle, L. The outside   **Fic**
Brande, R. Evolution, me, & other freaks of nature   **Fic**
Crossley-Holland, K. Crossing to Paradise   **Fic**
Despain, B. The dark Divine   **Fic**
Dickerson, M. The merchant's daughter   **Fic**
Fixmer, E. Saint training   **Fic**
Galante, C. The patron saint of butterflies   **Fic**
Gee Whiz   **Fic**
The great good summer   **Fic**
Grimes, N. A girl named Mister   **Fic**
Hemphill, H. Long gone daddy   **Fic**
Hilmo, T. With a name like Love   **Fic**
Jaden, D. Losing Faith   **Fic**
Lopez, D. Ask my mood ring how I feel   **Fic**
McCrite, K. D. In front of God and everybody **Fic**
Nelson, R. A. Days of Little Texas   **Fic**
Parry, R. Heart of a shepherd   **Fic**
Paterson, K. Preacher's boy   **Fic**
Pie in the Sky   **Fic**
Rupp, R. Octavia Boone's big questions about life, the universe, and everything   **Fic**
Shoemaker, T. Back before dark   **Fic**
Shoemaker, T. Code of silence   **Fic**
Smiley, J. The Georges and the Jewels   **Fic**
Smiley, J. A good horse   **Fic**
Smiley, J. True Blue   **Fic**
Watson, R. What Momma left me   **Fic**
White, R. A month of Sundays   **Fic**
Zarr, S. Once was lost   **Fic**
Zielin, L. Donut days   **Fic**

CHRISTIAN MISSIONS
See also Christianity; Church history; Church work

CHRISTIAN MISSIONS -- FICTION
O'Dell, S. Zia   **Fic**

CHRISTIAN PHILOSOPHY
See also Philosophy

CHRISTIAN SAINTS
See also Saints

CHRISTIAN SECTS
See also Christianity; Church history; Sects

CHRISTIAN-OWNED BUSINESS ENTERPRISES
See also Business enterprises

Christianity. Hale, R. D.   **230**
Christianity. Nardo, D.   **230**

Cicada summer. Beaty, A. **Fic**

CIGARETTES
    See also Smoking; Tobacco

CIGARS
    See also Smoking; Tobacco

CINCO DE MAYO
    Mattern, J. Celebrate Cinco de Mayo **394.26**

CINCO DE MAYO (HOLIDAY)
    See also Holidays

Cinder. Meyer, M. **Fic**

**CINDERELLA (LEGENDARY CHARACTER)
-- FICTION**
    Barrett, T. The Stepsister's Tale **Fic**

CINDERELLA -- POETRY
    Whipple, L. If the shoe fits **811**

CINEMA *See* Motion pictures

CINEMATOGRAPHY
    Miller, R. Special effects **778.5**

CINEMATOGRAPHY
    See also Photography

CIPHER AND TELEGRAPH CODES
    See also Ciphers; Telegraph

CIPHERS
    Bell-Rehwoldt, S. Speaking secret codes **652**
    Blackwood, G. L. Mysterious messages **652**
    Gregory, J. Breaking secret codes **652**
    Gregory, J. Making secret codes **652**
    Mitchell, S. K. Spy codes and ciphers **652**
    Pincock, S. Codebreaker **652**

CIPHERS
    See also Signs and symbols

CIPHERS -- FICTION
    Mone, G. Fish **Fic**
    Park, L. S. Storm warning **Fic**
    Riordan, R. The maze of bones **Fic**
    Riordan, R. Vespers rising **Fic**
    Stone, P. The Romeo and Juliet code **Fic**
    Watson, J. Beyond the grave **Fic**
    Watson, J. In too deep **Fic**

CIRCLE
    See also Geometry; Shape

Circle of flight. Marsden, J. **Fic**

The circle of gold. Prevost, G. **Fic**

Circle of heroes. **Fic**

Circle of magic [series]
    Pierce, T. Briar's book **Fic**
    Pierce, T. Daja's book **Fic**
    Pierce, T. Sandry's book **Fic**
    Pierce, T. Tris's book **Fic**

Circle of secrets. Little, K. G. **Fic**

The circuit: stories from the life of a migrant child.
Jimenez, F. **Fic**

CIRCUITS, ELECTRIC *See* Electric circuits

Circulating life. Winner, C. **615**

Circulatory system. Bjorklund, R. **612.1**

CIRCULATORY SYSTEM *See* Cardiovascular
system

CIRCUMNAVIGATION *See* Voyages around the
world

CIRCUS
    Fleming, C. The great and only Barnum **92**
    Laidlaw, R. On parade **791.8**
    The magnificent Lizzie Brown and the mysterious
phantom **Fic**
    McCaughrean, G. The kite rider **Fic**
    Sullivan, G. Tom Thumb **92**

CIRCUS
    See also Amusements

CIRCUS -- FICTION
    Howard, J. J. That time I joined the circus **Fic**
    Oppel, K. The Boundless **Fic**
    Smith, R. Eruption **Fic**

CIRCUS EXECUTIVES
    Fleming, C. The great and only Barnum **92**
    Peck, R. Fair weather **Fic**

Circus Galacticus. Fagan, D. **Fic**

CIRCUS PERFORMERS
    Peck, R. Fair weather **Fic**
    Sullivan, G. Tom Thumb **92**

CIRCUS PERFORMERS -- FICTION
    Kelly, L. Chained **Fic**
    Larwood, K. Freaks **Fic**
    Wild boy and the black terror **Fic**

Cisneros, Sandra, 1954-
    Cisneros, S. The house on Mango Street **Fic**
        About
    Warrick, K. C. Sandra Cisneros **92**

Cities. Laidlaw, J. A. **307.7**

Cities. **307.76**

Cities. Lorinc, J. **307.7**

Cities and towns. Stefoff, R. **973.2**

CITIES AND TOWNS
    Cities **307.76**
    Hawkins, J. Atlantis and other lost worlds **001.94**
    Lorinc, J. Cities **307.7**
    Millard, A. A street through time **936**
    Spilsbury, R. Towns and cities **307.76**
    Stefoff, R. Cities and towns **973.2**

CITIES AND TOWNS -- GROWTH
    See also Internal migration; Population

CITIES AND TOWNS -- PLANNING *See* City
planning

CITIES AND TOWNS -- UNITED STATES
    Miller, C. C. Backlash **305.8**

CITIES AND TOWNS, MOVEMENT TO *See*
Cities and towns -- Growth; Urbanization

Citizen scientists. Burns, L. G. **590.72**

CitizenKid [series]
    This child, every child **305.23**

Citizenship. Raatma, L. **323.6**

CITIZENSHIP

Croswell, Ken
  The lives of stars   **523.8**
The **Crow**. Bial, R.   **970**
CROW INDIANS
  Bial, R. The Crow   **970**
Crowder, Melanie
  Parched   **Fic**
Crowe, Chris
  Getting away with murder: the true story of the Emmett Till case   **364.152**
  Mississippi trial, 1955   **Fic**
  More than a game   **810**
  Thurgood Marshall   **92**
Crowe, Felicity
  (ed) Illustrated dictionary of the Muslim world **297**
Crowe, Francis Trenholm, 1882-1946
About
  Aaseng, N. Construction: building the impossible   **624**
The **Crowfield** curse. Walsh, P.   **Fic**
The **Crowfield** demon. Walsh, P.   **Fic**
Crowley, Cath
  A little wanting song   **Fic**
Crowley, James
  Starfish   **Fic**
Crowley, Suzanne
  The stolen one   **Fic**
Crown of earth. Bell, H.   **Fic**
The **crown** of embers. Carson, R.   **Fic**
Crows & cards. Helgerson, J.   **Fic**
CROWS -- FICTION
  Bauer, A. C. E. Come Fall   **Fic**
CROWS -- GRAPHIC NOVELS
  McAdoo, D. Red moon   **741.5**
Crowther, Robert
  Robert Crowther's pop-up house of inventions **609**
Croy, Anita
  (ed) Ancient Aztec and Maya   **972**
  (ed) Ancient Egypt   **932**
  (ed) Ancient Greece   **938**
  (ed) Ancient Rome   **937**
  Ancient Pueblo   **978**
  Colombia   **986.1**
  Exploring the past   **930.1**
  Guatemala   **972.81**
  Spain   **946**
Croy, Elden
  United States   **973**
CRUDE OIL See Petroleum
Cruel Beauty. Hodge, R.   **Fic**
CRUELTY
  See also Ethics
CRUELTY TO ANIMALS See Animal welfare
CRUELTY TO CHILDREN See Child abuse
Cruise control. Trueman, T.   **Fic**
CRUISE SHIPS -- FICTION

De la Peña, M. The living   **Fic**
  Shusterman, N. Ship out of luck   **Fic**
The **Cruisers**. Myers, W. D.   **Fic**
Cruisers [series]
  Myers, W. D. A star is born   **Fic**
The **Cruisers**: checkmate. Myers, W. D.   **Fic**
CRUISES See Ocean travel
Crump, Marty
  The mystery of Darwin's frog   **597.8**
Crunch. Connor, L.   **Fic**
Crusade. Holder, N.   **Fic**
CRUSADES
  Crompton, S. The Third Crusade   **956**
  Currie, S. The Medieval crusades   **909.07**
  Lace, W. W. The unholy crusade   **956.1**
CRUSADES -- FICTION
  Cadnum, M. The book of the Lion   **Fic**
  Grant, K. M. Blood red horse   **Fic**
  Spradlin, M. P. Keeper of the Grail   **Fic**
Crush. Paulsen, G.   **Fic**
Crush: love poems.   **808.81**
CRUSHES
  See also Friendship; Love
CRUSHES -- FICTION
  Paulsen, G. Crush   **Fic**
Crust and spray. Larsen, C. S.   **612.8**
CRUSTACEA
  Gilpin, D. Lobsters, crabs & other crustaceans   **595.3**
Crutcher, Chris
  Athletic shorts   **S**
  Deadline   **Fic**
  Ironman   **Fic**
  King of the mild frontier: an ill-advised autobiography   **92**
  Running loose   **Fic**
  Staying fat for Sarah Byrnes   **Fic**
  Stotan!   **Fic**
  Whale talk   **Fic**
About
  Crutcher, C. King of the mild frontier: an ill-advised autobiography   **92**
  Sommers, M. A. Chris Crutcher   **92**
Cruz, Celia, 1929-2003
About
  Cartlidge, C. Celia Cruz   **92**
Cruzan v. Missouri. Perl, L.   **344**
Cruzan v. Missouri and the right to die debate. Fridell, R.   **344**
Cruzan, Joe, d. 1996
About
  Fridell, R. Cruzan v. Missouri and the right to die debate   **344**
  Perl, L. Cruzan v. Missouri   **344**
Cruzan, Nancy
About

LeVert, S. Ecstasy **362.29**

Parks, P. J. Bath salts and other synthetic drugs **362.29**

DESIGNER DRUGS

See also Drugs

DESIGNERS

See also Artists

Designing a school library media center for the future. Erikson, R. **027.8**

Desires of the dead. Derting, K. **Fic**

DESKTOP PUBLISHING

Todd, M. Whatcha mean, what's a zine? **070.5**

Desonie, Dana

Climate **551.6**

Geosphere **333.73**

Hydrosphere **551.48**

Oceans **551.46**

Despain, Bree

The dark Divine **Fic**

The **desperado** who stole baseball. Ritter, J. H. **Fic**

Desperate journey. Murphy, J. **Fic**

Despeyroux, Denise

The big book of vampires **Fic**

Despite all obstacles: La Salle and the conquest of the Mississippi. Goodman, J. E. **92**

DESPOTISM -- FICTION

Mourlevat Winter's end **Fic**

Desrocher, Jack

Doeden, M. Eat right! **613.2**

Donovan, S. Keep your cool! **616.85**

Golus, C. Take a stand! **302.3**

Johnson, R. L. Amazing DNA **572.8**

Johnson, R. L. Powerful plant cells **581.7**

Nelson, S. K. Stay safe! **613.6**

Dessen, Sarah, 1970-

The moon and more **Fic**

Along for the ride **Fic**

Lock and key **Fic**

That summer **Fic**

The truth about forever **Fic**

What happened to goodbye **Fic**

About

Glenn, W. J. Sarah Dessen **813**

DESSERTS

Carle, M. Teens cook dessert **641.8**

DESSERTS

See also Cooking

DeStefano, Lauren

Perfect ruin **Fic**

Destefano, Merrie

Butkus, M. How to draw zombies **743**

Destination unexpected: short stories. **S**

Destination Uranus, Neptune, and Pluto. Sparrow, G. **523.4**

Destiny's path. Jones, A. F. **Fic**

Destiny, rewritten. Fitzmaurice, K. **Fic**

DESTITUTION *See* Poverty

Destroy all cars. Nelson, B. **Fic**

DESTRUCTIVE INSECTS *See* Insect pests

DETECTIVE AND MYSTERY STORIES

Carter, A. Perfect scoundrels **Fic**

Gleason, C. The clockwork scarab **Fic**

McClintock, N. About that night **Fic**

Pastis, S. Timmy failure : now look what you've done **Fic**

Shouldn't you be in school? **Fic**

Teague, D. Saving Lucas Biggs **Fic**

Wild boy and the black terror **Fic**

DETECTIVE AND MYSTERY STORIES *See* Mystery fiction

DETECTIVE AND MYSTERY STORIES, ENG-LISH

Doyle, A. C. S. The adventures and the memoirs of Sherlock Holmes **Fic**

DETECTIVE FICTION *See* Mystery fiction

DETECTIVE STORIES *See* Mystery fiction

DETECTIVES

See also Police

DETECTIVES -- FICTION

Lawrence, C. P.K. Pinkerton and the pistol-packing widows **Fic**

Pastis, S. Timmy failure : now look what you've done **Fic**

DETECTOR DOGS

Castaldo, N. F. Sniffer dogs **636.7**

The **detention** club. Yoo, D. **Fic**

DETERGENT POLLUTION OF RIVERS, LAKES, ETC. *See* Water pollution

DETERMINATION (PERSONALITY TRAIT) -- FICTION

Eliza Bing is (not) a big, fat quitter **Fic**

Detorie, Rick

The accidental genius of Weasel High **Fic**

Detrick, Erin

(ed) Actor's choice **808.82**

DETROIT (MICH.) -- FICTION

Lupica, M. The batboy **Fic**

Whelan, G. See what I see **Fic**

DETROIT TIGERS (BASEBALL TEAM) -- FICTION

Lupica, M. The batboy **Fic**

Deuker, Carl

Gym candy **Fic**

High heat **Fic**

Night hoops **Fic**

Painting the black **Fic**

Payback time **Fic**

Swagger **Fic**

Devastated by a volcano! Person, S. **551.2**

DEVELOPING COUNTRIES

See also Economic conditions; Industrialization

Fleming, C. Ben Franklin's almanac **92**

Fleming, C. Our Eleanor **92**

Freedman, R. Eleanor Roosevelt **973.917**

MacDonald, B. The secret of the sealed room **Fic**

MacLeod, E. Eleanor Roosevelt **92**

McElligott, M. Benjamin Franklinstein lives! **Fic**

McElligott, M. Benjamin Franklinstein meets the Fright brothers **Fic**

Miller, B. M. Benjamin Franklin, American genius **92**

Ryan, P. M. The dreamer **Fic**

Shull, J. A. Pablo Neruda **92**

Woodruff, E. George Washington's spy **Fic**

DIPLOMATS

See also Diplomacy; International relations; Statesmen

DiPrimio, Pete

The sphinx **398.2**

We visit Iran **955**

DIRECT MARKETING

See also Mail-order business; Marketing

DIRECT SELLING

See also Marketing; Retail trade; Selling

Directing. Bezdecheck, B. **792.6**

DIRIGIBLE BALLOONS *See* Airships

Dirt road home. Key, W. **Fic**

Dirty little secrets. Omololu, C. J. **Fic**

DISABILITIES

See also Diseases; Wounds and injuries

DISABLED *See* People with disabilities

The **Disappeared.** Whelan, G. **Fic**

DISAPPOINTMENT

See also Emotions

Disaster in the Indian Ocean, Tsunami 2004. Torres, J. A. **909.83**

DISASTER PREPAREDNESS *See* Disaster relief

DISASTER RELIEF

Morley, D. Healing our world **610**

Robson, D. Disaster response **363.34**

Saul, L. Ways to help after a natural disaster **363.34**

See also Charities; Humanitarian intervention; Public welfare

Disaster response. Robson, D. **363.34**

DISASTER RESPONSE AND RECOVERY

Rusch, E. Eruption! **363.34**

Disaster survivors [series]

Aronin, M. Mangled by a hurricane! **551.55**

Aronin, M. Slammed by a tsunami! **551.46**

DeLallo, L. Hammered by a heat wave! **551.5**

Markovics, J. L. Blitzed by a blizzard! **551.55**

Person, S. Devastated by a volcano! **551.2**

Person, S. Struck by lightning! **551.56**

Reingold, A. Leveled by an earthquake! **551.2**

Rudolph, J. Erased by a tornado! **551.55**

Disasters. Guiberson, B. Z. **904**

DISASTERS

Blackwood, G. L. Enigmatic events **904**

Butts, E. SOS: stories of survival **363.34**

Garner, J. We interrupt this broadcast **070.1**

Guiberson, B. Z. Disasters **904**

Scott, E. Buried alive! **363.11**

Stefoff, R. Forensics and modern disasters **363.34**

DISC JOCKEYS

See also Musicians; Radio and music

DISC JOCKEYS -- FICTION

Sales, L. This song will save your life **Fic**

DISCIPLINE *See* Punishment

DISCIPLINE OF CHILDREN *See* Child rearing; School discipline

DISCOGRAPHY *See* Sound recordings

DISCOUNT STORES

Blumenthal, K. Mr. Sam **92**

DISCOUNT STORES

See also Retail trade; Stores

Discover animals [series]

Menon, S. Discover snakes **597.96**

Discover National Monuments, National Parks. Brown, C. L. **363.6**

Discover snakes. Menon, S. **597.96**

Discover the Amazon. Berkenkamp, L. **981**

Discover your world [series]

Brown, C. L. Discover National Monuments, National Parks **363.6**

DISCOVERERS *See* Explorers

DISCOVERIES AND EXPLORATION *See* Exploration

DISCOVERIES IN GEOGRAPHY

Into the unknown **910.4**

Lives of the explorers **920**

Kerley, B. The world is waiting for you **910**

DISCOVERIES IN GEOGRAPHY *See* Exploration

DISCOVERIES IN GEOGRAPHY -- EUROPEAN

Elliott, L. Exploration in the Renaissance **910**

DISCOVERIES IN MEDICINE

See also Discoveries in science; Medicine

DISCOVERIES IN SCIENCE

George, C. Biotech research **660.6**

Montgomery, H. L. Wild discoveries **590**

DISCOVERIES IN SCIENCE

See also Research; Science

DISCOVERIES IN SCIENCE -- EUROPE

Nardo, D. The scientific revolution **509**

DISCOVERIES IN SCIENCE -- FICTION

Blakemore, M. F. The Water Castle **Fic**

DISCOVERIES, SCIENTIFIC *See* Discoveries in science

Discovering atoms. Campbell, M. C. **539.7**

Discovering careers series

Food **647.95**

Discovering Central America [series]

West, K. Pivot point **Fic**
The **Divorce** Express. Danziger, P. **Fic**
DIVORCE MEDIATION
See also Divorce
DIVORCED FATHERS
See also Divorced parents; Divorced people;
Fathers
Dixon, Dougal
Meat-eating dinosaurs **567.912**
Plant-eating dinosaurs **567.9**
Prehistoric oceans **567.9**
Prehistoric skies **567.9**
Dixon, Heather
Entwined **Fic**
Dixon, Norma
Focus on flies **595.7**
Dizzy Gillespie. Boone, M. **788.9**
Dizzy in your eyes. Mora, P. **811**
DK biography [series]
Buckley, J. Pele **92**
Burgan, M. Ronald Reagan **92**
Krensky, S. Barack Obama **92**
Krensky, S. Clara Barton **92**
Sawyer, K. K. Harriet Tubman **92**
Wills, C. A. Annie Oakley: a photographic story of
a life **92**
DK children's illustrated encyclopedia. DK Publishing, I. **031**
DK eyewitness books [series]
Adams, S. World War I **940.3**
Adams, S. World War II **940.53**
Bender, L. Invention **609**
Burnie, D. Bird **598**
Byam, M. Arms & armor **355.8**
Clutton-Brock, J. Horse **636.1**
Cosgrove, B. Weather **551.5**
Cribb, J. Money **332.4**
Fortey, J. Great scientists **920**
Gamlin, L. Evolution **576.8**
Greenaway, T. Jungle **577.3**
Hornby, H. Soccer **796.334**
James, S. Ancient Rome **937**
Lane, B. Crime and detection **363.2**
Langley, A. Medieval life **940.1**
Langley, M. Religion **200**
McCarthy, C. Reptile **597.9**
Murdoch, D. H. North American Indian **970.004**
Nahum, A. Flying machine **629.133**
Newmark, A. Chemistry **540**
Parker, S. Seashore **577.7**
Redmond, I. Elephant **599.67**
Rowland-Warne, L. Costume **391**
Stott, C. Space exploration **629.4**
Taylor, P. D. Fossil **560**
Tubb, J. N. Bible lands **220.9**
Walker, R. Human body **612**

Woodward, J. Water **553.7**
DK Publishing, Inc.
DK children's illustrated encyclopedia **031**
(comp) The politics book **320.01**
(comp) Rocks and minerals **552**
(comp) Sharks **597.3**
(comp) Student atlas **912**
DNA. Silverstein, A. **572.8**
DNA. Ollhoff, J. **929**
DNA
Hall, L. E. DNA and RNA **611**
Johnson, R. L. Amazing DNA **572.8**
Polcovar, J. Rosalind Franklin and the structure of
life **92**
Rand, C. DNA and heredity **572.8**
Silverstein, A. DNA **572.8**
Vaughan, J. Who discovered DNA? **572.8**
See also Cells; Heredity; Nucleic acids
DNA -- HISTORY
Hartman, E. What are the issues with genetic technology? **660.6**
Yount, L. Rosalind Franklin **572.8**
DNA and body evidence. Innes, B. **363.2**
DNA and heredity. Rand, C. **572.8**
DNA and RNA. Hall, L. E. **611**
DNA FINGERPRINTING
Innes, B. DNA and body evidence **363.2**
Rainis, K. G. Blood & DNA evidence **363.2**
DNA FINGERPRINTING
See also Identification; Medical jurisprudence
DNA FINGERPRINTS *See* DNA fingerprinting
DNA IDENTIFICATION *See* DNA fingerprinting
DNA PROFILING *See* DNA fingerprinting
Do all Indians live in tipis? National Museum of the
American Indian (U.S.) **970.004**
Do not open. Farndon, J. **031.02**
Do not pass go. Hill, K. **Fic**
Do you know where your food comes from? Morris,
N. **363.8**
Do you love me? Harris, A. R. **613.9**
Do you read me? Webber, D. **363.2**
Doable renewables. Rigsby, M. **333.79**
Doak, Robin S.
Black Tuesday **330.9**
California, 1542-1850 **979.4**
Georgia, 1521-1776 **975.8**
Maryland, 1634-1776 **975.2**
New Jersey 1609-1776 **974.9**
South Carolina, 1540-1776 **975.7**
Struggling to become American **305.8**
Dobkin, Bonnie
Neptune's children **Fic**
Dobson, Clive
Wind power **333.9**
Dobson, Jolie
The duct tape book **745.5**

Greenwald, L. Dog Beach — **Fic**
Ibbotson, E. One dog and his boy — **Fic**
Larson, K. Dash — **Fic**
Larson, K. Lucky dog — **Fic**
Lean, S. A dog called Homeless — **Fic**
Martin, A. M. Rain Reign — **Fic**
Paulsen, G. Road trip — **Fic**
Pyron, B. The dogs of winter — **Fic**
Winget, D. D. A million ways home — **Fic**

DOGS -- GRAPHIC NOVELS
Kibuishi, K. Copper — **741.5**
McAdoo, D. Red moon — **741.5**

DOGS -- PSYCHOLOGY
See also Animal intelligence; Comparative psychology; Psychology

DOGS -- SENSE ORGANS
Castaldo, N. F. Sniffer dogs — **636.7**

DOGS -- TRAINING
Gewirtz, E. W. Fetch this book — **636.7**
Rogers, T. 4-H guide to dog training and dog tricks — **636.7**

DOGS -- WAR USE -- FICTION
Dogs of war — **741.5**

DOGS -- WAR USE -- UNITED STATES
Bausum, A. Stubby the War Dog — **940.4**
Dogs for kids! Mehus-Roe, K. — **636.7**

DOGS FOR THE BLIND *See* Guide dogs

DOGS IN ART
Ames, L. J. Draw 50 dogs — **743**
Dogs of war. — **741.5**
The **dogs** of winter. Pyron, B. — **Fic**

DOGSLEDDING -- FICTION
Johnson, T. L. Ice dogs — **Fic**
Kurtz, C. The adventures of a South Pole pig — **Fic**
Dogsong. Paulsen, G. — **Fic**
Dogtag summer. Partridge, E. — **Fic**
Doherty, Berlie
The girl who saw lions — **Fic**
Doherty, Kieran
To conquer is to live: the life of Captain John Smith of Jamestown — **973.2**
William Bradford — **974.4**
Doing it right. Pardes, B. — **613.9**
Doing social media so it matters. Solomon, L. — **302.3**
Dokey, Cameron
Hawes, J. Ghost hunt — **133.1**
Doktorski, Jennifer Salvato
Famous last words — **Fic**
Dolamore, Jaclyn
Magic under glass — **Fic**
Dolan, Edward F.
The American Indian wars — **970.004**
Careers in the U.S. Coast Guard — **363.2**
Careers in the U.S. Navy — **359**
George Washington — **92**
DOLL *See* Dolls

Doll bones. Black, H. — **Fic**
DOLL FURNITURE
See also Miniature objects; Toys
DOLLHOUSES
See also Miniature objects; Toys
DOLLMAKING
See also Dolls
DOLLS
Aranzi Aronzo Inc. Cute dolls — **745.592**
DOLLS
See also Toys
DOLLS -- FICTION
Black, H. Doll bones — **Fic**
DOLOMEDES
Markle, S. Fishing spiders — **595.4**
Dolphin song. St. John, L. — **Fic**
DOLPHINS
Christopherson, S. C. Top 50 reasons to care about whales and dolphins — **599.5**
Hall, H. A charm of dolphins — **599.5**
Turner, P. S. The dolphins of Shark Bay — **599.53**
Webb, S. Far from shore — **591.7**
DOLPHINS
See also Marine mammals
DOLPHINS -- FICTION
One white dolphin — **Fic**
St. John, L. Dolphin song — **Fic**
The **dolphins** of Shark Bay. Turner, P. S. — **599.53**
Domenic's war. Parkinson, C. — **Fic**
DOMESTIC ANIMALS
The horse and the Plains indians — **978**
Martin, C. Farming — **636**
Rothman, J. Farm anatomy — **630**
DOMESTIC ANIMALS
See also Animals
DOMESTIC ANIMALS -- DISEASES *See* Animals -- Diseases
DOMESTIC ANIMALS -- FICTION
Armstrong, A. Whittington — **Fic**
Blazanin, J. A & L do summer — **Fic**
DOMESTIC ARCHITECTURE
See also Architecture
DOMESTIC FINANCE *See* Household budgets; Personal finance
DOMESTIC RELATIONS
See also Interpersonal relations
DOMESTIC TERRORISM
See also Terrorism
DOMESTIC VIOLENCE
Domestic violence: opposing viewpoints — **362.82**
Gordon, S. M. Beyond bruises — **362.7**
Stewart, S. When Daddy hit Mommy — **362.82**
DOMESTIC VIOLENCE
See also Violence
DOMESTIC VIOLENCE -- FICTION
Oates, J. C. Freaky green eyes — **Fic**

Ellsworth, Loretta
  Unforgettable   **Fic**
Ellwood, Robert S.
  (ed) The encyclopedia of world religions   **200**
Elly. Gross, E. B.   **92**
ELOCUTION *See* Public speaking
Elsewhere. Zevin, G.   **Fic**
The Elsewhere chronicles [series]
  Bannister (Person) The shadow door   **741.5**
Elspeth. O'Hearn, K.   **Fic**
Elston, Ashley
  The rules for disappearing   **Fic**
ELVES
  See also Folklore
ELVES -- FICTION
  Springer, N. Rowan Hood, outlaw girl of Sherwood
    Forest   **Fic**
  Stewart, A. Dragonwood   **Fic**
Elvis. Collins, T.   **92**
Elvis Presley. Hampton, W.   **92**
Elvis Presley. Micklos, J.   **92**
ELY (ENGLAND) -- HISTORY -- 19TH CENTU-
  RY -- FICTION
  Berry, J. The scandalous sisterhood of Prickwillow
    Place   **Fic**
EMAIL *See* E-mail
EMAIL -- FICTION
  Rivers, K. Finding Ruby Starling   **Fic**
  Zarr, S. Roomies   **Fic**
Emako Blue. Woods, B.   **Fic**
EMANCIPATION OF SLAVES *See* Slaves --
  Emancipation
EMANCIPATION OF WOMEN *See* Women's
  rights
The Emancipation Proclamation. Woog, A. **973.7**
Emancipation Proclamation. Bolden, T.   **973.7**
EMANCIPATION PROCLAMATION (1863)
  Bolden, T. Emancipation Proclamation   **973.7**
  Woog, A. The Emancipation Proclamation   **973.7**
EMBARRASSMENT *See* Self-consciousness
Embassy row #1.   **Fic**
EMBLEMS *See* Decorations of honor; Heraldry;
  Insignia; Mottoes; National emblems; Seals (Nu-
  mismatics); Signs and symbols
EMBLEMS, NATIONAL
  Bateman, T. Red, white, blue, and Uncle who? **929.9**
Embracing, evaluating, and examining Afri-
  can American children's and young adult litera-
  ture.   **028.5**
EMBROIDERY
  See also Decoration and ornament; Needle-
    work; Sewing
EMBRYOLOGY
  See also Biology; Zoology
Emerald ash borer. Gray, S. H.   **595.7**
EMERALD ASH BORER

Gray, S. H. Emerald ash borer   **595.7**
The **emerald** atlas. Stephens, J.   **Fic**
Emerald green.   **Fic**
EMERGENCIES *See* Accidents; Disasters; First
  aid
EMERGENCY MEDICINE
  See also Medicine
EMERGENCY PREPAREDNESS *See* Disaster
  relief
EMERGENCY RELIEF *See* Disaster relief
EMERGENCY SURVIVAL *See* Survival skills
An **emerging** world power (1900-1929) Stanley, G.
  E.   **973.91**
Emerson, Ralph Waldo, 1803-1882
  About
  Caravantes, P. Self-reliance: the story of Ralph
    Waldo Emerson   **92**
Emerson, Sharon
  Zebrafish   **741.5**
Emert, Phyllis Raybin
  Art in glass   **748.2**
Emi and the rhino scientist. Carson, M. K. **599.66**
EMIGRANTS *See* Immigrants
EMIGRATION *See* Immigration and emigration
EMIGRATION AND IMMIGRATION -- FIC-
  TION
  Campoy, F. I. Yes! we are Latinos   **S**
  James, H. F. Paper son   **Fic**
EMIGRATION AND IMMIGRATION
  Senker, C. Immigrants and refugees   **304.8**
Emiko superstar. Tamaki, M.   **741.5**
Emil and Karl. Glatstein, J.   **Fic**
Emiliano Zapata and the Mexican Revolution. Stein,
  R. C.   **92**
Emily Dickinson. Meltzer, M.   **92**
Emily Goldberg learns to salsa. Ostow, M.   **Fic**
Emily Post prom and party etiquette. Senning, C.
  P.   **395**
Emily Post's table manners for kids. Post, P.   **395**
Emily Post's The guide to good manners for kids.
  Post, P.   **395**
The **Emily** sonnets.   **811**
Emily the Strange: dark times. Reger, R.   **Fic**
Emily the Strange: stranger and stranger. Reger,
  R.   **Fic**
Emily the Strange: the lost days. Reger, R.   **Fic**
EMINENT DOMAIN
  See also Constitutional law; Land use; Prop-
    erty
Emlyn's moon. Nimmo, J.   **Fic**
Emma-Jean Lazarus fell in love. Tarshis, L.   **Fic**
Emma-Jean Lazarus fell out of a tree. Tarshis,
  L.   **Fic**
Emmeluth, Donald
  Botulism   **616.9**
Emond, Stephen

EPISTOLARY FICTION

Moriarty, J. A corner of white   **Fic**

EPISTOLARY NOVELS *See* Epistolary fiction

EPISTOLARY POETRY

See also Poetry

EPITAPHS

See also Biography; Cemeteries; Inscriptions; Tombs

EPITHETS *See* Names; Nicknames

EPIZOA *See* Parasites

Epoch biographies [series]

Archer, J. They had a dream   **323.1**

Epstein, Adam Jay

Circle of heroes   **Fic**

Epstein, Robin

God is in the pancakes   **Fic**

EQUAL EMPLOYMENT OPPORTUNITY *See* Affirmative action programs; Discrimination in employment

EQUAL RIGHTS AMENDMENTS

See also Constitutions; Sex discrimination

EQUATIONS

See also Mathematics

EQUESTRIANISM *See* Horsemanship

EQUILIBRIUM (ECONOMICS)

See also Economics

ER vets. Jackson, D. M.   **636.089**

Eragon. Paolini, C.   **Fic**

Erak's ransom. Flanagan, J.   **Fic**

Erased by a tornado! Rudolph, J.   **551.55**

Erasing the ink. Spalding, F.   **391**

Erasing time. Hill, C. J.   **Fic**

Eratosthenes, 3rd cent. B.C.

About

Gow, M. Measuring the Earth   **92**

Erdoes, Richard

(ed) American Indian myths and legends   **398.2**

Brave Bird, M. Lakota woman   **92**

Erdrich, Louise

The birchbark house   **Fic**

Chickadee   **Fic**

The game of silence   **Fic**

The porcupine year   **Fic**

ERGONOMICS

Parks, D. Nature's machines   **92**

ERGONOMICS

See also Applied psychology; Engineering; Industrial design; Psychophysiology

Erickson, Paul

Daily life in the Pilgrim colony, 1636   **974.4**

Ericsson, Aprille, 1963-

About

Aerospace engineer Aprille Ericsson   **629.409**

ERIE CANAL (N.Y.)

Coleman, W. The amazing Erie Canal and how a big ditch opened up the West   **386**

ERIE CANAL (N.Y.) -- FICTION

Murphy, J. Desperate journey   **Fic**

Erikson, Rolf

Designing a school library media center for the future   **027.8**

Eritrea. NgCheong-Lum, R.   **963.5**

ERITREA

NgCheong-Lum, R. Eritrea   **963.5**

Erlbach, Arlene

The middle school survival guide   **373.1**

Ernest Hemingway. Reef, C.   **92**

Ernest Hemingway. Whiting, J.   **92**

Ernest J. Gaines. Abrams, D.   **92**

Ernest Rutherford and the birth of the atomic age. Baxter, R.   **530.092**

Ernest Shackleton. Johnson, R. L.   **92**

Ernesto Che Guevara. Abrams, D.   **92**

Ernst, Kathleen

Hearts of stone   **Fic**

Erosion. Stille, D. R.   **551.3**

EROSION

Stille, D. R. Erosion   **551.3**

EROTIC ART

See also Art; Erotica

EROTIC FILMS

See also Motion pictures

EROTIC LITERATURE

See also Erotica; Literature

EROTIC POETRY

See also Erotic literature; Poetry

Erratum. Sorrells, W.   **Fic**

Erskine, Kathryn

The absolute value of Mike   **Fic**

The badger knight   **Fic**

Quaking   **Fic**

Seeing red   **Fic**

Eruption. Smith, R.   **Fic**

Eruption! Rusch, E.   **363.34**

The **escape.** Lasky, K.   **Fic**

Escape and evasion. McIntosh, J. S.   **335.4**

Escape from Furnace [series]

Smith, A. G. Death sentence   **Fic**

Smith, A. G. Lockdown   **Fic**

Smith, A. G. Solitary   **Fic**

Escape from Mr. Lemoncello's library. Grabenstein, C.   **Fic**

Escape from Saigon. Warren, A.   **92**

Escape the mask. Ward, D.   **Fic**

Escape under the forever sky. Yohalem, E.   **Fic**

Escape velocity. Walden, M.   **Fic**

Escape velocity. Stevenson, R.   **Fic**

Escape! Fleischman, S.   **92**

Escape--teens on the run. Altman, L. J.   **940.53**

ESCAPES

See also Adventure and adventurers; Prisons

ESCAPES -- FICTION

EX-NUNS -- FICTION

Jarzab, A. The opposite of hallelujah   **Fic**

EXAMINATIONS

See also Questions and answers; Teaching

EXAMINATIONS -- FICTION

Charbonneau, J. The Testing   **Fic**

EXAMINATIONS -- STUDY GUIDES

Cunha, S. F. How to ace the National Geographic Bee   **372.63**

Fuhrken, C. What every middle school teacher needs to know about reading tests (from someone who has written them)   **428**

EXAMINATIONS -- STUDY GUIDES

See also Study skills

Examining energy [series]

Boyle, J. Examining geothermal energy   **621.44**

Examining geothermal energy. Boyle, J.   **621.44**

Examining issues through political cartoons [series]

Williams, M. E. Civil rights   **323.1**

Examining solar energy. Bright, S.   **621.47**

Excalibur.   **741.5**

EXCAVATION

See also Civil engineering; Tunnels

EXCAVATIONS (ARCHEOLOGY)

Aronson, M. The skull in the rock   **569.9**

Hansen, J. Breaking ground, breaking silence **974.7**

Rubalcaba, J. Every bone tells a story   **930.1**

Schlitz, L. A. The hero Schliemann   **92**

See also Archeology

EXCAVATIONS (ARCHAEOLOGY) -- CHINA -- CHANGSHA (HUNAN SHENG)

At home in her tomb   **931**

EXCAVATIONS (ARCHAEOLOGY) -- EGYPT -- VALLEY OF THE KINGS

Lace, W. King Tut's curse   **932**

EXCAVATIONS (ARCHAEOLOGY) -- SOUTH AFRICA -- WITWATERSRAND REGION

Aronson, M. The skull in the rock   **569.9**

EXCAVATIONS (ARCHAEOLOGY) -- TANZANIA -- OLDUVAI GORGE

Henderson, H. The Leakey family   **599.909**

EXCAVATIONS (ARCHAEOLOGY) -- TURKEY

Digging for Troy   **939**

Schlitz, L. A. The hero Schliemann   **92**

EXCAVATIONS (ARCHAEOLOGY) -- CANADA

Huey, L. M. American archaeology uncovers the Vikings   **970.01**

EXCAVATIONS (ARCHAEOLOGY) -- CHINA

At home in her tomb   **931**

EXCAVATIONS (ARCHAEOLOGY) -- EGYPT

Rubalcaba, J. Ancient Egypt   **932**

EXCAVATIONS (ARCHAEOLOGY) -- ENGLAND

Aronson, M. If stones could speak   **936**

EXCAVATIONS (ARCHAEOLOGY) -- EUROPE

Green, J. Ancient Celts   **936**

EXCAVATIONS (ARCHEOLOGY) -- GREECE

McGee, M. Ancient Greece   **938**

EXCAVATIONS (ARCHEOLOGY) -- INDONESIA

Goldenberg, L. Little people and a lost world **599.93**

EXCAVATIONS (ARCHEOLOGY) -- IRAQ

Gruber, B. Ancient Iraq   **935**

EXCAVATIONS (ARCHEOLOGY) -- ITALY

Sonneborn, L. Pompeii   **937**

EXCAVATIONS (ARCHEOLOGY) -- MEXICO

Cooke, T. Ancient Aztec   **972**

Harris, N. Ancient Maya   **972**

Kops, D. Palenque   **972**

Lourie, P. Hidden world of the Aztec   **972**

EXCAVATIONS (ARCHEOLOGY) -- PERU

Gruber, B. Ancient Inca   **985**

EXCAVATIONS (ARCHEOLOGY) -- UNITED STATES

Huey, L. M. American archaeology uncovers the Dutch colonies   **974.7**

Huey, L. M. American archaeology uncovers the earliest English colonies   **973.2**

Huey, L. M. American archaeology uncovers the Underground Railroad   **973.7**

Huey, L. M. American archaeology uncovers the Vikings   **970.01**

Huey, L. M. American archaeology uncovers the westward movement   **978**

Walker, S. M. Written in bone   **614**

EXCEPTIONAL CHILDREN

See also Children; Elementary education

The **exchange.** Joyce, G.   **Fic**

EXCHANGE OF PRISONERS OF WAR   *See* Prisoners of war

The **exchange** student. Gilmore, K.   **Fic**

EXCRETION

Klosterman, L. Excretory system   **612.4**

Excretory system. Klosterman, L.   **612.4**

EXCUSES

See also Etiquette; Manners and customs

EXECUTIONS AND EXECUTIONERS

See also Criminal law; Criminal procedure

EXECUTIVE DEPARTMENTS -- UNITED STATES

Bow, J. What is the executive branch?   **351**

EXECUTIVE POWER

Bow, J. What is the executive branch?   **351**

See also Constitutional law; Political science

EXECUTIVES

Gitlin, M. eBay   **338.7**

Exercise. Dicker, K.   **613.7**

EXERCISE

See also Health; Hygiene

Dicker, K. Exercise   **613.7**

Frederick, S. Strength training for teen athletes   **613.7**

B.   **Fic**

The familiars [series]
   Circle of heroes   **Fic**

FAMILIES -- BANGLADESH -- FICTION
   Tiger boy   **813.6**

FAMILIES -- HAITI -- FICTION
   Burg, A. E. Serafina's promise   **Fic**

FAMILIES -- INDIA
   Brahmachari, S. Jasmine Skies   **Fic**

FAMILIES
   Apelqvist, E. LGBTQ families   **306.87**

FAMILIES OF MILITARY PERSONNEL -- FICTION
   Fleming, D. The Saturday boy   **Fic**
   Gansworth, E. If I ever get out of here   **Fic**

FAMILY
   Bezdecheck, B. Relationships   **158**
   Fields, J. First-generation immigrant families   **325**
   Fields, J. Multiracial families   **306.8**
   Fox, A. What's up with my family?   **306.8**
   Harris, A. R. Is this really my family?   **646.7**
   Lynette, R. What makes us a family?   **306.8**
   McCaughrean, G. The kite rider   **Fic**
   Stewart, S. Growing up in religious communities   **305**
   Stewart, S. What is a family?   **306.8**

FAMILY
   See also Interpersonal relations; Sociology

FAMILY & RELATIONSHIPS -- LEARNING DISABILITIES
   The survival guide for kids with autism spectrum disorders (and their parents)   **618.92**

FAMILY -- FICTION
   Amato, M. Get happy   **Fic**
   Babbitt, N. The moon over High Street   **Fic**
   Backlash   **Fic**
   Berk, A. Mistle child   **Fic**
   Blakemore, M. F. The Water Castle   **Fic**
   Block, F. L. Love in the time of global warming   **Fic**
   Blumenthal, D. Mafia girl   **Fic**
   Brahmachari, S. Mira in the present tense   **Fic**
   Caine, R. Prince of Shadows   **Fic**
   Casanova, M. Frozen   **Fic**
   Catch you later, traitor   **Fic**
   Clifton, L. Freaky Fast Frankie Joe   **Fic**
   Erskine, K. Seeing red   **Fic**
   Friesner, E. Spirit's princess   **Fic**
   From the notebooks of a middle school princess   **Fic**
   Hemphill, S. Sisters of glass   **Fic**
   Hunt, L. M. One for the Murphys   **Fic**
   Levine, K. The paper cowboy   **Fic**
   Listen, Slowly   **Fic**
   Lockhart, E. We were liars   **Fic**
   My secret guide to Paris   **Fic**
   Knowles, J. See you at Harry's   **Fic**
   Mazer, H. Somebody, please tell me who I am   **Fic**

   McKay, H. Binny for short   **Fic**
   Potter, E. The humming room   **Fic**
   Red butterfly   **Fic**
   Rupp, R. After Eli   **Fic**
   Staniszewski, A. My sort of fairy tale ending   **Fic**
   Stone, P. Romeo blue   **Fic**
   Taub, M. Still star-crossed   **Fic**
   Thompson, J. E. The girl from Felony Bay   **Fic**

FAMILY BUDGET *See* Household budgets

FAMILY FARMS
   See also Farms

FAMILY FARMS -- FICTION
   MacLachlan, P. Kindred souls   **Fic**

FAMILY FINANCE *See* Personal finance

FAMILY HISTORIES *See* Genealogy

FAMILY LIFE
   Hart, J. Frequently asked questions about being part of a military family   **355.1**
   Lat Kampung boy   **741.5**
   Moore, W. Discovering Wes Moore   **975.2**
   Rosen, M. J. Our farm   **630**
   Sovern, M. J. The meaning of Maggie   **813.6**
   Tiger boy   **813.6**
   Telgemeier, R. Sisters   **741.5**
   See also Family

FAMILY LIFE -- ARKANSAS -- FICTION
   Levine, K. The lions of Little Rock   **Fic**

FAMILY LIFE -- BANGLADESH -- FICTION
   Tiger boy   **813.6**

FAMILY LIFE -- CALIFORNIA -- FICTION
   Blundell, J. A city tossed and broken   **Fic**
   Gee Whiz   **Fic**
   Leavitt, L. Going vintage   **Fic**
   Pie in the Sky   **Fic**
   Zarr, S. The Lucy variations   **Fic**
   Zarr, S. Roomies   **Fic**

FAMILY LIFE -- CALIFORNIA -- LOS ANGELES -- FICTION
   My life as a joke   **Fic**

FAMILY LIFE -- CANADA -- FICTION
   Hopkinson, N. The Chaos   **Fic**
   Johnston, E. K. The story of Owen   **Fic**
   Prairie fire   **Fic**

FAMILY LIFE -- COLORADO -- FICTION
   Mobley, J. Katerina's wish   **Fic**

FAMILY LIFE -- CONNECTICUT -- FICTION
   Hunt, L. M. One for the Murphys   **Fic**
   Matson, M. Since you've been gone   **Fic**

FAMILY LIFE -- ENGLAND -- FICTION
   Cooper, M. The FitzOsbornes at war   **Fic**
   Davies, K. The great dog disaster   **Fic**
   Emerald green   **Fic**
   Farrant, N. After Iris   **Fic**
   Ibbotson, E. One dog and his boy   **Fic**
   Lancaster, M. A. The future we left behind   **Fic**
   Terry, T. Slated   **Fic**

Matti, T. Mister Orange **Fic**
Stead, R. Liar & spy **Fic**
The Tapper twins go to war (with each other) **Fic**
Zevin, G. Because it is my blood **Fic**

FAMILY LIFE -- NEW YORK -- FICTION
Graff, L. A tangle of knots **Fic**

FAMILY LIFE -- NORTHWEST, PACIFIC -- FICTION
Alien encounter **Fic**

FAMILY LIFE -- PENNSYLVANIA -- FICTION
Andrews, J. Me & Earl & the dying girl **Fic**

FAMILY LIFE -- PENNSYLVANIA -- HERSHEY -- FICTION
Finneyfrock, K. The sweet revenge of Celia Door **Fic**

FAMILY LIFE -- RHODE ISLAND -- FICTION
Gray, C. Spellcaster **Fic**
Gray, C. Steadfast **Fic**

FAMILY LIFE -- RUSSIA -- FICTION
O'Brien, A. Lara's gift **Fic**

FAMILY LIFE -- TENNESSEE -- FICTION
Vawter, V. Paperboy **Fic**

FAMILY LIFE -- TEXAS -- FICTION
Gibbs, S. Poached **Fic**
Lopez, D. Ask my mood ring how I feel **Fic**
Wish girl **Fic**

FAMILY LIFE -- VIRGINIA -- FICTION
Erskine, K. Seeing red **Fic**
Harris, T. E. The perfect place **Fic**
Westrick, A. B. Brotherhood **Fic**

FAMILY LIFE -- WASHINGTON (STATE) -- FICTION
Flores-Scott, P. Jumped in **Fic**

FAMILY LIFE -- WASHINGTON (STATE) -- SEATTLE -- FICTION
Trueman, T. Life happens next **Fic**
Family matters. Meese, R. L. **011.6**

FAMILY MEDICINE
See also Medicine
A **family** of readers. Sutton, R. **809**

FAMILY PLANNING *See* Birth control

FAMILY PLANNING ADVOCATES
Bausum, A. Denied, detained, deported **325**

FAMILY PROBLEMS -- FICTION
Armistead, C. Being Henry David **Fic**
Black, H. Doll bones **Fic**
Blume, J. BFF* **Fic**
Burgis, S. Stolen magic **Fic**
Castan, M. Fighting for Dontae **Fic**
Chen, J. Return to me **Fic**
Cremer, A. Invisibility **Fic**
DeFelice, C. C. The ghost of Cutler Creek **Fic**
Deuker, C. High heat **Fic**
Golden, L. Every day after **Fic**
Harrington, K. Courage for beginners **Fic**
Harrington, K. Sure signs of crazy **Fic**

Hopkins, E. Rumble **Fic**
Horvath, P. One year in Coal Harbor **Fic**
Hunt, L. M. One for the Murphys **Fic**
Kehoe, S. W. The sound of letting go **Fic**
Kirby, J. Golden **Fic**
Knowles, J. See you at Harry's **Fic**
Levine, K. The paper cowboy **Fic**
Little, K. G. The time of the fireflies **Fic**
Loftin, N. Nightingale's nest **Fic**
Mazer, N. F. Girlhearts **Fic**
McCormick, P. Cut **Fic**
Nolan, H. A face in every window **Fic**
Peters, J. A. Define normal **Fic**
Peters, J. A. Luna **Fic**
Pitcher, A. My sister lives on the mantelpiece **Fic**
Pollock, T. The city's son **Fic**
Summers, C. This is not a test **Fic**
Sutton, K. Some quiet place **Fic**
Van Leeuwen, J. Lucy was there-- **Fic**
When reason breaks **Fic**
Willey, M. Beetle Boy **Fic**
Wish girl **Fic**

FAMILY RELATIONS *See* Domestic relations; Family life

FAMILY REUNIONS -- FICTION
Atkinson, E. J. I, Emma Freke **Fic**
The **family** Romanov. Fleming, C. **947.08**
A **family** secret. Heuvel, E. **741.5**

FAMILY SECRETS
See also Secrecy

FAMILY SECRETS -- FICTION
Brahmachari, S. Jasmine Skies **Fic**
Blakemore, M. F. The Water Castle **Fic**
Gone Crazy in Alabama **Fic**
Haddix, M. P. Full ride **Fic**
Infected **Fic**
Little, K. G. The time of the fireflies **Fic**

FAMILY SIZE
See also Family

FAMILY THERAPY
See also Counseling; Psychotherapy

FAMILY TRADITIONS
See also Family life; Manners and customs
Family tree [series]
Martin, A. M. Better to wish **Fic**

FAMILY TREES *See* Genealogy
Family trees [series]
Stefoff, R. The amphibian class **597.8**
Stefoff, R. The arachnid class **595.4**
Stefoff, R. The bird class **598**
Stefoff, R. The conifer division **585**
Stefoff, R. The fish classes **597**
Stefoff, R. The flowering plant division **580**
Stefoff, R. The fungus kingdom **579.5**
Stefoff, R. The marsupial order **599.2**
Stefoff, R. The Moneran kingdom **579**

The **Fog** diver.   **Fic**

Fogarty, Mignon
Grammar girl presents the ultimate writing guide for students   **428**

Fogelin, Adrian
The big nothing   **Fic**
The real question   **Fic**

Foiled. Yolen, J.   **741.5**

Foley, Erin
Costa Rica   **972.86**
Dominican Republic   **972.93**
Ecuador   **986.6**
El Salvador   **972.84**

Foley, Lizzie K.
Remarkable   **Fic**

Foley, Ryan
Stolen hearts   **741.5**

Folk. Handyside, C.   **781.62**

FOLK ART
Art from her heart: folk artist Clementine Hunter **92**
Govenar, A. B. Extraordinary ordinary people **745**

FOLK ART
See also Art; Art and society

FOLK ART, AMERICAN *See* American folk art

FOLK BELIEFS *See* Folklore; Superstition

FOLK DANCING
See also Dance

The **Folk** Keeper. Billingsley, F.   **Fic**

FOLK LITERATURE
Hearne, B. G. Beauties and beasts   **398.21**

FOLK LITERATURE
See also Folklore; Literature

FOLK LORE *See* Folklore

FOLK MUSIC
Handyside, C. Folk   **781.62**

FOLK MUSIC
See also Music

FOLK MUSICIANS
Orgill, R. Shout, sister, shout!   **920**
Partridge, E. This land was made for you and me **92**

FOLK SONGS
See also Folklore; Songs; Vocal music

FOLK SONGS -- UNITED STATES
See also American songs

Folk stories of the Hmong. Livo, N. J.   **398.2**

FOLK TALES *See* Folklore; Legends

FOLKLORE
The August House book of scary stories   **398.2**
Forest, H. Wisdom tales from around the world   **398.2**
Hausman, G. Horses of myth   **398.2**
Hearne, B. G. Beauties and beasts   **398.21**
Horowitz, A. Death and the underworld   **398.2**
Horowitz, A. Heroes and villains   **398.2**
Jaffe, N. The cow of no color: riddle stories and justice tales from around the world   **398.2**

Mitton, T. The storyteller's secrets   **398.2**
Norman, H. Between heaven and earth   **398.2**
Olson, A. N. Ask the bones: scary stories from around the world   **398.2**
Olson, A. N. More bones   **398.2**
Rapunzel and other magic fairy tales   **398.2**
San Souci, R. A terrifying taste of short & shivery   **398.2**
Schwartz, H. The day the Rabbi disappeared: Jewish holiday tales of magic   **398.2**
Tchana, K. H. Changing Woman and her sisters   **398.2**
Yolen, J. Mightier than the sword   **398.2**

FOLKLORE -- AFRICA
Abrahams, R. D. African folktales   **398.2**
African tales   **398.2**
Bryan, A. Ashley Bryan's African tales, uh-huh   **398.2**

FOLKLORE -- APPALACHIAN MOUNTAINS
Shelby, A. The adventures of Molly Whuppie and other Appalachian folktales   **398.2**

FOLKLORE -- CHINA
Bedard, M. The painted wall and other strange tales   **398.2**
Krasno, R. Cloud weavers   **398.2**
Yep, L. The rainbow people   **398.2**

FOLKLORE -- CUBA
Hayes, J. Dance, Nana, dance   **398.2**

FOLKLORE -- DICTIONARIES
Myths and legends   **398**

FOLKLORE -- EUROPE
Morpurgo, M. Beowulf   **398.2**
Raven, N. Beowulf   **398.2**
Rumford, J. Beowulf   **398.2**

FOLKLORE -- GERMANY
Gaiman, N. Hansel & Gretel   **741.5**
Zahler, D. The thirteenth princess   **Fic**

FOLKLORE -- GRAPHIC NOVELS
Trickster: Native American tales   **398.2**

FOLKLORE -- GREAT BRITAIN
English folktales   **398.2**
Philip, N. Celtic fairy tales   **398.2**
Pyle, H. The merry adventures of Robin Hood **398.2**

FOLKLORE -- GUATEMALA
Menchu, R. The secret legacy   **398.2**

FOLKLORE -- INDIA
Gavin, J. Tales from India   **398.2**

FOLKLORE -- IRAQ
The epic of Gilgamesh   **398.2**

FOLKLORE -- IRELAND
Burns, B. The king with horse's ears and other Irish folktales   **398.2**

FOLKLORE -- JAPAN -- GRAPHIC NOVELS
Ichiro   **741.5**

FOLKLORE -- LATIN AMERICA
Delacre, L. Golden tales   **398.209**

Geronimo, Apache Chief, 1829-1909
About
Brown, D. A. Bury my heart at Wounded
Knee **970.004**
Ehrlich, A. Wounded Knee: an Indian history of the
American West **970.004**
Sullivan, G. Geronimo **92**
Gerszak, Rafal, 1980-
About
Beyond bullets **958.1**
GESTALT PSYCHOLOGY
See also Consciousness; Perception; Psy-
chology; Senses and sensation; Theory of
knowledge
Get happy. Amato, M. **Fic**
Get into Art! Brooks, S. **704**
Get organized without losing it. Fox, J. S. **371.3**
Get real [series]
Tym, K. Coping with your emotions **152.4**
Tym, K. School survival **371.8**
Get smart with your money [series]
Byers, A. First credit cards and credit smarts **332.7**
Harmon, D. First car smarts **629.222**
Harmon, D. First job smarts **650.1**
Get the Scoop on Animal Puke. Cusick, D. **591.5**
Get well soon. Halpern, J. **Fic**
Getting away with murder: the true story of the Em-
mett Till case. Crowe, C. **364.152**
Getting graphic! Gorman, M. **741.5**
Getting inked. Gerber, L. **391**
Getting the girl. Juby, S. **Fic**
Gettysburg. Johnson, J. **973.7**
Gettysburg. Gregory, J. **973.7**
GETTYSBURG (PA.), BATTLE OF, 1863
Johnson, J. Gettysburg **973.7**
Murphy, J. The long road to Gettysburg **973.7**
Tarshis, L. I survived the Battle of Gettysburg,
1863 **E**
Weber, J. L. Summer's bloodiest days **973.7**
What was the Battle of Gettysburg? **973.7**
**GETTYSBURG (PA.), BATTLE OF, 1863 -- FIC-
TION**
Calkhoven, L. Will at the Battle of Gettysburg,
1863 **Fic**
Gutman, D. Abner & me **Fic**
Getzinger, Donna
George Frideric Handel and music for voices **92**
The Triangle Shirtwaist Factory fire **974.7**
Geus, Mireille
Piggy **Fic**
Gewirtz, Adina Rishe
Zebra forest **Fic**
Gewirtz, Elaine Waldorf
The bulldog **636.7**
Fetch this book **636.7**
Geyer, Mark

Moriarty, C. The inquisitor's apprentice **Fic**
GEYSERS
See also Geology; Geothermal resources;
Physical geography; Water
Ghana. Levy, P. **966.7**
GHANA
Levy, P. Ghana **966.7**
Weatherly, M. Teens in Ghana **966.7**
GHANA -- FICTION
Kittle, K. Reasons to be happy **Fic**
Mussi, S. The door of no return **Fic**
GHANA EMPIRE
Haywood, J. West African kingdoms **966**
McKissack, P. C. The royal kingdoms of Ghana,
Mali, and Songhay **966.2**
Gherman, Beverly
Anne Morrow Lindbergh **92**
Norman Rockwell **759.13**
Sparky: the life and art of Charles Schulz **92**
Ghetto cowboy. Neri, G. **Fic**
The **ghost** and Mrs. Hobbs. DeFelice, C. C. **Fic**
The **ghost** and the goth. Kade, S. **Fic**
Ghost canoe. Hobbs, W. **Fic**
GHOST DANCE
Ehrlich, A. Wounded Knee: an Indian history of the
American West **970.004**
Ghost girl. Ray, D. **Fic**
Ghost Hawk. Cooper, S. **Fic**
Ghost hunt. Hawes, J. **133.1**
Ghost hunt 2. Hawes, J. **133.1**
Ghost hunter. Paver, M. **Fic**
The **ghost** in the Tokaido Inn. Hoobler, D. **Fic**
Ghost letters. Alter, S. **Fic**
Ghost moon. Wilson, J. **Fic**
Ghost Mysteries [series]
DeFelice, C. C. The ghost of Fossil Glen **Fic**
The **ghost** of Crutchfield Hall. Hahn, M. D. **Fic**
The **ghost** of Cutler Creek. DeFelice, C. C. **Fic**
The **ghost** of Fossil Glen. DeFelice, C. C. **Fic**
The **ghost** of Poplar Point. DeFelice, C. C. **Fic**
Ghost of Spirit Bear. Mikaelsen, B. **Fic**
The **ghost** prison. Delaney, J. **Fic**
The **ghost** sitter. Griffin, P. R. **Fic**
GHOST STORIES
Abela, D. The ghosts of Gribblesea Pier **Fic**
Allison, J. Gilda Joyce, psychic investigator: the
bones of the holy **Fic**
Almond, D. Kit's wilderness **Fic**
Alter, S. Ghost letters **Fic**
Armstrong, K. The awakening **Fic**
Armstrong, K. The reckoning **Fic**
Armstrong, K. The summoning **Fic**
Auxier, J. The Night Gardener **Fic**
Avi The seer of shadows **Fic**
Barnholdt, L. Girl meets ghost **Fic**
Bauer, J. Peeled **Fic**

Damico, G. Rogue **Fic**

Delaney, J. The ghost prison **Fic**

Doyle, R. A greyhound of a girl **Fic**

McKay, H. Binny for short **Fic**

McNeal, T. Far far away **Fic**

Stroud, J. The screaming staircase **Fic**

Stroud, J. The whispering skull **Fic**

Winters, C. In the shadow of blackbirds **Fic**

GHOSTS -- FICTION *See* Ghost stories

GHOSTS -- GRAPHIC NOVELS

TenNapel, D. Ghostopolis **741.5**

Ghosts and spirits. Stefoff, R. **133.1**

Ghosts and spirits. Matthews, R. **133.1**

Ghosts in the fog. Seiple, S. **940.54**

The **ghosts** of Ashbury High. Moriarty, J. **Fic**

The **ghosts** of Gribblesea Pier. Abela, D. **Fic**

The **ghosts** of Kerfol. Noyes, D. **S**

The **ghosts** of Tupelo Landing. Turnage, S. **Fic**

Ghosts of war. Smithson, R. **956.7**

Ghoul strike! Newbound, A. **Fic**

The **giant** and how he humbugged America. Murphy, J. **974.7**

GIANT PANDA

Bortolotti, D. Panda rescue **599.78**

Firestone, M. Top 50 reasons to care about giant pandas **599.78**

Gish, M. Pandas **599.78**

Giant squid. Cerullo, M. M. **594**

GIANT SQUIDS

Cerullo, M. M. Giant squid **594**

Giant vs. giant. Bacchin, M. **567.9**

The **giant-slayer.** Lawrence, I. **Fic**

GIANTS

See also Folklore; Monsters

GIANTS -- FICTION

Aguiar, N. The lost island of Tamarind **Fic**

Gourlay, C. Tall story **Fic**

Lairamore, D. Ivy and the meanstalk **Fic**

Riordan, R. The house of Hades **Fic**

Trafton, J. The rise and fall of Mount Majestic **Fic**

Giants of science [series]

Krull, K. Albert Einstein **92**

Krull, K. Benjamin Franklin **92**

Krull, K. Charles Darwin **92**

Krull, K. Isaac Newton **92**

Krull, K. Leonardo da Vinci **92**

Krull, K. Marie Curie **92**

Gibbs, Stuart

Belly up **Fic**

The last musketeer **Fic**

Poached **Fic**

Spy camp **Fic**

Giblin, James

Giblin, J. C. The rise and fall of Senator Joe McCarthy **92**

Charles A. Lindbergh **629.13**

Good brother, bad brother **92**

The many rides of Paul Revere **92**

The riddle of the Rosetta Stone **493**

Gibson girls and suffragists. Gourley, C. **305.4**

Gibson, J. Phil

Plant diversity **580**

Gibson, Josh, 1911-1947

About

Twemlow, N. Josh Gibson **92**

Gibson, Julia Mary

Copper magic **Fic**

Gibson, Karen Bush

Native American history for kids **970.004**

The Obama view **92**

Gibson, Terri R.

Gibson, J. P. Plant diversity **580**

Giddings, Sharon

Cystic fibrosis **616.2**

Gidgets and women warriors. Gourley, C. **305.4**

Gidwitz, Adam

The Grimm conclusion **Fic**

A tale dark & Grimm **Fic**

Gier, Kerstin

Emerald green **Fic**

Ruby red **Fic**

Sapphire blue **Fic**

Giff, Patricia Reilly

Don't tell the girls **92**

Eleven **Fic**

Lily's crossing **Fic**

Maggie's door **Fic**

Nory Ryan's song **Fic**

Pictures of Hollis Woods **Fic**

R my name is Rachel **Fic**

Storyteller **Fic**

Water Street **Fic**

Winter sky **Fic**

About

Giff, P. R. Don't tell the girls **92**

Gifford, Clive

10 inventors who changed the world **920**

10 kings & queens who changed the world **920**

The arms trade **382**

Basketball **796.323**

Child labor **331.3**

Golf: from tee to green **796.352**

The Kingfisher geography encyclopedia **910.3**

The Kingfisher soccer encyclopedia **796.334**

Sports **796**

Swimming **797.2**

Tennis **796.342**

Track and field **796.42**

Track athletics **796.42**

Why did the Vietnam War happen? **959.704**

Giffords, Gabrielle D. (Gabrielle Dee), 1970-

About

Marsico, K. Ronald Reagan **92**
Marsico, K. Woodrow Wilson **92**
Matthews, T. L. Shots at sea **Fic**
Murphy, J. A savage thunder **973.7**
Panchyk, R. Franklin Delano Roosevelt for kids **92**
Petrillo, L. Sarah Palin **92**

GOVERNORS -- TEXAS -- BIOGRAPHY
Green, C. R. Sam Houston **976.4**

Gow, Mary
The great thinker: Aristotle and the foundations of
  science **92**
The greatest doctor of ancient times: Hippocrates
  and his oath **92**
Measuring the Earth **92**

Gownley, Jimmy
Amelia rules!: the whole world's crazy! **741.5**
The dumbest idea ever! **741.5**

Grabenstein, Chris
The black heart crypt **Fic**
The crossroads **Fic**
Escape from Mr. Lemoncello's library **Fic**
The Hanging Hill **Fic**
My brother the robot **Fic**
The smoky corridor **Fic**
Treasure hunters **Fic**

Grabowski, John
Television **621.388**

Grace, Amanda
In too deep **Fic**

Grace, gold and glory. Burford, M. **796.440**
Gracefully Grayson. Polonsky, A. **Fic**
Graceling. Cashore, K. **Fic**

GRADING AND MARKING (EDUCATION)
Strohmeyer, S. Smart girls get what they want **Fic**

GRADING AND MARKING (EDUCATION)
  See also Educational tests and measurements

GRADUATION (SCHOOL) -- FICTION
Charbonneau, J. The Testing **Fic**
Graduation day. Charbonneau, J. **Fic**
The **graduation** of Jake Moon. Park, B. **Fic**

Grady, Denise
Deadly invaders **614.4**

Graff, Lisa
Absolutely almost **Fic**
A tangle of knots **Fic**
Lost in the sun **Fic**

Graffiti. Uschan, M. V. **751.7**

GRAFFITI
Bingham, J. Graffiti **751.7**
Uschan, M. V. Graffiti **751.7**
Graffiti. Bingham, J. **751.7**

GRAFFITI -- FICTION
Bass, K. Graffiti knight **Fic**
Graffiti knight. Bass, K. **Fic**

GRAFT IN POLITICS *See* Political corruption
Graham Salisbury. Gill, D. M. **92**

Graham, Amy
Astonishing ancient world scientists **920**
Great Smoky Mountains National Park **976.8**

Graham, Bette Nesmith, 1924-1980
                About
Thimmesh, C. Girls think of everything **920**

Graham, Elspeth
(jt. auth) Peet, M. Mysterious traveler **Fic**

Graham, Ian
Fabulous bridges **624.2**
Forensic technology **363.2**
Robot technology **629.8**
Science rocks! **507.8**
Tremendous tunnels **624.1**

Graham, Martha
                About
Freedman, R. Martha Graham, a dancer's life **792.8**

GRAIL
  See also Folklore

GRAIL -- FICTION
Pyle, H. The story of the Grail and the passing of
  Arthur **398.2**
Spradlin, M. P. Keeper of the Grail **Fic**
Spradlin, M. P. Orphan of destiny **Fic**
Spradlin, M. P. Trail of fate **Fic**
Grail quest: the Camelot spell. Gilman, L. A. **Fic**
Grammar girl presents the ultimate writing guide
  for students. Fogarty, M. **428**

GRAMMAR SCHOOLS *See* Elementary education

GRAMMY AWARDS
  See also Sound recordings

GRAND CANYON (ARIZ.) -- FICTION
Hautman, P. Hole in the sky **Fic**
The **grand** plan to fix everything. Krishnaswami,
U. **Fic**

GRANDFATHERS
Crowe, C. Mississippi trial, 1955 **Fic**
Park, B. The graduation of Jake Moon **Fic**

GRANDFATHERS
  See also Grandparents

GRANDFATHERS -- FICTION
Brouwer, S. Devil's pass **Fic**
Gebhart, R. There will be bears **Fic**
Gleitzman, M. Now **Fic**
Half a man **Fic**
Holm, J. L. The fourteenth goldfish **Fic**
If you find this **Fic**
MacLachlan, P. Kindred souls **Fic**

Grandin, Temple
                About
Montgomery, S. Temple Grandin **636**

Grandits, John
Blue lipstick **811**
Technically, it's not my fault **811**

GRANDMOTHERS

Nardo, D. Migrant mother **973.917**

Ruggiero, A. American voices from The Great Depression **973.917**

Stanley, J. Children of the Dust Bowl **371.9**

GREAT DEPRESSION, 1929-1939

   See also Depressions; Economic conditions

GREAT DEPRESSION, 1929-1939 -- FICTION

Ayres, K. Macaroni boy **Fic**

Blume, L. M. M. Tennyson **Fic**

Brown, D. The train jumper **Fic**

Curtis, C. P. Bud, not Buddy **Fic**

Fusco, K. N. The wonder of Charlie Anne **Fic**

Giff, P. R. R my name is Rachel **Fic**

Hale, M. The truth about sparrows **Fic**

Hesse, K. Out of the dust **Fic**

Ingold, J. Hitch **Fic**

Jackson, A. Rainmaker **Fic**

Laskas, G. M. The miner's daughter **Fic**

Lottridge, C. B. The listening tree **Fic**

Meltzer, M. Tough times **Fic**

Peck, R. A long way from Chicago **Fic**

Peck, R. A year down yonder **Fic**

Peterson, L. J. Silver rain **Fic**

Pinkney, A. D. Bird in a box **Fic**

Taylor, M. D. Let the circle be unbroken **Fic**

Vanderpool, C. Moon over Manifest **Fic**

Vollmar, R. The castaways **741.5**

Yep, L. Dragon road **Fic**

The **Great** Depression, 1929-1940. McNeese, T. **973.917**

The **great** dog disaster. Davies, K. **Fic**

Great episodes [series]

Rinaldi, A. Come Juneteenth **Fic**

Rinaldi, A. The fifth of March **Fic**

Great escapes [series]

Fradin, D. B. The Irish potato famine **941.508**

Great expectations. Geary, R. **741.5**

Great expeditions [series]

Bodden, V. Through the American West **917.804**

Bodden, V. To the heart of Africa **916**

Bodden, V. To the moon **629.45**

Bodden, V. To the ocean deep **551.46**

Bodden, V. To the South Pole **919.89**

Bodden, V. To the top of Mount Everest **796.52**

The **great** explainer. LeVine, H. **92**

Great explorations [series]

Calvert, P. Vasco da Gama **92**

Elish, D. Edmund Hillary **92**

Otfinoski, S. Henry Hudson **92**

Young, S. Richard Francis Burton **92**

Great explorers [series]

Crompton, S. Lewis and Clark **92**

Crompton, S. Robert de La Salle **92**

Crompton, S. Sir Edmund Hillary **92**

Goodman, J. E. Despite all obstacles: La Salle and the conquest of the Mississippi **92**

Goodman, J. E. A long and uncertain journey: the 27,000 mile voyage of Vasco da Gama **910**

Koestler-Grack, R. A. Ferdinand Magellan **92**

Koestler-Grack, R. A. Sir Ernest Shackleton **92**

Lace, W. W. Captain James Cook **92**

Lace, W. W. Sir Francis Drake **92**

Wagner, H. L. Hernan Cortes **92**

Woog, A. Jacques Cartier **92**

Great explorers of the world [series]

Aretha, D. Magellan **92**

DeFries, C. L. Leif Eriksson **92**

Feinstein, S. Captain Cook **92**

Feinstein, S. Columbus **92**

Feinstein, S. Marco Polo **92**

Young, J. C. Henry Hudson **92**

Young, J. C. Hernando de Soto **92**

Great extinctions of the past. Mehling, R. **576.8**

The **great** fire. Murphy, J. **977.3**

The **great** Gilly Hopkins. Paterson, K. **Fic**

The **great** god Pan. Napoli, D. J. **Fic**

The **great** good summer. **Fic**

The **great** Greene heist. Johnson, V. **Fic**

The great Hispanic heritage [series]

Abrams, D. America Ferrera **92**

Abrams, D. Ernesto Che Guevara **92**

Cartlidge, C. Celia Cruz **92**

Darraj, S. M. Gabriel Garcia Marquez **92**

Darraj, S. M. Oscar de la Renta **92**

Friedman, I. C. Manny Ramirez **92**

Lange, B. Antonio Lopez de Santa Anna **92**

McNeese, T. Jorge Luis Borges **92**

McNeese, T. Salvador Dali **92**

McNeese, T. Tito Puente **92**

Reis, R. A. Simon Bolivar **92**

Slavicek, L. C. Carlos Santana **92**

Great historic debates and speeches [series]

Porterfield, J. The Lincoln-Douglas senatorial debates of 1858 **973.7**

Great historic disasters [series]

Bennie, P. The great Chicago fire of 1871 **363.1**

Koestler-Grack, R. A. The Johnstown flood of 1889 **974.8**

Kupperberg, P. The influenza pandemic of 1918-1919 **614.5**

Lace, W. W. The Hindenburg disaster of 1937 **363.1**

Lace, W. W. The Indian Ocean tsunami of 2004 **909.83**

Pietras, J. Hurricane Katrina **363.34**

Reis, R. A. The Dust Bowl **978**

Slavicek, L. C. The Black Death **614.5**

Slavicek, L. C. The San Francisco earthquake and fire of 1906 **979.4**

A great idea [series]

Mooney, C. Pilotless planes **623.7**

Woog, A. SCRATCHbot **629.8**

Great ideas of science [series]

C. **595.78**

How to ruin a summer vacation. Elkeles, S. **Fic**

How to ruin my teenage life. Elkeles, S. **Fic**

How to ruin your boyfriend's reputation. Elkeles, S. **Fic**

How to save a life. Zarr, S. **Fic**

How to say no to drugs. Kreske, D. P. **362.29**

How to speak cat. Whitehead, S. **636.8**

How to speak dog. Whitehead, S. **636.7**

How to steal a car. Hautman, P. **Fic**

How to steal a dog. O'Connor, B. **Fic**

HOW TO STUDY *See* Study skills

How to survive anything. Buchholz, R. **646.7**

How to survive in Antarctica. Bledsoe, L. J. **998**

How to survive middle school. Gephart, D. **Fic**

How to talk to an autistic kid. **616.85**

How to use waste energy to heat and light your home. O'Neal, C. **621.1**

How to use wind power to light and heat your home. O'Neal, C. **621.31**

How to write your life story. Fletcher, R. **808**

How video game designers use math. Egan, J. **794.8**

How we know what we know about our changing climate. Cherry, L. **363.7**

How weird is it. Hillman, B. **500**

How writers work. Fletcher, R. **808**

How Zoe made her dreams (mostly) come true. Strohmeyer, S. **Fic**

How-to-do-it manuals for librarians [series]

Alire, C. Serving Latino communities **027.6**

Gorman, M. Connecting young adults and libraries **027.62**

Martin, B. S. Fundamentals of school library media management **025.1**

Martin, H. J. Serving lesbian, gay, bisexual, transgender, and questioning teens **027.62**

Tallman, J. I. Making the writing and research connection with the I-search process **025.5**

HOW-TO-STOP-SMOKING PROGRAMS *See* Smoking cessation programs

Howard, Ellen

The crimson cap **Fic**

Howard, J. J.

That time I joined the circus **Fic**

Howard, Todd

(ed) Mark Twain **818**

Howe, Ian

Jennings, M. Soccer step-by-step **796.334**

Howe, James

(ed) 13 **S**

Addie on the inside **Fic**

Also known as Elvis **Fic**

The misfits **Fic**

Totally Joe **Fic**

Howe, Katherine

Conversion **Fic**

Howe, Peter

Waggit again **Fic**

Waggit's tale **Fic**

Howe, Samuel Gridley, 1801-1876

About

Alexander, S. H. She touched the world: Laura Bridgman, deaf-blind pioneer **92**

Howe, William Howe, 5th Viscount, 1729-1814

About

Murphy, J. The crossing **973.3**

Howell, Brian

Sports **796**

Howell, Troy

The dragon of Cripple Creek **Fic**

Howes, Kelly King

The roaring twenties almanac and primary sources **973.91**

Howl's moving castle. Jones, D. W. **Fic**

Howland, Leila

Forget-me-not summer **Fic**

Nantucket blue **Fic**

Howling at the moon. Etingoff, K. **398**

Howse, Jennifer

The Civil War **973.7**

Hoyt, Erich

Weird sea creatures **591.77**

HPV. **362.1**

Hrdlitschka, Shelley

Allegra **Fic**

Sister wife **Fic**

Hsüan-tsang, ca. 596-664

About

Galloway, P. Adventures on the ancient Silk Road **950**

Hubbard, Amanda

Ripple **Fic**

Hubbard-Brown, Janet

Chaucer **92**

Condoleezza Rice **92**

Hubble imaging space and time. DeVorkin, D. H. **522**

HUBBLE SPACE TELESCOPE

Cole, M. D. Eye on the universe **522**

DeVorkin, D. H. Hubble imaging space and time **522**

Scott, E. Space, stars, and the beginning of time **522**

See also Telescopes

Hubble, Edwin Powell, 1889-1953

About

Datnow, C. L. Edwin Hubble **92**

Hudmon, Andrew

Learning and memory **153.1**

Hudson. **92**

HUDSON RIVER (N.Y. AND N.J.)

Talbott, H. River of dreams **974.7**

Hudson, Don

HYPERACTIVITY DISORDER *See* Attention deficit disorder

HYPERKINESIA *See* Attention deficit disorder; Hyperactivity

HYPOCHONDRIA -- FICTION

Raf, M. The symptoms of my insanity   **Fic**

I

I am (not) the walrus. Briant, E.   **Fic**

I am a SEAL Team Six warrior. Wasdin, H. E.   **92**

I am Malala.   **92**

I am Mordred. Springer, N.   **Fic**

I am Morgan le Fay. Springer, N.   **Fic**

I am not Joey Pigza. Gantos, J.   **Fic**

I am phoenix: poems for two voices. Fleischman, P.   **811**

I am Rembrandt's daughter. Cullen, L.   **Fic**

I am Scout: the biography of Harper Lee. Shields, C. J.   **92**

I am the cheese. Cormier, R.   **Fic**

I am the darker brother.   **811**

I and I. Medina, T.   **92**

I can cook! [series]

Blaxland, W. Mexican food   **641.59**

I can't keep my own secrets.   **808.8**

I did it without thinking. Hugel, B.   **155.5**

I don't want to be crazy. Schutz, S.   **92**

I feel a little jumpy around you.   **808.81**

I found a dead bird. Thornhill, J.   **306.9**

I found it on the Internet. Harris, F. J.   **025.042**

I have lived a thousand years. Bitton-Jackson, L.   **940.53**

I have the right to be a child.   **323.3**

I heard God talking to me. Spires, E.   **811**

I kissed a zombie, and I liked it. Selzer, A.   **Fic**

I know what you did last summer. Duncan, L.   **Fic**

I lived on Butterfly Hill. Agosín, M.   **Fic**

I love him to pieces.   **741.5**

--I never saw another butterfly-- Volavkova, H. **741.9**

I once was a monkey. Lee, J. M.   **294.3**

I put a spell on you. Selzer, A.   **Fic**

I shall wear midnight. Pratchett, T.   **Fic**

I survived the Battle of Gettysburg, 1863. Tarshis, L.   **E**

I wanna be your shoebox. Garcia, C.   **Fic**

I want to live. Lugovskaia, N.   **92**

I was dreaming to come to America. Lawlor, V. **304.8**

I was Jane Austen's best friend. Harrison, C.   **Fic**

I will plant you a lilac tree. Hillman, L.   **940.53**

I'll ask you three times, are you ok? Nye, N. S. **92**

I'll be there. Sloan, H. G.   **Fic**

I'll get there, it better be worth the trip. Donovan, J.   **Fic**

I'll pass for your comrade. Silvey, A.   **973.7**

I'm a vegetarian. Schwartz, E.   **613.2**

I'm glad I did.   **Fic**

I'm not her. Gurtler, J.   **Fic**

I'm with stupid. Herbach, G.   **Fic**

I, Coriander. Gardner, S.   **Fic**

I, Emma Freke. Atkinson, E. J.   **Fic**

I, Q.: book one, Independence Hall. Smith, R.   **Fic**

I, robot. Asimov, I.   **S**

I, too, sing America.   **811**

I. Q.: book two, The White House. Smith, R.   **Fic**

I.M. Pei. Slavicek, L. C.   **92**

I.M. Pei. Rubalcaba, J.   **92**

Ibbitson, John

The Landing   **Fic**

Ibbotson, Eva

The beasts of Clawstone Castle   **Fic**

The dragonfly pool   **Fic**

The Ogre of Oglefort   **Fic**

One dog and his boy   **Fic**

The star of Kazan   **Fic**

Ibn al-Haytham. Steffens, B.   **92**

Ice. Durst, S. B.   **Fic**

ICE

Berlatsky, N. Water and ice   **551.4**

Glaciers, sea ice, and ice formation   **551.3**

Pringle, L. Ice!   **621.5**

ICE

See also Cold; Frost; Physical geography; Water

ICE -- FICTION

Kirby, M. J. Icefall   **Fic**

ICE AGE

See also Earth

Ice age Neanderthals. Stefoff, R.   **599.93**

Ice claw. Gilman, D.   **Fic**

The **ice** cream con. Docherty, J.   **Fic**

ICE CREAM, ICES, ETC.

See also Desserts; Frozen foods

Ice dogs. Johnson, T. L.   **Fic**

ICE FISHING

See also Fishing; Winter sports

Ice hockey. Sharp, A. W.   **796.962**

ICE HOCKEY *See* Hockey

Ice island. Shahan, S.   **Fic**

Ice scientist. Latta, S. L.   **998**

ICE SKATERS

Koestler-Grack, R. A. Michelle Kwan   **92**

ICE SKATING

McDougall, C. Figure skating   **796.91**

ICE SKATING -- BIOGRAPHY

Koestler-Grack, R. A. Michelle Kwan   **92**

ICE SKATING -- FICTION

Messner, K. Sugar and ice   **Fic**

ICE SKATING -- GRAPHIC NOVELS

Nakajo, H. Sugar Princess volume 1: skating to win   **741.5**

Ice time. McKinley, M.   **796.962**

Ice! Pringle, L.   **621.5**

Houts, M. The Beef Princess of Practical County **Fic**

Lasky, K. Chasing Orion **Fic**

Peck, R. Here lies the librarian **Fic**

Peck, R. The teacher's funeral **Fic**

Trigiani, A. Viola in reel life **Fic**

Woodworth, C. Double-click for trouble **Fic**

Woodworth, C. When Ratboy lived next door **Fic**

INDIANA -- POETRY

Crisler, C. L. Tough boy sonatas **811**

INDIANAPOLIS (CRUISER)

Nelson, P. Left for dead **940.54**

INDIANS OF NORTH AMERICA *See* Native Americans; Native Americans -- North America; Native Americans -- United States

INDIANS OF NORTH AMERICA -- ALASKA -- FICTION

Bell, H. Traitor's son **Fic**

INDIANS OF NORTH AMERICA -- ART *See* Native American art

INDIANS OF NORTH AMERICA -- CHILDREN *See* Native American children

INDIANS OF NORTH AMERICA -- COSTUME *See* Native American costume

INDIANS OF NORTH AMERICA -- DOMESTIC ANIMALS -- GREAT PLAINS

The horse and the Plains indians **978**

INDIANS OF NORTH AMERICA -- FICTION

Knutsson, C. Shadows cast by stars **Fic**

INDIANS OF NORTH AMERICA -- GREAT PLAINS -- HISTORY -- 19TH CENTURY -- CHRONOLOGY

Langley, A. The Plains Indian wars 1864-1890 **978.004**

INDIANS OF NORTH AMERICA -- HISTORY -- COLONIAL PERIOD, CA. 1600-1775

The Countryside in colonial America **973.2**

INDIANS OF NORTH AMERICA -- MISSISSIPPI -- FICTION

Robinson, G. Little Brother of War **Fic**

INDIANS OF NORTH AMERICA -- NEW YORK (STATE) -- FICTION

Abrahams, P. The outlaws of Sherwood Street **Fic**

Gansworth, E. If I ever get out of here **Fic**

INDIANS OF NORTH AMERICA -- NORTHWEST, PACIFIC -- FICTION

Parry, R. Written in stone **Fic**

INDIANS OF NORTH AMERICA -- RELATIONS WITH EARLY SETTLERS *See* Native Americans -- Relations with early settlers

INDIANS OF NORTH AMERICA -- SOUTHWEST, NEW -- FICTION

Bruchac, J. Killer of enemies **Fic**

INDIANS OF NORTH AMERICA -- TEXAS -- FICTION

Tingle, T. Danny Blackgoat, Navajo prisoner **Fic**

INDIANS OF NORTH AMERICA -- WARS -- 1866-1895

Langley, A. The Plains Indian wars 1864-1890 **978.004**

INDIANS OF NORTH AMERICA -- WASHINGTON (STATE) -- ANTIQUITIES

Owsley, D. W. Their skeletons speak **970.01**

Indians, cowboys, and farmers and the battle for the Great Plains, 1865-1910. Collier, C. **978**

INDIC ART

Ram-Prasad, C. Exploring the life, myth, and art of India **954**

INDIC COOKING

Ejaz, K. Recipe and craft guide to India **641.5**

INDIC MYTHOLOGY

Ollhoff, J. Indian mythology **294**

Ram-Prasad, C. Exploring the life, myth, and art of India **954**

Schomp, V. Ancient India **294.5**

Indie girl. Daswani, K. **Fic**

INDIGENOUS PEOPLES -- AMERICA *See* Native Americans

INDIGENOUS PEOPLES -- FICTION

Khoury, J. Origin **Fic**

INDIGESTION

See also Digestion

The **indigo** king. Owen, J. A. **Fic**

The **indigo** notebook. Resau, L. **Fic**

Indigo's star. McKay, H. **Fic**

Indira Gandhi. Schupack, S. **954.04**

The **indispensable** librarian. **025.1**

INDIVIDUALISM

See also Economics; Equality; Political science; Sociology

INDIVIDUALISM -- FICTION

Austen, C. All good children **Fic**

Philbin, J. The daughters take the stage **Fic**

Wolitzer, M. The fingertips of Duncan Dorfman **Fic**

INDIVIDUALITY

Spinelli, J. Jake and Lily **Fic**

Spinelli, J. Stargirl **Fic**

Voigt, C. It's not easy being bad **Fic**

INDIVIDUALITY

See also Consciousness; Psychology

Indiviglio, Frank

The everything aquarium book **639.34**

Indivisible. **811**

INDOCTRINATION, FORCED *See* Brainwashing

Indonesia. Cooper, R. **959.8**

INDONESIA

Cooper, R. Indonesia **959.8**

INDONESIA -- FICTION

Fama, E. Overboard **Fic**

INDONESIAN COOKING

Reusser, K. Recipe and craft guide to Indone-

JEOPARDY (TELEVISION PROGRAM) -- FIC-TION

Gephart, D. Olivia Bean, trivia queen **Fic**

Jepp, who defied the stars. Marsh, K. **Fic**

Jeremy Fink and the meaning of life. Mass, W. **Fic**

Jermyn, Leslie

Belize **972.82**

Foley, E. Dominican Republic **972.93**

Foley, E. Ecuador **986.6**

Guyana **988.1**

NgCheong-Lum, R. Haiti **972.94**

Paraguay **989.2**

Sheehan, S. Cuba **972.91**

Uruguay **989.5**

Jerome, Kate Boehm

Atomic universe **539.7**

Jersey tomatoes are the best. Padian, M. **Fic**

JERUSALEM -- FICTION

Abdel-Fattah, R. Where the streets had a name **Fic**

Jeschonek, Robert T.

My favorite band does not exist **Fic**

Jesse Owens. Burlingame, J. **92**

Jesse Owens. McDougall, C. **92**

Jesse Owens. Gigliotti, J. **92**

Jessica's guide to dating on the dark side. Fantaskey, B. **Fic**

Jessie's mountain. Madden, K. **Fic**

Jesus. Spirin, G. **232.9**

Jesus Christ

About

Fletcher, S. Alphabet of dreams **Fic**

Grimes, N. At Jerusalem's gate **811**

Lottridge, C. B. Stories from the life of Jesus **232.9**

Spirin, G. Jesus **232.9**

JESUS CHRIST -- ART

See also Christian art

Jesus Jackson. Daley, J. R. **Fic**

JET PLANES

See also Airplanes

Jeter, Derek, 1974-

The contract **Fic**

About

Rappoport, K. Derek Jeter **796.357**

The **Jewel** of the Kalderash. Rutkoski, M. **Fic**

The **jeweler's** art. Macfarlane, K. **739.27**

JEWELRY

Macfarlane, K. The jeweler's art **739.27**

JEWELRY

See also Clothing and dress; Costume; Decorative arts; Fashion accessories

JEWELRY -- FICTION

Watson, J. Loot **Fic**

JEWELS *See* Gems; Jewelry; Precious stones

JEWISH CHILDREN

Freedman, P. J. My basmati bat mitzvah **Fic**

JEWISH CHILDREN IN THE HOLOCAUST

Hodge, D. Rescuing the children **940.53**

Prins, M. Hidden like Anne Frank **92**

JEWISH CHILDREN IN THE HOLOCAUST

See also Holocaust, 1939-1945

JEWISH CHILDREN IN THE HOLOCAUST -- BIOGRAPHY

Anne Frank **92**

JEWISH CHILDREN IN THE HOLOCAUST -- NETHERLANDS -- BIOGRAPHY

Prins, M. Hidden like Anne Frank **92**

JEWISH CHILDREN IN THE HOLOCAUST -- POLAND -- KRAKÓW -- BIOGRAPHY

Leyson, L. The boy on the wooden box **92**

JEWISH CIVILIZATION

See also Civilization

JEWISH COOKING

Bloomfield, J. Jewish holidays cookbook **641.5**

JEWISH DIASPORA

See also Human geography; Jews

JEWISH ETHICS

See also Ethics

Jewish faith in America. Buxbaum, S. M. **296**

JEWISH FOLK LITERATURE

See also Folk literature; Jewish literature

Jewish holiday origami. Stern, J. **736**

JEWISH HOLIDAYS

Bloomfield, J. Jewish holidays cookbook **641.5**

Stern, J. Jewish holiday origami **736**

JEWISH HOLIDAYS

See also Judaism; Religious holidays

JEWISH HOLIDAYS -- FICTION

Schwartz, H. The day the Rabbi disappeared: Jewish holiday tales of magic **398.2**

Jewish holidays cookbook. Bloomfield, J. **641.5**

JEWISH HOLOCAUST (1933-1945) *See* Holocaust, 1939-1945

JEWISH LEADERS

Rubin, S. G. The Anne Frank Case: Simon Wiesenthal's search for the truth **92**

JEWISH LEGENDS

Chaikin, M. Angels sweep the desert floor **296.1**

Pinsker, M. In the days of sand and stars **296.1**

JEWISH LEGENDS

See also Legends

JEWISH LITERATURE

See also Literature; Religious literature

JEWISH REFUGEES

Fox, A. L. Ten thousand children **940.53**

Hoffman, B. N. Liberation **940.53**

Schloss, E. Eva's story **92**

JEWISH REFUGEES -- FICTION

Alban, A. Anya's war **Fic**

Chapman, F. S. Is it night or day? **Fic**

Friedman, D. D. Escaping into the night **Fic**

JEWISH RELIGION *See* Judaism

JEWISH WIT AND HUMOR

The **last** mall rat. Esckilsen, E. E.   **Fic**
The **last** Martin. Friesen, J.   **Fic**
The **last** mission. Mazer, H.   **Fic**
The **last** musketeer. Gibbs, S.   **Fic**
The **last** newspaper boy in America. Corbett, S. **Fic**
The **last** of the High Kings. Thompson, K.   **Fic**
The **last** of the sandwalkers.   **Fic**
The **last** Olympian. Riordan, R.   **Fic**
The **last** ride of Caleb O'Toole. Pierpoint, E.   **Fic**
Last shot. Feinstein, J.   **Fic**
The **last** sister. McKinney-Whitaker, C.   **Fic**
The **last** summer of the death warriors. Stork, F. X.   **Fic**
The **last** synapsid. Mason, T.   **Fic**
The **last** unicorn. Beagle, P. S.   **741.5**
Lat
  Kampung boy   **741.5**
  Town boy   **741.5**
Late medieval Europe. Morris, N.   **940.1**
The **latent** powers of Dylan Fontaine. Lurie, A. **Fic**
Latham, Don
  David Almond   **823**
Latham, Donna
  Amazing biome projects you can build yourself **577**
  Backyard Biology   **570.78**
  Canals and dams   **627.13**
  Ecology   **577**
Latham, Irene
  Leaving Gee's Bend   **Fic**
Latif, Zawiah Abdul
  Gish, S. Ethiopia   **963**
  Hassig, S. M. Somalia   **967.73**
  Heale, J. Madagascar   **969.1**
  Kagda, F. Algeria   **965**
  Kagda, S. Lithuania   **947.93**
  Levy, P. Sudan   **962.4**
  Sheehan, S. Lebanon   **956.92**
Latimer, Jonathan P.
  Backyard birds   **598**
  Birds of prey   **598.9**
  Caterpillars   **595.7**
  Songbirds   **598**
LATIN AMERICA
  Delacre, L. Salsa stories   **S**
LATIN AMERICA -- FICTION
  Delacre, L. Salsa stories   **S**
LATIN AMERICA -- HISTORY -- 1948-1980
  Kallen, S. A. Che Guevara   **92**
LATIN AMERICA -- POLITICS AND GOVERN-MENT
  See also Politics
Latin America and the Caribbean. Solway, A. **780.9**
LATIN AMERICAN ART
  Makosz, R. Latino arts and their influence on the United States   **700**
LATIN AMERICAN ART

  See also Art
LATIN AMERICAN LITERATURE
  See also Literature
LATIN AMERICAN LITERATURE -- BIBLIOG-RAPHY
  Schon, I. Recommended books in Spanish for children and young adults, 2004-2008   **011.6**
LATIN AMERICANS -- SOCIAL LIFE AND CUSTOMS
  Sanna, E. Latino folklore and culture   **398.2**
LATIN AMERICANS -- UNITED STATES -- FICTION
  Campoy, F. I. Yes! we are Latinos   **S**
LATIN LANGUAGE -- DICTIONARIES
  Simpson, D. P. Cassell's Latin dictionary   **473**
LATIN LITERATURE
  See also Literature
The **Latin** music scene. Tsoukanelis, E. A. **780.89**
Latino American history [series]
  Doak, R. S. Struggling to become American **305.8**
Latino arts and their influence on the United States. Makosz, R.   **700**
LATINO AUTHORS
  Amend, A. Hispanic-American writers   **810**
Latino biography library [series]
  Schraff, A. E. Ellen Ochoa   **92**
  Shull, J. A. Pablo Neruda   **92**
  Warrick, K. C. Sandra Cisneros   **92**
Latino folklore and culture. Sanna, E.   **398.2**
LATINOS (U.S.)
  Doak, R. S. Struggling to become American **305.8**
  Growing up Latino   **810**
  Hernandez, R. E. The Civil War, 1840s-1890s **973.7**
  Ortiz Cofer, J. Riding low on the streets of gold **860**
  Otfinoski, S. The new republic: 1760-1840s **973.3**
  Portraits of Hispanic American heroes   **920**
  Wachale! poetry and prose on growing up Latino in America   **810**
LATINOS (U.S.)
  See also Ethnic groups
LATITUDE
  See also Earth; Geodesy; Nautical astronomy
Latitude zero. Renn, D.   **Fic**
Latno, Mark
  The paper boomerang book   **745.54**
Latta, Sara L.
  The good, the bad, the slimy   **579**
  Ice scientist   **998**
  Lava scientist   **551.2**
LATTER-DAY SAINTS *See* Church of Jesus Christ of Latter-day Saints
Lau, Ruth
  Berg, E. Senegal   **966.3**
Laubach, Christyna M.
  Raptor! a kid's guide to birds of prey   **598**
Laubach, Rene

LIFE SKILLS--HANDBOOKS, MANUALS, ETC.

Bostick, N. Managing Money   **332**

Katz, A. Girl in the know   **612.6**

LIFE STYLES *See* Lifestyles

LIFE SUPPORT SYSTEMS (MEDICAL ENVIRONMENT)

  See also Hospitals; Terminal care

LIFE SUPPORT SYSTEMS (SPACE ENVIRONMENT)

  See also Ergonomics; Space medicine

LIFE SUPPORT SYSTEMS (SUBMARINE ENVIRONMENT)

  See also Ergonomics

Life under occupation. Samuels, C.   **940.53**

Life under slavery. DeFord, D. H.   **326**

Life, after. Littman, S.   **Fic**

LIFE, FUTURE *See* Future life

Life, the universe, and everything. Adams, D.   **Fic**

Lifeblood. Becker, T.   **Fic**

Lifeline biographies [series]

Krohn, K. E. Oprah Winfrey   **92**

Krohn, K. E. Vera Wang   **92**

Lesinski, J. M. Bill Gates   **92**

Roberts, J. Tiger Woods   **92**

Lifelines in world history.   **920.003**

LIFESAVING

Pratchett, T. Dodger   **Fic**

LIFESAVING

  See also Rescue work

LIFESTYLES

Hidalgo-Robert, A. Fat no more   **616.85**

LIFESTYLES

  See also Human behavior; Manners and customs

Lifeways [series]

Bial, R. The Apache   **970.004**

Bial, R. The Cree   **971**

Bial, R. The Crow   **970**

Bial, R. The Delaware   **974**

Bial, R. The Huron   **970.004**

Bial, R. The Menominee   **977.4**

Bial, R. The Shoshone   **970.004**

Lifeways [series] Bial, R.   **970.004**

Lifted. Toliver, W.   **Fic**

Liftoff. Mitchell, D.   **92**

Light.   **535**

LIGHT

Gardner, R. Easy genius science projects with light   **537**

Gardner, R. Light, sound, and waves science fair projects   **507.8**

Hartman, E. Light and sound   **530**

Meiani, A. Light   **535**

Sitarski, A. Cold light   **572**

Stille, D. R. Manipulating light   **535**

  See also Electromagnetic waves; Physics

LIGHT -- SPEED

Caes, C. J. Discovering the speed of light   **535**

Light   **535**

LIGHT -- STUDY AND TEACHING -- HISTORY

Caes, C. J. Discovering the speed of light   **535**

Light and sound. Hartman, E.   **530**

A **light** in the attic. Silverstein, S.   **811**

The **light** in the forest. Richter, C.   **Fic**

LIGHT PRODUCTION IN ANIMALS *See* Bioluminescence

LIGHT VERSE *See* Humorous poetry

Light years. Stein, T.   **Fic**

LIGHT, ELECTRIC *See* Electric lighting

Light, sound, and waves science fair projects. Gardner, R.   **507.8**

The **Light-Bearer's** daughter. Melling, O. R.   **Fic**

Light-gathering poems.   **808.81**

LIGHTHOUSES

Fletcher, S. Walk across the sea   **Fic**

House, K. L. Lighthouses for kids   **387.1**

LIGHTHOUSES

  See also Navigation

LIGHTHOUSES -- FICTION

Woodruff, E. Fearless   **Fic**

Lighthouses for kids. House, K. L.   **387.1**

LIGHTING

  See also Interior design; Light

LIGHTNING

Fleisher, P. Lightning, hurricanes, and blizzards   **551.55**

Person, S. Struck by lightning!   **551.56**

Stewart, M. Inside lightning   **551.56**

LIGHTNING

  See also Electricity; Meteorology; Thunderstorms

LIGHTNING -- FICTION

Lucky strike   **Fic**

The **Lightning** Dreamer. Engle, M.   **Fic**

The **lightning** key. Berkeley, J.   **Fic**

The **lightning** thief. Riordan, R.   **Fic**

The **lightning** thief: the graphic novel. Venditti, R.   **741.5**

Lightning, hurricanes, and blizzards. Fleisher, P.   **551.55**

Lights on the Nile. Napoli, D. J.   **Fic**

Lights, camera, action! O'Brien, L.   **791.43**

LIGHTSHIPS

  See also Lighthouses; Ships

Like a river.   **Fic**

Like men of war. Trudeau, N. A.   **973.7**

Like sisters on the homefront. Williams-Garcia, R.   **Fic**

Like water on stone. Walrath, D.   **Fic**

Likely story. Van Etten, D.   **Fic**

Likely story [series]

Riley, S. G. African Americans in the media today **920.003**

Sobel, D. What's the catch? **153.8**

MASS MEDIA

    See also Communication

MASS SPECTROMETRY

    See also Spectrum analysis

MASS SURVEILLANCE

    See also Intelligence service

Mass, Wendy

    Every soul a star **Fic**

    Gods and goddesses **201**

    Heaven looks a lot like the mall **Fic**

    Jeremy Fink and the meaning of life **Fic**

    A mango-shaped space **Fic**

    Pi in the sky **Fic**

Massachusetts. LeVert, S. **974.4**

MASSACHUSETTS

    Massachusetts **974.4**

Massachusetts. **974.4**

MASSACHUSETTS -- FICTION

    The Penderwicks in spring **Fic**

**MASSACHUSETTS -- HISTORY -- 1600-1775,
COLONIAL PERIOD**

    Aronson, M. John Winthrop, Oliver Cromwell, and
the Land of Promise **92**

    Doherty, K. William Bradford **974.4**

    Edwards, J. The Plymouth Colony and the Pilgrim
adventure in American history **974.4**

    Erickson, P. Daily life in the Pilgrim colony,
1636 **974.4**

    Harness, C. The adventurous life of Myles
Standish **92**

    Philbrick, N. The Mayflower and the Pilgrims'
New World **973.2**

    Stille, D. R. Anne Hutchinson **92**

**MASSACHUSETTS -- HISTORY -- 1600-1775,
COLONIAL PERIOD -- FICTION**

    Duble, K. B. The sacrifice **Fic**

**MASSACHUSETTS -- HISTORY -- NEW PLYM-
OUTH, 1620-1691 -- FICTION**

    Cooper, S. Ghost Hawk **Fic**

Massacre at Virginia Tech. Worth, R. **364.152**

MASSACRES

    See also Atrocities; History; Persecution

MASSAGE

    See also Physical therapy

Massie, Elizabeth

    Favor, L. J. Weighing in **613.2**

MASSIVE OPEN ONLINE COURSES

    See also Internet in education; University ex-
tension

Masson, Sophie

    The madman of Venice **Fic**

    Snow, fire, sword **Fic**

The **Master** of Misrule. Powell, L. **Fic**

Master, Irfan

    A beautiful lie **Fic**

The **mastermind** plot. Frazier, A. **Fic**

Masterpiece. Broach, E. **Fic**

Mastiff. Pierce, T. **Fic**

MASTODON

    Bardoe, C. Mammoths and mastodons **569**

MASTODON

    See also Extinct animals; Fossil mammals

Matas, Carol

    After the war **Fic**

    Sparks fly upward **Fic**

    The whirlwind **Fic**

Matched. Condie, A. B. **Fic**

Matched trilogy [series]

    Condie, A. Reached **Fic**

The **matchless** six. Hotchkiss, R. **796.48**

MATE SELECTION IN ANIMALS *See* Animal
courtship

MATERIA MEDICA

    See also Medicine; Therapeutics

Material changes and reactions. Oxlade, C. **540**

MATERIAL CULTURE

    See also Culture

**MATERIAL CULTURE -- CHINA -- CHANG-
SHA (HUNAN SHENG)**

    At home in her tomb **931**

MATERIALISM

    See also Philosophy; Positivism

MATERIALS

    Knapp, B. J. Materials science **620.1**

    Ward, D. J. Materials science **620.1**

Materials science. Knapp, B. J. **620.1**

Materials science. Ward, D. J. **620.1**

Materials that matter [series]

    Morris, N. Glass **620.1**

    Morris, N. Metals **620.1**

    Morris, N. Paper **676**

    Morris, N. Plastics **668.4**

    Morris, N. Textiles **677**

    Morris, N. Wood **634.9**

Math and science across cultures. Bazin, M. **510**

Math busters word problems [series]

    Wingard-Nelson, R. Graphing and probability
word problems **519.2**

Math doesn't suck. McKellar, D. **510**

Math games for middle school. Salvadori, M. G. **510**

Math in the real world [series]

    Arroyo, S. L. How chefs use math **641.5**

    Arroyo, S. L. How crime fighters use math **363.2**

    Arroyo, S. L. How deep sea divers use math **797.2**

    Arroyo, S. L. How race car drivers use math **796.72**

    Bertoletti, J. C. How baseball managers use
math **796.357**

    Bertoletti, J. C. How fashion designers use
math **746.9**

MAYAN ART

Laughton, T. Exploring the life, myth, and art of the
Maya **972.81**

MAYAS

Ancient Aztec and Maya **972**
George, C. Maya civilization **972**
Harris, N. Ancient Maya **972**
Kallen, S. A. Rigoberta Menchu, Indian rights activist **92**
Kops, D. Palenque **972**
Vanvoorst, J. F. The ancient Maya **972.81**

MAYAS -- ANTIQUITIES

Mann, E. Tikal **972.81**

MAYAS -- FICTION

Raedeke, C. The daykeeper's grimoire **Fic**
Rollins, J. Jake Ransom and the Skull King's shadow **Fic**
Voelkel, J. The end of the world club **Fic**
Voelkel, J. Middleworld **Fic**

MAYAS -- FOLKLORE

Laughton, T. Exploring the life, myth, and art of the
Maya **972.81**

Maydell, Natalie
Extraordinary women from the Muslim world **920**

Mayell, Mark
Newfoundland **971**
Saskatchewan **971**

Mayer, Brian
Libraries got game **025.2**

Mayer, Robert H.
When the children marched **323.1**

The **Mayflower** and the Pilgrims' New World. Philbrick, N. **973.2**

Maynard, John
(ed) Blake, W. William Blake **821**

Mayor, Adrienne
The Griffin and the Dinosaur **398.245**

MAYORS

Abrams, D. Nicolas Sarkozy **92**
Petrillo, L. Sarah Palin **92**

Mays, Carl, 1891-1971
About
Gutman, D. Ray & me **Fic**

A **maze** me. Nye, N. S. **811**
The **maze** of bones. Riordan, R. **Fic**
The **maze** runner. Dashner, J. **Fic**

Mazer, Anne
Spilling ink **808.3**

Mazer, Harry
A boy at war **Fic**
A boy no more **Fic**
Heroes don't run **Fic**
The last mission **Fic**
My brother Abe **Fic**
Snow bound **Fic**
Somebody, please tell me who I am **Fic**

Mazer, Norma Fox
After the rain **Fic**
Girlhearts **Fic**
The missing girl **Fic**

Mazorlig, Thomas
(ed) Boruchowitz, D. E. Sugar gliders **636.935**

McAdoo, David
Red moon **741.5**

McAllister, Ian
Salmon bears **599.78**
The sea wolves **599.77**

McAlpine, Margaret
Working in music and dance **780**
Working with animals **636**
Working with children **362.7**

McArthur, Debra
The Kansas-Nebraska Act and Bleeding Kansas in
American history **978.1**
A student's guide to Edgar Allan Poe **813**
A student's guide to William Faulkner **813**

McBride, Regina
The fire opal **Fic**

McCaffrey, Anne
Dragonflight **Fic**
Dragon's fire **Fic**

McCaffrey, Todd J.
McCaffrey, A. Dragon's fire **Fic**

McCahan, Erin
Love and other foreign words **Fic**

McCain, John S., 1936-
About
Robinson, T. John McCain **92**

Mccall, Guadalupe Garcia
Under the mesquite **Fic**

McCallum, Ann
Eat your science homework **507.8**

McCampbell, Darlene Z.
(ed) Leaving home: stories **808.8**
(comp) Who do you think you are? **S**

McCann, Jim
Return of the Dapper Men **741.5**

McCann, Michelle Roehm
Girls who rocked the world **920.72**
The **McCarthy** hearings. **973.921**

McCarthy, Colin
Reptile **597.9**

McCarthy, Joseph, 1908-1957
About
Fitzgerald, B. McCarthyism **973.921**
Giblin, J. C. The rise and fall of Senator Joe McCarthy **92**
The McCarthy hearings **973.921**

McCarthy, Maureen
When you wish upon a rat **Fic**

McCarthy, Tom
About

MEMBERS OF PARLIAMENT

MEMBERS OF PARLIAMENT See Legislators

Meminger, Neesha

MEMOIRISTS

MENTAL DEPRESSION *See* Depression (Psychology)

MENTAL DISEASES *See* Abnormal psychology; Mental illness

Mental disorders. Farrell, C.   **362.1**

MENTAL HEALING

   See also Alternative medicine

MENTAL HEALTH

  Bellenir, K.   Mental health information for teens   **616.89**

MENTAL HEALTH

   See also Happiness; Health

Mental health information for teens. Bellenir, K.   **616.89**

MENTAL HEALTH LAWS -- UNITED STATES

  Houser, A. Tragedy in Tucson   **364.152**

MENTAL HEALTH SERVICES

   See also Medical care

MENTAL HOSPITALS *See* Psychiatric hospitals

MENTAL HYGIENE *See* Mental health

Mental Illness.   **362.2**

MENTAL ILLNESS

  Binstock, M. Nourishment   **92**

  Farrell, C. Mental disorders   **362.1**

  Kent, D. Snake pits, talking cures, & magic bullets   **616.89**

  Mental Illness   **362.2**

  Monaque, M. Trouble in my head   **92**

  Patterson, J. Med head   **92**

   See also Abnormal psychology; Diseases; Sick

MENTAL ILLNESS -- FICTION

  Collomore, A. The ruining   **Fic**

  Graves, K. The orphan of Awkward Falls   **Fic**

  Halpern, J. Have a nice day   **Fic**

  Kuehn, S. Complicit   **Fic**

  Michaels, R. Nobel genes   **Fic**

  Trueman, T. Inside out   **Fic**

  Vaught, S. Freaks like us   **Fic**

  White, R. Memories of Summer   **Fic**

  Wunder, W. The museum of intangible things   **Fic**

MENTAL ILLNESS -- GRAPHIC NOVELS

  White, T. How I made it to eighteen   **741.5**

MENTAL ILLNESS -- PHYSIOLOGICAL ASPECTS

   See also Physiology

MENTAL PATIENTS *See* Mentally ill

MENTAL STEREOTYPE *See* Stereotype (Social psychology)

MENTAL STRESS *See* Stress (Psychology)

MENTAL SUGGESTION

   See also Mind and body; Parapsychology; Subconsciousness

MENTAL TESTS *See* Intelligence tests; Psychological tests

MENTALLY DEPRESSED *See* Depression (Psychology)

MENTALLY DERANGED *See* Mentally ill

MENTALLY HANDICAPPED -- FICTION

  Hamilton, K. R. Tyger tyger   **Fic**

  Hooper, M. Fallen Grace   **Fic**

  Lowry, L. The silent boy   **Fic**

  Mackall, D. D. The silence of murder   **Fic**

  Magnin, J. Carrying Mason   **Fic**

  Martin, A. M. A corner of the universe   **Fic**

  Nolan, H. A face in every window   **Fic**

  Nuzum, K. A. A small white scar   **Fic**

  Sturtevant, K. The brothers story   **Fic**

  Williams, M. Now is the time for running   **Fic**

  Wood, J. R. The man who loved clowns   **Fic**

MENTORING

   See also Counseling

MENTORING -- FICTION

  McMullan, M. Cashay   **Fic**

  Myers, W. D. Kick   **Fic**

MENUS

   See also Cooking; Diet

Menzel, Peter

  What the world eats   **641.3**

Mercado, Nancy E.

  (ed) Baseball crazy: ten short stories that cover all the bases   **S**

  (ed) Every man for himself   **S**

Mercator, Gerardus, 1512-1594

          About

  Heinrichs, A. Gerardus Mercator   **92**

MERCENARY SOLDIERS

   See also Military personnel; Soldiers

MERCENARY SOLDIERS -- FICTION

  Arnett, M. Avalon   **Fic**

  Taylor, L. Silksinger   **Fic**

Mercer, Bobby

  The flying machine book   **745.592**

  Junk drawer physics   **530**

  The Robot book   **629.8**

MERCHANDISING *See* Marketing; Retail trade

MERCHANT MARINE

   See also Maritime law; Sailors; Ships; Transportation

The merchant of death. MacHale, D. J.   **Fic**

The merchant of Venice. Hinds, G.   **741.5**

The merchant of Venice.   **741.5**

The merchant's daughter. Dickerson, M.   **Fic**

MERCHANTS

   See also Businesspeople

Mercian triology [series]

  Wignall, K. J. Blood   **Fic**

Mercury. Larson, H.   **741.5**

Mercury. Colligan, L. H.   **523.4**

MERCURY

   See also Chemical elements; Metals

MERCURY (PLANET)

  Colligan, L. H. Mercury   **523.4**

Torres, J. A. The Battle of Midway   **940.54**

The **midwife's** apprentice. Cushman, K.   **Fic**

MIDWIFERY *See* Midwives

Midwinterblood. Sedgwick, M.   **S**

MIDWIVES

Let it shine   **920**

Wells, R. Mary on horseback   **92**

MIDWIVES

     See also Childbirth; Natural childbirth; Nurses

MIDWIVES -- FICTION

Cushman, K. The midwife's apprentice   **Fic**

Hathaway, B. Missy Violet & me   **Fic**

O'Brien, C. M. Birthmarked   **Fic**

Mierka, Gregg A.

Nathanael Greene   **92**

Mieville, China

Railsea   **Fic**

Un Lun Dun   **Fic**

Mightier than the sword. Yolen, J.   **398.2**

The **mighty** 12. Smith, C. R.   **398.209**

The **mighty** Mars rovers. Rusch, E.   **523.43**

The **mighty** Quinn.   **Fic**

MIGRANT AGRICULTURAL LABORERS

Stavans, I. Cesar Chavez   **92**

MIGRANT LABOR

Cooper, M. L. Dust to eat   **973.917**

Ouellette, J. A day without immigrants   **331.6**

Stanley, J. Children of the Dust Bowl   **371.9**

MIGRANT LABOR -- FICTION

Engle, M. Silver people   **Fic**

Migrant mother. Nardo, D.   **973.917**

MIGRATION *See* Animals -- Migration; Immigration and emigration

Migration Nation.   **591.56**

MIGRATION, INTERNAL *See* Internal migration

MIGRATIONS OF NATIONS

Helget, N. Barbarians   **940.1**

MIGRATORY WORKERS *See* Migrant labor

Mikaelsen, Ben

Ghost of Spirit Bear   **Fic**

Touching Spirit Bear   **Fic**

Miki Falls, Book One: Spring. Crilley, M.   **741.5**

Miklowitz, Gloria D.

The enemy has a face   **Fic**

Milagros. Medina, M.   **Fic**

MILAN (ITALY) -- FICTION

Beyer, K. The demon catchers of Milan   **Fic**

Mileham, Rebecca

Global pollution   **363.7**

Miles Davis. Orr, T.   **788.9**

Miles from ordinary. Williams, C. L.   **Fic**

Miles to go for freedom. Osborne, L. B.   **305.896**

Miles, Lisa

Ballet spectacular   **792.8**

Miles, Liz

Louis Pasteur   **509.2**

Writing a screenplay   **808**

Milestones in American history [series]

Crompton, S. Sputnik/Explorer 1   **629.4**

Crompton, S. The Wright brothers   **92**

Davenport, J. The internment of Japanese Americans during World War II   **940.53**

Lange, B. The Stock Market Crash of 1929   **330.9**

McNeese, T. The Donner Party   **979.4**

Renehan, E. J. The Monroe doctrine   **327**

Renehan, E. J. The Transcontinental Railroad   **385**

Renehan, E. J. The Treaty of Paris   **973.3**

Sonneborn, L. The electric light   **621.32**

Woog, A. The Emancipation Proclamation   **973.7**

Milestones in discovery and invention [series]

Henderson, H. Artificial intelligence   **006.3**

Henderson, H. Communications and broadcasting   **384**

Henderson, H. Mathematics: powerful patterns in nature and society   **510**

Yount, L. Modern astronomy   **520**

Yount, L. Modern genetics   **576.5**

Yount, L. Modern marine science   **551.46**

Milestones in modern world history [series]

Allport, A. The Battle of Britain   **940.54**

Slavicek, L. C. The Chinese Cultural Revolution   **951.05**

Sonneborn, L. The end of apartheid in South Africa   **968.06**

Wagner, H. L. The Algerian war   **965**

Wagner, H. L. The Iranian Revolution   **955**

Milford, Kate

The Boneshaker   **Fic**

The Broken Lands   **Fic**

Greenglass House   **Fic**

Military. Grayson, R.   **355.4**

MILITARY AERONAUTICS

Mooney, C. Pilotless planes   **623.7**

MILITARY AERONAUTICS

     See also Aeronautics; Military art and science; War

MILITARY AIR BASES *See* Air bases

MILITARY AIRPLANES

     See also Airplanes; Military aeronautics

MILITARY ART AND SCIENCE

Chapman, C. Battles & weapons: exploring history through art   **355**

Collier, J. L. Gunpowder and weaponry   **623.4**

Cooke, T. Weapons, tactics, and strategy   **973.7**

Durman, L. Siege   **355.4**

McIntosh, J. S. Escape and evasion   **335.4**

Nardo, D. The Civil War   **973.3**

MILITARY ART AND SCIENCE -- HISTORY

Gunderson, J. Conquistadors   **970.01**

Helget, N. Mongols   **950**

MISSING CHILDREN -- FICTION

Button Hill   **Fic**
Starmer, A. The Riverman   **Fic**
Valentine, J. Double   **Fic**
The **missing** girl. Mazer, N. F.   **Fic**
Missing in action. Hughes, D.   **Fic**

MISSING IN ACTION

See also Prisoners of war; Soldiers

Missing link trilogy [series]
Thompson, K. Origins   **Fic**
Missing May. Rylant, C.   **Fic**

MISSING PERSONS

The Book of Storms   **Fic**
Borden, L. His name was Raoul Wallenberg   **92**
Brown, J. K. Amelia Earhart   **92**
Fleming, C. Amelia lost: the life and disappearance
   of Amelia Earhart   **92**
Littke, L. Lake of secrets   **Fic**
Micklos, J. Unsolved: what really happened to
   Amelia Earhart?   **92**
Miklowitz, G. D. The enemy has a face   **Fic**
Olson, K. M. The D.B. Cooper hijacking   **364.1**
Tanaka, S. Amelia Earhart   **92**

MISSING PERSONS

See also Criminal investigation

MISSING PERSONS -- FICTION

Crockett, S. D. After the snow   **FIC**
Dubosarsky, U. The golden day   **Fic**
Fisher, C. Obsidian mirror   **Fic**
Goeglein, T. M. Cold fury   **Fic**
Mackey, H. Dreamwood   **Fic**
McClintock, N. About that night   **Fic**
Mister Max   **Fic**
Moriarty, J. The cracks in the kingdom   **Fic**
Roecker, L. The lies that bind   **Fic**
Rosoff, M. Picture me gone   **Fic**
Sedgwick, M. She is not invisible   **Fic**
Smith, R. C. Mutation   **Fic**
Vaught, S. Freaks like us   **Fic**
When did you see her last?   **Fic**
Mission control, this is Apollo. Chaikin, A.   **629.45**
Mission to Mars. Hartman, E.   **629.45**
Mission unstoppable. Gutman, D.   **Fic**
Mission: planet Earth. Ride, S. K.   **525**
Mission: Science [series]
BishopRoby, J. Animal kingdom   **590**
Cregan, E. R. The atom   **539.7**
Cregan, E. R. Marie Curie   **92**
Fuoco, G. D. Earth   **333.72**
Greathouse, L. E. Skygazers   **920**
Greathouse, L. E. Solar system   **523.2**
Herweck, D. Robert Fulton   **92**
Housel, D. J. Ecologists   **920**
Housel, D. J. Ecosystems   **577**
Jankowski, C. Astronomers   **920**
Jankowski, C. Space exploration   **520**

Lee, K. F. Cells   **571.6**
Van Gorp, L. Antoine Lavoisier   **92**
Van Gorp, L. Elements   **540**
Van Gorp, L. Gregor Mendel   **92**
Weir, J. Matter   **530**
Weir, J. Max Planck   **92**
Zamosky, L. Louis Pasteur   **92**
Zamosky, L. Simple organisms   **579**

MISSIONARIES

Harness, C. The tragic tale of Narcissa Whitman
   and a faithful history of the Oregon Trail   **92**
Slavicek, L. C. Mother Teresa   **92**

MISSIONARIES, MEDICAL -- BIOGRAPHY

Bodden, V. To the heart of Africa   **916**
Kidder, T. Mountains beyond mountains   **92**
Mississippi. Shirley, D.   **976.2**
Mississippi.   **976.2**

MISSISSIPPI

Mississippi   **976.2**

MISSISSIPPI -- FICTION

McMullan, M. How I found the Strong   **Fic**
McMullan, M. Sources of light   **Fic**
McMullan, M. When I crossed No-Bob   **Fic**
Robinson, G. Little Brother of War   **Fic**
Taylor, M. D. The friendship   **Fic**
Taylor, M. D. Let the circle be unbroken   **Fic**
Taylor, M. D. The road to Memphis   **Fic**
Taylor, M. D. Roll of thunder, hear my cry   **Fic**
Taylor, M. D. The well   **Fic**
Wiles, D. The Aurora County All-Stars   **Fic**

MISSISSIPPI -- POETRY

Lewis, J. P. Black cat bone   **811**
A wreath for Emmett Till   **811**

MISSISSIPPI -- RACE RELATIONS

Aretha, D. Freedom Summer   **323.1**
Aretha, D. The murder of Emmett Till   **364.152**
Bowers, R. The spies of Mississippi   **323.1**
Coleman, W. Racism on trial   **345**
Crowe, C. Getting away with murder: the true story
   of the Emmett Till case   **364.152**
Crowe, C. Mississippi trial, 1955   **Fic**
Wright, S. Simeon's story   **305.8**

MISSISSIPPI -- RACE RELATIONS -- HISTO-RY -- 20TH CENTURY

Mitchell, D. The Freedom Summer Murders   **323.1**

MISSISSIPPI FREEDOM PROJECT

Aretha, D. Freedom Summer   **323.1**
Mitchell, D. The Freedom Summer Murders   **323.1**
Rubin, S. G. Freedom Summer   **323.11**
Mississippi Jack. Meyer, L. A.   **Fic**

MISSISSIPPI RIVER

Waldman, N. Voyages   **92**

MISSISSIPPI RIVER -- FICTION

Gray, D. E. Tomorrow, the river   **Fic**
Helgerson, J. Horns & wrinkles   **Fic**
Meyer, L. A. Mississippi Jack   **Fic**

The **moon.** Carlowicz, M. J.   **523.3**
Moon & sun [series]
   Lisle, H. The Ruby Key   **Fic**
   Lisle, H. The silver door   **Fic**
MOON -- EXPLORATION
   Carlowicz, M. J. The moon   **523.3**
   Simon, S. The moon   **523.3**
MOON -- EXPLORATION
   See also Space flight to the moon
MOON -- FICTION
   The Girl Who Soared over Fairyland and Cut the
     Moon in Two   **Fic**
   Hickam, H. H. Crater   **Fic**
   Hickam, H. Crescent   **Fic**
   Lin, G. Starry River of the Sky   **Fic**
MOON -- MAPS
   See also Maps
The **moon** and more. Dessen, S.   **Fic**
Moon bear.   **Fic**
Moon landing. Platt, R.   **629.45**
The **moon** over High Street. Babbitt, N.   **Fic**
Moon over Manifest. Vanderpool, C.   **Fic**
MOON ROCKS
   See also Lunar geology; Petrology
Moon without magic. Tunnell, M. O.   **Fic**
MOON WORSHIP
   See also Religion
MOON, VOYAGES TO *See* Space flight to the
   moon
Moon: science, history, and mystery. Ross, S. **629.45**
Moonbird. Hoose, P.   **598.072**
Mooney, Bel
   (ed) You never did learn to knock   **S**
Mooney, Carla
   Amazing Africa   **960**
   Explorers of the New World   **970.01**
   Genetics   **576.5**
   George Washington   **92**
   The Industrial Revolution   **330.9**
   Junk food junkies   **613.2**
   Mood disorders   **616.85**
   Oil spills and offshore drilling   **333.8**
   Online predators   **004.6**
   Pilotless planes   **623.7**
   Surviving in cold places   **363.34**
   Thinking critically   **303.48**
Mooney, Maggie
   Benjamin, M. Nobel's women of peace   **920**
Moonglass. Kirby, J.   **Fic**
Moonrunner. Thomason, M.   **Fic**
Moonshadow. Higgins, S.   **Fic**
Moonshadow [series]
   Higgins, S. The nightmare ninja   **Fic**
Moonshine express. Norville, R.   **Fic**
MOONSHINING -- FICTION
   Norville, R. Moonshine express   **Fic**

The **moorchild.** McGraw, E. J.   **Fic**
Moore, Ann
     About
   Thimmesh, C. Girls think of everything   **920**
Moore, Carley
   The stalker chronicles   **Fic**
Moore, Charles, 1931-2010
     About
   Nardo, D. Birmingham 1963   **323.1**
Moore, Christopher, 1957-
   From then to now   **909**
Moore, Derrick
   Always upbeat / All that   **Fic**
Moore, Inga
   Burnett, F. H. The secret garden   **Fic**
Moore, Kate
   The Battle of Britain   **940.54**
Moore, Perry
   Hero   **Fic**
Moore, Peter
   Red moon rising   **Fic**
   V is for villain   **Fic**
Moore, Peter D.
   Wetlands   **578.7**
Moore, Sarah W.
   The rap scene   **781.66**
Moore, Stephanie Perry
   (jt. auth) Moore, D. Always upbeat / All that   **Fic**
Moore, Wes, 1975-
     About
   Moore, W. Discovering Wes Moore   **975.2**
Moore, Willamarie
   All about Japan   **952**
MOORS *See* Muslims
Moose. Gish, M.   **599.65**
MOOSE
   Gish, M. Moose   **599.65**
Mora, Pat
   Dizzy in your eyes   **811**
     About
   Marcovitz, H. Pat Mora   **92**
Moragne, Wendy
   Depression   **616.85**
   New Jersey   **974.9**
MORAL AND PHILOSOPHIC STORIES *See*
   Didactic fiction; Fables; Parables
MORAL EDUCATION
   See also Education; Ethics
MORAL PHILOSOPHY *See* Ethics
MORALE
   See also Courage
MORALITY *See* Ethics
MORALITY PLAYS
   See also Drama; English drama; Religious
   drama; Theater

MORALS *See* Conduct of life; Ethics; Human behavior; Moral conditions

Moran, Katy
Bloodline — Fic
Bloodline rising — Fic

Mordan, C. B.
Dendy, L. A. Guinea pig scientists — 616
Marrin, A. Oh, rats! — 599.35

Mordecai, Martin
Blue Mountain trouble — Fic

Morden, Simon
The lost art — Fic

MORDRED (LEGENDARY CHARACTER) -- FICTION
Springer, N. I am Mordred — Fic
Vande Velde, V. The book of Mordred — Fic

More about Boy. Dahl, R. — 92
More bones. Olson, A. N. — 398.2
More bullies in more books. Bott, C. J. — 371.5
More scary stories to tell in the dark. Schwartz, A. — 398.2
More short scenes and monologues for middle school students. Surface, M. H. — 808.82
More telescope power. Matloff, G. L. — 522
More than a game. Crowe, C. — 810
More than friends. Holbrook, S. — 811
More than the blues? Lucas, E. — 616.85
More word histories and mysteries. — 422

Moreillon, Judi
Collaborative strategies for teaching reading comprehension — 372.4

MORGAN LE FAY (LEGENDARY CHARACTER) -- FICTION
McKenzie, N. Guinevere's gamble — Fic
Service, P. F. Tomorrow's magic — Fic
Service, P. F. Yesterday's magic — Fic
Springer, N. I am Morgan le Fay — Fic

Morgan, Jennifer
Cells of the nervous system — 611

Morgan, Nicola
The highwayman's footsteps — Fic

Morgan, Page
The beautiful and the cursed — Fic

Morgan, Sally
Focus on Pakistan — 954.91
From Greek atoms to quarks — 530
From Mendel's peas to genetic fingerprinting — 576.5
From sea urchins to dolly the sheep — 571.8

Morganelli, Adrianna
Formula One — 796.72

Morgenstern, Julie
Organizing from the inside out for teens — 646.7

Morgenstern, Susie Hoch
Secret letters from 0 to 10 — Fic

Morgenstern-Colon, Jessi
Morgenstern, J. Organizing from the inside out for

teens — 646.7

The **morgue** and me. Ford, J. C. — Fic

Moriarty, Chris
The inquisitor's apprentice — Fic
The watcher in the shadows — Fic

Moriarty, Jaclyn
A corner of white — Fic
The cracks in the kingdom — Fic
The ghosts of Ashbury High — Fic
The murder of Bindy Mackenzie — Fic
The year of secret assignments — Fic

Moribito. — Fic
Moribito II. Uehashi, N. — Fic

Morley, David
Healing our world — 610

MORMON CHURCH *See* Church of Jesus Christ of Latter-day Saints

MORMONS
Bial, R. Nauvoo — 289.3
Book of Mormon The Book of Mormon — 289.3
Bushman, C. L. Mormons in America — 289.3

MORMONS -- FICTION
Smith, E. W. Back when you were easier to love — Fic
Smith, E. W. The way he lived — Fic

Mormons in America. Bushman, C. L. — 289.3

Morn, September B.
The pug — 636.7

Morning Girl. Dorris, M. — Fic
Morning in a different place. McGuigan, M. A. — Fic
Morocco. Seward, P. — 964

MOROCCO
Donovan, S. Teens in Morocco — 305.235
Seward, P. Morocco — 964

MORPHINE
See also Narcotics

Morpurgo, Michael
The amazing story of Adolphus Tips — Fic
Beowulf — 398.2
An elephant in the garden — Fic
Half a man — Fic
Kensuke's kingdom — Fic
The Mozart question — Fic
Private Peaceful — Fic
Singing for Mrs. Pettigrew — S
Sir Gawain and the Green Knight — 398.2
War horse — Fic

Morrice, Polly Alison
Iowa — 977.7

Morris dictionary of word and phrase origins. Morris, W. — 422

Morris, Betty J.
Administering the school library media center — 027.8

Morris, Gerald
The ballad of Sir Dinadan — Fic
The legend of the king — Fic
The lioness & her knight — Fic

MOTOR VEHICLE INDUSTRY *See* Automobile industry

MOTORBOATS
> *See also* Boats and boating

MOTORBOATS -- MODELS
Gabrielson, C. Kinetic contraptions **621.46**

MOTORBOATS -- MODELS
> *See also* Models and modelmaking

MOTORCYCLES
Amado, E. High riders, saints and death cars **709.2**
Smedman, L. From boneshakers to choppers **629.227**
Woods, B. Hottest motorcycles **629.227**

MOTORCYCLES
> *See also* Bicycles

MOTORCYCLING
> *See also* Cycling

MOTORING *See* Automobile travel

MOTORS *See* Electric motors; Engines

Moulton, Courtney Allison
Angelfire **Fic**

Mouly, Françoise
The TOON treasury of classic children's comics **741.5**

MOUNDS AND MOUND BUILDERS
> *See also* Archeology; Burial; Tombs

MOUNT EVEREST (CHINA AND NEPAL)
Berne, E. C. Summiting Everest **796.522**
Bodden, V. To the top of Mount Everest **796.52**
> *See also* Mountains

MOUNT EVEREST (CHINA AND NEPAL) -- FICTION
Smith, R. Peak **Fic**

MOUNT RAINIER (WASH.)
> *See also* Mountains

MOUNTAIN ANIMALS
> *See also* Animals

MOUNTAIN BIKES
> *See also* All terrain vehicles; Bicycles

MOUNTAIN BIKING
> *See also* Cycling

MOUNTAIN BIKING -- FICTION
Davis, R. F. Chasing AllieCat **Fic**

MOUNTAIN CLIMBING *See* Mountaineering

MOUNTAIN ECOLOGY
Lynch, W. Rocky Mountains **577.4**

MOUNTAIN ECOLOGY
> *See also* Ecology

MOUNTAIN LIFE
> *See also* Country life

MOUNTAIN LIFE -- FICTION
Dowell, F. O. Dovey Coe **Fic**
Hemingway, E. M. Road to Tater Hill **Fic**
Mordecai, M. Blue Mountain trouble **Fic**

MOUNTAIN PLANTS
> *See also* Plant ecology; Plants

Mountain pose. Wilson, N. H. **Fic**
Mountain solo. Ingold, J. **Fic**

MOUNTAINEERING
Athans, S. K. Secrets of the sky caves **796.522**
Berne, E. C. Summiting Everest **796.522**
Brennan, K. Sir Edmund Hillary, modern day explorer **796.52**
Cleare, J. Epic climbs **796.52**
Crompton, S. Sir Edmund Hillary **92**
Elish, D. Edmund Hillary **92**
Helfand, L. Conquering Everest **741.5**
Skreslet, L. To the top of Everest **796.52**
Wurdinger, S. D. Rock climbing **796.52**

MOUNTAINEERING
> *See also* Outdoor life

MOUNTAINEERING EXPEDITIONS -- EVEREST, MOUNT (CHINA AND NEPAL) -- PICTORIAL WORKS
Berne, E. C. Summiting Everest **796.522**

MOUNTAINEERING -- EVEREST, MOUNT (CHINA AND NEPAL) -- HISTORY
Bodden, V. To the top of Mount Everest **796.52**

MOUNTAINEERING -- FICTION
Birdseye, T. Storm Mountain **Fic**
Carbone, E. Jump **Fic**
Patneaude, D. A piece of the sky **Fic**
Smith, R. Peak **Fic**

MOUNTAINEERING -- NEPAL -- MUSTANG (DISTRICT)
Athans, S. K. Secrets of the sky caves **796.522**

MOUNTAINEERS
Bredeson, C. After the last dog died **92**
Brennan, K. Sir Edmund Hillary, modern day explorer **796.52**
Crompton, S. Sir Edmund Hillary **92**
Elish, D. Edmund Hillary **92**
Helfand, L. Conquering Everest **741.5**
Mortenson, G. Three cups of tea **371.82**

MOUNTAINEERS -- EVEREST, MOUNT (CHINA AND NEPAL) -- BIOGRAPHY
Bodden, V. To the top of Mount Everest **796.52**

Mountains. Aleshire, P. **551.4**

MOUNTAINS
Aleshire, P. Mountains **551.4**
Collier, M. Over the mountains **557**
> *See also* Landforms; Physical geography

MOUNTAINS -- FICTION
Hale, S. Princess Academy **Fic**
Princess Academy **Fic**

Mountains beyond mountains. Kidder, T. **92**

Mountjoy, Shane
Causes of the Civil War **973.7**
Engel v. Vitale **344**
Technology and the Civil War **973.7**

Mourlevat, Jean-Claude
The pull of the ocean **Fic**

Islamic beliefs, practices, and cultures 297

Modern Muslim societies 297

MUSLIMS

Clinton, C. A stone in my hand **Fic**

Lat Kampung boy 741.5

MUSLIMS -- FICTION

Fama, E. Overboard **Fic**

MUSLIMS -- GRAPHIC NOVELS

Lat Kampung boy 741.5

MUSLIMS -- UNITED STATES

Hafiz, D. The American Muslim teenager's handbook 297

Islam in America 297

Musolf, Nell

Teens in Greece 305.23

Mussari, Mark

Amy Tan 92

Haruki Murakami 92

Othello 822.3

Musser, Susan

(ed) Abortion: opposing viewpoints 363.46

(ed) The attack on Pearl Harbor 940.54

(ed) Can the War on Terrorism be won? 363.32

(ed) Epidemics: opposing viewpoints 614.4

(ed) Global warming: opposing viewpoints 363.7

(ed) The Middle East: opposing viewpoints 956

(ed) Religion in America: opposing viewpoints 200.9

Mussi, Sarah

The door of no return **Fic**

Must love black. McClymer, K. **Fic**

MUSTANG (NEPAL : DISTRICT) -- ANTIQUITIES

Athans, S. K. Secrets of the sky caves 796.522

Mutation. Smith, R. C. **Fic**

MUTATION (BIOLOGY) *See* Evolution; Variation (Biology)

MUTATION (BIOLOGY) -- FICTION

Reeve, P. Scrivener's moon **Fic**

MUTUAL FUNDS

See also Investments

MUTUALISM (BIOLOGY) *See* Symbiosis

My America. 811

My anxious mind. Tompkins, M. A. 616.85

My basmati bat mitzvah. Freedman, P. J. **Fic**

My big mouth. Hannan, P. **Fic**

My black me. 811

My bonny light horseman. Meyer, L. A. **Fic**

My book of life by Angel. Leavitt, M. **Fic**

My boyfriend bites. Jolley, D. 741.5

My boyfriend is a monster [series]

I love him to pieces 741.5

Jolley, D. My boyfriend bites 741.5

Storrie, P. D. Made for each other 741.5

My bridges of hope. Bitton-Jackson, L. 940.53

My brother Abe. Mazer, H. **Fic**

My brother Sam is dead. Collier, J. L. **Fic**

My brother the robot. Grabenstein, C. **Fic**

My brother's book. Sendak, M. 811

My brother's keeper. McCormick, P. **Fic**

My brother's shadow. Schroeder, M. **Fic**

My brother, my sister, and I. Watkins, Y. K. **Fic**

My childhood under fire. Halilbegovich, N. 949.7

My contract with Henry. Vaupel, R. **Fic**

My dad's a punk. **S**

My daily diet. 613.2

My Daniel. Conrad, P. **Fic**

My fake boyfriend is better than yours. Springer, K. **Fic**

My favorite band does not exist. Jeschonek, R. T. **Fic**

My future career [series]

McAlpine, M. Working in music and dance 780

McAlpine, M. Working with animals 636

McAlpine, M. Working with children 362.7

My gender workbook. Bornstein, K. 305.3

My Havana. Wells, R. **Fic**

My heartbeat. Freymann-Weyr, G. **Fic**

My kind of sad. Scowen, K. 616.85

My last skirt. Durrant, L. **Fic**

My letter to the world and other poems. 811

My life as a book. **Fic**

My life as a cartoonist. **Fic**

My life as a joke. **Fic**

My life as a stuntboy. Tashjian, J. **Fic**

My life in black and white. Friend, N. **Fic**

My life in dog years. Paulsen, G. 813

My life in pink and green. Greenwald, L. **Fic**

My Life Is A Zoo [series]

Keating, J. How to outrun a crocodile when your shoes are untied **Fic**

My life the musical. Wood, M. **Fic**

My life undecided. Brody, J. **Fic**

My life with the Lincolns. Brandeis, G. **Fic**

My life, the theater, and other tragedies. Zadoff, A. **Fic**

My misadventures as a teenage rock star. Raskin, J. **Fic**

My most excellent year. Kluger, S. **Fic**

My mother the cheerleader. Sharenow, R. **Fic**

My name is Mina. Almond, D. **Fic**

My name is not easy. Edwardson, D. D. **Fic**

My name is Parvana. Ellis, D. **Fic**

My name is Sally Little Song. Woods, B. **Fic**

My new gender workbook. Bornstein, K. 305.3

My one hundred adventures. Horvath, P. **Fic**

My Own Revolution. Marsden, C. **Fic**

My parent has cancer and it really sucks. Silver, M. 616.99

My perfect life. Sheldon, D. **Fic**

My secret guide to Paris. **Fic**

My sister lives on the mantelpiece. Pitcher, A. **Fic**

MYSTERY FICTION

Abbott, T. The postcard	Fic
Abrahams, P. Behind the curtain	Fic
Abrahams, P. Down the rabbit hole	Fic
Abrahams, P. Into the dark	Fic
Adam, P. Max Cassidy: escape from Shadow Island	Fic
Allison, J. Gilda Joyce, psychic investigator	Fic
Allison, J. Gilda Joyce, psychic investigator: the bones of the holy	Fic
Allison, J. Gilda Joyce: the dead drop	Fic
Allison, J. Gilda Joyce: the ghost sonata	Fic
Allison, J. Gilda Joyce: the Ladies of the Lake	Fic
Angleberger, T. Horton Halfpott	Fic
Archer, J. Through her eyes	Fic
Armistead, C. Being Henry David	Fic
Aronson, S. Beyond lucky	Fic
Avi City of orphans	Fic
Avi The man who was Poe	Fic
Baccalario, P. City of wind	Fic
Baccalario, P. Star of Stone	Fic
Bachmann, S. The Cabinet of Curiosities	S
Balliett, B. The Calder game	Fic
Balliett, B. Chasing Vermeer	Fic
Balliett, B. Hold fast	Fic
Balliett, B. The Wright 3	Fic
Banghart, T. E. Shattered Veil	813.6
Baratz-Logsted, L. Twin's daughter	Fic
Barnholdt, L. Girl meets ghost	Fic
Barrett, T. The 100-year-old secret	Fic
Barrett, T. The Beast of Blackslope	Fic
Barrett, T. The case that time forgot	Fic
Baucom, I. Through the skylight	Fic
Beaufrand, M. J. The river	Fic
Beil, M. D. The Red Blazer Girls: the ring of Rocamadour	Fic
Beil, M. D. The Red Blazer Girls: The vanishing violin	Fic
Beil, M. The Red Blazer Girls: the mistaken masterpiece	Fic
Bell, J. Kepler's dream	Fic
Bellairs, J. The curse of the blue figurine	Fic
Berk, J. Guy Langman, crime scene procrastinator	Fic
Berk, J. Strike three, you're dead	Fic
Berlin, E. The potato chip puzzles	Fic
Berlin, E. The puzzling world of Winston Breen	Fic
Bernard, R. Find me	Fic
Berry, J. The scandalous sisterhood of Prickwillow Place	Fic
Blakemore, M. F. The spy catchers of Maple Hill	Fic
Blundell, J. What I saw and how I lied	Fic
Bradbury, J. Wrapped	Fic
Brennan, J. H. The secret prophecy	Fic
Brennan, S. R. Unspoken	Fic

Broach, E. Masterpiece	Fic
Broach, E. Shakespeare's secret	Fic
Bryant, J. Kaleidoscope eyes	Fic
Bunce, E. C. Liar's moon	Fic
Buzbee, L. The haunting of Charles Dickens	Fic
Byars, B. C. The dark stairs	Fic
Carey, B. Poison most vial	Fic
Carey, B. The unknowns	Fic
Catch you later, traitor	Fic
Chari, S. Vanished	Fic
Chatterton, M. The Brain finds a leg	Fic
Chatterton, M. The Brain full of holes	Fic
Choldenko, G. Al Capone does my homework	Fic
Coben, H. Seconds away	Fic
Coben, H. Shelter	Fic
Colfer, E. Half-Moon investigations	Fic
Corbett, S. The last newspaper boy in America	Fic
Cotler, S. Cheesie Mack is not a genius or anything	Fic
Cox, S. The Dead Girls Detective Agency	Fic
Daley, J. R. Jesus Jackson	Fic
Damico, G. Croak	FIC
DeFelice, C. C. The ghost of Cutler Creek	Fic
DeFelice, C. C. The ghost and Mrs. Hobbs	Fic
Derting, K. The body finder	Fic
Dionne, E. Moxie and the art of rule breaking	Fic
Dionne, E. Ollie and the science of treasure hunting	Fic
Dowd, S. The London Eye mystery	Fic
Doyle, A. C. S. The adventures and the memoirs of Sherlock Holmes	Fic
Doyle, M. Courtship and curses	Fic
Draanen, W. v. Sammy Keyes and the hotel thief	Fic
Dubosarsky, U. The golden day	Fic
Duncan, L. I know what you did last summer	Fic
Duncan, L. Locked in time	Fic
Dunlap, S. E. The musician's daughter	Fic
Edge, C. Twelve minutes to midnight	Fic
Evans, L. Horten's miraculous mechanisms	Fic
Fairlie, E. The lost treasure of Tuckernuck	Fic
Fantaskey, B. Buzz kill	Fic
Feinstein, J. Change up	Fic
Feinstein, J. Cover-up	Fic
Feinstein, J. Last shot	Fic
Feinstein, J. The rivalry	Fic
Feinstein, J. Vanishing act	Fic
Ferraiolo, J. D. The big splash	Fic
File under: 13 suspicious incidents	Fic
Ford, J. C. The morgue and me	Fic
Frazier, A. The mastermind plot	Fic
Frazier, A. The midnight tunnel	Fic
Fusilli, J. Marley Z and the bloodstained violin	Fic
Gagnon, M. Strangelets	Fic
Gantos, J. From Norvelt to nowhere	Fic
Gavin, R. Knightley and son	Fic

Gibbs, S. Belly up	**Fic**	
Gibbs, S. Poached	**Fic**	
Gilman, D. Blood sun	**Fic**	
Gilman, D. Ice claw	**Fic**	
Gleason, C. The clockwork scarab	**Fic**	
Goeglein, T. M. Cold fury	**Fic**	
Goelman, A. The path of names	**Fic**	
Grabenstein, C. The black heart crypt	**Fic**	
Grant, V. Quid pro quo	**Fic**	
Grant, V. Res judicata	**Fic**	
Graves, K. The orphan of Awkward Falls	**Fic**	
Grisham, J. Theodore Boone: kid lawyer	**Fic**	
Hahn, M. D. Mister Death's blue-eyed girls	**Fic**	
Haines, K. M. The girl is murder	**Fic**	
Haines, K. M. The girl is trouble	**Fic**	
Hamilton, V. The house of Dies Drear	**Fic**	
Harrison, M. 13 treasures	**Fic**	
Harvey, A. Haunting Violet	**Fic**	
Hautman, P. Doppelganger	**Fic**	
Hautman, P. Skullduggery	**Fic**	
Hautman, P. Snatched	**Fic**	
Healey, K. The shattering	**Fic**	
Higgins, F. E. The Eyeball Collector	**Fic**	
Hilmo, T. With a name like Love	**Fic**	
Hoobler, D. The demon in the teahouse	**Fic**	
Hoobler, D. The ghost in the Tokaido Inn	**Fic**	
Hoobler, D. Seven paths to death	**Fic**	
Hoobler, D. The sword that cut the burning grass	**Fic**	
Horowitz, A. The Falcon's Malteser	**Fic**	
Horowitz, A. The Greek who stole Christmas	**Fic**	
Horowitz, A. Public enemy number two	**Fic**	
Horowitz, A. South by southeast	**Fic**	
Horowitz, A. Three of diamonds	**Fic**	
Ibbotson, E. The star of Kazan	**Fic**	
Jarzab, A. All unquiet things	**Fic**	
Jinks, C. The abused werewolf rescue group	**Fic**	
Jinks, C. The reformed vampire support group	**Fic**	
Johnson, M. The madness underneath	**Fic**	
Juby, S. Getting the girl	**Fic**	
Kelsey, M. A recipe 4 robbery	**Fic**	
Kirby, J. Golden	**Fic**	
Klise, K. Letters from camp	**Fic**	
Konigsburg, E. L. Silent to the bone	**Fic**	
Lacey, J. Island of Thieves	**Fic**	
Lane, A. Black ice	**Fic**	
Lane, A. Rebel fire	**Fic**	
Larwood, K. Freaks	**Fic**	
Lawrence, C. The case of the deadly desperados	**Fic**	
Lawrence, C. P.K. Pinkerton and the petrified man	**Fic**	
Lawrence, C. P.K. Pinkerton and the pistol-packing widows	**Fic**	
Lawrence, I. The seance	**Fic**	
Leck, J. The adventures of Jack Lime	**Fic**	

Lee, Y. S. The body at the tower	**Fic**	
Lee, Y. S. A spy in the house	**Fic**	
Leonard, J. P. Cold case	**Fic**	
Levine, G. C. A tale of Two Castles	**Fic**	
Littke, L. Lake of secrets	**Fic**	
Little, K. G. The time of the fireflies	**Fic**	
Lloyd Jones, R. Wild boy	**Fic**	
MacColl, M. Nobody's secret	**Fic**	
MacDonald, B. The secret of the sealed room	**Fic**	
MacDonald, B. Wicked Will	**Fic**	
Mack, T. The fall of the Amazing Zalindas	**Fic**	
Mack, T. The mystery of the conjured man	**Fic**	
Mackall, D. D. The silence of murder	**Fic**	
Madison, B. Lulu Dark and the summer of the Fox	**Fic**	
The magnificent Lizzie Brown and the mysterious phantom	**Fic**	
Margolis, L. Girl's best friend	**Fic**	
Marina	**Fic**	
Matthews, T. L. Danger in the dark	**Fic**	
Matthews, T. L. Frame-up on the Bowery	**Fic**	
Matthews, T. L. Shots at sea	**Fic**	
McClintock, N. Masked	**Fic**	
McLoughlin, J. At Yellow Lake	**Fic**	
McMann, L. Cryer's Cross	**Fic**	
McNamee, G. Acceleration	**Fic**	
Milford, K. Greenglass House	**Fic**	
Miller, K. Kiki Strike: inside the shadow city	**Fic**	
Miller, K. Kiki Strike: the Empress's tomb	**Fic**	
Mills, R. Charlie's key	**Fic**	
Morton-Shaw, C. The hunt for the seventh	**Fic**	
Mulligan, A. Trash	**Fic**	
Murder is bad manners	**Fic**	
Nayeri, D. Straw house, Wood house, Brick house, Blow	**S**	
Newbery, L. Lost boy	**Fic**	
Nixon, J. L. Nightmare	**Fic**	
Nooks & crannies	**Fic**	
Osterlund, A. Aurelia	**Fic**	
Park, L. S. Trust no one	**Fic**	
Parker, R. B. The Edenville Owls	**Fic**	
Patron, S. Behind the masks	**Fic**	
Pauley, K. Cat Girl's day off	**Fic**	
Peacock, S. Death in the air	**Fic**	
Peacock, S. The dragon turn	**Fic**	
Peacock, S. Eye of the crow	**Fic**	
Peacock, S. The secret fiend	**Fic**	
Peacock, S. Vanishing girl	**Fic**	
Perez, M. Dead is a killer tune	**Fic**	
Pieces and players	**Fic**	
Poblocki, D. The nightmarys	**Fic**	
Princess Academy	**Fic**	
Pullman, P. Two crafty criminals!	**Fic**	
Reichs, K. J. Virals	**Fic**	
Renn, D. Latitude zero	**Fic**	
Renn, D. Tokyo heist	**Fic**	

Chotjewitz, D. Daniel half human **Fic**
Dowswell, P. The Auslander **Fic**
Falkner, B. The project **Fic**
Lasky, K. Ashes **Fic**
Sharenow, R. The Berlin Boxing Club **Fic**
Wolf, J. M. Someone named Eva **Fic**

NATIONAL SOCIALISM -- HISTORY -- FICTION
The watcher **Fic**

NATIONAL SONGS
National anthems of the world **782.42**

NATIONAL SONGS
See also Songs

NATIONAL SONGS -- UNITED STATES
See also American songs

NATIONAL SYMBOLS *See* National emblems

National Wildlife Federation
Evans, A. V. National Wildlife Federation field guide to insects and spiders & related species of North America **595.7**
National Wildlife Federation field guide to insects and spiders & related species of North America. Evans, A. V. **595.7**

NATIONALISM
See also International relations; Political science

NATIONALITY (CITIZENSHIP) *See* Citizenship

NATIONS
Wojtanik, A. The National Geographic Bee ultimate fact book **910**

NATIVE AMERICAN ARCHITECTURE
See also Architecture

NATIVE AMERICAN ART
January, B. Native American art & culture **704**

NATIVE AMERICAN ART
See also Art

Native American art & culture. January, B. **704**

NATIVE AMERICAN AUTHORS
See also Authors

NATIVE AMERICAN CHILDREN
Ellis, D. Looks Like Daylight **970.1**
Walking on earth and touching the sky **810**

NATIVE AMERICAN CHILDREN
See also Children

NATIVE AMERICAN COSTUME
McEvoy, A. The American West **391**

NATIVE AMERICAN COSTUME
See also Costume

NATIVE AMERICAN GAMES
See also Games; Native Americans -- Social life and customs

Native American history for kids. Gibson, K. B. **970.004**

NATIVE AMERICAN LITERATURE
See also Literature

NATIVE AMERICAN LITERATURE -- HISTORY AND CRITICISM
Otfinoski, S. Native American writers **810**

NATIVE AMERICAN MEDICINE
See also Medicine

NATIVE AMERICAN MUSIC
See also Music

NATIVE AMERICAN NAMES
See also Names

Native American religion. Martin, J. **299.7**
Native American religions. Hartz, P. **299.7**

NATIVE AMERICAN SIGN LANGUAGE
See also Sign language

NATIVE AMERICAN WOMEN
See also Women

NATIVE AMERICAN WOMEN -- DICTIONARIES
Sonneborn, L. A to Z of American Indian women **920.003**

Native American writers. Otfinoski, S. **810**
The **Native** Americans. Schomp, V. **970.004**

NATIVE AMERICANS
Bial, R. The Apache **970.004**
Bial, R. The Cree **971**
Bial, R. The Crow **970**
Bial, R. The Delaware **974**
Bial, R. The Huron **970.004**
Bial, R. Lifeways [series] **970.004**
Bial, R. The Menominee **977.4**
Dreaming in Indian **704.03**
Frost, H. Salt **Fic**
Gansworth, E. If I ever get out of here **Fic**
Gibson, K. B. Native American history for kids **970.004**
Goble, P. All our relatives **970.004**
January, B. Native American art & culture **704**
Katz, W. L. Black Indians **305.8**
Keoke, E. D. American Indian contributions to the world **970.004**
King, D. C. First people **970.004**
Kirkpatrick, K. Mysterious bones **979.7**
McNeese, T. The fascinating history of American Indians **970.004**
Murdoch, D. H. North American Indian **970.004**
National Museum of the American Indian (U.S.) Do all Indians live in tipis? **970.004**
Philbrick, N. The Mayflower and the Pilgrims' New World **973.2**
Philip, N. The great circle **970.004**
Schomp, V. The Native Americans **970.004**
Weber, E. N. R. Rattlesnake Mesa **92**

NATIVE AMERICANS -- AGRICULTURE
See also Agriculture

NATIVE AMERICANS -- ALASKA -- FICTION
Bell, H. Traitor's son **Fic**

NATIVE AMERICANS -- ANTIQUITIES

NATIVE AMERICANS -- WARS

Brown, D. A. Bury my heart at Wounded Knee **970.004**

Dolan, E. F. The American Indian wars **970.004**

Ehrlich, A. Wounded Knee: an Indian history of the American West **970.004**

Langley, A. The Plains Indian wars 1864-1890 **978.004**

Zimmerman, D. J. Saga of the Sioux **970.004**

NATIVE AMERICANS -- WARS -- ENCYCLO-PEDIAS

Encyclopedia of Native American wars and warfare **970.004**

NATIVE AMERICANS -- WARS -- FICTION

McKinney-Whitaker, C. The last sister **Fic**

NATIVE AMERICANS -- WEST (U.S.)

Brown, D. A. Bury my heart at Wounded Knee **970.004**

Ehrlich, A. Wounded Knee: an Indian history of the American West **970.004**

Gitlin, M. Wounded Knee Massacre **970.004**

NATIVE AMERICANS -- WEST INDIES -- FICTION

Engle, M. Hurricane dancers **Fic**

NATIVE AMERICANS IN ART

Reich, S. Painting the wild frontier: the art and adventures of George Catlin **92**

NATIVE PLANTS

See also Plants

Native son: the story of Richard Wright. Hart, J. **92**

Natterson, Cara

The care & keeping of you 2 **613**

NATURAL CHILDBIRTH

See also Childbirth

Natural disasters. **363.34**

NATURAL DISASTERS

See also Disasters

NATURAL DISASTERS

Bailey, G. Fragile planet **363.34**

Engelbert, P. Dangerous planet **363.34**

Garbe, S. The Worst wildfires of all time **363.34**

Guiberson, B. Z. Disasters **904**

Hile, L. Animal survival **591.5**

Langley, A. Hurricanes, tsunamis, and other natural disasters **363.34**

Natural disasters **363.34**

Rusch, E. Eruption! **363.34**

Sanna, E. Nature's wrath **363.34**

Trammel, H. K. Wildfires **634.9**

NATURAL DISASTERS -- FICTION

Dashner, J. The kill order **Fic**

De la Peña, M. The living **Fic**

NATURAL FOODS

Apte, S. Eating green **630**

Johanson, P. Fake foods **613.2**

Miller, D. A. Organic foods **641.3**

Organic food and farming **641.3**

Rau, D. M. Going organic **613.2**

See also Food

NATURAL FOODS INDUSTRY

Miller, D. A. Organic foods **641.3**

NATURAL GAS

See also Fuel; Gases

NATURAL HISTORY

Calhoun, Y. Plant and animal science fair projects **570.7**

Kelsey, E. Strange new species **578**

Quinlan, S. E. The case of the monkeys that fell from the trees **577.3**

NATURAL HISTORY

See also Science

NATURAL HISTORY -- AFRICA

Woods, M. Seven natural wonders of Africa **508**

NATURAL HISTORY -- ASIA

Woods, M. Seven natural wonders of Asia and the Middle East **508**

NATURAL HISTORY -- AUSTRALIA

Woods, M. Seven natural wonders of Australia and Oceania **508**

NATURAL HISTORY -- CENTRAL AMERICA

Woods, M. Seven natural wonders of Central and South America **508**

NATURAL HISTORY -- EUROPE

Woods, M. Seven natural wonders of Europe **508**

NATURAL HISTORY -- FICTION

Meyer, C. The true adventures of Charley Darwin **Fic**

NATURAL HISTORY -- FLORIDA

Lynch, W. The Everglades **508**

NATURAL HISTORY -- GALAPAGOS ISLANDS

Chin, J. Island **508**

Hague, B. Alien deep **551.2**

NATURAL HISTORY -- MASSACHUSETTS

McCurdy, M. Walden then & now **818**

NATURAL HISTORY -- MIDDLE EAST

Woods, M. Seven natural wonders of Asia and the Middle East **508**

NATURAL HISTORY -- NORTH AMERICA

Woods, M. Seven natural wonders of North America **508**

NATURAL HISTORY -- ROCKY MOUNTAINS

Lynch, W. Rocky Mountains **577.4**

NATURAL HISTORY -- SONORAN DESERT

Lynch, W. Sonoran Desert **577.5**

NATURAL HISTORY -- SOUTH AMERICA

Woods, M. Seven natural wonders of Central and South America **508**

Natural History Museum (London, England) (comp) Rocks & minerals **552**

NATURAL LAW

See also Ethics; Law

A **natural** man. Soto, G. **811**

River of words 808.81
The tree that time built 808.81
    See also Poetry
NATURE PROTECTION *See* Nature conservation
Nature science experiments. Bardhan-Quallen, S. 508
NATURE STUDY
Art, H. W. Woodswalk 508
Bardhan-Quallen, S. Nature science experiments 508
Lee, D. Biomimicry 608
Nature's art box. Martin, L. C. 745.5
Nature's machines. Parks, D. 92
Nature's wonders [series]
Heinrichs, A. The Amazon rain forest 981
Heinrichs, A. The Nile 962
Heinrichs, A. The Sahara 966
Kras, S. L. The Galapagos Islands 986.6
Kummer, P. K. The Great Barrier Reef 578.7
Kummer, P. K. The Great Lakes 977
Nature's wrath. Sanna, E. 363.34
NATURECRAFT *See* Nature craft
NATUROPATHY
    See also Alternative medicine; Therapeutics
NAUTICAL ALMANACS
    See also Almanacs; Navigation
NAUTICAL ASTRONOMY
    See also Astronomy
NAUTICAL CHARTS
    See also Maps; Navigation
Nauvoo. Bial, R. 289.3
NAVAHO INDIANS *See* Navajo Indians
NAVAJO CHILDREN
    See also Native American children; Navajo Indians
NAVAJO INDIANS
Bial, R. The Long Walk 970.004
Denetdale, J. The Long Walk 970.004
Ehrlich, A. Wounded Knee: an Indian history of the American West 970.004
NAVAJO INDIANS -- FICTION
Tingle, T. Danny Blackgoat, Navajo prisoner Fic
NAVAJO LONG WALK, 1863-1867 -- FICTION
Tingle, T. Danny Blackgoat, Navajo prisoner Fic
NAVAJO WOMEN
    See also Native American women; Navajo Indians
NAVAL AERONAUTICS *See* Military aeronautics
NAVAL AIR BASES *See* Air bases
NAVAL ARCHITECTURE
    See also Architecture
NAVAL HISTORY
    See also History
NAVAL OFFICERS
Blumberg, R. Commodore Perry in the land of the Shogun 952

Brager, B. L. John Paul Jones 92
Cooper, M. L. Hero of the high seas 92
Feinstein, S. Captain Cook 92
Knowles, J. Jacques Cousteau 92
Lace, W. W. Captain James Cook 92
Lawlor, L. Magnificent voyage 910.4
Nelson, P. Left for dead 940.54
Olmstead, K. A. Jacques Cousteau 92
NAVAL PERSONNEL *See* Sailors
NAVIES
    See also Armed forces; Military personnel
NAVIGATION
Williams, L. D. Navigational aids 623.89
Young, K. R. Across the wide ocean 623.89
NAVIGATION (AERONAUTICS)
    See also Aeronautics
NAVIGATION (ASTRONAUTICS)
    See also Astrodynamics; Astronautics
NAVIGATION -- FICTION
Frederick, H. V. The voyage of Patience Goodspeed Fic
Wilson, J. The alchemist's dream Fic
Navigational aids. Williams, L. D. 623.89
The **Navigator.** McNamee, E. Fic
Navigator trilogy [series]
McNamee, E. City of Time Fic
McNamee, E. The Frost Child Fic
McNamee, E. The Navigator Fic
NAVIGATORS *See* Explorers; Sailors
Navigators [series]
Smith, M. Ancient Egypt 932
Navy SEALs. McIntosh, J. S. 359.9
Nayeri, Daniel
Straw house, Wood house, Brick house, Blow S
Naylor, Phyllis Reynolds
Alice in April Fic
Alice in lace Fic
Alice in rapture, sort of Fic
Alice in-between Fic
Alice on her way Fic
Alice the brave Fic
All but Alice Fic
Almost Alice Fic
Cricket man Fic
Dangerously Alice Fic
Faith, hope, and Ivy June Fic
Incredibly Alice Fic
Intensely Alice Fic
Outrageously Alice Fic
Reluctantly Alice Fic
Saving Shiloh Fic
Shiloh Fic
Shiloh season Fic
Simply Alice Fic
The **Nazi** hunters. Bascomb, N. 364.15
NAZI HUNTERS

NOTE-TAKING

Green, J. Write it down **371.3**

NOTE-TAKING

See also Reporters and reporting; Study skills

NOTEBOOKS, ARTISTS' *See* Artists' notebooks

Notes from a liar and her dog. Choldenko, G. **Fic**

Notes from a totally lame vampire. Collins, T. **Fic**

Notes from the dog. Paulsen, G. **Fic**

Notes from the midnight driver. Sonnenblick, J. **Fic**

Nothing. **Fic**

Nothing but ghosts. Kephart, B. **Fic**

Nothing but the truth. Avi **Fic**

Nothing Can Possibly Go Wrong. **Fic**

Nothing here but stones. Oswald, N. **Fic**

Nothing special. Herbach, G. **Fic**

The **notorious** Benedict Arnold. Sheinkin, S. **92**

Nouraee, Andisheh

(jt. auth) Anderson, J. L. Americapedia **320**

Nourishment. Binstock, M. **92**

Nouvian, Claire

(ed) The Deep **591.7**

NOVA SCOTIA -- GRAPHIC NOVELS

Larson, H. Mercury **741.5**

Novak, Amy

Glenn Beck **92**

NOVELISTS

See also Authors

NOVELS IN LETTERS *See* Epistolary fiction

NOVELS IN VERSE

Agard, J. The young inferno **Fic**

Applegate, K. Home of the brave **Fic**

Bingham, K. Shark girl **Fic**

Bryant, J. Kaleidoscope eyes **Fic**

Bryant, J. Ringside, 1925 **Fic**

Burg, A. E. All the broken pieces **Fic**

Chaltas, T. Because I am furniture **Fic**

Cheng, A. Brushing Mom's hair **Fic**

Creech, S. Hate that cat **Fic**

Crossan, S. The Weight of Water **Fic**

Engle, M. Firefly letters **Fic**

Engle, M. Hurricane dancers **Fic**

Engle, M. Silver people **Fic**

Engle, M. The surrender tree **811**

Engle, M. Tropical secrets **Fic**

Engle, M. The wild book **Fic**

Fehler, G. Beanball **Fic**

Frost, H. The braid **Fic**

Frost, H. Crossing stones **Fic**

Frost, H. Diamond Willow **Fic**

Frost, H. Hidden **Fic**

Grimes, N. Dark sons **Fic**

Grimes, N. A girl named Mister **Fic**

Grimes, N. Planet Middle School **Fic**

Hemphill, S. Hideous love **Fic**

Hemphill, S. Sisters of glass **Fic**

Hemphill, S. Wicked girls **Fic**

Hesse, K. Out of the dust **Fic**

Hesse, K. Witness **Fic**

Hopkins, E. Rumble **Fic**

Howe, J. Addie on the inside **Fic**

Koertge, R. Shakespeare makes the playoffs **Fic**

Lai, T. Inside out and back again **Fic**

Leavitt, M. My book of life by Angel **Fic**

LeZotte, A. C. T4 **Fic**

Macdonald, M. Odette's secrets **Fic**

MacLean, J. Nix Minus One **Fic**

Marcus, K. Exposed **Fic**

Myers, W. D. Amiri & Odette **Fic**

Myers, W. D. Street love **Fic**

Ostlere, C. Karma **Fic**

Richards, J. Three rivers rising **Fic**

Rose, C. S. May B. **Fic**

Saller, C. F. Eddie's war **Fic**

Schroeder, L. Chasing Brooklyn **Fic**

Smith, H. A. Keeping the night watch **Fic**

Smith, H. A. The way a door closes **Fic**

Sones, S. What my mother doesn't know **Fic**

Thompson, H. The language inside **Fic**

Thompson, H. Orchards **Fic**

Tregay, S. Love and leftovers **Fic**

Turner, A. W. Hard hit **Fic**

Venkatraman, P. A time to dance **Fic**

Weatherford, C. B. Becoming Billie Holiday **Fic**

Weston, R. P. Zorgamazoo **Fic**

Williams, C. L. Glimpse **Fic**

Wolf, A. The watch that ends the night **Fic**

Wolff, V. E. Make lemonade **Fic**

Wolff, V. E. This full house **Fic**

Wolff, V. E. True believer **Fic**

Woodson, J. Locomotion **Fic**

Yeomans, E. Rubber houses **Fic**

Zimmer, T. V. 42 miles **Fic**

Zimmer, T. V. Reaching for sun **Fic**

November blues. Draper, S. M. **Fic**

November, Alan C.

Empowering students with technology **371.3**

November, Sharyn

(ed) Firebirds **S**

(ed) Firebirds rising **S**

(ed) Firebirds soaring **S**

Novio boy. Soto, G. **812**

Now. Gleitzman, M. **Fic**

Now is the time for running. Williams, M. **Fic**

Now playing. Koertge, R. **Fic**

Now starring Vivien Leigh Reid: Diva in training.
Collins, Y. **Fic**

Nowhere girl. Paquette **Fic**

Nowhere to run. Griffin, C. J. **Fic**

Noyes, Alfred

The highwayman **821**

Noyes, Deborah

(ed) Gothic! **S**

(ed) Fitzmaurice, K. Destiny, rewritten **Fic**

O'Reilly, Bill, 1949-
Kennedy's last days **973.922**

O'Reilly, Gillian
Lee, C. The great number rumble **510**

O'Rourke, Erica
Tangled **Fic**
Torn **Fic**

O'Shaughnessy, Tam
Ride, S. K. Mission: planet Earth **525**

O'Shea, Clare
Llewellyn, C. Cooking with fruits and vegetables **641.3**
Llewellyn, C. Cooking with meat and fish **641.6**

O'Shea, Maria
Kuwait **953.67**

O'Sullivan, Joanne
Migration Nation **591.56**

OAK
See also Trees; Wood

Oakes, Cory Putman
Dinosaur boy **Fic**

Oakley, Annie, 1860-1926
About
Koestler-Grack, R. A. Annie Oakley **92**
Wills, C. A. Annie Oakley: a photographic story of a life **92**

Oaks, J. Adams
Why I fight **Fic**

Oates, Joyce Carol
Big Mouth & Ugly Girl **Fic**
Freaky green eyes **Fic**
Oath breaker. Paver, M. **Fic**

OAXACA DE JUÁREZ (MEXICO) -- FICTION
Zevin, G. Because it is my blood **Fic**
Obama. Abramson, J. **92**
The **Obama** view. Gibson, K. B. **92**
Obama, Barack, 1961-
About
Abramson, J. Obama **92**
Burgan, M. Barack Obama **92**
Gibson, K. B. The Obama view **92**
Krensky, S. Barack Obama **92**
Obama, B. Dreams from my father **92**
Thomas, G. E. Yes we can: a biography of Barack Obama **92**
Zeiger, J. Barack Obama **973.932**

Obama, Michelle
About
Brophy, D. Michelle Obama **92**
Colbert, D. Michelle Obama **92**
Uschan, M. V. Michelle Obama **92**

Obata, Takeshi
Hotta, Y. Hikaru No Go, Volume 1 **741.5**

OBELISKS
See also Archeology; Architecture; Monu-

ments

Oberman, Sheldon
Solomon and the ant **398.2**

Obesity. **616.3**

OBESITY
Allman, T. Obesity **616.3**
Edwards, H. Talking about your weight **613.2**
Fast food **362.1**
Favor, L. J. Weighing in **613.2**
Fredericks, C. Obesity **616.3**
Heller, T. Overweight **613.2**
Hicks, T. A. Obesity **616.3**
Hidalgo-Robert, A. Fat no more **616.85**
Holt, K. W. When Zachary Beaver came to town **Fic**
Libal, A. Fats, sugars, and empty calories **613.2**
Obesity **616.3**
Zahensky, B. A. Diet fads **613.2**
Obesity. Allman, T. **616.3**
Obesity. Fredericks, C. **616.3**
Obesity. Hicks, T. A. **616.3**

OBESITY -- FICTION
Brande, R. Fat Cat **Fic**
Cohn, R. You know where to find me **Fic**
Crutcher, C. Staying fat for Sarah Byrnes **Fic**
Deuker, C. Payback time **Fic**
Dionne, E. Models don't eat chocolate cookies **Fic**
Does this book make me look fat? **S**
George, M. Looks **Fic**
Holt, K. W. When Zachary Beaver came to town **Fic**
Lange, E. J. Butter **Fic**
Lipsyte, R. One fat summer **Fic**
Mackler, C. The earth, my butt, and other big, round things **Fic**
Paley, S. Huge **Fic**
Peters, J. A. By the time you read this, I'll be dead **Fic**
Potter, E. Slob **Fic**
Vande Velde, V. Remembering Raquel **Fic**
Zadoff, A. Food, girls, and other things I can't have **Fic**

OBESITY -- FICTION
Going, K. L. Fat kid rules the world **Fic**
OBESITY IN CHILDREN
Currie-McGhee, L. K. Childhood obesity **618.92**
Obesity: modern day epidemic [series]
Libal, A. Fats, sugars, and empty calories **613.2**
OBITUARIES
See also Biography
OBSESSION (PSYCHOLOGY) See Obsessive-compulsive disorder
Obsessive-compulsive disorder. Parks, P. J. **616.85**
OBSESSIVE-COMPULSIVE DISORDER
Binstock, M. Nourishment **92**
Parks, P. J. Anxiety disorders **616.85**

Kops, D. Racial profiling **363.2**

Naden, C. J. Patients' rights **362.1**

Stefoff, R. The right to die **179.7**

OPEN HEART SURGERY *See* Heart -- Surgery

Open me up. Buller, L. **612**

The **open** ocean. Walker, P. **578.7**

Open the door to liberty!: a biography of Toussaint L'Ouverture. Rockwell, A. F. **92**

Open the unusual door. **920**

Openly straight. Konigsberg, B. **Fic**

OPERA

Siberell, A. Bravo! brava! a night at the opera **782.1**

OPERA

See also Drama; Musical form; Performing arts; Vocal music

OPERA -- SOUND RECORDINGS

See also Sound recordings

OPERA SINGERS

Freedman, R. The voice that challenged a nation **92**

Jones, V. G. Marian Anderson **92**

OPERAS *See* Opera

OPERATION FRESHMAN, 1942

Sheinkin, S. Bomb **623.4**

OPERATION OVERLORD

Drez, R. J. Remember D-day **940.54**

Operation Yes. Holmes, S. L. **Fic**

OPERATIONS RESEARCH

See also Research; System theory

OPERATIONS, SURGICAL *See* Surgery

OPERETTA

See also Musical form; Opera; Vocal music

Ophelia and the marvelous boy. Foxlee, K. **Fic**

Ophelia speaks. Shandler, S. **305.235**

OPIATES *See* Narcotics

Opini, Bathseba

(jt. auth) Lee, R. B. Africans thought of it! **609**

OPIUM

See also Narcotics

OPIUM -- PHYSIOLOGICAL EFFECT

See also Drugs -- Physiological effect

Oppel, Kenneth

Airborn **Fic**

The Boundless **Fic**

Darkwing **Fic**

Firewing **Fic**

Half brother **Fic**

Silverwing **Fic**

Skybreaker **Fic**

Starclimber **Fic**

Such wicked intent **Fic**

Sunwing **Fic**

This dark endeavor **Fic**

Oppenheim, Joanne

Dear Miss Breed **940.53**

Oppong, Joseph R.

Africa South of the Sahara **967**

Opposing viewpoints in world history [series]

Slavery **326**

Opposing viewpoints [series]

Abortion: opposing viewpoints **363.46**

Addiction: opposing viewpoints **362.29**

Africa: opposing viewpoints **960**

America's prisons: opposing viewpoints **365**

The death penalty: opposing viewpoints **364.66**

Discrimination: opposing viewpoints **305.8**

Domestic violence: opposing viewpoints **362.82**

Endangered oceans: opposing viewpoints **333.95**

Endangered species: opposing viewpoints **578.68**

The environment: opposing viewpoints **363.7**

Epidemics: opposing viewpoints **614.4**

Euthanasia: opposing viewpoints **179.7**

Global warming: opposing viewpoints **363.7**

Israel: opposing viewpoints **956.94**

The Middle East: opposing viewpoints **956**

Paranormal phenomena: opposing viewpoints **133**

Pollution: opposing viewpoints **363.7**

Race relations: opposing viewpoints **305.8**

Religion in America: opposing viewpoints **200.9**

Suicide: opposing viewpoints **362.28**

Terrorism **363.32**

Tobacco and Smoking **362.29**

War: opposing viewpoints **355**

The **opposite** of hallelujah. Jarzab, A. **Fic**

Oprah Winfrey. Krohn, K. E. **92**

Oprah Winfrey. Cooper, I. **92**

OPTICAL ILLUSIONS

Jarrow, G. The amazing Harry Kellar **793.809**

Vry, S. Trick of the eye **152.14**

Wick, W. Walter Wick's optical tricks **152.14**

OPTICAL ILLUSIONS

See also Hallucinations and illusions; Psychophysiology; Vision

OPTICS

See also Physics

The **oracle** betrayed. Fisher, C. **Fic**

ORACLE CORP.

Ehrenhaft, D. Larry Ellison **338.7**

Oracle prophecies [series]

Fisher, C. Day of the scarab **Fic**

Fisher, C. The oracle betrayed **Fic**

Fisher, C. The sphere of secrets **Fic**

ORACLES

See also Occultism

ORAL HISTORY

See also History

ORAL HISTORY -- FICTION

The Tapper twins go to war (with each other) **Fic**

ORANGUTAN

Russon, A. E. Orangutans: wizards of the rainforest **599.8**

Orangutans: wizards of the rainforest. Russon, A. E. **599.8**

ORATIONS *See* Speeches

ORATORS

Shecter, V. A. Cleopatra's moon **Fic**

ORATORY *See* Public speaking

Orb weavers. Markle, S. **595.4**

ORBITAL LABORATORIES *See* Space stations

ORBITAL RENDEZVOUS (SPACE FLIGHT)

See also Space flight; Space stations; Space vehicles

ORBITING VEHICLES *See* Artificial satellites; Space stations

Orca currents [series]

Butcher, K. Cheat **Fic**

Peterson, L. J. Beyond repair **Fic**

Walters, E. Special Edward **Fic**

Watson, C. Benched **Fic**

Orca footprints [series]

Mulder, M. Every last drop **333.91**

Orca limelights [series]

Lieberman, L. Off pointe **Fic**

Orca soundings [series]

McClintock, N. Masked **Fic**

Rodman, S. Infiltration **Fic**

Schwartz, E. Cellular **Fic**

Tullson, D. Riley Park **Fic**

Van Tol, A. Knifepoint **Fic**

Yee, P. Learning to fly **Fic**

Orca sports [series]

Barwin, S. Hardball **Fic**

Muller, R. D. Squeeze **Fic**

Ross, J. The drop **Fic**

Stevenson, R. H. Dead in the water **Fic**

Thomas, E. Boarder patrol **Fic**

Orchards. Thompson, H. **Fic**

ORCHESTRA

Ganeri, A. The young person's guide to the orchestra **784.2**

ORCHESTRAL MUSIC

See also Instrumental music; Music; Orchestra

The **Order** of Odd-Fish. Kennedy, J. **Fic**

ORDERLINESS

Morgenstern, J. Organizing from the inside out for teens **646.7**

Ordinary miracles. Aspin, D. **S**

ORDNANCE

See also Military art and science

Oregon. **979.5**

OREGON

Oregon **979.5**

OREGON -- FICTION

Beaufrand, M. J. The river **Fic**

Forman, G. If I stay **Fic**

The mighty Quinn **Fic**

Olson, G. Call me Hope **Fic**

Parry, R. Heart of a shepherd **Fic**

Patneaude, D. A piece of the sky **Fic**

Platt, R. B. Hellie Jondoe **Fic**

OREGON NATIONAL HISTORIC TRAIL -- FICTION

Pierpoint, E. The last ride of Caleb O'Toole **Fic**

OREGON TRAIL

Dallas, S. The quilt walk **Fic**

Olson, T. How to get rich on the Oregon Trail **978**

Pierpoint, E. The last ride of Caleb O'Toole **Fic**

See also Overland journeys to the Pacific; United States

Orenstein, Denise Gosliner

The secret twin **Fic**

Unseen companion **Fic**

ORES

See also Minerals

ORGAN MUSIC

See also Church music; Instrumental music; Music

Organ transplants. Foran, R. **617.9**

ORGAN TRANSPLANTS *See* Transplantation of organs, tissues, etc.

Organ transplants. Campbell, A. **617.9**

Organ transplants. Schwartz, T. P. **617.9**

ORGANIC AGRICULTURE *See* Organic farming

ORGANIC CHEMISTRY

Gardner, R. Organic chemistry science fair projects **547**

ORGANIC CHEMISTRY

See also Chemistry

Organic chemistry science fair projects. Gardner, R. **547**

ORGANIC COMPOUNDS

See also Chemicals; Organic chemistry

ORGANIC FARMING

Organic food and farming **641.3**

Rau, D. M. Going organic **613.2**

ORGANIC FARMING

See also Agriculture

Organic food and farming. **641.3**

Organic foods. Miller, D. A. **641.3**

ORGANIC FOODS *See* Natural foods

ORGANIC GARDENING

See also Gardening; Horticulture

ORGANIC WASTE AS FUEL *See* Waste products as fuel

ORGANICALLY GROWN FOODS *See* Natural foods

ORGANICULTURE *See* Organic farming; Organic gardening

ORGANIZATION OFFICIALS

Brimner, L. D. Black & white **323.1**

Byrnes, P. Environmental pioneers **363.7**

Let it shine **920**

Organizational storytelling for librarians. Marek, K. **025.1**

ORGANIZED CRIME

Korman, G. Son of the mob   **Fic**

ORGANIZED CRIME

See also Crime

ORGANIZED CRIME -- FICTION

Black, H. Black heart   **FIC**

Gavin, R. Knightley and son   **Fic**

Renn, D. Latitude zero   **Fic**

ORGANIZED LABOR *See* Labor unions

Organizing from the inside out for teens. Morgenstern, J.   **646.7**

ORGANS (MUSICAL INSTRUMENTS)

See also Musical instruments

ORGANS, ARTIFICIAL *See* Artificial organs

Orgill, Roxane

Shout, sister, shout!   **920**

ORIENT *See* Asia; East Asia; Middle East

ORIENTAL ARCHITECTURE *See* Asian architecture

ORIENTEERING

Champion, N. Finding your way   **613.6**

ORIENTEERING

See also Hiking; Racing; Running; Sports

ORIGAMI

Boursin, D. Easy origami   **736**

Nguyen, D. Zombigami   **736**

Stern, J. Jewish holiday origami   **736**

Temko, F. Origami holiday decorations for Christmas, Hanukkah, and Kwanzaa   **736**

ORIGAMI

See also Paper crafts

ORIGAMI -- FICTION

Angleberger, T. Emperor Pickletine rides the bus   **Fic**

Origami holiday decorations for Christmas, Hanukkah, and Kwanzaa. Temko, F.   **736**

Origin. Khoury, J.   **Fic**

ORIGIN OF MAN *See* Human origins

ORIGIN OF SPECIES *See* Evolution

The **Originals.** Patrick, C.   **Fic**

Origins. Thompson, K.   **Fic**

The **origins** of the Holocaust. Downing, D.   **940.53**

Orlev, Uri

Run, boy, run   **Fic**

The song of the whales   **Fic**

ORNITHOLOGISTS

Sherman, P. John James Audubon   **92**

ORNITHOLOGISTS -- UNITED STATES -- BIOGRAPHY

This strange wilderness   **92**

The **orphan** army.   **Fic**

ORPHAN DRUGS

See also Drugs

The **orphan** of Awkward Falls. Graves, K.   **Fic**

Orphan of destiny. Spradlin, M. P.   **Fic**

Orphan train rider. Warren, A.   **362.7**

ORPHAN TRAINS -- FICTION

MacColl, M. Rory's promise   **Fic**

ORPHANAGES

See also Charities; Children -- Institutional care

ORPHANAGES -- FICTION

Barnaby, H. Wonder show   **Fic**

Stewart, T. L. The extraordinary education of Nicholas Benedict   **Fic**

ORPHANS

Blackwood, G. L. Shakespeare's scribe   **Fic**

Ellis, D. Our stories, our songs   **362.7**

Hahn, M. D. Promises to the dead   **Fic**

Hansen, J. One true friend   **Fic**

Horowitz, A. Eagle Strike   **Fic**

Horowitz, A. Stormbreaker   **Fic**

Hurst, C. O. Through the lock   **Fic**

Lowry, L. Gathering blue   **Fic**

Mazer, N. F. Girlhearts   **Fic**

Skrypuch, M. F. Last airlift   **959.704**

Skrypuch, M. F. One Step at a Time   **618.927**

Warren, A. Orphan train rider   **362.7**

Warren, A. We rode the orphan trains   **362.73**

Woodson, J. Locomotion   **Fic**

See also Children

ORPHANS -- FICTION

Almond, D. The Boy who swam with piranhas **Fic**

Black, P. J. Urban outlaws   **Fic**

Clare, C. Clockwork prince   **Fic**

Creech, S. The great unexpected   **Fic**

Edge, C. Twelve minutes to midnight   **Fic**

Fforde, J. The Eye of Zoltar   **Fic**

From the notebooks of a middle school princess **Fic**

Fusco, K. N. Beholding Bee   **Fic**

Gaiman, N. The graveyard book graphic novel Volume 1   **741.5**

Graff, L. A tangle of knots   **Fic**

The graveyard book graphic novel Volume 2 **741.5**

Hickam, H. H. Crater   **Fic**

Hopkinson, D. The Great Trouble   **Fic**

Hughes, G. Unhooking the moon   **Fic**

Kinsey-Warnock, N. True colors   **Fic**

Kuehn, S. Complicit   **Fic**

Larson, K. Hattie ever after   **Fic**

Lawrence, C. The case of the deadly desperados   **Fic**

MacColl, M. Rory's promise   **Fic**

McQuein, J. L. Arclight   **Fic**

Nielsen, J. A. The false prince   **Fic**

Paper things   **Fic**

Parry, R. Written in stone   **Fic**

Price, L. Starters   **Fic**

Rooftoppers   **Fic**

Schlitz, L. A. Splendors and glooms   **Fic**

Schrefer, E. Threatened   **Fic**

Sloan, H. G. Counting by 7s   **Fic**

POLAR BEAR -- FICTION

Pastis, S. Timmy failure   **Fic**

Pastis, S. Timmy failure : now look what you've done   **Fic**

Waluk   **741.5**

Polar Bears. Lockwood, S.   **599.78**

Polar bears. Ovsyanikov, N.   **599.78**

POLAR EXPEDITIONS *See* Antarctica -- Exploration; Arctic regions -- Exploration; Scientific expeditions

Polar explorations. Nardo, D.   **910.4**

POLAR REGIONS

Conlan, K. Under the ice   **578.7**

Woodford, C. Arctic tundra and polar deserts   **577**

POLAR REGIONS -- ENVIRONMENTAL CONDITIONS

Mooney, C. Surviving in cold places   **363.34**

POLAR REGIONS -- EXPLORATION

Nardo, D. Polar explorations   **910.4**

Polar worlds. Wade, R.   **998**

Polcovar, Jane

Rosalind Franklin and the structure of life   **92**

Police. Mezzanotte, J.   **363.2**

POLICE

    See also Administration of criminal justice; Law enforcement

POLICE

Busby, C. The year we disappeared   **92**

Newton, M. Bomb squad   **363.2**

Newton, M. SWAT teams   **363.2**

POLICE -- FICTION

Myers, W. D. Kick   **Fic**

Pierce, T. Bloodhound   **Fic**

Pierce, T. Mastiff   **Fic**

Pierce, T. Terrier   **Fic**

White, K. Paranormalcy   **Fic**

POLICE -- HISTORY -- 20TH CENTURY

Samuels, C. Spying and security   **940.54**

POLICE -- LOS ANGELES (CALIF.)

Worth, R. Los Angeles Police Department   **363.2**

POLICE -- NEW YORK (N.Y.)

Evans, C. New York Police Department   **363.2**

POLICE BRUTALITY

    See also Police

POLICE BRUTALITY -- FICTION

Kephart, B. Dr. Radway's Sarsaparilla Resolvent   **Fic**

POLICE CORRUPTION

    See also Misconduct in office; Police

POLICE OFFICERS *See* Police

POLICE OFFICIALS

Brimner, L. D. Black & white   **323.1**

Rosenberg, A. The Civil War   **920**

POLICEMEN *See* Police

POLICEWOMEN

    See also Police; Women

POLIOMYELITIS

Skrypuch, M. F. One Step at a Time   **618.927**

    See also Diseases

POLIOMYELITIS -- FICTION

Durbin, W. The Winter War   **Fic**

Lasky, K. Chasing Orion   **Fic**

Lawrence, I. The giant-slayer   **Fic**

Tooke, W. King of the mound   **Fic**

POLIOMYELITIS VACCINE

Sherrow, V. Jonas Salk   **92**

    See also Vaccination

POLISH AMERICANS -- FICTION

Cushman, K. Rodzina   **Fic**

Friesner, E. M. Threads and flames   **Fic**

Sternberg, L. The case against my brother   **Fic**

Polisner, Gae

The pull of gravity   **Fic**

POLITENESS *See* Courtesy; Etiquette

POLITICAL ACTIVISTS

Brave Bird, M. Lakota woman   **92**

Chemerka, W. R. Juan Seguin   **976.4**

Levinson, C. Y. We've got a job   **323.1**

O'Keefe, S. Champion of freedom   **92**

Tashjian, J. Vote for Larry   **Fic**

POLITICAL ACTIVISTS -- FICTION

Nye, N. S. Going going   **Fic**

Schröder, M. My brother's shadow   **Fic**

Tashjian, J. Larry and the meaning of life   **Fic**

POLITICAL ACTIVISTS -- PAKISTAN

Aretha, D. Malala Yousafzai and the girls of Pakistan   **92**

POLITICAL AND SOCIAL PHILOSOPHERS

Rossig, W. Karl Marx   **92**

Scott, M. The magician   **Fic**

Scott, M. The sorceress   **Fic**

Scott, M. The warlock   **Fic**

POLITICAL ATROCITIES -- CAMBODIA

Sonneborn, L. The Khmer Rouge   **959.604**

POLITICAL CAMPAIGNS *See* Politics

Political corruption. Miller, D. A.   **364.1**

POLITICAL CORRUPTION

Miller, D. A. Political corruption   **364.1**

    See also Conflict of interests; Political crimes and offenses; Political ethics; Politics

POLITICAL CORRUPTION -- FICTION

Mulligan, A. Trash   **Fic**

Singer, N. Gem X   **Fic**

POLITICAL CRIMES AND OFFENSES

    See also Criminal law; Political ethics; Subversive activities

POLITICAL DEFECTORS *See* Defectors

POLITICAL ECONOMY *See* Economics

POLITICAL ETHICS

Stearman, K. Freedom of information   **342**

    See also Ethics; Political science; Politics; Social ethics

Mulligan, A. Trash **Fic**
Newton, R. Runner **Fic**
Qamar, A. Beneath my mother's feet **Fic**
Shulman, M. Scrawl **Fic**
Steinbeck, J. The pearl **Fic**
Stellings, C. The contest **Fic**
Strasser, T. If I grow up **Fic**
Strasser, T. No place **Fic**
Uchida, Y. The best bad thing **Fic**
Wolff, V. E. Make lemonade **Fic**
Wolff, V. E. True believer **Fic**
Poverty and hunger. Senker, C. **362.5**
Powder monkey. Dowswell, P. **Fic**
POWDER, SMOKELESS *See* Gunpowder
Powell, Anton
  Ancient Greece **938**
Powell, Barbara Johns, 1935-1991
    About
  Kanefield, T. The girl from the tar paper school **92**
Powell, Ben
  Skateboarding skills **796.22**
  Stock, C. Skateboarding step-by-step **796.22**
Powell, Colin L., 1937-
    About
  Shichtman, S. H. Colin Powell **92**
  Vander Hook, S. Colin Powell **92**
Powell, Jillian
  Alcohol and drug abuse **362.29**
  Explaining cystic fibrosis **616.3**
  Self-harm and suicide **616.85**
Powell, Laura
  Burn mark **Fic**
  The game of triumphs **Fic**
  The Master of Misrule **Fic**
Powell, Randy
  Swiss mist **Fic**
  Three clams and an oyster **Fic**
Powell, Ransom J., 1849-1899
    About
  Wisler, G. C. Red Cap **Fic**
Powell, William Campbell
  Expiration day **Fic**
Power. Ravilious, K. **179**
POWER (MECHANICS)
    See also Mechanical engineering; Mechanics
The **power** of reading. Krashen, S. D. **028.5**
POWER PLANTS, HYDROELECTRIC *See* Hydroelectric power plants
POWER PLANTS, NUCLEAR *See* Nuclear power plants
POWER POLITICS *See* Balance of power; Cold war
POWER RESOURCES *See* Energy resources
POWER RESOURCES -- ARCTIC REGIONS
  McPherson, S. S. Arctic thaw **333.79**

POWER RESOURCES CONSERVATION *See* Energy conservation
POWER SUPPLY *See* Energy resources
The **power** to prevent suicide. Galas, J. C. **362.28**
POWER TOOLS
    See also Tools
Power tools recharged. Valenza, J. K. **027.8**
POWER TRANSMISSION
    See also Mechanical engineering; Power (Mechanics)
POWER TRANSMISSION, ELECTRIC *See* Electric lines; Electric power distribution
Powerful medicine [series]
  Markle, S. Bad burns **617.1**
  Markle, S. Faulty hearts **612.1**
  Markle, S. Leukemia **616.99**
  Markle, S. Lost sight **617.7**
  Markle, S. Shattered bones **617.1**
  Markle, S. Wounded brains **617**
Powerful plant cells. Johnson, R. L. **581.7**
Powerful words. Hudson, W. **081**
Powering the future. Thaddeus, E. **333.79**
Powerless. Cody, M. **Fic**
Powers. Le Guin, U. K. **Fic**
Powers, J. L.
  This thing called the future **Fic**
Powers, Ron
  Bradley, J. Flags of our fathers **940.54**
POWHATAN INDIANS
  Jones, V. G. Pocahontas **92**
POWHATAN INDIANS -- FICTION
  Carbone, E. L. Blood on the river **Fic**
POWS *See* Prisoners of war
POWWOWS
    See also Festivals; Native Americans -- Rites and ceremonies; Native Americans -- Social life and customs
Poynter, Margaret
  Doomsday rocks from space **523.4**
The **practical** astronomer. Gater, W. **520**
PRACTICAL JOKES
  Hargrave, J. Sir John Hargrave's mischief maker's manual **818**
  The terrible two **Fic**
PRACTICAL JOKES
    See also Jokes; Wit and humor
PRACTICAL JOKES -- FICTION
  The Tapper twins go to war (with each other) **Fic**
  Waiting for Gonzo **Fic**
PRACTICAL NURSES
    See also Nurses
PRACTICAL POLITICS *See* Politics
PRACTICE TEACHING *See* Student teaching
Praetor war [series]
  Mark of the thief **Fic**
Prager, Ellen J.

Kennedy, J. E. Puppet planet **791.5**
   See also Drama; Folk drama; Theater
PUPPETS AND PUPPET PLAYS -- FICTION
Schlitz, L. A. Splendors and glooms **Fic**
PUPPIES *See* Dogs
Pure grit. Farrell, M. C. **940.54**
Pure Spring. Doyle, B. **Fic**
PURIFICATION OF WATER *See* Water purification
PURITANS
Aronson, M. John Winthrop, Oliver Cromwell, and the Land of Promise **92**
Stille, D. R. Anne Hutchinson **92**
PURITANS -- FICTION
Duble, K. B. The sacrifice **Fic**
Speare, E. G. The witch of Blackbird Pond **Fic**
Purperhart, Helen
Yoga exercises for teens **613.7**
Purple Heart. McCormick, P. **Fic**
The **pushcart** war. Merrill, J. **Fic**
Put it all together. Cornwall, P. **808**
Put your best foot forward. Schorer, S. **792.8**
Putin, Vladimir
About
Shields, C. J. Vladimir Putin **92**
Putting it all together. Barnett, D. **025.04**
Putting makeup on the fat boy. Wright, B. **Fic**
PUYALLUP ASSEMBLY CENTER (PUYALLUP, WASH.) -- FICTION
Larson, K. Dash **Fic**
Patt, B. Best friends forever **Fic**
PUZZLES
   See also Amusements
PUZZLES -- FICTION
Beil, M. D. The Red Blazer Girls: the ring of Rocamadour **Fic**
Beil, M. The Red Blazer Girls: the mistaken masterpiece **Fic**
Berlin, E. The potato chip puzzles **Fic**
Berlin, E. The puzzling world of Winston Breen **Fic**
Ephron, D. Frannie in pieces **Fic**
The **puzzling** world of Winston Breen. Berlin, E. **Fic**
PX! Book one: a girl and her panda. Anderson, E. A. **741.5**
Pyers, Greg
The biodiversity of coral reefs **577.7**
PYGMIES
Goldenberg, L. Little people and a lost world **599.93**
Pyle, Howard
The merry adventures of Robin Hood **398.2**
The story of King Arthur and his knights **398.2**
The story of Sir Launcelot and his companions **398.2**
The story of the champions of the Round Table **398.2**

The story of the Grail and the passing of Arthur **398.2**
Pyle, Kevin C.
Katman **741.5**
Pyle, Robert Michael
The Audubon Society field guide to North American butterflies **595.7**
Pyramid. Macaulay, D. **726**
PYRAMIDS
Aaseng, N. Construction: building the impossible **624**
George, C. The pyramids of Giza **932**
Macaulay, D. Pyramid **726**
   See also Ancient architecture; Archeology; Monuments
The **pyramids** of Giza. George, C. **932**
Pyron, Bobbie
Lucky strike **Fic**
The dogs of winter **Fic**
A dog's way home **Fic**
Python. Somervill, B. A. **597.96**
PYTHONS
Somervill, B. A. Python **597.96**

Q

QAIDA (ORGANIZATION)
Hillstrom, K. The September 11 terrorist attacks **973.931**
Lusted, M. A. The capture and killing of Osama bin Laden **958.1**
   See also Terrorism
Qamar, Amjed
Beneath my mother's feet **Fic**
Qatar. Orr, T. **953.6**
QATAR
Orr, T. Qatar **953.6**
QEB changes in . . . [series]
Parker, S. Climate **551.6**
Parker, S. Food and farming **630**
Parker, S. Population **363.7**
Qi Shufang
About
Major, J. S. Caravan to America **745**
QUACKS AND QUACKERY
   See also Impostors and imposture; Medicine; Swindlers and swindling
QUAKERS *See* Society of Friends
Quaking. Erskine, K. **Fic**
QUALITY OF LIFE
   See also Economic conditions; Social conditions
Qualls, Sean
Hudson, W. Powerful words **081**
Pinkney, A. D. Bird in a box **Fic**
QUANTITY COOKING
   See also Cooking

RADIO AUTHORSHIP
  See also Authorship; Radio broadcasting

RADIO BROADCASTING
Novak, A. Glenn Beck   **92**
  See also Broadcasting; Mass media

RADIO BROADCASTING -- FICTION
Pinkney, A. D. Bird in a box   **Fic**

RADIO BROADCASTING OF SPORTS
  See also Broadcast journalism; Radio broadcasting

RADIO IN AERONAUTICS
  See also Aeronautics; Navigation (Aeronautics); Radio

RADIO IN EDUCATION
  See also Audiovisual education; Radio; Teaching -- Aids and devices

RADIO INDUSTRY *See* Radio broadcasting; Radio supplies industry

RADIO JOURNALISM *See* Broadcast journalism

RADIO PERSONALITIES -- UNITED STATES -- BIOGRAPHY
Novak, A. Glenn Beck   **92**

RADIO PROGRAMS
  See also Radio broadcasting

RADIO PROGRAMS -- FICTION
Cooney, C. B. The voice on the radio   **Fic**

RADIO STATIONS
  See also Radio broadcasting
Radio-controlled car experiments. Sobey, E. **796.1**

RADIOACTIVE FALLOUT
  See also Atomic bomb; Hydrogen bomb; Radioactive pollution

RADIOACTIVE POLLUTION
  See also Pollution; Radioactivity

RADIOACTIVE SUBSTANCES *See* Radioactivity

RADIOACTIVE WASTE DISPOSAL
Scarborough, K. Nuclear waste   **363.7**

RADIOACTIVE WASTE DISPOSAL
  See also Nuclear engineering; Nuclear power plants -- Environmental aspects; Radioactivity; Refuse and refuse disposal

RADIOACTIVITY
Henderson, H. The Curie family   **539.7**
Jerome, K. B. Atomic universe   **539.7**
  See also Physics; Radiation

RADIOACTIVITY -- HISTORY
Henderson, H. The Curie family   **539.7**

RADIOBIOLOGY
  See also Biology; Biophysics; Nuclear physics; Radioactivity

RADIOCARBON DATING
  See also Archeology

RADIOCARBON DATING -- NORTH AMERICA
Deem, J. M. Faces from the past   **599.9**

RADIOCHEMISTRY
  See also Physical chemistry; Radioactivity

RADIOECOLOGY -- UKRAINE -- CHORNOBYL
Johnson, R. L. Chernobyl's wild kingdom **590.94**

RADIOISOTOPES
  See also Isotopes; Nuclear engineering

RADIOLOGISTS
  See also Physicians

RADIOTHERAPY
  See also Electrotherapeutics; Physical therapy; Radioactivity; Therapeutics

RADIUM
  See also Chemical elements; Radiation

Raedeke, Christy
The daykeeper's grimoire   **Fic**
The serpent's coil   **Fic**

Raf, Mindy
The symptoms of my insanity   **Fic**

Rafferty, John P.
(ed) Glaciers, sea ice, and ice formation **551.3**
(ed) Plate tectonics, volcanoes, and earthquakes **551**

The **raft.** Bodeen, S. A.   **Fic**

RAFTING (SPORTS) -- FICTION
Woods, R. The hero   **Fic**

RAGE *See* Anger

Rage of the fallen. Delaney, J.   **Fic**
Rage within. Roberts, J.   **Fic**
Raggin', jazzin', rockin' VanHecke, S. **784.19**

Raicht, Mike
Dezago, T. Spider-man: Spidey strikes back Vol. 1 digest   **741.5**

Raiders' ransom. Diamand, E.   **Fic**
Raiders' ransom [series]
Diamand, E. Flood and fire   **Fic**

RAILROAD ACCIDENTS
  See also Accidents; Disasters

RAILROAD ENGINEERING
  See also Civil engineering; Engineering; Railroads

RAILROAD TRAINS -- FICTION
Oppel, K. The Boundless   **Fic**

RAILROAD TRAVEL
  See also Transportation; Travel; Voyages and travels

RAILROAD WORKERS
Anderson, W. Brown v. Board of Education **344**
Fleischman, J. Phineas Gage: a gruesome but true story about brain science   **362.1**
Gold, S. D. Brown v. Board of Education **344**
Nelson, S. R. Ain't nothing but a man   **92**

RAILROADS
Collier, C. Indians, cowboys, and farmers and the battle for the Great Plains, 1865-1910 **978**
Haugen, B. The Great Train Robbery **364.1**
McMahon, P. Ultimate trains   **385**

REACTORS (NUCLEAR PHYSICS) *See* Nuclear reactors

Read all about it! **808.8**

Read, Nicholas
City critters **591.75**
McAllister, I. Salmon bears **599.78**
(jt. auth) McAllister, I. The sea wolves **599.77**

Read, Tracy C.
Exploring the world of raccoons **599.74**

READER SERVICES (LIBRARIES) *See* Library services

A **reader's** guide to Amy Tan's The joy luck club. Loos, P. **813**

A **reader's** guide to Chinua Achebe's Things fall apart. Shea, G. **823**

A **reader's** guide to Gary Soto's Taking sides. Jones, J. **813**

A **reader's** guide to Lorraine Hansberry's A raisin in the sun. Loos, P. **812**

A **reader's** guide to Marjane Satrapi's Persepolis. Schroeder, H. L. **813**

A **reader's** guide to Richard Wright's Black boy. Hinds, M. J. **813**

A **reader's** guide to Zora Neale Hurston's Their eyes were watching god. Litwin, L. B. **813**

READERS AND LIBRARIES *See* Library services

Readers theatre [series]
Black, A. N. Readers theatre for middle school boys **812**

Readers theatre for middle school boys. Black, A. N. **812**

The **readers'** advisory guide to graphic novels. Goldsmith, F. **025.2**

READERS' THEATER
Black, A. N. Readers theatre for middle school boys **812**
See also Theater

READINESS FOR SCHOOL
See also Elementary education; Preschool education

READING
Bacon, P. S. 100+ literacy lifesavers **428**
Bernadowski, C. Research-based reading strategies in the library for adolescent learners **372.4**
Kajder, S. B. Bringing the outside in **028.5**
Krashen, S. D. The power of reading **028.5**
Ostenson, J. W. Integrating young adult literature through the common core standards **418**
See also Language arts

READING (MIDDLE SCHOOL) -- ABILITY TESTING
Fuhrken, C. What every middle school teacher needs to know about reading tests (from someone who has written them) **428**

READING (SECONDARY)

Farwell, S. M. Supporting reading in grades 6-12 **428**
Ostenson, J. W. Integrating young adult literature through the common core standards **418**

READING -- FICTION
Castan, M. Fighting for Dontae **Fic**
Charlie Joe Jackson's guide to summer vacation **Fic**

READING -- PHONETIC METHOD
See also English language -- Pronunciation; Reading

READING -- STUDY AND TEACHING *See* Reading

READING -- UNITED STATES
Grover, S. Listening to learn **372.4**

READING COMPREHENSION
Grimes, S. Reading is our business **027.8**
Moreillon, J. Collaborative strategies for teaching reading comprehension **372.4**

READING COMPREHENSION
See also Psychology of learning; Reading; Verbal learning

READING DISABILITY
See also Learning disabilities; Reading

READING INTERESTS
Zbaracki, M. D. Best books for boys **028.5**

READING INTERESTS *See* Books and reading

READING INTERESTS OF CHILDREN *See* Children -- Books and reading

READING INTERESTS OF TEENAGERS *See* Teenagers -- Books and reading

READING INTERESTS OF YOUNG ADULTS *See* Teenagers -- Books and reading

Reading is our business. Grimes, S. **027.8**

READING MATERIALS
See also Children's literature

READING READINESS
See also Reading

Ready to make music [series]
Landau, E. Are the drums for you? **786.9**
Landau, E. Is singing for you? **783**
Landau, E. Is the flute for you? **788**
Landau, E. Is the guitar for you? **787.87**
Landau, E. Is the trumpet for you? **788**
Landau, E. Is the violin for you? **787.2**

Ready to wear. Taylor, C. **Fic**

Reagan, Ronald, 1911-2004
About
Brill, M. T. America in the 1980s **973.927**
Burgan, M. Ronald Reagan **92**
Marsico, K. Ronald Reagan **92**
The **real** Alice in Wonderland. Rubin, C. M. **92**
The **real** Benedict Arnold. Murphy, J. **92**
Real courage. Don, K. **813**

REAL ESTATE
See also Land use; Property

REAL ESTATE DEVELOPERS

Roselius, J. C. Magic Johnson   **92**

REAL ESTATE INVESTMENT

   See also Investments; Real estate; Speculation

Real food, real fast. Stern, S.   **641.5**

Real friends vs. the other kind. Fox, A.   **158**

Real pirates. Clifford, B.   **910.4**

The **real** question. Fogelin, A.   **Fic**

The **real** revolution. Aronson, M.   **973.3**

The **real** spy's guide to becoming a spy. Earnest, P.   **327.12**

Real teen voices [series]

   Vicious   **302.34**

REAL WORLD (TELEVISION PROGRAM) --
   GRAPHIC NOVELS

   Winick, J. Pedro & me   **362.1**

Real world data [series]

   Rand, C. Graphing sports   **796**

   Solway, A. Graphing immigration   **325**

   Solway, A. Graphing war and conflict   **355**

   Somervill, B. A. Graphing crime   **364**

Real world economics [series]

   Brezina, C. How deflation works   **332.4**

   Brezina, C. How stimulus plans work   **338.5**

   Furgang, K. How the stock market works   **332.6**

   La Bella, L. How taxation works   **336.2**

Real-life story [series]

   Macy, S. Sally Ride   **92**

   Nelson Mandela   **92**

Realism. Gunderson, J.   **709.03**

REALISM

   See also Philosophy

REALISM IN ART

   Gunderson, J. Realism   **709.03**

   See also Art

REALISM IN LITERATURE

   See also Literature

REALITY

   See also Philosophy; Truth

The **reality** bug. MacHale, D. J.   **Fic**

Reality check. Abrahams, P.   **Fic**

Reality rules II. Fraser, E.   **028.5**

Reality rules! Fraser, E.   **028.5**

REALITY TELEVISION PROGRAMS -- FIC-
   TION

   Williams, K. Pizza, love, and other stuff that made me famous   **Fic**

A **really** short history of nearly everything. Bryson, B.   **500**

Really, really big questions. Law, S.   **100**

REASON

   See also Intellect; Rationalism

REASONING

   See also Psychology; Reason; Thought and thinking

Reasons to be happy. Kittle, K.   **Fic**

Reaves, Michael

   Gaiman, N. Interworld   **Fic**

Rebel fire. Lane, A.   **Fic**

Rebel McKenzie. Ransom, C.   **Fic**

Rebellion. Sandler, K.   **Fic**

Rebels of rock [series]

   Aberback, B. Black Sabbath   **781.66**

   Bowe, B. J. The Ramones   **781.66**

   Burlingame, J. Aerosmith   **781.66**

Reber, Deborah

   (comp) Chicken soup for the teenage soul's the real deal   **158**

   Chill   **613**

REBIRTH *See* Reincarnation

Rebman, Renee C.

   Euthanasia and the right to die   **179.7**

Rebora, Piero

   (comp) Cassell's Italian dictionary   **453**

Rebuilding the body. Fullick, A.   **617.9**

RECESSIONS

   Brezina, C. America's recession   **330.9**

   Brezina, C. How stimulus plans work   **338.5**

   Heinrichs, A. The great recession   **330.9**

   See also Business cycles

A **recipe** 4 robbery. Kelsey, M.   **Fic**

Recipe and craft guide to China. Mattern, J.   **641.5**

Recipe and craft guide to France. LaRoche, A.   **641.5**

Recipe and craft guide to India. Ejaz, K.   **641.5**

Recipe and craft guide to Indonesia. Reusser, K.   **641.5**

Recipe and craft guide to Japan. Mofford, J. H.   **641.5**

Recipe and craft guide to the Caribbean. Mofford, J. H.   **641.5**

Recipe for disaster. Fergus, M.   **Fic**

RECIPES *See* Cooking

Reckless.   **Fic**

The **reckoning.** Armstrong, K.   **Fic**

RECLAMATION OF LAND

   See also Agriculture; Civil engineering; Hydraulic engineering; Land use

RECOMBINANT DNA

   See also DNA; Genetic engineering; Genetic recombination

Recommended books in Spanish for children and young adults, 2004-2008. Schon, I.   **011.6**

Reconstruction. McNeese, T.   **973.8**

Reconstruction. Fitzgerald, S.   **973.8**

RECONSTRUCTION (1865-1876)

   Barney, W. L. The Civil War and Reconstruction   **973.7**

   Bartoletti, S. C. They called themselves the K.K.K.   **322.4**

   Bolden, T. Cause: Reconstruction America, 1863-1877   **973.7**

   Carlisle, R. P. Civil War and Reconstruction   **973.7**

   Fitzgerald, S. Reconstruction   **973.8**

REFERENCE BOOKS -- BIBLIOGRAPHY

REFERENCE SERVICES (LIBRARIES)

REFERENCE SERVICES (LIBRARIES)

Reference shelf [series]

Reference sources and services for youth. Harper, M.   025.5

REFERENCE WORK (LIBRARIES) See Reference services (Libraries)

REFERENDUM

Reflections. Jones, D. W.   823

Reflections on a gift of watermelon pickle--and other modern verse.   811

REFLEXOLOGY

REFORESTATION

Reform movements in American history [series]

REFORM, SOCIAL See Social problems

REFORMATION

REFORMATORIES

REFORMATORIES -- FICTION

RIGHTS OF LESBIANS *See* Gay rights

RIGHTS OF MAN *See* Human rights

RIGHTS OF WOMEN *See* Women's rights

RIGHTS, HUMAN *See* Human rights

Rigoberta Menchu, Indian rights activist. Kallen, S. A. **92**

Rigsby, Mike

Amazing rubber band cars **745.592**

Doable renewables **333.79**

Rikers High. Volponi, P. **Fic**

RIKERS ISLAND PRISON (NEW YORK, N.Y.) -- FICTION

Volponi, P. Rikers High **Fic**

Riley Park. Tullson, D. **Fic**

Riley, James

Half upon a time **Fic**

Story thieves **Fic**

Riley, Sam G.

African Americans in the media today **920.003**

Riley, Tracy L.

Karnes, F. A. Competitions for talented kids **371.95**

Rimoli, Ana Paula

Amigurumi world **746.43**

Rinaldi, Ann

Come Juneteenth **Fic**

The fifth of March **Fic**

Girl in blue **Fic**

The redheaded princess **Fic**

An unlikely friendship **Fic**

Ring of fire. Baccalario, P. **Fic**

The **ring** of Solomon. Stroud, J. **Fic**

Ringside, 1925. Bryant, J. **Fic**

Riordan, Rick

(jt. auth) Collar, O. The Red Pyramid **Fic**

The battle of the Labyrinth **Fic**

The blood of Olympus **Fic**

The house of Hades **Fic**

The last Olympian **Fic**

The lightning thief **Fic**

The lost hero **Fic**

The maze of bones **Fic**

Percy Jackson's Greek Gods **Fic**

The red pyramid **741.5**

The Sea of Monsters **Fic**

The Serpent's Shadow **Fic**

The son of Neptune **Fic**

The throne of fire **Fic**

The Titan's curse **Fic**

Vespers rising **Fic**

Venditti, R. The lightning thief: the graphic novel **741.5**

Riot. Myers, W. D. **Fic**

RIOTS

See also Crime; Freedom of assembly; Offenses against public safety

RIOTS -- FICTION

Myers, A. Tulsa burning **Fic**

Myers, W. D. Riot **Fic**

RIOTS -- UNITED STATES

Miller, C. C. Backlash **305.8**

RIOTS -- UNITED STATES -- HISTORY -- 20TH CENTURY

Miller, C. C. Backlash **305.8**

Rip tide. Falls, K. **Fic**

RIPOFFS *See* Fraud

Ripple. Hubbard, A. **Fic**

Riptide. Scheibe, L. **Fic**

The **rise** and fall of Mount Majestic. Trafton, J. **Fic**

The **rise** and fall of Senator Joe McCarthy. Giblin, J. C. **92**

Rise of a hero. Bell, H. **Fic**

Rise of the huntress. **Fic**

The **Rise** of the Soviet Union. **947.084**

Rise of the thinking machines. VanVoorst, J. **629.8**

The **rise** of the wolf. Jobling, C. **Fic**

The **rising** star of Rusty Nail. Blume, L. M. M. **Fic**

Rising storm. Hunter, E. **Fic**

RISK

See also Economics

RISK-TAKING (PSYCHOLOGY)

Braun, L. W. Risky business **027.62**

Hugel, B. I did it without thinking **155.5**

See also Psychology

Risked. Haddix, M. P. **Fic**

Risky business. Braun, L. W. **027.62**

Rissa Bartholomew's declaration of independence. Comerford, L. B. **Fic**

Ritchie, Donald A.

Our Constitution **342**

The **rites** & wrongs of Janice Wills. Pearson, J. **Fic**

Rites of passage. Hensley, J. N. **Fic**

The **Rithmatist.** Sanderson, B. **Fic**

Ritschel, John

The kickboxing handbook **796.8**

Ritter, John H.

The boy who saved baseball **Fic**

Choosing up sides **Fic**

The desperado who stole baseball **Fic**

The **rivalry.** Feinstein, J. **Fic**

Rivals. Green, T. **Fic**

The **river.** Beaufrand, M. J. **Fic**

The **river.** Paulsen, G. **Fic**

The **river** between us. Peck, R. **Fic**

RIVER ECOLOGY

Lynette, R. River food chains **577.6**

See also Ecology

River food chains. Lynette, R. **577.6**

River of dreams. Talbott, H. **974.7**

River of words. **808.81**

RIVER POLLUTION *See* Water pollution

River roads west. Roop, P. **386**

River secrets. Hale, S. **Fic**

Strikes; Subversive activities; Terrorism

Sabotaged. Haddix, M. P.   **Fic**

Sabriel. Nix, G.   **Fic**

Sabuda, Robert

  Sharks and other sea monsters   **560**

Sacagawea. Green, C. R.   **978.004**

Sacagawea. Crosby, M. T.   **92**

Sacagawea. Berne, E. C.   **92**

Sacagawea, b. 1786

About

  Berne, E. C. Sacagawea   **92**

  Crosby, M. T. Sacagawea   **92**

  Green, C. R. Sacagawea   **978.004**

  O'Dell, S. Streams to the river, river to the sea **Fic**

Saccardi, Marianne

  Books that teach kids to write   **028.5**

Sachar, Louis

  The cardturner   **Fic**

  Holes   **Fic**

  Small steps   **Fic**

SACRED ART *See* Religious art

Sacred mountain. Taylor-Butler, C.   **954.9**

Sacred places. Yolen, J.   **811**

Sacred scars. Duey, K.   **Fic**

Sacred texts [series]

  Brown, A. The Bible and Christianity   **220**

  Ganeri, A. The Ramayana and Hinduism   **294.5**

The **sacrifice.** Duble, K. B.   **Fic**

Sadek, Ademola O.

  (jt. auth) Indovino, S. C. Italy   **945**

Saenz, Benjamin Alire

  He forgot to say good-bye   **Fic**

SAFARIS

  See also Adventure and adventurers; Outdoor recreation; Scientific expeditions; Travel

Safe. Shaw, S.   **Fic**

Safe house. Heneghan, J.   **Fic**

SAFE SEX IN AIDS PREVENTION

  See also AIDS (Disease) -- Prevention; Sexual hygiene

Safe social networking. Schwartz, H. E.   **302.302**

Safekeeping. Hesse, K.   **Fic**

SAFETY EDUCATION

  Doeden, M. Safety smarts   **613.6**

  Nelson, S. K. Stay safe!   **613.6**

  Raatma, L. Safety in your neighborhood   **613.6**

Safety in your neighborhood. Raatma, L.   **613.6**

Safety smarts. Doeden, M.   **613.6**

Safford, Barbara Ripp

  Guide to reference materials for school library media centers   **011.6**

Saffy's angel. McKay, H.   **Fic**

Safire, William

  (comp) Lend me your ears   **808.85**

Saga. Kostick, C.   **Fic**

Saga of the Sioux. Zimmerman, D. J.   **970.004**

SAGAS

  See also Folklore; Literature; Old Norse literature; Scandinavian literature

Sage, Angie

  Darke   **Fic**

  Flyte   **Fic**

  Magyk   **Fic**

  The Magykal papers   **Fic**

  Pathfinder   **Fic**

  Physik   **Fic**

  Queste   **Fic**

  Syren   **Fic**

The **Sahara.** Heinrichs, A.   **966**

SAHARA DESERT

  Heinrichs, A. The Sahara   **966**

SAHARA DESERT -- FICTION

  Peet, M. Mysterious traveler   **Fic**

Sahwira. Marsden, C.   **Fic**

Sailing. Storey, R.   **797.1**

SAILING

  Storey, R. Sailing   **797.1**

  See also Ships; Water sports

SAILING -- FICTION

  Appelt, K. Keeper   **Fic**

  Bukiet, M. J. Undertown   **Fic**

  Herlong, M. The great wide sea   **Fic**

  Stevenson, R. H. Dead in the water   **Fic**

  Welsh, M. L. Heart of stone   **Fic**

  Welsh, M. L. Mistress of the Storm   **Fic**

Sailing the unknown.   **Fic**

SAILORS

  Kraske, R. Marooned   **92**

  Llanas, S. G. Women of the U.S. Navy   **359**

  See also Military personnel; Naval art and science; Navies

SAILORS -- FICTION

  Russell, K. Chasing the Nightbird   **Fic**

SAILORS -- FICTION *See* Sea stories

SAILORS' LIFE *See* Sailors; Seafaring life

SAINT LOUIS (MO.) -- FICTION

  Helgerson, J. Crows & cards   **Fic**

Saint Lucia. Orr, T.   **972.98**

SAINT LUCIA

  Orr, T. Saint Lucia   **972.98**

SAINT PETERSBURG (RUSSIA) -- SIEGE, 1941-1944 -- FICTION

  Whelan, G. Burying the sun   **Fic**

Saint training. Fixmer, E.   **Fic**

Saint-Exupery, Antoine de

  The little prince   **Fic**

About

  Sfar, J. The little prince   **741.5**

Saint-Georges, Joseph Boulogne, chevalier de, 1745-1799

About

  Brewster, H. The other Mozart   **92**

Sammy Keyes and the hotel thief. Draanen, W. v. **Fic**

SAMPLING (STATISTICS)
    See also Probabilities; Statistics

Sampson, Deborah, 1760-1827
             About
  Klass, S. S. Soldier's secret **Fic**
Samuel Adams. Irvin, B. **973.3**
Samuel Houston. Bodden, V. **92**
Samuel Taylor Coleridge. **821**
Samuels, Charlie
  Home front **940.53**
  Iraq **956.7**
  Life under occupation **940.53**
  Propaganda **940.54**
  Soldiers **940.54**
  Spying and security **940.54**
Samurai. Niz, X. **952**
SAMURAI
  Hoobler, D. The demon in the teahouse **Fic**
  Hoobler, D. The ghost in the Tokaido Inn **Fic**
  Niz, X. Samurai **952**
  Turnbull, S. R. The most daring raid of the samurai **952**
SAMURAI -- FICTION
  Bradford, C. Young samurai: the way of the sword **Fic**
  Bradford, C. Young samurai: the way of the warrior **Fic**
  Hoobler, D. Seven paths to death **Fic**
  Matthews, A. The way of the warrior **Fic**
  Snow, M. Chasing the secret **Fic**
  Snow, M. Journey through fire **Fic**
  Snow, M. Sisters of the sword **Fic**
Samurai shortstop. Gratz, A. **Fic**
SAN ANTONIO (TEX.) -- FICTION
  Lopez, D. Ask my mood ring how I feel **Fic**
  Nye, N. S. Going going **Fic**
  Villareal, R. Body slammed! **Fic**
SAN DIEGO (CALIF.) -- FICTION
  Scheibe, L. Riptide **Fic**
SAN DIEGO (CALIF.) -- HISTORY -- 20TH CENTURY -- FICTION
  Winters, C. In the shadow of blackbirds **Fic**
SAN FRANCISCO (CALIF.) -- FICTION
  Bullen, A. Wish **Fic**
  Childs, T. L. Sweet venom **Fic**
  Doctorow, C. Little brother **Fic**
  Hopkinson, D. Into the firestorm **Fic**
  Lavender, W. Aftershocks **Fic**
  Scott, M. The alchemyst **Fic**
  Scott, M. The warlock **Fic**
  Snyder, Z. K. The magic nation thing **Fic**
  Yep, L. Dragonwings **Fic**
  Yep, L. The star maker **Fic**
  Zarr, S. The Lucy variations **Fic**

SAN FRANCISCO (CALIF.) -- HISTORY
  Hopkinson, D. Into the firestorm **Fic**
  Slavicek, L. C. The San Francisco earthquake and fire of 1906 **979.4**
SAN FRANCISCO (CALIF.) -- HISTORY -- 20TH CENTURY -- FICTION
  Blundell, J. A city tossed and broken **Fic**
  Larson, K. Hattie ever after **Fic**
SAN FRANCISCO BAY AREA (CALIF.) -- EMIGRATION AND IMMIGRATION -- HISTORY
  Angel Island **979.4**
The **San** Francisco earthquake and fire of 1906. Slavicek, L. C. **979.4**
SAN JOSE MINE ACCIDENT, CHILE, 2010
  Scott, E. Buried alive! **363.11**
SAN NICOLAS ISLAND (CALIF.) -- FICTION
  O'Dell, S. Island of the Blue Dolphins **Fic**
San Souci, Robert
  Dare to be scared **S**
  Cut from the same cloth **398.2**
  Dare to be scared 4 **S**
  Haunted houses **S**
  A terrifying taste of short & shivery **398.2**
Sanchez, Alex
  Bait **Fic**
  So hard to say **Fic**
SANCTUARY MOVEMENT
    See also Asylum; Church and social problems; Social movements
SAND CREEK, BATTLE OF, 1864
  Ehrlich, A. Wounded Knee: an Indian history of the American West **970.004**
Sand dollar summer. Jones, K. K. **Fic**
SAND DUNES
    See also Seashore
SAND SCULPTURE
    See also Nature craft; Sculpture
Sandell, Lisa Ann
  A map of the known world **Fic**
Sanders, Nancy I.
  America's black founders **973.3**
  Frederick Douglass for kids **973.8**
Sanders, Ronald
  Storming the tulips **940.53**
Sanders, Scott Loring
  Gray baby **Fic**
Sanders, Shelly
  Rachel's secret **Fic**
Sanderson, Brandon
  Alcatraz versus the evil Librarians **Fic**
  Alcatraz versus the Knights of Crystallia **Fic**
  Alcatraz versus the Scrivener's Bones **Fic**
  Alcatraz versus the shattered lens **Fic**
  The Rithmatist **Fic**
Sandifer, Robert, d. 1994

SCHOOL PLAYS *See* Children's plays; College and school drama

SCHOOL PRINCIPALS *See* School superintendents and principals

SCHOOL PROSE *See* Children's writings

SCHOOL PSYCHOLOGISTS
> *See also* Psychologists

School reform and the school library media specialist. Hughes-Hassell, S. **027.8**

SCHOOL REPORTS
> *See also* Report writing

SCHOOL SHOOTINGS
Mackay, J. The Columbine School shooting **364.152**
Marsico, K. The Columbine High School massacre **364.152**
Simons, R. Students in danger **371.7**
> *See also* Crime; School violence

SCHOOL SONGBOOKS
> *See also* Songbooks; Songs

SCHOOL SPORTS
Fay, G. Sports **796**
> *See also* Sports; Student activities

SCHOOL SPORTS -- FICTION
Barwin, S. Hardball **Fic**

SCHOOL STORIES
Abdel-Fattah, R. Does my head look big in this? **Fic**
Abdel-Fattah, R. Ten things I hate about me **Fic**
Abrahams, P. Reality check **Fic**
Ackley, A. Sign language **Fic**
Adler, E. Sweet 15 **Fic**
Alender, K. Bad girls don't die **Fic**
Alexie, S. The absolutely true diary of a part-time Indian **Fic**
Allison, J. Gilda Joyce: the Ladies of the Lake **Fic**
Alvarez, J. How Tia Lola learned to teach **Fic**
Amato, M. Invisible lines **Fic**
Anderson, K. D. Kiss & Make Up **Fic**
Anderson, L. H. Speak **Fic**
Angleberger, T. Darth Paper strikes back **Fic**
Angleberger, T. The strange case of Origami Yoda **Fic**
Angleberger, T. Emperor Pickletine rides the bus **Fic**
Angleberger, T. Princess Labelmaker to the rescue! **Fic**
Appelt, K. Kissing Tennessee and other stories from the Stardust Dance **S**
Archer, J. Through her eyes **Fic**
Armstrong, K. The gathering **Fic**
Ashby, A. Fairy bad day **Fic**
Ashby, A. Zombie queen of Newbury High **Fic**
Asher, J. The future of us **Fic**
Asher, J. Thirteen reasons why **Fic**
Atkins, C. Alt ed **Fic**
Atkinson, E. From Alice to Zen and everyone in between **Fic**

Avi Nothing but the truth **Fic**
Ayres, K. Macaroni boy **Fic**
Balliett, B. The Wright 3 **Fic**
Bancks, T. Mac Slater hunts the cool **Fic**
Baratz-Logsted, L. Crazy beautiful **Fic**
Barnes, J. L. The Squad: perfect cover **Fic**
Barnes, J. The Squad: killer spirit **Fic**
Barnholdt, L. Girl meets ghost **Fic**
Barnholdt, L. Sometimes it happens **Fic**
Baskin, N. R. Anything but typical **Fic**
Baskin, N. R. Runt **Fic**
Basye, D. E. Heck **Fic**
Bates, M. Awkward **Fic**
Bauer, A. C. E. Come Fall **Fic**
Bauer, J. Peeled **Fic**
Beil, M. D. The Red Blazer Girls: the ring of Rocamadour **Fic**
Beil, M. The Red Blazer Girls: the mistaken masterpiece **Fic**
Bennett, O. The Allegra Biscotti collection **Fic**
Benoit, C. You **Fic**
Benway, R. Also known as **Fic**
Benway, R. The extraordinary secrets of April, May and June **Fic**
Berk, J. The dark days of Hamburger Halpin **Fic**
Berry, J. The scandalous sisterhood of Prickwillow Place **Fic**
Bigelow, L. J. Starting from here **Fic**
Blackbird fly **Fic**
Block, F. L. The waters & the wild **Fic**
Bloor, E. London calling **Fic**
Bloor, E. A plague year **Fic**
Boie, K. The princess trap **Fic**
Booraem, E. Texting the underworld **Fic**
Boyd, M. Will **Fic**
Brande, R. Evolution, me, & other freaks of nature **Fic**
Brande, R. Fat Cat **Fic**
Brauner, B. The magic mistake **Fic**
Brennan, S. R. Team Human **Fic**
Brewer, H. The chronicles of Vladimir Tod: eighth grade bites **Fic**
Brewer, H. The chronicles of Vladimir Tod: ninth grade slays **Fic**
Brewer, H. Eleventh grade burns **Fic**
Brewer, H. Tenth grade bleeds **Fic**
Brody, J. My life undecided **Fic**
Brown, J. Star Wars **741.5**
Budhos, M. Ask me no questions **Fic**
Burton, R. Leaving Jetty Road **Fic**
Butcher, K. Cheat **Fic**
Butler, D. H. The truth about Truman School **Fic**
Buyea, R. Because of Mr. Terupt **Fic**
Buyea, R. Mr. Terupt falls again **Fic**
Calloway, C. Confessions of a First Daughter **Fic**

Carriger, G. Etiquette & espionage **Fic**
Carvell, M. Sweetgrass basket **Fic**
Carvell, M. Who will tell my brother? **Fic**
Castan, M. The price of loyalty **Fic**
Castellucci, C. Rose sees red **Fic**
Castle, J. You look different in real life **Fic**
Cerra, K. O. Just a drop of water **Fic**
Chaltas, T. Because I am furniture **Fic**
Chapman, L. Flawless **Fic**
Chatterton, M. The Brain finds a leg **Fic**
Cheva, C. DupliKate **Fic**
Childs, T. L. Oh. My. Gods. **Fic**
Clark, C. G. Secrets of Greymoor **Fic**
Cleary, B. Dear Mr. Henshaw **Fic**
Coben, H. Shelter **Fic**
Cody, M. Powerless **Fic**
Colasanti, S. So much closer **Fic**
Colasanti, S. Something like fate **Fic**
Collins, T. Notes from a totally lame vampire **Fic**
Comerford, L. B. Rissa Bartholomew's declaration of independence **Fic**
Cooney, C. B. Code orange **Fic**
Cooper, I. Angel in my pocket **Fic**
Cormier, R. Beyond the chocolate war **Fic**
Cormier, R. The chocolate war **Fic**
Cornered **S**
Corrigan, E. Accomplice **Fic**
Coy, J. Box out **Fic**
Coy, J. Crackback **Fic**
Coy, J. Love of the game **Fic**
Crawford, B. Carter finally gets it **Fic**
Crawford, B. Carter's unfocused, one-track mind **Fic**
Creech, S. Bloomability **Fic**
Creech, S. Hate that cat **Fic**
Creech, S. Love that dog **Fic**
Crewe, M. Give up the ghost **Fic**
Crossan, S. The Weight of Water **Fic**
Crutcher, C. Deadline **Fic**
Crutcher, C. Ironman **Fic**
Crutcher, C. Running loose **Fic**
Crutcher, C. Whale talk **Fic**
Cummings, P. Blindsided **Fic**
Cushman, K. The loud silence of Francine Green **Fic**
Daly, C. Flirt Club **Fic**
Daneshvari, G. Class is not dismissed! **Fic**
Daneshvari, G. School of Fear **Fic**
Danziger, P. The cat ate my gymsuit **Fic**
De Goldi, K. The 10 p.m. question **Fic**
De Lint, C. The blue girl **Fic**
Delsol, W. Frost **Fic**
Delsol, W. Stork **Fic**
Derting, K. Desires of the dead **Fic**
Despain, B. The dark Divine **Fic**
Dessen, S. What happened to goodbye **Fic**

Deuker, C. Gym candy **Fic**
Deuker, C. High heat **Fic**
Deuker, C. Painting the black **Fic**
Deuker, C. Payback time **Fic**
DeVillers, J. Lynn Visible **Fic**
Dionne, E. The total tragedy of a girl named Hamlet **Fic**
Dowell, F. O. R. Ten miles past normal **Fic**
Dowell, F. O. The kind of friends we used to be **Fic**
Drama **741.5**
Draper, S. M. The Battle of Jericho **Fic**
Draper, S. M. Fire from the rock **Fic**
Draper, S. M. Just another hero **Fic**
Draper, S. M. November blues **Fic**
Duey, K. Sacred scars **Fic**
Duncan, L. Killing Mr. Griffin **Fic**
Edwardson, D. D. My name is not easy **Fic**
Ellis, A. D. This is what I did **Fic**
Ellis, D. Bifocal **Fic**
Ellsworth, L. Unforgettable **Fic**
Emond, S. Happyface **Fic**
Erskine, K. Quaking **Fic**
Fehler, G. Beanball **Fic**
Ferraiolo, J. D. The big splash **Fic**
Finneyfrock, K. The sweet revenge of Celia Door **Fic**
Fitzgerald, D. Soccer chick rules **Fic**
Fixmer, E. Saint training **Fic**
Flake, S. G. The broken bike boy and the Queen of 33rd Street **Fic**
Flake, S. G. The skin I'm in **Fic**
Fleming, D. The Saturday boy **Fic**
Forester, V. The girl who could fly **Fic**
Fredericks, M. Head games **Fic**
Fredericks, M. Love **Fic**
Freitas, D. The possibilities of sainthood **Fic**
From the notebooks of a middle school princess **Fic**
Fry, M. The Odd Squad **Fic**
Fusilli, J. Marley Z and the bloodstained violin **Fic**
Gale, E. K. The Bully Book **Fic**
Gantos, J. Heads or tails **Fic**
Gantos, J. Jack on the tracks **Fic**
Gantos, J. Joey Pigza swallowed the key **Fic**
Garcia, K. Beautiful creatures **Fic**
Garden, N. Endgame **Fic**
Gensler, S. The revenant **Fic**
George, M. Looks **Fic**
Gephart, D. How to survive middle school **Fic**
Gilman, C. Professor Gargoyle **Fic**
Gorman, C. Games **Fic**
Gosselink, J. The defense of Thaddeus A. Ledbetter **Fic**
Grabenstein, C. My brother the robot **Fic**
Grabenstein, C. The smoky corridor **Fic**
Gratz, A. Samurai shortstop **Fic**
Green, T. New kid **Fic**

Mangaman **741.5**

Marcus, K. Exposed **Fic**

Margolis, L. Everybody bugs out **Fic**

Margolis, L. Girls acting catty **Fic**

Margolis, L. Girl's best friend **Fic**

Mariz, R. The Unidentified **Fic**

Martinez, C. G. The smell of old lady perfume **Fic**

Mass, W. Heaven looks a lot like the mall **Fic**

Mass, W. A mango-shaped space **Fic**

Matthews, L. S. The outcasts **Fic**

McDaniel, L. Hit and run **Fic**

McDonald, A. The anti-prom **Fic**

McKissack, F. Shooting star **Fic**

McMann, L. Fade **Fic**

McMann, L. Wake **Fic**

McNish, C. Angel **Fic**

McPhee, P. New blood **Fic**

Meminger, N. Shine, coconut moon **Fic**

Meyer, S. Eclipse **Fic**

Meyer, S. New moon **Fic**

Meyer, S. Twilight **Fic**

Meyerhoff, J. Queen of secrets **Fic**

Middle school, the worst years of my life **Fic**

The mighty Quinn **Fic**

Mikaelsen, B. Ghost of Spirit Bear **Fic**

Mlynowski, S. Gimme a call **Fic**

Monaghan, A. A girl named Digit **Fic**

A monster calls **Fic**

Moore, C. The stalker chronicles **Fic**

Morgenstern, S. H. Secret letters from 0 to 10 **Fic**

Moriarty, J. The ghosts of Ashbury High **Fic**

Moriarty, J. The murder of Bindy Mackenzie **Fic**

Moriarty, J. The year of secret assignments **Fic**

Murder is bad manners **Fic**

My life as a cartoonist **Fic**

My life as a joke **Fic**

Myers, W. D. The Cruisers: checkmate **Fic**

Myers, W. D. A star is born **Fic**

Myers, W. D. Game **Fic**

Myers, W. D. Slam! **Fic**

Myracle, L. Luv ya bunches **Fic**

Myracle, L. Thirteen **Fic**

Myracle, L. Violet in bloom **Fic**

Nails, J. Next to Mexico **Fic**

Naylor, P. R. Alice in April **Fic**

Naylor, P. R. Alice in lace **Fic**

Naylor, P. R. Alice on her way **Fic**

Naylor, P. R. All but Alice **Fic**

Naylor, P. R. Almost Alice **Fic**

Naylor, P. R. Cricket man **Fic**

Naylor, P. R. Dangerously Alice **Fic**

Naylor, P. R. Faith, hope, and Ivy June **Fic**

Naylor, P. R. Incredibly Alice **Fic**

Naylor, P. R. Outrageously Alice **Fic**

Naylor, P. R. Reluctantly Alice **Fic**

Naylor, P. R. Simply Alice **Fic**

Neely, C. Unearthly **Fic**

Neff, H. H. The fiend and the forge **Fic**

Neff, H. H. The hound of Rowan **Fic**

Neff, H. H. The second siege **Fic**

Nelson, B. Destroy all cars **Fic**

Nichols, J. Messed up **Fic**

Nimmo, J. Charlie Bone and the beast **Fic**

Nimmo, J. Charlie Bone and the castle of mirrors **Fic**

Nimmo, J. Charlie Bone and the hidden king **Fic**

Nimmo, J. Charlie Bone and the invisible boy **Fic**

Nimmo, J. Charlie Bone and the Red Knight **Fic**

Nimmo, J. Charlie Bone and the shadow **Fic**

Nimmo, J. Charlie Bone and the time twister **Fic**

Nimmo, J. Midnight for Charlie Bone **Fic**

Nixon, J. L. Laugh till you cry **Fic**

Nolan, H. Crazy **Fic**

Northrop, M. Trapped **Fic**

Nothing **Fic**

Oates, J. C. Big Mouth & Ugly Girl **Fic**

O'Connell, T. True love, the sphinx, and other unsolvable riddles **Fic**

O'Connor, B. Fame and glory in Freedom, Georgia **Fic**

O'Dell, K. Agnes Parker . . . girl in progress **Fic**

O'Dell, K. Agnes Parker . . . keeping cool in middle school **Fic**

Okimoto, J. D. Maya and the cotton candy boy **Fic**

Omololu, C. J. Dirty little secrets **Fic**

Ostow, M. So punk rock (and other ways to disappoint your mother) **Fic**

Padian, M. Brett McCarthy: work in progress **Fic**

Patrick, C. Forgotten **Fic**

Paulsen, G. Liar, liar **Fic**

Paulsen, G. The Schernoff discoveries **Fic**

Paulsen, G. Vote **Fic**

Pearce, J. As you wish **Fic**

Pearsall, S. All of the above **Fic**

Pearson, J. The rites & wrongs of Janice Wills **Fic**

Perez, M. Dead is a state of mind **Fic**

Perez, M. Dead is just a rumor **Fic**

Perez, M. Dead is not an option **Fic**

Perez, M. Dead is the new black **Fic**

Perkins, S. Anna and the French kiss **Fic**

Peters, J. A. Define normal **Fic**

Petrucha, S. The Rule of Won **Fic**

Philbin, J. The daughters **Fic**

Philbin, J. The daughters break the rules **Fic**

Philbin, J. The daughters take the stage **Fic**

Pike, A. Illusions **Fic**

Pinkney, A. D. With the might of angels **Fic**

Pixley, M. Freak **Fic**

Poblocki, D. The haunting of Gabriel Ashe **Fic**

Polonsky, A. Gracefully Grayson **Fic**

Preller, J. Bystander **Fic**

Princess Academy **Fic**

Aretha, D. Malala Yousafzai and the girls of Pakistan **92**

SEX EDUCATION

Bailey, J. Sex, puberty, and all that stuff **612.6**
Bell, R. Changing bodies, changing lives **613.9**
Bornstein, K. My new gender workbook **305.3**
Brynie, F. H. 101 questions about reproduction **612.6**
Cole, J. Asking about sex & growing up **613.9**
Forssberg, M. Sex for guys **306.7**
It's perfectly normal **613.9**
Jukes, M. The guy book **305.235**
Madaras, L. The what's happening to my body? book for boys **612.6**
Madaras, L. The what's happening to my body? book for girls **612.6**
McCoy, K. The teenage body book **613**
Murray, C. Sexpectations **613.9**
Pardes, B. Doing it right **613.9**
Rand, C. Human reproduction **612.6**
Sexual health information for teens **613.9**
Sex for guys. Forssberg, M. **306.7**

SEX IN MASS MEDIA

See also Mass media

SEX IN POPULAR CULTURE

See also Popular culture

SEX IN THE WORKPLACE

See also Sex

SEX INSTRUCTION *See* Sex education

SEX INSTRUCTION FOR CHILDREN WITH MENTAL DISABILITIES

Couwenhoven, T. The boys' guide to growing up **613**

SEX ORGANS *See* Reproductive system

SEX PRESELECTION

See also Reproduction

SEX REASSIGNMENT SURGERY

See also Surgery

SEX REASSIGNMENT SURGERY -- FICTION

Farizan, S. If you could be mine **Fic**

SEX ROLE

The Full spectrum **306.76**
Macy, S. Wheels of change **796.6**
McKissack, P. C. Nzingha, warrior queen of Matamba **Fic**
Pierce, T. Page **Fic**
Pierce, T. Squire **Fic**
Prince, L. Tomboy **741.5**
Rinaldi, A. Girl in blue **Fic**
Springer, N. Rowan Hood, outlaw girl of Sherwood Forest **Fic**
Whelan, G. Chu Ju's house **Fic**
See also Gender role

SEX ROLE -- FICTION

Blacker, T. Boy2girl **Fic**
Brothers, M. Debbie Harry sings in French **Fic**

Bunting, E. The pirate captain's daughter **Fic**
Chibbaro, J. Deadly **Fic**
Cochrane, M. The girl who threw butterflies **Fic**
Day, K. No cream puffs **Fic**
Durrant, L. My last skirt **Fic**
Engle, M. Firefly letters **Fic**
Friesner, E. M. Nobody's princess **Fic**
Friesner, E. M. Nobody's prize **Fic**
Friesner, E. Spirit's princess **Fic**
Goodman, A. Eon: Dragoneye reborn **Fic**
Haddix, M. P. Just Ella **Fic**
Hale, S. Princess Academy **Fic**
Hensley, J. N. Rites of passage **Fic**
Holm, J. L. Our only May Amelia **Fic**
Khan, R. Wanting Mor **Fic**
Lavender, W. Aftershocks **Fic**
Lee, T. Piratica **Fic**
Lee, T. Piratica II: return to Parrot Island **Fic**
Meyer, L. A. Bloody Jack **Fic**
Meyer, L. A. Under the Jolly Roger **Fic**
Meyer, L. A. Viva Jacquelina! **Fic**
Meyer, L. A. The wake of the Lorelei Lee **Fic**
Mobley, J. Searching for Silverheels **Fic**
Namioka, L. Ties that bind, ties that break **Fic**
Napoli, D. J. Bound **Fic**
O'Brien, A. Lara's gift **Fic**
Pierce, T. First test **Fic**
Qamar, A. Beneath my mother's feet **Fic**
Quick, B. A golden web **Fic**
Reedy, T. Words in the dust **Fic**
Reeve, P. Fever Crumb **Fic**
Rinaldi, A. Girl in blue **Fic**
Snow, M. Chasing the secret **Fic**
Snow, M. Journey through fire **Fic**
Snow, M. Sisters of the sword **Fic**
Spinelli, J. There's a girl in my hammerlock **Fic**
Staples, S. F. Haveli **Fic**
Staples, S. F. The house of djinn **Fic**
Staples, S. F. Shabanu **Fic**
Stolz, J. The shadows of Ghadames **Fic**
Thomson, S. L. The secret of the Rose **Fic**
The trouble with May Amelia **Fic**
Waller, S. B. A mad, wicked folly **Fic**
Whelan, G. Chu Ju's house **Fic**
Williams, S. Wind rider **Fic**
Wilson, D. L. Firehorse **Fic**
Yang, D. J. Daughter of Xanadu **Fic**
Zielin, L. Donut days **Fic**

SEX ROLE -- GRAPHIC NOVELS

Takako, S. Wandering son **Fic**
Sex, brains, and video games. Burek Pierce, J. **027.62**
Sex, puberty, and all that stuff. Bailey, J. **612.6**

SEXISM

See also Attitude (Psychology); Prejudices
Sexpectations. Murray, C. **613.9**

SEXUAL ABSTINENCE

The **shadow** society. Rutkoski, M.   **Fic**

The **shadow** speaker. Okorafor, N.   **Fic**

The **shadow** throne. Nielsen, J. A.   **Fic**

Shadow wolf. Lasky, K.   **Fic**

Shadowcry. Burtenshaw, J.   **Fic**

Shadoweyes.   **741.5**

Shadowfell. Marillier, J.   **Fic**

The **Shadowhand** Covenant. Farrey, B.   **Fic**

The **Shadowing**: Hunted. Slater, A.   **Fic**

SHADOWPACT (FICTIONAL CHARACTERS)

> *See also* Fictional characters; Superheroes

Shadows cast by stars. Knutsson, C.   **Fic**

Shadows in the twilight. Mankell, H.   **Fic**

The **shadows** of Ghadames. Stolz, J.   **Fic**

Shahan, Sherry

  Death mountain   **Fic**

  Ice island   **Fic**

Shake, rattle, & roll. George-Warren, H.   **781.66**

SHAKERS

  Peck, R. N. A day no pigs would die   **Fic**

SHAKERS -- FICTION

  Durrant, L. Imperfections   **Fic**

  Higgins, J. Waiting for the queen   **Fic**

  Peck, R. N. A day no pigs would die   **Fic**

Shakespeare explained [series]

  Krueger, S. H. The tempest   **822.3**

  Mussari, M. Othello   **822.3**

Shakespeare kids. Cox, C.   **792.9**

Shakespeare makes the playoffs. Koertge, R.   **Fic**

The **Shakespeare** stealer. Blackwood, G. L.   **Fic**

SHAKESPEARE'S GLOBE (LONDON, ENG-
LAND)

  Aliki William Shakespeare & the Globe   **792.09**

Shakespeare's scribe. Blackwood, G. L.   **Fic**

Shakespeare's secret. Broach, E.   **Fic**

Shakespeare's spy. Blackwood, G. L.   **Fic**

Shakespeare, William, 1564-1616

  One hundred and eleven Shakespeare monologues   **822.3**

About

  Aliki William Shakespeare & the Globe   **792.09**

  All the world's a stage   **Fic**

  Appignanesi, R. As you like it   **741.5**

  Appignanesi, R. Hamlet   **741.5**

  Appignanesi, R. A midsummer night's dream   **741.5**

  Appignanesi, R. Romeo and Juliet   **741.5**

  Appignanesi, R. The tempest   **741.5**

  Blackwood, G. L. The Shakespeare stealer   **Fic**

  Blackwood, G. L. Shakespeare's scribe   **Fic**

  Cooper, S. King of shadows   **Fic**

  Coville, B. William Shakespeare's A midsummer
night's dream   **822.3**

  Coville, B. William Shakespeare's Romeo and Juliet   **822.3**

  Cox, C. Shakespeare kids   **792.9**

  Harper, S. The Juliet club   **Fic**

  Hinds, G. King Lear   **741.5**

  Hinds, G. The merchant of Venice   **741.5**

  Klein, L. M. Lady Macbeth's daughter   **Fic**

  Krueger, S. H. The tempest   **822.3**

  Macbeth   **741.5**

  MacDonald, B. Wicked Will   **Fic**

  McDermott, K. William Shakespeare   **822.3**

  McKeown, A. Julius Caesar   **822.3**

  The merchant of Venice   **741.5**

  The most excellent and lamentable tragedy of Romeo & Juliet   **741.5**

  Mussari, M. Othello   **822.3**

  Nettleton, P. H. William Shakespeare   **822.3**

  Packer, T. Tales from Shakespeare   **822.3**

  Raum, E. Twenty-first-century Shakespeare   **822.3**

  Rees, C. The fool's girl   **Fic**

  Schmidt, G. D. The Wednesday wars   **Fic**

  Selfors, S. Saving Juliet   **Fic**

  Sobran, J. A midsummer night's dream   **822.3**

  Stanley, D. Bard of Avon: the story of William
Shakespeare   **822.3**

  Twelfth night   **741.5**

SHAKESPEARE, WILLIAM, 1564-1616 -- AU-
THORSHIP

> *See also* Authorship

SHAKESPEARE, WILLIAM, 1564-1616 -- DIC-
TIONARIES

> *See also* Encyclopedias and dictionaries

SHAKESPEARE, WILLIAM, 1564-1616 -- FIC-
TION

  The secrets of Shakespeare's grave   **Fic**

Shaking the foundation. Johnson, S. A.   **576.8**

Shakur, Tupac

About

  Golus, C. Tupac Shakur   **92**

  Harris, A. R. Tupac Shakur   **92**

  Woodson, J. After Tupac and D Foster   **Fic**

SHALE GAS

  Squire, A. O. Hydrofracking   **622**

SHAMANISM

  Kallen, S. A. Shamans   **201**

> *See also* Religions

Shamans. Kallen, S. A.   **201**

SHAMANS

  Nelson, S. D. Black Elk's vision   **92**

SHAMANS -- FICTION

  Friesner, E. Spirit's princess   **Fic**

SHAME

> *See also* Emotions

Shan, Darren

  Bec   **Fic**

  Blood beast   **Fic**

  Dark calling   **Fic**

  Death's Shadow   **Fic**

  Demon apocalypse   **Fic**

  Demon thief   **Fic**

Lord Loss **Fic**
Slawter **Fic**
Wolf Island **Fic**
Shanahan, Lisa
The sweet, terrible, glorious year I truly, completely lost it **Fic**
Shandler, Sara
Ophelia speaks **305.235**
Shang, Wendy Wan-Long
The way home looks now **Fic**
Shange, Ntozake
Freedom's a-callin' me **811**
We troubled the waters **811**
SHANGHAI (CHINA) -- FICTION
Alban, A. Anya's war **Fic**
Shanghai shadows. Ruby, L. **Fic**
SHAPE
See also Concepts; Geometry; Perception
Shapera, Paul M.
Iran's religious leaders **955**
Shapers of America [series]
Crosby, M. T. Sacagawea **92**
Shapeshifter. Bennett, H. **Fic**
Shapeshifters. **292**
SHAPESHIFTING -- COMIC BOOKS, STRIPS, ETC.
Nimona **741.5**
SHAPESHIFTING -- FICTION
Bell, H. Traitor's son **Fic**
Kagawa, J. Talon **Fic**
Marr, M. Loki's wolves **Fic**
Marr, M. Odin's ravens **Fic**
Rossetti, R. The girl with borrowed wings **Fic**
Shaping modern science [series]
Cohen, M. What is cell theory? **571.6**
Hyde, N. What is germ theory? **615**
McLean, A. What is atomic theory? **539.7**
O'Leary, D. What are Newton's laws of motion? **531**
Saunders, C. What is the theory of plate tectonics? **551.1**
Walker, R. What is the theory of evolution? **576.8**
Shapiro, Ouisie
Bullying and me **302.3**
Shards and Ashes. **S**
SHARED HOUSING
See also Housing
Sharenow, Rob
Sharenow, R. The Berlin Boxing Club **Fic**
My mother the cheerleader **Fic**
SHARES OF STOCK *See* Stocks
Shark. Macquitty, M. **597.3**
Shark girl. Bingham, K. **Fic**
Shark life. Benchley, P. **597**
Sharks. **597.3**
SHARKS

Benchley, P. Shark life **597**
Capuzzo, M. Close to shore **597**
Cerullo, M. M. The truth about great white sharks **597**
Cerullo, M. M. Searching for Great white sharks **597.3**
Hamilton, S. L. Eaten by a shark **597**
Journey to shark island **597.309**
Mallory, K. Swimming with hammerhead sharks **597.3**
Macquitty, M. Shark **597.3**
Seeking giant sharks **597.3**
Sharks **597.3**
Sharks of the deep **597.3**
Sharks & boys. Tracy, K. **Fic**
SHARKS -- FICTION
Monninger, J. Wish **Fic**
Sharks and other sea monsters. Sabuda, R. **560**
Sharks of the deep. **597.3**
Sharon Creech. Baptiste, T. **92**
Sharon Creech. Carroll, P. S. **813**
Sharon Creech. Tighe, M. A. **813**
Sharon M. Draper. Hinton, K. **813**
Sharp shot. Higgins, J. **Fic**
Sharp, Anne Wallace
Ice hockey **796.962**
Malcolm X and Black pride **92**
Separate but equal **379**
Sharrar, Jack F.
(ed) Great monologues for young actors **808.82**
(ed) Great scenes for young actors from the stage **808.82**
Shattered bones. Markle, S. **617.1**
Shattered Veil. Banghart, T. E. **813.6**
Shattered youth in Nazi Germany. Altman, L. J. **940.53**
Shattered: stories of children and war. **S**
The **shattering.** Healey, K. **Fic**
Shaughnessy, Edward L.
Exploring the life, myth, and art of ancient China **931**
Shaw, Daniel
Eco-tracking **577**
Shaw, Elizabeth M.
(ed) Brannen, D. E. Supreme Court drama **347**
Shaw, Liane
Fostergirls **Fic**
Shaw, Susan
One of the survivors **Fic**
Safe **Fic**
Tunnel vision **Fic**
SHAWNEE INDIANS
Zimmerman, D. J. Tecumseh **92**
She dared. Butts, E. **920**
She is not invisible. Sedgwick, M. **Fic**
She said/she saw. McClintock, N. **Fic**

Slavin, Bill
Transformed **670**
Slavin, Jim
Slavin, B. Transformed **670**
Slawter. Shan, D. **Fic**
The Slayer chronicles [series]
Brewer, H. First kill **Fic**
Slayers. Hill, C. J. **Fic**
Slayton, Fran Cannon
When the whistle blows **Fic**
Sleator, William
The duplicate **Fic**
Interstellar pig **Fic**
Oddballs **S**
Singularity **Fic**
SLED DOG RACERS
Blasingame, J. B. Gary Paulsen **813**
Paulsen, G. Caught by the sea **818**
Paulsen, G. Guts **813**
Paulsen, G. How Angel Peterson got his name **813**
Paulsen, G. My life in dog years **813**
Paulsen, G. Woodsong **796.5**
SLED DOG RACING -- FICTION
Paulsen, G. Dogsong **Fic**
Shahan, S. Ice island **Fic**
SLED DOGS -- FICTION
Johnson, T. L. Ice dogs **Fic**
Kurtz, C. The adventures of a South Pole pig **Fic**
SLEDDING -- FICTION
Doyle, R. Wilderness **Fic**
SLEDS
See also Vehicles
SLEEP
Brynie, F. H. 101 questions about sleep and dreams that kept you awake nights . . . until now **612.8**
Scott, E. All about sleep from A to ZZZZ **612.8**
See also Health; Hygiene; Mind and body; Psychophysiology; Rest; Subconsciousness
SLEEP -- FICTION
Hulme, J. The glitch in sleep **Fic**
Pierson, D. C. The boy who couldn't sleep and never had to **Fic**
SLEEP APNEA
See also Sleep
Sleep disorders. Marcovitz, H. **616.8**
SLEEP DISORDERS
Colligan, L. H. Sleep disorders **616.8**
Marcovitz, H. Sleep disorders **616.8**
Sleep disorders. Colligan, L. H. **616.8**
SLEEP DISORDERS -- FICTION
Pierson, D. C. The boy who couldn't sleep and never had to **Fic**
Sleeper code. Sniegoski, T. **Fic**
Sleeper conspiracy [series]
Sniegoski, T. Sleeper code **Fic**
Sleeping freshmen never lie. Lubar, D. **Fic**

SLEIGHT OF HAND *See* Juggling; Magic tricks
SLIDES (PHOTOGRAPHY)
See also Photography
Slipping. Bell, C. D. **Fic**
Sloan, Christopher
Tracking Tyrannosaurs **567.91**
Sloan, Christopher
Bizarre dinosaurs **567.9**
The human story **599.93**
Mummies **393**
Sloan, Holly Goldberg
Counting by 7s **Fic**
I'll be there **Fic**
Slob. Potter, E. **Fic**
Slog's dad. Almond, D. **Fic**
Slovey, Christine
(ed) Pendergast, T. Westward expansion: almanac **978**
SLOW FOOD MOVEMENT
See also Gastronomy; Social movements
SLUMDOG MILLIONAIRE (MOTION PICTURE)
Ali, R. Slumgirl dreaming **92**
Slumgirl dreaming. Ali, R. **92**
Small acts of amazing courage. Whelan, G. **Fic**
SMALL AND LARGE *See* Size
SMALL ARMS *See* Guns
Small as an elephant. Jacobson, J. R. **Fic**
SMALL BUSINESS
Bielagus, P. G. Quick cash for teens **658.1**
Bochner, A. B. The new totally awesome business book for kids (and their parents) **658**
SMALL BUSINESS -- FICTION
Nye, N. S. Going going **Fic**
A **small** free kiss in the dark. Millard, G. **Fic**
Small Indian Mongoose. Somervill, B. A. **599.74**
Small persons with wings. Booraem, E. **Fic**
Small steps. Sachar, L. **Fic**
A **small** white scar. Nuzum, K. A. **Fic**
Small wildcats. Bonar, S. **599.75**
Small, David
Appelt, K. The underneath **Fic**
Smalley, Carol Parenzan
Green changes you can make around your home **333.72**
Smallpox. Reingold, A. **614.5**
SMALLPOX
Peters, S. T. Smallpox in the new world **614.5**
Reingold, A. Smallpox **614.5**
SMALLPOX -- FICTION
Cooney, C. B. Code orange **Fic**
Spooner, M. Last Child **Fic**
Smallpox in the new world. Peters, S. T. **614.5**
Smallwood, Carol
(ed) The frugal librarian **025.1**
(ed) Writing and publishing **808**

The **smart** aleck's guide to American history. Selzer, A. **973**

The **smart** girl's guide to going vegetarian. Warren, R. M. **641.5**

Smart girls get what they want. Strohmeyer, S. **Fic**

Smart, Denise
The cookbook for girls **641.5**

SMARTPHONES
See also Cellular telephones; Portable computers

Smedman, Lisa
From boneshakers to choppers **629.227**

Smek for president! Rex, A. **Fic**

Smelcer, John E.
The Great Death **Fic**
The trap **Fic**

SMELL
Castaldo, N. F. Sniffer dogs **636.7**
See also Senses and sensation

The **smell** of old lady perfume. Martinez, C. G. **Fic**

Smells like dog. Selfors, S. **Fic**

Smells like treasure. Selfors, S. **Fic**

Smelt, Roselynn
New Zealand **993**

Smibert, Angie
Memento Nora **Fic**

Smile. Telgemeier, R. **741.5**

The **smile.** Napoli, D. J. **Fic**

Smiles to go. Spinelli, J. **Fic**

Smiles, Eileen Michaelis
Yolen, J. Apple for the teacher **782.42**

Smiley, Jane
The Georges and the Jewels **Fic**
Gee Whiz **Fic**
A good horse **Fic**
Pie in the Sky **Fic**
True Blue **Fic**

Smith, Adam, 1723-1790
About
Crain, C. D. Adam Smith **92**

Smith, Alan
Jennings, M. Baseball step-by-step **796.357**

Smith, Alexander Gordon
Death sentence **Fic**
Lockdown **Fic**
Solitary **Fic**

Smith, Bessie, 1894-1937
About
Orgill, R. Shout, sister, shout! **920**

Smith, Carter
Ochoa, G. Atlas of Hispanic-American history **305.8**

Smith, Charles R., 1969-
Kipling, R. If **821**
Pick-up game **S**
Hoop queens **811**

The mighty 12 **398.209**

Twelve rounds to glory: the story of Muhammad Ali **92**

Smith, Charles W. G.
Laubach, C. M. Raptor! a kid's guide to birds of prey **598**

Smith, Chris
Twitter **92**

Smith, Cynthia Leitich
Feral nights **Fic**
Rain is not my Indian name **Fic**

Smith, D. J.
It was September when we ran away the first time **Fic**

Smith, D. James
The boys of San Joaquin **Fic**
Probably the world's best story about a dog and the girl who loved me **Fic**

Smith, David J.
This child, every child **305.23**

Smith, Emily Wing
Back when you were easier to love **Fic**
The way he lived **Fic**

Smith, Hope Anita
Keeping the night watch **Fic**
Mother poems **811**
The way a door closes **Fic**

Smith, Hugh L.
(comp) Reflections on a gift of watermelon pickle--and other modern verse **811**

Smith, Icy
Half spoon of rice **Fic**

Smith, Jeff
Bone: out from Boneville **741.5**
Bone: Rose **741.5**
Bone: tall tales **741.5**
Sniegoski, T. Quest for the spark **Fic**

Smith, Jennifer E.
The geography of you and me **Fic**

Smith, Jennifer E.
The comeback season **Fic**

Smith, John, 1580-1631
About
Doherty, K. To conquer is to live: the life of Captain John Smith of Jamestown **973.2**

Smith, Karen Lynn
Popular dance **793.3**

Smith, Larry
(ed) I can't keep my own secrets **808.8**

Smith, Laura Lee
Cook, J. Natural writer: a story about Marjorie Kinnan Rawlings **813**

Smith, Lindsay
Sekret **Fic**

Smith, Marilyn E.
(jt. auth) Lily, H. M. School violence and conflict

So, you want to work in fashion? Wooster, P. **746.9**
So, you want to work in sports? Mattern, J. **796**
SOAP SCULPTURE
> *See also* Modeling; Sculpture

Sobel, David
What's the catch? **153.8**
Sobey, Ed
Electric motor experiments **621**
Radio-controlled car experiments **796.1**
Robot experiments **629.8**
Solar cell and renewable energy experiments **333.79**
Sobol, Richard
Breakfast in the rainforest **599.8**
The life of rice **633.1**
Sobran, Joseph
A midsummer night's dream **822.3**
Soccer. Kassouf, J. **796.334**
SOCCER
Bazemore, S. Soccer: how it works **796.334**
Crisfield, D. Winning soccer for girls **796.334**
Goodstein, M. Goal! science projects with soccer **507.8**
Hornby, H. Soccer **796.334**
Jennings, M. Soccer step-by-step **796.334**
Jokulsson, I. Stars of the World Cup **920**
Kassouf, J. Soccer **796.334**
Stewart, M. Goal!: the fire and fury of soccer's greatest moment **796.334**
> *See also* Ball games; Football; Sports

Soccer. Hornby, H. **796.334**
SOCCER -- BIOGRAPHY
Buckley, J. Pele **92**
SOCCER -- ENCYCLOPEDIAS
Gifford, C. The Kingfisher soccer encyclopedia **796.334**
SOCCER -- FICTION
Aronson, S. Beyond lucky **Fic**
Bloor, E. Tangerine **Fic**
Choat, B. Soccerland **Fic**
Fitzgerald, D. Soccer chick rules **Fic**
Halpin, B. Shutout **Fic**
Myers, W. D. Kick **Fic**
Walliams, D. The boy in the dress **Fic**
Williams, M. Now is the time for running **Fic**
Soccer chick rules. Fitzgerald, D. **Fic**
SOCCER COACHES
St. John, W. Outcasts united **796.334**
SOCCER COACHES -- GEORGIA -- CLARKSTON -- BIOGRAPHY
St. John, W. Outcasts united **796.334**
SOCCER PLAYERS
Buckley, J. Pele **92**
SOCCER PLAYERS -- BIOGRAPHY
Jokulsson, I. Stars of the World Cup **920**
Soccer step-by-step. Jennings, M. **796.334**
SOCCER TEAMS

Jokulsson, I. Stars of the World Cup **920**
St. John, W. Outcasts united **796.334**
Soccer: how it works. Bazemore, S. **796.334**
Soccerland. Choat, B. **Fic**
SOCIAL ACTION
Drake, J. Yes you can! **361.2**
Dublin, A. June Callwood **92**
Halpin, M. It's your world--if you don't like it, change it **361.2**
Houle, M. E. Lindsey Williams **92**
Rubel, D. If I had a hammer **363.5**
Saul, L. Ways to help disadvantaged youth **362.7**
Woog, A. Jyotirmayee Mohapatra **92**
SOCIAL ACTION -- FICTION
Myers, W. D. On a clear day **Fic**
SOCIAL ACTIVISM *See* Social action
SOCIAL ACTIVISTS
Dublin, A. June Callwood **92**
Fleming, C. Our Eleanor **92**
Freedman, R. Eleanor Roosevelt **973.917**
MacLeod, E. Eleanor Roosevelt **92**
Murphy, A. G. Chico Mendes **92**
SOCIAL ADJUSTMENT
> *See also* Human behavior; Interpersonal relations; Social psychology

SOCIAL ADVOCACY
> *See also* Social work

SOCIAL BEHAVIOR *See* Human behavior
SOCIAL CASE WORK
> *See also* Social work

SOCIAL CHANGE
Hill, L. C. America dreaming **303.4**
> *See also* Anthropology; Social sciences; Sociology

SOCIAL CHANGE -- FICTION
Levithan, D. Two boys kissing **Fic**
SOCIAL CHANGE -- UNITED STATES -- HISTORY
Pinkney, A. D. Hand in hand **973**
SOCIAL CLASSES
Nardo, D. Government and social class in colonial America **973.2**
SOCIAL CLASSES -- FICTION
Glewwe, E. Sparkers **Fic**
London, A. Guardian **Fic**
Smith, J. E. The geography of you and me **Fic**
SOCIAL CONFLICT -- FICTION
Harland, R. Liberator **Fic**
SOCIAL DISTINCTIONS *See* Social classes
SOCIAL DRINKING *See* Drinking of alcoholic beverages
SOCIAL ECOLOGY *See* Human ecology
SOCIAL ETHICS
Our country's founders **973**
> *See also* Ethics; Sociology

SOCIAL EVOLUTION *See* Social change

SWEDISH LITERATURE

See also Literature; Scandinavian literature

Sweeney, Joyce

The guardian **Fic**

Sweeney, Mary Ellen

Wood, K. The 101 best tropical fishes **639.34**

Sweeney, Michael S.

Dau, J. B. Lost boy, lost girl **962.4**

Sweet 15. Adler, E. **Fic**

The **sweet** revenge of Celia Door. Finneyfrock, K. **Fic**

Sweet Thang. Whittenberg, A. **Fic**

Sweet treats, secret crushes. Greenwald, L. **Fic**

Sweet venom. Childs, T. L. **Fic**

Sweet! Love, A. **641.8**

Sweet, hereafter. Johnson, A. **Fic**

The **sweet,** terrible, glorious year I truly, completely lost it. Shanahan, L. **Fic**

Sweetblood. Hautman, P. **Fic**

The **sweetest** spell. Selfors, S. **Fic**

Sweetgrass basket. Carvell, M. **Fic**

The **sweetheart** of Prosper County. Alexander, J. S. **Fic**

Sweethearts. Zarr, S. **Fic**

Sweethearts of rhythm. Nelson, M. **811**

SWEETS *See* Candy; Confectionery

Swift, Jonathan

Gulliver's travels **Fic**

Swift, Richard

Gangs **364.1**

Swifter, higher, stronger. Macy, S. **796.48**

A **swiftly** tilting planet. L'Engle, M. **Fic**

Swim that rock. **Fic**

Swimming. Gifford, C. **797.2**

SWIMMING

Crutcher, C. Whale talk **Fic**

Gifford, C. Swimming **797.2**

Hoblin, P. Swimming & diving **797.2**

Swimming & diving. Hoblin, P. **797.2**

SWIMMING -- FICTION

Crossan, S. The Weight of Water **Fic**

Crutcher, C. Staying fat for Sarah Byrnes **Fic**

Crutcher, C. Stotan! **Fic**

Crutcher, C. Whale talk **Fic**

Mayall, B. Mermaid Park **Fic**

Swimming to America. Mead, A. **Fic**

Swimming upstream. George, K. O. **811**

Swimming with hammerhead sharks. Mallory, K. **597.3**

Swinburne, Stephen R.

Sea turtle scientist **597.92**

Swinburne, Stephen R.

Saving manatees **599.5**

Wiff and Dirty George: the Z.E.B.R.A. Incident **Fic**

Swindle. Korman, G. **Fic**

Swindle [series]

Korman, G. Swindle **Fic**

Swindlers. Blackwood, G. L. **364.16**

SWINDLERS AND SWINDLING

Blackwood, G. L. Swindlers **364.16**

Schroeder, A. Scams! **364.1**

See also Crime; Criminals

SWINDLERS AND SWINDLING -- FICTION

Cushman, K. Will Sparrow's road **Fic**

Farrey, B. The Grimjinx rebellion **Fic**

Farrey, B. The Vengekeep prophecies **Fic**

SWINE *See* Pigs

SWINE INFLUENZA

Parks, P. J. Influenza **616.2**

Swinney, Geoff

Fish facts **597**

Swish. Stewart, M. **796.323**

Swiss mist. Powell, R. **Fic**

Swissler, Becky

Winning lacrosse for girls **796.34**

Switch. Snow, C. **Fic**

Switched. Wollman, J. **Fic**

Switched at birthday. Standiford, N. **Fic**

SWITZERLAND -- FICTION

Chatterton, M. The Brain full of holes **Fic**

Creech, S. Bloomability **Fic**

Creech, S. The unfinished angel **Fic**

Henderson, J. Vampire rising **Fic**

Henderson, J. Voice of the undead **Fic**

Young, E. L. STORM: The Black Sphere **Fic**

SWITZERLAND -- HISTORY -- 20TH CENTURY -- FICTION

Haddix, M. P. Caught **Fic**

A **sword** in her hand. Sage, A. **Fic**

The **Sword** of Darrow. Malchow, A. **Fic**

Sword of waters. Bell, H. **Fic**

Sword song. Sutcliff, R. **Fic**

The **sword** that cut the burning grass. Hoobler, D. **Fic**

Swords. Boos, B. **623.4**

SWORDS

Boos, B. Swords **623.4**

SWORDS

See also Weapons

Sykes, Judith A.

Conducting action research to evaluate your school library **027.8**

SYLO. MacHale, D. J. **Fic**

Sylvester, Kelvin

(jt. auth) Hlinka, M. Follow Your Money **330**

Sylvie and the songman. Binding, T. **Fic**

Symbiosis. Silverstein, A. **577.8**

SYMBIOSIS

Silverstein, A. Symbiosis **577.8**

See also Biology; Ecology

SYMBOLIC LOGIC

See also Logic; Mathematics

SYMBOLISM
    See also Art; Mythology
SYMBOLISM IN LITERATURE
    See also Literature; Symbolism
SYMBOLS *See* Signs and symbols
Symes, R. F.
    Rocks & minerals   **552**
SYMPATHY
    See also Conduct of life; Emotions
The **symptoms** of my insanity. Raf, M.   **Fic**
SYNAGOGUES
    See also Buildings; Religious institutions;
    Temples
SYNCHRONIZED SWIMMING
    See also Swimming
SYNESTHESIA -- FICTION
    Ellsworth, L. Unforgettable   **Fic**
    Mass, W. A mango-shaped space   **Fic**
    Parkinson, S. Blue like Friday   **Fic**
SYNTHETIC DRUGS
    Parks, P. J. Bath salts and other synthetic
    drugs   **362.29**
SYNTHETIC DRUGS OF ABUSE *See* Designer
    drugs
SYNTHETIC FABRICS
    See also Fabrics; Synthetic products
SYNTHETIC RUBBER
    See also Plastics; Synthetic products
SYPHILIS
    Uschan, M. V. Forty years of medical racism **174.2**
SYPHILIS
    See also Sexually transmitted diseases
Syren. Sage, A.   **Fic**
Syria. Yomtov, N.   **956.91**
SYRIA
    Gelfand, D. E. Syria   **956.91**
    Yomtov, N. Syria   **956.91**
Syria. Gelfand, D. E.   **956.91**
SYRIA -- FICTION
    Jolin, P. In the name of God   **Fic**
SYRUPS
    See also Sugar
SYSTEM THEORY
    See also Science
SYSTEMS ENGINEERING
    See also Automation; Cybernetics; Engineer-
    ing; Industrial design; System analysis; Sys-
    tem theory
Szpirglas, Jeff
    You just can't help it!   **599.9**
Szulhan, Rebecca
    Contemporary achievements   **305.8**
Szumski, Bonnie
    (jt. auth) Karson, J. Are cell phones danger-
    ous?   **615.9**
    (jt. auth) Karson, J. Is medical marijuana neces-

sary?   **615.7**
    Thinking critically   **615.7**
Szynkowski, Liz
    Ferry, S. Yukon Territory   **971**

T

T-Minus: the race to the moon. Ottaviani, J. **629.45**
T-SHIRTS
    See also Clothing and dress
T. rex and the great extinction. Bacchin, M.   **567.9**
T4. LeZotte, A. C.   **Fic**
TABLE ETIQUETTE
    See also Eating customs; Etiquette
TABLE TENNIS
    See also Ball games
Tabletop scientist [series]
    Parker, S. The science of air   **533**
    Parker, S. The science of water   **532**
Tabula rasa.   **Fic**
TACTICS
    See also Military art and science; Strategy
Tadjo, Veronique
    Talking drums   **808**
TADPOLES *See* Frogs
Tae kwon do. Haney-Withrow, A.   **796.8**
TAE KWON DO
    Haney-Withrow, A. Tae kwon do   **796.8**
    Pawlett, M. The tae kwon do handbook   **796.8**
    See also Karate; Martial arts; Self-defense
TAE KWON DO -- FICTION
    Eliza Bing is (not) a big, fat quitter   **Fic**
    The **tae** kwon do handbook. Pawlett, M.   **796.8**
Taft, Robert A., 1889-1953
          About
    Kennedy, J. F. Profiles in courage   **920**
Tag, toss & run. Rowell, V.   **790.1**
Tahiti. NgCheong-Lum, R.   **996**
TAHITI (FRENCH POLYNESIA)
    NgCheong-Lum, R. Tahiti   **996**
TAI CHI
    Jennings, M. Tai chi step-by-step   **613.7**
    See also Exercise; Martial arts
Tai chi step-by-step. Jennings, M.   **613.7**
TAI JI QUAN *See* Tai chi
TAICHI *See* Tai chi
TAILORING
    See also Clothing and dress; Clothing indus-
    try
TAINO INDIANS -- FICTION
    Dorris, M. Morning Girl   **Fic**
Tait, Noel
    Insects & spiders   **595.7**
Taj Mahal. Arnold, C.   **954**
Taj Mahal. Mann, E.   **954**
TAJ MAHAL (AGRA, INDIA)
    Arnold, C. Taj Mahal   **954**

Tanaka, Shelley
  Augustyn, F. Footnotes **792.8**
  Amelia Earhart **92**
Tangerine. Bloor, E. **Fic**
A **tangle** of knots. Graff, L. **Fic**
Tangled. O'Rourke, E. **Fic**
Tangled. Mackler, C. **Fic**
Tanglewreck. Winterson, J. **Fic**
Tanguay, Bridget
  Kenya **967.62**
Tank man. Burgan, M. **951.05**
TANK WARFARE
  See also War
Tankborn. Sandler, K. **Fic**
Tankborn [series]
  Sandler, K. Rebellion **Fic**
TANKS (MILITARY SCIENCE) *See* Military
  tanks
Tanner, Lian
  City of lies **Fic**
  Museum of thieves **Fic**
Tanner, Mike
  Flat-out rock **781.66**
Tanzania. Heale, J. **967.8**
Tanzania. **967.8**
TANZANIA
  Tanzania **967.8**
TANZANIA -- FICTION
  Doherty, B. The girl who saw lions **Fic**
  Sullivan, T. Golden boy **Fic**
TAO
  See also Philosophy
TAOISM
  Demi The legend of Lao Tzu and the Tao te ch-
    ing **299.5**
  Hartz, P. Daoism **299.5**
  Osborne, M. P. One world, many religions **200**
    See also Religions
TAP DANCING
  See also Dance
TAPE RECORDINGS, AUDIO *See* Sound record-
  ings
TAPESTRY
  See also Decoration and ornament; Decora-
    tive arts; Interior design; Needlework
The tapestry [series]
  Neff, H. H. The fiend and the forge **Fic**
  Neff, H. H. The hound of Rowan **Fic**
  Neff, H. H. The second siege **Fic**
TAPESTRY -- FICTION
  Guibord, M. Warped **Fic**
The **tapir** scientist. **599.66**
TAPIRS
  The tapir scientist **599.66**
TAPIRS -- BRAZIL
  The tapir scientist **599.66**

Tapper twins [series]
  The Tapper twins go to war (with each other) **Fic**
  The **Tapper** twins go to war (with each other) **Fic**
Taran Wanderer. Alexander, L. **Fic**
A **tarantula** in my purse. George, J. C. **639.9**
The **tarantula** scientist. Montgomery, S. **595.4**
Tarantulas. Markle, S. **595.4**
TARANTULAS
  Markle, S. Tarantulas **595.4**
  Montgomery, S. The tarantula scientist **595.4**
Tarbell, Ida M. (Ida Minerva), 1857-1944
          About
  Bausum, A. Muckrakers **070.4**
  McCully, E. A. Ida M. Tarbell **92**
TARGET MARKETING
  See also Marketing
Tarnowska, Wafa'
  Arabian nights **398.2**
TAROT -- FICTION
  Powell, L. The Master of Misrule **Fic**
Tarshis, Lauren
  Emma-Jean Lazarus fell in love **Fic**
  Emma-Jean Lazarus fell out of a tree **Fic**
  I survived the Battle of Gettysburg, 1863 **E**
Tarshis, Thomas Paul
  Living with peer pressure and bullying **303.3**
Taschek, Karen
  The Civil War **391**
  Daughters of liberty **305.4**
  Hanging with bats **599.4**
Tashjian, Janet
  My life as a book **Fic**
  My life as a cartoonist **Fic**
  My life as a joke **Fic**
  The gospel according to Larry **Fic**
  Larry and the meaning of life **Fic**
  My life as a stuntboy **Fic**
  Vote for Larry **Fic**
TASTE
  See also Senses and sensation
TASTE (AESTHETICS) *See* Aesthetics
A **taste** for rabbit. Zuckerman, L. **Fic**
A **taste** for red. Harris, L. **Fic**
A **taste** of culture [series]
  Sheen, B. Foods of Chile **641.5**
  Sheen, B. Foods of Cuba **641.5**
  Sheen, B. Foods of Egypt **641.5**
  Sheen, B. Foods of Ireland **641.5**
  Sheen, B. Foods of Kenya **641.5**
  Sheen, B. Foods of Korea **641.5**
  Sheen, B. Foods of Peru **641.5**
The **Tasters** Guild. Appelbaum, S. **Fic**
Tasting the sky. Barakat, I. **92**
Tate, Eleanora E.
  African American musicians **920**
  Celeste's Harlem Renaissance **Fic**

Wachtel, A. September 11   **973.931**
Weinberg, L. What is terrorism?   **303.6**
Williams, B. The war on terror   **973.931**
Terrorism [series]
Bedell, J. M. Combating terrorism   **363.32**
Burgan, M. Terrorist groups   **363.32**
Nardo, D. The history of terrorism   **363.32**
Tougas, S. What makes a terrorist?   **363.32**
TERRORISM -- FICTION
Monaghan, A. A girl named Digit   **Fic**
Sandler, K. Rebellion   **Fic**
Terry, T. Fractured   **Fic**
TERRORISM -- PREVENTION -- FICTION
The Worst class trip ever   **Fic**
TERRORISM -- RELIGIOUS ASPECTS
Is Islam a religion of war or peace?   **297**
TERRORISM -- UNITED STATES
Benoit, P. September 11 we will never forget   **973.931**
Frank, M. Understanding September 11th   **973.931**
Hillstrom, K. The September 11 terrorist attacks   **973.931**
TERRORIST ACTS *See* Terrorism
Terrorist attacks. Friedman, L. S.   **363.32**
TERRORIST ATTACKS, SEPTEMBER 11, 2001
  See September 11 terrorist attacks, 2001
TERRORIST BOMBINGS *See* Bombings
Terrorist groups. Burgan, M.   **363.32**
The **terrorist** trial of the 1993 bombing of the World
  Trade Center. Pellowski, M.   **974.7**
TERRORISTS
Burgan, M. Terrorist groups   **363.32**
Frank, M. Understanding September 11th   **973.931**
Lusted, M. A. The capture and killing of Osama bin
  Laden   **958.1**
Tougas, S. What makes a terrorist?   **363.32**
  See also Criminals
TERRORISTS -- BIOGRAPHY
Lunis, N. The takedown of Osama bin Laden   **958.104**
Terry, Chris L.
Zero fade   **Fic**
Terry, Michael Bad Hand
Daily life in a Plains Indian village, 1868   **970.004**
Terry, Teri
Fractured   **Fic**
Slated   **Fic**
Tesla's attic. Elfman, E.   **Fic**
Tesla, Nikola, 1856-1943
    About
Burgan, M. Nikola Tesla   **92**
Elfman, E. Tesla's attic   **Fic**
Watson, G. Edison's gold   **Fic**
Weyn, S. Distant waves   **Fic**
Yount, L. Nikola Tesla   **621.309**
TEST BIAS

  See also Discrimination in education; Educational tests and measurements
TEST PILOTS *See* Air pilots; Airplanes -- Testing
TEST PREPARATION GUIDES *See* Examinations -- Study guides
Test tube babies. Fullick, A.   **618.1**
TEST TUBE BABIES
Fullick, A. Test tube babies   **618.1**
  See also Fertilization in vitro
TEST TUBE FERTILIZATION *See* Fertilization
  in vitro
Testa, Dom
The Cassini code   **Fic**
The comet's curse   **Fic**
Cosmic storm   **Fic**
The dark zone   **Fic**
The web of Titan   **Fic**
Testa, Maria
Something about America   **811**
The **Testing**. Charbonneau, J.   **Fic**
The **testing** [series]
Charbonneau, J. Independent study   **Fic**
TESTING FOR DRUG ABUSE *See* Drug testing
TESTS *See* Educational tests and measurements;
  Examinations
TETON INDIANS -- LITERARY COLLECTIONS
Walking on earth and touching the sky   **810**
TEUTONIC PEOPLES
Helget, N. Barbarians   **940.1**
TEUTONIC RACE *See* Teutonic peoples
Texas.   **976.4**
TEXAS
Texas   **976.4**
TEXAS -- BIOGRAPHY
Henrietta King, la patrona   **976.4**
TEXAS -- FICTION
Harrington, K. Courage for beginners   **Fic**
TEXAS -- HISTORY
Chemerka, W. R. Juan Seguin   **976.4**
**TEXAS -- POLITICS AND GOVERNMENT --
1951-**
Raatma, L. Barbara Jordan   **92**
Texas gothic. Clement-Moore, R.   **Fic**
The **Texas** polygamist raid. Marsico, K.   **364.1**
The **Texas** Rangers. Newton, M.   **976.4**
TEXAS RANGERS
Alter, J. John Barclay Armstrong   **92**
Newton, M. The Texas Rangers   **976.4**
The **Texas** war of independence: the 1800s. Worth,
  R.   **976.4**
Texas, 1527-1836. Teitelbaum, M.   **976.4**
TEXT MESSAGING
  See also Wireless communication systems
TEXTILE CHEMISTRY
  See also Industrial chemistry; Textile industry

How I became a ghost   **Fic**

Tingle, Tim

   Spirits dark and light   **398.2**

   Walking the Choctaw road   **398.2**

Tiny Tyrant. Trondheim, L.   **741.5**

Tiny yarn animals. Snow, T.   **746.43**

Tips and other bright ideas for elementary school libraries.   **025.1**

TISSUES -- TRANSPLANTATION See Transplantation of organs, tissues, etc.

The **Titan's** curse. Riordan, R.   **Fic**

Titanic. Hopkinson, D.   **910.4**

TITANIC (STEAMSHIP)

   Hopkinson, D. Titanic   **910.4**

TITANIC (STEAMSHIP) -- FICTION

   Watts, I. N. No moon   **Fic**

   Weyn, S. Distant waves   **Fic**

   Wolf, A. The watch that ends the night   **Fic**

Titanic sinks! Denenberg, B.   **910.4**

The **Titanic** tragedy. Burlingame, J.   **910.4**

Titanium. Woodford, C.   **546**

TITANIUM

   Woodford, C. Titanium   **546**

Titans of business [series]

   Spilsbury, R. Jay-Z   **92**

Tito Puente. McNeese, T.   **92**

Tjia, Sherwin

   Lawson, J. Black stars in a white night sky   **811**

TLINGIT INDIANS

   Mikaelsen, B. Touching Spirit Bear   **Fic**

To come and go like magic. Fawcett, K. P.   **Fic**

To conquer is to live: the life of Captain John Smith of Jamestown. Doherty, K.   **973.2**

To dare mighty things.   **92**

To darkness fled. Williamson, J.   **Fic**

To every thing there is a season. Dillon, L.   **223**

To kill a mockingbird. Lee, H.   **Fic**

To the heart of Africa. Bodden, V.   **916**

To the moon. Bodden, V.   **629.45**

To the mountaintop! Hunter-Gault, C.   **070.92**

To the ocean deep. Bodden, V.   **551.46**

To the South Pole. Bodden, V.   **919.89**

To the top of Everest. Skreslet, L.   **796.52**

To the top of Mount Everest. Bodden, V.   **796.52**

To the young writer. Nuwer, H.   **808**

TOADS

   Beltz, E. Frogs: inside their remarkable world **597.8**

   Somervill, B. A. Cane toad   **597.8**

TOADS -- FICTION

   Williams, L. A. The witches' kitchen   **Fic**

Toads and diamonds. Tomlinson, H.   **Fic**

TOADSTOOLS See Mushrooms

TOASTS

   See also Epigrams; Speeches

TOBACCO

   Hyde, M. O. Smoking 101   **616.86**

TOBACCO

   See also Plants

Tobacco and Smoking.   **362.29**

TOBACCO HABIT

   Hunter, D. Born to smoke   **616.86**

   Merino, N. Smoking   **362.29**

   Miller, H. Smoking   **616.86**

   Naff, C. F. Nicotine and tobacco   **362.29**

   Price, S. Nicotine   **616.86**

   Tobacco information for teens   **362.29**

TOBACCO HABIT

   See also Habit; Smoking

TOBACCO INDUSTRY

   Tobacco and Smoking   **362.29**

   Tobacco information for teens.   **362.29**

TOBACCO PIPES

   See also Smoking

Tobacco: the deadly drug [series]

   Esherick, J. No more butts   **616.86**

   Hunter, D. Born to smoke   **616.86**

Toby alone. Fombelle, T. d.   **Fic**

Toby and the secrets of the tree. Fombelle, T. d. **Fic**

Tocci, Salvatore

   Gardner, R. Ace your chemistry science project   **540.7**

   Gardner, R. Ace your ecology and environmental science project   **577**

   Gardner, R. Ace your exercise and nutrition science project: great science fair ideas   **613**

   Gardner, R. Ace your food science project   **664**

   Gardner, R. Ace your weather science project **551.5**

   The chaparral   **577.3**

   Life in the tropical forests   **577.3**

Tocher, Timothy

   Bill Pennant, Babe Ruth, and me   **Fic**

   Chief Sunrise, John McGraw, and me   **Fic**

Today [series]

   Ponsford, S. The European Union today **341.242**

Today I will. Spinelli, E.   **808.8**

Today the world is watching you. Magoon, K. **379**

Today's writers and their works [series]

   Axelrod-Contrada, J. Isabel Allende   **92**

   Mussari, M. Amy Tan   **92**

   Mussari, M. Haruki Murakami   **92**

   Stefoff, R. Stephen King   **92**

Todd, Anne M.

   Susan B. Anthony   **92**

   Vera Wang   **92**

Todd, Mark

   Whatcha mean, what's a zine?   **070.5**

Todd, Pamela

   The blind faith hotel   **Fic**

TODD, SWEENEY (LEGENDARY CHARACTER) -- FICTION

   Pratchett, T. Dodger   **Fic**

Todras, Ellen H.

Childress, D. Marco Polo's journey to China 92

Claybourne, A. Who discovered natural selection? **576.8**

Demi. Marco Polo 92

Diorio, M. A. L. A student's guide to Mark Twain **813**

Doherty, K. To conquer is to live: the life of Captain John Smith of Jamestown **973.2**

Eldredge, N. Charles Darwin and the mystery of mysteries 92

Ellis, S. From reader to writer **372.62**

Feiler, B. S. Walking the Bible **222**

Feinstein, S. Captain Cook 92

Feinstein, S. Marco Polo 92

Finkelstein, N. H. Three across **629.13**

Fleischman, S. The trouble begins at 8 92

Galloway, P. Adventures on the ancient Silk Road **950**

Heiligman, D. Charles and Emma 92

Houle, M. M. Mark Twain 92

Klein, L. M. Cate of the Lost Colony **Fic**

Krull, K. Charles Darwin 92

Lace, W. W. Captain James Cook 92

Lawlor, L. Magnificent voyage **910.4**

Lourie, P. On the Texas trail of Cabeza de Vaca 92

Mark Twain **818**

Meyer, C. The true adventures of Charley Darwin **Fic**

Murphy, J. Across America on an emigrant train **385**

Schanzer, R. What Darwin saw 92

Sonneborn, L. Mark Twain 92

Stefoff, R. Charles Darwin and the evolution revolution **575**

Twist, C. Marco Polo 92

Walker, R. What is the theory of evolution? **576.8**

Wood, A. J. Charles Darwin and the Beagle adventure **508**

Yang, D. J. Daughter of Xanadu **Fic**

Young, S. Richard Francis Burton 92

TRAVEL WRITING

   See also Authorship

TRAVELERS

Armstrong, A. Looking for Marco Polo **Fic**

Childress, D. Marco Polo's journey to China 92

Demi. Marco Polo 92

Feinstein, S. Marco Polo 92

Galloway, P. Adventures on the ancient Silk Road **950**

Twist, C. Marco Polo 92

Yang, D. J. Daughter of Xanadu **Fic**

   See also Voyages and travels

Traveling green. Ball, J. A. **790.1**

Traveling photographer [series]

Sobol, R. The life of rice **633.1**

Traveling the freedom road. Osborne, L. B. **973.7**

TRAVELS *See* Voyages and travels

Travers, P. L. (Pamela L.), 1899-1996
About

Ellis, S. From reader to writer **372.62**

The **treachery** of beautiful things. Long, R. F. **Fic**

TREASON

   See also Crime; Political crimes and offenses; Subversive activities

Treaster, Joseph B.

Hurricane force **551.55**

TREASURE HUNT (GAME) -- FICTION

Holczer, T. The secret hum of a daisy **Fic**

Treasure hunters. **Fic**

Treasure hunters [series]

Ancient treasures **930.1**

Barber, N. Lost cities **930.1**

Barber, N. Tomb explorers **930.1**

Guillain, C. Great art thefts **364.16**

Treasure hunters **Fic**

Treasure Island. Stevenson, R. L. **Fic**

Treasure Island. Stevenson, R. L. **Fic**

The **treasure** of Way Down Deep. White, R. **Fic**

TREASURE TROVE *See* Buried treasure

TREASURE TROVES

Ancient treasures **930.1**

Barber, N. Tomb explorers **930.1**

Hunter, N. Pirate treasure **910.4**

TREASURE TROVES -- CHINA -- CHANGSHA (HUNAN SHENG)

At home in her tomb **931**

Treasury of Egyptian Mythology. **299.31**

Treasury of Greek mythology. Napoli, D. J. **398.2**

TREATIES

I have the right to be a child **323.3**

   See also Diplomacy; International law; International relations

The **Treaty** of Paris. Renehan, E. J. **973.3**

TREATY OF PARIS (1783)

Renehan, E. J. The Treaty of Paris **973.3**

Tree frogs, mud puppies, & other amphibians. Gilpin, D. **597.8**

TREE HOUSES

   See also Buildings

The **Tree** is older than you are. **860**

TREE KANGAROOS

Montgomery, S. Quest for the tree kangaroo **599.2**

TREE PLANTING

   See also Forests and forestry

Tree shaker. Keller, B. 92

The **tree** that time built. **808.81**

Trees. Ridsdale, C. **582.16**

TREES

Branching out **582.16**

Ridsdale, C. Trees **582.16**

   See also Plants

TREES -- FICTION

The **twilight** prisoner. Marsh, K. **Fic**

TWILIGHT ZONE (TELEVISION PROGRAM) -- GRAPHIC NOVELS

Serling, R. The Twilight Zone: the after hours **741.5**

Serling, R. The Twilight Zone: walking distance **741.5**

The **Twilight** Zone: the after hours. Serling, R. **741.5**

The **Twilight** Zone: walking distance. Serling, R. **741.5**

The **Twin** Towers. Abbott, D. **973.931**

Twin's daughter. Baratz-Logsted, L. **Fic**

The **twinning** project. Lipsyte, R. **Fic**

TWINS

Kor, E. M. Surviving the Angel of Death **92**

Schuman, M. Scarlet Johansson **92**

See also Multiple birth; Siblings

TWINS -- FICTION

Clayton, E. The Whisper **Fic**

Lipsyte, R. The twinning project **Fic**

Mack, W. C. Athlete vs. mathlete **Fic**

Rivers, K. Finding Ruby Starling **Fic**

Spinelli, J. Jake and Lily **Fic**

The Tapper twins go to war (with each other) **Fic**

Watson, J. Loot **Fic**

Wrede, P. C. The Far West **Fic**

Zhang, K. What's left of me **Fic**

Twist, Clint

Steer, D. The mythology handbook **292**

Marco Polo **92**

Wood, A. J. Charles Darwin and the Beagle adventure **508**

TWISTERS (TORNADOES) *See* Tornadoes

Twitter. Smith, C. **92**

TWITTER, INC.

Gilbert, S. D. The story of Twitter **006.7**

Lusted, M. A. Social networking: MySpace, Facebook, & Twitter **302.3**

Smith, C. Twitter **92**

Two boys kissing. Levithan, D. **Fic**

Two crafty criminals! Pullman, P. **Fic**

Twomey, Cathleen

Beachmont letters **Fic**

Txt me l8r. Harris, A. R. **303.4**

Tycho Brahe. Nardo, D. **92**

Tyger tyger. Hamilton, K. R. **Fic**

Tym, Kate

Coping with your emotions **152.4**

School survival **371.8**

Tyme [series]

Grounded **Fic**

TYPHOID FEVER

Fatal fever **614.51**

See also Diseases

TYPHOID FEVER -- FICTION

Chibbaro, J. Deadly **Fic**

Typhoid Mary, 1869-1938

About

Chibbaro, J. Deadly **Fic**

Fatal fever **614.51**

TYPHOONS

Longshore, D. Encyclopedia of hurricanes, typhoons, and cyclones **551.55**

See also Cyclones; Storms; Winds

TYPHOONS -- ENCYCLOPEDIAS

Longshore, D. Encyclopedia of hurricanes, typhoons, and cyclones **551.55**

TYPOLOGY (PSYCHOLOGY)

See also Personality; Psychology; Temperament

TYRANNOSAURUS REX

Tracking Tyrannosaurs **567.91**

See also Dinosaurs

Tyranny. Fairfield, L. **741.5**

The **tyrant's** daughter. Carleson, J. C. **Fic**

Tyson, Edith S.

Orson Scott Card **813**

Tyson, Neil deGrasse

Tyson, N. D. G. The Pluto files **523.4**

About

Explore the cosmos like Neil DeGrasse Tyson **520.92**

U

U-X-L Asian American voices. **815**

U-X-L encyclopedia of biomes. **577.8**

U-X-L encyclopedia of world mythology. **201**

The U.S. Armed Forces and military careers [series]

Gray, J. S. The U.S. Coast Guard and military careers **359.9**

The **U.S.** Coast Guard and military careers. Gray, J. S. **359.9**

U.S. involvement in Vietnam. Gitlin, M. **959.704**

U.S. marshals. Newton, M. **363.2**

U.S. SPACE CAMP (HUNTSVILLE, ALA.)

Goodman, S. Ultimate field trip 5 **629.45**

U.S. v. Nixon. Stefoff, R. **342**

UAVS (UNMANNED AERIAL VEHICLES) *See* Drone aircraft

Uchida, Yoshiko

The best bad thing **Fic**

A jar of dreams **Fic**

Journey to Topaz **Fic**

Udvardy, Miklos D. F.

National Audubon Society field guide to North American birds, Western region **598**

Uehashi, Nahoko

Moribito **Fic**

Moribito II **Fic**

UFOs. Stewart, G. **001.9**

UFOS *See* Unidentified flying objects

Uganda. Barlas, R. **967.61**

UNITED STATES MILITARY ACADEMY

Efaw, A. Battle dress **Fic**

See also Colleges and universities

UNITED STATES MILITARY ACADEMY -- FICTION

Efaw, A. Battle dress **Fic**

UNITED STATES NAVAL EXPEDITION TO JAPAN (1852-1854)

Blumberg, R. Commodore Perry in the land of the Shogun **952**

UNITED STATES PENITENTIARY, ALCATRAZ ISLAND, CALIFORNIA -- FICTION

Choldenko, G. Al Capone does my homework **Fic**

United States presidents [series]

Allen, M. G. Calvin Coolidge **973.91**

United States v. Amistad. Gold, S. D. **326**

UNITED STATES. AIR FORCE

Earl, S. Benjamin O. Davis, Jr. **92**

Schwartz, H. E. Women of the U.S. Air Force **358.4**

Vanderhoof, G. Air Force **358.4**

UNITED STATES. AIR FORCE -- FICTION

Lynch, C. Casualties of war **Fic**

UNITED STATES. ARMY

Allen, R. M. Mr. Lincoln's High-Tech War **973.7**

Stone, T. L. Courage has no color, the true story of the Triple Nickles **940.54**

See also Armies; Military history; United States -- Armed forces

UNITED STATES. ARMY -- AFRICAN AMERICAN TROOPS -- HISTORY

Howse, J. The Civil War **973.7**

UNITED STATES. ARMY -- CAVALRY

Uschan, M. V. The cavalry during the Civil War **973.7**

UNITED STATES. ARMY -- DELTA FORCE

Haney, E. L. Inside Delta Force **356**

UNITED STATES. ARMY -- MOUNTAIN DIVISION, 10TH -- FICTION

Duble, K. B. Phantoms in the snow **Fic**

UNITED STATES. ARMY -- RANGER BATTALION, 2ND

Zaloga, S. J. The most daring raid of World War II **940.54**

UNITED STATES. ARMY -- RANGERS

Earl, C. F. Army Rangers **356**

UNITED STATES. ARMY -- SPECIAL FORCES

Earl, C. F. Green Berets **356**

McIntosh, J. S. Elite forces selection **356**

McIntosh, J. S. Escape and evasion **335.4**

UNITED STATES. ARMY -- WOMEN'S ARMY CORPS -- FICTION

Davis, T. S. Mare's war **Fic**

UNITED STATES. ARMY NURSE CORPS

Kuhn, B. Angels of mercy **940.54**

UNITED STATES. ARMY -- BIOGRAPHY

See also Biography

UNITED STATES. ARMY -- MILITARY LIFE

See also Military personnel; Soldiers

UNITED STATES. ARMY -- OFFICERS

See also Military personnel; Soldiers

UNITED STATES. ARMY -- PARACHUTE TROOPS

See also Parachute troops

UNITED STATES. ARMY -- SONGS

See also Songs

UNITED STATES. ARMY. AIR CORPS

First flight around the world **910.4**

UNITED STATES. ARMY. INFANTRY REGIMENT, 102ND -- MASCOTS

Bausum, A. Stubby the War Dog **940.4**

UNITED STATES. ARMY. PARACHUTE INFANTRY BATTALION, 555TH -- FICTION

Pearsall, S. Jump into the sky **Fic**

UNITED STATES. ARTICLES OF CONFEDERATION

Feinberg, B. S. The Articles of Confederation **342**

Sonneborn, L. The Articles of Confederation **342.73**

UNITED STATES. BORDER PATROL

Weir, W. Border patrol **363.2**

UNITED STATES. CENTRAL INTELLIGENCE AGENCY

Goodman, M. E. The CIA and other American spies **327.127**

UNITED STATES. CENTRAL INTELLIGENCE AGENCY -- FICTION

Whyman, M. Goldstrike **Fic**

UNITED STATES. CONGRESS

Bow, J. What is the legislative branch? **328.73**

See also Legislative bodies

UNITED STATES. CONGRESS. HOUSE -- BIOGRAPHY

Green, C. R. Davy Crockett **976.8**

Raatma, L. Barbara Jordan **92**

UNITED STATES. CONGRESS. SENATE -- BIOGRAPHY

Green, C. R. Sam Houston **976.4**

UNITED STATES. CONSTITUTION

D'Agnese, J. Signing their rights away **920**

Fradin, D. B. The founders **920**

Ritchie, D. A. Our Constitution **342**

Sonneborn, L. The United States Constitution **342.73**

Vile, J. R. The United States Constitution **342**

UNITED STATES. CONSTITUTION. 1ST-10TH AMENDMENTS

Baxter, R. The Bill of Rights **342.73**

UNITED STATES. DECLARATION OF INDEPENDENCE

Driver, S. S. Understanding the Declaration of Independence **973.3**

Fradin, D. B. The signers **973.3**

Worth, R. Louisiana, 1682-1803 **976.3**

Worth, R. New France, 1534-1763 **971.01**

Voices in first person. **S**

Voices of dragons. Vaughn, C. **Fic**

Voigt, Cynthia

Bad girls in love **Fic**

Dicey's song **Fic**

Homecoming **Fic**

It's not easy being bad **Fic**

Izzy, willy-nilly **Fic**

A solitary blue **Fic**

Volavkova, Hana

--I never saw another butterfly-- **741.9**

Volcanic eruptions, earthquakes, and tsunamis. McCollum, S. **551.2**

A **volcano** beneath the snow. Marrin, A. **92**

Volcano! Fradin, J. B. **551.2**

Volcanoes. Silverstein, A. **551.2**

VOLCANOES

> See also Geology; Mountains; Physical geography

VOLCANOES

Fradin, J. B. Volcano! **551.2**

Fradin, J. B. Volcanoes **551.2**

Latta, S. L. Lava scientist **551.2**

Levy, M. Earthquakes, volcanoes, and tsunamis **551.2**

McCollum, S. Volcanic eruptions, earthquakes, and tsunamis **551.2**

Nardo, D. Volcanoes **551.2**

Person, S. Devastated by a volcano! **551.2**

Plate tectonics, volcanoes, and earthquakes **551**

Prager, E. J. Earthquakes and volcanoes **551.2**

Rooney, A. Volcanoes **551.2**

Rusch, E. Eruption! **363.34**

Silverstein, A. Volcanoes **551.2**

Stewart, M. Inside Volcanoes **551.2**

Winchester, S. The day the world exploded **551.2**

Volcanoes. Nardo, D. **551.2**

Volcanoes. Fradin, J. B. **551.2**

Volcanoes. Rooney, A. **551.2**

VOLCANOES -- FICTION

Nelson, J. On the volcano **Fic**

Smith, R. Eruption **Fic**

Volleyball. McDougall, C. **796.325**

VOLLEYBALL

Crisfield, D. Winning volleyball for girls **796.325**

McDougall, C. Volleyball **796.325**

> See also Ball games; Sports

Vollmar, Rob

The castaways **741.5**

Volponi, Paul

Black and white **Fic**

The hand you're dealt **Fic**

Homestretch **Fic**

Hurricane song **Fic**

Rikers High **Fic**

Rucker Park setup **Fic**

VOLUME (CUBIC CONTENT)

> See also Geometry; Measurement; Weights and measures

VOLUNTARISM

Laidlaw, R. Cat champions **636.8**

VOLUNTARISM See Volunteer work

VOLUNTEER WORK

Gay, K. Volunteering **361.3**

Gillespie, K. M. Teen volunteer services in libraries **021.2**

O'Neal, C. Volunteering in your school **361.3**

O'Neal, C. Ways to help in your community **361.3**

Saul, L. Ways to help after a natural disaster **363.34**

Teens and volunteerism **302**

VOLUNTEER WORK -- FICTION

Kephart, B. The heart is not a size **Fic**

Reinhardt, D. How to build a house **Fic**

Rhuday-Perkovich, O. 8th grade superzero **Fic**

Volunteering. Gay, K. **361.3**

VOLUNTEERING See Volunteer work

Volunteering in your school. O'Neal, C. **361.3**

VOMITING

Cusick, D. Get the Scoop on Animal Puke **591.5**

Von Braun, Wernher, 1912-1977

About

Richie, J. Space flight **629**

VOODOOISM

> See also Religions

Voorhees, Coert

Lucky fools **Fic**

Vote. Paulsen, G. **Fic**

Vote for Larry. Tashjian, J. **Fic**

VOTER REGISTRATION

> See also Elections; Suffrage

VOTING See Elections; Suffrage

VOTING RIGHTS ACT OF 1965

Aretha, D. Selma and the Voting Rights Act **324.6**

VOYA guides [series]

Gillespie, K. M. Teen volunteer services in libraries **021.2**

The **voyage** of Patience Goodspeed. Frederick, H. V. **Fic**

The **voyage** of the Dawn Treader. Lewis, C. S. **Fic**

VOYAGERS See Explorers; Travelers

Voyages. Waldman, N. **92**

VOYAGES AND TRAVELS

Childress, D. Marco Polo's journey to China **92**

Demi Marco Polo **92**

Feinstein, S. Marco Polo **92**

Galloway, P. Adventures on the ancient Silk Road **950**

Hagglund, B. Epic treks **910.4**

Nye, N. S. I'll ask you three times, are you ok? **92**

Phelan, M. Around the world **741.5**

Watch wolf. Lasky, K.   **Fic**

The **watcher**.   **Fic**

The **watcher** in the shadows.   **Fic**

WATCHES See Clocks and watches

Watching Jimmy. Hartry, N.   **Fic**

Water. Laidlaw, J. A.   **333.91**

Water. Workman, J. G.   **363.6**

WATER

    See also Earth sciences; Hydraulics

WATER

    Burgan, M. Not a drop to drink   **363.6**

    Gardner, R. Water   **551.48**

    Goodstein, M. Water science fair projects   **546**

    Just add water   **546**

    Knapp, B. J. Materials science   **620.1**

    Laidlaw, J. A. Water   **333.91**

    Parker, S. The science of water   **532**

    Woodward, J. Water   **553.7**

Water. Woodward, J.   **553.7**

Water. Gardner, R.   **551.48**

Water. Warhol, T.   **577.6**

WATER -- FICTION

    LaFaye, A. Water steps   **Fic**

    Park, L. S. A long walk to water   **Fic**

WATER -- POLLUTION

    Desonie, D. Hydrosphere   **551.48**

    Running dry   **333.91**

WATER -- PURIFICATION See Water purification

Water and atmosphere. Casper, J. K.   **553.7**

Water and ice. Berlatsky, N.   **551.4**

WATER ANIMALS See Aquatic animals

Water balloon. Vernick, A.   **Fic**

WATER BIRDS

    Webb, S. Far from shore   **591.7**

    Wolny, P. Waterfowl   **799.2**

WATER BIRDS

    See also Birds

The **Water** Castle. Blakemore, M. F.   **Fic**

WATER CONSERVATION

    Cousteau, P. Make a splash!   **577.7**

    Fridell, R. Protecting Earth's water supply   **363.7**

    Mulder, M. Every last drop   **333.91**

    Running dry   **333.91**

    Workman, J. G. Water   **363.6**

    See also Conservation of natural resources

WATER FLUORIDATION

    See also Water supply

WATER FOWL See Water birds

The **water** mirror. Meyer, K.   **Fic**

WATER PLANTS See Freshwater plants; Marine plants

WATER POLLUTION

    Bryan, N. Danube   **363.7**

    Desonie, D. Hydrosphere   **551.48**

    Fridell, R. Protecting Earth's water supply   **363.7**

    Geiger, B. Clean water   **363.7**

    Kurlansky, M. The world without fish   **333.95**

WATER POLLUTION

    See also Environmental health; Pollution; Public health

WATER POWER

    See also Energy resources; Hydraulics; Power (Mechanics); Renewable energy resources; Rivers; Water resources development

WATER PURIFICATION

    Desonie, D. Hydrosphere   **551.48**

WATER PURIFICATION

    See also Sanitation; Water supply

WATER QUALITY MANAGEMENT

    Mulder, M. Every last drop   **333.91**

WATER RESOURCES DEVELOPMENT

    Mulder, M. Every last drop   **333.91**

Water science fair projects. Goodstein, M.   **546**

The **water** seeker. Holt, K. W.   **Fic**

WATER SPORTS

    See also Sports

Water steps. LaFaye, A.   **Fic**

Water Street. Giff, P. R.   **Fic**

WATER SUPPLY

    Burgan, M. Not a drop to drink   **363.6**

    Casper, J. K. Water and atmosphere   **553.7**

    Geiger, B. Clean water   **363.7**

    Laidlaw, J. A. Water   **333.91**

    Running dry   **333.91**

    Workman, J. G. Water   **363.6**

    See also Natural resources; Public utilities

WATER SUPPLY ENGINEERING

    See also Civil engineering; Engineering

Water: tales of elemental spirits. McKinley, R.   **S**

WATERCOLOR PAINTING

    See also Painting

WATERCOLOR PAINTING -- TECHNIQUE

    Lanza, B. Enchanting elves   **758**

Waterfalls. Carrigan, P.   **551.48**

WATERFALLS

    Carrigan, P. Waterfalls   **551.48**

Waterfowl. Wolny, P.   **799.2**

WATERGATE AFFAIR, 1972-1974

    Stefoff, R. U.S. v. Nixon   **342**

The **waterless** sea. Constable, K.   **Fic**

The **waters** & the wild. Block, F. L.   **Fic**

Waters, Dan

    Generation dead   **Fic**

Waters, Rosa

    My daily diet   **613.2**

Waters, Sophie

    The female reproductive system   **612.6**

    Seeing the gynecologist   **618.1**

Waters, Zack C.

    Blood moon rider   **Fic**

Watership Down. Adams, R.   **Fic**

Lockhart, E. We were liars **Fic**
WEALTHY PEOPLE See Rich
WEAPONRY See Weapons
WEAPONS
Byam, M. Arms & armor **355.8**
WEAPONS
See also Tools; Weapons
WEAPONS -- HISTORY
Collier, J. L. Gunpowder and weaponry **623.4**
Diagram Group The new weapons of the world encyclopedia **623.4**
WEAPONS INDUSTRY See Defense industry; Firearms industry
WEAPONS, ATOMIC See Nuclear weapons
WEAPONS, NUCLEAR See Nuclear weapons
Weapons, tactics, and strategy. Cooke, T. **973.7**
Wearing, Judy
Bacteria **579.3**
Fungi **579**
Weather. Banqueri, E. **551.5**
WEATHER
Banqueri, E. Weather **551.5**
Carson, M. K. Weather projects for young scientists **551.5**
Cosgrove, B. Weather **551.5**
Gaffney, T. R. Storm scientist **551.5**
Gardner, R. Ace your weather science project **551.5**
Gardner, R. Easy genius science projects with weather **551.5**
Gardner, R. Weather science fair projects **551.6**
Henningfeld, D. A. Health and disease **363.7**
Natural disasters **363.34**
Streissguth, T. Extreme weather **551.5**
Vogt, G. The atmosphere **551.5**
Weather. Cosgrove, B. **551.5**
WEATHER -- FICTION
Williams, A. The deep freeze of Bartholomew Tullock **Fic**
WEATHER -- FOLKLORE
See also Folklore; Meteorology; Weather forecasting
WEATHER -- GRAPHIC NOVELS
Evans, K. Weird weather **363.7**
WEATHER CONTROL
See also Meteorology; Weather
WEATHER FORECASTING
Evans, B. It's raining fish and spiders **551.6**
Fleisher, P. Doppler radar, satellites, and computer models **551.63**
Gardner, R. Meteorology projects with a weather station you can build **551.5**
See also Forecasting; Meteorology; Weather
Weather projects for young scientists. Carson, M. K. **551.5**
Weather science fair projects. Gardner, R. **551.6**
Weatherford, Carole Boston

Becoming Billie Holiday **Fic**
Remember the bridge **811**
Weatherly, Lee
Angel burn **Fic**
Kat got your tongue **Fic**
Weatherly, Myra
Elizabeth I **92**
Teens in Ghana **966.7**
Women of the sea **910.4**
Weatherwise [series]
Fleisher, P. Doppler radar, satellites, and computer models **551.63**
Fleisher, P. Lightning, hurricanes, and blizzards **551.55**
Weaver, Janice
Hudson **92**
It's your room **747**
Mirror with a memory **971**
Weaver, Will
Defect **Fic**
Full service **Fic**
Saturday night dirt **Fic**
Super stock rookie **Fic**
WEAVING
See also Handicraft; Textile industry
Web 2.0. Kling, A. A. **006.7**
WEB 2.0
Berger, P. Choosing Web 2.0 tools for learning and teaching in a digital world **025.04**
Brooks-Young, S. Teaching with the tools kids really use **372**
WEB LOGS See Weblogs
A **Web** of Air. Reeve, P. **Fic**
Web of lies. Naidoo, B. **Fic**
The **web** of Titan. Testa, D. **Fic**
WEB PAGES See Web sites
WEB RESEARCH See Internet research
WEB SEARCH ENGINES
Hamen, S. E. Google **338.7**
Henderson, H. Larry Page and Sergey Brin **920**
Randolph, R. P. New research techniques **001.4**
Sapet, K. Google founders: Larry Page and Sergey Brin **92**
WEB SEARCH ENGINES
See also Internet searching; World Wide Web
WEB SEARCHING See Internet searching; Web search engines
WEB SITES
Tashjian, J. The gospel according to Larry **Fic**
See also Internet resources; World Wide Web
WEB SITES -- DESIGN
Selfridge, B. A teen's guide to creating Web pages and blogs **006.7**
Smith, S. S. Web-based instruction **025.5**
WEB SITES -- FICTION
Bancks, T. Mac Slater vs. the city **Fic**

Morris, N. Global warming **363.7**

Senker, C. Poverty **362.5**

Sheehan, S. Endangered species **333.95**

What is a family? Stewart, S. **306.8**

What is art? [series]

Hosack, K. Buildings **720**

What is atomic theory? McLean, A. **539.7**

What is cell theory? Cohen, M. **571.6**

What is germ theory? Hyde, N. **615**

What is terrorism? Weinberg, L. **303.6**

What is the executive branch? Bow, J. **351**

What is the future of alternative energy cars? Bjorn-lund, L. **388.3**

What is the future of fossil fuels? Marcovitz, H. **553.2**

What is the judicial branch? Rodger, E. **347.73**

What is the legislative branch? Bow, J. **328.73**

What is the theory of evolution? Walker, R. **576.8**

What is the theory of plate tectonics? Saunders, C. **551.1**

What it's like. Belanger, J. **179**

What Janie found. Cooney, C. B. **Fic**

What makes a terrorist? Tougas, S. **363.32**

What makes us a family? Lynette, R. **306.8**

What Momma left me. Watson, R. **Fic**

What my girlfriend doesn't know. Sones, S. **Fic**

What my mother doesn't know. Sones, S. **Fic**

What the birds see. Hartnett, S. **Fic**

What the Heart Knows. Sidman, J. **811**

What the moon saw. Resau, L. **Fic**

What the world eats. Menzel, P. **641.3**

What they found. Myers, W. D. **S**

What to do when you're sad & lonely. Crist, J. J. **158**

What to do when you're scared & worried. Crist, J. J. **158**

What was the Battle of Gettysburg? **973.7**

What we found in the sofa (and how it saved the world) Clark, H. **Fic**

What will happen to me? Zehr, H. **362.82**

What world is left. Polak, M. **Fic**

What would Joey do? Gantos, J. **Fic**

What you must think of me. Ford, E. **616.85**

What you wish for. Book Wish Foundation **S**

What's black and white and Reid all over? Reid, R. **027.62**

What's cooking? Whitman, S. **394.1**

The **what's** happening to my body? book for boys. Madaras, L. **612.6**

The **what's** happening to my body? book for girls. Madaras, L. **612.6**

What's left of me. Zhang, K. **Fic**

What's the catch? Sobel, D. **153.8**

What's up with my family? Fox, A. **306.8**

What-the-Dickens. Maguire, G. **Fic**

Whatcha mean, what's a zine? Todd, M. **070.5**

Whatever happened to Janie? Cooney, C. B. **Fic**

WHEELCHAIR BASKETBALL

See also Basketball; Wheelchair sports

WHEELCHAIR SPORTS

See also Sports for people with disabilities

WHEELCHAIRS -- FICTION

My life as a cartoonist **Fic**

Wheels of change. Macy, S. **796.6**

Whelan, Gloria

After the train **Fic**

All my noble dreams and then what happens **Fic**

Burying the sun **Fic**

Chu Ju's house **Fic**

The Disappeared **Fic**

Goodbye, Vietnam **Fic**

Homeless bird **Fic**

Listening for lions **Fic**

The locked garden **Fic**

See what I see **Fic**

Small acts of amazing courage **Fic**

When a friend dies. Gootman, M. E. **155.9**

When Daddy hit Mommy. Stewart, S. **362.82**

When did you see her last? **Fic**

When dinos dawned, mammals got munched, and Pterosaurs took flight. Bonner, H. **567.9**

When elephants fight. Walters, E. **920**

When I crossed No-Bob. McMullan, M. **Fic**

When I was a boy Neruda called me Policarpo. Delano, P. **92**

When I was a soldier. Zenatti, V. **92**

When I was Joe. David, K. **Fic**

When is a planet not a planet? Scott, E. **523.4**

When life stinks. Piquemal, M. **158**

When love comes to town. Lennon, T. **Fic**

When lunch fights back. Johnson, R. L. **591.47**

When Molly was a Harvey Girl. Wood, F. **Fic**

When my name was Keoko. Park, L. S. **Fic**

When nothing matters anymore. Cobain, B. **616.85**

When Ratboy lived next door. Woodworth, C. **Fic**

When reason breaks. **Fic**

When the black girl sings. Wright, B. **Fic**

When the children marched. Mayer, R. H. **323.1**

When the snow fell. Mankell, H. **Fic**

When the stars threw down their spears. Hamilton, K. **Fic**

When the Tripods came. Christopher, J. **Fic**

When the whistle blows. Slayton, F. C. **Fic**

When we wake. Healey, K. **Fic**

When will I stop hurting? Myers, E. **155.9**

When you reach me. Stead, R. **Fic**

When you were here. Whitney, D. **Fic**

When you wish. Harmel, K. **Fic**

When you wish upon a rat. McCarthy, M. **Fic**

When Zachary Beaver came to town. Holt, K. W. **Fic**

Where do you stay? Cheng, A. **Fic**

WOMEN SCIENTISTS -- BIOGRAPHY

Di Domenico, K. Women scientists who changed the world **509.2**

Montgomery, S. Temple Grandin **636**

WOMEN SCIENTISTS -- DICTIONARIES

Yount, L. A to Z of women in science and math **920.003**

WOMEN SCIENTISTS -- GRAPHIC NOVELS

Ottaviani, J. Dignifying science **920**

Women scientists who changed the world. Di Domenico, K. **509.2**

WOMEN SOCIAL REFORMERS -- PAKISTAN

Aretha, D. Malala Yousafzai and the girls of Pakistan **92**

WOMEN SOLDIERS

Crew, H. S. Women engaged in war in literature for youth **016**

Silvey, A. I'll pass for your comrade **973.7**

Zenatti, V. When I was a soldier **92**

WOMEN SPIES -- FICTION

Avi Sophia's war **Fic**

Women win the vote. VanMeter, L. A. **305.4**

Women's adventures in science [series]

Bortz, F. Beyond Jupiter **92**

Ebersole, R. Gorilla mountain **92**

Hopping, L. J. Bone detective **92**

Hopping, L. J. Space rocks **92**

Parks, D. Nature's machines **92**

WOMEN'S CLOTHING

See also Clothing and dress

WOMEN'S FRIENDSHIP See Female friendship

Women's hall of fame [series]

Benjamin, M. Nobel's women of peace **920**

Dublin, A. Dynamic women dancers **920**

Simoni, S. Fantastic women filmmakers **920**

WOMEN'S MOVEMENT

See also Women -- Social conditions; Women's rights

Women's right to vote. Marsico, K. **305.4**

WOMEN'S RIGHTS

Gelletly, L. A woman's place in early America **305.4**

Norgren, J. Belva Lockwood **92**

Senker, C. Strength in numbers **305.4**

See also Civil rights; Sex discrimination

WOMEN'S RIGHTS -- FICTION

Feldman, R. T. Blue thread **Fic**

WOMEN'S RIGHTS -- HISTORY

Bausum, A. With courage and cloth **305.4**

WOMEN'S RIGHTS -- UNITED STATES -- HISTORY

Hollihan, K. L. Rightfully ours **324.6**

Sigerman, H. Elizabeth Cady Stanton **92**

WOMEN'S SUFFRAGE See Women -- Suffrage

Wonder. Palacio, R. J. **Fic**

Wonder beasts. Nigg, J. **398.24**

Wonder girl. Van Natta, D. **92**

The wonder of Charlie Anne. Fusco, K. N. **Fic**

Wonder show. Barnaby, H. **Fic**

WONDER WOMAN (FICTIONAL CHARACTER)

Fisch, S. Super friends: for justice! **741.5**

WONDER WOMAN (FICTIONAL CHARACTER)

See also Fictional characters; Superheroes

Wonderful wikis. Truesdell, A. **006.7**

Wonderland. Kovac, T. **741.5**

WONDERS See Curiosities and wonders

Wonders and miracles. Kimmel, E. A. **296.4**

Wonders of the world. Dumont-Le Cornec, E. **910**

Wonders of the world [series]

Mann, E. Hoover Dam **627**

Mann, E. The Parthenon **726**

Mann, E. The Roman Colosseum **937**

Mann, E. Statue of Liberty **974.7**

Mann, E. Taj Mahal **954**

Mann, E. Tikal **972.81**

Wonderstruck. Selznick, B. **Fic**

Wong, Janet S., 1962-

(ed) The Poetry Friday Anthology for Middle School **808.1**

Wong, Nicole E.

Cheng, A. Brushing Mom's hair **Fic**

Wong, Stephen

Baseball treasures **796.357**

Wong, Winnie

Heale, J. Tanzania **967.8**

Holmes, T. Zambia **968.94**

Jermyn, L. Uruguay **989.5**

Levy, P. Ghana **966.7**

Woo, Howie

Isabella, J. Hoaxed! **500**

Wood. Morris, N. **634.9**

WOOD

Knapp, B. J. Materials science **620.1**

Morris, N. Wood **634.9**

WOOD

See also Building materials; Forest products; Fuel; Trees

WOOD CARVING -- FICTION

Bow, E. Plain Kate **Fic**

Wood, A. J.

Charles Darwin and the Beagle adventure **508**

Wood, Don

Into the volcano **741.5**

Wood, Elaine

Walker, P. The continental shelf **578.7**

Walker, P. The coral reef **577.7**

Walker, P. Ecosystem science fair projects **577**

Walker, P. Environmental science experiments **507.8**

Walker, P. Forensic science experiments **363.2**

Alma, A. Brave deeds   **940.53**
Sanders, R. Storming the tulips   **940.53**
WORLD WAR, 1939-1945 -- NETHERLANDS --
FICTION
Polak, M. What world is left   **Fic**
WORLD WAR, 1939-1945 -- NETHERLANDS --
PERSONAL NARRATIVES
Prins, M. Hidden like Anne Frank   **92**
WORLD WAR, 1939-1945 -- NORWAY -- FIC-
TION
Casanova, M. The klipfish code   **Fic**
WORLD WAR, 1939-1945 -- OCCUPIED TER-
RITORIES
Samuels, C. Life under occupation   **940.53**
WORLD WAR, 1939-1945 -- OCCUPIED TER-
RITORIES
    See also Military occupation;   World War,
    1939-1945 -- Territorial questions
WORLD WAR, 1939-1945 -- PACIFIC AREA
Samuels, C. Life under occupation   **940.53**
WORLD WAR, 1939-1945 -- PARTICIPATION,
AFRICAN AMERICAN
Myers, W. D. Invasion!   **Fic**
WORLD WAR, 1939-1945 -- PERSONAL NAR-
RATIVES
Allen, T. B. Remember Pearl Harbor   **940.54**
Altman, L. J. Hidden teens, hidden lives **940.53**
Byers, A.   Trapped--youth in the Nazi ghet-
tos   **940.53**
DeMallie, H. R. Behind enemy lines   **940.54**
Layson, A. H. Lost childhood   **92**
Opdyke, I. G. In my hands   **940.53**
WORLD WAR, 1939-1945 -- PERSONAL NAR-
RATIVES
    See also Autobiographies; Biography
WORLD WAR, 1939-1945 -- PERSONAL NAR-
RATIVES, AMERICAN
McMullan, J. Leaving China   **92**
WORLD WAR, 1939-1945 -- PHILIPPINES --
FICTION
Salisbury, S. Hunt for the bamboo rat   **Fic**
WORLD WAR, 1939-1945 -- POETRY
    See also Historical poetry; War poetry
WORLD WAR, 1939-1945 -- POLAND
Opdyke, I. G. In my hands   **940.53**
The secret of the village fool   **Fic**
WORLD WAR, 1939-1945 -- PRISONERS AND
PRISONS
    See also Concentration camps; Prisoners of
    war; Prisons
WORLD WAR, 1939-1945 -- PRISONERS AND
PRISONS, JAPANESE
Farrell, M. C. Pure grit   **940.54**
WORLD WAR, 1939-1945 -- PROPAGANDA
Samuels, C. Propaganda   **940.54**

WORLD WAR, 1939-1945 -- PROTEST MOVE-
MENTS
    See also Protest movements
WORLD WAR, 1939-1945 -- REFUGEES
Hodge, D. Rescuing the children   **940.53**
WORLD WAR, 1939-1945 -- REFUGEES
    See also Political refugees
WORLD WAR, 1939-1945 -- REFUGEES -- FIC-
TION
Deep sea   **Fic**
Perl, L. Isabel's War   **Fic**
WORLD WAR, 1939-1945 -- RESISTANCE
MOVEMENTS *See* World War, 1939-1945 --
    Underground movements
WORLD WAR, 1939-1945 -- SECRET SERVICE
Code name Pauline   **940.54**
Samuels, C. Spying and security   **940.54**
WORLD WAR, 1939-1945 -- SECRET SERVICE
-- GREAT BRITAIN
Sheinkin, S. Bomb   **623.4**
WORLD WAR, 1939-1945 -- SECRET SERVICE
-- SOVIET UNION
Sheinkin, S. Bomb   **623.4**
WORLD WAR, 1939-1945 -- THEATER AND
THE WAR
    See also Theater
WORLD WAR, 1939-1945 -- TRANSPORTA-
TION
    See also Transportation
WORLD WAR, 1939-1945 -- TREATIES
    See also Treaties
WORLD WAR, 1939-1945 -- UNDERGROUND
MOVEMENTS -- DENMARK
The boys who challenged Hitler   **940.53**
WORLD WAR, 1939-1945 -- UNDERGROUND
MOVEMENTS -- FICTION
Casanova, M. The klipfish code   **Fic**
Couloumbis, A. War games   **Fic**
Jablonski, C. Defiance   **741.5**
WORLD WAR, 1939-1945 -- UNDERGROUND
MOVEMENTS -- FRANCE
Code name Pauline   **940.54**
WORLD WAR, 1939-1945 -- UNDERGROUND
MOVEMENTS -- FRANCE -- FICTION
Jablonski, C. Victory   **741.5**
WORLD WAR, 1939-1945 -- UNDERGROUND
MOVEMENTS -- FRANCE
Calkhoven, L. Michael at the invasion of France,
1943   **Fic**
Elliott, L. Under a war-torn sky   **Fic**
WORLD WAR, 1939-1945 -- UNDERGROUND
MOVEMENTS -- GERMANY -- FICTION
The watcher   **Fic**
WORLD WAR, 1939-1945 -- UNDERGROUND
MOVEMENTS -- GRAPHIC NOVELS
Jablonski, C. Resistance, book 1   **741.5**

APPENDIX

APPENDIX

The following charts lists Newbery medalists in the collection and their locations in the Classified Collection.

Newbery Medal Award Winners

Author	Title	Dewey Location
Alexander, K.	*The crossover*	Fic
Applegate, K.	*The one and only Ivan*	Fic
Armstrong, W. H.	*Sounder*	Fic
Avi.	*Crispin: the cross of lead*	Fic
Byars, B. C.	*The summer of the swans*	Fic
Cleary, B.	*Dear Mr. Henshaw*	Fic
Creech, S.	*Walk two moons*	Fic
Curtis, C. P.	*Bud, not Buddy*	Fic
Cushman, K.	*The midwife's apprentice*	Fic
DiCamillo, K.	*Flora & Ulysses*	Fic
Fleischman, P.	*Joyful noise: poems for two voices*	811
Fleischman, S.	*The whipping boy*	Fic
Freedman, R.	*Lincoln: a photobiography*	92
Gaiman, N.	*The graveyard book*	Fic
Gantos, J.	*Dead end in Norvelt*	Fic
George, J. C.	*Julie of the wolves*	Fic
Hesse, K.	*Out of the dust*	Fic
Kadohata, C.	*Kira-Kira*	Fic
Konigsburg, E. L.	*The view from Saturday*	Fic
L'Engle, M.	*A wrinkle in time*	Fic
Lowry, L.	*The giver*	Fic
Lowry, L.	*Number the stars*	Fic
McKinley, R.	*The hero and the crown*	Fic
Naylor, P. R.	*Shiloh*	Fic
O'Brien, R. C.	*Mrs. Frisby and the rats of NIMH*	Fic
O'Dell, S.	*Island of the Blue Dolphins*	Fic
Park, L. S.	*A single shard*	Fic
Paterson, K.	*Bridge to Terabithia*	Fic
Peck, R. N.	*A year down yonder*	Fic
Perkins, L. R.	*Criss cross*	Fic
Rylant, C.	*Missing May*	Fic
Sachar, L.	*Holes*	Fic
Schlitz, L. A.	*Good masters! Sweet ladies!*	940.1
Speare, E. G.	*The witch of Blackbird Pond*	Fic
Stead, R.	*When you reach me*	Fic
Spinelli, J.	*Maniac Magee*	Fic
Taylor, M. D.	*Roll of thunder, hear my cry*	Fic
Vanderpool, C.	*Moon over Manifest*	Fic
Voigt, C.	*Dicey's song*	Fic
Yates, E.	*Amos Fortune, free man*	92

O'Brien, R.C	Mrs. Frisby and the rats of NIMH	Fic
O'Dell, S	Island of the Blue Dolphins	Fic
Park, L.S	A single shard	Fic
Paterson, K.	Bridge to Terabithia	Fic
Peck, R.N	A year down yonder	Fic
Perkins, L.R.	Criss cross	Fic
Rylant, C	Missing May	Fic
Sachar, L.	Holes	Fic
Selznick, B.A.	Good masters! Sweet ladies	398.1
Speare, E.G	The witch of Blackbird Pond	Fic
Stead, R.	When you reach me	Fic
Spinelli, J	Maniac Magee	Fic
Taylor, M.D.	Roll of thunder, hear my cry	Fic
Vanderpool, C.	Moon over Manifest	Fic
Voigt, C	Dicey's song	Fic
Yates, E	Amos Fortune, free man	92